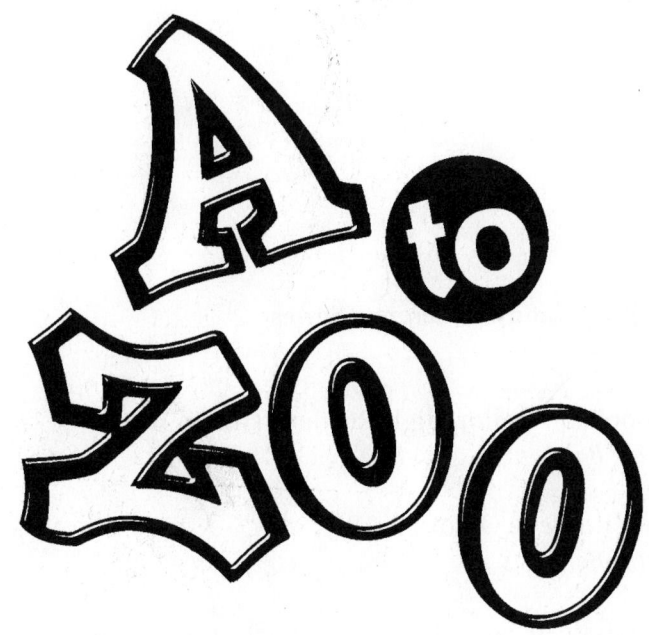

Recent Titles in the
Children's and Young Adult Literature Reference Series
Catherine Barr, Series Editor

Best Books for Middle School and Junior High Readers, Grades 6–9
John T. Gillespie and Catherine Barr

Best Books for High School Readers, Grades 9–12
John T. Gillespie and Catherine Barr

Popular Series Fiction for K-6 Readers: A Reading and Selection Guide
Rebecca L. Thomas and Catherine Barr

Popular Series Fiction for Middle School and Teen Readers: A Reading and Selection Guide
Rebecca L. Thomas and Catherine Barr

Fantasy Literature for Children and Young Adults: A Comprehensive Guide, Fifth Edition
Ruth Nadelman Lynn

The Children's and Young Adult Literature Handbook: A Research and Reference Guide
John T. Gillespie

Subject Access to Children's Picture Books

Seventh Edition

Carolyn W. Lima and John A. Lima

Children's and Young Adult Literature Reference Series
Catherine Barr, Series Editor

LIBRARIES
U N L I M I T E D
A Member of the Greenwood Publishing Group

Westport, Connecticut • London

Library of Congress Cataloging-in-Publication Data

Lima, Carolyn W.
   A to zoo : subject access to children's picture books / by Carolyn W.
Lima and John A. Lima. – 7th ed.
     p. cm. – (Children's and young adult literature reference series)
   Includes bibliographical references and index.
   ISBN 1-59158-232-6 (alk. paper)
   1. Picture books for children—Indexes. 2. Children's literature,
English—Indexes. I. Lima, John A. II. Title. III. Series.
Z1037.L715   2006
011.62—dc22   2005030879

British Library Cataloguing in Publication Data is available.

Library of Congress Catalog Card Number: 2005030879
ISBN: 1-59158-232-6

First published in 2006

Libraries Unlimited, 88 Post Road West, Westport, CT 06881
A Member of the Greenwood Publishing Group, Inc.
www.lu.com

Printed in the United States of America

The paper used in this book complies with the
Permanent Paper Standard issued by the National
Information Standards Organization (Z39.48–1984).

10 9 8 7 6 5 4 3 2 1

Dedication

To the loving memory of my mother, Bonnie Womack,
who taught me the value of all kinds of books

Contents

Preface

The importance of the picture book, long a source of delight and learning for young readers, continues today with an increasing emphasis on early childhood education and on reading, and with the need for supervised childcare for working parents. Teachers, librarians, and parents are finding the picture book an important learning and entertainment tool. Choosing the right book for a particular situation or need can be time-consuming and frustrating without some guidance. Many responsible professionals and parents have neither the time nor the materials to develop an intimate familiarity with the field. Rather than simply choosing the first title that appears to treat a specific subject from among the many thousands of books available, the user can now confidently identify a book that will cover the desired subject, using this seventh edition of *A to Zoo: Subject Access to Children's Picture Books.* This edition of *A to Zoo* has more than 28,000 titles cataloged under more than 1,350 subjects.

Recent editions of *A to Zoo* have outgrown most large collections. In an effort to ensure that the most up-to-date information is included in this edition, the authors consulted many sources. Large public and university library collections, review copies from various publishers, published reviews, and the authors' personal searches of titles and literature provided an information base. Out-of-print titles are included because school and public library collections are largely retrospective, consisting mostly of out-of-print materials. Additionally, many use *A to Zoo* as a resource for research.

The picture book, as it is broadly defined within the scope of this book, is a fiction or nonfiction title with illustrations occupying as much or more space than the text and with text, vocabulary, or concepts suitable for preschool through grade two. It is noted, however that picture books appeal to a wider audience; adults, older children, and others often find picture books enjoyable, useful, and informative.[1]

The "Introduction: Genesis of the English-Language Picture Book" has been reviewed, and additional sources and reference works have been added to the list of suggested titles for further reading. Some historically important developments have been identified in the last few years. Studies have been made of the gender bias found in children's picture books; this bias seems to be lessening, with improved representation of women and girls in leadership roles that aid children in defining standards for gender behavior.[2] There has been considerable emphasis on the immigrant experience, both for new American citizens and for non-immigrant children.[3] Another development is the prevalence of controversy regarding picture books. Picture books are the subject of challenges, censorship, political rancor, and theft (especially as a form of censorship). Books such as *Heather Has Two Mommies* have engendered particularly bitter debates and action.[4] Abuse is a subject encountered now in picture books.[5] Picture books, then, can be controversial on the basis of political, moral, and religious convictions, with stereotypes, race, violence, and sex prominently alleged. Children must be protected from the presentation of things violent, unsettling, or "inappropriate" for children.[6] Inappropriateness is, sadly, a growing phenomenon in children's picture books. Almost anything goes — including war, suicide, and violence — whether it is a subject that can or cannot be resolved in 32 pages.[7] Other, older trends, continue as previously noted; mechanical and "pop-up" books remain prolific; board books, for the very young, are plentiful; and "educational" books, or those with a "lesson" designed to accomplish some social purpose other than mere entertainment of the young reader, remain in evidence.[8]

Trends in education, particularly for illiterate or second-language students, highlight picture books as a beginning point for adults because of the controlled vocabulary and concepts.[9] These "crossover" books, which appeal to two markets, are popular with publishers.[10] Serious fine artists continue to contribute to picture books; the effect has been a general improvement and sophistication in the art depicted.

Picture books also continue to dwell in the realm of the e-book, accessible for reading or viewing in cyberspace at www.ipicturebooks.com.[11]

HOW TO USE THIS BOOK

A to Zoo can be used to obtain information about children's picture books in two ways: to learn the titles, authors, and illustrators of books on a particular subject, such as "dragons" or "weddings"; or to ascertain the subject (or subjects) when only the title, author and title, or illustrator and title are known. For example, if the title *Wild About Books* is known, this volume will enable the user to discover that *Wild About Books* is written by Judy Sierra, illustrated by Marc Tolon Brown, and published by Knopf in 2004, and that its subject areas are Animals; Books, reading; Careers – librarians; Libraries; Rhyming text; and Zoos.

For ease and convenience of reference use, *A to Zoo* is divided into five sections:

> Subject Headings
> Subject Guide
> Bibliographic Guide
> Title Index
> Illustrator Index

SUBJECT HEADINGS: This section contains an alphabetical list of the subjects cataloged in this book. The subject headings reflect the established terms used commonly in public libraries, originally based on questions asked by parents and teachers and then modified and adapted by librarians. To facilitate reference use, and because subjects are requested in a variety of terms, the list of subject headings contains numerous cross-references. Subheadings are arranged alphabetically under each general topic, for example:

> Animals (general topic)
> Animals – aardvarks (subheading)
> Animals – anteaters (subheading)
> Animals – antelopes (subheading)
> Animals – apes *see* Animals – baboons; Animals – chimpanzees; Animals – gorillas; Animals – monkeys (cross-reference)

SUBJECT GUIDE: This guide to more than 28,000 picture books for preschool children through second graders is cataloged under more than 1,350 subjects. The guide reflects the arrangement in the Subject Headings, alphabetically arranged by subject heading and subheading. Many books, of course, relate to more than one subject, and this comprehensive list provides a means of identifying all those books that may contain any information or material on a particular subject.

If, for example, the user wants books on crabs (crustaceans), the Subject Headings section will show that Crustaceans is a subject classification. A look in the Subject Guide reveals that under Crustaceans there are 6 titles listed alphabetically by author, plus an additional 33 titles under 4 related subheadings.

BIBLIOGRAPHIC GUIDE: Each book is listed with full bibliographic information. This section is arranged alphabetically by author, or by title when the author is unknown, or by uniform (classic) title. Each entry contains bibliographic information in order: author, title, illustrator, publisher and date of publication, miscellaneous notes when given, International Standard Book Number (ISBN), and subjects, listed according to the alphabetical classification in the Subject Headings section. Where ISBNs appear they probably indicate entries new to the third and subsequent editions, and are the library binding edition or the next best quality edition available. However, many older books have been given ISBNs retrospectively, and where these were available, the entries have been updated.

The user can consult the Bibliographic Guide to find complete data on each of the titles listed in the Subject Guide under the subheading of Crustaceans – crabs, as for example:

Boyce, Katie. *Hector the hermit crab* ill. by author. Bloomsbury, 2003. ISBN 1-58234-800-6 Subj: Character traits – confidence. Crustaceans – crabs. Friendship. Self-concept.

In the case of joint authors, the second author is listed in alphabetical order, followed by the book title and the name of the primary author or main entry. The user can then locate the first-named author for complete bibliographic information. For example:

Stoker, Wayne. *I can be a welder* (Lillegard, Dee)

Bibliographic information for this title will be found in the Bibliographic Guide section under "Lillegard, Dee."

Titles for an author who is both a single author and a joint author are interfiled alphabetically. Where the author is not known, the entry is listed alphabetically by title with complete bibliographic information following the same format as given above.

Library of Congress conventions regarding the cataloged name of the author(s) have been followed in this edition. Thus, books published under the name "Aliki" are listed in alphabetical order under Aliki; a cross-reference with the name "Brandenberg, Aliki" refers the user to the name preferred.

TITLE INDEX: This section contains an alphabetical list of all titles in the book with authors in parentheses, followed by the page number of the full listing in the Bibliographic Guide, such as:

Albert's story (Long, Claudia), 1023

If a title has no known author, the name of the illustrator is given if available. When multiple versions of the same title are listed, the illustrator's name is given with the author's name (when known) in parentheses:

The night before Christmas, ill. by Michael Foreman (Moore, Clement C.), 1079
The night before Christmas, ill. by Gyo Fujikawa (Moore, Clement C.), 1079

ILLUSTRATOR INDEX: This section contains an alphabetical list of illustrators with titles and authors, followed by the page number of the full listing in the Bibliographic Guide. For example:

Glasser, Judy. *Albert's story* (Long, Claudia), 1023

Titles listed under an illustrator's name appear in alphabetical sequence. When the author is the same as the illustrator the author's name is not repeated.

Notes:

1. Hearne, Betsy Gould, and Deborah Stevenson. *Choosing Books for Children: A Commonsense Guide.* Urbana, Ill.: Univ. of Illinois Press, 1999.

2. Tepper, Clary A., and Kimberly Wright Cassidy. "Gender Differences in Emotional Language in Children's Picture Books." *Sex Roles* 40. 3–4 (Fall 1999): 265–80.

3. Lamme, Linda Leonard. "Immigrants as Portrayed in Children's Picture Books." *The Social Studies* 95:3 (May–June 2004), p. 123(7).

4. Leslea Newman. " 'Heather' and Her Critics" (Controversy over the Children's Book *Heather Has Two Mommies*). *The Horn Book Magazine* 73:2 (March–April 1997), p. 149(5).

5. "Children's Picture Books Tackle Abuse by Adults". *Yomiuri Shimbun/Daily Yomiuri*, August 16, 2001 p. YOSH18356835.

6. "Controversial Books for Children." In *Children's Books and Their Creators*, Anita Silvey, ed. Houghton Mifflin, 1995. pp. 162–5.

7. Sutton, Roger. "Why Is This a Picture Book? Inappropriate Themes for Children's Picture Books" (editorial). *The Horn Book Magazine* 72:4 (July–August 1996), p. 390(2).

8. Horning, Kathleen T. *From Cover to Cover: Evaluating and Reviewing Children's Books.* New York: HarperCollins, 1997.

9. Ammon, Bette D., and Gale W. Sherman. *Worth a Thousand Words: An Annotated Guide to Picture Books for Older Readers.* Libraries Unlimited, 1996.

10. *Publishers Weekly* (Nov. 24, 1992). p. 38.

11. Maughan, Shannon. *Publishers Weekly* (Jan. 29, 2001), pp. 30–32.

Acknowledgments

The authors wish to express their thanks for the assistance provided by many people in bringing this book together. Special thanks to our editor, Barbara Ittner at Libraries Unlimited. Special thanks also to Julia C. Miller, Catherine Barr, and Christine McNaull, who did much work on the database, sorting, and typesetting for both this and the previous edition.

We also wish to thank many publishers for providing review copies of their picture books, especially HarperCollins; Harcourt Brace; Firefly Books; Little, Brown; Crowell; Lothrop; Lippincott; Holiday House, Greenwillow and Morrow; and Hyperion Books.

Introduction
Genesis of the English-Language Picture Book

Picture books are a genre generally devoted to children's literature, usually presented in a book form consisting of 32 pages, in which pictures and words combine to tell a story — an art form in itself.[1]

Increasing numbers of children's books are published each year, each one touched in some way by those that preceded it. Consumer awareness is on the rise, books are being mass marketed, and the Internet is being used to market, promote, and even display children's picture books.[2] In the 1990s, 5,000 to 6,000 children's books were published each year in the United States, and perhaps even more in the United Kingdom.[3] Even a casual observer would note that a substantial percentage of these books were picture books.

Probably the roots of what we know as children's literature lie in the stories and folktales told and retold through the centuries in every civilization since human beings first learned to speak. These stories were narrated over and over as a sort of oral history, literature, and education.[4] But they were not intended, either primarily or exclusively, for children. It was only through the passing years, as the children who were part of any audience responded with interest and delight to these tales and as adults found less leisure time in an increasingly busy world, that the stories and folktales came to be regarded as belonging to the world of the child. These were repeated or retold often by traveling storytellers. Some tales were written down, printed, and spread throughout England and Europe. Early fairy tales, stories about miraculous encounters, transformations, and lessons, often written in Latin and other high languages, were not intended for children or for ordinary people, as most people were then illiterate.[5] In the nineteenth century, the brothers Grimm (Jacob and Wilhelm) invited storytellers to their home to narrate the folktales of Germany, and to collect them and refine them. They altered stories to make them more acceptable for children or for adults who were concerned about what children read and heard, creating a stylistic ideal for fairy tales "more proper and prudent for bourgeois audiences."[6]

Book art or book illustration began with manuscripts — handwritten on parchment or other materials, rolled or scrolled, and later loosely bound into books — that were illuminated or "decorated in lively, vigorous and versatile styles."[7] In time, these decorations — some realistic, some intricate, some imaginative — took on the technological advances of other art forms, notably stained glass, and color was introduced to illustrated texts.[8] The children's books that existed in the Middle Ages, before the invention of movable type, were rarely intended to amuse the reader. They were, instead, mostly instructional and moralizing. Monastic teachers, writing essentially for the children of wealthy families, usually wrote in Latin and "began the tradition of didacticism that was to dominate children's books for hundreds of years."[9] Children's books of that day frequently follow either the rhymed format or the question-and-answer format, both attributed to Aldhelm, abbot of Malmesbury.[10] An early encyclopedia, thought to be the work of Anselm (1033–1109), archbishop of Canterbury, addressed such subjects as "manners and customs, natural science, children's duties, morals, and religious precepts."[11] The books were intended for instruction and indoctrination in the principles of moral and religious belief and behavior,[12] an intent that persisted even after the invention of movable type. Indeed, "children were not born to live happy but to die holy, and true education lay in preparing the soul to meet its maker."[13] A contemporary general view is that children's books have changed "from didacticism to freedom," or maybe "from strictness to corruption." Modern writers, like those early writers, know their power to influence children, and also their responsibility to children.[14]

Perhaps the first printed book that was truly intended for children, other than elementary Latin grammar texts, was the French *Les Contenances de la Table*, on the courtesies and manners of dining.[15] Printed and illustrated children's books in Europe followed the invention of printing in the fifteenth century. Those first books were printed in lowercase letters, and "blank spaces were left on the page for initials and marginal decorations to be added in color by hand. In general, the effect was the same as in manuscript."[16] Some well-known and important artists of the time did the illustrations, using woodcuts, engravings, and lithographic processes.[17] This combination of pictures and printed text, still with the intent of teaching and incorporating the earlier but persistent dedication to moral and religious education, finally resulted in what is often assumed to be the first real children's picture book in 1657 — the *Orbis Pictus of John Amos Comenius*.[18] The simple idea of this Czech author was that a child could be taught most quickly by naming and showing the object at the same time, a seventeenth-century ABC! Noted for its many illustrations, the book contained the seeds of future children's publications, softening somewhat the earlier "harshness with which, in the unsympathetic age, the first steps of learning were always associated."[19]

In the English language, children's books followed a parallel pattern. William Caxton, England's first printer, was responsible for printing many books that, although intended for adults, were often adopted by children as their own. One, *Æsop's Fables* (about 1484), featured woodcut illustrations and is an early "milestone" in history of children's literature.[20] His stories, the first for English children in their own language, gave the lessons of "The Fox and the Grapes" and "The Tortoise and the Hare" to children of the fifteenth century and all who followed thereafter.

Later, American authors and books in English for American children began to appear. Like English publications before them, these books reflected a basic profile of moral and religious education. American John Cotton's *Spiritual Milk for Boston Babes* (1646) was not an especially easy text for the young minds that had to master its difficult Puritan lessons. Later came similar books such as *Pilgrim's Progress* by John Bunyan (1678), *The New England Primer* with its rhyming alphabet and illustrations (since children were understood to learn better from pictures[21] (1691), and *Divine and Moral Songs for Children* by Isaac Watts (1715).

In the early eighteenth century, a significant movement began in English children's books with the publication of *Robinson Crusoe* by Daniel Defoe (1715), a narrative that delighted children as well as adults. This innovation, utilizing children's books to carry more intricate messages, perhaps aimed at adults as well as older children, reflected a growing sophistication of society and perhaps some shifting of purely religious or moral bases toward political morality. An all-time favorite with young readers, *Gulliver's Travels* by Jonathan Swift, published in 1726, illustrates this dual thrust. This work, embellished with a wit and rather pointed sarcasm that is sure to escape the young, nonetheless delighted children with the inhabitants of mythical lands and has survived through the years. Perhaps the ultimate development of this trend is found in Lewis Carroll's *Alice's Adventures in Wonderland* (1865), which manages to be perfectly palatable and interesting to children, yet contains subtle lessons for adult society. Although based on earlier plays and vignettes that had been written only for the purpose of entertainment and use of imagination, *Alice*, and other books of the time, began to reflect a change in society's view of children and of reading materials suitable for children.

The English translation of *Tales of Mother Goose* by Charles Perrault in 1729 made moral lessons for young readers less didactic, but it was 1744 that "saw the real foundation of something today everywhere taken for granted — the production of books for children's enjoyment."[22] This book from a small bookstall in London was *A Little Pretty Pocket-Book*, "now famous as the first book for children published by John Newbery."[23] It may indeed be the first book recognizing children as people with intelligence and human needs, notably the need for humor and entertainment.[24] While John Newbery is often thought to have originated publishing of children's literature, his legacy is even more important as beginning "the serious *business* of publishing for children."[25]

For the next 20 years or so, Newbery published well-illustrated and inexpensive little books for young readers. Soon other books designed especially for children followed this trend. Pictures became an essential and integral component, somewhat downplaying the soul-saving educational harshness of earlier books and promoting amusement and enlightened education. Thomas Bewick's first book specifically intended for children, *A Pretty Book of Pictures for Little Masters and Misses, or Tommy Trip's*

History of Beasts and Birds, was published in 1779 and represented a major stride in the refinement of woodcuts used for book illustration. Bewick "developed better tools for this work, made effective use of the white line, and carried the woodcut to a high level of artistic achievement."[26] His efforts and those of his brother John had a more lasting effect on illustrators and illustrations for children's books. As a result of Bewick's contributions, "artists of established reputations began to sign their pictures for children's books."[27]

Some talented artists lovingly produced children's books with special artistic achievement, although their principal skills were directed toward adults. For example, William Blake, an artist and poet of considerable renown, published *Songs-of-Innocence* in 1789.[28] An engraver, he produced this "first great original picture book" using etched plates in which the garlands and scrolls of his own original design were lovingly engraved and hand-colored after printing.[29]

Some efforts were also great commercial successes. When John Harris published, in 1805, *The Comic Adventures of Old Mother Hubbard and her Dog,* by "S.C.M." [Sarah Catherine Martin], he sold some 10,000 copies in a few months. Within a year, twenty editions had been issued. Adults as well as children enjoyed the humor of Old Mother Hubbard.[30] The serious business of writing and illustrating children's books was now respectable and worthwhile, and those books had a feeling of class. But such loving dedication as that of William Blake and others did not long enjoy a singular place in publishing history. Commercialism soon entered the scene and, although some very dedicated people in America and England alike continued to develop books for children, some hackwork also appeared. "Publishers, realizing that children formed a new and somewhat undiscriminating market, were quick to take advantage of the fact. Having chosen a suitable title, and having available some spare woodcut blocks that might be sufficiently relevant for a juvenile book, a publisher would commission a story or series of tales to be woven around the illustrations. One of the results of this was that illustrations of different proportions might be used in the same story, while on other occasions it was clear that the pictures were by different hands. Sometimes the inclusion of a picture was obviously forced. A good example occurs in one of the editions of *Goody Two-Shoes,*" attributed to Oliver Goldsmith.[31]

Fortunately, under the guidance of innovative and bold publishers, carefully designed works, crafted with an eye toward the complete and final unit and with special consideration for the means of production, appeared in the field of children's picture books. Beautiful printing became the mark of publishers such as Edmund Evans, printer and artist in his own right, who with his special skill in color engraving published the works of Walter Crane, Randolph Caldecott, and Kate Greenaway. The work of the three great English picture-book artists of the nineteenth century represents the best to be found in picture books for children in any era; the strength of design and richness of color and detail of Walter Crane's pictures; the eloquence, humor, vitality, and movement of Randolph Caldecott's art; and the tenderness, dignity, and grace of the very personal interpretation of Kate Greenaway's enchanted land of childhood."[32]

These three were indeed great names in the history of children's picture books. The first nursery picture books of Walter Crane, an apprentice wood engraver, were *Sing a Song for Sixpence, The House That Jack Built, Dame Trot and Her Comical Cat,* and *The History of Cock Robin and Jenny Wren,* published by the firm of Warne in 1865 and 1866. Crane was one of the first of the modern illustrators who believed that text and illustrations should be in harmony, forming a complete unit. Randolph Caldecott, who began drawing at age six, could make animals come alive on a page. During his short life (1846–1886), he illustrated numerous books for children, producing fine examples of fun and good humor including *The Diverting History of John Gilpin* and *The Babes in the Wood.* His preeminence in the art of the children's picture book has been acknowledged by many more recent artists, and is certainly a seminal factor in the establishment of the English style as a standard by which to measure picture book art.[33]

Kate Greenaway's simple verses made an appropriate accompaniment to her lovely drawings. *Under the Window* was her first picture book, published by Routledge in 1878. Everywhere in her books are the flowers she so loved. She is probably best known for her *Almanacs,* published between 1883 and 1897. Like those of Crane, Caldecott, and Greenaway, the works of Britain's Beatrix Potter became well known to American children. Potter, a self-taught artist specializing in animals with charming characteristics, produced a number of tales for young children, the best known being *The Tale of Peter Rabbit* (1901), which presented the illustrations as an integral part of the story and marked a pivotal point in the development of the modern picture book in Europe. The excellence of the growing children's book field in England eclipsed the technologically inferior American product, virtually driving American efforts from the marketplace until nearly fifteen years after World War I.[34]

Meanwhile, the books of such English artists as L. Leslie Brooke, Arthur Rackham, Edmund Dulac, Charles Folkard, and others continued the tradition of excellence through the first three decades of the twentieth century. Despite the superior English publications, "a self-conscious and systematic concern for children and the books they read had been growing in the United States."[35] Children's libraries and children's librarians appeared around the turn of the century. In 1916, the Bookshop for Boys and Girls was founded in Boston.[36] In 1924, the Bookshop published *The Horn Book Magazine*, "the first journal in the world to be devoted to the critical appraisal of children's books."[37] Another publication, *Junior Libraries*, made its appearance in 1954; this periodical later became *School Library Journal*, published by R. R. Bowker. In this area, the Americans were ten years ahead of Europeans.

Publishers and editors were becoming more and more oriented toward children's literature. In 1919, Macmillan established a Children's Book Department separate from its adult publishing line; other publishing houses began to do the same. Children's Book Week was instituted, an idea that started with Franklin K. Mathews and was supported by Frederic G. Melcher. A landmark in children's book publishing was established in the United States in 1922 when Melcher, then chief editor of *Publishers Weekly*, proposed at the 1921 American Library Association meeting that a medal be awarded each year for the year's most distinguished contribution to American literature for children written by an American citizen or resident and published in the United States. Named for John Newbery, the medal was first awarded to Hendrik Willem von Loon for *The Story of Mankind*.

Melcher, who was always aware of the significance of books in the lives of children, later proposed the establishment of a similar award for picture books, named in honor of Randolph Caldecott, whose pictures still delight today's children. Since 1938, the Caldecott Medal has been awarded annually by an awards committee of the American Library Association's Association for Library Service to Children to the illustrator of the most distinguished American picture book for children published in the United States during the preceding year. Again, the recipient must reside in or be a citizen of the United States.

The end of the 1920s marked the newly emerging prominence of the modern children's picture book in America. Mainly imported from Europe until that time, children's picture books now began to be published in America. William Nicholson's *Clever Bill* (1927) was followed the next year by one of the most successful picture books of all time, *Millions of Cats* by Wanda Gág. The near perfect marriage of the rhythmic prose and flowing movement of her dramatic black-and-white illustrations presents a simple, direct story with a folk flavor. This title is still included in the repertoire of today's storytellers and continues to be taken from the shelves by young readers; it ushered in the "Golden Thirties" of children's book publishing.[38]

By 1930, many publishers had set up separate editorial departments expressly for the purpose of publishing children's materials. The White House Conference on Child Health and Protection was held that year to study the plight of the child.[39] Improved technologies accelerated and economized book production. The stage was set for the modern picture book with its profuse illustrations. Until this time, there were only a few great children's books, illustrated with pictures that were largely an extension of the text. "Yet in a very few years, in respect to the books for the younger children, the artist has attained a place of equal importance with the writer."[40]

The period between World War I and World War II saw many authors and illustrators collaborate on picture books. Their talents and varied backgrounds contributed immensely to the changes in the picture book in America, which truly came into its own in this period of lower production costs. The "Golden Thirties" and the 1940s produced a spectacular number and variety of profusely illustrated books for young children.[41] Many of the new authors and illustrators then beginning their careers in this developing field have continued to keep their places in the hearts of children: such familiar names as Marjorie Flack, Maud and Miska Petersham, Ingri and Edgar d'Aulaire, Ludwig Bemelmans, Theodor Geisel (Dr. Seuss), Marcia Brown, Feodor Rojankovsky, James Daugherty, Robert Lawson, Marguerite de Angeli, Virginia Lee Burton, Robert McCloskey, and many, many more.

The war years affected the progress of children's picture books, with shortages of materials, poor quality paper, narrow margins, inferior bindings, and less color and illustration. However, the postwar years began a boom in children's publishing, adding to the list of talented authors and illustrators such names as Maurice Sendak, Brian Wildsmith, Trina Schart Hyman, Paul Galdone, Leo Politi, Ezra Jack Keats, Gyo Fujikawa, Arnold Lobel, and so many more.

Through the years, many factors have contributed to the growth, even explosion, of children's picture books: society's changing attitudes toward the child; the development of children's libraries, awards, councils, and studies; increasing interest in children's reading on the part of publishers, educators, and literary critics; changing technologies; and the development of American artists and authors. More recently, new directions in publishing — challenging the library as the principal outlet for children's books, seeking consumer markets, and applying modern marketing strategies — have affected the nature of the children's picture book.[42] Children's books, including picture books, have found a natural marketing presence on the Internet; the Web features publishers' sites, promotions, information on individual books, and even sample pages.[43] Today the picture book is a part of growing up, a teaching tool, an entertainment medium, a memory to treasure. Perhaps only imagination and the talent of the artist and author can define its limits.

Emphasizing the value of good materials and the quality of art as an essential standard of good picture books, some have recognized the late twentieth century as the "day of the artist" in children's books.[44] Perhaps this heyday will continue well into the twenty-first century. Among notable features are the graphic trends in children's picture books, including the treatment of black as an actual color, the spatial relations of objects, and the use of technologies that lend new life to collages and other media.[45] Some have noted the coming of age of children's books as an art form.[46] Certainly, some of the modern trends give one pause. Spectacular color, shading, and texture are all very evident today, along with broader subject perspectives, picture books that are aimed more at older children (and adults) than at the traditional audience, and a generally higher level of sophistication. More mechanical books (pop-ups) reminiscent of the Victorian age are reappearing, as are gimmicks, and the trading on the familiarity of existing themes.[47]

Many old favorites are being reissued, often showcasing a new illustrator's talents. Many collections or compendiums of an author's or illustrator's works are being published, often in large formats with 60 to 120 or more pages, straining the definition and concept of "picture book." At times, these appear in what can only be called a large "coffee-table" format; impressive but hardly "child-friendly." Other trends include the large number of "board" books and other unusual formats, and the development of themes that emphasize reality, such as everyday situations, misbehavior or mischievous behavior, and multicultural or multi-ethnic experiences.

Professionalism, curiosity on all subjects, and freedom of expression have brought the children's picture book into the twenty-first century with a bewildering array of materials from which to choose. Imaginary animals of the past and future line the shelves with the cats, dogs, horses, and dolphins of the modern day. Fantasy lands compete with tales of spaceships and astronauts; dreams of the future can be found alongside the realities of the past; picture books of all kinds for all kinds of children — and adults — to enjoy!

For the teacher, librarian, or parent who wishes to open this fantastic world of color and imagination for the child, some tool is necessary that will provide access to the great number of possibilities for enjoyment in the picture book field today. *A to Zoo: Subject Access to Children's Picture Books* is designed with just this purpose in mind. For those interested in exploring more deeply the world of children's publishing and the children's picture book, a list of suggested titles for further reading begins on page xx.

Notes

1. Latrobe, Kathy, Carolyn Brodie, and Maureen White. *The Children's Literature Dictionary: Definitions, Desources, and Learning Activities.* New York: Neal-Schuman, 2002, p. 129.

2. Rosen, Judith. "Children's Books Make Strong Internet Showing." *Publishers Weekly*, 244:2 (Jan. 13, 1997): 32.

3. Watkins, Tony, and Zena Sutherland. "Contemporary Children's Literature," in *Children's Literature: An Illustrated History*, ed. by Peter Hunt. Oxford: Oxford Univ. Pr., 1995. p. 290.

4. Hewins, Caroline M. "The History of Children's Books (1988)," in *Children and Literature: Views and Reviews*, comp.

by Virginia Haviland. New York: Lothrop, 1974, p. 30.

5. Zipes, Jack, ed. "Introduction," in *The Oxford Companion to Fairy Tales.* Oxford: Oxford Univ. Pr., 2002, p. xxi.

6. Zipes, Jack, tr. "Once There Were Two Brothers Named Grimm," in *The Complete Fairy Tales of the Brothers Grimm.*" New York: Bantam, 1992, pp. xvii–xxxi.

7. MacCann, Donnarae, and Olga Richard. *The Child's First Books: A Critical Study of Pictures and Texts.* New York: Wilson, 1973, p. 11.

8. Ibid.

9. Sutherland, Zena. *Children and Books*, 9th ed. New York: Longman, 1997, p. 42.

10. Ibid.

11. Ibid.

12. Ibid.

13. Hürlimann, Bettina. *Three Centuries of Children's Books in Europe*, tr. and ed. by Brian Alderson. London: Oxford Univ. Press, 1967, p. xii.

14. Hunt, Peter, ed. "Editor's Preface," in *Children's Literature: An Illustrated History*, Oxford: Oxford Univ. Pr., 1995. p. xii.

15. Sutherland, op. cit., p. 42.

16. MacCann and Richard, op. cit., p. 11.

17. Ibid.

18. Hürlimann, op. cit., pp. 127–129.

19. Freeman, Ruth Sunderlin. *Children's Picture Books, Yesterday and Today.* Watkins Glen, N.Y.: Century House, 1967, p. 12.

20. Sutherland, op. cit., pp. 42, 122, 170.

21. MacLeod, Anne Scott. "Children's Literature in America: From the Puritan Beginnings to 1870," in *Children's Literature: An Illustrated History*, ed. by Peter Hunt. Oxford: Oxford Univ. Pr., 1995, p. 103.

22. Newbery, John. *Little Pretty Pocket-Book: A Facsimile.* London: Oxford Univ. Press, 1966.

23. Ibid., p. 3.

24. Ibid., p. 2.

25. Kinnell, Margaret. "Publishing for Children," in *Children's

Literature: An Illustrated History*, ed. by Peter Hunt. Oxford: Oxford Univ. Pr., 1995, p. 34.

26. Sutherland, op. cit., p. 123.

27. Ibid.

28. Ibid., p. 138.

29. Alderson, Brian. *Sing a Song for Sixpence: The English Picture Book Tradition and Randolph Caldecott.* Cambridge, England: Cambridge Univ. Press, 1986, p. 46.

30. Ibid., pp. 49–51.

31. Whalley, Joyce Irene. *Cobwebs to Catch Flies: Illustrated Books for the Nursery and Schoolroom 1700–1900.* Berkeley: Univ. of California Press, 1975, p. 7.

32. Alderson, op. cit., p. 8.

33. Viguers, Ruth Hill. "Introduction," in Kate Greenaway, *The Kate Greenaway Treasury.* World, 1967, p. 13.

34. Bader, Barara. *American Picturebooks from Noah's Ark to the Beast Within.* New York: Macmillan, 1976.

35. Viguers, loc. cit., p. 39.

36. Ibid.

37. Ibid.

38. Sutherland, op. cit., p. 127.

39. Wilkin, Binnie Tate. *Survival Themes in Fiction for Children and Young People.* Metuchen, N.J.: Scarecrow, 1978, p. 21.

40. Meigs, Cornelia, et al. *A Critical History of Children's Literature*, rev. ed. New York: Macmillan, 1969, p. 649.

41. Ibid., 402.

42. Elleman, Barbara. "Current Trends in Literature for Children," *Library Trends* 35: 3 (Winter 1987): 32.

43. Rosen, Judith, "Children's Books Make Strong Internet Showing," *Publishers Weekly* (Jan. 13, 1997): 32.

44. Sutherland, op. cit., p. 147.

45. Hale, Robert D. "Musings," Horn Book Magazine 70:3 (May/June 1994): 356.

46. Hearne, Betsy Gould. *Choosing Books for Children: A Commonsense Guide.* Urbana: Univ., of Illinois Press, 1999, p. 29.

47. Elleman, loc. cit., pp. 415, 421.

Further Reading

Alderson, Brian. *The Brothers Grimm: Popular Folk Tales.* London: Victor Gollancz Ltd., 1978.

———. *Looking at Picture Books 1973.* Chicago: Children's Book Council, 1974.

*———. *Sing a Song for Sixpence: The English Picture Book Tradition and Randolph Caldecott.* Cambridge, England: Cambridge Univ. Press, 1986.

Ammon, Bette D., and Gale W. Sherman. *Worth a Thousand Words: An Annotated Guide to Picture Books for Older Readers.* Englewood, Colo.: Libraries Unlimited, 1996.

Andersson, Theodore. *A Guide to Family Reading in Two Lan-

guages: The Preschool Years.* Wheaton, Md.: National Clearinghouse for Bilingual Education, 1981.

Arbuthnot, May Hill, et al. *The Arbuthnot Anthology of Children's Literature*, 4th ed. Glenview, Ill.: Scott, Foresman, 1976.

*Bader, Barbara. *American Picturebooks from Noah's Ark to the Beast Within.* New York: Macmillan, 1976.

Barchilon, Jacques, and Henry Pettit. *The Authentic Mother Goose Fairy Tales and Nursery Rhymes.* Athens, Ohio: Swallow Press, 1960.

Barr, John. *Illustrated Children's Books.* London; Dover, N.H.: British Library, 1986.

Barry, Florence V. *A Century of Children's Books.* London: Methuen, 1922.

Bauer, Caroline Feller. *Read for the Fun of It: Active Programming with Books for Children.* New York: Wilson, 1992.

Beyond Words: Picture Books for Older Readers and Writers, ed. by Susan Benedict and Lenore Carlisle. Portsmouth, N.H.: Heinemann, 1992.

Bingham, Jane, ed. *Writers for Children.* New York: Scribner's, 1987.

*———, and Grayce Scholt, eds. *Fifteen Centuries of Children's Literature: An Annotated Chronology of British and American Works in Historical Context.* Westport, Conn.: Greenwood Press, 1980.

Bland, David. *A History of Book Illustration,* 2nd ed. London: Faber & Faber, 1969.

———. *The Illustration of Books.* London: Faber & Faber, 1962.

Bodger, Joan. *How the Heather Looks.* New York: Viking, 1965.

Bottigheimer, Ruth B. *Grimms' Bad Girls and Bold Boys.* New Haven, Conn.: Yale Univ. Press, 1987.

Braun, Saul. "Sendak Raises the Shade on Childhood." *New York Times Magazine* (June 7, 1970): 34+.

Bush, Margaret A. *Children's Literature: A Guide to Reference Services and Monographs.* Englewood, Colo.: Libraries Unlimited, 1988.

Butler, Dorothy. *Babies Need Books.* New York: Atheneum, 1980.

Butler, Francelia, and Richard W. Robert, eds. *Reflections on Literature for Children.* Hamden, Conn.: Shoe String Press, 1984.

———. *Triumphs of the Spirit in Children's Literature.* Hamden, Conn.: Library Professional Publications, 1986.

Carroll, Frances Laverne, and Mary Meacham. *Exciting, Funny, Scary, Short, Different, and Sad Books Kids Like About Animals, Science, Sports, Families, Songs, and Other Things.* Chicago: American Library Association, 1984.

Children's Book Illustration and Design, ed. by Julie Cummins. New York: Library of Applied Design, PBC International, 1991.

Cianciola, Patricia. *Illustrations in Children's Books,* 2nd ed. Dubuque, Iowa: William C. Brown, 1976.

———. *Picture Books for Children,* 3rd ed. Chicago: American Library Association, 1990.

Clay, Marie. "Introduction." In *Cushla and Her Books,* by Dorothy Butler, Boston: Horn Book, 1980.

———, and Dorothy Butler. *Reading Begins at Home,* 2nd ed. Exeter, N.H.: Heinemann, 1987.

Cohn, Amy L., Compiler. *From Sea to Shining Sea: A Treasury of American Folklore and Folk Songs.* New York: Scholastic. 1993.

Comenius, John Amos. *The Orbis Pictus of John Amos Comenius.* Detroit: Singing Tree, 1968.

Crouch, Marcus. *Treasure Seekers and Borrowers: Children's Books in Britain 1900–1960.* London: Library Association, 1962.

Dahl, Svend. *Dahl's History of the Book,* 3rd English ed. Ed. by Bill Katz. Metuchen, N.J.: Scarecrow Press, 1995.

Dalby, Richard. *The Golden Age of Children's Book Illustrations.* London: M. O'Mara Books, 1991.

Daniel, Eloise. *A Treasury of Books for Family Enjoyment: Books for Children from Infancy to Grade 2.* Pontiac, Mich.: Blue Engine Press, 1983.

Darling, Richard L. *The Rise of Children's Book Reviewing in America, 1865–1881.* New York: R. R. Bowker, 1968.

Darrell, Margery, ed. *Once Upon a Time: The Fairy-Tale World of Arthur Rackham.* New York: Viking, 1972.

*Darton, F. J. H. *Children's Books in England: Five Centuries of Social Life,* 3rd ed. Ed. by Brian Alderson. New York: Cambridge Univ. Press, 1982.

Datlow, Ellen, and Terri Windling, eds. *Snow White and Blood Red.* New York: Morrow, 1993.

Day, Alexandra; Cooper Edens; and Welleran Poltarnees. *Children from the Golden Age, 1880–1930.* San Diego: Green Tiger Press, 1987.

*Delamar, Gloria T. *Mother Goose: From Nursery to Literature.* Jefferson, N.C.: McFarland, 1987.

Demers, Patricia, ed. *A Garland from the Golden Age: Children's Literature from 1850–1900.* New York: Oxford Univ. Press, 1984.

———, and Gordon Moyles, eds. *From Instruction to Delight: An Anthology of Children's Literature to 1850.* New York: Oxford Univ. Press, 1982.

Duvoisin, Roger. "Children's Book Illustration: The Pleasure and Problems." *Top of the News* 22 (Nov. 1965): 30.

Earle, Alice Morse. *Child Life in Colonial Days.* New York: Macmillan, 1899.

Eckenstein, Lina. *Comparative Studies in Nursery Rhymes.* London: Duckworth, 1906; Detroit: Singing Tree, 1968.

Egoff, Sheila A.; G. T. Stubbs; and L. F. Ashley, eds. *Only Connect: Readings on Children's Literature,* 2nd ed. New York: Oxford Univ. Press, 1980.

———. *Worlds Within: Children's Fantasy from the Middle Ages to Today.* Chicago: American Library Association, 1988.

Ellis, Alec. *A History of Children's Reading and Literature.* Elmsford, N.Y.: Pergamon Press, 1968.

Estes, Glen, ed. *American Writers for Children Since 1960.* Detroit: Gale, 1987.

Ettlinger, John R. T., and Diana L. Spirt. *Choosing Books for Young People,* Vol. 2. Phoenix: Oryx, 1987.

Eyre, Frank. *British Children's Books in the Twentieth Century.* New York: Dutton, 1973.

———. *Twentieth Century Children's Books.* Cambridge, Mass.: Robert Bentley, 1953.

Fiction, Folklore, Fantasy and Poetry for Children, 1976–1985, 2 vols. New York: R. R. Bowker, 1986.

Field, Louise F. *The Child and His Book: Some Account of the History and Progress of Children's Literature in England.* Detroit: Singing Tree, 1968.

Fisher, Margery Turner. *Intent upon Reading: A Critical Appraisal of Modern Fiction for Children.* Leicester, England: Brockhampton Press, 1961.

———. *Who's Who in Children's Books: A Treasury of the Familiar Characters of Childhood.* New York: Holt, 1975.

Fox, Geoffrey Percival, et al., eds. *Writers, Critics, and Children: Articles from Children's Literature in Education.* New York: Agathon Press, 1976.

Freeman, Judy. *More Books Kids Will Sit Still For.* New Providence, N.J.: R. R. Bowker, 1995.

*Freeman, Ruth Sunderlin, *Children's Picture Books, Yesterday and Today.* Watkins Glen, N.Y.: Century House, 1967.

Galinsky, Ellen, and Judy David. *The Preschool Years: Family Strategies That Work—From Experts and Parents.* New York: Times Books, 1988.

*Gillespie, John T. *Best Books for Children: Preschool Through the Middle Grades,* 7th ed. Westport, Conn.: Bowker-Greenwood 2001.

Gillespie, Margaret C., and John W. Connor. *Creative Growth Through Literature for Children and Adolescents*. Columbus, Ohio: Merrill, 1975.

Gottlieb, Gerald. *Early Children's Books and Their Illustration*. Boston: Godine, 1975.

Green, Percy B. *A History of Nursery Rhymes*. Detroit: Singing Tree, 1968.

Green, Roger Lancelyn. *Tellers of Tales: British Authors of Children's Books from 1800 to 1964*. New York: Watts, 1965.

*Greenaway, Kate. *The Kate Greenaway Treasury*. Cleveland: World, 1967.

Halsey, Rosalie V. *Forgotten Books of the American Nursery*. Detroit: Singing Tree, 1969.

Harrison, Barbara G., and Gregory Maguire. *Innocence and Experience: Essays and Conversations on Children's Literature*. New York: Lothrop, 1987.

*Haviland, Virginia, comp. *Children and Literature: Views and Reviews*. New York: Lothrop, 1974.

———. *Children's Literature: A Guide to Reference Sources*. Washington, D.C.: Library of Congress, 1966; first supplement, 1972.

*Hearne, Betsy Gould, with Deborah Stevenson. *Choosing Books for Children: A Commonsense Guide*. Urbana, Ill.: Univ. of Illinois Press, 1999.

Hendrickson, Linnea. *Children's Literature: A Guide to the Criticism*. Boston: G. K. Hall, 1987.

Horning, Kathleen T. *From Cover to Cover: Evaluating and Reviewing Children's Books*. New York: HarperCollins Children's Books, 1997.

Huber, Miriam Blanton. *Story and Verse for Children*, 3rd ed. New York: Macmillan, 1965.

*Hürlimann, Bettina. *Three Centuries of Children's Books in Europe*. Ed. and tr. by Brian Alderson. London: Oxford Univ. Press, 1967; Cleveland: World, 1968.

Inglis, Fred. *The Promise of Happiness*. New York: Cambridge Univ. Press, 1981.

James, Philip. *Children's Books of Yesterday*. Ed. by C. Geoffrey Holme. London and New York: Studio, 1933; Detroit: Gale, 1976.

Jan, Isabelle. *On Children's Literature*. Ed. by Catherine Storr. New York: Schocken Books, 1974.

Katz, Bill, ed. *A History of Book Illustration: 29 Points of View*. Metuchen, N.J.: Scarecrow Press, 1994.

Katz, Lillian G., ed. *Current Topics in Early Childhood Education*, Vol. 6. Norwood, N.J.: Ablex, 1986.

Kiefer, Monica. *American Children Through Their Books, 1700–1835*. Philadelphia: Univ. of Pennsylvania Press, 1948, 1970.

Klemin, Diana. *The Art of Art for Children's Books*. Greenwich, Conn.: Murton Press, 1966, 1982.

———. *The Illustrated Book*. Greenwich, Conn.: Murton Press, 1970, 1983.

Lanes, Selma G. "The Art of Maurice Sendak: A Diversity of Influences Inform an Art for Children," *Artforum* IX (May 1971): 70–73.

Leif, Irving P. *Children's Literature: A Historical and Contemporary Bibliography*. Troy, N.Y.: Whitston, 1977.

Lewis, John. *The Twentieth Century Book: Its Illustration and Design*. New York: Van Nostrand Reinhold, 1967.

Linder, Leslie L. *The Art of Beatrix Potter*, 6th rev. ed. London: Warne, 1972.

*Lipson, Eden Ross. *The New York Times Parent's Guide to the Best Books for Children*, 3rd ed. Three Rivers Press, 2000.

Lukens, Rebecca J. *A Critical Handbook of Children's Literature*, 2nd ed. Glenview, Ill.: Scott, Foresman, 1981.

Lynn, Ruth Nadelman. *Fantasy Literature for Children and Young Adults: An Annotated Bibliography*, 5th ed. Westport, Conn.: Libraries Unlimited, 2005.

Lystad, Mary. *From Dr. Mather to Dr. Seuss: Two Hundred Years of American Books for Children*. Cambridge, Mass.: Schenkman, 1980.

*MacCann, Donnarae, and Olga Richard. *The Child's First Books*. New York: Wilson, 1973.

MacCann, Donnarae, and Gloria Woodard, eds. *The Black American in Books for Children: Readings in Racism*, 2nd ed. Metuchen, N.J.: Scarecrow Press, 1985.

MacDonald, Margaret Read. *The Storyteller's Sourcebook: A Subject, Title, and Motif Index to Folklore Collections for Children*. Detroit: Neal-Schuman Publishers, Inc., in association with Gale Research Co., 1982.

MacDonald, Ruth K. *Dr. Seuss*. Boston: Twayne, 1988.

*McTigue, Bernard, ed. *A Child's Garden of Delights: Pictures, Poems, and Stories for Children from the Collection of the New York Public Library*. New York: Abrams, 1987.

Mahoney, Ellen, and Leah Wilcox. *Ready, Set, Read: Best Books to Prepare Preschoolers*. Metuchen, N.J.: Scarecrow, 1985.

Mahony, Bertha E.; Latimer, Louise P.; and Folmsbee, Beulah, comps. *Illustrators of Children's Books, 1744–1945*. Boston: Horn Book, 1947.

Marantz, Sylvia S. *Artists of the Page: Interviews with Children's Book Illustrators*. Jefferson, N.C.: McFarland, 1992.

———. *Picture Books for Looking and Learning: Awakening Visual Perceptions Through the Art of Children's Books*. Phoenix, Ariz.: Oryx Press, 1992.

——— and Kenneth A. Marantz. *The Art of Children's Picture Books*. New York: Garland Pub., 1995.

Martin, Douglas. *The Telling Line: Essays on Fifteen Contemporary Book Illustrators*. New York: Delacorte Press, 1990.

Maughan, Shannon. "A Revolution Waiting to Happen?" *Publishers Weekly* 248:5 (Jan. 29, 2001): 30+.

Meacham, Mary. *Information Sources in Children's Literature*. New York: Macmillan, 1953; rev. ed., 1969.

Monson, Diane L., ed. *Adventuring with Books: A Booklist for Pre-K–Grade 6*. Urbana, Ill.: NCTE, 1985.

Moore, Anne Carroll. *My Roads to Childhood*. Boston: Horn Book, 1961.

Moransee, Jesse R., ed. *Children's Prize Books*. Ridgewood, N.J.: K. G. Saur, 1983.

Muir, Percy. *English Children's Books, 1600–1900*. New York: Praeger, 1969.

*Newbery, John. *A Little Pretty Pocket-Book: A Facsimile*. London: Oxford Univ. Press, 1966.

*Nodelman, Perry. *Words About Pictures: The Narrative Art of Children's Picture Books*. Athens, Ga.: Univ. of Georgia Press, 1989.

Norby, Shirley, and Gregory Ryan. *Famous Illustrators of Children's Literature*. Minneapolis, Minn.: T.S. Denison, 1992.

Opie, Iona, and Peter Opie. *A Family Book of Nursery Rhymes*. New York: Oxford Univ. Press, 1964.

———. *A Nursery Companion*. New York: Oxford Univ. Press, 1964.

———. *The Oxford Dictionary of Nursery Rhymes.* New York: Oxford Univ. Press, 1951.

Oppenheim, Joanne F., et al. *Choosing Books for Kids.* New York: Ballantine, 1986.

The Original Mother Goose's Melody, As First Issued by John Newbery, of London, about A.D. 1760. Reproduced in facsimile from the edition as reprinted by Isaiah Thomas of Worcester, Mass., about A.D. 1785, with introductory notes by William H. Whitmore. Detroit: Singing Tree, 1969.

Paterson, Katherine. *The Spying Heart: More Thoughts on Reading and Writing Books for Children.* New York: Dutton, 1988.

*Pellowski, Anne. *The Family Storytelling Handbook.* New York: Watson-Guptill, 1963.

Potter, Beatrix. *Beatrix Potter: The V and A Collection.* London: Warne, 1986.

Prentice, Jeffrey, and Bettina Bird. *Dromkeen: A Journey into Children's Literature.* New York: Henry Holt, 1988.

Preschool Services and Parent Education Committee, Association for Library Service to Children. *Opening Doors for Preschool Children and Their Parents,* 2nd ed. Chicago: American Library Association, 1981.

Richard, Olga. "The Visual Language of the Picture Book." *Wilson Library Bulletin* (Dec. 1969).

Roback, Diane, ed. "Arnold Lobel's Three Years with Mother Goose." *Publishers Weekly* 230: 8 (Aug. 22, 1986).

Roberts, Ellen E. M. *The Children's Picture Book.* Cincinnati, Ohio: Writer's Digest, 1981, 1987.

Roberts, Patricia L. *Counting Books Are More Than Numbers: An Annotated Action Bibliography.* Hamden, Conn.: Library Professional Publications, 1990.

Rosenbach, Abraham S. W. *Early American Children's Books by A. S. W. Rosenbach, with Bibliographical Descriptions of the Books in His Private Collection.* Foreword by A. Edward Newton. Portland, Maine: Southworth Press, 1933.

Russell, David L. *Literature for Children: A Short Introduction,* 3rd ed. White Plains, N.Y.: Longman, 1997.

Sadker, Myra, and David Miller Sadker. *Now Upon a Time: A Contemporary View of Children's Literature.* New York: Harper, 1977.

Salway, Lance, ed. *A Peculiar Gift.* New York: Penguin, 1976.

San Diego Museum of Art Staff, eds. *Dr. Seuss from Then to Now.* New York: Random House, 1987.

Sendak, Maurice. *Caldecott & Co.: Notes on Books and Pictures.* New York: Farrar, Straus & Giroux, 1988.

———. "Mother Goose's Garnishings." *Book Week* Fall Children's Issue (Oct. 31, 1965): 5, 38–40; also printed in Haviland, *Children and Literature,* pp. 188–195.

Senick, Gerald J., ed. *Children's Literature Review,* Vols. 12, 13. Detroit: Gale, 1987.

Smith, Dora V. *Fifty Years of Children's Books, 1910–1960.* Urbana, Ill.: NCTE, 1963.

*Smith, Elva S. *The History of Children's Literature: A Syllabus with Selected Bibliographies,* rev. and enlarged by Margaret Hodges and Susan Steinfirst. Chicago: American Library Association, 1980.

Stott, Jon. *Children's Literature from A to Z: A Guide for Parents and Teachers.* New York: McGraw-Hill, 1984.

Sutherland, Zena, ed. *The Best in Children's Books: The University of Chicago Guide to Children's Literature, 1979–1984.* Chicago: Univ. of Chicago Press, 1986.

*———. *Children and Books,* 9th ed. New York: Longman, 1997.

Targ, William, ed. *Bibliophile in the Nursery.* Metuchen, N.J.: Scarecrow, 1969.

Taylor, Ina. *The Art of Kate Greenaway: A Nostalgic Portrait of Childhood.* Gretna, La.: Pelican Pub. Co., 1991.

*Taylor, Judy. *Beatrix Potter: Artist, Storyteller and Countrywoman.* London: Warne, 1986.

——— et al. *Beatrix Potter, 1866–1943: The Artist and Her World.* London: Warne, 1987.

Thomas, Katherine Elwes. *The Real Personages of Mother Goose.* New York: Lothrop, 1930.

Thomson, Susan Ruth, ed. *Kate Greenaway: A Catalogue of the Kate Greenaway Collection, Rare Book Room, Detroit Public Library.* Detroit: Wayne State Univ. Press, 1977.

Thwaite, Mary. *From Primer to Pleasure in Reading,* 2nd ed. London: The Library Association, 1972.

Townsend, John Rowe. *Written for Children: An Outline of English-Language Children's Literature,* 3rd rev. ed. New York: Harper, 1988.

Very Best of Children's Book Illustration, comp. by the Society of Illustrators. Cincinnati, Ohio: North Light Books, 1993.

Viguers, Ruth Hill; Marcia Dalphin; and Bertha Mahony Miller, comps. *Illustrators of Children's Books, 1946–1956.* Boston: Horn Book, 1958.

Vries, Leonard de. *A Treasury of Illustrated Children's Books: Early Nineteenth-Century Classics from the Osborne Collection.* New York: Abbeville Press, 1989.

Warner, Marina. *From the Beast to the Blonde: On Fairy Tales and Their Tellers.* New York: Farrar, Straus and Giroux, 1995.

Weitenkampf, Frank. *The Illustrated Book.* Cambridge, Mass.: Harvard Univ. Press, 1938.

Welch, D'Alte A. *A Bibliography of American Children's Books Printed Prior to 1821.* Worcester, Mass.: American Antiquarian Society, 1972.

*Whalley, Joyce Irene. *Cobwebs to Catch Flies: Illustrated Books for the Nursery and Schoolroom 1700–1900.* Berkeley, Calif.: Univ. of California Press, 1975.

——— and Tessa Rose Chester. *The Bright Stream: A History of Children's Book Illustration.* Boston: D. R. Godine, 1994, c1988.

White, Burton L. *Educating the Infant and Toddler.* Lexington, Mass.: Lexington Bks., 1987.

White, Dorothy M. Neal. *Books Before Five.* New York: Oxford Univ. Press, 1954.

White, Mary Lou. *Adventuring with Books: A Booklist for Pre-K–Grade 6.* Chicago: American Library Association, 1981.

———. *Children's Literature: Criticism and Response.* Columbus, Ohio: Merrill, 1976.

*Wilkin, Binnie Tate. *Survival Themes in Fiction for Children and Young People.* Metuchen, N.J.: Scarecrow, 1978.

Williams, Helen E. *Books by African-American Authors and Illustrators for Children and Young Adults.* Chicago: American Library Association, 1991.

Wilson, Elizabeth L. *Books Children Love.* Westchester, Ill.: Good News, 1987.

Winkel, Lois, and Sue Kimmel. *Mother Goose Comes First: An Annotated Guide to the Best Books and Recordings for Your Preschool Child.* New York: Henry Holt, 1990.

*Zipes, Jack, tr. *The Complete Fairy Tales of the Brothers Grimm.* New York: Bantam, 1992.

Subject Headings

Main headings, subheadings, and cross-references are arranged alphabetically and provide a quick reference to the subjects used in the Subject Guide section, where author and title names appear under appropriate headings.

Aardvarks *see* Animals – aardvarks
ABC books
Abnaki Indians *see* Indians of North America – Abnaki
Aborigines, Australian *see* Australian aborigines
Abused children *see* Child abuse
Acadians *see* Ethnic groups in the U.S. – Cajun
Accidents
Accordion books *see* Format, unusual
Accordions *see* Musical instruments – accordions
Accountants *see* Careers – accountants
Acrobats *see* Careers – acrobats
Activities
Activities – babysitting
Activities – baking, cooking
Activities – ballooning
Activities – bargaining *see* Activities – trading
Activities – bartering *see* Activities – trading
Activities – bathing
Activities – cooking *see* Activities – baking, cooking
Activities – dancing
Activities – digging
Activities – drawing
Activities – driving
Activities – eating *see* Food
Activities – flying
Activities – gardening *see* Gardens, gardening
Activities – jumping
Activities – kissing *see* Kissing
Activities – knitting
Activities – making things
Activities – painting
Activities – photographing
Activities – picnicking
Activities – playing
Activities – quilting
Activities – reading *see* Books, reading
Activities – running
Activities – sewing
Activities – shopping *see* Shopping
Activities – singing
Activities – storytelling
Activities – swapping *see* Activities – trading
Activities – swimming *see* Sports – swimming
Activities – swinging
Activities – talking
Activities – trading
Activities – traveling
Activities – vacationing
Activities – walking

Activities – weaving
Activities – whistling
Activities – wishing
Activities – wood carving
Activities – working
Activities – writing
Actors *see* Careers – actors
ADD *see* Handicaps – ADD
Adoption
Aerialists *see* Careers – aerialists
Afghanistan *see* Foreign lands – Afghanistan
Africa *see* Foreign lands – Africa
African Americans *see* Ethnic groups in the U.S. – African Americans
Aged *see* Old age
AIDS *see* Illness – AIDS
Airplane pilots *see* Careers – airplane pilots
Airplanes, airports
Airports *see* Airplanes, airports
Alaska
Albatrosses *see* Birds – albatrosses
Alcoholism *see* Illness – alcoholism
Aleuts *see* Indians of North America – Aleuts
Algonquin Indians *see* Indians of North America – Algonquin
Aliens
All Souls' Day *see* Holidays – Day of the Dead
Allergies *see* Illness – allergies
Alligators *see* Reptiles – alligators, crocodiles
Alphabet books *see* ABC books
Alzheimer's *see* Illness – Alzheimer's
Amazon *see* Foreign lands – Amazon
Ambition *see* Character traits – ambition
American Indians *see* Indians of Central America; Indians of North America; Indians of Central America
Amish *see* Ethnic groups in the U.S. – Amish
Amphibians
Amusement parks *see* Parks – amusement
Anasazi Indians *see* Indians of North America – Anasazi
Anatomy
Anatomy – belly buttons *see* Anatomy – navels
Anatomy – brain
Anatomy – ears
Anatomy – eyes
Anatomy – faces
Anatomy – feet
Anatomy – fingers
Anatomy – fins
Anatomy – hands
Anatomy – heads

Anatomy – legs
Anatomy – mouths
Anatomy – navels
Anatomy – noses
Anatomy – skeletons
Anatomy – skin
Anatomy – tails
Anatomy – teeth *see* Teeth
Anatomy – thumbs *see* thumb sucking
Anatomy – toes
Anatomy – tongues
Anatomy – wings
Angels
Anger *see* Emotions – anger
Animals
Animals – aardvarks
Animals – anteaters
Animals – antelopes
Animals – apes *see* Animals – baboons; Animals – chimpanzees; Animals – gorillas; Animals – monkeys
Animals – armadillos
Animals – babies
Animals – baboons
Animals – badgers
Animals – bandicoots
Animals – bats
Animals – bears
Animals – beavers
Animals – bison *see* Animals – buffaloes
Animals – bobcats
Animals – brush wolves *see* Animals – coyotes
Animals – buffaloes
Animals – bulls, cows
Animals – bushbabies
Animals – camels
Animals – caribou *see* Animals – reindeer
Animals – cats
Animals – cheetahs
Animals – chimpanzees
Animals – chipmunks
Animals – cougars
Animals – cows *see* Animals – bulls, cows
Animals – coyotes
Animals – deer
Animals – dislike of *see* Behavior – animals, dislike of
Animals – dogs
Animals – dolphins
Animals – donkeys
Animals – dormice
Animals – elephants
Animals – elk
Animals – endangered animals
Animals – ferrets
Animals – foxes
Animals – gerbils
Animals – giraffes

Animals – goats
Animals – gorillas
Animals – groundhogs
Animals – guinea pigs
Animals – hamsters
Animals – hedgehogs
Animals – hippopotamuses
Animals – horses, ponies
Animals – hyenas
Animals – jackals
Animals – jaguars
Animals – kangaroos
Animals – kindness to animals *see* Character traits – kindness to animals
Animals – koalas
Animals – leeches
Animals – lemmings
Animals – lemurs
Animals – leopards
Animals – lions
Animals – llamas
Animals – lorises
Animals – lynx
Animals – manatees
Animals – meerkats
Animals – mice
Animals – migration *see* Migration
Animals – minks
Animals – moles
Animals – mongooses
Animals – monkeys
Animals – moose
Animals – mountain lions *see* Animals – cougars
Animals – mules
Animals – muskrats
Animals – octopuses *see* Octopuses
Animals – opossums *see* Animals – possums
Animals – orangutans
Animals – otters
Animals – oxen
Animals – pack rats
Animals – pandas
Animals – panthers *see* Animals – leopards
Animals – pigs
Animals – platypuses
Animals – polar bears
Animals – porcupines
Animals – possums
Animals – prairie dogs
Animals – prairie wolves *see* Animals – coyotes
Animals – pumas *see* Animals – cougars
Animals – rabbits
Animals – raccoons
Animals – rats
Animals – reindeer
Animals – rhinoceros
Animals – salamanders *see* Reptiles – salamanders
Animals – sea lions
Animals – seals
Animals – service animals
Animals – sheep
Animals – shrews
Animals – skunks
Animals – sloths
Animals – slugs
Animals – snails
Animals – snow leopards *see* Animals – leopards
Animals – sponges
Animals – squirrels
Animals – starfish
Animals – swine *see* Animals – pigs
Animals – tapirs

Animals – tigers
Animals – walruses
Animals – warthogs
Animals – water buffaloes
Animals – weasels
Animals – whales
Animals – wildebeests
Animals – wolves
Animals – wombats
Animals – woodchucks *see* Animals – groundhogs
Animals – woolly mammoths
Animals – worms
Animals – yaks
Animals – zebras
Antarctic *see* Foreign lands – Antarctic
Anteaters *see* Animals – anteaters
Antelopes *see* Animals – antelopes
Anti-violence *see* Violence, nonviolence
Ants *see* Insects – ants
Apache *see* Indians of North America – Apache
Apartments *see* Homes, houses
Apes *see* Animals – baboons; Animals – chimpanzees; Animals – gorillas; Animals – monkeys
Appearance *see* Character traits – appearance
April Fools' Day *see* Holidays – April Fools' Day
Aprons *see* Clothing – aprons
Aquariums
Arab Americans *see* Ethnic groups in the U.S. – Arab Americans
Arabia *see* Foreign lands – Arabia
Arachnids *see* Spiders
Archaeologists *see* Careers – archaeologists
Archery *see* Sports – archery
Architects *see* Careers – architects
Arctic *see* Foreign lands – Arctic
Argentina *see* Foreign lands – Argentina
Arguing *see* Behavior – fighting, arguing
Arithmetic *see* Counting, numbers
Armadillos *see* Animals – armadillos
Armenia *see* Foreign lands – Armenia
Art
Artists *see* Careers – artists
Asia *see* Foreign lands – Asia
Asian Americans *see* Ethnic groups in the U.S. – Asian Americans
Assertiveness *see* Character traits – assertiveness
Asthma *see* Illness – asthma
Astrology *see* Zodiac
Astronauts *see* Careers – astronauts; Space & space ships
Astronomers *see* Careers – astronomers
Astronomy
Athabascan Indians *see* Indians of North America – Athabascan
Aunts *see* Family life – aunts, uncles
Aurora Borealis *see* Northern lights
Australia *see* Foreign lands – Australia
Australian aborigines
Austria *see* Foreign lands – Austria
Authors *see* Careers – authors
Authors, children *see* Children as authors
Autism *see* Handicaps – autism
Automobiles
Autumn *see* Seasons – fall
Award-winning books *see* Caldecott award books; Caldecott award honor books
Aztec Indians *see* Indians of North America – Aztec

Babies
Babies, new *see* Family life – new sibling
Baboons *see* Animals – baboons
Babysitting *see* Activities – babysitting
Bad day *see* Behavior – bad day
Badgers *see* Animals – badgers
Bagpipes *see* Musical instruments – bagpipes
Bakers *see* Careers – bakers
Baking *see* Activities – baking, cooking
Balalaikas *see* Musical instruments – balalaikas
Bali *see* Foreign lands – Bali
Ballerinas *see* Ballet; Careers – dancers
Ballet
Ballooning *see* Activities – ballooning
Balloons *see* Toys – balloons
Balls *see* Toys – balls
Bandicoots *see* Animals – bandicoots
Bands *see* Musical instruments – bands
Banjos *see* Musical instruments – banjos
Barbers *see* Careers – barbers
Barns
Bartering *see* Activities – trading
Baseball *see* Sports – baseball
Bashfulness *see* Character traits – shyness
Basketball *see* Sports – basketball
Bathing *see* Activities – bathing
Bats *see* Animals – bats
Bavaria *see* Foreign lands – Austria; Foreign lands – Germany
Beaches *see* Sea & seashore – beaches
Bears *see* Animals – bears
Beasts *see* Monsters
Beauty shops
Beavers *see* Animals – beavers
Beds *see* Furniture – beds
Bedtime
Bedwetting *see* Behavior – bedwetting
Beekeepers *see* Careers – beekeepers
Bees *see* Insects – bees
Beetles *see* Insects – beetles
Beggars *see* Careers – beggars
Behavior
Behavior – animals, dislike of
Behavior – bad day
Behavior – bedwetting
Behavior – boasting
Behavior – boredom
Behavior – bossy
Behavior – bullying
Behavior – carelessness
Behavior – cheating
Behavior – collecting things
Behavior – disbelief
Behavior – dissatisfaction
Behavior – fidgeting
Behavior – fighting, arguing
Behavior – forgetfulness
Behavior – forgiving
Behavior – gossip
Behavior – greed
Behavior – growing up
Behavior – hiding
Behavior – hiding things
Behavior – hurrying
Behavior – imitation
Behavior – indecision
Behavior – indifference
Behavior – lost
Behavior – lost & found possessions
Behavior – lying
Behavior – messy
Behavior – misbehavior
Behavior – mistakes
Behavior – misunderstanding
Behavior – nagging

Behavior – name calling
Behavior – naughty *see* Behavior – misbehavior
Behavior – needing someone
Behavior – potty training *see* Toilet training
Behavior – promptness, tardiness
Behavior – resourcefulness
Behavior – running away
Behavior – saving things
Behavior – secrets
Behavior – seeking better things
Behavior – sharing
Behavior – solitude
Behavior – stealing
Behavior – talking to strangers
Behavior – teasing
Behavior – toilet training *see* Toilet training
Behavior – trickery
Behavior – unnoticed, unseen
Behavior – wishing
Behavior – worrying
Being different *see* Character traits – being different
Belize *see* Foreign lands – Belize
Belly buttons *see* Anatomy – navels
Bereavement *see* Death; Emotions – grief
Bible *see* Religion
Bicycling *see* Sports – bicycling
Bigotry *see* Prejudice
Birds
Birds – albatrosses
Birds – blackbirds
Birds – bluebirds
Birds – bluejays
Birds – boobys
Birds – buzzards
Birds – canaries
Birds – cardinals
Birds – chickadees
Birds – chickens
Birds – cockatoos
Birds – condors
Birds – cormorants
Birds – cranes
Birds – crows
Birds – cuckoos
Birds – dodos
Birds – doves
Birds – ducks
Birds – eagles
Birds – egrets
Birds – emus
Birds – falcons
Birds – flamingos
Birds – geese
Birds – guinea fowl
Birds – hawks
Birds – herons
Birds – hornbills
Birds – humming birds
Birds – ibis
Birds – kestrels
Birds – larks
Birds – loons
Birds – macaws
Birds – magpies
Birds – mockingbirds
Birds – nightingales
Birds – ostriches
Birds – owls
Birds – parakeets, parrots
Birds – peacocks, peahens
Birds – pelicans
Birds – penguins
Birds – pigeons

Birds – plovers
Birds – ptarmigans
Birds – puffins
Birds – quail
Birds – ravens
Birds – roadrunners
Birds – robins
Birds – sandpipers
Birds – seagulls
Birds – sparrows
Birds – spoonbills
Birds – storks
Birds – swallows
Birds – swans
Birds – toucans
Birds – turkeys
Birds – vultures
Birds – wood-hoopoes
Birds – woodpeckers
Birds – wrens
Birth
Birthdays
Bison *see* Animals – buffaloes
Black Americans *see* Ethnic groups in the U.S. – African Americans
Black Carib *see* Indians of Central America – Black Carib
Blackbirds *see* Birds – blackbirds
Blackfoot Indians *see* Indians of North America – Blackfoot
Blackouts *see* Power failure
Blindness *see* Handicaps – blindness; Senses – sight
Blizzards *see* Weather – blizzards
Blocks *see* Toys – blocks
Bluejays *see* Birds – bluejays
Board books *see* Format, unusual – board books
Boasting *see* Behavior – boasting
Boat builders *see* Careers – boat builders
Boats, ships
Bobcats *see* Animals – bobcats
Bombs *see* Weapons
Boobys *see* Birds – boobys
Boogy man *see* Monsters
Books
Boots *see* Clothing – boots; Clothing – shoes
Boredom *see* Behavior – boredom
Borneo *see* Foreign lands – Borneo
Bossy *see* Behavior – bossy
Botswana *see* Foreign lands – Botswana
Bowling *see* Sports – bowling
Boxing *see* Sports – boxing
Bravery *see* Character traits – bravery
Brazil *see* Foreign lands – Brazil
Bridges
Brothers *see* Family life; Family life – brothers; Family life – brothers & sisters; Family life - sisters; Sibling rivalry
Brownies *see* Mythical creatures – elves
Brush wolf *see* Animals – coyotes
Bubbles
Buddhism *see* Religion – Buddhism
Buffaloes *see* Animals – buffaloes
Bugs *see* Insects
Buildings
Bulldozers *see* Machines
Bulls *see* Animals – bulls, cows
Bullying *see* Behavior – bullying
Bumble bees *see* Insects – bees
Bungee Indians *see* Indians of North America – Bungee
Burglars *see* Crime
Burma *see* Foreign lands – Burma
Burros *see* Animals – donkeys

Bus drivers *see* Careers – bus drivers
Buses
Bushbabies *see* Animals – bushbabies
Butchers *see* Careers – butchers
Butterflies *see* Insects – butterflies, caterpillars
Buzzards *see* Birds – buzzards

Cab drivers *see* Careers – taxi drivers
Cable cars, trolleys
Cabs *see* Taxis
Cafés *see* Restaurants
Caldecott award books
Caldecott award honor books
Calendars
Cambodia *see* Foreign lands – Cambodia
Cambodian Americans *see* Ethnic groups in the U.S. – Cambodian Americans
Camels *see* Animals – camels
Cameroon *see* Foreign lands – Cameroon
Camouflages *see* Disguises
Camps, camping
Canada *see* Foreign lands – Canada
Canada Day *see* Holidays – Canada Day
Canaries *see* Birds – canaries
Cancer *see* Illness – cancer
Canoes & canoeing
Canyons
Capes *see* Clothing – coats
Caps *see* Clothing – hats
Cardboard page books *see* Format, unusual – board books
Cardinals *see* Birds – cardinals
Cards *see* Letters, cards
Careers
Careers – accountants
Careers – acrobats
Careers – actors
Careers – aerialists
Careers – airplane pilots
Careers – archaeologists
Careers – architects
Careers – artists
Careers – astronauts
Careers – astronomers
Careers – authors
Careers – bakers
Careers – barbers
Careers – beekeepers
Careers – beggars
Careers – blacksmiths
Careers – boat builders
Careers – bookbinders
Careers – bus drivers
Careers – butchers
Careers – cab drivers *see* Careers – taxi drivers
Careers – carpenters
Careers – cartographers
Careers – chefs, cooks
Careers – clergy
Careers – clockmakers
Careers – coaches
Careers – comedians
Careers – composers
Careers – conductors (music)
Careers – construction workers
Careers – cooks *see* Careers – chefs, cooks
Careers – custodians, janitors
Careers – dancers
Careers – dentists
Careers – detectives
Careers – doctors
Careers – doormen
Careers – electricians
Careers – emergency medical technicians

Careers – engineers
Careers – entertainers
Careers – explorers
Careers – farmers
Careers – firefighters
Careers – fishermen
Careers – forest rangers *see* Careers – park rangers
Careers – fortune tellers
Careers – garbage collectors *see* Careers – sanitation workers
Careers – geologists
Careers – handymen
Careers – harpists
Careers – hatters
Careers – housekeepers
Careers – illustrators
Careers – inventors
Careers – janitors *see* Careers – custodians, janitors
Careers – journalists
Careers – judges
Careers – lawyers
Careers – librarians
Careers – lifeguards
Careers – lumberjacks
Careers – magicians
Careers – mail carriers *see* Careers – postal workers
Careers – mayors
Careers – mechanics
Careers – messengers
Careers – meteorologists
Careers – migrant workers
Careers – military
Careers – miners
Careers – models
Careers – motion picture producers
Careers – museum workers
Careers – musicians
Careers – nuns
Careers – nurses
Careers – opera singers
Careers – opticians, optometrists
Careers – organists
Careers – ornithologists
Careers – painters
Careers – paleontologists
Careers – park rangers
Careers – peddlers
Careers – pharmacists
Careers – photographers
Careers – physicians *see* Careers – doctors
Careers – plasterers
Careers – plumbers
Careers – poets
Careers – police officers
Careers – postal workers
Careers – potters
Careers – preachers *see* Careers – clergy, preachers, etc.
Careers – principals *see* Careers – school principals
Careers – printers
Careers – puppeteers
Careers – race car drivers
Careers – railroad engineers
Careers – ranchers
Careers – rangers *see* Careers – park rangers
Careers – sailors *see* Careers – military; Sailors
Careers – salesmen
Careers – sanitation workers
Careers – school principals
Careers – scientists
Careers – sculptors
Careers – seamstresses

Careers – shepherds
Careers – sheriffs
Careers – shoe shiners
Careers – shoemakers
Careers – sign painters
Careers – singers
Careers – soldiers *see* Careers – military
Careers – storekeepers
Careers – tailors
Careers – taxi drivers
Careers – teachers
Careers – telephone operators
Careers – toy makers
Careers – train engineers *see* Careers – railroad engineers
Careers – truck drivers
Careers – veterinarians
Careers – waiters, waitresses
Careers – weather reporters *see* Careers – meteorologists
Careers – weavers
Careers – welders
Careers – whalers
Careers – window cleaners
Careers – woodcarvers
Careers – writers
Careers – zookeepers
Carelessness *see* Behavior – carelessness
Caribbean Islands *see* Foreign lands – Caribbean Islands
Caribou *see* Animals – reindeer
Carnivals *see* Fairs
Carousels *see* Merry-go-rounds
Carpenters *see* Careers – carpenters
Carrier Indians *see* Indians of North America – Carrier
Cars *see* Automobiles
Cartographers *see* Careers – cartographers
Castles
Caterpillars *see* Insects – butterflies, caterpillars
Cats *see* Animals – cats
Cave drawings *see* Petroglyphs
Cavemen
Caves
Cellos *see* Musical instruments – cellos
Centipedes *see* Crustaceans – centipedes, millipedes
Central America *see* Foreign lands – Central America
Cerebral palsy *see* Handicaps – cerebral palsy
Chairs *see* Furniture – chairs
Chameleons *see* Reptiles – chameleons
Change *see* Concepts – change
Chanukah *see* Holidays – Hanukkah
Character traits
Character traits – ambition
Character traits – appearance
Character traits – assertiveness
Character traits – being different
Character traits – bravery
Character traits – cleanliness
Character traits – cleverness
Character traits – clumsiness
Character traits – completing things
Character traits – compromising
Character traits – conceit
Character traits – confidence
Character traits – cooperation
Character traits – courage *see* Character traits – bravery
Character traits – cruelty to animals *see* Character traits – kindness to animals
Character traits – curiosity
Character traits – flattery
Character traits – foolishness

Character traits – fortune *see* Character traits – luck
Character traits – freedom
Character traits – generosity
Character traits – helpfulness
Character traits – honesty
Character traits – incentive *see* Character traits – ambition
Character traits – individuality
Character traits – kindness
Character traits – kindness to animals
Character traits – laziness
Character traits – loyalty
Character traits – luck
Character traits – meanness
Character traits – optimism
Character traits – orderliness
Character traits – ostracism *see* Character traits – being different
Character traits – patience
Character traits – perfectionism
Character traits – perseverance
Character traits – persistence
Character traits – practicality
Character traits – pride
Character traits – questioning
Character traits – responsibility
Character traits – selfishness
Character traits – shyness
Character traits – smallness
Character traits – stubbornness
Character traits – vanity
Character traits – willfulness
Character traits – wisdom
Cheating *see* Behavior – cheating
Cheerleading
Cheetahs *see* Animals – cheetahs
Chefs *see* Careers – chefs, cooks
Cherokee Indians *see* Indians of North America – Cherokee
Cherubs *see* Angels
Cheyenne (Sioux) Indians *see* Indians of North America – Cheyenne (Sioux)
Chickasaw Indians *see* Indians of North America – Chickasaw
Chicken pox *see* Illness – chicken pox
Chickens *see* Birds – chickens
Child abuse
Children as authors
Children as illustrators
Children as inventors
Chile *see* Foreign lands – Chile
Chimpanzees *see* Animals – chimpanzees
China *see* Foreign lands – China
Chinese Americans *see* Ethnic groups in the U.S. – Chinese Americans
Chinese New Year *see* Holidays – Chinese New Year
Chinook Indians *see* Indians of North America – Chinook
Chipmunks *see* Animals – chipmunks
Chippewa Indians *see* Indians of North America – Chippewa
Chol Indians *see* Indians of North America – Chol
Christmas *see* Holidays – Christmas
Chumash Indians *see* Indians of North America – Chumash
Cinco de Mayo *see* Holidays – Cinco de Mayo
Circular tales
Circus
Cities, towns
Clallam Indians *see* Indians of North America – Clallam
Clarinets *see* Musical instruments – clarinets

Ears *see* Anatomy – ears; Handicaps – deafness; Senses – hearing
Earth
Earthquakes
East Indian Americans *see* Ethnic groups in the U.S. – East Indian Americans
Easter *see* Holidays – Easter
Eating *see* Food
Ecology
Ecuador *see* Foreign lands – Ecuador
Education *see* School
Eggs
Egrets *see* Birds – egrets
Egypt *see* Foreign lands – Egypt
Egyptian language *see* Hieroglyphics
El Salvador *see* Foreign lands – El Salvador
Elderly *see* Old age
Electricians *see* Careers – electricians
Elephant seals *see* Animals – seals
Elephants *see* Animals – elephants
Elevators, escalators
Elk *see* Animals – elk
Elves *see* Mythical creatures – elves
Embarrassment *see* Emotions – embarrassment
Emergency medical technicians *see* Careers – emergency medical technicians
Emotions
Emotions – anger
Emotions – embarrassment
Emotions – envy, jealousy
Emotions – fear
Emotions – grief
Emotions – happiness
Emotions – hate
Emotions – jealousy *see* Emotions – envy, jealousy
Emotions – loneliness
Emotions – love
Emotions – sadness
Emotions – unhappiness *see* Emotions – happiness; Emotions – sadness
Emperors *see* Royalty – emperors
Emus *see* Birds – emus
Endangered animals *see* Animals – endangered animals
Engineered books *see* Format, unusual – toy & movable books
Engineers *see* Careers – engineers
England *see* Foreign lands – England
Entertainers *see* Careers – entertainers
Entertainment *see* Theater
Environment *see* Ecology
Envy *see* Emotions – envy, jealousy
Epilepsy *see* Illness – epilepsy
Escalators *see* Elevators, escalators
Eskimos
Estonia *see* Foreign lands – Estonia
Ethiopia *see* Foreign lands – Ethiopia
Ethnic groups in the U.S.
Ethnic groups in the U.S. – Acadians *see* Ethnic groups in the U.S. – Cajuns
Ethnic groups in the U.S. – African Americans
Ethnic groups in the U.S. – Amish
Ethnic groups in the U.S. – Arab Americans
Ethnic groups in the U.S. – Asian Americans
Ethnic groups in the U.S. – Black Americans *see* Ethnic groups in the U.S. – African Americans
Ethnic groups in the U.S. – Cajuns
Ethnic groups in the U.S. – Cambodian Americans
Ethnic groups in the U.S. – Chinese Americans

Ethnic groups in the U.S. – Cuban Americans
Ethnic groups in the U.S. – Czechoslovakian Americans
Ethnic groups in the U.S. – Dutch Americans
Ethnic groups in the U.S. – East Indian Americans
Ethnic groups in the U.S. – Filipino Americans
Ethnic groups in the U.S. – French Americans
Ethnic groups in the U.S. – German Americans
Ethnic groups in the U.S. – Greek Americans
Ethnic groups in the U.S. – Guatemalan Americans
Ethnic groups in the U.S. – Hispanic Americans
Ethnic groups in the U.S. – Hmong Americans
Ethnic groups in the U.S. – Hungarian Americans
Ethnic groups in the U.S. – Indian Americans
Ethnic groups in the U.S. – Irish Americans
Ethnic groups in the U.S. – Italian Americans
Ethnic groups in the U.S. – Japanese Americans
Ethnic groups in the U.S. – Jewish Americans
Ethnic groups in the U.S. – Korean Americans
Ethnic groups in the U.S. – Lebanese Americans
Ethnic groups in the U.S. – Lithuanian Americans
Ethnic groups in the U.S. – Mexican Americans
Ethnic groups in the U.S. – Pakistani Americans
Ethnic groups in the U.S. – Polish Americans
Ethnic groups in the U.S. – Puerto Rican Americans
Ethnic groups in the U.S. – Russian Americans
Ethnic groups in the U.S. – Shakers
Ethnic groups in the U.S. – Swedish Americans
Ethnic groups in the U.S. – Vietnamese Americans
Etiquette
Europe *see* Foreign lands – Europe
Evening *see* Twilight
Exercise *see* Health & Fitness – exercise
Experiments *see* Science
Explorers *see* Careers – explorers
Extraterrestrial beings *see* Aliens
Eye glasses *see* Glasses
Eyes *see* Anatomy – eyes; Glasses; Handicaps – blindness; Senses – sight

Fables *see* Folk & fairy tales
Faces *see* Anatomy – faces
Fairies
Fairs, festivals
Fairy tales *see* Folk & fairy tales
Falcons *see* Birds – falcons
Fall *see* Seasons – fall
Family life
Family life – aunts, uncles
Family life – brothers
Family life – brothers & sisters

Family life – cousins
Family life – daughters
Family life – fathers
Family life – grandfathers
Family life – grandmothers
Family life – grandparents
Family life – great-grandparents
Family life – mothers
Family life – new sibling
Family life – only child
Family life – parents
Family life – single-parent families
Family life – sisters
Family life – sons
Family life – stepfamilies
Family life – stepchildren *see* Divorce; Family life – stepfamilies
Family life – stepparents *see* Divorce; Family life – stepfamilies
Farmers *see* Careers – farmers
Farms
Father's Day *see* Holidays – Father's Day
Fathers *see* Family life – fathers
Fear *see* Emotions – fear
Feathers
Feeling *see* Senses – touch
Feelings *see* Emotions
Feet *see* Anatomy – feet
Ferrets *see* Animals – ferrets
Fidgeting *see* Behavior – fidgeting
Fighting *see* Behavior – fighting, arguing
Fiji *see* Foreign lands – Fiji
Fingers *see* Anatomy – hands
Finishing things *see* Character traits – completing things
Finland *see* Foreign lands – Finland
Fins *see* Anatomy – fins
Fire
Fire engines *see* Careers – firefighters; Trucks
Firefighters *see* Careers – firefighters
Fires *see* Fire
Fish
Fish – seahorses
Fish – sharks
Fishermen *see* Careers – fishermen
Fishing *see* Sports – fishing
Fitness *see* Health & fitness
Flags
Flamingos *see* Birds – flamingos
Flattery *see* Character traits – flattery
Fleas *see* Insects – fleas
Flies *see* Insects – flies
Floods *see* Weather – floods
Flowers
Flowers – roses
Flutes *see* Musical instruments – flutes
Flying *see* Activities – flying
Fog *see* Weather – fog
Fold-out books *see* Format, unusual – toy & movable books
Folk & fairy tales
Folk & fairy tales – pourquoi tales
Food
Foolishness *see* Character traits – foolishness
Football *see* Sports – football
Foreign lands
Foreign lands – Afghanistan
Foreign lands – Africa
Foreign lands – Amazon
Foreign lands – Antarctic
Foreign lands – Arabia
Foreign lands – Arctic
Foreign lands – Argentina
Foreign lands – Armenia
Foreign lands – Asia
Foreign lands – Australia

Foreign lands – Austria
Foreign lands – Bali
Foreign lands – Bavaria *see* Foreign lands
  – Austria; Foreign lands – Germany
Foreign lands – Belgium
Foreign lands – Belize
Foreign lands – Borneo
Foreign lands – Bosnia-Herzegovina
Foreign lands – Botswana
Foreign lands – Brazil
Foreign lands – British Columbia
Foreign lands – Burma
Foreign lands – Cambodia
Foreign lands – Cameroon
Foreign lands – Canada
Foreign lands – Caribbean Islands
Foreign lands – Central America
Foreign lands – Chile
Foreign lands – China
Foreign lands – Colombia
Foreign lands – Congo (Democratic
  Republic)
Foreign lands – Costa Rica
Foreign lands – Cuba
Foreign lands – Czechoslovakia
Foreign lands – Denmark
Foreign lands – Dominican Republic
Foreign lands – Ecuador
Foreign lands – Egypt
Foreign lands – El Salvador
Foreign lands – England
Foreign lands – Estonia
Foreign lands – Ethiopia
Foreign lands – Europe
Foreign lands – Fiji
Foreign lands – Finland
Foreign lands – France
Foreign lands – French Guiana
Foreign lands – Galapagos Islands
Foreign lands – Galilee
Foreign lands – Gambia
Foreign lands – Germany
Foreign lands – Ghana
Foreign lands – Gilbert Islands
Foreign lands – Great Britain
Foreign lands – Greece
Foreign lands – Greenland
Foreign lands – Guatemala
Foreign lands – Guyana
Foreign lands – Haiti
Foreign lands – Himalayas
Foreign lands – Holland
Foreign lands – Hungary
Foreign lands – Iceland
Foreign lands – India
Foreign lands – Indonesia
Foreign lands – Iran
Foreign lands – Iraq
Foreign lands – Ireland
Foreign lands – Israel
Foreign lands – Italy
Foreign lands – Jamaica
Foreign lands – Japan
Foreign lands – Kenya
Foreign lands – Korea
Foreign lands – Korea (North)
Foreign lands – Kurdistan
Foreign lands – Laos
Foreign lands – Lapland
Foreign lands – Latin America
Foreign lands – Latvia
Foreign lands – Lebanon
Foreign lands – Liberia
Foreign lands – Madagascar
Foreign lands – Malaysia
Foreign lands – Mali
Foreign lands – Martinique
Foreign lands – Mexico

Foreign lands – Middle East
Foreign lands – Mongolia
Foreign lands – Morocco
Foreign lands – Namibia
Foreign lands – Nepal
Foreign lands – Netherlands *see* Foreign
  lands – Holland
Foreign lands – New Guinea
Foreign lands – New Zealand
Foreign lands – Newfoundland
Foreign lands – Nicaragua
Foreign lands – Nigeria
Foreign lands – Nkandla
Foreign lands – Norway
Foreign lands – Pakistan
Foreign lands – Palestine
Foreign lands – Panama
Foreign lands – Persia
Foreign lands – Peru
Foreign lands – Philippines
Foreign lands – Poland
Foreign lands – Portugal
Foreign lands – Puerto Rico
Foreign lands – Romania
Foreign lands – Russia
Foreign lands – Rwanda
Foreign lands – Sahara Desert
Foreign lands – Scandinavia
Foreign lands – Scotland
Foreign lands – Serbia
Foreign lands – Siam *see* Foreign lands –
  Thailand
Foreign lands – Siberia
Foreign lands – South Africa
Foreign lands – South America
Foreign lands – South Sea Islands
Foreign lands – Soviet Union
Foreign lands – Spain
Foreign lands – Sri Lanka
Foreign lands – Sudan
Foreign lands – Suriname
Foreign lands – Sweden
Foreign lands – Switzerland
Foreign lands – Taiwan
Foreign lands – Tanzania
Foreign lands – Tasmania
Foreign lands – Thailand
Foreign lands – Tibet
Foreign lands – Trinidad
Foreign lands – Turkey
Foreign lands – Tyrol
Foreign lands – Uganda
Foreign lands – Ukraine
Foreign lands – Uzbekistan
Foreign lands – Venezuela
Foreign lands – Vietnam
Foreign lands – Wales
Foreign lands – West Indies
Foreign lands – Yukon Territory
Foreign lands – Zaire
Foreign lands – Zambia
Foreign lands – Zanzibar
Foreign lands – Zimbabwe
Foreign languages
Forest, woods
Forgetfulness *see* Behavior – forgetfulness
Forgiving *see* Behavior – forgiving
Format, unusual
Format, unusual – board books
Format, unusual – toy & movable books
Fortune *see* Character traits – luck
Fortune tellers *see* Careers – fortune
  tellers
Fossils
Fourth of July *see* Holidays – Fourth of
  July
Foxes *see* Animals – foxes
France *see* Foreign lands – France

Freedom *see* Character traits – freedom
French Americans *see* Ethnic groups in
  the U.S. – French Americans
French Guiana *see* Foreign lands – French
  Guiana
Friendship
Frogs & toads
Frontier life *see* U.S. history – frontier &
  pioneer life
Fungi, molds
Furniture
Furniture – beds
Furniture – chairs
Furniture – couches, sofas
Furniture – cradles
Furniture – dressers
Furniture – tables

Galapagos Islands *see* Foreign lands –
  Galapagos Islands
Galilee *see* Foreign lands – Galilee
Gambia *see* Foreign lands – Gambia
Games
Gangs *see* Clubs, gangs
Garage sales, rummage sales
Garbage collectors *see* Careers – sanitation
  workers
Gardens, gardening
Geese *see* Birds – geese
Gender roles
Genealogy
Generosity *see* Character traits –
  generosity
Genies *see* Mythical creatures – genies
Geography
Geologists *see* Careers – geologists
Gerbils *see* Animals – gerbils
German Americans *see* Ethnic groups in
  the U.S. – German Americans
Germany *see* Foreign lands – Germany
Ghana *see* Foreign lands – Ghana
Ghosts
Giants
Gifts
Gilbert Islands *see* Foreign lands – South
  Sea Islands
Giraffes *see* Animals – giraffes
Glasses
Gloves *see* Clothing – gloves, mittens
Gnats *see* Insects – gnats
Gnomes *see* Mythical creatures – gnomes
Goats *see* Animals – goats
Goblins *see* Mythical creatures – goblins
Golf *see* Sports – golf
Gorillas *see* Animals – gorillas
Goshute Indians *see* Indians of North
  America – Goshute
Gossip *see* Behavior – gossip
Gourds *see* Musical instruments – gourds
Grammar *see* Language
Grandfathers *see* Family life –
  grandfathers; Family life –
  grandparents
Grandmothers *see* Family life –
  grandmothers; Family life –
  grandparents
Grandparents *see* Family life –
  grandfathers; Family life –
  grandmothers; Family life –
  grandparents
Grasshoppers *see* Insects – grasshoppers
Great Plains Indians *see* Indians of North
  America – Great Plains
Great-grandparents *see* Family life – great-
  grandparents
Greece *see* Foreign lands – Greece
Greed *see* Behavior – greed

Greek Americans *see* Ethnic groups in the U.S. – Greek Americans
Greenland *see* Foreign lands – Greenland
Grief *see* Emotions – grief
Griffins *see* Mythical creatures – griffins
Grocery stores *see* Shopping; Stores
Groundhog Day *see* Holidays – Groundhog Day
Groundhogs *see* Animals – groundhogs
Growing up *see* Behavior – growing up
Guatemala *see* Foreign lands – Guatemala
Guinea fowl *see* Birds – guinea fowl
Guinea pigs *see* Animals – guinea pigs
Guns *see* Weapons
Guy Fawkes Day *see* Holidays – Guy Fawkes Day
Guyana *see* Foreign lands – Guyana
Gymnastics *see* Sports – gymnastics
Gypsies

Habits *see* Thumb sucking
Haida Indians *see* Indians of North America – Haida
Hair
Haiti *see* Foreign lands – Haiti
Halloween *see* Holidays – Halloween
Hamsters *see* Animals – hamsters
Handbags *see* Clothing – handbags, purses
Handicaps
Handicaps – ADD
Handicaps – autism
Handicaps – blindness
Handicaps – cerebral palsy
Handicaps – deafness
Handicaps – Down syndrome
Handicaps – dyslexia
Handicaps – mental handicaps
Handicaps – physical handicaps
Handicaps – stuttering
Hands *see* Anatomy – hands
Handymen *see* Careers – handymen
Hanukkah *see* Holidays – Hanukkah
Happiness *see* Emotions – happiness
Hares *see* Animals – rabbits
Harmonicas *see* Musical instruments – harmonicas
Harps *see* Musical instruments – harps
Harpsichords *see* Musical instruments – harpsichords
Hats *see* Clothing – hats
Hatters *see* Careers – hatters
Hawaii
Hawks *see* Birds – hawks
Heads *see* Anatomy – heads
Health & fitness
Health & fitness – exercise
Health & safety
Hearing *see* Anatomy – ears; Handicaps – deafness; Senses – hearing
Heat *see* Concepts – cold & heat
Heavy equipment *see* Machines
Hedgehogs *see* Animals – hedgehogs
Helicopters
Helpfulness *see* Character traits – helpfulness
Hens *see* Birds – chickens
Herons *see* Birds – herons
Hibernation
Hiccups
Hiding *see* Behavior – hiding
Hiding things *see* Behavior – hiding things
Hieroglyphics
Hiking *see* Sports – hiking
Himalayas *see* Foreign lands – Himalayas
Hinduism *see* Religion – Hinduism
Hippopotamuses *see* Animals – hippopotamuses

Hispanic Americans *see* Ethnic groups in the U.S. – Hispanic Americans
Hmong Americans *see* Ethnic groups in the U.S. – Hmong Americans
Hobby horses *see* Toys – rocking horses
Hockey *see* Sports – hockey
Hogs *see* Animals – pigs
Hohokam Indians *see* Indians of North America – Hohokam
Holidays
Holidays – April Fools' Day
Holidays – Canada Day
Holidays – Chanukah *see* Holidays – Hanukkah
Holidays – Chinese New Year
Holidays – Christmas
Holidays – Cinco de Mayo
Holidays – Columbus Day
Holidays – Day of the Dead
Holidays – Divali
Holidays – Earth Day
Holidays – Easter
Holidays – Father's Day
Holidays – Fourth of July
Holidays – Groundhog Day
Holidays – Guy Fawkes Day
Holidays – Halloween
Holidays – Hanukkah
Holidays – Independence Day *see* Holidays – Fourth of July
Holidays – Juneteenth
Holidays – Kwanzaa
Holidays – Mardi Gras *see* Mardi Gras
Holidays – Martin Luther King, Jr. Day
Holidays – May Day
Holidays – Memorial Day
Holidays – Mother's Day
Holidays – New Year's
Holidays – Passover
Holidays – Purim
Holidays – Ramadan
Holidays – Rosh Hashanah
Holidays – Seder
Holidays – Shavuot
Holidays – St. Patrick's Day
Holidays – Sukkot
Holidays – Thanksgiving
Holidays – Tu B'Shevat
Holidays – Valentine's Day
Holidays – Washington's Birthday
Holidays – Yom Kippur
Holland *see* Foreign lands – Holland
Holocaust
Homeless
Homes, houses
Homework
Homosexuality
Honesty *see* Character traits – honesty
Honey bees *see* Insects – bees
Hope
Hopi Indians *see* Indians of North America – Hopi
Hornbills *see* Birds – hornbills
Hornets *see* Insects – hornets
Horses *see* Animals – horses, ponies
Horses, rocking *see* Toys – rocking horses
Hospitals
Hotels
Housekeepers *see* Careers – housekeepers
Houses *see* Homes, houses
Hugging
Huichol Indians *see* Indians of North America – Huichol
Humming birds *see* Birds – humming birds
Humorous stories
Hungary *see* Foreign lands – Hungary

Hunting *see* Sports – hunting
Hurdy-gurdies *see* Musical instruments – hurdy-gurdies
Huron Indians *see* Indians of North America – Huron
Hurricanes *see* Weather – hurricanes
Hurrying *see* Behavior – hurrying
Hyenas *see* Animals – hyenas
Hygiene

Ibis *see* Birds – ibis
Ice skating *see* Sports – ice skating
Iceland *see* Foreign lands – Iceland
Identity *see* Self-concept
Iguanas *see* Reptiles – iguanas
Illness
Illness – AIDS
Illness – alcoholism
Illness – allergies
Illness – Alzheimer's
Illness – asthma
Illness – cancer
Illness – chicken pox
Illness – cold (disease)
Illness – diabetes
Illness – drug addiction
Illness – epilepsy
Illness – influenza
Illness – measles
Illness – mental illness
Illness – mumps
Illness – muscular dystrophy
Illness – poliomyelitis
Illness – tonsillectomy
Illusions, optical *see* Optical illusions
Illustrators *see* Careers – illustrators
Illustrators, children *see* Children as illustrators
Imaginary friends *see* Imagination – imaginary friends
Imagination
Imagination – imaginary friends
Imitation *see* Behavior – imitation
Immigrants
Imps *see* Mythical creatures – imps
In & out *see* Concepts – in & out
Incas *see* Indians of South America – Incas
Incentive *see* Character traits – ambition
Indecision *see* Behavior – indecision
Independence Day *see* Holidays – Fourth of July
India *see* Foreign lands – India
Indians, American *see* Indians of Central America; Indians of North America; Indians of South America
Indians of Central America
Indians of Central America – Black Carib
Indians of Central America – Maya
Indians of Central America – Taino
Indians of North America
Indians of North America – Abnaki
Indians of North America – Aleuts
Indians of North America – Algonquin
Indians of North America – Anasazi
Indians of North America – Apache
Indians of North America – Athabascan
Indians of North America – Aztec
Indians of North America – Blackfoot
Indians of North America – Bungee
Indians of North America – Carrier
Indians of North America – Cherokee
Indians of North America – Cheyenne (Sioux)
Indians of North America – Chickasaw
Indians of North America – Chinook
Indians of North America – Chippewa
Indians of North America – Chol

Indians of North America – Chumash
Indians of North America – Clallam
Indians of North America – Comanche
Indians of North America – Coquelle
Indians of North America – Cora
Indians of North America – Cree
Indians of North America – Creek
Indians of North America – Crow
Indians of North America – Dakota (Sioux)
Indians of North America – Delaware
Indians of North America – Goshute
Indians of North America – Great Basin
Indians of North America – Great Plains
Indians of North America – Haida
Indians of North America – Hohokam
Indians of North America – Hopi
Indians of North America – Huichol
Indians of North America – Huron
Indians of North America – Inuit
Indians of North America – Inuk
Indians of North America – Iroquois
Indians of North America – Karok
Indians of North America – Kato
Indians of North America – Kutenai
Indians of North America – Lakota (Sioux)
Indians of North America – Lenape
Indians of North America – Maidu
Indians of North America – Micmac
Indians of North America – Missisauga
Indians of North America – Miwok
Indians of North America – Modoc
Indians of North America – Mohawk
Indians of North America – Muskogee
Indians of North America – Nanticoke
Indians of North America – Narragansett
Indians of North America – Navajo
Indians of North America – Nez Perce
Indians of North America – Nishnawbe
Indians of North America – Nisqually
Indians of North America – Nobscusset
Indians of North America – Ojibwa
Indians of North America – Paiute
Indians of North America – Papago
Indians of North America – Pawnee
Indians of North America – Penobscot
Indians of North America – Pima
Indians of North America – Potawatomi
Indians of North America – Powhatan
Indians of North America – Pueblo
Indians of North America – Seminole
Indians of North America – Seneca
Indians of North America – Shawnee
Indians of North America – Shoshone
Indians of North America – Siksika
Indians of North America – Sioux
Indians of North America – Southwest
Indians of North America – Suquamish
Indians of North America – Taino
Indians of North America – Tarascan
Indians of North America – Tewa
Indians of North America – Tlingit
Indians of North America – Tohono O'Odham
Indians of North America – Tsimshian
Indians of North America – Twa
Indians of North America – Ute
Indians of North America – Wampanoag
Indians of North America – Windigos
Indians of North America – Yana
Indians of North America – Yupik
Indians of North America – Zapotec
Indians of North America – Zuni
Indians of South America
Indians of South America – Incas
Indians of South America – Karina

Indians of South America – Quechua
Indians of South America – Yanomamo
Indifference *see* Behavior – indifference
Individuality *see* Character traits – individuality
Indonesia *see* Foreign lands – Indonesia
Indonesian Archipelago *see* Foreign lands – South Sea Islands
Influenza *see* Illness – influenza
Insects
Insects – ants
Insects – bees
Insects – beetles
Insects – butterflies, caterpillars
Insects – cockroaches
Insects – crickets
Insects – damselflies
Insects – dragonflies
Insects – fireflies
Insects – fleas
Insects – flies
Insects – gnats
Insects – grasshoppers
Insects – hornets
Insects – lady birds *see* Insects – ladybugs
Insects – ladybugs
Insects – lice
Insects – lightning bugs *see* Insects – fireflies
Insects – mosquitoes
Insects – moths
Insects – praying mantis
Insects – termites
Insects – wasps
Interracial marriage *see* Marriage, interracial
Inuit Indians *see* Indians of North America – Inuit
Inuk Indians *see* Indians of North America – Inuk
Inventions
Inventors *see* Careers – inventors
Iran *see* Foreign lands – Iran
Iraq *see* Foreign lands – Iraq
Ireland *see* Foreign lands – Ireland
Irish Americans *see* Ethnic groups in the U.S. – Irish Americans
Iroquois Indians *see* Indians of North America – Iroquois
Islam *see* Foreign lands – Israel
Islands
Israel *see* Foreign lands – Israel
Italian Americans *see* Ethnic groups in the U.S. – Italian Americans
Italy *see* Foreign lands – Italy

Jackals *see* Animals – jackals
Jackets *see* Clothing – coats
Jaguars *see* Animals – jaguars
Jails *see* Prisons
Jamaica *see* Foreign lands – Jamaica
Janitors *see* Careers – custodians, janitors
Japan *see* Foreign lands – Japan
Japanese Americans *see* Ethnic groups in the U.S. – Asian Americans; Ethnic groups in the U.S. – Japanese Americans
Jealousy *see* Emotions – envy, jealousy
Jesters *see* Clowns, jesters
Jewelry
Jewish culture
Jobs *see* Careers
Jokes *see* Riddles & jokes
Jonah *see* Religion – Jonah
Journalists *see* Careers – journalists
Judges *see* Careers – judges
Jumping *see* Activities – jumping

Jumping rope *see* Sports – jumping rope
Juneteenth *see* Holidays – Juneteenth
Jungle

Kangaroos *see* Animals – kangaroos
Karate *see* Sports – karate
Karok Indians *see* Indians of North America – Karok
Kato Indians *see* Indians of North America – Kato
Kelpies *see* Mythical creatures – kelpies
Kenya *see* Foreign lands – Kenya
Khans *see* Royalty – khans
Kindness *see* Character traits – kindness
Kindness to animals *see* Character traits – kindness to animals
Kings *see* Royalty – kings
Kissing
Kites
Knights
Knitting *see* Activities – knitting
Koalas *see* Animals – koalas
Komodo dragons *see* Reptiles – Komodo dragons
Korea *see* Foreign lands – Korea
Korea (North) *see* Foreign lands – Korea (North)
Korean Americans *see* Ethnic groups in the U.S. – Korean Americans
Kurdistan *see* Foreign lands – Kurdistan
Kutenai Indians *see* Indians of North America – Kutenai
Kwanzaa *see* Holidays – Kwanzaa

Lady birds *see* Insects – ladybugs
Ladybugs *see* Insects – ladybugs
Lakes, ponds
Lakota (Sioux) Indians *see* Indians of North America – Lakota (Sioux)
Lambs *see* Animals – babies; Animals – sheep
Language
Language – sign language *see* Sign language
Language, foreign *see* Foreign languages
Laos *see* Foreign lands – Laos
Lapland *see* Foreign lands – Lapland
Larks *see* Birds – larks
Latin America *see* Foreign lands – Latin America
Latvia *see* Foreign lands – Latvia
Laundry
Law *see* Careers – judges; Careers – lawyers; Careers – police officers; Crime; Prisons
Lawyers *see* Careers – lawyers
Laziness *see* Character traits – laziness
Lebanese Americans *see* Ethnic groups in the U.S. – Lebanese Americans
Lebanon *see* Foreign lands – Lebanon
Leeches *see* Animals – leeches
Left & right *see* Concepts – left & right
Left-handedness
Legends *see* Folk & fairy tales
Legs *see* Anatomy – legs
Lemmings *see* Animals – lemmings
Lemurs *see* Animals – lemurs
Lenape Indians *see* Indians of North America – Lenape
Leopards *see* Animals – leopards
Leprechauns *see* Mythical creatures – leprechauns
Letters, cards
Leverage *see* Concepts – leverage
Liberia *see* Foreign lands – Liberia
Librarians *see* Careers – librarians

Nagging *see* Behavior – nagging
Name calling *see* Behavior – name calling
Names
Namibia *see* Foreign lands – Namibia
Nanticoke Indians *see* Indians of North
America – Nanticoke
Napping *see* Sleep
Narragansett Indians *see* Indians of North
America – Narragansett
Native Americans *see* Eskimos; Indians of
Central America; Indians of North
America; Indians of South America
Nativity *see* Religion – Nativity
Nature
Naughty *see* Behavior – misbehavior
Navajo Indians *see* Indians of North
America – Navajo
Navels *see* Anatomy – navels
Neckties *see* Clothing – neckties
Needing someone *see* Behavior – needing
someone
Negotiation *see* Activities – trading
Neighborhoods *see* Communities,
neighborhoods
Nepal *see* Foreign lands – Nepal
Netherlands *see* Foreign lands – Holland
New Guinea *see* Foreign lands – New
Guinea
New Year's *see* Holidays – New Year's
New Zealand *see* Foreign lands – New
Zealand
Nez Perce Indians *see* Indians of North
America – Nez Perce
Nicaragua *see* Foreign lands – Nicaragua
Nigeria *see* Foreign lands – Nigeria
Night
Nightingales *see* Birds – nightingales
Nightmares
Nishnawbe Indians *see* Indians of North
America – Nishnawbe
Nisqually Indians *see* Indians of North
America – Nisqually
No text *see* Wordless
Noah *see* Religion – Noah
Nobscusset Indians *see* Indians of North
America – Nobscusset
Noise, sounds
Noise, sounds – snoring *see* Sleep –
snoring
North Pole *see* Foreign lands – Arctic
Northern lights
Norway *see* Foreign lands – Norway
Noses *see* Anatomy – noses; Senses – smell
Numbers *see* Counting, numbers
Nuns *see* Careers – nuns
Nursery rhymes
Nursery school *see* School – nursery
Nurses *see* Careers – nurses

Occupations *see* Careers
Oceans *see* Sea & seashore
Octopuses
Odors *see* Senses – smell
Ogres *see* Mythical creatures – ogres
Oil
Ojibwa Indians *see* Indians of North
America – Ojibwa
Old age
Olympics *see* Sports – Olympics
Only child *see* Family life – only child
Opera singers *see* Careers – opera singers;
Careers – singers
Opossums *see* Animals – possums
Opposites *see* Concepts – opposites
Optical illusions
Opticians, optometrists *see* Careers –
opticians, optometrists

Optimism *see* Character traits – optimism
Orangutans *see* Animals – orangutans
Orchestras *see* Musical instruments –
orchestras
Orderliness *see* Character traits –
orderliness
Organists *see* Careers – organists
Organs *see* Musical instruments – organs
Orphans
Ostriches *see* Birds – ostriches
Otters *see* Animals – otters
Outer space *see* Space ships
Outlaws *see* Crime
Owls *see* Birds – owls
Oxen *see* Animals – oxen

Pack rats *see* Animals – pack rats
Pageants *see* Theater
Painters *see* Activities – painting; Careers –
painters
Painting *see* Activities – painting
Paiute Indians *see* Indians of North
America – Paiute
Pajamas *see* Clothing – pajamas
Pakistan *see* Foreign lands – Pakistan
Paleontologists *see* Careers –
paleontologists
Palestine *see* Foreign lands – Palestine
Panama *see* Foreign lands – Panama
Pandas *see* Animals – pandas
Panthers *see* Animals – leopards
Pants *see* Clothing – pants
Papago *see* Indians of North America –
Papago
Paper
Parades
Parakeets *see* Birds – parakeets, parrots
Parks
Parks – amusement
Participation
Parties
Passover *see* Holidays – Passover
Patience *see* Character traits – patience
Patterns *see* Concepts – patterns
Pawnee Indians *see* Indians of North
America – Pawnee
Peacocks, peahens *see* Birds – peacocks,
peahens
Peddlers *see* Careers – peddlers
Pegasus *see* Mythical creatures – Pegasus
Pelicans *see* Birds – pelicans
Pen pals
Penguins *see* Birds – penguins
Penobscot Indians *see* Indians of North
America – Penobscot
Perfectionism *see* Character traits –
perfectionism
Perseverance *see* Character traits –
perseverance
Persia *see* Foreign lands – Persia
Persistence *see* Character traits –
persistence
Perspective *see* Concepts – perspective
Peru *see* Foreign lands – Peru
Petroglyphs
Petroleum *see* Oil
Pets
Pharaohs *see* Royalty – pharaohs
Philippines *see* Foreign lands –
Philippines
Phoenix *see* Mythical creatures – phoenix
Photographers *see* Careers –
photographers
Photography *see* Activities –
photographing
Physical handicaps *see* Handicaps –
physical handicaps

Physicians *see* Careers – doctors
Pianos *see* Musical instruments – pianos
Picnics *see* Activities – picnicking
Picture puzzles
Pigeons *see* Birds – pigeons
Pigs *see* Animals – pigs
Pilgrims
Pilots *see* Careers – airplane pilots
Pima Indians *see* Indians of North
America – Pima
Pioneer life *see* U.S. history – frontier &
pioneer life
Pirates
Pixies *see* Mythical creatures – pixies
Planes *see* Airplanes, airports
Planets
Plants
Plasterers *see* Careers – plasterers
Playing *see* Activities – playing
Plays *see* Theater
Plovers *see* Birds – plovers
Plumbers *see* Careers – plumbers
Pockets *see* Clothing
Poetry
Poland *see* Foreign lands – Poland
Polar bears *see* Animals – polar bears
Police officers *see* Careers – police officers
Polio *see* Illness – poliomyelitis
Polish Americans *see* Ethnic groups in the
U.S. – Polish Americans
Poltergeists *see* Ghosts
Ponds *see* Lakes, ponds
Ponies *see* Animals – horses, ponies
Pooka spirit *see* Mythical creatures –
pooka spirit
Poor *see* Homeless; Poverty
Pop-up books *see* Format, unusual – toy &
movable books
Porcupines *see* Animals – porcupines
Porpoises *see* Animals – dolphins
Portugal *see* Foreign lands – Portugal
Possums *see* Animals – possums
Post office
Postal workers *see* Careers – postal
workers
Potawatomi Indians *see* Indians of North
America – Potawatomi
Potty training *see* Toilet training
Pourquoi tales *see* Folk & fairy tales –
pourquoi tales
Poverty
Pow-wows
Power failures
Powhatan Indians *see* Indians of North
America – Powhatan
Practicality *see* Character traits –
practicality
Prairie dogs *see* Animals – prairie dogs
Prairie wolves *see* Animals – coyotes
Prayers *see* Religion
Praying mantis *see* Insects – praying
mantis
Preachers *see* Careers – clergy
Pregnancy *see* Birth
Prehistoric man *see* Cavemen
Prehistory
Prejudice
Preschool *see* School – nursery
Pride *see* Character traits – pride
Priests *see* Careers – clergy
Princes *see* Royalty – princes
Princesses *see* Royalty – princesses
Printers *see* Careers – printers
Prisons
Problem solving
Progress
Promptness *see* Behavior – promptness
Proverbs

Ptarmigans *see* Birds – ptarmigans
Pueblo Indians *see* Indians of North America – Pueblo
Puerto Rico *see* Foreign lands – Puerto Rico
Puffins *see* Birds – puffins
Pumas *see* Animals – cougars
Punchball *see* Sports – punchball
Punctuality *see* Behavior – promptness
Puppeteers *see* Careers – puppeteers
Puppets
Purim *see* Holidays – Purim
Purses *see* Clothing – handbags, purses
Puzzles

Quail *see* Birds – quail
Quechua Indians *see* Indians of South America – Quechua
Queens *see* Royalty – queens
Questioning *see* Character traits – questioning
Quicksand *see* Sand
Quilts

Rabbis *see* Careers – clergy
Rabbits *see* Animals – rabbits
Raccoons *see* Animals – raccoons
Race car drivers *see* Careers – race car drivers
Race relations *see* Prejudice
Racing *see* Sports – racing
Radios
Railroad engineers *see* Careers – railroad engineers
Railroads *see* Trains
Rain *see* Weather – rain
Rainbows *see* Weather – rainbows
Rajahs *see* Royalty – rajahs
Ramadan *see* Holidays – Ramadan
Ranchers *see* Careers – ranchers
Rangers *see* Careers – park rangers
Rats *see* Animals – rats
Ravens *see* Birds – ravens
Reading *see* Books, reading
Rebuses
Reindeer *see* Animals – reindeer
Religion
Religion – Buddhism
Religion – Daniel
Religion – David
Religion – Hinduism
Religion – Islam
Religion – Jonah
Religion – Moses
Religion – Nativity
Religion – Noah
Remembering *see* Memories, memory
Repetitive stories *see* Cumulative tales
Reptiles
Reptiles – alligators, crocodiles
Reptiles – chameleons
Reptiles – crocodiles *see* Reptiles – alligators, crocodiles
Reptiles – iguanas
Reptiles – Komodo dragons
Reptiles – lizards
Reptiles – monitor lizards
Reptiles – salamanders
Reptiles – snakes
Reptiles – turtles, tortoises
Resourcefulness *see* Behavior – resourcefulness
Responsibility *see* Character traits – responsibility
Rest *see* Sleep
Restaurants

Rhinoceros *see* Animals – rhinoceros
Rhyming text
Riddles & jokes
Right & left *see* Concepts – left & right
Riots
Rivers
Roads
Robbers *see* Crime
Robins *see* Birds – robins
Robots
Rock climbing *see* Sports – rock climbing
Rockets *see* Space & space ships
Rocking chairs *see* Furniture – chairs
Rocking horses *see* Toys – rocking horses
Rocks
Rodeos
Roller skating *see* Sports – roller skating
Romania *see* Foreign lands – Romania
Roosters *see* Birds – chickens
Rosh Hashanah *see* Holidays – Rosh Hashanah
Royalty
Royalty – emperors
Royalty – khans
Royalty – kings
Royalty – pharaohs
Royalty – princes
Royalty – princesses
Royalty – queens
Royalty – rajahs
Royalty – sultans
Royalty – tsars
Rummage sales *see* Garage sales, rummage sales
Running *see* Activities – running; Sports – racing
Running away *see* Behavior – running away
Russia *see* Foreign lands – Russia
Russian Americans *see* Ethnic groups in the U.S. – Russian Americans
Rwanda *see* Foreign lands – Rwanda

Sadness *see* Emotions – sadness
Safety
Sahara Desert *see* Foreign lands – Sahara Desert
Sailing *see* Sports – sailing
Sailors
Saint Patrick's Day *see* Holidays – St. Patrick's Day
Salamanders *see* Reptiles – salamanders
Salesmen *see* Careers – salesmen
Sand
Sandcastles *see* Sand
Sandman *see* Mythical creatures – sandman
Sandpipers *see* Birds – sandpipers
Sandstorms *see* Weather – sandstorms
Sanitation workers *see* Careers – sanitation workers
Santa Claus
Saving things *see* Behavior – saving things
Saxophones *see* Musical instruments – saxophones
Scandinavia *see* Foreign lands – Scandinavia
Scarecrows
School
School – field trips
School – first day
School – nursery
School principals *see* Careers – school principals
School teachers *see* Careers – teachers
Science
Scientists *see* Careers – scientists

Scotland *see* Foreign lands – Scotland
Scuba diving *see* Sports – skin diving
Sculptors *see* Careers – sculptors
Sea & seashore
Sea & seashore – beaches
Sea lions *see* Animals – sea lions
Sea serpents *see* Monsters; Mythical creatures
Seagulls *see* Birds – seagulls
Seahorses *see* Fish – seahorses
Seals *see* Animals – seals
Seamstresses *see* Careers – seamstresses
Seashore *see* Sand; Sea & seashore – beaches
Seasons
Seasons – fall
Seasons – spring
Seasons – summer
Seasons – winter
Secret codes
Secrets *see* Behavior – secrets
Seeds
Seeing *see* Anatomy – eyes; Glasses; Handicaps – blindness; Senses – sight
Seeing eye dogs *see* Animals – service animals
Seeking better things *see* Behavior – seeking better things
Self-concept
Self-esteem *see* Self-concept
Self-image *see* Self-concept
Self-reliance *see* Character traits – confidence
Selfishness *see* Character traits – selfishness
Selkies *see* Mythical creatures – selkies
Seminole Indians *see* Indians of North America – Seminole
Seneca Indians *see* Indians of North America – Seneca
Senses
Senses – hearing
Senses – sight
Senses – smell
Senses – taste
Senses – touch
Serbia *see* Foreign lands – Serbia
Service animals *see* Animals – service animals
Sewing *see* Activities – sewing
Sex instruction
Sex roles *see* Gender roles
Sextuplets *see* Multiple births – sextuplets
Shadows
Shakers *see* Ethnic groups in the U.S. – Shakers
Shakespeare
Shape *see* Concepts – shape
Shaped books *see* Format, unusual
Sharing *see* Behavior – sharing
Sharks *see* Fish – sharks
Shavuot *see* Holidays – Shavuot
Shawnee Indians *see* Indians of North America – Shawnee
Sheep *see* Animals – sheep
Shells *see* Sea & seashore
Shepherds *see* Careers – shepherds
Sheriffs *see* Careers – sheriffs
Ships *see* Boats, ships
Shirts *see* Clothing – shirts
Shopping
Shops *see* Stores
Shoshone Indians *see* Indians of North America – Shoshone
Shows *see* Theater
Shrews *see* Animals – shrews
Shrimp *see* Crustaceans – shrimp
Shyness *see* Character traits – shyness

Siam *see* Foreign lands – Thailand
Siberia *see* Foreign lands – Siberia
Sibling rivalry
Siblings *see* Family life – brothers; Family life – brothers & sisters; Family life – sisters; Family life – stepfamilies
Sickness *see* Health & fitness; Illness
Sight *see* Anatomy – eyes; Glasses; Handicaps – blindness; Senses – sight
Sign language
Sign painters *see* Careers – sign painters
Signs & signboards
Siksika Indians *see* Indians of North America – Siksika
Singers *see* Careers – opera singers; Careers – singers
Singing *see* Activities – singing
Single-parent families *see* Family life – single-parent families
Sioux Indians *see* Indians of North America – Cheyenne (Sioux); Indians of North America – Dakota (Sioux); Indians of North America – Lakota (Sioux); Indians of North America – Sioux
Sisters *see* Family life; Family life – brothers; Family life – brothers & sisters; Family life – sisters; Sibling rivalry
Size *see* Concepts – size
Skateboarding *see* Sports – skateboarding
Skating *see* Sports – ice skating; Sports – hockey; Sports – roller skating
Skeletons *see* Anatomy – skeletons
Skiing *see* Sports – skiing
Skin *see* Anatomy – skin
Skin diving *see* Sports – skin diving
Skunks *see* Animals – skunks
Sky
Slavery
Sledding *see* Sports – sledding
Sleep
Sleep – snoring
Sleepovers
Sleight-of-hand *see* Magic
Sloths *see* Animals – sloths
Slugs *see* Animals – slugs
Smallness *see* Character traits – smallness
Smell *see* Anatomy – noses; Senses – smell
Smiles, smiling *see* Anatomy – faces
Snails *see* Animals – snails
Snakes *see* Reptiles – snakes
Snoring *see* Noise, sounds; Sleep – snoring
Snow *see* Weather – blizzards; Weather – snow
Snow plows *see* Machines
Snowmen
Soccer *see* Sports – soccer
Society Islands *see* Foreign lands – South Sea Islands
Socks *see* Clothing – socks
Sofas *see* Furniture – couches, sofas
Soldiers *see* Careers – military
Soldiers, toy *see* Toys – soldiers
Solitude *see* Behavior – solitude
Songs
Sons *see* Family life – sons
Sorcerers *see* Wizards
Sounds *see* Noise, sounds
South Africa *see* Foreign lands – South Africa
South America *see* Foreign lands – South America
South Pole *see* Foreign lands – Antarctic
South Sea Islands *see* Foreign lands – South Sea Islands
Southwest Indians *see* Indians of North America – Southwest

Soviet Union *see* Foreign lands – Soviet Union
Space & space ships
Spain *see* Foreign lands – Spain
Sparrows *see* Birds – sparrows
Special Olympics *see* Sports – Special Olympics
Spectacles *see* Glasses
Speech *see* Handicaps – stuttering; Language
Speed *see* Concepts – speed
Spelunking *see* Caves
Spiders
Split page books *see* Format, unusual
Sponges *see* Animals – sponges
Spooks *see* Ghosts; Mythical creatures – goblins
Spoonbills *see* Birds – spoonbills
Sports
Sports – archery
Sports – baseball
Sports – basketball
Sports – bicycling
Sports – bowling
Sports – boxing
Sports – camping *see* Camps, camping
Sports – fishing
Sports – football
Sports – golf
Sports – gymnastics
Sports – hiking
Sports – hockey
Sports – hunting
Sports – ice skating
Sports – jumping rope
Sports – karate
Sports – mountain climbing
Sports – Olympics
Sports – punchball
Sports – racing
Sports – rock climbing
Sports – roller skating
Sports – sailing
Sports – skateboarding
Sports – skiing
Sports – skin diving
Sports – sledding
Sports – snowboarding
Sports – soccer
Sports – Special Olympics
Sports – surfing
Sports – swimming
Sports – T-ball
Sports – Tae Kwon Do
Sports – volleyball
Sports – wrestling
Sportsmanship
Spring *see* Seasons – spring
Squirrels *see* Animals – squirrels
Stage *see* Theater
Starfish *see* Animals – starfish
Stars
Stealing *see* Behavior – stealing; Crime
Steam shovels *see* Machines
Steamrollers *see* Machines
Stepfamilies *see* Divorce; Family life – stepfamilies
Stepchildren *see* Divorce; Family life – stepfamilies
Stepparents *see* Divorce; Family life – stepfamilies
Stones *see* Rocks
Storekeepers *see* Careers – storekeepers
Stores
Stories in rhyme *see* Rhyming text
Storks *see* Birds – storks
Storms *see* Weather – storms
Storytelling *see* Activities – storytelling

Strangers *see* Behavior – talking to strangers
Streams *see* Rivers
Streets *see* Roads
String
Stubbornness *see* Character traits – stubbornness
Stuttering *see* Handicaps – stuttering
Submarines *see* Boats, ships
Suits *see* Clothing – suits
Sukkot *see* Holidays – Sukkot
Sullivan Islands *see* Foreign lands – South Sea Islands
Sultans *see* Royalty – sultans
Summer *see* Seasons – summer
Sun
Superstition
Surfing *see* Sports – surfing
Suriname *see* Foreign lands – Suriname
Swallows *see* Birds – swallows
Swamps
Swans *see* Birds – swans
Swapping *see* Activities – trading
Sweaters *see* Clothing – sweaters
Sweden *see* Foreign lands – Sweden
Swimming *see* Sports – swimming
Swinging *see* Activities – swinging
Switzerland *see* Foreign lands – Switzerland
Symbiosis

T-ball *see* Sports – T-ball
Tables *see* Furniture – tables
Tae Kwon Do *see* Sports – Tae Kwon Do
Tailors *see* Careers – tailors
Tails *see* Anatomy – tails
Taiwan *see* Foreign lands – Taiwan
Talking *see* Activities – talking
Talking to strangers *see* Behavior – talking to strangers
Tall tales
Tanzania *see* Foreign lands – Tanzania
Tapirs *see* Animals – tapirs
Tarascan Indians *see* Indians of North America – Tarascan
Tardiness *see* Behavior – promptness, tardiness
Taste *see* Senses – taste
Taxi drivers *see* Careers – taxi drivers
Taxis
Teachers *see* Careers – teachers
Teasing *see* Behavior – bullying
Teddy bears *see* Toys – bears
Teeth
Telephone
Telephone operators *see* Careers – telephone operators
Television
Telling stories *see* Activities – storytelling
Telling time *see* Clocks, watches; Time
Temper tantrums *see* Emotions – anger
Texas
Textless *see* Wordless
Thailand *see* Foreign lands – Thailand
Thanksgiving *see* Holidays – Thanksgiving
Theater
Thieves *see* Crime
Thumb sucking
Thunder *see* Weather – lightning, thunder; Weather – storms
Tibet *see* Foreign lands – Tibet
Tigers *see* Animals – tigers
Time
Tin soldiers *see* Toys – soldiers
Tlingit Indians *see* Indians of North America – Tlingit
Toads *see* Frogs & toads

Toes *see* Anatomy – toes
Toilet training
Tongue twisters
Tongues *see* Anatomy – tongues
Tonsillectomy *see* Illness – tonsillectomy
Tools
Tooth fairy *see* Fairies; Teeth
Tornadoes *see* Weather – tornadoes
Tortoises *see* Reptiles – turtles, tortoises
Toucans *see* Birds – toucans
Touch *see* Senses – touch
Towns *see* Cities, towns
Toy & movable books *see* Format, unusual – toy & movable books
Toy makers *see* Careers – toy makers
Toys
Toys – balloons
Toys – balls
Toys – bears
Toys – blocks
Toys – dolls
Toys – hobby horses *see* Toys – rocking horses
Toys – pandas *see* Toys – bears
Toys – rocking horses
Toys – soldiers
Toys – teddy bears *see* Toys – bears
Toys – tin soldiers *see* Toys – soldiers
Toys – trains
Toys – wagons
Tractors
Trading *see* Activities – trading
Traffic, traffic signs
Train engineers *see* Careers – railroad engineers
Trains
Trains, toy *see* Toys – trains
Transportation
Traveling *see* Activities – traveling
Trees
Trickery *see* Behavior – trickery
Tricks *see* Magic
Trinidad *see* Foreign lands – Trinidad
Trolleys *see* Cable cars, trolleys
Trolls *see* Mythical creatures – trolls
Trombones *see* Musical instruments – trombones
Truck drivers *see* Careers – truck drivers
Trucks
Tsars *see* Royalty – tsars
Tsimshian Indians *see* Indians of North America – Tsimshian
Tsunamis
Tu B'Shevat *see* Holidays – Tu B'Shevat
Turkey *see* Foreign lands – Turkey
Turkeys *see* Birds – turkeys
Turtles *see* Reptiles – turtles, tortoises
TV *see* Television
Twa Indians *see* Indians of North America – Twa
Twilight
Twins *see* Multiple births – twins
Tyrol *see* Foreign lands – Tyrol

U.S. history
U.S. history – frontier & pioneer life
Ukraine *see* Foreign lands – Ukraine
Umbrellas
Uncles *see* Family life – aunts, uncles
Unhappiness *see* Emotions – happiness; Emotions – sadness
UNICEF
Unicorns *see* Mythical creatures – unicorns
Unnoticed *see* Behavior – unnoticed, unseen
Unusual format *see* Format, unusual

Up & down *see* Concepts – up & down
Ute Indians *see* Indians of North America – Ute
Uzbekistan *see* Foreign lands – Uzbekistan

Vacationing *see* Activities – vacationing
Vacuum cleaners *see* Machines – vacuum cleaners
Valentine's Day *see* Holidays – Valentine's Day
Values
Vampires *see* Monsters – vampires
Vanity *see* Character traits – vanity
Vatican City *see* Foreign lands – Vatican City
Venezuela *see* Foreign lands – Venezuela
Veterinarians *see* Careers – veterinarians
Vietnam *see* Foreign lands – Vietnam
Vietnamese Americans *see* Ethnic groups in the U.S. – Vietnamese Americans
Vikings
Violence, nonviolence
Violins *see* Musical instruments – violins
Volcanoes
Vultures *see* Birds – vultures

Wagons *see* Toys – wagons
Waiters *see* Careers – waiters, waitresses
Waitresses *see* Careers – waiters, waitresses
Wales *see* Foreign lands – Wales
Walking *see* Activities – walking
Walruses *see* Animals – walruses
Wampanoag Indians *see* Indians of North America – Wampanoag
War
Warthogs *see* Animals – warthogs
Washboards *see* Musical instruments – washboards
Washing machines *see* Machines
Washington's Birthday *see* Holidays – Washington's Birthday
Wasps *see* Insects – wasps
Watches *see* Clocks, watches
Water
Water buffaloes *see* Animals – water buffaloes
Weapons
Weasels *see* Animals – weasels
Weather
Weather – blizzards
Weather – clouds
Weather – cold
Weather – droughts
Weather – floods
Weather – fog
Weather – hurricanes
Weather – lightning, thunder
Weather – mist *see* Weather – fog
Weather – rain
Weather – rainbows
Weather – sandstorms
Weather – snow
Weather – storms
Weather – thunder *see* Weather – lightning, thunder
Weather – tornadoes
Weather – wind
Weather reporters *see* Careers – meteorologists
Weavers *see* Careers – weavers
Weaving *see* Activities – weaving
Weddings
Weekdays *see* Days of the week, months of the year
Weight *see* Concepts – weight
Welders *see* Careers – welders

Werewolves *see* Mythical creatures – werewolves
West *see* U.S. history – frontier & pioneer life
West Indies *see* Foreign lands – West Indies
Whalers *see* Careers – whalers
Whales *see* Animals – whales
Wheelchairs *see* Handicaps – physical handicaps
Wheels
Whistles
Whistling *see* Activities – whistling
Wildebeests *see* Animals – wildebeests
Willfulness *see* Character traits – willfulness
Wind *see* Weather – wind
Windigos Indians *see* Indians of North America – Windigos
Windmills
Window cleaners *see* Careers – window cleaners
Wings *see* Anatomy – wings
Winter *see* Seasons – winter
Wisdom *see* Character traits – wisdom
Wishing *see* Behavior – wishing
Witches
Wizards
Wolves *see* Animals – wolves
Wombats *see* Animals – wombats
Wood-hoopoe *see* Birds – wood-hoopoes
Woodcarvers *see* Careers – woodcarvers
Woodchucks *see* Animals – groundhogs
Woodpeckers *see* Birds – woodpeckers
Woods *see* Forest, woods
Word games *see* Language
Wordless
Working *see* Activities – working; Careers
World
Worms *see* Animals – worms
Worrying *see* Behavior – worrying
Wrecking machines *see* Machines
Wrens *see* Birds – wrens
Wrestling *see* Sports – wrestling
Writers *see* Careers – writers; Children as authors
Writing *see* Activities – writing
Writing letters *see* Letters, cards

Yaks *see* Animals – yaks
Yana Indians *see* Indians of North America – Yana
Yanomamo Indians *see* Indians of South America – Yanomamo
Yom Kippur *see* Holidays – Yom Kippur
Yukon Territory *see* Foreign lands – Yukon Territory
Yupik Indians *see* Indians of North America – Yupik

Zaire *see* Foreign lands – Zaire
Zanzibar *see* Foreign lands – Zanzibar
Zapotec Indians *see* Indians of North America – Zapotec
Zebras *see* Animals – zebras
Zodiac
Zookeepers *see* Careers – zookeepers
Zoos
Zuni Indians *see* Indians of North America – Zuni

Subject Guide

This is a subject-arranged guide to picture books. Under appropriate subject headings and subheadings, titles appear alphabetically by author name, or by title when author is unknown. Complete bibliographic information for each title cited will be found in the Bibliographic Guide.

Aardvarks *see* Animals – aardvarks

ABC books

A is for alphabet
ABC school riddles
ABCDEFGHIJKLMNOPQRSTUVWXYZ in English and Spanish
Abrams, Pam. *Now I eat my ABC's*
Abrons, Mary. *For Alice a palace*
Ackerman, Karen. *Flannery Row*
Ada, Alma Flor. *Gathering the sun*
Agee, Jon. *Z goes home*
Alda, Arlene. *Arlene Alda's ABC*
Alexander, Anne (Anna Barbara Cooke). *ABC of cars and trucks*
Allen, Susan. *Read anything good lately?*
Allington, Richard L. *Letters*
Andersen, Karen Born. *An alphabet in five acts*
Anglund, Joan Walsh. *A is for always*
Anno, Mitsumasa. *Anno's alphabet*
    Anno's magical ABC
Argent, Kerry. *Animal capers*
Arnosky, Jim. *Mouse letters*
    Mouse numbers and letters
    Mouse writing
Asch, Frank. *The alphabet zoo*
    Little Devil's ABC
Ashley Bryan's abc of African American poetry
Ashton, Elizabeth Allen. *An old-fashioned ABC book*
Aylesworth, Jim. *The folks in the valley*
    Old Black Fly
Azarian, Mary. *A farmer's alphabet*
    A gardener's alphabet
Babson, Jane F. *Babson's bestiary*
Baker, Alan. *Black and White Rabbit's ABC*
Balian, Lorna. *Humbug potion*
Balog, James. *James Balog's animals A to Z*
Bannatyne-Cugnet, Jo. *A prairie alphabet*
Barron, Rex. *Fed up!*
Barry, Katharina. *A is for anything*
Barry, Robert E. *Animals around the world*
Base, Graeme. *Animalia*
Baseball ABC
Baskin, Leonard. *Hosie's alphabet*
Bayer, Jane. *A my name is Alice*
Bea, Holly. *My spiritual alphabet book*
Beaton, Clare. *Zoë and her zebra*
Beller, Janet. *A-B-C-ing*
Bender, Robert. *The A to Z beastly jamboree*
Berenstain, Stan. *The Berenstains' B book*
Berger, Terry. *Ben's ABC day*

Bernhard, Durga. *Alphabeasts*
Bishop, Ann. *Riddle-iculous rid-alphabet book*
Black, Floyd. *Alphabet cat*
Blake, Quentin. *Quentin Blake's ABC*
Bond, Jean Carey. *A is for Africa*
Bond, Michael. *Paddington's ABC*
Borlenghi, Patricia. *From albatross to zoo*
Bourke, Linda. *Eye count*
Bove, Linda. *Sign language ABC with Linda Bove*
Bowen, Betsy. *Antler, bear, canoe*
Boxer, Devorah. *26 ways to be somebody else*
Boynton, Sandra. *A is for angry*
Bridwell, Norman. *Clifford's ABC*
Bronson, Linda. *The circus alphabet*
Brown, Judith Gwyn. *Alphabet dreams*
Brown, Marc Tolon. *Arthur's animal adventure*
Brown, Marcia. *All butterflies*
    Peter Piper's alphabet
Brown, Margaret Wise. *Sleepy ABC*
Brown, Ruth. *Alphabet times four*
Bruce, Lisa. *Oliver's alphabets*
Bruchac, Joseph. *Many nations*
Bruna, Dick. *B is for bear*
Brunhoff, Laurent de. *Babar's ABC*
Brusca, María Cristina. *When jaguars ate the moon*
Budd, Lillian. *The pie wagon*
Budney, Blossom. *N is for nursery school*
Bullard, Lisa. *Not enough beds!*
Bunting, Jane. *My first ABC*
Burnard, Damon. *I spy in the ocean*
Burningham, John. *First steps*
    John Burningham's ABC
Burnstein, Chaya M. *The Jewish kids' Hebrew-English wordbook*
Burton, Jane. *ABC*
Burton, Marilee Robin. *Aaron awoke*
Calmenson, Stephanie. *ABC*
    It begins with an A
Capucilli, Alyssa Satin. *Mrs. McTats and her houseful of cats*
Carlson, Nancy L. *ABC, I like me!*
Catalanotto, Peter. *Matthew A.B.C.*
Chandra, Deborah. *A is for Amos*
Chaplin, Susan Gibbons. *I can sign my ABCs*
Chardiet, Bernice. *C is for circus*
Charles, Donald. *Shaggy dog's animal alphabet*
Charlip, Remy. *Handtalk*
Chase, Catherine. *An alphabet book*
    Baby mouse learns his ABC's
Chess, Victoria. *Alfred's alphabet walk*
Chial, Debra. *M is for Minnesota*
A child's picture English-Hebrew dictionary
Chin-Lee, Cynthia. *A is for Asia*
Chouinard, Roger. *The amazing animal alphabet book*
Chwast, Seymour. *Alphabet parade*
    Still another alphabet book
Cleary, Beverly. *The hullabaloo ABC*, ill. by Ted Rand
    The hullabaloo ABC, ill. by Earl Thollander
Cleaver, Elizabeth. *ABC*
Cline-Ransome, Lesa. *Quilt alphabet*
Coats, Laura Jane. *Alphabet garden*

Cohen, Nora. *From apple to zipper*
Cohen, Peter Zachary. *Authorized autumn charts of the Upper Red Canoe River country*
Coletta, Irene. *From A to Z*
Conran, Sebastian. *My first ABC book*
Cooney, Barbara. *A garland of games and other diversions*
Cousins, Lucy. *Maisy's ABC*
Cox, Lynn. *Crazy alphabet*
Cremins, Robert. *My animal ABC*
Crews, Donald. *We read*
Crowther, Robert. *The most amazing hide-and-seek alphabet book*
　My pop-up surprise ABC
Cushman, Doug. *The ABC mystery*
Daleo, Morgan Simone. *A spirited alphabet*
Darling, Kathy (Mary Kathleen). *ABC cats*
　ABC dogs
　Amazon A B C
Dauphin, Francine Legrand. *A French A. B. C.*
DeLage, Ida. *ABC Christmas*
　ABC Easter bunny
　ABC fire dogs
　ABC Halloween witch
　ABC pigs go to market
　ABC pirate adventure
　ABC Santa Claus
　ABC triplets at the zoo
Delaunay, Sonia. *Sonia Delaunay's alphabet*
Demarest, Chris L. *The cowboy ABC*
　Firefighters A to Z
De Mejo, Oscar. *Oscar de Mejo's ABC*
Demi. *Demi's find the animals A B C*
　The peek-a-boo ABC
De Vicq de Cumptich, Roberto. *Bembo's zoo*
Dodd, Emma. *Dog's ABC*
Dodd, Lynley. *The minister's cat: ABC*
Domanska, Janina. *A was an angler*
Doolittle, Eileen. *The ark in the attic*
Doubilet, Anne. *Under the sea from A to Z*
Downie, Jill. *Alphabet puzzle*
Dragonwagon, Crescent. *Alligator arrived with apples*
Dreamer, Sue. *Circus ABC*
Drucker, Malka. *A Jewish holiday ABC*
Duke, Kate. *The guinea pig ABC*
Duvoisin, Roger Antoine. *A for the ark*
Eastman, P. D. (Philip D.). *The alphabet book*
Edens, Cooper. *An ABC of fashionable animals*
Edwards, Michelle. *Alef-bet*
Edwards, Pamela Duncan. *The wacky wedding*
Ehlert, Lois. *Eating the alphabet*
Eichenberg, Fritz. *Ape in cape*
Elliott, David. *An alphabet of rotten kids!*
Elting, Mary. *Q is for duck*
Emberley, Ed (Edward Randolph). *Ed Emberley's ABC*
Ernst, Lisa Campbell. *The letters are lost!*
Eschbacher, Roger. *Nonsense! He yelled*
Falls, C. B. (Charles Buckles). *ABC book*
Farber, Norma. *As I was crossing Boston Common*
Farley, Carol J. *The king's secret*
Faulkenberry, Lauren. *What do animals do on the weekend?*
Feelings, Muriel. *Jambo means hello*
Feldman, Judy. *The alphabet in nature*
Ferguson, Don. *Winnie the Pooh's A to Zzzz*
Fife, Dale. *Adam's ABC*
Fisher, Leonard Everett. *The ABC exhibit*
Fisher, Valorie. *Ellsworth's extraordinary electric ears and other amazing alphabet anecdotes*
Fleming, Denise. *Alphabet under construction*
Floyd, Lucy. *Agatha's alphabet, with her very own dictionary*
Ford, Juwanda G. *K is for Kwanzaa*
Frampton, David. *My beastie book of ABC*
Freeman, Don. *Add-a-line alphabet*
Fujikawa, Gyo. *Gyo Fujikawa's A to Z picture book*
Gabler, Mirko. *The alphabet soup*
Gág, Wanda. *ABC bunny*
Gallup, Joan. *Silly animal ABCs*
Gantz, David. *The genie bear with the light brown hair word book*
Gardner, Beau. *Have you ever seen . . . ?*

Garten, Jan. *The alphabet tale*
Geringer, Laura. *The cow is mooing anyhow*
Gerstein, Mordicai. *The absolutely awful alphabet*
Ghigna, Charles. *The alphabet parade*
Girnis, Margaret. *ABC for you and me*
Glyman, Caroline A. *Learning your ABC's of nutrition*
Goennel, Heidi. *Heidi's zoo*
Golding, Kim. *Alphababies*
Good, Phyllis Pellman. *Plain Pig's ABCs*
Greenaway, Kate. *A apple pie*
Gretz, Susanna. *Teddy bears ABC*
Grimes, Nikki. *C is for city*
Groening, Maggie. *Maggie Simpson's alphabet book*
Grossbart, Francine. *A big city*
Grossman, Bill. *My little sister hugged an ape*
Grover, Max. *The accidental zucchini*
Gundersheimer, Karen. *A B C, say with me*
Gunning, Monica. *The two Georges = Los dos Jorges*
Haas, Jessie. *Appaloosa zebra*
Hague, Kathleen. *Alphabears*
Hallinan, P. K. (Patrick K.). *When I grow up*
Hansen, Biruta Akerbergs. *Parading with piglets*
Harada, Joyce. *It's the ABC book*
Harness, Cheryl. *Midnight in the cemetery*
Harrison, Ted. *A northern alphabet*
Hausman, Bonnie. *A to Z, do you ever feel like me?*
Hausman, Gerald. *Turtle Island ABC*
Hawkins, Colin. *Busy ABC*
Hayward, Linda. *Alphabet School*
　D is for doll
Heller, Nicholas. *Goblins in green*
Hepworth, Catherine. *ANTics! an alphabetical anthology*
Hill, Susan. *Simba's A-Z*
Hillman, Priscilla. *A Merry-Mouse Christmas A B C*
Hindley, Judy. *Crazy ABC*
Hoban, Tana. *A B See!*
　26 letters and 99 cents
Hobbie, Holly. *Toot and Puddle, Puddle's ABC*
Hoberman, Mary Ann. *Nuts to you and nuts to me*
Hoguet, Susan Ramsay. *I unpacked my grandmother's trunk*
Holabird, Katharine. *The little mouse ABC*
Holl, Adelaide. *The ABC of cars, trucks and machines*
Hooper, Patricia. *A bundle of beasts*
Hopkins, Lee Bennett. *Alphathoughts*
　April, bubbles, chocolate
Horenstein, Henry. *A is for – ?*
　Arf! beg! catch!
Howard-Gibbon, Amelia Frances. *An illustrated comic alphabet*
Howell, Will C. *Zoo flakes ABC*
Howland, Naomi. *ABCDrive!*
Hubbard, Woodleigh Marx. *C is for curious*
Hudson, Cheryl Willis. *Afro-Bets ABC book*
Hudson, Wade. *Afro-Bets Kids I'm gonna be*
Hughes, Langston. *The sweet and sour animal book*
Hughes, Shirley. *Alfie's ABC*
　Lucy and Tom's A.B.C.
Hyman, Trina Schart. *A little alphabet*
Ilsley, Velma. *A busy day for Chris*
　M is for moving
Inkpen, Mick. *Kipper's A to Z*
Ipcar, Dahlov (Zorach). *I love my anteater with an A*
Isadora, Rachel. *ABC pop!*
　City seen from A to Z
J. Paul Getty Museum. *A is for artist*
Jefferds, Vincent. *Disney's elegant ABC book*
Jewell, Nancy. *ABC cat*
Johnson, Crockett. *Harold's ABC*
Johnson, Jean. *Teachers A to Z*
Johnson, Odette. *Apples, alligators, and also alphabets*
Johnson, Stephen T. *Alphabet city*
Jonas, Ann. *Aardvarks, disembark!*
Jordan, Martin. *Amazon alphabet*
Joyce, Susan. *ABC animal riddles*
　ABC nature riddles
　Alphabet riddles
Kalman, Maira. *What Pete ate from A-Z*
Keith, Adrienne. *Fairies from A to Z*

Kelley, Marty. *Summer stinks*
Kellogg, Steven (Stephen). *Aster Aardvark's alphabet adventures*
Kightley, Rosalinda. *ABC*
King-Smith, Dick. *Dick King-Smith's Alphabeasts*
Kirk, David. *Miss Spider's ABC*
Kitamura, Satoshi. *From acorn to zoo and everything in between in alphabetical order*
    What's inside?
Kitchen, Bert. *Animal alphabet*
Krull, Kathleen. *M is for music*
Kuskin, Karla. *ABCDEFGHIJKLMNOPQRSTUVWXYZ*
Kutner, Merrily. *Z is for zombie*
Laidlaw, Ken. *The amazing I spy ABC*
Lalicki, Barbara. *If there were dreams to sell*
Lalli, Judy. *Feelings alphabet*
Lauture, Denizé. *Running the road to ABC*
Leander, Ed. *Q is for crazy*
Lear, Edward. *A was once an apple pie*
    ABC
    An Edward Lear alphabet, ill. by Carol Newsom
    An Edward Lear alphabet, ill. by Vladimir Radunsky
    Edward Lear's ABC
    Nonsense alphabet
Lecourt, Nancy. *Abracadabra to zigzag*
Leonard, Marcia. *Alphabet bandits*
Lester, Alison. *Alice and Aldo*
Lester, Mike. *A is for salad*
Lillie, Patricia. *One very, very quiet afternoon*
Lindbergh, Reeve. *The awful aardvarks go to school*
Linscott, Jody. *Once upon A to Z*
Lionni, Leo. *The alphabet tree*
    Letters to talk about
Lippman, Sidney. *A you're adorable*
A little ABC book
Little, Mary E. *ABC for the library*
Livingston, Myra Cohn. *B is for baby*
Lobel, Anita. *Alison's zinnia*
    Away from home
    Pierrot's ABC garden
Lobel, Arnold. *On Market Street*
Low, Joseph. *Adam's book of odd creatures*
Lyne, Alice. *A, my name is . . .*
Lyon, George Ella. *A B Cedar*
McCurdy, Michael. *The sailor's alphabet*
MacDonald, Ross. *Achoo! Bang! Crash!*
MacDonald, Suse. *Alphabatics*
McDonnell, Flora. *Flora McDonnell's ABC*
McGinley, Phyllis. *All around the town*
McKenzie, Ellen Kindt. *The perfectly orderly house*
MacKinnon, Debbie. *My first ABC*
McKissack, Patricia C. *Big bug book of the alphabet*
    My Bible ABC book
McLean, Dirk. *Play mas'! a carnival ABC*
McMillan, Bruce. *The alphabet symphony*
McPhail, David M. *Animals A to Z*
Magee, Doug. *All aboard ABC*
    Let's fly from A to Z
Mahurin, Tim. *Jeremy Kooloo*
Major, Kevin. *Eh to zed?*
Manson, Beverlie. *The fairies' alphabet book*
Margalit, Avishai. *The Hebrew alphabet book*
Markes, Julie. *Sidewalk ABC*
Martin, Bill (William Ivan). *Chicka chicka boom boom*
    Chicka chicka boom boom [board book]
    Chicka chicka sticka sticka
Martin, Mary Jane. *From Anne to Zach*
Marzollo, Jean. *Baby's alphabet*
    I spy little letters
Mayer, Marianna. *The Brambleberrys animal alphabet*
    The unicorn alphabet
Mayer, Mercer. *Little Monster's alphabet book*
Mayers, Florence Cassen. *Egyptian art from the Brooklyn Museum*
    The Museum of Fine Arts, Boston
    The Museum of Modern Art, New York
    The National Air and Space Museum
Melmed, Laura Krauss. *Capital! Washington D.C. from A to Z*
Mendoza, George. *The alphabet boat*

Alphabet sheep
    Norman Rockwell's Americana ABC
Merriam, Eve. *Goodnight to Annie*, ill. by Carol Schwartz
    Goodnight to Annie, ill. by John Wallner
    Halloween ABC
    Where is everybody?
Metaxas, Eric. *Bible ABC*
    The birthday ABC
Miles, Miska. *Apricot ABC*
Milich, Zoran. *The city ABC book*
Miller, Edna. *Mousekin's ABC*
Miller, Jane. *Farm alphabet book*
Milne, A. A. (Alan Alexander). *Pooh's alphabet book*
Miranda, Anne. *Alphabet fiesta*
    Pignic
Mitter, Matt. *ABC: alphabet rhymes*
Moak, Allan. *A big city ABC*
Mockford, Caroline. *Cleo's alphabet book*
Montresor, Beni. *A for angel*
Morice, Dave. *A visit from St. Alphabet*
Morse, Samuel French. *All in a suitcase*
Moss, Jeffrey. *The Sesame Street ABC storybook*
Most, Bernard. *ABC T-Rex*
Mother Goose. *ABC rhymes*
    In a pumpkin shell
Moxley, Sheila. *ABCD an alphabet book of cats and dogs*
Mullins, Patricia. *V for vanishing*
Munari, Bruno. *ABC*
Murphy, Chuck. *Chuck Murphy's alphabet magic*
Murphy, Mary. *The Alphabet Keeper*
Musgrove, Margaret. *Ashanti to Zulu*
Napier, Matt. *Z is for zamboni*
Nathan, Cheryl. *Bugs and beasties ABC*
Neumeier, Marty. *Action alphabet*
Newberry, Clare Turlay. *The kittens' ABC*
Nichol, Barbara. *Trunks all aboard*
Niland, Deborah. *ABC of monsters*
Obligado, Lilian. *Faint frogs feeling feverish and other terrifically tantalizing tongue twisters*
Ogle, Lucille. *A B See*
Oliver, Dexter. *I want to be . . .*
O'Shell, Marcia. *Alphabet Annie announces an all-American album*
Owens, Mary Beth. *A caribou alphabet*
Oxenbury, Helen. *Helen Oxenbury's ABC of things*
Page, Robin. *The alphabet sticker book*
Pallotta, Jerry. *The airplane alphabet book*
    The jet alphabet book
Paul, Ann Whitford. *Eight hands round*
    Everything to spend the night . . . from A to Z
Peaceable kingdom
Pearson, Debora. *Alphabeep*
Pearson, Tracey Campbell. *A apple pie*
Pelham, David. *A is for animals*
Pelletier, David. *The graphic alphabet*
Penner, Lucille Recht. *Slowpoke*
Penney, Ian. *Ian Penney's ABC*
Peppé, Rodney. *The alphabet book*
Petersham, Maud. *An American ABC*
Pfister, Marcus. *Rainbow fish ABC*
Phillips, Tamara. *Day care ABC*
Piatti, Celestino. *Celestino Piatti's animal ABC*
Piers, Helen. *Puppy's ABC*
Pittman, Helena Clare. *Miss Hindy's cats*
Pomeroy, Diana. *Wildflower ABC*
Potter, Beatrix. *Peter Rabbit's ABC*
Poulin, Stéphane. *Ah! belle cité = A beautiful city*
Powell, Consie. *A bold carnivore*
Pratt, Kristin Joy. *A fly in the sky*
    A swim through the sea
Raschka, Christopher. *Talk to me about the alphabet*
Rash, Andy. *Agent A to Agent Z*
Reed, Lynn Rowe. *Pedro, his perro, and the alphabet sombrero*
Reeves, James. *Ragged Robin*
Ressmeyer, Roger. *Astronaut to zodiac*
Rey, H. A. (Hans Augusto). *Curious George learns the alphabet*
    Look for the letters
Rice, James. *Cajun alphabet*

Roache, Gordon. *A Halifax ABC*
Roe, Richard. *Animal ABC*
Rogers, Jacqueline. *Kindergarten ABC*
Rojankovsky, Feodor. *ABC, an alphabet of many things*
    Animals in the zoo
Rosario, Idalia. *Idalia's project ABC*
Rose, Deborah Lee. *Into the A, B, sea*
Rosen, Michael J. (1954–). *Avalanche*
Rosenberg, Liz. *A big and little alphabet*
Ruben, Patricia. *Apples to zippers*
Rubin, Cynthia Elyce. *ABC Americana from the National Gallery of Art*
Rumford, James. *Sequoyah*
    There's a monster in the alphabet
Rutherford, Erica. *An Island alphabet*
Ruurs, Margriet. *Animal alphabet*
    A mountain alphabet
    A Pacific alphabet
Ryden, Hope. *Wild animals of Africa ABC*
Sabuda, Robert James. *ABC Disney*
    The Christmas alphabet
Samton, Sheila White. *Amazing Aunt Agatha*
Sanders, Marilyn. *What's your name?*
Sandved, Kjell Bloch. *The butterfly alphabet*
Sardegna, Jill. *K is for kiss good night*
Scarry, Richard. *Richard Scarry's ABC word book*
Schaefer, Lola M. *Homes ABC*
Schafer, Kevin. *Penguins A B C*
Schnur, Steven. *Autumn*
    Spring
    Summer
    Winter
The Sea World alphabet book
Sendak, Maurice. *Alligators all around*
Sesame Street. *The Sesame Street book of letters*
Seuss, Dr. *Dr. Seuss's ABC*
    Hooper Humperdink . . . ? Not him!
Shahan, Sherry. *The jazzy alphabet*
Shannon, George. *Tomorrow's alphabet*
Shelby, Anne. *Potluck*
Shepard, E. H. (Ernest Howard). *Winnie-the-Pooh's ABC*
Shuttlesworth, Dorothy Edwards. *ABC of buses*
Sierra, Judy. *There's a zoo in room 22*
Silverman, Maida. *Bunny's ABC*
Simpson, Gretchen Dow. *Gretchen's ABC*
Slate, Joseph. *Miss Bindergarten gets ready for kindergarten*
    Miss Bindergarten stays home from kindergarten
    Miss Bindergarten takes a field trip with kindergarten
Sloat, Teri. *From letter to letter*
    Patty's pumpkin patch
Smith, William Jay (1918–). *Puptents and pebbles*
Sneed, Brad. *Picture a letter*
Snow, Alan. *The monster book of ABC sounds*
Staake, Bob. *My little ABC book*
Steiner, Charlotte. *ABC*
Stevenson, James. *Grandpa's great city tour*
Stock, Catherine. *Alexander's midnight snack*
Stonem, Tanya Lee. *D is for dreidel*
Stutson, Caroline. *Prairie primer A to Z*
Tapahonso, Luci. *Navajo ABC*
Testa, Fulvio. *A long trip to Z*
Teyssèdre, Fabienne. *Joseph wants to read*
Thornhill, Jan. *Wildlife ABC*
The Timbertoes ABC alphabet book
Tobias, Tobi. *A world of words*
Troll, Ray. *Sharkabet*
Tryon, Leslie. *Albert's alphabet*
Tucker, Sian. *A is for astronaut*
Turner, Priscilla. *Among the odds and evens*
Van Allsburg, Chris. *The Z was zapped*
Vidrine, Beverly Barras. *Easter Day alphabet*
Viorst, Judith. *The Alphabet from Z to A*
Waber, Bernard. *An anteater named Arthur*
Walters, Marguerite. *The city-country ABC*
Walton, Rick. *So many bunnies*
Watson, Clyde. *Applebet*
Watson, Nancy Dingman. *What does A begin with?*

Wells, Rosemary. *Letters and sounds*
Wethered, Peggy. *Touchdown Mars!*
Whitehouse, Patricia. *Seasons ABC*
    What's awake? A B C
Wilbur, Richard. *The disappearing alphabet*
Wild, Robin. *The bears' ABC book*
Williams, Garth. *The big golden animal ABC*
Williams, Laura E. *ABC kids*
Wilner, Isabel. *A garden alphabet*
Wilson, Barbara Ker. *ABC and 123*
Wilson-Max, Ken. *A book of letters*
Winnie-the-Pooh's ABC
Wojtowycz, David. *David Wojtowycz presents Animal ABC*
Wolf, Janet. *Adelaide to Zeke*
Wood, Audrey. *Alphabet adventure*
Wormell, Christopher. *The new alphabet of animals*
Yolen, Jane. *All in the woodland early*
    Elfabet

Abnaki Indians *see* Indians of North America – Abnaki

Aborigines, Australian *see* Australian aborigines

Abused children *see* Child abuse

Acadians *see* Indians of North America – Acadians; Ethnic groups in the U.S. – Cajun

Accidents

Bauer, Marion Dane. *Uh-oh!*
Biro, Val. *Gumdrop and the steamroller*
Bond, Michael. *Paddington Bear goes to the hospital*
Brown, Marc Tolon. *D. W. thinks big [board book]*
Carlson, Nancy L. *Arnie and the new kid*
Carrick, Carol. *The accident*
French, Vivian. *Oh no, Anna!*
Harder, Dan (Dan Wymbs). *Colliding with Chris*
Hindley, Judy. *The big red bus*
How Raggedy Ann got her candy heart
Hurd, Thacher. *Santa Mouse and the ratdeer*
Keeshan, Robert. *Itty Bitty Kitty makes a big splash*
Lange, Willem. *John and Tom*
Lawson, Julie. *Emma and the silk train*
Loewen, Nancy. *Emergencies*
McPhail, David M. *Big brown bear*
Marzollo, Jean. *What's the matter with Mother Goose?*
Mattern, Joanne. *Safety in public places*
O'Connor, Jane. *Nina, Nina ballerina*
Perrow, Angeli. *Captain's castaway*
Polacco, Patricia. *In Enzo's splendid gardens*
Porter, Sue. *Parsnip and the runaway tractor*
Rand, Gloria. *Baby in a basket*
    Little Flower
Rylant, Cynthia. *Silver packages*
Singer, Marilyn. *Boo hoo boo-boo*
Sykes, Julie. *Careful, Santa*
Wardlaw, Lee. *The chair where bear sits*
Weller, Frances Ward. *The angel of Mill Street*
Wild, Margaret. *The pocket dogs*
Wood, Audrey. *A cowboy Christmas*

Accordion books *see* Format, unusual

Accordions *see* Musical instruments – accordions

Accountants *see* Careers – accountants

Acrobats *see* Careers – acrobats

Activities

Accorsi, William. *Short short short stories*
Ahlberg, Allan. *Me and my friend*
Ajmera, Maya. *To be a kid*

Alborough, Jez. *Can you jump like a kangaroo?*
Alderson, Sue Ann. *Bonnie McSmithers is at it again!*
Aliki. *All by myself!*
    Overnight at Mary Bloom's
Allard, Harry. *The Stupids step out*
Allington, Richard L. *Feelings*
    Hearing
    Looking
    Smelling
    Tasting
    Touching
Andre, Evelyn M. *Places I like to be*
Anno, Mitsumasa. *All in a day*
Arnold, Caroline. *How do we have fun?*
Arquette, Kerry. *What did you do today?*
Asch, Frank. *The alphabet zoo*
    Gia and the one hundred dollars worth of bubblegum
    Like a windy day
Aylesworth, Jim. *Wake up, little children*
Azarian, Mary. *A farmer's alphabet*
Baird, Anne. *The guppies of Hilly Dale House*
Bantock, Nick. *Runners, sliders, bouncers, climbers*
Barasch, Lynne. *Radio rescue*
Behrens, June. *Can you walk the plank?*
Beller, Janet. *A-B-C-ing*
Bender, Robert. *The A to Z beastly jamboree*
Beni, Ruth. *Sir Baldergog the great*
Benjamin, Alan. *Busy bunnies*
Bennett, Jill. *Days are where we live and other poems*
Blackstone, Stella. *You and me*
Bowie, C. W. *Busy toes*
Boyd, Lizi. *I love Daddy*
    I love Mommy
    The not-so-wicked stepmother
Brandenberg, Franz. *Otto is different*
Brann, Esther. *A book for baby*
Bridges, Margaret Park. *Edna elephant*
Brown, Elinor. *The little story book*
Brown, Margaret Wise. *The little fur family*
Brown, Ruth. *Our cat Flossie*
Bryant, Dean. *Here am I*
Bulla, Clyde Robert. *Daniel's duck*
Bundey, Nikki. *In the park*
    In the snow
    In the water
Bunting, Jane. *My first word book*
Burdekin, Harold. *A child's grace*
Burke, Jennifer S. *Cloudy days*
    Ovals
    Rainy days
    Sunny days
Burningham, John. *The school*
    Skip trip
    Sniff shout
    Wobble pop
Bush, Timothy. *Teddy bear, teddy bear*
Calmenson, Stephanie. *The kindergarten book*
    Meet Penny
    Meet Timmy
Carle, Eric. *From head to toe*
Carlson, Nancy L. *Arnie goes to camp*
    Bunnies and their hobbies
    Look out kindergarten, here I come!
Carr, Jan. *Frozen noses*
Cartlidge, Michelle. *The bear's bazaar*
    A mouse's diary
Carton, Lonnie Caming. *Mommies*
Cauley, Lorinda Bryan. *Clap your hands*
Chernoff, Goldie Taub. *Clay-dough, play-dough*
    Just a box?
    Pebbles and pods
    Puppet party
Chorao, Kay. *Peekaboo! Was it you?*
Cole, Joanna. *Fun on wheels,* ill. by Whitney Darrow
    Fun on wheels, ill. by Don Gauthier
Costa, Nicoletta. *The grown-up dog*
Cote, Nancy. *Flip-flops*

Creighton, Jill. *One day there was nothing to do*
Crews, Nina. *A high, low, near, far, loud, quiet story*
Cronin, Doreen. *Wiggle*
Crume, Marion W. *Let me see you try*
    Listen!
    What do you say?
Curtiss, A. B. *In the company of bears*
Dahl, Tessa. *The same but different*
Davies, Kay. *My balloon*
    My mirror
Day, Alexandra. *Boswell wide-awake*
Delton, Judy. *I'm telling you now*
Denim, Sue. *Make way for Dumb Bunnies*
Denslow, Sharon Phillips. *Night owls*
    Dinosaurs and monsters
Dodds, Siobhan. *Words and pictures*
Doyle, Malachy. *Well, a crocodile can!*
Dunn, Phoebe. *Busy, busy toddlers*
Dwight, Laura. *We can do it!*
Edwards, Richard. *Fly with the birds*
Ehrlich, Amy. *Bunnies all day long*
Ernst, Lisa Campbell. *Sam Johnson and the blue ribbon quilt*
Erskine, Jim. *Bert and Susie's messy tale*
Facklam, Margery. *So can I*
Fair, Sylvia. *The bedspread*
Falconer, Ian. *Olivia*
Faulkenberry, Lauren. *What do animals do on the weekend?*
Faunce-Brown, Daphne. *Snuffles' house*
Fitz-Gibbon, Sally. *Two shoes, blue shoes, new shoes!*
Flournoy, Valerie. *The best time of day*
Foord, Jo. *The book of babies*
Ford, Miela. *Watch us play*
Freeman, Don. *The day is waiting*
Friend, Catherine. *Eddie the raccoon*
    Funny Ruby
Fujikawa, Gyo. *My favorite thing*
    Surprise! Surprise!
Gentieu, Penny. *Baby! Talk!*
George, Jean Craighead. *Morning, noon, and night*
Gerstein, Mordicai. *The man who walked between the towers*
Gibbons, Gail. *The missing maple syrup sap mystery*
Giff, Patricia Reilly. *Ronald Morgan goes to camp*
Giovanni, Nikki. *The genie in the jar*
Gipson, Morrell. *Hello, Peter*
Gliori, Debi. *Mr. Bear babysits*
Goennel, Heidi. *My day*
    Sometimes I like to be alone
    While I am little
Gomi, Taro. *My friends*
    Seeing, saying, doing, playing
Good, Merle. *Amos and Susie*
Goor, Ron. *In the driver's seat*
Gore, Sheila. *My shadow*
Gove, Doris. *My mother talks to trees*
Grambling, Lois G. *Daddy will be there*
Grejniec, Michael. *Good morning, good night*
Grindley, Sally. *Mucky Duck*
Gugler, Laurel Dee. *Muddle cuddle*
Haddon, Mark. *At home*
    At playgroup
    In the garden
    On vacation
Hafner, Marylin. *A year with Molly and Emmett*
Haley, Amanda. *It's a baby's world*
Hallinan, P. K. (Patrick K.). *I'm glad to be me*
    Just being alone
Hanly, Shelia. *Toddler's book of fun things to do*
Harper, Dan. *Sit, Truman*
Harper, Piers. *If you love a bear*
Hawkins, Colin. *Busy ABC*
Hayles, Marsha. *He saves the day*
Heiligman, Deborah. *On the move*
Helldorfer, M. C. (Mary Claire). *Carnival*
Henley, Claire. *At the zoo*
Hennessy, B. G. (Barbara G.). *Busy Dinah Dinosaur*
Herkert, Barbara. *Birds in your backyard*
Hest, Amy. *How to get famous in Brooklyn*

Hindley, Judy. *What's in baby's morning*
Hines, Anna Grossnickle. *What can we do in the rain?*
  What can you do in the snow?
  What can you do in the sun?
  What can you do in the wind?
Holzenthaler, Jean. *My feet do*
  My hands can
Hooks, Bell. *Be boy buzz*
Hooks, William H. *How do you make a bubble?*
Hubbard, Woodleigh Marx. *2 is for dancing*
Hughes, Shirley. *Annie Rose is my little sister*
  Bouncing
Hynard, Julia. *Percival's party*
Hynard, Stephen. *Snowy the rabbit*
Ingman, Bruce. *A night on the tiles*
Isadora, Rachel. *Babies*
  Friends
Iverson, Diane. *Discover the seasons*
Jabar, Cynthia. *Bored blue? Think what you can do!*
Jennings, Sharon. *When Jeremiah found Mrs. Ming*
Jensen, Helen Zane. *When Panda came to our house*
Johnson, Doug. *Substitute teacher plans*
Johnson, Paul Brett. *The pig who ran a red light*
Jonas, Ann. *When you were a baby*
Kaufman, Curt. *Hotel boy*
Kavanagh, Peter. *I love my mama*
Kelley, True. *Look, baby! Listen, baby! Do, baby!*
Kilroy, Sally. *Busy babies*
Kitchen, Bert. *Somewhere today*
Koller, Jackie French. *Bouncing on the bed*
Konigsburg, E. L. (Elaine Lobl). *Amy Elizabeth explores Bloomingdale's*
Krasilovsky, Phyllis. *The very little boy*
Krementz, Jill. *Katharine goes to nursery school*
Kroll, Virginia L. *Boy, you're amazing!*
Kunhardt, Edith. *Which one would you choose?*
  Which pig would you choose?
Kunnas, Mauri. *The nighttime book*
Lachner, Dorothea. *Smoky's special Easter present*
Lavis, Steve. *Jump!*
Lawson, Carol. *Teddy bear, teddy bear*
Lawston, Lisa. *Can you hop?*
Leavy, Una. *Harry's stormy night*
Leblanc, Anne. *Benjamin's busy day*
Lee, Ho Baek. *While we were out*
Leedy, Loreen. *A dragon Christmas*
Leonard, Marcia. *Busy babies*
Lester, Alison. *Celeste sails to Spain*
  Clive eats alligators
  Tessa snaps snakes
  Yikes!
Le-Tan, Pierre. *The afternoon cat*
Levine, Abby. *Daddies give you horsey rides*
Liatsos, Sandra Olson. *Bicycle riding and other poems*
Lilly, Kenneth. *Animal builders*
  Animal climbers
  Animal jumpers
  Animal runners
  Animal swimmers
Lionni, Leo. *Let's make rabbits*
Loomis, Christine. *At the laundromat*
Lyon, George Ella. *A sign*
MacDonald, Amy. *Let's do it*
  Let's try
McGuirk, Leslie. *Tucker off his rocker*
McKié, Roy. *Snow*
MacKinnon, Debbie. *My day: I can do it!*
McMillan, Bruce. *Step by step*
McNaughton, Colin. *Autumn*
  Winter
McPhail, David M. *A bug, a bear, and a boy*
  A girl, a goat, and a goose
  Those can-do pigs
McQuade, Jacqueline. *Good times with Teddy Bear*
Maestro, Betsy. *Busy day*
Mainwaring, Jane. *My feather*
Maitland, Barbara. *My bear and me*

Mangin, Marie-France. *Suzette and Nicholas and the seasons clock*
Markes, Julie. *Good thing you're not an octopus!*
Martin, David. *Piggy and Dad*
Masks and puppets
Mazer, Anne. *Watch me*
Meyers, Susan. *Everywhere babies*
Milios, Rita. *Yo soy = I am*
Miller, Margaret. *Every day*
  Happy days
Moncure, Jane Belk. *Now I am five!*
  Now I am four!
  Now I am three!
Monfried, Lucia. *Dishes all done*
Moser, Barry. *Tucker Pfeffercorn*
Most, Bernard. *A pair of protoceratops*
  A trio of triceratops
Motyka, Sally Mitchell. *An ordinary day*
Munsch, Robert N. *Up, up, down!*
Murkoff, Heidi Eisenberg. *What to expect at preschool*
Murphy, Mary. *I like it when . . .*
  I like it when . . .
  Some things change
My busy day
Myers, Arthur. *Kids do amazing things*
Nelson, Brenda. *Mud for sale*
Neumeier, Marty. *Action alphabet*
Newman, Lesléa. *Dogs, dogs, dogs*
Nobisso, Josephine. *The moon's lullaby*
Noble, Trinka Hakes. *The day Jimmy's boa ate the wash*
Noll, Sally. *Jiggle wiggle prance*
Numeroff, Laura Joffe. *Chimps don't wear glasses*
  If you take a mouse to the movies
O'Brien, Anne Sibley. *Come play with us*
O'Brien, Claire. *Sam's sneaker search*
O'Mara, Carmel. *Good morning*
  Good night
Ormerod, Jan. *Who's whose?*
Oxenbury, Helen. *I can*
  Tom and Pippo's day
Paradis, Susan. *My Daddy*
Parish, Peggy. *I can – can you?*
Pelham, David. *Worms wiggle*
Peyo. *What do smurfs do all day?*
Pirotta, Saviour. *Little bird*
Pitcher, Caroline. *Animals*
  Cars and boats
Pizer, Abigail. *Harry's night out*
Pluckrose, Henry Arthur. *Join it!*
Pomerantz, Charlotte. *Serena Katz*
Pomeroy, Diana. *Wildflower ABC*
Ray, Karen. *Sleep song*
Reasoner, Charles. *Who pretends?*
Regan, Dian Curtis. *Daddies*
Regan, Lara Jo (Michael P.). *A Winkle in time*
Reinen, Judy. *Bow wow*
  Meow
Rhyme time around the day
Rice, Eve. *Aren't you coming too?*
Roberts, Bethany. *Fourth of July mice*
Rockwell, Anne F. *In our house*
Rockwell, Harlow. *I did it*
  Look at this
Rosenberry, Vera. *Run, jump, whiz, splash*
Ross, H. L. *Not counting monsters*
Ross, Tony. *Treasure of Cozy Cove*
Rotner, Shelley. *What can you do?*
Rubel, Nicole. *Me and my kitty*
Rukeyser, Muriel. *More night*
Rylant, Cynthia. *In November*
Sage, Chris. *That's mine, that's yours*
Samuels, Barbara. *Duncan and Dolores*
Schindel, John. *Busy penguins*
Schwartz, Amy. *The boys teams*
Schweninger, Ann. *Summertime*
Senisi, Ellen B. *Hurray for pre-K!*
Seven spunky monkeys
Shields, Carol Diggory. *Day by day a week goes round*

Silbaugh, Elizabeth. *Raggedy Ann's birthday party book*
Simmons, Jane. *Daisy says, "Here we go round the mulberry bush"*
Simon, Francesca. *Toddler time*
Simon, Norma. *I'm busy, too*
    What do I do?
Siomades, Lorianne. *Kangaroo and cricket*
Spetter, Jung-Hee. *Lily and Trooper's winter*
Spinelli, Eileen. *What do angels wear?*
Spinelli, Jerry. *My daddy and me*
Stanley, Mandy. *Bloomer, the dog you can play with*
Stevenson, James. *Rolling Rose*
Stickland, Paul. *A child's book of things*
Stock, Catherine. *Halloween monster*
Swinburne, Stephen R. *Go, go, go!*
Taberski, Sharon. *Morning, noon, and night*
Tafuri, Nancy. *Do not disturb*
Takeshita, Fumiko. *The park bench*
Taylor, Barbara. *Zooming and creeping*
Thompson, Carol. *Baby days*
Thomson, Ruth. *My bear: I can . . . can you?*
Thorne, Jenny. *My uncle*
Tirabosco, Tom. *At the same time*
Türk, Hanne. *The rope skips Max*
Uff, Caroline. *Lulu's busy day*
Van Laan, Nancy. *People, people, everywhere*
Vasiliu, Mircea. *What's happening?*
Voake, Charlotte. *First things first*
Vulliamy, Clara. *Wide awake*
Walsh, Melanie. *Do donkeys dance?*
Warnick, Elsa. *Bedtime*
Weiss, Nicki. *On a hot, hot day*
Wellington, Monica. *All my little ducklings*
    Night city
Wells, Rosemary. *Night sounds, morning colors*
What we do
Williams, Jenny (Jennifer). *Playtime 1 2 3*
Williams, Sam. *The baby's word book*
Willis, Jeanne. *Susan laughs*
Winch, John. *Keeping up with Grandma*
Winn, Chris. *Archie's acrobats*
    Helping
Winteringham, Victoria. *Penguin day*
Wood, Audrey. *King Bidgood's in the bathtub*
Yolen, Jane. *Elfabet*
Zalben, Jane Breskin. *Oliver and Alison's week*
Ziefert, Harriet. *Baby Ben's busy book*
    Baby Ben's noisy book
    Bear's busy morning
    Piggety Pig from morn 'til night
    A polar bear can swim
    Rockheads
    Toes have wiggles, kids have giggles
Zimelman, Nathan. *How the second grade got $8,205.50 to visit the Statue of Liberty*
Zolotow, Charlotte (Shapiro). *Wake up and goodnight*

Activities – babysitting

Abel, Ruth. *The new sitter*
Anderson, Peggy Perry. *Time for bed, the babysitter said*
Berenstain, Stan. *The Berenstain bears and the sitter*
Berman, Linda. *The goodbye painting*
Blaustein, Muriel. *Baby Mabu and Auntie Moose*
Brown, Marc Tolon. *Arthur babysits*
Bush, Timothy. *Benjamin McFadden and the robot babysitter*
Carlson, Natalie Savage. *Marie Louise's heyday*
Carrick, Carol. *The climb*
Cazet, Denys. *Big shoe, little shoe*
Chalmers, Mary. *Be good, Harry*
Child, Lauren. *Clarice Bean, guess who's babysitting?*
Christelow, Eileen. *Jerome and the Witchcraft kids*
    Jerome the babysitter
Cole, William. *What's good for a three-year-old?*
Crowley, Arthur. *Bonzo Beaver*
Day, Alexandra. *Carl makes a scrapbook*
    Carl pops up
    Carl's afternoon in the park
    Carl's birthday
    Carl's Christmas
    Follow Carl!
    Good dog, Carl
Finfer, Celentha. *Grandmother dear*
Gardner, Sally. *Mama, don't go out tonight*
Gliori, Debi. *Mr. Bear babysits*
Gordon, Margaret. *Frogs' holiday*
Greenberg, Barbara. *The bravest babysitter*
Gretz, Susanna. *Roger takes charge!*
Grimes, Nikki. *Someone's baby-sitting*
Harris, Robie H. *Don't forget to come back*, ill.by Harry Bliss
    Don't forget to come back, ill. by Tony DeLuna
Hellard, Susan. *Eleanor and the babysitter*
Hest, Amy. *Nannies for hire*
Himmelman, John. *J.J. versus the babysitter*
Hindley, Judy. *Mrs. Mary Malarky's seven cats*
Hines, Anna Grossnickle. *Grandma gets grumpy*
Hughes, Shirley. *An evening at Alfie's*
    George the babysitter
Hunter, Dette. *38 ways to entertain your babysitter*
Hurd, Edith Thacher. *Hurry, hurry!*
    Stop, stop
Impey, Rose. *Joe's café*
Johnson, Angela. *Shoes like Miss Alice's*
Johnson, Dolores. *What kind of baby-sitter is this?*
Johnson, Doug. *Never babysit the hippopotamuses!*
Joyce, William. *George shrinks*
Keller, Holly. *Geraldine and Mrs. Duffy*
    What Alvin wanted
Lawson, Annetta. *The lucky yak*
Loomis, Christine. *My new baby-sitter*
McAllister, Angela. *The babies of Cockle Bay*
McCourt, Lisa. *Chicken soup for little souls: The never-forgotten doll*
McCully, Emily Arnold. *The grandma mix-up*
Martin, C. L. G. *The dragon nanny*
Miranda, Anne. *Baby-sit*
Moore, Lilian. *Little Raccoon and no trouble at all*
Mueller, Virginia. *Monster and the baby*
Nelson, Nan Ferring. *My day with Anka*
Newberry, Clare Turlay. *T-Bone, the baby-sitter*
Nilsson, Ulf. *Little sister rabbit*
Olofsdotter, Marie. *Frej the fearless*
Ovenell-Carter, Julie. *Adam's daycare*
Paterson, Bettina. *Bun and Mrs. Tubby*
Paton, Priscilla. *Howard and the sitter surprise*
Puner, Helen Walker. *The sitter who didn't sit*
Quackenbush, Robert M. *Henry babysits*
Rayner, Mary. *Mr. and Mrs. Pig's evening out*
Richardson, Jean. *Thomas's sitter*
Robbins, Beth. *Tom, Ally, and the baby-sitter*
Rubel, Nicole. *Uncle Henry and Aunt Henrietta's honeymoon*
Schick, Eleanor. *Peter and Mr. Brandon*
Sendak, Maurice. *Outside over there*
Simon, Charnan. *Click and the kids go sailing*
Simon, Francesca. *The Topsy-Turvies*
Steel, Danielle. *Max and the baby sitter*
Sykes, Julie. *Robbie Rabbit and the little ones*
Teague, Mark. *Baby tamer*
Tsutsui, Yoriko. *Anna in charge*
Van den Honert, Dorry. *Demi the baby sitter*
Van Laan, Nancy. *Mama rocks, Papa sings*
Viorst, Judith. *The good-bye book*
Waggoner, Karen. *The lemonade babysitter*
Wahl, Jan. *Peter and the troll baby*
Wardlaw, Lee. *Saturday night jamboree*
Watson, Jane Werner. *My friend the babysitter*
Watson, Pauline. *Curley Cat baby-sits*
Wells, Rosemary. *Max's dragon shirt*
    Shy Charles
    Stanley and Rhoda
Weninger, Brigitte. *Davy in the middle*
    Will you mind the baby, Davy?
Williams, Barbara. *Jeremy isn't hungry*
Winthrop, Elizabeth. *Bear and Mrs. Duck*
    Bear and Roly-Poly
    Bear's Christmas surprise

Yolen, Jane. *Baby Bear's bedtime book*
Young, Ruth. *My baby-sitter*
Zweifel, Frances W. *Animal baby-sitters*

Activities – baking, cooking

Abolafia, Yossi. *A fish for Mrs. Gardenia*
Adinolfi, JoAnn. *Tina's diner*
Andersen, H. C. (Hans Christian). *The nightingale*, ill. by Christopher Santoro
Armstrong, Jennifer. *Little Salt Lick and the Sun King*
Auch, Mary Jane. *The princess and the pizza*
Axelrod, Amy. *Pigs in the pantry*
Bastin, Marjolein. *Vera in the kitchen*
Beck, Andrea. *Elliot bakes a cake*
    Elliot bakes a cake
Beil, Karen Magnuson. *A cake all for me!*
Blackstone, Stella. *Making minestrone*
Blundell, Tony. *Beware of boys*
Brink, Carol Ryrie. *Goody O'Grumpity*
Brown, Marcia. *Skipper John's cook*
Brunhoff, Laurent de. *Babar learns to cook*
Bugni, Alice. *Moose racks, bear tracks and other Alaska kidsnacks*
Bunting, Eve (Anne Evelyn). *Barney the Beard*
Butler, Daphne. *What happens when food cooks?*
Cauley, Lorinda Bryan. *The bake-off*
    Pease porridge hot
Chandra, Deborah. *Miss Mabel's table*
Charlip, Remy. *Peanut butter party*
Chavarría-Cháirez, Becky. *Magda's tortillas = Las tortillas de Magada*
Christelow, Eileen. *Don't wake up Mama!*
Cocca-Leffler, Maryann. *Wednesday is spaghetti day*
Compestine, Ying Chang. *The story of noodles*
Cooper, Helen (Helen F.). *Pumpkin soup*
Cousins, Lucy. *Maisy makes gingerbread*
Cunliffe, John. *The king's birthday cake*
Czernecki, Stefan. *The sleeping bread*
Da Rif, Andrea. *The blueberry cake that little fox baked*
Darling, Abigail. *Teddy bears' picnic cookbook*
Darling, Benjamin. *Valerie and the silver pear*
De Paola, Tomie (Thomas Anthony). *Pancakes for breakfast*
    The popcorn book
    Things to make and do for Valentine's Day
De Regniers, Beatrice Schenk. *Sam and the impossible thing*
DeRubertis, Barbara. *Lulu's lemonade*
Devlin, Wende. *Old Black Witch!*
    Old Witch and the polka-dot ribbon
    Old Witch rescues Halloween
Dodds, Siobhan. *Grandpa Bud*
Donohue, Dorothy. *Veggie soup*
Dooley, Norah. *Everybody bakes bread*
    Everybody serves soup
Douglass, Barbara. *The chocolate chip cookie contest*
Dragonwagon, Crescent. *This is the bread I baked for Ned*
Dumas, Bianca. *Tia Luisa, the magical cook*
Edwards, Frank B. *Is the spaghetti ready?*
Edwards, Pamela Duncan. *Four famished foxes and Fosdyke*
    Warthogs in the kitchen
Elya, Susan Middleton. *Eight animals bake a cake*
English, Karen. *Just right stew*
Erdrich, Louise. *The range eternal*
Ericsson, Jennifer A. *Out and about at the bakery*
Ernst, Lisa Campbell. *Little Red Riding Hood*
Everitt, Betsy. *Mean soup*
Falwell, Cathryn. *Feast for ten*
Fearnley, Jan. *Mr. Wolf and the three bears*
    Mr. Wolf's pancakes
Feder, Harriet K. *What can you do with a bagel?*
Florian, Douglas. *A chef*
Fox, Christyan. *Count to ten, PiggyWiggy!*
Gabler, Mirko. *The alphabet soup*
Geeslin, Campbell. *How Nanita learned to make flan*
Gelsanliter, Wendy. *Dancin' in the kitchen*
Gibbons, Gail. *Apples*
    The berry book
    The too-great bread bake book

Gilchrist, Theo E. *Halfway up the mountain*
Glaser, Linda. *Mrs. Greenberg's messy Hanukkah*
Goldin, Barbara Diamond. *Cakes and miracles*
Greenberg, Melanie Hope. *My father's luncheonette*
Gregory, Valiska. *Riddle soup*
Gretz, Susanna. *Teddybears cookbook*
Hall, Margaret. *Corn*
    Peanuts
Harris, Lee. *Never let your cat make lunch for you*
Head, Judith. *Mud soup*
Heath, Amy. *Sofie's role*
Hedderwick, Mairi. *The big Katie Morag storybook*
Hill, Eric. *Spot bakes a cake*
Hill, Mary (1977–). *Let's make pizza*
    Let's make tacos
Hill, Susan. *Ruby bakes a cake*
Hippely, Hilary Horder. *A song for Lena*
Hoban, Lillian. *Arthur's Christmas cookies*
Holub, Joan. *The pizza that we made*
Hooper, Meredith. *A cow, a bee, a cookie, and me*
Hoopes, Lyn Littlefield. *The unbeatable bread*
Hopkinson, Deborah. *Fannie in the kitchen*
Hunter, Dette. *38 ways to entertain your babysitter*
    38 ways to entertain your grandparents
Jacobs, Laurie A. *So much in common*
Kahl, Virginia. *The Duchess bakes a cake*
Kidd, Richard. *Monsieur Thermidor*
Krasilovsky, Phyllis. *The man who cooked for himself*
    The man who entered a contest
Krensky, Stephen. *The pizza book*
Laminack, Lester L. *Saturdays and teacakes*
Lasker, Joe. *Lentil soup*
Latimer, Jim. *James Bear's pie*
Lemerise, Bruce. *Sheldon's lunch*
Leonard, Marcia. *Food is fun!*
Levitin, Sonia. *Nobody stole the pie*
Lewin, Ted. *Big Jimmy's Kum Kau Chinese take out*
Lin, Grace. *Dim sum for everyone*
Lindman, Maj. *Flicka, Ricka, Dicka bake a cake*
Lindsey, Treska. *When Batistine made bread*
The little red hen. *The cock, the mouse and the little red hen*, ill. by Lorinda Bryan Cauley
    The cock, the mouse and the little red hen, ill. by Graham Percy
    The little red hen, ill. by Byron Barton
    The little red hen, ill. by Emily Bolam
    The little red hen, ill. by Janina Domanska
    The little red hen, ill. by Paul Galdone
    The little red hen, ill. by Dennis Hockerman
    Little red hen, ill. by Norman Messenger
    The little red hen, ill. by Mel Pekarsky
    The little red hen, ill. by William Stobbs
    The little red hen, ill. by Annie West
    The little red hen, ill. by Margot Zemach
    The little red hen and the ear of wheat, ill. by Elisabeth Bell
    The Little Red Hen makes a pizza
Long, Earlene. *Johnny's egg*
Loomis, Christine. *In the diner*
Maccarone, Grace. *Pizza party*
MacDonald, Elizabeth. *Miss Poppy and the honey cake*
    Mr. Badger's birthday pie
MacDonald, Maryann. *Hedgehog bakes a cake*
McKissack, Patricia C. *Messy Bessey's holidays*
Malkin, Michele. *Pinky's sweet tooth*
Many, Paul. *The great pancake escape*
Mayer, Marianna. *Marcel the pastry chef*
Meddaugh, Susan. *Hog-eye*
Meijer, Marie. *The bake-a-cake book*
Meister, Cari. *Skinny and fats, best friends*
Millen, C. M. *Blue bowl down*
Miller, Alice P. *The mouse family's blueberry pie*
Moon, Nicola. *Alligator tails and crocodile cakes*
Mora, Pat. *The bakery lady = La señora de la panadería*
Moss, Marissa. *Mel's diner*
Müller, Birte. *Finn cooks*
Murphy, Stuart J. *A fair bear share*
Myers, Edward. *Forri the baker*
Nakagawa, Rieko. *Guri and Gura*

Guri and Gura's special gift
Nelson, Nan Ferring. *My day with Anka*
Nixon, Joan Lowery. *Beats me, Claude*
Nolen, Jerdine. *In my momma's kitchen*
Oxenbury, Helen. *It's my birthday*
Park, Frances. *Where on earth is my bagel?*
Parker, Nancy Winslow. *Love from Aunt Betty*
Patron, Susan. *Burgoo stew*
Pelham, David. *Sam's pizza*
Petie, Haris. *The seed the squirrel dropped*
Powell, Jillian. *Eggs*
Priceman, Marjorie. *How to make an apple pie and see the world*
Reiser, Lynn. *Cherry pies and lullabies*
Rex, Michael. *The pie is cherry*
Rice, Eve. *Benny bakes a cake*
Robbins, Ken. *Apples*
Rockwell, Anne F. *The Mother Goose cookie-candy book*
Root, Phyllis. *Turnover Tuesday*
Rotner, Shelley. *Hold the anchovies!*
Rylant, Cynthia. *The cookie-store cat*
   Mr. Putter and Tabby bake the cake
Sanger, Amy Wilson. *First book of sushi*
Schwalje, Marjory. *Mr. Angelo*
Sharmat, Marjorie Weinman. *Nate the Great and the monster mess*
Shecter, Ben. *The big stew*
Shiefman, Vicky. *Sunday potatoes, Monday potatoes*
Shohet, Marti. *Market days*
Smith, Linda. *Mrs. Biddlebox*
Smothers, Ethel Footman. *Auntee Edna*
Speed, Toby. *Brave potatoes*
   Hattie baked a wedding cake
Spilsbury, Louise. *Carrots*
   Oranges
   Peas
Spohn, Kate. *Ruth's bake shop*
Stevens, Jan Romero. *Carlos digs to China = Carlos excava hasta la China*
Stevens, Janet. *Cook-a-doodle-doo!*
Stewig, John Warren. *Making plum jam*
Swendson, Patsy. *The potluck adventures of Mrs. Marmalade*
Tomchek, Ann Heinrichs. *I can be a chef*
Tornborg, Pat. *The Sesame Street cookbook*
Torres, Leyla. *Saturday sancocho*
Tzannes, Robin. *Sanji and the baker*
Ungar, Richard. *Rachel's gift*
Ungerer, Tomi. *Zeralda's ogre*
Von Königslöw, Andrea Wayne. *Bing and Chutney*
Wagner, Karen. *Chocolate chip cookies*
Wallace, Ian. *Duncan's way*
Wallace, Nancy Elizabeth. *Apples, apples, apples*
Wallis, Diz. *Pip's adventure*
Wellington, Monica. *Mr. Cookie Baker*
Wells, Rosemary. *Bunny cakes*
Willard, Nancy. *The high rise glorious skittle skat roarious sky pie angel food cake*
Wilson-Kelly, Becky. *Mother Grumpy's dog biscuits*
Yee, Paul. *Roses sing on new snow*
Yorinks, Arthur. *Company's going*
Young, Miriam Burt. *The sugar mouse cake*
Zolkower, Edie Stoltz. *Too many cooks*
Zweifel, Frances W. *The Make-Something Club*

Activities – ballooning

Adams, Adrienne. *The great Valentine's Day balloon race*
Appelt, Kathi. *Elephants aloft*
Bansemer, Roger. *Rachael's splendifilous adventure*
Bynum, Janie. *Altoona Baboona*
Calhoun, Mary. *Hot-air Henry*
Coerr, Eleanor. *The big balloon race*
Curious George and the hot air balloon
De Beer, Hans. *Little Polar Bear and the big balloon*
Delacre, Lulu. *Nathan's balloon adventure*
DeLage, Ida. *The old witch gets a surprise*
Gibbons, Gail. *Flying*
Goffe, Toni. *Toby's animal rescue service*
Haseley, Dennis. *Horses with wings*

Hayes, Sarah. *The grumpalump*
Johnson, Neil. *Fire and silk*
Lenssen, Ann. *A rainbow balloon*
McGrory, Anik. *Mouton's impossible dream*
McPhail, David M. *Henry Bear's park*
Mayhew, James. *Miranda the explorer*
Mott, Evelyn Clarke. *Balloon ride*
Peppé, Rodney. *The mice and the flying basket*
Quin-Harkin, Janet. *Benjamin's balloon*
Rogers, Paul (Patrick). *What can you see?*
Wade, Alan. *I'm flying!*
Wallner, Alexandra. *The first air voyage in the United States*
Wegen, Ron. *The balloon trip*
Wildsmith, Brian. *Bear's adventure*

Activities – bargaining *see* Activities – trading

Activities – bartering *see* Activities – trading

Activities – bathing

Alborough, Jez. *Bare bear*
Allen, Pamela. *Mr. Archimedes' bath*
Ambrus, Victor G. *The Sultan's bath*
Anderson, Lena. *Bunny bath*
Anderson, Peggy Perry. *To the tub*
Arnold, Tedd. *No more water in the tub!*
Aulaire, Ingri Mortenson d'. *Children of the northlights*
Beck, Andrea. *Elliot's bath*
Bedford, David. *Shaggy Dog and the terrible itch*
Bethell, Jean. *Bathtime*
Blocksma, Mary. *Rub-a-dub-dub*
Brouillard, Anne. *The bathtub prima donna*
Brown, Margaret Wise. *The dirty little boy*
Burningham, John. *Time to get out of the bath, Shirley*
Buxbaum, Susan Kovacs. *Splash!*
Capucilli, Alyssa Satin. *Bathtime for Biscuit*
   Biscuit visits the pumpkin patch
Carlstrom, Nancy White. *Jesse Bear's tra-la tub*
Cartlidge, Michelle. *Good night, Teddy*
Conrad, Pam. *The Tub People*
Cottle, Joan. *Emily's shoes*
DeFelice, Cynthia C. *Casey in the bath*
Demarest, Chris L. *My blue boat*
Dickens, Lucy. *Dirty Henry*
Dodds, Dayle Ann. *Pet wash*
Dodds, Siobhan. *Ting-a-ling!*
Dowling, Paul. *You need a bath, Mustard*
Edwards, Frank B. *Mortimer Mooner stopped taking a bath*
   Troubles with bubbles
Faulkner, Matt. *The amazing voyage of Jackie Grace*
The fish is me
Goodman, Joan Elizabeth. *Bernard's bath*
Hall, Derek. *Elephant bathes*
Hazen, Barbara Shook. *The me I see*
Hedderwick, Mairi. *Katie Morag and the two grandmothers*
Henkes, Kevin. *Clean enough*
Hughes, Shirley. *Bathwater's hot*
Inkpen, Mick. *Kipper's bathtime*
Jackson, Ellen B. *The bear in the bathtub*
Janovitz, Marilyn. *Is it time?*
Johansen, K. V. (Krista V.). *Pippin takes a bath*
Jonell, Lynne. *Mommy go away!*
Josephs, Rhoda. *The baby bubble book*
Kopper, Lisa. *Daisy knows best*
Kroll, Steven. *The pigrates clean up*
Krosoczka, Jarrett J. *Bubble bath pirates*
Kudrna, C. Imbior. *To bathe a boa*
Lauber, Patricia. *What you never knew about tubs, toilets and showers*
Lindbloom, Steven. *Let's give kitty a bath!*
Lindgren, Barbro. *Sam's bath*
Lobb, Janice. *Splash! Splosh! Why do we wash?*
McDonald, Megan. *Bedbugs*
McDonnell, Flora. *I love boats*
MacKinnon, Debbie. *Daniel's duck*
McLeod, Emilie Warren. *One snail and me*

McNeal, Tom. *The dog who lost his Bob*
McPhail, David M. *Andrew's bath*
Manushkin, Fran. *Bubblebath!*
Meister, Cari. *Tiny's bath*
Miller, Margaret. *Where's Jenna?*
Nayer, Judy. *Bath*
Nomura, Takaaki. *Grandpa's town*
Noonan, Julia. *Bath day*
Palatini, Margie. *Tub-boo-boo*
Pallotta, Jerry. *The dory story*
Paterson, Diane. *The bathtub ocean*
Pryor, Ainslie. *The baby blue cat and the dirty dog brothers*
Puttock, Simon. *Squeaky clean*
Reavin, Sam. *Hurray for Captain Jane!*
Ripley, Catherine. *Why is soap so slippery?*
Roffey, Maureen. *Bathtime*
Sayre, April Pulley. *Splish! splash! animal baths*
Schotter, Roni. *Captain Bob sets sail*
Shannon, Terry Miller. *Tub toys*
Shott, Steve (Stephen). *Bathtime*
Slangerup, Erik Jon. *Dirt Boy*
Slate, Joseph. *The mean, clean, giant canoe machine*
Smith, Janice Lee. *Jess and the stinky cowboys*
Spinelli, Eileen. *Summerbath, winterbath*
Spohn, Kate. *Piglet's bath*
Stevens, Kathleen. *The beast in the bathtub*
Stuart, Chad. *The Ballymara flood*
Sutherland, Harry A. *Dad's car wash*
Sykes, Julie. *I don't want to take a bath!*
Thompson, Kay. *Kay Thompson's Eloise takes a bawth [sic]*
Thompson, Richard. *Effie's bath*
Varekamp, Marjolein. *Little Sam takes a bath*
Wabbes, Marie. *Rose's bath*
Watanabe, Shigeo. *I can take a bath!*
Weeks, Sarah. *Splish splash*
Wells, Rosemary. *Max's bath*
Willis, Jeanne. *The tale of Georgie Grub*
Wilson, Sarah. *Uncle Albert's flying birthday*
Wood, Audrey. *King Bidgood's in the bathtub*
Woodruff, Elvira. *Tubtime*
Yolen, Jane. *No bath tonight*
Ziefert, Harriet. *Harry takes a bath*
Zion, Gene. *Harry, the dirty dog*

Activities – cooking *see* Activities – baking, cooking

Activities – dancing

Ackerman, Karen. *Song and dance man*
Allen, Debbie. *Brothers of the knight*
  Dancing in the wings
Allen, Pamela. *Bertie and the bear*
Ambrus, Victor G. *The seven skinny goats*
Ancona, George. *Dancing is*
  Let's dance!
Andersen, H. C. (Hans Christian). *The red shoes*
Andreae, Giles. *Giraffes can't dance*
Andrews, Sylvia. *Dancing in my bones*
Appelt, Kathi. *The Alley Cat's Meow*
  Bats around the clock
Arnosky, Jim. *Rattlesnake dance*
Asch, Frank. *Moondance*
  Moongame
Asher, Sandy. *Stella's dancing days*
Auch, Mary Jane. *Hen lake*
  Peeping Beauty
Axelrod, Amy. *Pigs in the corner*
Babbitt, Natalie. *Nellie, a cat on her own*
Backx, Patsy. *Skippy and Jack*
Baron, Alan. *Red Fox dances*
Baumgardner, Mary Alice. *Alexandra, keeper of dreams*
Bazilian, Barbara. *The red shoes*
Bell, Anthea. *Swan Lake*
Berger, Barbara Helen. *The jewel heart*
Bianco, Margery Williams. *The hurdy-gurdy man*
Blocksma, Mary. *The best dressed bear*
Bornstein, Ruth Lercher. *The dancing man*

Bottner, Barbara. *Messy*
  Myra
Boynton, Sandra. *Barnyard dance!*
Brandenberg, Alexa. *Ballerina flying*
Brighton, Catherine. *Nijinsky*
Brown, Margaret Wise. *Sailor boy jig*
Bunting, Eve (Anne Evelyn). *The day before Christmas*
Burstein, Fred. *The dancer*
Cazet, Denys. *Dancing*
Charlot, Martin. *Felisa and the magic tikling bird*
Chevance, Audrey. *Tutu*
Childress, Mark. *Joshua and Bigtooth*
Clayton, Elaine. *Ella's trip to the museum*
Corey, Shana. *Ballerina bear*
Cox, David. *Ayu and the perfect moon*
Crimi, Carolyn. *Tessa's tip-tapping toes*
Cristaldi, Kathryn. *Baseball ballerina*
  Baseball ballerina strikes out
Daly, Niki. *Papa Lucky's shadow*
Dawavendewa, Gerald. *The butterfly dance*
De Anda, Diane. *Dancing Miranda = Baila, Miranda, baila*
Deetlefs, Rene. *Tabu and the dancing elephants*
De Paola, Tomie (Thomas Anthony). *Oliver Button is a sissy*
Dickens, Lucy. *Dancing class*
Edelman, Elaine. *Boom-de-boom*
Edwards, Pamela Duncan. *Bravo, Livingstone Mouse!*
  Honk!
Esbensen, Barbara Juster. *Dance with me*
Evans, Richard Paul. *The dance*
Eversole, Robyn Harbert. *The magic house*
Fern, Eugene. *Pepito's story*
Fonteyn, Margot, Dame. *Coppélia*
French, Vivian. *One ballerina two*
Gallwey, Kay. *Dancing Daisy*
Gauch, Patricia Lee. *Bravo, Tanya*
  Dance, Tanya
  Presenting Tanya, the Ugly Duckling
  Tanya and Emily in a dance for two
  Tanya and the magic wardrobe
  Tanya steps out
Gelsanliter, Wendy. *Dancin' in the kitchen*
Geras, Adèle. *Giselle*
  The nutcracker
  Sleeping beauty
  Swan Lake
  Time for ballet
Geringer, Laura. *Molly's new washing machine*
Getz, Arthur. *Humphrey, the dancing pig*
Gliori, Debi. *Polar Bolero*
Goble, Paul. *Star boy*
Gollub, Matthew. *Gobble, quack, moon*
Graves, Keith. *Frank was a monster who wanted to dance*
Gray, Libba Moore. *My mama had a dancing heart*
Greene, Carol. *Katherine Dunham*
Grimm, Jacob. *The twelve dancing princesses*, ill. by Kinuko Y. Craft
  The twelve dancing princesses, ill. by Anne Dalton
  The twelve dancing princesses, ill. by Dennis Hockerman
  The twelve dancing princesses, ill. by Errol Le Cain
  The twelve dancing princesses, ill. by Gerald McDermott
  The twelve dancing princesses, ill. by Jane Ray
  The twelve dancing princesses, ill. by Uri Shulevitz
  The twelve dancing princesses, ill. by Suçie Stevenson
  The twelve princesses, ill. by Gordon Fitchett
Hague, Michael. *The nutcracker*
Hallworth, Grace. *Sing me a story*
Hampshire, Susan. *Rosie's ballet slippers*
Hannert, Todd. *Morning dance*
Hayward, Linda. *A day in the life of a dancer*
Hazen, Barbara Shook. *Turkey in the straw*
Heidbreder, Robert. *Drumheller dinosaur dance*
Hesse, Karen. *Come on, rain*
Hest, Amy. *Mabel dancing*
Hoban, Russell. *Charlie Meadows*
  The dancing tigers
Hobbs, Will. *Beardream*
Hoffmann, E. T. A. *The nutcracker*, ill. by Francesca Crespi
  The nutcracker, ill. by Renée Graef

The nutcracker, ill. by Rachel Isadora
The nutcracker, ill. by Joanna Isles
The nutcracker, ill. by Maurice Sendak
The nutcracker, ill. by Lisbeth Zwerger
The nutcracker ballet, ill. by Carolyn Ewing
The nutcracker ballet, ill. by Vladimir Vasilévich Vagin
Holabird, Katharine. *Angelina and the princess*
   Angelina ballerina
   Angelina dances
   Angelina on stage
   Angelina's ballet class
Hurd, Edith Thacher. *I dance in my red pajamas*
Inkpen, Mick. *Wibbly Pig can dance!*
Isadora, Rachel. *Lili at ballet*
   Lili on stage
   Max
   My ballet class
   My ballet diary
   Not just tutus
   Opening night
Jabar, Cynthia. *Shimmy shake earthquake*
Jennings, Linda M. *Coppelia*
   Crispin and the dancing piglet
   The sleeping beauty
Jennings, Sharon. *Priscilla's paw de deux*
Jonas, Ann. *Color dance*
Jones, Bill T. *Dance*
Kajikawa, Kimiko. *Yoshi's feast*
Kinerk, Robert. *Clorinda*
Kingsland, Robin. *Bus stop bop*
Kleven, Elisa. *The dancing deer and the foolish hunter*
Klingel, Cynthia Fitterer. *Dancers*
Komaiko, Leah. *Aunt Elaine does the dance from Spain*
Kraus, Robert. *Dance, Spider, dance!*
Kroll, Virginia L. *Can you dance, Dalila?*
Kuklin, Susan. *Going to my ballet class*
Landström, Olof. *Boo and Baa in a party mood*
La Prise, Larry. *The hokey pokey*
Lasky, Kathryn. *The solo*
   Starring Lucille
Lattimore, Deborah Nourse. *Punga the goddess of ugly*
Lee, Jeanne M. *Silent lotus*
Leiner, Katherine. *Mama does the mambo*
Lemaître, Pascal. *Zelda's secret*
Lemieux, Margo. *The fiddle ribbon*
Lewison, Wendy Cheyette. *I wear my tutu everywhere!*
   Ten little ballerinas
Lifton, Betty Jean. *Tell me a real adoption story*
Lillegard, Dee. *The Big Bug Ball*
London, Jonathan. *Who bop*
Loredo, Elizabeth. *Boogie Bones*
McCoy, Karen Kawamoto. *Bon Odori dancer*
McKissack, Patricia C. *Mirandy and brother wind*
McLerran, Alice. *The ghost dance*
McMullan, Kate (Hall). *Noel the first*
   Nutcracker Noel
Maiorano, Robert. *A little interlude*
Manson, Ainslie. *Ballerinas don't wear glasses*
Marshall, James. *The Cut-Ups carry on*
   George and Martha encore
   Swine lake
Martin, Bill (William Ivan). *Barn dance!*
Martin, Nora. *The stone dancers*
Marzollo, Jean. *Shanna's ballerina show*
Mathers, Petra. *Sophie and Lou*
Mayer, Mercer. *The queen always wanted to dance*
Medearis, Angela Shelf. *Dancing with the Indians*
Medina, Nina. *Have you ever noticed that rabbits don't sing?*
Mellor, Corinne. *Bruce the balding moose*
Mills, Judith Christine. *The painted chest*
Mitton, Tony. *Dinosaurumpus*
   Down by the cool of the pool
Moers, Hermann. *Annie's dancing day*
Morris, Ann. *Little ballerinas*
Murphy, Kelly. *The boll weevil ball*
Nelson, Esther L. *Holiday singing and dancing games*
Newsome, Jill. *Dream dancer*

Norman, Philip Ross. *Dancing dogs*
O'Connor, Jane. *Nina, Nina and the copycat ballerina*
   Nina, Nina ballerina
   Nina, Nina, star ballerina
Ormerod, Jan. *Emily dances*
Oxenbury, Helen. *The dancing class*
Palazzo-Craig, Janet. *Ballet dancer*
Pancheri, Jan. *The twelve poodle princess*
Paraskevas, Betty. *Marvin, the tap-dancing horse*
Pavlova, Anna. *I dreamed I was a ballerina*
Paxton, Tom. *Engelbert the elephant*
Pinkney, Andrea Davis. *Alvin Ailey*
Pulver, Robin. *Alicia's tutu*
Puttock, Simon. *A ladder to the stars*
Quin-Harkin, Janet. *Peter Penny's dance*
Raczek, Linda Theresa. *The night the grandfathers danced*
Richardson, Jean. *The bear who went to the ballet*
   Clara's dancing feet
   The sleeping beauty
Riddell, Chris. *The bear dance*
Rose, Emma. *Ballet magic*
Ryder, Joanne. *Big bear ball*
Satterfield, Barbara. *The story dance*
Schaefer, Jackie Jasina. *Miranda's day to dance*
Scheffrin-Falk, Gladys. *Another celebrated dancing bear*
Schertle, Alice. *Bill and the google-eyed goblins*
Schick, Eleanor. *I have another language*
Schneider, Christine M. *Saxophone Sam and his snazzy jazz band*
Schomp, Virginia. *If you were a . . . ballet dancer*
Schroeder, Alan. *Ragtime Tumpie*
Schumaker, Ward. *Dance!*
Shannon, George. *April showers*
   Dancing the breeze
Shields, Carol Diggory. *Saturday night at the dinosaur stomp*
Simon, Carly. *Amy the dancing bear*
Sis, Peter. *Ballerina*
Smith, Cynthia Leitich. *Jingle dancer*
Sorine, Stephanie Riva. *Our ballet class*
Stanley, Mandy. *Lettice, the dancing rabbit*
Stapler, Sarah. *Cordellia, dance!*
Stickland, Paul. *Dinosaur stomp!*
Stower, Adam. *Two left feet*
Stroud, Bettye. *Dance y'all*, ill. by Cornelious Van Wright & Ying-
   Hwa Hu
Sutton, Jane. *What should a hippo wear?*
Taylor, Ann. *Baby dance*
Thorpe, Kiki. *Time to cha-cha-cha!*
Tilden, Ruth. *Sophie's dance class*
Tompert, Ann. *Savina, the gypsy dancer*
Turner, Nancy Byrd. *When young Melissa sweeps*
Vaughan, Marcia Kapok. *Night dancer*
Von Königslöw, Andrea Wayne. *Bing and Chutney*
Waboose, Jan Bourdeau. *Firedancers*
Walton, Rick. *Dance, pioneer, dance!*
   How can you dance?
   Noah's square dance
Wardlaw, Lee. *Saturday night jamboree*
Warner, Sunny. *Madison finds a line*
Waters, Kate. *Lion dancer*
Welch, Willy. *Dancing with Daddy*
Westman, Barbara. *Dancing dogs*
Whittington, Mary K. *Carmina, come dance!*
Wild, Margaret. *Midnight babies*
Wilkes, Angela. *The best book of ballet*
Wilkes, Larry. *The king's egg dance*
Wolkstein, Diane. *Bouki dances the Kokioko*
Wood, Audrey. *Little Penguin's tale*
Wright, Jill. *The old woman and the Willy Nilly Man*
Yee, Wong Herbert. *The Officers' Ball*
Young, Amy. *Belinda, the ballerina*
Ziefert, Harriet. *Dancing*
Zwerger, Lisbeth. *Swan Lake*

Activities – digging

Agard, John. *Dig away two-hole Tim*
Aliki. *Digging up dinosaurs*

Ayres, Pam. *When dad fills in the garden pond*
Baynton, Martin. *Fifty gets the picture*
Brown, Margaret Wise. *The diggers*
Cleary, Beverly. *The real hole*
Crowther, Robert. *Dump trucks and diggers*
Duke, Kate. *Archaeologists dig for clues*
Gibbons, Gail. *Tunnels*
Harrison, Troon. *Don't dig so deep, Nicholas!*
Hoban, Tana. *Dig, drill, dump, fill*
Krauss, Ruth. *A hole is to dig*
Kumin, Maxine W. *Speedy digs downside up*
Paraskevas, Betty. *Maggie and the Ferocious Beast, the big carrot*
Perkins, Al. *The digging-est dog*
Rawlins, Donna. *Digging to China*
Rex, Michael. *Who digs?*
Royston, Angela. *Diggers and dump trucks*
Stevens, Jan Romero. *Carlos digs to China = Carlos excava hasta la China*
Stickland, Paul. *All about diggers*
Tyler, Jenny. *Big Pig on a dig*

Activities – drawing

Alexander, Martha G. *I'll never share you, Blackboard Bear*
Asch, Frank. *Monkey face*
Baker, Liza. *Dinosaur days*
Berlan, Kathryn Hook. *Andrew's amazing monsters*
Bloom, Becky. *Mice make trouble*
Bornstein, Ruth Lercher. *That's how it is when we draw*
Carle, Eric. *Draw me a star*
Emberlcy, Ed (Edward Randolph). *Ed Emberley's drawing book of trucks and trains*
   Ed Emberley's fingerprint drawing book
Engel, Diana. *The shelf-paper jungle*
Fain, Moira. *Snow day*
Falwell, Cathryn. *David's drawing*
Gilliland, Judith Heide. *Not in the house, Newton!*
Greenblat, Rodney Alan. *Thunder Bunny*
Hamsa, Bobbie. *Fast-draw Freddie*
Hoban, Russell. *Monsters*
Hutchins, H. J. (Hazel J.). *The sidewalk rescue*
Inkpen, Mick. *Wibbly Pig makes pictures*
Jagtenberg, Yvonne. *Jack's rabbit*
Jennings, Linda M. *Franklin's neighborhood*
Kamish, Daniel. *The night scary beasties popped out of my head*
Kleven, Elisa. *The paper princess*
Kroll, Steven. *Patches*
   Patches lost and found
Levine, Arthur A. *The boy who drew cats*
Littlesugar, Amy. *Josiah True and the art maker*
McClintock, Barbara. *The fantastic drawings of Danielle*
McPhail, David M. *Drawing lessons from a bear*
   Moony B. Finch, fastest draw in the West
Moss, Marissa. *Regina's big mistake*
Nikola-Lisa, W. *Can you top that?*
Pericoli, Matteo. *See the city*
Poydar, Nancy. *Cool Ali*
Priest, Robert H. *The pirate's eye*
Rey, Margret (Margret Elisabeth Waldstein). *Billy's picture*
Russo, Marisabina. *Under the table*
Say, Allen. *Emma's rug*
Thomson, Ruth. *Drawing*
Van Allsburg, Chris. *Bad day at Riverbend*
Wallner, Alexandra. *Beatrix Potter*
Walsh, Patricia. *Cars*
   Dinosaurs
Wilson, April. *April Wilson's magpie magic*

Activities – driving

Aylesworth, Jim. *Through the night*
Gibbons, Faye. *Mama and me and the Model-T*
Greenfield, Eloise. *Kia Tanisha drives her car*

Activities – eating *see* Food

Activities – flying

Aardema, Verna. *Jackal's flying lesson*
Abolafia, Yossi. *Yanosh's Island*
Adoff, Arnold. *Flamboyan*
Allard, Harry. *The Stupids take off*
Allen, Laura Jean. *Where is Freddy?*
Anderson, Joan. *Harry's helicopter*
Anderson, Lonzo. *Mr. Biddle and the birds*
Arabian Nights. *The flying carpet*
Arvetis, Chris. *Why does it fly?*
Aulaire, Ingri Mortenson d'. *Wings for Per*
Ayal, Ora. *The adventures of Chester the chest*
Ayres, Becky Hickox. *Victoria flies high*
Balian, Lorna. *Wilbur's space machine*
Bang, Molly. *Goose*
Benchley, Nathaniel. *The flying lessons of Gerald Pelican*
Berger, Melvin. *How do airplanes fly?*
Blake, Robert J. *Fledgling*
Blathwayt, Benedict. *Tangle and the silver bird*
Borden, Louise. *Goodbye, Charles Lindbergh*
Bradfield, Roger (Jolly Roger). *The flying hockey stick*
Breathed, Berke (Berkeley). *A wish for wings that work*
Brenner, Barbara A. *The flying patchwork quilt*
Brimner, Larry Dane. *If dogs had wings*
Brock, Emma Lillian. *Surprise balloon*
Brown, Marc Tolon. *Wings on things*
Brown, Margaret Wise. *Streamlined pig*
Bruna, Dick. *The happy apple*
   Miffy goes flying
Buchanan, Heather S. *George Mouse learns to fly*
Buckingham, Simon. *Alec and his flying bed*
Cave, Kathryn. *The boy who became an eagle*
Cherry, Lynne. *The armadillo from Amarillo*
Clearman, Deborah. *The goose's tale*
Collicott, Sharleen. *Seeing stars*
Collins, Pat Lowery. *Tomorrow, up and away!*
Conover, Chris. *The lion's share*
Corbalis, Judy. *Porcellus, the flying pig*
Crebbin, June. *Fly by night*
Crews, Donald. *Flying*
Dabcovich, Lydia. *Ducks fly*
De Beer, Hans. *Little Polar Bear and the big balloon*
Demarest, Chris L. *Lindbergh*
   Smokejumpers one to ten
Dollinger, Renate. *The rabbi who flew*
Dorros, Arthur. *Abuela*
Drawson, Blair. *Flying Dimitri*
Dunbar, Joyce. *Baby bird*
Duvoisin, Roger Antoine. *Petunia takes a trip*
Edwards, Pamela Duncan. *The Wright brothers*
Erlbruch, Wolf. *Mrs. Meyer, the bird*
Finn, Isobel. *The very lazy ladybug*
Florian, Douglas. *Airplane ride*
Foreman, Michael. *The little reindeer*
Fort, Patrick. *Redbird*
French, Vivian. *Little Ghost*
Garland, Michael. *Icarus Swinebuckle*
Gay, Michel. *Bibi takes flight*
Gerrard, Roy. *Jocasta Carr, movie star*
Gibbons, Gail. *Flying*
Glass, Andrew. *The wondrous whirligig*
Gorbachev, Valeri. *The fool of the world and the flying ship*
Graham, Bob. *Max*
Gramatky, Hardie. *Loopy*
Gregorowski, Christopher. *Fly, eagle, fly!*
Grist, Julie. *Flying, just plane fun*
Hays, Hoffman Reynolds. *Charley sang a song*
Heller, Nicholas. *Elwood and the witch*
Hill, Eric. *Up there*
Hoban, Russell. *Ace Dragon Ltd.*
Hughes, Shirley. *Up and up*
Jackson, Carolyn. *The flying ark*
James, J. Alison. *Eucalyptus wings*
Jenkins, Steve. *Animals in flight*
Jenny, Anne. *The fantastic story of King Brioche the First*
Jeschke, Susan. *Perfect the pig*

Johnson, Neil. *Fire and silk*
Johnson, Paul Brett. *The cow who wouldn't come down*
Joyce, William. *Santa calls*
Jukes, Mavis. *I'll see you in my dreams*
Kaufmann, John. *Flying giants of long ago*
King, Christopher L. *The boy who ate the moon*
Kleven, Elisa. *The paper princess*
Kojima, Naomi. *The flying grandmother*
Kotzwinkle, William. *Walter, the farting dog: rough weather ahead*
Krauss, Ruth. *I can fly*
Kuskin, Karla. *Just like everyone else*
Lang, Andrew. *The flying ship*
Lewis, Kim. *Here we go Harry*
Liddell, Janice. *Imani and the Flying Africans*
Lies, Brian. *Hamlet and the enormous Chinese dragon kite*
Lindbergh, Reeve. *Nobody owns the sky*
Lindgren, Barbro. *Shorty takes off*
Lobato, Arcadio. *Paper bird*
Loux, Lynn C. *The day I could fly*
McConnachie, Brian. *Flying boy*
McDermott, Gerald. *Coyote*
McKee, David. *Elmer and the wind*
   Elmer takes off
McLellan, Stephanie Simpson. *The chicken cat*
McPhail, David M. *First flight*
Maizlish, Lisa. *The ring*
Mara, Wil. *Amelia Earhart*
Metaxas, Eric. *The fool and the flying ship*
Mills, Lauren A. *Fairy wings*
Minshull, Evelyn White. *Eaglet's world*
Munsch, Robert N. *Angela's airplane*
Murphy, Pat. *Pigasus*
Myers, Bernice. *The flying shoes*
Myers, Christopher A. *Wings*
Myers, Walter Dean. *How Mr. Monkey saw the whole world*
Nones, Eric Jon. *Angela's wings*
Noyes, Deborah. *It's Vladimir!*
O'Malley, Kevin. *Little buggy*
Osborne, Mary Pope. *Moonhorse*, ill. by David McPhail
   Moonhorse, ill. by S. M. Saelig
Pacovská, Kveta. *Flying*
Peet, Bill (William Bartlett). *The kweeks of Kookatumdee*
   Merle the high flying squirrel
Pinkney, J. Brian. *The adventures of sparrowboy*
Pirotta, Saviour. *Little bird*
Pomerantz, Charlotte. *Flap your wings and try*
Potok, Chaim. *The sky of now*
Priceman, Marjorie. *Princess Picky*
Priestley, Alice. *Someone is reading this book*
Provensen, Alice. *The glorious flight*
Ransome, Arthur. *The fool of the world and the flying ship*
Rigby, Rodney. *Hello, this is your penguin speaking*
Ringgold, Faith. *Tar Beach*
Ross, Pat. *Your first airplane trip*
Rühmann, Karl. *Filbert flies*
Ryan, Pam Muñoz. *Amelia and Eleanor go for a ride*
Ryder, Joanne. *Rainbow wings*
Schomp, Virginia. *If you were a . . . pilot*
Schotter, Roni. *Captain Bob takes flight*
Schulz, Walter A. *Will and Orv*
Schumacher, Claire. *Nutty's birthday*
Scruton, Clive. *Pig in the air*
Scuderi, Lucia. *To fly*
Seibold, J. Otto. *Mr. Lunch takes a plane ride*
   Penguin dreams
Simont, Marc. *The goose that almost got cooked*
Smith, Lane. *Flying Jake*
Spurr, Elizabeth. *Mrs. Minetta's car pool*
Stadler, John. *Three cheers for hippo!*
Stevenson, James. *The castaway*
   Grandpa's great city tour
Tarpley, Natasha Anastasia. *Joe-Joe's first flight*
Taylor, Judy. *Dudley goes flying*
Testa, Fulvio. *The paper airplane*
Thompson, Colin (Colin Edward). *Falling angels*
Tibo, Gilles. *The cowboy kid*
Titus, Eve. *Anatole over Paris*

Trez, Denise. *Maila and the flying carpet*
Uhlberg, Myron. *Flying over Brooklyn*
Ungerer, Tomi. *Adelaide*
   The Mellops go flying
Valens, Evans G. *Wingfin and Topple*
Walter, Mildred Pitts. *Brother to the wind*
Ward, Helen. *The dragon machine*
   The king of the birds
Waterton, Betty. *Orff, 27 dragons (and a snarkel)*
Watson, Clyde. *Midnight moon*
Wende, Philip. *Bird boy*
West, Ian. *Silas, the first pig to fly*
Wheeling, Lynn. *When you fly*
Wiesner, David. *Tuesday*
Winer, Yvonne. *Butterflies fly*
Wolkstein, Diane. *The cool ride in the sky*
   The magic wings
Woodruff, Elvira. *The wing shop*
Yolen, Jane. *Wings*
Young, Miriam Burt. *If I flew a plane*

Activities – gardening *see* Gardens, gardening

Activities – jumping

Akass, Susan. *Number nine duckling*
Bright, Robert. *My hopping bunny*
Cain, Sheridan. *Look out for the big bad fish!*
Cole, Joanna. *Norma Jean, jumping bean*
Easton, Violet. *Elephants never jump*
Esbensen, Barbara Juster. *Jumping day*
King, Stephen Michael. *Emily loves to bounce*
Lyne, Alice. *A, my name is . . .*
Most, Bernard. *The very boastful kangaroo*
Murphy, Stuart J. *Ready, set, hop!*
Powell, Jillian. *Jumpers*
Scruggs, Afi. *Jump rope magic*
Stephens, Karen. *Jumping*

Activities – kissing *see* Kissing

Activities – knitting

Aber, Linda Williams. *Carrie measures up!*
Anholt, Catherine. *Tom's rainbow walk*
Blackwood, Mary. *Derek the knitting dinosaur*
Hilton, Nette. *The long red scarf*
Hissey, Jane. *Jolly Tall*
Holl, Adelaide. *Mrs. McGarrity's peppermint sweater*
Laurin, Anne. *Little things*
Lecher, Doris. *Angelita's magic yarn*
Martinez, Ruth. *Mrs. McDockerty's knitting*
Shannon, Margaret. *The red wolf*
Smee, Nicola. *The Tusk Fairy*
Storr, Catherine (Cole). *Hugo and his grandma*
Wild, Margaret. *Mr. Nick's knitting*
Ziefert, Harriet. *With love from Grandma*

Activities – making things

Ahlberg, Allan. *Miss Brick, the builder's baby*
Arnold, Tedd. *The simple people*
Balterman, Lee. *Girders and cranes*
Bartels, Alice L. *The grandmother doll*
The big Peter Rabbit book
Blocksma, Mary. *Easy-to-make spaceships that really fly*
Blos, Joan W. *The grandpa days*
Boucher, Jerry. *Fire truck nuts and bolts*
Calder, Lyn. *Walt Disney's Alice's tea party*
Crowley, Michael. *New kid on Spurwick Ave.*
Curtis, Neil. *How paper is made*
Dalmais, Anne-Marie. *And may the best animal win!*
   Petey the puppy
Day, Alexandra. *Carl makes a scrapbook*
De Paola, Tomie (Thomas Anthony). *Things to make and do for*
   Valentine's Day
Ehlert, Lois. *Hands*

Engel, Diana. *The little lump of clay*
Falwell, Cathryn. *Nicky and Alex*
Fleming, Denise. *Alphabet under construction*
Flint, Russ. *Let's build a house*
Florian, Douglas. *A potter*
Fox, Perla. *The Wooodles*
Gibbons, Gail. *How a house is built*
Ginsburg, Mirra. *Clay boy*
Gliori, Debi. *New big house*
Graham, Thomas. *Mr. Bear's chair*
Grossman, Bill. *The banging book*
Hall, Donald. *Lucy's Christmas*
Halperin, Wendy Anderson. *Once upon a company*
Himmelman, John. *The day-off machine*
   The great leaf blast-off
Hindley, Judy. *The little train*
Hoban, Tana. *Construction zone*
Howell, Will C. *Zoo flakes ABC*
Huff, Vivian. *Let's make paper dolls*
Hughes, Shirley. *The big concrete lorry*
Hunter, Dette. *38 ways to entertain your babysitter*
   38 ways to entertain your grandparents
Inkpen, Mick. *Wibbly Pig can make a tent*
Iverson, Diane. *Discover the seasons*
Johnson, Angela. *Those building men*
Johnson, Stephen T. *My little blue robot*
Kiser, Kevin. *Buzzy Widget*
Kiser, SuAnn. *The birthday thing*
Kreye, Walter. *The giant from the little island*
Kroll, Steven. *Will you be my valentine?*
Kuklin, Susan. *From head to toe*
Kunhardt, Edith. *Danny's Christmas star*
Lanteigne, Helen. *The seven chairs*
Leedy, Loreen. *A dragon Christmas*
Lohf, Sabine. *Things I can make with buttons*
   Things I can make with cloth
   Things I can make with cork
   Things I can make with paper
Lopshire, Robert. *How to make snop snappers and other fine things*
Lum, Kate. *What! cried Granny*
McCain, Becky R. (Becky Ray). *Grandmother's dreamcatcher*
Martin, Jacqueline Briggs. *Good times on Grandfather Mountain*
Maurer-Mathison, Diane V. *Make your own spectacular Valentines*
Miller, Cameron. *Woodlore*
Miller, Margaret. *I can make it!*
Moffatt, Judith. *Snow shapes*
Moon, Nicola. *Lucy's picture*
Moss, Marissa. *Knick knack paddywack*
Neitzel, Shirley. *The house I'll build for the wrens*
Oates, Eddie Hershel. *Making music*
Parker, Steve. *I wonder why tunnels are round*
Pfanner, Louise. *Louise builds a boat*
   Louise builds a house
Pilkey, Dav. *The Silly Gooses build a house*
Radford, Derek. *Harry builds a house*
Ransom, Candice F. *The promise quilt*
Ray, Mary Lyn. *Basket moon*
Rockwell, Anne F. *What we like*
Rosenberg, Liz. *The scrap doll*
Rumford, James. *The cloudmakers*
Shaw, Mary. *Brady Brady and the great rink*
Sohi, Morteza E. *Look what I did with a leaf!*
Swinburne, Stephen R. *Swallows in the birdhouse*
Tafuri, Nancy. *Counting to Christmas*
Thelen, Gerda. *The toy maker*
Thomson, Ruth. *Printing*
   The Rainforest Indians
Tryon, Leslie. *Albert's alphabet*
Vainio, Pirkko. *The dream house*
Wallace, John. *Building a house with Mr. Bumble*
Weller, Frances Ward. *Matthew Wheelock's wall*
Wood, Audrey. *The flying dragon room*
Ziefert, Harriet. *Before I was born*
Zweifel, Frances W. *The Make-Something Club*

Activities – painting *see also* Careers – artists; Careers – painters

Adams, Adrienne. *The Easter egg artists*
Agee, Jon. *The incredible painting of Felix Clousseau*
Asch, Frank. *Bread and honey*
Baker, Alan. *Benjamin's portrait*
   Black and White Rabbit's ABC
   White Rabbit's color book
Baker, Keith. *Little Green*
Bang, Molly. *Tye May and the magic brush*
Bassède, Francine. *George paints his house*
Becker, Edna. *Nine hundred buckets of paint*
Beim, Jerrold. *Jay's big job*
Bilgrami, Shaheen. *Farmyard painting party*
   Jungle art show
Black, Harley. *Magic art class*
Bond, Michael. *Paddington's art exhibit*
Bromhall, Winifred. *Mary Ann's first picture*
Caple, Kathy. *Worm gets a job*
Carrick, Donald. *Morgan and the artist*
Catalanotto, Peter. *The painter*
Coats, Laura Jane. *Marcella and the moon*
Craven, Carolyn. *What the mailman brought*
Day, Marie. *Quennu and the cave bear*
Decker, Dorothy W. *Stripe visits New York*
Demi. *Liang and the magic paintbrush*
De Paola, Tomie (Thomas Anthony). *The legend of the Indian paintbrush*
Dionetti, Michelle V. *Painting the wind*
Duvoisin, Roger Antoine. *The house of four seasons*
Edwards, Pamela Duncan. *Warthogs paint*
Ernst, Lisa Campbell. *Hamilton's art show*
Flanagan, Alice K. *The Wilsons, a house-painting team*
Florian, Douglas. *A painter*
Freeman, Don. *The chalk box story*
Geoghegan, Adrienne. *All your own teeth*
Helldorfer, M. C. (Mary Claire). *Cabbage Rose*
Hest, Amy. *Jamaica Louise James*
Himmelman, John. *Ellen and the goldfish*
Hurd, Thacher. *Art dog*
Johnston, Tony. *Pages of music*
Kelley, True. *Claude Monet*
Kessler, Leonard P. *Mr. Pine's purple house*
Kidd, Richard. *Almost famous Daisy!*
Leaf, Margaret. *Eyes of the dragon*
Leonard, Marcia. *Paintbox penguins*
Lindsay, Elizabeth. *A letter for Maria*
McClintock, Barbara. *The fantastic drawings of Danielle*
MacLachlan, Patricia. *Painting the wind*
McPhail, David M. *Big brown bear*
   Lorenzo
   Something special
Martin, Charles E. *For rent*
Menter, Ian. *The Albany Road mural*
Miller, Warren. *Pablo paints a picture*
Molarsky, Osmond. *A sky full of kites*
Morris, Jill. *The boy who painted the sun*
Muller, Robin. *The magic paintbrush*
Nerlove, Miriam. *Flowers on the wall*
   If all the world were paper
Nez, Redwing T. *Forbidden talent*
Partridge, Elizabeth. *Pig's eggs*
Pinkwater, Daniel Manus. *The big orange splot*
   The picture of Morty and Ray
Pittman, Helena Clare. *Still-life stew*
Rinder, Lenore. *A big mistake*
Rogers, Paul (Patrick). *Don't blame me!*
Romanelli, Serena. *Little Bobo saves the day*
Roth, Roger. *The sign painter's dream*
Rylant, Cynthia. *All I see*
   Mr. Putter and Tabby paint the porch
Segal, Lore Groszmann. *Morris the artist*
Sharratt, Nick. *The time it took Tom*
Silsbe, Brenda. *Just one more color*
Skorpen, Liesel Moak. *We were tired of living in a house*
Snyder, Carol. *We're painting*

Spier, Peter. *Oh, were they ever happy!*
Tamar, Erika. *The garden of happiness*
Thomas, Abigail. *Pearl paints*
Thomson, Ruth. *Painting*
Voigt, Hannelore. *Not now, Sara!*
Wabbes, Marie. *Rose's picture*
Walsh, Ellen Stoll. *Mouse paint*
Walsh, Jill Paton. *Pepi and the secret names*
Walsh, Melanie. *Ned's rainbow*
Weisgard, Leonard. *Mr. Peaceable paints*
Wilhelm, Hans. *Quacky Ducky's Easter fun*
Williams, Karen Lynn. *Painted dreams*
Woodhouse, Jayne. *Pieter Bruegel*
Ziefert, Harriet. *Elemenopeo*
    Lunchtime for a purple snake

Activities – photographing

Brimner, Larry Dane. *Max and Felix*
Castle, Caroline. *Grandpa Baxter and the photographs*
Hest, Amy. *Guess who, Baby Duck*
    Weekend girl
Johnson, Dinah. *All around town*
Levinson, Riki. *I go with my family to Grandma's*
McClintock, Barbara. *The fantastic drawings of Danielle*
McPhail, David M. *Pig Pig and the magic photo album*
Manushkin, Fran. *The perfect Christmas picture*
Marshall, Janet Perry. *My camera*
Morrow, Barbara. *Edward's portrait*
Plourde, Lynn. *School picture day*
Roche, Denis (Denis M.). *The best class picture ever*
Seguin-Fontes, Marthe. *A wedding book*
Swinburne, Stephen R. *Guess whose shadow?*
Talley, Linda. *Jackson's plan*
Tison, Annette. *Animal hide-and-seek*
Trimble, Marcia. *Hello sun*
Türk, Hanne. *Snapshot Max*
Villarejo, Mary. *The tiger hunt*
Vincent, Gabrielle. *Smile, Ernest and Celestine*
Watts, Mabel (Pizzey). *Weeks and weeks*
Willard, Nancy. *Simple pictures are best*
Wyllie, Stephen. *Snappity snap*

Activities – picnicking

Alborough, Jez. *It's the bear*
Asch, Frank. *Sand cake*
Ashforth, Camilla. *Willow on the river*
Benjamin, Alan. *A change of plans*
Berger, Terry. *The turtles' picnic and other nonsense stories*
Bertrand, Diane Gonzales. *Uncle Chente's picnic = El picnic de Tío Chente*
Binnamin, Vivian. *The case of the anteater's missing lunch*
Bishop, Bonnie. *Ralph rides away*
Bowden, Joan Chase. *The Ginghams and the backward picnic*
Bratton, John. *The teddy bears' picnic*, ill. by Renate Kozikowski
Brown, Ruth. *The picnic*
Browne, Eileen. *Where's that bus?*
Brunhoff, Laurent de. *Babar's picnic*
Bunting, Eve (Anne Evelyn). *A picnic in October*
    Someday a tree
Butler, Dorothy. *Higgledy, piggledy, hobbledy hoy*
Butterworth, Nick. *All together now!*
    The rescue party
Capucilli, Alyssa Satin. *Biscuit's picnic*
Cauley, Lorinda Bryan. *Treasure hunt*
Chalmers, Mary. *Here comes the trolley*
    Mr. Cat's wonderful surprise
Christelow, Eileen. *Five little monkeys sitting in a tree*
Christian, Mary Blount. *Go west, swamp monsters*
Claverie, Jean. *The picnic*
Darling, Abigail. *Teddy bears' picnic cookbook*
Daugherty, James Henry. *The picnic*
Delton, Judy. *On a picnic*
Denton, Kady MacDonald. *The picnic*
Dickinson, Mary. *Alex's outing*
Dubanevich, Arlene. *Pig William*

Dunham, Meredith. *Picnic*
Du Quette, Keith. *Ripping day for a picnic*
Eilenberg, Max. *Squeak's good idea*
Ernst, Lisa Campbell. *Up to ten and down again*
Ets, Marie Hall. *In the forest*
Freschet, Berniece. *The ants go marching*
Gackenbach, Dick. *Claude has a picnic*
Garcia, Jerry. *The teddy bears' picnic*
Garland, Sarah. *Having a picnic*
Gliori, Debi. *Mr. Bear's picnic*
Goldstone, Bruce. *The beastly feast*
Goodall, John S. *The surprise picnic*
Gordon, Margaret. *Wilberforce goes on a picnic*
Graham, Bob. *Jethro Byrd, fairy child*
    Libby, Oscar and me
Graham, Thomas. *Mr. Bear's boat*
Granowsky, Alvin. *Can I help?*
Hamilton, Richard. *Polly's picnic*
Hayes, Sarah. *This is the bear and the picnic lunch*
Hest, Amy. *Weekend girl*
Higham, Jon Atlas. *Aardvark's picnic*
Hill, Eric. *Spot's first picnic*
Hill, Susan. *Stuart sets sail*
Hines, Anna Grossnickle. *Come to the meadow*
    The greatest picnic in the world
Hurd, Edith Thacher. *No funny business*
Ichikawa, Satomi. *Nora's surprise*
Inkpen, Mick. *Picnic*
Iwamura, Kazuo. *The fourteen forest mice and the spring meadow picnic*
Jarrett, Clare. *The best picnic ever*
Kasza, Keiko. *The pigs' picnic*
Keller, Holly. *Henry's Fourth of July*
Kennedy, Jimmy. *The teddy bears' picnic*, ill. by Alexandra Day
    The teddy bears' picnic, ill. by Michael Hague
    The teddy bears' picnic, ill. by Prue Theobalds
Killingback, Julia. *Busy Bears' picnic*
King, Bob. *Sitting on the farm*
Knox-Wagner, Elaine. *The oldest kid*
Kroll, Steven. *It's Groundhog Day!*
Landström, Olof. *Boo and Baa in the woods*
Lathrop, Dorothy Pulis. *Who goes there?*
Lewis, J. Patrick. *The la-di-da hare*
Little, Jean. *Once upon a golden apple*
Livingston, Irene. *Finklehopper Frog cheers*
London, Jonathan. *Let's go, Froggy!*
Losi, Carol A. *The 512 ants on Sullivan Street*
McCully, Emily Arnold. *Picnic*
MacGregor, Marilyn. *Helen the hungry bear*
Maestro, Betsy. *The perfect picnic*
Mahy, Margaret. *The rattlebang picnic*
Manzano, Sonia. *No dogs allowed*
Maris, Ron. *In my garden*
Marshall, Edward. *Three by the sea*
Matje, Martin. *Celeste*
Miranda, Anne. *Pignic*
Morton, Christine. *Picnic farm*
Murphy, Stuart J. *More or less*
Naylor, Phyllis Reynolds. *The picnic*
    Please do feed the bears
Numeroff, Laura Joffe. *What mommies do best*
Polacco, Patricia. *Picnic at Mudsock Meadow*
Prater, John. *Once upon a picnic*
Radlauer, Ruth Shaw. *Molly*
    Molly goes hiking
Rappus, Gerhard. *When the sun was shining*
Robertson, Lilian. *Picnic woods*
Rodgers, Richard. *A real nice clambake*
Roffey, Maureen. *Mealtime*
Rogers, Paul (Patrick). *Lily's picnic*
Rowinski, Kate. *L. L. Bear's island adventure*
Samton, Sheila White. *On the river*
Saunders, Susan. *Charles Rat's picnic*
    Fish fry
Scarry, Richard. *My first word book*
Schaap, Martine. *Mop and the birthday picnic*
Schroeder, Binette. *Tuffa and the picnic*

Shapiro, Arnold L. *Square*
Spetter, Jung-Hee. *Lily and Trooper's spring*
Steig, William. *Toby, who are you?*
Szekeres, Cyndy. *Ladybug, ladybug, where are you?*
Taylor, Judy. *Sophie and Jack*
Tether, Graham. *Skunk and possum*
Thomas, Jane Resh. *Celebration!*
Tsutsui, Yoriko. *Before the picnic*
Vaës, Alain. *The porcelain pepper pot*
Van Stockum, Hilda. *A day on skates*
Vincent, Gabrielle. *Ernest and Celestine's picnic*
Von Königslöw, Andrea Wayne. *Bing and Chutney off to Moosonee*
Waddell, Martin. *Mimi and the picnic*
Wasmuth, Eleanor. *The picnic basket*
Watson, Clyde. *Hickory stick rag*
The weekend
Wells, Rosemary. *McDuff saves the day*
Westcott, Nadine Bernard. *The giant vegetable garden*
Weston, Martha. *Bea's four bears*
Wheeler, Cindy. *Marmalade's picnic*
Wood, Joyce. *Grandmother Lucy goes on a picnic*
Woodson, Jacqueline. *We had a picnic this Sunday past*
Yeoman, John. *The bear's water picnic*
Yolen, Jane. *Picnic with Piggins*

Activities – playing

Adam, Barbara. *The big, big box*
Adorjan, Carol Madden. *I can! Can you?*
Agee, Jon. *Ellsworth*
Ahlberg, Allan. *Me and my friend*
Ahlberg, Janet. *Funnybones*
Playmates
Ajmera, Maya. *Come out and play*
Alberts, Nancy Markham. *No toys on Sunday*
Alborough, Jez. *Hide and seek*
Alexander, Martha G. *Blackboard Bear*
Good night, Lily
I'll be the horse if you'll play with me
Lily and Willy
Where's Willy?
Willy's boot
Aliki. *Overnight at Mary Bloom's*
Allen, Pamela. *I wish I had a pirate suit*
Allen, Robert. *Ten little babies play*
Anglund, Joan Walsh. *The brave cowboy*
Apperley, Dawn. *Flip and Flop*
Arnold, Caroline. *How do we have fun?*
Playtime for zoo animals
Splashtime for zoo animals
Arnosky, Jim. *Watching foxes*
Artis, Vicki Kimmel. *Pajama walking*
Asch, Frank. *Rebecka*
Aulaire, Ingri Mortenson d'. *Children of the northlights*
Ayal, Ora. *Ugbu*
Bailey, Debbie. *The playground*
Baillie, Allan. *Drac and the gremlin*
Baillie, Marilyn. *Nose to toes*
Baker, Leslie A. *You bad dog!*
Bang, Molly. *One fall day*
Yellow ball
Barclay, Jane. *Going on a journey to the sea*
Baron, Alan. *Little Pig's bouncy ball*
Batchelor, Louise. *Whoops!*
Bauer, Helen. *Good times at the park*
Baugh, Dolores M. *Slides*
Swings
Beck, Andrea. *Elliot's shipwreck*
Benét, William Rose. *Timothy's angels*
Bergman, Donna. *Timmy Green's blue lake*
Berkowitz, Linda. *Alfonse, where are you?*
Berry, Holly. *Busy Lizzie*
Best, Cari. *Last licks*
Taxi! Taxi!
Bethell, Jean. *Playmates*
Blegvad, Lenore. *Rainy day Kate*
Blizzard, Gladys S. *Come look with me*

Bogacki, Tomasz. *Cat and mouse in the snow*
Bonsall, Crosby Newell. *And I mean it, Stanley*
Bottner, Barbara. *Bootsie Barker bites*
Boyd, Lizi. *Willy and the cardboard boxes*
Bram, Elizabeth. *Saturday morning lasts forever*
Breeze, Lynn. *This little baby's morning*
Breinburg, Petronella. *Doctor Shawn*
Brimner, Larry Dane. *The big, beautiful, brown box*
Brinckloe, Julie. *Playing marbles*
Brown, Myra Berry. *First night away from home*
Brown, Ruth. *Our puppy's vacation*
Browne, Anthony. *Things I like*
Bruna, Dick. *Miffy at the playground*
Miffy's dream
Bruzzone, Catherine. *Puppy finds a friend = Cachorrito encuentra un amigo*
Puppy finds a friend = Le petit chien se trouve un ami
Buck, Nola. *Oh, cats!*
Sid and Sam
Buckley, Helen Elizabeth. *"Take care of things," Edward said*
Burningham, John. *Where's Julius?*
Burns, Maurice. *Go ducks, go!*
Burstein, Fred. *Whispering in the park*
Butterworth, Nick. *When we play together*
Cabban, Vanessa. *Bertie and Small and the fast bike ride*
Cabrera, Jane. *Monkey's play time*
Cader, Lisa Lebowitz. *When I wear my crown*
When I wear my tiara
Capucilli, Alyssa Satin. *Biscuit wants to play*
Carlstrom, Nancy White. *Heather hiding*
Carrier, Lark. *Scout and Cody*
Carroll, Ruth. *Where's the bunny?*
Cartlidge, Michelle. *Pippin and Pod*
Teddy's friends
Caseley, Judith. *The noisemakers*
Castle, Caroline. *Naughty!*
Cauley, Lorinda Bryan. *Clap your hands*
Chichester Clark, Emma. *More!*
Chorao, Kay. *Annie and cousin Precious*
Christian, Mary Blount. *The sand lot*
Cimarusti, Marie Torres. *Peek-a-moo*
Coffelt, Nancy. *Good night, Sigmund*
Cole, Joanna. *Sharing is fun*
Cole, William. *What's good for a four-year-old?*
What's good for a six-year-old?
Cooney, Nancy Evans. *Chatter-box Jamie*
Cousins, Lucy. *Doctor Maisy*
Maisy goes to the playground
Creighton, Jill. *Maybe a monster*
Crews, Donald. *Cloudy day/sunny day*
Crews, Nina. *Snowball*
Cuneo, Mary Louise. *Mail for Husher Town*
Dahlbäck-Lutteman, Helena. *My sister Lotta and me*
Dale, Penny. *All about Alice*
Day, Alexandra. *Carl goes to daycare*
Follow Carl!
DeBear, Kirsten. *Be quiet, Marina!*
DeLage, Ida. *Frannie's flower*
De Paola, Tomie (Thomas Anthony). *Katie, Kit and cousin Tom*
Deprisco, Dorothea. *Snowbear's winter day*
Derby, Sally. *My steps*
Dewan, Ted. *Baby gets the zapper*
Crispin, the pig who had it all
Dickens, Lucy. *At the beach*
Our day
Outside
Playtime
Donaldson, Joan. *The real pretend*
Donovan, Mary Lee. *Won't you come and play with me?*
Doyle, Charlotte Lackner. *You can't catch me*
Dubowski, Cathy East. *Snug Bug's play day*
Duke, Kate. *One guinea pig is not enough*
The playground
Eaton, Deborah. *The rainy day grump*
Ehrlich, H. M. *Gotcha, Louie!*
Emecheta, Buchi. *Nowhere to play*
Ets, Marie Hall. *Play with me*

Falwell, Cathryn. *Nicky and Alex*
  Nicky and grandpa
  Where's Nicky?
Fitzhugh, Louise. *Bang, bang, you're dead*
Fitzpatrick, Marie-Louise. *I'm a tiger, too!*
Ford, Christine. *Snow!*
Ford, Miela. *Follow the leader*
  Mom and me
  My day in the garden
French, Vivian. *Little Ghost*
Fuge, Charles. *I know a rhino*
Fujikawa, Gyo. *That's not fair!*
Gardiner, Lindsey. *Here come Poppy and Max*
  When Poppy and Max grow up
Gay, Marie-Louise. *Stella, queen of the snow*
Gebert, Warren. *The old ball and the sea*
George, Jean Craighead. *Snow bear*
Gibbons, Gail. *Playgrounds*
Gliori, Debi. *Mr. Bear says peek-a-boo*
  The snowchild
Godwin, Laura. *The best fall of all*
  Happy and Honey
Goffstein, M. B. (Marilyn Brooke). *Our snowman*
Gorbachev, Valeri. *Big Little Elephant*
  Chicken chickens
Greenfield, Eloise. *Big friend, little friend*
  My doll, Keshia
Gretz, Susanna. *Duck takes off*
  Teddy bears stay indoors
Grindley, Sally. *Can we play too, Piglittle?*
Gundersheimer, Karen. *Find cat, wear hat*
  Splish splash bang crash!
Hallinan, P. K. (Patrick K.). *Let's play as a team*
Hallworth, Grace. *Down by the river*
Halpern, Julie. *Toby and the snowflakes*
Halpern, Shari. *What shall we do when we all go out?*
Hann, Jacquie. *Follow the leader*
Hartman, Gail. *For sand castles or seashells*
Haus, Felice. *Beep! Beep! I'm a jeep*
Havill, Juanita. *Jamaica Tag-Along*
Hawkins, Colin. *Dip, dip, dip*
  One finger, one thumb
  Oops-a-Daisy
  Where's bear?
Heap, Sue. *What shall we play?*
Heidbreder, Robert. *I wished for a unicorn*
Henderson, Kathy. *Bounce, bounce, bounce*
Hendrickson, Karen. *Baby and I can play*
  Fun with toddlers
Henkes, Kevin. *Oh!*
  A weekend with Wendell
Henley, Claire. *Playtime*
Hill, Eric. *Spot and friends play*
  Spot at play
  Spot goes to the beach
  Spot goes to the park
  Spot sleeps over
  Spot's walk in the woods
Hillert, Margaret. *Play ball*
  What is it?
Hines, Anna Grossnickle. *Bethany for real*
  It's just me, Emily
  Keep your old hat
  They really like me!
Hines-Stephens, Sarah. *Bean's games*
Hirschi, Ron. *A time for playing*
Hissey, Jane. *Jolly snow*
Hoffman, Phyllis. *We play*
Houghton, Eric. *The backwards watch*
  The crooked apple tree
Hru, Dakari. *The magic moonberry jump ropes*
  Tickle, tickle
Hubbell, Patricia. *Pots and pans*
Hudelhoff, Allen H. *Cats and kids*
Hughes, Sarah. *Let's play hopscotch*
  Let's play jacks
Hughes, Shirley. *Alfie's feet*

  Playing
Hulme, Joy N. *Bubble trouble*
Hunter, Sally. *Humphrey's corner*
Hutchins, H. J. (Hazel J.). *Norman's snowball*
Ichikawa, Satomi. *Isabela's ribbons*
  Let's play
  Suzanne and Nicholas in the garden
Impey, Rose. *Joe's café*
Inkpen, Mick. *Kipper's playtime*
  Kipper's snowy day
  Swing!
  Wibbly Pig can dance!
  Wibbly Pig can make a tent
Jackson, Ellen B. *Monsters in my mailbox*
Jakob, Donna. *My new sandbox*
  Tiny toes
Jaramillo, Raquel. *Ride, baby, ride!*
Jarrett, Clare. *The best picnic ever*
Jensen, Patricia. *The mess*
Jewell, Nancy. *Try and catch me*
Jocelyn, Marthe. *A day with Nellie*
Johnson, Mildred D. *Wait, skates!*
Kasza, Keiko. *Dorothy and Mikey*
Keats, Ezra Jack. *Skates*
  The snowy day
  The snowy day [board book]
Keeping, Charles. *Willie's fire-engine*
Kennedy, Kim. *Napoleon*
Kent, Jack. *Joey*
Keown, Elizabeth. *Emily's snowball*
King, Stephen Michael. *Emily loves to bounce*
Kline, Suzy. *Don't touch!*
Knutson, Kimberley. *Muddigush*
Kobayashi, Yuji. *Miss Josephine's secret walk*
Krahn, Fernando. *Robot-bot-bot*
Kraus, Robert. *Come out and play, little mouse*
  Springfellow
Krauss, Ruth. *I can fly*
Krementz, Jill. *Lily goes to the playground*
Krupp, Robin Rector. *Get set to wreck!*
Kvasnosky, Laura McGee. *One, two, three, play with me!*
Lacome, Julie. *I'm a jolly farmer*
  Ruthie's big old coat
Lakin, Pat (Patricia). *Play*
Landa, Norbert. *Rabbit and chicken play hide and seek*
LaRochelle, David. *The evening king*
Lasky, Kathryn. *Pond year*
Lebrun, Claude. *Little Brown Bear learns to share*
Lenski, Lois. *Let's play house*
Leonard, Marcia. *Dress-up*
  Hop, skip, run
Leslie, Amanda. *Who's that scratching at my door?*
Lester, Alison. *Alice and Aldo*
Lewis, Kim. *Floss*
Lewison, Wendy Cheyette. *Mud*
Lia, Simone. *Red's great chase*
Lindgren, Barbro. *Rosa*
  The wild baby goes to sea
Lipkind, William. *Sleepyhead*
London, Jonathan. *Puddles*
  Sun dance, water dance
Loomis, Christine. *Cowboy bunnies*
Lopshire, Robert. *New tricks I can do!*
Luenn, Nancy. *Otter play*
McAllister, Angela. *Harry's box*
McCarthy, Ruth. *Katie and the smallest bear*
McClintock, Barbara. *Dahlia*
McCord, David. *Every time I climb a tree*
McCully, Emily Arnold. *First snow*
MacDonald, Amy. *Let's go*
  Let's play
  Let's pretend
McGuirk, Leslie. *Tucker flips!*
McHenry, E. B. *Poodlena*
McKay, Hilary. *Pirates ahoy!*
McKee, David. *Elmer in the snow*
MacKinnon, Debbie. *Let's play: I can do it!*

What am I?
McLerran, Alice. *Roxaboxen*
McMillan, Bruce. *Play day*
McNulty, Faith. *When a boy wakes up in the morning*
McPhail, David M. *Pig Pig rides*
Maestro, Betsy. *Harriet at play*
Major, Beverly. *Playing sardines*
Mallat, Kathy. *Just ducky*
    Trouble on the tracks
Manushkin, Fran. *The best toy of all*
    Swinging and swinging
Marino, Dorothy. *Edward and the boxes*
Marshall, James. *Three up a tree*
Martin, David. *Lizzie and her friend*
    Lizzie and her puppy
Mayers, Patrick. *Just one more block*
Mayper, Monica. *Oh snow*
Medearis, Angela Shelf. *Here comes the snow*
    We play on a rainy day
Meeks, Esther K. *The hill that grew*
Merriam, Eve. *Boys and girls, girls and boys*
Meryl, Debra. *Baby's peek-a-boo album*
Miller, Margaret. *Let's play!*
    Playtime
    Water play
Miller, Ruth. *I went to the farm*
Miller, Virginia. *In a minute!*
Mills, Judith Christine. *The painted chest*
Miranda, Anne. *Baby walk*
Mitchell, Cynthia. *Halloweena Hecatee*
    Playtime
Moers, Hermann. *Rufus and Max*
Moffett, Martha A. *A flower pot is not a hat*
Morgan-Vanroyen, Mary. *Wild Rosie*
Morozumi, Atsuko. *Playing*
Morris, Ann. *Play*
Moss, Elaine. *Polar*
Moss, Marissa. *Want to play?*
Moss, Miriam. *The snow bear*
Mueller, Virginia. *A playhouse for Monster*
Munsch, Robert N. *Mud puddle*
Murkoff, Heidi Eisenberg. *What to expect at a play date*
Murphy, Jill. *All for one*
Narahashi, Keiko. *Is that Josie?*
Naylor, Phyllis Reynolds. *King of the playground*
Neitzel, Shirley. *I'm taking a trip on my train*
Newcome, Zita. *Pop-up toddlerobics*
    Toddlerobics
Newman, Lesléa. *A fire engine for Ruthie*
Nikola-Lisa, W. *Bein' with you this way*
Nobisso, Josephine. *Hot-cha-cha!*
Northway, Jennifer. *Get lost, Laura!*
Ochiltree, Dianne. *Pillow pup*
Offen, Hilda. *The sheep made a leap*
O'Malley, Kevin. *The box*
O'Mara, Carmel. *Rainy day*
    Sunny day
Oppenheim, Joanne. *James will never die*
Oram, Hiawyn. *In the attic*
Ormerod, Jan. *Midnight pillow fight*
    Miss Mouse's day
    The saucepan game
Owen, Annie. *Playtime duck*
Oxenbury, Helen. *All fall down*
    Clap hands
    Grandma and Grandpa
    Playing
    Say goodnight
    Tickle, tickle
    Tom and Pippo and the dog
Packard, Mary. *Bubble trouble*
    Where is Jake?
Paré, Roger. *Summer days*
Paschkis, Julie. *Play all day*
Paul, Ann Whitford. *Hello toes! Hello feet!*
Pearson, Susan. *That's enough for one day!*
Pfister, Marcus. *Chris and Croc*

Pirani, Felix. *Abigail at the beach*
Pocock, Rita. *Annabelle and the big slide*
Pollock, Penny. *Water is wet*
Powell, Alma. *My little wagon [board book]*
Poydar, Nancy. *Snip, snip . . . snow!*
Pragoff, Fiona. *It's fun to be one*
    It's great to be two
Priest, Robert H. *The old pirate of Central Park*
Pringle, Laurence P. *Octopus hug*
Quinlan, Patricia. *Emma's sea journey*
Raebeck, Lois. *Who am I?*
Raney, Ken. *Stick horse*
Ray, Mary Lyn. *Red rubber boot day*
Reid, Rob. *Wave goodbye*
Reiser, Lynn. *Best friends think alike*
Ring, Elizabeth. *Some stuff*
Roche, Harriet. *Pete's puddles*
Rockwell, Anne F. *At the beach*
    I play in my room
    My back yard
Roddie, Shen. *Toes are to tickle*
Rogers, Fred. *Making friends*
Rosner, Ruth. *Arabba gah zee, Marissa and Me!*
Rowan, Paula S. *Rick and Rocky*
Russ, Lavinia. *Alec's sand castle*
Russo, Marisabina. *The big brown box*
    The line up book
    Where is Ben?
Ryan, Pam Muñoz. *Mud is cake*
Sato, Satoru. *I wish I had a big, big tree*
Schaap, Martine. *Mop's mountain adventure*
Schaefer, Carole Lexa. *Snow pumpkin*
Schwartz, Roslyn. *The mole sisters and the fairy ring*
Sendak, Maurice. *Maurice Sendak's Really Rosie*
    The sign on Rosie's door
Shearer, Marilyn J. *I like to play*
Shirotani, Hideo. *Let's play*
Shott, Steve (Stephen). *Playtime*
Siddals, Mary McKenna. *I'll play with you*
Silverman, Erica. *Follow the leader*
Simmons, Jane. *Little Fern's first winter*
Simon, Charnan. *Mud!*
Simon, Francesca. *Calling all toddlers*
Snyder, Zilpha Keatley. *Come on, Patsy*
Spetter, Jung-Hee. *Lily and Trooper's fall*
    Lily and Trooper's spring
    Lily and Trooper's summer
Standon, Anna. *Three little cats*
Steig, William. *Pete's a pizza*
    Toby, what are you?
    Toby, where are you?
Steiner, Charlotte. *Kiki's play house*
    Look what Tracy found
Steptoe, John. *Baby says*
Stevenson, Robert Louis. *Where go the boats?*
Stevenson, Suçie. *Do I have to take Violet?*
Stine, Jovial Bob. *Pork and beans*
Stinson, Kathy. *The dressed up book*
Swanson-Natsues, Lyn. *Days of adventure*
Sykes, Julie. *Wait for me, Little Tiger*
Thompson, Lauren. *Little Quack's new friend*
Thompson, Richard. *Jenny's neighbours*
Thwaites, Lyndsay. *Super Adam and Rosie Wonder*
Tibo, Gilles. *Simon's disguise*
Todd, Kathleen. *Snow*
Tompert, Ann. *Just a little bit*
Townson, Hazel. *What on earth . . . ?*
Trimble, Marcia. *Malinda Martha and her stepping stones*
Turkle, Brinton. *Obadiah the Bold*
Turner, Ann Warren. *Let's be animals*
Turner, Charles. *The turtle and the moon*
Udry, Janice May. *Mary Ann's mud day*
Van Allsburg, Chris. *Zathura*
Van der Meer, Mara. *Can we play?*
Vasiliu, Mircea. *A day at the beach*
Veldkamp, Tjibbe. *22 orphans*
Vigna, Judith. *Boot weather*

Viorst, Judith. *Sunday morning*
Vulliamy, Clara. *Bang and shout*
　　Boo baby boo!
Waber, Bernard. *Ira sleeps over*
Waddell, Martin. *Snow bears*
　　Squeak-a-lot
　　Tom Rabbit
Wahl, Jan. *Push Kitty*
Wallace, John. *Little Bean's friend*
Walsh, Jill Paton. *Connie came to play*
Wasmuth, Eleanor. *An alligator day*
Watanabe, Shigeo. *Daddy, play with me!*
　　I can build a house!
　　I can ride it!
　　I'm the king of the castle!
Waters, Jennifer. *Summer fun*
Weatherford, Carole Boston. *Jazz baby*
Wells, Philip. *Daddy Island*
Wells, Rosemary. *A lion for Lewis*
Whybrow, Ian. *Harry and the bucketful of dinosaurs*
Williams, Sherley Anne. *Girls together*
Williams, Sophy. *Nana's garden*
Winn, Chris. *Playing*
Winter, Jeanette. *Cowboy Charlie*
Winthrop, Elizabeth. *Bunk beds*
　　That's mine
Wood, Audrey. *The Tickleoctopus*
Wood, Jakki. *Dads are such fun*
Yee, Patrick. *Let's play*
Yim, Natasha. *Otto's rainy day*
Yolen, Jane. *Before the storm*
Young, Miriam Burt. *Jellybeans for breakfast*
Zehler, Antonia. *Two fine ladies have a tiff*
　　Two fine ladies: tea for three
Ziefert, Harriet. *Baby Ben's go-go book*
　　Come out, Jessie!
　　Lewis the fire fighter
　　Strike four!
Zimelman, Nathan. *Walls are to be walked*
Ziner, Feenie. *Counting carnival*
Zinnemann-Hope, Pam. *Let's play ball, Ned*
Zolotow, Charlotte (Shapiro). *The park book*
　　The white marble

Activities – quilting

Hammersmith, Craig. *Patterns*

Activities – reading see Books, reading

Activities – running

Adoff, Arnold. *I am the running girl*
Cartier, Wesley. *Marco's run*
Emerson, Carl. *Marion Jones*
Greenfield, Eloise. *Kia Tanisha*
Livingston, Irene. *Finklehopper Frog*

Activities – sewing

Armstrong, Jennifer. *Pockets*
Beck, Andrea. *Elliot's emergency*
Brown, Craig McFarland. *Patchwork farmer*
Gibbons, Gail. *The quilting bee*
Green, Stephanie. *Betsy Ross and the silver thimble*
Hoffman, Christine. *Sewing by hand*
Hopkinson, Deborah. *Sweet Clara and the freedom quilt*
Johnston, Tony. *My best friend Bear*
Kuskin, Karla. *Patchwork island*
Leedahl, Shelley A. (Shelley Ann). *The bone talker*
Leonard, Marcia. *Violet and the pirates*
Paul, Ann Whitford. *The seasons sewn*
Ransom, Candice F. *The promise quilt*
Sabuda, Robert James. *The Blizzard's robe*
Shea, Pegi Deitz. *The whispering cloth*
Wallner, Alexandra. *Betsy Ross*
Warner, Sunny. *The magic sewing machine*

Woolf, Virginia. *Nurse Lugton's curtain*
Yolen, Jane. *Old Dame Counterpane*

Activities – shopping see Shopping

Activities – singing

Allamand, Pascale. *The pop rooster*
Aroner, Miriam. *The kingdom of singing birds*
Auch, Mary Jane. *Bantam of the opera*
Birdseye, Tom. *She'll be comin' round the mountain*
Brouillard, Anne. *The bathtub prima donna*
Buck, Nola. *Sid and Sam*
Cave, Kathryn. *Henry's song*
Cazet, Denys. *Dancing*
Cowley, Joy. *Singing down the rain*
Crimi, Carolyn. *Tessa's tip-tapping toes*
Czernecki, Stefan. *The singing snake*
D'Arc, Karen Scourby. *My grandmother is a singing Yaya*
Dodds, Dayle Ann. *Sing, Sophie!*
Downey, Lynn. *Sing, Henrietta! Sing!*
Fleming, Candace. *Westward ho, Carlotta!*
Fowler, Susi Gregg. *Fog*
Gibbons, Faye. *Emma Jo's song*
Goble, Paul. *I sing for the animals*
Gold, Julie. *From a distance*
Goss, Linda. *The frog who wanted to be a singer*
Grigg, Carol. *The singing snow bear*
Himmelman, John. *Simpson Snail sings*
Hirschi, Ron. *A time for singing*
Howe, James. *Horace and Morris join the chorus (but what about Dolores?)*
Jewell, Nancy. *Sailor song*
Kraus, Robert. *Screamy Mimi*
Kushner, Tony. *Brundibar*
Latimer, Jim. *James Bear and the goose gathering*
Lucado, Max. *Alabaster's song*
McCully, Emily Arnold. *The orphan singer*
Peterson, Jeanne Whitehouse. *My mama sings*
Saul, Carol P. *Peter's song*
Sikundar, Sylvia. *Forest singer*
Sproule, Gail. *Singing the dark*
Stenmark, Victoria. *The singing chick*
Sundgaard, Arnold. *The bear who loved Puccini*
Taylor, Ann. *Baby dance*
Wahl, Jan. *The singing geese*
Weaver, Tess. *Opera cat*
Wright, Catherine (Catherine E.). *Steamboat Annie and the thousand-pound catfish*

Activities – storytelling

Ahlberg, Allan. *The snail house*
Ahlberg, Janet. *It was a dark and stormy night*
Blackstone, Stella. *How big is a pig?*
Bouchard, Dave. *The song within my heart*
Brillhart, Julie. *Story hour – starring Megan!*
Brutschy, Jennifer. *Just one more story*
Cazet, Denys. *The octopus*
Davol, Marguerite W. *The snake's tales*
De Paola, Tomie (Thomas Anthony). *The Prince of the Dolomites*
Dwyer, Mindy. *Coyote in love*
Farley, Carol J. *Mr. Pak buys a story*
Foreman, Michael. *Grandfather's pencil and the room of stories*
Hanson, Regina. *A season for mangoes*
Harley, Bill. *Sarah's story*
Hest, Amy. *The babies are coming!*
Hughes, Vi. *Aziz, the story teller*
Lester, Helen. *Help! I'm stuck!*
Le Tord, Bijou. *God's little seeds*
Lewin, Ted. *The storytellers*
McDonald, Megan. *Tundra mouse*
Mahoney, Daniel J. *The Saturday escape*
Martin, Rafe. *The storytelling princess*
Mayr, Diane. *Littlebat's Halloween story*
Nash, Scott. *Tuff Fluff*
Nolan, Janet. *The St. Patrick's Day shillelagh*

O'Malley, Kevin. *Velcome*
Paton, Priscilla. *Howard and the sitter surprise*
Reiser, Lynn. *Little clam*
Roberts, Bethany. *Gramps and the fire dragon*
Rochelle, Belinda. *Jewels*
Ruurs, Margriet. *Ms. Bee's magical bookcase*
Schaefer, Carole Lexa. *Down in the woods at sleepytime*
  Down in the woods at sleepytime [board book]
Schwartz, Amy. *Some babies*
Scrimger, Richard. *Eugene's story*
Simms, Laura. *Rotten teeth*
Slate, Joseph. *Story time for Little Porcupine*
Spalding, Andrea. *Solomon's tree*
Van Leeuwen, Jean. *The tickle stories*
Velasquez, Eric. *Grandma's records*
Wallen, Ila. *The moon in my room*
Walsh, Ellen Stoll. *Jack's tale*
Watts, Jeri Hanel. *Keepers*
Yolen, Jane. *Miz Berlin walks*
Zeman, Ludmila. *Sindbad in the land of giants*
  Sindbad's secret

Activities – swapping *see* Activities – trading

Activities – swimming *see* Sports – swimming

Activities – swinging

Anderson, Robin. *Sinabouda Lily*
Baugh, Dolores M. *Swings*
Manushkin, Fran. *Swinging and swinging*
Marks, Marcia Bliss. *Swing me, swing tree*

Activities – talking

Ziefert, Harriet. *Talk, baby!*

Activities – trading

Andersen, H. C. (Hans Christian). *The old man is always right*
Burdick, Margaret. *Bobby Otter and the blue boat*
Bushey, Jerry. *The barge book*
Chorao, Kay. *The cherry pie baby*
  Pig and Crow
Davidson, Jill A. *And that's what happened to little Lucy*
De Regniers, Beatrice Schenk. *Was it a good trade?*
Dick Whittington and his cat. *Dick Whittington*, ill. by Edward Ardizzone
  Dick Whittington, ill. by Antony Maitland
  Dick Whittington and his cat, ill. by Marcia Brown
  Dick Whittington and his cat, ill. by Kurt Werth
Edwards, Pamela Duncan. *Livingstone Mouse*
Fowler, Susi Gregg. *I'll see you when the moon is full*
Gardella, Tricia. *Blackberry booties*
Gill, Bob. *A balloon for a blunderbuss*
Hale, Irina. *The lost toys*
Hirsh, Marilyn. *The pink suit*
Hughes, Shirley. *David and dog*
  Dogger
Inkpen, Mick. *Penguin small*
Jennings, Sharon. *Franklin makes a deal*
Johnson, Paul Brett. *Bearhide and crow*
Kimmel, Eric A. *Onions and garlic*
Langstaff, John M. *The swapping boy*
Levine, Abby. *Ollie knows everything*
Lichtveld, Noni. *I lost my arrow in a kankan tree*
McAllister, Angela. *Matepo*
McKay, Lawrence. *Caravan*
Martin, Jacqueline Briggs. *On Sand Island*
Murphy, Stuart J. *Dinosaur deals*
O'Neill, Alexis. *Estela's swap*
Shannon, George. *The Piney Woods peddler*
Stroyer, Poul. *It's a deal*
Suen, Anastasia. *Window music*
Torres, Leyla. *Saturday sancocho*
Watts, Mabel (Pizzey). *Something for you, something for me*
Weigelt, Udo. *Mole's journey*

Activities – traveling

Aardema, Verna. *Traveling to Tondo*
Aksakov, Sergei. *The scarlet flower*
Anderson, Scoular. *MacPelican's American adventure*
Arnold, Caroline. *How do we travel?*
Axelrod, Amy. *Pigs on the move*
Aylesworth, Jim. *My sister's rusty bike*
Ball, Duncan. *Jeremy's tail*
Ballard, Robin. *When we get home*
Bansemer, Roger. *Rachael's splendifilous adventure*
Barklem, Jill. *The high hills*
Barracca, Debra. *Maxi, the star*
Bate, Lucy. *How Georgina drove the car very carefully from Boston to New York*
Baum, Louis. *JuJu and the pirate*
Beatty, Hetty Burlingame. *Moorland pony*
Bemelmans, Ludwig. *Quito express*
Best, Cari. *When Catherine the Great and I were eight!*
Billout, Guy. *By camel or by car*
Blech, Dietlind. *Hello Irina*
Bolognese, Don. *A new day*
Borchers, Elisabeth. *Dear Sarah*
Brandenberg, Franz. *Everyone ready?*
Brann, Esther. *'Round the world*
Bridgman, Elizabeth. *How to travel with grownups*
  Nanny bear's cruise
Brisson, Pat. *Kate on the coast*
  Magic carpet
  Your best friend, Kate
Bröger, Achim. *Bruno takes a trip*
Bromhall, Winifred. *Johanna arrives*
Brown, Don. *Alice Ramsey's grand adventure*
Brown, Laurie Krasny. *Dinosaurs travel*
Brown, Marc Tolon. *Arthur meets the president*
Brown, Margaret Wise. *Three little animals*
Brown, Tricia. *The city by the bay*
Bruna, Dick. *The sailor*
Brunhoff, Jean de. *The travels of Babar*
Brutschy, Jennifer. *Just one more story*
Buchanan, Heather S. *George Mouse's covered wagon*
Buffett, Jimmy. *The jolly mon*
Bunting, Eve (Anne Evelyn). *Ducky*
  Peepers
  The traveling men of Ballycoo
Bursik, Rose. *Amelia's fantastic flight*
Butler, Dorothy. *A happy tale*
  My brown bear Barney
Cabban, Vanessa. *Bertie and Small and the brave sea journey*
Caines, Jeannette. *Just us women*
Calmenson, Stephanie. *Zip, whiz, zoom!*
Carle, Eric. *The rooster who set out to see the world*
  Rooster's off to see the world
Cech, John. *My grandmother's journey*
Chalmers, Mary. *Here comes the trolley*
Chancellor, Deborah. *Traveling on land*
Chwast, Seymour. *Tall city, wide country*
Cocca-Leffler, Maryann. *Bus route to Boston*
Coerr, Eleanor. *The Josefina story quilt*
Conrad, Donna. *See you soon, Moon*
Conway, Celeste. *Where is Papa now?*
Cooney, Barbara. *Miss Rumphius*
Coy, John. *Night driving*
  Vroomaloom zoom
Crampton, Gertrude. *Scuffy the tugboat*
Cummings, Pat. *My aunt came back*
Czernecki, Stefan. *Zorah's magic carpet*
Davis, Kenneth C. *Don't know much about the pioneers*
Davis, Maggie S. *The best way to Ripton*
Day, Edward C. *John Tabor's ride*
De Beer, Hans. *Little polar bear, take me home!*
Demarest, Chris L. *My little red car*
Demi. *The adventures of Marco Polo*
Denslow, Sharon Phillips. *Riding with Aunt Lucy*
Denton, Terry. *Home is the sailor*
Derby, Sally. *The mouse who owned the sun*
DeSaix, Deborah Durland. *In the back seat*

Dickson, Louise. *The vanishing cat*
Diller, Harriett. *Grandaddy's highway*
Dugan, Barbara. *Leaving home with a pickle jar*
Dupre, Kelly. *The raven's gift*
Eisenstein, Marilyn. *Periwinkle isn't Paris*
Ekker, Ernest A. *What is beyond the hill?*
Fairclough, Chris. *Take a trip to China*
    Take a trip to England
    Take a trip to Holland
    Take a trip to Israel
    Take a trip to Italy
    Take a trip to West Germany
Feldman, Barbara. *Going, going*
Field, Rachel Lyman. *A road might lead to anywhere*
Fitzpatrick, Marie-Louise. *You, me and the big blue sea*
Fox, Mem. *Possum magic*
Gackenbach, Dick. *With love from Gran*
Gammell, Stephen. *How about going for a ride*
Gans, Roma. *How do birds find their way?*
Gantschev, Ivan. *The train to Grandma's*
Garay, Luis. *The long road*
Gay, Michel. *Night ride*
Gerrard, Roy. *Jocasta Carr, movie star*
    Wagons west!
Gikow, Louise. *Follow that Fraggle!*
Gomi, Taro. *Bus stop*
Goodall, John S. *Paddy goes traveling*
Grahame, Kenneth. *The open road*
    The wind in the willows: the open road:
Gray, Genevieve. *How far, Felipe?*
Greenblat, Rodney Alan. *Thunder Bunny*
Greene, Carla. *A motor holiday*
Gretz, Susanna. *Teddy bears take the train*
Gutman, Anne. *Lisa's airplane trip*
Haley, Patrick. *The little person*
Hammerschlag, Carl A. *The go away doll*
Handford, Martin. *Find Waldo now*
    The great Waldo search
    Where's Waldo?
    Where's Waldo? In Hollywood
    Where's Waldo now?
    Where's Waldo? The fantastic journey
    Where's Waldo? The wonder book
Hannan, Peter. *Sillyville or bust*
Harrison, Troon. *Lavender Moon*
Harshman, Marc. *Roads*
Harvey, Brett. *Cassie's journey*
Hayashi, Akiko. *Aki and the fox*
Heckman, Philip. *The moon is following me*
Helldorfer, M. C. (Mary Claire). *Hog music*
Heuck, Sigrid. *Who stole the apples?*
Hobbie, Holly. *Toot and Puddle*
    Toot and Puddle, I'll be home for Christmas
    Toot and Puddle, top of the world
Hodges, Margaret. *The legend of Saint Christopher*
Holabird, Katharine. *Alexander and the magic boat*
Houk, Randy. *Chessie, the travelin' man*
Howard, Elizabeth Fitzgerald. *The train to Lulu's*
Howland, Naomi. *ABCDrive!*
Hughes, Shirley. *Abel's moon*
Hume, Stephen Eaton. *Red moon follows truck*
Hurd, Thacher. *Hobo dog*
Hutchins, H. J. (Hazel J.). *Beneath the bridge*
Isadora, Rachel. *No, Agatha!*
    Over the green hills
Isele, Elizabeth. *Pooks*
Jacobs, Leland B. (Leland Blair). *Is somewhere always far away?*, ill. by John E. Johnson
    Is somewhere always far away?, ill. by Jeff Kaufman
Janosch. *The trip to Panama*
Jonas, Ann. *Round trip*
Joosse, Barbara M. *Lewis and papa*
Joslin, Mary. *The shore beyond*
Kaczman, James. *A bird and his worm*
Kalman, Maira. *Sayonara, Mrs. Kackleman*
Karmi, Giora. *And Shira imagined*
Kasparavicius, Kestutis. *The bear family's world tour Christmas*

Kay, Verla. *Covered wagons, bumpy trails*
Kellogg, Steven (Stephen). *Johnny Appleseed*
Kelly, Mij. *William and the night train*
Kesselman, Wendy Ann. *There's a train going by my window*
Kessler, Leonard P. *Mrs. Pine takes a trip*
Kidd, Richard. *Almost famous Daisy!*
Kilroy, Sally. *On the road*
Kimmel, Eric A. *Pumpkinhead*
Knapp, Jennifer. *The go go dogs*
Koralek, Jenny. *Night ride to Nanna's*
Krementz, Jill. *Jamie goes on an airplane*
    A visit to Washington, D.C.
Lasky, Kathryn. *The Gates of the Wind*
Lawlor, Laurie. *Old Crump*
Leedy, Loreen. *Blast off to Earth!*
Le Guin, Ursula K. *Tom Mouse*
Leighton, Maxinne Rhea. *An Ellis Island Christmas*
Lenski, Lois. *Davy goes places*
Leonard, Marcia. *Bye-bye, Baby-boo*
Lester, Alison. *The journey home*
Leventhal, Debra. *What is your language?*
Levitin, Sonia. *Nine for California*
Lewin, Hugh. *Jafta – the journey*
Lewis, Thomas P. *Clipper ship*
Liddell, Janice. *Imani and the Flying Africans*
Lin, Grace. *Olvina flies*
Lindbergh, Reeve. *Johnny Appleseed*
Lobel, Anita. *Away from home*
Locker, Thomas. *Sailing with the wind*
Lodge, Bernard. *Cloud Cuckoo Land (and other odd spots)*
London, Jonathan. *Moshi moshi*
Lööf, Jan. *Uncle Louie's fantastic sea voyage*
Loomis, Christine. *We're going on a trip*
Lyndon, Kerry Raines. *A birthday for Blue*
Lyon, George Ella. *A regular rolling Noah*
    A traveling cat
McAllister, Angela. *Jessie's journey*
McCarthy, Meghan. *The adventures of Patty and the big red bus*
McCarty, Peter. *Little bunny on the move*
McCormack, John E. *Rabbit travels*
McCourt, Lisa. *I miss you, Stinky Face*
McDonald, Megan. *The night Iguana left home*
McKay, Lawrence. *Caravan*
    Journey home
McKissack, Patricia C. *Big bug book of places to go*
McToots, Rudi. *The kid's book of games for cars, trains and planes*
Maestro, Betsy. *Ferryboat*
Mahy, Margaret. *A busy day for a good grandmother*
    The three-legged cat
Manson, Christopher. *Two travelers*
Margolin, H. Ellen. *Goin' to Boston*
Marshak, S. (Samuil). *The pup grew up!*
Martin, C. L. G. *The blueberry train*
Martin, Charles E. *Sam saves the day*
Mauner, Claudia. *Zoe Sophia's scrapbook*
May, Charles Paul. *High-noon rocket*
Mayhew, James. *Miranda the explorer*
Meddaugh, Susan. *Maude and Claude go abroad*
Miller, Edna. *Mousekin takes a trip*
Miller, Sara Swan. *Cat in the bag*
Milton, Nancy. *The giraffe that walked to Paris*
Moss, Marissa. *In America*
Munro, Roxie. *The inside-outside book of Texas*
    The inside-outside book of Washington, D.C.
    Mazescapes
Nayer, Judy. *The happy little engine*
Neitzel, Shirley. *The bag I'm taking to Grandma's*
Nixon, Joan Lowery. *If you say so, Claude*
Nordqvist, Sven. *Willie in the big world*
Norling, Beth. *The stone baby*
Nye, Naomi Shihab. *Come with me*
Oechsli, Helen. *Fly away!*
O'Kelley, Mattie Lou. *Moving to town*
Ormerod, Jan. *Miss Mouse takes off*
Owen, Annie. *Bumper to bumper*
Pattison, Darcy. *The journey of Oliver K. Woodman*
Patz, Nancy. *Gina Farina and the Prince of Mintz*

Peters, Lisa Westberg. *This way home*
Petty, Kate. *On a plane*
Piepmeier, Charlotte. *Lucy's journey to the wild west*
Piers, Helen. *Is there room on the bus?*
Pinkney, Gloria Jean. *The Sunday outing*
Potter, Giselle. *The year I didn't go to school*
Poulin, Stéphane. *Travels for two*
Priceman, Marjorie. *How to make an apple pie and see the world*
Quackenbush, Robert M. *Henry's world tour*
Quattlebaum, Mary. *Underground train*
Rabe, Berniece. *A smooth move*
Raney, Ken. *Stick horse*
Rey, Margret (Margret Elisabeth Waldstein). *Whiteblack the penguin sees the world*
Robbins, Ken. *City/country*
Roberts, Bethany. *Camel caravan*
Rogers, Fred. *Going on an airplane*
Rohmann, Eric. *Pumpkinhead*
Rose, Gerald. *PB takes a holiday*
Rosenberg, Liz. *Grandmother and the runaway shadow*
Rosenblum, Richard. *Journey to the golden land*
Rovetch, Lissa. *Cora and the elephants*
Rumford, James. *The Island-below-the-star*
Rush, Ken. *Friday's journey*
Rylant, Cynthia. *The relatives came*
    Tulip sees America
Salter, Mary Jo. *The moon comes home*
Say, Allen. *Grandfather's journey*
Schneider, Howie. *No dogs allowed*
Schories, Pat. *Mouse around*
Schulz, Charles M. *Bon voyage, Charlie Brown (and don't come back!!)*
Seuss, Dr. *I had trouble getting to Solla Sollew*
Sharratt, Nick. *Mrs. Pirate*
Sheldon, Dyan. *Love, your bear, Pete*
Silvano, Wendi J. *Just one more*
Sis, Peter. *Tibet through the red box*
Slater, Teddy. *The fabulous fish from Lake Wiggawalla*
Slavin, Bill. *The cat came back*
Smith, Barry. *The first voyage of Christopher Columbus*
Smith, Maggie (Margaret C.). *Counting our way to Maine*
Smyth, Gwenda. *A pet for Mrs. Arbuckle*
Sorensen, Henri. *New Hope*
Stanley, Diane. *Joining the Boston Tea Party*
    Thanksgiving on Plymouth Plantation
Steel, Danielle. *Freddie's trip*
Steger, Hans-Ulrich. *Traveling to Tripiti*
Stem, J. David. *Kay Thompson's Eloise in Hollywood*
Steptoe, Javaka. *The Jones family express*
Stevenson, Harvey. *Grandpa's house*
Stevenson, James. *All aboard!*
    Are we almost there?
Storm, Theodor. *Little Hobbin*
Suben, Eric. *Pigeon takes a trip*
Swain, Gwenyth. *Johnny Appleseed*
Tapio, Pat Decker. *The lady who saw the good side of everything*
Tews, Susan. *Lizard sees the world*
Thompson, Kay. *Kay Thompson's Eloise in Moscow*
Tibo, Gilles. *The grand journey of Mr. Man*
Tomlinson, Theresa. *Little stowaway*
Trevelyan, Kathy. *Don't be surprised!*
Trimble, Marcia. *Hello sun*
Trottier, Maxine. *Little dog Moon*
Türk, Hanne. *Max packs*
Turner, Ann Warren. *Nettie's trip south*
Tzannes, Robin. *Sanji and the baker*
Uhlberg, Myron. *Lemuel, the fool*
Ungerer, Tomi. *Adelaide*
Valfre, Edward. *Backseat buckaroo*
Van Leeuwen, Jean. *Across the wide dark sea*
Vevers, Gwynne. *Animals that travel*
Waddell, Martin. *Small Bear lost*
Wallace, Ivy. *Pookie*
Walters, Virginia. *Are we there yet, Daddy?*
Watson, Mary. *The butterfly seeds*
Waugh, Peter. *The great cannon beach mouse caper*
Weston, Martha. *The dinosaurs meet Dr. Clock*
Whitcher, Susan. *Something for everyone*

Wiesmüller, Dieter. *The adventures of Marco and Polo*
Wild, Margaret. *Going home*
Willard, Nancy. *The voyage of the Ludgate Hill*
Willis, Jeanne. *Earth mobiles as explained by Professor Xargle*
Wong, Janet S. *The trip back home*
Wood, Audrey. *Silly Sally*
Woodtor, Dee. *Big meeting*
Wright, Courtni Crump. *Wagon train*
Yee, Paul. *Let's eat*
Ziefert, Harriet. *A car trip for Mole and Mouse*
    Keeping daddy awake on the way home from the beach

Activities – vacationing

Adams, Adrienne. *The Easter egg artists*
Ahlberg, Allan. *Skeleton crew*
Bemelmans, Ludwig. *Hansi*
Berenstain, Stan. *The Berenstain bears and too much vacation*
Best, Cari. *Montezuma's revenge*
Blades, Ann. *Back to the cabin*
Bond, Michael. *Paddington at the seaside*
Bornstein, Ruth Lercher. *I'll draw a meadow*
Brandenberg, Franz. *A fun weekend*
Briggs, Raymond. *Father Christmas goes on holiday*
Bright, Robert. *Georgie and the noisy ghost*
Brisson, Pat. *Kate on the coast*
    Your best friend, Kate
Brode, Robyn. *August*
Brown, Marc Tolon. *Arthur's family vacation*
Brown, Ruth. *Our puppy's vacation*
Brunhoff, Laurent de. *Babar's cousin, that rascal Arthur*
    Babar's mystery
Buchanan, Heather S. *George Mouse's covered wagon*
Carlstrom, Nancy White. *The moon came too*
Carrick, Carol. *The washout*
Chall, Marsha Wilson. *Up north at the cabin*
Cole, Joanna. *The Clown-Arounds go on vacation*
Cottle, Joan. *Miles away from home*
Dalmais, Anne-Marie. *Henry the hedgehog*
De Paola, Tomie (Thomas Anthony). *Strega Nona takes a vacation*
Dodd, Lynley. *Schnitzel von Krumm forget-me-not*
Du Bois, William Pène. *Otto and the magic potatoes*
Duvoisin, Roger Antoine. *Petunia takes a trip*
Everton, Macduff. *Finding the magic circus = El circo magico modelo*
Fatio, Louise. *The happy lion's vacation*
Florian, Douglas. *A summer day*
Gili, Phillida. *Fanny and Charles*
Goodall, John S. *Paddy Pork's holiday*
Goyder, Alice. *Holiday in Catland*
Graham, Bob. *Greetings from Sandy Beach*
Gutman, Anne. *Gaspard on vacation*
Haddon, Mark. *On vacation*
Hale, Kathleen. *Orlando and the water cats*
Hänel, Wolfram. *Mia the beach cat*
Hayward, Linda. *Grover's summer vacation*
Hill, Eric. *Spot goes on holiday*
Hundal, Nancy. *Camping*
Jocelyn, Marthe. *Mayfly*
Joyce, William. *Dinosaur Bob*
Kellogg, Steven (Stephen). *Ralph's secret weapon*
Kessler, Leonard P. *Are we lost, daddy?*
Khalsa, Dayal Kaur. *My family vacation*
Laden, Nina. *Clowns on vacation*
Lawson, Julie. *Midnight in the mountains*
Lazard, Naomi. *What Amanda saw*
Lester, Alison. *Magic beach*
Lindman, Maj. *Snipp, Snapp, Snurr and the red shoes*
Lippman, Peter. *The Know-It-Alls take a winter vacation*
Loomis, Christine. *We're going on a trip*
McPhail, David M. *Emma's pet*
    Emma's vacation
Maestro, Betsy. *The pandas take a vacation*
Marshall, James. *George and Martha 'round and 'round*
Martin, Charles E. *Sam saves the day*
Maynard, Bill. *Santa's time off*
Meddaugh, Susan. *Martha calling*
Monfried, Lucia. *The Daddies Boat*

Murdocca, Sal (Salvatore). *Lucy takes a holiday*
Murphy, Stuart J. *The best vacation ever*
Nethery, Mary. *Hannah and Jack*
Newton, Patricia Montgomery. *Vacation surprise*
Njeng, Pierre Yves. *Vacation in the village*
Noll, Sally. *Lucky morning*
Pohrt, Tom. *Having a wonderful time*
Rand, Gloria. *The cabin key*
Reiss, Mike. *Santa claustrophobia*
Rockwell, Anne F. *On our vacation*
Rodda, Emily. *Yay!*
Roffey, Maureen. *I spy on vacation*
Samuels, Barbara. *Aloha, Dolores*
Schneider, Howie. *No dogs allowed*
Shea, Pegi Deitz. *Bungalow fungalow*
Steel, Danielle. *Freddie's trip*
Stephens, Helen. *Ahoyty-toyty*
Stevenson, James. *The castaway*
    The Sea View Hotel
Tafuri, Nancy. *The brass ring*
Thomson, Ruth. *Peabody all at sea*
Tobias, Tobi. *At the beach*
Valfre, Edward. *Vacationers from outer space*
Van Leeuwen, Jean. *Touch the sky summer*
Wallace, Karen. *City pig*
Weiss, Nicki. *Weekend at Muskrat Lake*
Williams, Jay. *The city witch and the country witch*
Ziefert, Harriet. *Pushkin minds the bundle*

Activities – walking

Ackerman, Karen. *Walking with Clara Belle*
Alexander, Martha G. *Where does the sky end, Grandpa?*
Arnosky, Jim. *Crinkleroot's guide to walking in wild places*
    Outdoors on foot
Aylesworth, Jim. *Siren in the night*
Bax, Martin. *Edmond went far away*
Berry, Christine. *Mama went walking*
Bodsworth, Nan. *A nice walk in the jungle*
Brown, Margaret Wise. *Four fur feet*
Buchanan, Joan. *It's a good thing*
Buckley, Helen Elizabeth. *Grandfather and I*
Bullock, Kathleen. *It chanced to rain*
Davidson, Jill A. *And that's what happened to little Lucy*
De Regniers, Beatrice Schenk. *Going for a walk*
Devine, Monica. *Carry me, Mama*
Dowling, Paul. *Where are you going, Jimmy?*
Duncan, Lois. *I walk at night*
Edwards, Pamela Duncan. *The worrywarts*
Falwell, Cathryn. *Nicky loves daddy*
    Nicky's walk
Florian, Douglas. *Nature walk*
George, Lindsay Barrett. *In the woods*
Greenfield, Karen R. *Sister Yessa's story*
Haughton, Emma. *Rainy day*
Hertz, Grete Janus. *Olie's bedtime walk*
Hill, Eric. *The park*
    Spot's first walk
Hindley, Judy. *Funny walks*
    Into the jungle
Hoban, Tana. *I walk and read*
Hubbell, Patricia. *Sidewalk trip*
Inches, Alison. *Corduroy's hike*
Johnson, D. B. (Donald B.). *Henry hikes to Fitchburg*
    Henry works
Jonas, Ann. *The trek*
    Watch William walk
Kingman, Lee. *Peter's long walk*
Klein, Leonore. *Henri's walk to Paris*
Komaiko, Leah. *Great Aunt Ida and her Great Dane, Doc*
Krupinski, Loretta. *Into the woods*
Lenski, Lois. *I went for a walk*
Lewis, Kim. *One summer day*
Lobe, Mira. *The snowman who went for a walk*
London, Jonathan. *Wiggle, waggle*
Luenn, Nancy. *Squish!*
McNaughton, Colin. *Walk rabbit walk*

Manuel, Lynn. *The night the moon blew kisses*
Oxenbury, Helen. *Our dog*
Pearson, Susan. *Silver morning*
Pfister, Marcus. *Penguin Pete and Little Tim*
Radlauer, Ruth Shaw. *Molly*
    Molly goes hiking
Ray, Deborah Kogan. *The cloud*
Rockwell, Anne F. *Willy can count*
Sarton, May. *A walk through the woods*
Sharmat, Marjorie Weinman. *Burton and Dudley*
Shirotani, Hideo. *Let's take a walk = Vamos a caminar*
Showers, Paul. *The listening walk*
Singer, Marilyn. *Didi and Daddy on the Promenade*
Smalls-Hector, Irene. *Jonathan and his mommy*
Stevenson, James. *Rolling Rose*
Stynes, Barbara White. *Walking with mama*
Sullivan, Paula. *Todd's box*
Thomas, Ianthe. *Walk home tired, Billy Jenkins*
Thompson, Richard. *I have to see this*
Tobias, Tobi. *The dawdlewalk*
Türk, Hanne. *Rainy day Max*
Turner, Ethel. *Walking to school*
Tworkov, Jack. *The camel who took a walk*
Viorst, Judith. *Try it again, Sam*
Watanabe, Shigeo. *I can take a walk!*
Williams, David. *Walking to the creek*
Williams, Sue. *I went walking*
    I went walking [board book]
Wood, Joyce. *Grandmother Lucy goes on a picnic*
Yolen, Jane. *Miz Berlin walks*
Zolotow, Charlotte (Shapiro). *One step, two . . .*
    Say it!
    The summer night

Activities – weaving

Bang, Molly. *Dawn*
Blood, Charles L. *The goat in the rug*
Bodkin, Odds. *The crane wife*
Brill, Marlene Targ. *Margaret Knight, girl inventor*
Castaneda, Omar S. *Abuela's weave*
Chanin, Michael. *Chief's blanket*
Coombs, Patricia. *Tilabel*
Czernecki, Stefan. *Zorah's magic carpet*
Duncan, Lois. *The magic of Spider Woman*
Ernst, Lisa Campbell. *Nattie Parsons' good-luck lamb*
Gill, Janet. *Basket Weaver and Catches Many Mice*
Hamilton, Virginia. *The girl who spun gold*
Heyer, Marilee. *The weaving of a dream*
Keo, Ena. *The crane wife*
Khan, Rukhsana. *The roses in my carpets*
Kherdian, David. *The golden bracelet*
Lattimore, Deborah Nourse. *The dragon's robe*
Le Tord, Bijou. *Picking and weaving*
London, Jonathan. *The village basket weaver*
Medearis, Angela Shelf. *Seven spools of thread*
Murphy, Shirley Rousseau. *Wind child*
Musgrove, Margaret. *The spider weaver*
Oughton, Jerrie. *The magic weaver of rugs*
Radley, Gail. *The spinner's gift*
San Souci, Robert D. *The enchanted tapestry*
    A weave of words
Trân-Khánh-Tuyê. *The little weaver of Thái-Yên Village*
Tseng, Grace. *White tiger, blue serpent*
Yagawa, Sumiko. *The crane wife*

Activities – whistling

Alexander, Anne (Anna Barbara Cooke). *I want to whistle*
Ambrus, Victor G. *The three poor tailors*
Bason, Lillian. *Pick a raincoat, pick a whistle*
Blackwood, Gladys Rourke. *Whistle for Cindy*
Egielski, Richard. *Three magic balls*
Honeycutt, Natalie. *Whistle home*
Keats, Ezra Jack. *Whistle for Willie*
Watts, Bernadette. *The Christmas bird*

Activities – wishing

Jackson, Shirley. *9 magic wishes*

Activities – wood carving

Dorros, Arthur. *Julio's magic*

Activities – working

Ackerman, Karen. *By the dawn's early light*
Ackerman, Karen. *When mama retires*
Æsop. *The ant and the grasshopper*, ill. by Amy Lowry Poole
   The ant and the grasshopper, ill. by Sara Rojo
Ahlberg, Allan. *Mrs. Wobble the waitress*
Alda, Arlene. *Sonya's mommy works*
Allen, Jeffrey. *Mary Alice, operator number 9*
Altman, Linda Jacobs. *Amelia's road*
Ardizzone, Edward. *Paul, the hero of the fire*
Arkin, Alan. *Tony's hard work day*
Asch, Frank. *Good lemonade*
Aylesworth, Jim. *Shenandoah Noah*
Bach, Othello. *Lilly, Willy and the mail-order witch*
Ballard, Robin. *My day, your day*
Banks, Kate (Katherine A.). *Mama's coming home*
   The night worker
Barber, Barbara E. *Saturday at the new you*
Bartoletti, Susan Campbell. *Silver at night*
Barton, Byron. *Machines at work*
Basso, Bill. *The top of the pizzas*
Batt, Tanya Robyn. *The faerie's gift*
Beim, Jerrold. *Jay's big job*
Bethell, Jean. *Three cheers for Mother Jones!*
Blance, Ellen. *Monster gets a job*
Bloom, Becky. *Crackers*
Bond, Michael. *Paddington cleans up*
Brooks, Ben. *Lemonade parade*
Buehner, Caralyn. *A job for Wittilda*
Bunting, Eve (Anne Evelyn). *A day's work*
Burke, Timothy. *Tugboats in action*
Burton, Virginia Lee. *Mike Mulligan and his steam shovel*
Butterworth, Nick. *When there's work to do*
Caple, Kathy. *The purse*
Carle, Eric. *Walter the baker*
Civardi, Anne. *Things people do*
Clark, Ann Nolan. *The little Indian basket maker*
   The little Indian pottery maker
Claverie, Jean. *Working*
Cole, Babette. *The trouble with Dad*
Dahl, Roald. *The giraffe and the pelly and me*
DeGross, Monalisa. *Granddaddy's street songs*
Delaney, Ned. *Terrible things could happen*
Delton, Judy. *Hired help for Rabbit*
   My mother lost her job today
De Paola, Tomie (Thomas Anthony). *Boss for a day*
Duke, Kate. *Clean-up day*
Dumbleton, Mike. *Dial-a-croc*
Dupasquier, Philippe. *A busy day at the garage*
Eisenberg, Phyllis Rose. *You're my Nikki*
Euvremer, Teryl. *Sun's up*
Fleischman, Paul. *The animal hedge*
Florian, Douglas. *People working*
   A potter
Gág, Wanda. *Gone is gone*
Gallo, Giovanni. *The lazy beaver*
Garland, Michael. *Circus girl*
Gibbons, Gail. *Deadline!*
   Zoo
Goffstein, M. B. (Marilyn Brooke). *An actor*
   A writer
Goodall, John S. *Paddy Pork*
Grossman, Patricia. *The night ones*
Haley, Gail E. *Two bad boys*
Hall, Donald. *The ox-cart man*
Harper, Anita. *How we work*
Harvey, Brett. *My prairie year*
Hautzig, Deborah. *It's not fair!*

Hazen, Barbara Shook. *Mommy's office*
Heide, Florence Parry. *The day of Ahmed's secret*
Heine, Helme. *Merry-go-round*
Henderson, Kathy. *In the middle of the night*
Hertz, Grete Janus. *Olie's bedtime walk*
Hoban, Julia. *Buzby to the rescue*
Hoban, Russell. *Charlie the tramp*
Horvath, Betty F. *Jasper makes music*
Johnson, Angela. *I dream of trains*
Johnson, D. B. (Donald B.). *Henry works*
Joseph, Lynn. *Jasmine's parlour day*
Killingback, Julia. *Monday is washing day*
Komaiko, Leah. *A million moms and mine*
   On Sally Perry's farm
Krahn, Fernando. *Robot-bot-bot*
Kroll, Steven. *Howard and Gracie's luncheonette*
Lasker, Joe. *Mothers can do anything*
Leiner, Katherine. *Both my parents work*
Lewis, Kim. *Floss*
Lindsey, Treska. *When Batistine made bread*
Lockwood, Primrose. *Cissy Lavender*
London, Jonathan. *Hip cat*
Look, Lenore. *Love as strong as ginger*
Loomis, Christine. *Rush hour*
Love, Ann. *Fishing*
Lum, Kate. *Princesses are not quitters!*
Lyon, David. *The biggest truck*
Lyon, George Ella. *Mama is a miner*
McCunn, Ruthanne L. *Pie-Biter*
McGowen, Tom (Thomas). *The only glupmaker in the U.S. Navy*
McPhail, David M. *Annie and Co.*
   Pig Pig gets a job
Maestro, Betsy. *Harriet at work*
Marshall, James. *Fox on the job*
Maynard, Joyce. *New house*
Medearis, Angela Shelf. *Picking peas for a penny*
Merriam, Eve. *Mommies at work*
Mills, Judith Christine. *The painted chest*
Mitchell, Joyce Slayton. *My mommy makes money*
Modesitt, Jeanne. *Lunch with Milly*
Morck, Irene. *Old bird*
Morris, Ann. *Work*
Murphy, Stuart J. *Sluggers' car wash*
Nethery, Mary. *Hannah and Jack*
100 words about working
Paterson, Diane. *Soap and suds*
Paulsen, Gary. *Worksong*
Pedersen, Marika. *Mommy works, Daddy works*
Peterson, Cris. *Horsepower*
Petrides, Heidrun. *Hans and Peter*
Pilkey, Dav. *The paperboy*
Pryor, Bonnie. *The dream jar*
Puner, Helen Walker. *Daddys, what they do all day*
Purdy, Carol. *Least of all*
Quinlan, Patricia. *My dad takes care of me*
Relf, Patricia. *Tonka trucks night and day*
Rodriguez, Anita. *Jamal and the angel*
Rose, Deborah Lee. *Meredith's mother takes the train*
Ross, Jessica. *Ms. Klondike*
Rotner, Shelley. *Everybody works*
Rylant, Cynthia. *Mr. Griggs' work*
Sandberg, Inger. *Come on out, Daddy!*
San Souci, Robert D. *The hired hand*
Sathre, Vivian. *On Grandpa's farm*
Shaw, Mary. *Brady Brady and the great rink*
Shipton, Jonathan. *Busy! Busy! Busy!*
Simon, Norma. *I'm busy, too*
Singer, Marilyn. *Chester, the out-of-work dog*
Skurzynski, Gloria. *Martin by himself*
Spinelli, Eileen. *Night shift daddy*
Stolz, Mary (Mary Slattery). *Zekmet, the stone carver*
Thayer, Tanya. *Earning money*
Thomas, Mark. *Work in Colonial America*
Türk, Hanne. *Raking leaves with Max*
Turner, Nancy Byrd. *When young Melissa sweeps*
Valens, Amy. *Jesse's day care*
Waber, Bernard. *Lyle at the office*

Wahl, Jan. *Three pandas*
Wheeler, Lisa. *Jam & jelly by Holly & Nellie*
Williams, Sherley Anne. *Working cotton*
Wittmann, Patricia. *Go ask Giorgio!*
Ye, Ting-xing. *Three monks, no water*
Yee, Wong Herbert. *Hamburger Heaven*
Yeoman, John. *The wild washerwomen*

Activities – writing

Aliki. *Communication*
Allington, Richard L. *Writing*
Arnosky, Jim. *Mouse writing*
Battle-Lavert, Gwendolyn. *Papa's mark*
Brown, Marc Tolon. *Arthur writes a story*
Caseley, Judith. *Dear Annie*
Cech, John. *The southernmost cat*
Cobb, Vicki. *Writing it down*
Cronin, Doreen. *Click, clack, moo*
   Diary of a worm
Dewey, Jennifer Owings. *Stories on stone*
Fain, Moira. *Snow day*
Felt, Sue. *Rosa-too-little*
Foreman, Michael. *Grandfather's pencil and the room of stories*
Greenblat, Rodney Alan. *Thunder Bunny*
Greene, Carol. *Margaret Wise Brown, author of Goodnight moon*
Harrison, Joanna. *Dear bear*
Heide, Florence Parry. *The day of Ahmed's secret*
Hoban, Lillian. *Arthur's pen pal*
Hughes, Shirley. *Abel's moon*
Inches, Alison. *Corduroy writes a letter*
Johnson, D. B. (Donald B.). *Henry works*
Joslin, Sesyle. *Dear dragon*
Kraus, Robert. *The adventures of Wise Old Owl*
Krauss, Ruth. *I write it*
Lattimore, Deborah Nourse. *The sailor who captured the sea*
Leedy, Loreen. *The Furry News*
   Messages in the mailbox
Linch, Tanya. *My duck*
Lionni, Leo. *The alphabet tree*
Lockwood, Primrose. *Cissy Lavender*
McElroy, Lisa Tucker. *Meet my grandmother. She's a children's book
   author*
Miles, Miska. *The pointed brush . . .*
Nixon, Joan Lowery. *If you were a writer*
Oakley, Graham. *The diary of a church mouse*
Rockwell, Anne F. *Father's Day*
Rylant, Cynthia. *Best wishes*
Schotter, Roni. *Nothing ever happens on 90th Street*
Seuss, Dr. *I can write!*
Spurr, Elizabeth. *The long, long letter*
Stewart, Sarah. *The journey*
Teague, Mark. *Dear Mrs. LaRue*
   Detective LaRue
Van Nutt, Julia. *Skyrockets and snickerdoodles*

Actors *see* Careers – actors

ADD *see* Handicaps – ADD

Adoption

Banish, Roslyn. *A forever family*
Bawden, Nina. *Princess Alice*
Bloom, Suzanne. *A family for Jamie*
Brodzinsky, Anne Braff. *The mulberry bird*
Bunin, Catherine. *Is that your sister?*
Bunting, Eve (Anne Evelyn). *Jin Woo*
Caines, Jeannette. *Abby*
Chapman, Noralee. *The story of Barbara*
Cole, Joanna. *How I was adopted: Samantha's story*
Curtis, Jamie Lee. *Tell me again about the night I was born*
Czech, Jan M. *An American face*
D'Antonio, Nancy. *Our baby from China*
De Paola, Tomie (Thomas Anthony). *A new Barker in the house*
Fisher, Iris L. *Katie-Bo*

Fowler, Susi Gregg. *When Joel comes home*
Freudberg, Judy. *Susan and Gordon adopt a baby*
Gabel, Susan L. *Where the sun kisses the sea*
Ginsburg, Mirra. *We adopted you, Benjamin Koo*
Girard, Linda Walvoord. *Adoption is for always*
Greenberg, Judith E. *Adopted*
Hess, Edith. *Peter and Susie find a family*
Hodge, Deborah. *Emma's story*
Höjer, Dan. *Heart of mine*
Hutchins, Pat. *Our baby is best*
Kasza, Keiko. *A mother for Choco*
Katz, Karen. *Over the moon*
Keller, Holly. *Horace*
Koehler, Phoebe. *The day we met you*
Koski, Mary. *Impatient Pamela wants a bigger family*
Kroll, Virginia L. *Beginnings*
Lapsley, Susan. *I am adopted*
Lewis, Rose A. *I love you like crazy cakes*
Livingston, Carole. *"Why was I adopted?"*
London, Jonathan. *A koala for Katie*
Lottridge, Celia Barker. *Berta, a remarkable dog*
McCully, Emily Arnold. *My real family*
McCutcheon, John. *Happy adoption day!*
MacKay, Jed. *The big secret*
Milgram, Mary. *Brothers are all the same*
Miller, Kathryn Ann. *Did my first mother love me?*
Molnar-Fenton, Stephan. *An Mei's strange and wondrous journey*
Mora, Pat. *Pablo's tree*
Nixon, Joan Lowery. *That's the spirit, Claude*
   You bet your britches, Claude
Okimoto, Jean Davies. *The White Swan express*
Peacock, Carol Antoinette. *Mommy far, Mommy near*
Pellegrini, Nina. *Families are different*
Rogers, Fred. *Adoption*
Rondell, Florence. *The family that grew*
Rosen, Michael J. (1954–). *Bonesy and Isabel*
Rosenberg, Liz. *We wanted you*
Rosenberg, Maxine B. *Being adopted*
Rovetch, Lissa. *Cora and the elephants*
Say, Allen. *Allison*
Schnitter, Jane. *William is my brother*
Schreck, Karen Halvorsen. *Lucy's family tree*
Sobol, Harriet Langsam. *We don't look like our mom and dad*
Stanek, Muriel. *My little foster sister*
Stein, Sara Bonnett. *The adopted one*
Stein, Stephanie. *Lucy's feet*
Turner, Ann Warren. *Through moon and stars and night skies*
Udry, Janice May. *Theodore's parents*
Voake, Charlotte. *Mrs. Goose's baby*
Wasson, Valentina Pavlovna. *The chosen baby*
Zisk, Mary. *The best single mom in the world*

Aerialists *see* Careers – aerialists

Afghanistan *see* Foreign lands – Afghanistan

Africa *see* Foreign lands – Africa

African Americans *see* Ethnic groups in the U.S. – African
Americans

Aged *see* Old age

AIDS *see* Illness – AIDS

Airplane pilots *see* Careers – airplane pilots

Airplanes, airports

Bagwell, Richard. *This is an airport*
Baker, Donna. *I want to be a pilot*
Barton, Byron. *Airplanes*
   Airport
Baumann, Kurt. *The paper airplane*
Berger, Melvin. *How do airplanes fly?*

Bingham, Caroline. *DK big book of airplanes*
Brenner, Anita. *I want to fly*
Brown, Don. *Ruth Law thrills a nation*
Brown, Margaret Wise. *Streamlined pig*
Browne, Eileen. *No problem*
Browne, Gerard. *The aircraft lift-the-flap book*
Buchanan, Heather S. *George Mouse learns to fly*
Bunting, Eve (Anne Evelyn). *Fly away home*
Bursik, Rose. *Amelia's fantastic flight*
Butler, Dorothy. *A happy tale*
Cave, Ron. *Airplanes*
Cotler, Joanna. *Sky above earth below*
Crews, Donald. *Flying*
Demarest, Chris L. *Lindbergh*
    Plane
Duchess of York. *Budgie at Bendick's Point*
    Budgie the little helicopter
Edwards, Pamela Duncan. *The Wright brothers*
Emberley, Ed (Edward Randolph). *Cars, boats, and planes*
Flanagan, Alice K. *Flying an agricultural plane with Mr. Miller*
Floca, Brian. *Five trucks*
Florian, Douglas. *Airplane ride*
Fort, Patrick. *Redbird*
Gay, Michel. *Bibi takes flight*
    Little plane
Gibbons, Gail. *Flying*
Gordon, David. *The ugly truckling*
Gramatky, Hardie. *Loopy*
Grist, Julie. *Flying, just plane fun*
Gutman, Anne. *Lisa's airplane trip*
I want to be a pilot
Ingoglia, Gina. *The big book of real airplanes*
Joseph, Lynn. *Fly, Bessie, fly*
Kallen, Stuart A. *The airport*
Krementz, Jill. *Jamie goes on an airplane*
Lenski, Lois. *The little airplane*
Lin, Grace. *Olvina flies*
Lindbergh, Reeve. *Nobody owns the sky*
Loomis, Christine. *We're going on a trip*
McPhail, David M. *First flight*
Magee, Doug. *Let's fly from A to Z*
Mantegazza, Giovanna. *Look inside an airplane*
Morgan, Allen. *Matthew and the midnight pilot*
Munsch, Robert N. *Angela's airplane*
Nolan, Dennis. *Wizard McBean and his flying machine*
O'Donnell, Peter. *Dizzy*
Oechsli, Helen. *Fly away!*
Olschewski, Alfred. *We fly*
Ormerod, Jan. *Miss Mouse takes off*
Pallotta, Jerry. *The airplane alphabet book*
    The jet alphabet book
Petty, Kate. *On a plane*
Planes
Potter, Tony. *See how it works: planes*
Provensen, Alice. *The glorious flight*
Rand, Gloria. *Salty takes off*
Raven, Margot Theis. *Mercedes and the chocolate pilot*
Richards, Jon. *Jetliners*
Rockwell, Anne F. *Planes*
Rogers, Fred. *Going on an airplane*
Rogers, Hal. *Airplanes*
Ross, Pat. *Your first airplane trip*
Royston, Angela. *Planes*
Ryan, Pam Muñoz. *Amelia and Eleanor go for a ride*
Schaefer, Lola M. *Airport*
    The Wright brothers
Schulz, Charles M. *Snoopy's facts and fun book about planes*
Schulz, Walter A. *Will and Orv*
Seibold, J. Otto. *Mr. Lunch takes a plane ride*
Seymour, Peter S. *Pilots*
Siebert, Diane. *Plane song*
Simon, Seymour. *Amazing aircraft*
Spier, Peter. *Bored – nothing to do!*
Struges, Philemon. *I love planes*
Suen, Anastasia. *Air show*
Testa, Fulvio. *The paper airplane*
Thompson, Brenda. *Famous planes*

Ungerer, Tomi. *The Mellops go flying*
Wheeling, Lynn. *When you fly*
Wilson-Max, Ken. *Little red plane*
Yolen, Jane. *My brothers' flying machine*
Young, Miriam Burt. *If I flew a plane*
Zaffo, George J. *The book of real airplanes*
    The giant nursery book of things that go

Airports *see* Airplanes, airports

Alaska

Bania, Michael. *Kumak's house*
Blake, Robert J. *Akiak*
Boyle, Doe. *Gray wolf pup*
Carlstrom, Nancy White. *Midnight dance of the snowshoe hare*
    Raven and river
Chamberlin-Calamar, Pat. *Alaska's twelve days of summer*
Dixon, Ann. *The blueberry shoe*
Dwyer, Mindy. *Aurora, a tale of the Northern Lights*
Fowler, Susi Gregg. *Circle of thanks*
Griese, Arnold A. *Anna's Athabaskan summer*
Guenther, James. *Turnagain, Ptarmigan, where did you go?*
Laverde, Arlene. *Alaska's three pigs*
Magdanz, James S. *Go home, river*
Martin, Rafe. *The eagle's gift*
Miller, Debbie S. *A caribou journey*
    River of life
Nicolai, Margaret. *Kitaq goes ice fishing*
Rand, Gloria. *Baby in a basket*
    Prince William
    Salty sails north
    Salty takes off
Schoenherr, John. *Bear*
Seibert, Patricia. *Mush!*
Senshu, Noriko. *Sonny's dream*
Stihler, Chérie B. *The giant cabbage turnip*
Williams, Maria. *How Raven stole the sun*

Albatrosses *see* Birds – albatrosses

Alcoholism *see* Illness – alcoholism

Aleuts *see* Indians of North America – Aleuts

Algonquin Indians *see* Indians of North America – Algonquin

Aliens

Breathed, Berke (Berkeley). *Edwurd Fudwupper fibbed big*
Butterworth, Nick. *QPootle 5*
Camp, Lindsay. *Why?*
Cazet, Denys. *Minnie and Moo and the potato from Planet X*
    Minnie and Moo save the earth
Corey, Shana. *First graders from Mars: Horus's horrible day*
    First graders from Mars: Nergal and the Great Space Race
    First graders from Mars: Tera, star student
    First graders from Mars: The problem with Pelly
Karas, G. Brian. *Bebe's bad dream*
Kirk, Daniel. *Hush, little alien*
Layton, Neal. *Smile if you're human*
McNaughton, Colin. *Here come the aliens!*
McPhail, David M. *Tinker and Tom and the Star Baby*
Mooser, Stephen. *Funnyman meets the monster from outer space*
Pallotta, Jerry. *Twizzlers percentages book*
Passen, Lisa. *Attack of the 50-foot teacher*
Pinkwater, Daniel Manus. *Guys from space*
Porto, Tony. *Blue aliens*
    Get red
Pryor, Bonnie. *Mr. Munday and the space creatures*
Rix, Jamie. *The last chocolate cookie*
Rosen, Michael (1946–). *Mission Ziffoid*
Scieszka, Jon. *Baloney, Henry P.*
Shields, Carol Diggory. *Martian rock*
Valfre, Edward. *Vacationers from outer space*

Weston, Martha. *Space guys!*
Whatley, Bruce. *Captain Pajamas*
Willis, Jeanne. *The long blue blazer*
Wood, Audrey. *The Christmas adventure of Space Elf Sam*
   New pet
Yorinks, Arthur. *Company's going*
Ziegler, Ursina. *Squaps the moonling*

All Souls' Day *see* Holidays – Day of the Dead

Allergies *see* Illness – allergies

Alligators *see* Reptiles – alligators, crocodiles

Alphabet books *see* ABC books

Alzheimer's *see* Illness – Alzheimer's

Amazon *see* Foreign lands – Amazon

Ambition *see* Character traits – ambition

American Indians *see* Indians of Central America; Indians of North America; Indians of Central America

Amish *see* Ethnic groups in the U.S. – Amish

Amphibians *see also* Frogs & toads; Reptiles

Florian, Douglas. *Lizards, frogs, and polliwogs*

Amusement parks *see* Parks – amusement

Anasazi Indians *see* Indians of North America – Anasazi

Anatomy

Allen, Robert. *Ten little babies eat*
Andrews, Sylvia. *Dancing in my bones*
Anholt, Catherine. *One, two, three, count with me*
Arnold, Tedd. *More parts*
   Parts
Artell, Mike. *Legs*
Barner, Bob. *Dem bones*
Bauer, Marion Dane. *If you had a nose like an elephant's trunk*
   Toes, ears, and nose!
The best part of me
Bilgrami, Shaheen. *Amazing dinosaur discovery*
   Incredible animal discovery
Blegvad, Lenore. *This is me*
Boynton, Sandra. *Horns to toes and in between*
Brown, Laurie Krasny. *What's the big secret?*
Campbell, Rod. *It's mine*
Caputo, Robert. *More than just pets*
Carle, Eric. *From head to toe*
   My very first book of heads and tails
Castle, Sue. *Face talk, hand talk, body talk*
Cho, Shinta. *The gas we pass*
Clark, Sue. *Bodies*
Cole, Brock. *The giant's toe*
Cole, Joanna. *The magic school bus inside the human body*
   Your insides
Collard, Sneed B. *Beaks!*
Cummings, Phil. *Goodness gracious!*
Elkin, Benjamin. *Gillespie and the guards*
Facklam, Margery. *But not like mine*
Faulkner, Keith. *This is me*
Hazen, Barbara Shook. *The me I see*
Hickling, Meg. *Boys, girls and body science*
Hindley, Judy. *Eyes, nose, fingers and toes*
Hirschmann, Linda. *In a lick of a flick of a tongue*
Hooks, William H. *Read-a-rebus*
Jackson, Ellen B. *The book of slime*

Jenkins, Steve. *Actual size*
   What do you do with a tail like this?
Kates, Bobbi Jane. *We're different, we're the same*
Kelley, True. *Look, baby! Listen, baby! Do, baby!*
Kilroy, Sally. *Babies' bodies*
Krauss, Ruth. *Eyes, nose, fingers, toes*
MacKinnon, Debbie. *All about me*
Maloney, Peter (1955–). *His mother's nose*
Manning, Mick. *My body, your body*
Markle, Sandra. *Outside and inside alligators*
   Outside and inside bats
   Outside and inside dinosaurs
   Outside and inside you
Martin, Bill (William Ivan). *Here are my hands*
Martin, David. *We've all got bellybuttons*
Moon, Nicola. *At the beginning of a pig*
Munsch, Robert N. *Good families don't*
My body
Pluckrose, Henry Arthur. *Fur and feathers*
   Paws and claws
Pratt, Pierre. *I see . . . my mom/I see . . . my dad*
   I see . . . my sister/I see . . . my cat
Rauzon, Mark J. *Feet, flippers, hooves, and hands*
Rice, Melanie. *My first body book*
Rothman, Joel. *This can lick a lollipop = esto goza chupando un caramelo*
Rotner, Shelley. *The body book*
Royston, Angela. *My body*
Serfozo, Mary. *A head is for hats*
Seuling, Barbara. *From head to toe*
Sharmat, Marjorie Weinman. *Helga high-up*
Shott, Steve (Stephen). *Look at me*
Showers, Paul. *A drop of blood*
   Hear your heart
   How you talk
   You can't make a move without your muscles
Singer, Marilyn. *The one and only me*
Smallman, Clare. *Outside in*
Stinson, Kathy. *The bare naked book*
Waters, Jennifer. *All kinds of people*
Waxman, Stephanie. *What is a girl? What is a boy?*
Wilkes, Angela. *Me and my body*
Wright, Rachel. *My amazing body*

Anatomy – belly buttons *see* Anatomy – navels

Anatomy – brain

O'Connor, Teddy. *A new brain for Igor*

Anatomy – ears

Bolliger, Max. *The rabbit with the sky blue ears*
Davison, Martine. *Robby visits the doctor*
Genechten, Guido Van. *Flop-Ear*
Greenway, Shirley. *Here's ears*
Hartley, Karen. *Hearing in living things*
Harvey, Amanda. *Dog-eared*
Irbinskas, Heather. *How Jackrabbit got his very long ears*
Miles, Elizabeth J. *Ears*
Nelson, Robin. *Hearing*
Perkins, Al. *The ear book*
Rauzon, Mark J. *Eyes and ears*
Rowe, Jeannette. *Whose ears?*
Showers, Paul. *Ears are for hearing*

Anatomy – eyes

Bailey, Jill. *Eyes*
Cobb, Vicki. *Open your eyes*
Glaser, Jason. *Pinkeye*
Gordon, Sharon. *Pinkeye*
   Seeing
Hartley, Karen. *Seeing in living things*
Naylor, Phyllis Reynolds. *Jennifer Jean, the Cross-Eyed Queen*
Nelson, Robin. *Seeing*
Patterson, Elizabeth Burman. *Whose eyes are these?*

Priest, Robert H. *The pirate's eye*
Rauzon, Mark J. *Eyes and ears*
Rice, Judith. *Those ooey gooey winky-blinky but – invisible pinkeye germs = Esos pringosos viscosos pestañeantes parpadeantes pero – invisibles gérmenes que causan conjuntivitis*
Seuss, Dr. *The eye book*
Showers, Paul. *Look at your eyes*
Thomson, Ruth. *Eyes*
Wiesmüller, Dieter. *In the blink of an eye*
Worthy, Judith. *Eyes*

Anatomy – faces

Anno, Mitsumasa. *Anno's faces*
Brenner, Barbara A. *Faces, faces, faces*
Butterworth, Nick. *Making faces*
Clark, Sue. *Faces*
Emberley, Ed (Edward Randolph). *Ed Emberley's crazy mixed-up face game*
Intrater, Roberta Grobel. *Two eyes, a nose, and a mouth*
Isaacs, Gwynne L. *Baby face*
Miller, Margaret. *Baby faces*
Pieńkowski, Jan. *Faces*
Rotner, Shelley. *Faces*
Smith, Patty. *Faces*
Swain, Gwenyth. *Smiling*
Yep, Laurence. *The city of dragons*
Yudell, Lynn Deena. *Make a face*

Anatomy – feet

Aliki. *My feet*
Bailey, Jill. *Feet*
Blanchard, Arlene. *Sounds my feet make*
Chase, Catherine. *Feet*
Goor, Ron. *All kinds of feet*
Hamm, Diane Johnston. *How many feet in the bed?*
Holzenthaler, Jean. *My feet do*
Koski, Mary. *Impatient Pamela asks, "Why are my feet so huge?"*
Machotka, Hana. *What neat feet!*
Morgenstern, Constance. *Good night, feet*
Neidigh, Sherry. *Creatures at my feet*
Paul, Ann Whitford. *Hello toes! Hello feet!*
Rauzon, Mark J. *Feet, flippers, hooves, and hands*
Rowe, Jeannette. *Whose feet?*
Schertle, Alice. *My two feet*
Schubert, Ingrid. *Little big feet*
Seuss, Dr. *The foot book*
Waller, Barrett. *New feet for old*
Walton, Rick. *My two hands, my two feet*
Weiss, Leatie. *Funny feet!*
Whittaker, Nicola. *Feet*
Young, Amy. *Belinda, the ballerina*

Anatomy – fingers

Bowie, C. W. *Busy fingers*
Emberley, Ed (Edward Randolph). *Ed Emberley's fingerprint drawing book*

Anatomy – fins

Miles, Elizabeth J. *Wings, fins, and flippers*

Anatomy – hands

Aliki. *My hands*
Baer, Edith. *The wonder of hands*
Blume, Karin. *My new friends*
Calmenson, Stephanie. *Kinderkittens, show-and-tell*
Ehlert, Lois. *Hands*
Holzenthaler, Jean. *My hands can*
Kroll, Virginia L. *Hands!*
Lasky, Kathryn. *Mommy's hands*
Perkins, Al. *Hand, hand, fingers, thumb*
Price, Hope Lynne. *These hands*
Rauzon, Mark J. *Feet, flippers, hooves, and hands*

Ryder, Joanne. *My father's hands*
Walton, Rick. *My two hands, my two feet*

Anatomy – heads

Bishop, Claire Huchet. *The man who lost his head*
Kimmel, Eric A. *Pumpkinhead*
Miller, Margaret. *What's on my head?*
Swanson, Diane. *Headgear that hides and plays*

Anatomy – legs

Greenway, Shirley. *Legs and all*
Mead, Katherine. *How spiders got eight legs*

Anatomy – mouths

Bailey, Jill. *Mouths*
Miles, Elizabeth J. *Mouths and teeth*

Anatomy – navels

Batten, Mary. *Who has a belly button?*
Jeram, Anita. *Bill's belly button*
Maloney, Peter (1955–). *Belly button boy*
Martin, David. *We've all got bellybuttons*
Nanao, Jun. *Contemplating your bellybutton*
Pringle, Laurence P. *Everybody has a bellybutton*
Schoen, Mark. *Bellybuttons are navels*
Willis, Jeanne. *The boy who lost his bellybutton*

Anatomy – noses

Bailey, Jill. *Noses*
Bentley, Nancy. *I've got your nose!*
Boujon, Claude. *The fairy with the long nose*
Brown, Marc Tolon. *Arthur's nose*
Caple, Kathy. *The biggest nose*
Cullen, Lynn. *Little Scraggly Hair*
Dubov, Christine Salac. *Aleksandra, where is your nose?*
Eaton, Jason. *The day my runny nose ran away*
Faulkner, Keith. *The long-nosed pig*
Fazzi, Maura. *The circus of mystery*
Freymann, Saxton. *Dr. Pompo's nose*
Gordon, Sharon. *Smelling*
Hartley, Karen. *Smelling in living things*
Hawcock, David. *Whose nose?*
Hutton, Warwick. *The nose tree*
Johnston, Tony. *The badger and the magic fan*
Krüss, James. *Johnny Longnose*
Levine, Deb. *Parker picks*
Machotka, Hana. *Breathtaking noses*
May, Robert Lewis. *Rudolph the red-nosed reindeer*, ill. by Diana Magnuson
  Rudolph the red-nosed reindeer, ill. by David Wenzel
Miles, Elizabeth J. *Noses*
Moncure, Jane Belk. *What your nose knows!*
Nelson, Robin. *Smelling*
Ormerod, Jan. *This little nose*
Perkins, Al. *The nose book*
Richards, Jean. *How the elephant got his trunk*
Rowe, Jeannette. *Whose nose?*
Samuels, Jenny. *A nose like a hose*
Schwarz, Viviane. *The adventures of a nose*
Swanson, Diane. *Noses that plow and poke*
Warrick, Karen Clemens. *Who needs that nose?*
Whittaker, Nicola. *Noses*

Anatomy – skeletons

Ahlberg, Allan. *The black cat*
Ahlberg, Allan. *Dinosaur dreams*
  The ghost train
  Mystery tour
  The pet shop
  Skeleton crew
Ahlberg, Janet. *Funnybones*

Balestrino, Philip. *The skeleton inside you*
Bunting, Eve (Anne Evelyn). *The bones of Fred Mcfee*
Esbensen, Barbara Juster. *Sponges are skeletons*
Faulkner, Keith. *Basil Rattlebones*
Glaser, Byron. *Bonz, inside-out*
Gross, Ruth Belov. *A book about your skeleton*
Johansen, K. V. (Krista V.). *Pippin and the bones*
Johnston, Tony. *The ghost of Nicholas Greebe*
    Soup bone
Loredo, Elizabeth. *Boogie Bones*
McDonald, Megan. *The bone keeper*
McMullan, Kate (Hall). *Skeletons! Skeletons! All about bones*
San Souci, Robert D. *Cinderella Skeleton*
Schertle, Alice. *The skeleton in the closet*
Spohn, David. *Nate's treasure*
Stevenson, James. *The most amazing dinosaur*
Villoldo, Alberto. *Skeleton woman*

Anatomy – skin

Grossman, Bill. *The bear whose bones were Jezebel Jones*
Hawcock, David. *Whose coat?*
Kipling, Rudyard. *How the rhinoceros got his skin*
Machotka, Hana. *Outstanding outsides*
Pinkney, Sandra L. *A rainbow all around me*
Pluckrose, Henry Arthur. *Skin, shell and scale*
Sandeman, Anna. *Skin, teeth, and hair*
Showers, Paul. *Your skin and mine*
Swanson, Diane. *Skin that slimes and scares*

Anatomy – tails

Ashman, Linda. *The tale of Wagmore Gently*
Bechtold, Lisze. *Edna's tale*
Garrett, Ann. *Tales of tails*
Greenway, Shirley. *A tale of tails*
Gregg, Andy. *Great Rabbit and the long-tailed Wildcat*
Kawata, Ken. *Animal tails*
Machotka, Hana. *Terrific tails*
Milne, A. A. (Alan Alexander). *Eeyore loses a tail*
Warrick, Karen Clemens. *If I had a tail*
Whittaker, Nicola. *Tails*

Anatomy – teeth *see* Teeth

Anatomy – thumbs *see* thumb sucking

Anatomy – toes

Bowie, C. W. *Busy toes*
Crum, Shutta. *Who took my hairy toe?*
Dubov, Christine Salac. *Aleksandra, where are your toes?*
Elias, Joyce. *Whose toes are those?*
Hawkins, Colin. *This little pig*
Jakob, Donna. *Tiny toes*
Paul, Ann Whitford. *Hello toes! Hello feet!*
Wallace, Ian. *The true story of Trapper Jack's left big toe*

Anatomy – tongues

Bonsignore, Joan. *Stick out your tongue*
Hartley, Karen. *Tasting in living things*
Nelson, Robin. *Tasting*

Anatomy – wings

Miles, Elizabeth J. *Wings, fins, and flippers*
Myers, Christopher A. *Wings*

Angels

Absolutely angels
Aichinger, Helga. *The shepherd*
Andersen, H. C. (Hans Christian). *The red shoes*
Arnold, Mary. *The fussy angel*
Benét, William Rose. *Timothy's angels*
Brown, Abbie Farwell. *The Christmas angel*

Brown, Ruth. *The shy little angel*
Clements, Andrew. *Bright Christmas*
Cole, Brock. *Larky Mavis*
Collington, Peter. *The angel and the soldier boy*
Cowen-Fletcher, Jane. *Baby angels*
Downes, Belinda. *Every little angel's handbook*
Garland, Michael. *Angel cat*
Greenfield, Eloise. *Angels*
Greeson, Janet. *The stingy baker*
Gregory, Valiska. *Looking for angels*
Hoffman, Mary. *An angel just like me*
I imagine angels
Ives, Penny. *The golden angel*
    The snow angel
Judd, Naomi. *Naomi Judd's guardian angels*
Kavanaugh, James J. *The crooked angel*
Knight, Hilary. *Angels and berries and candy canes*
Krahn, Fernando. *A funny friend from heaven*
Lathrop, Dorothy Pulis. *An angel in the woods*
Lester, Julius. *What a truly cool world*
    Why heaven is far away
Lucado, Max. *Alabaster's song*
McAllister, Angela. *The snow angel*
Magnier, Thierry. *Isabelle and the angel*
Martin, Judith. *The tree angel*
Marzollo, Jean. *Snow angel*
Myers, Walter Dean. *Brown angels*
    Glorious angels
Norris, Leslie. *Albert and the angels*
Paterson, Katherine. *The angel and the donkey*
Pieńkowski, Jan. *Bel and Bub and the baby bird*
    Bel and Bub and the bad snowball
    Bel and Bub and the big brown box
    Bel and Bub and the black hole
Pittman, Helena Clare. *The angel tree*
Prose, Francine. *The angel's mistake*
    Dybbuk
Ragz, M. M. *Lost little angel*
Rodriguez, Anita. *Jamal and the angel*
Rylant, Cynthia. *Dog Heaven*
Safran, Sheri. *The musical cherub*
    The painted cherub
Sawyer, Ruth. *The Christmas Anna angel*
Shannon, Mark. *The acrobat and the angel*
Sloat, Teri. *Hark! The aardvark angels sing*
Spinelli, Eileen. *What do angels wear?*
Stone, Phoebe. *What night do the angels wander?*
Tangvald, Christine Harder. *Hey, Mr. Angel!*
Tazewell, Charles. *The littlest angel*, ill. by Deborah Lanino
    The littlest angel, ill. by Paul Micich
    The littlest angel, ill. by Rebecca Thornburgh
Thomas, Kathy. *The angel's quest*
Tolan, Stephanie S. *Bartholomew's blessing*
Turner, Ann Warren. *Angel hide and seek*
Vainio, Pirkko. *The Christmas angel*
Wallace, Ian. *Morgan the magnificent*
Wangerin, Walter. *Probity Jones and the Fear Not Angel*
Warfel, Elizabeth Stuart. *The blue pearls*
Weller, Frances Ward. *The angel of Mill Street*
Willard, Nancy. *The high rise glorious skittle skat roarious sky pie angel*
    food cake
Williams, Sam. *Angel's Christmas cookies*
    Snowy magic
Zimelman, Nathan. *The star of Melvin*

Anger *see* Emotions – anger

Animals *see also* Birds; Frogs & toads; Reptiles

Aardema, Verna. *Princess Gorilla and a new kind of water*
    Rabbit makes a monkey of lion
    Traveling to Tondo
    The vingananee and the tree toad
    What's so funny, Ketu?
    Who's in Rabbit's house?
    Why mosquitoes buzz in people's ears
Abisch, Roz. *The clever turtle*

Abolafia, Yossi. *Fox tale*
Ackerman, Karen. *This old house*
Ada, Alma Flor. *Dear Peter Rabbit*
   The unicorn of the west
Adler, David A. *The carsick zebra and other riddles*
Adlerman, Daniel. *Africa calling*
Æsop. *Animal fables from Æsop*
   The donkey in the lion's skin
   Seven fables from Æsop
   The lion and the mouse and other Æsop fables, ill. by Bert Kitchen
Agee, Jon. *Dmitri the astronaut*
Agell, Charlotte. *To the island*
Ahlberg, Allan. *Big bad pig*
Aitken, Amy. *Kate and Mona in the jungle*
   Wanda's circus
Ajmera, Maya. *Animal friends*
Akass, Susan. *Number nine duckling*
Albert, Richard E. *Alejandro's gift*
Alborough, Jez. *Beaky*
   Can you jump like a kangaroo?
   Can you peck like a hen?
   Captain Duck
   Clothesline
   Duck in the truck
   Fix-It Duck
   Hide and seek
   Hug
   There's something at the mail slot
   Watch out! Big Bro's coming!
Alda, Arlene. *Pig, horse, or cow, don't wake me now*
   Sheep, sheep, sheep, help me fall asleep
Aldridge, Josephine Haskell. *The best of friends*
   A possible tree
Alexander, Cecil Frances. *All things bright and beautiful*, ill. by Anna Vojtech
Alexander, Martha G. *Pigs say oink*
Aliki. *My visit to the aquarium*
   My visit to the zoo
   Wild and woolly mammoths
Allamand, Pascale. *The animals who changed their colors*
   The camel who left the zoo
Allard, Harry. *Bumps in the night*
Allen, Gertrude E. *Everyday animals*
Allen, Jeffrey. *Mary Alice, operator number 9*
   Nosey Mrs. Rat
Allen, Jonathan. *A bad case of animal nonsense*
   Two by two by two
Allen, Linda. *Mrs. Simkin's bed*
Allen, Marjorie N. *One, two, three – ah-choo!*
Allen, Martha Dickson. *Real life monsters*
Allen, Pamela. *Mr. Archimedes' bath*
   Who sank the boat?
Allen, Robert. *The zoo book*
Alphabestiary
Amery, H. *At the zoo*
   The farm picture book
   The zoo picture book
Amusing moments in the wild
Anastas, Margaret. *A hug for you*
   Mommy's best kisses
Anaya, Rudolfo A. *Roadrunner's dance*
Ancona, George. *Handtalk zoo*
Andersen, H. C. (Hans Christian). *The emperor's new clothes*, ill. by Robert Byrd
Anderson, Laurie Halse. *Ndito runs*
Anderson, Lena. *Bunny story*
   Tick-tock
Anderson, Stephen Axel. *I know the moon*
Andreae, Giles. *Cock-a-doodle-doo!*
   The pop-up Rumble in the jungle
   Rumble in the jungle
Anholt, Catherine. *Chaos at Cold Custard Farm*
   Chimp and Zee's noisy book
   A kiss like this
   Twins, two by two
Animal nursery rhymes
Animal 123's

Anno, Mitsumasa. *Anno's animals*
   Anno's masks
Aoki, Hisako. *Santa's favorite story*
Apperley, Dawn. *Good night, sleep tight, little bunnies*
   In the jungle
   Santa Claus will come tonight
Apple, Margot. *Blanket*
Applebaum, Stan. *Going my way?*
Archambault, John. *Counting sheep*
Argent, Kerry. *Animal capers*
Armour, Richard Willard. *Animals on the ceiling*
   Have you ever wished you were something else?
Arnold, Caroline. *Australian animals*
   Five nests
   Mealtime for zoo animals
   Mother and baby zoo animals
   Noisytime for zoo animals
   Playtime for zoo animals
   Sleepytime for zoo animals
   Splashtime for zoo animals
   A walk by the seashore
   A walk in the desert
   A walk in the woods
   A walk on the Great Barrier Reef
   A walk up the mountain
Arnold, Katya. *The adventures of Snowwoman*
   Let's find it!
   Meow!
Arnold, Tedd. *Sounds*
Arnosky, Jim. *Crinkleroot's guide to knowing animal habitats*
   Crinkleroot's 25 mammals every child should know
   Every autumn comes the bear
   I see animals hiding
   Wild and swampy
Arquette, Kerry. *What did you do today?*
Artell, Mike. *Legs*
   Petite Rouge
Aruego, José. *Look what I can do*
   We hide, you seek
   Weird friends
Arvetis, Chris. *Why does it fly?*
   Why is it dark?
Asbjørnsen, P. C. (Peter Christen). *The man who kept house*
Asch, Frank. *Barnyard lullaby*
   Bread and honey
   I can blink
   I can roar
   Monkey face
   Moonbear's dream
Ashabranner, Brent. *I'm in the zoo, too*
Ashforth, Camilla. *Calamity*
   Willow by the sea
Ashman, Linda. *Castles, caves, and honeycombs*
Asimov, Isaac. *Animals of the Bible*
Aston, Dianna Hutts. *Loony Little*
Atwell, Debby. *Humphrey Thud*
Atwood, Margaret. *Anna's pet*
Auch, Mary Jane. *The nutquacker*
   Poultrygeist
   Souperchicken
Aulaire, Ingri Mortenson d'. *Animals everywhere*
   Children of the northlights
Auld, Mary. *Noah's ark*
Austin, Margot. *A friend for Growl Bear*
Austin, Virginia. *Say please*
Axworthy, Anni. *Guess what I am*
   Guess what I'll be
Aylesworth, Jim. *The good-night kiss*
   One crow
Azore, Barbara. *Wanda and the wild hair*
B. B. Blacksheep and Company
Babson, Jane F. *Babson's bestiary*
Backovsky, Jan. *Trouble in Paradise*
Bahr, Robert. *Blizzard at the zoo*
Bailey, Jill. *Eyes*
   Feet
   Mouths

Noses
Baillie, Marilyn. *Nose to toes*
  Side by side
Baker, Alan. *Gray Rabbit's one, two, three*
  Two tiny mice
  Where's mouse?
Baker, Betty. *Sonny-Boy Sim*
Baker, Eugene H. *Bicycles*
  Fire
  Home
  Outdoors
  School
  Water
Baker, Jeffrey J. W. *Patterns of nature*
Baker, Laura Nelson. *The friendly beasts*
Ballart, Elisabet. *Let's count*
Balmer, Helen. *Jungle adventure*
Balog, James. *James Balog's animals A to Z*
Bancroft, Henrietta. *Animals in winter*
Bandes, Hanna. *Sleepy river*
Bang, Betsy. *The old woman and the red pumpkin*
  The old woman and the rice thief
Bang, Molly. *Delphine*
Banks, Merry. *Animals of the night*
Bannon, Laura. *The best house in the world*
  Little people of the night
  Red mittens
  The scary thing
Bantock, Nick. *Runners, sliders, bouncers, climbers*
Barasch, Marc Ian. *No plain pets!*
Barbosa, Rogério Andrade. *African animal tales*
Barbot, Daniel. *A bicycle for Rosaura*
Bare, Colleen Stanley. *Who comes to the water hole?*
Barnes, Laura T. *Ernest's special Christmas*
Baron, Alan. *Little Pig's bouncy ball*
  Red Fox dances
Barrett, Judi. *Animals should definitely not act like people*
  Animals should definitely not wear clothing
  Snake is totally tail
Barry, Robert E. *Animals around the world*
Barton, Byron. *Zoo animals*
Baruch, Dorothy. *Kappa's tug-of-war with the big brown horse*
Base, Graeme. *Animalia*
  Jungle drums
  My grandma lived in Gooligulch
  The water hole
Baskin, Leonard. *Hosie's zoo*
Bason, Lillian. *Castles and mirrors and cities of sand*
Bassett, Lisa. *A clock for Beany*
Bateman, Robert. *Safari*
Bateman, Teresa. *Farm flu*
Bates, Ivan. *All by myself*
Batherman, Muriel. *Animals live here*
Batten, Mary. *Who has a belly button?*
Battles, Edith. *What does the rooster say, Yoshio?*
Bauer, Marion Dane. *Frog's best friend*
  If you had a nose like an elephant's trunk
  If you were born a kitten
  My mother is mine
  Sleep, little one, sleep
  Why do kittens purr?
Baugh, Dolores M. *Let's see the animals*
Baumann, Hans. *Chip has many brothers*
Bax, Martin. *Edmond went far away*
Bayer, Jane. *A my name is Alice*
Bayley, Nicola. *One old Oxford ox*
Baylor, Byrd. *Desert voices*
  We walk in sandy places
Beach, Stewart. *Good morning, sun's up!*
Beames, Margaret. *Night cat*
Beaton, Clare. *How loud is a lion?*
  One moose, twenty mice
  One moose, twenty mice [board book]
Beaumont, Karen. *Duck, duck, goose!*
Beautiful moments in the wild
Beck, Andrea. *Elliot bakes a cake*
  Elliot digs for treasure

  Elliot gets stuck
  Elliot's bath
  Elliot's Christmas surprise
  Elliot's emergency
  Elliot's shipwreck
Becker, Bonny. *An ant's day off*
  Tickly prickly
Becker, Helaine. *Mama likes to mambo*
Beeke, Jemma. *The Rickety Barn show*
Beeke, Tiphanie. *Roar like a lion!*
Beifuss, John. *Armadillo Ray*
Beil, Karen Magnuson. *A cake all for me!*
Beim, Jerrold. *Eric on the desert*
Belling the cat and other stories
Belloc, Hilaire. *The bad child's book of beasts*
  The bad child's book of beasts, and more beasts for worse children
  The bad child's pop-up book of beasts
  More beasts for worse children
Bellville, Rod. *Large animal veterinarians*
Belpré, Pura. *Dance of the animals*
Bemelmans, Ludwig. *Rosebud*
Bender, Robert. *The A to Z beastly jamboree*
Bendick, Jeanne. *Why can't I?*
Benevelli, Alberto. *The colors of the chameleon*
Bennett, David. *One cow moo moo*
Bennett, Jill. *Animal fair*
Berends, Polly Berrien. *I heard said the bird*
Berger, Barbara Helen. *Animalia*
Berger, Melvin. *Brrr! a book about polar animals*
  Dive! a book of deep sea creatures
  Prehistoric mammals
Berger, Terry. *The turtles' picnic and other nonsense stories*
Berkes, Marianne Collins. *Marsh music*
Berkowitz, Linda. *Alfonse, where are you?*
Bernhard, Durga. *Alphabeasts*
  Earth, sky, wet, dry
Bernhard, Emery. *How Snowshoe Hare rescued the sun*
Bernstein, Joanne E. *Creepy crawly critter riddles*
Bernstein, Margery. *Coyote goes hunting for fire*
  The first morning
Berson, Harold. *I'm bored, Ma!*
  Why the jackal won't speak to the hedgehog
Bester, Roger. *Guess what?*
Bethell, Jean. *Bathtime*
  Playmates
Bible, Charles. *Hamdaani*
Bible. Old Testament. Noah. *Noah and the ark*, ill. by Pauline Baynes
  Noah and the ark, ill. by Jim Cummins
Bierhorst, John. *Doctor Coyote*
Big, bad, and a little bit scary
The big Peter Rabbit book
Bilgrami, Shaheen. *Amazing dinosaur discovery*
  Farmyard painting party
  Incredible animal discovery
  Jungle art show
Binzen, Bill. *Alfred goes house hunting*
Birchmore, Daniel A. *Pilly, Polly, and Wee*
Biro, Val. *Gumdrop and the farmyard caper*
  Gumdrop and the great sausage caper
Bischoff-Miersch, Andrea. *Do you know the difference?*
Bishop, Roma. *Animals*
  My first pop-up book of prehistoric animals
  On a safari
Black, Charles C. *The royal nap*
Black, Harley. *Amazing magic school*
Blackstone, Stella. *How big is a pig?*
  Secret seahorse
  Secret seahorse [board book]
  Who are you?
Blaich, Ute. *The star*
Blake, Quentin. *Fantastic Daisy Artichoke*
  Zagazoo
Blathwayt, Benedict. *Tangle and the silver bird*
Bless the beasts
Bloom, Becky. *Mr. Cuckoo*
  Wolf

Blough, Glenn O. *Who lives in this meadow?*
Bock, Lee. *Oh, crumps! = Ay, caramba!*
Bodsworth, Nan. *Monkey business*
Bogacki, Tomasz. *I hate you! I like you!*
Bograd, Larry. *Egon*
Bohdal, Susi. *1, 2, 3, what do you see?*
   Tom cat
Bolliger, Max. *Noah and the rainbow*
Bond, Felicia. *Tumble bumble*
Bonfils, Bolette. *Peter joins the circus*
Bonino, Louise. *The cozy little farm*
Bonning, Tony. *Another fine mess*
Boon, Emilie. *1 2 3 how many animals can you see?*
   Peterkin's very own garden
   Peterkin's wet walk
Borden, Beatrice Brown. *Wild animals of Africa*
Borg, Inga. *Plupp builds a house*
Borlenghi, Patricia. *From albatross to zoo*
Bosca, Francesca. *The apple king*
Bottner, Barbara. *Zoo song*
Bourgeois, Paulette. *Franklin and Harriet*
   Franklin and the thunderstorm
   Franklin rides a bike
   Franklin's class trip
   Franklin's secret club
   Too many chickens
Bowden, Miriam. *The adventure of Paz in the land of numbers*
Bowen, Betsy. *Tracks in the wild*
Bowman, Pete. *I wish I were big*
Boyd, Lizi. *Lulu Crow's garden*
Boyd, Selma. *I met a polar bear*
Boynton, Sandra. *A is for angry*
   Barnyard dance!
   The going to bed book
   Good night, good night
   Moo, baa, la la la!
Bozylinsky, Hannah Heritage. *Lala Salama*
Bradman, Tony. *See you later, alligator*
Brandenberg, Franz. *Aunt Nina and her nephews and nieces*
   Cock-a-doodle-doo
Brasch, Kate. *Prehistoric monsters*
Breebaart, Joeri. *When I die, will I get better?*
Breeze, Lynn. *Baby's animals*
Brennan, John. *Zoo day*
Brenner, Barbara A. *One small place by the sea*
   Ostrich feathers
Brenner, Emily. *On the first day of grade school*
Brent, Isabelle. *Noah's ark*
Brett, Jan. *Annie and the wild animals*
   Armadillo rodeo
   Berlioz the bear
   The hat
Brett, Jessica. *Animals on the go*
Brice, Tony. *Baby animals*
Brierley, Louise. *King Lion and his cooks*
Bright, Paul. *Quiet!*
Brimner, Larry Dane. *Dinosaurs dance*
Brisson, Pat. *Hobbledy-clop*
Bro, Marguerite (Harmon). *The animal friends of Peng-u*
Brock, Emma Lillian. *Nobody's mouse*
   Surprise balloon
Brooke, L. Leslie (Leonard Leslie). *Johnny Crow's garden*
   Johnny Crow's new garden
   Johnny Crow's party
Brooks, Alan. *Frogs jump*
Brown, Andrew. *Armored animals*
   Dangerous animals
Brown, Craig McFarland. *My barn*
Brown, Jo. *Where's my mommy?*
Brown, Ken (Ken James). *Mucky Pup*
   What's the time, Grandma Wolf?
Brown, Marc Tolon. *Arthur and the true Francine*
   Arthur goes to camp
   Arthur's animal adventure
   Arthur's April fool
   Arthur's Christmas
   Arthur's eyes

   Arthur's Halloween
   Arthur's perfect Christmas
   Arthur's teacher moves in
   Arthur's teacher trouble
   Arthur's Thanksgiving
   Arthur's tooth
   Arthur's underwear
   Arthur's Valentine
   The bionic bunny show
   The silly tail book
Brown, Marcia. *The blue jackal*
   The bun
   Once a mouse . . .
Brown, Margaret Wise. *Baby animals*, ill. by Mary Cameron
   Baby animals, ill. by Susan Jeffers
   The big fur secret
   Big red barn, ill. by Felicia Bond
   Big red barn, ill. by Rosella Hartman
   A child's good morning book
   The days before now
   The diggers
   The dirty little boy
   Don't frighten the lion
   The duck
   Fox eyes
   The friendly book
   The golden birthday book
   The Golden sleepy book
   The little fur family
   Once upon a time in pigpen and three other stories
   Streamlined pig
   They all saw it
   Three little animals
   Wait till the moon is full
   Where have you been?, ill. by Barbara Cooney
   Where have you been?, ill. by Leo and Diane Dillon
Brown, Richard Eric. *One hundred words about animals*
Brown, Rick. *Who built the ark?*
Brown, Ruth. *Copycat*
   The grizzly revenge
   One stormy night
   The picnic
Browne, Anthony. *Animal fair*
   Bear goes to town
   The little bear book
   Zoo
Browne, Eileen. *No problem*
Browne, Philippa-Alys. *A gaggle of geese*
Brownell, Barbara. *Spin's really wild U.S.A. tour*
Browner, Richard. *Everyone has a name*
Bruchac, Joseph. *The great ball game*
Brunhoff, Laurent de. *Babar's counting book*
   Babar's little circus star
   The rescue of Babar
Brusca, María Cristina. *When jaguars ate the moon*
Bruss, Deborah. *Book! book! book!*
Brutschy, Jennifer. *Celeste and Crabapple Sam*
Bryant-Mole, Karen. *Moving*
Buck, Frank. *Jungle animals*
Buck, Nola. *Creepy crawly critters and other Halloween tongue twisters*
Buehner, Caralyn. *I did it, I'm sorry*
Buff, Mary (Marsh). *Forest folk*
Buller, Jon. *Toad on the road*
Bullock, Kathleen. *It chanced to rain*
Bunting, Eve (Anne Evelyn). *Happy birthday, dear duck*
   Little Badger's just-about birthday
   Night tree
   Swan in love
   Terrible things
   We need a bigger zoo!
   We were there
Burdick, Margaret. *Bobby Otter and the blue boat*
   Sara Raccoon and the secret place
Burgess, Thornton. *Old Mother West Wind*
Burnard, Damon. *I spy in the jungle*
   I spy in the ocean
Burningham, John. *Cluck baa*

Hey! Get off our train
Mr. Gumpy's outing
The shopping basket
Burns, Diane L. *Backyard beasties*
Burns, Kate. *In the snow*
Burton, Jane. *Animals at home*
Animals at night
Animals at rest
Animals at work
Animals eating
Animals fighting
Animals keeping clean
Animals keeping cool
Animals keeping safe
Animals keeping warm
Animals learning
Animals talking
Burton, Katherine. *One gray mouse*
Burton, Marilee Robin. *The elephant's nest*
Tail toes eyes ears nose
Bush, John. *The giraffe who got in a knot*
Bush, Timothy. *Three at sea*
Butler, Dorothy. *Higgledy, piggledy, hobbledy hoy*
Butler, John. *While you were sleeping*
Butler, M. Christina. *One snowy night*
Butler, Stephen. *The mouse and the apple*
Butterworth, Nick. *One blowy night*
One snowy night
The rescue party
The secret path
Byars, Betsy Cromer. *The groober*
The lace snail
Bynum, Janie. *Altoona Baboona*
Cabrera, Jane. *Monkey's play time*
Calhoun, Mary. *Euphonia and the flood*
Calmenson, Stephanie. *The after school book*
All aboard the goodnight train
Dinner at the Panda Palace
The kindergarten book
One little monkey
Where will the animals stay?
Campbell, Rod. *Dear zoo*
It's mine
My pop-up garden friends
Caple, Kathy. *Worm gets a job*
Capucilli, Alyssa Satin. *Biscuit visits the pumpkin patch*
Inside a barn in the country
Inside a house that is haunted
Inside a zoo in the city
Carle, Eric. *Does a kangaroo have a mother, too?*
From head to toe
Hello, red fox
1, 2, 3 to the zoo
"Slowly, slowly, slowly," said the sloth
10 little rubber ducks
Today is Monday
The very busy spider
Carlson, Nancy L. *Arnie and the new kid*
Arnie and the skateboard gang
Arnie and the stolen markers
Arnie goes to camp
How about a hug?
Louanne Pig in making the team
The talent show
Carlson, Natalie Savage. *Surprise in the mountains*
Carlstrom, Nancy White. *Midnight dance of the snowshoe hare*
Raven and river
Rise and shine!
The way to Wyatt's house
What would you do if you lived at the zoo?
Carrick, Carol. *In the moonlight, waiting*
Patrick's dinosaurs
Carrick, Malcolm. *I can squash elephants!*
Carrier, Lark. *A Christmas promise*
Carroll, Kathleen Sullivan. *One red rooster*
Carryl, Charles E. (Charles Edward). *The camel's lament*
Carter, David A. *Old MacDonald had a farm*

Carter, Noelle. *I'm a little mouse*
My house
My pet
Cartlidge, Michelle. *Bear in the forest*
Duck in the pond
Elephant in the jungle
Cartwright, Ann. *Norah's ark*
Casanova, Mary. *One-dog canoe*
Caseley, Judith. *Mickey's class play*
Casey, Patricia. *Beep! Beep! Oink! Oink! animals in the city*
Cluck cluck
One day at Wood Green Animal Shelter
Cash, Megan Montague. *I saw the sea and the sea saw me*
Cassedy, Sylvia. *Red dragonfly on my shoulder*
Cassidy, Dianne. *Circus animals*
Cassie, Brian. *Say it again*
Castle, Caroline. *Herbert Binns and the flying tricycle*
Catalanotto, Peter. *Mr. Mumble*
Catchpole, Clive. *Deserts*
Grasslands
Jungles
Mountains
Cathon, Laura E. *Tot Botot and his little flute*
Cauley, Lorinda Bryan. *The animal kids*
The bake-off
Causley, Charles. *"Quack!" said the billy-goat*
Cave, Kathryn. *Henry's song*
Out for the count
Cazet, Denys. *Are there any questions?*
The duck with squeaky feet
Frosted glass
Lucky me
Minnie and Moo go to Paris
Minnie and Moo: the night of the living bed
Minnie and Moo: will you be my Valentine?
Minnie and Moo: the attack of the Easter bunnies
Mother night
Never poke a squid
Never spit on your shoes
Nothing at all
Sunday
Cech, John. *Django*
Cecil, Laura. *Noah and the space ark*
Chalmers, Audrey. *Hundreds and hundreds of pancakes*
Chalmers, Mary. *A Christmas story*
Easter parade
Chamberlin-Calamar, Pat. *Alaska's twelve days of summer*
Chapman, Cheryl. *Pass the fritters, critters*
Charles, Donald. *Calico Cat at the zoo*
Shaggy dog's animal alphabet
Chase, Catherine. *Noah's ark*
Chen, Tony. *Animals showing off*
Cherry, Lynne. *The great kapok tree*
Who's sick today?
Chichester Clark, Emma. *Follow the leader!*
Little Miss Muffet's count-along surprise
Chicken Little. *Chicken Licken,* ill. by Jutta Ash
Chicken Licken, ill. by Gavin Bishop
Chicken Little, ill. by Sally Hobson
Henny Penny, ill. by Emily Bolam
Henny Penny, ill. by Stephen Butler
Henny Penny, ill. by Paul Galdone
Henny Penny, ill. by William Stobbs
Henny-Penny, ill. by Jane Wattenberg
The sky is falling
The story of Chicken Licken
Child, Lauren. *I am not sleepy and I will not go to bed*
Chinery, Michael. *Desert animals*
Grassland animals
Chitwood, Suzanne Tanner. *Wake up, big barn!*
Cho, Shinta. *The gas we pass*
Chocolate, Deborah M. Newton. *Imani in the belly*
Chorao, Kay. *Carousel round and round*
Lemon moon
Number one number fun
Chottin, Ariane. *A home for Little Turtle*
Chouinard, Roger. *The amazing animal alphabet book*

One magic box
Christelow, Eileen. *Glenda Feathers casts a spell*
    Olive and the magic hat
    The robbery at the diamond dog diner
    Where's the big bad wolf?
Christensen, Gardell Dano. *Mrs. Mouse needs a house*
Christiana, David. *White nineteens*
Christmas in the stable, ill. by Beverly K. Duncan
Chukovskii, Kornei Ivanovich. *Telephone*, ill. by Vladimir Radunsky
Chwast, Seymour. *Mr. Merlin and the turtle*
    The twelve circus rings
Cimarusti, Marie Torres. *Peek-a-moo*
Clément, Claude. *The hungry duckling*
Clement, Rod. *Just another ordinary day*
Clewes, Dorothy. *Henry Hare's boxing match*
    The wild wood
Climo, Shirley. *The cobweb Christmas*
    The little red ant and the great big crumb
Clymer, Ted. *The horse and the bad morning*
Cneut, Carll. *The amazing love story of Mr. Morf*
Coats, Laura Jane. *Ten little animals*
Coatsworth, Elizabeth. *A peaceable kingdom, and other poems*
Cober, Alan E. *Cober's choice*
Cocca-Leffler, Maryann. *Jungle Halloween*
Cock Robin. *The courtship, merry marriage, and feast of Cock Robin and Jenny Wren*
    Who killed Cock Robin?, ill. by William Stobbs
Coffey, Maria. *A cat in a kayak*
Cohen, Caron Lee. *Digger Pig and the turnip*
    Pigeon, pigeon
Cohen, Peter Zachary. *Boris's glasses*
Cohn, Diana. *Dream carver*
Colby, C. B. (Carroll Burleigh). *Who lives there?*
    Who went there?
Cole, Babette. *Tarzanna!*
Cole, Joanna. *Animal sleepyheads*
    Evolution
    It's too noisy
    Large as life daytime animals
    Large as life nighttime animals
Cole, Michael. *Head in the sand*
Cole, Sheila. *The hen that crowed*
    When the tide is low
Cole, William. *I went to the animal fair*
    A zooful of animals
Coleman, Michael. *Lazy Ozzie*
Collard, Sneed B. *Animal dads*
    Animals asleep
    Creepy creatures
    Making animal babies
Collicott, Sharleen. *Seeing stars*
    Toestomper and the caterpillars
Collins, Pat Lowery. *Tomorrow, up and away!*
Colman, Hila. *Watch that watch*
Cone, Molly. *Squishy, misty, damp & muddy*
Conklin, Gladys. *I caught a lizard*
Conover, Chris. *The lion's share*
Conrad, Pam. *Animal lingo*
    Animal lullabies
Cooper, Ann (Ann C.). *In the forest*
Cooper, Helen (Helen F.). *Pumpkin soup*
Cooper, Melrose. *Pets!*
Cooper, Susan. *Matthew's dragon*
Coplans, Peta. *Spaghetti for Suzy*
Corey, Dorothy. *A shot for baby bear*
    Will it ever be my birthday?
Cormack, M. Grant. *Animal tales from Ireland*
Cortesi, Wendy W. *Explore a spooky swamp*
Cosgrove, Margaret. *Wintertime for animals*
Cotten, Cynthia. *At the edge of the woods*
Cousins, Lucy. *Country animals*
    Doctor Maisy
    Farm animals
    Garden animals
    Happy birthday, Maisy
    Jazzy in the jungle

    Katy Cat and Beaky Boo
    Maisy at the fair
    Maisy dresses up
    Maisy's bedtime
    Maisy's big flap book
    Maisy's farm
    Maisy's halloween
    Maisy's morning on the farm
    Maisy's noisy day
    Maisy's pool
    Noah's ark
    Noah's ark [board book]
    Pet animals
    What can rabbit hear?
    What can rabbit see?
Coville, Bruce. *Sarah's unicorn*
Cowcher, Helen. *Rain forest*
Cowell, Cressida. *What shall we do with the Boo-Hoo Baby?*
Cowen-Fletcher, Jane. *Farmer Will*
Cowley, Stewart. *Down Ladybug Lane*
    In dragonfly forest
    In songbird jungle
    On Butterfly Farm
    What's that sound?
Coxe, Molly. *Bunny and the beast*
    Whose footprints?
Craig, M. Jean. *Spring is like the morning*
Craighead, Charles. *The eagle and the river*
Craver, Mike. *Beaver ball at the bug club*
Crawford, Ron. *Pet?*
Crawford, Sheryl Ann. *The baby who changed the world*
Crebbin, June. *Cows in the kitchen*
Creighton, Jill. *One day there was nothing to do*
Cremins, Robert. *My animal ABC*
    My animal Mother Goose
Crimi, Carolyn. *Don't need friends*
Crisp, Marty. *Black and white*
Cristini, Ermanno. *In the pond*
    In the woods
Cronin, Doreen. *Giggle, giggle, quack*
Cross, Genevieve. *A trip to the yard*
Crowe, Robert L. *Tyler Toad and the thunder*
Crowther, Robert. *Animal rap!*
    Animal snap!
    Who lives in the country?
    Who lives in the garden?
Croxford, Vera. *All kinds of animals*
Cruickshank, Margrit. *We're going to feed the ducks*
Crum, Shutta. *The bravest of the brave*
Crump, Donald J. *Creatures small and furry*
Cullen, Lynn. *Little Scraggly Hair*
Cummings, Pat. *Ananse and the lizard*
    Carousel
Curle, Jock J. *The four good friends*
Curry, Peter. *Animals*
Cushman, Doug. *The ABC mystery*
    The mystery of the monkey's maze
Cutler, Ivor. *The animal house*
    Herbert
Cuyler, Margery. *The biggest, best snowman*
    Road signs
    That's good! that's bad!
Czernecki, Stefan. *The singing snake*
Dahl, Michael. *One giant splash*
    Starry arms
Dahl, Roald. *The enormous crocodile*
    The giraffe and the pelly and me
Dale, Penny. *Daisy Rabbit's tree house*
    The elephant tree
Dallas-Conte, Juliet. *Cock-a-moo-moo*
Dalmais, Anne-Marie. *And may the best animal win!*
    The Elephant's airplane and other machines
Daly, Catherine. *Whiskers*
Daly, Kathleen N. *Today's biggest animals*
    Unusual animals
Damjan, Mischa. *The big squirrel and the little rhinoceros*
Darling, Kathy (Mary Kathleen). *Amazon A B C*

Arctic babies
Desert babies
Pecos Bill finds a horse
Rain forest babies
Seashore babies
Davenier, Christine. *Leon and Albertine*
Davidson, Jill A. *And that's what happened to little Lucy*
Davis, Douglas F. *There's an elephant in the garage*
Davis, Katie (Katie I.). *Who hoots?*
  Who hops?
Davis, Lee. *Feeding time*
  The lifesize animal opposites book
Davol, Marguerite W. *Batwings and the curtain of night*
  How snake got his hiss
Davoll, Barbara. *Dusty Mole, private eye*
Day, Alexandra. *The Christmas we moved to the barn*
  Helping the animals
  Helping the flowers and trees
  Helping the night
  Helping the sun
  Special deliveries
Day, David. *King of the woods*
Day, Marie. *Dragon in the rocks*
Day, Trevor. *Youch! it bites!*
Deacon, Alexis. *Slow Loris*
Deady, Kathleen W. *It's time!*
  Out and about at the zoo
DeBoer, Jesslyn. *Getting ready for Christmas*
De Groat, Diane. *Happy birthday to you, you belong in a zoo*
  Jingle bells, homework smells
  Roses are pink, your feet really stink
  Trick or treat, smell my feet
DeLage, Ida. *ABC triplets at the zoo*
  Good morning, lady
Delamare, David. *The Christmas secret*
Delessert, Etienne. *The endless party*
Delton, Judy. *The perfect Christmas gift*
Demarest, Chris L. *Farmer Nat*
  Kitman and Willy at sea
Demi. *A Chinese zoo*
  Demi's basket of books
  Demi's Christmas surprise
  Demi's count the animals 1-2-3
  Demi's dragons and fantastic creatures
  Demi's find the animals A B C
  Demi's opposites
  Find Demi's baby animals
  Find Demi's sea creatures
  Three little elephants
Demuth, Patricia Brennan. *Ornery morning*
Denim, Sue. *The Dumb Bunnies go to the zoo*
Dennard, Deborah. *Bullfrog at Magnolia Circle*
  Do cats have nine lives?
  Koala country
  Travis and the better mousetrap
Dennis, Suzanne E. *Answer me that*
Dennis, Wesley. *Flip*
Denton, Terry. *Home is the sailor*
De Paola, Tomie (Thomas Anthony). *Bill and Pete to the rescue*
  Country farm
  The hunter and the animals
  Jingle, the Christmas clown
  Noah and the ark
De Posadas Mane, Carmen. *Mister North Wind*
Deprisco, Dorothea. *Snowbear's winter day*
De Regniers, Beatrice Schenk. *Going for a walk*
  It does not say meow!
  May I bring a friend?
  What did you put in your pocket?
Desmoinaux, Christel. *Mrs. Hen's big surprise*
De Vicq de Cumptich, Roberto. *Bembo's zoo*
De Zutter, Hank. *Who says a dog goes bow-wow?*
DiFiori, Lawrence. *Baby animals*
Dijs, Carla. *Are you my daddy?*
  Are you my mommy?
  Mommy, what if—?
  Mommy, would you love me if . . . ?

Dionetti, Michelle V. *The day Eli went looking for bear*
DiPucchio, Kelly S. *What's the magic word?*
Dixon, Ann. *The blueberry shoe*
Dodd, Emma. *Dog's noisy day*
Dodd, Lynley. *Find me a tiger*
  Wake up, bear
Dodds, Dayle Ann. *Do bunnies talk?*
  Pet wash
Dodds, Siobhan. *Charles Tiger*
  Elizabeth Hen
Domanska, Janina. *What do you see?*
Domestic animals
Donahue, Shari Faden. *The zebra-striped whale with the polka-dot tail*
Donaldson, Julia. *The gruffalo*
  Room on the broom
Donohue, Dorothy. *Big and little on the farm*
  Veggie soup
Doolittle, Bev. *Reading the wild*
Doray, Malika. *One more Wednesday*
Dorros, Arthur. *City chicken*
Dowling, Paul. *Happy birthday, Owl*
  Where are you going, Jimmy?
  You need a bath, Mustard
Downey, Lynn. *The flea's sneeze*
Downs, Mike. *Pig giggles and rabbit rhymes*
Doyle, Malachy. *Well, a crocodile can!*
Dragonwagon, Crescent. *Alligator arrived with apples*
  Alligators and others all year long!
Dryden, Emma. *Good morning – good night*
Dubois, Muriel L. *I like animals: what can I be?*
Du Bois, William Pène. *Bear circus*
  Bear party
Dubov, Christine Salac. *Oink! and other sounds*
Duff, Maggie (Margaret K.). *Dancing turtle*
Duffy, Dee Dee (Deborah). *Barnyard tracks*
Duke, Kate. *Aunt Isabel tells a good one*
  If you walk down this road
Dunbar, Joyce. *Baby bird*
  Eggday
Duncan, Riana. *A nutcracker in a tree*
  When Emily woke up angry
Dunn, Judy. *The animals of Buttercup Farm*
Dunn, Phoebe. *Baby's animal friends*
Dunnick, Regan. *Sweet dreams, Douglas*
Dunphy, Madeleine. *Here is the Arctic winter*
  Here is the tropical rain forest
Dunrea, Olivier. *Bear Noel*
  Deep down underground
Dupasquier, Philippe. *1 2 3, follow me!*
Duplaix, Georges. *Animal stories*
Du Quette, Keith. *Hotel Animal*
  Ripping day for a picnic
  They call me Woolly
Durant, Alan. *Mouse party*
  Snake supper
Durrell, Julie. *Mouse tails*
Duvoisin, Roger Antoine. *A for the ark*
  The crocodile in the tree
  Jasmine
  Our Veronica goes to Petunia's farm
  Petunia
  Petunia and the song
  Petunia, beware!
  Petunia takes a trip
  Petunia, the silly goose
  Petunia's treasure
Dyer, Sarah. *Clementine and Mungo*
Easter babies
Easton, Violet. *Elephants never jump*
Edens, Cooper. *An ABC of fashionable animals*
  The Animal Mall
Edwards, Frank B. *New at the zoo*
Edwards, Pamela Duncan. *Bravo, Livingstone Mouse!*
  The grumpy morning
  McGillycuddy could
  Roar
  Some smug slug

The worrywarts
Edwards, Richard. *The forest child*
   Good night, Copycub
   Moon frog
Egan, Tim. *The blunder of the Rogues*
   Friday night at Hodges' café
   Metropolitan cow
   Serious farm
   The trial of Cardigan Jones
Egg-napped!
Ehrlich, Amy. *Lucy's winter tale*
   Parents in the pigpen, pigs in the tub
Eichenberg, Fritz. *Dancing in the moon*
Elborn, Andrew. *Noah and the ark and the animals*
Elias, Joyce. *Whose toes are those?*
Elkin, Benjamin. *Why the sun was late*
Elliott, David. *And here's to you!*
Elting, Mary. *Q is for duck*
Elya, Susan Middleton. *Eight animals bake a cake*
   Eight animals on the town
Emberley, Barbara. *One wide river to cross*
Emberley, Ed (Edward Randolph). *Animals*
   Thanks, Mom!
Emberley, Rebecca. *My animals = Mis animales*
Emmett, Jonathan. *Bringing down the moon*
   No place like home
Enderle, Judith (Ann) Ross. *A pile of pigs*
   Six snowy sheep
   Upstairs
Erdrich, Liselotte. *Bears make rock soup and other stories*
Erickson, Russell E. *Warton's Christmas eve adventure*
Ernst, Lisa Campbell. *Hamilton's art show*
   Wake up, it's Spring!
Ets, Marie Hall. *Another day*
   Beasts and nonsense
   Elephant in a well
   In the forest
   Just me
   Mister Penny
   Mister Penny's circus
   Play with me
Eure, Wesley. *A fish out of water*
Euvremer, Teryl. *The thieves of Peck's pocket*
Evans, Eva Knox. *Sleepy time*
   Where do you live?
Facklam, Margery. *But not like mine*
   I eat dinner
   I go to sleep
   Only a star
   So can I
Falda, Dominique. *The treasure chest*
Farber, Norma. *All those mothers at the manger*
   As I was crossing Boston Common
   How the hibernators came to Bethlehem
   How the left-behind beasts built Ararat
   How to ride a tiger
   When it snowed that night
   Without wings, mother, how can I fly?
Farm animals [Macmillan, 1991]
Farm animals, photos sel. by Debby Slier
Farm house
Farris, Pamela J. *Young Mouse and Elephant*
Faulkenberry, Lauren. *What do animals do on the weekend?*
Faulkner, Keith. *Do you have my quack?*
   The giraffe who cock-a-doodle-doo'd
   Jumbled jungle
   My pets
   The tallest shortest longest greenest brownest animal in the jungle!
   The wide-mouthed frog
Fay, Hermann. *My zoo*
Fearnley, Jan. *Little Robin's Christmas*
   A perfect day for it
Fecher, Sarah. *Wild animals*
Feczko, Kathy. *Umbrella parade*
Feldman, Eve B. *Animals don't wear pajamas*
Fernandes, Eugenie. *Busy Little Mouse*
Fiddle-i-fee

Fife, Dale. *The little park*
Finn, Isobel. *The very lazy ladybug*
Finzel, Julia. *Large as life*
Fischer, Hans. *The birthday*
Fischetto, Laura. *Inside Noah's ark*
   The jungle is my home
Fisher, Aileen Lucia. *Anybody home?*
   Do bears have mothers too?
   We went looking
   Where does everyone go?
Fisher, Carolyn. *A twisted tale*
Fitzpatrick, Marie-Louise. *I'm a tiger, too!*
Flack, Marjorie. *Ask Mr. Bear*
Flanagan, Alice K. *Dr. Friedman helps animals*
   Soil
Flanders, Michael. *Creatures great and small*
Fleming, Candace. *Gator gumbo*
   Who invited you?
Fleming, Denise. *Barnyard banter*
   Count!
   In the small, small pond
   Where once there was a wood
Fletcher, Elizabeth. *What am I?*
Floca, Brian. *The frightful story of Harry Walfish*
Flora, James. *The day the cow sneezed*
Florian, Douglas. *At the zoo*
   Beast feast
   A bird can fly
   In the swim
Flynn, Kitson. *Carrot in my pocket*
Foreman, Michael. *Look! Look!*
   Panda and the bushfire
   Rock-a-doodle-do!
Foster, John. *Pet poems*
Fournier, Catharine. *The coconut thieves*
Fowler, Allan. *Cubs and colts and calves and kittens*
   Hard-to-see animals
Fowler, Richard. *Cat's cake*
   Cat's car
   Happy birthday, Mouse!
   Little Chick's big adventure
   Mr. Little's noisy car
   Mr. Little's noisy fire engine
   Mr. Little's noisy truck
Fowler, Susi Gregg. *Circle of thanks*
Fox, Charles Philip. *Mr. Stripes the gopher*
Fox, Mem. *Hattie and the fox*
   Time for bed
   Wombat divine
   Zoo-looking
Frampton, David. *My beastie book of ABC*
Francis, Frank. *The magic wallpaper*
Frascino, Edward. *My cousin the king*
Fraser, Mary Ann. *Where are the night animals?*
Fredericks, Anthony D. *In one tidepool*
Freedman, Claire. *Where's your smile, crocodile?*
Freedman, Russell. *Farm babies*
   Hanging on
   Tooth and claw
   When winter comes
Freeman, Don. *Add-a-line alphabet*
Freeman, Mylo. *Potty*
Freeman, Tor. *Hooray! I'm five today!*
French, Fiona. *Anancy and Mr. Dry-Bone*
French, Vivian. *Little Tiger goes shopping*
Freschet, Berniece. *Owl in the garden*
   Where's Henrietta's hen?
Friedrich, Priscilla. *The wishing well in the woods*
The friendly beasts
Fries, Claudia. *A pig is moving in*
Frith, Michael K. *Some of us walk, some fly, some swim*
A frog he would a-wooing go (folk-song). *Frog went a-courtin'*, ill. by Feodor Rojankovsky
   The frog went a-courting, ill. by Dominic Catalano
   Froggie went a-courting, ill. by Chris Conover
   Froggie went a courting, ill. by Marjorie Priceman
   Mr. Frog went a-courting

Wendy Watson's frog went a-courting
From King Boggen's hall to nothing-at-all
Fromm, Lilo. *Muffel and Plums*
Fuchshuber, Annegert. *Two peas in a pod*
Fuge, Charles. *I know a rhino*
Fussenegger, Gertrud. *Noah's ark*
Futamata, Eigoro. *How not to catch a mouse*
Gackenbach, Dick. *Supposes*
Gaffney, Michael. *Secret forests*
Galdone, Paul. *Cat goes fiddle-i-fee*
Galko, Francine. *Cave animals*
Gallo, Frank. *Night sounds*
Gallup, Joan. *Silly animal ABCs*
Gambill, Henrietta D. *Little Christmas animals*
Gamble, Isobel. *Who's that?*
Gammell, Stephen. *Once upon MacDonald's farm*
Ganeri, Anita. *Animal hideaways*
    The hunt for food
Gantos, Jack (John, Jr.). *The perfect pal*
Gardam, Catharine. *The animals' Christmas*
Gardner, Beau. *Can you imagine . . . ?*
    Guess what?
Garelick, May. *Look at the moon*, ill. by Barbara Garrison
    Look at the moon, ill. by Leonard Weisgard
Garelli, Cristina. *Farm friends clean up*
Garland, Michael. *Last night at the zoo*
Garland, Sarah. *Billy and Belle*
Garrett, Ann. *Tales of tails*
    What's for lunch?
Garten, Jan. *The alphabet tale*
Gauch, Patricia Lee. *Noah*
Gay, Marie-Louise. *On my island*
    Stella, fairy of the forest
Gay, Michel. *Bibi's birthday surprise*
    Night ride
Gay, Zhenya. *Look!*
Geis, Jacqueline. *Where the buffalo roam*
Geisert, Arthur. *After the flood*
    The ark
Geoghegan, Adrienne. *All your own teeth*
George, Jean Craighead. *Morning, noon, and night*
George, Lindsay Barrett. *Around the pond*
    In the woods
George, William T. *Christmas at Long Pond*
    Fishing at Long Pond
Geraghty, Paul. *The great green forest*
    The hoppameleon
    Over the steamy swamp
    Stop that noise!
Geras, Adèle. *My wishes for you*
Gerber, Carole. *Arctic dreams*
Geringer, Laura. *The cow is mooing anyhow*
Gerrard, Roy. *Mik's mammoth*
Gershator, Phillis. *When it starts to snow*
Gerstein, Mordicai. *The absolutely awful alphabet*
    Daisy's garden
    Noah and the great flood
    William, where are you?
Gervais, Bernadette. *Voyage under the stars*
Ghigna, Charles. *Animal trunk*
Gibbons, Gail. *Nature's green umbrella*
    Prehistoric animals
    Say woof!
    Zoo
Gibert, Bruno. *The king is naked!*
Giffard, Hannah. *Hens say cluck*
    Striped zebra
Gilbert, Suzie. *Hawk Hill*
Gilman, Rita Golden. *Mole in a hole*
    Rice is life
Ginsburg, Mirra. *The fox and the hare*
    Mushroom in the rain
Gipson, Morrell. *Whose tracks are these?*
Gleeson, Brian. *The tiger and the Brahmin*
Gliori, Debi. *Mr. Bear says, "Are you there, Baby Bear?"*
    Mr. Bear to the rescue
Goble, Paul. *The great race of the birds and animals*

Godard, Alex. *Idora*
Godwin, Laura. *Barnyard prayers*
    Little white dog
Goennel, Heidi. *Heidi's zoo*
    If I were a penguin . . .
Goffe, Toni. *Toby's animal rescue service*
Goffin, Josse. *Yes*
Goffstein, M. B. (Marilyn Brooke). *Natural history*
Goldin, David. *Go-Go-Go!*
Goldsmith, Howard. *Sleepy little owl*
Goldstone, Bruce. *The beastly feast*
Gollub, Matthew. *Gobble, quack, moon*
Gomi, Taro. *Guess who?*
    My friends
    Santa through the window
Goode, Diane. *The little book of farm friends*
Goode, Molly. *Mama loves*
Goodhart, Pippa. *Noah makes a boat*
    Row, row, row your boat
Goodman, Susan E. *What do you do – at the zoo?*
Goodspeed, Peter. *A rhinoceros wakes me up in the morning*
Goor, Ron. *All kinds of feet*
Gorbachev, Valeri. *Chicken chickens*
    Chicken chickens go to school
    One rainy day
    Where is the apple pie?
    Whose hat is it?
Gordon, Shirley. *Grandma zoo*
Grabianski, Janusz. *Grabianski's wild animals*
Graham Barber, Lynda. *Spy hops and belly flops*
Graham, Bob. *First there was Frances*
Graham, John. *A crowd of cows*
    I love you, mouse
Grahame, Kenneth. *The open road*
    The wind in the willows, ill. by Joanne Moss
    A wind in the willows Christmas
    The wind in the willows: home sweet home
    The wind in the willows: the open road
    The wind in the willows: the river bank
    The wind in the willows: the wild wood
Grambling, Lois G. *This whole Tooth Fairy thing's nothing but a big rip-off!*
Gray, Kes. *The "Get well soon" book*
Gray, Libba Moore. *Is there room on the feather bed?*
Greaves, Margaret. *The naming*
Greeley, Valerie. *Animals*
    Farm animals
    Field animals
    Pets
    Where's my share?
    White is the moon
    Zoo animals
Greenaway, Shirley. *Forests*
    Jungles
Greene, Ellin. *The legend of the cranberry*
Greene, Rhonda Gowler. *Barnyard song*
    Jamboree day
Greenfield, Karen R. *Sister Yessa's story*
Greenway, Shirley. *Animal homes: burrows*
    Can you see me?
    Color me bright
    Here's ears
    How big am I?
    How do I move?
    Legs and all
    A tale of tails
    Two's company . . .
    What do I eat?
    Where do I live?
    Whose baby am I?
Gregory, Valiska. *When stories fell like shooting stars*
Gretz, Susanna. *Duck takes off*
    Frog, duck, and rabbit
    Frog in the middle
    Rabbit rambles on
Greydanus, Rose. *Animals at the zoo*
Griffith, Helen V. *Grandaddy's place*

How many candles?
Grimes, Nikki. *Minnie's new friend*
Grimm, Jacob. *The Bremen town band*
　The Bremen town musicians, ill. by Donna Diamond
　The Bremen town musicians, ill. by Bill Dickson
　The Bremen town musicians, ill. by Janina Domanska
　The Bremen town musicians, ill. by Paul Galdone
　The Bremen town musicians, ill. by David Johnson
　Bremen town musicians, ill. by Josef Palecek
　The Bremen town musicians, ill. by Ilse Plume
　The Bremen town musicians, ill. by Janet Stevens
　The Bremen town musicians, ill. by Bernadette Watts
　Little Red Riding Hood, ill. by John S. Goodall
　The musicians of Bremen, ill. by John Segal
　The musicians of Bremen, ill. by Svend Otto S
　The musicians of Bremen, ill. by Martin Ursell
　The traveling musicians of Bremen
Grindley, Sally. *Where are my chicks?*
Grobler, Piet. *Hey, frog!*
Groening, Maggie. *Maggie Simpson's book of animals*
Grossman, Bill. *The bear whose bones were Jezebel Jones*
Grosvenor, Donna. *Zoo babies*
Grupper, Jonathan. *Destination – Rocky Mountains*
Gryspeerdt, Rebecca. *Counting friends*
Guarino, Deborah. *Is your mama a llama?*
Gugler, Laurel Dee. *There's a billy goat in the garden*
Gullikson, Sandy. *Trouble for breakfast*
Gundersheimer, Karen. *Colors to know*
Guthrie, Donna. *Nobiah's well*
Haas, Irene. *A summertime song*
Haley, Gail E. *Noah's ark*
Hall, Donald. *Andrew the lion farmer*
Hall, Malcolm. *CariCATures*
Halpern, Shari. *My river*
Hamanaka, Sheila. *I look like a girl*
Hamberger, John. *The day the sun disappeared*
Hamilton, Richard. *Polly's picnic*
Hamilton, Virginia. *Jaguarundi*
Hamm, Diane Johnston. *Rock-a-bye farm*
Han, Oki S. *Kongi and Potgi*
Hands, Hargrave. *Duckling sees*
　Little lamb sees
Hanna, Jack. *Jungle Jack Hanna's safari adventure*
　The petting zoo
Hannant, Judith Stuller. *The doorknob collection of pets and pals*
Hansen, Biruta Akerbergs. *Parading with piglets*
Hargrove, Linda. *Wings across the moon*
Harker, Lesley. *Annie's ark*
Harley, Bill. *Bear's all-night party*
Harris, Joel Chandler. *Jump!*
　Jump again!
Harris, Susan. *Creatures that look alike*
Harrison, David Lee. *The animals' song*
　Wake up, sun!
Harrison, Sarah. *In granny's garden*
Harrison, Troon. *Don't dig so deep, Nicholas!*
Harter, Debbie. *Walking through the jungle*
Hartley, Karen. *The sixth sense and other special senses*
Hartman, Gail. *As the crow flies*
　As the roadrunner runs
Hartmann, Wendy. *One sun rises*
Haseley, Dennis. *The cave of snores*
Hassett, John. *Mouse in the house*
Haubensak-Tellenbach, Margrit. *The story of Noah's ark*
Hausman, Gerald. *How Chipmunk got tiny feet*
Hawcock, David. *Whose coat?*
　Whose home?
　Whose nose?
Hawkins, Colin. *Max and the magic word*
　Where's my mommy?
Hawkinson, John. *Robins and rabbits*
Hayashi, Leslie Ann. *Fables from the sea*
Hayes, Ann. *Meet the Marching Smithereens*
　Meet the orchestra
Hayes, Sarah. *The grumpalump*
Hayles, Karen. *What is stuck*
Hayles, Marsha. *A pet of a pet*

Hays, Anna Jane. *The pup speaks up*
Haywood, Carolyn. *Hello, star*
Hazelaar, Cor. *Zoo dreams*
Hazen, Barbara Shook. *Where do bears sleep?*, ill. by Mary Morgan-Vanroyen
　Where do bears sleep?, ill. by Ian E. Staunton
Heatwole, Marsha. *Jambo, watoto!*
Heiligman, Deborah. *On the move*
Heine, Helme. *Friends*
　Friends go adventuring
　Mollywoop
　Three little friends: the alarm clock
　Three little friends: the racing cart
　Three little friends: the visitor
Heinz, Brian J. *Butternut Hollow Pond*
Hellard, Susan. *Time to get up*
Hellen, Nancy. *Animals of the jungle*
　Circle farm
　A visit to the farm
　A visit to the zoo
Heller, Nicholas. *Mathilda the dream bear*
Heller, Ruth. *Animals born alive and well*
　How to hide a gray treefrog and other amphibians
　How to hide a polar bear
　How to hide an octopus
Helmer, Marilyn. *Three barnyard tales*
　Three tales of three
Helweg, Hans. *Farm animals*
Henderson, Kathy. *Counting farm*
　I can be a rancher
Hendra, Sue. *Oliver's wood*
Hendrick, Mary Jean. *If anything ever goes wrong at the zoo*
Henkes, Kevin. *Chrysanthemum*
　Oh!
Henley, Claire. *At the zoo*
　Dinnertime
　Farm day
　In the ocean
　Jungle day
　Playtime
　Quack, quack
Henley, Karyn. *Hatch!*
Hennessy, B. G. (Barbara G.). *Corduroy at the zoo*
　Eeney, Meeney, Miney, Mo
Herriot, James. *Only one woof*
Hersom, Kathleen. *The copycat*
Hess, Paul. *Farmyard animals*
　Polar animals
　Rainforest animals
　Safari animals
Heuck, Sigrid. *Who stole the apples?*
Hewitt, Sally. *All year round*
　Animal homes
　Face to face safari
　Woods and meadows
Higham, Jon Atlas. *Aardvark's picnic*
Hightower, Susan. *Twelve snails to one lizard*
Hill, Eric. *Spot at play*
　Spot at the fair
　Spot counts from 1 to 10
　Spot goes to the farm
　Spot on the farm
　Spot's favorite baby animals
Hill, Susan. *Ruby bakes a cake*
　Simba's A-Z
Hillenbrand, Will. *Fiddle-i-fee*
Himmelman, John. *Amanda and the magic garden*
　A guest is a guest
　Montigue on the high seas
Hindley, Judy. *Does a cow say boo?*
　Funny walks
　Into the jungle
　One by one
　Ten bright eyes
Hines, Anna Grossnickle. *I'll tell you what they say*
　Miss Emma's wild garden
Hippely, Hilary Horder. *Adventure on Klickitat Island*

The Hippopotamus's birthday and other poems about animals and birds
Hirschi, Ron. *Faces in the forest*
  Fall
  Forest
  Loon Lake
  Mountain
  Ocean
  Spring
  Summer
  A time for babies
  A time for playing
  A time for singing
  A time for sleeping
  When morning comes
  When night comes
  Who lives in . . . Alligator Swamp?
  Who lives in . . . the forest?
  Winter
Hirschmann, Linda. *In a lick of a flick of a tongue*
Hiscock, Bruce. *Coyote and badger*
Hiskey, Iris. *I like a snack on an iceberg*
Ho, Minfong. *Brother Rabbit*
  Hush!
Hoban, Julia. *Quick chick*
Hoban, Lillian. *The case of the two masked robbers*
Hoban, Russell. *The marzipan pig*
Hoban, Tana. *Big ones, little ones*
  A children's zoo
  Who are they?
Hoberman, Mary Ann. *A fine fat pig and other animal poems*
  "It's simple," said Simon
Hodge, Deborah. *Deer, moose, elk and caribou*
Hoff, Carol. *The four friends*
Hogrogian, Nonny. *Noah's ark*
Hol, Coby. *Tippy Bear's Christmas*
  A visit to the farm
Holder, Heidi. *Carmine the crow*
Holl, Adelaide. *The rain puddle*
  Small Bear builds a playhouse
Holm, Mayling Mack. *A forest Christmas*
Holmes, Anita. *Can you find us?*
  Who dug that hole?
Holmes, Efner Tudor. *Deer in the hollow*
Holsonback, Anita. *Monkey see, monkey do*
Holub, Joan. *Turkeys never gobble*
Hood, Thomas. *Before I go to sleep*
Hooks, William H. *Rough, tough, Rowdy*
Hooper, Patricia. *A bundle of beasts*
  Where do you sleep, little one?
Hoopes, Lyn Littlefield. *My own home*
Hopkins, Lee Bennett. *Animals from Mother Goose*
  To the zoo
Hoppe, Matthias. *Mouse and elephant*
Horácek, Petr. *When the moon smiled*
Horenstein, Henry. *A is for – ?*
Horn, Peter. *The best father of all*
Horowitz, Ruth. *Crab moon*
Hort, Lenny. *We're going on a treasure hunt*
  We're going on safari
Hosta, Dar. *I love the night*
Houston, John A. *A room full of animals*
Howard, Jane R. *When I'm hungry*
Howe, James. *Hot fudge*
Howell, Will C. *Zoo flakes ABC*
Hubbard, Woodleigh Marx. *2 is for dancing*
Hubbell, Patricia. *Earthmates*
Hudson, Cheryl Willis. *Animal sounds for baby*
Hughes, Langston. *The sweet and sour animal book*
Hull, Rod. *Mr. Betts and Mr. Potts*
Hulme, Joy N. *Sea squares*
  What if?
Huneck, Stephen. *Sally goes to the farm*
Hunt, Jonathan. *One is a mouse*
Hunter, Anne. *Possum and the peeper*
  Possum's harvest moon
  What's in the meadow?
  What's in the pond

What's in the tide pool?
Hurd, Edith Thacher. *Christmas eve*
Hurd, Thacher. *A night in the swamp*
Hurford, John. *The dormouse*
Hurwitz, Johanna. *Ethan out and about*
Hutchins, Pat. *Little pink pig*
  1 hunter
  Rosie's walk [board book]
  Shrinking mouse
  The silver Christmas tree
  The surprise party
  Ten red apples
  What game shall we play?
Hutton, Warwick. *Noah and the great flood*
Ichikawa, Satomi. *Nora's castle*
  Nora's duck
Ife, Elaine. *Noah and the ark*
Inkpen, Mick. *Anything cuddly will do!*
  Billy's beetle
  The great pet sale
  Kipper's A to Z
  Kipper's book of counting
  Kipper's book of numbers
  Meow!
  One bear at bedtime
  Picnic
  Splosh!
Ipcar, Dahlov (Zorach). *Animal hide and seek*
  Bright barnyard
  Brown cow farm
  The calico jungle
  A flood of creatures
  I like animals
  I love my anteater with an A
  Lost and found
  My wonderful Christmas tree
  Wild and tame animals
Irbinskas, Heather. *How Jackrabbit got his very long ears*
Irvine, Georgeanne. *The nursery babies*
  Tully the tree kangaroo
Isadora, Rachel. *A South African night*
Isenbart, Hans-Heinrich. *Baby animals on the farm*
Isherwood, Shirley. *Something for James*
Jackson, Bobby L. *Makimba's animal world*
Jackson, Carolyn. *The flying ark*
Jackson, Ellen B. *The precious gift*
Jacobs, Joseph. *Hereafterthis*
  The three sillies, ill. by Kathryn Hewitt
  The three sillies, ill. by Steven Kellogg
Jacobson, Jennifer Richard. *Moon sandwich mom*
Jahn-Clough, Lisa. *On the hill*
  1 2 3 yippie
Jakob, Donna. *My new sandbox*
Janisch, Heinz. *Noah's ark*
Janosch. *Tonight at nine*
Janovitz, Marilyn. *Look out, bird!*
Jarrett, Clare. *The best picnic ever*
Jaynes, Ruth M. *Tell me please! What's that?*
Jenkin-Pearce, Susie. *Bad Boris goes to school*
Jenkins, Steve. *Actual size*
  Animals in flight
  Big and little
  Biggest, strongest, fastest
  Duck's breath and mouse pie
  I see a kookaburra
  Slap, squeak, and scatter
  What do you do when something wants to eat you?
  What do you do with a tail like this?
Jennings, Linda M. *Easy peasy!*
  Franklin's neighborhood
  Hide and seek birthday treat
Jennings, Sharon. *Franklin forgives*
  Franklin makes a deal
  Franklin stays up
  Franklin wants a badge
  Franklin's music lessons
  Franklin's reading lesson

Franklin's surprise
Franklin's trading cards
Jensen, Patricia. *Little Squirrel's special nest*
Jewell, Nancy. *Christmas lullaby*
Joerns, Consuelo. *Oliver's escape*
Johnson, Amy Crane. *Cinnamon and the April shower = Canela y el aguacero de abril*
Johnson, Angela. *The girl who wore snakes*
Johnson, Crockett. *We wonder what will Walter be? When he grows up*
Johnson, Russell. *Trouble at Christmas*
Johnston, Deborah. *Mathew Michael's beastly day*
Johnston, Tony. *Desert song*
Goblin walk
Jolivet, Joëlle. *Zoo-ology*
Jonas, Ann. *Aardvarks, disembark!*
Splash!
The trek
Jones, Carol. *What's the time, Mr. Wolf?*
Jones, Jennifer Berry. *Who lives in the snow?*
Jordan, Martin. *Amazon alphabet*
Jungle days, jungle nights
Jordan, Sandra. *Down on Casey's farm*
Frog hunt
Jorgensen, Gail. *Crocodile Beat*
Gotcha!
Joyce, Susan. *ABC animal riddles*
Kajikawa, Kimiko. *Sweet dreams*
Kalan, Robert. *Stop, thief!*
Kallen, Stuart A. *The zoo*
Kamen, Gloria. *"Paddle," said the swan*
The ringdoves
Kane, Henry B. *Wings, legs, or fins*
Karim, Roberta. *This is a hospital, not a zoo!*
Karlin, Nurit. *I see, you saw*
Kastner, Jill. *Barnyard big top*
Kasza, Keiko. *A mother for Choco*
When the elephant walks
Katz, Bobbi. *The creepy crawly book*
Kaufmann, John. *Flying giants of long ago*
Kaufmann, Nancy. *Bye, Bye*
Kawata, Ken. *Animal tails*
Keats, Ezra Jack. *Pet show!*
Keller, Emily Snowell. *Sleeping Bunny*
Keller, Holly. *Cecil's garden*
Furry
That's mine, Horace
Too big
Will it rain?
Kelley, True. *Look again at funny animals*
Kellogg, Steven (Stephen). *Aster Aardvark's alphabet adventures*
Chicken Little
Kemp, Anthea. *Mr. Percy's magic greenhouse*
Kemp, Moira. *Lift-the-flap chick*
Lift-the-flap kitten
Kenah, Katharine. *Predator attack!*
Kennaway, Adrienne. *Little elephant's walk*
Kennedy, Marge M. *The book of boo!*
Kennedy, X. J. *The beasts of Bethlehem*
Kent, Jack. *Joey runs away*
Little Peep
Kepes, Juliet. *Five little monkeys*
Kerins, Tony (Anthony). *The brave ones*
Kessler, Brad. *Brer Rabbit and Boss Lion*
Kessler, Ethel. *Are there hippos on the farm?*
Do baby bears sit in chairs?
Is there an elephant in your kitchen?
Kessler, Leonard P. *The big mile race*
Do you have any carrots?
Kharms, Daniil. *The story of a boy named Will, who went sledding down the hill*
Kherdian, David. *The animal*
The cat's midsummer jamboree
Kidd, Richard. *Monsieur Thermidor*
Kilroy, Sally. *Animal noises*
Babies' zoo
Kimmel, Eric A. *Anansi and the moss-covered rock*
Anansi and the talking melon

I took my frog to the library
The rooster's antlers
King, Bob. *Sitting on the farm*
King, Thomas. *Coyote sings to the moon*
Kingman, Lee. *Peter's long walk*
Kipling, Rudyard. *The elephant's child*, ill. by Louise Brierley
The elephant's child, ill. by Lorinda Bryan Cauley
The elephant's child, ill. by Tim Raglin
The elephant's child, ill. by John A. Rowe
How the camel got his hump, ill. by Quentin Blake
How the camel got his hump, ill. by Tim Raglin
How the camel got his hump, ill. by Lisbeth Zwerger
The miracle of the mountain
Kirn, Ann. *Beeswax catches a thief*
Kitchen, Bert. *And so they build*
Animal alphabet
Animal numbers
Pig in a barrow
Somewhere today
Tenrec's twigs
When hunger calls
Kleven, Elisa. *Sun bread*
Klingel, Cynthia Fitterer. *Deserts*
Forests
Oceans
Knight, Bertram T. *Working at a zoo*
Knowles, Sheena. *Edward the emu*
Knüppel, Helga. *The adventures of Christabel Crocodile*
Knutson, Barbara. *How the guinea fowl got her spots*
Kobayashi, Robert. *Maria Mazaretti loves spaghetti*
Kobayashi, Yuji. *Miss Josephine's secret walk*
Koch, Michelle. *Hoot, howl, hiss*
Koelling, Caryl. *Animal mix and match*
Koide, Tan. *May we sleep here tonight?*
Kolar, Bob. *Stomp, stomp!*
Koller, Jackie French. *Fish fry tonight*
Mole and Shrew step out
Komori, Atsushi. *Animal mothers*
Koopmans, Loek. *The woodcutter's mitten*
Koralek, Jenny. *The friendly fox*
Koscielniak, Bruce. *Euclid Bunny delivers the mail*
Krahn, Fernando. *The biggest Christmas tree on earth*
Kramer, Anthony Penta. *Numbers on parade*
Kranking, Kathy. *The ocean is . . .*
Kraus, Robert. *The adventures of Wise Old Owl*
Animal families
Buggy Bear cleans up
Ella the bad speller
Good morning, Miss Gator
Here comes Tardy Toad
How Spider saved Easter
Klunky Monkey, new kid in class
Robert Kraus' a sunny day in Babytown
Springfellow's parade
Squirmy's big secret
The three friends
Wise Old Owl's Christmas adventure
Krauze, Andrzej. *What's so special about today?*
Krischanitz, Raoul. *Nobody likes me!*
Kroll, Steven. *It's Groundhog Day!*
Queen of the May
Kroll, Virginia L. *Lunching and munching*
Sweet Magnolia
Krüss, James. *3 X 3*
Kubler, Susanne. *The three friends*
Kuchalla, Susan. *Baby animals*
Kuhn, Dwight. *Hungry little frog*
Kuklin, Susan. *Taking my dog to the vet*
Kulling, Monica. *Waiting for Amos*
Kunhardt, Edith. *I'm going to be a vet*
Kuskin, Karla. *The animals and the ark*
James and the rain
Roar and more
Something sleeping in the hall
Kvasnosky, Laura McGee. *Pink, red, blue, what are you?*
Kwitz, Mary DeBall. *When it rains*
Lacome, Julie. *Garden*

Seashore
 Walking through the jungle
Lady Eden's School. *Just how stories*
Laird, Elizabeth. *The day the ducks went skating*
 The day Veronica was nosy
Lake, Mary Dixon. *The royal drum*
LaMarche, Jim. *The raft*
Langstaff, John M. *Over in the meadow*
Lapp, Eleanor. *The mice came in early this year*
Larson, Bonnie. *When animals were people = Cuando los animales*
 eran personas
Lass, Bonnie. *Who took the cookies from the cookie jar?*
Lathrop, Dorothy Pulis. *Who goes there?*
Latimer, Jim. *James Bear and the goose gathering*
 Moose and friends
 When moose was young
Laurencin, Geneviève. *I wish I were*
Lavies, Bianca. *Lily pad pond*
 Tree trunk traffic
Lavis, Steve. *Cock-a-doodle-doo*
 Jump!
 On the farm
Lawrence, John. *This little chick*
Lawrence, Michael (Michael C.). *The caterpillar that roared*
Layton, Neal. *Hot, hot, hot*
 Smile if you're human
Lazard, Naomi. *What Amanda saw*
Ledwon, Peter. *Midnight math twelve terrific math games*
Lee, Chinlun. *Good dog, Paw*
Lee, Jeanne M. *I once was a monkey*
 Toad is the uncle of heaven
Leedy, Loreen. *Fraction action*
 The Furry News
 The great trash bash
 Mission – addition
 There's a frog in my throat
 Who's who in my family?
Leeson, Christine. *Molly and the storm*
Leigh, Oretta. *The merry-go-round*
Lemaître, Pascal. *Zelda's secret*
Lenski, Lois. *Animals for me*
 Big little Davy
 The Easter Rabbit's parade
 Mr. and Mrs. Noah
Leonard, Marcia. *Animal talk*
 King Lionheart's castle
 Noisy neighbors
 What's that, Baby-boo?
Léonard, Marie. *Tibili, the little boy who didn't want to go to school*
Leslie, Amanda. *Alfie and Betty Bug*
 Animal noises
 Are chickens stripy?
 Do crocodiles moo?
 Flappy, waggy, wiggly
 Play kitten play
 Play puppy play
 Who's that scratching at my door?
Lesser, Carolyn. *The goodnight circle*
 What a wonderful day to be a cow
Lester, Alison. *Imagine*
Lester, Helen. *Hooway for Wodney Wat*
 It wasn't my fault
 Lin's backpack
Lester, Julius. *Ackamarackus*
 Albidaro and the mischievous dream
Le Tord, Bijou. *Noah's trees*
Levine, Arthur A. *Bono and Nonno*
Lewandowski, Frrich. *It's Christmas again*
Lewin, Betsy. *Animal snackers*
Lewin, Ted. *Nilo and the tortoise*
 When the rivers go home
Lewis, J. Patrick. *The boat of many rooms*
 Earth and me, our family tree
 Good mousekeeping
 A hippopotamusn't
 The la-di-da hare
 Long was the winter road they traveled

Two-legged, four-legged, no-legged rhymes
Lewis, Kim. *Here we go Harry*
Lewis, Naomi. *Hare and badger go to town*
Lewis, Shari. *Baby Lamb Chop loves animals*
Lewis, Stephen (Stephen Paul). *Zoo city*
Lewison, Wendy Cheyette. *"Buzz," said the bee*
 Going to sleep on the farm
 The rooster who lost his crow
Liersch, Anne. *A house is not a home*
The Lifesize animal counting book
Lillegard, Dee. *The hee-haw river*
 My yellow ball
 Sitting in my box
 Tortoise brings the mail
Lillie, Patricia. *When the rooster crowed*
Lilly, Kenneth. *Animal builders*
 Animal climbers
 Animal jumpers
 Animal runners
 Animal swimmers
 Animals at the zoo
 Animals in the country
 Animals in the jungle
 Animals on the farm
Lind, Mecka. *Cackle goes a-courting*
Lindbergh, Reeve. *Benjamin's barn*
 The day the goose got loose
 Midnight farm
 North country spring
 There's a cow in the road!
Lionni, Leo. *The biggest house in the world*
 Frederick's fables
Lipkind, William. *The boy and the forest*
Lippman, Peter. *New at the zoo*
Lishak, Anthony. *Row your boat*
Lithgow, John. *Carnival of the animals*
Little Bear's Valentine
The little red hen. The cock, the mouse and the little red hen, ill. by
 Lorinda Bryan Cauley
 The cock, the mouse and the little red hen, ill. by Graham Percy
 The little red hen, ill. by Byron Barton
 The little red hen, ill. by Emily Bolam
 The little red hen, ill. by Janina Domanska
 The little red hen, ill. by Paul Galdone
 The little red hen, ill. by Dennis Hockerman
 Little red hen, ill. by Norman Messenger
 The little red hen, ill. by Mel Pekarsky
 The little red hen, ill. by William Stobbs
 The little red hen, ill. by Annie West
 The little red hen, ill. by Margot Zemach
 The Little Red Hen makes a pizza
Little, Jean. *Pippin the Christmas pig*
Livingston, Myra Cohn. *Valentine poems*
Livinson, Nancy Smiler. *North Pole, South Pole*
Lloyd, David. *Duck*
 Hello, goodbye
Lobel, Anita. *King Rooster, Queen Hen*
Lobel, Arnold. *Fables*
 A holiday for Mister Muster
 A zoo for Mister Muster
Lodge, Jo. *Happy birthday, Moo Moo*
Loewer, H. Peter. *The moonflower*
Löfgren, Ulf. *Alvin the zookeeper*
 One-two-three
London, Jonathan. *Crunch munch*
 Fireflies, fireflies, light my way
 Froggy plays in the band
 Froggy plays soccer
 Froggy's first Christmas
 Gone again ptarmigan
 Loon Lake
 The owl who became the moon
 What the animals were waiting for
 Who bop
 Wiggle, waggle
Longfellow, Layne. *Imaginary menagerie*
Loomans, Diane. *The lovables in the kingdom of self-esteem*

Loomis, Christine. *The Hippo Hop*
    One cow coughs
    Scuba bunnies
Lorenz, Lee. *Hugo and the spacedog*
    A weekend in the city
Lorian, Nicole. *A birthday present for Mama*
Losordo, Stephen. *Cow moo me*
Lottridge, Celia Barker. *Berta, a remarkable dog*
Low, Joseph. *Adam's book of odd creatures*
Lowell, Susan. *The tortoise and the jackrabbit*
Lumry, Amanda. *Safari in South Africa*
Lunsford, Annie. *Who lives here?*
Lüton, Mildred. *Little chicks' mothers and all the others*
Luttrell, Ida. *Mattie and the chicken thief*
    The star counters
    Three good blankets
Lyfick, Warren. *Animal tales*
Lynn, Sara. *Big animals*
    Farm animals
    Garden animals
    Jungle friends
    1 2 3
    Small animals
Lyon, George Ella. *Mother to tigers*
    A regular rolling Noah
McAllister, Angela. *Matepo*
McBratney, Sam. *Just you and me*
McCall, Francis X. *A huge hog is a big pig*
Maccarone, Grace. *The class trip*
    Oink! moo! how do you do?
    Pumpkin faces
McCarthy, Bobette. *Dreaming*
McCarthy, Michael. *The story of Noah and the ark*
McCarty, Peter. *Little bunny on the move*
McCaughrean, Geraldine. *The story of Noah and the ark*
McCauley, Jane R. *The way animals sleep*
McClung, Robert. *How animals hide*
McConnachie, Brian. *Lily of the forest*
McCourt, Lisa. *The rainforest counts!*
McCrea, Lilian. *Mother hen*
McCurry, Kristen. *Ocean babies*
    Safari babies
MacDonald, Elizabeth. *My aunt and the animals*
    The wolf is coming!
MacDonald, Maryann. *Hedgehog bakes a cake*
MacDonald, Suse. *Look whooo's counting*
    Nanta's lion
    Peck, slither and slide
    Sea shapes
McDonnell, Flora. *Giddy-up! Let's ride!*
    I love animals
    Splash!
McFall, Gardner. *Naming the animals*
McFarlane, Sheryl. *On the farm*
McGee, Marni. *The noisy farm*
    The quiet farmer
McGill, Alice. *Sure as sunrise*
MacGill-Callahan, Sheila. *When Solomon was king*
McGinley-Nally, Sharon. *The friendly beasts*
Machotka, Hana. *Breathtaking noses*
    Outstanding outsides
    Terrific tails
    What do you do at a petting zoo?
    What neat feet!
McKee, David. *Elmer's friends*
    I can too!
    The sad story of Veronica who played the violin
    Zebra's hiccups
MacKeen, Leslie Ann. *Who can fix it?*
McKié, Roy. *Noah's ark*
MacLeod, Elizabeth. *I heard a little baa*
McLeod, Emilie Warren. *One snail and me*
McMullan, Kate (Hall). *Supercat*
McNally, Darcie. *In a cabin in a wood*
McNaught, Harry. *Baby animals*
McNaughton, Colin. *If dinosaurs were cats and dogs*
McNeer, May Yonge. *Little Baptiste*

McPhail, David M. *Andrew's bath*
    Animals A to Z
    The day the dog said, "Cock-a-doodle doo!"
    The day the sheep showed up
    Edward in the jungle
    Farm morning
    The Glerp
    The great race
    Lorenzo
    The party
    The puddle
    Where can an elephant hide?
McQuade, Jacqueline. *At the petting zoo with Teddy Bear*
    Big babies
    Small babies
    Snow babies
Madgwick, Wendy. *Animaze!*
Mado, Michio. *The animals*
Maestro, Giulio. *Leopard is sick*
    One more and one less
Maestro, Marco. *Geese find the missing piece*
Maggi, María Elena. *The great canoe*
Mahoney, Daniel J. *The perfect clubhouse*
    The Saturday escape
Mahy, Margaret. *Boom Baby boom, boom*
    The Christmas tree tangle
    17 kings and 42 elephants
    Simply delicious!
    A summery Saturday morning
    When the king rides by
Maitland, Barbara. *Moo in the morning*
Mallory, Kenneth. *Families of the deep blue sea*
Mann, Peggy. *King Laurence, the alarm clock*
Manning, Linda. *Animal hours*
Manning, Mick. *My body, your body*
    Supermom
Manson, Christopher. *A farmyard song*
Manushkin, Fran. *My Christmas safari*
Mari, Iela. *Eat and be eaten*
Maris, Ron. *Bernard's boring day*
    Better move on, frog!
    Ducks quack
    Frogs jump
    I wish I could fly
    In my garden
    Runaway rabbit
Markes, Julie. *Good thing you're not an octopus!*
Marks, Burton. *Animals*
Marsh, T. J. *Way out in the desert*
Marshall, Edward. *Fox all week*
Marshall, James. *Eugene*
    Four little troubles
    Hey, diddle, daddle
    Sing out, Irene
    Willis
Marshall, Janet Perry. *A honey of a day*
    My camera
Martin, Bill (William Ivan). *Chicken Chuck*
    Polar bear, polar bear, what do you hear?
Martin, C. L. G. *Down Dairy Farm Road*
Martin, David. *We've all got bellybuttons*
Martin, Francesca. *Clever Tortoise*
    The honey hunters
Martin, Rafe. *Will's mammoth*
Marzollo, Jean. *Home sweet home*
    I spy little animals
    Mama, Mama
    Papa, papa
    Pretend you're a cat
    Sun song
    Ten cats have hats
    What's the matter with Mother Goose?
Massie, Diane Redfield. *The baby beebee bird*
Mathers, Petra. *A cake for Herbie*
Mathews, Judith. *Nathaniel Willy, scared silly*
Mathis, Melissa Bay. *Animal house*
Maxner, Joyce. *Nicholas Cricket*

Mayer, Marianna. *Beauty and the beast*
  The Brambleberrys animal alphabet
  The Brambleberrys animal book of big and small shapes
  The Brambleberrys animal book of colors
  The Brambleberrys animal book of counting
  The little jewel box
Mayer, Mercer. *Appelard and Liverwurst*
  What do you do with a kangaroo?
Mayne, William. *Come, come to my corner*
Meade, Holly. *A place to sleep*
Meddaugh, Susan. *The best place*
Medearis, Angela Shelf. *Barry and Bennie*
Meeker, Clare Hodgson. *Who wakes rooster?*
Meeks, Esther K. *Friendly farm animals*
  Something new at the zoo
Meeuwissen, Tony. *Remarkable animals*
Mellor, Corinne. *Bruce the balding moose*
Melmed, Laura Krauss. *I love you as much . . .*
Mendoza, George. *Need a house? Call Ms. Mouse*
  Traffic jam
Meres, Jonathan. *The big bad rumor*
Merriam, Eve. *The birthday cow*
  Goodnight to Annie, ill. by Carol Schwartz
  What in the world?
  Where is everybody?
Metaxas, Eric. *The birthday ABC*
Meyer, Brigit. *Little Easter surprise*
Michels, Tilde. *Who's that knocking at my door?*
Michelson, Richard. *Animals that ought to be*
  Ten times better
Miklowitz, Gloria D. *The zoo that moved*
Miles, Elizabeth J. *Ears*
  Mouths and teeth
  Noses
  Wings, fins, and flippers
Miles, Miska. *Noisy gander*
  Sylvester Jones and the voice in the forest
Miller, David. *Just like you and me*
Miller, Edna. *Mousekin's Thanksgiving*
Miller, J. P. (John Parr). *Farmer John's animals*
Miller, Jane. *Farm noises*
  Seasons on the farm
Miller, Margaret. *I love colors*
Miller, Ruth. *I went to the bay*
  I went to the farm
Millhouse, Nicholas. *Blue-footed booby*
Minarik, Else Holmelund. *Am I beautiful?*
  The little girl and the dragon
Miranda, Anne. *Alphabet fiesta*
  Does a mouse have a house?
  To market, to market
Miryam. *The happy man and his dump truck*
Mitchell, Adrian. *Our mammoth*
  Twice my size
Mitter, Matt. *ABC: alphabet rhymes*
  Once upon a rhyme
  1, 2, 3, counting rhymes
Mitton, Tony. *Down by the cool of the pool*
Mizumura, Kazue. *If I were a cricket . . .*
Modesitt, Jeanne. *Lunch with Milly*
  The night call
  Vegetable soup
Moffatt, Judith. *Who stole the cookies?*
Mogensen, Jan. *Teddy's birthday bugle*
Mollel, Tololwa M. (Tololwa Marti). *Dume's roar*
  The king and the tortoise
  Rhinos for lunch and elephants for supper
  To dinner, for dinner
Moncure, Jane Belk. *Riddle me a riddle*
Monsell, Mary Elise. *Underwear!*
Montanari, Eva. *The crocodile's true colors*
Moon, Nicola. *At the beginning of a pig*
Moore, Elaine. *Grandma's house*
Moore, Eva. *Franklin and the baby*
Moore, John. *Granny Stickleback*
Moore, Karen Ann. *The baby king*
Mora, Emma. *Animals of the forest*

Mora, Pat. *Delicious hullabaloo = Pachanga deliciosa*
  Listen to the desert = Oye al desierto
  The race of toad and deer
  This big sky
Moran, Alex. *Boots for Beth*
  Come here, tiger
Morehead, Debby. *A special place for Charlee*
Moreton, Daniel. *La Cucaracha Martina*
Morgan, Michaela. *Edward gets a pet*
Morley, Carol. *Farmyard song*
Morozumi, Atsuko. *One gorilla*
Morpurgo, Michael. *Wombat goes walkabout*
Morris, Ann. *The animal book*
Morris, Johnny. *Animal-go-round*
Morris, Linda Lowe. *Morning milking*
Morrison, Sean. *Is that a happy hippopotamus?*
Morrow, Tara Jaye. *Mommy loves her baby; Daddy loves his baby*
Morse, Samuel French. *All in a suitcase*
Morton, Christine. *Picnic farm*
Moser, Erwin. *The crow in the snow and other bedtime stories*
Moser, Madeline. *Ever heard of an aardwolf?*
Moses, Amy. *At the zoo*
Moss, Miriam. *Bad hare day*
  This is the tree
Most, Bernard. *Catbirds and dogfish*
  Cock-a-doodle-moo!
  The cow that went oink
  Dinosaur cousins?
  Peek-a-moo!
  Row, row, row your goat
  Zoodles
Mother Goose. *Hey, diddle, diddle*, ill. by Linda Bronson
  Hey, diddle, diddle, ill. by Heather Collins
  Hey, diddle, diddle, ill. by Marilyn Janovitz
  Hey, diddle, diddle, ill. by Moira Kemp
  Hey, diddle, diddle, ill. by Marc Mongeau
  Hey, diddle, diddle, ill. by Nita Sowter
  Hey, diddle, diddle, ill. by Eleanor Wasmuth
  Hey, diddle, diddle picture book, ill. by Randolph Caldecott
  Hickory, dickory, dock, ill. by Suzanne Duranceau
  Pat-a-cake, ill. by Marilyn Janovitz
Mozelle, Shirley. *The pig is in the pantry, the cat is on the shelf*
Mudd-Ruth, Maria. *The ultimate ocean book*
Mullins, Edward S. *Animal limericks*
Munari, Bruno. *Animals for sale*
  Bruno Munari's zoo
  The elephant's wish
  Who's there? Open the door
Munsch, Robert N. *Alligator baby*
Munsterberg, Peggy. *Beastly banquet*
Murdocca, Sal (Salvatore). *Tuttle's shell*
Murdock, Laurette. *Someone is talking about Hortense*
Murphy, Mary. *How kind*
  Koala and the flower
  My puffer train
Murphy, Stuart J. *Animals on board*
Murray, Marjorie Dennis. *The stars are waiting*
Musicant, Elke. *The night vegetable eater*
Muth, Jon J. *The three questions*
Mwenye Hadithi. *Crafty chameleon*
  Lazy lion
  Tricky tortoise
My first book of baby animals
Myers, Bernice. *The flying shoes*
Myers, Walter Dean. *The story of the three kingdoms*
Nail, James T. *Whose tracks are these?*
Nakabayashi, Ei. *The rainy day puddle*
Nakamura, Katherine Riley. *Song of night*
Nakano, Hirotaka. *Elephant blue*
Nakatani, Chiyoko. *The zoo in my garden*
Narahashi, Keiko. *Is that Josie?*
Nash, Ogden. *Custard the dragon*
Nathan, Cheryl. *Bugs and beasties ABC*
  The long and short of it
Nayer, Judy. *Jungle life*
  Night animals
  Sea creatures

Naylor, Phyllis Reynolds. *The picnic*
Neidigh, Sherry. *Creatures at my feet*
Nelson, Robert Lyn. *Ocean friends*
Nerlove, Miriam. *I made a mistake*
Neugebauer, Charise. *Santa's gift*
Newcome, Zita. *Rosie goes exploring*
Newman, Jeff. *Reginald*
Newton, Patricia Montgomery. *The frog who drank the waters of the world*
Nichol, B. P. *Once, a lullaby*
Nichols, Grace. *Asana and the animals*
Nicholson, Nicholas B. A. *Little girl in a red dress with cat and dog*
Nikola-Lisa, W. *Can you top that?*
  No babies asleep
Nilsén, Anna. *Let's all hang and dangle*
  Where are Percy's friends?
  Where is Percy's dinner?
Nixon, Joan Lowery. *Gus and Gertie and the missing pearl*
Noble, Kate. *Bubble gum*
  Oh look, it's a nosserus
Noll, Sally. *Jiggle wiggle prance*
  Lucky morning
Norman, Charles. *The hornbean tree and other poems*
Norman, Philip Ross. *A mammoth imagination*
Novak, Matt. *Mr. Floop's lunch*
Numeroff, Laura Joffe. *The Chicken sisters*
  Chimps don't wear glasses
  The hope tree
  What grandmas do best; What grandpas do best
Nye, Naomi Shihab. *Lullaby raft*
Nygaard, Elizabeth. *Snake alley band*
Obligado, Lilian. *Faint frogs feeling feverish and other terrifically tantalizing tongue twisters*
O'Brien, Claire. *Sam's sneaker search*
O'Donnell, Elizabeth Lee. *Winter visitors*
O'Donnell, Peter. *Carnegie's excuse*
  Moonlit journey
Offen, Hilda. *As quiet as a mouse*
  A fox got my socks
  The sheep made a leap
Old MacDonald had a farm. *E I E I O*
  Old MacDonald, ill. by Rosemary Wells
  Old MacDonald had a farm, ill. by Holly Berry
  Old MacDonald had a farm, ill. by Lorinda Bryan Cauley
  Old MacDonald had a farm, ill. by Mel Crawford
  Old MacDonald had a farm, ill. by Tracey English
  Old MacDonald had a farm, ill. by David Frankland
  Old MacDonald had a farm, ill. by Abner Graboff
  Old MacDonald had a farm, ill. by Nancy Hellen
  Old MacDonald had a farm, ill. by Carol Jones
  Old MacDonald had a farm, ill. by Tracey Campbell Pearson
  Old MacDonald had a farm, ill. by Robert M. Quackenbush
  Old MacDonald had a farm, ill. by Glen Rounds
  Old McDonald had a farm, ill. by Iain Smith
  Old MacDonald had a farm, ill. by Jessica Souhami
  Old MacDonald had a farm, ill. by William Stobbs
  Old MacDonald had a farm, ill. by Prue Theobalds
Oppenheim, Joanne. *"Not now!" said the cow*
  "Uh-oh!" said the crow
  You can't catch me!
Oppenheim, Shulamith Levey. *What is the full moon full of?*
Oram, Hiawyn. *Badger's bad mood*
  Badger's bring something party
  Mole's moon
Ormerod, Jan. *If you're happy and you know it!*
  Joe can count
  Ms. MacDonald has a class
  When we went to the zoo
Ostheeren, Ingrid. *Jonathan Mouse, detective*
Otto, Carolyn. *What color is camouflage?*
Over in the grasslands
Over in the meadow, ill. by Paul Galdone
Over in the meadow, ill. by Ezra Jack Keats
Owen, Roy. *My night forest*
Oxenbury, Helen. *Friends*
  It's my birthday
  Monkey see, monkey do

  Pippo gets lost
  729 curious creatures
  729 merry mix-ups
Pack, Robert. *Then what did you do?*
Packard, Mary. *Same and different*
Pacovská, Kveta. *Flying*
Palatini, Margie. *Earthquack*
  Moo who?
Palazzo, Tony (Anthony D.). *Animal babies*
  Animals 'round the mulberry bush
Palazzo-Craig, Janet. *Little Danny Dinosaur*
Paley, Joan. *One more river*
Pallotta, Jerry. *The dory story*
  Underwater counting
Palmer, Mary Babcock. *No-sort-of-animal*
Paraskevas, Betty. *Junior Kroll and Company*
Paré, Roger. *Animal capers*
  Circus days
  Play time
  Summer days
Park, W. B. *Bakery business*
  The costume party
Parker, Nancy Winslow. *Working frog*
Parker, Victoria. *Bearum scarum*
Parnall, Peter. *Alfalfa Hill*
  Winter barn
Parsons, Alexandra. *Amazing mammals*
Partridge, Elizabeth. *Moon glowing*
Partridge, Jenny. *Colonel Grunt*
  Grandma Snuffles
  Hopfellow
  Mr. Squint
  Peterkin Pollensnuff
Paschkis, Julie. *So happy/So sad*
Patent, Dorothy Hinshaw. *Bold and bright, black-and-white animals*
Paterson, Bettina. *My first wild animals*
Paterson, Brian. *Zigby camps out*
Paterson, Diane. *If I were a toad*
Patterson, Elizabeth Burman. *Whose eyes are these?*
Patterson, Geoffrey. *The lion and the gypsy*
Paul, Jan S. *Hortense*
Paul, Korky. *Winnie in winter*
Paxton, Tom. *Belling the cat and other Æsop fables*
  Going to the zoo
Payne, Joan Balfour. *The stable that stayed*
Peaceable kingdom
Peaceful moments in the wild: animals and their homes
Pearce, Q. L. *In the African grasslands*
  In the desert
Pearson, Tracey Campbell. *Bob*
Peek, Merle. *The balancing act*
  Mary wore her red dress and Henry wore his green sneakers
Peet, Bill (William Bartlett). *The ant and the elephant*
  Cock-a-doodle Dudley
  Farewell to Shady Glade
  The gnats of knotty pine
  No such things
Pelham, David. *A is for animals*
  Crawlies creep
  Worms wiggle
Peppé, Rodney. *Little circus*
Percy, Graham. *24 strange little animals in a haunted house*
A pet for me
Peters, Lisa Westberg. *The hayloft*
Peters, Sharon. *Animals at night*
Peterson, Esther Allen. *Frederick's alligator*
Peterson, Stephanie True. *Where do the animals live?*
Pevear, Richard. *Mister Cat-and-a-Half*
Peyo. *The Smurfs and their woodland friends*
Pfister, Marcus. *Hopper hunts for spring*
  How Leo learned to be king
  Just the way you are
Phillips, Mildred. *And the cow said, "moo"!*
Piatti, Celestino. *Celestino Piatti's animal ABC*
Pieńkowski, Jan. *Farm*
  Homes
  Pizza!

Zoo
Piers, Helen. *Is there room on the bus?*
  Who's in my bed?
Pilkey, Dav. *The Moonglow Roll-O-Rama*
Pinkney, Jerry. *Noah's ark*
Pinkwater, Daniel Manus. *Rainy morning*
Pirotta, Saviour. *Little bird*
Pitcher, Caroline. *Animals*
  Are you spring?
Pittman, Helena Clare. *Once when I was scared*
Piven, Hanokh. *The perfect purple feather*
Pizer, Abigail. *It's a perfect day*
Plante, Patricia. *The turtle and the two ducks*
Please, Mr. Crocodile!
Pluckrose, Henry Arthur. *Fur and feathers*
  Paws and claws
  Skin, shell and scale
Pomerantz, Charlotte. *The birthday letters*
Poole, Valerie. *Obadiah Coffee and the music contest*
Porter, Sue. *One potato*
Porter-Gaylord, Laurel. *I love my daddy because . . .*
  I love my mommy because . . .
Potter, Beatrix. *Appley Dapply's nursery rhymes*
  Cecily Parsley's nursery rhymes
  Ginger and Pickles
  More tales from Beatrix Potter
  Peter Rabbit's ABC
  The tale of Jemima Puddle-Duck and other farmyard tales
  The tale of Peter Rabbit and other stories
  A treasury of Peter Rabbit and other stories
  Yours affectionately, Peter Rabbit
Pouyanne, Rési. *What I see hidden by the pond*
Pow, Tom. *Who is the world for?*
Powell, Consie. *A bold carnivore*
Powell, Jillian. *Jumpers*
Powzyk, Joyce Ann. *Tasmania*
Prater, John. *On top of the world*
Pratt, Kristin Joy. *A fly in the sky*
Pratt, Pierre. *Car*
  Park
Prelutsky, Jack. *Beneath a blue umbrella*
  The pack rat's day and other poems
Price, Kathy (Kathy Z.). *The Bourbon Street musicians*
Price, Mathew. *Do you see what I see?*
  Don't worry, Alfie
Price-Thomas, Brian. *The magic ark*
Provensen, Alice. *Our animal friends at Maple Hill Farm*
  The year at Maple Hill Farm
Pryor, Bonnie. *Greenbrook farm*
The pudgy book of farm animals
Purcell, John Wallace. *African animals*
Puttock, Simon. *Big bad wolf is good*
Quackenbush, Robert M. *Pete Pack Rat*
Raatma, Lucia. *Veterinarians*
Rankin, Joan. *First day*
  You're somebody special, Walliwigs!
Raschka, Christopher. *Moosey Moose*
Raskin, Ellen. *And it rained*
  Who, said Sue, said whoo?
Rathmann, Peggy. *Good night, Gorilla*
Rauzon, Mark J. *Eyes and ears*
  Feet, flippers, hooves, and hands
Rayner, Shoo. *My first picture joke book*
Reasoner, Charles. *Who drives this?*
Rechner, Amy. *Out and about at the aquarium*
Reddix, Valerie. *Millie and the mudhole*
Reeves, Mona Rabun. *I had a cat*
Reider, Katja. *The big little sneeze*
  Snail started it!
Reidy, Hannah. *Crazy creature contrasts*
Reinhart, Matthew. *Animal popposites*
Reiser, Lynn. *Little clam*
  Night thunder and the Queen of the Wild Horses
Rex, Michael. *Who digs?*
Rey, H. A. (Hans Augusto). *Tit for tat*
  Where's my baby?
Rey, Margret (Margret Elisabeth Waldstein). *Billy's picture*

Whiteblack the penguin sees the world
Rice, Eve. *Sam who never forgets*
Rich, Scharlotte. *Who made the wild woods?*
Richards, Jean. *How the elephant got his trunk*
Richardson, John. *Ten bears in a bed*
Richter, Mischa. *Quack?*
Riddell, Chris. *Bird's new shoes*
Riddle, Tohby. *The great escape from City Zoo*
Riley, Linda Capus. *Elephants swim*
Robbins, Beth. *Tom's first day at school*
  Tom's new haircut
Roberts, Bethany. *Birthday mice*
  Valentine mice!
Robinson, Irene Bowen. *Picture book of animal babies*
Robinson, W. W. (William Wilcox). *On the farm*
Rockwell, Anne F. *Big bad goat*
  Chip and the karate kick
  The good llama
  Honk honk!
  Katie Catz makes a splash
  Morgan plays soccer
  Poor Goose
  Root-a-toot-toot
Roddie, Shen. *Animal stew*
Roe, Richard. *Animal ABC*
Roffey, Maureen. *I spy at the zoo*
Rogers, Paul (Patrick). *Quacky Duck*
Rojankovsky, Feodor. *Animals in the zoo*
  Animals on the farm
  The great big animal book
  The great big wild animal book
Root, Barry. *Gumbrella*
Root, Phyllis. *Moon tiger*
  One duck stuck
  One duck stuck [board book]
  One windy Wednesday
Roscoe, William. *The butterfly's ball and the grasshopper's feast*
Rose, Anne K. *Spider in the sky*
Rose, Deborah Lee. *Birthday zoo*
  Into the A, B, sea
Rose, Gerald. *Trouble in the ark*
Rosen, Michael (1946–). *How the animals got their colors*
  Little rabbit Foo Foo
Rosen, Michael J. (1954–). *All eyes on the pond*
  With a dog like that, a kid like me . . .
Rosenberg, Liz. *A big and little alphabet*
Rosenberry, Vera. *Who is in the garden?*
Ross, Eileen. *The Halloween showdown*
Roth, Carol. *The little school bus*
Rotner, Shelley. *Pick a pet*
Roughsey, Dick. *The giant devil-dingo*
Rouillard, Wendy. *Barnaby's bunny*
Rounds, Glen. *Washday on Noah's ark*
Rovetch, Lissa. *Crocs in shirts, hippos in skirts*
Rowan, James P. *I can be a zoo keeper*
Rowe, Jeannette. *Whose ears?*
  Whose feet?
  Whose nose?
Rowe, John A. *Jasper the terror*
  Smudge
Rowinski, Kate. *L. L. Bear's island adventure*
Royston, Angela. *Baby animals*
  Jungle animals
  Night-time animals
  Sea animals
  Small animals
Rumford, James. *Nine animals and the well*
Runcie, Jill. *Cock-a-doodle-doo*
Rupprecht, Siegfried P. *The tale of the vanishing rainbow*
Ruschak, Lynette. *The counting zoo*
Rusling, Albert. *The mouse and Mrs. Proudfoot*
Russell, Solveig Paulson. *What good is a tail?*
Rutherford, Meg. *Animal poems*
Ruurs, Margriet. *Animal alphabet*
  Emma's cold day
  A mountain alphabet
Ryan, Pam Muñoz. *Armadillos sleep in dugouts*

Ryder, Joanne. *Big bear ball*
  Each living thing
  A fawn in the grass
  Fog in the meadow
  A house by the sea
  The night flight
Rylant, Cynthia. *Night in the country*
Sabuda, Robert James. *The movable Mother Goose*
Sadler, Marilyn. *Elizabeth, Larry, and Ed*
Sage, Angie. *Monkeys in the jungle*
Saleh, Harold J. *Even tiny ants must sleep*
Salley, Coleen. *Epossumondas*
Samton, Sheila White. *Ten tiny monsters*
San Diego Zoological Society. *Families*
  A visit to the zoo
Sandberg, Inger. *Nicholas' favorite pet*
San Souci, Robert D. *Two bear cubs*
Santore, Charles. *A stowaway on Noah's Ark*
Sasso, Sandy Eisenberg. *A prayer for the earth*
Saunders, Dave. *Snowtime*
  So slow!
Savage, Stephen. *Making tracks*
Sayre, April Pulley. *Dig, wait, listen*
  Home at last
  If you should hear a honey guide
  Splish! splash! animal baths
Scarry, Richard. *Is this the house of Mistress Mouse?*
  Pie rats ahoy!
  Richard Scarry's all around Busytown
  Richard Scarry's animal nursery tales
  Richard Scarry's great big mystery book
  Richard Scarry's Mr. Frumble's biggest hat flap book ever
  Richard Scarry's mix or match storybook
  Richard Scarry's Postman Pig and his busy neighbors
Schaefer, Carole Lexa. *Down in the woods at sleepytime*
  Down in the woods at sleepytime [board book]
Schaefer, Jackie Jasina. *Miranda's day to dance*
Scharer, Niko. *Emily's house*
Schatz, Letta. *The extraordinary tug-of-war*
Scheidl, Gerda Marie. *Can we help you, Saint Nicholas?*
Schertle, Alice. *Advice for a frog and other poems*
Schick, Eleanor. *A surprise in the forest*
Schimmel, Schim. *The family of earth*
Schindel, John. *What did they see?*
Schindler, Regina. *The bear's cave*
Schlein, Miriam. *Hello, hello!*
  Sleep safe, little whale
Schmid, Eleonore. *Farm animals*
Schofield, Jennifer. *Animal babies in grasslands*
  Animal babies in polar lands
  Animal babies in ponds and rivers
  Animal babies in rain forests
Schomp, Virginia. *If you were a . . . veterinarian*
  If you were a . . . zookeeper
Schongut, Emanuel. *Look kitten*
Schrecker, Judie. *Santa's new reindeer*
Schubert, Ingrid. *There's always room for one more*
Schulman, Janet. *Countdown to spring*
Schultz, Sam. *Animal antics: the beast jokes ever*
Schumacher, Claire. *King of the zoo*
  Nutty's birthday
  Tim and Jim
Schumaker, Ward. *Dance!*
Schwartz, David M. *If you hopped like a frog*
Schwartz, Roslyn. *The mole sisters and the cool breeze*
  The mole sisters and the question
Schweitzer, Iris. *Hilda's restful chair*
Scruton, Clive. *Mary's pets*
Seignobosc, Françoise. *The big rain*
  The story of Colette
Selberg, Ingrid. *Nature's hidden world*
Selkowe, Valrie M. *Happy birthday to me!*
  Spring green
Selsam, Millicent E. *All kinds of babies*
  A first look at kangaroos, koalas and other animals with pouches
  A first look at seashells
  Hidden animals

How to be a nature detective
  Keep looking!
  Night animals
Sendak, Maurice. *Very far away*
Sensel, Joni. *Bears barge in*
Seuling, Barbara. *Spring song*
  Winter lullaby
Seuss, Dr. *Mr. Brown can moo! Can you?*
  Would you rather be a bullfrog?
Severn, Jeffrey. *George and his giant shadow*
Sewall, Marcia. *Animal song*
Seymour, Peter S. *Animals in disguise*
Seymour, Tres. *I love my buzzard*
Shannon, David. *Duck on a bike*
Shapiro, Arnold L. *Who says that?*
Sharmat, Marjorie Weinman. *Bartholomew the bossy*
  Taking care of Melvin
  The 329th friend
  Walter the wolf
Sharratt, Nick. *Shark in the park*
Shea, Kitty. *Out and about at the vet clinic*
Sheppard, Jeff. *Splash, splash*
Shields, Carol Diggory. *Colors*
  Homes
  On the go
  Patterns
Short, Mayo. *Andy and the wild ducks*
Showers, Paul. *Sleep is for everyone*
Sidman, Joyce. *Just us two*
  Son of the water boatman
Sierra, Judy. *Preschool to the rescue*
  There's a zoo in room 22
  Wild about books
Sill, Cathryn P. *About mammals*
Simmons, Jane. *Daisy and the Beastie*
  Daisy says Coo!
  Daisy's favorite things
  Daisy's hide-and-seek
  Little Fern's first winter
Simon, Carly. *Midnight farm*
Simon, Francesca. *But what does the hippopotamus say?*
Simon, Mina Lewiton. *If you were an eel, how would you feel?*
Simon, Paul. *At the zoo*
Simon, Seymour. *Animal fact – animal fable*
Simple gifts
Singer, Isaac Bashevis. *Why Noah chose the dove*
Singer, Marilyn. *Creature carnival*
  Fred's bed
  Quiet night
  Turtle in July
Siomades, Lorianne. *Cuckoo can't find you*
  Kangaroo and cricket
  My box of color
Siracusa, Catherine. *No mail for Mitchell*
Skaar, Grace Marion. *What do the animals say?*
Skofield, James. *Crow moon, worm moon*
Skorpen, Liesel Moak. *All the Lassies*
Slate, Joseph. *Little Porcupine's Christmas*
  Miss Bindergarten celebrates the 100th day of kindergarten
  Miss Bindergarten gets ready for kindergarten
  Miss Bindergarten stays home from kindergarten
  Miss Bindergarten takes a field trip with kindergarten
  Who is coming to our house?
Slingsby, Janet. *Hush-a-bye babies*
Sloat, Teri. *Farmer Brown goes round and round*
  Pieces of Christmas
  Rib-ticklers
  There was an old lady who swallowed a trout
  The thing that bothered Farmer Brown
Slobodkin, Louis. *Friendly animals*
  Melvin, the moose child
  Our friendly friends
Slobodkina, Esphyr. *The wonderful feast*
Small, David. *George Washington's cows*
  Imogene's antlers
Smath, Jerry. *The animals' Christmas carol*
Smith, Donald. *Who's wearing my baseball cap?*

Tolstoy, Aleksey Nikolayevich. *The enormous turnip*
   The great big enormous turnip
Tomkins, Jasper. *The catalog*
Tomlinson, Jill. *The owl who was afraid of the dark*
Tompert, Ann. *The hungry black bag*
Trapani, Iza. *Baa baa black sheep*
   Baa baa black sheep [board book]
   Row, row, row your boat
   What am I?
Tresselt, Alvin R. *The mitten*
   Wake up, farm!, ill. by author
   Wake up, farm!, ill. by Carolyn Ewing
Trinca, Rod. *One woolly wombat*
Tripp, Valerie. *Happy, happy Mother's Day*
Trottier, Maxine. *Dreamstones*
Troughton, Joanna. *Make-believe tales*
   Mouse-Deer's market
Tryon, Leslie. *Albert's birthday*
   Albert's Christmas
   Albert's Halloween
   Albert's play
   Patsy says
Tudor, Tasha. *A tale for Easter*
Tufts, Mary L. *The wee kitten who sucked her thumb*
Tulloch, Shirley. *Who made me?*
Turnbull, Ann. *Too tired*
Turner, Ann Warren. *Let's be animals*
Turner, Gwenda. *Over on the farm*
Twinem, Neecy. *Changing colors*
   High in the trees
   In the air
Tworkov, Jack. *The camel who took a walk*
Tyers, Jenny. *When it is night and when it is day*
Udry, Janice May. *Is Susan here?*, ill. by Peter Edwards
   Is Susan here?, ill. by Karen Gundersheimer
Ueno, Noriko. *Elephant buttons*
Underhill, Liz. *The lucky coin*
Unwin, Pippa. *The great zoo hunt!*
Upper, Jonathan. *Spin's really wild Africa tour*
Upton, Pat. *Who lives in the woods?*
Uribe, Verónica. *Buzz buzz buzz*
Vagin, Vladimir Vasilévich. *The enormous carrot*
Vail, Rachel. *Over the moon*
Van Caster, Nancy. *An alligator lives in Benjamin's house*
Van Eerbeek. *The world of farm animals*
   The world of wild animals
Van Fleet, Matthew. *Fuzzy yellow ducklings*
   One yellow lion
   Spotted yellow frogs
Van Kampen, Vlasta. *It couldn't be worse*
Van Laan, Nancy. *The big fat worm*
   Little Fish lost
   Moose tales
   A mouse in my house
   Sleep, sleep, sleep
   This is the hat
   A tree for me
   When winter comes
Van Vorst, M. L. *A Norse lullaby*
Van Woerkom, Dorothy. *The rat, the ox and the zodiac*
Varga, Judy. *The monster behind Black Rock*
Vaughan, Marcia Kapok. *The lemonade stand*
   Snap!
   Whistling Dixie
   Wombat stew
Velthuijs, Max. *Frog and the birdsong*
   Frog is a hero
   Frog is frightened
Venino, Suzanne. *Animals helping people*
Verboven, Agnes. *Ducks like to swim*
VerDorn, Bethea. *Day breaks*
   Moon glows
Vevers, Gwynne. *Animal homes*
   Animal parents
   Animals of the dark
   Animals that store food
   Animals that travel

Vigna, Judith. *Couldn't we have a turtle instead?*
Villarejo, Mary. *The tiger hunt*
A visit to a pond
Voce, Louise. *Over in the meadow*
Von Königslöw, Andrea Wayne. *Bing and Chutney off to Moosonee*
   Bing finds Chutney
   Would you love me?
Vozar, David. *M. C. Turtle and the hip hop hare*
Vrombaut, An. *Clarabella's teeth*
Vulliamy, Clara. *Yum yum*
Waber, Bernard. *Bearsie Bear and the surprise sleepover party*
   Fast food! gulp! gulp!
   "You look ridiculous," said the rhinoceros to the hippopotamus
Waddell, Martin. *Farmer Duck*
   The happy hedgehog band
   The pig in the pond
   Webster J. Duck
Wadsworth, Ginger. *One tiger growls*
Wagner, Karen. *Silly Fred*
Wahl, Jan. *Pleasant Fieldmouse*
   Pleasant Fieldmouse's Halloween party
   The sleepytime book
Waldron, Kathleen Cook. *Rough day at Loon Lake*
Walker, Sally M. *Seahorse reef*
Wallace, Ivy. *Pookie*
   Pookie believes in Santa Claus
   Pookie puts the world right
Wallace, John. *Building a house with Mr. Bumble*
Wallace, Karen. *A bed for winter*
Wallen, Ila. *The moon in my room*
Wallis, Diz. *Battle of the beasts*
Wallner, Alexandra. *Beatrix Potter*
Wallner, John C. *Old MacDonald had a farm*
Wallwork, Amanda. *Find the fish that looks like this*
Walsh, Ellen Stoll. *Pip's magic*
Walsh, Jill Paton. *Pepi and the secret names*
Walsh, Melanie. *Do donkeys dance?*
   Do monkeys tweet?
Walter, Virginia. *"Hi, pizza man!"*
Walton, Rick. *Little dogs say "Rough!"*
   Noah's square dance
Ward, Helen. *Old shell, new shell*
   The tin forest
Ward, Lynd. *Nic of the woods*
Ward, Nanda Weedon. *The black sombrero*
   The elephant that ga-lumped
Ward, Nick. *Farmer George and the fieldmice*
   Farmer George and the hungry guests
   Farmer George and the lost chick
Wardlaw, Lee. *The chair where bear sits*
Warrick, Karen Clemens. *If I had a tail*
   Who needs that nose?
Watkins, Hope (Brister). *The cunning fox and other tales*
Watts, Barrie. *Bird's nest*
Watts, Bernadette. *Harvey Hare's Christmas*
Webb, Clifford. *The story of Noah*
Weeks, Sarah. *Crocodile smile*
   My somebody special
   Splish splash
Wegen, Ron. *Where can the animals go?*
Weigelt, Udo. *Bear's last journey*
   Old Beaver
   Who stole the gold?
Weil, Ann. *Animal families*
Weird pet poems
Weiss, Nicki. *Dog boy cap skate*
   Where does the brown bear go?
   Where does the brown bear go? [board book]
Welber, Robert. *Goodbye, hello*
Welch, Willy. *Dancing with Daddy*
Welling, Peter J. *Shawn O'Hisser, the last snake in Ireland*
Wellington, Monica. *Bunny's first snowflake*
   Bunny's rainbow day
Wells, Rosemary. *The germ busters*
   Hazel's amazing mother
   My kindergarten
   The school play

Weninger, Brigitte. *The elf's hat*
   Merry Christmas, Davy!
West, Colin. *Go tell it to the toucan*
   I brought my love a tabby cat
   One day in the jungle
   "Pardon?" said the giraffe
West, Judy. *Have you got my purr?*
Westcott, Nadine Bernard. *There's a hole in the bucket*
Whippo, Walt. *Little white duck*
White, Kathryn (Kathryn Ivy). *Nutty nut chase*
Whitehouse, Patricia. *What's awake? A B C*
   What's awake? 1 2 3
Whitfield, Susan. *The animals of the Chinese zodiac*
Whitney, Dorothy B. *Creatures of an exceptional kind*
Whittaker, Nicola. *Feet*
   Hair
   Noses
   Tails
Whybrow, Ian. *Good night, monster*
   Parcel for Stanley
   Quacky quack-quack!
Wick, Walter. *Can you see what I see? Cool collections*
   Can you see what I see? Seymour and the juice box boat
Wiesmüller, Dieter. *In the blink of an eye*
Wiesner, William. *Noah's ark*
Wild, Margaret. *Nighty night*
Wilds, Kazumi Inose. *Hajime in the North Woods*
Wildsmith, Brian. *Animal games*
   Animal homes
   Animal shapes
   Animal tricks
   Goat's trail
   Professor Noah's spaceship
   Python's party
   What the moon saw
   Wild animals
Wilkes, Angela. *Rain forest animals*
Willard, Nancy. *The voyage of the Ludgate Hill*
Willey, Margaret. *Clever Beatrice and the best little pony*
Williams, Garth. *The big golden animal ABC*
Williams, Jenny (Jennifer). *Ride a cockhorse*
Williams, Linda. *Horse in the pigpen*
Williams, Sue. *I went walking*
   I went walking [board book]
   Let's go visiting
Williams, Suzanne. *Old MacDonald in the city*
Willis, Jeanne. *Be gentle, Python!*
   The boy who lost his bellybutton
   No biting, Puma!
   Sloth's shoes
   Take turns, Penguin!
Wilner, Isabel. *A garden alphabet*
Wilson, Anna. *Over in the grasslands*
Wilson, Anne. *Noah's ark*
Wilson, Karma. *Bear stays up for Christmas*
Wilson, Sarah. *Love and kisses*
Winch, Madeleine. *Come by chance*
Windham, Sophie. *Noah's ark*
Winnick, Karen B. *Barn sneeze*
Winter, Jeanette. *The girl and the moon man*
Winter, Rick. *Dirty birdy feet*
Winters, Kay. *Wolf watch*
Wiseman, Bernard. *Doctor Duck and Nurse Swan*
   Little new kangaroo
   Tails are not for painting
Witte, Anna. *The parrot Tico Tango*
Wojtowycz, David. *Animal antics from 1 to 10*
   David Wojtowycz presents Animal ABC
   Dudley's birthday party
Wolcott, Patty. *Eeeeeek!*
Wolf, Jake. *Daddy, could I have an elephant?*
Wolfe, Art. *1, 2, 3 moose*
Wolfe, Frances. *It is the wind*
Wolff, Ashley. *A year of beasts*
Wolkstein, Diane. *Little Mouse's painting*
Wood, A. J. *Amazing animals*
Wood, Audrey. *Little Penguin's tale*

   The napping house
   The napping house wakes up
   Silly Sally
Wood, Douglas. *Old Turtle*
Wood, Jacqueline. *Never say boo to a goose!*
Wood, Jakki. *Across the big blue sea*
   Dads are such fun
   Fiddle-i-fee
   Moo moo, brown cow
Wood, Jenny. *The animal kingdom*
   I wonder why kangaroos have pouches and other questions about baby animals
Wood, John Norris. *Jungles*
Woolf, Virginia. *Nurse Lugton's curtain*
Wormell, Christopher. *Blue Rabbit and friends*
   Blue Rabbit and the runaway wheel
   The new alphabet of animals
   Puff, puff, chugga-chugga
Wormell, Mary. *Bernard the angry rooster*
   Hilda Hen's happy birthday
   Why not?
Worthington, Phoebe. *Teddy bear farmer*
Worthy, Judith. *Eyes*
Wright-Frierson, Virginia. *An island scrapbook*
Wundrow, Deanna. *Jungle drum*
Wyler, Rose. *Puddles and ponds*
Wyllie, Stephen. *The great race*
   Snappity snap
Yabuuchi, Masayuki. *Animals sleeping*
   Whose baby?
   Whose footprints?
Yaccarino, Dan. *Deep in the jungle*
   Five little ducks
   An octopus followed me home
   So big
Yee, Wong Herbert. *Eek! There's a mouse in the house*
   Fireman Small
   Fireman Small, fire down below
   Fireman Small to the rescue
   Hamburger Heaven
   Mrs. Brown went to town
   The Officers' Ball
   A small Christmas
Yen, Clara. *Why rat comes first*
Yep, Laurence. *Tiger woman*
Ylla. *Animal babies*
Yolen, Jane. *Animal train*
   Dragon night and other lullabies
   How beastly!
   An invitation to the butterfly ball
   Jane Yolen's Old MacDonald songbook
   Nocturne
   Picnic with Piggins
   Piggins
   Welcome to the icehouse
   Welcome to the river of grass
   Welcome to the sea of sand
Yoon, Salina. *Wild animals*
Yorinks, Arthur. *Quack!*
Yoshi. *Who's hiding here?*
Yoshida, Toshi. *Elephant crossing*
   Rhinoceros mother
Young animals in the zoo
Young domestic animals
Young, Ruth. *Who says moo?*
Youngs, Betty Ferrell. *One panda*
   Pink pigs in mud
Zabar, Abbie. *Fifty-five friends*
Zadrzynska, Ewa. *The peaceable kingdom*
Zalben, Jane Breskin. *Basil and Hillary*
   Norton's nighttime
Ziefert, Harriet. *All clean!*
   All gone!
   Animal music
   Animals of the Bible
   Baby Ben's bow-wow book
   Cock-a-doodle-doo!

Cow in the house
Dancing
Egad, alligator!
Happy birthday, Grandpa!
I swapped my dog
Listen! Piggety Pig
Oh, what a noisy farm!
On our way to the barn
On our way to the zoo
A polar bear can swim
Run! Run!
The turnip
What do ducks dream?
Zoehfeld, Kathleen Weidner. *What lives in a shell?*
What's alive?
Zoll, Max Alfred. *Animal babies*
Zolotow, Charlotte (Shapiro). *The sleepy book,* ill. by Vladimir Bobri
The sleepy book, ill. by Ilse Plume
Wake up and goodnight
Zoo animals [board book]
Zoo animals
Zweifel, Frances W. *Animal baby-sitters*

Animals – aardvarks

Brown, Marc Tolon. *Arthur babysits*
Arthur goes to school
Arthur lost and found
Arthur meets the president
Arthur tricks the tooth fairy
Arthur writes a story
Arthur's animal adventure
Arthur's baby
Arthur's birthday
Arthur's chicken pox
Arthur's computer disaster
Arthur's family vacation
Arthur's first sleepover
Arthur's neighborhood
Arthur's new puppy
Arthur's new puppy [board book]
Arthur's nose
Arthur's perfect Christmas
Arthur's pet business
Arthur's really helpful word book
Arthur's spookiest Halloween
Arthur's teacher moves in
Arthur's TV trouble
Arthur's underwear
D. W., go to your room!
D. W. rides again!
D. W., the picky eater
D. W. thinks big [board book]
D. W.'s library card
D. W.'s lost blankie
Glasses for D. W.
Marc Brown's Boat book
The true Francine
Caple, Kathy. *Inspector Aardvark and the perfect cake*
Higham, Jon Atlas. *Aardvark's picnic*
Kellogg, Steven (Stephen). *Aster Aardvark's alphabet adventures*
Lindbergh, Reeve. *The awful aardvarks go to school*
The awful aardvarks shop for school
Moodie, Fiona. *Noko and the night monster*
Mwalimu. *Awful aardvark*
Schaffer, Libor. *Arthur sets sail*
Sloat, Teri. *Hark! The aardvark angels sing*

Animals – anteaters

Binnamin, Vivian. *The case of the anteater's missing lunch*
Brown, Marc Tolon. *D. W. all wet*
D. W. flips!
Hall, Malcolm. *The friends of Charlie Ant Bear*
Hellard, Susan. *Eleanor and the babysitter*
Waber, Bernard. *An anteater named Arthur*

Animals – antelopes

Jensen, Patricia. *Be careful, Little Antelope*
Lacapa, Michael. *Antelope Woman*

Animals – apes *see* Animals – baboons; Animals – chimpanzees; Animals – gorillas; Animals – monkeys

Animals – armadillos

Allard, Harry. *The cactus flower bakery*
Arnosky, Jim. *Armadillo's orange*
Beifuss, John. *Armadillo Ray*
Brett, Jan. *Armadillo rodeo*
Cherry, Lynne. *The armadillo from Amarillo*
David, Lawrence. *The land of the hungry armadillos*
Ketteman, Helen. *Armadillo tattletale*
Armadilly chili
Kipling, Rudyard. *The beginning of the armadillos,* ill. by Lorinda Bryan Cauley
The beginning of the armadillos, ill. by Charles Keeping
Lewis, Rob. *Aunt Armadillo*
Monsell, Mary Elise. *Armadillo*
Patton, Don. *Armadillos*
Radunsky, Vladimir. *One*
Ten
Saunders, Susan. *Charles Rat's picnic*
Simon, Sidney B. *The armadillo who had no shell*
Singer, Marilyn. *Archer Armadillo's secret room*

Animals – babies

Abercrombie, Barbara. *Bad dog, Dodger*
Alexander, Martha G. *When the new baby comes, I'm moving out*
Aliki. *At Mary Bloom's*
Arbeit, Eleanor Werner. *Mrs. Cat hides something*
Arnold, Caroline. *Mother and baby zoo animals*
Asch, Frank. *Baby Bird's first nest*
Ashman, Linda. *Babies on the go*
Baby animals
Bauer, Marion Dane. *If you were born a kitten*
Blake, Quentin. *Zagazoo*
Blomgren, Jennifer. *Where do I sleep?*
Brandenberg, Franz. *Aunt Nina and her nephews and nieces*
Brenner, Barbara A. *What the elephant told*
Brown, Andrew. *Baby animals*
Brown, Craig McFarland. *In the spring*
Bruzzone, Catherine. *Puppy finds a friend = Cachorrito encuentra un amigo*
Puppy finds a friend = Le petit chien se trouve un ami
Bunting, Eve (Anne Evelyn). *Sing a song of piglets*
Burton, Jane. *Caper the kid*
Dizzie the pony
Fancy the fox
Ginger the kitten
Gipper the guinea pig
Hoppy the toad
Jack the puppy
Pacer, the pony
Surfer the seal
Butler, John. *Hush, little ones*
Pi-shu, the little panda
Whose baby am I?
Calmenson, Stephanie. *Kinderkittens, who took the cookie from the cookie jar?*
Perfect puppy
Capucilli, Alyssa Satin. *Biscuit wants to play*
Biscuit's new trick
Biscuit's Valentine's Day
Cartlidge, Michelle. *Baby mice at home*
Castle, Caroline. *Naughty!*
Chwast, Seymour. *Harry, I need you!*
Traffic jam
Clements, Andrew. *Slippers at home*
Coats, Lucy. *One hungry baby*
Cole, Babette. *Lady Lupin's book of etiquette*
Cole, Joanna. *A calf is born*

Collard, Sneed B. *Leaving home*
Costello, Emily. *Realm of the panther*
Coxe, Molly. *Big egg*
Darling, Kathy (Mary Kathleen). *Desert babies*
Davis, Kate (1951–). *Barnyard babies*
Deady, Kathleen W. *It's time!*
Doepker, David. *Animal babies*
　　Farm babies
Donohue, Dorothy. *Big and little on the farm*
Dowson, Nick. *Tigress*
Doyle, Malachy. *Baby see, baby do!*
Edwards, Nicola. *Goodnight Baxter*
Edwards, Pamela Duncan. *Wake-up kisses*
Falconer, Ian. *Olivia counts*
　　Olivia's opposites
Fearnley, Jan. *Just like you*
Fisher, Aileen Lucia. *You don't look like your mother*
Fleming, Denise. *Mama cat has three kittens*
Fraggalosch, Audrey. *Trails above the tree line*
Fraser, Mary Ann. *How animal babies stay safe*
French, Vivian. *Growing frogs*
Friedman, Mel. *Kitten castle*
Fuchshuber, Annegert. *Two peas in a pod*
Gentle, Victor. *Baby sharks*
George, Jean Craighead. *Look to the north*
Godwin, Laura. *What the baby hears*
Goode, Molly. *Mama loves*
Goodhart, Pippa. *Pudgy, a puppy to love*
Gréban, Quentin. *Nestor*
Grindley, Sally. *Little Elephant Thunderfoot*
　　Polar Star
Gulbis, Stephen. *Cowgirl Rosie and her five baby bison*
Halls, Kelly Milner. *I bought a baby chicken*
Hamsa, Bobbie. *Animal babies*
Hellard, Susan. *Baby lemur*
Henkes, Kevin. *Kitten's first full moon*
Henley, Claire. *I'm a baby, too!*
Herman, Gail. *Lucky goes to school*
Hewett, Joan. *A flamingo chick grows up*
　　A giraffe calf grows up
　　A harbor seal pup grows up
　　A kangaroo joey grows up
　　A koala joey grows up
　　A monkey baby grows up
　　A penguin chick grows up
　　A tiger cub grows up
Hillenbrand, Will. *Down by the station*
Hindley, Judy. *The best thing about a puppy*
Hirschi, Ron. *A time for babies*
Howe, James. *Pinky and Rex and the just-right pet*
Hutchins, H. J. (Hazel J.). *One dark night*
James, Betsy. *Tadpoles*
Jensen, Patricia. *Be patient, Little Chick*
Johnson, Paul Brett. *The goose who went off in a huff*
Jonovitz, Marilyn. *Maybe, my baby*
Kaizuki, Kiyonori. *A calf is born*
Kessler, Cristina. *Jubela*
Kopper, Lisa. *Daisy is a mommy*
　　Daisy knows best
　　Good dog, Daisy
　　I'm a baby, you're a baby
Kroll, Virginia L. *Motherlove*
Kuiper, Nannie. *Bailey the bear cub*
Kunhardt, Katharine. *Let's count the puppies*
Labatt, Mary. *Pizza for Sam*
Landa, Norbert. *Cubs*
　　Kittens
　　Puppies
Lang, Aubrey. *The adventures of Baby Bear*
　　Baby elephant
　　Baby fox
　　Baby lion
　　Baby penguin
Lawrence, John. *This little chick*
Lewis, Kim. *Just like Floss*
　　Little Baa
　　Little calf

Little lamb
Little puppy
Lilly, Kenneth. *Baby animals*
Llewellyn, Claire. *Crocodile*
　　Duck
London, Jonathan. *Baby whale's journey*
　　Snuggle wuggle
Lunsford, Annie. *What will I become?*
McCurry, Kristen. *Ocean babies*
　　Safari babies
MacDonald, Elizabeth. *Dilly-Dally and the nine secrets*
McGeorge, Constance W. *Boomer's big surprise*
Macken, JoAnn Early. *Kittens*
　　Puppies
McLellan, Stephanie Simpson. *The chicken cat*
McMullan, Kate (Hall). *If you were my bunny*
　　Supercat
McQuade, Jacqueline. *Big babies*
　　Farm babies
　　Small babies
　　Snow babies
Magloff, Lisa. *Bear*
　　Butterfly
　　Duckling
　　Elephant
　　Frog
　　Kitten
　　Penguin
　　Rabbit
Marciano, John Bemelmans. *Delilah*
Markle, Sandra. *Creepy, crawly baby bugs*
Marsh, T. J. *Way out in the desert*
Miller, Margaret. *Me and my bear*
Murphy, Stuart J. *Pepper's journal*
Murray, Marjorie Dennis. *Little Wolf and the moon*
Nakamura, Katherine Riley. *Song of night*
Nolan, Lucy A. *Jack Quack*
Otto, Carolyn. *Our puppies are growing*
Partis, Joanne. *Stripe*
Pfeffer, Wendy. *Mallard duck at Meadow View Pond*
Plummer, David. *Counting kittens*
Porter, Sue. *Parsnip*
　　Parsnip and the pink blanket
　　Parsnip and the runaway tractor
Purmell, Ann. *Where wild babies sleep*
Radcliffe, Theresa. *Bashi, elephant baby*
Ring, Susan. *Polar babies*
Robinson, Sue. *I want to play*
Roddie, Shen. *Not now, Mrs. Wolf*
Root, Phyllis. *Oliver finds his way*
Rovetch, Lissa. *Sweet dreams, little one*
Ruurs, Margriet. *Wild babies*
Ryan, Pam Muñoz. *A pinky is a baby mouse, and other baby animal names*
Ryder, Joanne. *Little panda*
Saltzberg, Barney. *Baby animal kisses*
Schneider, Howie. *Chewy Louie*
Schofield, Jennifer. *Animal babies in grasslands*
　　Animal babies in polar lands
　　Animal babies in ponds and rivers
　　Animal babies in rain forests
Sidman, Joyce. *Just us two*
Singer, Marilyn. *Tough beginnings*
Slepian, Jan. *Lost moose*
Starke, Katherine. *Dogs and puppies*
Stone, Lynn M. *Chickens have chicks*
　　Pigs and piglets
Swinburne, Stephen R. *Safe, warm, and snug*
Tafolla, Carmen. *Baby Coyote and the old woman = El coyotito y la viejita*
Tafuri, Nancy. *I love you, little one*
Tanner, Suzy-Jane. *Tinyflock Nursery School*
Tatham, Betty. *Penguin chick*
Tender moments in the wild
Thompson, Lauren. *Little Quack*
　　Little Quack [board book]
Tildes, Phyllis Limbacher. *Baby animals black and white*

Van Eerbeek. *The world of baby animals*
Volkmann, Roy. *Curious kittens*
Waddell, Martin. *It's quacking time*
Walters, Catherine. *Are you there, Baby Bear?*
Ward, Jennifer. *Somewhere in the ocean*
Watt, Fiona. *Kittens*
Weare, Tim. *I'm a little penguin*
    I'm a little puppy
Weeks, Sarah. *Baa-choo!*
Wolfe, Art. *Northwest animal babies*
Wood, Jenny. *I wonder why kangaroos have pouches and other questions about baby animals*
Wormell, Mary. *Why not?*
Wright, Cliff. *Santa's ark*
Yolen, Jane. *Off we go!*
Ziefert, Harriet. *A dozen ducklings lost and found*

Animals – baboons

Banks, Kate (Katherine A.). *Baboon*
Bynum, Janie. *Altoona up north*
Ching. *The baboon's umbrella*
Field, Susan. *The sun, the moon, and the silver baboon*
Noble, Kate. *Bubble gum*
Olaleye, Isaac. *Bitter bananas*

Animals – badgers

Baker, Betty. *Partners*
Brewster, Patience. *Two bushy badgers*
Bunting, Eve (Anne Evelyn). *Can you do this, Old Badger?*
    Little Badger, terror of the seven seas
    Little Badger's just-about birthday
Carlstrom, Nancy White. *No nap for Benjamin Badger*
Cox, Paul. *The case of the botched book*
    The great eucalyptus mystery
    The riddle of the floating island
Grahame, Kenneth. *The wind in the willows*, ill. by Joanne Moss
Hiscock, Bruce. *Coyote and badger*
Hoban, Russell. *A baby sister for Frances*
    A bargain for Frances
    Bedtime for Frances
    Best friends for Frances
    A birthday for Frances
    Bread and jam for Frances
Johnston, Tony. *The badger and the magic fan*
Liersch, Anne. *A house is not a home*
Linders, Clara. *The very best door of all*
MacDonald, Elizabeth. *Mr. Badger's birthday pie*
Muller, Robin. *Badger's new house*
Oram, Hiawyn. *Badger's bad mood*
    Badger's bring something party
Potter, Beatrix. *The tale of Mr. Tod*
Schuurmans, Hilde. *Sydney won't swim*
Silverman, Erica. *Warm in winter*
Tompert, Ann. *Badger on his own*
Varley, Susan. *Badger's parting gifts*
Wells, Rosemary. *Hazel's amazing mother*

Animals – bandicoots

Argent, Kerry. *Wombat and Bandicoot*

Animals – bats

Appelt, Kathi. *Bats around the clock*
    Bats on parade
Berman, Ruth. *Squeaking bats*
Cannon, Annie. *The bat in the boot*
Cannon, Janell. *Stellaluna*
    Stellaluna: a pop-up book and mobile
Carlson, Natalie Savage. *Spooky and the wizard's bats*
Davies, Nicola. *Bat loves the night*
Davol, Marguerite W. *Batwings and the curtain of night*
Dragonwagon, Crescent. *Bat in the dining room*
Freeman, Don. *Hattie the backstage bat*
Gibbons, Gail. *Bats*

Glaser, Linda. *Beautiful bats*
Heinrichs, Ann. *Bats*
Hoban, Russell. *Lavina bat*
Horowitz, Ruth. *Bat time*
Jarrell, Randall. *A bat is born*
Laschütza, Susanne. *Nat the bat*
McMullan, Kate (Hall). *Batty riddles*
Maestro, Betsy. *Bats*
Markle, Sandra. *Outside and inside bats*
Mayr, Diane. *Littlebat's Halloween story*
Medearis, Angela Shelf. *Barry and Bennie*
Mitchard, Jacquelyn. *Baby bat's lullaby*
Mollel, Tololwa M. (Tololwa Marti). *A promise to the sun*
Quackenbush, Robert M. *Batbaby*
    Batbaby finds a home
Ungerer, Tomi. *Rufus*
Whitehouse, Patricia. *Bats*

Animals – bears

Adelson, Leone. *The mystery bear*
Agee, Jon. *Milo's hat trick*
Ahlberg, Allan. *Bravest ever bear*
Alborough, Jez. *Ice cream bear*
    It's the bear
    My friend bear
    Where's my teddy?
Alderson, Sue Ann. *Wherever bears be*
Alexander, Martha G. *And my mean old mother will be sorry, Blackboard Bear*
    Blackboard Bear
    I sure am glad to see you, Blackboard Bear
    I'll never share you, Blackboard Bear
    We're in big trouble, Blackboard Bear
    You're a genius, Blackboard Bear
Alexander, Sally Hobart. *Maggie's whopper*
Allen, Pamela. *Bertie and the bear*
Ambrus, Victor G. *Never laugh at bears*
Amoit, Pierre. *Bijou, the little bear*
Andreae, Giles. *Love is a handful of honey*
Anglund, Joan Walsh. *Cowboy and his friend*
    The cowboy's Christmas
Appelt, Kathi. *Where, where is Swamp Bear?*
Apperley, Dawn. *Blossom and Boo*
    Blossom and Boo stay up late
Arnosky, Jim. *Every autumn comes the bear*
Asch, Frank. *Bear shadow*
    Bear's bargain
    Bread and honey
    Good night, Baby Bear
    Goodbye house
    Happy birthday, moon!
    Just like daddy
    Milk and cookies
    Moonbear
    Moonbear's books
    Moonbear's canoe
    Moonbear's dream
    Moonbear's friend
    Moonbear's pet
    Mooncake
    Moondance
    Moongame
    Popcorn
    Sand cake
    Skyfire
Austin, Margot. *A friend for Growl Bear*
Bach, Alice. *Millicent the magnificent*
    The smartest bear and his brother Oliver
    Warren Weasel's worse than measles
Bailey, Linda. *Gordon Loggins and the three bears*
Baker, Jill. *Basil of Bywater Hollow*
Bardill, Linard. *The great golden thing*
Barrett, John M. *The bear who slept through Christmas*
    The Easter bear
Barto, Emily Newton. *Chubby bear*
Bartoli, Jennifer. *Snow on bear's nose*

Bassett, Lisa. *Beany and Scamp*
   Beany wakes up for Christmas
   A clock for Beany
Bauer, Marion Dane. *Jason's bears*
The bear
Bearcub and Mama
Beck, Martine. *Rescue of Brown Bear and White Bear*
   The wedding of Brown Bear and White Bear
Bedford, David. *Big bears can!*
Bellows, Cathy. *The Grizzly sisters*
Bentley, Dawn. *Fuzzy bear*
   Fuzzy Bear's potty book
Benton, Robert. *Don't ever wish for a 7-foot bear*
Berenstain, Stan. *After the dinosaurs*
   The bear detectives
   Bears in the night
   Bears on wheels
   The Berenstain bears and mama's new job
   The Berenstain bears and the bad dream
   The Berenstain bears and the bad habit
   The Berenstain bears and the big road race
   The Berenstain bears and the double dare
   The Berenstain bears and the ghost of the forest
   The Berenstain bears and the messy room
   The Berenstain bears and the missing dinosaur bone
   The Berenstain bears and the missing honey
   The Berenstain bears and the prize pumpkin
   The Berenstain bears and the real Easter eggs
   The Berenstain bears and the sitter
   The Berenstain bears and the slumber party
   The Berenstain bears and the spooky old tree
   The Berenstain bears and the trouble with friends
   The Berenstain bears and the truth
   The Berenstain bears and the week at grandma's
   The Berenstain bears and the wild, wild honey
   The Berenstain bears and too much birthday
   The Berenstain bears and too much junk food
   The Berenstain bears and too much TV
   The Berenstain bears and too much vacation
   The Berenstain bears blaze a trail
   The Berenstain bears' Christmas tree
   The Berenstain bears' counting book
   The Berenstain bears don't pollute anymore
   The Berenstain bears forget their manners
   The Berenstain bears get in a fight
   The Berenstain bears get stage fright
   The Berenstain bears get the gimmies
   The Berenstain bears go out for the team
   The Berenstain bears go to camp
   The Berenstain bears go to school
   The Berenstain bears go to the doctor
   The Berenstain bears in the dark
   The Berenstain bears learn about strangers
   The Berenstain bears meet Santa Bear
   The Berenstain bears' moving day
   The Berenstain bears no girls allowed
   The Berenstain bears on the moon
   The Berenstain bears ready, set, go!
   The Berenstain bears' report card trouble
   The Berenstain bears' science fair
   The Berenstain bears' that stump must go!
   The Berenstain bears trick or treat
   The Berenstain bears' trouble at school
   The Berenstain bears' trouble with money
   The Berenstain bears' trouble with pets
   The Berenstain bears visit the dentist
   The Berenstains' B book
   He bear, she bear
   Inside outside upside down
   Old hat, new hat
Berman, Ruth. *Fishing bears*
Bird, E. J. *How do bears sleep?*
Bishop, Claire Huchet. *Twenty-two bears*
Bittner, Wolfgang. *Wake up, Grizzly!*
Blackaby, Susan. *Rembrandt's hat*
Blackstone, Stella. *Bear at home*
   Bear in a square

Bear in sunshine
   Bear on a bike
   Bear's busy family
Blathwayt, Benedict. *Bear's adventure*
Blocksma, Mary. *The best dressed bear*
Bodnar, Judit Z. *Tale of a tail*
Boegehold, Betty. *Bear underground*
Boehm, Arlene P. *Jack in search of Art*
Boelts, Maribeth. *Looking for Sleepy*
Bond, Michael. *Paddington and the knickerbocker rainbow*
   Paddington at the circus
   Paddington at the fair
   Paddington at the palace
   Paddington at the seaside
   Paddington at the tower
   Paddington at the zoo
   Paddington Bear, ill. by R. W. Alley
   Paddington Bear, ill. by John Lobban
   Paddington Bear and the Busy Bee Carnival
   Paddington Bear and the Christmas surprise
   Paddington cleans up
   Paddington's ABC
   Paddington's art exhibit
   Paddington's colors
   Paddington's garden
   Paddington's lucky day
   Paddington's 1 2 3
   Paddington's opposites
Boon, Emilie. *Belinda's balloon*
Bos, Burny. *Alexander the great*
Bowden, Joan Chase. *The bear's surprise party*
Bradman, Tony. *A bad week for the three bears*
Brandenberg, Franz. *A fun weekend*
Braun, Sebastien. *I love my daddy*
Brenner, Barbara A. *Two orphan cubs*
Brett, Jan. *Berlioz the bear*
Brian, Janeen. *Where does Thursday go?*
Bridgman, Elizabeth. *Nanny bear's cruise*
Bright, Robert. *Me and the bears*
Brimner, Larry Dane. *Country Bear's good neighbor*
   Country Bear's surprise
Brinckloe, Julie. *Gordon's house*
Brown, Margaret Wise. *Love songs of the little bear*
Browne, Anthony. *Bear goes to town*
   Bear hunt
   The little bear book
Bunting, Eve (Anne Evelyn). *The Valentine bears*
Butterfield, Moira. *Brown, fierce, and furry*
Cabrera, Jane. *Bear's good night*
Cahill, Chris. *Bear magic*
Caple, Kathy. *Fox and bear*
Capucilli, Alyssa Satin. *Bear hugs*
   What kind of kiss?
Carleton, Barbee Oliver. *Benny and the bear*
Carlstrom, Nancy White. *Better not get wet, Jesse Bear*
   Guess who's coming, Jesse Bear
   Happy birthday, Jesse Bear!
   How do you say it today, Jesse Bear?
   It's about time, Jesse Bear
   Jesse Bear, what will you wear?
   Jesse Bear's tra-la tub
   Jesse Bear's tum-tum tickle
   Jesse Bear's wiggle-jiggle jump-up
   Jesse Bear's yum-yum crumble
   Let's count it out, Jesse Bear
   What a scare, Jesse Bear!
   Where is Christmas, Jesse Bear?
Carmichael, Clay. *Bear at the beach*
Carrick, Carol. *The polar bears are hungry*
Carson, Jo. *The great shaking*
Cartlidge, Michelle. *Bear in the forest*
   The bear's bazaar
   Bears on the go
   Teddy trucks
Catalano, Dominic. *Santa and the three bears*
Cauley, Lorinda Bryan. *Treasure hunt*
Chambless, Jane. *Tucker and the bear*

Cherry, Lynne. *Grizzly bear*
Chevalier, Christa. *The little bear who forgot*
Christian, Peggy. *Chocolate, a glacier grizzly*
Cocca-Leffler, Maryann. *Bravery soup*
Collins, Billy. *Daddy's little boy*
Compton, Joanne. *Sody Sallyratus*
Cooper, Helen (Helen F.). *The bear under the stairs*
Corey, Shana. *Ballerina bear*
Crespi, Francesca. *Little Bear and the oompah-pah*
Crewe, Sabrina. *The bear*
Dabcovich, Lydia. *Sleepy bear*
Dalmais, Anne-Marie. *The Best bedtime stories of Mother Bear*
Davis, Aubrey. *Sody salleratus*
Day, Alexandra. *Boswell wide-awake*
    Frank and Ernest
    Frank and Ernest on the road
    Frank and Ernest play ball
Day, Marie. *Quennu and the cave bear*
De Beer, Hans. *Bernard Bear's amazing adventure*
Degen, Bruce. *Jamberry*
DeLage, Ida. *The old witch and the snores*
Delton, Judy. *Bear and Duck on the run*
    Brimhall comes to stay
    Brimhall turns detective
    Brimhall turns to magic
    The elephant in Duck's garden
    No time for Christmas
    A pet for Duck and Bear
    Rabbit finds a way
    Two good friends
Dennis, Morgan. *Burlap*
Deprisco, Dorothea. *Snowbear's winter day*
De Regniers, Beatrice Schenk. *How Joe the bear and Sam the mouse got together*
Dewey, Ariane. *Splash!*
Dierssen, Andreas. *Timmy's new friend*
Dodd, Lynley. *Wake up, bear*
Dorian, Marguerite. *When the snow is blue*
Dowling, Paul. *You need a bath, Mustard*
Dubar, Joyce. *The very small*
Dubois, Claude K. *He's my jumbo!*
    Looking for Ginny
Dunbar, Joyce. *A cake for Barney*
Dunrea, Olivier. *Bear Noel*
Duplaix, Georges. *The big brown bear*
Durant, Alan. *Brown Bear gets in shape*
Duvoisin, Roger Antoine. *Snowy and Woody*
Edwards, Richard. *Always Copycub*
    Copy me, Copycub
    Good night, Copycub
Edwards, Roberta. *Anna Bear's first winter*
Egan, Tim. *A mile from Ellington station*
Ernst, Lisa Campbell. *Goldilocks returns*
Faglia, Maeto. *Happy birthday, I'm 4*
Falk, Barbara Bustetter. *Grusha*
Fatio, Louise. *The happy lion and the bear*
Fearnley, Jan. *Mr. Wolf and the three bears*
    A perfect day for it
Flack, Marjorie. *Ask Mr. Bear*
Fleishman, Seymour. *Too hot in Potzburg*
Fleming, Denise. *Time to sleep*
Flory, Jane. *The bear on the doorstep*
Foreman, Michael. *Moose*
Fox, Mem. *Sleepy bears*
Fraggalosch, Audrey. *Great grizzly wilderness*
    Grizzly bear family
Freeman, Don. *Bearymore*
Gabriel, Ashala. *Night night toes*
Gage, Wilson. *Cully Cully and the bear*
Galdone, Joanna. *The little girl and the big bear*
Gammell, Stephen. *Wake up, bear . . . It's Christmas!*
Gantschev, Ivan. *Otto the bear*
    RumpRump
Gantz, David. *The genie bear with the light brown hair word book*
George, Jean Craighead. *The grizzly bear with the golden ears*
Gerstein, Mordicai. *Anytime Mapleson and the hungry bears*
Gibbons, Gail. *Grizzly bears*

Gifford, Kathie Lee. *Giff the scaredy bear*
    Giff's big game
Gilks, Helen. *Bears*
Ginsburg, Mirra. *Two greedy bears*
Glass, Andrew. *Bewildered for three days*
Glicksman, Caroline. *Eric the math bear*
Gliori, Debi. *Can I have a hug?*
    Mr. Bear babysits
    Mr. Bear says, "Are you there, Baby Bear?"
    Mr. Bear says peek-a-boo
    Mr. Bear to the rescue
    Mr. Bear's new baby
    Mr. Bear's picnic
    Tickly under there
    Willie Bear and the Wish Fish
Goldman, Dara. *There's no such thing!*
Goldstein, Bobbye S. *Bear in mind*
Goodings, Lennie. *When you grow up*
Gordon, Margaret. *Wilberforce goes on a picnic*
    Wilberforce goes to a party
Gordon, Sharon. *Christmas surprise*
Graham, Thomas. *Mr. Bear's boat*
    Mr. Bear's chair
Greaves, Margaret. *Little Bear and the Papagini circus*
Gregory, Valiska. *Through the mickle woods*
Greydanus, Rose. *Bedtime story*
    Climb aboard
Grimm, Jacob. *The bear and the kingbird*
    Rose Red and the bear prince
    Snow White and Rose Red, ill. by Adrienne Adams
    Snow White and Rose Red, ill. by John Wallner
    Snow White and Rose Red, ill. by Bernadette Watts
    Snow-White and Rose-Red, ill. by Barbara Cooney
Grindley, Sally. *What are friends for?*
    What will I do without you?
Grossman, Bill. *The bear whose bones were Jezebel Jones*
Guilfoile, Elizabeth. *Nobody listens to Andrew*
Hague, Kathleen. *Calendarbears*
    Ten little bears
Hamsa, Bobbie. *Your pet bear*
Hansen, Carla. *Barnaby Bear builds a boat*
    Barnaby Bear visits the farm
Hansen, Felicity. *The first bear*
Hanson, Mary Elizabeth. *Snug*
Harley, Bill. *Bear's all-night party*
Harper, Piers. *If you love a bear*
Harrison, Joanna. *Dear bear*
Harvey, Bev. *The bear family*
Haseley, Dennis. *A story for Bear*
Hawkins, Colin. *Dip, dip, dip*
    I'm not sleepy!
    One finger, one thumb
    Oops-a-Daisy
    Where's bear?
Hayes, Geoffrey. *Christmas in Puttyville*
    Patrick and his grandpa
    Patrick and Ted
    Patrick at the circus
    The secret inside
Heap, Sue. *Four friends in the garden*
Heine, Helme. *Prince Bear*
Heller, Nicholas. *Mathilda the dream bear*
Hellsing, Lennart. *The wonderful pumpkin*
Hest, Amy. *Kiss good night*
    You can do it, Sam
Heuck, Sigrid. *Pony and Bear are friends*
Hill, Eric. *At home*
    Baby Bear's bedtime
    Good morning, baby bear
    My pets
    Up there
Hillert, Margaret. *The three bears*
Hirschi, Ron. *Where are my bears?*
Hobbs, Will. *Beardream*
    Howling Hill
Hodge, Deborah. *Bears*
Hoff, Syd. *Bernard on his own*

Grizzwold
Hol, Coby. *Tippy Bear and little Sam*
  Tippy Bear goes to a party
  Tippy Bear hunts for honey
  Tippy Bear's Christmas
Holl, Adelaide. *Small Bear builds a playhouse*
  Small Bear solves a mystery
Hooks, William H. *Snowbear Whittington, an Appalachian Beauty and the Beast*
Irwin, Michael. *Bears in my bed*
Isenberg, Barbara. *The adventures of Albert, the running bear*
  Albert the running bear gets the jitters
  Albert the running bear's exercise book
Isherwood, Shirley. *The band over the hill*
Itaya, Satoshi. *Buttons and Bo*
Jackson, Ellen B. *The bear in the bathtub*
Janice. *Little Bear marches in the St. Patrick's Day parade*
  Little Bear's Christmas
  Little Bear's New Year's party
  Little Bear's pancake party
  Little Bear's Sunday breakfast
  Little Bear's Thanksgiving
Jennings, Michael. *The bears who came to breakfix*
Jeschke, Susan. *Angela and Bear*
  The devil did it
Johnson, D. B. (Donald B.). *Henry builds a cabin*
  Henry climbs a mountain
  Henry works
Johnston, Tony. *Little bear sleeping*
Jonas, Ann. *Two bear cubs*
Jorgensen, Gail. *Gotcha!*
Jukes, Mavis. *You're a bear*
Kangas, Juli. *Hello, Honey Bear*
Kasparavicius, Kestutis. *The bear family's world tour Christmas*
Kasza, Keiko. *Don't laugh, Joe*
  The mightiest
Keller, Holly. *Jacob's tree*
Kelley, True. *Buggly Bear's hiccup cure*
Killingback, Julia. *Busy Bears at the fire station*
  Busy Bears' picnic
  Monday is washing day
  What time is it, Mrs. Bear?
Kimmel, Eric A. *Bearhead*
Kinsey-Warnock, Natalie. *The bear that heard crying*
Klingel, Cynthia Fitterer. *Grizzly bears*
Koscielniak, Bruce. *Bear and Bunny grow tomatoes*
Kraus, Robert. *Buggy Bear cleans up*
Krause, Ute. *Nora and the great bear*
Krauss, Ruth. *Bears*
Krensky, Stephen. *The big time bears*
Kuchalla, Susan. *Bears*
Kuiper, Nannie. *Bailey the bear cub*
Kuratomi, Chizuko. *Mr. Bear and the robbers*
Landa, Norbert. *Little Bear's Christmas*
Lang, Aubrey. *The adventures of Baby Bear*
Langreuter, Jutta. *Little Bear and the big fight*
  Little Bear brushes his teeth
  Little Bear goes to kindergarten
  Little Bear won't go to bed
Langsen, Richard C. *When someone in the family drinks too much*
Lansky, Vicki. *It's not your fault, KoKo Bear*
Lapp, Eleanor. *The blueberry bears*
Lasky, Kathryn. *Fourth of July bear*
Latimer, Jim. *The fox under first base*
  James Bear and the goose gathering
  James Bear's pie
Lawson, Julie. *Bear on the train*
Leblanc, Anne. *Benjamin finds a friend*
  Benjamin in the snow
  Benjamin takes care of Mommy
  Benjamin's busy day
Lebrun, Claude. *Little Brown Bear does not want to eat*
  Little Brown Bear learns to share
Lemieux, Michèle. *What's that noise?*
Leonard, Marcia. *Bear's busy year*
Le Tord, Bijou. *Good wood bear*
Lewis, Paeony. *I'll always love you*

Lipkind, William. *Nubber bear*
Lisowski, Gabriel. *Roncalli's magnificent circus*
Little Bear's Valentine
London, Jonathan. *Count the ways, Little Brown Bear*
  Honey Paw and Lightfoot
Lowell, Susan. *Dusty Locks and the three bears*
Lucas, Barbara (Barbara M.). *Sleeping over*
Ludwig, Warren. *Good morning, Granny Rose*
Lundell, Margo. *The furry bedtime book*
Lyon, David. *The crumbly coast*
McCarthy, Ruth. *Katie and the smallest bear*
McCloskey, Robert. *Blueberries for Sal*
McCully, Emily Arnold. *The evil spell*
  My real family
  Speak up, Blanche!
  Zaza's big break
MacDonald, Alan. *Beware of the bears!*
MacGregor, Marilyn. *Helen the hungry bear*
Mack, Stanley (Stan). *Ten bears in my bed*
McMullan, Kate (Hall). *Papa's song*
McPhail, David M. *The bear's toothache*
  Big brown bear
  A bug, a bear, and a boy
  A bug, a bear, and a boy go to school
  Drawing lessons from a bear
  Emma's pet
  Emma's vacation
  Henry Bear's Christmas
  Henry Bear's park
  Jack and Rick
  Lost
  Stanley: Henry Bear's friend
  Tinker and Tom and the Star Baby
Magloff, Lisa. *Bear*
Maitland, Barbara. *The bear who didn't like honey*
Mallat, Kathy. *Brave bear*
Mangan, Anne. *Browny, the smallest bear of all*
Margolis, Richard J. *Big bear, spare that tree*
Marino, Dorothy. *Buzzy Bear and the rainbow*
  Buzzy Bear goes camping
  Buzzy Bear in the garden
  Buzzy Bear's busy day
Maris, Ron. *Hold tight, bear!*
Marshall, James. *What's the matter with Carruthers?*
Martin, Bill (William Ivan). *Brown bear, brown bear, what do you see?*
Martin, Claire. *The race of the golden apples*
Mayer, Mercer. *Two moral tales*
Medearis, Angela Shelf. *Barry and Bennie*
Miller, Margaret. *Me and my bear*
Miller, Ruth. *The bear on the bed*
Miller, Virginia. *Be gentle!*
  Eat your dinner!
  Go to bed!
  I love you just the way you are
  In a minute!
  On your potty!
  Ten red apples
Minarik, Else Holmelund. *Father Bear comes home*
  Father's flying flapjacks
  A kiss for Little Bear
  Little Bear
  Little Bear's friend
  Little Bear's new friend
  Little Bear's visit
Moers, Hermann. *Katie and the big, brave bear*
Monsell, Helen Albee. *Paddy's Christmas*
Moore, Eva. *Franklin and the baby*
Moret, Brigitte Frey. *The bear's Christmas*
Moroney, Lynn. *The boy who loved bears*
Muntean, Michaela. *Bicycle bear*
  Bicycle Bear rides again
  The house that bear built
Murdocca, Sal (Salvatore). *Christmas bear*
Murphy, Jill. *Peace at last*
  What next, baby bear!
Murphy, Jim. *Backyard bear*
Murphy, Stuart J. *A fair bear share*

Myers, Bernice. *Herman and the bears and the giants*
Namm, Diane. *Little bear*
Nash, Ogden. *The adventures of Isabel*, ill. by Walter Lorraine
    The adventures of Isabel, ill. by James Marshall
Nayer, Judy. *Little bear's first Christmas*
Naylor, Phyllis Reynolds. *Old Sadie and the Christmas bear*
    Please do feed the bears
Newman, Nanette. *There's a bear in the bath!*
Nims, Bonnie Larkin. *Where is the bear in the city?*
Nordqvist, Sven. *Porker finds a chair*
    Porker's taxi
Novak, Matt. *Jazzbo and Googy*
    Jazzbo goes to school
Obrist, Jürg. *Bear business*
Oliviero, Jamie. *The day Sun was stolen*
O'Mara, Carmel. *Good morning*
    Good night
    Rainy day
    Sunny day
Oppenheim, Joanne. *Could it be?*
Oram, Hiawyn. *Going to Grandpa's*
    Kiss it better
Ørdal, Stina Langlo. *Princess Aasta*
Owen, Annie. *Goodnight bear!*
Pallandt, Nicholas van. *The butterfly night of Old Brown Bear*
Parker, Victoria. *Bearum scarum*
Paton, Priscilla. *Howard and the sitter surprise*
Patz, Nancy. *Sarah Bear and Sweet Sidney*
Peek, Merle. *Mary wore her red dress and Henry wore his green sneakers*
Peet, Bill (William Bartlett). *Big bad Bruce*
Petty, Dini. *The queen, the bear and the bumblebee*
Pfister, Marcus. *Make a wish, Honey Bear!*
Phillips, Joan. *Peek-a-boo! I see you!*
Pinkwater, Daniel Manus. *The bear's picture*
    Bongo Larry
Pitcher, Caroline. *Are you spring?*
Pluckrose, Henry Arthur. *Bears*
Polisar, Barry Louis. *The trouble with Ben*
Pomerantz, Charlotte. *Where's the bear?*
Poppy Bear
Powell, Alma. *My little wagon* [board book]
Prater, John. *Hold tight!*
Price, Mathew. *Don't worry, Alfie*
    Where's Alfie?
Pringle, Laurence P. *Bear hug*
Raphael, Elaine. *Turnabout*
Rascal. *Oregon's journey*
    Orson
Ratnett, Michael. *Jenny's bear*
Reider, Katja. *The big little sneeze*
Reit, Seymour. *Rebus bears*
Ressner, Phil. *August explains*
Richardson, John. *Ten bears in a bed*
Riddell, Chris. *The bear dance*
    Ben and the bear
Rikys, Bodel. *Red bear*
Robbins, Maria Polushkin. *Bubba and Babba*
Rockwell, Anne F. *A bear, a bobcat and three ghosts*
    Bear Child's book of hours
    Boats
    Come to town
    First comes spring
    In our house
    Morgan plays soccer
    On our vacation
Roddie, Shen. *Sandbear*
Root, Phyllis. *Oliver finds his way*
Rosales, Melodye Benson. *Leola and the honeybears*
Rosen, Michael (1946–). *We're going on a bear hunt*
Ross, Christine. *Lily and the bears*
Rouillard, Wendy. *Barnaby's bunny*
Rowinski, Kate. *L. L. Bear's island adventure*
Rucki, Ani. *When the Earth wakes*
Ruck-Pauquèt, Gina. *Mumble bear*
Ryder, Joanne. *Bears out there*
    Big bear ball
Rylant, Cynthia. *Bear day*

San Souci, Robert D. *Two bear cubs*
Scheffler, Ursel. *Taking care of Sister Bear*
    Who has time for Little Bear?
Scheffrin-Falk, Gladys. *Another celebrated dancing bear*
Schindel, John. *Who are you?*
Schneider, Antonie. *The birthday bear*
Schoenherr, John. *Bear*
Schubert, Ingrid. *Bear's eggs*
    Beaver's lodge
Senshu, Noriko. *Sonny's dream*
Shannon, George. *Laughing all the way*
    Lizard's song
Sharmat, Marjorie Weinman. *I'm terrific*
    Lucretia the unbearable
Siewert, Margaret. *Bear hunt*
Simon, Carly. *Amy the dancing bear*
Simon, Seymour. *Wild bears*
Sivulich, Sandra Stroner. *I'm going on a bear hunt*
Skorpen, Liesel Moak. *Outside my window*
Smith, Wendy. *Say hello, Tilly*
Spelman, Cornelia Maude. *Mama and Daddy Bear's divorce*
    When I care about others
    When I feel scared
Spohn, Kate. *Snow play*
Stanley, Diane. *Goldie and the three bears*
Stapler, Sarah. *Trilby's trumpet*
Steiner, Jörg. *The bear who wanted to be a bear*
Steptoe, John. *Jeffrey Bear cleans up his act*
Stevens, Janet. *Tops and bottoms*
Stickland, Paul. *Bears*
Stoddard, Sandol. *Bedtime for bear*
Stubbs, Joanna. *Happy Bear's day*
Sundgaard, Arnold. *The bear who loved Puccini*
Tafuri, Nancy. *Mama's little bears*
Taylor, Mark. *Henry the explorer*
Tejima, Keizaburo. *The bears' autumn*
Thomas, Frances. *The Bear and Mr. Bear*
Thompson, Carol. *Time*
Thorpe, Kiki. *A comfy, cozy Thanksgiving*
    Time to cha-cha-cha!
The three bears. *Goldilocks*, ill. by Janice Russell
    Goldilocks, ill. by Christopher Santoro
    Goldilocks and the three bears, ill. by H. Amery
    Goldilocks and the three bears, ill. by Yvette Banek
    Goldilocks and the three bears, ill. by Jan Brett
    Goldilocks and the three bears, ill. by Lorinda Bryan Cauley
    Goldilocks and the three bears, ill. by Jane Dyer
    Goldilocks and the three bears, ill. by Lynn Bywaters Ferris
    Goldilocks and the three bears, ill. by Valeri Gorbachev
    Goldilocks and the three bears, ill. by Steven Guarnaccia
    Goldilocks and the three bears, ill. by Madelaine Gill Linden
    Goldilocks and the three bears, ill. by David McPhail
    Goldilocks and the three bears, ill. by James Marshall
    Goldilocks and the three bears, ill. by Laura Rader
    Goldilocks and the three bears, ill. by Tony Ross
    Goldilocks and the three bears, ill. by Kristina Stephenson
    Goldilocks and the three bears, ill. by Janet Stevens
    Goldilocks and the three bears, ill. by Bernadette Watts
    Goldilocks and the three bears, ill. by Bari Weissman
    The story of the three bears, ill. by L. Leslie Brooke
    The story of the three bears, ill. by William Stobbs
    The three bears, ill. by Byron Barton
    The three bears, ill. by Paul Galdone
    The three bears, ill. by Feodor Rojankovsky
    The three bears, ill. by Robin Spowart
    The three bears [board book], ill. by Thea Kliros
Tokuda, Wendy. *Samson the hot tub bear*
Tolhurst, Marilyn. *Somebody and the three Blairs*
Trapani, Iza. *Row, row, row your boat*
Turkle, Brinton. *Deep in the forest*
Upham, Elizabeth. *Little brown bear loses his clothes*
Vainio, Pirkko. *The best of friends*
Van Kampen, Vlasta. *Bear tales*
Van Woerkom, Dorothy. *Becky and the bear*
Venable, Alan. *The checker players*
Vincent, Gabrielle. *Bravo, Ernest and Celestine!*
    Breakfast time, Ernest and Celestine

Ernest and Celestine
Ernest and Celestine at the circus
Ernest and Celestine's patchwork quilt
Ernest and Celestine's picnic
Merry Christmas, Ernest and Celestine
Smile, Ernest and Celestine
Where are you, Ernest and Celestine?
Waddell, Martin. *Can't you sleep, Little Bear?*
  Good job, Little Bear!
  Let's go home, Little Bear
  Night night Cuddly Bear
  Snow bears
  Yum, yum, yummy
Wahl, Jan. *Sylvester Bear overslept*
Wallace, John. *Anything for you*
Wallace, Karen. *Bears in the forest*
Wallen, Ila. *The moon in my room*
Walters, Catherine. *Are you there, Baby Bear?*
  Play gently, Alfie Bear
  When will it be spring?
Walton, Rick. *The bear came over to my house*
Ward, Andrew. *Baby bear and the long sleep*
Ward, Lynd. *The biggest bear*
Wardlaw, Lee. *The chair where bear sits*
Warren, Cathy. *Springtime bears*
Watanabe, Shigeo. *Daddy, play with me!*
  How do I put it on?
  I can build a house!
  I can ride it!
  I can take a bath!
  I can take a walk!
  Ice cream is falling!
  I'm the king of the castle!
  It's my birthday
  Let's go swimming
  What a good lunch!
  Where's my daddy?
Weedn, Flavia. *The little snow bear*
Weigelt, Udo. *Bear's last journey*
Weinberg, Larry (Lawrence). *The Forgetful Bears*
  The Forgetful Bears help Santa
  The Forgetful Bears meet Mr. Memory
Wells, Rosemary. *The bear went over the mountain*
White, Carolyn. *The adventure of Louey and Frank*
Wijngaard, Juan. *Bear*
Wild, Robin. *The bears' ABC book*
  The bears' counting book
Wildsmith, Brian. *Bear's adventure*
  The lazy bear
Williams, Leslie. *A bear in the air*
Williams, Sam. *Angel's Christmas cookies*
Wilson, Karma. *Bear stays up for Christmas*
Winter, Paula. *The bear and the fly*
Winthrop, Elizabeth. *Bear and Mrs. Duck*
  Bear's Christmas surprise
Wiseman, Bernard. *Christmas with Morris and Borris*
  Morris and Boris at the circus
  Morris has a birthday party!
Wood, Audrey. *Oh my baby bear!*
Wood, Jakki. *One bear with bees in his hair*
Woodman, Allen. *The bear who came to stay*
Yee, Patrick. *Baby bear*
Yee, Wong Herbert. *Big black bear*
Yektai, Niki. *Bears at the beach*
  Bears in pairs
Yeoman, John. *The bear's water picnic*
Ylla. *Two little bears*
Yolen, Jane. *Baby Bear's bedtime book*
  The three bears holiday rhyme book
  The three bears rhyme book
Yulya. *Bears are sleeping*
Zalben, Jane Breskin. *Beni's first Chanukah*
  Beni's first wedding
  Happy Passover, Rosie
  Leo and Blossom's Sukkah
Zehler, Antonia. *Two fine ladies: tea for three*
Ziefert, Harriet. *Bear all year*

Bear gets dressed
Bear goes shopping
Bear's busy morning
Zimnik, Reiner. *The bear on the motorcycle*
Zirbes, Laura. *How many bears?*
Zoehfeld, Kathleen Weidner. *Apples, apples*

Animals – beavers

Arnosky, Jim. *Beaver pond, moose pond*
Barr, Cathrine. *Little Ben*
Bentley, Dawn. *Busy little beaver*
Bernstein, Margery. *How the sun made a promise and kept it*
Bowen, Vernon. *The lazy beaver*
Carlson, Nancy L. *Take time to relax*
  A visit to grandma's
Chottin, Ariane. *Beaver gets lost*
Crowley, Arthur. *Bonzo Beaver*
Dabcovich, Lydia. *Busy beavers*
Gallo, Giovanni. *The lazy beaver*
George, William T. *Beaver at Long Pond*
Gibson, Kari Smalley. *Mooki's secret*
Hamsa, Bobbie. *Your pet beaver*
Himmelman, John. *The Clover County carrot contest*
  The day-off machine
  The great leaf blast-off
  The super camper caper
Hoban, Russell. *Charlie the tramp*
Hodge, Deborah. *Beavers*
Johnson, Amy Crane. *Mason moves away = Mason se muda*
Kalas, Sybille. *The beaver family book*
Kuiper, Nannie. *Bravo, brave beavers*
MacDonald, Amy. *Little Beaver and the echo*
Minarik, Else Holmelund. *Percy and the five houses*
Pryor, Bonnie. *The beaver boys*
Schubert, Ingrid. *Beaver's lodge*
  There's always room for one more
Sheehan, Angela. *The beaver*
Tresselt, Alvin R. *The beaver pond*
Van Laan, Nancy. *Moose tales*
Weigelt, Udo. *Old Beaver*

Animals – bison see Animals – buffaloes

Animals – bobcats

Hodge, Deborah. *Wild cats*
Rockwell, Anne F. *A bear, a bobcat and three ghosts*

Animals – brush wolves *see* Animals – coyotes

Animals – buffaloes

Baker, Olaf. *Where the buffaloes begin*
Brandon, Siobhán. *The bird's story*
Esbensen, Barbara Juster. *The great buffalo race*
Glasscock, Sarah. *My prairie summer*
Goble, Paul. *Her seven brothers*
  The return of the buffaloes
Grimsdell, Jeremy. *Kalinzu*
Gulbis, Stephen. *Cowgirl Rosie and her five baby bison*
Kershen, L. Michael (Lloyd Michael). *Why buffalo roam*
Latimer, Jim. *Snail and Buffalo*
McCarthy, Bobette. *Buffalo girls*
Midge, Tiffany. *Buffalo*
Roop, Peter. *The buffalo jump*
Stilz, Carol Curtis. *Grandma Buffalo, May, and me*
Waldman, Neil. *They came from the Bronx*
Wiebe, Rudy. *Hidden buffalo*
Wittmann, Patricia. *Buffalo Thunder*

Animals – bulls, cows

Abel, Simone. *How now, cow?*
Aliki. *Milk from cow to carton*
Allen, Pamela. *Belinda*
Asch, Frank. *Oats and wild apples*

Babcock, Chris. *No moon, no milk!*
Barker, Melvern J. *Country fair*
Bulla, Clyde Robert. *Dandelion Hill*
Carlson, Natalie Savage. *Time for the white egret*
Carrick, Donald. *The deer in the pasture*
    Milk
Cazet, Denys. *Minnie and Moo and the musk of Zorro*
    Minnie and Moo and the potato from Planet X
    Minnie and Moo and the Thanksgiving tree
    Minnie and Moo go to Paris
    Minnie and Moo meet Frankenswine
    Minnie and Moo save the earth
    Minnie and Moo: the night before Christmas
    Minnie and Moo: the night of the living bed
    Minnie and Moo: will you be my Valentine?
    Minnie and Moo: the attack of the Easter bunnies
Choldenko, Gennifer. *Moonstruck*
Climo, Shirley. *The Irish Cinderlad*
Cole, Babette. *Supermoo!*
Cole, Joanna. *A calf is born*
Coulter, Hope Norman. *Uncle Chuck's truck*
Cronin, Doreen. *Click, clack, moo*
Cushman, Jerome. *Marvella's hobby*
Dennis, Wesley. *Flip and the cows*
Doyle, Malachy. *Cow*
Dreier, Ted. *Moozie's kind adventure*
Drescher, Henrik. *Looking for Santa Claus*
Dubanevich, Arlene. *Calico cows*
Du Bois, William Pène. *Elisabeth, the cow ghost*
Duffield, Katy. *Farmer McPeepers and his missing milk cows*
Ericsson, Jennifer A. *No milk!*
Ernst, Lisa Campbell. *When Bluebell sang*
Ets, Marie Hall. *The cow's party*
Flanagan, Alice K. *Raising cows on the Koebels' farm*
Forrester, Victoria. *The magnificent moo*
    Poor Gabriella
Fox, Mem. *Because of the bloomers*
Gibbons, Gail. *Yippee-yay!*
Glass, Andrew. *Chickpea and the talking cow*
Gollub, Matthew. *Gobble, quack, moon*
Gomi, Taro. *Spring is here*
Greene, Ellin. *Billy Beg and his bull*
Greenstein, Elaine. *Emily and the crows*
Hader, Berta Hoerner. *The story of Pancho and the bull with the crooked tail*
Hancock, Sibyl. *Old Blue*
Harrison, David Lee. *When cows come home*
Herriot, James. *Blossom comes home*
Hurd, Thacher. *Moo Cow Kaboom!*
Jackson, Woody. *Counting cows*
Johnson, Paul Brett. *The cow who wouldn't come down*
Johnston, Tony. *The bull and the fire truck*
    The promise
Kaizuki, Kiyonori. *A calf is born*
Kent, Jack. *Mrs. Mooley*
Ketteman, Helen. *Bubba the cowboy prince*
Kinerk, Robert. *Clorinda*
Kirby, David K. *Cows are going to Paris*
Koch, Dorothy Clarke. *When the cows got out*
Kovalski, Maryann. *Queen Nadine*
Krasilovsky, Phyllis. *The cow who fell in the canal*
Kroll, Virginia L. *The Christmas cow*
Laden, Nina. *When Pigasso met Mootisse*
Leaf, Munro. *The story of Ferdinand the bull*
Lent, Blair. *Pistachio*
Le Tord, Bijou. *A brown cow*
Lewis, Kim. *Little calf*
Lindgren, Astrid. *A calf for Christmas*
Ling, Mary. *Calf*
Lodge, Jo. *Moo Moo goes to the city*
Lowell, Susan. *Little Red Cowboy Hat*
Macaulay, David. *Black and white*
MacFarland, Cynthia. *Cows in the parlor*
Martin, Bill (William Ivan). *White Dynamite and Curly Kidd*
Mathews, Judith. *There's nothing to d-o-o-o!*
Meeks, Esther K. *The curious cow*
Merrill, Jean. *Tell about the cowbarn, Daddy*

Milgrim, David. *Cows can't fly*
Milway, Katie Smith. *Cappuccina goes to town*
Miranda, Anne. *Counting*
Moers, Hermann. *Camomile heads for home*
Morck, Irene. *Tyler's new boots*
Morris, Linda Lowe. *Morning milking*
Most, Bernard. *Moo-ha!*
    Peek-a-moo!
Murphy, Andy. *Out and about at the dairy farm*
Newman, Jeff. *Reginald*
Nikola-Lisa, W. *Wheels go round*
Palatini, Margie. *Moo who?*
Pedersen, Janet. *Millie wants to play*
Pellowski, Michael. *Clara joins the circus*
Peterson, Cris. *Amazing grazing*
    Extra cheese, please!
Poskanzer, Susan Cornell. *Dairy farmer*
Rogers, Hal. *Milking machines*
Root, Phyllis. *Kiss the cow*
Royston, Angela. *Cow*
Schertle, Alice. *How now, brown cow?*
Schnitzler, Pattie L. *Widdermaker*
Schuh, Mari C. *Cows on the farm*
Scruton, Clive. *Circus cow*
Sewall, Marcia. *The wee, wee mannie and the big, big coo*
Smith, Linda. *When Moon fell down*
Speed, Toby. *Two cool cows*
Talley, Carol. *Clarissa*
Thomas, Patricia. *"There are rocks in my socks!" said the ox to the fox*
Weidt, Maryann N. *Daddy played music for the cows*
Wheeler, Lisa. *Sixteen cows*
Whishaw, Iona. *Henry and the cow problem*
Whybrow, Ian. *Parcel for Stanley*
Wiseman, Bernard. *Morris the moose*
    Oscar is a mama
Woodworth, Viki. *Daisy the dancing cow*
    Daisy the firecow
Wright, Dare. *Look at a calf*
Ziefert, Harriet. *Cow in the house*
Zullo, Germano. *Marta and the bicycle*

Animals – bushbabies

Kennaway, Adrienne. *Bushbaby*

Animals – camels

Bailey, Donna. *Camels*
Carryl, Charles E. (Charles Edward). *The camel's lament*
Coatsworth, Elizabeth. *Song of the camels*
Eduar, Gilles. *Dream journey*
Goodenow, Earle. *The last camel*
Hamsa, Bobbie. *Your pet camel*
Kipling, Rudyard. *How the camel got his hump*, ill. by Quentin Blake
    How the camel got his hump, ill. by Tim Raglin
    How the camel got his hump, ill. by Lisbeth Zwerger
Lewin, Betsy. *What's the matter, Habibi?*
McKee, David. *The day the tide went out and out and out*
Manuel, Lynn. *Camels always do*
Oppenheim, Shulamith Levey. *The hundredth name*
Parker, Nancy Winslow. *The Christmas camel*
Peet, Bill (William Bartlett). *Pamela Camel*
Roberts, Bethany. *Camel caravan*
Rubinetti, Donald. *Cappy the lonely camel*
Simon, Francesca. *Camels don't ski*
Thury, Frederick. *The last straw*
Tworkov, Jack. *The camel who took a walk*
Wells, Rosemary. *Abdul*

Animals – caribou *see* Animals – reindeer

Animals – cats

Abercrombie, Barbara. *Charlie Anderson*
    Michael and the cats
Abley, Mark. *Ghost cat*
Adam, Barbara. *The big, big box*

Adoff, Arnold. *Daring Dog and Captain Cat*
Æsop. *Belling the cat*
    Town mouse, country mouse, ill. by Jan Brett
Aggs, Patrice. *The visitor*
Ahlberg, Allan. *The black cat*
Alcantara, Ricardo. *Dog and cat*
Alexander, Lloyd. *The house Gobbaleen*
    How the cat swallowed thunder
Aliki. *Tabby*
Allen, Jeffrey. *Up the steps, down the slide*
Allen, Jonathan. *My cat*
    Purple sock, pink sock
Allen, Pamela. *My cat Maisie*
Alter, Anna. *Estelle and Lucy*
Althea. *Jeremy Mouse and cat*
Ambrus, Victor G. *Grandma, Felix, and Mustapha Biscuit*
Amoore, Susannah. *Motley the cat*
Anderson, Douglas. *Let's draw a story*
Appelt, Kathi. *The Alley Cat's Meow*
Apple, Margot. *Brave Martha*
Aralan, Haydé. *Milton*
    Milton's Christmas
Arbeit, Eleanor Werner. *Mrs. Cat hides something*
Archambault, John. *A beautiful feast for a big king cat*
Armitage, Ronda. *The lighthouse keeper's catastrophe*
Armstrong, Jennifer. *Chin Yu Min and the ginger cat*
Arnold, Katya. *Meow!*
Arnold, Marsha Diane. *Metro cat*
Asare, Meshack. *Cat . . . in search of a friend*
Asch, Frank. *Mr. Maxwell's mouse*
Asher, Sandy. *Stella's dancing days*
Astley, Judy. *When one cat woke up*
Aulaire, Ingri Mortenson d'. *Foxie, the singing dog*
Austin, Patricia. *The cat who loved Mozart*
Averill, Esther. *The fire cat*
Axworthy, Anni. *Along came Toto*
Aylesworth, Jim. *McGraw's Emporium*
    Mother Halverson's new cat
Baba, Noboru. *Eleven cats and a pig*
    Eleven cats and albatrosses
    Eleven cats in a bag
    Eleven hungry cats
Babbitt, Natalie. *Nellie, a cat on her own*
Bahous, Sally. *Sitti and the cats*
Bailey, Mary Bryant. *Jeoffry's Christmas*
Baker, Barbara. *Digby and Kate*
    Digby and Kate again
    Digby and Kate and the beautiful day
Baker, Keith. *Cat tricks*
Baker, Leslie A. *The antique store cat*
    Paris cat
    The third-story cat
Balian, Lorna. *Amelia's nine lives*
    Leprechauns never lie
Ballard, Robin. *Cat and Alex and the magic flying carpet*
Barbaresi, Nina. *Firemouse*
Barber, Antonia. *Catkin*
    The mousehole cat
Barbero, Maria. *The bravest mouse*
Bare, Colleen Stanley. *Critter, the class cat*
    To love a cat
Barnes-Murphy, Rowan. *Numbers*
Barrows, Marjorie Wescott. *Fraidy cat*
Bartoletti, Susan Campbell. *Nobody's nosier than a cat*
Barton, Byron. *The wee little woman*
Bascom, Joe. *Malcolm Softpaws*
    Malcolm's job
Bassède, Francine. *George paints his house*
Bayley, Nicola. *Crab cat*
    Elephant cat
    Parrot cat
    Polar bear cat
    Spider cat
Beames, Margaret. *Night cat*
Beaton, Clare. *One moose, twenty mice*
    One moose, twenty mice [board book]
Bechtold, Lisze. *Edna's tale*

Beecroft, John. *What? Another cat!*
Beisner, Monika. *Catch that cat!*
Berg, Jean Horton. *The O'Learys and friends*
    The wee little man
Bergman, Tamar. *Where is?*
Bernhard, Durga. *What's Maggie up to?*
Bernhard, Josephine Butkowska. *Lullaby*
Berson, Harold. *Raminagrobis and the mice*
The best cat in the world
Bibbel, Mark. *Oh, Harry!*
Bible. Old Testament. Jonah. *Jonah*, ill. by Kurt Mitchell
Bingham, Mindy. *Minou*
Birnbaum, Abe. *Green eyes*
Black, Floyd. *Alphabet cat*
Blegvad, Lenore. *Mr. Jensen and cat*
    Mittens for kittens and other rhymes about cats
Bloom, Becky. *Crackers*
Boegehold, Betty. *In the castle of cats*
    Pawpaw's run
    Three to get ready
Bogacki, Tomasz. *Cat and mouse in the night*
    Cat and mouse in the snow
Bogan, Paulette. *Momma's magical purse*
Bohdal, Susi. *Tom cat*
Bonners, Susan. *Why does the cat do that?*
Bonsall, Crosby Newell. *The amazing the incredible super dog*
    Listen, listen!
Borton, Lady. *Fat chance!*
Bos, Burny. *Alexander the great*
Boxall, Ed. *Francis the scaredy cat*
Boyd, Lizi. *Baby play*
Boynton, Sandra. *Chloë and Maude*
Bradford, Karleen. *You can't rush a cat*
Bradman, Tony. *A goodnight kind of feeling*
Brandenberg, Franz. *Aunt Nina and her nephews and nieces*
    Aunt Nina's visit
    No school today!
    A robber! A robber!
    What's wrong with a van?
Brenner, Barbara A. *Where's that cat?*
Brent, Isabelle. *Cameo cats*
Brett, Jan. *Annie and the wild animals*
    Comet's nine lives
Brewster, Patience. *Ellsworth and the cats from Mars*
Bright, Robert. *Miss Pattie*
Brimner, Larry Dane. *Cat on wheels*
Brown, Marc Tolon. *The cloud over Clarence*
Brown, Marcia. *Felice*
Brown, Margaret Wise. *House of a hundred windows*
    Night and day
    A pussycat's Christmas, ill. by Anne Mortimer
    Pussycat's Christmas, ill. by Helen Stone
    Sneakers
    Sneakers, the seaside cat
    When the wind blew
Brown, Myra Berry. *Benjy's blanket*
Brown, Ruth. *Copycat*
    Holly, the true story of a cat
    Our cat Flossie
Bruna, Dick. *Kitten Nell*
Bryan, Ashley. *The cat's purr*
Buck, Nola. *Oh, cats!*
Buck, Pearl S. (Pearl Sydenstricker). *The Chinese story teller*
Buckmaster, Henrietta. *Lucy and Loki*
Bulla, Clyde Robert. *Valentine cat*
Burch, Robert. *Joey's cat*
Burns, Theresa. *You're not my cat*
Burton, Jane. *Ginger the kitten*
    Kitten
Butterworth, Nick. *Jasper's beanstalk*
    Jingle bells
    Just like Jasper
Byrd, Robert. *Marcella was bored*
Calder, S. J. *If you were a cat*
Calhoun, Mary. *Audubon cat*
    Blue-ribbon Henry
    Cross-country cat

Henry the Christmas cat
Henry the sailor cat
High-wire Henry
Hot-air Henry
The nine lives of Homer C. Cat
Tonio's cat
The witch of Hissing Hill
The witch who lost her shadow
Wobble the witch cat
Calmenson, Stephanie. *Kinderkittens, show-and-tell*
   Kinderkittens, who took the cookie from the cookie jar?
Cameron, Alice. *The cat sat on the mat*
Cameron, John. *If mice could fly*
Cameron, Polly. *The cat who thought he was a tiger*
Campbell, Rod. *Misty's mischief*
Caple, Kathy. *Hillary to the rescue*
   Starring Hillary
Capucilli, Alyssa Satin. *Biscuit wants to play*
   Happy birthday, Biscuit!
   Mrs. McTats and her houseful of cats
   Only my mom and me
Carle, Eric. *Have you seen my cat?*
Carlson, Nancy L. *Arnie and the skateboard gang*
   Arnie goes to camp
Carlson, Natalie Savage. *Spooky and the bad luck raven*
   Spooky and the ghost cat
   Spooky and the witch's goat
   Spooky and the wizard's bats
   Spooky night
Carlstrom, Nancy White. *What does the rain play?*
Carroll, Ruth. *Old Mrs. Billups and the black cats*
Carter, Anne Laurel. *Bella's secret garden*
Carter, Noelle. *Where's my squishy ball?*
Cartlidge, Michelle. *Teddy's cat*
Casey, Patricia. *My cat Jack*
Cash, Megan Montague. *What makes the seasons?*
Cass, Joan E. *The cat thief*
   The cats go to market
Cassedy, Sylvia. *The best cat suit of all*
Cate, Rikki. *A cat's tale*
Cazet, Denys. *Are there any questions?*
   Good morning, Maxine!
   Never spit on your shoes
Cech, John. *The southernmost cat*
Cecil, Mirabel. *Lottie's cats*
Chalmers, Audrey. *Fancy be good*
Chalmers, Mary. *Be good, Harry*
   Boots finds a house
   The cat who liked to pretend
   Come to the doctor, Harry
   George Appleton
   Merry Christmas, Harry
   Mr. Cat's wonderful surprise
   Take a nap, Harry
   Throw a kiss, Harry
Chapman, Jean. *Moon-Eyes*
Charles, Donald. *Calico Cat at school*
   Calico Cat at the zoo
   Calico Cat meets bookworm
   Calico Cat's exercise book
   Calico Cat's year
   Time to rhyme with Calico Cat
Chenery, Janet. *Pickles and Jake*
Cherry, Lynne. *Archie, follow me*
Chittum, Ida. *The cat's pajamas*
Choi, Yangsook. *New cat*
Chorao, Kay. *Ida and Betty and the secret eggs*
   Knock at the door and other baby action rhymes
Chottin, Ariane. *Little Mouse's rescue*
Christian, Mary Blount. *Scarabee, the witch's cat*
Chwast, Seymour. *Harry, I need you!*
   Traffic jam
Cleary, Beverly. *Two dog biscuits*
Clements, Andrew. *Dolores and the big fire*
   Temple cat, ill. by Kate Kiesler
   Temple cat, ill. by Alan Marks
Cleveland-Peck, Patricia. *City cat, country cat*

Coats, Laura Jane. *City cat*
Coatsworth, Elizabeth. *The giant golden book of cat stories*
Cocca-Leffler, Maryann. *Wednesday is spaghetti day*
Coffelt, Nancy. *The dog who cried woof*
   Good night, Sigmund
Coffey, Maria. *A cat adrift*
   A cat in a kayak
   A seal in the family
Cohen, Caron Lee. *Whiffle Squeek*
Cohn, Norma. *Brother and sister*
Cole, Joanna. *My new kitten*
Collington, Peter. *Clever cat*
   My darling kitten
Cook, Bernadine. *Looking for Susie*
Coombs, Patricia. *The magician and McTree*
Cooper, Elisha. *Magic thinks big*
Cooper, Helen (Helen F.). *Pumpkin soup*
Cooper, Jacqueline. *Angus and the Mona Lisa*
Coplans, Peta. *Cat and dog*
Corrin, Ruth. *Mister cat*
Costa, Nicoletta. *The birthday party [board book]*
   Dressing up
   A friend comes to play
   The missing cat
   Molly and Tom, the birthday party
Cousins, Lucy. *Katy Cat and Beaky Boo*
Cowley, Stewart. *Five little kittens*
Coxon, Michèle. *The cat who lost his purr*
Craft, Ruth. *Carrie Hepple's garden*
Crawford, Phyllis. *The blot*
Cretan, Gladys Yessayan. *Lobo and Brewster*
Crimi, Carolyn. *Tessa's tip-tapping toes*
Crozat, François. *I am a little cat*
Cushman, Doug. *Space cat*
da Costa, Deborah. *Snow in Jerusalem*
Daily, Don. *The twelve days of Christmas cats*
Dalmais, Anne-Marie. *Best bedtime stories of Mother Cat*
   Kelly the kitten
Damjan, Mischa. *The little prince and the tiger cat*
Darling, Kathy (Mary Kathleen). *ABC cats*
Dauer, Rosamond. *The 300 pound cat*
Daugherty, Charles Michael. *Wisher*
Davis, David (David R.). *Jazz cats*
Davis, Douglas F. *There's an elephant in the garage*
Day, Nancy Raines. *A kitten's year*
Deeter, Catherine. *Seymour Bleu*
Degen, Bruce. *Aunt Possum and the pumpkin man*
DeJong, David Cornel. *Looking for Alexander*
DeLage, Ida. *The old witch and the wizard*
Demarest, Chris L. *Kitman and Willy at sea*
   The lunatic adventure of Kitman and Willy
Demi. *So soft kitty*
Dennis, Morgan. *Skit and Skat*
De Paola, Tomie (Thomas Anthony). *Bonjour, Mister Satie*
   Katie, Kit and cousin Tom
   Kit and Kat
De Regniers, Beatrice Schenk. *Cats cats cats*
   Everyone is good for something
   Picture book theater
   So many cats!
Desimini, Lisa. *I am running away today*
Dick Whittington and his cat. *Dick Whittington*, ill. by Edward Ardizzone
   Dick Whittington, ill. by Antony Maitland
   Dick Whittington and his cat, ill. by Marcia Brown
   Dick Whittington and his cat, ill. by Kurt Werth
Dickson, Louise. *The vanishing cat*
Dillon, Eilis. *The cats' opera*
Disher, Garry. *Switch cat*
Diska, Pat. *Andy says . . . Bonjour!*
Dodd, Lynley. *Hairy Maclary from Donaldson's dairy*
   Hairy Maclary, Scattercat
   Hairy Maclary's caterwaul caper
   Hairy Maclary's showbusiness
   The minister's cat: ABC
   Slinky Malinki
   Slinky Malinki catflaps

Slinky Malinki, open the door
Doherty, Berlie. *Paddiwak and cozy*, ill. by Alison Bartlett
    Paddiwak and cozy, ill. by Teresa O'Brien
Douglas, Michael. *Round, round world*
Dowling, Paul. *Are you sleepy, Puff?*
Doyle, Malachy. *Storm cats*
Drake, John. *The beginning of the river*
Driscoll, Laura. *The bravest cat!*
Dubanevich, Arlene. *Tom's tail*
Duncan, Lois. *I walk at night*
Duvoisin, Roger Antoine. *Veronica and the birthday present*
Egielski, Richard. *Slim and Jim*
Ehlert, Lois. *Feathers for lunch*
    Top cat
Eisler, Colin. *Cats know best*
Eliot, T. S. (Thomas Stearns). *Mr. Mistoffelees with Mungojerrie and
    Rumpelteazer*
Elsdale, Bob. *Mac side up*
Elzbieta. *Brave Babette and sly Tom*
Emberley, Michael. *Ruby*
Ernst, Lisa Campbell. *The rescue of Aunt Pansy*
Ets, Marie Hall. *Mr. T. W. Anthony Woo*
Evans, Eva Knox. *That lucky Mrs. Plucky*
Evans, Mark. *Kitten*
Faglia, Maeto. *Happy birthday, I'm 3*
Farish, Terry. *The cat who liked potato soup*
Farjeon, Eleanor. *Cats*
    Cats sleep anywhere, ill. by Mary Price Jenkins
    Cats sleep anywhere, ill. by Anne Mortimer
The fat cat
Fatio, Louise. *Marc and Pixie and the walls in Mrs. Jones's garden*
Faunce-Brown, Daphne. *Snuffles' house*
Feder, Jane. *Beany*
Fehlner, Paul. *Dog and cat*
Field, Eugene. *The gingham dog and the calico cat*, ill. by Janet
    Street
    The gingham dog and the calico cat, ill. by Johanna Westerman
Fischer-Nagel, Heiderose. *A kitten is born*
Fish, Hans. *Pitschi, the kitten who always wanted to do something else*
Flack, Marjorie. *Angus and the cat*
    William and his kitten
Fleming, Denise. *Mama cat has three kittens*
Florian, Douglas. *Bow wow meow meow, it's rhyming cats and dogs*
Flory, Jane. *We'll have a friend for lunch*
Foreman, Michael. *Cat and canary*
    Cat in the manger
Forrester, Victoria. *The magnificent moo*
Fowler, Richard. *Cat's story*
Frascino, Edward. *My cousin the king*
    Nanny Noony and the dust queen
    Nanny Noony and the magic spell
French, Vivian. *Christmas kitten*
    A present for mom
Freschet, Berniece. *Furlie Cat*
Friedman, Mel. *Kitten castle*
Fujikawa, Gyo. *Shags finds a kitten*
Funakoshi, Canna. *One morning*
Gág, Flavia. *Chubby's first year*
Gág, Wanda. *Millions of cats*
Galdone, Paul. *King of the cats*
Gantos, Jack (John, Jr.). *Back to school for Rotten Ralph*
    Happy birthday, Rotten Ralph
    Not so Rotten Ralph
    Rotten Ralph
    Rotten Ralph's Halloween howl
    Rotten Ralph's rotten Christmas
    Rotten Ralph's rotten romance
    Rotten Ralph's show and tell
    Rotten Ralph's trick or treat
    Wedding bells for Rotten Ralph
    Worse than Rotten Ralph
Garland, Michael. *Angel cat*
Gay, Marie-Louise. *Moonbeam on a cat's ear*
Gay, Michel. *Rabbit express*
Geraghty, Paul. *Slobcat*
Geras, Adèle. *Sleep tight, Ginger Kitten*
Gerstein, Mordicai. *The new creatures*

Ghigna, Charles. *Good cats/Bad cats*
Gibbon, David. *Kittens*
Gibbons, Gail. *Cats*
Giff, Patricia Reilly. *Good luck, Ronald Morgan*
Gill, Janet. *Basket Weaver and Catches Many Mice*
Ginsburg, Mirra. *Kitten from one to ten*
    Three kittens
Godwin, Laura. *The best fall of all*
    Happy and Honey
    Happy Christmas, Honey
    Honey helps
Gollub, Matthew. *The twenty-five Mixtec cats*
Goodall, John S. *The surprise picnic*
Gordon, Gaelyn. *Duckat*
Gordon, Margaret. *The supermarket mice*
Goyder, Alice. *Holiday in Catland*
    Party in Catland
Grabianski, Janusz. *Cats*
Graham, Bob. *Libby, Oscar and me*
Graham-Yooll, Liz. *Timothy Tib*
Gravdahl, John. *Curious catwalk*
Gray, Nigel. *The dog show*
Greaves, Margaret. *Henry's wild morning*
    The witch cat
Greenburg, Dan. *Great-Grandpa's in the litter box*
Greene, Carol. *The old ladies who liked cats*
    Where is that cat?
Griessman, Annette. *Jenny's prayer*
Griffith, Helen V. *Alex and the cat*
    Alex remembers
    More Alex and the cat
Grimm, Jacob. *The fisherman and his wife*, ill. by Eleanor Hubbard
    Godfather Cat and Mousie
Haas, Jessie. *Chipmunk!*
Hafner, Marylin. *Molly and Emmett's camping adventure*
    Molly and Emmett's surprise garden
    A year with Molly and Emmett
Hains, Harriet. *Our new kitten*
Hale, Kathleen. *Orlando and the water cats*
    Orlando buys a farm
    Orlando, the frisky housewife
Haley, Gail E. *The post office cat*
Hall, Donald. *I am the dog, I am the cat*
Hamilton, DeWitt. *Sad days, glad days*
Hamley, Dennis. *Tigger and friends*
Hänel, Wolfram. *Mia the beach cat*
Hannant, Judith Stuller. *Three little kittens*
Hardy, Tad. *Lost cat*
Harjo, Joy. *The good luck cat*
Harper, Dan. *Telling time with Big Mama Cat*
Harper, Jessica. *I'm not going to chase the cat today*
Harris, Lee. *Never let your cat make lunch for you*
Harvey, Amanda. *Dog days*
Harvey, Bev. *The cat family*
Hasler, Eveline. *Winter magic*
Hassett, John. *Cat up a tree*
Hausherr, Rosmarie. *My first kitten*
Hautzig, Deborah. *Ernie and Bert's new kitten*
Hawkins, Colin. *Pat the cat*
Hayes, Geoffrey. *Elroy and the witch's child*
Hayes, Sarah. *The cats of Tiffany Street*
Hayward, Linda. *Alphabet School*
Hazen, Barbara Shook. *The Fat Cats, Cousin Scraggs and the monster
    mice*
    Tight times
Hearn, Diane Dawson. *Bad luck Boswell*
Hearn, Michael Patrick. *The porcelain cat*
Heilbroner, Joan. *Tom the TV cat*
Helmer, Diana Star. *The cat who came for tacos*
Helmer, Marilyn. *Mr. McGratt and the ornery cat*
    Three cat and mouse tales
Hendry, Diana. *Back soon!*
Henkes, Kevin. *Kitten's first full moon*
Henry, Steve. *Nobody asked me!*
Herman, Gail. *Fievel's big showdown*
    The haunted house
    Otto the cat

Pizza cats
Herriot, James. *Christmas Day kitten*
  Moses the kitten
Hesse, Karen. *Lester's dog*
Hill, Susan. *Stuart hides out*
Hiller, Catherine. *Abracatabby*
Hillert, Margaret. *The little runaway*
Hindley, Judy. *Mrs. Mary Malarky's seven cats*
Hines-Stephens, Sarah. *Bean's games*
Hirschi, Ron. *What is a cat?*
Hiskey, Iris. *Cassandra who?*
Hoban, Julia. *Buzby to the rescue*
Hoban, Russell. *Flat cat*
Hoban, Tana. *One little kitten*
Hoberman, Mary Ann. *The looking book*
  The two sillies
Hodge, Deborah. *Wild cats*
Hoff, Syd. *Captain Cat*
Hofsepian, Sylvia A. *Why not?*
Hogrogian, Nonny. *The cat who loved to sing*
Holmes, Efner Tudor. *The Christmas cat*
Holub, Joan. *Cinderdog and the wicked stepcat*
  Scat cats
  Why do cats meow?
Hood, Susan. *Meet Trouble*
Horn, Emily. *Excuse me – are you a witch?*
Howe, James. *Creepy-crawly birthday*
  Pinky and Rex and the just-right pet
  Rabbit-Cadabra!
  Scared silly
Howell, Lynn. *Winifred's new bed*
Hubbell, Patricia. *Wrapping paper romp*
Hudelhoff, Allen H. *Cats and kids*
Hughes, Shirley. *Alfie and the birthday surprise*
Huling, Jan. *Puss in cowboy boots*
Hulse, Gillian. *Morris, where are you?*
Hurd, Edith Thacher. *Come and have fun*
  No funny business
  The so-so cat
Hurd, Thacher. *Axle the freeway cat*
  Cat's pajamas
  Tomato soup
Hürlimann, Ruth. *The proud white cat*
Hutchins, H. J. (Hazel J.). *One dark night*
Imai, Miko. *Lilly's secret*
Imoto, Yoko. *Skipper at the beach*
  Skipper is the daddy
Ingman, Bruce. *A night on the tiles*
Inkiow, Dimiter. *Me and Clara and Casimir the cat*
Inkpen, Mick. *Meow!*
Ipcar, Dahlov (Zorach). *The cat at night*
  The cat came back
Isaacs, Anne. *Cat up a tree*
Ivory, Lesley Anne. *The birthday cat*
  Cats in the sun
  Meet my cats
Jack Sprat. *The life of Jack Sprat, his wife and his cat*
James, Betsy. *He wakes me*
Jane, Pamela. *Milo and the greatest trick ever*
Janice. *Minette*
Jenkin-Pearce, Susie. *Bad Boris and the new kitten*
Jenkins, Emily. *Five creatures*
Jennings, Linda M. *Easy peasy!*
Jennings, Sharon. *Priscilla's paw de deux*
Jensen, Patricia. *Kitty's special job*
Jeschke, Susan. *Lucky's choice*
Jessell, Camilla. *The kitten book*
Jewell, Nancy. *ABC cat*
  Five little kittens
Jobling, Curtis. *Frankenstein's cat*
Johansen, K. V. (Krista V.). *Pippin and Pudding*
Johnson, Diana F. *Princesa and Friskie*
Johnson, Paul Brett. *Mr. Persnickety and Cat Lady*
Johnston, Tony. *The old lady and the birds*
Jonathan, Langley. *Missing*
Jones, Elizabeth. *Sunshine and Storm*
Jonovitz, Marilyn. *Three little kittens*

Joosse, Barbara M. *Nugget and Darling*
Jung, Minna. *William's ninth life*
Jungman, Ann. *When the people are away*
Kahl, Virginia. *Whose cat is that?*
Kamen, Gloria. *Second-hand cat*
Kanao, Keiko. *Kitten up a tree*
Kangas, Juli. *Ginger Kitten's surprise*
Karlin, Nurit. *The fat cat sat on the mat*
Kay, Helen. *A stocking for a kitten*
Keats, Ezra Jack. *Hi, cat!*
  Kitten for a day
  Pssst! doggie
Keens-Douglas, Richard. *The Miss Meow pageant*
Keeshan, Robert. *Itty Bitty Kitty*
  Itty Bitty Kitty makes a big splash
Keillor, Garrison. *Cat, you better come home*
Keller, Holly. *A bed full of cats*
Kellogg, Steven (Stephen). *A rose for Pinkerton*
  Tallyho, Pinkerton!
Kemp, Moira. *Lift-the-flap kitten*
Kennedy, Joseph. *Lucy goes to the country*
Kent, Lorna. *No, no, Charlie Rascal!*
Kerr, Judith. *Mog and bunny*
  Mog, the forgetful cat
  Mog's bad thing
  Mog's Christmas
Ketteman, Helen. *Grandma's cat*
Kettner, Christine. *An ordinary cat*
Khalsa, Dayal Kaur. *Green cat*
  The snow cat
Kherdian, David. *The cat's midsummer jamboree*
  Country cat, city cat
Killilea, Marie (Marie Lyons). *Newf*
Kimmel, Eric A. *Ten suns*
King, Deborah. *Cloudy*
Kinsey-Warnock, Natalie. *Wilderness cat*
Kitamura, Satoshi. *Captain Toby*
  Comic adventures of Boots
  Me and my cat?
Knotts, Howard. *The summer cat*
  The winter cat
Kocí, Marta. *Katie's kitten*
Koehler, Phoebe. *Making room*
Koenig, Marion. *The tale of fancy Nancy*
  The wonderful world of night
Komoda, Beverly. *Simon's soup*
Koontz, Robin Michal. *Chicago and the cat*
  Chicago and the cat, the camping trip
  Chicago and the cat, the family reunion
  Pussycat ate the dumplings
Koralek, Jenny. *Cat and Kit*
Krahn, Fernando. *Catch that cat!*
Krasilovsky, Phyllis. *Scaredy cat*
Kraus, Robert. *Big Squeak, Little Squeak*
  Come out and play, little mouse
Krensky, Stephen. *Fraidy Cats*
Kroll, Steven. *Branigan's cat and the Halloween ghost*
  It's April Fools' Day!
Kunhardt, Dorothy. *Kitty's new doll*
Kunhardt, Edith. *Pat the cat*
Kuskin, Karla. *The upstairs cat*
Kyte, Dennis. *Mattie and Cataragus*
Lachner, Dorothea. *Look out, Cinder!*
Lakin, Patricia. *Clarence the copy cat*
Landa, Norbert. *Kittens*
Landalf, Helen. *The secret night world of cats*
Landshoff, Ursula. *Cats are good company*
Lansdown, Brenda. *Galumph*
Larrick, Nancy. *Cats are cats*
Laskowski, Jerzy. *Master of the royal cats*
Lasson, Robert. *Orange Oliver*
Lawrence, John. *Rabbit and pork*
Lawson, Janet (Janet M.). *Audrey and Barbara*
Lear, Edward. *Of pelicans and pussycats*
  The owl and the pussy cat, ill. by Ian Beck
  The owl and the pussycat, ill. by Jan Brett
  The owl and the pussycat, ill. by Lorinda Bryan Cauley

The owl and the pussy-cat, ill. by Barbara Cooney
The owl and the pussycat, ill. by Emma Crosby
The owl and the pussy-cat, ill. by William Pène Du Bois
The owl and the pussycat, ill. by Lori Farbanish
The owl and the pussy-cat, ill. by Gwen Fulton
The owl and the pussy-cat, ill. by Paul Galdone
The owl and the pussycat, ill. by Elaine Muis
The owl and the pussycat, ill. by Erica Rutherford
The owl and the pussycat, ill. by Janet Stevens
The owl and the pussy-cat, ill. by Louise Voce
The owl and the pussycat, ill. by Colin West
The owl and the pussy-cat, ill. by Owen Wood
Le Guin, Ursula K. *A visit from Dr. Katz*
Leman, Jill. *Ten little pussy cats*
Lent, Blair. *Ruby and Fred*
Leonard, Marcia. *The kitten twins*
   Violet and the pirates
Leslie, Amanda. *Play kitten play*
Le-Tan, Pierre. *The afternoon cat*
Levine, Arthur A. *The boy who drew cats*
Levitin, Sonia. *All the cats in the world*
Lewin, Betsy. *Cat count*
Lewis, J. Patrick. *The Fat-Cats at sea*
Lewis, Naomi. *The stepsister*
Lexau, Joan M. *Come here, cat*
Lillie, Patricia. *Jake and Rosie*
Lindbloom, Steven. *Let's give kitty a bath!*
Lindgren, Barbro. *Sam's ball*
Lindman, Maj. *Flicka, Ricka, Dicka and the three kittens*
Lipkind, William. *Russet and the two reds*
   The two reds
The little book of cats
Little Robin Redbreast
Lively, Penelope. *The cat, the crow, and the banyan tree*
Livermore, Elaine. *Find the cat*
   Three little kittens lost their mittens
Livingston, Myra Cohn. *Cat poems*
Lloyd, David. *Cat and dog*
Lobel, Anita. *One lighthouse, one moon*
Lobel, Arnold. *The rose in my garden*
   Whiskers and rhymes
Lockwood, Primrose. *Cat boy!*
London, Jonathan. *Hip cat*
Luttrell, Ida. *Mattie's little possum pet*
Lyon, George Ella. *A traveling cat*
MacArthur-Onslow, Annette Rosemary. *Minnie*
McBratney, Sam. *The dark at the top of the stairs*
McCarty, Peter. *Hondo and Fabian*
McClintock, Barbara. *The battle of Luke and Longnose*
McClure, Gillian. *Tom Finger*
McCully, Emily Arnold. *Four hungry kittens*
MacDonald, Margaret Read. *Fat cat*
   Mabela the clever
McFarland, Lyn Rossiter. *Widget & the puppy*
McGraw, Sheila. *Pussycats everywhere*
McGuinness-Kelly, Tracy-Lee. *Bad Cat puts on his top hat*
McGurn, Patty. *Me and Marie*
Macken, JoAnn Early. *Cats on Judy*
   Kittens
MacKinnon, Debbie. *Ken's kitten*
   My kitty!
MacLachlan, Patricia. *Bittle*
   Who loves me?
McLaren, Chesley. *Zat cat*
McLellan, Stephanie Simpson. *The chicken cat*
McLerran, Alice. *I want to go home*
McMillan, Bruce. *Kitten can . . .*
McMullan, Kate (Hall). *Kitty riddles*
   No no Jo
   Supercat
   Supercat to the rescue
McPhail, David M. *Great cat*
McQuade, Jacqueline. *Good times with Teddy Bear*
Macsolis. *Dance moon = Baile de luna*
Magloff, Lisa. *Kitten*
Mahurin, Tim. *Jeremy Kooloo*
Mahy, Margaret. *The Christmas tree tangle*

The three-legged cat
Maitland, Barbara. *The bookstore burglar*
   The bookstore ghost
   The bookstore valentine
Malkovych, Ivan. *The cat and the rooster*
Mallat, Kathy. *Trouble on the tracks*
Mandry, Kathy. *The cat and the mouse and the mouse and the cat*
Mantegazza, Giovanna. *The cat*
Manuel, Lynn. *Lucy Maud and the Cavendish cat*
Maris, Ron. *My book*
Mark, Jan. *Fun with Mrs. Thumb*
   Fur
Martin, Ann M. *Leo the Magnificat*
Martin, David. *Lizzie and her kitty*
Martinez, Ruth. *Mrs. McDockerty's knitting*
Marzollo, Jean. *Christmas cats*
   Thanksgiving cats
   Uproar on Hollercat Hill
   Valentine cats
Maschler, Fay. *T. G. and Moonie go shopping*
   T. G. and Moonie have a baby
   T. G. and Moonie move out of town
Masurel, Claire. *A cat and a dog*
Matthias, Catherine. *I love cats*
Mayer, Mercer. *The great cat chase*
Mayne, William. *Pandora*
   The patchwork cat
   Tibber
Meddaugh, Susan. *Too short Fred*
Meggs, Libby Phillips. *Go home!*
Merriam, Eve. *The birthday door*
   Where's that cat?
Metaxas, Eric. *Puss in boots*
   The white cat
Micklethwait, Lucy. *Spot a cat*
Micucci, Charles. *A little night music*
Miller, Edna. *Patches finds a new home*
Miller, Sara Swan. *Cat in the bag*
Miller, Virginia. *Be gentle!*
   Ten red apples
Minarik, Else Holmelund. *Cat and dog*
   It's spring!
Mockford, Caroline. *Cleo and Caspar*
   Cleo in the snow
   Cleo on the move
   Cleo the cat
   Cleo's alphabet book
   Cleo's counting book
   Come here, Cleo
Modell, Frank. *Seen any cats?*
Mole, John. *Copy cat*
Moncure, Jane Belk. *The talking tabby cat*
Monks, Lydia. *The cat barked?*
Monson, A. M. *Wanted . . . best friend*
Moore, Inga. *Six dinner Sid*
Moore, Lilian. *See my lovely poison ivy, and other verses about witches,*
   ghosts and things
Mooser, Stephen. *The fat cat*
Mora, Pat. *A birthday basket for Tia*
Moran, Alex. *Come here, tiger*
   Sam and Jack
Morris, Ann. *Hello Peter = Bonjour, Rémy*
Morris, Bob. *Crispin the Terrible*
Morris, Dewi. *Sandy's street*
Moskin, Marietta D. *Lysbet and the fire kittens*
Mother Goose. *Cats by Mother Goose*
   Hickory dickory dock, ill. by Doug Cushman
   Hickory dickory dock, ill. by Marilyn Janovitz
   Kitten rhymes
   The three little kittens, ill. by Lorinda Bryan Cauley
   The three little kittens, ill. by Paul Galdone
   The three little kittens, ill. by Dorothy Stott
   The three little kittens, ill. by Shelley Thornton
Mott, Evelyn Clarke. *Cool cat*
The moving adventures of Old Dame Trot and her comical cat
Moxley, Sheila. *ABCD an alphabet book of cats and dogs*
Murphey, Sara. *The animal hat shop*

Murphy, Chuck. *Black cat, white cat*
Murphy, Stuart J. *Pepper's journal*
Murray, Andrew. *Have you seen Chester?*
Namioka, Lensey. *The loyal cat*
Napoli, Donna Jo. *Rocky, the cat who barks*
Nethery, Mary. *Hannah and Jack*
    Orange cat goes to market
Newberry, Clare Turlay. *April's kittens*
    The kittens' ABC
    Marshmallow
    Pandora
    Percy, Polly and Pete
    Smudge
    T-Bone, the baby-sitter
    Widget
Newman, Lesléa. *Cats, cats, cats*
Newton, Jill. *Cat-fish*
Nicoll, Helen. *Meg and Mog*
    Meg at sea
    Meg on the moon
    Meg's eggs
    Mog's box
Nightingale, Sandy. *Cat's knees and bee's whiskers*
Nishimura, Kae. *Dinah*
Noll, Sally. *Surprise!*
Nones, Eric Jon. *Wendell*
Nordqvist, Sven. *Festus and Mercury go camping*
    Festus and Mercury: ruckus in the garden
    Festus and Mercury wishing to go fishing
    The fox hunt
    Pancake pie
Norman, Philip Ross. *Dancing dogs*
Northrup, Mili. *The watch cat*
Norwich, William D. *Molly and the magic dress*
Oakley, Graham. *The church cat abroad*
    The church mice and the moon
    The church mice and the ring
    The church mice at bay
    The church mice spread their wings
    The church mouse
    The diary of a church mouse
Oana, Kay D. *Shasta and the shebang machine*
Oates, Joyce Carol. *Come meet Muffin!*
Obrist, Jürg. *Fluffy*
Oh, Jiwon. *Cat and mouse*
Okimoto, Jean Davies. *Blumpoe the grumpoe meets Arnold the cat*
Oller, Erika. *The cabbage soup solution*
Olson, Arielle North. *Noah's cats and the devil's fire*
Oppenheim, Joanne. *Do you like cats?*
    No way, Slippery Slick!
Oram, Hiawyn. *Just Dog*
Ormerod, Jan. *Come back, kittens*
    Kitten day
    The saucepan game
Otto, Margaret Glover. *The little brown horse*
Palazzo-Craig, Janet. *Muffy and Fluffy*
Panek, Dennis. *Catastrophe Cat*
    Catastrophe Cat at the zoo
Paré, Roger. *A friend like you*
Parish, Peggy. *The cats' burglar*
    Scruffy
Parker, Nancy Winslow. *Puddums, the Cathcarts' orange cat*
Passen, Lisa. *Grammy and Sammy*
Peacock, Carol Antoinette. *Pilgrim cat*
Pearson, Tracey Campbell. *The storekeeper*
Peet, Bill (William Bartlett). *Jennifer and Josephine*
Penner, Lucille Recht. *Where's that bone?*
Peppé, Rodney. *Cat and mouse*
    The color catalog
Perkins, Lynne Rae. *The broken cat*
Perrault, Charles. *Puss in boots*, ill. by Marcia Brown
    Puss in boots, ill. by Lorinda Bryan Cauley
    Puss in boots, ill. by Jean Claverie
    Puss in boots, ill. by Andrea Da Rif
    Puss in boots, ill. by Stasys Eidrigevicius
    Puss in boots, ill. by Hans Fischer
    Puss in boots, ill. by Paul Galdone

    Puss in boots, retold and ill. by John S. Goodall
    Puss in boots, retold and ill. by Gail E. Haley
    Puss in boots, ill. by Steve Light
    Puss in boots, ill. by Giuliano Lunelli
    Puss in boots, ill. by Fred Marcellino [pub. by Farrar, 1990]
    Puss in boots, ill. by Fred Marcellino [pub. by Farrar, 1998]
    Puss in boots, ill. by Julia Noonan
    Puss in boots, ill. by Tony Ross
    Puss in boots, ill. by William Stobbs
    Puss in boots, ill. by Yan Thomas
    Puss in boots, ill. by Alain Vaës
    Puss in boots, ill. by Barry Wilkinson
Peters, Lisa Westberg. *The hayloft*
Petersen-Fleming, Judy. *Kitten training and critters, too!*
Pevear, Richard. *Mister Cat-and-a-Half*
Pfloog, Jan. *Kittens*
Pilkey, Dav. *Dragon's fat cat*
    When cats dream
Pinkwater, Daniel Manus. *The phantom of the lunch wagon*
    Roger's umbrella
Pittman, Helena Clare. *Miss Hindy's cats*
Pizer, Abigail. *Harry's night out*
    Nosey Gilbert
Plummer, David. *Counting kittens*
Pohrt, Tom. *Having a wonderful time*
Polacco, Patricia. *Mrs. Katz and Tush*
    Tikvah means hope
Polette, Nancy. *The little old woman and the hungry cat*
Politi, Leo. *Lito and the clown*
Pomerantz, Charlotte. *The ballad of the long-tailed rat*
    Buffy and Albert
Potter, Beatrix. *The pie and the patty-pan*
    Rolly-polly pudding
    The sly old cat
    The story of Miss Moppet
    The tale of Tom Kitten
Poulin, Stéphane. *Can you catch Josephine?*
    Have you seen Josephine?
Powell, Roxanne Dyer. *Cat, mouse and moon*
Pratt, Pierre. *I see . . . my sister/I see . . . my cat*
Price, Mathew. *Patch finds a friend*
Priceman, Marjorie. *My nine lives / by Clio*
Pringle, Laurence P. *Naming the cat*
Pryor, Ainslie. *The baby blue cat and the dirty dog brothers*
    The baby blue cat and the smiley worm doll
    The baby blue cat who said no
Pullman, Philip. *Puss in boots*, ill. by Ian Beck
Pulver, Robin. *Christmas for a kitten*
Puppies and kittens
Purdy, Carol. *Mrs. Merriwether's musical cat*
Rae, Jennifer. *Dog tales*
Rankin, Joan. *The little cat and the greedy old woman*
Raschka, Christopher. *John Coltrane's giant steps*
Rathmann, Peggy. *Ruby the copycat*
Redies, Rainer. *The cats' party*
Reinen, Judy. *Meow*
Reiser, Lynn. *Bedtime cat*
    Dog and cat
    My cat Tuna
Reynolds, Marilynn. *A present for Mrs. Kazinski*
Richard, Françoise. *On Cat Mountain*
Ridlon, Marcia. *Kittens and more kittens*
Robbins, Beth. *Tom, Ally, and the baby-sitter*
    Tom, Ally, and the new baby
    Tom and Ally visit the doctor
    Tom's afraid of the dark
    Tom's first day at school
    Tom's new haircut
Robbins, Maria Polushkin. *Here's that kitten*
    Kitten in trouble
    Who said meow?, ill. by Giulio Maestro
    Who said meow?, ill. by Ellen Weiss
Roberts, Bethany. *Christmas mice*
Robertus, Polly M. *The dog who had kittens*
Robinson, Sue. *I want to play*
Robinson, Thomas P. *Buttons*
Robledo, Honorio. *Nico visits the moon*

Rockwell, Anne F. *Katie Catz makes a splash*
  Space vehicles
  The way to Captain Yankee's
Roffey, Maureen. *Here, kitty kitty!*
Rohmann, Eric. *The cinder-eyed cats*
Rose, Agatha. *Hide-and-seek in the yellow house*
Ross, Eileen. *The Halloween showdown*
Ross, George Maxim. *When Lucy went away*
Ross, Tony. *I want a cat*
  Treasure of Cozy Cove
Rowan, Paula S. *Rick and Rocky*
Rowinski, Kate. *Cats in the dark*
Rubel, Nicole. *Me and my kitty*
  Sam and Violet are twins
  Sam and Violet go camping
Ruelle, Karen Gray. *April fool*
  Easter egg disaster
  Easy as apple pie
  Snow Valentines
  Spookier than a ghost
Rylant, Cynthia. *The cookie-store cat*
  Mr. Putter and Tabby bake the cake
  Mr. Putter and Tabby paint the porch
  Mr. Putter and Tabby pick the pears
  Mr. Putter and Tabby pour the tea
  Mr. Putter and Tabby walk the dog
  Moonlight, the Halloween cat
Sage, James. *Farmer Smart's fat cat*
Samuels, Barbara. *Aloha, Dolores*
  Duncan and Dolores
Sanderson, Ruth. *Papa Gatto*
San Souci, Robert D. *The white cat*
Sara. *Across town*
Saul, Carol P. *Barn cat*
Say, Allen. *Allison*
Scamell, Ragnhild. *Solo plus one*
  The wish come true cat
Schachner, Judith Byron. *The Grannyman*
Schaffer, Marion. *I love my cat*
Schatz, Letta. *Whiskers, my cat*
Schertle, Alice. *I am the cat*
  That Olive!
Schilling, Betty. *Two kittens are born*
Scruton, Clive. *Scaredy cat*
Seguin-Fontes, Marthe. *The cat's surprise*
Seidler, Rosalie. *Grumpus and the Venetian cat*
Seignobosc, Françoise. *Minou*
Selsam, Millicent E. *A first look at cats*
  How kittens grow
Seuss, Dr. *The cat in the hat*
  The cat in the hat comes back!
Shaw, Richard. *The kitten in the pumpkin patch*
Siekkinen, Raija. *Mister King*
Silverman, Erica. *Mrs. Peachtree and the Eighth Avenue cat*
Simmie, Lois. *Mister got to go*
  Mister got to go and Arnie
Simmonds, Posy. *Fred*
Simon, Norma. *Cats do, dogs don't*
  Mama cat's year
  Oh, that cat!
  Where does my cat sleep?
Simon, Seymour. *Cats*
Siomades, Lorianne. *Three little kittens*
Skaar, Grace Marion. *Nothing but (cats) and all about (dogs)*
  The very little dog
Slate, Joseph. *Lonely Lula cat*
Slavin, Bill. *The cat came back*
Sloan, Carolyn. *Carter is a painter's cat*
Slobodkin, Louis. *Colette and the princess*
Slobodkina, Esphyr. *Billy, the condominium cat*
  Pinky and the petunias
Smart, Christopher. *For I will consider my cat Jeoffry*
Smith, Maggie (Margaret C.). *Desser, the best ever cat*
Smyth, Gwenda. *A pet for Mrs. Arbuckle*
Sneed, Brad. *Lucky Russell*
Snow, Alan. *The truth about cats*
So, Meilo. *Gobble, gobble, slip, slop*

Soto, Gary. *Chato and the party animals*
  Chato's kitchen
Spanner, Helmut. *I am a little cat*
Spier, Peter. *Little cats*
Spires, Elizabeth. *The big meow*
Spohn, Kate. *Clementine's winter wardrobe*
Stadler, John. *Catilda*
  The cats of Mrs. Calamari
Stainton, Sue. *The lighthouse cat*
  Santa's snow cat
Standon, Anna. *Three little cats*
Stanley, Diane. *Captain Whiz-Bang*
  A country tale
  Siegfried
Steel, Danielle. *Max and the baby sitter*
Steig, William. *Solomon the rusty nail*
Stein, Sara Bonnett. *Cat*
Steiner, Charlotte. *Kiki and Muffy*
Stephens, Helen. *I'm too busy*
  What about me?
Stern, Peter. *Floyd, a cat's story*
Stevens, Cat. *Teaser and the firecat*
Stevens, Janet. *My big dog*
Stock, Catherine. *Sampson the Christmas cat*
Stoddard, Sandol. *My very own special particular private and personal cat*
Stone, Bernard. *The charge of the mouse brigade*
Stratemeyer, Clara Georgeanna. *Pepper*
Sturgis, Matthew. *Tosca's surprise*
Sumiko. *Kittymouse*
Sutton, Eve. *My cat likes to hide in boxes*
Sykes, Julie. *This and that*
Szekeres, Cyndy. *Suppertime for Frieda Fuzzypaws*
Taber, Anthony. *Cats' eyes*
Tan, Amy. *The Chinese Siamese cat*
Tapio, Pat Decker. *The lady who saw the good side of everything*
Taylor, Mark. *The case of the missing kittens*
Teague, Mark. *Detective LaRue*
  The trouble with the Johnsons
Thayer, Jane. *The cat that joined the club*
Thompson, Harwood. *The witch's cat*
Thornhill, Jan. *Wild in the city*
Tiller, Ruth. *Cats vanish slowly*
Titus, Eve. *Anatole and the cat*
  The kitten who couldn't purr
Tufts, Mary L. *The wee kitten who sucked her thumb*
Turkle, Brinton. *Do not open*
Turnbull, Ann. *The tapestry cats*
Uchida, Yoshiko. *The two foolish cats*
Udry, Janice May. *"Oh no, cat!"*
Ungerer, Tomi. *Flix*
  No kiss for mother
Untermeyer, Louis. *The kitten who barked*
Unwin, Pippa. *Tomcat takes a walk*
Vagin, Vladimir Vasilévich. *Here comes the cat*
Vainio, Pirkko. *The dream house*
Van Haeringen, Annemarie. *The cats' tale*
Van Horn, William. *Harry Hoyle's giant jumping bean*
Vesey, A. *Merry Christmas, Thomas!*
Viorst, Judith. *The tenth good thing about Barney*
Voake, Charlotte. *Ginger*
  Pizza kittens
  Tom's cat
Volkmann, Roy. *Curious kittens*
Waber, Bernard. *Lyle at Christmas*
  Mice on my mind
  Rich cat, poor cat
Waddell, Martin. *A kitten called Moonlight*
  Who do you love?
Wagner, Jenny. *John Brown, Rose and the midnight cat*
Wahl, Jan. *Dracula's cat*
  Dracula's cat and Frankenstein's dog
  My cat Ginger
  Push Kitty
Waite, Judy. *Mouse, look out!*
  The stray kitten
Wallace-Brodeur, Ruth. *Goodbye, Mitch*

Wallis, Diz. *Pip's adventure*
Ward, Cindy. *Cookie's week*
Wardlaw, Lee. *The tales of Grandpa Cat*
Warner, Sunny. *Madison finds a line*
    The moon quilt
Washington, Donna L. *The big, spooky house*
Watson, Pauline. *Curley Cat baby-sits*
Watson, Wendy. *Happy Easter day!*
Watt, Fiona. *Kittens*
Weaver, Tess. *Opera cat*
Weigelt, Udo. *Ben and the Buccaneers*
Weihs, Erika. *Count the cats*
Weilerstein, Sadie Rose. *K'tonton's Yom Kippur kitten*
Welch, Martha McKeen. *Will that wake mother?*
Wellington, Monica. *Night city*
    Squeaking of art, the mice go to the museum
Wells, Rosemary. *Mama, don't go!*
    The school play
    Yoko
    Yoko's paper cranes
West, Judy. *Have you got my purr?*
Westell, Kerry. *Amanda's book*
Wethered, Peggy. *Touchdown Mars!*
Wezel, Peter. *The naughty bird*
Wheeler, Cindy. *Marmalade's Christmas present*
    Marmalade's nap
    Marmalade's picnic
    Marmalade's snowy day
    Marmalade's yellow leaf
Whitmore, Adam. *Max in America*
    Max in Australia
    Max in India
    Max leaves home
Whitney, Alma Marshak. *Leave Herbert alone*
Whittle, Emily. *Sailor cats*
Whybrow, Ian. *Parcel for Stanley*
Wijngaard, Juan. *Cat*
Wild, Margaret. *Big cat dreaming*
    The very best of friends
Wild, Robin. *Spot's dogs and the alley cats*
Wilkon, Piotr. *The brave little kittens*
    Rosie the cool cat
Willard, Nancy. *The mouse, the cat and Grandmother's hat*
Willis, Jeanne. *Earth tigerlets as explained by Professor Xargle*
Wilson, Budge. *The fear of Angelina Domino*
Wilson, Joyce Lancaster. *Tobi*
Wishinsky, Frieda. *Give Maggie a chance*
Withers, Carl. *The tale of a black cat*
Woelfle, Gretchen. *Katje the windmill cat*
Wolff, Ashley. *Only the cat saw*
Wood, Jacqueline. *Never say boo to a goose!*
Wood, Jakki. *Moo moo, brown cow*
Wooding, Sharon L. *The painter's cat*
Woods, Noah. *Tom cat*
Wormell, Mary. *Why not?*
Wright, Betty Ren. *The cat next door*
    Pet detectives!
Wright, Dare. *The doll and the kitten*
    The lonely doll learns a lesson
    Look at a kitten
Wright, Josephine Lord. *Cotton Cat and Martha Mouse*
Wynne-Jones, Tim. *Zoom upstream*
Yashima, Mitsu. *Momo's kitten*
Yeoman, John. *Mouse trouble*
Ylla. *I'll show you cats*
Young, Ed (Edward). *Cat and Rat*
    Up a tree
Young, James. *Penelope and the pirates*
Ziefert, Harriet. *Elemenopeo*
    Nicky upstairs and down
    Nicky's Christmas surprise
    Nicky's friends
    Nicky's noisy night
    No kiss for Grandpa!
    No, no, Nicky!
    Wee G.
    Where's the cat?

Zimelman, Nathan. *The great adventure of Wo Ti*
    Mean Murgatroyd and the ten cats

Animals – cheetahs

Adamson, Joy. *Pippa the cheetah and her cubs*
Camp, Lindsay. *Keeping up with Cheetah*
Conklin, Gladys. *Cheetahs, the swift hunters*
Heatwole, Marsha. *Jambo, watoto!*
Irvine, Georgeanne. *Sasha the cheetah*
Milton, Joyce. *Big cats*
Morrison, Taylor. *Cheetah*
St. Pierre, Stephanie. *Cheetahs*

Animals – chimpanzees

Alborough, Jez. *Hug*
Anholt, Catherine. *Chimp and Zee and the big storm*
    Chimp and Zee's noisy book
    Monkey around with Chimp and Zee [board book]
Blaustein, Muriel. *Jim chimp's story*
Browne, Anthony. *I like books*
    I like books [board book]
    Things I like
    Willy and Hugh
    Willy the champ
    Willy the dreamer
    Willy the wimp
    Willy the wizard
    Willy's pictures
Durant, Alan. *Brown Bear gets in shape*
Faulkner, Keith. *Charlie Chimp's Christmas*
Hoban, Lillian. *Arthur's back to school day*
    Arthur's birthday party
    Arthur's Christmas cookies
    Arthur's funny money
    Arthur's great big Valentine
    Arthur's pen pal
    Arthur's prize reader
Hurd, Edith Thacher. *The mother chimpanzee*
Oram, Hiawyn. *The wrong overcoat*
Parish, Peggy. *Jumper goes to school*

Animals – chipmunks

Angelo, Valenti. *The acorn tree*
Berenstain, Michael. *Peat Moss and Ivy and the birthday present*
    Peat Moss and Ivy's backyard adventure
Bruchac, Joseph. *How Chipmunk got his stripes*
Conger, Marion. *The chipmunk that went to church*
Haas, Jessie. *Chipmunk!*
Moore, Lilian. *Little Raccoon and no trouble at all*
Price, Dorothy E. *Speedy gets around*
Ryder, Joanne. *Chipmunk song*
Stevenson, James. *Wilfred the rat*
Williams, Barbara. *Chester Chipmunk's Thanksgiving*

Animals – cougars

Anderson, C. W. (Clarence Williams). *Blaze and the mountain lion*
Costello, Emily. *Realm of the panther*
Gouck, Maura. *Mountain lions*
Gregg, Andy. *Great Rabbit and the long-tailed Wildcat*
Hodge, Deborah. *Wild cats*
London, Jonathan. *Panther, shadow of the swamp*
Milton, Joyce. *Big cats*

Animals – cows *see* Animals – bulls, cows

Animals – coyotes

Aardema, Verna. *Borreguita and the coyote*
Baker, Betty. *And me, coyote!*
    Partners
Baylor, Byrd. *Coyote cry*
    Moon song
Beaumont, Karen. *Duck, duck, goose!*

Bernstein, Margery. *Coyote goes hunting for fire*
Bierhorst, John. *Doctor Coyote*
Carey, Valerie Scho. *Quail song*
Carrick, Carol. *Two coyotes*
Cornette. *Purple coyote*
Covault, Ruth M. *Pablo and Pimienta*
Czernecki, Stefan. *Huevos rancheros*
De Montaño, Martha Kreipe. *Coyote in love with a star*
Dwyer, Mindy. *Coyote in love*
French, Fiona. *Lord of the animals*
Goble, Paul. *Iktomi and the ducks*
Hausman, Gerald. *Coyote walks on two legs*
Hiscock, Bruce. *Coyote and badger*
Johnston, Tony. *The tale of Rabbit and Coyote*
King, Thomas. *Coyote sings to the moon*
Levy, Elizabeth. *Cleo and the coyote*
London, Jonathan. *At the edge of the forest*
    Fire race
Lowell, Susan. *The three little javelinas*
Lund, Jillian. *Two cool coyotes*
McDermott, Gerald. *Coyote*
Nunes, Susan Miho. *Coyote dreams*
Pia Toya
Pohrt, Tom. *Coyote goes walking*
Ruurs, Margriet. *Emma and the coyote*
Sage, James. *Coyote makes man*
Stevens, Janet. *Old bag of bones*
Tafolla, Carmen. *Baby Coyote and the old woman = El coyotito y la
    viejita*
Taylor, Harriet Peck. *Coyote and the laughing butterflies*
Whitehouse, Patricia. *Coyotes*

Animals – deer

Aragon, Jane Chelsea. *Salt hands*
    Winter harvest
Arnosky, Jim. *All about deer*
    Deer at the brook
Asch, Frank. *Oats and wild apples*
Bare, Colleen Stanley. *Never grab a deer by the ear*
Bemelmans, Ludwig. *Parsley*
Boegehold, Betty. *Small Deer's magic tricks*
Buff, Mary (Marsh). *Dash and Dart*
    Forest folk
Carrick, Donald. *The deer in the pasture*
    Harold and the great stag
Eberle, Irmengarde. *Fawn in the woods*
Frankel, Bernice. *Half-As-Big and the tiger*
Helldorfer, M. C. (Mary Claire). *Night of the white stag*
Henderson, Kathy. *Disney's Bambi: the winter trail*
Hodge, Deborah. *Deer, moose, elk and caribou*
Hodges, Margaret. *The golden deer*
Holmes, Efner Tudor. *Deer in the hollow*
Ikeda, Daisaku. *Kanta and the deer*
Kleven, Elisa. *The dancing deer and the foolish hunter*
Lindman, Maj. *Snipp, Snapp, Snurr and the reindeer*
Marzollo, Jean. *Once upon a springtime*
Oates, Joyce Carol. *Come meet Muffin!*
Prusski, Jeffrey. *Bring back the deer*
San Souci, Daniel. *In the moonlight mist*
Schlein, Miriam. *Deer in the snow*
Soros, Barbara. *Tenzin's deer*
Taylor, Harriet Peck. *Two days in May*
Townsend, Emily Rose. *Deer*
Troughton, Joanna. *Mouse-Deer's market*

Animals – dislike of *see* Behavior – animals, dislike of

Animals – dogs

Abercrombie, Barbara. *Bad dog, Dodger*
Adams, Jean Ekman. *Clarence and the great surprise*
Adoff, Arnold. *Daring Dog and Captain Cat*
    The return of Rex and Ethel
Æsop. *The dog and the wolf*
Agee, Jon. *Ellsworth*
Ajmera, Maya. *A kid's best friend*

Alcantara, Ricardo. *Dog and cat*
Alden, Joan. *A boy's best friend*
Alexander, Martha G. *Bobo's dream*
    Maggie's moon
Allen, Jeffrey. *The secret life of Mr. Weird*
Allen, Jonathan. *My dog*
Allen, Pamela. *Bertie and the bear*
Aller, Susan B. *Emma and the night dogs*
Ambler, C. Gifford (Christopher Gifford). *Ten little foxhounds*
Anderson, Douglas. *Let's draw a story*
Anholt, Laurence. *The new puppy*
Annett, Cora. *The dog who thought he was a boy*
Ardizzone, Edward. *Tim's friend Towser*
Argueta, Manlio. *The magic dogs of the volcanoes*
Armstrong, Jennifer. *Little Salt Lick and the Sun King*
Arnold, Katya. *Meow!*
Asare, Meshack. *Sosu's call*
Asch, Frank. *The last puppy*
    Rebecka
Ashman, Linda. *The tale of Wagmore Gently*
Auch, Mary Jane. *Bird dogs can't fly*
Aulaire, Ingri Mortenson d'. *Foxie, the singing dog*
Autry, Gene. *Here comes Santa Claus*
Axworthy, Anni. *Along came Toto*
Aylesworth, Jim. *The bad dream*
Backx, Patsy. *Josie and Mr. Fernandez*
    Skippy and Jack
Bacon, Ethel. *To see the moon*
Bailey, Linda. *Stanley's party*
Baker, Barbara. *Digby and Kate*
    Digby and Kate again
    Digby and Kate and the beautiful day
Baker, Charlotte. *Little brother*
Baker, Jeannie. *Home in the sky*
Baker, Leslie A. *You bad dog!*
Baker, Margaret. *A puppy called Spinach*
Barasch, Lynne. *Old friends*
Bare, Colleen Stanley. *Sammy, dog detective*
    To love a dog
Barner, Bob. *Elevator escalator book*
Baron, Alan. *Little Pig's bouncy ball*
Barr, Cathrine. *Hound dog's bone*
Barracca, Debra. *Maxi, the hero*
    Maxi, the star
    A taxi dog Christmas
Barracca, Sal. *The adventures of taxi dog*
Barton, Byron. *Jack and Fred*
    Where's Al?
Bastin, Marjolein. *A little dog for Vera*
Batherman, Muriel. *Some things you should know about my dog*
Battles, Edith. *The terrible terrier*
Bauer, Steven. *The strange and wonderful tale of Robert McDoodle*
Baumann, Kurt. *Piro and the fire brigade*
Baumgart, Klaus. *Don't be afraid, Tommy*
Baylor, Byrd. *Coyote cry*
Baynes, Pauline. *How dog began*
Bedford, David. *Shaggy Dog and the terrible itch*
Beim, Lorraine. *The little igloo*
Belting, Natalia Maree. *Verity Mullens and the Indian*
Bemelmans, Ludwig. *Madeline's rescue*
Benchley, Peter. *Jonathan visits the White House*
Berends, Polly Berrien. *Ladybug and dog and the night walk*
Berenstain, Stan. *The Berenstain bears on the moon*
Beresford, Elisabeth. *Snuffle to the rescue*
Bergen, Lara Rice. *Blue's world of words*
Bertrand, Cécile. *Let's pretend!*
Best, Cari. *Montezuma's revenge*
Bettina (Bettina Ehrlich). *Pantaloni*
Bingham, Mindy. *My way Sally*
Biro, Val. *Gumdrop and the secret switches*
Black, Irma (Simonton). *Big puppy and little puppy*
Blackstone, Stella. *An island in the sun*
Blackwood, Gladys Rourke. *Whistle for Cindy*
Blades, Ann. *Mary of mile 18*
Blake, Quentin. *Mrs. Armitage and the big wave*
    Mrs. Armitage: queen of the road
Blake, Robert J. *Akiak*

Blegvad, Lenore. *Hark! Hark! The dogs do bark, and other poems about dogs*
Bliss, Corinne Demas. *That dog Melly!*
Blocksma, Mary. *The pup went up*
    Rub-a-dub-dub
Boase, Susan. *Lucky boy*
Bogan, Paulette. *Momma's magical purse*
    Spike in the city
Boland, Janice. *A dog named Sam*
Bolognese, Elaine. *The sleepy watchdog*
Bonsall, Crosby Newell. *The amazing the incredible super dog*
    And I mean it, Stanley
    Listen, listen!
    Who's afraid of the dark?
Bontemps, Arna Wendell. *The fast sooner hound*
Bornstein, Ruth Lercher. *I'll draw a meadow*
    Jim
Bottner, Barbara. *Horrible Hannah*
Bowden, Joan Chase. *Boo and the flying flews*
Boyd, Lizi. *Black dog red house*
Boynton, Sandra. *Doggies*
Bradford, Ann. *The mystery of the blind writer*
    The mystery of the missing dogs
Brenner, Barbara A. *A dog I know*
Brett, Jan. *Comet's nine lives*
    The first dog
    The trouble with trolls
Bridgman, Elizabeth. *A new dog next door*
Bridwell, Norman. *Clifford counts bubbles*
    Clifford goes to Hollywood
    Clifford's ABC
    Clifford's good deeds
    Clifford's Halloween
    Clifford's neighborhood
    Glow-in-the-dark Halloween
Bright, Robert. *Georgie and the little dog*
Brimner, Larry Dane. *Dinosaurs dance*
    If dogs had wings
Bröger, Achim. *Francie's paper puppy*
Brown, Ken (Ken James). *Mucky Pup*
    Mucky Pup's Christmas
Brown, Marc Tolon. *Arthur's new puppy*
    Arthur's new puppy [board book]
    Arthur's pet business
Brown, Margaret Wise. *Big dog, little dog*
    The country noisy book
    Don't frighten the lion
    The indoor noisy book
    The quiet noisy book
    Sailor boy jig
    The seashore noisy book
    The summer noisy book
    The winter noisy book
Brown, Ruth. *The ghost of Greyfriar's Bobby*
    I don't like it!
    Our puppy's vacation
Browne, Anthony. *Voices in the park*
Bruce, Lisa. *Fran's friend*
Bruna, Dick. *Snuffy*
    Snuffy and the fire
Bruzzone, Catherine. *Puppy finds a friend = Cachorrito encuentra un amigo*
    Puppy finds a friend = Le petit chien se trouve un ami
Bryan, Dorothy. *Friendly little Jonathan*
    Just Tammie!
Buck, Pearl S. (Pearl Sydenstricker). *The Chinese story teller*
Buckley, Helen Elizabeth. *Josie's Buttercup*
Buckmaster, Henrietta. *Lucy and Loki*
Buehner, Caralyn. *Superdog, the heart of a hero*
Bunting, Eve (Anne Evelyn). *Ghost's hour, spook's hour*
    Jane Martin, dog detective
Burningham, John. *Cannonball Simp*
    Courtney
    The dog
Burton, Jane. *Jack the puppy*
    Puppy
Bushey, Jeanne. *A sled dog for Moshi*

Butler, Kristi T. *Rip's secret spot*
Calhoun, Mary. *High-wire Henry*
    Houn' dog
    Mrs. Dog's own house
Calmenson, Stephanie. *Fido*
    My dog's the best
    Perfect puppy
    Rosie, a visiting dog's story
    Shaggy, waggy dogs (and others)
Campbell, Rod. *Henry's busy day*
Capucilli, Alyssa Satin. *Bathtime for Biscuit*
    Biscuit
    Biscuit finds a friend
    Biscuit gives a gift
    Biscuit goes to school
    Biscuit loves school
    Biscuit wants to play
    Biscuit wins a prize
    Biscuit's big friend
    Biscuit's new trick
    Biscuit's picnic
    Biscuit's Valentine's Day
    Happy birthday, Biscuit!
    Happy Hanukkah, Biscuit
    Hello, Biscuit!
    Merry Christmas, from Biscuit
Carlson, Nancy L. *Harriet and George's Christmas treat*
    Harriet and the garden
    Harriet and the roller coaster
    Harriet and Walt
    Harriet's Halloween candy
    Harriet's recital
    Poor Carl
Carrick, Carol. *The accident*
    Ben and the porcupine
    The foundling
    Lost in the storm
Carrier, Lark. *Scout and Cody*
Carroll, Ruth. *What Whiskers did*
    Where's the bunny?
Carter, Debby L. *Clipper*
Cartlidge, Michelle. *Doggy days*
Catalano, Dominic. *Mr. Bassett plays*
Catalanotto, Peter. *Dylan's day out*
Cazet, Denys. *Frosted glass*
    The octopus
    Saturday
Chall, Marsha Wilson. *Bonaparte*
Chalmers, Audrey. *Hector and Mr. Murfit*
Chapman, Cheryl. *Snow on snow on snow*
Chapman, Nancy Kapp. *Doggie dreams*
Charles, Donald. *Shaggy dog's birthday*
    Shaggy dog's Halloween
    Shaggy dog's tall tale
    Time to rhyme with Calico Cat
Charlton, Nancy Lee. *Derek's dog days*
Chase, Catherine. *Pete, the wet pet*
Chenery, Janet. *Pickles and Jake*
Chorao, Kay. *Annie and cousin Precious*
    The cherry pie baby
Christelow, Eileen. *The five-dog night*
    Gertrude, the bulldog detective
    Not until Christmas, Walter!
Christian, Mary Blount. *The green thumb thief*
    No dogs allowed, Jonathan!
Ciardi, John. *Scrappy, the pup*
Clayton, Elaine. *Pup in school*
Cleary, Beverly. *Two dog biscuits*
Clement, Rod. *Frank's great museum adventure*
Clements, Andrew. *Brave Norman*
    Circus family dog
    Slippers at home
    Tara and Tiree, fearless friends
Cneut, Carll. *The amazing love story of Mr. Morf*
Coffelt, Nancy. *The dog who cried woof*
    Dogs in space
Cohen, Caron Lee. *Bronco dogs*

Three yellow dogs
Cohen, Miriam. *Jim's dog Muffins*
Cole, Babette. *Dr. Dog*
   Lady Lupin's book of etiquette
   Truelove
Cole, Joanna. *Monster and Muffin*
   My puppy is born
Cole, William. *Have I got dogs!*
Cook, Marion B. *Waggles and the dog catcher*
Coontz, Otto. *The quiet house*
Copeland, Eric. *Milton, my father's dog*
Coplans, Peta. *Cat and dog*
Costa, Nicoletta. *The clever dog*
   The grown-up dog
   The naughty puppy
   The new puppy
Cottle, Joan. *Miles away from home*
Cowley, Joy. *Agapanthus Hum and Major Bark*
Cowley, Stewart. *Hide-and-seek puppies*
Cretan, Gladys Yessayan. *Lobo and Brewster*
Crimi, Carolyn. *Don't need friends*
Crisp, Marty. *Black and white*
Cronin, Doreen. *Wiggle*
Crozat, François. *I am a little dog*
Crunk, Tony. *Grandpa's overalls*
Cullen, Lynn. *Little Scraggly Hair*
   The mightiest heart
Curious George and the puppies
Cuyler, Margery. *Freckles and Jane*
   Freckles and Willie
   Shadow's baby
Czarnecki, Lois R. *The six wrinkled Woos*
Dale, Penny. *Wake up, Mr. B.!*
Dale, Ruth Bluestone. *Benjamin . . . and Sylvester also*
Dalgleish, Sharon. *Working dogs*
Dalmais, Anne-Marie. *Petey the puppy*
Daly, Kathleen N. *The Giant little Golden Book of dogs*
Daly, Maureen. *Patrick visits the library*
Damjan, Mischa. *Atuk*
Darling, Kathy (Mary Kathleen). *ABC dogs*
Day, Alexandra. *Carl goes shopping*
   Carl goes to daycare
   Carl makes a scrapbook
   Carl pops up
   Carl's afternoon in the park
   Carl's birthday
   Carl's Christmas
   Carl's masquerade
   Darby, the special-order pup
   Follow Carl!
   Good dog, Carl
   Paddy's pay-day
Deady, Kathleen W. *It's time!*
De Beer, Hans. *Little polar bear and the husky pup*
   Oh no, Ono!
DeLage, Ida. *ABC fire dogs*
   What does a witch need?
Delaney, Ned. *Bad dog!*
Delton, Judy. *I'll never love anything ever again*
Demers, Dominique. *Old Thomas and the little fairy*
Demi. *Fuzzy wuzzy puppy*
Denchfield, Nick. *Desmond the dog*
   Desmond the dog, a wag-the-tail pop-up book
Denison, Carol. *A part-time dog for Nick*
Dennis, Morgan. *Burlap*
   The pup himself
   The sea dog
   Skit and Skat
De Paola, Tomie (Thomas Anthony). *Boss for a day*
   Hide-and-seek all week
   Meet the Barkers
   A new Barker in the house
Desimini, Lisa. *Dot the Firedog*
Dickens, Lucy. *Dirty Henry*
Dickson, Louise. *The vanishing cat*
DiSalvo-Ryan, DyAnne. *A dog like Jack*
Dodd, Emma. *Dog's ABC*

Dog's colorful day
Dog's noisy day
Dodd, Lynley. *A dragon in a wagon*
   Hairy Maclary from Donaldson's dairy
   Hairy Maclary, Scattercat
   Hairy Maclary, sit
   Hairy Maclary's bone
   Hairy Maclary's caterwaul caper
   Hairy Maclary's rumpus at the vet
   Hairy Maclary's showbusiness
   Schnitzel von Krumm forget-me-not
   Schnitzel von Krumm's basketwork
Dodds, Dayle Ann. *The Kettles get new clothes*
   Where's Pup?
Domanska, Janina. *Spring is*
Doughtie, Charles. *Gabriel Wrinkles, the bloodhound who couldn't smell*
Dowling, Paul. *Jimmy's snowy book*
Doyle, Malachy. *Sleepy Pendoodle*
Drescher, Joan E. *Max and Rufus*
Du Bois, William Pène. *Giant Otto*
   Otto and the magic potatoes
   Otto at sea
   Otto in Africa
   Otto in Texas
Dubowski, Cathy East. *A cake for Jake*
Dumas, Philippe. *Laura, Alice's new puppy*
   Laura and the bandits
   Laura loses her head
   Laura on the road
Dunbar, Polly. *Dog Blue*
Dunn, Judy. *The little puppy*
Dunnick, Regan. *Sweet dreams, Douglas*
Dunrea, Olivier. *Fergus and Bridey*
Dupré, Ramona Dorrel. *Too many dogs*
Duvoisin, Roger Antoine. *Day and night*
Eagle, Ellen. *Gypsy's cleaning day*
Eastman, P. D. (Philip D.). *Go, dog, go!*
Edwards, Nicola. *Goodnight Baxter*
Edwards, Pamela Duncan. *Ed and Fred Flea*
   Muldoon
Egan, Tim. *Burnt toast on Davenport Street*
   A mile from Ellington station
Ehrlich, Amy. *Maggie and Silky and Joe*
Ellwand, David. *Alfred's camera*
   Alfred's party
Enderle, Judith (Ann) Ross. *Francis, the earthquake dog*
Enell, Trinka. *Roll over, Rosie*
Erickson, Phoebe. *Just follow me*
Erlbruch, Wolf. *Leonard*
Ernst, Lisa Campbell. *Duke, the Dairy Delight dog*
   Ginger jumps
   Walter's tail
Ets, Marie Hall. *Mr. T. W. Anthony Woo*
Evans, Katie. *Hunky Dory ate it*
Evans, Mark. *Puppy*
Faglia, Maeto. *Happy birthday, I'm 2*
Falwell, Cathryn. *P.J. & Puppy*
Fanelli, Sara. *The doggy book*
Fechner, Amrei. *I am a little dog*
Fehlner, Paul. *Dog and cat*
Feiffer, Jules. *Bark, George*
Ferns, Ronald. *Osbert and Lucy*
Field, Eugene. *The gingham dog and the calico cat*, ill. by Janet Street
   The gingham dog and the calico cat, ill. by Johanna Westerman
Fischer-Nagel, Heiderose. *A puppy is born*
Fisher, Aileen Lucia. *I like weather*
Flack, Marjorie. *Angus and the cat*
   Angus and the ducks
   Angus lost
Flather, Lisa. *Ten silly dogs*
Florian, Douglas. *Bow wow meow meow, it's rhyming cats and dogs*
Foster, Sally. *A pup grows up*
Fox, Mem. *Night noises*
Francia, Silvia. *Roberta's vacation*
Frank, John. *The toughest cowboy, Or, How the Wild West was tamed*

Freeman, Don. *Ski pup*
Frith, Michael K. *I'll teach my dog 100 words*
Fuge, Charles. *Yip! Snap! Yap!*
Fujikawa, Gyo. *Millie's secret*
    Shags finds a kitten
Furchgott, Terry. *Phoebe and the hot water bottles*
Gackenbach, Dick. *A bag full of pups*
    Barker's crime
    Beauty, brave and beautiful
    Claude and Pepper
    Claude has a picnic
    Claude the dog
    The dog and the deep dark woods
    Dog for a day
    Pepper and all the legs
    What's Claude doing?
Gág, Wanda. *Nothing at all*
Gannett, Ruth Stiles. *Katie and the sad noise*
Gardiner, Lindsey. *Good night, Poppy and Max*
    Here come Poppy and Max
    When Poppy and Max grow up
Geoghegan, Adrienne. *Dogs don't wear glasses*
George, Jean Craighead. *Cliff hanger*
    Little Dog and Duncan
Gerrard, Roy. *Jocasta Carr, movie star*
Gerson, Corinne. *Good dog, bad dog*
Gerstein, Mordicai. *The new creatures*
Ghigna, Charles. *Good dogs/Bad dogs*
Gibbie, Mike. *Small Brown Dog's bad remembering day*
Gibbons, Gail. *Dogs*
Giff, Patricia Reilly. *Good luck, Ronald Morgan*
Giglio, Judy. *The tapping tale*
Gikow, Louise. *Follow that Fraggle!*
Gill-Brown, Vanessa. *Rufferella*
Gliori, Debi. *The snow lambs*
Godwin, Laura. *The best fall of all*
    Happy and Honey
    Happy Christmas, Honey
    Honey helps
Goennel, Heidi. *My dog*
Goldsmith, Howard. *Little lost dog*
Golembe, Carla. *Annabelle's big move*
Goode, Diane. *Mama's perfect present*
    Tiger trouble
Goodhart, Pippa. *Pudgy, a puppy to love*
Goodspeed, Peter. *Hugh and Fitzhugh*
Gordon, Sharon. *What a dog!*
Gottfried, Maya. *Good dog*
Graeber, Charlotte Towner. *Nobody's Dog*
Graham, Amanda. *Who wants Arthur?*
Graham, Bob. *Benny*
    "Let's get a pup!" said Kate
    Libby, Oscar and me
Graham, Margaret Bloy. *Benjy and his friend Fifi*
    Benjy and the barking bird
    Benjy's boat trip
    Benjy's dog house
Grambling, Lois G. *Big Dog*
Granowsky, Alvin. *At the park*
Gray, Nigel. *The dog show*
Green, Phyllis. *Bagdad ate it*
Green-Armytage, Stephen. *Dudley, the little terrier that could*
Gregoire, Caroline. *Uglypuss*
Gregory, Nan. *How Smudge came*
Gregory, Valiska. *The oatmeal cookie giant*
    Riddle soup
    Sunny side up
    Terribly wonderful
Gretz, Susanna. *Teddy bears at the seaside*
Griffith, Helen V. *Alex and the cat*
    Alex remembers
    Dream meadow
    Mine will, said John
    More Alex and the cat
    Pluck's dreams
Grimm, Jacob. *The horse, the fox, and the lion*
Grindley, Sally. *Four black puppies*

Gutman, Anne. *Gaspard and Lisa, friends forever*
    Gaspard and Lisa's Christmas surprise
    Gaspard and Lisa's rainy day
    Gaspard at the seashore
    Gaspard in the hospital
    Gaspard on vacation
    Lisa in New York
    Lisa in the jungle
    Lisa's airplane trip
    Lisa's baby sister
Gwynne, Fred. *Easy to see why*
Haas, Jessie. *Busybody Brandy*
Hains, Harriet. *My new puppy*
Hall, Donald. *I am the dog, I am the cat*
Hamberger, John. *Hazel was an only pet*
    The lazy dog
Hänel, Wolfram. *Mary and the mystery dog*
Hansard, Peter. *Wag, wag, wag*
Harper, Dan. *Sit, Truman*
Harper, Isabelle. *My dog Rosie*
    Our new puppy
Harper, Jessica. *I'm not going to chase the cat today*
Harriott, Ted. *Coming home*
Harrison, David Lee. *Farmer's garden*
Harrison, Troon. *The dream collector*
Harsh, Fred. *Alfie*
Harvey, Amanda. *Dog days*
    Dog gone
    Dog-eared
Harvey, Bev. *The dog family*
Hassett, John. *Charles of the wild*
Hausherr, Rosmarie. *My first puppy*
Hawkins, Colin. *Tog the dog*
Hayes, Sarah. *This is the bear and the bad little girl*
    This is the bear and the picnic lunch
Hays, Anna Jane. *The pup speaks up*
Hazelaar, Cor. *Dogs everywhere*
Hazen, Barbara Shook. *Digby*
    Fang
    The new dog
    Stay, Fang
Heine, Helme. *Mr. Miller, the dog*
Heller, Nicholas. *Happy birthday, Moe dog*
Hendry, Diana. *Dog Donovan*
Henkes, Kevin. *Circle dogs*
Herman, Gail. *Lucky goes to school*
    My dog talks
    Otto the cat
    The puppy who went to school
    What a hungry puppy!
Herriot, James. *Only one woof*
Hesse, Karen. *Lester's dog*
Hewett, Joan. *Rosalie*
Hill, Eric. *Puppy love*
    Spot and friends dress up
    Spot and friends play
    Spot at home
    Spot at play
    Spot at the fair
    Spot bakes a cake
    Spot counts from 1 to 10
    Spot goes on holiday
    Spot goes to a party
    Spot goes to school
    Spot goes to the beach
    Spot goes to the circus
    Spot goes to the farm
    Spot goes to the park
    Spot in the garden
    Spot looks at colors
    Spot looks at opposites
    Spot looks at shapes
    Spot looks at weather
    Spot on the farm
    Spot sleeps over
    Spot visits his grandparents
    Spot visits the hospital

Spot's baby sister
Spot's big book of colors, shapes and numbers = El libro grande de Spot
Spot's big book of colours, shapes, and numbers
Spot's big book of words = El libro grande de las palabras de Spot
Spot's favorite baby animals
Spot's favorite colors
Spot's favorite numbers
Spot's favorite words
Spot's first Christmas
Spot's first Easter
Spot's first 1, 2, 3 frieze
Spot's first picnic
Spot's first walk
Spot's first words
Spot's magical Christmas
Spot's toy box
Spot's walk in the woods
Hillert, Margaret. *What is it?*
Himmelman, John. *The talking tree*
Hindley, Judy. *The best thing about a puppy*
Hines, Anna Grossnickle. *I'll tell you what they say*
No, no Jack!
Hoban, Lillian. *The laziest robot in zone one*
Hoban, Russell. *The stone doll of Sister Brute*
Hoberman, Mary Ann. *One of each*
Hoff, Syd. *Barkley*
Lengthy
Holmes, Efner Tudor. *Carrie's gift*
Holub, Joan. *Cinderdog and the wicked stepcat*
Why do dogs bark?
Honeycutt, Natalie. *Whistle home*
Hood, Susan. *Pup and Hound*
Pup and Hound move in
Hooks, William H. *A dozen dizzy dogs*
Where's Lulu?
Hooper, Meredith. *Dogs' Night*
Hopkins, Lee Bennett. *A dog's life*
Horenstein, Henry. *Arf! beg! catch!*
Howard, Arthur. *Cosmo zooms*
Howard, Ellen. *Murphy and Kate*
Howe, James. *Creepy-crawly birthday*
Rabbit-Cadabra!
Scared silly
Hume, Stephen Eaton. *Red moon follows truck*
Huneck, Stephen. *Sally goes to the beach*
Sally goes to the farm
Sally goes to the mountains
Hurd, Edith Thacher. *The black dog who went into the woods*
Little dog, dreaming
Hurd, Thacher. *Art dog*
Hobo dog
Hürlimann, Bettina. *Barry*
Ingman, Bruce. *Lost property*
Inkiow, Dimiter. *Me and Clara and Snuffy the dog*
Inkpen, Mick. *Arnold*
Butterfly
Hissss!
Honk!
Kipper
Kipper and Roly
Kipper's A to Z
Kipper's bathtime
Kipper's bedtime
Kipper's birthday
Kipper's book of colors
Kipper's book of counting
Kipper's book of numbers
Kipper's book of opposites
Kipper's book of weather
Kipper's Christmas eve
Kipper's monster
Kipper's playtime
Kipper's rainy day
Kipper's snacktime
Kipper's snowy day
Kipper's sunny day
Kipper's toybox

Meow!
Picnic
Splosh!
Swing!
Thing
Where, oh where, is Kipper's bear?
Ipcar, Dahlov (Zorach). *Black and white*
Isele, Elizabeth. *Pooks*
Iwamura, Kazuo. *Ton and Pon: big and little*
Ton and Pon: two good friends
Iwasaki, Chihiro. *What's fun without a friend?*
Jacka, Martin. *Waiting for Billy*
James, Brian. *The Supertwins meet the bad dogs from space*
Jane, Pamela. *Milo and the fire engine parade*
Janice. *Angélique*
Mr. and Mrs. Button's wonderful watchdogs
Janovitz, Marilyn. *Bowl patrol!*
Jeram, Anita. *It was Jake*
Jessell, Camilla. *The puppy book*
Jobling, Curtis. *Frankenstein's cat*
Joerns, Consuelo. *Oliver's escape*
Johansen, K. V. (Krista V.). *Pippin and Pudding*
Pippin takes a bath
Johnson, Crockett. *The blue ribbon puppies*
Terrible terrifying Toby
Johnson, David. *Oh, that Nuzzle!*
Johnson, Diana F. *Princesa and Friskie*
Johnson, Gillian. *My sister Gracie*
Johnson, Janet P. *How Mr. Dog got tame*
Johnson, Paul Brett. *Lost*
Johnston, Tony. *Desert dog*
The ghost of Nicholas Greebe
Jonas, Ann. *Watch William walk*
Jonell, Lynne. *It's my birthday, too!*
Jones, Elizabeth. *Sunshine and Storm*
Jones, Rebecca C. *The biggest, meanest, ugliest dog in the whole wide world*
Joosse, Barbara M. *Bad dog school*
Better with two
Nugget and Darling
Jordan, June. *Kimako's story*
Kahl, Virginia. *Away went Wolfgang*
Maxie
Kalman, Maira. *What Pete ate from A-Z*
Kanome, Kayoko. *Little Mop lost*
Kastner, Jill. *Princess Dinosaur*
Katschke, Judy. *Take a hike, Snoopy*
Keats, Ezra Jack. *Kitten for a day*
My dog is lost!
Pssst! doggie
Skates
Whistle for Willie
Keller, Holly. *Goodbye, Max*
Kelley, Anne. *Daisy's discovery*
Kellogg, Steven (Stephen). *Best friends*
Give the dog a bone
A penguin pup for Pinkerton
Pinkerton, behave!
Prehistoric Pinkerton
A rose for Pinkerton
Tallyho, Pinkerton!
Kemp, Moira. *Lift-the-flap puppy*
Kennedy, Kim. *Napoleon*
Keyser, Marcia. *Roger on his own*
Khalsa, Dayal Kaur. *I want a dog*
Killilea, Marie (Marie Lyons). *Newf*
Kimmel, Eric A. *Sirko and the wolf*
Kimmel, Haven. *Orville, a dog story*
Kimmelman, Leslie. *Frannie's fruits*
Kimura, Yasuko. *Fergus and the sea monster*
King, Deborah. *Sirius and Saba*
King-Smith, Dick. *Puppy love*
Kirk, Daniel. *Moondogs*
Kitamura, Satoshi. *Lily takes a walk*
Knapp, Jennifer. *The go go dogs*
Kocí, Marta. *Blackie and Marie*
Koehler, Phoebe. *Making room*

Kolar, Bob. *Racer dogs*
Komaiko, Leah. *Great Aunt Ida and her Great Dane, Doc*
Kopczynski, Anna. *Jerry and Ami*
Kopper, Lisa. *Daisy is a mommy*
    Daisy knows best
    Daisy thinks she is a baby
    Good dog, Daisy
Kotzwinkle, William. *Walter, the farting dog*
    Walter, the farting dog: rough weather ahead
    Walter, the farting dog: trouble at the yard sale
Kovalski, Maryann. *Brenda and Edward*
Kraus, Robert. *The detective of London*
    Ludwig the dog who snored symphonies
Krischanitz, Raoul. *Nobody likes me!*
Kroll, Steven. *Don't get me in trouble*
    The magic rocket
    Oh, Tucker!
    Woof, woof!
Kumin, Maxine W. *What color is Caesar?*
Kunhardt, Edith. *Pat the puppy*
Kunhardt, Katharine. *Let's count the puppies*
Kuskin, Karla. *City dog*
    Watson, the smartest dog in the U.S.A.
Labatt, Mary. *A friend for Sam*
    Pizza for Sam
    Sam finds a monster
    Sam gets lost
    Sam goes to school
    Sam's first Halloween
Lacome, Julie. *Funny business*
    I'm a jolly farmer
Laden, Nina. *Bad dog*
Laird, Elizabeth. *The day Patch stood guard*
Lamm, C. Drew. *Anniranni and Mollymishi, the wild-haired doll*
Lamont, Priscilla. *Out to lunch*
Landa, Norbert. *Puppies*
Lane, Judith. *Buster, where are you?*
Lang, Glenna. *Looking out for Sarah*
Langdo, Bryan. *The dog who loved the good life*
Laschütza, Susanne. *Nat the bat*
Laskowski, Jerzy. *Master of the royal cats*
Lathrop, Dorothy Pulis. *Puppies for keeps*
Lawlor, Laurie. *Second-grade dog*
Lawrence, Jennifer B. *Sad doggy*
Leaf, Munro. *Noodle*
Lears, Laurie. *Ben has something to say*
Lebentritt, Julia. *The Kooken*
Lee, Chinlun. *Good dog, Paw*
    The very kind rich lady and her one hundred dogs
Leedy, Loreen. *Mapping Penny's world*
Leemis, Ralph. *Smart dog*
Leichman, Seymour. *Shaggy dogs and spotty dogs and shaggy and spotty dogs*
Lemberg, Stephen H. *Scaredy dog*
L'Engle, Madeleine. *The other dog*
Lenski, Lois. *Davy and his dog*
    Debbie and her dolls
    A dog came to school
    The little sailboat
Lent, Blair. *Ruby and Fred*
Leonard, Marcia. *Get the ball, Slim*
    Laura Jean the yard sale queen
Lerman, Rory S. *Charlie's checklist*
Leslie, Amanda. *Play puppy play*
    Who's that scratching at my door?
Let me call you sweetheart
Levine, Evan. *Not the piano, Mrs. Medley!*
Levinson, Riki. *Country dawn to dusk*
Levy, Elizabeth. *Cleo and the coyote*
Lewis, Kim. *First snow*
    Floss
    Just like Floss
    Little puppy
Lewis, Thomas P. *Call for Mr. Sniff*
    Mr. Sniff and the motel mystery
Lewis, Wendy A. *In Abby's hands*
Lewison, Wendy Cheyette. *My new puppy*

Raindrop, plop
Lexau, Joan M. *The dog food caper*
    Go away, dog, ill. by Crosby Newell Bonsall
    Go away, dog, ill. by Paul Meisel
    I'll tell on you
Lidz, Jane. *Zak, the one-of-a-kind dog*
Lillegard, Dee. *My yellow ball*
Lindenbaum, Pija. *Boodil, my dog*
Lindgren, Barbro. *Rosa*
    Sam's bath
    Sam's wagon
    The wild baby gets a puppy
Lindman, Maj. *Flicka, Ricka, Dicka and a little dog*
    Snipp, Snapp, Snurr and the seven dogs
    Snipp, Snapp, Snurr and the yellow sled
Lipkind, William. *Even Steven*
    Finders keepers
Lish, Ted. *The three little puppies and the big bad flea*
Livingston, Myra Cohn. *Dog poems*
Lloyd, David. *Cat and dog*
    Polly Molly Woof Woof
Lockwood, Primrose. *One winter's night*
Lohans, Alison. *Sundog rescue*
London, Jonathan. *Shawn and Keeper and the birthday party*
    Shawn and Keeper: show-and-tell
    What do you love?
    What do you love? [board book]
Lopshire, Robert. *New tricks I can do!*
    Put me in the zoo
Lorenz, Lee. *Hugo and the spacedog*
Lottridge, Celia Barker. *Berta, a remarkable dog*
Loupy, Christophe. *Don't worry, Wags*
Low, Joseph. *My dog, your dog*
Ludwig, Warren. *Good morning, Granny Rose*
Luttrell, Ida. *Mattie's little possum pet*
Lyon, George Ella. *Ada's pal*
McAllister, Angela. *Harry's box*
McCarty, Peter. *Hondo and Fabian*
McCutcheon, Marc. *Grandfather's Christmas camp*
McDonnell, Flora. *Sparky*
McFarland, Lyn Rossiter. *Widget & the puppy*
McGeorge, Constance W. *Boomer goes to school*
    Boomer's big day
    Boomer's big surprise
McGough, Roger. *Until I met Dudley*
McGuirk, Leslie. *Tucker flips!*
    Tucker off his rocker
    Tucker over the top
McHenry, E. B. *Poodlena*
Machetanz, Sara. *A puppy named Gia*
Macken, JoAnn Early. *Puppies*
McKinley, Robin. *Rowan*
MacKinnon, Debbie. *Pippa's puppy*
MacLachlan, Patricia. *Bittle*
    Three names
    Who loves me?
McLean, Janet. *Dog tales*
    Josh
McMullan, Kate (Hall). *Puppy riddles*
McNeal, Tom. *The dog who lost his Bob*
Mahy, Margaret. *Making friends*
Manushkin, Fran. *Walt Disney's one hundred one dalmations*
Manzano, Sonia. *No dogs allowed*
Marie, Geraldine. *The magic box*
Markoe, Merrill. *The day my dogs became guys*
Marshak, S. (Samuel). *In the van*
    The pup grew up!
Marshall, James. *Miss Dog's Christmas*
    Speedboat
Martin, Charles E. *Dunkel takes a walk*
Martin, David. *Lizzie and her puppy*
Martin, Sarah Catherine. *The comic adventures of Old Mother Hubbard and her dog*
    Old Mother Hubbard, ill. by Jane Cabrera
    Old Mother Hubbard, ill. by Colin Hawkins
    Old Mother Hubbard and her dog, ill. by Lisa Amoroso
    Old Mother Hubbard and her dog, ill. by Paul Galdone

Old Mother Hubbard and her dog, ill. by Evaline Ness
Old Mother Hubbard and her wonderful dog
Martinez, Ruth. *Mrs. McDockerty's knitting*
Mason, Adrienne. *Lu and Clancy sound off*
  Lu and Clancy's spy stuff
Mason, Jane B. *The wee puppy who wouldn't go to sleep*
Masurel, Claire. *A cat and a dog*
  No, no, Titus!
  Ten dogs in the window
Mathers, Petra. *Theodor and Mr. Balbini*
Mauner, Claudia. *Zoe Sophia's scrapbook*
Mayer, Mercer. *A boy, a dog, a frog and a friend*
  A boy, a dog and a frog
Meddaugh, Susan. *Martha and Skits*
  Martha blah blah
  Martha calling
  Martha speaks
  Martha walks the dog
  Perfectly Martha
  The witches' supermarket
Meister, Cari. *Tiny goes to the library*
  Tiny the snow dog
  Tiny's bath
  When Tiny was tiny
Meserve, Adria. *Smog, the city dog*
Micklethwait, Lucy. *Spot a dog*
Miles, Miska. *Show and tell . . .*
  Somebody's dog
Milgrim, David. *Dog brain*
  My friend Lucky
  Why Benny barks
Mills, Lauren A. *The dog prince*
Minarik, Else Holmelund. *Cat and dog*
Mockford, Caroline. *Cleo and Caspar*
  Cleo in the snow
  Cleo on the move
Modell, Frank. *Skeeter and the computer*
  Tooley! Tooley!
Moers, Hermann. *Rufus and Max*
Monks, Lydia. *The cat barked?*
Moore, Elaine. *Roly-poly puppies*
Moore, Inga. *Little dog lost*
Morris, Terry Nell. *Lucky puppy! Lucky boy!*
Moss, Marissa. *Knick knack paddywack*
Mostacchi, Massimo. *A dog's best friend*
Mother Goose. *Baa baa, black sheep*, ill. by Marilyn Janovitz
Mott, Evelyn Clarke. *Hot dog*
Moxley, Sheila. *ABCD an alphabet book of cats and dogs*
Moyer, Marshall M. *Rollo Bones, canine hypnotist*
Muller, Robin. *Little Wonder*
Murdocca, Sal (Salvatore). *Lucy takes a holiday*
Murphy, Mary. *Here comes spring, and summer and fall and winter*
  I feel happy, and sad, and angry, and glad
  You smell and taste and feel and see and hear
Murphy, Stuart J. *Get up and go!*
  Henry the fourth
Murray, Andrew. *Have you seen Chester?*
Myers, Walter Dean. *The blues of Flats Brown*
Myller, Rolf. *A very noisy day*
Mystery manor
Nakatani, Chiyoko. *The day Chiro was lost*
Napoli, Donna Jo. *Rocky, the cat who barks*
Nayer, Judy. *Tricky puppies*
Newberry, Clare Turlay. *Barkis*
Newman, Lesléa. *Dogs, dogs, dogs*
Nichol, Barbara. *Biscuits in the cupboard*
Nilsén, Anna. *Where are Percy's friends?*
  Where is Percy's dinner?
Noble, Sheilagh. *More*
Nolan, Dennis. *Shadow of the dinosaurs*
Noonan, Julia. *Bath day*
  Breakfast time
Norman, Philip Ross. *Dancing dogs*
Norris, Leslie. *Albert and the angels*
Novak, Matt. *The Pillow War*
Numeroff, Laura Joffe. *Sherman Crunchley*
Oakley, Graham. *The church mice and the ring*

O'Brien, John (1953–). *Mother Hubbard's Christmas*
  Sam and Spot
Ochiltree, Dianne. *Pillow pup*
O'Connor, Jane. *The perfect puppy for me*
Okimoto, Jean Davies. *A place for Grace*
O'Neill, Catharine. *Mrs. Dunphy's dog*
Oram, Hiawyn. *Just Dog*
Ormerod, Jan. *Come back, puppies*
Osborne, Mary Pope. *Molly and the prince*
Osofsky, Audrey. *My buddy*
Ostheeren, Ingrid. *The blue monster*
  The new dog
Ottley, Matt. *What Faust saw*
Otto, Carolyn. *Our puppies are growing*
Overbeck, Cynthia. *Rusty the Irish setter*
Oxenbury, Helen. *Our dog*
  Tom and Pippo and the dog
Pancheri, Jan. *The twelve poodle princess*
Pape, D. L. (Donna Lugg). *Doghouse for sale*
Paraskevas, Betty. *Hoppy and Joe*
  A very Kroll Christmas
Parker, Marjorie. *Jasper's day*
Parker, Nancy Winslow. *Cooper, the McNallys' big black dog*
  Poofy loves company
Patent, Dorothy Hinshaw. *Maggie, a sheep dog*
Paterson, Katherine. *Celia and the sweet, sweet water*
Paul, Ann Whitford. *Hello toes! Hello feet!*
Pearson, Tracey Campbell. *The howling dog*
Peet, Bill (William Bartlett). *The Whingdingdilly*
Penner, Lucille Recht. *Where's that bone?*
Perkins, Al. *The digging-est dog*
Perrault, Charles. *Cinderella*, ill. by Diane Goode
Perrow, Angeli. *Captain's castaway*
  Lighthouse dog to the rescue
  Sirius, the dog star
Petersen-Fleming, Judy. *Puppy training and critters, too!*
Pfloog, Jan. *Puppies*
Phillips, Joan. *My new boy*
Pickering, Jimmy. *It's fall*
  It's winter
Piepmeier, Charlotte. *Lucy's journey to the wild west*
Piers, Helen. *Puppy's ABC*
Pilkey, Dav. *The Hallo-wiener*
Pinkwater, Daniel Manus. *Aunt Lulu*
Pizer, Abigail. *Charlie the puppy*
  Nosey Gilbert
Politi, Leo. *Emmet*
  The nicest gift
Pomerantz, Charlotte. *The outside dog*
Porte, Barbara Ann. *Harry's dog*
Posthuma, Sieb. *Benny*
Potter, Beatrix. *The pie and the patty-pan*
Powell, Consie. *Old dog Cora and the Christmas tree*
Prather, Ray. *Double dog dare*
Price, Mathew. *Patch and the rabbits*
  Patch finds a friend
Pryor, Ainslie. *The baby blue cat and the dirty dog brothers*
Pulver, Robin. *Homer and the house next door*
Puppies and kittens
Rae, Jennifer. *Dog tales*
Rand, Gloria. *Aloha, Salty!*
  Salty dog
  Salty sails north
  Salty takes off
Rankin, Joan. *First day*
Ranville, Myralene. *Tex*
Rascal. *Socrates*
Raschka, Christopher. *Can't sleep*
Rathmann, Peggy. *Officer Buckle and Gloria*
Rayner, Mary. *Marathon and Steve*
Reed, Lynn Rowe. *Pedro, his perro, and the alphabet sombrero*
Regan, Lara Jo. *What is Mr. Winkle?*
Regan, Lara Jo (Michael P.). *A Winkle in time*
Reinen, Judy. *Bow wow*
Reiser, Lynn. *Any kind of dog*
  Dog and cat
  My dog Truffle

Reneaux, J. J. *Why Alligator hates Dog*
Rey, Margret (Margret Elisabeth Waldstein). *Pretzel*
  Pretzel and the puppies
Rice, Eve. *Benny bakes a cake*
  Papa's lemonade and other stories
Richardson, Bill. *Sally Dog Little*
Robbins, Maria Polushkin. *Who said meow?*, ill. by Giulio Maestro
  Who said meow?, ill. by Ellen Weiss
Robertus, Polly M. *The dog who had kittens*
Robins, Joan. *Addie meets Max*
Rockwell, Anne F. *Fire engines*
  Hugo at the park
  Hugo at the window
  When Hugo went to school
  Willy runs away
Roffey, Maureen. *Quick, catch Dan!*
Rogers, Paul (Patrick). *What can you see?*
Rose, Gerald. *Scruff*
Rose, Mitchell. *Norman*
Rosen, Michael (1946–). *Howler*
Rosen, Michael J. (1954–). *Avalanche*
  Bonesy and Isabel
  The dog who walked with God
  With a dog like that, a kid like me . . .
Ross, Tony. *This old man*
  Towser and the terrible thing
Rotenberg, Lisa. *Rodeo pup*
Round, Graham. *Hangdog*
Rowand, Phyllis. *George*
  George goes to town
Ruby-Spears Enterprises. *The puppy's new adventures*
Russell, Joan Plummer. *Aero and Officer Mike*
Rylant, Cynthia. *The bookshop dog*
  Dog Heaven
  The great Gracie chase
  Mr. Putter and Tabby paint the porch
  Mr. Putter and Tabby walk the dog
  Tulip sees America
Sadler, Judy Ann. *Sandwiches for Duke*
Saltzberg, Barney. *Cromwell*
Sampson, Michael R. *Caddie, the golf dog*
Sandberg, Inger. *Nicholas' favorite pet*
San Souci, Robert D. *The Hobyahs*
  The silver charm
Sarrazin, Johan. *Tootle*
Saunders, Susan. *Wales' tale*
Saxon, Charles D. *Don't worry about Poopsie*
Schaap, Martine. *Mop and the birthday picnic*
  Mop's backyard concert
  Mop's mountain adventure
  Mop's treasure hunt
Scheidl, Gerda Marie. *Pickle and Patch*
Schneider, Elisa. *The merry-go-round dog*
Schneider, Howie. *Chewy Louie*
  No dogs allowed
Schroeder, Binette. *Tuffa and her friends*
  Tuffa and the bone
  Tuffa and the ducks
  Tuffa and the picnic
  Tuffa and the snow
Schubert, Leda. *Winnie all day long*
  Winnie plays ball
Schulman, Janet. *The great big dummy*
Schulz, Charles M. *Snoopy's facts and fun book about boats*
  Snoopy's facts and fun book about farms
  Snoopy's facts and fun book about houses
  Snoopy's facts and fun book about nature
  Snoopy's facts and fun book about planes
  Snoopy's facts and fun book about seashores
  Snoopy's facts and fun book about seasons
  Snoopy's facts and fun book about trucks
Schwartz, Amy. *Oma and Bobo*
Schweninger, Ann. *Autumn days*
  Summertime
  Wintertime
Scott, Sally. *Little Wiener*
  There was Timmy!

Seeber, Dorothea P. *A pup just for me . . . A boy just for me*
Seibert, Patricia. *Mush!*
Seibold, J. Otto. *Mr. Lunch borrows a canoe*
Seligson, Susan. *The amazing Amos and the greatest couch on earth*
  Amos ahoy
  Amos camps out
  Amos
Selsam, Millicent E. *A first look at dogs*
  How puppies grow
Sendak, Maurice. *Some swell pup*
Serfozo, Mary. *What's what?*
Sewall, Marcia. *The little wee tyke*
Sewell, Helen Moore. *Birthdays for Robin*
  Ming and Mehitable
Shannon, George. *Tippy-toe chick, go*
Sharmat, Andrew. *Smedge*
Sharmat, Marjorie Weinman. *I'm the best*
  Nate the Great and the fishy prize
  Sasha the silly
Sharratt, Nick. *Monday run-day*
Shibano, Tamizo. *The old man who made the trees bloom*
Shields, Carol Diggory. *I wish my brother was a dog*
Shortall, Leonard W. *Andy, the dog walker*
Shyer, Marlene Fanta. *Stepdog*
Simmie, Lois. *Mister got to go and Arnie*
Simmons, Jane. *Ebb and Flo and the greedy gulls*
  Ebb and Flo and the new friend
Simon, Charnan. *Show-and-tell Sam*
Simon, Norma. *Cats do, dogs don't*
Simon, Seymour. *Dogs*
Simont, Marc. *The stray dog*
Singer, Marilyn. *Chester, the out-of-work dog*
  The dog who insisted he wasn't
Skaar, Grace Marion. *Nothing but (cats) and all about (dogs)*
  The very little dog
Skorpen, Liesel Moak. *All the Lassies*
  His mother's dog
  Old Arthur
Smith, Charles R. *Loki and Alex*
Smith, Janice Lee. *Jess and the stinky cowboys*
Snoopy on wheels
Snow, Alan. *Woof!*
Soto, Gary. *Chato's kitchen*
Spetter, Jung-Hee. *Lily and Trooper's fall*
  Lily and Trooper's spring
  Lily and Trooper's summer
  Lily and Trooper's winter
Spiegelman, Art. *I'm a dog!*
Spier, Peter. *Little dogs*
Spires, Elizabeth. *The big meow*
Spooner, J. B. *The story of the little Black Dog*
Stadler, John. *The cats of Mrs. Calamari*
  Hector, the accordion-nosed dog
  Ready, set, go!
Stanley, Mandy. *Bloomer, the dog you can play with*
Stanton, Karen. *Mr. K and Yudi*
Starke, Katherine. *Dogs and puppies*
Steig, William. *Caleb and Kate*
  Tiffky Doofky
Steiner, Charlotte. *Lulu*
  Pete and Peter
Stephens, Helen. *Poochie-poo*
  Ruby and the muddy dog
Stern, Mark. *It's a dog's life*
Stevens, Janet. *My big dog*
Stevenson, James. *Are we almost there?*
  Worse than the worst
Stevenson, Suçie. *Jessica the blue streak*
Stratemeyer, Clara Georgeanna. *Tuggy*
Suen, Anastasia. *Willie's birthday*
Sugita, Yutaka. *My friend Little John and me*
Surany, Anico. *Kati and Kormos*
Svend Otto S (Svend Otto Sorensen). *Taxi dog*
Sweeney, Joan. *Suzette and the puppy*
Sykes, Julie. *Smudge*
Szekeres, Cyndy. *Nothing-to-do puppy*
Tabler, Judith. *The new puppy*

Tafuri, Nancy. *Who's counting?*
Tallon, Robert. *Latouse my moose*
Tanaka, Hideyuki. *The happy dog*
Taylor, Alastair. *Swollobog*
Taylor, Mark. *The case of the missing kittens*
   Old Blue, you good dog you
Taylor, Sydney. *The dog who came to dinner*
Teague, Mark. *Dear Mrs. LaRue*
   Detective LaRue
Thaler, Mike. *My puppy*
Thayer, Jane. *Part-time dog*
   The puppy who wanted a boy, ill. by Seymour Fleishman
   The puppy who wanted a boy, ill. by Lisa McCue
Thomas, Jane Resh. *Scaredy dog*
Thompson, Colin (Colin Edward). *Unknown*
Thomson, Ruth. *Peabody all at sea*
   Peabody's first case
Titus, Eve. *Anatole and the poodle*
Tracqui, Valérie. *The dog*
Trapani, Iza. *How much is that doggie in the window?*
Trimble, Marcia. *Peppy's shadow*
Trottier, Maxine. *Little dog Moon*
Turkle, Brinton. *The sky dog*
Turnbull, Ann. *Rob goes a-hunting*
Turner, Pamela S. *Hachiko*
Turner, Sandy. *Silent night*
Udry, Janice May. *Alfred*
   What Mary Jo wanted
Uhlberg, Myron. *Mad Dog McGraw*
Ungerer, Tomi. *Flix*
Untermeyer, Louis. *The kitten who barked*
Updike, David. *A winter's journey*
U'Ren, Andrea. *Pugdog*
Van Allsburg, Chris. *The garden of Abdul Gasazi*
Van den Honert, Dorry. *Demi the baby sitter*
Van Dusen, Chris. *Down to the sea with Mr. Magee*
Van Leeuwen, Jean. *The strange adventures of Blue Dog*
Vincent, Gabrielle. *A day, a dog*
Voake, Charlotte. *Mr. Davies and the baby*
Waber, Bernard. *Bernard*
Waddell, Martin. *We love them*
Wagner, Jenny. *John Brown, Rose and the midnight cat*
Wahl, Jan. *The adventures of Underwater Dog*
   Dracula's cat and Frankenstein's dog
   Frankenstein's dog
Wahl, Mats. *Grandfather's laika*
Waite, Judy. *Mouse, look out!*
Waite, Michael P. *Jojofu*
Wallace, John. *Little Bean's friend*
Wallner, Alexandra. *The first air voyage in the United States*
Walt Disney Productions. *Tod and Copper*
   Tod and Vixey
Walton, Rick. *Bertie was a watchdog*
Ward, Barbara Briggs. *The really really hairy flight of Snarly Sally*
Ward, Lynd. *Nic of the woods*
Wardlaw, Lee. *Bow-wow birthday*
Weare, Tim. *I'm a little puppy*
Weeks, Sarah. *Oh my gosh, Mrs. McNosh!*
Weiss, Harvey. *The sooner hound*
Weller, Frances Ward. *The angel of Mill Street*
   Riptide
Wellington, Monica. *The sheep follow*
Wells, Rosemary. *Bingo*
   Lucy comes to stay
   McDuff and the baby
   McDuff comes home
   McDuff goes to school
   McDuff moves in
   McDuff saves the day
   McDuff's hide-and-seek
   McDuff's new friend
Westman, Barbara. *Dancing dogs*
   The day before Christmas
Weston, Martha. *Jack and Jill and Big Dog Bill*
Whatley, Bruce. *Captain Pajamas*
   That magnetic dog
White, Amanda. *Rip and Rap*

White, Ellen Emerson. *Santa paws*
White, Marsha. *Hooper has lost his owner*
Widerberg, Siv. *The boy and the dog*
Wiese, Kurt. *The dog, the fox and the fleas*
Wijngaard, Juan. *Dog*
Wild, Margaret. *Big cat dreaming*
   Fox
   The pocket dogs
   Toby
Wild, Robin. *Spot's dogs and the alley cats*
Wildsmith, Brian. *Give a dog a bone*
   Hunter and his dog
Wilhelm, Hans. *Don't cut my hair*
   I lost my tooth!
   I'll always love you
   It's too windy!
   A new home, a new friend
   Schnitzel's first Christmas
Williams, Suzanne. *My dog never says please*
Williamson, Stan. *The no-bark dog*
Willis, Jeanne. *The boy who lost his bellybutton*
Willoughby, Elaine Macmann. *Boris and the monsters*
Wilson-Kelly, Becky. *Mother Grumpy's dog biscuits*
Winthrop, Elizabeth. *I'm the Boss!*
Wirth, Beverly. *Margie and me*
Wittbold, Maureen. *Mending Peter's heart*
Wold, Jo Anne. *Well! Why didn't you say so?*
Wood, Leslie. *A dog called Mischief*
Wright, Betty Ren. *Pet detectives!*
Yaccarino, Dan. *Oswald*
   Unlovable
Yee, Wong Herbert. *Did you see Chip?*
Yeoman, John. *Old Mother Hubbard's dog dresses up*
   Old Mother Hubbard's dog learns to play
   Old Mother Hubbard's dog needs a doctor
   Old Mother Hubbard's dog takes up sport
Yolen, Jane. *Nocturne*
Yorinks, Arthur. *Harry and Lulu*
   Hey, Al
Ziefert, Harriet. *A dozen dogs*
   I swapped my dog
   Pushkin meets the bundle
   Pushkin minds the bundle
   Sam and Lucy
   Sleepy dog
   Where's the dog?
Zimelman, Nathan. *Mean Murgatroyd and the ten cats*
Zimmerman, Andrea Griffing. *My dog Toby*
Zion, Gene. *Harry, the dirty dog*
   No roses for Harry
Zolotow, Charlotte (Shapiro). *The old dog*
   The poodle who barked at the wind

Animals – dolphins

Anderson, Lonzo. *Arion and the dolphins*
Bailey, Donna. *Dolphins*
Behrens, June. *Whales of the world*
Canyon, Christopher. *John Denver's Ancient rhymes*
Chottin, Ariane. *The curious little dolphin*
Cousteau Society. *Dolphins*
DeSaix, Frank. *The girl who danced with dolphins*
Fowler, Allan. *Friendly dolphins*
Gordon, Sharon. *Dolphins and porpoises*
Harvey, Bev. *The dolphin family*
Jacka, Martin. *Waiting for Billy*
Lilly, Kenneth. *Animals of the ocean*
McKenna, Virginia. *Back to the blue*
Nakatani, Chiyoko. *Fumio and the dolphins*
Nelson, Robert Lyn. *Ocean friends*
Orstadius, Brita. *The dolphin journey*
Pfeffer, Wendy. *Dolphin talk*
Wallace, Karen. *Diving dolphin*
Waxman, Laura Hamilton. *Diving dolphins*
Winton, Tim. *The deep*
Wood, Audrey. *The rainbow bridge*

Animals – donkeys

Æsop. *The donkey in the lion's skin*
  The miller, his son and their donkey, ill. by Roger Antoine
    Duvoisin
  The miller, his son and their donkey, ill. by Eugen Sopko
Barnes, Laura T. *Ernest and the big itch*
  Ernest's special Christmas
  Teeny tiny Ernest
  Twist and Ernest
Barton, Bob. *Paul Gallico's The small miracle*
Bates, H. E. (Herbert Ernest). *Achilles and Diana*
  Achilles the donkey
Berger, Barbara Helen. *The donkey's dream*
Bettina (Bettina Ehrlich). *Cocolo comes to America*
  Cocolo's home
  Piccolo
Brown, Katherine. *The Small One*
Brown, Marcia. *Tamarindo!*
Brown, Margaret Wise. *Little Donkey close your eyes*
Byrd, Robert. *Saint Francis and the Christmas donkey*
Calhoun, Mary. *Old man Whickutt's donkey*
Clark, Elizabeth. *Father Christmas and the donkey*
Cohen, Barbara. *The donkey's story*
Crawford, Sheryl Ann. *The baby who changed the world*
Daugherty, Sonia (Medvedeva). *Vanka's donkey*
DeVajay, Szabolcs. *The animals' gift*
Devlin, Wende. *Cranberry summer*
Dumas, Philippe. *Lucy, a tale of a donkey*
  The story of Edward
Duvoisin, Roger Antoine. *Donkey-donkey*
Evans, Katherine. *The man, the boy and the donkey*
Gramatky, Hardie. *Bolivar*
Gray, Genevieve. *How far, Felipe?*
Grimm, Jacob. *The donkey prince*
Grindley, Sally. *Why is the sky blue?*
Hale, Irina. *Donkey's dreadful day*
Hol, Coby. *Niki's little donkey*
Hurd, Edith Thacher. *Under the lemon tree*
Jensen, Patricia. *Little Donkey learns to help*
La Fontaine, Jean de. *The miller, the boy and the donkey*, adapt. and
    ill. by Brian Wildsmith
McCrea, James. *The king's procession*
McGee, Marni. *The colt and the king*
Maris, Ron. *Hold tight, bear!*
Morpurgo, Michael. *Jo-Jo the melon donkey*
Ness, Evaline. *Josefina February*
Oppenheim, Joanne. *Donkey's tale*
Oppenheim, Shulamith Levey. *Yanni rubbish*
Quintero-Spongberg, Emily. *Hannibal and the king*
Raphael, Elaine. *Donkey and Carlo*
  Donkey, it's snowing
Seignobosc, Françoise. *Chouchou*
Showalter, Jean B. *The donkey ride*
Silver, Jody. *Isadora*
Smith, Kathryn. *Little Donkey's Christmas story*
Spang, Günter. *The ox and the Donkey*
Steig, William. *Farmer Palmer's wagon ride*
  Sylvester and the magic pebble
Tafuri, Nancy. *The donkey's Christmas song*
Tangvald, Christine Harder. *The Rinky Dinky Donkey*
Van Woerkom, Dorothy. *Abu Ali counts his donkeys*
  Donkey Ysabel
Wildsmith, Brian. *A Christmas story*
  The Easter story
Winter, Paula. *Sir Andrew*
Young, Ed (Edward). *Donkey trouble*

Animals – dormice

Alexander, Sue. *Dear Phoebe*
Allancé, Mireille d'. *How long?*
Dale, Elizabeth. *How long?*
De Beer, Hans. *Bernard Bear's amazing adventure*
Ezra, Mark. *The sleepy dormouse*
Fuchshuber, Annegert. *Giant story – Mouse tale*
Ravilious, Robin. *Two in a pocket*

San José, Christine. *Sleeping Beauty*
Wallace, Karen. *A bed for winter*

Animals – elephants

Alborough, Jez. *Esther's trunk*
Allen, Judy. *Elephant*
Allinson, Beverley. *Effie*
Ambrus, Victor G. *Mishka*
Appelt, Kathi. *Elephants aloft*
Backstein, Karen. *The blind men and the elephant*
Balian, Lorna. *Elephant?*
Barner, Bob. *Elephant facts*
Barry, David. *The Rajah's rice*
Bates, Ivan. *All by myself*
Beeler, Selby B. *How many Elephants?*
Berry, James. *Don't leave an elephant to go and chase a bird*
Bishop, Ann. *The Ella Fannie elephant riddle book*
Blumberg, Rhoda. *Jumbo*
Bohman, Nils Axel Erik. *Jim, Jock and Jumbo*
Bos, Burny. *Ollie the elephant*
Boynton, Sandra. *If at first . . .*
Brenner, Barbara A. *What the elephant told*
Bridges, Margaret Park. *Edna elephant*
Brown, Ken (Ken James). *Nellie's knot*
Brunhoff, Jean de. *Babar and Father Christmas*
  Babar and his children
  Babar and Zephir
  Babar the king
  Babar the king, facsimile ed
  The story of Babar, the little elephant
  The travels of Babar
Brunhoff, Laurent de. *Babar and the ghost*
  Babar and the succotash bird
  Babar and the Wully-Wully
  Babar comes to America
  Babar learns to cook
  Babar the magician
  Babar visits another planet
  Babar's ABC
  Babar's battle
  Babar's birthday surprise
  Babar's book of color
  Babar's castle
  Babar's counting book
  Babar's cousin, that rascal Arthur
  Babar's fair will be opened next Sunday
  Babar's little circus star
  Babar's little girl
  Babar's Museum of Art: (closed Mondays)
  Babar's mystery
  Babar's picnic
  Babar's visit to Bird Island
  Meet Babar and his family
  The rescue of Babar
Burns, Diane L. *Elephants never forget!*
Cantieni, Benita. *Little Elephant and Big Mouse*
Caple, Kathy. *The biggest nose*
Cartlidge, Michelle. *Elephant in the jungle*
Chorao, Kay. *George told Kate*
  Kate's box
  Kate's car
  Kate's quilt
  Kate's snowman
Cole, Babette. *Nungu and the elephant*
Cole, Joanna. *Aren't you forgetting something, Fiona?*
Cousins, Lucy. *Maisy makes lemonade*
Dale, Penny. *The elephant tree*
D'Amico, Carmela. *Ella, the elegant elephant*
Davies, Gill. *Tiny's big wish*
Day, Alexandra. *Frank and Ernest*
  Frank and Ernest on the road
  Frank and Ernest play ball
Deetlefs, Rene. *Tabu and the dancing elephants*
Delacre, Lulu. *Nathan and Nicholas Alexander*
  Nathan's balloon adventure
  Nathan's fishing trip

Time for school, Nathan!
Delton, Judy. *The elephant in Duck's garden*
  Penny wise, fun foolish
Demi. *Three little elephants*
Dijs, Carla. *Mommy, what if—?*
DiVito, Anna. *Elephants on ice*
Domanska, Janina. *Why so much noise?*
DuBois, Ivy. *Baby Jumbo*
Durant, Alan. *Mouse party*
Easton, Violet. *Elephants never jump*
Eilenberg, Max. *Squeak's good idea*
Ets, Marie Hall. *Elephant in a well*
Farris, Pamela J. *Young Mouse and Elephant*
Fechner, Amrei. *I am a little elephant*
Fern, Eugene. *What's he been up to now?*
Foulds, Elfrida Vipont. *The elephant and the bad baby*
Fowler, Allan. *The biggest animal on land*
Freschet, Berniece. *Elephant and friends*
Froese, Deborah L. *The wise washerman*
Geraghty, Paul. *The hunter*
Goodman, Joan Elizabeth. *Bernard goes to school*
  Bernard's bath
  Bernard's nap
Gorbachev, Valeri. *Big Little Elephant*
Gréban, Quentin. *Nestor*
Greene, Carol. *The insignificant elephant*
Grindley, Sally. *Little Elephant Thunderfoot*
Hall, Derek. *Elephant bathes*
Hallensleben, Georg. *Pauline*
Hamsa, Bobbie. *Your pet elephant*
Hänel, Wolfram. *Little elephant's song*
Hart, Christopher. *Merwin, master of disguise*
Havill, Juanita. *Sato and the elephants*
Hawkins, Colin. *The elephant*
Hewett, Joan. *The mouse and the elephant*
Hoberman, Mary Ann. *Miss Mary Mack*
Hoff, Syd. *Oliver*
Hoffman, Mary. *Animals in the wild: elephant*
Hogan, Inez. *About Nono, the baby elephant*
Hoppe, Matthias. *Mouse and elephant*
Hunter, Sally. *Humphrey's bedtime*
  Humphrey's birthday
  Humphrey's Christmas
  Humphrey's corner
Irvine, Georgeanne. *Elmer the elephant*
Jackson, Kathryn. *The saggy baggy elephant*
James, Ellen Foley. *Little Bull*
Jenkin-Pearce, Susie. *Bad Boris and the new kitten*
  Bad Boris goes to school
  Boris's big ache
Jeram, Anita. *Bill's belly button*
Johnson, Paul Brett. *The goose who went off in a huff*
Joslin, Sesyle. *Baby elephant and the secret wishes*
  Baby elephant goes to China
  Baby elephant's trunk
  Brave Baby Elephant
  Señor Baby Elephant, the pirate
Kasza, Keiko. *The mightiest*
Kavanagh, Peter. *I love my mama*
Kennaway, Adrienne. *Little elephant's walk*
Kent, Jack. *The biggest shadow in the zoo*
Kimmel, Eric A. *Anansi and the talking melon*
Kipling, Rudyard. *The elephant's child*, ill. by Louise Brierley
  The elephant's child, ill. by Lorinda Bryan Cauley
  The elephant's child, ill. by Tim Raglin
  The elephant's child, ill. by John A. Rowe
Klein, Suzanne. *An elephant in my bed*
Kraus, Robert. *Boris bad enough*
  Ella the bad speller
Kroll, Steven. *Doctor on an elephant*
Lang, Aubrey. *Baby elephant*
Lawrence, John. *Pope Leo's elephant*
Lemaître, Pascal. *Zelda's secret*
Leslie, Amanda. *Alfie and Betty Bug*
Lester, Helen. *Hurty feelings*
  Tacky in trouble
Levitin, Sonia. *When Elephant goes to a party*

Lewin, Betsy. *Chubbo's pool*
Lewin, Hugh. *An elephant came to swim*
Lewis, Kim. *Good night, Harry*
  Here we go Harry
  My friend Harry
Lipkind, William. *Chaga*
Lobel, Arnold. *Uncle Elephant*
Löfgren, Ulf. *The traffic stopper that became a grandmother visitor*
Ludwig, Warren. *Old Noah's elephants*
MacDonald, Suse. *Elephants on board*
McDonnell, Flora. *Splash!*
McKee, David. *Elmer*
  Elmer again
  Elmer and the kangaroo
  Elmer and the lost teddy
  Elmer and the wind
  Elmer and Wilbur
  Elmer in the snow
  Elmer takes off
  Elmer's colors
  Elmer's day
  Elmer's friends
  Elmer's weather
  I can too!
  Tusk tusk
McPhail, David M. *Where can an elephant hide?*
Maestro, Betsy. *Around the clock with Harriet*
  Harriet at home
  Harriet at play
  Harriet at school
  Harriet at work
  Harriet goes to the circus
  Harriet reads signs and more signs
  On the go
  On the town
  Through the year with Harriet
  Where is my friend?
Magloff, Lisa. *Elephant*
Manson, Christopher. *Two travelers*
Martin, Bill (William Ivan). *Smoky Poky*
Mayer, Mercer. *Ah-choo*
Melmed, Laura Krauss. *Jumbo's lullaby*
Miranda, Anne. *The elephant at the Waldorf*
Mitra, Annie. *Tusk! Tusk!*
Mogensen, Jan. *The tiger's breakfast*
Moser, Erwin. *Wilma the elephant*
Mueller, Doris L. *Small One's adventure*
Murphy, Jill. *All in one piece*
  Five minutes' peace
  A piece of cake
  A quiet night in
Nakano, Hirotaka. *Elephant blue*
Nichol, Barbara. *Trunks all aboard*
Noble, Kate. *The blue elephant*
O'Donnell, Peter. *Dizzy*
  Oscar
Offen, Hilda. *Elephant pie*
Oyibo, Papa. *Big brother, little sister*
Paterson, Bettina. *Bun and Mrs. Tubby*
  Bun's birthday
Patz, Nancy. *No thumpin' no bumpin' no rumpus tonight!*
  Pumpernickel tickle and mean green cheese
Paxton, Tom. *Engelbert the elephant*
Pearce, Philippa. *Emily's own elephant*
Peek, Merle. *The balancing act*
Peet, Bill (William Bartlett). *The ant and the elephant*
  Ella
  Encore for Eleanor
Percy, Graham. *Elephants never forget*
Perkins, Al. *Tubby and the lantern*
  Tubby and the Poo-Bah
Petersham, Maud. *The circus baby*
Pluckrose, Henry Arthur. *Elephants*
Pratt, Pierre. *Car*
  Home
  Park
  Shopping

Price, Mathew. *Dumbo*
Propp, James. *Tuscanini*
Quigley, Lillian Fox. *The blind men and the elephant*
Radcliffe, Theresa. *Bashi, elephant baby*
Richards, Jean. *How the elephant got his trunk*
Richardson, Judith Benét. *The way home*
Riddell, Chris. *The trouble with elephants*
Robinson, Bruce. *The obvious elephant*
Rodda, Emily. *Where do you hide two elephants?*
Rogers, Edmund. *Elephants*
Root, Barry. *Gumbrella*
Rovetch, Lissa. *Cora and the elephants*
Sadler, Marilyn. *Alistair's elephant*
Samuels, Jenny. *A nose like a hose*
Saxe, John Godfrey. *The blind men and the elephant*
Schlein, Miriam. *Elephant herd*
Schwartz, Amy. *How to catch an elephant*
Schwartz, Roslyn. *Rose and Dorothy*
Seuss, Dr. *Horton hatches the egg*
    Horton hears a Who!
Sheppard, Jeff. *The right number of elephants*
Simont, Marc. *How come elephants?*
Slobodkina, Esphyr. *Circus caps for sale*
    Pezzo the peddler and the circus elephant
Smath, Jerry. *But no elephants*
    Elephant goes to school
Smith, Maggie (Margaret C.). *Paisley*
Steig, William. *Doctor De Soto goes to Africa*
    An eye for elephants
Stock, Catherine. *Alexander's midnight snack*
Sutherland, Tui. *Meet Mo and Ella*
Talbot, John. *Pins and needles*
Tompert, Ann. *Just a little bit*
Tresselt, Alvin R. *Smallest elephant in the world*
Turner, Sandy. *Otto's trunk*
Velthuijs, Max. *Crocodile's masterpiece*
Vere, Ed. *Everyone's little*
Von Königslöw, Andrea Wayne. *Bing and Chutney*
    Bing and Chutney off to Moosonee
    Bing finds Chutney
Vries, Anke de. *My elephant can do almost anything*
Wahl, Jan. *Hello, elephant*
Wallace, Joseph E. *Big and noisy Simon*
Ward, Nanda Weedon. *The elephant that ga-lumped*
Weedn, Flavia. *The elephant prince*
Weinberg, Lawrence. *The Forgetful Bears meet Mr. Memory*
Weisgard, Leonard. *Silly Willy Nilly*
Weiss, Leatie. *My teacher sleeps in school*
Wells, H. G. (Herbert George). *The adventures of Tommy*
Westcott, Nadine Bernard. *Peanut butter and jelly*
Whitehouse, Patricia. *Elephants*
Williamson, Hamilton. *Little elephant*
Wilson-Max, Ken. *Max's starry night*
Worth, Bonnie. *Jumbo*
Yee, Patrick. *Little Buddy meets Bobo*
Ylla. *The little elephant*
Yoshida, Toshi. *Elephant crossing*
Young, Ed (Edward). *Seven blind mice*
Young, Miriam Burt. *If I rode an elephant*
Zeman, Ludmila. *Sindbad's secret*
Ziefert, Harriet. *April Fool*

Animals – elk

Hausman, Gerald. *The story of Blue Elk*
Hodge, Deborah. *Deer, moose, elk and caribou*

Animals – endangered animals

Ackerman, Diane. *Monk seal hideaway*
Aliki. *My visit to the zoo*
Allen, Judy. *Eagle*
    Elephant
    Panda
    Seal
    Tiger
    Whale

Balog, James. *James Balog's animals A to Z*
Beeke, Tiphanie. *Roar like a lion!*
Butler, John. *Pi-shu, the little panda*
Coville, Bruce. *The prince of butterflies*
Cowcher, Helen. *Tigress*
Cromie, William J. *Steven and the green turtle*
Davis, Maggie S. *A garden of whales*
Dobson, David. *Can we save them?*
Fowler, Allan. *The biggest animal on land*
    It could still be endangered
Gibbons, Gail. *Giant pandas*
    Grizzly bears
Greene, Carol. *Reading about the gray wolf*
    Reading about the peregrine falcon
    Reading about the river otter
Hall, Derek. *Baby animals*
Hamilton, Virginia. *Jaguarundi*
Havill, Juanita. *Sato and the elephants*
Heinz, Brian J. *The wolves*
Hirschi, Ron. *Where are my bears?*
    Where are my prairie dogs and black-footed ferrets?
    Where are my puffins, whales, and seals?
    Where are my swans, whooping cranes, and singing loons?
Jacobs, Francine. *Lonesome George, the giant tortoise*
Jenkins, Priscilla Belz. *Falcons nest on skyscrapers*
Jonas, Ann. *Aardvarks, disembark!*
Kalman, Benjamin. *Animals in danger*
Lee, Sandra. *Giant pandas*
London, Jonathan. *Condor's egg*
McCully, Emily Arnold. *Hurry!*
McFarlane, Sheryl. *Eagle dreams*
Mullins, Patricia. *V for vanishing*
Noonan, Diana. *The crocodile*
Paladino, Catherine. *Our vanishing farm animals*
Raffi. *Baby beluga*
Sackett, Elisabeth. *Danger on the African grassland*
    Danger on the Arctic ice
Schertle, Alice. *Advice for a frog and other poems*
Steele, Philip. *The blue whale*
    The giant panda
Taylor, Barbara. *Going, going, gone*
Theodorou, Rod. *Bengal tiger*
    Black rhino
    Blue whale
    Florida manatee
    Giant panda
    Mountain gorilla
Thomson, Sarah L. *Tigers*
Turbak, Gary. *Mountain animals in danger*
    Ocean animals in danger
Weeks, Sarah. *Crocodile smile*

Animals – ferrets

Elsdale, Bob. *Mac side up*
Hirschi, Ron. *Where are my prairie dogs and black-footed ferrets?*
London, Jonathan. *Phantom of the prairie*
Weigelt, Udo. *It wasn't me*

Animals – foxes

Abolafia, Yossi. *Fox tale*
Æsop. *The donkey in the lion's skin*
    The fox and the grapes
    The raven and the fox
    Three Æsop fox fables
Ambrus, Victor G. *Country wedding*
Anderson, Paul S. *Red fox and the hungry tiger*
Anno, Mitsumasa. *Anno's Æsop*
Arnosky, Jim. *Watching foxes*
Auch, Mary Jane. *Peeping Beauty*
Ayers, Rebecca Hickox. *Zorro and Quwi*
Baker, Liza. *I love you because you're you*
Baron, Alan. *Red Fox dances*
Barr, Cathrine. *Hound dog's bone*
Baynton, Martin. *Fifty and the fox*
Beck, Ian. *Five little ducks*

Bemelmans, Ludwig. *Welcome home!*
Bergman, Donna. *City fox*
Berson, Harold. *Henry Possum*
    Joseph and the snake
Bingham, Mindy. *My way Sally*
Blyler, Allison. *Finding foxes*
Bodnar, Judit Z. *Tale of a tail*
    A wagonload of fish
Bonning, Tony. *Another fine mess*
    Fox tale soup
Brown, Marcia. *The neighbors*
Brown, Margaret Wise. *Fox eyes*
Brutschy, Jennifer. *The winter fox*
Buck, Pearl S. (Pearl Sydenstricker). *The little fox in the middle*
Bunting, Eve (Anne Evelyn). *Box, fox, ox, and the peacock*
    Red fox running
Burningham, John. *Harquin*
Burton, Jane. *Fancy the fox*
    Trill the fox cub
Calhoun, Mary. *Houn' dog*
Campoy, F. Isabel. *Rosa Raposa*
Caple, Kathy. *Fox and bear*
Carroll, Ruth. *What Whiskers did*
Carter, Anne Laurel. *Ruff leaves home*
Chaucer, Geoffrey. *Chanticleer and the fox*
Christelow, Eileen. *Henry and the red stripes*
Cocca-Leffler, Maryann. *Bravery soup*
Conover, Chris. *Mother Goose and the sly fox*
Cox, Judy. *Rabbit pirates*
Cox, Phil Roxbee. *Fox on a box*
Crum, Shutta. *Fox and Fluff*
Cunningham, Julia. *The vision of François the fox*
Davis, Lavinia (Riker). *Roger and the fox*
Delton, Judy. *Duck goes fishing*
Domanska, Janina. *The best of the bargain*
DuBois, Ivy. *Mother fox*
Edwards, Pamela Duncan. *Four famished foxes and Fosdyke*
Ehlert, Lois. *Mole's hill*
    Moon rope = Un lazo a la luna
Enderle, Judith (Ann) Ross. *What would Mama do?*
Fatio, Louise. *The red bantam*
Firmin, Peter. *Basil Brush and the windmills*
The fox went out on a chilly night
Fox, Charles Philip. *A fox in the house*
French, Vivian. *Red Hen and Sly Fox*
Giffard, Hannah. *Red Fox*
    Red Fox on the move
Ginsburg, Mirra. *Across the stream*
    The fox and the hare
    Mushroom in the rain
    Two greedy bears
Gliori, Debi. *No matter what*
Grimm, Jacob. *The golden bird*, ill. by Isabelle Brent
    The golden bird, ill. by Sandro Nardini
    The horse, the fox, and the lion
    Mrs. Fox's wedding
Grindley, Sally. *Silly Goose and Dizzy Duck play hide-and-seek*
    What are friends for?
    What will I do without you?
Guzzo, Sandra E. *Fox and Heggie*
Hartley, Deborah. *Up north in the winter*
Havard, Christian. *The fox, playful prowler*
Hayes, Sarah. *Nine ducks nine*
Hayward, Linda. *All stuck up*
Hindley, Judy. *Do like a duck does*
Hogrogian, Nonny. *One fine day*
Houck, Eric L. *Rabbit surprise*
Hurd, Edith Thacher. *Under the lemon tree*
Hutchins, Pat. *Rosie's walk*
    Rosie's walk [board book]
Isami, Ikuyo. *The fox's egg*
Jacobson, Jennifer Richard. *Moon sandwich mom*
Janovitz, Marilyn. *Little Fox*
Jonovitz, Marilyn. *Good morning, Little Fox*
Kent, Jack. *Silly goose*
Komaiko, Leah. *Fritzi Fox flew in from Florida*
Koralek, Jenny. *The friendly fox*

Kraus, Robert. *All my chickens*
Kvasnosky, Laura McGee. *Zelda and Ivy*
    Zelda and Ivy and the boy next door
    Zelda and Ivy one Christmas
Lang, Aubrey. *Baby fox*
Langston, Laura. *The fox's kettle*
Latimer, Jim. *The fox under first base*
Leverich, Kathleen. *The hungry fox and the foxy duck*
Levine, Michelle. *Red foxes*
Lifton, Betty Jean. *The many lives of Chio and Goro*
Lindgren, Astrid. *The tomten and the fox*
Ling, Mary. *Fox*
Lionni, Leo. *In the rabbitgarden*
Lipkind, William. *The Christmas bunny*
    The little tiny rooster
Livermore, Elaine. *Follow the fox*
London, Jonathan. *Gray fox*
    Ice Bear and Little Fox
McBratney, Sam. *I'll always be your friend*
McDermott, Gerald. *The fox and the stork*
McKissack, Patricia C. *Flossie and the fox*
McPhail, David M. *The blue door*
Malkovych, Ivan. *The cat and the rooster*
Marshall, Edward. *Fox all week*
    Fox and his friends
    Fox at school
    Fox in love
    Fox on wheels
Marshall, James. *Fox on the job*
    Rapscallion Jones
    Wings
Marston, Elsa. *The fox maiden*
Mayne, William. *A house in town*
Meddaugh, Susan. *Maude and Claude go abroad*
Miles, Miska. *The fox and the fire*
Miller, Edward. *Frederick Ferdinand Fox*
Myers, Tim (Tim Brian). *Basho and the fox*
Nikola-Lisa, W. *The dancin' fox*
Nordqvist, Sven. *The fox hunt*
Numeroff, Laura Joffe. *What daddies do best*
Palatini, Margie. *Zoom Broom*
Pevear, Richard. *Mister Cat-and-a-Half*
Potter, Beatrix. *The tale of Mr. Tod*
Preston, Edna Mitchell. *Squawk to the moon, little goose*
Rankin, Joan. *Wow! It's great being a duck*
Riordan, James. *Little Bunny Bobkin*
Roach, Marilynne K. *Dune fox*
Rockwell, Anne F. *Big boss*
San Souci, Robert D. *The silver charm*
Sara. *The rabbit, the fox, and the wolf*
Schami, Rafik. *Albert and Lila*
Schlein, Miriam. *The four little foxes*
Selsam, Millicent E. *A first look at dogs*
Sharmat, Marjorie Weinman. *The best Valentine in the world*
Small, David. *Eulalie and the hopping head*
Steig, William. *Doctor De Soto*
    Roland, the minstrel pig
Szekeres, Cyndy. *Good night, Sammy*
Taylor, Harriet Peck. *Ulaq and the northern lights*
Tejima, Keizaburo. *Fox's dream*
Thomas, Patricia. *"There are rocks in my socks!" said the ox to the fox*
Threadgall, Colin. *Proud rooster and the fox*
The three little pigs. *The three little pigs and the fox*
Tolan, Stephanie S. *Bartholomew's blessing*
Tompert, Ann. *Grandfather Tang's story*
    Little Fox goes to the end of the world
Townsend, Emily Rose. *Arctic foxes*
Turner, Ann Warren. *Hedgehog for breakfast*
Varga, Judy. *The mare's egg*
Wallace, Karen. *Red fox*
Walsh, Ellen Stoll. *You silly goose*
Walt Disney Productions. *Tod and Copper*
    Tod and Vixey
Ward, Helen. *The rooster and the fox*
Ward, Nick. *Farmer George and the hungry guests*
Waring, Richard (Richard M. N.). *Hungry hen*
Watson, Clyde. *Father Fox's feast of songs*

Tom Fox and the apple pie
Valentine foxes
Watson, Wendy. *Tales for a winter's eve*
Weil, Lisl. *Gillie and the flattering fox*
Wells, Rosemary. *Don't spill it again, James*
Westwood, Jennifer. *Going to Squintum's*
Wiese, Kurt. *The dog, the fox and the fleas*
Wild, Margaret. *Fox*
Wilhelm, Hans. *More bunny trouble*
Williams, Sue. *Dinnertime*
Wyllie, Stephen. *Dinner with fox*

Animals – gerbils

Petty, Kate. *Gerbils*
Roth, Susan L. *Cinnamon's day out*

Animals – giraffes

Aggs, Patrice. *The visitor*
Andreae, Giles. *Giraffes can't dance*
Bailey, Donna. *Giraffes*
Brenner, Barbara A. *Mr. Tall and Mr. Small*
Brunhoff, Laurent de. *Serafina the giraffe*
Bush, John. *The giraffe who got in a knot*
Collier, Mary Jo. *The king's giraffe*
Cooke, Ann. *Giraffes at home*
Doughtie, Charles. *High Henry . . . the cowboy who was too tall to ride a horse*
Duvoisin, Roger Antoine. *Periwinkle*
George, Jean Craighead. *Giraffe trouble*
Godard, Alex. *Idora*
Hamsa, Bobbie. *Your pet giraffe*
Hewett, Joan. *A giraffe calf grows up*
Horowitz, Dave. *A monkey among us*
Irvine, Georgeanne. *Georgie the giraffe*
Le Guin, Ursula K. *Solomon Leviathan's nine hundred and thirty-first trip around the world*
Lemaître, Pascal. *Emily the giraffe*
Lin, Grace. *Okie-dokie, Artichokie*
Markert, Jenny. *Giraffes*
Milton, Nancy. *The giraffe that walked to Paris*
Rey, H. A. (Hans Augusto). *Cecily G and the nine monkeys*
Riches, Judith. *Giraffes have more fun*
Sharmat, Marjorie Weinman. *Helga high-up*
Spanyol, Jessica. *Carlo likes counting*
Weare, Tim. *I'm a little giraffe*
Weedn, Flavia. *The enchanted tree*

Animals – goats

Ada, Alma Flor. *Jordi's star*
Alakija, Polly. *Catch that goat!*
Allamand, Pascale. *The little goat in the mountains*
Ambrus, Victor G. *The seven skinny goats*
The three poor tailors
Asbjørnsen, P. C. (Peter Christen). *Billy goats Gruff*, ill. by Wendy Edelson
Billy goats Gruff, ill. by Susan Hellard
The three billy goats Gruff, ill. by Tim Arnold
The three billy goats Gruff, ill. by Robert Bender
The three billy goats Gruff, ill. by Marcia Brown
The three billy goats Gruff, ill. by Stephen Carpenter
Three billy goats Gruff, ill. by Tom Dunnington
The three billy goats Gruff, ill. by Paul Galdone
The three billy goats Gruff, ill. by David Jorgensen
The three billy goats Gruff, ill. by Dennis Kendrick
The three billygoats Gruff, ill. by Eric Kincaid
Three billy goats Gruff, ill. by Thea Kliros
The three billy goats Gruff, ill. by Jonathan Langley
The three billy goats Gruff, ill. by Loretta Lustig
The three billy goats Gruff, ill. by Thomas Newbury
The three billy goats Gruff, ill. by Lilian Obligado
The three billy goats Gruff, ill. by Ed Parker
The three billy goats Gruff, ill. by Heidi Petach
The three billy goats Gruff, ill. by Laura Rader
The three billy goats Gruff, ill. by Glen Rounds

The three billy goats Gruff, ill. by Janet Stevens
The three billy goats Gruff, ill. by William Stobbs
The three billy goats Gruff, ill. by Svend Otto S
The truth about three billy goats Gruff
Berson, Harold. *Balarin's goat*
Blood, Charles L. *The goat in the rug*
Bornstein, Ruth Lercher. *Of course a goat*
Burton, Jane. *Caper the kid*
Carigiet, Alois. *Anton the goatherd*
Carlson, Natalie Savage. *Spooky and the witch's goat*
Chandoha, Walter. *A baby goat for you*
Chiefari, Janet. *Kids are baby goats*
Chottin, Ariane. *Little Goat's new horns*
Damjan, Mischa. *The wolf and the kid*
Daudet, Alphonse. *The brave little goat of Monsieur Séguin*
Dunn, Judy. *The little goat*
Edwards, Julie Andrews. *Dumpy to the rescue!*
Emberley, Rebecca. *Three cool kids*
Fletcher, Elizabeth. *The little goat*
Gage, Wilson. *Mrs. Gaddy and the fast-growing vine*
Gorbachev, Valeri. *One rainy day*
Grimm, Jacob. *Nanny goat and the seven little kids*
The wolf and the seven kids, ill. by Kinuko Y. Craft
The wolf and the seven little kids, ill. by Svend Otto S
The wolf and the seven little kids, ill. by Martin Ursell
Gugler, Laurel Dee. *There's a billy goat in the garden*
Hillert, Margaret. *The three goats*
Hoberman, Mary Ann. *Bill Grogan's goat*
Hoff, Syd. *Happy birthday, Henrietta!*
Hooks, William H. *The Gruff brothers*
Jacobs, Laurie A. *So much in common*
Johnston, Tony. *Desert dog*
Keefer, Janice Kulyk. *Anna's goat*
Kessler, Cristina. *One night*
Kimmel, Eric A. *One Eye, Two Eyes, Three Eyes*
Kimura, Yuichi. *One stormy night . . .*
One sunny day . . .
Kinsey-Warnock, Natalie. *The summer of Stanley*
Kroll, Steven. *The goat parade*
Leaf, Munro. *Gordon, the goat*
Lewis, J. Patrick. *The night of the goat children*
Lipkind, William. *Billy the kid*
McBrier, Page. *Beatrice's goat*
McPhail, David M. *A girl, a goat, and a goose*
Mahy, Margaret. *The queen's goat*
Miller, Heather. *My goats*
Mills, Alan. *The hungry goat*
Morris, Ann. *700 kids on Grandpa's farm*
Pizer, Abigail. *Hattie the goat*
Polacco, Patricia. *Oh, look!*
Rappus, Gerhard. *When the sun was shining*
Royston, Angela. *The goat*
Salley, Coleen. *Who's that tripping over my bridge?*
Sattler, Helen Roney. *No place for a goat*
Seignobosc, Françoise. *Biquette, the white goat*
Springtime for Jeanne-Marie
Sharmat, Mitchell. *Gregory, the terrible eater*
Siddiqui, Ashraf. *Bhombal Dass, the uncle of lion*
Slobodkin, Louis. *The polka-dot goat*
Up high and down low
Suhl, Yuri. *The Purim goat*
Tompert, Ann. *The hungry black bag*
Tudor, Tasha. *Corgiville fair*
Wade, Barrie. *The three billy goats gruff*
Watson, Nancy Dingman. *The birthday goat*
Wildsmith, Brian. *Goat's trail*
Wolkstein, Diane. *The banza*
Youngquist, Cathrene Valente. *The three Billygoats Gruff and Mean Calypso Joe*
Ziefert, Harriet. *Pumpkin Pie*

Animals – gorillas

Aardema, Verna. *Princess Gorilla and a new kind of water*
Browne, Anthony. *Gorilla*
Voices in the park
Willy and Hugh

Willy the champ
Willy the wimp
Buehner, Caralyn. *The escape of Marvin the ape*
Conklin, Gladys. *Little apes*
Delton, Judy. *On a picnic*
George, Jean Craighead. *Gorilla gang*
Hall, Derek. *Gorilla builds*
Harrison, David Lee. *Detective Bob and the great ape escape*
Hazen, Barbara Shook. *The gorilla did it!*
   Gorilla wants to be the baby
Hoff, Syd. *Julius*
Howe, James. *The day the teacher went bananas*
Kessler, Ethel. *Is there a gorilla in the band?*
Krahn, Fernando. *The great ape*
Layton, Neal. *Smile if you're human*
Meyers, Susan. *The truth about gorillas*
Morozumi, Atsuko. *My friend gorilla*
   One gorilla
Most, Bernard. *There's an ape behind the drape*
Palatini, Margie. *Ding dong ding dong*
Schertle, Alice. *The gorilla in the hall*
Selsam, Millicent E. *A first look at monkeys*
Theodorou, Rod. *Mountain gorilla*
Weller, Frances Ward. *The closet gorilla*
Zimelman, Nathan. *Positively no pets allowed*

Animals – groundhogs

Balian, Lorna. *A garden for a groundhog*
Bang, Molly. *Goose*
Bond, Felicia. *Wake up, Vladimir*
Cherry, Lynne. *How Groundhog's garden grew*
Cohen, Carol L. *Wake up, groundhog!*
Coombs, Patricia. *Tilabel*
Cox, Judy. *Go to sleep, Groundhog*
Delton, Judy. *Groundhog's Day at the doctor*
Freeman, Don. *Gregory's Shadow*
Glass, Marvin. *What happened today, Freddy Groundhog?*
Groundhog at Evergreen Road
Hamberger, John. *This is the day*
Hiskey, Iris. *The secret of the first one up*
Jensen, Patricia. *Go to sleep, little groundhog*
Johnson, Crockett. *Will spring be early or will spring be late?*
Kesselman, Wendy Ann. *Time for Jody*
Koscielniak, Bruce. *Geoffrey Groundhog predicts the weather*
Levine, Abby. *Gretchen Groundhog, it's your day!*
Lewin, Betsy. *Groundhog day*
McNulty, Faith. *Woodchuck*
Palazzo, Tony (Anthony D.). *Waldo the woodchuck*
Stanovich, Betty Jo. *Hedgehog adventures*
Tompert, Ann. *Nothing sticks like a shadow*
Watson, Wendy. *Has winter come?*
Welling, Peter J. *Andrew McGroundhog and his shady shadow*

Animals – guinea pigs

Ayers, Rebecca Hickox. *Zorro and Quwi*
Bare, Colleen Stanley. *Guinea pigs don't read books*
Brooks, Andrea. *The guinea pigs' adventure*
Burton, Jane. *Dazy the guinea pig*
   Gipper the guinea pig
Cooper, Patrick. *Never trust a squirrel*
Duke, Kate. *Bedtime*
   Clean-up day
   The guinea pig ABC
   Guinea pigs far and near
   One guinea pig is not enough
   The playground
   Twenty is too many
   What bounces?
Evans, Mark. *Guinea pigs*
King-Smith, Dick. *I love guinea pigs*
Knutson, Barbara. *Love and roast chicken*
Kroll, Steven. *Patches*
   Patches lost and found
Liersch, Anne. *Nell and Fluffy*
Macken, JoAnn Early. *Guinea pigs*

Mayne, William. *Barnabas walks*
Meade, Holly. *John Willy and Freddy McGee*
Meshover, Leonard. *The guinea pigs that went to school*
Miller, Michaela. *Guinea pigs*
Nelson, Robin. *Pet guinea pig*
Potter, Beatrix. *The tale of Tuppeny*
Pursell, Margaret Sanford. *Polly the guinea pig*
Royston, Angela. *Life cycle of a guinea pig*
Rylant, Cynthia. *Little Whistle*
   Little Whistle's Christmas
   Little Whistle's dinner party
   Little Whistle's medicine
Shannon, Margaret. *Gullible's troubles*
Spelman, Cornelia Maude. *When I feel sad*
   When I miss you
Ziefert, Harriet. *Where's the guinea pig?*

Animals – hamsters

Ambrus, Victor G. *Grandma, Felix, and Mustapha Biscuit*
Baker, Alan. *Benjamin and the box*
   Benjamin bounces back
   Benjamin's balloon
   Benjamin's book
   Benjamin's dreadful dream
   Benjamin's portrait
Blacker, Terence. *Herbie Hamster, where are you?*
Blegvad, Lenore. *The great hamster hunt*
Brandenberg, Franz. *The hit of the party*
Brook, Judy. *Hector and Harriet the night hamsters*
Claude-Lafontaine, Pascale. *Monsieur Bussy, the celebrated hamster*
Cohen, Peter Zachary. *Boris's glasses*
Gregory, Valiska. *A Valentine for Norman Noggs*
Inkpen, Deborah. *Harriet and the little fat fairy*
Inkpen, Mick. *Kipper and Roly*
Kirk, Daniel. *Bus stop, bus go*
Leonard, Marcia. *Hannah the hamster hunter*
Meredith, Susan. *Hamsters*
Nelson, Robin. *Pet hamster*
Norac, Carl. *Hello, sweetie pie*
   I love to cuddle
   I love you so much
Petty, Kate. *Hamsters*
Rathmann, Peggy. *10 minutes till bedtime*
Rockwell, Anne F. *My pet hamster*
Saltzberg, Barney. *Crazy hair day*
Suen, Anastasia. *Hamster chase*
Vaës, Alain. *The wild hamster*
Walsh, Ellen Stoll. *Hamsters to the rescue*
Watts, Barrie. *Hamster*
Weigelt, Udo. *Who stole the gold?*

Animals – hedgehogs

Berson, Harold. *Why the jackal won't speak to the hedgehog*
Bodecker, N. M. (Nils Mogens). *Miss Jaster's garden*
Brett, Jan. *Christmas trolls*
   The hat
   Hedgie's surprise
Brook, Judy. *Tim mouse goes down the stream*
   Tim mouse visits the farm
Cartwright, Ann. *The winter hedgehog*
Dalmais, Anne-Marie. *Henry the hedgehog*
Dennard, Deborah. *Hedgehog haven*
Domanska, Janina. *The best of the bargain*
Flot, Jeannette B. *Princess Kalina and the hedgehog*
Guzzo, Sandra E. *Fox and Heggie*
Holden, Edith. *The hedgehog feast*
McClure, Gillian. *Prickly pig*
MacDonald, Maryann. *Hedgehog bakes a cake*
   Rabbit's birthday kite
Millais, Raoul. *Elijah and Pin-Pin*
Myller, Lois. *No! No!*
Pfister, Marcus. *The happy hedgehog*
Potter, Beatrix. *The tale of Mrs. Tiggy-Winkle*
Ruck-Pauquèt, Gina. *Little hedgehog*
Schubert, Ingrid. *Bear's eggs*

Beaver's lodge
Stanovich, Betty Jo. *Hedgehog adventures*
Stewart, Paul. *The birthday presents*
    A little bit of winter
    Rabbit's wish
Stott, Rowena. *The hedgehog feast*
Turner, Ann Warren. *Hedgehog for breakfast*
Waddell, Martin. *The happy hedgehog band*
Wheeler, Lisa. *Porcupining*
Yeoman, John. *The bear's water picnic*

Animals – hippopotamuses

Alexander, Sue. *Ellsworth and Millicent*
    What's wrong now, Millicent?
Allen, Frances Charlotte. *Little hippo*
Bennett, Rainey. *The secret hiding place*
Bohman, Nils Axel Erik. *Jim, Jock and Jumbo*
Bos, Claire. *Maurice the hippo*
Boynton, Sandra. *But not the hippopotamus*
    Hester in the wild
    Hippos go berserk
Brown, Marcia. *How, hippo!*
Calmenson, Stephanie. *The birthday hat*
    Where is Grandma Potamus?
Camp, Lindsay. *Keeping up with Cheetah*
Caple, Kathy. *The coolest place in town*
Castle, Caroline. *Naughty!*
Cole, Babette. *Nungu and the hippopotamus*
Croswell, Volney. *How to hide a hippopotamus*
Dijs, Carla. *Pretend you're a hippo*
Duvoisin, Roger Antoine. *Lonely Veronica*
    Our Veronica goes to Petunia's farm
    Veronica
    Veronica and the birthday present
    Veronica's smile
Flanders, Michael. *The hippopotamus song*
Grambling, Lois G. *This whole Tooth Fairy thing's nothing but a big rip-off!*
Grejniec, Michael. *Albert's nap*
Heide, Florence Parry. *The bigness contest*
Hill, Eric. *Spot's baby sister*
Horowitz, Dave. *A monkey among us*
Jacobs, Laurie A. *So much in common*
Jenkin-Pearce, Susie. *Percy Short and Cuthbert*
Johnson, Doug. *Never babysit the hippopotamuses!*
Kasza, Keiko. *Dorothy and Mikey*
Kishida, Eriko. *The hippo boat*
Kraus, Robert. *Musical Max*
Landström, Lena. *The little hippos' adventure*
Lasher, Faith B. *Hubert Hippo's world*
Lee, Hector Viveros. *I had a hippopotamus*
Leemis, Ralph. *Mister Momboo's hat*
Leonard, Marcia. *Swimming in the sand*
Lester, Helen. *Hurty feelings*
Lewin, Betsy. *Chubbo's pool*
    Hip, hippo, hooray!
McCarthy, Bobette. *Happy hiding hippos*
    Ten little hippos
MacDonald, Maryann. *Little Hippo gets glasses*
    Little Hippo starts school
Mahy, Margaret. *The boy who was followed home*
Mantegazza, Giovanna. *The hippopotamus*
Marshall, James. *George and Martha*
    George and Martha back in town
    George and Martha encore
    George and Martha one fine day
    George and Martha rise and shine
    George and Martha 'round and 'round
    George and Martha, tons of fun
Martin, Bill (William Ivan). *The happy hippopotami*
Mayer, Marianna. *Marcel the pastry chef*
Mayer, Mercer. *Hiccup*
    Oops
Minarik, Else Holmelund. *Am I beautiful?*
Morgan, Michaela. *Helpful Betty solves a mystery*
    Helpful Betty to the rescue

Most, Bernard. *Hippopotamus hunt*
Mwenye Hadithi. *Hot hippo*
Neugebauer, Charise. *The real winner*
Panek, Dennis. *Matilda Hippo has a big mouth*
Parker, Nancy Winslow. *Love from Uncle Clyde*
Patz, Nancy. *To Annabella Pelican from Thomas Hippopotamus*
Paxton, Tom. *The jungle baseball game*
Pouyanne, Thérèse. *The hippo*
Puttock, Simon. *A story for Hippo*
Radford, Derek. *Harry at the garage*
Raschka, Christopher. *The blushful hippopotamus*
Saltzberg, Barney. *Hip, hip, hooray day!*
    The problem with pumpkins
Shipton, Jonathan. *How to be a happy hippo*
Slobodkin, Louis. *Hustle and bustle*
Stadler, John. *Three cheers for hippo!*
Stephens, Helen. *Ruby and the noisy hippo*
Sugita, Yutaka. *Helena the unhappy hippopotamus*
Sutton, Jane. *What should a hippo wear?*
Taylor, Judy. *Sophie and Jack*
    Sophie and Jack help out
Thaler, Mike. *Hippo lemonade*
    It's me, hippo!
    There's a hippopotamus under my bed
    What could a hippopotamus be?
Tyler, Linda Wagner. *Waiting for mom*
    When daddy comes home
Waber, Bernard. *Evie & Margie*
    "You look ridiculous," said the rhinoceros to the hippopotamus
Wahl, Jan. *Old Hippo's Easter egg*
Wharton, Thomas. *Hildegard sings*
Whitehouse, Patricia. *Hippopotamus*
Woychuk, Denis. *The other side of the wall*
    Pirates
Yee, Wong Herbert. *The Officers' Ball*
Young, Miriam Burt. *Please don't feed Horace*
Ziefert, Harriet. *Harry takes a bath*

Animals – horses, ponies

Aarle, Thomas Van. *Don't put your cart before the horse race*
Adams, Jean Ekman. *Clarence and the great surprise*
    Clarence and the purple horse bounce into town
Addy, Sharon Hart. *When wishes were horses*
All the pretty little horses
Ammon, Richard. *Amish horses*
Anderson, C. W. (Clarence Williams). *Billy and Blaze*
    Blaze and the forest fire
    Blaze and the gray spotted pony
    Blaze and the gypsies
    Blaze and the Indian cave
    Blaze and the lost quarry
    Blaze and the mountain lion
    Blaze and Thunderbolt
    Blaze finds forgotten roads
    Blaze finds the trail
    Blaze shows the way
    The crooked colt
    Linda and the Indians
    Lonesome little colt
    A pony for Linda
    A pony for three
    The rumble seat pony
Anderson, Peggy Perry. *We go in a circle*
Arundel, Jocelyn. *Shoes for Punch*
Asch, Frank. *Goodnight horsey*
Ayers, Rebecca Hickox. *Per and the Dala horse*
Baker, Betty. *Three fools and a horse*
Baker, Karen Lee. *Seneca*
Balet, Jan B. *Five Rollatinis*
Barnes, Laura T. *Twist and Ernest*
Barr, Cathrine. *A horse for Sherry*
Barrett, Lawrence Louis. *Twinkle, the baby colt*
Beatty, Hetty Burlingame. *Bucking horse*
    Little Owl Indian
    Moorland pony
Bemelmans, Ludwig. *Madeline in London*

Blech, Dietlind. *Hello Irina*
Boegehold, Betty. *A horse called Starfire*
Bowden, Joan Chase. *A new home for Snow Ball*
Brett, Jan. *Fritz and the beautiful horses*
Brill, Marlene Targ. *Bronco Charlie and the Pony Express*
Brimner, Larry Dane. *Cowboy up!*
Burningham, John. *Humbert, Mister Firkin and the Lord Mayor of London*
Burton, Jane. *Dizzie the pony*
    Pacer, the pony
Callan, Elizabeth Koda. *Good luck pony*
Chan, Chin-Yi. *Good luck horse*
Chandler, Edna Walker. *Pony rider*
Chandra, Deborah. *A is for Amos*
Charmatz, Bill. *The Troy St. bus*
Choldenko, Gennifer. *Moonstruck*
Christiansen, Candace. *The ice horse*
Clement-Davies, David. *Spirit: stallion of the Cimarron*
Climo, Lindee. *Clyde*
Coerr, Eleanor. *Chang's paper pony*
Cohen, Caron Lee. *The mud pony*
Cole, Babette. *Babette Cole's ponies*
    Winni Allfours
Cole, Joanna. *Riding Silver Star*
Collington, Peter. *The midnight circus*
Cotten, Cynthia. *Snow ponies*
Couture, Susan Arkin. *The biggest horse I ever did see*
Cowley, Joy. *Where horses run free*
Cox, David. *Tin Lizzie and Little Nell*
Cretien, Paul D. *Sir Henry and the dragon*
Cummings, W. T. (Walter Thies). *The kid*
Damrell, Liz. *With the wind*
Darling, Kathy (Mary Kathleen). *Pecos Bill finds a horse*
Darrow, Sharon. *Old Thunder and Miss Raney*
Demi. *The hallowed horse*
Dennis, Wesley. *Flip and the cows*
    Flip and the morning
    Tumble, the story of a mustang
Doherty, Berlie. *Snowy*
Dragonwagon, Crescent. *Margaret Ziegler is horse-crazy*
Duncan, Lois. *Horses of dreamland*
Ehrlich, Amy. *Emma's new pony*
Elborn, Andrew. *Noah and the ark and the animals*
Ets, Marie Hall. *Mr. Penny's race horse*
Fain, James W. *Rodeos*
Farley, Walter. *Black stallion*
Fatio, Louise. *Anna, the horse*
Felton, Harold W. *Pecos Bill and the mustang*
Fregosi, Claudia. *The happy horse*
Friskey, Margaret (Margaret Richards). *Indian Two Feet and his horse*
Frost, Robert. *The runaway*
Garbutt, Bernard. *Roger, the rosin back*
Gaston, Susan. *New boots for Salvador*
Glass, Andrew. *The sweetwater run*
Goble, Paul. *Adopted by the eagles*
    The gift of the sacred dog
    The girl who loved wild horses
    Mystic horse
Grabianski, Janusz. *Horses*
Greaves, Margaret. *The star horse*
Greenfield, Eloise. *On my horse*
Greydanus, Rose. *Horses*
Grimm, Jacob. *The horse, the fox, and the lion*
Gross, Ruth Belov. *The girl who wouldn't get married*
Haas, Jessie. *Appaloosa zebra*
    Getting ready to drive a horse and cart
    No foal yet
    Sugaring
Harvey, Bev. *The horse family*
Hasler, Eveline. *Martin is our friend*
Hawkinson, John. *Where the wild apples grow*
Hayden, Kate. *Horse show*
Heilbroner, Joan. *Robert the rose horse*
Herman, R. A. (Ronnie Ann). *Pal the pony*
Herriot, James. *Bonny's big day*
Herzig, Alison Cragin. *Bronco busters*

Heuck, Sigrid. *Pony and Bear are friends*
High, Linda Oatman. *The girl on the high-diving horse*
    Winter shoes for Shadow Horse
Hirschi, Ron. *What is a horse?*
    Where do horses live?
Hoban, Russell. *The rain door*
Hoberman, Mary Ann. *Mr. and Mrs. Muddle*
Hoff, Syd. *Chester*
    The horse in Harry's room
Hoffman, Mary. *Clever Katya*
Hol, Coby. *Henrietta saves the show*
Honda, Tetsuya. *Wild horse winter*
Inkiow, Dimiter. *Me and Clara and Baldwin the pony*
Ipcar, Dahlov (Zorach). *One horse farm*
    World full of horses
Jacka, Martin. *Waiting for Billy*
James, Shirley Kerby. *Going to a horse farm*
Jauck, Andrea. *Assateague*
Jeffers, Susan. *All the pretty horses*
Jeppson, Ann-Sofie. *Here comes Pontus*
    You're growing up, Pontus
Karim, Roberta. *Mandy Sue Day*
Keeping, Charles. *Molly o' the moors*
Kessler, Ethel. *Is there a horse in your house?*
King, Deborah. *Custer*
Kinsey-Warnock, Natalie. *The wild horses of Sweetbriar*
Kraus, Robert. *Springfellow*
    Springfellow's parade
Krauss, Ruth. *Charlotte and the white horse*
Krum, Charlotte. *The four riders*
La Farge, Phyllis. *Joanna runs away*
Lange, Willem. *John and Tom*
Lasell, Fen. *Michael grows a wish*
Le Guin, Ursula K. *A ride on the red mare's back*
Lester, Julius. *Black cowboy, wild horses*
Libby, Barbara. *I rode the red horse*
Ling, Mary. *Foal*
Lobel, Arnold. *Lucille*
Locker, Thomas. *The mare on the hill*
London, Jonathan. *If I had a horse*
    Mustang canyon
London, Sara. *Firehorse Max*
Low, Alice. *David's windows*
McDonnell, Flora. *Giddy-up! Let's ride!*
McGinley, Phyllis. *The horse who lived upstairs*
McMillan, Bruce. *Gletta the foal*
Marshall, James. *Hey, diddle, daddle*
Martin, Bill (William Ivan). *Chicken Chuck*
Martin, Jacqueline Briggs. *The finest horse in town*
Mayer, Marianna. *The black horse*
Medearis, Angela Shelf. *The zebra-riding cowboy*
Meeks, Esther K. *Playland pony*
Metaxas, Eric. *The gardener's apprentice*
Miles, Miska. *Friend of Miguel*
Miller, Heather. *My horses*
Morck, Irene. *Old bird*
Mullins, Patricia. *One horse waiting for me*
Nelson, S. D. *Gift horse*
Osborne, Mary Pope. *Moonhorse*, ill. by David McPhail
    Moonhorse, ill. by S. M. Saelig
Otsuka, Yuzo. *Suho and the white horse*
Otto, Margaret Glover. *The little brown horse*
Paraskevas, Betty. *Marvin, the tap-dancing horse*
Paterson, A. B. (Andrew Barton). *Mulga Bill's bicycle*
Patterson, Geoffrey. *The naughty boy and the strawberry horse*
Peet, Bill (William Bartlett). *Cowardly Clyde*
Pender, Lydia. *Barnaby and the horses*
Peterson, Cris. *Horsepower*
Peterson, Jeanne Whitehouse. *Sometimes I dream horses*
Pitcher, Caroline. *Run with the wind*
Pluckrose, Henry Arthur. *Horses*
Polacco, Patricia. *Mrs. Mack*
Porter, Sue. *Parsnip and the pink blanket*
Primavera, Elise. *Basil and Maggie*
Rabinowitz, Sandy. *A colt named mischief*
    What's happening to Daisy?
Richards, Jane. *A horse grows up*

Robbins, Sandra. *The firefly star*
Rosenberg, Liz. *The carousel*
Rounds, Glen. *Once we had a horse*
    The strawberry roan
Royston, Angela. *The pony*
Sanderson, Ruth. *The golden mare, the firebird, and the magic ring*
Saville, Lynn. *Horses in the circus ring*
Scheidl, Gerda Marie. *Pickle and Patch*
Schnitzler, Pattie L. *Widdermaker*
Scott, Ann Herbert. *Someday rider*
Sewall, Marcia. *Ridin' that strawberry roan*
Sewell, Helen Moore. *Peggy and the pony*
Slobodkina, Esphyr. *The wonderful feast*
Sonberg, Lynn. *A horse named Paris*
Springer, Nancy. *Music of their hooves*
Steers, Billy. *Tractor Mac*
Sutton, Elizabeth Henning. *A pony for keeps*
Thayer, Jane. *Andy and the runaway horse*
    The horse with the Easter bonnet
Thompson, Vivian Laubach. *The horse that liked sandwiches*
Tibo, Gilles. *The cowboy kid*
Tinkelman, Murray. *Cowgirl*
Tracqui, Valérie. *The horse*
Van Camp, Richard. *What's the most beautiful thing you know about horses?*
Ward, Lynd. *The silver pony*
Watson, Esther (Pearl). *The adventures of Jules and Gertie*
    Trouble at Sugar Dip Well
Wells, Rosemary. *Abdul*
Willey, Margaret. *Clever Beatrice and the best little pony*
Winnick, Karen B. *Sybil's night ride*
Winthrop, Elizabeth. *The little humpbacked horse*
Wondriska, William. *The stop*
Wright, Dare. *Look at a colt*
Yeoman, John. *The young performing horse*
Yolen, Jane. *Sky dogs*
Young, Ed (Edward). *The lost horse*
Young, Miriam Burt. *If I rode a horse*
Zimnik, Reiner. *The proud circus horse*
Zolotow, Charlotte (Shapiro). *I have a horse of my own*

Animals – hyenas

Grimsdell, Jeremy. *Kalinzu*
Kimmel, Eric A. *Anansi and the magic stick*
Prelutsky, Jack. *The mean old mean hyena*

Animals – jackals

Aardema, Verna. *Jackal's flying lesson*
Alexander, Sue. *Peacocks are very special*

Animals – jaguars

Brusca, María Cristina. *When jaguars ate the moon*
Campoy, F. Isabel. *Rosa Raposa*
Cowcher, Helen. *Jaguar*
Hamilton, Virginia. *Jaguarundi*
Milton, Joyce. *Big cats*
Ryder, Joanne. *Jaguar in the rain forest*
St. Pierre, Stephanie. *Jaguars*
Woods, Theresa. *Jaguars*

Animals – kangaroos

Bonnett-Rampersaud, Louise. *Polly Hopper's pouch*
Braun, Kathy. *Kangaroo and kangaroo*
Bridges, Margaret Park. *Will you take care of me?*
Brown, Margaret Wise. *Young kangaroo*
Chichester Clark, Emma. *Where are you, Blue Kangaroo?*
Chottin, Ariane. *Little Kangaroo finds his way*
Cole, Joanna. *Norma Jean, jumping bean*
Edwards, Pamela Duncan. *McGillycuddy could*
Hague, Michael. *The perfect present*
Hamsa, Bobbie. *Your pet kangaroo*
Harper, Anita. *It's not fair!*
Hewett, Joan. *A kangaroo joey grows up*

Hurd, Edith Thacher. *The mother kangaroo*
Johnson, Crockett. *Upside down*
Katz, Avner. *The little pickpocket*
Kent, Jack. *Joey*
    Joey runs away
Kipling, Rudyard. *The sing-song of old man kangaroo*
Leonard, Marcia. *Counting kangaroos*
Levitin, Sonia. *When Kangaroo goes to school*
Lithgow, John. *Marsupial Sue*
    Marsupial Sue presents "The Runaway Pancake"
McKee, David. *Elmer and the kangaroo*
Most, Bernard. *The very boastful kangaroo*
Murphy, Stuart J. *Too many kangaroo things to do!*
Pape, D. L. (Donna Lugg). *Where is my little Joey?*
Payne, Emmy. *Katy no-pocket*
Sanchez, Jose Louis Garcia. *Kangaroo*
Schlein, Miriam. *Big talk*, ill. by Joan Auclair
    Big talk, ill. by Laura Lydecker
Selig, Sylvie. *Kangaroo*
Stonehouse, Bernard. *Kangaroos*
Townsend, Anita. *The kangaroo*
Ungerer, Tomi. *Adelaide*
Vaughan, Marcia Kapok. *Snap!*
Wiseman, Bernard. *Little new kangaroo*

Animals – kindness to animals *see* Character traits – kindness to animals

Animals – koalas

Armitage, Ronda. *Harry hates shopping!*
Backker, Vera de. *Coco the koala*
Bassett, Lisa. *Koala Christmas*
Bowden, Miriam. *The adventure of Paz in the land of numbers*
Broome, Errol. *The smallest koala*
Cox, Paul. *The case of the botched book*
    The great eucalyptus mystery
    The riddle of the floating island
Dennard, Deborah. *Koala country*
Du Bois, William Pène. *Bear circus*
    Bear party
Fox, Mem. *Koala Lou*
Gelman, Rita Golden. *A koala grows up*
Hellard, Susan. *Eleanor and the babysitter*
Hewett, Joan. *A koala joey grows up*
Irvine, Georgeanne. *Sydney the koala*
Krings, Antoon. *Oliver's bicycle*
    Oliver's pool
    Oliver's strawberry patch
Levens, George. *Kippy the koala*
London, Jonathan. *A koala for Katie*
Murphy, Mary. *Koala and the flower*
Nobisso, Josephine. *For the sake of a cake*
Quackenbush, Robert M. *I don't want to go, I don't know how to act*
Ruck-Pauquèt, Gina. *Oh, that koala!*
Snyder, Dick. *One day at the zoo*
Sotzek, Hannelore. *A koala is not a bear!*
Walsh, Grahame L. *Didane the koala*

Animals – leeches

Merrick, Patrick. *Leeches*

Animals – lemmings

Steig, Jeanne. *Consider the lemming*

Animals – lemurs

Chichester Clark, Emma. *Lunch with Aunt Augusta*
Cousins, Lucy. *Jazzy in the jungle*
Dennard, Deborah. *Lemur landing*
Hellard, Susan. *Baby lemur*
Lester, Helen. *Something might happen*

Animals – leopards

Aardema, Verna. *Half-a-ball-of-kenki*
Cherry, Lynne. *Snow leopard*
Frampton, David. *The whole night through*
Ipcar, Dahlov (Zorach). *Stripes and spots*
Irvine, Georgeanne. *Lindi the leopard*
Jennings, Linda M. *Hide and seek birthday treat*
Keller, Holly. *Brave Horace*
    Horace
Kepes, Juliet. *Run little monkeys, run, run, run*
Kipling, Rudyard. *How the leopard got his spots*, ill. by Caroline
    Ebborn
    How the leopard got his spots, ill. by Lori Lohstoeter
Livermore, Elaine. *Looking for Henry*
McDonald, Mary Ann. *Leopards*
Maestro, Giulio. *Leopard is sick*
Milton, Joyce. *Big cats*
Mollel, Tololwa M. (Tololwa Marti). *To dinner, for dinner*
Nagda, Anne Whitehead. *World above the clouds*
Radcliffe, Theresa. *The snow leopard*
Robertson, Janet. *Oscar's spots*
St. Pierre, Stephanie. *Leopards*
Souhami, Jessica. *The leopard's drum*

Animals – lions

Aardema, Verna. *The lonely lioness and the ostrich chicks*
Adamson, Joy. *Elsa*
    Elsa and her cubs
Æsop. *Androcles and the lion*, ill. by Janusz Grabianski
    Androcles and the lion, ill. by Dennis Nolan
    Androcles and the lion, ill. by Robert Rayevsky
    Androcles and the lion, ill. by Janet Stevens
    The lion and the mouse, ill. by Carol Jones
    The lion and the mouse, ill. by Lisa McCue
    The lion and the mouse, ill. by Sara Rojo
    The lion and the mouse, ill. by Gerald Rose
    The lion and the mouse, ill. by Bernadette Watts
    The lion and the mouse, ill. by Ed Young
Allen, Pamela. *A lion in the night*
Anholt, Catherine. *A kiss like this*
Balet, Jan B. *Ned and Ed and the lion*
Bannerman, Helen. *The story of the teasing monkey*
Belloc, Hilaire. *Jim, who ran away from his nurse, and was eaten by a
    lion*
Bennett, Barbara. *Lion's precious gift*
Bible. Old Testament. Daniel. *Daniel in the lions' den*, ill. by Leon
    Baxter
    Daniel in the lions' den, ill. by Jim Cummins
    Daniel in the lions' den, ill. by Diana Mayo
Bohman, Nils Axel Erik. *Jim, Jock and Jumbo*
Brenner, Barbara A. *Lion and Lamb*
Bridges, William. *Lion Island*
Bright, Paul. *Quiet!*
Brown, Margaret Wise. *The sleepy little lion*
Cabrera, Jane. *Rory and the lion*
Chichester Clark, Emma. *The story of Horrible Hilda and Henry*
Cohen, Caron Lee. *Martin and the giant lions*
Conover, Chris. *The lion's share*
Cottringer, Anne. *Ella and the naughty lion*
Daugherty, James Henry. *Andy and the lion*
    The picnic
Davies, Andrew. *Poonam's pets*
Davis, Douglas F. *The lion's tail*
Day, Nancy Raines. *The lion's whiskers*
Delton, Judy. *On a picnic*
Demarest, Chris L. *Clemens' kingdom*
Devlin, Wende. *Aunt Agatha, there's a lion under the couch!*
Dineen, Jacqueline. *Lions*
Du Bois, William Pène. *Lion*
Edwards, Pamela Duncan. *Roar*
Fatio, Louise. *The happy lion*
    The happy lion and the bear
    The happy lion in Africa
    The happy lion roars
    The happy lion's quest

    The happy lion's rabbits
    The happy lion's treasure
    The happy lion's vacation
    The three happy lions
Fechner, Amrei. *I am a little lion*
Ford, Miela. *Watch us play*
Freeman, Don. *Dandelion*
Galdone, Paul. *Androcles and the lion*
Gay, Zhenya. *I'm tired of lions*
George, Jean Craighead. *Giraffe trouble*
Gibert, Bruno. *The king is naked!*
Gliori, Debi. *A lion at bedtime*
Goldsboro, Bobby. *Jonah and the whale; and, Daniel in the lion's den*
Goodhart, Pippa. *Row, row, row your boat*
Greaves, Margaret. *Sarah's lion*
Grimm, Jacob. *The horse, the fox, and the lion*
Hancock, Joy Elizabeth. *The loudest little lion*
Hawkins, Mark. *A lion under her bed*
Hill, Susan. *Simba's A-Z*
Hoban, Russell. *The rain door*
Hodges, Margaret. *St. Jerome and the lion*
Hurd, Edith Thacher. *Johnny Lion's bad day*
    Johnny Lion's book
    Johnny Lion's rubber boots
Jensen, Patricia. *Gentle Little Lion*
Kasza, Keiko. *The mightiest*
Kishida, Eriko. *The lion and the bird's nest*
Kleven, Elisa. *The lion and the little red bird*
La Fontaine, Jean de. *The lion and the rat*
Lang, Aubrey. *Baby lion*
    Lions
McCarthy, Michael. *The story of Daniel in the lions' den*
MacDonald, Suse. *Nanta's lion*
McKean, Thomas. *Hooray for Grandma Jo!*
Mahy, Margaret. *A lion in the meadow*
Makower, Sylvia. *Samson's breakfast*
Mann, Peggy. *King Laurence, the alarm clock*
Marzollo, Jean. *Daniel in the lion's den*
May, Kara. *Joe Lion's big boots*
Michael, Emory H. *Androcles and the lion*
Michel, Anna. *Little wild lion cub*
Milton, Joyce. *Big cats*
Moers, Hermann. *Evie to the rescue!*
    Hugo's baby brother
Mollel, Tololwa M. (Tololwa Marti). *Dume's roar*
Montenegro, Laura Nyman. *Sweet Tooth*
Mostacchi, Massimo. *The beast and the boy*
Mwenye Hadithi. *Lazy lion*
Ness, Evaline. *Fierce*
Newberry, Clare Turlay. *Herbert the lion*
Peet, Bill (William Bartlett). *Eli*
    Hubert's hair-raising adventures
    Randy's dandy lions
Pfister, Marcus. *How Leo learned to be king*
Pitcher, Caroline. *The time of the lion*
Pluckrose, Henry Arthur. *Lions and tigers*
Presencer, Alain. *Roaring lion tales*
Scheffler, Ursel. *Be brave, little lion!*
Schneider, Antonie. *Luke the Lionhearted*
Siddiqui, Ashraf. *Bhombal Dass, the uncle of lion*
Siepmann, Jane. *The lion on Scott Street*
Skorpen, Liesel Moak. *If I had a lion*
Stephenson, Dorothy. *How to scare a lion*
Stewart, Elizabeth Laing. *The lion twins*
Townsend, Kenneth. *Felix, the bald-headed lion*
Trimble, Marcia. *Hello sun*
Varga, Judy. *Miss Lollipop's lion*
Waber, Bernard. *A lion named Shirley Williamson*
Wagener, Gerda. *Leo the lion*
Wolf, Gita. *The very hungry lion*
Yaccarino, Dan. *Deep in the jungle*
Yee, Patrick. *Baby lion*
Yoshida, Toshi. *Young lions*
Zelinsky, Paul O. *The lion and the stoat*
Zimelman, Nathan. *Treed by a pride of irate lions*

Animals – llamas

Alexander, Ellen. *Llama and the great flood*
Guarino, Deborah. *Is your mama a llama?*
Livingstone, Star. *Harley*
Rockwell, Anne F. *The good llama*

Animals – lorises

Deacon, Alexis. *Slow Loris*

Animals – lynx

Bonners, Susan. *Hunter in the snow*
Hodge, Deborah. *Wild cats*
London, Jonathan. *Let the lynx come in*
St. Pierre, Stephanie. *Lynx*

Animals – manatees

Arnosky, Jim. *A manatee morning*
Cousteau Society. *Manatees*
Harms, John, II. *The saving of Sly Manatee*
Houk, Randy. *Chessie, the travelin' man*
Klingel, Cynthia Fitterer. *Manatees*
Lithgow, John. *I'm a manatee*
Theodorou, Rod. *Florida manatee*

Animals – meerkats

Paterson, Brian. *Zigby camps out*
    Zigby hunts for treasure

Animals – mice

Ada, Alma Flor. *Friend frog*
Æsop. *Belling the cat*
    The country mouse and the city mouse, ill. by Laura Lydecker
    The country mouse and the city mouse, ill. by Diane Silverman
    The lion and the mouse, ill. by Carol Jones
    The lion and the mouse, ill. by Lisa McCue
    The lion and the mouse, ill. by Sara Rojo
    The lion and the mouse, ill. by Gerald Rose
    The lion and the mouse, ill. by Bernadette Watts
    The lion and the mouse, ill. by Ed Young
    The town mouse and the country mouse, ill. by Lorinda Bryan Cauley
    The town mouse and the country mouse, ill. by Helen Craig
    The town mouse and the country mouse, ill. by Paul Galdone
    The town mouse and the country mouse, ill. by Tom Garcia
    The town mouse and the country mouse, ill. by Janet Stevens
    The town mouse and the country mouse, ill. by Bernadette Watts
    Town mouse, country mouse, ill. by Jan Brett
    Town mouse, country mouse, ill. by Carol Jones
Albert, Shirley. *Doll party*
Alborough, Jez. *Watch out! Big Bro's coming!*
Aliki. *At Mary Bloom's*
Allen, Laura Jean. *Rollo and Tweedy and the case of the missing cheese*
Allen, Linda. *The mouse bride*
Alter, Anna. *Estelle and Lucy*
Althea. *Jeremy Mouse and cat*
Angelo, Nancy Carolyn Harrison. *Camembert*
Angelo, Valenti. *The candy basket*
Aragon, Jane Chelsea. *The major and the mousehole mice*
Archambault, John. *A beautiful feast for a big king cat*
Arnosky, Jim. *Mouse letters*
    Mouse numbers and letters
    Mouse writing
Asch, Frank. *Dear brother*
    Mr. Maxwell's mouse
Augarde, Steve (Stephen). *Barnaby Shrew, Black Dan and . . . the mighty wedgwood*
Aylesworth, Jim. *The completed hickory dickory dock*
    Two terrible frights
Baehr, Patricia. *Mouse in the house*
Baker, Alan. *Two tiny mice*
    Where's mouse?

Balian, Lorna. *Mother's Mother's Day*
Balzano, Jeanne. *The wee moose*
Barbaresi, Nina. *Firemouse*
Barbero, Maria. *The bravest mouse*
Barkan, Joanne. *Whiskerville bake shop*
    Whiskerville firehouse
    Whiskerville post office
    Whiskerville school
Barklem, Jill. *Autumn story*
    The big book of Brambly Hedge
    The high hills
    The secret staircase
    Spring story
    Summer story
    Winter story
Barner, Bob. *Which way to the Revolution?*
Barnes-Murphy, Rowan. *Numbers*
Barringer, William. *Gregory and Alexander*
Barrows, Marjorie Wescott. *Muggins' big balloon*
    Muggins Mouse
    Muggins takes off
    The Rand McNally book of favorite Muggins Mouse stories
Bastin, Marjolein. *A little dog for Vera*
    My name is Vera
    Vera and her friends
    Vera dresses up
    Vera in the kitchen
    Vera the mouse
    Vera's special hobbies
Bedford, David. *Ella's games*
Belpré, Pura. *Pérez and Martina*
Benjamin, A. H. *It could have been worse*
    Mouse, mole and the falling star
Berson, Harold. *A moose is not a mouse*
    Raminagrobis and the mice
Bible. Old Testament. Jonah. *Jonah*, ill. by Kurt Mitchell
Bloom, Becky. *Crackers*
    Mice make trouble
Boegehold, Betty. *Pippa Mouse*
    Pippa pops out!
Bogacki, Tomasz. *Cat and mouse in the night*
    Cat and mouse in the snow
Bond, Felicia. *The Halloween performance*
    The Halloween play
Bos, Burny. *Alexander the great*
Bottner, Barbara. *Wallace's lists*
Boyd, Lizi. *Mouse in a house*
Boynton, Sandra. *If at first . . .*
Brady, Irene. *Wild mouse*
Brady, Susan. *Find my blanket*
Brandenberg, Franz. *Everyone ready?*
    Six new students
Brenner, Barbara A. *Mr. Tall and Mr. Small*
Bright, Robert. *Georgie and the runaway balloon*
Brook, Judy. *Tim mouse goes down the stream*
    Tim mouse visits the farm
Brooks, Nigel. *Country mouse cottage*
    Town mouse house
Brown, Palmer. *Something for Christmas*
Buchanan, Heather S. *Emily Mouse saves the day*
    Emily Mouse's beach house
    Emily Mouse's first adventure
    Emily Mouse's garden
    George and Matilda Mouse and the floating school
    George and Matilda Mouse and the moon rocket
    George Mouse learns to fly
    George Mouse's covered wagon
    George Mouse's first summer
    George Mouse's riverboat band
Bullock, Kathleen. *A surprise for Mitzi Mouse*
Bunting, Eve (Anne Evelyn). *The Mother's Day mice*
Burningham, John. *Trubloff*
Burton, Katherine. *One gray mouse*
Butler, Stephen. *The mouse and the apple*
Butterworth, Nick. *Jingle bells*
Cameron, Alice. *The cat sat on the mat*
Cameron, John. *If mice could fly*

Cantieni, Benita. *Little Elephant and Big Mouse*
Carle, Eric. *Do you want to be my friend?*
Carlson, Nancy L. *Look out kindergarten, here I come!*
Carlstrom, Nancy White. *I'm not moving, mama!*
Carter, Noelle. *I'm a little mouse*
   Where's my squishy ball?
Cartlidge, Michelle. *Baby mice at home*
   Fairy letters
   A house for Lily Mouse
   Michelle Cartlidge's book of words
   Mouse birthday
   Mouse Christmas
   Mouse in the house
   Mouse letters
   Mouse theater
   Mouse time
   A mouse's diary
   Mouse's scrapbook
   Pippin and Pod
Castle, Caroline. *Herbert Binns and the flying tricycle*
Charles, Donald. *Calico Cat's exercise book*
Chase, Catherine. *Baby mouse goes shopping*
   Baby mouse learns his ABC's
   The mouse in my house
Choi, Yangsook. *New cat*
Chorao, Kay. *Cathedral mouse*
Chottin, Ariane. *Little Mouse's rescue*
Christensen, Gardell Dano. *Mrs. Mouse needs a house*
Christian, Mary Blount. *The bookstore mouse*
Claret, Maria. *Melissa Mouse*
Collicott, Sharleen. *Mildred and Sam*
Coombs, Patricia. *Mouse Café*
Cousins, Lucy. *Count with Maisy*
   Doctor Maisy
   Happy birthday, Maisy
   Maisy at the fair
   Maisy at the farm
   Maisy cleans up
   Maisy dresses up
   Maisy goes shopping
   Maisy goes swimming
   Maisy goes to bed
   Maisy goes to school
   Maisy goes to the playground
   Maisy makes gingerbread
   Maisy makes lemonade
   Maisy's ABC
   Maisy's bedtime
   Maisy's big flap book
   Maisy's colors
   Maisy's farm
   Maisy's first clock
   Maisy's halloween
   Maisy's morning on the farm
   Maisy's noisy day
   Maisy's pirate treasure hunt
   Maisy's pool
   Maisy's pop-up playhouse
   Maisy's rainbow dream
   Maisy's twinkly, crinkly counting book
Coxe, Molly. *6 sticks*
Craig, Helen. *Charlie and Tyler at the seashore*
Cressey, James. *Max the mouse*
Crimi, Carolyn. *Tessa's tip-tapping toes*
Cunningham, Julia. *A mouse called Junction*
Currey, Anna. *Tickling tigers*
   Truffle's Christmas
Cushman, Doug. *Mouse and Mole and the Christmas walk*
Dahlie, Elizabeth. *Bernelly & Harriet*
Dalmais, Anne-Marie. *Best bedtime stories of Mother Mouse*
   Molly and Mimi the mouse twins
Dauer, Rosamond. *Bullfrog grows up*
Daugherty, James Henry. *The picnic*
Delacre, Lulu. *Nathan and Nicholas Alexander*
   Nathan's balloon adventure
   Nathan's fishing trip
Delaney, Ned. *Two strikes, four eyes*

Delessert, Etienne. *How the mouse was hit on the head by a stone and so discovered the world*
Demarest, Chris L. *Kitman and Willy at sea*
   The lunatic adventure of Kitman and Willy
Dennard, Deborah. *Travis and the better mousetrap*
De Paola, Tomie (Thomas Anthony). *Charlie needs a cloak*
Derby, Sally. *The mouse who owned the sun*
De Regniers, Beatrice Schenk. *How Joe the bear and Sam the mouse got together*
   Picture book theater
Dominguez, Angel. *Diary of a Victorian mouse*
Donaldson, Julia. *The gruffalo*
Doty, Roy. *Old-one-eye meets his match*
Dubanevich, Arlene. *Tom's tail*
Duke, Kate. *Aunt Isabel makes trouble*
   Aunt Isabel tells a good one
Dupré, Judith. *The mouse bride*
Durant, Alan. *Mouse party*
Durrell, Julie. *Mouse tails*
Edwards, Pamela Duncan. *Bravo, Livingstone Mouse!*
   Livingstone Mouse
Egielski, Richard. *Slim and Jim*
Ellwand, David. *Midas Mouse*
Elzbieta. *Brave Babette and sly Tom*
Emberley, Ed (Edward Randolph). *Thanks, Mom!*
Emberley, Michael. *Ruby*
Engel, Diana. *Eleanor, Arthur, and Claire*
   Gino Badino
Ernst, Lisa Campbell. *The rescue of Aunt Pansy*
Esbensen, Barbara Juster. *The dream mouse*
Ets, Marie Hall. *Mr. T. W. Anthony Woo*
Ezra, Mark. *The sleepy dormouse*
Farris, Pamela J. *Young Mouse and Elephant*
Fearnley, Jan. *Just like you*
   Watch out!
Félix, Monique. *The further adventures of the little mouse trapped in a book*
   The story of a little mouse trapped in a book
Fernandes, Eugenie. *Big week for little mouse*
   Busy Little Mouse
   Sleepy little mouse
Field, Rachel Lyman. *A road might lead to anywhere*
Fisher, Aileen Lucia. *The house of a mouse*
   Sing, little mouse
Fleming, Denise. *Alphabet under construction*
   Lunch
Fontes, Justine Korman. *Signs of spring*
Forward, Toby. *Ben's Christmas carol*
Fowler, Richard. *Happy birthday, Mouse!*
Fraser, Mary Ann. *I.Q. goes to school*
   I.Q. goes to the library
Freeman, Don. *The guard mouse*
   Norman the doorman
Freeman, Lydia. *Pet of the Met*
Freschet, Berniece. *Bear mouse*
   Bernard of Scotland Yard
Futamata, Eigoro. *How not to catch a mouse*
Gackenbach, Dick. *The perfect mouse*
Gág, Wanda. *Snippy and Snappy*
Gantz, David. *The genie bear with the light brown hair word book*
Garland, Michael. *The mouse before Christmas*
Gay, Marie-Louise. *Moonbeam on a cat's ear*
Geraghty, Paul. *Look out, Patrick!*
   Stop that noise!
Geras, Adèle. *The nutcracker*
Ghigna, Charles. *Mice are nice*
Gifford, Kathie Lee. *Moochie's surprise*
Gili, Phillida. *Fanny and Charles*
Ginsburg, Mirra. *Four brave sailors*
Goldsboro, Bobby. *Noah and the ark; and, David and Goliath*
Goodall, John S. *Creepy castle*
   Naughty Nancy goes to school
Gordon, Margaret. *The supermarket mice*
Goundaud, Karen Jo. *A very mice joke book*
Graham, John. *I love you, mouse*
Greaves, Margaret. *The mice of Nibbling Village*
Greene, Carol. *A computer went a-courting*

Grimm, Jacob. *Godfather Cat and Mousie*
  Little Red Riding Hood, ill. by John S. Goodall
Guest, C. Z. *Tiny green thumbs*
Gundersheimer, Karen. *1, 2, 3, play with me*
  Shapes to show
Hague, Michael. *The nutcracker*
Hale, Irina. *Chocolate mouse and sugar pig*
Hale, Linda. *The glorious Christmas soup party*
Hall, Malcolm. *And then the mouse . . .*
Harper, Jessica. *I'm not going to chase the cat today*
Harris, Leon A. *The great diamond robbery*
  The great picture robbery
Harris, Robie H. *Goodbye, Mousie*
Hawkinson, John. *The old stump*
Hazen, Barbara Shook. *The Fat Cats, Cousin Scraggs and the monster mice*
Heling, Kathryn. *Mouse makes magic*
  Mouse's hide-and-seek words
Hellings, Colette. *Too little, too big*
Helmer, Marilyn. *Three cat and mouse tales*
Hendry, Diana. *The very noisy night*
Henkes, Kevin. *Chester's way*
  Lilly's purple plastic purse
  Owen
  Sheila Rae, the brave
  Sheila Rae's peppermint stick
  A weekend with Wendell
  Wimberly worried
Henrietta. *A mouse in the house*
Herman, Gail. *Fievel's big showdown*
Hewett, Joan. *The mouse and the elephant*
Hill, Susan. *Stuart at the fun house*
  Stuart hides out
  Stuart sets sail
Hillman, Priscilla. *A Merry-Mouse book of favorite poems*
  A Merry-Mouse book of months
  A Merry-Mouse book of nursery rhymes
  The Merry-Mouse book of opposites
  The Merry-Mouse book of toys
  A Merry-Mouse Christmas A B C
  The Merry-Mouse counting and colors book
  The Merry-Mouse schoolhouse
Himmelman, John. *Montigue on the high seas*
Hines, Anna Grossnickle. *Whose shoes?*
Hoban, Lillian. *It's really Christmas*
  The sugar snow spring
Hoban, Russell. *Charlie Meadows*
  Flat cat
Hoberman, Mary Ann. *Marvelous mouse man*
  The two sillies
Hoff, Carol. *The four friends*
Hoff, Syd. *Mrs. Brice's mice*
Hoffman, Elizabeth Stokes. *Miss Renée's mice*
  Miss Renée's mice go to an exhibition
Hoffmann, E. T. A. *The nutcracker*, ill. by Francesca Crespi
  The nutcracker, ill. by Renée Graef
  The nutcracker, ill. by Rachel Isadora
  The nutcracker, ill. by Joanna Isles
  The nutcracker, ill. by Maurice Sendak
  The nutcracker, ill. by Lisbeth Zwerger
  The nutcracker ballet, ill. by Carolyn Ewing
  The nutcracker ballet, ill. by Vladimir Vasilévich Vagin
Holabird, Katharine. *Angelina and Alice*
  Angelina and Henry
  Angelina and the princess
  Angelina at the fair
  Angelina ballerina
  Angelina dances
  Angelina ice skates
  Angelina on stage
  Angelina's baby sister
  Angelina's ballet class
  Angelina's birthday surprise
  Angelina's Christmas
  Angelina's Halloween
  Christmas with Angelina
  The little mouse ABC

Holl, Adelaide. *A mouse story*
  Sylvester, the mouse with the musical ear
Hopkins, Margaret. *Sleepytime for baby mouse*
Hoppe, Matthias. *Mouse and elephant*
House mouse, photos by David Thompson
Houston, John A. *A mouse in my house*
Howard, Jean G. *Of mice and mice*
Howe, James. *Horace and Morris but mostly Dolores*
  Horace and Morris join the chorus (but what about Dolores?)
Hurd, Edith Thacher. *Come and have fun*
Hurd, Thacher. *Blackberry ramble*
  Little Mouse's big Valentine
  Little Mouse's birthday cake
  The pea patch jig
  Santa Mouse and the ratdeer
  Tomato soup
Hurford, John. *The dormouse*
Hürlimann, Ruth. *The mouse with the daisy hat*
Inkpen, Mick. *Kipper's toybox*
Irving, John. *A sound like someone trying not to make a sound*
Ivimey, John William. *The complete story of the three blind mice*, ill. by Paul Galdone
  The complete version of ye three blind mice, ill. by Walton Corbould
  Three blind mice, ill. by Lorinda Bryan Cauley
  Three blind mice, ill. by Victoria Chess
Iwamura, Kazuo. *The fourteen forest mice and the harvest moon watch*
  The fourteen forest mice and the spring meadow picnic
  The fourteen forest mice and the summer laundry day
  The fourteen forest mice and the winter sledding day
Jensen, Patricia. *Kitty's special job*
Jeram, Anita. *All together now*
  Birthday happy, Contrary Mary
  Bunny, my Honey
  Contrary Mary
  Daisy Dare
Joerns, Consuelo. *The foggy rescue*
  The lost and found house
Johnson, Pamela. *A mouse's tale*
Johnson, Paul Brett. *Mr. Persnickety and Cat Lady*
Joly-Berbesson, Fanny. *Marceau Bonappetit*
Jones, Jennifer Berry. *Heetunka's harvest*
Karlin, Nurit. *Little big mouse*
Keenan, Martha. *The mannerly adventures of Little Mouse*
Keller, Holly. *The new boy*
Kelley, True. *Blabber Mouse*
Kellogg, Steven (Stephen). *The island of the skog*
Kemp, Moira. *Lift-the-flap mouse*
Kerr, Phyllis Forbes. *I tricked you*
Kimmel, Eric A. *The greatest of all*
Knight, Hilary. *A firefly in a fir tree*
Koenig, Marion. *The tale of fancy Nancy*
Koller, Jackie French. *Fish fry tonight*
Kraus, Robert. *Another mouse to feed*
  Big Squeak, Little Squeak
  Come out and play, little mouse
  Dr. Mouse, Bungle Jungle doctor
  I, Mouse
  Mouse in love
  Mouse work
  Where are you going, little mouse?
  Whose mouse are you?
Krupinski, Loretta. *Christmas in the city*
Kumin, Maxine W. *Joey and the birthday present*
Kuskin, Karla. *What did you bring me?*
Kwitz, Mary DeBall. *Mouse at home*
Lakin, Patricia. *Clarence the copy cat*
Larios, Julie Hofstrand. *On the stairs*
Layton, Aviva. *The squeakers*
Leeson, Christine. *Molly and the storm*
Le Guin, Ursula K. *Tom Mouse*
Levine, Arthur A. *The boardwalk princess*
Lewison, Wendy Cheyette. *Happy Thanksgiving!*
  Shy Vi
Lexau, Joan M. *The dog food caper*
Linch, Elizabeth Johanna. *Samson*
Lionni, Leo. *Alexander and the wind-up mouse*
  A busy year

Colors to talk about
Frederick
Geraldine, the music mouse
The greentail mouse
In the rabbitgarden
Letters to talk about
Matthew's dream
Mr. McMouse
Mouse days
Nicholas, where have you been?
Numbers to talk about
Theodore and the talking mushroom
Tillie and the wall
What?
When?
Where?
Who?
Words to talk about
The Little book of mice
The little red hen. The little red hen and the ear of wheat, ill. by Elisabeth Bell
Little, Mary E. Ricardo and the puppets
Lobel, Arnold. Martha, the movie mouse
Mouse soup
Mouse tales
The rose in my garden
Low, Joseph. The Christmas grump
Mice twice
Lubin, Leonard B. Christmas gift-bringers
McBratney, Sam. The dark at the top of the stairs
McCully, Emily Arnold. The Christmas gift
First snow
Monk camps out
Mouse practice
New baby
Picnic
School
MacDonald, Margaret Read. Fat cat
Mabela the clever
McDonald, Megan. Tundra mouse
McKissack, Patricia C. Country mouse and city mouse
McMillan, Bruce. Mouse views
McMullan, Kate (Hall). Supercat to the rescue
McNulty, Faith. Mouse and Tim
Maisner, Heather. Find Mouse in the house
Find Mouse in the yard
Maitland, Barbara. The bookstore burglar
The bookstore ghost
Majewski, Joe. A friend for Oscar Mouse
Mandry, Kathy. The cat and the mouse and the mouse and the cat
Manson, Christopher. Here begins the tale of the marvellous blue mouse
Mantinband, Gerda. Three clever mice
Manushkin, Fran. Moon dragon
Martin, Bill (William Ivan). A beasty story
Martin, Jacqueline Briggs. Bizzy Bones and Moosemouse
Bizzy Bones and the lost quilt
Bizzy Bones and Uncle Ezra
Masters, Anthony. Ricky's rat gang
Mathers, Petra. Sophie and Lou
Mayer, Marianna. Alley oop!
Mayne, William. Mousewing
Medoff, Francine. The mouse in the matzah factory
Mendoza, George. Henri Mouse
Henri Mouse, the juggler
Need a house? Call Ms. Mouse
Merski, P. K. Roaring, boring, Alice
Miles, Miska. Mouse six and the happy birthday
Miller, Alice P. The mouse family's blueberry pie
Miller, Edna. Mousekin finds a friend
Mousekin takes a trip
Mousekin's ABC
Mousekin's Christmas eve
Mousekin's close call
Mousekin's Easter basket
Mousekin's fables
Mousekin's family

Mousekin's frosty friend
Mousekin's golden house
Mousekin's lost woodland
Mousekin's mystery
Mousekin's Thanksgiving
Miller, Moira. Oscar Mouse finds a home
The proverbial mouse
Modesitt, Jeanne. It's Hanukkah!
Mogensen, Jan. The tiger's breakfast
Mollel, Tololwa M. (Tololwa Marti). Kitoto the mighty
Monsell, Mary Elise. Crackle Creek
Monson, A. M. Wanted . . . best friend
Moore, Clement Clarke. The night before Christmas, ill. by Loretta Krupinski
Moore, Inga. The vegetable thieves
Moore, Lilian. Adam Mouse's book of poems
Moran, Alex. Sam and Jack
Morgan, Michaela. Brave, brave mouse
Morgan-Vanroyen, Mary. Curious Rosie
Gentle Rosie
Guess who I love?
Patient Rosie
The Pudgy Merry Christmas book
Sleep tight, little mouse
Wild Rosie
Morimoto, Junko. Mouse's marriage
Morris, Ann. Eleanora Mousie catches a cold
Eleanora Mousie in the dark
Eleanora Mousie makes a mess
Eleanora Mousie's gray day
Moss, Marissa. But not Kate
Moss, Miriam. I'll be your friend, Smudge
It's my turn, Smudge
A new house for Smudge
Mother Goose. Hickory dickory dock, ill. by Doug Cushman
Hickory dickory dock, ill. by Marilyn Janovitz
Hickory, dickory, dock, ill. by Moira Kemp
Mouse house, ill. by Zokeisha
Muller, Robin. Badger's new house
Nakagawa, Rieko. Guri and Gura
Guri and Gura's special gift
Nayer, Judy. Mice are nice
Nivola, Claire A. The forest
Noll, Sally. Watch where you go
Noonan, Julia. Mouse by mouse
Novak, Matt. Mouse TV
Numeroff, Laura Joffe. If you give a mouse a cookie
If you take a mouse to school
If you take a mouse to the movies
What mommies do best
Oakley, Graham. The church cat abroad
The church mice adrift
The church mice and the moon
The church mice and the ring
The church mice at bay
The church mice at Christmas
The church mice in action
The church mice spread their wings
The church mouse
The diary of a church mouse
Oh, Jiwon. Cat and mouse
Olson, Arielle North. Noah's cats and the devil's fire
Oram, Hiawyn. Princess Chamomile gets her way
Ormerod, Jan. Miss Mouse's day
Ormondroyd, Edward. Broderick
Ostheeren, Ingrid. Jonathan Mouse
Jonathan Mouse and the baby bird
Jonathan Mouse and the magic box
Jonathan Mouse at the circus
Jonathan Mouse, detective
Oyibo, Papa. Big brother, little sister
Palmer, Todd Starr. Rhino and Mouse
Paraskevas, Betty. Maggie and the Ferocious Beast, the big carrot
Maggie and the Ferocious Beast, the big scare
Peguero, Leone. Lionel and Amelia
Peppé, Rodney. Cat and mouse
The kettleship pirates

The mice and the clockwork bus
The mice and the flying basket
The mice who lived in a shoe
Pfister, Marcus. *Milo and the magical stones*
   Milo and the mysterious island
Piers, Helen. *The mouse book*
Pomerantz, Charlotte. *The mousery*
Popov, Nikolai. *Why?*
Potter, Beatrix. *The tailor of Gloucester*
   The tale of Johnny Town-Mouse
   The tale of Mrs. Tittlemouse
   The tale of Mrs. Tittlemouse and other mouse stories
   The tale of two bad mice
   The two bad mice
Powell, Roxanne Dyer. *Cat, mouse and moon*
Pratt, Pierre. *Car*
   Home
   Park
   Shopping
Provencher, Rose-Marie. *Mouse cleaning*
Pryor, Bonnie. *Louie and Dan are friends*
   The porcupine mouse
Quackenbush, Robert M. *Chuck lends a paw*
Rand, Gloria. *Prince William*
   Willie takes a hike
Randall, Ronne. *The Hanukkah mice*
Reiser, Lynn. *Two mice in three fables*
Reitman, Andrea. *Mouse in the house*
Reynolds, Peter H. *Sydney's star*
Riley, Linnea Asplind. *Mouse mess*
Ring, Elizabeth. *Lucky mouse*
Roach, Marilynne K. *Two Roman mice*
Robbins, Maria Polushkin. *Mother, Mother, I want another*
   Mother, Mother I want another
Robbins, Sandra. *The firefly star*
Roberts, Bethany. *Birthday mice*
   Christmas mice
   Easter mice
   Fourth of July mice
   Valentine mice!
Roche, P. K. (Patrick K.). *Good-bye, Arnold!*
   Webster and Arnold go camping
Rodell, Susanna. *Dear Fred*
Rogers, Paul (Patrick). *Ruby's dinnertime*
   Ruby's potty
Rohmann, Eric. *My friend Rabbit*
Ross, Tony. *Hugo and Oddsock*
   Hugo and the bureau of holidays
   Hugo and the man who stole colors
Ryder, Joanne. *Mouse tail moon*
Sabuda, Robert James. *The mummy's tomb*
Sage, James. *Farmer Smart's fat cat*
San Souci, Robert D. *The silver charm*
Santore, Charles. *A stowaway on Noah's Ark*
Schermer, Judith. *Mouse in house*
Schlein, Miriam. *Home, the tale of a mouse*
Schoenherr, John. *The barn*
Schories, Pat. *Mouse around*
Schumacher, Claire. *Tommy the winner*
Schwartz, Roslyn. *Rose and Dorothy*
Scruton, Clive. *Bubble and squeak*
Seidler, Rosalie. *Grumpus and the Venetian cat*
Seignobosc, Françoise. *Small-Trot*
Selden, George. *The mice, the monks and the Christmas tree*
Sharratt, Nick. *Mouse moves house*
Shepard, Aaron. *The princess mouse*
Sierra, Judy. *The beautiful butterfly*
   'Twas the fright before Christmas
Silverman, Maida. *Mouse's shape book*
Simon, Charnan. *Click and the kids go sailing*
Simon, Sidney B. *Henry, the uncatchable mouse*
Siomades, Lorianne. *Three little kittens*
Slate, Joseph. *Who is coming to our house?*
Smith, Jim. *The frog band and Durrington Dormouse*
Smith, Mavis. *'Twas the day after Thanksgiving*
Smith, Wendy. *The lonely, only mouse*
   Twice mice

Snell, Gordon. *'Twas the day after Christmas*
Soto, Gary. *Chato's kitchen*
Spohn, Kate. *By word of mouse*
Spurling, Margaret. *Bilby moon*
Standiford, Natalie. *Dollhouse mouse*
Stanley, Diane. *The conversation club*
Steig, William. *Abel's Island*
   Doctor De Soto
   Doctor De Soto goes to Africa
Stein, Sara Bonnett. *Mouse*
Steptoe, John. *The story of jumping mouse*
Stern, Peter. *Max the dragon*
Stevens, Harry. *Fat mouse*
Stevenson, James. *All aboard!*
   The castaway
   The Sea View Hotel
   The stowaway
Stoddard, Sandol. *Bedtime mouse*
Stone, Bernard. *The charge of the mouse brigade*
   Emergency mouse
Stortz, Diane M. *Barnaby Mouse, detective, and the mystery of the big book*
Sumiko. *Kittymouse*
Summers, Kate. *Milly and Tilly*
   Milly's wedding
Sutherland, Tui. *Meet Mo and Ella*
Szekeres, Cyndy. *Cyndy Szekeres' counting book, 1 to 10*
   Ladybug, ladybug, where are you?
   The mouse that Jack built
   Toby!
   Toby's please and thank you
Takao, Yuko. *A winter concert*
Talbot, John. *Pins and needles*
Taylor, Judy. *Dudley and the monster*
   Dudley and the strawberry shake
   Dudley goes flying
   Dudley in a jam
Thompson, Lauren. *Mouse's first Christmas*
   Mouse's first Christmas [board book]
   Mouse's first Halloween
Titus, Eve. *Anatole*
   Anatole and the cat
   Anatole and the piano
   Anatole and the pied piper
   Anatole and the poodle
   Anatole and the robot
   Anatole and the thirty thieves
   Anatole and the toyshop
   Anatole in Italy
   Anatole over Paris
Tolan, Stephanie S. *Bartholomew's blessing*
Tompert, Ann. *A carol for Christmas*
   Just a little bit
   The pied piper of Peru
Trapani, Iza. *Shoo fly!*
Tsultim, Yeshe. *The mouse king*
Türk, Hanne. *Goodnight Max*
   Happy birthday Max
   Max packs
   Max the artlover
   Max versus the cube
   Merry Christmas Max
   Rainy day Max
   Raking leaves with Max
   The rope skips Max
   Snapshot Max
   A surprise for Max
Udry, Janice May. *Thump and Plunk*, ill. by Ann Schweninger
Vagin, Vladimir Vasilévich. *Here comes the cat*
Vincent, Gabrielle. *Bravo, Ernest and Celestine!*
   Breakfast time, Ernest and Celestine
   Ernest and Celestine
   Ernest and Celestine at the circus
   Ernest and Celestine's patchwork quilt
   Ernest and Celestine's picnic
   Merry Christmas, Ernest and Celestine
   Smile, Ernest and Celestine

Where are you, Ernest and Celestine?
Vinson, Pauline. *Willie goes to the seashore*
Vreeken, Elizabeth. *Henry*
Vries, Anke de. *Grey mouse*
Vulliamy, Clara. *Small*
Waber, Bernard. *Do you see a mouse?*
   Mice on my mind
   The mouse that snored
Waddell, Martin. *Mimi and the dream house*
   Mimi and the picnic
   Mimi's Christmas
   Sam Vole and his brothers
   Squeak-a-lot
Wagner, Karen. *Bravo, Mildred and Ed!*
   A friend like Ed
Wahl, Jan. *The field mouse and the dinosaur named Sue*
   Old Hippo's Easter egg
   Pleasant Fieldmouse
   Pleasant Fieldmouse's Halloween party
Waite, Judy. *Mouse, look out!*
Wallis, Diz. *Pip's adventure*
Walsh, Ellen Stoll. *Dot and Jabber and the great acorn mystery*
   Dot and Jabber and the mystery of the missing stream
   Mouse count
   Mouse magic
   Mouse paint
   You silly goose
Ward, Nick. *Farmer George and the fieldmice*
Waters, Tony. *Sailor's bride*
Watson, Clyde. *How Brown Mouse kept Christmas*
Watts, Barrie. *Mouse*
Waugh, Peter. *The great cannon beach mouse caper*
Wax, Wendy. *A very mice Christmas*
Weeks, Sarah. *Drip, drop*
Weigelt, Udo. *It wasn't me*
Wellington, Monica. *Night city*
   Squeaking of art, the mice go to the museum
Wells, Joel. *The manger mouse*
Wells, Rosemary. *Noisy Nora*
   Shy Charles
   Stanley and Rhoda
Wenning, Elisabeth. *The Christmas mouse*
Willard, Nancy. *The mouse, the cat and Grandmother's hat*
Willems, Mo. *Time to pee*
Williams, Juliet. *Mouse house*
   Mouse house [board book]
Wilson, Ron. *Mice*
Wisniewski, David. *Sumo Mouse*
Wolkstein, Diane. *Little Mouse's painting*
Wood, Don. *Merry Christmas, big hungry bear*
Wooding, Sharon L. *Arthur's Christmas wish*
Woychuk, Denis. *The other side of the wall*
   Pirates
Wright, Josephine Lord. *Cotton Cat and Martha Mouse*
Yamashita, Haruo. *Mice at the beach*
Yeoman, John. *Mouse trouble*
Yolen, Jane. *Beneath the ghost moon*
   Little Mouse and Elephant
Young, Ed (Edward). *Mouse match*
   Seven blind mice
Young, Miriam Burt. *The sugar mouse cake*
Zelinsky, Paul O. *The maid and the mouse and the odd-shaped house*
Ziefert, Harriet. *A car trip for Mole and Mouse*
   A clean house for Mole and Mouse
   Let's go! Piggety Pig
   A new house for Mole and Mouse
   No more! Piggety Pig
   Presents for Santa
Zimmermann, H. Werner (Heinz Werner). *Alphonse knows . . .*
   twelve months make a year

Animals – migration *see* Migration

Animals – minks

Holder, Heidi. *Crows*
Lyon, David. *The crumbly coast*

Animals – moles

Benjamin, A. H. *Mouse, mole and the falling star*
Bos, Burny. *Fun with the Molesons*
   Meet the Molesons
Browne, Eileen. *Where's that bus?*
Carter, Anne Laurel. *Molly in danger*
Coursen, Valerie. *Mordant's wish*
Cushman, Doug. *Mouse and Mole and the Christmas walk*
Davoll, Barbara. *Dusty Mole, private eye*
Delaney, Ned. *A worm for dinner*
Ehlert, Lois. *Mole's hill*
   Moon rope = Un lazo a la luna
Emmett, Jonathan. *Bringing down the moon*
   No place like home
Firmin, Peter. *Basil Brush and the windmills*
French, Vivian. *It's a go-to-the-park day*
Gantschev, Ivan. *Where is Mr. Mole?*
Gilman, Rita Golden. *Mole in a hole*
Grahame, Kenneth. *The wind in the willows*, ill. by Joanne Moss
   A wind in the willows Christmas
Gukova, Julia. *Mole's daughter*
Himmelman, John. *Montigue on the high seas*
Hoban, Lillian. *Silly Tilly and the Easter bunny*
   Silly Tilly's Valentine
Hoban, Russell. *The mole family's Christmas*
Honigsberg, Peter Jan. *Pillow of dreams*
Johnston, Tony. *Mole and Troll trim the tree*
Jonell, Lynne. *When Mommy was mad*
Koller, Jackie French. *Mole and Shrew*
   Mole and Shrew are two
   Mole and Shrew step out
Kwon, Holly H. *The moles and the mireuk*
McPhail, David M. *Mole music*
Millais, Raoul. *Elijah and Pin-Pin*
Moon, Nicola. *Tick-tock, drip-drop*
Murschetz, Luis. *Mister Mole*
Newman, Marjorie. *Mole and the baby bird*
   Mole and the baby bird [board book]
Obrist, Jürg. *They do things right in Albern*
Oram, Hiawyn. *Badger's bad mood*
   Mole's moon
Potter, Tessa. *Digger, the story of a mole in the fall*
Schwartz, Roslyn. *The mole sisters and the cool breeze*
   The mole sisters and the fairy ring
   The mole sisters and the piece of moss
   The mole sisters and the question
   The mole sisters and the rainy day
Shannon, George. *Heart to heart*
Takihara, Koji. *Rolli*
Walt Disney Productions. *Walt Disney's The adventures of Mr. Toad*
Weigelt, Udo. *Mole's journey*
Wouters, Anne. *This book is for us*
   This book is too small
Yolen, Jane. *Eeny, meeny, miney mole*
Ziefert, Harriet. *A car trip for Mole and Mouse*
   A clean house for Mole and Mouse
   A new house for Mole and Mouse

Animals – mongooses

Aardema, Verna. *The lonely lioness and the ostrich chicks*
Carlson, Natalie Savage. *Marie Louise and Christophe at the carnival*
   Marie Louise's heyday
   Runaway Marie Louise
Kipling, Rudyard. *Rikki-tikki-tavi*, ill. by Lambert Davis
   Rikki-tikki-tavi, ill. by Jerry Pinkney
Mwalimu. *Awful aardvark*

Animals – monkeys

Ahlberg, Allan. *Monkey do!*
Banks, Kate (Katherine A.). *The bird, the monkey, and the snake in the jungle*
Bannerman, Helen. *The story of the teasing monkey*
Borovsky, Paul. *Nico*
Browne, Anthony. *Animal fair*

Brunhoff, Jean de. *Babar and Zephir*
Brunhoff, Laurent de. *Babar the magician*
Bulette, Sara. *The splendid belt of Mr. Big*
Bunting, Eve (Anne Evelyn). *Monkey in the middle*
Cabrera, Jane. *Monkey's play time*
Calmenson, Stephanie. *One little monkey*
Christelow, Eileen. *Don't wake up Mama!*
    Five little monkeys jumping on the bed
    Five little monkeys sitting in a tree
    Five little monkeys wash the car
    Five little monkeys with nothing to do
Curious George and the dinosaur
Curious George and the dump truck (1984)
Curious George and the dump truck (1999)
Curious George and the hot air balloon
Curious George and the pizza
Curious George and the puppies
Curious George at the fire station
Curious George goes camping
Curious George goes hiking
Curious George goes sledding
Curious George goes to a chocolate factory
Curious George goes to a movie
Curious George goes to an ice cream shop
Curious George goes to school
Curious George goes to the aquarium
Curious George goes to the circus
Curious George goes to the dentist
Curious George in the big city
Curious George in the snow
Curious George makes pancakes
Curious George takes a train
Curious George visits a toy store
Curious George visits the zoo
Curious George's 1 to 10 and back again
DeLuise, Dom. *Charlie the caterpillar*
DePalma, Mary Newell. *The strange egg*
Dodds, Dayle Ann. *The color box*
Drescher, Henrik. *Look-alikes*
    The yellow umbrella
Elkin, Benjamin. *Such is the way of the world*
Elliott, George. *The boy who loved bananas*
Franklin, Kristine L. *When the monkeys came back*
Galdone, Paul. *The monkey and the crocodile*
Goodall, John S. *Jacko*
Gréban, Quentin. *Nestor*
Gugler, Laurel Dee. *Monkey tales*
Guy, Rosa. *Mother crocodile*
Hansard, Peter. *I like monkeys because . . .*
Hewett, Joan. *A monkey baby grows up*
Hoffman, Mary. *Animals in the wild: monkey*
Horio, Seishi. *The monkey and the crab*
Horowitz, Dave. *A monkey among us*
Hurd, Edith Thacher. *Last one home is a green pig*
Irvine, Georgeanne. *Bo the orangutan*
Iwamura, Kazuo. *Tan Tan's hat*
    Tan Tan's suspenders
Jendresen, Erik. *Hanuman*
Jeyaveeran, Ruth. *The road to Mumbai*
Jiang, Ji-li. *The magical Monkey King, mischief in heaven*
Kaye, Geraldine. *The sea monkey*
Keeshan, Robert. *Alligator in the basement*
Kepes, Juliet. *Five little monkeys*
    Run little monkeys, run, run, run
Knight, Hilary. *Where's Wallace?*
Koller, Jackie French. *One monkey too many*
Komoda, Beverly. *Simon's soup*
Kraus, Robert. *Klunky Monkey, new kid in class*
Lin, Grace. *Okie-dokie, Artichokie*
London, Jonathan. *Little Red Monkey*
McAllister, Angela. *Matepo*
MacKinnon, Debbie. *Meg's monkey*
McKissack, Patricia C. *Who is coming?*
Mangan, Anne. *The monkey who wanted the moon*
Martin, David. *Monkey business*
    Monkey trouble
Martin, Rafe. *The monkey bridge*

Mathiesen, Egon. *Oswald, the monkey*
Meshover, Leonard. *The monkey that went to school*
Metaxas, Eric. *The monkey people*
Moore, Inga. *Fifty red night-caps*
Morgan, Michaela. *Helpful Betty to the rescue*
Myers, Walter Dean. *How Mr. Monkey saw the whole world*
Olds, Helen Diehl. *Miss Hattie and the monkey*
Oxenbury, Helen. *Tom and Pippo and the dog*
    Tom and Pippo go shopping
    Tom and Pippo in the garden
    Tom and Pippo on the beach
    Tom and Pippo see the moon
    Tom and Pippo's day
P'an, Ts'ai-ying. *Monkey creates havoc in heaven*
Paxton, Tom. *The jungle baseball game*
Phillips, Betty Lou. *Emily goes wild*
Preston, Edna Mitchell. *Monkey in the jungle*
Puttock, Simon. *A story for Hippo*
Regan, Dana. *Monkey see, monkey do*
Reitveld, Jane Klatt. *Monkey island*
Rey, H. A. (Hans Augusto). *Cecily G and the nine monkeys*
    Curious George
    Curious George gets a medal
    Curious George learns the alphabet
    Curious George rides a bike
    Curious George takes a job
    The original Curious George
Rey, Margret (Margret Elisabeth Waldstein). *Curious George flies a kite*
    Curious George goes to the hospital
Rockwell, Anne F. *The stolen necklace*
Rowe, John A. *Monkey trouble*
San Souci, Robert D. *Pedro and the monkey*
Schubert, Dieter. *Where's my monkey?*
Selsam, Millicent E. *A first look at monkeys*
Seven spunky monkeys
Shi, Zhang Xiu. *Monkey and the white bone demon*
Sierra, Judy. *Counting crocodiles*
Silvano, Wendi. *Counting coconuts = Contando cocos*
Slobodkina, Esphyr. *Caps for sale*
Souhami, Jessica. *Rama and the demon king*
Stanley, Sanna. *Monkey Sunday*
Suba, Susanne. *The monkeys and the pedlar*
Teleki, Geza. *Aerial apes*
Temple, Frances. *Tiger soup*
Teyssèdre, Fabienne. *Joseph wants to read*
Thaler, Mike. *Moonkey*
Van Laan, Nancy. *So say the little monkeys*
Wiesmüller, Dieter. *The adventures of Marco and Polo*
Williamson, Hamilton. *Monkey tale*
Wolkstein, Diane. *The cool ride in the sky*
Woodruff, Elvira. *Mrs. McCloskey's monkeys*
Yee, Patrick. *Baby monkey*
Young, Ed (Edward). *Monkey King*

Animals – moose

Alexander, Martha G. *Even that moose won't listen to me*
Allen, Jonathan. *Mucky moose*
Arnosky, Jim. *Beaver pond, moose pond*
Beck, Andrea. *Elliot bakes a cake*
    Elliot digs for treasure
    Elliot gets stuck
    Elliot's bath
    Elliot's Christmas surprise
    Elliot's emergency
    Elliot's great big lift-the-flap book
    Elliot's noisy night
    Elliot's shipwreck
Bloxam, Frances. *Antlers forever!*
Bourgeois, Paulette. *Franklin's new friend*
Brown, Marc Tolon. *Moose and goose*
Bunting, Eve (Anne Evelyn). *A turkey for Thanksgiving*
Capucilli, Alyssa Satin. *Biscuit visits the pumpkin patch*
Carlstrom, Nancy White. *Moose in the garden*
Egan, Tim. *The trial of Cardigan Jones*
Foreman, Michael. *Moose*

Freschet, Berniece. *Moose baby*
Green, Stephanie. *Not just another moose*
Guthrie, Arlo. *Mooses come walking*
Hodge, Deborah. *Deer, moose, elk and caribou*
Hoff, Syd. *Santa's moose*
Kasperson, James. *Little brother moose*
Kelley, True. *Buggly Bear's hiccup cure*
Latimer, Jim. *Going the moose way home*
    Moose and friends
    When moose was young
McNeer, May Yonge. *My friend Mac*
Marshall, James. *The guest*
Mellor, Corinne. *Bruce the balding moose*
Murray, Martine. *A moose called Mouse*
Numeroff, Laura Joffe. *If you give a moose a muffin*
Palatini, Margie. *Moosetache*
Prøysen, Alf. *Mrs. Pepperpot and the moose*
Raschka, Christopher. *Moosey Moose*
Seuss, Dr. *Thidwick, the big-hearted moose*
Slepian, Jan. *Lost moose*
Slobodkin, Louis. *Melvin, the moose child*
Stadler, John. *The ballad of Wilbur and the moose*
Stapler, Sarah. *Spruce the moose cuts loose*
Stern, Maggie. *Acorn magic*
Stihler, Chérie B. *The giant cabbage turnip*
Van Laan, Nancy. *Moose tales*
Wiseman, Bernard. *Christmas with Morris and Borris*
    Morris and Boris at the circus
    Morris has a birthday party!
    Morris the moose

Animals – mountain lions *see* Animals – cougars

Animals – mules

Beatty, Hetty Burlingame. *Droopy*
Bishop, Brett. *Clayton's path*
Brown, Kathryn. *Muledred*
Edwards, Pamela Duncan. *Rude mule*
Sharmat, Marjorie Weinman. *Hooray for Father's Day!*
Snyder, Anne. *The old man and the mule*
Yezerski, Thomas F. *A full hand*
Zemach, Margot. *Jake and Honeybunch go to heaven*

Animals – muskrats

Arnosky, Jim. *Come out, muskrats*
Hoban, Russell. *Harvey's hideout*
Savageau, Cheryl. *Muskrat will be swimming*
Wilson, Sarah. *Muskrat, muskrat, eat your peas!*

Animals – octopuses *see* Octopuses

Animals – opossums *see* Animals – possums

Animals – orangutans

Carrick, Carol. *Banana beer*
Cherry, Lynne. *Orangutan*
Grindley, Sally. *Little Sibu*
Romanelli, Serena. *Little Bobo saves the day*

Animals – otters

Allen, Laura Jean. *Ottie and the star*
Berger, Barbara Helen. *A lot of otters*
Boyle, Doe. *Otter on his own*
Burdick, Margaret. *Bobby Otter and the blue boat*
Carlstrom, Nancy White. *Swim the silver sea, Joshie Otter*
Cousteau Society. *Otters*
Galvin, Laura Gates. *River Otter at Autumn Lane*
Godkin, Celia. *Sea Otter Inlet*
Greene, Carol. *Reading about the river otter*
Hall, Derek. *Otter swims*
Harshman, Terry Webb. *Porcupine's pajama party*
Hoban, Lillian. *Big Little Otter*

Hoban, Russell. *Emmet Otter's jug-band Christmas*
Luenn, Nancy. *Otter play*
Murray, Peter. *Sea otters*
Shaw, Evelyn S. *Sea otters*
Sheehan, Angela. *The otter*
Simms, Laura. *Moon and Otter and Frog*
Tompert, Ann. *Little Otter remembers and other stories*
Wisbeski, Dorothy Gross. *Pícaro, a pet otter*

Animals – oxen

Balcziak, Bill. *Paul Bunyan*
Bunting, Eve (Anne Evelyn). *Box, fox, ox, and the peacock*
DeVajay, Szabolcs. *The animals' gift*
Emberley, Barbara. *The story of Paul Bunyan*
Gleeson, Brian. *Paul Bunyan*
Hong, Lily Toy. *How the ox star fell from heaven*
Kellogg, Steven (Stephen). *Paul Bunyan*
Lawlor, Laurie. *Old Crump*
Spang, Günter. *The ox and the Donkey*

Animals – pack rats

Miller, Edna. *Pebbles, a pack rat*
Quackenbush, Robert M. *Pete Pack Rat*
Van Horn, William. *Harry Hoyle's giant jumping bean*

Animals – pandas

Allen, Judy. *Panda*
Butler, John. *Pi-shu, the little panda*
Cabrera, Jane. *Panda Big and Panda Small*
Calmenson, Stephanie. *Dinner at the Panda Palace*
Carr, Jan. *Sweet hearts*
Conover, Chris. *Sam Panda and Thunder Dragon*
Dunbar, Joyce. *Gander's pond*
    The secret friend
Foreman, Michael. *Dad! I can't sleep*
    Look! Look!
    Panda and the bunyips
    Panda and the bushfire
    Panda's puzzle, and his voyage of discovery
    Surprise! Surprise!
Gibbons, Gail. *Giant pandas*
Granfield, Linda. *The legend of the panda*
Greaves, Margaret. *Once there were no pandas*
Grosvenor, Donna. *Pandas*
Hall, Derek. *Panda climbs*
Hoban, Tana. *Panda, panda*
Hoffman, Mary. *Animals in the wild: panda*
Jensen, Helen Zane. *When Panda came to our house*
Kraus, Robert. *Milton the early riser*
Lee, Sandra. *Giant pandas*
Leedy, Loreen. *Pingo the plaid panda*
Maestro, Betsy. *The pandas take a vacation*
Mayer, Marianna. *The Brambleberrys animal book of colors*
Nagda, Anne Whitehead. *A home for panda*
Owen, Annie. *Hungry panda*
Pluckrose, Henry Arthur. *Bears*
Rigby, Shirley Lincoln. *Smaller than most*
Ryder, Joanne. *Little panda*
Steele, Philip. *The giant panda*
Stimson, Joan. *Big Panda, Little Panda*
Theodorou, Rod. *Giant panda*
Wahl, Jan. *Three pandas*
Wild, Margaret. *Tom goes to kindergarten*

Animals – panthers *see* Animals – leopards

Animals – pigs

Adams, Jean Ekman. *Clarence and the great surprise*
    Clarence and the purple horse bounce into town
Ahlberg, Allan. *Half a pig*
Alarcón, Karen Beaumont. *Louella Mae, she's run away!*
Allard, Harry. *There's a party at Mona's tonight*
Anholt, Catherine. *Truffles in trouble*

Truffles is sick
Aruego, José. *Rockabye crocodile*
Asch, Frank. *Ziggy Piggy and the three little pigs*
Augarde, Steve (Stephen). *Pig*
Axelrod, Amy. *Pigs in the corner*
　Pigs in the pantry
　Pigs on a blanket
　Pigs on the ball
　Pigs on the move
　Pigs will be pigs
Aylesworth, Jim. *Hanna's hog*
Ayres, Becky Hickox. *Victoria flies high*
Ayres, Pam. *Piggo and the nosebag*
　Piggo has a train ride
Baldner, Gaby. *Joba and the wild boar = Joba und das wildschwein*
Baron, Alan. *Little Pig's bouncy ball*
Bassède, Francine. *A day with the Bellyflops*
Beck, Scott. *A mud pie for mother*
Beil, Karen Magnuson. *A cake all for me!*
Berson, Harold. *Truffles for lunch*
Bianchi, John. *Swine snafu*
Bishop, Claire Huchet. *The truffle pig*
Blake, Jon. *Wriggly Pig*
Blegvad, Lenore. *This little pig-a-wig and other rhymes about pigs*
Bloom, Suzanne. *No place for a pig*
　Piggy Monday
　We keep a pig in the parlor
Boegehold, Betty. *You are much too small*
Boland, Janice. *Annabel*
　Annabel again
Bond, Felicia. *Mary Betty Lizzie McNutt's birthday*
　Poinsettia and her family
　Poinsettia and the firefighters
The book of Pooh: Biglet
Boynton, Sandra. *Hester in the wild*
Brand, Millen. *This little pig named Curly*
Branford, Henrietta. *Little Pig Figwort can't get to sleep*
Brimner, Larry Dane. *Nana's hog*
Brock, Emma Lillian. *Pig with a front porch*
Brown, Judith Gwyn. *Max and the truffle pig*
Brown, Ken (Ken James). *Mucky Pup's Christmas*
Brown, Marc Tolon. *Perfect pigs*
Brown, Margaret Wise. *The good little bad little pig*
Browne, Anthony. *Piggybook*
Bruna, Dick. *Poppy Pig goes to market*
Bunting, Eve (Anne Evelyn). *Sing a song of piglets*
Bynum, Janie. *Otis*
Calhoun, Mary. *The witch's pig*
Calmenson, Stephanie. *Never take a pig to lunch and other funny poems about animals*
Caple, Kathy. *The wimp*
Carlson, Nancy L. *How about a hug?*
　Louanne Pig in making the team
　Louanne Pig in the mysterious Valentine
　Louanne Pig in the perfect family
　Witch lady
Cazet, Denys. *Mud baths for everyone*
Chataway, Carol. *The perfect pet*
Chorao, Kay. *Pig and Crow*
Christelow, Eileen. *The great pig escape*
　The great pig search
　Mr. Murphy's marvelous invention
Cibula, Matt S. *Slumgullion, the executive pig*
Cole, Brock. *Nothing but a pig*
Coontz, Otto. *Starring Rosa*
Corbalis, Judy. *Porcellus, the flying pig*
Cort, Ben. *Pigs can't fly!*
Craig, Helen. *The night of the paper bag monsters*
　Susie and Alfred in a busy day in town
　Susie and Alfred in the knight, the princess and the dragon
　A welcome for Annie
Cushman, Doug. *Once upon a pig*
Dahl, Michael. *Pie for piglets*
Dakos, Kalli. *Our principal promised to kiss a pig*
Dalmais, Anne-Marie. *Best bedtime stories of Mother Pig*
Davenier, Christine. *Leon and Albertine*
Davis, Maggie S. *The rinky-dink café*

Degen, Bruce. *Sailaway home*
DeLage, Ida. *ABC pigs go to market*
Denslow, Sharon Phillips. *Riding with Aunt Lucy*
Dewan, Ted. *Crispin and the 3 little piglets*
　Crispin, the pig who had it all
Dorros, Arthur. *When the pigs took over*
Dotlich, Rebecca Kai. *Mama loves*
　Papa loves
Dubanevich, Arlene. *Pig William*
　The piggest show on earth
　Pigs at Christmas
　Pigs in hiding
Dunbar, Joyce. *The pig who wished*
Dunrea, Olivier. *Eddy B, pigboy*
Dyke, John. *Pigwig*
　Pigwig and the pirates
Edwards, Frank B. *Melody Mooner stayed up all night*
　Mortimer Mooner stopped taking a bath
Egan, Tim. *The experiments of Doctor Vermin*
Enderle, Judith (Ann) Ross. *A pile of pigs*
Eriksson, Ake. *Joel, Jasper, and Julia*
Ernst, Lisa Campbell. *The prize pig surprise*
Erskine, Jim. *Bert and Susie's messy tale*
Falconer, Ian. *Olivia*
　Olivia – and the missing toy
　Olivia counts
　Olivia saves the circus
　Olivia's opposites
Faulkner, Keith. *The long-nosed pig*
Fine, Howard. *A piggie Christmas*
Fischetto, Laura. *All pigs on deck*
Fox, Christyan. *Astronaut PiggyWiggy*
　Count to ten, PiggyWiggy!
　Fire fighter PiggyWiggy
　What color is that, PiggyWiggy?
　What shape is that, PiggyWiggy?
Gackenbach, Dick. *Harvey, the foolish pig*
　Hurray for Hattie Rabbit!
　The pig who saw everything
Galdone, Paul. *The amazing pig*
Garland, Michael. *Icarus Swinebuckle*
Geisert, Arthur. *The giant ball of string*
　Mystery
　Nursery crimes
　Oink
　Oink oink
　Pigaroons
　Pigs from 1 to 10
Getz, Arthur. *Humphrey, the dancing pig*
Gibbons, Gail. *Pigs*
Gikow, Louise. *Bye-bye, pacifier*
Gliori, Debi. *A present for Big Pig*
Good, Phyllis Pellman. *Plain Pig's ABCs*
Goodall, Jane. *Dr. White*
Goodall, John S. *The adventures of Paddy Pork*
　The ballooning adventures of Paddy Pork
　Paddy goes traveling
　Paddy Pork
　Paddy Pork's holiday
　Paddy to the rescue
　Paddy under water
　Paddy's evening out
　Paddy's new hat
Gorbachev, Valeri. *One rainy day*
Gralley, Jean. *Hogula, dread pig of night*
Gray, Nigel. *Little pig's tale*
　Pigs can't fly
Gretz, Susanna. *It's your turn, Roger*
　Roger loses his marbles!
　Roger takes charge!
Grindley, Sally. *Can we play too, Piglittle?*
Grossman, Bill. *Tommy at the grocery store*
Guthrie, Donna. *This little pig stayed home*
Hale, Irina. *Chocolate mouse and sugar pig*
Hammar, Asa. *Fit for pigs*
Haswell, Peter. *Pog*
　Pog climbs Mount Everest

Hauptmann, Tatjana. *A day in the life of Petronella Pig*
Hawkins, Colin. *Mig the pig*
  This little pig
Heine, Helme. *The pigs' wedding*
Hellard, Susan. *This little piggy*
Heller, Nicholas. *A book for Woody*
  Elwood and the witch
  Woody
Hiskey, Iris. *Cassandra who?*
Hoban, Lillian. *Mr. Pig and family*
  Mr. Pig and Sonny too
Hobbie, Holly. *Toot and Puddle*
  Toot and Puddle, a present for Toot
  Toot and Puddle, I'll be home for Christmas
  Toot and Puddle, Puddle's ABC
  Toot and Puddle, top of the world
  Toot and Puddle, you are my sunshine
Hoff, Syd. *Happy birthday, Henrietta!*
Hofstrand, Mary. *Albion pig*
  By the sea
Horning, Sandra. *The giant hug*
Hutchins, Pat. *Little pink pig*
Inkpen, Mick. *Arnold*
  Gumboot's chocolatey day
  If I had a pig
  Kipper and Roly
  Kipper's A to Z
  Wibbly Pig can dance!
  Wibbly Pig can make a tent
  Wibbly Pig is upset
  Wibbly Pig likes bananas
  Wibbly Pig makes pictures
  Wibbly Pig opens his presents
Jackson, Ellen B. *Boris the boring boar*
Jacobs, Joseph. *The three sillies*, ill. by Kathryn Hewitt
  The three sillies, ill. by Steven Kellogg
Jennings, Linda M. *Crispin and the dancing piglet*
  Tom's tail
Jeschke, Susan. *Perfect the pig*
Johnson, Angela. *Julius*
Johnson, Paul Brett. *A perfect pork stew*
  The pig who ran a red light
Johnston, Tony. *Farmer Mack measures his pig*
Jolley, Mike. *Grunter, a pig with an attitude!*
Kasza, Keiko. *The pigs' picnic*
Kaufmann, Nancy. *Bye, Bye*
Keller, Holly. *Geraldine and Mrs. Duffy*
  Geraldine first
  Geraldine's baby brother
  Geraldine's big snow
  Geraldine's blanket
  Merry Christmas, Geraldine
Kent, Jack. *Piggy Bank Gonzalez*
King-Smith, Dick. *All pigs are beautiful*
  The spotty pig
Kirk, David. *Little pig, Biddle pig*
Kiser, SuAnn. *The hog call to end all!*
Kneen, Maggie. *The Christmas surprise*
Korth-Sander, Irmtraut. *Will you be my friend?*
Koscielniak, Bruce. *Hector and Prudence*
  Hector and Prudence – all aboard!
Kranendonk, Anke. *Just a minute*
Krause, Ute. *Pig surprise*
Kroll, Steven. *The pigrates clean up*
  Pigs in the house
Laden, Nina. *When Pigasso met Mootisse*
Laird, Donivee Martin. *The three little Hawaiian pigs and the magic shark*
Laird, Elizabeth. *The day Sidney ran off*
Lasky, Kathryn. *Lucille camps in*
  Lucille's snowsuit
  Starring Lucille
Laverde, Arlene. *Alaska's three pigs*
Lawrence, John. *Rabbit and pork*
Leonard, Marcia. *Birthday in a bathtub*
Lester, Helen. *Me first*
  Score one for the sloths

Levine, Abby. *You push, I ride*
Lewis, Bobby. *Home before midnight*
Lies, Brian. *Hamlet and the enormous Chinese dragon kite*
  Hamlet and the magnificent sandcastle
Lin, Grace. *Olvina flies*
Lindgren, Barbro. *Benny and the binky*
  Benny's had enough
Ling, Mary. *Pig*
The Little book of pigs
Little, Jean. *Gruntle Piggle takes off*
  Pippin the Christmas pig
Lobel, Arnold. *Small pig*
  A treeful of pigs
Lorenz, Lee. *Pig and duck buy a truck*
  A weekend in the country
Lowell, Susan. *The three little javelinas*
Luttrell, Ida. *Milo's toothache*
McClenathan, Louise. *The Easter pig*
MacDonald, Allan. *The pig in a wig*
MacDonald, Elizabeth. *Miss Poppy and the honey cake*
McLarey, Kristina Thermaenius. *When you take a pig to a party*
MacLean, Kerry Lee. *Peaceful piggy meditation*
McNaughton, Colin. *Boo!*
  Little boo!
  Little goal!
  Little oops!
  Little suddenly!
  Oomph!
  Oops!
  Preston's goal!
  Shh! (Don't tell Mr. Wolf!)
  Suddenly!
  Yum!
McPhail, David M. *Big Pig and Little Pig*
  Pig Pig and the magic photo album
  Pig Pig gets a job
  Pig Pig goes to camp
  Pig Pig grows up
  Pig Pig rides
  Pigs ahoy
  Pigs aplenty, pigs galore!
  Those can-do pigs
McQueen, Lucinda. *Tidy pig*
Maestro, Betsy. *The guessing game*
Magnier, Thierry. *Isabelle and the angel*
Marshall, James. *Portly McSwine*
  Swine lake
  Yummers!
  Yummers too
Martin, David. *Five little piggies*
  Piggy and Dad
  Piggy and Dad go fishing
Martin, Jacqueline Briggs. *The water gift and the pig of the pig*
Martinez, Ruth. *Mrs. McDockerty's knitting*
Martín Larrañaga, Ana. *Pepo and Lolo and the red apple*
  Pepo and Lolo are friends
Mathews, Louise. *The great take-away*
Mayne, William. *Lady Muck*
Meddaugh, Susan. *Hog-eye*
Meister, Cari. *Skinny and fats, best friends*
Miles, Miska. *This little pig*
Miller, Heather. *My pigs*
Milord, Susan. *Willa the wonderful*
Miranda, Anne. *Pignic*
  To market, to market
Moon, Cliff. *Pigs on the farm*
Moore, Inga. *The truffle hunter*
Moran, Alex. *Boots for Beth*
Morley, Carol. *A spider and a pig*
Most, Bernard. *Oink-ha!*
  Z-Z-Zoink!
Mother Goose. *This little pig*, ill. by Leonard Lubin
  This little pig went to market, ill. by L. Leslie Brooke
  This little piggy, ill. by Moira Kemp
Munsch, Robert N. *Pigs*
Murphy, Pat. *Pigasus*
Nayer, Judy. *Pig in a wig*

Newman, Lesléa. *Pigs, pigs, pigs*
Newton, Patricia Montgomery. *Vacation surprise*
Newton-John, Olivia. *A pig tale*
Nightingale, Sandy. *Pink pigs aplenty*
Novak, Matt. *Jazzbo and Googy*
Numeroff, Laura Joffe. *If you give a pig a pancake*
Offen, Hilda. *Nice work, little wolf!*
Ostheeren, Ingrid. *Fabian Youngpig sails the world*
Oxenbury, Helen. *Pig tale*
Palatini, Margie. *Piggie pie*
Paraskevas, Betty. *The ferocious beast with the polka-dot hide*
    Maggie and the Ferocious Beast, the big carrot
    Maggie and the Ferocious Beast, the big scare
Partridge, Elizabeth. *Pig's eggs*
Patterson, Geoffrey. *A pig's tale*
Peck, Robert Newton. *Hamilton*
Peet, Bill (William Bartlett). *Chester the worldly pig*
Petach, Heidi. *Wee three pigs*
Philpot, Graham. *Where is Little Harry?*
Pizer, Abigail. *Penelope pig*
Plourde, Lynn. *Pigs in the mud in the middle of the rud*
Pomerantz, Charlotte. *The piggy in the puddle*
Potter, Beatrix. *The tale of Little Pig Robinson*
    The tale of Pigling Bland
Pryor, Bonnie. *Amanda and April*
    Merry Christmas, Amanda and April
Puttock, Simon. *Squeaky clean*
Rader, Laura. *Tea for me, tea for you*
Rand, Gloria. *Little Flower*
Rayner, Mary. *Garth Pig and the ice cream lady*
    Mr. and Mrs. Pig's evening out
    Mrs. Pig gets cross and other stories
    Mrs. Pig's bulk buy
    One by one
    Ten pink piglets
Reddix, Valerie. *Millie and the mudhole*
Richardson, John. *Grunt*
Robb, Laura. *Snuffles and snouts*
Roche, Denis (Denis M.). *Little Pig is capable*
Root, Phyllis. *Mrs. Potter's pig*
Ross, Tony. *The enchanted pig*
Roth, Carol. *Ten dirty pigs / Ten clean pigs*
Royston, Angela. *The pig*
Rusackas, Francesca. *Daddy all day long*
    I love you all day long
Samton, Sheila White. *Frogs in clogs*
Saul, Carol P. *Peter's song*
Scarry, Richard. *Mr. Frumble's worst day ever!*
    Pig Will and Pig Won't
    Pig Will and Pig Won't: 2-in-1 turn-around books
    Richard Scarry's Mr. Frumble's biggest hat flap book ever
    Richard Scarry's Peasant Pig and the terrible dragon
Schaffer, Libor. *Arthur sets sail*
Schami, Rafik. *Albert and Lila*
Schotter, Roni. *That extraordinary pig of Paris*
Schroeder, Alan. *Smoky Mountain Rose*
Schuh, Mari C. *Pigs on the farm*
Schwartz, Mary. *Spiffen*
Scieszka, Jon. *The true story of the three little pigs by A. Wolf, as told to Jon Scieszka*
Scruton, Clive. *Pig in the air*
Sharmat, Mitchell. *The seven sloppy days of Phineas Pig*
Shecter, Ben. *Partouche plants a seed*
Slate, Joseph. *The mean, clean, giant canoe machine*
Snow, Alan. *Oink!*
Spinelli, Eileen. *Six hogs on a scooter*
Spohn, Kate. *Piglet's bath*
Spurr, Elizabeth. *A pig named Perrier*
Stadler, John. *The ballad of Wilbur and the moose*
Steer, Dougald. *Just one more story*
Steig, William. *The amazing bone*
    Farmer Palmer's wagon ride
    Roland, the minstrel pig
    Zeke Pippin
Stepto, Michele. *Snuggle Piggy and the magic blanket*
Stevens, Carla. *Hooray for pig!*
    Pig and the blue flag

Stine, Jovial Bob. *Pork and beans*
Stobbs, William. *This little piggy*
Stolz, Mary (Mary Slattery). *Emmett's pig*
Stone, Lynn M. *Pigs and piglets*
Teague, Mark. *Pigsty*
Tharlet, Eve. *Little pig, big trouble*
Thiesing, Lisa. *The Viper*
Thompson, Carol. *Piggy goes to bed*
The three little pigs. *The original three little pigs re-told*, ill. by Jonathan Smith
    The story of the three little pigs, ill. by L. Leslie Brooke
    The story of the three little pigs, ill. by William Stobbs
    Three little pigs [Facsimile ed]
    The three little pigs, ill. by Val Biro
    The three little pigs, ill. by Gavin Bishop
    The three little pigs, ill. by Erik Blegvad
    The three little pigs, ill. by Caroline Bucknall
    The three little pigs, ill. by Stephen Cartwright
    The three little pigs, ill. by Lorinda Bryan Cauley
    The three little pigs, ill. by Jean Claverie
    The three little pigs, ill. by Doug Cushman
    The three little pigs, ill. by William Pène Du Bois
    The three little pigs, ill. by Paul Galdone
    The three little pigs, ill. by Madelaine Gill
    The three little pigs, ill. by Rob Hefferan
    The three little pigs, ill. by Steven Kellogg
    The three little pigs, ill. by David McPhail
    The three little pigs, ill. by James Marshall
    The three little pigs, ill. by Paul Meisel
    The three little pigs, ill. by Rodney Peppé
    The three little pigs, ill. by Edda Reinl
    The three little pigs, ill. by John Wallner
    The three little pigs, ill. by Irma Wilde
    The three little pigs, ill. by Margot Zemach
    The three little pigs and the big bad wolf
    The three little pigs and the fox
    The three little pigs [board book], ill. by Thea Kliros
    The three pigs, ill. by Tony Ross
    Who's at the door?
Tripp, Wallace. *The tale of a pig*
Trivizas, Eugenios. *The three little wolves and the big bad pig*
Tryon, Leslie. *Patsy says*
Tyler, Jenny. *Big Pig on a dig*
Tyler, Linda Wagner. *The sick-in-bed birthday book*
Ungerer, Tomi. *Christmas eve at the Mellops*
    The Mellops go diving for treasure
    The Mellops go flying
    The Mellops go spelunking
    The Mellops strike oil
Uttley, Alison. *The Christmas box*
    Sam Pig and the dragon
    Sam Pig and the hurdy-gurdy man
    Sam Pig and the wind
Van der Meer, Ron. *Pigs at home*
Van Leeuwen, Jean. *More tales of Oliver Pig*
Van Nutt, Julia. *The mystery of Mineral Gorge*
    Pignapped!
    Pumpkins from the sky?
Varekamp, Marjolein. *Little Sam takes a bath*
Vernon, Tannis. *Little Pig and the blue-green sea*
Von Königslöw, Andrea Wayne. *Bing and Chutney*
    Bing and Chutney off to Moosonee
    Bing finds Chutney
Wabbes, Marie. *Rose is hungry*
    Rose is muddy
    Rose's bath
    Rose's picture
Waddell, Martin. *The pig in the pond*
Waechter, Friedrich Karl. *Three is company*
Wagner, Karen. *Silly Fred*
Wahl, Jan. *Mrs. Owl and Mr. Pig*
Waldron, Jan L. *Angel Pig and the hidden Christmas*
    John Pig's Halloween
Walker, Barbara K. (Barbara Kerlin). *Pigs and pirates*
Wallace, Karen. *City pig*
Walton, Rick. *Pig, Pigger, Piggest*
Watson, Pauline. *Wriggles, the little wishing pig*

Weiss, Ellen. *Pigs in space*
Wells, Rosemary. *The little lame prince*
West, Ian. *Silas, the first pig to fly*
West, Keith. *Little Pig's special day*
Weston, Martha. *Peony's rainbow*
    Tuck in the pool
    Tuck's haunted house
Whatley, Bruce. *Wait! No paint!*
Wheeler, Cindy. *Rose*
White, Carolyn. *Whuppity Stoorie*
Whybrow, Ian. *Wish, change, friend*
Wild, Margaret. *Old Pig*
Wild, Robin. *Little Pig and the big bad wolf*
Wilhelm, Hans. *Oh, what a mess*
Winthrop, Elizabeth. *Sloppy kisses*
Wiseman, Bernard. *Don't make fun!*
Wojtowycz, David. *Dudley helps out*
    Dudley's birthday party
Wondriska, William. *Mr. Brown and Mr. Gray*
Wood, David. *Piggies*
    Piggies [board book]
Yee, Wong Herbert. *Fireman Small*
    Fireman Small, fire down below
    Fireman Small to the rescue
    Hamburger Heaven
Yeoman, John. *The bear's water picnic*
Yolen, Jane. *Picnic with Piggins*
    Piggins
Zakhoder, Boris Vladimirovich. *How a piglet crashed the Christmas party*
Zalben, Jane Breskin. *Basil and Hillary*
Ziefert, Harriet. *Let's go! Piggety Pig*
    No more! Piggety Pig
    Piggety Pig from morn 'til night

Animals – platypuses

Clarke, Ginjer L. *Platypus!*
Riddell, Chris. *Platypus*
    Platypus and the lucky day

Animals – polar bears

Adinolfi, JoAnn. *The Egyptian polar bear*
Alborough, Jez. *Bare bear*
    Running Bear
Aulaire, Ingri Mortenson d'. *East of the sun and west of the moon*
Bedford, David. *Touch the sky, my little bear*
Bishop, Adela. *The Christmas polar bear*
Briggs, Raymond. *The bear*
Brooks, Erik. *The practically perfect pajamas*
Bushey, Jeanne. *The polar bear's gift*
Carrick, Carol. *The polar bears are hungry*
Cotton, Jacqueline S. *Polar bears*
Curtiss, A. B. *In the company of bears*
Dabcovich, Lydia. *The polar bear son*
Dasent, George W. *East o' the sun, west o' the moon*
De Beer, Hans. *Ahoy there, little polar bear*
    Little polar bear
    Little Polar Bear and the big balloon
    Little polar bear and the brave little hare
    Little polar bear and the husky pup
    Little polar bear finds a friend
    Little polar bear, take me home!
Dickens, Lucy. *Go fish*
Duvoisin, Roger Antoine. *Snowy and Woody*
Ford, Miela. *Follow the leader*
    Mom and me
George, Jean Craighead. *Snow bear*
Gibbons, Gail. *Polar bears*
Gliori, Debi. *Polar Bolero*
Graber, Janet. *Jacob and the polar bears*
Grigg, Carol. *The singing snow bear*
Grindley, Sally. *Polar Star*
Hall, Derek. *Polar bear leaps*
Harlow, Joan Hiatt. *Shadow bear*
Heinz, Brian J. *Nanuk, lord of the ice*

Heller, Ruth. *How to hide a polar bear*
Hodge, Deborah. *Bears*
Inkpen, Mick. *Penguin small*
Jane, Cabrera. *The lonesome polar bear*
Just like father
Karas, G. Brian. *Skidamarink*
Kern, Noris. *I love you with all my heart*
Lesser, Carolyn. *Great crystal bear*
Lilly, Kenneth. *Animals of the ocean*
London, Jonathan. *Ice Bear and Little Fox*
Mercer, Lynn. *Schubert's snowflakes*
Moss, Miriam. *The snow bear*
Newton, Jill. *Polar bear scare*
Ørdal, Stina Langlo. *Princess Aasta*
Pinkwater, Daniel Manus. *At the Hotel Larry*
    Bad bears and a bunny
    Bad bears in the big city
    Bongo Larry
    Ice-cream Larry
    Irving and Muktuk
    Young Larry
Pluckrose, Henry Arthur. *Bears*
Ring, Susan. *Polar babies*
Rives. *If I were a polar bear*
Rockhill, Dennis. *Polar slumber = Sueño polar*
Rose, Gerald. *PB takes a holiday*
Ryder, Joanne. *White bear, ice bear*
Stafford, Liliana. *The snow bear*
Townsend, Emily Rose. *Polar bears*
Wahl, Jan. *"I remember," cried Grandma Pinky*
Wild, Margaret. *Thank you, Santa*
Wojtowycz, David. *A cuddle for Claude*
Wouters, Anne. *This book is for us*
    This book is too small
Ylla. *Polar bear brothers*

Animals – porcupines

Annett, Cora. *When the porcupine moved in*
Carrick, Carol. *Ben and the porcupine*
Haines, Mike. *Countdown to bedtime*
Harshman, Terry Webb. *Porcupine's pajama party*
Joly, Fanny. *Mr. Fine, porcupine*
Lester, Helen. *A porcupine named Fluffy*
Lies, Brian. *Hamlet and the enormous Chinese dragon kite*
    Hamlet and the magnificent sandcastle
Linders, Clara. *The very best door of all*
Lipson, Beth Weiner. *Benjamin's perfect solution*
Massie, Diane Redfield. *Tiny pin*
Moodie, Fiona. *Noko and the night monster*
Morgan-Vanroyen, Mary. *Benjamin's bugs*
Pfister, Marcus. *Where is my friend?*
The porcupine
Schlein, Miriam. *Lucky porcupine!*
Slate, Joseph. *Little Porcupine's Christmas*
    Story time for Little Porcupine
Stevenson, James. *The castaway*
Stren, Patti. *Hug me*
Thomas, Patricia. *The one and only, super-duper, golly-whopper, jim-dandy, really-handy clock-tock-stopper*
Wheeler, Lisa. *Porcupining*

Animals – possums

Berson, Harold. *Henry Possum*
Burch, Robert. *Joey's cat*
Carlson, Natalie Savage. *Marie Louise's heyday*
Conford, Ellen. *Eugene the brave*
    Impossible, possum
    Just the thing for Geraldine
Cushman, Doug. *Possum stew*
Degen, Bruce. *Aunt Possum and the pumpkin man*
De Groat, Diane. *Good night, sleep tight, don't let the bedbugs bite*
    Jingle bells, homework smells
    Liar, liar, pants on fire
    Lola the elf
DeLage, Ida. *Good morning, lady*

Dodd, Lynley. *The apple tree*
Fontenot, Mary Alice. *Tah-Tye*
Fox, Mem. *Possum magic*
Freschet, Berniece. *Possum baby*
Glaser, Linda. *Keep your socks on, Albert!*
Hoban, Russell. *Nothing to do*
Hunter, Anne. *Possum and the peeper*
  Possum's harvest moon
Hurd, Thacher. *Mama don't allow*
Kasza, Keiko. *Don't laugh, Joe*
Keller, Holly. *Henry's Fourth of July*
Lipson, Beth Weiner. *Benjamin's perfect solution*
Luttrell, Ida. *Mattie's little possum pet*
Salley, Coleen. *Epossumondas*
Swendson, Patsy. *The potluck adventures of Mrs. Marmalade*
Taylor, Mark. *Old Blue, you good dog you*
Tether, Graham. *Skunk and possum*
Van Laan, Nancy. *Possum come a-knocking*
Whitehouse, Patricia. *Opossums*
Winthrop, Elizabeth. *Potbellied possums*
Young, James. *Everyone loves the moon*

Animals – prairie dogs

Baylor, Byrd. *Amigo*
Casey, Denise. *The friendly prairie dog*
Hirschi, Ron. *Where are my prairie dogs and black-footed ferrets?*
Luttrell, Ida. *Lonesome Lester*

Animals – prairie wolves *see* Animals – coyotes

Animals – pumas *see* Animals – cougars

Animals – rabbits

Adams, Adrienne. *The Christmas party*
  The Easter egg artists
  The great Valentine's Day balloon race
Adler, David A. *Bunny rabbit rebus*
Æsop. *The hare and the frogs*
  The hare and the tortoise, ill. by Paul Galdone
  The hare and the tortoise, ill. by Carol Jones
  The hare and the tortoise, ill. by Gerald Rose
  The hare and the tortoise, ill. by Helen Ward
  The hare and the tortoise, ill. by Peter Weevers
  The tortoise and the hare, ill. by Sara Rojo
  The tortoise and the hare, adapt. & ill. by Janet Stevens
Anderson, Lena. *Bunny bath*
  Bunny box
  Bunny fun
  Bunny party
  Bunny story
  Bunny surprise
Anderson, Lonzo. *Two hundred rabbits*
Annett, Cora. *When the porcupine moved in*
Apperley, Dawn. *Blossom and Boo*
  Blossom and Boo stay up late
Araki, Mie. *The magic toolbox*
Arnosky, Jim. *Rabbits and raindrops*
Baby's first book of colors
Baker, Alan. *Black and White Rabbit's ABC*
  Brown Rabbit's shape book
  Gray Rabbit's one, two, three
  Little Rabbit's first number book
  Little Rabbit's first word book
  White Rabbit's color book
Balian, Lorna. *Humbug rabbit*
Barasch, Lynne. *Rodney's inside story*
Bardill, Linard. *The great golden thing*
Barrett, John M. *The Easter bear*
Bartoli, Jennifer. *In a meadow, two hares hide*
Barton, Byron. *Jack and Fred*
Bate, Lucy. *Little rabbit's loose tooth*
Baumann, Hans. *The hare's race*
Becker, John Leonard. *Seven little rabbits*
Benjamin, Alan. *Busy bunnies*

Bergström, Gunilla. *Is that a monster, Alfie Atkins?*
Berlin, Irving. *Easter parade*
Berson, Harold. *Pop! goes the turnip*
Bianco, Margery Williams. *The velveteen rabbit*, ill. by Allen Atkinson
  The velveteen rabbit, ill. by Monique Félix
  The velveteen rabbit, ill. by Michael Green
  The velveteen rabbit, ill. by Michael Hague
  The velveteen rabbit, ill. by Estella Hickman
  The velveteen rabbit, ill. by Steve Johnson & Lou Fancher
  The velveteen rabbit, ill. by David Jorgensen
  The velveteen rabbit, ill. by Thea Kliros
  The velveteen rabbit, ill. by Elizabeth Miles
  The velveteen rabbit, ill. by William Nicholson
  The velveteen rabbit, ill. by Robyn Officer
  The velveteen rabbit, ill. by Ilse Plume
  The velveteen rabbit, ill. by S. D. Schindler
  The velveteen rabbit, ill. by Tien
Birchall, Mark. *Rabbit's birthday surprise*
  Rabbit's wooly sweater
Bishop, Adela. *The Easter wolf*
Bishop, Gavin. *Little Rabbit and the sea*
Blake, Jon. *You're a hero, Daley B.!*
Blau, Judith. *Bunny Mitten's book*
Boelts, Maribeth. *Little Bunny's cool tool set*
  Little Bunny's pacifier plan
  Little Bunny's preschool countdown
  You're a brother, Little Bunny!
Bolliger, Max. *The rabbit with the sky blue ears*
Bonfils, Bolette. *Peter joins the circus*
Bornstein, Ruth Lercher. *Indian bunny*
  Rabbit's good news
Bourguignon, Laurence. *A friend for Tiger*
Bowden, Joan Chase. *The bouncy baby bunny*
  Bouncy baby bunny finds his bed
  Little grey rabbit
Boyd, Lizi. *Bunny hop*
Boyle, Doe. *Summer coat, winter coat*
Brewster, Patience. *Rabbit Inn*
Bright, Robert. *My hopping bunny*
Brophy, Nannette. *The color of my fur*
Brown, Marc Tolon. *The bionic bunny show*
  One, two buckle my shoe
  What do you call a dumb bunny? and other rabbit riddles, games, jokes and cartoons
Brown, Marcia. *The neighbors*
Brown, Margaret Wise. *Bunny's noisy book*
  Bunny's noisy book [board book]
  The golden egg book
  Goodnight moon
  Little chicken
  My world
  The runaway bunny
  The runaway bunny [board book]
  The whispering rabbit
Browne, Eileen. *Where's that bus?*
Bruna, Dick. *Miffy*
  Miffy at the beach
  Miffy at the playground
  Miffy at the seaside
  Miffy at the zoo
  Miffy goes flying
  Miffy goes to school
  Miffy in the hospital
  Miffy in the snow
  Miffy loves New York City!
  Miffy the ghost
  Miffy's bicycle
  Miffy's birthday
  Miffy's dream
Brutschy, Jennifer. *The winter fox*
Bryant, Donna. *My rabbit Roberta*
Bullock, Kathleen. *Rabbits are coming*
Burke, Bobby. *Daddy's little girl*
Burningham, John. *The rabbit*
Burton, Jane. *Freckles the rabbit*
Cahill, Chris. *Bunny magic*

Cain, Sheridan. *Why so sad, Brown Rabbit?*
Caldwell, Mary. *Morning, rabbit, morning*
Calmenson, Stephanie. *One red shoe (the other's blue!)*
    Wanted
Campbell, Alison. *Are you asleep, rabbit?*
Capucilli, Alyssa Satin. *Only my dad and me*
    Peekaboo bunny
Carlson, Nancy L. *Bunnies and their hobbies*
    Bunnies and their sports
    Harriet and George's Christmas treat
    Loudmouth George and the big race
    Loudmouth George and the cornet
    Loudmouth George and the fishing trip
    Loudmouth George and the new neighbors
    Loudmouth George and the sixth-grade bully
Carlstrom, Nancy White. *Kiss your sister, Rose Marie*
    Midnight dance of the snowshoe hare
    Who gets the sun out of bed?
Carrick, Carol. *A rabbit for Easter*
Carroll, Ruth. *What Whiskers did*
    Where's the bunny?
Carter, Anne Laurel. *Bella's secret garden*
Cartlidge, Michelle. *Bunny's birthday*
Cazet, Denys. *Big shoe, little shoe*
    Christmas moon
    December 24th
    You make the angels cry
Chadwick, Tim. *Cabbage moon*
Chalmers, Mary. *Come for a walk with me*
    Kevin
Chandoha, Walter. *A baby bunny for you*
Christelow, Eileen. *Henry and the dragon*
    Henry and the red stripes
Claret, Maria. *The chocolate rabbit*
Cleveland, David. *The April rabbits*
Coatsworth, Elizabeth. *Pika and the roses*
Cocca-Leffler, Maryann. *Missing: one stuffed rabbit*
Coldrey, Jennifer. *The world of rabbits*
Compton, Joanne. *Little Rabbit's Easter surprise*
Cooper, Helen (Helen F.). *Tatty-Ratty*
Cosgrove, Stephen (Edward). *Sleepy time bunny*
Cousins, Lucy. *What can Pinky hear?*
    What can Pinky see?
    What can rabbit hear?
    What can rabbit see?
Cowley, Stewart. *Little bunny*
    Little lost rabbit
Cox, Judy. *Rabbit pirates*
Cross, Genevieve. *My bunny book*
Crummel, Susan Stevens. *Tumbleweed stew*
Cuyler, Margery. *Road signs*
Dale, Penny. *Daisy Rabbit's tree house*
Dalmais, Anne-Marie. *Betsy the bunny*
Darling, Kathy (Mary Kathleen). *The Easter bunny's secret*
De Beer, Hans. *Little polar bear and the brave little hare*
Delacre, Lulu. *Peter Cottontail's Easter book*
DeLage, Ida. *ABC Easter bunny*
    Am I a bunny?
    A bunny ride
    Bunny school
Delton, Judy. *Brimhall turns detective*
    Brimhall turns to magic
    Hired help for Rabbit
    Rabbit finds a way
    Rabbit goes to night school
    Three friends find spring
Demi. *Fleecy bunny*
    Little bitty bunny
Denim, Sue. *The Dumb Bunnies*
    The Dumb Bunnies' Easter
    The Dumb Bunnies go to the zoo
    Make way for Dumb Bunnies
Dennis, Lynne. *Raymond Rabbit's early morning*
De Paola, Tomie (Thomas Anthony). *Too many Hopkins*
Diakité, Baba Wagué. *The magic gourd*
Dierssen, Andreas. *Timid Timmy*
    Timmy's new friend

Dieterlé, Nathalie. *I am the king!*
Dodds, Dayle Ann. *Do bunnies talk?*
Donohue, Dorothy. *Veggie soup*
Dorsky, Blanche. *Harry, a true story*
Doucet, Sharon Arms. *Why Lapin's ears are long and other stories of the Louisiana bayou*
Dowling, Paul. *You can do it, Rabbit*
Doyle, Charlotte Lackner. *Where's Bunny's mommy?*
Du Bois, William Pène. *The hare and the tortoise and the tortoise and the hare = La liebre y la tortuga and La tortuga y la liebre*
Dunbar, Joyce. *Lollopy*
    Tell me something happy before I go to sleep
Dunn, Judy. *The little rabbit*
Durant, Alan. *Big Bad Bunny*
    Brown Bear gets in shape
Dutton, Sandra. *The cinnamon hen's autumn day*
Dyjak, Elisabeth. *Bertha's garden*
Easterling, Bill. *Prize in the snow*
Edvall, Lilian. *The rabbit who longed for home*
Ehrlich, Amy. *Bunnies all day long*
    Bunnies and their grandma
    Bunnies at Christmastime
    Bunnies on their own
Elzbieta. *Jon-Jon and Annette*
Ernst, Lisa Campbell. *Miss Penny and Mr. Grubbs*
Evans, Mark. *Rabbit*
Faglia, Maeto. *Happy birthday, I'm 1*
Fatio, Louise. *The happy lion's rabbits*
Ferns, Ronald. *Osbert and Lucy*
Fisher, Aileen Lucia. *Listen, rabbit*
    Rabbits, rabbits
Fleming, Candace. *Muncha! Muncha! Muncha!*
Flory, Jane. *The bear on the doorstep*
Floyd, Lucy. *Rabbit and turtle go to school*
Freedman, Claire. *Hushabye Lily*
Friskey, Margaret (Margaret Richards). *Mystery of the gate sign*
Gackenbach, Dick. *Hattie be quiet, Hattie be good*
    Hattie rabbit
    Hurray for Hattie Rabbit!
    Mother Rabbit's son Tom
Gág, Wanda. *ABC bunny*
Galdone, Paul. *A strange servant*
Gay, Michel. *Rabbit express*
Gay, Zhenya. *Small one*
Genechten, Guido Van. *Flop-Ear*
George, Lindsay Barrett. *My bunny and me*
Geras, Adèle. *My wishes for you*
Geringer, Laura. *Molly's new washing machine*
Gill, Madelaine. *The spring hat*
Ginsburg, Mirra. *The fox and the hare*
Gliori, Debi. *Flora's blanket*
    Flora's surprise
Gorbachev, Valeri. *Nicky and the big, bad wolves*
    Nicky and the fantastic birthday gift
    Nicky and the rainy day
Gordon, Sharon. *Easter Bunny's lost egg*
Got, Yves. *Sam's big book of words*
    Sam's little sister
Green, Adam. *The funny bunny factory*
Greenblat, Rodney Alan. *Thunder Bunny*
Greene, Carol. *The insignificant elephant*
Gretz, Susanna. *Rabbit food*
    Rabbit rambles on
Greydanus, Rose. *Climb aboard*
Grimm, Jacob. *The rabbit's bride*
Grindley, Sally. *Why is the sky blue?*
Grossman, Virginia. *Ten little rabbits*
Guest, C. Z. *Tiny green thumbs*
Hands, Hargrave. *Bunny sees*
Hayward, Linda. *All stuck up*
    Hello, house!
    Sunny Day Bunny
Heap, Sue. *Four friends in the garden*
Heine, Helme. *Superhare*
Henkes, Kevin. *Bailey goes camping*
Herford, Oliver. *The most timid in the land*
Heyward, Du Bose. *The country bunny and the little gold shoes*

Hide-and-seek bunnies
Ho, Minfong. *Brother Rabbit*
Hoban, Lillian. *Harry's song*
Hoban, Tana. *Where is it?*
Hogrogian, Nonny. *Carrot cake*
Honigsberg, Peter Jan. *Pillow of dreams*
Hooks, William H. *Rough, tough, Rowdy*
   Three rounds with rabbit
Hooper, Meredith. *Tom's rabbit*
Horse, Harry. *Little rabbit lost*
Houck, Eric L. *Rabbit surprise*
Howe, James. *Bunnicula escapes!*
   Rabbit-Cadabra!
   Scared silly
Hubbell, Patricia. *Rabbit moon*
Huriet, Genevieve. *Dandelion's vanishing vegetable garden*
Hynard, Stephen. *Snowy the rabbit*
Ichikawa, Satomi. *La La Rose*
Ikeda, Daisaku. *The princess and the moon*
Irbinskas, Heather. *How Jackrabbit got his very long ears*
Ivory, Lesley Anne. *The birthday cat*
Jabar, Cynthia. *Party day!*
Jagtenberg, Yvonne. *Jack's rabbit*
Jaquith, Priscilla. *Bo Rabbit smart for true*
Jennings, Linda M. *The brave little bunny*
Jennings, Sharon. *Franklin and the scooter*
Jeram, Anita. *All together now*
   Bunny, my Honey
   I love my little storybook
Jewell, Nancy. *The snuggle bunny*
Johnson, Jane. *My dear Noel*
Johnson, Paul Brett. *Little Bunny Foo Foo*
Johnston, Mary Anne. *Sing me a song*
Johnston, Tony. *Little Rabbit goes to sleep*
   The tale of Rabbit and Coyote
Julian, Alison. *Brave as a bunny can be*
Kangas, Juli. *Fluffy Bunny's friend*
Karlin, Nurit. *Ten little bunnies*
Keller, Emily Snowell. *Sleeping Bunny*
Keller, Holly. *Cecil's garden*
   Cromwell's glasses
   Maxine in the middle
Keller, Irene. *Benjamin Rabbit and the stranger danger*
Kelley, True. *A Valentine for Fuzzboom*
Kenyon, Tony. *Hyacinth Hop has the hic-hops*
Kirk, David. *Little bunny, Biddle bunny*
Kirn, Ann. *The tale of a crocodile*
Komoda, Beverly. *The too hot day*
   The winter day
Koontz, Robin Michal. *Chicago and the cat*
   Chicago and the cat, the camping trip
   Chicago and the cat, the family reunion
Koscielniak, Bruce. *Bear and Bunny grow tomatoes*
   Euclid Bunny delivers the mail
Kraus, Robert. *Big brother*
   Daddy Long Ears
   Good night Richard Rabbit
   The littlest rabbit
   Phil the ventriloquist
Kroll, Steven. *The big bunny and the Easter eggs*
   The big bunny and the magic show
Kuratomi, Chizuko. *Mr. Bear and the robbers*
Kwitz, Mary DeBall. *Rabbits' search for a little house*
Lachner, Dorothea. *Smoky's special Easter present*
Lacome, Julie. *Hocus pocus*
   Ruthie's big old coat
La Fontaine, Jean de. *The hare and the tortoise*
Landa, Norbert. *Rabbit and chicken count eggs*
   Rabbit and chicken find a box
   Rabbit and chicken play hide and seek
   Rabbit and chicken play with colors
Lasky, Kathryn. *Lunch bunnies*
   Science fair bunnies
   Show and tell bunnies
Lawrence, John. *Rabbit and pork*
Lawston, Lisa. *Can you hop?*
Leach, Michael. *Rabbits*

Lee, Ho Baek. *While we were out*
Leedy, Loreen. *The bunny play*
   The race
Leonard, Alain. *Barnaby and the big gorilla*
Leonard, Marcia. *Shopping for snowflakes*
Lester, Helen. *Listen, Buddy*
Le Tord, Bijou. *Rabbit seeds*
Levine, Abby. *Ollie knows everything*
Lewis, Rob. *Friends*
Lewison, Wendy Cheyette. *Say thank you, Theodore*
Lifton, Betty Jean. *The rice-cake rabbit*
Lionni, Leo. *Let's make rabbits*
Lipkind, William. *The Christmas bunny*
Littlefield, William. *The whiskers of Ho Ho*
Livingston, Irene. *Finklehopper Frog*
   Finklehopper Frog cheers
London, Jonathan. *Jackrabbit*
   Liplap's wish
Long, Sylvia. *Deck the hall*
Loomis, Christine. *Astro Bunnies*
   Cowboy bunnies
   Scuba bunnies
Lorian, Nicole. *A birthday present for Mama*
Lowell, Susan. *The tortoise and the jackrabbit*
McAllister, Angela. *The little blue rabbit*
   Night-night, little one
McBratney, Sam. *Guess how much I love you*
McCarty, Peter. *Little bunny on the move*
McCormack, John E. *Rabbit tales*
   Rabbit travels
McCullough, Sharon Pierce. *Bunbun at bedtime*
   Bunbun, the middle one
McDermott, Gerald. *Zomo the rabbit*
MacDonald, Elizabeth. *The wolf is coming!*
MacDonald, Margaret Read. *Pickin' peas*
MacDonald, Maryann. *Rabbit's birthday kite*
   Rosie and the poor rabbits
   Rosie runs away
   Rosie's baby tooth
Machado, Ana Maria. *Nina Bonita*
Macken, JoAnn Early. *Rabbits*
McLenighan, Valjean. *Turtle and rabbit*
McMullan, Kate (Hall). *Bunny riddles*
McNaughton, Colin. *Walk rabbit walk*
McPhail, David M. *The blue door*
   Jack and Rick
Magloff, Lisa. *Rabbit*
Mangas, Brian. *A nice surprise for Father Rabbit*
Manushkin, Fran. *Be brave, baby rabbit*
   Little rabbit's baby brother
Maril, Lee. *Mr. Bunny paints the eggs*
Maris, Ron. *Runaway rabbit*
Martin, Rafe. *Foolish rabbit's big mistake*
Marzollo, Jean. *I spy little bunnies*
Mathews, Louise. *Bunches and bunches of bunnies*
Mayne, William. *Come, come to my corner*
Medina, Nina. *Have you ever noticed that rabbits don't sing?*
Meister, Cari. *Skinny and fats, best friends*
Mendelson, S. T. *Stupid Emilien*
Meroux, Felix. *The prince of the rabbits*
Merrick, Patrick. *Easter bunnies*
Meyer, Brigit. *Easter bunny saves the day*
Michels, Tilde. *Rabbit spring*
Miles, Miska. *Rabbit garden*
   Small rabbit
Miller, J. P. (John Parr). *Good night, Little Rabbit*
   Learn to count with Little Rabbit
Milne, A. A. (Alan Alexander). *Prince Rabbit*
Minters, Frances. *Too big, too small, just right*
Modesitt, Jeanne. *Little Bunny's Easter surprise*
   Mama, if you had a wish
   Vegetable soup
Molk, Laurel. *Good job, Oliver!*
Mollel, Tololwa M. (Tololwa Marti). *To dinner, for dinner*
Moon, Nicola. *Tick-tock, drip-drop*
Moore, Elaine. *Grammy, do you love me?*
Moore, Inga. *A big day for Little Jack*

Oh, little Jack
Mora, Jo (Joseph Jacinto). *Budgee Budgee Cottontail*
Moremen, Grace E. *No, no, Natalie*
Moss, Miriam. *Bad hare day*
Murphy, Stuart J. *Just enough carrots*
  Rabbit's pajama party
Mussenbrock, Anne. *Easter Bunny saves the day*
  The little Easter surprise
Namm, Diane. *Bunny's bedtime*
Nayer, Judy. *Funny bunnies*
Newberry, Clare Turlay. *Marshmallow*
Newsome, Jill. *Shadow*
Newton, Jill. *Polar bear scare*
Nilsson, Ulf. *Little sister rabbit*
Noonan, Julia. *Hare and Rabbit, friends forever*
Norman, Philip Ross. *The carrot war*
O'Keefe, Susan Heyboer. *Love me, love you*
Oller, Erika. *The cabbage soup solution*
O'Mara, Carmel. *Rainy day*
  Sunny day
Ostheeren, Ingrid. *Coriander's Easter adventure*
Packard, Mary. *Don't make a sound*
Paraskevas, Betty. *Maggie and the Ferocious Beast, the big carrot*
  Nibbles O'Hare
Parish, Peggy. *Too many rabbits*
Parry, Marian. *King of the fish*
Patchett, Fiona. *Rabbits*
Peet, Bill (William Bartlett). *Huge Harold*
Petach, Heidi. *Goldilocks and the three hares*
Peters, Sharon. *Ready, get set, go!*
  Stop that rabbit
Petty, Kate. *Rabbits*
Pfister, Marcus. *Hang on, Hopper!*
  Hopper
  Hopper hunts for spring
  Hopper's treetop adventure
Pinkwater, Daniel Manus. *Bad bears and a bunny*
  Irving and Muktuk
Pizer, Abigail. *Loppylugs*
Poole, Valerie. *Obadiah Coffee and the music contest*
Porter, Sue. *My little rabbit tale*
Posey, Lee. *Night rabbits*
Potter, Beatrix. *The complete adventures of Peter Rabbit*
  Peter Rabbit's one two three
  The story of fierce bad rabbit
  The tale of Benjamin Bunny
  The tale of Mr. Tod
  The tale of Peter Rabbit, ill. by Margot Apple
  The tale of Peter Rabbit, ill. by author
  The tale of the Flopsy Bunnies
  Where's Peter Rabbit?
Price, Mathew. *Patch and the rabbits*
The pudgy bunny book
Quackenbush, Robert M. *First grade jitters*
  Funny bunnies
  Funny bunnies on the run
Ratnett, Michael. *Marmaduke and the scary story*
Ratz de Tagyos, Paul. *A coney tale*
Ray, Mary Lyn. *All aboard*
Repchuk, Caroline. *The race*
Rey, Margret (Margret Elisabeth Waldstein). *Spotty*
Riordan, James. *Little Bunny Bobkin*
Robbins, Beth. *Tom, Ally, and the baby-sitter*
Roberts, Bethany. *Waiting-for-Christmas stories*
  Waiting-for-Papa stories
  Waiting-for-spring stories
Rockwell, Anne F. *Chip and the karate kick*
Roddie, Shen. *Sandbear*
Rohmann, Eric. *My friend Rabbit*
Rosen, Michael (1946–). *Little rabbit Foo Foo*
Roth, Carol. *Little Bunny's sleepless night*
Rowe, John A. *Rabbit moon*
Ryder, Joanne. *Hello, first grade*
Rylant, Cynthia. *Bunny bungalow*
Sadler, Marilyn. *It's not easy being a bunny*
Saltzberg, Barney. *Hip, hip, hooray day!*
  The problem with pumpkins

San Souci, Daniel. *The rabbit and the dragon king*
Sara. *The rabbit, the fox, and the wolf*
Schlein, Miriam. *Little Rabbit, the high jumper*
Schmid, Eleonore. *Hare's Christmas gift*
Schotter, Roni. *Bunny's night out*
Schulman, Janet. *A bunny for all seasons*
Schweninger, Ann. *Birthday wishes*
  Christmas secrets
  Halloween surprises
  The hunt for rabbit's galosh
  Off to school!
  Valentine friends
Selby, Jennifer. *Beach bunny*
Selkowe, Valrie M. *Happy birthday to me!*
Seuss, Dr. *The eye book*
Sharmat, Marjorie Weinman. *Thornton, the worrier*
Silverman, Erica. *Warm in winter*
Silverman, Maida. *Bunny's ABC*
Simmons, Jane. *Little Fern's first winter*
Smith, Barry. *Grandma Rabbitty's visit*
Smith, Cara Lockhart. *Twenty-six rabbits run riot*
Solotareff, Grégoire. *Don't call me little bunny*
Sonnenschein, Harriet. *Harold's hideaway thumb*
  Harold's runaway nose
Spelman, Cornelia Maude. *When I feel angry*
Spier, Peter. *Little rabbits*
Stanley, Mandy. *Lettice, the dancing rabbit*
Steig, William. *Solomon the rusty nail*
  Which would you rather be?
Steiner, Charlotte. *My bunny feels soft*
Steiner, Jörg. *Rabbit Island*
Stevens, Janet. *Tops and bottoms*
Stevenson, James. *Monty*
Stevenson, Suçie. *Christmas eve*
  Do I have to take Violet?
Stewart, Paul. *The birthday presents*
  A little bit of winter
  Rabbit's wish
Sykes, Julie. *Robbie Rabbit and the little ones*
Szekeres, Cyndy. *Cyndy Szekeres' learn to count, funny bunnies*
  Hide-and-seek duck
  I can count 100 bunnies, and so can you!
Tafuri, Nancy. *Rabbit's morning*
  Where did Bunny go?
  Will you be my friend?
Tarrant, Graham. *Rabbits*
Taylor, Shirley. *The cross in the egg*
Tegen, Katherine Brown. *The story of the Easter Bunny*
Tejima, Keizaburo. *Ho-limlim*
Thomas, Patricia. *The one and only, super-duper, golly-whopper, jim-dandy, really-handy clock-tock-stopper*
Thornhill, Jan. *The rumor*
Tidd, Louise Vitellaro. *The best pet yet*
Tompert, Ann. *Nothing sticks like a shadow*
Tresselt, Alvin R. *The rabbit story*, ill. by Carolyn Ewing
  Rabbit story, ill. by Leonard Weisgard
Trez, Denise. *Rabbit country*
Tripp, Wallace. *My Uncle Podger*
Troughton, Joanna. *How rabbit stole the fire*
Vainio, Pirkko. *The best of friends*
Van Emst, Charlotte. *Little Rabbit's big day*
Van Woerkom, Dorothy. *Harry and Shelburt*
Velthuijs, Max. *Little Man to the rescue*
Vozar, David. *M. C. Turtle and the hip hop hare*
Wabbes, Marie. *Good night, Little Rabbit*
  Happy birthday, Little Rabbit
  It's snowing, Little Rabbit
  Little Rabbit's garden
Waddell, Martin. *Tom Rabbit*
  We love them
Wahl, Jan. *Carrot nose*
  Doctor Rabbit's foundling
  The five in the forest
  Rabbits on roller skates!
Wallace, Ivy. *Pookie*
  Pookie believes in Santa Claus
  Pookie puts the world right

Wallace, John. *Tiny Rabbit goes to a birthday party*
Wallace, Nancy Elizabeth. *Apples, apples, apples*
  Count down to clean up
  Paperwhite
  Pumpkin day
  Rabbit's bedtime
  Snow
  Tell-a-bunny
Walton, Rick. *One more bunny*
Watson, Carol. *Rabbit*
Watson, Wendy. *The bunnies' Christmas eve*
  Lollipop
Watts, Barrie. *Rabbit*
Watts, Bernadette. *Harvey Hare, postman extraordinaire*
  Harvey Hare's Christmas
Wayland, April Halprin. *To Rabbittown*
Weigelt, Udo. *The Easter Bunny's baby*
Weil, Lisl. *The candy egg bunny*
Welch, Willy. *Grumpy Bunnies*
Wellington, Monica. *Bunny's first snowflake*
  Bunny's rainbow day
  Night rabbits
Wells, Rosemary. *Bunny cakes*
  Bunny money
  Bunny party
  Emily's first 100 days of school
  First tomato
  Goodnight Max
  Hooray for Max
  The island light
  McDuffs hide-and-seek
  Max and Ruby's Midas
  Max cleans up
  Max's bath
  Max's bedtime
  Max's birthday
  Max's breakfast
  Max's chocolate chicken
  Max's Christmas
  Max's dragon shirt
  Max's first word
  Max's new suit
  Max's ride
  Max's toys
  Morris's disappearing bag
  Moss pillows
  My kindergarten
  Read to your bunny
  Ruby's beauty shop
Weninger, Brigitte. *Davy in the middle*
  Happy birthday, Davy
  Happy Easter, Davy
  Merry Christmas, Davy!
  What's the matter, Davy?
  Why are you fighting, Davy?
  Will you mind the baby, Davy?
White, Carolyn. *The adventure of Louey and Frank*
Whybrow, Ian. *Parcel for Stanley*
Wiese, Kurt. *Happy Easter*
Wild, Margaret. *Rosie and Tortoise*
Wilhelm, Hans. *Bunny trouble*
  More bunny trouble
Williams, Garth. *Benjamin's treasure*
  The rabbits' wedding
Williams, Sue. *Dinnertime*
Wolf, Ann. *The rabbit and the turtle*
Wolf, Winfried. *The Easter bunny*
Wood, Douglas. *Rabbit and the moon*
Wormell, Christopher. *The big ugly monster and the little stone rabbit*
  Blue Rabbit and friends
  Blue Rabbit and the runaway wheel
Worth, Bonnie. *Peter Cottontail's surprise*
Wyllie, Stephen. *White Rabbit builds a dream house*
Wynne-Jones, Tim. *On Tumbledown Hill*
Yee, Patrick. *Bedtime for Rosie Rabbit*
  Little Buddy meets Bobo
  Rosie Rabbit's colors

  Rosie Rabbit's numbers
  Rosie Rabbit's opposites
  Rosie Rabbit's shapes
  Winter rabbit
Zakhoder, Boris Vladimirovich. *Rosachok*
Zalben, Jane Breskin. *Miss Violet's shining day*
Ziefert, Harriet. *Breakfast time!*
  Bye-bye, daddy!
  Good morning, sun!
  Happy birthday, Grandpa!
  Happy Easter, Grandma!
  Let's get dressed!
  Rabbit and Hare divide an apple
Zolotow, Charlotte (Shapiro). *The bunny who found Easter*
  Mr. Rabbit and the lovely present

Animals – raccoons

Arnosky, Jim. *Raccoon on his own*
  Raccoons and ripe corn
Bellows, Cathy. *The royal raccoon*
Bradford, Ann. *The mystery at Misty Falls*
  The mystery of the missing raccoon
Brown, Margaret Wise. *Wait till the moon is full*
Burdick, Margaret. *Sara Raccoon and the secret place*
Calmenson, Stephanie. *Come to my party*
Cocca-Leffler, Maryann. *Bravery soup*
Cummings, Pat. *Petey Moroni's Camp Runamok diary*
Duvoisin, Roger Antoine. *Petunia, I love you*
Elliott, David. *Hunter's best friend at school*
Freschet, Berniece. *Five fat raccoons*
Friend, Catherine. *Eddie the raccoon*
Glass, Andrew. *Bewildered for three days*
Haines, Mike. *Countdown to bedtime*
Hill, Susan. *Ruby bakes a cake*
Hoban, Lillian. *The case of the two masked robbers*
  Here come raccoons
Johnson, Donna Kay. *Brighteyes*
Leedy, Loreen. *The race*
Leonard, Marcia. *Alphabet bandits*
Lewison, Wendy Cheyette. *Where is Sammy's smile?*
McPhail, David M. *Henry Bear's Christmas*
  Something special
  Stanley: Henry Bear's friend
Miklowitz, Gloria D. *Save that raccoon!*
Miles, Miska. *The raccoon and Mrs. McGinnis*
Moore, Lilian. *Little Raccoon and no trouble at all*
  Little Raccoon and the outside world
  Little Raccoon and the thing in the pool
Morgan, Allen. *Molly and Mr. Maloney*
Nelson, Kristin L. *Clever raccoons*
Neugebauer, Charise. *The real winner*
Noguere, Suzanne. *Little raccoon*
St. George, Judith. *The Halloween pumpkin smasher*
Sharmat, Marjorie Weinman. *The 329th friend*
Shaw, Nancy (Nancy E.). *Raccoon tune*
Steiner, Barbara (Annette). *But not Stanleigh*
Thayer, Jane. *The clever raccoon*
Wells, Rosemary. *Timothy goes to school*
  Yoko
Whelan, Gloria. *A week of raccoons*
Whitehouse, Patricia. *Raccoons*
Young, James. *Everyone loves the moon*
Zweifel, Frances W. *The Make-Something Club*

Animals – rats

Annixter, Jane. *Brown rats, black rats*
Augarde, Steve (Stephen). *Barnaby Shrew, Black Dan and . . . the mighty wedgwood*
  Barnaby Shrew goes to sea
Bartos-Hoppner, Barbara. *The pied piper of Hamelin*
Baynton, Martin. *Fifty saves his friend*
Bellows, Cathy. *Four fat rats*
Berson, Harold. *The rats who lived in the delicatessen*
Bianchi, John. *The lab rats of Doctor Eclair*
Biro, Val. *The pied piper of Hamelin*

Black, Floyd. *Alphabet cat*
Browning, Robert. *The pied piper of Hamelin*, ill. by Patricia and Robin DeWitt
   The pied piper of Hamelin, ill. by Kate Greenaway
   The pied piper of Hamelin, ill. by Anatoly Ivanov
   The pied piper of Hamelin, ill. by Errol Le Cain
   The pied piper of Hamelin, ill. by Drahos Zak
Bryan, Ashley. *The cat's purr*
Child, Lauren. *That pesky rat*
Coffey, Maria. *A cat adrift*
Cohen, Barbara. *The chocolate wolf*
Cole, Babette. *Hurray for Ethelyn*
   Three cheers for Errol!
Cook, Joel. *The rat's daughter*
Cressey, James. *Fourteen rats and a rat-catcher*
Crimi, Carolyn. *Don't need friends*
Cunningham, Julia. *A mouse called Junction*
Doty, Roy. *Old-one-eye meets his match*
Egielski, Richard. *Slim and Jim*
Emberley, Rebecca. *Three cool kids*
Erickson, Russell E. *Warton and the traders*
Grahame, Kenneth. *The wind in the willows*, ill. by Joanne Moss
   A wind in the willows Christmas
Harris, Marian. *Tuesday in Arizona*
Hearn, Michael Patrick. *The porcelain cat*
Hoban, Russell. *Flat cat*
Hurd, Thacher. *Mystery on the docks*
Jennings, Sharon. *Priscilla and Rosy*
   Priscilla's paw de deux
Johnston, Tony. *Sparky and Eddie, trouble with rats*
Karlin, Nurit. *The fat cat sat on the mat*
Kasza, Keiko. *The rat and the tiger*
Knüppel, Helga. *Christabel Crocodile's birthday egg*
Kouts, Anne. *Kenny's rat*
La Fontaine, Jean de. *The lion and the rat*
Lager, Claude. *A tale of two rats*
Latimer, Jim. *The Irish piper*
Lester, Helen. *Hooway for Wodney Wat*
McNaughton, Colin. *The rat race*
Mayer, Mercer. *The pied piper of Hamelin*
Meddaugh, Susan. *Cinderella's rat*
Miles, Miska. *Wharf rat*
Moore, Inga. *Aktil's big swim*
Oakley, Graham. *The church mice adrift*
Peppé, Rodney. *The mice and the clockwork bus*
   The mice and the flying basket
Pomerantz, Charlotte. *The ballad of the long-tailed rat*
Potter, Beatrix. *The sly old cat*
Root, Phyllis. *Sam, who was swallowed by a shark*
Ross, Tony. *The pied piper of Hamelin*
Rowe, John A. *Smudge*
Saunders, Susan. *Charles Rat's picnic*
Schiller, Barbara. *The white rat's tale*
Sharmat, Marjorie Weinman. *Mooch the messy*
Snow, Alan. *The monster book of ABC sounds*
Stevenson, James. *The most amazing dinosaur*
   Wilfred the rat
Van Woerkom, Dorothy. *The rat, the ox and the zodiac*
Walt Disney Productions. *Walt Disney's The adventures of Mr. Toad*
Whitehouse, Patricia. *Rats*
Young, Ed (Edward). *Cat and Rat*
Zemach, Kaethe. *The beautiful rat*

Animals – reindeer

Bernhard, Emery. *Reindeer*
Brett, Jan. *The wild Christmas reindeer*
Cleaver, Elizabeth. *The enchanted caribou*
Dwyer, Mindy. *Aurora, a tale of the Northern Lights*
Foreman, Michael. *The little reindeer*
Haywood, Carolyn. *How the reindeer saved Santa*
Hodge, Deborah. *Deer, moose, elk and caribou*
Hoff, Syd. *Where's Prancer?*
Janovitz, Marilyn. *What could be keeping Santa?*
Jessell, Tim. *Amorak*
McCaughrean, Geraldine. *How the reindeer got their antlers*

May, Robert Lewis. *Rudolph the red-nosed reindeer*, ill. by Diana Magnuson
   Rudolph the red-nosed reindeer, ill. by David Wenzel
Miller, Debbie S. *A caribou journey*
Okrend, Elise. *Blintzes for Blitzen*
Owens, Mary Beth. *A caribou alphabet*
Root, Phyllis. *If you want to see a caribou*
Schrecker, Judie. *Santa's new reindeer*
Wright, Cliff. *Santa's ark*

Animals – rhinoceros

Araki, Mie. *The magic toolbox*
Ardizzone, Edward. *Diana and her rhinoceros*
Brunhoff, Laurent de. *Babar's battle*
Bush, John. *The cross-with-us rhinoceros*
Cazet, Denys. *Great-Uncle Felix*
George, Jean Craighead. *Rhino romp*
Heine, Helme. *The boxer and the princess*
Johnson, Louise. *Malunda*
Kessler, Cristina. *Jubela*
Kipling, Rudyard. *How the rhinoceros got his skin*
Maestro, Giulio. *Just enough Rosie*
Mammano, Julie. *Rhinos who play soccer*
   Rhinos who skateboard
   Rhinos who snowboard
Noble, Kate. *Oh look, it's a nosserus*
O'Malley, Kevin. *Bud*
Palmer, Todd Starr. *Rhino and Mouse*
Sackett, Elisabeth. *Danger on the African grassland*
Sis, Peter. *Rainbow Rhino*
Standon, Anna. *The singing rhinoceros*
Terry, Michael. *Rhino's horns*
Theodorou, Rod. *Black rhino*
Yoshida, Toshi. *Rhinoceros mother*

Animals – salamanders *see* Reptiles – salamanders

Animals – sea lions

Hamsa, Bobbie. *Your pet sea lion*
Olds, Elizabeth. *Plop plop ploppie*
Schreiber, Georges. *Bambino the clown*
Tafuri, Nancy. *Follow me!*
Whitehouse, Patricia. *Sea lion*

Animals – seals

Ackerman, Diane. *Monk seal hideaway*
Allen, Judy. *Seal*
Bare, Colleen Stanley. *Elephants on the beach*
Barr, Cathrine. *Sammy seal ov the sircus*
Bos, Claire. *Webster's wardrobe*
Burton, Jane. *Surfer the seal*
Cherry, Lynne. *Seal*
Coffey, Maria. *A seal in the family*
Cooper, Susan. *The Selkie girl*
Cousteau Society. *Seals*
Duran, Bonté. *The adventures of Arthur and Edmund*
Foreman, Michael. *Seal surfer*
Freeman, Don. *The seal and the slick*
Gerstein, Mordicai. *The seal mother*
Hewett, Joan. *A harbor seal pup grows up*
Hirschi, Ron. *Where are my puffins, whales, and seals?*
Hoff, Syd. *Sammy the seal*
Hollenbeck, Kathleen M. *Islands of ice*
Kessler, Ethel. *Are there seals in the sandbox?*
Lilly, Kenneth. *Animals of the ocean*
McClure, Gillian. *Selkie*
MacGill-Callahan, Sheila. *The seal prince*
Rotter, Charles. *Seals*
Rühmann, Karl. *Filbert flies*
Rumford, James. *Dog-of-the-Sea-Waves*
Sackett, Elisabeth. *Danger on the Arctic ice*
Townsend, Emily Rose. *Seals*
Yolen, Jane. *Greyling*

Animals – service animals

Dalgleish, Sharon. *Working dogs*
Lang, Glenna. *Looking out for Sarah*
Russell, Joan Plummer. *Aero and Officer Mike*

Animals – sheep

Aardema, Verna. *Borreguita and the coyote*
Æsop. *The wolf in sheep's clothing*
Alborough, Jez. *The grass is always greener*
Alda, Arlene. *Sheep, sheep, sheep, help me fall asleep*
Baird, Anne. *The Christmas lamb*
Ballart, Elisabet. *Let's count*
Beskow, Elsa Maartman. *Pelle's new suit*
Blanchard, Arlene. *The naughty lamb*
Brenner, Barbara A. *Lion and Lamb*
Brown, Margaret Wise. *Little lost lamb*
    Sheep don't count sheep
Butterworth, Nick. *The lost sheep*
Calhoun, Mary. *Henry the Christmas cat*
Carlstrom, Nancy White. *Ten Christmas sheep*
Carrick, Carol. *Valentine*
Cazzola, Gus. *The bells of Santa Lucia*
Clayton, Gordon. *Lamb*
Coe, Lloyd. *Charcoal*
Dalmais, Anne-Marie. *Best bedtime stories of Mother Sheep*
Demi. *Fleecy lamb*
    Little baby lamb
De Paola, Tomie (Thomas Anthony). *Charlie needs a cloak*
    Haircuts for the Woolseys
Duncan, Jane. *Brave Janet Reachfar*
Dunn, Judy. *The little lamb*
Enderle, Judith (Ann) Ross. *Six creepy sheep*
    Six sandy sheep
Ernst, Lisa Campbell. *Nattie Parsons' good-luck lamb*
Eversole, Robyn Harbert. *Red berry wool*
Fleetwood, Jenni. *While shepherds watched*
Fox, Mem. *Where is the green sheep?*
Fraggalosch, Audrey. *Trails above the tree line*
Friend, Catherine. *Funny Ruby*
Galdone, Paul. *Little Bo-Peep*
Ginsburg, Mirra. *The strongest one of all*
Gliori, Debi. *The snow lambs*
Gordon, Jeffie Ross. *Six sleepy sheep*
Grejniec, Michael. *When I open my eyes*
Hale, Sarah Josepha Buell. *Mary had a little lamb*, ill. by Tomie de Paola
    Mary had a little lamb, photos. by Bruce McMillan
    Mary had a little lamb, ill. by Salley Mavor
    Mary had a little lamb, ill. by Ann Schweninger
    Mary had a little lamb, ill. by Iza Trapani
    Mary had a little lamb, ill. by Suzanne Vasilak
    Mary had a little lamb [board book], ill. by Iza Trapani
Heap, Sue. *Four friends in the garden*
Heck, Elisabeth. *The black sheep*
Hedderwick, Mairi. *Katie Morag and the two grandmothers*
Helldorfer, M. C. (Mary Claire). *Daniel's gift*
Hoberman, Mary Ann. *Mary had a little lamb*, ill. by Nadine Bernard Westcott
Ichikawa, Satomi. *Nora's surprise*
Inkpen, Mick. *If I had a sheep*
Ipcar, Dahlov (Zorach). *The land of flowers*
Johnston, Tony. *Three little bikers*
Kiser, Kevin. *Sherman the sheep*
Kitamura, Satoshi. *Sheep in wolves' clothing*
    When sheep cannot sleep
Kraus, Robert. *Strudwick, a sheep in wolf's clothing*
Landström, Olof. *Boo and Baa at sea*
    Boo and Baa get wet
    Boo and Baa in a party mood
    Boo and Baa in the woods
    Boo and Baa in windy weather
    Boo and Baa on a cleaning spree
Levine, Arthur A. *Sheep dreams*
Levine, Gail Carson. *Betsy who cried wolf*
Lewis, Kim. *Emma's lamb*

First snow
Little Baa
Little lamb
The shepherd boy
Lewis, Rob. *Friska, the sheep that was too small*
Livingstone, Star. *Harley*
London, Jonathan. *At the edge of the forest*
Lunn, Janet Louise Swoboda. *Amos's sweater*
McCully, Emily Arnold. *My real family*
    Speak up, Blanche!
McGee, Barbara. *Counting sheep*
McGinty, Alice B. *Ten little lambs*
MacGregor, Marilyn. *On top*
McGrory, Anik. *Mouton's impossible dream*
McMullan, Kate (Hall). *Sheepish riddles*
McPhail, David M. *The day the sheep showed up*
Mallat, Kathy. *Seven stars, more!*
Marciano, John Bemelmans. *Delilah*
Mendoza, George. *Alphabet sheep*
    Silly sheep and other sheepish rhymes
Mills, Claudia. *One small lost sheep*
Mother Goose. *Baa baa, black sheep*, ill. by Marilyn Janovitz
    Baa, baa, black sheep, ill. by Moira Kemp
Novak, Matt. *While the shepherd slept*
O'Brien, Mary. *Counting sheep to sleep*
Oram, Hiawyn. *Where are you hiding, little lamb?*
Patent, Dorothy Hinshaw. *Maggie, a sheep dog*
Peet, Bill (William Bartlett). *Buford the little bighorn*
Porter, Sue. *Parsnip*
    Parsnip and the pink blanket
    Parsnip and the runaway tractor
Rogers, Paul (Patrick). *Sheepchase*
Root, Phyllis. *Ten sleepy sheep*
Rothstein, Gloria. *Sheep asleep*
Royston, Angela. *The sheep*
Russell, Betty. *Run sheep run*
Ryder, Joanne. *Beach party*
Sanders, Scott R. (Scott Russell). *Warm as wool*
Schuh, Mari C. *Sheep on the farm*
Scotton, Rob. *Russell the sheep*
Shaw, Nancy (Nancy E.). *Sheep in a jeep*
    Sheep in a shop
    Sheep on a ship
    Sheep out to eat
    Sheep take a hike
    Sheep trick or treat
Sloat, Teri. *Farmer Brown shears his sheep*
Slobodkin, Louis. *Up high and down low*
Smith, Kathryn. *Little Lamb's Christmas story*
Snyder, Zilpha Keatley. *The changing maze*
Steiner, Charlotte. *Red Ridinghood's little lamb*
Stickland, Paul. *Bears*
Strete, Craig Kee. *Big thunder magic*
Sundgaard, Arnold. *The lamb and the butterfly*
Tanner, Suzy-Jane. *Tinyflock Nursery School*
Trapani, Iza. *Baa baa black sheep*
    Baa baa black sheep [board book]
Wallace, Barbara Brooks. *Argyle*
Weeks, Sarah. *Baa-choo!*
Weiss, Ellen. *Clara the fortune-telling chicken*
Wellington, Monica. *The sheep follow*
Wheeler, Lisa. *Wool gathering*
Widman, Christine. *The star grazers*
Wild, Jocelyn. *Florence and Eric take the cake*
Zalben, Jane Breskin. *Pearl plants a tree*
    Pearl's eight days of Chanukah
    Pearl's marigolds for grandpa

Animals – shrews

Augarde, Steve (Stephen). *Barnaby Shrew, Black Dan and . . . the mighty wedgwood*
    Barnaby Shrew goes to sea
Goodall, John S. *Shrewbettina's birthday*
Koller, Jackie French. *Mole and Shrew*
    Mole and Shrew are two
    Mole and Shrew step out

Olsen, Alfa-Betty. *Gabby the shrew*

Animals – skunks

Crum, Shutta. *The bravest of the brave*
De Regniers, Beatrice Schenk. *A special birthday party for someone very special*
Fair, David. *The fabulous four skunks*
Gray, Libba Moore. *Is there room on the feather bed?*
Greenberg, David (David T.). *Skunks*
Hoban, Brom. *Skunk Lane*
Jones, Chuck. *William the backwards skunk*
Latimer, Jim. *James Bear's pie*
Reeves, Mona Rabun. *The spooky eerie night noise*
Schlein, Miriam. *What's wrong with being a skunk?*
Schoenherr, John. *The barn*
Stevens, Jan Romero. *Carlos and the skunk = Carlos y el zorrillo*
Tether, Graham. *Skunk and possum*
Wells, Rosemary. *Fritz and the mess fairy*

Animals – sloths

Carle, Eric. *"Slowly, slowly, slowly," said the sloth*
Knight, Hilary. *Sylvia the sloth*
Lester, Helen. *Score one for the sloths*
Sharmat, Mitchell. *Sherman is a slowpoke*
Turnbull, Ann. *Too tired*
Willis, Jeanne. *Sloth's shoes*

Animals – slugs

Colborn, Mary Palenick. *Rainy day slug*
Edwards, Pamela Duncan. *Some smug slug*
Raschka, Christopher. *Sluggy Slug*

Animals – snails

Ahlberg, Allan. *The snail house*
Allen, Judy. *Are you a snail?*
Byars, Betsy Cromer. *The lace snail*
Cutler, Jane. *Mr. Carey's garden*
Dorros, Arthur. *When the pigs took over*
Greenberg, David (David T.). *Slugs*
Hartley, Karen. *Snail*
Hightower, Susan. *Twelve snails to one lizard*
Himmelman, John. *Simpson Snail sings*
Jackson, Ellen B. *The precious gift*
Janovitz, Marilyn. *Look out, bird!*
Latimer, Jim. *Snail and Buffalo*
Lord, John Vernon. *Mr. Mead and his garden*
McAllister, Angela. *Snail's birthday problem*
McGuirk, Leslie. *Snail boy*
Marshall, James. *The guest*
O'Connor, Jane. *Snail City*
O'Hagan, Caroline. *It's easy to have a snail visit you*
Oleson, Jens. *Snail*
Reider, Katja. *Snail started it!*
Rockwell, Anne F. *The story snail*
Ryder, Joanne. *Snail in the woods*
  The snail's spell
Saunders, Dave. *So slow!*
Stadler, John. *Hooray for snail!*
  Snail saves the day
Ungerer, Tomi. *Snail, where are you?*

Animals – snow leopards *see* Animals – leopards

Animals – sponges

Esbensen, Barbara Juster. *Sponges are skeletons*

Animals – squirrels

Alexander, Sue. *There's more . . . much more*
Angelo, Valenti. *The acorn tree*
Apperley, Dawn. *Don't wake the baby*
Ashabranner, Brent. *I'm in the zoo, too*

Bare, Colleen Stanley. *Busy, busy squirrels*
  Tree squirrels
Bassett, Lisa. *Beany and Scamp*
  Beany wakes up for Christmas
Bowers, Tim. *A new home*
Braun, Sebastien. *I love my mommy*
Browne, Eileen. *Tick-tock*
  Where's that bus?
Buff, Mary (Marsh). *Hurry, Skurry and Flurry*
Carey, Valerie Scho. *Harriet and William and the terrible creature*
Carter, Anne Laurel. *Scurry's treasure*
Cherry, Lynne. *How Groundhog's garden grew*
Chottin, Ariane. *Beaver gets lost*
Coldrey, Jennifer. *The world of squirrels*
Collins, Pat Lowery. *Tomorrow, up and away!*
Cooper, Helen (Helen F.). *Pumpkin soup*
Cooper, Patrick. *Never trust a squirrel*
Crane, Donn. *Flippy and Skippy*
DeLage, Ida. *The squirrel's tree party*
Drummond, Violet H. *Phewtus the squirrel*
Earle, Olive L. *Squirrels in the garden*
Ehlert, Lois. *Nuts to you!*
Ernst, Lisa Campbell. *Squirrel Park*
Falda, Dominique. *The treasure chest*
Grindley, Sally. *What will I do without you?*
Harper, Charise Mericle. *The trouble with normal*
James, Simon. *The wild woods*
Jango-Cohen, Judith. *Flying squirrels*
Jensen, Patricia. *Little Squirrel's special nest*
Jones, Penelope. *I didn't want to be nice*
Kimmel, Eric A. *Pumpkinhead*
Kroll, Steven. *The squirrels' Thanksgiving*
Lane, Margaret. *The squirrel*
Lithgow, John. *Micawber*
McBratney, Sam. *Just one!*
Miller, Edna. *Scamper*
Mills, Joyce C. *Gentle Willow*
Oxford Scientific Films. *Grey squirrel*
Peet, Bill (William Bartlett). *Merle the high flying squirrel*
Peterson, Hans. *Erik has a squirrel*
Pfister, Marcus. *Hopper's treetop adventure*
Potter, Beatrix. *The tale of Squirrel Nutkin*
  The tale of Timmy Tiptoes
Quackenbush, Robert M. *Batbaby*
Roberts, Bethany. *Rosie to the rescue*
Ryden, Hope. *The raggedy red squirrel*
Schmid, Eleonore. *The squirrel and the moon*
Schumacher, Claire. *Nutty's birthday*
  Nutty's Christmas
Shannon, George. *Heart to heart*
  The surprise
Sharmat, Marjorie Weinman. *Attila the angry*
  Sophie and Gussie
  The trip
Stage, Mads. *The lonely squirrel*
Stern, Maggie. *The missing sunflowers*
Stevenson, James. *Wilfred the rat*
Townsend, Emily Rose. *Squirrels*
Waldron, Kathleen Cook. *Loon Lake fishing derby*
Walsh, Ellen Stoll. *Dot and Jabber and the great acorn mystery*
Weigelt, Udo. *There's room in the forest for everyone*
Yeoman, John. *The bear's water picnic*
Young, Miriam Burt. *Miss Suzy's Easter surprise*
Zion, Gene. *The meanest squirrel I ever met*
Zweifel, Frances W. *Bony*
  The Make-Something Club

Animals – starfish

Heyduck-Huth, Hilde. *The starfish*
Hurd, Edith Thacher. *Starfish*
Zuchora-Walske, Christine. *Spiny sea stars*

Animals – swine *see* Animals – pigs

Animals – tapirs

Maestro, Giulio. *The tortoise's tug of war*

Animals – tigers

Adams, Richard (Richard Newbold). *The tyger voyage*
Allen, Judy. *Tiger*
Anderson, Paul S. *Red fox and the hungry tiger*
Baker, Keith. *Who is the beast?*
Banks, Kate (Katherine A.). *Close your eyes*
Bannerman, Helen. *Little Black Sambo*, Platt & Munk, 1933
   Little Black Sambo, ill. by Nina R. Jordan
   Little Black Sambo, ill. by Gladys Turkey Mitchell
   Little Black Sambo, ill. by Robert Moore
   Little Black Sambo, ill. by Fern Bisel Peat
   Little Black Sambo, ill. by Mary LaFetra Russell
   Little Black Sambo, ill. by Cobb X. Shinn
   Little Black Sambo, ill. by Terry & Mary Smith
   Little Black Sambo, ill. by Suzanne
   Little Black Sambo, ill. by Gustaf Tenggren
   Little Black Sambo, ill. by Keith Ward
   Little Black Sambo, ill. by Julian Wehr
   The Little Black Sambo story book
   The story of Little Babaji
   The story of Little Black Sambo, Reilly, 1905
   The story of Little Black Sambo, Lippincott, 1915
   The story of Little Black Sambo, Stokes, 1923
   The story of Little Black Sambo, Altemus, 1931
   The story of Little Black Sambo, Lippincott, 1943
   The story of Little Black Sambo, Greenhouse, 1986
   The story of Little Black Sambo, HarperCollins, 1990
   The story of little black Sambo, Applewood, 1996
   The story of Little Black Sambo, ill. by Christopher Bing
   The story of Little Black Sambo, "pop-up" picture by C. Carey Cloud
   The story of Little Black Sambo, ill. by Judith Russell
Barrows, Marjorie Wescott. *Timothy Tiger*
Blake, William. *The tyger*
Blaustein, Muriel. *Bedtime, Zachary!*
   Make friends, Zachary!
Bohdal, Susi. *Tiger baby*
Bourguignon, Laurence. *A friend for Tiger*
Bunting, Eve (Anne Evelyn). *Riding the tiger*
Butterfield, Moira. *Fast, strong, and striped*
Canning, Kate. *A painted tale*
Chichester Clark, Emma. *Follow the leader!*
Choi, Yangsook. *The sun girl and the moon boy*
Cowcher, Helen. *Tigress*
Currey, Anna. *Tickling tigers*
Davies, Gill. *Wilbur waited*
De Beer, Hans. *Little polar bear, take me home!*
Dines, Glen. *A tiger in the cherry tree*
Dodds, Siobhan. *Charles Tiger*
Domanska, Janina. *Why so much noise?*
Dowson, Nick. *Tigress*
Duncan, Lois. *Song of the circus*
Edwards, Roland. *Tigers*
Egan, Tim. *Friday night at Hodges' café*
Farber, Norma. *How to ride a tiger*
Fenner, Carol. *Tigers in the cellar*
Frankel, Bernice. *Half-As-Big and the tiger*
French, Vivian. *Little Tiger finds a friend*
   Little Tiger goes shopping
   Tiger and the new baby
   Tiger and the temper tantrum
Gleeson, Brian. *The tiger and the Brahmin*
Goode, Diane. *Tiger trouble*
Hall, Derek. *Tiger runs*
Hewett, Joan. *A tiger cub grows up*
   Tiger, tiger, growing up
Hoban, Russell. *The dancing tigers*
Hoberman, Mary Ann. *"It's simple," said Simon*
Hoffman, Eric. *No fair to tigers = No es justo para los tigres*
Hoffman, Mary. *Animals in the wild: tiger*
Hogrogian, Nonny. *The tiger of Turkestan*
Ipcar, Dahlov (Zorach). *Stripes and spots*

Justice, Jennifer. *The tiger*
Kasza, Keiko. *The rat and the tiger*
Kepes, Juliet. *Cock-a-doodle-doo*
Kerr, Judith. *The tiger who came to tea*
Kraus, Robert. *Leo the late bloomer*
   Little Louie the baby bloomer
Lester, Julius. *Sam and the tigers*
Lewis, Sharon. *Tiger!*
Milton, Joyce. *Big cats*
Nagda, Anne Whitehead. *A tiger tale*
O'Donnell, Peter. *Carnegie's excuse*
Offen, Hilda. *Good girl, Gracie Growler!*
Palecek, Libuse. *Brave as a tiger*
Parkison, Jami. *Amazing Mallika*
Partis, Joanne. *Stripe*
   Stripe's naughty sister
Paul, Anthony. *The tiger who lost his stripes*
Pluckrose, Henry Arthur. *Lions and tigers*
Prelutsky, Jack. *The terrible tiger*
Rockwell, Anne F. *Big boss*
Root, Phyllis. *Moon tiger*
Rose, Gerald. *The tiger-skin rug*
Round, Graham. *Hangdog*
St. Pierre, Stephanie. *Siberian tigers*
Seuss, Dr. *I can lick 30 tigers today and other stories*
Sykes, Julie. *I don't want to take a bath!*
   Little Tiger's big surprise
   Wait for me, Little Tiger
Taylor, Mark. *Henry explores the jungle*
Temple, Frances. *Tiger soup*
Theodorou, Rod. *Bengal tiger*
Thomson, Sarah L. *Tigers*
Tseng, Grace. *White tiger, blue serpent*
Tworkov, Jack. *The camel who took a walk*
Villarejo, Mary. *The tiger hunt*
Wahl, Jan. *Tiger watch*
Wallace, Karen. *Imagine you are a tiger*
Wersba, Barbara. *Do tigers ever bite kings?*
Whitehouse, Patricia. *Tiger*
Whitney, Alex. *Once a bright red tiger*
Winters, Kay. *Tiger trail*
Wolkstein, Diane. *The banza*
Wolski, Slawomir. *Tiger cat*
Xiong, Blia. *Nine-in-one Grr! Grr!*

Animals – walruses

Bridges, William. *Ookie, the walrus who likes people*
Hoff, Syd. *Walpole*
Rotter, Charles. *Walruses*
Stevenson, James. *Winston, Newton, Elton, and Ed*

Animals – warthogs

Base, Graeme. *Jungle drums*
Edwards, Pamela Duncan. *Slop goes the soup*
   Warthogs in a box
   Warthogs in the kitchen
   Warthogs paint
Hazen, Barbara Shook. *Wally the worry-warthog*

Animals – water buffaloes

Gobhai, Mehlli. *Lakshmi, the water buffalo who wouldn't*

Animals – weasels

Bach, Alice. *Warren Weasel's worse than measles*
Blake, Jon. *You're a hero, Daley B.!*
Ernst, Lisa Campbell. *Zinnia and Dot*
Ezra, Mark. *The sleepy dormouse*
Grant, Rose Marie. *Andiamo, Weasel*
Hallensleben, Georg. *Pauline*
Holder, Heidi. *Crows*
Lobel, Arnold. *Mouse soup*
Mathews, Louise. *Cluck one*
Zelinsky, Paul O. *The lion and the stoat*

Animals – whales

Allen, Judy. *Whale*
Appelbaum, Neil. *Is there a hole in your head?*
Archambault, John. *The birth of a whale*
Armitage, Ronda. *The lighthouse keeper's rescue*
Armour, Richard Willard. *Sea full of whales*
Auld, Mary. *The story of Jonah*
Baumann, Kurt. *The story of Jonah*
Behrens, June. *Whales of the world*
   Whalewatch!
Bellamy, David. *How green are you?*
Benchley, Nathaniel. *The deep dives of Stanley Whale*
Bible. Old Testament. Jonah. *The Book of Jonah*
   Jonah, ill. by Kurt Mitchell
   Jonah and the great fish, ill. by Leon Baxter
   Jonah and the great fish, ill. by Jim Cummins
Borovsky, Paul. *The fish that wasn't*
Bulla, Clyde Robert. *Jonah and the great fish*
Burton, Martin Nelson. *The whale comedian*
Cech, John. *The southernmost cat*
Clark, Harry. *The first story of the whale*
Climo, Shirley. *The adventure of Walter*
Conklin, Gladys. *Journey of the gray whales*
Cousteau Society. *Whales*
Davies, Nicola. *Big blue whale*
Davis, Maggie S. *A garden of whales*
Day, Edward C. *John Tabor's ride*
Drummond, Allan. *Moby Dick*
Dunbar, Joyce. *Indigo and the whale*
Duvoisin, Roger Antoine. *The Christmas whale*
Edwardson, Debby Dahl. *Whale snow*
Engle, Joanna. *Cap'n kid goes to the South Pole*
Fowler, Allan. *The biggest animal ever*
   Friendly dolphins
Franklin, Kristine L. *The gift*
French, Vivian. *Whale journey*
Gentle, Victor. *Orcas, killer whales*
Gerstein, Mordicai. *Jonah and the two great fish*
Gibbons, Gail. *Whales*
Goldsboro, Bobby. *Jonah and the whale; and, Daniel in the lion's den*
Grigg, Carol. *The singing snow bear*
Haiz, Danah. *Jonah's journey*
Hanze. *Yann and the whale*
Hayles, Karen. *What is stuck*
Hennessy, B. G. (Barbara G.). *Meet Winslow whale*
Himmelman, John. *Ibis*
Hirschi, Ron. *Where are my puffins, whales, and seals?*
Hudson, Eleanor. *A whale of a rescue*
Hurd, Edith Thacher. *What whale? Where?*
Hutton, Warwick. *Jonah and the great fish*
If you ever meet a whale
James, Simon. *Dear Mr. Blueberry*
   My friend whale
Johnston, Johanna. *Whale's way*
Johnston, Tony. *Whale song*
King, Patricia. *Mable the whale*
Lawson, Julie. *A morning to polish and keep*
Le Guin, Ursula K. *Solomon Leviathan's nine hundred and thirty-first trip around the world*
Lent, Blair. *John Tabor's ride*
Lewis, Paul Owen. *Storm boy*
Lewis, Sharon. *Orca! The killer whale*
Lilly, Kenneth. *Animals of the ocean*
Lobato, Arcadio. *The greatest treasure*
London, Jonathan. *Baby whale's journey*
McAllister, Angela. *The whales' tale*
McCloskey, Robert. *Bert Dow, deep-water man*
McDermott, Beverly Brodsky. *Jonah*
McFarlane, Sheryl. *Waiting for the whales*
McMillan, Bruce. *Going on a whale watch*
Maestro, Giulio. *The tortoise's tug of war*
Metaxas, Eric. *The boy and the whale*
Nobisso, Josephine. *Shh! the whale is smiling*
O'Neill, Alexis. *Loud Emily*
Oppel, Kenneth. *Peg and the whale*
Patterson, Geoffrey. *Jonah and the whale*

Pfister, Marcus. *Rainbow fish and the big blue whale*
Pitcher, Caroline. *The snow whale*
Pluckrose, Henry Arthur. *Whales*
Postgate, Oliver. *Noggin and the whale*
Raff, Courtney Granet. *Giant of the sea*
Raffi. *Baby beluga*
Raschka, Christopher. *Whaley Whale*
Roy, Ronald. *A thousand pails of water*
Ryder, Joanne. *Winter whale*
Rylant, Cynthia. *The whales*
Schlein, Miriam. *Sleep safe, little whale*
Schuch, Steve. *A symphony of whales*
Selsam, Millicent E. *A first look at whales*
Sheldon, Dyan. *The whales' song*
Siberell, Anne. *Whale in the sky*
Sis, Peter. *An ocean world*
Sobol, Richard. *Adelina's whales*
Stansfield, Ian. *The legend of the whale*
Steele, Philip. *The blue whale*
Steiner, Barbara (Annette). *The whale brother*
Strange, Florence. *Rock-a-bye whale*
Theodorou, Rod. *Blue whale*
Thomson, Sarah L. *Amazing whales*
Thorne, Jenny. *Jonah and the whale*
Tokuda, Wendy. *Humphrey the lost whale*
Van Dusen, Chris. *Down to the sea with Mr. Magee*
Watanabe, Yuichi. *Wally the whale who loved balloons*
   Whales
Williams, Marcia. *Jonah and the whale*
Wilson, Bob. *Stanley Bagshaw and the twenty-two ton whale*
Wilson, Lynn. *Baby whale*
Wood, Audrey. *Little Penguin's tale*

Animals – wildebeests

Berliner, Franz. *Wildebeest*

Animals – wolves

Æsop. *The boy who cried wolf*, ill. by Dianne Silverman
   The dog and the wolf
   The wolf in sheep's clothing
Allen, Jonathan. *Mucky moose*
Ambrus, Victor G. *Country wedding*
Asch, Frank. *Ziggy Piggy and the three little pigs*
Baynes, Pauline. *How dog began*
Bedard, Michael. *The wolf of Gubbio*
Berman, Ruth. *Watchful wolves*
Bishop, Adela. *The Easter wolf*
Blades, Ann. *Mary of mile 18*
Bloom, Becky. *Wolf*
Blundell, Tony. *Beware of boys*
Boyle, Doe. *Gray wolf pup*
Bradman, Tony. *Look out, he's behind you*
Brandenburg, Jim. *Scruffy*
Brett, Jan. *The first dog*
Brimner, Larry Dane. *The littlest wolf*
Brown, Ken (Ken James). *What's the time, Grandma Wolf?*
Bruna, Dick. *Dick Bruna's Little Red Riding Hood*
Bunting, Eve (Anne Evelyn). *On Call Back Mountain*
Child, Lauren. *Beware of the storybook wolves*
Christelow, Eileen. *Where's the big bad wolf?*
Cohen, Barbara. *The chocolate wolf*
Curti, Anna. *Seasons*
Damjan, Mischa. *Atuk*
   The wolf and the kid
Daudet, Alphonse. *The brave little goat of Monsieur Séguin*
Delaney, A. *The gunnywolf*
De Marolles, Chantal. *The lonely wolf*
De Regniers, Beatrice Schenk. *Red Riding Hood*
Dinardo, Jeffrey. *The wolf who cried boy*
Douzou, Olivier. *Wolf's lunch*
Dyjak, Elisabeth. *Bertha's garden*
Egan, Tim. *The experiments of Doctor Vermin*
Ernst, Lisa Campbell. *Little Red Riding Hood*
Evans, Katherine. *The boy who cried wolf*
Fearnley, Jan. *Mr. Wolf and the three bears*

Mr. Wolf's pancakes
Firmin, Peter. *Chicken stew*
Friskey, Margaret (Margaret Richards). *Indian Two Feet and the wolf cubs*
Gackenbach, Dick. *Harvey, the foolish pig*
Gay, Michel. *The Christmas wolf*
George, Jean Craighead. *Look to the north*
   Nutik and Amaroq play ball
   Nutik, the wolf pup
Goble, Paul. *The friendly wolf*
Gorbachev, Valeri. *Nicky and the big, bad wolves*
Grant, Rose Marie. *Andiamo, Weasel*
Greene, Carol. *Reading about the gray wolf*
Grimm, Jacob. *Little red cap*
   Little Red Riding Hood, ill. by Frank E. Aloise
   Little Red Riding Hood, ill. by Gwen Connelly
   Little Red Riding Hood, ill. by Paul Galdone
   Little Red Riding Hood, ill. by John S. Goodall
   Little Red Riding Hood, ill. by Trina Schart Hyman
   Little Red Riding Hood, ill. by Mireille Levert
   Little Red Riding Hood, ill. by David M. McPhail
   Little Red Riding Hood, ill. by Jean-François Martin
   Little Red Riding Hood, ill. by Bernadette Watts
   Nanny goat and the seven little kids
   The wolf and the seven kids, ill. by Kinuko Y. Craft
   The wolf and the seven little kids, ill. by Svend Otto S
   The wolf and the seven little kids, ill. by Martin Ursell
Gunthrop, Karen. *Adam and the wolf*
Guthrie, Donna. *This little pig stayed home*
Harper, Wilhelmina. *The gunniwolf*
Hartman, Bob. *The wolf who cried boy*
Hawkins, Colin. *What time is it, Mr. Wolf?*
Hayward, Linda. *Hello, house!*
Heinz, Brian J. *The wolves*
Hobbs, Will. *Howling Hill*
Hoffman, Alice. *Fireflies*
Jackson, Ellen B. *Boris the boring boar*
Jagtenberg, Yvonne. *Jack the wolf*
Janovitz, Marilyn. *Can I help?*
   Is it time?
Jessell, Tim. *Amorak*
Johnson, Janet P. *How Mr. Dog got tame*
Jones, Carol. *What's the time, Mr. Wolf?*
Judes, Marie-Odile. *Max, the stubborn little wolf*
Kasza, Keiko. *The wolf's chicken stew*
Kimmel, Eric A. *Sirko and the wolf*
Kimura, Yuichi. *One stormy night . . .*
   One sunny day . . .
Kitamura, Satoshi. *Sheep in wolves' clothing*
Klingel, Cynthia Fitterer. *Timber wolves*
Kraus, Robert. *Strudwick, a sheep in wolf's clothing*
Lairla, Sergio. *Abel and the wolf*
Lester, Helen. *Tacky the penguin*
Levine, Gail Carson. *Betsy who cried wolf*
Lewis, Rob. *Friska, the sheep that was too small*
Lindbergh, Reeve. *Bridget and the gray wolves*
London, Jonathan. *The eyes of Gray Wolf*
   Red wolf country
Lowell, Susan. *Little Red Cowboy Hat*
McClure, Gillian. *What's the time, Rory Wolf?*
MacDonald, Elizabeth. *The wolf is coming!*
McDonald, Megan. *The bone keeper*
McNaughton, Colin. *Oomph!*
   Oops!
   Preston's goal!
   Shh! (Don't tell Mr. Wolf!)
   Suddenly!
   Yum!
McPhail, David M. *A wolf story*
Marshall, James. *Red Riding Hood*
   Swine lake
Meddaugh, Susan. *The best place*
   Hog-eye
Moore, Maggie. *Little Red Riding Hood*
Morris, Ann. *The Little Red Riding Hood rebus book*
Murphy, Jim. *The call of the wolves*
Murray, Marjorie Dennis. *Little Wolf and the moon*

Novak, Matt. *Little Wolf, Big Wolf*
Offen, Hilda. *Nice work, little wolf!*
Palatini, Margie. *Piggie pie*
Parish, Peggy. *Granny, the baby and the big gray thing*
Peck, Robert Newton. *Hamilton*
Pinkwater, Daniel Manus. *Wolf Christmas*
Porter, Sue. *Little Wolf and the giant*
Prokofiev, Sergei Sergeievitch. *Peter and the wolf*, ill. by Reg Cartwright
   Peter and the wolf, ill. by Warren Chappell
   Peter and the wolf, ill. by Barbara Cooney
   Peter and the wolf, ill. by Julia Gukova
   Peter and the wolf, ill. by Frans Haacken
   Peter and the wolf, ill. by Alan Howard
   Peter and the wolf, ill. by Charles Mikolaycak
   Peter and the wolf, ill. by Jörg Müller
   Peter and the wolf, ill. by Josef Palecek
   Peter and the wolf, ill. by Kozo Shimizu
   Peter and the wolf, retold and ill. by Vladimir Vagin
   Peter and the wolf, ill. by Erna Voigt
Prusski, Jeffrey. *Bring back the deer*
Puttock, Simon. *Big bad wolf is good*
Rayner, Mary. *Garth Pig and the ice cream lady*
   Mr. and Mrs. Pig's evening out
Roche, Denis (Denis M.). *Little Pig is capable*
Rockwell, Anne F. *Romulus and Remus*
   The wolf who had a wonderful dream
Roddie, Shen. *Not now, Mrs. Wolf*
Ross, Gayle. *How Turtle's back was cracked*
Ross, Tony. *The boy who cried wolf*
   Stone soup
Roth, Susan L. *Kanahena*
Santangelo, Colony Elliott. *Brother Wolf of Gubbio*
Sara. *The rabbit, the fox, and the wolf*
Scamell, Ragnhild. *Who likes Wolfie?*
Schick, Alice. *Just this once*
Scieszka, Jon. *The true story of the three little pigs by A. Wolf, as told to Jon Scieszka*
Selsam, Millicent E. *A first look at dogs*
Sharmat, Marjorie Weinman. *Walter the wolf*
Sheehan, Patty. *Shadow and the ready time*
Souhami, Jessica. *No dinner!*
Spinelli, Eileen. *Thanksgiving at the Tappletons'*
Stevenson, Harvey. *Big scary wolf*
Storr, Catherine (Cole). *Clever Polly and the stupid wolf*
Sweeten, Sami. *Wolf*
The three little pigs. *The original three little pigs re-told*, ill. by Jonathan Smith
   The story of the three little pigs, ill. by L. Leslie Brooke
   The story of the three little pigs, ill. by William Stobbs
   Three little pigs [Facsimile ed]
   The three little pigs, ill. by Val Biro
   The three little pigs, ill. by Gavin Bishop
   The three little pigs, ill. by Erik Blegvad
   The three little pigs, ill. by Caroline Bucknall
   The three little pigs, ill. by Stephen Cartwright
   The three little pigs, ill. by Lorinda Bryan Cauley
   The three little pigs, ill. by Jean Claverie
   The three little pigs, ill. by Doug Cushman
   The three little pigs, ill. by William Pène Du Bois
   The three little pigs, ill. by Paul Galdone
   The three little pigs, ill. by Madelaine Gill
   The three little pigs, ill. by Rob Hefferan
   The three little pigs, ill. by Steven Kellogg
   The three little pigs, ill. by David McPhail
   The three little pigs, ill. by James Marshall
   The three little pigs, ill. by Paul Meisel
   The three little pigs, ill. by Rodney Peppé
   The three little pigs, ill. by Edda Reinl
   The three little pigs, ill. by John Wallner
   The three little pigs, ill. by Irma Wilde
   The three little pigs, ill. by Margot Zemach
   The three little pigs and the big bad wolf
   The three little pigs [board book], ill. by Thea Kliros
   The three pigs, ill. by Tony Ross
   Who's at the door?
Trivizas, Eugenios. *The three little wolves and the big bad pig*

Vozar, David. *Yo, hungry wolf!*
Whatley, Bruce. *Wait! No paint!*
Wild, Robin. *Little Pig and the big bad wolf*
Winters, Kay. *Wolf watch*
Wyllie, Stephen. *Dinner with fox*
Young, Ed (Edward). *Lon Po Po*
Ziefert, Harriet. *Little Red Riding Hood*

Animals – wombats

Argent, Kerry. *Happy birthday wombat!*
   Wombat and Bandicoot
Churchill, Vicki. *Sometimes I like to curl up in a ball*
Cushman, Doug. *The mystery of King Karfu*
Elks, Wendy. *Charles B. Wombat and the very strange thing*
Fox, Mem. *Wombat divine*
French, Jackie. *Diary of a wombat*
Morpurgo, Michael. *Wombat goes walkabout*

Animals – woodchucks *see* Animals – groundhogs

Animals – woolly mammoths

Miller, Debbie S. *Woolly mammoth journey*

Animals – worms

Ahlberg, Janet. *The little worm book*
Bailey, Jill. *Worm*
Barwin, Gary. *The racing worm brothers*
Caple, Kathy. *Worm gets a job*
Cronin, Doreen. *Diary of a worm*
Demi. *Where is Willie Worm?*
Glaser, Linda. *Wonderful worms*
Hayward, Linda. *The city worm and the country worm*
James, Brian. *Supertwins and the sneaky, slimy book worms*
Kaczman, James. *A bird and his worm*
Kraus, Robert. *Squirmy's big secret*
Lackner, Michelle Myers. *Toil in the soil*
Lindgren, Barbro. *A worm's tale*
Martin, David. *Piggy and Dad go fishing*
O'Callahan, Jay. *Herman and Marguerite*
O'Hagan, Caroline. *It's easy to have a worm visit you*
Pfeffer, Wendy. *Wiggling worms at work*
Pinczes, Elinor J. *Inchworm and a half*
Raschka, Christopher. *Wormy Worm*
San Souci, Robert D. *Two bear cubs*
Scarry, Richard. *Richard Scarry's busy houses*
Thayer, Jane. *Andy and the wild worm*
Wong, Herbert H. *Our earthworms*

Animals – yaks

Berger, Barbara Helen. *All the way to Lhasa*
Johnston, Tony. *Go track a yak*
Lawson, Annetta. *The lucky yak*

Animals – zebras

Castle, Caroline. *Naughty!*
Cousins, Lucy. *Za-Za's baby brother*
Gay, Michel. *Zee is not scared*
Goodall, Daphne Machin. *Zebras*
McKee, David. *Zebra's hiccups*
Miranda, Anne. *Alphabet fiesta*
Mwenye Hadithi. *Greedy zebra*
Padt, Maartje. *Shanti*
Paterson, Brian. *Zigby camps out*
   Zigby dives in
   Zigby hunts for treasure
Peet, Bill (William Bartlett). *Zella, Zack, and Zodiac*

Antarctic *see* Foreign lands – Antarctic

Anteaters *see* Animals – anteaters

Antelopes *see* Animals – antelopes

Anti-violence *see* Violence, nonviolence

Ants *see* Insects – ants

Apache *see* Indians of North America – Apache

Apartments *see* Homes, houses

Apes *see* Animals – baboons; Animals – chimpanzees; Animals – gorillas; Animals – monkeys

Appearance *see* Character traits – appearance

April Fools' Day *see* Holidays – April Fools' Day

Aprons *see* Clothing – aprons

Aquariums

Aliki. *My visit to the aquarium*
Binnamin, Vivian. *The case of the mysterious mermaid*
Calder, S. J. *If you were a fish*
Collins, Pat Lowery. *Don't tease the guppies*
Curious George goes to the aquarium
Rechner, Amy. *Out and about at the aquarium*

Arab Americans *see* Ethnic groups in the U.S. – Arab Americans

Arabia *see* Foreign lands – Arabia

Arachnids *see* Spiders

Archaeologists *see* Careers – archaeologists

Archery *see* Sports – archery

Architects *see* Careers – architects

Arctic *see* Foreign lands – Arctic

Argentina *see* Foreign lands – Argentina

Arguing *see* Behavior – fighting, arguing

Arithmetic *see* Counting, numbers

Armadillos *see* Animals – armadillos

Armenia *see* Foreign lands – Armenia

Art

Agee, Jon. *The incredible painting of Felix Clousseau*
Anderson, Douglas. *Let's draw a story*
Andrews-Goebel, Nancy. *The pot that Juan built*
Angelo, Nancy Carolyn Harrison. *Camembert*
Angelou, Maya. *My painted house, my friendly chicken, and me*
Anholt, Laurence. *Camille and the sunflowers*
Auch, Mary Jane. *Eggs mark the spot*
Baker, Jeannie. *Grandmother*
Baylor, Byrd. *When clay sings*
Bilgrami, Shaheen. *Jungle art show*
Black, Harley. *Amazing magic school*
Blizzard, Gladys S. *Come look with me*
   Come look with me
Boehm, Arlene P. *Jack in search of Art*
Bond, Michael. *Paddington's art exhibit*
Bornstein, Ruth Lercher. *That's how it is when we draw*
Borten, Helen. *Do you see what I see?*

Voigt, Hannelore. *Not now, Sara!*
Wabbes, Marie. *Rose's picture*
Waddell, Martin. *Alice the artist*
Waldman, Neil. *The starry night*
Wallace, Ian. *The naked lady*
Wallner, Alexandra. *Beatrix Potter*
Weitzman, Jacqueline Preiss. *You can't take a balloon into the Metropolitan Museum*
    You can't take a balloon into the National Gallery
Wellington, Monica. *Squeaking of art, the mice go to the museum*
Wheatley, Nadia. *Luke's way of looking*
Williams, Vera B. *Cherries and cherry pits*
Winter, Jeanette. *Cowboy Charlie*
    My baby
Winter, Jonah. *Diego*
Wolf, Janet. *The best present is me*
Wood, Michele. *Going back home*
Woodhouse, Jayne. *Pieter Bruegel*
Wooding, Sharon L. *The painter's cat*
Zadrzynska, Ewa. *The peaceable kingdom*
Zelinsky, Paul O. *The lion and the stoat*
Zelver, Patricia. *The wonderful Towers of Watts*

Artists *see* Careers – artists

Asia *see* Foreign lands – Asia

Asian Americans *see* Ethnic groups in the U.S. – Asian Americans

Assertiveness *see* Character traits – assertiveness

Asthma *see* Illness – asthma

Astrology *see* Zodiac

Astronauts *see* Careers – astronauts; Space & space ships

Astronomers *see* Careers – astronomers

Astronomy

Alberti, Theresa Jarosz. *Out and about at the planetarium*
Asch, Frank. *The sun is my favorite star*
Barlowe, Sy. *A child's book of stars*
Barner, Bob. *Stars, stars, stars*
Carpenter, Mary-Chapin. *Halley came to Jackson*
Crew, Gary. *Bright star*
Dussling, Jennifer. *Stars*
Fisher, Aileen Lucia. *Sing of the earth and sky*
Gibbons, Gail. *The planets*
    Stargazers
Hirst, Robin. *My place in space*
Holland, Simon. *Space*
Jones, Brian. *Space*
Leedy, Loreen. *Postcards from Pluto*
Markoe, Merrill. *The day my dogs became guys*
Ressmeyer, Roger. *Astronaut to zodiac*
Rockwell, Anne F. *Our stars*
Rosen, Sidney. *Where's the big dipper?*
Sis, Peter. *Starry messenger*
Sykes, Julie. *Little Rocket's special star*
Tomecek, Steve. *Stars*

Athabascan Indians *see* Indians of North America – Athabascan

Aunts *see* Family life – aunts, uncles

Aurora Borealis *see* Northern lights

Australia *see* Foreign lands – Australia

Australian aborigines

Germein, Katrina. *Big rain coming*
Lester, Alison. *Ernie dances to the didgeridoo*
Wolkstein, Diane. *Sun Mother wakes the world*

Austria *see* Foreign lands – Austria

Authors *see* Careers – authors

Authors, children *see* Children as authors

Autism *see* Handicaps – autism

Automobiles

Aldag, Kurt. *Some things never change*
Alexander, Anne (Anna Barbara Cooke). *ABC of cars and trucks*
Aulaire, Ingri Mortenson d'. *The two cars*
Barton, Byron. *My car*
Baugh, Dolores M. *Trucks and cars to ride*
Bell, Babs. *The bridge is up!*
Best, Cari. *When Catherine the Great and I were eight!*
Biro, Val. *Gumdrop and the birthday surprise*
    Gumdrop and the farmyard caper
    Gumdrop and the great sausage caper
    Gumdrop and the secret switches
    Gumdrop and the steamroller
    Gumdrop at the zoo
    Gumdrop beats the clock
    Gumdrop catches a cold
    Gumdrop finds a friend
    Gumdrop finds a ghost
    Gumdrop floats away
    Gumdrop gets a lift
    Gumdrop gets his wings
    Gumdrop goes to school
    Gumdrop has a birthday
    Gumdrop in double trouble
    Gumdrop is the best
    Gumdrop on the Brighton run
    Gumdrop races a train
    Gumdrop, the adventures of a vintage car
Blake, Quentin. *Mrs. Armitage: queen of the road*
Braithwaite, Jill. *Police cars*
Brandenberg, Franz. *What's wrong with a van?*
Bridwell, Norman. *Clifford's good deeds*
Broekel, Ray. *I can be an auto mechanic*
Brown, Don. *Alice Ramsey's grand adventure*
Bullard, Lisa. *Stock cars*
Buller, Jon. *Toad on the road*
Burningham, John. *Mr. Gumpy's motor car*
    Slam bang
Caines, Jeannette. *Just us women*
Campbell, Rod. *Funwheels with moving parts!*
Cars and trucks
Cars and trucks and other vehicles
Cartlidge, Michelle. *Bears on the go*
Cave, Ron. *Automobiles*
Christelow, Eileen. *Five little monkeys wash the car*
Collicutt, Paul. *This car*
Coy, John. *Night driving*
    Vroomaloom zoom
Cummings, W. T. (Walter Thies). *Miss Esta Maude's secret*
Dahl, Michael. *One checkered flag*
Demarest, Chris L. *My little red car*
DeSaix, Deborah Durland. *In the back seat*
DiFiori, Lawrence. *If I had a little car*
Dupasquier, Philippe. *A busy day at the garage*
Emberley, Ed (Edward Randolph). *Cars, boats, and planes*
Ets, Marie Hall. *Little old automobile*
Feldman, Barbara. *Going, going*
Flanagan, Alice K. *Mr. Yee fixes cars*
Florian, Douglas. *An auto mechanic*
Fowler, Richard. *Cat's car*
    Mr. Little's noisy car

Gammell, Stephen. *How about going for a ride*
Gay, Michel. *Little auto*
Gibbons, Faye. *Mama and me and the Model-T*
Gibbons, Gail. *Fill it up!*
Giffard, Hannah. *Fast car*
Greenblat, Rodney Alan. *Uncle Wizzmo's new used car*
Greene, Carla. *A motor holiday*
Greenfield, Eloise. *Kia Tanisha drives her car*
Greve, Andreas. *Christopher's dream car*
Hannan, Peter. *Sillyville or bust*
Harshman, Marc. *Roads*
Holl, Adelaide. *The ABC of cars, trucks and machines*
Howland, Naomi. *ABCDrive!*
Hurd, Thacher. *Zoom City*
Janosch. *The magic auto*
Jordan, Jennifer. *Albert goes to town*
Kirk, Daniel. *Lucky's twenty-four hour garage*
Kirk, David. *Miss Spider's new car*
Kolar, Bob. *Racer dogs*
Koralek, Jenny. *Night ride to Nanna's*
Lenski, Lois. *The little auto*
Leslie, Amanda. *Let's look inside the red car*
Löfgren, Ulf. *The traffic stopper that became a grandmother visitor*
Loomis, Christine. *We're going on a trip*
Maccarone, Grace. *Cars! Cars! Cars!*
MacKeen, Leslie Ann. *Who can fix it?*
McPartland, Suzy. *Zoom, car, zoom*
Mahy, Margaret. *The rattlebang picnic*
Mantegazza, Giovanna. *Look inside a car*
Manzano, Sonia. *No dogs allowed*
Marshall, James. *The Cut-Ups crack up*
Meister, Cari. *Busy, busy city street*
Mendoza, George. *Traffic jam*
Miranda, Anne. *Beep! beep!*
　　Vroom, chugga, vroom-vroom
Mitgutsch, Ali. *From rubber tree to tire*
Murphy, Stuart J. *Beep beep, vroom vroom!*
Nayer, Judy. *The happy little engine*
Newton, Laura P. *William the vehicle king*
Nilsén, Anna. *Drive your car*
Nobles, Kristen M. *Drive this book*
Osborne, Victor. *Rex, the most special car in the world*
Owen, Annie. *Bumper to bumper*
Oxenbury, Helen. *The car trip*
Parish, Herman. *Good driving, Amelia Bedelia*
Patron, Susan. *Dark cloud strong breeze*
Pearson, Debora. *Alphabeep*
Peet, Bill (William Bartlett). *Jennifer and Josephine*
Peppé, Rodney. *Little wheels*
Perry, Michael. *Daniel's ride*
Petrie, Catherine. *Hot Rod Harry*
Piehl, Janet. *Formula One race cars*
Pinkwater, Daniel Manus. *Tooth-gnasher superflash*
Pitcher, Caroline. *Cars and boats*
Potter, Tony. *See how it works: cars*
Pratt, Pierre. *Car*
Radford, Derek. *Harry at the garage*
Reasoner, Charles. *Who drives this?*
Rex, Michael. *My race car*
Robbins, Ken. *City/country*
Rockwell, Anne F. *Cars*
Rogers, Hal. *Cars*
Root, Phyllis. *Rattletrap car*
　　Rattletrap car [board book]
Royston, Angela. *Cars*
Rylant, Cynthia. *Tulip sees America*
Scarry, Huck. *On the road*
Scarry, Richard. *The great big car and truck book*
The scrubbly-bubbly car wash
Shuter, Jane. *Henry Ford*
Spier, Peter. *Bill's service station*
Spurr, Elizabeth. *Mrs. Minetta's car pool*
Stanley, Mandy. *On the move*
Steel, Danielle. *Freddie's trip*
Steen, Sandra. *Car wash*
Stille, Darlene R. *Police cars*
Stobbs, William. *A car called beetle*

Suen, Anastasia. *Red light, green light*
Todd, Mark. *Start your engines*
Walsh, Patricia. *Cars*
Walters, Virginia. *Are we there yet, Daddy?*
Wilkinson, Sylvia. *Automobiles*
　　I can be a race car driver
Wood, Tim. *Motor racing*
Young, Miriam Burt. *If I drove a car*
Ziefert, Harriet. *A car trip for Mole and Mouse*
　　Where's daddy's car?

Autumn *see* Seasons – fall

Award-winning books *see* Caldecott award books;
　　Caldecott award honor books

Aztec Indians *see* Indians of North America – Aztec

Babies *see also* Animals – babies; Birds – babies

Ahlberg, Allan. *Miss Brick, the builder's baby*
　　Mockingbird
Ahlberg, Janet. *The baby's catalogue*
　　Bye-bye, baby
　　Peek-a-boo!
Alexander, Martha G. *Nobody asked me if I wanted a baby sister*
Aliki. *Welcome, little baby*
Allen, Pamela. *A lion in the night*
Allen, Robert. *Ten little babies count*
　　Ten little babies dress
　　Ten little babies eat
　　Ten little babies play
Ancona, George. *It's a baby!*
Andreae, Giles. *There's a house inside my mommy*
Andry, Andrew C. *Hi, new baby*
　　How babies are made
Anglund, Joan Walsh. *Baby brother*
　　How many days has Baby to play?
　　Love is a baby
Anholt, Catherine. *Aren't you lucky!*
　　Here come the babies
　　Toddlers
　　What makes me happy?
　　When I was a baby
Anholt, Laurence. *Sophie and the new baby*
Appelt, Kathi. *Someone's come to our house*
Apperley, Dawn. *Don't wake the baby*
Arnstein, Helene S. *Billy and our new baby*
Asch, Frank. *Baby in the box*
　　Starbaby
Auch, Mary Jane. *Monster brother*
Baby's words
Baicker, Karen. *Pea pod babies*
Baird, Anne. *Baby socks*
　　Kiss, kiss
Baker, Charlotte. *Little brother*
Baker, Gayle. *Special delivery*
Ballard, Robin. *I used to be the baby*
　　When I am a sister
Banish, Roslyn. *Let me tell you about my baby*
Bauer, Marion Dane. *Grandmother's song*
Bendick, Jeanne. *What made you you?*
Bennett, Barbara. *Lion's precious gift*
Berends, Polly Berrien. *I heard said the bird*
Birdseye, Tom. *Waiting for baby*
Blackstone, Stella. *Baby high, baby low*
Boelts, Maribeth. *You're a brother, Little Bunny!*
Bogart, Jo Ellen. *Daniel's dog*

Bolognese, Don. *A new day*
Bond, Rebecca. *Just like a baby*
Bourgeois, Paulette. *Franklin's baby sister*
Bowen, Anne. *I loved you before you were born*
    When you visit Grandma and Grandpa
Boyd, Lizi. *Baby play*
    Baby's journal
    Sam is my half brother
Bradman, Tony. *Billy and the baby*
    This little baby
Brann, Esther. *A book for baby*
Breeze, Lynn. *Baby's animals*
    Baby's clothes
    Baby's food
    Baby's toys
    This little baby goes out
    This little baby's bedtime
    This little baby's morning
Brenner, Barbara A. *What the elephant told*
Brice, Tony. *Baby animals*
Brooks, Robert B. *So that's how I was born*
Brown, Craig McFarland. *In the spring*
Brown, Marc Tolon. *Arthur's baby*
Browne, Anthony. *The big baby*
    Changes
Brownlow, Michael. *Way out West – with a baby!*
Buck, Nola. *Hey, little baby!*
    How a baby grows
Bunting, Eve (Anne Evelyn). *Our teacher's having a baby*
    Twinnies
Burningham, John. *Avocado baby*
    The baby
Busy baby
Byars, Betsy Cromer. *Go and hush the baby*
Byers, Rinda M. *Mycca's baby*
Byrne, David. *Stay up late*
Calmenson, Stephanie. *Good for you!*
    Welcome, baby!
Carlson, Nancy L. *Poor Carl*
Carlstrom, Nancy White. *Before you were born*
    Kiss your sister, Rose Marie
Carter, Alden R. *Big brother Dustin*
Caseley, Judith. *Mama, coming and going*
    Silly baby
Cazet, Denys. *Dancing*
Chaffin, Lillie D. *Tommy's big problem*
Charlip, Remy. *Baby hearts and baby flowers*
    Sleepytime rhyme
Chess, Victoria. *Poor Esmé*
Chorao, Kay. *Baby's Christmas treasury*
    The baby's good morning book
    The cherry pie baby
    Knock at the door and other baby action rhymes
Christenson, Larry. *The wonderful way that babies are made*
Clarke, Gus. *Along came Eric*
Clifton, Lucille. *Everett Anderson's nine months long*
Coats, Lucy. *One hungry baby*
Cohen, Caron Lee. *Happy to you!*
Cohn, Janice I. *Molly's rosebush*
Cole, Babette. *Mommy laid an egg!*
    Truelove
Cole, Brock. *Larky Mavis*
Cole, Joanna. *How you were born*
    I'm a big brother
    I'm a big sister
    The new baby at your house
    When you were inside mommy
Collicott, Sharleen. *Mildred and Sam*
Collins, Pat Lowery. *Waiting for baby Joe*
Cooke, Trish. *So much*
Cooper, Helen (Helen F.). *Little monster did it!*
Corey, Dorothy. *Will there be a lap for me?*
Cottringer, Anne. *Ella and the naughty lion*
Cowell, Cressida. *What shall we do with the Boo-Hoo Baby?*
Cowen-Fletcher, Jane. *Baby angels*
Cuetara, Mittie. *Baby business*
Cullen, Catherine Ann. *Thirsty baby*

Cummings, Pat. *Angel baby*
Curtis, Jamie Lee. *Tell me again about the night I was born*
    When I was little
Cutler, Jane. *Darcy and Gran don't like babies*
Cuyler, Margery. *Shadow's baby*
Dahl, Tessa. *Babies, babies, babies*
Davies, Gill. *Wilbur waited*
Davis, Jennifer. *Before you were born*
Day, Alexandra. *Carl's masquerade*
Dedieu, Thierry. *Baby clown*
Delacre, Lulu. *Good times with baby*
De Paola, Tomie (Thomas Anthony). *The baby sister*
    Baby's first Christmas
Dewan, Ted. *Baby gets the zapper*
    Crispin and the 3 little piglets
Dilley, Becki. *Sixty fingers, sixty toes*
Dixon, Ann. *Waiting for Noël*
Douglas, Ann. *Baby science*
    Before you were born
Doyle, Malachy. *Baby see, baby do!*
Dragonwagon, Crescent. *Wind Rose*
Drescher, Henrik. *The strange appearance of Howard Cranebill, Jr.*
Driscoll, Debbie. *Baby comes home*
Dunn, Phoebe. *Baby's animal friends*
    Busy, busy toddlers
    I'm a baby!
Dunrea, Olivier. *It's snowing*
Edelman, Elaine. *I love my baby sister (most of the time)*
Falwell, Cathryn. *Nicky and Alex*
    Nicky and grandpa
    Nicky loves daddy
    Nicky, 1-2-3
    Nicky's walk
    We have a baby
    Where's Nicky?
Fearnley, Jan. *A special something*
Ferguson, Alane. *That new pet!*
Fisher, Iris L. *Katie-Bo*
Foord, Jo. *The book of babies*
Foreman, Michael. *Ben's baby*
Foulds, Elfrida Vipont. *The elephant and the bad baby*
Fowler, Susi Gregg. *When Joel comes home*
Franklin, Jonathan. *Don't wake the baby*
Frasier, Debra. *On the day you were born*
French, Simon. *Guess the baby*
French, Vivian. *Tiger and the new baby*
Fujikawa, Gyo. *Ten little babies*
Galbraith, Kathryn Osebold. *Roommates*
    Waiting for Jennifer
Garland, Sarah. *All gone!*
    Billy and Belle
    Oh, no!
    Polly's puffin
Gauch, Patricia Lee. *Christina Katerina and the great bear train*
Geddes, Anne. *Shapes*
Gelbard, Jane. *My bye-bye bottle book*
    My dressing book
    My eating book
    My sharing book
Gentieu, Penny. *Baby! Talk!*
    Grow! babies!
Gerstein, Mordicai. *The gigantic baby*
Gewing, Lisa. *Mama, daddy, baby and me*
Gikow, Louise. *Baby Kermit's Christmas*
    Bye-bye, pacifier
Gill, Joan. *Hush, Jon!*
Girard, Linda Walvoord. *You were born on your very first birthday*
Gliori, Debi. *Mr. Bear's new baby*
    New big sister
    Penguin post
Golding, Kim. *Alphababies*
Gorog, Judith. *Zilla Sasparilla and the mud baby*
Graham, Bob. *Crusher is coming!*
Graham, Richard. *Jack and the monster*
Grambling, Lois G. *Grandma tells a story*
Green, Jen. *Our new baby*
Greenberg, Barbara. *The bravest babysitter*

Greenberg, Judith E. *Adopted*
Greenfield, Eloise. *She come bringing me that little baby girl*
    Sweet baby coming
Greenfield, Monica. *The baby*
Greenstein, Elaine. *As big as you*
Grimes, Nikki. *Baby's bedtime*
Gutman, Anne. *Lisa's baby sister*
Haarhoff, Dorian. *Desert December*
Hains, Harriet. *My baby brother*
Haley, Amanda. *It's a baby's world*
Hamilton-Merritt, Jane. *Our new baby*
Hamm, Diane Johnston. *Rock-a-bye farm*
Hanson, Joan. *I don't like Timmy*
Hanson, Mary Elizabeth. *The difference between babies and cookies*
Harper, Anita. *It's not fair!*
Harris, Robie H. *Hi, new baby*
Hathorn, Libby (Elizabeth). *Freya's fantastic surprise*
Hayes, Sarah. *Eat up, Gemma*
Hayward, Linda. *Baby Moses*
Hazen, Barbara Shook. *Why couldn't I be an only kid like you, Wigger?*
Heap, Sue. *Cowboy Baby*
Hedderwick, Mairi. *Katie Morag and the tiresome Ted*
Heiligman, Deborah. *Babies*
Hello, baby
Helmering, Doris Wild. *We're going to have a baby*
Henderson, Kathy. *The baby dances*
    Baby knows best
    The baby's book of babies
    Bumpety bump
    Newborn
Hendrickson, Karen. *Baby and I can play*
    Fun with toddlers
Henley, Claire. *I'm a baby, too!*
Herter, Jonina. *Eighty-eight kisses*
Hesse, Karen. *Lavender*
Hest, Amy. *The babies are coming!*
    In the rain with Baby Duck
    Nannies for hire
    Off to school, Baby Duck
    You're the boss, Baby Duck
Hiatt, Fred. *Baby talk*
Hill, Susan. *King of kings*
Hillenbrand, Will. *Fiddle-i-fee*
Hindley, Judy. *What's in baby's morning*
Hines, Anna Grossnickle. *Big like me*
Hirsh, Marilyn. *Leela and the watermelon*
    Where is Yonkela?
Hobson, Laura Z. *"I'm going to have a baby!"*
Hoffman, Mary. *Henry's baby*
Hoffman, Phyllis. *Baby's first year*
Hoffman, Rosekrans. *Sister Sweet Ella*
Höjer, Dan. *Heart of mine*
Hol, Coby. *Tippy Bear and little Sam*
Holabird, Katharine. *Angelina's baby sister*
Holland, Viki. *We are having a baby*
Horowitz, Ruth. *Mommy's lap*
Hort, Lenny. *We're going on a treasure hunt*
    We're going on safari
Horton, Barbara Savadge. *What comes in spring?*
Hru, Dakari. *Tickle, tickle*
Hubbell, Patricia. *Bouncing time*
    Wrapping paper romp
Hudson, Cheryl Willis. *Animal sounds for baby*
    Good morning baby
    Good night baby
Hughes, Shirley. *Angel Mae*
    Being together
    Olly and me
Hurwitz, Johanna. *Russell's secret*
Hush little baby. *Hush little baby*, ill. by Aliki
    Hush, little baby, ill. by Marla Frazee
    Hush little baby, ill. by Shari Halpern
    Hush little baby, ill. by Jeanette Winter
    Hush little baby, ill. by Margot Zemach
Hutchins, H. J. (Hazel J.). *Two so small*
Hutchins, Pat. *Our baby is best*

    Where's the baby?
Hutton, Warwick. *Moses in the bulrushes*
Ife, Elaine. *Moses in the bulrushes*
Intrater, Roberta Grobel. *Peek-a-boo!*
    Smile!
Isaacs, Gwynne L. *Baby face*
Isadora, Rachel. *Babies*
I hear
I see
Jam, Teddy. *Night cars*
Jaramillo, Raquel. *Ride, baby, ride!*
Jarrell, Mary. *The knee baby*
Josephs, Rhoda. *The baby bubble book*
Kallok, Emma. *Gem*
Katz, Karen. *Over the moon*
    Where is baby's mommy?
Keats, Ezra Jack. *Peter's chair*
Keller, Holly. *Geraldine's baby brother*
    What Alvin wanted
Kelley, True. *Look, baby! Listen, baby! Do, baby!*
Kilroy, Sally. *Babies' bodies*
    Baby colors
    Busy babies
Kleven, Elisa. *A monster in the house*
Knight, Joan. *Opal in the closet*
Knight, Margy Burns. *Welcoming babies*
Knowlton, Laurie Lazzaro. *The Nativity*
Koehler, Phoebe. *The day we met you*
    Making room
Koller, Jackie French. *Baby for sale*
Komaiko, Leah. *Where can Daniel be?*
Kopper, Lisa. *Daisy is a mommy*
    Daisy knows best
    Daisy thinks she is a baby
    Good dog, Daisy
    I'm a baby, you're a baby
    Ten little babies
Krasilovsky, Phyllis. *The very little boy*
    The very little girl
Kraus, Robert. *Big brother*
    Robert Kraus' a sunny day in Babytown
    Robert Kraus' Babytown express
    Robert Kraus' meet the babies
    Robert Kraus' welcome to Babytown
Kroll, Virginia L. *She is born*
Kunhardt, Edith. *Where's Peter?*
Lagerlöf, Selma. *The changeling*
Lakin, Pat (Patricia). *Don't touch my room*
Langstaff, Nancy. *A tiny baby for you*
Lasky, Kathryn. *A baby for Max*
    Baby love
Lawrence, Michael (Michael C.). *Baby loves*
L'Engle, Madeleine. *The other dog*
Leonard, Marcia. *Babies help out*
    Busy babies
    Bye-bye, Baby-boo
    Night-night, Baby-boo
    Peek-a-boo, baby!
    What's that, Baby-boo?
    Where's Baby-boo?
Leuck, Laura. *My baby brother has ten tiny toes*
Levi, Dorothy Hoffman. *A very special sister*
Levine, Abby. *What did mommy do before you?*
Levinson, Riki. *Me baby!*
Levitin, Sonia. *Taking charge*
Lewis, Rose A. *I love you like crazy cakes*
Lewison, Wendy Cheyette. *Baby has a boo-boo*
    Bye-bye, baby
    Don't wake the baby!
    Our new baby
    Uh oh, baby
    Where's baby?
Lexau, Joan M. *Finders keepers, losers weepers*
Lindgren, Astrid. *I want a brother or sister*
Lindgren, Barbro. *Benny and the binky*
Lippman, Sidney. *A you're adorable*
Livingston, Myra Cohn. *B is for baby*

Shapp, Martha. *Let's find out about babies*
Shea, Pegi Deitz. *I see me!*
Sheffield, Margaret. *Before you were born*
   Where do babies come from?
Shields, Carol Diggory. *I wish my brother was a dog*
Showers, Paul. *Before you were a baby*
Slepian, Jan. *Lost moose*
Smith, Charles R. *I'll be there*
   My gal
Smith, Peter. *Jenny's baby brother*
Steel, Danielle. *Max's new baby*
Stein, Sara Bonnett. *Oh, baby!*
   That new baby
Steptoe, John. *Baby says*
Stevenson, James. *Rolling Rose*
   Worse than Willy!
Stimson, Joan. *Big Panda, Little Panda*
Stoeke, Janet Morgan. *A friend for Minerva Louise*
Stuve-Bodeen, Stephanie. *Mama Elizabeti*
Suen, Anastasia. *Baby born*
   Baby born [board book]
Tabby, Abigail. *Baby face*
Tafuri, Nancy. *The ball bounced*
   My friends
Taylor, Ann. *Baby dance*
Thayer, Jane. *Gus and the baby ghost*
Thomas, Iolette. *Janine and the new baby*
Thomas, Joyce Carol. *You are my perfect baby*
Thomas, Shelley Moore. *A baby's coming to your house*
Thompson, Carol. *Baby days*
Titherington, Jeanne. *Baby's boat*
   Baby's boat [board book]
   A place for Ben
Tucker, Sian. *At home*
   Going out
   My clothes
   My toys
Van der Beek, Deborah. *Superbabe!*
Van Laan, Nancy. *Mama rocks, Papa sings*
Vigna, Judith. *Couldn't we have a turtle instead?*
Voake, Charlotte. *Mr. Davies and the baby*
Von Königslöw, Andrea Wayne. *That's my baby?*
Vulliamy, Clara. *Bang and shout*
   Blue hat, red coat
   Boo baby boo!
   Ellen and Penguin and the new baby
   Good night, baby
   Yum yum
Waddell, Martin. *When the teddy bears came*
Wahl, Jan. *Mabel ran away with the toys*
   The sleepytime book
Wangerin, Walter. *Water come down*
Wardlaw, Lee. *The chair where bear sits*
Wattenberg, Jane. *Mrs. Mustard's baby faces*
Watts, Bernadette. *David's waiting day*
Weeks, Sarah. *Bite me, I'm a shape*
   Bite me, I'm a book
Wellington, Monica. *Baby at home*
   Baby in a buggy
   Baby in a car
Wells, Rosemary. *McDuff and the baby*
   Max cleans up
Weninger, Brigitte. *Will you mind the baby, Davy?*
West, Keith. *Little Pig's special day*
Weston, Martha. *Bad baby brother*
What do babies do?
What do toddlers do?
Wheeler, Lisa. *Jazz baby*
Whybrow, Ian. *A baby for Grace*
Wild, Margaret. *Midnight babies*
Wilds, Kazumi Inose. *Hajime in the North Woods*
Wilhelm, Hans. *It's too windy!*
Wilkes, Angela. *See how I grow*
Wilkowski, Susan. *Baby's Bris*
Williams, Barbara. *Jeremy isn't hungry*
Williams, Sam. *The baby's word book*
Williams, Susan. *Poppy's first year*

Williams, Vera B. *"More more more," said the baby*
Willis, Jeanne. *Earthlets as explained by Professor Xargle*
   What did I look like when I was a baby?
Wilner, Isabel. *The baby's game book*
Winter, Jeanette. *My baby*
Winter, Susan. *A baby just like me*
Wishinsky, Frieda. *Oonga boonga*, ill. by Suçie Stevenson
   Oonga boonga, ill. by Carol Thompson
Wong, Janet S. *Grump*
Yee, Wong Herbert. *A drop of rain*
Young, Ruth. *My blanket*
   The new baby
Zalben, Jane Breskin. *Baby Babka*
Ziefert, Harriet. *Baby Ben's bow-wow book*
   Baby Ben's busy book
   Baby Ben's go-go book
   Baby Ben's noisy book
   Before I was born
   Breakfast time!
   Bye-bye, daddy!
   Getting ready for new baby
   Good morning, sun!
   Let's get dressed!
   Pushkin meets the bundle
   Pushkin minds the bundle
   Talk, baby!
   Waiting for baby
Zolotow, Charlotte (Shapiro). *But not Billy*
   Do you know what I'll do?

Babies, new *see* Family life – new sibling

Baboons *see* Animals – baboons

Babysitting *see* Activities – babysitting

Bad day *see* Behavior – bad day

Badgers *see* Animals – badgers

Bagpipes *see* Musical instruments – bagpipes

Bakers *see* Careers – bakers

Baking *see* Activities – baking, cooking

Balalaikas *see* Musical instruments – balalaikas

Bali *see* Foreign lands – Bali

Ballerinas *see* Ballet; Careers – dancers

Ballet

Allen, Debbie. *Dancing in the wings*
Auch, Mary Jane. *Hen lake*
   Peeping Beauty
Baumgardner, Mary Alice. *Alexandra, keeper of dreams*
Bell, Anthea. *Swan Lake*
Berger, Barbara Helen. *The jewel heart*
Brandenberg, Alexa. *Ballerina flying*
Brighton, Catherine. *Nijinsky*
Burstein, Fred. *The dancer*
Chevance, Audrey. *Tutu*
Corey, Shana. *Ballerina bear*
Cristaldi, Kathryn. *Baseball ballerina*
   Baseball ballerina strikes out
De Paola, Tomie (Thomas Anthony). *Oliver Button is a sissy*
Edwards, Pamela Duncan. *Honk!*
Ellwand, David. *Cinderlily*
Eversole, Robyn Harbert. *The magic house*
The firebird. The firebird, ill. by Reg Cartwright
   The firebird, ill. by Francesca Crespi
   The firebird, ill. by Demi

The firebird, adapt. and ill. by Rachel Isadora
The firebird, ill. by Moira Kemp
The firebird, ill. by Kris Waldherr
The firebird, ill. by Boris Zvorykin
The tale of the firebird, ill. by Gennady Spirin
Fonteyn, Margot, Dame. *Coppélia*
French, Vivian. *One ballerina two*
Gallwey, Kay. *Dancing Daisy*
Gauch, Patricia Lee. *Bravo, Tanya*
   Dance, Tanya
   Presenting Tanya, the Ugly Duckling
   Tanya and Emily in a dance for two
   Tanya and the magic wardrobe
   Tanya steps out
Geras, Adèle. *Giselle*
   The nutcracker
   Sleeping beauty
   Swan Lake
   Time for ballet
Gray, Libba Moore. *My mama had a dancing heart*
Greaves, Margaret. *Petrushka*
Hague, Michael. *The nutcracker*
Hampshire, Susan. *Rosie's ballet slippers*
Hayward, Linda. *A day in the life of a dancer*
Hoffmann, E. T. A. *The nutcracker*, ill. by Francesca Crespi
   The nutcracker, ill. by Renée Graef
   The nutcracker, ill. by Rachel Isadora
   The nutcracker, ill. by Joanna Isles
   The nutcracker, ill. by Maurice Sendak
   The nutcracker, ill. by Lisbeth Zwerger
   The nutcracker ballet, ill. by Carolyn Ewing
   The nutcracker ballet, ill. by Vladimir Vasilévich Vagin
Holabird, Katharine. *Angelina and the princess*
   Angelina ballerina
   Angelina dances
   Angelina on stage
   Angelina's ballet class
Isadora, Rachel. *Lili at ballet*
   Lili on stage
   Max
   My ballet class
   My ballet diary
   Not just tutus
Jennings, Linda M. *Coppelia*
   The sleeping beauty
Jennings, Sharon. *Priscilla's paw de deux*
Kinerk, Robert. *Clorinda*
Kroll, Virginia L. *Can you dance, Dalila?*
Kuklin, Susan. *Going to my ballet class*
Lasky, Kathryn. *Starring Lucille*
Lemaître, Pascal. *Zelda's secret*
Lewison, Wendy Cheyette. *I wear my tutu everywhere!*
   Ten little ballerinas
Littlesugar, Amy. *Marie in fourth position*
McMullan, Kate (Hall). *Noel the first*
   Nutcracker Noel
Maiorano, Robert. *A little interlude*
Manson, Ainslie. *Ballerinas don't wear glasses*
Marshall, James. *Swine lake*
Marzollo, Jean. *Shanna's ballerina show*
Mills, Elaine. *Marinetta at the ballet*
Moers, Hermann. *Annie's dancing day*
Morris, Ann. *Little ballerinas*
Newsome, Jill. *Dream dancer*
O'Connor, Jane. *Nina, Nina and the copycat ballerina*
   Nina, Nina ballerina
   Nina, Nina, star ballerina
Oxenbury, Helen. *The dancing class*
Palazzo-Craig, Janet. *Ballet dancer*
Pavlova, Anna. *I dreamed I was a ballerina*
Pulver, Robin. *Alicia's tutu*
Richardson, Jean. *The bear who went to the ballet*
   Clara's dancing feet
   The sleeping beauty
Rose, Emma. *Ballet magic*
Schomp, Virginia. *If you were a . . . ballet dancer*
Sis, Peter. *Ballerina*

Sorine, Stephanie Riva. *Our ballet class*
Stanley, Mandy. *Lettice, the dancing rabbit*
Tilden, Ruth. *Sophie's dance class*
Wilkes, Angela. *The best book of ballet*
Yolen, Jane. *The firebird*
Young, Amy. *Belinda, the ballerina*
Ziefert, Harriet. *Dancing*
Zwerger, Lisbeth. *Swan Lake*

Ballooning *see* Activities – ballooning

Balloons *see* Toys – balloons

Balls *see* Toys – balls

Bandicoots *see* Animals – bandicoots

Bands *see* Musical instruments – bands

Banjos *see* Musical instruments – banjos

Barbers *see* Careers – barbers

Barns

Atwell, Debby. *Barn*
Brown, Craig McFarland. *My barn*
Brown, Margaret Wise. *Big red barn*, ill. by Felicia Bond
   Big red barn, ill. by Rosella Hartman
Carrick, Carol. *The old barn*
Climo, Lindee. *Chester's barn*
High, Linda Oatman. *Barn savers*
Johnston, Tony. *The barn owls*
Lindbergh, Reeve. *Benjamin's barn*
Martin, Bill (William Ivan). *Barn dance!*
Merrill, Jean. *Tell about the cowbarn, Daddy*
Miles, Miska. *The raccoon and Mrs. McGinnis*
Oppenheim, Joanne. *"Uh-oh!" said the crow*
Parnall, Peter. *Winter barn*
Schoenherr, John. *The barn*
Sewell, Helen Moore. *Blue barns*
Tafuri, Nancy. *The barn party*
Yolen, Jane. *Raising Yoder's barn*

Bartering *see* Activities – trading

Baseball *see* Sports – baseball

Bashfulness *see* Character traits – shyness

Basketball *see* Sports – basketball

Bathing *see* Activities – bathing

Bats *see* Animals – bats

Bavaria *see* Foreign lands – Austria; Foreign lands – Germany

Beaches *see* Sea & seashore – beaches

Bears *see* Animals – bears

Beasts *see* Monsters

Beauty shops

Barber, Barbara E. *Saturday at the new you*
Munsch, Robert N. *Makeup mess*
Wells, Rosemary. *Ruby's beauty shop*

Beavers *see* Animals – beavers

Beds *see* Furniture – beds

Bedtime

Alda, Arlene. *Sheep, sheep, sheep, help me fall asleep*
Alexander, Martha G. *Good night, Lily*
Allison, Diane Worfolk. *In window eight, the moon is late*
Anderson, Lena. *Bunny box*
   Bunny story
Anderson, Peggy Perry. *Time for bed, the babysitter said*
Anholt, Catherine. *Twins, two by two*
Appelt, Kathi. *Bayou lullaby*
   Cowboy dreams
Apperley, Dawn. *Blossom and Boo stay up late*
   Good night, sleep tight, little bunnies
Apple, Margot. *Blanket*
   Brave Martha
Archambault, John. *Counting sheep*
Arnold, Tedd. *No jumping on the bed!*
Asch, Frank. *Good night, Baby Bear*
   Goodnight horsey
   Milk and cookies
Asher, Sandy. *Princess Bee and the royal good-night story*
Ashforth, Camilla. *Horatio's bed*
Ashman, Linda. *How to make a night*
Atnip, Linda. *Miranda's magic garden*
Auch, Mary Jane. *Monster brother*
Aylesworth, Jim. *The good-night kiss*
   Teddy bear tears
   Tonight's the night
Baird, Anne. *No sheep*
Baker, Ken. *Brave little monster*
Ballard, Robin. *Tonight and tomorrow*
   When we get home
Bang, Molly. *One fall day*
   Ten, nine, eight
   Wiley and the hairy man
Banks, Kate (Katherine A.). *And if the moon could talk*
Barasch, Lynne. *Rodney's inside story*
Baring-Gould, S. (Sabine). *Now the day is over*
Barrett, Judi. *I hate to go to bed*
Bauer, Marion Dane. *Sleep, little one, sleep*
Baum, Louis. *I want to see the moon*
Bea, Holly. *Bless your heart*
Beck, Andrea. *Elliot's noisy night*
Beckman, Kaj. *Lisa cannot sleep*
Bedtime
Berenstain, Stan. *Bears in the night*
   The Berenstain bears and the slumber party
Bergman, Mara. *Musical beds*
Berridge, Celia. *Grandmother's tales*
Berry, Holly. *Busy Lizzie*
Bertrand, Lynne. *Dragon naps*
Blaustein, Muriel. *Bedtime, Zachary!*
Blocksma, Mary. *Did you hear that?*
Boelts, Maribeth. *Looking for Sleepy*
Bogan, Paulette. *Goodnight Lulu*
Bond, Felicia. *Poinsettia and the firefighters*
Bottner, Barbara. *There was nobody there*
Bowden, Joan Chase. *Bouncy baby bunny finds his bed*
Bowers, Kathleen Rice. *At this very minute*
Bowman, Pete. *Goodnight, teddy bear*
Boyd, Lizi. *Sweet dreams, Willy*
Boynton, Sandra. *Dinosaur's binkit*
   The going to bed book
   Good night, good night
Bozylinsky, Hannah Heritage. *Lala Salama*
Bradley, Kimberly Brubaker. *Favorite things*
Brandenberg, Franz. *Aunt Nina, good night*
Branford, Henrietta. *Little Pig Figwort can't get to sleep*
Breeze, Lynn. *This little baby's bedtime*
Briggs, Kelly Paul. *Lighthouse lullaby*
Brisson, Pat. *Star blanket*
Brown, Margaret Wise. *A child's good night book*
   Goodnight moon
   Little Donkey close your eyes
   Sleepy ABC

   The sleepy men
Buchholz, Quint. *Sleep well, little bear*
Bullard, Lisa. *Not enough beds!*
Bunting, Eve (Anne Evelyn). *No nap*
Burleigh, Robert. *It's funny where Ben's train takes him*
Butler, John. *While you were sleeping*
Butterworth, Nick. *When it's time for bed*
Cabrera, Jane. *Bear's good night*
Calhoun, Mary. *While I sleep*
Callen, Larry. *Dashiel and the night*
Calmenson, Stephanie. *All aboard the goodnight train*
Cameron, Ann. *Harry (the monster)*
Camp, Lindsay. *The biggest bed in the world*
Campbell, Alison. *Are you asleep, rabbit?*
Capucilli, Alyssa Satin. *Biscuit*
Carlstrom, Nancy White. *Northern lullaby*
   Swim the silver sea, Joshie Otter
Carpenter, Mary-Chapin. *Dreamland*
Cartlidge, Michelle. *Good night, Teddy*
Caseley, Judith. *Slumber party!*
Castle, Caroline. *Naughty!*
Catalanotto, Peter. *Christmas always . . .*
Cave, Kathryn. *Out for the count*
Cazet, Denys. *I'm not sleepy*
   Mother night
   Night lights
Charlip, Remy. *Baby hearts and baby flowers*
Chevalier, Christa. *Spence and the sleepytime monster*
Child, Lauren. *I am not sleepy and I will not go to bed*
Chislett, Gail. *Whump*
Chorao, Kay. *Lemon moon*
Christelow, Eileen. *Five little monkeys jumping on the bed*
   Henry and the dragon
Cleary, Beverly. *Petey's bedtime story*
Clise, Michele Durkson. *Ophelia's bedtime book*
Coats, Lucy. *One hungry baby*
Coatsworth, Elizabeth. *Good night*
Cole, Joanna. *Sweet dreams, Clown-Arounds!*
Cole, William. *Frances face-maker*
Compton, Kenn. *Granny Greenteeth and the noise in the night*
Corddry, Thomas I. *Kibby's big feat*
Cosgrove, Stephen (Edward). *Sleepy time bunny*
Count in the dark with Glo Worm
Cousins, Lucy. *Maisy goes to bed*
   Maisy's bedtime
Coy, John. *Vroomaloom zoom*
Crum, Shutta. *All on a sleepy night*
Dahl, Roald. *Dirty beasts*
Dale, Penny. *Bet you can't*
   Ten out of bed
   Ten play hide-and-seek
Dalmais, Anne-Marie. *The Best bedtime stories of Mother Bear*
   Best bedtime stories of Mother Cat
   Best bedtime stories of Mother Hen
   Best bedtime stories of Mother Mouse
   Best bedtime stories of Mother Pig
   Best bedtime stories of Mother Sheep
Damjan, Mischa. *How do dinosaurs say goodnight?*
Davis, Katie (Katie I.). *I hate to go to bed!*
Davol, Marguerite W. *Batwings and the curtain of night*
Denton, Kady MacDonald. *Granny is a darling*
De Paola, Tomie (Thomas Anthony). *Fight the night*
   Pajamas for Kit
De Vries, Maggie. *How sleep found Tabitha*
Dowling, Paul. *Are you sleepy, Puff?*
   Splodger
The drowsy hours
Dubowski, Cathy East. *Snug Bug*
Duke, Kate. *Aunt Isabel tells a good one*
   Bedtime
Dunbar, Joyce. *Tell me something happy before I go to sleep*
Dunnick, Regan. *Sweet dreams, Douglas*
Edwards, Frank B. *Melody Mooner stayed up all night*
Edwards, Nicola. *Goodnight Baxter*
Edwards, Richard. *Good night, Copycub*
Eilenberg, Max. *Cowboy Kid*
Emberley, Ed (Edward Randolph). *Go away, big green monster!*

Engel, Diana. *Circle song*
Engvick, William. *Lullabies and night songs*
Eriksson, Eva. *Hocus-pocus*
Erskine, Jim. *Bedtime story*
Facklam, Margery. *I go to sleep*
Faulkner, Keith. *The scared little bear*
Fearnley, Jan. *Just like you*
Feldman, Eve B. *Animals don't wear pajamas*
Flattinger, Hubert. *Stormy night*
Foreman, Michael. *Dad! I can't sleep*
Foster, Karen Sharp. *Good night my little chicks = Buenas noches mis pollitos*
Fox, Mem. *A bedtime story*
　Time for bed
Fox, Siv Cedering. *The blue horse and other night poems*
Freedman, Claire. *Hushabye Lily*
　Night-night, Emily
Freedman, Sally. *Devin's new bed*
Gabriel, Ashala. *Night night toes*
Gackenbach, Dick. *Poppy the panda*
Galouchko, Annouchka. *Shô and the demons of the deep*
Gamble, Isobel. *Who's that?*
Gardiner, Lindsey. *Good night, Poppy and Max*
Garland, Sherry. *Goodnight, cowboy*
Gay, Marie-Louise. *Moonbeam on a cat's ear*
Gay, Michel. *Zee is not scared*
Gerstein, Mordicai. *Bedtime, everybody!*
　William, where are you?
Ginsburg, Mirra. *Asleep, asleep*
　Which is the best place?
Gliori, Debi. *Flora's blanket*
　A lion at bedtime
　Polar Bolero
　When I'm big
Goffstein, M. B. (Marilyn Brooke). *Sleepy people*
Goldsmith, Howard. *Sleepy little owl*
Goode, Diane. *I hear a noise*
Goodman, Joan Elizabeth. *Bernard's nap*
Goodspeed, Peter. *A rhinoceros wakes me up in the morning*
Gorbachev, Valeri. *Nicky and the big, bad wolves*
Gordon, Jeffie Ross. *Two badd babies*
Graff, Nancy Price. *In the hush of the evening*
Grambling, Lois G. *Night sounds*
Greenberg, Dan. *The bed who ran away from home*
Greenleaf, Ann. *No room for Sarah*
Greenstein, Elaine. *Dreaming*
Gregory, Valiska. *Kate's giants*
Gretz, Susanna. *Hide-and-seek*
　I'm not sleepy
　Ready for bed
　Too dark!
Greydanus, Rose. *Bedtime story*
Grimes, Nikki. *Baby's bedtime*
Grindley, Sally. *Knock, knock! Who's there?*
Gurney, John. *Dinosaur train*
Hague, Kathleen. *Good night, fairies*
Haines, Mike. *Countdown to bedtime*
Hamm, Diane Johnston. *How many feet in the bed?*
　Rock-a-bye farm
Hancock, Joy Elizabeth. *The loudest little lion*
Harley, Bill. *Nothing happened*
Harris, Dorothy Joan. *Goodnight Jeffrey*
Harshman, Marc. *All the way to morning*
Harshman, Terry Webb. *Porcupine's pajama party*
Hawkins, Colin. *Dip, dip, dip*
　I'm not sleepy!
　One finger, one thumb
　Oops-a-Daisy
　Where's bear?
Hawkins, Mark. *A lion under her bed*
Hazelaar, Cor. *Zoo dreams*
Heap, Sue. *Cowboy Baby*
Heiligman, Deborah. *Into the night*
Heller, Nicholas. *This little piggy*
Hendra, Sue. *Oliver's wood*
Hendry, Diana. *The very noisy night*
Hennessy, B. G. (Barbara G.). *Sleep tight*

Hest, Amy. *Kiss good night*
　Mabel dancing
Hill, Eric. *Baby Bear's bedtime*
Himmelman, John. *Lights out!*
Hindley, Judy. *Maybe it's a pirate*
　The sleepy book
Hines, Anna Grossnickle. *Rumble thumble boom!*
Hissey, Jane. *Hoot*
　Little bear's bedtime
Hoban, Russell. *Bedtime for Frances*
　Goodnight
Holabird, Katharine. *Alexander and the dragon*
Hood, Thomas. *Before I go to sleep*
Hopkins, Lee Bennett. *Go to bed!*
Hopkins, Margaret. *Sleepytime for baby mouse*
Horowitz, Ruth. *Bat time*
Hudson, Cheryl Willis. *Good night baby*
Hunter, Sally. *Humphrey's bedtime*
Hutchins, Pat. *Little pink pig*
Imbody, Amy. *Snug as a bug?*
Impey, Rose. *The flat man*
Inkpen, Mick. *Kipper's bedtime*
　Lullabyhullaballoo!
　One bear at bedtime
　Wibbly Pig can dance!
Ipcar, Dahlov (Zorach). *The calico jungle*
Irving, John. *A sound like someone trying not to make a sound*
Janovitz, Marilyn. *Is it time?*
Jeffers, Susan. *All the pretty horses*
Jennings, Sharon. *No monsters here*
Johnson, Jane. *Today I thought I'd run away*
Johnston, Tony. *Little bear sleeping*
　Little Rabbit goes to sleep
Jonas, Ann. *The quilt*
Joslin, Sesyle. *Brave Baby Elephant*
Joyce, William. *Sleepy time Olie*
Kalman, Maira. *Hey Willy, see the pyramids!*
Kamen, Gloria. *"Paddle," said the swan*
Kamish, Daniel. *The night scary beasties popped out of my head*
Katz, Avner. *The little pickpocket*
Keller, Holly. *Ten sleepy sheep*
Kellogg, Steven (Stephen). *A-hunting we will go!*
Kelly, Mij. *William and the night train*
Kent, Jack. *The once-upon-a-time dragon*
Khalsa, Dayal Kaur. *Sleepers*
Khan, Rukhsana. *Bedtime ba-a-a-lk*
King, Christopher L. *The vegetables go to bed*
Kirk, Daniel. *Hush, little alien*
Kitamura, Satoshi. *When sheep cannot sleep*
Knutson, Kimberley. *Bed bouncers*
Koide, Tan. *May we sleep here tonight?*
Koller, Jackie French. *No such thing*
Kotzwinkle, William. *The nap master*
Krahn, Fernando. *Sleep tight, Alex Pumpernickel*
Kramsky, Jerry. *The cranky sun*
Kraus, Robert. *Good night little one*
　Good night Richard Rabbit
Krauss, Ruth. *Goodnight, goodnight, sleepyhead*
Krensky, Stephen. *Fraidy Cats*
Krosoczka, Jarrett J. *Good night, Monkey Boy*
Kuskin, Karla. *The Dallas Titans get ready for bed*
　Night again
　A space story
Laimgruber, Monika. *Susannah and the Sandman*
Langreuter, Jutta. *Little Bear won't go to bed*
Lansky, Bruce. *Sweet dreams*
Larrick, Nancy. *When the dark comes dancing*
Leaf, Munro. *Boo, who used to be scared of the dark*
Leonard, Marcia. *Night-night, Baby-boo*
Lesser, Carolyn. *The goodnight circle*
Lester, Alison. *Ruby*
Lesynski, Loris. *Night school*
Leuck, Laura. *Goodnight, baby monster*
Levine, Joan. *A bedtime story*
Lewis, Kim. *Good night, Harry*
Lewison, Wendy Cheyette. *Going to sleep on the farm*
　My favorite doll

Lifton, Betty Jean. *Goodnight orange monster*
Lipniacka, Ewa. *To bed . . . or else!*
Lippman, Peter. *New at the zoo*
Litowinsky, Olga. *Boats for bedtime*
Lively, Penelope. *Good night, sleep tight*
Lloyd, Errol. *Nandy's bedtime*
Lobe, Mira. *Valerie and the good-night swing*
London, Jonathan. *Froggy goes to bed*
Lullaby and goodnight
Lum, Kate. *What! cried Granny*
Lundell, Margo. *The furry bedtime book*
Lundgren, Mary Beth. *Seven scary monsters*
McAllister, Angela. *Night-night, little one*
    Sleepy Ella
McBratney, Sam. *The caterpillow fight*
    The dark at the top of the stairs
    Guess how much I love you
    In the light of the moon and other bedtime stories
Maccarone, Grace. *A child's good night prayer*
McCarthy, Bobette. *Dreaming*
McCourt, Lisa. *Good night, Princess Pruney Toes*
    I love you, Stinky Face
McCullough, Sharon Pierce. *Bunbun at bedtime*
MacDonald, Margaret Read. *Tuck-me-in tales*
McDonald, Megan. *Bedbugs*
McGee, Marni. *Sleepy me*
McGuire, Leslie. *Baby night owl*
Mack, Stanley (Stan). *Ten bears in my bed*
MacKinnon, Debbie. *Find monkey!*
McMullan, Kate (Hall). *Good night, Stella*
    If you were my bunny
McPartland, Suzy. *Sleepy-time moon*
McPhail, David M. *The dream child*
Mählqvist, Stefan. *I'll take care of the crocodiles*
Maitland, Barbara. *My bear and me*
Mallat, Kathy. *Seven stars, more!*
Marcin, Marietta. *A zoo in her bed*
Maris, Ron. *My book*
Marshall, James. *What's the matter with Carruthers?*
Marshall, Margaret. *Mike*
Marzollo, Jean. *Close your eyes*
Mason, Jane B. *The wee puppy who wouldn't go to sleep*
Mathews, Judith. *Nathaniel Willy, scared silly*
Matura, Mustapha. *Moon jump*
Mayer, Mercer. *Little Monster's bedtime book*
    There's a nightmare in my closet
    There's an alligator under my bed
Mayper, Monica. *After good-night*
Meade, Holly. *A place to sleep*
Melmed, Laura Krauss. *The first song ever sung*
    Jumbo's lullaby
Merriam, Eve. *Goodnight to Annie*, ill. by Carol Schwartz
    Goodnight to Annie, ill. by John Wallner
Michelson, Richard. *Did you say ghosts?*
Miles, Sally. *Alfi and the dark*
Miller, J. P. (John Parr). *Good night, Little Rabbit*
Miller, Virginia. *Go to bed!*
Mitchard, Jacquelyn. *Baby bat's lullaby*
Montgomery, Michael G. *'Night, America*
Montresor, Beni. *Bedtime!*
Moon, Nicola. *Tick-tock, drip-drop*
The moon's the north wind's cooky
Moore, Julia. *While you sleep*
Morgan, Allen. *Nicole's boat*
Morgan, Mary. *My good night book*
Morgan-Vanroyen, Mary. *Sleep tight, little mouse*
Morgenstern, Constance. *Good night, feet*
Morozumi, Atsuko. *Time for bed*
Morris, Ann. *Cuddle up*
    Kiss time
    Night counting
    Sleepy, sleepy
Morris, Terry Nell. *Good night, dear monster!*
Morris, Winifred. *What if the shark wears tennis shoes?*
Morton, Lone. *Hurry up, Molly = Apúrate, Molly*
    Hurry up, Molly = Dépêche-toi, Molly
Mother Goose. *Hush-a-bye baby*, ill. by Nicola Bayley

Mueller, Virginia. *Monster can't sleep*
Munsch, Robert N. *Mortimer*
Muntean, Michaela. *Kermit and Robin's scary story*
Murphy, Jill. *A quiet night in*
    What next, baby bear!
Murray, Marjorie Dennis. *The stars are waiting*
Nakamura, Katherine Riley. *Song of night*
Namm, Diane. *Bunny's bedtime*
Nichol, B. P. *On the merry-go-round*
    Once, a lullaby
Nixon, Joan Lowery. *Will you give me a dream?*
Nobisso, Josephine. *The moon's lullaby*
    Shh! the whale is smiling
O'Brien, Mary. *Counting sheep to sleep*
O'Donnell, Elizabeth Lee. *Sing me a window*
Ogburn, Jacqueline K. *Noise lullaby*
Ohi, Ruth. *Pants off first*
O'Keefe, Susan Heyboer. *Good night, God bless*
Oppenheim, Joanne. *The story book prince*
Oppenheim, Shulamith Levey. *What is the full moon full of?*
Orgel, Doris. *Little John*
Ormerod, Jan. *Moonlight*
Otto, Carolyn. *Dinosaur chase*
Owen, Annie. *Goodnight bear!*
Owen, Roy. *My night forest*
Oxenbury, Helen. *Good night, good morning*
Packard, Mary. *We are monsters*
Paul, Ann Whitford. *Everything to spend the night . . . from A to Z*
Pearson, Susan. *When baby went to bed*
Peck, Richard. *Monster night at Grandma's house*
Pedersen, Judy. *When night time comes near*
Penner, Lucille Recht. *Lights out!*
Petersham, Maud. *Off to bed*
Pfister, Marcus. *I see the moon*
Piers, Helen. *Who's in my bed?*
Pierson, Judith Patterson. *The always moon*
Plath, Sylvia. *The bed book*
Plotz, Helen. *A week of lullabies*
Plourde, Lynn. *Wild child*
Pomerantz, Charlotte. *All asleep*
    Posy
Pow, Tom. *Tell me one thing, Dad*
Preston, Edna Mitchell. *Monkey in the jungle*
Pryor, Ainslie. *The baby blue cat who said no*
Pumphrey, Jerome. *Creepy things are scaring me*
Purmell, Ann. *Where wild babies sleep*
Quackenbush, Robert M. *Batbaby*
Raschka, Christopher. *Can't sleep*
Rathmann, Peggy. *10 minutes till bedtime*
Ray, Karen. *Sleep song*
Rees, Mary. *Ten in a bed*
Reiser, Lynn. *Bedtime cat*
    Little clam
    Night thunder and the Queen of the Wild Horses
Rice, Eve. *Goodnight, goodnight*
Richardson, Bill. *But if they do*
Richardson, John. *Ten bears in a bed*
Richter, Mischa. *To bed, to bed!*
Riddell, Chris. *Mr. Underbed*
Ripley, Catherine. *Why do stars twinkle?*
Robbins, Beth. *Tom's afraid of the dark*
Robbins, Maria Polushkin. *Mother, Mother, I want another*
    Mother, Mother I want another
Roberts, Bethany. *Gramps and the fire dragon*
    Waiting-for-Christmas stories
Robison, Deborah. *No elephants allowed*
Rock, Lois. *God bless me, God bless you*
Rockwell, Anne F. *Buster and the bogeyman*
Rogers, Paul (Patrick). *Somebody's sleepy*
Rohmann, Eric. *The cinder-eyed cats*
Root, Phyllis. *Ten sleepy sheep*
Rosen, Michael (1946–). *Under the bed*
Rosenberg, Liz. *Adelaide and the night train*
    Eli's night-light
Roth, Carol. *Ten dirty pigs / Ten clean pigs*
Roth, Susan L. *Night-time numbers*
Rothstein, Gloria. *Sheep asleep*

Rusackas, Francesca. *Daddy all day long*
Russo, Marisabina. *Why do grownups have all the fun?*
Rydell, Katy. *Wind says good night*
Sage, James. *To sleep*
Saltzberg, Barney. *It must have been the wind*
Sanromán, Susana. *Señora Regañona*
Sardegna, Jill. *K is for kiss good night*
Schaefer, Carole Lexa. *Down in the woods at sleepytime*
    Down in the woods at sleepytime [board book]
    Someone says
Schertle, Alice. *Goodnight, Hattie, my dearie, my dove*, ill. by Linda
    Strauss Edwards
    Goodnight, Hattie, my dearie, my dove, ill. by Ted Rand
Schindel, John. *Who are you?*
Schlein, Miriam. *Sleep safe, little whale*
Schneider, Nina. *While Susie sleeps*
Schotter, Roni. *Bunny's night out*
Schreier, Joshua. *Luigi's all-night parking lot*
Schubert, Ingrid. *There's a crocodile under my bed!*
Schwartz, Amy. *Some babies*
Scotton, Rob. *Russell the sheep*
Shannon, David. *David gets in trouble*
Sharmat, Marjorie Weinman. *Go to sleep, Nicholas Joe*
    Goodnight, Andrew. Goodnight, Craig
Shepperson, Rob. *The sandman*
Shipton, Jonathan. *In the night*
Showers, Paul. *Sleep is for everyone*
Silverman, Erica. *Follow the leader*
Simmons, Jane. *The dreamtime fairies*
    Go to sleep, Daisy
Simms, Laura. *The squeaky door*
Simon, Carly. *Midnight farm*
Skorpen, Liesel Moak. *Outside my window*
Slate, Joseph. *The star rocker*
Slingsby, Janet. *Hush-a-bye babies*
Smee, Nicola. *Finish the story, dad*
Smith, Edward Biko. *A lullaby for Daddy*
Smith, Robert Paul. *Nothingatall, nothingatall, nothingatall*
Spinelli, Eileen. *When Mama comes home tonight*
    Where is the night train going?
Sproule, Gail. *Singing the dark*
Staub, Leslie. *Bless this house*
Steer, Dougald. *Just one more story*
Steiner, Charlotte. *The sleepy quilt*
Stevens, Kathleen. *The beast in the bathtub*
Stevenson, Harvey. *Big scary wolf*
Stevenson, James. *We can't sleep*
    What's under my bed?
Stickland, Paul. *Bears*
Stock, Catherine. *Alexander's midnight snack*
Stoddard, Sandol. *Bedtime for bear*
    Bedtime mouse
    Turtle time
Stone, Kazuko G. *Goodnight Twinklegator*
Storm, Theodor. *Little Hobbin*
Strahl, Rudi. *Sandman in the lighthouse*
Strand, Mark. *The planet of lost things*
Sugita, Yutaka. *Good night 1, 2, 3*
Sussman, Susan. *Hippo thunder*
Sutherland, Harry A. *Dad's car wash*
Swados, Elizabeth. *Lullaby*
Swain, Ruth Freeman. *Bedtime!*
Sweeney, Jacqueline. *Katie and the night noises*
Tafuri, Nancy. *What the sun sees / What the moon sees*
Takamado no Miya Hisako. *Katie and the dream-eater*
Taylor, Livingston. *Pajamas*
Thomas, Shelley Moore. *Good night, Good Knight*
    Putting the world to sleep
Thompson, Lauren. *Little Quack's bedtime*
Titherington, Jeanne. *Baby's boat*
    Baby's boat [board book]
    A child's prayer
Tobias, Tobi. *Chasing the goblins away*
Trez, Denise. *Good night, Veronica*
Trottier, Maxine. *Dreamstones*
Türk, Hanne. *Goodnight Max*
Twining, Edith. *Sandman*

Van Leeuwen, Jean. *The tickle stories*
Velthuijs, Max. *Frog is frightened*
Viorst, Judith. *My mama says there aren't any zombies, ghosts, vam-
    pires, creatures, demons, monsters, fiends, goblins, or things*
Vulliamy, Clara. *Good night, baby*
Wabbes, Marie. *Good night, Little Rabbit*
Waber, Bernard. *Bearsie Bear and the surprise sleepover party*
    Ira sleeps over
Waddell, Martin. *Can't you sleep, Little Bear?*
    Night night Cuddly Bear
    Tom Rabbit
    Who do you love?
Wahl, Jan. *Elf night*
    Humphrey's bear
    The sleepytime book
Wallace, John. *Anything for you*
Wallace, Nancy Elizabeth. *Rabbit's bedtime*
Wallen, Ila. *The moon in my room*
Wallwork, Amanda. *Sleep songs*
Walsh, Melanie. *Hide and sleep*
Walty, Margaret. *Rock-a-bye baby*
Warnick, Elsa. *Bedtime*
Watson, Clyde. *Fisherman lullabies*
    Midnight moon
Weedn, Flavia. *I feel happy*
Weir, Alison. *Peter, good night*
Weiss, Nicki. *Where does the brown bear go?*
    Where does the brown bear go? [board book]
Wells, Rosemary. *Goodnight Max*
    Max's bedtime
Westcott, Nadine Bernard. *Going to bed*
Whishaw, Iona. *Henry and the cow problem*
Whiteside, Karen. *Lullaby of the wind*
Whitman, Candace. *The night is like an animal*
Wick, Walter. *Can you see what I see? Dream machine*
Wiesner, David. *Free fall*
Wild, Margaret. *Nighty night*
Willis, Jeanne. *The monster bed*
Winthrop, Elizabeth. *Bunk beds*
    Maggie and the monster
Wolfe, Frances. *It is the wind*
Wood, Audrey. *Moonflute*
    Oh my baby bear!
    Sweet dream pie
Wright, Christine. *Bedtime prayers*
Yaccarino, Dan. *Good night, Mr. Night*
Yee, Patrick. *Bedtime for Rosie Rabbit*
Yolen, Jane. *Baby Bear's bedtime book*
    Dragon night and other lullabies
    How do dinosaurs say good night?
    The lullaby songbook
    Moon ball
Zalben, Jane Breskin. *Norton's nighttime*
Ziefert, Harriet. *Clara Ann Cookie go to bed!*
    Good night everyone!
    I want to sleep in your bed!
    I won't go to bed!
    Moonride
    Say good night!
    What do ducks dream?
Zinnemann-Hope, Pam. *Time for bed, Ned*
Zolotow, Charlotte (Shapiro). *Flocks of birds*
    The sleepy book, ill. by Vladimir Bobri
    The sleepy book, ill. by Ilse Plume
    The summer night
    Wake up and goodnight
    When the wind stops
    Who is Ben?

Bedwetting *see* Behavior – bedwetting

Beekeepers *see* Careers – beekeepers

Bees *see* Insects – bees

Beetles *see* Insects – beetles

Beggars *see* Careers – beggars

Behavior

Armitage, Ronda. *Harry hates shopping!*
Arnold, Tedd. *Mother Goose's words of wit and wisdom*
Auch, Mary Jane. *Poultrygeist*
Babbitt, Lorraine. *Pink like the geranium*
Bauer, Marion Dane. *Why do kittens purr?*
Beim, Jerrold. *The swimming hole*
Belloc, Hilaire. *The bad child's book of beasts*
Berenstain, Stan. *The Berenstain bears' trouble at school*
Bertrand, Cécile. *Mr. and Mrs. Smith have only one child, but what a child!*
Birchall, Mark. *Rabbit's wooly sweater*
Blake, Jon. *Wriggly Pig*
Blundell, Tony. *Joe on Sunday*
Bluthenthal, Diana Cain. *Matilda the moocher*
Boegehold, Betty. *Three to get ready*
Bond, Felicia. *Poinsettia and her family*
Bonners, Susan. *Why does the cat do that?*
Brandon, Siobhán. *The bird's story*
Brown, Marc Tolon. *The true Francine*
Brown, Ruth. *Copycat*
Buehner, Caralyn. *I did it, I'm sorry*
Bunting, Eve (Anne Evelyn). *My backpack*
Butler, Geoff. *The hangashore*
Carle, Eric. *The grouchy ladybug*
Carlson, Nancy L. *Life is fun*
Caseley, Judith. *The noisemakers*
Caudill, Rebecca. *Contrary Jenkins*
Cecil, Ivon. *Kirby Kelvin and the not laughing lessons*
Chorao, Kay. *Pig and Crow*
Cibula, Matt S. *What's up with you, Taquandra Fu?*
Cohen, Miriam. *Eddy's dream*
Cole, Joanna. *Don't tell the whole world*
Collard, Sneed B. *Animal dads*
    Leaving home
Collicott, Sharleen. *Toestomper and the bad butterflies*
Corey, Shana. *First graders from Mars: Tera, star student*
Cowell, Cressida. *What shall we do with the Boo-Hoo Baby?*
Cuetara, Mittie. *Terrible Teresa and other very short stories*
Cuneo, Diane. *Mary Louise loses her manners*
Curious George and the hot air balloon
Curtis, Jamie Lee. *I'm gonna like me*
Cyrus, Kurt. *Slow train to Oxmox*
David, Lawrence. *Peter Claus and the naughty list*
Delton, Judy. *I'm telling you now*
Donnelly, Jennifer. *Humble pie*
Doyle, Malachy. *Well, a crocodile can!*
Edwards, Pamela Duncan. *Rude mule*
Egan, Tim. *Metropolitan cow*
Elliott, David. *An alphabet of rotten kids!*
    Hunter's best friend at school
Erickson, Karen. *Do I have to go home?*
Ets, Marie Hall. *Bad boy, good boy*
    Play with me
Falconer, Ian. *Olivia*
    Olivia's opposites
Fearnley, Jan. *Watch out!*
Fernandes, Eugenie. *Sleepy little mouse*
Foreman, Michael. *The angel and the wild animal*
French, Vivian. *Lazy Jack*
    Tiger and the temper tantrum
Gackenbach, Dick. *Hattie be quiet, Hattie be good*
Gaeddert, LouAnn Bigge. *Noisy Nancy Norris*
Gambill, Henrietta D. *Self-control*
Gibbons, Gail. *Bats*
Graham Barber, Lynda. *Spy hops and belly flops*
Gray, Nigel. *The grocer's daughter*
Greaves, Margaret. *Sarah's lion*
Griffin, Kitty. *The foot-stomping adventures of Clementine Sweet*
Grimes, Nikki. *Someone's baby-sitting*
Grindley, Sally. *I don't want to!*
Gutman, Anne. *Lisa's baby sister*
Gwynne, Fred. *Easy to see why*
Haddix, Margaret Peterson. *Say what?*

Hannan, Peter. *The battle of Sillyville*
Hanson, Mary Elizabeth. *Snug*
Harber, Frances. *The brothers' promise*
Harper, Jamie. *Don't grown-ups ever have fun?*
Harper, Jessica. *Lizzy's do's and don'ts*
Harris, Robie H. *Don't forget to come back*, ill. by Harry Bliss
    Don't forget to come back, ill. by Tony DeLuna
Haugaard, Erik Christian. *Princess Horrid*
Hautzig, Deborah. *Little Witch's bad dream*
Hayward, Linda. *A day in the life of Oscar the Grouch*
Hazen, Barbara Shook. *The new dog*
Himmelman, John. *Wanted: perfect parents*
Hines, Anna Grossnickle. *Mean old Uncle Jack*
Hoban, Russell. *Dinner at Alberta's*
Hogrogian, Nonny. *Carrot cake*
Hood, Susan. *The new kid*
Horvath, Betty F. *Be nice to Josephine*
Hubbard, Woodleigh. *Whoa, jealousy*
Hutchins, Pat. *Tidy Titch*
Ikeda, Daisaku. *The princess and the moon*
Inwald, Robin. *Cap it off with a smile*
Irbinskas, Heather. *How Jackrabbit got his very long ears*
Jackson, Jean. *Thorndike and Nelson*
James, Betsy. *Tadpoles*
Jeram, Anita. *Birthday happy, Contrary Mary*
    Contrary Mary
Johnson, Paul Brett. *The pig who ran a red light*
Johnston, Marianne. *Dealing with anger*
Jolley, Mike. *Grunter, a pig with an attitude!*
Kasza, Keiko. *Don't laugh, Joe*
Keller, Holly. *The new boy*
    That's mine, Horace
Kelley, Marty. *The rules*
Kerr, Phyllis Forbes. *I tricked you*
Kettner, Christine. *An ordinary cat*
Knowlton, Laurie Lazzaro. *Why cowgirls are such sweet talkers*
Kopelke, Lisa. *Excuse me!*
Kroll, Steven. *That makes me mad*
Kurtz, Jane. *Rain romp*
Kyle, Kathryn. *Respect*
Lakin, Pat (Patricia). *A good sport*
Lester, Helen. *Hurty feelings*
    Me first
    Tacky in trouble
Lester, Julius. *Albidaro and the mischievous dream*
Levine, Deb. *Parker picks*
Livingston, Myra Cohn. *Higgledy-Piggledy*
Low, Joseph. *Don't drag your feet . . .*
    My dog, your dog
Lucado, Max. *All you ever need*
Luttrell, Ida. *Ottie Slockett*
McCarthy, Meghan. *George upside down*
MacDonald, Amy. *Quentin Fenton Herter three*
Macdonald, Anne. *Wickiup walkingstick*
MacDonald, Suse. *Peck, slither and slide*
McGee, Marni. *Wake up, me!*
Mahoney, Daniel J. *The Saturday escape*
Markoe, Merrill. *The day my dogs became guys*
Masurel, Claire. *No, no, Titus!*
Meyer, Eleanor Walsh. *The keeper of ugly sounds*
Mills, Lauren A. *The dog prince*
Morgan-Vanroyen, Mary. *Gentle Rosie*
    Wild Rosie
Murkoff, Heidi Eisenberg. *What to expect at a play date*
Muth, Jon J. *The three questions*
Myller, Lois. *No! No!*
Naylor, Phyllis Reynolds. *Sweet strawberries*
Niner, Holly L. *Mr. Worry*
Noyes, Deborah. *It's Vladimir!*
O'Callahan, Jay. *Orange cheeks*
Pace, David. *Shouting Sharon*
Panek, Dennis. *Matilda Hippo has a big mouth*
Parker, Nancy Winslow. *Puddums, the Cathcarts' orange cat*
Parr, Todd. *Do's and don'ts*
Paterson, Diane. *Wretched Rachel*
Paterson, Geoffrey. *The naughty boy and the strawberry horse*
Pfister, Marcus. *How Leo learned to be king*

Milo and the magical stones
Pilkey, Dav. *The Silly Gooses*
Pinkwater, Daniel Manus. *Bad bears and a bunny*
Puttock, Simon. *Big bad wolf is good*
Quackenbush, Robert M. *I don't want to go, I don't know how to act*
Reider, Katja. *Snail started it!*
Remkiewicz, Frank. *Greedyanna*
Rice, David L. *Because Brian hugged his mother*
Ringi, Kjell (Arne Sorensen). *The winner*
Roberts, David (1970–). *Dirty Bertie*
Rotner, Shelley. *The A.D.D. book for kids*
Scarry, Richard. *Pig Will and Pig Won't*
    Pig Will and Pig Won't: 2-in-1 turn-around books
Shannon, David. *A bad case of stripes*
    The rain came down
Sharmat, Marjorie Weinman. *Scarlet Monster lives here*
Spelman, Cornelia Maude. *When I feel angry*
Stem, J. David. *Kay Thompson's Eloise in Hollywood*
Stevenson, James. *Don't make me laugh*
Stover, Jo Ann. *If everybody did*
Supraner, Robyn. *Would you rather be a tiger?*
Svendsen, Carol. *Hulda*
Swain, Ruth Freeman. *Bedtime!*
Sweetland, Nancy Rose. *Yelly Kelly*
Swope, Sam. *The Araboolies of Liberty Street*
Tabor, Nancy (Maria Grande). *Bottles break*
Teague, Mark. *Baby tamer*
Thomas, Karen. *The good thing . . . the bad thing*
Thompson, Kay. *Kay Thompson's Eloise*
Van Laan, Nancy. *A mouse in my house*
Waggoner, Karen. *The lemonade babysitter*
Wahl, Jan. *Little Johnny Buttermilk*
Wahl, Robert. *Pyxx*
Walker, Alice. *Finding the green stone*
Wallace, Joseph E. *Big and noisy Simon*
Wheeler, Lisa. *Old Cricket*
Willis, Jeanne. *Do little mermaids wet their beds*
Winer, Yvonne. *Frogs sing songs*
Wisdom, Jude. *Whatever Wanda wanted*
Wittels, Harriet. *Things I hate!*
Yaccarino, Dan. *If I had a robot*
Yolen, Jane. *How do dinosaurs say good night?*
Zimmett, Debbie. *Eddie enough*
Zolotow, Charlotte (Shapiro). *When I have a little girl; When I have a little boy*

Behavior – animals, dislike of

Bemelmans, Ludwig. *Madeline and the bad hat*
Kay, Helen. *An egg is for wishing*
Udry, Janice May. *Alfred*

Behavior – bad day

Alborough, Jez. *Running Bear*
Andrews, F. Emerson (Frank Emerson). *Nobody comes to dinner*
Baker, Alan. *Benjamin's portrait*
Balzola, Asun. *Munia and the day things went wrong*
Berenstain, Stan. *The Berenstain bears get in a fight*
Birdseye, Tom. *A regular flood of mishap*
Corey, Shana. *First graders from Mars: Horus's horrible day*
Demuth, Patricia Brennan. *Ornery morning*
Duncan, Jane. *Janet Reachfar and Chickabird*
Everitt, Betsy. *Mean soup*
Fernandes, Eugenie. *A difficult day*
Fujikawa, Gyo. *Sam's all-wrong day*
Gammell, Stephen. *Is that you, winter?*
Giff, Patricia Reilly. *Today was a terrible day*
Griffith, Helen V. *Nata*
Grindley, Sally. *The sulky vulture*
Haywood, Carolyn. *Santa Claus forever!*
Hoban, Russell. *The sorely trying day*
Hurd, Edith Thacher. *Johnny Lion's bad day*
Hurd, Thacher. *Mystery on the docks*
    Santa Mouse and the ratdeer
Jackson, Ellen B. *Sometimes bad things happen*
Johnston, Deborah. *Mathew Michael's beastly day*

Keith, Eros. *Bedita's bad day*
Kline, Suzy. *Ooops!*
Krahn, Fernando. *Here comes Alex Pumpernickel!*
Lexau, Joan M. *I should have stayed in bed*
Martin, Jane Read. *Now everybody really hates me*
    Now I will never leave the dinner table
Miller, Virginia. *I love you just the way you are*
Morris, Ann. *Eleanora Mousie's gray day*
Moss, Miriam. *Smudge's grumpy day*
Murphy, Stuart J. *Probably pistachio*
Oram, Hiawyn. *Badger's bad mood*
    Kiss it better
Oxenbury, Helen. *The car trip*
Prater, John. *The perfect day*
Riddell, Chris. *Platypus and the lucky day*
Robins, Joan. *Addie's bad day*
Rockwell, Anne F. *No! No! No!*
Scarry, Richard. *Mr. Frumble's worst day ever!*
Shannon, George. *Laughing all the way*
Simon, Charnan. *The good bad day*
Simon, Francesca. *Spider school*
Smath, Jerry. *Mr. Digby's bad day*
Sondheimer, Ilse. *The boy who could make his mother stop yelling*
Van Leeuwen, Jean. *Too hot for ice cream*
Viorst, Judith. *Alexander and the terrible, horrible, no good, very bad day*
Vreeken, Elizabeth. *One day everything went wrong*
Wells, Rosemary. *Unfortunately Harriet*
Wight, Tamra. *The three grumpies*
Wormell, Mary. *Bernard the angry rooster*

Behavior – bedwetting

Willis, Jeanne. *Do little mermaids wet their beds*

Behavior – boasting

Augarde, Steve (Stephen). *Barnaby Shrew, Black Dan and . . . the mighty wedgwood*
Bonsall, Crosby Newell. *The amazing the incredible super dog*
    Mine's the best
Browne, Anthony. *Look what I've got!*
Butterworth, Nick. *My dad is awesome*
    My grandpa is amazing
Carlson, Nancy L. *Loudmouth George and the big race*
    Loudmouth George and the cornet
    Loudmouth George and the fishing trip
    Loudmouth George and the new neighbors
    Loudmouth George and the sixth-grade bully
Collins, Pat Lowery. *My friend Andrew*
Currey, Anna. *Tickling tigers*
Diot, Alain. *Better, best, bestest*
Duvoisin, Roger Antoine. *See what I am*
Ellentuck, Shan. *A sunflower as big as the sun*
Farris, Pamela J. *Young Mouse and Elephant*
Gretz, Susanna. *Rabbit rambles on*
Harshman, Marc. *Uncle James*
Hayes, Joe. *A spoon for every bite*
Johnston, Tony. *Farmer Mack measures his pig*
Kajpust, Melissa. *The peacock's pride*
Kepes, Juliet. *The story of a bragging duck*
Knutson, Barbara. *Why the crab has no head*
Lopshire, Robert. *I am better than you*
Lund, Doris Herold. *You ought to see Herbert's house*
May, Kara. *Big brave brother Ben*
Miller, Moira. *The moon dragon*
Miller, Warren. *The goings on at Little Wishful*
Oppenheim, Joanne. *You can't catch me!*
Parker, Kristy. *My dad the magnificent*
Pavey, Peter. *I'm Taggarty Toad*
Peterson, Esther Allen. *Frederick's alligator*
Raphael, Elaine. *Turnabout*
Ross, Gayle. *How Turtle's back was cracked*
Schindler, Regina. *The bear's cave*
Schlein, Miriam. *Big talk*, ill. by Joan Auclair
    Big talk, ill. by Laura Lydecker
Schwartz, Amy. *Her Majesty, Aunt Essie*

Simmonds, Posy. *The chocolate wedding*
Slater, Teddy. *The cow that could tap dance*
    The fabulous fish from Lake Wiggawalla
Yolen, Jane. *Little Mouse and Elephant*

Behavior – boredom

Alexander, Martha G. *We never get to do anything*
Anholt, Catherine. *Come back, Jack!*
Arqués, Isabel M. *Ken's cloud*
Ayal, Ora. *The adventures of Chester the chest*
Berson, Harold. *I'm bored, Ma!*
Christelow, Eileen. *Five little monkeys with nothing to do*
Creighton, Jill. *One day there was nothing to do*
Delton, Judy. *My mom hates me in January*
Duvoisin, Roger Antoine. *Veronica's smile*
Eriksson, Eva. *One short week*
Gay, Marie-Louise. *On my island*
Geoghegan, Adrienne. *There's a wardrobe in my monster!*
Graves, Keith. *Pet boy*
Gutman, Anne. *Gaspard and Lisa's rainy day*
Hannan, Peter. *Sillyville or bust*
Henkes, Kevin. *Once around the block*
Hoban, Russell. *Nothing to do*
Ichikawa, Satomi. *Nora's roses*
Jennings, Sharon. *When Jeremiah found Mrs. Ming*
Krauss, Ruth. *A good man and his good wife*
Lawlor, Laurie. *Second-grade dog*
McConnachie, Brian. *Lily of the forest*
McGovern, Ann. *Nicholas Bentley Stoningpot III*
McKee, David. *Elmer again*
McLaughlin, Lissa. *Why won't winter go?*
Maris, Ron. *Bernard's boring day*
Meroux, Felix. *The prince of the rabbits*
Modarressi, Mitra. *The parent thief*
Noble, Trinka Hakes. *Meanwhile back at the ranch*
Oram, Hiawyn. *In the attic*
Raskin, Ellen. *Nothing ever happens on my block*
Reit, Seymour. *The king who learned to smile*
Seymour, Tres. *Too quiet for these old bones*
Spier, Peter. *Bored – nothing to do!*
Stevenson, James. *There's nothing to do!*
Szekeres, Cyndy. *Toby!*
Thayer, Jane. *Mr. Turtle's magic glasses*
Watts, Marjorie-Ann. *Crocodile medicine*

Behavior – bossy

De Paola, Tomie (Thomas Anthony). *Boss for a day*

Behavior – bullying

Alden, Joan. *A boy's best friend*
Alexander, Martha G. *I sure am glad to see you, Blackboard Bear*
    Move over, Twerp
Anaya, Rudolfo A. *Roadrunner's dance*
Anderson, Laurie Halse. *The big cheese of Third Street*
Bateman, Teresa. *The Bully Blockers Club*
Berquist, Grace. *The boy who couldn't roar*
Bible. Old Testament. David. *David and the giant*
Bottner, Barbara. *Bootsie Barker bites*
Boyd, Lizi. *Bailey the big bully*
Browne, Anthony. *Willy the champ*
Bryant, Bernice. *Follow the leader*
Caple, Kathy. *The wimp*
Carlson, Nancy L. *Loudmouth George and the sixth-grade bully*
Carter, Anne Laurel. *The F team*
Caseley, Judith. *Bully*
Cauley, Lorinda Bryan. *The trouble with Tyrannosaurus Rex*
Cazet, Denys. *Mud baths for everyone*
Chapman, Carol. *Herbie's troubles*
Charlton, Elizabeth. *Terrible tyrannosaurus*
Christelow, Eileen. *Jerome camps out*
Clayton, Elaine. *Pup in school*
Cohen, Miriam. *Tough Jim*
Cole, Babette. *Hurray for Ethelyn*
Cole, Joanna. *Bully trouble*

    Don't call me names!
Collicott, Sharleen. *Toestomper and the caterpillars*
Couric, Katie. *The brand new kid*
Cristaldi, Kathryn. *Baseball ballerina strikes out*
D'Amico, Carmela. *Ella, the elegant elephant*
De Paola, Tomie (Thomas Anthony). *Katie, Kit and cousin Tom*
    Kit and Kat
Dodd, Lynley. *Hairy Maclary, Scattercat*
Freschet, Berniece. *Furlie Cat*
Gretz, Susanna. *Roger takes charge!*
Hassett, John. *The three silly girls Grubb*
Henkes, Kevin. *Chester's way*
Hooks, William H. *Rough, tough, Rowdy*
Isenberg, Barbara. *Albert the running bear gets the jitters*
Janice. *Angélique*
Johnston, Marianne. *Dealing with bullying*
Karas, G. Brian. *Home on the bayou*
Kasza, Keiko. *The rat and the tiger*
Keats, Ezra Jack. *Goggles*
Kliphuis, Christine. *Robbie and Ronnie*
Kroll, Steven. *It's April Fools' Day!*
Kushner, Tony. *Brundibar*
Lagercrantz, Rose. *Brave little Pete of Geranium Street*
Laurencin, Geneviève. *I wish I were*
Lester, Helen. *Hooway for Wodney Wat*
Liersch, Anne. *A house is not a home*
Little, Jean. *Jess was the brave one*
Lovell, Patty. *Stand tall, Molly Lou Melon*
McCain, Becky R. (Becky Ray). *Nobody knew what to do*
McCully, Emily Arnold. *Grandmas trick-or-treat*
McMullan, Kate (Hall). *Hey, Pipsqueak!*
Mahy, Margaret. *Beaten by a balloon*
Marton, Jirina. *Flowers for mom*
Masters, Anthony. *Ricky's rat gang*
Mayer, Mercer. *Just big enough*
Meddaugh, Susan. *Martha walks the dog*
Minarik, Else Holmelund. *The little girl and the dragon*
Modarressi, Mitra. *The beastly visits*
Montanari, Eva. *Dino bikes*
Morimoto, Junko. *The two bullies*
Morrison, Toni. *The book of mean people*
Moss, Peggy. *Say something*
Mwenye Hadithi. *Crafty chameleon*
    Tricky tortoise
Naylor, Phyllis Reynolds. *King of the playground*
Nickle, John. *The ant bully*
Nolen, Jerdine. *Plantzilla goes to camp*
O'Neill, Alexis. *The Recess Queen*
Passen, Lisa. *Fat, fat Rose Marie*
Peet, Bill (William Bartlett). *Big bad Bruce*
Pieńkowski, Jan. *Bel and Bub and the bad snowball*
Pinkney, J. Brian. *The adventures of sparrowboy*
Polacco, Patricia. *Mr. Lincoln's way*
Rayner, Mary. *Crocodarling*
Robberecht, Thierry. *Stolen smile*
Roche, Denis (Denis M.). *Mim, gym, and June*
Roche, P. K. (Patrick K.). *Plaid bear and the rude rabbit gang*
Schafer, Milton. *That crazy Barb'ra*
Shipton, Jonathan. *No biting, horrible crocodile!*
Sorel, Edward. *The Saturday kid*
Staunton, Ted. *Taking care of Crumley*
Taylor, Scott. *Dinosaur James*
Waddell, Martin. *Yum, yum, yummy*
Wagner, Jenny. *Amy's monster*
Wilhelm, Hans. *Tyrone the horrible*
Wishinsky, Frieda. *Give Maggie a chance*

Behavior – carelessness

Aliki. *Keep your mouth closed, dear*
Biro, Val. *Gumdrop gets a lift*
Bottner, Barbara. *Messy*
Brett, Jan. *Comet's nine lives*
Brimner, Larry Dane. *Cat on wheels*
Brown, Marc Tolon. *The cloud over Clarence*
Brunhoff, Laurent de. *Babar's little girl*
Buchanan, Joan. *It's a good thing*

Carrick, Carol. *A rabbit for Easter*
Chislett, Gail. *The rude visitors*
Claret, Maria. *The chocolate rabbit*
Cleary, Beverly. *Lucky Chuck*
De Paola, Tomie (Thomas Anthony). *The quicksand book*
    Strega Nona's magic lessons
Gackenbach, Dick. *Binky gets a car*
Gantos, Jack (John, Jr.). *Aunt Bernice*
Haas, Jessie. *Chipmunk!*
Harris, Robie H. *Messy Jessie*
Ilsley, Velma. *The pink hat*
Kline, Suzy. *Ooops!*
Koscielniak, Bruce. *Euclid Bunny delivers the mail*
Mayer, Mercer. *Oops*
Moskin, Marietta D. *Lysbet and the fire kittens*
Novak, Matt. *Elmer Blunt's open house*
Oram, Hiawyn. *Reckless Ruby*
Panek, Dennis. *Catastrophe Cat*
Pender, Lydia. *Barnaby and the horses*
Reader, Dennis. *Butterfingers*
Roberts, Sarah. *Ernie's big mess*
Serfozo, Mary. *Dirty Kurt*
Sommers, Tish. *Bert and the broken teapot*
Whatley, Bruce. *Wait! No paint!*

Behavior – cheating

Havill, Juanita. *Jamaica and the substitute teacher*

Behavior – collecting things

Armstrong-Ellis, Carey. *Prudy's problem and how she solved it*
Bauer, Caroline Feller. *Too many books!*
Beim, Lorraine. *Lucky Pierre*
Blumenthal, Deborah. *Aunt Claire's yellow beehive hair*
Bram, Elizabeth. *Woodruff and the clocks*
Braun, Kathy. *Kangaroo and kangaroo*
Bunting, Eve (Anne Evelyn). *Anna's table*
Carlstrom, Nancy White. *The moon came too*
Cleary, Beverly. *Janet's thingamajigs*
Couture, Susan Arkin. *The block book*
Enderle, Judith (Ann) Ross. *Good junk*
Engel, Diana. *Josephina, the great collector*
Evans, Eva Knox. *That lucky Mrs. Plucky*
Gans, Roma. *Let's go rock collecting*
    Rock collecting
Geringer, Laura. *A three hat day*
Greenblat, Rodney Alan. *Aunt Ippy's museum of junk*
Hayward, Linda. *Ernie and Bert's summer project*
Heller, Nicholas. *Ten old pails*
Heyduck-Huth, Hilde. *The starfish*
    The strawflower
Horse, Harry. *A friend for Little Bear*
Hurst, Carol Otis. *Rocks in his head*
Jennings, Sharon. *Franklin's trading cards*
Jocelyn, Marthe. *Hannah's Collections*
Johnson, Pamela. *A mouse's tale*
Kleven, Elisa. *The puddle pail*
Krasilovsky, Phyllis. *The woman who saved things*
Lewis, Naomi. *The butterfly collector*
Lillie, Patricia. *When this box is full*
McDonald, Megan. *Insects are my life*
Penner, Fred. *Proud*
Pfeffer, Wendy. *Marta's magnets*
Sullivan, Paula. *Todd's box*
Thompson, Richard. *The night walker*
Tusa, Tricia. *Stay away from the junkyard!*
Van Horn, William. *Harry Hoyle's giant jumping bean*
Weil, Lisl. *To sail a ship of treasures*
Westell, Kerry. *Amanda's book*
Zelver, Patricia. *The wonderful Towers of Watts*

Behavior – disbelief

Alexander, Martha G. *Even that moose won't listen to me*
Brisson, Pat. *Wanda's roses*
Cole, Brock. *The king at the door*

Gunthrop, Karen. *Adam and the wolf*
Jackson, Ellen B. *Ants can't dance*
Norman, Howard A. *The owl-scatterer*
Turner, Ann Warren. *Nettie's trip south*
Waber, Bernard. *Do you see a mouse?*

Behavior – dissatisfaction

Alexander, Sue. *Ellsworth and Millicent*
    What's wrong now, Millicent?
Aliki. *The twelve months*
    The wish workers
Allen, Jeffrey. *The secret life of Mr. Weird*
Asch, Frank. *Monkey face*
Balet, Jan B. *The king and the broom maker*
Bauer, Steven. *The strange and wonderful tale of Robert McDoodle*
Bentley, Nancy. *I've got your nose!*
Best, Cari. *Montezuma's revenge*
Brewster, Patience. *Nobody*
Brock, Emma Lillian. *Pig with a front porch*
Brothers, Aileen. *Sad Mrs. Sam Sack*
Butterworth, Nick. *Jasper's beanstalk*
Byars, Betsy Cromer. *The groober*
Chapman, Carol. *The tale of Meshka the Kvetch*
Clymer, Ted. *The horse and the bad morning*
Coffey, Maria. *A cat in a kayak*
Cole, Babette. *King Change-A-Lot*
Cronin, Doreen. *Click, clack, moo*
Crowley, Arthur. *The boogey man*
Cushman, Doug. *Nasty Kyle the crocodile*
Dale, Ruth Bluestone. *Benjamin . . . and Sylvester also*
Day, Shirley. *Waldo's back yard*
Duvoisin, Roger Antoine. *Petunia, beware!*
Elborn, Andrew. *Bird Adalbert*
Ets, Marie Hall. *The cow's party*
Fish, Hans. *Pitschi, the kitten who always wanted to do something else*
Fowler, Richard. *Cat's cake*
Gackenbach, Dick. *Mother Rabbit's son Tom*
Gay, Zhenya. *I'm tired of lions*
Getz, Arthur. *Humphrey, the dancing pig*
Grindley, Sally. *The sulky vulture*
Hautzig, Deborah. *It's not fair!*
Hazen, Barbara Shook. *The Fat Cats, Cousin Scraggs and the monster mice*
Heide, Florence Parry. *Oh, grow up!*
Herman, Gail. *Flower girl*
Hest, Amy. *The mommy exchange*
Hille-Brandts, Lene. *The little black hen*
Hoban, Lillian. *Stick-in-the-mud turtle*
Jenkin-Pearce, Susie. *Percy Short and Cuthbert*
Johnson, Evelyne. *The cow in the kitchen*
Jolin, Dominique. *It's not fair!*
Keats, Ezra Jack. *Jennie's hat*
McDermott, Gerald. *The stonecutter*
MacDonald, Margaret Read. *The old woman who lived in a vinegar bottle*
McDonald, Megan. *The night Iguana left home*
McGinley, Phyllis. *The horse who lived upstairs*
Massie, Diane Redfield. *Walter was a frog*
May, Kara. *Creepy crawly caterpillar*
Meddaugh, Susan. *The best place*
Milstein, Linda Breiner. *Amanda's perfect hair*
Newton, Jill. *Cat-fish*
Nightingale, Sandy. *The witch's spell*
O'Donnell, Elizabeth Lee. *Maggie doesn't want to move*
Olsen, Alfa-Betty. *Gabby the shrew*
Olujic, Grozdana. *Rose of Mother-of-Pearl*
Oram, Hiawyn. *Jenna and the troublemaker*
Palatini, Margie. *Good as Goldie*
Palmer, Mary Babcock. *No-sort-of-animal*
Peet, Bill (William Bartlett). *The caboose who got loose*
    The luckiest one of all
    The Whingdingdilly
Pogorelsky, Antony. *The black hen, or, The underground inhabitants*
    The little black hen
Price, Roger. *The last little dragon*
Roberts, Bethany. *Camel caravan*

Roth, Carol. *Little Bunny's sleepless night*
Russo, Marisabina. *Why do grownups have all the fun?*
Sadler, Marilyn. *It's not easy being a bunny*
Sarnoff, Jane. *That's not fair*
Sharmat, Marjorie Weinman. *Grumley the grouch*
Simon, Francesca. *Camels don't ski*
Testa, Fulvio. *Never satisfied*
Turnage, Sheila. *Trout the magnificent*
Waller, Barrett. *New feet for old*
Weedn, Flavia. *The ragged peddler*
White, Linda Arms. *Too many pumpkins*
Wiesner, William. *Turnabout*
Yaccarino, Dan. *Deep in the jungle*
Yaffe, Alan. *The magic meatballs*
Zakhoder, Boris Vladimirovich. *Rosachok*
Zolotow, Charlotte (Shapiro). *It's not fair*

Behavior – fidgeting

Carlson, Nancy L. *Sit still!*

Behavior – fighting, arguing

Alexander, Martha G. *I'll be the horse if you'll play with me*
Bassett, Jeni. *The chicks' trick*
Beim, Lorraine. *Two is a team*
Berry, Joy Wilt. *Fighting*
Boegehold, Betty. *The fight*
Bruchac, Joseph. *The great ball game*
Bunting, Eve (Anne Evelyn). *Box, fox, ox, and the peacock*
Burdett, Lois. *Macbeth for kids*
    Romeo and Juliet for kids
Burningham, John. *Mr. Gumpy's outing*
Burton, Jane. *Animals fighting*
Christian, Mary Blount. *The sand lot*
Dayton, Mona. *Earth and sky*
Edwards, Pamela Duncan. *Gigi and Lulu's gigantic fight*
Ernst, Lisa Campbell. *Zinnia and Dot*
Field, Eugene. *The gingham dog and the calico cat*, ill. by Janet
    Street
    The gingham dog and the calico cat, ill. by Johanna Westerman
Foreman, Michael. *The two giants*
Gekiere, Madeleine. *The frilly lily and the princess*
Gilchrist, Theo E. *Halfway up the mountain*
Goffin, Josse. *Who is the boss?*
Grimes, Nikki. *Someone's fighting*
Harvey, Amanda. *Stormy weather*
Hoban, Russell. *Harvey's hideout*
    The sorely trying day
    Tom and the two handles
Hodges, Margaret. *The kitchen knight*
Holabird, Katharine. *Alexander and the dragon*
Hooks, William H. *Peach boy*
Keller, Holly. *Cecil's garden*
Lasker, Joe. *A tournament of knights*
Levitin, Sonia. *Who owns the moon?*
Lionni, Leo. *It's mine!*
McBratney, Sam. *I'm sorry*
McCully, Emily Arnold. *Grandmas trick-or-treat*
McFarland, Lyn Rossiter. *The pirate's parrot*
McKee, David. *Tusk tusk*
    Two monsters
Martin, Francesca. *The honey hunters*
Masurel, Claire. *A cat and a dog*
Merriam, Eve. *Fighting words*
Minarik, Else Holmelund. *No fighting, no biting!*
Morrison, Toni. *The book of mean people*
Murray, Andrew. *Have you seen Chester?*
Novak, Matt. *The Pillow War*
O'Malley, Kevin. *Little Buggy runs away*
Pfister, Marcus. *Rainbow fish and the big blue whale*
Rose, Gerald. *Trouble in the ark*
St. Germain, Sharon. *The terrible fight*
Sharmat, Marjorie Weinman. *I'm not Oscar's friend any more*
    Rollo and Juliet . . . forever!
    Sometimes mama and papa fight
Shute, Linda. *Momotaro, the peach boy*

Slobodkin, Louis. *Hustle and bustle*
Souhami, Jessica. *Mrs. McCool and the giant Cuhullin*
Steadman, Ralph. *The bridge*
Stevenson, James. *Are we almost there?*
Tusa, Tricia. *Sisters*
Udry, Janice May. *Let's be enemies*
    Thump and Plunk, ill. by Geoffrey Hayes
    Thump and Plunk, ill. by Ann Schweninger
Van Kampen, Vlasta. *It couldn't be worse*
Van Leeuwen, Jean. *Sorry*
Venable, Alan. *The checker players*
Waggoner, Karen. *Dad Gummit and Ma Foot*
Wallis, Diz. *Battle of the beasts*
Weninger, Brigitte. *Why are you fighting, Davy?*
White, Kathryn (Kathryn Ivy). *Nutty nut chase*
    When they fight
Widman, Christine. *Housekeeper of the wind*
Williams, Arlene. *Dragon soup*
Winthrop, Elizabeth. *That's mine*
Yorinks, Arthur. *Oh, brother*
Zehler, Antonia. *Two fine ladies have a tiff*
Zolotow, Charlotte (Shapiro). *The quarreling book*
    The unfriendly book

Behavior – forgetfulness

Alexander, Sue. *Witch, Goblin and sometimes Ghost*
Aliki. *Use your head, dear*
Arnold, Tedd. *Ollie forgot*
Birdseye, Tom. *Soap! Soap! Don't forget the soap!*
Brown, Ken (Ken James). *Nellie's knot*
Cole, Joanna. *Aren't you forgetting something, Fiona?*
Copp, James (Andrew James). *Martha Matilda O'Toole*
De Paola, Tomie (Thomas Anthony). *Strega Nona*
Dines, Glen. *A tiger in the cherry tree*
Dodd, Lynley. *Schnitzel von Krumm forget-me-not*
Domanska, Janina. *Palmiero and the ogre*
Fox, Mem. *Wilfrid Gordon McDonald Partridge*
Galdone, Joanna. *Gertrude, the goose who forgot*
Galdone, Paul. *The magic porridge pot*
Guthrie, Donna. *Grandpa doesn't know it's me*
Hale, Irina. *The lost toys*
Hutchins, Pat. *Don't forget the bacon!*
Kerr, Judith. *Mog, the forgetful cat*
King-Smith, Dick. *Farmer Bungle forgets*
MacGregor, Ellen. *Theodor Turtle*
Marshak, S. (Samuil). *The absentminded fellow*
Miles, Miska. *Chicken forgets*
Nikly, Michelle. *The perfume of memory*
Parish, Peggy. *Be ready at eight*
Patz, Nancy. *Pumpernickel tickle and mean green cheese*
Rogers, Paul (Patrick). *Forget-me-not*
Schatell, Brian. *The McGoonys have a party*
Schweninger, Ann. *The hunt for rabbit's galosh*
Stevenson, Suçie. *I forgot*
Sutherland, Colleen. *Jason goes to show-and-tell*
Van Allsburg, Chris. *The stranger*
Wahl, Jan. *"I remember," cried Grandma Pinky*
Weinberg, Larry (Lawrence). *The Forgetful Bears*
    The Forgetful Bears help Santa
    The Forgetful Bears meet Mr. Memory
Weisgard, Leonard. *Silly Willy Nilly*
Wild, Margaret. *Remember me*

Behavior – forgiving

Bower, Gary. *Ivy's icicle*
Dierssen, Andreas. *Timmy's new friend*
Jennings, Sharon. *Franklin forgives*

Behavior – gossip

Allen, Jeffrey. *Nosey Mrs. Rat*
Andersen, H. C. (Hans Christian). *It's perfectly true!*
Aston, Dianna Hutts. *Loony Little*
Berson, Harold. *The thief who hugged a moonbeam*
Brenner, Barbara A. *Good news*

Chicken Little. *Chicken Licken*, ill. by Jutta Ash
  Chicken Licken, ill. by Gavin Bishop
  Chicken Little, ill. by Sally Hobson
  Henny Penny, ill. by Emily Bolam
  Henny Penny, ill. by Stephen Butler
  Henny Penny, ill. by Paul Galdone
  Henny Penny, ill. by William Stobbs
  Henny-Penny, ill. by Jane Wattenberg
  The sky is falling
  The story of Chicken Licken
Holl, Adelaide. *The runaway giant*
Hutchins, Pat. *The surprise party*
Ketteman, Helen. *Armadillo tattletale*
Kraus, Robert. *Mert the blurt*
Love, Ann. *The prince who wrote a letter*
Mantinband, Gerda. *Blabbermouths*
Meres, Jonathan. *The big bad rumor*
Stevens, Harry. *Parrot told snake*
Varga, Judy. *The monster behind Black Rock*
Zolotow, Charlotte (Shapiro). *The hating book*

Behavior – greed

Aardema, Verna. *Sebgugugu the glutton*
Æsop. *The goose that laid the golden egg*
Afanas'ev, Aleksandr N. *Salt*
Aliki. *The eggs*
Allen, Pamela. *Hidden treasure*
Andersen, H. C. (Hans Christian). *The woman with the eggs*
Angelo, Valenti. *The candy basket*
Arnold, Caroline. *The terrible Hodag*
Aulaire, Ingri Mortenson d'. *Don't count your chicks*
Aylesworth, Jim. *Mary's mirror*
Barker, Inga-Lil. *Why teddy bears are brown*
Bascom, Joe. *Malcolm Softpaws*
Battles, Edith. *The terrible terrier*
  The terrible trick or treat
Bellows, Cathy. *Four fat rats*
Berenstain, Stan. *The Berenstain bears get the gimmies*
Berson, Harold. *Larbi and Leila*
  The rats who lived in the delicatessen
Bohdal, Susi. *The magic honey jar*
Bolliger, Max. *The golden apple*
Bonsall, Crosby Newell. *It's mine! A greedy book*
Borovsky, Paul. *Nico*
Brenner, Barbara A. *Ostrich feathers*
The brothers gruesome
Brown, Marcia. *The bun*
Buckley, Richard. *The greedy python*
Bunting, Eve (Anne Evelyn). *The man who could call down owls*
Carlson, Nancy L. *Harriet's Halloween candy*
Carter, Anne Laurel. *Bella's secret garden*
Chichester Clark, Emma. *More!*
Christian, Mary Blount. *The devil take you, Barnabas Beane!*
Coco, Eugene Bradley. *The wishing well*
Cooper, Susan. *The silver cow*
Corbalis, Judy. *The cuckoo bird*
Dauer, Rosamond. *The 300 pound cat*
David, Lawrence. *The land of the hungry armadillos*
De Paola, Tomie (Thomas Anthony). *Andy (that's my name)*
Diakité, Baba Wagué. *The magic gourd*
Donnelly, Jennifer. *Humble pie*
Edwards, Pamela Duncan. *Ed and Fred Flea*
  The leprechaun's gold
Ernst, Lisa Campbell. *The prize pig surprise*
Evans, Katherine. *The maid and her pail of milk*
Faulkner, William J. *Brer Tiger and the big wind*
Forward, Toby. *Ben's Christmas carol*
Gackenbach, Dick. *Barker's crime*
Gantschev, Ivan. *The moon lake*
Gerson, Mary-Joan. *Why the sky is far away*
Gifaldi, David. *The boy who spoke colors*
Ginsburg, Mirra. *Two greedy bears*
Green, Phyllis. *Bagdad ate it*
Gregory, Valiska. *When stories fell like shooting stars*
Grimm, Jacob. *The fisherman and his wife*, ill. by Eleanor Hubbard
  The fisherman and his wife, ill. by Monika Laimgruber

The fisherman and his wife, ill. by Alan Marks
  The fisherman and his wife, ill. by Todd Ouren
  The fisherman and his wife, ill. by Laurinda Spear
  The fisherman and his wife, ill. by Margot Tomes
  The fisherman and his wife, ill. by Margot Zemach
  The golden bird, ill. by Isabelle Brent
  The golden bird, ill. by Sandro Nardini
  The golden goose, ill. by Dennis McDermott
  Mother Holly
  One gift deserves another
Grobler, Piet. *Hey, frog!*
Hamilton, Virginia. *The girl who spun gold*
Hausman, Gerald. *Coyote walks on two legs*
Henwood, Simon. *A piece of luck*
Hewitt, Kathryn. *King Midas and the golden touch*
Heyer, Carol. *Robin Hood*
Ishii, Momoko. *The tongue-cut sparrow*
Jacobs, Joseph. *Hudden and Dudden and Donald O'Neary*
Johnson, Paul Brett. *Bearhide and crow*
Kennedy, Richard. *The lost kingdom of Karnica*
Kimmel, Eric A. *Onions and garlic*
Kinter, Judith. *King of magic, man of glass*
Kismaric, Carole. *The rumor of Pavel and Paali*
Krudop, Walter Lyon. *The man who caught fish*
Kuskin, Karla. *What did you bring me?*
Levy, Janice. *The man who lived in a hat*
Lewis, J. Patrick. *The tsar and the amazing cow*
Lind, Michael. *Bluebonnet girl*
Lionni, Leo. *The biggest house in the world*
Lorenz, Lee. *Pinchpenny John*
Luenn, Nancy. *Miser on the mountain*
Lussert, Anneliese. *The farmer and the moon*
Luttrell, Ida. *The star counters*
McClenathan, Louise. *My mother sends her wisdom*
McKissack, Patricia C. *King Midas and his gold*
McLenighan, Valjean. *Three strikes and you're out*
Mahy, Margaret. *Rooms for rent*
Mangan, Anne. *The monkey who wanted the moon*
Manson, Christopher. *Here begins the tale of the marvellous blue mouse*
Mark, Jan. *The Midas touch*
Marshall, James. *Yummers too*
Matsutani, Miyoko. *How the withered trees blossomed*
Mayne, William. *Lady Muck*
Mollel, Tololwa M. (Tololwa Marti). *The flying tortoise*
Muller, Robin. *The magic paintbrush*
Mwenye Hadithi. *Greedy zebra*
Obrist, Jürg. *The miser who wanted the sun*
Paraskevas, Betty. *The ferocious beast with the polka-dot hide*
Peet, Bill (William Bartlett). *Kermit the hermit*
  The kweeks of Kookatumdee
Peppé, Rodney. *The mice and the flying basket*
Perkins, Al. *King Midas and the golden touch*
Porter, David Lord. *Mine!*
Roffey, Maureen. *Look, there's my hat!*
Rohmer, Harriet. *The invisible hunters*
Ross, Tony. *The greedy little cobbler*
Sanderson, Ruth. *Papa Gatto*
Sanfield, Steve. *Just rewards, or, Who is that man in the moon and what's he doing up there anyway?*
San Souci, Robert D. *The enchanted tapestry*
Schlessinger, Laura. *But I waaannt it!*
Schroeder, Alan. *The stone lion*
Selway, Martina. *Greedyguts*
Shibano, Tamizo. *The old man who made the trees bloom*
Smath, Jerry. *The animals' Christmas carol*
So, Meilo. *Gobble, gobble, slip, slop*
Solotareff, Grégoire. *Never trust an ogre*
Stadler, John. *Animal café*
Stage, Mads. *The greedy blackbird*
Stanley, Diane. *Rumpelstiltskin's daughter*
Stewig, John Warren. *King Midas*
Storr, Catherine (Cole). *King Midas*
Tolstoy, Leo. *How much land does a man need?*
Tompert, Ann. *The hungry black bag*
Vaës, Alain. *The princess and the pea*
Waddell, Martin. *Yum, yum, yummy*

Watson, Esther (Pearl). *Trouble at Sugar Dip Well*
Wells, Rosemary. *The little lame prince*
   Max and Ruby's Midas
Winthrop, Elizabeth. *That's mine*
Witte, Anna. *The parrot Tico Tango*
Yep, Laurence. *Tiger woman*

Behavior – growing up

Alexander, Sue. *Dear Phoebe*
Aliki. *I'm growing!*
Allison, Alida. *The toddler's potty book*
Anholt, Catherine. *When I was a baby*
Anholt, Laurence. *Billy and the big new school*
Appell, Clara. *Now I have a daddy haircut*
Ardizzone, Edward. *Paul, the hero of the fire*
Aseltine, Lorraine. *First grade can wait*
Atkins, Jeannine. *Robin's home*
Aulaire, Ingri Mortenson d'. *Too big*
Balzola, Asun. *Munia and the red shoes*
Barrett, Judi. *I hate to take a bath*
   I'm too small, you're too big
Bat-Ami, Miriam. *Sea, salt, and air*
Baumgart, Klaus. *Don't be afraid, Tommy*
Bedford, David. *Touch the sky, my little bear*
Bentley, Dawn. *Fuzzy Bear's potty book*
Boelts, Maribeth. *Little Bunny's pacifier plan*
Bogot, Howard. *I'm growing*
Bolliger, Max. *The magic bird*
Bonnici, Peter. *The festival*
Borden, Louise. *Albie the lifeguard*
Bourgeois, Paulette. *Big Sarah's little boots*
Brentano, Clemens. *Schoolmaster Whackwell's wonderful sons*
Brimner, Larry Dane. *The littlest wolf*
Brinckloe, Julie. *Fireflies!*
Bromhall, Winifred. *Bridget's growing day*
Brown, Margaret Wise. *Another important book*
Brown, Myra Berry. *Benjy's blanket*
Bruchac, Joseph. *A boy called Slow*
Bruna, Dick. *I can dress myself*
Bryant, Bernice. *Follow the leader*
Buck, Nola. *Hey, little baby!*
Buckley, Kate. *Love notes*
Bulla, Clyde Robert. *Dandelion Hill*
Burton, Jane. *Caper the kid*
   Dizzie the pony
   Fancy the fox
   Ginger the kitten
   Gipper the guinea pig
   Hoppy the toad
   Jack the puppy
   Pacer, the pony
   Snowy, the barn owl
   Surfer the seal
   Taddy the toad
Cannon, Janell. *Verdi*
Carle, Eric. *My very first book of growth*
Carrier, Lark. *Scout and Cody*
Carter, Dorothy (Dorothy A.). *Wilhe'mina Miles after the stork night*
Caseley, Judith. *Annie's potty*
Chaffin, Lillie D. *Tommy's big problem*
Ciardi, John. *Scrappy, the pup*
Civardi, Anne. *Potty time*
Clayton, Gordon. *Lamb*
Cleary, Beverly. *The growing-up feet*
   Janet's thingamajigs
Coats, Laura Jane. *Mr. Jordan in the park*
Cobb, Vicki. *Feeding yourself*
   Getting dressed
Cohen, Miriam. *Jim meets the thing*
Cole, Joanna. *My big boy potty*
   My big girl potty
   Your new potty
Collard, Sneed B. *Leaving home*
Cooke, Trish. *When I grow bigger*
Cooney, Nancy Evans. *The blanket that had to go*
   Donald says thumbs down

Corey, Dorothy. *Tomorrow you can*
Curtis, Jamie Lee. *It's hard to be five*
   When I was little
Dauer, Rosamond. *Bullfrog grows up*
Davies, Gill. *Tiny's big wish*
Delton, Judy. *The best mom in the world*
DeLuise, Dom. *Charlie the caterpillar*
De Paola, Tomie (Thomas Anthony). *Katie's good idea*
Devine, Monica. *Carry me, Mama*
Douglas, Ann. *Baby science*
Dowson, Nick. *Tigress*
Drescher, Joan E. *I'm in charge!*
Ernst, Kathryn F. *Danny and his thumb*
Esbensen, Barbara Juster. *Who shrank my grandmother's house?*
Faison, Eleanora. *Becoming*
Fassler, Joan. *Don't worry dear*
   The man of the house
Felt, Sue. *Rosa-too-little*
Fontenot, Mary Alice. *Tah-Tye*
Fox, Mem. *Shoes from grandpa*
Fraggalosch, Audrey. *Grizzly bear family*
Freedman, Sally. *Devin's new bed*
Freeman, Mylo. *Potty*
Fribourg, Marjorie G. *Ching-Ting and the ducks*
Galbraith, Kathryn Osebold. *Roommates*
Galvin, Laura Gates. *River Otter at Autumn Lane*
Garelick, May. *Just my size*
Gelbard, Jane. *My bye-bye bottle book*
   My dressing book
   My eating book
   My sharing book
Gentieu, Penny. *Grow! babies!*
George, Jean Craighead. *Look to the north*
Gikow, Louise. *Bye-bye, pacifier*
Goennel, Heidi. *When I grow up . . .*
   While I am little
Goodings, Lennie. *When you grow up*
Gould, Deborah. *Aaron's shirt*
Graham, Bob. *The red woolen blanket*
Greenstein, Elaine. *As big as you*
Grifalconi, Ann. *Flyaway girl*
Grimes, Nikki. *It's raining laughter*
   Something on my mind
Grindley, Sally. *Little Sibu*
Groundhog at Evergreen Road
Hale, Irina. *Small big bad boy*
Hall, Derek. *Elephant bathes*
   Gorilla builds
   Polar bear leaps
Hänel, Wolfram. *Little elephant's song*
Hanson, Joan. *I won't be afraid*
Harper, Charise Mericle. *When I grow up*
Harris, Robie H. *Go! Go! Maria!*
   I hate kisses
Hayes, Geoffrey. *Patrick and Ted*
Heide, Florence Parry. *Oh, grow up!*
Heiligman, Deborah. *Babies*
Heitler, Susan M. (Susan McCrensky). *David decides, no more thumb-sucking*
Hellard, Susan. *Baby lemur*
Henderson, Kathy. *The baby dances*
Henkes, Kevin. *Owen*
Hewett, Joan. *A flamingo chick grows up*
   A giraffe calf grows up
   A harbor seal pup grows up
   A kangaroo joey grows up
   A koala joey grows up
   A monkey baby grows up
   A penguin chick grows up
   A tiger cub grows up
Hines, Anna Grossnickle. *All by myself*
   Big like me
Ho, Minfong. *The two brothers*
Hoban, Brom. *Skunk Lane*
Hoban, Lillian. *Big Little Otter*
Hobbs, Will. *Howling Hill*
Hoffman, Don. *Billy is a big boy*

Hoffman, Phyllis. *Baby's first year*
Hopkins, Lee Bennett. *Through our eyes*
Horn, Peter. *When I grow up . . .*
Horner, Althea J. *Little big girl*
Howard, Arthur. *When I was five*
Howard, Ellen. *The big seed*
Iverson, Genie. *I want to be big*
Jenkin-Pearce, Susie. *Boris's big ache*
Jensen, Patricia. *Be patient, Little Chick*
    Gentle Little Lion
Jeppson, Ann-Sofie. *You're growing up, Pontus*
Johnson, Crockett. *We wonder what will Walter be? When he grows up*
Johnson, Marion. *Caillou, new shoes*
Jonas, Ann. *When you were a baby*
Joosse, Barbara M. *Fourth of July*
Jorgensen, Richard. *Reading with Dad*
Joslin, Mary. *The shore beyond*
Joyce, William. *Big time Olie*
Kandoian, Ellen. *Maybe she forgot*
Karon, Jan. *The trellis and the seed*
Keller, Holly. *Jacob's tree*
Kessler, Cristina. *One night*
Khalsa, Dayal Kaur. *I want a dog*
Kirk, Daniel. *Bigger*
Klinting, Lars. *Regal the golden eagle*
Koralek, Jenny. *Cat and Kit*
Krasilovsky, Phyllis. *The very little boy*
    The very little girl
Kraus, Robert. *Leo the late bloomer*
Krauss, Ruth. *The growing story*
Krensky, Stephen. *Children of the wind and water*
Kuiper, Nannie. *Bailey the bear cub*
Lakin, Pat (Patricia). *Growing up*
Lebrun, Claude. *Little Brown Bear does not want to eat*
    Little Brown Bear learns to share
Lester, Alison. *When Frank was four*
Levine, Abby. *What did mommy do before you?*
Lewison, Wendy Cheyette. *The princess and the potty*
Lexau, Joan M. *I hate red rover*
Lindgren, Barbro. *Sam's potty*
London, Jonathan. *Old salt, young salt*
Maccarone, Grace. *My tooth is about to fall out*
McCarty, Peter. *Baby steps*
McCully, Emily Arnold. *The ballot box battle*
MacDonald, Amy. *Cousin Ruth's tooth*
MacKinnon, Debbie. *Baby's first year*
McPhail, David M. *Pig Pig grows up*
Magloff, Lisa. *Bear*
    Butterfly
    Duckling
    Elephant
    Frog
    Kitten
    Penguin
    Rabbit
Marshak, S. (Samuil). *The pup grew up!*
Martin, C. L. G. *The blueberry train*
Mason, Jane B. *Hello, two-wheeler!*
Massie, Diane Redfield. *Tiny pin*
Mayer, Marianna. *The prince and the pauper*
Mayer, Mercer. *Bun Bun's birthday*
    Just big enough
Meddaugh, Susan. *Martha and Skits*
Meister, Cari. *When Tiny was tiny*
Mellage, Nanette. *See me grow, head to toe*
Miller, Virginia. *On your potty!*
Minshull, Evelyn White. *Eaglet's world*
Moers, Hermann. *Camomile heads for home*
    Little Ben
Moncure, Jane Belk. *Now I am five!*
    Now I am four!
    Now I am three!
Monnier, Miriam. *Just right*
Mordvinoff, Nicolas. *Coral Island*
Morgan, Richard. *Zoo poo*
Morris, Johnny. *Animal-go-round*
Moss, Thylias. *I want to be*

Mueller, Doris L. *Small One's adventure*
Munsch, Robert N. *Andrew's loose tooth*
    I have to go!
Murphy, Jill. *The last noo-noo*
My potty book for boys
My potty book for girls
Nelson, S. D. *Gift horse*
Newberry, Clare Turlay. *Percy, Polly and Pete*
Nicholls, Judith. *Billywise*
Noll, Sally. *I have a loose tooth*
    That bothered Kate
Nordlicht, Lillian. *I love to laugh*
Once I was . . .
Otto, Carolyn. *Our puppies are growing*
Packard, Mary. *When I am big*
Parish, Peggy. *I can – can you?*
Patrick, Denise Lewis. *No diapers for baby!*
Pearson, Debora. *Leo's tree*
Pellowski, Anne. *Stairstep farm*
Pfeffer, Wendy. *Mallard duck at Meadow View Pond*
Piggy and Bear in their underwear
Pinkwater, Daniel Manus. *Young Larry*
Pitcher, Caroline. *Run with the wind*
Poulin, Stéphane. *My mother's loves*
Power, Barbara. *I wish Laura's mommy was my mommy*
Reichmeier, Betty. *Potty time!*
Rockwell, Anne F. *Growing like me*
Rogers, Fred. *Going to the potty*
Rogers, Paul (Patrick). *Ruby's dinnertime*
    Ruby's potty
Rosman, Steven M. *Deena the damselfly*
Ross, Anna. *I did it!*
    I have to go
Ross, Katharine (1954–). *When you were a baby*
Ross, Tony. *I want my potty*
Schertle, Alice. *Maisie*
Schlein, Miriam. *Billy, the littlest one*
    Herman McGregor's world
    When will the world be mine?
Schlessinger, Laura. *Dr. Laura Schlessinger's Growing up is hard*
Schwartz, Amy. *Begin at the beginning*
    Things I learned in second grade
Scott, Ann Herbert. *Someday rider*
Scuderi, Lucia. *To fly*
Sears, William, M.D. *You can go to the potty*
Senshu, Noriko. *Sonny's dream*
Sharmat, Marjorie Weinman. *Bartholomew the bossy*
Shavick, Andrea. *You'll grow soon, Alex*
Sheehan, Patty. *Shadow and the ready time*
Sis, Peter. *Madlenka*
Slepian, Jan. *Emily just in time*
Smith, Robert Paul. *When I am big*
Snyder, Zilpha Keatley. *Come on, Patsy*
Solomon, Chuck. *Moving up from kindergarten to first grade*
Sonnenschein, Harriet. *Harold's hideaway thumb*
Stanley, Diane. *Captain Whiz-Bang*
Stevenson, James. *Higher on the door*
    I meant to tell you
Stimson, Joan. *Big Panda, Little Panda*
Strub, Susanne. *Lulu goes swimming*
    Lulu on her bike
Suen, Anastasia. *Baby born*
    Baby born [board book]
Svend Otto S (Svend Otto Sorensen). *The giant fish and other stories*
Tildes, Phyllis Limbacher. *Billy's big-boy bed*
Turkle, Brinton. *Obadiah the Bold*
Turner, Sandy. *Grow up*
Van Leeuwenm, Jean. *"Wait for me!" said Maggie McGee*
Waber, Bernard. *You're a little kid with a big heart*
Waddell, Martin. *Once there were giants*
Waite, Judy. *The stray kitten*
Wallace, Karen. *Diving dolphin*
    Imagine you are a tiger
Watts, Barrie. *Mouse*
Waxman, Stephanie. *What is a girl? What is a boy?*
Weiss, Nicki. *Barney is big*

Welber, Robert. *Goodbye, hello*
Wells, Rosemary. *Timothy goes to school*
Weninger, Brigitte. *Davy in the middle*
Wilhelm, Hans. *I lost my tooth!*
Wilkes, Angela. *See how I grow*
Willis, Jeanne. *What did I look like when I was a baby?*
Willis, Val. *Silly little chick*
Wilson, Gina. *Ignis*
Winter, Jeanette. *My baby*
Winters, Kay. *Tiger trail*
    Wolf watch
Wittman, Sally. *A special trade*
Wood, Audrey. *Oh my baby bear!*
Yoshida, Toshi. *Young lions*
Young, Helen. *A throne for Sesame*
Young, Ruth. *My potty chair*
Zagone, Theresa. *No nap for me*
Zagwÿn, Deborah Turney. *The pumpkin blanket*
Zimelman, Nathan. *If I were strong enough . . .*
Zolotow, Charlotte (Shapiro). *But not Billy*
    Do you know what I'll do?
    I like to be little
    May I visit?
    Someone new
    When I have a son

Behavior – hiding

Adler, David A. *Hiding from the Nazis*
Ahlberg, Allan. *Master Salt the sailor's son*
Alborough, Jez. *Hide and seek*
Aldis, Dorothy (Keeley). *Hiding*
Apperley, Dawn. *In the jungle*
Arnosky, Jim. *I see animals hiding*
Aruego, José. *We hide, you seek*
Asch, Frank. *Moongame*
Bernhard, Durga. *Alphabeasts*
Blacker, Terence. *Herbie Hamster, where are you?*
Blake, Quentin. *Cockatoos*
Blanchard, Arlene. *The naughty lamb*
Brutschy, Jennifer. *Celeste and Crabapple Sam*
Burns, Kate. *In the snow*
Chorao, Kay. *Kate's box*
Cole, Michael. *Head in the sand*
Dale, Penny. *Ten play hide-and-seek*
Dodd, Lynley. *Find me a tiger*
Dubanevich, Arlene. *Pigs in hiding*
Ganeri, Anita. *Animal hideaways*
Gerstein, Mordicai. *William, where are you?*
Gomi, Taro. *Where's the fish?*
Greene, Carol. *Where is that cat?*
Gretz, Susanna. *Hide-and-seek*
Greydanus, Rose. *My secret hiding place*
Grifalconi, Ann. *The village that vanished*
Heller, Ruth. *How to hide a butterfly*
    How to hide a polar bear
Hughes, Shirley. *Hiding*
Hulse, Gillian. *Morris, where are you?*
Humphries, Tudor. *Hiding*
Hutchins, Pat. *Titch and Daisy*
Jahn-Clough, Lisa. *Missing Molly*
Jennings, Linda M. *Hide and seek birthday treat*
Koralek, Jenny. *The cobweb curtain*
Kudrna, C. Imbior. *To bathe a boa*
Livermore, Elaine. *Looking for Henry*
Love, Pamela. *A loon alone*
McCarthy, Bobette. *Happy hiding hippos*
McClung, Robert. *How animals hide*
McNaughton, Colin. *Shh! (Don't tell Mr. Wolf!)*
McPhail, David M. *Where can an elephant hide?*
Major, Beverly. *Playing sardines*
Matus, Greta. *Where are you, Jason?*
Milios, Rita. *Sneaky Pete*
Mintzberg, Yvette. *Sally, where are you?*
Nims, Bonnie Larkin. *Where is the bear in the city?*
Oppenheim, Shulamith Levey. *The lily cupboard*
Oram, Hiawyn. *Where are you hiding, little lamb?*

Oxford Scientific Films. *Danger colors*
    Hide and seek
Philpot, Graham. *Where is Little Harry?*
Polacco, Patricia. *The butterfly*
Price, Mathew. *Where's Alfie?*
Raschka, Christopher. *Whaley Whale*
Santore, Charles. *A stowaway on Noah's Ark*
Schertle, Alice. *Jeremy Bean's St. Patrick's Day*
    That Olive!
Sowler, Sandie. *Amazing animal disguises*
Steig, William. *Toby, where are you?*
Stoeke, Janet Morgan. *Hide and seek*
Szekeres, Cyndy. *Hide-and-seek duck*
Tafuri, Nancy. *Where did Bunny go?*
Tulloch, Richard. *Danny in the toybox*
Unwin, Pippa. *The great zoo hunt!*
Vigna, Judith. *The hiding house*
Walsh, Ellen Stoll. *Mouse paint*
Walsh, Melanie. *Hide and sleep*
Warren, Cathy. *Springtime bears*
Weare, Tim. *Hide-and-seek with Leo*
Wood, John Norris. *Jungles*
    Oceans
Ziefert, Harriet. *Where's the cat?*
    Where's the dog?
    Where's the guinea pig?
    Where's the turtle?
Zion, Gene. *Hide and seek day*

Behavior – hiding things

Allen, Pamela. *Hidden treasure*
Bason, Lillian. *Those foolish Molboes!*
Baylor, Byrd. *Your own best secret place*
Beck, Andrea. *Elliot digs for treasure*
Brady, Susan. *Find my blanket*
Croswell, Volney. *How to hide a hippopotamus*
Demi. *Demi's find the animals A B C*
Henwood, Simon. *A piece of luck*
Hines, Anna Grossnickle. *No, no Jack!*
Ivory, Lesley Anne. *The birthday cat*
Micklethwait, Lucy. *Spot a cat*
    Spot a dog
Modesitt, Jeanne. *Little Bunny's Easter surprise*
Penner, Lucille Recht. *Where's that bone?*
Rodda, Emily. *Where do you hide two elephants?*
Wood, Leslie. *A dog called Mischief*

Behavior – hurrying

Alda, Arlene. *Hurry Granny Annie*
Biro, Val. *Gumdrop beats the clock*
Gomi, Taro. *First comes Harry*
Greydanus, Rose. *Willie the slowpoke*
Hurd, Edith Thacher. *Hurry, hurry!*
McCully, Emily Arnold. *Hurry!*
Myers, Bernice. *It happens to everyone*
Pfister, Marcus. *Wake up, Santa Claus!*
Steiner, Charlotte. *What's the hurry, Harry?*
Thoreau, Henry D. *What befell at Mrs. Brooks's*

Behavior – imitation

Allamand, Pascale. *The animals who changed their colors*
Aruego, José. *Look what I can do*
Asch, Frank. *Just like daddy*
Barrett, Judi. *Animals should definitely not act like people*
    Animals should definitely not wear clothing
Bendick, Jeanne. *Why can't I?*
Blake, Quentin. *Zagazoo*
Blakeley, Peggy. *What shall I be tomorrow?*
Buckmaster, Henrietta. *Lucy and Loki*
Calhoun, Mary. *The nine lives of Homer C. Cat*
Canning, Kate. *A painted tale*
Cauley, Lorinda Bryan. *The animal kids*
Charlton, Elizabeth. *Terrible tyrannosaurus*
Clewes, Dorothy. *Henry Hare's boxing match*

Cole, Brock. *Nothing but a pig*
Cort, Ben. *Pigs can't fly!*
Elliott, George. *The boy who loved bananas*
Farber, Norma. *There goes feathertop!*
Gauch, Patricia Lee. *Dance, Tanya*
Gill-Brown, Vanessa. *Rufferella*
Graham, Amanda. *Who wants Arthur?*
Hallinan, P. K. (Patrick K.). *Where's Michael?*
Harrison, David Lee. *Dylan, the eagle-hearted chicken*
Heine, Helme. *Mr. Miller, the dog*
Hersom, Kathleen. *The copycat*
Inkpen, Mick. *Kipper*
Jones, Chuck. *William the backwards skunk*
Kellogg, Steven (Stephen). *A rose for Pinkerton*
Kent, Jack. *The once-upon-a-time dragon*
Lavis, Steve. *Jump!*
Lawrence, Michael (Michael C.). *The caterpillar that roared*
Marzollo, Jean. *Pretend you're a cat*
Mole, John. *Copy cat*
Moore, Inga. *Fifty red night-caps*
Munsch, Robert N. *Stephanie's ponytail*
Newcome, Zita. *Animal fun*
Noll, Sally. *That bothered Kate*
Numeroff, Laura Joffe. *If you give a mouse a cookie*
O'Connor, Jane. *Nina, Nina and the copycat ballerina*
Ostheeren, Ingrid. *I'm the real Santa Claus!*
Packard, Mary. *When I am big*
Rathmann, Peggy. *Ruby the copycat*
Riddell, Chris. *Bird's new shoes*
Ross, Christine. *Lily and the bears*
Ruurs, Margriet. *Emma's cold day*
Saltzberg, Barney. *The yawn*
Schwartz, Amy. *Bea and Mr. Jones*
Shields, Carol Diggory. *I am really a princess*
Steig, William. *Toby, what are you?*
Van Caster, Nancy. *An alligator lives in Benjamin's house*

Behavior – indecision

Cooper, Elisha. *Magic thinks big*

Behavior – indifference

Blos, Joan W. *Old Henry*
Dubanevich, Arlene. *Pig William*
Hogrogian, Nonny. *The hermit and Harry and me*
Kroll, Steven. *Will you be my valentine?*
Roy, Ronald. *Three ducks went wandering*
Sendak, Maurice. *Pierre*
Sharmat, Marjorie Weinman. *I don't care*
Watts, Mabel (Pizzey). *The day it rained watermelons*

Behavior – lost

Alborough, Jez. *Hug*
Alexander, Liza. *Ernie gets lost*
Allen, Laura Jean. *Where is Freddy?*
Aller, Susan B. *Emma and the night dogs*
Anderson, C. W. (Clarence Williams). *Blaze finds forgotten roads*
    Blaze finds the trail
Anderson, Scoular. *MacPelican's American adventure*
Anholt, Catherine. *Chimp and Zee and the big storm*
Arnosky, Jim. *Armadillo's orange*
Ayer, Jacqueline. *Little Silk*
Bacheller, Irving. *Lost in the fog*
Baker, Leslie A. *Paris cat*
Balian, Lorna. *Amelia's nine lives*
Barklem, Jill. *Autumn story*
Bartoli, Jennifer. *Snow on bear's nose*
Barton, Byron. *Where's Al?*
Bassett, Lisa. *Beany and Scamp*
Beck, Ian. *Home before dark*
    Teddy's snowy day
Belting, Natalia Maree. *Verity Mullens and the Indian*
Bemelmans, Ludwig. *Madeline and the gypsies*
Beni, Ruth. *Sir Baldergog the great*
Benjamin, Alan. *Ribtickle Town*

Bergen, Lara Rice. *Washington Irving's Rip Van Winkle*
Berger, Barbara Helen. *A lot of otters*
Berson, Harold. *Henry Possum*
Bliss, Corinne Demas. *The littlest matryoshka*
Boegehold, Betty. *Pawpaw's run*
Bograd, Larry. *Lost in the store*
Bolliger, Max. *Sandy at the children's zoo*
Bornstein, Ruth Lercher. *Annabelle*
    Jim
Bothwell, Jean. *Paddy and Sam*
Brett, Jan. *Daisy comes home*
Brewster, Patience. *Ellsworth and the cats from Mars*
Brown, Jane Clark. *Whonk, and whonk again*
Brown, Judith Gwyn. *Max and the truffle pig*
Brown, Marc Tolon. *Arthur lost and found*
Brown, Marcia. *Tamarindo!*
Brown, Margaret Wise. *Little lost lamb*
    Three little animals
Bruna, Dick. *Snuffy*
Brunhoff, Laurent de. *Babar's little girl*
Buffett, Jimmy. *Trouble dolls*
Bunting, Eve (Anne Evelyn). *Jane Martin, dog detective*
Bush, Timothy. *Teddy bear, teddy bear*
Butterworth, Nick. *The lost sheep*
Calmenson, Stephanie. *Where is Grandma Potamus?*
Carigiet, Alois. *Anton the goatherd*
Carle, Eric. *Have you seen my cat?*
Carrick, Carol. *The highest balloon on the common*
    Left behind
Carter, Anne Laurel. *Ruff leaves home*
Carter, Noelle. *I'm a little mouse*
Cartlidge, Michelle. *Pippin and Pod*
Chottin, Ariane. *Beaver gets lost*
Cocca-Leffler, Maryann. *Missing: one stuffed rabbit*
Cohen, Miriam. *Lost in the museum*
Cole, Joanna. *The Clown-Arounds go on vacation*
Corddry, Thomas I. *Kibby's big feat*
Cousins, Lucy. *Jazzy in the jungle*
Cowley, Stewart. *Little lost rabbit*
Cummings, Betty Sue. *Turtle*
Dalmais, Anne-Marie. *Betsy the bunny*
Daly, Niki. *The boy on the beach*
De Beer, Hans. *Little polar bear*
    Little polar bear, take me home!
Deetlefs, Rene. *Tabu and the dancing elephants*
Delaney, Ned. *Bad dog!*
Donovan, Gail. *Lost at sea*
Drummond, Violet H. *Phewtus the squirrel*
Dubanevich, Arlene. *Calico cows*
Dubar, Joyce. *The very small*
Dwyer, Mindy. *Aurora, a tale of the Northern Lights*
Edwards, Richard. *Always copycub*
Enderle, Judith (Ann) Ross. *Where are you, little Zack?*
Erickson, Phoebe. *Just follow me*
Escudie, René. *Paul and Sebastian*
Farber, Norma. *Where's Gomer?*
Fitzpatrick, Marie-Louise. *Lizzy and Skunk*
Flack, Marjorie. *Angus lost*
Fleischman, Paul. *Lost!*
Fletcher, Elizabeth. *The little goat*
Fletcher, Ralph J. *The circus surprise*
Fowler, Richard. *Little Chick's big adventure*
Francis, Frank. *The magic wallpaper*
Freschet, Gina. *Naty's parade*
Gantschev, Ivan. *The Christmas teddy bear*
Gay, Michel. *Take me for a ride*
Gay, Zhenya. *Small one*
George, Jean Craighead. *Rhino romp*
Gliori, Debi. *Mr. Bear says, "Are you there, Baby Bear?"*
Goble, Paul. *The friendly wolf*
Goldsmith, Howard. *Little lost dog*
Gomi, Taro. *I lost my dad*
Goode, Diane. *Where's our mama?*
Grimm, Jacob. *Hansel and Gretel*, ill. by Adrienne Adams
    Hansel and Gretel, ill. by Anthony Browne
    Hansel and Gretel, ill. by Susan Jeffers
    Hansel and Gretel, ill. by Winslow P. Pels

Hansel and Gretel, ill. by Jane Ray
Hansel and Gretel, ill. by Conxita Rodriguez
Hansel and Gretel, ill. by Christopher Santoro
Hansel and Gretel, ill. by John Wallner
Hansel and Gretel, ill. by Claudia Wolf
Hansel and Gretel, ill. by Paul O. Zelinsky
Hansel and Gretel, ill. by Lisbeth Zwerger
Grimsdell, Jeremy. *Kalinzu*
Grindley, Sally. *Where are my chicks?*
Grossman, Bill. *Tommy at the grocery store*
Guilfoile, Elizabeth. *Have you seen my brother?*
Guthrie, Donna. *Grandpa doesn't know it's me*
Gutman, Anne. *Lisa in New York*
Hader, Berta Hoerner. *Lost in the zoo*
Hamm, Diane Johnston. *Laney's lost momma*
Hänel, Wolfram. *Little elephant runs away*
Hardy, Tad. *Lost cat*
Hassett, John. *Junior*
Hawkins, Colin. *Tog the dog*
Hayes, Sarah. *This is the bear*
Henderson, Kathy. *Disney's Pooh's grand adventure: the search for Christopher Robin*
Henkes, Kevin. *Sheila Rae, the brave*
Hill, Eric. *Where's Spot?*
Hines, Anna Grossnickle. *Don't worry, I'll find you*
Hirsh, Marilyn. *Where is Yonkela?*
Hoban, Lillian. *The laziest robot in zone one*
Hobbs, Will. *Howling Hill*
Hoff, Syd. *Bernard on his own*
Holabird, Katharine. *Angelina and Henry*
Horse, Harry. *Little rabbit lost*
Hurd, Edith Thacher. *Johnny Lion's book*
Hutchins, Pat. *Where's the baby?*
Ichikawa, Satomi. *La La Rose*
Inches, Alison. *Corduroy's hike*
Irving, Washington. *Rip Van Winkle*, ill. by John Howe
Rip Van Winkle, ill. by Thomas Locker
Rip Van Winkle, ill. by Peter Wingham
Itaya, Satoshi. *Buttons and Bo*
Jaques, Faith. *Tilly's rescue*
Jeram, Anita. *Bunny, my Honey*
Joerns, Consuelo. *The foggy rescue*
The forgotten bear
Johnson, Paul Brett. *Lost*
Jonas, Ann. *Two bear cubs*
Jonathan, Langley. *Missing*
Kanome, Kayoko. *Little Mop lost*
Keats, Ezra Jack. *My dog is lost!*
Kemp, Moira. *Lift-the-flap chick*
Kessler, Leonard P. *Are we lost, daddy?*
Kinsey-Warnock, Natalie. *The bear that heard crying*
Knüppel, Helga. *The adventures of Christabel Crocodile*
Christabel Crocodile's birthday egg
Kocí, Marta. *Katie's kitten*
Komaiko, Leah. *Where can Daniel be?*
Kovalski, Maryann. *Brenda and Edward*
Krause, Ute. *Nora and the great bear*
Labatt, Mary. *Sam gets lost*
Lambert, Martha Lewis. *I won't get lost*
Lane, Judith. *Buster, where are you?*
Lears, Laurie. *Ian's walk*
Levine, Abby. *Ollie knows everything*
Lewis, J. Patrick. *The Christmas of the reddle moon*
Lewison, Wendy Cheyette. *Princess Buttercup*
Lindbergh, Reeve. *Bridget and the gray wolves*
Lisker, Sonia O. *Lost*
Livermore, Elaine. *Follow the fox*
Lobel, Arnold. *Uncle Elephant*
London, Jonathan. *Ali, child of the desert*
Loupy, Christophe. *Don't worry, Wags*
Lubell, Winifred. *Rosalie, the bird market turtle*
Maccarone, Grace. *The class trip*
McCloskey, Robert. *Blueberries for Sal*
McCully, Emily Arnold. *Picnic*
McFarland, Lyn Rossiter. *Widget & the puppy*
McGraw, Sheila. *Pussycats everywhere*
McKee, David. *Elmer and Wilbur*

McKelvey, Douglas Kaine. *A child's Christmas at St. Nicholas Circle*
McPhail, David M. *The blue door*
Lost
Maisner, Heather. *Find Mouse in the house*
Maris, Ron. *Are you there, bear?*
Marks, Alan. *Nowhere to be found*
Marshall, James. *Hansel and Gretel*
Martin, Jacqueline Briggs. *Bizzy Bones and Moosemouse*
Marzollo, Jean. *Snow angel*
Mathews, Judith. *There's nothing to d-o-o-o!*
Tuti, Blue Horse, and the Nipnope Man
Mauner, Claudia. *Zoe Sophia's scrapbook*
Melmed, Laura Krauss. *Little Oh*
Mendoza, George. *Alphabet sheep*
Miles, Miska. *This little pig*
Miller, M. L. *The enormous snore*
Minarik, Else Holmelund. *Little Bear's new friend*
Modell, Frank. *Tooley! Tooley!*
Moerbeek, Kees. *The diary of Hansel and Gretel*
Moers, Hermann. *Annie's dancing day*
Mogensen, Jan. *Lost and found Teddy*
When Teddy woke early
Montresor, Beni. *Hansel and Gretel*
Morley, Carol. *A spider and a pig*
Morpurgo, Michael. *Wombat goes walkabout*
Moser, Erwin. *Wilma the elephant*
Moss, Miriam. *The snow bear*
Nakatani, Chiyoko. *The day Chiro was lost*
Naylor, Phyllis Reynolds. *Ducks disappearing*
Nims, Bonnie Larkin. *Where is the bear?*
Nishimura, Kae. *Dinah*
Oates, Joyce Carol. *Come meet Muffin!*
Offen, Hilda. *Elephant pie*
Olsen, Ib Spang. *Cat alley*
Parenteau, Shirley. *I'll bet you thought I was lost*
Paul, Jan S. *Hortense*
Peet, Bill (William Bartlett). *Ella*
Politi, Leo. *The nicest gift*
Ragz, M. M. *Lost little angel*
Rand, Gloria. *Willie takes a hike*
Remkiewicz, Frank. *The last time I saw Harris*
Rey, Margret (Margret Elisabeth Waldstein). *Curious George goes to the hospital*
Root, Phyllis. *Oliver finds his way*
Ross, Tony. *Hansel and Gretel*
Rubel, Nicole. *It came from the swamp*
Salat, Cristina. *Peanut's emergency*
Sauer, Julia Lina. *Mike's house*
Saxon, Charles D. *Don't worry about Poopsie*
Scheffler, Ursel. *Taking care of Sister Bear*
Schertle, Alice. *Little Frog's song*
Schneider, Antonie. *Luke the Lionhearted*
Schumacher, Claire. *Tim and Jim*
Seignobosc, Françoise. *Minou*
Springtime for Jeanne-Marie
Shortall, Leonard W. *Andy, the dog walker*
Simmons, Jane. *Come along, Daisy!*
Quack, Daisy, quack!
Singer, Marilyn. *Chester, the out-of-work dog*
Slepian, Jan. *Lost moose*
Slobodkin, Louis. *Yasu and the strangers*
Smith, Cara Lockhart. *Twenty-six rabbits run riot*
Standon, Anna. *Little duck lost*
Stevenson, James. *Howard*
Sykes, Julie. *Dora's chicks*
Taylor, Mark. *The case of the missing kittens*
Henry the castaway
Henry the explorer
Titherington, Jeanne. *Where are you going, Emma?*
Tokuda, Wendy. *Humphrey the lost whale*
Trimble, Patti. *Lost!*
Trottier, Maxine. *Dreamstones*
Storm at Batoche
Tsutsui, Yoriko. *Anna in charge*
Turnbull, Ann. *Rob goes a-hunting*
Vincent, Gabrielle. *Where are you, Ernest and Celestine?*
Vreeken, Elizabeth. *The boy who would not say his name*

Waddell, Martin. *A kitten called Moonlight*
   Sailor Bear
   Small Bear lost
   Webster J. Duck
Waite, Judy. *The stray kitten*
Ward, Heather Patricia. *I promise I'll find you*
Ward, Nick. *Farmer George and the lost chick*
Waring, Richard (Richard M. N.). *Alberto the dancing alligator*
Watanabe, Shigeo. *Where's my daddy?*
Waters, Tony. *Sailor's bride*
Wells, Rosemary. *McDuff comes home*
   Max's dragon shirt
Wild, Margaret. *The pocket dogs*
Wold, Jo Anne. *Well! Why didn't you say so?*
Ylla. *Two little bears*
Young, Evelyn. *The tale of Tai*
Ziefert, Harriet. *Wee G.*

Behavior – lost & found possessions

Abolafia, Yossi. *A fish for Mrs. Gardenia*
Ackerman, Karen. *Araminta's paint box*
Ahlberg, Allan. *Mystery tour*
Alarcón, Karen Beaumont. *Louella Mae, she's run away!*
Amoss, Berthe. *What did you lose, Santa?*
Ardizzone, Edward. *The little girl and the tiny doll*
Armitage, Ronda. *The lighthouse keeper's catastrophe*
Ayer, Jacqueline. *Nu Dang and his kite*
Baker, Alan. *Where's mouse?*
Baker, Leslie A. *Paris cat*
Banks, Kate (Katherine A.). *Peter and the talking shoes*
Bannon, Laura. *Red mittens*
Barrows, Marjorie Wescott. *The funny hat*
Bassett, Lisa. *Beany and Scamp*
Birchall, Mark. *Rabbit's birthday surprise*
Birdseye, Tom. *Airmail to the moon*
Blackaby, Susan. *Rembrandt's hat*
Blos, Joan W. *Hello, shoes!*
Bogan, Paulette. *Spike in the city*
Bond, Michael. *Paddington at the zoo*
Bottner, Barbara. *Big boss! Little boss!*
   Pish and Posh
Bowden, Joan Chase. *Who took the top hat trick?*
Boyle, Constance. *The story of Little Owl*
Brandle, Bine. *Flusi, the sock monster*
Brett, Jan. *The mitten*
Bromhall, Winifred. *Middle Matilda*
Brown, Marc Tolon. *D. W.'s lost blankie*
Burningham, John. *The blanket*
Butler, Kristi T. *Rip's secret spot*
Carmichael, Clay. *Lonesome bear*
Carter, Noelle. *Where's my squishy ball?*
Chorao, Kay. *Maudie's umbrella*
   Molly's lies
   Molly's Moe
Coman, Carolyn. *Losing things at Mr. Mudd's*
Coombs, Patricia. *The lost playground*
Cooper, Helen (Helen F.). *Tatty-Ratty*
Craft, Ruth. *The day of the rainbow*
Davidson, Amanda. *Teddy in the garden*
Denton, Terry. *The school for laughter*
Derby, Sally. *Two fools and a horse*
Dixon, Ann. *The blueberry shoe*
Dodds, Siobhan. *Charles Tiger*
Donaldson, Julia. *Room on the broom*
Dornbusch, Erica. *Finding Kate's shoes*
Dunrea, Olivier. *The trow-wife's treasure*
Eagle, Ellen. *Gypsy's cleaning day*
Edwards, Julie Andrews. *Dumpy to the rescue!*
Egg-napped!
Ellwand, David. *Alfred's camera*
   Alfred's party
Eriksson, Eva. *The tooth trip*
Ernst, Lisa Campbell. *Stella Louella's runaway book*
Falconer, Ian. *Olivia – and the missing toy*
Feiffer, Jules. *I lost my bear*
Findlay, Lisa. *What's in Oscar's trashcan?*

Fitzgerald, Ella. *A-tisket, a-tasket*
Flynn, Kitson. *Carrot in my pocket*
Freedman, Claire. *Night-night, Emily*
Garland, Sarah. *Polly's puffin*
Gay, Michel. *Little shoe*
Geisert, Arthur. *The giant ball of string*
Gillerlain, Gayle. *Reverend Thomas's false teeth*
Gliori, Debi. *Flora's blanket*
Gorbachev, Valeri. *Whose hat is it?*
Gulbis, Stephen. *Cowgirl Rosie and her five baby bison*
Guthrie, Donna. *Grandpa doesn't know it's me*
Haddon, Mark. *Gilbert's gobstopper*
Handford, Martin. *Where's Waldo?*
   Where's Waldo? The wonder book
Hannant, Judith Stuller. *Three little kittens*
Harranth, Wolf. *The flute concert*
Hassett, John. *Junior*
Havill, Juanita. *Jamaica's find*
Hayes, Sarah. *A bad start for Santa*
   Lucy Anna and the Finders
Hayward, Linda. *The case of the missing Duckie*
Herman, Gail. *What a hungry puppy!*
Hines, Anna Grossnickle. *Moompa, Toby, and Bomp*
Hissey, Jane. *Little Bear lost*
Hoberman, Mary Ann. *The looking book*
Hoff, Syd. *Arturo's baton*
Hutchins, H. J. (Hazel J.). *Leanna builds a genie trap*
   Norman's snowball
Ichikawa, Satomi. *The first bear in Africa!*
Ingman, Bruce. *Lost property*
Inkpen, Mick. *Billy's beetle*
   Where, oh where, is Kipper's bear?
Jeram, Anita. *Bill's belly button*
Johnson, B. J. *My blanket Burt*
Johnson, G. Francis. *Has anybody lost a glove?*
Jonas, Ann. *Where can it be?*
Jonovitz, Marilyn. *Three little kittens*
Kako, Satoshi. *Little Daruma and little Kaminari*
Kay, Helen. *One mitten Lewis*
Keenen, George. *The preposterous week*
Keller, Holly. *A bed full of cats*
Kelley, Anne. *Daisy's discovery*
Kellogg, Steven (Stephen). *The mystery of the magic green ball*
   The mystery of the missing red mitten
Ketteman, Helen. *I remember papa*
Kroll, Steven. *Patches*
   Patches lost and found
Lakin, Pat (Patricia). *Trash and treasure*
Lewis, Kim. *First snow*
Lewison, Wendy Cheyette. *Where's my teddy?*
Lexau, Joan M. *Finders keepers, losers weepers*
Livermore, Elaine. *Lost and found*
   Three little kittens lost their mittens
London, Jonathan. *Let's go, Froggy!*
Low, Alice. *Aunt Lucy went to buy a hat*
Luciani, Brigitte. *Those messy Hempels*
Lyon, George Ella. *Basket*
McCourt, Lisa. *Chicken soup for little souls: The never-forgotten doll*
MacDonald, Amy. *Cousin Ruth's tooth*
McElmurry, Jill. *Mad about plaid*
McGinley, Phyllis. *Lucy McLockett*
McKean, Thomas. *Hooray for Grandma Jo!*
McKee, David. *Elmer and the lost teddy*
MacKinnon, Debbie. *Billy's boots*
   Cathy's cake
   Ken's kitten
   Meg's monkey
McLean-Carr, Carol. *Fairy dreams*
McNeely, Jeannette. *Where's Izzy?*
McPhail, David M. *The teddy bear*
Marcus, Susan. *The missing button adventure*
Marks, Alan. *Nowhere to be found*
Marshak, S. (Samuel). *The pup grew up!*
Martin, Jacqueline Briggs. *Bizzy Bones and the lost quilt*
Morgan, Allen. *Matthew and the midnight money van*
Moss, Miriam. *Wibble wobble*
Mother Goose. *The three little kittens*, ill. by Lorinda Bryan Cauley

The three little kittens, ill. by Paul Galdone
The three little kittens, ill. by Dorothy Stott
The three little kittens, ill. by Shelley Thornton
Munari, Bruno. *Jimmy has lost his cap*
Murdocca, Sal (Salvatore). *Tuttle's shell*
Murrow, Liza Ketchum. *Good-bye, Sammy*
Norris, Leslie. *Albert and the angels*
O'Brien, Anne Sibley. *Where's my truck?*
O'Brien, Claire. *Sam's sneaker search*
Oxenbury, Helen. *Pippo gets lost*
Parr, Letitia. *A man and his hat*
Porter, Sue. *Parsnip and the pink blanket*
Poydar, Nancy. *Busy Bea*
Precek, Katharine Wilson. *Penny in the road*
Price, Mathew. *Do you see what I see?*
Priest, Robert H. *The pirate's eye*
Pryor, Ainslie. *The baby blue cat and the smiley worm doll*
The baby blue cat and the whole batch of cookies
Rabe, Berniece. *Where's Chimpy?*
Rickert, Janet Elizabeth. *Russ and the almost perfect day*
Rogers, Jean. *Runaway mittens*
Rogers, Paul (Patrick). *Forget-me-not*
Ryder, Eileen. *Winston's new cap*
Schubert, Dieter. *Where's my monkey?*
Scott, C. Anne (Cynthia Anne). *Old Jake's skirts*
Sharmat, Marjorie Weinman. *Nate the Great and the monster mess*
Nate the Great, San Francisco detective
The trip
Shaw, Mary. *Brady Brady and the big mistake*
Siomades, Lorianne. *Cuckoo can't find you*
Three little kittens
Slonim, David. *Oh, Ducky*
Smith, Barry. *Cumberland Road*
Sonnenschein, Harriet. *Harold's runaway nose*
Stadler, John. *Catilda*
One seal
Stainton, Sue. *Santa's snow cat*
Teague, Mark. *The Lost and found*
Upham, Elizabeth. *Little brown bear loses his clothes*
Wallace, John. *Little Bean's friend*
Walsh, Ellen Stoll. *Hamsters to the rescue*
Walsh, Jill Paton. *Lost and found*
Weninger, Brigitte. *What's the matter, Davy?*
West, Judy. *Have you got my purr?*
White, Florence Meiman. *How to lose your lunch money*
White, Marsha. *Hooper has lost his owner*
Wood, Audrey. *Alphabet adventure*
Yee, Wong Herbert. *Did you see Chip?*
Yorinks, Arthur. *Christmas in July*
Zander, Hans. *My blue chair*
Ziefert, Harriet. *Good night, Jessie!*
Zinnemann-Hope, Pam. *Find your coat, Ned*

Behavior – lying

Æsop. *The boy who cried wolf*, ill. by Dianne Silverman
Wolf! Wolf!
Belloc, Hilaire. *Matilda who told lies and was burned to death*
Berenstain, Stan. *The Berenstain bears and the truth*
Brown, Marc Tolon. *Arthur and the true Francine*
Chorao, Kay. *Molly's lies*
Cohen, Miriam. *Liar, liar, pants on fire!*
Collodi, Carlo. *The adventures of Pinocchio*
Pinocchio
De Groat, Diane. *Liar, liar, pants on fire*
Diakité, Baba Wagué. *The hunterman and the crocodiles*
Dinardo, Jeffrey. *The wolf who cried boy*
Elliott, Dan. *Ernie's little lie*
Elzbieta. *Dikou the little troon who walks at night*
Evans, Katherine. *The boy who cried wolf*
Gackenbach, Dick. *Crackle, Gluck and the sleeping toad*
Hayes, Joe. *Juan Verdades, the man who could not tell a lie*
Helena, Ann. *The lie*
Jeram, Anita. *It was Jake*
Lexau, Joan M. *Finders keepers, losers weepers*
Lloyd, David. *The ridiculous story of Gammer Gurton's needle*
McKissack, Patricia C. *The honest-to-goodness truth*

Parsons, Virginia. *Pinocchio and Gepetto*
Pearson, Kit. *The singing basket*
Ross, Tony. *The boy who cried wolf*
Saltzberg, Barney. *Phoebe and the spelling bee*
Sharmat, Marjorie Weinman. *A big fat enormous lie*
Turkle, Brinton. *The adventures of Obadiah*
Wright, Dare. *Edith and Mr. Bear*

Behavior – messy

Ericsson, Jennifer A. *She did it!*
Jensen, Patricia. *The mess*
McKissack, Patricia C. *Messy Bessey*
Messy Bessey = Ada, la desordenada
Messy Bessey's closet
Provencher, Rose-Marie. *Mouse cleaning*
Riley, Linnea Asplind. *Mouse mess*
Ward, Barbara Briggs. *The really really hairy flight of Snarly Sally*

Behavior – misbehavior

Adams, Lisa K. *Dealing with teasing*
Agard, John. *Dig away two-hole Tim*
Ahlberg, Allan. *Monkey do!*
Alexander, Lloyd. *How the cat swallowed thunder*
Alexander, Martha G. *We're in big trouble, Blackboard Bear*
Allard, Harry. *Miss Nelson is back*
Miss Nelson is missing!
Anderson, Peggy Perry. *Out to lunch*
Aralan, Haydé. *Milton's Christmas*
Archambault, John. *A beautiful feast for a big king cat*
Arnold, Tedd. *Huggly takes a bath*
No jumping on the bed!
The signmaker's assistant
Asch, Frank. *Moonbear's dream*
Ashforth, Camilla. *Monkey tricks*
Ashley, Bernard. *Dinner ladies don't count*
Auer, Martin. *Now, now Markus*
Baba, Noboru. *Eleven cats and a pig*
Eleven cats and albatrosses
Eleven cats in a bag
Eleven hungry cats
Baker, Alan. *Benjamin's book*
Benjamin's dreadful dream
Baker, Leslie A. *You bad dog!*
Baker, Margaret. *A puppy called Spinach*
Baumann, Kurt. *The story of Jonah*
Baumgart, Klaus. *Anna and the little green dragon*
Beech, Caroline. *Peas again for lunch*
Beim, Jerrold. *The taming of Toby*
Belloc, Hilaire. *Jim, who ran away from his nurse, and was eaten by a lion*
Matilda who told lies and was burned to death
Bellows, Cathy. *The Grizzly sisters*
Bemelmans, Ludwig. *Madeline and the bad hat*
Berenstain, Stan. *The Berenstain bears and the truth*
Berridge, Celia. *Hannah's temper*
Berry, Joy Wilt. *Being destructive*
Being selfish
Disobeying
Fighting
Throwing tantrums
Whining
Birchman, David Francis. *Jigsaw Jackson*
Biro, Val. *Gumdrop goes to school*
Blake, Robert J. *Yudonsi*
Blaustein, Muriel. *Baby Mabu and Auntie Moose*
Bedtime, Zachary!
Boland, Janice. *A dog named Sam*
Boyd, Lizi. *Half wild and half child*
Bradman, Tony. *The bad babies' book of colors*
The bad babies' counting book
A bad week for the three bears
Michael
Brown, Ken (Ken James). *Mucky Pup's Christmas*
Brown, Marc Tolon. *Arthur's computer disaster*
Arthur's first sleepover

Brown, Margaret Wise. *Sneakers*
 Sneakers, the seaside cat
Browne, Eileen. *Tick-tock*
Brunhoff, Laurent de. *Babar's cousin, that rascal Arthur*
Calhoun, Mary. *The goblin under the stairs*
Campbell, Rod. *Henry's busy day*
 Misty's mischief
Carlson, Nancy L. *How to lose all your friends*
Carr, Jan. *The nature of the beast*
Cartlidge, Michelle. *Pippin and Pod*
Chalmers, Audrey. *Fancy be good*
Chapman, Carol. *Herbie's troubles*
Chess, Victoria. *Alfred's alphabet walk*
Chichester Clark, Emma. *The story of Horrible Hilda and Henry*
Childress, Mark. *Joshua and the big bad blue crabs*
Christelow, Eileen. *Five little monkeys jumping on the bed*
 Five little monkeys sitting in a tree
 Jerome and the Witchcraft kids
Christian, Mary Blount. *Go west, swamp monsters*
Claverie, Jean. *The party*
Cohen, Miriam. *Starring first grade*
Cole, Babette. *Bad habits! or, The taming of Lucretzia Crum*
 Tarzanna!
Cole, William. *That pest Jonathan*
Colette, Sidonie Gabrielle. *The boy and the magic*
Collington, Peter. *Little pickle*
Collins, Pat Lowery. *Taking care of Tucker*
Collodi, Carlo. *The adventures of Pinocchio*
 Pinocchio
Cooper, Helen (Helen F.). *Little monster did it!*
Costa, Nicoletta. *The naughty puppy*
 The new puppy
Couture, Susan Arkin. *Melanie Jane*
Cowell, Cressida. *Don't do that, Kitty Kilroy*
Cowley, Stewart. *The naughty ducklings*
Craig, Helen. *A welcome for Annie*
Crebbin, June. *Cows in the kitchen*
Crowley, Arthur. *The boogey man*
 Curious George and the puppies
 Curious George goes to a chocolate factory
 Curious George goes to a movie
 Curious George in the snow
Dauer, Rosamond. *My friend, Jasper Jones*
David, Lawrence. *The good little girl*
Davies, Gill. *Can't, don't, won't*
Day, Alexandra. *Carl's birthday*
Debecker, Benoît. *The naughty prince*
De Groat, Diane. *Roses are pink, your feet really stink*
Delaney, A. *The gunnywolf*
Delaney, Ned. *Bad dog!*
 Rufus the doofus
Denchfield, Nick. *Desmond the dog*
 Desmond the dog, a wag-the-tail pop-up book
De Paola, Tomie (Thomas Anthony). *Stagestruck*
Dieterlé, Nathalie. *I am the king!*
Dodd, Lynley. *Hairy Maclary's rumpus at the vet*
 Slinky Malinki, open the door
Douglass, Barbara. *Good as new*
Dowling, Paul. *Splodger*
Durant, Alan. *Big Bad Bunny*
Eastman, P. D. (Philip D.). *Are you my mother?*
Enright, Elizabeth. *Zeee*
Faulkner, Keith. *The monster in my bathroom*
 The monster in my toybox
Flack, Marjorie. *The story about Ping*
Floca, Brian. *The frightful story of Harry Walfish*
Froment, Eugène. *The story of a round loaf*
Gackenbach, Dick. *Pepper and all the legs*
Gág, Wanda. *The sorcerer's apprentice*
Galbraith, Kathryn Osebold. *Katie did!*
Gantos, Jack (John, Jr.). *Happy birthday, Rotten Ralph*
 Not so Rotten Ralph
 Rotten Ralph
 Rotten Ralph's rotten romance
 Wedding bells for Rotten Ralph
 Worse than Rotten Ralph
Garland, Sarah. *Oh, no!*

Geisert, Arthur. *Oink*
 Oink oink
Gerson, Corinne. *Good dog, bad dog*
Gerstein, Mordicai. *Stop those pants!*
Ghigna, Charles. *Good cats/Bad cats*
 Good dogs/Bad dogs
Gliori, Debi. *Mr. Bear babysits*
Goodall, John S. *Naughty Nancy*
 Naughty Nancy goes to school
Gordon, Margaret. *Wilberforce goes to a party*
Graham, Bob. *Has anyone here seen William?*
Grindley, Sally. *Four black puppies*
Gullikson, Sandy. *Trouble for breakfast*
Gutman, Anne. *Gaspard and Lisa's rainy day*
Hale, Sarah Josepha Buell. *Mary had a little lamb [board book]*, ill.
 by Iza Trapani
Harper, Wilhelmina. *The gunniwolf*
Havill, Juanita. *Jamaica and the substitute teacher*
 Magic fort
Hawkes, Kevin. *Then the troll heard the squeak*
Hayes, Sarah. *Bad egg*
Hedderwick, Mairi. *Katie Morag and the big boy cousins*
 Katie Morag and the tiresome Ted
 Katie Morag delivers the mail
Helmer, Marilyn. *Mr. McGratt and the ornery cat*
Henkes, Kevin. *A weekend with Wendell*
Heo, Yumi. *The green frogs*
Hill, Eric. *Spot visits the hospital*
 Spot's first picnic
Hiller, Catherine. *Argentaybee and the boonie*
Hilton, Nette. *Prince Lachlan*
Himmelman, John. *Amanda and the witch switch*
Hirsh, Marilyn. *Deborah the dybbuk*
Hoban, Russell. *How Tom beat Captain Najork and his hired sports-
 men*
Hodeir, André. *Warwick's 3 bottles*
Hogan, Inez. *About Nono, the baby elephant*
Hood, Susan. *Meet Trouble*
Hort, Lenny. *The boy who held back the sea*
Hughes, Shirley. *The snow lady*
Humphries, Tudor. *Hiding*
Hutchins, Pat. *Three-star Billy*
 Where's the baby?
Inkiow, Dimiter. *Me and Clara and Baldwin the pony*
 Me and Clara and Snuffy the dog
 Me and my sister Clara
Jeffers, Susan. *Wild Robin*
Jeram, Anita. *It was Jake*
Johnson, Paul Brett. *Little Bunny Foo Foo*
Johnston, Tony. *Lorenzo the naughty parrot*
Joosse, Barbara M. *The thinking place*
Keller, Beverly. *When mother got the flu*
Keller, Holly. *A bear for Christmas*
Kellogg, Steven (Stephen). *Prehistoric Pinkerton*
Kent, Jack. *The scribble monster*
Kent, Lorna. *No, no, Charlie Rascal!*
Kipling, Rudyard. *How the camel got his hump*, ill. by Quentin Blake
 How the camel got his hump, ill. by Tim Raglin
 How the camel got his hump, ill. by Lisbeth Zwerger
Kline, Suzy. *Don't touch!*
Koenig, Marion. *The wonderful world of night*
Kranendonk, Anke. *Just a minute*
Krasilovsky, Phyllis. *The man who entered a contest*
Kraus, Robert. *Boris bad enough*
Krause, Ute. *Pig surprise*
Kroll, Steven. *Otto*
 Pigs in the house
Laden, Nina. *Bad dog*
Langreuter, Jutta. *Little Bear and the big fight*
Lattimore, Deborah Nourse. *Punga the goddess of ugly*
Leach, Norman. *My wicked stepmother*
Leaf, Munro. *A flock of watchbirds*
Levinson, Riki. *Touch! Touch!*
Lexau, Joan M. *I'll tell on you*
Lieberman, Syd. *The wise shoemaker of Studena*
Lillie, Patricia. *One very, very quiet afternoon*
Lindbergh, Reeve. *The awful aardvarks go to school*

The awful aardvarks shop for school
The day the goose got loose
Lindgren, Barbro. *The wild baby*
Lipkind, William. *Nubber bear*
Lippman, Peter. *The Know-It-Alls go to sea*
 The Know-It-Alls help out
 The Know-It-Alls mind the store
 The Know-It-Alls take a winter vacation
Littlewood, Valerie. *The season clock*
Lobel, Arnold. *Prince Bertram the bad*
London, Jonathan. *Froggy eats out*
 Shawn and Keeper: show-and-tell
Lorimer, Janet. *The biggest bubble in the world*
Luttrell, Ida. *Mattie and the chicken thief*
McBratney, Sam. *The caterpillow fight*
MacDonald, Amy. *Quentin Fenton Herter three*
McGuire, Richard. *What goes around comes around*
McNaughton, Colin. *Captain Abdul's pirate school*
McPhail, David M. *Andrew's bath*
Mahiri, Jabari. *The day they stole the letter J*
Mahy, Margaret. *The boy with two shadows*
Malloy, Judy. *Bad Thad*
Manning, Linda. *Dinosaur days*
Marshall, Edward. *Fox and his friends*
 Fox on wheels
Marshall, James. *The Cut-Ups*
 The Cut-Ups at Camp Custer
 The Cut-Ups crack up
 The Cut-Ups cut loose
 Fox on the job
 George and Martha back in town
Martin, David. *Monkey trouble*
Marzollo, Jean. *Uproar on Hollercat Hill*
Mayer, Mercer. *Appelard and Liverwurst*
Mazer, Anne. *The Fixits*
Milgrim, David. *Dog brain*
Moremen, Grace E. *No, no, Natalie*
Morgan, Allen. *Molly and Mr. Maloney*
Moss, Marissa. *Who was it?*
Moss, Miriam. *Bad hare day*
Mozelle, Shirley. *The pig is in the pantry, the cat is on the shelf*
Munsch, Robert N. *Angela's airplane*
 Good families don't
 Moira's birthday
Murphy, Jill. *All in one piece*
Murphy, Patti Beling. *Elinor and Violet*
Myller, Lois. *No! No!*
Nones, Eric Jon. *Wendell*
Oana, Kay D. *Shasta and the shebang machine*
Obrist, Jürg. *Bear business*
O'Kelley, Mattie Lou. *Circus!*
Oldfield, Pamela. *Melanie Brown climbs a tree*
Olson, Helen Kronberg. *The strange thing that happened to Oliver Wendell Iscovitch*
O'Malley, Kevin. *Carl caught a flying fish*
Oram, Hiawyn. *Ned and the Joybaloo*
Oxenbury, Helen. *The car trip*
 The important visitor
Parker, Nancy Winslow. *Cooper, the McNallys' big black dog*
 Poofy loves company
Parsons, Virginia. *Pinocchio and Gepetto*
Partis, Joanne. *Stripe*
Paterson, Diane. *Soap and suds*
Paton, Priscilla. *Howard and the sitter surprise*
Pearson, Tracey Campbell. *The howling dog*
 Sing a song of sixpence
Phillips, Betty Lou. *Emily goes wild*
Pinkwater, Daniel Manus. *Bad bears in the big city*
 Ice-cream Larry
 Irving and Muktuk
 The picture of Morty and Ray
Potter, Beatrix. *The complete adventures of Peter Rabbit*
 The tale of Benjamin Bunny
 The tale of Peter Rabbit, ill. by Margot Apple
 The tale of Peter Rabbit, ill. by author
 The tale of two bad mice
 The two bad mice

Where's Peter Rabbit?
Poulin, Stéphane. *Can you catch Josephine?*
Prater, John. *"No!" said Joe*
 On Friday something funny happened
 You can't catch me!
Preston, Edna Mitchell. *Horrible Hepzibah*
 Squawk to the moon, little goose
Provensen, Alice. *Punch in New York*
Quackenbush, Robert M. *Mouse feathers*
Rabinowitz, Sandy. *A colt named mischief*
Rappus, Gerhard. *When the sun was shining*
Rice, Eve. *Benny bakes a cake*
Richardson, Jean. *Thomas's sitter*
Robbins, Maria Polushkin. *Kitten in trouble*
Robison, Deborah. *Your turn, doctor*
Rockwell, Anne F. *The boy who wouldn't obey*
 Honk honk!
Ross, Tony. *Oscar got the blame*
Rovetch, Lissa. *Trigwater did it*
Rubel, Nicole. *Goldie's nap*
Ruck-Pauquèt, Gina. *Oh, that koala!*
Russo, Marisabina. *Under the table*
Sadler, Marilyn. *Alistair's elephant*
Sandberg, Inger. *Dusty wants to help*
 Nicholas' red day
Sarrazin, Johan. *Tootle*
Say, Allen. *Allison*
Schatell, Brian. *Farmer Goff and his turkey Sam*
Schroeder, Binette. *Tuffa and the picnic*
Schumacher, Claire. *King of the zoo*
Schwartz, Amy. *Camper of the week*
Sendak, Maurice. *Where the wild things are*
Shannon, David. *David gets in trouble*
 David goes to school
 No, David!
Sharratt, Nick. *The time it took Tom*
Shaw, Mary. *Brady Brady and the big mistake*
Sherrow, Victoria. *There goes the ghost*
Simmonds, Posy. *The chocolate wedding*
Simmons, Steven J. *Alice and Greta's color magic*
 Greta's revenge
Small, David. *Paper John*
Smith, Barry. *A child's guide to bad behavior*
Smith, Cara Lockhart. *Twenty-six rabbits run riot*
Smith, Janice Lee. *The monster in the third dresser drawer and other stories about Adam Joshua*
Solotareff, Grégoire. *Don't call me little bunny*
Standon, Anna. *Three little cats*
Stephens, Helen. *Poochie-poo*
Stevenson, James. *Worse than the worst*
Stevenson, Suçie. *Jessica the blue streak*
Sykes, Julie. *Robbie Rabbit and the little ones*
Tharlet, Eve. *Little pig, big trouble*
Tierney, Hanne. *Where's your baby brother, Becky Bunting?*
Trivizas, Eugenios. *The three little wolves and the big bad pig*
Van Allsburg, Chris. *The garden of Abdul Gasazi*
Veldkamp, Tjibbe. *22 orphans*
Vidal, Beatriz A. *Federico and the Magi's gift*
Vigna, Judith. *Anyhow, I'm glad I tried*
 She's not my real mother
Vincent, Gabrielle. *Breakfast time, Ernest and Celestine*
Waddell, Martin. *Amy said*
Wade, Barrie. *Little monster*
Wahl, Jan. *Little Eight John*
Wallace, Ian. *Morgan the magnificent*
 The sparrow's song
Ward, Cindy. *Cookie's week*
Ward, Nick. *Giant*
Ward, Sally G. *Charlie and Grandma*
Watanabe, Yuichi. *Wally the whale who loved balloons*
Watson, Wendy. *Lollipop*
We wish you a merry Christmas
Weilerstein, Sadie Rose. *K'tonton's Yom Kippur kitten*
Wells, Rosemary. *Fritz and the mess fairy*
 Good night, Fred
 Hazel's amazing mother
White, Florence Meiman. *How to lose your lunch money*

Wild, Margaret. *Toby*
Willard, Nancy. *The well-mannered balloon*
Williams, Barbara. *Whatever happened to Beverly Bigler's birthday?*
Willis, Jeanne. *Be gentle, Python!*
  Be quiet, Parrot!
  No biting, Puma!
  Take turns, Penguin!
Wiseman, Bernard. *Don't make fun!*
Wood, Audrey. *Elbert's bad word*
Woodruff, Elvira. *Mrs. McCloskey's monkeys*
Wright, Jill. *The old woman and the jar of ums*
Yee, Wong Herbert. *Big black bear*
Yeoman, John. *The wild washerwomen*
Zemach, Margot. *Jake and Honeybunch go to heaven*
Zemke, Deborah. *The shadow of Matilda Hunt*
Ziefert, Harriet. *Strike four!*

Behavior – mistakes

Aliki. *Jack and Jake*
Becker, Bonny. *The Christmas crocodile*
Boehm, Arlene P. *Jack in search of Art*
Boyd, Selma. *The how: making the best of a mistake*
Brandenberg, Franz. *No school today!*
Brett, Jan. *Armadillo rodeo*
Bridwell, Norman. *Clifford's good deeds*
Burdett, Lois. *Twelfth night*
Chevalier, Christa. *Spence makes circles*
Cohen, Peter Zachary. *Olson's meat pies*
Cowley, Joy. *Big moon tortilla*
Cresswell, Helen. *Two hoots and the king*
  Two hoots in the snow
Demi. *The leaky umbrella*
Erickson, Karen. *No one is perfect*
Gág, Wanda. *Gone is gone*
Galdone, Paul. *Obedient Jack*
Geringer, Laura. *Molly's new washing machine*
Hoban, Julia. *Buzby to the rescue*
Hoff, Syd. *Henrietta, the early bird*
Inkpen, Mick. *Kipper's birthday*
Jacobs, Joseph. *Hereafterthis*
Lexau, Joan M. *It all began with a drip, drip, drip*
Lindbergh, Reeve. *If I'd known then what I know now*
Lipson, Beth Weiner. *Benjamin's perfect solution*
McFarland, Lyn Rossiter. *The pirate's parrot*
Martin, Rafe. *Foolish rabbit's big mistake*
Medearis, Angela Shelf. *Poppa's new pants*
Pilkey, Dav. *The Silly Gooses build a house*
Prager, Annabelle. *The baseball birthday party*
Prose, Francine. *The angel's mistake*
Rinder, Lenore. *A big mistake*
Root, Phyllis. *Contrary bear*
Rowe, John A. *Monkey trouble*
Saltzberg, Barney. *Crazy hair day*
Spinelli, Eileen. *Somebody loves you, Mr. Hatch*
Springstubb, Tricia. *The magic guinea pig*
Stoeke, Janet Morgan. *A friend for Minerva Louise*
  Minerva Louise at the fair
Waber, Bernard. *Nobody is perfick*
Walker, Barbara K. (Barbara Kerlin). *New patches for old*
Weigelt, Udo. *The Easter Bunny's baby*
Wiseman, Bernard. *Tails are not for painting*
Yee, Wong Herbert. *A drop of rain*

Behavior – misunderstanding

Adelson, Leone. *The mystery bear*
Allard, Harry. *The Stupids die*
Baron, Alan. *Little Pig's bouncy ball*
Berg, Jean Horton. *The O'Learys and friends*
Berson, Harold. *Kassim's shoes*
Boyd, Lizi. *The not-so-wicked stepmother*
Brown, Don. *Odd boy out*
Bryant, Sara Cone. *Epaminondas and his auntie*
Bush, John. *The cross-with-us rhinoceros*
Carrick, Carol. *Old Mother Witch*
Catalanotto, Peter. *Mr. Mumble*

Cohen, Barbara. *Make a wish, Molly*
Cottle, Joan. *Miles away from home*
Demuth, Patricia Brennan. *Max, the bad-talking parrot*
Dickinson, Mike. *My dad doesn't even notice*
Donaldson, Joan. *The real pretend*
Ericsson, Jennifer A. *No milk!*
Gackenbach, Dick. *Arabella and Mr. Crack*
  King Wacky
Harper, Jo. *Prairie dog pioneers*
Henkes, Kevin. *Kitten's first full moon*
Hopkins, Lee Bennett. *I loved Rose Ann*
Knight, Joan. *Bon appetit, Bertie!*
Komaiko, Leah. *Earl's too cool for me*
Kraus, Robert. *Ladybug, ladybug!*
Krause, Ute. *Pig surprise*
Lionni, Leo. *Fish is fish*
McClintock, Marshall. *A fly went by*
Mayer, Marianna. *The prince and the pauper*
Mayer, Mercer. *Bun Bun's birthday*
Morgan, Michaela. *Helpful Betty to the rescue*
Nixon, Joan Lowery. *Bigfoot makes a movie*
Nordqvist, Sven. *Porker finds a chair*
Robbins, Maria Polushkin. *Mother, Mother, I want another*
  Mother, Mother I want another
Roberts, Sarah. *Bert and the missing mop mix-up*
Salley, Coleen. *Epossumondas*
Schatell, Brian. *The McGoonys have a party*
Shannon, David. *The rain came down*
Sharmat, Marjorie Weinman. *Gila monsters meet you at the airport*
Simmons, Jane. *Ebb and Flo and the greedy gulls*
Stoeke, Janet Morgan. *A hat for Minerva Louise*
  Minerva Louise
  Minerva Louise at school
Thornhill, Jan. *The rumor*
Turner, Ann Warren. *Hedgehog for breakfast*
Tusa, Tricia. *Chicken*
Waber, Bernard. *Funny, funny Lyle*
Wild, Jocelyn. *Florence and Eric take the cake*
Wiseman, Bernard. *Morris has a birthday party!*
  Morris the moose
Wold, Jo Anne. *Well! Why didn't you say so?*
Yorinks, Arthur. *Company's coming*
Young, Ed (Edward). *Donkey trouble*
Zemke, Deborah. *The way it happened*

Behavior – nagging

Dickinson, Mary. *Alex's outing*
Mahy, Margaret. *Mrs. Discombobulous*
Stalder, Valerie. *Even the devil is afraid of a shrew*

Behavior – name calling

Merriam, Eve. *Fighting words*
Waber, Bernard. *But names will never hurt me*

Behavior – naughty *see* Behavior – misbehavior

Behavior – needing someone

Aardema, Verna. *The lonely lioness and the ostrich chicks*
Ahlberg, Janet. *Bye-bye, baby*
Alborough, Jez. *Hug*
Aruego, José. *Weird friends*
Asare, Meshack. *Cat . . . in search of a friend*
Asher, Sandy. *Princess Bee and the royal good-night story*
Austin, Margot. *A friend for Growl Bear*
Axworthy, Anni. *Along came Toto*
Billam, Rosemary. *Fuzzy rabbit*
Bingham, Mindy. *Minou*
Biro, Val. *Gumdrop gets a lift*
Boase, Susan. *Lucky boy*
Bulla, Clyde Robert. *The stubborn old woman*
Cain, Sheridan. *Why so sad, Brown Rabbit?*
Chichester Clark, Emma. *I love you, Blue Kangaroo!*
Collins, Pat Lowery. *Taking care of Tucker*
Corey, Dorothy. *Will there be a lap for me?*

You go away
Coxon, Michèle. *The cat who lost his purr*
Crimi, Carolyn. *Don't need friends*
David, Lawrence. *The good little girl*
Farber, Norma. *The boy who longed for a lift*
Fine, Anne. *Poor Monty*
Gauch, Patricia Lee. *Christina Katerina and the time she quit the family*
Godard, Álex. *Mama, across the sea*
Goodhart, Pippa. *Pudgy, a puppy to love*
Graeber, Charlotte Towner. *Nobody's Dog*
Guilfoile, Elizabeth. *Nobody listens to Andrew*
Hassett, John. *Cat up a tree*
Hawkins, Colin. *Where's my mommy?*
Hayes, Sarah. *Mary Mary*
Herriot, James. *Blossom comes home*
Hippely, Hilary Horder. *The crimson ribbon*
Hughes, Richard. *Gertrude's child*
Hughes, Shirley. *Alfie gives a hand*
Jacobs, Kate. *A sister's wish*
Jane, Cabrera. *The lonesome polar bear*
Jensen, Patricia. *Little Donkey learns to help*
Jeschke, Susan. *Lucky's choice*
Jonell, Lynne. *Bravemole*
    Mom pie
Keats, Ezra Jack. *Louie's search*
Kent, Jack. *There's no such thing as a dragon*
Kiser, Kevin. *Buzzy Widget*
Lewis, Kim. *Emma's lamb*
Lindgren, Barbro. *Andrei's search*
Livermore, Elaine. *Follow the fox*
Lobel, Anita. *A birthday for the princess*
Lottridge, Celia Barker. *Berta, a remarkable dog*
McAllister, Angela. *The little blue rabbit*
McBratney, Sam. *Once there was a Hoodie*
McCormick, Wendy. *Daddy, will you miss me?*
McGinnis, Lila Sprague. *If Daddy only knew me*
McGuirk, Leslie. *Snail boy*
McLerran, Alice. *The mountain that loved a bird*
McPhail, David M. *Emma's pet*
    Great cat
Mayer, Mercer. *Whinnie the lovesick dragon*
Meggs, Libby Phillips. *Go home!*
Morris, Terry Nell. *Lucky puppy! Lucky boy!*
Moser, Erwin. *Wilma the elephant*
Munsch, Robert N. *Millicent and the wind*
Olsen, Ib Spang. *The grown-up trap*
Oppenheim, Joanne. *On the other side of the river*
Paraskevas, Betty. *The tangerine bear*
Peet, Bill (William Bartlett). *Zella, Zack, and Zodiac*
Pelton, Mindy L. *When Dad's at sea*
Ranville, Myralene. *Tex*
Rayner, Mary. *Crocodarling*
Roberts, Sarah. *I want to go home!*
Robertson, M. P. *The egg*
Rodell, Susanna. *Dear Fred*
Schindel, John. *Dear Daddy*
Schneider, Christine M. *Horace P. Tuttle, magician extraordinaire*
Schubert, Dieter. *Where's my monkey?*
Scott, Ann Herbert. *On mother's lap*
    On mother's lap [board book]
    Sam
Seeber, Dorothea P. *A pup just for me . . . A boy just for me*
Sendak, Maurice. *Very far away*
Singer, Marilyn. *Pickle plan*
Skorpen, Liesel Moak. *Charles*
Smith, Maggie (Margaret C.). *Paisley*
Stehr, Frédéric. *Quack-quack*
Strauss, Gwen. *The night shimmy*
Sugita, Yutaka. *Helena the unhappy hippopotamus*
Tennyson, Noel. *The lady's chair and the ottoman*
Thompson, Colin (Colin Edward). *Unknown*
Tibo, Gilles. *The grand journey of Mr. Man*
Tokuda, Wendy. *Humphrey the lost whale*
Tompert, Ann. *Will you come back for me?*
Vigna, Judith. *Mommy and me by ourselves again*
Vincent, Gabrielle. *A day, a dog*

Weigelt, Udo. *The Sandman*
Wells, Rosemary. *McDuff moves in*
    Noisy Nora
Wheeler, Lisa. *Porcupining*
Wilhelm, Hans. *Schnitzel's first Christmas*
Wolde, Gunilla. *Betsy and the chicken pox*
Wyeth, Sharon Dennis. *Always my dad*

Behavior – potty training *see* Toilet training

Behavior – promptness, tardiness

Axelrod, Amy. *Pigs on a blanket*
Boyd, Selma. *I met a polar bear*
Burningham, John. *John Patrick Norman McHennessy – the boy who was always late*
Dalmais, Anne-Marie. *Danny the duck*
Edwards, Pamela Duncan. *The grumpy morning*
Gregory, Nan. *Amber waiting*
Grossman, Bill. *The guy who was five minutes late*
Herman, Gail. *Ice cream soup*
Hines, Anna Grossnickle. *What Joe saw*
Hutchins, Pat. *Little pink pig*
Johns, Linda. *Sarah's secret plan*
Kraus, Robert. *Here comes Tardy Toad*
Lachtman, Ofelia Dumas. *Pepita takes time = Pepita, siempre tarde*
Lamont, Priscilla. *Out to lunch*
O'Donnell, Peter. *Carnegie's excuse*
Reiss, Mike. *Late for school*
Sykes, Julie. *Hurry, Santa!*
Teague, Mark. *The secret shortcut*
Tidd, Louise Vitellaro. *I'll do it later*
Wallace-Brodeur, Ruth. *Home by five*
Willis, Jeanne. *Sloth's shoes*

Behavior – resourcefulness

Hayes, Sarah. *Lucy Anna and the Finders*
Layton, Neal. *Hot, hot, hot*
Meisel, Paul. *Zara's hats*
Ørdal, Stina Langlo. *Princess Aasta*
Perrow, Angeli. *Sirius, the dog star*

Behavior – running away

Ackerman, Karen. *Bingleman's midway*
Adoff, Arnold. *Where wild Willie?*
Ahlberg, Allan. *Monkey do!*
Alexander, Martha G. *And my mean old mother will be sorry, Blackboard Bear*
Allamand, Pascale. *The camel who left the zoo*
Baker, Leslie A. *The antique store cat*
    The third-story cat
Barrett, Lawrence Louis. *Twinkle, the baby colt*
Barton, Byron. *The wee little woman*
Bates, H. E. (Herbert Ernest). *Achilles the donkey*
Bauer, Steven. *The strange and wonderful tale of Robert McDoodle*
Belloc, Hilaire. *Jim, who ran away from his nurse, and was eaten by a lion*
Bond, Felicia. *Wake up, Vladimir*
Brimner, Larry Dane. *Elliot Fry's good-bye*
Brown, Margaret Wise. *The runaway bunny*
    The runaway bunny [board book]
Brunhoff, Jean de. *The story of Babar, the little elephant*
Burton, Virginia Lee. *Choo choo*
Byrd, Robert. *Marcella was bored*
Carlson, Natalie Savage. *Runaway Marie Louise*
Carroll, Ruth. *What Whiskers did*
Charles, Veronika Martenova. *The crane girl*
Christelow, Eileen. *The great pig escape*
    The great pig search
Christian, Mary Blount. *Go west, swamp monsters*
Clayton, Elaine. *The yeoman's daring daughter and the princes in the tower*
Clements, Andrew. *Temple cat*, ill. by Kate Kiesler
    Temple cat, ill. by Alan Marks
Clifton, Lucille. *My brother fine with me*

Cohen, Barbara. *The chocolate wolf*
Coombs, Patricia. *Lisa and the grompet*
Davies, Gill. *Can't, don't, won't*
Davy's scary journey
Desimini, Lisa. *I am running away today*
Dumas, Philippe. *Lucy, a tale of a donkey*
Dupasquier, Philippe. *The great escape*
Duvoisin, Roger Antoine. *The missing milkman*
Dyer, Heather. *Tina and the penguin*
Eaton, Jason. *The day my runny nose ran away*
Edwards, Pamela Duncan. *Barefoot*
Egan, Tim. *Metropolitan cow*
Eisenstein, Marilyn. *Periwinkle isn't Paris*
Elzbieta. *Dikou and the mysterious moon sheep*
Dikou and the Snivelly Snoak
Farber, Norma. *The boy who longed for a lift*
Return of the shadows
Ferns, Ronald. *Osbert and Lucy*
Freeman, Don. *Beady Bear*
French, Vivian. *It's a go-to-the-park day*
Gackenbach, Dick. *Claude and Pepper*
Galbraith, Richard. *Reuben runs away*
Garland, Michael. *Last night at the zoo*
Gianni, Peg. *Alex, the amazing juggler*
The gingerbread boy. *Gingerbread baby*, ill. by Jan Brett
The gingerbread boy, ill. by Emily Bolam
The gingerbread boy, ill. by Scott Cook
The gingerbread boy, ill. by Richard Egielski
The gingerbread boy, ill. by Paul Galdone
The gingerbread boy, ill. by Joan Elizabeth Goodman
The gingerbread boy, ill. by William Curtis Holdsworth
The gingerbread man, ill. by Carol Jones
The gingerbread man, ill. by Megan Lloyd
The gingerbread man, ill. by Barbara McClintock
The gingerbread man, ill. by Diana Mayo
The gingerbread man, ill. by Gerald Rose
The gingerbread man, ill. by Bonnie & Bill Rutherford
The pancake boy
Whiff, sniff, nibble and chew
Goodall, John S. *The adventures of Paddy Pork*
Goodhart, Pippa. *Pudgy, a puppy to love*
Gray, Nigel. *I'll take you to Mrs. Cole!*
Running away from home
Greenberg, Dan. *The bed who ran away from home*
Greene, Graham. *The little train*
Hale, Irina. *Chocolate mouse and sugar pig*
Hamilton, Morse. *My name is Emily*
Hänel, Wolfram. *Little elephant runs away*
Hanson, Joan. *I'm going to run away*
Hassett, John. *Charles of the wild*
Hayward, Linda. *The runaway Christmas toy*
Heck, Elisabeth. *The black sheep*
Heller, Nicholas. *Up the wall*
Heller, Wendy. *Clementine and the cage*
Herman, Gail. *Teddy bear for sale*
Hillert, Margaret. *The little runaway*
Hoban, Russell. *A baby sister for Frances*
Hooks, William H. *The rainbow ribbon*
Howe, James. *Bunnicula escapes!*
Howland, Naomi. *The matzah man*
Hughes, Richard. *Gertrude's child*
Hyman, Robin. *Casper and the rainbow bird*
Isenberg, Barbara. *The adventures of Albert, the running bear*
Jagtenberg, Yvonne. *Jack's rabbit*
Jeschke, Susan. *Lucky's choice*
Joerns, Consuelo. *Oliver's escape*
Johnson, Dolores. *Seminole diary*
Johnson, Jane. *Today I thought I'd run away*
Keller, Holly. *Maxine in the middle*
Kent, Jack. *Joey runs away*
Kimmel, Eric A. *The runaway tortilla*
Kimmelman, Leslie. *The runaway latkes*
Kiser, SuAnn. *The catspring somersault flying one-handed flip-flop*
Knight, Hilary. *Where's Wallace?*
Kraus, Robert. *Where are you going, little mouse?*
La Farge, Phyllis. *Joanna runs away*
Langner, Nola. *By the light of the silvery moon*

Lasker, Joe. *The do-something day*
Lindgren, Barbro. *Benny's had enough*
Lisowski, Gabriel. *Roncalli's magnificent circus*
Lobel, Arnold. *The man who took the indoors out*
Small pig
Lobel, Gillian. *Does anybody love me?*
McClure, Gillian. *Fly home McDoo*
McConnachie, Brian. *Lily of the forest*
McCully, Emily Arnold. *My real family*
MacDonald, Maryann. *Rosie runs away*
McKissack, Patricia C. *Who is coming?*
McNeal, Tom. *The dog who lost his Bob*
McPhail, David M. *Stanley: Henry Bear's friend*
Maris, Ron. *Runaway rabbit*
Marol, Jean-Claude. *Vagabul escapes*
Martín Larrañaga, Ana. *Woo! The not-so-scary Ghost*
Mayne, William. *Pandora*
Meade, Holly. *John Willy and Freddy McGee*
Miles, Miska. *This little pig*
Modarressi, Mitra. *The parent thief*
Mogensen, Jan. *Teddy runs away*
Moore, Inga. *Little dog lost*
Mora, Jo (Joseph Jacinto). *Budgee Budgee Cottontail*
Moss, Miriam. *Smudge's grumpy day*
Mostacchi, Massimo. *The beast and the boy*
A dog's best friend
Moyer, Marshall M. *Rollo Bones, canine hypnotist*
Munsch, Robert N. *Aaron's hair*
Murray, Andrew. *Have you seen Chester?*
Oakley, Graham. *Hetty and Harriet*
O'Donnell, Elizabeth Lee. *Maggie doesn't want to move*
O'Malley, Kevin. *Little Buggy runs away*
Parker, Nancy Winslow. *The crocodile under Louis Finneberg's bed*
Patterson, Geoffrey. *A pig's tale*
Paxton, Tom. *Jennifer's rabbit*
Pearson, Susan. *Saturday, I ran away*
Peet, Bill (William Bartlett). *Pamela Camel*
Pittaway, Margaret. *The rainforest children*
Pizer, Abigail. *Loppylugs*
Poulin, Stéphane. *Have you seen Josephine?*
Prater, John. *You can't catch me!*
Ravilious, Robin. *The runaway chick*
Robins, Joan. *Addie runs away*
Rockwell, Anne F. *Willy runs away*
Rogers, Paul (Patrick). *Sheepchase*
Rosen, Michael (1946–). *Crow and Hawk*
Rosenberry, Vera. *Vera runs away*
Roth, Susan L. *Cinnamon's day out*
Schneider, Antonie. *Luke the Lionhearted*
Seligman, Dorothy Halle. *Run away home*
Sendak, Maurice. *Very far away*
Sharmat, Marjorie Weinman. *Rex*
Singer, Marilyn. *Archer Armadillo's secret room*
Slangerup, Erik Jon. *Dirt Boy*
Steig, William. *Zeke Pippin*
Stevens, Janet. *And the dish ran away with the spoon*
My big dog
Svend Otto S (Svend Otto Sorensen). *Taxi dog*
Sykes, Julie. *I don't want to take a bath!*
Van Laan, Nancy. *Little baby Bobby*
Vernon, Tannis. *Little Pig and the blue-green sea*
Voake, Charlotte. *Ginger*
Waber, Bernard. *Bernard*
A lion named Shirley Williamson
Wahl, Jan. *Mabel ran away with the toys*
Weeks, Sarah. *Oh my gosh, Mrs. McNosh!*
Whitmore, Adam. *Max leaves home*
Wilkon, Piotr. *Rosie the cool cat*
Wojtowycz, David. *A cuddle for Claude*
Wooding, Sharon L. *The painter's cat*
Woolaver, Lance. *From Ben Loman to the sea*
Wright, Dare. *Edith and Mr. Bear*
Yep, Laurence. *The city of dragons*
Yolen, Jane. *The girl who loved the wind*
Yorinks, Arthur. *Hey, Al*
Ziefert, Harriet. *Sam and Lucy*
Zimnik, Reiner. *The bear on the motorcycle*

The proud circus horse
Zion, Gene. *Harry, the dirty dog*
Zolotow, Charlotte (Shapiro). *Big sister and little sister*

Behavior – saving things

Calhoun, Mary. *The traveling ball of string*
Ciardi, John. *John J. Plenty and Fiddler Dan*
Delton, Judy. *Penny wise, fun foolish*
Foster, Doris Van Liew. *A pocketful of seasons*
Mayne, William. *The patchwork cat*
Thayer, Tanya. *Saving money*

Behavior – secrets

Aardema, Verna. *What's so funny, Ketu?*
Allard, Harry. *Miss Nelson has a field day*
Auerbach, Marjorie. *King Lavra and the barber*
Bahr, Amy C. *Sometimes it's ok to tell secrets*
Bang, Molly. *Dawn*
Barklem, Jill. *The secret staircase*
Baylor, Byrd. *Your own best secret place*
Beisner, Monika. *Secret spells and curious charms*
Brandenberg, Franz. *A secret for grandmother's birthday*
Brighton, Catherine. *Five secrets in a box*
Christelow, Eileen. *The robbery at the diamond dog diner*
Cole, Joanna. *Don't tell the whole world*
Compton, Kenn. *Happy Christmas to all!*
Coombs, Patricia. *The magician and McTree*
Cummings, W. T. (Walter Thies). *Miss Esta Maude's secret*
Davis, Maggie S. *Grandma's secret letter*
Emberley, Rebecca. *My mother's secret life*
Farley, Carol J. *The king's secret*
Galbraith, Kathryn Osebold. *Waiting for Jennifer*
Giff, Patricia Reilly. *I love Saturday*
Gretz, Susanna. *Frog in the middle*
Griffin, Kitty. *Cowboy Sam and those confounded secrets*
Guthrie, Donna. *One hundred and two steps*
Hayes, Sarah. *This is the bear*
Heide, Florence Parry. *The day of Ahmed's secret*
Hest, Amy. *In the rain with Baby Duck*
Hines, Anna Grossnickle. *The secret keeper*
Hughes, Shirley. *Sally's secret*
Kelley, True. *Blabber Mouse*
Krahn, Fernando. *The secret in the dungeon*
Lakin, Pat (Patricia). *Don't forget*
Lemaître, Pascal. *Zelda's secret*
Lifton, Betty Jean. *The secret seller*
Murdock, Laurette. *Someone is talking about Hortense*
Naylor, Phyllis Reynolds. *Keeping a Christmas secret*
Olofsdotter, Marie. *Frej the fearless*
Oppenheim, Shulamith Levey. *The hundredth name*
Pevear, Richard. *Our king has horns!*
Polacco, Patricia. *The butterfly*
Prose, Francine. *You never know*
Rappaport, Doreen. *The long-haired girl*
Riggio, Anita. *Secret signs*
Russell, Pamela. *Do you have a secret?*
San Souci, Robert D. *The snow wife*
Senisi, Ellen B. *Secrets*
Theroux, Phyllis. *Serefina under the circumstances*
Thomson, Peggy. *The king has horse's ears*
Wadsworth, Ginger. *Tomorrow is Daddy's birthday*
Willis, Val. *The secret in the matchbox*
Zemke, Deborah. *The way it happened*

Behavior – seeking better things

Abolafia, Yossi. *Yanosh's Island*
Alborough, Jez. *The grass is always greener*
Allen, Jeffrey. *The secret life of Mr. Weird*
Altman, Linda Jacobs. *Amelia's road*
Bradby, Marie. *More than anything else*
Brandenberg, Franz. *What's wrong with a van?*
Buckley, Richard. *The foolish tortoise*
Carmichael, Clay. *Bear at the beach*
Carter, Anne Laurel. *The fisherwoman*

Carter, Penny. *A new house for the Morrisons*
Chichester Clark, Emma. *More!*
Climo, Lindee. *Clyde*
Cole, Brock. *Nothing but a pig*
Cummings, W. T. (Walter Thies). *The kid*
Damjan, Mischa. *The clown said no*
Demarest, Chris L. *Benedict finds a home*
Gackenbach, Dick. *Little bug*
Gage, Wilson. *Mrs. Gaddy and the fast-growing vine*
Gantschev, Ivan. *Where is Mr. Mole?*
Ganz, Yaffa. *The story of Mimmy and Simmy*
Giff, Patricia Reilly. *Next year I'll be special*
Hamilton, Virginia. *Jaguarundi*
Heilbroner, Joan. *Tom the TV cat*
Hopkinson, Deborah. *Sweet Clara and the freedom quilt*
Ivanov, Anatoly. *Ol' Jake's lucky day*
Jennings, Linda M. *Crispin and the dancing piglet*
Joly-Berbesson, Fanny. *Marceau Bonappetit*
Keillor, Garrison. *Cat, you better come home*
Kent, Jack. *Joey runs away*
Kraus, Robert. *Where are you going, little mouse?*
Kwon, Holly H. *The moles and the mireuk*
Lasky, Kathryn. *Sea swan*
Le Guin, Ursula K. *Solomon Leviathan's nine hundred and thirty-first trip around the world*
Lindgren, Astrid. *My nightingale is singing*
Lionni, Leo. *Tillie and the wall*
Lopshire, Robert. *I want to be somebody new!*
McCunn, Ruthanne L. *Pie-Biter*
McKee, David. *The hill and the rock*
Mahy, Margaret. *The man whose mother was a pirate*
Marshall, James. *Rapscallion Jones*
Miller, Moira. *Oscar Mouse finds a home*
Moore, Inga. *The truffle hunter*
Nixon, Joan Lowery. *If you say so, Claude*
Pittaway, Margaret. *The rainforest children*
Rose, Anne K. *As right as right can be*
Stanley, Diane. *A country tale*
Watts, Bernadette. *St. Francis and the proud crow*
Williams, Vera B. *A chair for my mother*
Yorinks, Arthur. *Bravo, Minski*

Behavior – sharing

Albert, Burton. *Mine, yours, ours*
Alexander, Martha G. *I'll never share you, Blackboard Bear*
Allan, Nicholas. *The bird*
Allen, Jonathan. *Two by two by two*
Arnold, Katya. *That apple is mine!*
Azaad, Meyer (Mahmud). *Half for you*
Backx, Patsy. *Josie and Mr. Fernandez*
Banks, Kate (Katherine A.). *The bird, the monkey, and the snake in the jungle*
Beim, Jerrold. *The smallest boy in the class*
Benjamin, A. H. *Mouse, mole and the falling star*
Berliner, Franz. *Wildebeest*
Bernard, Robin. *Juma and the honey-guild*
Blegvad, Lenore. *First friends*
Boelts, Maribeth. *Little Bunny's cool tool set*
Bosca, Francesca. *The apple king*
Brett, Jan. *Christmas trolls*
Brownridge, William Roy. *The final game*
Buckley, Helen Elizabeth. *Moonlight kite*
Cameron, C. C. *One for me, one for you*
Caudill, Rebecca. *A pocketful of cricket*
Cleveland-Peck, Patricia. *City cat, country cat*
Cohen, Caron Lee. *Digger Pig and the turnip*
Cohen, Miriam. *Don't eat too much turkey!*
Cole, Joanna. *Sharing is fun*
Corey, Dorothy. *Everybody takes turns*
    We all share
Cote, Nancy. *It feels like snow*
Cousins, Lucy. *Maisy makes lemonade*
Croll, Carolyn. *Too many babas*
Curry, Jane Louise. *The Christmas knight*
Davis, Aubrey. *The enormous potato*
Davis, Gibbs. *The other Emily*

Delacre, Lulu. *Nathan and Nicholas Alexander*
DeLage, Ida. *Beware! Beware! A witch won't share*
De Lynam, Alicia Garcia. *It's mine!*
Demarest, Chris L. *Morton and Sidney*
Devlin, Wende. *Cranberry Christmas*
Dowling, Paul. *Meg and Jack's new friends*
Dubar, Joyce. *The very small*
Dubois, Claude K. *He's my jumbo!*
Dubowski, Cathy East. *Snug Bug's play day*
Dunbar, Joyce. *Gander's pond*
Ehlert, Lois. *Top cat*
Ets, Marie Hall. *The cow's party*
Flory, Jane. *The unexpected grandchildren*
Forest, Heather. *Stone soup*
Forward, Toby. *Ben's Christmas carol*
Fox, Mem. *Feathers and fools*
French, Vivian. *Little Tiger goes shopping*
Gackenbach, Dick. *Claude the dog*
Galdone, Paul. *The magic porridge pot*
Gantschev, Ivan. *Where the moon lives*
Gelbard, Jane. *My sharing book*
Gervais, Bernadette. *Voyage under the stars*
Gikow, Louise. *Jim Henson's Muppets in What's fair is fair*
Glaser, Linda. *The borrowed Hanukkah latkes*
Goldin, Barbara Diamond. *Just enough is plenty*
Gould, Deborah. *Brendan's best-timed birthday*
Gretz, Susanna. *It's your turn, Roger*
Grindley, Sally. *Can we play too, Piglittle?*
Grosz, Peter. *The special gifts*
Hallinan, P. K. (Patrick K.). *Let's care about sharing!*
Hamilton, Richard. *Polly's picnic*
Henkes, Kevin. *Sheila Rae's peppermint stick*
Heuck, Sigrid. *Who stole the apples?*
Hoberman, Mary Ann. *One of each*
Holder, Heidi. *Carmine the crow*
Hooker, Ruth. *Sara loves her big brother*
Houston, John A. *The bright yellow rope*
Hughes, Monica. *A handful of seeds*
Hutchins, Pat. *The doorbell rang*
  It's my birthday!
Jakob, Donna. *My new sandbox*
Jennings, Sharon. *Franklin and the scooter*
Johnston, Tony. *Mole and Troll trim the tree*
Kadono, Eiko. *Grandpa's soup*
Karon, Jan. *Miss Fannie's hat*
Kasza, Keiko. *The rat and the tiger*
Keats, Ezra Jack. *Peter's chair*
Ketteman, Helen. *Armadilly chili*
Klein, Norma. *Visiting Pamela*
Koehler, Phoebe. *Making room*
Lacoe, Addie. *Just not the same*
Lakin, Pat (Patricia). *Don't touch my room*
  Growing up
Lebrun, Claude. *Little Brown Bear does not want to eat*
  Little Brown Bear learns to share
Lesikin, Joan. *Down the road*
Lester, Helen. *The wizard, the fairy and the magic chicken*
Lindgren, Barbro. *Sam's car*
  Sam's cookie
Lister, Mary. *The Winter King and the Summer Queen*
The little red hen. *The cock, the mouse and the little red hen*, ill. by
  Lorinda Bryan Cauley
  The cock, the mouse and the little red hen, ill. by Graham Percy
  The little red hen, ill. by Byron Barton
  The little red hen, ill. by Emily Bolam
  The little red hen, ill. by Janina Domanska
  The little red hen, ill. by Paul Galdone
  The little red hen, ill. by Dennis Hockerman
  Little red hen, ill. by Norman Messenger
  The little red hen, ill. by Mel Pekarsky
  The little red hen, ill. by William Stobbs
  The little red hen, ill. by Annie West
  The little red hen, ill. by Margot Zemach
  The little red hen and the ear of wheat, ill. by Elisabeth Bell
  The Little Red Hen makes a pizza
Littledale, Freya. *The farmer in the soup*
Luthardt, Kevin. *Mine*

Luttrell, Ida. *Three good blankets*
McAllister, Angela. *The battle of Sir Cob and Sir Filbert*
Maccarone, Grace. *Sharing time troubles*
MacDonald, Maryann. *Rosie and the poor rabbits*
Maiorano, Robert. *A little interlude*
Masurel, Claire. *Christmas is coming*
Medina, Tony. *Christmas makes me think*
Meserve, Adria. *Smog, the city dog*
Mills, Lauren A. *The rag coat*
Moss, Miriam. *It's my turn, Smudge*
Munsch, Robert N. *We share everything!*
Murphy, Stuart J. *Give me half!*
  Let's fly a kite
  Seaweed soup
Nakagawa, Rieko. *Guri and Gura*
  Guri and Gura's special gift
Nanji, Shenaaz. *Treasure for lunch*
Noble, June. *Two homes for Lynn*
Novak, Matt. *Mr. Floop's lunch*
O'Brien, Anne Sibley. *I want that!*
O'Connor, Jane. *Kate skates*
Oram, Hiawyn. *Mine!*
Ormerod, Jan. *101 things to do with a baby*
Pacilio, V. J. *Ling Cho and his three friends*
Palazzo-Craig, Janet. *Muffy and Fluffy*
Parkinson, Kathy. *The enormous turnip*
Paterson, Bettina. *Bun's birthday*
Peck, Jan. *The giant carrot*
Pfister, Marcus. *The rainbow fish*
Pieńkowski, Jan. *Bel and Bub and the big brown box*
Pinkwater, Daniel Manus. *Doodle flute*
Porte, Barbara Ann. *Harry's visit*
Rankin, Joan. *The little cat and the greedy old woman*
Rathmann, Peggy. *Officer Buckle and Gloria*
Riddell, Chris. *Ben and the bear*
Ring, Elizabeth. *Some stuff*
Rosen, Michael (1946–). *This is our house*
Russo, Marisabina. *The big brown box*
Rylant, Cynthia. *Birthday presents*
Sage, Chris. *That's mine, that's yours*
Sasso, Sandy Eisenberg. *God said amen*
Sawyer, Ruth. *The remarkable Christmas of the cobbler's sons*
Sharmat, Marjorie Weinman. *The trip*
Sherman, Ivan. *I do not like it when my friend comes to visit*
Simmons, Jane. *Ebb and Flo and the new friend*
Siomades, Lorianne. *A place to bloom*
Smalls-Hector, Irene. *Because you're lucky*
Smith, Wendy. *The lonely, only mouse*
Spelman, Cornelia Maude. *When I care about others*
Spinelli, Eileen. *Thanksgiving at the Tappletons'*
Spurr, Elizabeth. *The biggest birthday cake in the world*
Stadler, John. *Gorman and the treasure chest*
Stage, Mads. *The greedy blackbird*
Stanek, Muriel. *My little foster sister*
Stewart, Paul. *The birthday presents*
Stone, Lynn M. *Partners*
Swartz, Nancy Sohn. *In our image*
Thayer, Jane. *Part-time dog*
Turkle, Brinton. *Rachel and Obadiah*
Vigna, Judith. *The hiding house*
Vincent, Gabrielle. *Bravo, Ernest and Celestine!*
  Ernest and Celestine's patchwork quilt
Waber, Bernard. *Bernard*
Wahl, Jan. *Mrs. Owl and Mr. Pig*
Wallner, Alexandra. *An Alcott family Christmas*
Walsh, Jill Paton. *Connie came to play*
Watson, Clyde. *Tom Fox and the apple pie*
Watts, Mabel (Pizzey). *Something for you, something for me*
Weigelt, Udo. *There's room in the forest for everyone*
Weninger, Brigitte. *Merry Christmas, Davy!*
Weston, Martha. *Bea's four bears*
Wezel, Peter. *The good bird*
White, Kathryn (Kathryn Ivy). *Nutty nut chase*
Willis, Jeanne. *Take turns, Penguin!*
Wilson, Christopher Bernard. *Hobnob*
Winthrop, Elizabeth. *That's mine*
Wolff, Ferida. *The emperor's garden*

Wood, Don. *Merry Christmas, big hungry bear*
Wright, Josephine Lord. *Cotton Cat and Martha Mouse*
Yolen, Jane. *Spider Jane*
Ziefert, Harriet. *Me, too! Me, too!*
   Rabbit and Hare divide an apple
Zolotow, Charlotte (Shapiro). *The new friend*

Behavior – solitude

Alborough, Jez. *Cuddly Dudley*
Bennett, Rainey. *The secret hiding place*
Bulla, Clyde Robert. *Keep running, Allen!*
Burdick, Margaret. *Sara Raccoon and the secret place*
Carrick, Carol. *Sleep out*
Dragonwagon, Crescent. *Katie in the morning*
   When light turns into night
Ehrlich, Amy. *The everyday train*
Goennel, Heidi. *Sometimes I like to be alone*
Hall, Donald. *The man who lived alone*
Hallinan, P. K. (Patrick K.). *Just being alone*
Hayes, Geoffrey. *Bear by himself*
Henkes, Kevin. *All alone*
Huck, Charlotte S. *Secret places*
Keller, Beverly. *Pimm's place*
Keyser, Marcia. *Roger on his own*
Luttrell, Ida. *Lonesome Lester*
Morris, Jill. *The boy who painted the sun*
Reesink, Marijke. *The princess who always ran away*
Schertle, Alice. *In my treehouse*
Stubbs, Joanna. *Happy Bear's day*
Sweetland, Nancy Rose. *God's quiet things*
Tresselt, Alvin R. *I saw the sea come in*
Yezback, Steven A. *Pumpkinseeds*

Behavior – stealing

Ada, Alma Flor. *The gold coin*
Ahlberg, Janet. *Jeremiah in the dark wood*
Alborough, Jez. *It's the bear*
Aylesworth, Jim. *Hanna's hog*
Barr, Cathrine. *Hound dog's bone*
Barton, Byron. *The wee little woman*
Brennan, Patricia D. *Hitchety hatchety up I go!*
Brett, Jan. *Christmas trolls*
Carlson, Nancy L. *Arnie and the stolen markers*
   Loudmouth George and the sixth-grade bully
Cass, Joan E. *The cat thief*
Cate, Rikki. *A cat's tale*
Christian, Mary Blount. *The doggone mystery*
   The green thumb thief
Cohn, Janice I. *"Why did it happen?"*
Cole, Joanna. *The secret box*
Collington, Peter. *The angel and the soldier boy*
Cooper, Jacqueline. *Angus and the Mona Lisa*
De Gerez, Toni. *Louhi, witch of North Farm*
De Paola, Tomie (Thomas Anthony). *Bill and Pete go down the Nile*
Devlin, Wende. *Cranberry Halloween*
Dodd, Lynley. *The apple tree*
Dyke, John. *Pigwig*
Enderle, Judith (Ann) Ross. *Nell Nugget and the cow caper*
Euvremer, Teryl. *The thieves of Peck's pocket*
Fagan, Cary. *Gogol's coat*
Farmer, Nancy. *Runnery granary*
Fine, Edith Hope. *Under the lemon moon*
The firebird. *The firebird*, ill. by Reg Cartwright
   The firebird, ill. by Francesca Crespi
   The firebird, ill. by Demi
   The firebird, adapt. and ill. by Rachel Isadora
   The firebird, ill. by Moira Kemp
   The firebird, ill. by Kris Waldherr
   The firebird, ill. by Boris Zvorykin
   The tale of the firebird, ill. by Gennady Spirin
Foulds, Elfrida Vipont. *The elephant and the bad baby*
Freschet, Berniece. *Owl in the garden*
Ginsburg, Mirra. *Striding slippers*
Goodall, John S. *Paddy to the rescue*
Hare, Norma Q. *Mystery at mouse house*

Helldorfer, M. C. (Mary Claire). *The darling boys*
Hennessy, B. G. (Barbara G.). *The missing tarts*
Hogrogian, Nonny. *Rooster brother*
Hooks, William H. *The rainbow ribbon*
Kimmel, Eric A. *The tale of Ali Baba and the forty thieves*
Kroll, Steven. *Amanda and the giggling ghost*
Moffatt, Judith. *Who stole the cookies?*
Moore, Inga. *Fifty red night-caps*
Murphy, Pat. *Pigasus*
My first Raggedy Ann, Raggedy Ann's wishing pebble
Pyle, Howard. *The Swan Maiden*
Ross, Tony. *Hugo and the man who stole colors*
Tompert, Ann. *The hungry black bag*
Weigelt, Udo. *It wasn't me*
   Who stole the gold?
Yolen, Jane. *Piggins*

Behavior – talking to strangers

Bahr, Amy C. *It's ok to say no*
Berenstain, Stan. *The Berenstain bears learn about strangers*
Boegehold, Betty. *Hurray for Pippa!*
Bradman, Tony. *Look out, he's behind you*
Bruna, Dick. *Dick Bruna's Little Red Riding Hood*
Chlad, Dorothy. *Strangers*
Choi, Yangsook. *The sun girl and the moon boy*
Conover, Chris. *Mother Goose and the sly fox*
Davoll, Barbara. *Dusty Mole, private eye*
De Regniers, Beatrice Schenk. *Red Riding Hood*
Emberley, Michael. *Ruby*
Ernst, Lisa Campbell. *Little Red Riding Hood*
Girard, Linda Walvoord. *Who is a stranger, and what should I do?*
Grimm, Jacob. *Little red cap*
   Little Red Riding Hood, ill. by Frank E. Aloise
   Little Red Riding Hood, ill. by Gwen Connelly
   Little Red Riding Hood, ill. by Paul Galdone
   Little Red Riding Hood, ill. by John S. Goodall
   Little Red Riding Hood, ill. by Trina Schart Hyman
   Little Red Riding Hood, ill. by Mireille Levert
   Little Red Riding Hood, ill. by David M. McPhail
   Little Red Riding Hood, ill. by Jean-François Martin
   Little Red Riding Hood, ill. by Bernadette Watts
Hooks, William H. *The monster from the sea*
Joyce, Irma. *Never talk to strangers*
Kaczman, James. *A bird and his worm*
Keller, Irene. *Benjamin Rabbit and the stranger danger*
Kevi. *Don't talk to strangers*
Marshall, James. *Red Riding Hood*
Meyer, Linda D. *Safety zone*
Moore, Maggie. *Little Red Riding Hood*
Morris, Ann. *The Little Red Riding Hood rebus book*
Petty, Kate. *Being careful with strangers*
Potter, Beatrix. *The tale of Little Pig Robinson*
Raschka, Christopher. *Elizabeth imagined an iceberg*
Vogel, Carole Garbuny. *The dangers of strangers*
Wood, Audrey. *Heckedy Peg*
Ziefert, Harriet. *Little Red Riding Hood*

Behavior – teasing

Brooks, Erik. *The practically perfect pajamas*

Behavior – toilet training *see* Toilet training

Behavior – trickery

Aardema, Verna. *Anansi finds a fool*
   Borreguita and the coyote
   Jackal's flying lesson
   Rabbit makes a monkey of lion
Abolafia, Yossi. *Fox tale*
Æsop. *The boy who cried wolf*, ill. by Dianne Silverman
   The donkey in the lion's skin
   Three Æsop fox fables
   The wolf in sheep's clothing
   Wolf! Wolf!
Alexander, Lloyd. *The house Gobbaleen*

Wright, Jill. *The old woman and the Willy Nilly Man*
Yep, Laurence. *The man who tricked a ghost*
Yerxa, Leo. *A fish tale, or, The little one that got away*
Young, Ed (Edward). *Monkey King*
Zemach, Harve. *The tricks of Master Dabble*
Zimelman, Nathan. *The great adventure of Wo Ti*

Behavior – unnoticed, unseen

Bishop, Bonnie. *No one noticed Ralph*
Jones, Diana Wynne. *Yes, dear*
Kroll, Steven. *The candy witch*
Krudop, Walter Lyon. *Something is growing*
Levinson, Riki. *Me baby!*
Mwenye Hadithi. *Crafty chameleon*
Scott, Ann Herbert. *Hi!*
Udry, Janice May. *How I faded away*

Behavior – wishing

Addy, Sharon Hart. *When wishes were horses*
Aliki. *The wish workers*
Allen, Pamela. *I wish I had a pirate suit*
    A lion in the night
Anawalt, Paula Bonnier. *The crystal palace*
Ayer, Jacqueline. *A wish for little sister*
Baker, Betty. *My sister says*
Baruch, Dorothy. *I would like to be a pony and other wishes*
Base, Graeme. *Jungle drums*
Baumgart, Klaus. *Laura's secret*
Bazilian, Barbara. *The red shoes*
Bentley, Nancy. *I've got your nose!*
Benton, Robert. *Don't ever wish for a 7-foot bear*
Beresford, Elisabeth. *Jack and the magic stove*
Berson, Harold. *Truffles for lunch*
Bodsworth, Nan. *Monkey business*
Bos, Burny. *Ollie the elephant*
Bowman, Pete. *I wish I were big*
Brandenberg, Franz. *I wish I was sick, too!*
Breathed, Berke (Berkeley). *A wish for wings that work*
Brenner, Barbara A. *Rosa and Marco and the three wishes*
Brett, Jan. *Fritz and the beautiful horses*
Bright, Robert. *Me and the bears*
Brown, Margaret Wise. *The fierce yellow pumpkin*
Bruchac, Joseph. *Gluskabe and the four wishes*
Bruna, Dick. *The happy apple*
Buehner, Caralyn. *Fanny's dream*
Bush, John. *The fish who could wish*
Bush, Timothy. *Benjamin McFadden and the robot babysitter*
Butcher, Julia. *The sheep and the rowan tree*
Carlstrom, Nancy White. *Wishing at dawn in summer*
Chapman, Carol. *Barney Bipple's magic dandelions*
Chess, Victoria. *Poor Esmé*
Christensen, Jack. *The forgotten rainbow*
Clifton, Lucille. *Three wishes*, ill. by Stephanie Douglas
    Three wishes, ill. by Michael Hays
Coco, Eugene Bradley. *The wishing well*
Cole, Joanna. *Mixed-up magic*
Coopersmith, Jerome. *A Chanukah fable for Christmas*
Coursen, Valerie. *Mordant's wish*
Damjan, Mischa. *The big squirrel and the little rhinoceros*
Daugherty, Charles Michael. *Wisher*
Davis, Karen. *Star light, star bright*
Demi. *The stonecutter*
Dragonwagon, Crescent. *Coconut*
    Diana, maybe
Dunbar, Joyce. *The pig who wished*
Duncan, Lois. *The longest hair in the world*
Dupré, Rick. *The wishing chair*
Egan, Tim. *Burnt toast on Davenport Street*
Elborn, Andrew. *Bird Adalbert*
Ellwand, David. *Midas Mouse*
Erlbruch, Wolf. *Leonard*
Fox, Mem. *Possum magic*
Friedrich, Priscilla. *The wishing well in the woods*
Fuchshuber, Annegert. *The wishing hat*
Gackenbach, Dick. *Hattie rabbit*

Geras, Adèle. *My wishes for you*
Gliori, Debi. *Willie Bear and the Wish Fish*
Greaves, Margaret. *The star horse*
Greenberg, Polly. *Oh, Lord, I wish I was a buzzard*
Griffith, Helen V. *Emily and the enchanted frog*
Haas, Irene. *The Maggie B*
Haddon, Mark. *Toni and the tomato soup*
Hale, Irina. *Small big bad boy*
Harshman, Marc. *A little excitement*
Heidbreder, Robert. *I wished for a unicorn*
Heller, Nicholas. *Woody*
Hermes, Patricia. *When snow lay soft on the mountain*
Himmelman, John. *Amanda and the witch switch*
Hines, Anna Grossnickle. *Moon's wish*
Hoban, Lillian. *It's really Christmas*
Horn, Sandra Ann. *The dandelion wish*
Howe, James. *I wish I were a butterfly*
Hru, Dakari. *Joshua's Masai mask*
Iwasaki, Chihiro. *The birthday wish*
Jacobs, Kate. *A sister's wish*
Jaffe, Rona. *Last of the wizards*
Janosch. *Just one apple*
Kay, Helen. *An egg is for wishing*
Kent, Jack. *Knee-high Nina*
Kirk, Daniel. *Jack and Jill*
Kojima, Naomi. *The flying grandmother*
Kovalski, Maryann. *Pizza for breakfast*
Krauss, Ruth. *Mama, I wish I was snow. Child, you'd be very cold*
Krensky, Stephen. *A good knight's sleep*
    The youngest fairy godmother ever
Kreye, Walter. *The giant from the little island*
Lasell, Fen. *Michael grows a wish*
Laurencin, Geneviève. *I wish I were*
Leemis, Ralph. *Smart dog*
Lesynski, Loris. *Rocksy*
Lewis, J. Patrick. *At the wish of the fish*
Lillegard, Dee. *My yellow ball*
Lipp, Frederick. *The caged birds of Phnom Penh*
Littledale, Freya. *The snow child*
Lobato, Arcadio. *Just one wish*
McAllister, Angela. *The Christmas wish*
    Sleepy Ella
McClintock, Barbara. *Molly and the magic wishbone*
McGrory, Anik. *Mouton's impossible dream*
McKee, David. *The monster and the teddy bear*
McKissack, Patricia C. *King Midas and his gold*
Maris, Ron. *I wish I could fly*
Mark, Jan. *The Midas touch*
Mayer, Marianna. *The spirit of the blue light*
Mike, Jan M. *Juan Bobo and the horse of seven colors*
Mitra, Annie. *Penguin moon*
Modesitt, Jeanne. *Mama, if you had a wish*
Mollel, Tololwa M. (Tololwa Marti). *Big boy*
Munari, Bruno. *The elephant's wish*
Munsch, Robert N. *Millicent and the wind*
    Wait and see
Murphy, Mary. *Caterpillar's wish*
My first Raggedy Ann, Raggedy Ann's wishing pebble
Myers, Bernice. *Sidney Rella and the glass sneaker*
Orbach, Ruth. *Please send a panda*
Osborne, Mary Pope. *Moonhorse*, ill. by David McPhail
    Moonhorse, ill. by S. M. Saelig
Ostheeren, Ingrid. *Coriander's Easter adventure*
Paterson, Diane. *If I were a toad*
Perkins, Al. *King Midas and the golden touch*
Petty, Dini. *The queen, the bear and the bumblebee*
Pfister, Marcus. *Make a wish, Honey Bear!*
Polacco, Patricia. *Luba and the wren*
Power, Barbara. *I wish Laura's mommy was my mommy*
Prater, John. *The gift*
Proimos, James. *Joe's wish*
Pulver, Robin. *Alicia's tutu*
Puttock, Simon. *A ladder to the stars*
Ratnett, Michael. *Jenny's bear*
Recknagel, Friedrich. *Meg's wish*
Reed, Kit. *When we dream*
Riddell, Chris. *The wish factory*

Robertson, M. P. *The sandcastle*
Rock, Lois. *I wish tonight*
Rodriguez, Anita. *Jamal and the angel*
Rosen, Winifred. *Henrietta and the day of the iguana*
Roth, Susan L. *Happy birthday Mr. Kang*
Sachs, Marilyn. *Fleet-footed Florence*
Scamell, Ragnhild. *The wish come true cat*
Schweninger, Ann. *Birthday wishes*
Seignobosc, Françoise. *Jeanne-Marie counts her sheep*
Seuss, Dr. *I wish that I had duck feet*
    Please try to remember the first of Octember!
Sewell, Helen Moore. *Peggy and the pony*
Shecter, Ben. *The discontented mother*
Shepard, Aaron. *The gifts of Wali Dad*
Shields, Carol Diggory. *I wish my brother was a dog*
Shimin, Symeon. *I wish there were two of me*
Simon, Norma. *I wish I had my father*
Stevenson, James. *The wish card ran out!*
Storr, Catherine (Cole). *King Midas*
Tan, Amy. *The moon lady*
Thaler, Mike. *Hippo lemonade*
Tobias, Tobi. *Jane wishing*
    Wishes for you
Tornqvist, Rita. *The Christmas carp*
Turkle, Brinton. *Do not open*
Turnbull, Ann. *The tapestry cats*
Varga, Judy. *Janko's wish*
Vigna, Judith. *I wish my daddy didn't drink so much*
Waber, Bernard. *You're a little kid with a big heart*
Wallace, Ivy. *Pookie puts the world right*
Watson, Pauline. *Wriggles, the little wishing pig*
Weisgard, Leonard. *Who dreams of cheese?*
Whybrow, Ian. *Wish, change, friend*
Willard, Nancy. *The marzipan moon*
Williams, Barbara. *Someday, said Mitchell*
Williams, Suzanne. *My dog never says please*
Wolfe, Frances. *One wish*
Wolkstein, Diane. *The magic wings*
Wood, Audrey. *Jubal's wish*
Wooding, Sharon L. *Arthur's Christmas wish*
Wooldridge, Connie Nordhielm. *Wicked Jack*
Zemach, Margot. *The three wishes*
Zimelman, Nathan. *To sing a song as big as Ireland*
Zolotow, Charlotte (Shapiro). *Someday*

Behavior – worrying

Benedek, Elissa P. *The secret worry*
Boelts, Maribeth. *Little Bunny's preschool countdown*
Bourgeois, Paulette. *Franklin says "I love you"*
Brown, Marc Tolon. *Arthur's underwear*
Carlson, Nancy L. *What if it never stops raining?*
Cuyler, Margery. *Stop drop and roll*
Delton, Judy. *The elephant in Duck's garden*
    On a picnic
Devlin, Wende. *Cranberry Easter*
Edwards, Pamela Duncan. *The worrywarts*
Erlbruch, Wolf. *Mrs. Meyer, the bird*
Gackenbach, Dick. *Where are Momma, Poppa, and Sister June?*
Gorog, Judith. *Zilla Sasparilla and the mud baby*
Greene, Carol. *The golden locket*
Gross, Alan. *Sometimes I worry . . .*
    What if the teacher calls on me?
Hanson, Regina. *The tangerine tree*
Hazen, Barbara Shook. *Wally the worry-warthog*
Heide, Florence Parry. *Timothy Twinge*
Henkes, Kevin. *Wimberly worried*
Herman, Charlotte. *My mother didn't kiss me good-night*
Jackson, Kathryn. *The saggy baggy elephant*
Komaiko, Leah. *Where can Daniel be?*
Lasky, Kathryn. *Lunch bunnies*
Lerner, Harriet Goldhor. *What's so terrible about swallowing an apple seed?*
Lester, Helen. *Something might happen*
Levitin, Sonia. *A piece of home*
    A single speckled egg
Lewis, Paeony. *I'll always love you*

Lindenbaum, Pija. *Else-Marie and her seven little daddies*
Loupy, Christophe. *Don't worry, Wags*
MacDonald, Maryann. *Sam's worries*
Magorian, Michelle. *Who's going to take care of me?*
Marshall, James. *Portly McSwine*
Pennypacker, Sara. *Stuart's cape*
Raschka, Christopher. *Waffle*
Roche, Denis (Denis M.). *Little Pig is capable*
Segal, Lore Groszmann. *The story of old Mrs. Brubeck and how she looked for trouble and where she found him*
Sewall, Marcia. *The cobbler's song*
Sharmat, Marjorie Weinman. *Lucretia the unbearable*
    Thornton, the worrier
Stadler, Alexander. *Beverly Billingsly borrows a book*
Tyler, Linda Wagner. *Waiting for mom*
Waddell, Martin. *Mimi's Christmas*
Williams, Marcia. *Not a worry in the world*
Yin. *Dear Santa, please come to the 19th floor*

Being different *see* Character traits – being different

Belize *see* Foreign lands – Belize

Belly buttons *see* Anatomy – navels

Bereavement *see* Death; Emotions – grief

Bible *see* Religion

Bicycling *see* Sports – bicycling

Bigotry *see* Prejudice

Birds

Aardema, Verna. *Jackal's flying lesson*
Ada, Alma Flor. *The malachite palace*
Adoff, Arnold. *Birds*
Alborough, Jez. *Beaky*
Alexander, Martha G. *Out! Out! Out!*
Aliki. *My visit to the zoo*
    The wish workers
Allred, Mary. *Grandmother Poppy and the funny-looking bird*
Anderson, Lonzo. *Mr. Biddle and the birds*
Anholt, Laurence. *Billy and the big new school*
Apperley, Dawn. *Good night, sleep tight, little bunnies*
Arnold, Caroline. *Five nests*
Arnosky, Jim. *Crinkleroot's 25 birds every child should know*
    Mouse writing
Aroner, Miriam. *The kingdom of singing birds*
Asch, Frank. *Baby Bird's first nest*
    Bear's bargain
    Moonbear
    Moonbear's dream
    Moonbear's pet
    Mooncake
Ash, Jutta. *Wedding birds*
Ayer, Jacqueline. *A wish for little sister*
Azaad, Meyer (Mahmud). *Half for you*
Bailey, Jill. *Eyes*
    Feet
    Mouths
Baker, Jeffrey J. W. *Patterns of nature*
Bancroft, Henrietta. *Animals in winter*
Bang, Betsy. *Tuntuni the tailor bird*
Banks, Kate (Katherine A.). *The bird, the monkey, and the snake in the jungle*
Barber, Antonia. *The enchanter's daughter*
Barnes, Laura T. *Ernest and the big itch*
Bash, Barbara. *Urban roosts*
Baskin, Leonard. *Hosie's aviary*
Baum, Willi. *Birds of a feather*
Beck, Scott. *Pepito the brave*
Beisert, Heide Helene. *Poor fish*
Berends, Polly Berrien. *I heard said the bird*

Berkes, Marianne Collins. *Marsh music*
Berliner, Franz. *Miserable Marabou*
Bernard, Robin. *Juma and the honey-guild*
Bernhard, Durga. *What's Maggie up to?*
Borden, Beatrice Brown. *Wild animals of Africa*
Boyle, Constance. *Little Owl and the weed*
Brian, Janeen. *Where does Thursday go?*
Bright, Robert. *Georgie and the baby birds*
Brillhart, Julie. *The dino expert*
Brock, Emma Lillian. *The birds' Christmas tree*
Brodzinsky, Anne Braff. *The mulberry bird*
Browne, Philippa-Alys. *A gaggle of geese*
Browne, Vee. *Monster birds*
Bruchac, Joseph. *The great ball game*
Bruna, Dick. *The little bird*
    Little bird tweet
Brunhoff, Laurent de. *Babar and the succotash bird*
    Babar's visit to Bird Island
Burstein, Fred. *Anna's rain*
Burton, Robert. *The egg*
Cannon, Janell. *Stellaluna*
    Stellaluna: a pop-up book and mobile
Carney, Margaret (Margaret Rose). *Where does a tiger-heron spend the night?*
Chönz, Selina. *Florina and the wild bird*
Christelow, Eileen. *The robbery at the diamond dog diner*
Climo, Shirley. *King of the birds*
Coatsworth, Elizabeth. *Under the green willow*
Colby, C. B. (Carroll Burleigh). *Who lives there?*
    Who went there?
Cole, Michael. *Head in the sand*
Collard, Sneed B. *Beaks!*
Conklin, Gladys. *If I were a bird*
Cortesi, Wendy W. *Explore a spooky swamp*
Cousins, Lucy. *Doctor Maisy*
    Portly's hat
Cowley, Stewart. *"Tweet, tweet, tweet"*
Cristini, Ermanno. *In the woods*
Cronin, Doreen. *Click, clack, moo*
Cross, Diana Harding. *Some birds have funny names*
Cross, Genevieve. *A trip to the yard*
Crowther, Kitty. *Jack and Jim*
Cruickshank, Margrit. *We're going to feed the ducks*
Cutler, Ivor. *Doris*
Dalmais, Anne-Marie. *The butterfly book of birds*
Damjan, Mischa. *Goodbye little bird*
Darby, Gene. *What is a bird?*
Darling, Kathy (Mary Kathleen). *Arctic babies*
Davies, Jacqueline. *The boy who drew birds*
Day, David. *King of the woods*
Delaney, Ned. *A worm for dinner*
Demarest, Chris L. *Benedict finds a home*
DePalma, Mary Newell. *The strange egg*
Did dinosaurs have feathers?
DiPucchio, Kelly S. *What's the magic word?*
Dobson, Clive. *Fred's TV*
Dodd, Lynley. *Slinky Malinki, open the door*
Doolittle, Bev. *Reading the wild*
Dunbar, Joyce. *Baby bird*
    Eggday
Eastman, P. D. (Philip D.). *Are you my mother?*
    Flap your wings
Egan, Tim. *Distant Feathers*
Ehlert, Lois. *Cuckoo, a Mexican folktale = Cucú: un cuento folklórico mexicano*
    Feathers for lunch
Elbling, Peter. *Aria*
Elborn, Andrew. *Bird Adalbert*
Elliott, David. *And here's to you!*
Elzbieta. *Brave Babette and sly Tom*
Erlbruch, Wolf. *Mrs. Meyer, the bird*
Eure, Wesley. *A fish out of water*
Fender, Kay. *Odette!*
Fisher, Aileen Lucia. *We went looking*
Fitzsimons, Cecilia. *My first birds*
Flanders, Michael. *Creatures great and small*
Fleming, Candace. *When Agnes caws*

Flora. *Feathers like a rainbow*
Florian, Douglas. *On the wing*
Fowler, Allan. *It could still be a bird*
Freeman, Don. *Fly high, fly low*
French, Fiona. *The blue bird*
Freschet, Berniece. *The little woodcock*
    Owl in the garden
Friskey, Margaret (Margaret Richards). *Birds we know*
Fujita, Tamao. *The boy and the bird*
Gallo, Frank. *Bird calls*
Gans, Roma. *How do birds find their way?*
    Hummingbirds in the garden
    When birds change their feathers
Ginsburg, Mirra. *The old man and his birds*
Givens, Janet Eaton. *Just two wings*
Goble, Paul. *The great race of the birds and animals*
Goodall, Jane. *The eagle and the wren*
Goode, Molly. *Mama loves*
Gray, Samantha. *Birds*
Greeley, Valerie. *Where's my share?*
Green, Jen. *Birds*
Greene, Ellin. *Ling-li and the phoenix fairy*
Grimm, Jacob. *The bear and the kingbird*
    The golden bird, ill. by Isabelle Brent
    The golden bird, ill. by Sandro Nardini
Hader, Berta Hoerner. *Mister Billy's gun*
Hague, Kathleen. *The legend of the Veery bird*
Haley, Gail E. *Birdsong*
Hautzig, Deborah. *Get well, Granny Bird*
Hawkinson, Lucy (Ozone). *Birds in the sky*
Hayles, Marsha. *The feathered crown*
Heller, Ruth. *How to hide a parakeet and other birds*
    How to hide a whip-poor-will and other birds
Helmer, Marilyn. *Three barnyard tales*
Helweg, Hans. *Farm animals*
Henley, Claire. *Quack, quack*
Herkert, Barbara. *Birds in your backyard*
Hindley, Judy. *Ten bright eyes*
Hines, Anna Grossnickle. *Miss Emma's wild garden*
Hirschi, Ron. *Faces in the forest*
    What is a bird?
    When morning comes
    When night comes
    Where do birds live?
    Who lives in . . . the forest?
Hoban, Lillian. *No, no, Sammy Crow*
Hoban, Tana. *A children's zoo*
Hooks, William H. *Feed me!*
Hunter, Anne. *What's in the meadow?*
Hurd, Edith Thacher. *Look for a bird*
Ipcar, Dahlov (Zorach). *Bright barnyard*
    The song of the day birds and the night birds
James, Simon. *The birdwatchers*
Janovitz, Marilyn. *Look out, bird!*
Jenkins, Steve. *Animals in flight*
Jenny, Anne. *The fantastic story of King Brioche the First*
John, Naomi. *Roadrunner*
Johnson, Angela. *Mama bird, baby birds*
Johnston, Tony. *The old lady and the birds*
Jonas, Ann. *Bird talk*
Kaczman, James. *A bird and his worm*
Kamal, Aleph. *The bird who was an elephant*
Kantrowitz, Mildred. *When Violet died*
Kasza, Keiko. *A mother for Choco*
Katschke, Judy. *Take a hike, Snoopy*
Kaufmann, John. *Birds are flying*
    Flying giants of long ago
Kellogg, Steven (Stephen). *Aster Aardvark's alphabet adventures*
Kimmel, Eric A. *The birds' gift*
Kirk, David. *Little bird, Biddle bird*
Kishida, Eriko. *The lion and the bird's nest*
Kleven, Elisa. *The dancing deer and the foolish hunter*
    The lion and the little red bird
Krauss, Ruth. *The happy egg*
Kroll, Virginia L. *Sweet Magnolia*
Kuchalla, Susan. *Birds*
Kumin, Maxine W. *Mittens in May*

Langton, Jane. *The queen's necklace*
Lavis, Steve. *Jump!*
Lent, Blair. *Ruby and Fred*
Lerner, Harriet Goldhor. *Franny B. Kranny, there's a bird in your hair*
Lifton, Betty Jean. *Joji and the Amanojaku*
   Joji and the dragon
   Joji and the fog
Lionni, Leo. *Inch by inch*
   Tico and the golden wings
Lipp, Frederick. *The caged birds of Phnom Penh*
Lobato, Arcadio. *Paper bird*
Louie, Therese On. *Raymond's perfect present*
Lubell, Winifred. *Rosalie, the bird market turtle*
Lyfick, Warren. *The little book of fowl jokes*
McCauley, Jane R. *Baby birds and how they grow*
McGrory, Anik. *Mouton's impossible dream*
McLerran, Alice. *The mountain that loved a bird*
McPhail, David M. *Farm morning*
Mallat, Kathy. *Brave bear*
Marshak, S. (Samuil). *The merry starlings*
Martchenko, Michael. *Bird feeder banquet*
Marzollo, Jean. *Ten little eggs*
Massie, Diane Redfield. *The baby beebee bird*
Mathers, Petra. *Herbie's secret Santa*
   Lottie's new friend
Mayer, Marianna. *The little jewel box*
Mayer, Mercer. *Two moral tales*
Mazzola, Frank. *Counting is for the birds*
Mead, Alice. *Billy and Emma*
Meddaugh, Susan. *Tree of birds*
Meeker, Clare Hodgson. *A tale of two rice birds*
Meres, Jonathan. *The big bad rumor*
Meyer, Brigit. *Little Easter surprise*
Millhouse, Nicholas. *Blue-footed booby*
Mitchell, Adrian. *Twice my size*
Mollel, Tololwa M. (Tololwa Marti). *A promise to the sun*
   Song bird
Most, Bernard. *Zoodles*
Munari, Bruno. *Bruno Munari's zoo*
   Tic, Tac and Toc
Myers, Christopher A. *Sparrows*
Napoli, Donna Jo. *Albert*
Nathan, Emma. *What do you call a group of turkeys?*
Neitzel, Shirley. *The house I'll build for the wrens*
Nesbit, Edith. *Cockatoucan*
Ness, Evaline. *Pavo and the princess*
Newman, Marjorie. *Mole and the baby bird*
   Mole and the baby bird [board book]
Norling, Beth. *The stone baby*
Norman, Charles. *The hornbean tree and other poems*
Oana, Kay D. *Robbie and the raggedy scarecrow*
Oberman, Sheldon. *The wisdom bird*
O Huigin, Sean. *King of the birds*
Okimoto, Jean Davies. *No dear, not here*
Olds, Elizabeth. *Feather mountain*
Oppenheim, Joanne. *Have you seen birds?*
Paraskevas, Betty. *Junior Kroll and Company*
Parnall, Peter. *Alfalfa Hill*
Parsons, Alexandra. *Amazing birds*
Paulsen, Gary. *Canoe days*
Pearson, Susan. *Lenore's big break*
Pearson, Tracey Campbell. *The purple hat*
Pedersen, Judy. *The tiny patient*
Peet, Bill (William Bartlett). *The kweeks of Kookatumdee*
   The pinkish, purplish, bluish egg
Peters, Lisa Westberg. *This way home*
Pieńkowski, Jan. *Bel and Bub and the baby bird*
Pirotta, Saviour. *Little bird*
Polacco, Patricia. *Mr. Lincoln's way*
Pomerantz, Charlotte. *Flap your wings and try*
Postgate, Oliver. *Noggin the king*
Potter, Beatrix. *The tale of Jemima Puddle-Duck and other farmyard tales*
Powell, Consie. *A bold carnivore*
Pratt, Kristin Joy. *A fly in the sky*
Pratt, Pierre. *Car*

Riddle, Tohby. *The singing hat*
Ringgold, Faith. *Bonjour, Lonnie*
Robinson, Tim. *Tobias, the quig, and the rumplenut tree*
Rockwell, Anne F. *Honk honk!*
   Our yard is full of birds
Rohmann, Eric. *Time flies*
Rose, Gerald. *The bird garden*
Rossetti, Christina Georgina. *Fly away, fly away over the sea*
Roth, Susan L. *Happy birthday Mr. Kang*
Rowe, John A. *Smudge*
Ryder, Joanne. *Wild birds*
Rylant, Cynthia. *The bird house*
San Souci, Robert D. *The birds of Killingworth*
Sayre, April Pulley. *If you should hear a honey guide*
Scamell, Ragnhild. *Who likes Wolfie?*
Schaefer, Carole Lexa. *Two scarlet songbirds*
Schumacher, Claire. *Alto and Tango*
Scuderi, Lucia. *To fly*
Seidler, Rosalie. *Grumpus and the Venetian cat*
Selsam, Millicent E. *A first look at bird nests*
   A first look at owls, eagles and other hunters of the sky
Seuss, Dr. *Horton hatches the egg*
   Thidwick, the big-hearted moose
Seymour, Tres. *The gulls of the Edmund Fitzgerald*
Sharratt, Nick. *Shark in the park*
Shulevitz, Uri. *What is a wise bird like you doing in a silly tale like this?*
Simmons, Al. *Counting feathers*
Simple gifts
Sis, Peter. *Rainbow Rhino*
Smith, Lane. *Flying Jake*
Smith, William Jay (1918–). *Birds and beasts*
Snoopy on wheels
Stage, Mads. *The greedy blackbird*
Stanley, Diane. *Birdsong lullaby*
Stone, A. Harris. *The last free bird*
Tafuri, Nancy. *Where did Bunny go?*
   Will you be my friend?
Taylor, Sydney. *Mr. Barney's beard*
Thornhill, Jan. *Wild in the city*
Troughton, Joanna. *How the birds changed their feathers*
Tusa, Tricia. *Maebelle's suitcase*
Twinem, Neecy. *In the air*
Van den Berg, Marinus. *The three birds*
Van Fleet, Matthew. *Fuzzy yellow ducklings*
Van Laan, Nancy. *The big fat worm*
Varley, Dimitry. *The whirly bird*
Velthuijs, Max. *Frog is frightened*
   The painter and the bird
Vyner, Sue. *The stolen egg*
Waechter, Friedrich Karl. *Three is company*
Wallis, Diz. *Battle of the beasts*
Walsh, Grahame L. *The goori goori bird*
Ward, Helen. *The king of the birds*
Watts, Barrie. *Bird's nest*
Watts, Bernadette. *The Christmas bird*
Weatherill, Stephen. *The very first Lucy Goose book*
West, Colin. *Have you seen the crocodile?*
Wezel, Peter. *The good bird*
   The naughty bird
Wildsmith, Brian. *Brian Wildsmith's birds*
Williams, Julie Stewart. *And the birds appeared*
Winer, Yvonne. *Birds build nests*
Winter, Rick. *Dirty birdy feet*
Wolff, Ashley. *A year of birds*
Wood, A. J. *Beautiful birds*
Wood, Audrey. *Birdsong*
   Little Penguin's tale
Yolen, Jane. *Bird watch*
   Spider Jane
   Welcome to the river of grass
Yoshida, Toshi. *Rhinoceros mother*
Ziefert, Harriet. *Happy Easter, Grandma!*
Zirkel, Lynn. *The shell dragon*
Zolotow, Charlotte (Shapiro). *Flocks of birds*

Birds – albatrosses

Cousteau Society. *Albatross*
Hoff, Syd. *Albert the albatross*

Birds – blackbirds

Bryan, Ashley. *Beautiful blackbird*
Duff, Maggie (Margaret K.). *Rum pum pum*
Murphy, Pat. *Pigasus*

Birds – bluebirds

Ketteman, Helen. *Armadilly chili*

Birds – bluejays

Angelo, Valenti. *The acorn tree*
Margolis, Richard J. *Big bear, spare that tree*
Newton, Patricia Montgomery. *The frog who drank the waters of the world*
Rockwell, Anne F. *Two blue jays*

Birds – boobys

Lewin, Betsy. *Booby hatch*

Birds – buzzards

Goble, Paul. *Iktomi and the buzzard*
Myers, Walter Dean. *How Mr. Monkey saw the whole world*
Sandburg, Helga. *Anna and the baby buzzard*
Wolkstein, Diane. *The cool ride in the sky*

Birds – canaries

Chase, Jan Brinckerhoff. *The golden song*
Foreman, Michael. *Cat and canary*
Freeman, Don. *Quiet! There's a canary in the library*
Heller, Wendy. *Clementine and the cage*
Nones, Eric Jon. *Canary prince*
Schneider, Antonie. *Good-bye, Vivi!*

Birds – cardinals

Galinsky, Ellen. *The baby cardinal*
Maloney, Peter (1955–). *Redbird at Rockefeller Center*
Preller, James. *Cardinal and sunflower*

Birds – chickadees

Ziefert, Harriet. *Birdhouse for rent*

Birds – chickens

Abel, Simone. *Follow that chicken!*
Ada, Alma Flor. *The rooster who went to his uncle's wedding*
Allamand, Pascale. *The pop rooster*
Allard, Harry. *I will not go to market today*
Allen, Pamela. *Fancy that!*
Ambrus, Victor G. *The little cockerel*
Auch, Mary Jane. *Bantam of the opera*
    The Easter egg farm
    Eggs mark the spot
    Hen lake
    Peeping Beauty
    Poultrygeist
    Souperchicken
Aulaire, Ingri Mortenson d'. *Don't count your chicks*
    Foxie, the singing dog
Back, Christine. *Chicken and egg*
Barber, Antonia. *Gemma and the baby chick*
Barbot, Daniel. *A bicycle for Rosaura*
Bassett, Jeni. *The chicks' trick*
Belpré, Pura. *Santiago*
Berkowitz, Linda. *Alfonse, where are you?*
Berquist, Grace. *Speckles goes to school*
Birchall, Mark. *Hen goes shopping*

Bishop, Adela. *The Easter wolf*
Bishop, Ann. *Chicken riddle*
Bogan, Paulette. *Goodnight Lulu*
Bond, Felicia. *Christmas in the chicken coop*
Bourgeois, Paulette. *Too many chickens*
Bourke, Linda. *Ethel's exceptional egg*
Boutwell, Edna. *Red rooster*
Brett, Jan. *Daisy comes home*
    Hedgie's surprise
Brothers, Aileen. *Jiffy, Miss Boo and Mr. Roo*
Brown, Jo. *Where's my mommy?*
Brown, Ken (Ken James). *The scarecrow's hat*
Brown, Margaret Wise. *Little chicken*
Burton, Jane. *Chester the chick*
    Chick
Carle, Eric. *The rooster who set out to see the world*
    Rooster's off to see the world
Casey, Patricia. *Cluck cluck*
    Quack quack
Cazet, Denys. *Elvis the rooster almost goes to heaven*
    Lucky me
    Minnie and Moo and the musk of Zorro
    Minnie and Moo: the night before Christmas
Chaucer, Geoffrey. *Chanticleer and the fox*
Chicken Little. *Chicken Licken*, ill. by Jutta Ash
    Chicken Licken, ill. by Gavin Bishop
    Chicken Little, ill. by Sally Hobson
    Henny Penny, ill. by Emily Bolam
    Henny Penny, ill. by Stephen Butler
    Henny Penny, ill. by Paul Galdone
    Henny Penny, ill. by William Stobbs
    Henny-Penny, ill. by Jane Wattenberg
    The sky is falling
    The story of Chicken Licken
Chukovskii, Kornei Ivanovich. *Good morning, chick*
Coerr, Eleanor. *The Josefina story quilt*
Coldrey, Jennifer. *The world of chickens*
Cole, Joanna. *A chick hatches*
Cole, Sheila. *The hen that crowed*
Conrad, Pam. *The rooster's gift*
Cousins, Lucy. *Hen on the farm*
Cowley, Stewart. *Little chick*
Coxe, Molly. *Big egg*
Crum, Shutta. *Fox and Fluff*
Czernecki, Stefan. *Huevos rancheros*
Dabcovich, Lydia. *Mrs. Huggins and her hen Hannah*
Dallas-Conte, Juliet. *Cock-a-moo-moo*
Dalmais, Anne-Marie. *Best bedtime stories of Mother Hen*
Daly, Niki. *What's cooking, Jamela?*
Davenier, Christine. *Leon and Albertine*
Delaney, Ned. *Cosmic chickens*
Demi. *Cuddly chick*
    Little chick chick
Denslow, Sharon Phillips. *Hazel's circle*
Desmoinaux, Christel. *Mrs. Hen's big surprise*
Dodds, Siobhan. *Elizabeth Hen*
Dorros, Arthur. *City chicken*
Dumas, Philippe. *Caesar, cock of the village*
Dutton, Sandra. *The cinnamon hen's autumn day*
Edwards, Dorothy. *A wet Monday*
Edwards, Michelle. *Chicken Man*
Ehrhardt, Reinhold. *Kikeri*
Ernst, Lisa Campbell. *Zinnia and Dot*
Fatio, Louise. *The red bantam*
Feldman, Thea. *Who you callin' chicken?*
Firmin, Peter. *Chicken stew*
Foster, Karen Sharp. *Good night my little chicks = Buenas noches mis pollitos*
Fowler, Richard. *Little Chick's big adventure*
Fox, Mem. *Hattie and the fox*
French, Vivian. *Red Hen and Sly Fox*
Freschet, Berniece. *Where's Henrietta's hen?*
Froissart, Bénédicte. *Uncle Henry's dinner guests*
Gershator, David. *Moon rooster*
Ginsburg, Mirra. *Across the stream*
    The chick and the duckling
The golden goose, ill. by William Stobbs

Stevens, Janet. *Cook-a-doodle-doo!*
Stoeke, Janet Morgan. *A friend for Minerva Louise*
  A hat for Minerva Louise
  Hide and seek
  Minerva Louise
  Minerva Louise and the red truck
  Minerva Louise at school
  Minerva Louise at the fair
Stone, Lynn M. *Chickens have chicks*
Sykes, Julie. *Dora's chicks*
  Dora's eggs
Threadgall, Colin. *Proud rooster and the fox*
The three little pigs. *The three little pigs and the fox*
Tripp, Valerie. *Sillyhen's big surprise*
Tusa, Tricia. *Chicken*
Van Horn, Grace. *Little red rooster*
Van Woerkom, Dorothy. *Something to crow about*
Voake, Charlotte. *Mrs. Goose's baby*
Waber, Bernard. *How to go about laying an egg*
Wallace, Karen. *My hen is dancing*
Walton, Rick. *Dumb clucks!*
Ward, Helen. *The rooster and the fox*
Ward, Nick. *Farmer George and the lost chick*
Waring, Richard (Richard M. N.). *Hungry hen*
Weil, Lisl. *Gillie and the flattering fox*
Weiss, Ellen. *Clara the fortune-telling chicken*
Williams, Garth. *The chicken book*
Willis, Val. *Silly little chick*
Wormell, Mary. *Bernard the angry rooster*
  Hilda Hen's happy birthday
  Hilda Hen's search

Birds – cockatoos

Blake, Quentin. *Cockatoos*
Cummings, W. T. (Walter Thies). *Wickford of Beacon Hill*
Pershall, Mary K. *Hello, Barney!*

Birds – condors

London, Jonathan. *Condor's egg*

Birds – cormorants

Bunting, Eve (Anne Evelyn). *Magic and the night river*

Birds – cranes

Bang, Molly. *Dawn*
  The paper crane
Bodkin, Odds. *The crane wife*
Charles, Veronika Martenova. *The crane girl*
Chen, Kerstin. *Lord of the cranes*
Coerr, Eleanor. *Sadako*
Hirschi, Ron. *Where are my swans, whooping cranes, and singing loons?*
Keller, Holly. *Grandfather's dream*
Keo, Ena. *The crane wife*
Laurin, Anne. *Perfect crane*
Owens, Mary Beth. *Counting cranes*
The peasant's pea patch
Wells, Rosemary. *Yoko's paper cranes*
Yagawa, Sumiko. *The crane wife*

Birds – crows

Æsop. *The crow and the pitcher*
Armstrong, Jennifer. *King crow*
Boyd, Lizi. *Lulu Crow's garden*
Chorao, Kay. *Pig and Crow*
Cunningham, David. *A crow's journey*
DeFelice, Cynthia C. *Clever crow*
DeLage, Ida. *The old witch and the crows*
Dillon, Jana. *Jeb Scarecrow's pumpkin patch*
Frascino, Edward. *Nanny Noony and the magic spell*
Freeman, Don. *Cyrano the crow*
Gage, Wilson. *The crow and Mrs. Gaddy*

Goble, Paul. *Crow chief*
Grant, Rose Marie. *Andiamo, Weasel*
Greenstein, Elaine. *Emily and the crows*
Guy, Ginger Foglesong. *Black crow, black crow*
Hale, Irina. *The naughty crow*
Harsh, Fred. *Alfie*
Hazelton, Elizabeth Baldwin. *Sammy, the crow who remembered*
Holder, Heidi. *Carmine the crow*
  Crows
Hyman, Robin. *Casper and the rainbow bird*
Johnson, Paul Brett. *Bearhide and crow*
Latimer, Jim. *James Bear's pie*
Lionni, Leo. *Six crows*
Lively, Penelope. *The cat, the crow, and the banyan tree*
Loux, Lynn C. *The day I could fly*
McDermott, Gerald. *Coyote*
Marion, Jeff Daniel. *Hello, Crow*
Oppenheim, Joanne. *"Not now!" said the cow*
Orgel, Doris. *Two crows counting*
Pringle, Laurence P. *Crows*
Rosen, Michael (1946–). *Crow and Hawk*
Rowe, John A. *Baby Crow*
Schami, Rafik. *The crow who stood on his beak*
Singer, Marilyn. *The company of crows*
Van Laan, Nancy. *Rainbow crow*
Wheeler, Lisa. *Old Cricket*

Birds – cuckoos

Bloom, Becky. *Mr. Cuckoo*
Corbalis, Judy. *The cuckoo bird*
Ehlert, Lois. *Cuckoo, a Mexican folktale = Cucú: un cuento folklórico mexicano*

Birds – dodos

Lehan, Daniel. *This is not a book about dodos*
Mathers, Petra. *Dodo gets married*

Birds – doves

Æsop. *The ant and the dove*
Agostinelli, Maria Enrica. *On wings of love*
Baker, Keith. *The dove's letter*
Freeman, Don. *The turtle and the dove*
Peet, Bill (William Bartlett). *The pinkish, purplish, bluish egg*
Potter, Beatrix. *The tale of the faithful dove*
Sage, James. *The boy and the dove*
Singer, Isaac Bashevis. *Why Noah chose the dove*
Wells, Rosemary. *The language of doves*
Wolff, Ashley. *The bells of London*

Birds – ducks

Akass, Susan. *Number nine duckling*
Alborough, Jez. *Captain Duck*
  Duck in the truck
  Fix-It Duck
Allen, Jeffrey. *Mary Alice, operator number 9*
  Mary Alice returns
Anastas, Margaret. *A hug for you*
Andersen, H. C. (Hans Christian). *The ugly duckling*, ill. by Adrienne Adams
  The ugly duckling, ill. by Lorinda Bryan Cauley
  The ugly duckling, ill. by Charlene DeLage
  The ugly duckling, ill. by Troy Howell
  The ugly duckling, ill. by Tadasu Izawa and Shigemi Hijikata
  The ugly duckling, ill. by Monika Laimgruber
  The ugly duckling, ill. by Johannes Larsen
  The ugly duckling, ill. by Thomas Locker
  The ugly duckling, ill. by Alan Marks
  The ugly duckling, ill. by Josef Palecek
  The ugly duckling, ill. by Jerry Pinkney
  The ugly duckling, ill. by Maria Ruis
  The ugly duckling, ill. by Daniel San Souci
  The ugly duckling, ill. by Meilo So
  The ugly duckling, ill. by Robert Van Nutt

The ugly duckling, ill. by Bernadette Watts
The ugly little duck, ill. by Peggy Perry Anderson
Arnosky, Jim. *All night near the water*
Asch, Frank. *Baby Duck's new friend*
Auch, Mary Jane. *The nutquacker*
Barnhart, Peter. *The wounded duck*
Barry, Frances. *Duckie's rainbow*
Bassède, Francine. *George paints his house*
Baumgardner, Mary Alice. *Alexandra, keeper of dreams*
Beck, Ian. *Five little ducks*
Bedard, Michael. *Sitting ducks*
Benjamin, A. H. *A duck so small*
Blocksma, Mary. *Where's that duck?*
Bothwell, Jean. *Paddy and Sam*
Boyd, Lizi. *The not-so-wicked stepmother*
Brown, Margaret Wise. *The duck*
   The golden egg book
Bunting, Eve (Anne Evelyn). *Happy birthday, dear duck*
Burton, Jane. *Dabble the duckling*
Cain, Sheridan. *Why so sad, Brown Rabbit?*
Capucilli, Alyssa Satin. *Biscuit finds a friend*
Carle, Eric. *10 little rubber ducks*
Cartlidge, Michelle. *Duck in the pond*
Caseley, Judith. *Mickey's class play*
Casey, Patricia. *Quack quack*
Cazet, Denys. *The duck with squeaky feet*
Chen, Chih-Yuan. *Guji Guji*
Clément, Claude. *The hungry duckling*
Coats, Laura Jane. *Marcella and the moon*
Conover, Chris. *Six little ducks*
Cooper, Helen (Helen F.). *Pumpkin soup*
Cowley, Stewart. *The naughty ducklings*
Cox, Phil Roxbee. *Ted in a red bed*
Cronin, Doreen. *Giggle, giggle, quack*
Cruickshank, Margrit. *We're going to feed the ducks*
Curious George and the dump truck
Dabcovich, Lydia. *Ducks fly*
Dalmais, Anne-Marie. *Danny the duck*
Davy's scary journey
Delton, Judy. *Bear and Duck on the run*
   Duck goes fishing
   The elephant in Duck's garden
   The perfect Christmas gift
   A pet for Duck and Bear
   Three friends find spring
   Two good friends
Demi. *Downy duckling*
   Little lucky ducky
Dreier, Ted. *Moozie's kind adventure*
Duckling
Dunn, Judy. *The little duck*
Duvoisin, Roger Antoine. *Two lonely ducks*
Egan, Tim. *Friday night at Hodges' café*
Ellis, Anne Leo. *Dabble Duck*
Enderle, Judith (Ann) Ross. *Where are you, little Zack?*
Faulkner, Keith. *Do you have my quack?*
Fierstein, Harvey. *The sissy duckling*
Flack, Marjorie. *Angus and the ducks*
   The story about Ping
Freschet, Berniece. *Wood duck baby*
Fribourg, Marjorie G. *Ching-Ting and the ducks*
Friskey, Margaret (Margaret Richards). *Seven diving ducks*
Gantschev, Ivan. *Where the moon lives*
Garland, Sarah. *Having a picnic*
Garland, Sherry. *Why ducks sleep on one leg*
Georgiady, Nicholas P. *Gertie the duck*
Gerstein, Mordicai. *Follow me!*
Gibbons, Gail. *Ducks*
Gibson, Betty. *The story of Little Quack*
Ginsburg, Mirra. *Across the stream*
   The chick and the duckling
Goble, Paul. *Iktomi and the ducks*
Goldin, Augusta. *Ducks don't get wet*
Goldsboro, Bobby. *Noah and the ark; and, David and Goliath*
Gordon, Gaelyn. *Duckat*
Grahame, Kenneth. *Duck song*
Gretz, Susanna. *Duck takes off*

Grimm, Jacob. *The twelve princesses*, ill. by Gordon Fitchett
Grindley, Sally. *Mucky Duck*
   Silly Goose and Dizzy Duck play hide-and-seek
Hader, Berta Hoerner. *Cock-a-doodle doo*
Hayes, Sarah. *Nine ducks nine*
Herman, Gail. *The littlest duckling*
Hest, Amy. *Baby Duck and the bad eyeglasses*
   Baby Duck and the cozy blanket
   Guess who, Baby Duck
   In the rain with Baby Duck
   Make the team, Baby Duck
   Off to school, Baby Duck
   You're the boss, Baby Duck
Hillert, Margaret. *The funny baby*
Hindley, Judy. *Do like a duck does*
Hurd, Edith Thacher. *Last one home is a green pig*
Hutchins, H. J. (Hazel J.). *One duck*
Ichikawa, Satomi. *Nora's duck*
Inkpen, Mick. *Gumboot's chocolatey day*
Isenbart, Hans-Heinrich. *A duckling is born*
James, Simon. *Little One Step*
Janice. *Angélique*
Jeram, Anita. *All together now*
   Bunny, my Honey
Jonas, Ann. *Watch William walk*
Joyce, William. *Bently and egg*
Kepes, Juliet. *The story of a bragging duck*
Laird, Elizabeth. *The day the ducks went skating*
Leverich, Kathleen. *The hungry fox and the foxy duck*
Linch, Tanya. *My duck*
Llewellyn, Claire. *Duck*
Lloyd, David. *Duck*
Loomis, Jennifer A. *A duck in a tree*
Lorenz, Lee. *Pig and duck buy a truck*
   A weekend in the country
Lunn, Janet Louise Swoboda. *Duck cakes for sale*
McCloskey, Robert. *Make way for ducklings*
MacDonald, Elizabeth. *Dilly-Dally and the nine secrets*
MacKinnon, Debbie. *Daniel's duck*
McMillan, Bruce. *Days of the ducklings*
Magloff, Lisa. *Duckling*
Mallat, Kathy. *Just ducky*
Mamin-Sibiryak, D. N. *Grey Neck*
Mathers, Petra. *A cake for Herbie*
Matje, Martin. *Celeste*
Mendoza, George. *Were you a wild duck, where would you go?*
Miles, Miska. *Noisy gander*
Moore, Sheila. *Samson Svenson's baby*
Naylor, Phyllis Reynolds. *Ducks disappearing*
Nethery, Mary. *Mary Veronica's egg*
Nolan, Lucy A. *Jack Quack*
Otto, Carolyn. *Ducks, ducks, ducks*
Owen, Annie. *Playtime duck*
Palatini, Margie. *Earthquack*
Paparone, Pamela. *Five little ducks*
Paterson, Katherine. *The tale of the Mandarin ducks*
Peters, Lisa Westberg. *Cold little duck, duck, duck*
Pfeffer, Wendy. *Mallard duck at Meadow View Pond*
Pizer, Abigail. *Percy the duck*
Pomerantz, Charlotte. *One duck, another duck*
Potter, Beatrix. *The tale of Jemima Puddle-Duck*
Quackenbush, Robert M. *Henry babysits*
   Henry's world tour
Rankin, Joan. *Wow! It's great being a duck*
Reiser, Lynn. *The surprise family*
Reynolds, Adrian. *Pete and Polo's farmyard adventure*
Richter, Mischa. *Eric and Matilda*
   Quack?
Roddie, Shen. *Not now, Mrs. Wolf*
Rogers, Paul (Patrick). *Quacky Duck*
Root, Phyllis. *One duck stuck*
   One duck stuck [board book]
Roy, Ronald. *Three ducks went wandering*
Saunders, Dave. *Snowtime*
Scamell, Ragnhild. *Solo plus one*
Schroeder, Binette. *Tuffa and the ducks*
Scruton, Clive. *Bubble and squeak*

Seignobosc, Françoise. *Springtime for Jeanne-Marie*
Sewell, Helen Moore. *Blue barns*
Shannon, David. *Duck on a bike*
Shannon, George. *Laughing all the way*
Shapes
Shaw, Evelyn S. *Nest of wood ducks*
Sheehan, Angela. *The duck*
Simmons, Jane. *Bouncy bouncy Daisy*
   Come along, Daisy!
   Daisy and the Beastie
   Daisy and the egg
   Daisy says Coo!
   Daisy says, "Here we go round the mulberry bush"
   Daisy says, "If you're happy and you know it"
   Daisy, the little duck with big feet
   Daisy's day out
   Daisy's favorite things
   Daisy's hide-and-seek
   Go to sleep, Daisy
   Quack, Daisy, quack!
   Splish splash Daisy
Sizes
Smith, Mavis. *Fred, is that you?*
Snow, Alan. *Quack!*
Sondergaard, Arensa. *Biddy and the ducks*
Spier, Peter. *Little ducks*
Standon, Anna. *Little duck lost*
Stehr, Frédéric. *Quack-quack*
Stevenson, James. *Howard*
   Monty
Stott, Dorothy. *Little Duck's bicycle ride*
   Too much
Sweeney, Jacqueline. *What about Bettie?*
Szekeres, Cyndy. *Hide-and-seek duck*
Tafuri, Nancy. *Have you seen my duckling?*
Thiele, Colin. *Farmer Schulz's ducks*
Thompson, Lauren. *Little Quack*
   Little Quack [board book]
   Little Quack's bedtime
   Little Quack's hide and seek
   Little Quack's new friend
Tryon, Leslie. *Albert's alphabet*
   Albert's birthday
   Albert's Christmas
   Albert's Halloween
Tudor, Bethany. *Samuel's tree house*
   Skiddycock Pond
Turska, Krystyna. *The woodcutter's duck*
Udry, Janice May. *Thump and Plunk*, ill. by Geoffrey Hayes
Van Laan, Nancy. *Shingebiss*
Velthuijs, Max. *Frog in love*
Verboven, Agnes. *Ducks like to swim*
Waddell, Martin. *Farmer Duck*
   It's quacking time
   Webster J. Duck
Wahl, Jan. *Old Hippo's Easter egg*
Ward, Nick. *Come on Baby Duck*
Watson, Jane Werner. *The fuzzy duckling*
Watts, Barrie. *Duck*
Wellington, Monica. *All my little ducklings*
Wells, Rosemary. *The itsy-bitsy spider*
Whippo, Walt. *Little white duck*
Whybrow, Ian. *Parcel for Stanley*
Wijngaard, Juan. *Duck*
Wildsmith, Brian. *The little wood duck*
Wilhelm, Hans. *Quacky Ducky's Easter egg*
   Quacky Ducky's Easter fun
Winthrop, Elizabeth. *Bear and Mrs. Duck*
   Bear's Christmas surprise
Withers, Carl. *The wild ducks and the goose*
Wright, Dare. *Edith and the duckling*
Yaccarino, Dan. *Five little ducks*
Yorinks, Arthur. *Quack!*
Ziefert, Harriet. *A dozen ducklings lost and found*

Birds – eagles

Allen, Judy. *Eagle*
The bear
Bernhard, Emery. *Eagles*
   Spotted Eagle and Black Crow
Craighead, Charles. *The eagle and the river*
Foreman, Michael. *Moose*
Gibbons, Gail. *Soaring with the wind*
Goble, Paul. *Adopted by the eagles*
Gregorowski, Christopher. *Fly, eagle, fly!*
Harrison, David Lee. *Dylan, the eagle-hearted chicken*
Hausman, Gerald. *Eagle boy*
Hodge, Deborah. *Eagles*
Klinting, Lars. *Regal the golden eagle*
McFarlane, Sheryl. *Eagle dreams*
Martin, Rafe. *The eagle's gift*
Martin-James, Kathleen. *Soaring bald eagles*
Mason, Jane B. *River day*
Melville, Herman. *Catskill eagle*
Minshull, Evelyn White. *Eaglet's world*
Morrison, Gordon. *Bald eagle*
Paraskevas, Betty. *On the day the tall ships sailed*
Vaughan, Richard Lee. *Eagle boy*

Birds – egrets

Carlson, Natalie Savage. *Time for the white egret*

Birds – emus

Knowles, Sheena. *Edward the emu*

Birds – falcons

George, Jean Craighead. *Frightful's daughter*
Greene, Carol. *Reading about the peregrine falcon*
Jenkins, Priscilla Belz. *Falcons nest on skyscrapers*

Birds – flamingos

Carlstrom, Nancy White. *Fish and flamingo*
Damjan, Mischa. *The fake flamingos*
Grambling, Lois G. *Miss Hildy's missing cape caper*
Hewett, Joan. *A flamingo chick grows up*
Keller, Holly. *Island baby*
McCloskey, Kevin. *Mrs. Fitz's flamingos*
Rossetti, Christina Georgina. *What is pink?*
Walsh, Ellen Stoll. *For Pete's sake*
Whitehouse, Patricia. *Flamingo*
Zoll, Max Alfred. *A flamingo is born*

Birds – geese

Æsop. *The goose that laid the golden egg*
Asch, Frank. *MacGooses's grocery*
Auch, Mary Jane. *Bird dogs can't fly*
Bacheller, Irving. *Lost in the fog*
Bang, Molly. *Goose*
Berkowitz, Linda. *Alfonse, where are you?*
Braun, Trudi. *My goose Betsy*
Brenner, Barbara A. *Good news*
Brown, Marc Tolon. *Moose and goose*
Bunting, Eve (Anne Evelyn). *Goose dinner*
Burningham, John. *Borka*
Cauley, Lorinda Bryan. *The goose and the golden coins*
Chandoha, Walter. *A baby goose for you*
Clearman, Deborah. *The goose's tale*
Conover, Chris. *Mother Goose and the sly fox*
Cox, Phil Roxbee. *Goose on the loose*
Day, Betsy. *Stefan and Olga*
Deedy, Carmen Agra. *Agatha's feather bed*
Delton, Judy. *On a picnic*
Demarest, Chris L. *Honk!*
Dunbar, Joyce. *Gander's pond*
   The secret friend
Dunrea, Olivier. *Ollie*

Ollie the stomper
Peedie
Duvoisin, Roger Antoine. *Petunia*
  Petunia and the song
  Petunia, beware!
  Petunia, I love you
  Petunia takes a trip
  Petunia, the silly goose
  Petunia's Christmas
  Petunia's treasure
Egg-napped!
Enderle, Judith (Ann) Ross. *What would Mama do?*
Fox, Mem. *Boo to a goose*
Fredericks, Anthony D. *In one tidepool*
Freeman, Don. *Will's quill*
Galdone, Joanna. *Gertrude, the goose who forgot*
George, Lindsay Barrett. *William and Boomer*
Gervais, Bernadette. *Voyage under the stars*
Grimm, Jacob. *The golden goose*, ill. by Dennis McDermott
Grindley, Sally. *Silly Goose and Dizzy Duck play hide-and-seek*
Holmes, Efner Tudor. *Amy's goose*
Houston, James. *Kiviok's magic journey*
Ichikawa, Satomi. *Nora's surprise*
Illyés, Gyula. *Matt the gooseherd*
Inkpen, Mick. *Honk!*
Jackson, Chris. *The Gaggle sisters river tour*
Johnson, Paul Brett. *The goose who went off in a huff*
Johnson, Ryerson. *Kenji and the magic geese*
Kalas, Sybille. *The goose family book*
Kasperson, James. *Little brother moose*
Kent, Jack. *Silly goose*
Kerr, Judith. *The other goose*
King, Deborah. *The flight of the snow geese*
Koch, Dorothy Clarke. *Gone is my goose*
Lasell, Fen. *Fly away goose*
Latimer, Jim. *James Bear and the goose gathering*
Lears, Laurie. *Waiting for Mr. Goose*
Le Tord, Bijou. *Good wood bear*
Lindbergh, Reeve. *The day the goose got loose*
Low, Joseph. *Benny rabbit and the owl*
  Boo to a goose
McBratney, Sam. *Just you and me*
McPhail, David M. *A girl, a goat, and a goose*
Mahy, Margaret. *A summery Saturday morning*
Manning, Mick. *Honk! honk!*
Mother Goose. *The golden goose book*, ill. by L. Leslie Brooke
Oram, Hiawyn. *Gerda the goose*
Pilkey, Dav. *The Silly Gooses*
  The Silly Gooses build a house
Pizer, Abigail. *Nosey Gilbert*
Polacco, Patricia. *I can hear the sun*
  Rechenka's eggs
Preston, Edna Mitchell. *Squawk to the moon, little goose*
Rockwell, Anne F. *Poor Goose*
Rong, Yu. *A lovely day for Amelia Goose*
Root, Phyllis. *Grandmother Winter*
Rossiter, Nan Parson. *The way home*
Ryder, Joanne. *Catching the wind*
Sanfield, Steve. *The girl who wanted a song*
Sansone, Adele. *The little green goose*
Saunders, Dave. *Snowtime*
Schoenherr, John. *Rebel*
Schubert, Ingrid. *Bear's eggs*
Sewell, Helen Moore. *Blue barns*
Simmons, Jane. *Ebb and Flo and the new friend*
Simont, Marc. *The goose that almost got cooked*
Stevens, Kathleen. *Aunt Skilly and the stranger*
Strand, Keith. *Grandfather's Christmas tree*
Tafuri, Nancy. *Silly little goose!*
Voake, Charlotte. *Mrs. Goose's baby*
Wahl, Jan. *The singing geese*
Walsh, Ellen Stoll. *You silly goose*
Weatherill, Stephen. *The very first Lucy Goose book*
Wood, Jacqueline. *Never say boo to a goose!*
Zeman, Ludmila. *The first red maple leaf*
Zijlstra, Tjerk. *Benny and his geese*

Birds – guinea fowl

Knutson, Barbara. *How the guinea fowl got her spots*
Paterson, Brian. *Zigby camps out*

Birds – hawks

Baylor, Byrd. *Hawk, I'm your brother*
Bliss, Corinne Demas. *Matthew's meadow*
Gilbert, Suzie. *Hawk Hill*
Harvey, Bev. *The hawk family*
Hayes, Joe. *Little Gold Star = Estrellita de oro*
Houk, Randy. *Rico's hawk*
Pia Toya
Rosen, Michael (1946–). *Crow and Hawk*

Birds – herons

Brandon, Siobhán. *The bird's story*
McGaw, Wayne T. *T-boy of the bayou*
Owen, Roy. *The ibis and the egret*

Birds – hornbills

Shepard, Steve. *Elvis Hornbill, international business bird*

Birds – humming birds

Allard, Harry. *The hummingbirds' day*
Baker, Keith. *Little Green*
Czernecki, Stefan. *The hummingbird's gift*
Hausman, Gerald. *Doctor Bird*
Ryder, Joanne. *Dancers in the garden*
Sayre, April Pulley. *The hungry hummingbird*

Birds – ibis

Owen, Roy. *The ibis and the egret*

Birds – kestrels

Blake, Robert J. *Fledgling*

Birds – larks

Czernecki, Stefan. *The singing snake*

Birds – loons

Aston, Dianna Hutts. *Loony Little*
Hassett, John. *Junior*
Hirschi, Ron. *Loon Lake*
  Where are my swans, whooping cranes, and singing loons?
London, Jonathan. *Loon Lake*
Love, Pamela. *A loon alone*
Martin, Jacqueline Briggs. *Washing the willow tree loon*
Santucci, Barbara. *Loon summer*

Birds – macaws

Mead, Alice. *Billy and Emma*

Birds – magpies

Wild, Margaret. *Fox*
Wilson, April. *April Wilson's magpie magic*

Birds – mockingbirds

Ryder, Joanne. *Mockingbird morning*

Birds – nightingales

Andersen, H. C. (Hans Christian). *The emperor and the nightingale*, ill. by Meilo So
  The emperor and the nightingale, ill. by James Watling
  The emperor's nightingale, ill. from the Disney archives
  The emperor's nightingale, ill. by Georges Lemoine

The nightingale, ill. by Harold Berson
The nightingale, ill. by Nancy Ekholm Burkert
The nightingale, ill. by Alison Claire Darke
The nightingale, ill. by Demi
The nightingale, ill. by Beni Montresor
The nightingale, ill. by Josef Palecek
The nightingale, ill. by Regolo Ricci
The nightingale, ill. by Christopher Santoro
The nightingale, ill. by Lisbeth Zwerger
Chase, Catherine. *The nightingale and the fool*
Maugham, W. Somerset (William Somerset). *Princess September and the nightingale*
Moore, Inga. *Rose and the nightingale*

Birds – ostriches

Aardema, Verna. *The lonely lioness and the ostrich chicks*
Burton, Marilee Robin. *Oliver's birthday*
Coxe, Molly. *Big egg*
Delton, Judy. *Penny wise, fun foolish*
Peet, Bill (William Bartlett). *Zella, Zack, and Zodiac*
Weigelt, Udo. *The Easter Bunny's baby*
Whitehouse, Patricia. *Ostrich*
Ylla. *Look who's talking*

Birds – owls

Æsop. *Town mouse, country mouse*, ill. by Jan Brett
Beifuss, John. *Armadillo Ray*
Bennett, Rainey. *After the sun goes down*
Bernhard, Emery. *The girl who wanted to hunt*
Blaich, Ute. *The star*
Boyle, Constance. *The story of Little Owl*
Bright, Robert. *Georgie to the rescue*
Brown, Alan. *Hoot and Holler*
Bunting, Eve (Anne Evelyn). *The man who could call down owls*
Burton, Jane. *Buffy the barn owl*
    Snowy, the barn owl
Carey, Mary. *The owl who loved sunshine*
Coleman, Michael. *Lazy Ozzie*
Crebbin, June. *Fly by night*
Cresswell, Helen. *Two hoots and the king*
    Two hoots in the snow
DeLage, Ida. *The old witch and the crows*
Delton, Judy. *Duck goes fishing*
Dowling, Paul. *Happy birthday, Owl*
Duvoisin, Roger Antoine. *Day and night*
Eastman, P. D. (Philip D.). *Sam and the firefly*
Flower, Phyllis. *Barn owl*
Foster, Doris Van Liew. *Tell me, Mr. Owl*
Freschet, Berniece. *Owl in the garden*
Funazaki, Yasuko. *Baby owl*
Gantschev, Ivan. *Where is Mr. Mole?*
Gates, Frieda. *Owl eyes*
Goldsmith, Howard. *Sleepy little owl*
Goodenow, Earle. *The owl who hated the dark*
Harshman, Terry Webb. *Porcupine's pajama party*
Hendra, Sue. *Oliver's wood*
Hissey, Jane. *Hoot*
Hoban, Russell. *Charlie Meadows*
Hoopes, Lyn Littlefield. *My own home*
Houk, Randy. *Ruffle, Coo and Hoo Doo*
Hutchins, Pat. *Good night owl*
Johnston, Tony. *The barn owls*
Kirn, Ann. *I spy*
Kraus, Robert. *The adventures of Wise Old Owl*
    Owliver
    Wise Old Owl's canoe trip adventure
    Wise Old Owl's Christmas adventure
Lamm, C. Drew. *Screech Owl at Midnight Hollow*
Lear, Edward. *The owl and the pussy cat*, ill. by Ian Beck
    The owl and the pussycat, ill. by Jan Brett
    The owl and the pussycat, ill. by Lorinda Bryan Cauley
    The owl and the pussy-cat, ill. by Barbara Cooney
    The owl and the pussy-cat, ill. by Emma Crosby
    The owl and the pussy-cat, ill. by William Pène Du Bois
    The owl and the pussycat, ill. by Lori Farbanish

The owl and the pussy-cat, ill. by Gwen Fulton
The owl and the pussycat, ill. by Paul Galdone
The owl and the pussy-cat, ill. by Elaine Muis
The owl and the pussycat, ill. by Erica Rutherford
The owl and the pussycat, ill. by Janet Stevens
The owl and the pussycat, ill. by Louise Voce
The owl and the pussycat, ill. by Colin West
The owl and the pussy-cat, ill. by Owen Wood
Leonard, Marcia. *Little owl leaves the nest*
Lionni, Leo. *Six crows*
Lobel, Arnold. *Owl at home*
London, Jonathan. *The owl who became the moon*
McDonald, Megan. *Whoo-oo is it?*
McGuire, Leslie. *Baby night owl*
McKeever, Katherine. *A family for Minerva*
Maschler, Fay. *T. G. and Moonie go shopping*
    T. G. and Moonie have a baby
    T. G. and Moonie move out of town
Most, Bernard. *Z-Z-Zoink!*
Nicholls, Judith. *Billywise*
Nicoll, Helen. *Meg at sea*
    Meg's eggs
Norman, Howard A. *The owl-scatterer*
O'Malley, Kevin. *Who killed Cock Robin?*
Panek, Dennis. *Detective Whoo*
Pfister, Marcus. *The sleepy owl*
Piatti, Celestino. *The happy owls*
Potter, Beatrix. *The tale of Squirrel Nutkin*
Riley, Joelle. *Quiet owls*
Schären, Beatrix. *Tillo*
Schoenherr, John. *The barn*
Shles, Larry. *Moths and mothers, feathers and fathers*
Slobodkin, Louis. *Wide-awake owl*
Smith, Jim. *The frog band and the owlnapper*
Tejima, Keizaburo. *Owl lake*
Thaler, Mike. *Owley*
Tomlinson, Jill. *The owl who was afraid of the dark*
Tompert, Ann. *Badger on his own*
Townsend, Emily Rose. *Owls*
Waddell, Martin. *Owl babies*
Wahl, Jan. *Mrs. Owl and Mr. Pig*
Whitehouse, Patricia. *Barn owls*
Wildsmith, Brian. *The owl and the woodpecker*
Yolen, Jane. *Owl moon*

Birds – parakeets, parrots

Asch, Frank. *George's store*
Augarde, Steve (Stephen). *Barnaby Shrew, Black Dan and . . . the mighty wedgwood*
Banchek, Linda. *Snake in, snake out*
Baum, Louis. *JuJu and the pirate*
Best, Cari. *Top banana*
Bishop, Bonnie. *No one noticed Ralph*
    Ralph rides away
Blegvad, Lenore. *The parrot in the garret and other rhymes about dwellings*
Bradford, Ann. *The mystery of the tree house*
Cressey, James. *Pet parrot*
Davis, Patricia Anne. *Brian's bird*
Demuth, Patricia Brennan. *Max, the bad-talking parrot*
Dragonwagon, Crescent. *Coconut*
Fox, Mem. *Tough Boris*
Gál, László. *The parrot*
Gordon, Sharon. *Pete the parakeet*
Graham, Bob. *Pete and Roland*
Graham, Margaret Bloy. *Benjy and the barking bird*
Hamsa, Bobbie. *Polly wants a cracker*
Heller, Ruth. *How to hide a parakeet and other birds*
Holman, Felice. *Victoria's castle*
Houk, Randy. *Ruffle, Coo and Hoo Doo*
Hyman, Robin. *Casper and the rainbow bird*
Johnston, Tony. *Little wild parrot*
    Lorenzo the naughty parrot
Lester, Helen. *Princess Penelope's parrot*
McDermott, Gerald. *Papagayo, the mischief maker*
McFarland, Lyn Rossiter. *The pirate's parrot*

Macken, JoAnn Early. *Parakeets*
Mahy, Margaret. *The horrendous hullabaloo*
Meddaugh, Susan. *Martha walks the dog*
Potter, Stephen. *Squawky, the adventures of a clasperchoice*
Rankin, Joan. *You're somebody special, Walliwigs!*
Remkiewicz, Frank. *The last time I saw Harris*
Steig, William. *Wizzil*
Willis, Jeanne. *Be quiet, Parrot!*
Witte, Anna. *The parrot Tico Tango*
Zacharias, Thomas. *But where is the green parrot?*
Zusman, Evelyn. *The Passover parrot*

Birds – peacocks, peahens

Alan, Sandy. *The plaid peacock*
Alexander, Sue. *Peacocks are very special*
Auch, Mary Jane. *Hen lake*
Bunting, Eve (Anne Evelyn). *Box, fox, ox, and the peacock*
Daniel, Doris Temple. *Pauline and the peacock*
Fox, Mem. *Feathers and fools*
Hamberger, John. *The peacock who lost his tail*
Kajpust, Melissa. *The peacock's pride*
Kepes, Juliet. *The seed that peacock planted*
Peet, Bill (William Bartlett). *The spooky tail of Prewitt Peacock*
Polacco, Patricia. *Just plain Fancy*
Schami, Rafik. *The crow who stood on his beak*
Wittman, Sally. *Pelly and Peak*
    Plenty of Pelly and Peak

Birds – pelicans

Benchley, Nathaniel. *The flying lessons of Gerald Pelican*
Crane, Alan. *Pepita bonita*
Freeman, Don. *Come again, pelican*
Hewett, Joan. *Fly away free*
Jenkin-Pearce, Susie. *Percy Short and Cuthbert*
Lear, Edward. *Of pelicans and pussycats*
    The pelican chorus, ill. by Harold Berson
    The pelican chorus and the quangle wangle's hat, ill. by Kevin W. Maddison
O'Reilly, Edward. *Brown pelican at the pond*
Patz, Nancy. *To Annabella Pelican from Thomas Hippopotamus*
Wildsmith, Brian. *Pelican*
Wittman, Sally. *Pelly and Peak*
    Plenty of Pelly and Peak

Birds – penguins

Alborough, Jez. *Cuddly Dudley*
Apperley, Dawn. *Flip and Flop*
Arrhenius, Peter. *The Penguin Quartet*
Benson, Patrick. *Little penguin*
Breathed, Berke (Berkeley). *A wish for wings that work*
Bright, Robert. *Which is Willy?*
Chester, Jonathan. *Splash!*
Coldrey, Jennifer. *Penguins*
Cousins, Lucy. *Portly's hat*
Cousteau Society. *Penguins*
Davies, Gill. *Can't, don't, won't*
Duquennoy, Jacques. *North Pole, South Pole*
Dyer, Heather. *Tina and the penguin*
Fatio, Louise. *Hector and Christina*
    Hector penguin
Faulkner, Keith. *The puzzled penguin*
Gay, Michel. *Bibi takes flight*
    Bibi's birthday surprise
Geraghty, Paul. *Solo*
Gibbons, Gail. *Penguins!*
Gliori, Debi. *Penguin post*
Guiberson, Brenda Z. *The emperor lays an egg*
Hamsa, Bobbie. *Your pet penguin*
Hewett, Joan. *A penguin chick grows up*
Hogan, Paula Z. *The penguin*
Horáček, Petr. *Flip's day*
Howe, Caroline Walton. *Counting penguins*
Inkpen, Mick. *Penguin small*
Jenkins, Martin. *The emperor's egg*

Johnston, Johanna. *Penguin's way*
Karas, G. Brian. *Skidamarink*
Kellogg, Steven (Stephen). *A penguin pup for Pinkerton*
Kessler, Ethel. *Is there a penguin at your party?*
Kimmel, Elizabeth Cody. *My penguin Osbert*
Knüppel, Helga. *Christabel Crocodile's birthday egg*
Lang, Aubrey. *Baby penguin*
Leonard, Marcia. *Paintbox penguins*
Lester, Helen. *Tacky and the Emperor*
    Tacky in trouble
    Tacky the penguin
    Tackylocks and the three bears
    Three cheers for Tacky
Lilly, Kenneth. *Animals of the ocean*
McDonald, Megan. *Penguin and Little Blue*
McMillan, Bruce. *Puffins climb, penguins rhyme*
Magloff, Lisa. *Penguin*
Mitra, Annie. *Penguin moon*
Murphy, Mary. *I like it when . . .*
    I like it when . . . [board book]
    My puffer train
    Please be quiet!
    Some things change
Nichols, Cathy. *Tuxedo Sam*
Nixon, Joan Lowery. *Gus and Gertie and the missing pearl*
O'Donnell, Peter. *Pinkie goes south*
Perlman, Janet. *The Emperor Penguin's new clothes*
    The penguin and the pea
Pfister, Marcus. *Penguin Pete and Little Tim*
Radcliffe, Theresa. *Nanu, penguin chick*
Rey, Margret (Margret Elisabeth Waldstein). *Whiteblack the penguin sees the world*
Rigby, Rodney. *Hello, this is your penguin speaking*
Robinson, Claire. *Penguins*
Rühmann, Karl. *Filbert flies*
Schafer, Kevin. *Penguins A B C*
    Penguins 1 2 3
Schindel, John. *Busy penguins*
Seibold, J. Otto. *Penguin dreams*
Sheehan, Angela. *The penguin*
Shields, Carol Diggory. *Martian rock*
Somme, Lauritz. *The penguin family book*
Stevenson, James. *Winston, Newton, Elton, and Ed*
Tatham, Betty. *Penguin chick*
Townsend, Emily Rose. *Penguins*
Walker, Jane. *Ten little penguins*
Waterhouse, Stephen A. *Get busy this Christmas*
Weare, Tim. *I'm a little penguin*
Weeks, Sarah. *Without you*
Weiss, Leatie. *Funny feet!*
Whybrow, Ian. *Wish, change, friend*
Wiesmüller, Dieter. *The adventures of Marco and Polo*
Willis, Jeanne. *Take turns, Penguin!*
Winteringham, Victoria. *Penguin day*
Wood, Audrey. *Little Penguin's tale*
Yee, Patrick. *Baby penguin*

Birds – pigeons

Allan, Nicholas. *The bird*
Baker, Jeannie. *Home in the sky*
    Millicent
Benchley, Nathaniel. *Walter the homing pigeon*
Erdrich, Louise. *Grandmother's pigeon*
Kingman, Lee. *Pierre Pigeon*
Kurtz, Jane. *Only a pigeon*
Macaulay, David. *Angelo*
McClure, Gillian. *Fly home McDoo*
Peet, Bill (William Bartlett). *Fly, Homer, fly*
Shulman, Milton. *Prep, the little pigeon of Trafalgar Square*
Suben, Eric. *Pigeon takes a trip*
Wells, Rosemary. *The language of doves*
Willems, Mo. *Don't let the pigeon drive the bus*

Birds – plovers

De Paola, Tomie (Thomas Anthony). *Bill and Pete*

Bill and Pete go down the Nile
Bill and Pete to the rescue

Birds – ptarmigans

Guenther, James. *Turnagain, Ptarmigan, where did you go?*
London, Jonathan. *Gone again ptarmigan*

Birds – puffins

Bentley, Dawn. *Welcome back, Puffin*
De Beer, Hans. *Little Polar Bear and the big balloon*
Drew, Patricia. *Spotter Puff*
Hall, Pam. *On the edge of the eastern ocean*
Hirschi, Ron. *Where are my puffins, whales, and seals?*
Lawson, Annetta. *The lucky yak*
Lewis, Naomi. *Puffin*
McMillan, Bruce. *Nights of the pufflings*
    Puffins climb, penguins rhyme

Birds – quail

Carey, Valerie Scho. *Quail song*
Troughton, Joanna. *The quail's egg*

Birds – ravens

Æsop. *The raven and the fox*
Aiken, Joan. *Arabel and Mortimer*
Battle-Lavert, Gwendolyn. *The shaking bag*
Carlstrom, Nancy White. *Raven and river*
Dixon, Ann. *How raven brought light to people*
Dupre, Kelly. *The raven's gift*
Grimm, Jacob. *The seven ravens*, ill. by Felix Hoffmann
    The seven ravens, ill. by Lisbeth Zwerger
Johnson, Amy Crane. *Cinnamon and the April shower = Canela y el aguacero de abril*
    Mason moves away = Mason se muda
Luenn, Nancy. *Song for the ancient forest*
McDermott, Gerald. *Raven*
Weigelt, Udo. *It wasn't me*
Williams, Maria. *How Raven stole the sun*

Birds – roadrunners

Anaya, Rudolfo A. *Roadrunner's dance*

Birds – robins

Atkins, Jeannine. *Robin's home*
Calder, S. J. *If you were a bird*
Cock Robin. *The courtship, merry marriage, and feast of Cock Robin and Jenny Wren*
    Who killed Cock Robin?, ill. by William Stobbs
Fearnley, Jan. *Little Robin's Christmas*
Fisher, Aileen Lucia. *You don't look like your mother*
Flack, Marjorie. *The restless robin*
Hawkinson, John. *Robins and rabbits*
Holmes, Anita. *Where robins fly*
Jenkins, Priscilla Belz. *A nest full of eggs*
Kent, Jack. *Round Robin*
Ketcham, Sallie. *The Christmas bird*
Kraus, Robert. *The first robin*
Little Robin Redbreast
O'Malley, Kevin. *Who killed Cock Robin?*
Posada, Mia. *Robins*
Rockwell, Anne F. *My spring robin*
Stern, Elsie-Jean. *Wee Robin's Christmas song*
Tresselt, Alvin R. *Hi, Mister Robin*

Birds – sandpipers

Hurd, Edith Thacher. *Sandpipers*
Mendoza, George. *The scribbler*

Birds – seagulls

Armitage, Ronda. *The lighthouse keeper's lunch*

Carrick, Carol. *Beach bird*
    Melanie
Duvoisin, Roger Antoine. *Snowy and Woody*
Engels-Fietzek, Petra. *Sophie and the seagull*
Gibbons, Gail. *Gulls – gulls – gulls*
Hoff, Syd. *The lighthouse children*
Ness, Evaline. *Do you have the time, Lydia?*
Paraskevas, Betty. *Hoppy and Joe*
Pursell, Margaret Sanford. *Shelley the sea gull*
Rühmann, Karl. *Filbert flies*
Simmons, Jane. *Ebb and Flo and the greedy gulls*
Turkle, Brinton. *Thy friend, Obadiah*
Walsh, Ellen Stoll. *Hamsters to the rescue*
Waugh, Peter. *The great cannon beach mouse caper*

Birds – sparrows

Cowley, Joy. *The video shop sparrow*
Crabtree, Judith. *The sparrow's story at the king's command*
Fregosi, Claudia. *The pumpkin sparrow*
Gerstein, Mordicai. *Prince Sparrow*
Ishii, Momoko. *The tongue-cut sparrow*
Myers, Christopher A. *Sparrows*
Ostheeren, Ingrid. *Jonathan Mouse and the baby bird*
Selden, George. *Sparrow socks*
Wallace, Ian. *The sparrow's song*
Weigelt, Udo. *Ben and the Buccaneers*

Birds – spoonbills

Guiberson, Brenda Z. *Spoonbill swamp*

Birds – storks

Berliner, Franz. *Miserable Marabou*
Bos, Burny. *Prince Valentino*
Brown, Margaret Wise. *Wheel on the chimney*
Damjan, Mischa. *The fake flamingos*
Drescher, Henrik. *The strange appearance of Howard Cranebill, Jr.*
Gantschev, Ivan. *Journey of the storks*
McDermott, Gerald. *The fox and the stork*

Birds – swallows

Politi, Leo. *Song of the swallows*
Swinburne, Stephen R. *Swallows in the birdhouse*

Birds – swans

Andersen, H. C. (Hans Christian). *The ugly duckling*, ill. by Adrienne Adams
    The ugly duckling, ill. by Lorinda Bryan Cauley
    The ugly duckling, ill. by Charlene DeLage
    The ugly duckling, ill. by Troy Howell
    The ugly duckling, ill. by Tadasu Izawa and Shigemi Hijikata
    The ugly duckling, ill. by Monika Laimgruber
    The ugly duckling, ill. by Johannes Larsen
    The ugly duckling, ill. by Thomas Locker
    The ugly duckling, ill. by Alan Marks
    The ugly duckling, ill. by Josef Palecek
    The ugly duckling, ill. by Jerry Pinkney
    The ugly duckling, ill. by Maria Ruis
    The ugly duckling, ill. by Daniel San Souci
    The ugly duckling, ill. by Meilo So
    The ugly duckling, ill. by Robert Van Nutt
    The ugly duckling, ill. by Bernadette Watts
    The ugly little duck, ill. by Peggy Perry Anderson
    The wild swans, ill. by Angela Barrett
    The wild swans, ill. by Susan Jeffers
Auer, Martin. *Now, now Markus*
Bell, Anthea. *Swan Lake*
Bunting, Eve (Anne Evelyn). *Swan in love*
Canfield, Jane White. *Swan cove*
Clément, Claude. *The painter and the wild swans*
Day, David. *The swan children*
DeChristopher, Marlowe. *Greencoat and the swanboy*
Edwards, Pamela Duncan. *Honk!*

Fox, Mem. *Feathers and fools*
Gantschev, Ivan. *Where the moon lives*
Geras, Adèle. *Swan Lake*
Grimm, Jacob. *The six swans*, ill. by Dorothée Duntze
    The six swans, ill. by Daniel San Souci
    The six swans, ill. by Margot Tomes
Hillert, Margaret. *The funny baby*
Hirschi, Ron. *Where are my swans, whooping cranes, and singing loons?*
Hogan, Paula Z. *The black swan*
Lemberg, Stephen H. *Scaredy dog*
Lewis, Naomi. *Swan*
MacGill-Callahan, Sheila. *The children of Lir*
Morpurgo, Michael. *The silver swan*
Pyle, Howard. *The Swan Maiden*
Seabrooke, Brenda. *The swan's gift*
Swan flyway
Tejima, Keizaburo. *Swan sky*
Willington, Monica. *Seasons of swans*
Zwerger, Lisbeth. *Swan Lake*

Birds – toucans

McKee, David. *Two can toucan*

Birds – turkeys

Arnosky, Jim. *All about turkeys*
Balian, Lorna. *Sometimes it's turkey*
Bateman, Teresa. *A plump and perky turkey*
Bunting, Eve (Anne Evelyn). *A turkey for Thanksgiving*
Cowley, Joy. *Gracias, the Thanksgiving turkey*
Kraus, Robert. *How Spider saved Turkey*
Kroll, Steven. *One tough turkey*
Morgan, Allen. *Matthew and the midnight ball game*
    Matthew and the midnight turkeys
Nathan, Emma. *What do you call a group of turkeys?*
Nikola-Lisa, W. *The dancin' fox*
Pilkey, Dav. *'Twas the night before Thanksgiving*
Pollock, Penny. *The turkey girl*
Schatell, Brian. *Farmer Goff and his turkey Sam*
    Sam's no dummy, Farmer Goff
Spirn, Michele. *I am the turkey*
Wheeler, Lisa. *Turk and Runt*
Wickstrom, Sylvie (Sylvie Kantrovitz). *Turkey on the loose!*

Birds – vultures

Allard, Harry. *Crash helmet*
Duvoisin, Roger Antoine. *Petunia, I love you*
Grindley, Sally. *The sulky vulture*
Peet, Bill (William Bartlett). *Eli*
Ungerer, Tomi. *Orlando, the brave vulture*
Wolkstein, Diane. *The cool ride in the sky*

Birds – wood-hoopoes

Kroll, Virginia L. *Wood-hoopoe Willie*

Birds – woodpeckers

Tejima, Keizaburo. *Woodpecker forest*
Townsend, Emily Rose. *Woodpeckers*
Wildsmith, Brian. *The owl and the woodpecker*

Birds – wrens

Brock, Emma Lillian. *Mr. Wren's house*
Cock Robin. *The courtship, merry marriage, and feast of Cock Robin and Jenny Wren*
    Who killed Cock Robin?, ill. by William Stobbs
O'Malley, Kevin. *Who killed Cock Robin?*
Polacco, Patricia. *Luba and the wren*
Ravilious, Robin. *Two in a pocket*

Birth

Alexander, Sue. *One more time, Mama*
Andreae, Giles. *There's a house inside my mommy*
Andry, Andrew C. *Hi, new baby*
    How babies are made
Anholt, Laurence. *Sophie and the new baby*
Archambault, John. *The birth of a whale*
Baker, Gayle. *Special delivery*
Banish, Roslyn. *Let me tell you about my baby*
Batten, Mary. *Who has a belly button?*
Bauer, Marion Dane. *Grandmother's song*
Berry, James. *Celebration song*
Brooks, Robert B. *So that's how I was born*
Brown, Craig McFarland. *In the spring*
Burton, Jane. *Chick*
    Kitten
    Puppy
Carlstrom, Nancy White. *Before you were born*
Carrick, Carol. *In the moonlight, waiting*
Carter, Dorothy (Dorothy A.). *Wilhe'mina Miles after the stork night*
Christenson, Larry. *The wonderful way that babies are made*
Clayton, Gordon. *Lamb*
Cole, Babette. *Mommy laid an egg!*
Cole, Joanna. *A calf is born*
    How you were born
    My puppy is born
    When you were inside mommy
Corrin, Ruth. *Mister cat*
Dahl, Tessa. *Babies, babies, babies*
Davis, Jennifer. *Before you were born*
Dixon, Ann. *Waiting for Noël*
Douglas, Ann. *Before you were born*
Farber, Norma. *All those mothers at the manger*
Fearnley, Jan. *A special something*
Fischer-Nagel, Heiderose. *A kitten is born*
    A puppy is born
Foreman, Michael. *Seal surfer*
Fox, Mem. *Sophie*
Frasier, Debra. *On the day you were born*
Fuchshuber, Annegert. *Two peas in a pod*
Girard, Linda Walvoord. *You were born on your very first birthday*
Gliori, Debi. *New big sister*
Grambling, Lois G. *Grandma tells a story*
Haas, Jessie. *No foal yet*
Hariton, Anca. *Egg story*
Helldorfer, M. C. (Mary Claire). *Silver Rain Brown*
Hobson, Laura Z. *"I'm going to have a baby!"*
Horton, Barbara Savadge. *What comes in spring?*
Isenbart, Hans-Heinrich. *A duckling is born*
Jarrell, Randall. *A bat is born*
Jessell, Camilla. *The kitten book*
    The puppy book
Kaizuki, Kiyonori. *A calf is born*
Kallok, Emma. *Gem*
Lohans, Alison. *Waiting for the sun*
Lund, Deb. *Tell me my story, Mama*
MacLachlan, Patricia. *All the places to love*
Mantegazza, Giovanna. *Look how a baby grows*
Manushkin, Fran. *Baby, come out!*
Mark, Jan. *Fur*
Nanao, Jun. *Contemplating your bellybutton*
Oppenheim, Shulamith Levey. *Waiting for Noah*
Overend, Jenni. *Welcome with love*
Padt, Maartje. *Shanti*
Pringle, Laurence P. *Everybody has a bellybutton*
Pursell, Margaret Sanford. *A look at birth*
Rabinowitz, Sandy. *What's happening to Daisy?*
Radunsky, Vladimir. *Ten*
Rockwell, Lizzy. *Hello baby!*
Roddie, Shen. *Hatch, egg, hatch!*
Rosenberg, Maxine B. *Mommy's in the hospital having a baby*
Russo, Marisabina. *Waiting for Hannah*
Schilling, Betty. *Two kittens are born*
Schlein, Miriam. *The story about me*
Sears, William, M.D. *Baby on the way*
Selsam, Millicent E. *Egg to chick*

Sheffield, Margaret. *Before you were born*
    Where do babies come from?
Showers, Paul. *Before you were a baby*
Sykes, Julie. *Dora's eggs*
    This and that
Taylor, Kim. *Frog*
Watts, Barrie. *Duck*
    Rabbit
Willington, Monica. *Seasons of swans*

Birthdays

Abrons, Mary. *For Alice a palace*
Alexander, Sue. *World famous Muriel*
Aliki. *June 7!*
    Use your head, dear
Amoss, Berthe. *It's not your birthday*
Anderson, C. W. (Clarence Williams). *Billy and Blaze*
Anderson, Lena. *Stina's visit*
Anholt, Catherine. *Snow fairy and the spaceman*
Annett, Cora. *The dog who thought he was a boy*
Argent, Kerry. *Happy birthday wombat!*
Armitage, Ronda. *The bossing of Josie*
Arnold, Caroline. *Everybody has a birthday*
Arthur, Catherine. *My sister's silent world*
Asch, Frank. *Happy birthday, moon!*
Ashley, Bernard. *Dinner ladies don't count*
Ashman, Linda. *Maxwell's magic mix-up*
Awdry, W. *Happy birthday, Thomas!*
Ayer, Jacqueline. *A wish for little sister*
Balan, Bruce. *Pie in the sky*
Bannon, Laura. *Manuela's birthday*
Barbot, Daniel. *A bicycle for Rosaura*
Barklem, Jill. *Spring story*
Barrett, Judi. *Benjamin's 365 birthdays*
Bassett, Lisa. *A clock for Beany*
Bauer, Helen. *Good times at the park*
Bauer, Steven. *The strange and wonderful tale of Robert McDoodle*
Baum, Arline. *Opt*
Beck, Andrea. *Elliot bakes a cake*
    Elliot bakes a cake
Beck, Scott. *A mud pie for mother*
Bell, Norman. *Linda's airmail letter*
Bemelmans, Ludwig. *Madeline in London*
Benchley, Peter. *Jonathan visits the White House*
Berenstain, Michael. *Peat Moss and Ivy and the birthday present*
Berenstain, Stan. *The Berenstain bears and too much birthday*
Bergel, Colin. *Mail by the pail*
Bertrand, Diane Gonzales. *The last doll = La última muñeca*
Beskow, Elsa Maartman. *Peter in Blueberry Land*
    Peter's adventures in Blueberry Land
Best, Cari. *Three cheers for Catherine the Great!*
Bible, Charles. *Jennifer's new chair*
Billam, Rosemary. *Fuzzy rabbit*
Biro, Val. *Gumdrop has a birthday*
Bliss, Corinne Demas. *The boy who was generous with salt*
    The disappearing island
Blocksma, Mary. *Grandma Dragon's birthday*
Bond, Felicia. *Mary Betty Lizzie McNutt's birthday*
Borden, Louise. *A. Lincoln and me*
Borovsky, Paul. *The fish that wasn't*
Bourgeois, Paulette. *Franklin says "I love you"*
    Postal workers
Boynton, Sandra. *Birthday monsters!*
Bradman, Tony. *The bad babies' book of colors*
Brandenberg, Franz. *Aunt Nina and her nephews and nieces*
    A secret for grandmother's birthday
Brillhart, Julie. *When daddy came to school*
Brimner, Larry Dane. *Country Bear's surprise*
Bromhall, Winifred. *Mary Ann's first picture*
Brown, Marc Tolon. *Arthur's birthday*
Brown, Margaret Wise. *The golden birthday book*
Brown, Tricia. *Hello, amigos!*
Browne, Anthony. *Gorilla*
Browne, Eileen. *No problem*
Bruna, Dick. *Miffy's birthday*
    Tilly and Tess

Brunhoff, Laurent de. *Babar's birthday surprise*
    Serafina the giraffe
Buntain, Ruth Jaeger. *The birthday story*
Bunting, Eve (Anne Evelyn). *Flower garden*
    Happy birthday, dear duck
    Little Badger's just-about birthday
    A picnic in October
    The robot birthday
    The Wednesday surprise
Burton, Marilee Robin. *Oliver's birthday*
Butler, Dorothy. *My brown bear Barney at the party*
Calmenson, Stephanie. *The birthday hat*
    Come to my party
    Zip, whiz, zoom!
Capucilli, Alyssa Satin. *Happy birthday, Biscuit!*
Carle, Eric. *Hello, red fox*
    The secret birthday message
Carlstrom, Nancy White. *Happy birthday, Jesse Bear!*
Carrick, Carol. *Paul's Christmas birthday*
Cartlidge, Michelle. *Bunny's birthday*
    Mouse birthday
Caseley, Judith. *Slumber party!*
    Three happy birthdays
Cazet, Denys. *December 24th*
    A fish in his pocket
Chalmers, Mary. *A hat for Amy Jean*
Charles, Donald. *Shaggy dog's birthday*
Charlip, Remy. *Handtalk birthday*
Chavarría-Cháirez, Becky. *Magda's piñata magic = Magda y la piñata mágica*
    Magda's tortillas = Las tortillas de Magada
Chichester Clark, Emma. *Little Miss Muffet's count-along surprise*
Christelow, Eileen. *Don't wake up Mama!*
Clarke, Gus. *How many days to my birthday?*
Clifton, Lucille. *Don't you remember?*
Coats, Lucy. *Neil's numberless world*
Cocca-Leffler, Maryann. *Ice-cold birthday*
Cohen, Barbara. *Make a wish, Molly*
Cole, Babette. *Babette Cole's beastly birthday book*
Cole, William. *What's good for a three-year-old?*
Cooke, Trish. *So much*
Corey, Dorothy. *Will it ever be my birthday?*
Costa, Nicoletta. *The birthday party [board book]*
    Molly and Tom, the birthday party
Cousins, Lucy. *Happy birthday, Maisy*
Cummings, Pat. *Carousel*
Cunliffe, John. *The king's birthday cake*
Dalmais, Anne-Marie. *Molly and Mimi the mouse twins*
Daly, Maureen. *Patrick visits the library*
Da Rif, Andrea. *The blueberry cake that little fox baked*
Davidson, Amanda. *Teddy's birthday*
Davis, Lavinia (Riker). *The wild birthday cake*
Davis, Lee. *P. B. Bear's birthday party*
Day, Alexandra. *Carl's birthday*
Dayton, Laura. *LeRoy's birthday circus*
De Groat, Diane. *Happy birthday to you, you belong in a zoo*
De Paola, Paula. *Rosie and the yellow ribbon*
De Regniers, Beatrice Schenk. *A special birthday party for someone very special*
Díaz, Katacha. *Carolina's gift*
Dixon, Ann. *Waiting for Noël*
Dowling, Paul. *Happy birthday, Owl*
Dragonwagon, Crescent. *Annie flies the birthday bike*
Drawson, Blair. *Flying Dimitri*
Dubowski, Cathy East. *A cake for Jake*
    Cave boy
Duncan, Lois. *Birthday moon*
    The longest hair in the world
Duvoisin, Roger Antoine. *Veronica and the birthday present*
Eberstadt, Isabel (Nash). *What is for my birthday?*
Eccles, Jane. *Maxwell's birthday*
Edwards, Pamela Duncan. *Rosie's roses*
Ellwand, David. *Alfred's party*
Emberley, Michael. *The present*
Eriksson, Eva. *One short week*
Estes, Kristyn Rehling. *Manuela's gift*
Faglia, Maeto. *Happy birthday, I'm 1*

McNeill, Janet. *The giant's birthday*
Madrigal, Antonio Hernandez. *Erandi's braids*
Marie, Geraldine. *The magic box*
Martin, Bill (William Ivan). *Fire! Fire! said Mrs. McGuire*
Martin, David. *Monkey business*
Mayer, Mercer. *Bun Bun's birthday*
Merriam, Eve. *The birthday door*
Metaxas, Eric. *The birthday ABC*
Miklowitz, Gloria D. *Bearfoot boy*
Miles, Miska. *Mouse six and the happy birthday*
Miller, Margaret. *My birthday*
Minarik, Else Holmelund. *Little Bear*
Miranda, Anne. *Alphabet fiesta*
    Counting
    Monster math
Modarressi, Mitra. *The dream pillow*
Modell, Frank. *Ice cream soup*
Mogensen, Jan. *Teddy's birthday bugle*
Moon, Grace Purdie. *One little Indian*
Mora, Pat. *A birthday basket for Tía*
    One, two, three = Uno, dos, tres
    Pablo's tree
Morice, Dave. *The happy birthday handbook*
Moss, Miriam. *I'll be your friend, Smudge*
Mother Goose. *Pat-a-cake*, ill. by Marilyn Janovitz
Mueller, Virginia. *Monster's birthday hiccups*
Munari, Bruno. *The birthday present*
Munsch, Robert N. *Moira's birthday*
    Wait and see
Murdock, Laurette. *Someone is talking about Hortense*
Murphy, Stuart J. *Too many kangaroo things to do!*
Myers, Bernice. *Charlie's birthday present*
Myller, Rolf. *How big is a foot?*
Myrick, Jean Lockwood. *Ninety-nine pockets*
Ness, Evaline. *Josefina February*
Nightingale, Sandy. *I'm a little monster*
Nixon, Joan Lowery. *When I am eight*
Noble, Trinka Hakes. *Jimmy's boa and the big splash birthday bash*
Noll, Sally. *Surprise!*
O'Donnell, Elizabeth Lee. *Patrick's day*
Oppenheim, Shulamith Levey. *Waiting for Noah*
Ostheeren, Ingrid. *The blue monster*
Owen, Annie. *Bumper to bumper*
Oxenbury, Helen. *The birthday party*
    It's my birthday
Parish, Peggy. *Be ready at eight*
    Scruffy
    Snapping turtle's all wrong day
Park, W. B. *Bakery business*
Parker, Nancy Winslow. *Love from Uncle Clyde*
Paterson, Bettina. *Bun's birthday*
Patz, Nancy. *No thumpin' no bumpin' no rumpus tonight!*
Pearson, Susan. *Happy birthday, Grampie*
Peek, Merle. *Mary wore her red dress and Henry wore his green sneakers*
Peppé, Rodney. *The kettleship pirates*
Perkins, Al. *Tubby and the lantern*
Peters, Sharon. *Happy birthday*
Peterson, Esther Allen. *Penelope gets wheels*
Pittman, Helena Clare. *A dinosaur for Gerald*
Polacco, Patricia. *Some birthday!*
Pomerantz, Charlotte. *The half-birthday party*
    You're not my best friend anymore
Prager, Annabelle. *The surprise party*
The pudgy fingers counting book
Quin-Harkin, Janet. *Helpful Hattie*
Radlauer, Ruth Shaw. *Breakfast by Molly*
Reed, Lynn Rowe. *Pedro, his perro, and the alphabet sombrero*
Reynolds, Marilynn. *A present for Mrs. Kazinski*
Rice, Eve. *Benny bakes a cake*
Roberts, Bethany. *Birthday mice*
Robins, Joan. *Addie's bad day*
Rockwell, Anne F. *Happy birthday to me*
    Hugo at the window
Rodda, Emily. *Power and glory*
Roffey, Maureen. *Mealtime*
Rollings, Susan. *New shoes, red shoes*

Root, Phyllis. *Gretchen's grandma*
Rose, Deborah Lee. *Birthday zoo*
Russo, Marisabina. *Only six more days*
Rylant, Cynthia. *Birthday presents*
Sáenz, Benjamin Alire. *A gift from papá Diego = Un regalo de papá Diego*
    Grandma Fina and her wonderful umbrellas = La abuelita Fina y sus sombrillas maravillosas
Sage, Angie. *Molly and the birthday party*
Saltzberg, Barney. *The Flying Garbanzos*
    Hip, hip, hooray day!
Samuels, Barbara. *Happy birthday, Dolores*
Sandberg, Inger. *Nicholas' favorite pet*
Sandburg, Carl (Charles August). *Not everyday an aurora borealis for your birthday*
Sawicki, Norma Jean. *Something for mom*
Sayre, April Pulley. *It's my city*
Schaap, Martine. *Mop and the birthday picnic*
Schachner, Judith Byron. *Yo, Vikings*
Schneider, Antonie. *The birthday bear*
Schubert, Leda. *Winnie plays ball*
Schumacher, Claire. *Nutty's birthday*
Schweninger, Ann. *Birthday wishes*
Segal, Lore Groszmann. *Morris the artist*
Selkowe, Valrie M. *Happy birthday to me!*
Seuss, Dr. *Happy birthday to you!*
    Hooper Humperdink . . . ? Not him!
Sewell, Helen Moore. *Birthdays for Robin*
Shannon, George. *The surprise*
Sherrow, Victoria. *Wilbur waits*
Shimin, Symeon. *A special birthday*
Silbaugh, Elizabeth. *Raggedy Ann's birthday party book*
Simpson, Lesley. *The Purim surprise*
Singer, Marilyn. *Minnie's Yom Kippur birthday*
Sis, Peter. *Going up!*
Smith, Wendy. *Say hello, Tilly*
Soto, Gary. *Chato and the party animals*
Spinelli, Eileen. *In my new yellow shirt*
Spurr, Elizabeth. *The biggest birthday cake in the world*
Stapler, Sarah. *Spruce the moose cuts loose*
Starr, Meg. *Alicia's happy day*
Steiner, Charlotte. *Birthdays are for everyone*
Steptoe, John. *Birthday*
Stevenson, Suçie. *I forgot*
Stewart, Paul. *The birthday presents*
Stewart, Sarah. *The journey*
Stock, Catherine. *The birthday present*
Stolz, Mary (Mary Slattery). *Emmett's pig*
Supraner, Robyn. *Sam Sunday and the mystery at the Ocean Beach Hotel*
Sutton, Elizabeth Henning. *A pony for keeps*
Swanson, Susan Marie. *The first thing my mama told me*
Sykes, Julie. *Little Rocket's special star*
Tafuri, Nancy. *The barn party*
Tatcheva, Eva. *Witch Zelda's birthday cake*
Theroux, Phyllis. *Serefina under the circumstances*
Thomas, Naturi. *Uh-oh! It's Mama's birthday!*
Trimble, Patti. *What day is it?*
Tryon, Leslie. *Albert's birthday*
Türk, Hanne. *Happy birthday Max*
Turnbull, Ann. *The tapestry cats*
Tyler, Linda Wagner. *The sick-in-bed birthday book*
Uchida, Yoshiko. *Sumi's special happening*
Uff, Caroline. *Happy birthday, Lulu*
Van der Beek, Deborah. *Alice's blue cloth*
Vigna, Judith. *Mommy and me by ourselves again*
    My two uncles
Wabbes, Marie. *Happy birthday, Little Rabbit*
Waber, Bernard. *Lyle and the birthday party*
Wadsworth, Ginger. *Tomorrow is Daddy's birthday*
Wallace, John. *Tiny Rabbit goes to a birthday party*
Wallace, Nancy Elizabeth. *Tell-a-bunny*
Wardlaw, Lee. *Bow-wow birthday*
Watanabe, Shigeo. *It's my birthday*
Watson, Nancy Dingman. *The birthday goat*
    Tommy's mommy's fish, ill. by Aldren Auld Watson
    Tommy's mommy's fish, ill. by Thomas Aldren Dingman Watson

Watts, Jeri Hanel. *Keepers*
Weeks, Sarah. *Happy birthday, Frankie*
Weiss, Ellen. *Mokey's birthday present*
Wells, Rosemary. *Bunny party*
    Max's birthday
    Yoko's paper cranes
Weninger, Brigitte. *Happy birthday, Davy*
West, Colin. *Go tell it to the toucan*
White, Linda Arms. *Comes a wind*
Whittington, Mary K. *The patchwork lady*
Wickstrom, Sylvie (Sylvie Kantrovitz). *Mothers can't get sick*
Wilcox, Brian. *Full moon*
Willard, Nancy. *The high rise glorious skittle skat roarious sky pie angel food cake*
    The marzipan moon
    The mouse, the cat and Grandmother's hat
Williams, Barbara. *Whatever happened to Beverly Bigler's birthday?*
Williams, Vera B. *Something special for me*
Willis, Jeanne. *Sloth's shoes*
Wilson, Sarah. *Uncle Albert's flying birthday*
Wojtowycz, David. *Dudley's birthday party*
Wormell, Mary. *Hilda Hen's happy birthday*
Worth, Bonnie. *Peter Cottontail's surprise*
Wright, Betty Ren. *The blizzard*
Yaroshevskaya, Kim. *Little Kim's doll*
Yashima, Taro. *Umbrella*
Yezerski, Thomas F. *Queen of the world*
Yolen, Jane. *Picnic with Piggins*
Ziefert, Harriet. *Happy birthday, Grandpa!*
    Surprise!
Zimelman, Nathan. *Once when I was five*
Zolotow, Charlotte (Shapiro). *Mr. Rabbit and the lovely present*

Bison *see* Animals – buffaloes

Black Americans *see* Ethnic groups in the U.S. – African Americans

Black Carib *see* Indians of Central America – Black Carib

Blackbirds *see* Birds – blackbirds

Blackfoot Indians *see* Indians of North America – Blackfoot

Blackouts *see* Power failure

Blindness *see* Handicaps – blindness; Senses – sight

Blizzards *see* Weather – blizzards

Blocks *see* Toys – blocks

Bluejays *see* Birds – bluejays

Board books *see* Format, unusual – board books

Boasting *see* Behavior – boasting

Boat builders *see* Careers – boat builders

Boats, ships

Agell, Charlotte. *The sailor's book*
Ahlberg, Allan. *Skeleton crew*
Alborough, Jez. *Captain Duck*
Alexander, Anne (Anna Barbara Cooke). *Boats and ships from A to Z*
Allen, Jonathan. *Two by two by two*
Allen, Pamela. *Who sank the boat?*
Amoss, Berthe. *Old Hannibal and the hurricane*
Anderson, Joan. *Sally's submarine*
Anderson, Lonzo. *Arion and the dolphins*
Ardizzone, Edward. *Little Tim and the brave sea captain*

Ship's cook Ginger
Tim all alone
Tim and Charlotte
Tim and Ginger
Tim and Lucy go to sea
Tim in danger
Tim to the rescue
Tim's friend Towser
Tim's last voyage
Arro, Lena. *By geezers and galoshes!*
Augarde, Steve (Stephen). *Barnaby Shrew goes to sea*
Auld, Mary. *Noah's ark*
Baker, Betty. *My sister says*
Barton, Byron. *Boats*
Bate, Norman. *What a wonderful machine is a submarine*
Beck, Andrea. *Elliot's shipwreck*
Beck, Ian. *Emily and the golden acorn*
Benjamin, Alan. *A change of plans*
Berenstain, Michael. *The ship book*
Bergel, Colin. *Mail by the pail*
Berger, Melvin. *Dive! a book of deep sea creatures*
Bible. Old Testament. Noah. *Noah and the ark*, ill. by Pauline Baynes
    Noah and the ark, ill. by Jim Cummins
Blake, Robert J. *Spray*
Bliss, Corinne Demas. *The disappearing island*
Bolliger, Max. *Noah and the rainbow*
Brent, Isabelle. *Noah's ark*
Bridgman, Elizabeth. *Nanny bear's cruise*
Brown, Jane Clark. *Whonk, and whonk again*
Brown, Judith Gwyn. *The happy voyage*
Brown, Marc Tolon. *Marc Brown's Boat book*
Brown, Marcia. *Skipper John's cook*
Brown, Rick. *Who built the ark?*
Bruna, Dick. *The sailor*
Buchanan, Heather S. *George Mouse's riverboat band*
Bullard, Lisa. *Powerboats*
Bunting, Eve (Anne Evelyn). *Swan in love*
Burchard, Peter. *The Carol Moran*
Burdett, Lois. *Twelfth night*
Burke, Timothy. *Tugboats in action*
Burningham, John. *Mr. Gumpy's outing*
Bushey, Jerry. *The barge book*
Calhoun, Mary. *Euphonia and the flood*
    Henry the sailor cat
Campbell, Ann-Jeanette. *Let's find out about boats*
Carrick, Carol. *The washout*
Carryl, Charles E. (Charles Edward). *A capital ship*
    The walloping window-blind, ill. by Jim LaMarche
    The walloping window blind, ill. by Ted Rand
Carter, Katharine. *Ships and seaports*
Chalmers, Mary. *Boots finds a house*
Chan, Arlene. *Awakening the dragon*
Chase, Catherine. *Noah's ark*
Cohen, Peter Zachary. *Authorized autumn charts of the Upper Red Canoe River country*
Conrad, Pam. *The lost sailor*
Conway, Celeste. *Where is Papa now?*
Corey, Shana. *Boats!*
Cousins, Lucy. *Noah's ark*
    Noah's ark [board book]
Crampton, Gertrude. *Scuffy the tugboat*
Crews, Donald. *Harbor*
    Sail away
Cullen, Lynn. *Little Scraggly Hair*
Day, Alexandra. *River parade*
Deedy, Carmen Agra. *The secret of Old Zeb*
DeLage, Ida. *Pilgrim children on the Mayflower*
Delessert, Etienne. *The endless party*
Demarest, Chris L. *My blue boat*
    Ship
Demi. *The magic boat*
Dennis, Morgan. *The sea dog*
Denton, Terry. *Home is the sailor*
De Paola, Tomie (Thomas Anthony). *Four stories for four seasons*
    Noah and the ark
DeRubertis, Barbara. *Columbus Day*

Devlin, Harry. *The walloping window blind*, ill. by author
Dickson, Louise. *The vanishing cat*
Diller, Harriett. *The waiting day*
Doherty, Berlie. *Snowy*
Domanska, Janina. *I saw a ship a-sailing*
Dorros, Arthur. *Pretzels*
Du Bois, William Pène. *Otto at sea*
Duke, Kate. *Twenty is too many*
Dunrea, Olivier. *Fergus and Bridey*
Dupasquier, Philippe. *Dear Daddy . . .*
    Jack at sea
Duvoisin, Roger Antoine. *A for the ark*
Elborn, Andrew. *Noah and the ark and the animals*
Elting, Mary. *The big book of real boats and ships*
Emberley, Ed (Edward Randolph). *Cars, boats, and planes*
Farber, Norma. *How the left-behind beasts built Ararat*
    Where's Gomer?
Faulkner, Matt. *The amazing voyage of Jackie Grace*
Figley, Marty Rhodes. *Noah's wife*
Fischetto, Laura. *All pigs on deck*
    Inside Noah's ark
Fitzpatrick, Marie-Louise. *You, me and the big blue sea*
Flack, Marjorie. *The boats on the river*
Flanagan, Alice K. *Riding the ferry with Captain Cruz*
Flora, James. *Fishing with dad*
Foreman, Michael. *Jack's fantastic voyage*
French, Fiona. *Rise and shine*
Fry, Christopher. *The boat that mooed*
Fussenegger, Gertrud. *Noah's ark*
Garland, Sherry. *My father's boat*
Gauch, Patricia Lee. *Noah*
Gay, Michel. *Little boat*
Gedin, Birgitta. *The little house from the sea*
Geisert, Arthur. *After the flood*
    The ark
Gerrard, Roy. *Sir Francis Drake*
Gerstein, Mordicai. *Noah and the great flood*
Gibbons, Gail. *Boat book*
    Exploring the deep, dark sea
Ginsburg, Mirra. *Four brave sailors*
Goffstein, M. B. (Marilyn Brooke). *My Noah's ark*
Goldsboro, Bobby. *Noah and the ark; and, David and Goliath*
Gomboli, Mario. *Look inside a ship*
Goodall, John S. *Jacko*
Goodhart, Pippa. *Noah makes a boat*
    Row, row, row your boat
Gorbachev, Valeri. *The fool of the world and the flying ship*
Graham, Lorenz B. *God wash the world and start again*
Graham, Margaret Bloy. *Benjy's boat trip*
Graham, Thomas. *Mr. Bear's boat*
Gramatky, Hardie. *Little Toot*
    Little Toot and the Loch Ness monster
    Little Toot on the Mississippi
    Little Toot on the Thames
    Little Toot through the Golden Gate
Greene, Carol. *Sunflower Island*
Gutman, Anne. *Gaspard on vacation*
Haas, Irene. *The Maggie B*
Halak, Glenn. *A grandmother's story*
Haley, Gail E. *Noah's ark*
Hansen, Carla. *Barnaby Bear builds a boat*
Harker, Lesley. *Annie's ark*
Harness, Cheryl. *Mark Twain and the queens of the Mississippi*
Harrison, Troon. *The floating orchard*
Haubensak-Tellenbach, Margrit. *The story of Noah's ark*
Hayward, Linda. *Noah's ark*
Helldorfer, M. C. (Mary Claire). *Sailing to the sea*
Henderson, Kathy. *The little boat*
Henrioud, Charles. *Mr. Noah and the animals*
Hest, Amy. *A sort-of sailor*
Hewitt, Kathryn. *Two by two*
Hill, Susan. *Stuart sets sail*
Hillert, Margaret. *The yellow boat*
Hogrogian, Nonny. *Noah's ark*
Holabird, Katharine. *Alexander and the magic boat*
Hooper, Meredith. *Tom's rabbit*
Hoopes, Lyn Littlefield. *Half a button*

Hunt, Jonathan. *Leif's saga*
Hurd, Edith Thacher. *What whale? Where?*
Hutchins, H. J. (Hazel J.). *Beneath the bridge*
Hutton, Warwick. *Noah and the great flood*
Ife, Elaine. *Noah and the ark*
Isadora, Rachel. *No, Agatha!*
Janisch, Heinz. *Noah's ark*
Joerns, Consuelo. *The foggy rescue*
Johnson, Pamela. *A mouse's tale*
Jonas, Ann. *Aardvarks, disembark!*
Kellogg, Steven (Stephen). *The island of the skog*
    Mike Fink
Kimmel, Eric A. *The Erie Canal pirates*
Kovacs, Deborah. *Moonlight on the river*
Kroll, Steven. *The pigrates clean up*
Kuskin, Karla. *The animals and the ark*
LaMarche, Jim. *The raft*
Landström, Olof. *Boo and Baa at sea*
Lang, Andrew. *The flying ship*
Lawson, Julie. *A morning to polish and keep*
Lenski, Lois. *The little sailboat*
    Mr. and Mrs. Noah
Leonard, Marcia. *Violet and the pirates*
Le Tord, Bijou. *Noah's trees*
Lewin, Ted. *Amazon boy*
    Nilo and the tortoise
Lewis, J. Patrick. *The boat of many rooms*
    The Fat-Cats at sea
Lewis, Thomas P. *Clipper ship*
Lindman, Maj. *Sailboat time*
Lippman, Peter. *The Know-It-Alls go to sea*
Litowinsky, Olga. *Boats for bedtime*
Locker, Thomas. *Sailing with the wind*
London, Jonathan. *Old salt, young salt*
    Where the big fish are
Lööf, Jan. *Uncle Louie's fantastic sea voyage*
Ludwig, Warren. *Old Noah's elephants*
Maass, Robert. *Tugboats*
MacBeth, George. *Noah's journey*
McCarthy, Bobette. *Dreaming*
McCarthy, Michael. *The story of Noah and the ark*
McCaughrean, Geraldine. *The story of Noah and the ark*
McCloskey, Robert. *Bert Dow, deep-water man*
McCully, Emily Arnold. *The pirate queen*
McDonnell, Flora. *I love boats*
MacGill-Callahan, Sheila. *To capture the wind*
McGovern, Ann. *Nicholas Bentley Stoningpot III*
McGowan, Alan. *Sailing ships*
McKié, Roy. *Noah's ark*
McMillan, Bruce. *Going on a whale watch*
McNeil, Florence. *Sail away*
McPhail, David M. *Pigs ahoy*
Maestro, Betsy. *Big city port*
    Ferryboat
Mahy, Margaret. *Sailor Jack and the twenty orphans*
Marshall, James. *Speedboat*
Marston, Elsa. *Cynthia and the runaway gazebo*
Martin, Charles E. *Noah's ark*
Martin, Jacqueline Briggs. *On Sand Island*
Meddaugh, Susan. *Harry on the rocks*
    Maude and Claude go abroad
Mee, Charles L. *Noah*
Mendoza, George. *The alphabet boat*
Metaxas, Eric. *The fool and the flying ship*
    Stormalong, the legendary sea captain
Miles, Miska. *No, no, Rosina*
Miller, Ruth. *I went to the bay*
Mills, Judith Christine. *The stonehook schooner*
Modarressi, Mitra. *The parent thief*
Monfried, Lucia. *The Daddies Boat*
Morgan, Allen. *Nicole's boat*
Morrissey, Dean. *The Christmas ship*
Most, Bernard. *Row, row, row your goat*
Nakawatari, Harutaka. *The sea and I*
O'Hearn, Michael. *Hercules the harbor tug*
Olson, Arielle North. *Noah's cats and the devil's fire*
O'Neill, Alexis. *Loud Emily*

Oppel, Kenneth. *Peg and the whale*
Ostheeren, Ingrid. *Fabian Youngpig sails the world*
Palazzo, Tony (Anthony D.). *Noah's ark*
Paley, Joan. *One more river*
Pallotta, Jerry. *The dory story*
Paraskevas, Betty. *On the day the tall ships sailed*
Partridge, Jenny. *Hopfellow*
Peacock, Carol Antoinette. *Pilgrim cat*
Pelton, Mindy L. *When Dad's at sea*
Peppé, Rodney. *The kettleship pirates*
Perkins, Al. *Tubby and the Poo-Bah*
Perrow, Angeli. *Sirius, the dog star*
Pfanner, Louise. *Louise builds a boat*
Philip, Neil. *Noah and the devil*
Pinkney, Jerry. *Noah's ark*
Pitcher, Caroline. *Cars and boats*
Potter, Beatrix. *The tale of Little Pig Robinson*
Priest, Robert H. *The old pirate of Central Park*
Rand, Gloria. *Aloha, Salty!*
   Sailing home
   Salty dog
   Salty sails north
Ransome, Arthur. *The fool of the world and the flying ship*
Rassmus, Jens. *Farmer Enno and his cow*
Reavin, Sam. *Hurray for Captain Jane!*
Reesink, Marijke. *The golden treasure*
Rettich, Margret. *The voyage of the jolly boat*
Reynolds, Peter H. *Sydney's star*
Rockwell, Anne F. *Boats*
   Ferryboat ride!
Rohmann, Eric. *The cinder-eyed cats*
Root, Phyllis. *Sam, who was swallowed by a shark*
Rose, Gerald. *Trouble in the ark*
Rotner, Shelley. *Boats afloat*
Round, Graham. *Hangdog*
Rounds, Glen. *Washday on Noah's ark*
Royston, Angela. *Ships and boats*
Rubel, Nicole. *Uncle Henry and Aunt Henrietta's honeymoon*
Rumford, James. *The Island-below-the-star*
Samton, Sheila White. *Jenny's journey*
San Souci, Robert D. *Brave Margaret*
Santore, Charles. *A stowaway on Noah's Ark*
Sasso, Sandy Eisenberg. *A prayer for the earth*
Scarry, Richard. *Pie rats ahoy!*
Schachner, Judith Byron. *Yo, Vikings*
Schaefer, Lola M. *Tugboats*
Schaffer, Libor. *Arthur sets sail*
Schulz, Charles M. *Snoopy's facts and fun book about boats*
Seibold, J. Otto. *Mr. Lunch borrows a canoe*
Seymour, Tres. *The gulls of the Edmund Fitzgerald*
Shaw, Nancy (Nancy E.). *Sheep on a ship*
Shecter, Ben. *If I had a ship*
Shortall, Leonard W. *Tod on the tugboat*
Singer, Isaac Bashevis. *Why Noah chose the dove*
Sis, Peter. *Ship ahoy!*
Slawski, Wolfgang. *Captain Jonathan sails the sea*
Smith, Barry. *The first voyage of Christopher Columbus*
Smith, Elmer Boyd. *The story of Noah's ark*
Smith, Roger. *How the animals saved the ark and put two and two together*
Spier, Peter. *Noah's ark*
Spooner, J. B. *The story of the little Black Dog*
Stafford, Liliana. *Just dragon*
Stephens, Helen. *Ahoyty-toyty*
Stevenson, James. *The stowaway*
Stevenson, Jocelyn. *Jim Henson's Muppets at sea*
Sting (Musician). *Rock steady*
Surany, Anico. *Ride the cold wind*
Swift, Hildegarde Hoyt. *The little red lighthouse and the great gray bridge*
Tagore, Rabindranath. *Paper boats*
Taylor, Mark. *Henry the castaway*
Thomson, Ruth. *Peabody all at sea*
Thorne, Jenny. *Noah's ark*
Titherington, Jeanne. *Baby's boat*
   Baby's boat [board book]
Trapani, Iza. *Row, row, row your boat*

Tudor, Bethany. *Skiddycock Pond*
Twining, Edith. *Sandman*
Van Allsburg, Chris. *The wreck of the Zephyr*
Van Dusen, Chris. *Down to the sea with Mr. Magee*
Van Leeuwen, Jean. *Across the wide dark sea*
Venable, Alan. *The checker players*
Vernon, Tannis. *Little Pig and the blue-green sea*
Waddell, Martin. *Sailor Bear*
Walton, Rick. *Noah's square dance*
Waters, Tony. *Sailor's bride*
Webb, Clifford. *The story of Noah*
White, Carolyn. *The adventure of Louey and Frank*
Wick, Walter. *Can you see what I see? Seymour and the juice box boat*
Wiesner, William. *Noah's ark*
Willard, Nancy. *The voyage of the Ludgate Hill*
Williams, Vera B. *Three days on a river in a red canoe*
Wilson, Anne. *Noah's ark*
Windham, Sophie. *Noah's ark*
Winter, Jeanette. *The Christmas tree ship*
Wood, Jakki. *Across the big blue sea*
Yezerski, Thomas F. *A full hand*
Young, James. *Penelope and the pirates*
Young, Miriam Burt. *If I sailed a boat*
Young, Ruth. *Daisy's taxi*
Zaffo, George J. *The giant nursery book of things that go*
Zagwÿn, Deborah Turney. *The sea house*
Ziefert, Harriet. *My sister says nothing ever happens when we go sailing*

Bobcats *see* Animals – bobcats

Bombs *see* Weapons

Boobys *see* Birds – boobys

Boogy man *see* Monsters

Books *see* Books, reading; Libraries

Books, reading *see also* Libraries

Aliki. *How a book is made*
Allen, Susan. *Read anything good lately?*
Allington, Richard L. *Reading*
Anholt, Catherine. *Come back, Jack!*
Asch, Frank. *Dear brother*
   Moonbear's books
Auch, Mary Jane. *Souperchicken*
Austin, Virginia. *Say please*
Baggette, Susan K. *Jonathan goes to the library*
Baker, Betty. *Worthington Botts and the steam machine*
Bank Street College of Education. *People read*
Barasch, Lynne. *Rodney's inside story*
Battle-Lavert, Gwendolyn. *Papa's mark*
Bauer, Caroline Feller. *Too many books!*
Baumgart, Klaus. *The little green dragon steps out*
Bertram, Debbie. *The best place to read*
Black, Irma (Simonton). *The little old man who could not read*
Bloom, Becky. *Wolf*
Boatfield, Jonny. *The twilight book*
Bogart, Jo Ellen. *Jeremiah learns to read*
Borden, Louise. *The day Eddie met the author*
Bradby, Marie. *More than anything else*
Brillhart, Julie. *Story hour – starring Megan!*
Brimner, Larry Dane. *Aggie and Will*
Brown, Ken (Ken James). *The scarecrow's hat*
Brown, Marc Tolon. *Arthur's really helpful word book*
   D. W.'s library card
Browne, Anthony. *I like books*
   I like books [board book]
Browne, Eileen. *No problem*
Bruna, Dick. *I can read*
   I can read difficult words
   I can read more
Bruss, Deborah. *Book! book! book!*
Bunting, Eve (Anne Evelyn). *The Wednesday surprise*

Burleigh, Robert. *I love going through this book*
Caseley, Judith. *Sophie and Sammy's library sleepover*
Charlip, Remy. *Why I will never ever ever ever have enough time to read this book*
Cheng, Andrea. *Anna the bookbinder*
Christian, Mary Blount. *The bookstore mouse*
Cohen, Miriam. *When will I read?*
Collins, Pat Lowery. *Don't tease the guppies*
Conover, Chris. *The lion's share*
Cowley, Joy. *Mrs. Goodstory*
Dakos, Kalli. *Our principal promised to kiss a pig*
Daly, Niki. *Once upon a time*
DeFelice, Cynthia C. *The real, true Dulcie Campbell*
DiFiori, Lawrence. *My first book*
Duvoisin, Roger Antoine. *Petunia*
Faulkner, Keith. *The monster who loved books*
Feiffer, Jules. *Meanwhile . . .*
Flanagan, Alice K. *Librarians*
   Ms. Davison, our librarian
Fox, Mem. *A bedtime story*
Friskey, Margaret (Margaret Richards). *Mystery of the gate sign*
Funk, Tom (Thompson). *I read signs*
Furtado, Jo. *Sorry, Miss Folio!*
Garland, Michael. *Miss Smith's incredible storybook*
Giff, Patricia Reilly. *The beast in Ms. Rooney's room*
Gile, John. *Oh, how I wished I could read!*
Gillham, Bill. *The early words picture book*
Goor, Ron. *Signs*
Grifalconi, Ann. *Electric Yancy*
Haley, Gail E. *Dream peddler*
Hall, Patricia. *Hooray for reading!*
Hallinan, P. K. (Patrick K.). *Just open a book*
Haseley, Dennis. *A story for Bear*
Heller, Nicholas. *A book for Woody*
Herman, Gail. *Fievel's big showdown*
Hoban, Lillian. *Arthur's prize reader*
Hoban, Tana. *I read signs*
   I read symbols
   I walk and read
Holl, Adelaide. *Most-of-the-time Maxie*
Holleyman, Sonia. *Mona the vampire*
Hood, Susan. *Look! I can read!*
Hopkins, Lee Bennett. *Good books, good times*
Huff, Barbara A. *Once inside the library*
Hurd, Edith Thacher. *Johnny Lion's book*
Hutchins, H. J. (Hazel J.). *Nicholas at the library*
Hutchins, Pat. *The tale of Thomas Mead*
Jennings, Sharon. *Franklin's reading lesson*
Jeram, Anita. *I love my little storybook*
Johnson, Dolores. *Papa's stories*
Johnston, Tony. *Amber on the mountain*
Jorgensen, Richard. *Reading with Dad*
Krull, Kathleen. *The boy on Fairfield Street*
Kuskin, Karla. *Watson, the smartest dog in the U.S.A.*
Lakin, Patricia. *Fat chance Thanksgiving*
Lamm, C. Drew. *Pirates*
Lattimore, Deborah Nourse. *The sailor who captured the sea*
Lehman, Barbara. *The red book*
Léonard, Marie. *Tibili, the little boy who didn't want to go to school*
Levinson, Nancy Smiler. *Clara and the bookwagon*
Lexau, Joan M. *Olaf reads*
Lillegard, Dee. *Sitting in my box*
Little, Jean. *Gruntle Piggle takes off*
   Once upon a golden apple
Lyon, George Ella. *Book*
McDonald, Megan. *Lucky star*
McGill, Alice. *Molly Bannaky*
McLenighan, Valjean. *One whole doughnut, one doughnut hole*
McPhail, David M. *Edward and the pirates*
   Fix-it
   Santa's book of names
Maestro, Betsy. *Harriet reads signs and more signs*
Mahoney, Daniel J. *The Saturday escape*
Maitland, Barbara. *The bookstore burglar*
   The bookstore valentine
Marshall, James. *Wings*
Meddaugh, Susan. *Hog-eye*

Meister, Cari. *Tiny goes to the library*
Miller, William. *Richard Wright and the library card*
Minsberg, David. *The book monster*
Mora, Pat. *A library for Juana*
   Tomás and the library lady
Most, Bernard. *There's an ant in Anthony*
Olofsson, Helena. *The little jester*
O'Neill, Catharine. *Mrs. Dunphy's dog*
Ormerod, Jan. *Reading*
Ormondroyd, Edward. *Broderick*
Parlato, Stephen. *The world that loved books*
Paterson, Katherine. *Marvin one too many*
Patschke, Steve. *The spooky book*
Pearson, Susan. *That's enough for one day!*
Pinczes, Elinor J. *My full moon is square*
Polacco, Patricia. *Aunt Chip and the great Triple Creek dam affair*
   Thank you, Mr. Falker
Porazinska, Janina. *The enchanted book*
Purdy, Carol. *Least of all*
Radabaugh, Melinda Beth. *Going to the library*
Radlauer, Ruth Shaw. *Molly at the library*
Rahaman, Vashanti. *Read for me, Mama*
Rau, Dana Meachen. *The secret code*
Robb, Diane Burton. *The alphabet war*
Rockwell, Anne F. *Father's Day*
Rogers, Jacqueline. *Kindergarten ABC*
Rowe, John A. *Tommy DoLittle*
Ruurs, Margriet. *Ms. Bee's magical bookcase*
Seuss, Dr. *I can read with my eyes shut*
Sharmat, Marjorie Weinman. *My mother never listens to me*
Sierra, Judy. *Wild about books*
Smalls, Irene. *Don't say ain't*
Stadler, Alexander. *Beverly Billingsly borrows a book*
Stadler, John. *What's so scary?*
Stanley, Diane. *Raising Sweetness*
Steer, Dougald. *Just one more story*
Stewart, Sarah. *The library*
Stortz, Diane M. *Barnaby Mouse, detective, and the mystery of the big book*
Tirabosco, Tom. *At the same time*
Viorst, Judith. *The good-bye book*
Waller, Curt. *Baby's first signs*
   More baby's first signs
Weeks, Sarah. *Bite me, I'm a book*
Wells, Rosemary. *Read to your bunny*
Whybrow, Ian. *Wish, change, friend*
Wiesner, David. *Free fall*
Williams, Suzanne. *Library Lil*
Winters, Kay. *Abe Lincoln, the boy who loved books*
Wishinsky, Frieda. *Give Maggie a chance*
Zemach, Kaethe. *The character in the book*

Boots *see* Clothing – boots; Clothing – shoes

Boredom *see* Behavior – boredom

Borneo *see* Foreign lands – Borneo

Bossy *see* Behavior – bossy

Botswana *see* Foreign lands – Botswana

Bowling *see* Sports – bowling

Boxing *see* Sports – boxing

Bravery *see* Character traits – bravery

Brazil *see* Foreign lands – Brazil

Bridges

Bell, Babs. *The bridge is up!*
Buckley, Helen Elizabeth. *The leftover bridge*
Carlisle, Norman. *Bridges*

Hunter, Ryan Ann. *Cross a bridge*
Lobel, Anita. *Sven's bridge*
McCully, Emily Arnold. *Crossing the new bridge*
Neville, Emily Cheney. *The bridge*
Oppenheim, Joanne. *On the other side of the river*
Steadman, Ralph. *The bridge*
Swift, Hildegarde Hoyt. *The little red lighthouse and the great gray bridge*
Yagelski, Robert. *The day the lifting bridge stuck*

Brothers *see* Family life – brothers; Family life – brothers & sisters; Sibling rivalry

Brownies *see* Mythical creatures – elves

Brush wolf *see* Animals – coyotes

Bubbles

Anastasio, Dina. *Baby Piggy and giant bubble*
Anawalt, Paula Bonnier. *The crystal palace*
Bradley, Kimberly Brubaker. *Pop!*
Bridwell, Norman. *Clifford counts bubbles*
De Paola, Tomie (Thomas Anthony). *The bubble factory*
  Strega Nona takes a vacation
Edwards, Frank B. *Troubles with bubbles*
Hooks, William H. *How do you make a bubble?*
Hulme, Joy N. *Bubble trouble*
Inkpen, Mick. *Thing*
Josephs, Rhoda. *The baby bubble book*
Lorimer, Janet. *The biggest bubble in the world*
Manushkin, Fran. *Bubblebath!*
Mayer, Mercer. *Bubble bubble*
O'Connor, Jane. *Benny's big bubble*
Packard, Mary. *Bubble trouble*
Schubert, Ingrid. *The magic bubble trip*
Woodruff, Elvira. *Show and tell*
  Tubtime
Zager, Karen. *Bubbles*

Buddhism *see* Religion – Buddhism

Buffaloes *see* Animals – buffaloes

Bugs *see* Insects

Buildings

Balterman, Lee. *Girders and cranes*
Barkan, Joanne. *Whiskerville bake shop*
  Whiskerville firehouse
  Whiskerville post office
  Whiskerville school
Bunting, Eve (Anne Evelyn). *Night of the gargoyles*
Cooper, Elisha. *Building*
Czernecki, Stefan. *The cricket's cage*
Gibbons, Gail. *Up goes the skyscraper!*
Henri, Adrian. *The postman's palace*
Hunter, Ryan Ann. *Into the sky*
Lewis, Kevin. *The lot at the end of my block*
Merriam, Eve. *Bam, bam, bam*
Numeroff, Laura Joffe. *What daddies do best*
Otto, Carolyn. *Pioneer church*
Parker, Steve. *I wonder why tunnels are round*
Pluckrose, Henry Arthur. *Walls*
Reasoner, Charles. *The big busy building*
Rex, Michael. *Who builds?*
Stone, Lynn M. *Farm buildings*
Suen, Anastasia. *Raise the roof*
Tarsky, Sue. *The busy building book*
Zelver, Patricia. *The wonderful Towers of Watts*

Bulldozers *see* Machines

Bulls *see* Animals – bulls, cows

Bullying *see* Behavior – bullying

Bumble bees *see* Insects – bees

Bungee Indians *see* Indians of North America – Bungee

Burglars *see* Crime

Burma *see* Foreign lands – Burma

Burros *see* Animals – donkeys

Bus drivers *see* Careers – bus drivers

Buses

Blance, Ellen. *Monster on the bus*
Brillhart, Julie. *Molly rides the school bus*
Brown, Marc Tolon. *Arthur lost and found*
Browne, Eileen. *Where's that bus?*
Bus-a-saurus bop
Cazet, Denys. *Minnie and Moo go to Paris*
Cocca-Leffler, Maryann. *Bus route to Boston*
Cole, Joanna. *The magic school bus in the time of the dinosaurs*
  The magic school bus inside a beehive
  The magic school bus lost in the solar system
  The magic school bus on the ocean floor
Cossi, Olga. *Gus the bus*
Crews, Donald. *School bus*
  School bus [board book]
Demarest, Chris L. *Bus*
Denslow, Sharon Phillips. *Bus riders*
Foreman, Michael. *The perfect present*
Fuller, Ted. *Barney the bus*
Giffard, Hannah. *Red bus*
Gomi, Taro. *Bus stop*
Helakoski, Leslie. *The smushy bus*
Hellen, Nancy. *Bus stop*
Hindley, Judy. *The big red bus*
Hirst, Robin. *My place in space*
Jewell, Nancy. *Bus ride*
Kilroy, Sally. *On the road*
Kingsland, Robin. *Bus stop bop*
Kirk, Daniel. *Bus stop, bus go*
Kovalski, Maryann. *The wheels on the bus*
McCarthy, Meghan. *The adventures of Patty and the big red bus*
McMahon, Patricia. *Listen for the bus*
Matthias, Catherine. *Out the door*
Muntean, Michaela. *The very bumpy bus ride*
Nichols, Paul. *Big Paul's school bus*
Owen, Ann (1953–). *Taking your places*
Peppé, Rodney. *The mice and the clockwork bus*
Piers, Helen. *Is there room on the bus?*
Rogers, Hal. *Buses*
Roth, Carol. *The little school bus*
Shuttlesworth, Dorothy Edwards. *ABC of buses*
Silvano, Wendi J. *Just one more*
Wolcott, Patty. *Double-decker, double-decker, double-decker bus*
Young, Miriam Burt. *If I drove a bus*
Zelinsky, Paul O. *The wheels on the bus*
Ziefert, Harriet. *Jason's bus ride*

Bushbabies *see* Animals – bushbabies

Butchers *see* Careers – butchers

Butterflies *see* Insects – butterflies, caterpillars

Buzzards *see* Birds – buzzards

Cab drivers *see* Careers – taxi drivers

Cable cars, trolleys

Burton, Virginia Lee. *Maybelle, the cable car*
Caen, Herb. *The cable car and the dragon*
Chalmers, Mary. *Here comes the trolley*
Gramatky, Hardie. *Sparky*
McMillan, Bruce. *Grandfather's trolley*
Taniuchi, Kota. *Trolley*

Cabs *see* Taxis

Cafés *see* Restaurants

Caldecott award books

Aardema, Verna. *Why mosquitoes buzz in people's ears*
Ackerman, Karen. *Song and dance man*
Alger, Leclaire Gowans. *Always room for one more*
Aulaire, Ingri Mortenson d'. *Abraham Lincoln*
Bemelmans, Ludwig. *Madeline's rescue*
Brown, Marcia. *Once a mouse . . .*
Brown, Margaret Wise. *The little island*
Bunting, Eve (Anne Evelyn). *Smoky night*
Burton, Virginia Lee. *The little house*
Cendrars, Blaise. *Shadow*
Chaucer, Geoffrey. *Chanticleer and the fox*
De Regniers, Beatrice Schenk. *May I bring a friend?*
Emberley, Barbara. *Drummer Hoff*
Ets, Marie Hall. *Nine days to Christmas*
Field, Rachel Lyman. *Prayer for a child*
A frog he would a-wooing go (folk-song). *Frog went a-courtin'*, ill. by Feodor Rojankovsky
Gerstein, Mordicai. *The man who walked between the towers*
Goble, Paul. *The girl who loved wild horses*
Grimm, Jacob. *Rapunzel*, ill. by Paul O. Zelinsky
Hader, Berta Hoerner. *The big snow*
Haley, Gail E. *A story, a story*
Hall, Donald. *The ox-cart man*
Handforth, Thomas. *Mei Li*
Henkes, Kevin. *Kitten's first full moon*
Hodges, Margaret. *Saint George and the dragon*
Hogrogian, Nonny. *One fine day*
Keats, Ezra Jack. *The snowy day*
    The snowy day [board book]
Lawson, Robert. *They were strong and good*
Lipkind, William. *Finders keepers*
Lobel, Arnold. *Fables*
Macaulay, David. *Black and white*
McCloskey, Robert. *Make way for ducklings*
    Time of wonder
McCully, Emily Arnold. *Mirette on the high wire*
McDermott, Gerald. *Arrow to the sun*
Martin, Jacqueline Briggs. *Snowflake Bentley*
Milhous, Katherine. *The egg tree*
Mosel, Arlene. *The funny little woman*
Musgrove, Margaret. *Ashanti to Zulu*
Ness, Evaline. *Sam, Bangs, and moonshine*
Perrault, Charles. *Cinderella*, ill. by Marcia Brown
Petersham, Maud. *The rooster crows*
Politi, Leo. *Song of the swallows*
Provensen, Alice. *The glorious flight*
Ransome, Arthur. *The fool of the world and the flying ship*
Rathmann, Peggy. *Officer Buckle and Gloria*
Robbins, Ruth. *Baboushka and the three kings*
Rohmann, Eric. *My friend Rabbit*
St. George, Judith. *So you want to be president?*

Sendak, Maurice. *Where the wild things are*
Spier, Peter. *Noah's ark*
Steig, William. *Sylvester and the magic pebble*
Taback, Simms. *Joseph had a little overcoat*
Thurber, James. *Many moons*, ill. by Louis Slobodkin
Tresselt, Alvin R. *White snow, bright snow*
Udry, Janice May. *A tree is nice*
Van Allsburg, Chris. *Jumanji*
    The polar express
Ward, Lynd. *The biggest bear*
Wiesner, David. *Tuesday*
Yolen, Jane. *Owl moon*
Yorinks, Arthur. *Hey, Al*
Young, Ed (Edward). *Lon Po Po*
Zemach, Harve. *Duffy and the devil*

Caldecott award honor books

Alger, Leclaire Gowans. *All in the morning early*
Andersen, H. C. (Hans Christian). *The ugly duckling*, ill. by Jerry Pinkney
Armer, Laura Adams. *The forest pool*
Artzybasheff, Boris. *Seven Simeons*
Baker, Olaf. *Where the buffaloes begin*
Bang, Molly. *The grey lady and the strawberry snatcher*
    Ten, nine, eight
    When Sophie gets angry – really, really angry . . .
Bartone, Elisa. *Peppe the lamplighter*
Baskin, Leonard. *Hosie's alphabet*
Baylor, Byrd. *The desert is theirs*
    Hawk, I'm your brother
    The way to start a day
    When clay sings
Belting, Natalia Maree. *The sun is a golden earring*
Bemelmans, Ludwig. *Madeline*
Birnbaum, Abe. *Green eyes*
Brown, Marcia. *Henry fisherman*
    Skipper John's cook
    Stone soup
Brown, Margaret Wise. *A child's good night book*
    Little lost lamb
    Wheel on the chimney
Buff, Mary (Marsh). *Dash and Dart*
Cathon, Laura E. *Tot Botot and his little flute*
Caudill, Rebecca. *A pocketful of cricket*
Chan, Chin-Yi. *Good luck horse*
A child's calendar
Chodos-Irvine, Margaret. *Ella Sarah gets dressed*
Clark, Ann Nolan. *In my mother's house*
Crews, Donald. *Freight train*
    Truck
Cronin, Doreen. *Click, clack, moo*
Dalgliesh, Alice. *The Thanksgiving story*
Daugherty, James Henry. *Andy and the lion*
Davis, Lavinia (Riker). *Roger and the fox*
    The wild birthday cake
Dayrell, Elphinstone. *Why the sun and the moon live in the sky*
De Angeli, Marguerite. *The book of nursery and Mother Goose rhymes*
    Yonie Wondernose
De Paola, Tomie (Thomas Anthony). *Strega Nona*
Dick Whittington and his cat. *Dick Whittington and his cat*, ill. by Marcia Brown
Domanska, Janina. *If all the seas were one sea*
Du Bois, William Pène. *Bear party*
    Lion
Ehlert, Lois. *Color zoo*
Eichenberg, Fritz. *Ape in cape*
Elkin, Benjamin. *Gillespie and the guards*
Emberley, Barbara. *One wide river to cross*
Ets, Marie Hall. *In the forest*
    Just me
    Mister Penny
    Mr. Penny's race horse
    Mr. T. W. Anthony Woo
    Play with me
Falconer, Ian. *Olivia*
Feelings, Muriel. *Jambo means hello*

Yolen, Jane. *The emperor and the kite*
Young, Ed (Edward). *Seven blind mice*
Zemach, Harve. *The judge*
Zemach, Margot. *It could always be worse*
Zion, Gene. *All falling down*
Zolotow, Charlotte (Shapiro). *Mr. Rabbit and the lovely present*
  The storm book

Calendars

A child's calendar
Hague, Kathleen. *Calendarbears*
Murphy, Stuart J. *Pepper's journal*

Cambodia *see* Foreign lands – Cambodia

Cambodian Americans *see* Ethnic groups in the U.S. – Cambodian Americans

Camels *see* Animals – camels

Cameroon *see* Foreign lands – Cameroon

Camouflages *see* Disguises

Camps, camping

Armitage, Ronda. *One moonlit night*
Baker, Keith. *Meet Mr. and Mrs. Green*
Bauer, Marion Dane. *When I go camping with Grandma*
The bear
Berenstain, Stan. *The Berenstain bears go to camp*
Birdseye, Tom. *Oh yeah!*
Blaustein, Muriel. *Make friends, Zachary!*
Boynton, Sandra. *Hester in the wild*
Brillhart, Julie. *When Daddy took us camping*
Brown, Marc Tolon. *Arthur goes to camp*
  Arthur's first sleepover
Brown, Myra Berry. *Pip camps out*
Bunting, Eve (Anne Evelyn). *I don't want to go to camp*
Carrick, Carol. *Sleep out*
Chesworth, Michael. *Archibald Frisby*
Christelow, Eileen. *Jerome camps out*
Cummings, Pat. *Petey Moroni's Camp Runamok diary*
Cummins, Julie. *Country kid, city kid*
Curious George goes camping
De Groat, Diane. *Good night, sleep tight, don't let the bedbugs bite*
Delton, Judy. *My mom made me go to camp*
Gifaldi, David. *Ben, king of the river*
Giff, Patricia Reilly. *Ronald Morgan goes to camp*
Gould, Deborah. *Camping in the Temple of the Sun*
Graham, Bob. *Greetings from Sandy Beach*
Gutman, Anne. *Gaspard at the seashore*
Hafner, Marylin. *Molly and Emmett's camping adventure*
Hannan, Peter. *Escape from Camp Wannabarf*
Hayward, Linda. *Elmo goes to day camp*
Henkes, Kevin. *Bailey goes camping*
Himmelman, John. *Lights out!*
  The super camper caper
Hoff, Syd. *Danny and the dinosaur go to camp*
Holabird, Katharine. *Angelina and Henry*
Hume, Stephen Eaton. *Red moon follows truck*
Hundal, Nancy. *Camping*
Huneck, Stephen. *Sally goes to the mountains*
Inkpen, Mick. *Kipper's monster*
  Wibbly Pig can make a tent
Jagtenberg, Yvonne. *Jack's kite*
Johnson, Paul Brett. *Lost*
Katschke, Judy. *Take a hike, Snoopy*
Koontz, Robin Michal. *Chicago and the cat, the camping trip*
Lasky, Kathryn. *Lucille camps in*
Leonard, Marcia. *My camp-out*
London, Jonathan. *The waterfall*
Lyon, George Ella. *A day at damp camp*
McCully, Emily Arnold. *Monk camps out*
McCutcheon, Marc. *Grandfather's Christmas camp*

McPhail, David M. *Pig Pig goes to camp*
Maestro, Betsy. *Camping out*
Marino, Dorothy. *Buzzy Bear goes camping*
Marshall, James. *The Cut-Ups at Camp Custer*
Mayer, Mercer. *Just me and my dad*
  You're the scaredy cat
Maynard, Joyce. *Camp-out*
Nolen, Jerdine. *Plantzilla goes to camp*
Nordqvist, Sven. *Festus and Mercury go camping*
Osofsky, Audrey. *My buddy*
Paterson, Brian. *Zigby camps out*
Peters, Sharon. *Fun at camp*
Price, Dorothy E. *Speedy gets around*
Pringle, Laurence P. *Bear hug*
Robins, Joan. *Addie runs away*
Roche, P. K. (Patrick K.). *Webster and Arnold go camping*
Rockwell, Anne F. *The night we slept outside*
  On our vacation
Rubel, Nicole. *Sam and Violet go camping*
Ruurs, Margriet. *When we go camping*
Schulman, Janet. *Camp Kee Wee's secret weapon*
Schwartz, Amy. *Camper of the week*
Schwartz, Henry. *How I captured a dinosaur*
Seligson, Susan. *Amos camps out*
Shulevitz, Uri. *Dawn*
Singer, Marilyn. *Quiet night*
Spohn, David. *Starry night*
Spohn, Kate. *Turtle and Snake go camping*
Stern, Maggie. *Acorn magic*
Stock, Catherine. *Sophie's knapsack*
Tafuri, Nancy. *Do not disturb*
Thompson, Vivian Laubach. *Camp-in-the-yard*
Warren, Cathy. *The ten-alarm camp-out*
Weiss, Nicki. *Battle day at Camp Delmont*
Williams, Vera B. *Three days on a river in a red canoe*
Wolff, Ashley. *Stella and Roy go camping*
Yolen, Jane. *The giants go camping*

Canada *see* Foreign lands – Canada

Canada Day *see* Holidays – Canada Day

Canaries *see* Birds – canaries

Cancer *see* Illness – cancer

Canoes & canoeing

Asch, Frank. *Moonbear's canoe*
Baker, Sanna Anderson. *Mississippi going north*
Casanova, Mary. *One-dog canoe*
Drawson, Blair. *All along the river*
Kraus, Robert. *Wise Old Owl's canoe trip adventure*
London, Jonathan. *Loon Lake*
Maggi, María Elena. *The great canoe*
Mason, Jane B. *River day*
Paterson, Brian. *Zigby hunts for treasure*
Paulsen, Gary. *Canoe days*

Canyons

Cameron, Eileen. *Canyon*
London, Jonathan. *Mustang canyon*

Capes *see* Clothing – coats

Caps *see* Clothing – hats

Cardboard page books *see* Format, unusual – board books

Cardinals *see* Birds – cardinals

Cards *see* Letters, cards

Careers

Aitken, Amy. *Ruby!*
Arnold, Caroline. *What is a community?*
    Who keeps us safe?
    Who works here?
Azaad, Meyer (Mahmud). *Half for you*
Baker, Eugene H. *I want to be a computer operator*
Bank Street College of Education. *People read*
Barber, Barbara E. *Saturday at the new you*
Bauer, Caroline Feller. *My mom travels a lot*
Berenstain, Stan. *The Berenstain bears and mama's new job*
Bond, Michael. *Paddington Bear and the Christmas surprise*
Bond, Rebecca. *Bravo, Maurice!*
Boxer, Devorah. *26 ways to be somebody else*
Brandenberg, Alexa. *I am me!*
Brentano, Clemens. *Schoolmaster Whackwell's wonderful sons*
Brott, Ardyth. *Jeremy's decision*
Bunting, Eve (Anne Evelyn). *Girls A to Z*
Butterworth, Nick. *Busy people*
Calmenson, Stephanie. *Fido*
Civardi, Anne. *Things people do*
Davis, Gary. *Working at a TV station*
Dubois, Muriel L. *I like animals: what can I be?*
    I like computers: what can I be?
    I like sports: what can I be?
Dupasquier, Philippe. *Dear Daddy . . .*
Florian, Douglas. *People working*
Freeman, Don. *The night the lights went out*
Gardiner, Lindsey. *When Poppy and Max grow up*
Gibbons, Gail. *Emergency!*
    Farming
    Fill it up!
    The pottery place
Gibson, Karen Bush. *Child care workers*
    Emergency medical technicians
Glassman, Peter. *My dad's job*
Goffstein, M. B. (Marilyn Brooke). *An actor*
Goodings, Lennie. *When you grow up*
Greenberg, Melanie Hope. *My father's luncheonette*
Greene, Carol. *I can be a baseball player*
Grossman, Patricia. *The night ones*
Hallinan, P. K. (Patrick K.). *When I grow up*
Halperin, Wendy Anderson. *Once upon a company*
Harper, Anita. *How we work*
Harris, Steven Michael. *This is my trunk*
Hazen, Barbara Shook. *Mommy's office*
High, Linda Oatman. *The last chimney of Christmas eve*
Ipcar, Dahlov (Zorach). *I like animals*
Jensen, Patricia. *Kitty's special job*
Jordan, Roslyn M. *Salt in his shoes*
Judes, Marie-Odile. *Max, the stubborn little wolf*
Ketteman, Helen. *Shoeshine Whittaker*
Kherdian, David. *The golden bracelet*
Klein, Norma. *Girls can be anything*
Kraus, Robert. *Owliver*
Krensky, Stephen. *How Santa got his job*
    How Santa lost his job
Kroll, Steven. *Howard and Gracie's luncheonette*
Lasker, Joe. *Mothers can do anything*
Lenski, Lois. *Lois Lenski's big book of Mr. Small*
Le-Tan, Pierre. *Timothy's dream book*
Liebman, Daniel. *I want to be a cowboy*
MacKinnon, Debbie. *What am I?*
McNaughton, Colin. *Yum!*
McPhail, David M. *Pig Pig gets a job*
Mara, Wil. *Jackie Robinson*
Matthias, Catherine. *I can be a computer operator*
Mayer, Mercer. *Little Monster at work*
Maynard, Christopher. *Jobs people do*
Mellage, Nanette. *Coming home*
Merriam, Eve. *Mommies at work*
Miller, Heather. *Cowboy*
Miller, Margaret. *Who uses this?*
    Whose hat?
Mitchell, Joyce Slayton. *My mommy makes money*
Moore, Elaine. *Good morning, city*

Morris, Ann. *Work*
Morrison, Bill. *Louis James hates school*
Myers, Bernice. *The gold watch*
Nettleton, Pamela Hill. *George Washington*
Nichols, Paul. *Big Paul's school bus*
Nolen, Jerdine. *Raising dragons*
O'Book, Irene. *Maybe my baby*
Oliver, Dexter. *I want to be . . .*
100 words about working
Oppenheim, Joanne. *On the other side of the river*
Oppenheim, Shulamith Levey. *Yanni rubbish*
Paulsen, Gary. *Worksong*
Portnoy, Mindy Avra. *Ima on the Bima*
Puner, Helen Walker. *Daddys, what they do all day*
Ray, Mary Lyn. *Basket moon*
Reasoner, Charles. *Who drives this?*
Relf, Patricia. *Tonka trucks night and day*
Robinson, Aminah Brenda Lynn. *A street called home*
Rockwell, Anne F. *Career day*
Rotner, Shelley. *Everybody works*
Rowan, James P. *I can be a zoo keeper*
Rowe, Jeanne A. *City workers*
Sandberg, Inger. *Come on out, Daddy!*
Sava, Donna Lynn. *Teddy bear dreams*
Scarry, Richard. *Richard Scarry's busiest people ever*
    Richard Scarry's Postman Pig and his busy neighbors
Schaefer, Lola M. *Airport*
Schomp, Virginia. *If you were a . . . ballplayer*
Seignobosc, Françoise. *What do you want to be?*
Sesame Street. *The Sesame Street book of people and things*
Shank, Ned. *The sanyasin's first day*
Sharmat, Marjorie Weinman. *I'm Santa Claus and I'm famous*
Shepard, Steve. *Elvis Hornbill, international business bird*
Stevenson, James. *Sam the Zamboni man*
Stewart, Robert S. *The daddy book*
Thaler, Mike. *What could a hippopotamus be?*
Turner, Sandy. *Grow up*
Upton, Pat. *Who does this job?*
Williams, Barbara. *I know a salesperson*
Wittmann, Patricia. *Go ask Giorgio!*

Careers – accountants

Hudson, Wade. *Jamal's busy day*
Lasky, Kathryn. *Marven of the Great North Woods*

Careers – acrobats

Filleul, Liz. *Tumbler*
Saltzberg, Barney. *The Flying Garbanzos*

Careers – actors

Ackerman, Karen. *Bean's big day*
Dunrea, Olivier. *Appearing tonight! Mary Heather Elizabeth Livingstone*
Gerrard, Roy. *Jocasta Carr, movie star*
Krementz, Jill. *A very young actress*
Littlesugar, Amy. *Tree of hope*
McCully, Emily Arnold. *Zaza's big break*
McKissack, Patricia C. *Paul Robeson*
Philpot, Graham. *Fabulous fairy tale follies*
Waber, Bernard. *Evie & Margie*

Careers – aerialists

Gerstein, Mordicai. *The man who walked between the towers*
McCully, Emily Arnold. *Mirette and Bellini cross Niagara Falls*

Careers – airplane pilots

Adler, David A. *A picture book of Amelia Earhart*
Baker, Donna. *I want to be a pilot*
Barton, Byron. *Airport*
Behrens, June. *I can be a pilot*
Borden, Louise. *Goodbye, Charles Lindbergh*
Brown, Don. *Ruth Law thrills a nation*

Duble, Kathleen Benner. *Pilot mom*
Edwards, Pamela Duncan. *The Wright brothers*
Flanagan, Alice K. *Flying an agricultural plane with Mr. Miller*
   I want to be a pilot
Joseph, Lynn. *Fly, Bessie, fly*
Krementz, Jill. *Jamie goes on an airplane*
Lenski, Lois. *The little airplane*
Lindbergh, Reeve. *A view from the air*
Mara, Wil. *Amelia Earhart*
Morgan, Allen. *Matthew and the midnight pilot*
Pelton, Mindy L. *When Dad's at sea*
Raven, Margot Theis. *Mercedes and the chocolate pilot*
Schomp, Virginia. *If you were a . . . pilot*
Seymour, Peter S. *Pilots*
Tarpley, Natasha Anastasia. *Joe-Joe's first flight*
Yolen, Jane. *My brothers' flying machine*
Young, Miriam Burt. *If I flew a plane*

Careers – archaeologists

Addy, Sharon Hart. *Right here on this spot*
Brighton, Catherine. *The fossil girl*
Cole, Joanna. *The magic school bus shows and tells*
Duke, Kate. *Archaeologists dig for clues*

Careers – architects

Clinton, Susan. *I can be an architect*
Cooper, Elisha. *Building*
Demi. *The artist and the architect*
Hudson, Wade. *Jamal's busy day*
Hunter, Ryan Ann. *Into the sky*
Laden, Nina. *Roberto, the insect architect*

Careers – artists *see also* Activities – painting; Careers – painters

Adams, Adrienne. *The great Valentine's Day balloon race*
Angelo, Nancy Carolyn Harrison. *Camembert*
Anholt, Laurence. *Camille and the sunflowers*
Baker, Alan. *Benjamin's portrait*
Baynton, Martin. *Fifty gets the picture*
Belton, Sandra. *Pictures for Miss Josie*
Brenner, Barbara A. *The boy who loved to draw*
Browne, Anthony. *Willy's pictures*
Carrick, Donald. *Morgan and the artist*
Catalanotto, Peter. *Emily's art*
Christelow, Eileen. *What do authors do?*
Collins, Pat Lowery. *I am an artist*
Davies, Jacqueline. *The boy who drew birds*
Deeter, Catherine. *Seymour Bleu*
Demi. *The artist and the architect*
DeNoble, Augustine. *Brother Joseph*
Dunrea, Olivier. *The painter who loved chickens*
Edwards, Michelle. *A baker's portrait*
   Eve and Smithy
Ekoomiak, Normee. *Arctic memories*
Everett, Gwen. *Li'l Sis and Uncle Willie*
Flanagan, Alice K. *Mrs. Scott's beautiful art*
Florian, Douglas. *A painter*
Frith, Margaret. *Frida Kahlo*
Galli, Letizia. *Mona Lisa*
Gardner, Jane Mylum. *Henry Moore*
Gibbons, Gail. *The art box*
Goffstein, M. B. (Marilyn Brooke). *An artist*
Green, Donna. *My little artist*
Guarnieri, Paolo. *A boy named Giotto*
Havill, Juanita. *Sato and the elephants*
Heller, Nicholas. *The giant*
Hershenhorn, Esther. *Fancy that*
Hest, Amy. *Nana's birthday party*
Holub, Joan. *Vincent van Gogh*
Hyde, Margaret E. *Matisse for kids*
   Van Gogh for kids
Isom, Joan Shaddox. *The first starry night*
Johnson, Angela. *Daddy calls me man*
Kelley, True. *Claude Monet*

Kleven, Elisa. *The lion and the little red bird*
Laden, Nina. *When Pigasso met Mootisse*
Lager, Claude. *A tale of two rats*
Lakin, Pat (Patricia). *Subway sonata*
Leaf, Margaret. *Eyes of the dragon*
Lehan, Daniel. *This is not a book about dodos*
Le Tord, Bijou. *A bird or two*
Levine, Arthur A. *The boy who drew cats*
Lionni, Leo. *Matthew's dream*
Lithgow, John. *Micawber*
Littlesugar, Amy. *Jonkonnu*
   Josiah True and the art maker
   Marie in fourth position
Locker, Thomas. *The man who paints nature*
   Miranda's smile
   The young artist
McClintock, Barbara. *The fantastic drawings of Danielle*
MacLachlan, Patricia. *Painting the wind*
MacLean, Kerry Lee. *Peaceful piggy meditation*
McPhail, David M. *Drawing lessons from a bear*
Magnier, Thierry. *Isabelle and the angel*
Mayhew, James. *Katie and the Mona Lisa*
   Katie meets the Impressionists
Maynard, Bill. *Incredible Ned*
Merberg, Julie. *In the garden with Van Gogh*
   A magical day with Matisse
Miller, Warren. *Pablo paints a picture*
Moss, Marissa. *Regina's big mistake*
Nicholson, Nicholas B. A. *Little girl in a red dress with cat and dog*
Nickens, Bessie. *Walking the log*
Nikola-Lisa, W. *The year with Grandma Moses*
Parillo, Tony. *Michelangelo's surprise*
Payne, Joan Balfour. *The stable that stayed*
Pinkwater, Daniel Manus. *The bear's picture*
Porte, Barbara Ann. *Chickens! Chickens!*
Raczka, Bob. *No one saw*
Ross, Tom. *Eggbert, the slightly cracked egg*
Rubin, Susan Goldman. *The yellow house*
Schaefer, A. R. (Adam Richard). *Alexander Calder*
   Diego Rivera
   Grandma Moses
Segal, Lore Groszmann. *Morris the artist*
Sharon, Mary Bruce. *Scenes from childhood*
Sloan, Carolyn. *Carter is a painter's cat*
Spohn, Kate. *By word of mouse*
Stadler, John. *What's so scary?*
Stevenson, James. *Fun, no fun*
   I meant to tell you
Stock, Catherine. *Gugu's house*
Sweeney, Joan. *Suzette and the puppy*
Thomas, Abigail. *Pearl paints*
Tunnell, Michael O. *The joke's on George*
Turnbull, Ann. *The sand horse*
Vande Griek, Susan. *The art room*
Velthuijs, Max. *Crocodile's masterpiece*
   The painter and the bird
Ventura, Piero. *The painter's trick*
Waddell, Martin. *Alice the artist*
Waldman, Neil. *The starry night*
Wallace, Ian. *The naked lady*
Walsh, Jill Paton. *Pepi and the secret names*
Warhola, James. *Uncle Andy's*
Weisgard, Leonard. *Mr. Peaceable paints*
Wheatley, Nadia. *Luke's way of looking*
Willard, Nancy. *Pish posh, said Hieronymous Bosch*
Winter, Jeanette. *Cowboy Charlie*
Winter, Jonah. *Diego*
Wolkstein, Diane. *Little Mouse's painting*
Wood, Michele. *Going back home*
Woodhouse, Jayne. *Pieter Bruegel*
Wooding, Sharon L. *The painter's cat*
Wynne-Jones, Tim. *On Tumbledown Hill*
Yacowitz, Caryn. *The jade stone*
Ziefert, Harriet. *Lunchtime for a purple snake*

Careers – astronauts

Agee, Jon. *Dmitri the astronaut*
Anderson, Joan. *Richie's rocket*
Barton, Byron. *I want to be an astronaut*
Bartram, Simon. *Man on the moon*
Behrens, June. *I can be an astronaut*
Branley, Franklyn M. (Mansfield). *Floating in space*
Bredeson, Carmen. *Getting ready for space*
    Liftoff!
    Living on a space shuttle
Brown, Don. *One giant leap*
Catalanotto, Peter. *Dad and me*
Eco, Umberto. *The three astronauts*
Fox, Christyan. *Astronaut PiggyWiggy*
Greene, Carol. *Astronauts work in space*
Nettleton, Pamela Hill. *Sally Ride*
Rau, Dana Meachen. *Neil Armstrong*
Schomp, Virginia. *If you were an . . . astronaut*

Careers – astronomers

Crew, Gary. *Bright star*
Hopkinson, Deborah. *Maria's comet*
Pinkney, Andrea Davis. *Dear Benjamin Banneker*

Careers – authors

Borden, Louise. *The day Eddie met the author*
Browne, Anthony. *The shape game*
Bunting, Eve (Anne Evelyn). *My special day at third street school*
Dunlap, Julie. *Louisa May and Mr. Thoreau's flute*
Krull, Kathleen. *The boy on Fairfield Street*
Lynch, Wendy. *Dr. Seuss*
    Janet and Allan Ahlberg
McElroy, Lisa Tucker. *Meet my grandmother. She's a children's book author*
MacLean, Kerry Lee. *Peaceful piggy meditation*
Manuel, Lynn. *Lucy Maud and the Cavendish cat*
Mara, Wil. *Laura Ingalls Wilder*
Mora, Pat. *A library for Juana*
Myers, Walter Dean. *Harlem*
Rau, Dana Meachen. *Dr. Seuss*
Steig, William. *When everybody wore a hat*
Walsh, Ellen Stoll. *Jack's tale*

Careers – bakers

Allard, Harry. *The cactus flower bakery*
Barkan, Joanne. *Whiskerville bake shop*
Bunting, Eve (Anne Evelyn). *Barney the Beard*
Caple, Kathy. *Inspector Aardvark and the perfect cake*
Carle, Eric. *Walter the baker*
Craig, M. Jean. *The man whose name was not Thomas*
De Paola, Tomie (Thomas Anthony). *Tony's bread*
Edwards, Michelle. *A baker's portrait*
Ericsson, Jennifer A. *Out and about at the bakery*
Flanagan, Alice K. *Mr. Santizo's tasty treats!*
Forest, Heather. *The baker's dozen*
Green, Melinda. *Bembelman's bakery*
Greeson, Janet. *The stingy baker*
Hartman, Bob. *Who brought the bread?*
Hayward, Linda. *Baker, baker, cookie maker*
    The biggest cookie in the world
Heath, Amy. *Sofie's role*
Helldorfer, M. C. (Mary Claire). *The darling boys*
Kessler, Leonard P. *Soup for the king*
Kleven, Elisa. *Sun bread*
Langford, Sondra Gordon. *Mishka and Plishka*
Levitin, Sonia. *Boom town*
Lillegard, Dee. *I can be a baker*
Mathers, Petra. *Herbie's secret Santa*
Mayer, Marianna. *Marcel the pastry chef*
Pinkwater, Daniel Manus. *The Frankenbagel monster*
Rylant, Cynthia. *The cookie-store cat*
Schwartz, Ellen. *Mr. Belinsky's bagels*
Shepard, Aaron. *The baker's dozen*

Stewart, Sarah. *The gardener*
Sundvall, Viveca. *Mimi and the biscuit factory*
Tzannes, Robin. *Sanji and the baker*
Westcott, Nadine Bernard. *Peanut butter and jelly*
Willey, Margaret. *Clever Beatrice and the best little pony*
Worthington, Phoebe. *Teddy bear baker*
Young, Miriam Burt. *The sugar mouse cake*
Ziegler, Sandra. *A visit to the bakery*

Careers – barbers

Appell, Clara. *Now I have a daddy haircut*
Auerbach, Marjorie. *King Lavra and the barber*
Barry, Robert E. *Next please*
Battle-Lavert, Gwendolyn. *The barber's cutting edge*
Burnard, Damon. *Dave's haircut*
Cole, Kenneth, Dr. *No bad news*
Freeman, Don. *Mop Top*
Koren, Edward. *Very hairy Harry*
Kunhardt, Dorothy. *Billy the barber*
Mahiri, Jabari. *The day they stole the letter J*
Mitchell, Margaree King. *Uncle Jed's barbershop*
Peet, Bill (William Bartlett). *Hubert's hair-raising adventures*
Portlock, Rob. *Someone's trying to cut off my head*
Radabaugh, Melinda Beth. *Getting a haircut*
Robbins, Beth. *Tom's new haircut*
Rockwell, Anne F. *My barber*
Tarpley, Natasha Anastasia. *Bippity Bop barbershop*

Careers – beekeepers

Flanagan, Alice K. *Learning about bees from Mr. Krebs*
Krebs, Laurie. *The Beeman*

Careers – beggars

Oppenheim, Shulamith Levey. *Ali and the magic stew*
Scott, Sally. *The three wonderful beggars*

Careers – blacksmiths

High, Linda Oatman. *Winter shoes for Shadow Horse*

Careers – boat builders

Hunt, Jonathan. *Leif's saga*
Rand, Gloria. *Salty dog*

Careers – bookbinders

Cheng, Andrea. *Anna the bookbinder*

Careers – bus drivers

Brown, Marc Tolon. *Arthur lost and found*
Denslow, Sharon Phillips. *Bus riders*
Flanagan, Alice K. *Riding the school bus with Mrs. Kramer*
Harrison, Troon. *Lavender Moon*
Helakoski, Leslie. *The smushy bus*
Lakin, Pat (Patricia). *Up a tree*
Owen, Ann (1953–). *Taking your places*
Poydar, Nancy. *First day, hooray!*
Pulver, Robin. *Axle Annie*
Willems, Mo. *Don't let the pigeon drive the bus*
Young, Miriam Burt. *If I drove a bus*

Careers – butchers

Kobayashi, Robert. *Maria Mazaretti loves spaghetti*
Yorinks, Arthur. *Louis the fish*

Careers – cab drivers *see* Careers – taxi drivers

Careers – carpenters

Baker, Keith. *The magic fan*
Denslow, Sharon Phillips. *At Taylor's place*

Florian, Douglas. *A carpenter*
Greene, Carla. *I want to be a carpenter*
Hest, Amy. *The ring and the window seat*
Lillegard, Dee. *I can be a carpenter*
Lucado, Max. *Jacob's gift*
Pickthall, Marjorie L. C. (Marjorie Lowry Christie). *The worker in sandalwood*
Prøysen, Alf. *Christmas eve at Santa's*
Snyder, Inez. *Building tools*

Careers – cartographers

Chancellor, Deborah. *Maps and mapping*

Careers – chefs, cooks

Bliss, Corinne Demas. *The boy who was generous with salt*
Dumas, Bianca. *Tia Luisa, the magical cook*
Egan, Tim. *The experiments of Doctor Vermin*
Florian, Douglas. *A chef*
Guthrie, Donna. *This little pig stayed home*
Harrison, Troon. *Lavender Moon*
Kidd, Richard. *Monsieur Thermidor*
Loomis, Christine. *In the diner*
Medearis, Angela Shelf. *The ghost of Sifty-Sifty Sam*
Moss, Marissa. *Mel's diner*
Myers, Edward. *Forri the baker*
Pillar, Marjorie. *Pizza man*
Poskanzer, Susan Cornell. *What's it like to be a chef?*
Radabaugh, Melinda Beth. *Going to a restaurant*
Tomchek, Ann Heinrichs. *I can be a chef*
Wellington, Monica. *Mr. Cookie Baker*

Careers – clergy

DeNoble, Augustine. *Brother Joseph*
Dollinger, Renate. *The rabbi who flew*
Frost, Helen. *Martin Luther King, Jr. Day*
Gillerlain, Gayle. *Reverend Thomas's false teeth*
Hirsh, Marilyn. *The Rabbi and the twenty-nine witches*
I've seen the promised land
Johnson, Paul Brett. *Old Dry Fry*
Kimmel, Eric A. *Zigazak!*
McKissack, Patricia C. *Booker T. Washington*
Muth, Jon J. *Stone soup*
Nettleton, Pamela Hill. *Martin Luther King, Jr.*
Norris, Kathleen. *The holy twins: Benedict and Scholastica*
Olofsson, Helena. *The little jester*
Rappaport, Doreen. *Martin's big words*
Sexton, Colleen A. *Let's meet Martin Luther King, Jr.*
Swain, Gwenyth. *I wonder as I wander*

Careers – clockmakers

Ardizzone, Edward. *Johnny the clockmaker*
Henwood, Simon. *The clock shop*

Careers – coaches

Finchler, Judy. *You're a good sport, Miss Malarkey*
Flanagan, Alice K. *Coach John and his soccer team*

Careers – comedians

Burton, Martin Nelson. *The whale comedian*

Careers – composers

Anderson, M. T. *Strange Mr. Satie*
Brighton, Catherine. *Mozart*
Celenza, Anna Harwell. *The farewell symphony*
Dineen, Jacqueline. *Frédéric Chopin*
Lasker, David. *The boy who loved music*
Lynch, Wendy. *Bach*
Schaefer, Carole Lexa. *Two scarlet songbirds*
Swain, Gwenyth. *I wonder as I wander*

Careers – conductors (music)

Lithgow, John. *The remarkable Farkle McBride*

Careers – construction workers

Banks, Kate (Katherine A.). *The night worker*
Big noisy trucks and diggers
Copeland, Cynthia L. *What are you waiting for?*
Flanagan, Alice K. *Mr. Paul and Mr. Luecke build communities*
Hayward, Linda. *A day in the life of a builder*
Hennessy, B. G. (Barbara G.). *Road builders*
Hill, Lee Sullivan. *Earthmovers*
Johnson, Angela. *Those building men*
Kilby, Don. *At a construction site*
Lewis, Kevin. *The lot at the end of my block*
Liebman, Daniel. *I want to be a builder*
Rex, Michael. *Who builds?*
    Who digs?
Schaefer, Lola M. *Construction site*
Schomp, Virginia. *If you were a . . . construction worker*
Stoeke, Janet Morgan. *Minerva Louise and the red truck*
Suen, Anastasia. *Raise the roof*
Wallace, Karen. *Big machines*

Careers – cooks *see* Careers – chefs, cooks

Careers – custodians, janitors

Flanagan, Alice K. *Call Mr. Vasquez, he'll fix it!*
Lakin, Pat (Patricia). *Trash and treasure*

Careers – dancers

Hayward, Linda. *A day in the life of a dancer*
Isadora, Rachel. *Lili on stage*
Klingel, Cynthia Fitterer. *Dancers*
Komaiko, Leah. *Aunt Elaine does the dance from Spain*
Pavlova, Anna. *I dreamed I was a ballerina*
Pinkney, Andrea Davis. *Alvin Ailey*
Schomp, Virginia. *If you were a . . . ballet dancer*
Sis, Peter. *Ballerina*
Woodworth, Viki. *Daisy the dancing cow*

Careers – dentists

Ambrus, Victor G. *What's the time, Dracula?*
Barnett, Naomi. *I know a dentist*
Berenstain, Stan. *The Berenstain bears visit the dentist*
Curious George goes to the dentist
Davis, Katie (Katie I.). *Mabel the Tooth Fairy and how she got her job*
Duvoisin, Roger Antoine. *Crocus*
Flanagan, Alice K. *Dr. Kanner, dentist with a smile*
Gomi, Taro. *The crocodile and the dentist*
Hallinan, P. K. (Patrick K.). *My dentist, my friend*
Keller, Laurie. *Open wide: tooth school inside*
Krementz, Jill. *Taryn goes to the dentist*
Kuklin, Susan. *When I see my dentist*
Lapp, Carolyn. *The dentists' tools*
Linn, Margot. *A trip to the dentist*
Luttrell, Ida. *Milo's toothache*
Mitra, Annie. *Tusk! Tusk!*
Murkoff, Heidi Eisenberg. *What to expect when you go to the dentist*
Richter, Alice Numeroff. *You can't put braces on spaces*
Rockwell, Harlow. *My dentist*
Rosenberry, Vera. *Vera goes to the dentist*
Schaefer, Lola M. *Dental office*
Steig, William. *Doctor De Soto goes to Africa*
Swanson, Diane. *The dentist and you*
Watson, Jane Werner. *My friend the dentist*
Whybrow, Ian. *Harry and the dinosaurs say "Raahh"*
Wolf, Bernard. *Michael and the dentist*
Zalben, Jane Breskin. *Buster gets braces*

Careers – detectives

Allen, Laura Jean. *Rollo and Tweedy and the case of the missing cheese*

Rollo and Tweedy and the ghost of Dougal Castle
Where is Freddy?
Berenstain, Stan. *The bear detectives*
Bunting, Eve (Anne Evelyn). *Jane Martin, dog detective*
Christelow, Eileen. *Gertrude, the bulldog detective*
Where's the big bad wolf?
Cox, Paul. *The case of the botched book*
The great eucalyptus mystery
The riddle of the floating island
Cushman, Doug. *The ABC mystery*
The mystery of King Karfu
The mystery of the monkey's maze
Dickson, Louise. *The vanishing cat*
Geisert, Arthur. *Mystery*
Harrison, David Lee. *Detective Bob and the great ape escape*
Jeffrey, Sean. *Franklin's big search-and-solve flap book*
Kitamura, Satoshi. *Sheep in wolves' clothing*
Kraus, Robert. *The detective of London*
Latimer, Jim. *The fox under first base*
Lawrence, James. *Binky Brothers and the fearless four*
Binky Brothers, detectives
Mason, Adrienne. *Lu and Clancy sound off*
Lu and Clancy's spy stuff
Meddaugh, Susan. *Perfectly Martha*
Nash, Scott. *Tuff Fluff*
Nixon, Joan Lowery. *Gus and Gertie and the missing pearl*
O'Malley, Kevin. *Who killed Cock Robin?*
Ostheeren, Ingrid. *Jonathan Mouse, detective*
Palatini, Margie. *The web files*
Panek, Dennis. *Detective Whoo*
Rash, Andy. *Agent A to Agent Z*
Schaefer, Lola M. *Police station*
Sharmat, Marjorie Weinman. *Nate the Great*
Nate the Great and the lost list
Nate the Great and the monster mess
Nate the Great and the phony clue
Nate the Great goes undercover
Nate the Great, San Francisco detective
Stortz, Diane M. *Barnaby Mouse, detective, and the mystery of the big book*
Supraner, Robyn. *Sam Sunday and the mystery at the Ocean Beach Hotel*
Teague, Mark. *Detective LaRue*
Thomson, Ruth. *Peabody all at sea*
Peabody's first case
Tryon, Leslie. *Albert's Halloween*

Careers – doctors

Arnold, Caroline. *Who keeps us healthy?*
Baggette, Susan K. *Jonathan goes to the doctor*
Berenstain, Stan. *The Berenstain bears go to the doctor*
Bertrand, Lynne. *One day, two dragons*
Breckler, Rosemary K. *Sweet dried apples*
Breinburg, Petronella. *Doctor Shawn*
Charlip, Remy. *"Mother, mother I feel sick"*
Chislett, Gail. *Melinda's no's cold*
Cobb, Vicki. *How the doctor knows you're fine*
Corey, Dorothy. *A shot for baby bear*
Davison, Martine. *Robby visits the doctor*
DeSantis, Kenny. *A doctor's tools*
Fine, Anne. *Poor Monty*
Freeman, Don. *Corduroy's busy street and Corduroy goes to the doctor*
Gilbert, Helen Earle. *Dr. Trotter and his big gold watch*
Goodsell, Jane. *Katie's magic glasses*
Greene, Carla. *Doctors and nurses*
Hallinan, P. K. (Patrick K.). *My doctor, my friend*
Hanklin, Rebecca. *I can be a doctor*
Kraus, Robert. *Boris bad enough*
Dr. Mouse, Bungle Jungle doctor
Kroll, Steven. *Doctor on an elephant*
Kuklin, Susan. *When I see my doctor*
Lerner, Marguerite Rush. *Doctors' tools*
Liebman, Daniel. *I want to be a doctor*
Linn, Margot. *A trip to the doctor*
London, Jonathan. *Froggy goes to the doctor*
Marcus, Susan. *Casey visits the doctor*

Murkoff, Heidi Eisenberg. *What to expect when you go to the doctor*
My doctor's bag
Owen, Ann (1953–). *Keeping you healthy*
Oxenbury, Helen. *The checkup*
Piumini, Roberto. *Doctor Me Di Cin*
Robbins, Beth. *Tom and Ally visit the doctor*
Robison, Deborah. *Your turn, doctor*
Rockwell, Harlow. *My doctor*
Rogers, Fred. *Going to the doctor*
Roop, Peter. *Stick out your tongue!*
Rylant, Cynthia. *Silver packages*
Schaefer, Lola M. *Hospital*
Schomp, Virginia. *If you were a . . . doctor*
Stein, Sara Bonnett. *A hospital story*
Swanson, Diane. *The doctor and you*
Viorst, Judith. *The tenth good thing about Barney*
Wahl, Jan. *Doctor Rabbit's foundling*
Watson, Jane Werner. *My friend the doctor*
Wolde, Gunilla. *Betsy and the doctor*

Careers – doormen

Grimm, Edward. *The doorman*

Careers – electricians

Cole, Joanna. *The magic school bus and the electric field trip*
Lillegard, Dee. *I can be an electrician*

Careers – emergency medical technicians

Koski, Mary. *Impatient Pamela calls 9-1-1*
Levine, Michelle. *Ambulances*
Mayo, Margaret. *Emergency!*

Careers – engineers

Drummond, Allan. *Casey Jones*
Highet, Alistair. *The yellow train*
Moss, Marissa. *True heart*
Shuter, Jane. *Henry Ford*

Careers – entertainers

Ahlberg, Allan. *Mr. and Mrs. Hay the horse*
Newman, Lesléa. *Pigs, pigs, pigs*

Careers – explorers

Brown, Don. *Uncommon traveler*
Conrad, Pam. *Call me Ahnighito*
DeRubertis, Barbara. *Columbus Day*
Edwards, Pamela Duncan. *Livingstone Mouse*
Hunt, Jonathan. *Leif's saga*
Jendresen, Erik. *The first story ever told*
Kroll, Steven. *Lewis and Clark*
Mayhew, James. *Miranda the explorer*
Schachner, Judith Byron. *Yo, Vikings*
Sis, Peter. *Follow the dream*
Thomas, Frances. *One day, Daddy*
Yorinks, Arthur. *The Miami giant*

Careers – farmers

Ackerman, Karen. *Bingleman's midway*
Æsop. *The goose that laid the golden egg*
Aliki. *Milk from cow to carton*
Allen, Pamela. *Belinda*
Ambrus, Victor G. *Never laugh at bears*
Anderson, Janet S. *Sunflower Sal*
Asch, Frank. *Barnyard lullaby*
Aylesworth, Jim. *My son John*
Birchman, David Francis. *Jigsaw Jackson*
Bock, Lee. *Oh, crumps! = Ay, caramba!*
Booth, David. *The dust bowl*
Brown, Craig McFarland. *City sounds*
Patchwork farmer

Buehner, Caralyn. *Fanny's dream*
Carlson, Melody. *Farmer Brown's field trip*
Carney, Margaret (Margaret Rose). *At Grandpa's sugar bush*
Carter, David A. *Old MacDonald had a farm*
Chorao, Kay. *Little farm by the sea*
Christelow, Eileen. *The great pig escape*
Cowley, Joy. *The rusty, trusty tractor*
Crebbin, June. *Cows in the kitchen*
Cronin, Doreen. *Click, clack, moo*
Crunk, Tony. *Grandpa's overalls*
Demarest, Chris L. *Farmer Nat*
Demuth, Patricia Brennan. *Ornery morning*
Douglas, Erin. *Get that pest!*
Duffield, Katy. *Farmer McPeepers and his missing milk cows*
Dunrea, Olivier. *The trow-wife's treasure*
Egan, Tim. *Serious farm*
Ehrlich, Amy. *Parents in the pigpen, pigs in the tub*
A farmer boy birthday
The farmer in the dell. *The farmer in the dell*, ill. by John O'Brien
   The farmer in the dell, ill. by Kathy Parkinson
   The farmer in the dell, ill. by Mary Maki Rae
   The farmer in the dell, ill. by Diane Stanley
   The farmer in the dell, ill. by Alexandra Wallner
Flanagan, Alice K. *Farmers*
   Raising cows on the Koebels' farm
   A visit to the Gravesens' farm
   The Zieglers and their apple orchard
Friedrich, Elizabeth. *Leah's pony*
Goodhart, Pippa. *Arthur's tractor*
Haas, Jessie. *Hurry!*
Hall, Donald. *The milkman's boy*
Hamm, Diane Johnston. *Rock-a-bye farm*
Hazen, Barbara Shook. *Turkey in the straw*
Henderson, Kathy. *I can be a farmer*
Henley, Claire. *Farm day*
Hutchins, H. J. (Hazel J.). *One duck*
Johnson, Angela. *Casey Jones*
Johnson, Paul Brett. *Farmers' market*
Kallen, Stuart A. *The farm*
Kaufman, Jeff. *Milk rock*
Ketteman, Helen. *I remember papa*
Kightley, Rosalinda. *The farmer*
Klingel, Cynthia Fitterer. *Farmers*
Kunhardt, Edith. *I'm going to be a farmer*
Laird, Elizabeth. *The day the ducks went skating*
   The day Veronica was nosy
Lasky, Kathryn. *The emperor's old clothes*
Love, Ann. *Farming*
Ludy, Mark. *The farmer*
Lunn, Janet Louise Swoboda. *Come to the fair*
Maccarone, Grace. *Oink! moo! how do you do?*
Maguire, Gregory. *Crabby Cratchitt*
Marciano, John Bemelmans. *Delilah*
Most, Bernard. *Cock-a-doodle-moo!*
Nettleton, Pamela Hill. *George Washington*
Nordqvist, Sven. *The fox hunt*
Old MacDonald had a farm. *E I E I O*
   Old MacDonald, ill. by Rosemary Wells
   Old MacDonald had a farm, ill. by Holly Berry
   Old MacDonald had a farm, ill. by Lorinda Bryan Cauley
   Old MacDonald had a farm, ill. by Mel Crawford
   Old MacDonald had a farm, ill. by Tracey English
   Old MacDonald had a farm, ill. by David Frankland
   Old MacDonald had a farm, ill. by Abner Graboff
   Old MacDonald had a farm, ill. by Nancy Hellen
   Old MacDonald had a farm, ill. by Carol Jones
   Old MacDonald had a farm, ill. by Tracey Campbell Pearson
   Old MacDonald had a farm, ill. by Robert M. Quackenbush
   Old MacDonald had a farm, ill. by Glen Rounds
   Old McDonald had a farm, ill. by Iain Smith
   Old MacDonald had a farm, ill. by Jessica Souhami
   Old MacDonald had a farm, ill. by William Stobbs
   Old MacDonald had a farm, ill. by Prue Theobalds
Parks, Carmen. *Farmers market*
Peterson, Cris. *Extra cheese, please!*
Poskanzer, Susan Cornell. *Dairy farmer*
Powell, Consie. *Amazing apples*

Purmell, Ann. *Apple cider making days*
Riecken, Nancy. *Today is the day*
Sandburg, Carl (Charles August). *The Huckabuck family and how they raised popcorn in Nebraska and quit and came back*, ill. by David Small
Schomp, Virginia. *If you were a . . . farmer*
Scott, C. Anne (Cynthia Anne). *Old Jake's skirts*
Skrypuch, Marsha Forchuk. *Enough*
Slate, Joseph. *The great big wagon that rang*
Sloat, Teri. *The thing that bothered Farmer Brown*
Steig, William. *Wizzil*
Sugar snow
Tafuri, Nancy. *This is the farmer*
Taylor, Joanne. *Full moon rising*
Trottier, Maxine. *Prairie willow*
Van Leeuwen, Jean. *Nothing here but trees*
   Sorry
Waddell, Martin. *Farmer Duck*
   The pig in the pond
Ward, Nick. *Farmer George and the fieldmice*
   Farmer George and the hungry guests
   Farmer George and the lost chick
Waters, Jennifer. *Harvest time*
Wellington, Monica. *Apple farmer Annie*
Yee, Wong Herbert. *Fireman Small to the rescue*
Yolen, Jane. *The flying witch*
   Harvest home

Careers – firefighters

Averill, Esther. *The fire cat*
Barbaresi, Nina. *Firemouse*
Barkan, Joanne. *Whiskerville firehouse*
Barr, Jene. *Fire snorkel number 7*
Baumann, Kurt. *Piro and the fire brigade*
Bester, Roger. *Fireman Jim*
Bingham, Caroline. *Big book of rescue vehicles*
Boucher, Jerry. *Fire truck nuts and bolts*
Bourgeois, Paulette. *Fire fighters*
Bridwell, Norman. *Clifford's good deeds*
Brown, Margaret Wise. *Five little firemen*
   The little fireman
Bundt, Nancy. *The fire station book*
Bunting, Eve (Anne Evelyn). *On Call Back Mountain*
Bushey, Jerry. *Building a fire truck*
Carabine, Sue. *A firefighter's night before Christmas*
Chalmers, Mary. *Throw a kiss, Harry*
Child, Lauren. *Clarice Bean, guess who's babysitting?*
Curious George at the fire station
Cutlip, Kimbra L. *Firefighter's night before Christmas*
DeLage, Ida. *ABC fire dogs*
Demarest, Chris L. *Firefighters A to Z*
   Hotshots!
   Smokejumpers one to ten
Desimini, Lisa. *Dot the Firedog*
Dubois, Muriel L. *Out and about at the fire station*
Dubowski, Cathy East. *Fire engine to the rescue*
Elliott, Dan. *A visit to the Sesame Street firehouse*
Emergency!
Fast rolling fire trucks
Firehouse
Fisher, Leonard Everett. *Pumpers, boilers, hooks and ladders*
Flanagan, Alice K. *Ms. Murphy fights fires*
Fowler, Richard. *Mr. Little's noisy fire engine*
Fox, Christyan. *Fire fighter PiggyWiggy*
Gergely, Tibor. *The great big fire engine book*
Gibbons, Gail. *Fire! Fire!*
Gramatky, Hardie. *Hercules*
Greydanus, Rose. *Big red fire engine*
Hammar, Asa. *Fit for pigs*
Hanklin, Rebecca. *I can be a fire fighter*
Hansen, Jeff. *Being a fire fighter isn't just squirtin' water*
Hayward, Linda. *A day in the life of a firefighter*
Hill, Mary Lou. *My dad's a smokejumper*
Homme, Bob. *The friendly giant's book of fire engines*
Jane, Pamela. *Milo and the fire engine parade*
Jango-Cohen, Judith. *Fire trucks*

Kallen, Stuart A. *The fire station*
Keeping, Charles. *Willie's fire-engine*
Killingback, Julia. *Busy Bears at the fire station*
Klingel, Cynthia Fitterer. *Firefighters*
Kuklin, Susan. *Fighting fires*
Kunhardt, Edith. *I'm going to be a fire fighter*
Lenski, Lois. *The little fire engine*
Leonard, Marcia. *Jeffrey Lee, future fireman*
Lewison, Wendy Cheyette. *A trip to the firehouse*
Liebman, Daniel. *I want to be a firefighter*
Lukasewich, Lori. *The night fire*
Marston, Hope Irvin. *Fire trucks*
Martin, Ann M. *Fire truck to the rescue*
Martin, Bill (William Ivan). *Fire! Fire! said Mrs. McGuire*
Mayer, Mercer. *Fireman critter*
Mayo, Margaret. *Emergency!*
Mitton, Tony. *Flashing fire engines*
Morgan, Allen. *Matthew and the midnight firemen*
Munsch, Robert N. *The fire station*
Osborne, Mary Pope. *New York's bravest*
Owen, Ann (1953–). *Protecting your home*
Rex, Michael. *My fire engine*
Rey, H. A. (Hans Augusto). *Curious George*
    The original Curious George
Robinson, Nancy K. *Firefighters!*
Rockwell, Anne F. *At the firehouse*
    Fire engines
Royston, Angela. *Fire fighters*
Santoro, Scott. *Isaac the Ice Cream Truck*
Sis, Peter. *Fire truck*
Spiegel, Doris. *Danny and Company 92*
Spier, Peter. *Firehouse*
Steel, Danielle. *Max's daddy goes to the hospital*
Weiss, Harvey. *The sooner hound*
Wilson-Max, Ken. *Big red fire truck*
Winkleman, Katherine K. *Firehouse*
Woodworth, Viki. *Daisy the firecow*
Yee, Wong Herbert. *Fireman Small*
    Fireman Small, fire down below
    Fireman Small to the rescue
    A small Christmas
Zaffo, George J. *Big book of real fire engines*

Careers – fishermen

Adams, Jeanie. *Going for oysters*
Aldridge, Josephine Haskell. *Fisherman's luck*
Bateman, Teresa. *The merbaby*
Beim, Lorraine. *Lucky Pierre*
Bliss, Corinne Demas. *The boy who was generous with salt*
Brown, Marcia. *Henry fisherman*
Brown, Margaret Wise. *The little fisherman*
Bunting, Eve (Anne Evelyn). *Magic and the night river*
Demers, Dominique. *Old Thomas and the little fairy*
Dunbar, Joyce. *Indigo and the whale*
Edwards, Roberta. *Five silly fishermen*
Flora, James. *Fishing with dad*
Florian, Douglas. *A fisher*
Galchutt, David. *There was magic inside*
Garland, Sherry. *My father's boat*
Garne, S. T. *By a blazing blue sea*
Gibbons, Gail. *Surrounded by sea*
Gramatky, Hardie. *Nikos and the sea god*
Guiberson, Brenda Z. *Lobster boat*
Le Tord, Bijou. *Joseph and Nellie*
Lewin, Ted. *Nilo and the tortoise*
Love, Ann. *Fishing*
McGaw, Wayne T. *T-boy of the bayou*
Matsutani, Miyoko. *The fisherman under the sea*
Miles, Miska. *No, no, Rosina*
Mills, Patricia. *On an island in the bay*
Mitchell, Barbara. *Waterman's child*
Moxley, Susan. *Abdul's treasure*
Nakawatari, Harutaka. *The sea and I*
Napoli, Guillier. *Adventure at Mont-Saint-Michel*
Pallotta, Jerry. *Going lobstering*
Parker, Dorothy D. *Liam's catch*

Rettich, Margret. *The voyage of the jolly boat*
San Souci, Robert D. *Nicholas Pipe*
Sunami, Kitoba. *How the fisherman tricked the genie*
Tomlinson, Theresa. *Little stowaway*
Weil, Lisl. *Gertie and Gus*
Williams, Laura E. *Torch fishing with the sun*
Yolen, Jane. *Greyling*

Careers – forest rangers *see* Careers – park rangers

Careers – fortune tellers

Alexander, Lloyd. *Fortune tellers*
Jeschke, Susan. *Firerose*
Shepard, Aaron. *Forty fortunes*
Weiss, Ellen. *Clara the fortune-telling chicken*

Careers – garbage collectors *see* Careers – sanitation workers

Careers – geologists

Cole, Joanna. *The magic school bus inside the earth*
Sipiera, Paul P. *I can be a geologist*

Careers – handymen

Flanagan, Alice K. *Call Mr. Vasquez, he'll fix it!*
Mazer, Anne. *The Fixits*
Rockwell, Anne F. *Handy Hank will fix it*

Careers – harpists

Edwards, Pamela Duncan. *The leprechaun's gold*

Careers – hatters

Chetwin, Grace. *Box and Cox*

Careers – housekeepers

McKissack, Patricia C. *Ma Dear's aprons*
Widman, Christine. *Housekeeper of the wind*

Careers – illustrators

Browne, Anthony. *The shape game*
Krull, Kathleen. *The boy on Fairfield Street*
Locker, Thomas. *The man who paints nature*
Lynch, Wendy. *Dr. Seuss*
    Janet and Allan Ahlberg
Myers, Walter Dean. *Harlem*
Rau, Dana Meachen. *Dr. Seuss*
Steig, William. *When everybody wore a hat*
Whatley, Bruce. *Wait! No paint!*

Careers – inventors

Brill, Marlene Targ. *Margaret Knight, girl inventor*
Denslow, Sharon Phillips. *Radio boy*
Glass, Andrew. *The wondrous whirligig*
Himmelman, John. *The Clover County carrot contest*
    The super camper caper
Krensky, Stephen. *Ben Franklin and his first kite*
Lustig, Michael. *Willy Whyner, cloud designer*
Nettleton, Pamela Hill. *Benjamin Franklin*
Priceman, Marjorie. *It's me, Marva!*
Reynolds, Peter H. *Sydney's star*
Schaefer, Lola M. *The Wright brothers*
Schanzer, Rosalyn. *How Ben Franklin stole the lightning*
Taylor, Barbara. *I wonder why zippers have teeth and other questions about inventions*
Yolen, Jane. *My brothers' flying machine*

Careers – janitors *see* Careers – custodians, janitors

Careers – journalists

Hawkins, Colin. *Fairytale news*
Leedy, Loreen. *The Furry News*
Shea, Kitty. *Out and about at the newspaper*
Wishinsky, Frieda. *What's the matter with Albert?*

Careers – judges

Flanagan, Alice K. *A day in court with Mrs. Trinh*
Mirkovic, Irene. *The greedy shopkeeper*
Zemach, Harve. *The judge*

Careers – lawyers

Flanagan, Alice K. *A day in court with Mrs. Trinh*

Careers – librarians

Baggette, Susan K. *Jonathan goes to the library*
Baker, Donna. *I want to be a librarian*
Brillhart, Julie. *Story hour – starring Megan!*
Ernst, Lisa Campbell. *Stella Louella's runaway book*
Flanagan, Alice K. *Librarians*
    Ms. Davison, our librarian
Greene, Carol. *I can be a librarian*
Lakin, Pat (Patricia). *Information, please*
Liebman, Daniel. *I want to be a librarian*
Mann, Pamela. *The frog princess?*
Miller, Heather. *Librarian*
Mora, Pat. *Tomás and the library lady*
Pinkwater, Daniel Manus. *Aunt Lulu*
Porte, Barbara Ann. *Harry in trouble*
Radabaugh, Melinda Beth. *Going to the library*
Ruurs, Margriet. *Ms. Bee's magical bookcase*
Shea, Kitty. *Out and about at the public library*
Sierra, Judy. *Wild about books*
Stadler, Alexander. *Beverly Billingsly borrows a book*
Williams, Suzanne. *Library Lil*

Careers – lifeguards

Bingham, Caroline. *Big book of rescue vehicles*
Borden, Louise. *Albie the lifeguard*
Pinkwater, Daniel Manus. *At the Hotel Larry*
    Young Larry

Careers – lumberjacks

Balcziak, Bill. *Paul Bunyan*
Emberley, Barbara. *The story of Paul Bunyan*
Gleeson, Brian. *Paul Bunyan*
Hines, Gary. *The day of the high climber*
Kellogg, Steven (Stephen). *Paul Bunyan*
Lange, Willem. *John and Tom*
Lasky, Kathryn. *Marven of the Great North Woods*

Careers – magicians

Agee, Jon. *Milo's hat trick*
Ashman, Linda. *Maxwell's magic mix-up*
Bardill, Linard. *The great golden thing*
Geras, Adèle. *Swan Lake*
Graham, Bob. *Benny*
Grejniec, Michael. *Who is my neighbor?*
Hodges, Margaret. *Comus*
Howe, James. *Rabbit-Cadabra!*
Many, Paul. *The great pancake escape*
My first Raggedy Ann, Raggedy Ann and Andy and the nice police officer
Schneider, Christine M. *Horace P. Tuttle, magician extraordinaire*
Seeger, Pete. *Abiyoyo returns*

Careers – mail carriers *see* Careers – postal workers

Careers – mayors

Flanagan, Alice K. *Mayors*

Careers – mechanics

Aldag, Kurt. *Some things never change*
Augarde, Steve (Stephen). *Garage*
Broekel, Ray. *I can be an auto mechanic*
Dupasquier, Philippe. *A busy day at the garage*
Flanagan, Alice K. *Mr. Yee fixes cars*
Florian, Douglas. *An auto mechanic*
Kirk, Daniel. *Lucky's twenty-four hour garage*
Liebman, Daniel. *I want to be a mechanic*
Radford, Derek. *Harry at the garage*

Careers – messengers

Burleigh, Robert. *Messenger, messenger*

Careers – meteorologists

Bahr, Mary. *My brother loved snowflakes*
Kespert, Deborah. *Rain and shine*

Careers – migrant workers

Altman, Linda Jacobs. *Amelia's road*
Covault, Ruth M. *Pablo and Pimienta*
Dorros, Arthur. *Radio Man = Don Radio*
Hanson, Regina. *The tangerine tree*
Mora, Pat. *Tomás and the library lady*
Pérez, L. King. *First day in grapes*
Thomas, Jane Resh. *Lights on the river*
Williams, Sherley Anne. *Working cotton*

Careers – military

Ambrus, Victor G. *Brave soldier Janosch*
Aragon, Jane Chelsea. *The major and the mousehole mice*
Brown, Marcia. *Stone soup*
Bunting, Eve (Anne Evelyn). *The wall*
Chin, Charlie. *China's bravest girl*
Conrad, Pam. *The lost sailor*
Duble, Kathleen Benner. *Pilot mom*
Emberley, Barbara. *Drummer Hoff*
Hoff, Syd. *Captain Cat*
Jewell, Nancy. *Sailor song*
Kimmel, Eric A. *Billy Lazroe and the King of the Sea*
Langstaff, John M. *Soldier, soldier, won't you marry me?*
Lee, Jeanne M. *The song of Mu Lan*
Little, Mimi Otey. *Yoshiko and the foreigner*
Littlesugar, Amy. *Lisette's angel*
McGowen, Tom (Thomas). *The only glupmaker in the U.S. Navy*
McKinley, Robin. *My father is in the Navy*
Mahy, Margaret. *Sailor Jack and the twenty orphans*
Nettleton, Pamela Hill. *George Washington*
Pelton, Mindy L. *When Dad's at sea*
Van Rynbach, Iris. *The soup stone*

Careers – miners

Amsden, Janet. *Grizzly Pete and the ghosts*
Bartoletti, Susan Campbell. *Silver at night*
Brown, Margaret Wise. *Two little miners*
Eversole, Robyn Harbert. *The gift stone*
Harris, Marian. *Tuesday in Arizona*
Kay, Verla. *Gold fever*
Levitin, Sonia. *Boom town*
Lyon, George Ella. *Mama is a miner*
Nixon, Joan Lowery. *Fat chance, Claude*

Careers – models

Greene, Carol. *I can be a model*
Littlesugar, Amy. *Marie in fourth position*

Careers – motion picture producers

Brown, Don. *Mack made movies*

Careers – museum workers

L'Hommedieu, Arthur John. *Working at a museum*

Careers – musicians

Arrhenius, Peter. *The Penguin Quartet*
Battle-Lavert, Gwendolyn. *The music in Derrick's heart*
Birchman, David Francis. *A green horn blowing*
Brighton, Catherine. *Mozart*
Burleigh, Robert. *Lookin' for Bird in the big city*
Carter, Don. *Heaven's all-star jazz band*
Chocolate, Deborah M. Newton. *The piano man*
Christensen, Bonnie. *Woody Guthrie, poet of the people*
Cox, Judy. *My family plays music*
Cutler, Jane. *The cello of Mr. O*
DeFelice, Cynthia C. *Cold feet*
Dubois, Muriel L. *I like music: what can I be?*
Edwards, Julie Andrews. *Simeon's gift*
England, Linda. *The old cotton blues*
    3 kids dreamin'
Foreman, Michael. *Rock-a-doodle-do!*
Francis, Panama. *David gets his drum*
Gillmor, Don. *The fabulous song*
Grimm, Jacob. *The Bremen town band*
    The Bremen town musicians, ill. by Donna Diamond
    The Bremen town musicians, ill. by Bill Dickson
    The Bremen town musicians, ill. by Janina Domanska
    The Bremen town musicians, ill. by Paul Galdone
    The Bremen town musicians, ill. by David Johnson
    Bremen town musicians, ill. by Josef Palecek
    The Bremen town musicians, ill. by Ilse Plume
    The Bremen town musicians, ill. by Janet Stevens
    The Bremen town musicians, ill. by Bernadette Watts
    The musicians of Bremen, ill. by John Segal
    The musicians of Bremen, ill. by Svend Otto S
    The musicians of Bremen, ill. by Martin Ursell
    The traveling musicians of Bremen
Harranth, Wolf. *The flute concert*
Hoff, Syd. *Arturo's baton*
Isherwood, Shirley. *The band over the hill*
Johnson, Angela. *Violet's music*
Komaiko, Leah. *Broadway Banjo Bill*
Krementz, Jill. *A very young musician*
Leonard, Marcia. *Big Ben*
Liebman, Daniel. *I want to be a musician*
Linscott, Jody. *Once upon A to Z*
Lithgow, John. *The remarkable Farkle McBride*
London, Jonathan. *Hip cat*
McKee, David. *The sad story of Veronica who played the violin*
Martin, Bill (William Ivan). *Maestro plays*
Orgill, Roxane. *If I only had a horn*
Pinkney, Andrea Davis. *Duke Ellington*
Pinkwater, Daniel Manus. *Bongo Larry*
Poole, Valerie. *Obadiah Coffee and the music contest*
Price, Kathy (Kathy Z.). *The Bourbon Street musicians*
Raschka, Christopher. *Charlie Parker played be bop*
    Mysterious Thelonious
Ray, Mary Lyn. *Pianna*
Schomp, Virginia. *If you were a . . . musician*
Shepard, Aaron. *The sea king's daughter*
Troupe, Quincy. *Little Stevie Wonder*
Turner, Barbara J. *Out and about at the orchestra*
Ungerer, Tomi. *Tortoni Tremelo the cursed musician*
Weller, Frances Ward. *The angel of Mill Street*
Winter, Jeanette. *Once upon a time in Chicago*

Careers – nuns

Mora, Pat. *A library for Juana*
Norris, Kathleen. *The holy twins: Benedict and Scholastica*
Ransom, Candice F. *Mother Teresa*
Routh, Jonathan. *The Nuns go to Africa*

Careers – nurses

Arnold, Caroline. *Who keeps us healthy?*
Behrens, June. *I can be a nurse*
Davison, Martine. *Kevin and the school nurse*
Flanagan, Alice K. *Ask Nurse Pfaff, she'll help you!*
Greene, Carla. *Doctors and nurses*
Karim, Roberta. *This is a hospital, not a zoo!*
Kraus, Robert. *Rebecca Hatpin*
Lakin, Pat (Patricia). *The mystery illness*
Liebman, Daniel. *I want to be a nurse*
Schaefer, Lola M. *Hospital*
Stein, Sara Bonnett. *A hospital story*
Vickers, Rebecca. *Florence Nightingale*
Whitney, Alma Marshak. *Just awful*
Wohlrabe, Sarah C. *Helping you heal, a book about nurses*
Woolf, Virginia. *Nurse Lugton's curtain*

Careers – opera singers *see also* Careers – singers

Fleming, Candace. *Westward ho, Carlotta!*
Weaver, Tess. *Opera cat*

Careers – opticians, optometrists

Flanagan, Alice K. *Choosing eyeglasses with Mrs. Koutris*

Careers – organists

Ketcham, Sallie. *Bach's big adventure*

Careers – ornithologists

Davies, Jacqueline. *The boy who drew birds*

Careers – painters *see also* Activities – painting; Careers – artists

Flanagan, Alice K. *The Wilsons, a house-painting team*

Careers – paleontologists

Atkins, Jeannine. *Mary Anning and the sea dragon*
Barner, Bob. *Dinosaur bones*
Brown, Don. *Rare treasure*
Day, Marie. *Dragon in the rocks*
Hawcock, David. *Dinosaur hunt*

Careers – park rangers

Bunting, Eve (Anne Evelyn). *On Call Back Mountain*
Butterworth, Nick. *The rescue party*
    The secret path
Christian, Peggy. *Chocolate, a glacier grizzly*
Flanagan, Alice K. *Exploring parks with Ranger Dockett*
Greene, Carol. *I can be a forest ranger*
Hill, Mary Lou. *My dad's a park ranger*
Muller, Gerda. *Around the oak*

Careers – peddlers

Crossley-Holland, Kevin. *The pedlar of Swaffham*
DeGross, Monalisa. *Granddaddy's street songs*
DeLage, Ida. *Good morning, lady*
Derby, Sally. *Two fools and a horse*
Haley, Gail E. *Dream peddler*
Jacobs, Joseph. *The crock of gold*
Johnson, Angela. *The Rolling Store*
Lewis, J. Patrick. *The moonbow of Mr. B. Bones*
London, Sara. *Firehorse Max*
McDonald, Megan. *The potato man*
Miller, William. *Jenny and the peddler*
Rockwell, Anne F. *A bear, a bobcat and three ghosts*
Shefelman, Janice Jordan. *A peddler's dream*
Slobodkina, Esphyr. *Caps for sale*
    Circus caps for sale
    Pezzo the peddler and the circus elephant
    Pezzo the peddler and the thirteen silly thieves

Suba, Susanne. *The monkeys and the pedlar*
Waller, Barrett. *New feet for old*

Careers – pharmacists

Gibson, Karen Bush. *Pharmacists*

Careers – photographers

Bahr, Mary. *My brother loved snowflakes*
Bibbons, Faye. *The day the picture man came*
High, Linda Oatman. *The girl on the high-diving horse*
Johnson, Dinah. *All around town*
Martin, Jacqueline Briggs. *Snowflake Bentley*

Careers – physicians *see* Careers – doctors

Careers – plasterers

Carle, Eric. *My apron*

Careers – plumbers

Adinolfi, JoAnn. *Tina's diner*
Ahlberg, Allan. *Mrs. Plug the plumber*
Duvall, Jill. *Who keeps the water clean? Ms. Schindler!*
Morgan, Allen. *Matthew and the midnight flood*

Careers – poets

Burleigh, Robert. *Langston's train ride*
Gollub, Matthew. *Cool melons – turn to frogs*
Perdorno, Willie. *Visiting Langston*

Careers – police officers

Adelson, Leone. *Who blew that whistle?*
Ahlberg, Allan. *Cops and robbers*
Baker, Donna. *I want to be a police officer*
Bare, Colleen Stanley. *Sammy, dog detective*
Bourgeois, Paulette. *Police officers*
Braithwaite, Jill. *Police cars*
Brown, David. *Someone always needs a policeman*
Carter, Anne Laurel. *Under a prairie sky*
Chapin, Cynthia. *Squad car 55*
Chwast, Seymour. *Traffic jam*
Erdoes, Richard. *Policemen around the world*
Flanagan, Alice K. *Officer Brown keeps neighborhoods safe*
 Police officers
Goodall, John S. *Paddy's new hat*
Guilfoile, Elizabeth. *Have you seen my brother?*
Kallen, Stuart A. *The police station*
Keats, Ezra Jack. *My dog is lost!*
Kunhardt, Edith. *I'm going to be a police officer*
Lakin, Pat (Patricia). *Aware and alert*
Lattin, Anne. *Peter's policeman*
Lenski, Lois. *Policeman Small*
Liebman, Daniel. *I want to be a police officer*
McCloskey, Robert. *Make way for ducklings*
Mayer, Mercer. *Policeman critter*
My first Raggedy Ann, Raggedy Ann and Andy and the nice police officer
Numeroff, Laura Joffe. *Sherman Crunchley*
Owen, Ann (1953–). *Keeping you safe*
Rathmann, Peggy. *Officer Buckle and Gloria*
Russell, Joan Plummer. *Aero and Officer Mike*
Schaefer, Lola M. *Police station*
Schlein, Miriam. *The amazing Mr. Pelgrew*
Schomp, Virginia. *If you were a . . . police officer*
Smith, Janice Lee. *Jess and the stinky cowboys*
Stille, Darlene R. *Police cars*
Vreeken, Elizabeth. *The boy who would not say his name*
Yee, Wong Herbert. *The Officers' Ball*

Careers – postal workers

Ahlberg, Janet. *The jolly Christmas postman*
 The jolly pocket postman
 The jolly postman
Barkan, Joanne. *Whiskerville post office*
Beim, Jerrold. *Country mailman*
Boelts, Maribeth. *Grace and Joe*
Bourgeois, Paulette. *Postal workers*
Bradby, Marie. *The longest wait*
Brandt, Betty. *Special delivery*
Brill, Marlene Targ. *Bronco Charlie and the Pony Express*
Buchheimer, Naomi. *Let's go to a post office*
Carter, Don. *Send it!*
Craven, Carolyn. *What the mailman brought*
Cuneo, Mary Louise. *Mail for Husher Town*
Day, Alexandra. *Special deliveries*
Drummond, Violet H. *The flying postman*
Flanagan, Alice K. *Here comes Mr. Eventoff with the mail!*
 Letter carriers
Gibbons, Gail. *The post office book*
Glass, Andrew. *The sweetwater run*
Grindley, Sally. *The giant postman*
Haley, Gail E. *The post office cat*
Hedderwick, Mairi. *Katie Morag delivers the mail*
Henkes, Kevin. *Good-bye, Curtis*
Henri, Adrian. *The postman's palace*
Holabird, Katharine. *Angelina's Christmas*
Horning, Sandra. *The giant hug*
Kightley, Rosalinda. *The postman*
Klingel, Cynthia Fitterer. *Postal workers*
Koscielniak, Bruce. *Euclid Bunny delivers the mail*
Lakin, Pat (Patricia). *Red letter day*
Lillegard, Dee. *Tortoise brings the mail*
Marshak, S. (Samuil). *Hail to mail*
Maury, Inez. *My mother the mail carrier = Mi mama la cartera*
Morgan, Allen. *Matthew and the midnight ball game*
Owen, Ann (1953–). *Delivering your mail*
Pryor, Bonnie. *Mr. Munday and the space creatures*
Rylant, Cynthia. *Mr. Griggs' work*
Scarry, Richard. *Richard Scarry's all around Busytown*
 Richard Scarry's Postman Pig and his busy neighbors
Schneider, Howie. *Fast 'n Snappy*
Shea, Kitty. *Out and about at the post office*
Siracusa, Catherine. *No mail for Mitchell*
Skurzynski, Gloria. *Here comes the mail*
Spinelli, Eileen. *Somebody loves you, Mr. Hatch*
Tunnell, Michael O. *Mailing May*
Watts, Bernadette. *Harvey Hare, postman extraordinaire*
 Harvey Hare's Christmas

Careers – potters

Andrews-Goebel, Nancy. *The pot that Juan built*

Careers – preachers *see* Careers – clergy

Careers – principals *see* Careers – school principals

Careers – printers

Chetwin, Grace. *Box and Cox*
Edwards, Michelle. *Dora's book*
Fisher, Leonard Everett. *Gutenberg*
Monsell, Mary Elise. *Crackle Creek*
Nettleton, Pamela Hill. *Benjamin Franklin*

Careers – puppeteers

Poskanzer, Susan Cornell. *Puppeteer*

Careers – race car drivers

Rex, Michael. *My race car*
Wilkinson, Sylvia. *I can be a race car driver*

Careers – railroad engineers

Lenski, Lois. *The little train*
O'Brien, Patrick. *Steam, smoke, and steel*

Rex, Michael. *My freight train*

Careers – ranchers

Henderson, Kathy. *I can be a rancher*
Peterson, Cris. *Amazing grazing*

Careers – rangers *see* Careers – park rangers

Careers – sailors *see* Careers – military; Sailors

Careers – salesmen

Palatini, Margie. *Ding dong ding dong*

Careers – sanitation workers

Bourgeois, Paulette. *Garbage collectors*
Glaser, Linda. *Stop that garbage truck!*
Hartmann, Wendy. *All the magic in the world*
Kirk, Daniel. *Trash trucks!*
Maass, Robert. *Garbage*
McMullan, Kate (Hall). *I stink!*
Showers, Paul. *Where does the garbage go?*
Steig, William. *Tiffky Doofky*
Testa, Fulvio. *Too much garbage*
Zimmerman, Andrea Griffing. *Trashy town*
Zion, Gene. *Dear garbage man*

Careers – school principals

Calmenson, Stephanie. *The frog principal*
    The principal's new clothes
Cocca-Leffler, Maryann. *Mr. Tanen's ties*
Creech, Sharon. *A fine, fine school*
Dakos, Kalli. *Our principal promised to kiss a pig*
Polacco, Patricia. *Mr. Lincoln's way*
Poydar, Nancy. *First day, hooray!*

Careers – scientists

Accorsi, William. *Rachel Carson*
Brown, Don. *Odd boy out*
Chambers, Roland. *Rooftop rocket party*
Elliott, David. *Hazel Nutt, mad scientist*
James, Brian. *Supertwins meet the dangerous dino-robots*
Krensky, Stephen. *Ben Franklin and his first kite*
Lehn, Barbara. *What is a scientist?*
Martin, Jacqueline Briggs. *Snowflake Bentley*
Nettleton, Pamela Hill. *Benjamin Franklin*
O'Connor, Teddy. *A new brain for Igor*
Schanzer, Rosalyn. *How Ben Franklin stole the lightning*
Weston, Martha. *The dinosaurs meet Dr. Clock*
Wishinsky, Frieda. *What's the matter with Albert?*

Careers – sculptors

Schaefer, A. R. (Adam Richard). *Alexander Calder*
Stevenson, Harvey. *Looking at liberty*

Careers – seamstresses

Brown, Margaret Wise. *Bunny's noisy book*
    Bunny's noisy book [board book]
Chevance, Audrey. *Tutu*
Olds, Helen Diehl. *Miss Hattie and the monkey*

Careers – shepherds

Ada, Alma Flor. *Jordi's star*
Aichinger, Helga. *The shepherd*
Ben-´Ezer, Ehud. *Hosni the dreamer*
Calhoun, Mary. *A shepherd's gift*
Eversole, Robyn Harbert. *Red berry wool*
Gantschev, Ivan. *The moon lake*
Garaway, Margaret Kahn. *Ashkii and his grandfather*
Guarnieri, Paolo. *A boy named Giotto*

Levine, Gail Carson. *Betsy who cried wolf*
Lewis, Kim. *The shepherd boy*
Mills, Claudia. *One small lost sheep*
Safran, Sheri. *The musical cherub*
Wellington, Monica. *The sheep follow*

Careers – sheriffs

Yorinks, Arthur. *Whitefish Will rides again*

Careers – shoe shiners

Quattlebaum, Mary. *The shine man*

Careers – shoemakers

Aiken, Joan. *The shoemaker's boy*
Dollinger, Renate. *The rabbi who flew*
Gilbert, Helen Earle. *Mr. Plum and the little green tree*
Grimm, Jacob. *The elves and the shoemaker*, ill. by Doug Cushman
    The elves and the shoemaker, ill. by Paul Galdone
    The elves and the shoemaker, ill. by Margaret Walty
    The elves and the shoemaker, ill. by Bernadette Watts
    The shoemaker and his elves, ill. by Bill Dickson
    The shoemaker and the elves, ill. by Adrienne Adams
    The shoemaker and the elves, ill. by Cynthia and William Birrer
    The shoemaker and the elves, ill. by Ilse Plume
Hodges, Margaret. *The hero of Bremen*
Johnson, Grace. *The candle in the window*
Lieberman, Syd. *The wise shoemaker of Studena*
Light, Steve. *The shoemaker extraordinaire*
Lowell, Susan. *The bootmaker and the elves*
Madonna. *Yakov and the seven thieves*
Oppenheim, Joanne. *Left and right*
Prose, Francine. *You never know*
Ross, Tony. *The greedy little cobbler*
San Souci, Robert D. *The red heels*
Sheldon, Aure. *Of cobblers and kings*

Careers – sign painters

Roth, Roger. *The sign painter's dream*

Careers – singers *see also* Careers – opera singers

Fisher, Mary M. *Rosita's bridge*
Littlesugar, Amy. *Shake Rag*
McKissack, Patricia C. *Paul Robeson*

Careers – soldiers *see* Careers – military

Careers – storekeepers

Asch, Frank. *George's store*
Carling, Amelia Lau. *Mama and Papa have a store*
Flanagan, Alice K. *A busy day at Mr. Kang's grocery store*
    Buying a pet from Ms. Chavez
    Choosing eyeglasses with Mrs. Koutris
Fleming, Candace. *The hatmaker's sign*
Heo, Yumi. *Father's rubber shoes*
Kimmelman, Leslie. *Frannie's fruits*
Melmed, Laura Krauss. *The Marvelous Market on Mermaid*
Pearson, Tracey Campbell. *The storekeeper*
Schaefer, Lola M. *Supermarket*
Shea, Kitty. *Out and about at the supermarket*
Shefelman, Janice Jordan. *A peddler's dream*
Shelby, Anne. *We keep a store*
Wisniewski, David. *Sumo Mouse*

Careers – tailors

Ackerman, Karen. *Just like Max*
Ambrus, Victor G. *The three poor tailors*
Armstrong, Jennifer. *Pockets*
Calmenson, Stephanie. *The principal's new clothes*
Galdone, Paul. *The monster and the tailor*
Green, Stephanie. *Betsy Ross and the silver thimble*

Grimm, Jacob. *The brave little tailor*, ill. by Mark Corcoran
   The brave little tailor, ill. by Olga Dugina & Andrej Dugin
   The brave little tailor, ill. by Daniel San Souci
   The brave little tailor, ill. by David Shaw
   The brave little tailor, ill. by Svend Otto S
   The brave little tailor, ill. by Eve Tharlet
   The brave little tailor, ill. by James Warhola
   Seven at one blow
   The valiant little tailor
Hest, Amy. *The purple coat*
Hilton, Nette. *Dirty Dave*
Osborne, Mary Pope. *The brave little seamstress*
Potter, Beatrix. *The tailor of Gloucester*
Sanfield, Steve. *Bit by bit*
Schotter, Roni. *Dreamland*
West, Colin. *I brought my love a tabby cat*
Yorinks, Arthur. *Oh, brother*

Careers – taxi drivers

Moore, Lilian. *Papa Albert*
Ross, Jessica. *Ms. Klondike*
Svend Otto S (Svend Otto Sorensen). *Taxi dog*

Careers – teachers

Allard, Harry. *Miss Nelson is back*
   Miss Nelson is missing!
Amper, Thomas. *Booker T. Washington*
Arnold, Caroline. *Where do you go to school?*
Barkan, Joanne. *Whiskerville school*
Beckman, Beatrice. *I can be a teacher*
Bognomo, Joel Eboueme. *Madoulina*
Borden, Louise. *Good luck, Mrs. K!*
Brandt, Amy. *When Katie was our teacher = Cuando Katie era muestra maestra*
Brenner, Emily. *On the first day of grade school*
Brillhart, Julie. *Anna's goodbye apron*
Brown, Marc Tolon. *Arthur's teacher moves in*
Bunting, Eve (Anne Evelyn). *Our teacher's having a baby*
Calmenson, Stephanie. *The teeny tiny teacher*
Cole, Joanna. *The magic school bus in the time of the dinosaurs*
   The magic school bus inside a beehive
   The magic school bus lost in the solar system
   The magic school bus on the ocean floor
Cummings, W. T. (Walter Thies). *Miss Esta Maude's secret*
Daniel, Kira. *Teacher*
Danneberg, Julie. *First day jitters*
   First year letters
Denslow, Sharon Phillips. *On the trail with Miss Pace*
Feder, Paula Kurzband. *Where does the teacher live?*
Figley, Marty Rhodes. *The schoolchildren's blizzard*
Finchler, Judy. *Miss Malarkey won't be in today*
   Testing Miss Malarkey
   You're a good sport, Miss Malarkey
Flanagan, Alice K. *Learning is fun with Mrs. Perez*
   Teachers
Garland, Michael. *Miss Smith's incredible storybook*
Glennon, Karen M. *Miss Eva and the red balloon*
Greene, Carol. *Teachers help us learn*
Hallinan, P. K. (Patrick K.). *My teacher's my friend*
Havill, Juanita. *Jamaica and the substitute teacher*
Hayward, Linda. *A day in the life of a teacher*
Henkes, Kevin. *Lilly's purple plastic purse*
Houston, Gloria. *My Great-Aunt Arizona*
James, Simon. *Dear Mr. Blueberry*
Johnson, Doug. *Substitute teacher plans*
Johnson, Jean. *Teachers A to Z*
Kraus, Robert. *Good morning, Miss Gator*
Krensky, Stephen. *My teacher's secret life*
Lehn, Barbara. *What is a teacher?*
Liebman, Daniel. *I want to be a teacher*
Linch, Tanya. *My duck*
Lorbiecki, Marybeth. *Sister Anne's hands*
McKissack, Patricia C. *Booker T. Washington*
McKissack, Robert L. *Try your best*
Marshall, James. *Eugene*

Marzollo, Jean. *Shanna's teacher show*
Munsch, Robert N. *Thomas' snowsuit*
Myers, Bernice. *It happens to everyone*
Nolen, Jerdine. *Plantzilla*
Paraskevas, Betty. *Gracie Graves and the kids from room 402*
Passen, Lisa. *Attack of the 50-foot teacher*
   The incredible shrinking teacher
Pattou, Edith. *Mrs. Spitzer's garden*
Polacco, Patricia. *Thank you, Mr. Falker*
Powers, Mary E. *Our teacher's in a wheelchair*
Poydar, Nancy. *First day, hooray!*
Priceman, Marjorie. *Emeline at the circus*
Pulver, Robin. *Mrs. Toggle and the dinosaur*
   Mrs. Toggle's beautiful blue shoe
   Mrs. Toggle's zipper
Radabaugh, Melinda Beth. *Going to school*
Reynolds, Marilynn. *The magnificent piano recital*
Roche, Denis (Denis M.). *The best class picture ever*
Schomp, Virginia. *If you were a . . . teacher*
Tabor, Nancy (Maria Grande). *Bottles break*
Teyssèdre, Fabienne. *Joseph wants to read*
Vande Velde, Vivian. *Troll teacher*
Weiss, Leatie. *My teacher sleeps in school*
Wheatley, Nadia. *Luke's way of looking*
Wilson, Troy. *Perfect man*
Wohlrabe, Sarah C. *Helping you learn, a book about teachers*
Wood, Douglas. *What teachers can't do*

Careers – telephone operators

Allen, Jeffrey. *Mary Alice, operator number 9*
   Mary Alice returns

Careers – toy makers

Gallaz, Christophe. *Threadbear*
Geras, Adèle. *The nutcracker*
Hague, Michael. *The nutcracker*
Hoffmann, E. T. A. *The nutcracker*, ill. by Francesca Crespi
   The nutcracker, ill. by Renée Graef
   The nutcracker, ill. by Rachel Isadora
   The nutcracker, ill. by Joanna Isles
   The nutcracker, ill. by Maurice Sendak
   The nutcracker, ill. by Lisbeth Zwerger
   The nutcracker ballet, ill. by Carolyn Ewing
   The nutcracker ballet, ill. by Vladimir Vasilévich Vagin
McMullan, Kate (Hall). *Nutcracker Noel*
Thurber, James. *The great Quillow*
Waddell, Martin. *The toymaker*

Careers – train engineers *see* Careers – railroad engineers

Careers – truck drivers

Behrens, June. *I can be a truck driver*
Cartlidge, Michelle. *Teddy trucks*
Cowley, Joy. *Gracias, the Thanksgiving turkey*
Day, Alexandra. *Frank and Ernest on the road*
Gibson, Karen Bush. *Truck drivers*
Horenstein, Henry. *Sam goes trucking*
Liebman, Daniel. *I want to be a truck driver*
Mitchell, Joyce Slayton. *Tractor-trailer trucker*
Royston, Angela. *Truck trouble*
Schomp, Virginia. *If you were a . . . truck driver*
Sturges, Philemon. *I love trucks!*
Young, Miriam Burt. *If I drove a truck*

Careers – veterinarians

Bellville, Rod. *Large animal veterinarians*
Coffey, Maria. *A seal in the family*
Dodd, Lynley. *Hairy Maclary's rumpus at the vet*
Dubois, Muriel L. *I like animals: what can I be?*
Flanagan, Alice K. *Dr. Friedman helps animals*
Gibbons, Gail. *Say woof!*
Herriot, James. *Moses the kitten*
   Only one woof

Hewett, Joan. *Fly away free*
Hull, Rod. *Mr. Betts and Mr. Potts*
Kuklin, Susan. *Taking my dog to the vet*
Kunhardt, Edith. *I'm going to be a vet*
Lee, Chinlun. *Good dog, Paw*
Leonard, Marcia. *The pet vet*
Liebman, Daniel. *I want to be a vet*
Lumley, Katheryn Wentzel. *I can be an animal doctor*
Martin, C. L. G. *Down Dairy Farm Road*
Owen, Ann (1953–). *Caring for your pet*
Perkins, Lynne Rae. *The broken cat*
Polhamus, Jean Burt. *Doctor Dinosaur*
Raatma, Lucia. *Veterinarians*
Schomp, Virginia. *If you were a . . . veterinarian*
Shea, Kitty. *Out and about at the vet clinic*

Careers – waiters, waitresses

Ahlberg, Allan. *Mrs. Wobble the waitress*
Krementz, Jill. *Benjy goes to a restaurant*
Loomis, Christine. *In the diner*
Mooser, Stephen. *Funnyman's first case*
Moss, Marissa. *Mel's diner*
Peters, Sharon. *Happy Jack*
Radabaugh, Melinda Beth. *Going to a restaurant*

Careers – weather reporters *see* Careers – meteorologists

Careers – weavers

Musgrove, Margaret. *The spider weaver*
Wilhelm, Hans. *All for the best*

Careers – welders

Lillegard, Dee. *I can be a welder*

Careers – whalers

Drummond, Allan. *Moby Dick*

Careers – window cleaners

Dahl, Roald. *The giraffe and the pelly and me*
Rey, H. A. (Hans Augusto). *Curious George takes a job*
Thiesing, Lisa. *The Viper*

Careers – woodcarvers

Cohn, Diana. *Dream carver*
Dorros, Arthur. *Julio's magic*
Rosen, Michael J. (1954–). *Elijah's angel*
Steven, Kenneth C. *The bearer of gifts*
Wojciechowski, Susan. *The Christmas miracle of Jonathan Toomey*

Careers – writers

Broekel, Ray. *I can be an author*
Brown, Margaret Wise. *The days before now*
Christelow, Eileen. *What do authors do?*
Corpi, Lucha. *Where fireflies dance = Ahí, donde bailan las luciérnagas*
Davidson, Rebecca Piatt. *All the world's a stage*
Edwards, Michelle. *Dora's book*
Findon, Joanne. *Auld lang syne*
Goffstein, M. B. (Marilyn Brooke). *A writer*
Harness, Cheryl. *Mark Twain and the queens of the Mississippi*
Hurwitz, Johanna. *A dream come true*
Johnson, Jane. *My dear Noel*
Lester, Helen. *Author*
London, Jonathan. *Tell me a story*
Lyon, George Ella. *A sign*
Muntean, Michaela. *Kermit and Robin's scary story*
Rylant, Cynthia. *Best wishes*
Schotter, Roni. *Nothing ever happens on 90th Street*
Stevenson, James. *Fun, no fun*
   I meant to tell you
Wallner, Alexandra. *Beatrix Potter*

Wilson, Troy. *Perfect man*

Careers – zookeepers

Goodman, Susan E. *What do you do – at the zoo?*
Knight, Bertram T. *Working at a zoo*
Liebman, Daniel. *I want to be a zookeeper*
Löfgren, Ulf. *Alvin the zookeeper*
Lyon, George Ella. *Mother to tigers*
Miller, Heather. *Zookeeper*
Rathmann, Peggy. *Good night, Gorilla*
Schomp, Virginia. *If you were a . . . zookeeper*

Carelessness *see* Behavior – carelessness

Caribbean Islands *see* Foreign lands – Caribbean Islands

Caribou *see* Animals – reindeer

Carnivals *see* Fairs

Carousels *see* Merry-go-rounds

Carpenters *see* Careers – carpenters

Carrier Indians *see* Indians of North America – Carrier

Cars *see* Automobiles

Cartographers *see* Careers – cartographers

Castles

Allen, Laura Jean. *Rollo and Tweedy and the ghost of Dougal Castle*
Anawalt, Paula Bonnier. *The crystal palace*
Brunhoff, Laurent de. *Babar and the ghost*
Clavel, Bernard. *Castle of books*
Crebbin, June. *Into the castle*
Duquennoy, Jacques. *The ghosts in the cellar*
Dürr, Ursula. *The secret of Trembleton Hall*
Gabler, Mirko. *Brakus, Krakus . . . Or the incredible adventure of Mr. Skola's Tourist Club*
Hawkins, Colin. *Creepy castle*
Krensky, Stephen. *We just moved!*
Leonard, Marcia. *King Lionheart's castle*
Love, Ann. *Ice cream at the castle*
Oberman, Sheldon. *The white stone in the castle wall*
Walton, Rick. *Pig, Pigger, Piggest*
Yee, Brenda Shannon. *Sand castle*

Caterpillars *see* Insects – butterflies, caterpillars

Cats *see* Animals – cats

Cave drawings *see* Petroglyphs

Cavemen

Baylor, Byrd. *One small blue bead*
Hoff, Syd. *Stanley*
Seyton, Marion. *The hole in the hill*
Slobodkin, Louis. *Dinny and Danny*
Wood, Audrey. *The Tickleoctopus*

Caves

Baynes, Pauline. *How dog began*
Brett, Jan. *The first dog*
Day, Marie. *Quennu and the cave bear*
DeLage, Ida. *The old witch and the snores*
Galko, Francine. *Cave animals*
Galloway, Ruth. *Fidgety fish*
Harrison, David Lee. *Caves*
Pfister, Marcus. *Rainbow fish and the sea monsters' cave*

Rau, Dana Meachen. *Explore in a cave*
Siebert, Diane. *Cave*
Taylor, Harriet Peck. *Secrets of the stone*
Tettelbaum, Michael. *The cave of the lost Fraggle*
Ungerer, Tomi. *The Mellops go spelunking*

Cellos *see* Musical instruments – cellos

Centipedes *see* Crustaceans – centipedes, millipedes

Central America *see* Foreign lands – Central America

Cerebral palsy *see* Handicaps – cerebral palsy

Chairs *see* Furniture – chairs

Chameleons *see* Reptiles – chameleons

Change *see* Concepts – change

Chanukah *see* Holidays – Hanukkah

Character traits

Buehner, Caralyn. *I did it, I'm sorry*
Burdett, Lois. *Twelfth night*
Johnson, Crockett. *The emperor's gifts*
Seignobosc, Françoise. *Jeanne-Marie in gay Paris*
Wahl, Jan. *Mrs. Owl and Mr. Pig*
Walker, Alice. *Finding the green stone*
Wilson-Kelly, Becky. *Mother Grumpy's dog biscuits*

Character traits – ambition

Balet, Jan B. *Joanjo*
Barton, Byron. *I want to be an astronaut*
Chottin, Ariane. *Beaver gets lost*
Claude-Lafontaine, Pascale. *Monsieur Bussy, the celebrated hamster*
Dunrea, Olivier. *The painter who loved chickens*
Evans, Richard Paul. *The spyglass*
Graham, Al. *Timothy Turtle*
Gramatky, Hardie. *Little Toot*
Greaves, Margaret. *Henry's wild morning*
Herman, R. A. (Ronnie Ann). *Pal the pony*
Horwitz, Elinor Lander. *Sometimes it happens*
Kumin, Maxine W. *Speedy digs downside up*
Lester, Helen. *Score one for the sloths*
Pavlova, Anna. *I dreamed I was a ballerina*
Ringi, Kjell (Arne Sorensen). *My father and I*
Root, Phyllis. *Sam, who was swallowed by a shark*
Seignobosc, Françoise. *What do you want to be?*
Shecter, Ben. *Hester the jester*
Shefelman, Janice Jordan. *A peddler's dream*
Spirin, Gennady. *Philipok*
Turska, Krystyna. *The magician of Cracow*
Uchida, Yoshiko. *Sumi's prize*

Character traits – appearance

Andersen, H. C. (Hans Christian). *The ugly duckling*, ill. by Adrienne Adams
   The ugly duckling, ill. by Lorinda Bryan Cauley
   The ugly duckling, ill. by Charlene DeLage
   The ugly duckling, ill. by Troy Howell
   The ugly duckling, ill. by Tadasu Izawa and Shigemi Hijikata
   The ugly duckling, ill. by Monika Laimgruber
   The ugly duckling, ill. by Johannes Larsen
   The ugly duckling, ill. by Thomas Locker
   The ugly duckling, ill. by Alan Marks
   The ugly duckling, ill. by Josef Palecek
   The ugly duckling, ill. by Jerry Pinkney
   The ugly duckling, ill. by Maria Ruis
   The ugly duckling, ill. by Daniel San Souci
   The ugly duckling, ill. by Meilo So
   The ugly duckling, ill. by Robert Van Nutt

   The ugly duckling, ill. by Bernadette Watts
   The ugly little duck, ill. by Peggy Perry Anderson
Asch, Frank. *I can blink*
Balestrino, Philip. *Fat and skinny*
Beim, Jerrold. *Freckle face*
Bonsall, Crosby Newell. *Listen, listen!*
Boyle, Vere. *Beauty and the beast*
Butterworth, Nick. *Making faces*
Carter, Anne Laurel. *Beauty and the beast*
Caseley, Judith. *Molly Pink goes hiking*
Charles, Donald. *Shaggy dog's Halloween*
   Ugly bug
Chevalier, Christa. *Spence isn't Spence anymore*
Cohen, Burton. *Nelson makes a face*
Collins, Judith Graham. *Josh's scary dad*
Crowley, Arthur. *The ugly book*
Dellinger, Annetta. *You are special to Jesus*
De Paola, Tomie (Thomas Anthony). *Big Anthony and the magic ring*
Eco, Umberto. *The three astronauts*
Edwards, Lisa. *Disney's Beauty and the beast, a book of manners*
Elborn, Andrew. *Big Al*
   Bird Adalbert
Fatio, Louise. *The happy lion and the bear*
Freeman, Don. *Dandelion*
Ginsburg, Mirra. *The Chinese mirror*
Girion, Barbara. *The boy with the special face*
Goble, Paul. *Star boy*
Greenfield, Eloise. *Grandpa's face*
Hale, Irina. *Brown bear in a brown chair*
Heine, Helme. *The most wonderful egg in the world*
Hillert, Margaret. *The funny baby*
Hutton, Warwick. *Beauty and the beast*
Iké, Jane Hori. *A Japanese fairy tale*
Joly, Fanny. *Mr. Fine, porcupine*
Kasza, Keiko. *The pigs' picnic*
Keller, Irene. *The Thingumajig book of manners*
Lieberman, Syd. *The wise shoemaker of Studena*
Lindenbaum, Pija. *Boodil, my dog*
McDermott, Gerald. *The magic tree*
Maestro, Betsy. *On the town*
Mayer, Marianna. *Beauty and the beast*
Mayer, Mercer. *How the trollusk got his hat*
Moore, Sheila. *Samson Svenson's baby*
Munsch, Robert N. *Makeup mess*
   The paper bag princess
   Stephanie's ponytail
Myers, Amy. *I know a monster*
Nesbit, Edith. *Beauty and the beast*
Ness, Evaline. *The girl and the goatherd*
Numeroff, Laura Joffe. *Amy for short*
   Why a disguise?
Ormerod, Jan. *Just like me*
   Our Ollie
   Silly goose
Ormondroyd, Edward. *Theodore*
Otto, Carolyn. *What color is camouflage?*
Palatini, Margie. *Piggie pie*
Paraskevas, Betty. *The tangerine bear*
Park, Ruth. *When the wind changed*
Pfister, Marcus. *The rainbow fish*
   Rainbow fish to the rescue!
Primavera, Elise. *Basil and Maggie*
Quinsey, Mary Beth. *Why does that man have such a big nose?*
Ring, Elizabeth. *Tiger lilies and other beastly plants*
Salus, Naomi Panush. *My daddy's mustache*
Schaffer, Libor. *Arthur sets sail*
Scott, Natalie (Anderson). *Firebrand, push your hair out of your eyes*
Small, David. *Imogene's antlers*
Stern, Ellen. *I saw a bullfrog*
Stren, Patti. *Mountain Rose*
Thomson, Peggy. *The king has horse's ears*
Willis, Jeanne. *What did I look like when I was a baby?*
Wright, Freire. *Beauty and the beast*
Yep, Laurence. *The city of dragons*

Character traits – assertiveness

Dunbar, Joyce. *A cake for Barney*
Ingoglia, Gina. *The art class*
Lindgren, Astrid. *Pippi Longstocking's after-Christmas party*
Martchenko, Michael. *Bird feeder banquet*
Moss, Marissa. *After-school monster*
Winthrop, Elizabeth. *I'm the Boss!*

Character traits – being different

Aggs, Patrice. *The visitor*
Alborough, Jez. *Cuddly Dudley*
Allinson, Beverley. *Effie*
Andersen, H. C. (Hans Christian). *The ugly duckling*, ill. by Adrienne Adams
    The ugly duckling, ill. by Lorinda Bryan Cauley
    The ugly duckling, ill. by Charlene DeLage
    The ugly duckling, ill. by Troy Howell
    The ugly duckling, ill. by Tadasu Izawa and Shigemi Hijikata
    The ugly duckling, ill. by Monika Laimgruber
    The ugly duckling, ill. by Johannes Larsen
    The ugly duckling, ill. by Thomas Locker
    The ugly duckling, ill. by Alan Marks
    The ugly duckling, ill. by Josef Palecek
    The ugly duckling, ill. by Jerry Pinkney
    The ugly duckling, ill. by Maria Ruis
    The ugly duckling, ill. by Daniel San Souci
    The ugly duckling, ill. by Meilo So
    The ugly duckling, ill. by Robert Van Nutt
    The ugly duckling, ill. by Bernadette Watts
    The ugly little duck, ill. by Peggy Perry Anderson
Arnold, Tedd. *Green Wilma*
Aulaire, Ingri Mortenson d'. *Nils*
Baumann, Hans. *Mischa and his brothers*
Beim, Jerrold. *Freckle face*
Blos, Joan W. *Old Henry*
Blue, Rose. *I am here = Yo estoy aqui*
Brandenberg, Franz. *Otto is different*
Brightman, Alan. *Like me*
Brown, Margaret Wise. *Robin's room*
Burningham, John. *Borka*
Cannon, Janell. *Stellaluna*
    Stellaluna: a pop-up book and mobile
Caple, Kathy. *The biggest nose*
Carle, Eric. *The mixed-up chameleon*
Carrick, Carol. *Two very little sisters*
Chapman, Elizabeth. *Suzy*
Cibula, Matt S. *The contrary kid*
Clément, Claude. *The hungry duckling*
Cohen, Miriam. *It's George!*
Coombs, Patricia. *The lost playground*
Corbalis, Judy. *Porcellus, the flying pig*
Counsel, June. *But Martin!*
Crossley-Holland, Kevin. *The green children*
De Veaux, Alexis. *An enchanted hair tale*
Dinan, Carolyn. *Say cheese!*
Drescher, Henrik. *The strange appearance of Howard Cranebill, Jr.*
Dubanevich, Arlene. *Pigs at Christmas*
Duvoisin, Roger Antoine. *Our Veronica goes to Petunia's farm*
    Veronica
Emberley, Ed (Edward Randolph). *Rosebud*
Escudie, René. *Paul and Sebastian*
Fern, Eugene. *Pepito's story*
Fleming, Denise. *Mama cat has three kittens*
Frieden, Sarajo. *The care and feeding of fish*
Garcia, Carolyn. *Moonboy*
Hayes, Sarah. *Mary Mary*
Heine, Helme. *Superhare*
Hennessy, B. G. (Barbara G.). *Meet Winslow whale*
Hillert, Margaret. *The funny baby*
Hoff, Syd. *Mrs. Brice's mice*
Imai, Miko. *Lilly's secret*
Jeram, Anita. *Daisy Dare*
Johnson, D. B. (Donald B.). *Henry climbs a mountain*
Kaczman, James. *A bird and his worm*
Karlin, Nurit. *The blue frog*

Keller, Holly. *Horace*
Krasilovsky, Phyllis. *The very tall little girl*
Kuklin, Susan. *Thinking big*
Leech, Bryan Jeffery. *John Jeremy Colton*
Leedy, Loreen. *Pingo the plaid panda*
Lerner, Marguerite Rush. *Lefty, the story of left-handedness*
Levine, Rhoda. *Harrison loved his umbrella*
Lionni, Leo. *Cornelius*
McGovern, Ann. *Mr. Skinner's skinny house*
Machado, Ana Maria. *Nina Bonita*
McKee, David. *Elmer*
McKelvey, David. *Bobby the mostly silky*
Mills, Lauren A. *Fin and the imp*
Modarressi, Mitra. *The beastly visits*
Mora, Pat. *The rainbow tulip*
Moser, Madeline. *Ever heard of an aardwolf?*
Murphy, Pat. *Pigasus*
Myers, Christopher A. *Wings*
Nanji, Shenaaz. *An alien in my house*
Nimmo, Jenny. *Something wonderful*
Nones, Eric Jon. *Angela's wings*
Nordlicht, Lillian. *I love to laugh*
Novak, Matt. *Little Wolf, Big Wolf*
O'Connor, Jane. *Snail City*
Ostrow, Vivian. *My brother is from outer space*
Paek, Min. *Aekyung's dream*
Passen, Lisa. *Fat, fat Rose Marie*
Payne, Sherry Neuwirth. *A contest*
Peet, Bill (William Bartlett). *The spooky tail of Prewitt Peacock*
Polacco, Patricia. *I can hear the sun*
Polisar, Barry Louis. *The trouble with Ben*
Quinsey, Mary Beth. *Why does that man have such a big nose?*
Rankin, Joan. *You're somebody special, Walliwigs!*
Reesink, Marijke. *The princess who always ran away*
Reidy, Hannah. *Crazy creature contrasts*
Rey, Margret (Margret Elisabeth Waldstein). *Spotty*
Riddell, Chris. *Bird's new shoes*
Rohmann, Eric. *Pumpkinhead*
Rubinetti, Donald. *Cappy the lonely camel*
Sansone, Adele. *The little green goose*
Schertle, Alice. *Jeremy Bean's St. Patrick's Day*
Schotter, Roni. *Captain Snap and the children of Vinegar Lane*
Sharmat, Marjorie Weinman. *Helga high-up*
Shles, Larry. *Moths and mothers, feathers and fathers*
Shub, Elizabeth. *Dragon Franz*
Simon, Francesca. *The Topsy-Turvies*
Simon, Norma. *Why am I different?*
Simon, Sidney B. *The armadillo who had no shell*
Slyder, Ingrid. *The Fabulous Flying Fandinis*
Stapler, Sarah. *Cordellia, dance!*
Sweeney, Jacqueline. *What about Bettie?*
Thurber, James. *The great Quillow*
Uegaki, Chieri. *Suki's kimono*
Voake, Charlotte. *Mrs. Goose's baby*
Wadhams, Margaret. *Anna*
Wallace, Barbara Brooks. *Argyle*
Wallace, Ivy. *Pookie*
Walsh, Ellen Stoll. *For Pete's sake*
Watt, Mélanie. *Leon the chameleon*
Weedn, Flavia. *The enchanted tree*
Wells, Rosemary. *Abdul*
Whitcomb, Mary E. *Odd Velvet*
Whitmore, Adam. *Max in America*
    Max in Australia
    Max in India
    Max leaves home
Wilkon, Piotr. *Rosie the cool cat*
Willis, Jeanne. *The long blue blazer*
Wood, Audrey. *Weird parents*
Yep, Laurence. *The city of dragons*

Character traits – bravery

Aitken, Amy. *Ruby, the red knight*
Alborough, Jez. *There's something at the mail slot*
Aliki. *George and the cherry tree*

Andersen, H. C. (Hans Christian). *The snow queen*, ill. by Angela Barrett
  The snow queen, ill. by Toma Bogdanovic
  The snow queen, ill. by June Atkin Corwin
  The snow queen, ill. by Sally Holmes
  The snow queen, ill. by Susan Jeffers
  The snow queen, ill. by Errol Le Cain
  The snow queen, ill. by Bernadette Watts
  The snow queen, ill. by Arieh Zeldich
Anglund, Joan Walsh. *The brave cowboy*
Ardizzone, Edward. *Little Tim and the brave sea captain*
  Paul, the hero of the fire
  Peter the wanderer
  Tim and Charlotte
  Tim to the rescue
Arnold, Marsha Diane. *The bravest of us all*
Asare, Meshack. *Sosu's call*
Aulaire, Ingri Mortenson d'. *Wings for Per*
Bailey, Linda. *When Addie was scared*
Baillie, Allan. *Rebel!*
Baldner, Gaby. *Joba and the wild boar = Joba und das wildschwein*
Bannon, Laura. *Hat for a hero*
Barbero, Maria. *The bravest mouse*
Barr, Cathrine. *Little Ben*
Barrows, Marjorie Wescott. *Fraidy cat*
Baumann, Kurt. *Piro and the fire brigade*
Bawden, Nina. *William Tell*
Beck, Scott. *Pepito the brave*
Beim, Jerrold. *Eric on the desert*
Benchley, Nathaniel. *The deep dives of Stanley Whale*
Benjamin, Anne. *Young Pocahontas*
Birdseye, Tom. *Oh yeah!*
Blegvad, Lenore. *Anna Banana and me*
Bornstein, Ruth Lercher. *Jim*
Brook, Judy. *Tim mouse goes down the stream*
Brown, Margaret Wise. *Streamlined pig*
Burgert, Hans-Joachim. *Samulo and the giant*
Cameron, Ann. *Harry (the monster)*
Carleton, Barbee Oliver. *Benny and the bear*
Carlson, Nancy L. *Arnie and the skateboard gang*
  Harriet and the roller coaster
Chaffin, Lillie D. *We be warm till springtime comes*
Chapouton, Anne-Marie. *Billy the brave*
Charlton, Elizabeth. *Jeremy and the ghost*
Chocolate, Deborah M. Newton. *Imani in the belly*
Church, Kristine. *My brother John*
Coles, Robert. *The story of Ruby Bridges*
Conford, Ellen. *Eugene the brave*
Coombs, Patricia. *Molly Mullett*
Coville, Bruce. *The foolish giant*
Cowell, Cressida. *Hiccup the seasick Viking*
Craft, Ruth. *Carrie Hepple's garden*
Crum, Shutta. *The bravest of the brave*
Cutler, Jane. *The cello of Mr. O*
De Beer, Hans. *Little polar bear and the brave little hare*
Deedy, Carmen Agra. *The yellow star*
De La Mare, Walter (Walter John). *Molly Whuppie*
De Posadas Mane, Carmen. *Mister North Wind*
Derby, Sally. *King Kenrick's splinter*
Dierssen, Andreas. *Timid Timmy*
Dreifus, Miriam W. *Brave Betsy*
Driscoll, Laura. *The bravest cat!*
Duncan, Jane. *Brave Janet Reachfar*
Duncan, Lois. *Song of the circus*
Dyke, John. *Pigwig*
Ehlert, Lois. *Cuckoo, a Mexican folktale = Cucú: un cuento folklórico mexicano*
Erickson, Karen. *I'm brave!*
Fatio, Louise. *The red bantam*
Fern, Eugene. *The most frightened hero*
Fuchshuber, Annegert. *Giant story – Mouse tale*
Furchgott, Terry. *Phoebe and the hot water bottles*
Gackenbach, Dick. *Beauty, brave and beautiful*
Gantschev, Ivan. *The Christmas train*
Ginsburg, Mirra. *The strongest one of all*
Golenbock, Peter. *Hank Aaron*
Goodall, John S. *Paddy to the rescue*

Grant, Joan. *The monster that grew small*
Grasshopper to the rescue
Greaves, Margaret. *Once there were no pandas*
Grimm, Jacob. *The brave little tailor*, ill. by Mark Corcoran
  The brave little tailor, ill. by Olga Dugina & Andrej Dugin
  The brave little tailor, ill. by Daniel San Souci
  The brave little tailor, ill. by David Shaw
  The brave little tailor, ill. by Svend Otto S
  The brave little tailor, ill. by Eve Tharlet
  The brave little tailor, ill. by James Warhola
  Seven at one blow
  The valiant little tailor
Haley, Gail E. *Jack and the fire dragon*
Harris, Leon A. *The great diamond robbery*
Harrison, Troon. *Courage to fly*
Harshman, Marc. *A little excitement*
Hayes, Sarah. *This is the bear and the scary night*
Hazen, Barbara Shook. *Fang*
  The new dog
Hearne, Betsy Gould. *Seven brave women*
Heide, Florence Parry. *Timothy Twinge*
Helldorfer, M. C. (Mary Claire). *The mapmaker's daughter*
Henkes, Kevin. *Sheila Rae, the brave*
Herman, Gail. *Fievel's big showdown*
Heyer, Carol. *Robin Hood*
Hiser, Berniece T. *The adventure of Charlie and his wheat-straw hat*
Hoban, Lillian. *No, no, Sammy Crow*
Holl, Adelaide. *Sir Kevin of Devon*
Hooks, William H. *Peach boy*
Hort, Lenny. *The boy who held back the sea*
Horvath, Betty F. *Jasper and the hero business*
Howard, Elizabeth Fitzgerald. *Papa tells Chita a story*
Hughes, Monica. *Little Fingerling*
Hulpach, Vladimir. *Ahaiyute and Cloud Eater*
Hürlimann, Bettina. *Barry*
Jackson, Shelley. *The old woman and the wave*
Jakes, John. *Susanna of the Alamo*
James, J. Alison. *The drums of Noto Hanto*
Jaques, Faith. *Tilly's rescue*
Jeram, Anita. *Daisy Dare*
Jonell, Lynne. *When Mommy was mad*
Julian, Alison. *Brave as a bunny can be*
Keens-Douglas, Richardo. *The nutmeg princess*
Keller, Beverly. *Pimm's place*
Keller, Holly. *Brave Horace*
Kerins, Tony (Anthony). *The brave ones*
Kimmel, Eric A. *The four gallant sisters*
Kipling, Rudyard. *Rikki-tikki-tavi*, ill. by Lambert Davis
  Rikki-tikki-tavi, ill. by Jerry Pinkney
Kurtz, Jane. *Miro in the kingdom of the sun*
Lagercrantz, Rose. *Brave little Pete of Geranium Street*
Lears, Laurie. *Becky the brave*
Lee, Jeanne M. *The song of Mu Lan*
Le Guin, Ursula K. *A ride on the red mare's back*
Lemaître, Pascal. *Emily the giraffe*
Leonard, Alain. *Barnaby and the big gorilla*
Lewis, Rob. *Friska, the sheep that was too small*
Lexau, Joan M. *It all began with a drip, drip, drip*
Little, Jean. *Jess was the brave one*
Little, Lessie Jones. *I can do it by myself*
Littlewood, Valerie. *The season clock*
Low, Joseph. *Benny rabbit and the owl*
  Boo to a goose
Lunge-Larsen, Lise. *The legend of the lady slipper*
Maitland, Barbara. *The bear who didn't like honey*
Mallat, Kathy. *Brave bear*
Manushkin, Fran. *Be brave, baby rabbit*
Marshak, S. (Samuil). *The tale of a hero nobody knows*
Martin, Bill (William Ivan). *Knots on a counting rope*
Martin, Rafe. *The monkey bridge*
Masini, Beatrice. *A brave little princess*
Matsutani, Miyoko. *The witch's magic cloth*
May, Kara. *Big brave brother Ben*
Mayer, Marianna. *The unicorn and the lake*
Mayer, Mercer. *Liverwurst is missing*
  Liza Lou and the Yeller Belly Swamp
Milne, A. A. (Alan Alexander). *Winnie-the-Pooh: a pop-up book*

Mitchell, Margaree King. *Granddaddy's gift*
Morgan, Michaela. *Brave, brave mouse*
Moss, Marissa. *After-school monster*
Namioka, Lensey. *The loyal cat*
Nash, Ogden. *The adventures of Isabel*, ill. by Walter Lorraine
   The adventures of Isabel, ill. by James Marshall
   Custard the dragon
   Custard the dragon and the wicked knight, ill. by Lynn Munsinger
   Custard the dragon and the wicked knight, ill. by Linell Nash
Nishikawa, Osamu. *Alexander and the blue ghost*
Nobisso, Josephine. *John Blair and the great Hinckley fire*
Olson, Arielle North. *The lighthouse keeper's daughter*
Oppenheim, Shulamith Levey. *The lily cupboard*
Osborne, Mary Pope. *The brave little seamstress*
   New York's bravest
Palecek, Libuse. *Brave as a tiger*
Peet, Bill (William Bartlett). *Cowardly Clyde*
Pieńkowski, Jan. *Bel and Bub and the black hole*
Pryor, Bonnie. *The porcupine mouse*
Raglus, Jeff. *Schnorky the wave puncher*
Rappaport, Doreen. *The long-haired girl*
Raschka, Christopher. *Waffle*
Reynolds, Marilynn. *The name of the child*
Robbins, Maria Polushkin. *The little hen and the giant*
Roth, Susan L. *Brave Martha and the dragon*
San Souci, Robert D. *The enchanted tapestry*
   The samurai's daughter
Scarry, Richard. *Richard Scarry's Peasant Pig and the terrible dragon*
Scheffler, Ursel. *Be brave, little lion!*
Schertle, Alice. *The gorilla in the hall*
Schmid, Eleonore. *Hare's Christmas gift*
Schumacher, Claire. *Brave Lily*
Sewell, Helen Moore. *Jimmy and Jemima*
Shannon, George. *Tippy-toe chick, go*
Shire, Ellen. *The mystery at number seven, Rue Petite*
Shute, Linda. *Momotaro, the peach boy*
Small, Terry. *The legend of William Tell*
Stanek, Muriel. *All alone after school*
Steig, William. *Brave Irene*
Stevenson, Drew. *The ballad of Penelope Lou . . . and me*
Taylor, Mark. *Henry explores the jungle*
   Henry explores the mountains
   Henry the explorer
Thompson, Lauren. *Little Quack*
   Little Quack [board book]
Titus, Eve. *Anatole and the cat*
Uchida, Yoshiko. *The magic purse*
Va, Leong. *A letter to the king*
Van Woerkom, Dorothy. *Becky and the bear*
Waber, Bernard. *Courage*
Weigelt, Udo. *Miranda's ghosts*
Wells, H. G. (Herbert George). *The adventures of Tommy*
Wetterer, Margaret K. *Kate Shelley and the midnight express*
   The snow walker
Wilkon, Piotr. *The brave little kittens*
Wishinsky, Frieda. *Give Maggie a chance*
Wolkstein, Diane. *The banza*
Yolen, Jane. *Beneath the ghost moon*

Character traits – cleanliness

Adelborg, Ottilia. *Clean Peter and the children of Grubbylea*
Ahlberg, Allan. *Mrs. Lather's laundry*
Allen, Jonathan. *Mucky moose*
Bonning, Tony. *Another fine mess*
Bottner, Barbara. *Two messy friends*
Bowling, David Louis. *Dirty Dingy Daryl*
Brown, Margaret Wise. *The dirty little boy*
Bucknall, Caroline. *One bear in the picture*
Burch, Robert. *The jolly witch*
Bynum, Janie. *Otis*
Carlstrom, Nancy White. *Jesse Bear's yum-yum crumble*
Cobb, Vicki. *Keeping clean*
Cole, Babette. *Dr. Dog*
Conrad, Pam. *This mess*
Cummings, Pat. *Clean your room, Harvey Moon!*
De Paola, Tomie (Thomas Anthony). *Marianna May and Nursey*

Dickinson, Mary. *Alex's bed*
Eagle, Ellen. *Gypsy's cleaning day*
Edwards, Frank B. *Mortimer Mooner stopped taking a bath*
Ernst, Lisa Campbell. *Duke, the Dairy Delight dog*
Flot, Jeannette B. *Princess Kalina and the hedgehog*
Gantos, Jack (John, Jr.). *Swampy alligator*
Garelli, Cristina. *Farm friends clean up*
Grindley, Sally. *Mucky Duck*
Groves-Raines, Antony. *The tidy hen*
Hamsa, Bobbie. *Dirty Larry*
Hare, Lorraine. *Who needs her?*
Haseley, Dennis. *The soap bandit*
Hickman, Martha Whitmore. *Eeps creeps, it's my room!*
Howells, Mildred. *The woman who lived in Holland*
Hurd, Edith Thacher. *Stop, stop*
Hutchins, Pat. *Where's the baby?*
Jackson, Ellen B. *The bear in the bathtub*
Kamish, Daniel. *Diggy Dan*
Kirk, David. *Little pig, Biddle pig*
Krasilovsky, Phyllis. *The man who didn't wash his dishes*
Kraus, Robert. *Buggy Bear cleans up*
Krensky, Stephen. *What a mess!*
Kroll, Steven. *The pigrates clean up*
Landström, Olof. *Boo and Baa on a cleaning spree*
Lattimore, Deborah Nourse. *Cinderhazel*
Lauber, Patricia. *What you never knew about tubs, toilets and showers*
Lindbergh, Anne. *Tidy lady*
Lobb, Janice. *Splish! Splash! Why do we wash?*
Loomis, Christine. *The cleanup surprise*
Luciani, Brigitte. *Those messy Hempels*
McElmurry, Jill. *Mess pets*
McHenry, E. B. *Poodlena*
McKay, Hilary. *Where's bear?*
McKissack, Patricia C. *Messy Bessey*
   Messy Bessey = Ada, la desordenada
   Messy Bessey and the birthday overnight
   Messy Bessey's family reunion
   Messy Bessey's holidays
McQueen, Lucinda. *Tidy pig*
Madden, Don. *The Wartville wizard*
Mahy, Margaret. *Keeping house*
Maloney, Peter (1955–). *Belly button boy*
Miller, Edward. *The curse of Claudia*
Moon, Nicola. *Alligator tails and crocodile cakes*
Morris, Ann. *Eleanora Mousie makes a mess*
Munsch, Robert N. *Mud puddle*
Nerlove, Miriam. *I meant to clean my room today*
Noonan, Julia. *Hare and Rabbit, friends forever*
Peters, Sharon. *Messy Mark*
Potter, Beatrix. *The tale of Mrs. Tittlemouse*
Provencher, Rose-Marie. *Mouse cleaning*
Robbins, Maria Polushkin. *Bubba and Babba*
Roberts, David (1970–). *Dirty Bertie*
Rockwell, Anne F. *Nice and clean*
Root, Phyllis. *Mrs. Potter's pig*
Rounds, Glen. *Washday on Noah's ark*
Schwartz, Mary. *Spiffen*
Serfozo, Mary. *Dirty Kurt*
Sharmat, Marjorie Weinman. *Mooch the messy*
Sharmat, Mitchell. *The seven sloppy days of Phineas Pig*
Smith, Janice Lee. *Jess and the stinky cowboys*
Stanton, Elizabeth. *The very messy room*
Stephens, Helen. *Ruby and the muddy dog*
Teague, Mark. *Pigsty*
Viorst, Judith. *Super-completely and totally the messiest*
Wabbes, Marie. *Rose is muddy*
Wallace, Nancy Elizabeth. *Count down to clean up*
Wells, Rosemary. *Fritz and the mess fairy*
   The germ busters
   Max cleans up
Wilhelm, Hans. *Oh, what a mess*
Willis, Jeanne. *The tale of Georgie Grub*
Wilson, Sarah. *The day that Henry cleaned his room*
Wojtowycz, David. *Dudley helps out*
Ziefert, Harriet. *A clean house for Mole and Mouse*
   Hurry up, Jessie!

Character traits – cleverness

Æsop. *The crow and the pitcher*
Ahlberg, Janet. *It was a dark and stormy night*
Alberts, Nancy Markham. *No toys on Sunday*
Alderson, Sue Ann. *Ida and the wool smugglers*
Alexander, Sue. *Peacocks are very special*
Aliki. *The eggs*
Andersen, H. C. (Hans Christian). *The swineherd*, ill. by Erik Blegvad
   The swineherd, ill. by Dorothée Duntze
   The swineherd, ill. by Deborah Hahn
   The swineherd, ill. by Lisbeth Zwerger
Anderson, Paul S. *Red fox and the hungry tiger*
Ardizzone, Edward. *Peter the wanderer*
Arnold, Katya. *Baba Yaga and the little girl*
Asbjørnsen, P. C. (Peter Christen). *Billy goats Gruff*, ill. by Wendy Edelson
   Billy goats Gruff, ill. by Susan Hellard
   The three billy goats Gruff, ill. by Tim Arnold
   The three billy goats Gruff, ill. by Robert Bender
   The three billy goats Gruff, ill. by Marcia Brown
   The three billy goats Gruff, ill. by Stephen Carpenter
   Three billy goats Gruff, ill. by Tom Dunnington
   The three billy goats Gruff, ill. by Paul Galdone
   The three billy goats Gruff, ill. by David Jorgensen
   The three billy goats Gruff, ill. by Dennis Kendrick
   The three billygoats Gruff, ill. by Eric Kincaid
   Three billy goats Gruff, ill. by Thea Kliros
   The three billy goats Gruff, ill. by Jonathan Langley
   The three billy goats Gruff, ill. by Loretta Lustig
   The three billy goats Gruff, ill. by Thomas Newbury
   The three billy goats Gruff, ill. by Lilian Obligado
   The three billy goats Gruff, ill. by Ed Parker
   The three billy goats Gruff, ill. by Heidi Petach
   The three billy goats Gruff, ill. by Laura Rader
   The three billy goats Gruff, ill. by Glen Rounds
   The three billy goats Gruff, ill. by Janet Stevens
   The three billy goats Gruff, ill. by William Stobbs
   The three billy goats Gruff, ill. by Svend Otto S
   The truth about three billy goats Gruff
Asch, Frank. *Ziggy Piggy and the three little pigs*
Baker, Betty. *And me, coyote!*
   Partners
Bang, Betsy. *The old woman and the red pumpkin*
   The old woman and the rice thief
Bang, Molly. *Wiley and the hairy man*
Bannerman, Helen. *Little Black Sambo*, Platt & Munk, 1933
   Little Black Sambo, ill. by Nina R. Jordan
   Little Black Sambo, ill. by Gladys Turkey Mitchell
   Little Black Sambo, ill. by Robert Moore
   Little Black Sambo, ill. by Fern Bisel Peat
   Little Black Sambo, ill. by Mary LaFetra Russell
   Little Black Sambo, ill. by Cobb X. Shinn
   Little Black Sambo, ill. by Terry & Mary Smith
   Little Black Sambo, ill. by Suzanne
   Little Black Sambo, ill. by Gustaf Tenggren
   Little Black Sambo, ill. by Keith Ward
   Little Black Sambo, ill. by Julian Wehr
   The Little Black Sambo story book
   The story of Little Babaji
   The story of Little Black Sambo, Reilly, 1905
   The story of Little Black Sambo, Lippincott, 1915
   The story of Little Black Sambo, Stokes, 1923
   The story of Little Black Sambo, Altemus, 1931
   The story of Little Black Sambo, Lippincott, 1943
   The story of Little Black Sambo, Greenhouse, 1986
   The story of Little Black Sambo, HarperCollins, 1990
   The story of little black Sambo, Applewood, 1996
   The story of Little Black Sambo, ill. by Christopher Bing
   The story of Little Black Sambo, "pop-up" picture by C. Carey Cloud
   The story of Little Black Sambo, ill. by Judith Russell
Barbosa, Rogério Andrade. *African animal tales*
Barry, David. *The Rajah's rice*
Bason, Lillian. *Those foolish Molboes!*
Bell, Anthea. *The wise queen*

Bemelmans, Ludwig. *Welcome home!*
Berson, Harold. *How the devil gets his due*
   Joseph and the snake
   Why the jackal won't speak to the hedgehog
Bishop, Claire Huchet. *The five Chinese brothers*
Blundell, Tony. *Beware of boys*
Bodnar, Judit Z. *A wagonload of fish*
Boegehold, Betty. *Pawpaw's run*
Bonning, Tony. *Fox tale soup*
Brett, Jan. *Fritz and the beautiful horses*
   Hedgie's surprise
   The trouble with trolls
Brown, Marcia. *The bun*
   Stone soup
Brown, Margaret Wise. *Don't frighten the lion*
Buchanan, Heather S. *George Mouse's first summer*
Buchanan, Sue. *Mud Pie Annie*
Burningham, John. *Harquin*
   The shopping basket
Byfield, Barbara Ninde. *The haunted churchbell*
Calhoun, Mary. *Cross-country cat*
   Jack and the whoopee wind
Cameron, John. *If mice could fly*
Caseley, Judith. *Ada potato*
Castle, Caroline. *Herbert Binns and the flying tricycle*
Cauley, Lorinda Bryan. *The trouble with Tyrannosaurus Rex*
Christelow, Eileen. *Jerome the babysitter*
Climo, Shirley. *King of the birds*
Coatsworth, Elizabeth. *Pika and the roses*
Cohen, Caron Lee. *Renata, Whizbrain and the ghost*
Cole, Joanna. *Doctor Change*
Collington, Peter. *Clever cat*
Compton, Kenn. *Jack the giant chaser*
Costa, Nicoletta. *The clever dog*
Crompton, Anne Eliot. *The lifting stone*
Czernecki, Stefan. *Huevos rancheros*
Damjan, Mischa. *The wolf and the kid*
Daniels, Guy. *The Tsar's riddles*
Dee, Ruby. *Two ways to count to ten*
DeFelice, Cynthia C. *Clever crow*
   Three perfect peaches
De La Mare, Walter (Walter John). *Molly Whuppie*
Demi. *One grain of rice*
   Under the shade of the mulberry tree
De Regniers, Beatrice Schenk. *Catch a little fox*
Dickens, Frank. *Boffo*
Dines, Glen. *Gilly and the wicharoo*
Dodd, Lynley. *Hairy Maclary's bone*
Domanska, Janina. *The best of the bargain*
   King Krakus and the dragon
   Why so much noise?
Dos Santos, Joyce Audy. *The diviner*
Elkin, Benjamin. *Gillespie and the guards*
   Lucky and the giant
Erickson, Russell E. *Warton and the traders*
Ernst, Lisa Campbell. *The prize pig surprise*
Forest, Heather. *Stone soup*
Frankel, Bernice. *Half-As-Big and the tiger*
Frascino, Edward. *My cousin the king*
French, Vivian. *Red Hen and Sly Fox*
Freschet, Berniece. *Elephant and friends*
Galdone, Paul. *The monkey and the crocodile*
   What's in fox's sack?
Ginsburg, Mirra. *The fisherman's son*
Goldman, Dara. *There's no such thing!*
Gorbachev, Valeri. *The fool of the world and the flying ship*
Greeson, Janet. *An American army of two*
Grimm, Jacob. *The four clever brothers*
   The rabbit's bride
Harrison, David Lee. *Little boy soup*
Hayes, Sarah. *Nine ducks nine*
Hazen, Barbara Shook. *The Fat Cats, Cousin Scraggs and the monster mice*
Helldorfer, M. C. (Mary Claire). *The darling boys*
   Jack, Skinny Bones, and the golden pancakes
Hillert, Margaret. *The three goats*
Hirsh, Marilyn. *The Rabbi and the twenty-nine witches*

Hogrogian, Nonny. *Rooster brother*
Hooks, William H. *The Gruff brothers*
    Three rounds with rabbit
Huck, Charlotte S. *Princess Furball*
Hughes, Monica. *Little Fingerling*
Huling, Jan. *Puss in cowboy boots*
Hutton, Warwick. *The nose tree*
Jackson, Ellen B. *The impossible riddle*
Jaffe, Rona. *Last of the wizards*
Jameson, Cynthia. *The house of five bears*
Kennedy, Richard. *The contests at Cowlick*
Kimmel, Eric A. *Count Silvernose*
Kipling, Rudyard. *Rikki-tikki-tavi*, ill. by Lambert Davis
    Rikki-tikki-tavi, ill. by Jerry Pinkney
Kraus, Robert. *Big Squeak, Little Squeak*
Laroche, Michel. *The snow rose*
Lester, Julius. *Sam and the tigers*
Leverich, Kathleen. *The hungry fox and the foxy duck*
Lieberman, Syd. *The wise shoemaker of Studena*
Lobel, Anita. *The straw maid*
Lobel, Arnold. *How the rooster saved the day*
    Mouse soup
Logue, Christopher. *The magic circus*
Lorenz, Lee. *The feathered ogre*
Lowell, Susan. *The three little javelinas*
McClenathan, Louise. *My mother sends her wisdom*
McCormack, John E. *Rabbit tales*
McCurdy, Michael. *The devils who learned to be good*
McNaughton, Colin. *Oops!*
Mahy, Margaret. *The seven Chinese brothers*
Mantinband, Gerda. *Three clever mice*
Martin, Charles E. *Dunkel takes a walk*
Mathers, Petra. *Lottie's new beach towel*
Metaxas, Eric. *The fool and the flying ship*
    Puss in boots
Mogensen, Jan. *The tiger's breakfast*
Muth, Jon J. *Stone soup*
Myers, Edward. *Forri the baker*
Obrist, Jürg. *The miser who wanted the sun*
Olaleye, Isaac. *Bitter bananas*
Parish, Peggy. *Zed and the monsters*
Parry, Marian. *King of the fish*
Paterson, A. B. (Andrew Barton). *The man from Ironbark*
Patron, Susan. *Burgoo stew*
Paul, Anthony. *The tiger who lost his stripes*
Perrault, Charles. *Puss in boots*, ill. by Marcia Brown
    Puss in boots, ill. by Lorinda Bryan Cauley
    Puss in boots, ill. by Jean Claverie
    Puss in boots, ill. by Andrea Da Rif
    Puss in boots, ill. by Stasys Eidrigevicius
    Puss in boots, ill. by Hans Fischer
    Puss in boots, ill. by Paul Galdone
    Puss in boots, retold and ill. by John S. Goodall
    Puss in boots, retold and ill. by Gail E. Haley
    Puss in boots, ill. by Steve Light
    Puss in boots, ill. by Giuliano Lunelli
    Puss in boots, ill. by Fred Marcellino [pub. by Farrar, 1990]
    Puss in boots, ill. by Fred Marcellino [pub. by Farrar, 1998]
    Puss in boots, ill. by Julia Noonan
    Puss in boots, ill. by Tony Ross
    Puss in boots, ill. by William Stobbs
    Puss in boots, ill. by Yan Thomas
    Puss in boots, ill. by Alain Vaës
    Puss in boots, ill. by Barry Wilkinson
Peterson, Julienne. *Caterina, the clever farm girl*
Pittman, Helena Clare. *A grain of rice*
Potter, Beatrix. *The sly old cat*
    The tale of the Flopsy Bunnies
Prokofiev, Sergei Sergeievitch. *Peter and the wolf*, ill. by Reg Cartwright
    Peter and the wolf, ill. by Warren Chappell
    Peter and the wolf, ill. by Barbara Cooney
    Peter and the wolf, ill. by Julia Gukova
    Peter and the wolf, ill. by Frans Haacken
    Peter and the wolf, ill. by Alan Howard
    Peter and the wolf, ill. by Charles Mikolaycak
    Peter and the wolf, ill. by Jörg Müller

Peter and the wolf, ill. by Josef Palecek
Peter and the wolf, ill. by Kozo Shimizu
Peter and the wolf, retold and ill. by Vladimir Vagin
Peter and the wolf, ill. by Erna Voigt
Pullman, Philip. *Puss in boots*, ill. by Ian Beck
Ransome, Arthur. *The fool of the world and the flying ship*
Reneaux, J. J. *Why Alligator hates Dog*
Rockwell, Anne F. *Big boss*
    The bump in the night
    The stolen necklace
Ross, Tony. *Stone soup*
Ruurs, Margriet. *Emma and the coyote*
Salley, Coleen. *Who's that tripping over my bridge?*
San Souci, Robert D. *Callie Ann and Mistah Bear*
    Little Pierre
Schatell, Brian. *Sam's no dummy, Farmer Goff*
Schatz, Letta. *The extraordinary tug-of-war*
Shannon, George. *Laughing all the way*
    Lizard's home
Sheldon, Aure. *Of cobblers and kings*
Siddiqui, Ashraf. *Bhombal Dass, the uncle of lion*
Sierra, Judy. *Wiley and the Hairy Man*
Simon, Sidney B. *Henry, the uncatchable mouse*
Singh, Jacquelin. *Fat Gopal*
Small, David. *Paper John*
Souhami, Jessica. *Mrs. McCool and the giant Cuhullin*
Steig, William. *Doctor De Soto*
Stevens, Janet. *Tops and bottoms*
Stewig, John Warren. *Clever Gretchen*
    Stone soup
Storr, Catherine (Cole). *Clever Polly and the stupid wolf*
Tchana, Katrin. *Sense Pass King*
Threadgall, Colin. *Proud rooster and the fox*
The three little pigs. *The original three little pigs re-told*, ill. by Jonathan Smith
    The story of the three little pigs, ill. by L. Leslie Brooke
    The story of the three little pigs, ill. by William Stobbs
    Three little pigs [Facsimile ed]
    The three little pigs, ill. by Val Biro
    The three little pigs, ill. by Gavin Bishop
    The three little pigs, ill. by Erik Blegvad
    The three little pigs, ill. by Caroline Bucknall
    The three little pigs, ill. by Stephen Cartwright
    The three little pigs, ill. by Lorinda Bryan Cauley
    The three little pigs, ill. by Jean Claverie
    The three little pigs, ill. by Doug Cushman
    The three little pigs, ill. by William Pène Du Bois
    The three little pigs, ill. by Paul Galdone
    The three little pigs, ill. by Madelaine Gill
    The three little pigs, ill. by Rob Hefferan
    The three little pigs, ill. by Steven Kellogg
    The three little pigs, ill. by David McPhail
    The three little pigs, ill. by James Marshall
    The three little pigs, ill. by Paul Meisel
    The three little pigs, ill. by Rodney Peppé
    The three little pigs, ill. by Edda Reinl
    The three little pigs, ill. by John Wallner
    The three little pigs, ill. by Irma Wilde
    The three little pigs, ill. by Margot Zemach
    The three little pigs and the big bad wolf
    The three little pigs and the fox
    The three little pigs [board book], ill. by Thea Kliros
    The three pigs, ill. by Tony Ross
    Who's at the door?
Thurber, James. *The great Quillow*
Troughton, Joanna. *Mouse-Deer's market*
Van Rynbach, Iris. *The soup stone*
Van Woerkom, Dorothy. *The rat, the ox and the zodiac*
Wade, Barrie. *The three billy goats gruff*
Wahl, Jan. *Little Johnny Buttermilk*
Walker, Barbara K. (Barbara Kerlin). *Teeny-Tiny and the witch-woman*
Walsh, Ellen Stoll. *Jack's tale*
Ward, Helen. *The king of the birds*
    The rooster and the fox
Westwood, Jennifer. *Going to Squintum's*
Wetterer, Margaret K. *Patrick and the fairy thief*

Wheeler, Lisa. *Turk and Runt*
Wild, Robin. *Little Pig and the big bad wolf*
Willey, Margaret. *Clever Beatrice, an Upper Peninsula conte*
   Clever Beatrice and the best little pony
   Clever Beatrice Christmas
Williams, Jay. *School for sillies*
Winthrop, Elizabeth. *The little humpbacked horse*
Wolkstein, Diane. *The cool ride in the sky*
Wood, Audrey. *Heckedy Peg*
Yohannes, Gebregeorgis. *Silly Mammo = Kilu Mammo*
Yolen, Jane. *The flying witch*
Young, Ed (Edward). *Little Plum*
   The terrible Nung Gwama
Youngquist, Cathrene Valente. *The three Billygoats Gruff and Mean Calypso Joe*
Zakhoder, Boris Vladimirovich. *The good stepmother*
Zemach, Harve. *Nail soup*

Character traits – clumsiness

Dewey, Ariane. *Splash!*
Edwards, Pamela Duncan. *Slop goes the soup*
Fox, Mem. *Harriet, you'll drive me wild*
Kroll, Steven. *Oh, Tucker!*
McNaughton, Colin. *Preston's goal!*
Naylor, Phyllis Reynolds. *"I can't take you anywhere!"*
Stower, Adam. *Two left feet*
Wardlaw, Lee. *The chair where bear sits*

Character traits – completing things

Flack, Marjorie. *Angus and the cat*
Ness, Evaline. *Do you have the time, Lydia?*
Petrides, Heidrun. *Hans and Peter*

Character traits – compromising

Eure, Wesley. *A fish out of water*
Hogrogian, Nonny. *Carrot cake*
Wildsmith, Brian. *The owl and the woodpecker*

Character traits – conceit

Bellows, Cathy. *The royal raccoon*
Brenner, Barbara A. *Mr. Tall and Mr. Small*
Flack, Marjorie. *Angus and the ducks*
Goble, Paul. *Iktomi and the boulder*
   Iktomi and the buffalo skull
Grimm, Jacob. *King Grisly-Beard*
Martin, Ann M. *Rachel Parker, kindergarten show-off*
Modarressi, Mitra. *The dream pillow*
Peet, Bill (William Bartlett). *Ella*
Sharmat, Marjorie Weinman. *I'm terrific*
Williams, Barbara. *So what if I'm a sore loser?*

Character traits – confidence

Alexander, Martha G. *My outrageous friend Charlie*
Aliki. *All by myself!*
Asch, Frank. *Baby Duck's new friend*
Barrett, Joyce Durham. *Willie's not the hugging kind*
Boyce, Katie. *Hector the hermit crab*
Callan, Elizabeth Koda. *Good luck pony*
Caseley, Judith. *Harry and Willy and Carrothead*
Chottin, Ariane. *Little Kangaroo finds his way*
Corey, Shana. *Ballerina bear*
Gibbons, Faye. *Emma Jo's song*
Gorbachev, Valeri. *Chicken chickens*
Grant, Rose Marie. *Andiamo, Weasel*
Hest, Amy. *Make the team, Baby Duck*
   You can do it, Sam
Hoff, Syd. *Stanley*
Lasky, Kathryn. *The solo*
Lewis, Wendy A. *In Abby's hands*
Pérez, L. King. *First day in grapes*
Pocock, Rita. *Annabelle and the big slide*
Seed, Jenny. *Ntombi's song*

Waddell, Martin. *Good job, Little Bear!*
Wagner, Karen. *Bravo, Mildred and Ed!*
Wilhelm, Hans. *A cool kid – like me!*

Character traits – cooperation

Brimner, Larry Dane. *The big, beautiful, brown box*
Domanska, Janina. *The turnip*
Geisert, Arthur. *The giant ball of string*
Goodall, Jane. *The eagle and the wren*
Hewett, Anita. *The tale of the turnip*
Hiscock, Bruce. *Coyote and badger*
Hudelhoff, Allen H. *Cats and kids*
Jennings, Sharon. *Priscilla's paw de deux*
Kako, Satoshi. *Little Daruma and little Daikoku*
Kuiper, Nannie. *Bravo, brave beavers*
McPhail, David M. *Jack and Rick*
Mahoney, Daniel J. *The perfect clubhouse*
Martín Larrañaga, Ana. *Pepo and Lolo and the red apple*
Milhous, Katherine. *The turnip*
Parkinson, Kathy. *The enormous turnip*
Paye, Won-Ldy. *Head, body, legs*
Rouss, Sylvia A. *The littlest pair*
Stihler, Chérie B. *The giant cabbage turnip*
Suen, Anastasia. *The clubhouse*
Tolstoy, Aleksey Nikolayevich. *The enormous turnip*
   The gigantic turnip, ill. by Niamh Sharkey
   The great big enormous turnip
Ziefert, Harriet. *The turnip*

Character traits – courage *see* Character traits – bravery

Character traits – cruelty to animals *see* Character traits – kindness to animals

Character traits – curiosity

Adamson, Gareth. *Old man up a tree*
Alden, Laura. *When?*
Allen, Jeffrey. *Nosey Mrs. Rat*
Ames, Mildred. *The wonderful box*
Arnosky, Jim. *Raccoon on his own*
Bang, Molly. *Dawn*
Bird, E. J. *How do bears sleep?*
Bograd, Larry. *Egon*
Bohdal, Susi. *Tiger baby*
Bonnett-Rampersaud, Louise. *Polly Hopper's pouch*
Broome, Errol. *The smallest koala*
Campbell, Rod. *Buster's afternoon*
   Buster's morning
Chottin, Ariane. *The curious little dolphin*
Clark, Roberta. *Why?*
Climo, Shirley. *The adventure of Walter*
Cooper, Patrick. *Never trust a squirrel*
Cornette. *Purple coyote*
Curious George and the dump truck
Curious George and the pizza
Curious George at the fire station
Curious George goes hiking
Curious George goes sledding
Curious George goes to the aquarium
Curious George goes to the circus
Curious George in the big city
Curious George takes a train
Curious George visits a toy store
Curious George visits the zoo
De Beer, Hans. *Oh no, Ono!*
Demarest, Chris L. *Clemens' kingdom*
Domanska, Janina. *Spring is*
Fisher, Aileen Lucia. *Anybody home?*
Flack, Marjorie. *Angus and the cat*
   Angus and the ducks
Gackenbach, Dick. *The pig who saw everything*
Gottlieb, Dale. *Seeing Eye Willie*
Gravdahl, John. *Curious catwalk*
Kanao, Keiko. *Kitten up a tree*

Kipling, Rudyard. *The elephant's child*, ill. by Louise Brierley
　The elephant's child, ill. by Lorinda Bryan Cauley
　The elephant's child, ill. by Tim Raglin
　The elephant's child, ill. by John A. Rowe
McBratney, Sam. *The dark at the top of the stairs*
MacGregor, Marilyn. *Baby takes a trip*
Meeks, Esther K. *The curious cow*
Moncure, Jane Belk. *Where?*
Morgan-Vanroyen, Mary. *Curious Rosie*
Murphy, Mary. *Koala and the flower*
Napoli, Guillier. *Adventure at Mont-Saint-Michel*
Parker, Steve. *I wonder why tunnels are round*
Pinkwater, Daniel Manus. *Devil in the drain*
Ravilious, Robin. *The runaway chick*
Reece, Colleen L. *What?*
Rey, H. A. (Hans Augusto). *Curious George*
　Curious George gets a medal
　Curious George learns the alphabet
　Curious George rides a bike
　Curious George takes a job
　The original Curious George
Rey, Margret (Margret Elisabeth Waldstein). *Curious George flies a kite*
　Curious George goes to the hospital
Richards, Jean. *How the elephant got his trunk*
Rylant, Cynthia. *Miss Maggie*
Sandberg, Inger. *Dusty wants to borrow everything*
Schoenherr, John. *Rebel*
Waber, Bernard. *Lorenzo*
Weil, Lisl. *Pandora's box*
Yolen, Jane. *Eeny, meeny, miney mole*

Character traits – flattery

Æsop. *Three Æsop fox fables*
Chaucer, Geoffrey. *Chanticleer and the fox*

Character traits – foolishness

Aardema, Verna. *Sebgugugu the glutton*
Alexander, Lloyd. *The house Gobbaleen*
Bason, Lillian. *Those foolish Molboes!*
Bradman, Tony. *Not like this, like that*
Brenner, Barbara A. *Rosa and Marco and the three wishes*
Butterworth, Nick. *The house on the rock*
Carlson, Nancy L. *Arnie and the skateboard gang*
Gackenbach, Dick. *Harvey, the foolish pig*
Gammell, Stephen. *The story of Mr. and Mrs. Vinegar*
Ginsburg, Mirra. *The king who tried to fry an egg on his head*
Gordon, Ruth. *Feathers*
Grimm, Jacob. *Hans in luck*, ill. by Paul Galdone
　Hans in luck, ill. by Felix Hoffmann
　Jack in luck
　Lucky Hans
Jacobs, Joseph. *The three sillies*, ill. by Kathryn Hewitt
　The three sillies, ill. by Steven Kellogg
Johnson, Evelyne. *The cow in the kitchen*
Keenen, George. *The preposterous week*
Lazy Jack. *Lazy Jack*, ill. by Barry Wilkinson
Maitland, Antony. *Idle Jack*
Mike, Jan M. *Juan Bobo and the horse of seven colors*
Miller, William. *The knee-high man*
Morgan, Michaela. *Helpful Betty to the rescue*
Phillips, Louis. *The brothers Wrong and Wrong Again*
San Souci, Robert D. *Six foolish fishermen*
Schwartz, Amy. *Yossel Zissel and the wisdom of Chelm*
Scruton, Clive. *Circus cow*
Uhlberg, Myron. *Lemuel, the fool*
Van Nutt, Julia. *Pignapped!*
Zemach, Margot. *The three wishes*

Character traits – fortune *see* Character traits – luck

Character traits – freedom

Æsop. *The dog and the wolf*

Andersen, H. C. (Hans Christian). *The emperor and the nightingale*, ill. by Meilo So
　The emperor and the nightingale, ill. by James Watling
　The emperor's nightingale, ill. from the Disney archives
　The emperor's nightingale, ill. by Georges Lemoine
　The nightingale, ill. by Harold Berson
　The nightingale, ill. by Nancy Ekholm Burkert
　The nightingale, ill. by Alison Claire Darke
　The nightingale, ill. by Demi
　The nightingale, ill. by Beni Montresor
　The nightingale, ill. by Josef Palecek
　The nightingale, ill. by Regolo Ricci
　The nightingale, ill. by Christopher Santoro
　The nightingale, ill. by Lisbeth Zwerger
Babbitt, Natalie. *Nellie, a cat on her own*
Bayar, Steven. *Rachel and Mischa*
Baylor, Byrd. *Hawk, I'm your brother*
Benjamin, Anne. *Young Harriet Tubman*
Blaustein, Muriel. *Baby Mabu and Auntie Moose*
Bradford, Ann. *The mystery of the missing raccoon*
Buehner, Caralyn. *The escape of Marvin the ape*
Bunting, Eve (Anne Evelyn). *How many days to America?*
Crew, Gary. *Bright star*
De Beer, Hans. *Little polar bear finds a friend*
Dennis, Wesley. *Tumble, the story of a mustang*
Drummond, Allan. *Liberty*
Fatio, Louise. *Hector and Christina*
Fujita, Tamao. *The boy and the bird*
Hawkinson, John. *Where the wild apples grow*
McKenna, Virginia. *Back to the blue*
McPhail, David M. *A wolf story*
Maugham, W. Somerset (William Somerset). *Princess September and the nightingale*
Meade, Holly. *John Willy and Freddy McGee*
Murphy, Mary. *The Alphabet Keeper*
Nelson, Vaunda Micheaux. *Almost to freedom*
Oram, Hiawyn. *Princess Chamomile gets her way*
Park, Frances. *My freedom trip*
Polacco, Patricia. *The butterfly*
Rascal. *Oregon's journey*
Riddle, Tohby. *The great escape from City Zoo*
Roth, Susan L. *Happy birthday Mr. Kang*
Sanders, Scott R. (Scott Russell). *A place called Freedom*
Shulevitz, Uri. *What is a wise bird like you doing in a silly tale like this?*
Siegelson, Kim L. *In the time of the drums*
Steiner, Jörg. *Rabbit Island*
Stern, Mark. *It's a dog's life*
Stroud, Bettye. *The patchwork path*
Sundgaard, Arnold. *The lamb and the butterfly*
Trottier, Maxine. *Little dog Moon*
Wright, Courtni Crump. *Journey to freedom*

Character traits – generosity

Ainsworth, Ruth. *The mysterious Baba and her magic caravan*
Alborghetti, Marci. *Miracle of the myrrh*
Aliki. *The story of Johnny Appleseed*
Anglund, Joan Walsh. *Christmas is a time of giving*
Battle-Lavert, Gwendolyn. *The shaking bag*
Bawden, Nina. *St. Francis of Assisi*
Beck, Scott. *A mud pie for mother*
Behrens, June. *Christmas-magic wagon*
Bliss, Corinne Demas. *The magic apple*
Bohanon, Paul. *Golden Kate*
Bowen, Keith. *Katy's gift*
Brown, Palmer. *Something for Christmas*
Butler, M. Christina. *One snowy night*
Chalmers, Mary. *A hat for Amy Jean*
Chinn, Karen. *Sam and the lucky money*
Christian, Mary Blount. *The devil take you, Barnabas Beane!*
Chute, Beatrice Joy. *Journey to Christmas*
Cohen, Barbara. *Even higher*
Cohen, Miriam. *Liar, liar, pants on fire!*
Compestine, Ying Chang. *The runaway rice cake*
Davis, Aubrey. *Bone button borscht*
DiSalvo-Ryan, DyAnne. *A castle on Viola Street*

Emberley, Michael. *The present*
Erickson, Russell E. *Warton and the traders*
Evans, Richard Paul. *The Christmas candle*
Farjeon, Eleanor. *Mrs. Malone*
Fearnley, Jan. *Little Robin's Christmas*
Fine, Edith Hope. *Under the lemon moon*
Fleming, Candace. *Boxes for Katje*
Fontane, Theodor. *Nick Ribbeck of Ribbeck of Havelland*
  Sir Ribbeck of Ribbeck of Havelland
Fox, Mem. *With love, at Christmas*
French, Vivian. *Why the sea is salt*
Grimm, Jacob. *The falling stars*
  One gift deserves another
Hänel, Wolfram. *The gold at the end of the rainbow*
Hayes, Geoffrey. *Christmas in Puttyville*
Henry, O. *The gift of the Magi*
Hoban, Russell. *Emmet Otter's jug-band Christmas*
  The mole family's Christmas
Hodges, Margaret. *Saint Patrick and the peddler*
Houston, John A. *The bright yellow rope*
Hughes, Shirley. *Giving*
Hush little baby. *Hush little baby*, ill. by Aliki
  Hush, little baby, ill. by Marla Frazee
  Hush little baby, ill. by Shari Halpern
  Hush little baby, ill. by Jeanette Winter
  Hush little baby, ill. by Margot Zemach
Janice. *Little Bear's Christmas*
Johnson, Crockett. *The emperor's gifts*
Kasza, Keiko. *The wolf's chicken stew*
Kunnas, Mauri. *Twelve gifts for Santa Claus*
Kvasnosky, Laura McGee. *Zelda and Ivy one Christmas*
Lattimore, Deborah Nourse. *The dragon's robe*
Lexau, Joan M. *A house so big*
Lindman, Maj. *Snipp, Snapp, Snurr and the red shoes*
Lionni, Leo. *Tico and the golden wings*
Lucado, Max. *All you ever need*
Lussert, Anneliese. *The Christmas visitor*
McBratney, Sam. *Just one!*
McClenathan, Louise. *The Easter pig*
McCourt, Lisa. *Chicken soup for little souls: The best night out with Dad*
MacDonald, Maryann. *Rosie and the poor rabbits*
Marton, Jirina. *Flowers for mom*
Mitchell, Marianne. *Gullywasher gulch*
Munsch, Robert N. *Ribbon rescue*
Muntean, Michaela. *Mokey and the festival of the bells*
Ness, Evaline. *Josefina February*
Patron, Susan. *Five bad boys, Billy Que, and the dustdobbin*
Pilkey, Dav. *Dragon's merry Christmas*
Pomerantz, Charlotte. *The mousery*
Priest, Robert H. *The pirate's eye*
Quattlebaum, Mary. *The shine man*
Rockwell, Anne F. *Gogo's pay day*
Rodanas, Kristina. *The story of Wali Dâd*
Ross, Christine. *Lily and the present*
Roth, Roger. *The sign painter's dream*
Rylant, Cynthia. *Silver packages*
Sandman, Rochel. *Perfect porridge*
Schotter, Roni. *Captain Snap and the children of Vinegar Lane*
Shecter, Ben. *If I had a ship*
Shepard, Aaron. *The baker's dozen*
Shollar, Leah. *A thread of kindness*
Silverstein, Shel. *The giving tree*
Tada, Joni Eareckson. *The incredible discovery of Lindsey Renee*
Testa, Fulvio. *Wolf's favor*
Timmermans, Felix. *A gift from Saint Nicholas*
Tolstoy, Aleksey Nikolayevich. *Shoemaker Martin*
Wallner, Alexandra. *An Alcott family Christmas*
Wang, Rosalind C. *The fourth question*
  The treasure chest
Ward, Sally G. *What goes around comes around*
Yep, Laurence. *The junior thunder lord*

Character traits – helpfulness

Adelson, Leone. *Who blew that whistle?*
Adshead, Gladys L. *Brownies – hush!*

  Brownies – they're moving
Æsop. *Androcles and the lion*, ill. by Janusz Grabianski
  Androcles and the lion, ill. by Dennis Nolan
  Androcles and the lion, ill. by Robert Rayevsky
  Androcles and the lion, ill. by Janet Stevens
  The ant and the dove
  The lion and the mouse, ill. by Carol Jones
  The lion and the mouse, ill. by Lisa McCue
  The lion and the mouse, ill. by Sara Rojo
  The lion and the mouse, ill. by Gerald Rose
  The lion and the mouse, ill. by Bernadette Watts
  The lion and the mouse, ill. by Ed Young
Aliki. *The two of them*
Aller, Susan B. *Emma and the night dogs*
Ancona, George. *Helping out*
Asch, Frank. *Baby Bird's first nest*
  Monsieur Saguette and his baguette
Aylesworth, Jim. *Mr. McGill goes to town*
Baillie, Marilyn. *Side by side*
Baker, Betty. *Partners*
Bakken, Harold. *The special string*
Barnes, Laura T. *Ernest's special Christmas*
Beard, Darleen Bailey. *Twister*
Beim, Jerrold. *Country mailman*
Best, Cari. *Top banana*
Biro, Val. *Gumdrop and the birthday surprise*
  Gumdrop beats the clock
Bogacki, Tomasz. *Circus girl*
Borovsky, Paul. *Nico*
Bourgeois, Paulette. *Franklin and Harriet*
Bridwell, Norman. *Clifford's good deeds*
Bright, Robert. *Georgie and the baby birds*
  Georgie and the ball of yarn
  Georgie and the little dog
  Georgie and the runaway balloon
Brown, Myra Berry. *Company's coming for dinner*
Buchanan, Heather S. *Emily Mouse saves the day*
Bunting, Eve (Anne Evelyn). *December*
Burningham, John. *Harvey Slumfenburger's Christmas present*
Bushey, Jeanne. *The polar bear's gift*
Butterworth, Nick. *The two sons*
Calhoun, Mary. *Blue-ribbon Henry*
  Euphonia and the flood
  Jack the wise and the Cornish cuckoos
Calmenson, Stephanie. *The little witch sisters*
Cannon, Janell. *Crickwing*
Carey, Valerie Scho. *Harriet and William and the terrible creature*
Chevalier, Christa. *Spence is small*
Clements, Andrew. *Santa's secret helper*
Clifton, Lucille. *My friend Jacob*
Cole, William. *Aunt Bella's umbrella*
Collier, Ethel. *Who goes there in my garden?*
Collington, Peter. *A small miracle*
Cooper, Susan. *Danny and the Kings*
Cousins, Lucy. *Maisy makes lemonade*
Curle, Jock J. *The four good friends*
Cuyler, Margery. *Fat Santa*
Daly, Niki. *Thank you Henrietta*
Davis, Alice Vaught. *Timothy Turtle*
Day, Alexandra. *Frank and Ernest*
  Helping the animals
  Helping the flowers and trees
  Helping the night
  Helping the sun
Day, Shirley. *Waldo's back yard*
De Groat, Diane. *Lola the elf*
DeLage, Ida. *What does a witch need?*
Devlin, Wende. *Cranberry autumn*
  Cranberry Christmas
Dowling, Paul. *You can do it, Rabbit*
Du Bois, William Pène. *Bear circus*
Edwards, Michelle. *Eve and Smithy*
Erickson, Karen. *I like to help*
Ethan, Eric. *Helicopters*
Ets, Marie Hall. *Elephant in a well*
Galdone, Paul. *Androcles and the lion*
Gibbons, Gail. *Emergency!*

Godwin, Laura. *Honey helps*
Graham, Al. *Timothy Turtle*
Graham, Margaret Bloy. *Benjy and his friend Fifi*
Granowsky, Alvin. *Can I help?*
Gray, Genevieve. *Send Wendell*
Green, Norma B. *The hole in the dike*
Greene, Laura. *Help*
Grimm, Jacob. *The elves and the shoemaker*, ill. by Doug Cushman
    The elves and the shoemaker, ill. by Paul Galdone
    The elves and the shoemaker, ill. by Margaret Walty
    The elves and the shoemaker, ill. by Bernadette Watts
    Mother Holly
    The shoemaker and his elves, ill. by Bill Dickson
    The shoemaker and the elves, ill. by Adrienne Adams
    The shoemaker and the elves, ill. by Cynthia and William Birrer
    The shoemaker and the elves, ill. by Ilse Plume
Hague, Kathleen. *The legend of the Veery bird*
Haley, Gail E. *Birdsong*
Han, Oki S. *Kongi and Potgi*
Hassett, John. *Cat up a tree*
Hayes, Sarah. *This is the bear and the bad little girl*
Herold, Ann Bixby. *The helping day*
Hill, Elizabeth Starr. *Evan's corner*
Hol, Coby. *Tippy Bear hunts for honey*
Holmes, Efner Tudor. *Amy's goose*
Houston, John A. *The bright yellow rope*
Hürlimann, Bettina. *Barry*
Jackson, Ellen B. *Sometimes bad things happen*
Janovitz, Marilyn. *Can I help?*
Jensen, Patricia. *Little Donkey learns to help*
    Little Squirrel's special nest
Joyce, William. *Bently and egg*
    The Leaf Men and the brave good bugs
Kishida, Eriko. *The lion and the bird's nest*
Kraus, Robert. *Herman the helper*
    Rebecca Hatpin
La Fontaine, Jean de. *The lion and the rat*
Laminack, Lester L. *Saturdays and teacakes*
Landa, Norbert. *Rabbit and chicken find a box*
Lewis, Eils Moorhouse. *The snug little house*
Lindman, Maj. *Flicka, Ricka, Dicka and the new dotted dress*
    Snipp, Snapp, Snurr and the red shoes
Lively, Penelope. *One, two, three, jump!*
Lloyd, Errol. *Nini at carnival*
Loki. *Jake Greenthumb*
Lowell, Susan. *The bootmaker and the elves*
Ludy, Mark. *The farmer*
McConnachie, Brian. *Flying boy*
McKissack, Patricia C. *Messy Bessey and the birthday overnight*
McMullan, Kate (Hall). *No no Jo*
McPhail, David M. *Santa's book of names*
Marcus, Susan. *The missing button adventure*
Marshall, James. *What's the matter with Carruthers?*
Mayer, Mercer. *Just for you*
Mayne, William. *The blue book of Hob stories*
    The green book of Hob stories
    The red book of Hob stories
    The yellow book of Hob stories
Michael, Emory H. *Androcles and the lion*
Miller, M. L. *The enormous snore*
Monsell, Mary Elise. *Crackle Creek*
Morgan, Michaela. *Helpful Betty solves a mystery*
    Helpful Betty to the rescue
Nakano, Hirotaka. *Elephant blue*
Ness, Evaline. *Pavo and the princess*
Okimoto, Jean Davies. *A place for Grace*
Oxenbury, Helen. *Mother's helper*
Oyibo, Papa. *Big brother, little sister*
Paraskevas, Betty. *Maggie and the Ferocious Beast, the big carrot*
Parker, Nancy Winslow. *Cooper, the McNallys' big black dog*
Partridge, Jenny. *Peterkin Pollensnuff*
Paul, Sherry. *2-B and the rock 'n roll band*
Peet, Bill (William Bartlett). *The ant and the elephant*
    Cyrus the unsinkable sea serpent
Porte, Barbara Ann. *Harry in trouble*
Potter, Beatrix. *The tailor of Gloucester*
Quackenbush, Robert M. *Chuck lends a paw*

Rau, Dana Meachen. *In the yard*
Rayner, Mary. *The rain cloud*
Reider, Katja. *The big little sneeze*
Rockwell, Anne F. *Big bad goat*
    The bump in the night
    Can I help?
    Handy Hank will fix it
Rosa-Casanova, Sylvia. *Mama Provi and the pot of rice*
Rylant, Cynthia. *Mr. Putter and Tabby walk the dog*
Schuch, Steve. *A symphony of whales*
Schwartz, Roslyn. *The mole sisters and the piece of moss*
Schweiger-Dmi'el, Itzhak. *Hanna's Sabbath dress*
Seuss, Dr. *Horton hatches the egg*
Shah, Idries. *The clever boy and the terrible, dangerous animal*
Sierra, Judy. *Preschool to the rescue*
Simon, Norma. *What do I do?*
Slawski, Wolfgang. *Captain Jonathan sails the sea*
Slobodkin, Louis. *Dinny and Danny*
Snow, Pegeen. *Mrs. Periwinkle's groceries*
Soto, Gary. *The old man and his door*
Stevenson, James. *Will you please feed our cat?*
Strauss, Anna. *Hush, Mama loves you*
Suhl, Yuri. *The Purim goat*
Thomas, Shelley Moore. *Somewhere today*
Thorpe, Kiki. *A comfy, cozy Thanksgiving*
Tregebov, Rhea. *What-if Sara*
Trottier, Maxine. *Little dog Moon*
Udry, Janice May. *Is Susan here?*, ill. by Peter Edwards
    Is Susan here?, ill. by Karen Gundersheimer
Venino, Suzanne. *Animals helping people*
Waber, Bernard. *Lyle, Lyle Crocodile*
Waddell, Martin. *Farmer Duck*
    Good job, Little Bear!
Watson, Wendy. *Holly's Christmas eve*
Weller, Frances Ward. *Madaket Millie*
Weninger, Brigitte. *Davy in the middle*
Wetterer, Margaret K. *The snow walker*
Wheeler, Lisa. *Old Cricket*
White, Ellen Emerson. *Santa paws*
Williams, Barbara. *Someday, said Mitchell*
Wittmann, Patricia. *Go ask Giorgio!*
Wojtowycz, David. *Dudley helps out*
Wolde, Gunilla. *Betsy's fixing day*
Zemach, Margot. *To Hilda for helping*
Ziefert, Harriet. *Ode to Humpty Dumpty*

Character traits – honesty

Aardema, Verna. *Pedro and the padre*
Alexander, Lloyd. *The truthful harp*
Aliki. *Diogenes*
Ardizzone, Edward. *Peter the wanderer*
Breathed, Berke (Berkeley). *Edwurd Fudwupper fibbed big*
Bunting, Eve (Anne Evelyn). *A day's work*
De Groat, Diane. *Liar, liar, pants on fire*
Demi. *Chen Ping and his magic axe*
    The empty pot
Dierssen, Andreas. *Timid Timmy*
Donovan, Gail. *A fishy story*
Gallant, Kathryn. *The flute player of Beppu*
Gikow, Louise. *Jim Henson's Muppets in Rowlf's big test*
Goldsmith, Howard. *Little lost dog*
Grambling, Lois G. *The witch who wanted to be a princess*
Gretz, Susanna. *Rabbit rambles on*
Gutman, Anne. *Lisa in the jungle*
Hathorn, Libby (Elizabeth). *Freya's fantastic surprise*
Havill, Juanita. *Jamaica's find*
Heyer, Carol. *Robin Hood*
Himmelman, John. *Honest Tulio*
Keller, Holly. *That's mine, Horace*
Kyle, Kathryn. *Honesty*
Langton, Jane. *The hedgehog boy*
McKissack, Patricia C. *The honest-to-goodness truth*
McLenighan, Valjean. *I know you cheated*
Mathers, Petra. *Herbie's secret Santa*
Matsuno, Masako. *A pair of red clogs*
    Taro and the Tofu

Mayer, Mercer. *How the trollusk got his hat*
Moss, Marissa. *Who was it?*
O'Connor, Jane. *Nina, Nina, star ballerina*
Schroeder, Alan. *The stone lion*
Stephens, Helen. *Ruby and the muddy dog*
Torre, Betty L. *The luminous pearl*
Turkle, Brinton. *The adventures of Obadiah*
Wilson, Julia. *Becky*

Character traits – incentive *see* Character traits – ambition

Character traits – individuality

Abolafia, Yossi. *My three uncles*
Alderson, Sue Ann. *Bonnie McSmithers is at it again!*
Aliki. *All by myself!*
    Jack and Jake
Allamand, Pascale. *The animals who changed their colors*
Andreae, Giles. *Giraffes can't dance*
Anglund, Joan Walsh. *Look out the window*
Anholt, Catherine. *Kids*
    What I like
Appelt, Kathi. *Incredible me!*
Azore, Barbara. *Wanda and the wild hair*
Baicker, Karen. *Pea pod babies*
Baker, Jeannie. *Millicent*
Baker, Roberta. *No ordinary Olive*
Bass, Jules. *Herb, the vegetarian dragon*
Bates, Ivan. *All by myself*
Beim, Jerrold. *Country train*
    Freckle face
Berliner, Franz. *Wildebeest*
Boland, Janice. *Annabel*
Bowen, Keith. *Katy's gift*
Boynton, Sandra. *Yay, you! : moving out, moving up, moving on*
Bradman, Tony. *Michael*
Bright, Robert. *Which is Willy?*
Brimner, Larry Dane. *Nana's hog*
Brown, Don. *Odd boy out*
Brumbeau, Jeff. *Miss Hunnicutt's hat*
Burke-Weiner, Kimberly. *The maybe garden*
Bynum, Janie. *Otis*
Carey, Mary. *The owl who loved sunshine*
Carey, Valerie Scho. *Tsugele's broom*
Carlson, Nancy L. *I like me*
Caseley, Judith. *Cousins*
Cave, Kathryn. *Henry's song*
Charlip, Remy. *Hooray for me!*
Chodos-Irvine, Margaret. *Ella Sarah gets dressed*
Cibula, Matt S. *What's up with you, Taquandra Fu?*
Collington, Peter. *Clever cat*
Conford, Ellen. *Impossible, possum*
Corey, Shana. *First graders from Mars: The problem with Pelly*
Cowan, Catherine. *My life with the wave*
Delaney, Ned. *One dragon to another*
Dellinger, Annetta. *You are special to Jesus*
Delton, Judy. *I'm telling you now*
De Paola, Tomie (Thomas Anthony). *Oliver Button is a sissy*
Dobkin, Bonnie. *Everybody says*
Duvoisin, Roger Antoine. *Jasmine*
Eduar, Gilles. *Jooka saves the day*
Fatio, Louise. *Hector penguin*
Friedman, Laurie B. *A style all her own*
Fuchshuber, Annegert. *Two peas in a pod*
Genechten, Guido Van. *Flop-Ear*
Gerrard, Roy. *Mik's mammoth*
Gilbert, Jane. *Indescribably Arabella*
Gramatky, Hardie. *Little Toot through the Golden Gate*
Grejniec, Michael. *What do you like?*
Guy, Rosa. *Billy the Great*
Hallinan, P. K. (Patrick K.). *A rainbow of friends*
Henderson, Alicia Terry. *Call me black, call me beautiful*
Hendry, Diana. *Back soon!*
Hines, Anna Grossnickle. *What Joe saw*
Hogrogian, Nonny. *The tiger of Turkestan*

Horvath, Betty F. *Will the real Tommy Wilson please stand up?*
Jaynes, Ruth M. *What is a birthday child?*
Jeffery, Graham. *Thomas the tortoise*
Jeram, Anita. *Contrary Mary*
Katz, Karen. *The colors of us*
Keens-Douglas, Richardo. *The Miss Meow pageant*
Keller, Holly. *Harry and Tuck*
King, Stephen Michael. *Henry and Amy (right-way-round and upside down)*
Knowles, Sheena. *Edward the emu*
Kraus, Robert. *Owliver*
Kuskin, Karla. *I am me*
    Which horse is William?
Lachner, Dorothea. *Meredith, the witch who wasn't*
Lampert, Emily. *A little touch of monster*
Latimer, Jim. *Snail and Buffalo*
Leaf, Munro. *The story of Ferdinand the bull*
Leonard, Marcia. *Best friends*
Lester, Alison. *Celeste sails to Spain*
    Clive eats alligators
    Tessa snaps snakes
Lester, Helen. *Tacky the penguin*
    Three cheers for Tacky
Levine, Rhoda. *Harrison loved his umbrella*
Lewison, Wendy Cheyette. *Shy Vi*
Lidz, Jane. *Zak, the one-of-a-kind dog*
Lionni, Leo. *A color of his own*
    Pezzettino
    Tico and the golden wings
Littledale, Freya. *The magic plum tree*
Livingston, Irene. *Finklehopper Frog*
Lopshire, Robert. *I want to be somebody new!*
Lucas, David. *Halibut Jackson*
Lystad, Mary H. *That new boy*
McCarthy, Meghan. *George upside down*
McCaughrean, Geraldine. *How the reindeer got their antlers*
McConnachie, Brian. *Flying boy*
McCormack, John E. *Rabbit tales*
MacGregor, Marilyn. *On top*
Maguire, Arlene H. *Special people, special ways*
Maguire, John. *People*
Maloney, Peter (1955–). *His mother's nose*
Manning, Mick. *My body, your body*
Manushkin, Fran. *Shirleybird*
Marciano, John Bemelmans. *Delilah*
Martin, Bill (William Ivan). *Chicken Chuck*
Mayer, Marianna. *The prince and the pauper*
Mills, Lauren A. *Tatterhood and the hobgoblins*
Mitchell, Lori. *Different just like me*
Modesitt, Jeanne. *Mama, if you had a wish*
Morris, Ann. *Families*
Moss, Marissa. *But not Kate*
Newman, Lesléa. *Belinda's bouquet*
Numeroff, Laura Joffe. *Sherman Crunchley*
Ogburn, Jacqueline K. *The Masked Maverick*
Olsen, Alfa-Betty. *Gabby the shrew*
Oram, Hiawyn. *Ned and the Joybaloo*
    The wrong overcoat
Parkinson, Curtis. *Emily's eighteen aunts*
Parr, Todd. *The okay book*
Peet, Bill (William Bartlett). *Buford the little bighorn*
    The spooky tail of Prewitt Peacock
Percy, Graham. *24 strange little animals in a haunted house*
Pinkwater, Daniel Manus. *The big orange splot*
Rand, Gloria. *Salty dog*
Rankin, Joan. *You're somebody special, Walliwigs!*
Redies, Rainer. *The cats' party*
Richardson, John. *Grunt*
Rockwell, Anne F. *Show and tell day*
Rogers, Fred. *If we were all the same*
Rohmann, Eric. *Pumpkinhead*
Ross, Tom. *Eggbert, the slightly cracked egg*
Rotner, Shelley. *Faces*
    What can you do?
Rubel, Nicole. *Sam and Violet are twins*
    Sam and Violet go camping
Ruck-Pauquèt, Gina. *Mumble bear*

Schami, Rafik. *Albert and Lila*
   The crow who stood on his beak
Schotter, Roni. *Dreamland*
Sendak, Maurice. *Pierre*
Seskin, Steve. *Don't laugh at me*
Seuling, Barbara. *The triplets*
Seuss, Dr. *I can draw it myself*
Shannon, David. *A bad case of stripes*
Sharmat, Marjorie Weinman. *What are we going to do about Andrew?*
Sharmat, Mitchell. *Sherman is a slowpoke*
Silverstein, Shel. *The missing piece*
Simon, Norma. *All kinds of children*
   I know what I like
   Why am I different?
Simont, Marc. *The goose that almost got cooked*
Singer, Marilyn. *The dog who insisted he wasn't*
   The one and only me
   Pickle plan
Slobodkin, Louis. *Millions and millions and millions*
Tafuri, Nancy. *Have you seen my duckling?*
Thomas, Joyce Carol. *Cherish me*
Thomson, Pat. *Beware of the aunts!*
Tusa, Tricia. *Camilla's new hairdo*
Tyrrell, Anne. *Mary Ann always can*
Viorst, Judith. *Try it again, Sam*
Waber, Bernard. *"You look ridiculous," said the rhinoceros to the hippopotamus*
Wallace, John. *The twins*
Walsh, Ellen Stoll. *For Pete's sake*
Waters, Jennifer. *All kinds of people*
Waxman, Stephanie. *What is a girl? What is a boy?*
Wells, Rosemary. *Shy Charles*
Weninger, Brigitte. *Why are you fighting, Davy?*
Wheatley, Nadia. *Luke's way of looking*
White, Amanda. *Rip and Rap*
Whitney, Dorothy B. *Creatures of an exceptional kind*
Woods, Noah. *Tom cat*

Character traits – kindness

Æsop. *The lion and the mouse*, ill. by Sara Rojo
Aliki. *The story of William Penn*
Bang, Molly. *The paper crane*
Barber, Antonia. *Satchelmouse and the doll's house*
Barbour, Karen. *Mr. Bow Tie*
Barrett, Mary Brigid. *The man of the house at Huffington Row*
Baumann, Kurt. *The prince and the lute*
Bishop, Adela. *The Easter wolf*
Blaich, Ute. *The star*
Bloom, Becky. *Crackers*
Brown, Margaret Wise. *Dr. Squash the doll doctor*
Butterworth, Nick. *Amanda's butterfly*
Calhoun, Mary. *The thieving dwarfs*
Caswell, Helen Rayburn. *Parable of the good Samaritan*
Cazet, Denys. *A fish in his pocket*
Chmielarz, Sharon. *Down at Angel's*
Cole, Brock. *The king at the door*
Cole, Joanna. *A gift from Saint Francis*
Compton, Joanne. *Ashpet*
Coville, Bruce. *The foolish giant*
   Sarah and the dragon
Curry, Jane Louise. *The Christmas knight*
Davis, Maggie S. *Grandma's secret letter*
DeArmond, Dale. *The seal oil lamp*
Edwards, Nancy. *Glenna's seeds*
Elzbieta. *Dikou and the baby star*
   Dikou the little troon who walks at night
Evans, Richard Paul. *The light of Christmas*
Fatio, Louise. *The happy lion's rabbits*
Fleischman, Sid. *The scarebird*
Fuchshuber, Annegert. *Carly*
Fyleman, Rose. *A fairy went a-marketing*
Gannett, Ruth Stiles. *Katie and the sad noise*
Gerstein, Mordicai. *The wild boy*
Goodsell, Jane. *Toby's toe*
Grimm, Jacob. *The golden goose*, ill. by Dorothée Duntze

The golden goose, ill. by Dennis McDermott
The golden goose, ill. by Isadore Seltzer
The golden goose, ill. by Martin Ursell
Hasler, Eveline. *Martin is our friend*
Hastings, Selina. *The singing ringing tree*
Heyward, Du Bose. *The country bunny and the little gold shoes*
Holmquist, Delano. *SantaSaurus*
Jiménez, Francisco. *The Christmas gift = El regalo de Navidad*
Johnson, Grace. *The candle in the window*
Karlin, Nurit. *The tooth witch*
Kent, Jack. *Clotilda*
Kraus, Robert. *The first robin*
Lamstein, Sarah Marwil. *I like your buttons!*
LaRochelle, David. *A Christmas guest*
Lee, Jeanne M. *Ba-Nam*
Lipkind, William. *The magic feather duster*
McCourt, Lisa. *Chicken soup for little souls: The Goodness Gorillas*
   Chicken soup for little souls: The never-forgotten doll
MacDonald, Margaret Read. *Slop!*
McKinley, Cindy. *One smile*
McNaughton, Janet. *Brave Jack and the unicorn*
Martin, Nora. *The stone dancers*
Mayer, Marianna. *The little jewel box*
Meddaugh, Susan. *Beast*
Mizumura, Kazue. *If I built a village*
Munsch, Robert N. *David's father*
Murphy, Mary. *How kind*
Nesbit, Edith. *The last of the dragons*
Newton, Patricia Montgomery. *The five sparrows*
Noble, Trinka Hakes. *Hansy's mermaid*
Ormondroyd, Edward. *Theodore*
Paterson, Katherine. *Celia and the sweet, sweet water*
Peterson, Hans. *Erik and the Christmas horse*
Postgate, Oliver. *Noggin the king*
Rice, David L. *Because Brian hugged his mother*
Richard, Françoise. *On Cat Mountain*
Rider, Joanne. *First grade valentines*
Rohmer, Harriet. *Atariba and Niguayona*
San Souci, Robert D. *The talking eggs*
Schaefer, Carole Lexa. *Under the midsummer sky*
Schnur, Steven. *The tie man's miracle*
Schotter, Roni. *Captain Snap and the children of Vinegar Lane*
Schroeder, Alan. *The stone lion*
Seuss, Dr. *Horton hears a Who!*
Shibano, Tamizo. *The old man who made the trees bloom*
Silverman, Erica. *Gittel's hands*
Simmons, Steven J. *Alice and Greta*
Singer, Marilyn. *The maiden on the moor*
Small, David. *Eulalie and the hopping head*
Spelman, Cornelia Maude. *When I care about others*
Steig, William. *Wizzil*
Steptoe, John. *Mufaro's beautiful daughters*
Stevens, Carla. *Stories from a snowy meadow*
Stock, Catherine. *Secret Valentine*
Stroud, Bettye. *Down home at Miss Dessa's*
Tolstoy, Aleksey Nikolayevich. *Shoemaker Martin*
Torre, Betty L. *The luminous pearl*
Ungar, Richard. *Rachel's gift*
Ungerer, Tomi. *Zeralda's ogre*
Vigna, Judith. *Anyhow, I'm glad I tried*
Warren, Cathy. *Saturday belongs to Sara*
Weedn, Flavia. *The giant's garden*
Wells, H. G. (Herbert George). *The adventures of Tommy*
Wilde, Oscar. *Fairy tales of Oscar Wilde*
   The selfish giant, ill. by S. Saelig Gallagher
   The selfish giant, ill. by Dom Mansell
   The selfish giant, ill. by Fabian Negrin
   The selfish giant, ill. by Lisbeth Zwerger
Wittman, Sally. *The boy who hated Valentine's Day*
Wojciechowski, Susan. *A fine St. Patrick's Day*
Yep, Laurence. *The junior thunder lord*
Zolotow, Charlotte (Shapiro). *I know a lady*

Character traits – kindness to animals

Aardema, Verna. *Koi and the kola nuts*
Æsop. *Androcles and the lion*, ill. by Janusz Grabianski

Androcles and the lion, ill. by Dennis Nolan
Androcles and the lion, ill. by Robert Rayevsky
Androcles and the lion, ill. by Janet Stevens
Albert, Richard E. *Alejandro's gift*
Allred, Mary. *Grandmother Poppy and the funny-looking bird*
Anderson, C. W. (Clarence Williams). *Lonesome little colt*
  The rumble seat pony
Aragon, Jane Chelsea. *Winter harvest*
Armstrong, Jennifer. *King crow*
Baker, Jeannie. *Home in the sky*
Barnhart, Peter. *The wounded duck*
Baumann, Hans. *Chip has many brothers*
Beatty, Hetty Burlingame. *Moorland pony*
Bergman, Donna. *City fox*
Berson, Harold. *Joseph and the snake*
Bianchi, John. *The lab rats of Doctor Eclair*
Birrer, Cynthia. *The lady and the unicorn*
Bodkin, Odds. *The crane wife*
Bolliger, Max. *The magic bird*
Boon, Emilie. *It's spring, Peterkin*
Brenner, Barbara A. *Two orphan cubs*
Brighton, Catherine. *Hope's gift*
Brock, Emma Lillian. *The birds' Christmas tree*
Brown, Katherine. *The Small One*
Brown, Ruth. *The grizzly revenge*
Brunhoff, Laurent de. *Babar's little girl*
Brutschy, Jennifer. *The winter fox*
Bryan, Ashley. *Sh-ko and his eight wicked brothers*
Buchanan, Heather S. *Emily Mouse's first adventure*
Bunting, Eve (Anne Evelyn). *Night tree*
Burch, Robert. *The hunting trip*
Butterworth, Nick. *One blowy night*
  One snowy night
Cannon, Annie. *The bat in the boot*
Carey, Mary. *The owl who loved sunshine*
Carter, Anne Laurel. *Bella's secret garden*
Chase, Jan Brinckerhoff. *The golden song*
Clark, Elizabeth. *Father Christmas and the donkey*
Clewes, Dorothy. *The wild wood*
Coffey, Maria. *A seal in the family*
Collicott, Sharleen. *Toestomper and the caterpillars*
Cowcher, Helen. *Tigress*
Cowley, Joy. *The video shop sparrow*
Curle, Jock J. *The four good friends*
Daugherty, James Henry. *Andy and the lion*
De Beer, Hans. *Little polar bear and the husky pup*
De Marolles, Chantal. *The lonely wolf*
Devlin, Wende. *Cranberry summer*
Dobson, Clive. *Fred's TV*
Dragonwagon, Crescent. *Bat in the dining room*
Drew, Patricia. *Spotter Puff*
Dunn, Judy. *The little lamb*
Duvoisin, Roger Antoine. *The happy hunter*
Easterling, Bill. *Prize in the snow*
Elbling, Peter. *Aria*
Falk, Barbara Bustetter. *Grusha*
Fowler, Susi Gregg. *Circle of thanks*
Freeman, Don. *The seal and the slick*
Galdone, Paul. *Androcles and the lion*
Gantschev, Ivan. *Otto the bear*
Georgiady, Nicholas P. *Gertie the duck*
Geraghty, Paul. *The hunter*
Gilbert, Suzie. *Hawk Hill*
Gleeson, Brian. *Koi and the kola nuts*
Goffstein, M. B. (Marilyn Brooke). *Natural history*
The good-hearted youngest brother
Graham, Bob. *Pete and Roland*
  Queenie, one of the family
Grant, Joan. *The monster that grew small*
Haas, Jessie. *Mowing*
Hader, Berta Hoerner. *Mister Billy's gun*
Harriott, Ted. *Coming home*
Harrison, David Lee. *Little turtle's big adventure*
Hendry, Diana. *Dog Donovan*
Herriot, James. *Christmas Day kitten*
Hewett, Joan. *Rosalie*
Himmelman, John. *Ibis*

Hirsh, Marilyn. *Deborah the dybbuk*
Hodges, Margaret. *The golden deer*
  St. Jerome and the lion
Hol, Coby. *Niki's little donkey*
Holmes, Efner Tudor. *Amy's goose*
  Carrie's gift
Hoose, Philip M. *Hey little ant*
Houk, Randy. *Rico's hawk*
Hutchins, H. J. (Hazel J.). *The catfish palace*
  One duck
Ichikawa, Satomi. *Nora's duck*
Ikeda, Daisaku. *Kanta and the deer*
  The snow country prince
Ishii, Momoko. *The tongue-cut sparrow*
Jeffery, Graham. *Thomas the tortoise*
Joosse, Barbara M. *Nugget and Darling*
Keats, Ezra Jack. *Jennie's hat*
Keller, Holly. *Island baby*
Keo, Ena. *The crane wife*
Kimmel, Eric A. *The birds' gift*
Kroll, Steven. *Queen of the May*
Kroll, Virginia L. *Sweet Magnolia*
Kumin, Maxine W. *Mittens in May*
Laird, Elizabeth. *The day the ducks went skating*
Lathrop, Dorothy Pulis. *Who goes there?*
Lears, Laurie. *Waiting for Mr. Goose*
Levitin, Sonia. *All the cats in the world*
Lewis, Paul Owen. *Frog girl*
Lipkind, William. *The boy and the forest*
London, Jonathan. *Jackrabbit*
Macaulay, David. *Angelo*
McClure, Gillian. *Selkie*
McDonnell, Flora. *I love animals*
McFarlane, Sheryl. *Eagle dreams*
McMillan, Bruce. *Nights of the pufflings*
McNally, Darcie. *In a cabin in a wood*
McNulty, Faith. *The lady and the spider*
  Mouse and Tim
McPhail, David M. *The bear's toothache*
  A wolf story
Mamin-Sibiryak, D. N. *Grey Neck*
Martchenko, Michael. *Bird feeder banquet*
Martin, Jacqueline Briggs. *Washing the willow tree loon*
Martin, Rafe. *The language of birds*
  The Shark God
Meddaugh, Susan. *Tree of birds*
Michael, Emory H. *Androcles and the lion*
Miklowitz, Gloria D. *Save that raccoon!*
Miller, Edna. *Mousekin's frosty friend*
Mogensen, Jan. *Teddy's Christmas gift*
Moore, Inga. *Rose and the nightingale*
Moore, Sheila. *Samson Svenson's baby*
Nakatani, Chiyoko. *Fumio and the dolphins*
Newberry, Clare Turlay. *Percy, Polly and Pete*
Novak, Matt. *Mr. Floop's lunch*
Numeroff, Laura Joffe. *If you give a moose a muffin*
  If you give a mouse a cookie
  If you give a pig a pancake
Orstadius, Brita. *The dolphin journey*
Pedersen, Judy. *The tiny patient*
Peet, Bill (William Bartlett). *Huge Harold*
Pinkwater, Daniel Manus. *Rainy morning*
Root, Barry. *Gumbrella*
Rossiter, Nan Parson. *The way home*
Roy, Ronald. *A thousand pails of water*
Rumford, James. *Dog-of-the-Sea-Waves*
Ryder, Joanne. *Each living thing*
Rylant, Cynthia. *The bookshop dog*
Sampson, Michael R. *Caddie, the golf dog*
Sandburg, Helga. *Anna and the baby buzzard*
Sayre, April Pulley. *Turtle, turtle, watch out!*
Schlein, Miriam. *Deer in the snow*
Sheldon, Dyan. *The whales' song*
Simont, Marc. *The stray dog*
Soros, Barbara. *Tenzin's deer*
Strand, Keith. *Grandfather's Christmas tree*
Strete, Craig Kee. *The lost boy and the monster*

Tada, Satoshi. *Mr. Beetle*
Thayer, Jane. *Part-time dog*
Thomas, Frances. *The Bear and Mr. Bear*
Thomas, Jane Resh. *Scaredy dog*
Tompert, Ann. *The pied piper of Peru*
Turkle, Brinton. *Thy friend, Obadiah*
Turska, Krystyna. *The woodcutter's duck*
Tyler, Linda Wagner. *After Christmas tree*
Van West, Patricia E. *The crab man*
Varley, Dimitry. *The whirly bird*
Velthuijs, Max. *Little Man to the rescue*
Vincent, Gabrielle. *A day, a dog*
Wallace, Ian. *The sparrow's song*
Ward, Lynd. *The biggest bear*
Waterton, Betty. *A salmon for Simon*
Wersba, Barbara. *Do tigers ever bite kings?*
Whitney, Alma Marshak. *Leave Herbert alone*
Wildsmith, Brian. *Hunter and his dog*
Wondriska, William. *The stop*
Yagawa, Sumiko. *The crane wife*

Character traits – laziness

Armstrong, Jennifer. *Pierre's dream*
Aylesworth, Jim. *Hush up!*
Baker, Betty. *Partners*
Bolognese, Elaine. *The sleepy watchdog*
Bowen, Vernon. *The lazy beaver*
Bright, Robert. *Gregory, the noisiest and strongest boy in Grangers Grove*
Cohen, Caron Lee. *Digger Pig and the turnip*
Coleman, Michael. *Lazy Ozzie*
Davies, Gill. *Can't, don't, won't*
De Paola, Tomie (Thomas Anthony). *Jamie O'Rourke and the big potato*
    Jamie O'Rourke and the pooka
Du Bois, William Pène. *Lazy Tommy pumpkinhead*
Finn, Isobel. *The very lazy ladybug*
Geraghty, Paul. *Slobcat*
Grimm, Jacob. *Mother Holly*
    The three spinning fairies
Holding, James. *The lazy little Zulu*
Ketteman, Helen. *Armadilly chili*
Koscielniak, Bruce. *Bear and Bunny grow tomatoes*
Krasilovsky, Phyllis. *The man who didn't wash his dishes*
    The man who tried to save time
    The man who was too lazy to fix things
Lazy Jack. *Lazy Jack*, ill. by Bert Dodson
    Lazy Jack, ill. by Tony Ross
    Lazy Jack, ill. by Kurt Werth
    Lazy Jack, ill. by Barry Wilkinson
Lester, Helen. *Score one for the sloths*
The little red hen. *The cock, the mouse and the little red hen*, ill. by Lorinda Bryan Cauley
    The cock, the mouse and the little red hen, ill. by Graham Percy
    The little red hen, ill. by Byron Barton
    The little red hen, ill. by Emily Bolam
    The little red hen, ill. by Janina Domanska
    The little red hen, ill. by Paul Galdone
    The little red hen, ill. by Dennis Hockerman
    Little red hen, ill. by Norman Messenger
    The little red hen, ill. by Mel Pekarsky
    The little red hen, ill. by William Stobbs
    The little red hen, ill. by Annie West
    The little red hen, ill. by Margot Zemach
    The little red hen and the ear of wheat, ill. by Elisabeth Bell
    The Little Red Hen makes a pizza
Lobel, Arnold. *A treeful of pigs*
Lorenz, Lee. *Big Gus and Little Gus*
Martin, Antoinette Truglio. *Famous seaweed soup*
Mathews, Louise. *The great take-away*
Melmed, Laura Krauss. *Prince Nautilus*
Metaxas, Eric. *The monkey people*
Mwenye Hadithi. *Lazy lion*
Namioka, Lensey. *The laziest boy in the world*
Nobisso, Josephine. *For the sake of a cake*
Oppenheim, Joanne. *"Not now!" said the cow*

Pack, Robert. *How to catch a crocodile*
Papas, William. *Taresh the tea planter*
Root, Phyllis. *Aunt Nancy and Cousin Lazybones*
Rowe, John A. *Tommy DoLittle*
San Souci, Robert D. *The hired hand*
Schmidt, Eric von. *The young man who wouldn't hoe corn*
Sharmat, Marjorie Weinman. *Burton and Dudley*
Snyder, Dianne. *The boy of the three-year nap*
Taylor, Sydney. *Mr. Barney's beard*
Wells, Ruth. *The farmer and the poor god*
Wildsmith, Brian. *The lazy bear*
Wolf, Gita. *The very hungry lion*

Character traits – loyalty

Aliki. *The two of them*
Ardizzone, Edward. *Tim to the rescue*
Boyle, Vere. *Beauty and the beast*
Bridwell, Norman. *Clifford goes to Hollywood*
Calhoun, Mary. *The witch who lost her shadow*
Carter, Anne Laurel. *Beauty and the beast*
Collodi, Carlo. *The adventures of Pinocchio*
    Pinocchio
Cooney, Barbara. *Little brother and little sister*
Crompton, Anne Eliot. *The winter wife*
Cullen, Lynn. *The mightiest heart*
Edwards, Lisa. *Disney's Beauty and the beast, a book of manners*
Gregory, Nan. *How Smudge came*
Grimm, Jacob. *Little brother and little sister*
Hautzig, Deborah. *Beauty and the beast*
Haywood, Carolyn. *How the reindeer saved Santa*
Hurd, Edith Thacher. *Under the lemon tree*
Hutton, Warwick. *Beauty and the beast*
Ichikawa, Satomi. *Fickle Barbara*
Jennings, Sharon. *Priscilla and Rosy*
Lasker, Joe. *He's my brother*
McCrea, James. *The king's procession*
McLerran, Alice. *The mountain that loved a bird*
Mayer, Marianna. *Beauty and the beast*
Montenegro, Laura Nyman. *Sweet Tooth*
Nesbit, Edith. *Beauty and the beast*
Parsons, Virginia. *Pinocchio and Gepetto*
Pollock, Penny. *The turkey girl*
Potter, Beatrix. *The tale of the faithful dove*
Stanovich, Betty Jo. *Hedgehog adventures*
Va, Leong. *A letter to the king*
Waite, Michael P. *Jojofu*
Whittier, John Greenleaf. *Barbara Frietchie*
Wright, Freire. *Beauty and the beast*

Character traits – luck

Aldridge, Josephine Haskell. *Fisherman's luck*
Alexander, Lloyd. *The house Gobbaleen*
Aliki. *Three gold pieces*
Beim, Lorraine. *Lucky Pierre*
Benjamin, A. H. *It could have been worse*
Bond, Michael. *Paddington's lucky day*
Breckler, Rosemary K. *Hoang breaks the lucky teapot*
Brown, Margaret Wise. *Wheel on the chimney*
Butler, Dorothy. *Another happy tale*
    A happy tale
Callan, Elizabeth Koda. *Good luck pony*
Cazet, Denys. *Lucky me*
Chausse, Sylvie. *The egg and I*
Cocca-Leffler, Maryann. *Ice-cold birthday*
Conrad, Pam. *The lost sailor*
Delton, Judy. *I never win!*
    It happened on Thursday
Dillon, Jana. *Lucky O'Leprechaun*
Elkin, Benjamin. *Lucky and the giant*
Gackenbach, Dick. *Harvey, the foolish pig*
Geraghty, Paul. *Look out, Patrick!*
Grimm, Jacob. *Hans in luck*, ill. by Paul Galdone
    Hans in luck, ill. by Felix Hoffmann
    Lucky Hans
Hann, Jacquie. *Up day, down day*

Harjo, Joy. *The good luck cat*
Hearn, Diane Dawson. *Bad luck Boswell*
Henwood, Simon. *A piece of luck*
Hodges, Margaret. *Saint Patrick and the peddler*
Holland, Janice. *You never can tell*
Ivanov, Anatoly. *Ol' Jake's lucky day*
Lecher, Doris. *Angelita's magic yarn*
Lin, Grace. *Fortune cookie fortunes*
Long, Jan Freeman. *The bee and the dream*
Mayer, Marianna. *The little jewel box*
Moeri, Louise. *The unicorn and the plow*
Riddell, Chris. *Platypus and the lucky day*
Russell, Betty. *Big store, funny door*
Seuss, Dr. *Did I ever tell you how lucky you are?*
Stafford, Kay. *Ling Tang and the lucky cricket*
Stanley, Diane. *The good-luck pencil*
Tobias, Tobi. *Serendipity*
Underhill, Liz. *The lucky coin*
Velthuijs, Max. *Little Man's lucky day*
Walsh, Jill Paton. *Lost and found*
Ziefert, Harriet. *Good luck, bad luck*

Character traits – meanness

Bellows, Cathy. *Four fat rats*
Bottner, Barbara. *Mean Maxine*
Brown, Marc Tolon. *D. W., go to your room!*
Burningham, John. *Borka*
Carey, Valerie Scho. *The devil and mother Crump*
Carlson, Nancy L. *How to lose all your friends*
Carr, Jan. *Dark day, light night*
Carrick, Carol. *Old Mother Witch*
Clayton, Elaine. *Pup in school*
Coville, Bruce. *Sarah's unicorn*
David, Lawrence. *The good little girl*
Debecker, Benoît. *The naughty prince*
Edwards, Richard. *The forest child*
Euvremer, Teryl. *Triple whammy*
Freeman, Don. *Tilly Witch*
Gantos, Jack (John, Jr.). *Rotten Ralph's rotten Christmas*
  Rotten Ralph's show and tell
  Rotten Ralph's trick or treat
  Worse than Rotten Ralph
Glazer, Lee. *Cookie Becker casts a spell*
Goble, Paul. *The lost children*
Goodsell, Jane. *Toby's toe*
Himmelman, John. *Amanda and the witch switch*
Hoban, Russell. *Big John Turkle*
  The little Brute family
Jones, Rebecca C. *The biggest, meanest, ugliest dog in the whole wide world*
Kidd, Bruce. *Hockey showdown*
Kismaric, Carole. *The rumor of Pavel and Paali*
Kraus, Robert. *The Christmas cookie sprinkle snitcher*
McCrea, James. *The magic tree*
McCully, Emily Arnold. *Little Kit, or, The Industrious Flea Circus girl*
Mahy, Margaret. *The boy with two shadows*
Manushkin, Fran. *Hocus and Pocus at the circus*
Morrison, Toni. *The book of mean people*
Nickl, Peter. *Ra ta ta tam*
O'Malley, Kevin. *Humpty Dumpty egg-splodes*
Patz, Nancy. *Gina Farina and the Prince of Mintz*
Prelutsky, Jack. *The mean old mean hyena*
Price, Michelle. *Mean Melissa*
Roberts, Lynn (Lynn M.). *Rapunzel, a groovy fairy tale*
San Souci, Robert D. *Sootface*
Seuss, Dr. *How the Grinch stole Christmas*
Shibano, Tamizo. *The old man who made the trees bloom*
Silverman, Erica. *Gittel's hands*
Simmons, Steven J. *Alice and Greta*
Snyder, Anne. *The old man and the mule*
Somers, Kevin. *Meaner than meanest*
Steptoe, John. *Mufaro's beautiful daughters*
Stevenson, James. *Fried feathers for Thanksgiving*
  Happy Valentine's Day, Emma!
  The worst person's Christmas
Udry, Janice May. *The mean mouse and other mean stories*

Wooldridge, Connie Nordhiem. *Wicked Jack*
Zimelman, Nathan. *Mean Murgatroyd and the ten cats*
Zion, Gene. *The meanest squirrel I ever met*

Character traits – optimism

Alexander, Sue. *Marc the Magnificent*
Aliki. *The twelve months*
Anglund, Joan Walsh. *Rainbow love*
Atwood, Margaret. *Anna's pet*
Ayer, Jacqueline. *The paper-flower tree*
Brisson, Pat. *Wanda's roses*
Butterworth, Nick. *One blowy night*
Carey, Valerie Scho. *Maggie Mab and the bogey beast*
Carlson, Nancy L. *Smile a lot!*
Delton, Judy. *My mother lost her job today*
Dionetti, Michelle V. *Coal mine peaches*
Gregory, Valiska. *Sunny side up*
  Terribly wonderful
Hall, Malcolm. *The friends of Charlie Ant Bear*
Hoff, Syd. *Oliver*
Hubbard, Woodleigh Marx. *All that you are*
Krauss, Ruth. *The carrot seed*
Lindgren, Astrid. *Of course Polly can do almost everything*
Lionni, Leo. *Theodore and the talking mushroom*
Martin, Jacqueline Briggs. *Good times on Grandfather Mountain*
Peet, Bill (William Bartlett). *The Whingdingdilly*
Piatti, Celestino. *The happy owls*
Rice, Inez. *A long long time*
Saltzman, David. *The jester has lost his jingle*
Schwartz, Roslyn. *The mole sisters and the piece of moss*
Seuss, Dr. *Would you rather be a bullfrog?*
Tapio, Pat Decker. *The lady who saw the good side of everything*
Wiesner, William. *Happy-Go-Lucky*
Wilhelm, Hans. *All for the best*
Zakhoder, Boris Vladimirovich. *Rosachok*

Character traits – orderliness

Bottner, Barbara. *Two messy friends*
  Wallace's lists
Braybrooks, Ann. *Plenty of pockets*
Dale, Penny. *Bet you can't*
Dubowski, Cathy East. *Megan's messy room*
Duncan, Alice Faye. *Miss Viola and Uncle Ed Lee*
Glaser, Linda. *Mrs. Greenberg's messy Hanukkah*
Grohmann, Susan. *The dust under Mrs. Merriweather's bed*
Hassett, John. *Mouse in the house*
Kamish, Daniel. *Diggy Dan*
Leonard, Marcia. *I like mess*
Lillie, Patricia. *Everything has a place*
MacDonald, Alan. *Beware of the bears!*
McElmurry, Jill. *Mess pets*
McKenzie, Ellen Kindt. *The perfectly orderly house*
McKissack, Patricia C. *Messy Bessey*
Miller, Margaret. *Where does it go?*
O'Malley, Kevin. *Bud*
Peguero, Leone. *Lionel and Amelia*
Perkins, Lynne Rae. *Clouds for dinner*
Piers, Helen. *Who's in my bed?*
Prigger, Mary Skillings. *Aunt Minnie McGranahan*
Root, Phyllis. *Mrs. Potter's pig*
Schotter, Roni. *Captain Bob takes flight*
Schwab, Eva. *Robert and the Robot*
Sutherland, Colleen. *Jason goes to show-and-tell*
Teague, Mark. *Pigsty*
Viorst, Judith. *Super-completely and totally the messiest*
Yolen, Jane. *How do dinosaurs clean their rooms?*

Character traits – ostracism *see* Character traits – being different

Character traits – patience

Appelt, Kathi. *Watermelon day*
Barbosa, Rogério Andrade. *African animal tales*
Barton, Byron. *Hester*

Butler, Stephen. *The mouse and the apple*
Clarke, Gus. *How many days to my birthday?*
Cyrus, Kurt. *Slow train to Oxmox*
Dunrea, Olivier. *Ollie*
Erickson, Karen. *Waiting my turn*
Gerstein, Mordicai. *The wild boy*
Grindley, Sally. *Why is the sky blue?*
Grunwald, Lisa. *Now, soon, later*
Hellen, Nancy. *Bus stop*
Jensen, Patricia. *Be patient, Little Chick*
Ketteman, Helen. *Not yet, Yvette*
Kibbey, Marsha. *My grammy*
Koski, Mary. *Impatient Pamela calls 9-1-1*
    Impatient Pamela wants a bigger family
Kulling, Monica. *Waiting for Amos*
Laurin, Anne. *Little things*
Ludy, Mark. *The farmer*
Mollel, Tololwa M. (Tololwa Marti). *Subira subira*
Morgan-Vanroyen, Mary. *Patient Rosie*
Poydar, Nancy. *Mailbox magic*
Rockwell, Anne F. *Chip and the karate kick*
Steiner, Charlotte. *What's the hurry, Harry?*
Walters, Catherine. *When will it be spring?*
Weiss, Nicki. *Waiting*
Wells, Rosemary. *Max's breakfast*

Character traits – perfectionism

Harris, Peter. *Perfect Prudence*

Character traits – perseverance

Abisch, Roz. *Sweet Betsy from Pike*
Æsop. *The miller, his son and their donkey*, ill. by Roger Antoine
    Duvoisin
    The miller, his son and their donkey, ill. by Eugen Sopko
Alexander, Martha G. *Move over, Twerp*
    We never get to do anything
Aliki. *A weed is a flower*
Ambrus, Victor G. *The little cockerel*
    Mishka
Balcziak, Bill. *John Henry*
Barber, Barbara E. *Allie's basketball dream*
Baumgardner, Mary Alice. *Alexandra, keeper of dreams*
Bethell, Jean. *Hooray for Henry*
Blades, Ann. *Mary of mile 18*
Boynton, Sandra. *If at first . . .*
Brennan, Joseph Killorin. *Gobo and the river*
Calhoun, Mary. *Old man Whickutt's donkey*
Carle, Eric. *The very clumsy click beetle*
Carter, Anne Laurel. *The F team*
Choldenko, Gennifer. *Moonstruck*
Conford, Ellen. *Just the thing for Geraldine*
Day, Shirley. *Ruthie's big tree*
Erickson, Karen. *I'll try*
Gray, Genevieve. *How far, Felipe?*
Hoff, Syd. *Slugger Sal's slump*
Jensen, Virginia Allen. *Sara and the door*
Kahl, Virginia. *Maxie*
Keats, Ezra Jack. *John Henry*
Kent, Jack. *Mrs. Mooley*
Kinerk, Robert. *Clorinda*
Lester, Julius. *John Henry*
Lindgren, Astrid. *Of course Polly can do almost everything*
London, Jonathan. *Where the big fish are*
Ludy, Mark. *The farmer*
Mitchell, Margaree King. *Uncle Jed's barbershop*
Pinkney, J. Brian. *Jojo's flying side kick*
Piper, Watty. *The little engine that could*
Riordan, James. *The three magic gifts*
Saunders, Dave. *So slow!*
Shearer, Marilyn J. *The crown of fools*
Shine, Deborah. *The little engine that could pudgy word book*
Skorpen, Liesel Moak. *All the Lassies*
Spinelli, Eileen. *Sophie's masterpiece*
Steig, William. *Brave Irene*
Thomas, Jane Resh. *Scaredy dog*

Thomas, Kathy. *The angel's quest*
Ungerer, Tomi. *The Mellops go spelunking*
Watanabe, Shigeo. *I can build a house!*
    I can ride it!
    Where's my daddy?
Waterton, Betty. *Orff, 27 dragons (and a snarkel)*
Weedn, Flavia. *The elephant prince*
Weller, Frances Ward. *Madaket Millie*

Character traits – persistence

Adler, David A. *Helen Keller*
Anderson, Laurie Halse. *The big cheese of Third Street*
Birdseye, Tom. *Airmail to the moon*
Brown, Ruth. *The ghost of Greyfriar's Bobby*
Brutschy, Jennifer. *Celeste and Crabapple Sam*
Bulla, Clyde Robert. *The stubborn old woman*
Czernecki, Stefan. *Paper lanterns*
Day, Marie. *Dragon in the rocks*
Glass, Andrew. *Charles T. McBiddle*
Gray, Kes. *Eat your peas*
Hodges, Margaret. *Hidden in sand*
Howe, James. *Horace and Morris join the chorus (but what about
    Dolores?)*
Lattimore, Deborah Nourse. *The sailor who captured the sea*
Lexau, Joan M. *Go away, dog*, ill. by Crosby Newell Bonsall
    Go away, dog, ill. by Paul Meisel
McCully, Emily Arnold. *The ballot box battle*
    Mouse practice
Marsh, Jeri. *Hurrah for Alexander*
Palatini, Margie. *The perfect pet*
Patz, Nancy. *Gina Farina and the Prince of Mintz*
Rigby, Rodney. *Hello, this is your penguin speaking*
Ross, Tony. *I want a cat*
Schachner, Judith Byron. *Yo, Vikings*
Siomades, Lorianne. *The itsy bitsy spider*
Trapani, Iza. *The itsy bitsy spider*
Van Leeuwen, Jean. *Sorry*
Ward, Sally G. *Molly and Grandpa*
West, Colin. *"Pardon?" said the giraffe*
Zagwÿn, Deborah Turney. *Apple batter*

Character traits – practicality

Aylesworth, Jim. *Mother Halverson's new cat*
Evans, Katherine. *The man, the boy and the donkey*
Gág, Wanda. *Millions of cats*
Gretz, Susanna. *Roger loses his marbles!*
La Fontaine, Jean de. *The miller, the boy and the donkey*, adapt. and
    ill. by Brian Wildsmith
Modell, Frank. *One zillion valentines*
Oppenheim, Joanne. *Donkey's tale*
Schlein, Miriam. *The pile of junk*

Character traits – pride

Andersen, H. C. (Hans Christian). *The emperor's new clothes*, ill. by
    Angela Barrett
    The emperor's new clothes, ill. by Erik Blegvad
    The emperor's new clothes, ill. by Virginia Lee Burton
    The emperor's new clothes, ill. by Robert Byrd
    The emperor's new clothes, ill. by Charlene DeLage
    The emperor's new clothes, ill. by Jack and Irene Delano
    The emperor's new clothes, ill. by Demi
    The emperor's new clothes, ill. by Hélène Desputeaux
    The emperor's new clothes, ill. by Birte Dietz
    The emperor's new clothes, ill. by Dorothée Duntze
    The emperor's new clothes, ill. by Pamela Baldwin Ford
    The emperor's new clothes, ill. by Jack Kent
    The emperor's new clothes, ill. by Monika Laimgruber
    The emperor's new clothes, ill. by Anne F. Rockwell
    The emperor's new clothes, ill. by Janet Stevens
    The emperor's new clothes, ill. by Eve Tharlet
    The emperor's new clothes, ill. by Robert Van Nutt
    The emperor's new clothes, ill. by Nadine Bernard Westcott
    The red shoes
Armstrong, Jennifer. *Chin Yu Min and the ginger cat*

Atkins, Jeannine. *Get set! Swim!*
Balcziak, Bill. *John Henry*
Bazilian, Barbara. *The red shoes*
Bemelmans, Ludwig. *Rosebud*
Birch, David. *The king's chessboard*
Burningham, John. *Humbert, Mister Firkin and the Lord Mayor of London*
Calhoun, Mary. *The runaway brownie*
Calmenson, Stephanie. *The principal's new clothes*
Clifton, Lucille. *All us come cross the water*
Conrad, Pam. *The rooster's gift*
Crary, Elizabeth. *I'm proud*
DeLuise, Dom. *King Bob's new clothes*
Dionetti, Michelle V. *Thalia Brown and the blue bug*
Duvoisin, Roger Antoine. *Crocus Petunia*
Edwards, Dorothy. *A wet Monday*
Ehrhardt, Reinhold. *Kikeri*
Evans, Richard Paul. *The tower*
Friskey, Margaret (Margaret Richards). *Indian Two Feet rides alone*
Gackenbach, Dick. *The dog and the deep dark woods*
Goode, Diane. *The dinosaur's new clothes*
Grifalconi, Ann. *Osa's pride*
Hamberger, John. *The peacock who lost his tail*
Hürlimann, Ruth. *The proud white cat*
Jackson, Chris. *The Gaggle sisters river tour*
Keats, Ezra Jack. *John Henry*
Lester, Julius. *John Henry*
McCaughrean, Geraldine. *How the reindeer got their antlers*
McKissack, Patricia C. *The king's new clothes*
McLenighan, Valjean. *What you see is what you get*
McMullan, Kate (Hall). *Noel the first*
Perlman, Janet. *The Emperor Penguin's new clothes*
Pomerantz, Charlotte. *The ballad of the long-tailed rat*
Radunsky, Vladimir. *One*
Rogasky, Barbara. *The water of life*
Ross, Anna. *I did it!*
Rumford, James. *Nine animals and the well*
Rylant, Cynthia. *Mr. Griggs' work*
Sasso, Sandy Eisenberg. *God said amen*
Schwartz, Amy. *Annabelle Swift, kindergartner*
Sharmat, Marjorie Weinman. *I'm terrific*
Tettelbaum, Michael. *The cave of the lost Fraggle*
Threadgall, Colin. *Proud rooster and the fox*
Ward, Helen. *The rooster and the fox*
Whitney, Alex. *Once a bright red tiger*
Wilde, Oscar. *The star child*, ill. by Fiona French
Winthrop, Elizabeth. *Tough Eddie*
Yolen, Jane. *King Long Shanks*
Zimnik, Reiner. *The proud circus horse*

Character traits – questioning

Adler, David A. *A little at a time*
Alden, Laura. *When?*
Alexander, Martha G. *Where does the sky end, Grandpa?*
Allard, Harry. *May I stay?*
Anholt, Catherine. *All about you*
Baynton, Martin. *Why do you love me?*
Bird, E. J. *How do bears sleep?*
Brown, Margaret Wise. *Wait till the moon is full*
Camp, Lindsay. *Why?*
Carlstrom, Nancy White. *Goodbye geese*
Clark, Roberta. *Why?*
Clarke, Gus. *How many days to my birthday?*
De Veaux, Alexis. *Na-ni*
Dunbar, Joyce. *Why is the sky up?*
Gorbachev, Valeri. *Where is the apple pie?*
Haswell, Peter. *Pog*
Hazen, Barbara Shook. *Santa clues*
Hines, Anna Grossnickle. *Even if I spill my milk?*
Holub, Joan. *Why do cats meow?*
    Why do dogs bark?
Hopkins, Lee Bennett. *Animals from Mother Goose*
    People from Mother Goose
    Questions
Hulbert, Jay. *Armando asked "Why?"*

Jacobs, Leland B. (Leland Blair). *Is somewhere always far away?*, ill. by John E. Johnson
    Is somewhere always far away?, ill. by Jeff Kaufman
Keven, Elisa. *Ernest*
Krauze, Andrzej. *What's so special about today?*
Lindbergh, Reeve. *What is the sun?*
Lionni, Leo. *Tico and the golden wings*
McKaughan, Larry. *Why are your fingers cold?*
Mahood, Kenneth. *Why are there more questions than answers, Grandad?*
Miller, M. L. *Dizzy from fools*
Miller, Margaret. *Can you guess?*
Moncure, Jane Belk. *Where?*
Murphy, Mary. *Koala and the flower*
Reece, Colleen L. *What?*
Ripley, Catherine. *Why do stars twinkle?*
    Why is soap so slippery?
Schertle, Alice. *That's what I thought*
Simont, Marc. *How come elephants?*
Slater, Teddy. *The cow that could tap dance*
Stover, Jo Ann. *Why? Because*
Taylor, Barbara. *I wonder why zippers have teeth and other questions about inventions*
Thaler, Mike. *Owley*
Tucker, Kathy. *Do cowboys ride bikes?*
Vance, Eleanor Graham. *Jonathan*
Weeks, Sarah. *My somebody special*
Williams, Barbara. *If he's my brother*
Wormell, Mary. *Why not?*
Young, Ruth. *Who says moo?*
Ziefert, Harriet. *Sarah's questions*

Character traits – responsibility

Graves, Keith. *Pet boy*
Gregory, Valiska. *When stories fell like shooting stars*
Haas, Jessie. *Busybody Brandy*
Liersch, Anne. *Nell and Fluffy*
Mahoney, Daniel J. *The Saturday escape*
Oberman, Sheldon. *King Solomon, Sheba, and the hoopoe bird*
Park, Linda Sue. *The firekeeper's son*
Schachner, Judith Byron. *The Grannyman*
Stephens, Helen. *Ruby and the muddy dog*

Character traits – selfishness

Andersen, H. C. (Hans Christian). *The swineherd*, ill. by Erik Blegvad
    The swineherd, ill. by Dorothée Duntze
    The swineherd, ill. by Deborah Hahn
    The swineherd, ill. by Lisbeth Zwerger
Angelo, Valenti. *The acorn tree*
Baba, Noboru. *Eleven cats and a pig*
    Eleven cats and albatrosses
    Eleven cats in a bag
    Eleven hungry cats
Bahous, Sally. *Sitti and the cats*
Barrett, John M. *Oscar the selfish octopus*
Bascom, Joe. *Malcolm Softpaws*
Berquist, Grace. *The boy who couldn't roar*
Berry, Joy Wilt. *Being selfish*
Bryant, Bernice. *Follow the leader*
Carlson, Nancy L. *How to lose all your friends*
Chang, Margaret Scrogin. *The beggar's magic*
Christian, Mary Blount. *The devil take you, Barnabas Beane!*
Coombs, Patricia. *Mouse Café*
Demi. *One grain of rice*
Egan, Tim. *Chestnut Cove*
Elkin, Benjamin. *Lucky and the giant*
Gantos, Jack (John, Jr.). *Back to school for Rotten Ralph*
Garrett, Jennifer. *The queen who stole the sky*
Grindley, Sally. *Can we play too, Piglittle?*
Henkes, Kevin. *A weekend with Wendell*
Hooks, William H. *The rainbow ribbon*
Kahl, Virginia. *The perfect pancake*
Keens-Douglas, Richardo. *The nutmeg princess*
Kraus, Robert. *Rebecca Hatpin*

Lattimore, Deborah Nourse. *The dragon's robe*
Lester, Helen. *Me first*
    Princess Penelope's parrot
Lewin, Betsy. *Chubbo's pool*
Lipkind, William. *Even Steven*
    Finders keepers
Martin, Jane Read. *Now everybody really hates me*
Mollel, Tololwa M. (Tololwa Marti). *The princess who lost her hair*
Peet, Bill (William Bartlett). *The ant and the elephant*
Rankin, Joan. *The little cat and the greedy old woman*
Reader, Dennis. *I want one!*
Reesink, Marijke. *The golden treasure*
Remkiewicz, Frank. *Greedyanna*
Rosen, Michael (1946–). *This is our house*
Sanfield, Steve. *Just rewards, or, Who is that man in the moon and what's he doing up there anyway?*
Schroeder, Alan. *The stone lion*
Warburton, Nick. *Mr. Tite's belongings*
Ward, Helen. *The moonrat and the white turtle*
Weedn, Flavia. *The giant's garden*
Wilde, Oscar. *Fairy tales of Oscar Wilde*
    The selfish giant, ill. by S. Saelig Gallagher
    The selfish giant, ill. by Dom Mansell
    The selfish giant, ill. by Fabian Negrin
    The selfish giant, ill. by Lisbeth Zwerger
    The star child, ill. by Fiona French
Winthrop, Elizabeth. *The Best Friends Club*
Wisdom, Jude. *Whatever Wanda wanted*
Wojtowycz, David. *Dudley's birthday party*
Yep, Laurence. *Tiger woman*

Character traits – shyness

Aboff, Marcie. *The giant jelly bean jar*
Blaustein, Muriel. *Jim chimp's story*
Brice, Tony. *The bashful goldfish*
Cooney, Nancy Evans. *Chatter-box Jamie*
Devlin, Wende. *Cranberry Valentine*
Dines, Glen. *A tiger in the cherry tree*
Glaser, Linda. *Stop that garbage truck!*
Goble, Paul. *Love flute*
Goffstein, M. B. (Marilyn Brooke). *Neighbors*
Gorbachev, Valeri. *Chicken chickens go to school*
Hamilton, Morse. *How do you do, Mr. Birdsteps?*
Hogrogian, Nonny. *Carrot cake*
Hutchins, Pat. *Titch and Daisy*
Keats, Ezra Jack. *Louie*
Keller, Beverly. *Fiona's bee*
Krasilovsky, Phyllis. *The shy little girl*
Lester, Helen. *The shy people's picnic*
Levine, Arthur A. *Sheep dreams*
Lewison, Wendy Cheyette. *Shy Vi*
Lexau, Joan M. *Benjie*
Lucas, David. *Halibut Jackson*
McCourt, Lisa. *Chicken soup for little souls: The new kid and the cookie thief*
McCully, Emily Arnold. *Speak up, Blanche!*
Mathers, Petra. *Sophie and Lou*
Metcalf, Paula. *Norma No Friends*
Montenegro, Laura Nyman. *A bird about to sing*
Moore, Inga. *A big day for Little Jack*
Richardson, Jean. *Clara's dancing feet*
Rosenberry, Vera. *Vera's first day of school*
Schaefer, Charles E. *Cat's got your tongue?*
Smith, Wendy. *Say hello, Tilly*
Udry, Janice May. *What Mary Jo shared*
Wold, Jo Anne. *Tell them my name is Amanda*
Yashima, Taro. *Crow boy*
    The youngest one
Zalben, Jane Breskin. *Miss Violet's shining day*
Zolotow, Charlotte (Shapiro). *A tiger called Thomas*, ill. by Catherine Stock
    A tiger called Thomas, ill. by Kurt Werth

Character traits – smallness

Andersen, H. C. (Hans Christian). *Thumbelina*, ill. by Adrienne Adams
    Thumbelina, ill. by Wayne Anderson
    Thumbelina, ill. by Emma Chichester Clark
    Thumbelina, ill. by Alison Claire Darke
    Thumbelina, ill. by Charlene DeLage
    Thumbelina, ill. by Demi
    Thumbelina, ill. by Arlene Graston
    Thumbelina, ill. by Susan Jeffers
    Thumbelina, ill. by Kaarina Kaila
    Thumbelina, ill. by Christine Willis Nigognossian
    Thumbelina, ill. by Gustaf Tenggren
    Thumbelina, ill. by Lisbeth Zwerger
    Thumbeline, ill. by Lisbeth Zwerger; tr. by Anthea Bell
Bang, Betsy. *The cucumber stem*
Beim, Jerrold. *The smallest boy in the class*
Benjamin, A. H. *A duck so small*
Bromhall, Winifred. *Bridget's growing day*
Burgess, Gelett. *The little father*
Chevalier, Christa. *Spence is small*
Cooper, Susan. *The silver cow*
Cuneo, Mary Louise. *Inside a sandcastle and other secrets*
Curry, Jane Louise. *Little, little sister*
De Paola, Tomie (Thomas Anthony). *Andy (that's my name)*
Gay, Michel. *Little helicopter*
Glass, Andrew. *Chickpea and the talking cow*
Hoff, Syd. *The littlest leaguer*
Horvath, Betty F. *Hooray for Jasper*
Johnston, Johanna. *Sugarplum*
Kraus, Robert. *The littlest rabbit*
Kumin, Maxine W. *Sebastian and the dragon*
Kuskin, Karla. *Herbert hated being small*
Lindgren, Barbro. *Shorty takes off*
Lipkind, William. *The little tiny rooster*
Lurie, Morris. *The story of Imelda, who was small*
Meddaugh, Susan. *Too short Fred*
Miles, Miska. *No, no, Rosina*
Moore, Inga. *Oh, little Jack*
Orgel, Doris. *On the sand dune*
Prøysen, Alf. *Mrs. Pepperpot and the moose*
Rigby, Shirley Lincoln. *Smaller than most*
Schlein, Miriam. *Billy, the littlest one*
Stanley, John. *It's nice to be little*
Tresselt, Alvin R. *Smallest elephant in the world*
Williams, Barbara. *Someday, said Mitchell*
Yolen, Jane. *The emperor and the kite*
Young, Ed (Edward). *Little Plum*

Character traits – stubbornness

Beatty, Hetty Burlingame. *Droopy*
Bulla, Clyde Robert. *The stubborn old woman*
Coplans, Peta. *Spaghetti for Suzy*
Garrett, Jennifer. *The queen who stole the sky*
Keller, Holly. *Merry Christmas, Geraldine*
Leaf, Margaret. *Eyes of the dragon*
Minarik, Else Holmelund. *The little girl and the dragon*
O'Brien, Anne Sibley. *I'm not tired*
Plourde, Lynn. *Pigs in the mud in the middle of the rud*
Priceman, Marjorie. *Princess Picky*
Steig, William. *Spinky sulks*
Tarbescu, Edith. *The boy who stuck out his tongue*
Tusa, Tricia. *Miranda*
Viorst, Judith. *Alexander, who's not (Do you hear me? I mean it!) going to move*

Character traits – vanity

Andersen, H. C. (Hans Christian). *The emperor's new clothes*, ill. by Angela Barrett
    The emperor's new clothes, ill. by Erik Blegvad
    The emperor's new clothes, ill. by Virginia Lee Burton
    The emperor's new clothes, ill. by Robert Byrd
    The emperor's new clothes, ill. by Charlene DeLage
    The emperor's new clothes, ill. by Jack and Irene Delano

The emperor's new clothes, ill. by Demi
The emperor's new clothes, ill. by Hélène Desputeaux
The emperor's new clothes, ill. by Birte Dietz
The emperor's new clothes, ill. by Dorothée Duntze
The emperor's new clothes, ill. by Pamela Baldwin Ford
The emperor's new clothes, ill. by Jack Kent
The emperor's new clothes, ill. by Monika Laimgruber
The emperor's new clothes, ill. by Anne F. Rockwell
The emperor's new clothes, ill. by Janet Stevens
The emperor's new clothes, ill. by Eve Tharlet
The emperor's new clothes, ill. by Robert Van Nutt
The emperor's new clothes, ill. by Nadine Bernard Westcott
It's perfectly true!
Armstrong, Jennifer. *Chin Yu Min and the ginger cat*
Brown, Marcia. *Once a mouse . . .*
Brown, Margaret Wise. *The duck*
Browne, Anthony. *The big baby*
Calmenson, Stephanie. *The principal's new clothes*
DeLuise, Dom. *King Bob's new clothes*
Elborn, Andrew. *Bird Adalbert*
Evans, Richard Paul. *The tower*
Fleming, Candace. *Madame LaGrande and her so high, to the sky, uproarious pompadour*
Frascino, Edward. *My cousin the king*
Goode, Diane. *The dinosaur's new clothes*
Hausman, Gerald. *Coyote walks on two legs*
Kajpust, Melissa. *The peacock's pride*
Kepes, Juliet. *The story of a bragging duck*
McCormack, John E. *Rabbit tales*
MacDonald, Margaret Read. *The girl who wore too much*
McKissack, Patricia C. *The king's new clothes*
Marshall, James. *George and Martha, tons of fun*
Peppé, Rodney. *The color catalog*
Perlman, Janet. *The Emperor Penguin's new clothes*
Radunsky, Vladimir. *One*
Rumford, James. *Nine animals and the well*
Sasso, Sandy Eisenberg. *God said amen*
Sharmat, Marjorie Weinman. *Sasha the silly*
Shields, Carol Diggory. *I am really a princess*
Wall, Lina Mao. *Judge Rabbit and the tree spirit*
Ward, Helen. *The rooster and the fox*
Winter, Paula. *Sir Andrew*
Yolen, Jane. *King Long Shanks*
    Pegasus, the flying horse

Character traits – willfulness

Albert, Shirley. *Doll party*
Alexander, Sue. *Nadia the willful*
Boyd, Lizi. *Half wild and half child*
Cox, David. *Bossyboots*
Grimm, Jacob. *The princess and the frog*, ill. by Rachel Isadora
    The princess and the frog, ill. by Will Eisner
Lattimore, Deborah Nourse. *The prince and the golden ax*
Lester, Helen. *Pookins gets her way*
Quin-Harkin, Janet. *Benjamin's balloon*
Vesey, A. *The princess and the frog*

Character traits – wisdom

Bell, Anthea. *The wise queen*
Calhoun, Mary. *Jack the wise and the Cornish cuckoos*
Delton, Judy. *Penny wise, fun foolish*
Elkin, Benjamin. *The wisest man in the world*
Froese, Deborah L. *The wise washerman*
Hoffman, Mary. *Three wise women*
Kraus, Robert. *The adventures of Wise Old Owl*
    Wise Old Owl's canoe trip adventure
    Wise Old Owl's Christmas adventure
Lieberman, Syd. *The wise shoemaker of Studena*
McClenathan, Louise. *My mother sends her wisdom*
Oberman, Sheldon. *The wisdom bird*
Sherman, Josepha. *Vassilisa the wise*
Uchida, Yoshiko. *The wise old woman*
Wisniewski, David. *The warrior and the wise man*

Cheating *see* Behavior – cheating

Cheerleading

Carlson, Nancy L. *Louanne Pig in making the team*
Lester, Helen. *Three cheers for Tacky*

Cheetahs *see* Animals – cheetahs

Chefs *see* Careers – chefs, cooks

Cherokee Indians *see* Indians of North America – Cherokee

Cherubs *see* Angels

Cheyenne (Sioux) Indians *see* Indians of North America – Cheyenne (Sioux)

Chickasaw Indians *see* Indians of North America – Chickasaw

Chicken pox *see* Illness – chicken pox

Chickens *see* Birds – chickens

Child abuse

Caines, Jeannette. *Chilly stomach*
Clifton, Lucille. *One of the problems of Everett Anderson*
Kleven, Sandy. *The right touch*
Sherman, Joanne. *Because it's my body*
Spelman, Cornelia Maude. *Your body belongs to you*
Trottier, Maxine. *A safe place*

Children as authors

Baskin, Leonard. *Hosie's alphabet*
    Hosie's aviary
The best part of me
Burdett, Lois. *Hamlet for kids*
    Macbeth for kids
    A midsummer night's dream for kids
    Romeo and Juliet for kids
    The tempest for kids
    Twelfth night
Children's prayers from around the world
Haidle, Elizabeth. *Elmer the grump*
Harper, Isabelle. *My dog Rosie*
Jay, Betsy. *Swimming lessons*
Kallok, Emma. *Gem*
Kershen, L. Michael (Lloyd Michael). *Why buffalo roam*
Komaiko, Leah. *A million moms and mine*
Krauss, Ruth. *Somebody else's nut tree, and other tales from children*
Kroll, Steven. *Patches*
Lady Eden's School. *Just how stories*
MacKeen, Leslie Ann. *Who can fix it?*
Michels-Gualtieri, Akaela S. *I was born to be a sister*
Night time
Noah, build your boat
O'Reilly, Edward. *Brown pelican at the pond*
The palm of my heart
Phumla. *Nomi and the magic fish*
Pia Toya
Poems for the very young
St. Pierre, Wendy. *Henry finds a home*
Salter, Heidi. *Taddy McFinley and the great grey grimly*
Waldman, Sarah. *Light*
Wiener, Lori. *Be a friend*

Children as illustrators

Arnold, Lynda. *My Mommy has AIDS*
Burdett, Lois. *Hamlet for kids*
    Macbeth for kids
    A midsummer night's dream for kids
    Romeo and Juliet for kids

Children as inventors

Chile *see* Foreign lands – Chile

Chimpanzees *see* Animals – chimpanzees

China *see* Foreign lands – China

Chinese Americans *see* Ethnic groups in the U.S. – Chinese Americans

Chinese New Year *see* Holidays – Chinese New Year

Chinook Indians *see* Indians of North America – Chinook

Chipmunks *see* Animals – chipmunks

Chippewa Indians *see* Indians of North America – Chippewa

Chol Indians *see* Indians of North America – Chol

Christmas *see* Holidays – Christmas

Chumash Indians *see* Indians of North America – Chumash

Cinco de Mayo *see* Holidays – Cinco de Mayo

Circular tales

Circus

Dreamer, Sue. *Circus ABC*
  Circus 1, 2, 3
Drescher, Henrik. *Klutz*
Dubanevich, Arlene. *The piggest show on earth*
Du Bois, William Pène. *Bear circus*
Duncan, Lois. *Song of the circus*
Ehlert, Lois. *Circus*
Ehrlich, Amy. *Lucy's winter tale*
Elks, Wendy. *Charles B. Wombat and the very strange thing*
Emberley, Ed (Edward Randolph). *Thanks, Mom!*
Emberley, Rebecca. *My mother's secret life*
Ernst, Lisa Campbell. *Ginger jumps*
Ets, Marie Hall. *Mister Penny's circus*
Everton, Macduff. *Finding the magic circus = El circo magico modelo*
Falconer, Ian. *Olivia saves the circus*
Falk, Barbara Bustetter. *Grusha*
Falwell, Cathryn. *Clowning around*
Fazzi, Maura. *The circus of mystery*
Flack, Marjorie. *Wait for William*
Fleischman, Paul. *Sidewalk circus*
Fletcher, Ralph J. *The circus surprise*
Fox, Charles Philip. *Come to the circus*
Freeman, Don. *Bearymore*
Garbutt, Bernard. *Roger, the rosin back*
Garland, Michael. *Circus girl*
Gascoigne, Bamber. *Why the rope went tight*
Gay, Michel. *Night ride*
Goennel, Heidi. *The circus*
Goodall, John S. *The adventures of Paddy Pork*
Gottfried, Maya. *Last night I dreamed a circus*
Gramatky, Hardie. *Homer and the circus train*
Greaves, Margaret. *Little Bear and the Papagini circus*
Hale, Irina. *Donkey's dreadful day*
Harris, Steven Michael. *This is my trunk*
Hayes, Geoffrey. *Patrick at the circus*
Herrmann, Frank. *The giant Alexander and the circus*
Hill, Eric. *Spot goes to the circus*
Hoff, Syd. *Barkley*
  Henrietta, circus star
  Oliver
Hol, Coby. *Henrietta saves the show*
Holl, Adelaide. *Mrs. McGarrity's peppermint sweater*
Hopkins, Lee Bennett. *Circus! Circus!*
The house that Jack built. *The house that Jack built*, ill. by Janet
  Stevens
Jackson, Kathryn. *The golden circus book*
Johnson, Crockett. *Harold's circus*
Johnson, Jane. *Bertie on the beach*
Johnson, Neil. *Big-top circus*
Karn, George. *Circus big and small*
  Circus colors
Kastner, Jill. *Barnyard big top*
Lacome, Julie. *Funny business*
Landry, Leo. *Eat your peas, Ivy Louise!*
Lent, Blair. *Pistachio*
Lipkind, William. *Circus rucus*
Lisowski, Gabriel. *Roncalli's magnificent circus*
Logue, Christopher. *The magic circus*
London, Jonathan. *Little Red Monkey*
Lopshire, Robert. *New tricks I can do!*
  Put me in the zoo
McCourt, Lisa. *Chicken soup for little souls: The best night out with*
  Dad
McCully, Emily Arnold. *Little Kit, or, The Industrious Flea Circus girl*
MacDonald, Suse. *Elephants on board*
McGuirk, Leslie. *Tucker over the top*
Maestro, Betsy. *Busy day*
  Harriet goes to the circus
Maley, Anne. *Have you seen my mother?*
Marokvia, Merelle. *A French school for Paul*
Martin, Bill (William Ivan). *Chicken Chuck*
Mayer, Mercer. *Liverwurst is missing*
Millman, Isaac. *Moses goes to the circus*
Miranda, Anne. *The elephant at the Waldorf*
Modell, Frank. *Seen any cats?*
Montenegro, Laura Nyman. *Sweet Tooth*
Munari, Bruno. *The circus in the mist*

Murphy, Stuart J. *Circus shapes*
Myers, Bernice. *Herman and the bears and the giants*
Ness, Evaline. *Fierce*
Nightingale, Sandy. *Pink pigs aplenty*
Nimmo, Jenny. *Esmeralda and the children next door*
Noonan, Julia. *Hare and Rabbit, friends forever*
O'Kelley, Mattie Lou. *Circus!*
Ostheeren, Ingrid. *Jonathan Mouse at the circus*
Panek, Dennis. *Detective Whoo*
Paré, Roger. *Circus days*
Peet, Bill (William Bartlett). *Chester the worldly pig*
  Ella
  Randy's dandy lions
Pellowski, Michael. *Clara joins the circus*
Peppé, Rodney. *Circus numbers*
  Little circus
  Thumbprint circus
Petersham, Maud. *The circus baby*
Pinkwater, Daniel Manus. *Rainy morning*
Piumini, Roberto. *The saint and the circus*
Prater, John. *The greatest show on earth*
Prelutsky, Jack. *Circus*
Price, Mathew. *Do you see what I see?*
  Dumbo
Priceman, Marjorie. *Emeline at the circus*
Quackenbush, Robert M. *The man on the flying trapeze*
Rascal. *Oregon's journey*
Rau, Dana Meachen. *Clown around*
Rey, H. A. (Hans Augusto). *Curious George rides a bike*
  See the circus
Robertson, Patrisha Grainger. *Cirque du Soleil*
Rounds, Glen. *The day the circus came to Lone Tree*
Saville, Lynn. *Horses in the circus ring*
Scheffrin-Falk, Gladys. *Another celebrated dancing bear*
Schulz, Charles M. *Life is a circus, Charlie Brown*
Seignobosc, Françoise. *Small-Trot*
Seligson, Susan. *The amazing Amos and the greatest couch on earth*
Seuss, Dr. *If I ran the circus*
Slobodkina, Esphyr. *Circus caps for sale*
  Pezzo the peddler and the circus elephant
Slocum, Rosalie. *Breakfast with the clowns*
Slyder, Ingrid. *The Fabulous Flying Fandinis*
Smith, Joseph A. (Joseph Anthony). *Circus train*
Spier, Peter. *Peter Spier's circus!*
Taylor, Mark. *Henry explores the jungle*
Teague, Mark. *Baby tamer*
Tester, Sylvia Root. *Parade!*
Tresselt, Alvin R. *Smallest elephant in the world*
Varga, Judy. *Circus cannonball*
  Miss Lollipop's lion
Vincent, Gabrielle. *Ernest and Celestine at the circus*
Wahl, Jan. *Sylvester Bear overslept*
  The toy circus
Wallace, Ian. *Morgan the magnificent*
Weil, Lisl. *Let's go to the circus*
Westman, Barbara. *Dancing dogs*
Wildsmith, Brian. *Brian Wildsmith's circus*
Winn, Chris. *Archie's acrobats*
Wiseman, Bernard. *Morris and Boris at the circus*
Worth, Bonnie. *Jumbo*
Yaccarino, Dan. *Deep in the jungle*
Zimnik, Reiner. *The bear on the motorcycle*
  The proud circus horse

Cities, towns

Ackerman, Karen. *Bean's big day*
Adams, Jean Ekman. *Clarence and the purple horse bounce into town*
Adinolfi, JoAnn. *Tina's diner*
Adoff, Arnold. *Street music*
  Where wild Willie?
Æsop. *The country mouse and the city mouse*, ill. by Laura Lydecker
  The country mouse and the city mouse, ill. by Diane Silverman
  The town mouse and the country mouse, ill. by Lorinda Bryan
    Cauley
  The town mouse and the country mouse, ill. by Helen Craig
  The town mouse and the country mouse, ill. by Paul Galdone

The town mouse and the country mouse, ill. by Tom Garcia
The town mouse and the country mouse, ill. by Janet Stevens
The town mouse and the country mouse, ill. by Bernadette Watts
Town mouse, country mouse, ill. by Jan Brett
Town mouse, country mouse, ill. by Carol Jones
Allamand, Pascale. *The pop rooster*
Asch, Frank. *City sandwich*
    Dear brother
Asch, George. *Linda*
Baker, Jeannie. *Home in the sky*
    Millicent
Bank Street College of Education. *Around the city*
    Green light, go
    In the city
    My city
    Uptown, downtown
Barracca, Debra. *Maxi, the hero*
    A taxi dog Christmas
Barracca, Sal. *The adventures of taxi dog*
Barrett, Judi. *Old MacDonald had an apartment house*
Bartone, Elisa. *Peppe the lamplighter*
Bash, Barbara. *Urban roosts*
Baum, Susan. *City shapes*
Baylor, Byrd. *The best town in the world*
Bemelmans, Ludwig. *Sunshine*
Berger, Barbara Helen. *Angels on a pin*
Bergere, Thea. *Paris in the rain with Jean and Jacqueline*
Bergman, Donna. *City fox*
Bernhard, Durga. *To and fro, fast and slow*
Bible. Old Testament. Psalms. *Psalm twenty-three*
Binzen, Bill. *Carmen*
Blake, Robert J. *Fledgling*
Blance, Ellen. *Monster comes to the city*
Blegvad, Lenore. *Once upon a time and Grandma*
Bloom, Suzanne. *No place for a pig*
Blue, Rose. *How many blocks is the world?*
Bogan, Paulette. *Spike in the city*
Bowden, Joan Chase. *Emilio's summer day*
Bozzo, Maxine Zohn. *Toby in the country, Toby in the city*
Bradby, Marie. *Momma, where are you from?*
Bright, Robert. *Georgie to the rescue*
Brock, Emma Lillian. *Nobody's mouse*
Brooks, Nigel. *Town mouse house*
Brown, Craig McFarland. *City sounds*
Brown, Jane Clark. *Whonk, and whonk again*
Brown, Marcia. *The little carousel*
Brown, Margaret Wise. *Three little animals*
Brown, Tricia. *The city by the bay*
Bruna, Dick. *Miffy loves New York City!*
Buehner, Caralyn. *The escape of Marvin the ape*
Bunting, Eve (Anne Evelyn). *Riding the tiger*
    Secret place
    Smoky night
Burke, Jennifer S. *Cold days*
    Hot days
    Ovals
    Rainy days
    Rectangles
    Squares
    Stars
    Triangles
    Windy days
Burleigh, Robert. *Lookin' for Bird in the big city*
    Messenger, messenger
Burstein, Fred. *The dancer*
Burton, Virginia Lee. *Katy and the big snow*
    The little house
    Maybelle, the cable car
Busch, Phyllis S. *City lots*
Calmenson, Stephanie. *Hotter than a hot dog!*
Cannon, Janell. *Trupp*
Carrick, Carol. *Left behind*
Casey, Patricia. *Beep! Beep! Oink! Oink! animals in the city*
Chall, Marsha Wilson. *Prairie train*
Chalmers, Mary. *Kevin*
Chapouton, Anne-Marie. *Ben finds a friend*
Christian, Mary Blount. *Christmas reflections*

Chwast, Seymour. *Tall city, wide country*
    Traffic jam
City, ill. by Roser Capdevila
Cleveland-Peck, Patricia. *City cat, country cat*
Clifton, Lucille. *The boy who didn't believe in spring*
    Everett Anderson's Christmas coming
Coats, Laura Jane. *City cat*
Cocca-Leffler, Maryann. *Bus route to Boston*
Cohen, Miriam. *Down in the subway*
Cole, Kenneth, Dr. *No bad news*
Collier, Bryan. *Uptown*
Colman, Hila. *Peter's brownstone house*
Come out to play
Corcos, Lucille. *The city book*
Corey, Shana. *Milly and the Macy's Parade*
Craft, Ruth. *The day of the rainbow*
Craig, Helen. *Susie and Alfred in a busy day in town*
Crews, Donald. *Parade*
Crews, Nina. *One hot summer day*
Crowell, Maryalicia. *A horse in the house*
Cummins, Julie. *Country kid, city kid*
Curious George in the big city
Dahlie, Elizabeth. *Bernelly & Harriet*
Daly, Niki. *Not so fast Songololo*
Decker, Dorothy W. *Stripe visits New York*
Demarest, Chris L. *Bus*
De Paola, Paula. *Rosie and the yellow ribbon*
De Veaux, Alexis. *Na-ni*
DiSalvo-Ryan, DyAnne. *City green*
Donnelly, Liza. *Dinosaur beach*
    Dinosaur garden
    Dinosaurs' Halloween
Dorros, Arthur. *Abuela*
    City chicken
Dunrea, Olivier. *The painter who loved chickens*
Duvoisin, Roger Antoine. *Lonely Veronica*
    Veronica
Ellis, Anne Leo. *Dabble Duck*
Emberley, Michael. *Ruby*
Emberley, Rebecca. *City sounds*
    My city = Mi cuidad
    Three cool kids
Enderle, Judith (Ann) Ross. *Upstairs*
    Where are you, little Zack?
Enderle, Judith Ross. *Something's happening on Calabash Street*
Fife, Dale. *Adam's ABC*
Finsand, Mary Jane. *The town that moved*
Fitzgerald, Joanne. *This is me and where I am*
Flanagan, Alice K. *Mayors*
Fleischman, Paul. *Sidewalk circus*
Florian, Douglas. *The city*
    City street
Fraser, Kathleen. *Adam's world, San Francisco*
Freeman, Don. *Fly high, fly low*
    The guard mouse
French, Fiona. *Snow White in New York*
Garhan Attebury, Nancy. *Out and about at city hall*
Garland, Sarah. *Polly's puffin*
Geisert, Bonnie. *Desert town*
    Mountain town
    Prairie town
Gibbons, Gail. *Up goes the skyscraper!*
Giff, Patricia Reilly. *I love Saturday*
Godwin, Laura. *Central Park serenade*
Goodall, John S. *The story of a main street*
    The story of an English village
Goode, Diane. *Tiger trouble*
Gramatky, Hardie. *Little Toot through the Golden Gate*
Greenberg, Melanie Hope. *My father's luncheonette*
Greenfield, Eloise. *Night on Neighborhood Street*
Grifalconi, Ann. *City rhythms*
Griffith, Helen V. *Grandaddy's stars*
Grimes, Nikki. *C is for city*
    Danitra Brown leaves town
    Meet Danitra Brown
    A pocketful of poems
Grossbart, Francine. *A big city*

Guilfoile, Elizabeth. *Have you seen my brother?*
Guthrie, Donna. *A rose for Abby*
Harrison, Troon. *Courage to fly*
Harvey, Brett. *Immigrant girl*
Hawkesworth, Jenny. *The lonely skyscraper*
Hayward, Linda. *The city worm and the country worm*
Hazelaar, Cor. *Dogs everywhere*
Helldorfer, M. C. (Mary Claire). *Silver Rain Brown*
Henderson, Kathy. *In the middle of the night*
  A year in the city
Henwood, Simon. *The hidden jungle*
Heo, Yumi. *One afternoon*
  One Sunday morning
Hest, Amy. *Nana's birthday party*
  Ruby's storm
  Weekend girl
High, Linda Oatman. *Under New York*
Himler, Ronald. *The girl on the yellow giraffe*
Hoban, Tana. *Is it red? Is it yellow? Is it blue?*
Holl, Adelaide. *A mouse story*
Hopkins, Lee Bennett. *I think I saw a snail*
  A song in stone
Hubbell, Patricia. *City kids*
  Sidewalk trip
Hughes, Shirley. *The big concrete lorry*
Hurd, Thacher. *Zoom City*
Ingle, Annie. *The big city book*
Isadora, Rachel. *City seen from A to Z*
  Listen to the city
Ivory, Lesley Anne. *A day in London*
  A day in New York
Jam, Teddy. *Night cars*
Jenkins, Priscilla Belz. *Falcons nest on skyscrapers*
Jocelyn, Marthe. *Mayfly*
Johnson, Dinah. *Sunday week*
Johnson, Stephen T. *Alphabet city*
Johnston, Tony. *How many miles to Jacksonville?*
Jonas, Ann. *Round trip*
Jones, Rebecca C. *Matthew and Tilly*
Joosse, Barbara M. *The morning chair*
Jordan, June. *Kimako's story*
Kahn, Joan. *Hi, Jock, run around the block*
Kanome, Kayoko. *Little Mop lost*
Karlins, Mark. *Music over Manhattan*
Kaufman, Curt. *Hotel boy*
Keats, Ezra Jack. *Apt. 3*
  Goggles
  Hi, cat!
  Pet show!
Keeping, Charles. *Alfie finds the other side of the world*
  Through the window
Kesselman, Wendy Ann. *Angelita*
Kightley, Rosalinda. *The postman*
Kilby, Don. *In the city*
Konigsburg, E. L. (Elaine Lobl). *Amy Elizabeth explores Blooming-dale's*
Koralek, Jenny. *Cat and Kit*
Kovalski, Maryann. *Jingle bells*
Krementz, Jill. *A visit to Washington, D.C.*
Kroll, Steven. *Mary McLean and the St. Patrick's Day parade*
Kroll, Virginia L. *Faraway drums*
Krudop, Walter Lyon. *Something is growing*
Krupinski, Loretta. *Christmas in the city*
Kuskin, Karla. *City noise*
  Jerusalem, shining still
Lakin, Pat (Patricia). *Subway sonata*
Lasky, Kathryn. *I have an aunt on Marlborough Street*
Lawrence, John. *Pope Leo's elephant*
Lenski, Lois. *Policeman Small*
  Sing a song of people
Lent, Blair. *Bayberry Bluff*
  Molasses flood
Lerman, Rory S. *Charlie's checklist*
Levine, Arthur A. *Pearl Moscowitz's last stand*
Levinson, Riki. *Our home is the sea*
Levitin, Sonia. *Boom town*
Lewin, Hugh. *Jafta – the town*

Lewin, Ted. *Amazon boy*
Lewis, Stephen (Stephen Paul). *Zoo city*
Lexau, Joan M. *Benjie on his own*
  Come here, cat
  Me day
Little, Jean. *Gruntle Piggle takes off*
Lodge, Jo. *Moo Moo goes to the city*
London, Jonathan. *Hip cat*
Loomis, Christine. *Rush hour*
Lorenz, Lee. *A weekend in the city*
Lotz, Karen E. *Can't sit still*
Low, Alice. *David's windows*
McCloskey, Kevin. *Mrs. Fitz's flamingos*
McCloskey, Robert. *Make way for ducklings*
McDermott, Gerald. *Tim O'Toole and the wee folk*
McFarlane, Sheryl. *In the city*
McGinley, Phyllis. *All around the town*
McKissack, Patricia C. *Country mouse and city mouse*
McPhail, David M. *The blue door*
Maestro, Betsy. *Big city port*
  Delivery van
  Taxi
Maestro, Giulio. *The remarkable plant in apartment 4*
Maitland, Barbara. *Moo in the morning*
Maizlish, Lisa. *The ring*
Mak, Kam. *My Chinatown*
Manushkin, Fran. *Let's go riding in our strollers*
Martin, Jacqueline Briggs. *The green truck garden giveaway*
Mathers, Petra. *Maria Theresa*
Mayer, Mercer. *Little Monster's neighborhood*
Medina, Tony. *DeShawn days*
Meister, Cari. *Busy, busy city street*
Melmed, Laura Krauss. *Capital! Washington D.C. from A to Z*
Mennen, Ingrid. *Somewhere in Africa*
Merriam, Eve. *Bam, bam, bam*
  Fighting words
  On my street
Miles, Miska. *No, no, Rosina*
  Rolling the cheese
Milich, Melissa. *Miz Fannie Mae's fine new Easter hat*
Milich, Zoran. *The city ABC book*
  City colors
  City 1 2 3
  City signs
Milway, Katie Smith. *Cappuccina goes to town*
Mizumura, Kazue. *If I built a village*
Moak, Allan. *A big city ABC*
Moore, Elaine. *Good morning, city*
Moore, Lilian. *Mural on Second Avenue, and other city poems*
Moreton, Daniel. *La Cucaracha Martina*
Morris, Jill. *The boy who painted the sun*
Muller, Gerda. *The garden in the city*
Munro, Roxie. *Christmastime in New York City*
  The inside-outside book of London
  The inside-outside book of New York City
  The inside-outside book of Paris
  The inside-outside book of Texas
  The inside-outside book of Washington, D.C.
  Mazescapes
Myers, Christopher A. *Sparrows*
Myers, Walter Dean. *Harlem*
Nichols, Cathy. *Tuxedo Sam*
Nims, Bonnie Larkin. *Where is the bear in the city?*
Numeroff, Laura Joffe. *What daddies do best*
O'Connor, Jane. *Snail City*
O'Donnell, Peter. *Oscar*
O'Kelley, Mattie Lou. *Moving to town*
Olds, Elizabeth. *Little Una*
Olsen, Ib Spang. *Cat alley*
Osborne, Mary Pope. *New York's bravest*
O'Shell, Marcia. *Alphabet Annie announces an all-American album*
Otto, Carolyn. *Ducks, ducks, ducks*
Our house
Peet, Bill (William Bartlett). *Fly, Homer, fly*
Perera, Lydia. *Frisky*
Pericoli, Matteo. *See the city*
Pinkwater, Daniel Manus. *Bad bears in the big city*

Clallam Indians *see* Indians of North America – Clallam

Clarinets *see* Musical instruments – clarinets

Cleanliness *see* Character traits – cleanliness

Clergy *see* Careers – clergy

Cleverness *see* Character traits – cleverness

Cloaks *see* Clothing – coats

Clockmakers *see* Careers – clockmakers

Clocks, watches

Clothing

Lattimore, Deborah Nourse. *I wonder what's under there?*
Lear, Edward. *The new vestments*
Leiner, Katherine. *Halloween*
Leonard, Marcia. *Getting dressed*
    No new pants!
Lester, Helen. *Tacky and the Emperor*
Lester, Julius. *Sam and the tigers*
Little, Mimi Otey. *Daddy has a pair of striped shorts*
Lloyd, Errol. *Nini at carnival*
London, Jonathan. *Froggy gets dressed*
    Froggy goes to school
Loomis, Christine. *At the laundromat*
Lottridge, Celia Barker. *The little rooster and the diamond button*
Lucas, David. *Halibut Jackson*
Lynn, Sara. *Clothes*
McClintock, Marshall. *What have I got?*
MacDonald, Margaret Read. *The girl who wore too much*
MacKinnon, Debbie. *Find my boots!*
McKissack, Patricia C. *The king's new clothes*
    Nettie Jo's friends
McLenighan, Valjean. *What you see is what you get*
Maestro, Betsy. *On the town*
Marshall, Janet Perry. *Ohmygosh, my pocket*
Mayer, Mercer. *Two moral tales*
Medearis, Angela Shelf. *Poppa's itchy Christmas*
    Poppa's new pants
Miklowitz, Gloria D. *Bearfoot boy*
Miller, Margaret. *My first words: me and my clothes*
    Where does it go?
Mills, Lauren A. *The rag coat*
Monsell, Mary Elise. *Underwear!*
Moore, Dessie. *Getting dressed*
Morris, Ann. *Weddings*
Mould, Wendy. *Ants in my pants*
Munsch, Robert N. *Thomas' snowsuit*
Mwenye Hadithi. *Greedy zebra*
Neitzel, Shirley. *The dress I'll wear to the party*
    The jacket I wear in the snow
Nielsen, Laura F. *Jeremy's muffler*
Oberman, Sheldon. *The always prayer shawl*
Offen, Hilda. *A fox got my socks*
Ohi, Ruth. *Pants off first*
Oliver, Stephen. *Clothes*
Ormerod, Jan. *Dad's back*
Oxenbury, Helen. *Dressing*
Parr, Todd. *Underwear do's and don'ts*
Partridge, Jenny. *Grandma Snuffles*
Paterson, Bettina. *My clothes*
Peppé, Rodney. *Little dolls*
Perlman, Janet. *The Emperor Penguin's new clothes*
Pochocki, Ethel. *Rosebud and red flannel*
Politi, Leo. *Little Leo*
Potter, Beatrix. *The tale of Mrs. Tiggy-Winkle*
Radley, Gail. *The spinner's gift*
Reidy, Hannah. *All sorts of clothes*
Rice, Inez. *The March wind*
Ricklen, Neil. *My clothes = Mi ropa*
Rothenberg, Joan Keller. *Inside-out grandma*
Rovetch, Lissa. *Crocs in shirts, hippos in skirts*
Samton, Sheila White. *Frogs in clogs*
Sanders, Scott R. (Scott Russell). *Warm as wool*
Sanfield, Steve. *Bit by bit*
Schertle, Alice. *The skeleton in the closet*
Schnur, Steven. *The tie man's miracle*
Scott, Ann Herbert. *Big Cowboy Western*
Scott, C. Anne (Cynthia Anne). *Old Jake's skirts*
Scott, Janine. *Let's get dressed*
Sharmat, Marjorie Weinman. *The trip*
Silver, Jody. *Isadora*
Sirois, Allen. *Dinosaur dress up*
Slobodkina, Esphyr. *Pezzo the peddler and the circus elephant*
    Pezzo the peddler and the thirteen silly thieves
Smith, Donald. *Who's wearing my bow tie?*
Spohn, Kate. *Clementine's winter wardrobe*
Stinson, Kathy. *The dressed up book*
Stoeke, Janet Morgan. *A hat for Minerva Louise*
Sutherland, Colleen. *Jason goes to show-and-tell*

Sutton, Jane. *What should a hippo wear?*
Szekeres, Cyndy. *The mouse that Jack built*
Thayer, Jane. *Gus was a gorgeous ghost*
Thomas, Mark. *Clothes in Colonial America*
Topek, Susan Remick. *A costume for Noah*
Townsend, Kenneth. *Felix, the bald-headed lion*
Tucker, Sian. *My clothes*
Tusa, Tricia. *Maebelle's suitcase*
Tyrrell, Anne. *Elizabeth Jane gets dressed*
Vigil-Piñón, Evangelina. *Marina's muumuu = el muumuu de Marina*
Vulliamy, Clara. *Blue hat, red coat*
Watanabe, Shigeo. *How do I put it on?*
Weiss, Nicki. *The world turns round and round*
Wells, Rosemary. *Max's dragon shirt*
    Max's new suit
West, Colin. *I brought my love a tabby cat*
Wild, Margaret. *The pocket dogs*
Winter, Jeanette. *My baby*
Wright, Jill. *The old woman and the Willy Nilly Man*
Yeoman, John. *Old Mother Hubbard's dog dresses up*
Yolen, Jane. *King Long Shanks*
Yorinks, Arthur. *Christmas in July*
Ziefert, Harriet. *Bear gets dressed*
    Clara Ann Cookie
    Let's get dressed!
Zion, Gene. *No roses for Harry*

Clothing – aprons

Brillhart, Julie. *Anna's goodbye apron*
Carle, Eric. *My apron*
McKissack, Patricia C. *Ma Dear's aprons*
Payne, Emmy. *Katy no-pocket*

Clothing – boots

DeFelice, Cynthia C. *Cold feet*
Dunrea, Olivier. *Ollie the stomper*
Emerson, Scott. *The magic boots*
Havill, Juanita. *Jamaica and Brianna*
Huling, Jan. *Puss in cowboy boots*
Hurd, Edith Thacher. *Johnny Lion's rubber boots*
Lewison, Wendy Cheyette. *So many boots*
London, Jonathan. *Puddles*
Lowell, Susan. *The bootmaker and the elves*
MacKinnon, Debbie. *Billy's boots*
May, Kara. *Joe Lion's big boots*
Mitchell, Marianne. *Joe Cinders*
Moran, Alex. *Boots for Beth*
Morck, Irene. *Tyler's new boots*
Perrault, Charles. *Puss in boots,* ill. by Steve Light
    Puss in boots, ill. by Barry Wilkinson
Ray, Mary Lyn. *Red rubber boot day*
Roche, Harriet. *Pete's puddles*

Clothing – coats

Bible. Old Testament. Joseph. *Joseph and his brothers*
De Paola, Tomie (Thomas Anthony). *Charlie needs a cloak*
Fagan, Cary. *Gogol's coat*
Fienberg, Anna. *Joseph*
Garelick, May. *Just my size*
Hest, Amy. *The purple coat*
Kassirer, Sue. *Joseph and his coat of many colors*
Lacome, Julie. *Ruthie's big old coat*
Milligan, Bryce. *Brigid's cloak*
Oram, Hiawyn. *The wrong overcoat*
Parton, Dolly. *Coat of many colors*
Pulver, Robin. *Mrs. Toggle's zipper*
Taback, Simms. *Joseph had a little overcoat*
Tafuri, Nancy. *One wet jacket*
Watson, Pauline. *The walking coat*
Wheeler, Lisa. *Jam & jelly by Holly & Nellie*
Williams, Marcia. *Joseph and his magnificent coat of many colors*
Wolff, Ferida. *The woodcutter's coat*
Woodruff, Elvira. *The memory coat*
Ziefert, Harriet. *A new coat for Anna*

Zinnemann-Hope, Pam. *Find your coat, Ned*

Clothing – costumes

Bos, Burny. *Alexander the great*
Cousins, Lucy. *Maisy dresses up*
David, Lawrence. *Superhero Max*
De Groat, Diane. *Trick or treat, smell my feet*
DeLage, Ida. *The old witch goes to the ball*
Ford, Miela. *My day in the garden*
Gauch, Patricia Lee. *Tanya and the magic wardrobe*
Geddes, Anne. *Shapes*
Gretz, Susanna. *Frog, duck, and rabbit*
Grey, Mini. *Traction Man is here*
Hasler, Eveline. *The giantess*
Hennessy, B. G. (Barbara G.). *Corduroy's Halloween*
Hort, Lenny. *We're going on a treasure hunt*
    We're going on safari
Kessler, Leonard P. *That's not Santa!*
London, Jonathan. *Froggy's Halloween*
McCue, Lisa. *Corduroy's best Halloween ever!*
McDonald, Megan. *Ant and Honey Bee*
Mayer, Pamela. *The scariest monster in the whole wide world*
Poydar, Nancy. *The perfectly horrible Halloween*
Rockwell, Anne F. *Halloween Day*
Ruelle, Karen Gray. *Spookier than a ghost*
Saltzberg, Barney. *The problem with pumpkins*
    Soccer mom from outer space
Tibo, Gilles. *Simon's disguise*
Todd, Mark. *What will you be for Halloween?*
Winter, Jeanette. *Niño's mask*
Wojciechowski, Susan. *The best Halloween of all*
Ziefert, Harriet. *On Halloween night*

Clothing – dresses

Daly, Niki. *Jamela's dress*
Dörrie, Doris. *Lottie's princess dress*
Friedman, Laurie B. *A style all her own*
Jocelyn, Marthe. *Hannah and the seven dresses*
Munsch, Robert N. *Ribbon rescue*
Norwich, William D. *Molly and the magic dress*
Schweiger-Dmi'el, Itzhak. *Hanna's Sabbath dress*
Seymour, Dorothy Z. *Ann likes red*
Spalding, Andrea. *Sarah May and the new red dress*

Clothing – gloves, mittens

Bannon, Laura. *Red mittens*
Hannant, Judith Stuller. *Three little kittens*
Johnson, G. Francis. *Has anybody lost a glove?*
Jonovitz, Marilyn. *Three little kittens*
Kay, Helen. *One mitten Lewis*
Kellogg, Steven (Stephen). *The mystery of the missing red mitten*
Kumin, Maxine W. *Mittens in May*
Livermore, Elaine. *Three little kittens lost their mittens*
Mother Goose. *The three little kittens*, ill. by Lorinda Bryan Cauley
    The three little kittens, ill. by Paul Galdone
    The three little kittens, ill. by Dorothy Stott
    The three little kittens, ill. by Shelley Thornton
Rogers, Jean. *Runaway mittens*
Siomades, Lorianne. *Three little kittens*

Clothing – handbags, purses

Bogan, Paulette. *Momma's magical purse*
Caple, Kathy. *The purse*
Hansen, P. (Paul H.). *My granny's purse*
Henkes, Kevin. *Lilly's purple plastic purse*
McElmurry, Jill. *Mad about plaid*
Uchida, Yoshiko. *The magic purse*
Westcott, Nadine Bernard. *The lady with the alligator purse*

Clothing – hats

Bailey, Debbie. *Hats*
Bancroft, Catherine. *Felix's hat*

Bannon, Laura. *Hat for a hero*
Barrett, Judi. *The wind thief*
Barrows, Marjorie Wescott. *The funny hat*
Blackaby, Susan. *Rembrandt's hat*
Blos, Joan W. *Martin's hats*
Bowden, Joan Chase. *A hat for the queen*
Boyd, Lizi. *Princess, cowboy, pirate, elf*
Brown, Ken (Ken James). *The scarecrow's hat*
Brumbeau, Jeff. *Miss Hunnicutt's hat*
Butler, M. Christina. *One snowy night*
Carlson, Laurie M. *Boss of the plains*
Carrick, Malcolm. *The extraordinary hatmaker*
Chalmers, Mary. *A hat for Amy Jean*
Christelow, Eileen. *Olive and the magic hat*
Cousins, Lucy. *Portly's hat*
D'Amico, Carmela. *Ella, the elegant elephant*
Demi. *Little bitty bunny*
Dunrea, Olivier. *Peedie*
Fisher, Leonard Everett. *A head full of hats*
Geringer, Laura. *A three hat day*
Gill, Madelaine. *The spring hat*
Gorbachev, Valeri. *Whose hat is it?*
Grifalconi, Ann. *Tiny's hat*
Hindley, Judy. *Uncle Harold and the green hat*
Hiser, Berniece T. *The adventure of Charlie and his wheat-straw hat*
Holland, Isabelle. *Kevin's hat*
Holm, Sharon Lane. *Zoe's hats*
Howard, Elizabeth Fitzgerald. *Aunt Flossie's hats (and crab cakes later)*
Hürlimann, Ruth. *The mouse with the daisy hat*
Iwamura, Kazuo. *Tan Tan's hat*
Jaynes, Ruth M. *Benny's four hats*
Johnson, B. J. *A hat like that*
Johnston, Tony. *The witch's hat*
Kahn, Rosemary. *Grandma's hat*
Karon, Jan. *Miss Fannie's hat*
Katz, Karen. *Twelve hats for Lena*
Keats, Ezra Jack. *Jennie's hat*
Keller, Holly. *Rosata*
Krisher, Trudy. *Kathy's hats*
Kroll, Steven. *Princess Abigail and the wonderful hat*
Landström, Olof. *Will's new cap*
Lattimore, Deborah Nourse. *The lady with the ship on her head*
Lear, Edward. *Of pelicans and pussycats*
    The quangle wangle's hat, ill. by Emma Crosby
    The quangle wangle's hat, ill. by Helen Oxenbury
    The quangle wangle's hat, ill. by Janet Stevens
    Two laughable lyrics
Leemis, Ralph. *Mister Momboo's hat*
Levy, Janice. *The man who lived in a hat*
Lexau, Joan M. *Who took the farmer's hat?*
Low, Alice. *Aunt Lucy went to buy a hat*
Lowell, Susan. *Little Red Cowboy Hat*
Luthardt, Kevin. *Hats*
Mayer, Mercer. *Two moral tales*
Meisel, Paul. *Zara's hats*
Milich, Melissa. *Miz Fannie Mae's fine new Easter hat*
Miller, Margaret. *What's on my head?*
    Whose hat?
Moore, Inga. *Fifty red night-caps*
Moore, Lilian. *While you were chasing a hat*
Morris, Ann. *Hats, hats, hats*
Morris, Neil. *Where's my hat?*
Murphey, Sara. *The animal hat shop*
Numeroff, Laura Joffe. *Sherman Crunchley*
Parr, Letitia. *A man and his hat*
Pearson, Tracey Campbell. *The purple hat*
Reed, Lynn Rowe. *Pedro, his perro, and the alphabet sombrero*
Riddle, Tohby. *The singing hat*
Roche, Hannah. *Sandra's sun hat*
Roy, Ronald. *Whose hat is that?*
Ryder, Eileen. *Winston's new cap*
Sadler, Judy Ann. *Sandwiches for Duke*
Scarry, Richard. *Richard Scarry's Mr. Frumble's biggest hat flap book ever*
Scheller, Melanie. *My grandfather's hat*
Slobodkina, Esphyr. *Caps for sale*

Circus caps for sale
Smath, Jerry. *A hat so simple*
Smith, Donald. *Who's wearing my baseball cap?*
Steig, William. *When everybody wore a hat*
 Which would you rather be?
Tafuri, Nancy. *Silly little goose!*
Thayer, Jane. *The horse with the Easter bonnet*
Ungerer, Tomi. *The hat*
Van der Meer, Ron. *Funny hats*
Van Laan, Nancy. *This is the hat*
Walbrecker, Dirk. *Benny's hat*
Ward, Nanda Weedon. *The black sombrero*
Weedn, Flavia. *The magic cap*
Weiss, Harvey. *My closet full of hats*
Weninger, Brigitte. *The elf's hat*
Westerberg, Christine. *The cap that mother made*
Williams, Karen Lynn. *Tap-tap*
Winthrop, Elizabeth. *Halloween hats*
Wittmann, Patricia. *Go ask Giorgio!*
Ziefert, Harriet. *Hats off for the Fourth of July!*

Clothing – kimonos

Uegaki, Chieri. *Suki's kimono*

Clothing – neckties

Cocca-Leffler, Maryann. *Mr. Tanen's ties*

Clothing – pajamas

Brooks, Erik. *The practically perfect pajamas*
De Paola, Tomie (Thomas Anthony). *Kit and Kat*
Graber, Janet. *Jacob and the polar bears*
Jackson, Isaac. *Somebody's new pajamas*

Clothing – pants

Andreae, Giles. *Pants*
Crunk, Tony. *Grandpa's overalls*
Gerstein, Mordicai. *Stop those pants!*
Good, Merle. *Dan's pants*
Hissey, Jane. *Little Bear's trousers*
Kraus, Robert. *The king's trousers*
Raschka, Christopher. *Moosey Moose*
Rice, Eve. *Peter's pockets*
Uttley, Alison. *Sam Pig and the wind*

Clothing – pockets

Armstrong, Jennifer. *Pockets*
Braybrooks, Ann. *Plenty of pockets*
Heiligman, Deborah. *Pockets*
Myrick, Jean Lockwood. *Ninety-nine pockets*
Payne, Emmy. *Katy no-pocket*
Rice, Eve. *Peter's pockets*
Scanlon, Elizabeth Garton. *A sock is a pocket for your toes*

Clothing – scarves

Wright, Dare. *A gift from the lonely doll*

Clothing – shirts

Anderson, Leone Castell. *The wonderful shrinking shirt*
Gould, Deborah. *Aaron's shirt*
Rudolph, Marguerita. *How a shirt grew in the field*, ill. by Erika
 Weihs
 How a shirt grew in the field, ill. by Yaroslava
Spinelli, Eileen. *In my new yellow shirt*

Clothing – shoes

Andersen, H. C. (Hans Christian). *The red shoes*
Bailey, Debbie. *Shoes*
Balzola, Asun. *Munia and the red shoes*
Banks, Kate (Katherine A.). *Peter and the talking shoes*
Bazilian, Barbara. *The red shoes*

Berridge, Celia. *Hannah's new boots*
Blos, Joan W. *Hello, shoes!*
Bourgeois, Paulette. *Big Sarah's little boots*
Brenner, Barbara A. *Somebody's slippers, somebody's shoes*
Browne, Anthony. *Willy the wizard*
Calmenson, Stephanie. *One red shoe (the other's blue!)*
Cote, Nancy. *Flip-flops*
Cottle, Joan. *Emily's shoes*
Denton, Kady MacDonald. *Christmas boot*
Dixon, Ann. *The blueberry shoe*
Dornbusch, Erica. *Finding Kate's shoes*
Fitz-Gibbon, Sally. *Two shoes, blue shoes, new shoes!*
Gay, Michel. *Little shoe*
Geeslin, Campbell. *How Nanita learned to make flan*
Grimes, Nikki. *Shoe magic*
Hampshire, Susan. *Rosie's ballet slippers*
Harper, Jessica. *I forgot my shoes*
Heo, Yumi. *Father's rubber shoes*
Hines, Anna Grossnickle. *Whose shoes?*
Hoe, Susan. *Which shoes would you choose?*
Hughes, Shirley. *Two shoes, new shoes*
Hurwitz, Johanna. *New shoes for Silvia*
Johnson, Angela. *Shoes like Miss Alice's*
Johnson, Marion. *Caillou, new shoes*
Komaiko, Leah. *Shoeshine Shirley*
Lawston, Lisa. *A pair of red sneakers*
LeRoy, Gen. *Billy's shoes*
Light, Steve. *The shoemaker extraordinaire*
Lodge, Bernard. *Shoe Shoe Baby*
Lunge-Larsen, Lise. *The legend of the lady slipper*
McKee, David. *King Rollo and the new shoes*
Matsuno, Masako. *A pair of red clogs*
Miller, Margaret. *Whose shoe?*
Morris, Ann. *Shoes, shoes, shoes*
Myers, Bernice. *The flying shoes*
Neidigh, Sherry. *Creatures at my feet*
Paul, Ann Whitford. *Hello toes! Hello feet!*
Pratt, Pierre. *Shopping*
Pulver, Robin. *Mrs. Toggle's beautiful blue shoe*
Rice, Eve. *New blue shoes*
Riddell, Chris. *Bird's new shoes*
Rollings, Susan. *New shoes, red shoes*
Ross, Tony. *Centipede's 100 shoes*
Roy, Ronald. *Whose shoes are these?*
Smith, Donald. *Who's wearing my sneakers?*
Tafuri, Nancy. *Two new sneakers*
Tucker, Kathy. *The leprechaun in the basement*
Uff, Caroline. *Hello, Lulu*
Vigna, Judith. *Boot weather*
Weiss, Leatie. *Funny feet!*
Wells, Ruth. *The farmer and the poor god*
Winthrop, Elizabeth. *Shoes*

Clothing – socks

Baird, Anne. *Baby socks*
Balian, Lorna. *The socksnatchers*
Brandle, Bine. *Flusi, the sock monster*
Daly, Niki. *Joseph's other red sock*
Glaser, Linda. *Keep your socks on, Albert!*
Mathews, Judith. *An egg and seven socks*
Murphy, Stuart J. *A pair of socks*
Selden, George. *Sparrow socks*

Clothing – suits

Rader, Laura. *Santa's new suit*

Clothing – sweaters

Birchall, Mark. *Rabbit's wooly sweater*
Diller, Harriett. *The faraway drawer*
Lunn, Janet Louise Swoboda. *Amos's sweater*

Clothing – underwear

Piggy and Bear in their underwear

Clouds *see* Weather – clouds

Clowns, jesters

Adler, David A. *You think it's fun to be a clown!*
Allen, Jeffrey. *Bonzini! the tattooed man*
Amoit, Pierre. *Bijou, the little bear*
Anno, Mitsumasa. *Dr. Anno's magical midnight circus*
Austin, Margot. *Barney's adventure*
Barr, Cathrine. *Sammy seal ov the sircus*
Bradford, Ann. *The mystery of the midget clown*
Burningham, John. *Cannonball Simp*
Cole, Joanna. *The Clown-Arounds*
    The Clown-Arounds go on vacation
    The Clown-Arounds have a party
    Get well, Clown-Arounds!
    Sweet dreams, Clown-Arounds!
Coontz, Otto. *A real class clown*
Daly, Niki. *Bravo, Zan Angelo!*
Damjan, Mischa. *The clown said no*
Dedieu, Thierry. *Baby clown*
De Paola, Tomie (Thomas Anthony). *Jingle, the Christmas clown*
    Sing, Pierrot, sing
Dodds, Dayle Ann. *Where's Pup?*
Douglass, Barbara. *The chocolate chip cookie contest*
Drescher, Henrik. *Klutz*
Faulkner, Nancy. *Small clown*
Fazzi, Maura. *The circus of mystery*
Fletcher, Ralph J. *The circus surprise*
Fox, Christyan. *What color is that, PiggyWiggy?*
Freeman, Don. *Forever laughter*
Garland, Michael. *Circus girl*
Harper, Jo. *Ollie Jolly, rodeo clown*
Harris, Steven Michael. *This is my trunk*
Hayes, Geoffrey. *Patrick at the circus*
Kotzwinkle, William. *Walter, the farting dog: trouble at the yard sale*
Krahn, Fernando. *A funny friend from heaven*
Lacome, Julie. *Funny business*
Laden, Nina. *Clowns on vacation*
Lent, Blair. *Pistachio*
Lobel, Anita. *Pierrot's ABC garden*
Long, Kathy. *Hallelujah the clown*
Lynn, Sara. *Colors*
McGuire, Richard. *What's wrong with this book?*
Marceau, Marcel. *The story of Bip*
Mendoza, George. *The Marcel Marceau counting book*
Miller, M. L. *Dizzy from fools*
Olds, Elizabeth. *Plop plop ploppie*
Olofsson, Helena. *The little jester*
Pellowski, Michael. *Clara joins the circus*
Petersham, Maud. *The circus baby*
Politi, Leo. *Lito and the clown*
Prater, John. *The greatest show on earth*
Quackenbush, Robert M. *The man on the flying trapeze*
Rascal. *Oregon's journey*
Rau, Dana Meachen. *Clown around*
Richardson, Jean. *Tall inside*
Rockwell, Anne F. *Gogo's pay day*
Salley, Coleen. *Epossumondas*
Saltzman, David. *The jester has lost his jingle*
Schreiber, Georges. *Bambino goes home*
    Bambino the clown
Shecter, Ben. *Hester the jester*
Slocum, Rosalie. *Breakfast with the clowns*
Sobol, Harriet Langsam. *Clowns*
Thurber, James. *Many moons*, ill. by Marc Simont
    Many moons, ill. by Louis Slobodkin

Clubs, gangs

Alexander, Sue. *Seymour the prince*
Bateman, Teresa. *The Bully Blockers Club*
Berenstain, Stan. *The Berenstain bears no girls allowed*
Bourgeois, Paulette. *Franklin's secret club*
Bradford, Ann. *The mystery at Misty Falls*
    The mystery in the secret club house
    The mystery of the blind writer
    The mystery of the midget clown
    The mystery of the missing dogs
    The mystery of the square footsteps
    The mystery of the tree house
Bunting, Eve (Anne Evelyn). *Riding the tiger*
Christian, Mary Blount. *The green thumb thief*
Collicott, Sharleen. *Toestomper and the caterpillars*
Crowley, Michael. *New kid on Spurwick Ave.*
    Shack and back
Hoffman, Mary. *Henry's baby*
Howe, James. *Horace and Morris but mostly Dolores*
Jackson, Ellen B. *Monsters in my mailbox*
Jennings, Sharon. *Franklin's reading lesson*
Johnson, Arden. *The Lost Tooth Club*
Kotzwinkle, William. *The day the gang got rich*
Leedy, Loreen. *The monster money book*
McCourt, Lisa. *Chicken soup for little souls: The Goodness Gorillas*
Mahoney, Daniel J. *The perfect clubhouse*
Murphy, Stuart J. *Treasure map*
Powell, Alma. *America's promise*
Stanley, Diane. *The conversation club*
Suen, Anastasia. *The clubhouse*
Thaler, Mike. *Pack 109*
Weigelt, Udo. *Ben and the Buccaneers*
Winthrop, Elizabeth. *The Best Friends Club*

Clumsiness *see* Character traits – clumsiness

Coaches *see* Careers – coaches

Coats *see* Clothing – coats

Cockatoos *see* Birds – cockatoos

Cockroaches *see* Insects – cockroaches

Codes *see* Secret codes

Cold *see* Concepts – cold & heat

Cold (disease) *see* Illness – cold (disease)

Collecting things *see* Behavior – collecting things

Colombia *see* Foreign lands – Colombia

Color *see* Concepts – color

Columbus Day *see* Holidays – Columbus Day

Comanche Indians *see* Indians of North America – Comanche

Communication

Acredolo, Linda P. *My first baby signs*
Allington, Richard L. *Talking*
    Words
Ancona, George. *Handtalk zoo*
Arnold, Caroline. *How do we communicate?*
Beeke, Tiphanie. *Roar like a lion!*
Bohdal, Susi. *Tom cat*
Borchers, Elisabeth. *Dear Sarah*
Brown, Margaret Wise. *The big fur secret*
Buchheimer, Naomi. *Let's go to a post office*
Charlip, Remy. *Handtalk*
Cheng, Andrea. *Grandfather counts*
Chukovskii, Kornei Ivanovich. *The telephone*, ill. by Blair Lent
Clifford, Eth. *A bear before breakfast*
Coleman, Evelyn. *The glass bottle tree*
Dewey, Jennifer Owings. *Stories on stone*
Dorros, Arthur. *Radio Man = Don Radio*
Elbling, Peter. *Aria*
Emberley, Ed (Edward Randolph). *Green says go*

Engdahl, Sylvia. *Our world is earth*
Ets, Marie Hall. *Talking without words*
Fisher, Leonard Everett. *Gutenberg*
Gibbons, Gail. *The post office book*
    Puff – flash – bang!
Goor, Ron. *Signs*
Heelan, Jamee Riggio. *Can you hear a rainbow?*
Hirschi, Ron. *A time for singing*
Hoban, Tana. *I read signs*
    I read symbols
Hughes, Shirley. *Chatting*
Jenkins, Steve. *Slap, squeak, and scatter*
Joslin, Sesyle. *Dear dragon*
Klove, Lars. *I see a sign*
Lachner, Dorothea. *Andrew's angry words*
Leedy, Loreen. *The Furry News*
LoMonaco, Palmyra. *Night letters*
Meres, Jonathan. *The big bad rumor*
Milich, Zoran. *City signs*
Millman, Isaac. *Moses goes to a concert*
    Moses goes to the circus
Pfeffer, Wendy. *Dolphin talk*
Potter, Beatrix. *Yours affectionately, Peter Rabbit*
Schlein, Miriam. *Hello, hello!*
Seuss, Dr. *Gerald McBoing Boing*
    Gerald McBoing Boing sound book
Sherman, Joanne. *Because it's my body*
Showers, Paul. *How you talk*
Stanley, Diane. *The conversation club*
Telephones
Tolkien, J. R. R. (John Ronald Reuel). *The Father Christmas letters*
Van Woerkom, Dorothy. *Hidden messages*
Walton, Rick. *My two hands, my two feet*
Wells, Rosemary. *Letters and sounds*
Wheeler, Cindy. *More simple signs*
    Simple signs

Communities, neighborhoods

Ahlberg, Allan. *Mr. Buzz the beeman*
Alda, Arlene. *Morning glory Monday*
Ancona, George. *Barrio*
Appelt, Kathi. *A red wagon year*
Arnold, Caroline. *What is a community?*
    Where do you go to school?
    Who works here?
Arnold, Tedd. *The simple people*
Baggette, Susan K. *Jonathan goes to the grocery store*
    Jonathan goes to the library
Bailey, Debbie. *The playground*
Barber, Barbara E. *Saturday at the new you*
Bartone, Elisa. *American, too*
Berridge, Celia. *On my street*
Best, Cari. *When Catherine the Great and I were eight!*
Blakeley, Peggy. *Two little ducks*
Block party today
Bourgeois, Paulette. *Fire fighters*
    Garbage collectors
    Police officers
    Postal workers
Brisson, Pat. *Wanda's roses*
Brown, Marc Tolon. *Arthur's neighborhood*
Bunting, Eve (Anne Evelyn). *Smoky night*
Caseley, Judith. *On the town*
Cole, Kenneth, Dr. *No bad news*
Crowley, Michael. *New kid on Spurwick Ave.*
Denslow, Sharon Phillips. *Hazel's circle*
DiSalvo-Ryan, DyAnne. *City green*
    Grandpa's corner store
Dooley, Norah. *Everybody bakes bread*
    Everybody brings noodles
Dowling, Paul. *Where are you going, Jimmy?*
Duke, Kate. *If you walk down this road*
Dupasquier, Philippe. *A busy day at the garage*
Eclare, Melanie. *A harvest of color*
Edwards, Michelle. *Chicken Man*
Edwards, Nancy. *Glenna's seeds*

Enderle, Judith Ross. *Something's happening on Calabash Street*
Flanagan, Alice K. *A busy day at Mr. Kang's grocery store*
    Buying a pet from Ms. Chavez
    Coach John and his soccer team
    Here comes Mr. Eventoff with the mail!
    Letter carriers
    Mayors
    Ms. Davison, our librarian
    Ms. Murphy fights fires
    Officer Brown keeps neighborhoods safe
    Police officers
    Riding the school bus with Mrs. Kramer
    A visit to the Gravesens' farm
Freeman, Don. *Corduroy's busy street and Corduroy goes to the doctor*
Freeman, Martha. *The trouble with babies*
Fries, Claudia. *A pig is moving in*
Gackenbach, Dick. *Claude has a picnic*
Gauch, Patricia Lee. *Christina Katerina and Fats and the Great Neighborhood War*
Geisert, Bonnie. *Prairie town*
Geras, Adèle. *The Cats of Cuckoo Square, Geejay the Hero*
Gibson, Karen Bush. *Child care workers*
    Emergency medical technicians
    Pharmacists
    Truck drivers
Gray, Libba Moore. *Miss Tizzy*
Greenfield, Eloise. *Night on Neighborhood Street*
Grejniec, Michael. *Look*
    Who is my neighbor?
Groner, Judyth Saypol. *My very own Jewish community*
Hartmann, Wendy. *All the magic in the world*
Haskins, Francine. *I remember "121"*
Helldorfer, M. C. (Mary Claire). *Silver Rain Brown*
Henkes, Kevin. *Good-bye, Curtis*
    Once around the block
Henwood, Simon. *The troubled village*
Heo, Yumi. *One afternoon*
Herrera, Juan Felipe. *Grandma and Me at the flea = Los meros meros remateros*
Hest, Amy. *How to get famous in Brooklyn*
Hubbell, Patricia. *Sidewalk trip*
Hughes, Shirley. *Chatting*
Isadora, Rachel. *Over the green hills*
Jennings, Linda M. *Franklin's neighborhood*
Johnson, G. Francis. *Has anybody lost a glove?*
Johnson, Paul Brett. *Mr. Persnickety and Cat Lady*
Kallen, Stuart A. *The farm*
    The fire station
    The museum
    The police station
Keats, Ezra Jack. *Pet show!*
Komaiko, Leah. *My perfect neighborhood*
Kraus, Robert. *Mouse in love*
Krensky, Stephen. *My teacher's secret life*
Lakin, Pat (Patricia). *Aware and alert*
    Information, please
    Red letter day
Lakin, Patricia. *Fat chance Thanksgiving*
Leedahl, Shelley A. (Shelley Ann). *The bone talker*
Leedy, Loreen. *The Furry News*
Lewis, Rob. *Friends*
Lewison, Wendy Cheyette. *A trip to the firehouse*
Liebman, Daniel. *I want to be a firefighter*
    I want to be a police officer
Loomis, Christine. *At the laundromat*
    At the mall
Louie, Therese On. *Raymond's perfect present*
Low, William. *Chinatown*
Martin, Jacqueline Briggs. *The green truck garden giveaway*
Medearis, Angela Shelf. *Rum-a-tum-tum*
Merriam, Eve. *On my street*
Miller, Margaret. *On my street*
Modarressi, Mitra. *Yard sale*
Modesitt, Jeanne. *Vegetable soup*
Nolan, Lucy A. *The Lizard Man of Crabtree County*
Novak, Matt. *The Robobots*
Owen, Ann (1953–). *Taking your places*

Pedersen, Judy. *When night time comes near*
Pinkney, J. Brian. *The adventures of sparrowboy*
Pittman, Helena Clare. *The angel tree*
Powell, Alma. *America's promise*
Ratz de Tagyos, Paul. *A coney tale*
Robinson, Aminah Brenda Lynn. *A street called home*
Rogers, Fred. *Moving*
Rosen, Michael (1946–). *A Thanksgiving wish*
Russo, Marisabina. *Mama talks too much*
SanAngelo, Ryan. *Eddie spaghetti*
Scheffler, Ursel. *Stop your crowing, Kasimir!*
Smalls-Hector, Irene. *Irene and the big, fine nickel*
    Jonathan and his mommy
Smith, Barry. *Cumberland Road*
Spinelli, Eileen. *Somebody loves you, Mr. Hatch*
Suen, Anastasia. *The clubhouse*
Sutherland, Marc. *MacMurtrey's wall*
Swope, Sam. *The Araboolies of Liberty Street*
Tamar, Erika. *The garden of happiness*
Taulbert, Clifton L. *Little Cliff and the porch people*
Thayer, Jane. *Part-time dog*
Ward, Sally G. *What goes around comes around*
Wells, Rosemary. *McDuff goes to school*
Wyeth, Sharon Dennis. *Something beautiful*
Yeoman, John. *Our village*
Yoaker, Harry. *The view*
Yolen, Jane. *Raising Yoder's barn*
Zarin, Cynthia. *Rose and Sebastian*

Competition *see* Sibling rivalry; Sports; Sportsmanship

Completing things *see* Character traits – completing
    things

Composers *see* Careers – composers

Compromising *see* Character traits – compromising

Computers

Baker, Eugene H. *I want to be a computer operator*
Brown, Marc Tolon. *Arthur's computer disaster*
Carrick, Carol. *Patrick's dinosaurs on the Internet*
D'Ignazio, Fred. *Katie and the computer*
Dubois, Muriel L. *I like computers: what can I be?*
Greene, Carol. *A computer went a-courting*
Lyon, David. *The brave little computer*
Matthias, Catherine. *I can be a computer operator*
Modell, Frank. *Skeeter and the computer*
Ross, Dave (David). *Space Monster Gorp and the runaway computer*
Skulavik, Mary Alys. *Bert*
Steadman, Ralph. *The little red computer*

Conceit *see* Character traits – conceit

Concepts

Ahlberg, Allan. *Big bad pig*
    Fee fi fo fum
    Happy worm
    Help!
Albert, Burton. *Mine, yours, ours*
Allen, Judy. *What is a wall, after all?*
Anholt, Catherine. *One, two, three, count with me*
Anno, Mitsumasa. *Anno's math games*
    Anno's math games II
    Anno's math games III
Arvetis, Chris. *Why is it dark?*
Balestrino, Philip. *Hot as an ice cube*
Bauman, A. F. *Guess where you're going, guess what you'll do*
Beisner, Monika. *Topsy turvy: the world of upside down*
Berenstain, Stan. *Inside outside upside down*
Berkley, Ethel S. *Ups and down*
Blackstone, Stella. *Baby high, baby low*
Blos, Joan W. *Hello, shoes!*
Bodger, Joan. *Belinda's ball*

Booth, Eugene. *At the circus*
    At the fair
    In the air
    In the garden
    In the jungle
    Under the ocean
Borten, Helen. *Do you see what I see?*
Brown, Marcia. *Touch will tell*
    Walk with your eyes
Brown, Margaret Wise. *Sailor boy jig*
Browne, Philippa-Alys. *A gaggle of geese*
Browner, Richard. *Look again!*
Bruna, Dick. *Dick Bruna's picture word book*
Bulloch, Ivan. *Patterns*
Burningham, John. *First steps*
Carle, Eric. *My very first book of motion*
Charosh, Mannis. *Number ideas through pictures*
Chase, Catherine. *Hot and cold*
Corey, Dorothy. *You go away*
Cousins, Lucy. *Katy Cat and Beaky Boo*
Crews, Donald. *Light*
    We read
Cushman, Doug. *Nasty Kyle the crocodile*
Dantzer-Rosenthal, Marya. *Some things are different, some things are the same*
Duke, Kate. *Guinea pigs far and near*
    What bounces?
Ehlert, Lois. *In my world*
Emberley, Ed (Edward Randolph). *Ed Emberley's amazing look through book*
Fisher, Leonard Everett. *Boxes! Boxes!*
Fleming, Denise. *The everything book*
    The everything book [board book]
Freudberg, Judy. *Some, more, most*
Froman, Robert. *Angles are easy as pie*
    A game of functions
Garland, Sarah. *All gone!*
Gillham, Bill. *Where does it go?*
Gomi, Taro. *Guess what?*
Green, Mary McBurney. *Is it hard? Is it easy?*
Greene, Laura. *Change*
Greenway, Shirley. *Two's company . . .*
Griest, Virginia. *In between*
Hammersmith, Craig. *Patterns*
Hartman, Gail. *For sand castles or seashells*
    For strawberry jam or fireflies
Hayward, Linda. *Wet foot, dry foot, low foot, high foot*
Heide, Florence Parry. *The bigness contest*
Heller, Nicholas. *Ten old pails*
Hennessy, B. G. (Barbara G.). *A, B, C, D, tummy, toes, hands, knee*
Hoban, Tana. *All about where*
    Black on white
    Dots, spots, speckles, and stripes
    Is it rough? Is it smooth? Is it shiny?
    Look! Look! Look!
    More, fewer, less
    Over, under and through
    Take another look
    White on black
Hughes, Shirley. *Lucy and Tom's 1, 2, 3*
Jenkins, Steve. *Biggest, strongest, fastest*
Jensen, Virginia Allen. *What's that?*
Johnson, Ryerson. *Upstairs and downstairs*
Johnson, Stephen T. *Alphabet city*
Jonas, Ann. *Reflections*
Killion, Bette. *Just think!*
Klove, Lars. *I see a sign*
Kulman, Andrew. *Red light stop, green light go*
Kuskin, Karla. *All sizes of noises*
Lember, Barbara Hirsch. *A book of fruit*
Leonard, Marcia. *Spots*
Lewis, Zoe. *Disney's Beauty and the beast teacup mix-up*
Lopshire, Robert. *The biggest, smallest, fastest, tallest things you've ever heard of*
McMillan, Bruce. *Becca backward, Becca forward*
    Dry or wet?
    One, two, one pair!

Sense suspense
Maestro, Betsy. *Temperature and you*
    Where is my friend?
Magnus, Erica. *Around me*
Marzollo, Jean. *I love you*
Matthias, Catherine. *Over and under = Arriba y abajo*
Matthiesen, Thomas. *Things to see*
Mayer, Mercer. *Mine!*
Mazer, Anne. *The yellow button*
Montanari, Eva. *The crocodile's true colors*
Murphy, Stuart J. *The greatest gymnast of all*
    Let's fly a kite
    Missing mittens
    Probably pistachio
Once I was . . .
Pelletier, David. *The graphic alphabet*
Peppé, Rodney. *Odd one out*
    Rodney Peppé's puzzle book
Pipe, Jim. *What makes it swing?*
Pluckrose, Henry Arthur. *Beginnings and endings*
Pragoff, Fiona. *Let's find Teddy*
    Odd one out
Rahn, Joan Elma. *Holes*
Rockwell, Anne F. *What we like*
Ross, Michael Elsohn. *Earth cycles*
Rotner, Shelley. *Parts*
Royston, Angela. *Heavy and light*
    Smooth and rough
Ruben, Patricia. *True or false?*
Scarry, Richard. *Richard Scarry's best first book ever!*
Schwartz, David M. *If you hopped like a frog*
Sesame Street. *The Sesame Street book of people and things*
Seuss, Dr. *Gerald McBoing Boing*
    Gerald McBoing Boing sound book
Shannon, George. *Tomorrow's alphabet*
Sis, Peter. *Beach ball*
Spohn, Kate. *The wet dry book*
Supraner, Robyn. *Giggly-wiggly, snickety-snick*
Swinburne, Stephen R. *What's a pair? What's a dozen?*
Tompert, Ann. *Just a little bit*
Wallner, John C. *Look and find*
Webb, Angela. *Talkabout light*
    Talkabout reflections
    Talkabout sound
Wells, Rosemary. *How many? How much?*
Wood, A. J. *Look! The ultimate spot-the-difference book*
Yektai, Niki. *Bears in pairs*
Zaslavsky, Claudia. *Zero! Is it something? Is it nothing?*
Ziefert, Harriet. *My getting-ready-for-school book*
    Rabbit and Hare divide an apple

Concepts – change

Murphy, Mary. *Some things change*

Concepts – cold & heat

Best, Cari. *When Catherine the Great and I were eight!*
Burke, Jennifer S. *Cold days*
    Hot days
Bynum, Janie. *Altoona up north*
Chambers, Catherine. *Heat wave*
McAllister, Angela. *The ice palace*
Rau, Dana Meachen. *Chilly Charlie*
Schwartz, Roslyn. *The mole sisters and the cool breeze*
Taulbert, Clifton L. *Little Cliff and the cold place*

Concepts – color

Abisch, Roz. *Open your eyes*
Adoff, Arnold. *Greens*
Allamand, Pascale. *The animals who changed their colors*
Allen, Jonathan. *Purple sock, pink sock*
Allen, Robert. *Ten little babies play*
Allington, Richard L. *Colors*
Anholt, Catherine. *Tom's rainbow walk*
Arnold, Tedd. *Colors*

Asch, Frank. *Yellow, yellow*
Baby's first book of colors
Baker, Alan. *Benjamin's portrait*
    White Rabbit's color book
Barasch, Lynne. *A winter walk*
Barry, Frances. *Duckie's rainbow*
Bassède, Francine. *George paints his house*
Beautiful moments in the wild
Beck, Andrea. *Elliot's great big lift-the-flap book*
Benevelli, Alberto. *The colors of the chameleon*
Berger, Judith. *Butterflies and rainbows*
Bilgrami, Shaheen. *Farmyard painting party*
    Jungle art show
Black, Harley. *Amazing magic school*
    Magic art class
Blackstone, Stella. *Bear's busy family*
Bond, Michael. *Paddington's colors*
Boyd, Lizi. *Black dog red house*
Bradman, Tony. *The bad babies' book of colors*
Brenner, Barbara A. *The color wizard*
Briggs, Raymond. *The snowman [a lift-the-flap board book]*
Bright, Robert. *I like red*
Brophy, Nannette. *The color of my fur*
Brown, Margaret Wise. *Afro-Bets book of colors*
    My world of color
    Red light, green light
Bruna, Dick. *My shirt is white*
Brunhoff, Laurent de. *Babar's book of color*
Burningham, John. *First steps*
    John Burningham's colors
Burton, Katherine. *One gray mouse*
Campbell, Ann-Jeanette. *Let's find out about color*
Can you see the red balloon?
Carle, Eric. *Hello, red fox*
    The mixed-up chameleon
    My very first book of colors
Carroll, Kathleen Sullivan. *One red rooster*
Charles, N. N. *What am I? Looking through shapes at apples and*
    grapes
Charlip, Remy. *Harlequin and the gift of many colors*
Chermayeff, Ivan. *Tomato and other colors*
Chocolate, Deborah M. Newton. *Kente colors*
Clifford, Eth. *Red is never a mouse*
Court, Rob. *Color*
Cousins, Lucy. *Maisy's colors*
    Maisy's rainbow dream
Cox, Phil Roxbee. *Ted in a red bed*
Crowther, Robert. *Colors*
Deeter, Catherine. *Seymour Bleu*
De Paola, Paula. *Rosie and the yellow ribbon*
De Paola, Tomie (Thomas Anthony). *Marcos: red, yellow, blue*
Dines, Glen. *Pitadoe, the color maker*
Dodd, Emma. *Dog's colorful day*
Dodds, Dayle Ann. *The color box*
Dunbar, Joyce. *Indigo and the whale*
Dunbar, Polly. *Dog Blue*
    Flyaway Katie
Dunham, Meredith. *Colors: how do you say it?*
Duvoisin, Roger Antoine. *The house of four seasons*
    See what I am
Dwyer, Mindy. *Aurora, a tale of the Northern Lights*
Edwards, Pamela Duncan. *Warthogs paint*
Ehlert, Lois. *Color farm*
    Color zoo
    Fish eyes
Emberley, Ed (Edward Randolph). *Green says go*
Emberley, Rebecca. *My colors = Mis colores*
Ernst, Lisa Campbell. *A colorful adventure of the bee who left home one*
    Monday morning and what he found along the way
Falwell, Cathryn. *Nicky's walk*
Feeney, Stephanie. *Hawaii is a rainbow*
Field, Susan. *The sun, the moon, and the silver baboon*
Fisher, Leonard Everett. *Boxes! Boxes!*
Fleming, Denise. *Lunch*
Flora. *Feathers like a rainbow*
Fosberg, John. *Ice cream colors*
Fowler, Allan. *Hard-to-see animals*

Fox, Christyan. *What color is that, PiggyWiggy?*
Freeman, Don. *The chalk box story*
  A rainbow of my own
French, Vivian. *Oh no, Anna!*
Garland, Sarah. *Seeing red*
Garne, S. T. *By a blazing blue sea*
Giffard, Hannah. *Red bus*
Gillham, Bill. *Let's look for colors*
Ginsburg, Mirra. *Three kittens*
Godwin, Laura. *Little white dog*
Goennel, Heidi. *Colors*
Goffstein, M. B. (Marilyn Brooke). *Artists' helpers enjoy the evening*
Gold-Vukson, Marji E. *The colors of my Jewish Year*
Graff, Nancy Price. *In the hush of the evening*
Graham, Amanda. *Picasso, the green tree frog*
Graham, Bob. *The red woolen blanket*
Greeley, Valerie. *White is the moon*
Greenway, Shirley. *Color me bright*
Groening, Maggie. *Maggie Simpson's book of colors and shapes*
Gundersheimer, Karen. *Colors to know*
Gunzi, Christiane. *Colors*
Haring, Keith. *Big*
Harshman, Marc. *Red are the apples*
Haskins, Ilma. *Color seems*
Hassett, John. *Father Sun, Mother Moon*
Heller, Ruth. *Color, color, color, color*
Hest, Amy. *The purple coat*
Hill, Eric. *Spot looks at colors*
  Spot's big book of colors, shapes and numbers = El libro grande de Spot
  Spot's big book of colours, shapes, and numbers
  Spot's favorite colors
Hillman, Priscilla. *The Merry-Mouse counting and colors book*
Hindley, Judy. *A song of colors*
Hoban, Tana. *Colors everywhere*
  Dots, spots, speckles, and stripes
  Is it red? Is it yellow? Is it blue?
  Of colors and things
  Red, blue, yellow shoe
Holm, Sharon Lane. *Zoe's hats*
Hooks, William H. *Read-a-rebus*
Horácek, Petr. *Strawberries are red*
  What is black and white?
Horwood, Annie. *Butterfly, butterfly what colors do you see?*
Hubbard, Patricia. *My crayons talk*
Hughes, Shirley. *Colors*
Imershein, Betsy. *Finding red, finding yellow*
Inkpen, Mick. *Kipper's book of colors*
Jackson, Ellen B. *Brown cow, green grass, yellow mellow sun*
Jenkins, Jessica. *Thinking about colors*
Johnston, Tony. *The bull and the fire truck*
Jonas, Ann. *Color dance*
Karn, George. *Circus colors*
Katz, Karen. *The colors of us*
Kessler, Leonard P. *Mr. Pine's purple house*
Kilroy, Sally. *Baby colors*
Kirkpatrick, Rena K. *Rainbow colors*
Kleven, Elisa. *The lion and the little red bird*
Konigsburg, E. L. (Elaine Lobl). *Samuel Todd's book of great colors*
Kumin, Maxine W. *What color is Caesar?*
Kunhardt, Edith. *Red day, green day*
Kvasnosky, Laura McGee. *Pink, red, blue, what are you?*
Lacome, Julie. *Funny business*
Landa, Norbert. *Rabbit and chicken play with colors*
Leonard, Marcia. *Favorite colors*
  Paintbox penguins
Leslie, Amanda. *Do crocodiles moo?*
Le Tord, Bijou. *A bird or two*
Levinson, Riki. *Country dawn to dusk*
Lewis, Naomi. *Once upon a rainbow*
Lionni, Leo. *A color of his own*
  Colors to talk about
  Little blue and little yellow
A little book of colors
Liu, Jae Soo. *Yellow umbrella*
Lobb, Janice. *Color and noise! Let's play with toys!*
Lobel, Arnold. *The great blueness and other predicaments*
Löfgren, Ulf. *The color trumpet*

Lopshire, Robert. *New tricks I can do!*
  Put me in the zoo
Lorenz, Lee. *Pig and duck buy a truck*
Lynn, Sara. *Colors*
Macdonald, Anne. *Wickiup walkingstick*
MacDonald, Maryann. *The pink party*
McGrath, Barbara Barbieri. *Kellogg's froot loops color fun book*
McKee, David. *Elmer's colors*
MacKinnon, Debbie. *Eye spy colors*
McMillan, Bruce. *Growing colors*
McPhail, David M. *Big brown bear*
Maisner, Heather. *Planet monster*
Marcos, subcomandante. *The story of colors = La historia de los colores*
Maril, Lee. *Mr. Bunny paints the eggs*
Marks, Burton. *Colors and numbers*
Martin, Bill (William Ivan). *Brown bear, brown bear, what do you see?*
Mayer, Marianna. *The Brambleberrys animal book of colors*
Milich, Zoran. *City colors*
Miller, J. P. (John Parr). *Do you know colors?*
  Learn about colors with Little Rabbit
Miller, Margaret. *I love colors*
  Me and my bear
Miller, Thomas Patton. *Can a coal scuttle fly?*
Munsch, Robert N. *Purple, green and yellow*
Murphy, Chuck. *Colors*
Oliver, Stephen. *My first look at colors*
Ostheeren, Ingrid. *Jonathan Mouse*
Oxford Scientific Films. *Danger colors*
  Hide and seek
Parr, Todd. *Black and white*
Pascoe, Gwen. *Deep in a rainforest*
Patent, Dorothy Hinshaw. *Bold and bright, black-and-white animals*
Peek, Merle. *Mary wore her red dress and Henry wore his green sneakers*
Peppé, Rodney. *The color catalog*
Phifer, Martha Nelson. *The colors of Christmas*
Pieńkowski, Jan. *Colors*
Pinkney, Sandra L. *A rainbow all around me*
Pinkwater, Daniel Manus. *The bear's picture*
  The big orange splot
Podendorf, Illa. *Color*
Porto, Tony. *Blue aliens*
  Get red
Priceman, Marjorie. *It's me, Marva!*
Priddy, Roger. *Baby's book of nature*
Raschka, Christopher. *Mysterious Thelonious*
Rau, Dana Meachen. *Lots of balloons*
Reiser, Lynn. *Best friends think alike*
Reiss, John J. *Colors*
Ricklen, Neil. *My colors = Mis colores*
Rikys, Bodel. *Red bear*
Robertson, Patrisha Grainger. *Cirque du Soleil*
Rogers, Margaret. *Green is beautiful*
Rosen, Michael (1946–). *How the animals got their colors*
Ross, Tony. *Hugo and the man who stole colors*
Rossetti, Christina Georgina. *Color*
  What is pink?
Ryan, Pam Muñoz. *The crayon counting book*
Sandberg, Inger. *Nicholas' red day*
Sawicki, Norma Jean. *The little red house*
Scott, Rochelle. *Colors, colors all around*
Selkowe, Valrie M. *Spring green*
Serfozo, Mary. *Who said red?*
Seymour, Dorothy Z. *Ann likes red*
Sharratt, Nick. *The green queen*
Shields, Carol Diggory. *Colors*
Shirotani, Hideo. *What color? = Qué color?*
Shub, Elizabeth. *Dragon Franz*
Siddals, Mary McKenna. *Tell me a season*
Sieveking, Anthea. *What color?*
Silsbe, Brenda. *Just one more color*
Silverman, Maida. *Ladybug's color book*
Simmons, Steven J. *Alice and Greta's color magic*
Siomades, Lorianne. *My box of color*
Sis, Peter. *Going up!*
Snyder, Carol. *We're painting*
Spafford, Suzy. *Witzy's colors*
Spier, Peter. *Oh, were they ever happy!*

Concepts – counting *see* Counting, numbers

Concepts – distance

Concepts – in & out

Concepts – left & right

Concepts – leverage

Concepts – measurement

Concepts – motion

Concepts – opposites

Hughes, Shirley. *Bathwater's hot*
Hunter, Tom. *Build it up and knock it down*
Inkpen, Mick. *Kipper's book of opposites*
Karn, George. *Circus big and small*
Kightley, Rosalinda. *Opposites*
King, Stephen Michael. *Henry and Amy (right-way-round and upside down)*
Koch, Michelle. *By the sea*
Lankford, Mary D. *Is it dark? Is it light?*
Leonard, Marcia. *The kitten twins*
    The opposite of stop is go
Lippman, Peter. *Peter Lippman's opposites*
Maccarone, Grace. *Pumpkin faces*
McKissack, Patricia C. *Big bug book of opposites*
McLenighan, Valjean. *Stop-go, fast-slow*
McMillan, Bruce. *Becca backward, Becca forward*
    Here a chick, there a chick
McNaughton, Colin. *At home*
    At playschool
    At the park
    At the party
    At the stores
Maestro, Betsy. *Traffic*
Matthias, Catherine. *Over-under*
Mendoza, George. *The Sesame Street book of opposites with Zero Mostel*
Milgrim, David. *My friend Lucky*
Milios, Rita. *Yo soy = I am*
Miller, Margaret. *Big and little*
    Playtime
Minters, Frances. *Too big, too small, just right*
Murphy, Chuck. *Black cat, white cat*
Oliver, Stephen. *Opposites*
Pragoff, Fiona. *Opposites*
Provensen, Alice. *Karen's opposites*
Reinhart, Matthew. *Animal popposites*
Serfozo, Mary. *What's what?*
Shirotani, Hideo. *Opposites*
Spier, Peter. *Fast-slow, high-low*
Staake, Bob. *My little opposites book*
Stevenson, James. *Fun, no fun*
Stickland, Paul. *Dinosaur roar!*
Swinburne, Stephen R. *What's opposite?*
Tullet, Hervé. *Night / day*
Wagner, Karen. *A friend like Ed*
Watson, Carol. *Opposites*
Wilbur, Richard. *Runaway opposites*
Wildsmith, Brian. *What the moon saw*
Yee, Patrick. *Rosie Rabbit's opposites*
Young, Ruth. *Daisy's taxi*
Ziefert, Harriet. *Let's go! Piggety Pig*

Concepts – patterns

Harris, Trudy. *Pattern bugs*
    Pattern fish
Harvey, Jayne. *Busy bugs*
Holm, Sharon Lane. *Zoe's hats*
Kassirer, Sue. *What's next, Nina?*
McElmurry, Jill. *Mad about plaid*
Masini, Beatrice. *A brave little princess*
Pallotta, Jerry. *Shapes and patterns*
Swinburne, Stephen R. *Lots and lots of zebra stripes*

Concepts – perspective

Adler, David A. *3D, 2D, 1D*
Cohen, Caron Lee. *Pigeon, pigeon*
    Where's the fly?
Davies, Kay. *My balloon*
    My mirror
Gore, Sheila. *My shadow*
Hutchins, Pat. *Shrinking mouse*
Mainwaring, Jane. *My feather*
Rotner, Shelley. *Close, closer, closest*
Testa, Fulvio. *The endless journey*
Titherington, Jeanne. *Big world, small world*
Wakefield, Joyce. *From where you are*

Yolen, Jane. *All those secrets of the world*

Concepts – self *see* Self-concept

Concepts – shape

Adler, David A. *3D, 2D, 1D*
Allen, Robert. *Round and square*
Allington, Richard L. *Shapes*
Anderson, Janet S. *Sunflower Sal*
Anno, Mitsumasa. *Anno's faces*
Atwood, Ann. *The little circle*
Axelrod, Amy. *Pigs on the ball*
Baker, Alan. *Brown Rabbit's shape book*
Baranski, Joan Sullivan. *Round is a pancake*
Barner, Bob. *Space race*
Baum, Susan. *City shapes*
Beck, Andrea. *Elliot's great big lift-the-flap book*
Berenstain, Stan. *Old hat, new hat*
Bishop, Roma. *Shapes*
Blackstone, Stella. *Bear in a square*
Brown, Marcia. *Listen to a shape*
Brown, Margaret Wise. *Afro-Bets book of shapes*
    The little fireman
Budney, Blossom. *A kiss is round*
Bulloch, Ivan. *Patterns*
Burke, Jennifer S. *Ovals*
    Rectangles
    Squares
    Stars
    Triangles
Carle, Eric. *Little cloud*
    Little cloud [board book]
    My very first book of shapes
Charles, N. N. *What am I? Looking through shapes at apples and grapes*
Charosh, Mannis. *The ellipse*
Chavarría-Cháirez, Becky. *Magda's tortillas = Las tortillas de Magada*
Coxe, Molly. *6 sticks*
Craig, M. Jean. *Boxes*
Crews, Donald. *Ten black dots*
Crowther, Robert. *Shapes*
De Mejo, Oscar. *La Bella Magellona and the little cavalier*
Dodds, Dayle Ann. *The shape of things*
Dotlich, Rebecca Kai. *What is a triangle?*
    What is round?
    What is square?
Dunbar, Fiona. *You'll never guess!*
Dunham, Meredith. *Shapes*
Ehlert, Lois. *Color farm*
    Color zoo
Emberley, Ed (Edward Randolph). *The wing on a flea*
Emberley, Rebecca. *My shapes = Mis formas*
Engel, Diana. *Circle song*
Esbensen, Barbara Juster. *Echoes for the eye*
Falwell, Cathryn. *Clowning around*
    Shape space
Feldman, Judy. *Shapes in nature*
Fisher, Leonard Everett. *Look around!*
Fosberg, John. *Cookie shapes*
Fowler, Allan. *What do you see in a cloud?*
Friedman, Mel. *Kitten castle*
Friskey, Margaret (Margaret Richards). *Three sides and the round one*
Gardner, Beau. *Guess what?*
    What is it?
Geddes, Anne. *Shapes*
Gerstein, Mordicai. *The gigantic baby*
Gillham, Bill. *Let's look for shapes*
Godwin, Laura. *Little white dog*
Goldblatt, Eli. *Leo loves round*
Gomi, Taro. *The big book of boxes*
Groening, Maggie. *Maggie Simpson's book of colors and shapes*
Gundersheimer, Karen. *Shapes to show*
Gunzi, Christiane. *Shapes*
Hatcher, Charles. *What shape is it?*

Hefter, Richard. *The strawberry book of shapes*
Heinst, Marie. *My first number book*
Henkes, Kevin. *The biggest boy*
 Circle dogs
Hill, Eric. *Spot looks at shapes*
 Spot's big book of colors, shapes and numbers = El libro grande de Spot
 Spot's big book of colours, shapes, and numbers
Hindley, Judy. *Ten bright eyes*
 The wheeling and whirling-around book
Hoban, Tana. *Circles, triangles, and squares*
 Cubes, cones, cylinders and spheres
 Dots, spots, speckles, and stripes
 Is it red? Is it yellow? Is it blue?
 Round and round and round
 Shapes and things
 Shapes, shapes, shapes
 So many circles, so many squares
 Spirals, curves, fanshapes and lines
Hughes, Peter. *The emperor's oblong pancake*
Hughes, Shirley. *All shapes and sizes*
Jensen, Virginia Allen. *Catching*
Joyce, William. *Rolie Polie Olie*
Kassirer, Sue. *Math fair blues*
Kightley, Rosalinda. *Shapes*
Kimmel, Eric A. *Ten suns*
Lacome, Julie. *Funny business*
Lionni, Leo. *Pezzettino*
Lopshire, Robert. *New tricks I can do!*
MacDonald, Suse. *Sea shapes*
MacKinnon, Debbie. *Eye spy shapes*
 What shape?
McMillan, Bruce. *Fire engine shapes*
Maisner, Heather. *Planet monster*
Mayer, Marianna. *The Brambleberrys animal book of big and small shapes*
Murphy, Stuart J. *Captain Invincible and the space shapes*
 Circus shapes
Newth, Philip. *Roly goes exploring*
Oliver, Stephen. *My first look at shapes*
Onyefulu, Ifeoma. *A triangle for Adaora*
Pallotta, Jerry. *Shapes and patterns*
Parker, Steve. *I wonder why tunnels are round*
Pieńkowski, Jan. *Shapes*
Pilegard, Virginia Walton. *The warlord's puzzle*
Pluckrose, Henry Arthur. *Shape*
Podendorf, Illa. *Shapes, sides, curves and corners*
Poydar, Nancy. *Cool Ali*
Pragoff, Fiona. *Shapes*
Priddy, Roger. *Baby's book of nature*
Radunsky, Eugenia. *Square, triangle, round, skinny*
Reiss, John J. *Shapes*
Reit, Seymour. *Round things everywhere*
Ribke, Simone T. *The shapes we eat*
Roberts, Cliff. *The dot*
 Start with a dot
Rogers, Paul (Patrick). *The shapes game*
Salazar, Violet. *Squares are not bad*
Santoro, Christopher. *Book of shapes*
Schlein, Miriam. *Shapes*
Serfozo, Mary. *There's a square*
Sesame Street. *The Sesame Street book of shapes*
Seuss, Dr. *The shape of me and other stuff*
Shapes
Shapiro, Arnold L. *Circle*
 Square
 Triangles
Shaw, Charles Green. *It looked like spilt milk*
Silverman, Maida. *Mouse's shape book*
Silverstein, Shel. *The missing piece*
Smith, Mavis. *Circles*
Smith-Moore, J. J. *Sally Small*
Snyder, Carol. *We're painting*
Stoddard, Sandol. *Curl up small*
Tafuri, Nancy. *The brass ring*
Testa, Fulvio. *If you look around*
Thong, Roseanne. *Round is a mooncake*
Turner, Gwenda. *Shapes*

Van Fleet, Matthew. *Fuzzy yellow ducklings*
 Spotted yellow frogs
Wallwork, Amanda. *Find the fish that looks like this*
Watson, Carol. *Shapes*
Weeks, Sarah. *Bite me, I'm a shape*
Wells, Tony. *Allsorts*
Wildsmith, Brian. *Animal shapes*
 Brian Wildsmith 1 2 3
Wilson, April. *April Wilson's magpie magic*
Yates, Irene. *All about pattern*
 All about shape
Yee, Patrick. *Rosie Rabbit's shapes*
Youldon, Gillian. *Shapes*
Ziefert, Harriet. *Squarehead*
Zimmermann, H. Werner (Heinz Werner). *Alphonse knows . . . a circle is not a Valentine*
Zwetchkenbaum, G. *The Peanuts shape circus puzzle book*

Concepts – size

Ahlberg, Allan. *The snail house*
Alborough, Jez. *Watch out! Big Bro's coming!*
Alexander, Martha G. *Blackboard Bear*
Allen, Jonathan. *Big owl, little towel*
Allington, Richard L. *Shapes*
Alter, Anna. *Estelle and Lucy*
Anderson, Janet S. *Sunflower Sal*
Anderson, Laurie Halse. *The big cheese of Third Street*
Anno, Mitsumasa. *The king's flower*
Aulaire, Ingri Mortenson d'. *Too big*
Balian, Lorna. *Where in the world is Henry?*
Barnes, Laura T. *Teeny tiny Ernest*
Barrett, Judi. *I hate to take a bath*
Bedford, David. *Big bears can!*
Benson, Patrick. *Little penguin*
Berenstain, Stan. *Old hat, new hat*
Berger, Barbara Helen. *Angels on a pin*
Black, Irma (Simonton). *Big puppy and little puppy*
Blackstone, Stella. *Bear in a square*
Blades, Ann. *Too small*
Blue, Rose. *How many blocks is the world?*
The book of Pooh: Biglet
Bowman, Pete. *I wish I were big*
Bridges, Margaret Park. *Am I big or little?*
Brown, Marcia. *Once a mouse . . .*
Brown, Margaret Wise. *Big dog, little dog*
 Bumble bugs and elephants
 The little fireman
Buehner, Caralyn. *Superdog, the heart of a hero*
Bulette, Sara. *The splendid belt of Mr. Big*
Cantieni, Benita. *Little Elephant and Big Mouse*
Chalmers, Audrey. *Hector and Mr. Murfit*
Clements, Andrew. *Big Al and Shrimpy*
Cole, Babette. *The trouble with Grandad*
Cole, Joanna. *Big Goof and Little Goof*
Cooke, Trish. *When I grow bigger*
Craig, M. Jean. *Boxes*
Croswell, Volney. *How to hide a hippopotamus*
Cuneo, Mary Louise. *What can a giant do?*
Cuyler, Margery. *The biggest, best snowman*
Damjan, Mischa. *The big squirrel and the little rhinoceros*
Davis, Lee. *The lifesize animal opposites book*
De Mejo, Oscar. *La Bella Magellona and the little cavalier*
Donohue, Dorothy. *Big and little on the farm*
Dubar, Joyce. *The very small*
Du Quette, Keith. *Hotel Animal*
Emmett, Jonathan. *Someone bigger*
Facklam, Margery. *The big bug book*
Finzel, Julia. *Large as life*
Florian, Douglas. *A pig is big*
French, Fiona. *Little Inchkin*
French, Vivian. *Molly in the middle*
Gackenbach, Dick. *Tiny for a day*
Gerstein, Mordicai. *The gigantic baby*
Gliori, Debi. *When I'm big*
Gorbachev, Valeri. *Big Little Elephant*
Gray, Nigel. *Pigs can't fly*

Green-Armytage, Stephen. *Dudley, the little terrier that could*
Greenway, Shirley. *How big am I?*
Grindley, Sally. *The giant postman*
  Too big bear
Gunzi, Christiane. *Sizes*
Haring, Keith. *Big*
Hellings, Colette. *Too little, too big*
Helmer, Marilyn. *Three teeny tiny tales*
Henkes, Kevin. *The biggest boy*
Herman, R. A. (Ronnie Ann). *Pal the pony*
Hill, Susan. *Stuart at the fun house*
Hindley, Judy. *Little and big*
Hoban, Tana. *Big ones, little ones*
  Is it larger? Is it smaller?
  Is it red? Is it yellow? Is it blue?
  Spirals, curves, fanshapes and lines
Hughes, Shirley. *All shapes and sizes*
Hutchins, H. J. (Hazel J.). *Two so small*
Hutchins, Pat. *Shrinking mouse*
  Titch
Ipcar, Dahlov (Zorach). *The biggest fish in the sea*
  The land of flowers
Iwamura, Kazuo. *Ton and Pon: big and little*
Jenkins, Steve. *Actual size*
  Big and little
Jensen, Patricia. *Be patient, Little Chick*
Jonell, Lynne. *Mommy go away!*
Jordan, Roslyn M. *Salt in his shoes*
Joyce, William. *Big time Olie*
  George shrinks
Kalan, Robert. *Blue sea*
Karlin, Nurit. *Little big mouse*
Keller, Holly. *Jacob's tree*
Kimmel, Eric A. *Ten suns*
Kirk, Daniel. *Bigger*
Kliphuis, Christine. *Robbie and Ronnie*
Koski, Mary. *Impatient Pamela asks, "Why are my feet so huge?"*
Kraus, Robert. *The little giant*
Krauss, Ruth. *Big and little*
  A bouquet of littles
Kuskin, Karla. *Herbert hated being small*
Lipkind, William. *Chaga*
Little, Jean. *Revenge of the small Small*
Long, Earlene. *Gone fishing*
McGuirk, Leslie. *Snail boy*
MacKinnon, Debbie. *What shape?*
  What size?
McPhail, David M. *A bug, a bear, and a boy*
Mangan, Anne. *Browny, the smallest bear of all*
Masurel, Claire. *Too big!*
May, Kara. *Joe Lion's big boots*
Mayer, Marianna. *The Brambleberrys animal book of big and small shapes*
Mayer, Mercer. *Just big enough*
Meister, Cari. *Tiny goes to the library*
  Tiny's bath
  When Tiny was tiny
Miller, Margaret. *Big and little*
  Now I'm big
Mitchell, Adrian. *Twice my size*
Moers, Hermann. *Little Ben*
Mogensen, Jan. *The Land of the Big*
Most, Bernard. *How big were the dinosaurs?*
Mueller, Doris L. *Small One's adventure*
Murphy, Kelly. *The boll weevil ball*
Murphy, Stuart J. *Bigger, better, best*
Nakabayashi, Ei. *The rainy day puddle*
Nathan, Cheryl. *The long and short of it*
Nickle, John. *The ant bully*
Nimmo, Jenny. *Esmeralda and the children next door*
Norac, Carl. *My daddy is a giant*
O'Brien, Patrick. *Gigantic!*
O'Connor, Jane. *Sir Small and the dragonfly*
Oliver, Stephen. *My first look at sizes*
Packard, Edward. *Big numbers*
Palazzo-Craig, Janet. *Little Danny Dinosaur*
Parr, Todd. *Big and little*

Passen, Lisa. *Attack of the 50-foot teacher*
  The incredible shrinking teacher
Patron, Susan. *Five bad boys, Billy Que, and the dustdobbin*
Peet, Bill (William Bartlett). *Huge Harold*
Pieńkowski, Jan. *Sizes*
Pluckrose, Henry Arthur. *Big and little*
Poydar, Nancy. *Cool Ali*
Pragoff, Fiona. *Shapes*
Prøysen, Alf. *Mrs. Pepperpot and the moose*
Rotner, Shelley. *Close, closer, closest*
Ruzzier, Sergio. *The little giant*
San Souci, Robert D. *Little Pierre*
Schwartz, David M. *How much is a million?*
Shapp, Martha. *Let's find out what's big and what's small*
Simon, Seymour. *Giant machines*
  Sizes
Smith, Mavis. *Circles*
Smith-Moore, J. J. *Sally Small*
Stickland, Paul. *Machines as big as monsters*
Stoddard, Sandol. *Curl up small*
Sutherland, Tui. *Meet Mo and Ella*
Tafuri, Nancy. *The brass ring*
Tangvald, Christine Harder. *The Rinky Dinky Donkey*
Turner, Sandy. *Otto's trunk*
Ueno, Noriko. *Elephant buttons*
Van Leeuwenm, Jean. *"Wait for me!" said Maggie McGee*
Van Emst, Charlotte. *Little Rabbit's big day*
Vere, Ed. *Everyone's little*
Wallwork, Amanda. *Find the fish that looks like this*
Walton, Rick. *Bertie was a watchdog*
Watson, Carol. *Sizes*
Wells, Tony. *Puzzle doubles*
Wheeler, Lisa. *Turk and Runt*
Wilson, April. *April Wilson's magpie magic*
Yaccarino, Dan. *So big*
Youldon, Gillian. *Sizes*
Zoehfeld, Kathleen Weidner. *Dinosaurs big and small*

Concepts – speed

Cartier, Wesley. *Marco's run*
Munsch, Robert N. *Zoom*
O'Connor, Jane. *Snail City*
Penner, Lucille Recht. *Slowpoke*
Saunders, Dave. *So slow!*
Schlein, Miriam. *Fast is not a ladybug*
Spier, Peter. *Fast-slow, high-low*

Concepts – up & down

Berkley, Ethel S. *Ups and down*
Harris, Trudy. *Up bear, down bear*
Hoban, Tana. *Look up, look down*
Johnson, Crockett. *Upside down*
Knight, Hilary. *Sylvia the sloth*
Matthias, Catherine. *Out the door = Sal y entra*
Seuss, Dr. *A great day for up*
Slobodkin, Louis. *Up high and down low*
Zion, Gene. *All falling down*

Concepts – weight

Cobb, Vicki. *I fall down*
Enderle, Judith (Ann) Ross. *What would Mama do?*
Fischer, Vera Kistiakowsky. *One way is down*
MacDonald, George. *The light princess*, ill. by Katie Thamer Treherne
Pluckrose, Henry Arthur. *Weight*
Royston, Angela. *Heavy and light*
Schlein, Miriam. *Heavy is a hippopotamus*
Schwartz, David M. *Ready! set! measure!*
Sweeney, Joan. *Me and the measure of things*

Condors *see* Birds – condors

Conductors *see* Careers – conductors (music)

Confidence *see* Character traits – confidence

Conservation *see* Ecology

Construction workers *see* Careers – construction workers

Contests

Aboff, Marcie. *The giant jelly bean jar*
Bliss, Corinne Demas. *Nina's waltz*
Bond, Michael. *Paddington Bear and the Busy Bee Carnival*
Caple, Kathy. *Worm gets a job*
Catalanotto, Peter. *Emily's art*
Cole, Joanna. *The Clown-Arounds*
Dalmais, Anne-Marie. *And may the best animal win!*
Darrow, Sharon. *Old Thunder and Miss Raney*
Dorros, Arthur. *Julio's magic*
Dunbar, Joyce. *Eggday*
Gray, Nigel. *The dog show*
Himmelman, John. *The Clover County carrot contest*
Jennings, Sharon. *Franklin and the contest*
Kerr, Judith. *Mog's bad thing*
Lattimore, Deborah Nourse. *The lady with the ship on her head*
London, Jonathan. *Froggy plays in the band*
Loredo, Elizabeth. *Boogie Bones*
Marshall, James. *The Cut-Ups carry on*
Mathers, Petra. *A cake for Herbie*
Most, Bernard. *The very boastful kangaroo*
Munsch, Robert N. *More pies*
Neugebauer, Charise. *The real winner*
Olaleye, Isaac. *In the Rainfield*
Park, Frances. *The royal bee*
Reynolds, Peter H. *Sydney's star*
Root, Phyllis. *Rosie's fiddle*
Sage, James. *Farmer Smart's fat cat*
Saltzberg, Barney. *Phoebe and the spelling bee*
Samuels, Barbara. *Aloha, Dolores*
Shields, Carol Diggory. *The bugliest bug*
Stower, Adam. *Two left feet*
Wells, Rosemary. *The Halloween parade*
White, Linda Arms. *Comes a wind*
Winters, Kay. *The teeny tiny ghost and the monster*
Wojciechowski, Susan. *A fine St. Patrick's Day*

Cooking *see* Activities – baking, cooking

Cooks *see* Careers – bakers; Careers – chefs, cooks

Cooperation *see* Character traits – cooperation

Coquelle Indians *see* Indians of North America – Coquelle

Cora Indians *see* Indians of North America – Cora

Coral Islands *see* Foreign lands – South Sea Islands

Cormorants *see* Birds – cormorants

Costa Rica *see* Foreign lands – Costa Rica

Costumes *see* Clothing – costumes

Couches, sofas *see* Furniture – couches, sofas

Cougars *see* Animals – cougars

Counting, numbers

Adams, Pam. *This old man*
Adler, David A. *Base five*
Ahlberg, Allan. *Fee fi fo fum*
Alakija, Polly. *Catch that goat!*
Alda, Arlene. *Arlene Alda's 1 2 3*

Arlene Alda's 1 2 3
Alexander, Anne (Anna Barbara Cooke). *My daddy and I*
Allbright, Viv. *Ten go hopping*
Allen, Jonathan. *One with a bun*
Allen, Robert. *Numbers*
  Ten little babies count
  Ten little babies dress
  Ten little babies eat
  Ten little babies play
Allington, Richard L. *Numbers*
Ambler, C. Gifford (Christopher Gifford). *Ten little foxhounds*
Ambrus, Victor G. *Count, Dracula*
Anholt, Catherine. *One, two, three, count with me*
Animal 123's
Anno, Mitsumasa. *Anno's counting book*
  Anno's counting house
  Anno's hat tricks
  Anno's magic seeds
  Anno's math games
  Anno's math games II
  Anno's math games III
Appelt, Kathi. *Bats on parade*
  Rain dance
Archambault, John. *Counting sheep*
Arnold, Tedd. *Bisnipian blast-off*
  Five ugly monsters
Arnosky, Jim. *Mouse numbers and letters*
Asch, Frank. *Little Devil's 123*
Ashton, Elizabeth Allen. *An old-fashioned one two three book*
Astley, Judy. *When one cat woke up*
Axelrod, Amy. *Pigs in the pantry*
  Pigs on the ball
Aylesworth, Jim. *The completed hickory dickory dock*
  One crow
Baker, Alan. *Gray Rabbit's one, two, three*
  Little Rabbit's first number book
Baker, Bonnie Jeanne. *A pear by itself*
Baker, Jeannie. *One hungry spider*
Ballart, Elisabet. *Let's count*
Bang, Molly. *Ten, nine, eight*
Barber, Patti. *First number book*
Barner, Bob. *Space race*
  Too many dinosaurs
Barnes-Murphy, Rowan. *Numbers*
Barry, David. *The Rajah's rice*
Base, Graeme. *The water hole*
Baseball 1-2-3
Bassède, Francine. *George's store at the shore*
Baum, Arline. *One bright Monday morning*
Bawden, Juliet. *One year old*
Bayley, Nicola. *One old Oxford ox*
Beaton, Clare. *One moose, twenty mice*
  One moose, twenty mice [board book]
Beck, Andrea. *Elliot's great big lift-the-flap book*
Beck, Ian. *Five little ducks*
Becker, John Leonard. *Seven little rabbits*
Beeler, Selby B. *How many Elephants?*
Bennett, David. *One cow moo moo*
Berenstain, Stan. *Bears on wheels*
  The Berenstain bears' counting book
Berkes, Marianne Collins. *Seashells by the seashore*
Bertrand, Lynne. *Dragon naps*
  One day, two dragons
Bishop, Claire Huchet. *Twenty-two bears*
Bishop, Roma. *Easter counting*
  Numbers
Blackstone, Stella. *Bear in a square*
Blake, Quentin. *Cockatoos*
Blegvad, Lenore. *One is for the sun*
Blumenthal, Nancy. *Count-a-saurus*
Bohdal, Susi. *1, 2, 3, what do you see?*
Bond, Felicia. *Tumble bumble*
Bond, Michael. *Paddington's 1 2 3*
Boon, Emilie. *1 2 3 how many animals can you see?*
Bourke, Linda. *Eye count*
Bowden, Miriam. *The adventure of Paz in the land of numbers*
Boynton, Sandra. *Hippos go berserk*

One, two, three!
Bradman, Tony. *The bad babies' counting book*
  Not like this, like that
Breeze, Lynn. *Baby's food*
Brenner, Barbara A. *The snow parade*
Bridgman, Elizabeth. *All the little bunnies*
Bridwell, Norman. *Clifford counts bubbles*
Briggs, Raymond. *The snowman [a lift-the-flap board book]*
Bright, Robert. *My red umbrella*
Brooks, Alan. *Frogs jump*
Brown, Marc Tolon. *Count to ten*
Brown, Rick. *Who built the ark?*
Bruce, Lisa. *Engines, engines*
Bruna, Dick. *I can count*
  I can count more
  I know more about numbers
  Poppy Pig goes to market
Brunhoff, Laurent de. *Babar's counting book*
Bucknall, Caroline. *One bear all alone*
Burningham, John. *Count up*
  First steps
  Five down
  John Burningham's 1 2 3
  Just cats
  Pigs plus
  Read one
  Ride off
Burton, Katherine. *One gray mouse*
Butler, John. *While you were sleeping*
Calmenson, Stephanie. *Come to my party*
  Dinner at the Panda Palace
  One little monkey
  Ten furry monsters
Cameron, C. C. *One for me, one for you*
Capucilli, Alyssa Satin. *Mrs. McTats and her houseful of cats*
Carle, Eric. *My very first book of numbers*
  1, 2, 3 to the zoo
  The rooster who set out to see the world
  Rooster's off to see the world
  10 little rubber ducks
Carlstrom, Nancy White. *Graham cracker animals 1-2-3*
  Let's count it out, Jesse Bear
Carroll, Kathleen Sullivan. *One red rooster*
Cave, Kathryn. *One child, one seed*
  Out for the count
Challoner, Jack. *The science book of numbers*
Chamberlin-Calamar, Pat. *Alaska's twelve days of summer*
Chandra, Deborah. *Miss Mabel's table*
Charles, Faustin. *A Caribbean counting book*
Charlip, Remy. *Thirteen*
Charosh, Mannis. *Number ideas through pictures*
Chester, Jonathan. *Splash!*
Chichester Clark, Emma. *Little Miss Muffet's count-along surprise*
Chorao, Kay. *Number one number fun*
Chouinard, Roger. *One magic box*
Christelow, Eileen. *Five little monkeys jumping on the bed*
  Five little monkeys sitting in a tree
Chwast, Seymour. *Still another number book*
  The twelve circus rings
Clarke, Gus. *Ten green monsters*
Clements, Andrew. *Mother Earth's counting book*
Cleveland, David. *The April rabbits*
Cline-Ransome, Lesa. *Quilt counting*
Coats, Laura Jane. *Ten little animals*
Coats, Lucy. *Neil's numberless world*
  One hungry baby
Cobb, Annie. *The long wait*
Cole, Joanna. *Animal sleepyheads*
Coleman, Michael. *One, two, three, oops!*
Conover, Chris. *Six little ducks*
Coplans, Peta. *Cat and dog*
Corbett, Grahame. *What number now?*
Cotten, Cynthia. *At the edge of the woods*
Count in the dark with Glo Worm
Count me in
Counting rhymes
Cousins, Lucy. *Count with Maisy*

Maisy's twinkly, crinkly counting book
Cowley, Stewart. *Down Ladybug Lane*
  Five little kittens
  Hide-and-seek puppies
  In dragonfly forest
  In songbird jungle
  Little chick
  Little lost rabbit
  The naughty ducklings
  On Butterfly Farm
Coxe, Molly. *6 sticks*
Cretan, Gladys Yessayan. *Ten brothers with camels*
Crews, Donald. *Bicycle race*
  Ten black dots
Crowther, Robert. *Hide and seek counting book*
  My pop-up surprise 1 2 3
Crum, Shutta. *The bravest of the brave*
Curious George's 1 to 10 and back again
Cuyler, Margery. *100th day worries*
Dahl, Michael. *Downhill fun*
  Eggs and legs
  Footprints in the snow
  From the garden
  Hands down
  Lots of ladybugs!
  On the launch pad
  One big building
  One checkered flag
  One giant splash
  Pie for piglets
  Starry arms
Daily, Don. *The twelve days of Christmas cats*
Dale, Penny. *Ten out of bed*
Dalmais, Anne-Marie. *In my garden*
Daniels, Teri. *Math man*
Dayton, Laura. *LeRoy's birthday circus*
DeCaprio, Annie. *One, two*
Deegan, Kim. *My first book of numbers*
Demarest, Chris L. *Smokejumpers one to ten*
Demi. *Demi's count the animals 1-2-3*
  One grain of rice
Denega, Danielle. *Numbers*
De Regniers, Beatrice Schenk. *So many cats!*
Dijs, Carla. *How many?*
Dodd, Emma. *Dog's colorful day*
Dodd, Lynley. *The nickle nackle tree*
Dodds, Dayle Ann. *The Great Divide*
Dodds, Siobhan. *Elizabeth Hen*
Doolittle, Eileen. *World of wonders*
Dreamer, Sue. *Circus 1, 2, 3*
Duckling
Duerrstein, Richard. *One Mickey Mouse, a Disney book of numbers = Un Ratón Mickey, un libro Disney de números*
Duke, Kate. *One guinea pig is not enough*
  Twenty is too many
Dunham, Meredith. *Numbers: how do you say it?*
Dunrea, Olivier. *Deep down underground*
Dupasquier, Philippe. *1 2 3, follow me!*
Duvoisin, Roger Antoine. *Two lonely ducks*
Edwards, Pamela Duncan. *Roar*
  Warthogs in the kitchen
Edwards, Richard. *Ten tall oaktrees*
Edwards, Roberta. *Five silly fishermen*
Ehlert, Lois. *Fish eyes*
Eichenberg, Fritz. *Dancing in the moon*
Elkin, Benjamin. *Six foolish fishermen*
Ellwand, David. *Ten in the bed*
Elya, Susan Middleton. *Eight animals on the town*
Emberley, Rebecca. *My numbers = Mis números*
Enderle, Judith (Ann) Ross. *Six creepy sheep*
  Six sandy sheep
  Six snowy sheep
  Where are you, little Zack?
Ernst, Lisa Campbell. *Up to ten and down again*
Evans, Lezlie. *Can you count ten toes?*
Everett, Percival L. *The one that got away*
Falconer, Ian. *Olivia counts*

Falwell, Cathryn. *Christmas for 10*
  Feast for ten
  Nicky, 1-2-3
  Turtle splash!
Fancher, Lou. *The quest for the One Big Thing*
Farber, Norma. *Up the down elevator*
Faulkner, Keith. *Pop! went another balloon!*
Fearrington, Ann. *Who sees the lighthouse?*
Feelings, Muriel. *Menjo means one*
Fisher, Leonard Everett. *Boxes! Boxes!*
Five little pumpkins
Flather, Lisa. *Ten silly dogs*
Fleming, Candace. *Who invited you?*
Fleming, Denise. *Count!*
Florian, Douglas. *A summer day*
Foreman, Michael. *Dad! I can't sleep*
Fowler, Richard. *Happy birthday, Mouse!*
Fox, Christyan. *Count to ten, PiggyWiggy!*
Freeman, Lydia. *Corduroy's day*
French, Vivian. *One ballerina two*
Freschet, Berniece. *The ants go marching*
  Where's Henrietta's hen?
Freymann, Saxton. *One lonely seahorse*
Friedman, Aileen. *The king's commissioners*
Friskey, Margaret (Margaret Richards). *Chicken Little, count-to-ten*
  Seven diving ducks
Fry, Jenny. *Building numbers*
Fuchshuber, Annegert. *Two peas in a pod*
Fujikawa, Gyo. *Ten little babies*
Gantz, David. *Captain Swifty counts to 50*
Gardiner, Lindsey. *Good night, Poppy and Max*
Gardner, Beau. *Can you imagine . . . ?*
Geisert, Arthur. *Pigs from 1 to 10*
George, Kristine O'Connell. *The great frog race and other poems*
Gerstein, Mordicai. *Guess what?*
  Roll over!
Giganti, Paul. *Each orange had eight slices*
  How many snails?
Gikow, Louise. *Count with me*
Gill, Shelley. *The big buck adventure*
Gillham, Bill. *Let's look for numbers*
Ginsburg, Mirra. *Kitten from one to ten*
Girnis, Margaret. *1, 2, 3 for you and me*
Glicksman, Caroline. *Eric the math bear*
Goennel, Heidi. *Odds and evens*
Gollub, Matthew. *Ten oni drummers*
Gorbachev, Valeri. *One rainy day*
Greenstein, Elaine. *Dreaming*
Gregor, Arthur S. *1, 2, 3, 4, 5*
Gretz, Susanna. *Teddy bears ABC*
  Teddy bears 1 – 10
Grimm, Jacob. *Mrs. Fox's wedding*
Grindley, Sally. *Where are my chicks?*
Groening, Maggie. *Maggie Simpson's counting book*
Grossman, Bill. *My little sister ate one hare*
Grossman, Virginia. *Ten little rabbits*
Gryspeerdt, Rebecca. *Counting friends*
Guettier, Bénédicte. *The father who had ten children*
Gundersheimer, Karen. *1, 2, 3, play with me*
Gunzi, Christiane. *Numbers*
Guy, Ginger Foglesong. *Fiesta*
Hague, Kathleen. *Numbears*
  Ten little bears
Halls, Kelly Milner. *I bought a baby chicken*
Halpern, Shari. *Moving from one to ten*
Hamm, Diane Johnston. *How many feet in the bed?*
Hamsa, Bobbie. *Polly wants a cracker*
Harada, Joyce. *It's the 0-1-2-3 book*
Haring, Keith. *10*
Harris, Trudy. *100 days of school*
Harshman, Marc. *Only one*
Hartmann, Wendy. *One sun rises*
Harvey, Jayne. *Busy bugs*
Haskins, Jim (James). *Count your way through Africa*
  Count your way through Brazil
  Count your way through Canada
  Count your way through China

Count your way through France
Count your way through Germany
Count your way through Greece
Count your way through India
Count your way through Ireland
Count your way through Israel
Count your way through Italy
Count your way through Japan
Count your way through Korea
Count your way through Mexico
Count your way through Russia
Count your way through the Arab world
Hassett, John. *Cat up a tree*
Hawkins, Colin. *One, two, guess who?*
  Take away monsters
Hay, Dean. *Now I can count*
Hayward, Linda. *Did I ever tell you how high you can count?*
  I can add upside down!
  I can count to ten and back again
  Oh, the things you can count from 1-10
Heinst, Marie. *My first number book*
Helakoski, Leslie. *The smushy bus*
Henderson, Kathy. *Counting farm*
Henley, Claire. *Joe's pool*
Hennessy, B. G. (Barbara G.). *One little, two little, three little pilgrims*
Hill, Eric. *Spot counts from 1 to 10*
  Spot's big book of colors, shapes and numbers = El libro grande de Spot
  Spot's big book of colours, shapes, and numbers
  Spot's favorite numbers
  Spot's first 1, 2, 3 frieze
Hillman, Priscilla. *The Merry-Mouse counting and colors book*
Hindley, Judy. *How many twos?*
  One by one
  Ten bright eyes
Hoban, Russell. *Ten what?*
Hoban, Tana. *Count and see*
  Let's count
  More, fewer, less
  1, 2, 3
  26 letters and 99 cents
Hoberman, Mary Ann. *The looking book*
Hoffman, Don. *A counting book with Billy and Abigail*
Holder, Heidi. *Crows*
Holland, Cheri. *Maccabee jamboree*
Holmes, Stephen. *Hidden numbers*
Hooks, William H. *A dozen dizzy dogs*
  Read-a-rebus
Hooper, Meredith. *Seven eggs*
Horácek, Petr. *When the moon smiled*
Howard, Katherine. *I can count to 100 . . . can you?*
Howe, Caroline Walton. *Counting penguins*
Hubbard, Patricia. *Trick or treat countdown*
Hubbard, Woodleigh Marx. *2 is for dancing*
Huck, Charlotte S. *A creepy countdown*
Hudson, Cheryl Willis. *Afro-Bets 123 book*
  Let's count, baby
Hughes, Shirley. *Lucy and Tom's 1, 2, 3*
  When we went to the park
Hulme, Joy N. *Sea squares*
  Sea sums
Hunt, Jonathan. *One is a mouse*
Hutchins, Pat. *1 hunter*
  Ten red apples
Inkpen, Mick. *Kipper's book of counting*
  Kipper's book of numbers
  Kipper's toybox
  One bear at bedtime
Ipcar, Dahlov (Zorach). *Brown cow farm*
  My wonderful Christmas tree
  Ten big farms
Isadora, Rachel. *123 pop!*
Jabar, Cynthia. *Party day!*
Jackson, Woody. *Counting cows*
Jahn-Clough, Lisa. *1 2 3 yippie*
Jane, Pamela. *Monster countdown*
Johnson, Odette. *One prickly porcupine*
Johnson, Stephen T. *City by numbers*

Johnston, Tony. *Whale song*
Jonas, Ann. *Splash!*
Jones, Carol. *This old man*
Joyce, William. *Rolie Polie Olie, how many howdys?*
Karlin, Nurit. *Ten little bunnies*
Kassirer, Sue. *Math fair blues*
Katz, Karen. *Counting kisses*
Katz, Michael Jay. *Ten potatoes in a pot and other counting rhymes*
Keats, Ezra Jack. *One red sun*
Kellogg, Steven (Stephen). *Give the dog a bone*
Kessler, Ethel. *Two, four, six, eight*
Kharms, Daniil. *First, second*
King, Dave. *Counting book*
Kitamura, Satoshi. *When sheep cannot sleep*
Kitchen, Bert. *Animal numbers*
Kneen, Maggie. *When you're not looking*
Koch, Michelle. *Just one more*
Koller, Jackie French. *One monkey too many*
Koontz, Robin Michal. *This old man*
Kopper, Lisa. *Ten little babies*
Kosowsky, Cindy. *Wordless counting book*
Kramer, Anthony Penta. *Numbers on parade*
Kraus, Robert. *Good night little one*
    Good night Richard Rabbit
Krebs, Laurie. *We all went on safari*
Krudwig, Vickie Leigh. *Cucumber soup*
Krüss, James. *3 X 3*
Kuhn, Dwight. *Hungry little frog*
Kunhardt, Katharine. *Let's count the puppies*
Kvasnosky, Laura McGee. *One, two, three, play with me!*
Landa, Norbert. *Rabbit and chicken count eggs*
Langstaff, John M. *Over in the meadow*
Larios, Julie Hofstrand. *On the stairs*
Lasker, Joe. *Lentil soup*
Lavis, Steve. *Cock-a-doodle-doo*
Ledwon, Peter. *Midnight math twelve terrific math games*
Lee, Huy Voun. *1, 2, 3 go!*
Leedy, Loreen. *Fraction action*
    Mission – addition
    A number of dragons
    2 x 2 = boo!
Leman, Jill. *Ten little pussy cats*
Leonard, Marcia. *Counting kangaroos*
Lester, Alison. *When Frank was four*
Let's count and count out
Leuck, Laura. *My baby brother has ten tiny toes*
    One witch
Lewin, Betsy. *Cat count*
    Hip, hippo, hooray!
Lewis, J. Patrick. *Arithme-tickle*
Lewis, Shari. *Baby Lamb Chop loves numbers*
Lewison, Wendy Cheyette. *Raindrop, plop*
Liebler, John. *Frog counts to ten*
The Lifesize animal counting book
Lindbergh, Reeve. *Midnight farm*
Linden, Ann Marie. *One smiling grandma*
Lionni, Leo. *Numbers to talk about*
Lippman, Peter. *Peter Lippman's numbers*
A little book of numbers
Livermore, Elaine. *One to ten, count again*
Lobel, Anita. *One lighthouse, one moon*
Lodge, Bernard. *How scary*
Löfgren, Ulf. *One-two-three*
London, Jonathan. *Count the ways, Little Brown Bear*
Loomis, Christine. *One cow coughs*
Losi, Carol A. *The 512 ants on Sullivan Street*
Luttrell, Ida. *The star counters*
Lynn, Sara. *1 2 3*
Lyon, George Ella. *Counting on the woods*
McCarthy, Bobette. *Ten little hippos*
McCourt, Lisa. *The rainforest counts!*
McCrea, Lilian. *Mother hen*
MacDonald, Elizabeth. *Dilly-Dally and the nine secrets*
    Mike's kite
    My aunt and the animals
MacDonald, Suse. *Look whooo's counting*
    Numblers

McGee, Barbara. *Counting sheep*
McGinty, Alice B. *Ten little lambs*
McGough, Roger. *Counting by numbers*
McGrath, Barbara Barbieri. *Kellogg's froot loops counting fun book*
McGuire, Richard. *The orange book*
Mack, Stanley (Stan). *Ten bears in my bed*
MacKinnon, Debbie. *How many?*
McKissack, Patricia C. *Big bug book of counting*
McLeod, Emilie Warren. *One snail and me*
McMillan, Bruce. *Counting wildflowers*
    Eating fractions
    Jelly beans for sale
    One, two, one pair!
Maestro, Betsy. *Dollars and cents for Harriet*
    Harriet goes to the circus
Maestro, Giulio. *One more and one less*
Magee, Doug. *Trucks you can count on*
Maisner, Heather. *Planet monster*
Mallat, Kathy. *Seven stars, more!*
Manning, Maurie J. *The aunts go marching*
Mannis, Celeste Davidson. *One leaf rides the wind*
Manushkin, Fran. *My Christmas safari*
    Walt Disney's one hundred one dalmations
Maris, Ron. *In my garden*
Markes, Julie. *Sidewalk 1 2 3*
Marks, Burton. *Colors and numbers*
Marsh, T. J. *Way out in the desert*
Marshall, Ray. *Pop-up numbers #1*
    Pop-up numbers #2
    Pop-up numbers #3
    Pop-up numbers #4
Martin, Bill (William Ivan). *Rock it, sock it, number line*
    Sounds I remember
    Sounds of numbers
Marzollo, Jean. *I spy little numbers*
    Ten cats have hats
    Ten little eggs
Masurel, Claire. *Ten dogs in the window*
Mathews, Louise. *Bunches and bunches of bunnies*
    Cluck one
    The great take-away
Matthias, Catherine. *Too many balloons*
Mayer, Marianna. *Alley oop!*
    The Brambleberrys animal book of counting
Mayer, Mercer. *Little Monster's counting book*
Mazzola, Frank. *Counting is for the birds*
Medearis, Angela Shelf. *The 100th day of school*
Meeks, Esther K. *One is the engine*, ill. by Ernie King
    One is the engine, ill. by Joe Rogers
Melmed, Laura Krauss. *1-2-3 Thanksgiving*
    This first Thanksgiving
Merriam, Eve. *Ten rosy roses*
    Train leaves the station
    12 ways to get to 11
Merrill, Jean. *How many kids are hiding on my block?*
Michelson, Richard. *Ten times better*
Milich, Zoran. *City 1 2 3*
Miller, J. P. (John Parr). *Learn to count with Little Rabbit*
Miller, Jane. *Farm counting book*
Miller, Virginia. *Ten red apples*
Milne, A. A. (Alan Alexander). *Pooh's counting book*
Milstein, Linda Breiner. *Coconut mon*
Min, Laura. *Mrs. Sato's hens*
Miranda, Anne. *Counting*
    Monster math
    Vroom, chugga, vroom-vroom
Mitter, Matt. *1, 2, 3, counting rhymes*
Mockford, Caroline. *Cleo's counting book*
Moore, Elaine. *Roly-poly puppies*
Mora, Pat. *One, two, three = Uno, dos, tres*
Morozumi, Atsuko. *One gorilla*
Morris, Ann. *Night counting*
Morse, Samuel French. *Sea sums*
Moss, Lloyd. *Zin! zin! zin! A violin*
Moss, Marissa. *Knick knack paddywack*
Mother Goose. *1, 2 buckle my shoe*, ill. by Sherry Neidigh
Mullins, Patricia. *One horse waiting for me*

Murphy, Stuart J. *Animals on board*
  Beep beep, vroom vroom!
  The best bug parade
  Betcha!
  Bug dance
  Captain Invincible and the space shapes
  Dave's down-to-earth rock shop
  Dinosaur deals
  Earth Day – hooray!
  Elevator magic
  Every buddy counts
  A fair bear share
  Give me half!
  The greatest gymnast of all
  Henry the fourth
  Just enough carrots
  Missing mittens
  Monster musical chairs
  More or less
  100 days of cool
  The penny pot
  Ready, set, hop!
  Seaweed soup
  Sluggers' car wash
  The sundae scoop
  Too many kangaroo things to do!
Namm, Diane. *Monsters!*
Nayer, Judy. *Funny bunnies*
  Tricky puppies
Naylor, Phyllis Reynolds. *Ducks disappearing*
Neuschwander, Cindy. *Amanda Bean's amazing dream*
Newman, Lesléa. *Dogs, dogs, dogs*
Nightingale, Sandy. *Pink pigs aplenty*
Nikola-Lisa, W. *Can you top that?*
  No babies asleep
  One hole in the road
  One, two, three Thanksgiving!
Noll, Sally. *Off and counting*
  Surprise!
Noonan, Julia. *Mouse by mouse*
Nordqvist, Sven. *Willie in the big world*
Numeroff, Laura Joffe. *Monster munchies*
O'Brien, Mary. *Counting sheep to sleep*
O'Donnell, Elizabeth Lee. *I can't get my turtle to move*
  The twelve days of summer
  Winter visitors
O'Keefe, Susan Heyboer. *One hungry monster*
Oliver, Stephen. *My first look at numbers*
Olyff, Clotilde. *1, 2, 3. One, two, three*
One rubber duckie
One, two, buckle my shoe, ill. by Rowan Barnes-Murphy
One, two, buckle my shoe, ill. by Gail E. Haley
One, two, skip a few!
Orgel, Doris. *Two crows counting*
Ormerod, Jan. *Come back, kittens*
  Come back, puppies
  Joe can count
  Young Joe
Over in the grasslands
Over in the meadow, ill. by Paul Galdone
Over in the meadow, ill. by Ezra Jack Keats
Owen, Annie. *From snowflakes to sandcastles*
Owens, Mary Beth. *Counting cranes*
Oxenbury, Helen. *Numbers of things*
Pace, David. *Shouting Sharon*
Packard, Edward. *Big numbers*
Pacovská, Kveta. *One, five, many*
Paley, Joan. *One more river*
Pallotta, Jerry. *Twizzlers percentages book*
  Underwater counting
Paparone, Pamela. *Five little ducks*
Parker, Victoria. *Bearum scarum*
Pavey, Peter. *One dragon's dream*
Pearson, Susan. *When baby went to bed*
Peek, Merle. *The balancing act*
Penner, Lucille Recht. *Lights out!*
Peppé, Rodney. *Circus numbers*

  Little numbers
Petie, Haris. *Billions of bugs*
Philpot, Lorna. *Amazing Anthony Ant*
Pieńkowski, Jan. *Numbers*
Piers, Helen. *Is there room on the bus?*
Pilegard, Virginia Walton. *The warlord's beads*
Pinczes, Elinor J. *Arctic fives arrive*
  Inchworm and a half
  A remainder of one
Pistoia, Sara. *Counting*
  Money
Pittman, Helena Clare. *Sunrise*
Pluckrose, Henry Arthur. *Counting*
  Numbers
Plummer, David. *Counting kittens*
Pomerantz, Charlotte. *One duck, another duck*
Pomeroy, Diana. *One potato*
Potter, Beatrix. *Peter Rabbit's one two three*
Prelutsky, Jack. *Halloween countdown*
  Wild witches' ball
Price, Christine. *One is God*
The pudgy fingers counting book
Rader, Laura. *Tea for me, tea for you*
Rand, Ann. *Little 1*
Rankin, Laura. *The handmade counting book*
Rayner, Mary. *One by one*
  Ten pink piglets
Rees, Mary. *Ten in a bed*
Reiser, Lynn. *Christmas counting*
Reiss, John J. *Numbers*
Reynolds, Adrian. *Pete and Polo's farmyard adventure*
Ribke, Simone T. *The shapes we eat*
Richardson, John. *Ten bears in a bed*
Ricklen, Neil. *My numbers = Mis números*
Riordan, James. *Little Bunny Bobkin*
Rockwell, Anne F. *100 school days*
  Willy can count
Rockwell, Norman. *Norman Rockwell's counting book*
Peek, Merle. *Roll over!*
Root, Phyllis. *One duck stuck*
  One duck stuck [board book]
Rose, Deborah Lee. *The twelve days of kindergarten*
Rosen, Michael J. (1954–). *Chanukah lights everywhere*
Ross, H. L. *Not counting monsters*
Ross, Tony. *This old man*
Roth, Carol. *Ten dirty pigs / Ten clean pigs*
Roth, Susan L. *Night-time numbers*
Rothstein, Gloria. *Sheep asleep*
Rumford, James. *Nine animals and the well*
Rusackas, Francesca. *Daddy all day long*
Ruschak, Lynette. *The counting zoo*
Ryan, Pam Muñoz. *The crayon counting book*
  One hundred is a family
Samton, Sheila White. *Moon to sun*
  On the river
  Ten tiny monsters
  The world from my window
Saul, Carol P. *Barn cat*
Sazer, Nina. *What do you think I saw?*
Scarry, Richard. *Richard Scarry's best counting book ever!*
Schaefer, Jackie Jasina. *Miranda's day to dance*
Schaefer, Lola M. *Homes 123*
Schafer, Kevin. *Penguins 1 2 3*
Schertle, Alice. *Goodnight, Hattie, my dearie, my dove*, ill. by Linda Strauss Edwards
  Goodnight, Hattie, my dearie, my dove, ill. by Ted Rand
Schnur, Steven. *Night lights*
Schulman, Janet. *Countdown to spring*
Schumaker, Ward. *In my garden*
Schwartz, David M. *How much is a million?*
  If you hopped like a frog
  Ready! set! measure!
Scott, Ann Herbert. *One good horse*
Scotton, Rob. *Russell the sheep*
Seignobosc, Françoise. *Jeanne-Marie counts her sheep*
Sendak, Maurice. *One was Johnny*
  Seven little monsters

Serfozo, Mary. *Who wants one?*
Sesame Street. *The Sesame Street book of numbers*
Seuss, Dr. *Ten apples up on top*
Seven spunky monkeys
Sharmat, Marjorie Weinman. *The 329th friend*
Sharratt, Nick. *Mouse moves house*
  Rocket countdown
Sheppard, Jeff. *The right number of elephants*
Shostak, Myra. *Rainbow candles*
Sierra, Judy. *Counting crocodiles*
Silvano, Wendi. *Counting coconuts = Contando cocos*
Silverman, Erica. *The Halloween house*
Simmons, Al. *Counting feathers*
Singer, Marilyn. *Quiet night*
Sis, Peter. *Fire truck*
  Going up!
  Waving
Sitomer, Mindel. *How did numbers begin?*
Skinner, Daphne. *Henry keeps score*
  Tightwad Tod
Slate, Joseph. *Miss Bindergarten celebrates the 100th day of kindergarten*
Smith, Donald. *Farm numbers*
Smith, Maggie (Margaret C.). *Counting our way to Maine*
  Dear Daisy, get well soon
Spanyol, Jessica. *Carlo likes counting*
Sper, Emily. *Hanukkah*
Spurr, Elizabeth. *Two bears beneath the stairs*
Staake, Bob. *My little 1 2 3 book*
Stanek, Muriel. *One, two, three for fun*
Steiner, Charlotte. *Five little finger playmates*
Stickland, Paul. *Ten terrible dinosaurs*
Stobbs, Joanna. *One sun, two eyes, and a million stars*
Stobbs, William. *This little piggy*
Sturges, Philemon. *Ten flashing fireflies*
Sugita, Yutaka. *Good night 1, 2, 3*
Sullivan, Charles. *Numbers at play*
Swinburne, Stephen R. *Water for one, water for everyone*
  What's a pair? What's a dozen?
Sykes, Julie. *Dora's chicks*
Szekeres, Cyndy. *Cyndy Szekeres' counting book, 1 to 10*
  Cyndy Szekeres' learn to count, funny bunnies
  I can count 100 bunnies, and so can you!
Tafuri, Nancy. *Counting to Christmas*
  Who's counting?
Tang, Greg. *Math appeal*
Testa, Fulvio. *If you take a pencil*
Thayer, Tanya. *Counting money*
Thompson, Lauren. *Little Quack*
  Little Quack [board book]
  Little Quack's hide and seek
  One riddle, one answer
Thompson, Susan L. *One more thing, dad*
Thornhill, Jan. *The wildlife 1-2-3*
The Timbertoes 1 2 3 counting book
Todd, Mark. *Start your engines*
Toft, Kim Michelle. *One less fish*
Trinca, Rod. *One woolly wombat*
Tudor, Tasha. *1 is one*
Turner, Gwenda. *Over on the farm*
Turner, Priscilla. *Among the odds and evens*
Two little eyes and other action rhymes
VanderKlipp, Michael A. *Joy to the world!*
Van der Meer, Ron. *Funny hats*
Van Fleet, Matthew. *One yellow lion*
Van Laan, Nancy. *Mama rocks, Papa sings*
  A tree for me
Van Woerkom, Dorothy. *Abu Ali counts his donkeys*
Voce, Louise. *Over in the meadow*
Wadsworth, Ginger. *One tiger growls*
Wadsworth, Olive A. *Over in the meadow*
Walker, Jane. *Ten little penguins*
Wallace, Nancy Elizabeth. *Count down to clean up*
Wallner, John C. *Look and find*
Walsh, Ellen Stoll. *Mouse count*
Walton, Rick. *How many?*
  One more bunny

  So many bunnies
Ward, Jennifer. *Over in the garden*
  Somewhere in the ocean
Warren, Cathy. *The ten-alarm camp-out*
Watson, Jane Werner. *The fuzzy duckling*
Watson, Nancy Dingman. *What is one?*
Weihs, Erika. *Count the cats*
Weiss, Monica. *Mmmm . . . cookies!*
Wells, Rosemary. *Emily's first 100 days of school*
  How many? How much?
  Max's toys
Weston, Martha. *Bea's four bears*
Whitehouse, Patricia. *Seasons 1 2 3*
  What's awake? 1 2 3
Wild, Robin. *The bears' counting book*
Wildsmith, Brian. *Brian Wildsmith 1 2 3*
Williams, Garth. *The chicken book*
Williams, Jenny (Jennifer). *One, two, buckle my shoe*
  Playtime 1 2 3
Williams, Rozanne Lanczak. *The coin counting book*
Williams, Sue. *Dinnertime*
  Let's go visiting
Williams, Suzanne. *Old MacDonald in the city*
Wilson, Anna. *Over in the grasslands*
Wilson, Barbara Ker. *ABC and 123*
Wojtowycz, David. *Animal antics from 1 to 10*
Wolfe, Art. *1, 2, 3 moose*
Wolff, Ferida. *On Halloween night*
Wood, Audrey. *Ten little fish*
Wood, Jakki. *Moo moo, brown cow*
  One bear with bees in his hair
Wyllie, Stephen. *Snappity snap*
Yates, Philip. *Ten little mummies*
Yee, Patrick. *Rosie Rabbit's numbers*
Yektai, Niki. *Bears at the beach*
Yolen, Jane. *How do dinosaurs count to ten?*
  An invitation to the butterfly ball
  Old Dame Counterpane
  Street rhymes around the world
Yoshi. *One, two, three*
Youldon, Gillian. *Counting*
  Numbers
Youngs, Betty Ferrell. *One panda*
Zabar, Abbie. *Fifty-five friends*
Zaslavsky, Claudia. *Count on your fingers African style*
  Zero! Is it something? Is it nothing?
Ziefert, Harriet. *A dozen dogs*
  A dozen ducklings lost and found
  Math riddles
  Mother Goose math
  Rabbit and Hare divide an apple
  Rockheads
  Two little witches
  You can't buy a dinosaur with a dime
Zimmermann, H. Werner (Heinz Werner). *Alphonse knows . . . zero is not enough*
Ziner, Feenie. *Counting carnival*
Zirbes, Laura. *How many bears?*
Zoller, Arthur David. *Fish counting*
Zolotow, Charlotte (Shapiro). *One step, two . . .*

Countries, foreign see Foreign lands

Country

Adams, Jean Ekman. *Clarence and the purple horse bounce into town*
Æsop. *The country mouse and the city mouse*, ill. by Laura Lydecker
  The country mouse and the city mouse, ill. by Diane Silverman
  The town mouse and the country mouse, ill. by Lorinda Bryan Cauley
  The town mouse and the country mouse, ill. by Helen Craig
  The town mouse and the country mouse, ill. by Paul Galdone
  The town mouse and the country mouse, ill. by Tom Garcia
  The town mouse and the country mouse, ill. by Janet Stevens
  The town mouse and the country mouse, ill. by Bernadette Watts
  Town mouse, country mouse, ill. by Jan Brett
  Town mouse, country mouse, ill. by Carol Jones

Alexander, Cecil Frances. *All things bright and beautiful*, ill. by Anna Vojtech
Anderson, Janet S. *Sunflower Sal*
Asch, Frank. *Country pie*
  Dear brother
Atwood, Margaret. *Anna's pet*
Aylesworth, Jim. *Wake up, little children*
Barklem, Jill. *The big book of Brambly Hedge*
Barton, Pat. *A week is a long time*
Bernhard, Durga. *To and fro, fast and slow*
Birdseye, Tom. *A regular flood of mishap*
  She'll be comin' round the mountain
Borden, Louise. *The watching game*
Bozzo, Maxine Zohn. *Toby in the country, Toby in the city*
Bröger, Achim. *Francie's paper puppy*
Brooks, Nigel. *Country mouse cottage*
Brown, Margaret Wise. *The country noisy book*
Browne, Caroline. *Mrs. Christie's farmhouse*
Burns, Maurice. *Go ducks, go!*
Burton, Virginia Lee. *The little house*
Carlstrom, Nancy White. *The snow speaks*
Caudill, Rebecca. *Contrary Jenkins*
Chall, Marsha Wilson. *Prairie train*
Chorao, Kay. *Ida and Betty and the secret eggs*
Christian, Mary Blount. *Christmas reflections*
Chwast, Seymour. *Tall city, wide country*
Cleveland-Peck, Patricia. *City cat, country cat*
Cline-Ransome, Lesa. *Quilt alphabet*
  Quilt counting
Cole, Sheila. *When the rain stops*
Cooper, Elisha. *Country fair*
Cousins, Lucy. *Country animals*
Crowther, Robert. *Who lives in the country?*
Cummins, Julie. *Country kid, city kid*
Dahlie, Elizabeth. *Bernelly & Harriet*
Dale, Ruth Bluestone. *Benjamin . . . and Sylvester also*
Day, Alexandra. *Paddy's pay-day*
DeFelice, Cynthia C. *When Grampa kissed his elbow*
Dennard, Deborah. *Hedgehog haven*
Dickinson, Mary. *Alex's outing*
Dorros, Arthur. *City chicken*
Florian, Douglas. *A year in the country*
Geisert, Bonnie. *Prairie town*
Gibbons, Faye. *Mountain wedding*
Gibbons, Gail. *County fair*
Goffstein, M. B. (Marilyn Brooke). *Our prairie home*
Gray, Rita. *Nonna's porch*
Griffith, Helen V. *Grandaddy's place*
Grimes, Nikki. *Danitra Brown leaves town*
Harshman, Marc. *A little excitement*
Hawkesworth, Jenny. *The lonely skyscraper*
Hayward, Linda. *The city worm and the country worm*
Hendershot, Judith. *Up the tracks to Grandma's*
Hirschi, Ron. *Harvest song*
Hodeir, André. *Warwick's 3 bottles*
Hoffman, Elizabeth Stokes. *Miss Renée's mice go to an exhibition*
Holl, Adelaide. *A mouse story*
Jam, Teddy. *The year of fire*
Jocelyn, Marthe. *Mayfly*
Johnson, Angela. *Down the winding road*
Kennedy, Joseph. *Lucy goes to the country*
Kilby, Don. *In the country*
Kingman, Lee. *Peter's long walk*
Kiser, SuAnn. *The hog call to end all!*
Kraus, Robert. *Robert Kraus' Babytown express*
Kuskin, Karla. *City dog*
Lawrence, Mary. *What's that sound?*
Levinson, Riki. *Country dawn to dusk*
Lewin, Ted. *Fair!*
Lewis, Kim. *One summer day*
Loomis, Christine. *Cowboy bunnies*
Lorenz, Lee. *A weekend in the city*
  A weekend in the country
Lunn, Janet Louise Swoboda. *Come to the fair*
McKissack, Patricia C. *Country mouse and city mouse*
MacLachlan, Patricia. *All the places to love*
  What you know first

McPartland, Suzy. *Zoom, car, zoom*
McPhail, David M. *Ed and me*
Maestro, Betsy. *Delivery van*
Martin, Bill (William Ivan). *Barn dance!*
Merriam, Eve. *Fighting words*
Miller, William. *Jenny and the peddler*
Mollel, Tololwa M. (Tololwa Marti). *Ananse's feast*
Moore, Elaine. *Grandma's house*
  Grandma's promise
Moore, Inga. *Little dog lost*
  The truffle hunter
Munro, Roxie. *The inside-outside book of Texas*
  Mazescapes
Nikola-Lisa, W. *Night is coming*
  Storm
  Till year's good end
Nolan, Lucy A. *The Lizard Man of Crabtree County*
Parks, Carmen. *Farmers market*
Payne, Joan Balfour. *The stable that stayed*
Pedersen, Judy. *Out in the country*
Pender, Lydia. *Barnaby and the horses*
Polacco, Patricia. *Meteor!*
Provensen, Alice. *Town and country*
Roach, Marilynne K. *Two Roman mice*
Rockwell, Anne F. *Willy can count*
Roe, Eileen. *Staying with Grandma*
Rylant, Cynthia. *Appalachia*
  Christmas in the country
  Night in the country
  Scarecrow
Scheffler, Ursel. *Stop your crowing, Kasimir!*
Schertle, Alice. *Down the road*
Sopko, Eugen. *Townsfolk and countryfolk*
Southwell, Jandelyn. *The little country town*
Spinelli, Eileen. *The best time of day*
Stanley, Diane. *A country tale*
Stevens, Kathleen. *Aunt Skilly and the stranger*
Summers, Kate. *Milly and Tilly*
Tucker, Kathy. *Do cowboys ride bikes?*
Van Allsburg, Chris. *The stranger*
Walters, Marguerite. *The city-country ABC*
  The weekend
Williams, David. *Walking to the creek*
Williams, Jay. *The city witch and the country witch*
Wyeth, Sharon Dennis. *Always my dad*
Yolen, Jane. *Letting Swift River go*

Courage *see* Character traits – bravery

Cousins *see* Family life – cousins

Cowboys, cowgirls

Anderson, C. W. (Clarence Williams). *Blaze and the Indian cave*
  Blaze and the lost quarry
  Blaze and the mountain lion
  Blaze and Thunderbolt
  Blaze finds forgotten roads
  Blaze finds the trail
Anglund, Joan Walsh. *The brave cowboy*
  Cowboy and his friend
  The cowboy's Christmas
  Cowboy's secret life
Antle, Nancy. *Sam's Wild West Show*
Appelt, Kathi. *Cowboy dreams*
Aulaire, Ingri Mortenson d'. *Nils*
Balcziak, Bill. *Pecos Bill*
Beatty, Hetty Burlingame. *Bucking horse*
Birney, Betty G. *Tyrannosaurus Tex*
Bishop, Ann. *Wild Bill Hiccup's riddle book*
Bright, Robert. *Georgie goes west*
Brimner, Larry Dane. *Cowboy up!*
Brownlow, Michael. *Way out West – with a baby!*
Carter, Anne Laurel. *Tall in the saddle*
Chandler, Edna Walker. *Cattle drive*
  Cowboy Andy

Pony rider
Secret tunnel
Cohen, Caron Lee. *Bronco dogs*
Cowley, Joy. *Where horses run free*
Darling, Kathy (Mary Kathleen). *Pecos Bill finds a horse*
Demarest, Chris L. *The cowboy ABC*
Denslow, Sharon Phillips. *On the trail with Miss Pace*
Dewey, Ariane. *Pecos Bill*
Doughtie, Charles. *High Henry . . . the cowboy who was too tall to ride a horse*
Enderle, Judith (Ann) Ross. *Nell Nugget and the cow caper*
Everett, Percival L. *The one that got away*
Fain, James W. *Rodeos*
Felton, Harold W. *Pecos Bill and the mustang*
Fitzhugh, Louise. *Bang, bang, you're dead*
Frank, John. *The toughest cowboy, Or, How the Wild West was tamed*
Gardella, Tricia. *Just like my dad*
Garland, Sherry. *Goodnight, cowboy*
Gerrard, Roy. *Rosie and the rustlers*
Gibbons, Gail. *Yippee-yay!*
Grossman, Bill. *Cowboy Ed*
Gulbis, Stephen. *Cowgirl Rosie and her five baby bison*
Hancock, Sibyl. *Old Blue*
Harper, Jo. *Ollie Jolly, rodeo clown*
Heap, Sue. *Cowboy Baby*
Herzig, Alison Cragin. *Bronco busters*
Hill, Eric. *Spot goes to a party*
Hillert, Margaret. *The little cowboy and the big cowboy*
Holub, Joan. *Cinderdog and the wicked stepcat*
Hooker, Ruth. *Matthew the cowboy*
Hopkins, Lee Bennett. *The horned toad prince*
Johnson, Neil. *Jack Creek cowboy*
Johnston, Tony. *The cowboy and the black-eyed pea*
Sparky and Eddie, wild, wild rodeo!
Karas, G. Brian. *Home on the bayou*
Kellogg, Steven (Stephen). *Pecos Bill*
Kennedy, Richard. *The contests at Cowlick*
Ketteman, Helen. *Bubba the cowboy prince*
Kimmel, Eric A. *Four dollars and fifty cents*
Grizz!
Kinerk, Robert. *Slim and Miss Prim*
Knowlton, Laurie Lazzaro. *Why cowgirls are such sweet talkers*
Krasilovsky, Phyllis. *The girl who was a cowboy*
Lawson, Julie. *Arizona Charlie and the Klondike Kid*
Lenski, Lois. *Cowboy Small*
Lester, Julius. *Black cowboy, wild horses*
Liebman, Daniel. *I want to be a cowboy*
Loomis, Christine. *Cowboy bunnies*
Lowell, Susan. *The bootmaker and the elves*
McAllister, Angela. *The clever cowboy*
Mayer, Mercer. *Cowboy critter*
Medearis, Angela Shelf. *The zebra-riding cowboy*
Miller, Heather. *Cowboy*
Miller, Robert H. (Robert Henry). *The story of Nat Love*
Mitchell, Marianne. *Joe Cinders*
Moon, Dolly M. *My very first book of cowboy songs*
Mora, Jo (Joseph Jacinto). *Budgee Budgee Cottontail*
Morck, Irene. *Tyler's new boots*
Munro, Roxie. *The inside-outside book of Texas*
Pinkney, Andrea Davis. *Bill Pickett, rodeo ridin' cowboy*
Quackenbush, Robert M. *Pete Pack Rat*
Roberts, Bethany. *Birthday mice*
Rounds, Glen. *Cowboys*
Rubel, Nicole. *A cowboy named Ernestine*
Sanfield, Steve. *The great turtle drive*
Schanzer, Rosalyn. *The Old Chisholm Trail*
Schnitzler, Pattie L. *Widdermaker*
Scott, Ann Herbert. *Big Cowboy Western*
One good horse
Someday rider
Sewall, Marcia. *Ridin' that strawberry roan*
Smith, Janice Lee. *Jess and the stinky cowboys*
Stadler, John. *The ballad of Wilbur and the moose*
Stutson, Caroline. *Cowpokes*
Sullivan, Silky. *Grandpa was a cowboy*
Tibo, Gilles. *The cowboy kid*
Tinkelman, Murray. *Cowgirl*

Tucker, Kathy. *Do cowboys ride bikes?*
Ulmer, Wendy K. *A campfire for cowboy Billy*
Ward, Nanda Weedon. *The black sombrero*
Watson, Esther (Pearl). *The adventures of Jules and Gertie*
Trouble at Sugar Dip Well
Wheeler, Lisa. *Sixteen cows*
Winter, Jeanette. *Cowboy Charlie*
Wood, Audrey. *A cowboy Christmas*
Wood, Nancy C. *Little wrangler*

Cows *see* Animals – bulls, cows

Coyotes *see* Animals – coyotes

Crabs *see* Crustaceans – crabs

Cradles *see* Furniture – cradles

Crafts *see* Activities – making things

Cranes (birds) *see* Birds – cranes

Creation

Alexander, Cecil Frances. *All things bright and beautiful*, ill. by Leo Politi
All things bright and beautiful, ill. by Bruce Whatley
Anaya, Rudolfo A. *Roadrunner's dance*
Aronow, Sara. *Seven days of creation*
Baker, Betty. *And me, coyote!*
Bernstein, Margery. *Earth namer*
Bible. Old Testament. Genesis. *Genesis*
The story of the creation
Bierhorst, John. *The woman who fell from the sky*
Blake, William. *The tyger*
Boroson, Martin. *Becoming me*
Bratton, Heidi. *Imagine*
Brown, Kerry. *Tupag the dreamer*
Carlstrom, Nancy White. *Glory*
Cassidy, Sheila. *The creation*
Caswell, Helen Rayburn. *God must like to laugh*
Cohen, Deborah Bodin. *The seventh day*
Cooner, Donna D. (Donna Danell). *The world God made*
Crespo, George. *How the sea began*
Davidson, Alice J. *The story of creation*
Davol, Marguerite W. *Batwings and the curtain of night*
Downey, Lynn. *This is the earth that God made*
Dwyer, Mindy. *Coyote in love*
Field, Edward. *Magic words*
Fisher, Leonard Everett. *The seven days of creation*
Foreman, Juli. *Great beginnings*
Frank, Penny. *In the beginning*
French, Fiona. *Lord of the animals*
Gates, Frieda. *Owl eyes*
Goble, Paul. *The great race of the birds and animals*
I sing for the animals
Remaking the earth
Goffe, Toni. *The story of creation*
Greene, Carol. *God's good creation*
Greene, Rhonda Gowler. *The beautiful world that God made*
Grimes, Nikki. *At break of day*
Haley, Gail E. *Two bad boys*
Hansen, Felicity. *The first bear*
Harper, Piers. *How the world was saved and other Native American tales*
Hartman, Bob. *The morning of the world*
Helldorfer, M. C. (Mary Claire). *Clap clap!*
Hickman, Martha Whitmore. *And God created squash*
Hofmeyr, Dianne. *The star-bearer*
Jackson, Ellen B. *The precious gift*
Jaffe, Nina. *The golden flower*
Jendresen, Erik. *The first story ever told*
Johnson, James Weldon. *The Creation*
Keams, Geri. *Snail girl brings water*
Kimmel, Eric A. *The rooster's antlers*

King, Thomas. *Coyote sings to the moon*
Lattimore, Deborah Nourse. *Why there is no arguing in heaven*
Lester, Julius. *What a truly cool world*
Le Tord, Bijou. *The deep blue sea*
Levin, Miriam Ramsfelder. *In the beginning*
Lewis, Jacqueline Janette. *You are so wonderful*
Lindbergh, Reeve. *The circle of days*
McDermott, Beverly Brodsky. *The dreamtime*
MacDonald, Amy. *The spider who created the world*
McFall, Gardner. *Naming the animals*
Maddern, Eric. *The fire children*
Matthews, Caitlin. *The blessing seed*
Neitzel, Shirley. *From the land of the white birch*
Oliviero, Jamie. *The day Sun was stolen*
Oppenheim, Shulamith Levey. *And the earth trembled*
   Iblis
Ortiz, Simon. *The people shall continue*
Pia Toya
Pohrt, Tom. *Coyote goes walking*
Poole, Amy Lowry. *How the rooster got his crown*
Quattlebaum, Mary. *In the beginning*
Reed, Allison. *Genesis*
Rich, Scharlotte. *Who made the wild woods?*
Riordan, James. *The coming of Night*
Rodanas, Kristina. *Follow the stars*
Rohmer, Harriet. *How we came to the fifth world*
Root, Phyllis. *Big Momma makes the world*
Rose, Anne K. *Spider in the sky*
Rosen, Michael J. (1954–). *The dog who walked with God*
Sage, James. *Coyote makes man*
Sattgast, L. J. *Look what God made*
Simms, Laura. *The bone man*
Slate, Joseph. *Story time for Little Porcupine*
Sneve, Virginia Driving Hawk. *The Cherokees*
   The Nez Perce
Strauss, Susan. *When woman became the sea*
Swartz, Nancy Sohn. *In our image*
Troughton, Joanna. *Who will be the sun?*
Van Kampen, Vlasta. *Bear tales*
Van Laan, Nancy. *Rainbow crow*
Waldman, Sarah. *Light*
Williams, Sheron. *And in the beginning . . .*
Wolkstein, Diane. *Sun Mother wakes the world*
Wood, Audrey. *The rainbow bridge*
Wood, Douglas. *Making the world*
Yolen, Jane. *Old Dame Counterpane*
Zeman, Ludmila. *The first red maple leaf*
Zhang, Song Nan. *The five heavenly emperors and other Chinese myths*
   from the creation
Ziefert, Harriet. *First He made the sun*

Creatures *see* Monsters; Mythical creatures

Cree Indians *see* Indians of North America – Cree

Creek Indians *see* Indians of North America – Creek

Creeks *see* Rivers

Crickets *see* Insects – crickets

Crime

Ada, Alma Flor. *The gold coin*
Adamson, Gareth. *Old man up a tree*
Ahlberg, Allan. *Cops and robbers*
Ahlberg, Janet. *Burglar Bill*
   It was a dark and stormy night
Alderson, Sue Ann. *Ida and the wool smugglers*
Allard, Harry. *It's so nice to have a wolf around the house*
Anderson, C. W. (Clarence Williams). *Blaze and the gypsies*
Antle, Nancy. *Sam's Wild West Show*
Auch, Mary Jane. *Eggs mark the spot*
Balouch, Kristen. *The king and the three thieves*
Barracca, Debra. *Maxi, the hero*
Berson, Harold. *The thief who hugged a moonbeam*

Biro, Val. *Gumdrop finds a friend*
   Gumdrop in double trouble
Blake, Quentin. *Snuff*
Bradford, Ann. *The mystery in the secret club house*
   The mystery of the blind writer
   The mystery of the tree house
Brandenberg, Franz. *A robber! A robber!*
Bright, Robert. *Georgie and the robbers*
Brunhoff, Laurent de. *Babar's mystery*
   The rescue of Babar
Burdett, Lois. *Hamlet for kids*
   Macbeth for kids
Calders, Pere. *Brush*
Carlson, Nancy L. *Arnie and the stolen markers*
Cass, Joan E. *The cat thief*
Christelow, Eileen. *The robbery at the diamond dog diner*
Christian, Mary Blount. *The doggone mystery*
Cohen, Caron Lee. *Bronco dogs*
Cohn, Janice I. *"Why did it happen?"*
Coltman, Paul. *Tinker Jim*
Cox, David. *Bossyboots*
Cressey, James. *Max the mouse*
   Pet parrot
Dahl, Roald. *The giraffe and the pelly and me*
Daly, Niki. *Vim, the rag mouse*
Derby, Sally. *Two fools and a horse*
Dixon, Chuck. *Batman*
Dodd, Lynley. *Slinky Malinki*
Douglas, Erin. *Get that pest!*
Dumas, Philippe. *Laura and the bandits*
Durant, Alan. *Big Bad Bunny*
Duvoisin, Roger Antoine. *Petunia and the song*
Egan, Tim. *The blunder of the Rogues*
   The trial of Cardigan Jones
Euvremer, Teryl. *The thieves of Peck's pocket*
Flanagan, Alice K. *A day in court with Mrs. Trinh*
   Officer Brown keeps neighborhoods safe
   Police officers
Foreman, Michael. *Look! Look!*
   Rock-a-doodle-do!
French, Fiona. *Snow White in New York*
Gage, Wilson. *Down in the boondocks*
Geisert, Arthur. *Mystery*
   Nursery crimes
   Pigaroons
Gerrard, Roy. *Jocasta Carr, movie star*
   Rosie and the rustlers
Glicksman, Caroline. *Eric the math bear*
Goodall, John S. *Paddy to the rescue*
Goode, Diane. *Tiger trouble*
Grimm, Jacob. *The Bremen town band*
   The Bremen town musicians, ill. by Donna Diamond
   The Bremen town musicians, ill. by Bill Dickson
   The Bremen town musicians, ill. by Janina Domanska
   The Bremen town musicians, ill. by Paul Galdone
   The Bremen town musicians, ill. by David Johnson
   Bremen town musicians, ill. by Josef Palecek
   The Bremen town musicians, ill. by Ilse Plume
   The Bremen town musicians, ill. by Janet Stevens
   The Bremen town musicians, ill. by Bernadette Watts
   The musicians of Bremen, ill. by John Segal
   The musicians of Bremen, ill. by Svend Otto S
   The musicians of Bremen, ill. by Martin Ursell
   The traveling musicians of Bremen
Harris, Leon A. *The great diamond robbery*
   The great picture robbery
Haseley, Dennis. *The thieves' market*
Heller, George. *Hiroshi's wonderful kite*
Heymans, Margriet. *Pippin and Robber Grumblecroak's big baby*
Hickman, Martha Whitmore. *When Andy's father went to prison*
High, Linda Oatman. *A Christmas Star*
Hilton, Nette. *Dirty Dave*
Hoffman, Eric. *Play Lady = La Señora Juguetona*
Hogrogian, Nonny. *The contest*
   Rooster brother
Jacobs, Joseph. *Hereafterthis*
James, Brian. *The Supertwins and tooth trouble*

Janice. *Mr. and Mrs. Button's wonderful watchdogs*
Johnson, Paul Brett. *Frank Fister's hidden talent*
Kimmel, Eric A. *Four dollars and fifty cents*
Kinerk, Robert. *Slim and Miss Prim*
Kirn, Ann. *I spy*
Kotzwinkle, William. *Walter, the farting dog: trouble at the yard sale*
Krahn, Fernando. *Mr. Top*
Kraus, Robert. *The detective of London*
Kroll, Steven. *Looking for Daniela*
   Woof, woof!
Lakin, Pat (Patricia). *Aware and alert*
Lawson, Julie. *Arizona Charlie and the Klondike Kid*
Levitin, Sonia. *Nobody stole the pie*
Lewis, J. Patrick. *The night of the goat children*
Lobel, Anita. *The straw maid*
Lobel, Arnold. *How the rooster saved the day*
McCully, Emily Arnold. *An outlaw Thanksgiving*
McKean, Thomas. *Hooray for Grandma Jo!*
McKee, David. *123456789 Benn*
McPhail, David M. *Moony B. Finch, fastest draw in the West*
   Stanley: Henry Bear's friend
Madonna. *Yakov and the seven thieves*
Mahy, Margaret. *Beaten by a balloon*
Maitland, Barbara. *The bookstore burglar*
Marzollo, Jean. *Jed and the space bandits*
Mathews, Louise. *The great take-away*
Mayer, Mercer. *Liverwurst is missing*
Mead, Alice. *Billy and Emma*
Miles, Miska. *The raccoon and Mrs. McGinnis*
Moore, John. *Granny Stickleback*
Mooser, Stephen. *Funnyman and the penny dodo*
Moss, P. Buckley (Pat Buckley). *Reuben and the quilt*
Myller, Rolf. *A very noisy day*
Nixon, Joan Lowery. *Gus and Gertie and the missing pearl*
Noyes, Alfred. *The highwayman*
Ogburn, Jacqueline K. *Scarlett Angelina Wolverton-Manning*
O'Malley, Kevin. *Who killed Cock Robin?*
Oram, Hiawyn. *Princess Chamomile gets her way*
Parish, Peggy. *The cats' burglar*
   Granny and the desperadoes
Partch, Virgil Franklin. *The Christmas cookie sprinkle snitcher*
Poffenberger, Nancy M. *September 11, 2001*
Politi, Leo. *Emmet*
Price, Kathy (Kathy Z.). *The Bourbon Street musicians*
Propp, James. *Tuscanini*
Pryor, Bonnie. *Mr. Munday and the rustlers*
Reidel, Marlene. *Jacob and the robbers*
Rose, Gerald. *The tiger-skin rug*
Rosenbloom, Joseph. *Deputy Dan and the bank robbers*
Ruby-Spears Enterprises. *The puppy's new adventures*
SanAngelo, Ryan. *Eddie spaghetti*
Scarry, Richard. *Richard Scarry's great big mystery book*
Schneider, Howie. *Fast 'n Snappy*
Seabrooke, Brenda. *The best burglar alarm*
Shire, Ellen. *The mystery at number seven, Rue Petite*
Skolsky, Mindy Warshaw. *Hannah and the whistling tea kettle*
Slobodkina, Esphyr. *Circus caps for sale*
   Pezzo the peddler and the thirteen silly thieves
Solotareff, Grégoire. *Don't call me little bunny*
Stevens, Kathleen. *Aunt Skilly and the stranger*
Thomson, Ruth. *Peabody all at sea*
   Peabody's first case
Titus, Eve. *Anatole and the thirty thieves*
Tompert, Ann. *The hungry black bag*
Ungerer, Tomi. *The three robbers*
Van Nutt, Julia. *The monster in the shadows*
Wahl, Jan. *The adventures of Underwater Dog*
Walton, Rick. *Bertie was a watchdog*
Watson, Esther (Pearl). *Trouble at Sugar Dip Well*
Watson, Nancy Dingman. *The birthday goat*
Weigelt, Udo. *It wasn't me*
Wisniewski, David. *Sumo Mouse*
Wolff, Ferida. *The woodcutter's coat*
Wright, Betty Ren. *Pet detectives!*
Yee, Wong Herbert. *The Officers' Ball*

Criminals *see* Crime; Prisons

Crippled *see* Handicaps – physical handicaps

Crocodiles *see* Reptiles – alligators, crocodiles

Crow Indians *see* Indians of North America – Crow

Crows *see* Birds – crows

Cruelty to animals *see* Character traits – kindness to animals

Crustaceans

Griffith, Helen V. *Emily and the enchanted frog*
Heller, Ruth. *How to hide an octopus*
Himmelman, John. *A pill bug's life*
James, Simon. *Sally and the limpet*
Pratt, Kristin Joy. *A swim through the sea*
Royston, Angela. *Sea animals*

Crustaceans – centipedes, millipedes

Greenaway, Theresa. *Centipedes and millipedes*
Merrick, Patrick. *Centipedes*
Ross, Tony. *Centipede's 100 shoes*

Crustaceans – crabs

Boyce, Katie. *Hector the hermit crab*
Carle, Eric. *A house for Hermit Crab*
Childress, Mark. *Joshua and the big bad blue crabs*
Coldrey, Jennifer. *The world of crabs*
Horio, Seishi. *The monkey and the crab*
Horowitz, Ruth. *Crab moon*
Kalan, Robert. *Moving day*
Kipling, Rudyard. *The crab that played with the sea*
Knutson, Barbara. *Why the crab has no head*
Krudop, Walter Lyon. *Blue claws*
Lewis, Paul Owen. *Grasper*
Maccarone, Grace. *The classroom pet*
McDonald, Megan. *Is this a house for Hermit Crab?*
Manson, Christopher. *The crab prince*
Mogensen, Jan. *Teddy in the undersea kingdom*
Nelson, Robin. *Pet hermit crab*
Peet, Bill (William Bartlett). *Kermit the hermit*
Riddell, Chris. *Platypus*
Spooner, Michael. *Old Meshikee and the little crabs*
Tafuri, Nancy. *Follow me!*
Van West, Patricia E. *The crab man*
Walsh, Ellen Stoll. *Hamsters to the rescue*
Ward, Helen. *Old shell, new shell*
Yamaguchi, Tohr. *Two crabs and the moonlight*

Crustaceans – lobsters

Carrick, Carol. *The blue lobster*
Guiberson, Brenda Z. *Lobster boat*
Hartman, Bob. *Lobster for lunch*
Kidd, Richard. *Monsieur Thermidor*
West, Colin. *"Only joking!" laughed the lobster*

Crustaceans – shrimp

McGaw, Wayne T. *T-boy of the bayou*

Crying *see* Emotions

Cuckoos *see* Birds – cuckoos

Cumulative tales

Aardema, Verna. *Bringing the rain to Kapiti Plain*
   The riddle of the drum
Ada, Alma Flor. *The gold coin*

The golden goose, ill. by William Stobbs
Gold-Vukson, Marji E. *Grandpa and me on Tu B'Shevat*
Grasshopper to the rescue
Gray, Libba Moore. *Is there room on the feather bed?*
Grimm, Jacob. *The table, the donkey and the stick*
    The wishing table
Grossman, Bill. *Donna O'Neeshuck was chased by some cows*
Harper, Charise Mericle. *There was a bold lady who wanted a star*
Harrison, David Lee. *The animals' song*
Hearn, Michael Patrick. *The porcelain cat*
Heilbroner, Joan. *This is the house where Jack lives*
Hewett, Anita. *The tale of the turnip*
Hill, Susanna Leonard. *The house that Mack built*
Hillenbrand, Will. *Down by the station*
    Fiddle-i-fee
Hillert, Margaret. *The three goats*
Himmelman, John. *Honest Tulio*
Hogrogian, Nonny. *The cat who loved to sing*
    One fine day
Hoguet, Susan Ramsay. *I unpacked my grandmother's trunk*
Hooper, Meredith. *Seven eggs*
Hoopes, Lyn Littlefield. *Wing-a-ding*
Horning, Sandra. *The giant hug*
Horsbrugh, Wilma. *The train to Glasgow*
The house that Jack built. *The house that Jack built,* ill. by Randolph Caldecott
    The house that Jack built, ill. by Seymour Chwast
    The house that Jack built, ill. by Diana Mayo
    The house that Jack built, ill. by Rodney Peppé
    The house that Jack built, ill. by Janet Stevens
    The house that Jack built, ill. by Jenny Stow
    The house that Jack built, ill. by Nadine Bernard Westcott
    The house that Jack built, ill. by Jeanette Winter
    The house that Jack built = la maison que Jacques a batie, ill. by Antonio Frasconi
    This is the house that Jack built, ill. by Simms Taback
    This is the house that Jack built, ill. by Liz Underhill
Houston, John A. *A mouse in my house*
Howland, Naomi. *The matzah man*
Hughes, Shirley. *Alfie gets in first*
Hush little baby. *Hush little baby,* ill. by Aliki
    Hush, little baby, ill. by Marla Frazee
    Hush little baby, ill. by Shari Halpern
    Hush little baby, ill. by Jeanette Winter
    Hush little baby, ill. by Margot Zemach
Hutchins, Pat. *Don't forget the bacon!*
    Good night owl
    Titch
Inkpen, Mick. *Billy's beetle*
Jackson, Alison. *I know an old lady who swallowed a pie*
Jacobs, Joseph. *Johnny-cake,* ill. by Emma Lillian Brock
    Johnny-cake, ill. by William Stobbs
Johnston, Tony. *Yonder*
Kahl, Virginia. *Whose cat is that?*
Kalan, Robert. *Jump, frog, jump!*
    Moving day
Kasza, Keiko. *When the elephant walks*
Kharms, Daniil. *First, second*
    The story of a boy named Will, who went sledding down the hill
Kimmel, Eric A. *The runaway tortilla*
King, Bob. *Sitting on the farm*
Krahn, Fernando. *The mystery of the giant footprints*
Krasilovsky, Phyllis. *The cow who fell in the canal*
Kroll, Steven. *The tyrannosaurus game*
Kuskin, Karla. *A boy had a mother who bought him a hat*
Lazy Jack. *Lazy Jack,* ill. by Bert Dodson
    Lazy Jack, ill. by Tony Ross
    Lazy Jack, ill. by Kurt Werth
Lear, Edward. *Whizz!*
Lenski, Lois. *Susie Mariar*
Lester, Helen. *It wasn't my fault*
Levine, Abby. *This is the pumpkin*
Lewis, Bobby. *Home before midnight*
Lewis, Kevin. *The lot at the end of my block*
Lewison, Wendy Cheyette. *"Buzz," said the bee*
    Going to sleep on the farm
Lexau, Joan M. *Crocodile and hen*

Lillegard, Dee. *Sitting in my box*
Lillie, Patricia. *When the rooster crowed*
Lindbergh, Anne. *Tidy lady*
Lindman, Maj. *Snipp, Snapp, Snurr and the buttered bread*
Little old lady who swallowed a fly. *Fancy that!*
    Golly Gump swallowed a fly
    I know an old lady, ill. by Abner Graboff
    I know an old lady, ill. by G. Brian Karas
    I know an old lady, ill. by Steve McInturff
    I know an old lady, ill. by Albert Miller
    I know an old lady who swallowed a fly, ill. by Stephen Gulbis
    I know an old lady who swallowed a fly, ill. by Glen Rounds
    I know an old lady who swallowed a fly, ill. by William Stobbs
    I know an old lady who swallowed a fly, ill. by Nadine Bernard Westcott
    There was an old lady, ill. by Nick Bantock
    There was an old lady who swallowed a fly, ill. by Pam Adams
    There was an old lady who swallowed a fly, ill. by Colin Hawkins
    There was an old lady who swallowed a fly, ill. by Simms Taback
    There was an old woman, ill. by Steven Kellogg
The little red hen. *The cock, the mouse and the little red hen,* ill. by Lorinda Bryan Cauley
    The cock, the mouse and the little red hen, ill. by Graham Percy
    The little red hen, ill. by Byron Barton
    The little red hen, ill. by Emily Bolam
    The little red hen, ill. by Janina Domanska
    The little red hen, ill. by Paul Galdone
    The little red hen, ill. by Dennis Hockerman
    Little red hen, ill. by Norman Messenger
    The little red hen, ill. by Mel Pekarsky
    The little red hen, ill. by William Stobbs
    The little red hen, ill. by Annie West
    The little red hen, ill. by Margot Zemach
    The little red hen and the ear of wheat, ill. by Elisabeth Bell
    The Little Red Hen makes a pizza
Little Tuppen
Lobel, Anita. *The pancake*
Lobel, Arnold. *The rose in my garden*
Lorenz, Lee. *Big Gus and Little Gus*
Losi, Carol A. *The 512 ants on Sullivan Street*
Lupton, Hugh. *Pirican Pic and Pirican Mor*
Macaulay, David. *Why the chicken crossed the road*
McClintock, Marshall. *A fly went by*
MacDonald, Amy. *Little Beaver and the echo*
MacDonald, Elizabeth. *Mike's kite*
    The wolf is coming!
Mahy, Margaret. *The Christmas tree tangle*
    When the king rides by
Manning, Linda. *Animal hours*
Manning, Maurie J. *The aunts go marching*
Manson, Christopher. *A farmyard song*
    The tree in the wood
Manushkin, Fran. *The matzah that Papa brought home*
    My Christmas safari
Margolin, H. Ellen. *Goin' to Boston*
Martin, Bill (William Ivan). *Brown bear, brown bear, what do you see?*
    Old devil wind
Martinez, Ruth. *Mrs. McDockerty's knitting*
Medearis, Angela Shelf. *Too much talk*
Melmed, Laura Krauss. *The Marvelous Market on Mermaid*
Milhous, Katherine. *The turnip*
Mollel, Tololwa M. (Tololwa Marti). *Rhinos for lunch and elephants for supper*
Moon, Pat. *This is the earth*
Morley, Carol. *Farmyard song*
Moss, Marissa. *Knick knack paddywack*
Munsch, Robert N. *Stephanie's ponytail*
Murphey, Sara. *The roly poly cookie*
Neitzel, Shirley. *The bag I'm taking to Grandma's*
    The dress I'll wear to the party
    The house I'll build for the wrens
    I'm not feeling well today
    I'm taking a trip on my train
    The jacket I wear in the snow
Noble, Trinka Hakes. *The king's tea*
Nolan, Dennis. *Wizard McBean and his flying machine*
Old MacDonald had a farm. *E I E I O*

Old MacDonald, ill. by Rosemary Wells
Old MacDonald had a farm, ill. by Holly Berry
Old MacDonald had a farm, ill. by Lorinda Bryan Cauley
Old MacDonald had a farm, ill. by Mel Crawford
Old MacDonald had a farm, ill. by Tracey English
Old MacDonald had a farm, ill. by David Frankland
Old MacDonald had a farm, ill. by Abner Graboff
Old MacDonald had a farm, ill. by Nancy Hellen
Old MacDonald had a farm, ill. by Carol Jones
Old MacDonald had a farm, ill. by Tracey Campbell Pearson
Old MacDonald had a farm, ill. by Robert M. Quackenbush
Old MacDonald had a farm, ill. by Glen Rounds
Old McDonald had a farm, ill. by Iain Smith
Old MacDonald had a farm, ill. by Jessica Souhami
Old MacDonald had a farm, ill. by William Stobbs
Old MacDonald had a farm, ill. by Prue Theobalds
The old woman and her pig. *The old woman and her pig*, ill. by Paul Galdone
   The old woman and her pig, ill. by Giyora Karmi
   The old woman and her pig, ill. by Rosanne Litzinger
   The troublesome pig
Oppenheim, Joanne. *"Not now!" said the cow*
   You can't catch me!
Ormerod, Jan. *Ms. MacDonald has a class*
Oxenbury, Helen. *It's my birthday*
Pace, David. *Shouting Sharon*
Pack, Robert. *Then what did you do?*
Parkinson, Kathy. *The enormous turnip*
Patron, Susan. *Dark cloud strong breeze*
Peet, Bill (William Bartlett). *The ant and the elephant*
Petie, Haris. *The seed the squirrel dropped*
Piers, Helen. *Is there room on the bus?*
   Who's in my bed?
Polacco, Patricia. *In Enzo's splendid gardens*
Polette, Nancy. *The little old woman and the hungry cat*
Prelutsky, Jack. *The terrible tiger*
Preston, Edna Mitchell. *One dark night*
Quackenbush, Robert M. *No mouse for me*
Raskin, Ellen. *Ghost in a four-room apartment*
Reider, Katja. *Snail started it!*
Reiser, Lynn. *Christmas counting*
Riddell, Chris. *Bird's new shoes*
Robart, Rose. *The cake that Mack ate*
Rockwell, Anne F. *Honk honk!*
   Poor Goose
   Root-a-toot-toot
Roddie, Shen. *Animal stew*
Rose, Anne K. *The talking turnip*
Rose, Deborah Lee. *The twelve days of kindergarten*
Rydell, Katy. *Wind says good night*
Rylant, Cynthia. *The great Gracie chase*
Sanfield, Steve. *Bit by bit*
Sawyer, Ruth. *Journey cake, ho!*
Schaefer, Lola M. *This is the sunflower*
Scieszka, Jon. *The book that Jack wrote*
Scott, William R. *This is the milk that Jack drank*
Seeger, Pete. *The foolish frog*
Segal, Lore Groszmann. *All the way home*
Seuss, Dr. *Green eggs and ham*
Seymour, Dorothy Z. *The tent*
Shannon, George. *Beanboy*
   Oh, I love!
Sierra, Judy. *The house that Drac built*
   'Twas the fright before Christmas
Silverman, Erica. *On the morn of Mayfest*
Silverstein, Shel. *A giraffe and a half*
Simms, Laura. *The squeaky door*
Skorpen, Liesel Moak. *All the Lassies*
   We were tired of living in a house
Sloat, Teri. *There was an old lady who swallowed a trout*
Snell, Gordon. *Twelve days, a Christmas countdown*
Snow, Pegeen. *Mrs. Periwinkle's groceries*
Steger, Hans-Ulrich. *Traveling to Tripiti*
Stevens, Jan Romero. *Twelve lizards leaping*
Stihler, Chérie B. *The giant cabbage turnip*
Stockdale, Susan. *Some sleep standing up*
Stoddard, Sandol. *Bedtime mouse*

Stojic, Manya. *Rain*
Stone, Rosetta. *Because a little bug went ka-choo!*
Stutson, Caroline. *By the light of the Halloween moon*
Suhl, Yuri. *Simon Boom gives a wedding*
Sutherland, Colleen. *Jason goes to show-and-tell*
Sutton, Eve. *My cat likes to hide in boxes*
Sweet, Melissa. *Fiddle-i-fee*
Szekeres, Cyndy. *The mouse that Jack built*
Tafuri, Nancy. *This is the farmer*
Tanaka, Beatrice. *The chase*
Thomas, Shelley Moore. *Putting the world to sleep*
Thompson, Richard. *The follower*
Thomson, Pat. *The squeaky, creaky bed*
Thornhill, Jan. *The rumor*
Tolstoy, Aleksey Nikolayevich. *The enormous turnip*
   The gigantic turnip, ill. by Niamh Sharkey
   The great big enormous turnip
Tompert, Ann. *Just a little bit*
Tresselt, Alvin R. *Rain drop splash*
Trosclair. *Cajun night before Christmas*
Troughton, Joanna. *The quail's egg*
The twelve days of Christmas. English folk song. *Brian Wildsmith's The twelve days of Christmas*
   Jack Kent's twelve days of Christmas
   The twelve days of Christmas, ill. by Jan Brett
   The twelve days of Christmas, ill. by Rachel Griffin
   The twelve days of Christmas, ill. by Ilonka Karasz
   The twelve days of Christmas, ill. by Ilse Plume
   The twelve days of Christmas, ill. by Erika Schneider
   The twelve days of Christmas, ill. by Vladimir Vagin
   The twelve days of Christmas, ill. by Sophie Windham
   The twelve days of Christmas [board book], ill. by Jan Brett
Tworkov, Jack. *The camel who took a walk*
Vagin, Vladimir Vasilévich. *The enormous carrot*
Van Laan, Nancy. *Mama rocks, Papa sings*
   Possum come a-knocking
Varga, Judy. *The monster behind Black Rock*
Waddell, Martin. *The pig in the pond*
Wahl, Jan. *Follow me cried Bee*
Wallner, John C. *Old MacDonald had a farm*
Wardlaw, Lee. *The chair where bear sits*
Weninger, Brigitte. *The elf's hat*
West, Colin. *Go tell it to the toucan*
   Have you seen the crocodile?
   The king of Kennelwick castle
   The king's toothache
   One day in the jungle
Wiesner, William. *Happy-Go-Lucky*
Wildsmith, Brian. *Goat's trail*
Williams, Linda. *The little old lady who was not afraid of anything*
Winter, Rick. *Dirty birdy feet*
Witte, Anna. *The parrot Tico Tango*
Wolkstein, Diane. *The magic wings*
Wood, Audrey. *The napping house*
   Silly Sally
Wood, Jakki. *Fiddle-i-fee*
Yee, Brenda Shannon. *Sand castle*
Yee, Wong Herbert. *Eek! There's a mouse in the house*
Yolen, Jane. *Jane Yolen's Old MacDonald songbook*
Young, Ed (Edward). *What about me?*
Zabar, Abbie. *Fifty-five friends*
Ziefert, Harriet. *I swapped my dog*
   On Halloween night
   The turnip
   When I first came to this land
Ziner, Feenie. *Counting carnival*
Zolotow, Charlotte (Shapiro). *The quarreling book*

Curiosity *see* Character traits – curiosity

Currency *see* Money

Custodians *see* Careers – custodians, janitors

Cycles *see* Motorcycles; Sports – bicycling

Czechoslovakia *see* Foreign lands – Czechoslovakia

Czechoslovakian Americans *see* Ethnic groups in the U.S.
  – Czechoslovakian Americans

Dakota (Sioux) Indians *see* Indians of North America –
  Dakota (Sioux)

Damselflies *see* Insects – damselflies

Dancers *see* Careers – dancers

Dancing *see* Activities – dancing; Ballet

Daniel *see* Religion – Daniel

Dark *see* Night; Power failures

Darkness – fear *see* Emotions – fear

Daughters *see* Family life – daughters

David and Goliath *see* Religion – David

Dawn *see* Morning

Day

Ashman, Linda. *Just another morning*
Ballard, Robin. *My day, your day*
Bradley, Kimberly Brubaker. *Favorite things*
Braun, Sebastien. *I love my daddy*
Charlip, Remy. *Why I will never ever ever ever have enough time to
  read this book*
George, Jean Craighead. *Morning, noon, and night*
Geras, Adèle. *My wishes for you*
Haley, Amanda. *It's a baby's world*
Kavanagh, Peter. *I love my mama*
McGee, Marni. *The noisy farm*
McLean, Janet. *Josh*
Melmed, Laura Krauss. *A hug goes around*
Nelson, Robin. *A day*
Rong, Yu. *A lovely day for Amelia Goose*
Ross, Michael Elsohn. *Earth cycles*
Schaefer, Carole Lexa. *Someone says*
Seven spunky monkeys
Spinelli, Eileen. *The best time of day*
Turner, Ann Warren. *In the heart*

Day care *see* School – nursery

Days of the week, months of the year

Alberts, Nancy Markham. *No toys on Sunday*
Anglund, Joan Walsh. *A child's year*
  How many days has Baby to play?
Anholt, Catherine. *One, two, three, count with me*
Appelt, Kathi. *A red wagon year*
Arnold, Tedd. *Mother Goose's words of wit and wisdom*
Baden, Robert. *And Sunday makes seven*
Boling, Katharine. *New year be coming!*
Boling, Ruth L. *Come worship with me*
Borchers, Elisabeth. *There comes a time*
Brian, Janeen. *Where does Thursday go?*
Brode, Robyn. *April*
  August
  December
  February
  January
  July
  June
  March
  May
  November
  October
  September
Bunting, Eve (Anne Evelyn). *Sing a song of piglets*
Butterworth, Nick. *Jasper's beanstalk*
Carle, Eric. *Today is Monday*
  The very hungry caterpillar
Carlstrom, Nancy White. *How do you say it today, Jesse Bear?*
Charles, Donald. *Calico Cat's year*
A child's calendar
Clarke, Gus. *How many days to my birthday?*
Clifton, Lucille. *Some of the days of Everett Anderson*
Cocca-Leffler, Maryann. *Wednesday is spaghetti day*
Coleridge, Sara. *January brings the snow*
Damjan, Mischa. *December's travels*
Day, Nancy Raines. *A kitten's year*
De Regniers, Beatrice Schenk. *Little Sister and the Month Brothers*
  What did you put in your pocket?
Dragonwagon, Crescent. *Alligators and others all year long!*
Fernandes, Eugenie. *Big week for little mouse*
Firmin, Josie. *My week*
Gág, Flavia. *Chubby's first year*
Gerstein, Mordicai. *The story of May*
Giff, Patricia Reilly. *I love Saturday*
Ginsburg, Mirra. *The old man and his birds*
Hague, Kathleen. *Calendarbears*
Halsey, Megan. *Jump for joy*
Harmer, Juliet. *Prayers for children*
Henderson, Kathy. *A year in the city*
Hillman, Priscilla. *A Merry-Mouse book of months*
Hooper, Meredith. *Seven eggs*
Howell, Lynn. *Winifred's new bed*
Hubbell, Patricia. *Rabbit moon*
Jackson, Ellen B. *April*
  August
  December
  February
  January
  July
  June
  March
  May
  November
  October
  September
Johnson, Dinah. *Sunday week*
Katz, Karen. *Twelve hats for Lena*
Keenen, George. *The preposterous week*
Lasker, Joe. *Lentil soup*
Lesser, Carolyn. *What a wonderful day to be a cow*
Lewis, J. Patrick. *July is a mad mosquito*
Lewis, Rob. *Hello, Mr. Scarecrow*
Lillie, Patricia. *When this box is full*
Llewellyn, Claire. *My first book of time*
Lobel, Anita. *One lighthouse, one moon*
Lord, Beman. *The days of the week*
McCurdy, Michael. *An Algonquian year*
MacDonald, Elizabeth. *My aunt and the animals*
Maestro, Betsy. *Through the year with Harriet*
Manning, Linda. *Dinosaur days*
Martin, Bill (William Ivan). *The turning of the year*
Martin, Rafe. *The twelve months*
Marzollo, Jean. *I spy, year-round challenger!*
Min, Laura. *Mrs. Sato's hens*
Molnar, Dorothy E. *Who will pick me up when I fall?*
Nelson, Robin. *A day*
  Months
  A week
Nikola-Lisa, W. *Till year's good end*
Otten, Charlotte F. *January rides the wind*

Owen, Annie. *From snowflakes to sandcastles*
Peters, Lisa Westberg. *October smiled back*
Plotz, Helen. *A week of lullabies*
Prater, John. *On Friday something funny happened*
Provensen, Alice. *The year at Maple Hill Farm*
Rau, Dana Meachen. *I'll make you a card*
Rylant, Cynthia. *Bless us all*
    Give me grace
Santos, Rosa. *Play date*
Scarry, Richard. *Richard Scarry's best first book ever!*
Sendak, Maurice. *Chicken soup with rice*
Sharratt, Nick. *Monday run-day*
Shiefman, Vicky. *Sunday potatoes, Monday potatoes*
Shields, Carol Diggory. *Day by day a week goes round*
    Month by month a year goes round
Shulevitz, Uri. *One Monday morning*
Singer, Marilyn. *Turtle in July*
Smith, Maggie (Margaret C.). *Dear Daisy, get well soon*
Smith, William Jay (1918–). *The sun is up*
Spinelli, Eileen. *Here comes the year*
Tafuri, Nancy. *All year long*
    Snowy flowy blowy
Taylor, Joanne. *Full moon rising*
Thomas, Joyce Carol. *Gingerbread days*
Thompson, Richard. *The follower*
Tudor, Tasha. *Around the year*
Tyrrell, Anne. *Elizabeth Jane gets dressed*
Van der Meer, Mara. *Can we play?*
Verdet, Andre. *All about time*
Vojtech, Anna. *Marushka and the Month Brothers*
Ward, Cindy. *Cookie's week*
Waysman, Dvora. *My Jewish days of the week*
Wells, Rosemary. *My kindergarten*
Winnick, Karen B. *A year goes round*
Wolff, Ashley. *A year of beasts*
    A year of birds
Wood, Audrey. *Heckedy Peg*
Yolen, Jane. *No bath tonight*
Zimmermann, H. Werner (Heinz Werner). *Alphonse knows . . .*
    twelve months make a year

Deafness *see* Anatomy – ears; Handicaps – deafness; Senses – hearing

Death

Abley, Mark. *Ghost cat*
Adoff, Arnold. *The return of Rex and Ethel*
Aliki. *Mummies made in Egypt*
Anaya, Rudolfo A. *Farolitos for Abuelo*
Anders, Rebecca. *A look at death*
Andersen, H. C. (Hans Christian). *It's perfectly true!*
    The little match girl, ill. by Rachel Isadora
    The little match girl, ill. by Blair Lent
    The little match girl, ill. by Jerry Pinkney
Anderson, Leone Castell. *It's O.K. to cry*
Arnold, Caroline. *What we do when someone dies*
Baker, Betty. *Rat is dead and ant is sad*
Barker, Peggy. *What happened when grandma died*
Barnhart, Peter. *The wounded duck*
Barron, T. A. *Where is Grandpa?*
Bartoli, Jennifer. *Nonna*
Beim, Jerrold. *With dad alone*
Bernstein, Joanne E. *When people die*
The best cat in the world
Boyden, Linda. *The blue roses*
Breckler, Rosemary K. *Sweet dried apples*
Breebaart, Joeri. *When I die, will I get better?*
Brown, Laurie Krasny. *When dinosaurs die*
Brown, Margaret Wise. *The dead bird*
Bunting, Eve (Anne Evelyn). *The big red barn*
    The day before Christmas
    The happy funeral
    On Call Back Mountain
    Rudi's pond

Burningham, John. *Grandpa*
Burrowes, Adjoa J. *Grandma's purple flowers*
Carlstrom, Nancy White. *Blow me a kiss, Miss Lilly*
Carrick, Carol. *The accident*
Carson, Jo. *You hold me and I'll hold you*
Caseley, Judith. *When Grandpa came to stay*
Cazet, Denys. *A fish in his pocket*
Cazzola, Gus. *The bells of Santa Lucia*
Clifton, Lucille. *Everett Anderson's goodbye*
Cock Robin. *The courtship, merry marriage, and feast of Cock Robin and Jenny Wren*
    Who killed Cock Robin?, ill. by William Stobbs
Coerr, Eleanor. *Sadako*
Cohen, Miriam. *Jim's dog Muffins*
Cohn, Janice I. *I had a friend named Peter*
    Molly's rosebush
Cooke, Trish. *The grandad tree*
Cooney, Barbara. *Island boy*
Coutant, Helen. *First snow*
Coville, Bruce. *My grandfather's house*
Dabcovich, Lydia. *Mrs. Huggins and her hen Hannah*
DeArmond, Dale. *The seal oil lamp*
De Paola, Tomie (Thomas Anthony). *Nana Upstairs and Nana Downstairs*, 1973
    Nana Upstairs and Nana Downstairs, 1998
DiSalvo-Ryan, DyAnne. *A dog like Jack*
Doray, Malika. *One more Wednesday*
Ehrlich, Amy. *Maggie and Silky and Joe*
Engel, Diana. *Eleanor, Arthur, and Claire*
Fassler, Joan. *My grandpa died today*
Fletcher, Ralph J. *Grandpa never lies*
Fowler, Susi Gregg. *Beautiful*
Fox, Louisa. *Every Monday in the mailbox*
Fox, Mem. *Sophie*
    With love, at Christmas
Fraustino, Lisa Rowe. *The hickory chair*
Fritts, Mary Bahr. *If Nathan were here*
Garland, Michael. *Angel cat*
Gerstein, Mordicai. *The mountains of Tibet*
    The shadow of a flying bird
Goble, Paul. *Beyond the ridge*
Gould, Deborah. *Grandpa's slide show*
Greenlee, Sharon. *When someone dies*
Gregory, Nan. *Wild Girl and Gran*
Gregory, Valiska. *Through the mickle woods*
Griffith, Helen V. *Dream meadow*
Grimm, Edward. *The doorman*
Grimm, Wilhelm. *Dear Mili*
Hallinan, P. K. (Patrick K.). *Three freckles past a hair*
Hanson, Regina. *A season for mangoes*
Harranth, Wolf. *My old grandad*
Harriott, Ted. *Coming home*
Harris, Robie H. *Goodbye, Mousie*
Harshman, Marc. *Uncle James*
Haseley, Dennis. *Ghost catcher*
Hastings, Selina. *The man who wanted to live forever*
Haynes, Max. *Grandma's gone to live in the stars*
Hazen, Barbara Shook. *Why did Grandpa die?*
Hesse, Karen. *Poppy's chair*
Heymans, Annemie. *The princess in the kitchen garden*
Hickox, Ruth. *Great-Grandmother's treasure*
Hill, Frances. *The bug cemetery*
Hines, Anna Grossnickle. *Remember the butterflies*
Hoffmann, E. T. A. *The strange child*
Hogan, Bernice. *My grandmother died but I won't forget her*
Hoopes, Lyn Littlefield. *Nana*
Hopkinson, Deborah. *Bluebird summer*
Horio, Seishi. *The monkey and the crab*
Howard, Ellen. *Murphy and Kate*
Hurd, Edith Thacher. *The black dog who went into the woods*
Hutton, Warwick. *Theseus and the Minotaur*
Jewell, Nancy. *Time for Uncle Joe*
Johnston, Tony. *That summer*
Joosse, Barbara M. *Better with two*
    Ghost wings
Joslin, Mary. *The goodbye boat*
Jukes, Mavis. *I'll see you in my dreams*

Kaldhol, Marit. *Goodbye Rune*
Kantrowitz, Mildred. *When Violet died*
Kaplan, Howard. *Waiting to sing*
Keats, Ezra Jack. *Maggie and the pirate*
Keller, Holly. *Goodbye, Max*
Kooharian, David. *Sammy's story*
Kroll, Virginia L. *Fireflies, peach pies, and lullabies*
    Helen the fish
Kübler-Ross, Elisabeth. *Remember the secret*
Lanton, Sandy. *Daddy's chair*
Leavy, Una. *Good-bye, Papa*
Le Tord, Bijou. *My Grandma Leonie*
Levete, Sarah. *When people die*
Limb, Sue. *Come back, Grandma*
London, Jonathan. *Gray fox*
    Liplap's wish
Luenn, Nancy. *A gift for Abuelita*
Lyon, George Ella. *Ada's pal*
McFarlane, Sheryl. *Waiting for the whales*
Madenski, Melissa. *Some of the pieces*
Maguire, Gregory. *Lucas Fishbone*
Maple, Marilyn J. *On the wings of a butterfly*
Mattingley, Christobel. *The angel with a mouth-organ*
Meeker, Clare Hodgson. *A tale of two rice birds*
Mendoza, George. *The hunter I might have been*
Mills, Joyce C. *Gentle Willow*
Monk, Isabell. *Blackberry stew*
Morehead, Debby. *A special place for Charlee*
Napoli, Donna Jo. *Flamingo dream*
Newman, Lesléa. *Too far away to touch*
Nobisso, Josephine. *Grandpa loved*
Nodar, Carmen Santiago. *Abuelita's paradise*
Old, Wendie C. *Stacy had a little sister*
Oliviero, Jamie. *Som See and the magic elephant*
Onyefulu, Ifeoma. *Saying goodbye*
Parker, Marjorie. *Jasper's day*
Peavy, Linda. *Allison's grandfather*
Pitcher, Caroline. *Nico's octopus*
Pollack, Eileen. *Whisper whisper Jesse, whisper whisper Josh*
Porte, Barbara Ann. *Harry's mom*
Portnoy, Mindy Avra. *Where do people go when they die?*
Puttock, Simon. *A story for Hippo*
Rappaport, Doreen. *Journey of Meng*
    The new king
Rogers, Fred. *When a pet dies*
Roper, Janice M. *Dancing on the moon*
Rosen, Michael (1946–). *A Thanksgiving wish*
Rosen, Michael J. (1954–). *Bonesy and Isabel*
Rosenberg, Liz. *The carousel*
Roth, Susan L. *Another Christmas*
Russo, Marisabina. *Grandpa Abe*
Rylant, Cynthia. *Dog Heaven*
Sanford, Doris. *David has AIDS*
Santucci, Barbara. *Anna's corn*
Scheller, Melanie. *My grandfather's hat*
Schick, Eleanor. *Mama*
Schneider, Antonie. *Good-bye, Vivi!*
Schotter, Roni. *In the piney woods*
Simmonds, Posy. *Fred*
Simon, Norma. *The saddest time*
Smith, Maggie (Margaret C.). *Desser, the best ever cat*
Smith-Ayala, Emilie. *Marisol and the yellow messenger*
Spohn, David. *Nate's treasure*
Stafford, Liliana. *Just dragon*
Stein, Sara Bonnett. *About dying*
Stevens, Carla. *Stories from a snowy meadow*
Stevens, Margaret (Dean). *When grandpa died*
Stiles, Norman. *I'll miss you, Mr. Hooper*
Stilz, Carol Curtis. *Kirsty's kite*
Taha, Karen T. *A gift for Tia Rose*
Tejima, Keizaburo. *Swan sky*
Thomas, Jane Resh. *Saying good-bye to grandma*
Tibo, Gilles. *The grand journey of Mr. Man*
Townsend, Maryann. *Pop's secret*
Trottier, Maxine. *Prairie willow*
Turner, Pamela S. *Hachiko*
Van den Berg, Marinus. *The three birds*

Varley, Susan. *Badger's parting gifts*
Velthuijs, Max. *Frog and the birdsong*
Vigna, Judith. *Saying goodbye to daddy*
Viorst, Judith. *The tenth good thing about Barney*
Wahl, Jan. *Tiger watch*
Wahl, Mats. *Grandfather's laika*
Walker, Alice. *To hell with dying*
Wallace, Ian. *The sparrow's song*
Wallace-Brodeur, Ruth. *Goodbye, Mitch*
Warfel, Elizabeth Stuart. *The blue pearls*
Warner, Sunny. *The moon quilt*
Weigelt, Udo. *Bear's last journey*
Weitzman, Elizabeth. *Let's talk about when a parent dies*
Wells, Rosemary. *The language of doves*
Whelan, Gloria. *Bringing the farmhouse home*
White Deer of Autumn. *The great change*
Wild, Margaret. *Old Pig*
    Toby
    The very best of friends
Wilhelm, Hans. *I'll always love you*
Williams, Laura E. *The long silk strand*
Wittbold, Maureen. *Mending Peter's heart*
Wood, Douglas. *Grandad's prayers of the earth*
Woodson, Jacqueline. *Sweet, sweet memory*
Wright, Betty Ren. *The cat next door*
Zalben, Jane Breskin. *Pearl's marigolds for grandpa*
Zolotow, Charlotte (Shapiro). *My grandson Lew*
    The old dog

Deer *see* Animals – deer

Delaware Indians *see* Indians of North America –
    Delaware

Demons *see* Devil; Monsters

Denmark *see* Foreign lands – Denmark

Dentists *see* Careers – dentists

Department stores *see* Shopping; Stores

Desert

Albert, Richard E. *Alejandro's gift*
Anaya, Rudolfo A. *Roadrunner's dance*
Apperley, Dawn. *In the sand*
Arnold, Caroline. *A walk in the desert*
Asch, Frank. *Cactus poems*
Bash, Barbara. *Desert giant*
Baylor, Byrd. *The desert is theirs*
    Desert voices
    I'm in charge of celebrations
    We walk in sandy places
Beim, Jerrold. *Eric on the desert*
Buchanan, Ken. *It rained on the desert today*
    This house is made of mud
Busch, Phyllis S. *Cactus in the desert*
Catchpole, Clive. *Deserts*
Caudill, Rebecca. *Wind, sand and sky*
Chinery, Michael. *Desert animals*
Clark, Ann Nolan. *Tia Maria's garden*
Córdova, Amy. *Abuelita's heart*
Cretan, Gladys Yessayan. *Ten brothers with camels*
Darling, Kathy (Mary Kathleen). *Desert babies*
Dunphy, Madeleine. *Here is the southwestern desert*
Geis, Jacqueline. *Where the buffalo roam*
Geisert, Bonnie. *Desert town*
Guiberson, Brenda Z. *Cactus hotel*
Haarhoff, Dorian. *Desert December*
Hiscock, Bruce. *Coyote and badger*
Holmes, Anita. *The 100-year-old cactus*
Irbinskas, Heather. *How Jackrabbit got his very long ears*
Jango-Cohen, Judith. *Desert iguanas*
John, Naomi. *Roadrunner*

Johnson, Paul Brett. *Lost*
Johnston, Tony. *Desert dog*
 Desert song
Keats, Ezra Jack. *Clementina's cactus*
Kessler, Cristina. *One night*
Klingel, Cynthia Fitterer. *Deserts*
Lawlor, Laurie. *Old Crump*
Levinson, Nancy Smiler. *Death Valley*
Levy, Elizabeth. *Cleo and the coyote*
London, Jonathan. *Ali, child of the desert*
Lowell, Susan. *The tortoise and the jackrabbit*
McDonald, Megan. *The bone keeper*
McKee, David. *The day the tide went out and out and out*
McLerran, Alice. *Roxaboxen*
 The year of the ranch
Marsh, T. J. *Way out in the desert*
Mora, Pat. *Delicious hullabaloo = Pachanga deliciosa*
 Listen to the desert = Oye al desierto
 The desert is my mother = El desierto es mi madre
 This big sky
Moreillon, Judi. *Sing down the rain*
Nunes, Susan Miho. *Coyote dreams*
Pearce, Q. L. *In the desert*
Pohrt, Tom. *Having a wonderful time*
Reynolds, Jan. *Sahara*
Roberts, Bethany. *Camel caravan*
Sayre, April Pulley. *Dig, wait, listen*
Siebert, Diane. *Mojave*
Silverman, Erica. *Fixing the crack of dawn*
Spurling, Margaret. *Bilby moon*
Ungerer, Tomi. *Orlando, the brave vulture*
Upper, Jonathan. *Spin's really wild Africa tour*
Vaughan, Marcia Kapok. *Night dancer*
Wondriska, William. *The stop*
Yolen, Jane. *Welcome to the sea of sand*
Young, Ed (Edward). *Donkey trouble*

Detective stories *see* Careers – detectives; Mystery stories;
 Problem solving

Detectives *see* Careers – detectives

Devil

Alger, Leclaire Gowans. *Kellyburn Braes*
Asch, Frank. *Little Devil's ABC*
 Little Devil's 123
Berson, Harold. *How the devil gets his due*
Carey, Valerie Scho. *The devil and mother Crump*
Coombs, Patricia. *The magic pot*
Elwell, Peter. *The king of the pipers*
Galdone, Joanna. *Amber day*
Grimm, Jacob. *The bearskinner*
 The devil with the green hairs
Helldorfer, M. C. (Mary Claire). *Jack, Skinny Bones, and the golden
 pancakes*
Joyce, James. *The cat and the devil*
Kimmel, Eric A. *Grizz!*
McCurdy, Michael. *The devils who learned to be good*
Magnus, Erica. *The boy and the devil*
Olson, Arielle North. *Noah's cats and the devil's fire*
Oppenheim, Shulamith Levey. *Iblis*
Philip, Neil. *Noah and the devil*
Pinkwater, Daniel Manus. *Devil in the drain*
Root, Phyllis. *Rosie's fiddle*
Scribner, Charles. *The devil's bridge*
Shute, Linda. *Momotaro, the peach boy*
Stalder, Valerie. *Even the devil is afraid of a shrew*
Stewig, John Warren. *Clever Gretchen*
Turska, Krystyna. *The magician of Cracow*
Wooldridge, Connie Nordhielm. *The legend of Strap Buckner*
 Wicked Jack
Zemach, Harve. *Duffy and the devil*

Diabetes *see* Illness – diabetes

Dictionaries

Ahlberg, Allan. *Me and my friend*
Bergen, Lara Rice. *Blue's world of words*
Bruna, Dick. *Dick Bruna's picture word book*
Bunting, Jane. *The children's visual dictionary*
 My first word book
Burnstein, Chaya M. *The Jewish kids' Hebrew-English wordbook*
Cartlidge, Michelle. *Michelle Cartlidge's book of words*
 A child's picture English-Hebrew dictionary
Daly, Kathleen N. *The Macmillan picture wordbook*
Day, Alexandra. *Frank and Ernest play ball*
Dodds, Siobhan. *Words and pictures*
Floyd, Lucy. *Agatha's alphabet, with her very own dictionary*
Got, Yves. *Sam's big book of words*
Halsey, William D. *The magic world of words*
Howard, Katherine. *My first picture dictionary*
Kelley, True. *Hammers and mops, pencils and pots*
Krensky, Stephen. *My first dictionary*
MacBean, Dilla Wittemore. *Picture book dictionary*
McIntire, Alta. *Follett beginning to read picture dictionary*
Parke, Margaret B. *Young reader's color-picture dictionary*
Priddy, Roger. *My big book of everything*
 Rand McNally picturebook dictionary
Scarry, Richard. *Richard Scarry's biggest word book ever!*
 Richard Scarry's storybook dictionary
Schulz, Charles M. *The Charlie Brown dictionary*
Seuss, Dr. *The cat in the hat dictionary*
Stanley, Mandy. *First word book*
Wilkes, Angela. *My first word book*
Williams, Sam. *The baby's word book*
Yates, Irene. *My ABC dictionary*

Diggers *see* Careers – construction workers; Machines

Digging *see* Activities – digging

Diners *see* Restaurants

Dinosaurs

Ahlberg, Allan. *Dinosaur dreams*
Aliki. *Digging up dinosaurs*
 Dinosaur bones
 Dinosaurs are different
 Fossils tell of long ago
 My visit to the dinosaurs
Alphin, Elaine Marie. *Dinosaur hunter*
Atkins, Jeannine. *Mary Anning and the sea dragon*
Baker, Liza. *Dinosaur days*
Barber, Antonia. *Satchelmouse and the dinosaurs*
Barner, Bob. *Dinosaur bones*
 Too many dinosaurs
Barton, Byron. *Bones, bones, dinosaur bones*
 Dinosaurs, dinosaurs
Bateman, Teresa. *Hunting the daddyosaurus*
Berenstain, Stan. *After the dinosaurs*
 The day of the dinosaur
Berger, Melvin. *Why did the dinosaurs disappear?*
Bilgrami, Shaheen. *Amazing dinosaur discovery*
Binnamin, Vivian. *The case of the snoring stegosaurus*
Birchman, David Francis. *Brother Billy Bronto's bygone blues band*
Birney, Betty G. *Tyrannosaurus Tex*
Bishop, Roma. *My first pop-up book of dinosaurs*
Blackwood, Mary. *Derek the knitting dinosaur*
Blumenthal, Nancy. *Count-a-saurus*
Bourgeois, Paulette. *Franklin's class trip*
Boynton, Sandra. *Dinosaur's binkit*
 Oh my oh my oh dinosaurs!
Bradman, Tony. *Dilly speaks up*
Brasch, Kate. *Prehistoric monsters*
Brenner, Barbara A. *Dinosaurium*
Brighton, Catherine. *The fossil girl*
Brillhart, Julie. *The dino expert*
Brown, Laurie Krasny. *Dinosaurs alive and well*
 Dinosaurs divorce

Shadow of the dinosaurs
O'Brien, Patrick. *Gigantic!*
Oram, Hiawyn. *A boy wants a dinosaur*
Otto, Carolyn. *Dinosaur chase*
Palazzo-Craig, Janet. *Little Danny Dinosaur*
Parish, Peggy. *Dinosaur time*
Penner, Lucille Recht. *Dinosaur babies*
Petersen, David. *Dinosaur National Monument*
Petty, Kate. *Dinosaurs*
Pfister, Marcus. *Dazzle the dinosaur*
Pittman, Helena Clare. *A dinosaur for Gerald*
Polhamus, Jean Burt. *Dinosaur do's and don'ts*
    Doctor Dinosaur
Prelutsky, Jack. *Tyrannosaurus was a beast*
Pulver, Robin. *Mrs. Toggle and the dinosaur*
Riehecky, Janet. *Apatosaurus*
Ripley, Catherine. *Two dozen dinosaurs*
Rohmann, Eric. *Time flies*
Royston, Angela. *Dinosaurs*
Rubel, Nicole. *Bruno Brontosaurus*
Ryder, Joanne. *Tyrannosaurus time*
Sansone, Adele. *The little green goose*
Sant, Laurent Sauveur. *Dinosaurs*
Schwartz, Henry. *Albert goes Hollywood*
    How I captured a dinosaur
Scott, Peter David. *Dinosaur*
See the dinosaurs
Selsam, Millicent E. *A first look at dinosaurs*
Sharmat, Marjorie Weinman. *Mitchell is moving*
Shields, Carol Diggory. *Saturday night at the dinosaur stomp*
Sibbick, John. *Creatures of long ago*
Silverman, Maida. *Dinosaur babies*
Simon, Seymour. *The largest dinosaurs*
    The smallest dinosaurs
Sirois, Allen. *Dinosaur dress up*
Sis, Peter. *Dinosaur!*
Slobodkin, Louis. *Dinny and Danny*
Smith, Jim. *Nimbus the explorer*
Stevenson, James. *The most amazing dinosaur*
Stewart, Frances Todd. *Dinosaurs and other creatures of long ago*
Stickland, Paul. *Dinosaur roar!*
    Dinosaur stomp!
    Ten terrible dinosaurs
Sundgaard, Arnold. *Jethro's difficult dinosaur*
Talbott, Hudson. *Going Hollywood! A dinosaur's dream*
Taylor, Scott. *Dinosaur James*
Teague, Mark. *The trouble with the Johnsons*
Thayer, Jane. *Quiet on account of dinosaur*
Torres, Daniel. *Tom*
Wahl, Jan. *The field mouse and the dinosaur named Sue*
    I met a dinosaur
Walsh, Patricia. *Dinosaurs*
Watson, Claire. *Big creatures from the past*
Watson, John. *We're the noisy dinosaurs!*
Weston, Martha. *The dinosaurs meet Dr. Clock*
Whybrow, Ian. *Harry and the bucketful of dinosaurs*
    Harry and the dinosaurs say "Raahh"
Wick, Walter. *Can you see what I see? Cool collections*
Wild, Margaret. *My dearest dinosaur*
Wilhelm, Hans. *Tyrone the horrible*
Wilkes, Angela. *The big book of dinosaurs*
Wise, William. *Dinosaurs forever*
Wood, Douglas. *What teachers can't do*
Yolen, Jane. *How do dinosaurs clean their rooms?*
    How do dinosaurs count to ten?
    How do dinosaurs get well soon?
    How do dinosaurs say good night?
Zalben, Jane Breskin. *Buster gets braces*
Zallinger, Peter. *Dinosaurs*
Zoehfeld, Kathleen Weidner. *Dinosaurs big and small*

Disabilities *see* Handicaps

Disbelief *see* Behavior – disbelief

Diseases *see* Illness

Disguises

Æsop. *The donkey in the lion's skin*
    The wolf in sheep's clothing
Cannon, Janell. *Little Yau*
Cazet, Denys. *Minnie and Moo and the musk of Zorro*
Gentle, Victor. *Shark camouflage and armor*
Hale, Irina. *Boxman*
Heller, Ruth. *How to hide a crocodile and other reptiles*
    How to hide a gray treefrog and other amphibians
    How to hide a parakeet and other birds
    How to hide a whip-poor-will and other birds
Holmes, Anita. *Can you find us?*
Hutchins, H. J. (Hazel J.). *I'd know you anywhere*
Kraus, Robert. *Strudwick, a sheep in wolf's clothing*
Lewis, J. Patrick. *The night of the goat children*
McNaughton, Colin. *Boo!*
Mason, Adrienne. *Lu and Clancy's spy stuff*
Riddle, Tohby. *The great escape from City Zoo*
Swinburne, Stephen R. *Lots and lots of zebra stripes*
The three little pigs. *Who's at the door?*
Tibo, Gilles. *Simon's disguise*
Tildes, Phyllis Limbacher. *Animals in camouflage*

Dissatisfaction *see* Behavior – dissatisfaction

Distance *see* Concepts – distance

Divali *see* Holidays – Divali

Diving *see* Sports – skin diving

Divorce

Ackerman, Karen. *In the park with dad*
Adams, Eric J. *On the day his daddy left*
Ballard, Robin. *Gracie*
Baum, Louis. *One more time*
Berger, Terry. *How does it feel when your parents get divorced?*
Bernhard, Durga. *To and fro, fast and slow*
Best, Cari. *Taxi! Taxi!*
Bienenfeld, Florence. *My mom and dad are getting a divorce*
Binch, Caroline. *Since Dad left*
Boegehold, Betty. *Daddy doesn't live here anymore*
Brown, Laurie Krasny. *Dinosaurs divorce*
Bunting, Eve (Anne Evelyn). *The days of summer*
Caines, Jeannette. *Daddy*
Christiansen, C. B. *My mother's house, my father's house*
Cole, Babette. *The un-wedding*
Cole, Julia. *My parents' divorce*
Coy, John. *Two old potatoes and me*
Dragonwagon, Crescent. *Always, always*
Girard, Linda Walvoord. *At Daddy's on Saturdays*
Goff, Beth. *Where's daddy?*
Grindley, Sally. *A new room for William*
Haughton, Emma. *Rainy day*
Hazen, Barbara Shook. *Two homes to live in*
Hickman, Martha Whitmore. *Robert lives with his grandparents*
Lansky, Vicki. *It's not your fault, KoKo Bear*
Lexau, Joan M. *Me day*
Lisker, Sonia O. *Two special cards*
Masurel, Claire. *Two homes*
Mayle, Peter. *Divorce can happen to the nicest people*
    Why are we getting a divorce?
Newman, Lesléa. *Saturday is Pattyday*
Noble, June. *Two homes for Lynn*
Norris, Lori P. (Peters). *D is for divorce*
Paris, Lena. *Mom is single*
Perry, Patricia. *Mommy and daddy are divorced*
Peterson, Jeanne Whitehouse. *That is that*
Pursell, Margaret Sanford. *A look at divorce*
Ransom, Jeanie Franz. *I don't want to talk about it*
Rodell, Susanna. *Dear Fred*
Rogers, Fred. *Divorce*
Rogers, Helen Spelman. *Morris and his brave lion*
Roy, Ronald. *Breakfast with my father*

Rush, Ken. *Friday's journey*
Santucci, Barbara. *Loon summer*
Schindel, John. *Dear Daddy*
Schotter, Roni. *Room for Rabbit*
Schuchman, Joan. *Two places to sleep*
Simon, Norma. *The daddy days*
Spelman, Cornelia Maude. *Mama and Daddy Bear's divorce*
Steel, Danielle. *Martha's new daddy*
Stein, Sara Bonnett. *On divorce*
Stinson, Kathy. *Mom and dad don't live together any more*
Tangvald, Christine Harder. *Mom and dad don't live together any-more*
Thomas, Pat (1959–). *My family's changing*
Vigna, Judith. *Daddy's new baby*
    Grandma without me
    She's not my real mother
Watson, Jane Werner. *Sometimes a family has to split up*
Weninger, Brigitte. *Good-bye, daddy!*
Willhoite, Michael. *Daddy's roommate*
Winthrop, Elizabeth. *As the crow flies*

Doctors *see* Careers – doctors

Dodos *see* Birds – dodos

Dogs *see* Animals – dogs

Dolls *see* Toys – dolls

Dolphins *see* Animals – dolphins

Donkeys *see* Animals – donkeys

Dormice *see* Animals – dormice

Doves *see* Birds – doves

Down & up *see* Concepts – up & down

Down syndrome *see* Handicaps – Down syndrome

Dragonflies *see* Insects – dragonflies

Dragons

Agell, Charlotte. *The sailor's book*
Alexander, Sue. *World famous Muriel and the scary dragon*
Anderson, Wayne. *Dragon*
Aruego, José. *The king and his friends*
Asch, Frank. *Milk and cookies*
Atkins, Jeannine. *Mary Anning and the sea dragon*
Bass, Jules. *Herb, the vegetarian dragon*
Baumgart, Klaus. *Anna and the little green dragon*
    The little green dragon steps out
Bertrand, Lynne. *Dragon naps*
    One day, two dragons
Biro, Val. *Tobias and the dragon*
Boswell, Stephen. *King Gorboduc's fabulous zoo*
Bradfield, Roger (Jolly Roger). *A good night for dragons*
Buckaway, C. M. *Alfred, the dragon who lost his flame*
Burnside, Julian. *Matilda and the dragon*
Carle, Eric. *Dragons dragons and other creatures that never were*
Cave, Kathryn. *You've got dragons*
Chalmers, Mary. *George Appleton*
Cherry, Lynne. *The dragon and the unicorn*
Christelow, Eileen. *Henry and the dragon*
Christian, Mary Blount. *The bookstore mouse*
Company González, Mercé. *Killian and the dragons*
Conover, Chris. *Sam Panda and Thunder Dragon*
Cooper, Susan. *Matthew's dragon*
Coville, Bruce. *Sarah and the dragon*
Craig, M. Jean. *The dragon in the clock box*
Cressey, James. *The dragon and George*
Cretien, Paul D. *Sir Henry and the dragon*

Davis, Reda. *Martin's dinosaur*
Day, Marie. *Dragon in the rocks*
DeLage, Ida. *The old witch and the dragon*
Delaney, Ned. *One dragon to another*
Demi. *Demi's dragons and fantastic creatures*
    Dragon kites and dragonflies
    The dragon's tale and other animal fables of the Chinese zodiac
De Paola, Tomie (Thomas Anthony). *The knight and the dragon*
Dewey, Ariane. *Dorin and the dragon*
Domanska, Janina. *King Krakus and the dragon*
Donaldson, Julia. *Room on the broom*
Dragon poems
Eduar, Gilles. *Jooka saves the day*
Emberley, Ed (Edward Randolph). *Klippity klop*
Enderle, Judith (Ann) Ross. *The good-for-something dragon*
Falwell, Cathryn. *Dragon tooth*
Fassler, Joan. *The man of the house*
Gág, Wanda. *The funny thing*
Galchutt, David. *There was magic inside*
Garrison, Christian. *The dream eater*
Goode, Diane. *I hear a noise*
Goodhart, Pippa. *Arthur's tractor*
Grahame, Kenneth. *The reluctant dragon*
Grimm, Jacob. *The four clever brothers*
Haley, Gail E. *Jack and the fire dragon*
Hillert, Margaret. *Happy birthday, dear dragon*
    Merry Christmas, dear dragon
Hillman, Elizabeth. *Min-Yo and the moon dragon*
Hoban, Russell. *Ace Dragon Ltd.*
Hodges, Margaret. *Saint George and the dragon*
Holabird, Katharine. *Alexander and the dragon*
Howe, James. *There's a dragon in my sleeping bag*
Hunter, Jana Novotny. *Little ones do*
Janosch. *Just one apple*
Jeschke, Susan. *Firerose*
Jonell, Lynne. *When Mommy was mad*
Jones, Maurice. *I'm going on a dragon hunt*
Joslin, Sesyle. *Dear dragon*
Kent, Jack. *The once-upon-a-time dragon*
    There's no such thing as a dragon
Kimmel, Eric A. *The four gallant sisters*
    The rooster's antlers
Kimmel, Margaret Mary. *Magic in the mist*
Krahn, Fernando. *The secret in the dungeon*
Kumin, Maxine W. *Sebastian and the dragon*
Lambert, Martha Lewis. *I won't get lost*
Lattimore, Deborah Nourse. *The dragon's robe*
Lawson, Julie. *The dragon's pearl*
Leaf, Margaret. *Eyes of the dragon*
Leedy, Loreen. *A dragon Christmas*
    The dragon Halloween party
    The dragon Thanksgiving feast
    A number of dragons
Lifton, Betty Jean. *Joji and the dragon*
Lindgren, Astrid. *The dragon with red eyes*
Lobel, Arnold. *Prince Bertram the bad*
Long, Claudia. *Albert's story*
McCaughrean, Geraldine. *Saint George and the dragon*
McCrea, James. *The story of Olaf*
McMullen, Eunice. *Dragon for breakfast*
Mahood, Kenneth. *The laughing dragon*
Mahy, Margaret. *The dragon of an ordinary family*
    A lion in the meadow
Manushkin, Fran. *Moon dragon*
Martin, C. L. G. *The dragon nanny*
Mathews, Judith. *An egg and seven socks*
Mayer, Mercer. *Whinnie the lovesick dragon*
Meddaugh, Susan. *Harry on the rocks*
Minarik, Else Holmelund. *The little girl and the dragon*
Mogensen, Jan. *Teddy and the Chinese dragon*
Munsch, Robert N. *The paper bag princess*
Murphy, Shirley Rousseau. *Valentine for a dragon*
Myers, Walter Dean. *The dragon takes a wife*
Nash, Ogden. *Custard the dragon*
    Custard the dragon and the wicked knight, ill. by Lynn Munsinger
    Custard the dragon and the wicked knight, ill. by Linell Nash
Nesbit, Edith. *The last of the dragons*

Noble, Kate. *The dragon of Navy Pier*
Nolan, Dennis. *The castle builder*
Nolen, Jerdine. *Raising dragons*
Nunes, Susan Miho. *The last dragon*
Oksner, Robert M. *The incompetent wizard*
Pattison, Darcy. *The river dragon*
Pavey, Peter. *One dragon's dream*
Peet, Bill (William Bartlett). *How Droofus the dragon lost his head*
Pendziwol, Jean. *No dragons for tea*
  A treasure at sea for dragon and me
Phillips, Louis. *The brothers Wrong and Wrong Again*
Pieńkowski, Jan. *Bel and Bub and the black hole*
Pilkey, Dav. *Dragon's fat cat*
  Dragon's merry Christmas
  A friend for Dragon
Price, Roger. *The last little dragon*
Reddix, Valerie. *Dragon kite of the autumn moon*
Robertson, M. P. *The egg*
Robinson, Fay. *Where did all the dragons go?*
Rosen, Winifred. *Dragons hate to be discreet*
Roth, Susan L. *Brave Martha and the dragon*
Rowe, John A. *Jasper the terror*
San Souci, Daniel. *The rabbit and the dragon king*
Scarry, Richard. *Richard Scarry's Peasant Pig and the terrible dragon*
Schotter, Richard. *There's a dragon about*
Scullard, Sue. *Miss Fanshawe and the great dragon adventure*
Sherman, Nancy. *Gwendolyn the miracle hen*
Shub, Elizabeth. *Dragon Franz*
Sierra, Judy. *'Twas the fright before Christmas*
Slote, Elizabeth. *Nelly's garden*
Stern, Peter. *Max the dragon*
Stern, Simon. *Vasily and the dragon*
Stock, Catherine. *Emma's dragon hunt*
Sutcliff, Rosemary. *The minstrel and the dragon pup*
Thayer, Jane. *The popcorn dragon*, ill. by Jay Hyde Barnum
  The popcorn dragon, ill. by Lisa McCue
Thomas, Shelley Moore. *Get well, good knight*
  Good night, Good Knight
Torre, Betty L. *The luminous pearl*
Trevelyan, Kathy. *Don't be surprised!*
Trez, Denise. *The little knight's dragon*
Tucker, Kathy. *The seven Chinese sisters*
Uttley, Alison. *Sam Pig and the dragon*
Van Woerkom, Dorothy. *Alexandra the rock-eater*
Vaughan, Marcia Kapok. *The dancing dragon*
Ward, Helen. *The dragon machine*
Waterton, Betty. *Orff, 27 dragons (and a snarkel)*
Wiesner, David. *Free fall*
  The loathsome dragon
Williams, Arlene. *Dragon soup*
Williams, Jay. *Everyone knows what a dragon looks like*
Willis, Val. *The secret in the matchbox*
Wilson, Gina. *Ignis*
Wilson, Sarah. *Beware the dragons!*
Wong, Benedict Norbert. *Lo & behold*
  Lo & behold, good enough to eat
Yep, Laurence. *Dragon prince*
Young, Russell. *Dragonsong*
Zirkel, Lynn. *The shell dragon*

Drawing *see* Activities – drawing

Drawing games *see* Games

Dreams

Adlerman, Daniel. *Africa calling*
Adoff, Arnold. *Flamboyan*
Ahlberg, Allan. *Dinosaur dreams*
Aichinger, Helga. *The shepherd*
Alborough, Jez. *Ice cream bear*
Alexander, Martha G. *Bobo's dream*
  You're a genius, Blackboard Bear
Allison, Diane Worfolk. *In window eight, the moon is late*
Anholt, Laurence. *Jack and the dreamsack*
Anrooy, Frans van. *The sea horse*

Appelt, Kathi. *Cowboy dreams*
Argueta, Jorge. *Trees are hanging from the sky*
Armstrong, Jennifer. *Pierre's dream*
Arnold, Tedd. *Green Wilma*
  No jumping on the bed!
Asch, Frank. *Milk and cookies*
  Moonbear's dream
Atnip, Linda. *Miranda's magic garden*
  Miranda's magic garden
Axworthy, Anni. *Ben's Wednesday*
Aylesworth, Jim. *The bad dream*
  Tonight's the night
Balet, Jan B. *Joanjo*
Balzola, Asun. *Munia and the orange crocodile*
Bancroft, Catherine. *Felix's hat*
Banks, Kate (Katherine A.). *And if the moon could talk*
  Close your eyes
Barasch, Lynne. *Old friends*
Baumgart, Klaus. *The little green dragon steps out*
Berenstain, Stan. *The Berenstain bears and the bad dream*
Berger, Barbara Helen. *The donkey's dream*
Bider, Djemma. *A drop of honey*
Bohdal, Susi. *The magic honey jar*
Bond, Felicia. *Wake up, Vladimir*
The book of Pooh: Biglet
Boyd, Lizi. *Sweet dreams, Willy*
Brown, M. K. (Mary K.). *Let's go swimming with Mr. Sillypants*
Brown, Margaret Wise. *Dream book*
  The little farmer
Brown, Ruth. *Mad summer night's dream*
Browne, Anthony. *Willy the dreamer*
Bruna, Dick. *Miffy's dream*
Buckley, Helen Elizabeth. *Someday with my father*
Burdett, Lois. *A midsummer night's dream for kids*
Burningham, John. *Hey! Get off our train*
  The magic bed
Burnside, Julian. *Matilda and the dragon*
Callen, Larry. *Dashiel and the night*
Carlson, Nancy L. *It's going to be perfect*
Carpenter, Mary-Chapin. *Dreamland*
Carroll, Lewis. *The nursery "Alice"*
Casler, Leigh. *The boy who dreamed of an acorn*
Cazet, Denys. *Daydreams*
  Minnie and Moo: the night of the living bed
Chapman, Nancy Kapp. *Doggie dreams*
Chesworth, Michael. *Rainy day dream*
Chorao, Kay. *Lemon moon*
Chwast, Seymour. *Still another children's book*
Cohen, Caron Lee. *Martin and the giant lions*
Cohen, Miriam. *Eddy's dream*
Cole, Babette. *The slimy book*
Collington, Peter. *Little pickle*
  The midnight circus
Cooper, Susan. *Matthew's dragon*
Cousins, Lucy. *Maisy's bedtime*
  Maisy's rainbow dream
Craig, M. Jean. *What did you dream?*
Crew, Gary. *Bright star*
Crossley-Holland, Kevin. *Sleeping Nanna*
Crowley, Arthur. *The wagon man*
Cuyler, Margery. *Fat Santa*
Dahl, Roald. *Dirty beasts*
Daugherty, Charles Michael. *Wisher*
Davis, Katie (Katie I.). *I hate to go to bed!*
Davis, Maggie S. *A garden of whales*
Davol, Marguerite W. *Batwings and the curtain of night*
Dennis, Wesley. *Flip*
DeSaix, Frank. *The girl who danced with dolphins*
Dewey, Ariane. *Dorin and the dragon*
Doherty, Berlie. *The midnight man*
Donaldson, Lois. *Karl's wooden horse*
Dragonwagon, Crescent. *Half a moon and one whole star*
Drescher, Henrik. *Simon's book*
Dunbar, Joyce. *The sand children*
  Tell me something happy before I go to sleep
Duncan, Lois. *Horses of dreamland*
Dunnick, Regan. *Sweet dreams, Douglas*

Dürr, Ursula. *The secret of Trembleton Hall*
Duvoisin, Roger Antoine. *The missing milkman*
Eduar, Gilles. *Dream journey*
Elzbieta. *Dikou and the mysterious moon sheep*
Emberley, Rebecca. *My mother's secret life*
Erskine, Jim. *Bedtime story*
Esbensen, Barbara Juster. *The dream mouse*
Farber, Norma. *I swim an ocean in my sleep*
Farmer, Bonnie. *Isaac's dreamcatcher*
Faulkner, Keith. *Amble has a dream*
Fazio, Brenda Lena. *Grandfather's story*
Field, Rachel Lyman. *A road might lead to anywhere*
Foreman, Michael. *Jack's fantastic voyage*
    Land of dreams
Francis, Anna B. *Pleasant dreams*
Francis, Frank. *The magic wallpaper*
Galouchko, Annouchka. *Shô and the demons of the deep*
Gantos, Jack (John, Jr.). *Greedy Greeny*
Garrison, Christian. *The dream eater*
Gay, Marie-Louise. *Moonbeam on a cat's ear*
Giff, Patricia Reilly. *Next year I'll be special*
Gile, John. *Oh, how I wished I could read!*
Ginsburg, Mirra. *Across the stream*
    Four brave sailors
Goldsmith, Howard. *Sleepy little owl*
Goodhart, Pippa. *Row, row, row your boat*
Goodman, Joan Elizabeth. *Bernard's nap*
Gorbachev, Valeri. *Nicky and the big, bad wolves*
Gottfried, Maya. *Last night I dreamed a circus*
Gould, Deborah. *Grandpa's slide show*
Greenfield, Eloise. *Africa dream*
Greenwood, Ann. *A pack of dreams*
Griffith, Helen V. *Pluck's dreams*
Hague, Kathleen. *Out of the nursery, into the night*
Hale, Irina. *Donkey's dreadful day*
Haley, Gail E. *Dream peddler*
Harrison, Troon. *The dream collector*
Hayes, Geoffrey. *The secret inside*
Hazelaar, Cor. *Zoo dreams*
Heckman, Philip. *Waking upside down*
Heine, Helme. *The marvelous journey through the night*
Heller, Nicholas. *Mathilda the dream bear*
    Peas
Henri, Adrian. *The postman's palace*
Hill, Susan. *Go away, bad dreams!*
Hodgetts, Blake Christopher. *Dream of the dinosaurs*
Honigsberg, Peter Jan. *Pillow of dreams*
Hurd, Edith Thacher. *Little dog, dreaming*
Hutchins, H. J. (Hazel J.). *Beneath the bridge*
Ipcar, Dahlov (Zorach). *Black and white*
Isadora, Rachel. *Caribbean dream*
Jacobs, Joseph. *The crock of gold*
James, Betsy. *The dream stair*
Jendresen, Erik. *The first story ever told*
Jennings, Michael. *The bears who came to breakfix*
Johnson, Angela. *I dream of trains*
Johnson, Jane. *Bertie on the beach*
Jonas, Ann. *The quilt*
Kamish, Daniel. *The night scary beasties popped out of my head*
Karlin, Nurit. *The dream factory*
Keats, Ezra Jack. *Dreams*
Keith, Eros. *Nancy's backyard*
Kenah, Katharine. *The dream shop*
Khan, Rukhsana. *Bedtime ba-a-a-lk*
Knotts, Howard. *The lost Christmas*
Koontz, Robin Michal. *Dinosaur dream*
Koralek, Jenny. *The boy and the cloth of dreams*
Kotzwinkle, William. *The nap master*
Krahn, Fernando. *Sebastian and the mushroom*
Kvasnosky, Laura McGee. *What shall I dream?*
Laimgruber, Monika. *Susannah and the Sandman*
Lester, Alison. *Isabella's bed*
    Ruby
Lester, Julius. *Albidaro and the mischievous dream*
Le-Tan, Pierre. *Visit to the North Pole*
Lindgren, Barbro. *The wild baby gets a puppy*
London, Jonathan. *Froggy goes to school*

    Into this night we are rising
Low, Joseph. *Don't drag your feet . . .*
Lyon, George Ella. *Dreamplace*
McAllister, Angela. *The ice palace*
McCain, Becky R. (Becky Ray). *Grandmother's dreamcatcher*
McCarthy, Bobette. *Dreaming*
McClintock, Barbara. *The battle of Luke and Longnose*
McDermott, Gerald. *Daniel O'Rourke*
MacDonald, Maryann. *Rosie and the poor rabbits*
MacDonald, Ross. *Another perfect day*
McLerran, Alice. *Dreamsong*
    The year of the ranch
McMullan, Kate (Hall). *The noisy giant's tea party*
Maconie, Robin. *Alice and her fabulous teeth*
McPhail, David M. *Adam's smile*
    The dream child
    Mistletoe
    The train
Mählqvist, Stefan. *I'll take care of the crocodiles*
Manning, Mick. *Honk! honk!*
Martin, Bill (William Ivan). *Barn dance!*
    Little granny quarterback
Martin, Jacqueline Briggs. *Grandmother Bryant's pocket*
Marton, Jirina. *I'll do it myself*
    Midnight visit at Molly's house
Mayer, Mercer. *The rocking horse angel*
    There's something in my attic
Mayper, Monica. *After good-night*
Melmed, Laura Krauss. *Jumbo's lullaby*
Mendes, Valerie. *Look at me, Grandma!*
Modarressi, Mitra. *The dream pillow*
Moers, Hermann. *Evie to the rescue!*
Montresor, Beni. *Bedtime!*
    The witches of Venice
Morgan, Allen. *Nicole's boat*
Musgrave, Susan. *Dreams are more real than bathtubs*
Nahas, Sylvaine. *Nicolo's unicorn*
Neuschwander, Cindy. *Amanda Bean's amazing dream*
Nightingale, Sandy. *A giraffe on the moon*
Nixon, Joan Lowery. *Will you give me a dream?*
Nobens, C. A. *Montgomery's time zone*
Nolan, Dennis. *Dinosaur dream*
Nunes, Susan Miho. *Coyote dreams*
Nye, Naomi Shihab. *Benito's dream bottle*
Oram, Hiawyn. *A boy wants a dinosaur*
Orgel, Doris. *Little John*
Osofsky, Audrey. *Dreamcatcher*
Pallandt, Nicholas van. *The butterfly night of Old Brown Bear*
Paraskevas, Betty. *Cecil Bunions and the midnight train*
Pavey, Peter. *One dragon's dream*
Paxton, Tom. *Jennifer's rabbit*
Pfister, Marcus. *Wake up, Santa Claus!*
Pierson, Judith Patterson. *The always moon*
Pilkey, Dav. *When cats dream*
Pinkwater, Daniel Manus. *Wallpaper from space*
Polacco, Patricia. *Appelemando's dreams*
Price, Mathew. *Patch and the rabbits*
Rassmus, Jens. *Farmer Enno and his cow*
Recknagel, Friedrich. *Meg's wish*
Reed, Kit. *When we dream*
Riddell, Chris. *The wish factory*
Ringgold, Faith. *My dream of Martin Luther King*
    Tar Beach
Rock, Lois. *I wish tonight*
Rockhill, Dennis. *Polar slumber = Sueño polar*
Rockwell, Anne F. *Buster and the bogeyman*
    The wolf who had a wonderful dream
Rohmann, Eric. *The cinder-eyed cats*
Roper, Janice M. *Dancing on the moon*
Ross, Lillian Hammer. *The little old man and his dreams*
Roth, Roger. *The sign painter's dream*
Rovetch, Lissa. *Sweet dreams, little one*
Ryder, Joanne. *The night flight*
Sage, James. *To sleep*
Sava, Donna Lynn. *Teddy bear dreams*
Say, Allen. *A river dream*
Schaefer, Carole Lexa. *Down in the woods at sleepytime*

Down in the woods at sleepytime [board book]
Schami, Rafik. *Fatima and the dream thief*
Schuch, Steve. *A symphony of whales*
Seibold, J. Otto. *Penguin dreams*
Sendak, Maurice. *In the night kitchen*
Senshu, Noriko. *Sonny's dream*
Shah, Idries. *The boy without a name*
Sheldon, Dyan. *Under the moon*
Shepperson, Rob. *The sandman*
Shimin, Symeon. *I wish there were two of me*
Showers, Paul. *Sleep is for everyone*
Shulevitz, Uri. *The treasure*
Simmonds, Posy. *The chocolate wedding*
Simmons, Jane. *Go to sleep, Daisy*
Simon, Carly. *Midnight farm*
Simon, Francesca. *Spider school*
Simons, Traute. *Paulino*
Singer, Marilyn. *The Morgans' dream*
Smee, Nicola. *Finish the story, dad*
Smith, Lane. *The big pets*
Smith-Moore, J. J. *Sally Small*
Spier, Peter. *Dreams*
Spinelli, Eileen. *Where is the night train going?*
Steig, William. *The Zabajaba Jungle*
Stevens, Janet. *Animal fair*
Storm, Theodor. *Little Hobbin*
Strand, Mark. *The planet of lost things*
Strauss, Gwen. *The night shimmy*
Strub, Susanne. *Lulu goes swimming*
 Lulu on her bike
Sutherland, Marc. *The waiting place*
Tafuri, Nancy. *Junglewalk*
 What the sun sees / What the moon sees
Takamado no Miya Hisako. *Katie and the dream-eater*
Tejima, Keizaburo. *Fox's dream*
Thorne, Jenny. *My uncle*
Tompert, Ann. *Will you come back for me?*
Trez, Denise. *Good night, Veronica*
Trottier, Maxine. *Dreamstones*
 Prairie willow
Troughton, Joanna. *Tortoise's dream*
Tudor, Tasha. *A tale for Easter*
Twining, Edith. *Sandman*
Updike, David. *A winter's journey*
Waddell, Martin. *Mimi and the dream house*
Wahl, Jan. *Elf night*
 Humphrey's bear
 The toy circus
Ward, Helen. *The tin forest*
Ward, Lynd. *The silver pony*
Waterton, Betty. *Orff, 27 dragons (and a snarkel)*
Weber, Linda Kay. *Louie Larkey and the bad dream patrol*
Weigelt, Udo. *Mole's journey*
Weisgard, Leonard. *Who dreams of cheese?*
Wende, Philip. *Bird boy*
Wersba, Barbara. *Amanda dreaming*
Wick, Walter. *Can you see what I see? Dream machine*
Wiebe, Rudy. *Hidden buffalo*
Wiesner, David. *Free fall*
Wild, Margaret. *Going home*
Wildsmith, Brian. *Carousel*
Willard, Nancy. *The mountains of quilt*
 Night story
Wood, Audrey. *Sweet dream pie*
Yaccarino, Dan. *Good night, Mr. Night*
Yolen, Jane. *Moon ball*
Yorinks, Arthur. *Hey, Al*
Young, Ed (Edward). *Night visitors*
Zemach, Kaethe. *The funny dream*
Ziefert, Harriet. *Moonride*
 Squarehead
 What do ducks dream?
Zolotow, Charlotte (Shapiro). *I have a horse of my own*
 Someday
 Wake up and goodnight
 Who is Ben?

Dresses *see* Clothing – dresses

Driving *see* Activities – driving

Droughts *see* Weather – droughts

Drug addiction *see* Illness – drug addiction

Drums *see* Musical instruments – drums

Ducks *see* Birds – ducks

Dutch Americans *see* Ethnic groups in the U.S. – Dutch Americans

Dwarfs, midgets

Bruna, Dick. *Dick Bruna's Snow-White and the seven dwarfs*
 Dick Bruna's Tom Thumb
Calhoun, Mary. *The thieving dwarfs*
Delessert, Etienne. *The seven dwarfs*
French, Fiona. *Snow White in New York*
Grimm, Jacob. *Rose Red and the bear prince*
 Snow White, ill. by Trina Schart Hyman
 Snow White, ill. by Bernadette Watts
 Snow White, ill. by Claudia Wolf
 Snow White and Rose Red, ill. by Adrienne Adams
 Snow White and Rose Red, ill. by John Wallner
 Snow White and Rose Red, ill. by Bernadette Watts
 Snow White and the seven dwarfs, ill. by Wanda Gág
 Snow White and the seven dwarves, ill. by Chihiro Iwasaki
Jennings, Michael. *Robin Goodfellow and the giant dwarf*
Ljungkvist, Laura. *Snow White and the seven dwarfts*
Lobel, Anita. *The dwarf giant*
Rascal. *Oregon's journey*
Ruzzier, Sergio. *The little giant*
Sikundar, Sylvia. *Forest singer*
Walt Disney Productions. *Walt Disney's Snow White and the seven dwarfs*

Dwellings *see* Buildings; Homes, houses

Dying *see* Death

Dyslexia *see* Handicaps – dyslexia

Eagles *see* Birds – eagles

Ears *see* Anatomy – ears; Handicaps – deafness; Senses – hearing

Earth

Anno, Mitsumasa. *Anno's sundial*
Asch, Frank. *The earth and I*
Asimov, Isaac. *The best new thing*
Benson, Laura Lee. *This is our earth*
Bernstein, Margery. *Earth namer*
Branley, Franklyn M. (Mansfield). *Earthquakes*
 The sun, our nearest star
 What makes day and night
Burningham, John. *Whaddayamean*
Cameron, Eileen. *Canyon*
Carson, Jo. *The great shaking*
Clements, Andrew. *Mother Earth's counting book*
Cole, Joanna. *The magic school bus inside the earth*

Dayton, Mona. *Earth and sky*
DeMunn, Michael. *The earth is good*
Elschner, Géraldine. *Moonchild, star of the sea*
Engdahl, Sylvia. *Our world is earth*
Fisher, Aileen Lucia. *Sing of the earth and sky*
Flanagan, Alice K. *Rocks*
   Soil
   Water
Glaser, Linda. *Our big home*
Greene, Rhonda Gowler. *The beautiful world that God made*
Jenkins, Steve. *Hottest, coldest, highest, deepest*
Johnston, Tony. *We love the dirt*
Lauber, Patricia. *How we learned the earth is round*
   You're aboard spaceship Earth
Leutscher, Alfred. *Earth*
Lewis, Claudia Louise. *When I go to the moon*
Lewis, J. Patrick. *Earth and me, our family tree*
   Earth and you, a closer view
Luenn, Nancy. *Mother earth*
Milgrim, David. *Here in space*
Reiser, Lynn. *Earthdance*
Ross, Michael Elsohn. *Earth cycles*
Rucki, Ani. *When the Earth wakes*
Schmid, Eleonore. *The living earth*
Simon, Seymour. *Beneath your feet*
Siomades, Lorianne. *A place to bloom*
Staub, Leslie. *Bless this house*
Wyler, Rose. *The starry sky*
Zoehfeld, Kathleen Weidner. *How mountains are made*

Earthquakes

Carson, Jo. *The great shaking*
Enderle, Judith (Ann) Ross. *Francis, the earthquake dog*
Givon, Hannah Gelman. *We shake in a quake*
Harrison, David Lee. *Earthquakes*
Lee, Milly. *Earthquake*
Palatini, Margie. *Earthquack*
Prager, Ellen J. *Earthquakes*
Simon, Seymour. *Danger! earthquakes*

East Indian Americans *see* Ethnic groups in the U.S. – East Indian Americans

Easter *see* Holidays – Easter

Eating *see* Food

Ecology

Accorsi, William. *Rachel Carson*
Albert, Toni. *I heard the willow weep*
Aldridge, Josephine Haskell. *A possible tree*
Alexander, Sue. *Behold the trees*
Aliki. *My visit to the zoo*
Allen, Judy. *Seal*
   Whale
Anholt, Laurence. *The forgotten forest*
Armentrout, David. *John Muir*
Arneson, D. J. *Secret places*
Arnold, Caroline. *A walk by the seashore*
   A walk in the desert
   A walk in the woods
   A walk on the Great Barrier Reef
   A walk up the mountain
Arnosky, Jim. *Crinkleroot's visit to Crinkle Cove*
Asch, Frank. *Cactus poems*
Atkins, Jeannine. *Aani and the tree huggers*
Atwell, Debby. *River*
Baker, Jeannie. *The story of rosy dock*
   Where the forest meets the sea
   Window
Balian, Lorna. *Wilbur's space machine*
Baylor, Byrd. *The desert is theirs*
Beisert, Heide Helene. *Poor fish*
Bellamy, David. *How green are you?*

   The roadside
   The rock pool
Benson, Laura Lee. *This is our earth*
Berenstain, Stan. *The Berenstain bears don't pollute anymore*
Berger, Melvin. *Oil spill!*
Bergman, Donna. *Timmy Green's blue lake*
Bloome, Enid. *The air we breathe!*
   The water we drink!
Brenner, Barbara A. *One small place by the sea*
Brown, Laurie Krasny. *Dinosaurs to the rescue*
Brown, Ruth. *The world that Jack built*
Bunting, Eve (Anne Evelyn). *Someday a tree*
Burningham, John. *Whaddayamean*
Burton, Virginia Lee. *The little house*
Busch, Phyllis S. *Puddles and ponds*
Caputo, Robert. *More than just pets*
Carrick, Carol. *A clearing in the forest*
Cecil, Laura. *Noah and the space ark*
Cherry, Lynne. *The dragon and the unicorn*
   The great kapok tree
   A river ran wild
Child, Lauren. *What planet are you from Clarice Bean?*
Cole, Babette. *Supermoo!*
Cone, Molly. *Squishy, misty, damp & muddy*
Craighead, Charles. *The eagle and the river*
Cushman, Doug. *Mouse and Mole and the Christmas walk*
Davies, Nicola. *Oceans and seas*
Dennard, Deborah. *Hedgehog haven*
De Paola, Tomie (Thomas Anthony). *Michael Bird-Boy*
Dobson, David. *Can we save them?*
Dunphy, Madeleine. *Here is the coral reef*
   Here is the southwestern desert
Duvoisin, Roger Antoine. *The happy hunter*
Ernst, Lisa Campbell. *Squirrel Park*
Fife, Dale. *The little park*
Firmin, Peter. *Basil Brush and the windmills*
Fischetto, Laura. *The jungle is my home*
Flanagan, Alice K. *Soil*
Foreman, Michael. *One world*
Franklin, Kristine L. *When the monkeys came back*
Fraser, Mary Ann. *Forest fire!*
Freeman, Don. *The seal and the slick*
Galko, Francine. *Cave animals*
Garland, Sherry. *Summer sands*
Garrett, Ann. *Keeper of the swamp*
George, Jean Craighead. *Everglades*
Gibbons, Gail. *Exploring the deep, dark sea*
   Nature's green umbrella
   Recycle!
Godkin, Celia. *Sea Otter Inlet*
   What about ladybugs?
Greene, Carol. *The old ladies who liked cats*
Greenway, Shirley. *Where do I live?*
Grindley, Sally. *Peter's place*
Grupper, Jonathan. *Destination, rain forest*
   Destination – Rocky Mountains
Guiberson, Brenda Z. *Cactus hotel*
Hader, Berta Hoerner. *The mighty hunter*
Haley, Gail E. *Noah's ark*
Hallinan, P. K. (Patrick K.). *For the love of our earth*
Halpern, Shari. *My river*
Hamanaka, Sheila. *Screen of frogs*
Hamberger, John. *The day the sun disappeared*
Hamilton, Virginia. *Drylongso*
   Jaguarundi
Hassett, John. *Junior*
Hazen, Barbara Shook. *World, world, what can I do?*
Heinz, Brian J. *Butternut Hollow Pond*
Henwood, Simon. *The hidden jungle*
Hewitt, Sally. *All year round*
   Woods and meadows
Hines, Gary. *A Christmas tree in the White House*
Hirschi, Ron. *Forest*
Hoff, Syd. *Grizzwold*
Hooks, William H. *Mr. Garbage*
Hurd, Edith Thacher. *Wilson's world*
Ichikawa, Satomi. *Suzanne and Nicholas in the garden*

James, Simon. *Sally and the limpet*
Jenkins, Steve. *I see a kookaburra*
Jewell, Nancy. *Try and catch me*
Johanasen, Heather. *About the rain forest*
Johnson, Amy Crane. *Mason moves away = Mason se muda*
Jordan, Sandra. *Christmas tree farm*
Joslin, Mary. *The tale of the heaven tree*
Kalman, Benjamin. *Animals in danger*
Karpin, Florence Baker. *Tree spirits*
Keister, Douglas. *Fernando's gift = El regalo de Fernando*
Kleven, Elisa. *The dancing deer and the foolish hunter*
Klingel, Cynthia Fitterer. *Underground*
Koch, Michelle. *World water watch*
Krull, Kathleen. *It's my earth too*
Lauber, Patricia. *Be a friend to trees*
   Who eats what?
Leedy, Loreen. *The great trash bash*
Le Tord, Bijou. *The river and the rain*
Leutscher, Alfred. *Water*
Levinson, Nancy Smiler. *Death Valley*
Lewin, Ted. *Amazon boy*
   When the rivers go home
Lewis, J. Patrick. *Earth and you, a closer view*
Lewis, Naomi. *Hare and badger go to town*
Lewis, Paul Owen. *Frog girl*
Lindbergh, Reeve. *A view from the air*
Locker, Thomas. *The land of gray wolf*
London, Jonathan. *Gone again ptarmigan*
Loomis, Christine. *The cleanup surprise*
Luenn, Nancy. *Mother earth*
   Song for the ancient forest
   Squish!
Lumry, Amanda. *Safari in South Africa*
Maass, Robert. *Garbage*
Mabey, Richard. *Oak and company*
Macdonald, Anne. *Wickiup walkingstick*
McKinney, Barbara Shaw. *Pass the energy, please*
McMillan, Bruce. *Days of the ducklings*
Mantegazza, Giovanna. *Look inside a rainforest*
Margolis, Richard J. *Big bear, spare that tree*
Martin, Jacqueline Briggs. *Washing the willow tree loon*
Mazer, Anne. *The salamander room*
Mendoza, George. *Were you a wild duck, where would you go?*
Meyer, Louis A. *The clean air and peaceful contentment dirigible air-*
   line
Michels, Tilde. *At the frog pond*
Miles, Miska. *Rabbit garden*
Miller, Debbie S. *Are trees alive?*
   River of life
Miller, Edna. *Mousekin's lost woodland*
Mizumura, Kazue. *If I built a village*
Moon, Pat. *This is the earth*
Moss, Miriam. *This is the tree*
Murphy, Stuart J. *Earth Day – hooray!*
Murschetz, Luis. *Mister Mole*
Muzik, Katharine. *At home in the coral reef*
Newton, James R. *Forest log*
Newton-John, Olivia. *A pig tale*
Pandell, Karen. *I love you sun, I love you moon*
Parnall, Peter. *The great fish*
   The rock
Pascoe, Gwen. *Deep in a rainforest*
Peet, Bill (William Bartlett). *The caboose who got loose*
   Farewell to Shady Glade
   Fly, Homer, fly
   The gnats of knotty pine
   The wump world
Peterson, Cris. *Amazing grazing*
Poppy Bear
Radley, Gail. *The spinner's gift*
Rand, Gloria. *Prince William*
Ray, Mary Lyn. *Pumpkins*
Reed-Jones, Carol. *The tree in the ancient forest*
Roach, Marilynne K. *Dune fox*
Robinson, Tim. *Tobias, the quig, and the rumplenut tree*
Roop, Connie. *Let's celebrate Earth Day*
Ryder, Joanne. *The waterfall's gift*

Sadler, Marilyn. *Elizabeth, Larry, and Ed*
Sanders, Scott R. (Scott Russell). *Crawdad Creek*
San Souci, Robert D. *The birds of Killingworth*
Santore, Charles. *William the Curious*
Sayre, April Pulley. *The shape of Betts Meadow*
Schmid, Eleonore. *The living earth*
Seattle, Chief. *Brother eagle, sister sky*
Selzer, Meyer. *Here comes the recycling truck!*
Sensel, Joni. *Bears barge in*
Seuss, Dr. *The Lorax*
Shields, Carol Diggory. *Homes*
Short, Mayo. *Andy and the wild ducks*
Showers, Paul. *Where does the garbage go?*
Siomades, Lorianne. *A place to bloom*
Snape, Juliet. *Frog odyssey*
Staub, Leslie. *Bless this house*
Stone, A. Harris. *The last free bird*
Stone, Lynn M. *Life of the kelp forest*
   Partners
Suzuki, David. *Salmon forest*
Swamp, Jake. *Giving thanks*
Tafolla, Carmen. *Baby Coyote and the old woman = El coyotito y la*
   viejita
Tate, Suzanne. *Crabby's water wish*
Testa, Fulvio. *Too much garbage*
Thornhill, Jan. *A tree in a forest*
   Wild in the city
Torgersen, Don Arthur. *The troll who lived in the lake*
Tresselt, Alvin R. *The beaver pond*
   The dead tree
   The gift of the tree
Van Laan, Nancy. *Round and round again*
Wahl, Jan. *Once when the world was green*
Waldman, Neil. *They came from the Bronx*
Ward, Helen. *The tin forest*
Wegen, Ron. *Where can the animals go?*
Weninger, Brigitte. *Precious water*
Wildsmith, Brian. *Professor Noah's spaceship*
Williams, Terry Tempest. *Between cattails*
Winer, Yvonne. *Frogs sing songs*
Winkelman, Barbara Gaines. *Sockeye's journey home*
Wood, Douglas. *Old Turtle*
Wright-Frierson, Virginia. *An island scrapbook*
Yardley, Thompson. *Buy now, pay later*
Yolen, Jane. *Welcome to the river of grass*
   Welcome to the sea of sand
   Where have the unicorns gone?

Ecuador *see* Foreign lands – Ecuador

Education *see* School

Eggs

Ada, Alma Flor. *Daniel's mystery egg*
Æsop. *The goose that laid the golden egg*
Andersen, H. C. (Hans Christian). *The woman with the eggs*
Asch, Frank. *MacGooses's grocery*
Auch, Mary Jane. *The Easter egg farm*
   Eggs mark the spot
Back, Christine. *Chicken and egg*
Balian, Lorna. *Humbug rabbit*
Barber, Antonia. *Gemma and the baby chick*
Bateson-Hill, Margaret. *Masha and the firebird*
Berenstain, Stan. *The Berenstain bears and the real Easter eggs*
Bourke, Linda. *Ethel's exceptional egg*
Brett, Jan. *Hedgie's surprise*
Brown, Margaret Wise. *The golden egg book*
Burton, Robert. *The egg*
Campbell, Rod. *Oh dear!*
Carter, David A. *Easter bugs*
Casey, Patricia. *Quack quack*
Chausse, Sylvie. *The egg and I*
Chorao, Kay. *Ida and Betty and the secret eggs*
Claret, Maria. *The chocolate rabbit*
Coontz, Otto. *The quiet house*

Dahl, Michael. *Eggs and legs*
Demi. *Little chick chick*
DePalma, Mary Newell. *The strange egg*
Desmoinaux, Christel. *Mrs. Hen's big surprise*
Dodds, Siobhan. *Elizabeth Hen*
Douglas, Erin. *Get that pest!*
Dunbar, Joyce. *Eggday*
Dunrea, Olivier. *Ollie*
    The trow-wife's treasure
Eastman, P. D. (Philip D.). *Flap your wings*
Egg-napped!
Eggs
Ernst, Lisa Campbell. *Zinnia and Dot*
Gill, Shelley. *The egg*
Goffin, Josse. *Yes*
Gordon, Sharon. *Easter Bunny's lost egg*
Halperin, Wendy Anderson. *When chickens grow teeth*
Hariton, Anca. *Egg story*
Hartmann, Wendy. *The dinosaurs are back and it's all your fault, Edward!*
Heller, Ruth. *Chickens aren't the only ones*
Hill, Eric. *Spot's first Easter*
Hoban, Lillian. *The case of the two masked robbers*
Hooks, William H. *Mr. Dinosaur*
Hooper, Meredith. *Seven eggs*
Howard, Reginald. *The big, big wall*
Imai, Miko. *Little Lumpty*
Isami, Ikuyo. *The fox's egg*
Jenkins, Priscilla Belz. *A nest full of eggs*
Joyce, William. *Bently and egg*
Kay, Helen. *An egg is for wishing*
Kellogg, Steven (Stephen). *A penguin pup for Pinkerton*
Kent, Jack. *The egg book*
Kimmel, Eric A. *The birds' gift*
Knüppel, Helga. *Christabel Crocodile's birthday egg*
Krauss, Ruth. *The happy egg*
Kumin, Maxine W. *Eggs of things*
Kwitz, Mary DeBall. *Little chick's story*
Landa, Norbert. *Rabbit and chicken count eggs*
    Rabbit and chicken play with colors
Lasell, Fen. *Fly away goose*
Lauber, Patricia. *What's hatching out of that egg?*
Leedy, Loreen. *Tracks in the sand*
Legg, Gerald. *From egg to chicken*
Levitin, Sonia. *A single speckled egg*
Lionni, Leo. *An extraordinary egg*
Lloyd, Megan. *Chicken tricks*
London, Jonathan. *Condor's egg*
Long, Earlene. *Johnny's egg*
Lorenz, Lee. *Dinah's egg*
McCrea, Lilian. *Mother hen*
MacDonald, Elizabeth. *Mr. MacGregor's breakfast egg*
McGovern, Ann. *Eggs on your nose*
Marzollo, Jean. *Ten little eggs*
Mathews, Louise. *Cluck one*
Meddaugh, Susan. *Harry on the rocks*
Merrick, Patrick. *Easter bunnies*
Meyer, Brigit. *Easter bunny saves the day*
    Little Easter surprise
Milgrom, Harry. *Egg-ventures*
Milhous, Katherine. *The egg tree*
Min, Laura. *Mrs. Sato's hens*
Mother Goose. *Humpty Dumpty*, ill. by Moira Kemp
Mussenbrock, Anne. *Easter Bunny saves the day*
    The little Easter surprise
Myers, Bernice. *The millionth egg*
Nakagawa, Rieko. *Guri and Gura*
Nethery, Mary. *Mary Veronica's egg*
Nicoll, Helen. *Meg's eggs*
Nolen, Jerdine. *Raising dragons*
O'Neill, Mary. *Big red hen*
Partridge, Elizabeth. *Pig's eggs*
Peet, Bill (William Bartlett). *The pinkish, purplish, bluish egg*
Polacco, Patricia. *Chicken Sunday*
    Just plain Fancy
    Rechenka's eggs
Potter, Beatrix. *The tale of Jemima Puddle-Duck*

Powell, Jillian. *Eggs*
Pursell, Margaret Sanford. *Jessie the chicken*
    Sprig the tree frog
Roberts, Bethany. *Easter mice*
Robertson, M. P. *The egg*
Rockwell, Anne F. *The gollywhopper egg*
    The wonderful eggs of Furicchia
Roddie, Shen. *Hatch, egg, hatch!*
Ross, Tom. *Eggbert, the slightly cracked egg*
Rouillard, Wendy. *Barnaby's bunny*
Ruelle, Karen Gray. *Easter egg disaster*
Ruurs, Margriet. *Emma's eggs*
San Souci, Robert D. *The talking eggs*
Scamell, Ragnhild. *Solo plus one*
Scarry, Richard. *Egg in the hole*
Schertle, Alice. *Down the road*
Schick, Eleanor. *A surprise in the forest*
Schubert, Ingrid. *Bear's eggs*
Selsam, Millicent E. *Egg to chick*
Seuss, Dr. *Horton hatches the egg*
Simmons, Jane. *Daisy and the egg*
Sklansky, Amy E. *Where do chicks come from?*
Smith, Mavis. *A snake mistake*
Standon, Anna. *Little duck lost*
Stevenson, James. *The great big especially beautiful Easter egg*
Sundgaard, Arnold. *Jethro's difficult dinosaur*
Sutcliff, Rosemary. *The minstrel and the dragon pup*
Sykes, Julie. *Dora's eggs*
Taylor, Shirley. *The cross in the egg*
Tildes, Phyllis Limbacher. *The magic babushka*
Tresselt, Alvin R. *The world in the candy egg*
Troughton, Joanna. *The quail's egg*
Tudor, Tasha. *A tale for Easter*
Vyner, Sue. *The stolen egg*
Waber, Bernard. *How to go about laying an egg*
Waddell, Martin. *It's quacking time*
Wahl, Jan. *The five in the forest*
Weigelt, Udo. *The Easter Bunny's baby*
Wilhelm, Hans. *More bunny trouble*
    Quacky Ducky's Easter egg
Wilkes, Larry. *The king's egg dance*
Wormell, Mary. *Hilda Hen's search*
Wright, Dare. *Edith and the duckling*
Ziefert, Harriet. *Happy Easter, Grandma!*

Egrets *see* Birds – egrets

Egypt *see* Foreign lands – Egypt

Egyptian language *see* Hieroglyphics

El Salvador *see* Foreign lands – El Salvador

Elderly *see* Old age

Electricians *see* Careers – electricians

Elephant seals *see* Animals – seals

Elephants *see* Animals – elephants

Elevators, escalators

Barner, Bob. *Elevator escalator book*
Farber, Norma. *Up the down elevator*
Murphy, Stuart J. *Elevator magic*
Reasoner, Charles. *The big busy building*
Sis, Peter. *Going up!*

Elk *see* Animals – elk

Elves *see* Mythical creatures – elves

Embarrassment *see* Emotions – embarrassment

Emergency medical technicians *see* Careers – emergency
medical technicians

Emotions

Aliki. *Feelings*

Allington, Richard L. *Feelings*

Alrawi, Karim. *The girl who lost her smile*

Ancona, George. *I feel*

Andersen, H. C. (Hans Christian). *The snow queen*, ill. by
Bernadette Watts

Andersen, Karen Born. *What's the matter, Sylvie, can't you ride?*

Anderson, Stephen Axel. *I know the moon*

Anholt, Catherine. *What I like*
What makes me happy?

Bach, Alice. *The day after Christmas*

Berger, Terry. *How does it feel when your parents get divorced?*
I have feelings
I have feelings too

Bienenfeld, Florence. *My mom and dad are getting a divorce*

Binch, Caroline. *Since Dad left*

Bluthenthal, Diana Cain. *I'm not invited?*

Bogacki, Tomasz. *I hate you! I like you!*

Borten, Helen. *Do you move as I do?*

Boyden, Linda. *The blue roses*

Brenner, Barbara A. *Faces, faces, faces*

Brown, Alan. *Hoot and Holler*

Brown, Laurie Krasny. *When dinosaurs die*

Brown, Tricia. *Someone special, just like you*

Brownridge, William Roy. *The moccasin goalie*

Bunting, Eve (Anne Evelyn). *I don't want to go to camp*
Sunshine home
Train to somewhere

Burdett, Lois. *The tempest for kids*

Burningham, John. *The baby*

Burrowes, Adjoa J. *Grandma's purple flowers*

Butterworth, Nick. *Making faces*

Cadnum, Michael. *The lost and found house*

Cain, Janan. *The way I feel*

Calhoun, Mary. *The witch who lost her shadow*

Campbell, Ann-Jeanette. *Dora's box*

Carter, David A. *If you're happy and you know it, clap your hands*

Castle, Sue. *Face talk, hand talk, body talk*

Christiansen, C. B. *My mother's house, my father's house*

Clark, Sue. *Feelings*

Clifford, Eth. *Your face is a picture*

Cole, William. *Frances face-maker*

Conta, Marcia Maher. *Feelings between brothers and sisters*
Feelings between friends
Feelings between kids and grownups
Feelings between kids and parents

Cowell, Cressida. *What shall we do with the Boo-Hoo Baby?*

Crary, Elizabeth. *I'm frustrated*

Cunningham, Julia. *A mouse called Junction*

Curtis, Gavin. *Grandma's baseball*

Curtis, Jamie Lee. *Today I feel silly and other moods that make my day*

Daly, Niki. *What's cooking, Jamela?*

Dragonwagon, Crescent. *Rainy day together*

Duerrstein, Richard. *Mickey is happy*

Dunbar, Polly. *Flyaway Katie*

Edvall, Lilian. *The rabbit who longed for home*

Edwards, Becky. *My first day at nursery school*

Eisenstein, Marilyn. *Periwinkle isn't Paris*

Emberley, Ed (Edward Randolph). *Glad monster, sad monster*

England, Linda. *The old cotton blues*

English, Karen. *Neeny coming, Neeny going*

Fernandes, Eugenie. *Sleepy little mouse*

Frame, Jeron Ashford. *Yesterday I had the blues*

Freedman, Claire. *Where's your smile, crocodile?*

Galdone, Paul. *The teeny-tiny woman*

Gallaz, Christophe. *Threadbear*

Got, Yves. *Sam loves kisses*

Grifalconi, Ann. *Kinda blue*

Grimes, Nikki. *Something on my mind*

Grossman, Bill. *My little sister hugged an ape*

Gugler, Laurel Dee. *Facing the day*

Hann, Jacquie. *Crybaby*

Harley, Bill. *Nothing happened*

Harper, Jessica. *Lizzy's ups and downs*

Harshman, Marc. *Moving days*

Hausman, Bonnie. *A to Z, do you ever feel like me?*

Hazen, Barbara Shook. *Good-bye/Hello*
Happy, sad, silly, mad
Two homes to live in

Heiligman, Deborah. *Mike Swan, sink or swim*

Helena, Ann. *The lie*

Hines, Anna Grossnickle. *Even if I spill my milk?*

Hoban, Russell. *La corona and the tin frog*
The marzipan pig
The stone doll of Sister Brute

Hobbie, Holly. *Toot and Puddle, you are my sunshine*

Hopkins, Lee Bennett. *I loved Rose Ann*

Hopkinson, Deborah. *Bluebird summer*

Horvath, Betty F. *Will the real Tommy Wilson please stand up?*

Hubbard, Woodleigh Marx. *C is for curious*

Hulme, Joy N. *Eerie feary feeling*

Inkpen, Mick. *Wibbly Pig is upset*

Isadora, Rachel. *At the crossroads*

Jackson, Ellen B. *Sometimes bad things happen*

Jenkins, Jessica. *Thinking about colors*

Johnson, Angela. *The leaving morning*

Johnson, Julie. *How do I feel about my stepfamily*

Johnston, Marianne. *Dealing with bullying*

Kaiser Johnson, Lee. *If I ran the family*

Karas, Jacqueline. *The doll house*

Keller, Holly. *Lizzie's invitation*

Kherdian, David. *Right now*

Kimmel, Haven. *Orville, a dog story*

Kiser, Kevin. *Buzzy Widget*

Knight, Joan. *Opal in the closet*

Knox-Wagner, Elaine. *My grandpa retired today*

Krauss, Ruth. *The bundle book*
You're just what I need

Lairla, Sergio. *Abel and the wolf*

Lalli, Judy. *Feelings alphabet*

Laskin, Pamela L. *Wish upon a star*

Lester, Helen. *Hurty feelings*

Levete, Sarah. *Looking after myself*

Lewin, Hugh. *Jafta*
Jafta – the homecoming
Jafta – the journey
Jafta – the town

McAllister, Angela. *The little blue rabbit*

Maccarone, Grace. *The lunch box surprise*

McCrea, James. *The magic tree*

McGovern, Ann. *Feeling mad, feeling sad, feeling bad, feeling glad*

MacLachlan, Patricia. *What you know first*

McLerran, Alice. *Hugs*

Mayer, Mercer. *Mine!*

Mayers, Patrick. *Just one more block*

Melmed, Laura Krauss. *A hug goes around*

Millen, C. M. *The low-down laundry line blues*

Miller, Kathryn Ann. *Did my first mother love me?*

Millward, David Wynn. *Jenny and Bob*

Mitchell, Cynthia. *Playtime*

Modesitt, Jeanne. *Sometimes I feel like a mouse*
The story of Z

Munsch, Robert N. *Aaron's hair*

Murdock, Laurette. *Someone is talking about Hortense*

Murphy, Mary. *I feel happy, and sad, and angry, and glad*

Musgrave, Susan. *Dreams are more real than bathtubs*

Napoli, Donna Jo. *Flamingo dream*

Nave, Yolanda. *Goosebumps and butterflies*

Ness, Evaline. *Pavo and the princess*

Nicholls, Judith. *Someone I like*

Norling, Beth. *The stone baby*

Numeroff, Laura Joffe. *The hope tree*

O'Donnell, Elizabeth Lee. *Maggie doesn't want to move*

Parr, Todd. *The feelings book*
Things that make you feel good, things that make you feel bad

Peacock, Carol Antoinette. *Mommy far, Mommy near*

Proimos, James. *The loudness of Sam*

Pursell, Margaret Sanford. *A look at divorce*

Ransom, Candice F. *When the whippoorwill calls*

Raschka, Christopher. *Ring! Yo?*
    Yo! Yes?
Robberecht, Thierry. *Stolen smile*
Rogers, Fred. *Adoption*
    Making friends
    Moving
Ross, Dave (David). *A book of hugs*
    A book of kisses
    More hugs!
Rotner, Shelley. *Feeling thankful*
Say, Allen. *Allison*
Selway, Martina. *Don't forget to write*
Senisi, Ellen B. *Hurray for pre-K!*
Sesame Street. *The Sesame Street book of people and things*
Sharratt, Nick. *I look like this*
Simon, Norma. *How do I feel?*
    I am not a crybaby!
Smith, Linda. *Mrs. Biddlebox*
Smith, Maggie (Margaret C.). *Desser, the best ever cat*
Smith, Wendy. *Twice mice*
Spelman, Cornelia Maude. *Mama and Daddy Bear's divorce*
    When I care about others
Stanton, Elizabeth. *Sometimes I like to cry*
Stevenson, James. *Fun, no fun*
Strauss, Anna. *Hush, Mama loves you*
Strauss, Gwen. *Trail of stones*
Sussman, Susan. *Hippo thunder*
Tabby, Abigail. *Baby face*
Taberski, Sharon. *Morning, noon, and night*
Thomas, Jane Resh. *Lights on the river*
Tobias, Tobi. *Moving day*
Tresselt, Alvin R. *What did you leave behind?*
Turner, Ethel. *Walking to school*
Vigna, Judith. *Saying goodbye to daddy*
Waber, Bernard. *Ira says goodbye*
Walsh, Ellen Stoll. *Two too much*
Weeks, Sarah. *My somebody special*
Wells, Rosemary. *Mama, don't go!*
Weninger, Brigitte. *Good-bye, daddy!*
Weston, Martha. *Bad baby brother*
Wight, Tamra. *The three grumpies*
Wild, Margaret. *Toby*
Willis, Jeanne. *Susan laughs*
Winthrop, Elizabeth. *Promises*
Wittels, Harriet. *Things I hate!*
Wolde, Gunilla. *This is Betsy*
Yudell, Lynn Deena. *Make a face*

Emotions – anger

Alexander, Martha G. *And my mean old mother will be sorry, Blackboard Bear*
Aliki. *We are best friends*
Andrews, F. Emerson (Frank Emerson). *Nobody comes to dinner*
Andrews, Jan. *The auction*
Aseltine, Lorraine. *I'm deaf and it's okay*
Bang, Molly. *When Sophie gets angry – really, really angry . . .*
Berridge, Celia. *Hannah's temper*
Boegehold, Betty. *Daddy doesn't live here anymore*
Bunting, Eve (Anne Evelyn). *Smoky night*
Carr, Jan. *Dark day, light night*
Cohn, Janice I. *"Why did it happen?"*
Cooper, Susan. *Jethro and the jumbie*
Couture, Susan Arkin. *Melanie Jane*
Craft, Ruth. *The day of the rainbow*
Crary, Elizabeth. *I'm mad*
    When you're mad and you know it
Cummings, Pat. *Carousel*
Demers, Dominique. *Old Thomas and the little fairy*
Du Bois, William Pène. *Bear party*
Duncan, Riana. *When Emily woke up angry*
Enright, Elizabeth. *Zeee*
Erickson, Karen. *I was so mad*
Everitt, Betsy. *Mean soup*
Fox, Mem. *Harriet, you'll drive me wild*
French, Vivian. *Tiger and the temper tantrum*
Frost, Helen. *Feeling angry*

Hapgood, Miranda. *Martha's mad day*
Harshman, Marc. *The storm*
Hautzig, Deborah. *Why are you so mean to me?*
Henkes, Kevin. *Lilly's purple plastic purse*
Hoban, Lillian. *Arthur's great big Valentine*
Howe, James. *Horace and Morris join the chorus (but what about Dolores?)*
Ikeda, Daisaku. *The princess and the moon*
Johnston, Marianne. *Dealing with anger*
Jones, Elizabeth. *Sunshine and Storm*
Joosse, Barbara M. *Dinah's mad, bad wishes*
Kroll, Steven. *That makes me mad*
Lachner, Dorothea. *Andrew's angry words*
    Danny, the angry lion
Langreuter, Jutta. *Little Bear and the big fight*
Lasky, Kathryn. *The tantrum*
Leonard, Marcia. *Angry*
Lester, Helen. *Princess Penelope's parrot*
Lewis, Kim. *Friends*
Lillie, Patricia. *Floppy teddy bear*
McBratney, Sam. *I'll always be your friend*
    I'm sorry
Mahy, Margaret. *Beaten by a balloon*
Morrison, Toni. *The book of mean people*
Moss, Miriam. *Smudge's grumpy day*
O'Malley, Kevin. *Humpty Dumpty egg-splodes*
Oram, Hiawyn. *Angry Arthur*
Palatini, Margie. *Goldie is mad*
Parkison, Jami. *Amazing Mallika*
Pieńkowski, Jan. *Bel and Bub and the bad snowball*
Rankin, Joan. *The little cat and the greedy old woman*
Sasso, Sandy Eisenberg. *Cain and Abel*
Shannon, David. *The amazing Christmas extravaganza*
Sharmat, Marjorie Weinman. *Attila the angry*
    I'm not Oscar's friend any more
    Rollo and Juliet . . . forever!
Shields, Carol Diggory. *I wish my brother was a dog*
Simon, Norma. *I was so mad!*
Small, David. *Paper John*
Spelman, Cornelia Maude. *When I feel angry*
Stein, Stephanie. *Lucy's feet*
Sunami, Kitoba. *How the fisherman tricked the genie*
Sykes, Julie. *Little Tiger's big surprise*
Tulloch, Richard. *Danny in the toybox*
Vail, Rachel. *Sometimes I'm Bombaloo*
Watson, Jane Werner. *Sometimes I get angry*
Widman, Christine. *Housekeeper of the wind*
Wilhelm, Hans. *Let's be friends again!*
Wormell, Mary. *Bernard the angry rooster*
Yorinks, Arthur. *Harry and Lulu*
Zolotow, Charlotte (Shapiro). *The quarreling book*

Emotions – embarrassment

Alexander, Martha G. *Sabrina*
Aylesworth, Jim. *Shenandoah Noah*
Boyd, Selma. *The how: making the best of a mistake*
Brown, Marc Tolon. *Arthur's underwear*
Bulla, Clyde Robert. *Daniel's duck*
Bunting, Eve (Anne Evelyn). *A picnic in October*
Carlson, Nancy L. *Loudmouth George and the big race*
Caseley, Judith. *Molly Pink*
Cazet, Denys. *Great-Uncle Felix*
Cooney, Nancy Evans. *Donald says thumbs down*
Corrigan, Kathy. *Emily Umily*
Davis, Gibbs. *Katy's first haircut*
Freeman, Don. *Quiet! There's a canary in the library*
Hirsh, Marilyn. *The pink suit*
Hoff, Syd. *A walk past Ellen's house*
Lexau, Joan M. *I should have stayed in bed*
Raschka, Christopher. *The blushful hippopotamus*
Shalev, Meir. *My father always embarrasses me*
Stanek, Muriel. *Left, right, left, right!*
Townsend, Kenneth. *Felix, the bald-headed lion*
Udry, Janice May. *How I faded away*
Wood, Audrey. *Weird parents*

Emotions – envy, jealousy

Abisch, Roz. *Mai-Ling and the mirror*
Alexander, Martha G. *Nobody asked me if I wanted a baby sister*
　When the new baby comes, I'm moving out
Armstrong, Jennifer. *King crow*
Asch, Frank. *Bear's bargain*
Aylesworth, Jim. *Mary's mirror*
Bach, Alice. *Millicent the magnificent*
Baker, Charlotte. *Little brother*
Beim, Jerrold. *Country mailman*
Best, Cari. *Top banana*
Brown, Ruth. *I don't like it!*
Bruna, Dick. *Dick Bruna's Snow-White and the seven dwarfs*
Buck, Pearl S. (Pearl Sydenstricker). *The Chinese story teller*
Bullock, Kathleen. *A surprise for Mitzi Mouse*
Bunting, Eve (Anne Evelyn). *Monkey in the middle*
Burningham, John. *Humbert, Mister Firkin and the Lord Mayor of London*
Caines, Jeannette. *I need a lunch box*
Calhoun, Mary. *High-wire Henry*
Carlson, Nancy L. *Poor Carl*
Castle, Caroline. *Herbert Binns and the flying tricycle*
Chottin, Ariane. *A home for Little Turtle*
　Little Goat's new horns
Chwast, Seymour. *Bushy bride*
Cole, Babette. *Hurray for Ethelyn*
Cole, Joanna. *The new baby at your house*
Conford, Ellen. *Why can't I be William?*
Cooper, Helen (Helen F.). *Little monster did it!*
Corey, Dorothy. *Will it ever be my birthday?*
Cottringer, Anne. *Ella and the naughty lion*
Cretan, Gladys Yessayan. *Lobo and Brewster*
Croft, Priscilla. *Dealing with jealousy*
Cutler, Jane. *Darcy and Gran don't like babies*
DeLage, Ida. *A bunny ride*
Demi. *The artist and the architect*
Doherty, Berlie. *Paddiwak and cozy*, ill. by Alison Bartlett
　Paddiwak and cozy, ill. by Teresa O'Brien
Drescher, Joan E. *My mother's getting married*
Egan, Tim. *A mile from Ellington station*
Eriksson, Eva. *Jealousy*
Ernst, Lisa Campbell. *Miss Penny and Mr. Grubbs*
Ferguson, Alane. *That new pet!*
Fienberg, Anna. *Joseph*
Fonteyn, Margot, Dame. *Coppélia*
Gantos, Jack (John, Jr.). *Back to school for Rotten Ralph*
　Rotten Ralph's rotten Christmas
Ganz, Yaffa. *The story of Mimmy and Simmy*
Gill, Joan. *Hush, Jon!*
Graham, Margaret Bloy. *Benjy and the barking bird*
Graham, Richard. *Jack and the monster*
Greenfield, Eloise. *She come bringing me that little baby girl*
Gretz, Susanna. *Frog in the middle*
Grimm, Jacob. *Snow White*, ill. by Trina Schart Hyman
　Snow White, ill. by Bernadette Watts
　Snow White, ill. by Claudia Wolf
　Snow White and Rose Red, ill. by Adrienne Adams
　Snow White and the seven dwarfs, ill. by Wanda Gág
　Snow White and the seven dwarves, ill. by Chihiro Iwasaki
Hathorn, Libby (Elizabeth). *Freya's fantastic surprise*
Hautzig, Deborah. *Grover's bad dream*
Havill, Juanita. *Jamaica and Brianna*
Hazen, Barbara Shook. *Why couldn't I be an only kid like you, Wigger?*
Hedderwick, Mairi. *Katie Morag and the tiresome Ted*
Hest, Amy. *You're the boss, Baby Duck*
Hoban, Russell. *A baby sister for Frances*
　A birthday for Frances
Hoffman, Rosekrans. *Sister Sweet Ella*
Howe, James. *I wish I were a butterfly*
Hubbard, Woodleigh. *Whoa, jealousy*
Jenkin-Pearce, Susie. *Bad Boris and the new kitten*
Joosse, Barbara M. *Nugget and Darling*
Joseph, Lynn. *Jump up time*
Keller, Holly. *Geraldine's baby brother*
Kellogg, Steven (Stephen). *Best friends*

Kimmel, Eric A. *Rimonah of the Flashing Sword*
Levete, Sarah. *Being jealous*
Levine, Abby. *Sometimes I wish I were Mindy*
Lindgren, Astrid. *I want a brother or sister*
Lionni, Leo. *Alexander and the wind-up mouse*
Ljungkvist, Laura. *Snow White and the seven dwarfs*
McAllister, Angela. *The battle of Sir Cob and Sir Filbert*
MacDonald, Maryann. *The pink party*
McGeorge, Constance W. *Boomer's big surprise*
McLenighan, Valjean. *You can go jump*
McMullan, Kate (Hall). *Nutcracker Noel*
Manushkin, Fran. *Little rabbit's baby brother*
Mario, Heidi Stetson. *I'd rather have an iguana*
Martin, Ann M. *Rachel Parker, kindergarten show-off*
Mathers, Petra. *Lottie's new friend*
Mayer, Mercer. *One frog too many*
Mayne, William. *Pandora*
Miller, Warren. *The goings on at Little Wishful*
Milligan, Bryce. *The prince of Ireland and the three magic stallions*
Mills, Claudia. *A visit to Amy-Claire*
Mills, Lauren A. *The goblin baby*
Moodie, Fiona. *Nabulela*
Moore, Liz. *Zizi and Tish*
Ormondroyd, Edward. *Theodore's rival*
Peet, Bill (William Bartlett). *The luckiest one of all*
Pushkin, Aleksandr Sergeevich. *The tale of Tsar Saltan*
Roop, Peter. *The buffalo jump*
Roper, Janice M. *Dancing on the moon*
Rosen, Michael (1946–). *Howler*
Russo, Marisabina. *The trouble with baby*
San Souci, Robert D. *Peter and the blue witch baby*
Satoshi, Kako. *Little Daruma and little Tengu*
Schick, Eleanor. *Peggy's new brother*
Shyer, Marlene Fanta. *Stepdog*
Skorpen, Liesel Moak. *His mother's dog*
Smalls-Hector, Irene. *Because you're lucky*
Stanley, Diane. *Siegfried*
Stephens, Helen. *What about me?*
Sykes, Julie. *Little Tiger's big surprise*
Velthuijs, Max. *Little Man to the rescue*
Vigna, Judith. *Couldn't we have a turtle instead?*
Voake, Charlotte. *Ginger*
Waber, Bernard. *Evie & Margie*
　Lyle and the birthday party
Wahl, Jan. *Mabel ran away with the toys*
Walt Disney Productions. *Walt Disney's Snow White and the seven dwarfs*
Watson, Jane Werner. *Sometimes I'm jealous*
Wild, Margaret. *Fox*
Winter, Susan. *A baby just like me*
Yep, Laurence. *Dragon prince*
Zemach, Margot. *To Hilda for helping*
Ziefert, Harriet. *Getting ready for new baby*
Zolotow, Charlotte (Shapiro). *It's not fair*

Emotions – fear

Aaron, Jane. *When I'm afraid*
Akass, Susan. *Number nine duckling*
Alborough, Jez. *It's the bear*
　Watch out! Big Bro's coming!
Alcantara, Ricardo. *Dog and cat*
Alderson, Sue Ann. *Wherever bears be*
Alexander, Anne (Anna Barbara Cooke). *Noise in the night*
Alexander, Martha G. *I'll protect you from the jungle beasts*
　Maybe a monster
Alexander, Sally Hobart. *Sarah's surprise*
Alexander, Sue. *Witch, Goblin and sometimes Ghost*
Anrooy, Frans van. *The sea horse*
Apple, Margot. *Brave Martha*
Arnold, Marsha Diane. *The bravest of us all*
Aseltine, Lorraine. *I'm deaf and it's okay*
Auch, Mary Jane. *Monster brother*
Aylesworth, Jim. *Siren in the night*
　Teddy bear tears
　Two terrible frights
Babbitt, Natalie. *The something*

Bailey, Linda. *When Addie was scared*
Baker, Ken. *Brave little monster*
Bannon, Laura. *Little people of the night*
    The scary thing
Barton, Byron. *Harry is a scaredy-cat*
Bauer, Marion Dane. *Jason's bears*
Baumgart, Klaus. *Don't be afraid, Tommy*
Beck, Scott. *Pepito the brave*
Benedek, Elissa P. *The secret worry*
Berenstain, Stan. *The Berenstain bears get stage fright*
    The Berenstain bears learn about strangers
Bergström, Gunilla. *Who's scaring Alfie Atkins?*
Berry, Christine. *Mama went walking*
Blegvad, Lenore. *Anna Banana and me*
Bonsall, Crosby Newell. *Who's afraid of the dark?*
Bourgeois, Paulette. *Franklin and the thunderstorm*
    Franklin in the dark
Boxall, Ed. *Francis the scaredy cat*
Bradbury, Ray. *Switch on the night*, ill. by Leo and Diane Dillion
    Switch on the night, ill. by Madeleine Gekiere
Brown, Margaret Wise. *Night and day*
Buck, Nola. *The basement stairs*
Bunting, Eve (Anne Evelyn). *Ghost's hour, spook's hour*
    Terrible things
Byfield, Barbara Ninde. *The haunted churchbell*
Caines, Jeannette. *Chilly stomach*
Callan, Elizabeth Koda. *Good luck pony*
Calmenson, Stephanie. *The kindergarten book*
    No stage fright for me!
Cameron, Ann. *Harry (the monster)*
Carlson, Melody. *When the creepy things come out*
Carlson, Nancy L. *Harriet's recital*
    There's a big, beautiful world out there!
    Witch lady
Carman, William. *What's that noise?*
Carrick, Carol. *Dark and full of secrets*
Cave, Kathryn. *You've got dragons*
Cazet, Denys. *Minnie and Moo meet Frankenswine*
    Mud baths for everyone
Chorao, Kay. *Lester's overnight*
    Shadow night
Church, Kristine. *My brother John*
Clifton, Lucille. *Amifika*
    Good, says Jerome
Cocca-Leffler, Maryann. *Bravery soup*
Cohen, Miriam. *Jim meets the thing*
    The real-skin rubber monster mask
Coles, Alison. *Michael and the sea*
    Michael in the dark
    Michael's first day
Company González, Mercé. *Killian and the dragons*
Compton, Kenn. *Granny Greenteeth and the noise in the night*
Conford, Ellen. *Eugene the brave*
Cooney, Nancy Evans. *Go away monsters, lickety split!*
Cooper, Helen (Helen F.). *The bear under the stairs*
Corey, Dorothy. *You go away*
Cowell, Cressida. *Hiccup the seasick Viking*
Credle, Ellis. *Big fraid, little fraid*
Crowe, Robert L. *Clyde monster*
Crum, Shutta. *The bravest of the brave*
Cunningham, Julia. *A mouse called Junction*
Cuyler, Margery. *Stop drop and roll*
Davis, Katie (Katie I.). *Scared stiff*
Devlin, Wende. *Aunt Agatha, there's a lion under the couch!*
Dickens, Lucy. *Go fish*
Dinardo, Jeffrey. *Timothy and the night noises*
Dodd, Lynley. *Hairy Maclary from Donaldson's dairy*
Dragonwagon, Crescent. *Will it be okay?*
Edwards, Michelle. *What's that noise?*
Egan, Tim. *The experiments of Doctor Vermin*
Emberley, Ed (Edward Randolph). *Go away, big green monster!*
Erickson, Karen. *It's dark – but I'm not scared*
Erlbruch, Wolf. *Leonard*
Farber, Werner. *Night lion*
Farmer, Bonnie. *Isaac's dreamcatcher*
Faulkner, Keith. *The scared little bear*
Figueredo, D. H. *When this world was new*

Fitzpatrick, Marie-Louise. *Lizzy and Skunk*
Flattinger, Hubert. *Stormy night*
Flood, Bo. *I'll go to school if . . .*
Foreman, Michael. *Surprise! Surprise!*
Frazee, Marla. *Roller coaster*
Freschet, Berniece. *Furlie Cat*
Frost, Helen. *Feeling scared*
Frost, Robert. *The runaway*
Gackenbach, Dick. *Harry and the terrible whatzit*
Gantos, Jack (John, Jr.). *Back to school for Rotten Ralph*
Gay, Michel. *Zee is not scared*
Gay, Zhenya. *Who's afraid?*
Gifford, Kathie Lee. *Giff the scaredy bear*
Gikow, Louise. *Boober Fraggle's ghosts*
Girard, Linda Walvoord. *Jeremy's first haircut*
Glaser, Linda. *Keep your socks on, Albert!*
Gliori, Debi. *A lion at bedtime*
Goldin, Barbara Diamond. *Night lights*
Goode, Diane. *I hear a noise*
Goodenow, Earle. *The owl who hated the dark*
Gorbachev, Valeri. *Nicky and the big, bad wolves*
Graham, Margaret Bloy. *Benjy and his friend Fifi*
Grant, Joan. *The monster that grew small*
Greenberg, Barbara. *The bravest babysitter*
Greene, Rhonda Gowler. *Eek! Creak! Snicker, sneak*
Gregory, Valiska. *Kate's giants*
Gretz, Susanna. *Hide-and-seek*
    Too dark!
Grifalconi, Ann. *Darkness and the butterfly*
Hall, Derek. *Otter swims*
    Panda climbs
    Tiger runs
Hamilton, Morse. *Who's afraid of the dark?*
Hanlon, Emily. *What if a lion eats me and I fall into a hippopotamus' mud hole?*
Hanson, Joan. *I won't be afraid*
Hanson, Regina. *The face at the window*
Harlow, Joan Hiatt. *Shadow bear*
Harrison, Joanna. *Dear bear*
Harshman, Marc. *The storm*
Hawkins, Colin. *Snap! Snap!*
Hazen, Barbara Shook. *Fang*
    The knight who was afraid of the dark
    The knight who was afraid to fight
    Wally the worry-warthog
Heide, Florence Parry. *Some things are scary*
    Timothy Twinge
Hendry, Diana. *Dog Donovan*
    The very noisy night
Hesse, Karen. *Lester's dog*
Hest, Amy. *Off to school, Baby Duck*
    A sort-of sailor
Higgs, Liz Curtis. *Go away, dark night*
Hill, Susan. *Go away, bad dreams!*
Himmelman, John. *Lights out!*
Hindley, Judy. *Maybe it's a pirate*
Hines, Anna Grossnickle. *My own big bed*
    Rumble thumble boom!
Hoban, Russell. *Bedtime for Frances*
    Goodnight
    Jim's lion
Honeycutt, Natalie. *Whistle home*
Hooks, William H. *The mighty Santa Fe*
Howe, James. *There's a monster under my bed*
Huth, Holly Young. *Darkfright*
Impey, Rose. *The ankle grabber*
    The flat man
    Jumble Joan
    Scare yourself to sleep
Inkpen, Mick. *Penguin small*
Jackson, Jean. *Big lips and hairy arms*
Jackson, Shelley. *The old woman and the wave*
Jacobson, Jennifer Richard. *A net of stars*
James, Betsy. *Flashlight*
Jay, Betsy. *Swimming lessons*
Jennings, Sharon. *No monsters here*
    Priscilla's paw de deux

Johnston, Tony. *Goblin walk*
  Little Rabbit goes to sleep
Jonas, Ann. *Holes and peeks*
Jones, Rebecca C. *Down at the bottom of the deep dark sea*
Joosse, Barbara M. *Spiders in the fruit cellar*
Julian, Alison. *Brave as a bunny can be*
Kasza, Keiko. *When the elephant walks*
Keller, Beverly. *Pimm's place*
Keller, Holly. *Brave Horace*
Kelley, True. *Day-care teddy bear*
Kimura, Yuichi. *One stormy night . . .*
  One sunny day . . .
Kinsey-Warnock, Natalie. *On a starry night*
Kirk, David. *Miss Spider's tea party*
Kitamura, Satoshi. *Lily takes a walk*
Klinting, Lars. *Regal the golden eagle*
Koller, Jackie French. *No such thing*
Koralek, Jenny. *The boy and the cloth of dreams*
Kraus, Robert. *Noel the coward*
Krensky, Stephen. *Fraidy Cats*
Lakin, Pat (Patricia). *Don't touch my room*
Laminack, Lester L. *Trevor's wiggly-wobbly tooth*
Lamm, C. Drew. *Pirates*
LaRose, Linda. *Jessica takes charge*
Layne, Steven L. *My brother Dan's delicious*
Leaf, Munro. *Boo, who used to be scared of the dark*
Lears, Laurie. *Ben has something to say*
Lemberg, Stephen H. *Scaredy dog*
Lester, Helen. *Something might happen*
Lifton, Betty Jean. *Goodnight orange monster*
Lin, Grace. *Olvina flies*
Lindbergh, Reeve. *Bridget and the gray wolves*
Lindgren, Astrid. *The ghost of Skinny Jack*
Little, Jean. *Jess was the brave one*
London, Jonathan. *Froggy learns to swim*
Lottridge, Celia Barker. *Something might be hiding*
Low, Joseph. *Benny rabbit and the owl*
  Boo to a goose
Lyon, George Ella. *Cecil's story*
McBratney, Sam. *The dark at the top of the stairs*
McCully, Emily Arnold. *The evil spell*
  Mirette on the high wire
McDonald, Megan. *Bedbugs*
McGhee, Alison. *Countdown to kindergarten*
McMullan, Kate (Hall). *Good night, Stella*
Mahy, Margaret. *Beaten by a balloon*
Maitland, Barbara. *The bear who didn't like honey*
Mallat, Kathy. *Brave bear*
Martin, C. L. G. *Three brave women*
Martin, Jacqueline Briggs. *Bizzy Bones and Uncle Ezra*
  Grandmother Bryant's pocket
Martín Larrañaga, Ana. *Woo! The not-so-scary Ghost*
Mathews, Judith. *Nathaniel Willy, scared silly*
Mayer, Mercer. *There's a nightmare in my closet*
  There's an alligator under my bed
  There's something in my attic
  You're the scaredy cat
Meredith, Carol. *Jamie Anderson wouldn't . . .*
Michelson, Richard. *Did you say ghosts?*
Milich, Melissa. *Can't scare me!*
Miller, William. *A house by the river*
Moers, Hermann. *Katie and the big, brave bear*
Mollel, Tololwa M. (Tololwa Marti). *Rhinos for lunch and elephants*
  for supper
Moodie, Fiona. *Noko and the night monster*
Moore, Inga. *A big day for Little Jack*
Moore, Lilian. *Little Raccoon and the thing in the pool*
Morgan, Michaela. *Brave, brave mouse*
Morris, Winifred. *What if the shark wears tennis shoes?*
Moss, Marissa. *After-school monster*
Most, Bernard. *Boo!*
Myers, Christopher A. *Turnip soup*
Myers, Walter Dean. *How Mr. Monkey saw the whole world*
Namioka, Lensey. *The loyal cat*
Nash, Ogden. *The adventures of Isabel*, ill. by Walter Lorraine
  The adventures of Isabel, ill. by James Marshall
Nivola, Claire A. *The forest*

O'Donnell, Peter. *Moonlit journey*
Olofsdotter, Marie. *Sofia and the Heartmender*
Oppenheim, Joanne. *"Uh-oh!" said the crow*
Oppenheim, Shulamith Levey. *The lily cupboard*
Ostheeren, Ingrid. *Martin and the Pumpkin Ghost*
Packard, Mary. *We are monsters*
Palecek, Libuse. *Brave as a tiger*
Paraskevas, Betty. *Maggie and the Ferocious Beast, the big scare*
Park, Barbara. *Psssst! It's me . . . the Bogeyman*
Patschke, Steve. *The spooky book*
Peck, Richard. *Monster night at Grandma's house*
Pfister, Marcus. *Rainbow fish to the rescue!*
Pittman, Helena Clare. *Once when I was scared*
Pizer, Abigail. *Nosey Gilbert*
Polacco, Patricia. *Thunder cake*
Potok, Chaim. *The sky of now*
Powell, Polly. *Just dessert*
Pryor, Bonnie. *The porcupine mouse*
Pumphrey, Jerome. *Creepy things are scaring me*
Rael, Elsa Okon. *When Zaydeh danced on Eldridge Street*
Raschka, Christopher. *Can't sleep*
  Waffle
Ratnett, Michael. *Marmaduke and the scary story*
Reed, Jonathan. *Do armadillos come in houses?*
Reeves, Mona Rabun. *The spooky eerie night noise*
Reynolds, Marilynn. *The name of the child*
Robbins, Beth. *Tom, Ally, and the baby-sitter*
  Tom and Ally visit the doctor
  Tom's afraid of the dark
  Tom's new haircut
Robison, Deborah. *No elephants allowed*
Rockwell, Anne F. *Katie Catz makes a splash*
  Welcome to kindergarten
Roddie, Shen. *Help, Mama, help!*
Rodgers, Frank. *Who's afraid of the ghost train?*
Rosenberry, Vera. *Vera's first day of school*
Ross, Pat. *Your first airplane trip*
Ross, Tony. *Happy blanket*
  I'm coming to get you!
Sabraw, John. *I wouldn't be scared*
Sanromán, Susana. *Señora Reganoña*
Schaefer, Charles E. *Cat's got your tongue?*
Scheffler, Ursel. *Be brave, little lion!*
Schertle, Alice. *The gorilla in the hall*
Schuurmans, Hilde. *Sydney won't swim*
Scruton, Clive. *Scaredy cat*
Senshu, Noriko. *Sonny's dream*
Seuss, Dr. *The Sneetches, and other stories*
Shah, Idries. *The clever boy and the terrible, dangerous animal*
Shortall, Leonard W. *Tony's first dive*
Simms, Laura. *The squeaky door*
Slepian, Jan. *Emily just in time*
Smith, Janice Lee. *The monster in the third dresser drawer and other*
  stories about Adam Joshua
Smith, Maggie (Margaret C.). *There's a witch under the stairs*
Spelman, Cornelia Maude. *When I feel scared*
Spinelli, Eileen. *A safe place called home*
  Wanda's monster
Spohn, Kate. *Turtle and Snake go camping*
Steel, Danielle. *Max and the baby sitter*
Stevenson, Drew. *The ballad of Penelope Lou . . . and me*
Stevenson, Harvey. *Big scary wolf*
Stevenson, James. *What's under my bed?*
Stewart, Shannon. *Sea crow*
Stock, Catherine. *Halloween monster*
Strand, Mark. *The night book*
Stroud, Bettye. *Dance y'all*, ill. by Cornelious Van Wright & Ying-
  Hwa Hu
Stubbs, Joanna. *With cat's eyes you'll never be scared of the dark*
Szilagyi, Mary. *Thunderstorm*
Taulbert, Clifton L. *Little Cliff's first day of school*
Taylor, Anelise. *Lights on, lights off*
Thiesing, Lisa. *The Viper*
This place I know
Thompson, Richard. *The night walker*
Thornhill, Jan. *The rumor*
Tomlinson, Jill. *The owl who was afraid of the dark*

Tompert, Ann. *The Tzar's bird*
    Will you come back for me?
Townson, Hazel. *Terrible Tuesday*
Trez, Denise. *The royal hiccups*
Tsutsui, Yoriko. *Anna in charge*
Tyger, Rory. *Newton*
Udry, Janice May. *Alfred*
Vigna, Judith. *Nobody wants a nuclear war*
Viorst, Judith. *My mama says there aren't any zombies, ghosts, vampires, creatures, demons, monsters, fiends, goblins, or things*
Vogel, Ilse-Margret. *The don't be scared book*
Waddell, Martin. *Can't you sleep, Little Bear?*
    Let's go home, Little Bear
    Owl babies
    Owl babies [board book]
    The park in the dark
    Tom Rabbit
Waldron, Jan L. *John Pig's Halloween*
Wallace, Ian. *Chin Chiang and the dragon's dance*
Wallen, Ila. *The moon in my room*
Walsh, Ellen Stoll. *Pip's magic*
Ward, Nick. *Come on Baby Duck*
Watson, Jane Werner. *Sometimes I'm afraid*
Weston, Martha. *Tuck in the pool*
Wharton, Thomas. *Hildegard sings*
Whishaw, Iona. *Henry and the cow problem*
Whybrow, Ian. *Harry and the dinosaurs say "Raahh"*
Widerberg, Siv. *The boy and the dog*
Williams, Gweneira Maureen. *Timid Timothy, the kitten who learned to be brave*
Williams, Linda. *The little old lady who was not afraid of anything*
Willis, Jeanne. *The monster bed*
    The monster storm
Wilson, Budge. *The fear of Angelina Domino*
Wilson-Max, Ken. *Max's starry night*
Winters, Kay. *The teeny tiny ghost*
    Whooo's haunting the teeny tiny ghost?
Winthrop, Elizabeth. *Potbellied possums*
Winton, Tim. *The deep*
Wishinsky, Frieda. *Give Maggie a chance*
    Nothing scares us
Wolf, Bernard. *Michael and the dentist*
Wondriska, William. *The stop*
Wynne-Jones, Tim. *On Tumbledown Hill*
Zarin, Cynthia. *Rose and Sebastian*
Ziefert, Harriet. *Egad, alligator!*
Zolotow, Charlotte (Shapiro). *The storm book*

Emotions – grief

Adoff, Arnold. *The return of Rex and Ethel*
Arnold, Caroline. *What we do when someone dies*
Baker, Betty. *Rat is dead and ant is sad*
Barker, Peggy. *What happened when grandma died*
Barron, T. A. *Where is Grandpa?*
Bartoli, Jennifer. *Nonna*
Bernstein, Joanne E. *When people die*
The best cat in the world
Boase, Susan. *Lucky boy*
Brown, Margaret Wise. *The dead bird*
Bunting, Eve (Anne Evelyn). *The memory string*
    Rudi's pond
Burningham, John. *Grandpa*
Carlstrom, Nancy White. *Blow me a kiss, Miss Lilly*
Carrick, Carol. *The accident*
Carson, Jo. *You hold me and I'll hold you*
Caseley, Judith. *When Grandpa came to stay*
Clifton, Lucille. *Everett Anderson's goodbye*
Cohen, Miriam. *Jim's dog Muffins*
Cohn, Janice I. *I had a friend named Peter*
    Molly's rosebush
Cooke, Trish. *The grandad tree*
Cooney, Barbara. *Island boy*
Coutant, Helen. *First snow*
Coville, Bruce. *My grandfather's house*
Dabcovich, Lydia. *Mrs. Huggins and her hen Hannah*

De Paola, Tomie (Thomas Anthony). *Nana Upstairs and Nana Downstairs*, 1973
    Nana Upstairs and Nana Downstairs, 1998
DiSalvo-Ryan, DyAnne. *A dog like Jack*
Doray, Malika. *One more Wednesday*
Edwards, Michelle. *Papa's latkes*
Ewart, Claire. *The giant*
Fassler, Joan. *My grandpa died today*
Fletcher, Ralph J. *Grandpa never lies*
Fox, Louisa. *Every Monday in the mailbox*
Fritts, Mary Bahr. *If Nathan were here*
Gould, Deborah. *Grandpa's slide show*
Greenlee, Sharon. *When someone dies*
Gregory, Nan. *Wild Girl and Gran*
Grifalconi, Ann. *Tiny's hat*
Grimm, Edward. *The doorman*
Hallinan, P. K. (Patrick K.). *Three freckles past a hair*
Hanson, Regina. *A season for mangoes*
Harranth, Wolf. *My old grandad*
Harriott, Ted. *Coming home*
Harris, Robie H. *Goodbye, Mousie*
Haynes, Max. *Grandma's gone to live in the stars*
Hazen, Barbara Shook. *Why did Grandpa die?*
Hesse, Karen. *Poppy's chair*
Heymans, Annemie. *The princess in the kitchen garden*
Hill, Frances. *The bug cemetery*
Hines, Anna Grossnickle. *Remember the butterflies*
Hoffmann, E. T. A. *The strange child*
Hogan, Bernice. *My grandmother died but I won't forget her*
Hoopes, Lyn Littlefield. *Nana*
Howard, Ellen. *Murphy and Kate*
Jewell, Nancy. *Time for Uncle Joe*
Johnston, Tony. *That summer*
Joslin, Mary. *The goodbye boat*
Kadono, Eiko. *Grandpa's soup*
Kaldhol, Marit. *Goodbye Rune*
Kantrowitz, Mildred. *When Violet died*
Kaplan, Howard. *Waiting to sing*
Keller, Holly. *Goodbye, Max*
Lanton, Sandy. *Daddy's chair*
Leavy, Una. *Good-bye, Papa*
Leiner, Katherine. *Mama does the mambo*
Le Tord, Bijou. *My Grandma Leonie*
Levete, Sarah. *When people die*
Limb, Sue. *Come back, Grandma*
London, Jonathan. *Liplap's wish*
Lyon, George Ella. *Ada's pal*
Madenski, Melissa. *Some of the pieces*
Maguire, Gregory. *Lucas Fishbone*
Maple, Marilyn J. *On the wings of a butterfly*
Martin, Jacqueline Briggs. *Grandmother Bryant's pocket*
Mendoza, George. *The hunter I might have been*
Monk, Isabell. *Blackberry stew*
Morehead, Debby. *A special place for Charlee*
Napoli, Donna Jo. *Flamingo dream*
Newman, Lesléa. *Too far away to touch*
Nickle, John. *TV Rex*
Nobisso, Josephine. *Grandpa loved*
Nodar, Carmen Santiago. *Abuelita's paradise*
Old, Wendie C. *Stacy had a little sister*
Oliviero, Jamie. *Som See and the magic elephant*
Onyefulu, Ifeoma. *Saying goodbye*
Parker, Marjorie. *Jasper's day*
Peavy, Linda. *Allison's grandfather*
Pollack, Eileen. *Whisper whisper Jesse, whisper whisper Josh*
Porte, Barbara Ann. *Harry's mom*
Puttock, Simon. *A story for Hippo*
Rappaport, Doreen. *The new king*
Recknagel, Friedrich. *Sarah's willow*
Rogers, Fred. *When a pet dies*
Roper, Janice M. *Dancing on the moon*
Rosen, Michael J. (1954–). *Bonesy and Isabel*
Rosenberg, Liz. *The carousel*
Roth, Susan L. *Another Christmas*
Russo, Marisabina. *Grandpa Abe*
Sanford, Doris. *David has AIDS*
Santucci, Barbara. *Anna's corn*

Scheller, Melanie. *My grandfather's hat*
Schick, Eleanor. *Mama*
Simmonds, Posy. *Fred*
Simon, Norma. *The saddest time*
Smith-Ayala, Emilie. *Marisol and the yellow messenger*
Stafford, Liliana. *Just dragon*
Stein, Sara Bonnett. *About dying*
Stevens, Margaret (Dean). *When grandpa died*
Stiles, Norman. *I'll miss you, Mr. Hooper*
Stilz, Carol Curtis. *Kirsty's kite*
This place I know
Thomas, Jane Resh. *Saying good-bye to grandma*
Tibo, Gilles. *The grand journey of Mr. Man*
Townsend, Maryann. *Pop's secret*
Trottier, Maxine. *Prairie willow*
Ulmer, Wendy K. *A campfire for cowboy Billy*
Van den Berg, Marinus. *The three birds*
Vigna, Judith. *Saying goodbye to daddy*
Viorst, Judith. *The tenth good thing about Barney*
Wahl, Mats. *Grandfather's laika*
Wallace-Brodeur, Ruth. *Goodbye, Mitch*
Warfel, Elizabeth Stuart. *The blue pearls*
Weigelt, Udo. *Bear's last journey*
Weitzman, Elizabeth. *Let's talk about when a parent dies*
Wilhelm, Hans. *I'll always love you*
Wittbold, Maureen. *Mending Peter's heart*
Wood, Douglas. *Grandad's prayers of the earth*
Woodson, Jacqueline. *Sweet, sweet memory*
Wright, Betty Ren. *The cat next door*
Zalben, Jane Breskin. *Pearl's marigolds for grandpa*
Ziefert, Harriet. *Ode to Humpty Dumpty*
Zolotow, Charlotte (Shapiro). *My grandson Lew*
The old dog

Emotions – happiness

Asch, George. *Linda*
Carlson, Nancy L. *Life is fun*
Cohen, Caron Lee. *Happy to you!*
Czernecki, Stefan. *Pancho's piñata*
Dodd, Lynley. *Schnitzel von Krumm's basketwork*
Frost, Helen. *Feeling happy*
Jackson, Ellen B. *Sometimes bad things happen*
Lloyd, David. *Polly Molly Woof Woof*
Low, Joseph. *The Christmas grump*
McBratney, Sam. *Once there was a Hoodie*
McCrea, James. *The magic tree*
McCully, Emily Arnold. *Crossing the new bridge*
Miller, Edward. *The curse of Claudia*
Miryam. *The happy man and his dump truck*
Ormerod, Jan. *If you're happy and you know it!*
Parr, Todd. *The feel good book*
Paschkis, Julie. *So happy/So sad*
Piatti, Celestino. *The happy owls*
Rice, Eve. *What Sadie sang*
Rylant, Cynthia. *The wonderful happens*
Schwarz, Viviane. *The adventures of a nose*
Starr, Meg. *Alicia's happy day*
Steig, William. *Spinky sulks*
Swain, Gwenyth. *Smiling*
Tapio, Pat Decker. *The lady who saw the good side of everything*
Thomas, Joyce Carol. *Joy*
Tobias, Tobi. *Jane wishing*
Tripp, Paul. *The strawman who smiled by mistake*
Weedn, Flavia. *I feel happy*
The ragged peddler
Wilcox, Brad. *Hip, hip, hooray for Annie McRae!*
Williams, Barbara. *Someday, said Mitchell*
Wondriska, William. *Mr. Brown and Mr. Gray*
Yabuki, Seiji. *I love the morning*
Ziefert, Harriet. *The snow child*

Emotions – hate

Udry, Janice May. *Let's be enemies*
Zolotow, Charlotte (Shapiro). *The hating book*

Emotions – jealousy *see* Emotions – envy, jealousy

Emotions – loneliness

Aardema, Verna. *The lonely lioness and the ostrich chicks*
Abley, Mark. *Ghost cat*
Alborough, Jez. *My friend bear*
Alexander, Sue. *Dear Phoebe*
Aliki. *We are best friends*
Allan, Nicholas. *The bird*
Allard, Harry. *Crash helmet*
Ardizzone, Edward. *Lucy Brown and Mr. Grimes*
Ballard, Robin. *My father is far away*
Battles, Edith. *One to teeter-totter*
Blegvad, Lenore. *Mr. Jensen and cat*
Bolliger, Max. *The lonely prince*
Brett, Jan. *Annie and the wild animals*
Bröger, Achim. *Francie's paper puppy*
Brown, Marcia. *The little carousel*
Buck, Pearl S. (Pearl Sydenstricker). *The little fox in the middle*
Buckley, Helen Elizabeth. *Moonlight kite*
Buntain, Ruth Jaeger. *The birthday story*
Bunting, Eve (Anne Evelyn). *The big cheese*
Burningham, John. *Aldo*
Chenault, Nell. *Parsifal the Poddley*
Chess, Victoria. *Poor Esmé*
Clewes, Dorothy. *Happiest day*
Coatsworth, Elizabeth. *Lonely Maria*
Conaway, Judith. *I'll get even*
Conger, Marion. *The chipmunk that went to church*
Coontz, Otto. *The quiet house*
Cort, Ben. *Pigs can't fly!*
Craven, Carolyn. *What the mailman brought*
Cummings, W. T. (Walter Thies). *The kid*
Delton, Judy. *Lee Henry's best friend*
My grandma's in a nursing home
Drawson, Blair. *Flying Dimitri*
Duvoisin, Roger Antoine. *Periwinkle*
Ellis, Anne Leo. *Dabble Duck*
Fatio, Louise. *The happy lion roars*
Fujikawa, Gyo. *Shags finds a kitten*
Funazaki, Yasuko. *Baby owl*
Gág, Wanda. *Nothing at all*
Gliori, Debi. *The snowchild*
Godard, Alex. *Idora*
Goffstein, M. B. (Marilyn Brooke). *Neighbors*
Golembe, Carla. *Annabelle's big move*
Gorbachev, Valeri. *Big Little Elephant*
Halpern, Julie. *Toby and the snowflakes*
Harranth, Wolf. *My old grandad*
Hobbs, Will. *Howling Hill*
Hofsepian, Sylvia A. *Why not?*
Hughes, Shirley. *Abel's moon*
Moving Molly
Jackson, Ellen B. *Boris the boring boar*
Jahn-Clough, Lisa. *On the hill*
James, J. Alison. *The bears' Christmas surprise*
Kadono, Eiko. *Grandpa's soup*
Keats, Ezra Jack. *The trip*
Kerr, Judith. *The other goose*
Kesselman, Wendy Ann. *Angelita*
Emma
Khalsa, Dayal Kaur. *How pizza came to Queens*
Knaff, Jean Christian. *Manhattan*
Labatt, Mary. *A friend for Sam*
Lachner, Dorothea. *Look out, Cinder!*
Levete, Sarah. *Making friends*
Levin, Miriam Ramsfelder. *In the beginning*
Lewin, Ted. *Nilo and the tortoise*
Lukesová, Milena. *The little girl and the rain*
Lund, Jillian. *Two cool coyotes*
Luttrell, Ida. *Lonesome Lester*
McClure, Gillian. *What's the time, Rory Wolf?*
McCormick, Wendy. *Daddy, will you miss me?*
McGovern, Ann. *Mr. Skinner's skinny house*
Nicholas Bentley Stoningpot III
McNeer, May Yonge. *My friend Mac*

Munthe, Adam John. *I believe in unicorns*
Murphy, Shirley Rousseau. *Valentine for a dragon*
Nomura, Takaaki. *Grandpa's town*
Norac, Carl. *I love to cuddle*
Norton, Natalie. *A little old man*
Norwich, William D. *Molly and the magic dress*
Novak, Matt. *Gertie and Gumbo*
Olsen, Ib Spang. *The grown-up trap*
Park, W. B. *The costume party*
Pearson, Tracey Campbell. *The howling dog*
Pfister, Marcus. *The rainbow fish*
Pilkey, Dav. *A friend for Dragon*
Ring, Elizabeth. *Some stuff*
Rylant, Cynthia. *Mr. Putter and Tabby pour the tea*
Sanfield, Steve. *The girl who wanted a song*
Sarton, May. *Punch's secret*
Scamell, Ragnhild. *Who likes Wolfie?*
Seignobosc, Françoise. *The story of Colette*
Siekkinen, Raija. *Mister King*
Skurzynski, Gloria. *Martin by himself*
Slate, Joseph. *Lonely Lula cat*
Smith, Wendy. *The lonely, only mouse*
Sonneborn, Ruth A. *Lollipop's party*
Spang, Günter. *Clelia and the little mermaid*
Spelman, Cornelia Maude. *When I miss you*
Spinelli, Eileen. *Somebody loves you, Mr. Hatch*
Spurr, Elizabeth. *The long, long letter*
Stage, Mads. *The lonely squirrel*
Stanek, Muriel. *All alone after school*
Stevenson, James. *Mr. Hacker*
Stren, Patti. *Hug me*
Sugita, Yutaka. *Helena the unhappy hippopotamus*
Surany, Anico. *Kati and Kormos*
Timlock, Jason. *Basil, the loneliest boy*
Titherington, Jeanne. *A place for Ben*
Vries, Anke de. *Grey mouse*
Waber, Bernard. *Gina*
Waddell, Martin. *The hidden house*
  Sam Vole and his brothers
Wagener, Gerda. *Leo the lion*
Wallner, Alexandra. *Beatrix Potter*
Walter, Mildred Pitts. *My mama needs me*
Ward, Helen. *The dragon machine*
Weigelt, Udo. *The Sandman*
Wells, Rosemary. *Small world of Binky Braverman*
Wheeler, Lisa. *Porcupining*
Wild, Margaret. *Fox*
Wormell, Christopher. *The big ugly monster and the little stone rabbit*
Wright, Dare. *A gift from the lonely doll*
  The lonely doll
Yashima, Taro. *Crow boy*
Zindel, Paul. *I love my mother*
Zolotow, Charlotte (Shapiro). *The bunny who found Easter*
  Janey
  Three funny friends
  A tiger called Thomas, ill. by Catherine Stock
  A tiger called Thomas, ill. by Kurt Werth

Emotions – love

Adoff, Arnold. *Love letters*
Agostinelli, Maria Enrica. *On wings of love*
Alexander, Sue. *Dear Phoebe*
  Nadia the willful
Allancé, Mireille d'. *How long?*
Anastas, Margaret. *A hug for you*
  Mommy's best kisses
Andersen, H. C. (Hans Christian). *The snow queen*, ill. by Angela Barrett
  The snow queen, ill. by Toma Bogdanovic
  The snow queen, ill. by June Atkin Corwin
  The snow queen, ill. by Sally Holmes
  The snow queen, ill. by Susan Jeffers
  The snow queen, ill. by Errol Le Cain
  The snow queen, ill. by Arieh Zeldich
Anglund, Joan Walsh. *Christmas is love*
  Love is a baby

  Love is a special way of feeling
Appelt, Kathi. *Oh my baby, little one*
Babbitt, Natalie. *Bub, or, The very best thing*
Baker, Keith. *The dove's letter*
Baker, Liza. *I love you because you're you*
Barrett, Joyce Durham. *Willie's not the hugging kind*
Bartoletti, Susan Campbell. *Silver at night*
Baynton, Martin. *Why do you love me?*
Berger, Barbara Helen. *The jewel heart*
Bergström, Gunilla. *You have a girlfriend, Alfie Atkins?*
Bianco, Margery Williams. *The velveteen rabbit*, ill. by Allen Atkinson
  The velveteen rabbit, ill. by Monique Félix
  The velveteen rabbit, ill. by Michael Green
  The velveteen rabbit, ill. by Michael Hague
  The velveteen rabbit, ill. by Estella Hickman
  The velveteen rabbit, ill. by Steve Johnson & Lou Fancher
  The velveteen rabbit, ill. by David Jorgensen
  The velveteen rabbit, ill. by Thea Kliros
  The velveteen rabbit, ill. by Elizabeth Miles
  The velveteen rabbit, ill. by William Nicholson
  The velveteen rabbit, ill. by Robyn Officer
  The velveteen rabbit, ill. by Ilse Plume
  The velveteen rabbit, ill. by S. D. Schindler
  The velveteen rabbit, ill. by Tien
Bible. New Testament. Corinthians, 1st, XIII. *Love is*
Billam, Rosemary. *Fuzzy rabbit*
Birdseye, Tom. *A song of stars*
Boegehold, Betty. *Pawpaw's run*
Boyle, Vere. *Beauty and the beast*
Brown, Palmer. *Something for Christmas*
Buckley, Helen Elizabeth. *Grandmother and I*
Bunting, Eve (Anne Evelyn). *Swan in love*
Burdett, Lois. *Romeo and Juliet for kids*
Calmenson, Stephanie. *Perfect puppy*
Capucilli, Alyssa Satin. *Bear hugs*
Carmichael, Clay. *Used-up Bear*
Carter, Anne Laurel. *Beauty and the beast*
Caseley, Judith. *Dear Annie*
Cazet, Denys. *Minnie and Moo: will you be my Valentine?*
Cheshire, Marc. *Love & kisses, Eloise*
Clifton, Lucille. *Everett Anderson's goodbye*
Cole, Babette. *Cupid*
  Truelove
Davenier, Christine. *Leon and Albertine*
De Mejo, Oscar. *La Bella Magellona and the little cavalier*
De Paola, Tomie (Thomas Anthony). *Helga's dowry*
Dragonwagon, Crescent. *Wind Rose*
Drummond, Allan. *The willow pattern story*
Dyke, John. *Pigwig*
Edwards, Lisa. *Disney's Beauty and the beast, a book of manners*
Edwards, Nicola. *Goodnight Baxter*
Eisenberg, Phyllis Rose. *You're my Nikki*
Elzbieta. *Jon-Jon and Annette*
Eure, Wesley. *A fish out of water*
Fatio, Louise. *The happy lion's treasure*
Flack, Marjorie. *Ask Mr. Bear*
Flanders, Michael. *The hippopotamus song*
Fowler, Susi Gregg. *Beautiful*
Fox, Mem. *Koala Lou*
  Sophie
Freedman, Florence B. *Brothers*
Freeman, Don. *Corduroy*
Gerstein, Mordicai. *Prince Sparrow*
Girard, Linda Walvoord. *At Daddy's on Saturdays*
Giuliano, Katie. *All the way to God*
Glass, Andrew. *Chickpea and the talking cow*
Gliori, Debi. *No matter what*
Goble, Paul. *Love flute*
Graham, Georgia. *The strongest man this side of Cremona*
Greene, Carol. *The golden locket*
Haseley, Dennis. *Ghost catcher*
Hautzig, Deborah. *Beauty and the beast*
Havill, Juanita. *I love you more*
Hazen, Barbara Shook. *Even if I did something awful*
Heine, Helme. *The boxer and the princess*
Hest, Amy. *The go-between*

Hill, Eric. *Puppy love*

Hines, Anna Grossnickle. *When we married Gary*

Hodges, Margaret. *The kitchen knight*

Hoopes, Lyn Littlefield. *When I was little*

Huss, Sally. *I love you with all my hearts*

Hutton, Warwick. *Beauty and the beast*

Jacobs, Joseph. *Tattercoats*

Jaffe, Nina. *The way meat loves salt*

Jenkins, Jordan. *Learning about love*

Jewell, Nancy. *The snuggle bunny*

Johnson, Dolores. *Grandma's hands*

Joosse, Barbara M. *Mama, do you love me?*

Karas, G. Brian. *Skidamarink*

Kasza, Keiko. *A mother for Choco*

Kern, Noris. *I love you with all my heart*

Kinerk, Robert. *Slim and Miss Prim*

King-Smith, Dick. *Puppy love*

Kirk, David. *Little Miss Spider*

Kocí, Marta. *Sarah's bear*

Kohlenberg, Sherry. *Sammy's mommy has cancer*

Kraus, Robert. *Buggy Bear cleans up*
  Mouse in love

Krauss, Ruth. *Big and little*

Lagerlöf, Selma. *The changeling*

Laird, Elizabeth. *A book of promises*

Lasky, Kathryn. *I have four names for my grandfather*

Lawrence, Michael (Michael C.). *Baby loves*

Lee, Chinlun. *Good dog, Paw*

Levitin, Sonia. *The man who kept his heart in a bucket*

Lexau, Joan M. *A house so big*

Lindbergh, Reeve. *Grandfather's lovesong*

London, Jonathan. *Count the ways, Little Brown Bear*
  Froggy's first kiss
  A koala for Katie
  What do you love?
  What do you love? [board book]

McBratney, Sam. *Guess how much I love you*

McCaughrean, Geraldine. *Beauty and the beast*

McCloskey, Kevin. *Mrs. Fitz's flamingos*

McCourt, Lisa. *I love you, Stinky Face*

Macken, JoAnn Early. *Cats on Judy*

MacLachlan, Patricia. *Who loves me?*

McNaughton, Colin. *Oomph!*

McPhail, David M. *Sisters*
  The teddy bear

Mangas, Brian. *A nice surprise for Father Rabbit*

Manna, Anthony L. *Mr. Semolina-Semolinus*

Marshall, Edward. *Fox in love*

Martin, Bill (William Ivan). *Knots on a counting rope*

Marzollo, Jean. *I love you*

Masurel, Claire. *Two homes*

Mayer, Marianna. *Beauty and the beast*

Mayer, Mercer. *Just for you*
  Whinnie the lovesick dragon

Mayne, William. *The patchwork cat*

Meeker, Clare Hodgson. *A tale of two rice birds*

Miles, Betty. *Around and around . . . love*

Mizumura, Kazue. *If I were a cricket . . .*

Moore, Elaine. *Grammy, do you love me?*

Morgan-Vanroyen, Mary. *Guess who I love?*

Morris, Ann. *Loving*

Morrow, Tara Jaye. *Mommy loves her baby; Daddy loves his baby*

Munsch, Robert N. *Love you forever*

Naylor, Phyllis Reynolds. *The baby, the bed, and the rose*

Nesbit, Edith. *Beauty and the beast*

Newman, Marjorie. *Mole and the baby bird*
  Mole and the baby bird [board book]

Newton, Laura P. *Me and my aunts*

Nobisso, Josephine. *Grandpa loved*

Norac, Carl. *I love you so much*

Noyes, Alfred. *The highwayman*

O'Keefe, Susan Heyboer. *Love me, love you*

Oppenheim, Shulamith Levey. *I love you, Bunny Rabbit*

Oram, Hiawyn. *Kiss it better*

Otsuka, Yuzo. *Suho and the white horse*

Paradis, Susan. *My mommy*

Paterson, Diane. *Wretched Rachel*

Pochocki, Ethel. *Rosebud and red flannel*

Porter-Gaylord, Laurel. *I love my daddy because . . .*
  I love my mommy because . . .

Pow, Tom. *Tell me one thing, Dad*

Price, Leontyne. *Aïda*

Rankin, Joan. *You're somebody special, Walliwigs!*

Ransom, Jeanie Franz. *I don't want to talk about it*

Reinl, Edda. *The little snake*

Reiser, Lynn. *The surprise family*

Rock, Lois. *Now we have a baby*

Rohmer, Harriet. *Mother scorpion country*

Rotner, Shelley. *Lots of grandparents*

Rowand, Phyllis. *Every day in the year*

Rusackas, Francesca. *Daddy all day long*

Samuels, Barbara. *Faye and Dolores*

Sandburg, Carl (Charles August). *Not everyday an aurora borealis for your birthday*

San Souci, Robert D. *Nicholas Pipe*

Schlessinger, Laura. *Why do you love me?*

Scott, Ann Herbert. *On mother's lap*
  On mother's lap [board book]

Shecter, Ben. *If I had a ship*

Shipton, Jonathan. *Busy! Busy! Busy!*

Silverman, Maida. *The magic well*

Spelman, Cornelia Maude. *Mama and Daddy Bear's divorce*

Steig, William. *Potch and Polly*
  Tiffky Doofky

Stuve-Bodeen, Stephanie. *Elizabeti's doll*

Summers, Kate. *Milly's wedding*

Tafuri, Nancy. *I love you, little one*

Tedesco, Donna. *Do you know how much I love you?*

Thompson, Kay. *Kay Thompson's Eloise's what I absolutely love love love*

Thompson, Richard. *Foo*

Tudor, Tasha. *Miss Kiss and the nasty beast*

Vaës, Alain. *The porcelain pepper pot*

Velthuijs, Max. *Frog in love*

Waddell, Martin. *The toymaker*
  Who do you love?

Wade, Barrie. *Little monster*

Wahl, Jan. *Old Hippo's Easter egg*

Ward, Heather Patricia. *I promise I'll find you*

Watson, Clyde. *Love's a sweet*

Watson, Wendy. *A Valentine for you*

Wilson, Sarah. *Love and kisses*

Woychuk, Denis. *The other side of the wall*

Wright, Freire. *Beauty and the beast*

Yezerski, Thomas F. *Together in Pinecone Patch*

Yorinks, Arthur. *Harry and Lulu*

Zalben, Jane Breskin. *A perfect nose for Ralph*

Ziefert, Harriet. *With love from Grandma*

Zindel, Paul. *I love my mother*

Zola, Meguido. *Only the best*

Zolotow, Charlotte (Shapiro). *Do you know what I'll do?*
  If you listen
  May I visit?
  A rose, a bridge, and a wild black horse
  Say it!
  The sky was blue
  Some things go together

Emotions – sadness

Abley, Mark. *Ghost cat*

Alexander, Sue. *Nadia the willful*

Allen, Frances Charlotte. *Little hippo*

Andrews, Jan. *The auction*

Baker, Betty. *Rat is dead and ant is sad*

Cole, Joanna. *The Clown-Arounds have a party*

Delton, Judy. *I'll never love anything ever again*

De Veaux, Alexis. *Na-ni*

Frost, Helen. *Feeling sad*

Hanson, Regina. *The tangerine tree*

Havill, Juanita. *Jamaica's blue marker*

Johnson, Angela. *The aunt in our house*

Lawrence, Jennifer B. *Sad doggy*

Lindgren, Astrid. *My nightingale is singing*

Low, Joseph. *The Christmas grump*
McLerran, Alice. *The mountain that loved a bird*
Monk, Isabell. *Blackberry stew*
Paschkis, Julie. *So happy/So sad*
Riggio, Anita. *Smack dab in the middle*
Sharmat, Marjorie Weinman. *I don't care*
Singer, Marilyn. *In the palace of the Ocean King*
Spelman, Cornelia Maude. *When I feel sad*
Sugita, Yutaka. *Helena the unhappy hippopotamus*
Wolff, Ashley. *The bells of London*

Emotions – unhappiness *see* Emotions – happiness;
Emotions – sadness

Emperors *see* Royalty – emperors

Emus *see* Birds – emus

Endangered animals *see* Animals – endangered animals

Engineered books *see* Format, unusual – toy & movable
books

Engineers *see* Careers – engineers

England *see* Foreign lands – England

Entertainers *see* Careers – entertainers

Entertainment *see* Theater

Environment *see* Ecology

Envy *see* Emotions – envy, jealousy

Epilepsy *see* Illness – epilepsy

Escalators *see* Elevators, escalators

Eskimos *see also* Indians of North America – Inuit; Indians
of North America – Inuk

Andrews, Jan. *Very last first time*
Bania, Michael. *Kumak's house*
Beim, Lorraine. *The little igloo*
Bernhard, Emery. *How Snowshoe Hare rescued the sun*
Brown, Kerry. *Tupag the dreamer*
Bushey, Jeanne. *A sled dog for Moshi*
Carlstrom, Nancy White. *Northern lullaby*
Conway, Diana Cohen. *Northern lights*
Dabcovich, Lydia. *The polar bear son*
Damjan, Mischa. *Atuk*
DeArmond, Dale. *The seal oil lamp*
Edwardson, Debby Dahl. *Whale snow*
Ekoomiak, Normee. *Arctic memories*
George, Jean Craighead. *Arctic son*
    Nutik and Amaroq play ball
    Nutik, the wolf pup
    Snow bear
Gerber, Carole. *Arctic dreams*
Harlow, Joan Hiatt. *Shadow bear*
Heinz, Brian J. *Nanuk, lord of the ice*
Hopkins, Marjorie. *Three visitors*
Houston, James. *Kiviok's magic journey*
Jessell, Tim. *Amorak*
Joosse, Barbara M. *Mama, do you love me?*
Kroll, Virginia L. *The seasons and someone*
Loverseed, Amanda. *Tikkatoo's journey*
Luenn, Nancy. *Nessa's fish*
    Nessa's story
McDonald, Megan. *Tundra mouse*
Machetanz, Sara. *A puppy named Gia*
Magdanz, James S. *Go home, river*
Martin, Rafe. *The eagle's gift*

Morrow, Suzanne Stark. *Inatuck's friend*
Munsch, Robert N. *A promise is a promise*
Nicolai, Margaret. *Kitaq goes ice fishing*
Parish, Peggy. *Ootah's lucky day*
San Souci, Robert D. *Song of Sedna*
Scott, Ann Herbert. *On mother's lap*
    On mother's lap [board book]
Sis, Peter. *A small tall tale from the far Far North*
Steiner, Barbara (Annette). *The whale brother*
Villoldo, Alberto. *Skeleton woman*

Estonia *see* Foreign lands – Estonia

Ethiopia *see* Foreign lands – Ethiopia

Ethnic groups in the U.S.

Appelt, Kathi. *Bayou lullaby*
Bailey, Debbie. *Grandma*
    Grandpa
Banish, Roslyn. *A forever family*
Barrett, Joyce Durham. *Willie's not the hugging kind*
Belpré, Pura. *Santiago*
Bettinger, Craig. *Follow me, everybody*
Blue, Rose. *I am here = Yo estoy aqui*
Brenner, Barbara A. *Faces, faces, faces*
Bunting, Eve (Anne Evelyn). *Smoky night*
Caseley, Judith. *Apple pie and onions*
Clifford, Eth. *Your face is a picture*
Cohen, Miriam. *Will I have a friend?*
Córdova, Amy. *Abuelita's heart*
Cox, Judy. *Now we can have a wedding!*
Crume, Marion W. *Listen!*
Cummings, Pat. *Petey Moroni's Camp Runamok diary*
Davol, Marguerite W. *Black, white, just right*
Dickens, Lucy. *Dancing class*
Dooley, Norah. *Everybody bakes bread*
    Everybody brings noodles
    Everybody cooks rice
    Everybody serves soup
Dorros, Arthur. *Abuela*
Edwards, Nancy. *Glenna's seeds*
Feldman, Eve B. *Animals don't wear pajamas*
Fisher, Iris L. *Katie-Bo*
Golding, Theresa Martin. *Memorial Day surprise*
Greene, Roberta. *Two and me makes three*
Heinst, Marie. *My first number book*
Hoffman, Phyllis. *Meatball*
Hogan, Paula Z. *The hospital scares me*
Hughes, Shirley. *The big concrete lorry*
James, Betsy. *The dream stair*
Jaynes, Ruth M. *Benny's four hats*
    Friends! friends! friends!
    Tell me please! What's that?
    That's what it is!
    What is a birthday child?
Jenkins, Jessica. *Thinking about colors*
Johnson, Angela. *The aunt in our house*
Kaiser Johnson, Lee. *If I ran the family*
Kallok, Emma. *Gem*
Katz, Karen. *The colors of us*
Keats, Ezra Jack. *My dog is lost!*
Kesselman, Wendy Ann. *Angelita*
Klein, Leonore. *Just like you*
Kroll, Virginia L. *New friends, true friends, stuck-like-glue friends*
Kuklin, Susan. *How my family lives in America*
Lansdown, Brenda. *Galumph*
Let's talk about race
Levy, Janice. *Totally uncool*
Lippman, Sidney. *A you're adorable*
MacKinnon, Debbie. *My first ABC*
Maestro, Betsy. *Coming to America*
May, Julian. *Why people are different colors*
Medearis, Angela Shelf. *The zebra-riding cowboy*
Merriam, Eve. *Boys and girls, girls and boys*
Merrill, Jean. *How many kids are hiding on my block?*

Miller, J. Philip. *We all sing with the same voice*
Moss, Jenny Jackson. *Cajun night after Christmas*
Moss, Marissa. *After-school monster*
Nikola-Lisa, W. *America: my land, your land, our land*
 Bein' with you this way
Paek, Min. *Aekyung's dream*
Pellegrini, Nina. *Families are different*
Pinkney, Sandra L. *A rainbow all around me*
Prager, Annabelle. *The baseball birthday party*
Reit, Seymour. *Round things everywhere*
Rosa-Casanova, Sylvia. *Mama Provi and the pot of rice*
Rosenberg, Maxine B. *Being adopted*
Rotner, Shelley. *Lots of moms*
Sage, James. *The little band*
Schaefer, Carole Lexa. *Snow pumpkin*
Shelby, Anne. *Potluck*
Simon, Norma. *I am not a crybaby!*
 What do I say?
Sobol, Harriet Langsam. *We don't look like our mom and dad*
Stanek, Muriel. *One, two, three for fun*
Swain, Gwenyth. *Smiling*
Udry, Janice May. *What Mary Jo shared*
Valentine, Johnny. *One dad, two dads, brown dad, blue dads*
Vigil-Piñón, Evangelina. *Marina's muumuu = el muumuu de Marina*
Watson, Mary. *The butterfly seeds*
Weiss, Nicki. *The world turns round and round*
Williams, Vera B. *"More more more," said the baby*
Wing, Natasha. *Jalapeño bagels*
Wong, Janet S. *This next New Year*
Zarin, Cynthia. *What do you see when you shut your eyes?*

Ethnic groups in the U.S. – African Americans

Ackerman, Karen. *By the dawn's early light*
Adler, David A. *A picture book of Martin Luther King, Jr.*
Adoff, Arnold. *Big sister tells me that I'm black*
 I am the running girl
 In for winter, out for spring
 Where wild Willie?
Alexander, Martha G. *Bobo's dream*
 The story grandmother told
Aliki. *A weed is a flower*
All night, all day
All the pretty little horses
Allen, Debbie. *Dancing in the wings*
Allison, Diane Worfolk. *This is the key to the kingdom*
Altman, Linda Jacobs. *The legend of Freedom Hill*
 Singing with Momma Lou
Altman, Susan. *Followers of the north star*
Amper, Thomas. *Booker T. Washington*
Ashley Bryan's abc of African American poetry
Balcziak, Bill. *John Henry*
Bang, Molly. *Ten, nine, eight*
 Wiley and the hairy man
Barber, Barbara E. *Allie's basketball dream*
 Saturday at the new you
Barber, Tiki. *By my brother's side*
Barner, Bob. *Dem bones*
Barnwell, Ysaye M. *No mirrors in my Nana's house*
Battle-Lavert, Gwendolyn. *The barber's cutting edge*
 The music in Derrick's heart
 Papa's mark
 The shaking bag
Beim, Jerrold. *The swimming hole*
Beim, Lorraine. *Two is a team*
Belton, Sandra. *Pictures for Miss Josie*
Benjamin, Anne. *Young Harriet Tubman*
Bennett, Kelly. *Not Norman*
Bible. New Testament. *The Lord's prayer*, ill. by Tim Ladwig
Bible. Old Testament. Psalms. *Psalm twenty-three*
Blackstone, Stella. *Bear on a bike*
Blue, Rose. *Black, black, beautiful black*
 How many blocks is the world?
Bogart, Jo Ellen. *Daniel's dog*
Bolden, Tonya. *Rock of ages*
Bradby, Marie. *Momma, where are you from?*
 More than anything else

Once upon a farm
Breinburg, Petronella. *Doctor Shawn*
 Shawn goes to school
 Shawn's red bike
Brown, Margaret Wise. *Afro-Bets book of colors*
 Afro-Bets book of shapes
Bryan, Ashley. *I'm going to sing*
Bunting, Eve (Anne Evelyn). *The blue and the gray*
Burch, Robert. *Joey's cat*
Burden-Patmon, Denise. *Carnival*
 Imani's gift at Kwanzaa
Burleigh, Robert. *Langston's train ride*
 Lookin' for Bird in the big city
Caines, Jeannette. *Abby*
 Daddy
 Just us women
Calhoun, Mary. *Big Sixteen*
Calloway, Northern J. *Northern J. Calloway presents Super-vroomer!*
Carlstrom, Nancy White. *Wild wild sunflower child Anna*
Carter, Don. *Heaven's all-star jazz band*
Cash, Megan Montague. *What makes the seasons?*
Chapman, Cheryl. *Snow on snow on snow*
Children go where I send thee
Chocolate, Deborah M. Newton. *Kwanzaa*
 The piano man
Clifton, Lucille. *All us come cross the water*
 Amifika
 The boy who didn't believe in spring
 Don't you remember?
 Everett Anderson's Christmas coming
 Everett Anderson's friend
 Everett Anderson's goodbye
 Everett Anderson's nine months long
 Everett Anderson's 1-2-3
 Everett Anderson's year
 Good, says Jerome
 My brother fine with me
 My friend Jacob
 One of the problems of Everett Anderson
 Some of the days of Everett Anderson
 Three wishes, ill. by Stephanie Douglas
 Three wishes, ill. by Michael Hays
Cole, Kenneth, Dr. *No bad news*
Coleman, Evelyn. *The glass bottle tree*
 To be a drum
 White socks only
Coles, Robert. *The story of Ruby Bridges*
Collier, Bryan. *Uptown*
Cooke, Trish. *Mr. Pam Pam and the Hullabazoo*
Cooper, Floyd. *Coming home*
Cooper, Melrose. *Gettin' through Thursday*
Cowley, Joy. *Singing down the rain*
Crews, Donald. *Cloudy day/sunny day*
 Shortcut
Crews, Nina. *A ghost story*
 One hot summer day
 You are here
Cummings, Pat. *Angel baby*
 Carousel
 Clean your room, Harvey Moon!
 Jimmy Lee did it
 My aunt came back
Curtis, Gavin. *The bat boy and his violin*
 Grandma's baseball
Dale, Penny. *Bet you can't*
DeFelice, Cynthia C. *Willy's silly grandma*
DeGross, Monalisa. *Granddaddy's street songs*
Derby, Sally. *My steps*
De Veaux, Alexis. *An enchanted hair tale*
Dionetti, Michelle V. *Thalia Brown and the blue bug*
Dobkin, Bonnie. *Everybody says*
Dragonwagon, Crescent. *Home place*
DuBurke, Randy. *The moon ring*
Duncan, Alice Faye. *Miss Viola and Uncle Ed Lee*
Dupré, Rick. *Agassu*
 The wishing chair
Edwards, Pamela Duncan. *Barefoot*

Elster, Jean Alicia. *Just call me Joe Joe*
Emerson, Carl. *Marion Jones*
Engel, Diana. *Circle song*
    Fishing
England, Linda. *The old cotton blues*
English, Karen. *Big wind coming!*
    Hot day on Abbott Avenue
    Just right stew
    Neeny coming, Neeny going
Evans, Mari. *Singing black*
Everett, Gwen. *Li'l Sis and Uncle Willie*
Falwell, Cathryn. *Christmas for 10*
    David's drawing
    Feast for ten
Fassler, Joan. *Don't worry dear*
Faulkner, William J. *Brer Tiger and the big wind*
Fife, Dale. *Adam's ABC*
Flournoy, Valerie. *The best time of day*
    The patchwork quilt
Ford, Juwanda G. *K is for Kwanzaa*
    Together for Kwanzaa
Frame, Jeron Ashford. *Yesterday I had the blues*
Fraser, Kathleen. *Adam's world, San Francisco*
Freeman, Don. *Corduroy*
    A pocket for Corduroy
Frost, Helen. *Martin Luther King, Jr. Day*
Gambill, Henrietta D. *Self-control*
George, Jean Craighead. *The wentletrap trap*
Gershwin, George. *Summertime from Porgy and Bess*
Gilchrist, Jan Spivey. *Indigo and moonlight gold*
Gill, Joan. *Hush, Jon!*
Giovanni, Nikki. *The genie in the jar*
    Spin a soft black song
    The sun is so quiet
Glaser, Linda. *Stop that garbage truck!*
Golenbock, Peter. *Hank Aaron*
Gray, Genevieve. *Send Wendell*
Gray, Libba Moore. *Miss Tizzy*
Gray, Nigel. *I'll take you to Mrs. Cole!*
Greenberg, Polly. *Oh, Lord, I wish I was a buzzard*
Greene, Carol. *Katherine Dunham*
Greenfield, Eloise. *Angels*
    Big friend, little friend
    Daddy and I
    Daydreamers
    Easter parade
    First pink light
    I make music
    Kia Tanisha
    Lisa's daddy and daughter day
    Me and Neesie, ill. by Moneta Barnett
    Me and Neesie, ill. by Jan Spivey Gilchrist
    My doll, Keshia
    Nathaniel talking
    Night on Neighborhood Street
    On my horse
    She come bringing me that little baby girl
    Sweet baby coming
    Water, water
    William and the good old days
Greenfield, Monica. *The baby*
    Waiting for Christmas
Grifalconi, Ann. *City rhythms*
    Electric Yancy
    Kinda blue
    Tiny's hat
    The village that vanished
Grimes, Nikki. *Baby's bedtime*
    Come Sunday
    Danitra Brown leaves town
    From a child's heart
    It's raining laughter
    Meet Danitra Brown
    My man Blue
    When Daddy prays
    Wild, wild hair
Guthrie, Donna. *A rose for Abby*

Guy, Rosa. *Billy the Great*
Hamilton, Virginia. *Drylongso*
Harrison, Troon. *Courage to fly*
Haseley, Dennis. *Crosby*
Haskins, Francine. *I remember "121"*
Hathorn, Libby (Elizabeth). *Sky sash so blue*
Havill, Juanita. *Jamaica and Brianna*
    Jamaica Tag-Along
    Jamaica's blue marker
    Jamaica's find
Hayes, Sarah. *Eat up, Gemma*
    Happy Christmas, Gemma
Hayward, Linda. *Hello, house!*
Heath, Amy. *Sofie's role*
Helldorfer, M. C. (Mary Claire). *Silver Rain Brown*
Henderson, Alicia Terry. *Call me black, call me beautiful*
Hesse, Karen. *Come on, rain*
Hest, Amy. *Jamaica Louise James*
Hill, Elizabeth Starr. *Evan's corner*
Hoffman, Mary. *Amazing Grace*
    An angel just like me
    Grace and family
Hoffman, Phyllis. *Steffie and me*
Hogan, Paula Z. *The hospital scares me*
Holman, Sandy Lynne. *Grandpa, is everything black bad?*
Hood, Susan. *Look! I can read!*
Hooks, Bell. *Be boy buzz*
    Happy to be nappy
Hooks, William H. *Where's Lulu?*
Hopkins, Lee Bennett. *I think I saw a snail*
Hort, Lenny. *How many stars in the sky*
Horvath, Betty F. *Hooray for Jasper*
    Jasper and the hero business
    Jasper makes music
Howard, Elizabeth Fitzgerald. *Aunt Flossie's hats (and crab cakes later)*
    Chita's Christmas tree
    Mac and Marie and the train toss surprise
    Papa tells Chita a story
    Virgie goes to school with us boys
    What's in Aunt Mary's room?
    When will Sarah come?
Hru, Dakari. *Joshua's Masai mask*
Hudson, Cheryl Willis. *Afro-Bets ABC book*
    Afro-Bets 123 book
    Animal sounds for baby
    Bright eyes, brown skin
    Good morning baby
    Good night baby
    Let's count, baby
Hudson, Wade. *Afro-Bets Kids I'm gonna be*
    I love my family
    Pass it on
Hughes, Langston. *Carol of the brown king*
Hulbert, Jay. *Armando asked "Why?"*
Hush songs
Hutchins, Pat. *My best friend*
I've seen the promised land
Igus, Toyomi. *Two Mrs. Gibsons*
    When I was little
In daddy's arms I am tall
Isadora, Rachel. *Ben's trumpet*
    Bring on that beat
    Peekaboo morning
Jackson, Bobby L. *Little Red Ronnika*
Jackson, Isaac. *Somebody's new pajamas*
Jaquith, Priscilla. *Bo Rabbit smart for true*
Jensen, Virginia Allen. *Sara and the door*
Johnson, Angela. *Casey Jones*
    Daddy calls me man
    Do like Kyla
    Down the winding road
    The girl who wore snakes
    Joshua by the sea
    Joshua's night whispers
    Julius
    The leaving morning

Mama bird, baby birds
One of three
Rain feet
The Rolling Store
Shoes like Miss Alice's
A sweet smell of roses
The wedding
When I am old with you
When mules flew on Magnolia Street
Johnson, Dinah. *All around town*
   Quinnie Blue
   Sunday week
Johnson, Dolores. *The best bug to be*
   Grandma's hands
   My mom is my show-and-tell
   Now let me fly
   Papa's stories
   Seminole diary
   What kind of baby-sitter is this?
   What will mommy do when I'm at school?
   Your dad was just like you
Johnson, James Weldon. *The Creation*
   Lift ev'ry voice and sing
Johnson, Janet P. *How Mr. Dog got tame*
   Keelboat Annie
Johnston, Tony. *The wagon*
Jonas, Ann. *Splash!*
Jones, Joy. *Tambourine moon*
Jones, Rebecca C. *Matthew and Tilly*
Joseph, Lynn. *Fly, Bessie, fly*
Kaufman, Curt. *Hotel boy*
Keats, Ezra Jack. *Apt. 3*
   Dreams
   Goggles
   Hi, cat!
   John Henry
   A letter to Amy
   Louie
   Pet show!
   Peter's chair
   Skates
   The snowy day
   The snowy day [board book]
   The trip
   Whistle for Willie
Kessler, Brad. *Brer Rabbit and Boss Lion*
Ketteman, Helen. *Not yet, Yvette*
Kirn, Ann. *Beeswax catches a thief*
Klingel, Cynthia Fitterer. *Rosa Parks*
Koplow, Lesley. *Tanya and the tobo man = Tanya y el hombre tobo*
Kroll, Virginia L. *Africa brothers and sisters*
   Can you dance, Dalila?
   Faraway drums
   Masai and I
   Sweet Magnolia
   Wood-hoopoe Willie
Kurtz, Jane. *Faraway home*
Lansdown, Brenda. *Galumph*
Lauture, Denizé. *Father and son*
Leonard, Marcia. *Get the ball, Slim*
   My camp-out
   My pal Al
Lester, Julius. *Black cowboy, wild horses*
   John Henry
   The knee-high man and other tales
   What a truly cool world
   Why heaven is far away
Lexau, Joan M. *Benjie*
   Benjie on his own
   I should have stayed in bed
   Me day
   The rooftop mystery
Liddell, Janice. *Imani and the Flying Africans*
Lillie, Patricia. *Jake and Rosie*
Lindbergh, Reeve. *Nobody owns the sky*
Lipkind, William. *Four-leaf clover*
Little, Lessie Jones. *Children of long ago*

Little, Mimi Otey. *Yoshiko and the foreigner*
Littlesugar, Amy. *Freedom school, yes!*
   Jonkonnu
   Shake Rag
   Tree of hope
Livingston, Myra Cohn. *Keep on singing*
Lorbiecki, Marybeth. *Sister Anne's hands*
Lotz, Karen E. *Can't sit still*
MacDonald, Margaret Read. *Pickin' peas*
McGhee, Alison. *In the hollow of your hand*
McGill, Alice. *Molly Bannaky*
   Sure as sunrise
McGovern, Ann. *Black is beautiful*
McKissack, Patricia C. *Booker T. Washington*
   Flossie and the fox
   Goin' someplace special
   The honest-to-goodness truth
   Ma Dear's aprons
   Messy Bessey
   Messy Bessey = Ada, la desordenada
   Messy Bessey's closet
   Messy Bessey's family reunion
   Messy Bessey's holidays
   Mirandy and brother wind
   Paul Robeson
McLellan, Stephanie Simpson. *The chicken cat*
Mandel, Peter. *Say hey*
Mara, Wil. *Jackie Robinson*
Martin, Ann M. *Rachel Parker, kindergarten show-off*
Marzollo, Jean. *Shanna's ballerina show*
May, Kathy. *Molasses man*
Mayer, Mercer. *Liza Lou and the Yeller Belly Swamp*
Medearis, Angela Shelf. *The adventures of Sugar and Junior*
   Annie's gifts
   Dancing with the Indians
   The freedom riddle
   The ghost of Sifty-Sifty Sam
   Kyle's first Kwanzaa
   Our people
   Picking peas for a penny
   Poppa's new pants
   Rum-a-tum-tum
   Tailypo
Medearis, Michael. *Daisy and the doll*
Medina, Tony. *Christmas makes me think*
   DeShawn days
Mellage, Nanette. *Coming home*
   See me grow, head to toe
Merriam, Eve. *Epaminondas*
Miles, Calvin. *Calvin's Christmas wish*
Milich, Melissa. *Can't scare me!*
   Miz Fannie Mae's fine new Easter hat
Miller, Thomas Patton. *Can a coal scuttle fly?*
Miller, William. *The bus ride*
   The conjure woman
   Frederick Douglass
   A house by the river
   Jenny and the peddler
   The knee-high man
   Night golf
   The piano
   Rent party jazz
   Richard Wright and the library card
Milstein, Linda Breiner. *Coconut mon*
Mitchell, Margaree King. *Granddaddy's gift*
   Susie Mae
   Uncle Jed's barbershop
Mitchell, Rhonda. *The talking cloth*
Monjo, F. N. *The drinking gourd*
Monk, Isabell. *Family*
   Hope
Moore, Dessie. *Getting dressed*
   Good morning
   Good night
   Let's pretend
Morris, Ann. *Grandma Lois remembers*
Moss, Marissa. *Mel's diner*

Moss, Thylias. *I want to be*
Myers, Christopher A. *Sparrows*
Myers, Walter Dean. *Brown angels*
   Glorious angels
   Harlem
   Young Martin's promise
Nelson, Vaunda Micheaux. *Almost to freedom*
Nettleton, Pamela Hill. *Martin Luther King, Jr.*
Nickens, Bessie. *Walking the log*
Nikola-Lisa, W. *Bein' with you this way*
   Hallelujah!
   Summer sun risin'
Nobisso, Josephine. *John Blair and the great Hinckley fire*
Nolan, Madeena Spray. *My daddy don't go to work*
Nolen, Jerdine. *Big Jabe*
   Thunder Rose
Oppenheim, Shulamith Levey. *Fireflies for Nathan*
Orgill, Roxane. *If I only had a horn*
The palm of my heart
Patrick, Denise Lewis. *No diapers for baby!*
Pegram, Laura. *Daughter's Day blues*
Perdorno, Willie. *Visiting Langston*
Perkins, Charles. *Swinging on a rainbow*
Peterson, Jeanne Whitehouse. *My mama sings*
Pinkney, Andrea Davis. *Alvin Ailey*
   Bill Pickett, rodeo ridin' cowboy
   Dear Benjamin Banneker
   Duke Ellington
   Mim's Christmas jam
Pinkney, Gloria Jean. *Back home*
   The Sunday outing
Pinkney, J. Brian. *The adventures of sparrowboy*
Pinkney, Sandra L. *Shades of black*
Polacco, Patricia. *Chicken Sunday*
   I can hear the sun
   Mrs. Katz and Tush
Poydar, Nancy. *Busy Bea*
   Rhyme time Valentine
Price, Hope Lynne. *These hands*
Rappaport, Doreen. *Martin's big words*
Raschka, Christopher. *Charlie Parker played be bop*
   Mysterious Thelonious
   Yo! Yes?
Riggio, Anita. *Secret signs*
Ringgold, Faith. *Bonjour, Lonnie*
   Cassie's word quilt
   Dinner at Aunt Connie's house
   If a bus could talk
   The invisible princesses
   My dream of Martin Luther King
   Tar Beach
Robinson, Aminah Brenda Lynn. *A street called home*
Rochelle, Belinda. *Jewels*
Rodriguez, Anita. *Jamal and the angel*
Romain, Trevor. *Jemma's journey*
Rosales, Melodye Benson. *Double Dutch and the voodoo shoes*
   Leola and the honeybears
   'Twas the night b'fore Christmas
Rosen, Michael J. (1954–). *Elijah's angel*
Sadu, Itah. *Christopher changes his name*
Saint James, Synthia. *The gifts of Kwanzaa*
   Sunday
Salat, Cristina. *Peanut's emergency*
Samton, Sheila White. *Amazing Aunt Agatha*
Samuels, Vyanne. *Carry go bring come*
Sanders, Scott R. (Scott Russell). *A place called Freedom*
San Souci, Robert D. *The boy and the ghost*
   Callie Ann and Mistah Bear
   The hired hand
   The secret of the stones
   Sukey and the mermaid
Schaefer, Lola M. *Kwanzaa*
Schertle, Alice. *Down the road*
Schrier, Jeffrey. *On the wings of eagles*
Schroeder, Alan. *Ragtime Tumpie*
Scott, Ann Herbert. *Big Cowboy Western*
   Let's catch a monster

   Sam
Scruggs, Afi. *Jump rope magic*
Serfozo, Mary. *What's what?*
Sexton, Colleen A. *Let's meet Martin Luther King, Jr.*
Shange, Ntozake. *Whitewash*
Sharmat, Marjorie Weinman. *I don't care*
Shelby, Anne. *We keep a store*
Showers, Paul. *Look at your eyes*
   Your skin and mine
Siegelson, Kim L. *In the time of the drums*
Sierra, Judy. *Wiley and the Hairy Man*
Singer, Marilyn. *In the palace of the Ocean King*
Smalls, Irene. *Don't say ain't*
Smalls-Hector, Irene. *Because you're lucky*
   Beginning school
   Irene and the big, fine nickel
   Irene Jennie and the Christmas masquerade
   Jenny Reen and the Jack Muh Lantern
   Jonathan and his mommy
   Kevin and his dad
   Louise's gift
Smith, Charles R. *Loki and Alex*
Smith, Edward Biko. *A lullaby for Daddy*
Smothers, Ethel Footman. *Auntee Edna*
Stephens, Helen. *What about me?*
Steptoe, Javaka. *The Jones family express*
Steptoe, John. *Birthday*
   Creativity
   My special best words
   Stevie
   Uptown
Stolz, Mary (Mary Slattery). *Storm in the night*
Straight, Susan. *Bear E. Bear*
Strom, Maria Diaz. *Rainbow Joe and me*
Stroud, Bettye. *Dance y'all*, ill. by Cornelious Van Wright & Ying-Hwa Hu
   Down home at Miss Dessa's
   The leaving
   The patchwork path
Suen, Anastasia. *The clubhouse*
   Hamster chase
   Loose tooth
   Willie's birthday
Swanson-Natsues, Lyn. *Days of adventure*
Tarpley, Natasha Anastasia. *Bippity Bop barbershop*
   I love my hair!
   Joe-Joe's first flight
Taulbert, Clifton L. *Little Cliff and the porch people*
   Little Cliff's first day of school
Taylor, Ann. *Baby dance*
Taylor, Sydney. *The dog who came to dinner*
Teague, Mark. *Baby tamer*
Temple, Charles A. *Train*
Thomas, Ianthe. *Lordy, Aunt Hattie*
   Walk home tired, Billy Jenkins
Thomas, Jane Resh. *Celebration!*
Thomas, Joyce Carol. *Brown honey in broomwheat tea*
   Cherish me
   Crowning glory
   Gingerbread days
   The gospel Cinderella
   Joy
   You are my perfect baby
Thomas, Naturi. *Uh-oh! It's Mama's birthday!*
Troupe, Quincy. *Little Stevie Wonder*
Turner, Ann Warren. *Nettie's trip south*
Udry, Janice May. *Mary Ann's mud day*
   Mary Jo's grandmother
   What Mary Jo shared
   What Mary Jo wanted
Vizurraga, Susan. *Miss Opal's auction*
Wahl, Jan. *The singing geese*
Walker, Alice. *Finding the green stone*
   To hell with dying
Walsh, Ellen Stoll. *Two too much*
Walter, Mildred Pitts. *My mama needs me*
Wangerin, Walter. *Probity Jones and the Fear Not Angel*

Washington, Donna L. *The story of Kwanzaa*
Watts, Jeri Hanel. *Keepers*
Weatherford, Carole Boston. *Juneteenth jamboree*
Wiles, Debbie. *Freedom summer*
Williams, Sherley Anne. *Girls together*
   Working cotton
Williams, Vera B. *Cherries and cherry pits*
Williams-Garcia, Rita. *Catching the wild waiyuuzee*
Williamson, Mel. *Walk on!*
Williamson, Stan. *The no-bark dog*
Wilson, Beth P. *Jenny*
Wilson, Julia. *Becky*
Wilson-Max, Ken. *Max's starry night*
Winne, Joanne. *Let's get ready for Kwanzaa*
Winter, Jeanette. *Follow the drinking gourd*
Wolfe, Frances. *It is the wind*
Wood, Michele. *Going back home*
Woodson, Jacqueline. *Coming on home soon*
   Sweet, sweet memory
   We had a picnic this Sunday past
Woodtor, Dee. *Big meeting*
Wright, Courtni Crump. *Journey to freedom*
   Jumping the broom
   Wagon train
Wyeth, Sharon Dennis. *Always my dad*
   Something beautiful
Yezback, Steven A. *Pumpkinseeds*
Yolen, Jane. *Miz Berlin walks*
Young, Ruth. *Golden Bear*
Zemach, Margot. *Jake and Honeybunch go to heaven*
Ziner, Feenie. *Counting carnival*
Zolotow, Charlotte (Shapiro). *Do you know what I'll do?*
   The old dog

Ethnic groups in the U.S. – Amish

Ammon, Richard. *An Amish Christmas*
   Amish horses
   An Amish wedding
   An Amish year
Bowen, Keith. *Katy's gift*
Good, Merle. *Amos and Susie*
   Reuben and the fire
Good, Phyllis Pellman. *Plain Pig's ABCs*
Gregory, Valiska. *Babysitting for Benjamin*
Mitchell, Barbara. *Down Buttermilk Lane*
Moss, P. Buckley (Pat Buckley). *Reuben and the quilt*
Smucker, Barbara Claasen. *Selina and the bear paw quilt*
Stewart, Sarah. *The journey*
Turkle, Brinton. *The adventures of Obadiah*
   Obadiah the Bold
   Rachel and Obadiah
   Thy friend, Obadiah
Wood, Douglas. *Northwoods cradle song*
Yolen, Jane. *Raising Yoder's barn*

Ethnic groups in the U.S. – Arab Americans

Nye, Naomi Shihab. *Sitti's secrets*

Ethnic groups in the U.S. – Asian Americans

Gabel, Susan L. *Where the sun kisses the sea*
Havill, Juanita. *Jamaica and Brianna*
Min, Laura. *Mrs. Sato's hens*
Molarsky, Osmond. *A sky full of kites*
Swanson-Natsues, Lyn. *Days of adventure*

Ethnic groups in the U.S. – Black Americans *see* Ethnic groups in the U.S. – African Americans

Ethnic groups in the U.S. – Cajuns

Collins, Sheila Hebert. *'T Pousette et 't Poulette*
Trosclair. *Cajun night before Christmas*

Ethnic groups in the U.S. – Cambodian Americans

Chiemruom, Sothea. *Dara's Cambodian New Year*

Ethnic groups in the U.S. – Chinese Americans

Behrens, June. *Soo Ling finds a way*
Bunting, Eve (Anne Evelyn). *The happy funeral*
Cheng, Andrea. *Grandfather counts*
Chin, Steven A. *Dragon Parade*
Chinn, Karen. *Sam and the lucky money*
Coerr, Eleanor. *Chang's paper pony*
D'Antonio, Nancy. *Our baby from China*
Flanagan, Alice K. *Chinese New Year*
Hoyt-Goldsmith, Diane. *Celebrating Chinese New Year*
Lee, Milly. *Earthquake*
   Nim and the war effort
Levine, Ellen. *I hate English!*
Lin, Grace. *Dim sum for everyone*
   Fortune cookie fortunes
   The ugly vegetables
Look, Lenore. *Henry's first-moon birthday*
   Love as strong as ginger
Louie, Therese On. *Raymond's perfect present*
Low, William. *Chinatown*
McCunn, Ruthanne L. *Pie-Biter*
Mak, Kam. *My Chinatown*
Molnar-Fenton, Stephan. *An Mei's strange and wondrous journey*
Morris, Ann. *Grandma Lai Goon remembers*
Nunes, Susan Miho. *The last dragon*
Okimoto, Jean Davies. *The White Swan express*
Partridge, Elizabeth. *Oranges on Golden Mountain*
Peacock, Carol Antoinette. *Mommy far, Mommy near*
Politi, Leo. *Moy Moy*
Pomeranc, Marion Hess. *The American Wei*
Quinn, Daniel P. *I am Buddhist*
Roth, Susan L. *Happy birthday Mr. Kang*
Schaefer, Lola M. *Chinese New Year*
Sing, Rachel. *Chinese New Year's dragon*
Thong, Roseanne. *Round is a mooncake*
Trottier, Maxine. *The tiny kite of Eddie Wing*
Vaughan, Marcia Kapok. *The dancing dragon*
Wallace, Ian. *Chin Chiang and the dragon's dance*
Waters, Kate. *Lion dancer*
Wong, Benedict Norbert. *Lo & behold*
   Lo & behold, good enough to eat
Yamate, Sandra S. *Char siu bao boy*
Ye, Ting-xing. *Share the sky*
Yee, Paul. *Roses sing on new snow*
Yee, Wong Herbert. *A drop of rain*
Yin. *Coolies*

Ethnic groups in the U.S. – Cuban Americans

Ada, Alma Flor. *With love, Little Red Hen*
Chapra, Mimi. *Amelia's show-and-tell fiesta = Amelia y la fiesta de "muestra y cuenta"*

Ethnic groups in the U.S. – Czechoslovakian Americans

Nelson, Nan Ferring. *My day with Anka*

Ethnic groups in the U.S. – Dutch Americans

Joosse, Barbara M. *The morning chair*

Ethnic groups in the U.S. – East Indian Americans

Gilmore, Rachna. *Lights for Gita*

Ethnic groups in the U.S. – Filipino Americans

Giles, Almira Astudillo. *Willie wins*
Yoder, Carolyn P. *Filipino Americans*

Ethnic groups in the U.S. – French Americans

McCully, Emily Arnold. *Mirette and Bellini cross Niagara Falls*

Ethnic groups in the U.S. – German Americans

Bodkin, Odds. *The Christmas cobwebs*
Jaspersohn, William. *The two brothers*
Nivola, Claire A. *Elisabeth*

Ethnic groups in the U.S. – Greek Americans

Bunting, Eve (Anne Evelyn). *I have an olive tree*
D'Arc, Karen Scourby. *My grandmother is a singing Yaya*

Ethnic groups in the U.S. – Guatemalan Americans

Flanagan, Alice K. *Mr. Santizo's tasty treats!*

Ethnic groups in the U.S. – Hispanic Americans

Aliki. *Tabby*
Ancona, George. *Barrio*
Carlson, Lori Marie. *Hurray for Three Kings' Day*
Carlstrom, Nancy White. *Barney is best*
Cisneros, Sandra. *Hairs = Pelitos*
De Anda, Diane. *Dancing Miranda = Baila, Miranda, baila*
De Paola, Tomie (Thomas Anthony). *A new Barker in the house*
English, Karen. *Speak English for us, Marisol*
Figueredo, D. H. *When this world was new*
Hayes, Joe. *A spoon for every bite*
Hughes, Monica. *A handful of seeds*
Lachtman, Ofelia Dumas. *Pepita takes time = Pepita, siempre tarde*
Lomas Garza, Carmen. *In my family*
Medearis, Angela Shelf. *The adventures of Sugar and Junior*
Miller, Elizabeth I. *Just like home = Como en mi tierra*
Morris, Ann. *Grandma Francisca remembers*
San Souci, Robert D. *Little gold star*
Shea, Pegi Deitz. *New moon*
Slate, Joseph. *The secret stars*
Starr, Meg. *Alicia's happy day*
Weiss, Nicki. *On a hot, hot day*
Yin. *Dear Santa, please come to the 19th floor*

Ethnic groups in the U.S. – Hmong Americans

Shea, Pegi Deitz. *The whispering cloth*

Ethnic groups in the U.S. – Hungarian Americans

Couric, Katie. *The brand new kid*

Ethnic groups in the U.S. – Indian Americans

Krishnaswami, Uma. *Chachaji's cup*

Ethnic groups in the U.S. – Irish Americans

Connor, Leslie. *Miss Bridie chose a shovel*
Dillon, Jana. *Lucky O'Leprechaun comes to America*
Hazen, Barbara Shook. *Katie's wish*
Kroll, Steven. *Mary McLean and the St. Patrick's Day parade*
Nolan, Janet. *The St. Patrick's Day shillelagh*
Weller, Frances Ward. *The angel of Mill Street*
Yezerski, Thomas F. *Together in Pinecone Patch*

Ethnic groups in the U.S. – Italian Americans

Alda, Arlene. *Morning glory Monday*
Bartoletti, Susan Campbell. *Silver at night*
Bartone, Elisa. *American, too*
    Peppe the lamplighter
Bunting, Eve (Anne Evelyn). *A picnic in October*
Dionetti, Michelle V. *Coal mine peaches*
Riggio, Anita. *A moon in my teacup*

Ethnic groups in the U.S. – Japanese Americans

Bunting, Eve (Anne Evelyn). *So far from the sea*
Copeland, Helen. *Meet Miki Takino*
Hawkinson, Lucy (Ozone). *Dance, dance, Amy-Chan!*
Igus, Toyomi. *Two Mrs. Gibsons*

Johnston, Tony. *Fishing Sunday*
Kroll, Virginia L. *Pink paper swans*
McCoy, Karen Kawamoto. *Bon Odori dancer*
Mochizuki, Ken. *Baseball saved us*
    Heroes
Noguchi, Rick. *Flowers from Mariko*
Sakai, Kimiko. *Sachiko means happiness*
Sanger, Amy Wilson. *First book of sushi*
Say, Allen. *Emma's rug*
    Grandfather's journey
    Tea with milk
Terasaki, Stanley Todd. *Ghosts for breakfast*
Trottier, Maxine. *Flags*
Uchida, Yoshiko. *The bracelet*
Uegaki, Chieri. *Suki's kimono*
Wells, Rosemary. *Yoko's paper cranes*
Yashima, Mitsu. *Momo's kitten*
Yashima, Taro. *Umbrella*
    The youngest one

Ethnic groups in the U.S. – Jewish Americans

Weitzman, Elizabeth. *I am Jewish American*

Ethnic groups in the U.S. – Korean Americans

Bercaw, Edna Coe. *Halmoni's day*
Bunting, Eve (Anne Evelyn). *Jin Woo*
Choi, Sook Nyul. *Halmoni and the picnic*
    Yunmi and Halmoni's trip
Choi, Yangsook. *The name jar*
Czech, Jan M. *An American face*
Flanagan, Alice K. *A busy day at Mr. Kang's grocery store*
Ginsburg, Mirra. *We adopted you, Benjamin Koo*
Heo, Yumi. *Father's rubber shoes*
Paek, Min. *Aekyung's dream*
Pak, Soyung. *Dear Juno*
    A place to grow
    Sumi's first day of school ever
Park, Frances. *Good-bye, 382 Shin Dang Dong*
Pellegrini, Nina. *Families are different*
Recorvits, Helen. *My name is Yoon*
Wong, Janet S. *The trip back home*

Ethnic groups in the U.S. – Lebanese Americans

Shefelman, Janice Jordan. *A peddler's dream*

Ethnic groups in the U.S. – Lithuanian Americans

Moss, Marissa. *In America*

Ethnic groups in the U.S. – Mexican Americans

Ada, Alma Flor. *I love Saturdays y domingos*
Anaya, Rudolfo A. *Farolitos for Abuelo*
Anzaldúa, Gloria. *Prietita and the ghost woman = Prietita y la llorona*
Behrens, June. *Fiesta!*
Bertrand, Diane Gonzales. *Family = familia*
    The last doll = La última muñeca
    Uncle Chente's picnic = El picnic de Tío Chente
Bolognese, Don. *A new day*
Brown, Tricia. *Hello, amigos!*
Bunting, Eve (Anne Evelyn). *A day's work*
    Going home
Calhoun, Mary. *Tonio's cat*
Cazet, Denys. *Born in the gravy*
Compos, Tito. *Muffler man = El hombre mofle*
Covault, Ruth M. *Pablo and Pimienta*
Cuyler, Margery. *From here to there*
Dorros, Arthur. *Radio Man = Don Radio*
    When the pigs took over
Ets, Marie Hall. *Bad boy, good boy*
    Gilberto and the wind
    Nine days to Christmas
Felt, Sue. *Rosa-too-little*
Fife, Dale. *Rosa's special garden*

Fisher, Mary M. *Rosita's bridge*
Flanagan, Alice K. *Cinco de Mayo*
Fraser, James Howard. *Los Posadas*
Freschet, Gina. *Beto and the bone dance*
Galindo, Mary Sue. *Icy watermelon = Sandía fría*
Havill, Juanita. *Treasure nap*
Head, Judith. *Mud soup*
Herrera, Juan Felipe. *Grandma and Me at the flea = Los meros meros remateros*
Jaynes, Ruth M. *Melinda's Christmas stocking*
  Tell me please! What's that?
  That's what it is!
  What is a birthday child?
Jiménez, Francisco. *The Christmas gift = El regalo de Navidad*
Johnston, Tony. *Uncle rain cloud*
Levy, Janice. *Abuelito eats with his fingers*
Lopez, Loretta. *The birthday swap*
Luenn, Nancy. *A gift for Abuelita*
Molnar, Joe. *Graciela*
Mora, Pat. *The bakery lady = La señora de la panadería*
  A birthday basket for Tía
  Confetti
  Pablo's tree
  The rainbow tulip
  Tomás and the library lady
O'Neill, Alexis. *Estela's swap*
Ormsby, Virginia H. *Twenty-one children plus ten*
Pérez, Amada Irma. *My very own room = Mi propio cuartito*
  My diary from here to there = Mi diario de aquí hasta allá
Pérez, L. King. *First day in grapes*
Politi, Leo. *Juanita*
  Pedro, the angel of Olvera Street
  Song of the swallows
Roe, Eileen. *With my brother = Con mi hermano*
Sáenz, Benjamin Alire. *A gift from papá Diego = Un regalo de papá Diego*
  Grandma Fina and her wonderful umbrellas = La abuelita Fina y sus sombrillas maravillosas
Schaefer, Lola M. *Cinco de Mayo*
Schreck, Karen Halvorsen. *Lucy's family tree*
Serfozo, Mary. *Welcome Roberto! Bienvenido, Roberto!*
Soto, Gary. *The old man and his door*
  Snapshots from the wedding
  Too many tamales
Taha, Karen T. *A gift for Tia Rose*
Thomas, Jane Resh. *Lights on the river*

Ethnic groups in the U.S. – Pakistani Americans

English, Karen. *Nadia's hands*

Ethnic groups in the U.S. – Polish Americans

Leighton, Maxinne Rhea. *An Ellis Island Christmas*
Levinson, Riki. *Soon, Annala*
Yezerski, Thomas F. *Together in Pinecone Patch*

Ethnic groups in the U.S. – Puerto Rican Americans

Atkins, Jeannine. *Get set! Swim!*
Belpré, Pura. *Santiago*
Blue, Rose. *I am here = Yo estoy aqui*
Bowden, Joan Chase. *Emilio's summer day*
Cowley, Joy. *Gracias, the Thanksgiving turkey*
Keats, Ezra Jack. *My dog is lost!*
Kesselman, Wendy Ann. *Angelita*
Manzano, Sonia. *No dogs allowed*
Simon, Norma. *What do I do?*
  What do I say?
Sonneborn, Ruth A. *Friday night is papa night*
  Lollipop's party
  Seven in a bed
Steptoe, John. *Creativity*
Velasquez, Eric. *Grandma's records*

Ethnic groups in the U.S. – Russian Americans

Best, Cari. *When Catherine the Great and I were eight!*
Broyles, Anne. *Shy Mama's Halloween*
Cohen, Barbara. *Make a wish, Molly*
Cohen, Miriam. *Mimmy and Sophie*
Levitin, Sonia. *A piece of home*
Polacco, Patricia. *The trees of the dancing goats*
Pryor, Bonnie. *The dream jar*
Rosenberg, Liz. *Grandmother and the runaway shadow*
Rosenblum, Richard. *Journey to the golden land*
Tarbescu, Edith. *Annushka's voyage*
Woodruff, Elvira. *The memory coat*

Ethnic groups in the U.S. – Shakers

Ray, Mary Lyn. *Shaker boy*

Ethnic groups in the U.S. – Swedish Americans

Peterson, Melissa. *Hanna's Christmas*

Ethnic groups in the U.S. – Vietnamese Americans

Breckler, Rosemary K. *Hoang breaks the lucky teapot*
Garland, Sherry. *The lotus seed*
  My father's boat
McKay, Lawrence. *Journey home*
Surat, Michele Maria. *Angel child, dragon child*
Trottier, Maxine. *The walking stick*

Etiquette

Ackley, Edith Flack. *Please*
  Thank you
Alden, Laura. *Saying I'm sorry*
Aliki. *Manners*
Anastasio, Dina. *Pass the peas, please*
Anderson, Peggy Perry. *Out to lunch*
Austin, Virginia. *Say please*
Behrens, June. *The manners book*
Berenstain, Stan. *The Berenstain bears forget their manners*
Betz, Betty. *Manners for moppets*
Bloom, Suzanne. *Piggy Monday*
Brown, Marc Tolon. *Perfect pigs*
Brown, Myra Berry. *Company's coming for dinner*
Buehner, Caralyn. *It's a spoon, not a shovel*
Carlson, Nancy L. *How to lose all your friends*
Chapman, Cheryl. *Pass the fritters, critters*
Charles, Donald. *Shaggy dog's birthday*
Cho, Shinta. *The gas we pass*
Cole, Babette. *The bad good manners book*
  Lady Lupin's book of etiquette
Cole, Joanna. *Monster manners*
Cuneo, Diane. *Mary Louise loses her manners*
Demuth, Patricia Brennan. *Max, the bad-talking parrot*
Duvoisin, Roger Antoine. *Periwinkle*
Edwards, Lisa. *Disney's Beauty and the beast, a book of manners*
Edwards, Pamela Duncan. *Rude mule*
Gardner, Martin. *Never make fun of a turtle, my son*
Gibbs, Lynne. *Don't slurp your soup!*
Gordon, Margaret. *Wilberforce goes to a party*
Hartman, Bob. *Aunt Mabel's table*
Hawkins, Colin. *Max and the magic word*
Helmer, Diana Star. *The cat who came for tacos*
Himmelman, John. *A guest is a guest*
Hoban, Russell. *Dinner at Alberta's*
  The little Brute family
Holub, Joan. *Turkeys never gobble*
Ichikawa, Satomi. *Nora's surprise*
Jefferds, Vincent. *Disney's elegant book of manners*
Joslin, Sesyle. *Dear dragon*
  What do you do, dear?
  What do you say, dear?
Kandoian, Ellen. *Is anybody up?*
Keenan, Martha. *The mannerly adventures of Little Mouse*
Keller, Irene. *The Thingumajig book of manners*

Keller, John G. *Krispin's fair*
Kopelke, Lisa. *Excuse me!*
Leaf, Munro. *A flock of watchbirds*
    How to behave and why
    Manners can be fun
Levitin, Sonia. *When Elephant goes to a party*
    When Kangaroo goes to school
Lewison, Wendy Cheyette. *Say thank you, Theodore*
Lexau, Joan M. *Cathy is company*
Marciano, John Bemelmans. *Madeline says merci*
Miller, Virginia. *On your potty!*
Montanari, Donata. *Children around the world*
Munsch, Robert N. *Good families don't*
Myller, Lois. *No! No!*
Parish, Peggy. *Mind your manners*
Parr, Todd. *Do's and don'ts*
Patterson, Geoffrey. *The naughty boy and the strawberry horse*
Paxton, Tom. *Engelbert the elephant*
Petersham, Maud. *The circus baby*
Polhamus, Jean Burt. *Dinosaur do's and don'ts*
Polisar, Barry Louis. *Don't do that!*
Potter, Beatrix. *The sly old cat*
Quackenbush, Robert M. *I don't want to go, I don't know how to act*
Rix, Jamie. *The last chocolate cookie*
Ross, Anna. *Say the magic word, please*
Scarry, Richard. *Richard Scarry's please and thank you book*
Seignobosc, Françoise. *The thank-you book*
Sherman, Ivan. *I do not like it when my friend comes to visit*
Slobodkin, Louis. *Thank you – you're welcome*
Smaridge, Norah. *You know better than that*
Smith, Barry. *A child's guide to bad behavior*
Stephens, Helen. *Ahoyty-toyty*
Stover, Jo Ann. *If everybody did*
Super, Gretchen. *Family traditions*
Sweetland, Nancy Rose. *Yelly Kelly*
Szekeres, Cyndy. *Toby's please and thank you*
Tryon, Leslie. *Patsy says*
Turner, Priscilla. *Among the odds and evens*
Weiss, Ellen. *Telephone time*
Yee, Wong Herbert. *Big black bear*
Ziefert, Harriet. *Someday we'll have very good manners*

Europe *see* Foreign lands – Europe

Evening *see* Twilight

Exercise *see* Health & Fitness – exercise

Experiments *see* Science

Explorers *see* Careers – explorers

Extraterrestrial beings *see* Aliens

Eye glasses *see* Glasses

Eyes *see* Anatomy – eyes; Glasses; Handicaps – blindness;
    Senses – sight

Fables *see* Folk & fairy tales

Faces *see* Anatomy – faces

Fairies

Allen, Jonathan. *Wake up, Sleeping Beauty*
Allingham, William. *The fairies*
Alper, Ann Fitzerald. *Harry McNairy, Tooth Fairy*
Anderson, Lonzo. *Two hundred rabbits*
Asch, Frank. *The flower faerie*
Barber, Antonia. *Catkin*
Barker, Cicely Mary. *Berry flower fairies*
    Blossom flower fairies
    Flower fairies of the garden
    Flower fairies of the seasons
    Flower fairies of the spring
    Flower fairies of the summer
    Flower fairies of the trees
    Flower fairies postcard book
    Spring flower fairies
    Summer flower fairies
Bate, Lucy. *Little rabbit's loose tooth*
Batt, Tanya Robyn. *The faerie's gift*
Beim, Lorraine. *Sasha and the samovar*
Bennett, Rowena. *Songs from around a toadstool table*
Bottner, Barbara. *Pish and Posh*
Bouchard, Dave. *Fairy*
Boujon, Claude. *The fairy with the long nose*
Briggs, Raymond. *The man*
Brown, Marc Tolon. *Arthur tricks the tooth fairy*
Butterworth, Nick. *Amanda's butterfly*
Carrick, Carol. *Norman fools the tooth fairy*
Carter, Angela. *The sleeping beauty and other favourite fairy tales*
Cartlidge, Michelle. *Fairy letters*
Cash, Rosanne. *Penelope Jane*
Chardiet, Bernice. *Martin and the tooth fairy*
Christiana, David. *A Tooth Fairy's tale*
    White nineteens
Clibbon, Meg. *Imagine you're a fairy!*
Climo, Shirley. *The Persian Cinderella*
Collington, Peter. *On Christmas eve*
    The tooth fairy
Coombs, Patricia. *Lisa and the grompet*
Davis, Katie (Katie I.). *Mabel the Tooth Fairy and how she got her job*
DeLage, Ida. *Weeny witch*
Demers, Dominique. *Old Thomas and the little fairy*
Durant, Alan. *Dear tooth fairy*
Edwards, Pamela Duncan. *Dear Tooth Fairy*
Elves, fairies and gnomes
Enright, Elizabeth. *Zeee*
Erlbruch, Wolf. *Leonard*
Fairies, trolls and goblins galore
Fairy poems for the very young
Forest, Heather. *The woman who flummoxed the fairies*
Fyleman, Rose. *A fairy went a-marketing*
Gardner, Mercedes. *Scooter and the magic star*
Gay, Marie-Louise. *Stella, fairy of the forest*
Graham, Bob. *Jethro Byrd, fairy child*
Grambling, Lois G. *This whole Tooth Fairy thing's nothing but a big rip-off!*
Griffith, Helen V. *Nata*
Grimm, Jacob. *The sleeping beauty*, ill. by Warwick Hutton
    The sleeping beauty, ill. by Trina Schart Hyman
    The sleeping beauty, ill. by Monika Laimgruber
    The sleeping beauty, ill. by Mercer Mayer
    Sleeping Beauty, ill. by Fina Rifa
    The sleeping beauty, ill. by Ruth Sanderson
    Sleeping Beauty, ill. by John Wallner
    The three spinning fairies
Gunther, Louise. *A tooth for the tooth fairy*
Hague, Kathleen. *Good night, fairies*
Heller, Nicholas. *The tooth tree*
Hollyn, Lynn. *Lynn Hollyn's Christmas toyland*
Hooks, William H. *The mystery of the missing tooth*
Hundal, Nancy. *Twilight fairies*
Inkpen, Deborah. *Harriet and the little fat fairy*
James, Brian. *The Supertwins and tooth trouble*
Jay, Betsy. *Jane vs. the Tooth Fairy*
Jennings, Linda M. *The sleeping beauty*
Jeschke, Susan. *Mia, Grandma and the genie*

Johnson, Paul Brett. *Little Bunny Foo Foo*
Karlin, Nurit. *The tooth witch*
Kaye, Marilyn. *The real tooth fairy*
Keith, Adrienne. *Fairies from A to Z*
Kennedy, Kim. *Mr. Bumble*
Kent, Jack. *Clotilda*
Kimmel, Eric A. *Asher and the capmakers*
Krensky, Stephen. *The youngest fairy godmother ever*
Kroll, Steven. *Loose tooth*
Lagerlöf, Selma. *The changeling*
Lester, Helen. *The wizard, the fairy and the magic chicken*
Lowell, Susan. *Cindy Ellen*
McClintock, Barbara. *Molly and the magic wishbone*
MacDonald, George. *Little Daylight*
MacDonald, Margaret Read. *Slop!*
MacDonald, Maryann. *Rosie's baby tooth*
McLean-Carr, Carol. *Fairy dreams*
Maconie, Robin. *Alice and her fabulous teeth*
Mahy, Margaret. *Pillycock's shop*
Manson, Beverlie. *The fairies' alphabet book*
Mayne, William. *The green book of Hob stories*
  The red book of Hob stories
  The yellow book of Hob stories
Metaxas, Eric. *The boy and the whale*
Mills, Lauren A. *Fairy wings*
  Fin and the imp
Milord, Susan. *Willa the wonderful*
Morris, Ann. *The Cinderella rebus book*
Munsch, Robert N. *Andrew's loose tooth*
Myers, Bernice. *Sidney Rella and the glass sneaker*
Myers, Walter Dean. *The dragon takes a wife*
Nesbit, Edith. *Melisande*
Newbolt, Henry John, Sir. *Rilloby-rill*
Nightingale, Sandy. *Cider apples*
Olson, Mary. *Nice try, Tooth Fairy*
Paxton, Tom. *The story of the Tooth Fairy*
Perrault, Charles. *Cinderella*, ill. by Diane Goode
  The sleeping beauty, ill. by David Walker
Peters, Stephanie True. *Raggedy Ann and Andy and the magic potion*
Pomeranc, Marion Hess. *The American Wei*
Prelutsky, Jack. *Monday's troll*
Ross, Tony. *A fairy tale*
Sierra, Judy. *The gift of the crocodile*
Silverman, Maida. *The magic well*
Simmons, Jane. *The dreamtime fairies*
Smee, Nicola. *The Tusk Fairy*
Smith, Lane. *Pinocchio, the boy*
Sperberg, Roger. *The story of the sleeping beauty, whose name was Briar Rose*
Taylor, Jane. *Twinkle, twinkle little star*, ill. by Heather Collins
  Twinkle, twinkle, little star, ill. by Michael Hague
Turnbull, Ann. *The tapestry cats*
Waddell, Martin. *The tough princess*
Wallace, Daisy. *Fairy poems*
Wallace, Ivy. *Pookie*
Wells, Rosemary. *Fritz and the mess fairy*
Weninger, Brigitte. *The elf's hat*
Wetterer, Margaret K. *Patrick and the fairy thief*
Wilder, Laura Ingalls. *Laura Ingalls Wilder's fairy poems*
Yolen, Jane. *Child of faerie, child of earth*

Fairs, festivals

Ackerman, Karen. *Bingleman's midway*
Amery, H. *Going to the fair*
Ancona, George. *Pablo remembers*
Aylesworth, Jim. *Mr. McGill goes to town*
Baker, Jill. *Basil of Bywater Hollow*
Baker, Keith. *Meet Mr. and Mrs. Green*
Ballard, Robin. *Carnival*
Barker, Melvern J. *Country fair*
Baynton, Martin. *Fifty and the great race*
Blumenthal, Deborah. *Ice palace*
Bond, Michael. *Paddington at the fair*
  Paddington Bear and the Busy Bee Carnival
Booth, Eugene. *At the fair*
Bourke, Linda. *Ethel's exceptional egg*

Browne, Anthony. *Animal fair*
Brunhoff, Laurent de. *Babar's fair will be opened next Sunday*
Bunting, Eve (Anne Evelyn). *Market day*
  The pumpkin fair
Burden-Patmon, Denise. *Carnival*
Calhoun, Mary. *Blue-ribbon Henry*
Calmenson, Stephanie. *Get well, gators!*
Carrick, Carol. *The highest balloon on the common*
Castaneda, Omar S. *Abuela's weave*
Cave, Kathryn. *The boy who became an eagle*
Chan, Arlene. *Awakening the dragon*
Chiefari, Janet. *Kids are baby goats*
Cooper, Elisha. *Country fair*
Cousins, Lucy. *Maisy at the fair*
Crews, Donald. *Night at the fair*
Crowther, Robert. *All the fun of the fair*
Daly, Niki. *Bravo, Zan Angelo!*
Darrow, Sharon. *Old Thunder and Miss Raney*
Delaney, A. *Pearl's first prize plant*
Delton, Judy. *Penny wise, fun foolish*
Devlin, Wende. *Old Witch and the polka-dot ribbon*
Dorros, Arthur. *Tonight is carnaval*
Enderle, Judith Ross. *Something's happening on Calabash Street*
Ernst, Lisa Campbell. *Miss Penny and Mr. Grubbs*
Ets, Marie Hall. *Mr. Penny's race horse*
Flanagan, Alice K. *Chinese New Year*
Gauch, Patricia Lee. *On to Widecombe Fair*
Geisert, Arthur. *Pigaroons*
Gibbons, Gail. *County fair*
Gikow, Louise. *Jim Henson's Muppets in What's fair is fair*
Greenstein, Elaine. *Mrs. Rose's garden*
Guy, Ginger Foglesong. *Fiesta*
Harshman, Marc. *Only one*
Hedderwick, Mairi. *Katie Morag and the two grandmothers*
Helldorfer, M. C. (Mary Claire). *Carnival*
Herriot, James. *Bonny's big day*
Hill, Eric. *Spot at the fair*
Hoff, Syd. *Henrietta goes to the fair*
Hoffman, Elizabeth Stokes. *Miss Renée's mice go to an exhibition*
Holabird, Katharine. *Angelina at the fair*
Horn, Sandra Ann. *The dandelion wish*
Jackson, Ellen B. *The autumn equinox*
Jacobson, Jennifer Richard. *A net of stars*
Joseph, Lynn. *Jump up time*
Kalman, Bobbie. *Celebrating the powwow*
Kassirer, Sue. *Math fair blues*
Kiser, SuAnn. *The hog call to end all!*
Krishnaswami, Uma. *Holi*
Kroll, Steven. *Queen of the May*
Landau, Elaine. *Mardi Gras*
Lasky, Kathryn. *Science fair bunnies*
Leech, Jay. *Bright Fawn and me*
Lewin, Ted. *Fair!*
Livingston, Myra Cohn. *Festivals*
Lunn, Janet Louise Swoboda. *Come to the fair*
McFarlane, Sheryl. *Going to the fair*
McLean, Dirk. *Play mas'! a carnival ABC*
Miles, Miska. *Jump frog jump*
Mitchell, Barbara. *Red Bird*
Moore, Elaine. *Grandma's smile*
Mott, Evelyn Clarke. *Dancing rainbows*
Muntean, Michaela. *The very bumpy bus ride*
Murphy, Stuart J. *The penny pot*
Nikola-Lisa, W. *Wheels go round*
O'Malley, Kevin. *Roller coaster*
Paraskevas, Betty. *Marvin, the tap-dancing horse*
Polacco, Patricia. *Oh, look!*
Sathre, Vivian. *Carnival time*
Schatell, Brian. *Farmer Goff and his turkey Sam*
Seignobosc, Françoise. *Jeanne-Marie at the fair*
Singer, Marilyn. *Will you take me to town on strawberry day?*
Speed, Toby. *Brave potatoes*
Stevens, Janet. *Animal fair*
Stevenson, James. *All aboard!*
Stihler, Chérie B. *The giant cabbage turnip*
Stoeke, Janet Morgan. *Minerva Louise at the fair*
Talley, Carol. *Clarissa*

Tudor, Tasha. *Corgiville fair*
Van Nutt, Julia. *Pumpkins from the sky?*
Watson, Clyde. *Applebet*
   Tom Fox and the apple pie
Watson, Nancy Dingman. *The birthday goat*
Widdecombe Fair
Wildsmith, Brian. *Carousel*
Winter, Jeanette. *Niño's mask*
Yacowitz, Caryn. *Pumpkin fiesta*
Ziefert, Harriet. *Pumpkin Pie*

Fairy tales *see* Folk & fairy tales

Falcons *see* Birds – falcons

Fall *see* Seasons – fall

Family life

Aaron, Jane. *When I'm afraid*
Abercrombie, Barbara. *Charlie Anderson*
Ackerman, Karen. *I know a place*
   In the park with dad
   Just like Max
   The sleeping porch
Adams, Eric J. *On the day his daddy left*
Adams, Jeanie. *Going for oysters*
Adler, David A. *Hiding from the Nazis*
Adoff, Arnold. *Big sister tells me that I'm black*
   Black is brown is tan
   In for winter, out for spring
   Ma nDa La
   Make a circle, keep us in
Agell, Charlotte. *Mud makes me dance in the spring*
Ahlberg, Allan. *Master Salt the sailor's son*
   Miss Brick, the builder's baby
   Mr. and Mrs. Hay the horse
   Mr. Biff the boxer
   Mr. Buzz the beeman
   Mockingbird
   Mrs. Plug the plumber
   Mrs. Wobble the waitress
   Mrs. Lather's laundry
Ahlberg, Janet. *The baby's catalogue*
   Bye-bye, baby
   Peek-a-boo!
Aitken, Amy. *Wanda's circus*
Ajmera, Maya. *To be a kid*
Alcott, Louisa May. *An old-fashioned Thanksgiving*
Aldis, Dorothy (Keeley). *Hiding*
Alexander, Martha G. *Even that moose won't listen to me*
   I'll be the horse if you'll play with me
   Marty McGee's space lab, no girls allowed
Alexander, Sue. *Dear Phoebe*
   Nadia the willful
Aliki. *Christmas tree memories*
   Jack and Jake
   June 7!
   Keep your mouth closed, dear
   Marianthe's story one: painted words; Marianthe's story two: spoken memories
   Those summers
   Welcome, little baby
Allard, Harry. *The Stupids have a ball*
   The Stupids step out
   The Stupids take off
Allen, Laura Jean. *Ottie and the star*
Allen, Thomas B. (Thomas Burt). *On grandaddy's farm*
Altman, Linda Jacobs. *Amelia's road*
Anderson, C. W. (Clarence Williams). *Billy and Blaze*
Anderson, Douglas. *Let's draw a story*
Anderson, Laurie Halse. *Turkey pox*
Anderson, Lonzo. *The day the hurricane happened*
Anderson, Peggy Perry. *Out to lunch*
Anholt, Catherine. *Catherine and Laurence Anholt's big book of families*

   Good days, bad days
   When I was a baby
Appelt, Kathi. *Someone's come to our house*
   Watermelon day
Arbeit, Eleanor Werner. *Mrs. Cat hides something*
Arcellana, Francisco. *The mats*
Arkin, Alan. *Tony's hard work day*
Armitage, Ronda. *The bossing of Josie*
   Don't forget, Matilda
   One moonlit night
Arnold, Marsha Diane. *The chicken salad club*
Arthur, Catherine. *My sister's silent world*
Asbjørnsen, P. C. (Peter Christen). *The man who kept house*
Asch, Frank. *Dear brother*
   Good night, Baby Bear
   Goodbye house
Asher, Sandy. *Princess Bee and the royal good-night story*
Atwell, Debby. *Pearl*
Aulaire, Ingri Mortenson d'. *Children of the northlights*
   Nils
Auld, Mary. *My aunt and uncle*
   My brother
   My dad
   My grandparents
   My mom
   My sister
Auzary-Luton, Sylvie. *1, 2, 3, music!*
Axelrod, Amy. *Pigs on the ball*
   Pigs will be pigs
   They'll believe me when I'm gone
Ayer, Jacqueline. *A wish for little sister*
Aylesworth, Jim. *The bad dream*
   Siren in the night
Babbitt, Lorraine. *Pink like the geranium*
Babbitt, Natalie. *Bub, or, The very best thing*
Bach, Alice. *Millicent the magnificent*
   The smartest bear and his brother Oliver
Bailey, Debbie. *My family*
   The playground
Baird, Anne. *Kiss, kiss*
Baisch, Cris. *When the lights went out*
Baker, Betty. *Sonny-Boy Sim*
Baker, Sanna Anderson. *Mississippi going north*
Balet, Jan B. *The fence*
   Five Rollatinis
Ballard, Robin. *Good-bye, house*
   Gracie
   Granny and me
   When we get home
Balzola, Asun. *Munia and the day things went wrong*
Banish, Roslyn. *A forever family*
Banks, Kate (Katherine A.). *Alphabet soup*
   Mama's coming home
Bannerman, Helen. *Little Black Sambo*, Platt & Munk, 1933
   Little Black Sambo, ill. by Nina R. Jordan
   Little Black Sambo, ill. by Gladys Turkey Mitchell
   Little Black Sambo, ill. by Robert Moore
   Little Black Sambo, ill. by Fern Bisel Peat
   Little Black Sambo, ill. by Mary LaFetra Russell
   Little Black Sambo, ill. by Cobb X. Shinn
   Little Black Sambo, ill. by Terry & Mary Smith
   Little Black Sambo, ill. by Suzanne
   Little Black Sambo, ill. by Gustaf Tenggren
   Little Black Sambo, ill. by Keith Ward
   Little Black Sambo, ill. by Julian Wehr
   The Little Black Sambo story book
   The story of Little Babaji
   The story of Little Black Sambo, Reilly, 1905
   The story of Little Black Sambo, Lippincott, 1915
   The story of Little Black Sambo, Stokes, 1923
   The story of Little Black Sambo, Altemus, 1931
   The story of Little Black Sambo, Lippincott, 1943
   The story of Little Black Sambo, Greenhouse, 1986
   The story of Little Black Sambo, HarperCollins, 1990
   The story of little black Sambo, Applewood, 1996
   The story of Little Black Sambo, ill. by Christopher Bing

The story of Little Black Sambo, "pop-up" picture by C. Carey Cloud

The story of Little Black Sambo, ill. by Judith Russell

Barasch, Lynne. *Old friends*

Barbato, Juli. *From bed to bus*

Barbour, Karen. *Little Nino's pizzeria*
  Mr. Bow Tie

Barrett, Joyce Durham. *Willie's not the hugging kind*

Barrett, Mary Brigid. *Day care days*

Bartoli, Jennifer. *Nonna*

Bascom, Joe. *Malcolm's job*

Bassett, Jeni. *The chicks' trick*

Bates, Artie Ann. *Ragsale*

Battles, Edith. *One to teeter-totter*

Bawden, Nina. *Princess Alice*

Baylor, Byrd. *The table where rich people sit*

Beard, Darleen Bailey. *Twister*

Beatty, Hetty Burlingame. *Moorland pony*

Beckman, Kaj. *Lisa cannot sleep*

Beim, Jerrold. *Jay's big job*

Beim, Lorraine. *Lucky Pierre*

Bemelmans, Ludwig. *Quito express*
  Sunshine

Benjamin, Alan. *A change of plans*

Bennett, Olivia. *A Turkish afternoon*

Benson, Ellen. *Philip's little sister*

Bentley, Dawn. *Busy little beaver*
  Welcome back, Puffin

Benton, Robert. *Little brother, no more*

Berenstain, Michael. *The dwarks*

Berenstain, Stan. *The Berenstain bears and the truth*
  The Berenstain bears and too much TV
  The Berenstain bears' Christmas tree
  The Berenstain bears forget their manners
  The Berenstain bears in the dark
  The Berenstain bears learn about strangers
  The Berenstain bears' moving day
  The Berenstain bears' report card trouble

Berger, Terry. *How does it feel when your parents get divorced?*

Bergman, Mara. *Musical beds*

Bernhard, Durga. *To and fro, fast and slow*
  What's Maggie up to?

Bernheim, Marc. *In Africa*

Berridge, Celia. *At my house*

Bertrand, Diane Gonzales. *Family = familia*

Bianchi, John. *Swine snafu*

Bible, Charles. *Jennifer's new chair*

Binch, Caroline. *Since Dad left*

Birdseye, Tom. *A regular flood of mishap*

Bishop, Claire Huchet. *The five Chinese brothers*

Bittner, Wolfgang. *Wake up, Grizzly!*

Blades, Ann. *Back to the cabin*
  Too small

Blaine, Marge (Margery Kay). *The terrible thing that happened at our house*

Blake, Claire. *The paper chain*

Blake, Jon. *Wriggly Pig*

Blake, Quentin. *Clown*

Blaustein, Muriel. *Bedtime, Zachary!*

Bloom, Suzanne. *A family for Jamie*

Blue, Rose. *How many blocks is the world?*

Blume, Judy. *The one in the middle is a green kangaroo*
  The Pain and The Great One

Blumenthal, Deborah. *Aunt Claire's yellow beehive hair*

Bodkin, Odds. *The Christmas cobwebs*

Boegehold, Betty. *Daddy doesn't live here anymore*
  You are much too small

Bogart, Jo Ellen. *Jeremiah learns to read*

Bograd, Larry. *Felix in the attic*

Boholm-Olsson, Eva. *Tuan*

Bolliger, Max. *The fireflies*
  The golden apple

Bolognese, Don. *A new day*

Bond, Felicia. *Poinsettia and her family*

Bond, Michael. *Paddington Bear*, ill. by John Lobban
  Paddington's garden

Bond, Rebecca. *Bravo, Maurice!*

Just like a baby

Bonsall, Crosby Newell. *The day I had to play with my sister*

Boon, Emilie. *Belinda's balloon*

Booth, David. *The dust bowl*

Bornstein, Ruth Lercher. *Of course a goat*

Bos, Burny. *Fun with the Molesons*
  Meet the Molesons
  Ollie the elephant

Bourgeois, Paulette. *Big Sarah's little boots*

Bowden, Joan Chase. *The bouncy baby bunny*

Bradman, Tony. *A bad week for the three bears*
  A goodnight kind of feeling
  That's not a fish
  Through my window
  Wait and see

Brady, Susan. *Find my blanket*

Brandenberg, Franz. *Everyone ready?*
  A fun weekend
  What's wrong with a van?

Brann, Esther. *A book for baby*

Breckler, Rosemary K. *Hoang breaks the lucky teapot*

Breeze, Lynn. *This little baby's bedtime*

Brennan, Jan. *Born two-gether*

Brenner, Barbara A. *The prince and the pink blanket*

Bresnick-Perry, Roslyn. *Leaving for America*

Brett, Jan. *Armadillo rodeo*

Bright, Robert. *Georgie*

Brimner, Larry Dane. *Elliot Fry's good-bye*

Brisson, Pat. *Your best friend, Kate*

Brock, Emma Lillian. *Mr. Wren's house*
  A pet for Barbie

Bromhall, Winifred. *Middle Matilda*

Brooks, Robert B. *So that's how I was born*

Brothers and sisters are like that!

Brothers, Aileen. *Sad Mrs. Sam Sack*

Brown, Jeff. *Flat Stanley*

Brown, Laurie Krasny. *What's the big secret?*
  When dinosaurs die

Brown, Marc Tolon. *Arthur's chicken pox*
  Arthur's family vacation
  D. W.'s lost blankie
  D. W., the picky eater

Brown, Margaret Wise. *The little scarecrow boy*
  My world
  On Christmas eve, ill. by Nancy Edwards Calder
  On Christmas eve, ill. by Beni Montresor
  Robin's room

Brown, Myra Berry. *Pip camps out*

Brown, Tricia. *Hello, amigos!*

Browne, Anthony. *Changes*
  Zoo

Broyles, Anne. *Shy Mama's Halloween*

Bruna, Dick. *Miffy*
  Miffy's birthday

Brunhoff, Laurent de. *Meet Babar and his family*

Brutschy, Jennifer. *The winter fox*

Buchanan, Heather S. *Emily Mouse saves the day*

Buck, Pearl S. (Pearl Sydenstricker). *The little fox in the middle*

Buckley, Helen Elizabeth. *Where did Josie go?*

Bunin, Catherine. *Is that your sister?*

Bunting, Eve (Anne Evelyn). *The big red barn*
  Ghost's hour, spook's hour
  Going home
  I have an olive tree
  My backpack
  Night tree
  The wall
  The Wednesday surprise

Burch, Robert. *The hunting trip*
  Joey's cat

Burden-Patmon, Denise. *Imani's gift at Kwanzaa*

Burdett, Lois. *Romeo and Juliet for kids*

Burningham, John. *Avocado baby*
  Courtney
  The snow
  Where's Julius?

Burns, Maurice. *Go ducks, go!*

Burstein, Fred. *Rebecca's nap*
Butler, Dorothy. *Another happy tale*
Byers, Rinda M. *Mycca's baby*
Byrd, Robert. *Marcella was bored*
Byrne, David. *Stay up late*
Cadnum, Michael. *The lost and found house*
Caffey, Donna. *Yikes-lice!*
Caines, Jeannette. *Abby*
　Chilly stomach
　I need a lunch box
Cairo, Shelley. *Our brother has Down's syndrome*
Calders, Pere. *Brush*
Calhoun, Mary. *Flood!*
Cameron, Polly. *"I can't," said the ant*
Camp, Lindsay. *The biggest bed in the world*
Campbell, Wayne. *What a catastrophe!*
Caple, Kathy. *The purse*
Capucilli, Alyssa Satin. *Bear hugs*
Carling, Amelia Lau. *Mama and Papa have a store*
　Mama and Papa have a store
Carlson, Nancy L. *It's going to be perfect*
　Louanne Pig in the perfect family
　Take time to relax
Carlstrom, Nancy White. *Baby-O*
　Barney is best
　Before you were born
　Heather hiding
　Jesse Bear, what will you wear?
　Thanksgiving Day at our house
　What does the rain play?
Carrick, Carol. *Banana beer*
Carson, Jo. *You hold me and I'll hold you*
Carter, Donna Renee. *Music in the family*
Carter, Penny. *A new house for the Morrisons*
Caseley, Judith. *Witch mama*
Castiglia, Julie. *Jill the pill*
Castle, Caroline. *Grandpa Baxter and the photographs*
Cazet, Denys. *Born in the gravy*
　Sunday
Chaffin, Lillie D. *Tommy's big problem*
Chall, Marsha Wilson. *Happy Birthday, America!*
　Sugarbush spring
Chalmers, Mary. *Mr. Cat's wonderful surprise*
　Take a nap, Harry
Chapman, Cheryl. *Snow on snow on snow*
Charles, Veronika Martenova. *The crane girl*
Charlip, Remy. *Hooray for me!*
Chase, Catherine. *Pete, the wet pet*
Cheng, Andrea. *Anna the bookbinder*
Chevalier, Christa. *The little bear who forgot*
Child, Lauren. *Clarice Bean, that's me*
　What planet are you from Clarice Bean?
Chislett, Gail. *Whump*
Chocolate, Deborah M. Newton. *Kwanzaa*
Chodos-Irvine, Margaret. *Ella Sarah gets dressed*
Choi, Sook Nyul. *Yunmi and Halmoni's trip*
Chorao, Kay. *Lester's overnight*
　Little farm by the sea
　Shadow night
Christelow, Eileen. *Five little monkeys with nothing to do*
Christenson, Larry. *The wonderful way that babies are made*
Christian, Mary Blount. *Christmas reflections*
Christiansen, C. B. *My mother's house, my father's house*
Cisneros, Sandra. *Hairs = Pelitos*
Clark, Ann Nolan. *In my mother's house*
Clavel, Bernard. *Castle of books*
Claverie, Jean. *Shopping*
Cleary, Beverly. *The growing-up feet*
　Janet's thingamajigs
　Petey's bedtime story
Clifton, Lucille. *Amifika*
　Don't you remember?
　Everett Anderson's goodbye
　Everett Anderson's 1-2-3
　Good, says Jerome
　My brother fine with me
　Some of the days of Everett Anderson

Cohen, Miriam. *Mimmy and Sophie*
Cohn, Janice I. *Molly's rosebush*
Cole, Babette. *Mommy laid an egg!*
　The un-wedding
　Winni Allfours
Cole, Barbara Hancock. *Texas star*
Cole, Joanna. *The Clown-Arounds*
　The Clown-Arounds have a party
　How I was adopted: Samantha's story
　How you were born
　Sweet dreams, Clown-Arounds!
Cole, Julia. *My parents' divorce*
Cole, William. *Frances face-maker*
　That pest Jonathan
Coleman, Michael. *Lazy Ozzie*
Collicott, Sharleen. *Mildred and Sam*
Collins, Pat Lowery. *Taking care of Tucker*
Condra, Estelle. *See the ocean*
Conford, Ellen. *Why can't I be William?*
Conrad, Pam. *Molly and the strawberry day*
　This mess
Conta, Marcia Maher. *Feelings between brothers and sisters*
　Feelings between kids and parents
Cook, Bernadine. *Looking for Susie*
Cooke, Trish. *So much*
　When I grow bigger
Coombs, Patricia. *Lisa and the grompet*
Cooney, Barbara. *Eleanor*
　Hattie and the wild waves
　Island boy
Cooper, Floyd. *Coming home*
Cooper, Helen (Helen F.). *Little monster did it!*
Cooper, Melrose. *I got a family*
Copeland, Eric. *Milton, my father's dog*
Corey, Dorothy. *Will there be a lap for me?*
Cornish, Sam. *Grandmother's pictures*
Corpi, Lucha. *Where fireflies dance = Ahí, donde bailan las luciérnagas*
Costa, Nicoletta. *The birthday party [board book]*
　Molly and Tom, the birthday party
Cousins, Lucy. *Za-Za's baby brother*
Cox, Judy. *My family plays music*
Coxe, Molly. *Whose footprints?*
Craig, M. Jean. *The dragon in the clock box*
Credle, Ellis. *Down, down the mountain*
Cressey, James. *Fourteen rats and a rat-catcher*
Crew, Gary. *Bright star*
Crews, Donald. *Sail away*
Crews, Nina. *A ghost story*
　You are here
Crompton, Margaret. *The house where Jack lives*
Crowley, Arthur. *The boogey man*
Cummings, Pat. *Carousel*
Curry, Jane Louise. *Little, little sister*
Curry, Nancy. *The littlest house*
Curti, Anna. *At home*
Curtis, Jamie Lee. *Tell me again about the night I was born*
　Today I feel silly and other moods that make my day
Cuyler, Margery. *Shadow's baby*
Dahl, Tessa. *Babies, babies, babies*
　The same but different
Dale, Penny. *Wake up, Mr. B.!*
Dalton, Anne. *This is the way*
Daly, Niki. *The boy on the beach*
　Bravo, Zan Angelo!
Daniel, Doris Temple. *Pauline and the peacock*
D'Antonio, Nancy. *Our baby from China*
David, Lawrence. *The good little girl*
Davis, Jennifer. *Before you were born*
Davis, Katie (Katie I.). *I hate to go to bed!*
Davis, Maggie S. *Something magic*
Davol, Marguerite W. *Black, white, just right*
Day, Alexandra. *The Christmas we moved to the barn*
De Angeli, Marguerite. *Yonie Wondernose*
Deedy, Carmen Agra. *The secret of Old Zeb*
Deetlefs, Rene. *Tabu and the dancing elephants*
DeFelice, Cynthia C. *The real, true Dulcie Campbell*
Delton, Judy. *Brimhall comes to stay*

Greaves, Margaret. *Little Bear and the Papagini circus*
Greenfield, Eloise. *I make music*
    Me and Neesie, ill. by Moneta Barnett
    Me and Neesie, ill. by Jan Spivey Gilchrist
Greenfield, Monica. *The baby*
    Waiting for Christmas
Grey, Mini. *Traction Man is here*
Griese, Arnold A. *Anna's Athabaskan summer*
Griffith, Helen V. *Mine will, said John*
Grimes, Nikki. *Come Sunday*
    Meet Danitra Brown
Grindley, Sally. *A new room for William*
    Wake up, dad!
Grossblatt, Ruby M. *Who's that sleeping on my sofabed?*
Gugler, Laurel Dee. *Facing the day*
Guiberson, Brenda Z. *The emperor lays an egg*
Guy, Rosa. *Billy the Great*
Hague, Kathleen. *The man who kept house*
Hale, Irina. *Boxman*
Hale, Kathleen. *Orlando and the water cats*
Hale, Lucretia. *The lady who put salt in her coffee*
Hall, Derek. *Elephant bathes*
    Gorilla builds
    Polar bear leaps
Hall, Donald. *Lucy's Christmas*
    Lucy's summer
Halperin, Wendy Anderson. *When chickens grow teeth*
Hamilton, DeWitt. *Sad days, glad days*
Hamm, Diane Johnston. *How many feet in the bed?*
Hammersmith, Craig. *What is a family?*
Hänel, Wolfram. *Little elephant's song*
Harley, Bill. *Nothing happened*
Harper, Jo. *Prairie dog pioneers*
Harris, Robie H. *Don't forget to come back*, ill.by Harry Bliss
    Don't forget to come back, ill. by Tony DeLuna
    Go! Go! Maria!
    Hot Henry
    Messy Jessie
Harrison, David Lee. *A thousand cousins, poems of family life*
Harshman, Marc. *Moving days*
Hartman, Bob. *Granny Mae's Christmas play*
    Lobster for lunch
Harvey, Amanda. *Stormy weather*
Harvey, Brett. *Cassie's journey*
    Immigrant girl
Haskins, Francine. *I remember "121"*
Hautzig, Esther (Rudomin). *At home*
Havill, Juanita. *Treasure nap*
Hayes, Sarah. *Happy Christmas, Gemma*
Hazelton, Elizabeth Baldwin. *Sammy, the crow who remembered*
Hazen, Barbara Shook. *Even if I did something awful*
    Tight times
Hearne, Betsy Gould. *Seven brave women*
Heath, Amy. *Sofie's role*
Heckman, Philip. *Waking upside down*
Hedderwick, Mairi. *Katie Morag and the big boy cousins*
    P. D. Pebbles' summer or winter book
Heide, Florence Parry. *Sami and the time of the troubles*
Heiligman, Deborah. *Mike Swan, sink or swim*
    Pockets
Helldorfer, M. C. (Mary Claire). *Harmonica night*
    Silver Rain Brown
Heller, Linda. *Lily at the table*
Heller, Nicholas. *The monster in the cave*
    Up the wall
Hendershot, Judith. *In coal country*
Henderson, Kathy. *Bumpety bump*
    Don't interrupt!
    Newborn
Hendrickson, Karen. *Fun with toddlers*
Hendry, Diana. *Back soon!*
    Not anywhere house
Henkes, Kevin. *Bailey goes camping*
    Julius, the baby of the world
    Shhhh
Hennessy, B. G. (Barbara G.). *A, B, C, D, tummy, toes, hands, knee*
Herman, Charlotte. *The memory cupboard*

Herman, Gail. *The littlest duckling*
Hershenhorn, Esther. *There goes Lowell's party!*
Hess, Edith. *Peter and Susie find a family*
Hessell, Jenny. *Staying at Sam's*
Hest, Amy. *The purple coat*
    The ring and the window seat
Heymans, Annemie. *The princess in the kitchen garden*
Hickman, Martha Whitmore. *When Andy's father went to prison*
Hill, Elizabeth Starr. *Evan's corner*
Hill, Eric. *At home*
    Spot goes to the beach
Hill, Susan. *Go away, bad dreams!*
Himmelman, John. *The Clover County carrot contest*
    The great leaf blast-off
    Wanted: perfect parents
Hindley, Judy. *What's in baby's morning*
Hines, Anna Grossnickle. *Big like me*
    Daddy makes the best spaghetti
    Even if I spill my milk?
    Moon's wish
    The secret keeper
    They really like me!
    Whose shoes?
Hines, Gary. *The day of the high climber*
Hippely, Hilary Horder. *The crimson ribbon*
Hirsh, Marilyn. *The pink suit*
Hoban, Julia. *Amy loves the rain*
    Amy loves the snow
    Amy loves the sun
Hoban, Lillian. *Arthur's prize reader*
    Mr. Pig and family
Hoban, Russell. *A baby sister for Frances*
    They came from Aargh!
Hoberman, Mary Ann. *Fathers, mothers, sisters, brothers*
Hodge, Deborah. *Emma's story*
Hodges, Margaret. *Silent night*
Hoffman, Don. *Good morning, good night Billy and Abigail*
Hoffman, Mary. *Grace and family*
Hoffman, Phyllis. *Steffie and me*
Hoffmann, E. T. A. *The strange child*
Hofstrand, Mary. *By the sea*
Höjer, Dan. *Heart of mine*
Hoke, Helen L. *The biggest family in the town*
Hol, Coby. *Tippy Bear and little Sam*
Holabird, Katharine. *Alexander and the magic boat*
Hooker, Ruth. *At Grandma and Grandpa's house*
Hoopes, Lyn Littlefield. *Daddy's coming home*
    Mommy, daddy, me
Hopkins, Margaret. *Sleepytime for baby mouse*
Hopkinson, Deborah. *Maria's comet*
Horton, Barbara Savadge. *What comes in spring?*
Horvath, Betty F. *Be nice to Josephine*
Houghton, Eric. *The crooked apple tree*
Houston, Gloria. *The year of the perfect Christmas tree*
Howard, Ellen. *The big seed*
    The log cabin Christmas
    The log cabin church
Hubbell, Patricia. *Bouncing time*
Hudson, Wade. *I love my family*
Hughes, Monica. *Little Fingerling*
Hughes, Shirley. *Bathwater's hot*
    Being together
    Chatting
    David and dog
    Dogger
    An evening at Alfie's
    Giving
    Lucy and Tom's A.B.C.
    Lucy and Tom's Christmas
    Lucy and Tom's 1, 2, 3
    Moving Molly
    Noisy
    Olly and me
    Out and about
    When we went to the park
Humphries, Tudor. *Hiding*
Hundal, Nancy. *Camping*

Layton, Neal. *Smile if you're human*
Lee, Milly. *Nim and the war effort*
Leedy, Loreen. *Who's who in my family?*
Le Guin, Ursula K. *Fish soup*
Leiner, Katherine. *Both my parents work*
Lenski, Lois. *At our house*
  Debbie and her family
  The little family
  Papa Small
Leonard, Marcia. *Angry*
  Getting dressed
Lerner, Harriet Goldhor. *Franny B. Kranny, there's a bird in your hair*
Lester, Alison. *Magic beach*
  My farm
  Rosie sips spiders
Lester, Julius. *Sam and the tigers*
Levine, Abby. *This is the turkey*
  You push, I ride
Levinson, Riki. *Grandpa's hotel*
  I go with my family to Grandma's
  Me baby!
  Our home is the sea
  Touch! Touch!
  Watch the stars come out
Levitin, Sonia. *Nine for California*
Lewin, Hugh. *Jafta*
  Jafta and the wedding
Lewis, Kim. *The last train*
Lewis, Rose A. *I love you like crazy cakes*
Lexau, Joan M. *Benjie*
  Every day a dragon
  Finders keepers, losers weepers
  Me day
Limb, Sue. *Come back, Grandma*
Lindman, Maj. *Flicka, Ricka, Dicka and a little dog*
  Flicka, Ricka, Dicka and the big red hen
  Flicka, Ricka, Dicka and the new dotted dress
  Flicka, Ricka, Dicka and the three kittens
  Flicka, Ricka, Dicka bake a cake
  Snipp, Snapp, Snurr and the buttered bread
  Snipp, Snapp, Snurr and the magic horse
  Snipp, Snapp, Snurr and the red shoes
  Snipp, Snapp, Snurr and the reindeer
  Snipp, Snapp, Snurr and the seven dogs
  Snipp, Snapp, Snurr and the yellow sled
Lindsay, Jeanne Warren. *Do I have a daddy?*
Lisker, Sonia O. *Two special cards*
Livingston, Carole. *"Why was I adopted?"*
Lomas Garza, Carmen. *In my family*
London, Jonathan. *Hurricane!*
  A koala for Katie
  The waterfall
Long, Melinda. *Hiccup snickup*
Loomis, Christine. *Across America, I love you*
Lopez, Loretta. *The birthday swap*
Lottridge, Celia Barker. *Something might be hiding*
Lotz, Karen E. *Can't sit still*
Lucas, Barbara (Barbara M.). *Snowed in*
Lyndon, Kerry Raines. *A birthday for Blue*
Lyon, George Ella. *Cecil's story*
  Come a tide
  Five live bongos
  One lucky girl
Macaulay, David. *Black and white*
Maccarone, Grace. *I shop with my daddy*
McCloskey, Robert. *Blueberries for Sal*
  One morning in Maine
McConnachie, Brian. *Lily of the forest*
McCully, Emily Arnold. *Monk camps out*
  My real family
McCutcheon, John. *Happy adoption day!*
MacDonald, Amy. *Cousin Ruth's tooth*
MacDonald, Maryann. *Rosie runs away*
McDonald, Megan. *Insects are my life*
McGinley, Phyllis. *Lucy McLockett*
MacGregor, Marilyn. *Helen the hungry bear*

Mack, Gail. *Yesterday's snowman*
McKaughan, Larry. *Why are your fingers cold?*
McKay, Hilary. *Where's bear?*
MacKay, Jed. *The big secret*
McKee, David. *The school bus comes at eight o'clock*
  Snow woman
MacKinnon, Debbie. *Let's play: I can do it!*
McKissack, Patricia C. *Messy Bessey's family reunion*
  Nettie Jo's friends
MacLachlan, Patricia. *All the places to love*
  Who loves me?
McLerran, Alice. *The year of the ranch*
McNaughton, Colin. *Guess who's just moved in next door?*
McPhail, David M. *The cereal box*
  Emma's pet
  Emma's vacation
McQuade, Jacqueline. *Good times with Teddy Bear*
Maestro, Betsy. *Bike trip*
Magdanz, James S. *Go home, river*
Mahy, Margaret. *Jam*
  Mrs. Discombobulous
  The rattlebang picnic
  The seven Chinese brothers
Mallett, Anne. *Here comes Tagalong*
Malloy, Judy. *Bad Thad*
Maloney, Peter (1955–). *His mother's nose*
Manes, Esther. *The bananas move to the ceiling*
Manushkin, Fran. *Baby*
  The best toy of all
  Bubblebath!
  The perfect Christmas picture
  Starlight and candles
Manzano, Sonia. *No dogs allowed*
Martel, Cruz. *Yagua days*
Martin, Bill (William Ivan). *White Dynamite and Curly Kidd*
Martin, C. L. G. *The blueberry train*
Martin, David. *Five little piggies*
Martin, Jacqueline Briggs. *On Sand Island*
Maschler, Fay. *T. G. and Moonie have a baby*
May, Kathy. *Molasses man*
Mayer, Gina. *This is my family*
Mayer, Mercer. *The rocking horse angel*
Mayle, Peter. *Divorce can happen to the nicest people*
  Why are we getting a divorce?
Maynard, Joyce. *Camp-out*
Mayper, Monica. *After good-night*
Mazer, Anne. *The No-Nothings and their baby*
  Watch me
Medina, Tony. *DeShawn days*
Melmed, Laura Krauss. *A hug goes around*
  Little Oh
Merriam, Eve. *The Christmas box*
Merrill, Jean. *Emily Emerson's moon*
Miles, Calvin. *Calvin's Christmas wish*
Milgram, Mary. *Brothers are all the same*
Miller, Edna. *Mousekin's family*
Miller, J. P. (John Parr). *Good night, Little Rabbit*
Miller, Kathryn Ann. *Did my first mother love me?*
Miller, M. L. *Those Bottles!*
Miller, Margaret. *At my house*
  Family time
  I can help
  I love colors
  I'm grown up!
  In my room
  My first words: me and my clothes
  Time to eat
Mills, Claudia. *A visit to Amy-Claire*
Millward, David Wynn. *Jenny and Bob*
Milord, Sue. *Maggie and the goodbye gift*
Minarik, Else Holmelund. *Father's flying flapjacks*
Mintzberg, Yvette. *Sally, where are you?*
Miranda, Anne. *Baby talk*
Mitchell, Barbara. *Red Bird*
  Waterman's child
Modarressi, Mitra. *The parent thief*
Moers, Hermann. *Hugo's baby brother*

Molnar, Dorothy E. *Who will pick me up when I fall?*
Monjo, F. N. *Rudi and the distelfink*
Monk, Isabell. *Family*
Moore, Inga. *Oh, little Jack*
Moore, Lilian. *Papa Albert*
Moorman, Margaret. *Light the lights!*
Morgan-Vanroyen, Mary. *Guess who I love?*
Morimoto, Junko. *The inch boy*
Morozumi, Atsuko. *Helping daddy*
Morris, Ann. *The baby book*
    Families
    Loving
Morrow, Barbara. *Edward's portrait*
Moses, Will. *Silent night*
Mosley, Francis. *The dinosaur eggs*
Moss, Marissa. *Mel's diner*
Motyka, Sally Mitchell. *An ordinary day*
Munsch, Robert N. *Good families don't*
    I have to go!
    Mmm, cookies!
Murphy, Jill. *All in one piece*
    Five minutes' peace
    The last noo-noo
    A quiet night in
Murphy, Stuart J. *The best vacation ever*
Myller, Lois. *No! No!*
Namioka, Lensey. *The laziest boy in the world*
Nayer, Judy. *The happy little engine*
Nelson, Vaunda Micheaux. *Always Gramma*
Nerlove, Miriam. *Easter*
Ness, Evaline. *Exactly alike*
Neville, Emily Cheney. *The bridge*
Neville, Mary. *The Christmas tree ride*
Newton, Jill. *Don't sit there!*
Nicholls, Judith. *Someone I like*
Nicholson, Nicholas B. A. *Little girl in a red dress with cat and dog*
Nikola-Lisa, W. *One, two, three Thanksgiving!*
    Summer sun risin'
Nilsson, Ulf. *Little sister rabbit*
Nivola, Claire A. *Elisabeth*
Nixon, Joan Lowery. *You bet your britches, Claude*
Noble, June. *Two homes for Lynn*
Nolan, Madeena Spray. *My daddy don't go to work*
Nolen, Jerdine. *In my momma's kitchen*
Nones, Eric Jon. *Wendell*
Norac, Carl. *I love you so much*
Novak, Matt. *Mouse TV*
O'Brien, John (1953–). *Poof!*
O'Brien, Patrick. *Steam, smoke, and steel*
O'Donnell, Elizabeth Lee. *Maggie doesn't want to move*
O'Kelley, Mattie Lou. *Circus!*
Olsen, Ib Spang. *The grown-up trap*
Oppenheim, Joanne. *Rooter remembers*
Oram, Hiawyn. *Reckless Ruby*
Ormerod, Jan. *Moonlight*
    Who's whose?
Osborne, Mary Pope. *Happy birthday, America*
Osofsky, Audrey. *Dreamcatcher*
Ostheeren, Ingrid. *The blue monster*
Ovenell-Carter, Julie. *Adam's daycare*
Overend, Jenni. *Welcome with love*
Oxenbury, Helen. *Beach day*
    Family
    Our dog
Palatini, Margie. *Tub-boo-boo*
Paraskevas, Betty. *The tangerine bear*
Paterson, Diane. *Wretched Rachel*
Pearce, Philippa. *Emily's own elephant*
Pearson, Susan. *Saturday, I ran away*
Pedersen, Judy. *Out in the country*
Pellegrini, Nina. *Families are different*
Pellowski, Anne. *Stairstep farm*
Pérez, Amada Irma. *My very own room = Mi propio cuartito*
    My diary from here to there = Mi diario de aquí hasta allá
Perkins, Lynne Rae. *The broken cat*
    Clouds for dinner
    Home lovely

Peterson, Jeanne Whitehouse. *Don't forget Winona*
Pfeffer, Wendy. *Mallard duck at Meadow View Pond*
Pilkey, Dav. *The Hallo-wiener*
Pinkney, Andrea Davis. *Mim's Christmas jam*
Pinkney, Gloria Jean. *Back home*
    The Sunday outing
Pinkney, J. Brian. *Jojo's flying side kick*
Pinkwater, Daniel Manus. *Wempires*
Politi, Leo. *Little Leo*
Pomerantz, Charlotte. *The mango tooth*
    Posy
Porte, Barbara Ann. *Harry's mom*
Portnoy, Mindy Avra. *Mommy never went to Hebrew school*
    Where do people go when they die?
Poulin, Stéphane. *My mother's loves*
    Travels for two
Powell, Consie. *Old dog Cora and the Christmas tree*
Powell, E. Sandy. *A chance to grow*
Prater, John. *Along came Tom*
    The greatest show on earth
Price, Mathew. *Peekaboo!*
Pringle, Laurence P. *Everybody has a bellybutton*
    Octopus hug
Provensen, Alice. *An owl and three pussycats*
Prøysen, Alf. *Christmas eve at Santa's*
Prusski, Jeffrey. *Bring back the deer*
Pryor, Bonnie. *The dream jar*
Pulver, Robin. *Alicia's tutu*
Purdy, Carol. *Iva Dunnit and the big wind*
    Least of all
Quackenbush, Robert M. *Funny bunnies on the run*
    Henry's world tour
    I don't want to go, I don't know how to act
    Mouse feathers
Quindlen, Anna. *The tree that came to stay*
Raffi. *One light, one sun*
Rand, Gloria. *Baby in a basket*
    The cabin key
    Sailing home
Ransom, Candice F. *When the whippoorwill calls*
Raphael, Elaine. *Turnabout*
Raskin, Ellen. *Ghost in a four-room apartment*
Raven, Margot Theis. *Angels in the dust*
Ray, Deborah Kogan. *Sunday morning we went to the zoo*
Rayner, Mary. *Mrs. Pig gets cross and other stories*
Redies, Rainer. *The cats' party*
Rees, Mary. *Ten in a bed*
Reid, Barbara. *The party*
Remkiewicz, Frank. *Greedyanna*
Reynolds, Marilynn. *The new land*
Rice, David L. *Because Brian hugged his mother*
Rice, Eve. *City night*
    Ebbie
    Papa's lemonade and other stories
Richardson, John. *Grunt*
Ricklen, Neil. *My family = Mi familia*
Rider, Alex. *At our house = Chez nous*
Rigby, Shirley Lincoln. *Smaller than most*
Riggio, Anita. *Smack dab in the middle*
    Wake up, William!
Ringgold, Faith. *Bonjour, Lonnie*
    Dinner at Aunt Connie's house
    The invisible princesses
Rippon, Penelope. *My day*
Robb, Brian. *My grandmother's djinn*
Roche, P. K. (Patrick K.). *Good-bye, Arnold!*
Rock, Lois. *Now we have a baby*
Rockwell, Anne F. *Blackout*
    In our house
    Long ago yesterday
    No! No! No!
    Once upon a time this morning
    The storm
Rodda, Emily. *Yay!*
Roffey, Maureen. *Bathtime*
    Family scramble
    Here, kitty kitty!

Mealtime

Quick, catch Dan!

Rogers, Fred. *Adoption*

Divorce

Moving

Rogers, Paul (Patrick). *Lily's picnic*

Ruby's dinnertime

Somebody's awake

Somebody's sleepy

Root, Phyllis. *Rattletrap car*

Rattletrap car [board book]

What Baby wants

Rosenberg, Liz. *On Christmas eve*

Rosenberg, Maxine B. *Being adopted*

Rosenberry, Vera. *Vera runs away*

Rosenblum, Richard. *Journey to the golden land*

Ross, Katharine (1954–). *When you were a baby*

Roth, Susan L. *Another Christmas*

Rounds, Glen. *Sod houses on the Great Plains*

Roy, Ronald. *Breakfast with my father*

Rubin, C. M. *Eleanor, Ellatony, Ellencake, and me*

Ruelle, Karen Gray. *The crunchy, munchy Christmas tree*

Ruffins, Reynold. *My brother never feeds the cat*

Russo, Marisabina. *The line up book*

Under the table

When mama gets home

Why do grownups have all the fun?

Ruurs, Margriet. *When we go camping*

Ryan, Pam Muñoz. *One hundred is a family*

Ryder, Joanne. *Beach party*

Rylant, Cynthia. *Best wishes*

Birthday presents

Bunny bungalow

The relatives came

When I was young in the mountains

Salley, Coleen. *Epossumondas*

Samuels, Vyanne. *Carry go bring come*

Sandburg, Carl (Charles August). *The Huckabuck family and how they raised popcorn in Nebraska and quit and came back,* ill. by David Small

Sansone, Adele. *The little green goose*

San Souci, Daniel. *In the moonlight mist*

Santos, Rosa. *Play date*

Sarnoff, Jane. *That's not fair*

Sasso, Sandy Eisenberg. *Naamah, Noah's wife*

Say, Allen. *Allison*

Grandfather's journey

A river dream

Schaefer, Carole Lexa. *The copper tin cup*

Schaefer, Lola M. *Loose tooth*

Scheffler, Ursel. *Be brave, little lion!*

Who has time for Little Bear?

Schermbrucker, Reviva. *Charlie's house*

Schermer, Judith. *Mouse in house*

Schertle, Alice. *Down the road*

That's what I thought

Schick, Eleanor. *A piano for Julie*

Schlein, Miriam. *Billy, the littlest one*

My family

My house

The story about me

Schoenherr, John. *Rebel*

Schreck, Karen Halvorsen. *Lucy's family tree*

Schuchman, Joan. *Two places to sleep*

Schumacher, Claire. *Brave Lily*

Schwartz, Amy. *Some babies*

Schweninger, Ann. *Summertime*

Valentine friends

Scott, Ann Herbert. *On mother's lap*

On mother's lap [board book]

Sam

Scuderi, Lucia. *To fly*

Seabrooke, Brenda. *The swan's gift*

Segal, Lore Groszmann. *Tell me a Mitzi*

Tell me a Trudy

Seligman, Dorothy Halle. *Run away home*

Senisi, Ellen B. *For my family, love, Allie*

Seuling, Barbara. *What kind of family is this?*

Seyton, Marion. *The hole in the hill*

Shannon, Margaret. *Gullible's troubles*

Sharmat, Marjorie Weinman. *Go to sleep, Nicholas Joe*

Goodnight, Andrew. Goodnight, Craig

Sometimes mama and papa fight

What are we going to do about Andrew?

Sharr, Christine. *Homes*

Shea, Pegi Deitz. *I see me!*

Shelby, Anne. *Homeplace*

We keep a store

Sherman, Eileen Bluestone. *The odd potato*

Shiefman, Vicky. *Sunday potatoes, Monday potatoes*

Shields, Carol Diggory. *I am really a princess*

Shyer, Marlene Fanta. *Stepdog*

Silverman, Erica. *Fixing the crack of dawn*

Simmons, Jane. *Come along, Daisy!*

Simon, Francesca. *The Topsy-Turvies*

Simon, Norma. *All families are special*

All kinds of families

How do I feel?

Oh, that cat!

What do I say?

Sing, Rachel. *Chinese New Year's dragon*

Singer, Marilyn. *The Morgans' dream*

The one and only me

Skorpen, Liesel Moak. *His mother's dog*

Skulavik, Mary Alys. *Bert*

Slobodkin, Louis. *Clear the track for Michael's magic train*

Magic Michael

Slyder, Ingrid. *The Fabulous Flying Fandinis*

Smalls, Irene. *Don't say ain't*

Smalls-Hector, Irene. *Irene and the big, fine nickel*

Louise's gift

Smith, Barry. *A child's guide to bad behavior*

Minnie and Ginger

Smith, Cynthia Leitich. *Jingle dancer*

Smith, Edward Biko. *A lullaby for Daddy*

Smith, Lucia B. *A special kind of sister*

Smith, Wendy. *Twice mice*

Sobol, Harriet Langsam. *We don't look like our mom and dad*

Sobol, Richard. *Adelina's whales*

Sonneborn, Ruth A. *Seven in a bed*

Sorensen, Henri. *New Hope*

Soto, Gary. *Snapshots from the wedding*

Speare, Jean. *A candle for Christmas*

Sperberg, Roger. *Real soon, raccoon*

Spinelli, Eileen. *The best time of day*

Six hogs on a scooter

Summerbath, winterbath

Thanksgiving at the Tappletons'

Stanton, Elizabeth. *The very messy room*

Steel, Danielle. *Freddie's trip*

Martha's new daddy

Max and the baby sitter

Steig, William. *Spinky sulks*

Sylvester and the magic pebble

Toby, what are you?

Toby, where are you?

Stein, Sara Bonnett. *The adopted one*

Oh, baby!

On divorce

That new baby

Steiner, Charlotte. *Daddy comes home*

Stepto, Michele. *Snuggle Piggy and the magic blanket*

Steptoe, John. *My special best words*

Stevenson, James. *"Could be worse!"*

When I was nine

Stevenson, Robert Louis. *The moon*

Stewart, Dana. *Friends from Galilee*

Stickland, Paul. *A child's book of things*

Stock, Catherine. *Sophie's bucket*

Sophie's knapsack

Stoddard, Sandol. *Curl up small*

The thinking book

Stone, Lynn M. *Farms old and new*

Straight, Susan. *Bear E. Bear*

Williams, Marcia. *Not a worry in the world*
Williams, Sherley Anne. *Working cotton*
Williams, Suzanne. *My dog never says please*
Williams, Vera B. *A chair for my mother*
  "More more more," said the baby
  Music, music for everyone
  Something special for me
Wilner, Isabel. *The baby's game book*
Wilson, Budge. *A fiddle for Angus*
Wilson, Sarah. *Big day on the river*
  Good zap, little grog
  Muskrat, muskrat, eat your peas!
Wing, Natasha. *Jalapeño bagels*
Winn, Chris. *My day*
Winter, Rick. *Dirty birdy feet*
Winthrop, Elizabeth. *Bunk beds*
  I think he likes me
  I'm the Boss!
Wittmann, Patricia. *Buffalo Thunder*
Wohl, Lauren L. *Matzoh mouse*
Wojtowycz, David. *Dudley helps out*
Wolde, Gunilla. *Betsy and Peter are different*
  Betsy and the vacuum cleaner
  Betsy's fixing day
  This is Betsy
Wolff, Ashley. *Only the cat saw*
  Stella and Roy go camping
Wong, Benedict Norbert. *Lo & behold*
  Lo & behold, good enough to eat
Wong, Janet S. *Buzz*
  This next New Year
  The trip back home
Wood, Audrey. *A cowboy Christmas*
  Elbert's bad word
  The Tickleoctopus
  Weird parents
Woodman, Allen. *The bear who came to stay*
Woodson, Jacqueline. *We had a picnic this Sunday past*
Yaccarino, Dan. *If I had a robot*
Yaffe, Alan. *The magic meatballs*
Yamashita, Haruo. *Mice at the beach*
Yardley, Joanna. *The red ball*
Yee, Paul. *The jade necklace*
Young, Evelyn. *Wu and Lu and Li*
Zagwÿn, Deborah Turney. *Apple batter*
Zalben, Jane Breskin. *Baby Babka*
  Beni's first Chanukah
  Beni's first wedding
  Happy Passover, Rosie
  Leo and Blossom's Sukkah
  Pearl's Passover
Zamorano, Ana. *Let's eat!*
Zemach, Kaethe. *The funny dream*
Zemach, Margot. *To Hilda for helping*
Ziefert, Harriet. *Before I was born*
  Birdhouse for rent
  Daddies are for catching fireflies
  Good night, Jessie!
  I want to sleep in your bed!
  Keeping daddy awake on the way home from the beach
  My sister says nothing ever happens when we go sailing
  A new coat for Anna
  Pushkin meets the bundle
  Pushkin minds the bundle
  Strike four!
Zimelman, Nathan. *If I were strong enough . . .*
Zinnemann-Hope, Pam. *Let's play ball, Ned*
Zolotow, Charlotte (Shapiro). *Big sister and little sister*
  Do you know what I'll do?
  If it weren't for you
  It's not fair
  May I visit?
  My grandson Lew
  The quiet mother and the noisy little boy
  A rose, a bridge, and a wild black horse
  The sky was blue
  Some things go together

  Someone new
  The summer night
  When I have a son
  William's doll
Zusman, Evelyn. *The Passover parrot*

Family life – aunts, uncles

Abercrombie, Barbara. *Michael and the cats*
Abolafia, Yossi. *My three uncles*
Alexander, Sally Hobart. *Maggie's whopper*
Allan, Nicholas. *The thing that ate Aunt Julia*
Anderson, Lena. *Tick-tock*
Anderson, Leone Castell. *It's O.K. to cry*
Arro, Lena. *By geezers and galoshes!*
Auld, Mary. *My aunt and uncle*
Austin, Heather. *Visiting Aunt Sylvia's*
Bertrand, Diane Gonzales. *Uncle Chente's picnic = El picnic de Tío Chente*
Bettina (Bettina Ehrlich). *Of uncles and aunts*
Blake, Quentin. *Mrs. Armitage: queen of the road*
Blaustein, Muriel. *Baby Mabu and Auntie Moose*
Brandenberg, Franz. *Aunt Nina and her nephews and nieces*
  Aunt Nina, good night
  Aunt Nina's visit
Brecht, Bertolt. *Uncle Eddie's moustache*
Brisson, Pat. *Magic carpet*
Brock, Emma Lillian. *A present for Auntie*
Bryant, Sara Cone. *Epaminondas and his auntie*
Bush, Timothy. *James in the house of Aunt Prudence*
Bynum, Janie. *Altoona up north*
Carle, Eric. *My apron*
Carr, Jan. *Dark day, light night*
Carson, Jo. *Pulling my leg*
Cazet, Denys. *Great-Uncle Felix*
Chichester Clark, Emma. *Lunch with Aunt Augusta*
Child, Lauren. *Clarice Bean, guess who's babysitting?*
Christiansen, Candace. *The ice horse*
Cole, Babette. *The trouble with Uncle*
Cole, William. *Aunt Bella's umbrella*
Coulter, Hope Norman. *Uncle Chuck's truck*
Crews, Nina. *A ghost story*
Cummings, Pat. *My aunt came back*
Degen, Bruce. *Aunt Possum and the pumpkin man*
Delton, Judy. *My Uncle Nikos*
Dennard, Deborah. *Travis and the better mousetrap*
Denslow, Sharon Phillips. *Riding with Aunt Lucy*
De Paola, Tomie (Thomas Anthony). *Bonjour, Mister Satie*
Devlin, Wende. *Aunt Agatha, there's a lion under the couch!*
Dillon, Jana. *Lucky O'Leprechaun*
  Lucky O'Leprechaun comes to America
Duke, Kate. *Aunt Isabel makes trouble*
  Aunt Isabel tells a good one
Edwards, Michelle. *A baker's portrait*
Edwards, Pamela Duncan. *Rosie's roses*
Edwards, Patricia Kier. *Chester and Uncle Willoughby*
Ehrlich, Amy. *Bunnies at Christmastime*
Ernst, Lisa Campbell. *The rescue of Aunt Pansy*
Everett, Gwen. *Li'l Sis and Uncle Willie*
Fowler, Susi Gregg. *Beautiful*
Froissart, Bénédicte. *Uncle Henry's dinner guests*
Gantos, Jack (John, Jr.). *Aunt Bernice*
Gauch, Patricia Lee. *Uncle Magic*
Go tell Aunt Rhody. *Go tell Aunt Rhody*, ill. by Aliki
  Go tell Aunt Rhody, ill. by Robert M. Quackenbush
Gray, Libba Moore. *When Uncle took the fiddle*
Green, Phyllis. *Uncle Roland, the perfect guest*
Greenblat, Rodney Alan. *Aunt Ippy's museum of junk*
  Uncle Wizzmo's new used car
Gregory, Valiska. *The oatmeal cookie giant*
Gretz, Susanna. *Rabbit food*
Grifalconi, Ann. *Kinda blue*
Guthrie, Donna. *One hundred and two steps*
Gutman, Anne. *Lisa in New York*
Hallinan, P. K. (Patrick K.). *We're very good friends, my aunt and I*
Harshman, Marc. *Uncle James*
Hartman, Bob. *Aunt Mabel's table*

Family life – brothers *see also* Family life; Family life – brothers & sisters; Sibling rivalry

Gifaldi, David. *Ben, king of the river*
Gordon, David. *The three little rigs*
Grimm, Jacob. *One gift deserves another*
Hanson, Joan. *I don't like Timmy*
Harber, Frances. *The brothers' promise*
Harley, Bill. *Nothing happened*
Hartmann, Wendy. *The dinosaurs are back and it's all your fault, Edward!*
Havill, Juanita. *Magic fort*
Henry, Steve. *Nobody asked me!*
Hiatt, Fred. *Baby talk*
Hill, Susan. *Stuart at the fun house*
Himmelman, John. *J.J. versus the babysitter*
Hoban, Russell. *Best friends for Frances*
 Harvey's hideout
Hoffman, Mary. *Henry's baby*
Hooker, Ruth. *Sara loves her big brother*
Hooks, William H. *Mr. Baseball*
 Mr. Dinosaur
 Mr. Monster
Howe, James. *There's a dragon in my sleeping bag*
Itaya, Satoshi. *Buttons and Bo*
Jacobs, Kate. *A sister's wish*
Jaffe, Nina. *Older brother, younger brother*
James, Simon. *Little One Step*
Jaspersohn, William. *The two brothers*
Johnston, Tony. *The iguana brothers, a perfect day*
 Slither McCreep and his brother, Joe
 That summer
Jonell, Lynne. *It's my birthday, too!*
Joosse, Barbara M. *I love you the purplest*
Keller, Holly. *Harry and Tuck*
Kleven, Elisa. *A monster in the house*
 The puddle pail
Kovacs, Deborah. *Moonlight on the river*
Kraus, Robert. *Little Louie the baby bloomer*
Kroll, Virginia L. *Helen the fish*
Kushner, Donn. *Peter's pixie*
Lakin, Pat (Patricia). *Just like me*
Lawson, Julie. *A morning to polish and keep*
Layne, Steven L. *My brother Dan's delicious*
Leuck, Laura. *My beastly brother*
Levine, Arthur A. *All the lights in the night*
London, Jonathan. *Moshi moshi*
Luthardt, Kevin. *Mine*
Maccarone, Grace. *Sharing time troubles*
MacKinnon, Debbie. *Tom's train*
Marzollo, Jean. *Baseball brothers*
Nixon, Joan Lowery. *When I am eight*
Olson, Mary. *An alligator ate my brother*
Oppenheim, Joanne. *Left and right*
Packard, Mary. *When I am big*
Palatini, Margie. *Tub-boo-boo*
Perry, Michael. *Daniel's ride*
Pinkwater, Daniel Manus. *Young Larry*
Pryor, Bonnie. *Louie and Dan are friends*
Robins, Joan. *My brother, Will*
Roche, P. K. (Patrick K.). *Webster and Arnold go camping*
Roe, Eileen. *With my brother = Con mi hermano*
Rossiter, Nan Parson. *Sugar on snow*
Rumford, James. *Dog-of-the-Sea-Waves*
 The Island-below-the-star
Russo, Marisabina. *The big brown box*
San Souci, Robert D. *The enchanted tapestry*
 Little Pierre
Sasso, Sandy Eisenberg. *Cain and Abel*
Schertle, Alice. *Witch Hazel*
Schnitter, Jane. *William is my brother*
Shields, Carol Diggory. *I wish my brother was a dog*
Silverman, Erica. *Follow the leader*
Spohn, David. *Starry night*
Steig, William. *The toy brother*
Stevenson, James. *That's exactly the way it wasn't*
Stuve-Bodeen, Stephanie. *Mama Elizabeti*
Titherington, Jeanne. *A place for Ben*
Van Allsburg, Chris. *Zathura*
Van Leeuwen, Jean. *Sorry*

Vulliamy, Clara. *Ellen and Penguin and the new baby*
Waddell, Martin. *Sam Vole and his brothers*
Wheeler, Lisa. *Turk and Runt*
White, Linda Arms. *Comes a wind*
Wilhelm, Hans. *More bunny trouble*
Woodruff, Elvira. *Mrs. McCloskey's monkeys*
Yin. *Coolies*
Yolen, Jane. *My brothers' flying machine*
Yorinks, Arthur. *Oh, brother*
 Ugh

Family life – brothers & sisters

Adoff, Arnold. *Today we are brother and sister*
Alborough, Jez. *Cuddly Dudley*
 Watch out! Big Bro's coming!
Alexander, Martha G. *Good night, Lily*
 Lily and Willy
 Where's Willy?
 Willy's boot
Andry, Andrew C. *Hi, new baby*
Anglund, Joan Walsh. *Baby brother*
Armitage, Ronda. *Harry hates shopping!*
Barrett, Mary Brigid. *The man of the house at Huffington Row*
Bartone, Elisa. *Peppe the lamplighter*
Bassède, Francine. *A day with the Bellyflops*
Baumgart, Klaus. *Laura's secret*
Beck, Ian. *Emily and the golden acorn*
Bedford, David. *Ella's games*
Berenstain, Stan. *The Berenstain bears no girls allowed*
Blake, Quentin. *Simpkin*
Boelts, Maribeth. *You're a brother, Little Bunny!*
Bogart, Jo Ellen. *Daniel's dog*
Bourgeois, Paulette. *Franklin and Harriet*
 Franklin's baby sister
Bowen, Anne. *When you visit Grandma and Grandpa*
Bowen, Keith. *Katy's gift*
Bower, Gary. *Ivy's icicle*
Breathed, Berke (Berkeley). *Edwurd Fudwupper fibbed big*
Brenner, Barbara A. *Rosa and Marco and the three wishes*
Brown, Laurie Krasny. *Rex and Lilly school time*
Brown, Marc Tolon. *Arthur tricks the tooth fairy*
 Arthur's first sleepover
 D. W. rides again!
 D. W. thinks big [board book]
 D. W.'s library card
 Glasses for D. W.
Browne, Anthony. *The tunnel*
Buck, Nola. *Hey, little baby!*
Burningham, John. *The baby*
Caple, Kathy. *The coolest place in town*
 The wimp
Carlstrom, Nancy White. *Wishing at dawn in summer*
Carter, Alden R. *Big brother Dustin*
Caseley, Judith. *Sophie and Sammy's library sleepover*
Chall, Marsha Wilson. *Mattie*
Chavarría-Cháirez, Becky. *Magda's piñata magic = Magda y la piñata mágica*
Child, Lauren. *I am too absolutely small for school*
Church, Kristine. *My brother John*
Collins, Pat Lowery. *Waiting for baby Joe*
Corpi, Lucha. *Where fireflies dance = Ahí, donde bailan las luciérnagas*
Craig, Helen. *Susie and Alfred in a busy day in town*
Crews, Nina. *A high, low, near, far, loud, quiet story*
Cummings, Pat. *Angel baby*
Dale, Penny. *Bet you can't*
Daly, Niki. *Monsters are like that*
David, Lawrence. *The land of the hungry armadillos*
Davies, Gill. *Wilbur waited*
Dealey, Erin. *Goldie Locks has chicken pox*
De Groat, Diane. *Trick or treat, smell my feet*
Denchfield, Nick. *Desmond the dog*
 Desmond the dog, a wag-the-tail pop-up book
De Paola, Tomie (Thomas Anthony). *Boss for a day*
 The bubble factory
 Marcos: red, yellow, blue
 Meet the Barkers

A new Barker in the house
Dewan, Ted. *Crispin and the 3 little piglets*
Dilley, Becki. *Sixty fingers, sixty toes*
Dixon, Ann. *Winter is . . .*
Driscoll, Debbie. *Baby comes home*
Dubois, Claude K. *Looking for Ginny*
Dunbar, Joyce. *Tell me something happy before I go to sleep*
Dyer, Sarah. *Clementine and Mungo*
Eaton, Deborah. *The rainy day grump*
Ellis, Sarah. *Big Ben*
Farmer, Patti. *What's he doing now?*
Fleming, Denise. *Mama cat has three kittens*
Ford, Juwanda G. *Together for Kwanzaa*
Franklin, Jonathan. *Don't wake the baby*
French, Vivian. *A Christmas star called Hannah*
    Molly in the middle
    Tiger and the new baby
Gammell, Stephen. *How about going for a ride*
Gay, Marie-Louise. *Good morning Sam*
    Stella, fairy of the forest
    Stella, queen of the snow
    Stella, star of the sea
George, Jean Craighead. *Nutik, the wolf pup*
Gerstein, Mordicai. *The gigantic baby*
Givens, Terryl. *Dragon scales and willow leaves*
Gliori, Debi. *My little brother*
Goode, Diane. *Mama's perfect present*
Gorbachev, Valeri. *Nicky and the rainy day*
Gordon, David. *The ugly truckling*
Got, Yves. *Sam's little sister*
Green, Jen. *Our new baby*
Grimm, Jacob. *The six swans*, ill. by Daniel San Souci
Haddix, Margaret Peterson. *Say what?*
Hains, Harriet. *My baby brother*
Hallinan, P. K. (Patrick K.). *Today is Easter!*
Hänel, Wolfram. *Little elephant runs away*
Harris, Robie H. *Hi, new baby*
Havill, Juanita. *Jamaica Tag-Along*
Helldorfer, M. C. (Mary Claire). *The darling boys*
Hendrickson, Karen. *Baby and I can play*
Herrick, Amy. *Kimbo's marble*
Hershenhorn, Esther. *Fancy that*
Hest, Amy. *You're the boss, Baby Duck*
Heymans, Annemie. *The princess in the kitchen garden*
Hiatt, Fred. *If I were queen of the world*
Hines, Anna Grossnickle. *Big help*
Hoban, Lillian. *Arthur's back to school day*
    No, no, Sammy Crow
Hoberman, Mary Ann. *And to think that we thought that we'd never be friends*
    The seven silly eaters
Hodges, Margaret. *Comus*
Hoffman, Rosekrans. *Sister Sweet Ella*
Holcomb, Nan. *Patrick and Emma Lou*
Hooks, William H. *The legend of the Christmas rose*
    Rough, tough, Rowdy
Horowitz, Ruth. *Mommy's lap*
Howard, Elizabeth Fitzgerald. *Mac and Marie and the train toss surprise*
    When will Sarah come?
Hughes, Shirley. *Alfie's ABC*
    Annie Rose is my little sister
    Olly and me
    Rhymes for Annie Rose
Hunter, Sally. *Humphrey's bedtime*
    Humphrey's Christmas
Hurwitz, Johanna. *Russell's secret*
Hutchins, Pat. *Silly Billy!*
Impey, Rose. *Joe's café*
    Jumble Joan
James, Brian. *Supertwins and the sneaky, slimy book worms*
    The Supertwins and tooth trouble
    The Supertwins meet the bad dogs from space
    Supertwins meet the dangerous dino-robots
Johnson, Angela. *Do like Kyla*
    When mules flew on Magnolia Street
Johnson, Gillian. *My sister Gracie*

Joyce, William. *Santa calls*
Karas, G. Brian. *Bebe's bad dream*
Kay, Verla. *Orphan train*
Keller, Holly. *Geraldine and Mrs. Duffy*
    Maxine in the middle
    What Alvin wanted
Kinsey-Warnock, Natalie. *The summer of Stanley*
Koller, Jackie French. *Baby for sale*
Komaiko, Leah. *Where can Daniel be?*
Kudler, David. *The Seven Gods of Luck*
Kurtz, Jane. *Fire on the mountain*
Kushner, Tony. *Brundibar*
Lamm, C. Drew. *Pirates*
Lasky, Kathryn. *Lucille's snowsuit*
    Starring Lucille
Lawlor, Laurie. *The biggest pest on Eighth Avenue*
Lears, Laurie. *Ian's walk*
Le Guin, Ursula K. *A ride on the red mare's back*
Leonard, Marcia. *Get the ball, Slim*
Lester, Alison. *The journey home*
Lester, Helen. *Help! I'm stuck!*
Leuck, Laura. *My baby brother has ten tiny toes*
Levine, Arthur A. *The boardwalk princess*
Lewison, Wendy Cheyette. *My baby brother*
    Our new baby
    Say thank you, Theodore
Little, Jean. *Revenge of the small Small*
Livingston, Myra Cohn. *Poems for brothers, poems for sisters*
Look, Lenore. *Henry's first-moon birthday*
McAllister, Angela. *The clever cowboy*
    The snow angel
McClintock, Barbara. *Molly and the magic wishbone*
McCormick, Wendy. *The night you were born*
McCullough, Sharon Pierce. *Bunbun, the middle one*
MacDonald, Maryann. *Ben at the beach*
Magorian, Michelle. *Who's going to take care of me?*
Manson, Ainslie. *Ballerinas don't wear glasses*
Manushkin, Fran. *Be brave, baby rabbit*
Mario, Heidi Stetson. *I'd rather have an iguana*
May, Kara. *Big brave brother Ben*
Mazer, Anne. *The Fixits*
Meddaugh, Susan. *Cinderella's rat*
Mendes, Valerie. *Look at me, Grandma!*
Michels-Gualtieri, Akaela S. *I was born to be a sister*
Mills, Claudia. *Phoebe's parade*
Mills, Lauren A. *The goblin baby*
Moon, Nicola. *Something special*
Munsch, Robert N. *Alligator baby*
Murdocca, Sal (Salvatore). *Baby wants the moon*
Murkoff, Heidi Eisenberg. *What to expect when the new baby comes home*
Naylor, Phyllis Reynolds. *The baby, the bed, and the rose*
Nelson, S. D. *The Star People*
Norris, Kathleen. *The holy twins: Benedict and Scholastica*
Novak, Matt. *The Pillow War*
Offen, Hilda. *Good girl, Gracie Growler!*
Packard, Mary. *Don't make a sound*
Palatini, Margie. *Goldie is mad*
    Good as Goldie
Partis, Joanne. *Stripe's naughty sister*
Pegram, Laura. *Daughter's Day blues*
Pelham, David. *Sam's pizza*
    Sam's sandwich
Pitcher, Caroline. *The snow whale*
Polacco, Patricia. *My rotten redheaded older brother*
Prigger, Mary Skillings. *Aunt Minnie McGranahan*
Pulver, Robin. *Way to go, Alex!*
Radunsky, Eugenia. *Yucka Drucka Droni*
Raschka, Christopher. *The blushful hippopotamus*
Reader, Dennis. *Butterfingers*
Robbins, Beth. *Tom, Ally, and the new baby*
    Tom and Ally visit the doctor
Rockwell, Lizzy. *Hello baby!*
Roddie, Shen. *Toes are to tickle*
Rodell, Susanna. *Dear Fred*
Rogers, Jacqueline. *Tiptoe into kindergarten*
Roper, Janice M. *Dancing on the moon*

Baum, Louis. *One more time*
Baynton, Martin. *Why do you love me?*
Beim, Jerrold. *With dad alone*
Bergel, Colin. *Mail by the pail*
Bergström, Gunilla. *Who's scaring Alfie Atkins?*
Bernard, Robin. *Juma and the honey-guild*
Best, Cari. *Taxi! Taxi!*
Bittner, Wolfgang. *Wake up, Grizzly!*
Blake, Robert J. *The perfect spot*
Blaustein, Muriel. *Play ball, Zachary!*
Bliss, Corinne Demas. *Nina's waltz*
Boelts, Maribeth. *Big Daddy, frog wrestler*
 Looking for Sleepy
Boyd, Lizi. *I love Daddy*
Bradman, Tony. *Daddy's lullaby*
 Not like this, like that
Braun, Sebastien. *I love my daddy*
Bridges, Margaret Park. *If I were your father*
Brillhart, Julie. *When daddy came to school*
 When Daddy took us camping
Brisson, Pat. *Star blanket*
Brooks, Ben. *Lemonade parade*
Browne, Anthony. *The big baby*
 Gorilla
 My dad
Brutschy, Jennifer. *Just one more story*
Buckley, Helen Elizabeth. *Someday with my father*
Bunting, Eve (Anne Evelyn). *Fly away home*
 A perfect Father's Day
Burgess, Gelett. *The little father*
Burke, Bobby. *Daddy's little girl*
Burstein, Fred. *Anna's rain*
 The dancer
Butterworth, Nick. *My dad is awesome*
 The two sons
Butterworth, Oliver. *A visit to the big house*
Caines, Jeannette. *Daddy*
Camp, Lindsay. *Why?*
Capucilli, Alyssa Satin. *Only my dad and me*
Carlstrom, Nancy White. *Goodbye geese*
Carter, Anne Laurel. *Tall in the saddle*
Catalanotto, Peter. *Dad and me*
 The painter
Cazet, Denys. *Dancing*
 I'm not sleepy
Chaconas, Don. *On a wintry morning*
Cheng, Andrea. *Anna the bookbinder*
Claverie, Jean. *Working*
Clifton, Lucille. *Amifika*
Cohen, Ron. *My dad's baseball*
Cole, Babette. *Dad*
 The trouble with Dad
Cole, Brock. *Buttons*
Cole, Sheila. *When the rain stops*
Collard, Sneed B. *Animal dads*
Collins, Billy. *Daddy's little boy*
Compos, Tito. *Muffler man = El hombre mofle*
Conway, Celeste. *Where is Papa now?*
Cowley, Joy. *Gracias, the Thanksgiving turkey*
Coy, John. *Night driving*
 Two old potatoes and me
Creech, Sharon. *Fishing in the air*
Croll, Carolyn. *The three brothers*
Crum, Shutta. *Fox and Fluff*
Daly, Niki. *My dad*
Day, Alexandra. *River parade*
Day, Jan. *The pirate, Pink*
 Pirate Pink and treasures of the reef
Diot, Alain. *Better, best, bestest*
DiTerlizzi, Tony. *Ted*
Dotlich, Rebecca Kai. *Papa loves*
Dragonwagon, Crescent. *The sun begun*
Drawson, Blair. *Flying Dimitri*
Dunbar, Joyce. *Indigo and the whale*
Dupasquier, Philippe. *Dear Daddy . . .*
Eckart, Edana. *I can bowl*
Edwards, Michelle. *Papa's latkes*

Eilenberg, Max. *Cowboy Kid*
Emmons, Chip. *Sammy wakes his dad*
Engel, Diana. *Circle song*
Ernst, Lisa Campbell. *Squirrel Park*
Evans, Richard Paul. *The dance*
Ewart, Claire. *The giant*
Falwell, Cathryn. *Dragon tooth*
 Nicky loves daddy
Fassler, Joan. *All alone with daddy*
Feiffer, Jules. *The daddy mountain*
Fienberg, Anna. *Joseph*
Foreman, Michael. *Dad! I can't sleep*
Fowler, Susi Gregg. *I'll see you when the moon is full*
Gardella, Tricia. *Just like my dad*
Gay, Michel. *Night ride*
George, Jean Craighead. *Cliff hanger*
George, William T. *Christmas at Long Pond*
Giles, Almira Astudillo. *Willie wins*
Giuliano, Katie. *All the way to God*
Glassman, Peter. *My dad's job*
Gliori, Debi. *Tickly under there*
Gomi, Taro. *I lost my dad*
Graham, Georgia. *The strongest man this side of Cremona*
Grambling, Lois G. *Daddy will be there*
Granowsky, Alvin. *At the park*
Gray, Nigel. *A balloon for grandad*
 Running away from home
Greenberg, Melanie Hope. *My father's luncheonette*
Greenfield, Eloise. *Daddy and I*
 First pink light
 Lisa's daddy and daughter day
Greydanus, Rose. *Bedtime story*
Grifalconi, Ann. *Tiny's hat*
Grimes, Nikki. *When Daddy prays*
Grindley, Sally. *Knock, knock! Who's there?*
Guettier, Bénédicte. *The father who had ten children*
Gugler, Laurel Dee. *Muddle cuddle*
Hanson, Regina. *The tangerine tree*
Hartman, Bob. *Who wrecked the roof?*
Haseley, Dennis. *Kite flier*
 My father doesn't know about the woods and me
Haughton, Emma. *Rainy day*
Hazen, Barbara Shook. *Katie's wish*
Heap, Sue. *Cowboy Baby*
Hearn, Diane Dawson. *Dad's dinosaur day*
Hendershot, Judith. *In coal country*
Heo, Yumi. *Father's rubber shoes*
 One Sunday morning
Hermes, Patricia. *When snow lay soft on the mountain*
High, Linda Oatman. *Barn savers*
 The girl on the high-diving horse
 Winter shoes for Shadow Horse
Hillert, Margaret. *The little cowboy and the big cowboy*
Hines, Anna Grossnickle. *Daddy makes the best spaghetti*
 Sky all around
Hinton, S. E. *Big David, Little David*
Hooks, William H. *Moss gown*
Hopkinson, Deborah. *Birdie's lighthouse*
Horenstein, Henry. *Sam goes trucking*
Horn, Peter. *The best father of all*
 When I grow up . . .
Horowitz, Ruth. *Bat time*
Hort, Lenny. *How many stars in the sky*
Howard, Elizabeth Fitzgerald. *Papa tells Chita a story*
Hru, Dakari. *Tickle, tickle*
Hudson, Wade. *Jamal's busy day*
Hughes, Shirley. *Abel's moon*
Hughes, Vi. *Aziz, the story teller*
Hundal, Nancy. *Number 21*
Hurwitz, Johanna. *Ethan out and about*
Hutchins, H. J. (Hazel J.). *I'd know you anywhere*
Impey, Rose. *My mom and our dad*
In daddy's arms I am tall
Irving, John. *A sound like someone trying not to make a sound*
Jaffe, Nina. *The way meat loves salt*
Jam, Teddy. *The kid line*
 Night cars

Janovitz, Marilyn. *Can I help?*
  Is it time?
Jennings, Sharon. *No monsters here*
Jensen, Patricia. *Be careful, Little Antelope*
Johnson, Angela. *Casey Jones*
  I dream of trains
  Joshua's night whispers
Johnson, Dolores. *Papa's stories*
  Your dad was just like you
Jolin, Dominique. *It's not fair!*
Jonovitz, Marilyn. *Good morning, Little Fox*
Joosse, Barbara M. *Lewis and papa*
Jorgensen, Richard. *Reading with Dad*
Judes, Marie-Odile. *Max, the stubborn little wolf*
Just like father
Kauffman, Lois. *What's that noise?*
Kaufmann, Nancy. *Bye, Bye*
Kessler, Leonard P. *Are we lost, daddy?*
Ketteman, Helen. *I remember papa*
  Not yet, Yvette
Kidd, Nina. *June Mountain secret*
Kilroy, Sally. *Market day*
Kinsey-Warnock, Natalie. *When spring comes*
Komaiko, Leah. *Just my dad and me*
Kraus, Robert. *Daddy Long Ears*
Kroll, Steven. *Happy Father's Day*
Kroll, Virginia L. *Africa brothers and sisters*
Kurtz, Jane. *Faraway home*
Lakin, Pat (Patricia). *Dad and me in the morning*
  Hurricane!
Langley, Karen. *Shine*
Lanton, Sandy. *Daddy's chair*
Lauture, Denizé. *Father and son*
Leblanc, Anne. *Benjamin in the snow*
Lenski, Lois. *Papa Small*
Leonard, Marcia. *The tin can man*
Levine, Abby. *Daddies give you horsey rides*
Levy, Janice. *Totally uncool*
Lewin, Hugh. *Jafta – the homecoming*
  Jafta's father
Lewin, Ted. *Big Jimmy's Kum Kau Chinese take out*
Lexau, Joan M. *Every day a dragon*
  Me day
Lindbergh, Reeve. *If I'd known then what I know now*
Lindenbaum, Pija. *Else-Marie and her seven little daddies*
Lindsay, Jeanne Warren. *Do I have a daddy?*
Little, Mimi Otey. *Daddy has a pair of striped shorts*
Livingston, Myra Cohn. *Poems for fathers*
Locker, Thomas. *Miranda's smile*
London, Jonathan. *At the edge of the forest*
  Loon Lake
  Old salt, young salt
Long, Earlene. *Gone fishing*
Lubell, Winifred. *Here comes daddy*
McAfee, Annalena. *The visitors who came to stay*
McAllister, Angela. *The ice palace*
McBratney, Sam. *Guess how much I love you*
McCaughrean, Geraldine. *One bright Penny*
McCormick, Wendy. *Daddy, will you miss me?*
McCourt, Lisa. *Chicken soup for little souls: The best night out with Dad*
  Good night, Princess Pruney Toes
McCully, Emily Arnold. *Popcorn at the palace*
McDonald, Megan. *Bedbugs*
McGee, Marni. *Sleepy me*
McGinnis, Lila Sprague. *If Daddy only knew me*
McKay, Lawrence. *Caravan*
McKee, David. *Prince Peter and the teddy bear*
McKinley, Robin. *My father is in the Navy*
MacLachlan, Patricia. *The sick day*
McMullan, Kate (Hall). *Papa's song*
McPhail, David M. *Ed and me*
  Henry Bear's park
  The party
McQuade, Jacqueline. *At preschool with Teddy Bear*
Madenski, Melissa. *Some of the pieces*
Mahy, Margaret. *Down the dragon's tongue*

Mangas, Brian. *A nice surprise for Father Rabbit*
Manushkin, Fran. *Peeping and sleeping*
Martin, David. *Piggy and Dad*
  Piggy and Dad go fishing
Marzollo, Jean. *Amy goes fishing*
  Close your eyes
  Papa, papa
Mayer, Mercer. *Just me and my dad*
  Shibumi and the kitemaker
Medearis, Angela Shelf. *Our people*
Meisel, Paul. *Zara's hats*
Meredith, Carol. *Jamie Anderson wouldn't . . .*
Micklos, John. *Daddy poems*
Milich, Melissa. *Miz Fannie Mae's fine new Easter hat*
Minarik, Else Holmelund. *Father Bear comes home*
Monjo, F. N. *The one bad thing about father*
Morgan, Allen. *Nicole's boat*
Morris, Ann. *The daddy book*
Morton, Lone. *Hurry up, Molly = Apúrate, Molly*
  Hurry up, Molly = Dépêche-toi, Molly
Munsch, Robert N. *Get me another one!*
  Something good
  Where is Gah-Ning?
Munson, Derek. *Enemy pie*
Myers, Bernice. *The gold watch*
Napoli, Donna Jo. *Flamingo dream*
Newton-John, Olivia. *A pig tale*
Nolan, Madeena Spray. *My daddy don't go to work*
Norac, Carl. *My daddy is a giant*
Novak, Matt. *Gertie and Gumbo*
Numeroff, Laura Joffe. *What daddies do best*
O'Donnell, Elizabeth Lee. *Sing me a window*
O'Malley, Kevin. *Little buggy*
  Little Buggy runs away
O'Neill, Alexis. *Estela's swap*
Oppenheim, Shulamith Levey. *Ali and the magic stew*
  Yanni rubbish
Ormerod, Jan. *Dad's back*
  Messy baby
  Reading
  Sleeping
Pak, Soyung. *A place to grow*
Paradis, Susan. *My Daddy*
Paris, Lena. *Mom is single*
Park, Linda Sue. *The firekeeper's son*
Parker, Kristy. *My dad the magnificent*
Parr, Todd. *The daddy book*
Paterson, Katherine. *Marvin one too many*
Patron, Susan. *Dark cloud strong breeze*
Paxton, Tom. *The marvelous toy*
Pelton, Mindy L. *When Dad's at sea*
Pettigrew, Eileen. *Night-time*
Pfister, Marcus. *Penguin Pete and Little Tim*
Pingry, Patricia. *Joseph's story*
Pitcher, Caroline. *The time of the lion*
Pittman, Helena Clare. *Uncle Phil's diner*
Polacco, Patricia. *My ol' man*
  Some birthday!
Porte, Barbara Ann. *Harry's dog*
  Harry's mom
Porter-Gaylord, Laurel. *I love my daddy because . . .*
Posey, Lee. *Night rabbits*
Pow, Tom. *Tell me one thing, Dad*
Pringle, Laurence P. *Bear hug*
Uhlberg, Myron. *The printer*
Puner, Helen Walker. *Daddys, what they do all day*
Quinlan, Patricia. *My dad takes care of me*
Rabe, Berniece. *Where's Chimpy?*
Radlauer, Ruth Shaw. *Molly at the library*
Rappaport, Doreen. *The new king*
Ray, Mary Lyn. *Basket moon*
Regan, Dian Curtis. *Daddies*
Repchuk, Caroline. *The forgotten garden*
Rice, Eve. *Swim!*
Riecken, Nancy. *Today is the day*
Ringi, Kjell (Arne Sorensen). *My father and I*
Roberts, Bethany. *Waiting-for-Papa stories*

Rockwell, Anne F. *Ducklings and pollywogs*
　Father's Day
Root, Phyllis. *Contrary bear*
Rusackas, Francesca. *Daddy all day long*
Rush, Ken. *Friday's journey*
Ryder, Joanne. *My father's hands*
Sachar, Louis. *Monkey soup*
Sandberg, Inger. *Come on out, Daddy!*
San Souci, Robert D. *The samurai's daughter*
Santucci, Barbara. *Loon summer*
Schindel, John. *Dear Daddy*
Schlessinger, Laura. *Dr. Laura Schlessinger's Growing up is hard*
Schotter, Roni. *Room for Rabbit*
Schwartz, Amy. *Bea and Mr. Jones*
The scrubbly-bubbly car wash
Shalev, Meir. *My father always embarrasses me*
Shannon, George. *Dancing the breeze*
Sharp, N. L. *Today I'm going fishing with my dad*
Shepard, Steve. *Elvis Hornbill, international business bird*
Shipton, Jonathan. *How to be a happy hippo*
Sidman, Joyce. *Just us two*
Simmonds, Posy. *Lulu and the flying babies*
Simon, Norma. *The daddy days*
　I wish I had my father
Singer, Marilyn. *Didi and Daddy on the Promenade*
　In the palace of the Ocean King
Slate, Joseph. *Story time for Little Porcupine*
Slater, Teddy. *Jan and Dan and the super dads*
Slawson, Michele Benoit. *Signs for sale*
Smalls-Hector, Irene. *Kevin and his dad*
Smee, Nicola. *Finish the story, dad*
Smith, Will (1968–). *Just the two of us*
Smith-Ayala, Emilie. *Marisol and the yellow messenger*
Sonneborn, Ruth A. *Friday night is papa night*
Spinelli, Eileen. *Night shift daddy*
Spinelli, Jerry. *My daddy and me*
Spohn, David. *Starry night*
　Winter wood
Stafford, Kim Robert. *We got here together*
Stanley, Sanna. *Monkey Sunday*
Stecher, Miriam B. *Daddy and Ben together*
Steel, Danielle. *Max's daddy goes to the hospital*
Steen, Sandra. *Car wash*
Steig, William. *Pete's a pizza*
Steiner, Charlotte. *Daddy comes home*
Steptoe, John. *Daddy is a monster . . . sometimes*
Stevens, Bryna. *Handel and the famous sword swallower of Halle*
Stevenson, James. *I meant to tell you*
　Sam the Zamboni man
Stevenson, Suçie. *Jessica the blue streak*
Stewart, Robert S. *The daddy book*
Stock, Catherine. *Christmas time*
Tarbescu, Edith. *Annushka's voyage*
Tarpley, Natasha Anastasia. *Bippity Bop barbershop*
Taylor, Ann. *Baby dance*
Thomas, Ianthe. *Willie blows a mean horn*
Thompson, Richard. *I have to see this*
Townson, Hazel. *What on earth . . . ?*
Trottier, Maxine. *A safe place*
Tyler, Linda Wagner. *When daddy comes home*
Udry, Janice May. *What Mary Jo shared*
Valentine, Johnny. *One dad, two dads, brown dad, blue dads*
Van Woerkom, Dorothy. *Something to crow about*
Vigna, Judith. *Daddy's new baby*
　I wish my daddy didn't drink so much
　Saying goodbye to daddy
Waboose, Jan Bourdeau. *Morning on the lake*
Waddell, Martin. *Can't you sleep, Little Bear?*
　Let's go home, Little Bear
　The toymaker
Wadsworth, Ginger. *Tomorrow is Daddy's birthday*
Wahl, Jan. *Once when the world was green*
Wallace, Ian. *Duncan's way*
Walters, Virginia. *Are we there yet, Daddy?*
Watanabe, Shigeo. *Daddy, play with me!*
　I can take a bath!
　Let's go swimming

　Where's my daddy?
Watson, Pauline. *Days with Daddy*
Weigel, Jeff. *Atomic Ace (he's just my dad)*
Welch, Willy. *Dancing with Daddy*
Wells, Philip. *Daddy Island*
Wells, Rosemary. *The island light*
Weninger, Brigitte. *Good-bye, daddy!*
Willhoite, Michael. *Daddy's roommate*
Winthrop, Elizabeth. *As the crow flies*
Wolf, Jake. *Daddy, could I have an elephant?*
Wood, Douglas. *What dads can't do*
Wood, Jakki. *Dads are such fun*
Worley, Daryl. *Billy and the attic adventure*
Wyeth, Sharon Dennis. *Always my dad*
Yezerski, Thomas F. *A full hand*
Yolen, Jane. *All those secrets of the world*
　The emperor and the kite
　Owl moon
Young, Ed (Edward). *Mouse match*
Zagwÿn, Deborah Turney. *Papa's latkes*
Ziefert, Harriet. *When daddy had the chicken pox*
Zimelman, Nathan. *Treed by a pride of irate lions*
Zola, Meguido. *Only the best*
Zolotow, Charlotte (Shapiro). *If you listen*
　The summer night

Family life – grandfathers

Ackerman, Karen. *Song and dance man*
Adams, Ken. *When I was your age*
Adler, David A. *A little at a time*
Alexander, Martha G. *Where does the sky end, Grandpa?*
Aliki. *The two of them*
Anaya, Rudolfo A. *Farolitos for Abuelo*
Anderson, Lena. *Stina*
　Stina's visit
Andrews, Jan. *The auction*
Appelt, Kathi. *Where, where is Swamp Bear?*
Arkin, Alan. *One present from Flekman's*
Auzary-Luton, Sylvie. *1, 2, 3, music!*
Bahr, Mary. *The memory box*
Bailey, Debbie. *Grandpa*
Balmer, Helen. *Jungle adventure*
Barrett, Judi. *Cloudy with a chance of meatballs*
Barron, T. A. *Where is Grandpa?*
Beardshaw, Rosalind. *Grandpa's surprise*
　Grandpa's surprise
Behrens, June. *Soo Ling finds a way*
Blades, Ann. *A boy of Taché*
Blos, Joan W. *The grandpa days*
　Hello, shoes!
Bond, Ruskin. *Cherry tree*
Borack, Barbara. *Grandpa*
Boyden, Linda. *The blue roses*
Bradford, Karleen. *You can't rush a cat*
Brady, Kimberley Smith. *Keeper for the sea*
Brooks, Ron. *Timothy and Gramps*
Brown, Kathryn. *Muledred*
Buckley, Helen Elizabeth. *Grandfather and I*
Bunting, Eve (Anne Evelyn). *Butterfly house*
　The day before Christmas
　A day's work
　The happy funeral
　Magic and the night river
　So far from the sea
Burningham, John. *Grandpa*
Butterworth, Nick. *My grandpa is amazing*
Carlson, Melody. *What Nick and Holly found in grandpa's attic*
Carlstrom, Nancy White. *Grandpappy*
Carney, Margaret (Margaret Rose). *The biggest fish in the lake*
Carrick, Carol. *Melanie*
Carter, Don. *Heaven's all-star jazz band*
Caseley, Judith. *Dear Annie*
　When Grandpa came to stay
Castle, Caroline. *Grandpa Baxter and the photographs*
Cazet, Denys. *Christmas moon*
　December 24th

Cheng, Andrea. *Grandfather counts*
Christian, Mary Blount. *Grandfathers, God's gift to children*
Clement, Rod. *Grandpa's teeth*
Coatsworth, Elizabeth. *Lonely Maria*
Cole, Babette. *The trouble with Grandad*
Conrad, Pam. *The Tub grandfather*
Cooke, Trish. *The grandad tree*
Coville, Bruce. *My grandfather's house*
Cowley, Joy. *The rusty, trusty tractor*
Crunk, Tony. *Grandpa's overalls*
Daly, Niki. *Old Bob's brown bear*
　　Papa Lucky's shadow
Darling, Benjamin. *Valerie and the silver pear*
Davis, Aubrey. *Bagels from Benny*
DeFelice, Cynthia C. *When Grampa kissed his elbow*
DeGross, Monalisa. *Granddaddy's street songs*
De Paola, Tomie (Thomas Anthony). *The bubble factory*
　　Kit and Kat
　　Now one foot, now the other
　　Tom
Diller, Harriett. *Grandaddy's highway*
Dionetti, Michelle V. *Coal mine peaches*
DiSalvo-Ryan, DyAnne. *Grandpa's corner store*
Dodds, Siobhan. *Grandpa Bud*
Douglass, Barbara. *Good as new*
Doyle, Malachy. *Jody's beans*
Drawson, Blair. *All along the river*
Dumas, Philippe. *Laura loses her head*
Edwards, Julie Andrews. *Dumpy the dump truck*
Engel, Diana. *Fishing*
Falwell, Cathryn. *Nicky and grandpa*
Farjeon, Eleanor. *Morning has broken*
Fassler, Joan. *My grandpa died today*
Fazio, Brenda Lena. *Grandfather's story*
Fletcher, Ralph J. *Grandpa never lies*
Flora, James. *Grandpa's farm*
　　Grandpa's ghost stories
Foreman, Michael. *Grandfather's pencil and the room of stories*
　　Jack's fantastic voyage
　　Seal surfer
Fox, Mem. *Shoes from grandpa*
　　Sophie
French, Vivian. *Caterpillar, caterpillar*
　　Oliver's fruit salad
Gantschev, Ivan. *The Christmas teddy bear*
Garaway, Margaret Kahn. *Ashkii and his grandfather*
Garrett, Ann. *Keeper of the swamp*
Geisert, Arthur. *Mystery*
George, William T. *Fishing at Long Pond*
Gerstein, Mordicai. *The new creatures*
Gibbons, Faye. *Full steam ahead*
Gillard, Denise. *Music from the sky*
Golding, Theresa Martin. *Memorial Day surprise*
Gold-Vukson, Marji E. *Grandpa and me on Tu B'Shevat*
Gray, Nigel. *A balloon for grandad*
Greenfield, Eloise. *Grandpa's face*
Griffith, Helen V. *Georgia music*
　　Grandaddy's place
　　Grandaddy's stars
Grindley, Sally. *A flag for Grandma*
Grist, Julie. *Flying, just plane fun*
Guthrie, Donna. *Grandpa doesn't know it's me*
Haas, Jessie. *Mowing*
Hallinan, P. K. (Patrick K.). *Three freckles past a hair*
Hänel, Wolfram. *The gold at the end of the rainbow*
Harper, Isabelle. *My dog Rosie*
　　Our new puppy
Harranth, Wolf. *My old grandad*
Hartley, Deborah. *Up north in the winter*
Hayes, Geoffrey. *Patrick and his grandpa*
Hazen, Barbara Shook. *Why did Grandpa die?*
Heiligman, Deborah. *Pockets*
Heller, Nicholas. *The giant*
Henkes, Kevin. *Grandpa and Bo*
Hest, Amy. *Baby Duck and the bad eyeglasses*
　　The crack-of-dawn walkers
　　Guess who, Baby Duck

　　In the rain with Baby Duck
　　Make the team, Baby Duck
　　Off to school, Baby Duck
　　The purple coat
　　Rosie's fishing trip
　　Ruby's storm
　　You're the boss, Baby Duck
High, Linda Oatman. *Beekeepers*
Highet, Alistair. *The yellow train*
Hilton, Nette. *The long red scarf*
Hines, Anna Grossnickle. *Moompa, Toby, and Bomp*
　　Remember the butterflies
Hines, Gary. *A ride in the crummy*
Holman, Sandy Lynne. *Grandpa, is everything black bad?*
Hoopes, Lyn Littlefield. *Half a button*
Hopkinson, Deborah. *Bluebird summer*
Houghton, Eric. *The backwards watch*
Hughes, Shirley. *When we went to the park*
Hutchins, Pat. *Happy birthday, Sam*
Igus, Toyomi. *When I was little*
Isadora, Rachel. *Jesse and Abe*
Jacobs, Joseph. *Tattercoats*
Jam, Teddy. *The year of fire*
James, Simon. *The birdwatchers*
　　The wild woods
Jessell, Tim. *Amorak*
Johnson, Angela. *Julius*
　　The Rolling Store
　　When I am old with you
Johnson, Dolores. *Your dad was just like you*
Johnston, Tony. *Fishing Sunday*
　　Grandpa's song
　　Little Rabbit goes to sleep
Jones, Joy. *Tambourine moon*
Kadono, Eiko. *Grandpa's soup*
Kastner, Jill. *Snake hunt*
Kasza, Keiko. *Grandpa Toad's last secret*
Keeshan, Robert. *Alligator in the basement*
Keller, Holly. *Grandfather's dream*
　　Island baby
Kinsey-Warnock, Natalie. *The fiddler of the Northern Lights*
Kirk, Barbara. *Grandpa, me and our house in the tree*
Knox-Wagner, Elaine. *My grandpa retired today*
Krebs, Laurie. *The Beeman*
Kroll, Virginia L. *Butterfly boy*
Krudop, Walter Lyon. *Blue claws*
Langner, Nola. *Freddy my grandfather*
Lapp, Eleanor. *In the morning mist*
Lasky, Kathryn. *I have four names for my grandfather*
Leavy, Una. *Good-bye, Papa*
LeBox, Annette. *Wild bog tea*
Legge, David. *Bamboozled*
Leonard, Marcia. *Dan and Dan*
Levine, Arthur A. *Bono and Nonno*
Levy, Janice. *Abuelito eats with his fingers*
Lindbergh, Reeve. *Grandfather's lovesong*
Little, Jean. *Gruntle Piggle takes off*
Lobel, Gillian. *Does anybody love me?*
Locker, Thomas. *The mare on the hill*
　　Where the river begins
London, Jonathan. *The village basket weaver*
Lyon, George Ella. *Basket*
McCully, Emily Arnold. *The Christmas gift*
McCutcheon, Marc. *Grandfather's Christmas camp*
McDonald, Megan. *The great pumpkin switch*
　　The potato man
McFarlane, Sheryl. *Waiting for the whales*
MacGill-Callahan, Sheila. *And still the turtle watched*
McMillan, Bruce. *Grandfather's trolley*
Mahood, Kenneth. *Why are there more questions than answers, Grandad?*
Marron, Carol A. *No trouble for Grandpa*
Martin, Bill (William Ivan). *Knots on a counting rope*
Martin, C. L. G. *Down Dairy Farm Road*
Martin, Jacqueline Briggs. *The water gift and the pig of the pig*
Mason, Jane B. *River day*
Matze, Claire Sidhom. *The stars in my Geddoh's sky*

May, Kathy. *Molasses man*
Mayer, Mercer. *Just big enough*
    Little Monster at work
Michaels, William. *Clare and her shadow*
Michelson, Richard. *Too young for Yiddish*
Mills, Claudia. *Gus and Grandpa and show-and-tell*
    Gus and Grandpa ride the train
Mitchell, Margaree King. *Granddaddy's gift*
Monk, Isabell. *Blackberry stew*
Moon, Nicola. *Lucy's picture*
Moore, Elaine. *Deep river*
Moore, Lilian. *While you were chasing a hat*
Mora, Pat. *Pablo's tree*
Morgan-Vanroyen, Mary. *Night ride*
Morris, Ann. *The grandpa book*
    700 kids on Grandpa's farm
Moss, Marissa. *In America*
Most, Bernard. *Catch me if you can!*
Mott, Evelyn Clarke. *Dancing rainbows*
Nanji, Shenaaz. *An alien in my house*
Nez, Redwing T. *Forbidden talent*
Nickle, John. *TV Rex*
Nicolai, Margaret. *Kitaq goes ice fishing*
Nikola-Lisa, W. *Night is coming*
Nobisso, Josephine. *Grandpa loved*
Noll, Sally. *Lucky morning*
Nomura, Takaaki. *Grandpa's town*
Numeroff, Laura Joffe. *What grandmas do best; What grandpas do best*
Oberman, Sheldon. *The always prayer shawl*
    By the Hanukkah light
Ogburn, Jacqueline K. *The jukebox man*
O'Malley, Kevin. *Bud*
Onyefulu, Ifeoma. *Grandfather's work*
Oram, Hiawyn. *A boy wants a dinosaur*
    Going to Grandpa's
Otto, Carolyn. *That sky, that rain*
Paraskevas, Betty. *Monster Beach*
Paterson, Diane. *Hey, cowboy!*
Paul, Ann Whitford. *Everything to spend the night . . . from A to Z*
Pearson, Susan. *Happy birthday, Grampie*
Peavy, Linda. *Allison's grandfather*
Pfister, Marcus. *The happy hedgehog*
Pomerantz, Charlotte. *Buffy and Albert*
    The outside dog
    Timothy Tall Feather
Pope, Geraldine. *The empty creel*
Prater, John. *Hold tight!*
Proimos, James. *Joe's wish*
Purmell, Ann. *Apple cider making days*
Raczek, Linda Theresa. *The night the grandfathers danced*
Radin, Ruth Yaffe. *High in the mountains*
Rael, Elsa Okon. *When Zaydeh danced on Eldridge Street*
Reddix, Valerie. *Dragon kite of the autumn moon*
Reynolds, Adrian. *Pete and Polo's farmyard adventure*
Rice, Eve. *Aren't you coming too?*
Rigby, Shirley Lincoln. *Smaller than most*
Roberts, Bethany. *Gramps and the fire dragon*
Rodgers, Frank. *Who's afraid of the ghost train?*
Roth, Susan L. *Happy birthday Mr. Kang*
    We'll ride elephants through Brooklyn
Rumford, James. *The cloudmakers*
Russo, Marisabina. *Grandpa Abe*
Sáenz, Benjamin Alire. *A gift from papá Diego = Un regalo de papá Diego*
Salter, Heidi. *Taddy McFinley and the great grey grimly*
Sandberg, Inger. *Dusty wants to help*
Santucci, Barbara. *Anna's corn*
Sathre, Vivian. *On Grandpa's farm*
Savageau, Cheryl. *Muskrat will be swimming*
Say, Allen. *Grandfather's journey*
Schaap, Martine. *Mop's treasure hunt*
Schaefer, Carole Lexa. *The little French whistle*
Scheller, Melanie. *My grandfather's hat*
Schlein, Miriam. *Go with the sun*
Schlessinger, Laura. *Dr. Laura Schlessinger's Where's God?*
Schotter, Roni. *In the piney woods*

Schwartz, David M. *Sugargrandpa*
Selway, Martina. *Don't forget to write*
Shields, Carol Diggory. *Lucky pennies and hot chocolate*
Shulevitz, Uri. *Dawn*
Stafford, Liliana. *Just dragon*
Stevens, Margaret (Dean). *When grandpa died*
Stevenson, Harvey. *Grandpa's house*
Stevenson, James. *Brr!*
    "Could be worse!"
    Grandpa's great city tour
    Grandpa's too-good garden
    The great big especially beautiful Easter egg
    No friends
    That dreadful day
    That terrible Halloween night
    That's exactly the way it wasn't
    There's nothing to do!
    We can't sleep
    What's under my bed?
    Will you please feed our cat?
    Worse than Willy!
Stiles, Martha Bennett. *Island magic*
Stilz, Carol Curtis. *Kirsty's kite*
Stock, Catherine. *Emma's dragon hunt*
    Thanksgiving treat
Stolz, Mary (Mary Slattery). *Storm in the night*
Sullivan, Silky. *Grandpa was a cowboy*
Tavares, Matt. *Oliver's game*
Titherington, Jeanne. *Where are you going, Emma?*
Tompert, Ann. *Grandfather Tang's story*
Townsend, Maryann. *Pop's secret*
Ulmer, Wendy K. *A campfire for cowboy Billy*
Valgardson, W. D. *Winter rescue*
Van Leeuwen, Jean. *The tickle stories*
Vigna, Judith. *My two uncles*
Wahl, Jan. *The fishermen*
Wahl, Mats. *Grandfather's laika*
Wallace, Ian. *Chin Chiang and the dragon's dance*
Wallace, Nancy Elizabeth. *Snow*
Walsh, Jill Paton. *Lost and found*
Ward, Sally G. *Molly and Grandpa*
    Punky goes fishing
Wardlaw, Lee. *Bow-wow birthday*
Webb, Denise. *The same sun was in the sky*
Wells, Rosemary. *The language of doves*
White Deer of Autumn. *The great change*
Williams, Laura E. *Torch fishing with the sun*
Winch, John. *Keeping up with Grandma*
Wood, Douglas. *Grandad's prayers of the earth*
Woodruff, Elvira. *Can you guess where we're going?*
Ye, Ting-xing. *Share the sky*
Zalben, Jane Breskin. *Pearl plants a tree*
    Pearl's marigolds for grandpa
Ziefert, Harriet. *Happy birthday, Grandpa!*
    Lunchtime for a purple snake
    No kiss for Grandpa!
Zolotow, Charlotte (Shapiro). *My grandson Lew*

Family life – grandmothers

Aber, Linda Williams. *Carrie measures up!*
Ackerman, Karen. *By the dawn's early light*
Addy, Sharon Hart. *A visit with great-grandma*
Ahlberg, Allan. *The snail house*
Alcott, Louisa May. *An old-fashioned Thanksgiving*
Alda, Arlene. *Hurry Granny Annie*
Alexander, Martha G. *The story grandmother told*
Allen, Linda. *Mr. Simkin's grandma*
Allred, Mary. *Grandmother Poppy and the children's tea party*
    Grandmother Poppy and the funny-looking bird
Altman, Linda Jacobs. *Singing with Momma Lou*
Ambrus, Victor G. *Grandma, Felix, and Mustapha Biscuit*
Anderson, Laurie Halse. *Turkey pox*
Anholt, Catherine. *Tom's rainbow walk*
Anholt, Laurence. *Summerhouse*
Bailey, Debbie. *Grandma*
Bailey, Linda. *When Addie was scared*

Baker, Jeannie. *Grandmother*
Balgassi, Haemi. *Peacebound trains*
Balian, Lorna. *Humbug rabbit*
Ballard, Robin. *Granny and me*
Barker, Peggy. *What happened when grandma died*
Barnwell, Ysaye M. *No mirrors in my Nana's house*
Bartoli, Jennifer. *Nonna*
Base, Graeme. *My grandma lived in Gooligulch*
Bauer, Marion Dane. *Grandmother's song*
   When I go camping with Grandma
Bea, Holly. *Where does God live?*
Beardshaw, Rosalind. *Grandma's beach*
Belton, Sandra. *May'naise sandwiches and sunshine tea*
Bercaw, Edna Coe. *Halmoni's day*
Berenstain, Stan. *The Berenstain bears and the week at grandma's*
Berridge, Celia. *Grandmother's tales*
Best, Cari. *Three cheers for Catherine the Great!*
   When Catherine the Great and I were eight!
Bible, Charles. *Jennifer's new chair*
Biro, Maureen Boyd. *Walking with Maga*
Blegvad, Lenore. *Once upon a time and Grandma*
Bliss, Corinne Demas. *The disappearing island*
Boon, Debbie. *My gran*
Borden, Louise. *The watching game*
Bottner, Barbara. *Nana Hannah's piano*
Bourgeois, Paulette. *Oma's quilt*
Bowen, Anne. *I loved you before you were born*
Bower, Gary. *Ivy's icicle*
Bowles, Brad. *Grandma's band*
Brandenberg, Franz. *A secret for grandmother's birthday*
Brenner, Barbara A. *Beef stew*
Brimner, Larry Dane. *Nana's hog*
Brisson, Pat. *Hobbledy-clop*
Brown, Ken (Ken James). *What's the time, Grandma Wolf?*
Bruna, Dick. *Dick Bruna's Little Red Riding Hood*
Bryan, Ashley. *Turtle knows your name*
Buckley, Helen Elizabeth. *Grandmother and I*
Bunting, Eve (Anne Evelyn). *A picnic in October*
   Sunshine home
   The Wednesday surprise
Burrowes, Adjoa J. *Grandma's purple flowers*
Butterworth, Nick. *My grandma is wonderful*
Caines, Jeannette. *Window wishing*
Calmenson, Stephanie. *Hotter than a hot dog!*
   Zip, whiz, zoom!
Carlson, Nancy L. *A visit to grandma's*
Carlstrom, Nancy White. *The moon came too*
Carrick, Carol. *Valentine*
Caseley, Judith. *Apple pie and onions*
Castaneda, Omar S. *Abuela's weave*
Cazzola, Gus. *The bells of Santa Lucia*
Cech, John. *My grandmother's journey*
Chall, Marsha Wilson. *Prairie train*
Chanin, Michael. *Chief's blanket*
Choi, Sook Nyul. *Halmoni and the picnic*
   Yunmi and Halmoni's trip
Chorao, Kay. *Lemon moon*
Christian, Mary Blount. *Grandmothers, God's gift to children*
Cole, Babette. *The trouble with Gran*
Coleman, Evelyn. *The glass bottle tree*
Collins, Ross. *Alvie eats soup*
Conrad, Donna. *See you soon, Moon*
Corbalis, Judy. *The cuckoo bird*
Cornish, Sam. *Grandmother's pictures*
Coutant, Helen. *First snow*
Cowley, Joy. *Big moon tortilla*
Crunk, Tony. *Big Mama*
Cutler, Jane. *Darcy and Gran don't like babies*
D'Arc, Karen Scourby. *My grandmother is a singing Yaya*
Daly, Niki. *Not so fast Songololo*
DeJong, David Cornel. *Looking for Alexander*
Delton, Judy. *My grandma's in a nursing home*
Denton, Kady MacDonald. *Granny is a darling*
De Paola, Tomie (Thomas Anthony). *The baby sister*
   Haircuts for the Woolseys
   Nana Upstairs and Nana Downstairs, 1973
   Nana Upstairs and Nana Downstairs, 1998

Devlin, Wende. *Cranberry autumn*
Dexter, Alison. *Grandma*
Díaz, Katacha. *Carolina's gift*
Dodd, Anne Westcott. *The story of the sea glass*
Doray, Malika. *One more Wednesday*
Dorros, Arthur. *Abuela*
Doyle, Malachy. *Splash, Joshua, splash!*
Drucker, Malka. *Grandma's latkes*
DuBurke, Randy. *The moon ring*
Dupré, Rick. *The wishing chair*
Dwyer, Mindy. *Quilt of dreams*
Easwaran, Eknath. *The monkey and the mango*
Ehrlich, Amy. *Bunnies and their grandma*
Eisenberg, Phyllis Rose. *A mitzvah is something special*
Erdrich, Louise. *Grandmother's pigeon*
Ernst, Lisa Campbell. *Little Red Riding Hood*
Farmer, Nancy. *Runnery granary*
Fellows, Rebecca Nevers. *A lei for Tutu*
Fernandes, Kim. *Visiting granny*
Finfer, Celentha. *Grandmother dear*
Fletcher, Ralph J. *Grandpa never lies*
Flournoy, Valerie. *The patchwork quilt*
Fraustino, Lisa Rowe. *The hickory chair*
Gackenbach, Dick. *With love from Gran*
Gammell, Stephen. *Twigboy*
Garland, Sherry. *The lotus seed*
George, Jean Craighead. *Dear Katie, the volcano is a girl*
   Dear Rebecca, winter is here
Godard, Alex. *Mama, across the sea*
Goffstein, M. B. (Marilyn Brooke). *Fish for supper*
Goldman, Susan. *Grandma is somebody special*
Gomi, Taro. *Coco can't wait!*
Goodman, Louise. *Ida's doll*
Gordon, Shirley. *Grandma zoo*
Gorog, Judith. *Zilla Sasparilla and the mud baby*
Gray, Rita. *Nonna's porch*
Green, Donna. *My little artist*
Greene, Rhonda Gowler. *At grandma's*
Greenfield, Eloise. *William and the good old days*
Gregory, Nan. *Wild Girl and Gran*
Grifalconi, Ann. *Osa's pride*
Grindley, Sally. *A flag for Grandma*
Guback, Georgia. *Luka's quilt*
Guest, C. Z. *Tiny green thumbs*
Halak, Glenn. *A grandmother's story*
Hamm, Diane Johnston. *Grandma drives a motor bed*
Hansen, P. (Paul H.). *My granny's purse*
Hanson, Regina. *A season for mangoes*
Hartman, Bob. *Granny Mae's Christmas play*
Hassett, John. *Mouse in the house*
Hautzig, Deborah. *Big Bird at the beach*
   Get well, Granny Bird
Hawxhurst, Joan C. *Bubbe and Gram, my two grandmothers*
Hayashi, Akiko. *Aki and the fox*
Hayes, Sarah. *Happy Christmas, Gemma*
Haynes, Max. *Grandma's gone to live in the stars*
Hayward, Linda. *Sunny Day Bunny*
Hedderwick, Mairi. *The big Katie Morag storybook*
   Katie Morag and the big boy cousins
   Katie Morag and the two grandmothers
   Katie Morag delivers the mail
Helldorfer, M. C. (Mary Claire). *Harmonica night*
Heller, Nicholas. *This little piggy*
Hendershot, Judith. *Up the tracks to Grandma's*
Henderson, Kathy. *And the good brown earth*
Hennessy, B. G. (Barbara G.). *When you were just a little girl*
Henriod, Lorraine. *Grandma's wheelchair*
Herman, Charlotte. *The memory cupboard*
Herrera, Juan Felipe. *Grandma and Me at the flea = Los meros meros remateros*
Hershey, Kathleen. *Cotton mill town*
Hest, Amy. *The Friday nights of Nana*
   The go-between
   Jamaica Louise James
   The midnight eaters
   Nana's birthday party
Hines, Anna Grossnickle. *Come to the meadow*

Gramma's walk
Grandma gets grumpy
My grandma is coming to town
Hippely, Hilary Horder. *A song for Lena*
Hirschi, Ron. *Harvest song*
Hiser, Berniece T. *The adventure of Charlie and his wheat-straw hat*
Hogan, Bernice. *My grandmother died but I won't forget her*
Hol, Coby. *Niki's little donkey*
Hoopes, Lyn Littlefield. *Nana*
Horning, Sandra. *The giant hug*
Howard, Elizabeth Fitzgerald. *When will Sarah come?*
Howard, Ellen. *The log cabin quilt*
Howard, Kim. *In wintertime*
Ichikawa, Satomi. *Nora's stars*
Igus, Toyomi. *Two Mrs. Gibsons*
Isadora, Rachel. *Over the green hills*
Jackson, Bobby L. *Little Red Ronnika*
James, Betsy. *The dream stair*
Jarrell, Mary. *The knee baby*
Jeschke, Susan. *Mia, Grandma and the genie*
Jessup, Harley. *Grandma summer*
Johnson, Dinah. *Quinnie Blue*
Johnson, Dolores. *Grandma's hands*
Johnston, Tony. *Goblin walk*
Jones, Diana Wynne. *Yes, dear*
Joosse, Barbara M. *Ghost wings*
    A houseful of Christmas
Kahn, Rosemary. *Grandma's hat*
Karkowsky, Nancy. *Grandma's soup*
Kay, Helen. *A stocking for a kitten*
Keller, Holly. *The best present*
Kessler, Cristina. *My great-grandmother's gourd*
Ketner, Mary Grace. *Ganzy remembers*
Ketteman, Helen. *Grandma's cat*
Khalsa, Dayal Kaur. *Tales of a gambling grandma*
Kibbey, Marsha. *My grammy*
Kimmelman, Leslie. *Me and Nana*
Kojima, Naomi. *The flying grandmother*
Konigsburg, E. L. (Elaine Lobl). *Amy Elizabeth explores Bloomingdale's*
Koralek, Jenny. *The boy and the cloth of dreams*
    Night ride to Nanna's
Kovalski, Maryann. *Take me out to the ball game*
    The wheels on the bus
Kraus, Robert. *Rebecca Hatpin*
Kroll, Steven. *Annie's four grannies*
    If I could be my grandmother
Kroll, Virginia L. *Sweet Magnolia*
Kunhardt, Edith. *Danny's mystery Valentine*
Kuskin, Karla. *Paul*
Lakin, Pat (Patricia). *Jet black pickup truck*
LaMarche, Jim. *The raft*
Laminack, Lester L. *Saturdays and teacakes*
    Trevor's wiggly-wobbly tooth
Lasky, Kathryn. *My island grandma*, ill. by Emily Arnold McCully
    My island grandma, ill. by Amy Schwartz
Leedahl, Shelley A. (Shelley Ann). *The bone talker*
Lenski, Lois. *Debbie and her grandma*
Lester, Alison. *Isabella's bed*
Le Tord, Bijou. *My Grandma Leonie*
Levine, Evan. *Not the piano, Mrs. Medley!*
Levinson, Riki. *I go with my family to Grandma's*
    Watch the stars come out
Lexau, Joan M. *Benjie*
    Benjie on his own
Limb, Sue. *Come back, Grandma*
Lindbergh, Reeve. *The hippie grandmother*
Linden, Ann Marie. *One smiling grandma*
Lindgren, Astrid. *The ghost of Skinny Jack*
Little, Jean. *Bats about baseball*
Lloyd, David. *Duck*
    Grandma and the pirate
    The stopwatch
London, Jonathan. *Liplap's wish*
    The sugaring-off party
Look, Lenore. *Henry's first-moon birthday*
    Love as strong as ginger

Love to mamá
Lovell, Patty. *Stand tall, Molly Lou Melon*
Low, Alice. *David's windows*
Low, William. *Chinatown*
Lowell, Susan. *Little Red Cowboy Hat*
Luenn, Nancy. *A gift for Abuelita*
    Nessa's fish
    Nessa's story
Lum, Kate. *What! cried Granny*
McCain, Becky R. (Becky Ray). *Grandmother's dreamcatcher*
McCaughrean, Geraldine. *My grandmother's clock*
McCully, Emily Arnold. *The grandma mix-up*
    Grandmas trick-or-treat
McElroy, Lisa Tucker. *Meet my grandmother. She's a children's book author*
McKay, Hilary. *Pirates ahoy!*
McKean, Thomas. *Hooray for Grandma Jo!*
McLeod, Elaine. *Lessons from Mother Earth*
McQueen, John Troy. *A world full of monsters*
Maguire, Gregory. *Lucas Fishbone*
Mahy, Margaret. *A busy day for a good grandmother*
Manuel, Lynn. *The night the moon blew kisses*
Martin, Bill (William Ivan). *Little granny quarterback*
Martin, C. L. G. *Three brave women*
Mason, Ann Maree. *The weird things in Nanna's house*
Mathews, Judith. *Nathaniel Willy, scared silly*
Mayer, Pamela. *The scariest monster in the whole wide world*
Mayhew, James. *Katie and the sunflowers*
Melmed, Laura Krauss. *The Marvelous Market on Mermaid*
Mendes, Valerie. *Look at me, Grandma!*
Milstein, Linda Breiner. *Grandma's jewelry box*
    Miami-Nanny stories
Mitchell, Lori. *Different just like me*
Moore, Elaine. *Grammy, do you love me?*
    Grandma's garden
    Grandma's house
    Grandma's promise
    Grandma's smile
Moore, Maggie. *Little Red Riding Hood*
Morris, Ann. *The grandma book*
    Grandma Esther remembers
    Grandma Francisca remembers
    Grandma Lai Goon remembers
    Grandma Lois remembers
    Grandma Maxine remembers
Morris, Winifred. *Just listen*
Mower, Nancy. *I visit my Tūtū and Grandma*
Murphy, Patti Beling. *Elinor and Violet*
Neasi, Barbara J. *Listen to me*
Nelson, S. D. *The Star People*
Nelson, Vaunda Micheaux. *Always Gramma*
Nethery, Mary. *Hannah and Jack*
Newman, Lesléa. *Matzo ball moon*
    Remember that
Newsome, Jill. *Dream dancer*
Nightingale, Sandy. *Cider apples*
Nobisso, Josephine. *Grandma's scrapbook*
Nodar, Carmen Santiago. *Abuelita's paradise*
Noll, Sally. *I have a loose tooth*
Numeroff, Laura Joffe. *What grandmas do best; What grandpas do best*
Nye, Naomi Shihab. *Benito's dream bottle*
    Sitti's secrets
O'Callahan, Jay. *Orange cheeks*
    Tulips
Ogburn, Jacqueline K. *The magic nesting doll*
Older, Effin. *My two grandmothers*
Olson, Arielle North. *Hurry home, Grandma!*
Oppenheim, Shulamith Levey. *Waiting for Noah*
Orbach, Ruth. *Please send a panda*
Pak, Soyung. *Dear Juno*
Palmisciano, Diane. *Garden partners*
Parish, Peggy. *Granny and the desperadoes*
    Granny and the Indians
    Granny, the baby and the big gray thing
Passen, Lisa. *Grammy and Sammy*
Peck, Richard. *Monster night at Grandma's house*

Pegram, Laura. *Daughter's Day blues*
Peters, Lisa Westberg. *Purple delicious blackberry jam*
Peterson, Jeanne Whitehouse. *Sometimes I dream horses*
Polacco, Patricia. *Babushka's Mother Goose*
    Chicken Sunday
    Thunder cake
Poskanzer, Susan Cornell. *Puppeteer*
Powers, Daniel. *Jiro's pearl*
Poydar, Nancy. *Busy Bea*
Pulver, Robin. *Alicia's tutu*
Reiser, Lynn. *Cherry pies and lullabies*
Roberts, Sarah. *I want to go home!*
Robertson, Joanne. *Sea witches*
Rockwell, Anne F. *When I go visiting*
Roe, Eileen. *Staying with Grandma*
Rogers, Paul (Patrick). *From me to you*
Romain, Trevor. *Jemma's journey*
Root, Phyllis. *Gretchen's grandma*
    The name quilt
Rosenberg, Liz. *Grandmother and the runaway shadow*
Roth, Susan L. *Another Christmas*
    Patchwork tales
Rothenberg, Joan Keller. *Inside-out grandma*
Rylant, Cynthia. *The ticky-tacky doll*
Sáenz, Benjamin Alire. *Grandma Fina and her wonderful umbrellas =*
    La abuelita Fina y sus sombrillas maravillosas
Sakai, Kimiko. *Sachiko means happiness*
Sasso, Sandy Eisenberg. *For heaven's sake*
Satterfield, Barbara. *The story dance*
Scheffler, Ursel. *A walk in the rain*
Schertle, Alice. *Maisie*
Schlein, Miriam. *The story about me*
Schneider, Antonie. *Good-bye, Vivi!*
Schwartz, Amy. *Oma and Bobo*
Scott, Ann Herbert. *Grandmother's chair*
Seymour, Tres. *Too quiet for these old bones*
Shea, Pegi Deitz. *The whispering cloth*
Shecter, Ben. *Grandma remembers*
Shelby, Anne. *Homeplace*
Sheldon, Dyan. *The whales' song*
Silverman, Erica. *On Grandma's roof*
Slate, Joseph. *The secret stars*
Slepian, Jan. *Emily just in time*
Smee, Nicola. *The Tusk Fairy*
Smith, Barry. *Grandma Rabbitty's visit*
Smith, Maggie (Margaret C.). *My grandma's chair*
Smucker, Barbara Claasen. *Selina and the bear paw quilt*
Sonneborn, Ruth A. *I love Gram*
Spalding, Andrea. *Sarah May and the new red dress*
Spinelli, Eileen. *Wanda's monster*
Spinner, Stephanie. *It's a miracle*
Spohn, Kate. *Snow play*
Stanovich, Betty Jo. *Big boy, little boy*
Steiner, Charlotte. *Kiki and Muffy*
Stilz, Carol Curtis. *Grandma Buffalo, May, and me*
Stock, Catherine. *Gugu's house*
Storr, Catherine (Cole). *Hugo and his grandma*
Stroud, Virginia A. *A walk to the Great Mystery*
Tan, Amy. *The moon lady*
Theroux, Phyllis. *Serefina under the circumstances*
Thomas, Jane Resh. *Saying good-bye to grandma*
Thompson, Colin (Colin Edward). *Falling angels*
Thompson, Mary. *Gran's bees*
Torres, Leyla. *Liliana's grandmothers*
    Saturday sancocho
Udry, Janice May. *Mary Jo's grandmother*
Uegaki, Chieri. *Suki's kimono*
Velasquez, Eric. *Grandma's records*
Vigil-Piñón, Evangelina. *Marina's muumuu = el muumuu de Marina*
Vigna, Judith. *Everyone goes as a pumpkin*
    Grandma without me
Vulliamy, Clara. *Small*
Waboose, Jan Bourdeau. *Firedancers*
Waddell, Martin. *Amy said*
Wahl, Jan. *"I remember," cried Grandma Pinky*
Waldman, Neil. *They came from the Bronx*
Walsh, Jill Paton. *When Grandma came*

    When I was little like you
Ward, Sally G. *Charlie and Grandma*
    What goes around comes around
Waterton, Betty. *Pettranella*
Watkins, Sherrin. *White Bead Ceremony*
Watts, Jeri Hanel. *Keepers*
Weitzman, Jacqueline Preiss. *You can't take a balloon into the Metro-*
    politan Museum
    You can't take a balloon into the National Gallery
Wells, Rosemary. *Bunny cakes*
    Bunny money
    Bunny party
    Ruby's beauty shop
    Yoko's paper cranes
Whelan, Gloria. *Bringing the farmhouse home*
Whitlock, Susan Love. *Donovan scares the monsters*
Whybrow, Ian. *Sammy and the robots*
Wilcox, Brian. *Full moon*
Wild, Margaret. *Big cat dreaming*
    Old Pig
    Our granny
    Remember me
Wilhelm, Hans. *A cool kid – like me!*
Willard, Nancy. *The mountains of quilt*
    The mouse, the cat and Grandmother's hat
Williams, Barbara. *Kevin's grandma*
Williams, Laura E. *The long silk strand*
Williams, Sophy. *Nana's garden*
Williams, Vera B. *Music, music for everyone*
Wilson, Beth P. *Jenny*
Winch, John. *Keeping up with Grandma*
Wojtowycz, David. *A cuddle for Claude*
Wolf, Janet. *The best present is me*
Wood, Audrey. *The napping house*
    The napping house wakes up
Wood, Joyce. *Grandmother Lucy goes on a picnic*
    Grandmother Lucy in her garden
Woodson, Jacqueline. *Coming on home soon*
Wright, Betty Ren. *The cat next door*
Wyse, Lois. *How to take your grandmother to the museum*
Yolen, Jane. *No bath tonight*
Zagwÿn, Deborah Turney. *The winter gift*
Zelinsky, Paul O. *The wheels on the bus*
Ziefert, Harriet. *Little Red Riding Hood*
    With love from Grandma
Zolotow, Charlotte (Shapiro). *William's doll*

Family life – grandparents

Ada, Alma Flor. *I love Saturdays y domingos*
Allen, Linda. *Mr. Simkin's grandma*
Auld, Mary. *My grandparents*
Baggette, Susan K. *Jonathan goes to the grocery store*
    Jonathan goes to the library
Barrett, Judi. *Pickles to Pittsburgh*
Bat-Ami, Miriam. *Sea, salt, and air*
Bate, Lucy. *How Georgina drove the car very carefully from Boston to*
    New York
Bateman, Teresa. *April foolishness*
Bergman, Tamar. *Where is?*
Bonners, Susan. *The wooden doll*
Bosak, Susan V. *Something to remember me by*
Bowen, Anne. *When you visit Grandma and Grandpa*
Bunting, Eve (Anne Evelyn). *The days of summer*
    Winter's coming
Carlson, Nancy L. *Hooray for Grandparent's Day!*
Caseley, Judith. *Grandpa's garden lunch*
Cazet, Denys. *Big shoe, little shoe*
    The octopus
    Saturday
Child, Lydia Maria. *Over the river and through the wood*
Chocolate, Deborah M. Newton. *The piano man*
Copeland, Helen. *Meet Miki Takino*
Crum, Shutta. *All on a sleepy night*
    My mountain song
Curtis, Gavin. *Grandma's baseball*
Dalmais, Anne-Marie. *Henry the hedgehog*

DeFelice, Cynthia C. *Willy's silly grandma*
De Paola, Tomie (Thomas Anthony). *Pajamas for Kit*
Dunbar, Joyce. *When I was young*
Eisenberg, Phyllis Rose. *A mitzvah is something special*
Engel, Diana. *Eleanor, Arthur, and Claire*
Eversole, Robyn Harbert. *The gift stone*
Farber, Norma. *How does it feel to be old?*
Feldman, Barbara. *Stephen's frog*
Flory, Jane. *The unexpected grandchildren*
French, Vivian. *Oliver's vegetables*
Galindo, Mary Sue. *Icy watermelon = Sandía fría*
Gantschev, Ivan. *The train to Grandma's*
Gould, Deborah. *Grandpa's slide show*
Grambling, Lois G. *Grandma tells a story*
A grand celebration
Greve, Andreas. *Christopher's dream car*
Haas, Irene. *A summertime song*
Haas, Jessie. *Hurry!*
    No foal yet
    Sugaring
Hamm, Diane Johnston. *Grandma drives a motor bed*
Harshman, Marc. *Roads*
Hawes, Judy. *Fireflies in the night*
Haywood, Carolyn. *Hello, star*
Hazen, Barbara Shook. *Katie's wish*
Heller, Linda. *The castle on Hester Street*
Hesse, Karen. *Poppy's chair*
Hest, Amy. *Gabby growing up*
    Weekend girl
Hickman, Martha Whitmore. *Robert lives with his grandparents*
Hill, Eric. *Spot visits his grandparents*
Hooker, Ruth. *At Grandma and Grandpa's house*
Hooper, Meredith. *A cow, a bee, a cookie, and me*
Hunter, Dette. *38 ways to entertain your grandparents*
Hurd, Edith Thacher. *I dance in my red pajamas*
Hutchins, H. J. (Hazel J.). *One dark night*
James, Betsy. *Flashlight*
Jennings, Sharon. *Franklin's Thanksgiving*
Joosse, Barbara M. *Jam day*
Joseph, Daniel M. *All dressed up and nowhere to go*
Kilroy, Sally. *Grandpa's garden*
Kitamura, Satoshi. *Captain Toby*
Kroll, Steven. *Toot! Toot!*
Kropf, Latifa Berry. *It's Hanukkah time!*
Kunhardt, Edith. *Pat the puppy*
Lakin, Pat (Patricia). *Grandparents*
Laminack, Lester L. *The sunsets of Miss Olivia Wiggins*
Lebentritt, Julia. *The Kooken*
Lemieux, Margo. *The fiddle ribbon*
Levinson, Riki. *Grandpa's hotel*
Lohans, Alison. *Sundog rescue*
Long, Melinda. *When Papa snores*
McAllister, Angela. *The wind garden*
Maccarone, Grace. *Baby visits grandma and grandpa*
Maris, Ron. *Is anyone home?*
Martin, Jacqueline Briggs. *Grandmother Bryant's pocket*
Minarik, Else Holmelund. *Little Bear's visit*
Mollel, Tololwa M. (Tololwa Marti). *Kele's secret*
Morgan, Michaela. *Visitors for Edward*
Moss, Marissa. *The ugly menorah*
Newman, Shirlee. *Tell me, grandma; tell me, grandpa*
Oechsli, Helen. *Fly away!*
Oppenheim, Shulamith Levey. *Fireflies for Nathan*
Oxenbury, Helen. *Grandma and Grandpa*
Palacios, Argentina. *A Christmas surprise for Chabelita*
Polacco, Patricia. *My rotten redheaded older brother*
    The trees of the dancing goats
Porte, Barbara Ann. *Harry's mom*
Raynor, Dorka. *Grandparents around the world*
Rice, Eve. *At Grammy's house*
Riggio, Anita. *A moon in my teacup*
Rockwell, Anne F. *When I go visiting*
Rosen, Michael (1946–). *A Thanksgiving wish*
Rosen, Winifred. *Henrietta and the gong from Hong Kong*
Rosenberg, Liz. *The silence in the mountains*
Rotner, Shelley. *Lots of grandparents*
Ruelle, Karen Gray. *Easy as apple pie*

Rylant, Cynthia. *Christmas in the country*
Saint James, Synthia. *Sunday*
Sandberg, Inger. *Dusty wants to borrow everything*
Scheffler, Ursel. *A walk in the rain*
Schneider, Antonie. *The birthday bear*
Shapiro, Jody Fickes. *Up, up, up! It's apple-picking time*
Skofield, James. *Snow country*
Skolsky, Mindy Warshaw. *Hannah and the whistling tea kettle*
Stevenson, James. *Higher on the door*
    July
Stojic, Manya. *Wet pebbles under our feet*
Thomson, Pat. *The squeaky, creaky bed*
Tsubakiyama, Margaret (Holloway). *Mei-Mei loves the morning*
Tunnell, Michael O. *Mailing May*
Uslander, Arlene. *That's what grandparents are for*
Van Haeringen, Annemarie. *The cats' tale*
Van Leeuwen, Jean. *Touch the sky summer*
Waddell, Martin. *Grandma's Bill*
Wardlaw, Lee. *The tales of Grandpa Cat*
Watanabe, Shigeo. *It's my birthday*
Watson, Mary. *The butterfly seeds*
Woodson, Jacqueline. *Sweet, sweet memory*
Woodtor, Dee. *Big meeting*
Wyeth, Sharon Dennis. *Always my dad*
Yolen, Jane. *Off we go!*
Ziefert, Harriet. *Chocolate mud cake*

Family life – great-grandparents

Arnold, Marsha Diane. *The chicken salad club*
Bornstein, Ruth Lercher. *A beautiful seashell*
Budd, Lillian. *The people on Long Ago Street*
Cross, Verda. *Great-grandma tells of threshing day*
De Paola, Tomie (Thomas Anthony). *Nana Upstairs and Nana Downstairs*, 1973
    Nana Upstairs and Nana Downstairs, 1998
Diller, Harriett. *The faraway drawer*
Greenburg, Dan. *Great-Grandpa's in the litter box*
Guthrie, Donna. *The secret admirer*
Herter, Jonina. *Eighty-eight kisses*
Hickcox, Ruth. *Great-Grandmother's treasure*
Hooks, William H. *The mighty Santa Fe*
Judd, Naomi. *Naomi Judd's guardian angels*
Ketner, Mary Grace. *Ganzy remembers*
Knotts, Howard. *Great-grandfather, the baby and me*
MacLachlan, Patricia. *Three names*
Matthews, Wendy. *The gift of a traveler*
Reiser, Lynn. *Cherry pies and lullabies*
Rochelle, Belinda. *Jewels*
Russo, Marisabina. *A visit to Oma*
Taulbert, Clifton L. *Little Cliff's first day of school*
Waddell, Martin. *My great grandpa*
Whittington, Mary K. *Carmina, come dance!*

Family life – mothers

Ackerman, Karen. *By the dawn's early light*
Ackerman, Karen. *When mama retires*
Albert, Shirley. *Doll party*
Alborough, Jez. *Hug*
    It's the bear
Alda, Arlene. *Morning glory Monday*
    Sonya's mommy works
Alexander, Sue. *One more time, Mama*
All the pretty little horses
Allancé, Mireille d'. *How long?*
Anastas, Margaret. *Mommy's best kisses*
Anderson, Laurie Halse. *No time for Mother's Day*
Anderson, Lena. *Bunny box*
Andreae, Giles. *There's a house inside my mommy*
Appelt, Kathi. *Oh my baby, little one*
Arnold, Lynda. *My Mommy has AIDS*
Asch, Frank. *Bread and honey*
Auld, Mary. *My mom*
Bailey, Debbie. *My mom*
Baker, Alan. *Where's mouse?*
Baker, Gayle. *Special delivery*

Baker, Liza. *I love you because you're you*
Balgassi, Haemi. *Peacebound trains*
Balian, Lorna. *Mother's Mother's Day*
Banks, Kate (Katherine A.). *Baboon*
 Close your eyes
 Mama's coming home
 Spider, spider
Barber, Antonia. *Gemma and the baby chick*
Barber, Barbara E. *Saturday at the new you*
Bassède, Francine. *A day with the Bellyflops*
Bauer, Caroline Feller. *My mom travels a lot*
Bauer, Marion Dane. *Grandmother's song*
 My mother is mine
Baum, Louis. *After dark*
Bearcub and Mama
Beck, Scott. *A mud pie for mother*
Bedford, David. *Touch the sky, my little bear*
Benjamin, Amanda. *Two's company*
Bergman, Tamar. *Where is?*
Berry, Christine. *Mama went walking*
Bertram, Debbie. *The best place to read*
Black, Sonia. *Hanging out with Mom*
Blaine, Marge (Margery Kay). *The terrible thing that happened at our house*
Blake, Claire. *The paper chain*
Bogan, Paulette. *Goodnight Lulu*
 Momma's magical purse
Bottner, Barbara. *Rosa's room*
Bourgeois, Paulette. *Franklin says "I love you"*
Boyd, Lizi. *I love Mommy*
Bradby, Marie. *Momma, where are you from?*
Bradley, Kimberly Brubaker. *Favorite things*
Brami, Elisbeth. *Mommy time*
Brandt, Amy. *Benjamin comes back = Benjamin regresa*
Braun, Sebastien. *I love my mommy*
Breeze, Lynn. *This little baby goes out*
 This little baby's morning
Bridges, Margaret Park. *Am I big or little?*
 Will you take care of me?
Brillhart, Julie. *Story hour – starring Megan!*
Brown, Jo. *Where's my mommy?*
Brown, Margaret Wise. *The runaway bunny*
 The runaway bunny [board book]
Browne, Anthony. *Piggybook*
Bulion, Leslie. *Fatuma's new cloth*
Bunting, Eve (Anne Evelyn). *The day before Christmas*
 Flower garden
 I don't want to go to camp
 Someday a tree
Burke-Weiner, Kimberly. *The maybe garden*
Butterworth, Nick. *My mom is excellent*
Cain, Sheridan. *Why so sad, Brown Rabbit?*
Campbell, Ann-Jeanette. *Queenie Farmer had fifteen daughters*
Cannon, Janell. *Stellaluna*
 Stellaluna: a pop-up book and mobile
Capucilli, Alyssa Satin. *Only my mom and me*
 What kind of kiss?
Carle, Eric. *Does a kangaroo have a mother, too?*
Carrick, Carol. *Valentine*
Carter, Dorothy (Dorothy A.). *Wilhe'mina Miles after the stork night*
Carton, Lonnie Caming. *Mommies*
Caseley, Judith. *Mama, coming and going*
Charlip, Remy. *Sleepytime rhyme*
Chichester Clark, Emma. *More!*
Christelow, Eileen. *Don't wake up Mama!*
Cohen, Caron Lee. *Happy to you!*
Cole, Babette. *Mum*
 The trouble with Mom
Cole, Joanna. *When you were inside mommy*
Cousins, Lucy. *Jazzy in the jungle*
Cowan, Catherine. *My friend the piano*
Cowell, Cressida. *Don't do that, Kitty Kilroy*
Cowen-Fletcher, Jane. *Mama zooms*
Coyne, Rachel. *Daughter, have I told you?*
Dale, Elizabeth. *How long?*
Daly, Niki. *Ben's gingerbread man*
 Teddy's ear

Damjan, Mischa. *How do dinosaurs say goodnight?*
De Anda, Diane. *Dancing Miranda = Baila, Miranda, baila*
Delton, Judy. *The best mom in the world*
 My mom made me go to camp
 My mom made me go to school
 My mom made me take piano lessons
 My mother lost her job today
Demarest, Chris L. *Honk!*
Dijs, Carla. *Mommy, what if—?*
 Mommy, would you love me if . . . ?
Dionetti, Michelle V. *The day Eli went looking for bear*
Dodds, Siobhan. *Ting-a-ling!*
Dornbusch, Erica. *Finding Kate's shoes*
Dörrie, Doris. *Lottie's princess dress*
Dotlich, Rebecca Kai. *Mama loves*
Douglas, Ann. *Before you were born*
Dowson, Nick. *Tigress*
Doyle, Charlotte Lackner. *Where's Bunny's mommy?*
Dragonwagon, Crescent. *Will it be okay?*
Drescher, Joan E. *My mother's getting married*
Duble, Kathleen Benner. *Pilot mom*
Dubowski, Cathy East. *Megan's messy room*
Dunrea, Olivier. *It's snowing*
Dwyer, Mindy. *Quilt of dreams*
Eastman, P. D. (Philip D.). *Are you my mother?*
Eccles, Jane. *Maxwell's birthday*
Eckart, Edana. *I can swim*
Edwards, Richard. *Copy me, Copycub*
Ehrlich, H. M. *Gotcha, Louie!*
Eisenberg, Phyllis Rose. *You're my Nikki*
Emberley, Ed (Edward Randolph). *Thanks, Mom!*
Emberley, Rebecca. *My mother's secret life*
English, Jennifer. *My mommy's special*
Evans, Lezlie. *If I were the wind*
Falwell, Cathryn. *Nicky's walk*
 P.J. & Puppy
Farber, Norma. *All those mothers at the manger*
 Without wings, mother, how can I fly?
Fassler, Joan. *The man of the house*
Fearnley, Jan. *Watch out!*
Feldman, Barbara. *Going, going*
Fine, Anne. *Poor Monty*
Fisher, Aileen Lucia. *Do bears have mothers too?*
 My mother and I
Fitzpatrick, Marie-Louise. *You, me and the big blue sea*
Flack, Marjorie. *Ask Mr. Bear*
Flattinger, Hubert. *Stormy night*
Ford, Miela. *Mom and me*
Foreman, Michael. *Surprise! Surprise!*
Fox, Mem. *Harriet, you'll drive me wild*
 Koala Lou
Fraggalosch, Audrey. *Grizzly bear family*
 Trails above the tree line
Frasier, Debra. *Out of the ocean*
Fruisen, Catherine Myler. *My mother's pearls*
Gackenbach, Dick. *Alice's special room*
 Hurray for Hattie Rabbit!
Galbraith, Kathryn Osebold. *Laura Charlotte*
Gardner, Sally. *Mama, don't go out tonight*
Geisert, Arthur. *Oink oink*
Gerber, Carole. *Arctic dreams*
Gibbons, Faye. *Mama and me and the Model-T*
Gilchrist, Jan Spivey. *Indigo and moonlight gold*
Giovanni, Nikki. *The genie in the jar*
Glassman, Peter. *My working mom*
Godard, Alex. *Mama, across the sea*
Goode, Diane. *Mama's perfect present*
 Where's our mama?
Goode, Molly. *Mama loves*
Goodings, Lennie. *When you grow up*
Gorbachev, Valeri. *Nicky and the fantastic birthday gift*
Gorog, Judith. *Zilla Sasparilla and the mud baby*
Gove, Doris. *My mother talks to trees*
Gray, Kes. *Eat your peas*
Gray, Libba Moore. *My mama had a dancing heart*
Greenstein, Elaine. *As big as you*
Grimes, Nikki. *My man Blue*

Guthrie, Donna. *Mrs. Gigglebelly is coming for tea*
Hafner, Marylin. *Mommies don't get sick*
Haggerty, Mary Elizabeth. *A crack in the wall*
Hague, Kathleen. *Good night, fairies*
Hamilton, DeWitt. *Sad days, glad days*
Hamm, Diane Johnston. *Laney's lost momma*
Hanson, Mary Elizabeth. *Snug*
Harper, Jessica. *Lizzy's do's and don'ts*
    Lizzy's ups and downs
Hawkins, Colin. *Where's my mommy?*
Haynes, Max. *Ticklemonster and me*
Hazen, Barbara Shook. *Mommy's office*
Heatwole, Marsha. *Jambo, watoto!*
Heiligman, Deborah. *Into the night*
Hellard, Susan. *Baby lemur*
Heo, Yumi. *One afternoon*
Hesse, Karen. *Come on, rain*
Hest, Amy. *Kiss good night*
    The mommy exchange
    You can do it, Sam
Hill, Susan. *Beware, beware*
Hines, Anna Grossnickle. *It's just me, Emily*
    Maybe a band-aid will help
Ho, Minfong. *Hush!*
Hoberman, Mary Ann. *The seven silly eaters*
Hubbell, Patricia. *Sea, sand, me!*
    Sidewalk trip
Hudson, Wade. *Jamal's busy day*
Hunter, Sally. *Humphrey's corner*
Hurd, Edith Thacher. *The mother chimpanzee*
Huss, Sally. *I love you with all my hearts*
Igus, Toyomi. *Two Mrs. Gibsons*
Imai, Miko. *Little Lumpty*
Impey, Rose. *My mom and our dad*
Jacobson, Jennifer Richard. *Moon sandwich mom*
Janowitz, Tama. *Hear that?*
Jenkins, Jordan. *Learning about love*
Jennings, Michael. *The bears who came to breakfix*
Jeram, Anita. *Bunny, my Honey*
Johnson, Angela. *Tell me a story, mama*
Johnson, Dolores. *My mom is my show-and-tell*
    What will mommy do when I'm at school?
Johnson, Marion. *Caillou, new shoes*
Johnson, Paul Brett. *The goose who went off in a huff*
Johnston, Tony. *My best friend Bear*
Jonas, Ann. *Two bear cubs*
Jonell, Lynne. *Bravemole*
    I need a snake
    Mom pie
    Mommy go away!
Joosse, Barbara M. *Dinah's mad, bad wishes*
    I love you the purplest
    Mama, do you love me?
Joseph, Lynn. *Jasmine's parlour day*
Kanao, Keiko. *Kitten up a tree*
Kandoian, Ellen. *Maybe she forgot*
Kaplan, Howard. *Waiting to sing*
Kaplan, John. *Mom and me*
Kasza, Keiko. *A mother for Choco*
Katz, Karen. *Where is baby's mommy?*
Kavanagh, Peter. *I love my mama*
Keller, Beverly. *When mother got the flu*
Keller, Holly. *When Francie was sick*
Kent, Jack. *Joey*
Kern, Noris. *I love you with all my heart*
Ketteman, Helen. *Not yet, Yvette*
Killion, Bette. *Just think!*
Kilroy, Sally. *On the road*
Kirk, David. *Little Miss Spider*
Kohlenberg, Sherry. *Sammy's mommy has cancer*
Kolar, Bob. *Stomp, stomp!*
Koller, Jackie French. *No such thing*
Komaiko, Leah. *A million moms and mine*
Kranendonk, Anke. *Just a minute*
Krauss, Ruth. *The bundle book*
    You're just what I need
Kroll, Steven. *That makes me mad*

Kroll, Virginia L. *Motherlove*
Krosoczka, Jarrett J. *Bubble bath pirates*
    Good night, Monkey Boy
Kuiper, Nannie. *Bailey the bear cub*
Lasker, Joe. *Mothers can do anything*
Lasky, Kathryn. *Mommy's hands*
Leblanc, Anne. *Benjamin takes care of Mommy*
Leonard, Marcia. *I like mess*
    My camp-out
    No new pants!
Leuck, Laura. *My monster mama loves me so*
Levine, Abby. *What did mommy do before you?*
Lewin, Hugh. *Jafta's mother*
Lewis, Paeony. *I'll always love you*
Lexau, Joan M. *A house so big*
Lindgren, Barbro. *Benny's had enough*
    The wild baby
    The wild baby gets a puppy
    The wild baby goes to sea
Lindsay, Jeanne Warren. *Do I have a daddy?*
Lish, Ted. *The three little puppies and the big bad flea*
Little Bear's Valentine
Livingston, Myra Cohn. *Poems for mothers*
London, Jonathan. *Count the ways, Little Brown Bear*
    What do you love?
    What do you love? [board book]
Love to mamá
Lyon, George Ella. *Mama is a miner*
McAllister, Angela. *Night-night, little one*
McBratney, Sam. *I'll always be your friend*
McCourt, Lisa. *I love you, Stinky Face*
    I miss you, Stinky Face
    It's time for school, Stinky Face
McKay, Lawrence. *Journey home*
McKee, David. *Prince Peter and the teddy bear*
MacLachlan, Patricia. *Mama one, Mama two*
McMullan, Kate (Hall). *If you were my bunny*
Madrigal, Antonio Hernandez. *Erandi's braids*
Mahy, Margaret. *Boom Baby boom, boom*
Maley, Anne. *Have you seen my mother?*
Manning, Mick. *Supermom*
Martin, C. L. G. *Three brave women*
Martin, David. *Monkey business*
Marton, Jirina. *I'll do it myself*
Marzollo, Jean. *Mama, Mama*
Mayer, Mercer. *Just for you*
Melmed, Laura Krauss. *I love you as much . . .*
Merriam, Eve. *Mommies at work*
    On my street
Micklos, John. *Mommy poems*
Miles, Miska. *Mouse six and the happy birthday*
Milich, Melissa. *Miz Fannie Mae's fine new Easter hat*
Miller, William. *A house by the river*
Minarik, Else Holmelund. *Am I beautiful?*
Miranda, Anne. *Baby-sit*
Mitchard, Jacquelyn. *Baby bat's lullaby*
Mitchell, Joyce Slayton. *My mommy makes money*
Mizumura, Kazue. *If I were a mother*
Modesitt, Jeanne. *Mama, if you had a wish*
Monfried, Lucia. *The Daddies Boat*
Monnier, Miriam. *Just right*
Morgan-Vanroyen, Mary. *Sleep tight, little mouse*
Morris, Ann. *Cuddle up*
    The mommy book
Moss, Marissa. *Who was it?*
Moss, Miriam. *The snow bear*
Müller, Birte. *Finn cooks*
Munsch, Robert N. *Love you forever*
Murphy, Mary. *Please be quiet!*
Murphy, Stuart J. *Rabbit's pajama party*
Neitzel, Shirley. *We're making breakfast for mother*
Newcome, Zita. *Rosie goes shopping*
Newman, Lesléa. *Heather has two mommies*
    Saturday is Pattyday
Nicholls, Judith. *Billywise*
Nixon, Joan Lowery. *Will you give me a dream?*
Noble, Sheilagh. *More*

Numeroff, Laura Joffe. *The hope tree*
Nye, Naomi Shihab. *Lullaby raft*
Ohi, Ruth. *Pants off first*
O'Keefe, Susan Heyboer. *Love me, love you*
Ormerod, Jan. *Bend and stretch*
    Making friends
    Mom's home
    This little nose
Oxenbury, Helen. *Mother's helper*
Palacios, Argentina. *A Christmas surprise for Chabelita*
Palatini, Margie. *Zak's lunch*
Palecek, Libuse. *Brave as a tiger*
Paradis, Susan. *My mommy*
Paris, Lena. *Mom is single*
Parkison, Jami. *Amazing Mallika*
Parr, Todd. *The mommy book*
Parton, Dolly. *Coat of many colors*
Paterson, Katherine. *Celia and the sweet, sweet water*
Patrick, Jean L. S. *If I had a snowplow*
Patz, Nancy. *No thumpin' no bumpin' no rumpus tonight!*
Peacock, Carol Antoinette. *Mommy far, Mommy near*
Pearson, Susan. *Silver morning*
Peterson, Jeanne Whitehouse. *My mama sings*
Pinkwater, Daniel Manus. *Young Larry*
Pitcher, Caroline. *Run with the wind*
Polacco, Patricia. *Betty Doll*
Pomerantz, Charlotte. *The chalk doll*
Porte, Barbara Ann. *Harry's mom*
Porter-Gaylord, Laurel. *I love my mommy because . . .*
Portnoy, Mindy Avra. *Ima on the Bima*
Posthuma, Sieb. *Benny*
Power, Barbara. *I wish Laura's mommy was my mommy*
Price, Hope Lynne. *These hands*
Price, Mathew. *Don't worry, Alfie*
    Where's Alfie?
Pulver, Robin. *Nobody's mother is in second grade*
Quinlan, Patricia. *Anna's red sled*
    My dad takes care of me
Radcliffe, Theresa. *Bashi, elephant baby*
Radlauer, Ruth Shaw. *Breakfast by Molly*
Raff, Courtney Granet. *Giant of the sea*
Rahaman, Vashanti. *Read for me, Mama*
Ransom, Candice F. *The Christmas dolls*
Ray, Deborah Kogan. *Stargazing sky*
Reimold, Mary Gallagher. *My mom is a runner*
Reiser, Lynn. *Any kind of dog*
    Cherry pies and lullabies
Reuter, Margaret. *My mother is blind*
Reyher, Rebecca (Hourwich). *My mother is the most beautiful*
    woman in the world
Reynolds, Marilynn. *The magnificent piano recital*
Rice, Eve. *New blue shoes*
Ring, Susan. *Polar babies*
Robbins, Maria Polushkin. *Mother, Mother, I want another*
    Mother, Mother I want another
Robinson, Sue. *I want to play*
Rockwell, Anne F. *Pumpkin day, pumpkin night*
    Willy can count
Roddie, Shen. *Help, Mama, help!*
    Not now, Mrs. Wolf
Rose, Deborah Lee. *Meredith's mother takes the train*
Rosenberg, Liz. *The carousel*
Rosselson, Leon. *Where's my mom?*
Rotner, Shelley. *Lots of moms*
Rowe, John A. *Smudge*
Rubel, Nicole. *No more vegetables!*
Rusackas, Francesca. *I love you all day long*
Russo, Marisabina. *Come back, Hannah*
    Mama talks too much
    Waiting for Hannah
    When mama gets home
Saltzberg, Barney. *Soccer mom from outer space*
Sawicki, Norma Jean. *Something for mom*
Say, Allen. *Tree of cranes*
Schaefer, Carole Lexa. *Down in the woods at sleepytime*
    Down in the woods at sleepytime [board book]
Schick, Eleanor. *Mama*

Schlessinger, Laura. *Why do you love me?*
Scott, Ann Herbert. *On mother's lap*
    On mother's lap [board book]
Selby, Jennifer. *Beach bunny*
Seymour, Tres. *I love my buzzard*
Sharmat, Marjorie Weinman. *My mother never listens to me*
Sheldon, Dyan. *Love, your bear, Pete*
Shipton, Jonathan. *Busy! Busy! Busy!*
Silverman, Maida. *The magic well*
Simpson, Lesley. *The Purim surprise*
Skurzynski, Gloria. *Martin by himself*
Slangerup, Erik Jon. *Dirt Boy*
Smalls-Hector, Irene. *Jonathan and his mommy*
Smith, Maggie (Margaret C.). *Dear Daisy, get well soon*
Sondheimer, Ilse. *The boy who could make his mother stop yelling*
Spinelli, Eileen. *When Mama comes home tonight*
Spurr, Elizabeth. *The long, long letter*
Standon, Anna. *Little duck lost*
Stanek, Muriel. *All alone after school*
Stehr, Frédéric. *Quack-quack*
Stephens, J. Moria. *Persephone, the ladybug*
Stilz, Carol Curtis. *Kirsty's kite*
Stimson, Joan. *Big Panda, Little Panda*
Stock, Catherine. *Easter surprise*
Strauss, Anna. *Hush, Mama loves you*
Stynes, Barbara White. *Walking with mama*
Suen, Anastasia. *Window music*
Sullivan, Paula. *Todd's box*
Swanson, Susan Marie. *The first thing my mama told me*
Sykes, Julie. *I don't want to take a bath!*
Tabor, Nancy (Maria Grande). *Bottles break*
Tafuri, Nancy. *I love you, little one*
    Mama's little bears
Tarpley, Natasha Anastasia. *I love my hair!*
Thaler, Mike. *Owley*
Thiesing, Lisa. *Me and you*
Thomas, Frances. *What if?*
Thomas, Jane Resh. *Scaredy dog*
Thomas, Joyce Carol. *Joy*
Thomas, Naturi. *Uh-oh! It's Mama's birthday!*
Thomas, Shelley Moore. *Get well, good knight*
Thompson, Lauren. *Little Quack's bedtime*
    Little Quack's hide and seek
The three little pigs. *The three little pigs*, ill. by Steven Kellogg
Titherington, Jeanne. *Big world, small world*
Tobias, Tobi. *The quitting deal*
Tompert, Ann. *Little Otter remembers and other stories*
Trottier, Maxine. *A safe place*
Turner, Ann Warren. *Stars for Sarah*
Tyler, Linda Wagner. *Waiting for mom*
Udry, Janice May. *Is Susan here?*, ill. by Peter Edwards
    Is Susan here?, ill. by Karen Gundersheimer
    Thump and Plunk, ill. by Geoffrey Hayes
    Thump and Plunk, ill. by Ann Schweninger
Ungerer, Tomi. *No kiss for mother*
Valens, Amy. *Jesse's day care*
Van Laan, Nancy. *Little Fish lost*
    Tickle tum
Vigna, Judith. *Couldn't we have a turtle instead?*
    Mommy and me by ourselves again
Viorst, Judith. *My mama says there aren't any zombies, ghosts, vam-*
    pires, creatures, demons, monsters, fiends, goblins, or things
Vulliamy, Clara. *Ellen and Penguin and the new baby*
Waber, Bernard. *Lyle finds his mother*
Waddell, Martin. *The big big sea*
    A kitten called Moonlight
    Owl babies
    Owl babies [board book]
    Rosie's babies
    Snow bears
    Webster J. Duck
    Yum, yum, yummy
Wallace, John. *Anything for you*
Walters, Catherine. *Play gently, Alfie Bear*
    When will it be spring?
Ward, Heather Patricia. *I promise I'll find you*
Warren, Cathy. *Saturday belongs to Sara*

Watson, Nancy Dingman. *Tommy's mommy's fish*, ill. by Aldren
    Auld Watson
    Tommy's mommy's fish, ill. by Thomas Aldren Dingman Watson
Weedn, Flavia. *I feel happy*
Weiss, Nicki. *On a hot, hot day*
Wells, Rosemary. *Hazel's amazing mother*
Weninger, Brigitte. *Special delivery*
Wetterer, Margaret K. *Patrick and the fairy thief*
Wheeler, Lisa. *Jam & jelly by Holly & Nellie*
White, Linda Arms. *Comes a wind*
Wickstrom, Sylvie (Sylvie Kantrovitz). *Mothers can't get sick*
Willard, Nancy. *The high rise glorious skittle skat roarious sky pie angel
    food cake*
    The tale I told Sasha
Williams, Karen Lynn. *Tap-tap*
Williams, Linda. *Horse in the pigpen*
Williams, Suzanne. *Mommy doesn't know my name*
Winthrop, Elizabeth. *Promises*
    A very noisy girl
Wong, Janet S. *Grump*
Wood, Douglas. *Northwoods cradle song*
    What moms can't do
Woodson, Jacqueline. *Coming on home soon*
Wynot, Jillian. *The Mother's Day sandwich*
Yezerski, Thomas F. *Queen of the world*
Yim, Natasha. *Otto's rainy day*
Yolen, Jane. *Nocturne*
Ziefert, Harriet. *Clara Ann Cookie*
    Home for Navidad
    Mommies are for counting stars
    Sarah's questions
    Surprise!
    Where's mommy's truck?
Zindel, Paul. *I love my mother*
Zinnemann-Hope, Pam. *Time for bed, Ned*
Zisk, Mary. *The best single mom in the world*
Zolotow, Charlotte (Shapiro). *I like to be little*
    Mr. Rabbit and the lovely present
    Say it!
    The seashore book
    This quiet lady

Family life – new sibling

Alexander, Martha G. *Nobody asked me if I wanted a baby sister*
    When the new baby comes, I'm moving out
Allen, Robert. *Ten little babies count*
Andry, Andrew C. *Hi, new baby*
Anholt, Catherine. *Aren't you lucky!*
    Here come the babies
Anholt, Laurence. *Sophie and the new baby*
Apperley, Dawn. *Don't wake the baby*
Arnstein, Helene S. *Billy and our new baby*
Auch, Mary Jane. *Monster brother*
Baker, Charlotte. *Little brother*
Banish, Roslyn. *Let me tell you about my baby*
Birdseye, Tom. *Waiting for baby*
Boelts, Maribeth. *You're a brother, Little Bunny!*
Bogart, Jo Ellen. *Daniel's dog*
Boyd, Lizi. *Sam is my half brother*
Bradman, Tony. *Billy and the baby*
Brown, Marc Tolon. *Arthur's baby*
Byars, Betsy Cromer. *Go and hush the baby*
Carlstrom, Nancy White. *Kiss your sister, Rose Marie*
Caseley, Judith. *Mama, coming and going*
    Silly baby
Chess, Victoria. *Poor Esmé*
Clarke, Gus. *Along came Eric*
Clifton, Lucille. *Everett Anderson's nine months long*
Cole, Joanna. *The new baby at your house*
Collins, Pat Lowery. *Waiting for baby Joe*
Corey, Dorothy. *Will there be a lap for me?*
Cottringer, Anne. *Ella and the naughty lion*
Cutler, Jane. *Darcy and Gran don't like babies*
Davies, Gill. *Wilbur waited*
De Paola, Tomie (Thomas Anthony). *The baby sister*
Dewan, Ted. *Crispin and the 3 little piglets*

Driscoll, Debbie. *Baby comes home*
Dunrea, Olivier. *Ollie*
Fearnley, Jan. *A special something*
Fisher, Iris L. *Katie-Bo*
Foreman, Michael. *Ben's baby*
Franklin, Jonathan. *Don't wake the baby*
Galbraith, Kathryn Osebold. *Waiting for Jennifer*
Garland, Sarah. *Billy and Belle*
Gewing, Lisa. *Mama, daddy, baby and me*
Gliori, Debi. *New big sister*
Graham, Richard. *Jack and the monster*
Greenfield, Eloise. *She come bringing me that little baby girl*
    Sweet baby coming
Gutman, Anne. *Lisa's baby sister*
Haarhoff, Dorian. *Desert December*
Hains, Harriet. *My baby brother*
Hamilton-Merritt, Jane. *Our new baby*
Hanson, Joan. *I don't like Timmy*
Hanson, Mary Elizabeth. *The difference between babies and cookies*
Harper, Anita. *It's not fair!*
Harris, Robie H. *Hi, new baby*
Hathorn, Libby (Elizabeth). *Freya's fantastic surprise*
Hedderwick, Mairi. *Katie Morag and the tiresome Ted*
Helmering, Doris Wild. *We're going to have a baby*
Henry, Steve. *Nobody asked me!*
Hobson, Laura Z. *"I'm going to have a baby!"*
Hoffman, Rosekrans. *Sister Sweet Ella*
Holabird, Katharine. *Angelina's baby sister*
Holland, Viki. *We are having a baby*
Hooker, Ruth. *Sara loves her big brother*
Horowitz, Ruth. *Mommy's lap*
Hughes, Shirley. *Angel Mae*
Hutchins, Pat. *Our baby is best*
Kallok, Emma. *Gem*
Keats, Ezra Jack. *Peter's chair*
Keller, Holly. *Geraldine's baby brother*
Knight, Joan. *Opal in the closet*
Krasilovsky, Phyllis. *The very little boy*
    The very little girl
Kushner, Donn. *Peter's pixie*
Lakin, Pat (Patricia). *Don't touch my room*
Lasky, Kathryn. *A baby for Max*
Levi, Dorothy Hoffman. *A very special sister*
Levinson, Riki. *Me baby!*
Lewison, Wendy Cheyette. *Our new baby*
Lindgren, Astrid. *I want a brother or sister*
Lohans, Alison. *Waiting for the sun*
McCormick, Wendy. *The night you were born*
Malecki, Maryann. *Mom and dad and I are having a baby!*
Manushkin, Fran. *Little rabbit's baby brother*
Mario, Heidi Stetson. *I'd rather have an iguana*
Mendes, Valerie. *Look at me, Grandma!*
Mills, Lauren A. *The goblin baby*
Moore, Eva. *Franklin and the baby*
Munsch, Robert N. *Alligator baby*
Murdocca, Sal (Salvatore). *Baby wants the moon*
Murkoff, Heidi Eisenberg. *What to expect when the new baby comes
    home*
Old, Wendie C. *Stacy had a little sister*
Reader, Dennis. *Butterfingers*
Rheingrover, Jean Sasso. *Veronica's first year*
Robbins, Beth. *Tom, Ally, and the new baby*
Robbins, Maria Polushkin. *Baby brother blues*
Robins, Joan. *My brother, Will*
Rock, Lois. *Now we have a baby*
Rockwell, Lizzy. *Hello baby!*
Rogers, Fred. *The new baby*
Rosenberg, Maxine B. *Mommy's in the hospital having a baby*
Ross, Christine. *Lily and the present*
Russo, Marisabina. *Hannah's baby sister*
Schick, Eleanor. *Peggy's new brother*
Schindel, John. *Frog face, my little sister and me*
Schlein, Miriam. *Laurie's new brother*
Sears, William, M.D. *What baby needs*
Shields, Carol Diggory. *I wish my brother was a dog*
Simmons, Jane. *Daisy and the egg*
Smith, Peter. *Jenny's baby brother*

Steel, Danielle. *Max's new baby*
Stevenson, James. *Worse than Willy!*
Stimson, Joan. *Big Panda, Little Panda*
Stuve-Bodeen, Stephanie. *Mama Elizabeti*
Sykes, Julie. *Little Tiger's big surprise*
Thomas, Iolette. *Janine and the new baby*
Thomas, Joyce Carol. *You are my perfect baby*
Thomas, Shelley Moore. *A baby's coming to your house*
Titherington, Jeanne. *A place for Ben*
Topek, Susan Remick. *A costume for Noah*
Vigna, Judith. *Couldn't we have a turtle instead?*
Vulliamy, Clara. *Ellen and Penguin and the new baby*
Waddell, Martin. *Rosie's babies*
   When the teddy bears came
Wahl, Jan. *Mabel ran away with the toys*
Walters, Catherine. *Are you there, Baby Bear?*
Watts, Bernadette. *David's waiting day*
Weninger, Brigitte. *Will you mind the baby, Davy?*
West, Keith. *Little Pig's special day*
Weston, Martha. *Bad baby brother*
Whybrow, Ian. *A baby for Grace*
Wild, Margaret. *Rosie and Tortoise*
Winter, Susan. *A baby just like me*
Young, Ruth. *The new baby*
Zagwÿn, Deborah Turney. *Turtle spring*
Ziefert, Harriet. *Getting ready for new baby*
   Talk, baby!
   Waiting for baby

Family life – only child

Bertrand, Cécile. *Mr. and Mrs. Smith have only one child, but what a child!*
Conford, Ellen. *Why can't I be William?*
Dragonwagon, Crescent. *Rainy day together*
Hallinan, P. K. (Patrick K.). *I'm glad to be me*
   Just being alone
Hamberger, John. *Hazel was an only pet*
Hazen, Barbara Shook. *Tight times*
   Why couldn't I be an only kid like you, Wigger?
Iwasaki, Chihiro. *Staying home alone on a rainy day*
Koski, Mary. *Impatient Pamela wants a bigger family*
Schick, Eleanor. *City in the winter*
Sharmat, Marjorie Weinman. *I want mama*
Shyer, Marlene Fanta. *Here I am, an only child*
Skorpen, Liesel Moak. *All the Lassies*
Smith, Wendy. *The lonely, only mouse*

Family life – parents

Anastas, Margaret. *A hug for you*
Baker, Roberta. *No ordinary Olive*
Ballard, Robin. *My day, your day*
Carlstrom, Nancy White. *Before you were born*
Cole, Joanna. *When Mommy and Daddy go to work*
Cusimano, Maryann K. *You are my I love you*
Fearnley, Jan. *Just like you*
Fraser, Mary Ann. *How animal babies stay safe*
Gay, Michel. *Zee is not scared*
Gellman, Marc. *Where does God live?*
Geras, Adèle. *My wishes for you*
Godwin, Laura. *What the baby hears*
Haddix, Margaret Peterson. *Say what?*
Harper, Jamie. *Don't grown-ups ever have fun?*
Hest, Amy. *Gabby growing up*
   Mabel dancing
Hunter, Jana Novotny. *Little ones do*
Iijima, Geneva Cobb. *The way we do it in Japan*
Jenkins, Martin. *The emperor's egg*
Johnston, Tony. *Go track a yak*
Jonovitz, Marilyn. *Maybe, my baby*
Kirk, Daniel. *The snow family*
Kurtz, Jane. *Rain romp*
Lobel, Gillian. *Does anybody love me?*
London, Jonathan. *Froggy eats out*
Lund, Deb. *Tell me my story, Mama*
McGee, Marni. *Wake up, me!*

Mack, Todd. *Princess Penelope*
Masurel, Claire. *Two homes*
Morrow, Tara Jaye. *Mommy loves her baby; Daddy loves his baby*
Murphy, Mary. *I like it when . . .*
   I like it when . . .
Okimoto, Jean Davies. *The White Swan express*
O'Mara, Carmel. *Good morning*
   Good night
Parks, Carmen. *Farmers market*
Pedersen, Marika. *Mommy works, Daddy works*
Pow, Tom. *Who is the world for?*
Pratt, Pierre. *I see . . . my mom/I see . . . my dad*
   I see . . . my sister/I see . . . my cat
Ransom, Jeanie Franz. *I don't want to talk about it*
Rau, Dana Meachen. *In the yard*
Roberts, Bethany. *Rosie to the rescue*
Robledo, Honorio. *Nico visits the moon*
Rockwell, Anne F. *Two blue jays*
Root, Phyllis. *Oliver finds his way*
Rosenberg, Liz. *We wanted you*
Spelman, Cornelia Maude. *When I miss you*
Steig, William. *Toby, who are you?*
Swinburne, Stephen R. *Safe, warm, and snug*
   Tender moments in the wild
Thomas, Frances. *One day, Daddy*
Tobias, Tobi. *Wishes for you*
Von Königslöw, Andrea Wayne. *Would you love me?*
Weeks, Sarah. *My somebody special*
   Without you
Weigelt, Udo. *The Easter Bunny's baby*
Wood, Jenny. *I wonder why kangaroos have pouches and other questions about baby animals*
Zolotow, Charlotte (Shapiro). *When I have a little girl; When I have a little boy*

Family life – single-parent families

Cooper, Melrose. *Gettin' through Thursday*
Edwards, Michelle. *Papa's latkes*

Family life – sisters *see also* Family life; Family life – brothers & sisters; Sibling rivalry

Ackerman, Karen. *Moveable Mabeline*
Adoff, Arnold. *Hard to be six*
Adorjan, Carol Madden. *I can! Can you?*
Alexander, Martha G. *Nobody asked me if I wanted a baby sister*
Alter, Anna. *Estelle and Lucy*
Anholt, Catherine. *Aren't you lucky!*
Arnold, Marsha Diane. *The bravest of us all*
Auld, Mary. *My sister*
Bang, Molly. *When Sophie gets angry – really, really angry . . .*
Barasch, Lynne. *The reluctant flower girl*
Blades, Ann. *Summer*
   Winter
Bliss, Corinne Demas. *The magic apple*
Blumenthal, Deborah. *Don't let the peas touch!*
Brown, Janet Allison. *Little women*
Brown, Marc Tolon. *Arthur meets the president*
   D. W., go to your room!
Brown, Ruth. *Cry baby*
Bullock, Kathleen. *A surprise for Mitzi Mouse*
Bunting, Eve (Anne Evelyn). *The days of summer*
   Twinnies
Calmenson, Stephanie. *The little witch sisters*
Carlstrom, Nancy White. *Kiss your sister, Rose Marie*
Caseley, Judith. *My sister Celia*
Cohen, Miriam. *Mimmy and Sophie*
Cole, Joanna. *I'm a big sister*
Curry, Jane Louise. *Little, little sister*
Dahlbäck-Lutteman, Helena. *My sister Lotta and me*
Dale, Penny. *All about Alice*
Delaney, Molly. *My sister*
De Paola, Tomie (Thomas Anthony). *The baby sister*
Edelman, Elaine. *I love my baby sister (most of the time)*
Ericsson, Jennifer A. *She did it!*
Eversole, Robyn Harbert. *The magic house*

Figley, Marty Rhodes. *The schoolchildren's blizzard*
Galbraith, Kathryn Osebold. *Roommates*
　Waiting for Jennifer
Garland, Sarah. *Billy and Belle*
Gauch, Patricia Lee. *Christina Katerina and the great bear train*
Glaser, Linda. *Keep your socks on, Albert!*
Goodman, Louise. *Ida's doll*
Greeson, Janet. *An American army of two*
Grossman, Bill. *My little sister hugged an ape*
Gutman, Anne. *Lisa's baby sister*
Hamilton, Morse. *Little sister for sale*
Hanrahan, Barbara. *My sisters love my clothes*
Hanson, Mary Elizabeth. *The difference between babies and cookies*
Harper, Isabelle. *Our new puppy*
Henkes, Kevin. *Sheila Rae, the brave*
　Sheila Rae's peppermint stick
Herman, Gail. *Flower girl*
　Keep your distance
Hines, Anna Grossnickle. *Jackie's lunch box*
Hoban, Russell. *Best friends for Frances*
　Harvey's hideout
Hodges, Margaret. *Up the chimney*
Holabird, Katharine. *Angelina's baby sister*
Howard, Elizabeth Fitzgerald. *The train to Lulu's*
　What's in Aunt Mary's room?
Hru, Dakari. *The magic moonberry jump ropes*
Hutchins, Pat. *Our baby is best*
Jackson, Chris. *The Gaggle sisters river tour*
Johnson, Angela. *One of three*
　A sweet smell of roses
　The wedding
Joseph, Lynn. *Jump up time*
Kalman, Maira. *Hey Willy, see the pyramids!*
Kassirer, Sue. *What's next, Nina?*
Keefer, Janice Kulyk. *Anna's goat*
Kroll, Virginia L. *Faraway drums*
　My sister, then and now
Kvasnosky, Laura McGee. *Zelda and Ivy*
　Zelda and Ivy and the boy next door
　Zelda and Ivy one Christmas
Lattimore, Deborah Nourse. *Punga the goddess of ugly*
Lears, Laurie. *Becky the brave*
Leech, Jay. *Bright Fawn and me*
Lerner, Harriet Goldhor. *What's so terrible about swallowing an apple seed?*
Levi, Dorothy Hoffman. *A very special sister*
Lillie, Patricia. *Floppy teddy bear*
Lindgren, Astrid. *Most beloved sister*
Little, Jean. *Jess was the brave one*
McCarthy, Meghan. *The adventures of Patty and the big red bus*
McElmurry, Jill. *Mess pets*
McGinnis, Lila Sprague. *If Daddy only knew me*
Martin, Jacqueline Briggs. *The finest horse in town*
Martin, Rafe. *The rough-face girl*
Mathews, Judith. *An egg and seven socks*
Mills, C. M. *The low-down laundry line blues*
Mills, Claudia. *A visit to Amy-Claire*
Montanari, Eva. *Tiff, Taff, and Lulu*
Moore, Liz. *Zizi and Tish*
Noll, Sally. *That bothered Kate*
Norling, Beth. *Sister night and sister day*
Northway, Jennifer. *Get lost, Laura!*
Numeroff, Laura Joffe. *The Chicken sisters*
O'Connor, Jane. *Kate skates*
Old, Wendie C. *Stacy had a little sister*
Oram, Hiawyn. *The second princess*
Peterson, Jeanne Whitehouse. *Don't forget Winona*
Plourde, Lynn. *Spring's sprung*
Porazinska, Janina. *The enchanted book*
Porte, Barbara Ann. *When Aunt Lucy rode a mule and other stories*
Prall, Jo. *My sister's special*
Price, Mathew. *Have you seen my sister?*
Pryor, Bonnie. *Amanda and April*
　Merry Christmas, Amanda and April
Rheingrover, Jean Sasso. *Veronica's first year*
Rosenberg, Liz. *The carousel*
Rothenberg, Joan Keller. *Matzah ball soup*

Sage, Chris. *That's mine, that's yours*
Samuels, Barbara. *Aloha, Dolores*
　Duncan and Dolores
　What's so great about Cindy Snappleby?
San Souci, Robert D. *Sootface*
Schindel, John. *Frog face, my little sister and me*
Schwartz, Roslyn. *The mole sisters and the cool breeze*
　The mole sisters and the fairy ring
　The mole sisters and the piece of moss
　The mole sisters and the question
　The mole sisters and the rainy day
Spohn, Kate. *By word of mouse*
Stevenson, Suçie. *Christmas eve*
Stewig, John Warren. *Mother Holly*
Stroud, Bettye. *Down home at Miss Dessa's*
Tarbescu, Edith. *Annushka's voyage*
Tucker, Kathy. *The seven Chinese sisters*
Viorst, Judith. *Super-completely and totally the messiest*
Waboose, Jan Bourdeau. *SkySisters*
Wallace, John. *The twins*
Weiss, Nicki. *A family story*
　Princess Pearl
Whybrow, Ian. *A baby for Grace*
Wilder, Laura Ingalls. *Going to town*
Wilhelm, Hans. *Let's be friends again!*
　More bunny trouble
Winter, Susan. *A baby just like me*
Yep, Laurence. *Dragon prince*
Yezerski, Thomas F. *Queen of the world*
Zehler, Antonia. *Two fine ladies have a tiff*
　Two fine ladies: tea for three

Family life – sons

Ambrus, Victor G. *Son of Dracula*
Bearcub and Mama
Boelts, Maribeth. *Looking for Sleepy*
Boyd, Lizi. *I love Daddy*
　I love Mommy
Braun, Sebastien. *I love my daddy*
Chichester Clark, Emma. *More!*
Collins, Billy. *Daddy's little boy*
Compos, Tito. *Muffler man = El hombre mofle*
Creech, Sharon. *Fishing in the air*
Fienberg, Anna. *Joseph*
Granowsky, Alvin. *At the park*
Hartman, Bob. *Who wrecked the roof?*
Jonovitz, Marilyn. *Good morning, Little Fox*
Joosse, Barbara M. *Lewis and papa*
Krosoczka, Jarrett J. *Good night, Monkey Boy*
Lakin, Pat (Patricia). *Dad and me in the morning*
Lauture, Denizé. *Father and son*
Lewin, Ted. *Big Jimmy's Kum Kau Chinese take out*
London, Jonathan. *At the edge of the forest*
　Loon Lake
McKay, Lawrence. *Caravan*
Newman, Lesléa. *Saturday is Pattyday*
Rusackas, Francesca. *Daddy all day long*
Schlessinger, Laura. *Dr. Laura Schlessinger's Growing up is hard*
　Why do you love me?
Smith, Will (1968–). *Just the two of us*
Spinelli, Jerry. *My daddy and me*
Sullivan, Paula. *Todd's box*
Tarpley, Natasha Anastasia. *Bippity Bop barbershop*
Thomas, Joyce Carol. *Joy*
Yezerski, Thomas F. *A full hand*

Family life – stepfamilies

Arnold, Katya. *Baba Yaga and the little girl*
Ballard, Robin. *When I am a sister*
Benjamin, Amanda. *Two's company*
Best, Cari. *Getting used to Harry*
Boyd, Lizi. *The not-so-wicked stepmother*
　Sam is my half brother
Brodzinsky, Anne Braff. *The mulberry bird*
Bruna, Dick. *Dick Bruna's Cinderella*

Bullard, Lisa. *Trick-or-treat on Milton Street*
Bunting, Eve (Anne Evelyn). *The memory string*
   Train to somewhere
Chwast, Seymour. *Bushy bride*
Cinderella
Climo, Shirley. *The Egyptian Cinderella*
   The Korean Cinderella
   The Persian Cinderella
Coburn, Jewell Reinhart. *Angkat*
   Jouanah
Daly, Jude. *Fair, Brown & Trembling*
Day, Nancy Raines. *The lion's whiskers*
Freeman, Martha. *The trouble with babies*
French, Fiona. *Snow White in New York*
Geras, Adèle. *Sleeping beauty*
Gibbons, Faye. *Mountain wedding*
Grimm, Jacob. *Cinderella*, ill. by Nonny Hogrogian
   Cinderella, ill. by Svend Otto S
   Little brother and little sister
Han, Oki S. *Kongi and Potgi*
Helmering, Doris Wild. *I have two families*
Hickox, Rebecca. *The golden sandal*
Hines, Anna Grossnickle. *When we married Gary*
Howard, Ellen. *The big seed*
Johnson, Julie. *How do I feel about my stepfamily*
Knight, Hilary. *Hilary Knight's Cinderella*
Kroll, Steven. *Annie's four grannies*
   Queen of the May
Leach, Norman. *My wicked stepmother*
Lewis, Naomi. *The stepsister*
Lowell, Susan. *Cindy Ellen*
McCaughrean, Geraldine. *Grandma Chickenlegs*
McKissack, Patricia C. *Cinderella*, ill. by Tom Dunnington
Perrault, Charles. *Cinderella*, ill. by Sheilah Beckett
   Cinderella, ill. by Marcia Brown
   Cinderella, ill. by Paul Galdone
   Cinderella, ill. by Diane Goode
   Cinderella, ill. by Susan Jeffers
   Cinderella, ill. by Loek Koopmans
   Cinderella, ill. by Emanuele Luzzati
   Cinderella, ill. by James Marshall
   Cinderella, ill. by Phil Smith
   Cinderella = Cenicienta
Roberts, Lynn (Lynn M.). *Cinderella, an Art Deco love story*
Sanderson, Ruth. *Cinderella*
San Souci, Robert D. *Cinderella Skeleton*
   Little gold star
Schotter, Roni. *Room for Rabbit*
Schroeder, Alan. *Smoky Mountain Rose*
Seuling, Barbara. *What kind of family is this?*
Sierra, Judy. *The gift of the crocodile*
Steel, Danielle. *Martha's new daddy*
Stewig, John Warren. *Mother Holly*
Thomas, Joyce Carol. *The gospel Cinderella*
Vojtech, Anna. *Marushka and the Month Brothers*
Wade, Barrie. *Cinderella*
Zakhoder, Boris Vladimirovich. *The good stepmother*

Family life – stepchildren *see* Divorce; Family life –
   stepfamilies

Family life – stepparents *see* Divorce; Family life –
   stepfamilies

Farmers *see* Careers – farmers

Farms

Adams, Pam. *This old man*
Addy, Sharon Hart. *Right here on this spot*
Akass, Susan. *Number nine duckling*
Alarcón, Karen Beaumont. *Louella Mae, she's run away!*
Alborough, Jez. *The grass is always greener*
Allen, Pamela. *Fancy that!*
Allen, Thomas B. (Thomas Burt). *On grandaddy's farm*
Amery, H. *The farm picture book*

Ammon, Richard. *Amish horses*
Andrews, Jan. *The auction*
Anholt, Catherine. *Chaos at Cold Custard Farm*
Arnosky, Jim. *Raccoons and ripe corn*
Ashforth, Camilla. *Willow at Christmas*
At the farm
Auch, Mary Jane. *The nutquacker*
Augarde, Steve (Stephen). *Pig*
Aulaire, Ingri Mortenson d'. *Wings for Per*
Ayers, Rebecca Hickox. *Per and the Dala horse*
Aylesworth, Jim. *My son John*
   One crow
Azarian, Mary. *A farmer's alphabet*
Bailey, Linda. *When Addie was scared*
Baker, Betty. *Partners*
Balian, Lorna. *A garden for a groundhog*
Balzano, Jeanne. *The wee moose*
Barber, Antonia. *Gemma and the baby chick*
Barr, Cathrine. *A horse for Sherry*
Barrett, Judi. *Old MacDonald had an apartment house*
Baruch, Dorothy. *Kappa's tug-of-war with the big brown horse*
Bateman, Teresa. *April foolishness*
   Farm flu
Bax, Martin. *Edmond went far away*
Baynton, Martin. *Fifty and the fox*
   Fifty and the great race
   Fifty gets the picture
   Fifty saves his friend
Beaumont, Karen. *Duck, duck, goose!*
Beeke, Jemma. *The Rickety Barn show*
Berends, Polly Berrien. *I heard said the bird*
Berkowitz, Linda. *Alfonse, where are you?*
Bibbons, Faye. *The day the picture man came*
Bilgrami, Shaheen. *Farmyard painting party*
Birchman, David Francis. *Jigsaw Jackson*
Biro, Val. *Gumdrop and the farmyard caper*
Blackstone, Stella. *How big is a pig?*
Blades, Ann. *Mary of mile 18*
   Summer
Blanchard, Arlene. *The naughty lamb*
Blocksma, Mary. *Where's that duck?*
Bloom, Suzanne. *We keep a pig in the parlor*
Bock, Lee. *Oh, crumps! = Ay, caramba!*
Bohanon, Paul. *Golden Kate*
Bonino, Louise. *The cozy little farm*
Bonning, Tony. *Fox tale soup*
Borton, Lady. *Fat chance!*
Boynton, Sandra. *Barnyard dance!*
Bradby, Marie. *Once upon a farm*
Brand, Millen. *This little pig named Curly*
Brandenberg, Franz. *Cock-a-doodle-doo*
Braun, Trudi. *My goose Betsy*
Bright, Robert. *Georgie*
Brook, Judy. *Tim mouse visits the farm*
Brown, Craig McFarland. *My barn*
   Patchwork farmer
Brown, Ken (Ken James). *Mucky Pup*
   Mucky Pup's Christmas
Brown, Margaret Wise. *Big red barn*, ill. by Felicia Bond
   Big red barn, ill. by Rosella Hartman
   Christmas in the barn
   The little farmer
   The summer noisy book
Brown, Ruth. *The big sneeze*
Browne, Caroline. *Mrs. Christie's farmhouse*
Bruna, Dick. *Farmer John*
   Little bird tweet
Budbill, David. *Christmas tree farm*
Buehner, Caralyn. *Fanny's dream*
Bulla, Clyde Robert. *Dandelion Hill*
Bunting, Eve (Anne Evelyn). *Goose dinner*
   Winter's coming
Burton, Marilee Robin. *Aaron awoke*
Butler, Dorothy. *Another happy tale*
Campbell, Rod. *Oh dear!*
Carle, Eric. *Dream snow*
Carlson, Natalie Savage. *Time for the white egret*

Carlstrom, Nancy White. *Rise and shine!*
  The way to Wyatt's house
Carr, Jan. *Big Truck and Little Truck*
Carrick, Carol. *In the moonlight, waiting*
Carrick, Donald. *The deer in the pasture*
  Harold and the giant knight
  Milk
Carter, David A. *Old MacDonald had a farm*
Cartwright, Ann. *Norah's ark*
Casey, Patricia. *Cluck cluck*
Caudill, Rebecca. *A pocketful of cricket*
Cazet, Denys. *Minnie and Moo: will you be my Valentine?*
  Minnie and Moo: the attack of the Easter bunnies
  Nothing at all
Chandra, Deborah. *A is for Amos*
Chaucer, Geoffrey. *Chanticleer and the fox*
Child, Lydia Maria. *Over the river and through the wood*
Chitwood, Suzanne Tanner. *Wake up, big barn!*
Chorao, Kay. *Little farm by the sea*
Cimarusti, Marie Torres. *Peek-a-moo*
Cleary, Beverly. *The hullabaloo ABC*, ill. by Ted Rand
  The hullabaloo ABC, ill. by Earl Thollander
Clewes, Dorothy. *Hide and seek*
Climo, Lindee. *Chester's barn*
Collier, Ethel. *I know a farm*
Cook, Bernadine. *Looking for Susie*
Coulter, Hope Norman. *Uncle Chuck's truck*
Cousins, Lucy. *Farm animals*
  Hen on the farm
  Maisy at the farm
  Maisy's farm
  Maisy's morning on the farm
Coxe, Molly. *Whose footprints?*
Crisp, Marty. *Black and white*
Croll, Carolyn. *The three brothers*
Cronin, Doreen. *Click, clack, moo*
  Giggle, giggle, quack
Cross, Verda. *Great-grandma tells of threshing day*
Crowther, Robert. *Who lives on the farm?*
Crum, Shutta. *My mountain song*
Crunk, Tony. *Grandpa's overalls*
Cummins, Julie. *Country kid, city kid*
Curry, Jane Louise. *Little, little sister*
Dalgleish, Sharon. *Working dogs*
Dalgliesh, Alice. *The little wooden farmer*
Dallas-Conte, Juliet. *Cock-a-moo-moo*
Daniel, Doris Temple. *Pauline and the peacock*
Davis, Aubrey. *The enormous potato*
Day, Betsy. *Stefan and Olga*
Deady, Kathleen W. *It's time!*
De Angeli, Marguerite. *Yonie Wondernose*
De Beer, Hans. *Oh no, Ono!*
Delaney, Ned. *Cosmic chickens*
Demarest, Chris L. *Farmer Nat*
Demuth, Patricia Brennan. *Ornery morning*
Dennis, Wesley. *Flip*
  Flip and the cows
Denslow, Sharon Phillips. *At Taylor's place*
De Paola, Tomie (Thomas Anthony). *Country farm*
De Regniers, Beatrice Schenk. *Going for a walk*
Dewey, Ariane. *Febold Feboldson*
DeWitt, Jamie. *Jamie's turn*
DiFiori, Lawrence. *The farm*
Dodd, Emma. *Dog's noisy day*
Dodds, Siobhan. *Elizabeth Hen*
Doepker, David. *Farm babies*
Domanska, Janina. *The turnip*
Donohue, Dorothy. *Big and little on the farm*
Dorros, Arthur. *Radio Man = Don Radio*
  Tonight is carnaval
Douglas, Erin. *Get that pest!*
Downey, Lynn. *The flea's sneeze*
Doyle, Malachy. *Cow*
Dragonwagon, Crescent. *Jemima remembers*
Dreier, Ted. *Moozie's kind adventure*
Duffield, Katy. *Farmer McPeepers and his missing milk cows*
Duncan, Jane. *Janet Reachfar and Chickabird*

Dunn, Judy. *The animals of Buttercup Farm*
  The little lamb
Dunrea, Olivier. *Eddy B, pigboy*
  The painter who loved chickens
Duvoisin, Roger Antoine. *The crocodile in the tree*
  Crocus
  Jasmine
  Our Veronica goes to Petunia's farm
  Petunia
  Petunia and the song
  Petunia, beware!
  Petunia, I love you
  Petunia, the silly goose
  Petunia's treasure
  Two lonely ducks
  Veronica
  Veronica and the birthday present
Edwards, Julie Andrews. *Dumpy the dump truck*
Edwards, Pamela Duncan. *The grumpy morning*
  McGillycuddy could
Egan, Tim. *Serious farm*
Ehlert, Lois. *Market day*
Ehrlich, Amy. *Maggie and Silky and Joe*
  Parents in the pigpen, pigs in the tub
English, Karen. *Big wind coming!*
Eriksson, Ake. *Joel, Jasper, and Julia*
Ets, Marie Hall. *Mister Penny*
  Mr. Penny's race horse
Euvremer, Teryl. *Sun's up*
Ewart, Claire. *The giant*
Farm animals [Macmillan, 1991]
Farm house
The farmer in the dell. *The farmer in the dell*, ill. by John O'Brien
  The farmer in the dell, ill. by Kathy Parkinson
  The farmer in the dell, ill. by Mary Maki Rae
  The farmer in the dell, ill. by Diane Stanley
  The farmer in the dell, ill. by Alexandra Wallner
Fatio, Louise. *The red bantam*
Faulkner, Keith. *Do you have my quack?*
Feldman, Barbara. *Stephen's frog*
Fernandes, Eugenie. *Busy Little Mouse*
Fiday, Beverly. *Time to go*
Fisher, Carolyn. *A twisted tale*
Flanagan, Alice K. *Farmers*
  Flying an agricultural plane with Mr. Miller
  Raising cows on the Koebels' farm
  A visit to the Gravesens' farm
  The Zieglers and their apple orchard
Fleischman, Paul. *The animal hedge*
Fleischman, Sid. *The scarebird*
Fleming, Denise. *Barnyard banter*
Flora, James. *Grandpa's farm*
Florian, Douglas. *A year in the country*
Flynn, Kitson. *Carrot in my pocket*
Fox, Mem. *Hattie and the fox*
Frascino, Edward. *Nanny Noony and the dust queen*
  Nanny Noony and the magic spell
Freedman, Russell. *Farm babies*
Freschet, Berniece. *Where's Henrietta's hen?*
Gackenbach, Dick. *Crackle, Gluck and the sleeping toad*
  The pig who saw everything
Galdone, Paul. *Cat goes fiddle-i-fee*
Gammell, Stephen. *Once upon MacDonald's farm*
Garelli, Cristina. *Farm friends clean up*
Garland, Michael. *My cousin Katie*
Geisert, Arthur. *Nursery crimes*
Gibbons, Gail. *Farming*
  The milk makers
Gibson, Betty. *The story of Little Quack*
Glass, Andrew. *Chickpea and the talking cow*
Glasscock, Sarah. *My prairie summer*
Good, Phyllis Pellman. *Plain Pig's ABCs*
Goodall, John S. *The story of a farm*
Goode, Diane. *The little book of farm friends*
Graham, Georgia. *The strongest man this side of Cremona*
Gray, Libba Moore. *Is there room on the feather bed?*
Greeley, Valerie. *Farm animals*

Green, Mary McBurney. *Everybody has a house and everybody eats*
Greenberg, Polly. *Oh, Lord, I wish I was a buzzard*
Greene, Rhonda Gowler. *Barnyard song*
Grifalconi, Ann. *Kinda blue*
Gunthrop, Karen. *Rina at the farm*
Haas, Jessie. *Busybody Brandy*
  Mowing
  No foal yet
Hader, Berta Hoerner. *Cock-a-doodle doo*
Hale, Kathleen. *Orlando buys a farm*
Hale, Sarah Josepha Buell. *Mary had a little lamb,* ill. by Iza Trapani
Hall, Donald. *Lucy's summer*
  The ox-cart man
Hall, Margaret. *Corn*
  Peanuts
Hamilton, Virginia. *Drylongso*
Hamm, Diane Johnston. *Rock-a-bye farm*
Hansen, Carla. *Barnaby Bear visits the farm*
Harranth, Wolf. *My old grandad*
Harshman, Marc. *A little excitement*
  The storm
  Uncle James
Harvey, Brett. *My prairie year*
Haseley, Dennis. *The old banjo*
Hawes, Judy. *Fireflies in the night*
Hayles, Marsha. *A pet of a pet*
Haywood, Carolyn. *Hello, star*
Hazen, Barbara Shook. *Turkey in the straw*
Hellen, Nancy. *Circle farm*
  A visit to the farm
Helweg, Hans. *Farm animals*
Henderson, Kathy. *Counting farm*
  I can be a farmer
Henley, Claire. *Farm day*
Herriot, James. *Blossom comes home*
  Bonny's big day
Hess, Paul. *Farmyard animals*
Hewett, Anita. *The tale of the turnip*
Hill, Eric. *Spot goes to the farm*
  Spot on the farm
Hillenbrand, Will. *Fiddle-i-fee*
Himmelman, John. *A guest is a guest*
Hindley, Judy. *Does a cow say boo?*
Hines, Anna Grossnickle. *I'll tell you what they say*
Hirschi, Ron. *Harvest song*
Hoban, Julia. *Quick chick*
Hol, Coby. *A visit to the farm*
Hopkins, Lee Bennett. *On the farm*
Hopkinson, Deborah. *Bluebird summer*
Houk, Randy. *Rico's hawk*
Hudson, Wade. *I love my family*
Huneck, Stephen. *Sally goes to the farm*
Huntington, Amy. *One Monday*
Hurd, Edith Thacher. *Under the lemon tree*
Hurd, Thacher. *Blackberry ramble*
  Moo Cow Kaboom!
  Tomato soup
Hutchins, H. J. (Hazel J.). *One duck*
Hutchins, Pat. *Rosie's walk*
  Rosie's walk [board book]
Ipcar, Dahlov (Zorach). *Bright barnyard*
  Brown cow farm
  Hard scrabble harvest
  One horse farm
  Ten big farms
Isenbart, Hans-Heinrich. *Baby animals on the farm*
Israel, Marion Louise. *The tractor on the farm*
Jackson, Ellen B. *Brown cow, green grass, yellow mellow sun*
Jacobs, Joseph. *Hereafterthis*
James, Shirley Kerby. *Going to a horse farm*
Jaspersohn, William. *The two brothers*
Jennings, Linda M. *Tom's tail*
Jensen, Patricia. *Kitty's special job*
Jeppson, Ann-Sofie. *Here comes Pontus*
Johnson, Angela. *Casey Jones*
Johnson, Dolores. *Grandma's hands*

Johnson, Paul Brett. *The cow who wouldn't come down*
  Farmers' market
Johnston, Tony. *Farmer Mack measures his pig*
  Once in the country
  The promise
  We love the dirt
Jones, Carol. *This old man*
Jordan, Sandra. *Christmas tree farm*
  Down on Casey's farm
Kallen, Stuart A. *The farm*
Karim, Roberta. *Mandy Sue Day*
Kastner, Jill. *Barnyard big top*
Kaufman, Jeff. *Milk rock*
Kent, Jack. *Little Peep*
Kessler, Ethel. *Are there hippos on the farm?*
Ketteman, Helen. *Heat wave*
  The year of no more corn
Kightley, Rosalinda. *The farmer*
Kimmel, Haven. *Orville, a dog story*
King-Smith, Dick. *Cuckoobush farm*
  Farmer Bungle forgets
Kinsey-Warnock, Natalie. *A Christmas like Helen's*
  A farm of her own
  From dawn till dusk
  The summer of Stanley
  When spring comes
Kiser, SuAnn. *The catspring somersault flying one-handed flip-flop*
  The hog call to end all!
Klingel, Cynthia Fitterer. *Farmers*
Koch, Dorothy Clarke. *When the cows got out*
Komaiko, Leah. *On Sally Perry's farm*
Koontz, Robin Michal. *This old man*
Koralek, Jenny. *Cat and Kit*
  The friendly fox
Kovalski, Maryann. *Queen Nadine*
Kunhardt, Edith. *I'm going to be a farmer*
  Which pig would you choose?
Kwitz, Mary DeBall. *Little chick's breakfast*
Lacome, Julie. *On the farm*
Laird, Elizabeth. *The day Patch stood guard*
  The day Sidney ran off
  The day the ducks went skating
  The day Veronica was nosy
Lapp, Eleanor. *The mice came in early this year*
Lasson, Robert. *Orange Oliver*
Lavis, Steve. *On the farm*
Lemieux, Margo. *The fiddle ribbon*
Lenski, Lois. *The little farm*
Lerman, Rory S. *Charlie's checklist*
Lesser, Carolyn. *What a wonderful day to be a cow*
Lester, Alison. *My farm*
Levitin, Sonia. *A single speckled egg*
Lewis, Kim. *Emma's lamb*
  First snow
  Friends
  Just like Floss
  Little Baa
  Little calf
  Little lamb
  Little puppy
Lewison, Wendy Cheyette. *Going to sleep on the farm*
  The rooster who lost his crow
Lexau, Joan M. *Who took the farmer's hat?*
Lillie, Patricia. *When the rooster crowed*
Lilly, Kenneth. *Animals on the farm*
Lindbergh, Reeve. *Benjamin's barn*
  The day the goose got loose
  Midnight farm
Lindgren, Astrid. *The dragon with red eyes*
  The tomten
Lindman, Maj. *Flicka, Ricka, Dicka and the big red hen*
  Snipp, Snapp, Snurr and the buttered bread
Ling, Mary. *Calf*
  Foal
  Pig
Lionni, Leo. *Six crows*

The little red hen. *The cock, the mouse and the little red hen*, ill. by
  Lorinda Bryan Cauley
  The cock, the mouse and the little red hen, ill. by Graham Percy
  The little red hen, ill. by Byron Barton
  The little red hen, ill. by Emily Bolam
  The little red hen, ill. by Janina Domanska
  The little red hen, ill. by Paul Galdone
  The little red hen, ill. by Dennis Hockerman
  Little red hen, ill. by Norman Messenger
  The little red hen, ill. by Mel Pekarsky
  The little red hen, ill. by William Stobbs
  The little red hen, ill. by Annie West
  The little red hen, ill. by Margot Zemach
  The little red hen and the ear of wheat, ill. by Elisabeth Bell
  The Little Red Hen makes a pizza
Little, Jean. *Gruntle Piggle takes off*
Littledale, Freya. *The farmer in the soup*
Lobel, Arnold. *Small pig*
  A treeful of pigs
Locker, Thomas. *Family farm*
  The mare on the hill
London, Jonathan. *At the edge of the forest*
  Like butter on pancakes
Lorenz, Lee. *Hugo and the spacedog*
Lottridge, Celia Barker. *Berta, a remarkable dog*
Love, Ann. *Farming*
Low, Joseph. *Benny rabbit and the owl*
  Boo to a goose
Lucas, Barbara (Barbara M.). *Snowed in*
Ludy, Mark. *The farmer*
Lüton, Mildred. *Little chicks' mothers and all the others*
Luttrell, Ida. *Be nice to Marilyn*
  Mattie's little possum pet
Maccarone, Grace. *Oink! moo! how do you do?*
McConnachie, Brian. *Elmer and the chickens vs. the big league*
McCrea, Lilian. *Mother hen*
McCue, Lisa. *The little chick*
McDonnell, Flora. *I love animals*
MacFarland, Cynthia. *Cows in the parlor*
McFarlane, Sheryl. *On the farm*
McGee, Marni. *The noisy farm*
  The quiet farmer
McGill, Alice. *Molly Bannaky*
MacLachlan, Patricia. *All the places to love*
  What you know first
McNeer, May Yonge. *Little Baptiste*
McPhail, David M. *The day the sheep showed up*
  Farm boy's year
  Farm morning
McQuade, Jacqueline. *Farm babies*
Maguire, Gregory. *Crabby Cratchitt*
Maitland, Barbara. *Moo in the morning*
Manson, Christopher. *A farmyard song*
Mantegazza, Giovanna. *Look inside a farm*
Marciano, John Bemelmans. *Delilah*
Maris, Ron. *Ducks quack*
  Is anyone home?
Martin, Bill (William Ivan). *Chicken Chuck*
Martin, C. L. G. *Down Dairy Farm Road*
Masurel, Claire. *No, no, Titus!*
Mayer, Mercer. *Appelard and Liverwurst*
Mayne, William. *Tibber*
Mayr, Diane. *Out and about at the apple orchard*
Medearis, Angela Shelf. *Picking peas for a penny*
Meeker, Clare Hodgson. *Who wakes rooster?*
Meeks, Esther K. *Friendly farm animals*
Merrill, Jean. *Tell about the cowbarn, Daddy*
Miles, Calvin. *Calvin's Christmas wish*
Miles, Miska. *Noisy gander*
  This little pig
Milhous, Katherine. *The turnip*
Miller, Heather. *My chickens*
  My goats
  My horses
  My pigs
Miller, J. P. (John Parr). *Farmer John's animals*
Miller, Jane. *Farm alphabet book*

Farm counting book
Farm noises
Seasons on the farm
Miller, Ruth. *I went to the farm*
Milord, Susan. *The ghost on the hearth*
Milway, Katie Smith. *Cappuccina goes to town*
Mitter, Matt. *1, 2, 3, counting rhymes*
Moeri, Louise. *The unicorn and the plow*
Moon, Cliff. *Pigs on the farm*
Morley, Carol. *Farmyard song*
Morris, Ann. *700 kids on Grandpa's farm*
Morris, Linda Lowe. *Morning milking*
Morton, Christine. *Picnic farm*
Most, Bernard. *Cock-a-doodle-moo!*
Mozelle, Shirley. *The pig is in the pantry, the cat is on the shelf*
Murphy, Andy. *Out and about at the dairy farm*
Murphy, Mary. *How kind*
My first farm
Nakatani, Chiyoko. *My day on the farm*
Nelson, Kristin L. *Farm tractors*
Nicholson, Nicholas B. A. *Little girl in a red dress with cat and dog*
Nikola-Lisa, W. *Summer sun risin'*
  Till year's good end
Nilsén, Anna. *Drive your tractor*
Noble, Trinka Hakes. *Apple tree Christmas*
Nodar, Carmen Santiago. *Abuelita's paradise*
Nolen, Jerdine. *Harvey Potter's balloon farm*
  Raising dragons
Numeroff, Laura Joffe. *The Chicken sisters*
O'Brien, Mary. *Counting sheep to sleep*
O'Kelley, Mattie Lou. *Circus!*
Old MacDonald had a farm. *E I E I O*
  Old MacDonald, ill. by Rosemary Wells
  Old MacDonald had a farm, ill. by Holly Berry
  Old MacDonald had a farm, ill. by Lorinda Bryan Cauley
  Old MacDonald had a farm, ill. by Mel Crawford
  Old MacDonald had a farm, ill. by Tracey English
  Old MacDonald had a farm, ill. by David Frankland
  Old MacDonald had a farm, ill. by Abner Graboff
  Old MacDonald had a farm, ill. by Nancy Hellen
  Old MacDonald had a farm, ill. by Carol Jones
  Old MacDonald had a farm, ill. by Tracey Campbell Pearson
  Old MacDonald had a farm, ill. by Robert M. Quackenbush
  Old MacDonald had a farm, ill. by Glen Rounds
  Old McDonald had a farm, ill. by Iain Smith
  Old MacDonald had a farm, ill. by Jessica Souhami
  Old MacDonald had a farm, ill. by William Stobbs
  Old MacDonald had a farm, ill. by Prue Theobalds
Oller, Erika. *The cabbage soup solution*
Olney, Ross R. *Farm giants*
Oppenheim, Joanne. *"Not now!" said the cow*
Ormerod, Jan. *Ms. MacDonald has a class*
Ostheeren, Ingrid. *Jonathan Mouse and the baby bird*
  The new dog
Otto, Carolyn. *That sky, that rain*
Paladino, Catherine. *Our vanishing farm animals*
Palatini, Margie. *The web files*
Patterson, Geoffrey. *A pig's tale*
Paul, Jan S. *Hortense*
Pearson, Susan. *Well, I never!*
Peck, Robert Newton. *Hamilton*
Peet, Bill (William Bartlett). *Cock-a-doodle Dudley*
Pellowski, Anne. *Stairstep farm*
Peters, Lisa Westberg. *The hayloft*
Peterson, Cris. *Extra cheese, please!*
Pfeffer, Wendy. *The big flood*
Phillips, Mildred. *And the cow said, "moo"!*
Pieńkowski, Jan. *Farm*
Piers, Helen. *Who's in my bed?*
Pinkney, Gloria Jean. *Back home*
  The Sunday outing
Pizer, Abigail. *Charlie the puppy*
  Hattie the goat
  It's a perfect day
  Penelope pig
  Percy the duck
Pluckrose, Henry Arthur. *On the farm*

Polacco, Patricia. *Just plain Fancy*
Poskanzer, Susan Cornell. *Dairy farmer*
Potter, Beatrix. *The tale of Peter Rabbit*, ill. by author
Prigger, Mary Skillings. *Aunt Minnie and the twister*
Provensen, Alice. *Our animal friends at Maple Hill Farm*
 An owl and three pussycats
 The year at Maple Hill Farm
Pryor, Bonnie. *Greenbrook farm*
 Lottie's dream
 Mr. Munday and the rustlers
The pudgy book of farm animals
Purmell, Ann. *Apple cider making days*
Raphael, Elaine. *Donkey and Carlo*
 Donkey, it's snowing
Rassmus, Jens. *Farmer Enno and his cow*
Raven, Margot Theis. *Angels in the dust*
Reddix, Valerie. *Millie and the mudhole*
Reynolds, Adrian. *Pete and Polo's farmyard adventure*
Reynolds, Marilynn. *The new land*
 The prairie fire
Rider, Alex. *A la ferme = At the farm*
Riecken, Nancy. *Today is the day*
Robart, Rose. *The cake that Mack ate*
Robbins, Ken. *Apples*
Robbins, Maria Polushkin. *Morning*
Robinson, W. W. (William Wilcox). *On the farm*
Rockwell, Anne F. *The gollywhopper egg*
Rogers, Hal. *Combines*
 Milking machines
 Plows
Rogers, Paul (Patrick). *Quacky Duck*
Rojankovsky, Feodor. *Animals on the farm*
 The great big animal book
Root, Phyllis. *One windy Wednesday*
 What Baby wants
Rosen, Michael J. (1954–). *Bonesy and Isabel*
Rossiter, Nan Parson. *Sugar on snow*
 The way home
Roth, Harold. *Let's look all around the farm*
Royston, Angela. *Cow*
 The goat
 The hen
 The pig
 The pony
 The sheep
Runcie, Jill. *Cock-a-doodle-doo*
Russell, Sandra Joanne. *A farmer's dozen*
Ruurs, Margriet. *Emma's cold day*
 Emma's eggs
Rylant, Cynthia. *Scarecrow*
Sadler, Judy Ann. *Sandwiches for Duke*
Sage, James. *Farmer Smart's fat cat*
Sandburg, Carl (Charles August). *From daybreak to good night*
 The Huckabuck family and how they raised popcorn in Nebraska and quit and came back, ill. by David Small
Sathre, Vivian. *On Grandpa's farm*
Scheidl, Gerda Marie. *Pickle and Patch*
Schertle, Alice. *Maisie*
Schlein, Miriam. *Something for now, something for later*
Schmid, Eleonore. *Farm animals*
Schmidt, Eric von. *The young man who wouldn't hoe corn*
Schnur, Steven. *Spring thaw*
Schoenherr, John. *The barn*
Schomp, Virginia. *If you were a . . . farmer*
Schuh, Mari C. *Chickens on the farm*
 Cows on the farm
 Pigs on the farm
 Sheep on the farm
Schulz, Charles M. *Snoopy's facts and fun book about farms*
Scott, C. Anne (Cynthia Anne). *Old Jake's skirts*
Seabrooke, Brenda. *The swan's gift*
Seignobosc, Françoise. *The big rain*
Selsam, Millicent E. *Keep looking!*
 More potatoes!
Selway, Martina. *Don't forget to write*
Sewell, Helen Moore. *Blue barns*
Shapiro, Jody Fickes. *Up, up, up! It's apple-picking time*

Sherman, Nancy. *Gwendolyn and the weathercock*
Short, Mayo. *Andy and the wild ducks*
Simmons, Jane. *Daisy and the Beastie*
Simon, Carly. *Midnight farm*
Simont, Marc. *The goose that almost got cooked*
Skofield, James. *Snow country*
Sloat, Teri. *Farmer Brown goes round and round*
 Farmer Brown shears his sheep
Slobodkina, Esphyr. *The wonderful feast*
Smith, Donald. *Farm numbers*
Smith, Mavis. *A snake mistake*
Sneed, Brad. *Lucky Russell*
Snow, Alan. *Cluck!*
 Oink!
 Quack!
 Woof!
Spinelli, Eileen. *The best time of day*
Staines, Bill. *All God's critters got a place in the choir*
Steers, Billy. *Tractor Mac*
Stevens, Jan Romero. *Carlos and the skunk = Carlos y el zorrillo*
Stevenson, James. *"Could be worse!"*
Stewig, John Warren. *Making plum jam*
Stoeke, Janet Morgan. *Hide and seek*
Stone, Lynn M. *Farm buildings*
 Farms old and new
Stott, Dorothy. *Little Duck's bicycle ride*
Strete, Craig Kee. *How the Indians bought the farm*
Stroud, Bettye. *Dance y'all*, ill. by Cornelious Van Wright & Ying-Hwa Hu
Stutson, Caroline. *Prairie primer A to Z*
Sweet, Melissa. *Fiddle-i-fee*
Sykes, Julie. *Dora's eggs*
 This and that
Tafuri, Nancy. *Early morning in the barn*
 This is the farmer
 Who's counting?
Talley, Carol. *Clarissa*
Tennyson, Alfred, Baron. *The brook*
Terasaki, Stanley Todd. *Ghosts for breakfast*
Thiele, Colin. *Farmer Schulz's ducks*
Thomas, Jane Resh. *Lights on the river*
Thompson, Mary. *Gran's bees*
Threadgall, Colin. *Proud rooster and the fox*
Tiller, Ruth. *Cats vanish slowly*
Tolstoy, Aleksey Nikolayevich. *The enormous turnip*
 The gigantic turnip, ill. by Niamh Sharkey
 The great big enormous turnip
Tompert, Ann. *The hungry black bag*
Torgersen, Don Arthur. *The girl who tricked the troll*
Tresselt, Alvin R. *Sun up*, ill. by author
 Sun up, ill. by Henri Sorensen
 Wake up, farm!, ill. by author
 Wake up, farm!, ill. by Carolyn Ewing
Tripp, Paul. *The strawman who smiled by mistake*
Tudor, Tasha. *Pumpkin moonshine*
Turner, Ann Warren. *Dakota dugout*
 Dust for dinner
Turner, Gwenda. *Over on the farm*
Twinem, Neecy. *Changing colors*
Udry, Janice May. *Emily's autumn*
Vaës, Alain. *The porcelain pepper pot*
Vagin, Vladimir Vasilévich. *The enormous carrot*
Van Eerbeek. *The world of farm animals*
Van Horn, Grace. *Little red rooster*
Van Leeuwen, Jean. *The strange adventures of Blue Dog*
Verboven, Agnes. *Ducks like to swim*
Waddell, Martin. *Farmer Duck*
 Tom Rabbit
Wallace, Ian. *The naked lady*
Wallace, Nancy Elizabeth. *Apples, apples, apples*
 Pumpkin day
Wallner, John C. *Old MacDonald had a farm*
Ward, Helen. *The rooster and the fox*
Ward, Nick. *Farmer George and the fieldmice*
 Farmer George and the lost chick
Waters, Jennifer. *Harvest time*
Watson, Jane Werner. *The fuzzy duckling*

Watson, Nancy Dingman. *What does A begin with?*
  What is one?
Weidt, Maryann N. *Daddy played music for the cows*
Wellington, Monica. *Apple farmer Annie*
  The sheep follow
Westcott, Nadine Bernard. *Skip to my Lou*
  There's a hole in the bucket
Wheeler, Cindy. *Rose*
Wiesner, William. *Happy-Go-Lucky*
Wild, Margaret. *The very best of friends*
Williams, Linda. *Horse in the pigpen*
Willis, Val. *Silly little chick*
Wolff, Ashley. *A year of beasts*
Wood, Jacqueline. *Never say boo to a goose!*
Wood, Jakki. *Moo moo, brown cow*
Wormell, Mary. *Hilda Hen's happy birthday*
  Hilda Hen's search
  Why not?
Worthington, Phoebe. *Teddy bear farmer*
Wright, Dare. *Look at a calf*
  Look at a colt
Yolen, Jane. *The giant's farm*
  Harvest home
  Jane Yolen's Old MacDonald songbook
  Raising Yoder's barn
Zalben, Jane Breskin. *Basil and Hillary*
Ziefert, Harriet. *I swapped my dog*
  Nicky's Christmas surprise
  Nicky's friends
  Oh, what a noisy farm!
  On our way to the barn
  Pumpkin Pie
  The turnip
  What do ducks dream?
Zwetchkenbaum, G. *The Snoopy farm puzzle book*

Father's Day *see* Holidays – Father's Day

Fathers *see* Family life – fathers

Fear *see* Emotions – fear

Feathers

Piven, Hanokh. *The perfect purple feather*

Feeling *see* Senses – touch

Feelings *see* Emotions

Feet *see* Anatomy – feet

Ferrets *see* Animals – ferrets

Fiddles *see* Musical instruments – violins

Fidgeting *see* Behavior – fidgeting

Fighting *see* Behavior – fighting, arguing

Fiji *see* Foreign lands – Fiji

Fingers *see* Anatomy – hands

Finishing things *see* Character traits – completing things

Finland *see* Foreign lands – Finland

Fins *see* Anatomy – fins

Fire

Anderson, C. W. (Clarence Williams). *Blaze and the forest fire*
Augarde, Steve (Stephen). *Pig*

Baker, Eugene H. *Fire*
Barr, Jene. *Fire snorkel number 7*
Baumann, Kurt. *Piro and the fire brigade*
Beatty, Hetty Burlingame. *Little Owl Indian*
Belloc, Hilaire. *Matilda who told lies and was burned to death*
Bernstein, Margery. *Coyote goes hunting for fire*
Bester, Roger. *Fireman Jim*
Bible, Charles. *Jennifer's new chair*
Blathwayt, Benedict. *Tangle and the firesticks*
Bond, Ruskin. *Flames in the forest*
Bourgeois, Paulette. *Fire fighters*
Brenner, Barbara A. *Mr. Tall and Mr. Small*
Brown, Margaret Wise. *The little fireman*
Bruna, Dick. *Snuffy and the fire*
Cash, Rosanne. *Penelope Jane*
Charles, Donald. *Chancay and the secret of fire*
Cuyler, Margery. *Stop drop and roll*
Demarest, Chris L. *Firefighters A to Z*
  Hotshots!
De Regniers, Beatrice Schenk. *Willy O'Dwyer jumped in the fire*
Driscoll, Laura. *The bravest cat!*
Dubois, Muriel L. *Out and about at the fire station*
Du Bois, William Pène. *Otto and the magic potatoes*
Dubowski, Cathy East. *Fire engine to the rescue*
Ehlert, Lois. *Cuckoo, a Mexican folktale = Cucú: un cuento folklórico mexicano*
Elliott, Dan. *A visit to the Sesame Street firehouse*
Emergency!
Fire
Firehouse
Flanagan, Alice K. *Ms. Murphy fights fires*
Foreman, Michael. *Panda and the bushfire*
Fraser, Mary Ann. *Forest fire!*
Garland, Michael. *Angel cat*
Good, Merle. *Reuben and the fire*
Gramatky, Hardie. *Hercules*
Greene, Graham. *The little fire engine*
Haines, Gail Kay. *Fire*
Hammar, Asa. *Fit for pigs*
Harshman, Marc. *A little excitement*
Hayward, Linda. *A day in the life of a firefighter*
Jam, Teddy. *The year of fire*
Kirn, Ann. *The tale of a crocodile*
Klingel, Cynthia Fitterer. *Firefighters*
Kraus, Robert. *Freddy, the fire engine*
Kuklin, Susan. *Lighting fires*
Lawrence, John. *Pope Leo's elephant*
Leech, Bryan Jeffery. *John Jeremy Colton*
Lemaître, Pascal. *Emily the giraffe*
Liebman, Daniel. *I want to be a firefighter*
London, Jonathan. *Fire race*
Mahood, Kenneth. *The laughing dragon*
Martin, Bill (William Ivan). *Fire! Fire! said Mrs. McGuire*
Martin, Jacqueline Briggs. *Grandmother Bryant's pocket*
Mike, Jan M. *Opossum and the great firemaker*
Miklowitz, Gloria D. *Save that raccoon!*
Miles, Miska. *The fox and the fire*
Moskin, Marietta D. *Lysbet and the fire kittens*
Nelson, S. D. *The Star People*
Newton, James R. *A forest is reborn*
Nobisso, Josephine. *John Blair and the great Hinckley fire*
Owen, Ann (1953–). *Protecting your home*
Pendziwol, Jean. *No dragons for tea*
Polacco, Patricia. *Tikvah means hope*
Uhlberg, Myron. *The printer*
Quackenbush, Robert M. *There'll be a hot time in the old town tonight*
Rex, Michael. *My fire engine*
Reynolds, Marilynn. *The prairie fire*
Roberts, Bethany. *Gramps and the fire dragon*
Roth, Susan L. *Fire came to the earth people*
Royston, Angela. *Fire fighters*
Sandburg, Carl (Charles August). *The Huckabuck family and how they raised popcorn in Nebraska and quit and came back*, ill. by David Small
Spiegel, Doris. *Danny and Company 92*
Taylor, Mark. *Henry explores the mountains*
Thompson, Colin (Colin Edward). *Unknown*

Troughton, Joanna. *How rabbit stole the fire*
Ungerer, Tomi. *The Mellops strike oil*
Van Laan, Nancy. *Rainbow crow*
Wilson, Gina. *Ignis*
Wilson-Max, Ken. *Big red fire truck*
Yee, Wong Herbert. *Fireman Small*
    Fireman Small, fire down below
    Fireman Small to the rescue
Ziefert, Harriet. *Lewis the fire fighter*

Fire engines *see* Careers – firefighters; Trucks

Firefighters *see* Careers – firefighters

Fires *see* Fire

Fish

Adams, Georgie. *Fish fish fish*
Aliki. *The long lost coelacanth and other living fossils*
    My visit to the aquarium
Arenson, Roberta. *Manu and the talking fish*
Arnosky, Jim. *Crinkleroot's 25 fish every child should know*
Aruego, José. *Pilyo the piranha*
    Weird friends
Asch, Frank. *Moonbear's pet*
Balet, Jan B. *Joanjo*
Beisert, Heide Helene. *Poor fish*
Bennett, Kelly. *Not Norman*
Berger, Melvin. *Dive! a book of deep sea creatures*
Borovsky, Paul. *The fish that wasn't*
Brenner, Barbara A. *Rosa and Marco and the three wishes*
Brice, Tony. *The bashful goldfish*
Broekel, Ray. *Dangerous fish*
Brown, Margaret Wise. *The little fisherman*
Bruna, Dick. *The fish*
Bunting, Eve (Anne Evelyn). *Gleam and Glow*
Burstein, Fred. *Whispering in the park*
Bush, John. *The fish who could wish*
Cain, Sheridan. *Look out for the big bad fish!*
Calder, S. J. *If you were a fish*
Carlstrom, Nancy White. *Fish and flamingo*
Clements, Andrew. *Big Al and Shrimpy*
Coatsworth, Elizabeth. *Under the green willow*
Cole, Joanna. *A fish hatches*
Cook, Bernadine. *The little fish that got away*
Cooper, Elizabeth K. *The fish from Japan*
Curious George goes to the aquarium
Dahl, Michael. *One giant splash*
Damjan, Mischa. *The little sea horse*
Darby, Gene. *What is a fish?*
Demi. *Find Demi's sea creatures*
Donovan, Gail. *The copycat fish*
    A fishy story
    Hidden treasures
    Lost at sea
Eastman, David. *What is a fish?*
Ehlert, Lois. *Fish eyes*
Elborn, Andrew. *Big Al*
Eure, Wesley. *A fish out of water*
Frieden, Sarajo. *The care and feeding of fish*
Galloway, Ruth. *Fidgety fish*
Gliori, Debi. *Willie Bear and the Wish Fish*
Goldfinger, Jennifer P. *A fish named Spot*
Gomi, Taro. *Where's the fish?*
Hall, Bill. *Fish tale*
Harris, Trudy. *Pattern fish*
Hawes, Judy. *Shrimps*
Henley, Claire. *In the ocean*
Himmelman, John. *Ellen and the goldfish*
Hirschi, Ron. *Ocean*
Hodge, Deborah. *Salmon*
Hogan, Paula Z. *The salmon*
Hutchins, H. J. (Hazel J.). *The catfish palace*
Ipcar, Dahlov (Zorach). *The biggest fish in the sea*
Jonas, Ann. *Splash!*

Kalan, Robert. *Blue sea*
Kelly, Irene. *Ebbie and Flo*
Kite, L. Patricia. *Down in the sea. The jellyfish*
Komaiko, Leah. *Just my dad and me*
Kroll, Virginia L. *A carp for Kimiko*
    Helen the fish
LeBox, Annette. *Salmon Creek*
Lewis, J. Patrick. *At the wish of the fish*
Lionni, Leo. *Fish is fish*
    Swimmy
London, Jonathan. *Where the big fish are*
Love, Ann. *Fishing*
Lubach, Peter. *Harry and the singing fish*
Lucado, Max. *Small gifts in God's hands*
McGaw, Wayne T. *T-boy of the bayou*
MacGill-Callahan, Sheila. *Finn MacCool and the talking fish*
Macken, JoAnn Early. *Goldfish*
McMullan, Kate (Hall). *Fishy riddles*
Maddern, Eric. *Curious clownfish*
Mallory, Kenneth. *Families of the deep blue sea*
Martin, David. *Piggy and Dad go fishing*
Mendoza, George. *The gillygoofang*
Metaxas, Eric. *Princess Scargo and the birthday pumpkin*
Mudd-Ruth, Maria. *The ultimate ocean book*
Muzik, Katharine. *At home in the coral reef*
Nayer, Judy. *Sea creatures*
Nelson, Robin. *Pet fish*
Newton, Jill. *Cat-fish*
O'Malley, Kevin. *Carl caught a flying fish*
Pallotta, Jerry. *The dory story*
Parnall, Peter. *The great fish*
Parry, Marian. *King of the fish*
Paulsen, Gary. *Canoe days*
Pfeffer, Wendy. *What's it like to be a fish?*
Pfister, Marcus. *The rainbow fish*
    Rainbow fish ABC
    Rainbow fish and the big blue whale
    Rainbow fish and the sea monsters' cave
    Rainbow fish board book and finger puppet
    The rainbow fish floor puzzle book
    Rainbow fish mini-book
    Rainbow fish to the rescue!
Pratt, Kristin Joy. *A swim through the sea*
Raschka, Christopher. *Arlene sardine*
Rechner, Amy. *Out and about at the aquarium*
Royston, Angela. *Life cycle of a salmon*
    Sea animals
Sayre, April Pulley. *Trout, trout, trout*
Schatell, Brian. *Midge and Fred*
Schlein, Miriam. *That's not Goldie!*
Schumacher, Claire. *Alto and Tango*
Seuss, Dr. *McElligot's pool*
    One fish, two fish, red fish, blue fish
Shaw, Evelyn S. *Fish out of school*
Sill, Cathryn P. *About fish*
Sloat, Teri. *There was an old lady who swallowed a trout*
Stevenson, James. *Which one is Whitney?*
Suzuki, David. *Salmon forest*
Toft, Kim Michelle. *One less fish*
Turnage, Sheila. *Trout the magnificent*
Valens, Evans G. *Wingfin and Topple*
Van Laan, Nancy. *Little Fish lost*
Waber, Bernard. *Lorenzo*
Waechter, Friedrich Karl. *Three is company*
Walton, Rick. *Something's fishy!*
Weeks, Sarah. *Splish splash*
Wezel, Peter. *The good bird*
Wilcox, Cathy. *Enzo the Wonderfish*
Wildsmith, Brian. *Fishes*
Winkelman, Barbara Gaines. *Puffer's surprise*
    Sockeye's journey home
Wong, Herbert H. *My goldfish*
Wood, Audrey. *Ten little fish*
Wood, John Norris. *Oceans*
Wright, Catherine (Catherine E.). *Steamboat Annie and the thousand-pound catfish*
Wyse, Lois. *Two guppies, a turtle and Aunt Edna*

Yerxa, Leo. *A fish tale, or, The little one that got away*
Yorinks, Arthur. *Louis the fish*
Zimelman, Nathan. *The great adventure of Wo Ti*
Zoller, Arthur David. *Fish colors*
　　Fish counting

Fish – seahorses

Blackstone, Stella. *Secret seahorse*
　　Secret seahorse [board book]
Damjan, Mischa. *The little seahorse and the Christmas pearl*
Freymann, Saxton. *One lonely seahorse*
Jango-Cohen, Judith. *Clinging sea horses*
Walker, Sally M. *Seahorse reef*

Fish – sharks

Arnold, Caroline. *Giant shark*
Clarke, Ginjer L. *Sharks!*
Cole, Joanna. *Hungry, hungry sharks*
Cox, Phil Roxbee. *Shark in the park*
Diffily, Deborah. *Jurassic shark*
Gay, Tenner Ottley. *Sharks in action*
Gentle, Victor. *Baby sharks*
　　Killer sharks, killer people
　　Shark camouflage and armor
　　Very big sharks
　　The world's strangest shark
Gibbons, Gail. *Sharks*
Griff (Andrew Griffin). *Shark-mad Stanley*
Laird, Donivee Martin. *The three little Hawaiian pigs and the magic shark*
Llewellyn, Claire. *The best book of sharks*
Mahy, Margaret. *The great white man-eating shark*
Martin, Rafe. *The Shark God*
Mellor, Corinne. *Clark the toothless shark*
O'Brien, Patrick. *Megatooth*
Pfister, Marcus. *Rainbow fish to the rescue!*
Selsam, Millicent E. *A first look at sharks*
Sharratt, Nick. *Shark in the park*
Troll, Ray. *Sharkabet*
Ward, Nick. *Don't eat the teacher*
West, Colin. *"Only joking!" laughed the lobster*
Zoehfeld, Kathleen Weidner. *Great white shark, ruler of the sea*

Fishermen *see* Careers – fishermen

Fishing *see* Sports – fishing

Fitness *see* Health & fitness

Flags

Bartoletti, Susan Campbell. *The flag maker*
Green, Stephanie. *Betsy Ross and the silver thimble*

Flamingos *see* Birds – flamingos

Flattery *see* Character traits – flattery

Fleas *see* Insects – fleas

Flies *see* Insects – flies

Floods *see* Weather – floods

Flowers

Aksakov, Sergei. *The scarlet flower*
Alda, Arlene. *Morning glory Monday*
Allison, Diane Worfolk. *This is the key to the kingdom*
Andersen, H. C. (Hans Christian). *Little Ida's flowers*
Anderson, Janet S. *Sunflower Sal*
Anno, Mitsumasa. *The king's flower*
Baker, Jeffrey J. W. *Patterns of nature*

Bardill, Linard. *The great golden thing*
Barker, Cicely Mary. *Berry flower fairies*
　　Blossom flower fairies
　　Flower fairies of the garden
　　Flower fairies of the seasons
　　Flower fairies of the spring
　　Flower fairies of the summer
　　Flower fairies of the trees
　　Flower fairies postcard book
　　Spring flower fairies
　　Summer flower fairies
Best, Cari. *Top banana*
Blossom tales
Brisson, Pat. *Wanda's roses*
Bruce, Lisa. *Fran's flower*
Bunting, Eve (Anne Evelyn). *Flower garden*
　　Sunflower house
Campbell, Rod. *Buster's afternoon*
Chapman, Carol. *Barney Bipple's magic dandelions*
Cooney, Barbara. *Miss Rumphius*
Cousins, Lucy. *Flower in the garden*
Day, Alexandra. *Helping the flowers and trees*
DeLage, Ida. *Frannie's flower*
Delaney, A. *The gunnywolf*
Denver, John. *The children and the flowers*
De Paola, Tomie (Thomas Anthony). *The legend of the bluebonnet*
　　The legend of the Indian paintbrush
Eclare, Melanie. *A handful of sunshine*
Ehlert, Lois. *Planting a rainbow*
Ellentuck, Shan. *A sunflower as big as the sun*
Ellwand, David. *Cinderlily*
Fellows, Rebecca Nevers. *A lei for Tutu*
Fish, Helen Dean. *When the root children wake up*, published by Lippincott, 1930
　　When the root children wake up, published by Green Tiger Pr., 1988
Fisher, Aileen Lucia. *And a sunflower grew*
　　Petals yellow and petals red
Ford, Miela. *Sunflower*
Givens, Janet Eaton. *Something wonderful happened*
Greene, Ellin. *Ling-li and the phoenix fairy*
Harper, Wilhelmina. *The gunniwolf*
Hearn, Diane Dawson. *Anna in the garden*
Heilbroner, Joan. *Robert the rose horse*
Heller, Ruth. *The reason for a flower*
Heyduck-Huth, Hilde. *The strawflower*
Hidaka, Masako. *Girl from the snow country*
Himmelman, John. *A dandelion's life*
Hines, Anna Grossnickle. *Miss Emma's wild garden*
Hoban, Julia. *Amy loves the sun*
Holmes, Anita. *Flowers and friends*
Ichikawa, Satomi. *Nora's roses*
　　Suzanne and Nicholas in the garden
Ipcar, Dahlov (Zorach). *The land of flowers*
Karon, Jan. *The trellis and the seed*
King, Elizabeth. *Backyard sunflower*
Kirkpatrick, Rena K. *Look at flowers*
Lagerlöf, Selma. *The legend of the Christmas rose*
Legg, Gerald. *From seed to sunflower*
Lerner, Carol. *Flowers of a woodland spring*
Lewison, Wendy Cheyette. *Princess Buttercup*
Lillegard, Dee. *The day the daisies danced*
Lin, Grace. *The ugly vegetables*
Lind, Michael. *Bluebonnet girl*
Lobel, Anita. *Alison's zinnia*
Lobel, Arnold. *The rose in my garden*
Loewer, H. Peter. *The moonflower*
Louie, Therese On. *Raymond's perfect present*
Lucht, Irmgard. *The red poppy*
Lunge-Larsen, Lise. *The legend of the lady slipper*
McMillan, Bruce. *Counting wildflowers*
Maris, Ron. *In my garden*
Marshall, Janet Perry. *A honey of a day*
Marton, Jirina. *Flowers for mom*
Marzollo, Jean. *I'm a seed*
Maurer, Tracy. *Growing flowers*
Medearis, Angela Shelf. *Seeds grow*

Merriam, Eve. *Ten rosy roses*
Milne, A. A. (Alan Alexander). *The magic hill*
Mockford, Caroline. *What's this?*
Montresor, Beni. *The witches of Venice*
Murphy, Mary. *Koala and the flower*
Newman, Lesléa. *Belinda's bouquet*
O'Callahan, Jay. *Tulips*
Olson, Arielle North. *The lighthouse keeper's daughter*
Pomeroy, Diana. *Wildflower ABC*
Posada, Mia. *Dandelions, stars in the grass*
Preller, James. *Cardinal and sunflower*
Ramirez, Melissa Bourbon. *The flight of the sunflower*
Rockwell, Anne F. *Bumblebee, bumblebee, do you know me?*
   My spring robin
Samson, Suzanne M. *Fairy dusters and blazing stars*
Schaefer, Lola M. *This is the sunflower*
Selsam, Millicent E. *A first look at flowers*
Shannon, George. *Dancing the breeze*
Slobodkina, Esphyr. *Pinky and the petunias*
Slote, Elizabeth. *Nelly's garden*
Spalding, Andrea. *Me and Mr. Mah*
Steig, William. *Rotten island*
Stephens, J. Moria. *Persephone, the ladybug*
Stern, Maggie. *The missing sunflowers*
Sugita, Yutaka. *The flower family*
Tamar, Erika. *The garden of happiness*
Trimble, Marcia. *Flower Green*
Turner, Ann Warren. *Red flower goes West*
Umezawa, Rui. *Aiko's flowers*
Waber, Bernard. *A lion named Shirley Williamson*
Wallace, Nancy Elizabeth. *Paperwhite*
Williams, Barbara. *Hello, dandelions!*
Wilson-Max, Ken. *Max loves sunflowers*
Wood, Audrey. *Birdsong*
   When the root children wake up

Flowers – roses

Edwards, Pamela Duncan. *Rosie's roses*
Hooks, William H. *The legend of the Christmas rose*

Flutes *see* Musical instruments – flutes

Flying *see* Activities – flying

Fog *see* Weather – fog

Fold-out books *see* Format, unusual – toy & movable
  books

Folk & fairy tales

Aardema, Verna. *Anansi does the impossible!*
  Anansi finds a fool
  Bimwili and the Zimwi
  Borreguita and the coyote
  Bringing the rain to Kapiti Plain
  Half-a-ball-of-kenki
  Jackal's flying lesson
  Ji-nongo-nongo means riddles
  Koi and the kola nuts
  The lonely lioness and the ostrich chicks
  Misoso
  Oh, Kojo! How could you!
  Pedro and the padre
  Princess Gorilla and a new kind of water
  The riddle of the drum
  Sebgugugu the glutton
  Traveling to Tondo
  The vinganan ee and the tree toad
  Who's in Rabbit's house?
  Why mosquitoes buzz in people's ears
Abisch, Roz. *The clever turtle*
  Mai-Ling and the mirror
  Sweet Betsy from Pike
Ada, Alma Flor. *Dear Peter Rabbit*

  The malachite palace
  The rooster who went to his uncle's wedding
Adshead, Gladys L. *Brownies – hush!*
Æsop. *Æsop*
  Æsop's fables, ill. by Gisela Dürr
  Æsop's fables, ill. by Michael Hague
  Æsop's fables, ill. by Heidi Holder
  Æsop's fables, ill. by Claire Littlejohn
  Æsop's fables, ill. by Jerry Pinkney
  Æsop's fables, ill. by Nick Price
  Æsop's fables, ill. by Lisbeth Zwerger
  Androcles and the lion, ill. by Janusz Grabianski
  Androcles and the lion, ill. by Dennis Nolan
  Androcles and the lion, ill. by Robert Rayevsky
  Androcles and the lion, ill. by Janet Stevens
  Animal fables from Æsop
  The ant and the dove
  The ant and the grasshopper, ill. by Amy Lowry Poole
  The ant and the grasshopper, ill. by Sara Rojo
  Belling the cat
  The best of Æsop's fables
  The boy who cried wolf, ill. by Dianne Silverman
  The children's Æsop
  The country mouse and the city mouse, ill. by Laura Lydecker
  The country mouse and the city mouse, ill. by Diane Silverman
  The crow and the pitcher
  The dog and the wolf
  Fables from Æsop, ill. by Tom Lynch
  The fables of Æsop
  The fox and the grapes
  The goose that laid the golden egg
  The hare and the frogs
  The hare and the tortoise, ill. by Paul Galdone
  The hare and the tortoise, ill. by Carol Jones
  The hare and the tortoise, ill. by Gerald Rose
  The hare and the tortoise, ill. by Helen Ward
  The hare and the tortoise, ill. by Peter Weevers
  The lion and the mouse, ill. by Carol Jones
  The lion and the mouse, ill. by Lisa McCue
  The lion and the mouse, ill. by Sara Rojo
  The lion and the mouse, ill. by Gerald Rose
  The lion and the mouse, ill. by Bernadette Watts
  The lion and the mouse, ill. by Ed Young
  The miller, his son and their donkey, ill. by Roger Antoine
    Duvoisin
  The miller, his son and their donkey, ill. by Eugen Sopko
  Once in a wood
  The raven and the fox
  Seven fables from Æsop
  Tales from Æsop
  The lion and the mouse and other Æsop fables, ill. by Bert Kitchen
  Three Æsop fox fables
  The tortoise and the hare, ill. by Sara Rojo
  The tortoise and the hare, adapt. & ill. by Janet Stevens
  The town mouse and the country mouse, ill. by Lorinda Bryan
    Cauley
  The town mouse and the country mouse, ill. by Helen Craig
  The town mouse and the country mouse, ill. by Paul Galdone
  The town mouse and the country mouse, ill. by Tom Garcia
  The town mouse and the country mouse, ill. by Janet Stevens
  The town mouse and the country mouse, ill. by Bernadette Watts
  Town mouse, country mouse, ill. by Jan Brett
  Town mouse, country mouse, ill. by Carol Jones
  Wolf! Wolf!
Afanas'ev, Aleksandr N. *Russian folk tales*
  Salt
Ahlberg, Allan. *Bravest ever bear*
  The Cinderella show
Aiken, Joan. *The shoemaker's boy*
Aleichem, Sholem. *Hanukah money*
Alexander, Ellen. *Llama and the great flood*
Alexander, Lloyd. *The king's fountain*
  The truthful harp
Alger, Leclaire Gowans. *All in the morning early*
  Always room for one more
Aliki. *Diogenes*
  The eggs

George and the cherry tree
Three gold pieces
The twelve months
The all-amazing ha ha book
Allard, Harry. *May I stay?*
Allen, Debbie. *Brothers of the knight*
Allen, Jonathan. *Wake up, Sleeping Beauty*
Allen, Linda. *The giant who had no heart*
The mouse bride
Alvarez, Julia. *The secret footprints*
Ambrus, Victor G. *The little cockerel*
Never laugh at bears
The seven skinny goats
The Sultan's bath
The three poor tailors
Anaya, Rudolfo A. *Maya's children*
Andersen, H. C. (Hans Christian). *The emperor and the nightingale*,
    ill. by Meilo So
The emperor and the nightingale, ill. by James Watling
The emperor's new clothes, ill. by Angela Barrett
The emperor's new clothes, ill. by Erik Blegvad
The emperor's new clothes, ill. by Virginia Lee Burton
The emperor's new clothes, ill. by Robert Byrd
The emperor's new clothes, ill. by Charlene DeLage
The emperor's new clothes, ill. by Jack and Irene Delano
The emperor's new clothes, ill. by Demi
The emperor's new clothes, ill. by Hélène Desputeaux
The emperor's new clothes, ill. by Birte Dietz
The emperor's new clothes, ill. by Dorothée Duntze
The emperor's new clothes, ill. by Pamela Baldwin Ford
The emperor's new clothes, ill. by Jack Kent
The emperor's new clothes, ill. by Monika Laimgruber
The emperor's new clothes, ill. by Anne F. Rockwell
The emperor's new clothes, ill. by Janet Stevens
The emperor's new clothes, ill. by Eve Tharlet
The emperor's new clothes, ill. by Robert Van Nutt
The emperor's new clothes, ill. by Nadine Bernard Westcott
The emperor's nightingale, ill. from the Disney archives
The emperor's nightingale, ill. by Georges Lemoine
The fir tree, ill. by Stephanie Britt
The fir tree, ill. by Nancy Elkholm Burkert
The fir tree, ill. by Diane Goode
The fir tree, ill. by Rita Marshall
The fir tree, ill. by Bernadette Watts
It's perfectly true!
Little Ida's flowers
The little match girl, ill. by Rachel Isadora
The little match girl, ill. by Blair Lent
The little match girl, ill. by Jerry Pinkney
The little mermaid, ill. by Charlene DeLage
The little mermaid, ill. by Edward Frascino
The little mermaid, ill. by Michael Hague
The little mermaid, ill. by Rachel Isadora
The little mermaid, ill. by Chihiro Iwasaki
The little mermaid, ill. by Dorothy Pulis Lathrop
The little mermaid, ill. by Darcy May
The little mermaid, ill. by Josef Palecek
The little mermaid, ill. by Daniel San Souci
The little mermaid, ill. by Katie Thamer Treherne
The nightingale, ill. by Harold Berson
The nightingale, ill. by Nancy Ekholm Burkert
The nightingale, ill. by Alison Claire Darke
The nightingale, ill. by Demi
The nightingale, ill. by Beni Montresor
The nightingale, ill. by Josef Palecek
The nightingale, ill. by Regolo Ricci
The nightingale, ill. by Christopher Santoro
The nightingale, ill. by Lisbeth Zwerger
The old man is always right
The princess and the pea, ill. by Emily Bolam
The princess and the pea, ill. by Charlene Delage
The princess and the pea, ill. by Dorothée Duntze
The princess and the pea, ill. by Dick Gackenbach
The princess and the pea, ill. by Paul Galdone
The princess and the pea, ill. by Camille Semelet
The princess and the pea, ill. by Janet Stevens
The princess and the pea, ill. by Suçie Stevenson

The princess and the pea, ill. by Eve Tharlet
The snow queen, ill. by Angela Barrett
The snow queen, ill. by Toma Bogdanovic
The snow queen, ill. by June Atkin Corwin
The snow queen, ill. by Sally Holmes
The snow queen, ill. by Susan Jeffers
The snow queen, ill. by Errol Le Cain
The snow queen, ill. by Bernadette Watts
The snow queen, ill. by Arieh Zeldich
The snow queen and other stories from Hans Andersen, ill. by
    Edmund Dulac
The steadfast tin soldier, ill. by Charlene DeLage
The steadfast tin soldier, ill. by Thomas di Grazia
The steadfast tin soldier, ill. by Paul Galdone
The steadfast tin soldier, ill. by Rachel Isadora
The steadfast tin soldier, ill. by David Jorgensen
The steadfast tin soldier, ill. by Monika Laimgruber
The steadfast tin soldier, ill. by P. J. Lynch
The steadfast tin soldier, ill. by Fred Marcellino
The steadfast tin soldier, ill. by Alain Vaës
The swineherd, ill. by Erik Blegvad
The swineherd, ill. by Dorothée Duntze
The swineherd, ill. by Deborah Hahn
The swineherd, ill. by Lisbeth Zwerger
Thumbelina, ill. by Adrienne Adams
Thumbelina, ill. by Wayne Anderson
Thumbelina, ill. by Emma Chichester Clark
Thumbelina, ill. by Alison Claire Darke
Thumbelina, ill. by Charlene DeLage
Thumbelina, ill. by Demi
Thumbelina, ill. by Arlene Graston
Thumbelina, ill. by Susan Jeffers
Thumbelina, ill. by Kaarina Kaila
Thumbelina, ill. by Christine Willis Nigognossian
Thumbelina, ill. by Gustaf Tenggren
Thumbelina, ill. by Lisbeth Zwerger
Thumbeline, ill. by Lisbeth Zwerger; tr. by Anthea Bell
The tinderbox, ill. by Warwick Hutton
The tinderbox, ill. by Barry Moser
The ugly duckling, ill. by Adrienne Adams
The ugly duckling, ill. by Lorinda Bryan Cauley
The ugly duckling, ill. by Charlene DeLage
The ugly duckling, ill. by Troy Howell
The ugly duckling, ill. by Tadasu Izawa and Shigemi Hijikata
The ugly duckling, ill. by Monika Laimgruber
The ugly duckling, ill. by Johannes Larsen
The ugly duckling, ill. by Thomas Locker
The ugly duckling, ill. by Alan Marks
The ugly duckling, ill. by Josef Palecek
The ugly duckling, ill. by Jerry Pinkney
The ugly duckling, ill. by Maria Ruis
The ugly duckling, ill. by Daniel San Souci
The ugly duckling, ill. by Meilo So
The ugly duckling, ill. by Robert Van Nutt
The ugly duckling, ill. by Bernadette Watts
The ugly little duck, ill. by Peggy Perry Anderson
The wild swans, ill. by Angela Barrett
The wild swans, ill. by Susan Jeffers
The woman with the eggs
Anderson, Lonzo. *Arion and the dolphins*
Anderson, Robin. *Sinabouda Lily*
Anglund, Joan Walsh. *Nibble nibble mousekin*
Anno, Mitsumasa. *Anno's Æsop*
In shadowland
Arabian Nights. *The first book of tales of ancient Araby*
The flying carpet
The tale of Aladdin and the wonderful lamp
Arenson, Roberta. *Manu and the talking fish*
Armitage, Marcia. *Lupatelli's favorite nursery tales*
Arnold, Caroline. *The terrible Hodag*
Arnold, Katya. *Baba Yaga and the little girl*
Knock, knock, teremok!
That apple is mine!
Arnott, Kathleen. *Spiders, crabs and creepy crawlers*
Aroner, Miriam. *The kingdom of singing birds*
Aronin, Ben. *The secret of the Sabbath fish*
Artell, Mike. *Petite Rouge*

Aruego, José. *A crocodile's tale*
  Look what I can do
  Rockabye crocodile
Asbjørnsen, P. C. (Peter Christen). *Billy goats Gruff*, ill. by Wendy Edelson
  Billy goats Gruff, ill. by Susan Hellard
  The man who kept house
  The three billy goats Gruff, ill. by Tim Arnold
  The three billy goats Gruff, ill. by Robert Bender
  The three billy goats Gruff, ill. by Marcia Brown
  The three billy goats Gruff, ill. by Stephen Carpenter
  Three billy goats Gruff, ill. by Tom Dunnington
  The three billy goats Gruff, ill. by Paul Galdone
  The three billy goats Gruff, ill. by David Jorgensen
  The three billy goats Gruff, ill. by Dennis Kendrick
  The three billygoats Gruff, ill. by Eric Kincaid
  Three billy goats Gruff, ill. by Thea Kliros
  The three billy goats Gruff, ill. by Jonathan Langley
  The three billy goats Gruff, ill. by Loretta Lustig
  The three billy goats Gruff, ill. by Thomas Newbury
  The three billy goats Gruff, ill. by Lilian Obligado
  The three billy goats Gruff, ill. by Ed Parker
  The three billy goats Gruff, ill. by Heidi Petach
  The three billy goats Gruff, ill. by Laura Rader
  The three billy goats Gruff, ill. by Glen Rounds
  The three billy goats Gruff, ill. by Janet Stevens
  The three billy goats Gruff, ill. by William Stobbs
  The three billy goats Gruff, ill. by Svend Otto S
  The truth about three billy goats Gruff
Asch, Frank. *The flower faerie*
  Ziggy Piggy and the three little pigs
Ata, Te. *Baby Rattlesnake*
Auch, Mary Jane. *The princess and the pizza*
Auerbach, Marjorie. *King Lavra and the barber*
Aulaire, Ingri Mortenson d'. *Children of the northlights*
  Don't count your chicks
  East of the sun and west of the moon
Ayers, Rebecca Hickox. *Per and the Dala horse*
  Zorro and Quwi
Aylesworth, Jim. *The full belly bowl*
Ayres, Becky Hickox. *Matreshka*
Azarian, Mary. *The tale of John Barleycorn or, From barley to beer*
Babbitt, Natalie. *Ouch!*
The babes in the woods. *The old ballad of the babes in the woods*
Backstein, Karen. *The blind men and the elephant*
Baden, Robert. *And Sunday makes seven*
Bahous, Sally. *Sitti and the cats*
Bailey, Linda. *Gordon Loggins and the three bears*
Baker, Betty. *And me, coyote!*
  Rat is dead and ant is sad
Baker, Olaf. *Where the buffaloes begin*
Balcziak, Bill. *John Henry*
Balducci, Rita. *Little Bear's timeless tales*
Balet, Jan B. *The fence*
Balian, Lorna. *Leprechauns never lie*
Balouch, Kristen. *The king and the three thieves*
Bang, Betsy. *The old woman and the red pumpkin*
  The old woman and the rice thief
  Tuntuni the tailor bird
Bang, Molly. *Dawn*
  The paper crane
  Wiley and the hairy man
Bannerman, Helen. *Sambo and the twins*
Barbosa, Rogério Andrade. *African animal tales*
Baring, Maurice. *The blue rose*
Barrie, J. M. (James M.). *Peter Pan*
Barry, David. *The Rajah's rice*
Bartels, Alice L. *The beast*
Bartos-Hoppner, Barbara. *The pied piper of Hamelin*
Baruch, Dorothy. *Kappa's tug-of-war with the big brown horse*
Basile, Giambattista. *Petrosinella*
Bason, Lillian. *Those foolish Molboes!*
Bateman, Teresa. *Harp o' gold*
  Leprechaun gold
  The princesses have a ball
Bateson-Hill, Margaret. *Lao Lao of Dragon Mountain*
  Masha and the firebird

Batt, Tanya Robyn. *The faerie's gift*
Baumann, Hans. *Chip has many brothers*
  The hare's race
Baumann, Kurt. *The prince and the lute*
Bawden, Nina. *William Tell*
Baylor, Byrd. *The desert is theirs*
  A God on every mountain top
  Moon song
  The way to start a day
Bazilian, Barbara. *Princess Lily*
  The red shoes
Bechstein, Ludwig. *The rabbit catcher and other fairy tales*
Bedard, Michael. *The wolf of Gubbio*
The bedtime book
Beeler, Selby B. *Throw your tooth on the roof*
Behan, Brendan. *The king of Ireland's son*
Bell, Anthea. *Swan Lake*
  The wise queen
Belling the cat and other stories
Belpré, Pura. *Dance of the animals*
  Pérez and Martina
Belting, Natalia Maree. *The sun is a golden earring*
Bemelmans, Ludwig. *Rosebud*
Ben-´Ezer, Ehud. *Hosni the dreamer*
Bennett, Jill. *Teeny tiny*
Berenstain, Michael. *The troll book*
Berenzy, Alix. *A frog prince*
  Rapunzel
Beresford, Elisabeth. *Jack and the magic stove*
Berg, Leila. *Folk tales for reading and telling*
Bergen, Lara Rice. *Washington Irving's Rip Van Winkle*
Berger, Barbara Helen. *All the way to Lhasa*
  Animalia
  Grandfather Twilight
Bernhard, Emery. *The girl who wanted to hunt*
  Spotted Eagle and Black Crow
  The tree that rains
Bernhard, Josephine Butkowska. *Lullaby*
  Nine cry-baby dolls
Bernstein, Margery. *Coyote goes hunting for fire*
  Earth namer
  The first morning
  How the sun made a promise and kept it
Bernstein, Robin. *Terrible, terrible!*
Berry, James. *Don't leave an elephant to go and chase a bird*
  First palm trees
Berson, Harold. *Balarin's goat*
  Barrels to the moon
  The boy, the baker, the miller and more
  Charles and Claudine
  How the devil gets his due
  Joseph and the snake
  Kassim's shoes
  Larbi and Leila
  Raminagrobis and the mice
  Why the jackal won't speak to the hedgehog
Bess, Clayton. *The truth about the moon*
Bianco, Margery Williams. *The velveteen rabbit*, ill. by Allen Atkinson
  The velveteen rabbit, ill. by Monique Félix
  The velveteen rabbit, ill. by Michael Green
  The velveteen rabbit, ill. by Michael Hague
  The velveteen rabbit, ill. by Estella Hickman
  The velveteen rabbit, ill. by Steve Johnson & Lou Fancher
  The velveteen rabbit, ill. by David Jorgensen
  The velveteen rabbit, ill. by Thea Kliros
  The velveteen rabbit, ill. by Elizabeth Miles
  The velveteen rabbit, ill. by William Nicholson
  The velveteen rabbit, ill. by Robyn Officer
  The velveteen rabbit, ill. by Ilse Plume
  The velveteen rabbit, ill. by S. D. Schindler
  The velveteen rabbit, ill. by Tien
Bible, Charles. *Hamdaani*
Bider, Djemma. *The buried treasure*
  A drop of honey
Bierhorst, John. *Doctor Coyote*
  The ring in the prairie

Don't tell the whole world
It's too noisy
Collins, Sheila Hebert. *'T Pousette et 't Poulette*
Collodi, Carlo. *The adventures of Pinocchio*
Pinocchio
Comissiong, Lynette. *Mind me good now!*
Compton, Joanne. *Ashpet*
Sody Sallyratus
Compton, Kenn. *Granny Greenteeth and the noise in the night*
Jack the giant chaser
Conger, Lesley. *Tops and bottoms*
Conover, Chris. *Mother Goose and the sly fox*
The wizard's daughter
Cook, Joel. *The rat's daughter*
Coombs, Patricia. *The magic pot*
Tilabel
Cooner, Donna D. (Donna Danell). *I know an old Texan who swallowed a fly*
Cooney, Barbara. *Little brother and little sister*
Cooper, Susan. *The Selkie girl*
The silver cow
Tam Lin
Coppinger, Tom. *Curse in reverse*
Cormack, M. Grant. *Animal tales from Ireland*
Costa, Nicoletta. *The mischievous princess*
Coville, Bruce. *Sarah and the dragon*
Coxe, Molly. *Bunny and the beast*
Craig, Helen. *The Random House book of nursery stories*
Credle, Ellis. *Big fraid, little fraid*
Croll, Carolyn. *The little snowgirl*
The three brothers
Crompton, Anne Eliot. *The lifting stone*
The winter wife
Crossley-Holland, Kevin. *The green children*
The pedlar of Swaffham
Crum, Shutta. *Who took my hairy toe?*
Cullen, Catherine Ann. *Thirsty baby*
Cullen, Lynn. *The mightiest heart*
Cummings, E. E. (Edward Estlin). *Fairy tales*
Fairy tales
Czernecki, Stefan. *The cricket's cage*
Pancho's piñata
The singing snake
Zorah's magic carpet
Dabcovich, Lydia. *The polar bear son*
Dadey, Debbie. *Shooting star: Annie Oakley, the legend*
Will Rogers: larger than life
Dahlie, Elizabeth. *Bernelly & Harriet*
Dalton, Anne. *Prince Starr*
Daly, Jude. *Fair, Brown & Trembling*
Daly, Niki. *Why the sun and moon live in the sky*
Daniels, Guy. *The Tsar's riddles*
Dasent, George W. *East o' the sun, west o' the moon*
Daugherty, Sonia (Medvedeva). *Vanka's donkey*
Davis, Aubrey. *Bagels from Benny*
Bone button borscht
The enormous potato
Sody salleratus
Davis, Douglas F. *The lion's tail*
Davol, Marguerite W. *Batwings and the curtain of night*
Day, David. *The swan children*
Day, Nancy Raines. *The lion's whiskers*
Dayrell, Elphinstone. *Why the sun and the moon live in the sky*
DeArmond, Dale. *The seal oil lamp*
DeChristopher, Marlowe. *Greencoat and the swanboy*
Dee, Ruby. *Tower to heaven*
Two ways to count to ten
Deetlefs, Rene. *Tabu and the dancing elephants*
DeFelice, Cynthia C. *Three perfect peaches*
De Gerez, Toni. *Louhi, witch of North Farm*
Delessert, Etienne. *The seven dwarfs*
Del Negro, Janice. *Lucy Dove*
DeLuise, Dom. *King Bob's new clothes*
De Mejo, Oscar. *La Bella Magellona and the little cavalier*
Demi. *The artist and the architect*
Chen Ping and his magic axe
A Chinese zoo

Demi's reflective fables
The dragon's tale and other animal fables of the Chinese zodiac
The empty pot
The greatest treasure
The hallowed horse
The magic boat
The magic tapestry
One grain of rice
The stonecutter
Under the shade of the mulberry tree
De Montaño, Martha Kreipe. *Coyote in love with a star*
De Paola, Tomie (Thomas Anthony). *Big Anthony, his story*
Favorite nursery tales
Fin M'Coul
Jamie O'Rourke and the big potato
The legend of Old Befana
The legend of the bluebonnet
The legend of the Indian paintbrush
The legend of the persian carpet
Little Grunt and the big egg
The mysterious giant of Barletta
The Prince of the Dolomites
Strega Nona meets her match
Tony's bread
De Regniers, Beatrice Schenk. *Everyone is good for something*
Little Sister and the Month Brothers
Red Riding Hood
DeSpain, Pleasant. *The dancing turtle*
Dewan, Ted. *The sorcerer's apprentice*
Dewey, Ariane. *The fish Peri*
Laffite, the pirate
Small Cloud
The thunder god's son
Diakité, Baba Wagué. *The hunterman and the crocodiles*
The magic gourd
Dick Whittington and his cat. *Dick Whittington*, ill. by Edward Ardizzone
Dick Whittington, ill. by Antony Maitland
Dick Whittington and his cat, ill. by Marcia Brown
Dick Whittington and his cat, ill. by Kurt Werth
Diller, Harriett. *The waiting day*
Dinardo, Jeffrey. *The wolf who cried boy*
Dobbs, Rose. *More once-upon-a-time stories*
Once-upon-a-time story book
Domanska, Janina. *The best of the bargain*
Busy Monday morning
King Krakus and the dragon
Look, there is a turtle flying
Marek, the little fool
Palmiero and the ogre
A scythe, a rooster and a cat
The tortoise and the tree
The turnip
Why so much noise?
Donnelly, Jennifer. *Humble pie*
Dos Santos, Joyce Audy. *The diviner*
Henri and the Loup-Garou
Doucet, Sharon Arms. *Why Lapin's ears are long and other stories of the Louisiana bayou*
Drummond, Allan. *The willow pattern story*
Du Bois, William Pène. *The hare and the tortoise and the tortoise and the hare = La liebre y la tortuga y La tortuga y la liebre*
Duff, Maggie (Margaret K.). *Dancing turtle*
The princess and the pumpkin
Rum pum pum
Dukas, P. (Paul Abraham). *The sorcerer's apprentice*
Duncan, Lois. *The magic of Spider Woman*
Dupré, Judith. *The mouse bride*
Dupré, Rick. *Agassu*
Durell, Ann. *The Diane Goode book of American folk tales and songs*
Dwyer, Mindy. *Coyote in love*
Easwaran, Eknath. *The monkey and the mango*
Edens, Cooper. *A present for Rose*
Edwards, Lisa. *Disney's Beauty and the beast, a book of manners*
Edwards, Pamela Duncan. *Dinorella*
Edwards, Roberta. *Five silly fishermen*

Ehlert, Lois. *Cuckoo, a Mexican folktale = Cucú: un cuento folklórico*
    mexicano
    Mole's hill
    Moon rope = Un lazo a la luna
Ehrlich, Amy. *Pome and Peel*
Eisner, Will. *Sundiata*
Elkin, Benjamin. *The king's wish and other stories*
    Six foolish fishermen
    Such is the way of the world
    The wisest man in the world
Ellwand, David. *Cinderlily*
Elwell, Peter. *The king of the pipers*
Elzbieta. *Dikou and the Snivelly Snoak*
Emberley, Barbara. *One wide river to cross*
Emberley, Rebecca. *Three cool kids*
Ernst, Lisa Campbell. *Goldilocks returns*
    Little Red Riding Hood
Esbensen, Barbara Juster. *The great buffalo race*
    Ladder to the sky
    The night rainbow
    The star maiden
Esterl, Arnica. *The fine round cake*
Evans, Katherine. *The boy who cried wolf*
    A bundle of sticks
    The maid and her pail of milk
    The man, the boy and the donkey
Eyvindson, Peter. *Backward brothers see the light*
Farley, Carol J. *Mr. Pak buys a story*
Farris, Pamela J. *Young Mouse and Elephant*
Faulkner, William J. *Brer Tiger and the big wind*
Fiddle-i-fee
Field, Edward. *Magic words*
The firebird. *The firebird*, ill. by Reg Cartwright
    The firebird, ill. by Francesca Crespi
    The firebird, ill. by Demi
    The firebird, adapt. and ill. by Rachel Isadora
    The firebird, ill. by Moira Kemp
    The firebird, ill. by Kris Waldherr
    The firebird, ill. by Boris Zvorykin
    The tale of the firebird, ill. by Gennady Spirin
Fisher, Leonard Everett. *Cyclops*
    Star signs
    Theseus and the Minotaur
    William Tell
Fleischman, Paul. *The animal hedge*
Flora. *Feathers like a rainbow*
Flot, Jeannette B. *Princess Kalina and the hedgehog*
Floyd, Lucy. *Rabbit and turtle go to school*
Foley, Bernice Williams. *The gazelle and the hunter*
    A walk among clouds
Foreman, Michael. *Rock-a-doodle-do!*
Forest, Heather. *The baker's dozen*
    Stone soup
    The woman who flummoxed the fairies
Fournier, Catharine. *The coconut thieves*
The fox went out on a chilly night
Francis, Frank. *Natasha's new doll*
Franco, Betsy. *Why the frog has big eyes*
Frasconi, Antonio. *The snow and the sun = la nieve y el sol*
Freedman, Florence B. *Brothers*
Fregosi, Claudia. *The pumpkin sparrow*
    Snow maiden
French, Fiona. *Anancy and Mr. Dry-Bone*
    King of another country
    Little Inchkin
    Lord of the animals
French, Vivian. *Lazy Jack*
    Red Hen and Sly Fox
    The thistle princess
    Why the sea is salt
Fritz, Jean. *The good giants and the bad Pukwudgies*
Froese, Deborah L. *The wise washerman*
Gackenbach, Dick. *Arabella and Mr. Crack*
    The perfect mouse
Gág, Wanda. *The sorcerer's apprentice*
Gál, László. *The parrot*
Galchutt, David. *There was magic inside*

Galdone, Joanna. *Amber day*
    The little girl and the big bear
Galdone, Paul. *The amazing pig*
    Androcles and the lion
    The greedy old fat man
    King of the cats
    The magic porridge pot
    The monkey and the crocodile
    Obedient Jack
    A strange servant
    The teeny-tiny woman
    What's in fox's sack?
Gammell, Stephen. *The story of Mr. and Mrs. Vinegar*
Garland, Sarah. *Seeing red*
Garland, Sherry. *Why ducks sleep on one leg*
Garner, Alan. *Once upon a time, though it wasn't in your time, and it*
    wasn't in my time, and it wasn't in anybody else's time . . .
Gates, Frieda. *Owl eyes*
Gauch, Patricia Lee. *The little friar who flew*
    On to Widecombe Fair
Geras, Adèle. *The nutcracker*
    Sleeping beauty
    Swan Lake
Gershator, Phillis. *Only one cowry*
    Zzzng! zzzng! zzzng!
Gerson, Mary-Joan. *Why the sky is far away*
Gerstein, Mordicai. *The seal mother*
    The shadow of a flying bird
Giannini, Enzo. *Little Parsley*
Gifaldi, David. *The boy who spoke colors*
Gill, Janet. *Basket Weaver and Catches Many Mice*
Gilleo, Alma. *Learning about monsters*
The gingerbread boy. *Gingerbread baby*, ill. by Jan Brett
    The gingerbread boy, ill. by Emily Bolam
    The gingerbread boy, ill. by Scott Cook
    The gingerbread boy, ill. by Richard Egielski
    The gingerbread boy, ill. by Paul Galdone
    The gingerbread boy, ill. by Joan Elizabeth Goodman
    The gingerbread boy, ill. by William Curtis Holdsworth
    The gingerbread man, ill. by Carol Jones
    The gingerbread man, ill. by Megan Lloyd
    The gingerbread man, ill. by Barbara McClintock
    The gingerbread man, ill. by Diana Mayo
    The gingerbread man, ill. by Gerald Rose
    The gingerbread man, ill. by Bonnie & Bill Rutherford
    The pancake boy
    Whiff, sniff, nibble and chew
Ginsburg, Mirra. *The Chinese mirror*
    Clay boy
    The fisherman's son
    The fox and the hare
    How the sun was brought back to the sky
    The king who tried to fry an egg on his head
    Pampalche of the silver teeth
    Striding slippers
Gleeson, Brian. *Anansi*
    Finn McCoul
    Koi and the kola nuts
    The tiger and the Brahmin
Go tell Aunt Rhody. *Go tell Aunt Rhody*, ill. by Aliki
Gobhai, Mehlli. *Usha, the mouse-maiden*
Goble, Paul. *Adopted by the eagles*
    Buffalo woman
    Crow chief
    The dream wolf
    The gift of the sacred dog
    The great race of the birds and animals
    Her seven brothers
    Iktomi and the berries
    Iktomi and the boulder
    Iktomi and the buffalo skull
    Iktomi and the buzzard
    Iktomi and the coyote
    Iktomi and the ducks
    The legend of the White Buffalo Woman
    The lost children
    Love flute

Mystic horse
Remaking the earth
The return of the buffaloes
Star boy
The golden goose, ill. by William Stobbs
Gollub, Matthew. *The twenty-five Mixtec cats*
The good-hearted youngest brother
Goodall, Jane. *The eagle and the wren*
Goode, Diane. *Diane Goode's book of silly stories & songs*
    The dinosaur's new clothes
Gorbachev, Valeri. *The fool of the world and the flying ship*
Gordon, Ruth. *Feathers*
Gramatky, Hardie. *Nikos and the sea god*
Grambling, Lois G. *The witch who wanted to be a princess*
Granfield, Linda. *The legend of the panda*
Grant, Joan. *The monster that grew small*
Gray, Nigel. *The frog prince*
Greaves, Margaret. *Kate Crackernuts*
    Mother Cuspen
    Petrushka
    The witch cat
    The witch's servant
Greene, Ellin. *Billy Beg and his bull*
    The legend of the cranberry
    Ling-li and the phoenix fairy
Greene, Jacqueline Dembar. *What his father did*
Greeson, Janet. *The stingy baker*
Gregg, Andy. *Great Rabbit and the long-tailed Wildcat*
Gregorowski, Christopher. *Fly, eagle, fly!*
Gregory, Valiska. *Through the mickle woods*
Grey, Mini. *The very smart pea and the princess-to-be*
Grieg, E. H. (Edvard Hagerup). *E. H. Grieg's Peer Gynt*
Grifalconi, Ann. *The village of round and square houses*
Grimm, Jacob. *The bear and the kingbird*
    The bearskinner
    The brave little tailor, ill. by Mark Corcoran
    The brave little tailor, ill. by Olga Dugina & Andrej Dugin
    The brave little tailor, ill. by Daniel San Souci
    The brave little tailor, ill. by David Shaw
    The brave little tailor, ill. by Svend Otto S
    The brave little tailor, ill. by Eve Tharlet
    The brave little tailor, ill. by James Warhola
    The Bremen town band
    The Bremen town musicians, ill. by Donna Diamond
    The Bremen town musicians, ill. by Bill Dickson
    The Bremen town musicians, ill. by Janina Domanska
    The Bremen town musicians, ill. by Paul Galdone
    The Bremen town musicians, ill. by David Johnson
    Bremen town musicians, ill. by Josef Palecek
    The Bremen town musicians, ill. by Ilse Plume
    The Bremen town musicians, ill. by Janet Stevens
    The Bremen town musicians, ill. by Bernadette Watts
    Cinderella, ill. by Nonny Hogrogian
    Cinderella, ill. by Svend Otto S
    Clever Kate
    The devil with the green hairs
    The donkey prince
    The earth gnome
    The elves and the shoemaker, ill. by Doug Cushman
    The elves and the shoemaker, ill. by Paul Galdone
    The elves and the shoemaker, ill. by Margaret Walty
    The elves and the shoemaker, ill. by Bernadette Watts
    The falling stars
    The fisherman and his wife, ill. by Eleanor Hubbard
    The fisherman and his wife, ill. by Monika Laimgruber
    The fisherman and his wife, ill. by Alan Marks
    The fisherman and his wife, ill. by Todd Ouren
    The fisherman and his wife, ill. by Laurinda Spear
    The fisherman and his wife, ill. by Margot Tomes
    The fisherman and his wife, ill. by Margot Zemach
    Fitcher's bird
    The four clever brothers
    The frog prince, ill. by Paul Galdone
    The frog prince, ill. by Todd Ouren
    The frog prince, ill. by Binette Schroeder
    The glass mountain, ill. by Louisa Bauer
    The glass mountain, ill. by Nonny Hogrogian

Godfather Cat and Mousie
The golden bird, ill. by Isabelle Brent
The golden bird, ill. by Sandro Nardini
The golden goose, ill. by Dorothée Duntze
The golden goose, ill. by Dennis McDermott
The golden goose, ill. by Isadore Seltzer
The golden goose, ill. by Martin Ursell
The goose girl, ill. by Sabine Bruntjen
The goose girl, ill. by Robert Sauber
Hans in luck, ill. by Paul Galdone
Hans in luck, ill. by Felix Hoffmann
Hansel and Gretel, ill. by Adrienne Adams
Hansel and Gretel, ill. by Anthony Browne
Hansel and Gretel, ill. by Susan Jeffers
Hansel and Gretel, ill. by Winslow P. Pels
Hansel and Gretel, ill. by Jane Ray
Hansel and Gretel, ill. by Conxita Rodriguez
Hansel and Gretel, ill. by Christopher Santoro
Hansel and Gretel, ill. by John Wallner
Hansel and Gretel, ill. by Claudia Wolf
Hansel and Gretel, ill. by Paul O. Zelinsky
Hansel and Gretel, ill. by Lisbeth Zwerger
The horse, the fox, and the lion
Iron Hans
Iron John, ill. by Trina Schart Hyman
Iron John, ill. by Winslow Pels
Jack in luck
Jorinda and Joringel, ill. by Adrienne Adams
Jorinda and Joringel, ill. by Jutta Ash
Jorinda and Joringel, ill. by Margot Tomes
King Grisly-Beard
Little brother and little sister
Little red cap
Little Red Riding Hood, ill. by Frank E. Aloise
Little Red Riding Hood, ill. by Gwen Connelly
Little Red Riding Hood, ill. by Paul Galdone
Little Red Riding Hood, ill. by John S. Goodall
Little Red Riding Hood, ill. by Trina Schart Hyman
Little Red Riding Hood, ill. by Mireille Levert
Little Red Riding Hood, ill. by David M. McPhail
Little Red Riding Hood, ill. by Jean-François Martin
Little Red Riding Hood, ill. by Bernadette Watts
Lucky Hans
Mother Holly
Mrs. Fox's wedding
The musicians of Bremen, ill. by John Segal
The musicians of Bremen, ill. by Svend Otto S
The musicians of Bremen, ill. by Martin Ursell
Nanny goat and the seven little kids
The princess and the frog, ill. by Rachel Isadora
The princess and the frog, ill. by Will Eisner
The rabbit's bride
Rapunzel, ill. by Jutta Ash
Rapunzel, ill. by Sheilah Beckett
Rapunzel, ill. by Bert Dodson
Rapunzel, ill. by Maja Dusíkova
Rapunzel, ill. by Michael Hague
Rapunzel, ill. by Trina Schart Hyman
Rapunzel, ill. by Kris Waldherr
Rapunzel, ill. by Bernadette Watts
Rapunzel, ill. by Paul O. Zelinsky
Rose Red and the bear prince
Rumpelstiltskin, ill. by Jacqueline Ayer
Rumpelstiltskin, ill. by Donna Diamond
Rumpelstiltskin, ill. by Paul Galdone
Rumpelstiltskin, ill. by Jonathan Langley
Rumpelstiltskin, ill. by David Shaw
Rumpelstiltskin, ill. by Gennady Spirin
Rumpelstiltskin, ill. by John Wallner
Rumpelstiltskin, ill. by Bernadette Watts
Rumpelstiltskin, ill. by Paul O. Zelinsky
Seven at one blow
The seven ravens, ill. by Felix Hoffmann
The seven ravens, ill. by Lisbeth Zwerger
The shoemaker and his elves, ill. by Bill Dickson
The shoemaker and the elves, ill. by Adrienne Adams
The shoemaker and the elves, ill. by Cynthia and William Birrer

The shoemaker and the elves, ill. by Ilse Plume
The six servants
The six swans, ill. by Dorothée Duntze
The six swans, ill. by Daniel San Souci
The six swans, ill. by Margot Tomes
The sleeping beauty, ill. by Warwick Hutton
The sleeping beauty, ill. by Trina Schart Hyman
The sleeping beauty, ill. by Monika Laimgruber
The sleeping beauty, ill. by Mercer Mayer
Sleeping Beauty, ill. by Fina Rifa
The sleeping beauty, ill. by Ruth Sanderson
Sleeping Beauty, ill. by John Wallner
Snow White, ill. by Trina Schart Hyman
Snow White, ill. by Bernadette Watts
Snow White, ill. by Claudia Wolf
Snow White and Rose Red, ill. by Adrienne Adams
Snow White and Rose Red, ill. by John Wallner
Snow White and Rose Red, ill. by Bernadette Watts
Snow White and the seven dwarfs, ill. by Wanda Gág
Snow White and the seven dwarves, ill. by Chihiro Iwasaki
Snow-White and Rose-Red, ill. by Barbara Cooney
The table, the donkey and the stick
Three Grimms' fairy tales
The three spinning fairies
The traveling musicians of Bremen
The twelve dancing princesses, ill. by Kinuko Y. Craft
The twelve dancing princesses, ill. by Anne Dalton
The twelve dancing princesses, ill. by Dennis Hockerman
The twelve dancing princesses, ill. by Errol Le Cain
The twelve dancing princesses, ill. by Gerald McDermott
The twelve dancing princesses, ill. by Jane Ray
The twelve dancing princesses, ill. by Uri Shulevitz
The twelve dancing princesses, ill. by Suçie Stevenson
The twelve princesses, ill. by Gordon Fitchett
The valiant little tailor
The wishing table
The wolf and the seven kids, ill. by Kinuko Y. Craft
The wolf and the seven little kids, ill. by Svend Otto S
The wolf and the seven little kids, ill. by Martin Ursell
Grimm, Wilhelm. Dear Mili
Grindley, Sally. The sorcerer's apprentice
    Who is it?
Groner, Judyth Saypol. All about Sukkot
Gross, Michael. The fable of the fig tree
Gross, Ruth Belov. The girl who wouldn't get married
Gugler, Laurel Dee. Monkey tales
    There's a billy goat in the garden
Gukova, Julia. Mole's daughter
Guthrie, Donna. Nobiah's well
Guy, Rosa. Mother crocodile
Hague, Kathleen. East of the sun and west of the moon
    The legend of the Veery bird
    The man who kept house
Hague, Michael. The nutcracker
Haley, Gail E. Birdsong
    Jack and the bean tree
    Jack and the fire dragon
    Sea tale
    A story, a story
Hall, Amanda. The gossipy wife
Hall, Malcolm. And then the mouse . . .
Hallinan, P. K. (Patrick K.). I'm thankful each day!
Hallworth, Grace. Sing me a story
Hamanaka, Sheila. Screen of frogs
Hamilton, Morse. Belching Hill
Hamilton, Virginia. The girl who spun gold
Han, Oki S. Kongi and Potgi
    Sir Whong and the golden pig
Hänel, Wolfram. The gold at the end of the rainbow
Harber, Frances. My king has donkey ears
Harness, Cheryl. The queen with bees in her hair
Harper, Charise Mericle. There was a bold lady who wanted a star
Harper, Jo. The legend of Mexicatl
Harper, Piers. How the world was saved and other Native American tales
Harris, Jim. Jack and the giant
Harris, Joel Chandler. Jump!

Jump again!
Harrison, David Lee. The book of giant stories
Harshman, Marc. Rocks in my pocket
Haseley, Dennis. The cave of snores
Hassett, John. The three silly girls Grubb
Hastings, Selina. The man who wanted to live forever
    The singing ringing tree
Haugaard, Erik Christian. Prince Boghole
    Princess Horrid
Hausman, Gerald. Coyote walks on two legs
    Doctor Bird
    Eagle boy
    How Chipmunk got tiny feet
    The story of Blue Elk
Hautzig, Deborah. Beauty and the beast
Haviland, Virginia. The talking pot
Havill, Juanita. Kentucky troll
Hawkins, Colin. Fairytale news
    One, two, guess who?
Hayes, Joe. Juan Verdades, the man who could not tell a lie
    Little Gold Star = Estrellita de oro
Hayward, Linda. All stuck up
    Hello, house!
    Pepe and Papa
Hazen, Barbara Shook. The sorcerer's apprentice
Hearn, Michael Patrick. The porcelain cat
Heins, Ethel L. The cat and the cook and other fables of Krylov
The Helen Oxenbury nursery collection
Helldorfer, M. C. (Mary Claire). Cabbage Rose
    Night of the white stag
Heller, Linda. Alexis and the golden ring
Helmer, Marilyn. Three barnyard tales
    Three cat and mouse tales
    Three prince charming tales
    Three royal tales
    Three tales of enchantment
    Three tales of three
    Three tales of trickery
    Three teeny tiny tales
    Three tuneful tales
Heo, Yumi. The green frogs
Herrick, Amy. Kimbo's marble
Hewett, Anita. The tale of the turnip
Hewitt, Kathryn. King Midas and the golden touch
Heyer, Carol. Robin Hood
Heyer, Marilee. The weaving of a dream
Hickox, Rebecca. The golden sandal
Hidaka, Masako. Girl from the snow country
Hill, Eric. Spot's birthday party
    Where's Spot?
Hille-Brandts, Lene. The little black hen
Hillert, Margaret. The funny baby
    The magic beans
    The three bears
    The three goats
Hillman, Elizabeth. Min-Yo and the moon dragon
Hirsh, Marilyn. Captain Jiri and Rabbi Jacob
    Joseph who loved the Sabbath
    One little goat
Ho, Minfong. Brother Rabbit
    The two brothers
Hobbs, Will. Beardream
Hoberman, Mary Ann. Marvelous mouse man
Hobzek, Mildred. We came a-marching . . . 1, 2, 3
Hodges, Margaret. Buried moon
    Comus
    The fire bringer
    The hero of Bremen
    Hidden in sand
    The kitchen knight
    Saint George and the dragon
    St. Jerome and the lion
    Saint Patrick and the peddler
    Up the chimney
    The voice of the great bell
    The wave
Hoffman, Mary. Clever Katya

Hoffmann, E. T. A. *The nutcracker*, ill. by Francesca Crespi
The nutcracker, ill. by Renée Graef
The nutcracker, ill. by Rachel Isadora
The nutcracker, ill. by Joanna Isles
The nutcracker, ill. by Maurice Sendak
The nutcracker, ill. by Lisbeth Zwerger
The nutcracker ballet, ill. by Carolyn Ewing
The nutcracker ballet, ill. by Vladimir Vasilévich Vagin
The strange child
Hofmeyr, Dianne. *The stone*
Hogrogian, Nonny. *The cat who loved to sing*
The contest
Rooster brother
Holland, Janice. *You never can tell*
Hong, Lily Toy. *How the ox star fell from heaven*
Hooks, William H. *Feed me!*
The Gruff brothers
Moss gown
Peach boy
Snowbear Whittington, an Appalachian Beauty and the Beast
Hopkins, Lee Bennett. *The horned toad prince*
Horn, Sandra Ann. *Babushka*
Hort, Lenny. *The boy who held back the sea*
Houston, James. *Kiviok's magic journey*
How the cock wrecked the manor
Howland, Naomi. *Latkes, latkes, good to eat*
Huck, Charlotte S. *Princess Furball*
Hughes, Monica. *Little Fingerling*
Huling, Jan. *Puss in cowboy boots*
Hulpach, Vladimir. *Ahaiyute and Cloud Eater*
Hunt, Angela Elwell. *The tale of three trees*
Hunt, Jonathan. *Leif's saga*
Hunter, C. W. *The green gourd*
Hürlimann, Ruth. *The proud white cat*
Hurst, Margaret M. *Grannie and the Jumbie*
Huth, Holly Young. *The son of the sun and the daughter of the moon*
Hutton, Warwick. *Beauty and the beast*
The nose tree
Perseus
The Trojan horse
Ichikawa, Satomi. *A child's book of seasons*
Sun through small leaves
Iké, Jane Hori. *A Japanese fairy tale*
Ikeda, Daisaku. *The snow country prince*
Illyés, Gyula. *Matt the gooseherd*
Irbinskas, Heather. *How Jackrabbit got his very long ears*
Irving, Washington. *Rip Van Winkle*, ill. by John Howe
Rip Van Winkle, ill. by Thomas Locker
Rip Van Winkle, ill. by Peter Wingham
Isele, Elizabeth. *The frog princess*
Ishii, Momoko. *The tongue-cut sparrow*
Ivanov, Anatoly. *Ol' Jake's lucky day*
I've been working on the railroad
Jack and the beanstalk. *The history of Mother Twaddle and the marvelous achievements of her son Jack*
Jack and the beanstalk, ill. by Val Biro
Jack and the beanstalk, ill. by Aljoscha Blau
Jack and the beanstalk, ill. by Lorinda Bryan Cauley
Jack and the beanstalk, ill. by Steve Cox
Jack and the beanstalk, ill. by Lydia Halverson
Jack and the beanstalk, ill. by Julek Heller
Jack and the beanstalk, ill. by John Howe
Jack and the beanstalk, ill. by Steven Kellogg
Jack and the beanstalk, ill. by Al Lorenz
Jack and the beanstalk, ill. by Ed Parker
Jack and the beanstalk, ill. by Tony Ross
Jack and the beanstalk, ill. by Niamh Sharkey
Jack and the beanstalk, ill. by Gennady Spirin
Jack and the beanstalk, ill. by William Stobbs
Jack and the beanstalk, ill. by James Warhola
Jack and the beanstalk, ill. by Anne Wilsdorf
Jack and the beanstalk = Juan y los frijoles magicos, ill. by Arnal Ballester
Jack the giant killer, ill. by Anne Wilsdorf
Jack the giantkiller, ill. by Tony Ross
Jackson, Alison. *I know an old lady who swallowed a pie*
Jackson, Bobby L. *Little Red Ronnika*

Jackson, Ellen B. *Cinder Edna*
Jacobs, Joseph. *The crock of gold*
Hereafterthis
Hudden and Dudden and Donald O'Neary
Johnny-cake, ill. by Emma Lillian Brock
Johnny-cake, ill. by William Stobbs
Master of all masters
Old Mother Wiggle-Waggle
Tattercoats
The three sillies, ill. by Paul Galdone
The three sillies, ill. by Kathryn Hewitt
The three sillies, ill. by Steven Kellogg
Jacobs, Shannon K. *The boy who loved morning*
Jaffe, Nina. *The golden flower*
In the month of Kislev
Older brother, younger brother
Tales for the seventh day
The way meat loves salt
Jagendorf, Moritz A. *Kwi-na the eagle*
Jameson, Cynthia. *The house of five bears*
Janisch, Heinz. *The merry pranks of Till Eulenspiegel*
A January fog will freeze a hog
Jaquith, Priscilla. *Bo Rabbit smart for true*
Jenkins, Steve. *Duck's breath and mouse pie*
Jennings, Linda M. *Coppelia*
The sleeping beauty
Jessell, Tim. *Amorak*
Jiang, Ji-li. *The magical Monkey King, mischief in heaven*
Johnson, Crockett. *Harold's fairy tale*
Johnson, Janet P. *How Mr. Dog got tame*
Keelboat Annie
Johnson, Paul Brett. *Jack outwits the giants*
Old Dry Fry
Johnston, Tony. *Alice Nizzy Nazzy, the Witch of Santa Fe*
The badger and the magic fan
Bigfoot Cinderrrrella
The cowboy and the black-eyed pea
Go track a yak
The tale of Rabbit and Coyote
Jones, Jennifer Berry. *Heetunka's harvest*
Juan Bobo goes to work
Kajikawa, Kimiko. *Yoshi's feast*
Kajpust, Melissa. *The peacock's pride*
Keams, Geri. *Snail girl brings water*
Keats, Ezra Jack. *John Henry*
Keens-Douglas, Richardo. *Anancy and the haunted house*
Keller, Emily Snowell. *Sleeping Bunny*
Kellogg, Steven (Stephen). *Chicken Little*
I was born about 10,000 years ago
Kent, Jack. *Jack Kent's happy-ever-after book*
Jack Kent's hokus pokus bedtime book
Keo, Ena. *The crane wife*
Kessler, Brad. *Brer Rabbit and Boss Lion*
Ketcham, Sallie. *The Christmas bird*
Ketteman, Helen. *Bubba the cowboy prince*
Kherdian, David. *The golden bracelet*
Kimmel, Eric A. *Anansi and the magic stick*
Anansi and the moss-covered rock
Anansi and the talking melon
Anansi goes fishing
Asher and the capmakers
Baba Yaga
Bearhead
Bernal and Florinda
Billy Lazroe and the King of the Sea
The birds' gift
Boots and his brothers
The Chanukkah tree
Count Silvernose
Easy work!
The Erie Canal pirates
The four gallant sisters
Gershon's monster
The greatest of all
Grizz!
The magic dreidels
One Eye, Two Eyes, Three Eyes

Lunge-Larsen, Lise. *The race of the Birkebeiners*
Lupton, Hugh. *Pirican Pic and Pirican Mor*
MacBeth, George. *Jonah and the Lord*
McCaughrean, Geraldine. *Beauty and the beast*
   Grandma Chickenlegs
   Saint George and the dragon
   Unicorns! Unicorns!
McClure, Gillian. *Selkie*
McCurdy, Michael. *The devils who learned to be good*
McDermott, Beverly Brodsky. *The crystal apple*
   The dreamtime
   The Golem
McDermott, Gerald. *Anansi the spider*
   Arrow to the sun
   Coyote
   Daniel O'Rourke
   Daughter of earth
   The fox and the stork
   Musicians of the sun
   Raven
   The stonecutter
   Tim O'Toole and the wee folk
   The voyage of Osiris
MacDonald, Amy. *Please, Malese!*
MacDonald, George. *The light princess*, ill. by Maurice Sendak
   The light princess, ill. by Katie Thamer Treherne
   Little Daylight
MacDonald, Margaret Read. *Fat cat*
   The girl who wore too much
   Mabela the clever
   The old woman who lived in a vinegar bottle
   Pickin' peas
   Slop!
   Tuck-me-in tales
MacDonald, Suse. *Once upon another*
McFarland, John. *The exploding frog and other fables from Æsop*
McGill, Alice. *Sure as sunrise*
MacGill-Callahan, Sheila. *And still the turtle watched*
   The children of Lir
   Finn MacCool and the talking fish
   The last snake in Ireland
   The seal prince
   To capture the wind
   When Solomon was king
McHale, Ethel Kharasch. *Son of thunder*
McKee, David. *The man who was going to mind the house*
McKissack, Patricia C. *Cinderella*, ill. by Tom Dunnington
   A million fish . . . more or less
   Mirandy and brother wind
McLenighan, Valjean. *Turtle and rabbit*
   What you see is what you get
   You are what you are
   You can go jump
McNaughton, Colin. *Guess who's just moved in next door?*
McNaughton, Janet. *Brave Jack and the unicorn*
Maddern, Eric. *The fire children*
Maestro, Giulio. *The tortoise's tug of war*
Maggi, María Elena. *The great canoe*
Magnus, Erica. *The boy and the devil*
   Old Lars
Mahy, Margaret. *The seven Chinese brothers*
Maitland, Antony. *Idle Jack*
Malkovych, Ivan. *The cat and the rooster*
Malotki, Ekkehart. *The magic hummingbird*
Mamin-Sibiryak, D. N. *Grey Neck*
Mann, Pamela. *The frog princess?*
Manna, Anthony L. *Mr. Semolina-Semolinus*
Manson, Christopher. *The crab prince*
   A gift for the king
   The tree in the wood
Mantinband, Gerda. *Blabbermouths*
Mark, Jan. *The Midas touch*
   The tale of Tobias
Marshall, James. *Hansel and Gretel*
   Red Riding Hood
Marston, Elsa. *The fox maiden*
Martin, Bill (William Ivan). *Sounds of laughter*

Martin, Claire. *Boots and the glass mountain*, ill. by Gennady Spirin
   The race of the golden apples
Martin, Francesca. *Clever Tortoise*
   The honey hunters
Martin, Rafe. *The eagle's gift*
   Foolish rabbit's big mistake
   The hungry tigress
   The language of birds
   The rough-face girl
   The Shark God
   The twelve months
Masini, Beatrice. *A brave little princess*
Mason, Jane B. *The flying horse*
Mathews, Judith. *Nathaniel Willy, scared silly*
Matsuno, Masako. *Taro and the bamboo shoot*
Matsutani, Miyoko. *The fisherman under the sea*
   The witch's magic cloth
Maugham, W. Somerset (William Somerset). *Princess September and the nightingale*
Mayer, Marianna. *Baba Yaga and Vasilisa the Brave*
   Beauty and the beast
   The black horse
   The little jewel box
   My first book of nursery tales
   Pegasus
   Perseus
   The spirit of the blue light
Mayer, Mercer. *The pied piper of Hamelin*
Mead, Katherine. *How spiders got eight legs*
Medearis, Angela Shelf. *The freedom riddle*
   Seven spools of thread
   The singing man
   Tailypo
   Too much talk
Medicine Crow, Joseph. *Brave Wolf and the Thunderbird*
Melmed, Laura Krauss. *Moishe's miracle*
   Prince Nautilus
   The rainbabies
Mendelson, S. T. *Stupid Emilien*
Merriam, Eve. *Epaminondas*
Meserve, Adria. *Smog, the city dog*
Metaxas, Eric. *The boy and the whale*
   The fool and the flying ship
   The gardener's apprentice
   The monkey people
   Puss in boots
   The white cat
Michael, Emory H. *Androcles and the lion*
Midge, Tiffany. *Buffalo*
Mike, Jan M. *The bird maiden*
   Clever Karlis
   Gift of the Nile
   Juan Bobo and the horse of seven colors
   Opossum and the great firemaker
Milhous, Katherine. *The turnip*
Miller, Edna. *Mousekin's fables*
Miller, Moira. *The moon dragon*
Miller, William. *The knee-high man*
Milligan, Bryce. *Brigid's cloak*
   The prince of Ireland and the three magic stallions
Mills, Lauren A. *Fairy wings*
   Tatterhood and the hobgoblins
Milne, A. A. (Alan Alexander). *The magic hill*
   Prince Rabbit
Minters, Frances. *Cinder-Elly*
   Sleepless Beauty
Mirkovic, Irene. *The greedy shopkeeper*
Mitchell, Marianne. *Joe Cinders*
Mobley, Jane. *The star husband*
Moerbeek, Kees. *The diary of Hansel and Gretel*
Moeri, Louise. *Star Mother's youngest child*
Mollel, Tololwa M. (Tololwa Marti). *Ananse's feast*
   Big boy
   Dume's roar
   The flying tortoise
   The king and the tortoise
   Kitoto the mighty

Pitre, Felix. *Paco and the witch*
Pittman, Helena Clare. *The gift of the willows*
   A grain of rice
Plante, Patricia. *The turtle and the two ducks*
Plume, Ilse. *The story of Befana*
Podwal, Mark H. *Golem*
Pogorelsky, Antony. *The black hen, or, The underground inhabitants*
   The little black hen
Pohrt, Tom. *Coyote goes walking*
Polacco, Patricia. *Babushka's Mother Goose*
   Luba and the wren
   Rechenka's eggs
Pollock, Penny. *The turkey girl*
   When the moon is full
Porazinska, Janina. *The enchanted book*
Powers, Daniel. *Jiro's pearl*
Prather, Ray. *The ostrich girl*
Presencer, Alain. *Roaring lion tales*
Preussler, Otfried. *The tale of the unicorn*
Price, Kathy (Kathy Z.). *The Bourbon Street musicians*
The prince who knew his fate
Prokofiev, Sergei Sergeievitch. *Peter and the wolf,* ill. by Reg
    Cartwright
   Peter and the wolf, ill. by Warren Chappell
   Peter and the wolf, ill. by Barbara Cooney
   Peter and the wolf, ill. by Julia Gukova
   Peter and the wolf, ill. by Frans Haacken
   Peter and the wolf, ill. by Alan Howard
   Peter and the wolf, ill. by Charles Mikolaycak
   Peter and the wolf, ill. by Jörg Müller
   Peter and the wolf, ill. by Josef Palecek
   Peter and the wolf, ill. by Kozo Shimizu
   Peter and the wolf, retold and ill. by Vladimir Vagin
   Peter and the wolf, ill. by Erna Voigt
Prose, Francine. *The angel's mistake*
   The demons' mistake
   Dybbuk
   You never know
Pullman, Philip. *Puss in boots,* ill. by Ian Beck
Pushkin, Aleksandr Sergeevich. *The tale of Tsar Saltan*
Pyle, Howard. *The Swan Maiden*
Quackenbush, Robert M. *Clementine*
   She'll be comin' 'round the mountain
   Skip to my Lou
   There'll be a hot time in the old town tonight
Quigley, Lillian Fox. *The blind men and the elephant*
Radunsky, Vladimir. *Manneken pis*
Rae, Jennifer. *Dog tales*
Ransome, Arthur. *The fool of the world and the flying ship*
Raphael, Elaine. *Turnabout*
Rappaport, Doreen. *Journey of Meng*
   The long-haired girl
   The new king
Rattigan, Jama Kim. *The woman in the moon*
Rayevsky, Inna. *The talking tree*
Reesink, Marijke. *The golden treasure*
   The princess who always ran away
Reit, Seymour. *Rebus bears*
Renberg, Dalia Hardof. *King Solomon and the bee*
Repchuk, Caroline. *The race*
Richard, Françoise. *On Cat Mountain*
Richardson, Jean. *The sleeping beauty*
Riggio, Anita. *Beware the Brindlebeast*
Ringgold, Faith. *The invisible princesses*
Riordan, James. *The coming of Night*
   The Snowmaiden
   The three magic gifts
Robbins, Maria Polushkin. *Bubba and Babba*
   The little hen and the giant
Robbins, Ruth. *Baboushka and the three kings*
Roberts, Lynn (Lynn M.). *Cinderella, an Art Deco love story*
   Rapunzel, a groovy fairy tale
Robertson, Joanne. *Sea witches*
Robins, Arthur. *The teeny tiny woman*
Robinson, Adjai. *Femi and old grandaddie*
Robinson, Fay. *Where did all the dragons go?*
Rockwell, Anne F. *The acorn tree and other folktales*

Bafana
The boy who wouldn't obey
The old woman and her pig and 10 other stories
Poor Goose
Romulus and Remus
The three bears and 15 other stories
Thump thump thump!
The wolf who had a wonderful dream
The wonderful eggs of Furicchia
Rodanas, Kristina. *The dragonfly's tale*
   Follow the stars
Rogasky, Barbara. *The water of life*
Rogers, Margaret. *Green is beautiful*
Rohmer, Harriet. *How we came to the fifth world*
   The invisible hunters
   Mother scorpion country
Ronay, Jadja. *Ginger*
Root, Phyllis. *Aunt Nancy and Old Man Trouble*
   Grandmother Winter
   Soup for supper
Rosales, Melodye Benson. *Leola and the honeybears*
Rose, Anne K. *Akimba and the magic cow*
   Pot full of luck
   Spider in the sky
   The talking turnip
   The triumphs of Fuzzy Fogtop
Rosen, Michael (1946–). *Crow and Hawk*
Ross, Gayle. *How Turtle's back was cracked*
   The legend of the Windigo
Ross, Tony. *The boy who cried wolf*
   The enchanted pig
   Hansel and Gretel
   The pied piper of Hamelin
   Stone soup
Roth, Susan L. *Brave Martha and the dragon*
   Fire came to the earth people
   Kanahena
   The story of light
Rothenberg, Joan Keller. *Inside-out grandma*
Roughsey, Dick. *The giant devil-dingo*
Rounds, Glen. *The boll weevil*
   Casey Jones
   Sweet Betsy from Pike
Rumford, James. *The cloudmakers*
   Nine animals and the well
Sage, James. *Coyote makes man*
Sahagun, Bernardino de. *Spirit child*
Salley, Coleen. *Epossumondas*
Sanderson, Ruth. *Cinderella*
   The enchanted wood
   The golden mare, the firebird, and the magic ring
   Papa Gatto
Sanfield, Steve. *Bit by bit*
   Just rewards, or, Who is that man in the moon and what's he doing
    up there anyway?
San José, Christine. *Sleeping Beauty*
San Souci, Daniel. *In the moonlight mist*
   The rabbit and the dragon king
San Souci, Robert D. *Brave Margaret*
   Callie Ann and Mistah Bear
   Cendrillon
   Cinderella Skeleton
   The enchanted tapestry
   The faithful friend
   The hired hand
   The Hobyahs
   The house in the sky
   The legend of Scarface
   The legend of Sleepy Hollow
   Little gold star
   Little Pierre
   Nicholas Pipe
   Pedro and the monkey
   Peter and the blue witch baby
   The red heels
   The samurai's daughter
   The secret of the stones

The story of the three bears, ill. by William Stobbs
The three bears, ill. by Byron Barton
The three bears, ill. by Paul Galdone
The three bears, ill. by Feodor Rojankovsky
The three bears, ill. by Robin Spowart
The three bears [board book], ill. by Thea Kliros
The three little pigs. *The original three little pigs re-told*, ill. by Jonathan Smith
The story of the three little pigs, ill. by L. Leslie Brooke
The story of the three little pigs, ill. by William Stobbs
Three little pigs [Facsimile ed]
The three little pigs, ill. by Val Biro
The three little pigs, ill. by Gavin Bishop
The three little pigs, ill. by Caroline Bucknall
The three little pigs, ill. by Stephen Cartwright
The three little pigs, ill. by Lorinda Bryan Cauley
The three little pigs, ill. by Jean Claverie
The three little pigs, ill. by Doug Cushman
The three little pigs, ill. by William Pène Du Bois
The three little pigs, ill. by Paul Galdone
The three little pigs, ill. by Madelaine Gill
The three little pigs, ill. by Rob Hefferan
The three little pigs, ill. by Steven Kellogg
The three little pigs, ill. by David McPhail
The three little pigs, ill. by James Marshall
The three little pigs, ill. by Paul Meisel
The three little pigs, ill. by Rodney Peppé
The three little pigs, ill. by Edda Reinl
The three little pigs, ill. by John Wallner
The three little pigs, ill. by Irma Wilde
The three little pigs, ill. by Margot Zemach
The three little pigs and the big bad wolf
The three little pigs and the fox
The three little pigs [board book], ill. by Thea Kliros
The three pigs, ill. by Tony Ross
Who's at the door?
Tildes, Phyllis Limbacher. *The magic babushka*
Tolhurst, Marilyn. *Somebody and the three Blairs*
Tolstoy, Aleksey Nikolayevich. *The enormous turnip*
The gigantic turnip, ill. by Niamh Sharkey
The great big enormous turnip
Tolstoy, Leo. *How much land does a man need?*
Tom Thumb. *The adventures of Tom Thumb*, ill. by Kinuko Y. Craft
Grimm Tom Thumb
Tom Thumb, ill. by L. Leslie Brooke
Tom Thumb, ill. by Dennis Hockerman
Tom Thumb, ill. by Felix Hoffmann
Tom Thumb, ill. by Lidia Postma
Tom Thumb, ill. by Richard Jesse Watson
Tom Thumb, ill. by William Wiesner
Tom Tit Tot. *Tom Tit Tot*
Tompert, Ann. *The jade horse, the cricket, and the peach stone*
Saint Nicholas
Tooinsky, Izzi. *The turkey prince*
Torre, Betty L. *The luminous pearl*
Towle, Faith M. *The magic cooking pot*
Toye, William. *Fire stealer*
How summer came to Canada
The loon's necklace
The mountain goats of Temlaham
Tresselt, Alvin R. *The mitten*
Tripp, Wallace. *The tale of a pig*
Trivizas, Eugenios. *The three little wolves and the big bad pig*
Troughton, Joanna. *Make-believe tales*
The quail's egg
Tortoise's dream
What made Tiddalik laugh
Who will be the sun?
Tseng, Grace. *White tiger, blue serpent*
Tsultim, Yeshe. *The mouse king*
Tune, Suelyn Ching. *How Maui slowed the sun*
Turkle, Brinton. *Deep in the forest*
Turska, Krystyna. *The magician of Cracow*
The woodcutter's duck
Uchida, Yoshiko. *The magic purse*
The two foolish cats
The wise old woman

Ungar, Richard. *Rachel captures the moon*
Va, Leong. *A letter to the king*
Vaës, Alain. *The princess and the pea*
Vagin, Vladimir Vasilévich. *The enormous carrot*
Valentine, Johnny. *The duke who outlawed jelly beans and other stories*
Van Kampen, Vlasta. *Bear tales*
It couldn't be worse
Van Laan, Nancy. *The legend of El Dorado*
The magic bean tree
Rainbow crow
Shingebiss
So say the little monkeys
Van Rynbach, Iris. *The soup stone*
Van Woerkom, Dorothy. *Alexandra the rock-eater*
The queen who couldn't bake gingerbread
The rat, the ox and the zodiac
Sea frog, city frog
Varga, Judy. *The mare's egg*
Vaughan, Richard Lee. *Eagle boy*
Verma, Jatinder Nath. *The story of Divaali*
Vernon, Adele. *The riddle*
Vesey, A. *The princess and the frog*
Villoldo, Alberto. *Skeleton woman*
Vojtech, Anna. *Marushka and the Month Brothers*
Volkmer, Jane Anne. *Song of Chirimia = La Musica de la Chirimia*
Vozar, David. *Yo, hungry wolf!*
Waddell, Martin. *The tough princess*
Wade, Barrie. *Cinderella*
The three billy goats gruff
Wahl, Jan. *Little Eight John*
Little Johnny Buttermilk
Waite, Michael P. *Jojofu*
Walburg, Lori. *The legend of the candy cane*
Walker, Barbara K. (Barbara Kerlin). *New patches for old*
Wall, Lina Mao. *Judge Rabbit and the tree spirit*
Wallis, Diz. *Battle of the beasts*
Walsh, Ellen Stoll. *Jack's tale*
Walsh, Grahame L. *Didane the koala*
The goori goori bird
Walsh, Jill Paton. *Pepi and the secret names*
Walt Disney Productions. *Walt Disney's Snow White and the seven dwarfs*
Walter, Mildred Pitts. *Ty's one-man band*
Wang, Rosalind C. *The fourth question*
The treasure chest
Ward, Helen. *The golden pear*
Watkins, Hope (Brister). *The cunning fox and other tales*
Watts, Bernadette. *St. Francis and the proud crow*
Weedn, Flavia. *The elephant prince*
The enchanted tree
The giant's garden
The magic cap
The moon maiden
The ragged peddler
The star gift
Weil, Lisl. *Pandora's box*
Weiss, Harvey. *The sooner hound*
Weiss, Nicki. *If you're happy and you know it*
Wells, Rosemary. *The little lame prince*
Wells, Ruth. *The farmer and the poor god*
Westcott, Nadine Bernard. *Skip to my Lou*
Westerberg, Christine. *The cap that mother made*
Westwood, Jennifer. *Going to Squintum's*
White, Carolyn. *Whuppity Stoorie*
Whitethorne, Baje. *Sunpainters*
Widdecombe Fair
Wiesner, David. *The loathsome dragon*
Wilde, Oscar. *Fairy tales of Oscar Wilde*
The happy prince
The selfish giant, ill. by S. Saelig Gallagher
The selfish giant, ill. by Dom Mansell
The selfish giant, ill. by Fabian Negrin
The selfish giant, ill. by Lisbeth Zwerger
The star child, ill. by Fiona French
Wildsmith, Brian. *The true cross*
Wilhelm, Hans. *All for the best*
Willard, Nancy. *Shadow story*

Willey, Margaret. *Clever Beatrice, an Upper Peninsula conte*
   Clever Beatrice and the best little pony
Williams, Arlene. *Dragon soup*
Williams, Jay. *The practical princess*
   The surprising things Maui did
Williams, Julie Stewart. *And the birds appeared*
Williams, Laura E. *The long silk strand*
   Torch fishing with the sun
Williams, Maria. *How Raven stole the sun*
Williams, Sheron. *And in the beginning . . .*
Wilson, Barbara Ker. *The turtle and the island*
Wilson, Sarah. *Beware the dragons!*
Winter, Jeanette. *The girl and the moon man*
Winthrop, Elizabeth. *The little humpbacked horse*
   Vasilissa the beautiful
Wisniewski, David. *Elfwyn's saga*
   Golem
   Sundiata
   The warrior and the wise man
Wolf, Ann. *The rabbit and the turtle*
Wolf, Gita. *The very hungry lion*
Wolff, Ferida. *The emperor's garden*
Wolfson, Margaret. *Turtle songs*
Wolkstein, Diane. *The banza*
   Bouki dances the Kokioko
   The cool ride in the sky
   The legend of Sleepy Hollow
   The magic wings
   Oom razoom; or, Go I know not where, Bring back I know not what
   Sun Mother wakes the world
   White wave
Wood, Audrey. *Heckedy Peg*
   The rainbow bridge
Wood, Douglas. *Rabbit and the moon*
Woodworth, Viki. *Fairy tale jokes*
Wooldridge, Connie Nordhielm. *The legend of Strap Buckner*
   Wicked Jack
Wright, Freire. *Beauty and the beast*
Wright, Jill. *The old woman and the Willy Nilly Man*
Wright, Sue (Sue M.). *The Christmas path*
Xiong, Blia. *Nine-in-one Grr! Grr!*
Yacowitz, Caryn. *The jade stone*
Yagawa, Sumiko. *The crane wife*
Yashima, Taro. *Seashore story*
Ye, Ting-xing. *Three monks, no water*
Yeoman, John. *The wild washerwomen*
Yep, Laurence. *Dragon prince*
   The junior thunder lord
   The Khan's daughter
   The shell woman and the king
   Tiger woman
Yohannes, Gebregeorgis. *Silly Mammo = Kilu Mammo*
Yolen, Jane. *Child of faerie, child of earth*
   The firebird
   The flying witch
   The girl in the golden bower
   Greyling
   King Long Shanks
   Little Mouse and Elephant
   Pegasus, the flying horse
   The sea king
   Sky dogs
   The three bears rhyme book
Young, Ed (Edward). *Cat and Rat*
   Donkey trouble
   High on a hill
   Little Plum
   Lon Po Po
   The lost horse
   Night visitors
   The rooster's horns
   The terrible Nung Gwama
   What about me?
Youngquist, Cathrene Valente. *The three Billygoats Gruff and Mean Calypso Joe*
Zelinsky, Paul O. *The maid and the mouse and the odd-shaped house*
Zemach, Harve. *Duffy and the devil*

Nail soup
Zemach, Kaethe. *The beautiful rat*
Zemach, Margot. *It could always be worse*
   Jake and Honeybunch go to heaven
   The little tiny woman
   The three wishes
Zeman, Ludmila. *Sindbad*
   Sindbad in the land of giants
   Sindbad's secret
Zhang, Song Nan. *The five heavenly emperors and other Chinese myths from the creation*
Ziefert, Harriet. *Cow in the house*
   Little Red Riding Hood
   The snow child
   The turnip
   When I first came to this land
Zijlstra, Tjerk. *Benny and his geese*
Zola, Meguido. *The dream of promise*
Zwerger, Lisbeth. *Swan Lake*

Folk & fairy tales – pourquoi tales

Alexander, Lloyd. *How the cat swallowed thunder*
Bernhard, Emery. *How Snowshoe Hare rescued the sun*
Bruchac, Joseph. *How Chipmunk got his stripes*
Crespo, George. *How the sea began*
Cummings, Pat. *Ananse and the lizard*
Dixon, Ann. *How raven brought light to people*
Dwyer, Mindy. *Aurora, a tale of the Northern Lights*
Kimmel, Eric A. *Why the snake crawls on its belly*
Kipling, Rudyard. *How the camel got his hump*, ill. by Quentin Blake
   How the camel got his hump, ill. by Tim Raglin
   How the camel got his hump, ill. by Lisbeth Zwerger
   How the leopard got his spots, ill. by Caroline Ebborn
   How the leopard got his spots, ill. by Lori Lohstoeter
   How the rhinoceros got his skin
Knutson, Barbara. *How the guinea fowl got her spots*
Larson, Bonnie. *When animals were people = Cuando los animales eran personas*
Lester, Julius. *Why heaven is far away*
Lunge-Larsen, Lise. *The legend of the lady slipper*
McDermott, Gerald. *Jabuti the tortoise*
McGuire-Turcotte, Casey A. *How Honu the turtle got his shell*
Marcos, subcomandante. *The story of colors = La historia de los colores*
Poole, Amy Lowry. *How the rooster got his crown*
Richards, Jean. *How the elephant got his trunk*
Robbins, Ruth. *How the first rainbow was made*
Rosen, Michael (1946–). *How the animals got their colors*
Shepard, Aaron. *Master man*
Sherman, Pat. *The sun's daughter*
Troughton, Joanna. *How rabbit stole the fire*
   How the birds changed their feathers
Wolkstein, Diane. *The day Ocean came to visit*

Food

Abrams, Pam. *Now I eat my ABC's*
Adams, Jean Ekman. *Clarence and the purple horse bounce into town*
Adler, David A. *Bunny rabbit rebus*
Æsop. *The fox and the grapes*
Ahlberg, Janet. *Yum yum*
Alborough, Jez. *Ice cream bear*
   It's the bear
Alcott, Louisa May. *An old-fashioned Thanksgiving*
Alderson, Sue Ann. *Wherever bears be*
Aliki. *Milk from cow to carton*
Allamand, Pascale. *Cocoa beans and daisies*
Allard, Harry. *The cactus flower bakery*
Allen, Laura Jean. *Rollo and Tweedy and the case of the missing cheese*
Allen, Robert. *Ten little babies eat*
Ambrus, Victor G. *Country wedding*
Andersen, H. C. (Hans Christian). *The nightingale*, ill. by Christopher Santoro
Andrews, Jan. *Very last first time*
Angelou, Maya. *Angelina of Italy*
Appelt, Kathi. *Watermelon day*
Armitage, Ronda. *Ice creams for Rosie*

The lighthouse keeper's lunch
Arnold, Caroline. *Mealtime for zoo animals*
Arnosky, Jim. *Raccoons and ripe corn*
Aronin, Ben. *The secret of the Sabbath fish*
Asch, Frank. *Good lemonade*
  Monsieur Saguette and his baguette
  Moonbear
  Popcorn
Auch, Mary Jane. *The princess and the pizza*
Axelrod, Amy. *Pigs in the pantry*
  Pigs will be pigs
Aylesworth, Jim. *The burger and the hot dog*
Azarian, Mary. *The tale of John Barleycorn or, From barley to beer*
Bach, Alice. *The smartest bear and his brother Oliver*
Backx, Patsy. *Josie and Mr. Fernandez*
Balan, Bruce. *Pie in the sky*
Banks, Kate (Katherine A.). *Alphabet soup*
Baranski, Joan Sullivan. *Round is a pancake*
Barasch, Lynne. *Rodney's inside story*
Barbato, Juli. *Mom's night out*
Barbour, Karen. *Little Nino's pizzeria*
Barklem, Jill. *The secret staircase*
Barrett, Judi. *An apple a day*
  Cloudy with a chance of meatballs
  Pickles to Pittsburgh
Barron, Rex. *Fed up!*
Bass, Jules. *Herb, the vegetarian dragon*
Basso, Bill. *The top of the pizzas*
Baugh, Dolores M. *Supermarket*
Beil, Karen Magnuson. *A cake all for me!*
Benchley, Nathaniel. *Walter the homing pigeon*
Benedictus, Roger. *Fifty million sausages*
Benjamin, Alan. *Ribtickle Town*
Berenstain, Stan. *The Berenstain bears and too much junk food*
Berson, Harold. *Pop! goes the turnip*
  The rats who lived in the delicatessen
Beskow, Elsa Maartman. *Peter in Blueberry Land*
  Peter's adventures in Blueberry Land
Bethell, Jean. *Hooray for Henry*
Biro, Val. *Gumdrop and the great sausage caper*
Black, Irma (Simonton). *Is this my dinner?*
Blackstone, Stella. *Making minestrone*
Bolliger, Max. *The giants' feast*
  The golden apple
Bond, Michael. *Paddington and the knickerbocker rainbow*
Bonning, Tony. *Fox tale soup*
Boutell, Clarence Burley. *The fat baron*
Brandenberg, Franz. *Fresh cider and apple pie*
Breeze, Lynn. *Baby's food*
Brenner, Barbara A. *Beef stew*
Brett, Jan. *Hedgie's surprise*
Brierley, Louise. *King Lion and his cooks*
Bright, Robert. *Gregory, the noisiest and strongest boy in Grangers Grove*
Brimner, Larry Dane. *Country Bear's good neighbor*
Broome, Errol. *The smallest koala*
Brown, Judith Gwyn. *Max and the truffle pig*
Brown, Marc Tolon. *D. W., the picky eater*
  Pickle things
Brown, Marcia. *Stone soup*
Bruna, Dick. *The fish*
Budd, Lillian. *The pie wagon*
Buehner, Caralyn. *A job for Wittilda*
Bugni, Alice. *Moose racks, bear tracks and other Alaska kidsnacks*
Burch, Robert. *The hunting trip*
Burnard, Damon. *The amazing adventures of Soupy Boy*
Burningham, John. *Avocado baby*
  The cupboard
  Where's Julius?
Burt, Olive (Woolley). *Let's find out about bread*
Burton, Jane. *Animals eating*
Butler, Daphne. *What happens when food cooks?*
Calhoun, Mary. *Audubon cat*
  The hungry leprechaun
Calmenson, Stephanie. *Dinner at the Panda Palace*
  Kinderkittens, who took the cookie from the cookie jar?
Capucilli, Karen. *The jelly bean fun book*

Carle, Eric. *My very first book of food*
  Pancakes, pancakes
  Today is Monday
  Walter the baker
Carlson, Nancy L. *Harriet and George's Christmas treat*
Carlstrom, Nancy White. *Moose in the garden*
Carney, Margaret (Margaret Rose). *At Grandpa's sugar bush*
Carrick, Donald. *Milk*
Caseley, Judith. *Grandpa's garden lunch*
Cauley, Lorinda Bryan. *Pease porridge hot*
Cazet, Denys. *Lucky me*
Chadwick, Tim. *Cabbage moon*
Chall, Marsha Wilson. *Sugarbush spring*
Chalmers, Audrey. *Hundreds and hundreds of pancakes*
Charlip, Remy. *Peanut butter party*
Chavarría-Cháirez, Becky. *Magda's tortillas = Las tortillas de Magada*
Chen, Chih-Yuan. *On my way to buy eggs*
Cherry, Lynne. *How Groundhog's garden grew*
Chichester Clark, Emma. *Lunch with Aunt Augusta*
Child, Lauren. *I will never not ever eat a tomato*
Childress, Mark. *Joshua and the big bad blue crabs*
Christelow, Eileen. *Don't wake up Mama!*
Clément, Claude. *The hungry duckling*
Coatsworth, Elizabeth. *Under the green willow*
Cocca-Leffler, Maryann. *Wednesday is spaghetti day*
Cohen, Peter Zachary. *Olson's meat pies*
Collins, Ross. *Alvie eats soup*
Coltman, Paul. *Tinker Jim*
Compestine, Ying Chang. *The runaway rice cake*
  The story of chopsticks
  The story of noodles
Conrad, Pam. *Molly and the strawberry day*
Coontz, Otto. *Starring Rosa*
Cooper, Elisha. *Ice cream*
Coplans, Peta. *Spaghetti for Suzy*
Cousins, Lucy. *Maisy makes gingerbread*
Cowley, Joy. *Big moon tortilla*
Cox, Judy. *Now we can have a wedding!*
  Rabbit pirates
  The West Texas chili monster
Coy, John. *Two old potatoes and me*
Croll, Carolyn. *Too many babas*
Crook, Connie Brummel. *Maple moon*
Cruickshank, Margrit. *We're going to feed the ducks*
Curious George and the pizza
Curious George goes to a chocolate factory
Curious George goes to an ice cream shop
Curious George makes pancakes
Cushman, Doug. *Possum stew*
Czernecki, Stefan. *The sleeping bread*
Dahl, Michael. *From the garden*
Daly, Niki. *Ben's gingerbread man*
Darling, Abigail. *Teddy bears' picnic cookbook*
Darrow, Sharon. *Old Thunder and Miss Raney*
Davies, Kay. *My apple*
Davis, Aubrey. *Bagels from Benny*
  Bone button borscht
  The enormous potato
  Sody salleratus
Davis, Lee. *Feeding time*
Davis, Maggie S. *The rinky-dink café*
Davison, Martine. *Kevin and the school nurse*
Degen, Bruce. *Jamberry*
Delton, Judy. *Rabbit finds a way*
Demarest, Chris L. *No peas for Nellie*
De Paola, Tomie (Thomas Anthony). *Pancakes for breakfast*
  The popcorn book
  Tony's bread
De Regniers, Beatrice Schenk. *Sam and the impossible thing*
  What did you put in your pocket?
DeRubertis, Barbara. *Lulu's lemonade*
Desimini, Lisa. *Moon soup*
Devlin, Wende. *Old Witch and the polka-dot ribbon*
DiTerlizzi, Tony. *Jimmy Zangwow's out-of-this-world, moon pie adventure*
Dixon, Ann. *The blueberry shoe*

Dodd, Lynley. *The apple tree*
Donnelly, Jennifer. *Humble pie*
Donohue, Dorothy. *Veggie soup*
Dooley, Norah. *Everybody bakes bread*
    Everybody brings noodles
    Everybody cooks rice
    Everybody serves soup
Downey, Lynn. *Sing, Henrietta! Sing!*
Doyle, Malachy. *Hungry! Hungry! Hungry!*
    Jody's beans
Dragonwagon, Crescent. *This is the bread I baked for Ned*
Drescher, Henrik. *The boy who ate around*
Drucker, Malka. *Grandma's latkes*
Dubowski, Cathy East. *Picky Nicky*
Dumas, Bianca. *Tia Luisa, the magical cook*
Du Quette, Keith. *Ripping day for a picnic*
Durant, Alan. *Snake supper*
Eclare, Melanie. *A harvest of color*
Edwards, Frank B. *Is the spaghetti ready?*
Edwards, Julie Andrews. *Dumpy's apple shop*
Edwards, Pamela Duncan. *Four famished foxes and Fosdyke*
Egan, Tim. *Chestnut Cove*
    The trial of Cardigan Jones
Ehlert, Lois. *Eating the alphabet*
    Growing vegetable soup
Elliott, George. *The boy who loved bananas*
Emberley, Ed (Edward Randolph). *Thanks, Mom!*
Emberley, Rebecca. *My food = Mi comida*
Enderle, Judith Ross. *Something's happening on Calabash Street*
Engel, Diana. *Gino Badino*
English, Karen. *Just right stew*
Esterl, Arnica. *The fine round cake*
Evans, Katie. *Hunky Dory ate it*
Everitt, Betsy. *Mean soup*
Facklam, Margery. *I eat dinner*
Faglia, Maeto. *Happy birthday, I'm 1*
    Happy birthday, I'm 2
    Happy birthday, I'm 3
    Happy birthday, I'm 4
Farber, Erica. *Ooey gooey*
Farish, Terry. *The cat who liked potato soup*
Faulkner, Keith. *The wide-mouthed frog*
Fearnley, Jan. *Mr. Wolf's pancakes*
Feder, Harriet K. *What can you do with a bagel?*
Fernandes, Kim. *Visiting granny*
Flanagan, Alice K. *The Zieglers and their apple orchard*
Fleming, Candace. *A big cheese for the White House*
    Gator gumbo
Fleming, Denise. *Lunch*
Flory, Jane. *We'll have a friend for lunch*
Fontaine, Jan. *The spaghetti tree*
Forest, Heather. *Stone soup*
    The woman who flummoxed the fairies
Fowler, Allan. *Corn . . . on and off the cob*
Fowler, Richard. *Cat's cake*
Fox, Christyan. *Count to ten, PiggyWiggy!*
Fox, Mem. *Possum magic*
French, Vivian. *Oliver's fruit salad*
    Oliver's vegetables
Frost, Helen. *Eating right*
    The fruit group
    The grain group
Gabler, Mirko. *The alphabet soup*
Gackenbach, Dick. *Barker's crime*
    Mother Rabbit's son Tom
Gág, Wanda. *The funny thing*
Galdone, Paul. *The magic porridge pot*
Ganeri, Anita. *The hunt for food*
Gantschev, Ivan. *RumpRump*
Garland, Michael. *The President and Mom's apple pie*
Garrett, Ann. *What's for lunch?*
Geeslin, Campbell. *How Nanita learned to make flan*
Gelbard, Jane. *My eating book*
Gershator, David. *Palampam Day*
Gibbons, Gail. *Apples*
    The berry book
    The honey makers

    The milk makers
    The missing maple syrup sap mystery
    The seasons of Arnold's apple tree
Giffard, Hannah. *Red Fox*
Gilman, Rita Golden. *Rice is life*
The gingerbread boy. *Gingerbread baby*, ill. by Jan Brett
    The gingerbread boy, ill. by Richard Egielski
    The gingerbread boy, ill. by Paul Galdone
    The gingerbread boy, ill. by Joan Elizabeth Goodman
    The gingerbread boy, ill. by William Curtis Holdsworth
    The gingerbread man, ill. by Carol Jones
    The gingerbread man, ill. by Barbara McClintock
    The gingerbread man, ill. by Diana Mayo
    The gingerbread man, ill. by Gerald Rose
    The gingerbread man, ill. by Bonnie & Bill Rutherford
    The pancake boy
Glaser, Linda. *Mrs. Greenberg's messy Hanukkah*
Glyman, Caroline A. *Learning your ABC's of nutrition*
Goble, Paul. *The return of the buffaloes*
Goldin, Barbara Diamond. *Cakes and miracles*
    A mountain of blintzes
Goldstein, Bobbye S. *What's on the menu?*
Goldstone, Bruce. *The beastly feast*
Goodall, John S. *The surprise picnic*
Gray, Kes. *Eat your peas*
Greeley, Valerie. *Where's my share?*
Greene, Carol. *The world's biggest birthday cake*
Greene, Ellin. *The pumpkin giant*
Greene, Jacqueline Dembar. *What his father did*
Greenway, Shirley. *What do I eat?*
Gretz, Susanna. *It's your turn, Roger*
    Rabbit food
    Teddy bears stay indoors
Gross, Ruth Belov. *What's on my plate?*
Gullikson, Sandy. *Trouble for breakfast*
Gunthrop, Karen. *Adam and the wolf*
Haas, Jessie. *Sugaring*
Haddon, Mark. *Toni and the tomato soup*
Hafner, Marylin. *Molly and Emmett's surprise garden*
Hale, Irina. *Chocolate mouse and sugar pig*
Hale, Linda. *The glorious Christmas soup party*
Hall, Donald. *The milkman's boy*
Hall, Margaret. *Corn*
    Peanuts
Hall, Zoe. *The apple pie tree*
Harper, Jo. *Jalapeno Hal*
Harris, Lee. *Never let your cat make lunch for you*
Hartman, Bob. *Aunt Mabel's table*
    Lobster for lunch
    Who brought the bread?
    The wolf who cried boy
Hayes, Sarah. *Eat up, Gemma*
Head, Judith. *Mud soup*
Heiligman, Deborah. *Mike Swan, sink or swim*
Heller, Linda. *Lily at the table*
Heller, Nicholas. *Ogres! ogres! ogres!*
    Peas
Hellsing, Lennart. *The wonderful pumpkin*
Helmer, Marilyn. *Yummy riddles*
Henkes, Kevin. *Sheila Rae's peppermint stick*
Henley, Claire. *Dinnertime*
Hennessy, B. G. (Barbara G.). *Jake baked the cake*
Hest, Amy. *You can do it, Sam*
Hill, Eric. *Spot bakes a cake*
Hill, Mary (1977–). *Let's make pizza*
    Let's make tacos
Hill, Susan. *Ruby bakes a cake*
Hippely, Hilary Horder. *A song for Lena*
Hirsh, Marilyn. *Leela and the watermelon*
    Potato pancakes all around
Hiskey, Iris. *I like a snack on an iceberg*
Hoban, Lillian. *Arthur's back to school day*
Hoban, Russell. *Bread and jam for Frances*
    Dinner at Alberta's
    The marzipan pig
Hoberman, Mary Ann. *The seven silly eaters*
Holden, Edith. *The hedgehog feast*

Holl, Adelaide. *Small Bear solves a mystery*
Holub, Joan. *The pizza that we made*
Hong, Lily Toy. *How the ox star fell from heaven*
Hoopes, Lyn Littlefield. *The unbeatable bread*
Hopkins, Lee Bennett. *How do you make an elephant float?*
Horácek, Petr. *Strawberries are red*
Hot potato
Houston, Gloria. *But no candy*
Howard, Jane R. *When I'm hungry*
Howe, James. *Hot fudge*
Howland, Naomi. *The matzah man*
Hughes, Monica. *A handful of seeds*
Hughes, Peter. *The emperor's oblong pancake*
  The king who loved candy
Hurwitz, Johanna. *Ethan out and about*
Hutchins, Pat. *Don't forget the bacon!*
  Ten red apples
Inkpen, Mick. *Gumboot's chocolatey day*
  Kipper's snacktime
  Wibbly Pig likes bananas
Jack Sprat. *The life of Jack Sprat, his wife and his cat*
Jackson, Alison. *I know an old lady who swallowed a pie*
Jackson, Ellen B. *Brown cow, green grass, yellow mellow sun*
  The impossible riddle
Jacobs, Joseph. *Johnny-cake*, ill. by Emma Lillian Brock
  Johnny-cake, ill. by William Stobbs
Janice. *Little Bear's pancake party*
  Little Bear's Sunday breakfast
Johnson, David. *Oh, that Nuzzle!*
Joly-Berbesson, Fanny. *Marceau Bonappetit*
Jonovitz, Marilyn. *Good morning, Little Fox*
Kadono, Eiko. *Grandpa's soup*
Kahl, Virginia. *The Duchess bakes a cake*
  The perfect pancake
  Plum pudding for Christmas
Kalz, Jill. *Fruits*
Kandoian, Ellen. *Is anybody up?*
Kantor, MacKinlay. *The preposterous week*
Kasza, Keiko. *The wolf's chicken stew*
Keillor, Garrison. *The old man who loved cheese*
Keller, Laurie. *Arnie the doughnut*
Kelley, True. *Let's eat*
Kennaway, Adrienne. *Bushbaby*
Kerr, Judith. *The tiger who came to tea*
Kessler, Leonard P. *Do you have any carrots?*
  Soup for the king
Ketteman, Helen. *Armadilly chili*
Khalsa, Dayal Kaur. *How pizza came to Queens*
Kilborne, Sarah S. *Peach and Blue*
King, Christopher L. *The vegetables go to bed*
Kirk, David. *Little bird, Biddle bird*
Kitchen, Bert. *When hunger calls*
Kleven, Elisa. *Sun bread*
Knight, Joan. *Bon appetit, Bertie!*
Kobayashi, Robert. *Maria Mazaretti loves spaghetti*
Koda-Callan, Elizabeth. *The squiggly Wigglys*
Koller, Jackie French. *Fish fry tonight*
Komoda, Beverly. *Simon's soup*
Kovalski, Maryann. *Pizza for breakfast*
Krasilovsky, Phyllis. *The man who cooked for himself*
Kraus, Robert. *Big Squeak, Little Squeak*
  The Christmas cookie sprinkle snitcher
  Klunky Monkey, new kid in class
Krensky, Stephen. *The pizza book*
Krings, Antoon. *Oliver's strawberry patch*
Kroll, Steven. *The Hokey-Pokey man*
Kroll, Virginia L. *Lunching and munching*
Krudwig, Vickie Leigh. *Cucumber soup*
Krull, Kathleen. *Supermarket*
Kwitz, Mary DeBall. *Little chick's breakfast*
Labatt, Mary. *Pizza for Sam*
Landry, Leo. *Eat your peas, Ivy Louise!*
Landström, Olof. *Boo and Baa in windy weather*
Lapp, Eleanor. *The blueberry bears*
Lasker, Joe. *Lentil soup*
Lass, Bonnie. *Who took the cookies from the cookie jar?*
Lauber, Patricia. *Who eats what?*

Lear, Edward. *The new vestments*
Leavitt, Melvin. *Grena and the magic pomegranate*
Leblanc, Anne. *Shopping with Benjamin*
Lebrun, Claude. *Little Brown Bear does not want to eat*
Lee, Hector Viveros. *I had a hippopotamus*
Leedy, Loreen. *The dragon Thanksgiving feast*
  The edible pyramid
Lember, Barbara Hirsch. *A book of fruit*
Lemerise, Bruce. *Sheldon's lunch*
Lent, Blair. *Molasses flood*
Leonard, Marcia. *Alphabet bandits*
  Food is fun!
  Rainboots for breakfast
Levert, Mireille. *An island in the soup*
Levine, Abby. *Too much mush!*
Levitin, Sonia. *Nobody stole the pie*
Lewin, Betsy. *Animal snackers*
Lillegard, Dee. *The wild bunch*
Lin, Grace. *Dim sum for everyone*
  Fortune cookie fortunes
  The ugly vegetables
Lindsey, Treska. *When Batistine made bread*
Ljungkvist, Laura. *Toni's topsy-turvy telephone day*
Llewellyn, Claire. *Tree*
Lobel, Anita. *The pancake*
London, Jonathan. *Candystore man*
  Crunch munch
  Froggy eats out
  Shawn and Keeper and the birthday party
  The sugaring-off party
Losi, Carol A. *The 512 ants on Sullivan Street*
Love, Ann. *Ice cream at the castle*
Lucado, Max. *Small gifts in God's hands*
Luciani, Brigitte. *Those messy Hempels*
Lurie, Morris. *The story of Imelda, who was small*
Lynn, Sara. *Food*
Lyon, David. *The crumbly coast*
Lyon, George Ella. *The outside inn*
Maccarone, Grace. *The lunch box surprise*
  Pizza party
McCloskey, Robert. *Blueberries for Sal*
McCully, Emily Arnold. *Popcorn at the palace*
McCurdy, Michael. *An Algonquian year*
MacDonald, Elizabeth. *Mr. MacGregor's breakfast egg*
MacDonald, Maryann. *Hedgehog bakes a cake*
McGovern, Ann. *Eggs on your nose*
McGrath, Barbara Barbieri. *Kellogg's froot loops color fun book*
  Kellogg's froot loops counting fun book
MacGregor, Marilyn. *Helen the hungry bear*
McGuire, Richard. *The orange book*
Machotka, Hana. *Pasta factory*
McKee, David. *King Rollo and the bread*
McKinney, Barbara Shaw. *Pass the energy, please*
MacKinnon, Debbie. *Cathy's cake*
  Find my cake!
McPhail, David M. *Pigs aplenty, pigs galore!*
Maestro, Betsy. *How do apples grow?*
Mahy, Margaret. *Boom Baby boom, boom*
  A busy day for a good grandmother
  Jam
  Simply delicious!
Manushkin, Fran. *The matzah that Papa brought home*
  Moon dragon
Many, Paul. *The great pancake escape*
Marcellino, Fred. *I, crocodile*
Marshall, James. *Miss Dog's Christmas*
  Yummers!
  Yummers too
Marshall, Janet Perry. *Banana moon*
Martchenko, Michael. *Bird feeder banquet*
Martin, Antoinette Truglio. *Famous seaweed soup*
Martin, Bill (William Ivan). *Rock it, sock it, number line*
  Trick or treat?
Martín Larrañaga, Ana. *Pepo and Lolo and the red apple*
Mayer, Mercer. *Frog goes to dinner*
Mayr, Diane. *Out and about at the apple orchard*
Meddaugh, Susan. *Martha blah blah*

Nate the Great and the lost list
Nate the Great and the monster mess
Nate the Great and the phony clue
Nate the Great goes undercover
Sharmat, Mitchell. *Gregory, the terrible eater*
Sharratt, Nick. *Ketchup on your cornflakes?*
Shaw, Nancy (Nancy E.). *Sheep out to eat*
Shea, Kitty. *Out and about at the supermarket*
Shecter, Ben. *The big stew*
Shelby, Anne. *Potluck*
Shiefman, Vicky. *Sunday potatoes, Monday potatoes*
Shirotani, Hideo. *Let's eat = Vamos a comer*
Shott, Steve (Stephen). *Mealtime*
Slepian, Jan. *The hungry thing returns*
Slobodkina, Esphyr. *The wonderful feast*
Slocum, Rosalie. *Breakfast with the clowns*
Slonim, David. *Oh, Ducky*
Smith, Linda. *Mrs. Biddlebox*
Smothers, Ethel Footman. *Auntee Edna*
Sobol, Harriet Langsam. *A book of vegetables*
Sokol, Edward. *Meet Stinky Magee*
Sondheimer, Ilse. *The magic of Pomme*
Soto, Gary. *Chato's kitchen*
 The old man and his door
 Too many tamales
Speed, Toby. *Hattie baked a wedding cake*
Spier, Peter. *Food market*
Spilsbury, Louise. *Carrots*
 Oranges
 Peas
Spohn, Kate. *Introducing Fanny*
Springer, Sally. *Let's make latkes*
Spurr, Elizabeth. *The biggest birthday cake in the world*
Stadler, John. *Animal café*
Stamaty, Mark Alan. *Minnie Maloney and Macaroni*
Steig, William. *Pete's a pizza*
Stevens, Janet. *Cook-a-doodle-doo!*
Stevenson, Jocelyn. *Red and the pumpkins*
Stewig, John Warren. *Making plum jam*
 Stone soup
Stock, Catherine. *Alexander's midnight snack*
Swain, Ruth Freeman. *How sweet it is (and was)*
Szekeres, Cyndy. *Suppertime for Frieda Fuzzypaws*
Tatcheva, Eva. *Witch Zelda's birthday cake*
Taulbert, Clifton L. *Little Cliff and the porch people*
Taylor, Judy. *Dudley and the strawberry shake*
 Dudley in a jam
Testa, Fulvio. *The land where the ice cream grows*
Thayer, Jane. *The popcorn dragon*, ill. by Jay Hyde Barnum
 The popcorn dragon, ill. by Lisa McCue
Thompson, Vivian Laubach. *The horse that liked sandwiches*
Torres, Leyla. *Saturday sancocho*
Towle, Faith M. *The magic cooking pot*
Tudor, Tasha. *Pumpkin moonshine*
Tunnell, Michael O. *Halloween pie*
Tusa, Tricia. *Sisters*
Uchida, Yoshiko. *The two foolish cats*
Van Laan, Nancy. *Tickle tum*
Van Rynbach, Iris. *The soup stone*
Van Woerkom, Dorothy. *Alexandra the rock-eater*
Vevers, Gwynne. *Animals that store food*
Voake, Charlotte. *Pizza kittens*
Vulliamy, Clara. *Yum yum*
Wabbes, Marie. *Rose is hungry*
Waber, Bernard. *Fast food! gulp! gulp!*
Waddell, Martin. *Yum, yum, yummy*
Walburg, Lori. *The legend of the candy cane*
Wallace, Karen. *Scarlette Beane*
Wallace, Nancy Elizabeth. *Pumpkin day*
Wallner, Alexandra. *Munch*
Ward, Nick. *Farmer George and the hungry guests*
Ward, Sally G. *Molly and Grandpa*
Wardlaw, Lee. *The chair where bear sits*
Wasmuth, Eleanor. *The picnic basket*
Watanabe, Shigeo. *What a good lunch!*
Watson, Clyde. *Tom Fox and the apple pie*
 Valentine foxes

Watson, Nancy Dingman. *Sugar on snow*
Weeks, Sarah. *Noodles*
Weir, Bob. *Panther dream*
Weiss, Monica. *Mmmm . . . cookies!*
Wellington, Monica. *Apple farmer Annie*
 Mr. Cookie Baker
Wells, Rosemary. *McDuff saves the day*
 Max and Ruby's Midas
 Yoko
Weninger, Brigitte. *Little apple*
Westcott, Nadine Bernard. *Peanut butter and jelly*
Wheeler, Lisa. *Jam & jelly by Holly & Nellie*
 Turk and Runt
White, Kathryn (Kathryn Ivy). *Nutty nut chase*
White, Linda Arms. *Too many pumpkins*
Who took the cookie?
Wikler, Madeline. *My first seder*
Willard, Nancy. *The marzipan moon*
 The Moon & Riddles Diner and the Sunnyside Café
Williams, Arlene. *Dragon soup*
Williams, Gweneira Maureen. *Timid Timothy, the kitten who learned to be brave*
Williams, Sam. *Angel's Christmas cookies*
Wilson, Sarah. *Muskrat, muskrat, eat your peas!*
Wilson-Kelly, Becky. *Mother Grumpy's dog biscuits*
Windham, Sophie. *Noah's ark*
Wing, Natasha. *Jalapeño bagels*
Winthrop, Elizabeth. *Potbellied possums*
Wisniewski, David. *Tough cookie*
Wong, Benedict Norbert. *Lo & behold*
 Lo & behold, good enough to eat
Wood, Audrey. *Heckedy Peg*
Wood, Leslie. *A dog called Mischief*
Wyllie, Stephen. *Dinner with fox*
Wynot, Jillian. *The Mother's Day sandwich*
Yaccarino, Dan. *The lima bean monster*
Yamate, Sandra S. *Char siu bao boy*
Yee, Patrick. *Let's go*
Yee, Wong Herbert. *Hamburger Heaven*
Young, Miriam Burt. *The sugar mouse cake*
Yummy! eating through a day
Zagwÿn, Deborah Turney. *Apple batter*
 Papa's latkes
Zalben, Jane Breskin. *Saturday night at the Beastro*
Zamorano, Ana. *Let's eat!*
Ziefert, Harriet. *Breakfast time!*
 Rabbit and Hare divide an apple
 Surprise!
Zoehfeld, Kathleen Weidner. *Apples, apples*
Zweifel, Frances W. *The Make-Something Club*

Foolishness *see* Character traits – foolishness

Football *see* Sports – football

Foreign lands

Ada, Alma Flor. *The rooster who went to his uncle's wedding*
Ajmera, Maya. *Back to school*
 Come out and play
 To be a kid
Aleichem, Sholem. *Hanukah money*
Aliki. *Marianthe's story one: painted words; Marianthe's story two: spoken memories*
Allen, Thomas B. (Thomas Burt). *Where children live*
Anglund, Joan Walsh. *Love one another*
Anno, Mitsumasa. *All in a day*
Baylor, Byrd. *The way to start a day*
Benjamin, Floella. *Skip across the ocean*
Berg, Leila. *Folk tales for reading and telling*
Berger, Barbara Helen. *Animalia*
Blossom tales
Borchers, Elisabeth. *Dear Sarah*
Brann, Esther. *'Round the world*
Bridgman, Elizabeth. *How to travel with grownups*
Bryson, Bernarda. *The twenty miracles of Saint Nicolas*

Climo, Shirley. *Stolen thunder*
Coburn, Jewell Reinhart. *Jouanah*
Darling, Kathy (Mary Kathleen). *Rain forest babies*
De Regniers, Beatrice Schenk. *Little Sister and the Month Brothers*
Domanska, Janina. *Marek, the little fool*
Dooley, Norah. *Everybody brings noodles*
Dorros, Arthur. *This is my house*
Douglas, Michael. *Round, round world*
Feldman, Eve B. *Birthdays!*
Gerrard, Roy. *Jocasta Carr, movie star*
　Sir Francis Drake
Goffstein, M. B. (Marilyn Brooke). *Across the sea*
Gray, Nigel. *A country far away*
Handford, Martin. *Where's Waldo?*
Hess, Paul. *Rainforest animals*
Höjer, Dan. *Heart of mine*
Knight, Margy Burns. *Talking walls*
Lesynski, Loris. *Dirty dog boogie*
Lewin, Ted. *Market!*
Listen to the storyteller
Low, Robert. *Peoples of the rain forest*
McDonald, Megan. *My house has stars*
Marlowe, Pete. *One Arabian morning*
Martin, Rafe. *The twelve months*
Mitchell, Cynthia. *Here a little child I stand*
Montanari, Donata. *Children around the world*
Morris, Ann. *Houses and homes*
　Loving
　On the go
　Play
　Work
Orstadius, Brita. *The dolphin journey*
Quackenbush, Robert M. *Henry's world tour*
Raffi. *Like me and you*
Rehnman, Mats. *The clay flute*
Robb, Brian. *My grandmother's djinn*
Schulz, Charles M. *Bon voyage, Charlie Brown (and don't come back!!)*
Scott, Sally. *The magic horse*
Sheldon, Dyan. *Love, your bear, Pete*
Shohet, Marti. *Market days*
Singer, Marilyn. *Nine o'clock lullaby*
Sis, Peter. *Madlenka*
Soto, Gary. *The old man and his door*
Svend Otto S (Svend Otto Sorensen). *The giant fish and other stories*
Trapani, Iza. *I'm a little teapot*
Van Laan, Nancy. *Sleep, sleep, sleep*
Van Woerkom, Dorothy. *Alexandra the rock-eater*
Yolen, Jane. *Street rhymes around the world*
Zeman, Ludmila. *Sindbad's secret*

Foreign lands – Afghanistan

Khan, Rukhsana. *The roses in my carpets*
McKay, Lawrence. *Caravan*

Foreign lands – Africa

Aardema, Verna. *Anansi does the impossible!*
　Bimwili and the Zimwi
　Bringing the rain to Kapiti Plain
　Half-a-ball-of-kenki
　Jackal's flying lesson
　Ji-nongo-nongo means riddles
　The lonely lioness and the ostrich chicks
　Misoso
　Oh, Kojo! How could you!
　Princess Gorilla and a new kind of water
　Rabbit makes a monkey of lion
　Sebgugugu the glutton
　The vinganee and the tree toad
　What's so funny, Ketu?
　Who's in Rabbit's house?
　Why mosquitoes buzz in people's ears
Abisch, Roz. *The clever turtle*
Adamson, Joy. *Elsa*
　Elsa and her cubs

Pippa the cheetah and her cubs
Adlerman, Daniel. *Africa calling*
Adoff, Arnold. *Ma nDa La*
Alakija, Polly. *Catch that goat!*
Alexander, Lloyd. *Fortune tellers*
Allen, Judy. *Elephant*
Appelt, Kathi. *Elephants aloft*
Arkin, David. *Black and white*
Arnott, Kathleen. *Spiders, crabs and creepy crawlers*
Aruego, José. *We hide, you seek*
Asare, Meshack. *Sosu's call*
Barbosa, Rogério Andrade. *African animal tales*
Bare, Colleen Stanley. *Who comes to the water hole?*
Base, Graeme. *Jungle drums*
Bateman, Robert. *Safari*
Bemelmans, Ludwig. *Rosebud*
Bernard, Robin. *Juma and the honey-guild*
Bernheim, Marc. *In Africa*
　A week in Aya's world
Bernstein, Margery. *The first morning*
Berson, Harold. *Kassim's shoes*
　Why the jackal won't speak to the hedgehog
Bess, Clayton. *The truth about the moon*
Bible, Charles. *Hamdaani*
Bishop, Roma. *On a safari*
Bond, Jean Carey. *A is for Africa*
Borden, Beatrice Brown. *Wild animals of Africa*
Bozylinsky, Hannah Heritage. *Lala Salama*
Brown, Don. *Uncommon traveler*
Bryan, Ashley. *Beat the story-drum, pum-pum*
　Lion and the ostrich chicks
　The story of lightning and thunder
Bulion, Leslie. *Fatuma's new cloth*
Butler, Andrea. *Mr. Sun and Mr. Sea*
Carrick, Malcolm. *I can squash elephants!*
Cendrars, Blaise. *Shadow*
Ching. *The baboon's umbrella*
Chocolate, Deborah M. Newton. *Imani in the belly*
　Kente colors
Cole, Babette. *Nungu and the elephant*
　Nungu and the hippopotamus
Coleman, Evelyn. *To be a drum*
Daly, Niki. *Not so fast Songololo*
Davis, Douglas F. *The lion's tail*
Davol, Marguerite W. *How snake got his hiss*
Dayrell, Elphinstone. *Why the sun and the moon live in the sky*
Dee, Ruby. *Two ways to count to ten*
De Paola, Tomie (Thomas Anthony). *Bill and Pete*
Diakité, Baba Wagué. *The hunterman and the crocodiles*
Diouf, Sylviane A, (Sylviane Anna). *Bintou's braids*
Domanska, Janina. *The tortoise and the tree*
Du Bois, William Pène. *Otto in Africa*
Dupré, Rick. *Agassu*
Economakis, Olga. *Oasis of the stars*
Eisner, Will. *Sundiata*
Elkin, Benjamin. *Such is the way of the world*
Ellis, Veronica Freeman. *Afro-Bets, first book about Africa*
Farris, Pamela J. *Young Mouse and Elephant*
Fatio, Louise. *The happy lion in Africa*
Fecher, Sarah. *Wild animals*
Feelings, Muriel. *Jambo means hello*
　Menjo means one
Fournier, Catharine. *The coconut thieves*
Franklin, Kristine L. *The old, old man and the very little boy*
French, Fiona. *King of another country*
Geraghty, Paul. *The hunter*
Gershator, Phillis. *Only one cowry*
　Zzzng! zzzng! zzzng!
Goldsmith, Howard. *Shy little turtle*
Graham, Lorenz B. *Song of the boat*
Greenfield, Eloise. *Africa dream*
Gregorowski, Christopher. *Fly, eagle, fly!*
Grifalconi, Ann. *Darkness and the butterfly*
　Flyaway girl
　Osa's pride
　The village of round and square houses
　The village that vanished

Grimsdell, Jeremy. *Kalinzu*
Guthrie, Donna. *Nobiah's well*
Guy, Rosa. *Mother crocodile*
Haley, Gail E. *A story, a story*
Hanna, Jack. *Jungle Jack Hanna's safari adventure*
Hartmann, Wendy. *One sun rises*
Haskins, Jim (James). *Count your way through Africa*
Heatwole, Marsha. *Jambo, watoto!*
Hess, Paul. *Safari animals*
Hetfield, Jamie. *The Yoruba of West Africa*
Hill, Susan. *Simba's A-Z*
Holding, James. *The lazy little Zulu*
Ichikawa, Satomi. *The first bear in Africa!*
Isadora, Rachel. *A South African night*
Jackson, Bobby L. *Makimba's animal world*
James, Ellen Foley. *Little Bull*
Kennaway, Adrienne. *Bushbaby*
   Little elephant's walk
Kessler, Cristina. *Jubela*
   One night
Kimmel, Eric A. *Anansi and the magic stick*
   Anansi and the talking melon
   Anansi goes fishing
Kipling, Rudyard. *The elephant's child*, ill. by Louise Brierley
   The elephant's child, ill. by Lorinda Bryan Cauley
   The elephant's child, ill. by Tim Raglin
   The elephant's child, ill. by John A. Rowe
   How the camel got his hump, ill. by Quentin Blake
   How the camel got his hump, ill. by Tim Raglin
   How the camel got his hump, ill. by Lisbeth Zwerger
Kirn, Ann. *The tale of a crocodile*
Kitchen, Bert. *Tenrec's twigs*
Knight, Margy Burns. *Africa is not a country*
Knutson, Barbara. *Why the crab has no head*
Kroll, Virginia L. *Africa brothers and sisters*
   Faraway drums
   Jaha and Jamil went down the hill
   Masai and I
Laskowski, Jerzy. *Master of the royal cats*
LaTeef, Nelda. *The hunter and the ebony tree*
Léonard, Marie. *Tibili, the little boy who didn't want to go to school*
Lester, Julius. *Shining*
Lewin, Hugh. *An elephant came to swim*
   Jafta
   Jafta and the wedding
   Jafta – the journey
   Jafta – the town
   Jafta's father
   Jafta's mother
Lexau, Joan M. *Crocodile and hen*
London, Jonathan. *What the animals were waiting for*
Lumry, Amanda. *Safari in South Africa*
McCormick, Wendy. *Daddy, will you miss me?*
McDermott, Gerald. *Anansi the spider*
   Zomo the rabbit
MacDonald, Margaret Read. *Mabela the clever*
MacDonald, Suse. *Nanta's lion*
McKissack, Patricia C. *Who is coming?*
Maddern, Eric. *The fire children*
Mantegazza, Giovanna. *The hippopotamus*
Manushkin, Fran. *My Christmas safari*
Martin, Francesca. *The honey hunters*
Melmed, Laura Krauss. *Jumbo's lullaby*
Mitchell, Rhonda. *The talking cloth*
Moers, Hermann. *Evie to the rescue!*
Mollel, Tololwa M. (Tololwa Marti). *Dume's roar*
   Kitoto the mighty
   The princess who lost her hair
   To dinner, for dinner
Montanari, Eva. *The crocodile's true colors*
Morozumi, Atsuko. *My friend gorilla*
Morrison, Taylor. *Cheetah*
Moss, Miriam. *This is the tree*
Musgrove, Margaret. *Ashanti to Zulu*
Mwalimu. *Awful aardvark*
Mwenye Hadithi. *Greedy zebra*
   Hot hippo

Noble, Kate. *Bubble gum*
   Oh look, it's a nosserus
Oberman, Sheldon. *The wisdom bird*
Olaleye, Isaac. *Bitter bananas*
   Lake of the Big Snake
Onyefulu, Ifeoma. *A triangle for Adaora*
Onyefulu, Obi. *Chinye*
   Over in the grasslands
Padt, Maartje. *Shanti*
Pearce, Q. L. *In the African grasslands*
Phumla. *Nomi and the magic fish*
Pitcher, Caroline. *The time of the lion*
Pohrt, Tom. *Having a wonderful time*
Prather, Ray. *The ostrich girl*
Purcell, John Wallace. *African animals*
Radcliffe, Theresa. *Bashi, elephant baby*
Richards, Jean. *How the elephant got his trunk*
Riordan, James. *The coming of Night*
Robinson, Adjai. *Femi and old grandaddie*
Rose, Anne K. *Akimba and the magic cow*
   Pot full of luck
Roth, Susan L. *Fire came to the earth people*
Routh, Jonathan. *The Nuns go to Africa*
Ryden, Hope. *Wild animals of Africa ABC*
Sackett, Elisabeth. *Danger on the African grassland*
San Souci, Robert D. *The secret of the stones*
Sayre, April Pulley. *If you should hear a honey guide*
Schatz, Letta. *The extraordinary tug-of-war*
Scheffler, Ursel. *Be brave, little lion!*
Schrier, Jeffrey. *On the wings of eagles*
Shepard, Steve. *Elvis Hornbill, international business bird*
Sikundar, Sylvia. *Forest singer*
Souhami, Jessica. *The leopard's drum*
Stanley, Sanna. *Monkey Sunday*
Steig, William. *Doctor De Soto goes to Africa*
Steptoe, John. *Mufaro's beautiful daughters*
Stojic, Manya. *Rain*
Swann, Brian. *The house with no door*
Swinburne, Stephen R. *Water for one, water for everyone*
Trimble, Marcia. *Hello sun*
Troughton, Joanna. *Tortoise's dream*
Tulloch, Shirley. *Who made me?*
Unobagha, Uzoamaka Chinyelu. *Off to the sweet shores of Africa and other talking drum rhymes*
Upper, Jonathan. *Spin's really wild Africa tour*
Van Laan, Nancy. *Little Fish lost*
Wallace, Joseph E. *Big and noisy Simon*
Walter, Mildred Pitts. *Brother to the wind*
Ward, Leila. *I am eyes, ni macho*
Weir, Bob. *Panther dream*
Williams, Karen Lynn. *Galimoto*
   When Africa was home
Williams, Sheron. *And in the beginning . . .*
Wilson, Anna. *Over in the grasslands*
Winter, Jeanette. *My baby*
Wolkstein, Diane. *The day Ocean came to visit*
Yoshida, Toshi. *Elephant crossing*
   Rhinoceros mother
   Young lions
Zaslavsky, Claudia. *Count on your fingers African style*
Zimelman, Nathan. *Treed by a pride of irate lions*

Foreign lands – Amazon

Darling, Kathy (Mary Kathleen). *Amazon A B C*
Gilliland, Judith Heide. *River*

Foreign lands – Antarctic

Benson, Patrick. *Little penguin*
Chester, Jonathan. *Splash!*
Duquennoy, Jacques. *North Pole, South Pole*
Dyer, Heather. *Tina and the penguin*
Faulkner, Keith. *The puzzled penguin*
Geraghty, Paul. *Solo*
Gibbons, Gail. *Penguins!*
Hooper, Meredith. *Tom's rabbit*

Inkpen, Mick. *Penguin small*
Livinson, Nancy Smiler. *North Pole, South Pole*
McDonald, Megan. *Penguin and Little Blue*
McQuade, Jacqueline. *Snow babies*
Radcliffe, Theresa. *Nanu, penguin chick*
Schofield, Jennifer. *Animal babies in polar lands*
Seibold, J. Otto. *Penguin dreams*
Townsend, Emily Rose. *Penguins*
Wood, Audrey. *Little Penguin's tale*
Yee, Patrick. *Baby penguin*

Foreign lands – Arabia

Alexander, Sue. *Nadia the willful*
Arabian Nights. *The first book of tales of ancient Araby*
Haskins, Jim (James). *Count your way through the Arab world*
Kimmel, Eric A. *The three princes*
Zeman, Ludmila. *Sindbad*
    Sindbad in the land of giants

Foreign lands – Arctic

Aston, Dianna Hutts. *Loony Little*
Berger, Melvin. *Brrr! a book about polar animals*
Brandenburg, Jim. *Scruffy*
Brown, Kerry. *Tupag the dreamer*
Carlstrom, Nancy White. *Swim the silver sea, Joshie Otter*
Dabcovich, Lydia. *The polar bear son*
Damjan, Mischa. *Atuk*
Darling, Kathy (Mary Kathleen). *Arctic babies*
De Beer, Hans. *Little polar bear and the brave little hare*
    Little polar bear finds a friend
Dunphy, Madeleine. *Here is the Arctic winter*
Duquennoy, Jacques. *North Pole, South Pole*
Dwyer, Mindy. *Aurora, a tale of the Northern Lights*
Foa, Maryclare. *Songs are thoughts*
Ford, Miela. *Mom and me*
George, Jean Craighead. *Arctic son*
    Nutik and Amaroq play ball
    Nutik, the wolf pup
    Snow bear
Gerber, Carole. *Arctic dreams*
Griese, Arnold A. *Anna's Athabaskan summer*
Grigg, Carol. *The singing snow bear*
Grindley, Sally. *Polar Star*
Hayles, Karen. *What is stuck*
Heinz, Brian J. *Nanuk, lord of the ice*
Hess, Paul. *Polar animals*
Inkpen, Mick. *Penguin small*
Kroll, Virginia L. *The seasons and someone*
Livinson, Nancy Smiler. *North Pole, South Pole*
London, Jonathan. *Gone again ptarmigan*
    Ice Bear and Little Fox
Low, Robert. *Peoples of the Arctic*
Luenn, Nancy. *Nessa's story*
McQuade, Jacqueline. *Snow babies*
Merski, P. K. *Roaring, boring, Alice*
Moss, Miriam. *The snow bear*
Newton, Jill. *Polar bear scare*
Pinczes, Elinor J. *Arctic fives arrive*
Primavera, Elise. *Auntie Claus*
    Auntie Claus and the key to Christmas
Raffi. *Baby beluga*
Reynolds, Jan. *Far north*
Ring, Susan. *Polar babies*
Rives. *If I were a polar bear*
Ryder, Joanne. *White bear, ice bear*
Sabuda, Robert James. *The Blizzard's robe*
Sackett, Elisabeth. *Danger on the Arctic ice*
Schofield, Jennifer. *Animal babies in polar lands*
Sis, Peter. *A small tall tale from the far Far North*
Taulbert, Clifton L. *Little Cliff and the cold place*
Taylor, Harriet Peck. *Ulaq and the northern lights*
Taylor, Theodore. *Hello, Arctic!*
Townsend, Emily Rose. *Arctic foxes*
    Polar bears
Trottier, Maxine. *Dreamstones*

Wild, Margaret. *Thank you, Santa*
Yolen, Jane. *Welcome to the icehouse*

Foreign lands – Argentina

Lamm, C. Drew. *Gauchada*
Van Laan, Nancy. *The magic bean tree*

Foreign lands – Armenia

Bider, Djemma. *A drop of honey*
Hogrogian, Nonny. *The contest*
Kherdian, David. *The golden bracelet*
San Souci, Robert D. *A weave of words*

Foreign lands – Asia

Chin-Lee, Cynthia. *A is for Asia*
Sierra, Judy. *Counting crocodiles*

Foreign lands – Australia

Adams, Jeanie. *Going for oysters*
The all-amazing ha ha book
Argent, Kerry. *Animal capers*
    Wombat and Bandicoot
Arnold, Caroline. *Australian animals*
    A walk on the Great Barrier Reef
Baker, Jeannie. *The story of rosy dock*
    Where the forest meets the sea
    Window
Base, Graeme. *My grandma lived in Gooligulch*
Bassett, Lisa. *Koala Christmas*
Bodsworth, Nan. *A nice walk in the jungle*
Bonnett-Rampersaud, Louise. *Polly Hopper's pouch*
Brown, Marc Tolon. *Arthur's animal adventure*
Cox, David. *Bossyboots*
    Tin Lizzie and Little Nell
Crew, Gary. *Bright star*
Czernecki, Stefan. *The singing snake*
Dennard, Deborah. *Koala country*
Dumbleton, Mike. *Dial-a-croc*
Eversole, Robyn Harbert. *The gift stone*
Factor, Jane. *Summer*
Foreman, Michael. *Panda and the bunyips*
    Panda and the bushfire
Fox, Mem. *Because of the bloomers*
    Possum magic
Gelman, Rita Golden. *A koala grows up*
Germein, Katrina. *Big rain coming*
Harrison, Troon. *Don't dig so deep, Nicholas!*
Hathorn, Libby (Elizabeth). *The tram to Bondi beach*
Henry, Lenny. *Charlie, queen of the desert*
Hilton, Nette. *Dirty Dave*
Jacka, Martin. *Waiting for Billy*
Katz, Avner. *The little pickpocket*
Kipling, Rudyard. *The sing-song of old man kangaroo*
Lester, Alison. *Ernie dances to the didgeridoo*
    My farm
    Rosie sips spiders
McDermott, Beverly Brodsky. *The dreamtime*
Morpurgo, Michael. *Wombat goes walkabout*
Niland, Kilmeny. *A bellbird in a flame tree*
Nunes, Susan Miho. *Tiddalick the frog*
Paterson, A. B. (Andrew Barton). *Mulga Bill's bicycle*
    Waltzing Matilda
Pershall, Mary K. *Hello, Barney!*
Pittaway, Margaret. *The rainforest children*
Powzyk, Joyce Ann. *Tasmania*
Reynolds, Jan. *Down under*
Rodda, Emily. *Yay!*
Roth, Susan L. *The biggest frog in Australia*
Roughsey, Dick. *The giant devil-dingo*
Spurling, Margaret. *Bilby moon*
Thiele, Colin. *Farmer Schulz's ducks*
Trinca, Rod. *One woolly wombat*
Troughton, Joanna. *What made Tiddalik laugh*

Turner, Ethel. *Walking to school*
Vaughan, Marcia Kapok. *Wombat stew*
Wagner, Jenny. *The bunyip of Berkeley's Creek*
Walsh, Grahame L. *Didane the koala*
    The goori goori bird
Ward, Helen. *Old shell, new shell*
Whitmore, Adam. *Max in Australia*
Wild, Margaret. *Thank you, Santa*
Wolkstein, Diane. *Sun Mother wakes the world*

Foreign lands – Austria

Granfield, Linda. *Silent night*
Kahl, Virginia. *Away went Wolfgang*
Tompert, Ann. *A carol for Christmas*
Wenning, Elisabeth. *The Christmas mouse*

Foreign lands – Bali

Cox, David. *Ayu and the perfect moon*

Foreign lands – Bavaria *see* Foreign lands – Austria; Foreign lands – Germany

Foreign lands – Belgium

Radunsky, Vladimir. *Manneken pis*
Woodhouse, Jayne. *Pieter Bruegel*

Foreign lands – Belize

London, Jonathan. *The village basket weaver*

Foreign lands – Borneo

Climo, Shirley. *The match between the winds*
Cushman, Doug. *The mystery of the monkey's maze*

Foreign lands – Bosnia-Herzegovina

Bunting, Eve (Anne Evelyn). *Gleam and Glow*

Foreign lands – Botswana

Lewin, Betsy. *Chubbo's pool*

Foreign lands – Brazil

Cherry, Lynne. *The great kapok tree*
DeSpain, Pleasant. *The dancing turtle*
Lewin, Ted. *Amazon boy*
    When the rivers go home
Machado, Ana Maria. *Nina Bonita*
Van Laan, Nancy. *So say the little monkeys*

Foreign lands – British Columbia

Manuel, Lynn. *Camels always do*

Foreign lands – Burma

Baillie, Allan. *Rebel!*
Froese, Deborah L. *The wise washerman*
Troughton, Joanna. *Make-believe tales*

Foreign lands – Cambodia

Coburn, Jewell Reinhart. *Angkat*
Ho, Minfong. *Brother Rabbit*
    The two brothers
Lee, Jeanne M. *Silent lotus*
Wall, Lina Mao. *Judge Rabbit and the tree spirit*

Foreign lands – Cameroon

Alexander, Lloyd. *Fortune tellers*
Bognomo, Joel Eboueme. *Madoulina*
Mollel, Tololwa M. (Tololwa Marti). *The king and the tortoise*

Njeng, Pierre Yves. *Vacation in the village*
Tchana, Katrin. *Sense Pass King*

Foreign lands – Canada

Andrews, Jan. *Very last first time*
Bannatyne-Cugnet, Jo. *A prairie alphabet*
Becker, Helaine. *Mama likes to mambo*
Blades, Ann. *A boy of Taché*
    Mary of mile 18
    Too small
Booth, David. *The dust bowl*
Bouchard, Dave. *Prairie born*
Brébeuf, Jean de, Saint. *The Huron carol*
Bushey, Jeanne. *The polar bear's gift*
Butler, Geoff. *The hangashore*
    Ode to Newfoundland
Carney, Margaret (Margaret Rose). *At Grandpa's sugar bush*
Carrier, Roch. *The longest home run*
Carter, Anne (1953–). *My home bay*
Carter, Anne Laurel. *Under a prairie sky*
Cleaver, Elizabeth. *The enchanted caribou*
Clements, Andrew. *Tara and Tiree, fearless friends*
Climo, Lindee. *Chester's barn*
Crook, Connie Brummel. *Maple moon*
Dos Santos, Joyce Audy. *The diviner*
    Henri and the Loup-Garou
Garay, Luis. *The long road*
Grassby, Donna. *A seaside alphabet*
Gregory, Nan. *Wild Girl and Gran*
Harrison, Ted. *O Canada*
Haskins, Jim (James). *Count your way through Canada*
Hodge, Deborah. *Emma's story*
Holling, Holling C. (Holling Clancy). *Paddle-to-the-sea*
Hume, Stephen Eaton. *Red moon follows truck*
Hutchins, H. J. (Hazel J.). *Tess*
Jam, Teddy. *The kid line*
    The year of fire
Jessell, Tim. *Amorak*
Kinsey-Warnock, Natalie. *The fiddler of the Northern Lights*
    Wilderness cat
Lawson, Julie. *Arizona Charlie and the Klondike Kid*
Lee, Dennis. *Bubblegum delicious*
Lipp, Frederick. *The caged birds of Phnom Penh*
Little old lady who swallowed a fly. *I know an old lady*, ill. by Abner Graboff
    I know an old lady who swallowed a fly, ill. by William Stobbs
    There was an old lady who swallowed a fly, ill. by Pam Adams
London, Jonathan. *The sugaring-off party*
McNaughton, Janet. *Brave Jack and the unicorn*
Major, Kevin. *Eh to zed?*
Marx, David F. *Canada*
Milord, Susan. *The ghost on the hearth*
Moak, Allan. *A big city ABC*
Munsch, Robert N. *From far away*
    Get me another one!
    Good families don't
    Love you forever
    Mud puddle
    Murmel, Murmel, Murmel
    A promise is a promise
    Thomas' snowsuit
    Wait and see
    Where is Gah-Ning?
Murphy, Patricia J. *Canada Day*
Nichol, Barbara. *Biscuits in the cupboard*
Norman, Howard A. *The owl-scatterer*
    Who-Paddled-Backward-With-Trout
Oberman, Sheldon. *The white stone in the castle wall*
Pearson, Kit. *The singing basket*
Pickthall, Marjorie L. C. (Marjorie Lowry Christie). *The worker in sandalwood*
Pinkwater, Daniel Manus. *Young Larry*
Poulin, Stéphane. *Ah! belle cité = A beautiful city*
    Can you catch Josephine?
    Have you seen Josephine?
Reynolds, Marilynn. *The name of the child*

Roache, Gordon. *A Halifax ABC*
Rutherford, Erica. *An Island alphabet*
Simmie, Lois. *Mister got to go and Arnie*
Smith-Ayala, Emilie. *Marisol and the yellow messenger*
Smucker, Barbara Claasen. *Selina and the bear paw quilt*
Speare, Jean. *A candle for Christmas*
Stuchner, Joan Betty. *The Kugel Valley Klezmer Band*
Thien, Madeleine. *The Chinese violin*
Thornhill, Jan. *A tree in a forest*
Toye, William. *How summer came to Canada*
   The loon's necklace
   The mountain goats of Temlaham
Trottier, Maxine. *Prairie willow*
   Storm at Batoche
Valgardson, W. D. *Winter rescue*
Van Camp, Richard. *What's the most beautiful thing you know about horses?*
Wallace, Ian. *The true story of Trapper Jack's left big toe*
Ward, Lynd. *The biggest bear*
   Nic of the woods
Waterton, Betty. *Pettranella*
Wiebe, Rudy. *Hidden buffalo*
Wilson, Budge. *A fiddle for Angus*
Wolfe, Frances. *Where I live*
Woolaver, Lance. *Christmas with the rural mail*
Yee, Paul. *The jade necklace*
Zagwÿn, Deborah Turney. *The pumpkin blanket*
Zeman, Ludmila. *The first red maple leaf*

Foreign lands – Caribbean Islands

Agard, John. *No hickory no dickory no dock*
Anderson, Lonzo. *The day the hurricane happened*
   Izzard
Appelbaum, Diana Karter. *Cocoa ice*
Berry, James. *First palm trees*
Bryan, Ashley. *Sing to the sun*
Buffett, Jimmy. *The jolly mon*
Carlstrom, Nancy White. *Baby-O*
Charles, Faustin. *A Caribbean counting book*
Cohen, Miriam. *Down in the subway*
Comissiong, Lynette. *Mind me good now!*
Cooper, Susan. *Jethro and the jumbie*
Dobrin, Arnold Jack. *Josephine's 'magination*
Garne, S. T. *By a blazing blue sea*
George, Jean Craighead. *The wentletrap trap*
Gershator, David. *Palampam Day*
Gershator, Phillis. *Sweet, sweet fig banana*
Godard, Alex. *Mama, across the sea*
Gottlieb, Dale. *Where Jamaica go?*
Greenfield, Eloise. *Under the Sunday tree*
Gunning, Monica. *Not a copper penny in me house*
Hallworth, Grace. *Down by the river*
   Sing me a story
Hurst, Margaret M. *Grannie and the Jumbie*
Huth, Holly Young. *Darkfright*
Isadora, Rachel. *Caribbean dream*
Jekyll, Walter. *I have a news*
Keens-Douglas, Richardo. *The nutmeg princess*
Lessac, Frané. *Caribbean canvas*
   My little island
Linden, Ann Marie. *One smiling grandma*
McLean, Dirk. *Play mas'! a carnival ABC*
McMillan, Bruce. *Sense suspense*
Milstein, Linda Breiner. *Coconut mon*
Moreton, Daniel. *La Cucaracha Martina*
Ness, Evaline. *Josefina February*
Rahaman, Vashanti. *O Christmas tree*
San Souci, Robert D. *Cendrillon*
   The faithful friend
   The house in the sky
Youngquist, Cathrene Valente. *The three Billygoats Gruff and Mean Calypso Joe*

Foreign lands – Central America

Ada, Alma Flor. *The gold coin*

Anaya, Rudolfo A. *Maya's children*
Tortillas and lullabies = Tortillas y cancioncitas
Wisniewski, David. *Rain player*

Foreign lands – Chile

Pitcher, Caroline. *Mariana and the merchild*

Foreign lands – China

Abisch, Roz. *Mai-Ling and the mirror*
Æsop. *The ant and the grasshopper*
Allen, Judy. *Panda*
   Tiger
Andersen, H. C. (Hans Christian). *The emperor and the nightingale,* ill. by Meilo So
   The emperor and the nightingale, ill. by James Watling
   The emperor's new clothes, ill. by Demi
   The emperor's new clothes, ill. by Eve Tharlet
   The emperor's nightingale, ill. from the Disney archives
   The emperor's nightingale, ill. by Georges Lemoine
   The nightingale, ill. by Harold Berson
   The nightingale, ill. by Nancy Ekholm Burkert
   The nightingale, ill. by Alison Claire Darke
   The nightingale, ill. by Demi
   The nightingale, ill. by Beni Montresor
   The nightingale, ill. by Josef Palecek
   The nightingale, ill. by Regolo Ricci
   The nightingale, ill. by Christopher Santoro
   The nightingale, ill. by Lisbeth Zwerger
Armstrong, Jennifer. *Chin Yu Min and the ginger cat*
Bateson-Hill, Margaret. *Lao Lao of Dragon Mountain*
Behrens, June. *Soo Ling finds a way*
Birdseye, Tom. *A song of stars*
Bishop, Claire Huchet. *The five Chinese brothers*
Brett, Jan. *Daisy comes home*
Bridges, Shirin Yim. *Ruby's wish*
Bright, Robert. *The travels of Ching*
Bro, Marguerite (Harmon). *The animal friends of Peng-u*
Buck, Pearl S. (Pearl Sydenstricker). *The Chinese story teller*
Casanova, Mary. *The hunter*
Chan, Arlene. *Awakening the dragon*
Chang, Margaret Scrogin. *The beggar's magic*
   The cricket warrior
Chen, Kerstin. *Lord of the cranes*
Cheng, Hou-Tien. *The Chinese New Year*
Chiang, Wei. *The legend of Mu Lan = La heroina Hua Mulan*
Chin, Charlie. *China's bravest girl*
Compestine, Ying Chang. *The runaway rice cake*
   The story of chopsticks
   The story of noodles
   The story of paper
Czernecki, Stefan. *The cricket's cage*
   Paper lanterns
D'Antonio, Nancy. *Our baby from China*
Dawson, Zöe. *China*
Demi. *The adventures of Marco Polo*
   The artist and the architect
   Chen Ping and his magic axe
   A Chinese zoo
   Demi's reflective fables
   Dragon kites and dragonflies
   The dragon's tale and other animal fables of the Chinese zodiac
   The empty pot
   The greatest treasure
   Happy, happy Chinese New Year
   Liang and the magic paintbrush
   The magic boat
   The magic tapestry
   The stonecutter
   Under the shade of the mulberry tree
Diller, Harriett. *The waiting day*
Drummond, Allan. *The willow pattern story*
Fairclough, Chris. *Take a trip to China*
Flack, Marjorie. *The story about Ping*
Foley, Bernice Williams. *A walk among clouds*
Fribourg, Marjorie G. *Ching-Ting and the ducks*

Gibbons, Gail. *Giant pandas*
Granfield, Linda. *The legend of the panda*
Greene, Ellin. *Ling-li and the phoenix fairy*
Handforth, Thomas. *Mei Li*
Haskins, Jim (James). *Count your way through China*
Heyer, Marilee. *The weaving of a dream*
Hillman, Elizabeth. *Min-Yo and the moon dragon*
Ho, Minfong. *Maples in the mist*
Hodge, Deborah. *Emma's story*
Hodges, Margaret. *The voice of the great bell*
Holland, Janice. *You never can tell*
Hong, Lily Toy. *How the ox star fell from heaven*
Jensen, Helen Zane. *When Panda came to our house*
Jiang, Ji-li. *The magical Monkey King, mischief in heaven*
Lattimore, Deborah Nourse. *The dragon's robe*
Lawson, Julie. *The dragon's pearl*
Leaf, Margaret. *Eyes of the dragon*
Lee, Jeanne M. *Legend of the Li River*
    The legend of the milky way
    The song of Mu Lan
Levinson, Riki. *Our home is the sea*
Lewis, Rose A. *I love you like crazy cakes*
Littlefield, William. *The whiskers of Ho Ho*
Lobel, Arnold. *Ming Lo moves the mountain*
Loo, Sanne te. *Ping-Li's kite*
Louie, Ai-Ling. *Yeh Shen*
Mahy, Margaret. *The seven Chinese brothers*
Miles, Miska. *The pointed brush . . .*
Miller, Moira. *The moon dragon*
Morimoto, Junko. *The two bullies*
Morris, Ann. *Grandma Lai Goon remembers*
Morris, Winifred. *The future of Yen-Tzu*
    The magic leaf
Mosel, Arlene. *Tikki Tikki Tembo*
Muth, Jon J. *Stone soup*
Nagda, Anne Whitehead. *A home for panda*
Namioka, Lensey. *The laziest boy in the world*
Okimoto, Jean Davies. *The White Swan express*
Pacilio, V. J. *Ling Cho and his three friends*
P'an, Ts'ai-ying. *Monkey creates havoc in heaven*
Partridge, Elizabeth. *Oranges on Golden Mountain*
Pattison, Darcy. *The river dragon*
Perkins, Al. *Tubby and the lantern*
Pilegard, Virginia Walton. *The warlord's beads*
    The warlord's puzzle
Pittman, Helena Clare. *A grain of rice*
Piumini, Roberto. *Doctor Me Di Cin*
Pluckrose, Henry Arthur. *China*
Poole, Amy Lowry. *How the rooster got his crown*
Porte, Barbara Ann. *Ma Jiang and the orange ants*
Rappaport, Doreen. *Journey of Meng*
    The long-haired girl
Rumford, James. *The cloudmakers*
Sanfield, Steve. *Just rewards, or, Who is that man in the moon and what's he doing up there anyway?*
San Souci, Robert D. *The enchanted tapestry*
Schaefer, Lola M. *Chinese New Year*
Shi, Zhang Xiu. *Monkey and the white bone demon*
Skipper, Mervyn. *The fooling of King Alexander*
Slobodkin, Louis. *Moon Blossom and the golden penny*
Stafford, Kay. *Ling Tang and the lucky cricket*
Stevens, Jan Romero. *Carlos digs to China = Carlos excava hasta la China*
Stone, Jon. *Big Bird in China*
Tan, Amy. *The Chinese Siamese cat*
    The moon lady
Tompert, Ann. *Grandfather Tang's story*
    The jade horse, the cricket, and the peach stone
Torre, Betty L. *The luminous pearl*
Tseng, Grace. *White tiger, blue serpent*
Tsubakiyama, Margaret (Holloway). *Mei-Mei loves the morning*
Tucker, Kathy. *The seven Chinese sisters*
Va, Leong. *A letter to the king*
Van Woerkom, Dorothy. *The rat, the ox and the zodiac*
Wang, Rosalind C. *The fourth question*
    The treasure chest
Whitfield, Susan. *The animals of the Chinese zodiac*

Wiese, Kurt. *Fish in the air*
Williams, Jay. *Everyone knows what a dragon looks like*
Wolff, Ferida. *The emperor's garden*
Wolkstein, Diane. *The magic wings*
    White wave
Yacowitz, Caryn. *The jade stone*
Ye, Ting-xing. *Share the sky*
    Three monks, no water
Yen, Clara. *Why rat comes first*
Yep, Laurence. *Dragon prince*
    The junior thunder lord
    The man who tricked a ghost
    The shell woman and the king
    Tiger woman
Yolen, Jane. *The emperor and the kite*
    The seeing stick
Young, Ed (Edward). *Cat and Rat*
    High on a hill
    Little Plum
    Lon Po Po
    The lost horse
    Monkey King
    Mouse match
    Night visitors
    The rooster's horns
    The terrible Nung Gwama
Young, Evelyn. *The tale of Tai*
    Wu and Lu and Li
Young, Russell. *Dragonsong*
Zhang, Song Nan. *The ballad of Mulan*
    The five heavenly emperors and other Chinese myths from the creation
Zimelman, Nathan. *The great adventure of Wo Ti*

Foreign lands – Colombia

Metaxas, Eric. *The monkey people*
Torres, Leyla. *Saturday sancocho*

Foreign lands – Congo (Democratic Republic)

Aardema, Verna. *Traveling to Tondo*

Foreign lands – Costa Rica

Baden, Robert. *And Sunday makes seven*
Franklin, Kristine L. *When the monkeys came back*
Keister, Douglas. *Fernando's gift = El regalo de Fernando*
Strauss, Susan. *When woman became the sea*

Foreign lands – Cuba

Leiner, Katherine. *Mama does the mambo*
Schreier, Alta. *Cuba*

Foreign lands – Czechoslovakia

Bolliger, Max. *The fireflies*
Cohen, Barbara. *Here come the Purim players!*, ill. by Shoshana Mekibel
Ginsburg, Mirra. *How the sun was brought back to the sky*
Marshak, S. (Samuil). *The Month-Brothers*
Peters, Andrew. *Salt is sweeter than gold*
Van Kampen, Vlasta. *Bear tales*
Vojtech, Anna. *Marushka and the Month Brothers*
Wisniewski, David. *Golem*

Foreign lands – Denmark

Andersen, H. C. (Hans Christian). *The snow queen*, ill. by Toma Bogdanovic
Bason, Lillian. *Those foolish Molboes!*
Blegvad, Lenore. *Mr. Jensen and cat*
Bodecker, N. M. (Nils Mogens). *"It's raining," said John Twaining*
Brande, Marlie. *Sleepy Nicholas*
Burdett, Lois. *Hamlet for kids*
A Christmas book
Conover, Chris. *The wizard's daughter*

Coombs, Patricia. *The magic pot*
Deedy, Carmen Agra. *The yellow star*
Haviland, Virginia. *The talking pot*
Kent, Jack. *Hoddy doddy*
Lobel, Anita. *King Rooster, Queen Hen*
MacDonald, Margaret Read. *Fat cat*

Foreign lands – Dominican Republic

Alvarez, Julia. *The secret footprints*

Foreign lands – Ecuador

Bemelmans, Ludwig. *Quito express*

Foreign lands – Egypt

Adinolfi, JoAnn. *The Egyptian polar bear*
Aliki. *Mummies made in Egypt*
Angeletti, Roberta. *Nefertari, princess of Egypt*
Auld, Mary. *Exodus from Egypt*
Bible. Old Testament. Joseph. *Joseph and his brothers*
Bower, Tamara. *The shipwrecked sailor*
Clements, Andrew. *Temple cat*, ill. by Kate Kiesler
    Temple cat, ill. by Alan Marks
Climo, Shirley. *The Egyptian Cinderella*
Cushman, Doug. *The mystery of King Karfu*
Daly, Niki. *Mary Malloy and the baby who wouldn't sleep*
De Paola, Tomie (Thomas Anthony). *Bill and Pete go down the Nile*
Gerrard, Roy. *Croco'nile*
Goodenow, Earle. *The last camel*
Grant, Joan. *The monster that grew small*
Hayward, Linda. *Baby Moses*
Heide, Florence Parry. *The day of Ahmed's secret*
Hofmeyr, Dianne. *The star-bearer*
Hutton, Warwick. *Moses in the bulrushes*
Ife, Elaine. *Moses in the bulrushes*
Kimmel, Eric A. *Rimonah of the Flashing Sword*
Laskowski, Jerzy. *Master of the royal cats*
Lewin, Betsy. *What's the matter, Habibi?*
McDermott, Gerald. *The voyage of Osiris*
McMullan, Kate (Hall). *Mummy riddles*
Marcellino, Fred. *I, crocodile*
Mayers, Florence Cassen. *Egyptian art from the Brooklyn Museum*
Mike, Jan M. *Gift of the Nile*
Oppenheim, Shulamith Levey. *The hundredth name*
Price, Leontyne. *Aïda*
The prince who knew his fate
Rouss, Sylvia A. *The littlest frog*
Sabuda, Robert James. *The mummy's tomb*
    Tutankhamen's gift
Stolz, Mary (Mary Slattery). *Zekmet, the stone carver*
Walsh, Jill Paton. *Pepi and the secret names*
Wynne-Jones, Tim. *Zoom upstream*
Yates, Philip. *Ten little mummies*

Foreign lands – El Salvador

Argueta, Jorge. *Trees are hanging from the sky*
Argueta, Manlio. *The magic dogs of the volcanoes*

Foreign lands – England

Ahlberg, Allan. *Cops and robbers*
Ambler, C. Gifford (Christopher Gifford). *Ten little foxhounds*
Anno, Mitsumasa. *Anno's Britain*
Ardizzone, Edward. *Lucy Brown and Mr. Grimes*
Armitage, Ronda. *Don't forget, Matilda*
Atkins, Jeannine. *Mary Anning and the sea dragon*
Azarian, Mary. *The tale of John Barleycorn or, From barley to beer*
Barber, Antonia. *The mousehole cat*
Beardshaw, Rosalind. *Grandpa's surprise*
    Grandpa's surprise
Beatty, Hetty Burlingame. *Moorland pony*
Belting, Natalia Maree. *Christmas folk*
    Summer's coming in
Bemelmans, Ludwig. *Madeline in London*

Bennett, Jill. *Teeny tiny*
Bennett, Olivia. *A Turkish afternoon*
Bentley, Anne. *The Groggs' day out*
    The Groggs have a wonderful summer
Blathwayt, Benedict. *The runaway train*
Bond, Michael. *Paddington and the knickerbocker rainbow*
    Paddington at the circus
    Paddington at the fair
    Paddington at the palace
    Paddington at the seaside
    Paddington at the tower
    Paddington at the zoo
    Paddington Bear, ill. by John Lobban
    Paddington cleans up
    Paddington's art exhibit
    Paddington's garden
    Paddington's lucky day
Brighton, Catherine. *The fossil girl*
Brooks, Nigel. *Country mouse cottage*
    Town mouse house
Brown, Don. *Rare treasure*
    Uncommon traveler
Brown, Janet Allison. *A little princess*
    The secret garden
Brown, Ruth. *A dark, dark tale*
Burnett, Frances Hodgson. *A little princess*
Burningham, John. *Borka*
Calhoun, Mary. *The pixy and the lazy housewife*
    The witch's pig
Carrick, Donald. *Harold and the great stag*
Christian, Mary Blount. *April fool*
Clayton, Elaine. *The yeoman's daring daughter and the princes in the tower*
Cole, Brock. *The king at the door*
Coltman, Paul. *Tinker Jim*
Conger, Lesley. *Tops and bottoms*
Cooper, Susan. *The silver cow*
Cressey, James. *The dragon and George*
Crompton, Margaret. *The house where Jack lives*
Crossley-Holland, Kevin. *The green children*
Davidson, Amanda. *Teddy at the seashore*
Davis, Reda. *Martin's dinosaur*
Dennard, Deborah. *Hedgehog haven*
Dick Whittington and his cat. *Dick Whittington*, ill. by Edward Ardizzone
    Dick Whittington, ill. by Antony Maitland
    Dick Whittington and his cat, ill. by Marcia Brown
    Dick Whittington and his cat, ill. by Kurt Werth
Dines, Glen. *Gilly and the wicharoo*
Dominguez, Angel. *Diary of a Victorian mouse*
Drummond, Violet H. *The flying postman*
Emecheta, Buchi. *Nowhere to play*
Esterl, Arnica. *The fine round cake*
Fairclough, Chris. *Take a trip to England*
Freeman, Don. *The guard mouse*
    Will's quill
Freschet, Berniece. *Bernard of Scotland Yard*
A frog he would a-wooing go (folk-song). *Mr. Frog went a-courting*
Ganly, Helen. *Jyoti's journey*
Garland, Sarah. *Seeing red*
Gauch, Patricia Lee. *On to Widecombe Fair*
Gerrard, Jean. *Matilda Jane*
Goodall, John S. *An Edwardian Christmas*
    An Edwardian summer
    Great days of a country house
    The story of a castle
    The story of a farm
    The story of an English village
Grahame, Kenneth. *The wind in the willows*, ill. by Joanne Moss
    The wind in the willows: home sweet home
Gramatky, Hardie. *Little Toot on the Thames*
Greaves, Margaret. *Kate Crackernuts*
    Mother Cuspen
    The witch cat
    The witch's servant
Haley, Gail E. *Dream peddler*
    The post office cat

Herrmann, Frank. *The giant Alexander*
  The giant Alexander and the circus
The Hippopotamus's birthday and other poems about animals and birds
Hodges, Margaret. *Molly Limbo*
  Saint George and the dragon
  Up the chimney
Hughes, Shirley. *Bathwater's hot*
  Lucy and Tom's A.B.C.
  Lucy and Tom's Christmas
  Noisy
  Out and about
  The snow lady
  When we went to the park
Ivory, Lesley Anne. *A day in London*
Jack and the beanstalk. *Jack and the beanstalk*, ill. by Aljoscha Blau
Jacobs, Joseph. *The crock of gold*
  Tattercoats
James, Simon. *Leon and Bob*
Keeping, Charles. *Alfie finds the other side of the world*
  Through the window
Kennedy, Cindy. *The star of Christmas*
Ketcham, Sallie. *The Christmas bird*
Laird, Elizabeth. *The day Patch stood guard*
  The day Sidney ran off
Lawrence, John. *The giant of Grabbist*
Lerman, Rory S. *Charlie's checklist*
Lewis, J. Patrick. *The Christmas of the reddle moon*
Lewis, Kim. *The last train*
Little old lady who swallowed a fly. *Fancy that!*
  I know an old lady, ill. by G. Brian Karas
  I know an old lady, ill. by Steve McInturff
  I know an old lady who swallowed a fly, ill. by Stephen Gulbis
  I know an old lady who swallowed a fly, ill. by Glen Rounds
  I know an old lady who swallowed a fly, ill. by Nadine Bernard Westcott
  There was an old lady, ill. by Nick Bantock
  There was an old lady who swallowed a fly, ill. by Colin Hawkins
Lodge, Bernard. *Door to door*
Long, Sylvia. *Deck the hall*
McCully, Emily Arnold. *Popcorn at the palace*
MacDonald, Margaret Read. *The old woman who lived in a vinegar bottle*
Menter, Ian. *Carnival*
Mother Goose. *London Bridge is falling down*, ill. by Ed Emberley
  London Bridge is falling down, ill. by Peter Spier
Muller, Robin. *Mollie Whuppie and the giant*
Munro, Roxie. *The inside-outside book of London*
Newcome, Zita. *Rosie goes shopping*
Nikola-Lisa, W. *Till year's good end*
Northway, Jennifer. *Lucy's day trip*
Oakley, Graham. *The church cat abroad*
  The church mice and the moon
  The church mice at bay
  The church mice spread their wings
  The church mouse
Oldfield, Pamela. *Melanie Brown climbs a tree*
Oxenbury, Helen. *The queen and Rosie Randall*
Penney, Ian. *Ian Penney's ABC*
Petty, Kate. *On a plane*
Riggio, Anita. *Beware the Brindlebeast*
Robins, Arthur. *The teeny tiny woman*
Rogers, Paul (Patrick). *Don't blame me!*
Ross, Diana. *The story of the little red engine*
San Souci, Robert D. *The Hobyahs*
Service, Pamela F. *The wizard of wind and rock*
Seuling, Barbara. *The teeny tiny woman*
Sewall, Marcia. *The Green Mist*
  The little wee tyke
Shannon, Mark. *Gawain and the Green Knight*
Shulman, Milton. *Prep, the little pigeon of Trafalgar Square*
Smith, Barry. *Minnie and Ginger*
Solomon, Joan. *A present for Mum*
Southey, Robert. *The cataract of Lodore*
Storr, Catherine (Cole). *Robin Hood*
Tennyson, Alfred, Baron. *The brook*
Thompson, Harwood. *The witch's cat*
Unwin, Pippa. *Tomcat takes a walk*

Vickers, Rebecca. *Florence Nightingale*
Wahl, Jan. *Little Johnny Buttermilk*
Widdecombe Fair
Willard, Barbara. *To London! To London!*
Wolff, Ashley. *The bells of London*
Wood, Joyce. *Grandmother Lucy in her garden*
Worthington, Phoebe. *Teddy bear baker*
  Teddy bear coalman
Zemach, Harve. *Duffy and the devil*

Foreign lands – Estonia

Moroney, Lynn. *Elinda who danced in the sky*

Foreign lands – Ethiopia

Day, Nancy Raines. *The lion's whiskers*
Kurtz, Jane. *Faraway home*
  Fire on the mountain
  Only a pigeon
Schrier, Jeffrey. *On the wings of eagles*
Schur, Maxine Rose. *Day of delight*

Foreign lands – Europe

Bornstein, Ruth Lercher. *The dancing man*
Dunrea, Olivier. *The trow-wife's treasure*
Jaffe, Nina. *The way meat loves salt*
Keefer, Janice Kulyk. *Anna's goat*
Sopko, Eugen. *Townsfolk and countryfolk*

Foreign lands – Fiji

Wolfson, Margaret. *Turtle songs*

Foreign lands – Finland

Allen, Linda. *The mouse bride*
De Gerez, Toni. *Louhi, witch of North Farm*
Shepard, Aaron. *The princess mouse*

Foreign lands – France

Aliki. *The king's day*
Allen, Laura Jean. *Rollo and Tweedy and the case of the missing cheese*
Anderson, M. T. *Strange Mr. Satie*
Angelo, Nancy Carolyn Harrison. *Camembert*
Arnold, Marsha Diane. *Metro cat*
Baker, Leslie A. *Paris cat*
Bemelmans, Ludwig. *Madeline*
  Madeline [pop-up book]
  Madeline and the bad hat
  Madeline and the gypsies
  Madeline's Christmas
  Madeline's rescue
Bergere, Thea. *Paris in the rain with Jean and Jacqueline*
Berson, Harold. *Barrels to the moon*
  Charles and Claudine
  How the devil gets his due
  Joseph and the snake
Bingham, Mindy. *Minou*
Bishop, Claire Huchet. *The truffle pig*
Brighton, Catherine. *My Napoleon*
Bring a torch, Jeannette, Isabella
Brown, Judith Gwyn. *Max and the truffle pig*
Brunhoff, Jean de. *The story of Babar, the little elephant*
Cazet, Denys. *Minnie and Moo go to Paris*
Chall, Marsha Wilson. *Bonaparte*
Charlip, Remy. *Harlequin and the gift of many colors*
Collier, Mary Jo. *The king's giraffe*
Cox, Judy. *Rabbit pirates*
Coxe, Molly. *Bunny and the beast*
Daudet, Alphonse. *The brave little goat of Monsieur Séguin*
Dauphin, Francine Legrand. *A French A. B. C.*
DeFelice, Cynthia C. *Three perfect peaches*
De Paola, Tomie (Thomas Anthony). *Bonjour, Mister Satie*
Diska, Pat. *Andy says . . . Bonjour!*

Dumas, Philippe. *Caesar, cock of the village*
   Laura loses her head
   The story of Edward
Eisenstein, Marilyn. *Periwinkle isn't Paris*
Ellwand, David. *Cinderlily*
Elzbieta. *Dikou and the Snivelly Snoak*
Fatio, Louise. *The happy lion*
   The happy lion and the bear
   The happy lion in Africa
   The happy lion roars
   The happy lion's quest
   The happy lion's rabbits
   The happy lion's treasure
   The three happy lions
Fender, Kay. *Odette!*
Fleming, Candace. *Madame LaGrande and her so high, to the sky, uproarious pompadour*
Froment, Eugène. *The story of a round loaf*
Gamgee, John. *Journey through France*
Goffstein, M. B. (Marilyn Brooke). *Artists' helpers enjoy the evening*
Goode, Diane. *Mama's perfect present*
   Where's our mama?
Harris, Leon A. *The great picture robbery*
Haseley, Dennis. *Horses with wings*
Haskins, Jim (James). *Count your way through France*
Hautzig, Esther (Rudomin). *At home*
   In the park
Hobbie, Holly. *Toot and Puddle, top of the world*
Hoestlandt, Jo. *Star of fear, star of hope*
Huling, Jan. *Puss in cowboy boots*
Ichikawa, Satomi. *La La Rose*
   Suzanne and Nicholas at the market
   Suzanne and Nicholas in the garden
Ingman, Bruce. *A night on the tiles*
Joslin, Sesyle. *Baby elephant's trunk*
Kelley, True. *Claude Monet*
Kimmel, Eric A. *Three sacks of truth*
Kirby, David K. *Cows are going to Paris*
Klein, Leonore. *Henri's walk to Paris*
Knight, Joan. *Bon appetit, Bertie!*
Le Tord, Bijou. *A bird or two*
Littlesugar, Amy. *Lisette's angel*
Lubell, Winifred. *Rosalie, the bird market turtle*
McCaughrean, Geraldine. *Beauty and the beast*
McCully, Emily Arnold. *Mirette on the high wire*
McLaren, Chesley. *Zat cat*
Manson, Christopher. *Here begins the tale of the marvellous blue mouse*
Marcellino, Fred. *I, crocodile*
Marokvia, Merelle. *A French school for Paul*
Meddaugh, Susan. *Maude and Claude go abroad*
Mendoza, George. *Henri Mouse, the juggler*
Milton, Nancy. *The giraffe that walked to Paris*
Moore, Inga. *The truffle hunter*
Moore, Lilian. *Papa Albert*
Morris, Ann. *The Cinderella rebus book*
   Hello Peter = Bonjour, Rémy
Munro, Roxie. *The inside-outside book of Paris*
Napoli, Guillier. *Adventure at Mont-Saint-Michel*
O'Callahan, Jay. *Tulips*
Olofsson, Helena. *The little jester*
Orgel, Doris. *Button soup*
Patron, Susan. *Burgoo stew*
Perrault, Charles. *Cinderella = Cenicienta*
   Puss in boots, ill. by Julia Noonan
Polacco, Patricia. *The butterfly*
Poole, Josephine. *Joan of Arc*
Pullman, Philip. *Puss in boots*, ill. by Ian Beck
Raffi. *Wheels on the bus*
Rider, Alex. *A la ferme = At the farm*
   At our house = Chez nous
Ringgold, Faith. *Bonjour, Lonnie*
Rockwell, Anne F. *Poor Goose*
   The wolf who had a wonderful dream
Rubin, Susan Goldman. *The yellow house*
Schiller, Barbara. *The white rat's tale*
Schotter, Roni. *That extraordinary pig of Paris*

Scribner, Charles. *The devil's bridge*
Seignobosc, Françoise. *The big rain*
   Biquette, the white goat
   Chouchou
   Jeanne-Marie at the fair
   Jeanne-Marie counts her sheep
   Jeanne-Marie in gay Paris
   Minou
   Noël for Jeanne-Marie
   Springtime for Jeanne-Marie
Shannon, Mark. *The acrobat and the angel*
Shecter, Ben. *Partouche plants a seed*
Slobodkin, Louis. *Colette and the princess*
Stevenson, Harvey. *Looking at liberty*
Sweeney, Joan. *Suzette and the puppy*
Titus, Eve. *Anatole*
   Anatole and the cat
   Anatole and the piano
   Anatole and the pied piper
   Anatole and the poodle
   Anatole and the robot
   Anatole and the thirty thieves
   Anatole and the toyshop
   Anatole over Paris
Ungerer, Tomi. *Adelaide*
   The beast of Monsieur Racine
Weelen, Guy. *The little red train*
Yorinks, Arthur. *Harry and Lulu*

Foreign lands – French Guiana

Ryder, Joanne. *Jaguar in the rain forest*

Foreign lands – Galapagos Islands

Jacobs, Francine. *Lonesome George, the giant tortoise*
Lewin, Ted. *Nilo and the tortoise*
Winkelman, Barbara Gaines. *Puffer's surprise*

Foreign lands – Galilee

Stewart, Dana. *Friends from Galilee*

Foreign lands – Gambia

Hoffman, Mary. *Grace and family*

Foreign lands – Germany

Allard, Harry. *May I stay?*
Allen, Debbie. *Brothers of the knight*
Attenberger, Walburga. *The little man in winter*
   Who knows the little man?
Babbitt, Natalie. *Ouch!*
Bartos-Hoppner, Barbara. *The pied piper of Hamelin*
Bechstein, Ludwig. *The rabbit catcher and other fairy tales*
Biro, Val. *The pied piper of Hamelin*
Browning, Robert. *The pied piper of Hamelin*, ill. by Patricia and Robin DeWitt
   The pied piper of Hamelin, ill. by Kate Greenaway
   The pied piper of Hamelin, ill. by Anatoly Ivanov
   The pied piper of Hamelin, ill. by Errol Le Cain
   The pied piper of Hamelin, ill. by Drahos Zak
Calhoun, Mary. *The thieving dwarfs*
Coombs, Patricia. *Tilabel*
Cooney, Barbara. *Little brother and little sister*
Croll, Carolyn. *The three brothers*
Delaney, A. *The gunnywolf*
Delessert, Etienne. *The seven dwarfs*
Fairclough, Chris. *Take a trip to West Germany*
Grimm, Jacob. *The brave little tailor*, ill. by Mark Corcoran
   The brave little tailor, ill. by Olga Dugina & Andrej Dugin
   The brave little tailor, ill. by Daniel San Souci
   The brave little tailor, ill. by David Shaw
   The brave little tailor, ill. by Svend Otto S
   The brave little tailor, ill. by Eve Tharlet
   The brave little tailor, ill. by James Warhola

The elves and the shoemaker, ill. by Doug Cushman
The elves and the shoemaker, ill. by Paul Galdone
The elves and the shoemaker, ill. by Margaret Walty
The elves and the shoemaker, ill. by Bernadette Watts
Iron Hans
Iron John, ill. by Trina Schart Hyman
Iron John, ill. by Winslow Pels
The rabbit's bride
Seven at one blow
The shoemaker and his elves, ill. by Bill Dickson
The shoemaker and the elves, ill. by Adrienne Adams
The shoemaker and the elves, ill. by Cynthia and William Birrer
The shoemaker and the elves, ill. by Ilse Plume
The three spinning fairies
Harper, Wilhelmina. *The gunniwolf*
Haskins, Jim (James). *Count your way through Germany*
Hoberman, Mary Ann. *Marvelous mouse man*
Hodges, Margaret. *The hero of Bremen*
Hürlimann, Ruth. *The proud white cat*
Janisch, Heinz. *The merry pranks of Till Eulenspiegel*
Johnson, Grace. *The candle in the window*
Kahl, Virginia. *Droopsi*
   Maxie
Kimmel, Eric A. *The four gallant sisters*
Kinter, Judith. *King of magic, man of glass*
Latimer, Jim. *The Irish piper*
Lynch, Wendy. *Bach*
Mayer, Marianna. *The spirit of the blue light*
Mayer, Mercer. *The pied piper of Hamelin*
Moore, Maggie. *Little Red Riding Hood*
Morgenstern, Elizabeth. *The little gardeners*
Norling, Beth. *Sister night and sister day*
Raven, Margot Theis. *Mercedes and the chocolate pilot*
Root, Phyllis. *Grandmother Winter*
Ross, Tony. *The pied piper of Hamelin*
Spang, Günter. *Clelia and the little mermaid*
Stewig, John Warren. *Mother Holly*
Van Woerkom, Dorothy. *The queen who couldn't bake gingerbread*

Foreign lands – Ghana

Angelou, Maya. *Kofi and his magic*
Appiah, Sonia. *Amoko and Efua Bear*
Berry, James. *Don't leave an elephant to go and chase a bird*
Cummings, Pat. *Ananse and the lizard*
Dee, Ruby. *Tower to heaven*
Lake, Mary Dixon. *The royal drum*
Medearis, Angela Shelf. *Seven spools of thread*
   Too much talk
Mollel, Tololwa M. (Tololwa Marti). *Ananse's feast*
Musgrove, Margaret. *The spider weaver*

Foreign lands – Gilbert Islands *see* Foreign lands – South Sea Islands

Foreign lands – Great Britain

Browne, Anthony. *The shape game*

Foreign lands – Greece

Aliki. *Diogenes*
Aliki. *The eggs*
   Three gold pieces
   The twelve months
Allen, Judy. *Seal*
Anderson, Lonzo. *Arion and the dolphins*
Birrer, Cynthia. *Song to Demeter*
Brown, Marcia. *Tamarindo!*
Bunting, Eve (Anne Evelyn). *I have an olive tree*
Delton, Judy. *My Uncle Nikos*
Haskins, Jim (James). *Count your way through Greece*
Hol, Coby. *Niki's little donkey*
Hutton, Warwick. *Persephone*
   Theseus and the Minotaur
   The Trojan horse

Manna, Anthony L. *Mr. Semolina-Semolinus*
Mason, Jane B. *The flying horse*
Mayer, Marianna. *Pegasus*
   Perseus
Oppenheim, Shulamith Levey. *Yanni rubbish*
Rumford, James. *There's a monster in the alphabet*
Steel, Barry. *Greek cities*
Stewig, John Warren. *King Midas*
Walker, Barbara K. (Barbara Kerlin). *Pigs and pirates*

Foreign lands – Greenland

Conrad, Pam. *Call me Ahnighito*
Dupre, Kelly. *The raven's gift*
Hertz, Ole. *Tobias catches trout*
   Tobias goes ice fishing
   Tobias goes seal hunting
   Tobias has a birthday

Foreign lands – Guatemala

Carling, Amelia Lau. *Mama and Papa have a store*
Carling, Amelia Lau. *Mama and Papa have a store*
Castaneda, Omar S. *Abuela's weave*
Czernecki, Stefan. *The sleeping bread*
Mora, Pat. *The race of toad and deer*

Foreign lands – Guyana

Agard, John. *Dig away two-hole Tim*

Foreign lands – Haiti

Lauture, Denizé. *Running the road to ABC*
MacDonald, Amy. *Please, Malese!*
Van Laan, Nancy. *Mama rocks, Papa sings*
Williams, Karen Lynn. *Painted dreams*
   Tap-tap
Wolkstein, Diane. *Bouki dances the Kokioko*

Foreign lands – Himalayas

Fleming, Candace. *When Agnes caws*
Nagda, Anne Whitehead. *World above the clouds*

Foreign lands – Holland

Anholt, Laurence. *Camille and the sunflowers*
Bouhuys, Mies. *The lady of Stavoren*
Bromhall, Winifred. *Johanna arrives*
Chasek, Judith. *Have you seen Wilhelmina Krumpf?*
Fairclough, Chris. *Take a trip to Holland*
Fleming, Candace. *Boxes for Katje*
Green, Norma B. *The hole in the dike*
Howells, Mildred. *The woman who lived in Holland*
Krasilovsky, Phyllis. *The cow who fell in the canal*
Oppenheim, Shulamith Levey. *The lily cupboard*
Reesink, Marijke. *The golden treasure*
Schubert, Ingrid. *The magic bubble trip*
Van Stockum, Hilda. *A day on skates*
Woelfle, Gretchen. *Katje the windmill cat*

Foreign lands – Hungary

Ambrus, Victor G. *Brave soldier Janosch*
Ambrus, Victor G. *The three poor tailors*
Bodnar, Judit Z. *A wagonload of fish*
Brown, Margaret Wise. *Wheel on the chimney*
Ginsburg, Mirra. *Two greedy bears*
The good-hearted youngest brother
Hippely, Hilary Horder. *A song for Lena*
Illyés, Gyula. *Matt the gooseherd*
Kimmel, Eric A. *The valiant red rooster*
Lieberman, Syd. *The wise shoemaker of Studena*
Lottridge, Celia Barker. *The little rooster and the diamond button*
Surany, Anico. *Kati and Kormos*
Varga, Judy. *Janko's wish*

Foreign lands – Iceland

Eyvindson, Peter. *Backward brothers see the light*
McMillan, Bruce. *Days of the ducklings*
    Gletta the foal
    Nights of the pufflings
Wisniewski, David. *Elfwyn's saga*

Foreign lands – India

Alan, Sandy. *The plaid peacock*
Ambrus, Victor G. *The Sultan's bath*
Appelt, Kathi. *Elephants aloft*
Arenson, Roberta. *Manu and the talking fish*
Atkins, Jeannine. *Aani and the tree huggers*
Backstein, Karen. *The blind men and the elephant*
Bang, Betsy. *The cucumber stem*
    The old woman and the red pumpkin
    The old woman and the rice thief
    Tuntuni the tailor bird
Bannerman, Helen. *Little Black Sambo*, Platt & Munk, 1933
    Little Black Sambo, ill. by Nina R. Jordan
    Little Black Sambo, ill. by Gladys Turkey Mitchell
    Little Black Sambo, ill. by Robert Moore
    Little Black Sambo, ill. by Fern Bisel Peat
    Little Black Sambo, ill. by Mary LaFetra Russell
    Little Black Sambo, ill. by Cobb X. Shinn
    Little Black Sambo, ill. by Terry & Mary Smith
    Little Black Sambo, ill. by Suzanne
    Little Black Sambo, ill. by Gustaf Tenggren
    Little Black Sambo, ill. by Keith Ward
    Little Black Sambo, ill. by Julian Wehr
    The Little Black Sambo story book
    Sambo and the twins
    The story of Little Babaji
    The story of Little Black Sambo, Reilly, 1905
    The story of Little Black Sambo, Lippincott, 1915
    The story of Little Black Sambo, Stokes, 1923
    The story of Little Black Sambo, Altemus, 1931
    The story of Little Black Sambo, Lippincott, 1943
    The story of Little Black Sambo, Greenhouse, 1986
    The story of Little Black Sambo, HarperCollins, 1990
    The story of little black Sambo, Applewood, 1996
    The story of Little Black Sambo, ill. by Christopher Bing
    The story of Little Black Sambo, "pop-up" picture by C. Carey
        Cloud
    The story of Little Black Sambo, ill. by Judith Russell
Barry, David. *The Rajah's rice*
Bond, Ruskin. *Cherry tree*
    Flames in the forest
Bonnici, Peter. *The festival*
Brown, Marcia. *The blue jackal*
    Once a mouse . . .
Bruce, Lisa. *Engines, engines*
Bush, Barbara. *In the heart of the village*
Cassedy, Sylvia. *Moon-uncle, moon-uncle*
Cathon, Laura E. *Tot Botot and his little flute*
Chase, Catherine. *The nightingale and the fool*
Demi. *The hallowed horse*
Domanska, Janina. *Why so much noise?*
Duff, Maggie (Margaret K.). *Rum pum pum*
Easwaran, Eknath. *The monkey and the mango*
Galdone, Paul. *The monkey and the crocodile*
Ganly, Helen. *Jyoti's journey*
Gardeski, Christina Mia. *Diwali*
Gleeson, Brian. *The tiger and the Brahmin*
Gobhai, Mehlli. *Lakshmi, the water buffalo who wouldn't*
    Usha, the mouse-maiden
Haskins, Jim (James). *Count your way through India*
Hirsh, Marilyn. *Leela and the watermelon*
Hodges, Margaret. *The golden deer*
    Hidden in sand
Jendresen, Erik. *Hanuman*
Jeyaveeran, Ruth. *The road to Mumbai*
Kajpust, Melissa. *The peacock's pride*
Kamal, Aleph. *The bird who was an elephant*
Kipling, Rudyard. *The miracle of the mountain*
    Rikki-tikki-tavi, ill. by Lambert Davis
    Rikki-tikki-tavi, ill. by Jerry Pinkney
Kroll, Steven. *Doctor on an elephant*
Lester, Julius. *Sam and the tigers*
Lexau, Joan M. *It all began with a drip, drip, drip*
Martin, Rafe. *The monkey bridge*
Myers, Walter Dean. *The golden serpent*
Newton, Patricia Montgomery. *The stonecutter*
Papas, William. *Taresh the tea planter*
Parkison, Jami. *Amazing Mallika*
Quigley, Lillian Fox. *The blind men and the elephant*
Rockwell, Anne F. *The stolen necklace*
Rodanas, Kristina. *The story of Wali Dâd*
Rumford, James. *Nine animals and the well*
Shank, Ned. *The sanyasin's first day*
Shepard, Aaron. *The gifts of Wali Dad*
Siberell, Anne. *A journey to paradise*
Singh, Jacquelin. *Fat Gopal*
Slobodkin, Louis. *The polka-dot goat*
So, Meilo. *Gobble, gobble, slip, slop*
Souhami, Jessica. *No dinner!*
    Rama and the demon king
Thornhill, Jan. *The rumor*
Towle, Faith M. *The magic cooking pot*
Trez, Denise. *Maila and the flying carpet*
Verma, Jatinder Nath. *The story of Divaali*
Villarejo, Mary. *The tiger hunt*
Wahl, Jan. *Tiger watch*
Ward, Nanda Weedon. *The elephant that ga-lumped*
Whitmore, Adam. *Max in India*
Wolf, Gita. *The very hungry lion*
Young, Ed (Edward). *Seven blind mice*

Foreign lands – Indonesia

Gilman, Rita Golden. *Rice is life*
Sierra, Judy. *The gift of the crocodile*

Foreign lands – Iran

Balouch, Kristen. *The king and the three thieves*
Hofmeyr, Dianne. *The stone*
Oppenheim, Shulamith Levey. *Ali and the magic stew*
Shepard, Aaron. *Forty fortunes*

Foreign lands – Iraq

Alrawi, Karim. *The girl who lost her smile*
Hickox, Rebecca. *The golden sandal*

Foreign lands – Ireland

Balian, Lorna. *Leprechauns never lie*
Behan, Brendan. *The king of Ireland's son*
Blazek, Sarah Kirwan. *An Irish Hallowe'en*
Bromhall, Winifred. *Bridget's growing day*
Bunting, Eve (Anne Evelyn). *Clancy's coat*
    Market day
Calhoun, Mary. *The hungry leprechaun*
Climo, Shirley. *The Irish Cinderlad*
Cooper, Susan. *The Selkie girl*
Cormack, M. Grant. *Animal tales from Ireland*
Daly, Jude. *Fair, Brown & Trembling*
Day, David. *The swan children*
De Paola, Tomie (Thomas Anthony). *Fin M'Coul*
    Jamie O'Rourke and the big potato
    Jamie O'Rourke and the pooka
    Patrick
Edwards, Pamela Duncan. *The leprechaun's gold*
Esckelson, Laura. *The copper braid of Shannon O'Shea*
Gerber, Carole. *Hush! a Gaelic lullaby*
Gleeson, Brian. *Finn McCoul*
Graham, Steve. *Dear old Donegal*
Greene, Ellin. *Billy Beg and his bull*
Hänel, Wolfram. *The gold at the end of the rainbow*
Haskins, Jim (James). *Count your way through Ireland*
Haugaard, Erik Christian. *Prince Boghole*

Hazen, Barbara Shook. *Katie's wish*
Hodges, Margaret. *Saint Patrick and the peddler*
Jacobs, Joseph. *Hudden and Dudden and Donald O'Neary*
Kennedy, Richard. *The leprechaun's story*
Lattimore, Deborah Nourse. *The sailor who captured the sea*
McCully, Emily Arnold. *The pirate queen*
McDermott, Gerald. *Daniel O'Rourke*
MacGill-Callahan, Sheila. *The children of Lir*
   Finn MacCool and the talking fish
   The last snake in Ireland
   To capture the wind
Milligan, Bryce. *Brigid's cloak*
   The prince of Ireland and the three magic stallions
Nolan, Janet. *The St. Patrick's Day shillelagh*
O'Donnell, Elizabeth Lee. *Patrick's day*
Parker, Dorothy D. *Liam's catch*
San Souci, Robert D. *Brave Margaret*
Souhami, Jessica. *Mrs. McCool and the giant Cuhullin*
Stuart, Chad. *The Ballymara flood*
Taylor, Alice. *A child's treasury of Irish rhymes*
Tompert, Ann. *Saint Patrick*
Welling, Peter J. *Shawn O'Hisser, the last snake in Ireland*
What do you feed your donkey on?
Zimelman, Nathan. *To sing a song as big as Ireland*

Foreign lands – Israel

Adler, David A. *A picture book of Israel*
Alexander, Sue. *Behold the trees*
Auld, Mary. *David and Goliath*
Bible. Old Testament. David. *David and Goliath*
Biers-Ariel, Matt. *Solomon and the trees*
Brin, Ruth F. *David and Goliath*
   The story of Esther
Carlstrom, Nancy White. *I am Christmas*
da Costa, Deborah. *Snow in Jerusalem*
De Regniers, Beatrice Schenk. *David and Goliath*, ill. by Scott
      Cameron
   David and Goliath, ill. by Richard M. Powers
Edwards, Michelle. *Chicken Man*
Elkin, Benjamin. *The wisest man in the world*
Fairclough, Chris. *Take a trip to Israel*
Fisher, Leonard Everett. *David and Goliath*
Goldsboro, Bobby. *Noah and the ark; and, David and Goliath*
Haskins, Jim (James). *Count your way through Israel*
Karmi, Giora. *And Shira imagined*
Kuskin, Karla. *Jerusalem, shining still*
Metaxas, Eric. *David and Goliath*
Oberman, Sheldon. *The wisdom bird*
Segal, Sheila. *Joshua's dream*
Waldman, Neil. *The never-ending greenness*

Foreign lands – Italy

Æsop. *Androcles and the lion*, ill. by Janusz Grabianski
Æsop. *Androcles and the lion*, ill. by Dennis Nolan
   Androcles and the lion, ill. by Robert Rayevsky
   Androcles and the lion, ill. by Janet Stevens
Angelou, Maya. *Angelina of Italy*
Anno, Mitsumasa. *Anno's Italy*
Atene, Ann (Anna). *The golden guitar*
Barton, Bob. *Paul Gallico's The small miracle*
Basile, Giambattista. *Petrosinella*
Bettina (Bettina Ehrlich). *Pantaloni*
Brighton, Catherine. *Five secrets in a box*
Brown, Marcia. *Felice*
Cauley, Lorinda Bryan. *The goose and the golden coins*
Cazzola, Gus. *The bells of Santa Lucia*
Cecil, Laura. *The frog princess*
Chafetz, Henry. *The legend of Befana*
Chapman, Jean. *Moon-Eyes*
Daly, Niki. *Bravo, Zan Angelo!*
De Paola, Tomie (Thomas Anthony). *Big Anthony, his story*
   The clown of God
   Jingle, the Christmas clown
   The legend of Old Befana
   Merry Christmas, Strega Nona

The mysterious giant of Barletta
The Prince of the Dolomites
Tony's bread
Ehrlich, Amy. *Pome and Peel*
Fairclough, Chris. *Take a trip to Italy*
Fleming, Candace. *Gabriella's song*
Gál, László. *The parrot*
Galdone, Paul. *Androcles and the lion*
Gerrard, Roy. *The Roman twins*
Giannini, Enzo. *Little Parsley*
Grant, Rose Marie. *Andiamo, Weasel*
Guarnieri, Paolo. *A boy named Giotto*
Gutman, Anne. *Gaspard on vacation*
Guy, Suzanne. *The music box*
Haskins, Jim (James). *Count your way through Italy*
Kimmel, Eric A. *Count Silvernose*
Kroll, Steven. *Looking for Daniela*
Lager, Claude. *A tale of two rats*
McCully, Emily Arnold. *The orphan singer*
Manson, Christopher. *The crab prince*
Mauner, Claudia. *Zoe Sophia's scrapbook*
Michael, Emory H. *Androcles and the lion*
Morpurgo, Michael. *Jo-Jo the melon donkey*
Nones, Eric Jon. *Canary prince*
Norris, Kathleen. *The holy twins: Benedict and Scholastica*
Parillo, Tony. *Michelangelo's surprise*
Peterson, Julienne. *Caterina, the clever farm girl*
Plume, Ilse. *The story of Befana*
Politi, Leo. *Little Leo*
Potter, Giselle. *The year I didn't go to school*
Rayevsky, Inna. *The talking tree*
Rockwell, Anne F. *Romulus and Remus*
   The wonderful eggs of Furicchia
Sanderson, Ruth. *Papa Gatto*
Seibold, J. Otto. *Mr. Lunch borrows a canoe*
Seidler, Rosalie. *Grumpus and the Venetian cat*
Titus, Eve. *Anatole in Italy*
Ungerer, Tomi. *The hat*
Weaver, Tess. *Opera cat*
Yorinks, Arthur. *The Miami giant*

Foreign lands – Jamaica

Belafonte, Harry. *Island in the sun*
Carter, Donna Renee. *Music in the family*
Gleeson, Brian. *Anansi*
Hanson, Regina. *A season for mangoes*
   The tangerine tree
Hausman, Gerald. *Doctor Bird*
Temple, Frances. *Tiger soup*
Van West, Patricia E. *The crab man*

Foreign lands – Japan

Baker, Keith. *The magic fan*
Bang, Molly. *Dawn*
Bartoli, Jennifer. *Snow on bear's nose*
Baruch, Dorothy. *Kappa's tug-of-war with the big brown horse*
Battles, Edith. *What does the rooster say, Yoshio?*
Bauld, Jane Scoggins. *Journey of the third seed*
Bodkin, Odds. *The crane wife*
Bryan, Ashley. *Sh-ko and his eight wicked brothers*
Bunting, Eve (Anne Evelyn). *Magic and the night river*
Cassedy, Sylvia. *Red dragonfly on my shoulder*
Charles, Veronika Martenova. *The crane girl*
Cocagnac, A. M. (Augustin Maurice). *The three trees of the Samurai*
Coerr, Eleanor. *Sadako*
Cook, Joel. *The rat's daughter*
Damjan, Mischa. *The little prince and the tiger cat*
Dawson, Zöe. *Japan*
DeForest, Charlotte B. *The prancing pony*
Demi. *The leaky umbrella*
Dines, Glen. *A tiger in the cherry tree*
Don't tell the scarecrow
Edens, Cooper. *A present for Rose*
Fazio, Brenda Lena. *Grandfather's story*
Fifield, Flora. *Pictures for the palace*

French, Fiona. *Little Inchkin*
Fujita, Tamao. *The boy and the bird*
Gackenbach, Dick. *The perfect mouse*
Galouchko, Annouchka. *Shô and the demons of the deep*
Garrison, Christian. *The dream eater*
Gollub, Matthew. *Cool melons – turn to frogs*
    Ten oni drummers
Hamanaka, Sheila. *Screen of frogs*
Hamilton, Morse. *Belching Hill*
Hanson, Regina. *The face at the window*
Haskins, Jim (James). *Count your way through Japan*
Heller, George. *Hiroshi's wonderful kite*
Hidaka, Masako. *Girl from the snow country*
Hodges, Margaret. *The wave*
Honda, Tetsuya. *Wild horse winter*
Hooks, William H. *Peach boy*
Hughes, Monica. *Little Fingerling*
Iijima, Geneva Cobb. *The way we do it in Japan*
Iké, Jane Hori. *A Japanese fairy tale*
Ikeda, Daisaku. *The cherry tree*
    Kanta and the deer
    The snow country prince
Ishii, Momoko. *The tongue-cut sparrow*
James, J. Alison. *The drums of Noto Hanto*
Johnson, Ryerson. *Kenji and the magic geese*
Johnston, Tony. *The badger and the magic fan*
Kajikawa, Kimiko. *Yoshi's feast*
Kako, Satoshi. *Little Daruma and little Daikoku*
    Little Daruma and little Kaminari
Kalman, Maira. *Sayonara, Mrs. Kackleman*
Keo, Ena. *The crane wife*
Kimmel, Eric A. *The greatest of all*
Kimura, Yuichi. *One stormy night . . .*
    One sunny day . . .
Kroll, Virginia L. *A carp for Kimiko*
Kudler, David. *The Seven Gods of Luck*
Langston, Laura. *The fox's kettle*
Laurin, Anne. *Perfect crane*
Levine, Arthur A. *The boy who drew cats*
Lifton, Betty Jean. *Joji and the Amanojaku*
    Joji and the dragon
    The many lives of Chio and Goro
    The rice-cake rabbit
Little, Mimi Otey. *Yoshiko and the foreigner*
Lobel, Anita. *The dwarf giant*
London, Jonathan. *Moshi moshi*
Long, Jan Freeman. *The bee and the dream*
Luenn, Nancy. *The dragon kite*
McDermott, Gerald. *The stonecutter*
Mado, Michio. *The magic pocket*
Marston, Elsa. *The fox maiden*
Matsuno, Masako. *A pair of red clogs*
    Taro and the bamboo shoot
    Taro and the Tofu
Matsutani, Miyoko. *The fisherman under the sea*
    How the withered trees blossomed
    The witch's magic cloth
Mayer, Mercer. *Shibumi and the kitemaker*
Melmed, Laura Krauss. *The first song ever sung*
Merrill, Jean. *The girl who loved caterpillars*
Morimoto, Junko. *The two bullies*
Mosel, Arlene. *The funny little woman*
Nakatani, Chiyoko. *Fumio and the dolphins*
Namioka, Lensey. *Hungriest boy in the world*
    The loyal cat
Newton, Patricia Montgomery. *The five sparrows*
Nomura, Takaaki. *Grandpa's town*
Paterson, Katherine. *The tale of the Mandarin ducks*
Pittman, Helena Clare. *The gift of the willows*
Powers, Daniel. *Jiro's pearl*
Richard, Françoise. *On Cat Mountain*
Roy, Ronald. *A thousand pails of water*
San Souci, Robert D. *The samurai's daughter*
    The silver charm
    The snow wife
Satoshi, Kako. *Little Daruma and little Tengu*
Say, Allen. *The bicycle man*

    Grandfather's journey
    Once under the cherry blossom tree
    Tea with milk
    Tree of cranes
Shannon, George. *Spring*
Shute, Linda. *Momotaro, the peach boy*
Sierra, Judy. *Tasty baby belly buttons*
Slobodkin, Louis. *Yasu and the strangers*
Takabayashi, Mari. *I live in Tokyo*
Takeshita, Fumiko. *The park bench*
Tejima, Keizaburo. *Ho-limlim*
Turner, Pamela S. *Hachiko*
Uchida, Yoshiko. *The magic purse*
    Sumi's prize
    Sumi's special happening
    The wise old woman
Van Woerkom, Dorothy. *Sea frog, city frog*
Waite, Michael P. *Jojofu*
Weedn, Flavia. *The moon maiden*
Wells, Rosemary. *Yoko's paper cranes*
Wells, Ruth. *The farmer and the poor god*
Williams, Laura E. *The long silk strand*
Wisniewski, David. *Sumo Mouse*
    The warrior and the wise man
Yagawa, Sumiko. *The crane wife*
Yashima, Mitsu. *Plenty to watch*
Yashima, Taro. *Crow boy*
    The village tree

Foreign lands – Kenya

Anderson, Laurie Halse. *Ndito runs*
Johnston, Tony. *A Kenya Christmas*
McLean, Virginia O. *Kenya, jambo!*
Mollel, Tololwa M. (Tololwa Marti). *Orphan boy*
    A promise to the sun
    Rhinos for lunch and elephants for supper
Wilson-Max, Ken. *Faraha means happy*

Foreign lands – Korea

Balgassi, Haemi. *Peacebound trains*
Choi, Sook Nyul. *Yunmi and Halmoni's trip*
Choi, Yangsook. *The sun girl and the moon boy*
Climo, Shirley. *The Korean Cinderella*
Farley, Carol J. *The king's secret*
    Mr. Pak buys a story
Fregosi, Claudia. *The pumpkin sparrow*
Ginsburg, Mirra. *The Chinese mirror*
Gukova, Julia. *Mole's daughter*
Han, Oki S. *Kongi and Potgi*
    Sir Whong and the golden pig
Haskins, Jim (James). *Count your way through Korea*
Heo, Yumi. *The green frogs*
Jaffe, Nina. *Older brother, younger brother*
Kwon, Holly H. *The moles and the mireuk*
Park, Frances. *Good-bye, 382 Shin Dang Dong*
    The royal bee
    Where on earth is my bagel?
Park, Linda Sue. *The firekeeper's son*
Parry, Marian. *King of the fish*
San Souci, Daniel. *In the moonlight mist*
    The rabbit and the dragon king
Wong, Janet S. *The trip back home*

Foreign lands – Korea (North)

Park, Frances. *My freedom trip*

Foreign lands – Kurdistan

Gerstein, Mordicai. *The shadow of a flying bird*

Foreign lands – Laos

Xiong, Blia. *Nine-in-one Grr! Grr!*

Foreign lands – Lapland

Aulaire, Ingri Mortenson d'. *Children of the northlights*
Borg, Inga. *Plupp builds a house*
Lindman, Maj. *Snipp, Snapp, Snurr and the red shoes*
McHale, Ethel Kharasch. *Son of thunder*
Reynolds, Jan. *Far north*
Stalder, Valerie. *Even the devil is afraid of a shrew*

Foreign lands – Latin America

Garay, Luis. *Pedrito's day*
Hurwitz, Johanna. *New shoes for Silvia*
Robbins, Sandra. *The firefly star*
Torres, Leyla. *Liliana's grandmothers*
Vidal, Beatriz A. *Federico and the Magi's gift*

Foreign lands – Latvia

Langton, Jane. *The hedgehog boy*
Mike, Jan M. *Clever Karlis*

Foreign lands – Lebanon

Heide, Florence Parry. *Sami and the time of the troubles*
Munsch, Robert N. *From far away*

Foreign lands – Liberia

Aardema, Verna. *Koi and the kola nuts*
Aardema, Verna. *The vingananee and the tree toad*
Gleeson, Brian. *Koi and the kola nuts*
Paye, Won-Ldy. *Head, body, legs*
  Mrs. Chicken and the hungry crocodile

Foreign lands – Madagascar

Dennard, Deborah. *Lemur landing*
Rappaport, Doreen. *The new king*

Foreign lands – Malaysia

Goodman, Susan E. *Chopsticks for my noodle soup*
Kaye, Geraldine. *The sea monkey*

Foreign lands – Mali

Diakité, Baba Wagué. *The magic gourd*
Eisner, Will. *Sundiata*
Wisniewski, David. *Sundiata*

Foreign lands – Martinique

San Souci, Robert D. *The faithful friend*

Foreign lands – Mexico

Aardema, Verna. *Borreguita and the coyote*
Aardema, Verna. *Pedro and the padre*
  The riddle of the drum
Alarcón, Francisco X. *From the bellybutton of the moon and other summer poems / poems = Del ombligo de la luna y otros poemas de verano / poemas*
Anaya, Rudolfo A. *Maya's children*
Ancona, George. *Pablo remembers*
Balet, Jan B. *The fence*
Bannon, Laura. *Hat for a hero*
  Manuela's birthday
Bernhard, Emery. *The tree that rains*
Blackmore, Vivien. *Why corn is golden*
Bunting, Eve (Anne Evelyn). *Going home*
Climo, Shirley. *The little red ant and the great big crumb*
Cohn, Diana. *Dream carver*
Corpi, Lucha. *Where fireflies dance = Ahí, donde bailan las luciérnagas*
Crane, Alan. *Pepita bonita*
Czernecki, Stefan. *The hummingbird's gift*
  Pancho's piñata
De Gerez, Toni. *My song is a piece of jade*

De Paola, Tomie (Thomas Anthony). *The Lady of Guadalupe*
Dorros, Arthur. *Julio's magic*
Dumas, Bianca. *Tia Luisa, the magical cook*
Dupré, Judith. *The mouse bride*
Ehlert, Lois. *Cuckoo, a Mexican folktale = Cucú: un cuento folklórico mexicano*
Estes, Kristyn Rehling. *Manuela's gift*
Ets, Marie Hall. *Nine days to Christmas*
Everton, Macduff. *Finding the magic circus = El circo magico modelo*
Fine, Edith Hope. *Under the lemon moon*
Flanagan, Alice K. *Cinco de Mayo*
Fraser, James Howard. *Los Posadas*
Frith, Margaret. *Frida Kahlo*
Geeslin, Campbell. *How Nanita learned to make flan*
Gollub, Matthew. *The twenty-five Mixtec cats*
Grifalconi, Ann. *The bravest flute*
  The toy trumpet
Grossman, Patricia. *Saturday market*
Guy, Ginger Foglesong. *Fiesta*
Hader, Berta Hoerner. *The story of Pancho and the bull with the crooked tail*
Harper, Jo. *The legend of Mexicatl*
Haskins, Jim (James). *Count your way through Mexico*
Johnston, Tony. *Day of the Dead*
  The iguana brothers, a perfect day
  Isabel's house of butterflies
  Lorenzo the naughty parrot
  My Mexico = México mío
  The old lady and the birds
  The tale of Rabbit and Coyote
Joosse, Barbara M. *Ghost wings*
Keep, Linda Lowery. *Day of the Dead*
Kent, Jack. *The Christmas piñata*
Kimmel, Eric A. *The two mountains*
  The witch's face
Kroll, Virginia L. *Butterfly boy*
Krull, Kathleen. *Maria Molina and the Days of the Dead*
Krupp, Robin Rector. *Let's go traveling in Mexico*
Larson, Bonnie. *When animals were people = Cuando los animales eran personas*
Lewis, Thomas P. *Hill of fire*
McDermott, Gerald. *Musicians of the sun*
Madrigal, Antonio Hernandez. *Erandi's braids*
Marcos, subcomandante. *The story of colors = La historia de los colores*
Martin, Bill (William Ivan). *My days are made of butterflies*
Mike, Jan M. *Opossum and the great firemaker*
Miles, Miska. *Friend of Miguel*
Mora, Pat. *A library for Juana*
  The night the moon fell
  The gift of the poinsettia = El regalo de la flor de nochebuena
Morrow, Elizabeth Cutter. *The painted pig*
Politi, Leo. *Lito and the clown*
  Rosa
Riecken, Nancy. *Today is the day*
Rohmer, Harriet. *How we came to the fifth world*
Ross, Michael Elsohn. *Mexican Christmas*
Sahagun, Bernardino de. *Spirit child*
Sanromán, Susana. *Señora Reganoña*
Schaefer, A. R. (Adam Richard). *Diego Rivera*
Schaefer, Lola M. *Cinco de Mayo*
Sobol, Richard. *Adelina's whales*
Swope, Sam. *Gotta go! Gotta go!*
Tompert, Ann. *The silver whistle*
Ungerer, Tomi. *Orlando, the brave vulture*
Van Laan, Nancy. *La boda*
Volkmer, Jane Anne. *Song of Chirimia = La Musica de la Chirimia*
Wade, Mary Dodson. *Cinco de Mayo*
Winter, Jeanette. *Niño's mask*
Wisniewski, David. *Rain player*
Yacowitz, Caryn. *Pumpkin fiesta*
Ziefert, Harriet. *Home for Navidad*

Foreign lands – Middle East

Figley, Marty Rhodes. *The story of Zacchaeus*
Kimmel, Eric A. *The tale of Ali Baba and the forty thieves*
Matze, Claire Sidhom. *The stars in my Geddoh's sky*

Shah, Idries. *The boy without a name*
   The clever boy and the terrible, dangerous animal
   The silly chicken
Weedn, Flavia. *The ragged peddler*
Young, Ed (Edward). *What about me?*

Foreign lands – Mongolia

Yep, Laurence. *The Khan's daughter*

Foreign lands – Morocco

Czernecki, Stefan. *Zorah's magic carpet*
Lewin, Ted. *The storytellers*
London, Jonathan. *Ali, child of the desert*

Foreign lands – Namibia

Aardema, Verna. *Jackal's flying lesson*
Haarhoff, Dorian. *Desert December*

Foreign lands – Nepal

Hobbie, Holly. *Toot and Puddle, top of the world*
Nagda, Anne Whitehead. *A tiger tale*
Reynolds, Jan. *Himalaya*

Foreign lands – Netherlands *see* Foreign lands – Holland

Foreign lands – New Guinea

Anderson, Robin. *Sinabouda Lily*
Wilson, Barbara Ker. *The turtle and the island*

Foreign lands – New Zealand

Bishop, Gavin. *Maui and the sun*
Lattimore, Deborah Nourse. *Punga the goddess of ugly*
Mahy, Margaret. *Bubble trouble and other poems and stories*
Turner, Gwenda. *Over on the farm*

Foreign lands – Newfoundland

Wallace, Ian. *Duncan's way*

Foreign lands – Nicaragua

Rohmer, Harriet. *The invisible hunters*
Rohmer, Harriet. *Mother scorpion country*

Foreign lands – Nigeria

Daly, Niki. *Why the sun and moon live in the sky*
Gerson, Mary-Joan. *Why the sky is far away*
Medearis, Angela Shelf. *The singing man*
Mollel, Tololwa M. (Tololwa Marti). *The flying tortoise*
Olaleye, Isaac. *Bikes for rent!*
   Bitter bananas
   The distant talking drum
   In the Rainfield
Onyefulu, Ifeoma. *Grandfather's work*
   Ogbo
   Saying goodbye
Shepard, Aaron. *Master man*

Foreign lands – Nkandla

Cave, Kathryn. *One child, one seed*

Foreign lands – Norway

Allard, Harry. *May I stay?*
Allen, Linda. *The giant who had no heart*
Asbjørnsen, P. C. (Peter Christen). *The man who kept house*
Aulaire, Ingri Mortenson d'. *East of the sun and west of the moon*
   Ola
   The terrible troll-bird
Brett, Jan. *Who's that knocking on Christmas eve?*

Chwast, Seymour. *Bushy bride*
Dasent, George W. *East o' the sun, west o' the moon*
Emberley, Michael. *Welcome back, Sun*
French, Vivian. *Why the sea is salt*
Grieg, E. H. (Edvard Hagerup). *E. H. Grieg's Peer Gynt*
Hague, Kathleen. *East of the sun and west of the moon*
   The man who kept house
Howard, Kim. *In wintertime*
Kimmel, Eric A. *Boots and his brothers*
   Easy work!
Lunge-Larsen, Lise. *The race of the Birkebeiners*
Magnus, Erica. *The boy and the devil*
   Old Lars
Martin, Claire. *Boots and the glass mountain*, ill. by Gennady Spirin
Mills, Lauren A. *Tatterhood and the hobgoblins*
Reynolds, Jan. *Far north*
The squire's bride
Wade, Barrie. *The three billy goats gruff*
Wiesner, William. *Happy-Go-Lucky*
   Turnabout

Foreign lands – Pakistan

Shepard, Aaron. *The gifts of Wali Dad*
Siddiqui, Ashraf. *Bhombal Dass, the uncle of lion*

Foreign lands – Palestine

Bahous, Sally. *Sitti and the cats*
Nye, Naomi Shihab. *Sitti's secrets*
Stewart, Dana. *Friends from Galilee*

Foreign lands – Panama

Janosch. *The trip to Panama*
Palacios, Argentina. *A Christmas surprise for Chabelita*
Sayre, April Pulley. *Army ant parade*

Foreign lands – Persia

Chaikin, Miriam. *Esther*
Climo, Shirley. *The Persian Cinderella*
De Paola, Tomie (Thomas Anthony). *The legend of the persian carpet*
Foley, Bernice Williams. *The gazelle and the hunter*
Manson, Christopher. *A gift for the king*

Foreign lands – Peru

Alexander, Ellen. *Chaska and the golden doll*
Alexander, Ellen. *Llama and the great flood*
Ayers, Rebecca Hickox. *Zorro and Quwi*
Charles, Donald. *Chancay and the secret of fire*
Dewey, Ariane. *The thunder god's son*
Díaz, Katacha. *Carolina's gift*
Dorros, Arthur. *Tonight is carnaval*
Ehlert, Lois. *Moon rope = Un lazo a la luna*
Loverseed, Amanda. *The thunder king*
Tompert, Ann. *The pied piper of Peru*

Foreign lands – Philippines

Allen, Judy. *Eagle*
Arcellana, Francisco. *The mats*
Aruego, José. *A crocodile's tale*
   Look what I can do
   Rockabye crocodile
Charlot, Martin. *Felisa and the magic tikling bird*
San Souci, Robert D. *Pedro and the monkey*
Walker, Sally M. *Seahorse reef*

Foreign lands – Poland

Adler, David A. *The children of Chelm*
Bernhard, Josephine Butkowska. *Lullaby*
   Nine cry-baby dolls
Carey, Valerie Scho. *Tsugele's broom*

Clement, Gary. *Just stay put*
Din dan don, it's Christmas
Domanska, Janina. *The best of the bargain*
   Busy Monday morning
   King Krakus and the dragon
   Look, there is a turtle flying
Gordon, Ruth. *Feathers*
Nerlove, Miriam. *Flowers on the wall*
Pellowski, Anne. *The nine crying dolls*
Porazinska, Janina. *The enchanted book*
Turska, Krystyna. *The magician of Cracow*
   The woodcutter's duck
Ungar, Richard. *Rachel's library*

Foreign lands – Portugal

Balet, Jan B. *The gift*
Balet, Jan B. *Joanjo*

Foreign lands – Puerto Rico

Belpré, Pura. *Dance of the animals*
Belpré, Pura. *Pérez and Martina*
Crespo, George. *How the sea began*
Gugler, Laurel Dee. *There's a billy goat in the garden*
Ichikawa, Satomi. *Isabela's ribbons*
Jaffe, Nina. *The golden flower*
Juan Bobo goes to work
London, Jonathan. *Hurricane!*
Martel, Cruz. *Yagua days*
Mike, Jan M. *Juan Bobo and the horse of seven colors*
Nodar, Carmen Santiago. *Abuelita's paradise*
Pitre, Felix. *Paco and the witch*
Pomerantz, Charlotte. *The outside dog*
Rohmer, Harriet. *Atariba and Niguayona*
Roth, Susan L. *Another Christmas*
Wallner, Alexandra. *Sergio and the hurricane*

Foreign lands – Romania

Matthews, Wendy. *The gift of a traveler*
Metaxas, Eric. *The gardener's apprentice*
Olson, Arielle North. *Noah's cats and the devil's fire*
Philip, Neil. *Noah and the devil*

Foreign lands – Russia

Afanas'ev, Aleksandr N. *Russian folk tales*
Afanas'ev, Aleksandr N. *Salt*
Aksakov, Sergei. *The scarlet flower*
Arnold, Katya. *Baba Yaga and the little girl*
   Knock, knock, teremok!
   That apple is mine!
Ayres, Becky Hickox. *Matreshka*
Bateson-Hill, Margaret. *Masha and the firebird*
Beim, Lorraine. *Sasha and the samovar*
Bernhard, Emery. *The girl who wanted to hunt*
   How Snowshoe Hare rescued the sun
Bider, Djemma. *The buried treasure*
Black, Algernon D. *The woman of the wood*
Bresnick-Perry, Roslyn. *Leaving for America*
Brighton, Catherine. *Nijinsky*
Brown, Marcia. *The neighbors*
   Stone soup
Campbell, M. Rudolph. *The talking crocodile*
Cech, John. *First snow, magic snow*
Cohen, Barbara. *The demon who would not die*
Cole, Joanna. *Bony-legs*
Croll, Carolyn. *The little snowgirl*
Daniels, Guy. *The Tsar's riddles*
Daugherty, Sonia (Medvedeva). *Vanka's donkey*
De Marolles, Chantal. *The lonely wolf*
De Regniers, Beatrice Schenk. *Everyone is good for something*
Domanska, Janina. *A scythe, a rooster and a cat*
   The turnip
Falk, Barbara Bustetter. *Grusha*
The firebird. *The firebird, ill. by Reg Cartwright*

The firebird, ill. by Francesca Crespi
The firebird, ill. by Demi
The firebird, adapt. and ill. by Rachel Isadora
The firebird, ill. by Moira Kemp
The firebird, ill. by Kris Waldherr
The firebird, ill. by Boris Zvorykin
The tale of the firebird, ill. by Gennady Spirin
Francis, Frank. *Natasha's new doll*
Fregosi, Claudia. *Snow maiden*
Galdone, Paul. *A strange servant*
Ginsburg, Mirra. *Clay boy*
   The fisherman's son
   The fox and the hare
   The king who tried to fry an egg on his head
   Pampalche of the silver teeth
   The strongest one of all
   Which is the best place?
Greaves, Margaret. *Petrushka*
Hall, Amanda. *The gossipy wife*
Haskins, Jim (James). *Count your way through Russia*
Hautzig, Esther (Rudomin). *At home*
   In the park
Heins, Ethel L. *The cat and the cook and other fables of Krylov*
Heller, Linda. *Alexis and the golden ring*
Hille-Brandts, Lene. *The little black hen*
Hoffman, Mary. *Clever Katya*
Horn, Sandra Ann. *Babushka*
Howland, Naomi. *Latkes, latkes, good to eat*
Huth, Holly Young. *The son of the sun and the daughter of the moon*
Isele, Elizabeth. *The frog princess*
Ivanov, Anatoly. *Ol' Jake's lucky day*
Jackson, Ellen B. *The impossible riddle*
Jameson, Cynthia. *The house of five bears*
Johnston, Tony. *Alice Nizzy Nazzy, the Witch of Santa Fe*
Kimmel, Eric A. *Baba Yaga*
   Bearhead
Lang, Andrew. *The flying ship*
Langford, Sondra Gordon. *Mishka and Plishka*
Levine, Arthur A. *All the lights in the night*
Lewis, J. Patrick. *At the wish of the fish*
   The frog princess
Lindgren, Barbro. *Andrei's search*
Lottridge, Celia Barker. *Music for the Tsar of the Sea*
McCaughrean, Geraldine. *Grandma Chickenlegs*
McDermott, Beverly Brodsky. *The crystal apple*
Marshak, S. (Samuil). *The tale of a hero nobody knows*
Martin, Rafe. *The language of birds*
Mayer, Marianna. *Baba Yaga and Vasilisa the Brave*
Mendelson, S. T. *Stupid Emilien*
Metaxas, Eric. *The fool and the flying ship*
Milhous, Katherine. *The turnip*
Odoyevsky, Vladimir. *Old Father Frost*
Oram, Hiawyn. *Baba Yaga and the wise doll*
Parkinson, Kathy. *The enormous turnip*
Pavlova, Anna. *I dreamed I was a ballerina*
The peasant's pea patch
Peck, Jan. *The giant carrot*
Pevear, Richard. *Our king has horns!*
Pogorelsky, Antony. *The black hen, or, The underground inhabitants*
   The little black hen
Polacco, Patricia. *Babushka's Mother Goose*
Prokofiev, Sergei Sergeievitch. *Peter and the wolf, ill. by Reg Cartwright*
   Peter and the wolf, ill. by Warren Chappell
   Peter and the wolf, ill. by Barbara Cooney
   Peter and the wolf, ill. by Julia Gukova
   Peter and the wolf, ill. by Frans Haacken
   Peter and the wolf, ill. by Alan Howard
   Peter and the wolf, ill. by Charles Mikolaycak
   Peter and the wolf, ill. by Jörg Müller
   Peter and the wolf, ill. by Josef Palecek
   Peter and the wolf, ill. by Kozo Shimizu
   Peter and the wolf, retold and ill. by Vladimir Vagin
   Peter and the wolf, ill. by Erna Voigt
Pushkin, Aleksandr Sergeevich. *The tale of Tsar Saltan*
Riordan, James. *The Snowmaiden*
Robbins, Maria Polushkin. *The little hen and the giant*

Robbins, Ruth. *Baboushka and the three kings*
Rosenblum, Richard. *Journey to the golden land*
Sanderson, Ruth. *The golden mare, the firebird, and the magic ring*
San Souci, Robert D. *Peter and the blue witch baby*
Schuch, Steve. *A symphony of whales*
Shepard, Aaron. *The sea king's daughter*
Sherman, Josepha. *Vassilisa the wise*
Slobodkina, Esphyr. *Boris and his balalaika*
Spirin, Gennady. *Philipok*
Stern, Simon. *Vasily and the dragon*
Thompson, Kay. *Kay Thompson's Eloise in Moscow*
Tolstoy, Aleksey Nikolayevich. *The enormous turnip*
  The gigantic turnip, ill. by Niamh Sharkey
  The great big enormous turnip
Tolstoy, Leo. *How much land does a man need?*
Tompert, Ann. *The Tzar's bird*
Trivas, Irene. *Annie . . . Anya*
Vagin, Vladimir Vasilévich. *The enormous carrot*
Van Kampen, Vlasta. *Bear tales*
Varga, Judy. *The mare's egg*
Winter, Jeanette. *The girl and the moon man*
Winthrop, Elizabeth. *The little humpbacked horse*
  Vasilissa the beautiful
Wiseman, Bernard. *Little new kangaroo*
Wolkstein, Diane. *Oom razoom; or, Go I know not where, Bring back I know not what*
Yaroshevskaya, Kim. *Little Kim's doll*
Yolen, Jane. *The firebird*
  The flying witch
  The sea king
Zakhoder, Boris Vladimirovich. *The good stepmother*
Ziefert, Harriet. *The snow child*
  The turnip
Zimmerman, Andrea Griffing. *Yetta, the trickster*

Foreign lands – Rwanda

Aardema, Verna. *Sebgugugu the glutton*

Foreign lands – Sahara Desert

Reynolds, Jan. *Sahara*

Foreign lands – Scandinavia

Manning, Mick. *What a Viking!*
Weedn, Flavia. *The elephant prince*

Foreign lands – Scotland

Alger, Leclaire Gowans. *All in the morning early*
Alger, Leclaire Gowans. *Always room for one more*
  Kellyburn Braes
Blegvad, Erik. *Burnie's hill*
Brown, Ruth. *The ghost of Greyfriar's Bobby*
Burdett, Lois. *Macbeth for kids*
Calhoun, Mary. *The runaway brownie*
Cate, Rikki. *A cat's tale*
Cooper, Susan. *The Selkie girl*
  Tam Lin
Del Negro, Janice. *Lucy Dove*
Duncan, Jane. *Janet Reachfar and Chickabird*
Duquennoy, Jacques. *The ghosts' trip to Loch Ness*
Fern, Eugene. *The most frightened hero*
Forest, Heather. *The woman who flummoxed the fairies*
A frog he would a-wooing go (folk-song). *Frog went a-courting*, retold & ill. by Dominic Catalano
Gramatky, Hardie. *Little Toot and the Loch Ness monster*
Hedderwick, Mairi. *Katie Morag and the big boy cousins*
  Katie Morag and the tiresome Ted
  Katie Morag and the two grandmothers
  Katie Morag delivers the mail
Jeffers, Susan. *Wild Robin*
Leaf, Munro. *Wee Gillis*
Lewis, Naomi. *Puffin*
Lupton, Hugh. *Pirican Pic and Pirican Mor*
MacGill-Callahan, Sheila. *The seal prince*

Manning, Mick. *A ruined house*
Robertson, Joanne. *Sea witches*
Sewall, Marcia. *The wee, wee mannie and the big, big coo*
White, Carolyn. *Whuppity Stoorie*
Yolen, Jane. *Greyling*

Foreign lands – Serbia

Mike, Jan M. *The bird maiden*

Foreign lands – Siam *see* Foreign lands – Thailand

Foreign lands – Siberia

Bernhard, Emery. *The girl who wanted to hunt*
Bernhard, Emery. *How Snowshoe Hare rescued the sun*

Foreign lands – South Africa

Angelou, Maya. *My painted house, my friendly chicken, and me*
Cave, Kathryn. *One child, one seed*
Daly, Niki. *The boy on the beach*
  Jamela's dress
  Not so fast Songololo
  Once upon a time
  What's cooking, Jamela?
Deetlefs, Rene. *Tabu and the dancing elephants*
Haarhoff, Dorian. *Desert December*
Isadora, Rachel. *At the crossroads*
  Over the green hills
  A South African night
Kahn, Rosemary. *Grandma's hat*
Lewin, Hugh. *Jafta – the homecoming*
Mennen, Ingrid. *Somewhere in Africa*
Moodie, Fiona. *Nabulela*
Schermbrucker, Reviva. *Charlie's house*
Seed, Jenny. *Ntombi's song*
Seeger, Pete. *Abiyoyo returns*
Wilson-Max, Ken. *Halala means welcome*

Foreign lands – South America

Alexander, Ellen. *Chaska and the golden doll*
Aruego, José. *Pilyo the piranha*
Brusca, María Cristina. *The cook and the king*
  When jaguars ate the moon
Campoy, F. Isabel. *Rosa Raposa*
Cherry, Lynne. *The shaman's apprentice*
Cowcher, Helen. *Rain forest*
Fischetto, Laura. *The jungle is my home*
Flora. *Feathers like a rainbow*
Frasconi, Antonio. *The snow and the sun = la nieve y el sol*
Gramatky, Hardie. *Bolivar*
Jordan, Martin. *Amazon alphabet*
  Jungle days, jungle nights
Knutson, Barbara. *Love and roast chicken*
McDermott, Gerald. *Jabutí the tortoise*
Maestro, Giulio. *The tortoise's tug of war*
Maiorano, Robert. *Francisco*
Reynolds, Jan. *Amazon*
Rockwell, Anne F. *The good llama*
Schaefer, Jackie Jasina. *Miranda's day to dance*
Silvano, Wendi J. *Just one more*
Smith-Ayala, Emilie. *Marisol and the yellow messenger*
Surany, Anico. *Ride the cold wind*
Thomson, Ruth. *The Rainforest Indians*
Troughton, Joanna. *How the birds changed their feathers*
Van Laan, Nancy. *The legend of El Dorado*

Foreign lands – South Sea Islands

Blackstone, Stella. *Secret seahorse*
Blackstone, Stella. *Secret seahorse [board book]*
Mordvinoff, Nicolas. *Coral Island*
Wood, Audrey. *Ten little fish*

Foreign lands – Soviet Union

Malkovych, Ivan. *The cat and the rooster*
Polacco, Patricia. *Luba and the wren*

Foreign lands – Spain

Davis, Aubrey. *Bagels from Benny*
Duff, Maggie (Margaret K.). *The princess and the pumpkin*
García Lorca, Federico. *The Lieutenant Colonel and the gypsy*
Greene, Jacqueline Dembar. *Butchers and bakers, rabbis and kings*
Hautzig, Esther (Rudomin). *At home*
    In the park
Kimmel, Eric A. *Bernal and Florinda*
    Squash it!
Leaf, Munro. *The story of Ferdinand the bull*
Oleson, Claire. *For Pipita, an orange tree*
Sierra, Judy. *The beautiful butterfly*
Vernon, Adele. *The riddle*
Zamorano, Ana. *Let's eat!*

Foreign lands – Sri Lanka

Troughton, Joanna. *The quail's egg*

Foreign lands – Sudan

Aardema, Verna. *What's so funny, Ketu?*
Kessler, Cristina. *My great-grandmother's gourd*

Foreign lands – Suriname

Lichtveld, Noni. *I lost my arrow in a kankan tree*

Foreign lands – Sweden

Ayers, Rebecca Hickox. *Per and the Dala horse*
Beskow, Elsa Maartman. *Children of the forest*
    Pelle's new suit
    Peter in Blueberry Land
    Peter's adventures in Blueberry Land
Hooks, William H. *The legend of the Christmas rose*
Langton, Jane. *The queen's necklace*
Lindgren, Astrid. *A calf for Christmas*
    Christmas in noisy village
    Christmas in the stable
    Do you know Pippi Longstocking?
    Lotta's Christmas surprise
    Pippi Longstocking in the park
    Pippi Longstocking's after-Christmas party
    The tomten
    The tomten and the fox
Lindman, Maj. *Flicka, Ricka, Dicka and a little dog*
    Flicka, Ricka, Dicka and the new dotted dress
    Flicka, Ricka, Dicka bake a cake
    Sailboat time
    Snipp, Snapp, Snurr and the buttered bread
    Snipp, Snapp, Snurr and the magic horse
    Snipp, Snapp, Snurr and the reindeer
    Snipp, Snapp, Snurr and the seven dogs
    Snipp, Snapp, Snurr and the yellow sled
Peterson, Hans. *Erik and the Christmas horse*
Schaefer, Carole Lexa. *Under the midsummer sky*
Schwartz, David M. *Sugargrandpa*
Sundvall, Viveca. *Mimi and the biscuit factory*
Weedn, Flavia. *The magic cap*
Westerberg, Christine. *The cap that mother made*
Zemach, Harve. *Nail soup*

Foreign lands – Switzerland

Allamand, Pascale. *Cocoa beans and daisies*
Baumann, Kurt. *Piro and the fire brigade*
Bawden, Nina. *William Tell*
Carigiet, Alois. *The pear tree, the birch tree and the barberry bush*
Chönz, Selina. *A bell for Ursli*
    Florina and the wild bird
    The snowstorm

Fisher, Leonard Everett. *William Tell*
Freeman, Don. *Ski pup*
Ostheeren, Ingrid. *The new dog*
Stone, Marti. *The singing fir tree*

Foreign lands – Taiwan

Chen, Chih-Yuan. *On my way to buy eggs*
Reddix, Valerie. *Dragon kite of the autumn moon*

Foreign lands – Tanzania

Grimes, Nikki. *Is it far to Zanzibar?*
Krebs, Laurie. *We all went on safari*
Martin, Francesca. *Clever Tortoise*
Mollel, Tololwa M. (Tololwa Marti). *Big boy*
    Kele's secret
    My rows and piles of coins
    Shadow dance
    Song bird
    Subira subira
Stuve-Bodeen, Stephanie. *Elizabeti's school*
    Elizabeti's doll
    Mama Elizabeti

Foreign lands – Tasmania

Baker, Jeannie. *The hidden forest*

Foreign lands – Thailand

Ayer, Jacqueline. *Nu Dang and his kite*
Ayer, Jacqueline. *The paper-flower tree*
    A wish for little sister
Ho, Minfong. *Hush!*
Krudop, Walter Lyon. *The man who caught fish*
MacDonald, Margaret Read. *The girl who wore too much*
Maugham, W. Somerset (William Somerset). *Princess September and the nightingale*
Northrup, Mili. *The watch cat*
Oliviero, Jamie. *Som See and the magic elephant*
Shea, Pegi Deitz. *The whispering cloth*

Foreign lands – Tibet

Berger, Barbara Helen. *All the way to Lhasa*
Schroeder, Alan. *The stone lion*
Sis, Peter. *Tibet through the red box*
Soros, Barbara. *Tenzin's deer*
Trottier, Maxine. *Little dog Moon*
Tsultim, Yeshe. *The mouse king*

Foreign lands – Trinidad

Joseph, Lynn. *Coconut kind of day*
Joseph, Lynn. *An island Christmas*
    Jasmine's parlour day
    Jump up time

Foreign lands – Turkey

Bennett, Olivia. *A Turkish afternoon*
Dewey, Ariane. *The fish Peri*
Walker, Barbara K. (Barbara Kerlin). *Teeny-Tiny and the witch-woman*
Yolen, Jane. *Little Mouse and Elephant*

Foreign lands – Tyrol

Bemelmans, Ludwig. *Hansi*
Sawyer, Ruth. *The remarkable Christmas of the cobbler's sons*

Foreign lands – Uganda

McBrier, Page. *Beatrice's goat*

Foreign lands – Ukraine

Brett, Jan. *The mitten*
Gorbachev, Valeri. *The fool of the world and the flying ship*
Hale, Irina. *The naughty crow*
Kay, Helen. *An egg is for wishing*
Kimmel, Eric A. *The birds' gift*
　　One Eye, Two Eyes, Three Eyes
　　Sirko and the wolf
Lisowski, Gabriel. *How Tevye became a milkman*
Malkovych, Ivan. *The cat and the rooster*
Ransome, Arthur. *The fool of the world and the flying ship*
Rudolph, Marguerita. *How a shirt grew in the field*, ill. by Erika
　　Weihs
　　How a shirt grew in the field, ill. by Yaroslava
Skrypuch, Marsha Forchuk. *Enough*
Tresselt, Alvin R. *The mitten*

Foreign lands – Uzbekistan

Sandman, Rochel. *Perfect porridge*

Foreign lands – Venezuela

Barbot, Daniel. *A bicycle for Rosaura*
Cowcher, Helen. *Jaguar*

Foreign lands – Vietnam

Boholm-Olsson, Eva. *Tuan*
Breckler, Rosemary K. *Sweet dried apples*
Garland, Sherry. *The lotus seed*
　　Why ducks sleep on one leg
Keller, Holly. *Grandfather's dream*
Lee, Jeanne M. *Ba-Nam*
McKay, Lawrence. *Journey home*
Shepard, Aaron. *The crystal heart*
Trân-Khánh-Tuyê. *The little weaver of Thái-Yên Village*

Foreign lands – Wales

Cullen, Lynn. *The mightiest heart*
MacDonald, Margaret Read. *Slop!*

Foreign lands – West Indies

Burgie, Irving. *Caribbean carnival*
Hamilton, Virginia. *The girl who spun gold*
Rahaman, Vashanti. *O Christmas tree*

Foreign lands – Yukon Territory

Wallace, Ian. *The true story of Trapper Jack's left big toe*

Foreign lands – Zaire

Aardema, Verna. *Traveling to Tondo*
Knutson, Barbara. *Why the crab has no head*

Foreign lands – Zambia

Bryan, Ashley. *Beautiful blackbird*

Foreign lands – Zanzibar

Aardema, Verna. *Bimwili and the Zimwi*
Grimes, Nikki. *Is it far to Zanzibar?*

Foreign lands – Zimbabwe

Stock, Catherine. *Gugu's house*

Foreign languages

ABCDEFGHIJKLMNOPQRSTUVWXYZ in English and Spanish
Ada, Alma Flor. *Gathering the sun*
　　The Christmas tree = El Arbol de Navidad
Aigner-Clark, Julie. *Language nursery*

Alarcón, Francisco X. *From the bellybutton of the moon and other sum-*
　　mer poems / poems = Del ombligo de la luna y otros poemas de ver-
　　ano / poemas
　　Iguanas in the snow and other winter poems / poemas = Iguanas en
　　la nieve y otros poemas de invierno / poemas
Alger, Leclaire Gowans. *Kellyburn Braes*
Anglund, Joan Walsh. *Love one another*
Anzaldúa, Gloria. *Prietita and the ghost woman = Prietita y la llorona*
Baden, Robert. *And Sunday makes seven*
Baldner, Gaby. *Joba and the wild boar = Joba und das wildschwein*
Bateson-Hill, Margaret. *Lao Lao of Dragon Mountain*
Beaton, Clare. *At home = A la maison*
Bernard, Robin. *Juma and the honey-guild*
Bertrand, Diane Gonzales. *Family = familia*
　　The last doll = La última muñeca
　　Uncle Chente's picnic = El picnic de Tío Chente
Blue, Rose. *I am here = Yo estoy aqui*
Bock, Lee. *Oh, crumps! = Ay, caramba!*
Borlenghi, Patricia. *From albatross to zoo*
Bowden, Miriam. *The adventure of Paz in the land of numbers*
Bozylinsky, Hannah Heritage. *Lala Salama*
Brandt, Amy. *Benjamin comes back = Benjamin regresa*
　　When Katie was our teacher = Cuando Katie era muestra maestra
Breckler, Rosemary K. *Hoang breaks the lucky teapot*
Brown, Ruth. *Alphabet times four*
Bruzzone, Catherine. *Puppy finds a friend = Cachorrito encuentra un*
　　amigo
　　Puppy finds a friend = Le petit chien se trouve un ami
Chapra, Mimi. *Amelia's show-and-tell fiesta = Amelia y la fiesta de*
　　"muestra y cuenta"
Chavarría-Cháirez, Becky. *Magda's piñata magic = Magda y la*
　　piñata mágica
　　Magda's tortillas = Las tortillas de Magada
Chiang, Wei. *The legend of Mu Lan = La heroina Hua Mulan*
A child's picture English-Hebrew dictionary
Cisneros, Sandra. *Hairs = Pelitos*
Compos, Tito. *Muffler man = El hombre mofle*
Conrad, Pam. *Animal lingo*
Córdova, Amy. *Abuelita's heart*
Corpi, Lucha. *Where fireflies dance = Ahí, donde bailan las luciérnagas*
Covault, Ruth M. *Pablo and Pimienta*
Dabcovich, Lydia. *The keys to my kingdom*
Dauphin, Francine Legrand. *A French A. B. C.*
De Anda, Diane. *Dancing Miranda = Baila, Miranda, baila*
De Gerez, Toni. *My song is a piece of jade*
Delacre, Lulu. *Arroz con leche*
　　Las Navidades
De Paola, Tomie (Thomas Anthony). *Marcos: red, yellow, blue*
De Zutter, Hank. *Who says a dog goes bow-wow?*
Diska, Pat. *Andy says . . . Bonjour!*
Dorros, Arthur. *Abuela*
Du Bois, William Pène. *The hare and the tortoise and the tortoise and*
　　the hare = La liebre y la tortuga and La tortuga y la liebre
Duerrstein, Richard. *In out, a Disney book of opposites = Dentro fuera,*
　　un libro Disney de opuestos
　　One Mickey Mouse, a Disney book of numbers = Un Ratón Mickey, un
　　libro Disney de números
Dumas, Bianca. *Tia Luisa, the magical cook*
Dunham, Meredith. *Colors: how do you say it?*
　　Numbers: how do you say it?
　　Picnic
　　Shapes
Edwards, Michelle. *Alef-bet*
Ehlert, Lois. *Cuckoo, a Mexican folktale = Cucú: un cuento folklórico*
　　mexicano
　　Moon rope = Un lazo a la luna
Elya, Susan Middleton. *Eight animals bake a cake*
　　Eight animals on the town
　　Say hola to Spanish
Emberley, Rebecca. *My animals = Mis animales*
　　My city = Mi cuidad
　　My clothes = Mi ropa
　　My colors = Mis colores
　　My food = Mi comida
　　My garden = Mi jardin
　　My house = Mi casa
　　My numbers = Mis números

My opposites = Mis opuestos
My room = Mi cuarto
My school = Mi escuela
My shapes = Mis formas
My toys = Mi juguetes
English, Karen. *Speak English for us, Marisol*
Evans, Lezlie. *Can you count ten toes?*
Everton, Macduff. *Finding the magic circus = El circo magico modelo*
Farley, Carol J. *The king's secret*
Faulkner, Keith. *My first one hundred words in French and English*
Feder, Jane. *Table, chair, bear*
Feelings, Muriel. *Jambo means hello*
Menjo means one
Flanagan, Alice K. *Learning is fun with Mrs. Perez*
Foster, Karen Sharp. *Good night my little chicks = Buenas noches mis pollitos*
Frasconi, Antonio. *See again, say again*
See and say
The snow and the sun = la nieve y el sol
Galindo, Mary Sue. *Icy watermelon = Sandía fría*
Geraty, Virginia Mixson. *Gullah night before Christmas*
Gerber, Carole. *Hush! a Gaelic lullaby*
Gershator, David. *Palampam Day*
Gollub, Matthew. *Ten oni drummers*
Gunning, Monica. *The two Georges = Los dos Jorges*
Guy, Ginger Foglesong. *Fiesta*
Hammond, Anna. *This home we have made*
Haring, Keith. *10*
Haskins, Jim (James). *Count your way through Africa*
Count your way through Brazil
Count your way through France
Count your way through Germany
Count your way through Greece
Count your way through India
Count your way through Israel
Count your way through Italy
Count your way through Korea
Count your way through Mexico
Hautzig, Esther (Rudomin). *At home*
In the park
Hayes, Joe. *Juan Verdades, the man who could not tell a lie*
Little Gold Star = Estrellita de oro
Head, Judith. *Mud soup*
Herrera, Juan Felipe. *Grandma and Me at the flea = Los meros meros remateros*
Hill, Eric. *Spot's big book of colors, shapes and numbers = El libro grande de Spot*
Spot's big book of words = El libro grande de las palabras de Spot
Hoffman, Eric. *No fair to tigers = No es justo para los tigres*
Play Lady = La Señora Juguetona
The house that Jack built. *The house that Jack built = la maison que Jacques a batie*, ill. by Antonio Frasconi
Iijima, Geneva Cobb. *The way we do it in Japan*
Jack and the beanstalk. *Jack and the beanstalk = Juan y los frijoles magicos*, ill. by Arnal Ballester
Jaynes, Ruth M. *Tell me please! What's that?*
Jiménez, Francisco. *The Christmas gift = El regalo de Navidad*
Johnson, Amy Crane. *Cinnamon and the April shower = Canela y el aguacero de abril*
Mason moves away = Mason se muda
Johnson, Diana F. *Princesa and Friskie*
Johnston, Tony. *My Mexico = México mío*
The old lady and the birds
Joslin, Sesyle. *Baby elephant goes to China*
Baby elephant's trunk
Señor Baby Elephant, the pirate
Kahn, Michèle. *My everyday Spanish word book*
Keats, Ezra Jack. *My dog is lost!*
Keister, Douglas. *Fernando's gift = El regalo de Fernando*
Koplow, Lesley. *Tanya and the tobo man = Tanya y el hombre tobo*
Krebs, Laurie. *We all went on safari*
Lachtman, Ofelia Dumas. *Pepita takes time = Pepita, siempre tarde*
Larson, Bonnie. *When animals were people = Cuando los animales eran personas*
Lee, Huy Voun. *1, 2, 3 go!*
Leventhal, Debra. *What is your language?*
Lomas Garza, Carmen. *In my family*

Love to mamá
Luenn, Nancy. *A gift for Abuelita*
McKissack, Patricia C. *Messy Bessey = Ada, la desordenada*
McLean, Dirk. *Play mas'! a carnival ABC*
Macsolis. *Dance moon = Baile de luna*
Mado, Michio. *The magic pocket*
Marcos, subcomandante. *The story of colors = La historia de los colores*
Matsutani, Miyoko. *How the withered trees blossomed*
Matthias, Catherine. *Out the door = Sal y entra*
Over and under = Arriba y abajo
Too many balloons = Demasiados globos
Maury, Inez. *My mother the mail carrier = Mi mama la cartera*
Milios, Rita. *Yo soy = I am*
Miller, Elizabeth I. *Just like home = Como en mi tierra*
Moore, Lilian. *Papa Albert*
Mora, Pat. *The bakery lady = La señora de la panadería*
Confetti
Delicious hullabaloo = Pachanga deliciosa
Listen to the desert = Oye al desierto
One, two, three = Uno, dos, tres
The race of toad and deer
The desert is my mother = El desierto es mi madre
The gift of the poinsettia = El regalo de la flor de nochebuena
Moreton, Daniel. *La Cucaracha Martina*
Morris, Ann. *Hello Peter = Bonjour, Rémy*
Morton, Lone. *Hurry up, Molly = Apúrate, Molly*
Hurry up, Molly = Dépêche-toi, Molly
Mother Goose. *Mother Goose in French*
Mother Goose in Spanish
Rimes de la Mere Oie
Nomura, Takaaki. *Grandpa's town*
Nye, Naomi Shihab. *Sitti's secrets*
On the little hearth
Pak, Soyung. *Dear Juno*
Pérez, Amada Irma. *My very own room = Mi propio cuartito*
My diary from here to there = Mi diario de aquí hasta allá
Perrault, Charles. *Cinderella = Cenicienta*
Pio peep!
Pomerantz, Charlotte. *If I had a Paka*
The tamarindo puppy and other poems
Rattigan, Jama Kim. *The woman in the moon*
Reasoner, Charles. *Who pretends?*
Reed, Lynn Rowe. *Pedro, his perro, and the alphabet sombrero*
Rice, Judith. *Those itsy-bitsy teeny-tiny not-so-nice head lice = Esos pequeñines, chiquitines, para nada simpáticos piojos*
Those ooey gooey winky-blinky but – invisible pinkeye germs = Esos pringosos viscosos pestañeantes parpadeantes pero – invisibles gérmenes que causan conjuntivitis
Ricklen, Neil. *My clothes = Mi ropa*
My colors = Mis colores
My family = Mi familia
My numbers = Mis números
Rider, Alex. *A la ferme = At the farm*
At our house = Chez nous
Roe, Eileen. *With my brother = Con mi hermano*
Rosa-Mendoza, Gladys. *What time is it? = Qué hora es?*
Rosario, Idalia. *Idalia's project ABC*
Rothman, Joel. *This can lick a lollipop = esto goza chupando un caramelo*
Rumford, James. *Dog-of-the-Sea-Waves*
Sequoyah
There's a monster in the alphabet
Ryan, Pam Muñoz. *Hello ocean = Hola mar*
Sáenz, Benjamin Alire. *A gift from papá Diego = Un regalo de papá Diego*
Grandma Fina and her wonderful umbrellas = La abuelita Fina y sus sombrillas maravillosas
San Souci, Robert D. *Little gold star*
Schaffer, Marion. *I love my cat*
Schotter, Roni. *That extraordinary pig of Paris*
Schreier, Alta. *Cuba*
Serfozo, Mary. *Welcome Roberto! Bienvenido, Roberto!*
Shirotani, Hideo. *Let's eat = Vamos a comer*
Let's take a walk = Vamos a caminar
What color? = Qué color?
Silvano, Wendi. *Counting coconuts = Contando cocos*
Simon, Norma. *What do I say?*

Soto, Gary. *Chato's kitchen*
  Too many tamales
Sper, Emily. *Hanukkah*
Standon, Anna. *Three little cats*
Steiner, Charlotte. *A friend is "Amie"*
Stevens, Cat. *Teaser and the firecat*
Stevens, Jan Romero. *Carlos and the skunk = Carlos y el zorrillo*
  Carlos digs to China = Carlos excava hasta la China
Sweetland, Nancy Rose. *If I could = Si yo pudiera*
Tafolla, Carmen. *Baby Coyote and the old woman = El coyotito y la viejita*
Takeshita, Fumiko. *The park bench*
  Tortillas and lullabies = Tortillas y cancioncitas
Va, Leong. *A letter to the king*
Vagin, Vladimir Vasilévich. *Here comes the cat*
Van Laan, Nancy. *La boda*
  Sleep, sleep, sleep
Vidal, Beatriz A. *Federico and the Magi's gift*
Vigil-Piñón, Evangelina. *Marina's muumuu = el muumuu de Marina*
Volkmer, Jane Anne. *Song of Chirimia = La Musica de la Chirimia*
Wells, Rosemary. *McDuff goes to school*
Wiese, Kurt. *You can write Chinese*
Wilson, Barbara Ker. *ABC and 123*
Wilson-Max, Ken. *Faraha means happy*
  Halala means welcome
Winter, Jonah. *Diego*
Yohannes, Gebregeorgis. *Silly Mammo = Kilu Mammo*
Yolen, Jane. *Street rhymes around the world*
Ziefert, Harriet. *Home for Navidad*
Zola, Meguido. *The dream of promise*

Forest, woods

Ada, Alma Flor. *The unicorn of the west*
Adler, David A. *Redwoods are the tallest trees in the world*
Ahlberg, Janet. *Jeremiah in the dark wood*
Alborough, Jez. *Where's my teddy?*
Allen, Gertrude E. *Everyday animals*
Anglund, Joan Walsh. *Nibble nibble mousekin*
Anholt, Laurence. *The forgotten forest*
Armer, Laura Adams. *The forest pool*
Arneson, D. J. *Secret places*
Arnold, Caroline. *The terrible Hodag*
  A walk in the woods
Arnosky, Jim. *Crinkleroot's guide to knowing the trees*
Baker, Jeannie. *Where the forest meets the sea*
Baumann, Hans. *Mischa and his brothers*
Berenstain, Stan. *The Berenstain bears and the ghost of the forest*
Beskow, Elsa Maartman. *Children of the forest*
Blake, Robert J. *The perfect spot*
Bond, Ruskin. *Flames in the forest*
Bowen, Betsy. *Antler, bear, canoe*
  Tracks in the wild
Bradman, Tony. *Look out, he's behind you*
Buff, Mary (Marsh). *Dash and Dart*
  Forest folk
Carrick, Carol. *A clearing in the forest*
Carrick, Donald. *Harold and the great stag*
Carrier, Lark. *A tree's tale*
Cartlidge, Michelle. *Bear in the forest*
Chall, Marsha Wilson. *Up north at the cabin*
Cherry, Lynne. *Archie, follow me*
  The shaman's apprentice
Christiana, David. *White nineteens*
Cooper, Ann (Ann C.). *In the forest*
Costello, Emily. *Realm of the panther*
Cotten, Cynthia. *At the edge of the woods*
Cowcher, Helen. *Rain forest*
Cristini, Ermanno. *In the woods*
Crum, Shutta. *The bravest of the brave*
Darling, Kathy (Mary Kathleen). *Rain forest babies*
Davidson, Jill A. *And that's what happened to little Lucy*
Day, David. *King of the woods*
Delessert, Etienne. *The seven dwarfs*
Demarest, Chris L. *Hotshots!*
  Smokejumpers one to ten
Dennard, Deborah. *Koala country*

  Lemur landing
Deprisco, Dorothea. *Snowbear's winter day*
Dunphy, Madeleine. *Here is the tropical rain forest*
Edwards, Richard. *The forest child*
Ets, Marie Hall. *Another day*
  In the forest
Franklin, Kristine L. *When the monkeys came back*
Fraser, Mary Ann. *Forest fire!*
Fredericks, Anthony D. *In one tidepool*
Frost, Robert. *Stopping by woods on a snowy evening*
Gaffney, Michael. *Secret forests*
Gammell, Stephen. *Twigboy*
Gay, Marie-Louise. *Stella, fairy of the forest*
George, Lindsay Barrett. *In the woods*
George, William T. *Christmas at Long Pond*
Geraghty, Paul. *The great green forest*
Gibbons, Gail. *Nature's green umbrella*
Gilliland, Judith Heide. *River*
Gliori, Debi. *Mr. Bear to the rescue*
Graham Barber, Lynda. *Spy hops and belly flops*
Grahame, Kenneth. *The wind in the willows: the wild wood:*
Greenaway, Shirley. *Forests*
Greene, Carol. *I can be a forest ranger*
Gregory, Valiska. *Through the mickle woods*
Grimm, Jacob. *Hansel and Gretel*, ill. by Adrienne Adams
  Hansel and Gretel, ill. by Anthony Browne
  Hansel and Gretel, ill. by Susan Jeffers
  Hansel and Gretel, ill. by Winslow P. Pels
  Hansel and Gretel, ill. by Jane Ray
  Hansel and Gretel, ill. by Conxita Rodriguez
  Hansel and Gretel, ill. by Christopher Santoro
  Hansel and Gretel, ill. by John Wallner
  Hansel and Gretel, ill. by Claudia Wolf
  Hansel and Gretel, ill. by Paul O. Zelinsky
  Hansel and Gretel, ill. by Lisbeth Zwerger
Grindley, Sally. *Little Sibu*
Grupper, Jonathan. *Destination, rain forest*
Hague, Kathleen. *The legend of the Veery bird*
Haseley, Dennis. *My father doesn't know about the woods and me*
Helldorfer, M. C. (Mary Claire). *Night of the white stag*
Hess, Paul. *Rainforest animals*
Hewitt, Sally. *Woods and meadows*
Hill, Eric. *Spot's walk in the woods*
Hill, Mary Lou. *My dad's a smokejumper*
Himmelman, John. *A wood frog's life*
Hines, Gary. *The day of the high climber*
Hirschi, Ron. *Faces in the forest*
  Forest
  Who lives in . . . Alligator Swamp?
  Who lives in . . . the forest?
Hodges, Margaret. *Buried moon*
  Comus
Holabird, Katharine. *Angelina and Henry*
Holder, Heidi. *Carmine the crow*
Holmes, Efner Tudor. *Deer in the hollow*
Hyman, Trina Schart. *The enchanted forest*
Itaya, Satoshi. *Buttons and Bo*
Iwamura, Kazuo. *The fourteen forest mice and the harvest moon watch*
  The fourteen forest mice and the spring meadow picnic
  The fourteen forest mice and the summer laundry day
  The fourteen forest mice and the winter sledding day
Jam, Teddy. *The year of fire*
Jaspersohn, William. *Timber!*
Johanasen, Heather. *About the rain forest*
Johnson, Amy Crane. *Cinnamon and the April shower = Canela y el aguacero de abril*
Johnston, Tony. *Bigfoot Cinderrrrella*
Jones, Chuck. *William the backwards skunk*
Keister, Douglas. *Fernando's gift = El regalo de Fernando*
Kerins, Tony (Anthony). *The brave ones*
Kleven, Elisa. *The dancing deer and the foolish hunter*
Klingel, Cynthia Fitterer. *Forests*
Krupinski, Loretta. *Into the woods*
Lairla, Sergio. *Abel and the wolf*
Landström, Olof. *Boo and Baa in the woods*
Lasky, Kathryn. *Marven of the Great North Woods*
Latimer, Jim. *Going the moose way home*

Leister, Mary. *The silent concert*
Lerner, Carol. *Flowers of a woodland spring*
Le Tord, Bijou. *The river and the rain*
Lipkind, William. *The boy and the forest*
Low, Robert. *Peoples of the rain forest*
Luenn, Nancy. *Song for the ancient forest*
Lukesová, Milena. *Julian in the autumn woods*
Lyon, George Ella. *Counting on the woods*
McConnachie, Brian. *Lily of the forest*
McCourt, Lisa. *The rainforest counts!*
Mantegazza, Giovanna. *Look inside a rainforest*
Maris, Ron. *Hold tight, bear!*
Marshall, Edward. *Troll country*
Marshall, James. *Hansel and Gretel*
Martin, Bill (William Ivan). *A beasty story*
Miklowitz, Gloria D. *Save that raccoon!*
Miles, Miska. *The fox and the fire*
    Sylvester Jones and the voice in the forest
Miller, Debbie S. *Are trees alive?*
Miller, Edna. *Mousekin's ABC*
    Mousekin's close call
    Mousekin's lost woodland
    Mousekin's Thanksgiving
Milne, A. A. (Alan Alexander). *Tigger comes to the forest and has breakfast*
Moerbeek, Kees. *The diary of Hansel and Gretel*
Montresor, Beni. *Hansel and Gretel*
Moore, Inga. *Fifty red night-caps*
Mora, Emma. *Animals of the forest*
    Gideon, the little bear cub
Muller, Gerda. *Around the oak*
Nail, James T. *Whose tracks are these?*
Newton, James R. *A forest is reborn*
    Forest log
Nivola, Claire A. *The forest*
O'Donnell, Peter. *Moonlit journey*
Olaleye, Isaac. *Lake of the Big Snake*
Osborne, Mary Pope. *Molly and the prince*
Owen, Roy. *My night forest*
Parnall, Peter. *The rock*
Pascoe, Gwen. *Deep in a rainforest*
Paul, Anthony. *The tiger who lost his stripes*
Pearson, Tracey Campbell. *The purple hat*
Peet, Bill (William Bartlett). *Big bad Bruce*
Peters, Lisa Westberg. *Meg and dad discover treasure in the air*
Peyo. *The Smurfs and their woodland friends*
Porter, Sue. *Little Wolf and the giant*
Prather, Ray. *The ostrich girl*
Prusski, Jeffrey. *Bring back the deer*
Reed-Jones, Carol. *The tree in the ancient forest*
Rich, Scharlotte. *Who made the wild woods?*
Ross, Tony. *Hansel and Gretel*
Ryder, Joanne. *Jaguar in the rain forest*
    The waterfall's gift
Sayre, April Pulley. *Army ant parade*
Schaefer, Carole Lexa. *Down in the woods at sleepytime*
    Down in the woods at sleepytime [board book]
Scheidl, Gerda Marie. *Can we help you, Saint Nicholas?*
Schick, Eleanor. *A surprise in the forest*
Schofield, Jennifer. *Animal babies in rain forests*
Schotter, Roni. *In the piney woods*
Seligson, Susan. *Amos camps out*
Seymour, Peter S. *What's in the prehistoric forest?*
Sikundar, Sylvia. *Forest singer*
Simple gifts
Slobodkin, Louis. *Melvin, the moose child*
Spohn, David. *Winter wood*
Stojic, Manya. *Snow*
Storr, Catherine (Cole). *Robin Hood*
Tejima, Keizaburo. *Fox's dream*
    Woodpecker forest
Thomson, Ruth. *The Rainforest Indians*
Thornhill, Jan. *A tree in a forest*
Tresselt, Alvin R. *The gift of the tree*
Upton, Pat. *Who lives in the woods?*
Waddell, Martin. *Let's go home, Little Bear*
Wahl, Jan. *The five in the forest*

Wallace, Karen. *Bears in the forest*
Wallen, Ila. *The moon in my room*
Ward, Helen. *The tin forest*
Ward, Lynd. *Nic of the woods*
Weigelt, Udo. *There's room in the forest for everyone*
Weir, Bob. *Panther dream*
Wells, Rosemary. *Moss pillows*
Wilds, Kazumi Inose. *Hajime in the North Woods*
Wilkes, Angela. *Rain forest animals*
Wilson, Karma. *Bear stays up for Christmas*
Witte, Anna. *The parrot Tico Tango*
Wood, Douglas. *Northwoods cradle song*
Woodman, Allen. *The bear who came to stay*
Yolen, Jane. *All in the woodland early*
    Owl moon
Zalben, Jane Breskin. *Norton's nighttime*
Ziefert, Harriet. *On our way to the forest*

Forgetfulness *see* Behavior – forgetfulness

Forgiving *see* Behavior – forgiving

Format, unusual

Adams, Pam. *This old man*
Ahlberg, Janet. *The jolly Christmas postman*
Aliki. *Marianthe's story one: painted words; Marianthe's story two: spoken memories*
Amery, H. *The zoo picture book*
Andersen, H. C. (Hans Christian). *The emperor's new clothes*, ill. by Robert Van Nutt
Anno, Mitsumasa. *Anno's faces*
    Anno's peekaboo
Axworthy, Anni. *Guess what I am*
    Guess what I'll be
Barker, Cicely Mary. *Berry flower fairies*
    Blossom flower fairies
    Spring flower fairies
    Summer flower fairies
Barrows, Marjorie Wescott. *Fraidy cat*
    The funny hat
Blake, William. *The tyger*
Boyd, Lizi. *Mouse in a house*
Brandon, Siobhán. *The bird's story*
Bratton, John. *The teddy bears' picnic*, ill. by Renate Kozikowski
Bridwell, Norman. *Glow-in-the-dark Halloween*
Brown, Margaret Wise. *The little fur family*
Brown, Rick. *Who built the ark?*
Burlson, Joe. *Space colony*
Burton, Jane. *ABC*
    Chick
Cahill, Chris. *Spider magic*
    Turtle magic
Cameron, Alice. *The cat sat on the mat*
Campbell, Rod. *Henry's busy day*
    Misty's mischief
Carle, Eric. *My very first book of colors*
    My very first book of growth
    My very first book of homes
    My very first book of motion
    My very first book of numbers
    My very first book of shapes
    My very first book of touch
    My very first book of words
    10 little rubber ducks
    The very hungry caterpillar
    The very quiet cricket
Carrier, Lark. *There was a hill . . .*
Cars and trucks and other vehicles
Carter, David A. *If you're happy and you know it, clap your hands*
Carter, Noelle. *I'm a little mouse*
Chwast, Seymour. *Tall city, wide country*
Count in the dark with Glo Worm
Cousins, Lucy. *Flower in the garden*
    Hen on the farm
    Kite in the park

Teddy in the house
Dennard, Deborah. *Hedgehog haven*
De Paola, Tomie (Thomas Anthony). *Country farm*
Dodds, Dayle Ann. *Wheel away!*
Donovan, Gail. *The copycat fish*
  A fishy story
  Lost at sea
Dryden, Emma. *Good morning – good night*
Durant, Alan. *Snake supper*
Dürr, Ursula. *The secret of Trembleton Hall*
Ehlert, Lois. *Color farm*
  Color zoo
  In my world
  Leaf man
Elias, Joyce. *Whose toes are those?*
Emberley, Ed (Edward Randolph). *Ed Emberley's amazing look*
  through book
Ernst, Lisa Campbell. *The rescue of Aunt Pansy*
Falwell, Cathryn. *Nicky and Alex*
  Nicky and grandpa
  Nicky loves daddy
  Nicky, 1-2-3
  Nicky's walk
  Where's Nicky?
Fanelli, Sara. *My map book*
Fort, Patrick. *Redbird*
Fowler, Richard. *Happy birthday, Mouse!*
Gantschev, Ivan. *The train to Grandma's*
  Where is Mr. Mole?
Garcia, Jerry. *The teddy bears' picnic*
Ghigna, Charles. *Good cats/Bad cats*
  Good dogs/Bad dogs
  Golden tales from long ago
Gomi, Taro. *Hi, butterfly!*
Goodall, John S. *The adventures of Paddy Pork*
  The ballooning adventures of Paddy Pork
  Creepy castle
  An Edwardian Christmas
  An Edwardian summer
  Jacko
  The midnight adventures of Kelly, Dot and Esmeralda
  Naughty Nancy
  Naughty Nancy goes to school
  Paddy goes traveling
  Paddy Pork
  Paddy Pork's holiday
  Paddy under water
  Paddy's evening out
  Paddy's new hat
  Shrewbettina's birthday
  The story of a castle
  The story of a farm
  The story of a main street
  The story of an English village
  The surprise picnic
Gorey, Edward (St. John). *The tunnel calamity*
Grimm, Jacob. *Little Red Riding Hood*, ill. by John S. Goodall
Grindley, Sally. *Shhh!*
Hague, Michael. *Michael Hague's world of unicorns*
Hannant, Judith Stuller. *Doorknob collection of nursery rhymes*
Hauptmann, Tatjana. *A day in the life of Petronella Pig*
Hayden, Lea. *Sunny day – rainy day*
Hedderwick, Mairi. *P. D. Pebbles' summer or winter book*
Hellard, Susan. *This little piggy*
Hellen, Nancy. *Bus stop*
Hill, Eric. *Spot's first 1, 2, 3 frieze*
Hoban, Tana. *Look! Look! Look!*
  26 letters and 99 cents
Hooper, Meredith. *Seven eggs*
Howell, Lynn. *Winifred's new bed*
Hyman, Trina Schart. *The enchanted forest*
Imershein, Betsy. *Finding red, finding yellow*
Inkpen, Mick. *The blue balloon*
  Threadbear
Jenkins, Martin. *Wings, stings, and wriggly things*
Jensen, Virginia Allen. *Catching*
  Red thread riddles

Jonas, Ann. *Reflections*
  The thirteenth clue
Jones, Carol. *This old man*
Kent, Lorna. *No, no, Charlie Rascal!*
Ladybug, ladybug, and other nursery rhymes
Lenski, Lois. *Sing a song of people*
Lewis, Stephen (Stephen Paul). *Zoo city*
Lewison, Wendy Cheyette. *Where is Sammy's smile?*
Little old lady who swallowed a fly. There was an old lady who swal-
  lowed a fly, ill. by Simms Taback
Llewellyn, Claire. *Crocodile*
  Duck
  Ladybug
  Tree
Lodge, Bernard. *Door to door*
  Rhyming Nell
MacDonald, Suse. *Nanta's lion*
  Once upon another
MacKinnon, Debbie. *Eye spy colors*
  Eye spy shapes
McNaughton, Colin. *Guess who's just moved in next door?*
Magnus, Erica. *Around me*
Mari, Iela. *Eat and be eaten*
Marshall, James. *Hey, diddle, daddle*
Martin, Jerome. *Carrot/parrot*
  Mitten/kitten
Meijer, Marie. *The bake-a-cake book*
Meyer, Brigit. *Little Easter surprise*
Miranda, Anne. *Baby walk*
Moffatt, Judith. *Christmas lights*
  Halloween frights
  Trick-or-treat faces
Monfried, Lucia. *Baby's world*
Morrow, Tara Jaye. *Mommy loves her baby; Daddy loves his baby*
Mother Goose. *Hickory dickory dock and other nursery rhymes*, ill. by
  Carol Jones
Munari, Bruno. *The circus in the mist*
My busy day
My doctor's bag
Newell, Peter. *Topsys and turvys*
Newth, Philip. *Roly goes exploring*
Nilsén, Anna. *Drive your car*
  Drive your tractor
  Let's all hang and dangle
Numeroff, Laura Joffe. *What grandmas do best; What grandpas do*
  best
Old MacDonald had a farm. Old MacDonald had a farm, ill. by
  Carol Jones
Ormerod, Jan. *Come back, kittens*
  Come back, puppies
Pacovská, Kveta. *One, five, many*
Padt, Maartje. *Shanti*
Page, Robin. *The alphabet sticker book*
Paschkis, Julie. *So happy/So sad*
Pericoli, Matteo. *See the city*
Peterson, Sue H. *Swim with me*
Pfister, Marcus. *Rainbow fish mini-book*
Potter, Beatrix. *Where's Peter Rabbit?*
Potter, Tony. *See how it works: cars*
  See how it works: earth movers
  See how it works: planes
  See how it works: trucks
Pratt, Pierre. *I see . . . my mom/I see . . . my dad*
  I see . . . my sister/I see . . . my cat
Price, Mathew. *Do you see what I see?*
  Have you seen my sister?
Radunsky, Eugenia. *Square, triangle, round, skinny*
Rey, H. A. (Hans Augusto). *Anybody at home?*
  How do you get there?
  See the circus
  Where's my baby?
Rice, Melanie. *My first body book*
Roddie, Shen. *Animal stew*
Roffey, Maureen. *Family scramble*
  Here, kitty kitty!
  Look, there's my hat!
  Quick, catch Dan!

Ross, Tony. *Happy blanket*
Roth, Carol. *Ten dirty pigs / Ten clean pigs*
Royston, Angela. *Shells*
　Small animals
Russell, Naomi. *The tree*
Scarry, Richard. *Egg in the hole*
　Pig Will and Pig Won't: 2-in-1 turn-around books
　Richard Scarry's biggest word book ever!
Scruton, Clive. *Mary's pets*
Scullard, Sue. *Miss Fanshawe and the great dragon adventure*
Seuss, Dr. *Gerald McBoing Boing sound book*
Sharratt, Nick. *I look like this*
　Look what I found!
Simmons, Jane. *Daisy, the little duck with big feet*
Steer, Dougald. *Just one more story*
Steiner, Charlotte. *The climbing book*
Tafuri, Nancy. *What the sun sees / What the moon sees*
Tarrant, Graham. *Rabbits*
The three bears. *Goldilocks and the three bears,* ill. by Madelaine Gill Linden
Tison, Annette. *The adventures of the three colors*
　Animal hide-and-seek
　Animals in color magic
　Inside and outside
The twelve days of Christmas. English folk song. *The twelve days of Christmas,* ill. by Erika Schneider
Vaughan, Marcia Kapok. *The dancing dragon*
Waber, Bernard. *The snake*
Wahl, Jan. *Dracula's cat and Frankenstein's dog*
Walters, Marguerite. *The city-country ABC*
Wattenberg, Jane. *Mrs. Mustard's baby faces*
Watts, Barrie. *Rabbit*
Wildsmith, Brian. *Give a dog a bone*
　Goat's trail
　Pelican
Wilson-Max, Ken. *Wake up; Sleep tight*
Windham, Sophie. *Noah's ark*
Wood, John Norris. *Jungles*
　Oceans
Wyllie, Stephen. *Ghost train*
　The great race
　White Rabbit builds a dream house
Youldon, Gillian. *Counting*
　Shapes
　Sizes
Young, Ed (Edward). *Mouse match*
Ziefert, Harriet. *Where's the cat?*
　Where's the dog?
　Where's the guinea pig?
　Where's the turtle?
Zolotow, Charlotte (Shapiro). *Wake up and goodnight*
　When I have a little girl; When I have a little boy

Format, unusual – board books

Abel, Simone. *Follow that chicken!*
Abel, Simone. *How now, cow?*
Abrams, Pam. *Now I eat my ABC's*
Acredolo, Linda P. *My first baby signs*
Aigner-Clark, Julie. *Language nursery*
Ajmera, Maya. *Animal friends*
Alexander, Martha G. *Good night, Lily*
　Lily and Willy
　Where's Willy?
　Willy's boot
Allen, Jonathan. *Big owl, little towel*
　One with a bun
　Purple sock, pink sock
Allen, Robert. *Ten little babies count*
　Ten little babies dress
　Ten little babies eat
　Ten little babies play
Alley, R. W. (Robert W.). *There once was a witch*
Anderson, Lena. *Bunny bath*
　Bunny box
　Bunny fun
　Bunny party

　Bunny story
　Bunny surprise
Anglund, Joan Walsh. *Christmas is here*
Anholt, Catherine. *Chimp and Zee's noisy book*
　Monkey around with Chimp and Zee [board book]
Arnold, Tedd. *Actions*
　Colors
　My first drawing book
　Opposites
　Sounds
Aronin, Ben. *The secret of the Sabbath fish*
Asch, Frank. *Moonbear's books*
　Moonbear's canoe
At the farm
Baby's first book of colors
Baby's words
Baggette, Susan K. *Jonathan goes to the doctor*
　Jonathan goes to the grocery store
Bailey, Debbie. *Clothes*
　Grandma
　Grandpa
　Hats
　My dad
　My family
　My mom
　The playground
　Shoes
　Toys
Bailey, Jill. *Eyes*
　Feet
　Mouths
　Noses
Baird, Anne. *Baby socks*
　Kiss, kiss
　Little tree
　No sheep
Bambi
Barack, Marcy. *Season song*
Barkan, Joanne. *Boxcar*
　Caboose
　Locomotive
　Passenger car
　Whiskerville bake shop
　Whiskerville firehouse
　Whiskerville post office
　Whiskerville school
Baseball ABC
Baseball 1-2-3
Beall, Pamela Conon. *Wee Sing if you're happy and you know it*
Beaton, Clare. *One moose, twenty mice [board book]*
Bedtime
Bible. Old Testament. Daniel. *Daniel in the lions' den,* ill. by Jim Cummins
Bible. Old Testament. Jonah. *Jonah and the great fish,* ill. by Jim Cummins
Bible. Old Testament. Joseph. *Joseph and his brothers*
Bishop, Roma. *Animals*
　Numbers
　Shapes
　Toys
Blackstone, Stella. *Secret seahorse [board book]*
　Who are you?
Blades, Ann. *Fall*
　Spring
　Summer
　Winter
Blegvad, Lenore. *This is me*
Blume, Karin. *Circus*
　My new friends
Bohdal, Susi. *Bobby the bear*
　Harry the hare
Boon, Emilie. *It's spring, Peterkin*
　Peterkin's very own garden
Bos, Claire. *Maurice the hippo*
　Webster's wardrobe
Bowman, Pete. *Goodnight, teddy bear*
Boyd, Lizi. *Baby play*

Bunny hop
Boynton, Sandra. *Barnyard dance!*
   Birthday monsters!
   But not the hippopotamus
   Dinosaur's binkit
   Doggies
   The going to bed book
   Horns to toes and in between
   Moo, baa, la la la!
   Oh my oh my oh dinosaurs!
   One, two, three!
   Opposites
Bratton, Heidi. *Imagine*
   Yes, I can!
Breeze, Lynn. *Baby's animals*
   Baby's clothes
   Baby's food
   Baby's toys
   This little baby goes out
   This little baby's bedtime
   This little baby's morning
Brett, Jan. *The mitten*
Brown, Marc Tolon. *Arthur goes to school*
   Arthur's animal adventure
   Arthur's new puppy [board book]
   Count to ten
   D. W. thinks big [board book]
   Marc Brown's Boat book
Brown, Margaret Wise. *Bumble bee*
   Bunny's noisy book [board book]
   The runaway bunny [board book]
Browne, Anthony. *I like books [board book]*
Bruna, Dick. *Miffy loves New York City!*
   Miffy the ghost
Buck, Nola. *How a baby grows*
Buehner, Caralyn. *Snowmen at night [board book]*
Burg, Ann. *Autumn walk*
Burnard, Damon. *I spy in the jungle*
   I spy in the ocean
Burningham, John. *Count up*
   The dog
   Five down
   Just cats
   Pigs plus
   Read one
   Ride off
Burton, Jane. *Kitten*
   Puppy
Busy baby
Butterworth, Nick. *When there's work to do*
   When we go shopping
   When we play together
Cabrera, Jane. *Monkey's play time*
   Panda Big and Panda Small
Cahill, Chris. *Bear magic*
   Bunny magic
   Spider magic
   Turtle magic
Calmenson, Stephanie. *Meet Penny*
   Meet Timmy
Campbell, Rod. *Look inside! All kinds of places*
   Look inside! Land, sea, air
Capucilli, Alyssa Satin. *Biscuit gives a gift*
Carle, Eric. *From head to toe*
   Little cloud [board book]
Carlstrom, Nancy White. *Jesse Bear's tra-la tub*
   Jesse Bear's tum-tum tickle
   Jesse Bear's wiggle-jiggle jump-up
   Jesse Bear's yum-yum crumble
Cars and trucks
Cartlidge, Michelle. *Baby mice at home*
   Bear in the forest
   Bears on the go
   Bunny's birthday
   Doggy days
   Duck in the pond
   Elephant in the jungle

Mouse in the house
Casalis, Anna. *Dinosaurs [board book]*
Cassidy, Dianne. *Circus animals*
   Circus people
   The caterpillar who turned into a butterfly
Cherry, Lynne. *Grizzly bear*
   Orangutan
   Seal
   Snow leopard
Children's Television Workshop. *Muppets in my neighborhood*
Chorao, Kay. *Peekaboo! Was it you?*
   Rock, rock, my baby
City, ill. by Roser Capdevila
Clark, Sue. *Bodies*
   Clothes
   Faces
   Feelings
Cock Robin. *Who killed Cock Robin?*, ill. by William Stobbs
Cole, Joanna. *Sharing is fun*
Collins, Heather. *Eensy weensy spider*
Come to the circus
Corbett, Grahame. *Guess who?*
   What number now?
   Who is hiding?
   Who is inside?
   Who is next?
Cosgrove, Stephen (Edward). *Sleepy time bunny*
Costa, Nicoletta. *The birthday party [board book]*
   Dressing up
   A friend comes to play
   The missing cat
Cousins, Lucy. *Count with Maisy*
   Country animals
   Farm animals
   Garden animals
   Humpty Dumpty and other nursery rhymes
   Jack and Jill
   Little Miss Muffet
   Maisy's halloween
   Maisy's noisy day
   Noah's ark [board book]
   Pet animals
   Wee Willie Winkie and other nursery rhymes
Cowley, Stewart. *Down Ladybug Lane*
   Five little kittens
   Hide-and-seek puppies
   In dragonfly forest
   In songbird jungle
   Little bunny
   Little chick
   Little lost rabbit
   The naughty ducklings
   On Butterfly Farm
   "Tweet, tweet, tweet"
   What's that sound?
Crary, Elizabeth. *When you're mad and you know it*
Crews, Donald. *School bus [board book]*
Crozat, François. *I am a little cat*
   I am a little caterpillar
   I am a little dog
Curious George's 1 to 10 and back again
Curti, Anna. *Seasons*
Daly, Kathleen N. *Jesus our friend*
Dann, Penny. *Eensy weensy spider*
Davidson, Amanda. *Teddy goes outside*
Davis, Caroline. *My little rocking horse lullabies*
   My little rowboat
Day, Alexandra. *Helping the animals*
   Helping the flowers and trees
   Helping the night
   Helping the sun
Deegan, Kim. *My first book of numbers*
   My first book of opposites
Demarest, Chris L. *Bus*
   Plane
   Train
Demi. *Cuddly chick*

Demi's Christmas surprise
Downy duckling
Fleecy bunny
Fleecy lamb
Fuzzy wuzzy puppy
Little baby lamb
Little bitty bunny
Little chick chick
Little lucky ducky
So soft kitty
De Paola, Tomie (Thomas Anthony). *Get dressed, Santa!*
Katie and Kit at the beach
Katie, Kit and cousin Tom
Katie's good idea
Marcos: red, yellow, blue
My first Chanukah
Pajamas for Kit
Dickens, Lucy. *At the beach*
Our day
Outside
Playtime
DiFiori, Lawrence. *Baby animals*
The farm
If I had a little car
My first book
My toys
Doepker, David. *Animal babies*
Farm babies
Domestic animals
Douzou, Olivier. *Wolf's lunch*
Dreamer, Sue. *Circus ABC*
Circus 1, 2, 3
Dubov, Christine Salac. *Aleksandra, where are your toes?*
Aleksandra, where is your nose?
Ding dong! and other sounds
Knock! and other sounds
Oink! and other sounds
Duckling
Duerrstein, Richard. *Mickey is happy*
Duke, Kate. *Bedtime*
Clean-up day
The playground
What bounces?
Dunn, Phoebe. *Baby's animal friends*
Busy, busy toddlers
I'm a baby!
Dupasquier, Philippe. *1 2 3, follow me!*
Edwards, Pamela Duncan. *Warthogs in a box*
Edwards, Roberta. *Anna Bear's first winter*
Eisenberg, Ann. *I can celebrate*
Ellwand, David. *Ten in the bed*
Emberley, Ed (Edward Randolph). *Animals*
Cars, boats, and planes
Home
Sounds
Emberley, Rebecca. *My animals = Mis animales*
My city = Mi cuidad
My clothes = Mi ropa
My colors = Mis colores
My food = Mi comida
My garden = Mi jardin
My house = Mi casa
My numbers = Mis números
My opposites = Mis opuestos
My room = Mi cuarto
My school = Mi escuela
My shapes = Mis formas
My toys = Mi juguetes
Emergency!
Faglia, Maeto. *Happy birthday, I'm 1*
Happy birthday, I'm 2
Happy birthday, I'm 3
Happy birthday, I'm 4
Falconer, Ian. *Olivia – and the missing toy*
Olivia counts
Olivia's opposites
Farjeon, Eleanor. *Cats*

Farm animals, photos sel. by Debby Slier
Farm house
Fast rolling fire trucks
Fast rolling work trucks
Fechner, Amrei. *I am a little dog*
I am a little elephant
I am a little lion
Firehouse
Fitzsimons, Cecilia. *My first birds*
My first butterflies
Five little pumpkins
Fleming, Denise. *The everything book [board book]*
Fosberg, John. *Cookie shapes*
Ice cream colors
Fowler, Richard. *Cat's story*
Fox, Christyan. *Count to ten, PiggyWiggy!*
What color is that, PiggyWiggy?
What shape is that, PiggyWiggy?
Freeman, Don. *Corduroy's busy street and Corduroy goes to the doctor*
Freeman, Lydia. *Corduroy's day*
Fujikawa, Gyo. *Let's grow a garden*
Millie's secret
My favorite thing
See what I can be!
Surprise! Surprise!
Fujita, Miho. *The little choo-choo*
Gardiner, Lindsey. *Good night, Poppy and Max*
Gelbard, Jane. *My bye-bye bottle book*
My dressing book
My eating book
My sharing book
Gellman, Ellie. *It's Chanukah!*
It's Rosh Hashanah!
Shai's Shabbat walk
Gergely, Tibor. *The great big fire engine book*
Giffard, Hannah. *Fast car*
Hens say cluck
Red bus
Striped zebra
Gikow, Louise. *Bye-bye, pacifier*
I am Kermit
Gliori, Debi. *Can I have a hug?*
Mr. Bear says peek-a-boo
Tickly under there
Gold-Vukson, Marji E. *The colors of my Jewish Year*
Gomboli, Mario. *Look inside a house*
Look inside a ship
Gomi, Taro. *Guess what?*
Guess who?
Good morning
Gorbaty, Norman. *Get up and go, little dinosaur!*
Got, Yves. *Sam loves kisses*
Sam's little sister
Grahame, Kenneth. *Duck song*
Greeley, Valerie. *Animals*
Farm animals
Field animals
Pets
Zoo animals
Greenfield, Eloise. *Big friend, little friend*
Daddy and I
I make music
My doll, Keshia
Sweet baby coming
Greenfield, Monica. *The baby*
Greenway, Shirley. *Color me bright*
Here's ears
Legs and all
A tale of tails
Gretz, Susanna. *Hide-and-seek*
I'm not sleepy
Ready for bed
Too dark!
Grimes, Nikki. *Baby's bedtime*
Groner, Judyth Saypol. *Where is the Afikomen?*
Gundersheimer, Karen. *Find cat, wear hat*
Haddon, Mark. *At home*

At playgroup
In the garden
On vacation
Haldane, Suzanne. *Teddies and machines*
  Teddies and trucks
Hale, Sarah Josepha Buell. *Mary had a little lamb [board book]*, ill.
  by Iza Trapani
Hands, Hargrave. *Bunny sees*
  Duckling sees
  Little lamb sees
Hannant, Judith Stuller. *Doorknob collection of nursery rhymes*
  The doorknob collection of pets and pals
  Three little kittens
Haring, Keith. *Big*
  10
Harris, Trudy. *Up bear, down bear*
Hathon, Elizabeth. *We go to school*
  We go to the zoo
Haus, Felice. *Beep! Beep! I'm a jeep*
Hawkins, Colin. *Hey, diddle, diddle*
Hayes, Geoffrey. *Patrick and his grandpa*
Hayward, Linda. *Sunny Day Bunny*
Hello, baby
Henkes, Kevin. *Lilly's chocolate heart*
  Sheila Rae's peppermint stick
Henley, Claire. *Dinnertime*
  I'm a baby, too!
  Playtime
  Quack, quack
Hest, Amy. *Baby Duck and the cozy blanket*
Hill, Eric. *Puppy love*
  Spot at home
  Spot at the fair
  Spot counts from 1 to 10
  Spot goes to the circus
  Spot goes to the farm
  Spot in the garden
  Spot looks at colors
  Spot looks at opposites
  Spot looks at shapes
  Spot looks at weather
  Spot on the farm
  Spot visits his grandparents
  Spot's favorite baby animals
  Spot's favorite colors
  Spot's favorite numbers
  Spot's favorite words
  Spot's first words
  Spot's magical Christmas
  Spot's toy box
Hines, Anna Grossnickle. *What can you do in the rain?*
  What can you do in the snow?
  What can you do in the sun?
  What can you do in the wind?
Hissey, Jane. *Little bear's bedtime*
  Little Bear's day
  Old Bear [board book]
Hoban, Lillian. *Big Little Otter*
Hoban, Tana. *1, 2, 3*
  Panda, panda
  Red, blue, yellow shoe
  What is it?
  What is that?
  White on black
  Who are they?
Hoe, Susan. *Which shoes would you choose?*
Hoffman, Don. *A counting book with Billy and Abigail*
  Good morning, good night Billy and Abigail
Holabird, Katharine. *Angelina dances*
Holub, Joan. *Turkeys never gobble*
Hopkins, Margaret. *Sleepytime for baby mouse*
Hubbell, Patricia. *Pots and pans*
  Wrapping paper romp
Hudson, Cheryl Willis. *Animal sounds for baby*
  Good morning baby
  Good night baby
  Let's count, baby

Hughes, Shirley. *Being together*
  Playing
Hurd, Thacher. *Cat's pajamas*
Hutchins, Pat. *Rosie's walk [board book]*
Hyde, Margaret E. *Matisse for kids*
  Van Gogh for kids
Imershein, Betsy. *Trucks*
Inkpen, Mick. *Wibbly Pig can make a tent*
  Wibbly Pig is upset
  Wibbly Pig likes bananas
  Wibbly Pig makes pictures
  Wibbly Pig opens his presents
Intrater, Roberta Grobel. *Peek-a-boo!*
  Smile!
Jackson, Kathryn. *The golden circus book*
Jaramillo, Raquel. *Ride, baby, ride!*
Johnson, Angela. *Joshua by the sea*
  Joshua's night whispers
  Mama bird, baby birds
  Rain feet
Johnson, John Emil. *My first book of things*
Josephs, Rhoda. *The baby bubble book*
Joyce, William. *Baseball Bob*
  Life with Bob
  Rolie Polie Olie, how many howdys?
Just like father
Kahn, Katherine Janus. *The shofar calls to us*
Kangas, Juli. *Fluffy Bunny's friend*
  Ginger Kitten's surprise
  Hello, Honey Bear
Karn, George. *Circus big and small*
  Circus colors
Keats, Ezra Jack. *One red sun*
  The snowy day [board book]
Keeshan, Robert. *Itty Bitty Kitty*
  Itty Bitty Kitty makes a big splash
Kelley, True. *Hammers and mops, pencils and pots*
Kemp, Moira. *I'm a little teapot*
  Knock at the door
  Round and round the garden
Kessler, Ethel. *Are there hippos on the farm?*
  Are there seals in the sandbox?
  Is there a gorilla in the band?
  Is there a horse in your house?
  Is there a penguin at your party?
  Is there an elephant in your kitchen?
Kilroy, Sally. *Animal noises*
  Babies' bodies
  Babies' homes
  Babies' outings
  Babies' zoo
  Baby colors
  Busy babies
  Noisy homes
Koelling, Caryl. *Animal mix and match*
  Mad monsters mix and match
  Silly stories mix and match
Koenner, Alfred. *Be quite quiet beside the lake*
  High flies the ball
Kraus, Robert. *Animal families*
  Freddy, the fire engine
  Mouse work
  Robert Kraus' a sunny day in Babytown
  Robert Kraus' Babytown express
  Robert Kraus' meet the babies
  Robert Kraus' welcome to Babytown
  Tony, the tow truck
Krauss, Ruth. *I can fly*
Krementz, Jill. *Benjy goes to a restaurant*
  Jack goes to the beach
  Jamie goes on an airplane
  Katharine goes to nursery school
  Lily goes to the playground
  Taryn goes to the dentist
Kress, Camille. *Purim*
  Tot Shabbat
Kvasnosky, Laura McGee. *One, two, three, play with me!*

Pink, red, blue, what are you?
Lacome, Julie. *Seashore*
Laden, Nina. *Peek-a-who?*
Landa, Norbert. *Rabbit and chicken count eggs*
   Rabbit and chicken find a box
   Rabbit and chicken play with colors
Lawrence, Michael (Michael C.). *Baby loves*
Leblanc, Anne. *Benjamin in the snow*
   Benjamin takes care of Mommy
   Benjamin's busy day
   Shopping with Benjamin
Leonard, Marcia. *Bye-bye, Baby-boo*
   What's that, Baby-boo?
   Where's Baby-boo?
Lewis, Shari. *Baby Lamb Chop loves animals*
   Baby Lamb Chop loves numbers
   Baby Lamb Chop loves nursery school
   Baby Lamb Chop loves the beach
   Baby Lamb Chop loves words
Lewison, Wendy Cheyette. *Baby has a boo-boo*
   Happy Thanksgiving!
   Nighty-night
Libney, Varda. *What I like about Passover*
Lilly, Kenneth. *Animal builders*
   Animal climbers
   Animal jumpers
   Animal runners
   Animal swimmers
   Animals at the zoo
   Animals in the country
   Animals in the jungle
   Animals of the ocean
   Animals on the farm
Lionni, Leo. *Colors to talk about*
   Letters to talk about
   Numbers to talk about
   What?
   When?
   Where?
   Who?
   Words to talk about
Lister, Clare. *My first Passover [board book]*
A little ABC book
A little book of colors
A little book of numbers
London, Jonathan. *What do you love? [board book]*
Losordo, Stephen. *Cow moo me*
Lundell, Margo. *Teddy bear's birthday*
Lynn, Sara. *Big animals*
   Clothes
   Farm animals
   Food
   Garden animals
   Home
   Jungle friends
   Small animals
   Toys
   Wheels
Maccarone, Grace. *Baby visits grandma and grandpa*
   Baby's toys
McCue, Lisa. *Corduroy's party*
   Corduroy's toys
   The little chick
McCurry, Kristen. *Ocean babies*
   Safari babies
MacDonald, Amy. *Let's do it*
   Let's go
   Let's make a noise
   Let's play
   Let's pretend
   Let's try
McFarlane, Sheryl. *In the city*
   On the farm
McGrath, Barbara Barbieri. *Kellogg's froot loops color fun book*
McKee, David. *Elmer's colors*
   Elmer's day
   Elmer's friends

Elmer's weather
McMullan, Kate (Hall). *Supercat*
McNaught, Harry. *Baby animals*
McNaughton, Colin. *At home*
   At playschool
   At the park
   At the party
   At the stores
   Autumn
   Spring
   Summer
   Winter
McQuade, Jacqueline. *At preschool with Teddy Bear*
   At the petting zoo with Teddy Bear
Maestro, Betsy. *Harriet at home*
   Harriet at play
   Harriet at school
   Harriet at work
Maier, Paul L. *The very first Christmas*
Mantegazza, Giovanna. *The cat*
   The hippopotamus
   Look how a baby grows
Maris, Ron. *Ducks quack*
   Frogs jump
Markes, Julie. *Sidewalk ABC*
   Sidewalk 1 2 3
Marshall, James. *Eugene*
   Sing out, Irene
Martin, Bill (William Ivan). *Chicka chicka boom boom [board book]*
   I pledge allegiance
Marzollo, Jean. *Do you know new?*
   I spy little animals
   I spy little book
   I spy little wheels
   Mama, Mama
   Papa, papa
Mayer, Mercer. *Astronaut critter*
   Cowboy critter
   Fireman critter
   Policeman critter
Mayo, Margaret. *Choo choo clickety-clack*
Medearis, Angela Shelf. *Bye-bye, babies!*
   Eat, babies, eat!
Melmed, Laura Krauss. *I love you as much . . .*
Merberg, Julie. *In the garden with Van Gogh*
   A magical day with Matisse
Merriam, Eve. *The hole story*
Miller, J. P. (John Parr). *Good night, Little Rabbit*
Miller, Margaret. *At my house*
   At the shore
   Baby faces
   Every day
   Family time
   Guess who?
   Happy days
   Here we go!
   I can help
   I can make it!
   I love colors
   I'm grown up!
   In my room
   Let's play!
   Let's pretend!
   Me and my bear
   My best friends
   My birthday
   My first words: me and my clothes
   On my street
   Playtime
   Time to eat
   Water play
   What's on my head?
   Wheels go 'round
Minarik, Else Holmelund. *Father's flying flapjacks*
Moore, Dessie. *Getting dressed*
   Good morning
   Good night

Let's pretend
Morgan-Vanroyen, Mary. *Guess who I love?*
   The Pudgy Merry Christmas book
Morozumi, Atsuko. *Helping daddy*
   In the park
   Playing
   Time for bed
Most, Bernard. *Moo-ha!*
   Oink-ha!
Mother Goose. *ABC rhymes*
   Baa, baa, black sheep, ill. by Moira Kemp
   Baa baa black sheep, ill. by Sue Porter
   Baa baa black sheep, ill. by Ferelith Eccles Williams
   Baby's first Mother Goose
   Hey, diddle, diddle, ill. by Moira Kemp
   Hey, diddle, diddle, ill. by Nita Sowter
   Hey, diddle, diddle, ill. by Eleanor Wasmuth
   Hey, diddle, diddle picture book, ill. by Randolph Caldecott
   Hickory, dickory, dock, ill. by Heather Collins
   Hickory, dickory, dock, ill. by Moira Kemp
   Humpty Dumpty, ill. by Colin and Jacqui Hawkins
   Humpty Dumpty and other rhymes, ill. by Rosemary Wells
   Jack and Jill, ill. by Heather Collins
   Jack and Jill, ill. by Eleanor Wasmuth
   Kate Greenaway's Mother Goose
   Kitten rhymes
   Little Boy Blue, ill. by Nita Sowter
   Little Boy Blue and other rhymes
   Little Miss Muffet, ill. by Heather Collins
   Mother Goose house
   My first real Mother Goose [board book], ill. by Blanche Fisher
     Wright
   The old woman in a shoe
   Pat-a-cake [board book], ill. by Heather Collins
   Pat-a-cake, pat-a-cake, ill. by Moira Kemp
   Pussy cat, pussy cat, ill. by Ferelith Eccles Williams
   Pussycat, pussycat and other rhymes
   The real Mother Goose [board book], ill. by Diane Muldrow
   Rock-a-bye baby [board book], ill. by Heather Collins
   Sing a song of sixpence, ill. by Margaret Chamberlain
   Sing a song of sixpence, ill. by Ferelith Eccles Williams
   This little pig, ill. by Eleanor Wasmuth
   This little pig went to market, ill. by Ferelith Eccles Williams
   This little piggy, ill. by Moira Kemp
   This little piggy [board book], ill. by Heather Collins
   The three little kittens, ill. by Dorothy Stott
   Wee Willie Winkie and other rhymes, ill. by Rosemary Wells
   Wee willie winkie [board book], ill. by Heather Collins
Mott, Evelyn Clarke. *Cool cat*
   Hot dog
Mouse house, ill. by Zokeisha
Murphy, Chuck. *Colors*
Murphy, Mary. *I like it when . . .*
My body
My first book of baby animals
My first Christmas [board book]
My first farm
My first word, touch and feel
Nayer, Judy. *Bath*
   Jungle life
   Night animals
   Reptiles
   Sea creatures
Newman, Marjorie. *Mole and the baby bird [board book]*
Nickl, Peter. *Ra ta ta tam*
Norac, Carl. *I love to cuddle*
O'Brien, Anne Sibley. *Come play with us*
   I want that!
   I'm not tired
   Where's my truck?
Ohi, Ruth. *Pants off first*
O'Mara, Carmel. *Rainy day*
   Sunny day
Our house
Owen, Annie. *Goodnight bear!*
   Hungry panda
   Playtime duck

Wake up Frog!
Oxenbury, Helen. *All fall down*
   Beach day
   Clap hands
   Dressing
   Family
   Friends
   I can
   I hear
   I see
   I touch
   Playing
   Say goodnight
   729 curious creatures
   729 merry mix-ups
   729 puzzle people
   The shopping trip
   Tickle, tickle
Parish, Peggy. *I can – can you?*
Parr, Todd. *Big and little*
   Black and white
Paterson, Bettina. *In my house*
   In my yard
   My clothes
   My toys
Patrick, Denise Lewis. *No diapers for baby!*
Pearson, Susan. *Baby and the bear*
   When baby went to bed
Pearson, Tracey Campbell. *Hector Protector [board book]*
Peppé, Rodney. *Little circus*
   Little dolls
   Little games
   Little numbers
   Little wheels
Peterson, Melissa. *Hanna's Christmas*
Pfister, Marcus. *Rainbow fish board book and finger puppet*
   Where is my friend?
Pfloog, Jan. *Kittens*
   Puppies
Phillips, Joan. *Peek-a-boo! I see you!*
Pieńkowski, Jan. *Faces*
   Food
Powell, Alma. *My little wagon [board book]*
Pragoff, Fiona. *Odd one out*
   Opposites
   Shapes
Pratt, Pierre. *Home*
   Park
   Shopping
Prelutsky, Jack. *Halloween countdown*
The pudgy book of babies
The pudgy book of farm animals
The pudgy book of here we go
The pudgy book of make-believe
The pudgy book of Mother Goose
The pudgy book of toys
The pudgy bunny book
The pudgy fingers counting book
The pudgy pals
The pudgy pat-a-cake book
The pudgy peek-a-boo book
The pudgy rock-a-bye book
Puppies and kittens
Reasoner, Charles. *Ants, ants, ants*
   The big busy building
Reidy, Hannah. *Crazy creature contrasts*
Ricklen, Neil. *My clothes = Mi ropa*
   My colors = Mis colores
   My family = Mi familia
   My numbers = Mis números
Rock, Lois. *Now we have a baby*
Roosevelt, Michelle Chopin. *Zoo animals*
Root, Phyllis. *One duck stuck [board book]*
   Rattletrap car [board book]
Rosa-Mendoza, Gladys. *What time is it? = Qué hora es?*
Roth, Harold. *Autumn days*
   A checkup

Nursery school
Winter days
Royston, Angela. *Cars*
Sage, Chris. *Happy baby*
Sleepy baby
Sanger, Amy Wilson. *First book of sushi*
Santa's little library of Christmas stories
Sasso, Sandy Eisenberg. *Naamah, Noah's wife*
Scarry, Richard. *My first word book*
Richard Scarry's busy houses
Richard Scarry's Lowly Worm word book
Schaefer, Carole Lexa. *Down in the woods at sleepytime [board book]*
Schanzer, Rosalyn. *In the synagogue*
Schindel, John. *Busy penguins*
Schmid, Eleonore. *Farm animals*
Schroeder, Binette. *Tuffa and her friends*
Tuffa and the bone
Tuffa and the ducks
Tuffa and the picnic
Tuffa and the snow
Scott, Ann Herbert. *On mother's lap [board book]*
Sesame Street. *Ernie and Bert can . . . can you?*
Shea, Pegi Deitz. *I see me!*
Shine, Deborah. *The little engine that could pudgy word book*
Shirotani, Hideo. *Let's eat = Vamos a comer*
Let's play
Let's take a walk = Vamos a caminar
What color? = Qué color?
Shostak, Myra. *Rainbow candles*
Shott, Steve (Stephen). *Bathtime*
Look at me
Mealtime
Playtime
Sieveking, Anthea. *Mary had a little lamb and other animal rhymes*
Polly put the kettle on and other play rhymes
Rub-a-dub-dub and other splashy rhymes
Twinkle, twinkle, little star and other bedtime rhymes
Silverman, Maida. *Bunny's ABC*
Ladybug's color book
Mouse's shape book
Simmons, Jane. *Daisy says Coo!*
Daisy says, "Here we go round the mulberry bush"
Daisy says, "If you're happy and you know it"
Daisy's day out
Daisy's favorite things
Splish splash Daisy
Smith, Charles R. *I'll be there*
My gal
Smith, Donald. *Who's wearing my baseball cap?*
Who's wearing my bow tie?
Who's wearing my sneakers?
Who's wearing my sunglasses?
Snow, Alan. *Cluck!*
Oink!
Quack!
Woof!
Spanner, Helmut. *I am a little cat*
Spier, Peter. *Bill's service station*
Firehouse
Food market
Little cats
Little dogs
Little ducks
Little rabbits
My school
The pet store
The toy shop
Spohn, Kate. *Piglet's bath*
Snow play
Springer, Sally. *Let's make latkes*
Staake, Bob. *My little ABC book*
My little color book
My little 1 2 3 book
My little opposites book
Stanley, Mandy. *At the pool*
In the park
On the move

Perfect pets
Stephens, Helen. *I'm too busy*
Stevens, Harry. *Fat mouse*
Parrot told snake
Stoeke, Janet Morgan. *Hide and seek*
Struppi
Suben, Eric. *Pigeon takes a trip*
Suen, Anastasia. *Baby born [board book]*
Szekeres, Cyndy. *Cyndy Szekeres' learn to count, funny bunnies*
Good night, Sammy
Hide-and-seek duck
Nothing-to-do puppy
Suppertime for Frieda Fuzzypaws
Toby's please and thank you
Tabler, Judith. *The new puppy*
Tafolla, Carmen. *Baby Coyote and the old woman = El coyotito y la viejita*
Tafuri, Nancy. *In a red house*
My friends
One wet jacket
Two new sneakers
Where we sleep
Tangvald, Christine Harder. *The best thing about Easter*
Taylor, Ann. *Baby dance*
Taylor, Jane. *Twinkle, twinkle little star*, ill. by Heather Collins
Taylor, Kim. *Frog*
Thomas, Joyce Carol. *Joy*
Thompson, Lauren. *Little Quack [board book]*
Mouse's first Christmas [board book]
The three bears. *Goldilocks and the three bears*, ill. by Jane Dyer
The three bears [board book], ill. by Thea Kliros
The three little pigs. *The three little pigs*, ill. by Val Biro
The three little pigs [board book], ill. by Thea Kliros
Tildes, Phyllis Limbacher. *Baby animals black and white*
Titherington, Jeanne. *Baby's boat [board book]*
Topek, Susan Remick. *Shalom, Shabbat*
Trapani, Iza. *Baa baa black sheep [board book]*
How much is that doggie in the window?
Tucker, Sian. *At home*
Going out
My clothes
My toys
The twelve days of Christmas. English folk song. *The twelve days of Christmas [board book]*, ill. by Jan Brett
Twinem, Neecy. *In the air*
VanderKlipp, Michael A. *Joy to the world!*
A visit to a pond
Vulliamy, Clara. *Bang and shout*
Blue hat, red coat
Boo baby boo!
Good night, baby
Wide awake
Yum yum
Waddell, Martin. *Owl babies [board book]*
Walker, Joni. *Tell me the Christmas story*
Waller, Curt. *Baby's first signs*
More baby's first signs
Waterhouse, Stephen A. *Get busy this Christmas*
Watson, Carol. *Rabbit*
Watts, Barrie. *Duck*
Wax, Wendy. *A very mice Christmas*
Weedn, Flavia. *I feel happy*
Weeks, Sarah. *Bite me, I'm a shape*
Bite me, I'm a book
Weiss, Nicki. *Where does the brown bear go? [board book]*
Wellington, Monica. *Baby at home*
Baby in a buggy
Baby in a car
Bunny's first snowflake
Bunny's rainbow day
Wells, Rosemary. *Bingo*
Hooray for Max
The itsy-bitsy spider
Max's bath
Max's bedtime
Max's birthday
Max's breakfast

Max's first word
 Max's new suit
 Max's ride
 Max's toys
What do babies do?
What do toddlers do?
White, Amanda. *Rip and Rap*
Who took the cookie?
Wijngaard, Juan. *Bear*
 Cat
 Dog
 Duck
Wikler, Madeline. *Let's build a Sukkah*
 My first seder
 The Purim parade
Wilhelm, Hans. *Quacky Ducky's Easter egg*
 Quacky Ducky's Easter fun
Williams, Sue. *I went walking [board book]*
Willis, Val. *The mystery in the bottle*
Winn, Chris. *Helping*
 Holiday
 My day
 Playing
Wood, David. *Piggies [board book]*
Yaccarino, Dan. *Five little ducks*
Yee, Patrick. *Baby bear*
 Baby lion
 Baby monkey
 Baby penguin
 Let's go
 Let's make friends
 Let's play
 Rosie Rabbit's colors
 Rosie Rabbit's numbers
 Rosie Rabbit's opposites
 Rosie Rabbit's shapes
Yee, Paul. *Let's eat*
Yolen, Jane. *How do dinosaurs clean their rooms?*
 How do dinosaurs count to ten?
 Time for naps
You can name 100 trucks!
Young animals in the zoo
Young domestic animals
Ziefert, Harriet. *Baby Ben's bow-wow book*
 Baby Ben's busy book
 Baby Ben's go-go book
 Baby Ben's noisy book
 My getting-ready-for-school book
 Nicky's friends
 No, no, Nicky!
 On our way to the barn
 On our way to the forest
 On our way to the water
 On our way to the zoo
 Where's the cat?
 Where's the dog?
 Where's the guinea pig?
 Where's the turtle?
Zoehfeld, Kathleen Weidner. *Apples, apples*
Zoller, Arthur David. *Fish colors*
 Fish counting
Zoo animals

Format, unusual – toy & movable books

Abel, Simone. *Follow that chicken!*
 How now, cow?
Æsop. *Æsop's fables*, ill. by Gisela Dürr
 Æsop's fables, ill. by Claire Littlejohn
 The children's Æsop
 The hare and the tortoise, ill. by Carol Jones
Ahlberg, Janet. *The bear nobody wanted*
 The jolly pocket postman
 The jolly postman
 Peek-a-boo!
 Playmates
 Yum yum

Alborough, Jez. *Can you jump like a kangaroo?*
 Can you peck like a hen?
 Clothesline
 Hide and seek
Alexander, Martha G. *3 magic flip books*
Andreae, Giles. *The pop-up Rumble in the jungle*
Anno, Mitsumasa. *Anno's magical ABC*
 Anno's masks
 Anno's sundial
Apperley, Dawn. *In the jungle*
 In the sand
Argent, Kerry. *Happy birthday wombat!*
Arnold, Tedd. *Bisnipian blast-off*
 My first drawing book
Arnosky, Jim. *Wild and swampy*
Artell, Mike. *Legs*
Asbjørnsen, P. C. (Peter Christen). *The three billy goats Gruff*, ill. by
  Thomas Newbury
 The three billy goats Gruff, ill. by Laura Rader
Asch, Frank. *I can blink*
 I can roar
 Short train, long train
Augarde, Steve (Stephen). *Garage*
Baby animals
Baker, Alan. *Where's mouse?*
Baker, Keith. *Cat tricks*
Balmer, Helen. *Jungle adventure*
Bannerman, Helen. *The story of Little Black Sambo*, "pop-up" pic-
 ture by C. Carey Cloud
Bantock, Nick. *Runners, sliders, bouncers, climbers*
Barnes-Murphy, Rowan. *Numbers*
Barry, Frances. *Duckie's rainbow*
Bauer, Marion Dane. *Toes, ears, and nose!*
 Uh-oh!
Beck, Andrea. *Elliot's great big lift-the-flap book*
Beeler, Selby B. *How many Elephants?*
Bees
Belloc, Hilaire. *The bad child's pop-up book of beasts*
Bemelmans, Ludwig. *Madeline [pop-up book]*
Benjamin, Alan. *1000 monsters*
Bentley, Dawn. *Fuzzy bear*
 Fuzzy Bear's potty book
Berger, Melvin. *Early humans*
 Prehistoric mammals
Big noisy trucks and diggers
Bilgrami, Shaheen. *Amazing dinosaur discovery*
 Farmyard painting party
 Incredible animal discovery
 Jungle art show
Birchall, Mark. *Hen goes shopping*
Bishop, Roma. *Animals*
 Christmas songs
 Easter counting
 Easter egg hunt
 Holiday cheer
 My first pop-up book of dinosaurs
 My first pop-up book of prehistoric animals
 Numbers
 On a safari
 Santa pays a visit
 Shapes
 Toys
Black, Harley. *Amazing magic school*
 Magic art class
Blum, Mark. *Big trucks and diggers in 3-D*
Bonfils, Bolette. *Peter joins the circus*
Bowman, Pete. *The Christmas songbook*
Boyd, Lizi. *Baby play*
 Bunny hop
Boynton, Sandra. *Dinosaur's binkit*
Bradman, Tony. *Look out, he's behind you*
 See you later, alligator
Breverton, David. *Here comes bulldozer*
 Here comes fire truck
 Here comes the dump truck
 Here comes the tow truck
Bridwell, Norman. *Clifford's neighborhood*

Briggs, Raymond. *The snowman [a lift-the-flap board book]*
    The snowman tell-the-time book
Brooks, Bruce. *Each a piece*
Brown, Marc Tolon. *Arthur goes to school*
    Arthur's neighborhood
    Arthur's spookiest Halloween
    Can you jump like a frog?
    Monster's lunchbox
    One, two buckle my shoe
    Teddy bear, teddy bear
    Two little monkeys
    What do you call a dumb bunny? and other rabbit riddles, games, jokes and cartoons
Brown, Ruth. *If at first you do not see*
Browne, Anthony. *Animal fair*
Browne, Gerard. *The aircraft lift-the-flap book*
Brownlow, Michael. *The big white book with almost nothing in it*
Bruna, Dick. *My toys*
Buck, Nola. *The basement stairs*
    Christmas in the manger
    Gotcha!
    Halloween parade
    The littlest witch
Burns, Kate. *How does your garden grow?*
    In the snow
Butler, Andrea. *Mr. Sun and Mr. Sea*
Butler, M. Christina. *One snowy night*
Butterfield, Moira. *Magic world of learning*
Butterworth, Nick. *All together now!*
    Making faces
    The rescue party
    When it's time for bed
Cabrera, Jane. *Bear's good night*
Campbell, Rod. *Buster gets dressed*
    Buster keeps warm
    Buster's afternoon
    Buster's morning
    Dear zoo
    Funwheels with moving parts!
    It's mine
    My pop-up garden friends
    Oh dear!
    Playwheels with moving parts!
Cannon, Janell. *Stellaluna: a pop-up book and mobile*
Capucilli, Alyssa Satin. *Biscuit loves school*
    Biscuit's Valentine's Day
    Happy Hanukkah, Biscuit
    Only my dad and me
    Only my mom and me
    Peekaboo bunny
Carle, Eric. *Dream snow*
    My very first book of food
    My very first book of heads and tails
    My very first book of sounds
    My very first book of tools
    Papa, please get the moon for me
    The secret birthday message
    The very lonely firefly
    Watch out! A giant!
Carlstrom, Nancy White. *Ten Christmas sheep*
    What would you do if you lived at the zoo?
Carney, Margaret (Margaret Rose). *Where does a tiger-heron spend the night?*
Carter, David A. *Chanukah bugs*
    Easter bugs
    Flapdoodle dinosaurs
    How many bugs in a box?
    In a dark, dark wood
    Old MacDonald had a farm
    Peekaboo bugs
    Who's under that hat?
Carter, Noelle. *My house*
    My pet
    Where's my squishy ball?
Cartlidge, Michelle. *Fairy letters*
    Mouse birthday
    Mouse Christmas

    Mouse letters
    Mouse theater
    Mouse time
    Mouse's scrapbook
Cassidy, Dianne. *Circus animals*
    Circus people
Charles, N. N. *What am I? Looking through shapes at apples and grapes*
Chen, Tony. *Animals showing off*
Cheshire, Marc. *Here comes Eloise!*
Child, Lauren. *My dream bed*
Chwast, Seymour. *Mr. Merlin and the turtle*
    Traffic jam
Cimarusti, Marie Torres. *Peek-a-moo*
Clarke, Gus. *Ten green monsters*
Cole, Babette. *Babette Cole's beastly birthday book*
    Babette Cole's brother
    Babette Cole's ponies
    Dad
    Don't go out tonight
    Mum
Cole, Henry. *I took a walk*
Cousins, Lucy. *Happy birthday, Maisy*
    Jazzy in the jungle
    Katy Cat and Beaky Boo
    Maisy at the farm
    Maisy goes swimming
    Maisy goes to bed
    Maisy goes to school
    Maisy goes to the playground
    Maisy's ABC
    Maisy's big flap book
    Maisy's farm
    Maisy's first clock
    Maisy's pirate treasure hunt
    Maisy's pop-up playhouse
    Maisy's twinkly, crinkly counting book
    What can Pinky hear?
    What can Pinky see?
    What can rabbit hear?
    What can rabbit see?
Cowley, Stewart. *Five little kittens*
    From my window
    Hide-and-seek puppies
    Little lost rabbit
    The naughty ducklings
Cox, Phil Roxbee. *Fox on a box*
    Goose on the loose
    Shark in the park
    Ted in a red bed
Cremins, Robert. *My animal ABC*
    My animal Mother Goose
    Pop up baby brontosaurus
    Pop up baby coelophysis
    Pop up baby pteranodon
    Pop up baby stegosaurus
    Pop up baby triceratops
    Pop up baby tyrannosaurus rex
Crespi, Francesca. *Make a joyful noise*
    Santa Claus is coming!
    Silent night
Crews, Donald. *Inside freight train*
Crowther, Robert. *All the fun of the fair*
    Animal rap!
    Animal snap!
    Colors
    Dump trucks and diggers
    Hide and seek counting book
    The most amazing hide-and-seek alphabet book
    The most amazing hide-and-seek opposites book
    My pop-up surprise ABC
    My pop-up surprise 1 2 3
    Pop goes the weasel!
    Shapes
    Who lives in the country?
    Who lives in the garden?
    Who lives on the farm?

Curtis, Jamie Lee. *Today I feel silly and other moods that make my day*
Davis, Jennifer. *Before you were born*
Davis, Kate (1951–). *Barnyard babies*
Davis, Lee. *The lifesize animal opposites book*
Day, Alexandra. *Carl pops up*
Day, Trevor. *Youch! it bites!*
DeBoer, Jesslyn. *Follow the star*
   Getting ready for Christmas
Dedieu, Thierry. *Baby clown*
De Groat, Diane. *Lola the elf*
Demarest, Chris L. *Fall*
   Farmer Nat
   Honk!
   Spring
   Summer
   Winter
Demi. *Cuddly chick*
   Demi's dragons and fantastic creatures
   Downy duckling
   Fuzzy wuzzy puppy
   Little bitty bunny
   Little chick chick
   The peek-a-boo ABC
   So soft kitty
   Three little elephants
   Where is Willie Worm?
Denchfield, Nick. *Desmond the dog, a wag-the-tail pop-up book*
Denega, Danielle. *Numbers*
   Rain or shine
Deprisco, Dorothea. *Snowbear's winter day*
Dijs, Carla. *Are you my daddy?*
   Are you my mommy?
   Big and small
   How many?
   Mommy, what if—?
   Mommy, would you love me if . . . ?
   Pretend you're a hippo
Dodds, Dayle Ann. *The color box*
   Where's Pup?
Dowley, Tim. *The shepherds' tale*
   The wise men's tale
Dowling, Paul. *Jimmy's snowy book*
   The night journey
Doyle, Malachy. *Baby see, baby do!*
   Well, a crocodile can!
Drescher, Henrik. *Pat the beastie*
Durant, Alan. *Dear tooth fairy*
Easter babies
Edwards, Richard. *Fly with the birds*
Ehlert, Lois. *Hands*
   Waiting for wings
Elson, Raymond. *Clothes*
   Pets
   Toys
Emberley, Ed (Edward Randolph). *Glad monster, sad monster*
   Go away, big green monster!
Facklam, Margery. *But not like mine*
   So can I
Faulkner, Keith. *Amble has a dream*
   Bertie's big blue binoculars
   Butterfly
   Charlie Chimp's Christmas
   David dreaming of dinosaurs
   Do you have my quack?
   Frog
   The giraffe who cock-a-doodle-doo'd
   Jumbled jungle
   The long-nosed pig
   The monster who loved books
   Munch looks for lunch
   My first one hundred words in French and English
   My pets
   Pop! went another balloon!
   The puzzled penguin
   Rexerella
   Rumble frightens himself
   Sam at the seaside

   Sam helps out
   The scared little bear
   Swoop flies too high
   The tallest shortest longest greenest brownest animal in the jungle!
   This is me
   A trick or a treat?
   The wide-mouthed frog
Ferguson, Don. *Winnie the Pooh's A to Zzzz*
Findlay, Lisa. *What's in Oscar's trashcan?*
Firmin, Josie. *My week*
Fowler, Richard. *Honeybee's busy day*
   Ladybug on the move
   Little Chick's big adventure
   Mr. Little's noisy car
   Mr. Little's noisy fire engine
   Mr. Little's noisy truck
   Pop-up trucks
French, Vivian. *Oh no, Anna!*
Fuchshuber, Annegert. *Giant story – Mouse tale*
Gabriel, Ashala. *Night night toes*
Gallo, Frank. *Bird calls*
   Night sounds
Gamble, Isobel. *Who's that?*
Ganeri, Anita. *Animal hideaways*
Gantschev, Ivan. *Where the moon lives*
Gardner, Beau. *What is it?*
   Whooo's a fright on Halloween night?
Garrett, Ann. *Tales of tails*
   What's for lunch?
Gauch, Patricia Lee. *Tanya steps out*
Gay, Tenner Ottley. *Dinosaurs and their relatives in action*
   Sharks in action
Gerrard, Roy. *A pocket full of posies*
Gerstein, Mordicai. *Guess what?*
   The man who walked between the towers
   William, where are you?
The gingerbread boy. *Gingerbread baby*, ill. by Jan Brett
Gliori, Debi. *Mr. Bear says, "Are you there, Baby Bear?"*
Goffin, Josse. *Oh!*
Gomi, Taro. *Santa through the window*
Gorbaty, Norman. *Tow truck*
Gordon, Lynn. *The witch's revenge*
Grimm, Jacob. *Sleeping Beauty*, ill. by John Wallner
Grindley, Sally. *Too big bear*
Gukova, Julia. *All mixed-up!*
Hague, Michael. *The perfect present*
Haines, Mike. *Countdown to bedtime*
Hanna, Jack. *The petting zoo*
Hansen, Biruta Akerbergs. *Parading with piglets*
Hansen, P. (Paul H.). *My granny's purse*
Harper, Dan. *Telling time with Big Mama Cat*
Hathon, Elizabeth. *We go to school*
   We go to the zoo
Hawcock, David. *Ant*
   Bee
   Beetle
   Brontosaurus
   Dinosaur hunt
   Fly
   Spider
   Stegosaurus
   Triceratops
   Tyrannosaurus
   Wasp
   Whose coat?
   Whose home?
   Whose nose?
Hawkins, Colin. *Come for a ride on the ghost train*
   Creepy castle
   The elephant
   Incy wincy spider
   Jen the hen
   Mig the pig
   One, two, guess who?
   Round the garden
   Take away monsters
   This little pig

Tog the dog
What time is it, Mr. Wolf?
Hellard, Susan. *Time to get up*
Hellen, Nancy. *Circle farm*
  Circle zoo
  A visit to the farm
  A visit to the zoo
Henderson, Kathy. *Don't interrupt!*
Hennessy, B. G. (Barbara G.). *Corduroy at the zoo*
  Corduroy's birthday
  Corduroy's Christmas
  Corduroy's Easter
  Corduroy's Halloween
Hergé. *Explorers on the moon*
Hernandez, Keith. *First-base hero*
Hewitt, Sally. *Face to face safari*
Hide-and-seek bunnies
Hill, Eric. *Spot and friends dress up*
  Spot and friends play
  Spot bakes a cake
  Spot goes on holiday
  Spot goes to a party
  Spot goes to school
  Spot goes to the beach
  Spot goes to the park
  Spot sleeps over
  Spot's baby sister
  Spot's birthday party
  Spot's first Christmas
  Spot's first Easter
  Spot's first walk
  Spot's walk in the woods
  Where's Spot?
Hill, Susanna Leonard. *The house that Mack built*
Hillman, Priscilla. *A Merry-Mouse book of months*
Hindley, Judy. *The big red bus*
  Ten bright eyes
Hines, Anna Grossnickle. *No, no Jack!*
  Whose shoes?
Hissey, Jane. *Old Bear, a pop-up book*
Hoban, Tana. *Just look*
  Look book
Holmes, Stephen. *Hidden numbers*
Horácek, Petr. *Flip's day*
  Strawberries are red
Horwood, Annie. *Butterfly, butterfly what colors do you see?*
The house that Jack built. *The house that Jack built*, ill. by Seymour Chwast
  The house that Jack built, ill. by Nadine Bernard Westcott
How much does God love me?
Howe, James. *Bunnicula escapes!*
Hulme, Joy N. *Eerie feary feeling*
Hurd, Thacher. *A night in the swamp*
Hutchins, H. J. (Hazel J.). *Two so small*
Inkpen, Mick. *Anything cuddly will do!*
  Crocodile!
  Kipper's bathtime
  Kipper's bedtime
  Kipper's Christmas eve
  Kipper's playtime
  Kipper's rainy day
  Kipper's snacktime
  Kipper's sunny day
  Lullabyhullaballoo!
  Penguin small
  This troll, that troll
  The very good dinosaur
  Where, oh where, is Kipper's bear?
Isaacs, Gwynne L. *Baby face*
It feels like Christmas!. *It feels like Christmas!*
Ives, Penny. *The golden angel*
  On Christmas eve
  The snow angel
Jeffrey, Sean. *Franklin's big search-and-solve flap book*
Johnson, B. J. *A hat like that*
  My blanket Burt
Johnson, Stephen T. *My little blue robot*

Jolley, Mike. *Grunter, a pig with an attitude!*
Jonas, Ann. *Where can it be?*
Jones, Carol. *What's the time, Mr. Wolf?*
Karas, G. Brian. *Skidamarink*
Katz, Karen. *Where is baby's mommy?*
Kemp, Moira. *Lift-the-flap chick*
  Lift-the-flap kitten
  Lift-the-flap mouse
  Lift-the-flap puppy
Koda-Callan, Elizabeth. *The squiggly Wigglys*
Kopper, Lisa. *Ten little babies*
Kraus, Robert. *See the Christmas lights*
  See the moon
Kunhardt, Edith. *Pat the cat*
  Pat the puppy
Kurokawa, Mitsuhiro. *Dinosaur valley*
Lacome, Julie. *Funny business*
  Garden
  Hocus pocus
Lagerlöf, Selma. *The changeling*
Laidlaw, Ken. *The amazing I spy ABC*
Lattimore, Deborah Nourse. *I wonder what's under there?*
Lavis, Steve. *On the farm*
Lawrence, Jennifer B. *Sad doggy*
Leonard, Marcia. *The best snowman ever*
Leslie, Amanda. *Alfie and Betty Bug*
  Are chickens stripy?
  Do crocodiles moo?
  Flappy, waggy, wiggly
  Let's look inside the red car
  Let's look inside the yellow truck
  Play kitten play
  Play puppy play
  Who's that scratching at my door?
Lewison, Wendy Cheyette. *Bye-bye, baby*
  My baby brother
  My favorite doll
  My new puppy
  Ten little ballerinas
  Uh oh, baby
  Where's baby?
  Where's my teddy?
Lions
Lippman, Peter. *Peter Lippman's numbers*
  Peter Lippman's opposites
Lishak, Anthony. *Row your boat*
Lithgow, John. *The remarkable Farkle McBride*
Little old lady who swallowed a fly. *Fancy that!*
  I know an old lady, ill. by Steve McInturff
  I know an old lady who swallowed a fly, ill. by Stephen Gulbis
  There was an old lady, ill. by Nick Bantock
  There was an old lady who swallowed a fly, ill. by Pam Adams
  There was an old lady who swallowed a fly, ill. by Colin Hawkins
Llewellyn, Claire. *My first book of time*
Lobel, Arnold. *The frog and toad pop-up book*
Lodge, Jo. *Happy birthday, Moo Moo*
  Moo Moo goes to the city
Longfellow, Layne. *Imaginary menagerie*
Lundell, Margo. *The furry bedtime book*
Lunsford, Annie. *What will I become?*
  Who lives here?
Maccarone, Grace. *Pumpkin faces*
McGowan, Alan. *Sailing ships*
McGuire, Richard. *What's wrong with this book?*
McKee, David. *I can too!*
MacKinnon, Debbie. *Billy's boots*
  Cathy's cake
  Daniel's duck
  Find monkey!
  Find my boots!
  Find my cake!
  Ken's kitten
  Let's play: I can do it!
  Meg's monkey
  My day: I can do it!
  My kitty!
  Pippa's puppy

Sarah's shovel
Tom's train
McMullan, Kate (Hall). *Hearty har har*
No no Jo
Trick or eeek!
McNaughton, Colin. *Shh! (Don't tell Mr. Wolf!)*
Who's that banging on the ceiling?
McPartland, Suzy. *Good morning, sun*
Sleepy-time moon
Toy-shop surprise
Zoom, car, zoom
Maisner, Heather. *Find Mouse in the house*
Find Mouse in the yard
Mantegazza, Giovanna. *Look how a baby grows*
Look inside a car
Look inside a farm
Look inside a rainforest
Maris, Ron. *Bernard's boring day*
Is anyone home?
Marshall, James. *Hey, diddle, diddle*
Marshall, Janet Perry. *Banana moon*
Marshall, Ray. *Pop-up numbers #1*
Pop-up numbers #2
Pop-up numbers #3
Pop-up numbers #4
The train
Martin, Bill (William Ivan). *Chicka chicka sticka sticka*
Martin, Sarah Catherine. *Old Mother Hubbard*, ill. by Colin
    Hawkins
Marzollo, Jean. *Ten little eggs*
Mason, Lura. *A book of boxes*
McMullan, Kate (Hall). *Back-to-school belly busters*
Hanukkah ha-has
Ho ho ho, ha ha ha
Meeuwissen, Tony. *Remarkable animals*
Meggendorfer, Lothar. *The genius of Lothar Meggendorfer*
Melcher, Mary. *Mommy, who does God love?*
Mellor, Corinne. *Bruce the balding moose*
Clark the toothless shark
Merriam, Eve. *What in the world?*
Meryl, Debra. *Baby's peek-a-boo album*
Meyer, Brigit. *Easter bunny saves the day*
Michelson, Richard. *Ten times better*
Milne, A. A. (Alan Alexander). *House at Pooh corner [a pop-up book]*
Pooh and some bees
Pooh goes visiting
Winnie-the-Pooh: a pop-up book
Milstein, Linda Breiner. *Grandma's jewelry box*
Miranda, Anne. *Baby talk*
Baby-sit
Moerbeek, Kees. *The diary of Hansel and Gretel*
Monfried, Lucia. *Dishes all done*
Moon, Nicola. *At the beginning of a pig*
Moore, Clement Clarke. *The night before Christmas*, ill. by Robert
    Sebuda
Moore, Karen Ann. *The baby king*
Morgan, Mary. *My good night book*
Morris, Dewi. *Sandy's street*
Morris, Johnny. *Animal-go-round*
Moseley, Keith. *Dinosaurs*
Most, Bernard. *Peek-a-moo!*
Mother Goose. *Humpty Dumpty*, ill. by Moira Kemp
Little Miss Muffet, ill. by Mary Morgan
1, 2 buckle my shoe, ill. by Sherry Neidigh
Sing a song of sixpence, ill. by Ray Marshall and Korky Paul
This little pig went to market, ill. by Denise Fleming
Mudd-Ruth, Maria. *The beetle*
The ultimate ocean book
Mullins, Patricia. *Dinosaur encore*
Munari, Bruno. *The elephant's wish*
Jimmy has lost his cap
Tic, Tac and Toc
Who's there? Open the door
Murphy, Chuck. *Black cat, white cat*
Chuck Murphy's alphabet magic
Mussenbrock, Anne. *Easter Bunny saves the day*
The little Easter surprise

Mystery manor
Nappa, Mike. *Do you see the star?*
Nayer, Judy. *Funny bunnies*
Mice are nice
Pig in a wig
Tricky puppies
Newell, Peter. *The slant book*
Nilsén, Anna. *Where are Percy's friends?*
Where is Percy's dinner?
Nobles, Kristen M. *Drive this book*
Noonan, Julia. *Mouse by mouse*
Oakley, Graham. *Graham Oakley's magical changes*
Old MacDonald had a farm. *Old McDonald had a farm*, ill. by Iain
    Smith
Old MacDonald had a farm, ill. by Jessica Souhami
Olyff, Clotilde. *1, 2, 3. One, two, three*
Ormerod, Jan. *Ben goes swimming*
Emily dances
Rock-a-baby
Pearson, Tracey Campbell. *A apple pie*
Pelham, David. *A is for animals*
Crawlies creep
Sam's pizza
Sam's sandwich
Worms wiggle
Peterson, Stephanie True. *Where do the animals live?*
Pfister, Marcus. *Just the way you are*
Milo and the magical stones
The rainbow fish floor puzzle book
Philpot, Graham. *Where is Little Harry?*
Philpot, Lorna. *Amazing Anthony Ant*
Pieńkowski, Jan. *Good night, a pop-up lullaby*
Haunted house
Pizza!
Piers, Helen. *Who's in my bed?*
Piggy and Bear in their underwear
Porter, Sue. *Parsnip*
Parsnip and the pink blanket
Parsnip and the runaway tractor
Potter, Beatrix. *The two bad mice*
Presencer, Alain. *Roaring lion tales*
Price, Mathew. *Patch and the rabbits*
Peekaboo!
Priestley, Alice. *Someone is reading this book*
Prokofiev, Sergei Sergeievitch. *Peter and the wolf*, ill. by Barbara
    Cooney
Reasoner, Charles. *The big busy building*
Who drives this?
Who pretends?
Regan, Dian Curtis. *How do you know it's Halloween?*
Reinhart, Matthew. *Animal popposites*
Reiser, Lynn. *My cat Tuna*
My dog Truffle
Reitman, Andrea. *Mouse in the house*
Rex, Michael. *Who builds?*
Who digs?
Richards, Kitty. *Merry Christmas, Rugrats!*
Richardson, John. *Ten bears in a bed*
Where's Jack?
Rives. *If I were a polar bear*
Robinson, Aminah Brenda Lynn. *A street called home*
Roddie, Shen. *Hatch, egg, hatch!*
Help, Mama, help!
Roffey, Maureen. *Home sweet home*
Rose, Emma. *Ballet magic*
Ross, Tony. *This old man*
Roth, Harold. *Let's look all around the farm*
Let's look all around the house
Let's look all around the town
Let's look for surprises all around
Rowe, Jeannette. *Whose ears?*
Whose feet?
Whose nose?
Ruby-Spears Enterprises. *The puppy's new adventures*
Ruschak, Lynette. *The counting zoo*
Sabuda, Robert James. *ABC Disney*
The Christmas alphabet

The movable Mother Goose
The mummy's tomb
Safran, Sheri. *The musical cherub*
   The painted cherub
Sage, Angie. *Molly and the birthday party*
Saltzberg, Barney. *Baby animal kisses*
Santa Claus is coming to town
Savage, Stephen. *Making tracks*
Scarry, Huck. *Looking into the Middle Ages*
Scarry, Richard. *Richard Scarry's all around Busytown*
   Richard Scarry's Mr. Frumble's biggest hat flap book ever
   Richard Scarry's mix or match storybook
Schindel, John. *What did they see?*
Schlein, Miriam. *Sleep safe, little whale*
Scuderi, Lucia. *To fly*
The secret princess handbook; or, How to be a little princess
See the dinosaurs
Seeber, Dorothea P. *A pup just for me*
Selberg, Ingrid. *Nature's hidden world*
Seymour, Peter S. *Animals in disguise*
   How the weather works
   Insects
   Pilots
   The pop-up book of big trucks
   What lives in the sea?
   What's in the deep blue sea?
   What's in the prehistoric forest?
Shapiro, Arnold L. *Circle*
   Square
   Triangles
Sharratt, Nick. *Ahoy, Pirate Pete*
   Ketchup on your cornflakes?
   Once upon a time . . .
   Rocket countdown
   Shark in the park
Shields, Carol Diggory. *Colors*
   Homes
   On the go
   Patterns
Shopping
Sibbick, John. *Creatures of long ago*
Simmons, Jane. *Bouncy bouncy Daisy*
   Daisy's hide-and-seek
Sis, Peter. *Fire truck*
   Trucks, trucks, trucks
Skwarek, Skip. *The horrors of Howling Hall*
   Mystery of Maggoty Mill
Smallman, Clare. *Outside in*
Smith, Kathryn. *Little Donkey's Christmas story*
   Little Lamb's Christmas story
   Smith, Mavis. *Fred, is that you?*
   'Twas the day after Thanksgiving
Spafford, Suzy. *Witzy's colors*
Sper, Emily. *The Passover seder*
Spiegelman, Art. *I'm a dog!*
Spurr, Elizabeth. *Two bears beneath the stairs*
Stanley, Mandy. *Bloomer, the dog you can play with*
Stapler, Sarah. *Trilby's trumpet*
Stickland, Paul. *Dinosaur stomp!*
   Truck jam
The Superman mix or match storybook
Tabby, Abigail. *Baby face*
Tagg, Christine. *Who will you meet on Scary Street?*
Tatcheva, Eva. *Witch Zelda's birthday cake*
Thomas's big railway pop-up book
The three little pigs. *The three little pigs, ill. by John Wallner*
   Who's at the door?
Tilden, Ruth. *Freddie works out*
   Sophie's dance class
Torres, Melissa A. *The great Christmas tree celebration*
Trevelyan, Kathy. *Don't be surprised!*
Tucker, Sian. *A is for astronaut*
Tullet, Hervé. *Night / day*
Underhill, Liz. *The lucky coin*
Van der Meer, Mara. *Can we play?*
Van der Meer, Ron. *Funny hats*
   Pigs at home

Van Fleet, Matthew. *Fuzzy yellow ducklings*
   One yellow lion
   Spotted yellow frogs
Varekamp, Marjolein. *Little Sam takes a bath*
Verdet, Andre. *All about time*
Vere, Ed. *Everyone's little*
Walker, Jane. *Ten little penguins*
Wallner, John C. *Look and find*
   Old MacDonald had a farm
Wallwork, Amanda. *Sleep songs*
Walsh, Melanie. *Monster, monster*
Watson, Claire. *Big creatures from the past*
Watson, Wendy. *The bunnies' Christmas eve*
Watt, Fiona. *Kittens*
Weare, Tim. *Hide-and-seek with Leo*
   I'm a little giraffe
   I'm a little penguin
   I'm a little puppy
Weeks, Sarah. *Noodles*
Wells, Rosemary. *Goodnight Max*
   McDuffs hide-and-seek
Weninger, Brigitte. *Special delivery*
Whales
White, Marsha. *Hooper has lost his owner*
Whybrow, Ian. *Good night, monster*
   Sammy and the robots
Williams, Juliet. *Mouse house [board book]*
Williams, Sam. *Spots and slots*
Wilson-Max, Ken. *Big blue engine*
   Big red fire truck
   A book of letters
   Little red plane
   Max loves sunflowers
Wojtowycz, David. *Dudley helps out*
   Dudley's birthday party
Wood, Audrey. *The napping house wakes up*
Wood, David. *Silly spider!*
Wyllie, Stephen. *Dinner with fox*
   Snappity snap
Yaccarino, Dan. *So big*
Yee, Patrick. *Bedtime for Rosie Rabbit*
   Little Buddy meets Bobo
Yolen, Jane. *Animal train*
Yoon, Salina. *Wild animals*
Yoshi. *Who's hiding here?*
Youldon, Gillian. *Colors*
   Numbers
Zager, Karen. *Bubbles*
Zelinsky, Paul O. *The wheels on the bus*
Ziefert, Harriet. *Animals of the Bible*
   Bear all year
   Bear gets dressed
   Bear goes shopping
   Bear's busy morning
   Daddies are for catching fireflies
   Dancing
   Mommies are for counting stars
   Nicky's noisy night
   People of the Bible
   Talk, baby!
   Where's daddy's car?
   Where's mommy's truck?

Fortune *see* Character traits – luck

Fortune tellers *see* Careers – fortune tellers

Fossils

Addy, Sharon Hart. *Right here on this spot*
Aliki. *Fossils tell of long ago*
   The long lost coelacanth and other living fossils
Alphin, Elaine Marie. *Dinosaur hunter*
Atkins, Jeannine. *Mary Anning and the sea dragon*
Barner, Bob. *Dinosaur bones*
Baylor, Byrd. *If you are a hunter of fossils*

Brighton, Catherine. *The fossil girl*
Brown, Don. *Rare treasure*
Cohen, Daniel. *Apatosaurus*
   Pteranodon
   Stegosaurus
   Triceratops
   Tyrannosaurus rex
   Velociraptor
Cole, Joanna. *The magic school bus shows and tells*
Day, Marie. *Dragon in the rocks*
Diffily, Deborah. *Jurassic shark*
Hawcock, David. *Dinosaur hunt*
Johansen, K. V. (Krista V.). *Pippin and the bones*
Markle, Sandra. *Outside and inside dinosaurs*
Pellant, Chris. *The best book of fossils, rocks, and minerals*
Taylor, Barbara. *Going, going, gone*

Fourth of July *see* Holidays – Fourth of July

Foxes *see* Animals – foxes

France *see* Foreign lands – France

Freedom *see* Character traits – freedom

French Americans *see* Ethnic groups in the U.S. – French Americans

French Guiana *see* Foreign lands – French Guiana

Friendship

Ada, Alma Flor. *Friend frog*
Ada, Alma Flor. *Jordi's star*
   The unicorn of the west
Adams, Jean Ekman. *Clarence and the purple horse bounce into town*
Adinolfi, JoAnn. *The Egyptian polar bear*
Æsop. *The ant and the dove*
Alborough, Jez. *My friend bear*
Alcantara, Ricardo. *Dog and cat*
Aldridge, Josephine Haskell. *The best of friends*
Alexander, Martha G. *My outrageous friend Charlie*
Alexander, Sue. *Ellsworth and Millicent*
   Small plays for you and a friend
   What's wrong now, Millicent?
   Witch, Goblin and sometimes Ghost
Aliki. *Best friends together again*
   Feelings
   Overnight at Mary Bloom's
   We are best friends
Allard, Harry. *The cactus flower bakery*
Allen, Pamela. *My cat Maisie*
Allinson, Beverley. *Effie*
Anastas, Margaret. *A hug for you*
Anderson, Lena. *Stina's visit*
Anderson, Leone Castell. *My friend next door*
Anderson, Paul S. *Red fox and the hungry tiger*
Anglund, Joan Walsh. *Cowboy and his friend*
   A friend is someone who likes you
Anholt, Catherine. *Snow fairy and the spaceman*
Anholt, Laurence. *Camille and the sunflowers*
Apperley, Dawn. *Blossom and Boo*
Ardizzone, Edward. *Tim and Lucy go to sea*
Argent, Kerry. *Wombat and Bandicoot*
Arnold, Caroline. *My friend from outer space*
Arnosky, Jim. *Armadillo's orange*
Artis, Vicki Kimmel. *Pajama walking*
Aruego, José. *The king and his friends*
Asare, Meshack. *Cat . . . in search of a friend*
Asch, Frank. *Moonbear's friend*
   Moonbear's pet
   Oats and wild apples
Auch, Mary Jane. *Bird dogs can't fly*
Aylesworth, Jim. *McGraw's Emporium*
   Mr. McGill goes to town

Baker, Alan. *Benjamin and the box*
Baker, Barbara. *Digby and Kate*
   Digby and Kate again
   Digby and Kate and the beautiful day
Baker, Betty. *Partners*
Balian, Lorna. *Wilbur's space machine*
Ballard, Robin. *Carnival*
Barasch, Lynne. *Old friends*
   The reluctant flower girl
Barbour, Karen. *Nancy*
Barnes, Laura T. *Ernest and the big itch*
   Ernest's special Christmas
   Twist and Ernest
Barrett, Joyce Durham. *Willie's not the hugging kind*
Barringer, William. *Gregory and Alexander*
Bassett, Lisa. *Beany wakes up for Christmas*
Bastin, Marjolein. *My name is Vera*
   Vera and her friends
Batchelor, Louise. *Whoops!*
Battles, Edith. *One to teeter-totter*
Bauer, Marion Dane. *Frog's best friend*
Baumgart, Klaus. *Laura's star*
Baylor, Byrd. *Guess who my favorite person is*
Baynton, Martin. *Fifty saves his friend*
Beck, Andrea. *Elliot's Christmas surprise*
   Elliot's emergency
   Elliot's shipwreck
Bedard, Michael. *Sitting ducks*
Begaye, Lisa Shook. *Building a bridge*
Beim, Jerrold. *The swimming hole*
Beim, Lorraine. *Two is a team*
Bell, Norman. *Linda's airmail letter*
Belton, Sandra. *May'naise sandwiches and sunshine tea*
   Pictures for Miss Josie
Bender, Robert. *A little witch magic*
Benjamin, A. H. *Mouse, mole and the falling star*
Bennett, Kelly. *Not Norman*
Berends, Polly Berrien. *Ladybug and dog and the night walk*
Berenstain, Stan. *The Berenstain bears and the trouble with friends*
   The Berenstain bears' moving day
Berger, Barbara Helen. *When the sun rose*
Berger, Terry. *Friends*
Bergman, Donna. *City fox*
Bergstrom, Corinne. *Losing your best friend*
Bianchi, John. *Swine snafu*
Binzen, Bill. *Carmen*
Birdseye, Tom. *She'll be comin' round the mountain*
Blake, Quentin. *Clown*
   Fantastic Daisy Artichoke
Blance, Ellen. *Monster looks for a friend*
Blaustein, Muriel. *Make friends, Zachary!*
Blegvad, Lenore. *First friends*
Bliss, Corinne Demas. *That dog Melly!*
Block party today
Bluthenthal, Diana Cain. *I'm not invited?*
   Matilda the moocher
Boelts, Maribeth. *Grace and Joe*
   Little Bunny's cool tool set
Bogacki, Tomasz. *Circus girl*
Bohdal, Susi. *Bobby the bear*
Bolliger, Max. *The lonely prince*
Bond, Felicia. *Four Valentines in a rainstorm*
Bonsall, Crosby Newell. *It's mine! A greedy book*
Bornstein, Ruth Lercher. *The seedling child*
Borton, Lady. *Junk pile!*
Bos, Burny. *Prince Valentino*
Bottner, Barbara. *Horrible Hannah*
   Mean Maxine
   Rosa's room
   Two messy friends
   Wallace's lists
Bourgeois, Paulette. *Franklin's new friend*
   Franklin's secret club
Bourguignon, Laurence. *A friend for Tiger*
Bowen, Keith. *Katy's gift*
Bowers, Tim. *A new home*
Boyce, Katie. *Hector the hermit crab*

Boyd, Lizi. *Black dog red house*
Boyd, Selma. *The how: making the best of a mistake*
Boynton, Sandra. *Chloë and Maude*
Bradbury, Ray. *Switch on the night*, ill. by Leo and Diane Dillion
 Switch on the night, ill. by Madeleine Gekiere
Breinburg, Petronella. *Shawn goes to school*
Brenner, Barbara A. *Beef stew*
 Lion and Lamb
Brewster, Patience. *Two bushy badgers*
Briggs, Raymond. *The snowman*
Bright, Robert. *Me and the bears*
Brimner, Larry Dane. *Aggie and Will*
 Dinosaurs dance
 Max and Felix
Brophy, Nannette. *The color of my fur*
Brown, Alan. *Hoot and Holler*
Brown, Laurie Krasny. *How to be a friend*
Brown, Marc Tolon. *Arthur's birthday*
 The cloud over Clarence
 The true Francine
Brown, Myra Berry. *Best friends*
 First night away from home
Browne, Anthony. *Willy and Hugh*
Browne, Eileen. *Where's that bus?*
Bruce, Lisa. *Fran's friend*
Bruna, Dick. *A story to tell*
Brutschy, Jennifer. *Celeste and Crabapple Sam*
Bruzzone, Catherine. *Puppy finds a friend = Cachorrito encuentra un amigo*
 Puppy finds a friend = Le petit chien se trouve un ami
Bryan, Dorothy. *Friendly little Jonathan*
Buck, Pearl S. (Pearl Sydenstricker). *The little fox in the middle*
Buntain, Ruth Jaeger. *The birthday story*
Bunting, Eve (Anne Evelyn). *The blue and the gray*
 Clancy's coat
 Monkey in the middle
 On Call Back Mountain
 Rudi's pond
 Summer wheels
Burdick, Margaret. *Sara Raccoon and the secret place*
Burningham, John. *Aldo*
 The friend
Bushey, Jeanne. *The polar bear's gift*
Butler, Dorothy. *My brown bear Barney in trouble*
Butterworth, Nick. *Albert the bear*
Byars, Betsy Cromer. *Ant plays bear*
Bynum, Janie. *Otis*
Cabrera, Jane. *Panda Big and Panda Small*
Calhoun, Mary. *Tonio's cat*
 The witch who lost her shadow
Calmenson, Stephanie. *Wanted*
Camp, Lindsay. *Keeping up with Cheetah*
Cannon, Janell. *Stellaluna*
 Stellaluna: a pop-up book and mobile
Caple, Kathy. *Fox and bear*
 Harry's smile
Capucilli, Alyssa Satin. *Biscuit finds a friend*
 Biscuit's big friend
Carle, Eric. *Do you want to be my friend?*
Carlson, Nancy L. *Arnie and the new kid*
 Hooray for Grandparent's Day!
 How to lose all your friends
 Louanne Pig in making the team
 My best friend moved away
 Snowden
Carlstrom, Nancy White. *Blow me a kiss, Miss Lilly*
 Fish and flamingo
 The way to Wyatt's house
Carmichael, Clay. *Bear at the beach*
Carr, Jan. *Frozen noses*
Carrier, Lark. *A Christmas promise*
Carter, Anne (1953–). *My home bay*
Cartlidge, Michelle. *Teddy's friends*
Caseley, Judith. *Field Day Friday*
 Harry and Willy and Carrothead
Cassedy, Sylvia. *The best cat suit of all*
Catalano, Dominic. *Mr. Bassett plays*

Cazet, Denys. *Never poke a squid*
Cech, John. *My grandmother's journey*
Chambless, Jane. *Tucker and the bear*
Chapouton, Anne-Marie. *Ben finds a friend*
Chase, Jan Brinckerhoff. *The golden song*
Chmielarz, Sharon. *Down at Angel's*
Chodos-Irvine, Margaret. *Ella Sarah gets dressed*
Chorao, Kay. *Ida and Betty and the secret eggs*
 Molly's lies
Chottin, Ariane. *Little Mouse's rescue*
Clarke, Gus. *Eddie and Teddy*
Clayton, Elaine. *Pup in school*
Clements, Andrew. *Big Al and Shrimpy*
Clifton, Lucille. *Everett Anderson's friend*
 My friend Jacob
 Three wishes, ill. by Stephanie Douglas
 Three wishes, ill. by Michael Hays
Cneut, Carll. *The amazing love story of Mr. Morf*
Cohen, Barbara. *Make a wish, Molly*
Cohen, Miriam. *Best friends*
 First grade takes a test
 Liar, liar, pants on fire!
 See you in second grade!
 Will I have a friend?
Cohn, Janice I. *I had a friend named Peter*
Cole, Babette. *The silly book*
Cole, Brock. *Nothing but a pig*
Cole, Joanna. *Don't call me names!*
 The missing tooth
 Monster and Muffin
 My new kitten
Collins, Pat Lowery. *Tumble, tumble, tumbleweed*
Conford, Ellen. *Why can't I be William?*
Conta, Marcia Maher. *Feelings between friends*
Coontz, Otto. *The quiet house*
Cooper, Helen (Helen F.). *Pumpkin soup*
Costa, Nicoletta. *A friend comes to play*
Coursen, Valerie. *Mordant's wish*
Cousins, Lucy. *Maisy cleans up*
Coville, Bruce. *The foolish giant*
Cox, Judy. *Rabbit pirates*
Craig, Helen. *The night of the paper bag monsters*
 A welcome for Annie
Crimi, Carolyn. *Don't need friends*
Crowley, Michael. *New kid on Spurwick Ave.*
Crowther, Kitty. *Jack and Jim*
Cunningham, Julia. *A mouse called Junction*
Cutler, Jane. *Mr. Carey's garden*
Cuyler, Margery. *Freckles and Jane*
 Freckles and Willie
Dabcovich, Lydia. *Mrs. Huggins and her hen Hannah*
Dalmais, Anne-Marie. *Kelly the kitten*
Daly, Kathleen N. *Making friends*
Daly, Niki. *Once upon a time*
Damjan, Mischa. *Goodbye little bird*
Dauer, Rosamond. *Bullfrog builds a house*
Davies, Sally. *When William went away*
Day, Betsy. *Stefan and Olga*
Day, Marie. *Edward the "crazy man"*
DeBear, Kirsten. *Be quiet, Marina!*
De Beer, Hans. *Little polar bear*
 Little polar bear and the brave little hare
 Little polar bear finds a friend
De Bruyn, Monica. *Lauren's secret ring*
Deeter, Catherine. *Seymour Bleu*
Degen, Bruce. *The little witch and the riddle*
De Groat, Diane. *Happy birthday to you, you belong in a zoo*
Delacre, Lulu. *Nathan's fishing trip*
 Time for school, Nathan!
Delamare, David. *The Christmas secret*
Delaney, Ned. *Bert and Barney*
 A worm for dinner
Delton, Judy. *Duck goes fishing*
 Lee Henry's best friend
 No time for Christmas
 The perfect Christmas gift
 A pet for Duck and Bear

Hennessy, B. G. (Barbara G.). *Meet Winslow whale*
Hesse, Karen. *Lavender*
Hest, Amy. *Best-ever good-bye party*
 The go-between
 Nannies for hire
Heuck, Sigrid. *Pony and Bear are friends*
Hickman, Martha Whitmore. *My friend William moved away*
Hill, Eric. *Spot and friends dress up*
 Spot and friends play
 Spot sleeps over
Hill, Susan. *Ruby bakes a cake*
Hilton, Nette. *Andrew Jessup*
Himmelman, John. *Ellen and the goldfish*
 Simpson Snail sings
Hissey, Jane. *Old Bear*
 Old Bear [board book]
Hoban, Lillian. *Arthur's great big Valentine*
Hoban, Russell. *A bargain for Frances*
 Best friends for Frances
Hobbie, Holly. *Toot and Puddle*
 Toot and Puddle, top of the world
 Toot and Puddle, you are my sunshine
Hoberman, Mary Ann. *And to think that we thought that we'd never*
  be friends
 One of each
Hoestlandt, Jo. *Star of fear, star of hope*
Hoff, Syd. *Happy birthday, Danny and the dinosaur!*
 Who will be my friends?
Hoffman, Phyllis. *Meatball*
 Steffie and me
Hogrogian, Nonny. *The hermit and Harry and me*
Holabird, Katharine. *Alexander and the dragon*
 Angelina and Alice
 Angelina at the fair
Holmes, Anita. *Flowers and friends*
Hood, Susan. *The new kid*
 Pup and Hound
 Pup and Hound move in
Hopkins, Lee Bennett. *Best friends*
 It's about time
Hoppe, Matthias. *Mouse and elephant*
Horse, Harry. *A friend for Little Bear*
Horvath, Betty F. *Will the real Tommy Wilson please stand up?*
Howard, Arthur. *When I was five*
Howard, Reginald. *The big, big wall*
Howe, James. *Horace and Morris but mostly Dolores*
 Horace and Morris join the chorus (but what about Dolores?)
Howell, Will C. *I call it sky*
Hru, Dakari. *The magic moonberry jump ropes*
Hughes, Shirley. *Moving Molly*
 Wheels
Hunter, Tom. *Build it up and knock it down*
Hurd, Thacher. *Axle the freeway cat*
Hutchins, Pat. *The doorbell rang*
 My best friend
 Titch and Daisy
Hutton, Warwick. *The nose tree*
Ichikawa, Satomi. *Fickle Barbara*
 Isabela's ribbons
Ikeda, Daisaku. *Over the deep blue sea*
Imai, Miko. *Lilly's secret*
Inkpen, Mick. *If I had a pig*
 If I had a sheep
 Kipper's Christmas eve
 Kipper's snowy day
 Swing!
Inwald, Robin. *Cap it off with a smile*
Isadora, Rachel. *Friends*
Iwamura, Kazuo. *Ton and Pon: big and little*
 Ton and Pon: two good friends
Iwasaki, Chihiro. *Will you be my friend?*
Jackson, Isaac. *Somebody's new pajamas*
Jackson, Jean. *Thorndike and Nelson*
Jacobs, Laurie A. *So much in common*
Jahn-Clough, Lisa. *Alicia's best friends*
 Missing Molly
 My friend and I

My happy birthday book
 Simon and Molly plus Hester
James, Betsy. *Mary Ann*
James, J. Alison. *Eucalyptus wings*
James, Simon. *Leon and Bob*
Jane, Cabrera. *The lonesome polar bear*
Jaques, Faith. *Tilly's rescue*
Jaynes, Ruth M. *Friends! friends! friends!*
Jenkin-Pearce, Susie. *Percy Short and Cuthbert*
Jennings, Sharon. *Franklin stays up*
 Franklin wants a badge
 Franklin's reading lesson
 Franklin's surprise
 Franklin's trading cards
 Priscilla and Rosy
Jeschke, Susan. *Lucky's choice*
Jewell, Nancy. *Try and catch me*
Joerns, Consuelo. *Oliver's escape*
Johansen, K. V. (Krista V.). *Pippin and Pudding*
Johnson, Angela. *Down the winding road*
 When mules flew on Magnolia Street
Johnson, Diana F. *Princesa and Friskie*
Johnson, Neil. *Jack Creek cowboy*
Johnston, Tony. *Amber on the mountain*
 The last snow of winter
 Soup bone
 Sparky and Eddie, the first day of school
 Sparky and Eddie, trouble with bugs
 Sparky and Eddie, trouble with rats
 Sparky and Eddie, wild, wild rodeo!
Jones, Elizabeth. *Sunshine and Storm*
Jones, Rebecca C. *The biggest, meanest, ugliest dog in the whole wide*
  world
 Matthew and Tilly
Joyce, William. *Santa calls*
Kajikawa, Kimiko. *Yoshi's feast*
Kako, Satoshi. *Little Daruma and little Daikoku*
 Little Daruma and little Kaminari
Kaldhol, Marit. *Goodbye Rune*
Kamen, Gloria. *The ringdoves*
Kangas, Juli. *Fluffy Bunny's friend*
 Ginger Kitten's surprise
 Hello, Honey Bear
Kantrowitz, Mildred. *I wonder if Herbie's home yet*
Karas, Jacqueline. *The doll house*
Kasza, Keiko. *Dorothy and Mikey*
 The rat and the tiger
Keats, Ezra Jack. *A letter to Amy*
 Peter's chair
Keller, Holly. *Lizzie's invitation*
 Rosata
Keller, John G. *Krispin's fair*
Kellogg, Steven (Stephen). *Best friends*
Kent, Jack. *Socks for supper*
Ketteman, Helen. *Armadilly chili*
Kilborne, Sarah S. *Peach and Blue*
Killilea, Marie (Marie Lyons). *Newf*
Kimmelman, Leslie. *Me and Nana*
Kimura, Yasuko. *Fergus and the sea monster*
Kimura, Yuichi. *One stormy night . . .*
 One sunny day . . .
King, Deborah. *Custer*
King, Larry L. *Because of Lozo Brown*
King, Stephen Michael. *Henry and Amy (right-way-round and upside*
  down)
Kingman, Lee. *Peter's long walk*
Kishida, Eriko. *The lion and the bird's nest*
Klein, Norma. *Visiting Pamela*
Kliphuis, Christine. *Robbie and Ronnie*
Knaff, Jean Christian. *Manhattan*
Knutson, Barbara. *How the guinea fowl got her spots*
Kocí, Marta. *Blackie and Marie*
Kolar, Bob. *Do you want to play?*
Koller, Jackie French. *Fish fry tonight*
 Mole and Shrew
 Mole and Shrew are two
 Mole and Shrew step out

Lottie's new friend
Mayer, Mercer. *A boy, a dog, a frog and a friend*
   A boy, a dog and a frog
   Frog, where are you?
Mead, Alice. *Billy and Emma*
Medearis, Angela Shelf. *The adventures of Sugar and Junior*
   Best friends in the snow
   We eat dinner in the bathtub
Meister, Cari. *Skinny and fats, best friends*
Mellor, Corinne. *Bruce the balding moose*
Merriam, Eve. *Boys and girls, girls and boys*
Metcalf, Paula. *Norma No Friends*
Miles, Betty. *Having a friend*
Miles, Sally. *Alfi and the dark*
Millais, Raoul. *Elijah and Pin-Pin*
Miller, Edna. *Mousekin finds a friend*
Mills, Lauren A. *The rag coat*
Min, Willemien. *Peter's patchwork dream*
Minarik, Else Holmelund. *Little Bear's friend*
   Little Bear's new friend
Mockford, Caroline. *Cleo and Caspar*
   Cleo in the snow
   Cleo on the move
   Cleo the cat
Modarressi, Mitra. *The beastly visits*
   The dream pillow
Moers, Hermann. *Katie and the big, brave bear*
Monsell, Mary Elise. *Armadillo*
Monson, A. M. *Wanted . . . best friend*
Montenegro, Laura Nyman. *Sweet Tooth*
Moon, Nicola. *Alligator tails and crocodile cakes*
Moore, Inga. *Little dog lost*
Moran, Alex. *Sam and Jack*
Morck, Irene. *Old bird*
Morozumi, Atsuko. *My friend gorilla*
Morris, Ann. *Eleanora Mousie's gray day*
Morrow, Suzanne Stark. *Inatuck's friend*
Moss, Miriam. *I'll be your friend, Smudge*
Mostacchi, Massimo. *A dog's best friend*
Munsch, Robert N. *Millicent and the wind*
   Murmel, Murmel, Murmel
   Wait and see
Munson, Derek. *Enemy pie*
Murkoff, Heidi Eisenberg. *What to expect at a play date*
   What to expect at preschool
Murphy, Jill. *All for one*
Murphy, Patti Beling. *Elinor and Violet*
Murphy, Stuart J. *Betcha!*
   Give me half!
Murray, Martine. *A moose called Mouse*
Mussenbrock, Anne. *Easter Bunny saves the day*
Napoli, Donna Jo. *Rocky, the cat who barks*
Narahashi, Keiko. *Two girls can!*
Naylor, Phyllis Reynolds. *King of the playground*
Nelson, Brenda. *Mud for sale*
Nelson, Nan Ferring. *My day with Anka*
Neuhaus, David. *His finest hour*
Neville, Mary. *The Christmas tree ride*
Newberry, Clare Turlay. *Marshmallow*
Newsome, Jill. *Shadow*
Nicholls, Judith. *Someone I like*
Nikly, Michelle. *The emperor's plum tree*
Nikola-Lisa, W. *Bein' with you this way*
Nilsén, Anna. *Where are Percy's friends?*
Nimmo, Jenny. *Esmeralda and the children next door*
Njeng, Pierre Yves. *Vacation in the village*
Nolen, Jerdine. *Raising dragons*
Nomura, Takaaki. *Grandpa's town*
Nones, Eric Jon. *Caleb's friend*
Noonan, Julia. *Hare and Rabbit, friends forever*
Novak, Matt. *Claude and Sun*
   Jazzbo and Googy
   Little Wolf, Big Wolf
Numeroff, Laura Joffe. *Amy for short*
Oakley, Graham. *The church mice and the ring*
O'Callahan, Jay. *Herman and Marguerite*
O'Donnell, Peter. *Pinkie goes south*

Ó Flatharta, Antoine. *Hurry and the monarch*
Oh, Jiwon. *Cat and mouse*
O'Mara, Carmel. *Rainy day*
Oppenheim, Shulamith Levey. *The lily cupboard*
Oram, Hiawyn. *Badger's bad mood*
   Badger's bring something party
   Mine!
Ørdal, Stina Langlo. *Princess Aasta*
Oxenbury, Helen. *First day of school*
   Friends
   Tom and Pippo and the dog
Oyibo, Papa. *Big brother, little sister*
Pacilio, V. J. *Ling Cho and his three friends*
Palmer, Todd Starr. *Rhino and Mouse*
Paraskevas, Betty. *The ferocious beast with the polka-dot hide*
   Hoppy and Joe
   Marvin, the tap-dancing horse
Paré, Roger. *A friend like you*
Parr, Todd. *The best friends book*
Passen, Lisa. *Fat, fat Rose Marie*
Paterson, Katherine. *Celia and the sweet, sweet water*
Patz, Nancy. *To Annabella Pelican from Thomas Hippopotamus*
Paxton, Tom. *The story of the Tooth Fairy*
Pearson, Susan. *Everybody knows that!*
Peet, Bill (William Bartlett). *Eli*
Peguero, Leone. *Lionel and Amelia*
Pendziwol, Jean. *No dragons for tea*
Perrow, Angeli. *Captain's castaway*
Peterson, Hans. *Erik has a squirrel*
Petty, Dini. *The queen, the bear and the bumblebee*
Pfeffer, Wendy. *Marta's magnets*
Pfister, Marcus. *Chris and Croc*
   Rainbow fish to the rescue!
   The sleepy owl
   Where is my friend?
Pieńkowski, Jan. *Bel and Bub and the black hole*
Pilkey, Dav. *A friend for Dragon*
Pinkwater, Daniel Manus. *Doodle flute*
Pitcher, Caroline. *The time of the lion*
Pittman, Helena Clare. *The angel tree*
   The snowman's path
Polacco, Patricia. *Chicken Sunday*
   Mrs. Katz and Tush
Pomerantz, Charlotte. *Serena Katz*
   You're not my best friend anymore
Postgate, Daniel. *The richest crocodile in the world*
Pratt, Pierre. *Home*
Price, Mathew. *Have you seen my sister?*
   Patch finds a friend
Priceman, Marjorie. *Friend or frog*
Pryor, Bonnie. *Louie and Dan are friends*
Puttock, Simon. *Big bad wolf is good*
   A story for Hippo
Quintero-Spongberg, Emily. *Hannibal and the king*
Raphael, Elaine. *Donkey and Carlo*
Rascal. *Orson*
Raschka, Christopher. *Ring! Yo?*
   Yo! Yes?
Raskin, Ellen. *A & The*
   Franklin Stein
Raven, Margot Theis. *Angels in the dust*
Ravilious, Robin. *Two in a pocket*
Recknagel, Friedrich. *Meg's wish*
Reiser, Lynn. *Best friends think alike*
   Two mice in three fables
Robins, Joan. *Addie meets Max*
   Addie's bad day
Robinson, Sue. *I want to play*
Roche, Denis (Denis M.). *Mim, gym, and June*
Roddie, Shen. *Sandbear*
Rogers, Fred. *Extraordinary friends*
   Making friends
   Moving
Rohmann, Eric. *My friend Rabbit*
Root, Phyllis. *Soup for supper*
Rosen, Michael J. (1954–). *Elijah's angel*
Rosner, Ruth. *Arabba gah zee, Marissa and Me!*

Ross, Dave (David). *A book of friends*
Ross, Pat. *Meet M and M*
Ross, Tony. *A fairy tale*
Roth, Carol. *Little Bunny's sleepless night*
Roth, Roger. *Fishing for Methuselah*
Round, Graham. *Hangdog*
Rowan, Paula S. *Rick and Rocky*
Rubin, Jeff. *Baseball brothers*
Rumford, James. *Dog-of-the-Sea-Waves*
Ruzzier, Sergio. *The little giant*
Rylant, Cynthia. *All I see*
   The bookshop dog
   Miss Maggie
   Mr. Putter and Tabby pick the pears
Sadler, Marilyn. *Elizabeth, Larry, and Ed*
St. Germain, Sharon. *The terrible fight*
Saltzberg, Barney. *Hip, hip, hooray day!*
   Phoebe and the spelling bee
   The problem with pumpkins
Samton, Sheila White. *Jenny's journey*
Sanromán, Susana. *Señora Reganoña*
Sarton, May. *Punch's secret*
Sasso, Sandy Eisenberg. *For heaven's sake*
Satoshi, Kako. *Little Daruma and little Tengu*
Saul, Carol P. *Peter's song*
Saunders, Susan. *Charles Rat's picnic*
Scheer, Julian. *By the light of the captured moon*
Scheffler, Ursel. *Who has time for Little Bear?*
Scheffrin-Falk, Gladys. *Another celebrated dancing bear*
Scheidl, Gerda Marie. *Pickle and Patch*
Schick, Eleanor. *Making friends*
   My Navajo sister
Schreiber, Georges. *Bambino goes home*
Schroeder, Binette. *Tuffa and her friends*
Schubert, Ingrid. *Beaver's lodge*
   There's always room for one more
Schulman, Janet. *The big hello*
   The great big dummy
Schumacher, Claire. *Alto and Tango*
   King of the zoo
   Tim and Jim
Schwartz, Amy. *Camper of the week*
Schwartz, Roslyn. *Rose and Dorothy*
Schweitzer, Iris. *Hilda's restful chair*
Scott, Elaine. *Friends!*
Scruton, Clive. *Bubble and squeak*
Seabrook, Elizabeth. *Cabbages and kings*
Shannon, George. *Heart to heart*
Sharmat, Marjorie Weinman. *Bartholomew the bossy*
   Burton and Dudley
   Gladys told me to meet her here
   I'm not Oscar's friend any more
   Mitchell is moving
   The pizza monster
   Rollo and Juliet . . . forever!
   Scarlet Monster lives here
   Sophie and Gussie
   Taking care of Melvin
   The 329th friend
   The trip
Shaw, Mary. *Brady Brady and the Twirlin' Torpedo goalie*
Sherman, Ivan. *I do not like it when my friend comes to visit*
Sherrow, Victoria. *Wilbur waits*
Shriver, Maria. *What's wrong with Timmy?*
Silverman, Erica. *Warm in winter*
Singer, Marilyn. *All we needed to say*
Sis, Peter. *Rainbow Rhino*
Slate, Joseph. *Lonely Lula cat*
Slobodkin, Louis. *Dinny and Danny*
Smalls-Hector, Irene. *Because you're lucky*
Smaridge, Norah. *Peter's tent*
Smith, Maggie (Margaret C.). *Dear Daisy, get well soon*
   Noly Poly Rabbit Tail and me
Snihura, Ulana. *I miss Franklin P. Shuckles*
Snyder, Zilpha Keatley. *Come on, Patsy*
Sommers, Tish. *Bert and the broken teapot*
Spalding, Andrea. *Me and Mr. Mah*

Spang, Günter. *Clelia and the little mermaid*
Spinelli, Eileen. *Somebody loves you, Mr. Hatch*
Spirn, Michele. *The Know-Nothings talk turkey*
Spohn, Kate. *Introducing Fanny*
Stafford, Liliana. *The snow bear*
Stanley, Diane. *A country tale*
   Goldie and the three bears
Steadman, Ralph. *The bridge*
Steel, Danielle. *Freddie's first night away*
   Martha's best friend
   Martha's new school
Steiner, Charlotte. *A friend is "Amie"*
Stephens, Helen. *Ahoyty-toyty*
   What about me?
Steptoe, John. *Creativity*
   Stevie
Stevens, Carla. *Stories from a snowy meadow*
Stevens, Janet. *My big dog*
Stevenson, James. *Howard*
   National worm day
   No friends
   The stowaway
   Wilfred the rat
   The worst person in the world
   The worst person in the world at Crab Beach
Stewart, Paul. *A little bit of winter*
   Rabbit's wish
Stihler, Chérie B. *The giant cabbage turnip*
Stone, Phoebe. *Go away, Shelley Boo!*
Strauss, Gwen. *The night shimmy*
Strete, Craig Kee. *Big thunder magic*
Strom, Maria Diaz. *Rainbow Joe and me*
Sugita, Yutaka. *Helena the unhappy hippopotamus*
Supraner, Robyn. *Sam Sunday and the mystery at the Ocean Beach Hotel*
Sutherland, Tui. *Meet Mo and Ella*
Tada, Joni Eareckson. *Forever friends*
Tada, Satoshi. *Mr. Beetle*
Tafuri, Nancy. *My friends*
   Where did Bunny go?
   Will you be my friend?
Taha, Karen T. *A gift for Tia Rose*
Talbott, Hudson. *Going Hollywood! A dinosaur's dream*
Taulbert, Clifton L. *Little Cliff and the porch people*
Taylor, Mark. *Old Blue, you good dog you*
Tegen, Katherine Brown. *Dracula and Frankenstein are friends*
Tether, Graham. *Skunk and possum*
Thaler, Mike. *It's me, hippo!*
   Moonkey
Tharlet, Ève. *Little pig, big trouble*
Thayer, Jane. *Gus was a friendly ghost*
   The popcorn dragon, ill. by Jay Hyde Barnum
   The popcorn dragon, ill. by Lisa McCue
Thomas, Shelley Moore. *Get well, good knight*
Thompson, Lauren. *Little Quack's new friend*
Thompson, Richard. *Effie's bath*
   Jenny's neighbours
Tibo, Gilles. *Simon and the snowflakes*
Titherington, Jeanne. *Bonkers Fellini*
Torres, Daniel. *Tom*
Trapani, Iza. *Baa baa black sheep*
   Baa baa black sheep [board book]
Trimble, Patti. *What day is it?*
Tripp, Paul. *The strawman who smiled by mistake*
Trivas, Irene. *Annie . . . Anya*
Tsutsui, Yoriko. *Anna's secret friend*
Tudor, Bethany. *Samuel's tree house*
Tunnell, Michael O. *The joke's on George*
Uchida, Yoshiko. *The bracelet*
Udry, Janice May. *Let's be enemies*
Uff, Caroline. *Hello, Lulu*
Vainio, Pirkko. *The best of friends*
Van Laan, Nancy. *Moose tales*
Van Woerkom, Dorothy. *Harry and Shelburt*
Varley, Susan. *Badger's parting gifts*
Velthuijs, Max. *Frog is a hero*
   Frog is frightened

Venable, Alan. *The checker players*
VerDorn, Bethea. *Day breaks*
Vigna, Judith. *The hiding house*
Vincent, Gabrielle. *Breakfast time, Ernest and Celestine*
  Ernest and Celestine's patchwork quilt
  Merry Christmas, Ernest and Celestine
Viorst, Judith. *Rosie and Michael*
Von Königslöw, Andrea Wayne. *Bing and Chutney*
  Bing and Chutney off to Moosonee
  Bing finds Chutney
Vrombaut, An. *Clarabella's teeth*
Waber, Bernard. *Evie & Margie*
  Gina
  Ira says goodbye
  Ira sleeps over
  Lovable Lyle
  Nobody is perfick
Waddell, Martin. *We love them*
Wade, Anne. *A promise is for keeping*
Waechter, Friedrich Karl. *Three is company*
Wagner, Karen. *Bravo, Mildred and Ed!*
  A friend like Ed
Walker, Alice. *To hell with dying*
Wallace, Nancy Elizabeth. *Paperwhite*
Walsh, Ellen Stoll. *Hamsters to the rescue*
Ward, Helen. *The golden pear*
Warren, Cathy. *Fred's first day*
Watson, Wendy. *Holly's Christmas eve*
Weedn, Flavia. *The little snow bear*
Weigelt, Udo. *Mole's journey*
  The Sandman
  Who stole the gold?
Weil, Lisl. *Gillie and the flattering fox*
Weiss, Ellen. *Mokey's birthday present*
Weiss, Nicki. *Battle day at Camp Delmont*
  A family story
  Maude and Sally
Weninger, Brigitte. *Why are you fighting, Davy?*
Whitcher, Susan. *Something for everyone*
White, Carolyn. *The adventure of Louey and Frank*
White, Linda Arms. *Too many pumpkins*
Wick, Walter. *Can you see what I see? Seymour makes new friends*
Wiesner, William. *Tops*
Wild, Margaret. *Fox*
  Mr. Nick's knitting
  The very best of friends
Wildsmith, Brian. *The lazy bear*
Wiles, Debbie. *Freedom summer*
Wilhelm, Hans. *Let's be friends again!*
  A new home, a new friend
  Quacky Ducky's Easter egg
Williams, Barbara. *Kevin's grandma*
Williams, Karen Lynn. *When Africa was home*
Williams, Sherley Anne. *Girls together*
Wilson, Jacqueline. *Mr. Cool*
Winthrop, Elizabeth. *The Best Friends Club*
  Katharine's doll
  Lizzie and Harold
  Sloppy kisses
Wishinsky, Frieda. *Jennifer Jones won't leave me alone*
  Nothing scares us
Wittbold, Maureen. *Mending Peter's heart*
Wittman, Sally. *The boy who hated Valentine's Day*
  Pelly and Peak
  Plenty of Pelly and Peak
  A special trade
  The wonderful Mrs. Trumbly
Wojciechowski, Susan. *The Christmas miracle of Jonathan Toomey*
Wolcott, Patty. *Double-decker, double-decker, double-decker bus*
Wolde, Gunilla. *Betsy and Peter are different*
Wolkstein, Diane. *Little Mouse's painting*
  Step by step
Wood, Audrey. *Jubal's wish*
Wormell, Christopher. *The big ugly monster and the little stone rabbit*
  Blue Rabbit and friends
Yaccarino, Dan. *Unlovable*
Yashima, Taro. *The youngest one*

Yee, Patrick. *Let's make friends*
Yee, Paul. *The boy in the attic*
Yee, Wong Herbert. *Did you see Chip?*
Yeoman, John. *Mouse trouble*
  You and me
Young, Ruth. *Golden Bear*
Zabar, Abbie. *Fifty-five friends*
Zalben, Jane Breskin. *Beni's first Chanukah*
  Oliver and Alison's week
Zarin, Cynthia. *Rose and Sebastian*
Zehler, Antonia. *Two fine ladies have a tiff*
  Two fine ladies: tea for three
Zelinsky, Paul O. *The lion and the stoat*
Ziefert, Harriet. *Mike and Tony*
  Nicky's friends
  39 uses for a friend
Zion, Gene. *The meanest squirrel I ever met*
Zolotow, Charlotte (Shapiro). *The hating book*
  Hold my hand
  Janey
  My friend John
  The new friend
  Three funny friends
  Timothy too!
  The unfriendly book
  The white marble

Frogs & toads

Ada, Alma Flor. *Friend frog*
Æsop. *The hare and the frogs*
Alexander, Martha G. *No ducks in our bathtub*
Allchin, Rosalind. *The frog princess*
Anderson, Peggy Perry. *Out to lunch*
  Time for bed, the babysitter said
  To the tub
Arnold, Tedd. *Green Wilma*
Arnosky, Jim. *All about frogs*
Asch, Frank. *Baby Bird's first nest*
  Moonbear's pet
Back, Christine. *Tadpole and frog*
Bancroft, Catherine. *Felix's hat*
Bauer, Marion Dane. *Frog's best friend*
Berenzy, Alix. *A frog prince*
Berkes, Marianne Collins. *Marsh music*
Berman, Ruth. *Climbing tree frogs*
Berson, Harold. *Charles and Claudine*
Boelts, Maribeth. *Big Daddy, frog wrestler*
Bos, Burny. *Prince Valentino*
Boyd, Lizi. *I love Daddy*
  I love Mommy
Brimner, Larry Dane. *Max and Felix*
Brown, Marc Tolon. *Can you jump like a frog?*
Brown, Ruth. *Toad*
Buller, Jon. *Toad on the road*
Burton, Jane. *Hoppy the toad*
  Taddy the toad
Bynum, Janie. *Otis*
Cain, Sheridan. *Look out for the big bad fish!*
Calmenson, Stephanie. *The frog principal*
Campbell, Wayne. *What a catastrophe!*
Canfield, Jane White. *The frog prince*
Carle, Eric. *Hello, red fox*
Carlson, Nancy L. *Smile a lot!*
Carmack, Lisa Jobe. *Philippe in Monet's garden*
Cecil, Laura. *The frog princess*
Charles, R. H. (Robert Henry). *The roundabout turn*
Chenery, Janet. *The toad hunt*
Chrustowski, Rick. *Hop frog*
Coldrey, Jennifer. *The world of frogs*
Cole, Joanna. *Don't call me names!*
Cooper, Susan. *Frog*
Cortesi, Wendy W. *Explore a spooky swamp*
Dauer, Rosamond. *Bullfrog builds a house*
  Bullfrog grows up
Debecker, Benoît. *The naughty prince*
Dennard, Deborah. *Bullfrog at Magnolia Circle*

Dewey, Jennifer Owings. *Poison dart frogs*
Dinardo, Jeffrey. *Timothy and the night noises*
Duke, Kate. *Seven froggies went to school*
Duvoisin, Roger Antoine. *Periwinkle*
Erickson, Russell E. *Warton and the traders*
    Warton's Christmas eve adventure
Faulkner, Keith. *Frog*
    The wide-mouthed frog
Feldman, Barbara. *Stephen's frog*
Flack, Marjorie. *Tim Tadpole and the great bullfrog*
Fleming, Denise. *In the small, small pond*
Florian, Douglas. *Lizards, frogs, and polliwogs*
Franco, Betsy. *Why the frog has big eyes*
French, Vivian. *Growing frogs*
    A song for little toad
Freschet, Berniece. *The old bullfrog*
A frog he would a-wooing go (folk-song). *Frog went a-courtin'*, ill.
    by Feodor Rojankovsky
    Frog went a-courting, retold & ill. by Dominic Catalano
    Froggie went a-courting, ill. by Chris Conover
    Froggie went a courting, ill. by Marjorie Priceman
    Mr. Frog went a-courting
    Wendy Watson's frog went a-courting
Gackenbach, Dick. *Crackle, Gluck and the sleeping toad*
Geraghty, Paul. *The hoppameleon*
Gibbons, Gail. *Frogs*
Gikow, Louise. *I am Kermit*
Gordon, Margaret. *Frogs' holiday*
Goss, Linda. *The frog who wanted to be a singer*
Graham, Amanda. *Picasso, the green tree frog*
Grahame, Kenneth. *The wind in the willows*, ill. by Joanne Moss
Gray, Nigel. *The frog prince*
Gretz, Susanna. *Frog in the middle*
Greydanus, Rose. *Freddie the frog*
Griffith, Helen V. *Emily and the enchanted frog*
Grimm, Jacob. *The frog prince*, ill. by Paul Galdone
    The frog prince, ill. by Todd Ouren
    The frog prince, ill. by Binette Schroeder
    The princess and the frog, ill. by Rachel Isadora
    The princess and the frog, ill. by Will Eisner
Grobler, Piet. *Hey, frog!*
Gwynne, Fred. *Pondlarker*
Hamanaka, Sheila. *Screen of frogs*
Harrison, David Lee. *The case of Og, the missing frog*
Hawes, Judy. *Spring peepers*
    Why frogs are wet
Hellard, Susan. *Froggie goes a-courting*
Heller, Ruth. *How to hide a gray treefrog and other amphibians*
Heo, Yumi. *The green frogs*
Himmelman, John. *Amanda and the witch switch*
    A wood frog's life
Hoban, Russell. *Jim Frog*
Hogan, Paula Z. *The frog*
Hopkins, Lee Bennett. *The horned toad prince*
Hunter, Anne. *Possum and the peeper*
Isele, Elizabeth. *The frog princess*
Isherwood, Shirley. *Flora the frog*
James, Betsy. *Tadpoles*
Johnson, Suzanne C. *Fribbity ribbit*
Jordan, Sandra. *Frog hunt*
Joyce, William. *Bently and egg*
Kalan, Robert. *Jump, frog, jump!*
Karlin, Nurit. *The blue frog*
Kasza, Keiko. *Grandpa Toad's last secret*
Keith, Eros. *Rrra-ah*
Kellogg, Steven (Stephen). *The mysterious tadpole*
Kent, Jack. *The caterpillar and the polliwog*
Kepes, Juliet. *Frogs, merry*
Ketteman, Helen. *Armadilly chili*
Kilborne, Sarah S. *Peach and Blue*
Kopelke, Lisa. *Excuse me!*
Kraus, Robert. *Here comes Tardy Toad*
    Mert the blurt
Kuhn, Dwight. *Hungry little frog*
Kulling, Monica. *Waiting for Amos*
Kumin, Maxine W. *Eggs of things*
Lane, Margaret. *The frog*

Lawston, Lisa. *Can you hop?*
Lee, Jeanne M. *Toad is the uncle of heaven*
Legg, Gerald. *From tadpole to frog*
Leonard, Marcia. *Rainboots for breakfast*
Lewis, J. Patrick. *The frog princess*
Lewis, Paul Owen. *Frog girl*
Liebler, John. *Frog counts to ten*
Lionni, Leo. *An extraordinary egg*
    Fish is fish
    It's mine!
Lively, Penelope. *One, two, three, jump!*
Livingston, Irene. *Finklehopper Frog*
    Finklehopper Frog cheers
Lobel, Arnold. *Days with Frog and Toad*
    Frog and Toad all year
    Frog and Toad are friends
    The frog and toad pop-up book
    Frog and Toad together
London, Jonathan. *Froggy eats out*
    Froggy gets dressed
    Froggy goes to bed
    Froggy goes to school
    Froggy goes to the doctor
    Froggy learns to swim
    Froggy plays in the band
    Froggy plays soccer
    Froggy's first Christmas
    Froggy's first kiss
    Froggy's Halloween
    Let's go, Froggy!
Lucas, Barbara (Barbara M.). *Sleeping over*
MacLachlan, Patricia. *Moon, stars, frogs and friends*
McLenighan, Valjean. *You are what you are*
McPhail, David M. *Captain Toad and the motorbike*
Magloff, Lisa. *Frog*
Mann, Pamela. *The frog princess?*
Manushkin, Fran. *Peeping and sleeping*
Maris, Ron. *Better move on, frog!*
    Frogs jump
Marshall, James. *Hey, diddle, daddle*
Martín Larrañaga, Ana. *The big wide-mouthed frog*
Massie, Diane Redfield. *Walter was a frog*
Mayer, Mercer. *A boy, a dog, a frog and a friend*
    A boy, a dog and a frog
    Frog goes to dinner
    Frog on his own
    Frog, where are you?
    One frog too many
McMullan, Kate (Hall). *Ribbit riddles*
Michels, Tilde. *At the frog pond*
Miles, Miska. *Jump frog jump*
Miller, Ruth. *I went to the bay*
Mitton, Tony. *Down by the cool of the pool*
Muntean, Michaela. *Kermit and Robin's scary story*
Murphy, Stuart J. *Ready, set, hop!*
Nelson, Robin. *Pet frog*
Newton, Patricia Montgomery. *The frog who drank the waters of the
    world*
Noll, Sally. *Off and counting*
Northey, Lawrence. *I'm a hop hop hoppity frog*
Nunes, Susan Miho. *Tiddalick the frog*
Ogburn, Jacqueline K. *The reptile ball*
Owen, Annie. *Wake up Frog!*
Parker, Nancy Winslow. *Working frog*
Partridge, Jenny. *Hopfellow*
Pavey, Peter. *I'm Taggarty Toad*
Pendery, Rosemary. *A home for Hopper*
Pfeffer, Wendy. *From tadpole to frog*
Pfister, Marcus. *Hopper hunts for spring*
Pinczes, Elinor J. *My full moon is square*
Policoff, Stephen Phillip. *Cesar's amazing journey*
Popov, Nikolai. *Why?*
Potter, Beatrix. *The tale of Mr. Jeremy Fisher*, ill. by author
    The tale of Mr. Jeremy Fisher, ill. by David Jorgensen
Priceman, Marjorie. *Friend or frog*
Pursell, Margaret Sanford. *Sprig the tree frog*
Robinson, Fay. *Fantastic frog*

Rockwell, Anne F. *Big boss*
    Toad
Rong, Yu. *A lovely day for Amelia Goose*
Roth, Susan L. *The biggest frog in Australia*
Rouss, Sylvia A. *The littlest frog*
Samton, Sheila White. *Frogs in clogs*
Samuels, Barbara. *What's so great about Cindy Snappleby?*
Santore, Charles. *William the Curious*
Saul, Carol P. *Peter's song*
Sayre, April Pulley. *Dig, wait, listen*
Schertle, Alice. *Advice for a frog and other poems*
    Little Frog's song
Schneider, Howie. *Fast 'n Snappy*
Schubert, Ingrid. *The magic bubble trip*
Schumacher, Claire. *Brave Lily*
Scieszka, Jon. *The frog prince, continued*
Seeger, Pete. *The foolish frog*
Seuss, Dr. *Would you rather be a bullfrog?*
Shannon, George. *April showers*
    Frog legs
Sill, Cathryn P. *About amphibians*
Simms, Laura. *Moon and Otter and Frog*
Small, David. *Eulalie and the hopping head*
Smith, Jim. *The frog band and Durrington Dormouse*
    The frog band and the onion seller
    The frog band and the owlnapper
Snape, Juliet. *Frog odyssey*
Solotareff, Grégoire. *The ogre and the frog king*
Steig, William. *Gorky rises*
Steptoe, John. *The story of jumping mouse*
Stevenson, James. *Monty*
Stratemeyer, Clara Georgeanna. *Frog fun*
    Tuggy
Tagholm, Sally. *The frog*
Talley, Linda. *Jackson's plan*
Taylor, Kim. *Frog*
Thayer, Mike. *In the middle of the puddle*
Thompson, Lauren. *Little Quack's new friend*
Tilden, Ruth. *Freddie works out*
Tresselt, Alvin R. *Frog in the well*
Troughton, Joanna. *What made Tiddalik laugh*
Turska, Krystyna. *The woodcutter's duck*
Van Woerkom, Dorothy. *Sea frog, city frog*
Velthuijs, Max. *Frog and the birdsong*
    Frog in love
    Frog is a hero
    Frog is frightened
    Little Man to the rescue
Vern, Alex. *Where do frogs come from?*
Vesey, A. *The princess and the frog*
Wahl, Jan. *Doctor Rabbit's foundling*
Walsh, Ellen Stoll. *Jack's tale*
Walt Disney Productions. *Walt Disney's The adventures of Mr. Toad*
Weiss, Monica. *Mmmm . . . cookies!*
West, Colin. *"Pardon?" said the giraffe*
Wiesner, David. *Tuesday*
Winer, Yvonne. *Frogs sing songs*
Wood, Audrey. *Jubal's wish*
Wynne-Jones, Tim. *The hour of the frog*
Yeoman, John. *The bear's water picnic*
Yolen, Jane. *King Long Shanks*
Zakhoder, Boris Vladimirovich. *Rosachok*

Frontier life *see* U.S. history – frontier & pioneer life

Fungi, molds

Royston, Angela. *Life cycle of a mushroom*

Furniture

Devlin, Wende. *Aunt Agatha, there's a lion under the couch!*
Hutchins, H. J. (Hazel J.). *Leanna builds a genie trap*
Lillegard, Dee. *Wake up house!*
Snyder, Inez. *Building tools*
Thompson, Carol. *Piggy goes to bed*

Furniture – beds

Allen, Linda. *Mrs. Simkin's bed*
Arnold, Tedd. *No jumping on the bed!*
Bibbel, Mark. *Oh, Harry!*
Bottner, Barbara. *Rosa's room*
Buckingham, Simon. *Alec and his flying bed*
Bullard, Lisa. *Not enough beds!*
Burningham, John. *The magic bed*
Camp, Lindsay. *The biggest bed in the world*
Child, Lauren. *My dream bed*
Cox, Phil Roxbee. *Ted in a red bed*
Deedy, Carmen Agra. *Agatha's feather bed*
Dickinson, Mary. *Alex's bed*
Dillon, Barbara. *The beast in the bed*
Freedman, Sally. *Devin's new bed*
Greenberg, Dan. *The bed who ran away from home*
Grindley, Sally. *Wake up, dad!*
Grossblatt, Ruby M. *Who's that sleeping on my sofabed?*
Hamm, Diane Johnston. *Grandma drives a motor bed*
Hawkins, Mark. *A lion under her bed*
Hines, Anna Grossnickle. *My own big bed*
Howe, James. *There's a monster under my bed*
Howell, Lynn. *Winifred's new bed*
Klein, Suzanne. *An elephant in my bed*
Knutson, Kimberley. *Bed bouncers*
Lewis, J. Patrick. *Isabella Abnormella and the very, very finicky Queen of Trouble*
Lum, Kate. *What! cried Granny*
Parker, Nancy Winslow. *The crocodile under Louis Finneberg's bed*
Pulver, Robin. *Alicia's tutu*
Rosen, Michael (1946–). *Under the bed*
Schubert, Ingrid. *There's a crocodile under my bed!*
Singer, Marilyn. *Fred's bed*
Stevenson, James. *What's under my bed?*
Storm, Theodor. *Little Hobbin*
Swain, Ruth Freeman. *Bedtime!*
Thaler, Mike. *There's a hippopotamus under my bed*
Thomson, Pat. *The squeaky, creaky bed*
Willis, Jeanne. *The monster bed*
Winthrop, Elizabeth. *Bunk beds*

Furniture – chairs

Bertram, Debbie. *The best place to read*
Bible, Charles. *Jennifer's new chair*
Cappetta, Cynthia. *Chairs, chairs, chairs!*
Graham, Thomas. *Mr. Bear's chair*
Hale, Irina. *Brown bear in a brown chair*
Jackson, Jean. *Mrs. Piccolo's easy chair*
Joosse, Barbara M. *The morning chair*
Keats, Ezra Jack. *Peter's chair*
Kessler, Ethel. *Do baby bears sit in chairs?*
Lanteigne, Helen. *The seven chairs*
Lanton, Sandy. *Daddy's chair*
Nordqvist, Sven. *Porker finds a chair*
Root, Phyllis. *The old red rocking chair*
Schweitzer, Iris. *Hilda's restful chair*
Scott, Ann Herbert. *Grandmother's chair*
Smith, Maggie (Margaret C.). *My grandma's chair*
Tennyson, Noel. *The lady's chair and the ottoman*
Williams, Vera B. *A chair for my mother*
Zander, Hans. *My blue chair*

Furniture – couches, sofas

Grossblatt, Ruby M. *Who's that sleeping on my sofabed?*
Newton, Jill. *Don't sit there!*
Seligson, Susan. *The amazing Amos and the greatest couch on earth*
    Amos ahoy
    Amos camps out
    Amos

Furniture – cradles

Bond, Rebecca. *Just like a baby*

Furniture – dressers

Montenegro, Laura Nyman. *One stuck drawer*

Furniture – tables

Grimm, Jacob. *The table, the donkey and the stick*
Grimm, Jacob. *The wishing table*
Heller, Linda. *Lily at the table*

Galapagos Islands *see* Foreign lands – Galapagos Islands

Galilee *see* Foreign lands – Galilee

Gambia *see* Foreign lands – Gambia

Games

Agostinelli, Maria Enrica. *I know something you don't know*
Ahlberg, Janet. *Each peach pear plum*
   Peek-a-boo!
Alexander, Martha G. *We never get to do anything*
   Where's Willy?
Allen, Jeffrey. *The secret life of Mr. Weird*
Allington, Richard L. *Letters*
Anderson, Douglas. *Let's draw a story*
Anglund, Joan Walsh. *The brave cowboy*
   Cowboy's secret life
Anno, Mitsumasa. *Anno's animals*
   Anno's Britain
   Anno's counting house
   Anno's flea market
   Anno's Italy
   Anno's journey
   Anno's magical ABC
   Anno's U.S.A.
   Topsy turvies: more pictures to stretch the imagination
   Topsy turvies: pictures to stretch the imagination
   Upside-downers
Appelbaum, Neil. *Is there a hole in your head?*
Aruego, José. *Look what I can do*
   We hide, you seek
Asch, Frank. *Goodnight horsey*
Baillie, Allan. *Drac and the gremlin*
Baker, Keith. *Hide and snake*
Ball, Duncan. *Jeremy's tail*
Battles, Edith. *One to teeter-totter*
Bauman, A. F. *Guess where you're going, guess what you'll do*
Baylor, Byrd. *Guess who my favorite person is*
Beach, Stewart. *Good morning, sun's up!*
Behrens, June. *Can you walk the plank?*
Berkowitz, Linda. *Alfonse, where are you?*
The big Peter Rabbit book
Blacker, Terence. *Herbie Hamster, where are you?*
Blake, Quentin. *Cockatoos*
Blanchard, Arlene. *The naughty lamb*
Blizzard, Gladys S. *Come look with me*
Boatfield, Jonny. *The twilight book*
Bonsall, Crosby Newell. *The day I had to play with my sister*
Booth, Eugene. *At the circus*
   At the fair
   In the air
   In the garden
   In the jungle
   Under the ocean
Brinckloe, Julie. *Playing marbles*
Brown, Marc Tolon. *Finger rhymes*

   Hand rhymes
   One, two buckle my shoe
   Play rhymes
   What do you call a dumb bunny? and other rabbit riddles, games, jokes and cartoons
Brown, Margaret Wise. *The indoor noisy book*
Buck, Nola. *Santa's short suit shrunk and other Christmas tongue twisters*
Buckley, Helen Elizabeth. *Where did Josie go?*
Burnard, Damon. *I spy in the jungle*
Butterfield, Moira. *Magic world of learning*
Byars, Betsy Cromer. *Go and hush the baby*
Capucilli, Alyssa Satin. *Peekaboo bunny*
Carroll, Ruth. *Where's the bunny?*
Carter, David A. *Peekaboo bugs*
Cauley, Lorinda Bryan. *Clap your hands*
Charlip, Remy. *Arm in arm*
   Where is everybody?
Chichester Clark, Emma. *Follow the leader!*
Chorao, Kay. *Peekaboo! Was it you?*
Civardi, Anne. *Things people do*
Clark, Harry. *The first story of the whale*
Cohen, Peter Zachary. *Authorized autumn charts of the Upper Red Canoe River country*
Cole, Joanna. *Pin the tail on the donkey and other party games*
Cowley, Stewart. *Hide-and-seek puppies*
Cox, Phil Roxbee. *Ted in a red bed*
Craig, M. Jean. *Boxes*
Dann, Penny. *Eensy weensy spider*
Delacre, Lulu. *Arroz con leche*
Delaney, Ned. *One dragon to another*
Delton, Judy. *I never win!*
Demi. *Demi's opposites*
De Paola, Tomie (Thomas Anthony). *Andy (that's my name)*
   Hide-and-seek all week
   Things to make and do for Valentine's Day
De Regniers, Beatrice Schenk. *What can you do with a shoe?*
Dubanevich, Arlene. *Pigs in hiding*
Duffy, Dee Dee (Deborah). *Barnyard tracks*
Dunbar, Fiona. *You'll never guess!*
Edwards, Richard. *Always copycub*
Elting, Mary. *Q is for duck*
Emberley, Ed (Edward Randolph). *Ed Emberley's crazy mixed-up face game*
   Klippity klop
Falwell, Cathryn. *Where's Nicky?*
The farmer in the dell. *The farmer in the dell*, ill. by John O'Brien
   The farmer in the dell, ill. by Kathy Parkinson
   The farmer in the dell, ill. by Mary Maki Rae
   The farmer in the dell, ill. by Diane Stanley
   The farmer in the dell, ill. by Alexandra Wallner
Finzel, Julia. *Large as life*
Fisher, Leonard Everett. *Look around!*
Fleisher, Robbin. *Quilts in the attic*
Fowler, Allan. *What do you see in a cloud?*
Fox, Dorothea Warren. *Follow me the leader*
French, Fiona. *Hunt the thimble*
Gardner, Beau. *Guess what?*
   What is it?
Gillham, Bill. *Can you see it?*
   What can you do?
   What's the difference?
   Where does it go?
Gliori, Debi. *Mr. Bear says peek-a-boo*
   Tickly under there
Go tell Aunt Rhody. *Go tell Aunt Rhody*, ill. by Aliki
   Go tell Aunt Rhody, ill. by Robert M. Quackenbush
Gomi, Taro. *Guess who?*
   Who ate it?
   Who hid it?
Gretz, Susanna. *Hide-and-seek*
   I'm not sleepy
Grindley, Sally. *Knock, knock! Who's there?*
   Silly Goose and Dizzy Duck play hide-and-seek
Hague, Michael. *Teddy bear, teddy bear*
Hahn, Hannelore. *Take a giant step*
Handford, Martin. *Find Waldo now*

The great Waldo search
Where's Waldo?
Where's Waldo? In Hollywood
Where's Waldo now?
Where's Waldo? The fantastic journey
Where's Waldo? The wonder book
Hann, Jacquie. *Follow the leader*
Hawkins, Colin. *Incy wincy spider*
   Round the garden
   This little pig
Hayes, Sarah. *Clap your hands*
Haynes, Max. *Sparky's rainbow repair*
   Ticklemonster and me
Heinst, Marie. *My first number book*
Henrietta. *A mouse in the house*
Hill, Susan. *Stuart hides out*
Hillert, Margaret. *Play ball*
Hines, Anna Grossnickle. *What can you do in the wind?*
Hissey, Jane. *Little Bear lost*
Hoban, Russell. *How Tom beat Captain Najork and his hired sports-men*
Hoff, Syd. *The littlest leaguer*
Hoguet, Susan Ramsay. *I unpacked my grandmother's trunk*
Holmes, Stephen. *Hidden numbers*
Hort, Lenny. *We're going on a treasure hunt*
Houghton, Eric. *The crooked apple tree*
Hru, Dakari. *Tickle, tickle*
Hughes, Sarah. *Let's play hopscotch*
   Let's play jacks
Hunter, Dette. *38 ways to entertain your babysitter*
   38 ways to entertain your grandparents
Hurd, Edith Thacher. *Last one home is a green pig*
Hutchins, Pat. *What game shall we play?*
   Which witch is which?
Intrater, Roberta Grobel. *Peek-a-boo!*
Isadora, Rachel. *Peekaboo morning*
Jahn-Clough, Lisa. *Missing Molly*
James, Simon. *Little One Step*
Jenkins, Steve. *What do you do with a tail like this?*
Jennings, Linda M. *Hide and seek birthday treat*
Johnson, Elizabeth. *All in free but Janey*
Jonas, Ann. *The trek*
Kahn, Joan. *Seesaw*
Katz, Karen. *Where is baby's mommy?*
Keeshan, Robert. *She loves me, she loves me not*
Kemp, Moira. *Knock at the door*
Khalsa, Dayal Kaur. *Tales of a gambling grandma*
Knight, Joan. *Tickle-toe rhymes*
Koch, Dorothy Clarke. *I play at the beach*
Kraus, Robert. *Mort the sport*
Krauss, Ruth. *The bundle book*
   Mama, I wish I was snow. Child, you'd be very cold
   You're just what I need
Kroll, Steven. *The tyrannosaurus game*
Kunhardt, Edith. *Where's Peter?*
Landa, Norbert. *Rabbit and chicken play hide and seek*
Ledwon, Peter. *Midnight math twelve terrific math games*
Leonard, Marcia. *Peek-a-boo, baby!*
   Where's Baby-boo?
Leslie, Amanda. *Hidden toys*
   Play kitten play
   Play puppy play
Let's count and count out
Lewis, J. Patrick. *The bookworm's feast*
Lexau, Joan M. *Every day a dragon*
   I hate red rover
Lipkind, William. *Sleepyhead*
Litchfield, Jo. *The Usborne book of everyday words*
Livermore, Elaine. *Find the cat*
   Lost and found
   One to ten, count again
   Three little kittens lost their mittens
Lopshire, Robert. *How to make snop snappers and other fine things*
McCall, Francis X. *A huge hog is a big pig*
McCarthy, Bobette. *Happy hiding hippos*
MacDonald, Amy. *Let's do it*
McGee, Shelagh. *I'm a little teapot*

Machotka, Hana. *Breathtaking noses*
   What neat feet!
MacKinnon, Debbie. *My kitty!*
McToots, Rudi. *The kid's book of games for cars, trains and planes*
Maestro, Giulio. *The tortoise's tug of war*
Maisner, Heather. *Find Mouse in the yard*
Major, Beverly. *Playing sardines*
Manning, Jane K. *My first baby games*
Marshall, Janet Perry. *My camera*
Martin, David. *Lizzie and her dolly*
Marzollo, Jean. *Shanna's ballerina show*
Merrill, Jean. *How many kids are hiding on my block?*
Meryl, Debra. *Baby's peek-a-boo album*
Miles, Miska. *Rolling the cheese*
Miller, Margaret. *Whose shoe?*
Milne, A. A. (Alan Alexander). *Pooh's quiz book*
Mitchell, Cynthia. *Halloweena Hecatee*
Monson, A. M. *Wanted . . . best friend*
Montgomerie, Norah. *This little pig went to market*
Moon, Nicola. *Alligator tails and crocodile cakes*
Morris, Neil. *Find the canary*
   Hide and seek
   Search for Sam
   Where's my hat?
Most, Bernard. *Peek-a-moo!*
   There's an ape behind the drape
Mother Goose. *London Bridge is falling down*, ill. by Ed Emberley
   London Bridge is falling down, ill. by Peter Spier
   Mother Goose in hieroglyphics
   Pat-a-cake, pat-a-cake, ill. by Moira Kemp
   This little pig went to market, ill. by Ferelith Eccles Williams
   The three little kittens, ill. by Lorinda Bryan Cauley
   The three little kittens, ill. by Shelley Thornton
Munari, Bruno. *The birthday present*
Munro, Roxie. *Mazescapes*
Murphy, Stuart J. *Monster musical chairs*
   More or less
Murray, Martine. *A moose called Mouse*
Myers, Amy. *I know a monster*
Nail, James T. *Whose tracks are these?*
Nayer, Judy. *Games*
Nelson, Esther L. *Holiday singing and dancing games*
Newman, Lesléa. *Runaway dreidel*
Nims, Bonnie Larkin. *Where is the bear at school?*
Offen, Hilda. *The sheep made a leap*
Oppenheim, Joanne. *The eency weency spider*
Oram, Hiawyn. *Skittlewonder and the wizard*
Ormerod, Jan. *To baby with love*
Oxenbury, Helen. *All fall down*
   The queen and Rosie Randall
Packard, Mary. *Where is Jake?*
Patterson, Elizabeth Burman. *Whose eyes are these?*
Patterson, Pat. *Hickory dickory duck*
Peppé, Rodney. *Little games*
   Odd one out
   Rodney Peppé's puzzle book
Philpot, Graham. *Fabulous fairy tale follies*
   Where is Little Harry?
Pow, Tom. *Tell me one thing, Dad*
Pragoff, Fiona. *Let's find Teddy*
   Odd one out
The pudgy pat-a-cake book
The pudgy peek-a-boo book
Ra, Carol F. *Trot, trot to Boston*
Raebeck, Lois. *Who am I?*
Ray, Karen. *Sleep song*
Ripley, Catherine. *Two dozen dinosaurs*
Rockwell, Norman. *Norman Rockwell's counting book*
Rodda, Emily. *Power and glory*
Roddie, Shen. *Toes are to tickle*
Rodriguez, Bobbie. *Sarah's sleepover*
Rogers, Paul (Patrick). *The shapes game*
Rosales, Melodye Benson. *Double Dutch and the voodoo shoes*
Rosen, Michael (1946–). *We're going on a bear hunt*
Russo, Marisabina. *The big brown box*
   The line up book
   Where is Ben?

Sandberg, Inger. *Little Anna saved*
Scruggs, Afi. *Jump rope magic*
Scruton, Clive. *Mary's pets*
Selsam, Millicent E. *Is this a baby dinosaur?*
Seymour, Tres. *We played marbles*
Sharratt, Nick. *I look like this*
Shaw, Charles Green. *The blue guess book*
　The guess book
　It looked like spilt milk
Siewert, Margaret. *Bear hunt*
Simmons, Jane. *Daisy's hide-and-seek*
　Little Fern's first winter
Sivulich, Sandra Stroner. *I'm going on a bear hunt*
Sperberg, Roger. *Real soon, raccoon*
Steig, William. *The bad speller*
　Pete's a pizza
　Toby, what are you?
Steiner, Charlotte. *Five little finger playmates*
　Red Ridinghood's little lamb
Stine, Jovial Bob. *Pork and beans*
Stoeke, Janet Morgan. *Hide and seek*
Sykes, Julie. *Robbie Rabbit and the little ones*
Tafuri, Nancy. *Where did Bunny go?*
Taylor, Mark. *Old Blue, you good dog you*
Thomas, Mark. *Fun and games in Colonial America*
Thompson, Lauren. *Little Quack's hide and seek*
Thwaite, Ann. *The day with the Duke*
Tison, Annette. *Animal hide-and-seek*
Trapani, Iza. *What am I?*
Ueno, Noriko. *Elephant buttons*
Ungerer, Tomi. *One, two, where's my shoe?*
　Snail, where are you?
Van Allsburg, Chris. *Jumanji*
　Zathura
Van Laan, Nancy. *Tickle tum*
Venable, Alan. *The checker players*
Viorst, Judith. *The Alphabet from Z to A*
Vulliamy, Clara. *Bang and shout*
　Boo baby boo!
Walsh, Melanie. *Hide and sleep*
Weare, Tim. *Hide-and-seek with Leo*
Weil, Lisl. *Owl and other scrambles*
Wells, Rosemary. *McDuffs hide-and-seek*
Wells, Tony. *Allsorts*
　Puzzle doubles
Weninger, Brigitte. *Special delivery*
Westcott, Nadine Bernard. *The lady with the alligator purse*
Wick, Walter. *Can you see what I see? Cool collections*
Wildsmith, Brian. *Animal games*
　Brian Wildsmith's puzzles
Williams, Jenny (Jennifer). *Ring around a rosy*
Wilner, Isabel. *The baby's game book*
Wisniewski, David. *Rain player*
Withers, Carl. *The tale of a black cat*
　The wild ducks and the goose
Wittington, Mary K. *Troll games*
Wood, A. J. *Look! The ultimate spot-the-difference book*
Wood, David. *Piggies*
　Piggies [board book]
Yaccarino, Dan. *So big*
Yektai, Niki. *What's missing?*
Yolen, Jane. *The lap-time song and play book*
　Street rhymes around the world
Yoon, Salina. *Wild animals*
Yudell, Lynn Deena. *Make a face*
Zacharias, Thomas. *But where is the green parrot?*
Ziefert, Harriet. *Bear all year*
　Bear gets dressed
　Bear goes shopping
　Bear's busy morning
Zion, Gene. *Hide and seek day*
　Jeffie's party

Gangs *see* Clubs, gangs

Garage sales, rummage sales

Devlin, Wende. *Cranberry autumn*
Kotzwinkle, William. *Walter, the farting dog: trouble at the yard sale*
Rockwell, Anne F. *Our garage sale*
Stevenson, James. *Yard sale*

Garbage collectors *see* Careers – sanitation workers

Gardens, gardening

Aliki. *Corn is maize*
Aliki. *The story of Johnny Appleseed*
Anno, Mitsumasa. *Anno's magic seeds*
Atnip, Linda. *Miranda's magic garden*
　Miranda's magic garden
Azarian, Mary. *A gardener's alphabet*
Baicker, Karen. *Pea pod babies*
Balian, Lorna. *A garden for a groundhog*
Barker, Cicely Mary. *Flower fairies of the garden*
Barrett, Judi. *Old MacDonald had an apartment house*
Bauld, Jane Scoggins. *Journey of the third seed*
Beames, Margaret. *Night cat*
Beck, Andrea. *Elliot digs for treasure*
Berson, Harold. *Pop! goes the turnip*
Bishop, Gavin. *Mrs. McGinty and the bizarre plant*
Bodecker, N. M. (Nils Mogens). *Miss Jaster's garden*
Bogacki, Tomasz. *My first garden*
Bond, Michael. *Paddington Bear in the garden*
　Paddington's garden
Boon, Emilie. *Peterkin's very own garden*
Boyd, Lizi. *Lulu Crow's garden*
Boyden, Linda. *The blue roses*
Boyle, Constance. *Little Owl and the weed*
Brenner, Barbara A. *Good morning, garden*
Brisson, Pat. *Wanda's roses*
Brown, Janet Allison. *The secret garden*
Brown, Marc Tolon. *Your first garden book*
Browne, Caroline. *Mrs. Christie's farmhouse*
Bruce, Lisa. *Fran's flower*
Bryan, Ashley. *The dancing granny*
Buchanan, Heather S. *Emily Mouse's garden*
Bunting, Eve (Anne Evelyn). *A day's work*
　Flower garden
　Sunflower house
Burke-Weiner, Kimberly. *The maybe garden*
Burns, Kate. *How does your garden grow?*
Butterworth, Nick. *The secret path*
Campbell, Rod. *My pop-up garden friends*
Carlstrom, Nancy White. *Moose in the garden*
Caseley, Judith. *Grandpa's garden lunch*
Cavagnaro, David. *The pumpkin people*
Cherry, Lynne. *How Groundhog's garden grew*
Coats, Laura Jane. *Alphabet garden*
Cole, Babette. *The trouble with Grandad*
Cole, Henry. *Jack's garden*
Collier, Ethel. *Who goes there in my garden?*
Cowley, Stewart. *From my window*
Craft, Ruth. *Carrie Hepple's garden*
Cristini, Ermanno. *In my garden*
Crowther, Robert. *Who lives in the garden?*
Cuneo, Mary Louise. *How to grow a picket fence*
Cutler, Jane. *Mr. Carey's garden*
Dahl, Michael. *From the garden*
Davidson, Amanda. *Teddy in the garden*
Davis, Maggie S. *A garden of whales*
Delaney, A. *Pearl's first prize plant*
Demi. *The empty pot*
De Paola, Tomie (Thomas Anthony). *Four stories for four seasons*
　Too many Hopkins
Dietl, Ulla. *The plant-and-grow project book*
DiSalvo-Ryan, DyAnne. *City green*
Domanska, Janina. *The best of the bargain*
Donnelly, Liza. *Dinosaur garden*
Downey, Lynn. *Sing, Henrietta! Sing!*
Doyle, Malachy. *Jody's beans*
Dyjak, Elisabeth. *Bertha's garden*

Eclare, Melanie. *A handful of sunshine*
   A harvest of color
Edwards, Michelle. *Eve and Smithy*
Ehlert, Lois. *Growing vegetable soup*
   Planting a rainbow
Emberley, Rebecca. *My garden = Mi jardin*
Ernst, Lisa Campbell. *Hamilton's art show*
   Miss Penny and Mr. Grubbs
Ezra, Mark. *The sleepy dormouse*
Farjeon, Eleanor. *Mr. Garden*
Fatio, Louise. *Marc and Pixie and the walls in Mrs. Jones's garden*
Fife, Dale. *Rosa's special garden*
Firmin, Peter. *Chicken stew*
Fisher, Aileen Lucia. *Mysteries in the garden*
Fleischman, Paul. *Weslandia*
Fleming, Candace. *Muncha! Muncha! Muncha!*
Florian, Douglas. *Vegetable garden*
Fontaine, Jan. *The spaghetti tree*
Ford, Miela. *Sunflower*
Fowler, Susi Gregg. *Beautiful*
French, Vivian. *Oliver's vegetables*
Fujikawa, Gyo. *Let's grow a garden*
Gage, Wilson. *Anna's garden songs*
   Mrs. Gaddy and the fast-growing vine
Gans, Roma. *Hummingbirds in the garden*
Gershator, Phillis. *Sweet, sweet fig banana*
Gerstein, Mordicai. *Daisy's garden*
Gibbons, Gail. *The pumpkin book*
Glaser, Linda. *Compost!*
   Spectacular spiders
Gliori, Debi. *Flora's surprise*
Godkin, Celia. *What about ladybugs?*
Goldin, Augusta. *Where does your garden grow?*
Greenstein, Elaine. *Mrs. Rose's garden*
Griffith, Helen V. *Georgia music*
Guest, C. Z. *Tiny green thumbs*
Haddon, Mark. *In the garden*
Hader, Berta Hoerner. *Mister Billy's gun*
Hafner, Marylin. *Molly and Emmett's surprise garden*
Hall, Fergus. *Groundsel*
Hall, Zoe. *The surprise garden*
Harrison, David Lee. *Farmer's garden*
Harshman, Marc. *Red are the apples*
Hawkins, Colin. *Round the garden*
Heap, Sue. *Four friends in the garden*
Hearn, Diane Dawson. *Anna in the garden*
Henderson, Kathy. *And the good brown earth*
Henterly, Jamichael. *Good night, garden gnome*
Higgs, Liz Curtis. *The parable of the lily*
Hill, Eric. *Spot in the garden*
Himmelman, John. *Amanda and the magic garden*
   The Clover County carrot contest
Hines, Anna Grossnickle. *Miss Emma's wild garden*
Hoffman, Eric. *Play Lady = La Señora Juguetona*
Holmes, Anita. *Flowers and friends*
Holub, Joan. *The garden that we grew*
Howard, Ellen. *The big seed*
Hubbell, Patricia. *Black earth, gold sun*
Hughes, Monica. *A handful of seeds*
Hurd, Thacher. *The pea patch jig*
Huriet, Genevieve. *Dandelion's vanishing vegetable garden*
Ichikawa, Satomi. *Suzanne and Nicholas in the garden*
Inches, Alison. *Corduroy's garden*
Ipcar, Dahlov (Zorach). *The land of flowers*
Jacobs, Laurie A. *So much in common*
Janovitz, Marilyn. *Can I help?*
Jenkin-Pearce, Susie. *The enchanted garden*
Johnston, Tony. *The old lady and the birds*
Jordan, Helene J. (Helene Jamieson). *How a seed grows*
Joslin, Mary. *The tale of the heaven tree*
Joyce, William. *The Leaf Men and the brave good bugs*
Keens-Douglas, Richardo. *The nutmeg princess*
Keeping, Charles. *Joseph's yard*
Kellogg, Steven (Stephen). *Johnny Appleseed*
Kemp, Anthea. *Mr. Percy's magic greenhouse*
Kemp, Moira. *Round and round the garden*
Kilroy, Sally. *Grandpa's garden*

King, Elizabeth. *Backyard sunflower*
   Pumpkin patch
Komaiko, Leah. *On Sally Perry's farm*
Koscielniak, Bruce. *Bear and Bunny grow tomatoes*
Krauss, Ruth. *The carrot seed*
Krementz, Jill. *A very young gardener*
Krings, Antoon. *Oliver's strawberry patch*
Krudop, Walter Lyon. *Something is growing*
Lacome, Julie. *Garden*
Legg, Gerald. *From seed to sunflower*
Leonard, Marcia. *Gregory and Mr. Grump*
Le Tord, Bijou. *Rabbit seeds*
   Sing a new song
Levenson, George. *Pumpkin circle*
Lin, Grace. *The ugly vegetables*
Lindbergh, Reeve. *Johnny Appleseed*
Lobel, Anita. *Pierrot's ABC garden*
Lobel, Arnold. *The rose in my garden*
Loki. *Jake Greenthumb*
Lord, John Vernon. *Mr. Mead and his garden*
Lynn, Sara. *Garden animals*
Maass, Robert. *Garden*
McAllister, Angela. *The wind garden*
MacDonald, Margaret Read. *Pickin' peas*
McLeod, Elaine. *Lessons from Mother Earth*
Maguire, Gregory. *Lucas Fishbone*
Mahy, Margaret. *The pumpkin man and the crafty creeper*
Mallett, David. *Inch by inch*
Mannis, Celeste Davidson. *One leaf rides the wind*
Marino, Dorothy. *Buzzy Bear in the garden*
Maris, Ron. *In my garden*
Marston, Elsa. *A griffin in the garden*
Martin, Jacqueline Briggs. *Button, bucket, sky*
   The green truck garden giveaway
Maurer, Tracy. *Growing flowers*
Medearis, Angela Shelf. *The friendship garden*
Miles, Miska. *Rabbit garden*
Mockford, Caroline. *What's this?*
Molk, Laurel. *Good job, Oliver!*
Moore, Elaine. *Grandma's garden*
Moore, Inga. *The vegetable thieves*
Morgenstern, Elizabeth. *The little gardeners*
Muller, Gerda. *The garden in the city*
Muntean, Michaela. *Alligator's garden*
Musicant, Elke. *The night vegetable eater*
Noguchi, Rick. *Flowers from Mariko*
Nordqvist, Sven. *Festus and Mercury: ruckus in the garden*
O'Callahan, Jay. *Tulips*
Oechsli, Helen. *In my garden*
O'Malley, Kevin. *Bud*
Oxenbury, Helen. *Tom and Pippo in the garden*
Pak, Soyung. *A place to grow*
Palmisciano, Diane. *Garden partners*
Paraskevas, Betty. *Maggie and the Ferocious Beast, the big carrot*
Pattou, Edith. *Mrs. Spitzer's garden*
Perkins, Lynne Rae. *Home lovely*
Pike, Norman. *The peach tree*
Pinczes, Elinor J. *Inchworm and a half*
Pittman, Helena Clare. *Still-life stew*
Poppy Bear
Primavera, Elise. *Plantpet*
Ray, Deborah Kogan. *Lily's garden*
Ray, Mary Lyn. *Pumpkins*
Repchuk, Caroline. *The forgotten garden*
Roberts, Bethany. *The wind's garden*
Rockwell, Anne F. *How my garden grew*
Rockwell, Harlow. *The compost heap*
Rosenberry, Vera. *Who is in the garden?*
Rubel, Nicole. *No more vegetables!*
Russo, Marisabina. *Waiting for Hannah*
Ryder, Joanne. *Dancers in the garden*
   First grade ladybugs
   My father's hands
Rylant, Cynthia. *This year's garden*
Schulman, Janet. *A bunny for all seasons*
Schumaker, Ward. *In my garden*
Seabrook, Elizabeth. *Cabbages and kings*

Selkowe, Valrie M. *Happy birthday to me!*
Sharpe, Sara. *Gardener George goes to town*
Shecter, Ben. *Partouche plants a seed*
Slote, Elizabeth. *Nelly's garden*
Smith, Maggie (Margaret C.). *This is your garden*
Snyder, Inez. *Gardening tools*
Sobol, Harriet Langsam. *A book of vegetables*
Spalding, Andrea. *Me and Mr. Mah*
Spurr, Elizabeth. *The gumdrop tree*
Stevens, Janet. *Tops and bottoms*
Stevenson, James. *Grandpa's too-good garden*
Stewart, Sarah. *The gardener*
Swain, Gwenyth. *Johnny Appleseed*
Tamar, Erika. *The garden of happiness*
Taylor, Judy. *Sophie and Jack help out*
Titherington, Jeanne. *Pumpkin pumpkin*
Trimby, Elisa. *Mr. Plum's paradise*
Trottier, Maxine. *Flags*
Van Haeringen, Annemarie. *The cats' tale*
Wabbes, Marie. *Little Rabbit's garden*
Waldherr, Kris. *Harvest*
Wallace, Karen. *Scarlette Beane*
Wallace, Nancy Elizabeth. *Paperwhite*
Ward, Jennifer. *Over in the garden*
Watts, Barrie. *Tomato*
Watts, Bernadette. *Tattercoats*
Weedn, Flavia. *The giant's garden*
Weeks, Sarah. *Mrs. McNosh and the great big squash*
Wells, Rosemary. *First tomato*
Westcott, Nadine Bernard. *The giant vegetable garden*
Wilde, Oscar. *Fairy tales of Oscar Wilde*
    The selfish giant, ill. by S. Saelig Gallagher
    The selfish giant, ill. by Dom Mansell
    The selfish giant, ill. by Fabian Negrin
    The selfish giant, ill. by Lisbeth Zwerger
Williams, Sophy. *Nana's garden*
Wilner, Isabel. *A garden alphabet*
Wolf, Janet. *The rosy fat magenta radish*
Wolff, Ferida. *The emperor's garden*
Yacowitz, Caryn. *Pumpkin fiesta*
Zagwÿn, Deborah Turney. *Apple batter*
    The pumpkin blanket
Zalben, Jane Breskin. *Pearl plants a tree*

Geese *see* Birds – geese

Gender roles

Alexander, Martha G. *Marty McGee's space lab, no girls allowed*
Banks, Kate (Katherine A.). *Mama's coming home*
Blackwood, Mary. *Derek the knitting dinosaur*
Bridges, Shirin Yim. *Ruby's wish*
Brown, Don. *Rare treasure*
Collard, Sneed B. *Animal dads*
Corey, Shana. *You forgot your skirt, Amelia Bloomer*
Cristaldi, Kathryn. *Baseball ballerina*
Ernst, Lisa Campbell. *Sam Johnson and the blue ribbon quilt*
Fierstein, Harvey. *The sissy duckling*
Fine, Anne. *Poor Monty*
Gág, Wanda. *Gone is gone*
Gibbons, Faye. *Mama and me and the Model-T*
Hilton, Nette. *The long red scarf*
Hines, Anna Grossnickle. *Daddy makes the best spaghetti*
Hooks, Bell. *Be boy buzz*
Howard, Elizabeth Fitzgerald. *Virgie goes to school with us boys*
Impey, Rose. *Who's a bright girl?*
Ives, Penny. *Mrs. Santa Claus*
Kroll, Virginia L. *A carp for Kimiko*
    Girl, you're amazing!
Lane, Megan Halsey. *Something to crow about*
Lattimore, Deborah Nourse. *Frida Maria*
Le Guin, Ursula K. *Fish soup*
Lyon, George Ella. *Mama is a miner*
Moss, Marissa. *True heart*
Numeroff, Laura Joffe. *What daddies do best*
    What mommies do best
Pearson, Susan. *Everybody knows that!*

Richardson, Jean. *Thomas's sitter*
San Souci, Robert D. *Brave Margaret*
    A weave of words
Schlank, Carol Hilgartner. *Elizabeth Cady Stanton*
Shaw, Mary. *Brady Brady and the Twirlin' Torpedo goalie*
Sierra, Judy. *Tasty baby belly buttons*
U'Ren, Andrea. *Pugdog*
Winthrop, Elizabeth. *Tough Eddie*
Wooldridge, Connie Nordhielm. *When Esther Morris headed west*
Yaroshevskaya, Kim. *Little Kim's doll*
Zhang, Song Nan. *The ballad of Mulan*

Genealogy

Dunbar, Joyce. *When I was young*
Schreck, Karen Halvorsen. *Lucy's family tree*
Sweeney, Joan. *Me and my family tree*

Generosity *see* Character traits – generosity

Genies *see* Mythical creatures – genies

Geography

Cuyler, Margery. *From here to there*
Holub, Joan. *Geogra-fleas*
Jenkins, Steve. *Hottest, coldest, highest, deepest*
Lewis, J. Patrick. *Earth and you, a closer view*
National Geographic Society (U.S.). *National Geographic our world: a child's first picture atlas*
Piepmeier, Charlotte. *Lucy's journey to the wild west*
Schuett, Stacey. *Somewhere in the world right now*
Vyner, Tim. *World team*

Geologists *see* Careers – geologists

Gerbils *see* Animals – gerbils

German Americans *see* Ethnic groups in the U.S. – German Americans

Germany *see* Foreign lands – Germany

Ghana *see* Foreign lands – Ghana

Ghosts

Ahlberg, Janet. *Funnybones*
Alexander, Sue. *More Witch, Goblin, and Ghost stories*
    Witch, Goblin and Ghost are back
    Witch, Goblin, and Ghost in the haunted woods
    Witch, Goblin and sometimes Ghost
Allard, Harry. *Bumps in the night*
Allen, Laura Jean. *Rollo and Tweedy and the ghost of Dougal Castle*
Amsden, Janet. *Grizzly Pete and the ghosts*
Anzaldúa, Gloria. *Prietita and the ghost woman = Prietita y la llorona*
Auch, Mary Jane. *Poultrygeist*
Bennett, Jill. *Teeny tiny*
Berenstain, Stan. *The Berenstain bears and the ghost of the forest*
Bergström, Gunilla. *Who's scaring Alfie Atkins?*
Birchman, David Francis. *Brother Billy Bronto's bygone blues band*
Biro, Val. *Gumdrop finds a ghost*
Bright, Robert. *Georgie*
    Georgie and the baby birds
    Georgie and the ball of yarn
    Georgie and the buried treasure
    Georgie and the little dog
    Georgie and the magician
    Georgie and the noisy ghost
    Georgie and the robbers
    Georgie and the runaway balloon
    Georgie goes west
    Georgie to the rescue
    Georgie's Christmas carol
    Georgie's Halloween

Brown, Marc Tolon. *Spooky riddles*
Brown, Ruth. *One stormy night*
Bruna, Dick. *Miffy the ghost*
Brunhoff, Laurent de. *Babar and the ghost*
    Babar and the ghost
Buck, Nola. *Gotcha!*
Bunting, Eve (Anne Evelyn). *In the haunted house*
Calmenson, Stephanie. *The teeny tiny teacher*
Capucilli, Alyssa Satin. *Inside a house that is haunted*
Carter, David A. *In a dark, dark wood*
Charlton, Elizabeth. *Jeremy and the ghost*
Chase, Mary. *The wicked, wicked ladies in the haunted house*
Cohen, Caron Lee. *Bronco dogs*
    Renata, Whizbrain and the ghost
Crews, Nina. *A ghost story*
Cutts, David. *I can read about creatures of the night*
Cuyler, Margery. *Sir William and the pumpkin monster*
DeFelice, Cynthia C. *Willy's silly grandma*
De Groat, Diane. *Good night, sleep tight, don't let the bedbugs bite*
DeLage, Ida. *The old witch and the ghost parade*
Diviny, Sean. *Halloween Motel*
Du Bois, William Pène. *Elisabeth, the cow ghost*
Duquennoy, Jacques. *The ghosts in the cellar*
    The ghosts' trip to Loch Ness
    Operation ghost
Dürr, Ursula. *The secret of Trembleton Hall*
Faulkner, Keith. *Hector Specter*
Flora, James. *Grandpa's ghost stories*
French, Vivian. *Little Ghost*
Friedrich, Priscilla. *The marshmallow ghosts*
Gabler, Mirko. *Brakus, Krakus . . . Or the incredible adventure of Mr. Skola's Tourist Club*
Gage, Wilson. *Mrs. Gaddy and the ghost*
Galdone, Joanna. *The tailypo*
Galdone, Paul. *King of the cats*
    The monster and the tailor
    The teeny-tiny woman
Gikow, Louise. *Boober Fraggle's ghosts*
Hancock, Sibyl. *Esteban and the ghost*
Harness, Cheryl. *Midnight in the cemetery*
Haseley, Dennis. *Ghost catcher*
Hawkins, Colin. *Come for a ride on the ghost train*
    Creepy castle
Hayes, Geoffrey. *The mystery of the pirate ghost*
Herman, Emily. *Hubknuckles*
Herman, Gail. *The haunted house*
Hirsh, Marilyn. *Deborah the dybbuk*
Hodges, Margaret. *Molly Limbo*
    Saint Patrick and the peddler
Johnston, Tony. *Four scary stories*
    The ghost of Nicholas Greebe
Khdir, Kate. *Little ghost*
Kraus, Robert. *Mummy knows best*
Kroll, Steven. *Amanda and the giggling ghost*
    Branigan's cat and the Halloween ghost
Kunnas, Mauri. *One spooky night and other scary stories*
Landry, Leo. *The snow ghosts*
Lewis, J. Patrick. *The house of Boo*
Lexau, Joan M. *Millicent's ghost*
Lindgren, Astrid. *The ghost of Skinny Jack*
McMillan, Bruce. *Ghost doll*
McMullan, Kate (Hall). *Creepy riddles*
Maitland, Barbara. *The bookstore ghost*
    The bookstore valentine
Martin, Bill (William Ivan). *Old devil wind*
Martín Larrañaga, Ana. *Woo! The not-so-scary Ghost*
Medearis, Angela Shelf. *The ghost of Sifty-Sifty Sam*
Michelson, Richard. *Did you say ghosts?*
Milich, Melissa. *Can't scare me!*
Milord, Susan. *The ghost on the hearth*
Mooser, Stephen. *The ghost with the Halloween hiccups*
Mystery manor
Nishikawa, Osamu. *Alexander and the blue ghost*
Nixon, Joan Lowery. *The Thanksgiving mystery*
O'Connor, Jane. *The teeny tiny woman*
Olson, Helen Kronberg. *The strange thing that happened to Oliver Wendell Iscovitch*

Ostheeren, Ingrid. *Martin and the Pumpkin Ghost*
Pieńkowski, Jan. *Haunted house*
Pinkwater, Daniel Manus. *The phantom of the lunch wagon*
Polisar, Barry Louis. *The haunted house party*
Prelutsky, Jack. *Halloween countdown*
Raskin, Ellen. *Ghost in a four-room apartment*
Reiner, Carl. *Tell me a scary story – but not too scary!*
Richardson, Bill. *Sally Dog Little*
Robins, Arthur. *The teeny tiny woman*
Rocklin, Joanne. *This book is haunted*
Rockwell, Anne F. *A bear, a bobcat and three ghosts*
Rodgers, Frank. *Who's afraid of the ghost train?*
Rubel, Nicole. *The ghost family meets its match*
Sandberg, Inger. *Little ghost Godfry*
San Souci, Robert D. *The boy and the ghost*
Seuling, Barbara. *The teeny tiny woman*
Sharmat, Marjorie Weinman. *Two ghosts on a bench*
Sherrow, Victoria. *There goes the ghost*
Silverman, Erica. *The Halloween house*
Skwarek, Skip. *The horrors of Howling Hall*
    Mystery of Maggoty Mill
Standiford, Natalie. *The headless horseman*
Terasaki, Stanley Todd. *Ghosts for breakfast*
Thayer, Jane. *Gus and the baby ghost*
    Gus loved his happy home
    Gus was a friendly ghost
    Gus was a gorgeous ghost
    Gus was a real dumb ghost
    What's a ghost going to do?
Vaughan, Marcia Kapok. *We're going on a ghost hunt*
Wallace, Daisy. *Ghost poems*
Weigelt, Udo. *Miranda's ghosts*
Wick, Walter. *I spy spooky night*
Williams, Sophy. *Nana's garden*
Winters, Kay. *The teeny tiny ghost*
    The teeny tiny ghost and the monster
    Whooo's haunting the teeny tiny ghost?
Wolkstein, Diane. *The legend of Sleepy Hollow*
Wyllie, Stephen. *Ghost train*
Yee, Paul. *The boy in the attic*
Yep, Laurence. *The man who tricked a ghost*
Zemach, Margot. *The little tiny woman*
Ziefert, Harriet. *Who can boo the loudest?*

Giants

Allen, Linda. *The giant who had no heart*
Auer, Martin. *Now, now Markus*
Auld, Mary. *David and Goliath*
Balian, Lorna. *A sweetheart for Valentine*
Benjamin, Alan. *Ribtickle Town*
Bible. Old Testament. David. *David and Goliath*
    David and the giant
Birdseye, Tom. *Look out, Jack! The giant is back*
Biro, Val. *Miranda's umbrella*
Bodwell, Gaile. *The long day of the giants*
Bolliger, Max. *The giants' feast*
    The magic bird
Bradfield, Roger (Jolly Roger). *Giants come in different sizes*
Briggs, Raymond. *Jim and the beanstalk*
Brin, Ruth F. *David and Goliath*
Carle, Eric. *Watch out! A giant!*
Christiana, David. *A Tooth Fairy's tale*
Cole, Brock. *The giant's toe*
Compton, Kenn. *Jack the giant chaser*
Coville, Bruce. *The foolish giant*
Cuneo, Mary Louise. *What can a giant do?*
Cunliffe, John. *Sara's giant and the upside down house*
Cushman, Doug. *Giants*
De La Mare, Walter (Walter John). *Molly Whuppie*
De Paola, Tomie (Thomas Anthony). *Fin M'Coul*
    The mysterious giant of Barletta
De Regniers, Beatrice Schenk. *David and Goliath*, ill. by Scott Cameron
    David and Goliath, ill. by Richard M. Powers
    The giant story
Desimini, Lisa. *Sun and moon*

Du Bois, William Pène. *Giant Otto*
  Otto and the magic potatoes
  Otto at sea
  Otto in Africa
  Otto in Texas
Dunbar, Joyce. *The sand children*
Elkin, Benjamin. *Lucky and the giant*
Farley, Jacqui. *Giant hiccups*
Fisher, Leonard Everett. *David and Goliath*
Foreman, Michael. *The two giants*
Fritz, Jean. *The good giants and the bad Pukwudgies*
Fuchshuber, Annegert. *Giant story – Mouse tale*
Gleeson, Brian. *Finn McCoul*
Goldsboro, Bobby. *Noah and the ark; and, David and Goliath*
Greene, Ellin. *The pumpkin giant*
Gregory, Valiska. *Kate's giants*
Grimm, Jacob. *The brave little tailor*, ill. by Mark Corcoran
  The brave little tailor, ill. by Olga Dugina & Andrej Dugin
  The brave little tailor, ill. by Daniel San Souci
  The brave little tailor, ill. by David Shaw
  The brave little tailor, ill. by Svend Otto S
  The brave little tailor, ill. by Eve Tharlet
  The brave little tailor, ill. by James Warhola
  The glass mountain, ill. by Nonny Hogrogian
  Seven at one blow
  The valiant little tailor
Grindley, Sally. *Shhh!*
Haley, Gail E. *Jack and the bean tree*
Harris, Jim. *Jack and the giant*
Harrison, David Lee. *The book of giant stories*
Hasler, Eveline. *The giantess*
Hawkes, Kevin. *His Royal Buckliness*
Hayes, Sarah. *Mary Mary*
Heller, Nicholas. *The giant*
Herrmann, Frank. *The giant Alexander*
  The giant Alexander and the circus
Hillert, Margaret. *The magic beans*
Homme, Bob. *The friendly giant's birthday*
  The friendly giant's book of fire engines
Hutchins, H. J. (Hazel J.). *Two so small*
Jack and the beanstalk. *The history of Mother Twaddle and the mar-
  velous achievements of her son Jack*
  Jack and the beanstalk, ill. by Val Biro
  Jack and the beanstalk, ill. by Aljoscha Blau
  Jack and the beanstalk, ill. by Lorinda Bryan Cauley
  Jack and the beanstalk, ill. by Steve Cox
  Jack and the beanstalk, ill. by Lydia Halverson
  Jack and the beanstalk, ill. by Julek Heller
  Jack and the beanstalk, ill. by John Howe
  Jack and the beanstalk, ill. by Steven Kellogg
  Jack and the beanstalk, ill. by Al Lorenz
  Jack and the beanstalk, ill. by Ed Parker
  Jack and the beanstalk, ill. by Tony Ross
  Jack and the beanstalk, ill. by Niamh Sharkey
  Jack and the beanstalk, ill. by Gennady Spirin
  Jack and the beanstalk, ill. by William Stobbs
  Jack and the beanstalk, ill. by James Warhola
  Jack and the beanstalk, ill. by Anne Wilsdorf
  Jack and the beanstalk = Juan y los frijoles magicos, ill. by Arnal
    Ballester
  Jack the giant killer, ill. by Anne Wilsdorf
  Jack the giantkiller, ill. by Tony Ross
Jennings, Michael. *Robin Goodfellow and the giant dwarf*
Johnson, Odette. *One prickly porcupine*
Johnson, Paul Brett. *Jack outwits the giants*
Kahl, Virginia. *Giants, indeed!*
Kasza, Keiko. *The mightiest*
Kraus, Robert. *The little giant*
Kreye, Walter. *The giant from the little island*
Kroll, Steven. *Big Jeremy*
Lawrence, John. *The giant of Grabbist*
Light, Steve. *The shoemaker extraordinaire*
Lobel, Anita. *The dwarf giant*
Lobel, Arnold. *Giant John*
Löfgren, Ulf. *The boy who ate more than the giant and other Swedish
  folktales*
McNeill, Janet. *The giant's birthday*

Metaxas, Eric. *David and Goliath*
Minarik, Else Holmelund. *The little giant girl and the elf boys*
Mollel, Tololwa M. (Tololwa Marti). *Big boy*
Muller, Robin. *Mollie Whuppie and the giant*
Munsch, Robert N. *David's father*
Nash, Ogden. *The adventures of Isabel*, ill. by Walter Lorraine
  The adventures of Isabel, ill. by James Marshall
O Huigin, Sean. *King of the birds*
Osborne, Mary Pope. *The brave little seamstress*
  Kate and the beanstalk
Podwal, Mark H. *Golem*
Pomerantz, Charlotte. *Mangaboom*
Porter, Sue. *Little Wolf and the giant*
Priestley, Alice. *Someone is reading this book*
Robbins, Maria Polushkin. *The little hen and the giant*
Roddie, Shen. *Animal stew*
Root, Phyllis. *Soup for supper*
Ruzzier, Sergio. *The little giant*
San Souci, Robert D. *Brave Margaret*
  Peter and the blue witch baby
Schami, Rafik. *Fatima and the dream thief*
Seeger, Pete. *Abiyoyo returns*
Selway, Martina. *Greedyguts*
Sherman, Ivan. *I am a giant*
Souhami, Jessica. *Mrs. McCool and the giant Cuhullin*
Spalding, Andrea. *It's raining, it's pouring*
Stanley, Diane. *The Giant and the beanstalk*
Still, James. *Jack and the wonder beans*
Thurber, James. *The great Quillow*
Tom Thumb. *The adventures of Tom Thumb*, ill. by Kinuko Y. Craft
Tompert, Ann. *Charlotte and Charles*
Ungerer, Tomi. *Zeralda's ogre*
Van Haeringen, Annemarie. *The cats' tale*
Wallace, Daisy. *Giant poems*
Ward, Nick. *Giant*
Weedn, Flavia. *The giant's garden*
Wiesner, William. *Tops*
Wilde, Oscar. *Fairy tales of Oscar Wilde*
  The selfish giant, ill. by S. Saelig Gallagher
  The selfish giant, ill. by Dom Mansell
  The selfish giant, ill. by Fabian Negrin
  The selfish giant, ill. by Lisbeth Zwerger
Willey, Margaret. *Clever Beatrice, an Upper Peninsula conte*
Yep, Laurence. *The city of dragons*
Yolen, Jane. *The giant's farm*
  The giants go camping
Yorinks, Arthur. *The Miami giant*
Zeman, Ludmila. *Sindbad in the land of giants*

Gifts

Albert, Richard E. *Alejandro's gift*
Anderson, Laurie Halse. *No time for Mother's Day*
Balet, Jan B. *The gift*
Beck, Andrea. *Elliot's Christmas surprise*
Beck, Scott. *A mud pie for mother*
Best, Cari. *Three cheers for Catherine the Great!*
Bohdal, Susi. *1, 2, 3, what do you see?*
Bourgeois, Paulette. *Franklin says "I love you"*
  Franklin's Christmas gift
Brighton, Catherine. *Hope's gift*
Brown, Marc Tolon. *Arthur's Christmas*
Bruce, Lisa. *Fran's friend*
Burden-Patmon, Denise. *Imani's gift at Kwanzaa*
Butler, M. Christina. *One snowy night*
Byars, Betsy Cromer. *The lace snail*
Calhoun, Mary. *A shepherd's gift*
Capucilli, Alyssa Satin. *Happy Hanukkah, Biscuit*
Charlip, Remy. *Harlequin and the gift of many colors*
Conrad, Pam. *The rooster's gift*
Czernecki, Stefan. *The hummingbird's gift*
De Groat, Diane. *Happy birthday to you, you belong in a zoo*
Delton, Judy. *No time for Christmas*
  The perfect Christmas gift
Díaz, Katacha. *Carolina's gift*
Dooley, Norah. *Everybody serves soup*
Dubowski, Cathy East. *Cave boy*

Edwards, Pamela Duncan. *Rosie's roses*
Engelbreit, Mary. *Queen of Christmas*
Estes, Kristyn Rehling. *Manuela's gift*
Fern, Eugene. *Birthday presents*
Frazee, Marla. *Santa Claus, the world's number one toy expert*
French, Vivian. *A present for mom*
Gardella, Tricia. *Blackberry booties*
Gerstein, Mordicai. *Guess what?*
Gliori, Debi. *A present for Big Pig*
    What can I give him?
Goble, Paul. *The gift of the sacred dog*
Gomi, Taro. *Santa through the window*
Grimm, Jacob. *One gift deserves another*
Grosz, Peter. *The special gifts*
Gutman, Anne. *Gaspard and Lisa's Christmas surprise*
Hague, Michael. *The perfect present*
Hayles, Marsha. *The feathered crown*
Helldorfer, M. C. (Mary Claire). *Daniel's gift*
    Hog music
Henry, O. *The gift of the Magi*
Higgs, Liz Curtis. *The parable of the lily*
High, Linda Oatman. *A Christmas Star*
Hobbie, Holly. *Toot and Puddle, a present for Toot*
Holmes, Efner Tudor. *Carrie's gift*
Hoopes, Lyn Littlefield. *Half a button*
Hubbell, Patricia. *Wrapping paper romp*
Hughes, Shirley. *Alfie and the birthday surprise*
Hutchins, Pat. *It's my birthday!*
Inkpen, Mick. *Kipper and Roly*
    Wibbly Pig opens his presents
Jackson, Ellen B. *The precious gift*
Johnson, Crockett. *The emperor's gifts*
Keats, Ezra Jack. *The little drummer boy*
Keister, Douglas. *Fernando's gift = El regalo de Fernando*
Keller, Holly. *A bear for Christmas*
Keselman, Gabriela. *The gift*
Kimmel, Elizabeth Cody. *My penguin Osbert*
Krahn, Fernando. *How Santa Claus had a long and difficult journey delivering his presents*
Kunnas, Mauri. *Twelve gifts for Santa Claus*
Linders, Clara. *The very best door of all*
Little, Jean. *Pippin the Christmas pig*
Louie, Therese On. *Raymond's perfect present*
Lubin, Leonard B. *Christmas gift-bringers*
McClure, Gillian. *Tom Finger*
McCourt, Lisa. *Chicken soup for little souls: The never-forgotten doll*
McCully, Emily Arnold. *The Christmas gift*
McKee, David. *Prince Peter and the teddy bear*
Manson, Christopher. *A gift for the king*
Mathers, Petra. *Lottie's new beach towel*
Medearis, Angela Shelf. *Annie's gifts*
Milord, Sue. *Maggie and the goodbye gift*
Mogensen, Jan. *Teddy's Christmas gift*
Mora, Pat. *A birthday basket for Tía*
    The gift of the poinsettia = El regalo de la flor de nochebuena
Morrissey, Dean. *The Christmas ship*
Naylor, Phyllis Reynolds. *Keeping a Christmas secret*
Neugebauer, Charise. *Santa's gift*
Politi, Leo. *The nicest gift*
Pomerantz, Charlotte. *You're not my best friend anymore*
Prater, John. *The gift*
Quattrocki, Carolyn. *The little drummer boy*
Radley, Gail. *The spinner's gift*
Riordan, James. *The three magic gifts*
Rodanas, Kristina. *The little drummer boy*
Rovetch, Lissa. *TLC grow with me*
Rumford, James. *Nine animals and the well*
Rylant, Cynthia. *Birthday presents*
Sabuda, Robert James. *Tutankhamen's gift*
Sage, Angie. *Molly and the birthday party*
Saint James, Synthia. *The gifts of Kwanzaa*
Seabrooke, Brenda. *The swan's gift*
Segal, Lore Groszmann. *Morris the artist*
Shepard, Aaron. *The gifts of Wali Dad*
Skolsky, Mindy Warshaw. *Hannah and the whistling tea kettle*
Smalls-Hector, Irene. *Louise's gift*
Speirs, John. *The little boy's Christmas gift*

Spinelli, Eileen. *In my new yellow shirt*
Steptoe, Javaka. *The Jones family express*
Steven, Kenneth C. *The bearer of gifts*
Stewart, Paul. *The birthday presents*
Taha, Karen T. *A gift for Tia Rose*
Tazewell, Charles. *The littlest angel*, ill. by Deborah Lanino
    The littlest angel, ill. by Paul Micich
    The littlest angel, ill. by Rebecca Thornburgh
Thomas, Naturi. *Uh-oh! It's Mama's birthday!*
Thury, Frederick. *The last straw*
Timmermans, Felix. *A gift from Saint Nicholas*
Uff, Caroline. *Happy birthday, Lulu*
Varley, Susan. *Badger's parting gifts*
Wallace, John. *Tiny Rabbit goes to a birthday party*
Watts, Bernadette. *Harvey Hare, postman extraordinaire*
Watts, Jeri Hanel. *Keepers*
Weedn, Flavia. *The star gift*
Wells, Rosemary. *Morris's disappearing bag*
Weninger, Brigitte. *Happy Easter, Davy*
Williams, Vera B. *Something special for me*
Wood, Don. *Merry Christmas, big hungry bear*
Wright, Dare. *A gift from the lonely doll*
Young, Russell. *Dragonsong*
Ziefert, Harriet. *Presents for Santa*

Gilbert Islands *see* Foreign lands – South Sea Islands

Giraffes *see* Animals – giraffes

Glasses *see also* Careers – opticians, optometrists

Brown, Marc Tolon. *Arthur's eyes*
    Glasses for D. W.
Carlson, Melody. *Farmer Brown's field trip*
Cohen, Peter Zachary. *Boris's glasses*
Cousins, Lucy. *What can rabbit see?*
Delaney, Ned. *Two strikes, four eyes*
Duffield, Katy. *Farmer McPeepers and his missing milk cows*
Flanagan, Alice K. *Choosing eyeglasses with Mrs. Koutris*
Geoghegan, Adrienne. *Dogs don't wear glasses*
Giff, Patricia Reilly. *Watch out, Ronald Morgan!*
Goodsell, Jane. *Katie's magic glasses*
Hest, Amy. *Baby Duck and the bad eyeglasses*
Keller, Holly. *Cromwell's glasses*
Kessler, Leonard P. *Mr. Pine's mixed-up signs*
Lasson, Robert. *Orange Oliver*
MacDonald, Maryann. *Little Hippo gets glasses*
McKean, Thomas. *Hooray for Grandma Jo!*
Marshall, James. *Willis*
Motomora, Mitchell. *Specs*
Paul, Korky. *Winnie flies again*
Rascal. *Socrates*
Raskin, Ellen. *Spectacles*
Smith, Donald. *Who's wearing my sunglasses?*
Smith, Lane. *Glasses . . . who needs 'em?*
Stadler, John. *The cats of Mrs. Calamari*
Thayer, Jane. *Mr. Turtle's magic glasses*
Tusa, Tricia. *Libby's new glasses*

Gloves *see* Clothing – gloves, mittens

Gnats *see* Insects – gnats

Gnomes *see* Mythical creatures – gnomes

Goats *see* Animals – goats

Goblins *see* Mythical creatures – goblins

Golf *see* Sports – golf

Gorillas *see* Animals – gorillas

Goshute Indians *see* Indians of North America – Goshute

Gossip *see* Behavior – gossip

Gourds *see* Musical instruments – gourds

Grammar *see* Language

Grandfathers *see* Family life – grandfathers; Family life – grandparents

Grandmothers *see* Family life – grandmothers; Family life – grandparents

Grandparents *see* Family life – grandfathers; Family life – grandmothers; Family life – grandparents

Grasshoppers *see* Insects – grasshoppers

Great-grandparents *see* Family life – great-grandparents

Great Plains Indians *see* Indians of North America – Great Plains

Greece *see* Foreign lands – Greece

Greed *see* Behavior – greed

Greek Americans *see* Ethnic groups in the U.S. – Greek Americans

Greenland *see* Foreign lands – Greenland

Grief *see* Emotions – grief

Griffins *see* Mythical creatures – griffins

Grocery stores *see* Shopping; Stores

Groundhog Day *see* Holidays – Groundhog Day

Groundhogs *see* Animals – groundhogs

Growing up *see* Behavior – growing up

Guatemala *see* Foreign lands – Guatemala

Guinea fowl *see* Birds – guinea fowl

Guinea pigs *see* Animals – guinea pigs

Guns *see* Weapons

Guy Fawkes Day *see* Holidays – Guy Fawkes Day

Guyana *see* Foreign lands – Guyana

Gymnastics *see* Sports – gymnastics

Gypsies

Anderson, C. W. (Clarence Williams). *Blaze and the gypsies*
Bemelmans, Ludwig. *Madeline and the gypsies*
García Lorca, Federico. *The Lieutenant Colonel and the gypsy*
Kellogg, Steven (Stephen). *The mystery of the magic green ball*
Mahy, Margaret. *Mrs. Discombobulous*
Oram, Hiawyn. *Skittlewonder and the wizard*
Patterson, Geoffrey. *The lion and the gypsy*
Tompert, Ann. *Savina, the gypsy dancer*

Habits *see* Thumb sucking

Haida Indians *see* Indians of North America – Haida

Hair

Abisch, Roz. *The Pumpkin Heads*
Appell, Clara. *Now I have a daddy haircut*
Azore, Barbara. *Wanda and the wild hair*
B-52's (Musical group). *Wig!*
Battle-Lavert, Gwendolyn. *The barber's cutting edge*
Bright, Robert. *I like red*
Burnard, Damon. *Dave's haircut*
Cisneros, Sandra. *Hairs = Pelitos*
Cole, Babette. *The hairy book*
Daly, Catherine. *Whiskers*
Davis, Gibbs. *Katy's first haircut*
De Veaux, Alexis. *An enchanted hair tale*
Diouf, Sylviane A, (Sylviane Anna). *Bintou's braids*
Duncan, Lois. *The longest hair in the world*
Esckelson, Laura. *The copper braid of Shannon O'Shea*
Fleming, Candace. *Madame LaGrande and her so high, to the sky, uproarious pompadour*
Girard, Linda Walvoord. *Jeremy's first haircut*
Goldin, Augusta. *Straight hair, curly hair*
Grimes, Nikki. *Wild, wild hair*
Grimm, Jacob. *Rapunzel*, ill. by Jutta Ash
   Rapunzel, ill. by Sheilah Beckett
   Rapunzel, ill. by Bert Dodson
   Rapunzel, ill. by Maja Dusíkova
   Rapunzel, ill. by Michael Hague
   Rapunzel, ill. by Trina Schart Hyman
   Rapunzel, ill. by Kris Waldherr
   Rapunzel, ill. by Bernadette Watts
   Rapunzel, ill. by Paul O. Zelinsky
Hair
Hest, Amy. *Gabby growing up*
Hooks, Bell. *Happy to be nappy*
Johnson, Lindsay Lee. *Hurricane Henrietta*
Joly, Fanny. *Mr. Fine, porcupine*
Koren, Edward. *Very hairy Harry*
Krisher, Trudy. *Kathy's hats*
Krosoczka, Jarrett J. *Baghead*
Kunhardt, Dorothy. *Billy the barber*
Landström, Olof. *Will gets a haircut*
Lerner, Harriet Goldhor. *Franny B. Kranny, there's a bird in your hair*
MacDonald, Allan. *The pig in a wig*
Madrigal, Antonio Hernandez. *Erandi's braids*
Marton, Jirina. *I'll do it myself*
Milstein, Linda Breiner. *Amanda's perfect hair*
Mollel, Tololwa M. (Tololwa Marti). *The princess who lost her hair*
Moss, Miriam. *Bad hare day*
Munsch, Robert N. *Aaron's hair*
   Stephanie's ponytail
Nesbit, Edith. *Melisande*
Palatini, Margie. *Bedhead*
   Moosetache
Parr, Todd. *This is my hair*
Portlock, Rob. *Someone's trying to cut off my head*
Quin-Harkin, Janet. *Helpful Hattie*
Radabaugh, Melinda Beth. *Getting a haircut*
Robbins, Beth. *Tom's new haircut*
Roberts, Lynn (Lynn M.). *Rapunzel, a groovy fairy tale*
Robins, Joan. *Addie's bad day*
Rockwell, Anne F. *My barber*
Saltzberg, Barney. *Crazy hair day*

Sandeman, Anna. *Skin, teeth, and hair*
Scott, Natalie (Anderson). *Firebrand, push your hair out of your eyes*
Tarpley, Natasha Anastasia. *Bippity Bop barbershop*
    I love my hair!
Tether, Graham. *The hair book*
Thomas, Joyce Carol. *Crowning glory*
Townsend, Kenneth. *Felix, the bald-headed lion*
Tusa, Tricia. *Camilla's new hairdo*
Whittaker, Nicola. *Hair*
Wilhelm, Hans. *Don't cut my hair*
Williams-Garcia, Rita. *Catching the wild waiyuuzee*

Haiti *see* Foreign lands – Haiti

Halloween *see* Holidays – Halloween

Hamsters *see* Animals – hamsters

Handbags *see* Clothing – handbags, purses

Handicaps

Alborghetti, Marci. *Miracle of the myrrh*
Anderson, Peggy Perry. *We go in a circle*
Arnold, Katrin. *Anna joins in*
Asare, Meshack. *Sosu's call*
Borton, Lady. *Junk pile!*
Bradford, Ann. *The mystery of the missing dogs*
Briscoe, Jill. *The innkeeper's daughter*
Brown, Tricia. *Someone special, just like you*
Brownridge, William Roy. *The moccasin goalie*
Cairo, Shelley. *Our brother has Down's syndrome*
Carter, Alden R. *Seeing things my way*
Charlot, Martin. *Felisa and the magic tikling bird*
Clifton, Lucille. *My friend Jacob*
Corrigan, Kathy. *Emily Umily*
Dwight, Laura. *We can do it!*
Eisner, Will. *Sundiata*
English, Jennifer. *My mommy's special*
Fanshawe, Elizabeth. *Rachel*
Fassler, Joan. *Howie helps himself*
Foreman, Michael. *Seal surfer*
Hamm, Diane Johnston. *Grandma drives a motor bed*
Hasler, Eveline. *Martin is our friend*
Henriod, Lorraine. *Grandma's wheelchair*
Hoffman, Alice. *Fireflies*
Kaufman, Curt. *Rajesh*
Kuklin, Susan. *Thinking big*
Larsen, Hanne. *Don't forget Tom*
Lasker, Joe. *He's my brother*
Lears, Laurie. *Waiting for Mr. Goose*
Lester, Helen. *Author*
    Hooway for Wodney Wat
Lester, Julius. *Shining*
Maguire, Arlene H. *Special people, special ways*
Marron, Carol A. *No trouble for Grandpa*
Naylor, Phyllis Reynolds. *Jennifer Jean, the Cross-Eyed Queen*
Polacco, Patricia. *Thank you, Mr. Falker*
Powers, Mary E. *Our teacher's in a wheelchair*
Prall, Jo. *My sister's special*
Pulver, Robin. *Way to go, Alex!*
Rabe, Berniece. *The balancing girl*
    Where's Chimpy?
Rogers, Fred. *Extraordinary friends*
Rosenberg, Maxine B. *My friend Leslie*
Schatell, Brian. *The McGoonys have a party*
Senisi, Ellen B. *Just kids*
Small, David. *Ruby Mae has something to say*
Smith, Lucia B. *A special kind of sister*
Stein, Sara Bonnett. *About handicaps*
Wahl, Jan. *Button eye's orange*
White, Paul. *Janet at school*
Whitney, Dorothy B. *Creatures of an exceptional kind*
Wisniewski, David. *Sundiata*
Wolf, Bernard. *Don't feel sorry for Paul*

Handicaps – ADD

Bishop, Brett. *Clayton's path*
Rotner, Shelley. *The A.D.D. book for kids*
Zimmett, Debbie. *Eddie enough*

Handicaps – autism

Amenta, Charles A. (Charles Anthony). *Russell is extra special*
Edwards, Becky. *My brother Sammy*
Ely, Lesley. *Looking after Louis*
Lears, Laurie. *Ian's walk*

Handicaps – blindness *see also* Anatomy – eyes

Adler, David A. *Helen Keller*
Armstrong, Jennifer. *King crow*
Backstein, Karen. *The blind men and the elephant*
Balian, Lorna. *Elephant?*
Bradford, Ann. *The mystery of the blind writer*
Brighton, Catherine. *My hands, my world*
Carrick, Carol. *Melanie*
Chapman, Elizabeth. *Suzy*
Clements, Andrew. *Brave Norman*
Cohen, Miriam. *See you tomorrow*
Condra, Estelle. *See the ocean*
Davis, Patricia Anne. *Brian's bird*
DeArmond, Dale. *The seal oil lamp*
Fraustino, Lisa Rowe. *The hickory chair*
Goldin, Barbara Diamond. *Cakes and miracles*
Herman, Bill. *Jenny's magic wand*
Jensen, Virginia Allen. *Catching*
    Red thread riddles
    What's that?
Johnson, Donna Kay. *Brighteyes*
Karim, Roberta. *Mandy Sue Day*
Keats, Ezra Jack. *Apt. 3*
Kroll, Virginia L. *Naomi knows it's springtime*
Lang, Glenna. *Looking out for Sarah*
Litchfield, Ada B. *A cane in her hand*
McMahon, Patricia. *Listen for the bus*
Martin, Bill (William Ivan). *Knots on a counting rope*
Moon, Nicola. *Lucy's picture*
Newth, Philip. *Roly goes exploring*
Quigley, Lillian Fox. *The blind men and the elephant*
Rau, Dana Meachen. *The secret code*
Reuter, Margaret. *My mother is blind*
Rodriguez, Bobbie. *Sarah's sleepover*
Sargent, Susan. *My favorite place*
Saxe, John Godfrey. *The blind men and the elephant*
Strom, Maria Diaz. *Rainbow Joe and me*
Troupe, Quincy. *Little Stevie Wonder*
Wisniewski, David. *Elfwyn's saga*
Yolen, Jane. *The seeing stick*
Young, Ed (Edward). *Seven blind mice*

Handicaps – cerebral palsy

DeBear, Kirsten. *Be quiet, Marina!*
Heelan, Jamee Riggio. *Rolling along, the story of Taylor and his wheelchair*
Moran, George. *Imagine me on a sit-ski!*
Payne, Sherry Neuwirth. *A contest*

Handicaps – deafness *see also* Anatomy – ears

Acredolo, Linda P. *My first baby signs*
Adams, Jean Ekman. *Clarence and the great surprise*
Adler, David A. *Helen Keller*
Ancona, George. *Handtalk zoo*
Arthur, Catherine. *My sister's silent world*
Aseltine, Lorraine. *I'm deaf and it's okay*
Baker, Pamela J. *My first book of sign*
Bove, Linda. *Sign language ABC with Linda Bove*
Chaplin, Susan Gibbons. *I can sign my ABCs*
Charlip, Remy. *Handtalk*
    Handtalk birthday

Gage, Wilson. *Down in the boondocks*
Greenberg, Judith E. *What is the sign for friend?*
Heelan, Jamee Riggio. *Can you hear a rainbow?*
Hesse, Karen. *Lester's dog*
Lee, Jeanne M. *Silent lotus*
Levi, Dorothy Hoffman. *A very special sister*
Litchfield, Ada B. *A button in her ear*
Millman, Isaac. *Moses goes to a concert*
   Moses goes to school
   Moses goes to the circus
Moore, Clement Clarke. *The night before Christmas in signed English*
Mother Goose. *Nursery rhymes from Mother Goose in signed English*
Okimoto, Jean Davies. *A place for Grace*
Pace, Elizabeth. *Chris gets ear tubes*
Uhlberg, Myron. *The printer*
Rankin, Laura. *The handmade counting book*
Wahl, Jan. *Jamie's tiger*
Waller, Curt. *Baby's first signs*
   More baby's first signs
Wheeler, Cindy. *More simple signs*
   Simple signs
Winnie-the-Pooh's ABC
Wolf, Bernard. *Anna's silent world*

Handicaps – Down syndrome

Butler, Geoff. *The hangashore*
Carter, Alden R. *Big brother Dustin*
DeBear, Kirsten. *Be quiet, Marina!*
Fleming, Virginia M. *Be good to Eddie Lee*
Girnis, Margaret. *ABC for you and me*
   1, 2, 3 for you and me
Gregory, Nan. *How Smudge came*
Rheingrover, Jean Sasso. *Veronica's first year*
Rickert, Janet Elizabeth. *Russ and the almost perfect day*
Stuve-Bodeen, Stephanie. *We'll paint the octopus red*

Handicaps – dyslexia

Robb, Diane Burton. *The alphabet war*

Handicaps – mental handicaps

Brightman, Alan. *Like me*
Fassler, Joan. *One little girl*
Gifaldi, David. *Ben, king of the river*
Rickert, Janet Elizabeth. *Russ and the almost perfect day*
Shriver, Maria. *What's wrong with Timmy?*

Handicaps – physical handicaps

Baggette, Susan K. *Jonathan goes to the grocery store*
Brown, Janet Allison. *The secret garden*
Carlson, Nancy L. *Arnie and the new kid*
Caseley, Judith. *Harry and Willy and Carrothead*
Cowen-Fletcher, Jane. *Mama zooms*
Damrell, Liz. *With the wind*
De Anda, Diane. *Dancing Miranda = Baila, Miranda, baila*
Edwards, Michelle. *Alef-bet*
Emmons, Chip. *Sammy wakes his dad*
Harshman, Marc. *The storm*
Heelan, Jamee Riggio. *The making of my special hand, Madison's story*
   Rolling along, the story of Taylor and his wheelchair
Hines, Anna Grossnickle. *Gramma's walk*
Hodges, Margaret. *The hero of Bremen*
Hoffman, Eric. *No fair to tigers = No es justo para los tigres*
Holcomb, Nan. *Patrick and Emma Lou*
Kirk, Daniel. *Breakfast at the Liberty Diner*
Lakin, Pat (Patricia). *Dad and me in the morning*
Lasker, Joe. *Nick joins in*
Lee, Jeanne M. *Silent lotus*
Moran, George. *Imagine me on a sit-ski!*
Munsch, Robert N. *Zoom*
Osofsky, Audrey. *My buddy*
Senisi, Ellen B. *All kinds of friends, even green*
Stewart, Shannon. *Sea crow*

Waddell, Martin. *My great grandpa*
Wells, Rosemary. *The little lame prince*
Willis, Jeanne. *Susan laughs*
Yin. *Dear Santa, please come to the 19th floor*

Handicaps – stuttering

Lears, Laurie. *Ben has something to say*

Hands *see* Anatomy – hands

Handymen *see* Careers – handymen

Hanukkah *see* Holidays – Hanukkah

Happiness *see* Emotions – happiness

Hares *see* Animals – rabbits

Harmonicas *see* Musical instruments – harmonicas

Harps *see* Musical instruments – harps

Harpsichords *see* Musical instruments – harpsichords

Hats *see* Clothing – hats

Hatters *see* Careers – hatters

Hawaii

Coste, Marion. *Honu*
Fellows, Rebecca Nevers. *A lei for Tutu*
Funai, Mamoru. *Moke and Poki in the rain forest*
George, Jean Craighead. *Dear Katie, the volcano is a girl*
Guback, Georgia. *Luka's quilt*
Hayashi, Leslie Ann. *Fables from the sea*
Laird, Donivee Martin. *The three little Hawaiian pigs and the magic shark*
Lewis, Richard. *In the night, still dark*
McGuire-Turcotte, Casey A. *How Honu the turtle got his shell*
Martin, Rafe. *The Shark God*
Mower, Nancy. *I visit my Tūtū and Grandma*
Rand, Gloria. *Aloha, Salty!*
Rattigan, Jama Kim. *The woman in the moon*
Rumford, James. *Dog-of-the-Sea-Waves*
   The Island-below-the-star
Samuels, Barbara. *Aloha, Dolores*
Stanley, Fay. *The last princess*
Tune, Suelyn Ching. *How Maui slowed the sun*
Vigil-Piñón, Evangelina. *Marina's muumuu = el muumuu de Marina*
Williams, Jay. *The surprising things Maui did*
Williams, Julie Stewart. *And the birds appeared*
Williams, Laura E. *Torch fishing with the sun*

Hawks *see* Birds – hawks

Heads *see* Anatomy – heads

Health & fitness

Arnold, Caroline. *Who keeps us healthy?*
Berger, Melvin. *Ouch! a book about cuts, scratches and scrapes*
Borten, Helen. *Do you move as I do?*
Bridge, Chris. *Andrew's story*
Brown, Laurie Krasny. *Dinosaurs alive and well*
Burnstein, John. *Slim Goodbody*
Cobb, Vicki. *How the doctor knows you're fine*
Cole, Babette. *Dr. Dog*
Corey, Shana. *First graders from Mars: Nergal and the Great Space Race*
Egielski, Richard. *Buz*
Fassler, David. *What's a virus, anyway?*
Frost, Helen. *Eating right*

The fruit group
The grain group
Glaser, Jason. *Pinkeye*
Glyman, Caroline A. *Learning your ABC's of nutrition*
Gordon, Sharon. *Asthma*
　Bruises
　Pinkeye
　Seeing
　Smelling
Gross, Ruth Belov. *A book about your skeleton*
Kalz, Jill. *Fruits*
Keller, Laurie. *Open wide: tooth school inside*
Kuklin, Susan. *When I see my dentist*
Leaf, Munro. *Health can be fun*
Leedy, Loreen. *The edible pyramid*
Levete, Sarah. *Looking after myself*
Lobb, Janice. *Splish! Splosh! Why do we wash?*
Loewen, Nancy. *School safety*
McElmurry, Jill. *Mess pets*
Marcus, Susan. *Casey visits the doctor*
Marshall, Lyn. *Yoga for your children*
Moncure, Jane Belk. *Happy healthkins*
　The healthkin food train
　Healthkins help
Morgan, Allen. *Matthew and the midnight hospital*
Müller, Birte. *Finn cooks*
Murkoff, Heidi Eisenberg. *What to expect when you go to the dentist*
　What to expect when you go to the doctor
Newcome, Zita. *Pop-up toddlerobics*
Newman, Leslèa. *Belinda's bouquet*
Onyefulu, Ifeoma. *Grandfather's work*
Owen, Ann (1953–). *Keeping you healthy*
Oxenbury, Helen. *The checkup*
Radlauer, Ruth Shaw. *Of course, you're a horse!*
Rice, Judith. *Those itsy-bitsy teeny-tiny not-so-nice head lice = Esos pequeñines, chiquitines, para nada simpáticos piojos*
　Those ooey gooey winky-blinky but – invisible pinkeye germs = Esos pringosos viscosos pestañeantes parpadeantes pero – invisibles gérmenes que causan conjuntivitis
Rockwell, Harlow. *My doctor*
Rosenberry, Vera. *Vera goes to the dentist*
Roth, Harold. *A checkup*
Sears, William, M.D. *Eat healthy, feel great*
Seuss, Dr. *The tooth book*
Sharmat, Marjorie Weinman. *Lucretia the unbearable*
Showers, Paul. *Sleep is for everyone*
Slangerup, Erik Jon. *Dirt Boy*
Spelman, Cornelia Maude. *Your body belongs to you*
Swanson, Diane. *The dentist and you*
　The doctor and you
Taylor, Sean. *Boing!*
Tilden, Ruth. *Freddie works out*
Watson, Jane Werner. *My friend the dentist*
　My friend the doctor
Yagya, Genichiro. *All about scabs*
Zamorano, Ana. *Let's eat!*

Health & fitness – exercise

Charles, Donald. *Calico Cat's exercise book*
Isenberg, Barbara. *Albert the running bear's exercise book*
Moncure, Jane Belk. *Healthkins exercise!*
Newcome, Zita. *Animal fun*
　Toddlerobics
Rockwell, Lizzy. *The busy body book*
Tsubakiyama, Margaret (Holloway). *Mei-Mei loves the morning*
Ziefert, Harriet. *Murphy meets the treadmill*

Health & safety

Gordon, Sharon. *Cuts and scrapes*

Hearing *see* Anatomy – ears; Handicaps – deafness; Senses – hearing

Heat *see* Concepts – cold & heat

Heavy equipment *see* Machines

Hedgehogs *see* Animals – hedgehogs

Helicopters

Anderson, Joan. *Harry's helicopter*
Budd, E. S. *Military helicopters*
Cartwright, Ann. *The winter hedgehog*
Drummond, Violet H. *The flying postman*
Duchess of York. *Budgie at Bendick's Point*
　Budgie the little helicopter
Ethan, Eric. *Helicopters*
Gay, Michel. *Little helicopter*
Glass, Andrew. *The wondrous whirligig*
Ingoglia, Gina. *The big book of real airplanes*
Taylor, Mark. *Henry explores the mountains*
Zaffo, George J. *The book of real airplanes*

Helpfulness *see* Character traits – helpfulness

Hens *see* Birds – chickens

Herons *see* Birds – herons

Hibernation

Arnosky, Jim. *Every autumn comes the bear*
Barrett, John M. *The bear who slept through Christmas*
Bartoli, Jennifer. *Snow on bear's nose*
Bassett, Lisa. *Beany wakes up for Christmas*
Bird, E. J. *How do bears sleep?*
Cohen, Carol L. *Wake up, groundhog!*
Cox, Judy. *Go to sleep, Groundhog*
De Beer, Hans. *Bernard Bear's amazing adventure*
DeLage, Ida. *The old witch and the snores*
De Paola, Tomie (Thomas Anthony). *Four stories for four seasons*
Evans, Eva Knox. *Sleepy time*
Fisher, Aileen Lucia. *Where does everyone go?*
Fleming, Denise. *Time to sleep*
Fraggalosch, Audrey. *Grizzly bear family*
Freeman, Don. *Bearymore*
Gammell, Stephen. *Wake up, bear . . . It's Christmas!*
Grindley, Sally. *What will I do without you?*
Hobbs, Will. *Beardream*
Janice. *Little Bear's Christmas*
Kepes, Juliet. *Frogs, merry*
Kesselman, Wendy Ann. *Time for Jody*
Krauss, Ruth. *The happy day*
Lawson, Julie. *Bear on the train*
London, Jonathan. *Froggy gets dressed*
Ludwig, Warren. *Good morning, Granny Rose*
McClure, Gillian. *Prickly pig*
Marshall, James. *What's the matter with Carruthers?*
Miller, Edna. *Mousekin's golden house*
Moret, Brigitte Frey. *The bear's Christmas*
Partridge, Elizabeth. *Moon glowing*
Patz, Nancy. *Sarah Bear and Sweet Sidney*
Piers, Helen. *Grasshopper and butterfly*
Rascal. *Orson*
Senshu, Noriko. *Sonny's dream*
Stewart, Paul. *A little bit of winter*
Stott, Rowena. *The hedgehog feast*
Wallace, Karen. *A bed for winter*
Walters, Catherine. *When will it be spring?*
Ward, Andrew. *Baby bear and the long sleep*
Watson, Wendy. *Has winter come?*
Welling, Peter J. *Andrew McGroundhog and his shady shadow*
Wilson, Karma. *Bear stays up for Christmas*
Yulya. *Bears are sleeping*
Zagwÿn, Deborah Turney. *Turtle spring*

Hiccups

Bains, Rae. *Hiccups, hiccups*
Berger, Melvin. *Why I sneeze, shiver, hiccup, and yawn*

Black, Charles C. *The royal nap*
Farley, Jacqui. *Giant hiccups*
Kelley, True. *Buggly Bear's hiccup cure*
Kenyon, Tony. *Hyacinth Hop has the hic-hops*
Long, Melinda. *Hiccup snickup*
McKee, David. *Zebra's hiccups*
Mayer, Mercer. *Hiccup*
Mooser, Stephen. *The ghost with the Halloween hiccups*
Mueller, Virginia. *Monster's birthday hiccups*
Trez, Denise. *The royal hiccups*

Hiding *see* Behavior – hiding

Hiding things *see* Behavior – hiding things

Hieroglyphics

Bower, Tamara. *The shipwrecked sailor*
Mother Goose. *Mother Goose in hieroglyphics*
The prince who knew his fate
Walsh, Jill Paton. *Pepi and the secret names*

Hiking *see* Sports – hiking

Himalayas *see* Foreign lands – Himalayas

Hinduism *see* Religion – Hinduism

Hippopotamuses *see* Animals – hippopotamuses

Hispanic Americans *see* Ethnic groups in the U.S. –
Hispanic Americans

Hmong Americans *see* Ethnic groups in the U.S. –
Hmong Americans

Hobby horses *see* Toys – rocking horses

Hockey *see* Sports – hockey

Hogs *see* Animals – pigs

Hohokam Indians *see* Indians of North America –
Hohokam

Holidays

Adler, David A. *The children's book of Jewish holidays*
A picture book of Jewish holidays
Alexander, Sue. *Small plays for special days*
Belting, Natalia Maree. *Summer's coming in*
Biers-Ariel, Matt. *Solomon and the trees*
Bonnici, Peter. *The festival*
Brode, Robyn. *April*
    August
    December
    February
    January
    July
    June
    March
    May
    November
    October
    September
Capucilli, Alyssa Satin. *Biscuit gives a gift*
Carle, Eric. *Hello, red fox*
Carlson, Lori Marie. *Hurray for Three Kings' Day*
Cazet, Denys. *December 24th*
Chaikin, Miriam. *Esther*
Chancellor, Deborah. *Holidays!*
Cohen, Barbara. *Even higher*
Conger, Marion. *The little golden holiday book*
Cooney, Barbara. *The story of Christmas*

Crespi, Francesca. *Little Bear and the oompah-pah*
Drucker, Malka. *A Jewish holiday ABC*
Eisenberg, Ann. *I can celebrate*
Emerman, Ellen. *Is it Shabbos yet?*
Fisher, Aileen Lucia. *Arbor day*
    Skip around the year
Fishman, Cathy Goldberg. *On Shabbat*
Forrester, Victoria. *Oddward*
Freschet, Gina. *Naty's parade*
Gellman, Ellie. *Shai's Shabbat walk*
Gold-Vukson, Marji E. *Grandpa and me on Tu B'Shevat*
Groner, Judyth Saypol. *Where is the Afikomen?*
Hest, Amy. *Gabby growing up*
Hopkins, Lee Bennett. *Ring out, wild bells*
Hubbell, Patricia. *Rabbit moon*
Jackson, Ellen B. *April*
    August
    The autumn equinox
    December
    February
    January
    July
    June
    March
    May
    November
    October
    September
    The spring equinox
    The summer solstice
    The winter solstice
Kimmelman, Leslie. *Dance, sing, remember*
Kress, Camille. *Tot Shabbat*
Kroll, Virginia L. *A carp for Kimiko*
Kumin, Maxine W. *Follow the fall*
Landau, Elaine. *Mardi Gras*
Livingston, Myra Cohn. *Celebrations*
McGee, Marni. *The colt and the king*
Mason, Lura. *A book of boxes*
Menter, Ian. *Carnival*
Meyer, Brigit. *Little Easter surprise*
Meyer, Elizabeth C. *The blue china pitcher*
Mora, Pat. *The bakery lady = La señora de la panadería*
Morris, Ann. *Light the candle! Bang the drum!*
Most, Bernard. *Happy holidaysaurus!*
Murphy, Stuart J. *Earth Day – hooray!*
Noll, Sally. *Surprise!*
Pandya, Meenal. *Here comes Diwali*
Pennington, Daniel. *Itse selu*
Podwal, Mark H. *A sweet year*
Rau, Dana Meachen. *I'll make you a card*
Reiss, Mike. *Santa claustrophobia*
Robbins, Sandra. *The firefly star*
Roop, Peter. *Holiday howlers*
    Let's celebrate!
Rosenfeld, Dina Herman. *Five alive*
Ross, Tony. *Hugo and the bureau of holidays*
Schaefer, Carole Lexa. *Under the midsummer sky*
Silverman, Maida. *My first book of Jewish holidays*
Stanley, Sanna. *Monkey Sunday*
Tunnell, Michael O. *Halloween pie*
Wikler, Madeline. *Let's build a Sukkah*
Winn, Chris. *Holiday*
Worth, Valerie. *At Christmastime*
Yolen, Jane. *The three bears holiday rhyme book*
Zolotow, Charlotte (Shapiro). *Over and over*

Holidays – April Fools' Day

Bateman, Teresa. *April foolishness*
Brown, Marc Tolon. *Arthur's April fool*
Christian, Mary Blount. *April fool*
Krahn, Fernando. *April fools*
Kroll, Steven. *It's April Fools' Day!*
Modell, Frank. *Look out, it's April Fools' Day*
Rockwell, Norman. *Norman Rockwell's counting book*
Ruelle, Karen Gray. *April fool*

Wegen, Ron. *Billy Gorilla*
Ziefert, Harriet. *April Fool*

Holidays – Canada Day

Murphy, Patricia J. *Canada Day*

Holidays – Chanukah *see* Holidays – Hanukkah

Holidays – Chinese New Year

Cheng, Hou-Tien. *The Chinese New Year*
Chin, Steven A. *Dragon Parade*
Chinn, Karen. *Sam and the lucky money*
Compestine, Ying Chang. *The runaway rice cake*
Demi. *Happy, happy Chinese New Year*
Flanagan, Alice K. *Chinese New Year*
Handforth, Thomas. *Mei Li*
Hoyt-Goldsmith, Diane. *Celebrating Chinese New Year*
Jango-Cohen, Judith. *Chinese New Year*
Low, William. *Chinatown*
Politi, Leo. *Moy Moy*
Schaefer, Lola M. *Chinese New Year*
Sing, Rachel. *Chinese New Year's dragon*
Vaughan, Marcia Kapok. *The dancing dragon*
Wallace, Ian. *Chin Chiang and the dragon's dance*
Waters, Kate. *Lion dancer*
Wong, Janet S. *This next New Year*
Young, Evelyn. *The tale of Tai*

Holidays – Christmas

Abisch, Roz. *'Twas in the moon of wintertime*
Ada, Alma Flor. *The Christmas tree = El Arbol de Navidad*
Adams, Adrienne. *The Christmas party*
Adams, Georgie. *The first Christmas*
Adshead, Gladys L. *Brownies – it's Christmas*
Ahlberg, Allan. *Cops and robbers*
Ahlberg, Janet. *The jolly Christmas postman*
Aichinger, Helga. *The shepherd*
Aldridge, Josephine Haskell. *A possible tree*
Aliki. *Christmas tree memories*
Allan, Nicholas. *Jesus' Christmas party*
Ambrus, Victor G. *Santa Claus takes off*
Ammon, Richard. *An Amish Christmas*
Amoss, Berthe. *What did you lose, Santa?*
Anaya, Rudolfo A. *Farolitos for Abuelo*
Andersen, H. C. (Hans Christian). *The fir tree*, ill. by Stephanie
   Britt
   The fir tree, ill. by Nancy Elkholm Burkert
   The fir tree, ill. by Diane Goode
   The fir tree, ill. by Rita Marshall
   The fir tree, ill. by Bernadette Watts
Anglund, Joan Walsh. *Christmas is a time of giving*
   Christmas is here
   Christmas is love
   The cowboy's Christmas
   Teddy bear tales
Aoki, Hisako. *Santa's favorite story*
Apperley, Dawn. *Santa Claus will come tonight*
Aralan, Haydé. *Milton's Christmas*
Ardizzone, Aingelda. *The night ride*
Armour, Richard Willard. *The year Santa went modern*
Arnold, Katya. *The adventures of Snowwoman*
Arnold, Mary. *The fussy angel*
Ashforth, Camilla. *Willow at Christmas*
Ashley, Jill. *Riddles about Christmas*
Auch, Mary Jane. *The nutquacker*
Autry, Gene. *Here comes Santa Claus*
Axelrod, Amy. *Pigs on the move*
Bach, Alice. *The day after Christmas*
Bach, Othello. *Hector McSnector and the mail-order Christmas witch*
Bailey, Mary Bryant. *Jeoffry's Christmas*
Baird, Anne. *The Christmas lamb*
Baker, Laura Nelson. *The friendly beasts*
   O children of the wind and pines
Balet, Jan B. *The gift*

Balian, Lorna. *Bah! Humbug?*
Barracca, Debra. *A taxi dog Christmas*
Barrett, John M. *The bear who slept through Christmas*
Barrett, Mary Brigid. *The man of the house at Huffington Row*
Barry, Robert E. *Mr. Willowby's Christmas tree*
Bartoletti, Susan Campbell. *The Christmas promise*
Bassett, Lisa. *Beany wakes up for Christmas*
   Koala Christmas
Baumgart, Klaus. *Laura's Christmas star*
Beck, Andrea. *Elliot's Christmas surprise*
Becker, Bonny. *The Christmas crocodile*
Behrens, June. *Christmas-magic wagon*
Belting, Natalia Maree. *Christmas folk*
Bemelmans, Ludwig. *Hansi*
   Madeline's Christmas
Berenstain, Stan. *The Berenstain bears' Christmas tree*
   The Berenstain bears meet Santa Bear
Berger, Barbara Helen. *The donkey's dream*
Bernardoni, Robert. *Christmas all over*
Berry, James. *Celebration song*
Bible. New Testament. Gospels. *Bethlehem*
   Christmas
   The Christmas story, ill. by James Bernardin
   The first Christmas
   The Nativity
   The story of Christmas, ill. by Jane Ray
Bishop, Adela. *The Christmas polar bear*
Bishop, Roma. *Christmas songs*
   Holiday cheer
   Santa pays a visit
Blaich, Ute. *The star*
Blough, Glenn O. *Christmas trees and how they grow*
Bodkin, Odds. *The Christmas cobwebs*
Bolognese, Don. *A new day*
Bond, Felicia. *Christmas in the chicken coop*
Bond, Michael. *Paddington Bear and the Christmas surprise*
Bourgeois, Paulette. *Franklin's Christmas gift*
Bowman, Pete. *The Christmas songbook*
Breathed, Berke (Berkeley). *A wish for wings that work*
Brébeuf, Jean de, Saint. *The Huron carol*
Brett, Jan. *Christmas trolls*
   Who's that knocking on Christmas eve?
   The wild Christmas reindeer
Briggs, Raymond. *Father Christmas*
   Father Christmas goes on holiday
Bright star shining
Bright, Robert. *Georgie's Christmas carol*
Bring a torch, Jeannette, Isabella
Briscoe, Jill. *The innkeeper's daughter*
Brock, Emma Lillian. *The birds' Christmas tree*
Bröger, Achim. *The Santa Clauses*
Brown, Abbie Farwell. *The Christmas angel*
Brown, Ken (Ken James). *Mucky Pup's Christmas*
Brown, Marc Tolon. *Arthur's Christmas*
   Arthur's perfect Christmas
Brown, Margaret Wise. *A child is born*
   Christmas in the barn
   Christmas in the barn
   The little fir tree
   On Christmas eve, ill. by Nancy Edwards Calder
   On Christmas eve, ill. by Beni Montresor
   A pussycat's Christmas, ill. by Anne Mortimer
   Pussycat's Christmas, ill. by Helen Stone
   The steamroller
Brown, Palmer. *Something for Christmas*
Brown, Ruth. *Holly, the true story of a cat*
Bruna, Dick. *Christmas*
   The Christmas book
Brunhoff, Jean de. *Babar and Father Christmas*
Bryson, Bernarda. *The twenty miracles of Saint Nicolas*
Buck, Nola. *Christmas in the manger*
   Santa's short suit shrunk and other Christmas tongue twisters
Budbill, David. *Christmas tree farm*
Bullard, Lisa. *Not enough beds!*
Bunting, Eve (Anne Evelyn). *Christmas cricket*
   The day before Christmas
   December

Going home
Night tree
We were there
Who was born this special day?
Burland, Brian. *St. Nicholas and the tub*
Burningham, John. *Harvey Slumfenburger's Christmas present*
Butler, M. Christina. *One snowy night*
Butterfield, Moira. *The Christmas story*
Butterworth, Nick. *Jingle bells*
The Nativity play
Byrd, Robert. *Saint Francis and the Christmas donkey*
Calhoun, Mary. *Henry the Christmas cat*
A shepherd's gift
Capucilli, Alyssa Satin. *Merry Christmas, from Biscuit*
Carabine, Sue. *A firefighter's night before Christmas*
Cardillo-Young, Donatella. *The yellow coat*
Carle, Eric. *Dream snow*
Carlson, Melody. *King of the stable*
What Nick and Holly found in grandpa's attic
Carlson, Nancy L. *Harriet and George's Christmas treat*
Carlson, Natalie Savage. *Surprise in the mountains*
Carlstrom, Nancy White. *I am Christmas*
Ten Christmas sheep
Where is Christmas, Jesse Bear?
Carrick, Carol. *Paul's Christmas birthday*
Carrier, Lark. *A Christmas promise*
Cartlidge, Michelle. *Mouse Christmas*
Teddy's Christmas
Catalano, Dominic. *Santa and the three bears*
Catalanotto, Peter. *Christmas always . . .*
Cazet, Denys. *Christmas moon*
Minnie and Moo: the night before Christmas
Chafetz, Henry. *The legend of Befana*
Chalmers, Mary. *A Christmas story*
Merry Christmas, Harry
Chambers, Catherine. *Christmas*
Chapman, Jean. *Moon-Eyes*
Chmielarz, Sharon. *Down at Angel's*
Chorao, Kay. *Baby's Christmas treasury*
The Christmas story
Christelow, Eileen. *Not until Christmas, Walter!*
Christian, Mary Blount. *Anna and the strangers*
Christmas reflections
A Christmas book
Christmas carols
Christmas in the stable, ill. by Beverly K. Duncan
Christmas presents
The Christmas story, paintings from the Metropolitan Museum of Art
Chute, Beatrice Joy. *Journey to Christmas*
Clark, Elizabeth. *Father Christmas and the donkey*
Clements, Andrew. *Bright Christmas*
Santa's secret helper
Clifton, Lucille. *Everett Anderson's Christmas coming*
Climo, Shirley. *The cobweb Christmas*
Coatsworth, Elizabeth. *The children come running*
Song of the camels
Cölle, Gisela. *The star tree*
Collington, Peter. *On Christmas eve*
A small miracle
Compton, Kenn. *Happy Christmas to all!*
Conrad, Pam. *The Tub People's Christmas*
Cooney, Barbara. *The little juggler*
The story of Christmas
Cooper, Susan. *Danny and the Kings*
Corey, Shana. *Milly and the Macy's Parade*
Crespi, Francesca. *Make a joyful noise*
Santa Claus is coming!
Silent night
Croll, Carolyn. *The little snowgirl*
Crossley-Holland, Kevin. *How many miles to Bethlehem?*
Cummings, E. E. (Edward Estlin). *Little tree*, ill. by Deborah Kogan Ray
Little tree, ill. by Mary C. Smith
Currey, Anna. *Truffle's Christmas*
Curry, Jane Louise. *The Christmas knight*
Cushman, Doug. *Mouse and Mole and the Christmas walk*

Cutlip, Kimbra L. *Firefighter's night before Christmas*
Cuyler, Margery. *Fat Santa*
Czernecki, Stefan. *Pancho's piñata*
Daffis-Felicelli, Christine. *The little star of Bethlehem*
Daily, Don. *The twelve days of Christmas cats*
Daly, Niki. *What's cooking, Jamela?*
Damjan, Mischa. *December's travels*
The little seahorse and the Christmas pearl
Darling, Kathy (Mary Kathleen). *The mystery in Santa's toyshop*
David, Lawrence. *Peter Claus and the naughty list*
Davidson, Amanda. *Teddy's first Christmas*
Day, Alexandra. *Carl's Christmas*
The Christmas we moved to the barn
DeBoer, Jesslyn. *Follow the star*
Getting ready for Christmas
Dedieu, Thierry. *The little Christmas soldier*
De Groat, Diane. *Jingle bells, homework smells*
Lola the elf
Delacre, Lulu. *Las Navidades*
DeLage, Ida. *ABC Christmas*
ABC Santa Claus
Delamare, David. *The Christmas secret*
Delton, Judy. *No time for Christmas*
The perfect Christmas gift
Demi. *Demi's Christmas surprise*
The legend of Saint Nicholas
Denim, Sue. *The Dumb Bunnies' Easter*
Denton, Kady MacDonald. *Christmas boot*
De Paola, Tomie (Thomas Anthony). *Baby's first Christmas*
The cat on the Dovrefell
The Christmas pageant
The clown of God
An early American Christmas
The family Christmas tree book
Get dressed, Santa!
Jingle, the Christmas clown
Merry Christmas, Strega Nona
The night of Las Posadas
The story of the three wise kings
DeVajay, Szabolcs. *The animals' gift*
Devlin, Wende. *Cranberry Christmas*
Dewan, Ted. *Crispin, the pig who had it all*
Din dan don, it's Christmas
Dixon, Ann. *Waiting for Noël*
Domanska, Janina. *I saw a ship a-sailing*
Donaldson, Lois. *Karl's wooden horse*
Dowley, Tim. *The shepherds' tale*
The wise men's tale
Drescher, Henrik. *Looking for Santa Claus*
Dubanevich, Arlene. *Pigs at Christmas*
Dubowski, Cathy East. *The Christmas Santa almost missed*
Dunrea, Olivier. *Bear Noel*
Duquennoy, Jacques. *North Pole, South Pole*
Duvoisin, Roger Antoine. *The Christmas whale*
One thousand Christmas beards
Petunia's Christmas
Edens, Cooper. *Nicholi*
Ehrlich, Amy. *Bunnies at Christmastime*
Enderle, Judith (Ann) Ross. *Six snowy sheep*
Engelbreit, Mary. *Queen of Christmas*
Ephron, Delia. *Santa and Alex*
Erickson, Russell E. *Warton's Christmas eve adventure*
Ets, Marie Hall. *Nine days to Christmas*
Evans, Richard Paul. *The Christmas candle*
The light of Christmas
Facklam, Margery. *Only a star*
Factor, Jane. *Summer*
Falwell, Cathryn. *Christmas for 10*
Farber, Norma. *All those mothers at the manger*
How the hibernators came to Bethlehem
When it snowed that night
Fatio, Louise. *Anna, the horse*
Faulkner, Keith. *Charlie Chimp's Christmas*
Fearnley, Jan. *Little Robin's Christmas*
Fenner, Carol. *Christmas tree on the mountain*
Fine, Howard. *A piggie Christmas*
Flanagan, Alice K. *Christmas*

Fleetwood, Jenni. *While shepherds watched*
Foote, Dan. *The cobbler, the princess, and the newborn King*
Foreman, Michael. *Cat in the manger*
  The little reindeer
  The perfect present
Forrester, Victoria. *Poor Gabriella*
Forward, Toby. *Ben's Christmas carol*
Fox, Mem. *With love, at Christmas*
  Wombat divine
Fraser, James Howard. *Los Posadas*
Frazee, Marla. *Santa Claus, the world's number one toy expert*
Freeman, Jean Todd. *Cynthia and the unicorn*
French, Vivian. *Christmas kitten*
  A Christmas star called Hannah
The friendly beasts
The friendly beasts and a partridge in a pear tree, ill. by Virginia Pearsons
Funakoshi, Canna. *One Christmas*
Gackenbach, Dick. *Claude the dog*
Gaffington, Urslan Judith. *Silver berries and Christmas magic*
Gambill, Henrietta D. *Little Christmas animals*
Gammell, Stephen. *Wake up, bear . . . It's Christmas!*
Ganeri, Anita. *The story of Christmas*
Gannett, Ruth Stiles. *Katie and the sad noise*
Gantos, Jack (John, Jr.). *Rotten Ralph's rotten Christmas*
Gantschev, Ivan. *The Christmas teddy bear*
  The Christmas train
Gardam, Catharine. *The animals' Christmas*
Garland, Michael. *Christmas City*
  Christmas magic
  The mouse before Christmas
Gay, Michel. *The Christmas wolf*
George, William T. *Christmas at Long Pond*
Geras, Adèle. *The nutcracker*
Geraty, Virginia Mixson. *Gullah night before Christmas*
Ghigna, Charles. *Christmas is coming!*
Gikow, Louise. *Baby Kermit's Christmas*
  Sprocket's Christmas tale
Ginolfi, Arthur. *The tiny star*
Gleeson, Brian. *The Savior is born*
Gliori, Debi. *What can I give him?*
Godwin, Laura. *Happy Christmas, Honey*
Goffin, Josse. *The Christmas story*
  Silent Christmas
Gomi, Taro. *Santa through the window*
Goodall, John S. *An Edwardian Christmas*
Gordon, Sharon. *Christmas surprise*
Grahame, Kenneth. *A wind in the willows Christmas*
  The wind in the willows: home sweet home
Granfield, Linda. *Silent night*
Greene, Rhonda Gowler. *The stable where Jesus was born*
Greenfield, Monica. *Waiting for Christmas*
Gutman, Anne. *Gaspard and Lisa's Christmas surprise*
Haarhoff, Dorian. *Desert December*
Hague, Michael. *Deck the halls*
  The nutcracker
  The perfect present
Hale, Linda. *The glorious Christmas soup party*
Hall, Donald. *Lucy's Christmas*
Harness, Cheryl. *Papa's Christmas gift*
Hartman, Bob. *The birthday of a king*
  Granny Mae's Christmas play
  A night the stars danced for joy
Harvey, Brett. *My prairie Christmas*
Hautzig, Deborah. *The Christmas story*
Hawxhurst, Joan C. *Bubbe and Gram, my two grandmothers*
Hayes, Geoffrey. *Christmas in Puttyville*
Hayes, Sarah. *Away in a manger*
  A bad start for Santa
  Happy Christmas, Gemma
Hayles, Marsha. *The feathered crown*
Hayward, Linda. *The runaway Christmas toy*
Haywood, Carolyn. *A Christmas fantasy*
  How the reindeer saved Santa
  Santa Claus forever!
Hazen, Barbara Shook. *Santa clues*
Heath, Amy. *Sofie's role*

Heck, Elisabeth. *The black sheep*
Helldorfer, M. C. (Mary Claire). *Daniel's gift*
  Night of the white stag
Heller, Nicholas. *The monster in the cave*
Hennessy, B. G. (Barbara G.). *Corduroy's Christmas*
  The first night
Henry, O. *The gift of the Magi*
Herriot, James. *Christmas Day kitten*
Hickman, Martha Whitmore. *A baby born in Bethlehem*
High, Linda Oatman. *A Christmas Star*
  The last chimney of Christmas eve
Hill, Eric. *Spot's first Christmas*
  Spot's magical Christmas
Hill, Susan. *Can it be true?*
  King of kings
Hillert, Margaret. *Merry Christmas, dear dragon*
Hillman, Priscilla. *A Merry-Mouse Christmas A B C*
Hines, Anna Grossnickle. *The secret keeper*
Hines, Gary. *A Christmas tree in the White House*
Hoban, Lillian. *Arthur's Christmas cookies*
  It's really Christmas
Hoban, Russell. *Emmet Otter's jug-band Christmas*
  The mole family's Christmas
Hobbie, Holly. *Toot and Puddle, I'll be home for Christmas*
Hodges, Margaret. *Silent night*
Hoff, Syd. *Merry Christmas, Henrietta!*
  Santa's moose
  Where's Prancer?
Hoffman, Mary. *An angel just like me*
  Three wise women
Hoffmann, E. T. A. *The nutcracker*, ill. by Francesca Crespi
  The nutcracker, ill. by Renée Graef
  The nutcracker, ill. by Rachel Isadora
  The nutcracker, ill. by Joanna Isles
  The nutcracker, ill. by Maurice Sendak
  The nutcracker, ill. by Lisbeth Zwerger
  The nutcracker ballet, ill. by Carolyn Ewing
  The nutcracker ballet, ill. by Vladimir Vasilévich Vagin
Hoffmann, Felix. *The story of Christmas*
Hogrogian, Nonny. *The first Christmas*
Hol, Coby. *Tippy Bear's Christmas*
Holabird, Katharine. *Angelina's Christmas*
  Christmas with Angelina
Holder, Mig. *The fourth wise man*
Hollyn, Lynn. *Lynn Hollyn's Christmas toyland*
Holm, Mayling Mack. *A forest Christmas*
Holmes, Efner Tudor. *The Christmas cat*
  Deer in the hollow
Holmquist, Delano. *SantaSaurus*
Hooks, William H. *The legend of the Christmas rose*
  The mighty Santa Fe
Hooper, Maureen Brett. *Silent night*
Hooper, Meredith. *Tom's rabbit*
Horn, Sandra Ann. *Babushka*
Houston, Gloria. *The year of the perfect Christmas tree*
Howard, Elizabeth Fitzgerald. *Chita's Christmas tree*
Howard, Ellen. *The log cabin Christmas*
Huffaker, Alice. *That first Christmas day*
Hughes, Langston. *Carol of the brown king*
Hughes, Shirley. *Angel Mae*
  Lucy and Tom's Christmas
Hunter, Sally. *Humphrey's Christmas*
Hurd, Edith Thacher. *Christmas eve*
Hurd, Thacher. *Santa Mouse and the ratdeer*
Hutchins, Pat. *King Henry's palace*
  The silver Christmas tree
Ichikawa, Satomi. *What the little fir tree wore to the Christmas party*
Inkpen, Deborah. *Harriet and the little fat fairy*
Inkpen, Mick. *Kipper's Christmas eve*
Ipcar, Dahlov (Zorach). *My wonderful Christmas tree*
It feels like Christmas!. *It feels like Christmas!*
Ives, Penny. *Mrs. Santa Claus*
  On Christmas eve
James, J. Alison. *The bears' Christmas surprise*
Janice. *Little Bear's Christmas*
Janovitz, Marilyn. *What could be keeping Santa?*
Jaques, Faith. *Tilly's rescue*

Jaynes, Ruth M. *Melinda's Christmas stocking*
Jiménez, Francisco. *The Christmas gift = El regalo de Navidad*
Johnson, Crockett. *Harold at the North Pole*
Johnson, Grace. *The candle in the window*
Johnson, Russell. *Trouble at Christmas*
Johnston, Tony. *A Kenya Christmas*
    Lorenzo the naughty parrot
    Mole and Troll trim the tree
Jones, Jessie Mae Orton. *A little child*
Joosse, Barbara M. *A houseful of Christmas*
Jordan, Sandra. *Christmas tree farm*
Joseph, Daniel M. *All dressed up and nowhere to go*
Joseph, Lynn. *An island Christmas*
Joslin, Sesyle. *Baby elephant and the secret wishes*
Jüchen, Aurel von. *The Holy Night*
Kahl, Virginia. *Plum pudding for Christmas*
Kajpust, Melissa. *A dozen silk diapers*
Kasparavicius, Kestutis. *The bear family's world tour Christmas*
Kastner, Jill. *Merry Christmas, Princess Dinosaur*
Keats, Ezra Jack. *The little drummer boy*
Keller, Holly. *A bear for Christmas*
    Merry Christmas, Geraldine
Kellogg, Steven (Stephen). *The Christmas witch*
    Santa Claus is comin' to town
Kennedy, Cindy. *The star of Christmas*
Kennedy, Jimmy. *The teddy bears' Christmas*
Kennedy, X. J. *The beasts of Bethlehem*
Kent, Jack. *The Christmas piñata*
Kerr, Judith. *Mog's Christmas*
Kessler, Leonard P. *That's not Santa!*
Ketcham, Sallie. *The Christmas bird*
Kimmel, Elizabeth Cody. *My penguin Osbert*
Kimpton, Diana. *The bear Santa Claus forgot*
King, B. A. *The very best Christmas tree*
Kinsey-Warnock, Natalie. *A Christmas like Helen's*
Kneen, Maggie. *The Christmas surprise*
Knight, Hilary. *Angels and berries and candy canes*
    A firefly in a fir tree
Knotts, Howard. *The lost Christmas*
Knowlton, Laurie Lazzaro. *The Nativity*
Koralek, Jenny. *The cobweb curtain*
Koscielniak, Bruce. *Hector and Prudence – all aboard!*
Kovalski, Maryann. *Jingle bells*
Krahn, Fernando. *The biggest Christmas tree on earth*
Kraus, Robert. *The Christmas cookie sprinkle snitcher*
    See the Christmas lights
    The tree that stayed up until next Christmas
    Wise Old Owl's Christmas adventure
Krensky, Stephen. *How Santa got his job*
    How Santa lost his job
Kroll, Steven. *Santa's crash-bang Christmas*
Kroll, Virginia L. *The Christmas cow*
Krupinski, Loretta. *Christmas in the city*
Kunhardt, Edith. *Danny's Christmas star*
Kunnas, Mauri. *Santa Claus and his elves*
    Twelve gifts for Santa Claus
Kvasnosky, Laura McGee. *Zelda and Ivy one Christmas*
Lachner, Dorothea. *The gift from Saint Nicholas*
Lagerlöf, Selma. *The legend of the Christmas rose*
Landa, Norbert. *Little Bear's Christmas*
Langley, Karen. *Shine*
Langstaff, John M. *On Christmas day in the morning*
LaRochelle, David. *A Christmas guest*
Lathrop, Dorothy Pulis. *An angel in the woods*
Laurence, Margaret. *The Christmas birthday story*
Lee, Quinlan B. *Crazy Christmas chaos*
Lee, Stan. *Stan Lee's superhero Christmas*
Leedy, Loreen. *A dragon Christmas*
Leighton, Maxinne Rhea. *An Ellis Island Christmas*
Leonard, Marcia. *The best snowman ever*
LeSourd, Nancy. *Christy, Christmastime at Cutter Gap*
Lewandowski, Frrich. *It's Christmas again*
Lewis, J. Patrick. *The Christmas of the reddle moon*
    Long was the winter road they traveled
Lin, Grace. *Okie-dokie, Artichokie*
Linch, Elizabeth Johanna. *Samson*
Lindgren, Astrid. *A calf for Christmas*

    Christmas in noisy village
    Christmas in the stable
    Lotta's Christmas surprise
    Of course Polly can do almost everything
    Pippi Longstocking's after-Christmas party
Lines, Kathleen. *Once in royal David's city*
Lipkind, William. *The Christmas bunny*
Little, Jean. *Pippin the Christmas pig*
London, Jonathan. *Froggy's first Christmas*
Long, Sylvia. *Deck the hall*
Low, Joseph. *The Christmas grump*
Lubin, Leonard B. *Christmas gift-bringers*
Lucado, Max. *Alabaster's song*
Lussert, Anneliese. *The Christmas visitor*
McAllister, Angela. *The Christmas wish*
Maccarone, Grace. *A child was born*
McCaughrean, Geraldine. *How the reindeer got their antlers*
    The story of the Nativity
McCully, Emily Arnold. *The Christmas gift*
McCutcheon, Marc. *Grandfather's Christmas camp*
McDermott, Gerald. *The light of the world*
MacDonald, Alan. *The not-so-wise man*
McGinley, Phyllis. *How Mrs. Santa Claus saved Christmas*
McGinley-Nally, Sharon. *The friendly beasts*
McKelvey, Douglas Kaine. *A child's Christmas at St. Nicholas Circle*
McKissack, Patricia C. *Messy Bessey's holidays*
McPhail, David M. *Henry Bear's Christmas*
    Mistletoe
    Santa's book of names
McQuade, Jacqueline. *Christmas with Teddy Bear*
Mahy, Margaret. *The Christmas tree tangle*
Maier, Paul L. *The very first Christmas*
Maloney, Peter (1955–). *Redbird at Rockefeller Center*
Mamchur, Carolyn Marie. *The popcorn tree*
Manushur, Fran. *My Christmas safari*
    The perfect Christmas picture
Mariana. *The journey of Bangwell Putt*
Marshall, James. *Merry Christmas, space case*
    Miss Dog's Christmas
Martin, Judith. *The tree angel*
Marzollo, Jean. *Christmas cats*
    I see a star
    I spy little Christmas
Masurel, Claire. *Christmas is coming*
Mathers, Petra. *Herbie's secret Santa*
Matthews, Wendy. *The gift of a traveler*
Mattingley, Christobel. *The angel with a mouth-organ*
Maxfield, Christine. *Christmas in Water Village*
May, Robert Lewis. *Rudolph the red-nosed reindeer*, ill. by Diana Magnuson
    Rudolph the red-nosed reindeer, ill. by David Wenzel
Mayper, Monica. *Come and see*
McMullan, Kate (Hall). *Ho ho ho, ha ha ha*
Medearis, Angela Shelf. *Poppa's itchy Christmas*
Medina, Tony. *Christmas makes me think*
Merriam, Eve. *The Christmas box*
Metaxas, Eric. *The boy and the whale*
    Uncle Mugsy and the terrible twins of Christmas
Miles, Calvin. *Calvin's Christmas wish*
Miller, Edna. *Mousekin's Christmas eve*
Moeri, Louise. *Star Mother's youngest child*
Moffatt, Judith. *Christmas lights*
Mogensen, Jan. *Teddy's Christmas gift*
Mohr, Joseph. *Silent night*
Monsell, Helen Albee. *Paddy's Christmas*
Moore, Clement Clarke. *The night before Christmas*, ill. by Jan Brett
    The night before Christmas, ill. by Tomie de Paola
    The night before Christmas, comp. by Cooper Edens and Harold Darling; ill. by various nineteenth- and twentieth-century artists
    The night before Christmas, ill. by Mary Engelbreit
    The night before Christmas, ill. by Michael Foreman
    The night before Christmas, ill. by Gyo Fujikawa
    The night before Christmas, ill. by Scott Gustafson
    The night before Christmas, ill. by Cheryl Harness
    The night before Christmas, ill. by Raquel Jaramillo
    The night before Christmas, ill. by Loretta Krupinski

The night before Christmas, ill. by Anita Lobel
The night before Christmas, ill. by James Marshall
The night before Christmas, ill. by Ted Rand
The night before Christmas, ill. by Jacqueline Rogers
The night before Christmas, ill. by Ruth Sanderson
The night before Christmas, ill. by Robert Sebuda
The night before Christmas, ill. by Robin Spowart
The night before Christmas, ill. by Gustaf Tenggren
The night before Christmas, ill. by Tasha Tudor
The night before Christmas, ill. by Wendy Watson
The night before Christmas, ill. by Bruce Whatley
The night before Christmas, ill. by Jody Wheeler
The night before Christmas in signed English
The teddy bears' night before Christmas
'Twas the night before Christmas, ill. by Matt Tavares
A visit from St. Nicholas
Moore, Karen Ann. *The baby king*
Moorman, Margaret. *Light the lights!*
Mora, Jo (Joseph Jacinto). *Budgee Budgee Cottontail*
Mora, Pat. *The gift of the poinsettia = El regalo de la flor de nochebuena*
Moret, Brigitte Frey. *The bear's Christmas*
Morgan-Vanroyen, Mary. *The Pudgy Merry Christmas book*
Morrissey, Dean. *The Christmas ship*
Moses, Will. *Silent night*
Moss, Jenny Jackson. *Cajun night after Christmas*
Munro, Roxie. *Christmastime in New York City*
Murdocca, Sal (Salvatore). *Christmas bear*
My first Christmas [board book]
Nayer, Judy. *Little bear's first Christmas*
Naylor, Phyllis Reynolds. *Keeping a Christmas secret*
    Old Sadie and the Christmas bear
Neale, J. M. (John Mason). *Good King Wenceslas*
Nerlove, Miriam. *Christmas*
Neugebauer, Charise. *Santa's gift*
Neville, Mary. *The Christmas tree ride*
Newland, Mary Reed. *Good King Wenceslas*
Nikola-Lisa, W. *Hallelujah!*
    To hear the angels sing
Niland, Kilmeny. *A bellbird in a flame tree*
Nixon, Joan Lowery. *That's the spirit, Claude*
Noble, Trinka Hakes. *Apple tree Christmas*
Norris, Leslie. *Albert and the angels*
Novak, Matt. *The last Christmas present*
Numeroff, Laura Joffe. *If you take a mouse to the movies*
Nussbaumer, Mares. *Away in a manger*
O Christmas tree
Oakley, Graham. *The church mice at Christmas*
O'Brien, John (1953–). *Mother Hubbard's Christmas*
O'Connor, Francine M. *The ABC's of Christmas*
Okrend, Elise. *Blintzes for Blitzen*
Older, Effin. *My two grandmothers*
Olson, Arielle North. *Hurry home, Grandma!*
Oppenheim, Joanne. *The Christmas witch*
Ostheeren, Ingrid. *I'm the real Santa Claus!*
Paraskevas, Betty. *A very Kroll Christmas*
Parker, Nancy Winslow. *The Christmas camel*
Partch, Virgil Franklin. *The Christmas cookie sprinkle snitcher*
Paxton, Tom. *The story of Santa Claus*
Pearson, Susan. *Karin's Christmas walk*
Peet, Bill (William Bartlett). *Countdown to Christmas*
Petach, Heidi. *Wee three pigs*
Peterson, Hans. *Erik and the Christmas horse*
Peterson, Melissa. *Hanna's Christmas*
Pfister, Marcus. *The Christmas star*
    Wake up, Santa Claus!
Phifer, Martha Nelson. *The colors of Christmas*
Pickthall, Marjorie L. C. (Marjorie Lowry Christie). *The worker in sandalwood*
Pierpont, James. *Jingle bells*
Pilkey, Dav. *Dragon's merry Christmas*
Pingry, Patricia. *Joseph's story*
Pinkney, Andrea Davis. *Mim's Christmas jam*
Pinkwater, Daniel Manus. *Wolf Christmas*
Pittman, Helena Clare. *The angel tree*
Plume, Ilse. *The story of Befana*
Polacco, Patricia. *The trees of the dancing goats*
    Welcome Comfort

Politi, Leo. *The nicest gift*
    Pedro, the angel of Olvera Street
    Rosa
Powell, Consie. *Old dog Cora and the Christmas tree*
Primavera, Elise. *Auntie Claus*
    Auntie Claus and the key to Christmas
Prøysen, Alf. *Christmas eve at Santa's*
Pryor, Bonnie. *Merry Christmas, Amanda and April*
Pulver, Robin. *Christmas for a kitten*
Quattlebaum, Mary. *The shine man*
Quattrocki, Carolyn. *The little drummer boy*
Quindlen, Anna. *The tree that came to stay*
Rabe, Berniece. *The first Christmas candy cane*
Rader, Laura. *Santa's new suit*
Rahaman, Vashanti. *O Christmas tree*
Ransom, Candice F. *The Christmas dolls*
Reiser, Lynn. *Christmas counting*
Reiss, Mike. *How Murray saved Christmas*
    Santa claustrophobia
Richards, Kitty. *Merry Christmas, Rugrats!*
Richardson, Jean. *Stephen's feast*
Richardson, John. *Where's Jack?*
Riggio, Anita. *A moon in my teacup*
Robbins, Ruth. *Baboushka and the three kings*
Roberts, Bethany. *Christmas mice*
    Waiting-for-Christmas stories
Rockwell, Anne F. *Bafana*
Rodanas, Kristina. *The little drummer boy*
Root, Phyllis. *All for the newborn baby*
Rosales, Melodye Benson. *'Twas the night b'fore Christmas*
Rosen, Michael J. (1954–). *Elijah's angel*
Rosenberg, Liz. *On Christmas eve*
Ross, Michael Elsohn. *Mexican Christmas*
Roth, Susan L. *Another Christmas*
Rowand, Phyllis. *Every day in the year*
Ruelle, Karen Gray. *The crunchy, munchy Christmas tree*
Rylant, Cynthia. *Christmas in the country*
    Little Whistle's Christmas
    Mr. Putter and Tabby bake the cake
    Silver packages
Sabuda, Robert James. *The Christmas alphabet*
Sahagun, Bernardino de. *Spirit child*
Santa Claus is coming to town
Santa's little library of Christmas stories
Sawyer, Ruth. *The Christmas Anna angel*
    The remarkable Christmas of the cobbler's sons
Say, Allen. *Tree of cranes*
Scarry, Richard. *Richard Scarry's best Christmas book ever!*
Scheidl, Gerda Marie. *Can we help you, Saint Nicholas?*
Schenk, Esther M. *Christmas time*
Schrecker, Judie. *Santa's new reindeer*
Schumacher, Claire. *Nutty's Christmas*
Schweninger, Ann. *Christmas secrets*
Seignobosc, Françoise. *Noël for Jeanne-Marie*
Selden, George. *The mice, the monks and the Christmas tree*
Seuss, Dr. *How the Grinch stole Christmas*
Shannon, David. *The amazing Christmas extravaganza*
Sharmat, Marjorie Weinman. *I'm Santa Claus and I'm famous*
Sierra, Judy. *'Twas the fright before Christmas*
Slate, Joseph. *Little Porcupine's Christmas*
Sleigh bells and snowflakes
Sloat, Teri. *Hark! The aardvark angels sing*
    Pieces of Christmas
A small treasury of Christmas poems and prayers
Smalls-Hector, Irene. *Irene Jennie and the Christmas masquerade*
Smath, Jerry. *The animals' Christmas carol*
Smith, Kathryn. *Little Donkey's Christmas story*
    Little Lamb's Christmas story
Snell, Gordon. *'Twas the day after Christmas*
    Twelve days, a Christmas countdown
Solheim, James. *Santa's secrets revealed*
Soto, Gary. *Too many tamales*
Spang, Günter. *The ox and the Donkey*
Speare, Jean. *A candle for Christmas*
Speirs, John. *The little boy's Christmas gift*
Spier, Peter. *Peter Spier's Christmas!*
Spinelli, Eileen. *Coming through the blizzard*

Spohn, Kate. *Turtle and Snake and the Christmas tree*
Stainton, Sue. *Santa's snow cat*
Steiner, Charlotte. *The climbing book*
Stephenson, Dorothy. *The night it rained toys*
Stern, Elsie-Jean. *Wee Robin's Christmas song*
Steven, Kenneth C. *The bearer of gifts*
Stevens, Jan Romero. *Twelve lizards leaping*
Stevenson, James. *Christmas at Mud Flat*
    The worst person's Christmas
Stevenson, Suçie. *Christmas eve*
Stock, Catherine. *Christmas time*
    Sampson the Christmas cat
Stone, Phoebe. *What night do the angels wander?*
Strand, Keith. *Grandfather's Christmas tree*
Sykes, Julie. *Careful, Santa*
    Hurry, Santa!
Tafuri, Nancy. *Counting to Christmas*
    The donkey's Christmas song
Tangvald, Christine Harder. *The best thing about Christmas*
    Hey, Mr. Angel!
Taylor, Jane. *Twinkle, twinkle little star*, ill. by Julia Noonan
Tazewell, Charles. *The littlest angel*, ill. by Deborah Lanino
    The littlest angel, ill. by Paul Micich
    The littlest angel, ill. by Rebecca Thornburgh
Teasdale, Sara. *Christmas carol*
Thayer, Jane. *The puppy who wanted a boy*, ill. by Seymour Fleishman
    The puppy who wanted a boy, ill. by Lisa McCue
Thompson, Kay. *Kay Thompson's Eloise at Christmastime*
Thompson, Lauren. *Mouse's first Christmas*
    Mouse's first Christmas [board book]
Thury, Frederick. *The last straw*
Timmermans, Felix. *A gift from Saint Nicholas*
Tippett, James Sterling. *Counting the days*
Tolan, Stephanie S. *Bartholomew's blessing*
Tolkien, J. R. R. (John Ronald Reuel). *The Father Christmas letters*
Tompert, Ann. *A carol for Christmas*
    The silver whistle
Tornqvist, Rita. *The Christmas carp*
Torres, Melissa A. *The great Christmas tree celebration*
Trent, Robbie. *The first Christmas*
Trimble, Marcia. *Moonbeams for Santa*
Trivas, Irene. *Emma's Christmas*
Trosclair. *Cajun night before Christmas*
Tryon, Leslie. *Albert's Christmas*
Tudor, Tasha. *The doll's Christmas*
    Snow before Christmas
Türk, Hanne. *Merry Christmas Max*
Turner, Ann Warren. *The Christmas house*
Turner, Sandy. *Silent night*
Tutt, Kay Cunningham. *And now we call him Santa Claus*
The twelve days of Christmas. English folk song. *Brian Wildsmith's The twelve days of Christmas*
    Jack Kent's twelve days of Christmas
    The twelve days of Christmas, ill. by Jan Brett
    The twelve days of Christmas, ill. by Rachel Griffin
    The twelve days of Christmas, ill. by Ilonka Karasz
    The twelve days of Christmas, ill. by Ilse Plume
    The twelve days of Christmas, ill. by Erika Schneider
    The twelve days of Christmas, ill. by Vladimir Vagin
    The twelve days of Christmas, ill. by Sophie Windham
    The twelve days of Christmas [board book], ill. by Jan Brett
Tyler, Linda Wagner. *After Christmas tree*
Ungerer, Tomi. *Christmas eve at the Mellops*
Uttley, Alison. *The Christmas box*
Vainio, Pirkko. *The Christmas angel*
Valgardson, W. D. *Winter rescue*
Van Allsburg, Chris. *The polar express*
Vesey, A. *Merry Christmas, Thomas!*
Vidal, Beatriz A. *Federico and the Magi's gift*
Vincent, Gabrielle. *Merry Christmas, Ernest and Celestine*
Waber, Bernard. *Lyle at Christmas*
Waddell, Martin. *Mimi's Christmas*
Wahl, Jan. *The Muffletumps' Christmas party*
Walburg, Lori. *The legend of the candy cane*
Waldron, Jan L. *Angel Pig and the hidden Christmas*
Walker, Joni. *Tell me the Christmas story*

Wallace, Ivy. *Pookie believes in Santa Claus*
Wallner, Alexandra. *An Alcott family Christmas*
Wangerin, Walter. *Angels and all children*
    Probity Jones and the Fear Not Angel
Waterhouse, Stephen A. *Get busy this Christmas*
Watson, Clyde. *How Brown Mouse kept Christmas*
Watson, Wendy. *The bunnies' Christmas eve*
    Holly's Christmas eve
Watts, Bernadette. *The Christmas bird*
    Harvey Hare's Christmas
Wax, Wendy. *A very mice Christmas*
We wish you a merry Christmas
Weil, Lisl. *Santa Claus around the world*
Weinberg, Larry (Lawrence). *The Forgetful Bears help Santa*
Weller, Frances Ward. *The angel of Mill Street*
Wells, Joel. *The manger mouse*
Wells, Rosemary. *McDuff's new friend*
    Max's Christmas
    Morris's disappearing bag
Weninger, Brigitte. *A letter to Santa Claus*
    Lumina
    Merry Christmas, Davy!
Wenning, Elisabeth. *The Christmas mouse*
Westman, Barbara. *The day before Christmas*
What a morning!
Wheeler, Cindy. *Marmalade's Christmas present*
White, Ellen Emerson. *Santa paws*
Wick, Walter. *Can you see what I see? The night before Christmas*
    I spy Christmas
Wijngaard, Juan. *The Nativity*
Wild, Margaret. *Thank you, Santa*
Wilder, Laura Ingalls. *Santa comes to little house*
Wildsmith, Brian. *A Christmas story*
Wilhelm, Hans. *Schnitzel's first Christmas*
Wilkon, Józef. *Lullaby for a newborn king*
Willey, Margaret. *Clever Beatrice Christmas*
Williams, Marcia. *The first Christmas*
Williams, Sam. *Angel's Christmas cookies*
    Snowy magic
Wilson, Karma. *Bear stays up for Christmas*
Wilson, Robina Beckles. *Merry Christmas!*
Wing, Natasha. *The night before the night before Christmas*
Winter, Jeanette. *The Christmas tree ship*
Winthrop, Elizabeth. *Bear's Christmas surprise*
    A child is born
Wiseman, Bernard. *Christmas with Morris and Boris*
Wojciechowski, Susan. *The Christmas miracle of Jonathan Toomey*
Wolff, Patricia Rae. *A new, improved Santa*
Wood, Audrey. *The Christmas adventure of Space Elf Sam*
    A cowboy Christmas
Wood, Don. *Merry Christmas, big hungry bear*
Wooding, Sharon L. *Arthur's Christmas wish*
Woolaver, Lance. *Christmas with the rural mail*
Worth, Valerie. *At Christmastime*
Wright, Cliff. *Santa's ark*
Wright, Dare. *A gift from the lonely doll*
Wright, Sue (Sue M.). *The Christmas path*
Yee, Wong Herbert. *A small Christmas*
Yeomans, Thomas. *For every child a star*
Yin. *Dear Santa, please come to the 19th floor*
Yorinks, Arthur. *Christmas in July*
Zagwÿn, Deborah Turney. *The winter gift*
Zakhoder, Boris Vladimirovich. *How a piglet crashed the Christmas party*
Ziefert, Harriet. *Home for Navidad*
    Nicky's Christmas surprise
    Presents for Santa
Zimelman, Nathan. *The star of Melvin*
Zolotow, Charlotte (Shapiro). *The beautiful Christmas tree*

Holidays – Cinco de Mayo

Behrens, June. *Fiesta!*
Flanagan, Alice K. *Cinco de Mayo*
Schaefer, Lola M. *Cinco de Mayo*
Wade, Mary Dodson. *Cinco de Mayo*

Holidays – Columbus Day

Showers, Paul. *Columbus Day*

Holidays – Day of the Dead

Ancona, George. *Pablo remembers*
Czernecki, Stefan. *The hummingbird's gift*
Freschet, Gina. *Beto and the bone dance*
Johnston, Tony. *Day of the Dead*
Joosse, Barbara M. *Ghost wings*
Keep, Linda Lowery. *Day of the Dead*
Krull, Kathleen. *Maria Molina and the Days of the Dead*
Luenn, Nancy. *A gift for Abuelita*

Holidays – Divali

Gardeski, Christina Mia. *Divali*
Gilmore, Rachna. *Lights for Gita*
Verma, Jatinder Nath. *The story of Divaali*

Holidays – Earth Day

Roop, Connie. *Let's celebrate Earth Day*

Holidays – Easter

Adams, Adrienne. *The Easter egg artists*
Armour, Richard Willard. *The adventures of Egbert the Easter egg*
Auch, Mary Jane. *The Easter egg farm*
Balian, Lorna. *Humbug rabbit*
Barrett, John M. *The Easter bear*
Berenstain, Stan. *The Berenstain bears and the real Easter eggs*
Berlin, Irving. *Easter parade*
Bible. New Testament. Gospels. *Easter*, ill. by Fiona French
Bishop, Adela. *The Easter wolf*
Bishop, Roma. *Easter counting*
    Easter egg hunt
Brown, Margaret Wise. *The golden egg book*
    The runaway bunny
Carlson, Melody. *The Easterville miracle*
Carrick, Carol. *A rabbit for Easter*
Carter, David A. *Easter bugs*
Cazet, Denys. *Minnie and Moo: the attack of the Easter bunnies*
Chalmers, Mary. *Easter parade*
Claret, Maria. *The chocolate rabbit*
Compton, Joanne. *Little Rabbit's Easter surprise*
Cross, Genevieve. *My bunny book*
Darling, Kathy (Mary Kathleen). *The Easter bunny's secret*
Delacre, Lulu. *Peter Cottontail's Easter book*
DeLage, Ida. *ABC Easter bunny*
Demi. *Demi's basket of books*
    Little bitty bunny
    Little chick chick
Denim, Sue. *The Dumb Bunnies' Easter*
Devlin, Wende. *Cranberry Easter*
Dunn, Judy. *The little rabbit*
Duvoisin, Roger Antoine. *Easter treat*
Easter babies
Fisher, Aileen Lucia. *The story of Easter*
Friedrich, Priscilla. *The Easter bunny that overslept*
Gibbons, Gail. *Easter*
Gordon, Sharon. *Easter Bunny's lost egg*
Green, Adam. *The funny bunny factory*
Greenfield, Eloise. *Easter parade*
Griest, Lisa. *Lost at the White House*
Hallinan, P. K. (Patrick K.). *The small town children's Easter*
    Today is Easter!
Hawxhurst, Joan C. *Bubbe and Gram, my two grandmothers*
Hennessy, B. G. (Barbara G.). *Corduroy's Easter*
Heyward, Du Bose. *The country bunny and the little gold shoes*
Higgs, Liz Curtis. *The parable of the lily*
Hill, Eric. *Spot's first Easter*
Hoban, Lillian. *Silly Tilly and the Easter bunny*
Hopkins, Lee Bennett. *Easter buds are springing*
Houselander, Caryll. *Petook*
Kay, Helen. *An egg is for wishing*

Kimmel, Eric A. *The birds' gift*
Kraus, Robert. *Daddy Long Ears*
    How Spider saved Easter
Kroll, Steven. *The big bunny and the Easter eggs*
    The big bunny and the magic show
Kunhardt, Edith. *Danny and the Easter egg*
Lachner, Dorothea. *Smoky's special Easter present*
Landa, Norbert. *Rabbit and chicken play with colors*
Lenski, Lois. *The Easter Rabbit's parade*
Littlefield, William. *The whiskers of Ho Ho*
McClenathan, Louise. *The Easter pig*
Maril, Lee. *Mr. Bunny paints the eggs*
Merrick, Patrick. *Easter bunnies*
Meyer, Brigit. *Easter bunny saves the day*
Milhous, Katherine. *The egg tree*
Milich, Melissa. *Miz Fannie Mae's fine new Easter hat*
Miller, Edna. *Mousekin's Easter basket*
Modesitt, Jeanne. *Little Bunny's Easter surprise*
Murphy, Elspeth Campbell. *Happy Easter, God*
Mussenbrock, Anne. *The little Easter surprise*
Nerlove, Miriam. *Easter*
Ostheeren, Ingrid. *Coriander's Easter adventure*
Paraskevas, Betty. *Nibbles O'Hare*
Pieńkowski, Jan. *Easter*
Polacco, Patricia. *Chicken Sunday*
Roberts, Bethany. *Easter mice*
Ruelle, Karen Gray. *Easter egg disaster*
A small treasury of Easter poems and prayers
Stock, Catherine. *Easter surprise*
Stohs, Anita. *An Easter alleluia*
Tangvald, Christine Harder. *The best thing about Easter*
Taylor, Shirley. *The cross in the egg*
Tegen, Katherine Brown. *The story of the Easter Bunny*
Thayer, Jane. *The horse with the Easter bonnet*
Thompson, Lauren. *Love one another*
Tildes, Phyllis Limbacher. *The magic babushka*
Tresselt, Alvin R. *The world in the candy egg*
Tudor, Tasha. *A tale for Easter*
Vidrine, Beverly Barras. *Easter Day alphabet*
Wahl, Jan. *The five in the forest*
Watson, Wendy. *Happy Easter day!*
Wedeven, Carol. *The Easter cave*
Weigelt, Udo. *The Easter Bunny's baby*
Weil, Lisl. *The candy egg bunny*
Wells, Rosemary. *Max's chocolate chicken*
Weninger, Brigitte. *Happy Easter, Davy*
Wiese, Kurt. *Happy Easter*
Wildsmith, Brian. *The Easter story*
Wilhelm, Hans. *More bunny trouble*
    Quacky Ducky's Easter egg
    Quacky Ducky's Easter fun
Winthrop, Elizabeth. *He is risen*
Wolf, Winfried. *The Easter bunny*
Young, Miriam Burt. *Miss Suzy's Easter surprise*
Ziefert, Harriet. *Happy Easter, Grandma!*
Zolotow, Charlotte (Shapiro). *The bunny who found Easter*
    Mr. Rabbit and the lovely present

Holidays – Father's Day

Bunting, Eve (Anne Evelyn). *A perfect Father's Day*
Butterworth, Nick. *My dad is awesome*
Kroll, Steven. *Happy Father's Day*
Livingston, Myra Cohn. *Poems for fathers*
Rockwell, Anne F. *Father's Day*
Sharmat, Marjorie Weinman. *Hooray for Father's Day!*
Simon, Norma. *I wish I had my father*

Holidays – Fourth of July

Bertrand, Diane Gonzales. *Uncle Chente's picnic = El picnic de Tío Chente*
Chall, Marsha Wilson. *Happy Birthday, America!*
Devlin, Wende. *Cranberry summer*
Hines, Anna Grossnickle. *Mean old Uncle Jack*
Houck, Eric L. *Rabbit surprise*
Joosse, Barbara M. *Fourth of July*

Keller, Holly. *Henry's Fourth of July*
Lasky, Kathryn. *Fourth of July bear*
Osborne, Mary Pope. *Happy birthday, America*
Paraskevas, Betty. *On the day the tall ships sailed*
Roberts, Bethany. *Fourth of July mice*
Shortall, Leonard W. *One way*
Thomas, Jane Resh. *Celebration!*
Van Nutt, Julia. *Skyrockets and snickerdoodles*
Watson, Wendy. *Hurray for the Fourth of July*
Wells, Rosemary. *McDuff saves the day*
Ziefert, Harriet. *Hats off for the Fourth of July!*
Zion, Gene. *The summer snowman*

Holidays – Groundhog Day

Balian, Lorna. *A garden for a groundhog*
Bartalos, Michael. *Shadowville*
Cohen, Carol L. *Wake up, groundhog!*
Cox, Judy. *Go to sleep, Groundhog*
Delton, Judy. *Groundhog's Day at the doctor*
Farber, Norma. *Return of the shadows*
Freeman, Don. *Gregory's Shadow*
Glass, Marvin. *What happened today, Freddy Groundhog?*
Hamberger, John. *This is the day*
Hiskey, Iris. *The secret of the first one up*
Johnson, Crockett. *Will spring be early or will spring be late?*
Kesselman, Wendy Ann. *Time for Jody*
Koscielniak, Bruce. *Geoffrey Groundhog predicts the weather*
Kroll, Steven. *It's Groundhog Day!*
Levine, Abby. *Gretchen Groundhog, it's your day!*
Lewin, Betsy. *Groundhog day*
Palazzo, Tony (Anthony D.). *Waldo the woodchuck*
Tompert, Ann. *Nothing sticks like a shadow*
Welling, Peter J. *Andrew McGroundhog and his shady shadow*

Holidays – Guy Fawkes Day

Buchanan, Heather S. *George and Matilda Mouse and the moon rocket*

Holidays – Halloween

Adams, Adrienne. *A Halloween happening*
    A woggle of witches
Agran, Rick. *Pumpkin shivaree*
Alexander, Sue. *Who goes out on Halloween?*
Alley, R. W. (Robert W.). *There once was a witch*
Anderson, Lonzo. *The Halloween party*
Asch, Frank. *Popcorn*
Auch, Mary Jane. *Poultrygeist*
Balian, Lorna. *Humbug witch*
Battles, Edith. *The terrible trick or treat*
Beim, Jerrold. *Sir Halloween*
Benarde, Anita. *The pumpkin smasher*
Bender, Robert. *A little witch magic*
Berenstain, Stan. *The Berenstain bears trick or treat*
Blazek, Sarah Kirwan. *An Irish Hallowe'en*
Bond, Felicia. *The Halloween performance*
    The Halloween play
Borten, Helen. *Halloween*
Bradford, Ann. *The mystery of the live ghosts*
Bridwell, Norman. *Clifford's Halloween*
    Glow-in-the-dark Halloween
Bright, Robert. *Georgie's Halloween*
Brown, Marc Tolon. *Arthur's Halloween*
    Arthur's spookiest Halloween
Brown, Margaret Wise. *The fierce yellow pumpkin*
Broyles, Anne. *Shy Mama's Halloween*
Buck, Nola. *Creepy crawly critters and other Halloween tongue twisters*
    Gotcha!
    Halloween parade
    The littlest witch
Bullard, Lisa. *Trick-or-treat on Milton Street*
Bunting, Eve (Anne Evelyn). *The bones of Fred Mcfee*
    In the haunted house
    Scary, scary Halloween
Calhoun, Mary. *The witch of Hissing Hill*

    Wobble the witch cat
Carlson, Melody. *When the creepy things come out*
Carlson, Natalie Savage. *Spooky and the ghost cat*
    Spooky and the wizard's bats
    Spooky night
Carlstrom, Nancy White. *What a scare, Jesse Bear!*
    Who said boo?
Carrick, Carol. *Old Mother Witch*
Caseley, Judith. *Witch mama*
Cassedy, Sylvia. *The best cat suit of all*
Cavagnaro, David. *The pumpkin people*
Cazet, Denys. *Minnie and Moo: the night of the living bed*
    Never poke a squid
Cecil, Mirabel. *Lottie's cats*
Charles, Donald. *Shaggy dog's Halloween*
Charlton, Elizabeth. *Jeremy and the ghost*
Chetkowski, Emily. *Pumpkin smile*
Christelow, Eileen. *Jerome and the Witchcraft kids*
Cocca-Leffler, Maryann. *Jungle Halloween*
Cohen, Miriam. *The real-skin rubber monster mask*
Cooper, Paulette. *Let's find out about Halloween*
Corey, Dorothy. *Will it ever be my birthday?*
Cousins, Lucy. *Maisy's halloween*
Crum, Shutta. *Who took my hairy toe?*
Cummings, E. E. (Edward Estlin). *Hist whist*
Cuyler, Margery. *Sir William and the pumpkin monster*
David, Lawrence. *Superhero Max*
Davis, Maggie S. *Rickety witch*
Degen, Bruce. *Aunt Possum and the pumpkin man*
De Groat, Diane. *Trick or treat, smell my feet*
DeLage, Ida. *ABC Halloween witch*
    The old witch and her magic basket
    The old witch goes to the ball
    The old witch's party
Desmoinaux, Christel. *"Hallo-what?"*
Devlin, Wende. *Cranberry Halloween*
    Old Witch rescues Halloween
Dillon, Jana. *Jeb Scarecrow's pumpkin patch*
Diviny, Sean. *Halloween Motel*
Donnelly, Liza. *Dinosaurs' Halloween*
Druce, Arden. *Halloween night*
Egan, Tim. *The experiments of Doctor Vermin*
Embry, Margaret. *The blue-nosed witch*
Enderle, Judith (Ann) Ross. *Six creepy sheep*
Faulkner, Keith. *A trick or a treat?*
Feczko, Kathy. *Halloween party*
Five little pumpkins
Flanagan, Alice K. *Halloween*
Foster, Doris Van Liew. *Tell me, Mr. Owl*
Freeman, Don. *Space witch*
    Tilly Witch
Friedrich, Priscilla. *The marshmallow ghosts*
Friskey, Margaret (Margaret Richards). *The perky little pumpkin*
Gantos, Jack (John, Jr.). *Rotten Ralph's Halloween howl*
    Rotten Ralph's trick or treat
Gardner, Beau. *Whooo's a fright on Halloween night?*
Ghigna, Charles. *Halloween night*
Gibbons, Gail. *Halloween*
    Halloween is . . .
Gordon, Lynn. *The witch's revenge*
Grambling, Lois G. *Miss Hildy's missing cape caper*
Greene, Carol. *The thirteen days of Halloween*
Greene, Ellin. *The pumpkin giant*
Guthrie, Donna. *The witch who lives down the hall*
Hall, Zoe. *It's pumpkin time!*
Hallinan, P. K. (Patrick K.). *Today is Halloween*
Halloweena
Heinz, Brian J. *The monsters' test*
Hellsing, Lennart. *The wonderful pumpkin*
Hennessy, B. G. (Barbara G.). *Corduroy's Halloween*
Herman, Emily. *Hubknuckles*
Hines, Anna Grossnickle. *When the goblins came knocking*
Hoff, Syd. *Henrietta's Halloween*
Holabird, Katharine. *Angelina's Halloween*
Holub, Joan. *The Halloween Queen*
Hopkins, Lee Bennett. *Ragged shadows*
Howe, James. *Scared silly*

Hubbard, Patricia. *Trick or treat countdown*
Hubbell, Patricia. *Boo! Halloween poems and limericks*
    Wrapping paper romp
Hubbell, Will. *Pumpkin Jack*
Huck, Charlotte S. *A creepy countdown*
Hurd, Edith Thacher. *The so-so cat*
Hutchins, Pat. *Which witch is which?*
Jane, Pamela. *Monster mischief*
Johnston, Tony. *Soup bone*
    The vanishing pumpkin
Keats, Ezra Jack. *The trip*
Keens-Douglas, Richardo. *Anancy and the haunted house*
Kellogg, Steven (Stephen). *The mystery of the flying orange pumpkin*
Khdir, Kate. *Little ghost*
King, Elizabeth. *Pumpkin patch*
Klingel, Cynthia Fitterer. *Halloween*
Kraus, Robert. *How Spider saved Halloween*
    Jack O'Lantern's scary Halloween
Kroll, Steven. *Branigan's cat and the Halloween ghost*
    The candy witch
Krosoczka, Jarrett J. *Annie was warned*
Kunhardt, Edith. *Trick or treat, Danny!*
Kunnas, Mauri. *One spooky night and other scary stories*
Kutner, Merrily. *Z is for zombie*
Labatt, Mary. *Sam's first Halloween*
Leedy, Loreen. *The dragon Halloween party*
    2 x 2 = boo!
Leiner, Katherine. *Halloween*
Leuck, Laura. *One witch*
Levine, Abby. *This is the pumpkin*
Lewis, J. Patrick. *The house of Boo*
Lewis, Kevin. *The runaway pumpkin*
London, Jonathan. *Froggy's Halloween*
Low, Alice. *The witch who was afraid of witches*
    Witch's holiday
Maccarone, Grace. *Pumpkin faces*
McCue, Lisa. *Corduroy's best Halloween ever!*
McCully, Emily Arnold. *Grandmas trick-or-treat*
McMullan, Kate (Hall). *Trick or eeek!*
Maestro, Giulio. *Halloween howls*
Manushkin, Fran. *Be brave, baby rabbit*
    Hocus and Pocus at the circus
Marshall, Edward. *Space case*
Martin, Bill (William Ivan). *The magic pumpkin*
    Old devil wind
    Trick or treat?
Massey, Jeanne. *The littlest witch*
Mayer, Pamela. *The scariest monster in the whole wide world*
Mayr, Diane. *Littlebat's Halloween story*
Meddaugh, Susan. *The witches' supermarket*
Melmed, Laura Krauss. *Fright night flight*
Merriam, Eve. *Halloween ABC*
Miller, Edna. *Mousekin's golden house*
Minor, Wendell. *Pumpkin heads*
Moffatt, Judith. *Halloween frights*
    The pumpkin man
    Trick-or-treat faces
Mooser, Stephen. *The ghost with the Halloween hiccups*
Mueller, Virginia. *A Halloween mask for Monster*
Nerlove, Miriam. *Halloween*
Nicoll, Helen. *Meg and Mog*
Nikola-Lisa, W. *Shake dem Halloween bones*
Nolan, Dennis. *Witch Bazooza*
Novak, Matt. *No zombies allowed*
Numeroff, Laura Joffe. *Emily's bunch*
O'Malley, Kevin. *Velcome*
Ott, John. *Peter Pumpkin*
Palatini, Margie. *Piggie pie*
Passen, Lisa. *Attack of the 50-foot teacher*
Paul, Sherry. *2-B and the space visitor*
Peters, Sharon. *Trick or treat Halloween*
Pilkey, Dav. *The Hallo-wiener*
Polacco, Patricia. *Picnic at Mudsock Meadow*
Polisar, Barry Louis. *The haunted house party*
Poydar, Nancy. *The perfectly horrible Halloween*
Prager, Annabelle. *The spooky Halloween party*
Prelutsky, Jack. *Halloween countdown*

    Wild witches' ball
Preston, Edna Mitchell. *One dark night*
Preston, Tim. *Pumpkin moon*
Racioppo, Larry. *Halloween*
Reeves, Howard W. *There was an old witch*
Regan, Dian Curtis. *How do you know it's Halloween?*
Rex, Michael. *Brooms are for flying*
Riggio, Anita. *Beware the Brindlebeast*
Rocklin, Joanne. *This book is haunted*
Rockwell, Anne F. *Apples and pumpkins*
    A bear, a bobcat and three ghosts
    Halloween Day
    Pumpkin day, pumpkin night
Rose, David S. *It hardly seems like Halloween*
Ross, Eileen. *The Halloween showdown*
Ruelle, Karen Gray. *Spookier than a ghost*
Rylant, Cynthia. *Moonlight, the Halloween cat*
St. George, Judith. *The Halloween pumpkin smasher*
Saltzberg, Barney. *The problem with pumpkins*
San Souci, Robert D. *Cinderella Skeleton*
    The legend of Sleepy Hollow
Schertle, Alice. *Bill and the google-eyed goblins*
    Hob Goblin and the skeleton
Schweninger, Ann. *Halloween surprises*
Scott, Ann Herbert. *Let's catch a monster*
Seinfeld, Jerry. *Halloween*
Shaw, Nancy (Nancy E.). *Sheep trick or treat*
Shaw, Richard. *The kitten in the pumpkin patch*
Shute, Linda. *Halloween party*
Sierra, Judy. *The house that Drac built*
Silverman, Erica. *The Halloween house*
Slobodkin, Louis. *Trick or treat*
Smalls-Hector, Irene. *Jenny Reen and the Jack Muh Lantern*
Spirn, Michele. *The Know-Nothing Halloween*
Standiford, Natalie. *The headless horseman*
Stevenson, James. *That terrible Halloween night*
Stock, Catherine. *Halloween monster*
Stutson, Caroline. *By the light of the Halloween moon*
Tagg, Christine. *Who will you meet on Scary Street?*
Tatcheva, Eva. *Witch Zelda's birthday cake*
Teague, Mark. *One Halloween night*
Tegen, Katherine Brown. *Dracula and Frankenstein are friends*
Thayer, Jane. *Gus was a gorgeous ghost*
Thompson, Lauren. *Mouse's first Halloween*
Titherington, Jeanne. *Pumpkin pumpkin*
Todd, Mark. *What will you be for Halloween?*
Tryon, Leslie. *Albert's Halloween*
Tudor, Tasha. *Pumpkin moonshine*
Van Rynbach, Iris. *Five little pumpkins*
Vaughan, Marcia Kapok. *We're going on a ghost hunt*
Vigna, Judith. *Everyone goes as a pumpkin*
Von Hippel, Ursula. *The craziest Halloween*
Wahl, Jan. *Pleasant Fieldmouse's Halloween party*
Waldron, Jan L. *John Pig's Halloween*
Watson, Jane Werner. *Which is the witch?*
Watson, Wendy. *Boo! It's Halloween*
Wegen, Ron. *The Halloween costume party*
Weigelt, Udo. *Miranda's ghosts*
Weller, Frances Ward. *The closet gorilla*
Wells, Rosemary. *The Halloween parade*
West, Kipling. *A rattle of bones*
Weston, Martha. *Tuck's haunted house*
Wick, Walter. *I spy spooky night*
Williams, Suzanne. *The witch casts a spell*
Winters, Kay. *The teeny tiny ghost*
    Whooo's haunting the teeny tiny ghost?
Winthrop, Elizabeth. *Halloween hats*
Wojciechowski, Susan. *The best Halloween of all*
Wolff, Ferida. *On Halloween night*
Wolkstein, Diane. *The legend of Sleepy Hollow*
Yolen, Jane. *Beneath the ghost moon*
    Child of faerie, child of earth
Ziefert, Harriet. *On Halloween night*
    Two little witches
Zimmer, Dirk. *The trick-or-treat trap*
Zolotow, Charlotte (Shapiro). *A tiger called Thomas*, ill. by Catherine Stock

A tiger called Thomas, ill. by Kurt Werth

Holidays – Hanukkah

Adler, David A. *A picture book of Hanukkah*
    A picture book of Jewish holidays
Aleichem, Sholem. *Hanukah money*
Behrens, June. *Hanukkah*
Bunting, Eve (Anne Evelyn). *One candle*
Capucilli, Alyssa Satin. *Happy Hanukkah, Biscuit*
Carter, David A. *Chanukah bugs*
Chaikin, Miriam. *Hanukkah*
Chanover, Hyman. *Happy Hanukah everybody*
Conway, Diana Cohen. *Northern lights*
Coopersmith, Jerome. *A Chanukah fable for Christmas*
De Paola, Tomie (Thomas Anthony). *My first Chanukah*
Drucker, Malka. *Grandma's latkes*
Edwards, Michelle. *Papa's latkes*
Fisher, Aileen Lucia. *My first Hanukkah book*
Fishman, Cathy Goldberg. *On Hanukkah*
Gellman, Ellie. *It's Chanukah!*
Glaser, Linda. *The borrowed Hanukkah latkes*
    Mrs. Greenberg's messy Hanukkah
Goffstein, M. B. (Marilyn Brooke). *Laughing latkes*
Goldin, Barbara Diamond. *Just enough is plenty*
Groner, Judyth Saypol. *All about Hanukkah*
Hanukkah lights
Hawxhurst, Joan C. *Bubbe and Gram, my two grandmothers*
Hirsh, Marilyn. *I love Hanukkah*
    Potato pancakes all around
Holland, Cheri. *Maccabee jamboree*
Howland, Naomi. *Latkes, latkes, good to eat*
Jaffe, Nina. *In the month of Kislev*
Kimmel, Eric A. *Asher and the capmakers*
    The Chanukkah guest
    The Chanukkah tree
    Hershel and the Hanukkah goblins
    The magic dreidels
    One winter night
    Ten suns
    Zigazak!
Kimmelman, Leslie. *Hanukkah lights, Hanukkah nights*
    The runaway latkes
Koralek, Jenny. *Hanukkah*
Kropf, Latifa Berry. *It's Hanukkah time!*
Krulik, Nancy E. *Is it Hanukkah yet?*
Kuskin, Karla. *A great miracle happened there*
Levine, Arthur A. *All the lights in the night*
Levoy, Myron. *The Hanukkah of Great-Uncle Otto*
McKissack, Patricia C. *Messy Bessey's holidays*
McMullan, Kate (Hall). *Hanukkah ha-has*
Manushkin, Fran. *Hooray for Hanukkah!*
    Latkes and applesauce
Melmed, Laura Krauss. *Moishe's miracle*
Modesitt, Jeanne. *It's Hanukkah!*
    Songs of Chanukah
Moorman, Margaret. *Light the lights!*
Moss, Marissa. *The ugly menorah*
Nayer, Judy. *The eight nights of Hanukka*
Nerlove, Miriam. *Hanukkah*
Newman, Lesléa. *Runaway dreidel*
Oberman, Sheldon. *By the Hanukkah light*
Okrend, Elise. *Blintzes for Blitzen*
Older, Effin. *My two grandmothers*
Podwal, Mark H. *The menorah story*
Polacco, Patricia. *The trees of the dancing goats*
Poskanzer, Susan Cornell. *Riddles about Hannukah*
Randall, Ronne. *The Hanukkah mice*
Rosen, Michael J. (1954–). *Chanukah lights everywhere*
    Elijah's angel
    Our eight nights of Hanukkah
Rothenberg, Joan Keller. *Inside-out grandma*
Schaefer, Lola M. *Hanukkah*
Schnur, Steven. *The tie man's miracle*
Schotter, Roni. *Hanukkah!*
Sherman, Eileen Bluestone. *The odd potato*
Shostak, Myra. *Rainbow candles*

Simon, Norma. *The story of Hanukkah*
Smith, Dian G. *Hanukkah lights*
Sper, Emily. *Hanukkah*
Spinner, Stephanie. *It's a miracle*
Stillerman, Marci. *Nine spoons*
Stonem, Tanya Lee. *D is for dreidel*
Zagwÿn, Deborah Turney. *Papa's latkes*
Zalben, Jane Breskin. *Beni's first Chanukah*
    Pearl's eight days of Chanukah

Holidays – Independence Day *see* Holidays – Fourth of July

Holidays – Juneteenth

Weatherford, Carole Boston. *Juneteenth jamboree*

Holidays – Kwanzaa

Burden-Patmon, Denise. *Imani's gift at Kwanzaa*
Chocolate, Deborah M. Newton. *Kente colors*
    Kwanzaa
Ford, Juwanda G. *K is for Kwanzaa*
    Together for Kwanzaa
Kroll, Virginia L. *Wood-hoopoe Willie*
McKissack, Patricia C. *Messy Bessey's holidays*
Medearis, Angela Shelf. *Kyle's first Kwanzaa*
    Seven spools of thread
Saint James, Synthia. *The gifts of Kwanzaa*
Schaefer, Lola M. *Kwanzaa*
Washington, Donna L. *The story of Kwanzaa*
Winne, Joanne. *Let's get ready for Kwanzaa*

Holidays – Mardi Gras *see* Mardi Gras

Holidays – Martin Luther King, Jr. Day

Frost, Helen. *Martin Luther King, Jr. Day*

Holidays – May Day

Mora, Pat. *The rainbow tulip*
Silverman, Erica. *On the morn of Mayfest*

Holidays – Memorial Day

Frost, Helen. *Memorial Day*
Golding, Theresa Martin. *Memorial Day surprise*
Scott, Geoffrey. *Memorial Day*

Holidays – Mother's Day

Anderson, Laurie Halse. *No time for Mother's Day*
Balian, Lorna. *Mother's Mother's Day*
Bauer, Marion Dane. *My mother is mine*
Bunting, Eve (Anne Evelyn). *The Mother's Day mice*
French, Vivian. *A present for mom*
Howe, James. *The case of the missing mother*
Kroll, Steven. *Happy Mother's Day*
Livingston, Myra Cohn. *Poems for mothers*
Morgan, Allen. *Matthew and the midnight money van*
Rockwell, Anne F. *Mother's Day*
Ruelle, Karen Gray. *Mother's Day mess*
Sharmat, Marjorie Weinman. *Hooray for Mother's Day!*
Tripp, Valerie. *Happy, happy Mother's Day*
Wynot, Jillian. *The Mother's Day sandwich*

Holidays – New Year's

Andersen, H. C. (Hans Christian). *The little match girl*, ill. by Rachel Isadora
    The little match girl, ill. by Blair Lent
    The little match girl, ill. by Jerry Pinkney
Chiemruom, Sothea. *Dara's Cambodian New Year*
Grifalconi, Ann. *The bravest flute*
Holabird, Katharine. *Angelina ice skates*
Janice. *Little Bear's New Year's party*

Kudler, David. *The Seven Gods of Luck*
Modell, Frank. *Goodbye old year, hello new year*
Ziefert, Harriet. *First Night*

Holidays – Passover

Adler, David A. *A picture book of Jewish holidays*
    A picture book of Passover
Auerbach, Julie Jaslow. *Everything's changing – It's pesach!*
Behrens, June. *Passover*
Feder, Harriet K. *Not yet, Elijah!*
Fishman, Cathy Goldberg. *On Passover*
Flanagan, Alice K. *Passover*
Geras, Adèle. *Rebecca's Passover*
Hawxhurst, Joan C. *Bubbe and Gram, my two grandmothers*
Hirsh, Marilyn. *I love Passover*
    One little goat
Howland, Naomi. *The matzah man*
Kimmelman, Leslie. *Hooray! it's Passover!*
Kropf, Latifa Berry. *It's seder time!*
Libney, Varda. *What I like about Passover*
Lister, Clare. *My first Passover [board book]*
Manushkin, Fran. *The matzah that Papa brought home*
    Miriam's cup
Newman, Lesléa. *Matzo ball moon*
Portnoy, Mindy Avra. *Matzah ball*
Rosen, Anne. *A family Passover*
Rothenberg, Joan Keller. *Matzah ball soup*
Rouss, Sylvia A. *Sammy Spider's first Passover*
Schotter, Roni. *Passover magic*
Schwartz, Lynne Sharon. *The four questions*
Shulevitz, Uri. *The magician*
Silverman, Erica. *Gittel's hands*
Simon, Norma. *The story of Passover*
Sper, Emily. *The Passover seder*
Swartz, Leslie. *A first Passover*
Ungar, Richard. *Rachel's gift*
Wikler, Madeline. *My first seder*
Wohl, Lauren L. *Matzoh mouse*
Zalben, Jane Breskin. *Happy Passover, Rosie*
    Pearl's Passover
Zolkower, Edie Stoltz. *Too many cooks*
Zucker, Jonny. *Four special questions*
Zusman, Evelyn. *The Passover parrot*

Holidays – Purim

Adelson, Leone. *The mystery bear*
Cohen, Barbara. *Here come the Purim players!*, ill. by Beverly Brodsky McDermott
    Here come the Purim players!, ill. by Shoshana Mekibel
Fishman, Cathy Goldberg. *On Purim*
Gerstein, Mordicai. *Queen Esther the morning star*
Kress, Camille. *Purim*
Nerlove, Miriam. *Purim*
Schotter, Roni. *Purim play*
Simpson, Lesley. *The Purim surprise*
Suhl, Yuri. *The Purim goat*
Topek, Susan Remick. *A costume for Noah*
Wikler, Madeline. *The Purim parade*
Zucker, Jonny. *It's party time*

Holidays – Ramadan

Ghazi, Suhaib Hamid. *Ramadan*
Marx, David F. *Ramadan*

Holidays – Rosh Hashanah

Fishman, Cathy Goldberg. *On Rosh Hashanah and Yom Kippur*
Gellman, Ellie. *It's Rosh Hashanah!*
Goldin, Barbara Diamond. *World's birthday*
Kahn, Katherine Janus. *The shofar calls to us*
Kimmel, Eric A. *Gershon's monster*
Kimmelman, Leslie. *Sound the shofar!*
Zucker, Jonny. *Apples and honey*

Holidays – St. Patrick's Day

Bunting, Eve (Anne Evelyn). *St. Patrick's Day in the morning*
Calhoun, Mary. *The hungry leprechaun*
Dillon, Jana. *Lucky O'Leprechaun*
Janice. *Little Bear marches in the St. Patrick's Day parade*
Kroll, Steven. *Mary McLean and the St. Patrick's Day parade*
Landau, Elaine. *St. Patrick's Day*
Nolan, Janet. *The St. Patrick's Day shillelagh*
O'Donnell, Elizabeth Lee. *Patrick's day*
Schertle, Alice. *Jeremy Bean's St. Patrick's Day*
Tucker, Kathy. *The leprechaun in the basement*
Wojciechowski, Susan. *A fine St. Patrick's Day*
Zimelman, Nathan. *To sing a song as big as Ireland*

Holidays – Seder

Kropf, Latifa Berry. *It's seder time!*

Holidays – Shavuot

Goldin, Barbara Diamond. *A mountain of blintzes*

Holidays – Sukkot

Goldin, Barbara Diamond. *Night lights*
Groner, Judyth Saypol. *All about Sukkot*
Lepon, Shoshana. *Hillel builds a house*
Polacco, Patricia. *Tikvah means hope*
Vorst, Rochel Groner. *The sukkah that I built*
Zalben, Jane Breskin. *Leo and Blossom's Sukkah*

Holidays – Thanksgiving

Alcott, Louisa May. *An old-fashioned Thanksgiving*
Anderson, Laurie Halse. *Thank you, Sarah*
    Turkey pox
Atwell, Debby. *The Thanksgiving door*
Balian, Lorna. *Sometimes it's turkey*
Bartlett, Robert Merrill. *The story of Thanksgiving*
Bateman, Teresa. *A plump and perky turkey*
Behrens, June. *The feast of Thanksgiving*
Berenstain, Stan. *The Berenstain bears and the prize pumpkin*
Borden, Louise. *Thanksgiving is . . .*
Brown, Marc Tolon. *Arthur's Thanksgiving*
Bruchac, Joseph. *Squanto's journey*
Bunting, Eve (Anne Evelyn). *How many days to America?*
    A turkey for Thanksgiving
Carlson, Nancy L. *A visit to grandma's*
Carlstrom, Nancy White. *Thanksgiving Day at our house*
Cazet, Denys. *Minnie and Moo and the Thanksgiving tree*
Child, Lydia Maria. *Over the river and through the wood*
Corey, Shana. *Milly and the Macy's Parade*
Cowley, Joy. *Gracias, the Thanksgiving turkey*
Dalgliesh, Alice. *The Thanksgiving story*
De Paola, Tomie (Thomas Anthony). *My first Thanksgiving*
Devlin, Wende. *Cranberry Thanksgiving*
Dragonwagon, Crescent. *Alligator arrived with apples*
Flanagan, Alice K. *Thanksgiving*
Geisert, Arthur. *Nursery crimes*
George, Jean Craighead. *The first Thanksgiving*
Gibbons, Gail. *Thanksgiving Day*
Greene, Rhonda Gowler. *The very first Thanksgiving Day*
Haugen, Brenda. *Thanksgiving*
Herman, Charlotte. *The memory cupboard*
Holub, Joan. *Turkeys never gobble*
Hopkins, Lee Bennett. *Merrily comes our harvest in*
Ipcar, Dahlov (Zorach). *Hard scrabble harvest*
Jackson, Alison. *I know an old lady who swallowed a pie*
Janice. *Little Bear's Thanksgiving*
Jennings, Sharon. *Franklin's Thanksgiving*
Kimmelman, Leslie. *Round the turkey*
Klingel, Cynthia Fitterer. *Thanksgiving*
Koller, Jackie French. *Nickommoh!*
Kraus, Robert. *How Spider saved Turkey*
Kroll, Steven. *Oh, what a Thanksgiving!*
    One tough turkey

The squirrels' Thanksgiving
Lakin, Patricia. *Fat chance Thanksgiving*
Leedy, Loreen. *The dragon Thanksgiving feast*
Levine, Abby. *This is the turkey*
Lowitz, Sadyebeth. *The pilgrims' party*
McCully, Emily Arnold. *An outlaw Thanksgiving*
Markes, Julie. *Thanks for Thanksgiving*
Marzollo, Jean. *Thanksgiving cats*
Melmed, Laura Krauss. *1-2-3 Thanksgiving*
   This first Thanksgiving
Metaxas, Eric. *Squanto and the miracle of Thanksgiving*
Miller, Edna. *Mousekin's Thanksgiving*
Myra, Harold Lawrence. *Thanksgiving*
Nerlove, Miriam. *Thanksgiving*
Nikola-Lisa, W. *One, two, three Thanksgiving!*
Nixon, Joan Lowery. *The Thanksgiving mystery*
Ott, John. *Peter Pumpkin*
Paraskevas, Betty. *A very Kroll Christmas*
Pilkey, Dav. *'Twas the night before Thanksgiving*
Pomeranc, Marion Hess. *The can-do Thanksgiving*
Quackenbush, Robert M. *Sheriff Sally Gopher and the Thanksgiving caper*
Rael, Elsa Okon. *Rivka's first Thanksgiving*
Rockwell, Anne F. *Thanksgiving Day*
Rosen, Michael (1946–). *A Thanksgiving wish*
Smith, Mavis. *'Twas the day after Thanksgiving*
Spinelli, Eileen. *Thanksgiving at the Tappletons'*
Spirn, Michele. *I am the turkey*
   The Know-Nothings talk turkey
Stanley, Diane. *Thanksgiving on Plymouth Plantation*
Stock, Catherine. *Thanksgiving treat*
Thorpe, Kiki. *A comfy, cozy Thanksgiving*
Tresselt, Alvin R. *Autumn harvest*
Watson, Wendy. *Thanksgiving at our house*
Wheeler, Lisa. *Turk and Runt*
Willey, Margaret. *Thanksgiving with me*
Williams, Barbara. *Chester Chipmunk's Thanksgiving*
Zion, Gene. *The meanest squirrel I ever met*

Holidays – Tu B'Shevat

Sammy Spider's first Tu B'Shevat

Holidays – Valentine's Day

Adams, Adrienne. *The great Valentine's Day balloon race*
Balian, Lorna. *A sweetheart for Valentine*
Blos, Joan W. *One very best Valentine's Day*
Bond, Felicia. *Four Valentines in a rainstorm*
Brown, Marc Tolon. *Arthur's Valentine*
Buckley, Kate. *Love notes*
Bulla, Clyde Robert. *The story of Valentine's Day*
   Valentine cat
Bunting, Eve (Anne Evelyn). *The Valentine bears*
Capucilli, Alyssa Satin. *Biscuit's Valentine's Day*
Carlson, Nancy L. *Louanne Pig in the mysterious Valentine*
Carr, Jan. *Sweet hearts*
Carrick, Carol. *Valentine*
Casey, Tina. *The runaway Valentine*
Cazet, Denys. *Minnie and Moo: will you be my Valentine?*
Cheshire, Marc. *Love & kisses, Eloise*
Cohen, Miriam. *Bee my Valentine!*
De Groat, Diane. *Roses are pink, your feet really stink*
De Paola, Tomie (Thomas Anthony). *Things to make and do for Valentine's Day*
Devlin, Wende. *Cranberry Valentine*
Flanagan, Alice K. *Valentine's Day*
Gantos, Jack (John, Jr.). *Rotten Ralph's rotten romance*
Geringer, Laura. *Yours 'til the ice cracks*
Gibbons, Gail. *Valentine's Day*
Greene, Carol. *A computer went a-courting*
Gregory, Valiska. *A Valentine for Norman Noggs*
Greydanus, Rose. *Someone's baby-sitting*
Guilfoile, Elizabeth. *Valentine's Day*
Guthrie, Donna. *The secret admirer*
Hallinan, P. K. (Patrick K.). *Today is Valentine's Day!*
Henkes, Kevin. *Lilly's chocolate heart*

Hoban, Lillian. *Arthur's great big Valentine*
   Silly Tilly's Valentine
Hurd, Thacher. *Little Mouse's big Valentine*
Jackson, Alison. *The ballad of Valentine*
Keeshan, Robert. *She loves me, she loves me not*
Kelley, True. *A Valentine for Fuzzboom*
Krahn, Fernando. *Little love story*
Kraus, Robert. *How Spider saved Valentine's Day*
Kroll, Steven. *Will you be my valentine?*
Kunhardt, Edith. *Danny's mystery Valentine*
Landau, Elaine. *Valentine's Day*
Let me call you sweetheart
Little Bear's Valentine
Livingston, Myra Cohn. *Valentine poems*
London, Jonathan. *Froggy's first kiss*
McMullan, Kate (Hall). *Hearty har har*
Maitland, Barbara. *The bookstore valentine*
Marzollo, Jean. *Valentine cats*
Maurer-Mathison, Diane V. *Make your own spectacular Valentines*
Modell, Frank. *One zillion valentines*
Murphy, Shirley Rousseau. *Valentine for a dragon*
Nerlove, Miriam. *Valentine's Day*
Nixon, Joan Lowery. *The Valentine mystery*
Poydar, Nancy. *Rhyme time Valentine*
Rider, Joanne. *First grade valentines*
Roberts, Bethany. *Valentine mice!*
Rockwell, Anne F. *Valentine's Day*, ill. by Lizzy Rockwell
Ruelle, Karen Gray. *Snow Valentines*
Sabuda, Robert James. *St. Valentine*
Schweninger, Ann. *The hunt for rabbit's galosh*
   Valentine friends
Shannon, George. *Heart to heart*
Sharmat, Marjorie Weinman. *The best Valentine in the world*
Spinelli, Eileen. *Somebody loves you, Mr. Hatch*
Spohn, Kate. *Turtle and Snake's Valentine's Day*
Stevenson, James. *Happy Valentine's Day, Emma!*
   A village full of valentines
Stock, Catherine. *Secret Valentine*
Watson, Clyde. *Valentine foxes*
Watson, Wendy. *A Valentine for you*
Wittman, Sally. *The boy who hated Valentine's Day*
Zimmermann, H. Werner (Heinz Werner). *Alphonse knows . . . a circle is not a Valentine*

Holidays – Washington's Birthday

Bulla, Clyde Robert. *Washington's birthday*

Holidays – Yom Kippur

Cohen, Barbara. *First fast*
Fishman, Cathy Goldberg. *On Rosh Hashanah and Yom Kippur*
Kimmelman, Leslie. *Sound the shofar!*
Singer, Marilyn. *Minnie's Yom Kippur birthday*
Weilerstein, Sadie Rose. *K'tonton's Yom Kippur kitten*

Holland *see* Foreign lands – Holland

Holocaust

Adler, David A. *Hiding from the Nazis*
Hoestlandt, Jo. *Star of fear, star of hope*
Lakin, Pat (Patricia). *Don't forget*
Lehman-Wilzig, Tami. *Keeping the promise*
Morris, Ann. *Grandma Esther remembers*
Nerlove, Miriam. *Flowers on the wall*
Oberman, Sheldon. *By the Hanukkah light*
Oppenheim, Shulamith Levey. *The lily cupboard*
Schnur, Steven. *The tie man's miracle*
Stillerman, Marci. *Nine spoons*

Homeless

Andersen, H. C. (Hans Christian). *The little match girl*, ill. by Rachel Isadora
   The little match girl, ill. by Blair Lent
   The little match girl, ill. by Jerry Pinkney

Barbour, Karen. *Mr. Bow Tie*
Bartoletti, Susan Campbell. *The Christmas promise*
Bunting, Eve (Anne Evelyn). *December*
 Fly away home
Cannon, Janell. *Trupp*
Chinn, Karen. *Sam and the lucky money*
Clément, Claude. *The man who lit the stars*
Coltman, Paul. *Tinker Jim*
Davis, Aubrey. *Bone button borscht*
Day, Marie. *Edward the "crazy man"*
Fuchshuber, Annegert. *Carly*
Gerstein, Mordicai. *The wild boy*
Gottlieb, Dale. *Seeing Eye Willie*
Guthrie, Donna. *A rose for Abby*
Hammond, Anna. *This home we have made*
Hughes, Monica. *A handful of seeds*
Khan, Rukhsana. *The roses in my carpets*
Komaiko, Leah. *Lenora O'Grady*
McPhail, David M. *The teddy bear*
Martin, Ann M. *Leo the Magnificat*
Meggs, Libby Phillips. *Go home!*
Myers, Christopher A. *Sparrows*
Polacco, Patricia. *I can hear the sun*
Powell, E. Sandy. *A chance to grow*
Rascal. *Socrates*
Rosen, Michael J. (1954–). *Home*
Tibo, Gilles. *The cowboy kid*
Vainio, Pirkko. *The Christmas angel*
Weninger, Brigitte. *Lumina*

Homes, houses

Ackerman, Karen. *I know a place*
 The sleeping porch
 This old house
Adler, David A. *The house on the roof*
Alger, Leclaire Gowans. *Always room for one more*
Altman, Linda Jacobs. *Amelia's road*
Angelou, Maya. *My painted house, my friendly chicken, and me*
Aragon, Jane Chelsea. *The major and the mousehole mice*
Arkin, Alan. *Tony's hard work day*
Arnold, Katya. *Knock, knock, teremok!*
Arnosky, Jim. *Armadillo's orange*
Ashman, Linda. *Castles, caves, and honeycombs*
Ayars, James Sterling. *Caboose on the roof*
Ballard, Robin. *Good-bye, house*
Bannon, Laura. *The best house in the world*
Barton, Byron. *Building a house*
Bassède, Francine. *George paints his house*
Beaton, Clare. *At home = A la maison*
Becker, Edna. *Nine hundred buckets of paint*
Bemelmans, Ludwig. *Sunshine*
Berridge, Celia. *At my house*
Binzen, Bill. *Alfred goes house hunting*
Blackstone, Stella. *Bear at home*
Blegvad, Lenore. *The parrot in the garret and other rhymes about dwellings*
Bloom, Suzanne. *No place for a pig*
Blos, Joan W. *Old Henry*
Boland, Janice. *Annabel again*
Borg, Inga. *Plupp builds a house*
Bour, Danièle. *The house from morning to night*
Boyd, Lizi. *Mouse in a house*
Brown, Marc Tolon. *There's no place like home*
Brown, Marcia. *The neighbors*
Brown, Margaret Wise. *House of a hundred windows*
 Robin's room
 The wonderful house
Buchanan, Ken. *This house is made of mud*
Bunting, Eve (Anne Evelyn). *In the haunted house*
Burton, Virginia Lee. *The little house*
Butterworth, Nick. *The house on the rock*
Calhoun, Mary. *Mrs. Dog's own house*
Calmenson, Stephanie. *Where will the animals stay?*
Campbell, Rod. *Buster's morning*
Carle, Eric. *A house for Hermit Crab*
 My very first book of homes

Carter, David A. *In a dark, dark wood*
Carter, Katharine. *Houses*
Carter, Noelle. *My house*
Carter, Penny. *A new house for the Morrisons*
Cartlidge, Michelle. *A house for Lily Mouse*
 Mouse in the house
Chase, Catherine. *The mouse in my house*
Chorao, Kay. *Cathedral mouse*
Christensen, Gardell Dano. *Mrs. Mouse needs a house*
Clements, Andrew. *Slippers at home*
Clymer, Eleanor Lowenton. *The tiny little house*
Colby, C. B. (Carroll Burleigh). *Who lives there?*
Collicott, Sharleen. *Mildred and Sam*
Colman, Hila. *Peter's brownstone house*
Cousins, Lucy. *Maisy's pop-up playhouse*
Crompton, Margaret. *The house where Jack lives*
Curry, Nancy. *The littlest house*
Cutler, Ivor. *The animal house*
Dale, Penny. *Daisy Rabbit's tree house*
Dalmais, Anne-Marie. *Petey the puppy*
Dauer, Rosamond. *Bullfrog builds a house*
De Regniers, Beatrice Schenk. *A little house of your own*
Desimini, Lisa. *My house*
DiSalvo-Ryan, DyAnne. *A castle on Viola Street*
Dorros, Arthur. *This is my house*
Dragonwagon, Crescent. *Home place*
Du Quette, Keith. *The house book*
Durant, Alan. *Mouse party*
Emberley, Ed (Edward Randolph). *Home*
Emberley, Rebecca. *My house = Mi casa*
 My room = Mi cuarto
Emerman, Ellen. *Just right*
Emmett, Jonathan. *No place like home*
Enderle, Judith (Ann) Ross. *Upstairs*
Erickson, Phoebe. *Just follow me*
Farm house
Feder, Paula Kurzband. *Where does the teacher live?*
Firehouse
Fisher, Aileen Lucia. *Best little house*
 The house of a mouse
Fitzgerald, Joanne. *This is me and where I am*
Flanagan, Alice K. *Call Mr. Vasquez, he'll fix it!*
 Mr. Paul and Mr. Luecke build communities
 The Wilsons, a house-painting team
Flint, Russ. *Let's build a house*
Flory, Jane. *The bear on the doorstep*
Fries, Claudia. *A pig is moving in*
Gamble, Isobel. *Who's that?*
Gedin, Birgitta. *The little house from the sea*
Gerstein, Mordicai. *The room*
Gibbons, Gail. *How a house is built*
Gliori, Debi. *Flora's surprise*
 Mr. Bear to the rescue
 New big house
Goffstein, M. B. (Marilyn Brooke). *A house, a home*
Gomboli, Mario. *Look inside a house*
Goodall, John S. *Great days of a country house*
Goode, Diane. *Tiger trouble*
Graham, Bob. *Spirit of Hope*
Grahame, Kenneth. *A wind in the willows Christmas*
 The wind in the willows: home sweet home
Green, Mary McBurney. *Everybody has a house and everybody eats*
Greenway, Shirley. *Animal homes: burrows*
Greydanus, Rose. *Tree house fun*
Grimm, Edward. *The doorman*
Grindley, Sally. *A new room for William*
Grosz, Peter. *The special gifts*
Groundhog at Evergreen Road
Guthrie, Woody. *Bling blang*
Hammer, Asa. *Fit for pigs*
Harper, Anita. *How we live*
Harper, Charise Mericle. *The trouble with normal*
Harrison, David Lee. *The alligator in the closet and other poems around the house*
 When cows come home
Hawcock, David. *Whose home?*
Hayward, Linda. *A day in the life of a builder*

In a people house
Shannon, George. *Lizard's home*
Shapp, Martha. *Let's find out about houses*
Sharr, Christine. *Homes*
Shecter, Ben. *Emily, girl witch of New York*
Shefelman, Janice Jordan. *Victoria House*
Shelby, Anne. *The someday house*
Sherrow, Victoria. *There goes the ghost*
Shields, Carol Diggory. *Homes*
Sierra, Judy. *The house that Drac built*
    'Twas the fright before Christmas
Silsbe, Brenda. *Just one more color*
Silverman, Erica. *On Grandma's roof*
Skorpen, Liesel Moak. *We were tired of living in a house*
Spinelli, Eileen. *A safe place called home*
    Sophie's masterpiece
Stanley, Diane. *Goldie and the three bears*
Stern, Simon. *Mrs. Vinegar*
Strathdee, Jean. *The house that grew*
Suen, Anastasia. *Raise the roof*
Swinburne, Stephen R. *Swallows in the birdhouse*
Tafuri, Nancy. *Silly little goose!*
Tallarico, Tony. *At home*
Testa, Fulvio. *The ideal home*
Thayer, Jane. *What's a ghost going to do?*
Thermes, Jennifer. *When I was built*
Tison, Annette. *Inside and outside*
Trivizas, Eugenios. *The three little wolves and the big bad pig*
Tudor, Bethany. *Samuel's tree house*
Turner, Ann Warren. *The Christmas house*
Vainio, Pirkko. *The dream house*
Van Allsburg, Chris. *Two bad ants*
Velthuijs, Max. *Little Man finds a home*
Vevers, Gwynne. *Animal homes*
Vizurraga, Susan. *Miss Opal's auction*
    Our old house
Waddell, Martin. *The hidden house*
    Mimi and the dream house
Waite, Judy. *Mouse, look out!*
Wallace, John. *Building a house with Mr. Bumble*
Ward, Nick. *Farmer George and the fieldmice*
Watanabe, Shigeo. *I can build a house!*
Waters, Jennifer. *Right at home*
Weeks, Sarah. *Drip, drop*
    Mrs. McNosh and the great big squash
Wellington, Monica. *Baby at home*
Wells, Rosemary. *The house in the mail*
Weston, Martha. *Tuck's haunted house*
Wildsmith, Brian. *Animal homes*
Williams, Juliet. *Mouse house*
    Mouse house [board book]
Winch, Madeleine. *Come by chance*
Winer, Yvonne. *Birds build nests*
Wolfe, Frances. *One wish*
Worley, Daryl. *Billy and the attic adventure*
Wormell, Christopher. *Blue Rabbit and friends*
Wyllie, Stephen. *White Rabbit builds a dream house*
Yee, Wong Herbert. *Eek! There's a mouse in the house*
    Mrs. Brown went to town
Yin. *Dear Santa, please come to the 19th floor*
Yoaker, Harry. *The view*
Zelinsky, Paul O. *The maid and the mouse and the odd-shaped house*
Ziefert, Harriet. *Birdhouse for rent*
    Cow in the house
    A new house for Mole and Mouse

Homework

De Groat, Diane. *Jingle bells, homework smells*

Homosexuality

Kennedy, Joseph. *Lucy goes to the country*
Newman, Lesléa. *Heather has two mommies*
    Saturday is Pattyday
Vigna, Judith. *My two uncles*
Willhoite, Michael. *Daddy's roommate*

Honesty *see* Character traits – honesty

Honey bees *see* Insects – bees

Hope

Ikeda, Daisaku. *The cherry tree*
Recknagel, Friedrich. *Sarah's willow*

Hopi Indians *see* Indians of North America – Hopi

Hornbills *see* Birds – hornbills

Hornets *see* Insects – hornets

Horses *see* Animals – horses, ponies

Horses, rocking *see* Toys – rocking horses

Hospitals

Baker, Gayle. *Special delivery*
Bemelmans, Ludwig. *Madeline*
    Madeline [pop-up book]
Blance, Ellen. *Monster goes to the hospital*
Bond, Michael. *Paddington Bear goes to the hospital*
Bruna, Dick. *Miffy in the hospital*
Bucknall, Caroline. *One bear in the hospital*
Carlstrom, Nancy White. *Barney is best*
Ciliotta, Claire. *"Why am I going to the hospital?"*
Collier, James Lincoln. *Danny goes to the hospital*
Cork, Barbara Taylor. *Katie goes to the hospital*
Curious George makes pancakes
Davison, Martine. *Maggie and the emergency room*
    Rita goes to the hospital
Dooley, Virginia. *Tubes in my ears*
Elliott, Ingrid Glatz. *Hospital roadmap*
Flanagan, Alice K. *Ask Nurse Pfaff, she'll help you!*
Garhan Attebury, Nancy. *Out and about at the hospital*
Goodall, Jane. *Dr. White*
Gutman, Anne. *Gaspard in the hospital*
Hatkoff, Juliana. *Good-bye tonsils*
Hautzig, Deborah. *A visit to the Sesame Street hospital*
Hill, Eric. *Spot visits the hospital*
Hoban, Russell. *Jim's lion*
Hogan, Paula Z. *The hospital scares me*
Jennings, Sharon. *Franklin goes to the hospital*
Karim, Roberta. *This is a hospital, not a zoo!*
Keller, Holly. *The best present*
Ketner, Mary Grace. *Ganzy remembers*
Marino, Barbara Pavis. *Eric needs stitches*
Martin, Charles E. *Island rescue*
Morgan, Allen. *Matthew and the midnight hospital*
Moses, Amy. *At the hospital*
Pace, Elizabeth. *Chris gets ear tubes*
Pirner, Connie White. *Even little kids get diabetes*
Pope, Billy N. *Your world*
Rey, Margret (Margret Elisabeth Waldstein). *Curious George goes to the hospital*
Rockwell, Anne F. *The emergency room*
Rogers, Fred. *Going to the hospital*
Rosenberg, Maxine B. *Mommy's in the hospital having a baby*
Schaefer, Lola M. *Hospital*
Shay, Arthur. *What happens when you go to the hospital*
Sobol, Harriet Langsam. *Jeff's hospital book*
Sonneborn, Ruth A. *I love Gram*
Steel, Danielle. *Max's daddy goes to the hospital*
Stein, Sara Bonnett. *A hospital story*
Stone, Bernard. *Emergency mouse*
Tamburine, Jean. *I think I will go to the hospital*
Watts, Marjorie-Ann. *Crocodile medicine*
    Crocodile plaster
Weber, Alfons. *Elizabeth gets well*
Whybrow, Ian. *Sammy and the robots*
Wild, Margaret. *Going home*

Mr. Nick's knitting
Wolde, Gunilla. *Betsy and the doctor*
Zonta, Pat. *Jessica's x-ray*

Hotels

Brewster, Patience. *Rabbit Inn*
Cheshire, Marc. *Here comes Eloise!*
Diviny, Sean. *Halloween Motel*
Du Quette, Keith. *Hotel Animal*
Keeshan, Robert. *Itty Bitty Kitty makes a big splash*
Knight, Joan. *Bon appetit, Bertie!*
Levinson, Riki. *Grandpa's hotel*
Mahy, Margaret. *Rooms for rent*
Naylor, Phyllis Reynolds. *Ducks disappearing*
Parkin, Rex. *The red carpet*
Pinkwater, Daniel Manus. *At the Hotel Larry*
  Bad bears and a bunny
Schneider, Howie. *No dogs allowed*
Simmie, Lois. *Mister got to go*
  Mister got to go and Arnie
Stem, J. David. *Kay Thompson's Eloise in Hollywood*
Stevens, Jan Romero. *Carlos digs to China = Carlos excava hasta la China*
Stevenson, James. *The Sea View Hotel*
Supraner, Robyn. *Sam Sunday and the mystery at the Ocean Beach Hotel*
Thompson, Kay. *Kay Thompson's Eloise*
  Kay Thompson's Eloise at Christmastime
  Kay Thompson's Eloise in Moscow
  Kay Thompson's Eloise takes a bawth [sic]
  Kay Thompson's Eloise's what I absolutely love love love
Vaughan, Marcia Kapok. *The Sea-Breeze Hotel*
Waber, Bernard. *Do you see a mouse?*
Wojtowycz, David. *Animal antics from 1 to 10*
Yee, Wong Herbert. *Fireman Small, fire down below*

Housekeepers *see* Careers – housekeepers

Houses *see* Homes, houses

Hugging

Horning, Sandra. *The giant hug*

Huichol Indians *see* Indians of North America – Huichol

Humming birds *see* Birds – humming birds

Humorous stories

Aardema, Verna. *Oh, Kojo! How could you!*
  What's so funny, Ketu?
  Who's in Rabbit's house?
Accorsi, William. *Short short short stories*
Adams, Richard (Richard Newbold). *The tyger voyage*
Adamson, Gareth. *Old man up a tree*
Adinolfi, JoAnn. *The Egyptian polar bear*
Adler, David A. *The children of Chelm*
Æsop. *The miller, his son and their donkey*, ill. by Roger Antoine Duvoisin
Ahlberg, Allan. *The adventures of Bert*
  A bit more Bert
  Bravest ever bear
  The ghost train
  Half a pig
  Mystery tour
Ahlberg, Janet. *The little worm book*
Alexander, Martha G. *Move over, Twerp*
  My outrageous friend Charlie
Alexander, Sue. *World famous Muriel*
Aliki. *Digging up dinosaurs*
  The eggs
The all-amazing ha ha book
Allamand, Pascale. *The animals who changed their colors*
Allard, Harry. *Miss Nelson has a field day*

Miss Nelson is back
Miss Nelson is missing!
The Stupids die
The Stupids have a ball
The Stupids step out
The Stupids take off
There's a party at Mona's tonight
Allen, Jonathan. *A bad case of animal nonsense*
Allen, Linda. *Mr. Simkin's grandma*
  Mrs. Simkin's bed
Allen, Marjorie N. *One, two, three – ah-choo!*
Allen, Pamela. *Mr. Archimedes' bath*
  Mr. McGee
Ambrus, Victor G. *Grandma, Felix, and Mustapha Biscuit*
Andersen, H. C. (Hans Christian). *The emperor's new clothes*, ill. by Erik Blegvad
  The emperor's new clothes, ill. by Virginia Lee Burton
  The emperor's new clothes, ill. by Robert Byrd
  The emperor's new clothes, ill. by Charlene DeLage
  The emperor's new clothes, ill. by Jack and Irene Delano
  The emperor's new clothes, ill. by Demi
  The emperor's new clothes, ill. by Hélène Desputeaux
  The emperor's new clothes, ill. by Birte Dietz
  The emperor's new clothes, ill. by Dorothée Duntze
  The emperor's new clothes, ill. by Pamela Baldwin Ford
  The emperor's new clothes, ill. by Jack Kent
  The emperor's new clothes, ill. by Monika Laimgruber
  The emperor's new clothes, ill. by Anne F. Rockwell
  The emperor's new clothes, ill. by Janet Stevens
  The emperor's new clothes, ill. by Eve Tharlet
  The emperor's new clothes, ill. by Nadine Bernard Westcott
  The old man is always right
Anderson, Leone Castell. *The wonderful shrinking shirt*
Andreae, Giles. *Pants*
Apperley, Dawn. *Don't wake the baby*
Armour, Richard Willard. *Animals on the ceiling*
Armstrong-Ellis, Carey. *Prudy's problem and how she solved it*
Arnosky, Jim. *Outdoors on foot*
Asch, Frank. *Sand cake*
  Turtle tale
Auch, Mary Jane. *Bantam of the opera*
  The princess and the pizza
Aulaire, Ingri Mortenson d'. *Don't count your chicks*
Axelrod, Amy. *They'll believe me when I'm gone*
Ayars, James Sterling. *Caboose on the roof*
Aylesworth, Jim. *Hush up!*
  Shenandoah Noah
Baker, Alan. *Benjamin and the box*
  Benjamin bounces back
  Benjamin's balloon
  Benjamin's book
  Benjamin's dreadful dream
  Benjamin's portrait
Baker, Betty. *Sonny-Boy Sim*
  Three fools and a horse
  Worthington Botts and the steam machine
Bakken, Harold. *The special string*
Balian, Lorna. *Leprechauns never lie*
Barr, Cathrine. *Hound dog's bone*
Barrett, John M. *The bear who slept through Christmas*
Behn, Harry. *What a beautiful noise*
Beisner, Monika. *Monika Beisner's book of riddles*
Belloc, Hilaire. *The bad child's book of beasts*
  The bad child's book of beasts, and more beasts for worse children
Bemelmans, Ludwig. *Rosebud*
  Sunshine
Benchley, Nathaniel. *Walter the homing pigeon*
Benedictus, Roger. *Fifty million sausages*
Benjamin, Alan. *1000 monsters*
Bennett, Jill. *Roger was a razor fish and other poems*
Benton, Robert. *Don't ever wish for a 7-foot bear*
Bishop, Ann. *Chicken riddle*
  The Ella Fannie elephant riddle book
  Hey riddle riddle
  Merry-go-riddle
  Noah riddle?
  Oh, riddlesticks!

The riddle ages
Riddle-iculous rid-alphabet book
Wild Bill Hiccup's riddle book
Bishop, Claire Huchet. *The man who lost his head*
Blake, Quentin. *Mister Magnolia*
  Mrs. Armitage on wheels
  Quentin Blake's nursery rhyme book
Bodecker, N. M. (Nils Mogens). *"It's raining," said John Twaining*
  "Let's marry" said the cherry, and other nonsense poems
  Snowman Sniffles and other verse
Bohman, Nils Axel Erik. *Jim, Jock and Jumbo*
Borten, Helen. *Do you go where I go?*
Bossom, Naomi. *A scale full of fish and other turnabouts*
Boynton, Sandra. *If at first . . .*
Bradfield, Roger (Jolly Roger). *The flying hockey stick*
Brecht, Bertolt. *Uncle Eddie's moustache*
Brenner, Barbara A. *A dog I know*
Bridwell, Norman. *The witch grows up*
Briggs, Raymond. *Jim and the beanstalk*
Brock, Emma Lillian. *Mr. Wren's house*
  Nobody's mouse
  Skipping Island
Brodmann, Aliana. *Such a noise!*
Bröger, Achim. *Little Harry*
  The Santa Clauses
Brothers, Aileen. *Sad Mrs. Sam Sack*
Brown, Jeff. *Flat Stanley*
Brown, Marc Tolon. *Spooky riddles*
  What do you call a dumb bunny? and other rabbit riddles, games, jokes and cartoons
Brown, Margaret Wise. *Once upon a time in pigpen and three other stories*
Brown, Ruth. *The big sneeze*
Browne, Caroline. *Mrs. Christie's farmhouse*
Bruna, Dick. *Kitten Nell*
Brunhoff, Laurent de. *Serafina the giraffe*
Bryant, Sara Cone. *Epaminondas and his auntie*
Buchanan, Joan. *It's a good thing*
Buehner, Caralyn. *It's a spoon, not a shovel*
Bunting, Eve (Anne Evelyn). *The big cheese*
Burnard, Damon. *The amazing adventures of Soupy Boy*
Burningham, John. *The shopping basket*
Burroway, Janet. *The truck on the track*
Burton, Marilee Robin. *The elephant's nest*
Byfield, Barbara Ninde. *The haunted churchbell*
Calhoun, Mary. *The nine lives of Homer C. Cat*
  Old man Whickutt's donkey
  The traveling ball of string
Cameron, Polly. *A child's book of nonsense*
Carrick, Donald. *Harold and the giant knight*
  Harold and the great stag
Carroll, Lewis. *Jabberwocky*, ill. by Graeme Base
  Jabberwocky, ill. from Disney archives
  Jabberwocky, ill. by Jane Breskin Zalben
  The walrus and the carpenter, ill. by Julian Doyle
  The walrus and the carpenter, ill. by Jane Breskin Zalben
Carroll, Ruth. *Old Mrs. Billups and the black cats*
Castle, Caroline. *Naughty!*
Caudill, Rebecca. *Contrary Jenkins*
Cauley, Lorinda Bryan. *The goose and the golden coins*
Causley, Charles. *"Quack!" said the billy-goat*
Cazet, Denys. *Elvis the rooster almost goes to heaven*
  Minnie and Moo go to Paris
  Minnie and Moo meet Frankenswine
  Minnie and Moo save the earth
  Minnie and Moo: the night before Christmas
  Minnie and Moo: the night of the living bed
Cerf, Bennett Alfred. *Bennett Cerf's book of animal riddles*
  Bennett Cerf's book of laughs
  Bennett Cerf's book of riddles
  More riddles
Chall, Marsha Wilson. *Rupa raises the sun*
Chalmers, Audrey. *Hundreds and hundreds of pancakes*
Chalmers, Mary. *Six dogs, twenty-three cats, forty-five mice, and one hundred sixteen spiders*
Charlip, Remy. *Arm in arm*
  Fortunately

"Mother, mother I feel sick"
Thirteen
Chetwin, Grace. *Box and Cox*
Chevalier, Christa. *Spence makes circles*
Child, Lauren. *What planet are you from Clarice Bean?*
Christelow, Eileen. *Where's the big bad wolf?*
Christian, Mary Blount. *Nothing much happened today*
Chukovskii, Kornei Ivanovich. *The telephone*, ill. by Blair Lent
Cibula, Matt S. *What's up with you, Taquandra Fu?*
Clement, Rod. *Just another ordinary day*
Clements, Andrew. *Double trouble in Walla Walla*
Cole, Babette. *Truelove*
Cole, Brock. *Buttons*
Cole, Joanna. *The Clown-Arounds*
  The Clown-Arounds go on vacation
  Get well, Clown-Arounds!
  It's too noisy
Collington, Peter. *Clever cat*
Collins, Judith Graham. *Josh's scary dad*
Cooke, Trish. *Mr. Pam Pam and the Hullabazoo*
Coontz, Otto. *Starring Rosa*
Copp, James (Andrew James). *Martha Matilda O'Toole*
Corey, Shana. *First graders from Mars: Horus's horrible day*
  First graders from Mars: Nergal and the Great Space Race
  First graders from Mars: Tera, star student
  First graders from Mars: The problem with Pelly
Coxe, Molly. *Big egg*
Craig, M. Jean. *The man whose name was not Thomas*
Crisp, Marty. *Totally polar*
Daugherty, James Henry. *Andy and the lion*
Davis, Katie (Katie I.). *Mabel the Tooth Fairy and how she got her job*
Davis, Maggie S. *The best way to Ripton*
Day, Edward C. *John Tabor's ride*
De Beer, Hans. *Oh no, Ono!*
Delaney, M. C. (Michael Clark). *The marigold monster*
Delaney, Ned. *Terrible things could happen*
Dennis, Suzanne E. *Answer me that*
De Paola, Tomie (Thomas Anthony). *Bill and Pete*
  Flicks
  Merry Christmas, Strega Nona
  Strega Nona
  Strega Nona meets her match
  Strega Nona's magic lessons
De Regniers, Beatrice Schenk. *May I bring a friend?*
Dillon, Jana. *Lucky O'Leprechaun comes to America*
Dorros, Arthur. *City chicken*
  Pretzels
  When the pigs took over
Downs, Mike. *Pig giggles and rabbit rhymes*
Drescher, Joan E. *Max and Rufus*
Duffield, Katy. *Farmer McPeepers and his missing milk cows*
Duvoisin, Roger Antoine. *Our Veronica goes to Petunia's farm*
  Petunia
  Petunia and the song
  Petunia, beware!
  Petunia, I love you
  Petunia takes a trip
  Petunia, the silly goose
  Petunia's Christmas
  Petunia's treasure
Easton, Violet. *Elephants never jump*
Edwards, Pamela Duncan. *Muldoon*
Egan, Tim. *Distant Feathers*
Ellentuck, Shan. *Did you see what I said?*
  A sunflower as big as the sun
Elliott, David. *Hazel Nutt, Alien Hunter*
  Hazel Nutt, mad scientist
Elliott, George. *The boy who loved bananas*
Elsdale, Bob. *Mac side up*
Ernst, Lisa Campbell. *Goldilocks returns*
Ets, Marie Hall. *Beasts and nonsense*
Evans, Katherine. *The maid and her pail of milk*
  The man, the boy and the donkey
Eyvindson, Peter. *Backward brothers see the light*
Farber, Norma. *There once was a woman who married a man*
Feiffer, Jules. *Bark, George*
Fenton, Edward. *The big yellow balloon*

Fisher, Carolyn. *A twisted tale*
Flora, James. *The day the cow sneezed*
   Grandpa's farm
Folsom, Marcia. *Easy as pie*
Frank, John. *The toughest cowboy, Or, How the Wild West was tamed*
Freeman, Don. *Forever laughter*
Frith, Michael K. *I'll teach my dog 100 words*
Fuchshuber, Annegert. *The wishing hat*
Gackenbach, Dick. *The pig who saw everything*
Gardner, Beau. *Have you ever seen . . . ?*
Garriel, Barbara S. *I know a shy fellow who swallowed a cello*
Gay, Marie-Louise. *Good morning Sam*
Gelman, Rita Golden. *Hey, kid*
The golden goose, ill. by William Stobbs
Goode, Diane. *Diane Goode's book of silly stories & songs*
Goodhart, Pippa. *Arthur's tractor*
Graber, Janet. *Jacob and the polar bears*
Green, Stephanie. *Not just another moose*
Griffin, Kitty. *Cowboy Sam and those confounded secrets*
   The foot-stomping adventures of Clementine Sweet
Grimm, Jacob. *Clever Kate*
   The golden goose, ill. by Dorothée Duntze
   The golden goose, ill. by Isadore Seltzer
   The golden goose, ill. by Martin Ursell
Grossman, Bill. *Timothy Tunny swallowed a bunny*
Hale, Lucretia. *The lady who put salt in her coffee*
Hale, Sarah Josepha Buell. *Mary had a little lamb*, ill. by Iza Trapani
Hall, Donald. *Andrew the lion farmer*
Hample, Stoo. *Stoo Hample's silly joke book*
Hannan, Peter. *The battle of Sillyville*
   Escape from Camp Wannabarf
   School after dark
   Sillyville or bust
Harrison, David Lee. *The boy who counted stars*
Hart, Christopher. *Merwin, master of disguise*
Hart, Jeanne McGahey. *Scareboy*
Hayward, Linda. *Pepe and Papa*
Heilbroner, Joan. *Robert the rose horse*
Helmer, Marilyn. *Critter riddles*
Helquist, Brett. *Roger, the jolly pirate*
Hindley, Judy. *Uncle Harold and the green hat*
Hirsh, Marilyn. *Could anything be worse?*
Hoban, Lillian. *Silly Tilly and the Easter bunny*
Hoban, Russell. *A near thing for Captain Najork*
Hoberman, Mary Ann. *"It's simple," said Simon*
Holman, Felice. *Victoria's castle*
Hort, Lenny. *Tie your socks and clap your feet*
Hunter, Norman. *Professor Branestawn's building bust-up*
Hutchins, Pat. *Clocks and more clocks*
   Don't forget the bacon!
   Rosie's walk
I invited a dragon to dinner
Jackson, Alison. *I know an old lady who swallowed a pie*
Jagtenberg, Yvonne. *Jack the wolf*
Jeschke, Susan. *Firerose*
Jobling, Curtis. *Frankenstein's cat*
Johnson, Crockett. *Harold and the purple crayon*
   Harold at the North Pole
   Harold's ABC
   Harold's circus
   Harold's fairy tale
   Harold's trip to the sky
   A picture for Harold's room
Johnson, Doug. *Substitute teacher plans*
Johnson, Lindsay Lee. *Hurricane Henrietta*
Johnson, Paul Brett. *Bearhide and crow*
   The goose who went off in a huff
   Little Bunny Foo Foo
Johnson, Suzanne C. *Fribbity ribbit*
Johnston, Tony. *Go track a yak*
   Goblin walk
Joslin, Sesyle. *What do you do, dear?*
   What do you say, dear?
Joyce, Irma. *Never talk to strangers*
Kantor, MacKinlay. *The preposterous week*
Karim, Roberta. *This is a hospital, not a zoo!*

Keats, Ezra Jack. *Skates*
Keenen, George. *The preposterous week*
Keller, Charles. *School daze*
Keller, Laurie. *Arnie the doughnut*
Kennedy, Richard. *The contests at Cowlick*
Kennedy, X. J. *Uncle Switch*
Kent, Jack. *Hoddy doddy*
Ketteman, Helen. *Bubba the cowboy prince*
Kimmel, Elizabeth Cody. *My penguin Osbert*
Kimmel, Eric A. *Four dollars and fifty cents*
King-Smith, Dick. *Farmer Bungle forgets*
Kirk, Daniel. *Jack and Jill*
Koelling, Caryl. *Silly stories mix and match*
Krahn, Fernando. *April fools*
Krauss, Ruth. *I'll be you and you be me*
   This thumbprint
Krosoczka, Jarrett J. *Baghead*
Kumin, Maxine W. *Eggs of things*
   Speedy digs downside up
Laden, Nina. *Bad dog*
   Private I. Guana, the case of the missing chameleon
La Fontaine, Jean de. *The miller, the boy and the donkey*, adapt. and ill. by Brian Wildsmith
Landström, Olof. *Boo and Baa at sea*
   Boo and Baa get wet
   Boo and Baa in a party mood
   Boo and Baa in the woods
   Boo and Baa in windy weather
   Boo and Baa on a cleaning spree
Lasky, Kathryn. *The emperor's old clothes*
Lattimore, Deborah Nourse. *The lady with the ship on her head*
Laurin, Anne. *Little things*
Lear, Edward. *A book of nonsense*
   The dong with a luminous nose
   Edward Lear's nonsense book
   A Learical lexicon
   Lear's nonsense verses
   The nutcrackers and the sugar-tongs
   The pelican chorus, ill. by Harold Berson
   The pelican chorus and the quangle wangle's hat, ill. by Kevin W. Maddison
   The pobble who has no toes, ill. by Emma Crosby
   The pobble who has no toes, ill. by Kevin W. Maddison
   The quangle wangle's hat, ill. by Emma Crosby
   The quangle wangle's hat, ill. by Helen Oxenbury
   The quangle wangle's hat, ill. by Janet Stevens
   Two laughable lyrics
   Whizz!
Lent, Blair. *John Tabor's ride*
LeRoy, Gen. *Lucky stiff!*
Lester, Julius. *Sam and the tigers*
Lesynski, Loris. *Dirty dog boogie*
Levitin, Sonia. *When Elephant goes to a party*
Levy, Janice. *The man who lived in a hat*
Lewis, J. Patrick. *The bookworm's feast*
Lindgren, Astrid. *Do you know Pippi Longstocking?*
Lionni, Leo. *Where?*
Ljungkvist, Laura. *Toni's topsy-turvy telephone day*
Lloyd, David. *The ridiculous story of Gammer Gurton's needle*
Lloyd, Megan. *Chicken tricks*
Lobel, Arnold. *Lucille*
   Mouse tales
   A treeful of pigs
Lodge, Bernard. *Cloud Cuckoo Land (and other odd spots)*
Löfgren, Ulf. *The boy who ate more than the giant and other Swedish folktales*
London, Jonathan. *Froggy goes to the doctor*
Low, Alice. *Aunt Lucy went to buy a hat*
Lowell, Susan. *The bootmaker and the elves*
Macaulay, David. *Why the chicken crossed the road*
MacDonald, Amy. *Quentin Fenton Herter three*
McGough, Roger. *What on earth can it be?*
McGovern, Ann. *Too much noise*
McGraw, Sheila. *Pussycats everywhere*
McKié, Roy. *The riddle book*
McKissack, Patricia C. *The king's new clothes*
McLarey, Kristina Thermaenius. *When you take a pig to a party*

McLenighan, Valjean. *What you see is what you get*
McNaughton, Colin. *Preston's goal!*
  Suddenly!
McPhail, David M. *Alligators are awful (and they have terrible manners, too)*
  The cereal box
Maestro, Giulio. *Just enough Rosie*
  A raft of riddles
  The remarkable plant in apartment 4
Mahood, Kenneth. *The laughing dragon*
Mahy, Margaret. *Beaten by a balloon*
  The boy who was followed home
  Bubble trouble and other poems and stories
  A summery Saturday morning
  The three-legged cat
Manes, Esther. *The bananas move to the ceiling*
Marcellino, Fred. *I, crocodile*
Marsh, Jeri. *Hurrah for Alexander*
Marshak, S. (Samuil). *The absentminded fellow*
Marshall, Edward. *Fox at school*
Marshall, James. *The Cut-Ups*
  The Cut-Ups at Camp Custer
  The Cut-Ups carry on
  The Cut-Ups crack up
  The Cut-Ups cut loose
  Sing out, Irene
Martin, Bill (William Ivan). *Sounds of laughter*
Mayer, Mercer. *The queen always wanted to dance*
  What do you do with a kangaroo?
Mazer, Anne. *The Fixits*
  The No-Nothings and their baby
McMullan, Kate (Hall). *Back-to-school belly busters*
  Hanukkah ha-has
Meddaugh, Susan. *Cinderella's rat*
Meeuwissen, Tony. *Remarkable animals*
Merriam, Eve. *The birthday cow*
  Epaminondas
Meyer, Louis A. *The clean air and peaceful contentment dirigible airline*
Miles, Miska. *Chicken forgets*
Mills, Alan. *The hungry goat*
Minters, Frances. *Princess Fishtail*
Mitchell, Adrian. *Our mammoth*
Mitter, Matt. *Once upon a rhyme*
Modell, Frank. *Tooley! Tooley!*
Moffett, Martha A. *A flower pot is not a hat*
Monsell, Mary Elise. *Underwear!*
Mooser, Stephen. *Funnyman and the penny dodo*
Morrison, Sean. *Is that a happy hippopotamus?*
Mother Goose. *The golden goose book*, ill. by L. Leslie Brooke
Mould, Wendy. *Ants in my pants*
Myller, Rolf. *How big is a foot?*
Nash, Ogden. *The animal garden*
  A boy is a boy
Newell, Peter. *Topsys and turvys*
Nikola-Lisa, W. *Tangletalk*
Nishimura, Kae. *Dinah*
Nixon, Joan Lowery. *Beats me, Claude*
  That's the spirit, Claude
  You bet your britches, Claude
Noble, Trinka Hakes. *The day Jimmy's boa ate the wash*
  Jimmy's boa and the big splash birthday bash
  Jimmy's boa bounces back
  Meanwhile back at the ranch
Nolan, Lucy A. *The Lizard Man of Crabtree County*
Nolen, Jerdine. *Plantzilla*
  Plantzilla goes to camp
Nordqvist, Sven. *Festus and Mercury go camping*
  Festus and Mercury wishing to go fishing
Numeroff, Laura Joffe. *Laura Numeroff's 10-step guide to living with your monster*
  Sometimes I wonder if poodles like noodles
Oller, Erika. *The cabbage soup solution*
Olson, Helen Kronberg. *The strange thing that happened to Oliver Wendell Iscovitch*
Oppenheim, Joanne. *Donkey's tale*
Oxenbury, Helen. *Tiny Tim*

Pack, Robert. *Then what did you do?*
Packard, Mary. *Same and different*
Palatini, Margie. *Ding dong ding dong*
  Earthquack
  The web files
Parish, Peggy. *Granny and the desperadoes*
  Granny and the Indians
  Granny, the baby and the big gray thing
Parkin, Rex. *The red carpet*
Parkinson, Curtis. *Emily's eighteen aunts*
Parr, Todd. *Underwear do's and don'ts*
Passen, Lisa. *The incredible shrinking teacher*
Paterson, Diane. *Eat*
  Smile for auntie
Patz, Nancy. *Pumpernickel tickle and mean green cheese*
Paul, Korky. *Winnie flies again*
Pearson, Tracey Campbell. *Bob*
  Sing a song of sixpence
Peet, Bill (William Bartlett). *Big bad Bruce*
  Buford the little bighorn
  Chester the worldly pig
  Countdown to Christmas
  Cowardly Clyde
  Eli
  Hubert's hair-raising adventures
  Huge Harold
  Jennifer and Josephine
  Jethro and Joel were a troll
  Kermit the hermit
  Merle the high flying squirrel
  Randy's dandy lions
Phillips, Louis. *The upside down riddle book*
Pilkey, Dav. *The Silly Gooses*
  The Silly Gooses build a house
Pinkney, J. Brian. *The adventures of sparrowboy*
Pinkwater, Daniel Manus. *At the Hotel Larry*
  Bad bears and a bunny
  Bad bears in the big city
  Bongo Larry
  Ice-cream Larry
  The picture of Morty and Ray
  Young Larry
Plourde, Lynn. *Pigs in the mud in the middle of the rud*
Polacco, Patricia. *In Enzo's splendid gardens*
Polisar, Barry Louis. *Insect soup*
Postgate, Oliver. *Noggin and the whale*
  Noggin the king
Potter, Beatrix. *The tale of Tom Kitten*
Prather, Ray. *Double dog dare*
Prelutsky, Jack. *The baby uggs are hatching*
  The queen of Eene
  The Random House book of poetry for children
  The snopp on the sidewalk and other poems
Preston, Edna Mitchell. *Horrible Hepzibah*
  Pop Corn and Ma Goodness
Pulver, Robin. *Mrs. Toggle's zipper*
Puner, Helen Walker. *The sitter who didn't sit*
Quackenbush, Robert M. *Funny bunnies*
  Pete Pack Rat
Rader, Laura. *Santa's new suit*
Ragz, M. M. *Lost little angel*
Raskin, Ellen. *Franklin Stein*
  Nothing ever happens on my block
Rayner, Shoo. *My first picture joke book*
Regan, Dian Curtis. *How do you know it's Halloween?*
Regan, Lara Jo. *What is Mr. Winkle?*
Reid, Alastair. *Supposing*
Reiss, Mike. *Late for school*
  Santa claustrophobia
Rey, H. A. (Hans Augusto). *Cecily G and the nine monkeys*
  Curious George
  Curious George gets a medal
  Curious George rides a bike
  Curious George takes a job
  Elizabite
  Elizabite, adventures of a carnivorous plant
  The original Curious George

Van der Meer, Ron. *Oh Lord!*
Van Kampen, Vlasta. *It couldn't be worse*
Van Laan, Nancy. *Little baby Bobby*
Van Woerkom, Dorothy. *Donkey Ysabel*
    The queen who couldn't bake gingerbread
Vaughan, Marcia Kapok. *The lemonade stand*
Viorst, Judith. *Sunday morning*
Vogel, Amos. *How little Lori visited Times Square*
Waber, Bernard. *How to go about laying an egg*
    Nobody is perfick
Wahl, Jan. *Cabbage moon*
Ward, Barbara Briggs. *The really really hairy flight of Snarly Sally*
Watanabe, Shigeo. *What a good lunch!*
Watson, Clyde. *Hickory stick rag*
Watson, Esther (Pearl). *The adventures of Jules and Gertie*
Weatherill, Stephen. *The very first Lucy Goose book*
Weeks, Sarah. *Bite me, I'm a book*
    Happy birthday, Frankie
    Mrs. McNosh hangs up her wash
    Oh my gosh, Mrs. McNosh!
Weinberg, Larry (Lawrence). *The Forgetful Bears help Santa*
Welling, Peter J. *Shawn O'Hisser, the last snake in Ireland*
Westcott, Nadine Bernard. *The lady with the alligator purse*
Wiese, Kurt. *Fish in the air*
Wiesner, William. *Happy-Go-Lucky*
    Turnabout
Willard, Nancy. *Simple pictures are best*
Willems, Mo. *Don't let the pigeon drive the bus*
Williams, Barbara. *Jeremy isn't hungry*
Williams, Jay. *School for sillies*
Williams, Juliet. *Mouse house*
    Mouse house [board book]
Wise, William. *Dinosaurs forever*
Wiseman, Bernard. *Tails are not for painting*
Wisniewski, David. *Tough cookie*
Wolkstein, Diane. *The legend of Sleepy Hollow*
Wood, Audrey. *King Bidgood's in the bathtub*
Wright, Jill. *The old woman and the Willy Nilly Man*
Yorinks, Arthur. *Company's coming*
    Company's going
Zemach, Harve. *The tricks of Master Dabble*
Zemach, Margot. *It could always be worse*
Ziefert, Harriet. *Math riddles*
Zimmerman, Andrea Griffing. *Yetta, the trickster*
Zullo, Germano. *Marta and the bicycle*

Hungary *see* Foreign lands – Hungary

Hunting *see* Sports – hunting

Hurdy-gurdies *see* Musical instruments – hurdy-gurdies

Huron Indians *see* Indians of North America – Huron

Hurricanes *see* Weather – hurricanes

Hurrying *see* Behavior – hurrying

Hyenas *see* Animals – hyenas

Hygiene *see also* Character traits – cleanliness; HIealth & fitness

Bottner, Barbara. *Two messy friends*
Cole, Babette. *Dr. Dog*
Garelli, Cristina. *Farm friends clean up*
Langreuter, Jutta. *Little Bear brushes his teeth*
Puttock, Simon. *Squeaky clean*
Wells, Rosemary. *The school play*
Yagya, Genichiro. *All about scabs*

Ibis *see* Birds – ibis

Ice skating *see* Sports – ice skating

Iceland *see* Foreign lands – Iceland

Identity *see* Self-concept

Iguanas *see* Reptiles – iguanas

Illness

Anholt, Catherine. *Truffles is sick*
Anzaldúa, Gloria. *Prietita and the ghost woman = Prietita y la llorona*
Arnold, Katrin. *Anna joins in*
Aylesworth, Jim. *McGraw's Emporium*
Baggette, Susan K. *Jonathan goes to the doctor*
Barrett, Judi. *An apple a day*
Bartels, Alice L. *The grandmother doll*
Bedford, David. *Shaggy Dog and the terrible itch*
Bemelmans, Ludwig. *Madeline's Christmas*
Berger, Melvin. *Germs make me sick!*
    Ouch! a book about cuts, scratches and scrapes
Bertrand, Lynne. *One day, two dragons*
Biro, Val. *Gumdrop catches a cold*
Borton, Lady. *Fat chance!*
Bradman, Tony. *Through my window*
Brandenberg, Franz. *I wish I was sick, too!*
Brown, Margaret Wise. *When the wind blew*
Bruna, Dick. *Miffy in the hospital*
Buckley, Helen Elizabeth. *Someday with my father*
Bucknall, Caroline. *One bear in the hospital*
Calmenson, Stephanie. *Get well, gators!*
    Rosie, a visiting dog's story
Cannon, Janell. *Little Yau*
Carrick, Carol. *Old Mother Witch*
Carter, Alden R. *Seeing things my way*
Cassedy, Sylvia. *The best cat suit of all*
Chalmers, Mary. *Come to the doctor, Harry*
Chanin, Michael. *Chief's blanket*
Charlip, Remy. *"Mother, mother I feel sick"*
Cherry, Lynne. *Who's sick today?*
Chislett, Gail. *Melinda's no's cold*
Christelow, Eileen. *Henry and the red stripes*
Ciliotta, Claire. *"Why am I going to the hospital?"*
Coerr, Eleanor. *Sadako*
Cole, Joanna. *Get well, Clown-Arounds!*
Cork, Barbara Taylor. *Katie goes to the hospital*
Cowell, Cressida. *Hiccup the seasick Viking*
Craven, Carolyn. *What the mailman brought*
Daly, Niki. *My dad*
Davison, Martine. *Maggie and the emergency room*
    Robby visits the doctor
De Groat, Diane. *Alligator's toothache*
Delton, Judy. *Groundhog's Day at the doctor*
    It happened on Thursday
Demuth, Patricia Brennan. *Achoo! all about colds*
Denslow, Sharon Phillips. *Bus riders*
De Paola, Tomie (Thomas Anthony). *Now one foot, now the other*
DeWitt, Jamie. *Jamie's turn*
Dooley, Virginia. *Tubes in my ears*
Duff, Maggie (Margaret K.). *The princess and the pumpkin*
Dugan, Barbara. *Loop the loop*
Duquennoy, Jacques. *Operation ghost*
Duvoisin, Roger Antoine. *The Christmas whale*
Eberstadt, Isabel (Nash). *What is for my birthday?*
Elliott, Ingrid Glatz. *Hospital roadmap*

Watson, Wendy. *Tales for a winter's eve*
Watts, Marjorie-Ann. *Crocodile medicine*
    Crocodile plaster
Weber, Alfons. *Elizabeth gets well*
Weigelt, Udo. *Mole's journey*
Wells, Rosemary. *The germ busters*
    The island light
West, Colin. *The king's toothache*
Whitney, Alma Marshak. *Just awful*
Whybrow, Ian. *Sammy and the robots*
Wickstrom, Sylvie (Sylvie Kantrovitz). *Mothers can't get sick*
Wild, Margaret. *Mr. Nick's knitting*
Wildsmith, Brian. *Carousel*
Williams, Barbara. *Albert's toothache*
Williams, Vera B. *Music, music for everyone*
Wolde, Gunilla. *Betsy and the chicken pox*
    Betsy and the doctor
Yolen, Jane. *How do dinosaurs get well soon?*
Ziefert, Harriet. *When daddy had the chicken pox*
Zonta, Pat. *Jessica's x-ray*

Illness – AIDS

Arnold, Lynda. *My Mommy has AIDS*
Newman, Lesléa. *Too far away to touch*
Pollack, Eileen. *Whisper whisper Jesse, whisper whisper Josh*
Wiener, Lori. *Be a friend*

Illness – alcoholism

Carrick, Carol. *Banana beer*
Langsen, Richard C. *When someone in the family drinks too much*
Oppenheim, Joanne. *No way, Slippery Slick!*
Tabor, Nancy (Maria Grande). *Bottles break*

Illness – allergies

Berger, Melvin. *Why I sneeze, shiver, hiccup, and yawn*
Geras, Adèle. *The Cats of Cuckoo Square, Geejay the Hero*
Harrison, Troon. *Aaron's awful allergies*
Wilson, Sarah. *Elmo says, achoo!*

Illness – Alzheimer's

Altman, Linda Jacobs. *Singing with Momma Lou*
Bahr, Mary. *The memory box*
Guthrie, Donna. *Grandpa doesn't know it's me*
Karkowsky, Nancy. *Grandma's soup*
Kroll, Virginia L. *Fireflies, peach pies, and lullabies*
Nelson, Vaunda Micheaux. *Always Gramma*
Sakai, Kimiko. *Sachiko means happiness*
Weitzman, Elizabeth. *Let's talk about when someone you love has Alzheimer's disease*

Illness – asthma

Berger, Melvin. *Why I sneeze, shiver, hiccup, and yawn*
Carter, Alden R. *I'm tougher than asthma!*
Gordon, Sharon. *Asthma*
London, Jonathan. *The lion who had asthma*

Illness – cancer

Blake, Claire. *The paper chain*
Borden, Louise. *Good luck, Mrs. K!*
Bridge, Chris. *Andrew's story*
Kohlenberg, Sherry. *Sammy's mommy has cancer*
Krisher, Trudy. *Kathy's hats*
Maple, Marilyn J. *On the wings of a butterfly*
Napoli, Donna Jo. *Flamingo dream*
Numeroff, Laura Joffe. *The hope tree*
Polacco, Patricia. *Betty Doll*
Tusa, Tricia. *Bunnies in my head*
Van den Berg, Marinus. *The three birds*
Winthrop, Elizabeth. *Promises*

Illness – chicken pox

Anderson, Laurie Halse. *Turkey pox*
Brown, Marc Tolon. *Arthur's chicken pox*
Cazet, Denys. *The octopus*
Dealey, Erin. *Goldie Locks has chicken pox*
Fine, Anne. *Poor Monty*
Kelley, True. *I've got chicken pox*
Maccarone, Grace. *Itchy, itchy chicken pox*
Rosa-Casanova, Sylvia. *Mama Provi and the pot of rice*
Rosenberry, Vera. *When Vera was sick*
Smith, Maggie (Margaret C.). *Dear Daisy, get well soon*

Illness – cold (disease)

Hest, Amy. *Guess who, Baby Duck*
Maccarone, Grace. *I have a cold*
Posthuma, Sieb. *Benny*
Slate, Joseph. *Miss Bindergarten stays home from kindergarten*
Weeks, Sarah. *Baa-choo!*

Illness – diabetes

Carter, Alden R. *I'm tougher than diabetes!*
Pirner, Connie White. *Even little kids get diabetes*

Illness – drug addiction

Oppenheim, Joanne. *No way, Slippery Slick!*

Illness – epilepsy

Lears, Laurie. *Becky the brave*

Illness – influenza

Bateman, Teresa. *Farm flu*
Reynolds, Marilynn. *The name of the child*

Illness – measles

Cole, Babette. *Don't go out tonight*
Duquennoy, Jacques. *Operation ghost*

Illness – mental illness

Day, Marie. *Edward the "crazy man"*
Houk, Randy. *Rico's hawk*
Niner, Holly L. *Mr. Worry*
Tooinsky, Izzi. *The turkey prince*

Illness – mumps

Lerner, Marguerite Rush. *Dear little mumps child*
Ostrovsky, Vivian. *Mumps!*
Showers, Paul. *No measles, no mumps for me*

Illness – muscular dystrophy

Osofsky, Audrey. *My buddy*

Illness – poliomyelitis

De Anda, Diane. *Dancing Miranda = Baila, Miranda, baila*

Illness – tonsillectomy

Carlstrom, Nancy White. *Barney is best*
Davison, Martine. *Rita goes to the hospital*
Hatkoff, Juliana. *Good-bye tonsils*

Illusions, optical *see* Optical illusions

Illustrators *see* Careers – illustrators

Illustrators, children *see* Children as illustrators

Imaginary friends *see* Imagination – imaginary friends

Imagination

Abisch, Roz. *Open your eyes*
Ada, Alma Flor. *Daniel's mystery egg*
Adam, Barbara. *The big, big box*
Adler, David A. *I know I'm a witch*
Adlerman, Daniel. *Africa calling*
Agee, Jon. *Ellsworth*
   The incredible painting of Felix Clousseau
Agell, Charlotte. *Mud makes me dance in the spring*
Aiken, Joan. *Arabel and Mortimer*
Aitken, Amy. *Kate and Mona in the jungle*
   Ruby!
   Ruby, the red knight
Alexander, Martha G. *Bobo's dream*
   Marty McGee's space lab, no girls allowed
Allan, Nicholas. *The thing that ate Aunt Julia*
Allen, Jeffrey. *The secret life of Mr. Weird*
Allen, Pamela. *I wish I had a pirate suit*
   A lion in the night
Anastasio, Dina. *Baby Piggy and giant bubble*
Andersen, H. C. (Hans Christian). *The emperor's new clothes*, ill. by Angela Barrett
   The emperor's new clothes, ill. by Erik Blegvad
   The emperor's new clothes, ill. by Virginia Lee Burton
   The emperor's new clothes, ill. by Robert Byrd
   The emperor's new clothes, ill. by Charlene DeLage
   The emperor's new clothes, ill. by Jack and Irene Delano
   The emperor's new clothes, ill. by Hélène Desputeaux
   The emperor's new clothes, ill. by Birte Dietz
   The emperor's new clothes, ill. by Dorothée Duntze
   The emperor's new clothes, ill. by Pamela Baldwin Ford
   The emperor's new clothes, ill. by Jack Kent
   The emperor's new clothes, ill. by Monika Laimgruber
   The emperor's new clothes, ill. by Anne F. Rockwell
   The emperor's new clothes, ill. by Janet Stevens
   The emperor's new clothes, ill. by Robert Van Nutt
   The emperor's new clothes, ill. by Nadine Bernard Westcott
Anderson, C. W. (Clarence Williams). *Linda and the Indians*
Anderson, Joan. *Harry's helicopter*
   Sally's submarine
Anderson, Lonzo. *The haganinny*
Anderson, Wayne. *Dragon*
Angeletti, Roberta. *Nefertari, princess of Egypt*
Anglund, Joan Walsh. *The brave cowboy*
   Cowboy's secret life
Anholt, Laurence. *Summerhouse*
Anno, Mitsumasa. *Anno's alphabet*
   Anno's animals
   Anno's Britain
   Anno's counting book
   Anno's counting house
   Anno's flea market
   Anno's Italy
   Anno's journey
   Anno's magical ABC
   Anno's U.S.A.
   Dr. Anno's magical midnight circus
   The king's flower
   Topsy turvies: more pictures to stretch the imagination
   Topsy turvies: pictures to stretch the imagination
   Upside-downers
Armour, Richard Willard. *Animals on the ceiling*
Armstrong, Jennifer. *Pockets*
Arnold, Caroline. *My friend from outer space*
Arnold, Tedd. *No jumping on the bed!*
   No more water in the tub!
Asch, Frank. *City sandwich*
   Goodnight horsey
   Rebecka
Ashman, Linda. *Just another morning*
Ayal, Ora. *The adventures of Chester the chest*
   Ugbu
Bach, Othello. *Lilly, Willy and the mail-order witch*
Baillie, Allan. *Drac and the gremlin*

Baillie, Marilyn. *Nose to toes*
Baker, Alan. *Benjamin bounces back*
Baker, Betty. *My sister says*
Baker, Keith. *The magic fan*
Baker, Roberta. *No ordinary Olive*
Balet, Jan B. *Ned and Ed and the lion*
Bang, Molly. *The grey lady and the strawberry snatcher*
Banks, Kate (Katherine A.). *Alphabet soup*
   Spider, spider
Bannon, Laura. *The best house in the world*
Barber, Antonia. *Satchelmouse and the dinosaurs*
Barrett, Judi. *Cloudy with a chance of meatballs*
   I hate to go to bed
Barry, Katharina. *A bug to hug*
Bartels, Alice L. *The grandmother doll*
Barthelme, Donald. *The slightly irregular fire engine*
Bate, Lucy. *How Georgina drove the car very carefully from Boston to New York*
Baumann, Kurt. *The paper airplane*
Bayley, Nicola. *Crab cat*
   Elephant cat
   Parrot cat
   Polar bear cat
   Spider cat
Beck, Ian. *Emily and the golden acorn*
Beech, Caroline. *Peas again for lunch*
Behrens, June. *Can you walk the plank?*
Beifuss, John. *Armadillo Ray*
Beim, Jerrold. *The taming of Toby*
Benedictus, Roger. *Fifty million sausages*
Benjamin, Alan. *Ribtickle Town*
Bennett, Rowena. *The day is dancing and other poems*
   Songs from around a toadstool table
Berenstain, Stan. *The Berenstain bears in the dark*
Bergman, Donna. *Timmy Green's blue lake*
Berry, Christine. *Mama went walking*
Berson, Harold. *I'm bored, Ma!*
Bertrand, Cécile. *Let's pretend!*
Bishop, Gavin. *Little Rabbit and the sea*
Bittner, Wolfgang. *Wake up, Grizzly!*
Blakeley, Peggy. *What shall I be tomorrow?*
Blathwayt, Benedict. *Tangle and the firesticks*
Blaustein, Muriel. *Jim chimp's story*
Blegvad, Lenore. *Anna Banana and me*
   Rainy day Kate
Blocksma, Mary. *The pup went up*
Blos, Joan W. *Martin's hats*
Blundell, Tony. *Joe on Sunday*
Bodsworth, Nan. *Monkey business*
Boegehold, Betty. *Hurray for Pippa!*
   In the castle of cats
Boon, Emilie. *Peterkin meets a star*
   Peterkin's wet walk
Bottner, Barbara. *Mean Maxine*
   Myra
   There was nobody there
Boutell, Clarence Burley. *The fat baron*
Bowdish, Lynea. *The carousel ride*
Bowers, Kathleen Rice. *At this very minute*
Boyd, Lizi. *Princess, cowboy, pirate, elf*
   Sweet dreams, Willy
   Willy and the cardboard boxes
Boyd, Selma. *I met a polar bear*
Bradley, Kimberly Brubaker. *Favorite things*
Brami, Elisabeth. *Mommy time*
Brenner, Anita. *I want to fly*
Brenner, Barbara A. *Dinosaurium*
Bridges, Margaret Park. *If I were your father*
Briggs, Raymond. *The bear*
   Walking in the air
Brimner, Larry Dane. *Cat on wheels*
Brisson, Pat. *Magic carpet*
Bröger, Achim. *Francie's paper puppy*
   Little Harry
Brooks, Gregory. *Monroe's island*
Brown, Calef. *Tippintown*
Browne, Anthony. *Bear goes to town*

Changes
Gorilla
The little bear book
Look what I've got!
Through the magic mirror
Bruce, Sheilah B. *The radish day jubilee*
Buckaway, C. M. *Alfred, the dragon who lost his flame*
Buckingham, Simon. *Alec and his flying bed*
Budd, Lillian. *The people on Long Ago Street*
Bulette, Sara. *The elf in the singing tree*
Bunting, Eve (Anne Evelyn). *Little Badger, terror of the seven seas*
Burke, Katie. *Lightning bug thunder*
Burke-Weiner, Kimberly. *The maybe garden*
Burleigh, Robert. *It's funny where Ben's train takes him*
Burnard, Damon. *The amazing adventures of Soupy Boy*
Burningham, John. *Cloudland*
    Come away from the water, Shirley
    John Patrick Norman McHennessy – the boy who was always late
    Time to get out of the bath, Shirley
    Where's Julius?
    Would you rather . . .
Bursik, Rose. *Amelia's fantastic flight*
Bush, Timothy. *James in the house of Aunt Prudence*
Cabban, Vanessa. *Bertie and Small and the brave sea journey*
Cader, Lisa Lebowitz. *When I wear my crown*
    When I wear my tiara
Calders, Pere. *Brush*
Callen, Larry. *Dashiel and the night*
Camp, Lindsay. *Dinosaurs at the supermarket*
Carle, Eric. *Little cloud*
    Little cloud [board book]
Carman, William. *What's that noise?*
Carrick, Carol. *Patrick's dinosaurs*
    Patrick's dinosaurs on the Internet
    What happened to Patrick's dinosaurs?
Carrier, Lark. *Scout and Cody*
    There was a hill . . .
Carroll, Lewis. *The nursery "Alice"*
Carter, Anne Laurel. *Circus play*
    Tall in the saddle
Cartier, Wesley. *Marco's run*
Catalanotto, Peter. *Dad and me*
Cazet, Denys. *Daydreams*
Chalmers, Mary. *The cat who liked to pretend*
Chapouton, Anne-Marie. *Sebastian is always late*
Charlton, Nancy Lee. *Derek's dog days*
Chen, Chih-Yuan. *On my way to buy eggs*
Chevalier, Christa. *Spence and the sleepytime monster*
Chichester Clark, Emma. *More!*
Child, Lauren. *I will never not ever eat a tomato*
Chislett, Gail. *The rude visitors*
Chorao, Kay. *Lester's overnight*
Chwast, Seymour. *Harry, I need you!*
Clibbon, Meg. *Imagine you're a fairy!*
    Imagine you're a mermaid!
    Imagine you're a pirate!
    Imagine you're a wizard!
Cohen, Caron Lee. *Martin and the giant lions*
Cohen, Miriam. *Down in the subway*
    Eddy's dream
Cole, Babette. *The trouble with Uncle*
Collier, John. *The backyard*
Collins, Pat Lowery. *My friend Andrew*
Cooper, Elizabeth K. *The fish from Japan*
Cooper, Helen (Helen F.). *The bear under the stairs*
    Tatty-Ratty
Couture, Susan Arkin. *The biggest horse I ever did see*
Cowen-Fletcher, Jane. *Farmer Will*
Cowley, Joy. *Mrs. Goodstory*
Coy, John. *Vroomaloom zoom*
Craig, Helen. *Susie and Alfred in the knight, the princess and the dragon*
Craig, M. Jean. *The dragon in the clock box*
Craven, Carolyn. *What the mailman brought*
Creech, Sharon. *Fishing in the air*
Creighton, Jill. *Maybe a monster*
    One day there was nothing to do

Crews, Nina. *I'll catch the moon*
    You are here
Crisp, Marty. *Totally polar*
Crowley, Michael. *New kid on Spurwick Ave.*
Cummings, E. E. (Edward Estlin). *Fairy tales*
Cuneo, Mary Louise. *How to grow a picket fence*
Cutler, Ivor. *Herbert*
Dale, Penny. *Wake up, Mr. B.!*
Damjan, Mischa. *The little sea horse*
Davis, Douglas F. *There's an elephant in the garage*
Day, Alexandra. *Mirror*
Degen, Bruce. *Sailaway home*
    Teddy bear towers
Delaney, A. *Monster tracks?*
Delessert, Etienne. *A long long song*
DeLuise, Dom. *King Bob's new clothes*
Demarest, Chris L. *My blue boat*
    My little red car
    No peas for Nellie
    Orville's odyssey
Dematons, Charlotte. *Let's go*
De Regniers, Beatrice Schenk. *Laura's story*
    A little house of your own
    Waiting for mama
    What can you do with a shoe?
DeSaix, Deborah Durland. *In the back seat*
Desimini, Lisa. *Moon soup*
De Veaux, Alexis. *An enchanted hair tale*
Devlin, Wende. *Aunt Agatha, there's a lion under the couch!*
De Vries, Maggie. *How sleep found Tabitha*
Dewan, Ted. *Baby gets the zapper*
Dickinson, Mary. *Alex and Roy*
Dickinson, Mike. *My dad doesn't even notice*
DiFiori, Lawrence. *If I had a little car*
D'Ignazio, Fred. *Katie and the computer*
Dijs, Carla. *Pretend you're a hippo*
Diller, Harriett. *The faraway drawer*
DiTerlizzi, Tony. *Jimmy Zangwow's out-of-this-world, moon pie adventure*
Diviny, Sean. *Snow inside the house*
Dobrin, Arnold Jack. *Josephine's 'magination*
Dodd, Lynley. *A dragon in a wagon*
Donahue, Shari Faden. *The zebra-striped whale with the polka-dot tail*
Doolittle, Eileen. *World of wonders*
Dorian, Marguerite. *When the snow is blue*
Dornbusch, Erica. *Finding Kate's shoes*
Dowling, Paul. *Splodger*
Dragonwagon, Crescent. *If you call my name*
Drawson, Blair. *All along the river*
    Flying Dimitri
    Mary Margaret's tree
Drescher, Henrik. *Looking for Santa Claus*
Drury, Tim. *When I'm big*
Dunbar, Polly. *Dog Blue*
    Flyaway Katie
Dunnick, Regan. *Sweet dreams, Douglas*
Eccles, Jane. *Maxwell's birthday*
Edmund and the White Witch
Edwards, Patricia Kier. *Chester and Uncle Willoughby*
Edwards, Roland. *Tigers*
Ekker, Ernest A. *What is beyond the hill?*
Elzbieta. *Dikou and the mysterious moon sheep*
Emerson, Scott. *The magic boots*
Etherington, Frank. *The spaghetti word race*
Ets, Marie Hall. *In the forest*
Evans, Lezlie. *If I were the wind*
Eversole, Robyn Harbert. *The magic house*
Falwell, Cathryn. *Word wizard*
Faulkner, Matt. *The amazing voyage of Jackie Grace*
Fazzi, Maura. *The circus of mystery*
Fearnley, Jan. *A special something*
Feiffer, Jules. *Meanwhile . . .*
Félix, Monique. *The further adventures of the little mouse trapped in a book*
    The story of a little mouse trapped in a book
Fenner, Carol. *Tigers in the cellar*
Fenton, Edward. *Fierce John*

Fitzpatrick, Marie-Louise. *I'm a tiger, too!*
Fleischman, Paul. *Rondo in C*
Fontaine, Jan. *The spaghetti tree*
Ford, Miela. *My day in the garden*
Fowler, Allan. *What do you see in a cloud?*
Fox, Christyan. *Astronaut PiggyWiggy*
    Fire fighter PiggyWiggy
Francis, Frank. *The magic wallpaper*
Franklin, Jonathan. *Don't wake the baby*
Freeman, Don. *The paper party*
    Quiet! There's a canary in the library
Fuge, Charles. *I know a rhino*
Fujikawa, Gyo. *See what I can be!*
Furtado, Jo. *Sorry, Miss Folio!*
Gackenbach, Dick. *Harry and the terrible whatzit*
    Mag the magnificent
    Supposes
Gage, Wilson. *Mrs. Gaddy and the ghost*
Galbraith, Kathryn Osebold. *Spots are special*
Gardiner, Lindsey. *Here come Poppy and Max*
    When Poppy and Max grow up
Gardner, Sally. *Mama, don't go out tonight*
Gay, Marie-Louise. *Rainy day magic*
George, Lindsay Barrett. *My bunny and me*
Geras, Adèle. *The nutcracker*
Gillham, Bill. *What can you do?*
Gilliland, Judith Heide. *Not in the house, Newton!*
Givens, Terryl. *Dragon scales and willow leaves*
Glass, Andrew. *My brother tries to make me laugh*
Glassman, Peter. *My dad's job*
    The wizard next door
Gliori, Debi. *When I'm big*
Godwin, Laura. *Little white dog*
Goennel, Heidi. *I pretend*
    If I were a penguin . . .
Goode, Diane. *The dinosaur's new clothes*
Gottlieb, Dale. *Seeing Eye Willie*
Graham, Bob. *Max*
Greenblat, Rodney Alan. *Thunder Bunny*
Greenburg, Dan. *Great-Grandpa's in the litter box*
    Through the medicine cabinet
Greenfield, Eloise. *I can draw a weeposaur and other dinosaurs*
    On my horse
Greenstein, Elaine. *Emily and the crows*
Gregory, Nan. *Wild Girl and Gran*
Grejniec, Michael. *When I open my eyes*
Greve, Andreas. *Christopher's dream car*
Greydanus, Rose. *Let's pretend*
Grifalconi, Ann. *Electric Yancy*
Griff (Andrew Griffin). *Shark-mad Stanley*
Guy, Ginger Foglesong. *Black crow, black crow*
Gwynne, Fred. *A chocolate moose for dinner*
    A little pigeon toad
Haas, Irene. *A summertime song*
Haggerty, Mary Elizabeth. *A crack in the wall*
Hague, Michael. *The nutcracker*
Hamanaka, Sheila. *I look like a girl*
Hamsa, Bobbie. *Your pet bear*
    Your pet beaver
    Your pet camel
    Your pet elephant
    Your pet giraffe
    Your pet kangaroo
    Your pet penguin
    Your pet sea lion
Handford, Martin. *Where's Waldo? The fantastic journey*
Hanlon, Emily. *What if a lion eats me and I fall into a hippopotamus' mud hole?*
Harper, Jessica. *Nora's room*
Harrison, Troon. *The dream collector*
Hartmann, Wendy. *All the magic in the world*
Haseley, Dennis. *My father doesn't know about the woods and me*
    The thieves' market
Haus, Felice. *Beep! Beep! I'm a jeep*
Hayles, Marsha. *He saves the day*
Heap, Sue. *What shall we play?*
Heckman, Philip. *Waking upside down*

Heidbreder, Robert. *I wished for a unicorn*
Heller, Nicholas. *An adventure at sea*
    The front hall carpet
    A troll story
    Up the wall
Hennessy, B. G. (Barbara G.). *The dinosaur who lived in my backyard*
Henry, Lenny. *Charlie and the big chill*
    Charlie, queen of the desert
Hiatt, Fred. *If I were queen of the world*
Hill, Susan. *Beware, beware*
Hillert, Margaret. *What is it?*
Himler, Ronald. *The girl on the yellow giraffe*
Himmelman, John. *Lights out!*
Hindley, Judy. *Maybe it's a pirate*
    Rosy's visitors
    Uncle Harold and the green hat
Hines, Anna Grossnickle. *Bethany for real*
    Gramma's walk
Hoban, Russell. *The flight of Bembel Rudzuk*
    Goodnight
    The great gum drop robbery
    Monsters
    The rain door
Hoffmann, E. T. A. *The nutcracker*, ill. by Francesca Crespi
    The nutcracker, ill. by Renée Graef
    The nutcracker, ill. by Rachel Isadora
    The nutcracker, ill. by Joanna Isles
    The nutcracker, ill. by Maurice Sendak
    The nutcracker, ill. by Lisbeth Zwerger
    The nutcracker ballet, ill. by Carolyn Ewing
    The nutcracker ballet, ill. by Vladimir Vasilévich Vagin
Holabird, Katharine. *Alexander and the magic boat*
Holl, Adelaide. *Most-of-the-time Maxie*
Holleyman, Sonia. *Mona the vampire*
Holman, Felice. *Victoria's castle*
Hood, Thomas. *Before I go to sleep*
Hooker, Ruth. *Matthew the cowboy*
Horwitz, Elinor Lander. *Sometimes it happens*
Howard, Jane R. *When I'm sleepy*
Hughes, Shirley. *Abel's moon*
    Up and up
Hurd, Edith Thacher. *The white horse*
Hutchins, H. J. (Hazel J.). *Nicholas at the library*
Ichikawa, Satomi. *Isabela's ribbons*
Imagine that! poems of never-was
Inkpen, Mick. *The blue balloon*
    If I had a pig
    If I had a sheep
    Lullabyhullaballoo!
    One bear at bedtime
Irwin, Michael. *Bears in my bed*
Isadora, Rachel. *The pirates of Bedford Street*
Ivanov, Anatoly. *Ol' Jake's lucky day*
James, Simon. *Dear Mr. Blueberry*
Janosch. *Hey Presto! You're a bear!*
Jenkin-Pearce, Susie. *The enchanted garden*
Jeram, Anita. *I love my little storybook*
Jeschke, Susan. *Tamar and the tiger*
Jewell, Nancy. *Try and catch me*
Jeyaveeran, Ruth. *The road to Mumbai*
Johnson, B. J. *A hat like that*
Johnson, Crockett. *The blue ribbon puppies*
    Ellen's lion
    Harold and the purple crayon
    Harold at the North Pole
    Harold's ABC
    Harold's circus
    Harold's fairy tale
    Harold's trip to the sky
    A picture for Harold's room
Johnson, D. B. (Donald B.). *Henry climbs a mountain*
Johnson, Elizabeth. *All in free but Janey*
Johnson, Jane. *Sybil and the blue rabbit*
Johnston, Deborah. *Mathew Michael's beastly day*
Jonas, Ann. *The trek*
Jonell, Lynne. *Mommy go away!*

Jones, Diana Wynne. *Yes, dear*
Jordan, Jennifer. *Albert goes to town*
Jordan, Sandra. *Down on Casey's farm*
Jukes, Mavis. *You're a bear*
Kalman, Maira. *Hey Willy, see the pyramids!*
Kamish, Daniel. *Diggy Dan*
Karim, Roberta. *This is a hospital, not a zoo!*
Karmi, Giora. *And Shira imagined*
Keats, Ezra Jack. *Dreams*
  Regards to the man in the moon
  The trip
Keeping, Charles. *Willie's fire-engine*
Keeshan, Robert. *Alligator in the basement*
Kellogg, Steven (Stephen). *Ralph's secret weapon*
King, Larry L. *Because of Lozo Brown*
Kitamura, Satoshi. *Lily takes a walk*
Knaff, Jean Christian. *Manhattan*
Knight, Hilary. *Hilary Knight's the owl and the pussy-cat*
Knutson, Kimberley. *Jungle jamboree*
Kojima, Naomi. *The flying grandmother*
Krahn, Fernando. *Amanda and the mysterious carpet*
Krauss, Ruth. *Everything under a mushroom*
  I can fly
  A moon or a button
  Open house for butterflies
  Somebody else's nut tree, and other tales from children
  This thumbprint
  A very special house
Krensky, Stephen. *Fraidy Cats*
Kroll, Steven. *Are you pirates?*
  The magic rocket
  Oh, what a Thanksgiving!
  Toot! Toot!
  The tyrannosaurus game
Kroll, Virginia L. *Faraway drums*
Kroninger, Stephen. *If I crossed the road*
Krupp, Robin Rector. *Get set to wreck!*
Kumin, Maxine W. *Follow the fall*
Kurjian, Judi. *In my own backyard*
Kuskin, Karla. *Paul*
  Which horse is William?
Lacome, Julie. *I'm a jolly farmer*
Landa, Norbert. *How does it feel?*
Landry, Leo. *Eat your peas, Ivy Louise!*
LaRochelle, David. *The evening king*
Lasell, Fen. *Fly away goose*
Lawson, Janet (Janet M.). *Audrey and Barbara*
Leemis, Ralph. *Smart dog*
Le Guin, Ursula K. *Fish soup*
Leonard, Marcia. *Dress-up*
Lester, Alison. *Celeste sails to Spain*
  Isabella's bed
  Magic beach
Le-Tan, Pierre. *Timothy's dream book*
  Visit to the North Pole
Levert, Mireille. *An island in the soup*
Lewis, J. Patrick. *The Christmas of the reddle moon*
Lewis, Kim. *The last train*
Lewis, Stephen (Stephen Paul). *Zoo city*
Lexau, Joan M. *A house so big*
Lifton, Betty Jean. *The secret seller*
Lindbergh, Reeve. *Benjamin's barn*
Lindgren, Astrid. *Most beloved sister*
Lindgren, Barbro. *The wild baby goes to sea*
Lionni, Leo. *Let's make rabbits*
Lithgow, John. *Carnival of the animals*
  I'm a manatee
Lively, Penelope. *The cat, the crow, and the banyan tree*
Lloyd, David. *Grandma and the pirate*
Löfgren, Ulf. *Alvin the pirate*
  The wonderful tree
London, Jonathan. *If I had a horse*
  Let the lynx come in
  The lion who had asthma
Long, Claudia. *Albert's story*
Longfellow, Layne. *Imaginary menagerie*
Loux, Lynn C. *The day I could fly*

Lucy steps through the wardrobe
Luenn, Nancy. *Nessa's story*
Lyon, George Ella. *Who came down that road?*
McAfee, Annalena. *Kirsty knows best*
McAllister, Angela. *Harry's box*
  Jessie's journey
  Sleepy Ella
McCarthy, Meghan. *The adventures of Patty and the big red bus*
McCaughrean, Geraldine. *Unicorns! Unicorns!*
McClintock, Barbara. *The fantastic drawings of Danielle*
McClintock, Marshall. *What have I got?*
McConnachie, Brian. *Elmer and the chickens vs. the big league*
McCormack, John E. *Rabbit tales*
McCourt, Lisa. *Good night, Princess Pruney Toes*
  I love you, Stinky Face
  It's time for school, Stinky Face
McDermott, Beverly Brodsky. *The crystal apple*
MacDonald, Amy. *Let's pretend*
McDonald, Megan. *Bedbugs*
McHargue, Georgess. *Private zoo*
McKay, Hilary. *Pirates ahoy!*
McKissack, Patricia C. *The king's new clothes*
McLenighan, Valjean. *What you see is what you get*
McLeod, Emilie Warren. *One snail and me*
McLerran, Alice. *Roxaboxen*
McMullan, Kate (Hall). *Good night, Stella*
  The noisy giant's tea party
McNaughton, Colin. *Who's that banging on the ceiling?*
McNeil, Florence. *Sail away*
McPhail, David M. *The cereal box*
  Edward and the pirates
  Edward in the jungle
  Mistletoe
  Moony B. Finch, fastest draw in the West
  Pig Pig and the magic photo album
  Pig Pig rides
  Tinker and Tom and the Star Baby
  The train
Magnus, Erica. *My secret place*
Maizlish, Lisa. *The ring*
Mansell, Dom. *If dinosaurs came to town*
Marceau, Marcel. *The story of Bip*
Mariotti, Mario. *Hands off!*
  Hanimations
Marlowe, Pete. *One Arabian morning*
Marshall, James. *George and Martha 'round and 'round*
  Three up a tree
Martin, David. *Little Chicken Chicken*
Martin, Rafe. *Will's mammoth*
Marzollo, Jean. *Pretend you're a cat*
  The silver bear
Massey, Ed. *Milton*
Matura, Mustapha. *Moon jump*
Matus, Greta. *Where are you, Jason?*
Mayer, Mercer. *Bubble bubble*
  I am a hunter
  Terrible troll
Mayhew, James. *Katie and the sunflowers*
  Miranda the explorer
Mazer, Anne. *The salamander room*
Michelson, Richard. *Animals that ought to be*
Milgrim, David. *Cows can't fly*
Miller, Margaret. *Let's pretend!*
Mills, Lauren A. *The goblin baby*
Min, Willemien. *Peter's patchwork dream*
Miranda, Anne. *Beep! beep!*
Modesitt, Jeanne. *Sometimes I feel like a mouse*
Moers, Hermann. *Annie's dancing day*
  Rufus and Max
Mogensen, Jan. *The forty-six little men*
Morgan, Michaela. *Edward gets a pet*
  Visitors for Edward
Morris, Ann. *Play*
Morris, Bob. *Crispin the Terrible*
Morris, Winifred. *What if the shark wears tennis shoes?*
Moser, Erwin. *The crow in the snow and other bedtime stories*
Most, Bernard. *If the dinosaurs came back*

Mould, Wendy. *Ants in my pants*
Murphy, Jill. *What next, baby bear!*
Narahashi, Keiko. *Is that Josie?*
Neitzel, Shirley. *I'm taking a trip on my train*
Nerlove, Miriam. *I meant to clean my room today*
   If all the world were paper
Nesbit, Edith. *Cockatoucan*
Ness, Evaline. *Sam, Bangs, and moonshine*
Newcome, Zita. *Rosie goes exploring*
Newton, Laura P. *William the vehicle king*
Nickle, John. *TV Rex*
Nightingale, Sandy. *I'm a little monster*
Nixon, Joan Lowery. *When I am eight*
Nolan, Dennis. *The castle builder*
Norman, Philip Ross. *A mammoth imagination*
Norwich, William D. *Molly and the magic dress*
Numeroff, Laura Joffe. *Chimps don't wear glasses*
Nunes, Susan Miho. *Coyote dreams*
Nygren, Tord. *The red thread*
Oakley, Graham. *Graham Oakley's magical changes*
Olofsdotter, Marie. *Frej the fearless*
Olsen, Ib Spang. *The grown-up trap*
O'Malley, Kevin. *The box*
   Straight to the pole
Oram, Hiawyn. *In the attic*
Ormerod, Jan. *Ben goes swimming*
   The saucepan game
Ottley, Matt. *What Faust saw*
Oxenbury, Helen. *729 curious creatures*
   729 merry mix-ups
   729 puzzle people
Pack, Robert. *How to catch a crocodile*
Palatini, Margie. *Zak's lunch*
Pallotta, Jerry. *The dory story*
Paolilli, Paul. *Silver seeds*
Park, Frances. *Where on earth is my bagel?*
Parlato, Stephen. *The world that loved books*
Paterson, Diane. *The bathtub ocean*
Pavey, Peter. *I'm Taggarty Toad*
Pennypacker, Sara. *Stuart's cape*
Peppé, Rodney. *The kettleship pirates*
Perkins, Charles. *Swinging on a rainbow*
Perlman, Janet. *The Emperor Penguin's new clothes*
Perry, Sarah. *If . . .*
Peters, Lisa Westberg. *Cold little duck, duck, duck*
Pfanner, Louise. *Louise builds a house*
Pinkwater, Daniel Manus. *I was a second grade werewolf*
   Tooth-gnasher superflash
   Wempires
Pirani, Felix. *Abigail at the beach*
Pittman, Helena Clare. *Once when I was scared*
Polacco, Patricia. *Appelemando's dreams*
   My ol' man
Pomerantz, Charlotte. *Timothy Tall Feather*
Ponti, Claude. *Adele's album*
Portlock, Rob. *Someone's trying to cut off my head*
Postma, Lidia. *The stolen mirror*
Powell, Polly. *Just dessert*
Prater, John. *Once upon a picnic*
   Once upon a time
Prelutsky, Jack. *The baby uggs are hatching*
   Ride a purple pelican
   The snopp on the sidewalk and other poems
Price, Mathew. *Have you seen my sister?*
Price-Thomas, Brian. *The magic ark*
Pringle, Laurence P. *Jesse builds a road*
The pudgy book of make-believe
Radlauer, Ruth Shaw. *Of course, you're a horse!*
Radley, Gail. *The night Stella hid the stars*
Raschka, Christopher. *Elizabeth imagined an iceberg*
Raskin, Ellen. *Franklin Stein*
   Spectacles
Ratnett, Michael. *Jenny's bear*
Reasoner, Charles. *Who pretends?*
Reavin, Sam. *Hurray for Captain Jane!*
Reid, Alastair. *Supposing*
Reiser, Lynn. *Any kind of dog*

   Best friends think alike
Renberg, Dalia Hardof. *Hello, clouds!*
Ressner, Phil. *Dudley Pippin*
Rex, Michael. *My fire engine*
Rice, Inez. *A long long time*
   The March wind
Riches, Judith. *Giraffes have more fun*
Riddle, Tohby. *Careful with that ball, Eugene!*
Rinder, Lenore. *A big mistake*
Ringgold, Faith. *Bonjour, Lonnie*
Ringi, Kjell (Arne Sorensen). *My father and I*
Robbins, Beth. *Tom's afraid of the dark*
Roberts, Bethany. *Gramps and the fire dragon*
   Rosie to the rescue
Roberts, Thom. *Pirates in the park*
Rodgers, Frank. *Who's afraid of the ghost train?*
Root, Phyllis. *Moon tiger*
Rosen, Michael J. (1954–). *With a dog like that, a kid like me . . .*
Rosen, Winifred. *Dragons hate to be discreet*
Rosenberg, Liz. *The carousel*
Rosner, Ruth. *Arabba gah zee, Marissa and Me!*
Rush, Ken. *Friday's journey*
Russ, Lavinia. *Alec's sand castle*
Russo, Marisabina. *The big brown box*
   Why do grownups have all the fun?
Ryan, Pam Muñoz. *Mud is cake*
Ryder, Joanne. *Bears out there*
   Tyrannosaurus time
Sabraw, John. *I wouldn't be scared*
Salter, Heidi. *Taddy McFinley and the great grey grimly*
Samton, Sheila White. *Jenny's journey*
SanAngelo, Ryan. *Eddie spaghetti*
Sato, Satoru. *I wish I had a big, big tree*
Sava, Donna Lynn. *Teddy bear dreams*
Say, Allen. *Emma's rug*
Schaap, Martine. *Mop's mountain adventure*
Schaefer, Carole Lexa. *Someone says*
Schoberle, Ceile. *Beyond the Milky Way*
Schotter, Roni. *Captain Bob sets sail*
   Captain Bob takes flight
   Dreamland
Schreier, Joshua. *Luigi's all-night parking lot*
Schrier, Jeffrey. *On the wings of eagles*
Scott, Ann Herbert. *Big Cowboy Western*
Seligson, Susan. *The amazing Amos and the greatest couch on earth*
   Amos ahoy
   Amos
Sendak, Maurice. *In the night kitchen*
   The sign on Rosie's door
   Where the wild things are
Seuss, Dr. *And to think that I saw it on Mulberry Street*
   McElligot's pool
   Oh say can you say?
   Oh, the thinks you can think!
Sharmat, Marjorie Weinman. *My mother never listens to me*
Sharratt, Nick. *Ahoy, Pirate Pete*
   Once upon a time . . .
Shaw, Charles Green. *It looked like spilt milk*
Shecter, Ben. *Conrad's castle*
   If I had a ship
Shelby, Anne. *The someday house*
Sheldon, Dyan. *Unicorn dreams*
Sherman, Ivan. *I am a giant*
Shields, Carol Diggory. *I am really a princess*
Shimin, Symeon. *I wish there were two of me*
Shipton, Jonathan. *What if?*
Shulevitz, Uri. *One Monday morning*
Sicotte, Virginia. *A riot of quiet*
Siepmann, Jane. *The lion on Scott Street*
Simmonds, Posy. *Lulu and the flying babies*
Sis, Peter. *Ballerina*
   Dinosaur!
   Madlenka
   Ship ahoy!
Skorpen, Liesel Moak. *If I had a lion*
Sleator, William. *That's silly*
Slobodkin, Louis. *Clear the track for Michael's magic train*

Magic Michael
Smith, Jim. *Nimbus the explorer*
Smith, Linda. *Sir Cassie to the rescue*
Smith, Maggie (Margaret C.). *My grandma's chair*
   There's a witch under the stairs
Spalding, Andrea. *It's raining, it's pouring*
Spinelli, Eileen. *In my new yellow shirt*
Stanley, Diane. *Birdsong lullaby*
Steig, William. *Pete's a pizza*
   Toby, who are you?
Steiner, Charlotte. *Look what Tracy found*
Stemp, Robin. *Guy and the flowering plum tree*
Stern, Ellen. *I saw a bullfrog*
Stevens, Cat. *Teaser and the firecat*
Stevenson, James. *Worse than Willy!*
Stevenson, Jocelyn. *Red and the pumpkins*
Stevenson, Robert Louis. *Block city*
   The little land
Stinson, Kathy. *The dressed up book*
   Those green things
Stoddard, Sandol. *Curl up small*
   The thinking book
Stone, Kazuko G. *Goodnight Twinklegator*
Stone, Phoebe. *Go away, Shelley Boo!*
Stuve-Bodeen, Stephanie. *Elizabeti's doll*
Sundgaard, Arnold. *Meet Jack Appleknocker*
Supraner, Robyn. *Would you rather be a tiger?*
Sutherland, Harry A. *Dad's car wash*
Sutherland, Marc. *The waiting place*
Swanson-Natsues, Lyn. *Days of adventure*
Sweeney, Jacqueline. *Katie and the night noises*
Sweetland, Nancy Rose. *If I could = Si yo pudiera*
Tafuri, Nancy. *Junglewalk*
Tamar, Erika. *Donnatalee*
Taniuchi, Kota. *Trolley*
Tarpley, Natasha Anastasia. *Joe-Joe's first flight*
Teague, Mark. *The Lost and found*
Testa, Fulvio. *The endless journey*
   The land where the ice cream grows
Thayer, Jane. *Andy and the wild worm*
Theroux, Phyllis. *Serefina under the circumstances*
Thomas, Frances. *What if?*
Thomas, Ianthe. *Walk home tired, Billy Jenkins*
Thompson, Colin (Colin Edward). *Falling angels*
Thompson, Richard. *Effie's bath*
   Gurgle, bubble, splash
   Jenny's neighbours
   Jesse on the night train
   The night walker
   Sky full of babies
Tibo, Gilles. *The cowboy kid*
   Simon's disguise
Tompert, Ann. *Little Fox goes to the end of the world*
Townson, Hazel. *Terrible Tuesday*
   What on earth . . . ?
Trapani, Iza. *I'm a little teapot*
Tregebov, Rhea. *What-if Sara*
Trottier, Maxine. *The tiny kite of Eddie Wing*
Turkle, Brinton. *The sky dog*
Turner, Ann Warren. *Let's be animals*
Turner, Sandy. *Grow up*
Tusa, Tricia. *Bunnies in my head*
   Camilla's new hairdo
Udry, Janice May. *Is Susan here?*, ill. by Peter Edwards
   Is Susan here?, ill. by Karen Gundersheimer
Ulmer, Wendy K. *A campfire for cowboy Billy*
Updike, David. *An autumn tale*
Utton, Peter. *Jennifer's room*
Valfre, Edward. *Backseat buckaroo*
   Vacationers from outer space
Van Allsburg, Chris. *Bad day at Riverbend*
   The garden of Abdul Gasazi
   Jumanji
   The mysteries of Harris Burdick
   The polar express
Van Caster, Nancy. *An alligator lives in Benjamin's house*
Vaughan, Marcia Kapok. *We're going on a ghost hunt*

Velthuijs, Max. *Crocodile's masterpiece*
   The painter and the bird
Vigna, Judith. *Boot weather*
Viorst, Judith. *The good-bye book*
   My mama says there aren't any zombies, ghosts, vampires, creatures, demons, monsters, fiends, goblins, or things
Vogel, Ilse-Margret. *The don't be scared book*
Vreeken, Elizabeth. *The boy who would not say his name*
Wahl, Jan. *I met a dinosaur*
   My cat Ginger
Wahl, Robert. *Pyxx*
Waldman, Neil. *The starry night*
Wallace, Karen. *Imagine you are a tiger*
Wallner, Alexandra. *Beatrix Potter*
Walsh, Jill Paton. *Connie came to play*
Walsh, Joanna. *What if?*
Ward, Helen. *The dragon machine*
Warner, Sunny. *Madison finds a line*
Watson, Clyde. *Midnight moon*
Wayland, April Halprin. *To Rabbittown*
Wells, Philip. *Daddy Island*
Wells, Rosemary. *Good night, Fred*
   A lion for Lewis
   Small world of Binky Braverman
Westell, Kerry. *Amanda's book*
Whatley, Bruce. *Captain Pajamas*
Wheatley, Nadia. *Luke's way of looking*
Whitcher, Susan. *The key to the cupboard*
Whittington, Mary K. *Carmina, come dance!*
Whybrow, Ian. *Harry and the bucketful of dinosaurs*
Wick, Walter. *I spy fantasy*
Wiesner, David. *Hurricane*
Willard, Nancy. *The tale I told Sasha*
   A visit to William Blake's inn
Williams, Vera B. *Cherries and cherry pits*
Williams-Garcia, Rita. *Catching the wild waiyuuzee*
Winthrop, Elizabeth. *Bunk beds*
   A very noisy girl
Wood, Audrey. *The flying dragon room*
Woodruff, Elvira. *Tubtime*
Woolf, Virginia. *Nurse Lugton's curtain*
Yardley, Joanna. *The red ball*
Yolen, Jane. *King Long Shanks*
Yorinks, Arthur. *Harry and Lulu*
   Hey, Al
   Louis the fish
Young, Miriam Burt. *Jellybeans for breakfast*
Young, Ruth. *Golden Bear*
   A trip to Mars
Zarin, Cynthia. *What do you see when you shut your eyes?*
Ziefert, Harriet. *Lewis the fire fighter*
Zimelman, Nathan. *Once when I was five*
Zolotow, Charlotte (Shapiro). *The seashore book*
   When I have a son

Imagination – imaginary friends

Alexander, Martha G. *And my mean old mother will be sorry, Blackboard Bear*
   Blackboard Bear
   I sure am glad to see you, Blackboard Bear
   I'll protect you from the jungle beasts
   We're in big trouble, Blackboard Bear
   You're a genius, Blackboard Bear
Andrews, F. Emerson (Frank Emerson). *Nobody comes to dinner*
Anglund, Joan Walsh. *Cowboy and his friend*
   The cowboy's Christmas
Berger, Barbara Helen. *When the sun rose*
Bogart, Jo Ellen. *Daniel's dog*
Bornstein, Ruth Lercher. *The seedling child*
Bram, Elizabeth. *There is someone standing on my head*
Brewster, Patience. *Nobody*
Brighton, Catherine. *My hands, my world*
Burningham, John. *Aldo*
Cottringer, Anne. *Ella and the naughty lion*
Cummings, Pat. *Jimmy Lee did it*
Cuneo, Mary Louise. *What can a giant do?*

Dauer, Rosamond. *My friend, Jasper Jones*
Dillon, Barbara. *The beast in the bed*
Dinan, Carolyn. *The lunch box monster*
DiTerlizzi, Tony. *Ted*
Geringer, Laura. *Look out, look out, it's coming!*
Greenfield, Eloise. *Me and Neesie,* ill. by Moneta Barnett
　Me and Neesie, ill. by Jan Spivey Gilchrist
Guthrie, Donna. *Mrs. Gigglebelly is coming for tea*
Hazen, Barbara Shook. *The gorilla did it!*
　Gorilla wants to be the baby
Henkes, Kevin. *Jessica*
Hiller, Catherine. *Argentaybee and the boonie*
Hoff, Syd. *The horse in Harry's room*
Howe, James. *There's a dragon in my sleeping bag*
James, Simon. *Leon and Bob*
Jeschke, Susan. *Angela and Bear*
　The devil did it
Joosse, Barbara M. *The thinking place*
Khalsa, Dayal Kaur. *The snow cat*
Kherdian, David. *By myself*
Kornblatt, Marc. *Eli and the Dimplemeyers*
Krahn, Fernando. *The creepy thing*
Krensky, Stephen. *The lion upstairs*
Langner, Nola. *By the light of the silvery moon*
Marx, Patricia (Patricia A.). *Meet my staff*
Moers, Hermann. *Katie and the big, brave bear*
Morris, Terry Nell. *Good night, dear monster!*
Noble, June. *Two homes for Lynn*
Oram, Hiawyn. *Ned and the Joybaloo*
Patz, Nancy. *No thumpin' no bumpin' no rumpus tonight!*
Pinkwater, Daniel Manus. *Pickle creature*
Ross, Tony. *Hugo and Oddsock*
Rovetch, Lissa. *Trigwater did it*
St. George, Judith. *The Halloween pumpkin smasher*
Steiner, Charlotte. *Lulu*
Strauss, Gwen. *The night shimmy*
Thaler, Mike. *My puppy*
Thayer, Jane. *Andy and his fine friends*
Titherington, Jeanne. *Bonkers Fellini*
Vries, Anke de. *My elephant can do almost anything*
Watts, Marjorie-Ann. *Zebra goes to school*
Williams, Rozanne Lanczak. *The purple snerd*
Zemke, Deborah. *The shadow of Matilda Hunt*
Zolotow, Charlotte (Shapiro). *Three funny friends*

Imitation *see* Behavior – imitation

Immigrants

Atwell, Debby. *The Thanksgiving door*
Avi. *Silent movie*
Broyles, Anne. *Shy Mama's Halloween*
Bunting, Eve (Anne Evelyn). *A picnic in October*
Carling, Amelia Lau. *Mama and Papa have a store*
　Mama and Papa have a store
Cohen, Miriam. *Mimmy and Sophie*
Connor, Leslie. *Miss Bridie chose a shovel*
Corey, Shana. *Milly and the Macy's Parade*
Figueredo, D. H. *When this world was new*
Garay, Luis. *The long road*
Hearne, Betsy Gould. *Seven brave women*
Jaspersohn, William. *The two brothers*
Jiménez, Francisco. *The Christmas gift = El regalo de Navidad*
Joosse, Barbara M. *The morning chair*
Levinson, Riki. *Soon, Annala*
McCully, Emily Arnold. *Mirette and Bellini cross Niagara Falls*
McGill, Alice. *Molly Bannaky*
Mak, Kam. *My Chinatown*
Miller, Elizabeth I. *Just like home = Como en mi tierra*
Nivola, Claire A. *Elisabeth*
Nolan, Janet. *The St. Patrick's Day shillelagh*
Oberman, Sheldon. *The always prayer shawl*
Ó Flatharta, Antoine. *The prairie train*
Pak, Soyung. *A place to grow*
Park, Frances. *My freedom trip*
Partridge, Elizabeth. *Oranges on Golden Mountain*

Pérez, Amada Irma. *My diary from here to there = Mi diario de aquí hasta allá*
Polacco, Patricia. *The keeping quilt*
Pomeranc, Marion Hess. *The American Wei*
Pryor, Bonnie. *The dream jar*
Rael, Elsa Okon. *Rivka's first Thanksgiving*
Recorvits, Helen. *My name is Yoon*
Reynolds, Marilynn. *The new land*
Rosenberg, Liz. *The silence in the mountains*
Sandman, Rochel. *Perfect porridge*
Steig, William. *When everybody wore a hat*
Stevenson, Harvey. *Looking at liberty*
Tarbescu, Edith. *Annushka's voyage*
Temple, Bob. *Ellis Island*
Tregebov, Rhea. *What-if Sara*
Trottier, Maxine. *The walking stick*
Woodruff, Elvira. *The memory coat*
Yee, Paul. *The jade necklace*
Yezerski, Thomas F. *Together in Pinecone Patch*
Yin. *Coolies*
Yoder, Carolyn P. *Filipino Americans*
Ziefert, Harriet. *When I first came to this land*

Imps *see* Mythical creatures – imps

In & out *see* Concepts – in & out

Incas *see* Indians of South America – Incas

Incentive *see* Character traits – ambition

Indecision *see* Behavior – indecision

Independence Day *see* Holidays – Fourth of July

India *see* Foreign lands – India

Indians of Central America – Black Carib

London, Jonathan. *The village basket weaver*

Indians of Central America – Maya

Dupré, Judith. *The mouse bride*
Ehlert, Lois. *Cuckoo, a Mexican folktale = Cucú: un cuento folklórico mexicano*
Grifalconi, Ann. *The bravest flute*
Lattimore, Deborah Nourse. *Why there is no arguing in heaven*
Marcos, subcomandante. *The story of colors = La historia de los colores*
Mora, Pat. *The night the moon fell*
Rockwell, Anne F. *The boy who wouldn't obey*
Volkmer, Jane Anne. *Song of Chirimia = La Musica de la Chirimia*
Wahl, Jan. *Once when the world was green*
Wisniewski, David. *Rain player*

Indians of Central America – Taino

Alvarez, Julia. *The secret footprints*

Indians of North America

Aliki. *Corn is maize*
Anderson, C. W. (Clarence Williams). *Linda and the Indians*
Anderson, Leone Castell. *Surprise at Muddy Creek*
Baker, Betty. *And me, coyote!*
Baker, Laura Nelson. *O children of the wind and pines*
Baker, Olaf. *Where the buffaloes begin*
Bandes, Hanna. *Sleepy river*
Baylor, Byrd. *A God on every mountain top*
　Hawk, I'm your brother
　Moon song
　When clay sings
Beatty, Hetty Burlingame. *Little Owl Indian*
Behrens, June. *Powwow*
Belting, Natalia Maree. *Verity Mullens and the Indian*
Benjamin, Anne. *Young Pocahontas*

Blake, Robert J. *Yudonsi*
Boegehold, Betty. *A horse called Starfire*
Bornstein, Ruth Lercher. *Indian bunny*
Bouchard, Dave. *The song within my heart*
Boyden, Linda. *The blue roses*
Brock, Emma Lillian. *One little Indian boy*
Brownridge, William Roy. *The moccasin goalie*
Bruchac, Joseph. *The circle of thanks*
    How Chipmunk got his stripes
    Many nations
    Thirteen moons on turtle's back
Clement-Davies, David. *Spirit: stallion of the Cimarron*
Doolittle, Bev. *The forest has eyes*
Ehrlich, Amy. *Zeek Silver Moon*
Esbensen, Barbara Juster. *The night rainbow*
Farmer, Bonnie. *Isaac's dreamcatcher*
Flöethe, Louise Lee. *The Indian and his pueblo*
Friskey, Margaret (Margaret Richards). *Indian Two Feet and his eagle feather*
    Indian Two Feet and his horse
    Indian Two Feet and the wolf cubs
    Indian Two Feet rides alone
Goble, Paul. *Buffalo woman*
    The girl who loved wild horses
Gorsline, Marie. *North American Indians*
Grossman, Virginia. *Ten little rabbits*
Hader, Berta Hoerner. *The mighty hunter*
Harjo, Joy. *The good luck cat*
Harper, Piers. *How the world was saved and other Native American tales*
Hausman, Gerald. *How Chipmunk got tiny feet*
    Turtle Island ABC
Hayes, Joe. *A spoon for every bite*
Jacobs, Shannon K. *The boy who loved morning*
Jagendorf, Moritz A. *Kwi-na the eagle*
Jones, Hettie. *The trees stand shining*
Kalman, Bobbie. *Celebrating the powwow*
Krensky, Stephen. *Children of the wind and water*
Kroll, Virginia L. *The seasons and someone*
Locker, Thomas. *The land of gray wolf*
London, Jonathan. *Fireflies, fireflies, light my way*
Luenn, Nancy. *Nessa's fish*
McDermott, Gerald. *Raven*
McLeod, Elaine. *Lessons from Mother Earth*
McLerran, Alice. *The ghost dance*
Mariana. *Doki, the lonely papoose*
Martin, Bill (William Ivan). *Brave little Indian*
    Knots on a counting rope
Midge, Tiffany. *Buffalo*
Moon, Grace Purdie. *One little Indian*
Native Americans
Ortiz, Simon. *The people shall continue*
Parish, Peggy. *Good hunting, Blue Sky*
    Good hunting, Little Indian
    Granny and the Indians
    Granny, the baby and the big gray thing
    Little Indian
    Snapping turtle's all wrong day
Parnall, Peter. *The great fish*
Pollock, Penny. *When the moon is full*
Pomerantz, Charlotte. *Timothy Tall Feather*
Prusski, Jeffrey. *Bring back the deer*
Rappaport, Doreen. *We are the many*
Robbins, Ruth. *How the first rainbow was made*
Rose, Anne K. *Spider in the sky*
Siberell, Anne. *Whale in the sky*
Smith, Cynthia Leitich. *Jingle dancer*
Speare, Jean. *A candle for Christmas*
Stan-Padilla, Viento. *Dream Feather*
Strete, Craig Kee. *How the Indians bought the farm*
Taylor, Harriet Peck. *Coyote and the laughing butterflies*
Toye, William. *The loon's necklace*
Troughton, Joanna. *How rabbit stole the fire*
Van Camp, Richard. *What's the most beautiful thing you know about horses?*
Vaughan, Marcia Kapok. *Night dancer*
Vaughan, Richard Lee. *Eagle boy*

Wheeler, M. J. (Mary Jane). *First came the Indians*
White Deer of Autumn. *The great change*
Wondriska, William. *The stop*
Wood, Douglas. *Northwoods cradle song*
Zeman, Ludmila. *The first red maple leaf*

Indians of North America – Abnaki

Bruchac, Joseph. *Gluskabe and the four wishes*
Crompton, Anne Eliot. *The winter wife*

Indians of North America – Aleuts

Villoldo, Alberto. *Skeleton woman*

Indians of North America – Algonquin

Gregg, Andy. *Great Rabbit and the long-tailed Wildcat*
McCurdy, Michael. *An Algonquian year*
Martin, Rafe. *The rough-face girl*
Ross, Gayle. *The legend of the Windigo*
Toye, William. *Fire stealer*

Indians of North America – Anasazi

James, Betsy. *The mud family*

Indians of North America – Apache

Baker, Betty. *Three fools and a horse*
Lacapa, Michael. *Antelope Woman*

Indians of North America – Athabascan

Griese, Arnold A. *Anna's Athabaskan summer*

Indians of North America – Aztec

Bierhorst, John. *Doctor Coyote*
Kimmel, Eric A. *The two mountains*
McDermott, Gerald. *Musicians of the sun*

Indians of North America – Blackfoot

Goble, Paul. *The lost children*
Roop, Peter. *The buffalo jump*
San Souci, Robert D. *The legend of Scarface*
Yolen, Jane. *Sky dogs*

Indians of North America – Bungee

Bernstein, Margery. *How the sun made a promise and kept it*

Indians of North America – Carrier

Blades, Ann. *A boy of Taché*

Indians of North America – Cherokee

Bruchac, Joseph. *The first strawberries*
Flanagan, Alice K. *Mrs. Scott's beautiful art*
Haley, Gail E. *Two bad boys*
Pennington, Daniel. *Itse selu*
Ross, Gayle. *How Turtle's back was cracked*
Roth, Susan L. *Kanahena*
    The story of light
Rumford, James. *Sequoyah*
Sneve, Virginia Driving Hawk. *The Cherokees*
Stroud, Virginia A. *A walk to the Great Mystery*

Indians of North America – Cheyenne (Sioux)

Bunting, Eve (Anne Evelyn). *Cheyenne again*
Goble, Paul. *Death of the iron horse*
    The great race of the birds and animals
    Her seven brothers
Leech, Jay. *Bright Fawn and me*

Indians of North America – Chickasaw

Ata, Te. *Baby Rattlesnake*

Indians of North America – Chinook

Casler, Leigh. *The boy who dreamed of an acorn*

Indians of North America – Chippewa

McCain, Becky R. (Becky Ray). *Grandmother's dreamcatcher*

Indians of North America – Chol

Dupré, Judith. *The mouse bride*

Indians of North America – Chumash

Wood, Audrey. *The rainbow bridge*

Indians of North America – Clallam

Hirschi, Ron. *Seya's song*

Indians of North America – Comanche

De Paola, Tomie (Thomas Anthony). *The legend of the bluebonnet*
Kershen, L. Michael (Lloyd Michael). *Why buffalo roam*
Lind, Michael. *Bluebonnet girl*
Waldman, Neil. *They came from the Bronx*

Indians of North America – Coquelle

Dwyer, Mindy. *Coyote in love*

Indians of North America – Cora

Mike, Jan M. *Opossum and the great firemaker*

Indians of North America – Cree

Ekoomiak, Normee. *Arctic memories*
Norman, Howard A. *Who-Paddled-Backward-With-Trout*
Oliviero, Jamie. *The fish skin*
Wiebe, Rudy. *Hidden buffalo*
Wood, Douglas. *Rabbit and the moon*

Indians of North America – Creek

Bruchac, Joseph. *The great ball game*

Indians of North America – Crow

Goble, Paul. *Crow chief*
Medicine Crow, Joseph. *Brave Wolf and the Thunderbird*
Sage, James. *Coyote makes man*

Indians of North America – Dakota (Sioux)

Bruchac, Joseph. *A boy called Slow*
Bunting, Eve (Anne Evelyn). *Moonstick*
Goble, Paul. *Iktomi and the boulder*
    Iktomi and the buzzard
    Love flute
Hays, Wilma Pitchford. *Little Yellow Fur*
Jones, Jennifer Berry. *Heetunka's harvest*
Nelson, S. D. *Gift horse*

Indians of North America – Delaware

Greene, Ellin. *The legend of the cranberry*
MacGill-Callahan, Sheila. *And still the turtle watched*

Indians of North America – Goshute

Pia Toya

Indians of North America – Great Basin

Pia Toya

Indians of North America – Great Plains

Bunting, Eve (Anne Evelyn). *Cheyenne again*
De Paola, Tomie (Thomas Anthony). *The legend of the Indian paintbrush*
Erdrich, Liselotte. *Bears make rock soup and other stories*
Goble, Paul. *Beyond the ridge*
    The dream wolf
    The friendly wolf
    The gift of the sacred dog
    Iktomi and the berries
    Iktomi and the boulder
    Iktomi and the buffalo skull
    Iktomi and the coyote
    Iktomi and the ducks
    Mystic horse
    Remaking the earth
Mobley, Jane. *The star husband*
Pohrt, Tom. *Coyote goes walking*

Indians of North America – Haida

Frantz, Jennifer. *Totem poles*
Oliviero, Jamie. *The day Sun was stolen*

Indians of North America – Hohokam

Webb, Denise. *The same sun was in the sky*

Indians of North America – Hopi

Dawavendewa, Gerald. *The butterfly dance*
Elting, Mary. *The Hopi way*
Malotki, Ekkehart. *The magic hummingbird*

Indians of North America – Huichol

Bernhard, Emery. *The tree that rains*
Larson, Bonnie. *When animals were people = Cuando los animales eran personas*

Indians of North America – Huron

Abisch, Roz. *'Twas in the moon of wintertime*
Brébeuf, Jean de, Saint. *The Huron carol*

Indians of North America – Inuit

Bania, Michael. *Kumak's house*
Bushey, Jeanne. *The polar bear's gift*
    A sled dog for Moshi
Cleaver, Elizabeth. *The enchanted caribou*
Edwardson, Debby Dahl. *Whale snow*
Field, Edward. *Magic words*
Foa, Maryclare. *Songs are thoughts*
George, Jean Craighead. *Arctic son*
Heinz, Brian J. *Nanuk, lord of the ice*
London, Jonathan. *Ice Bear and Little Fox*
Martin, Rafe. *The eagle's gift*
Sis, Peter. *A small tall tale from the far Far North*
Stafford, Liliana. *The snow bear*
Trottier, Maxine. *Dreamstones*

Indians of North America – Inuk

Ekoomiak, Normee. *Arctic memories*

Indians of North America – Iroquois

Bierhorst, John. *The woman who fell from the sky*
Longfellow, Henry Wadsworth. *Hiawatha*
    Hiawatha's childhood
Sherman, Pat. *The sun's daughter*

Indians of North America – Karok

London, Jonathan. *Fire race*

Indians of North America – Kato

Rosen, Michael J. (1954–). *The dog who walked with God*

Indians of North America – Kutenai

Tanaka, Beatrice. *The chase*
Troughton, Joanna. *Who will be the sun?*

Indians of North America – Lakota (Sioux)

Bateson-Hill, Margaret. *Shota and the star quilt*
Bernhard, Emery. *Spotted Eagle and Black Crow*
Bruchac, Joseph. *Crazy horse's vision*
Goble, Paul. *Adopted by the eagles*
    The legend of the White Buffalo Woman
    The return of the buffaloes
Nelson, S. D. *The Star People*

Indians of North America – Lenape

Van Laan, Nancy. *Rainbow crow*

Indians of North America – Maidu

Bernstein, Margery. *Earth namer*

Indians of North America – Micmac

Toye, William. *How summer came to Canada*

Indians of North America – Missisauga

Crook, Connie Brummel. *Maple moon*

Indians of North America – Miwok

French, Fiona. *Lord of the animals*
San Souci, Robert D. *Two bear cubs*

Indians of North America – Modoc

Simms, Laura. *The bone man*
    Moon and Otter and Frog

Indians of North America – Mohawk

Gates, Frieda. *Owl eyes*
Swamp, Jake. *Giving thanks*

Indians of North America – Muskogee

Bruchac, Joseph. *The great ball game*

Indians of North America – Nanticoke

Mitchell, Barbara. *Red Bird*

Indians of North America – Narragansett

Koller, Jackie French. *Nickommoh!*

Indians of North America – Navajo

Begaye, Lisa Shook. *Building a bridge*
Blood, Charles L. *The goat in the rug*
Browne, Vee. *Monster birds*
Chanin, Michael. *Chief's blanket*
Duncan, Lois. *The magic of Spider Woman*
Garaway, Margaret Kahn. *Ashkii and his grandfather*
Hausman, Gerald. *Coyote walks on two legs*
    Eagle boy
Jackson, Ellen B. *The precious gift*
Keams, Geri. *Snail girl brings water*

Nez, Redwing T. *Forbidden talent*
Oughton, Jerrie. *How the stars fell into the sky*
    The magic weaver of rugs
Perrine, Mary. *Salt boy*
Schick, Eleanor. *My Navajo sister*
Tapahonso, Luci. *Navajo ABC*
Whitethorne, Baje. *Sunpainters*

Indians of North America – Nez Perce

Kay, Verla. *Broken Feather*
Krupinski, Loretta. *Best friends*
Sneve, Virginia Driving Hawk. *The Nez Perce*

Indians of North America – Nishnawbe

Yerxa, Leo. *Last leaf first snowflake to fall*

Indians of North America – Nisqually

Luenn, Nancy. *Miser on the mountain*

Indians of North America – Nobscusset

Metaxas, Eric. *Princess Scargo and the birthday pumpkin*

Indians of North America – Ojibwa

Bernstein, Margery. *How the sun made a promise and kept it*
Esbensen, Barbara Juster. *Ladder to the sky*
    The star maiden
Larry, Charles. *Peboan and Seegwun*
Lunge-Larsen, Lise. *The legend of the lady slipper*
Neitzel, Shirley. *From the land of the white birch*
Osofsky, Audrey. *Dreamcatcher*
Rodanas, Kristina. *Follow the stars*
San Souci, Robert D. *Sootface*
Spooner, Michael. *Old Meshikee and the little crabs*
Van Laan, Nancy. *Shingebiss*
Waboose, Jan Bourdeau. *Firedancers*
    Morning on the lake
    SkySisters

Indians of North America – Paiute

Hodges, Margaret. *The fire bringer*

Indians of North America – Papago

Baylor, Byrd. *The desert is theirs*
Clark, Ann Nolan. *The little Indian basket maker*

Indians of North America – Pawnee

Cohen, Caron Lee. *The mud pony*
Goble, Paul. *Mystic horse*
Moroney, Lynn. *The boy who loved bears*

Indians of North America – Penobscot

Day, Michael E. *Berry Ripe Moon*

Indians of North America – Pima

Moreillon, Judi. *Sing down the rain*

Indians of North America – Potawatomi

De Montaño, Martha Kreipe. *Coyote in love with a star*

Indians of North America – Powhatan

Accorsi, William. *My name is Pocahontas*
Aulaire, Ingri Mortenson d'. *Pocahontas*
Nettleton, Pamela Hill. *Pocahontas*

Indians of North America – Pueblo

Baker, Betty. *Rat is dead and ant is sad*
Carey, Valerie Scho. *Quail song*
Clark, Ann Nolan. *The little Indian pottery maker*
Dewey, Jennifer Owings. *Stories on stone*
Hausman, Gerald. *The story of Blue Elk*
Lyon, George Ella. *Dreamplace*
McDermott, Gerald. *Arrow to the sun*
Rosen, Michael (1946–). *Crow and Hawk*
Strete, Craig Kee. *Big thunder magic*

Indians of North America – Seminole

Johnson, Dolores. *Seminole diary*
Medearis, Angela Shelf. *Dancing with the Indians*

Indians of North America – Seneca

Charles, Veronika Martenova. *The maiden of the mist*
Ehlert, Lois. *Mole's hill*
Esbensen, Barbara Juster. *The great buffalo race*
Savageau, Cheryl. *Muskrat will be swimming*

Indians of North America – Shawnee

Bierhorst, John. *The ring in the prairie*
Watkins, Sherrin. *White Bead Ceremony*

Indians of North America – Shoshone

Gleiter, Jan. *Sacagawea*
Morris, Ann. *Grandma Maxine remembers*
Stevens, Janet. *Old bag of bones*

Indians of North America – Siksika

Goble, Paul. *The lost children*
    Star boy
San Souci, Robert D. *The legend of Scarface*
Yolen, Jane. *Sky dogs*

Indians of North America – Sioux

Sheldon, Dyan. *Under the moon*

Indians of North America – Southwest

McDermott, Gerald. *Coyote*
Strete, Craig Kee. *The lost boy and the monster*
Taylor, Harriet Peck. *Secrets of the stone*

Indians of North America – Suquamish

Seattle, Chief. *Brother eagle, sister sky*

Indians of North America – Taino

Crespo, George. *How the sea began*
Jaffe, Nina. *The golden flower*

Indians of North America – Tarascan

Czernecki, Stefan. *The hummingbird's gift*

Indians of North America – Tewa

Clark, Ann Nolan. *In my mother's house*

Indians of North America – Tlingit

Dixon, Ann. *How raven brought light to people*
Lewis, Paul Owen. *Frog girl*
Sleator, William. *The angry moon*
Williams, Maria. *How Raven stole the sun*

Indians of North America – Tohono O'Odham

Cowley, Joy. *Big moon tortilla*

Indians of North America – Tsimshian

Spalding, Andrea. *Solomon's tree*
Toye, William. *The mountain goats of Temlaham*

Indians of North America – Twa

Mott, Evelyn Clarke. *Dancing rainbows*

Indians of North America – Ute

Hobbs, Will. *Beardream*
Raczek, Linda Theresa. *The night the grandfathers danced*

Indians of North America – Wampanoag

Bartlett, Robert Merrill. *The story of Thanksgiving*
Bruchac, Joseph. *Squanto's journey*
Fritz, Jean. *The good giants and the bad Pukwudgies*
Hennessy, B. G. (Barbara G.). *One little, two little, three little pilgrims*
Metaxas, Eric. *Squanto and the miracle of Thanksgiving*

Indians of North America – Windigos

Ross, Gayle. *The legend of the Windigo*

Indians of North America – Yana

Bernstein, Margery. *Coyote goes hunting for fire*

Indians of North America – Yupik

McDonald, Megan. *Tundra mouse*

Indians of North America – Zapotec

Grossman, Patricia. *Saturday market*
Johnston, Tony. *The tale of Rabbit and Coyote*
Van Laan, Nancy. *La boda*

Indians of North America – Zuni

Hulpach, Vladimir. *Ahaiyute and Cloud Eater*
Pollock, Penny. *The turkey girl*
Rodanas, Kristina. *The dragonfly's tale*

Indians of South America

Alexander, Ellen. *Chaska and the golden doll*
Flora. *Feathers like a rainbow*
Knutson, Barbara. *Love and roast chicken*
Metaxas, Eric. *The monkey people*
Reynolds, Jan. *Amazon*
Van Laan, Nancy. *The legend of El Dorado*

Indians of South America – Incas

Jendresen, Erik. *The first story ever told*
Kurtz, Jane. *Miro in the kingdom of the sun*

Indians of South America – Karina

Maggi, María Elena. *The great canoe*

Indians of South America – Quechua

Van Laan, Nancy. *The magic bean tree*

Indians of South America – Yanomamo

Thomson, Ruth. *The Rainforest Indians*

Indians, American *see* Indians of Central America;
    Indians of North America; Indians of South America

Indifference *see* Behavior – indifference

Individuality *see* Character traits – individuality

Indonesia *see* Foreign lands – Indonesia

Indonesian Archipelago *see* Foreign lands – South Sea Islands

Influenza *see* Illness – influenza

Insects

Adelson, Leone. *Please pass the grass*
Aldis, Dorothy (Keeley). *Quick as a wink*
Anastas, Margaret. *A hug for you*
Asch, Frank. *Insects from outer space*
Barrett, Judi. *Snake is totally tail*
Beall, Pamela Conon. *Wee Sing if you're happy and you know it*
Belpré, Pura. *Pérez and Martina*
Berger, Melvin. *Buzz! a book about insects*
Bernstein, Joanne E. *Creepy crawly critter riddles*
Boegehold, Betty. *Bear underground*
Bond, Felicia. *Tumble bumble*
Brouillette, Jeanne S. *Moths*
Buck, Nola. *Creepy crawly critters and other Halloween tongue twisters*
Bugs
Carter, David A. *Chanukah bugs*
   Easter bugs
   How many bugs in a box?
   Peekaboo bugs
Charles, Donald. *Ugly bug*
Claybourne, Anna. *Insects*
Colby, C. B. (Carroll Burleigh). *Who lives there?*
Cole, Joanna. *Find the hidden insect*
Conklin, Gladys. *I caught a lizard*
   We like bugs
   When insects are babies
Cristini, Ermanno. *In the pond*
Darling, Kathy (Mary Kathleen). *Bug circus*
Dennard, Deborah. *Bullfrog at Magnolia Circle*
Dubowski, Cathy East. *Snug Bug*
   Snug Bug's play day
Dussling, Jennifer. *Bugs! bugs! bugs!*
Edwards, Pamela Duncan. *Bravo, Livingstone Mouse!*
   The wacky wedding
Egielski, Richard. *Buz*
   Jazper
Facklam, Margery. *The big bug book*
Farber, Norma. *Never say ugh to a bug*
Fish, Helen Dean. *When the root children wake up*, published by Lippincott, 1930
   When the root children wake up, published by Green Tiger Pr., 1988
Fisher, Aileen Lucia. *When it comes to bugs*
Florian, Douglas. *Insectlopedia*
Gackenbach, Dick. *Little bug*
Gaffney, Michael. *Secret forests*
Gammell, Stephen. *Twigboy*
George, Jean Craighead. *All upon a stone*
Geraghty, Paul. *Over the steamy swamp*
Goudey, Alice E. *Red legs*
Greenberg, David (David T.). *Bugs!*
Griffen, Elizabeth. *A dog's book of bugs*
Harris, Trudy. *Pattern bugs*
Harvey, Jayne. *Busy bugs*
Heller, Ruth. *How to hide a butterfly*
Hepworth, Catherine. *Bug off!*
Hines, Anna Grossnickle. *Miss Emma's wild garden*
Holmes, Anita. *Insect detector*
Hopkins, Lee Bennett. *Flit, flutter, fly!*
Hunter, Anne. *What's in the meadow?*
   What's in the pond
Ipcar, Dahlov (Zorach). *Bug city*
Jaynes, Ruth M. *That's what it is!*
Jenkins, Martin. *Wings, stings, and wriggly things*

Jenkins, Steve. *Animals in flight*
Johnston, Tony. *Sparky and Eddie, trouble with bugs*
Joyce, William. *The Leaf Men and the brave good bugs*
Katz, Bobbi. *The creepy crawly book*
Kaufmann, John. *Flying giants of long ago*
Kirk, David. *Little Miss Spider at Sunny Patch School*
   Miss Spider's ABC
   Miss Spider's new car
Kraus, Robert. *How Spider saved Halloween*
   How Spider saved Valentine's Day
Krudwig, Vickie Leigh. *Cucumber soup*
Lavies, Bianca. *Tree trunk traffic*
Leslie, Amanda. *Alfie and Betty Bug*
Lewis, J. Patrick. *The little buggers*
Lewison, Wendy Cheyette. *So many boots*
Lifton, Betty Jean. *Tell me a real adoption story*
Lionni, Leo. *Inch by inch*
Llewellyn, Claire. *The best book of bugs*
   Some bugs glow in the dark
Lobel, Arnold. *Grasshopper on the road*
McDonald, Megan. *Bedbugs*
   Insects are my life
   Reptiles are my life
McKelvey, Douglas Kaine. *Locust pocus*
McKissack, Patricia C. *Big bug book of counting*
   Big bug book of opposites
   Big bug book of places to go
   Big bug book of the alphabet
McPhail, David M. *A bug, a bear, and a boy*
   A bug, a bear, and a boy go to school
Markle, Sandra. *Creepy, crawly baby bugs*
Martin, Bill (William Ivan). *The little squeegy bug*
Maxner, Joyce. *Lady Bugatti*
Milne, A. A. (Alan Alexander). *Pooh and some bees*
Miranda, Anne. *Does a mouse have a house?*
Mitchell, Adrian. *Twice my size*
Mogensen, Jan. *The Land of the Big*
Morgan-Vanroyen, Mary. *Benjamin's bugs*
Murawski, Darlyne A. *Bug faces*
Murphy, Stuart J. *The best bug parade*
   Bug dance
Nathan, Cheryl. *Bugs and beasties ABC*
O'Neil, Amanda. *I wonder why spiders spin webs*
Oppenheim, Joanne. *Have you seen bugs?*
Palatini, Margie. *The perfect pet*
Parker, Nancy Winslow. *Bugs*
Paulsen, Gary. *Canoe days*
Penner, Lucille Recht. *Monster bugs*
Petie, Haris. *Billions of bugs*
Peyo. *The Smurfs and their woodland friends*
Pieńkowski, Jan. *Pizza!*
Pin, Isabel. *The seed*
Pinczes, Elinor J. *A remainder of one*
Polisar, Barry Louis. *Insect soup*
Pratt, Kristin Joy. *A fly in the sky*
Rockwell, Anne F. *Bugs are insects*
   Bumblebee, bumblebee, do you know me?
Roop, Peter. *Going buggy!*
Rounds, Glen. *The boll weevil*
Ryder, Joanne. *My father's hands*
Sabuda, Robert James. *The movable Mother Goose*
Samton, Sheila White. *Frogs in clogs*
Sardegna, Jill. *The roly-poly spider*
Selsam, Millicent E. *Where do they go?*
Seymour, Peter S. *Insects*
Shields, Carol Diggory. *The bugliest bug*
Sidman, Joyce. *Son of the water boatman*
Sill, Cathryn P. *About insects*
Soya, Kiyoshi. *A house of leaves*
Stone, Rosetta. *Because a little bug went ka-choo!*
Sturges, Philemon. *I love bugs*
   What's that sound, Woolly Bear?
Tison, Annette. *Animal hide-and-seek*
Van Woerkom, Dorothy. *Hidden messages*
Ward, Jennifer. *Over in the garden*
Warner, Sunny. *Madison finds a line*
Williams, Suzanne. *Old MacDonald in the city*

Wood, Audrey. *When the root children wake up*
York, Penelope. *Bugs*

Insects – ants

Æsop. *The ant and the dove*
    The ant and the grasshopper, ill. by Amy Lowry Poole
    The ant and the grasshopper, ill. by Sara Rojo
Allen, Judy. *Are you an ant?*
Allinson, Beverley. *Effie*
Andreae, Giles. *The pop-up Rumble in the jungle*
    Rumble in the jungle
Becker, Bonny. *An ant's day off*
Byars, Betsy Cromer. *My brother, Ant*
Calder, S. J. *If you were an ant*
Cameron, Polly. *"I can't," said the ant*
Cannon, Janell. *Crickwing*
Ciardi, John. *John J. Plenty and Fiddler Dan*
Clay, Pat. *Ants*
Climo, Shirley. *The little red ant and the great big crumb*
Dorros, Arthur. *Ant cities*
Edwards, Pamela Duncan. *The wacky wedding*
Fancher, Lou. *The quest for the One Big Thing*
Fichter, George S. *Bees, wasps, and ants*
Freschet, Berniece. *The ants go marching*
Gomel, Luc. *The ant, energetic worker*
Harley, Bill. *Sarah's story*
Hartley, Karen. *Ant*
Hawcock, David. *Ant*
Hepworth, Catherine. *ANTics! an alphabetical anthology*
Hodge, Deborah. *Ants*
Hoose, Philip M. *Hey little ant*
Landström, Olof. *Boo and Baa in the woods*
Lass, Bonnie. *Who took the cookies from the cookie jar?*
Levy, Janice. *The man who lived in a hat*
Loewen, Nancy. *Tiny workers*
Losi, Carol A. *The 512 ants on Sullivan Street*
McDonald, Megan. *Ant and Honey Bee*
Nelson, Kristin L. *Busy ants*
Nickle, John. *The ant bully*
O'Connor, Jane. *Sir Small and the dragonfly*
O'Malley, Kevin. *Little Buggy runs away*
Peet, Bill (William Bartlett). *The ant and the elephant*
Philpot, Lorna. *Amazing Anthony Ant*
Pluckrose, Henry Arthur. *Ants*
Porte, Barbara Ann. *Ma Jiang and the orange ants*
Reasoner, Charles. *Ants, ants, ants*
Sayre, April Pulley. *Army ant parade*
Trimble, Patti. *Lost!*
    What day is it?
Van Allsburg, Chris. *Two bad ants*
Wells, Rosemary. *McDuff saves the day*
Wolkstein, Diane. *Step by step*
Young, Ed (Edward). *Night visitors*

Insects – bees

Ahlberg, Allan. *Mr. Buzz the beeman*
Baran, Tancy. *Bees*
Barton, Byron. *Buzz, buzz, buzz*
Bees
Brown, Margaret Wise. *Bumble bee*
    The whispering rabbit
Cole, Joanna. *The magic school bus inside a beehive*
Crewe, Sabrina. *The bee*
Duplaix, Georges. *The big brown bear*
Ernst, Lisa Campbell. *A colorful adventure of the bee who left home one Monday morning and what he found along the way*
Fichter, George S. *Bees, wasps, and ants*
Flanagan, Alice K. *Learning about bees from Mr. Krebs*
Fowler, Richard. *Honeybee's busy day*
Galdone, Joanna. *Honeybee's party*
Galvin, Laura Gates. *Bumblebee at Apple Tree Lane*
Gibbons, Faye. *Mountain wedding*
Gibbons, Gail. *The honey makers*
Gugler, Laurel Dee. *There's a billy goat in the garden*
Harley, Bill. *Sarah's story*

Hartley, Karen. *Bee*
Hawcock, David. *Bee*
Hawes, Judy. *Watch honeybees with me*
Heiligman, Deborah. *Honeybees*
High, Linda Oatman. *Beekeepers*
Hodge, Deborah. *Bees*
Hogan, Paula Z. *The honeybee*
Keller, Beverly. *Fiona's bee*
Kennedy, Kim. *Mr. Bumble*
Krebs, Laurie. *The Beeman*
Lobel, Arnold. *The rose in my garden*
Loewen, Nancy. *Busy buzzers*
Long, Jan Freeman. *The bee and the dream*
McDonald, Megan. *Ant and Honey Bee*
Neye, Emily. *Honeybees*
Petty, Dini. *The queen, the bear and the bumblebee*
Pizer, Abigail. *Nosey Gilbert*
Pluckrose, Henry Arthur. *Bees and wasps*
Polacco, Patricia. *In Enzo's splendid gardens*
Renberg, Dalia Hardof. *King Solomon and the bee*
Rockwell, Anne F. *Big bad goat*
    Bumblebee, bumblebee, do you know me?
    Honey in a hive
Sayre, April Pulley. *If you should hear a honey guide*
Stockton, Frank Richard. *The bee-man of Orn*
Thompson, Mary. *Gran's bees*
Wahl, Jan. *Follow me cried Bee*
Wallace, John. *Building a house with Mr. Bumble*
Wong, Janet S. *Buzz*

Insects – beetles

Carle, Eric. *The very clumsy click beetle*
Clay, Pat. *Beetles*
Conklin, Gladys. *I like beetles*
Hawcock, David. *Beetle*
Hoban, Russell. *Jim Frog*
Inkpen, Mick. *Billy's beetle*
Mudd-Ruth, Maria. *The beetle*
Murphy, Kelly. *The boll weevil ball*
Murray, Peter. *Beetles*
Tada, Satoshi. *Mr. Beetle*

Insects – butterflies, caterpillars

Aardema, Verna. *Who's in Rabbit's house?*
Abisch, Roz. *Let's find out about butterflies*
Allen, Judy. *Are you a butterfly?*
Arnosky, Jim. *Crinkleroot's guide to knowing butterflies and moths*
Barringer, William. *Gregory and Alexander*
Brown, Ruth. *If at first you do not see*
Bunting, Eve (Anne Evelyn). *Butterfly house*
Butterworth, Nick. *Amanda's butterfly*
Carle, Eric. *The very hungry caterpillar*
Carrick, Malcolm. *I can squash elephants!*
The caterpillar who turned into a butterfly
Collicott, Sharleen. *Toestomper and the bad butterflies*
    Toestomper and the caterpillars
Conklin, Gladys. *I like butterflies*
    I like caterpillars
Coville, Bruce. *The prince of butterflies*
Cowley, Stewart. *On Butterfly Farm*
Crozat, François. *I am a little caterpillar*
Cutts, David. *Look . . . a butterfly*
Darby, Gene. *What is a butterfly?*
Davol, Marguerite W. *Why butterflies go by on silent wings*
Delaney, A. *The butterfly*
Delaney, Ned. *One dragon to another*
DeLuise, Dom. *Charlie the caterpillar*
Denslow, Sharon Phillips. *Woollybear good-bye*
Edwards, Pamela Duncan. *Clara Caterpillar*
Ehlert, Lois. *Waiting for wings*
Ernst, Lisa Campbell. *Bubba and Trixie*
Faulkner, Keith. *Butterfly*
Fitzsimons, Cecilia. *My first butterflies*
Fleming, Denise. *In the tall, tall grass*
French, Vivian. *Caterpillar, caterpillar*

Garelick, May. *Where does the butterfly go when it rains?*, ill. by Leonard Weisgard
    Where does the butterfly go when it rains?, ill. by Nicholas Wilton
Gibbons, Gail. *Monarch butterfly*
Glaser, Linda. *Magnificent monarchs*
    Wonderful worms
Gomi, Taro. *Hi, butterfly!*
Grifalconi, Ann. *Darkness and the butterfly*
Hariton, Anca. *Butterfly story*
Heap, Sue. *Four friends in the garden*
Heiligman, Deborah. *From caterpillar to butterfly*
Heller, Ruth. *How to hide a butterfly*
Himmelman, John. *A monarch butterfly's life*
Hines, Anna Grossnickle. *Remember the butterflies*
Hogan, Paula Z. *The butterfly*
Horwood, Annie. *Butterfly, butterfly what colors do you see?*
Inkpen, Mick. *Butterfly*
Johnston, Tony. *Isabel's house of butterflies*
Joosse, Barbara M. *Ghost wings*
Kent, Jack. *The caterpillar and the polliwog*
Kotzwinkle, William. *Walter, the farting dog: rough weather ahead*
Kroll, Virginia L. *Butterfly boy*
Lawrence, Michael (Michael C.). *The caterpillar that roared*
Legg, Gerald. *From caterpillar to butterfly*
Lewis, Naomi. *The butterfly collector*
Ling, Mary. *Butterfly*
Lionni, Leo. *The alphabet tree*
McBratney, Sam. *The caterpillow fight*
McClung, Robert. *Sphinx*
Magloff, Lisa. *Butterfly*
Maple, Marilyn J. *On the wings of a butterfly*
Marzollo, Jean. *I'm a caterpillar*
May, Kara. *Creepy crawly caterpillar*
Merrill, Jean. *The girl who loved caterpillars*
Murphy, Mary. *Caterpillar's wish*
Neye, Emily. *Butterflies*
O'Callahan, Jay. *Herman and Marguerite*
Ó Flatharta, Antoine. *Hurry and the monarch*
O'Hagan, Caroline. *It's easy to have a caterpillar visit you*
Pallandt, Nicholas van. *The butterfly night of Old Brown Bear*
Patent, Dorothy Hinshaw. *Fabulous fluttering tropical butterflies*
Piers, Helen. *Grasshopper and butterfly*
Pluckrose, Henry Arthur. *Butterflies and moths*
Polacco, Patricia. *The butterfly*
Rockwell, Anne F. *Becoming butterflies*
Roscoe, William. *The butterfly's ball and the grasshopper's feast*
Ryder, Joanne. *Where butterflies grow*
Sandved, Kjell Bloch. *The butterfly alphabet*
Schubert, Ingrid. *There's always room for one more*
Selsam, Millicent E. *A first look at caterpillars*
Sierra, Judy. *The beautiful butterfly*
Sturges, Philemon. *What's that sound, Woolly Bear?*
Sundgaard, Arnold. *The lamb and the butterfly*
Swope, Sam. *Gotta go! Gotta go!*
Taylor, Harriet Peck. *Coyote and the laughing butterflies*
Thompson, Susan L. *Diary of a monarch butterfly*
Wallace, Karen. *Born to be a butterfly*
Watson, Mary. *The butterfly seeds*
Watts, Barrie. *Butterfly and caterpillar*
Winer, Yvonne. *Butterflies fly*
Wong, Herbert H. *Our caterpillars*
Yee, Paul. *The boy in the attic*

Insects – cockroaches

Cannon, Janell. *Crickwing*
Hartley, Karen. *Cockroach*
Merrick, Patrick. *Cockroaches*
Moreton, Daniel. *La Cucaracha Martina*
O'Malley, Kevin. *Leo Cockroach . . . toy tester*

Insects – crickets

Bunting, Eve (Anne Evelyn). *Christmas cricket*
Carle, Eric. *The very quiet cricket*
Caudill, Rebecca. *A pocketful of cricket*
Chang, Margaret Scrogin. *The cricket warrior*
Czernecki, Stefan. *The cricket's cage*
Kimmel, Eric A. *Why worry?*
Maxner, Joyce. *Nicholas Cricket*
Mizumura, Kazue. *If I were a cricket . . .*
Stafford, William. *The animal that drank up sound*
Wheeler, Lisa. *Old Cricket*

Insects – damselflies

Rosman, Steven M. *Deena the damselfly*

Insects – dragonflies

Bernhard, Emery. *Dragonfly*
Lively, Penelope. *One, two, three, jump!*
O'Connor, Jane. *Sir Small and the dragonfly*
Rodanas, Kristina. *The dragonfly's tale*

Insects – fireflies

Berends, Polly Berrien. *Ladybug and dog and the night walk*
Bolliger, Max. *The fireflies*
Brinckloe, Julie. *Fireflies!*
Buckley, Paul. *Amy Belligera and the fireflies*
Burke, Katie. *Lightning bug thunder*
Callen, Larry. *Dashiel and the night*
Carle, Eric. *The very lonely firefly*
Drachman, Eric. *Leo the lightning bug*
Eastman, P. D. (Philip D.). *Sam and the firefly*
Harris, Louise Dyer. *Flash, the life of a firefly*
Hawes, Judy. *Fireflies in the night*
Hoffman, Alice. *Fireflies*
Loewen, Nancy. *Living lights*
Oppenheim, Shulamith Levey. *Fireflies for Nathan*
Pinczes, Elinor J. *My full moon is square*
Robbins, Sandra. *The firefly star*
Ryder, Joanne. *Fireflies*
Sturges, Philemon. *Ten flashing fireflies*
Weedn, Flavia. *The moon maiden*

Insects – fleas

Cneut, Carll. *The amazing love story of Mr. Morf*
Downey, Lynn. *The flea's sneeze*
Edwards, Pamela Duncan. *Ed and Fred Flea*
Hanson, Mary Elizabeth. *The old man and the flea*
Kimmel, Eric A. *Squash it!*
Lish, Ted. *The three little puppies and the big bad flea*
McCully, Emily Arnold. *Little Kit, or, The Industrious Flea Circus girl*
Rogers, Paul (Patrick). *Tiny*
Weninger, Brigitte. *The elf's hat*
Wiese, Kurt. *The dog, the fox and the fleas*
Wood, Audrey. *The napping house wakes up*

Insects – flies

Aardema, Verna. *Half-a-ball-of-kenki*
Aylesworth, Jim. *Old Black Fly*
Brandenberg, Franz. *Fresh cider and apple pie*
Conklin, Gladys. *I watch flies*
Cooner, Donna D. (Donna Danell). *I know an old Texan who swallowed a fly*
Elkin, Benjamin. *Why the sun was late*
Gray, Nigel. *Fly*
Grejniec, Michael. *Albert's nap*
Hawcock, David. *Fly*
Howitt, Mary Botham. *Mary Howitt's The spider and the fly*
Jenkins, Martin. *Fly traps!*
Jorgensen, Gail. *Gotcha!*
Kraus, Robert. *How Spider saved Easter*
    The trouble with spider
Little old lady who swallowed a fly. *Fancy that!*
    Golly Gump swallowed a fly
    I know an old lady, ill. by Abner Graboff
    I know an old lady, ill. by G. Brian Karas
    I know an old lady, ill. by Steve McInturff
    I know an old lady, ill. by Albert Miller

I know an old lady who swallowed a fly, ill. by Stephen Gulbis
I know an old lady who swallowed a fly, ill. by Glen Rounds
I know an old lady who swallowed a fly, ill. by William Stobbs
I know an old lady who swallowed a fly, ill. by Nadine Bernard
   Westcott
There was an old lady, ill. by Nick Bantock
There was an old lady who swallowed a fly, ill. by Pam Adams
There was an old lady who swallowed a fly, ill. by Colin Hawkins
There was an old lady who swallowed a fly, ill. by Simms Taback
There was an old woman, ill. by Steven Kellogg
Lozoff, Bo. *The wonderful life of a fly who couldn't fly*
McClintock, Marshall. *A fly went by*
Merrick, Patrick. *Biting flies*
Oppenheim, Joanne. *You can't catch me!*
Pratt, Kristin Joy. *A fly in the sky*
Trapani, Iza. *Shoo fly!*
Winter, Paula. *The bear and the fly*
Yolen, Jane. *Spider Jane*

Insects – gnats

Peet, Bill (William Bartlett). *The gnats of knotty pine*

Insects – grasshoppers

Æsop. *The ant and the grasshopper*, ill. by Amy Lowry Poole
   The ant and the grasshopper, ill. by Sara Rojo
Allen, Judy. *Are you a grasshopper?*
Ciardi, John. *John J. Plenty and Fiddler Dan*
Du Bois, William Pène. *Bear circus*
Dugan, Barbara. *Leaving home with a pickle jar*
Grasshopper to the rescue
Heinrichs, Ann. *Grasshoppers*
Kimmel, Eric A. *Why worry?*
Lobel, Arnold. *Grasshopper on the road*
Loewen, Nancy. *Hungry hoppers*
Newbolt, Henry John, Sir. *Rilloby-rill*
Piers, Helen. *Grasshopper and butterfly*
Wolkstein, Diane. *Step by step*

Insects – hornets

Laird, Elizabeth. *The day Veronica was nosy*

Insects – lady birds *see* Insects – ladybugs

Insects – ladybugs

Allen, Judy. *Are you a ladybug?*
Berends, Polly Berrien. *Ladybug and dog and the night walk*
Bernhard, Emery. *Ladybug*
Bono, Mary. *Ugh! a bug*
Brown, Ruth. *Ladybug, ladybug*
Carle, Eric. *The grouchy ladybug*
Chrustowski, Rick. *Bright beetle*
Conklin, Gladys. *Lucky ladybugs*
Dahl, Michael. *Lots of ladybugs!*
Ernst, Lisa Campbell. *Bubba and Trixie*
Finn, Isobel. *The very lazy ladybug*
Finzel, Julia. *Large as life*
Fisher, Aileen Lucia. *We went looking*
Fowler, Richard. *Ladybug on the move*
Godkin, Celia. *What about ladybugs?*
Hartley, Karen. *Ladybug*
Hawes, Judy. *Ladybug, ladybug, fly away home*
Kepes, Juliet. *Lady bird, quickly*
Kraus, Robert. *How Spider saved Easter*
   Ladybug, ladybug!
Llewellyn, Claire. *Ladybug*
Loewen, Nancy. *Spotted beetles*
O'Malley, Kevin. *Little buggy*
   Little Buggy runs away
Posada, Mia. *Ladybugs*
Robbins, Sandra. *The firefly star*
Ryder, Joanne. *First grade ladybugs*
Schlein, Miriam. *Fast is not a ladybug*
Silverman, Maida. *Ladybug's color book*

Stephens, J. Moria. *Persephone, the ladybug*
Sueyoshi, Akiko. *Ladybird on a bicycle*
Szekeres, Cyndy. *Ladybug, ladybug, where are you?*
Tracqui, Valérie. *The ladybug*
Watts, Barrie. *Ladybug*
Wong, Herbert H. *My ladybug*

Insects – lice

Caffey, Donna. *Yikes-lice!*
Rice, Judith. *Those itsy-bitsy teeny-tiny not-so-nice head lice = Esos
   pequeñines, chiquitines, para nada simpáticos piojos*

Insects – lightning bugs *see* Insects – fireflies

Insects – mosquitoes

Aardema, Verna. *Why mosquitoes buzz in people's ears*
Gershator, Phillis. *Zzzng! zzzng! zzzng!*
Johnston, Tony. *The Chizzywink and the Alamagoozlum*
McDonald, Mary Ann. *Mosquitoes*
Ross, Gayle. *The legend of the Windigo*
Sloat, Teri. *The thing that bothered Farmer Brown*
Uribe, Verónica. *Buzz buzz buzz*

Insects – moths

Arnosky, Jim. *Crinkleroot's guide to knowing butterflies and moths*
Himmelman, John. *A luna moth's life*
Loewen, Nancy. *Night fliers*
Pluckrose, Henry Arthur. *Butterflies and moths*
Sandved, Kjell Bloch. *The butterfly alphabet*
Sturges, Philemon. *What's that sound, Woolly Bear?*

Insects – praying mantis

Conklin, Gladys. *Praying mantis*
James, Betsy. *Mary Ann*

Insects – termites

Laden, Nina. *Roberto, the insect architect*
Rouss, Sylvia A. *The littlest pair*

Insects – wasps

Fichter, George S. *Bees, wasps, and ants*
Hawcock, David. *Wasp*
Pluckrose, Henry Arthur. *Bees and wasps*

Interracial marriage *see* Marriage, interracial

Inuit Indians *see* Indians of North America – Inuit

Inuk Indians *see* Indians of North America – Inuk

Inventions

Christelow, Eileen. *Mr. Murphy's marvelous invention*
Dennard, Deborah. *Travis and the better mousetrap*
Dubowski, Cathy East. *Cave boy*
Fisher, Leonard Everett. *Gutenberg*
Frank, John. *Odds 'n' Ends Alvy*
Gackenbach, Dick. *Tiny for a day*
Harper, Charise Mericle. *Imaginative inventions*
Joyce, William. *Sleepy time Olie*
MacGill-Callahan, Sheila. *To capture the wind*
Perry, Andrea. *Here's what you do when you can't find your shoe*
Taylor, Barbara. *I wonder why zippers have teeth and other questions
   about inventions*

Inventors *see* Careers – inventors

Iran *see* Foreign lands – Iran

Iraq *see* Foreign lands – Iraq

Ireland *see* Foreign lands – Ireland

Irish Americans *see* Ethnic groups in the U.S. – Irish Americans

Iroquois Indians *see* Indians of North America – Iroquois

Islam *see* Foreign lands – Israel

Islands

Abolafia, Yossi. *Yanosh's Island*
Ackerman, Diane. *Monk seal hideaway*
Adoff, Arnold. *Flamboyan*
Agell, Charlotte. *To the island*
Ahlberg, Allan. *Master Salt the sailor's son*
Albert, Burton. *Where does the trail lead?*
Alderson, Sue Ann. *Ida and the wool smugglers*
Allan, Nicholas. *The bird*
Armitage, Ronda. *Ice creams for Rosie*
Backovsky, Jan. *Trouble in Paradise*
Beni, Ruth. *Sir Baldergog the great*
Blackstone, Stella. *An island in the sun*
Blake, Robert J. *Spray*
Bliss, Corinne Demas. *The disappearing island*
Brock, Emma Lillian. *Skipping Island*
Brown, Margaret Wise. *The little island*
Brunhoff, Laurent de. *Babar's visit to Bird Island*
Burdett, Lois. *The tempest for kids*
Buzzeo, Toni. *The sea chest*
Bynum, Janie. *Altoona Baboona*
Carrick, Carol. *Lost in the storm*
Civardi, Anne. *Things people do*
Coatsworth, Elizabeth. *Lonely Maria*
Cooney, Barbara. *Island boy*
Crossley-Holland, Kevin. *Sleeping Nanna*
English, Karen. *Neeny coming, Neeny going*
Farley, Walter. *Black stallion*
Field, Rachel Lyman. *If once you have slept on an island*
Gantschev, Ivan. *The train to Grandma's*
Gay, Marie-Louise. *On my island*
Gibbons, Gail. *Surrounded by sea*
Goodhart, Pippa. *Row, row, row your boat*
Greene, Carol. *The old ladies who liked cats*
    Sunflower Island
Greenfield, Eloise. *Under the Sunday tree*
Haynes, Max. *Dinosaur island*
Hedderwick, Mairi. *The big Katie Morag storybook*
    Katie Morag and the big boy cousins
    Katie Morag and the tiresome Ted
    Katie Morag and the two grandmothers
    Katie Morag delivers the mail
Hooks, William H. *The monster from the sea*
Hoopes, Lyn Littlefield. *Mommy, daddy, me*
Horse, Harry. *A friend for Little Bear*
Ichikawa, Satomi. *Isabela's ribbons*
Ikeda, Daisaku. *Over the deep blue sea*
Isadora, Rachel. *Caribbean dream*
Jauck, Andrea. *Assateague*
Jekyll, Walter. *I have a news*
Johnston, Tony. *Pages of music*
Joseph, Lynn. *Coconut kind of day*
    Jasmine's parlour day
Keller, Holly. *Island baby*
Kellogg, Steven (Stephen). *The island of the skog*
Kessler, Leonard P. *The pirates' adventure on Spooky Island*
King, Deborah. *Sirius and Saba*
Kinsey-Warnock, Natalie. *The wild horses of Sweetbriar*
Krahn, Fernando. *The great ape*
Lasky, Kathryn. *My island grandma*, ill. by Emily Arnold McCully
    My island grandma, ill. by Amy Schwartz
Lent, Blair. *Bayberry Bluff*
Lessac, Frané. *My little island*
Lewin, Betsy. *Booby hatch*
Lewin, Ted. *Nilo and the tortoise*
Lewis, J. Patrick. *The la-di-da hare*

McCloskey, Robert. *Time of wonder*
McClure, Gillian. *Selkie*
McGovern, Ann. *Nicholas Bentley Stoningpot III*
MacLachlan, Patricia. *Painting the wind*
McMillan, Bruce. *Days of the ducklings*
McPhail, David M. *Great cat*
Martin, Charles E. *For rent*
    Island rescue
    Island winter
Martin, Jacqueline Briggs. *On Sand Island*
Meddaugh, Susan. *Harry on the rocks*
Millhouse, Nicholas. *Blue-footed booby*
Mills, Patricia. *On an island in the bay*
Monfried, Lucia. *The Daddies Boat*
Mordvinoff, Nicolas. *Coral Island*
Morley, Carol. *A spider and a pig*
Olson, Arielle North. *The lighthouse keeper's daughter*
Pfister, Marcus. *Milo and the mysterious island*
Poulin, Stéphane. *Travels for two*
Raglus, Jeff. *Schnorky the wave puncher*
Rahaman, Vashanti. *O Christmas tree*
Rockwell, Anne F. *Ferryboat ride!*
    On our vacation
Rohmann, Eric. *The cinder-eyed cats*
Round, Graham. *Hangdog*
Rumford, James. *The Island-below-the-star*
Rutherford, Erica. *An Island alphabet*
Simon, Carly. *Midnight farm*
Smith, Roger. *The empty island*
Steig, William. *Abel's Island*
    Rotten island
Stevenson, James. *The castaway*
Stiles, Martha Bennett. *Island magic*
Stock, Catherine. *An island summer*
Stojic, Manya. *Wet pebbles under our feet*
Thaxter, Celia. *Celia's island journal*
Wallis, Lisa. *Island child*
Wallner, Alexandra. *Sergio and the hurricane*
Wells, Philip. *Daddy Island*
Williams, Garth. *Benjamin's treasure*
Wilson, Barbara Ker. *The turtle and the island*
Wisdom, Jude. *Whatever Wanda wanted*
Wright-Frierson, Virginia. *An island scrapbook*

Israel *see* Foreign lands – Israel

Italian Americans *see* Ethnic groups in the U.S. – Italian Americans

Italy *see* Foreign lands – Italy

Jackals *see* Animals – jackals

Jackets *see* Clothing – coats

Jaguars *see* Animals – jaguars

Jails *see* Prisons

Jamaica *see* Foreign lands – Jamaica

Janitors *see* Careers – custodians, janitors

Japan *see* Foreign lands – Japan

Japanese Americans *see* Ethnic groups in the U.S. – Asian Americans; Ethnic groups in the U.S. – Japanese Americans

Jealousy *see* Emotions – envy, jealousy

Jesters *see* Clowns, jesters

Jewelry

Fruisen, Catherine Myler. *My mother's pearls*
Kassirer, Sue. *What's next, Nina?*
Lamm, C. Drew. *Gauchada*
Langton, Jane. *The queen's necklace*
Vaës, Alain. *The princess and the pea*

Jewish culture

Adelson, Leone. *The mystery bear*
Adler, David A. *The children of Chelm*
   The children's book of Jewish holidays
   Hiding from the Nazis
   The house on the roof
   The number on my grandfather's arm
   A picture book of Hanukkah
   A picture book of Israel
   A picture book of Jewish holidays
   A picture book of Passover
Aleichem, Sholem. *Hanukah money*
Aronin, Ben. *The secret of the Sabbath fish*
Auerbach, Julie Jaslow. *Everything's changing – It's pesach!*
Bayar, Steven. *Rachel and Mischa*
Behrens, June. *Hanukkah*
   Passover
Bernstein, Robin. *Terrible, terrible!*
Biers-Ariel, Matt. *Solomon and the trees*
Bogot, Howard. *I'm growing*
Bresnick-Perry, Roslyn. *Leaving for America*
Brodmann, Aliana. *Such a noise!*
Buckley, Ray. *God's love is like . . .*
Burnstein, Chaya M. *The Jewish kids' Hebrew-English wordbook*
Burstein, Chaya M. *Joseph and Anna's time capsule*
Capucilli, Alyssa Satin. *Happy Hanukkah, Biscuit*
Caseley, Judith. *When Grandpa came to stay*
Chaikin, Miriam. *Esther*
   Exodus
   Hanukkah
Chanover, Hyman. *Happy Hanukah everybody*
Chapman, Carol. *The tale of Meshka the Kvetch*
A child's picture English-Hebrew dictionary
Clement, Gary. *Just stay put*
Cohen, Barbara. *Even higher*
   First fast
   Gooseberries to oranges
   Here come the Purim players!, ill. by Beverly Brodsky McDermott
   Here come the Purim players!, ill. by Shoshana Mekibel
   Make a wish, Molly
Cole, Joanna. *It's too noisy*
Conway, Diana Cohen. *Northern lights*
Coopersmith, Jerome. *A Chanukah fable for Christmas*
Davis, Aubrey. *Bagels from Benny*
   Bone button borscht
De Paola, Tomie (Thomas Anthony). *My first Chanukah*
Dollinger, Renate. *The rabbi who flew*
Drucker, Malka. *Grandma's latkes*
   A Jewish holiday ABC
Edwards, Michelle. *Alef-bet*
   A baker's portrait
   Papa's latkes
Ehrlich, Amy. *The story of Hannukah*
Eisenberg, Ann. *I can celebrate*
Eisenberg, Phyllis Rose. *A mitzvah is something special*
Emerman, Ellen. *Is it Shabbos yet?*
   Just right
Fass, David E. *The shofar that lost its voice*
Fassler, Joan. *My grandpa died today*

Feder, Harriet K. *Not yet, Elijah!*
   What can you do with a bagel?
Fisher, Aileen Lucia. *My first Hanukkah book*
Fishman, Cathy Goldberg. *On Hanukkah*
   On Passover
   On Purim
   On Rosh Hashanah and Yom Kippur
   On Shabbat
Flanagan, Alice K. *Passover*
Freedman, Florence B. *Brothers*
Ganz, Yaffa. *The story of Mimmy and Simmy*
Gellman, Ellie. *It's Chanukah!*
   It's Rosh Hashanah!
   Shai's Shabbat walk
Geras, Adèle. *Rebecca's Passover*
Gershator, Phillis. *Honi and his magic circle*
Gerstein, Mordicai. *Queen Esther the morning star*
   The shadow of a flying bird
Glaser, Linda. *The borrowed Hanukkah latkes*
   Mrs. Greenberg's messy Hanukkah
Goffstein, M. B. (Marilyn Brooke). *Laughing latkes*
Goldin, Barbara Diamond. *Cakes and miracles*
   Just enough is plenty
   A mountain of blintzes
   Night lights
   World's birthday
Gold-Vukson, Marji E. *The colors of my Jewish Year*
   Grandpa and me on Tu B'Shevat
Gordon, Ruth. *Feathers*
Greene, Jacqueline Dembar. *Butchers and bakers, rabbis and kings*
   What his father did
Groner, Judyth Saypol. *All about Hanukkah*
   All about Sukkot
   My very own Jewish community
   Thank you, God!
   Where is the Afikomen?
Gross, Michael. *The fable of the fig tree*
Grossblatt, Ruby M. *Who's that sleeping on my sofabed?*
Hanukkah lights
Harber, Frances. *The brothers' promise*
Harvey, Brett. *Immigrant girl*
Hawxhurst, Joan C. *Bubbe and Gram, my two grandmothers*
Hest, Amy. *Fancy Aunt Jess*
   The Friday nights of Nana
Hirsh, Marilyn. *Captain Jiri and Rabbi Jacob*
   Could anything be worse?
   I love Hanukkah
   I love Passover
   Joseph who loved the Sabbath
   One little goat
   The pink suit
   Potato pancakes all around
   The Rabbi and the twenty-nine witches
   Where is Yonkela?
Hoestlandt, Jo. *Star of fear, star of hope*
Holland, Cheri. *Maccabee jamboree*
Howland, Naomi. *Latkes, latkes, good to eat*
   The matzah man
Hutton, Warwick. *Moses in the bulrushes*
Ife, Elaine. *Moses in the bulrushes*
Jaffe, Nina. *In the month of Kislev*
   Tales for the seventh day
   The way meat loves salt
Kahn, Katherine Janus. *The shofar calls to us*
Karkowsky, Nancy. *Grandma's soup*
Karlinsky, Ruth Schild. *My first book of Mitzvos*
Kessler, Brad. *Moses in Egypt*
Kimmel, Eric A. *Asher and the capmakers*
   The Chanukkah guest
   The Chanukkah tree
   Gershon's monster
   Hershel and the Hanukkah goblins
   The magic dreidels
   One winter night
   Onions and garlic
   Ten suns
   Zigazak!

Woodruff, Elvira. *The memory coat*
Yorinks, Arthur. *The Miami giant*
Zagwÿn, Deborah Turney. *Papa's latkes*
Zalben, Jane Breskin. *Beni's first Chanukah*
    Beni's first wedding
    Happy Passover, Rosie
    Leo and Blossom's Sukkah
    Pearl's eight days of Chanukah
    Pearl's Passover
Zemach, Margot. *It could always be worse*
Zola, Meguido. *The dream of promise*
Zolkower, Edie Stoltz. *Too many cooks*
Zucker, Jonny. *Apples and honey*
    Four special questions
    It's party time
Zusman, Evelyn. *The Passover parrot*

Jobs *see* Careers

Jokes *see* Riddles & jokes

Jonah *see* Religion – Jonah

Journalists *see* Careers – journalists

Judges *see* Careers – judges

Jumping *see* Activities – jumping

Jumping rope *see* Sports – jumping rope

Juneteenth *see* Holidays – Juneteenth

Jungle

Aardema, Verna. *Rabbit makes a monkey of lion*
Aitken, Amy. *Kate and Mona in the jungle*
Allen, Judy. *Eagle*
Andreae, Giles. *The pop-up Rumble in the jungle*
    Rumble in the jungle
Apperley, Dawn. *In the jungle*
Baker, Liza. *Dinosaur days*
Balmer, Helen. *Jungle adventure*
Bare, Colleen Stanley. *Who comes to the water hole?*
Base, Graeme. *Jungle drums*
Beaton, Clare. *How loud is a lion?*
Bilgrami, Shaheen. *Jungle art show*
Bodsworth, Nan. *A nice walk in the jungle*
Bohdal, Susi. *Tiger baby*
Booth, Eugene. *In the jungle*
Bright, Paul. *Quiet!*
Burnard, Damon. *I spy in the jungle*
Bush, John. *The giraffe who got in a knot*
Calmenson, Stephanie. *One little monkey*
Campoy, F. Isabel. *Rosa Raposa*
Cannon, Janell. *Verdi*
Carle, Eric. *"Slowly, slowly, slowly," said the sloth*
Cartlidge, Michelle. *Elephant in the jungle*
Catchpole, Clive. *Jungles*
Cherry, Lynne. *The great kapok tree*
Chichester Clark, Emma. *Lunch with Aunt Augusta*
Cole, Babette. *Tarzanna!*
Corddry, Thomas I. *Kibby's big feat*
Cousins, Lucy. *Jazzy in the jungle*
Dale, Penny. *The elephant tree*
Demi. *Three little elephants*
Dijs, Carla. *Pretend you're a hippo*
Drescher, Henrik. *The yellow umbrella*
Edwards, Pamela Duncan. *Roar*
Elbling, Peter. *Aria*
Emberley, Rebecca. *Jungle sounds*
Engel, Diana. *The shelf-paper jungle*
Faulkner, Keith. *The giraffe who cock-a-doodle-doo'd*
    Jumbled jungle
    The tallest shortest longest greenest brownest animal in the jungle!

Fischetto, Laura. *The jungle is my home*
Frampton, David. *The whole night through*
Freeman, Mylo. *Potty*
Geoghegan, Adrienne. *All your own teeth*
Geraghty, Paul. *Stop that noise!*
Gibert, Bruno. *The king is naked!*
Greenaway, Shirley. *Jungles*
Greene, Rhonda Gowler. *Jamboree day*
Gutman, Anne. *Lisa in the jungle*
Harter, Debbie. *Walking through the jungle*
Hellen, Nancy. *Animals of the jungle*
Henley, Claire. *Jungle day*
Hennessy, B. G. (Barbara G.). *Eeney, Meeney, Miney, Mo*
Hewitt, Sally. *Face to face safari*
Hindley, Judy. *Into the jungle*
Isadora, Rachel. *A South African night*
Jennings, Linda M. *Hide and seek birthday treat*
Jordan, Martin. *Amazon alphabet*
    Jungle days, jungle nights
Kemp, Anthea. *Mr. Percy's magic greenhouse*
Kitchen, Bert. *Tenrec's twigs*
Lacome, Julie. *Walking through the jungle*
Lilly, Kenneth. *Animals in the jungle*
London, Jonathan. *Little Red Monkey*
Loomis, Christine. *The Hippo Hop*
Lynn, Sara. *Jungle friends*
McAllister, Angela. *Matepo*
MacDonald, Suse. *Nanta's lion*
McPhail, David M. *Edward in the jungle*
Mahy, Margaret. *17 kings and 42 elephants*
    Simply delicious!
Mangan, Anne. *The monkey who wanted the moon*
Morgan, Michaela. *Helpful Betty solves a mystery*
    Helpful Betty to the rescue
Most, Bernard. *Hippopotamus hunt*
Mwenye Hadithi. *Tricky tortoise*
Nayer, Judy. *Jungle life*
Newman, Jeff. *Reginald*
O'Donnell, Peter. *Oscar*
Parker, Victoria. *Bearum scarum*
Paterson, Brian. *Zigby camps out*
    Zigby hunts for treasure
Royston, Angela. *Jungle animals*
Sage, Angie. *Monkeys in the jungle*
Smith, Jim. *Nimbus the explorer*
Steig, William. *The Zabajaba Jungle*
Sykes, Julie. *Wait for me, Little Tiger*
Tafuri, Nancy. *Junglewalk*
Teyssèdre, Fabienne. *Joseph wants to read*
Upper, Jonathan. *Spin's really wild Africa tour*
Van Allsburg, Chris. *Jumanji*
Ward, Helen. *The tin forest*
West, Colin. *One day in the jungle*
Willis, Jeanne. *The boy who lost his bellybutton*
Wood, John Norris. *Jungles*
Wundrow, Deanna. *Jungle drum*

Kangaroos *see* Animals – kangaroos

Karok Indians *see* Indians of North America – Karok

Karate *see* Sports – karate

Kato Indians *see* Indians of North America – Kato

Kelpies *see* Mythical creatures – kelpies

Kenya *see* Foreign lands – Kenya

Khans *see* Royalty – khans

Kindness *see* Character traits – kindness

Kindness to animals *see* Character traits – kindness to animals

Kings *see* Royalty – kings

Kissing

Berenzy, Alix. *A frog prince*
Capucilli, Alyssa Satin. *What kind of kiss?*
Got, Yves. *Sam loves kisses*
Gray, Nigel. *The frog prince*
Grimm, Jacob. *The frog prince*, ill. by Paul Galdone
   The frog prince, ill. by Binette Schroeder
Hest, Amy. *Kiss good night*
Katz, Karen. *Counting kisses*
McLerran, Alice. *Kisses*
Oram, Hiawyn. *Kiss it better*
Root, Phyllis. *Kiss the cow*
Saltzberg, Barney. *Baby animal kisses*

Kites

Ayer, Jacqueline. *Nu Dang and his kite*
Baumgart, Klaus. *Laura's secret*
Brown, Marcia. *The little carousel*
Buckley, Helen Elizabeth. *Moonlight kite*
Cooper, Elizabeth K. *The fish from Japan*
Cousins, Lucy. *Kite in the park*
Emmett, Jonathan. *Someone bigger*
French, Vivian. *Little Tiger finds a friend*
Galouchko, Annouchka. *Shô and the demons of the deep*
Gerstein, Mordicai. *The mountains of Tibet*
Haseley, Dennis. *Crosby*
   Kite flier
Heller, George. *Hiroshi's wonderful kite*
How Raggedy Ann got her candy heart
Jagtenberg, Yvonne. *Jack's kite*
Krensky, Stephen. *Ben Franklin and his first kite*
Kroll, Virginia L. *A carp for Kimiko*
Lies, Brian. *Hamlet and the enormous Chinese dragon kite*
Lin, Grace. *Kite flying*
Lobato, Arcadio. *Paper bird*
Luenn, Nancy. *The dragon kite*
MacDonald, Elizabeth. *Mike's kite*
MacDonald, Maryann. *Rabbit's birthday kite*
Mayer, Mercer. *Shibumi and the kitemaker*
Miller, Moira. *The moon dragon*
Mitchell, Robin. *Windy*
Molarsky, Osmond. *A sky full of kites*
Murphy, Stuart J. *Let's fly a kite*
Packard, Mary. *The kite*
Peet, Bill (William Bartlett). *Merle the high flying squirrel*
Reddix, Valerie. *Dragon kite of the autumn moon*
Rey, Margret (Margret Elisabeth Waldstein). *Curious George flies a kite*
Roche, Hannah. *Corey's kite*
Romanelli, Serena. *Little Bobo saves the day*
Ruthstrom, Dorotha. *The big kite contest*
Stadler, John. *One seal*
Stafford, Liliana. *Just dragon*
Stilz, Carol Curtis. *Kirsty's kite*
Strauss, Gwen. *The night shimmy*
Thayer, Jane. *Gus loved his happy home*
Titus, Eve. *Anatole over Paris*
Trottier, Maxine. *The tiny kite of Eddie Wing*
Uchida, Yoshiko. *Sumi's prize*
Vaughan, Marcia Kapok. *The Sea-Breeze Hotel*
Wiese, Kurt. *Fish in the air*
Wisdom, Jude. *Whatever Wanda wanted*
Ye, Ting-xing. *Share the sky*

Yolen, Jane. *The emperor and the kite*

Knights

Blake, Quentin. *Snuff*
Boutell, Clarence Burley. *The fat baron*
Bradfield, Roger (Jolly Roger). *A good night for dragons*
Carrick, Donald. *Harold and the giant knight*
Cressey, James. *The dragon and George*
Cretien, Paul D. *Sir Henry and the dragon*
Curry, Jane Louise. *The Christmas knight*
De Paola, Tomie (Thomas Anthony). *The knight and the dragon*
Emberley, Ed (Edward Randolph). *Klippity klop*
Fradon, Dana. *Sir Dana – a knight*
Gerrard, Roy. *Sir Cedric*
   Sir Cedric rides again
Gibbons, Gail. *Knights in shining armor*
Goodall, John S. *Creepy castle*
Grahame, Kenneth. *The reluctant dragon*
Haley, Gail E. *The green man*
Hazen, Barbara Shook. *The knight who was afraid of the dark*
   The knight who was afraid to fight
Hodges, Margaret. *The hero of Bremen*
   The kitchen knight
Holl, Adelaide. *Sir Kevin of Devon*
Ipcar, Dahlov (Zorach). *Sir Addlepate and the unicorn*
Krensky, Stephen. *A good knight's sleep*
Lasker, Joe. *A tournament of knights*
Löfgren, Ulf. *Alvin the Knight*
McCrea, James. *The story of Olaf*
Mayer, Mercer. *Terrible troll*
Myers, Walter Dean. *The dragon takes a wife*
Nash, Ogden. *Custard the dragon and the wicked knight*, ill. by Lynn Munsinger
   Custard the dragon and the wicked knight, ill. by Linell Nash
Nolan, Dennis. *The castle builder*
O'Connor, Jane. *Sir Small and the dragonfly*
Peet, Bill (William Bartlett). *Cowardly Clyde*
   How Droofus the dragon lost his head
Scarry, Huck. *Looking into the Middle Ages*
Shannon, Mark. *Gawain and the Green Knight*
Smith, Linda. *Sir Cassie to the rescue*
Thomas, Shelley Moore. *Get well, good knight*
   Good night, Good Knight
Trez, Denise. *The little knight's dragon*
Tucker, Kathy. *Do knights take naps?*

Knitting *see* Activities – knitting

Koalas *see* Animals – koalas

Komodo dragons *see* Reptiles – Komodo dragons

Korea *see* Foreign lands – Korea

Korea (North) *see* Foreign lands – Korea (North)

Korean Americans *see* Ethnic groups in the U.S. – Korean Americans

Kurdistan *see* Foreign lands – Kurdistan

Kutenai Indians *see* Indians of North America – Kutenai

Kwanzaa *see* Holidays – Kwanzaa

Lady birds *see* Insects – ladybugs

Ladybugs *see* Insects – ladybugs

Lakes, ponds

Arnosky, Jim. *Beaver pond, moose pond*
Capucilli, Alyssa Satin. *Good morning, pond*
Cartlidge, Michelle. *Duck in the pond*
Fleming, Denise. *In the small, small pond*
Gantschev, Ivan. *The moon lake*
George, Lindsay Barrett. *Around the pond*
Heinz, Brian J. *Butternut Hollow Pond*
Hill, Susan. *Stuart sets sail*
Hunter, Anne. *What's in the pond*
Jordan, Sandra. *Frog hunt*
Lasky, Kathryn. *Pond year*
London, Jonathan. *Loon Lake*
Martin, Jacqueline Briggs. *On Sand Island*
Mills, Judith Christine. *The stonehook schooner*
Mitton, Tony. *Down by the cool of the pool*
Pfeffer, Wendy. *Mallard duck at Meadow View Pond*
Rockwell, Anne F. *Ducklings and pollywogs*
Root, Phyllis. *Rattletrap car*
　　Rattletrap car [board book]
Rosen, Michael J. (1954–). *All eyes on the pond*
Schoenherr, John. *Rebel*
Schofield, Jennifer. *Animal babies in ponds and rivers*
Seymour, Tres. *The gulls of the Edmund Fitzgerald*
Sidman, Joyce. *Son of the water boatman*
Taylor, Harriet Peck. *Coyote and the laughing butterflies*
Thompson, Lauren. *Little Quack's new friend*
Valgardson, W. D. *Winter rescue*
Van Leeuwen, Jean. *Touch the sky summer*
Waddell, Martin. *The pig in the pond*

Lakota (Sioux) Indians *see* Indians of North America – Lakota (Sioux)

Lambs *see* Animals – babies; Animals – sheep

Language

Abel, Simone. *Follow that chicken!*
Ada, Alma Flor. *I love Saturdays y domingos*
Ahlberg, Allan. *Big bad pig*
　　Fee fi fo fum
　　Happy worm
　　Help!
Aliki. *Communication*
　　Hello! Good-bye!
The all-amazing ha ha book
Allen, Susan. *Read anything good lately?*
Allington, Richard L. *Letters*
　　Talking
　　Words
Ancona, George. *Handtalk zoo*
Anglund, Joan Walsh. *The Adam book*
　　Emily and Adam book of opposites
　　The Emily book
Anholt, Catherine. *All about you*
　　First words and pictures
Antoine, Héloïse. *Curious kids go to preschool*
Arnold, Tedd. *More parts*
Asch, Frank. *Short train, long train*
Azarian, Mary. *A gardener's alphabet*
Baby's words
Baer, Edith. *Words are like faces*
Baker, Alan. *Little Rabbit's first word book*
Barrett, Judi. *The things that are most in the world*
Barton, Byron. *Tools*
Battle-Lavert, Gwendolyn. *The barber's cutting edge*
Battles, Edith. *What does the rooster say, Yoshio?*
Beaton, Clare. *Zoë and her zebra*
Bender, Robert. *The A to Z beastly jamboree*
Benjamin, Alan. *Rat-a-tat, pitter pat*
Bergen, Lara Rice. *Blue's world of words*
Berson, Harold. *A moose is not a mouse*

Bond, Michael. *Paddington and the knickerbocker rainbow*
Bossom, Naomi. *A scale full of fish and other turnabouts*
Bourke, Linda. *Eye count*
Brown, Marc Tolon. *Arthur's really helpful word book*
Bruce, Lisa. *Oliver's alphabets*
Buck, Nola. *Creepy crawly critters and other Halloween tongue twisters*
　　Oh, cats!
　　Santa's short suit shrunk and other Christmas tongue twisters
　　Sid and Sam
Bunting, Eve (Anne Evelyn). *Say it fast*
Bunting, Jane. *The children's visual dictionary*
　　My first ABC
　　My first word book
Burnstein, Chaya M. *The Jewish kids' Hebrew-English wordbook*
Carle, Eric. *My very first book of words*
Carlson, Nancy L. *ABC, I like me!*
Cartlidge, Michelle. *Michelle Cartlidge's book of words*
Cassie, Brian. *Say it again*
Chapman, Cheryl. *Snow on snow on snow*
Charlip, Remy. *Handtalk*
　　Handtalk birthday
Cheng, Andrea. *Grandfather counts*
Chislett, Gail. *Melinda's no's cold*
Clements, Andrew. *Double trouble in Walla Walla*
Clifford, Eth. *A bear before breakfast*
Cohen, Caron Lee. *Three yellow dogs*
Cole, Babette. *Tarzanna!*
Cox, Phil Roxbee. *Fox on a box*
　　Goose on the loose
　　Shark in the park
　　Ted in a red bed
Day, Alexandra. *Frank and Ernest*
　　Frank and Ernest on the road
　　Frank and Ernest play ball
DeRubertis, Barbara. *Janey Crane*
　　Joey Goat
　　Suzy Mule
　　Tiny Tiger
　　Zeely Zebra
Dodds, Dayle Ann. *Do bunnies talk?*
Dunham, Meredith. *Colors: how do you say it?*
　　Numbers: how do you say it?
　　Picnic
　　Shapes
Du Quette, Keith. *They call me Woolly*
Edwards, Richard. *Fly with the birds*
Ellentuck, Shan. *Did you see what I said?*
Everett, Percival L. *The one that got away*
Falwell, Cathryn. *Clowning around*
　　Word wizard
Folsom, Marcia. *Easy as pie*
Gibbons, Gail. *Weather words and what they mean*
Gifaldi, David. *The boy who spoke colors*
Gomi, Taro. *Seeing, saying, doing, playing*
Goodspeed, Peter. *Hugh and Fitzhugh*
Gordon, Jeffie Ross. *Six sleepy sheep*
Got, Yves. *Sam's big book of words*
Grover, Max. *The accidental zucchini*
Gwynne, Fred. *A chocolate moose for dinner*
　　A little pigeon toad
Haddix, Margaret Peterson. *Say what?*
Harris, Trudy. *Pattern bugs*
Hartman, Gail. *For strawberry jam or fireflies*
Hawkins, Colin. *Tog the dog*
Hayward, Linda. *Wet foot, dry foot, low foot, high foot*
Heelan, Jamee Riggio. *Can you hear a rainbow?*
Heling, Kathryn. *Mouse makes magic*
　　Mouse's hide-and-seek words
Heller, Ruth. *A cache of jewels and other collective nouns*
　　Fantastic! wow! and unreal!
　　Kites sail high
　　Many luscious lollipops
　　Merry-go-round
　　Mine, all mine
Hepworth, Catherine. *Bug off!*
Hiatt, Fred. *Baby talk*

Hill, Eric. *Spot's big book of words = El libro grande de las palabras de Spot*
　Spot's favorite words
　Spot's first words
Hill, Susan. *Simba's A-Z*
Hirschi, Ron. *Seya's song*
Hoban, Tana. *All about where*
　More than one
Hooper, Patricia. *A bundle of beasts*
Horenstein, Henry. *Arf! beg! catch!*
Hunt, Bernice Kohn. *Your ant is a which*
Hunter, Tom. *Build it up and knock it down*
Hurd, Thacher. *Cat's pajamas*
Hyman, Trina Schart. *A little alphabet*
Inkpen, Mick. *Kipper's book of opposites*
Jackson, Bobby L. *Makimba's animal world*
Johnston, Tony. *Uncle rain cloud*
Jonas, Ann. *Watch William walk*
Joyce, Susan. *ABC nature riddles*
Karlin, Nurit. *I see, you saw*
King-Smith, Dick. *Dick King-Smith's Alphabeasts*
Koch, Michelle. *By the sea*
　Just one more
Kopper, Lisa. *I'm a baby, you're a baby*
Kraus, Robert. *Ella the bad speller*
Krauss, Ruth. *A hole is to dig*
Krupp, Robin Rector. *Get set to wreck!*
Lachner, Dorothea. *Andrew's angry words*
Lacome, Julie. *My first book of words*
Leaf, Munro. *Grammar can be fun*
Leedy, Loreen. *There's a frog in my throat*
Leeton, Will C. *The Tower of Babel*
Lenssen, Ann. *A rainbow balloon*
Levine, Ellen. *I hate English!*
Levinson, Riki. *Soon, Annala*
Lewin, Betsy. *Wiley learns to spell*
Lewis, Shari. *Baby Lamb Chop loves words*
Lionni, Leo. *Words to talk about*
Litchfield, Jo. *The Usborne book of everyday words*
Little, Jean. *Bats about baseball*
MacCarthy, Patricia. *Herds of words*
MacDonald, Ross. *Achoo! Bang! Crash!*
McLean, Dirk. *Play mas'! a carnival ABC*
McMillan, Bruce. *One sun*
　Play day
　Super, super, superwords
McNaught, Harry. *Words to grow on*
Maestro, Betsy. *All aboard overnight*
　Camping out
　Delivery van
　On the go
　Taxi
Magee, Doug. *Let's fly from A to Z*
Marks, Alan. *Nowhere to be found*
Martin, Bill (William Ivan). *Words*
Martin, Jerome. *Carrot/parrot*
　Mitten/kitten
Maynard, Bill. *Quiet, Wyatt!*
Michelson, Richard. *Too young for Yiddish*
Milgrim, David. *My friend Lucky*
Miller, Margaret. *Every day*
　I'm grown up!
　My birthday
　On my street
　Playtime
　Where's Jenna?
Millman, Isaac. *Moses goes to a concert*
　Moses goes to school
　Moses goes to the circus
Moncure, Jane Belk. *Word Bird's fall words*
　Word Bird's spring words
　Word Bird's summer words
　Word Bird's winter words
Monfried, Lucia. *Baby's world*
Most, Bernard. *Hippopotamus hunt*
　Pets in trumpets and other word-play riddles
　There's an ape behind the drape

My first farm
My first word, touch and feel
Nathan, Emma. *What do you call a group of turkeys?*
Nayer, Judy. *Mice are nice*
　Pig in a wig
O'Brien, John (1953–). *Sam and Spot*
100 words about transportation
100 words about working
Owen, Annie. *From snowflakes to sandcastles*
Packard, Mary. *Same and different*
Parr, Todd. *Big and little*
　Black and white
Pluckrose, Henry Arthur. *Join it!*
Preiss, Byron. *The first crazy word book*
Rand, Ann. *Sparkle and spin*
Rankin, Laura. *The handmade counting book*
Rappaport, Doreen. *Martin's big words*
Reinhart, Matthew. *Animal popposites*
Richardson, Jack E. *Six in a mix*
Riddell, Edwina. *One hundred first words*
Ringgold, Faith. *Cassie's word quilt*
Rockwell, Anne F. *What we like*
Root, Phyllis. *Gretchen's grandma*
Rose, Gerald. *The bird garden*
Rovetch, Lissa. *Ook the book*
Rumford, James. *There's a monster in the alphabet*
Ruurs, Margriet. *A Pacific alphabet*
Sage, Michael. *If you talked to a boar*
Salt, Jane. *See and say picture word book*
Sattler, Helen Roney. *Train whistles*
Scarry, Richard. *Richard Scarry's biggest word book ever!*
Serfozo, Mary. *What's what?*
Sesame Street. *Sesame Street word book*
Sherman, Ivan. *Walking talking words*
Showers, Paul. *How you talk*
Small, David. *Ruby Mae has something to say*
Snell, Nigel. *A bird in hand . . .*
Snow, Alan. *My first dictionary*
Sper, Emily. *The Passover seder*
Sperberg, Roger. *Real soon, raccoon*
Stanley, Mandy. *At the pool*
　First word book
　In the park
Steig, William. *The bad speller*
Steptoe, John. *My special best words*
Tapahonso, Luci. *Navajo ABC*
Tester, Sylvia Root. *Never monkey with a monkey*
　What did you say?
Tobias, Tobi. *A world of words*
Trân-Khánh-Tuyê. *The little weaver of Thái-Yên Village*
Tullet, Hervé. *Night / day*
Viorst, Judith. *The Alphabet from Z to A*
Wall, Lina Mao. *Judge Rabbit and the tree spirit*
Wells, Rosemary. *Letters and sounds*
　Max's first word
　Max's ride
West, Kipling. *A rattle of bones*
Wiesner, William. *The Tower of Babel*
Wildsmith, Brian. *What the moon saw*
Wilkes, Angela. *My first word book*
Winnie-the-Pooh's ABC
Wood, Audrey. *Elbert's bad word*
Wynne-Jones, Tim. *On Tumbledown Hill*

Language – sign language *see* Sign language

Language, foreign *see* Foreign languages

Laos *see* Foreign lands – Laos

Lapland *see* Foreign lands – Lapland

Larks *see* Birds – larks

Latin America *see* Foreign lands – Latin America

Latvia *see* Foreign lands – Latvia

Laundry

Ahlberg, Allan. *Mrs. Lather's laundry*
Behrens, June. *Soo Ling finds a way*
Freeman, Don. *A pocket for Corduroy*
Iwamura, Kazuo. *The fourteen forest mice and the summer laundry day*
Ormondroyd, Edward. *Theodore*
Straight, Susan. *Bear E. Bear*
Weeks, Sarah. *Mrs. McNosh hangs up her wash*

Law *see* Careers – judges; Careers – lawyers; Careers – police officers; Crime; Prisons

Lawyers *see* Careers – lawyers

Laziness *see* Character traits – laziness

Lebanese Americans *see* Ethnic groups in the U.S. – Lebanese Americans

Lebanon *see* Foreign lands – Lebanon

Leeches *see* Animals – leeches

Left & right *see* Concepts – left & right

Left-handedness

Lerner, Marguerite Rush. *Lefty, the story of left-handedness*

Legends *see* Folk & fairy tales

Legs *see* Anatomy – legs

Lemmings *see* Animals – lemmings

Lemurs *see* Animals – lemurs

Lenape Indians *see* Indians of North America – Lenape

Leopards *see* Animals – leopards

Leprechauns *see* Mythical creatures – leprechauns

Letters, cards

Ada, Alma Flor. *Dear Peter Rabbit*
    With love, Little Red Hen
Adoff, Arnold. *Love letters*
Asch, Frank. *Dear brother*
Augustin, Barbara. *Antonella and her Santa Claus*
Baker, Keith. *The dove's letter*
Bauer, Marion Dane. *My mother is mine*
Bell, Norman. *Linda's airmail letter*
Brandt, Betty. *Special delivery*
Brisson, Pat. *Kate on the coast*
    Your best friend, Kate
Cartlidge, Michelle. *Fairy letters*
    Mouse letters
Caseley, Judith. *Dear Annie*
Cuneo, Mary Louise. *Mail for Husher Town*
Danneberg, Julie. *First year letters*
Dunbar, Joyce. *The secret friend*
Durant, Alan. *Dear tooth fairy*
Edwards, Pamela Duncan. *Dear Tooth Fairy*
Flanagan, Alice K. *Here comes Mr. Eventoff with the mail!*
    Letter carriers
Fox, Louisa. *Every Monday in the mailbox*
Harrison, Joanna. *Dear bear*
Hobbie, Holly. *Toot and Puddle*
Holub, Joan. *Pen pals*
Inches, Alison. *Corduroy writes a letter*

James, Simon. *Dear Mr. Blueberry*
Johnson, Jane. *My dear Noel*
Keats, Ezra Jack. *A letter to Amy*
Klingel, Cynthia Fitterer. *Postal workers*
Leedy, Loreen. *Messages in the mailbox*
Lester, Alison. *Ernie dances to the didgeridoo*
Lillegard, Dee. *Tortoise brings the mail*
Nolen, Jerdine. *Plantzilla*
    Plantzilla goes to camp
Olson, Mary. *Nice try, Tooth Fairy*
Owen, Ann (1953–). *Delivering your mail*
Pak, Soyung. *Dear Juno*
Pattison, Darcy. *The journey of Oliver K. Woodman*
Poydar, Nancy. *Mailbox magic*
Raffi. *Like me and you*
Rau, Dana Meachen. *I'll make you a card*
Ray, Deborah Kogan. *Lily's garden*
Rockwell, Anne F. *Valentine's Day*, ill. by Lizzy Rockwell
Rodell, Susanna. *Dear Fred*
Ross, Lillian Hammer. *Buba Leah and her paper children*
Rylant, Cynthia. *Little Whistle's Christmas*
Schindel, John. *Dear Daddy*
Schumacher, Claire. *Tommy the winner*
Selway, Martina. *Don't forget to write*
Seuss, Dr. *On beyond zebra*
Siracusa, Catherine. *No mail for Mitchell*
Skurzynski, Gloria. *Here comes the mail*
Sloat, Teri. *Pieces of Christmas*
Spurr, Elizabeth. *The long, long letter*
Stanley, Diane. *Raising Sweetness*
Steptoe, Javaka. *The Jones family express*
Stewart, Sarah. *The gardener*
Teague, Mark. *Dear Mrs. LaRue*
    Detective LaRue
Weninger, Brigitte. *A letter to Santa Claus*
Wild, Margaret. *Thank you, Santa*

Leverage *see* Concepts – leverage

Liberia *see* Foreign lands – Liberia

Librarians *see* Careers – librarians

Libraries

Alexander, Martha G. *How my library grew by Dinah*
Alexander, Sue. *World famous Muriel and the magic mystery*
Aliki. *How a book is made*
Baggette, Susan K. *Jonathan goes to the library*
Baker, Donna. *I want to be a librarian*
Bartlett, Susan. *Libraries*
Bauer, Caroline Feller. *Too many books!*
Baugh, Dolores M. *Let's take a trip*
Brillhart, Julie. *Story hour – starring Megan!*
Brimner, Larry Dane. *Aggie and Will*
Bruss, Deborah. *Book! book! book!*
Caseley, Judith. *The noisemakers*
    Sophie and Sammy's library sleepover
Charles, Donald. *Calico Cat meets bookworm*
Daly, Maureen. *Patrick visits the library*
Daugherty, James Henry. *Andy and the lion*
Demarest, Chris L. *Clemens' kingdom*
De Paola, Tomie (Thomas Anthony). *The knight and the dragon*
Ernst, Lisa Campbell. *Stella Louella's runaway book*
Felt, Sue. *Rosa-too-little*
Flanagan, Alice K. *Librarians*
    Ms. Davison, our librarian
Fraser, Mary Ann. *I.Q. goes to the library*
Freeman, Don. *Quiet! There's a canary in the library*
Furtado, Jo. *Sorry, Miss Folio!*
Gay, Zhenya. *Look!*
Gibbons, Gail. *Check it out!*
Hautzig, Deborah. *A visit to the Sesame Street library*
Hest, Amy. *The babies are coming!*
Horn, Emily. *Excuse me – are you a witch?*
Houghton, Eric. *Walter's magic wand*

Huff, Barbara A. *Once inside the library*
Hulbert, Jay. *Armando asked "Why?"*
Hutchins, H. J. (Hazel J.). *Nicholas at the library*
Jaspersohn, William. *My hometown library*
Kimmel, Eric A. *I took my frog to the library*
Lakin, Patricia. *Clarence the copy cat*
Levinson, Nancy Smiler. *Clara and the bookwagon*
Lewis, Rob. *Aunt Armadillo*
Little, Mary E. *ABC for the library*
   Ricardo and the puppets
Loomis, Christine. *At the library*
Mahoney, Daniel J. *The Saturday escape*
Mayr, Diane. *Littlebat's Halloween story*
Meister, Cari. *Tiny goes to the library*
Miller, Heather. *Librarian*
Miller, William. *Richard Wright and the library card*
Mora, Pat. *A library for Juana*
   Tomás and the library lady
Munro, Roxie. *The inside-outside book of libraries*
Murphy, Mary. *Koala and the flower*
Polacco, Patricia. *Aunt Chip and the great Triple Creek dam affair*
Radabaugh, Melinda Beth. *Going to the library*
Radlauer, Ruth Shaw. *Molly at the library*
Rahaman, Vashanti. *Read for me, Mama*
Rockwell, Anne F. *I like the library*
Sadler, Marilyn. *Alistair in outer space*
Sauer, Julia Lina. *Mike's house*
Shea, Kitty. *Out and about at the public library*
Sierra, Judy. *Wild about books*
Stadler, Alexander. *Beverly Billingsly borrows a book*
Stewart, Sarah. *The library*
Tudor, Tasha. *Mildred and the mummy*
Ungar, Richard. *Rachel's library*
Weil, Lisl. *Let's go to the library*
Woodruff, Elvira. *Can you guess where we're going?*

Lice *see* Insects – lice

Lifeguards *see* Careers – lifeguards

Light, lights

Baisch, Cris. *When the lights went out*
Berger, Melvin. *Switch on, switch off*
Crews, Donald. *Light*
Graham, Joan Bransfield. *Flicker flash*
Holderness, Jackie. *What is a shadow?*
Rosenberg, Liz. *Eli's night-light*
Schnur, Steven. *Night lights*
Swinburne, Stephen R. *Guess whose shadow?*
Weninger, Brigitte. *Lumina*
Wright, Sue (Sue M.). *The Christmas path*

Lighthouses

Armitage, Ronda. *The lighthouse keeper's catastrophe*
   The lighthouse keeper's lunch
   The lighthouse keeper's rescue
Barker, Melvern J. *Little island star*
Brett, Jan. *Comet's nine lives*
Briggs, Kelly Paul. *Lighthouse lullaby*
Buzzeo, Toni. *The sea chest*
Fearrington, Ann. *Who sees the lighthouse?*
Hoff, Syd. *The lighthouse children*
Hopkinson, Deborah. *Birdie's lighthouse*
Lobel, Anita. *One lighthouse, one moon*
Metaxas, Eric. *The boy and the whale*
Olson, Arielle North. *The lighthouse keeper's daughter*
Perrow, Angeli. *Captain's castaway*
   Lighthouse dog to the rescue
Rowinski, Kate. *Cats in the dark*
Stainton, Sue. *The lighthouse cat*
Strahl, Rudi. *Sandman in the lighthouse*
Swift, Hildegarde Hoyt. *The little red lighthouse and the great gray bridge*
Thaxter, Celia. *Celia's island journal*

Vaughan, Marcia Kapok. *Abbie against the storm*
Wells, Rosemary. *The island light*

Lightning *see* Weather – lightning, thunder

Lightning bugs *see* Insects – fireflies

Lions *see* Animals – lions

Lithuanian Americans *see* Ethnic groups in the U.S. – Lithuanian Americans

Little people

Barber, Antonia. *Catkin*
Berg, Jean Horton. *The wee little man*
Beskow, Elsa Maartman. *Peter in Blueberry Land*
   Peter's adventures in Blueberry Land
Brennan, Patricia D. *Hitchety hatchety up I go!*
Carrick, Carol. *Two very little sisters*
French, Fiona. *Little Inchkin*
Hughes, Monica. *Little Fingerling*
Krauss, Ruth. *Everything under a mushroom*
Mogensen, Jan. *The forty-six little men*
Morimoto, Junko. *The inch boy*
San Souci, Robert D. *Little Pierre*
Tom Thumb. *The adventures of Tom Thumb*, ill. by Kinuko Y. Craft
   Grimm Tom Thumb
   Tom Thumb, ill. by L. Leslie Brooke
   Tom Thumb, ill. by Dennis Hockerman
   Tom Thumb, ill. by Felix Hoffmann
   Tom Thumb, ill. by Lidia Postma
   Tom Thumb, ill. by Richard Jesse Watson
   Tom Thumb, ill. by William Wiesner

Littleness *see* Character traits – smallness

Lizards *see* Reptiles – lizards

Llamas *see* Animals – llamas

Lobsters *see* Crustaceans – lobsters

Loneliness *see* Emotions – loneliness

Loons *see* Birds – loons

Lorises *see* Animals – lorises

Losing things *see* Behavior – lost & found possessions

Lost *see* Behavior – lost

Love *see* Emotions – love

Loyalty *see* Character traits – loyalty

Luck *see* Character traits – luck

Lullabies

Ahlberg, Allan. *Mockingbird*
All the pretty little horses
Appelt, Kathi. *Bayou lullaby*
   I see the moon
Aragon, Jane Chelsea. *Lullaby*
Asch, Frank. *Barnyard lullaby*
Bang, Molly. *Ten, nine, eight*
Benjamin, Floella. *Skip across the ocean*
Bernhard, Josephine Butkowska. *Lullaby*
Blomgren, Jennifer. *Where do I sleep?*
Bozylinsky, Hannah Heritage. *Lala Salama*
Bradman, Tony. *Daddy's lullaby*

Calmenson, Stephanie. *All aboard the goodnight train*
Canyon, Christopher. *John Denver's Ancient rhymes*
Carlstrom, Nancy White. *Northern lullaby*
Carpenter, Mary-Chapin. *Dreamland*
Chorao, Kay. *Rock, rock, my baby*
Conrad, Pam. *Animal lullabies*
Davis, Caroline. *My little rocking horse lullabies*
The drowsy hours
Duncan, Lois. *Songs from dreamland*
Engvick, William. *Lullabies and night songs*
Fox, Mem. *Sleepy bears*
Frampton, David. *The whole night through*
French, Vivian. *A song for little toad*
Gerber, Carole. *Hush! a Gaelic lullaby*
Gilbert, Yvonne. *Baby's book of lullabies and cradle songs*
Ginsburg, Mirra. *Asleep, asleep*
Highwater, Jamake. *Moonsong lullaby*
Hindley, Judy. *The sleepy book*
Ho, Minfong. *Hush!*
Hopkins, Lee Bennett. *And God bless me*
Hush little baby. *Hush little baby*, ill. by Aliki
  Hush, little baby, ill. by Marla Frazee
  Hush little baby, ill. by Shari Halpern
  Hush little baby, ill. by Jeanette Winter
  Hush little baby, ill. by Margot Zemach
Hush songs
Khan, Rukhsana. *Bedtime ba-a-a-lk*
Kherdian, David. *Lullaby for Emily*
Kirk, Daniel. *Hush, little alien*
Lambert, Paulette Livers. *Evening*
Lansky, Bruce. *Sweet dreams*
London, Jonathan. *Fireflies, fireflies, light my way*
Lullaby and goodnight
Lullaby moons and a silver spoon
McGhee, Alison. *In the hollow of your hand*
McMullan, Kate (Hall). *If you were my bunny*
Marzollo, Jean. *Close your eyes*
Meigs, Mildred Plew. *Moon song*
Melmed, Laura Krauss. *Jumbo's lullaby*
Merriam, Eve. *Goodnight to Annie*, ill. by Carol Schwartz
Messenger, Jannat. *Lullabies and baby songs*
Millen, C. M. *Blue bowl down*
Miranda, Anne. *Night songs*
Mitchard, Jacquelyn. *Baby bat's lullaby*
Morgenstern, Christian. *Lullabies, lyrics and gallows songs*
Nichol, B. P. *Once, a lullaby*
Nye, Naomi Shihab. *Lullaby raft*
Ogburn, Jacqueline K. *Noise lullaby*
Pfister, Marcus. *I see the moon*
Pieńkowski, Jan. *Good night, a pop-up lullaby*
Plotz, Helen. *A week of lullabies*
Pomerantz, Charlotte. *All asleep*
Root, Phyllis. *All for the newborn baby*
  What Baby wants
Schlein, Miriam. *Sleep safe, little whale*
Slate, Joseph. *The star rocker*
Sleep, baby, sleep
Smith, Edward Biko. *A lullaby for Daddy*
Stanley, Diane. *Birdsong lullaby*
Staub, Leslie. *Bless this house*
Swados, Elizabeth. *Lullaby*
Taylor, Livingston. *Pajamas*
Titherington, Jeanne. *Baby's boat*
  Baby's boat [board book]
Van Laan, Nancy. *Sleep, sleep, sleep*
  When winter comes
Van Vorst, M. L. *A Norse lullaby*
Walty, Margaret. *Rock-a-bye baby*
Watson, Clyde. *Fisherman lullabies*
Whiteside, Karen. *Lullaby of the wind*
Wilkon, Józef. *Lullaby for a newborn king*
Wood, Douglas. *Northwoods cradle song*
Yolen, Jane. *Dragon night and other lullabies*
  The lullaby songbook

Lumberjacks *see* Careers – lumberjacks

Lutes *see* Musical instruments – lutes

Lutins *see* Mythical creatures – lutins

Lying *see* Behavior – lying

Lynx *see* Animals – lynx

Macaws *see* Birds – macaws

Machines

Adkins, Jan. *Heavy equipment*
Baker, Betty. *Worthington Botts and the steam machine*
Balterman, Lee. *Girders and cranes*
Barton, Byron. *Machines at work*
Bate, Norman. *Vulcan*
  Who built the bridge?
  Who built the highway?
Baugh, Dolores M. *Let's take a trip*
Benedictus, Roger. *Fifty million sausages*
Bennett, Jill. *Machine poems*
Big noisy trucks and diggers
Biro, Val. *Gumdrop and the steamroller*
Blum, Mark. *Big trucks and diggers in 3-D*
Bradfield, Roger (Jolly Roger). *The flying hockey stick*
Breverton, David. *Here comes bulldozer*
Brown, Margaret Wise. *The diggers*
  The steamroller
Burton, Virginia Lee. *Katy and the big snow*
  Mike Mulligan and his steam shovel
Calhoun, Mary. *Jack and the whoopee wind*
Carter, Don. *Get to work, trucks!*
Climo, Lindee. *Clyde*
Copeland, Cynthia L. *What are you waiting for?*
Cowcher, Helen. *Rain forest*
Cox, David. *Tin Lizzie and Little Nell*
Crowther, Robert. *Dump trucks and diggers*
Dahl, Michael. *One big building*
Du Bois, William Pène. *Lazy Tommy pumpkinhead*
Fleishman, Seymour. *Too hot in Potzburg*
Fleming, Candace. *Professor Fergus Fahrenheit and his wonderful
  weather machine*
Fowler, Allan. *Simple machines*
Fry, Jenny. *Building numbers*
Gackenbach, Dick. *Dog for a day*
Geringer, Laura. *Molly's new washing machine*
Goor, Ron. *In the driver's seat*
Gordon, David. *The three little rigs*
Granowsky, Alvin. *Diggers and cranes*
Haldane, Suzanne. *Teddies and machines*
  Teddies and trucks
Hennessy, B. G. (Barbara G.). *Road builders*
Henstra, Friso. *Wait and see*
Hill, Eric. *Spot goes to the farm*
Hill, Lee Sullivan. *Earthmovers*
Hoban, Tana. *Construction zone*
  Dig, drill, dump, fill
Holl, Adelaide. *The ABC of cars, trucks and machines*
Hopkins, Lee Bennett. *Click, rumble, roar*
Hunter, Norman. *Professor Branestawn's building bust-up*
Hutchings, Tony. *Things that go word book*
Ipcar, Dahlov (Zorach). *One horse farm*
Jacobs, Daniel. *What does it do?*
Kilby, Don. *At a construction site*
  In the city
  In the country
Kirk, David. *Nova's ark*

Löfgren, Ulf. *The traffic stopper that became a grandmother visitor*
Love, Ann. *Farming*
Lustig, Michael. *Willy Whyner, cloud designer*
MacDonald, Suse. *Elephants on board*
McGough, Roger. *Until I met Dudley*
Machotka, Hana. *Pasta factory*
Merriam, Eve. *Bam, bam, bam*
Munsch, Robert N. *Jonathan cleaned up – then he heard a sound*
Murphy, Andy. *Out and about at the dairy farm*
Neville, Emily Cheney. *The bridge*
Nikola-Lisa, W. *One hole in the road*
Olney, Ross R. *Construction giants*
    Farm giants
Parker, Steve. *I wonder why tunnels are round*
Patrick, Jean L. S. *If I had a snowplow*
Pluckrose, Henry Arthur. *On the farm*
    On the move
Potter, Tony. *See how it works: earth movers*
Pringle, Laurence P. *Jesse builds a road*
Radford, Derek. *Building machines and what they do*
    Cargo machines and what they do
Retan, Walter. *The snowplow that tried to go south*
    The steam shovel that wouldn't eat dirt
Rockwell, Anne F. *Big wheels*
    Machines
Rogers, Hal. *Combines*
    Milking machines
    Plows
Royston, Angela. *Big machines*
    Diggers and dump trucks
    Monster road builders
Sadler, Marilyn. *Alistair's time machine*
Simon, Seymour. *Giant machines*
Small, David. *Ruby Mae has something to say*
Smucker, Anna Egan. *No star nights*
Stevenson, James. *Sam the Zamboni man*
Stickland, Paul. *All about diggers*
    Machines as big as monsters
Walker, Sally M. *Levers*
Wallace, Karen. *Big machines*
Ward, Nick. *Farmer George and the fieldmice*
Watson, Wendy. *Holly's Christmas eve*
Weston, Martha. *The dinosaurs meet Dr. Clock*
Wolde, Gunilla. *Betsy and the vacuum cleaner*
Yagelski, Robert. *The day the lifting bridge stuck*
Zaffo, George J. *The giant nursery book of things that work*

Madagascar *see* Foreign lands – Madagascar

Magic

Agee, Jon. *Milo's hat trick*
Alexander, Martha G. *My outrageous friend Charlie*
    3 magic flip books
Alexander, Sue. *Marc the Magnificent*
    World famous Muriel and the magic mystery
Aliki. *The wish workers*
Andersen, H. C. (Hans Christian). *The tinderbox*, ill. by Warwick Hutton
    The tinderbox, ill. by Barry Moser
    The wild swans, ill. by Angela Barrett
    The wild swans, ill. by Susan Jeffers
Anderson, Lonzo. *Two hundred rabbits*
Anderson, Robin. *Sinabouda Lily*
Anno, Mitsumasa. *Anno's hat tricks*
Arabian Nights. *The flying carpet*
    The tale of Aladdin and the wonderful lamp
Araki, Mie. *The magic toolbox*
Argueta, Manlio. *The magic dogs of the volcanoes*
Armitage, Ronda. *The bossing of Josie*
Atwell, Debby. *Humphrey Thud*
Ayers, Rebecca Hickox. *Per and the Dala horse*
Aylesworth, Jim. *The full belly bowl*
Ayres, Becky Hickox. *Victoria flies high*
Babbitt, Samuel F. *The forty-ninth magician*
Bach, Othello. *Hector McSnector and the mail-order Christmas witch*
    Lilly, Willy and the mail-order witch

Balian, Lorna. *Humbug potion*
Ballard, Robin. *Cat and Alex and the magic flying carpet*
Banigan, Sharon Stearns. *Circus magic*
Barber, Antonia. *The enchanter's daughter*
    Satchelmouse and the dinosaurs
Base, Graeme. *Jungle drums*
Baumann, Hans. *Chip has many brothers*
Baumgart, Klaus. *Laura's Christmas star*
    Laura's secret
Behrens, June. *Christmas-magic wagon*
Beisner, Monika. *Secret spells and curious charms*
Bell, Anthea. *Swan Lake*
Bemelmans, Ludwig. *Madeline's Christmas*
Bentley, Nancy. *I've got your nose!*
Berenstain, Stan. *The Berenstain bears and the sitter*
Berson, Harold. *Charles and Claudine*
    The thief who hugged a moonbeam
Beskow, Elsa Maartman. *Peter in Blueberry Land*
    Peter's adventures in Blueberry Land
Bianco, Margery Williams. *The velveteen rabbit*, ill. by Allen Atkinson
    The velveteen rabbit, ill. by Monique Félix
    The velveteen rabbit, ill. by Michael Green
    The velveteen rabbit, ill. by Michael Hague
    The velveteen rabbit, ill. by Estella Hickman
    The velveteen rabbit, ill. by Steve Johnson & Lou Fancher
    The velveteen rabbit, ill. by David Jorgensen
    The velveteen rabbit, ill. by Thea Kliros
    The velveteen rabbit, ill. by Elizabeth Miles
    The velveteen rabbit, ill. by William Nicholson
    The velveteen rabbit, ill. by Robyn Officer
    The velveteen rabbit, ill. by Ilse Plume
    The velveteen rabbit, ill. by S. D. Schindler
    The velveteen rabbit, ill. by Tien
Birrer, Cynthia. *The lady and the unicorn*
Black, Harley. *Amazing magic school*
Blance, Ellen. *Monster and the magic umbrella*
Bloom, Becky. *Mice make trouble*
Bogan, Paulette. *Momma's magical purse*
Bottner, Barbara. *Pish and Posh*
Boujon, Claude. *The fairy with the long nose*
Bowden, Joan Chase. *Who took the top hat trick?*
Bower, Tamara. *The shipwrecked sailor*
Boyle, Vere. *Beauty and the beast*
Brenner, Barbara A. *The flying patchwork quilt*
Bridwell, Norman. *The witch grows up*
Bright, Robert. *Georgie and the magician*
Brown, Marcia. *Once a mouse . . .*
Browne, Anthony. *Through the magic mirror*
Bruna, Dick. *Dick Bruna's Snow-White and the seven dwarfs*
Brunhoff, Laurent de. *Babar the magician*
Buckaway, C. M. *Alfred, the dragon who lost his flame*
Buckley, Paul. *Amy Belligera and the fireflies*
Buffett, Jimmy. *Trouble dolls*
Bunting, Eve (Anne Evelyn). *The man who could call down owls*
Burdett, Lois. *The tempest for kids*
Burningham, John. *The magic bed*
Calmenson, Stephanie. *The frog principal*
    The little witch sisters
Carlson, Natalie Savage. *Spooky and the ghost cat*
    Spooky and the witch's goat
    Spooky and the wizard's bats
Carrier, Roch. *The longest home run*
Carter, Anne Laurel. *Beauty and the beast*
    The fisherwoman
Cecil, Laura. *The frog princess*
Chang, Margaret Scrogin. *The beggar's magic*
Chapman, Carol. *Barney Bipple's magic dandelions*
Chase, Mary. *The wicked, wicked ladies in the haunted house*
Chouinard, Roger. *One magic box*
Christelow, Eileen. *Olive and the magic hat*
Chwast, Seymour. *Mr. Merlin and the turtle*
Clayton, Elaine. *Ella's trip to the museum*
Cleaver, Elizabeth. *The enchanted caribou*
Climo, Shirley. *The cobweb Christmas*
Coats, Lucy. *Neil's numberless world*
Coco, Eugene Bradley. *The wishing well*

Cole, Babette. *Nungu and the elephant*
  Prince Cinders
Cole, Joanna. *Bony-legs*
  The magic school bus in the time of the dinosaurs
  The magic school bus inside a beehive
  The magic school bus lost in the solar system
  The magic school bus on the ocean floor
  Mixed-up magic
Colette, Sidonie Gabrielle. *The boy and the magic*
Coombs, Patricia. *The magic pot*
  The magician and McTree
Coville, Bruce. *The foolish giant*
  Sarah and the dragon
Cullen, Catherine Ann. *The magical, mystical, marvelous coat*
Czernecki, Stefan. *Zorah's magic carpet*
Day, Alexandra. *Mirror*
Degen, Bruce. *The little witch and the riddle*
DeLage, Ida. *The witchy broom*
Delton, Judy. *Brimhall turns to magic*
  Rabbit goes to night school
Demi. *Chen Ping and his magic axe*
  Liang and the magic paintbrush
  The magic boat
  The magic tapestry
De Paola, Tomie (Thomas Anthony). *Big Anthony and the magic ring*
  Merry Christmas, Strega Nona
  Strega Nona
  Strega Nona meets her match
  Strega Nona's magic lessons
Dewan, Ted. *The sorcerer's apprentice*
Dewey, Ariane. *Dorin and the dragon*
  The fish Peri
  The thunder god's son
Dickson, Louise. *The vanishing cat*
Dines, Glen. *A tiger in the cherry tree*
Domanska, Janina. *Palmiero and the ogre*
DuBurke, Randy. *The moon ring*
Dukas, P. (Paul Abraham). *The sorcerer's apprentice*
Dumas, Bianca. *Tia Luisa, the magical cook*
Edens, Cooper. *Nicholi*
Edmund and the White Witch
Edwards, Lisa. *Disney's Beauty and the beast, a book of manners*
Egielski, Richard. *Jazper*
  Three magic balls
Ehrlich, Amy. *Pome and Peel*
Evans, Richard Paul. *The Christmas candle*
The firebird. *The firebird*, ill. by Reg Cartwright
  The firebird, ill. by Francesca Crespi
  The firebird, ill. by Demi
  The firebird, adapt. and ill. by Rachel Isadora
  The firebird, ill. by Moira Kemp
  The firebird, ill. by Kris Waldherr
  The firebird, ill. by Boris Zvorykin
  The tale of the firebird, ill. by Gennady Spirin
Flot, Jeannette B. *Princess Kalina and the hedgehog*
Fox, Mem. *The magic hat*
Frascino, Edward. *Nanny Noony and the dust queen*
  Nanny Noony and the magic spell
French, Vivian. *Why the sea is salt*
Fuchshuber, Annegert. *The wishing hat*
Gabler, Mirko. *Brakus, Krakus . . . Or the incredible adventure of Mr. Skola's Tourist Club*
Gackenbach, Dick. *Ida Fanfanny*
Gaffington, Urslan Judith. *Silver berries and Christmas magic*
Gág, Wanda. *Nothing at all*
  The sorcerer's apprentice
Galchutt, David. *There was magic inside*
Galdone, Paul. *The magic porridge pot*
Garland, Michael. *Miss Smith's incredible storybook*
Gauch, Patricia Lee. *The little friar who flew*
  Uncle Magic
Geras, Adèle. *Swan Lake*
Gilliland, Judith Heide. *Not in the house, Newton!*
Ginsburg, Mirra. *The old man and his birds*
  Striding slippers
Glassman, Peter. *My working mom*

  The wizard next door
Glazer, Lee. *Cookie Becker casts a spell*
Glennon, Karen M. *Miss Eva and the red balloon*
Gollub, Matthew. *The twenty-five Mixtec cats*
The good-hearted youngest brother
Greaves, Margaret. *Kate Crackernuts*
Green, Marion. *The magician who lived on the mountain*
Greene, Ellin. *Billy Beg and his bull*
Greeson, Janet. *The stingy baker*
Grimm, Jacob. *The donkey prince*
  The earth gnome
  Fitcher's bird
  Rose Red and the bear prince
  Rumpelstiltskin, ill. by Jacqueline Ayer
  Rumpelstiltskin, ill. by Donna Diamond
  Rumpelstiltskin, ill. by Paul Galdone
  Rumpelstiltskin, ill. by Jonathan Langley
  Rumpelstiltskin, ill. by David Shaw
  Rumpelstiltskin, ill. by Gennady Spirin
  Rumpelstiltskin, ill. by John Wallner
  Rumpelstiltskin, ill. by Bernadette Watts
  Rumpelstiltskin, ill. by Paul O. Zelinsky
  The seven ravens, ill. by Felix Hoffmann
  The seven ravens, ill. by Lisbeth Zwerger
  The six servants
  The six swans, ill. by Dorothée Duntze
  The six swans, ill. by Daniel San Souci
  The six swans, ill. by Margot Tomes
  Snow White, ill. by Trina Schart Hyman
  Snow White, ill. by Bernadette Watts
  Snow White, ill. by Claudia Wolf
  Snow White and Rose Red, ill. by Adrienne Adams
  Snow White and Rose Red, ill. by John Wallner
  Snow White and Rose Red, ill. by Bernadette Watts
  Snow White and the seven dwarfs, ill. by Wanda Gág
  Snow White and the seven dwarves, ill. by Chihiro Iwasaki
Grindley, Sally. *The sorcerer's apprentice*
Guthrie, Donna. *The witch has an itch*
  The witch who lives down the hall
Haley, Gail E. *Jack and the bean tree*
Haller, Danita Ross. *Not just any ring*
Harrison, Troon. *The floating orchard*
Hartmann, Wendy. *All the magic in the world*
Haseley, Dennis. *The cave of snores*
Hastings, Selina. *The singing ringing tree*
Hausman, Gerald. *The story of Blue Elk*
Hautzig, Deborah. *Beauty and the beast*
Hayes, Joe. *Little Gold Star = Estrellita de oro*
Hazen, Barbara Shook. *The sorcerer's apprentice*
Hearn, Michael Patrick. *The porcelain cat*
Helldorfer, M. C. (Mary Claire). *The mapmaker's daughter*
Heller, Linda. *Alexis and the golden ring*
Helmer, Marilyn. *Three tales of enchantment*
Hiller, Catherine. *Abracatabby*
Himmelman, John. *Amanda and the magic garden*
Hindley, Judy. *Uncle Harold and the green hat*
Hodges, Margaret. *Comus*
Hoffman, Rosekrans. *Sister Sweet Ella*
Hoffmann, E. T. A. *The strange child*
Honigsberg, Peter Jan. *Pillow of dreams*
Hooks, William H. *Moss gown*
Houck, Eric L. *Rabbit surprise*
Houghton, Eric. *Walter's magic wand*
  How the cock wrecked the manor
Howland, Naomi. *Latkes, latkes, good to eat*
Hru, Dakari. *Joshua's Masai mask*
Hulpach, Vladimir. *Ahaiyute and Cloud Eater*
Hunter, C. W. *The green gourd*
Hutton, Warwick. *Beauty and the beast*
Isele, Elizabeth. *The frog princess*
Jackson, Shirley. *9 magic wishes*
James, J. Alison. *Eucalyptus wings*
Jane, Pamela. *Milo and the greatest trick ever*
Janosch. *Joshua and the magic fiddle*
  The magic auto
Jennings, Sharon. *Franklin and the magic show*
Jeschke, Susan. *Angela and Bear*

The talking eggs
The white cat
Saunders, Susan. *A sniff in time*
Scott, Sally. *The magic horse*
Seeger, Pete. *Abiyoyo*
    Abiyoyo returns
Shah, Idries. *The boy without a name*
Shecter, Ben. *Emily, girl witch of New York*
Shulevitz, Uri. *The magician*
Silverman, Maida. *The magic well*
Simmons, Steven J. *Alice and Greta*
    Alice and Greta's color magic
    Greta's revenge
Sleator, William. *That's silly*
Slobodkin, Louis. *Magic Michael*
Smith, Janice Lee. *Wizard and Wart in trouble*
Snyder, Zilpha Keatley. *The changing maze*
Sokol, Edward. *Meet Stinky Magee*
Somers, Kevin. *Meaner than meanest*
Sondheimer, Ilse. *The magic of Pomme*
Spiegelman, Art. *I'm a dog!*
Stanley, Diane. *The good-luck pencil*
Steig, William. *The amazing bone*
    Caleb and Kate
    Gorky rises
    Solomon the rusty nail
    Sylvester and the magic pebble
    Tiffky Doofky
    Zeke Pippin
Steptoe, John. *The story of jumping mouse*
Stevenson, James. *Yuck!*
Stewig, John Warren. *Clever Gretchen*
Stubbs, Joanna. *With cat's eyes you'll never be scared of the dark*
Taulbert, Clifton L. *Little Cliff and the porch people*
Teague, Mark. *One Halloween night*
Thaler, Mike. *Madge's magic show*
Thayer, Jane. *Mr. Turtle's magic glasses*
Thomas, Shelley Moore. *Good night, Good Knight*
Tibo, Gilles. *The cowboy kid*
Tom Tit Tot. *Tom Tit Tot*
Towle, Faith M. *The magic cooking pot*
Tresselt, Alvin R. *The world in the candy egg*
Trevelyan, Kathy. *Don't be surprised!*
Trez, Denise. *Maila and the flying carpet*
Tseng, Grace. *White tiger, blue serpent*
Tune, Suelyn Ching. *How Maui slowed the sun*
Tunnell, Michael O. *Halloween pie*
Turkle, Brinton. *The magic of Millicent Musgrave*
Turska, Krystyna. *The magician of Cracow*
Ungerer, Tomi. *The hat*
    Tortoni Tremelo the cursed musician
Vainio, Pirkko. *The dream house*
Van Allsburg, Chris. *The garden of Abdul Gasazi*
    The widow's broom
Varga, Judy. *Janko's wish*
Waber, Bernard. *You're a little kid with a big heart*
Wallace, Karen. *Scarlette Beane*
Walsh, Ellen Stoll. *Mouse magic*
    Pip's magic
Walt Disney Productions. *Walt Disney's Snow White and the seven dwarfs*
Wang, Rosalind C. *The treasure chest*
Weedn, Flavia. *The magic cap*
Whitcher, Susan. *The key to the cupboard*
Whybrow, Ian. *Parcel for Stanley*
Wiesner, David. *The loathsome dragon*
    Tuesday
Willard, Nancy. *The marzipan moon*
    The mountains of quilt
Williams, Sam. *Snowy magic*
Wisniewski, David. *Elfwyn's saga*
Wolkstein, Diane. *Oom razoom; or, Go I know not where, Bring back I know not what*
Wood, Audrey. *The flying dragon room*
Woodruff, Elvira. *Show and tell*
Wright, Freire. *Beauty and the beast*
Wright, Jill. *The old woman and the jar of ums*

Yaffe, Alan. *The magic meatballs*
Yep, Laurence. *The shell woman and the king*
Yolen, Jane. *The firebird*
Zwerger, Lisbeth. *Swan Lake*

Magicians *see* Careers – magicians

Magpies *see* Birds – magpies

Maidu Indians *see* Indians of North America – Maidu

Mail *see* Careers – postal workers; Letters, cards; Post office

Mail carriers *see* Careers – postal workers; Letters, cards; Post office

Making things *see* Activities – making things

Malaysia *see* Foreign lands – Malaysia

Mali *see* Foreign lands – Mali

Manatees *see* Animals – manatees

Mandolins *see* Musical instruments – mandolins

Manners *see* Etiquette

Maps

Barner, Bob. *Which way to the Revolution?*
Beck, Andrea. *Elliot digs for treasure*
Bredeson, Carmen. *Looking at maps and globes*
Chancellor, Deborah. *Maps and mapping*
Fanelli, Sara. *My map book*
Hartman, Gail. *As the crow flies*
    As the roadrunner runs
Helldorfer, M. C. (Mary Claire). *The mapmaker's daughter*
Keller, Laurie. *The scrambled states of America*
Leedy, Loreen. *Mapping Penny's world*
Murphy, Stuart J. *Treasure map*
National Geographic Society (U.S.). *National Geographic our world: a child's first picture atlas*
Paterson, Brian. *Zigby hunts for treasure*
Penner, Lucille Recht. *Where's that bone?*
Piepmeier, Charlotte. *Lucy's journey to the wild west*
Rockwell, Anne F. *The way to Captain Yankee's*
Schaap, Martine. *Mop's treasure hunt*
Singer, Marilyn. *On the same day in March*
Stroud, Bettye. *The patchwork path*
Tyler, Jenny. *Big Pig on a dig*
Walters, Virginia. *Are we there yet, Daddy?*

Mardi Gras

Landau, Elaine. *Mardi Gras*
Lionni, Leo. *The greentail mouse*
Moore, Elizabeth. *Mimi and Jean-Paul's Cajun Mardi Gras*

Marionettes *see* Puppets

Markets *see* Stores

Marriage, interracial

Adoff, Arnold. *Black is brown is tan*
Davol, Marguerite W. *Black, white, just right*
Igus, Toyomi. *Two Mrs. Gibsons*
McGill, Alice. *Molly Bannaky*
Northway, Jennifer. *Lucy's day trip*
Senisi, Ellen B. *For my family, love, Allie*

Marriages *see* Weddings

Mars *see* Planets

Martin Luther King, Jr. Day *see* Holidays – Martin Luther King, Jr. Day

Martinique *see* Foreign lands – Martinique

Masks

Anno, Mitsumasa. *Anno's masks*
Cohen, Miriam. *The real-skin rubber monster mask*
Emberley, Ed (Edward Randolph). *Glad monster, sad monster*
Hoban, Lillian. *The case of the two masked robbers*
Hru, Dakari. *Joshua's Masai mask*
Masks and puppets
Mueller, Virginia. *A Halloween mask for Monster*
Spalding, Andrea. *Solomon's tree*

Math *see* Counting, numbers

Maya Indians *see* Indians of Central America – Maya

Mazes

Madgwick, Wendy. *Animaze!*
Munro, Roxie. *Mazescapes*

Meanness *see* Character traits – meanness

Measles *see* Illness – measles

Measurement *see* Concepts – measurement

Mechanical men *see* Robots

Mechanics *see* Careers – mechanics

Medical technicians *see* Careers – emergency medical technicians

Memorial Day *see* Holidays – Memorial Day

Memories, memory

Ackerman, Karen. *Walking with Clara Belle*
Aliki. *Christmas tree memories*
Bahr, Mary. *The memory box*
Blumenthal, Deborah. *Aunt Claire's yellow beehive hair*
Bowen, Anne. *I loved you before you were born*
Brisson, Pat. *Star blanket*
Bunting, Eve (Anne Evelyn). *The memory string*
Clifton, Lucille. *Don't you remember?*
Cooke, Trish. *The grandad tree*
Doray, Malika. *One more Wednesday*
Dragonwagon, Crescent. *Jemima remembers*
Dunrea, Olivier. *Peedie*
Ekoomiak, Normee. *Arctic memories*
Esiason, Boomer. *A boy named Boomer*
Fitzpatrick, Marie-Louise. *You, me and the big blue sea*
Foreman, Michael. *Cat in the manger*
Gibbie, Mike. *Small Brown Dog's bad remembering day*
Griffith, Helen V. *Alex remembers*
Grindley, Sally. *A flag for Grandma*
Guthrie, Donna. *One hundred and two steps*
Hanson, Regina. *A season for mangoes*
Harper, Jessica. *I forgot my shoes*
Haskins, Francine. *I remember "121"*
Hazelton, Elizabeth Baldwin. *Sammy, the crow who remembered*
Hickcox, Ruth. *Great-Grandmother's treasure*
Hines, Anna Grossnickle. *Remember the butterflies*
When the goblins came knocking
Hines, Gary. *A ride in the crummy*
Hoban, Lillian. *Silly Tilly's Valentine*
Hoopes, Lyn Littlefield. *Half a button*

Hopkinson, Deborah. *Bluebird summer*
Johnson, Angela. *The Rolling Store*
Joosse, Barbara M. *Ghost wings*
Ketner, Mary Grace. *Ganzy remembers*
Kramlich, Carolyn Walz. *Mary's treasure box*
Krishnaswami, Uma. *Chachaji's cup*
Kroll, Virginia L. *Fireflies, peach pies, and lullabies*
Kübler-Ross, Elisabeth. *Remember the secret*
Kurtz, Jane. *Faraway home*
Laminack, Lester L. *The sunsets of Miss Olivia Wiggins*
Laser, Michael. *The rain*
Leedahl, Shelley A. (Shelley Ann). *The bone talker*
Lyon, George Ella. *A sign*
Marshak, S. (Samuil). *The absentminded fellow*
Martin, Bill (William Ivan). *Sounds I remember*
Martin, Jacqueline Briggs. *The finest horse in town*
Monk, Isabell. *Blackberry stew*
Morris, Ann. *Grandma Esther remembers*
Grandma Francisca remembers
Grandma Lai Goon remembers
Grandma Lois remembers
Grandma Maxine remembers
Newman, Lesléa. *Remember that*
Nobisso, Josephine. *Grandma's scrapbook*
Oppenheim, Joanne. *Rooter remembers*
Parker, Marjorie. *Jasper's day*
Perkins, Lynne Rae. *The broken cat*
Polacco, Patricia. *Betty Doll*
Mrs. Mack
Priceman, Marjorie. *My nine lives / by Clio*
Raven, Margot Theis. *Angels in the dust*
Repchuk, Caroline. *The forgotten garden*
Rochelle, Belinda. *Jewels*
Rowe, John A. *Smudge*
Santucci, Barbara. *Anna's corn*
Satterfield, Barbara. *The story dance*
Schaefer, Carole Lexa. *The copper tin cup*
Schick, Eleanor. *Mama*
Scott, Geoffrey. *Memorial Day*
Seinfeld, Jerry. *Halloween*
Seuss, Dr. *Please try to remember the first of Octember!*
Shecter, Ben. *Grandma remembers*
Spalding, Andrea. *Me and Mr. Mah*
Sarah May and the new red dress
Steig, William. *When everybody wore a hat*
Tompert, Ann. *Little Otter remembers and other stories*
Turner, Ann Warren. *Abe Lincoln remembers*
Vizurraga, Susan. *Miss Opal's auction*
Our old house
Wahl, Jan. *"I remember," cried Grandma Pinky*
Walsh, Jill Paton. *When I was little like you*
Warner, Sunny. *The moon quilt*
Watson, Mary. *The butterfly seeds*
Weinberg, Lawrence. *The Forgetful Bears meet Mr. Memory*
Wild, Margaret. *Remember me*
Woodruff, Elvira. *The memory coat*
Woodson, Jacqueline. *Sweet, sweet memory*
Zagwÿn, Deborah Turney. *The winter gift*
Zalben, Jane Breskin. *Pearl's marigolds for grandpa*

Menehunes *see* Mythical creatures – menehunes

Mental handicaps *see* Handicaps – mental handicaps

Mermaids *see* Mythical creatures – mermaids, mermen

Merry-go-rounds

Ardizzone, Edward. *Paul, the hero of the fire*
Bowdish, Lynea. *The carousel ride*
Brown, Marcia. *The little carousel*
Charles, R. H. (Robert Henry). *The roundabout turn*
Chorao, Kay. *Carousel round and round*
Clements, Andrew. *Workshop*
Crews, Donald. *Carousel*
Cummings, Pat. *Carousel*

Greaves, Margaret. *The star horse*
Leigh, Oretta. *The merry-go-round*
Martin, Bill (William Ivan). *Up and down on the merry-go-round*
Murphy, Stuart J. *Animals on board*
Noble, Kate. *The dragon of Navy Pier*
Perera, Lydia. *Frisky*
Rosenberg, Liz. *The carousel*
Schneider, Elisa. *The merry-go-round dog*
Thomas, Art. *Merry-go-rounds*
Wildsmith, Brian. *Carousel*

Messy *see* Behavior – messy

Metamorphosis

Abisch, Roz. *Let's find out about butterflies*
Barringer, William. *Gregory and Alexander*
Bunting, Eve (Anne Evelyn). *Butterfly house*
Carle, Eric. *The very hungry caterpillar*
The caterpillar who turned into a butterfly
Collicott, Sharleen. *Toestomper and the bad butterflies*
Crozat, François. *I am a little caterpillar*
Cutts, David. *Look . . . a butterfly*
Darby, Gene. *What is a butterfly?*
Delaney, Ned. *One dragon to another*
DeLuise, Dom. *Charlie the caterpillar*
Edwards, Pamela Duncan. *Clara Caterpillar*
Ernst, Lisa Campbell. *Bubba and Trixie*
French, Vivian. *Caterpillar, caterpillar*
Geras, Adèle. *Swan Lake*
Gibbons, Gail. *Monarch butterfly*
Glaser, Linda. *Wonderful worms*
Hariton, Anca. *Butterfly story*
Heiligman, Deborah. *From caterpillar to butterfly*
Hogan, Paula Z. *The butterfly*
Kent, Jack. *The caterpillar and the polliwog*
Legg, Gerald. *From caterpillar to butterfly*
McClung, Robert. *Sphinx*
Maple, Marilyn J. *On the wings of a butterfly*
Marzollo, Jean. *I'm a caterpillar*
May, Kara. *Creepy crawly caterpillar*
Murphy, Mary. *Caterpillar's wish*
O'Hagan, Caroline. *It's easy to have a caterpillar visit you*
Rockwell, Anne F. *Becoming butterflies*
Ryder, Joanne. *Where butterflies grow*
Selsam, Millicent E. *A first look at caterpillars*
Sturges, Philemon. *What's that sound, Woolly Bear?*
Thompson, Susan L. *Diary of a monarch butterfly*
Watts, Barrie. *Butterfly and caterpillar*
Wong, Herbert H. *Our caterpillars*

Mexican Americans *see* Ethnic groups in the U.S. –
    Mexican Americans

Mexico *see* Foreign lands – Mexico

Mice *see* Animals – mice

Micmac Indians *see* Indians of North America – Micmac

Middle Ages

Aiken, Joan. *The shoemaker's boy*
Althea. *Castle life*
Arnold, Tedd. *Ollie forgot*
Azarian, Mary. *The tale of John Barleycorn or, From barley to beer*
Babbitt, Natalie. *Bub, or, The very best thing*
Bahous, Sally. *Sitti and the cats*
Biro, Val. *The pied piper of Hamelin*
Bishop, Ann. *The riddle ages*
Black, Charles C. *The royal nap*
Carrick, Donald. *Harold and the great stag*
Cecil, Laura. *The frog princess*
Cohen, Barbara. *Here come the Purim players!*, ill. by Beverly Brodsky McDermott
Coombs, Patricia. *The magician and McTree*

Cressey, James. *The dragon and George*
Curry, Jane Louise. *The Christmas knight*
Dick Whittington and his cat. *Dick Whittington*, ill. by Edward Ardizzone
    Dick Whittington, ill. by Antony Maitland
    Dick Whittington and his cat, ill. by Marcia Brown
    Dick Whittington and his cat, ill. by Kurt Werth
Fradon, Dana. *Sir Dana – a knight*
Gerrard, Roy. *Sir Cedric*
    Sir Cedric rides again
Gibbons, Gail. *Knights in shining armor*
Hazen, Barbara Shook. *The knight who was afraid of the dark*
    The knight who was afraid to fight
Herford, Oliver. *The most timid in the land*
Hindley, Judy. *Princess Rosa's winter*
Hodges, Margaret. *The kitchen knight*
    Saint George and the dragon
Kahl, Virginia. *The Baron's booty*
    The Duchess bakes a cake
Krensky, Stephen. *We just moved!*
Löfgren, Ulf. *Alvin the Knight*
McAllister, Angela. *The battle of Sir Cob and Sir Filbert*
Manson, Christopher. *Here begins the tale of the marvellous blue mouse*
Mayer, Mercer. *Whinnie the lovesick dragon*
Olofsson, Helena. *The little jester*
Phillips, Louis. *The brothers Wrong and Wrong Again*
Richardson, Jean. *Stephen's feast*
Saltzman, David. *The jester has lost his jingle*
Scarry, Huck. *Looking into the Middle Ages*
Scarry, Richard. *Richard Scarry's Peasant Pig and the terrible dragon*
Shannon, Mark. *The acrobat and the angel*
    Gawain and the Green Knight
Singer, Marilyn. *The maiden on the moor*
Steig, William. *The toy brother*
Storr, Catherine (Cole). *Robin Hood*
Tompert, Ann. *Charlotte and Charles*
Tucker, Kathy. *Do knights take naps?*
Woychuk, Denis. *The other side of the wall*
Yep, Laurence. *The man who tricked a ghost*

Middle East *see* Foreign lands – Middle East

Migrant workers *see* Careers – migrant workers

Migration

Manning, Mick. *Honk! honk!*
Ó Flatharta, Antoine. *Hurry and the monarch*
Sayre, April Pulley. *Home at last*
    Turtle, turtle, watch out!
Swan flyway
Swope, Sam. *Gotta go! Gotta go!*
Winkelman, Barbara Gaines. *Sockeye's journey home*

Military *see* Careers – military

Millipedes *see* Crustaceans – centipedes, millipedes

Mimes *see* Clowns, jesters

Miners *see* Careers – miners

Ministers *see* Careers – clergy

Minks *see* Animals – minks

Minorities *see* Ethnic groups in the U.S.

Mirages *see* Optical illusions

Mirrors

Cobb, Vicki. *I see myself*
Day, Alexandra. *Mirror*

Schindel, John. *What did they see?*

Misbehavior *see* Behavior – misbehavior

Missions

Politi, Leo. *Song of the swallows*

Missisauga Indians *see* Indians of North America – Missisauga

Mist *see* Weather – fog

Mistakes *see* Behavior – mistakes

Misunderstanding *see* Behavior – misunderstanding

Mittens *see* Clothing – gloves, mittens

Miwok Indians *see* Indians of North America – Miwok

Mockingbirds *see* Birds – mockingbirds

Models *see* Careers – models

Modoc Indians *see* Indians of North America – Modoc

Mohawk Indians *see* Indians of North America – Mohawk

Molds *see* Fungi, molds

Moles *see* Animals – moles

Money

Arnold, Caroline. *What will we buy?*
Axelrod, Amy. *Pigs will be pigs*
Baylor, Byrd. *The table where rich people sit*
Berenstain, Stan. *The Berenstain bears' trouble with money*
Brenner, Barbara A. *The five pennies*
Brooks, Ben. *Lemonade parade*
Brown, Marc Tolon. *Arthur's TV trouble*
Brown, Marcia. *The little carousel*
Caple, Kathy. *The purse*
    Worm gets a job
Chardiet, Bernice. *Martin and the tooth fairy*
Cole, Joanna. *Don't tell the whole world*
Curious George and the puppies
Day, Alexandra. *Paddy's pay-day*
Garhan Attebury, Nancy. *Out and about at the bank*
    Out and about at the United States Mint
Gill, Shelley. *The big buck adventure*
Glass, Julie. *A dollar for Penny*
Hoban, Lillian. *Arthur's funny money*
Inkpen, Mick. *The great pet sale*
Jennings, Sharon. *Franklin and the scooter*
Kent, Jack. *Piggy Bank Gonzalez*
Kimmel, Eric A. *Four dollars and fifty cents*
Langford, Sondra Gordon. *Mishka and Plishka*
Leedy, Loreen. *Follow the money*
    The monster money book
Love, Ann. *Ice cream at the castle*
McCaughrean, Geraldine. *One bright Penny*
McMillan, Bruce. *Jelly beans for sale*
Maestro, Betsy. *Dollars and cents for Harriet*
Mantinband, Gerda. *Blabbermouths*
Mollel, Tololwa M. (Tololwa Marti). *My rows and piles of coins*
Murphy, Stuart J. *The penny pot*
    Sluggers' car wash
O'Neill, Alexis. *Estela's swap*
A paper of pins
Pistoia, Sara. *Money*
Rockwell, Anne F. *Gogo's pay day*
Rose, Anne K. *As right as right can be*

Skinner, Daphne. *Tightwad Tod*
Slobodkin, Louis. *Moon Blossom and the golden penny*
Smalls-Hector, Irene. *Irene and the big, fine nickel*
Stewart, Sarah. *The money tree*
Tada, Joni Eareckson. *The incredible discovery of Lindsey Renee*
Thayer, Tanya. *Counting money*
    Earning money
    Saving money
    Spending money
Turkle, Brinton. *Rachel and Obadiah*
Underhill, Liz. *The lucky coin*
Vaughan, Marcia Kapok. *The lemonade stand*
Vincent, Gabrielle. *Bravo, Ernest and Celestine!*
Viorst, Judith. *Alexander, who used to be rich last Sunday*
Wells, Rosemary. *Bunny money*
Williams, Rozanne Lanczak. *The coin counting book*
Wondriska, William. *Mr. Brown and Mr. Gray*
Yardley, Thompson. *Buy now, pay later*
Ziefert, Harriet. *You can't buy a dinosaur with a dime*
Zimelman, Nathan. *How the second grade got $8,205.50 to visit the Statue of Liberty*

Mongolia *see* Foreign lands – Mongolia

Mongooses *see* Animals – mongooses

Monitor lizards *see* Reptiles – monitor lizards

Monkeys *see* Animals – monkeys

Monsters

Ahlberg, Allan. *The ghost train*
    Me and my friend
Alexander, Lloyd. *The house Gobbaleen*
Alexander, Martha G. *Maybe a monster*
Alexander, Sue. *Who goes out on Halloween?*
Allen, Martha Dickson. *Real life monsters*
Ambrus, Victor G. *Count, Dracula*
    Son of Dracula
    What's the time, Dracula?
Apple, Margot. *Brave Martha*
Arnold, Caroline. *The terrible Hodag*
Arnold, Tedd. *Five ugly monsters*
    Huggly gets dressed
    Huggly takes a bath
Ashman, Linda. *The essential worldwide monster guide*
Auch, Mary Jane. *Monster brother*
Axworthy, Anni. *Ben's Wednesday*
Babbitt, Natalie. *The something*
Baggette, Susan K. *Jonathan goes to the library*
Baker, Ken. *Brave little monster*
Bang, Molly. *Wiley and the hairy man*
Barden, Rosalind. *TV monster*
Bartels, Alice L. *The beast*
Basso, Bill. *The top of the pizzas*
Benjamin, Alan. *1000 monsters*
Bennett, Jill. *Spooky poems*
Bergström, Gunilla. *Is that a monster, Alfie Atkins?*
Berlan, Kathryn Hook. *Andrew's amazing monsters*
Bird, Malcolm. *The school in Murky Wood*
Blake, Quentin. *Zagazoo*
Blance, Ellen. *Lady Monster has a plan*
    Lady Monster helps out
    Monster and the magic umbrella
    Monster and the mural
    Monster and the surprise cookie
    Monster at school
    Monster buys a pet
    Monster cleans his house
    Monster comes to the city
    Monster gets a job
    Monster goes around the town
    Monster goes to school
    Monster goes to the beach
    Monster goes to the circus

Monster goes to the hospital
Monster goes to the museum
Monster goes to the zoo
Monster has a party
Monster, Lady Monster and the bike ride
Monster looks for a friend
Monster looks for a house
Monster meets Lady Monster
Monster on the bus
Boxall, Ed. *Francis the scaredy cat*
Boynton, Sandra. *Birthday monsters!*
Brandle, Bine. *Flusi, the sock monster*
Brennan, Herbie. *Frankenstella and the video store monster*
The brothers gruesome
Brown, Marc Tolon. *Arthur's first sleepover*
    Marc Brown's full house
    Monster's lunchbox
    Spooky riddles
Browne, Vee. *Monster birds*
Bunting, Eve (Anne Evelyn). *Night of the gargoyles*
    Scary, scary Halloween
Calmenson, Stephanie. *Ten furry monsters*
Cameron, Ann. *Harry (the monster)*
Carey, Valerie Scho. *Harriet and William and the terrible creature*
Carr, Jan. *The nature of the beast*
Carrick, Carol. *Norman fools the tooth fairy*
Carrick, Malcolm. *I can squash elephants!*
Cazet, Denys. *Minnie and Moo meet Frankenswine*
Chapouton, Anne-Marie. *Billy the brave*
Cherry, Lynne. *The dragon and the unicorn*
Chevalier, Christa. *Spence and the sleepytime monster*
Christian, Mary Blount. *Go west, swamp monsters*
Church, Kristine. *My brother John*
Ciardi, John. *The monster den*
Clarke, Gus. *Ten green monsters*
Cohen, Barbara. *The demon who would not die*
Cohen, Caron Lee. *Whiffle Squeek*
Cohen, Daniel. *America's very own monsters*
Cohen, Miriam. *Jim meets the thing*
Cole, Joanna. *Monster manners*
Conger, Lesley. *Tops and bottoms*
Coombs, Patricia. *Molly Mullett*
Cooney, Nancy Evans. *Go away monsters, lickety split!*
Craig, Helen. *The night of the paper bag monsters*
Crebbin, June. *Into the castle*
Crowe, Robert L. *Clyde monster*
Crowley, Arthur. *The boogey man*
Crum, Shutta. *Who took my hairy toe?*
Cutts, David. *I can read about creatures of the night*
Dahl, Roald. *Dirty beasts*
Daly, Niki. *Monsters are like that*
David, Lawrence. *The land of the hungry armadillos*
Day, Trevor. *Youch! it bites!*
Delaney, M. C. (Michael Clark). *The marigold monster*
Del Negro, Janice. *Lucy Dove*
Demarest, Chris L. *Morton and Sidney*
Denton, Kady MacDonald. *Granny is a darling*
De Regniers, Beatrice Schenk. *Sam and the impossible thing*
Dillon, Barbara. *The beast in the bed*
Dinan, Carolyn. *The lunch box monster*
Dinosaurs and monsters
Diviny, Sean. *Halloween Motel*
Donaldson, Julia. *The gruffalo*
Dos Santos, Joyce Audy. *Henri and the Loup-Garou*
Doyle, Malachy. *Hungry! Hungry! Hungry!*
Drescher, Henrik. *The boy who ate around*
    Pat the beastie
    Simon's book
Duncan, Jane. *Janet Reachfar and the kelpie*
Duquennoy, Jacques. *The ghosts' trip to Loch Ness*
Dyer, Sarah. *Clementine and Mungo*
Eccles, Jane. *Maxwell's birthday*
Elliott, David. *Hazel Nutt, mad scientist*
Elzbieta. *Dikou and the Snively Snoak*
Emberley, Ed (Edward Randolph). *Glad monster, sad monster*
    Go away, big green monster!
Euvremer, Teryl. *Triple whammy*

Fassler, Joan. *The man of the house*
Faulkner, Keith. *The monster in my bathroom*
    The monster in my toybox
    The monster who loved books
    Velma Vampire
Flora, James. *Leopold, the see-through crumbpicker*
Florian, Douglas. *Monster Motel*
Francis, Anna B. *Pleasant dreams*
Freedman, Sally. *Monster birthday party*
Gackenbach, Dick. *Harry and the terrible whatzit*
    Mag the magnificent
Gág, Wanda. *The funny thing*
Galdone, Paul. *The monster and the tailor*
Gantos, Jack (John, Jr.). *Greedy Greeny*
    Rotten Ralph's Halloween howl
    The werewolf family
Geoghegan, Adrienne. *There's a wardrobe in my monster!*
Geringer, Laura. *Look out, look out, it's coming!*
Gerstein, Mordicai. *The absolutely awful alphabet*
Gilleo, Alma. *Learning about monsters*
Ginsburg, Mirra. *Ookie-Spooky*
Goodall, John S. *Creepy castle*
Goode, Diane. *I hear a noise*
Gorey, Edward (St. John). *The tunnel calamity*
Gramatky, Hardie. *Little Toot and the Loch Ness monster*
Grant, Joan. *The monster that grew small*
Graves, Keith. *Frank was a monster who wanted to dance*
Greene, Rhonda Gowler. *Eek! Creak! Snicker, sneak*
Grindley, Sally. *Knock, knock! Who's there?*
Harper, Charise Mericle. *The Monster Show*
Harshman, Terry Webb. *Porcupine's pajama party*
Hawkins, Colin. *Come for a ride on the ghost train*
    Creepy castle
    Snap! Snap!
    Take away monsters
Haynes, Max. *Ticklemonster and me*
Haywood, Carolyn. *The king's monster*
Heide, Florence Parry. *Grim and ghastly goings-on*
    A monster is coming! A monster is coming!
Heinz, Brian J. *The monsters' test*
Hellard, Susan. *Eleanor and the babysitter*
Heller, Nicholas. *The monster in the cave*
    Ogres! ogres! ogres!
Helmer, Marilyn. *Spooky riddles*
Herman, Gail. *Double-header*
Hoban, Russell. *Monsters*
Hooks, William H. *Mr. Monster*
    Peach boy
    Snowbear Whittington, an Appalachian Beauty and the Beast
Hopkins, Lee Bennett. *Creatures*
Howe, James. *There's a monster under my bed*
Hulpach, Vladimir. *Ahaiyute and Cloud Eater*
Hutchins, Pat. *It's my birthday!*
    Silly Billy!
    Three-star Billy
    The very worst monster
    Where's the baby?
Hutton, Warwick. *Theseus and the Minotaur*
Impey, Rose. *The ankle grabber*
    The flat man
    Scare yourself to sleep
Inkpen, Mick. *Kipper's monster*
Irving, John. *A sound like someone trying not to make a sound*
Jackson, Ellen B. *Monsters in my mailbox*
Jackson, Jean. *Big lips and hairy arms*
    Thorndike and Nelson
Jamison, Jocelyn. *Drac's night out*
Jane, Pamela. *Monster countdown*
    Monster mischief
Johnson, Jane. *Today I thought I'd run away*
Johnston, Tony. *Four scary stories*
Kahl, Virginia. *Giants, indeed!*
    How do you hide a monster?
Kamish, Daniel. *The night scary beasties popped out of my head*
Kasza, Keiko. *Grandpa Toad's last secret*
Kellogg, Steven (Stephen). *The island of the skog*
    The mysterious tadpole

Kimura, Yasuko. *Fergus and the sea monster*
Kleven, Elisa. *A monster in the house*
Koelling, Caryl. *Mad monsters mix and match*
Koller, Jackie French. *No such thing*
Krahn, Fernando. *The mystery of the giant footprints*
Kraus, Robert. *The phantom of Creepy Hollow*
Kunnas, Mauri. *One spooky night and other scary stories*
Labatt, Mary. *Sam finds a monster*
LaRose, Linda. *Jessica takes charge*
Laslett, Stephanie. *The monster party*
Layne, Steven L. *My brother Dan's delicious*
Leedy, Loreen. *The monster money book*
Lerner, Sharon. *Follow the monsters!*
Lesynski, Loris. *Night school*
Leuck, Laura. *Goodnight, baby monster*
    My beastly brother
    My monster mama loves me so
Lewin, Betsy. *Wiley learns to spell*
Lia, Simone. *Red's great chase*
Lichtenheld, Tom. *Everything I know about monsters*
Lifton, Betty Jean. *Goodnight orange monster*
Lodge, Bernard. *How scary*
Logue, Christopher. *The magic circus*
Lottridge, Celia Barker. *Something might be hiding*
Lundgren, Mary Beth. *Seven scary monsters*
McDonald, Megan. *Bedbugs*
MacGill-Callahan, Sheila. *The last snake in Ireland*
McKee, David. *The monster and the teddy bear*
    Two monsters
McMullan, Kate (Hall). *Creepy riddles*
McPhail, David M. *The Glerp*
McQueen, John Troy. *A world full of monsters*
Maisner, Heather. *Save Brave Ted*
Marshall, Edward. *Four on the shore*
Marshall, James. *Three up a tree*
Martin, Bill (William Ivan). *A beasty story*
Mason, Jane B. *The flying horse*
Mayer, Marianna. *Pegasus*
Mayer, Mercer. *Little Monster at home*
    Little Monster at school
    Little Monster at work
    Little Monster's alphabet book
    Little Monster's bedtime book
    Little Monster's counting book
    Little Monster's neighborhood
    Liza Lou and the Yeller Belly Swamp
    Mrs. Beggs and the wizard
    Terrible troll
    There's a nightmare in my closet
Mayer, Pamela. *The scariest monster in the whole wide world*
Meddaugh, Susan. *Beast*
Medearis, Angela Shelf. *Tailypo*
Medicine Crow, Joseph. *Brave Wolf and the Thunderbird*
Memling, Carl. *What's in the dark?*
Michelson, Richard. *Did you say ghosts?*
Miller, Edward. *The curse of Claudia*
Mills, Lauren A. *The dog prince*
Minsberg, David. *The book monster*
Miranda, Anne. *Monster math*
Modarressi, Mitra. *The beastly visits*
Moffatt, Judith. *Trick-or-treat faces*
Mollel, Tololwa M. (Tololwa Marti). *Song bird*
Monster poems
Monster soup and other spooky poems
Moodie, Fiona. *Nabulela*
    Noko and the night monster
Moore, Lilian. *See my lovely poison ivy, and other verses about witches, ghosts and things*
Mooser, Stephen. *Funnyman meets the monster from outer space*
Morris, Ann. *Eleanora Mousie in the dark*
Morris, Terry Nell. *Good night, dear monster!*
Mosel, Arlene. *The funny little woman*
Moss, Marissa. *After-school monster*
Most, Bernard. *Boo!*
Mueller, Virginia. *A Halloween mask for Monster*
    Monster and the baby
    Monster can't sleep

Monster goes to school
Monster's birthday hiccups
A playhouse for Monster
Murphy, Jill. *All for one*
    The last noo-noo
Murphy, Shirley Rousseau. *Valentine for a dragon*
Myers, Amy. *I know a monster*
Mystery manor
Namioka, Lensey. *Hungriest boy in the world*
Namm, Diane. *Monsters!*
Newsham, Wendy. *The monster hunt*
Nightingale, Sandy. *I'm a little monster*
Niland, Deborah. *ABC of monsters*
Nixon, Joan Lowery. *Bigfoot makes a movie*
Nolan, Lucy A. *The Lizard Man of Crabtree County*
Numeroff, Laura Joffe. *Laura Numeroff's 10-step guide to living with your monster*
    Monster munchies
O'Keefe, Susan Heyboer. *One hungry monster*
Olofsdotter, Marie. *Sofia and the Heartmender*
O'Malley, Kevin. *Velcome*
Packard, Mary. *We are monsters*
Paige, Rob. *Some of my best friends are monsters*
Paraskevas, Betty. *Cecil Bunions and the midnight train*
    Maggie and the Ferocious Beast, the big carrot
    Maggie and the Ferocious Beast, the big scare
    Monster Beach
Parish, Peggy. *No more monsters for me!*
    Zed and the monsters
Park, Barbara. *Psssst! It's me . . . the Bogeyman*
Parker, Nancy Winslow. *Love from Aunt Betty*
Peck, Richard. *Monster night at Grandma's house*
Peet, Bill (William Bartlett). *Cyrus the unsinkable sea serpent*
Pfister, Marcus. *Rainbow fish and the sea monsters' cave*
Pieńkowski, Jan. *Haunted house*
Pinkney, J. Brian. *Cosmo and the robot*
Pinkwater, Daniel Manus. *The Frankenbagel monster*
    I was a second grade werewolf
Polacco, Patricia. *Some birthday!*
Polisar, Barry Louis. *The haunted house party*
Prelutsky, Jack. *The baby uggs are hatching*
Prose, Francine. *The demons' mistake*
Reiner, Carl. *Tell me a scary story – but not too scary!*
Riddell, Chris. *Mr. Underbed*
    The wish factory
Riggio, Anita. *Beware the Brindlebeast*
Rix, Jamie. *The last chocolate cookie*
Robison, Nancy. *Ten tall soldiers*
Rockwell, Anne F. *The one-eyed giant and other monsters from the Greek Myths*
    Thump thump thump!
Root, Phyllis. *The hungry monster*
Ross, Dave (David). *Gorp and the space pirates*
    Space monster
    Space Monster Gorp and the runaway computer
Ross, Gayle. *The legend of the Windigo*
Ross, H. L. *Not counting monsters*
Ross, Tony. *I'm coming to get you!*
    Towser and the terrible thing
Sabraw, John. *I wouldn't be scared*
Salter, Heidi. *Taddy McFinley and the great grey grimly*
Samton, Sheila White. *Ten tiny monsters*
San Souci, Robert D. *The Hobyahs*
    Pedro and the monkey
Schnitzlein, Danny. *The monster who ate my peas*
Schroder, William. *Pea soup and serpents*
Schultz, Sam. *Monster mayhem*
Scrimger, Richard. *Princess Bun Bun*
Seeger, Pete. *Abiyoyo*
Selsam, Millicent E. *Sea monsters of long ago*
Sendak, Maurice. *Seven little monsters*
    Where the wild things are
Seymour, Peter S. *What's at the beach?*
Shannon, Margaret. *Gullible's troubles*
Shannon, Mark. *Gawain and the Green Knight*
Sharmat, Marjorie Weinman. *The pizza monster*
    Scarlet Monster lives here

Sierra, Judy. *The house that Drac built*
  Monster Goose
  'Twas the fright before Christmas
  Wiley and the Hairy Man
Silverman, Erica. *The Halloween house*
Simms, Laura. *The bone man*
Sis, Peter. *Ship ahoy!*
Skwarek, Skip. *Mystery of Maggoty Mill*
Smith, Janice Lee. *The monster in the third dresser drawer and other stories about Adam Joshua*
Snow, Alan. *The monster book of ABC sounds*
Solotareff, Grégoire. *The ogre and the frog king*
Spinelli, Eileen. *Wanda's monster*
Steig, William. *Rotten island*
Stephens, Helen. *Ruby and the noisy hippo*
Steptoe, John. *Daddy is a monster . . . sometimes*
Stern, Peter. *Max the dragon*
Stevens, Kathleen. *The beast in the bathtub*
Stevenson, James. *"Could be worse!"*
Stower, Adam. *Two left feet*
Strete, Craig Kee. *The lost boy and the monster*
Tagg, Christine. *Who will you meet on Scary Street?*
Taylor, Judy. *Dudley and the monster*
Tegen, Katherine Brown. *Dracula and Frankenstein are friends*
Thomas, Frances. *One day, Daddy*
  What if?
Todd, Mark. *What will you be for Halloween?*
Tunnell, Michael O. *Halloween pie*
Turkle, Brinton. *Do not open*
Ungerer, Tomi. *The beast of Monsieur Racine*
  Zeralda's ogre
Van Nutt, Julia. *The monster in the shadows*
Viorst, Judith. *My mama says there aren't any zombies, ghosts, vampires, creatures, demons, monsters, fiends, goblins, or things*
Wagner, Jenny. *Amy's monster*
  The bunyip of Berkeley's Creek
Wahl, Jan. *Dracula's cat*
  Dracula's cat and Frankenstein's dog
  Frankenstein's dog
Waldron, Jan L. *John Pig's Halloween*
Walsh, Melanie. *Monster, monster*
Watson, Pauline. *Wriggles, the little wishing pig*
Weare, Tim. *Hide-and-seek with Leo*
Weeks, Sarah. *Happy birthday, Frankie*
Weston, Martha. *Tuck's haunted house*
Whitlock, Susan Love. *Donovan scares the monsters*
Whybrow, Ian. *Good night, monster*
Willis, Jeanne. *The monster bed*
  The monster storm
Willoughby, Elaine Macmann. *Boris and the monsters*
Winters, Kay. *The teeny tiny ghost and the monster*
Winthrop, Elizabeth. *Maggie and the monster*
Wishinsky, Frieda. *Nothing scares us*
Wormell, Christopher. *The big ugly monster and the little stone rabbit*
Wynne-Jones, Tim. *On Tumbledown Hill*
Yaccarino, Dan. *The lima bean monster*
Yep, Laurence. *The Khan's daughter*
Young, Ed (Edward). *The terrible Nung Gwama*
Zalben, Jane Breskin. *Saturday night at the Beastro*
Zemach, Harve. *The judge*

Monsters – vampires

Gralley, Jean. *Hogula, dread pig of night*
Holleyman, Sonia. *Mona the vampire*
Noyes, Deborah. *It's Vladimir!*

Months of the year *see* Days of the week, months of the year

Moon

Agee, Jon. *Dmitri the astronaut*
Alexander, Martha G. *Maggie's moon*
Anderson, Stephen Axel. *I know the moon*
Appelt, Kathi. *I see the moon*
Arden, Carolyn. *Goose moon*

Asch, Frank. *Happy birthday, moon!*
  Moonbear
  Mooncake
  Moondance
  Moongame
Asimov, Isaac. *The moon*
Babcock, Chris. *No moon, no milk!*
Bacon, Ethel. *To see the moon*
Balet, Jan B. *Amos and the moon*
Balzola, Asun. *Munia and the moon*
Banks, Kate (Katherine A.). *And if the moon could talk*
Barlowe, Sy. *A child's book of stars*
Bartram, Simon. *Man on the moon*
Baum, Louis. *I want to see the moon*
Baylor, Byrd. *Moon song*
Beifuss, John. *Armadillo Ray*
Berenstain, Stan. *The Berenstain bears on the moon*
Berger, Barbara Helen. *Grandfather Twilight*
  A lot of otters
Bess, Clayton. *The truth about the moon*
Branley, Franklyn M. (Mansfield). *The moon seems to change*
  What the moon is like
Brown, Margaret Wise. *Goodnight moon*
  The sleepy men
  Wait till the moon is full
Buchanan, Heather S. *George and Matilda Mouse and the moon rocket*
Bunting, Eve (Anne Evelyn). *Moonstick*
Carle, Eric. *Papa, please get the moon for me*
Carlstrom, Nancy White. *Who gets the sun out of bed?*
Cazet, Denys. *Christmas moon*
Chadwick, Tim. *Cabbage moon*
Chambers, Roland. *Rooftop rocket party*
Choldenko, Gennifer. *Moonstruck*
Coats, Laura Jane. *Marcella and the moon*
Come out to play
Conrad, Donna. *See you soon, Moon*
Crews, Nina. *I'll catch the moon*
Daly, Niki. *Mary Malloy and the baby who wouldn't sleep*
  Why the sun and moon live in the sky
Dayrell, Elphinstone. *Why the sun and the moon live in the sky*
De Gerez, Toni. *Louhi, witch of North Farm*
Demarest, Chris L. *The lunatic adventure of Kitman and Willy*
De Paola, Tomie (Thomas Anthony). *The Prince of the Dolomites*
  The unicorn and the moon
De Regniers, Beatrice Schenk. *Willy O'Dwyer jumped in the fire*
Desimini, Lisa. *Moon soup*
  Sun and moon
Dillon, Jana. *Lucky O'Leprechaun in school*
DiTerlizzi, Tony. *Jimmy Zangwow's out-of-this-world, moon pie adventure*
Doherty, Berlie. *The midnight man*
DuBurke, Randy. *The moon ring*
Duncan, Lois. *Birthday moon*
Ehlert, Lois. *Moon rope = Un lazo a la luna*
Elschner, Géraldine. *Moonchild, star of the sea*
Emmett, Jonathan. *Bringing down the moon*
Fisher, Aileen Lucia. *Sing of the earth and sky*
Fletcher, Ralph J. *Hello, harvest moon*
Fowler, Allan. *So that's how the moon changes shape!*
Fowler, Susi Gregg. *I'll see you when the moon is full*
Freeman, Mae Blacker. *The sun, the moon and the stars*
  You will go to the moon
Fuchs, Erich. *Journey to the moon*
Gantschev, Ivan. *Good morning, good night*
  The moon lake
  Where the moon lives
Garcia, Carolyn. *Moonboy*
Garelick, May. *Look at the moon*, ill. by Barbara Garrison
  Look at the moon, ill. by Leonard Weisgard
Gay, Marie-Louise. *Moonbeam on a cat's ear*
Gershator, David. *Moon rooster*
Gillmor, Don. *Yuck, a love story*
Gollub, Matthew. *Gobble, quack, moon*
Gregory, Valiska. *When stories fell like shooting stars*
Griffith, Helen V. *Alex remembers*
Haddon, Mark. *The Sea of Tranquillity*

Hargrove, Linda. *Wings across the moon*
Harley, Bill. *Bear's all-night party*
Heckman, Philip. *The moon is following me*
Heller, Nicholas. *Elwood and the witch*
Henkes, Kevin. *Kitten's first full moon*
Hergé. *Explorers on the moon*
Hillert, Margaret. *Up, up and away*
Hillman, Elizabeth. *Min-Yo and the moon dragon*
Hines, Anna Grossnickle. *Moon's wish*
Hodges, Margaret. *Buried moon*
Horácek, Petr. *When the moon smiled*
Hughes, Shirley. *Abel's moon*
Hunter, Anne. *Possum's harvest moon*
Huth, Holly Young. *The son of the sun and the daughter of the moon*
Ikeda, Daisaku. *The princess and the moon*
Iwamura, Kazuo. *The fourteen forest mice and the harvest moon watch*
Janosch. *Joshua and the magic fiddle*
Jones, Joy. *Tambourine moon*
King, Christopher L. *The boy who ate the moon*
King, Thomas. *Coyote sings to the moon*
Kirk, Daniel. *Moondogs*
Kraus, Robert. *See the moon*
Kurt, Kemal. *The five fingers and the moon*
Lankford, Mary D. *Is it dark? Is it light?*
Lester, Robin. *Wuzzy takes off*
Levitin, Sonia. *Who owns the moon?*
Lewis, Claudia Louise. *When I go to the moon*
Lewis, J. Patrick. *The moonbow of Mr. B. Bones*
Lewison, Wendy Cheyette. *Nighty-night*
Lifton, Betty Jean. *The rice-cake rabbit*
Lindbergh, Reeve. *What is the sun?*
Little, Mimi Otey. *Blue moon soup spoon*
London, Jonathan. *Let the lynx come in*
Lussert, Anneliese. *The farmer and the moon*
McCarthy, Meghan. *The adventures of Patty and the big red bus*
McDermott, Gerald. *Anansi the spider*
    Papagayo, the mischief maker
McPartland, Suzy. *Sleepy-time moon*
Macsolis. *Dance moon = Baile de luna*
Mangan, Anne. *The monkey who wanted the moon*
Manuel, Lynn. *The night the moon blew kisses*
Manushkin, Fran. *Moon dragon*
Marton, Jirina. *Midnight visit at Molly's house*
Matura, Mustapha. *Moon jump*
Merrill, Jean. *Emily Emerson's moon*
Mitra, Annie. *Penguin moon*
Moché, Dinah L. *The astronauts*
Mora, Pat. *The night the moon fell*
Moroney, Lynn. *Moontellers*
Mother Goose. *Hey, diddle, diddle*, ill. by Linda Bronson
    Hey, diddle, diddle, ill. by Heather Collins
    Hey, diddle, diddle, ill. by Marilyn Janovitz
    Hey, diddle, diddle, ill. by Moira Kemp
    Hey, diddle, diddle, ill. by Marc Mongeau
    Hey, diddle, diddle, ill. by Nita Sowter
    Hey, diddle, diddle, ill. by Eleanor Wasmuth
    Hey, diddle, diddle picture book, ill. by Randolph Caldecott
Murray, Marjorie Dennis. *Little Wolf and the moon*
Nicoll, Helen. *Meg on the moon*
Oakley, Graham. *The church mice and the moon*
Olsen, Ib Spang. *The boy in the moon*
Oppenheim, Shulamith Levey. *What is the full moon full of?*
Oram, Hiawyn. *Mole's moon*
Oxenbury, Helen. *Tom and Pippo see the moon*
Pfister, Marcus. *I see the moon*
Pierson, Judith Patterson. *The always moon*
Pollock, Penny. *When the moon is full*
Powell, Roxanne Dyer. *Cat, mouse and moon*
Preston, Edna Mitchell. *Squawk to the moon, little goose*
Preston, Tim. *Pumpkin moon*
Raschka, Christopher. *Can't sleep*
Rattigan, Jama Kim. *The woman in the moon*
Robledo, Honorio. *Nico visits the moon*
Roper, Janice M. *Dancing on the moon*
Rosen, Sidney. *Where does the moon go?*
Rosenberg, Liz. *Window, mirror, moon*
Rowe, John A. *Rabbit moon*

Salter, Mary Jo. *The moon comes home*
Sanfield, Steve. *Just rewards, or, Who is that man in the moon and what's he doing up there anyway?*
Schaefer, Carole Lexa. *Sometimes moon*
Scheer, Julian. *By the light of the captured moon*
Scheidl, Gerda Marie. *The moon man*
Schertle, Alice. *Witch Hazel*
Schmid, Eleonore. *The squirrel and the moon*
Schweninger, Ann. *The man in the moon as he sails the sky and other moon verse*
Shea, Pegi Deitz. *New moon*
Simms, Laura. *Moon and Otter and Frog*
Skofield, James. *Crow moon, worm moon*
Sleator, William. *The angry moon*
Smith, Linda. *When Moon fell down*
Speed, Toby. *Two cool cows*
Spinelli, Eileen. *Rise the moon*
Spurling, Margaret. *Bilby moon*
Stevens, Cat. *Teaser and the firecat*
Stevenson, Robert Louis. *The moon*
Storm, Theodor. *Little Hobbin*
Suen, Anastasia. *Man on the moon*
The sun, the moon, and the stars
Tafuri, Nancy. *What the sun sees / What the moon sees*
Tan, Amy. *The moon lady*
Tarpley, Natasha Anastasia. *Joe-Joe's first flight*
Taylor, Joanne. *Full moon rising*
Thaler, Mike. *Moonkey*
Thurber, James. *Many moons*, ill. by Marc Simont
    Many moons, ill. by Louis Slobodkin
Trimble, Marcia. *Moonbeams for Santa*
Turner, Charles. *The turtle and the moon*
Turska, Krystyna. *The magician of Cracow*
Udry, Janice May. *The moon jumpers*
Ungar, Richard. *Rachel captures the moon*
Ungerer, Tomi. *Moon man*
Vail, Rachel. *Over the moon*
Vaughn, Jenny. *On the moon*
VerDorn, Bethea. *Moon glows*
Wahl, Jan. *Cabbage moon*
Ward, Helen. *The moonrat and the white turtle*
Watson, Clyde. *Midnight moon*
Weedn, Flavia. *The moon maiden*
Weigelt, Udo. *The Sandman*
Wilcox, Brian. *Full moon*
Wildsmith, Brian. *What the moon saw*
Willard, Nancy. *The nightgown of the sullen moon*
Winter, Jeanette. *The girl and the moon man*
Wolkstein, Diane. *The day Ocean came to visit*
Wood, Audrey. *Moonflute*
Wood, Douglas. *Rabbit and the moon*
Wynne-Jones, Tim. *Builder of the moon*
Yaccarino, Dan. *Zoom! Zoom! Zoom! I'm off to the moon!*
Yamaguchi, Tohr. *Two crabs and the moonlight*
Young, James. *Everyone loves the moon*
Ziefert, Harriet. *Moonride*
    Who can boo the loudest?
Ziegler, Ursina. *Squaps the moonling*
Zolotow, Charlotte (Shapiro). *The moon was the best*

Moose *see* Animals – moose

Mopeds *see* Motorcycles

Morning

Alda, Arlene. *Pig, horse, or cow, don't wake me now*
Anglund, Joan Walsh. *Morning is a little child*
Aylesworth, Jim. *Wake up, little children*
Barbato, Juli. *From bed to bus*
Beach, Stewart. *Good morning, sun's up!*
Brenner, Barbara A. *Good morning, garden*
Brown, Margaret Wise. *A child's good morning book*
    The quiet noisy book
Caldwell, Mary. *Morning, rabbit, morning*
Capucilli, Alyssa Satin. *Good morning, pond*

Carlstrom, Nancy White. *Who gets the sun out of bed?*
Chall, Marsha Wilson. *Rupa raises the sun*
Chase, Edith Newlin. *Secret dawn*
Chorao, Kay. *The baby's good morning book*
Christiansen, C. B. *Mara in the morning*
Conrad, Pam. *The rooster's gift*
Craig, M. Jean. *Spring is like the morning*
    What did you dream?
Dale, Penny. *Wake up, Mr. B.!*
Dennis, Lynne. *Raymond Rabbit's early morning*
Dennis, Wesley. *Flip and the morning*
Dragonwagon, Crescent. *Katie in the morning*
Dryden, Emma. *Good morning – good night*
Farjeon, Eleanor. *Morning has broken*
Funakoshi, Canna. *One morning*
Gay, Marie-Louise. *Good morning Sam*
Gleeson, Libby. *Cuddle time*
Good morning
Grindley, Sally. *Wake up, dad!*
Hannert, Todd. *Morning dance*
Harrison, David Lee. *Wake up, sun!*
Hellard, Susan. *Time to get up*
Henkes, Kevin. *Shhhh*
Hill, Eric. *Good morning, baby bear*
Himler, Ronald. *Wake up, Jeremiah*
Hirschi, Ron. *When morning comes*
Hoffman, Don. *Good morning, good night Billy and Abigail*
Hudson, Cheryl Willis. *Good morning baby*
Jacobs, Shannon K. *The boy who loved morning*
Johnston, Deborah. *Mathew Michael's beastly day*
Kandoian, Ellen. *Under the sun*
Lakin, Pat (Patricia). *Dad and me in the morning*
Lapp, Eleanor. *In the morning mist*
McGee, Marni. *Wake up, me!*
McNulty, Faith. *When a boy wakes up in the morning*
McPartland, Suzy. *Good morning, sun*
Mann, Peggy. *King Laurence, the alarm clock*
Meeker, Clare Hodgson. *Who wakes rooster?*
Moore, Dessie. *Good morning*
Moore, Elaine. *Good morning, city*
Most, Bernard. *Cock-a-doodle-moo!*
Mueller, Virginia. *In the morning*
Murphy, Stuart J. *Get up and go!*
O'Mara, Carmel. *Good morning*
Ormerod, Jan. *Sunshine*
Oxenbury, Helen. *Good night, good morning*
Pedersen, Janet. *Millie wants to play*
Pilkey, Dav. *The paperboy*
Pittman, Helena Clare. *Sunrise*
Raffi. *Rise and shine*
Ray, Deborah Kogan. *Fog drift morning*
Robbins, Maria Polushkin. *Morning*
Rogers, Paul (Patrick). *Somebody's awake*
Shulevitz, Uri. *Dawn*
Siddals, Mary McKenna. *Morning song*
Silverman, Erica. *Fixing the crack of dawn*
Tafuri, Nancy. *Early morning in the barn*
Tresselt, Alvin R. *Wake up, city!*
    Wake up, farm!, ill. by author
    Wake up, farm!, ill. by Carolyn Ewing
Tworkov, Jack. *The camel who took a walk*
VerDorn, Bethea. *Day breaks*
Westcott, Nadine Bernard. *Getting up*
Whitman, Candace. *Now it is morning*
Wick, Walter. *Can you see what I see? Dream machine*
Yabuki, Seiji. *I love the morning*
Ziefert, Harriet. *Good morning, sun!*
    Say good night!
Zolotow, Charlotte (Shapiro). *Something is going to happen*
    Wake up and goodnight

Morocco *see* Foreign lands – Morocco

Moses *see* Religion – Moses

Mosquitoes *see* Insects – mosquitoes

Mother Goose *see* Nursery rhymes

Mother's Day *see* Holidays – Mother's Day

Mothers *see* Family life – mothers; Family life – parents; Family life – stepfamilies

Moths *see* Insects – moths

Motion *see* Concepts – motion

Motion picture producers *see* Careers – motion picture producers

Motorcycles

Blake, Quentin. *Mrs. Armitage: queen of the road*
Cave, Ron. *Motorcycles*
Cleary, Beverly. *Lucky Chuck*
Dickens, Frank. *Boffo*
Hill, Lee Sullivan. *Motorcycles*
McPhail, David M. *Captain Toad and the motorbike*
Zimnik, Reiner. *The bear on the motorcycle*

Mountain climbing *see* Sports – mountain climbing

Mountain lions *see* Animals – cougars

Mountains

Arnold, Caroline. *A walk up the mountain*
Geisert, Bonnie. *Mountain town*
George, Jean Craighead. *Cliff hanger*
Grupper, Jonathan. *Destination – Rocky Mountains*
Hirschi, Ron. *Mountain*
Hoban, Russell. *Trouble on Thunder Mountain*
Huneck, Stephen. *Sally goes to the mountains*
Johnson, D. B. (Donald B.). *Henry climbs a mountain*
Kimmel, Eric A. *The two mountains*
Lasky, Kathryn. *The Gates of the Wind*
Lawson, Julie. *Midnight in the mountains*
Locker, Thomas. *Mountain dance*
Luenn, Nancy. *Miser on the mountain*
McCarthy, Meghan. *The adventures of Patty and the big red bus*
Nagda, Anne Whitehead. *World above the clouds*
Ray, Mary Lyn. *Basket moon*
Ruurs, Margriet. *A mountain alphabet*
Silvano, Wendi J. *Just one more*
Swanson, June. *Summit up*
Wells, Rosemary. *The bear went over the mountain*
Zoehfeld, Kathleen Weidner. *How mountains are made*

Mouths *see* Anatomy – mouths

Moving

Ackerman, Karen. *The sleeping porch*
Adshead, Gladys L. *Brownies – they're moving*
Aliki. *Best friends together again*
    We are best friends
Asch, Frank. *Goodbye house*
Ballard, Robin. *Good-bye, house*
Barbour, Karen. *Nancy*
Becker, Edna. *Nine hundred buckets of paint*
Berenstain, Stan. *The Berenstain bears' moving day*
Berg, Jean Horton. *The O'Learys and friends*
Blades, Ann. *Too small*
Bond, Felicia. *Poinsettia and her family*
Bottner, Barbara. *Horrible Hannah*
    Rosa's room
Bowers, Tim. *A new home*
Bresnick-Perry, Roslyn. *Leaving for America*
Bullard, Lisa. *Trick-or-treat on Milton Street*
Cadnum, Michael. *The lost and found house*
Carlson, Nancy L. *My best friend moved away*

Carlstrom, Nancy White. *I'm not moving, mama!*
Carter, Anne Laurel. *Molly in danger*
Carter, Penny. *A new house for the Morrisons*
Cartlidge, Michelle. *A house for Lily Mouse*
Cassedy, Sylvia. *The best cat suit of all*
Clifton, Lucille. *Good, says Jerome*
Clymer, Eleanor Lowenton. *A yard for John*
Cohen, Barbara. *Gooseberries to oranges*
D'Amico, Carmela. *Ella, the elegant elephant*
Davies, Sally. *When William went away*
Day, Alexandra. *The Christmas we moved to the barn*
DeLage, Ida. *The old witch finds a new house*
Delton, Judy. *Lee Henry's best friend*
Denslow, Sharon Phillips. *Woollybear good-bye*
Disher, Garry. *Switch cat*
Dowling, Paul. *Meg and Jack are moving*
    Meg and Jack's new friends
Dugan, Barbara. *Leaving home with a pickle jar*
Engel, Diana. *Fishing*
Felt, Sue. *Hello-goodbye*
Fiday, Beverly. *Time to go*
Figueredo, D. H. *When this world was new*
Finsand, Mary Jane. *The town that moved*
Fisher, Aileen Lucia. *Best little house*
Freeman, Martha. *The trouble with babies*
Giffard, Hannah. *Red Fox on the move*
Gilmore, Rachna. *Lights for Gita*
Graham, Bob. *First there was Frances*
    Spirit of Hope
Gretz, Susanna. *Teddy bears' moving day*
Grindley, Sally. *A new room for William*
Halpern, Shari. *Moving from one to ten*
Harper, Jo. *Prairie dog pioneers*
Harrison, Troon. *Courage to fly*
Harshman, Marc. *Moving days*
Havill, Juanita. *Jamaica's blue marker*
Hazen, Barbara Shook. *Good-bye/Hello*
Hendry, Diana. *Not anywhere house*
Hest, Amy. *Best-ever good-bye party*
Hickman, Martha Whitmore. *My friend William moved away*
Hilton, Nette. *Andrew Jessup*
Hoff, Syd. *Who will be my friends?*
Hood, Susan. *Pup and Hound*
Hughes, Shirley. *Moving Molly*
Hume, Stephen Eaton. *Red moon follows truck*
Ilsley, Velma. *M is for moving*
Isadora, Rachel. *The Potters' kitchen*
James, Betsy. *Mary Ann*
Jennings, Michael. *The bears who came to breakfix*
Johnson, Amy Crane. *Mason moves away = Mason se muda*
Johnson, Angela. *The leaving morning*
Johnston, Tony. *The quilt story*
    Sunsets of the West
Jones, Penelope. *I'm not moving!*
Kalan, Robert. *Moving day*
Karas, G. Brian. *Home on the bayou*
Keats, Ezra Jack. *The trip*
Keyworth, C. L. *New day*
Kinsey-Warnock, Natalie. *Wilderness cat*
Koller, Jackie French. *Mole and Shrew*
Komaiko, Leah. *Annie Bananie*
Krensky, Stephen. *We just moved!*
Lawlor, Laurie. *Old Crump*
Leighton, Maxinne Rhea. *An Ellis Island Christmas*
Lexau, Joan M. *The rooftop mystery*
Lobel, Arnold. *Ming Lo moves the mountain*
Lottridge, Celia Barker. *Something might be hiding*
Lystad, Mary H. *That new boy*
McCarthy, Bobette. *See you later, alligator*
McGeorge, Constance W. *Boomer's big day*
MacLachlan, Patricia. *What you know first*
McLerran, Alice. *I want to go home*
McNaughton, Colin. *Guess who's just moved in next door?*
Malone, Nola Langner. *A home*
Marshak, S. (Samuil). *In the van*
Maschler, Fay. *T. G. and Moonie move out of town*
Milord, Sue. *Maggie and the goodbye gift*

Mockford, Caroline. *Cleo on the move*
Moore, Inga. *Little dog lost*
Morris, Jill. *The boy who painted the sun*
Morrow, Barbara. *Help for Mr. Peale*
Moss, Miriam. *I'll be your friend, Smudge*
    A new house for Smudge
Munsch, Robert N. *From far away*
Newsome, Jill. *Shadow*
Obrist, Jürg. *Fluffy*
O'Donnell, Elizabeth Lee. *Maggie doesn't want to move*
O'Kelley, Mattie Lou. *Moving to town*
Park, Frances. *Good-bye, 382 Shin Dang Dong*
Patz, Nancy. *To Annabella Pelican from Thomas Hippopotamus*
Pedersen, Judy. *Out in the country*
Pennypacker, Sara. *Stuart's cape*
Pérez, Amada Irma. *My diary from here to there = Mi diario de aquí hasta allá*
Piepmeier, Charlotte. *Lucy's journey to the wild west*
Provensen, Alice. *Shaker Lane*
Pryor, Bonnie. *The beaver boys*
Pulver, Robin. *Homer and the house next door*
Rabe, Berniece. *A smooth move*
Ransom, Candice F. *When the whippoorwill calls*
Rodell, Susanna. *Dear Fred*
Rogers, Fred. *Moving*
Ross, Lillian Hammer. *Buba Leah and her paper children*
Schlein, Miriam. *My house*
Schulman, Janet. *The big hello*
Sharmat, Marjorie Weinman. *Gila monsters meet you at the airport*
    Mitchell is moving
    Scarlet Monster lives here
Shecter, Ben. *Grandma remembers*
Shefelman, Janice Jordan. *Victoria House*
Sherrow, Victoria. *There goes the ghost*
Simpson, Lesley. *The Purim surprise*
Singer, Marilyn. *Archer Armadillo's secret room*
Smith, Joseph A. (Joseph Anthony). *Circus train*
Snape, Juliet. *Frog odyssey*
Steel, Danielle. *Martha's new school*
Stevenson, James. *No friends*
Stewart, Shannon. *Sea crow*
Strathdee, Jean. *The house that grew*
Teague, Mark. *The trouble with the Johnsons*
Tobias, Tobi. *Moving day*
Tsutsui, Yoriko. *Anna's secret friend*
Turner, Ann Warren. *Dust for dinner*
    Stars for Sarah
Van Leeuwen, Jean. *Going west*
Viorst, Judith. *Alexander, who's not (Do you hear me? I mean it!) going to move*
Vizurraga, Susan. *Miss Opal's auction*
Waber, Bernard. *Gina*
    Ira says goodbye
Watson, Jane Werner. *Sometimes a family has to move*
Watson, Wendy. *Moving*
Whitcher, Susan. *Something for everyone*
Wilhelm, Hans. *A new home, a new friend*
Wishinsky, Frieda. *Jennifer Jones won't leave me alone*
Woodruff, Elvira. *The wing shop*
Yaccarino, Dan. *Oswald*
Yee, Wong Herbert. *Did you see Chip?*
Zagwÿn, Deborah Turney. *The winter gift*
Ziefert, Harriet. *A new house for Mole and Mouse*
Zolotow, Charlotte (Shapiro). *Janey*

Mules *see* Animals – mules

Multi-ethnic *see* Ethnic groups in the U.S.

Multiple births – sextuplets

Dilley, Becki. *Sixty fingers, sixty toes*

Multiple births – triplets

Abolafia, Yossi. *My three uncles*

Brunhoff, Jean de. *Babar and his children*
Lacoe, Addie. *Just not the same*
Lindman, Maj. *Flicka, Ricka, Dicka and a little dog*
  Flicka, Ricka, Dicka and the big red hen
  Flicka, Ricka, Dicka and the new dotted dress
  Flicka, Ricka, Dicka and the three kittens
  Flicka, Ricka, Dicka bake a cake
  Snipp, Snapp, Snurr and the buttered bread
  Snipp, Snapp, Snurr and the magic horse
  Snipp, Snapp, Snurr and the red shoes
  Snipp, Snapp, Snurr and the reindeer
  Snipp, Snapp, Snurr and the seven dogs
  Snipp, Snapp, Snurr and the yellow sled
Pirani, Felix. *Triplets*
Seuling, Barbara. *The triplets*

Multiple births – twins

Aliki. *Jack and Jake*
Anholt, Catherine. *Twins, two by two*
Balet, Jan B. *Ned and Ed and the lion*
Barber, Tiki. *By my brother's side*
Bos, Burny. *Meet the Molesons*
Brennan, Jan. *Born two-gether*
Brown, Marc Tolon. *Arthur babysits*
Browne, Vee. *Monster birds*
Bruna, Dick. *Lisa and Lynn*
  Tilly and Tess
Bunting, Eve (Anne Evelyn). *Twinnies*
Cleary, Beverly. *The growing-up feet*
  The real hole
  Two dog biscuits
Dalmais, Anne-Marie. *Molly and Mimi the mouse twins*
Denslow, Sharon Phillips. *On the trail with Miss Pace*
De Paola, Tomie (Thomas Anthony). *Boss for a day*
  The bubble factory
  Hide-and-seek all week
  Marcos: red, yellow, blue
  Meet the Barkers
  A new Barker in the house
Doro, Ann. *Twin pickle*
Fuchshuber, Annegert. *Two peas in a pod*
Gabler, Mirko. *The alphabet soup*
Gerrard, Roy. *The Roman twins*
Givens, Terryl. *Dragon scales and willow leaves*
Gliori, Debi. *New big sister*
Gordon, Jeffie Ross. *Two badd babies*
Greenberg, Dan. *The bed who ran away from home*
Himmelman, John. *J.J. versus the babysitter*
Hoban, Lillian. *Here come raccoons*
Hutchins, Pat. *Which witch is which?*
Impey, Rose. *My mom and our dad*
James, Brian. *Supertwins and the sneaky, slimy book worms*
  The Supertwins and tooth trouble
  The Supertwins meet the bad dogs from space
  Supertwins meet the dangerous dino-robots
Keller, Holly. *Harry and Tuck*
King-Smith, Dick. *Cuckoobush farm*
Kismaric, Carole. *The rumor of Pavel and Paali*
Lattimore, Deborah Nourse. *Punga the goddess of ugly*
Lawrence, James. *Binky Brothers and the fearless four*
  Binky Brothers, detectives
Leonard, Marcia. *Get the ball, Slim*
  The kitten twins
  Spots
Levi, Dorothy Hoffman. *A very special sister*
Lindgren, Astrid. *Most beloved sister*
McDermott, Gerald. *The magic tree*
McElmurry, Jill. *Mess pets*
MacKinnon, Debbie. *Tom's train*
McKissack, Patricia C. *Who is who?*
Mahy, Margaret. *Down the dragon's tongue*
Metaxas, Eric. *Uncle Mugsy and the terrible twins of Christmas*
Moore, Lilian. *Little Raccoon and no trouble at all*
Neasi, Barbara J. *Just like me*
Norling, Beth. *Sister night and sister day*
Norris, Kathleen. *The holy twins: Benedict and Scholastica*

Obrist, Jürg. *Bear business*
Perkins, Al. *Don and Donna go to bat*
Rockwell, Anne F. *Romulus and Remus*
Rubel, Nicole. *Sam and Violet are twins*
  Sam and Violet go camping
Saint James, Synthia. *Sunday*
Schaap, Martine. *Mop and the birthday picnic*
  Mop's backyard concert
  Mop's mountain adventure
  Mop's treasure hunt
Simon, Carly. *Midnight farm*
Simon, Norma. *How do I feel?*
Stanley, Diane. *Thanksgiving on Plymouth Plantation*
Steel, Danielle. *Max's new baby*
Stewart, Elizabeth Laing. *The lion twins*
Thompson, Vivian Laubach. *Camp-in-the-yard*
Wagner, Jenny. *Amy's monster*
Wagner, Karen. *Chocolate chip cookies*
Wallace, John. *The twins*
Walters, Catherine. *Are you there, Baby Bear?*
White, Amanda. *Rip and Rap*
Wisniewski, David. *The warrior and the wise man*
Yeoman, John. *The young performing horse*
Yorinks, Arthur. *Oh, brother*
Zehler, Antonia. *Two fine ladies have a tiff*
  Two fine ladies: tea for three

Mummies

Allard, Harry. *Crash helmet*
Yates, Philip. *Ten little mummies*

Mumps *see* Illness – mumps

Muppets *see* Puppets

Muscular dystrophy *see* Illness – muscular dystrophy

Museum workers *see* Careers – museum workers

Museums

Alexander, Liza. *A visit to the Sesame Street Museum*
Aliki. *My visit to the dinosaurs*
Armstrong-Ellis, Carey. *Prudy's problem and how she solved it*
Berenstain, Stan. *The Berenstain bears and the missing dinosaur bone*
Bilgrami, Shaheen. *Amazing dinosaur discovery*
Binnamin, Vivian. *The case of the snoring stegosaurus*
Blance, Ellen. *Monster goes to the museum*
Boehm, Arlene P. *Jack in search of Art*
Bourgeois, Paulette. *Franklin's class trip*
Brenner, Barbara A. *Dinosaurium*
Brown, Laurie Krasny. *Visiting the art museum*
Browne, Anthony. *The shape game*
Brunhoff, Laurent de. *Babar's Museum of Art: (closed Mondays)*
Bunting, Eve (Anne Evelyn). *Night of the gargoyles*
Butterworth, Nick. *The school trip*
Carmack, Lisa Jobe. *Philippe in Monet's garden*
The Christmas story, paintings from the Metropolitan Museum of
  Art
Clayton, Elaine. *Ella's trip to the museum*
Clement, Rod. *Frank's great museum adventure*
Cohen, Miriam. *Lost in the museum*
Cressy, Judith. *Can you find it?*
  Can you find it, too?
De Paola, Tomie (Thomas Anthony). *Bill and Pete go down the Nile*
Everett, Gwen. *Li'l Sis and Uncle Willie*
Faulkner, Keith. *David dreaming of dinosaurs*
Floca, Brian. *The frightful story of Harry Walfish*
Fradon, Dana. *Sir Dana – a knight*
Freeman, Don. *Norman the doorman*
Geisert, Arthur. *Mystery*
Gramatky, Hardie. *Hercules*
Hayward, Linda. *Ernie and Bert's summer project*
Hooper, Meredith. *Dogs' Night*
Hurd, Thacher. *Art dog*

J. Paul Getty Museum. *A is for artist*
Johansen, K. V. (Krista V.). *Pippin and the bones*
Kallen, Stuart A. *The museum*
Katz, Susan. *Mrs. Brown on exhibit*
Kellogg, Steven (Stephen). *Prehistoric Pinkerton*
Krementz, Jill. *A visit to Washington, D.C.*
L'Hommedieu, Arthur John. *Working at a museum*
Lionni, Leo. *Matthew's dream*
Lithgow, John. *Carnival of the animals*
    Micawber
Löfgren, Ulf. *Alvin the Knight*
Magnier, Thierry. *Isabelle and the angel*
Mayers, Florence Cassen. *Egyptian art from the Brooklyn Museum*
    The Museum of Fine Arts, Boston
    The Museum of Modern Art, New York
    The National Air and Space Museum
Mayhew, James. *Katie and the dinosaurs*
    Katie and the Mona Lisa
    Katie and the sunflowers
    Katie meets the Impressionists
Morrow, Barbara. *Help for Mr. Peale*
Munro, Roxie. *The inside-outside book of Texas*
    The inside-outside book of Washington, D.C.
Papajani, Janet. *Museums*
Rohmann, Eric. *Time flies*
Shea, Kitty. *Out and about at the science center*
Simmonds, Posy. *Lulu and the flying babies*
Stevenson, James. *The most amazing dinosaur*
Taylor, Barbara. *Going, going, gone*
Thayer, Jane. *Gus and the baby ghost*
Tunnell, Michael O. *The joke's on George*
Van Nutt, Julia. *Pignapped!*
Vincent, Gabrielle. *Where are you, Ernest and Celestine?*
Wahl, Jan. *The field mouse and the dinosaur named Sue*
    I met a dinosaur
Weil, Lisl. *Let's go to the museum*
Weitzman, Jacqueline Preiss. *You can't take a balloon into the Metropolitan Museum*
    You can't take a balloon into the National Gallery
Wellington, Monica. *Squeaking of art, the mice go to the museum*
Wheatley, Nadia. *Luke's way of looking*
Wyse, Lois. *How to take your grandmother to the museum*
Zadrzynska, Ewa. *The peaceable kingdom*

Music

Abisch, Roz. *Sweet Betsy from Pike*
    'Twas in the moon of wintertime
Alexander, Cecil Frances. *All things bright and beautiful*, ill. by Leo
    Politi
    All things bright and beautiful, ill. by Bruce Whatley
Alexander, Lloyd. *The truthful harp*
Alger, Leclaire Gowans. *Always room for one more*
    Kellyburn Braes
Aliki. *Ah, music!*
All night, all day
Alley, R. W. (Robert W.). *There once was a witch*
Ambrus, Victor G. *Mishka*
    The seven skinny goats
Appelt, Kathi. *Bats around the clock*
    Bats on parade
Arkin, David. *Black and white*
Asch, Frank. *Barnyard lullaby*
Ash, Jutta. *Wedding birds*
Atene, Ann (Anna). *The golden guitar*
Austin, Patricia. *The cat who loved Mozart*
Autry, Gene. *Here comes Santa Claus*
Auzary-Luton, Sylvie. *1, 2, 3, music!*
Azarian, Mary. *The tale of John Barleycorn or, From barley to beer*
Bach, Othello. *Lilly, Willy and the mail-order witch*
Baer, Gene. *Thump thump rat-a-tat-tat*
Baker, Laura Nelson. *The friendly beasts*
    O children of the wind and pines
Bascom, Joe. *Malcolm's job*
Bateman, Teresa. *Harp o' gold*
Bates, Katharine Lee. *America the beautiful*, ill. by Chris Gall
    America the beautiful, ill. by Wendell Minor

    America the beautiful, ill. by Neil Waldman
The bear
Behn, Harry. *What a beautiful noise*
Belafonte, Harry. *Island in the sun*
Berger, Barbara Helen. *The jewel heart*
Berlin, Irving. *Easter parade*
    God bless America
Bianco, Margery Williams. *The hurdy-gurdy man*
Birchman, David Francis. *Brother Billy Bronto's bygone blues band*
    A green horn blowing
Birdseye, Tom. *She'll be comin' round the mountain*
Bishop, Roma. *Christmas songs*
Black, Charles C. *The royal nap*
Bliss, Corinne Demas. *Nina's waltz*
Boesel, Ann Sterling. *Sing and sing again*
    Singing with Peter and Patsy
Bolliger, Max. *The most beautiful song*
Bottner, Barbara. *Nana Hannah's piano*
    Zoo song
Botwin, Esther. *A treasury of songs for little children*
Bowles, Brad. *Grandma's band*
Bowman, Pete. *The Christmas songbook*
Boynton, Sandra. *Good night, good night*
Bratton, John. *The teddy bears' picnic*, ill. by Renate Kozikowski
Brébeuf, Jean de, Saint. *The Huron carol*
Brett, Jan. *Berlioz the bear*
Bring a torch, Jeannette, Isabella
Brokering, Herbert F. *Earth and all stars*
Brott, Ardyth. *Jeremy's decision*
Brown, Marc Tolon. *Play rhymes*
Brown, Margaret Wise. *The little brass band*
Bruna, Dick. *The orchestra*
Buffett, Jimmy. *The jolly mon*
Bunting, Eve (Anne Evelyn). *The traveling men of Ballycoo*
Burden-Patmon, Denise. *Carnival*
Burgie, Irving. *Caribbean carnival*
Burke, Bobby. *Daddy's little girl*
Burleigh, Robert. *Lookin' for Bird in the big city*
Burningham, John. *Jangle twang*
    Trubloff
Butler, Geoff. *Ode to Newfoundland*
Canyon, Christopher. *John Denver's Ancient rhymes*
    John Denver's Sunshine on my shoulders
Carle, Eric. *I see a song*
Carryl, Charles E. (Charles Edward). *A capital ship*
Carter, David A. *If you're happy and you know it, clap your hands*
    Old MacDonald had a farm
Carter, Don. *Heaven's all-star jazz band*
Carter, Donna Renee. *Music in the family*
Caseley, Judith. *Ada potato*
Casterline, L. C. (Linda C.). *The sounds of music*
Cathon, Laura E. *Tot Botot and his little flute*
Causley, Charles. *Early in the morning*
Cech, John. *Django*
Celenza, Anna Harwell. *The farewell symphony*
Chalk, Gary. *Yankee Doodle*
Chanover, Hyman. *Happy Hanukah everybody*
Children go where I send thee
Chocolate, Deborah M. Newton. *The piano man*
Christensen, Bonnie. *Woody Guthrie, poet of the people*
Clément, Claude. *The voice of the wood*
Coco, Eugene Bradley. *The fiddler's son*
Colette, Sidonie Gabrielle. *The boy and the magic*
Collins, Billy. *Daddy's little boy*
Conover, Chris. *Six little ducks*
Count me in
Cowan, Catherine. *My friend the piano*
Craver, Mike. *Beaver ball at the bug club*
Crespi, Francesca. *Little Bear and the oompah-pah*
    Make a joyful noise
Cummings, W. T. (Walter Thies). *The kid*
Curtis, Gavin. *The bat boy and his violin*
Dallas-Smith, Peter. *Trumpets in Grumpetland*
Dalton, Alene. *My new picture book of songs*
Davies, Kay. *My drum*
Davis, David (David R.). *Jazz cats*
Davol, Marguerite W. *The heart of the wood*

Day, Betsy. *Stefan and Olga*

Delacre, Lulu. *Arroz con leche*
   Las Navidades

Delton, Judy. *My mom made me take piano lessons*

Diller, Harriett. *Big band sound*

Dillon, Eilis. *The cats' opera*

Dineen, Jacqueline. *Frédéric Chopin*

Domanska, Janina. *Busy Monday morning*

Donovan, Mary Lee. *Won't you come and play with me?*

Dubois, Muriel L. *I like music: what can I be?*

Dunbar, Joyce. *Indigo and the whale*

Duncan, Lois. *Songs from dreamland*

Durell, Ann. *The Diane Goode book of American folk tales and songs*

Elliott, David. *Hazel Nutt, mad scientist*

Ellwand, David. *Ten in the bed*

Emerson, Sally. *The Kingfisher nursery rhyme songbook*

England, Linda. *3 kids dreamin'*

Engvick, William. *Lullabies and night songs*

Fair, David. *The fabulous four skunks*

The farmer in the dell. *The farmer in the dell*, ill. by John O'Brien
   The farmer in the dell, ill. by Kathy Parkinson
   The farmer in the dell, ill. by Mary Maki Rae
   The farmer in the dell, ill. by Diane Stanley
   The farmer in the dell, ill. by Alexandra Wallner

Fine, Howard. *A piggie Christmas*

Fitzgerald, Ella. *A-tisket, a-tasket*

Flack, Marjorie. *The restless robin*

Flanders, Michael. *The hippopotamus song*

Fleischman, Paul. *Rondo in C*

Fleming, Candace. *Gabriella's song*

Fowler, Susi Gregg. *Fog*

Freeman, Lydia. *Pet of the Met*

The friendly beasts

The friendly beasts and a partridge in a pear tree, ill. by Virginia Pearsons

A frog he would a-wooing go (folk-song). *Frog went a-courting*, retold & ill. by Dominic Catalano
   Froggie went a-courting, ill. by Chris Conover
   Mr. Frog went a-courting
   Wendy Watson's frog went a-courting

Garcia, Jerry. *The teddy bears' picnic*

Gershwin, George. *Summertime from Porgy and Bess*

Gibbons, Faye. *Emma Jo's song*

Gilbert, Yvonne. *Baby's book of lullabies and cradle songs*

Go tell Aunt Rhody. *Go tell Aunt Rhody*, ill. by Robert M. Quackenbush

Goffstein, M. B. (Marilyn Brooke). *A little Schubert*

Gollub, Matthew. *Gobble, quack, moon*

Gomi, Taro. *Toot!*

Goode, Diane. *Diane Goode's book of silly stories & songs*

Goodhart, Pippa. *Row, row, row your boat*

Goss, Linda. *The frog who wanted to be a singer*

Graham, Steve. *Dear old Donegal*

Granfield, Linda. *Silent night*

Gray, Libba Moore. *When Uncle took the fiddle*

Greene, Carol. *A computer went a-courting*
   Hinny Winny Bunco
   The thirteen days of Halloween
   The world's biggest birthday cake

Greenfield, Eloise. *I make music*

Grifalconi, Ann. *The toy trumpet*

Griffith, Helen V. *Georgia music*

Grigg, Carol. *The singing snow bear*

Guthrie, Woody. *Bling blang*
   My dolly
   This land is your land
   Woody's 20 grow big songs

Guy, Suzanne. *The music box*

Hague, Michael. *Deck the halls*

Hale, Sarah Josepha Buell. *Mary had a little lamb*, ill. by Tomie de Paola
   Mary had a little lamb, photos. by Bruce McMillan
   Mary had a little lamb, ill. by Ann Schweninger
   Mary had a little lamb, ill. by Iza Trapani
   Mary had a little lamb, ill. by Suzanne Vasilak
   Mary had a little lamb [board book], ill. by Iza Trapani

Hallworth, Grace. *Sing me a story*

Halpern, Shari. *What shall we do when we all go out?*

Harranth, Wolf. *The flute concert*

Harrison, David Lee. *The animals' song*

Haseley, Dennis. *The old banjo*

Hayes, Ann. *Meet the Marching Smithereens*
   Meet the orchestra

Helmer, Marilyn. *Three tuneful tales*

Hoban, Russell. *Emmet Otter's jug-band Christmas*

Hoberman, Mary Ann. *Bill Grogan's goat*

Hodges, Margaret. *Silent night*

Hoff, Syd. *Arturo's baton*

Holl, Adelaide. *Sylvester, the mouse with the musical ear*

Hooper, Maureen Brett. *Silent night*

Hoose, Philip M. *Hey little ant*

Horvath, Betty F. *Jasper makes music*

Hot cross buns, and other old street cries

Howe, Caroline Walton. *Teddy Bear's bird and beast band*

Hurd, Thacher. *Mama don't allow*
   The pea patch jig

Hush little baby. *Hush little baby*, ill. by Aliki
   Hush, little baby, ill. by Marla Frazee
   Hush little baby, ill. by Shari Halpern
   Hush little baby, ill. by Jeanette Winter
   Hush little baby, ill. by Margot Zemach

Hush songs

Ipcar, Dahlov (Zorach). *The cat came back*
   The song of the day birds and the night birds

Isadora, Rachel. *Ben's trumpet*
   Bring on that beat

Isele, Elizabeth. *Pooks*

Isherwood, Shirley. *The band over the hill*

I've been working on the railroad

Ivimey, John William. *The complete story of the three blind mice*, ill. by Paul Galdone
   The complete version of ye three blind mice, ill. by Walton Corbould
   Three blind mice, ill. by Lorinda Bryan Cauley
   Three blind mice, ill. by Victoria Chess

James, J. Alison. *The drums of Noto Hanto*

Janosch. *Joshua and the magic fiddle*
   Tonight at nine

Jennings, Sharon. *Franklin and the magic show*

Johnson, Angela. *Violet's music*

Johnson, Paul Brett. *Little Bunny Foo Foo*

Johnston, Tony. *Pages of music*

Jones, Carol. *This old man*

Judd, Naomi. *Naomi Judd's guardian angels*

Kahl, Virginia. *Droopsi*

Kaplan, Howard. *Waiting to sing*

Kapp, Paul. *Cock-a-doodle-doo! Cock-a-doodle-dandy!*

Karlins, Mark. *Music over Manhattan*

Keats, Ezra Jack. *Apt. 3*
   The little drummer boy

Kellogg, Steven (Stephen). *Yankee Doodle*

Kepes, Juliet. *The seed that peacock planted*

Kessler, Ethel. *Is there a gorilla in the band?*

Ketcham, Sallie. *Bach's big adventure*

Kherdian, David. *The cat's midsummer jamboree*

Kimmel, Eric A. *The Erie Canal pirates*
   Why worry?

King, Bob. *Sitting on the farm*

Kingsland, Robin. *Bus stop bop*

Kinsey-Warnock, Natalie. *The fiddler of the Northern Lights*

Kirk, Daniel. *Go!*

Knight, Hilary. *A firefly in a fir tree*

Knutson, Kimberley. *Jungle jamboree*

Komaiko, Leah. *Broadway Banjo Bill*
   I like the music

Koontz, Robin Michal. *This old man*

Kovalski, Maryann. *Jingle bells*
   Take me out to the ball game
   The wheels on the bus

Kraus, Robert. *Ludwig the dog who snored symphonies*
   Musical Max

Krementz, Jill. *A very young musician*

Kroll, Steven. *By the dawn's early light*

Kroll, Virginia L. *Wood-hoopoe Willie*

Krull, Kathleen. *M is for music*

Songs of praise
Lambert, Paulette Livers. *Evening*
Langstaff, John M. *Oh, a-hunting we will go*
 Ol' Dan Tucker
 On Christmas day in the morning
 Soldier, soldier, won't you marry me?
 The swapping boy
 The two magicians
La Prise, Larry. *The hokey pokey*
Lasker, David. *The boy who loved music*
Lear, Edward. *Edward Lear's nonsense book*
 The pelican chorus, ill. by Harold Berson
 The pelican chorus and the quangle wangle's hat, ill. by Kevin W. Maddison
Lebentritt, Julia. *The Kooken*
Lemieux, Margo. *The fiddle ribbon*
Lenski, Lois. *At our house*
 Davy and his dog
 Davy goes places
 Debbie and her grandma
 A dog came to school
 I like winter
 I went for a walk
Lesynski, Loris. *Dirty dog boogie*
Levine, Evan. *Not the piano, Mrs. Medley!*
Lionni, Leo. *Frederick*
 Geraldine, the music mouse
Lippman, Sidney. *A you're adorable*
Listen to the storyteller
Little old lady who swallowed a fly. *I know an old lady,* ill. by Abner Graboff
Littlesugar, Amy. *Shake Rag*
Liu, Jae Soo. *Yellow umbrella*
Lobel, Anita. *The troll music*
Locker, Thomas. *Anna and the bagpiper*
Löfgren, Ulf. *The flying orchestra*
London, Sara. *Firehorse Max*
Long, Sylvia. *Deck the hall*
Lottridge, Celia Barker. *Music for the Tsar of the Sea*
Lynch, Wendy. *Bach*
Lyon, George Ella. *Five live bongos*
McAllister, Angela. *The enchanted flute*
McCarthy, Bobette. *Buffalo girls*
McCloskey, Robert. *Lentil*
McCully, Emily Arnold. *The orphan singer*
McCurdy, Michael. *The old man and the fiddle*
McDermott, Gerald. *Musicians of the sun*
McGinley-Nally, Sharon. *The friendly beasts*
McKee, David. *The sad story of Veronica who played the violin*
McMillan, Bruce. *The alphabet symphony*
McMullan, Kate (Hall). *Rock-a-baby band*
McNally, Darcie. *In a cabin in a wood*
McPhail, David M. *Mole music*
Maiorano, Robert. *A little interlude*
Mallett, David. *Inch by inch*
Manushkin, Fran. *My Christmas safari*
Margolin, H. Ellen. *Goin' to Boston*
Maril, Lee. *Mr. Bunny paints the eggs*
Maxner, Joyce. *Nicholas Cricket*
Mayer, Mercer. *The queen always wanted to dance*
Medearis, Angela Shelf. *The singing man*
 The zebra-riding cowboy
Micucci, Charles. *A little night music*
Miller, J. Philip. *We all sing with the same voice*
Miller, William. *The piano*
 Rent party jazz
Millman, Isaac. *Moses goes to a concert*
Mills, Alan. *The hungry goat*
Mills, Judith Christine. *The painted chest*
Modesitt, Jeanne. *Songs of Chanukah*
Morley, Carol. *Farmyard song*
Moss, Lloyd. *Our marching band*
 Zin! zin! zin! A violin
Mother Goose. *Hey, diddle, diddle,* ill. by Marilyn Janovitz
 The Mother Goose songbook
 Mother Goose's rhymes and melodies
 Pat-a-cake, ill. by Marilyn Janovitz

 Sing hey, diddle, diddle
 Thirty old-time nursery songs
Myers, Walter Dean. *The blues of Flats Brown*
Neale, J. M. (John Mason). *Good King Wenceslas*
Nelson, Esther L. *The funny songbook*
 Holiday singing and dancing games
 The silly songbook
Newbolt, Henry John, Sir. *Rilloby-rill*
Newland, Mary Reed. *Good King Wenceslas*
Nichol, B. P. *Once, a lullaby*
Niland, Kilmeny. *A bellbird in a flame tree*
Novak, Matt. *Gertie and Gumbo*
Nussbaumer, Mares. *Away in a manger*
Nygaard, Elizabeth. *Snake alley band*
Oates, Eddie Hershel. *Making music*
Ogburn, Jacqueline K. *The jukebox man*
Old MacDonald had a farm. *E I E I O*
 Old MacDonald had a farm, ill. by Holly Berry
 Old MacDonald had a farm, ill. by Lorinda Bryan Cauley
 Old MacDonald had a farm, ill. by Mel Crawford
 Old MacDonald had a farm, ill. by Tracey English
 Old MacDonald had a farm, ill. by David Frankland
 Old MacDonald had a farm, ill. by Abner Graboff
 Old MacDonald had a farm, ill. by Nancy Hellen
 Old MacDonald had a farm, ill. by Carol Jones
 Old MacDonald had a farm, ill. by Tracey Campbell Pearson
 Old MacDonald had a farm, ill. by Robert M. Quackenbush
 Old MacDonald had a farm, ill. by Glen Rounds
 Old MacDonald had a farm, ill. by William Stobbs
 Old MacDonald had a farm, ill. by Prue Theobalds
On the little hearth
Paker, Josephine. *I wonder why flutes have holes*
Paraskevas, Betty. *Junior Kroll and Company*
 On the day the tall ships sailed
Patterson, Geoffrey. *The lion and the gypsy*
Paxton, Tom. *Going to the zoo*
Peek, Merle. *The balancing act*
Perrault, Charles. *Cinderella,* ill. by Emanuele Luzzati
Peterson, Jeanne Whitehouse. *My mama sings*
Pierpont, James. *Jingle bells*
Pillar, Marjorie. *Join the band!*
Pinkney, Andrea Davis. *Duke Ellington*
Pinkwater, Daniel Manus. *Doodle flute*
Poole, Valerie. *Obadiah Coffee and the music contest*
Poston, Elizabeth. *Baby's song book*
Poulin, Stéphane. *Benjamin and the pillow saga*
Price, Leontyne. *Aïda*
Prokofiev, Sergei Sergeievitch. *Peter and the wolf,* ill. by Reg Cartwright
 Peter and the wolf, ill. by Warren Chappell
 Peter and the wolf, ill. by Barbara Cooney
 Peter and the wolf, ill. by Julia Gukova
 Peter and the wolf, ill. by Frans Haacken
 Peter and the wolf, ill. by Alan Howard
 Peter and the wolf, ill. by Charles Mikolaycak
 Peter and the wolf, ill. by Jörg Müller
 Peter and the wolf, ill. by Josef Palecek
 Peter and the wolf, ill. by Kozo Shimizu
 Peter and the wolf, retold and ill. by Vladimir Vagin
 Peter and the wolf, ill. by Erna Voigt
Purdy, Carol. *Mrs. Merriwether's musical cat*
Quackenbush, Robert M. *Clementine*
 The man on the flying trapeze
 Pop! goes the weasel and Yankee Doodle
 She'll be comin' 'round the mountain
 Skip to my Lou
 There'll be a hot time in the old town tonight
Quattrocki, Carolyn. *The little drummer boy*
Raffi. *Baby beluga*
 Down by the bay
 Everything grows
 Like me and you
 One light, one sun
 Rise and shine
 Shake my sillies out
 Wheels on the bus
Raposo, Joe. *The Sesame Street song book*

Raschka, Christopher. *Charlie Parker played be bop*
 John Coltrane's giant steps
Ray, Mary Lyn. *Pianna*
 Shaker boy
Rayner, Mary. *One by one*
 Ten pink piglets
Rehnman, Mats. *The clay flute*
Rey, H. A. (Hans Augusto). *Humpty Dumpty and other Mother Goose songs*
Richardson, Jean. *Stephen's feast*
Robbins, Ruth. *Baboushka and the three kings*
Rodanas, Kristina. *The little drummer boy*
Rodgers, Richard. *A real nice clambake*
Root, Phyllis. *Rosie's fiddle*
 Soup for supper
Ross, Tony. *This old man*
Rounds, Glen. *The boll weevil*
 Casey Jones
 The strawberry roan
 Sweet Betsy from Pike
Rubin, Mark. *The orchestra*
Safran, Sheri. *The musical cherub*
Sage, James. *The little band*
Santa Claus is coming to town
Schaaf, Peter. *The violin close up*
Schackburg, Richard. *Yankee Doodle*
Schaefer, Carole Lexa. *Two scarlet songbirds*
Schanzer, Rosalyn. *The Old Chisholm Trail*
Schick, Eleanor. *One summer night*
 A piano for Julie
Schneider, Christine M. *Saxophone Sam and his snazzy jazz band*
Scholey, Arthur. *Baboushka*
Schomp, Virginia. *If you were a . . . musician*
Schuch, Steve. *A symphony of whales*
Scott, Lesbia. *I sing a song of the saints of God*
Seeger, Pete. *The foolish frog*
Sendak, Maurice. *Maurice Sendak's Really Rosie*
Seskin, Steve. *Don't laugh at me*
Simple gifts
Singer, Marilyn. *Will you take me to town on strawberry day?*
Slavin, Bill. *The cat came back*
Sloat, Teri. *Hark! The aardvark angels sing*
Slobodkin, Louis. *Wide-awake owl*
Smith, Charles R. *I'll be there*
 My gal
Smith, Edward Biko. *A lullaby for Daddy*
Smith, Will (1968–). *Just the two of us*
Snell, Gordon. *Twelve days, a Christmas countdown*
Sorel, Edward. *The Saturday kid*
Spier, Peter. *The Erie Canal*
Stadler, Alexander. *Beverly Billingsly takes a bow*
Stadler, John. *Hector, the accordion-nosed dog*
Staines, Bill. *All God's critters got a place in the choir*
Stapler, Sarah. *Trilby's trumpet*
Stecher, Miriam B. *Max, the music-maker*
Steig, William. *Roland, the minstrel pig*
 Zeke Pippin
Stern, Elsie-Jean. *Wee Robin's Christmas song*
Stevens, Bryna. *Handel and the famous sword swallower of Halle*
Stevens, Jan Romero. *Twelve lizards leaping*
Stevenson, James. *Clams can't sing*
Stohs, Anita. *An Easter alleluia*
Strom, Maria Diaz. *Rainbow Joe and me*
Sweet, Melissa. *Fiddle-i-fee*
Takao, Yuko. *A winter concert*
Taylor, Mark. *The bold fisherman*
 Old Blue, you good dog you
Thien, Madeleine. *The Chinese violin*
Thomas, Ianthe. *Willie blows a mean horn*
Thomas, Joyce Carol. *The gospel Cinderella*
Titus, Eve. *Anatole and the piano*
 Anatole and the pied piper
Trapani, Iza. *I'm a little teapot*
 The itsy bitsy spider
 Shoo fly!
Tudor, Tasha. *Junior's tune*
Turner, Barbara J. *Out and about at the orchestra*

Tusa, Tricia. *Miranda*
The twelve days of Christmas. English folk song. *Brian Wildsmith's The twelve days of Christmas*
 Jack Kent's twelve days of Christmas
 The twelve days of Christmas, ill. by Jan Brett
 The twelve days of Christmas, ill. by Rachel Griffin
 The twelve days of Christmas, ill. by Ilonka Karasz
 The twelve days of Christmas, ill. by Ilse Plume
 The twelve days of Christmas, ill. by Erika Schneider
 The twelve days of Christmas, ill. by Vladimir Vagin
 The twelve days of Christmas, ill. by Sophie Windham
 The twelve days of Christmas [board book], ill. by Jan Brett
Ungerer, Tomi. *Tortoni Tremelo the cursed musician*
Uttley, Alison. *Sam Pig and the hurdy-gurdy man*
Vainio, Pirkko. *The Christmas angel*
Vaughan, Marcia Kapok. *Wombat stew*
Velasquez, Eric. *Grandma's records*
Vincent, Gabrielle. *Bravo, Ernest and Celestine!*
Waddell, Martin. *The happy hedgehog band*
Wallace, Nancy Elizabeth. *Apples, apples, apples*
Wallner, John C. *Old MacDonald had a farm*
Walter, Mildred Pitts. *Ty's one-man band*
Walty, Margaret. *Rock-a-bye baby*
Wangerin, Walter. *Angels and all children*
Ward, Jennifer. *Over in the garden*
Warner, Sunny. *Madison finds a line*
Watson, Clyde. *Father Fox's feast of songs*
 Fisherman lullabies
Weatherford, Carole Boston. *Jazz baby*
Weeks, Sarah. *Crocodile smile*
Weidt, Maryann N. *Daddy played music for the cows*
Weil, Lisl. *The magic of music*
Weiss, Nicki. *If you're happy and you know it*
Wells, Rosemary. *Bingo*
Wenning, Elisabeth. *The Christmas mouse*
Westcott, Nadine Bernard. *Skip to my Lou*
 There's a hole in the bucket
What a morning!
Wheeler, Lisa. *Jazz baby*
Wheeler, Opal. *Sing in praise*
 Sing Mother Goose
Whippo, Walt. *Little white duck*
Whittington, Mary K. *Carmina, come dance!*
Widdecombe Fair
Wilder, Laura Ingalls. *My little house songbook*
Williams, Suzanne. *The witch casts a spell*
Williams, Vera B. *Music, music for everyone*
Wilson, Budge. *A fiddle for Angus*
Winter, Jeanette. *The girl and the moon man*
 Once upon a time in Chicago
Wolkstein, Diane. *The banza*
Wood, Jakki. *Fiddle-i-fee*
Yeoman, John. *Old Mother Hubbard's dog learns to play*
Yolen, Jane. *Jane Yolen's Old MacDonald songbook*
 The lap-time song and play book
 The lullaby songbook
Yulya. *Bears are sleeping*
Zalben, Jane Breskin. *Miss Violet's shining day*
Zelinsky, Paul O. *The wheels on the bus*
Zemach, Harve. *Mommy, buy me a China doll*
Ziefert, Harriet. *Animal music*
Zimelman, Nathan. *To sing a song as big as Ireland*

Musical instruments

Behn, Harry. *What a beautiful noise*
Burningham, John. *Jangle twang*
Casterline, L. C. (Linda C.). *The sounds of music*
Cox, Judy. *My family plays music*
Kraus, Robert. *Musical Max*
Lithgow, John. *The remarkable Farkle McBride*
Oates, Eddie Hershel. *Making music*
Prokofiev, Sergei Sergeievitch. *Peter and the wolf*, ill. by Reg Cartwright
 Peter and the wolf, ill. by Warren Chappell
 Peter and the wolf, ill. by Barbara Cooney
 Peter and the wolf, ill. by Julia Gukova

Peter and the wolf, ill. by Frans Haacken
Peter and the wolf, ill. by Alan Howard
Peter and the wolf, ill. by Charles Mikolaycak
Peter and the wolf, ill. by Jörg Müller
Peter and the wolf, ill. by Josef Palecek
Peter and the wolf, ill. by Kozo Shimizu
Peter and the wolf, retold and ill. by Vladimir Vagin
Peter and the wolf, ill. by Erna Voigt
Shahan, Sherry. *The jazzy alphabet*
Stecher, Miriam B. *Max, the music-maker*
Stevens, Bryna. *Handel and the famous sword swallower of Halle*
Thorpe, Kiki. *Time to cha-cha-cha!*
Yeoman, John. *Old Mother Hubbard's dog learns to play*

Musical instruments – accordions

Stadler, John. *Hector, the accordion-nosed dog*
Williams, Vera B. *Music, music for everyone*

Musical instruments – bagpipes

DeFelice, Cynthia C. *Cold feet*
Locker, Thomas. *Anna and the bagpiper*

Musical instruments – balalaikas

Burningham, John. *Trubloff*

Musical instruments – bands

Appelt, Kathi. *Bats on parade*
Baer, Gene. *Thump thump rat-a-tat-tat*
Birchman, David Francis. *Brother Billy Bronto's bygone blues band*
Bowles, Brad. *Grandma's band*
Brett, Jan. *Berlioz the bear*
Brown, Margaret Wise. *The little brass band*
Carter, Don. *Heaven's all-star jazz band*
Crespi, Francesca. *Little Bear and the oompah-pah*
Diller, Harriett. *Big band sound*
England, Linda. *3 kids dreamin'*
Hoban, Russell. *Emmet Otter's jug-band Christmas*
Howe, Caroline Walton. *Teddy Bear's bird and beast band*
Hurd, Thacher. *Mama don't allow*
Johnson, Angela. *Violet's music*
Kassirer, Sue. *Math fair blues*
Kessler, Ethel. *Is there a gorilla in the band?*
London, Jonathan. *Froggy plays in the band*
McMullan, Kate (Hall). *Rock-a-baby band*
Maxner, Joyce. *Nicholas Cricket*
Moss, Lloyd. *Our marching band*
Nygaard, Elizabeth. *Snake alley band*
Orgill, Roxane. *If I only had a horn*
Pillar, Marjorie. *Join the band!*
Poole, Valerie. *Obadiah Coffee and the music contest*
Raschka, Christopher. *John Coltrane's giant steps*
Sage, James. *The little band*
Schaap, Martine. *Mop's backyard concert*
Stuchner, Joan Betty. *The Kugel Valley Klezmer Band*
Waddell, Martin. *The happy hedgehog band*
Walter, Mildred Pitts. *Ty's one-man band*
Wilson, Jacqueline. *Mr. Cool*
Winter, Jeanette. *Once upon a time in Chicago*
Ziefert, Harriet. *Animal music*

Musical instruments – banjos

Komaiko, Leah. *Broadway Banjo Bill*
Wolkstein, Diane. *The banza*

Musical instruments – cellos

Clément, Claude. *The voice of the wood*
Cutler, Jane. *The cello of Mr. O*
Garriel, Barbara S. *I know a shy fellow who swallowed a cello*
Lebentritt, Julia. *The Kooken*

Musical instruments – drums

Base, Graeme. *Jungle drums*
Davies, Kay. *My drum*
Davol, Marguerite W. *The loudest, fastest, best drummer in Kansas*
Francis, Panama. *David gets his drum*
Grace, Kayla. *Percussion instruments*
James, J. Alison. *The drums of Noto Hanto*
Keats, Ezra Jack. *The little drummer boy*
Kroll, Virginia L. *Wood-hoopoe Willie*
Lyon, George Ella. *Five live bongos*
Pinkwater, Daniel Manus. *Bongo Larry*
Quattrocki, Carolyn. *The little drummer boy*
Rodanas, Kristina. *The little drummer boy*

Musical instruments – fiddles *see* Musical instruments – violins

Musical instruments – flutes

Bolliger, Max. *The most beautiful song*
Cathon, Laura E. *Tot Botot and his little flute*
Day, Betsy. *Stefan and Olga*
Gillard, Denise. *Music from the sky*
Harranth, Wolf. *The flute concert*
Lionni, Leo. *Geraldine, the music mouse*
McAllister, Angela. *The enchanted flute*
Pillar, Marjorie. *Join the band!*
Rehnman, Mats. *The clay flute*

Musical instruments – gourds

Birchman, David Francis. *A green horn blowing*

Musical instruments – guitars

All night, all day
Atene, Ann (Anna). *The golden guitar*
Buffett, Jimmy. *The jolly mon*
Kingsland, Robin. *Bus stop bop*
Kovalski, Maryann. *The wheels on the bus*
Myers, Walter Dean. *The blues of Flats Brown*

Musical instruments – gusli

Lottridge, Celia Barker. *Music for the Tsar of the Sea*

Musical instruments – harmonicas

Battle-Lavert, Gwendolyn. *The music in Derrick's heart*
Griffith, Helen V. *Georgia music*
Keats, Ezra Jack. *Apt. 3*
McCloskey, Robert. *Lentil*
Steig, William. *Zeke Pippin*

Musical instruments – harps

Alexander, Lloyd. *The truthful harp*
Edwards, Pamela Duncan. *The leprechaun's gold*

Musical instruments – harpsichords

Guy, Suzanne. *The music box*

Musical instruments – hurdy-gurdies

Bianco, Margery Williams. *The hurdy-gurdy man*
Uttley, Alison. *Sam Pig and the hurdy-gurdy man*

Musical instruments – lutes

Steig, William. *Roland, the minstrel pig*

Musical instruments – mandolins

Kherdian, David. *The cat's midsummer jamboree*

Musical instruments – orchestras

Bruna, Dick. *The orchestra*
Hoff, Syd. *Arturo's baton*
Löfgren, Ulf. *The flying orchestra*
McMillan, Bruce. *The alphabet symphony*
Millman, Isaac. *Moses goes to a concert*
Rubin, Mark. *The orchestra*
Turner, Barbara J. *Out and about at the orchestra*

Musical instruments – organs

Ketcham, Sallie. *Bach's big adventure*
Wenning, Elisabeth. *The Christmas mouse*

Musical instruments – pianos

All night, all day
Austin, Patricia. *The cat who loved Mozart*
Bottner, Barbara. *Nana Hannah's piano*
Chocolate, Deborah M. Newton. *The piano man*
Cowan, Catherine. *My friend the piano*
Delton, Judy. *My mom made me take piano lessons*
Dineen, Jacqueline. *Frédéric Chopin*
Fleischman, Paul. *Rondo in C*
Guy, Suzanne. *The music box*
Jennings, Sharon. *Franklin's music lessons*
Kaplan, Howard. *Waiting to sing*
Levine, Evan. *Not the piano, Mrs. Medley!*
Maiorano, Robert. *A little interlude*
Miller, William. *The piano*
Pinkney, Andrea Davis. *Duke Ellington*
Pinkwater, Daniel Manus. *Doodle flute*
Purdy, Carol. *Mrs. Merriwether's musical cat*
Ray, Mary Lyn. *Pianna*
Reynolds, Marilynn. *The magnificent piano recital*
Schick, Eleanor. *A piano for Julie*
Takao, Yuko. *A winter concert*
Titus, Eve. *Anatole and the piano*
Tusa, Tricia. *Miranda*
Whittington, Mary K. *Carmina, come dance!*

Musical instruments – saxophones

Kallok, Emma. *Gem*
Paraskevas, Betty. *Junior Kroll and Company*
Raschka, Christopher. *Charlie Parker played be bop*
Strom, Maria Diaz. *Rainbow Joe and me*

Musical instruments – trombones

Zalben, Jane Breskin. *Miss Violet's shining day*

Musical instruments – trumpets

Burleigh, Robert. *Lookin' for Bird in the big city*
Dallas-Smith, Peter. *Trumpets in Grumpetland*
Gomi, Taro. *Toot!*
Grifalconi, Ann. *The toy trumpet*
Isadora, Rachel. *Ben's trumpet*
Karlins, Mark. *Music over Manhattan*
Krementz, Jill. *A very young musician*
Orgill, Roxane. *If I only had a horn*
Stapler, Sarah. *Trilby's trumpet*
Tudor, Tasha. *Junior's tune*

Musical instruments – violins

Ambrus, Victor G. *Mishka*
Berger, Barbara Helen. *The jewel heart*
Bottner, Barbara. *Zoo song*
Carle, Eric. *I see a song*
Caseley, Judith. *Ada potato*
Cech, John. *Django*
Curtis, Gavin. *The bat boy and his violin*
Davol, Marguerite W. *The heart of the wood*
Gray, Libba Moore. *When Uncle took the fiddle*
Greene, Carol. *Hinny Winny Bunco*

Janosch. *Joshua and the magic fiddle*
Kinsey-Warnock, Natalie. *The fiddler of the Northern Lights*
Kraus, Robert. *Mort the sport*
Lemieux, Margo. *The fiddle ribbon*
London, Sara. *Firehorse Max*
McCurdy, Michael. *The old man and the fiddle*
McKee, David. *The sad story of Veronica who played the violin*
McPhail, David M. *Mole music*
Micucci, Charles. *A little night music*
Moss, Lloyd. *Zin! zin! zin! A violin*
Root, Phyllis. *Rosie's fiddle*
Schaaf, Peter. *The violin close up*
Sorel, Edward. *The Saturday kid*
Thien, Madeleine. *The Chinese violin*
Vincent, Gabrielle. *Bravo, Ernest and Celestine!*
Wilson, Budge. *A fiddle for Angus*

Musical instruments – washboards

Bowles, Brad. *Grandma's band*

Musicians *see* Careers – musicians

Muskogee Indians *see* Indians of North America – Muskogee

Muskrats *see* Animals – muskrats

Mystery stories

Alexander, Sue. *World famous Muriel*
　　World famous Muriel and the magic mystery
Allen, Laura Jean. *Rollo and Tweedy and the case of the missing cheese*
　　Rollo and Tweedy and the ghost of Dougal Castle
　　Where is Freddy?
Amoore, Susannah. *Motley the cat*
Balian, Lorna. *The socksnatchers*
Berenstain, Stan. *The bear detectives*
　　The Berenstain bears and the messy room
　　The Berenstain bears and the missing dinosaur bone
　　The Berenstain bears and the missing honey
Binnamin, Vivian. *The case of the anteater's missing lunch*
　　The case of the planetarium puzzle
　　The case of the snoring stegosaurus
Boatfield, Jonny. *The twilight book*
Bradford, Ann. *The mystery at Misty Falls*
　　The mystery in the secret club house
　　The mystery of the blind writer
　　The mystery of the live ghosts
　　The mystery of the midget clown
　　The mystery of the missing dogs
　　The mystery of the missing raccoon
　　The mystery of the square footsteps
　　The mystery of the tree house
Bunting, Eve (Anne Evelyn). *Jane Martin, dog detective*
Christelow, Eileen. *Gertrude, the bulldog detective*
　　Where's the big bad wolf?
Christian, Mary Blount. *The doggone mystery*
Clement, Rod. *Grandpa's teeth*
Cox, Paul. *The case of the botched book*
　　The great eucalyptus mystery
　　The riddle of the floating island
Cushman, Doug. *The ABC mystery*
　　The mystery of King Karfu
　　The mystery of the monkey's maze
Darling, Kathy (Mary Kathleen). *The mystery in Santa's toyshop*
Davoll, Barbara. *Dusty Mole, private eye*
Fowler, Richard. *Inspector Smart gets the message!*
Freschet, Berniece. *Bernard of Scotland Yard*
Geisert, Arthur. *Mystery*
　　Nursery crimes
Gibbons, Gail. *The missing maple syrup sap mystery*
Grambling, Lois G. *Miss Hildy's missing cape caper*
Hare, Norma Q. *Mystery at mouse house*
Harrison, David Lee. *Detective Bob and the great ape escape*
Hayes, Geoffrey. *The mystery of the pirate ghost*

Hayward, Linda. *The case of the missing Duckie*
Hoban, Julia. *Buzby to the rescue*
Hoban, Lillian. *The case of the two masked robbers*
Holl, Adelaide. *Small Bear solves a mystery*
Hurd, Thacher. *Art dog*
  Mystery on the docks
Isherwood, Shirley. *Something for James*
Jonas, Ann. *The thirteenth clue*
Kellogg, Steven (Stephen). *The mystery of the flying orange pumpkin*
  The mystery of the magic green ball
  The mystery of the missing red mitten
  The mystery of the stolen blue paint
Kitamura, Satoshi. *Sheep in wolves' clothing*
Krahn, Fernando. *Arthur's adventure in the abandoned house*
  The mystery of the giant footprints
Kraus, Robert. *The detective of London*
  Mummy knows best
Laden, Nina. *Private I. Guana, the case of the missing chameleon*
Lass, Bonnie. *Who took the cookies from the cookie jar?*
Lawrence, James. *Binky Brothers and the fearless four*
  Binky Brothers, detectives
Lewis, Thomas P. *Call for Mr. Sniff*
  Mr. Sniff and the motel mystery
Lexau, Joan M. *The dog food caper*
  The rooftop mystery
McDonald, Megan. *The great pumpkin switch*
McKee, David. *123456789 Benn*
Mason, Jane B. *The shadow stealer*
Miller, Edna. *Mousekin's mystery*
Mooser, Stephen. *Funnyman and the penny dodo*
  Funnyman's first case
Morgan, Michaela. *Helpful Betty solves a mystery*
Musicant, Elke. *The night vegetable eater*
Nash, Scott. *Tuff Fluff*
Nixon, Joan Lowery. *Gus and Gertie and the missing pearl*
  The Thanksgiving mystery
  The Valentine mystery
O'Malley, Kevin. *Who killed Cock Robin?*
Ostheeren, Ingrid. *Jonathan Mouse, detective*
Panek, Dennis. *Detective Whoo*
Pape, D. L. (Donna Lugg). *Snoino mystery*
Sharmat, Marjorie Weinman. *Nate the Great*
  Nate the Great and the fishy prize
  Nate the Great and the lost list
  Nate the Great and the monster mess
  Nate the Great and the phony clue
  Nate the Great goes undercover
  Nate the Great, San Francisco detective
Shire, Ellen. *The mystery at number seven, Rue Petite*
Stern, Maggie. *The missing sunflowers*
Stortz, Diane M. *Barnaby Mouse, detective, and the mystery of the big book*
Supraner, Robyn. *Sam Sunday and the mystery at the Ocean Beach Hotel*
Taylor, Mark. *The case of the missing kittens*
Thompson, Richard. *The follower*
Thomson, Ruth. *Peabody all at sea*
  Peabody's first case
Tryon, Leslie. *Albert's Halloween*
Van Nutt, Julia. *The mystery of Mineral Gorge*
Ward, Nick. *Farmer George and the hungry guests*
Wick, Walter. *I spy treasure hunt*

Mythical creatures

Aardema, Verna. *Anansi finds a fool*
Ahlberg, Janet. *Jeremiah in the dark wood*
Arabian Nights. *The tale of Aladdin and the wonderful lamp*
Arnold, Tedd. *Bisnipian blast-off*
Aruego, José. *The king and his friends*
Ashman, Linda. *The essential worldwide monster guide*
Bartram, Simon. *Man on the moon*
Berenstain, Michael. *The dwarks*
Bryan, Ashley. *The dancing granny*
Bunting, Eve (Anne Evelyn). *Night of the gargoyles*
Campbell, Ann-Jeanette. *Dora's box*
Cannon, Janell. *Trupp*

Carle, Eric. *Dragons dragons and other creatures that never were*
Carroll, Lewis. *Jabberwocky*, ill. by Graeme Base
  Jabberwocky, ill. from Disney archives
  Jabberwocky, ill. by Jane Breskin Zalben
Chenault, Nell. *Parsifal the Poddley*
Child, Lauren. *Beware of the storybook wolves*
Climo, Shirley. *Stolen thunder*
Cole, Babette. *Cupid*
Conover, Chris. *The lion's share*
Cooper, Susan. *Jethro and the jumbie*
Coville, Bruce. *Sarah and the dragon*
Dallas-Smith, Peter. *Trumpets in Grumpetland*
Darling, Kathy (Mary Kathleen). *Pecos Bill finds a horse*
Decker, Dorothy W. *Stripe and the merbear*
De Paola, Tomie (Thomas Anthony). *The Prince of the Dolomites*
Dunrea, Olivier. *Ravena*
Elzbieta. *Dikou the little troon who walks at night*
Eschelson, Laura. *The copper braid of Shannon O'Shea*
Fairies, trolls and goblins galore
The firebird. *The firebird*, ill. by Reg Cartwright
  The firebird, ill. by Francesca Crespi
  The firebird, ill. by Demi
  The firebird, adapt. and ill. by Rachel Isadora
  The firebird, ill. by Moira Kemp
  The firebird, ill. by Kris Waldherr
  The firebird, ill. by Boris Zvorykin
  The tale of the firebird, ill. by Gennady Spirin
Fisher, Leonard Everett. *Cyclops*
  Theseus and the Minotaur
Foreman, Michael. *Panda and the bunyips*
  Panda and the bushfire
George, Jean Craighead. *Dear Katie, the volcano is a girl*
Gilleo, Alma. *Learning about monsters*
Goble, Paul. *Iktomi and the coyote*
Graham, Bob. *Max*
Gramatky, Hardie. *Nikos and the sea god*
Greenfield, Eloise. *I can draw a weeposaur and other dinosaurs*
Hayes, Sarah. *Lucy Anna and the Finders*
Hodges, Margaret. *Comus*
Hutton, Warwick. *Persephone*
  Perseus
  Theseus and the Minotaur
James, Brian. *The Supertwins meet the bad dogs from space*
Jendresen, Erik. *Hanuman*
Johnston, Tony. *Bigfoot Cinderrrrella*
Keeshan, Robert. *She loves me, she loves me not*
Kimmel, Eric A. *Billy Lazroe and the King of the Sea*
Krupp, Robin Rector. *Let's go traveling in Mexico*
Kurt, Kemal. *The five fingers and the moon*
McBratney, Sam. *Once there was a Hoodie*
McDonald, Megan. *The bone keeper*
McLenighan, Valjean. *You can go jump*
Mayer, Mercer. *Terrible troll*
Mayne, William. *The blue book of Hob stories*
  The green book of Hob stories
  The red book of Hob stories
  The yellow book of Hob stories
Medicine Crow, Joseph. *Brave Wolf and the Thunderbird*
Moore, Christopher J. *Ishtar and Tammuz*
Nones, Eric Jon. *Wendell*
Oram, Hiawyn. *Jenna and the troublemaker*
Osborne, Mary Pope. *Molly and the prince*
Peet, Bill (William Bartlett). *Cyrus the unsinkable sea serpent*
  No such things
  The pinkish, purplish, bluish egg
Plourde, Lynn. *Wild child*
  Winter waits
Richards, Jean. *The first Olympic games*
Robb, Brian. *My grandmother's djinn*
Rockwell, Anne F. *Buster and the bogeyman*
  The one-eyed giant and other monsters from the Greek Myths
Sabuda, Robert James. *The Blizzard's robe*
Schroder, William. *Pea soup and serpents*
Shepard, Aaron. *The sea king's daughter*
Sierra, Judy. *'Twas the fright before Christmas*
Singer, Marilyn. *Creature carnival*
Small, David. *Paper John*

Steiner, Charlotte. *Red Ridinghood's little lamb*
Takamado no Miya Hisako. *Katie and the dream-eater*
Todd, Barbara. *The rainmaker*
Vojtech, Anna. *Marushka and the Month Brothers*
Wagner, Jenny. *The bunyip of Berkeley's Creek*
Washington, Donna L. *The big, spooky house*
Williams, Suzanne. *The witch casts a spell*
Willis, Val. *The mystery in the bottle*
Wisniewski, David. *Golem*
Wood, Audrey. *The Bunyans*
   The Tickleoctopus
Yolen, Jane. *The firebird*
   Greyling
   Pegasus, the flying horse
   Wings
Zeman, Ludmila. *The first red maple leaf*
Zimelman, Nathan. *To sing a song as big as Ireland*

Mythical creatures – aliens *see* Aliens

Mythical creatures – elves

Adshead, Gladys L. *Brownies – hush!*
   Brownies – it's Christmas
   Brownies – they're moving
Bergen, Lara Rice. *Washington Irving's Rip Van Winkle*
Bernardoni, Robert. *Christmas all over*
Bulette, Sara. *The elf in the singing tree*
Calhoun, Mary. *The runaway brownie*
Cole, Joanna. *Mixed-up magic*
Compton, Kenn. *Happy Christmas to all!*
Cooper, Susan. *Tam Lin*
Cox, Palmer. *Another Brownie book*
   The Brownies
Davis, Maggie S. *Grandma's secret letter*
De Groat, Diane. *Lola the elf*
Dubowski, Cathy East. *The Christmas Santa almost missed*
Dürr, Ursula. *The secret of Trembleton Hall*
Elves, fairies and gnomes
Grimm, Jacob. *The elves and the shoemaker*, ill. by Doug Cushman
   The elves and the shoemaker, ill. by Paul Galdone
   The elves and the shoemaker, ill. by Margaret Walty
   The elves and the shoemaker, ill. by Bernadette Watts
   The shoemaker and his elves, ill. by Bill Dickson
   The shoemaker and the elves, ill. by Adrienne Adams
   The shoemaker and the elves, ill. by Cynthia and William Birrer
   The shoemaker and the elves, ill. by Ilse Plume
Haidle, Elizabeth. *Elmer the grump*
Irving, Washington. *Rip Van Winkle*, ill. by John Howe
   Rip Van Winkle, ill. by Thomas Locker
   Rip Van Winkle, ill. by Peter Wingham
Joyce, William. *The Leaf Men and the brave good bugs*
Krensky, Stephen. *How Santa lost his job*
Kunnas, Mauri. *Santa Claus and his elves*
   Twelve gifts for Santa Claus
Lowell, Susan. *The bootmaker and the elves*
Maconie, Robin. *Alice and her fabulous teeth*
May, Robert Lewis. *Rudolph the red-nosed reindeer*, ill. by Diana Magnuson
   Rudolph the red-nosed reindeer, ill. by David Wenzel
Minarik, Else Holmelund. *The little giant girl and the elf boys*
Norby, Lisa. *The Herself the elf storybook*
Novak, Matt. *The last Christmas present*
Smith, Mary. *Long ago elf*
Wahl, Jan. *Elf night*
Williams, Sam. *Angel's Christmas cookies*
   Snowy magic
Yolen, Jane. *Elfabet*

Mythical creatures – genies

Giovanni, Nikki. *The genie in the jar*
Hutchins, H. J. (Hazel J.). *Leanna builds a genie trap*
Jeschke, Susan. *Mia, Grandma and the genie*
Sunami, Kitoba. *How the fisherman tricked the genie*

Mythical creatures – gnomes

Elves, fairies and gnomes
Farmer, Nancy. *Runnery granary*
Grimm, Jacob. *The earth gnome*
Henterly, Jamichael. *Good night, garden gnome*
Lester, Helen. *Pookins gets her way*
Maris, Ron. *Bernard's boring day*
Smith, Mary. *Long ago elf*

Mythical creatures – goblins

Alexander, Lloyd. *The house Gobbaleen*
Alexander, Sue. *More Witch, Goblin, and Ghost stories*
   Who goes out on Halloween?
   Witch, Goblin and Ghost are back
   Witch, Goblin, and Ghost in the haunted woods
   Witch, Goblin and sometimes Ghost
Bang, Molly. *The goblins giggle and other stories*
Blazek, Sarah Kirwan. *An Irish Hallowe'en*
Bunting, Eve (Anne Evelyn). *Scary, scary Halloween*
Calhoun, Mary. *The goblin under the stairs*
De Paola, Tomie (Thomas Anthony). *Jamie O'Rourke and the pooka*
Doyle, Malachy. *Hungry! Hungry! Hungry!*
Haley, Gail E. *Go away, stay away*
Heller, Nicholas. *Goblins in green*
Impey, Rose. *The flat man*
Johnston, Tony. *Four scary stories*
   Goblin walk
Kimmel, Eric A. *Hershel and the Hanukkah goblins*
Lifton, Betty Jean. *Joji and the Amanojaku*
Mills, Lauren A. *Tatterhood and the hobgoblins*
Schertle, Alice. *Bill and the google-eyed goblins*
Sendak, Maurice. *Outside over there*
Tobias, Tobi. *Chasing the goblins away*

Mythical creatures – griffins

Marston, Elsa. *A griffin in the garden*

Mythical creatures – imps

Baruch, Dorothy. *Kappa's tug-of-war with the big brown horse*
Mills, Lauren A. *Fin and the imp*

Mythical creatures – kelpies

Duncan, Jane. *Janet Reachfar and the kelpie*

Mythical creatures – leprechauns

Balian, Lorna. *Leprechauns never lie*
Bateman, Teresa. *Leprechaun gold*
Calhoun, Mary. *The hungry leprechaun*
Chase, Mary. *The wicked, wicked ladies in the haunted house*
De Paola, Tomie (Thomas Anthony). *Jamie O'Rourke and the big potato*
Dillon, Jana. *Lucky O'Leprechaun*
   Lucky O'Leprechaun comes to America
   Lucky O'Leprechaun in school
Edwards, Pamela Duncan. *The leprechaun's gold*
Hänel, Wolfram. *The gold at the end of the rainbow*
Kennedy, Richard. *The leprechaun's story*
Landau, Elaine. *St. Patrick's Day*
Shub, Elizabeth. *Seeing is believing*
Shute, Linda. *Clever Tom and the leprechaun*
Tucker, Kathy. *The leprechaun in the basement*
Welling, Peter J. *Shawn O'Hisser, the last snake in Ireland*

Mythical creatures – lutins

Willey, Margaret. *Clever Beatrice and the best little pony*

Mythical creatures – menehunes

Funai, Mamoru. *Moke and Poki in the rain forest*

Mythical creatures – mermaids, mermen

Andersen, H. C. (Hans Christian). *The little mermaid*, ill. by Charlene DeLage
   The little mermaid, ill. by Edward Frascino
   The little mermaid, ill. by Michael Hague
   The little mermaid, ill. by Rachel Isadora
   The little mermaid, ill. by Chihiro Iwasaki
   The little mermaid, ill. by Dorothy Pulis Lathrop
   The little mermaid, ill. by Darcy May
   The little mermaid, ill. by Josef Palecek
   The little mermaid, ill. by Daniel San Souci
   The little mermaid, ill. by Katie Thamer Treherne
Bateman, Teresa. *The merbaby*
Binnamin, Vivian. *The case of the mysterious mermaid*
Clibbon, Meg. *Imagine you're a mermaid!*
Haley, Gail E. *Sea tale*
Minters, Frances. *Princess Fishtail*
Noble, Trinka Hakes. *Hansy's mermaid*
Nones, Eric Jon. *Caleb's friend*
Pitcher, Caroline. *Mariana and the merchild*
San Souci, Robert D. *Nicholas Pipe*
   Sukey and the mermaid
Spang, Günter. *Clelia and the little mermaid*
Tamar, Erika. *Donnatalee*
Willis, Jeanne. *Do little mermaids wet their beds*

Mythical creatures – ogres

Domanska, Janina. *Palmiero and the ogre*
Hamilton, Morse. *Belching Hill*
Heller, Nicholas. *Ogres! ogres! ogres!*
Lorenz, Lee. *The feathered ogre*
Prelutsky, Jack. *Awful Ogre's awful day*
San Souci, Robert D. *Little Pierre*
   The silver charm
Sierra, Judy. *Tasty baby belly buttons*
Solotareff, Grégoire. *Never trust an ogre*
   The ogre and the frog king
Ungerer, Tomi. *Zeralda's ogre*
Willard, Nancy. *Shadow story*

Mythical creatures – Pegasus

Mason, Jane B. *The flying horse*
Mayer, Marianna. *Pegasus*
Yolen, Jane. *Pegasus, the flying horse*

Mythical creatures – phoenix

Greene, Ellin. *Ling-li and the phoenix fairy*
Todaro, John. *Phillip the flower-eating phoenix*

Mythical creatures – pixies

Barrie, J. M. (James M.). *Peter Pan*
Calhoun, Mary. *The pixy and the lazy housewife*
Kushner, Donn. *Peter's pixie*

Mythical creatures – pooka spirit

De Paola, Tomie (Thomas Anthony). *Jamie O'Rourke and the big potato*
McDermott, Gerald. *Daniel O'Rourke*

Mythical creatures – sandman

Christiana, David. *A Tooth Fairy's tale*
Laimgruber, Monika. *Susannah and the Sandman*
Shepperson, Rob. *The sandman*
Strahl, Rudi. *Sandman in the lighthouse*
Twining, Edith. *Sandman*
Weigelt, Udo. *The Sandman*

Mythical creatures – selkies

Cooper, Susan. *The Selkie girl*
McClure, Gillian. *Selkie*

MacGill-Callahan, Sheila. *The seal prince*

Mythical creatures – trolls

Aardema, Verna. *Bimwili and the Zimwi*
Asbjørnsen, P. C. (Peter Christen). *Billy goats Gruff*, ill. by Wendy Edelson
   Billy goats Gruff, ill. by Susan Hellard
   The three billy goats Gruff, ill. by Tim Arnold
   The three billy goats Gruff, ill. by Robert Bender
   The three billy goats Gruff, ill. by Marcia Brown
   The three billy goats Gruff, ill. by Stephen Carpenter
   Three billy goats Gruff, ill. by Tom Dunnington
   The three billy goats Gruff, ill. by Paul Galdone
   The three billy goats Gruff, ill. by David Jorgensen
   The three billy goats Gruff, ill. by Dennis Kendrick
   The three billygoats Gruff, ill. Eric Kincaid
   Three billy goats Gruff, ill. by Thea Kliros
   The three billy goats Gruff, ill. by Jonathan Langley
   The three billy goats Gruff, ill. by Loretta Lustig
   The three billy goats Gruff, ill. by Thomas Newbury
   The three billy goats Gruff, ill. by Lilian Obligado
   The three billy goats Gruff, ill. by Ed Parker
   The three billy goats Gruff, ill. by Heidi Petach
   The three billy goats Gruff, ill. by Laura Rader
   The three billy goats Gruff, ill. by Glen Rounds
   The three billy goats Gruff, ill. by Janet Stevens
   The three billy goats Gruff, ill. by William Stobbs
   The three billy goats Gruff, ill. by Svend Otto S
   The truth about three billy goats Gruff
Aulaire, Ingri Mortenson d'. *The terrible troll-bird*
Ayers, Rebecca Hickox. *Per and the Dala horse*
Berenstain, Michael. *The troll book*
Brett, Jan. *Christmas trolls*
   Hedgie's surprise
   The trouble with trolls
   Who's that knocking on Christmas eve?
Carrick, Carol. *Melanie*
De Paola, Tomie (Thomas Anthony). *The cat on the Dovrefell*
   Helga's dowry
Dunrea, Olivier. *The trow-wife's treasure*
Grimm, Jacob. *The glass mountain*, ill. by Louisa Bauer
Havill, Juanita. *Kentucky troll*
Hawkes, Kevin. *Then the troll heard the squeak*
Heller, Nicholas. *A troll story*
Herrick, Amy. *Kimbo's marble*
Hillert, Margaret. *The three goats*
Hooks, William H. *The Gruff brothers*
Inkpen, Mick. *This troll, that troll*
Johnston, Tony. *Mole and Troll trim the tree*
Lagerlöf, Selma. *The changeling*
Leedy, Loreen. *The potato party and other troll tales*
Le Guin, Ursula K. *A ride on the red mare's back*
Lindgren, Astrid. *The tomten*
   The tomten and the fox
Lobel, Anita. *The troll music*
McMullan, Kate (Hall). *Hey, Pipsqueak!*
Marshall, Edward. *Troll country*
Martin, Claire. *Boots and the glass mountain*, ill. by Gennady Spirin
Mayer, Mercer. *Terrible troll*
Mills, Lauren A. *Fairy wings*
Minters, Frances. *Princess Fishtail*
Peet, Bill (William Bartlett). *Jethro and Joel were a troll*
Polacco, Patricia. *Oh, look!*
Prelutsky, Jack. *Monday's troll*
Salley, Coleen. *Who's that tripping over my bridge?*
Schertle, Alice. *Hob Goblin and the skeleton*
Svendsen, Carol. *Hulda*
Torgersen, Don Arthur. *The girl who tricked the troll*
   The troll who lived in the lake
Tudor, Tasha. *Corgiville fair*
Vande Velde, Vivian. *Troll teacher*
Wade, Barrie. *The three billy goats gruff*
Wahl, Jan. *Peter and the troll baby*
Walsh, Ellen Stoll. *Jack's tale*
Wittington, Mary K. *Troll games*
Wolff, Patricia Rae. *The toll-bridge troll*

Youngquist, Cathrene Valente. *The three Billygoats Gruff and Mean Calypso Joe*

Mythical creatures – unicorns

Ada, Alma Flor. *The unicorn of the west*
Birrer, Cynthia. *The lady and the unicorn*
Cherry, Lynne. *The dragon and the unicorn*
Coville, Bruce. *Sarah's unicorn*
De Paola, Tomie (Thomas Anthony). *The unicorn and the moon*
Freeman, Jean Todd. *Cynthia and the unicorn*
Greaves, Margaret. *The naming*
Hague, Michael. *Michael Hague's world of unicorns*
Heidbreder, Robert. *I wished for a unicorn*
Ipcar, Dahlov (Zorach). *Sir Addlepate and the unicorn*
McCaughrean, Geraldine. *Unicorns! Unicorns!*
McNaughton, Janet. *Brave Jack and the unicorn*
Mayer, Marianna. *The unicorn alphabet*
    The unicorn and the lake
Mitchell, Adrian. *Nobody rides the unicorn*
Moeri, Louise. *The unicorn and the plow*
Munthe, Adam John. *I believe in unicorns*
Nahas, Sylvaine. *Nicolo's unicorn*
Preussler, Otfried. *The tale of the unicorn*
Sheldon, Dyan. *Unicorn dreams*
Yolen, Jane. *Where have the unicorns gone?*

Mythical creatures – werewolves

Ogburn, Jacqueline K. *Scarlett Angelina Wolverton-Manning*

Nagging *see* Behavior – nagging

Name calling *see* Behavior – name calling

Names

Ackerman, Karen. *Flannery Row*
Alexander, Martha G. *Sabrina*
Bayer, Jane. *A my name is Alice*
Beim, Jerrold. *The smallest boy in the class*
Benton, Robert. *Little brother, no more*
Browner, Richard. *Everyone has a name*
Bryan, Ashley. *Turtle knows your name*
Bunting, Eve (Anne Evelyn). *Girls A to Z*
Capucilli, Alyssa Satin. *Hello, Biscuit!*
Carter, Alden R. *Big brother Dustin*
Catalanotto, Peter. *Matthew A.B.C.*
Child, Lauren. *That pesky rat*
Choi, Yangsook. *The name jar*
Cross, Diana Harding. *Some birds have funny names*
    Some plants have funny names
Davis, Gibbs. *The other Emily*
De Paola, Tomie (Thomas Anthony). *Andy (that's my name)*
    Tom
Dragonwagon, Crescent. *Wind Rose*
Du Quette, Keith. *They call me Woolly*
Engel, Diana. *Josephina hates her name*
Goffstein, M. B. (Marilyn Brooke). *School of names*
Greaves, Margaret. *The naming*
Henkes, Kevin. *Chrysanthemum*
Hinton, S. E. *Big David, Little David*
Hoban, Julia. *Quick chick*
Hogan, Inez. *About Nono, the baby elephant*
Inkpen, Mick. *Nothing*
Jacobs, Shannon K. *The boy who loved morning*
Johnson, Janice (Janice Kay). *Rosamund*
Kraus, Robert. *Squirmy's big secret*
Kroll, Virginia L. *The seasons and someone*

Lester, Helen. *A porcupine named Fluffy*
Lester, Robin. *Roy Foy's special name*
Low, Joseph. *Adam's book of odd creatures*
Lyne, Alice. *A, my name is . . .*
McFall, Gardner. *Naming the animals*
McKee, David. *Two can toucan*
MacLachlan, Patricia. *Three names*
McQuade, Jacqueline. *Big babies*
Martin, Mary Jane. *From Anne to Zach*
Monk, Isabell. *Hope*
Mosel, Arlene. *Tikki Tikki Tembo*
Moser, Barry. *Tucker Pfeffercorn*
Most, Bernard. *Catbirds and dogfish*
    A dinosaur named after me
Munsch, Robert N. *From far away*
Norac, Carl. *Hello, sweetie pie*
Norman, Howard A. *Who-Paddled-Backward-With-Trout*
Oppenheim, Shulamith Levey. *The hundredth name*
Parish, Peggy. *Little Indian*
Peterson, Scott K. *What's your name?*
Pitre, Felix. *Paco and the witch*
Pringle, Laurence P. *Naming the cat*
Raskin, Ellen. *A & The*
Recorvits, Helen. *My name is Yoon*
Reynolds, Marilynn. *The name of the child*
Rice, Eve. *Ebbie*
Root, Phyllis. *The name quilt*
Rubin, C. M. *Eleanor, Ellatony, Ellencake, and me*
Ryan, Pam Muñoz. *A pinky is a baby mouse, and other baby animal names*
Sadu, Itah. *Christopher changes his name*
Sanders, Marilyn. *What's your name?*
Sasso, Sandy Eisenberg. *In God's name*
Shah, Idries. *The boy without a name*
Swanson, Susan Marie. *The first thing my mama told me*
Tom Tit Tot. *Tom Tit Tot*
Vreeken, Elizabeth. *The boy who would not say his name*
Waber, Bernard. *But names will never hurt me*
    A lion named Shirley Williamson
Walsh, Jill Paton. *Pepi and the secret names*
Watkins, Sherrin. *White Bead Ceremony*
White, Carolyn. *Whuppity Stoorie*
Whybrow, Ian. *Harry and the bucketful of dinosaurs*
Wilkowski, Susan. *Baby's Bris*
Williams, Jay. *I wish I had another name*
Williams, Suzanne. *Mommy doesn't know my name*
Wilson, Sarah. *Good zap, little grog*
Wold, Jo Anne. *Tell them my name is Amanda*
Wolf, Janet. *Adelaide to Zeke*

Namibia *see* Foreign lands – Namibia

Nanticoke Indians *see* Indians of North America – Nanticoke

Napping *see* Sleep

Narragansett Indians *see* Indians of North America – Narragansett

Native Americans *see* Eskimos; Indians of Central America; Indians of North America; Indians of South America

Nativity *see* Religion – Nativity

Nature

Alarcón, Francisco X. *From the bellybutton of the moon and other summer poems / poemas = Del ombligo de la luna y otros poemas de verano / poemas*
Alexander, Cecil Frances. *All things bright and beautiful*, ill. by Leo Politi
    All things bright and beautiful, ill. by Anna Vojtech
    All things bright and beautiful, ill. by Bruce Whatley

Alexander, Martha G. *Where does the sky end, Grandpa?*
Alexander, Sue. *One more time, Mama*
Allen, Marjorie N. *Changes*
Aragon, Jane Chelsea. *Salt hands*
Arnold, Katya. *Let's find it!*
Arnosky, Jim. *Come out, muskrats*
   Crinkleroot's guide to knowing animal habitats
   Crinkleroot's guide to knowing the trees
   Crinkleroot's guide to walking in wild places
   Crinkleroot's 25 birds every child should know
   Crinkleroot's 25 fish every child should know
   Crinkleroot's 25 mammals every child should know
   Crinkleroot's visit to Crinkle Cove
   I see animals hiding
Asch, Frank. *The earth and I*
   Water
Ayres, Pam. *When dad cuts down the chestnut tree*
   When dad fills in the garden pond
Bailey, Jill. *The life cycle of a spider*
Baker, Alan. *Two tiny mice*
Baker, Sanna Anderson. *Mississippi going north*
Banks, Merry. *Animals of the night*
Bare, Colleen Stanley. *Never grab a deer by the ear*
Bash, Barbara. *Urban roosts*
Baskwill, Jane. *Somewhere*
Bastin, Marjolein. *Vera's special hobbies*
Baylor, Byrd. *I'm in charge of celebrations*
   The other way to listen
   The table where rich people sit
Bendick, Jeanne. *All around you*
Bennett, Rowena. *Songs from around a toadstool table*
Benson, Laura Lee. *This is our earth*
Berenstain, Stan. *The Berenstain bears and the wild, wild honey*
Berger, Melvin. *Look out for turtles!*
Bernhard, Durga. *Alphabeasts*
   Earth, sky, wet, dry
Bernhard, Emery. *Dragonfly*
   Eagles
   Ladybug
   The way of the willow branch
Biro, Maureen Boyd. *Walking with Maga*
Blake, Robert J. *The perfect spot*
Bliss, Corinne Demas. *Matthew's meadow*
Bloxam, Frances. *Antlers forever!*
Blyler, Allison. *Finding foxes*
Bornstein, Ruth Lercher. *Rabbit's good news*
Bowen, Betsy. *Antler, bear, canoe*
   Tracks in the wild
Boyle, Doe. *Summer coat, winter coat*
Brenner, Barbara A. *Two orphan cubs*
Brownell, Barbara. *Spin's really wild U.S.A. tour*
Bruchac, Joseph. *The circle of thanks*
Bryan, Ashley. *Sing to the sun*
Bunting, Eve (Anne Evelyn). *Anna's table*
   Moonstick
   Peepers
   Secret place
Burke, Katie. *Lightning bug thunder*
Burton, Jane. *Animals at home*
   Animals at night
   Animals at rest
   Animals at work
   Animals eating
   Animals fighting
   Animals keeping clean
   Animals keeping cool
   Animals keeping safe
   Animals keeping warm
   Animals learning
   Animals talking
Bush, Barbara. *In the heart of the village*
Campbell, Rod. *Buster's afternoon*
Capucilli, Alyssa Satin. *Good morning, pond*
Carlstrom, Nancy White. *Northern lullaby*
   What does the sky say?
Carter, Anne Laurel. *Molly in danger*
   Scurry's treasure

Chaikin, Miriam. *Don't step on the sky*
Chall, Marsha Wilson. *Up north at the cabin*
Cherry, Lynne. *A river ran wild*
Chester, Jonathan. *Splash!*
Clay, Pat. *Ants*
Cole, Babette. *Supermoo!*
Cole, Henry. *I took a walk*
Cooke, Trish. *The grandad tree*
Cooner, Donna D. (Donna Danell). *The world God made*
Cooper, Ann (Ann C.). *In the forest*
Cousins, Lucy. *Za-Za's baby brother*
Cousteau Society. *Albatross*
   Dolphins
   Manatees
   Otters
   Penguins
   Seals
   Turtles
   Whales
Crewe, Sabrina. *The bear*
   The bee
Davies, Kay. *My apple*
DeMunn, Michael. *The earth is good*
Diviny, Sean. *Snow inside the house*
Doolittle, Bev. *The forest has eyes*
   Reading the wild
Drawson, Blair. *Mary Margaret's tree*
Dunbar, Joyce. *Why is the sky up?*
Eaton, Deborah. *The rainy day grump*
Ernst, Lisa Campbell. *Wake up, it's Spring!*
Esbensen, Barbara Juster. *Dance with me*
   Echoes for the eye
Facklam, Margery. *Only a star*
Farjeon, Eleanor. *Between the earth and sun*
Feldman, Judy. *The alphabet in nature*
   Shapes in nature
Fife, Dale. *Empty lot*
Fish, Helen Dean. *When the root children wake up*, published by Lippincott, 1930
   When the root children wake up, published by Green Tiger Pr., 1988
Fisher, Aileen Lucia. *Like nothing at all*
Flatt, Lizann. *My first nature treasury*
Fleming, Denise. *In the tall, tall grass*
   Where once there was a wood
Fleming, Virginia M. *Be good to Eddie Lee*
Fletcher, Ralph J. *Hello, harvest moon*
Florian, Douglas. *Nature walk*
Ford, Miela. *Sunflower*
Gackenbach, Dick. *Mighty tree*
Ganeri, Anita. *The hunt for food*
Gans, Roma. *How do birds find their way?*
George, Jean Craighead. *Dear Rebecca, winter is here*
   Everglades
George, Kristine O'Connell. *The great frog race and other poems*
George, Lindsay Barrett. *Around the pond*
   In the woods
George, William T. *Beaver at Long Pond*
   Box turtle at Long Pond
   Christmas at Long Pond
Geraghty, Paul. *Over the steamy swamp*
Ghigna, Charles. *Haiku, the travelers of eternity*
Gill, Shelley. *The egg*
Giovanni, Nikki. *The sun is so quiet*
Glaser, Linda. *Compost!*
   It's fall
   It's spring
   It's summer
   It's winter
   Our big home
   Wonderful worms
Goble, Paul. *I sing for the animals*
Godkin, Celia. *What about ladybugs?*
Gomi, Taro. *Everyone poops*
Gouck, Maura. *Mountain lions*
Graham, Bob. *The wild*
Greeley, Valerie. *White is the moon*

Winter whale
San Souci, Robert D. *The birds of Killingworth*
Sarton, May. *A walk through the woods*
Schaefer, Lola M. *This is the sunflower*
Schimmel, Schim. *The family of earth*
Schnur, Steven. *Spring thaw*
Schoenherr, John. *Bear*
Schulz, Charles M. *Snoopy's facts and fun book about nature*
Schweninger, Ann. *Summertime*
Selsam, Millicent E. *How to be a nature detective*
Seymour, Peter S. *What's at the beach?*
Shulevitz, Uri. *Snow*
Siddals, Mary McKenna. *I'll play with you*
Siebert, Diane. *Sierra*
Simmons, Jane. *Come along, Daisy!*
Simon, Seymour. *Icebergs and glaciers*
Singer, Marilyn. *Turtle in July*
Skofield, James. *Crow moon, worm moon*
Sohi, Morteza E. *Look what I did with a leaf!*
The song of the Three Holy Children
Speed, Toby. *Watervoices*
Stafford, Kim Robert. *We got here together*
Stiles, Martha Bennett. *Island magic*
Stone, Phoebe. *When the Wind Bears go dancing*
Stroud, Virginia A. *A walk to the Great Mystery*
Suzuki, David. *Salmon forest*
Swamp, Jake. *Giving thanks*
Sweetland, Nancy Rose. *God's quiet things*
Swinburne, Stephen R. *Lots and lots of zebra stripes*
What color is nature?
Tafuri, Nancy. *What the sun sees / What the moon sees*
Taylor, Kim. *Too fast to see*
Too small to see
Tejima, Keizaburo. *Owl lake*
Woodpecker forest
Thornhill, Jan. *Wildlife ABC*
The wildlife 1-2-3
Tomecek, Steve. *Dirt*
Tucker, Sian. *Going out*
Waboose, Jan Bourdeau. *Morning on the lake*
Wahl, Jan. *My cat Ginger*
Wallace, Karen. *Bears in the forest*
Scarlette Beane
Walsh, Melanie. *Do donkeys dance?*
Walters, Catherine. *When will it be spring?*
Ward, Leila. *I am eyes, ni macho*
Watts, Barrie. *Apple tree*
Weiss, George (George David). *What a wonderful world*
Wells, Rosemary. *Forest of dreams*
Weninger, Brigitte. *Precious water*
Wildsmith, Brian. *Seasons*
Williams, David. *Walking to the creek*
Willington, Monica. *Seasons of swans*
Wilson, Ron. *Mice*
Winters, Kay. *Tiger trail*
Wolf watch
Winton, Tim. *The deep*
Wood, Audrey. *The Bunyans*
When the root children wake up
Wood, Douglas. *Grandad's prayers of the earth*
Making the world
Wood, Jakki. *Across the big blue sea*
Wood, Jenny. *The animal kingdom*
Wyler, Rose. *Puddles and ponds*
Yerxa, Leo. *Last leaf first snowflake to fall*
Yolen, Jane. *Welcome to the icehouse*
Yoshida, Toshi. *Rhinoceros mother*
Ziefert, Harriet. *Sarah's questions*
Zolotow, Charlotte (Shapiro). *Say it!*
The song
When the wind stops
Zoo animals
Zweifel, Frances W. *Animal baby-sitters*

Naughty *see* Behavior – misbehavior

Navajo Indians *see* Indians of North America – Navajo

Navels *see* Anatomy – navels

Neckties *see* Clothing – neckties

Needing someone *see* Behavior – needing someone

Negotiation *see* Activities – trading

Neighborhoods *see* Communities, neighborhoods

Nepal *see* Foreign lands – Nepal

Netherlands *see* Foreign lands – Holland

New Guinea *see* Foreign lands – New Guinea

New Year's *see* Holidays – New Year's

New Zealand *see* Foreign lands – New Zealand

Nez Perce Indians *see* Indians of North America – Nez Perce

Nicaragua *see* Foreign lands – Nicaragua

Nigeria *see* Foreign lands – Nigeria

Night

Ackerman, Karen. *The banshee*
Adlerman, Daniel. *Africa calling*
Adoff, Arnold. *Daring Dog and Captain Cat*
Make a circle, keep us in
Ahlberg, Allan. *Mystery tour*
Ahlberg, Janet. *Funnybones*
Alexander, Anne (Anna Barbara Cooke). *Noise in the night*
Alexander, Martha G. *Maggie's moon*
We're in big trouble, Blackboard Bear
You're a genius, Blackboard Bear
Aliki. *Overnight at Mary Bloom's*
Anholt, Laurence. *Jack and the dreamsack*
Anrooy, Frans van. *The sea horse*
Appelt, Kathi. *Bayou lullaby*
Cowboy dreams
Apperley, Dawn. *Blossom and Boo stay up late*
Good night, sleep tight, little bunnies
Apple, Margot. *Brave Martha*
Aragon, Jane Chelsea. *Salt hands*
Winter harvest
Ardizzone, Aingelda. *The night ride*
Armitage, Ronda. *One moonlit night*
Arnold, Tedd. *Huggly gets dressed*
Huggly takes a bath
Arnosky, Jim. *All night near the water*
Raccoons and ripe corn
Artis, Vicki Kimmel. *Pajama walking*
Asch, Frank. *Moonbear*
Ashman, Linda. *How to make a night*
Axworthy, Anni. *Ben's Wednesday*
Aylesworth, Jim. *The good-night kiss*
Through the night
Tonight's the night
Two terrible frights
Babbitt, Natalie. *The something*
Baker, Ken. *Brave little monster*
Ballard, Robin. *Tonight and tomorrow*
Balzola, Asun. *Munia and the moon*
Bandes, Hanna. *Sleepy river*
Banks, Kate (Katherine A.). *And if the moon could talk*
Banks, Merry. *Animals of the night*
Bannon, Laura. *Little people of the night*
Bartels, Alice L. *The beast*

Baumgart, Klaus. *The little green dragon steps out*
Beames, Margaret. *Night cat*
Beck, Andrea. *Elliot's noisy night*
Bennett, Rainey. *After the sun goes down*
Berends, Polly Berrien. *Ladybug and dog and the night walk*
Berenstain, Stan. *Bears in the night*
　The Berenstain bears in the dark
Berg, Jean Horton. *The wee little man*
Berlan, Kathryn Hook. *Andrew's amazing monsters*
Bilezikian, Gary. *While I slept*
Bird, Malcolm. *The school in Murky Wood*
Birdseye, Tom. *Oh yeah!*
Blocksma, Mary. *Did you hear that?*
Bogacki, Tomasz. *Cat and mouse in the night*
Bolliger, Max. *The fireflies*
Bond, Felicia. *Poinsettia and the firefighters*
Bonsall, Crosby Newell. *Who's afraid of the dark?*
Bourgeois, Paulette. *Franklin in the dark*
Bowman, Pete. *Goodnight, teddy bear*
Boyd, Lizi. *Sweet dreams, Willy*
Bradbury, Ray. *Switch on the night*, ill. by Leo and Diane Dillion
　Switch on the night, ill. by Madeleine Gekiere
Brandenberg, Franz. *A robber! A robber!*
Brown, Margaret Wise. *A child's good night book*
　Little Donkey close your eyes
　Night and day
　On Christmas eve, ill. by Nancy Edwards Calder
　On Christmas eve, ill. by Beni Montresor
　Wait till the moon is full
Brown, Myra Berry. *Pip camps out*
Brown, Ruth. *One stormy night*
Buchholz, Quint. *Sleep well, little bear*
Buckley, Paul. *Amy Belligera and the fireflies*
Budney, Blossom. *After dark*
Buehner, Caralyn. *Snowmen at night*
　Snowmen at night [board book]
Bunting, Eve (Anne Evelyn). *Ghost's hour, spook's hour*
Burningham, John. *The blanket*
Burnside, Julian. *Matilda and the dragon*
Burton, Jane. *Animals at night*
Butler, John. *Hush, little ones*
　While you were sleeping
Butterworth, Nick. *One snowy night*
Callen, Larry. *Dashiel and the night*
Carlson, Melody. *When the creepy things come out*
Carman, William. *What's that noise?*
Cass, Joan E. *The cat thief*
Cazet, Denys. *Mother night*
Chapouton, Anne-Marie. *Billy the brave*
Clise, Michele Durkson. *Ophelia's bedtime book*
Cohen, Caron Lee. *Martin and the giant lions*
Cole, Joanna. *Large as life nighttime animals*
Coles, Alison. *Michael in the dark*
Conford, Ellen. *Eugene the brave*
Conrad, Donna. *See you soon, Moon*
Cosgrove, Stephen (Edward). *Sleepy time bunny*
Coy, John. *Night driving*
Crebbin, June. *Fly by night*
Credle, Ellis. *Big fraid, little fraid*
Crews, Donald. *Night at the fair*
Crews, Nina. *I'll catch the moon*
Crowe, Robert L. *Clyde monster*
Cutts, David. *I can read about creatures of the night*
Dale, Penny. *Daisy Rabbit's tree house*
Davies, Nicola. *Bat loves the night*
Davol, Marguerite W. *Batwings and the curtain of night*
Day, Alexandra. *Boswell wide-awake*
　Helping the night
DeLage, Ida. *The old witch and the crows*
　Weeny witch
Delton, Judy. *A walk on a snowy night*
Denslow, Sharon Phillips. *Night owls*
Denton, Kady MacDonald. *Granny is a darling*
Dinardo, Jeffrey. *Timothy and the night noises*
Doherty, Berlie. *The midnight man*
Donaldson, Lois. *Karl's wooden horse*
Dowling, Paul. *The night journey*

Dragonwagon, Crescent. *Half a moon and one whole star*
　When light turns into night
The drowsy hours
Dryden, Emma. *Good morning – good night*
Duncan, Lois. *Horses of dreamland*
　I walk at night
Dupasquier, Philippe. *I can't sleep*
Duvoisin, Roger Antoine. *The missing milkman*
Edwards, Frank B. *Melody Mooner stayed up all night*
Edwards, Michelle. *What's that noise?*
Edwards, Pamela Duncan. *Wake-up kisses*
Edwards, Roland. *Tigers*
Emberley, Barbara. *Night's nice*
Erickson, Karen. *It's dark – but I'm not scared*
Erskine, Jim. *Bedtime story*
Esbensen, Barbara Juster. *The dream mouse*
Farber, Werner. *Night lion*
Faulkner, Keith. *A trick or a treat?*
Fenner, Carol. *Tigers in the cellar*
Field, Susan. *The sun, the moon, and the silver baboon*
Fisher, Aileen Lucia. *In the middle of the night*
Fletcher, Ralph J. *Hello, harvest moon*
Fox, Mem. *Night noises*
Fraser, Mary Ann. *Where are the night animals?*
Freeman, Don. *The night the lights went out*
Funakoshi, Canna. *One evening*
Gabriel, Ashala. *Night night toes*
Gallo, Frank. *Night sounds*
Garelick, May. *Sounds of a summer night*
Gay, Marie-Louise. *Moonbeam on a cat's ear*
Gay, Michel. *Night ride*
George, William T. *Beaver at Long Pond*
Gervais, Bernadette. *Voyage under the stars*
Gibbons, Gail. *Bats*
Gilchrist, Jan Spivey. *Indigo and moonlight gold*
Ginsburg, Mirra. *Asleep, asleep*
　The sun's asleep behind the hill
　Where does the sun go at night?
Goode, Diane. *I hear a noise*
Goodenow, Earle. *The owl who hated the dark*
Graber, Janet. *Jacob and the polar bears*
Grambling, Lois G. *Night sounds*
Greenfield, Eloise. *Night on Neighborhood Street*
Gregory, Valiska. *Kate's giants*
Gretz, Susanna. *Hide-and-seek*
　Too dark!
Grifalconi, Ann. *Darkness and the butterfly*
Grossman, Patricia. *The night ones*
Guthrie, Donna. *Not for babies*
Hague, Kathleen. *Out of the nursery, into the night*
Hamilton, Morse. *Who's afraid of the dark?*
Hamm, Diane Johnston. *Rock-a-bye farm*
Hannan, Peter. *School after dark*
Hargrove, Linda. *Wings across the moon*
Harley, Bill. *Nothing happened*
Harshman, Marc. *All the way to morning*
Haseley, Dennis. *The thieves' market*
Hasler, Eveline. *Winter magic*
Hawes, Judy. *Fireflies in the night*
Hawkins, Colin. *Snap! Snap!*
Hayes, Sarah. *This is the bear and the scary night*
Hazen, Barbara Shook. *The knight who was afraid of the dark*
Heine, Helme. *The marvelous journey through the night*
　Three little friends: the alarm clock
Helldorfer, M. C. (Mary Claire). *Harmonica night*
　Night of the white stag
Henderson, Kathy. *In the middle of the night*
Hendry, Diana. *The very noisy night*
Hertz, Grete Janus. *Olie's bedtime walk*
Hest, Amy. *The midnight eaters*
Higgs, Liz Curtis. *Go away, dark night*
Highwater, Jamake. *Moonsong lullaby*
Hill, Susan. *Beware, beware*
　Go away, bad dreams!
Himmelman, John. *Lights out!*
Hindley, Judy. *The sleepy book*
Hines, Anna Grossnickle. *Sky all around*

Hippely, Hilary Horder. *Adventure on Klickitat Island*
Hirschi, Ron. *When night comes*
Hissey, Jane. *Hoot*
Hoffman, Don. *Good morning, good night Billy and Abigail*
Horácek, Petr. *When the moon smiled*
Hort, Lenny. *How many stars in the sky*
Horwitz, Elinor Lander. *When the sky is like lace*
Hosta, Dar. *I love the night*
Howe, James. *There's a monster under my bed*
Hudson, Cheryl Willis. *Good night baby*
Hurd, Thacher. *A night in the swamp*
    The quiet evening
Huth, Holly Young. *Darkfright*
    Twilight
Impey, Rose. *The ankle grabber*
    The flat man
    Scare yourself to sleep
Ingman, Bruce. *A night on the tiles*
Ipcar, Dahlov (Zorach). *The cat at night*
    The song of the day birds and the night birds
Isadora, Rachel. *A South African night*
Jacobson, Jennifer Richard. *A net of stars*
Jam, Teddy. *Night cars*
James, Betsy. *Flashlight*
Johnson, Angela. *Joshua's night whispers*
Johnston, Tony. *The Chizzywink and the Alamagoozlum*
    Desert song
    Little Rabbit goes to sleep
Jones, Joy. *Tambourine moon*
Jukes, Mavis. *You're a bear*
Kamish, Daniel. *The night scary beasties popped out of my head*
Kandoian, Ellen. *Under the sun*
Kauffman, Lois. *What's that noise?*
Keats, Ezra Jack. *Dreams*
Kenah, Katharine. *The dream shop*
Kessler, Cristina. *One night*
Kinsey-Warnock, Natalie. *On a starry night*
Koenig, Marion. *The wonderful world of night*
Koralek, Jenny. *The boy and the cloth of dreams*
Kovacs, Deborah. *Moonlight on the river*
Kraus, Robert. *Good night little one*
    Good night Richard Rabbit
    See the moon
Krensky, Stephen. *Fraidy Cats*
Kunnas, Mauri. *The nighttime book*
Landalf, Helen. *The secret night world of cats*
LaRose, Linda. *Jessica takes charge*
Larrick, Nancy. *When the dark comes dancing*
Leaf, Munro. *Boo, who used to be scared of the dark*
Lesser, Carolyn. *The goodnight circle*
Lesynski, Loris. *Night school*
Lewison, Wendy Cheyette. *Nighty-night*
Lexau, Joan M. *Millicent's ghost*
Lifton, Betty Jean. *Goodnight orange monster*
Lindbergh, Reeve. *Midnight farm*
Lindgren, Barbro. *The wild baby gets a puppy*
Lionni, Leo. *When?*
Lipniacka, Ewa. *To bed . . . or else!*
Lively, Penelope. *Good night, sleep tight*
Lloyd, Errol. *Nandy's bedtime*
Loewer, H. Peter. *The moonflower*
LoMonaco, Palmyra. *Night letters*
London, Jonathan. *Fireflies, fireflies, light my way*
    Into this night we are rising
    Let the lynx come in
    The owl who became the moon
Lucht, Irmgard. *In this night*
Lullaby moons and a silver spoon
Lyon, David. *The biggest truck*
McDonald, Megan. *My house has stars*
    Whoo-oo is it?
McGinty, Alice B. *Ten little lambs*
McPartland, Suzy. *Sleepy-time moon*
McPhail, David M. *Adam's smile*
    The dream child
McQueen, John Troy. *A world full of monsters*
Maitland, Barbara. *The bear who didn't like honey*

Manushkin, Fran. *Peeping and sleeping*
Martin, Bill (William Ivan). *Barn dance!*
Marton, Jirina. *Midnight visit at Molly's house*
Matus, Greta. *Where are you, Jason?*
Mayer, Mercer. *There's something in my attic*
    You're the scaredy cat
Memling, Carl. *What's in the dark?*
Michelson, Richard. *Did you say ghosts?*
Micucci, Charles. *A little night music*
Miles, Sally. *Alfi and the dark*
Miranda, Anne. *Night songs*
Modesitt, Jeanne. *The night call*
Montgomery, Michael G. *'Night, America*
Moodie, Fiona. *Noko and the night monster*
The moon's the north wind's cooky
Moore, Dessie. *Good night*
Mora, Pat. *Delicious hullabaloo = Pachanga deliciosa*
Morgan, Mary. *My good night book*
Morgan-Vanroyen, Mary. *Night ride*
Morris, Ann. *Cuddle up*
    Eleanora Mousie in the dark
    Kiss time
    Night counting
    Sleepy, sleepy
Murphy, Jill. *What next, baby bear!*
Murphy, Jim. *Backyard bear*
Murray, Marjorie Dennis. *The stars are waiting*
Murray, Martine. *A moose called Mouse*
Mwalimu. *Awful aardvark*
Nayer, Judy. *Night animals*
Newman, Lesléa. *Cats, cats, cats*
Nichol, B. P. *On the merry-go-round*
    Once, a lullaby
Night time
Nikola-Lisa, W. *Night is coming*
Nobisso, Josephine. *The moon's lullaby*
    Shh! the whale is smiling
Nye, Naomi Shihab. *Lullaby raft*
O'Donnell, Peter. *Moonlit journey*
Olofsdotter, Marie. *Sofia and the Heartmender*
Oppenheim, Shulamith Levey. *What is the full moon full of?*
Ormerod, Jan. *Midnight pillow fight*
Osborne, Mary Pope. *Moonhorse*, ill. by David McPhail
    Moonhorse, ill. by S. M. Saelig
Ottley, Matt. *What Faust saw*
Owen, Annie. *Goodnight bear!*
Paraskevas, Betty. *Cecil Bunions and the midnight train*
Pearson, Tracey Campbell. *The howling dog*
Peck, Richard. *Monster night at Grandma's house*
Pedersen, Judy. *When night time comes near*
Percy, Graham. *24 strange little animals in a haunted house*
Peters, Sharon. *Animals at night*
Pettigrew, Eileen. *Night-time*
Pfister, Marcus. *I see the moon*
Pierson, Judith Patterson. *The always moon*
Pilkey, Dav. *The Moonglow Roll-O-Rama*
Pittman, Helena Clare. *Once when I was scared*
Pizer, Abigail. *Harry's night out*
A pocketful of stars
Posey, Lee. *Night rabbits*
Powell, Polly. *Just dessert*
Powell, Roxanne Dyer. *Cat, mouse and moon*
Prater, John. *On top of the world*
Preston, Edna Mitchell. *Monkey in the jungle*
Purmell, Ann. *Where wild babies sleep*
Raschka, Christopher. *Can't sleep*
Rathmann, Peggy. *Good night, Gorilla*
Ray, Deborah Kogan. *Stargazing sky*
Reeves, Mona Rabun. *The spooky eerie night noise*
Reidel, Marlene. *Jacob and the robbers*
Rice, Eve. *City night*
    Goodnight, goodnight
Riddell, Chris. *Mr. Underbed*
Riley, Linnea Asplind. *Mouse mess*
Riordan, James. *The coming of Night*
Ripley, Catherine. *Why do stars twinkle?*
Robbins, Beth. *Tom's afraid of the dark*

Rockwell, Anne F. *The night we slept outside*
Rodriguez, Bobbie. *Sarah's sleepover*
Rohmann, Eric. *The cinder-eyed cats*
Rosenberg, Liz. *Adelaide and the night train*
　Eli's night-light
　Window, mirror, moon
Ross, Michael Elsohn. *Earth cycles*
Roth, Susan L. *Night-time numbers*
Rowand, Phyllis. *It is night*
Rowinski, Kate. *Cats in the dark*
Royston, Angela. *Night-time animals*
Rukeyser, Muriel. *More night*
Ryan, Cheli Durán. *Hildilid's night*
Rydell, Katy. *Wind says good night*
Ryder, Joanne. *The night flight*
　The snail's spell
　Step into the night
Rylant, Cynthia. *Night in the country*
Salter, Mary Jo. *The moon comes home*
Sanromán, Susana. *Señora Reganoña*
Schlein, Miriam. *Here comes night*
Schneider, Nina. *While Susie sleeps*
Schnur, Steven. *Night lights*
Schotter, Roni. *Bunny's night out*
Selsam, Millicent E. *Night animals*
Shipton, Jonathan. *In the night*
Simmons, Jane. *Daisy's favorite things*
Singer, Marilyn. *Quiet night*
Sloat, Teri. *The thing that bothered Farmer Brown*
Somary, Wolfgang. *Night and the candlemaker*
Southwell, Jandelyn. *The little country town*
Spinelli, Eileen. *Night shift daddy*
　Rise the moon
Spohn, David. *Starry night*
Sproule, Gail. *Singing the dark*
Stanley, Diane. *Birdsong lullaby*
Stepto, Michele. *Snuggle Piggy and the magic blanket*
Stevens, Cat. *Teaser and the firecat*
Stevenson, Robert Louis. *The moon*
Stolz, Mary (Mary Slattery). *Storm in the night*
Stone, Kazuko G. *Goodnight Twinklegator*
Strand, Mark. *The night book*
Stubbs, Joanna. *With cat's eyes you'll never be scared of the dark*
Sturges, Philemon. *Ten flashing fireflies*
Tafuri, Nancy. *Do not disturb*
　What the sun sees / What the moon sees
Takamado no Miya Hisako. *Katie and the dream-eater*
Taylor, Anelise. *Lights on, lights off*
Tejima, Keizaburo. *Owl lake*
Thomas, Shelley Moore. *Putting the world to sleep*
Thompson, Lauren. *Little Quack's bedtime*
Thompson, Richard. *I have to see this*
　Jesse on the night train
　The night walker
Thornhill, Jan. *Wild in the city*
Tobias, Tobi. *Chasing the goblins away*
Tomlinson, Jill. *The owl who was afraid of the dark*
Tyers, Jenny. *When it is night and when it is day*
Updike, David. *An autumn tale*
Van Allsburg, Chris. *The polar express*
Vaughan, Marcia Kapok. *Night dancer*
VerDorn, Bethea. *Moon glows*
Vevers, Gwynne. *Animals of the dark*
Waboose, Jan Bourdeau. *Firedancers*
　SkySisters
Waddell, Martin. *The big big sea*
　Can't you sleep, Little Bear?
　Owl babies
　Owl babies [board book]
　The park in the dark
Wahl, Jan. *My cat Ginger*
　The sleepytime book
Wallace, Daisy. *Ghost poems*
Walsh, Ellen Stoll. *Pip's magic*
Walter, Mildred Pitts. *Darkness*
Weir, Alison. *Peter, good night*
Weiss, Nicki. *Where does the brown bear go?*

　Where does the brown bear go? [board book]
Wellington, Monica. *Night city*
　Night rabbits
Westcott, Nadine Bernard. *Going to bed*
Weston, Martha. *Space guys!*
Whatley, Bruce. *Captain Pajamas*
Whitehouse, Patricia. *What's awake? A B C*
　What's awake 1 2 3
Whitman, Candace. *The night is like an animal*
Wiesner, David. *Tuesday*
Wild, Margaret. *Midnight babies*
Willard, Nancy. *Night story*
　The nightgown of the sullen moon
　The well-mannered balloon
Williams, Laura E. *Torch fishing with the sun*
Winnick, Karen B. *Sybil's night ride*
Winthrop, Elizabeth. *Potbellied possums*
Wittington, Mary K. *Troll games*
Wolff, Ashley. *Only the cat saw*
Wood, Audrey. *Moonflute*
Wood, Douglas. *Northwoods cradle song*
Wouters, Anne. *This book is for us*
Wynne-Jones, Tim. *The hour of the frog*
Yaccarino, Dan. *Good night, Mr. Night*
Yeomans, Thomas. *For every child a star*
Yolen, Jane. *Nocturne*
　Owl moon
Zalben, Jane Breskin. *Norton's nighttime*
Ziefert, Harriet. *Hurry up, Jessie!*
　Moonride
　Nicky's noisy night
　Say good night!
Zolotow, Charlotte (Shapiro). *I have a horse of my own*
　Wake up and goodnight
　When the wind stops
　The white marble
　Who is Ben?

Nightingales *see* Birds – nightingales

Nightmares *see also* Bedtime; Monsters; Mythical creatures
　– goblins; Night; Sleep

Karas, G. Brian. *Bebe's bad dream*
Stadler, Alexander. *Beverly Billingsly borrows a book*

Nishnawbe Indians *see* Indians of North America –
　Nishnawbe

Nisqually Indians *see* Indians of North America –
　Nisqually

No text *see* Wordless

Noah *see* Religion – Noah

Nobscusset Indians *see* Indians of North America –
　Nobscusset

Noise, sounds

Ahlberg, Allan. *Crash, bang, wallop!*
Alda, Arlene. *Pig, horse, or cow, don't wake me now*
Alexander, Anne (Anna Barbara Cooke). *Noise in the night*
Alexander, Martha G. *Pigs say oink*
Allard, Harry. *Bumps in the night*
Allen, Pamela. *Bertie and the bear*
Anholt, Catherine. *Chimp and Zee's noisy book*
Arnold, Caroline. *Noisytime for zoo animals*
Arnold, Katya. *Meow!*
Arnold, Tedd. *Sounds*
Asch, Frank. *Barnyard lullaby*
　I can roar
Aylesworth, Jim. *Country crossing*
　Hush up!

Siren in the night
Bassett, Preston R. *Raindrop stories*
Beaton, Clare. *How loud is a lion?*
Beck, Andrea. *Elliot's noisy night*
Beeke, Tiphanie. *Roar like a lion!*
Behn, Harry. *What a beautiful noise*
Benjamin, Alan. *Rat-a-tat, pitter pat*
Bennett, David. *One cow moo moo*
Bennett, Jill. *Noisy poems*
Berenstain, Stan. *Bears in the night*
Berg, Jean Horton. *The noisy clock shop*
The wee little man
Berkes, Marianne Collins. *Marsh music*
Big noisy trucks and diggers
Bilezikian, Gary. *While I slept*
Blanchard, Arlene. *Sounds my feet make*
Blocksma, Mary. *Did you hear that?*
Bock, Lee. *Oh, crumps! = Ay, caramba!*
Bond, Felicia. *Poinsettia and the firefighters*
Bond, Rebecca. *Bravo, Maurice!*
Borten, Helen. *Do you hear what I hear?*
Boynton, Sandra. *Moo, baa, la la la!*
Brandenberg, Franz. *Cock-a-doodle-doo*
A robber! A robber!
Branley, Franklyn M. (Mansfield). *High sounds, low sounds*
Breeze, Lynn. *Baby's animals*
Baby's clothes
Bright, Paul. *Quiet!*
Bright, Robert. *Georgie and the noisy ghost*
Gregory, the noisiest and strongest boy in Grangers Grove
Brodmann, Aliana. *Such a noise!*
Brown, Craig McFarland. *City sounds*
Brown, Jane Clark. *Whonk, and whonk again*
Brown, Margaret Wise. *Bunny's noisy book*
Bunny's noisy book [board book]
The country noisy book
Five little firemen
The indoor noisy book
Noisy book
The quiet noisy book
The seashore noisy book
SHHhhh . . . . Bang
The summer noisy book
The winter noisy book
Bruss, Deborah. *Book! book! book!*
Burningham, John. *Cluck baa*
Jangle twang
Skip trip
Slam bang
Sniff shout
Wobble pop
Burton, Jane. *Animals talking*
Cabrera, Jane. *Rory and the lion*
Capucilli, Alyssa Satin. *Inside a barn in the country*
Carle, Eric. *My very first book of sounds*
The very quiet cricket
Carman, William. *What's that noise?*
Carter, David A. *Old MacDonald had a farm*
Caseley, Judith. *The noisemakers*
Casey, Patricia. *Beep! Beep! Oink! Oink! animals in the city*
Cluck cluck
Causley, Charles. *"Quack!" said the billy-goat*
Cazet, Denys. *Dancing*
Nothing at all
Christiansen, C. B. *Mara in the morning*
Chukovskii, Kornei Ivanovich. *Good morning, chick*
Cleary, Beverly. *The hullabaloo ABC*, ill. by Ted Rand
The hullabaloo ABC, ill. by Earl Thollander
Coffelt, Nancy. *The dog who cried woof*
Cole, Joanna. *It's too noisy*
Compton, Kenn. *Granny Greenteeth and the noise in the night*
Conrad, Pam. *Animal lingo*
Cousins, Lucy. *Maisy's noisy day*
What can Pinky hear?
What can rabbit hear?
Cowley, Stewart. *"Tweet, tweet, tweet"*
What's that sound?

Coy, John. *Vroomaloom zoom*
Crowe, Robert L. *Tyler Toad and the thunder*
Crowther, Robert. *Animal rap!*
Dallas-Conte, Juliet. *Cock-a-moo-moo*
Dalton, Cindy Devine. *Sound*
Davis, Katie (Katie I.). *Who hoots?*
Davol, Marguerite W. *The loudest, fastest, best drummer in Kansas*
Why butterflies go by on silent wings
DeLage, Ida. *The old witch and the snores*
Demarest, Chris L. *Farmer Nat*
Honk!
DeRubertis, Barbara. *Janey Crane*
Joey Goat
Suzy Mule
Tiny Tiger
Zeely Zebra
De Zutter, Hank. *Who says a dog goes bow-wow?*
Diller, Harriett. *Big band sound*
Dinardo, Jeffrey. *Timothy and the night noises*
Dodd, Emma. *Dog's noisy day*
Dodds, Dayle Ann. *Do bunnies talk?*
Doepker, David. *Farm babies*
Domanska, Janina. *Why so much noise?*
Dubov, Christine Salac. *Ding dong! and other sounds*
Knock! and other sounds
Oink! and other sounds
Durant, Alan. *Snake supper*
Duvoisin, Roger Antoine. *Petunia and the song*
Edwards, Michelle. *What's that noise?*
Edwards, Pamela Duncan. *Slop goes the soup*
Emberley, Ed (Edward Randolph). *Sounds*
Emberley, Rebecca. *City sounds*
Jungle sounds
Evans, Mel. *The tiniest sound*
Farber, Norma. *There once was a woman who married a man*
Faulkner, Keith. *Do you have my quack?*
Feiffer, Jules. *Bark, George*
Fernandes, Eugenie. *Busy Little Mouse*
Fleming, Candace. *When Agnes caws*
Fleming, Denise. *Barnyard banter*
Forrester, Victoria. *The magnificent moo*
Fowler, Richard. *Mr. Little's noisy car*
Mr. Little's noisy fire engine
Mr. Little's noisy truck
Fox, Mem. *Night noises*
Freedman, Claire. *Hushabye Lily*
Fuge, Charles. *Yip! Snap! Yap!*
Fujita, Miho. *The little choo-choo*
Gaeddert, LouAnn Bigge. *Noisy Nancy Norris*
Galdone, Paul. *Cat goes fiddle-i-fee*
Gallo, Frank. *Bird calls*
Night sounds
Gannett, Ruth Stiles. *Katie and the sad noise*
Garelick, May. *Sounds of a summer night*
Geisert, Arthur. *Oink*
Geraghty, Paul. *The great green forest*
Stop that noise!
Gershator, David. *Moon rooster*
Giffard, Hannah. *Hens say cluck*
Giglio, Judy. *The tapping tale*
Godwin, Laura. *What the baby hears*
Graff, Nancy Price. *In the hush of the evening*
Graham, John. *A crowd of cows*
Grambling, Lois G. *Night sounds*
Greene, Rhonda Gowler. *Barnyard song*
Grossman, Bill. *The banging book*
Gundersheimer, Karen. *Find cat, wear hat*
Splish splash bang crash!
Hancock, Joy Elizabeth. *The loudest little lion*
Hänel, Wolfram. *Little elephant's song*
Harper, Jessica. *Nora's room*
Harrison, David Lee. *The animals' song*
Harshman, Marc. *All the way to morning*
Hays, Anna Jane. *The pup speaks up*
Hendry, Diana. *The very noisy night*
Henley, Claire. *Quack, quack*
Heo, Yumi. *One afternoon*

Rowinski, Kate. *Cats in the dark*
Runcie, Jill. *Cock-a-doodle-doo*
Saltzberg, Barney. *It must have been the wind*
Scharer, Niko. *Emily's house*
Scheffler, Ursel. *Stop your crowing, Kasimir!*
Scruggs, Afi. *Jump rope magic*
Serfozo, Mary. *Rain talk*
Seuss, Dr. *Gerald McBoing Boing*
   Gerald McBoing Boing sound book
   Mr. Brown can moo! Can you?
Seymour, Tres. *Too quiet for these old bones*
Shapiro, Arnold L. *Who says that?*
Shaw, Nancy (Nancy E.). *Raccoon tune*
Sheppard, Jeff. *Splash, splash*
Shirotani, Hideo. *Sounds*
Showers, Paul. *Hear your heart*
   The listening walk
Sicotte, Virginia. *A riot of quiet*
Simmons, Jane. *Daisy says Coo!*
   Daisy says, "If you're happy and you know it"
   Daisy, the little duck with big feet
   Daisy's day out
   Daisy's hide-and-seek
   Go to sleep, Daisy
   Quack, Daisy, quack!
Simms, Laura. *The squeaky door*
Simon, Francesca. *But what does the hippopotamus say?*
Singer, Marilyn. *Quiet night*
Skaar, Grace Marion. *What do the animals say?*
Skolsky, Mindy Warshaw. *Hannah and the whistling tea kettle*
Slingsby, Janet. *Hush-a-bye babies*
Sloat, Teri. *Farmer Brown goes round and round*
   The thing that bothered Farmer Brown
Slobodkin, Louis. *Colette and the princess*
Smith, Barry. *Grandma Rabbitty's visit*
Snow, Alan. *Cluck!*
   The monster book of ABC sounds
   Oink!
   Quack!
   Woof!
Southwell, Jandelyn. *The little country town*
Spence, Robert, III. *Clickety clack*
Spier, Peter. *Crash! bang! boom!*
   Gobble, growl, grunt
Spires, Elizabeth. *The big meow*
Spohn, Kate. *Turtle and Snake go camping*
Spooner, Michael. *Old Meshikee and the little crabs*
Stafford, William. *The animal that drank up sound*
Stanley, Diane. *The conversation club*
Stapler, Sarah. *Trilby's trumpet*
Steiner, Charlotte. *Listen to my seashell*
Stephens, Helen. *Ruby and the noisy hippo*
Stevenson, Harvey. *Big scary wolf*
Stevenson, James. *Clams can't sing*
Strand, Mark. *The planet of lost things*
Sturges, Philemon. *What's that sound, Woolly Bear?*
Sweeney, Jacqueline. *Katie and the night noises*
Tafuri, Nancy. *Do not disturb*
   The donkey's Christmas song
Thayer, Jane. *Quiet on account of dinosaur*
Thomas, Patricia. *The one and only, super-duper, golly-whopper, jim-dandy, really-handy clock-tock-stopper*
Thompson, Richard. *The night walker*
Thomson, Pat. *The squeaky, creaky bed*
Titus, Eve. *The kitten who couldn't purr*
Tresselt, Alvin R. *Wake up, farm!*, ill. by author
   Wake up, farm!, ill. by Carolyn Ewing
Turner, Sandy. *Silent night*
Tyers, Jenny. *When it is night and when it is day*
Tyger, Rory. *Newton*
Velthuijs, Max. *Frog is frightened*
Verboven, Agnes. *Ducks like to swim*
Voake, Charlotte. *Tom's cat*
Waber, Bernard. *The mouse that snored*
Waddell, Martin. *Let's go home, Little Bear*
   Squeak-a-lot
Wadsworth, Ginger. *One tiger growls*

Wallace, Joseph E. *Big and noisy Simon*
Walsh, Melanie. *Do monkeys tweet?*
Walter, Virginia. *"Hi, pizza man!"*
Walton, Rick. *Little dogs say "Rough!"*
Watson, John. *We're the noisy dinosaurs!*
Webb, Angela. *Talkabout sound*
West, Colin. *One day in the jungle*
West, Judy. *Have you got my purr?*
Wheeler, Cindy. *Marmalade's nap*
Whybrow, Ian. *Quacky quack-quack!*
Wildsmith, Brian. *Goat's trail*
Winer, Yvonne. *Frogs sing songs*
Winnick, Karen B. *Barn sneeze*
Winthrop, Elizabeth. *A very noisy girl*
Wolfe, Frances. *It is the wind*
Wong, Janet S. *Buzz*
Wood, Jakki. *Fiddle-i-fee*
Wundrow, Deanna. *Jungle drum*
Wynne-Jones, Tim. *The hour of the frog*
Young, Ruth. *Who says moo?*
Zalben, Jane Breskin. *Norton's nighttime*
Zarin, Cynthia. *Rose and Sebastian*
Ziefert, Harriet. *Cow in the house*
   Listen! Piggety Pig
   Nicky's noisy night
   Oh, what a noisy farm!
   On our way to the barn
   On our way to the forest
   On our way to the water
   On our way to the zoo
Zolotow, Charlotte (Shapiro). *The poodle who barked at the wind*
   The quiet mother and the noisy little boy

Noise, sounds – snoring *see* Sleep – snoring

North Pole *see* Foreign lands – Arctic

Northern lights

Anawalt, Paula Bonnier. *The crystal palace*
Armentrout, Patricia. *Lights in the sky*
Barlowe, Sy. *A child's book of stars*
Conway, Diana Cohen. *Northern lights*
Dwyer, Mindy. *Aurora, a tale of the Northern Lights*
Esbensen, Barbara Juster. *The night rainbow*
Kalz, Jill. *Northern lights*
Kinsey-Warnock, Natalie. *The fiddler of the Northern Lights*
London, Jonathan. *Let the lynx come in*
McNally, John. *Northern lights*
Merski, P. K. *Roaring, boring, Alice*
Pinczes, Elinor J. *Arctic fives arrive*
Sabuda, Robert James. *The Blizzard's robe*
Sandburg, Carl (Charles August). *Not everyday an aurora borealis for your birthday*
Taylor, Harriet Peck. *Ulaq and the northern lights*
Waboose, Jan Bourdeau. *SkySisters*

Norway *see* Foreign lands – Norway

Noses *see* Anatomy – noses; Senses – smell

Numbers *see* Counting, numbers

Nuns *see* Careers – nuns

Nursery rhymes

Agard, John. *No hickory no dickory no dock*
Ahlberg, Janet. *The jolly Christmas postman*
Allison, Diane Worfolk. *This is the key to the kingdom*
Anholt, Catherine. *Come back, Jack!*
Animal nursery rhymes
Arnold, Tedd. *Actions*
   Colors
   Mother Goose's words of wit and wisdom
   Opposites

The complete version of ye three blind mice, ill. by Walton Corbould
Three blind mice, ill. by Lorinda Bryan Cauley
Three blind mice, ill. by Victoria Chess
Jack Sprat. *The life of Jack Sprat, his wife and his cat*
Jackson, Alison. *If the shoe fits*
Jekyll, Walter. *I have a news*
Jonovitz, Marilyn. *Three little kittens*
Kelley, Marty. *Fall is not easy*
Kemp, Moira. *Knock at the door*
Kepes, Juliet. *Lady bird, quickly*
Kessler, Leonard P. *The silly Mother Goose*
Kirk, Daniel. *Jack and Jill*
Knapp, John, II. *A pillar of pepper and other Bible nursery rhymes*
Knight, Joan. *Tickle-toe rhymes*
Koontz, Robin Michal. *Pussycat ate the dumplings*
Krensky, Stephen. *The missing Mother Goose*
Kroll, Virginia L. *Jaha and Jamil went down the hill*
Lacome, Julie. *Walking through the jungle*
Ladybug, ladybug, and other nursery rhymes
Lawson, Carol. *Teddy bear, teddy bear*
Lee, Dennis. *Alligator pie*
Levy, Sara G. *Mother Goose rhymes for Jewish children*
The little book of cats
The Little book of mice
The Little book of pigs
Little Robin Redbreast
Little Tom Tucker
Livermore, Elaine. *Three little kittens lost their mittens*
London, Jonathan. *I see the moon and the moon sees me*
Lord, Beman. *The days of the week*
McGee, Shelagh. *I'm a little teapot*
McMullan, Kate (Hall). *Baby Goose*
Manson, Christopher. *A farmyard song*
Marshak, S. (Samuil). *The merry starlings*
Marshall, James. *Hey, diddle, diddle*
Martin, Bill (William Ivan). *Fire! Fire! said Mrs. McGuire*
Sounds I remember
Martin, Sarah Catherine. *The comic adventures of Old Mother Hubbard and her dog*
Old Mother Hubbard, ill. by Jane Cabrera
Old Mother Hubbard, ill. by Colin Hawkins
Old Mother Hubbard and her dog, ill. by Lisa Amoroso
Old Mother Hubbard and her dog, ill. by Paul Galdone
Old Mother Hubbard and her dog, ill. by Evaline Ness
Old Mother Hubbard and her wonderful dog
Marzollo, Jean. *The rebus treasury*
Mendoza, George. *Silly sheep and other sheepish rhymes*
Miranda, Anne. *To market, to market*
Mitton, Tony. *Riddledy piggledy*
Montgomerie, Norah. *This little pig went to market*
Montgomery, Michael G. *Over the candlestick*
Morley, Carol. *Farmyard song*
Most, Bernard. *Four and twenty dinosaurs*
Mother Goose. *ABC rhymes*
The annotated Mother Goose
Arnold Lobel book of Mother Goose
As I was going up and down
Baa baa, black sheep, ill. by Marilyn Janovitz
Baa, baa, black sheep, ill. by Moira Kemp
Baa baa black sheep, ill. by Sue Porter
Baa baa black sheep, ill. by Ferelith Eccles Williams
Baby's first Mother Goose
The baby's lap book
Beatrix Potter's nursery rhyme book
Blessed Mother Goose
Brian Wildsmith's Mother Goose
Carolyn Wells' edition of Mother Goose
Cats by Mother Goose
The Charles Addams Mother Goose
A child's book of old nursery rhymes
The Chinese Mother Goose rhymes
The city and country Mother Goose
Frank Baber's Mother Goose
The gay Mother Goose
The glorious Mother Goose
Grafa' Grig had a pig
Gray goose and gander and other Mother Goose rhymes

Gregory Griggs and other nursery rhyme people
Hey, diddle, diddle, ill. by Linda Bronson
Hey, diddle, diddle, ill. by Heather Collins
Hey, diddle, diddle, ill. by Marilyn Janovitz
Hey, diddle, diddle, ill. by Moira Kemp
Hey, diddle, diddle, ill. by Marc Mongeau
Hey, diddle, diddle, ill. by Nita Sowter
Hey, diddle, diddle, ill. by Eleanor Wasmuth
Hey, diddle, diddle, and Baby bunting, ill. by Randolph Caldecott
Hey, diddle, diddle picture book, ill. by Randolph Caldecott
Hickory, dickory, dock, ill. by Heather Collins
Hickory dickory dock, ill. by Marilyn Janovitz
Hickory, dickory, dock, ill. by Moira Kemp
Hickory dickory dock and other nursery rhymes, ill. by Carol Jones
Humpty Dumpty, ill. by Colin and Jacqui Hawkins
Humpty Dumpty, ill. by Moira Kemp
Humpty Dumpty and other first rhymes, ill. by Betty Ferrell Youngs
Humpty Dumpty and other rhymes, ill. by Rosemary Wells
Hurrah, we're outward bound!
Hush-a-bye baby, ill. by Nicola Bayley
Ian Penney's book of nursery rhymes
In a pumpkin shell
Jack and Jill, ill. by Heather Collins
Jack and Jill, ill. by Eleanor Wasmuth
Jack Kent's merry Mother Goose
James Marshall's Mother Goose
Kate Greenaway's Mother Goose
Kitten rhymes
The Larousse book of nursery rhymes
Lavender's blue
Little Boy Blue, ill. by Nita Sowter
Little Boy Blue and other rhymes
Little Miss Muffet, ill. by Heather Collins
Little Miss Muffet, ill. by Mary Morgan
The little Mother Goose
London Bridge is falling down, ill. by Ed Emberley
London Bridge is falling down, ill. by Peter Spier
Michael Foreman's Mother Goose
Mother Goose, ill. by Scott Cook
Mother Goose, ill. by Roger Antoine Duvoisin
Mother Goose, ill. by Miss Elliott
Mother Goose, ill. by C. B. Falls
Mother Goose, ill. by Gyo Fujikawa
Mother Goose, ill. by Vernon Grant
Mother Goose, ill. by Kate Greenaway
Mother Goose, ill. by Michael Hague
Mother Goose, ill. by Violet La Mont
Mother Goose, ill. by Arthur Rackham
Mother Goose, ill. by Frederick Richardson, 1915
Mother Goose, ill. by Frederick Richardson, 1976
Mother Goose, ill. by Gustaf Tenggren
Mother Goose, ill. by Tasha Tudor
Mother Goose and nursery rhymes, ill. by Philip Reed
A Mother Goose book, ill. by Joan Walsh Anglund
The Mother Goose book, ill. by Alice and Martin Provensen
The Mother Goose book, ill. by Sonia Roetter
Mother Goose house
Mother Goose in French
Mother Goose in hieroglyphics
Mother Goose in Spanish
Mother Goose melodies
Mother Goose nursery rhymes, ill. by Arthur Rackham, 1969
Mother Goose nursery rhymes, ill. by Arthur Rackham, 1975
Mother Goose remembers
Mother Goose rhymes, ill. by Eulalie M. Banks & Lois Lenski
The Mother Goose songbook
The Mother Goose treasury, ill. by Raymond Briggs
Mother Goose's melodies
Mother Goose's melody
Mother Goose's nursery rhymes
Mother Goose's rhymes and melodies
My first real Mother Goose [board book], ill. by Blanche Fisher Wright
Nursery rhyme book
Nursery rhymes, ill. by Douglas W. Gorsline
Nursery rhymes, ill. by Eloise Wilkin
Nursery rhymes from Mother Goose in signed English

The old woman in a shoe
One I love, two I love, and other loving Mother Goose rhymes
One misty moisty morning
1, 2 buckle my shoe, ill. by Sherry Neidigh
One, two, buckle my shoe [board book], ill. by Heather Collins
The only true Mother Goose melodies
Over the moon
Pat-a-cake, ill. by Marilyn Janovitz
Pat-a-cake [board book], ill. by Heather Collins
Pat-a-cake, pat-a-cake, ill. by Moira Kemp
The piper's son, ill. by Emily Newton Barto
A pocket full of posies
Pussy cat, pussy cat, ill. by Ferelith Eccles Williams
Pussycat, pussycat and other rhymes
The rainbow Mother Goose
The real Mother Goose, ill. by Blanche Fisher Wright
The real Mother Goose [board book], ill. by Diane Muldrow
The real Mother Goose clock book
Richard Scarry's best Mother Goose ever
Richard Scarry's favorite Mother Goose rhymes
Rimes de la Mere Oie
Ring o' roses
Rock-a-bye baby [board book], ill. by Heather Collins
The Sesame Street players present Mother Goose
Sing a song of Mother Goose
Sing a song of sixpence, ill. by Randolph Caldecott; Barron's, 1988
Sing a song of sixpence, ill. by Randolph Caldecott; Hart, 1977
Sing a song of sixpence, ill. by Margaret Chamberlain
Sing a song of sixpence, ill. by Leonard Lubin
Sing a song of sixpence, ill. by Ray Marshall and Korky Paul
Sing a song of sixpence, ill. by Ferelith Eccles Williams
Sing hey, diddle, diddle
Songs for Mother Goose
The tall Mother Goose
Thirty old-time nursery songs
This little pig, ill. by Leonard Lubin
This little pig, ill. by Eleanor Wasmuth
This little pig went to market, ill. by L. Leslie Brooke
This little pig went to market, ill. by Denise Fleming
This little pig went to market, ill. by Ferelith Eccles Williams
This little piggy, ill. by Moira Kemp
This little piggy [board book], ill. by Heather Collins
The three jovial huntsmen
The three little kittens, ill. by Lorinda Bryan Cauley
The three little kittens, ill. by Paul Galdone
The three little kittens, ill. by Dorothy Stott
The three little kittens, ill. by Shelley Thornton
To market! To market!, ill. by Emma Lillian Brock
To market! To market!, ill. by Peter Spier
Tom, Tom the piper's son
Twenty nursery rhymes
Vernon Grant's Mother Goose
Wee Willie Winkie and other rhymes, ill. by Rosemary Wells
Wee willie winkie [board book], ill. by Heather Collins
Wendy Watson's Mother Goose
Will Moses Mother Goose
Willy Pogány's Mother Goose (1928)
Willy Pogány's Mother Goose (2000)
The moving adventures of Old Dame Trot and her comical cat
My first nursery rhymes
My first songs
Namm, Diane. *Favorite nursery rhymes*
Nayer, Judy. *Rhymes*
Nichols, Grace. *Asana and the animals*
Nursery rhymes, ill. by Gertrude Elliott
O'Malley, Kevin. *Humpty Dumpty egg-splodes*
One, two, buckle my shoe, ill. by Rowan Barnes-Murphy
One, two, buckle my shoe, ill. by Gail E. Haley
One, two, skip a few!
Ormerod, Jan. *To baby with love*
Over in the meadow, ill. by Paul Galdone
Palatini, Margie. *The web files*
Palazzo, Tony (Anthony D.). *Animals 'round the mulberry bush*
Paparone, Pamela. *Five little ducks*
Patterson, Pat. *Hickory dickory duck*

Patz, Nancy. *Moses supposes his toeses are roses and 7 other silly old rhymes*
Pearson, Tracey Campbell. *A apple pie*
   Hector Protector [board book]
   Sing a song of sixpence
Peppé, Rodney. *Cat and mouse*
   Hey, riddle, diddle
Percy, Graham. *Elephants never forget*
Petersham, Maud. *The rooster crows*
Pio peep!
Polacco, Patricia. *Babushka's Mother Goose*
Potter, Beatrix. *Appley Dapply's nursery rhymes*
   Cecily Parsley's nursery rhymes
The pudgy book of Mother Goose
Ragged Bear's book of nursery rhymes
Rey, H. A. (Hans Augusto). *Humpty Dumpty and other Mother Goose songs*
Robbins, Ruth. *The harlequin and Mother Goose*
Rosenberg, Liz. *Mama Goose*
Sabuda, Robert James. *The movable Mother Goose*
Scarry, Richard. *Richard Scarry's animal nursery tales*
Scieszka, Jon. *The book that Jack wrote*
Sendak, Maurice. *Hector Protector, and As I went over the water*
Sierra, Judy. *Monster Goose*
Sieveking, Anthea. *Mary had a little lamb and other animal rhymes*
   Polly put the kettle on and other play rhymes
   Rub-a-dub-dub and other splashy rhymes
   Twinkle, twinkle, little star and other bedtime rhymes
Simple Simon. *The adventures of Simple Simon*
   The history of Simple Simon
   Simple Simon
Siomades, Lorianne. *The itsy bitsy spider*
   Three little kittens
Stanley, Diane. *The Giant and the beanstalk*
Stevens, Janet. *And the dish ran away with the spoon*
Stobbs, William. *This little piggy*
Tarrant, Margaret. *The Margaret Tarrant nursery rhyme book*
Taylor, Alice. *A child's treasury of Irish rhymes*
Taylor, Jane. *Twinkle, twinkle little star*, ill. by Heather Collins
   Twinkle, twinkle, little star, ill. by Michael Hague
   Twinkle, twinkle little star, ill. by Julia Noonan
Thomson, Pat. *Rhymes around the day*
Trapani, Iza. *Baa baa black sheep*
   Baa baa black sheep [board book]
   The itsy bitsy spider
Tucker, Nicholas. *Mother Goose abroad*
Vail, Rachel. *Over the moon*
Voce, Louise. *Over in the meadow*
Wadsworth, Olive A. *Over in the meadow*
Wallwork, Amanda. *Sleep songs*
Walton, Rick. *How many?*
Watson, Wendy. *Thanksgiving at our house*
Weil, Lisl. *Mother Goose picture riddles*
What do you feed your donkey on?
Wheeler, Opal. *Sing Mother Goose*
Williams, Garth. *The chicken book*
Williams, Jenny (Jennifer). *Here's a ball for baby*
   One, two, buckle my shoe
   Ride a cockhorse
   Ring around a rosy
Williams, Sarah. *Ride a cock-horse*
Yolen, Jane. *The lap-time song and play book*
   Street rhymes around the world
Zemach, Margot. *Some from the moon, some from the sun*
Ziefert, Harriet. *Mother Goose math*
   Ode to Humpty Dumpty

Nursery school *see* School – nursery

Nurses *see* Careers – nurses

Occupations *see* Careers

Oceans *see* Sea & seashore

Octopuses

Barrett, John M. *Oscar the selfish octopus*
Brandenberg, Franz. *Otto is different*
Carrick, Carol. *Octopus*
Cazet, Denys. *The octopus*
Drdek, Richard E. *Horace the friendly octopus*
Heller, Ruth. *How to hide an octopus*
Kite, L. Patricia. *Down in the sea. The octopus*
Kraus, Robert. *Herman the helper*
Lauber, Patricia. *An octopus is amazing*
Most, Bernard. *My very own octopus*
Paterson, Brian. *Zigby dives in*
Pitcher, Caroline. *Nico's octopus*
Shaw, Evelyn S. *Octopus*
Spohn, Kate. *Ruth's bake shop*
Ungerer, Tomi. *Emile*
Waber, Bernard. *I was all thumbs*
Yaccarino, Dan. *An octopus followed me home*
    Oswald

Odors *see* Senses – smell

Ogres *see* Mythical creatures – ogres

Oil

Berger, Melvin. *Oil spill!*
Freeman, Don. *The seal and the slick*
Rand, Gloria. *Prince William*
Ungerer, Tomi. *The Mellops strike oil*

Ojibwa Indians *see* Indians of North America – Ojibwa

Old age

Ackerman, Karen. *Just like Max*
    Walking with Clara Belle
Allard, Harry. *It's so nice to have a wolf around the house*
Altman, Linda Jacobs. *Singing with Momma Lou*
Anderson, Lena. *Stina's visit*
Ardizzone, Edward. *Lucy Brown and Mr. Grimes*
Armitage, Ronda. *The lighthouse keeper's rescue*
Arnold, Marsha Diane. *The chicken salad club*
Arro, Lena. *By geezers and galoshes!*
Barasch, Lynne. *Old friends*
Bergman, Donna. *City fox*
Biro, Maureen Boyd. *Walking with Maga*
Bogart, Jo Ellen. *Jeremiah learns to read*
Bosak, Susan V. *Something to remember me by*
Briggs, Raymond. *Jim and the beanstalk*
Bunting, Eve (Anne Evelyn). *The big cheese*
    Can you do this, Old Badger?
    Sunshine home
Calmenson, Stephanie. *Rosie, a visiting dog's story*
Carlstrom, Nancy White. *Blow me a kiss, Miss Lilly*
Coats, Laura Jane. *Mr. Jordan in the park*
Collington, Peter. *A small miracle*
Delton, Judy. *My grandma's in a nursing home*
De Paola, Tomie (Thomas Anthony). *Nana Upstairs and Nana Downstairs*, 1973
    Nana Upstairs and Nana Downstairs, 1998
Dugan, Barbara. *Loop the loop*

Duncan, Alice Faye. *Miss Viola and Uncle Ed Lee*
Edelman, Elaine. *Boom-de-boom*
Farber, Norma. *How does it feel to be old?*
Fassler, Joan. *My grandpa died today*
Fender, Kay. *Odette!*
Fink, Dale Borman. *Mr. Silver and Mrs. Gold*
Foreman, Michael. *Rock-a-doodle-do!*
Fox, Louisa. *Every Monday in the mailbox*
Fox, Mem. *Wilfrid Gordon McDonald Partridge*
Franklin, Kristine L. *The gift*
    The old, old man and the very little boy
Gammell, Stephen. *Git along, old Scudder*
Glaser, Linda. *The borrowed Hanukkah latkes*
Goffstein, M. B. (Marilyn Brooke). *Fish for supper*
Graham, Bob. *Rose meets Mr. Wintergarten*
Greene, Carol. *The old ladies who liked cats*
Gregory, Valiska. *The oatmeal cookie giant*
Griffith, Helen V. *Dream meadow*
    Georgia music
    How many candles?
Grimm, Jacob. *The Bremen town band*
    The Bremen town musicians, ill. by Donna Diamond
    The Bremen town musicians
    The Bremen town musicians, ill. by Janina Domanska
    The Bremen town musicians, ill. by Paul Galdone
    The Bremen town musicians, ill. by David Johnson
    Bremen town musicians, ill. by Josef Palecek
    The Bremen town musicians, ill. by Ilse Plume
    The Bremen town musicians, ill. by Janet Stevens
    The Bremen town musicians, ill. by Bernadette Watts
    The horse, the fox, and the lion
    The musicians of Bremen, ill. by John Segal
    The musicians of Bremen, ill. by Svend Otto S
    The musicians of Bremen, ill. by Martin Ursell
    The traveling musicians of Bremen
Grosz, Peter. *The special gifts*
Guthrie, Donna. *Grandpa doesn't know it's me*
    The secret admirer
Hamm, Diane Johnston. *Grandma drives a motor bed*
Hazen, Barbara Shook. *Digby*
    Why did Grandpa die?
Herriot, James. *Blossom comes home*
Hest, Amy. *The midnight eaters*
Hewett, Joan. *Rosalie*
Hickcox, Ruth. *Great-Grandmother's treasure*
Hill, Susan. *King of kings*
Hindley, Judy. *The little train*
Hoff, Syd. *Barkley*
Holder, Heidi. *Carmine the crow*
Hughes, Shirley. *The snow lady*
Johnson, Angela. *When I am old with you*
Johnston, Tony. *Grandpa's song*
Jones, Rebecca C. *Great Aunt Martha*
Joyce, William. *The Leaf Men and the brave good bugs*
Jung, Minna. *William's ninth life*
Kahl, Virginia. *Maxie*
Karkowsky, Nancy. *Grandma's soup*
Keeping, Charles. *Molly o' the moors*
Ketner, Mary Grace. *Ganzy remembers*
Kibbey, Marsha. *My grammy*
Klein, Leonore. *Old, older, oldest*
Knox-Wagner, Elaine. *My grandpa retired today*
Krasilovsky, Phyllis. *The woman who saved things*
Kroll, Virginia L. *Fireflies, peach pies, and lullabies*
Kunhardt, Dorothy. *Billy the barber*
Kvasnosky, Laura McGee. *Zelda and Ivy one Christmas*
Lakin, Pat (Patricia). *Grandparents*
Laminack, Lester L. *The sunsets of Miss Olivia Wiggins*
Lasky, Kathryn. *Sea swan*
Leedahl, Shelley A. (Shelley Ann). *The bone talker*
Leonard, Marcia. *Gregory and Mr. Grump*
Lewis, J. Patrick. *The tsar and the amazing cow*
Littledale, Freya. *The snow child*
Martin, Bill (William Ivan). *Little granny quarterback*
Miller, William. *The piano*
Nanji, Shenaaz. *An alien in my house*
Nelson, Vaunda Micheaux. *Always Gramma*

Newman, Lesléa. *Remember that*
Nordqvist, Sven. *Festus and Mercury wishing to go fishing*
Peet, Bill (William Bartlett). *Smokey*
Peters, Lisa Westberg. *Good morning, river!*
Pomerantz, Charlotte. *Buffy and Albert*
Powell, Consie. *Old dog Cora and the Christmas tree*
Price, Kathy (Kathy Z.). *The Bourbon Street musicians*
Proimos, James. *Joe's wish*
Puttock, Simon. *A ladder to the stars*
Rawlins, Donna. *Digging to China*
Reynolds, Marilynn. *A present for Mrs. Kazinski*
Ross, Lillian Hammer. *The little old man and his dreams*
Rylant, Cynthia. *Mr. Putter and Tabby bake the cake*
    Mr. Putter and Tabby pick the pears
    Mr. Putter and Tabby pour the tea
    Mr. Putter and Tabby walk the dog
Sakai, Kimiko. *Sachiko means happiness*
Schachner, Judith Byron. *The Grannyman*
Schwartz, David M. *Sugargrandpa*
Seligson, Susan. *Amos*
Skorpen, Liesel Moak. *Old Arthur*
Slobodkina, Esphyr. *Billy, the condominium cat*
Smith, Barry. *Minnie and Ginger*
Snow, Pegeen. *Mrs. Periwinkle's groceries*
Sonneborn, Ruth A. *I love Gram*
Spalding, Andrea. *Me and Mr. Mah*
    Sarah May and the new red dress
Stanton, Karen. *Mr. K and Yudi*
Stevens, Janet. *Old bag of bones*
Stroud, Bettye. *Down home at Miss Dessa's*
Sullivan, Silky. *Grandpa was a cowboy*
Taber, Anthony. *Cats' eyes*
Tafolla, Carmen. *Baby Coyote and the old woman = El coyotito y la viejita*
Taylor, Mark. *Old Blue, you good dog you*
Tejima, Keizaburo. *Ho-limlim*
Tusa, Tricia. *Maebelle's suitcase*
Uchida, Yoshiko. *Sumi's special happening*
    The wise old woman
Vizurraga, Susan. *Miss Opal's auction*
Waggoner, Karen. *The lemonade babysitter*
Wahl, Jan. *"I remember," cried Grandma Pinky*
Watts, Jeri Hanel. *Keepers*
Weigelt, Udo. *Old Beaver*
Wild, Margaret. *Old Pig*
    Remember me
Wittman, Sally. *A special trade*
Wolfe, Frances. *One wish*
Yolen, Jane. *Miz Berlin walks*
Zolotow, Charlotte (Shapiro). *I know a lady*

Olympics *see* Sports – Olympics

Only child *see* Family life – only child

Opera singers *see* Careers – opera singers; Careers – singers

Opossums *see* Animals – possums

Opposites *see* Concepts – opposites

Optical illusions

Anno, Mitsumasa. *Anno's alphabet*
Anno, Mitsumasa. *Anno's counting book*
    Anno's counting house
    Anno's flea market
    Anno's Italy
    Anno's journey
    Anno's magical ABC
    Dr. Anno's magical midnight circus
    Topsy turvies: more pictures to stretch the imagination
    Topsy turvies: pictures to stretch the imagination
    Upside-downers
Baum, Arline. *Opt*

Doty, Roy. *Eye fooled you*
Gardner, Beau. *The look again . . . and again, and again, and again book*
    The turn about, think about, look about book
Mallat, Kathy. *Just ducky*
Noll, Sally. *Watch where you go*
Priceman, Marjorie. *It's me, Marva!*

Opticians, optometrists *see* Careers – opticians, optometrists

Optimism *see* Character traits – optimism

Orangutans *see* Animals – orangutans

Orchestras *see* Musical instruments – orchestras

Orderliness *see* Character traits – orderliness

Organists *see* Careers – organists

Organs *see* Musical instruments – organs

Orphans

Ardizzone, Edward. *Lucy Brown and Mr. Grimes*
The babes in the woods. *The old ballad of the babes in the woods*
Bemelmans, Ludwig. *Madeline*
    Madeline [pop-up book]
    Madeline and the bad hat
    Madeline and the gypsies
    Madeline in London
    Madeline's Christmas
    Madeline's rescue
Brown, Janet Allison. *A little princess*
Bulla, Clyde Robert. *Poor boy, rich boy*
Bunting, Eve (Anne Evelyn). *Train to somewhere*
Burnett, Frances Hodgson. *A little princess*
Burton, Jane. *Fancy the fox*
Calhoun, Mary. *A shepherd's gift*
Crunk, Tony. *Big Mama*
Gabel, Susan L. *Where the sun kisses the sea*
Gibson, Kari Smalley. *Mooki's secret*
Goble, Paul. *The lost children*
Hershenhorn, Esther. *Fancy that*
Jeram, Anita. *All together now*
Kay, Verla. *Orphan train*
Kessler, Cristina. *Jubela*
Lyon, David. *The crumbly coast*
McCully, Emily Arnold. *Little Kit, or, The Industrious Flea Circus girl*
    The orphan singer
McKay, Lawrence. *Journey home*
Mahy, Margaret. *Sailor Jack and the twenty orphans*
Martin, Jacqueline Briggs. *The water gift and the pig of the pig*
Mollel, Tololwa M. (Tololwa Marti). *Orphan boy*
Moore, Inga. *The vegetable thieves*
Polacco, Patricia. *Welcome Comfort*
Pomerantz, Charlotte. *The mousery*
Prigger, Mary Skillings. *Aunt Minnie McGranahan*
Rylant, Cynthia. *The bird house*
Sanfield, Steve. *The girl who wanted a song*
San Souci, Robert D. *The secret of the stones*
Stanley, Diane. *Raising Sweetness*
Sullivan, Silky. *Grandpa was a cowboy*
Thomas, Kathy. *The angel's quest*
Ungerer, Tomi. *The three robbers*
Warner, Sunny. *The magic sewing machine*
Weedn, Flavia. *The star gift*
Weninger, Brigitte. *Lumina*
Willard, Nancy. *Shadow story*
Yolen, Jane. *The girl in the golden bower*
Yorinks, Arthur. *Oh, brother*

Ostriches *see* Birds – ostriches

Otters *see* Animals – otters

Outer space *see* Space ships

Outlaws *see* Crime

Owls *see* Birds – owls

Oxen *see* Animals – oxen

Pack rats *see* Animals – pack rats

Pageants *see* Theater

Painters *see* Activities – painting; Careers – painters

Painting *see* Activities – painting

Paiute Indians *see* Indians of North America – Paiute

Pajamas *see* Clothing – pajamas

Pakistan *see* Foreign lands – Pakistan

Paleontologists *see* Careers – paleontologists

Palestine *see* Foreign lands – Palestine

Panama *see* Foreign lands – Panama

Pandas *see* Animals – pandas

Panthers *see* Animals – leopards

Pants *see* Clothing – pants

Papago *see* Indians of North America – Papago

Paper

Bateson-Hill, Margaret. *Lao Lao of Dragon Mountain*
Compestine, Ying Chang. *The story of paper*
Curtis, Neil. *How paper is made*
Czernecki, Stefan. *Paper lanterns*
Engel, Diana. *The shelf-paper jungle*
Gibbons, Gail. *Deadline!*
    Paper, paper everywhere
Howell, Will C. *Zoo flakes ABC*
Huff, Vivian. *Let's make paper dolls*
Jaspersohn, William. *Timber!*
Kleven, Elisa. *The paper princess*
Kroll, Virginia L. *Pink paper swans*
Lobato, Arcadio. *Paper bird*
Lohf, Sabine. *Things I can make with paper*
Melmed, Laura Krauss. *Little Oh*
Mitgutsch, Ali. *From wood to paper*
Moffatt, Judith. *Snow shapes*
Monsell, Mary Elise. *Crackle Creek*
Rumford, James. *The cloudmakers*
Small, David. *Paper John*
Tagore, Rabindranath. *Paper boats*
Testa, Fulvio. *The paper airplane*

Parades

Anderson, C. W. (Clarence Williams). *The rumble seat pony*
Appelt, Kathi. *Bats on parade*
Baer, Gene. *Thump thump rat-a-tat-tat*
Ballard, Robin. *Carnival*
Brenner, Barbara A. *The snow parade*
Butler, Dorothy. *Higgledy, piggledy, hobbledy hoy*
Chalmers, Mary. *Easter parade*
Chwast, Seymour. *Alphabet parade*
Corey, Shana. *Milly and the Macy's Parade*
Crews, Donald. *Parade*
Derby, Sally. *King Kenrick's splinter*
Emberley, Ed (Edward Randolph). *The parade book*
Ets, Marie Hall. *Another day*
    In the forest
Feczko, Kathy. *Umbrella parade*
Flack, Marjorie. *Wait for William*
Freschet, Gina. *Naty's parade*
Ghigna, Charles. *The alphabet parade*
Greenfield, Eloise. *Easter parade*
Gretz, Susanna. *Frog, duck, and rabbit*
Hayes, Ann. *Meet the Marching Smithereens*
Jane, Pamela. *Milo and the fire engine parade*
Janice. *Little Bear marches in the St. Patrick's Day parade*
Joosse, Barbara M. *Fourth of July*
Kraus, Robert. *Springfellow's parade*
Kroll, Steven. *The goat parade*
    Mary McLean and the St. Patrick's Day parade
Landau, Elaine. *St. Patrick's Day*
Lasky, Kathryn. *Fourth of July bear*
Lenski, Lois. *The Easter Rabbit's parade*
Leonard, Marcia. *The tin can man*
London, Jonathan. *Froggy plays in the band*
Mahy, Margaret. *When the king rides by*
Mills, Claudia. *Phoebe's parade*
Mora, Pat. *The rainbow tulip*
O'Donnell, Elizabeth Lee. *Patrick's day*
Richter, Mischa. *Eric and Matilda*
Roth, Susan L. *We'll ride elephants through Brooklyn*
Silverman, Erica. *On the morn of Mayfest*
Slobodkina, Esphyr. *Pezzo the peddler and the circus elephant*
Spier, Peter. *Crash! bang! boom!*
Wells, Rosemary. *The Halloween parade*
Winthrop, Elizabeth. *Halloween hats*
Ziefert, Harriet. *First Night*
Ziner, Feenie. *Counting carnival*

Parakeets *see* Birds – parakeets, parrots

Parks

Ackerman, Karen. *In the park with dad*
Bauer, Helen. *Good times at the park*
Black, Sonia. *Hanging out with Mom*
Browne, Anthony. *Voices in the park*
Burstein, Fred. *Whispering in the park*
Coats, Laura Jane. *Mr. Jordan in the park*
Cohen, Caron Lee. *Martin and the giant lions*
Cousins, Lucy. *Kite in the park*
Curious George and the dump truck
Ernst, Lisa Campbell. *Squirrel Park*
Fife, Dale. *The little park*
Flanagan, Alice K. *Exploring parks with Ranger Dockett*
Godwin, Laura. *Central Park serenade*
Gorbachev, Valeri. *Chicken chickens*
Granowsky, Alvin. *At the park*
Hautzig, Esther (Rudomin). *In the park*
Heo, Yumi. *One Sunday morning*
High, Linda Oatman. *The girl on the high-diving horse*
Hill, Eric. *The park*
    Spot goes to the park
Hill, Mary Lou. *My dad's a park ranger*
Hughes, Shirley. *When we went to the park*
Ichikawa, Satomi. *La La Rose*
Jones, Ursula. *The witch's children*
Kessler, Ethel. *Are there seals in the sandbox?*

Kolar, Bob. *Do you want to play?*
Lindgren, Astrid. *Pippi Longstocking in the park*
McKissack, Patricia C. *Messy Bessey's family reunion*
McNaughton, Colin. *At the park*
McPhail, David M. *Henry Bear's park*
Mahy, Margaret. *Down the dragon's tongue*
Matje, Martin. *Celeste*
Merriam, Eve. *Where's that cat?*
Morozumi, Atsuko. *In the park*
Noble, Sheilagh. *More*
Pratt, Pierre. *Park*
Roberts, Thom. *Pirates in the park*
Rockwell, Anne F. *Hugo at the park*
Sharratt, Nick. *Shark in the park*
Singer, Marilyn. *Didi and Daddy on the Promenade*
Sweeney, Joan. *Suzette and the puppy*
Takeshita, Fumiko. *The park bench*
Van der Beek, Deborah. *Superbabe!*
Waddell, Martin. *The park in the dark*
Weeks, Sarah. *Oh my gosh, Mrs. McNosh!*
Zolotow, Charlotte (Shapiro). *The park book*

Parks – amusement

Cobb, Annie. *The long wait*
Frazee, Marla. *Roller coaster*
Hill, Susan. *Stuart at the fun house*
Hoban, Russell. *Trouble on Thunder Mountain*
Horse, Harry. *Little rabbit lost*
O'Donnell, Peter. *Carnegie's excuse*
Rodda, Emily. *Yay!*

Participation

Agostinelli, Maria Enrica. *I know something you don't know*
Barrett, Judi. *What's left?*
Bauman, A. F. *Guess where you're going, guess what you'll do*
Bendick, Jeanne. *Why can't I?*
Berry, Holly. *Busy Lizzie*
Bester, Roger. *Guess what?*
Black, Irma (Simonton). *Is this my dinner?*
Blake, Quentin. *All join in*
Booth, Eugene. *At the circus*
   At the fair
   In the air
   In the garden
   In the jungle
   Under the ocean
Brown, Marc Tolon. *Finger rhymes*
Brown, Margaret Wise. *The country noisy book*
   The indoor noisy book
   Noisy book
   The quiet noisy book
   The seashore noisy book
   The summer noisy book
   The winter noisy book
Cameron, Polly. *"I can't," said the ant*
Carroll, Ruth. *Where's the bunny?*
Charlip, Remy. *Fortunately*
Cole, William. *Frances face-maker*
Corbett, Grahame. *Guess who?*
   What number now?
   Who is hiding?
   Who is inside?
   Who is next?
Craig, M. Jean. *Boxes*
Cronin, Doreen. *Wiggle*
Crume, Marion W. *Let me see you try*
   Listen!
   What do you say?
De Regniers, Beatrice Schenk. *It does not say meow!*
Elting, Mary. *Q is for duck*
Emberley, Ed (Edward Randolph). *Ed Emberley's amazing look through book*
   Klippity klop
Ets, Marie Hall. *Just me*
   Talking without words

Fowler, Allan. *What do you see in a cloud?*
French, Fiona. *Hunt the thimble*
Garten, Jan. *The alphabet tale*
Heilbroner, Joan. *This is the house where Jack lives*
Hewett, Anita. *The tale of the turnip*
Hoban, Tana. *Look again*
   Where is it?
The house that Jack built. *The house that Jack built*, ill. by Seymour Chwast
   The house that Jack built, ill. by Nadine Bernard Westcott
Hutchins, Pat. *Good night owl*
Ipcar, Dahlov (Zorach). *Lost and found*
Jaynes, Ruth M. *Benny's four hats*
Johnson, Ryerson. *Let's walk up the wall*
Kepes, Juliet. *Run little monkeys, run, run, run*
Kunhardt, Edith. *Which one would you choose?*
   Which pig would you choose?
Kuskin, Karla. *Roar and more*
Leonard, Marcia. *King Lionheart's castle*
Löfgren, Ulf. *One-two-three*
MacGregor, Ellen. *Theodor Turtle*
Martin, Bill (William Ivan). *Brave little Indian*
Montgomerie, Norah. *This little pig went to market*
Ogle, Lucille. *I hear*
Paterson, Diane. *If I were a toad*
Rosen, Michael (1946–). *We're going on a bear hunt*
Seignobosc, Françoise. *The things I like*
Seuss, Dr. *Gerald McBoing Boing sound book*
   Mr. Brown can moo! Can you?
   Wacky Wednesday
Shaw, Charles Green. *It looked like spilt milk*
Siewert, Margaret. *Bear hunt*
Simmons, Jane. *Daisy says, "Here we go round the mulberry bush"*
   Daisy says, "If you're happy and you know it"
Simon, Norma. *What do I say?*
Sivulich, Sandra Stroner. *I'm going on a bear hunt*
Skaar, Grace Marion. *What do the animals say?*
Skorpen, Liesel Moak. *All the Lassies*
Slobodkina, Esphyr. *Caps for sale*
   Circus caps for sale
   Pezzo the peddler and the circus elephant
   Pezzo the peddler and the thirteen silly thieves
Smith, Kathryn. *Little Donkey's Christmas story*
   Little Lamb's Christmas story
Spier, Peter. *Crash! bang! boom!*
   Gobble, growl, grunt
Steiner, Charlotte. *Five little finger playmates*
Sutton, Eve. *My cat likes to hide in boxes*
Trapani, Iza. *I'm a little teapot*
Two little eyes and other action rhymes
Ueno, Noriko. *Elephant buttons*
Watanabe, Shigeo. *How do I put it on?*
Weil, Lisl. *Owl and other scrambles*
Yudell, Lynn Deena. *Make a face*

Parties

Adams, Adrienne. *The Christmas party*
   A Halloween happening
Albert, Shirley. *Doll party*
Allard, Harry. *The Stupids have a ball*
   There's a party at Mona's tonight
Allred, Mary. *Grandmother Poppy and the children's tea party*
Anderson, Lena. *Bunny party*
Anderson, Lonzo. *The Halloween party*
Anholt, Catherine. *Snow fairy and the spaceman*
Asch, Frank. *Insects from outer space*
   Popcorn
Ashman, Linda. *Maxwell's magic mix-up*
Awdry, W. *Happy birthday, Thomas!*
Bailey, Linda. *Stanley's party*
Barbour, Karen. *Nancy*
Berenstain, Stan. *The Berenstain bears and the slumber party*
Berlan, Kathryn Hook. *Andrew's amazing monsters*
Bible, Charles. *Jennifer's new chair*
Birchall, Mark. *Rabbit's birthday surprise*
Blance, Ellen. *Monster has a party*

Millais, Raoul. *Elijah and Pin-Pin*
Miller, Margaret. *My birthday*
Miranda, Anne. *Alphabet fiesta*
    Monster math
Modell, Frank. *Ice cream soup*
Moore, Inga. *A big day for Little Jack*
Mora, Pat. *Delicious hullabaloo = Pachanga deliciosa*
Mother Goose. *Hickory, dickory, dock*, ill. by Suzanne Duranceau
Mueller, Virginia. *Monster's birthday hiccups*
Munsch, Robert N. *Moira's birthday*
Murdock, Laurette. *Someone is talking about Hortense*
Murphy, Stuart J. *Too many kangaroo things to do!*
Nikola-Lisa, W. *Shake dem Halloween bones*
Novak, Matt. *No zombies allowed*
Ogburn, Jacqueline K. *The reptile ball*
Older, Effin. *My two grandmothers*
Oram, Hiawyn. *Badger's bring something party*
Oxenbury, Helen. *The queen and Rosie Randall*
Park, W. B. *The costume party*
Passen, Lisa. *The incredible shrinking teacher*
Paterson, Bettina. *Bun's birthday*
Paxton, Tom. *Engelbert the elephant*
Pfister, Marcus. *Just the way you are*
Pinkwater, Daniel Manus. *Bad bears and a bunny*
Polacco, Patricia. *Some birthday!*
Polisar, Barry Louis. *The haunted house party*
Pomerantz, Charlotte. *The birthday letters*
Potter, Beatrix. *The sly old cat*
Prager, Annabelle. *The baseball birthday party*
    The spooky Halloween party
    The surprise party
Pryor, Bonnie. *Amanda and April*
Quackenbush, Robert M. *Funny bunnies on the run*
Quin-Harkin, Janet. *Helpful Hattie*
Radabaugh, Melinda Beth. *Sleeping over*
Rader, Laura. *Tea for me, tea for you*
Redies, Rainer. *The cats' party*
Reid, Barbara. *The party*
Roberts, Bethany. *Birthday mice*
Rollings, Susan. *New shoes, red shoes*
Rose, Deborah Lee. *Birthday zoo*
Rumford, James. *Nine animals and the well*
Ryder, Joanne. *Beach party*
Rylant, Cynthia. *Little Whistle's dinner party*
Sage, Angie. *Molly and the birthday party*
Samuels, Barbara. *Happy birthday, Dolores*
Schertle, Alice. *Jeremy Bean's St. Patrick's Day*
Schindel, John. *Who are you?*
Schweninger, Ann. *Birthday wishes*
Selkowe, Valrie M. *Spring green*
Shute, Linda. *Halloween party*
Silbaugh, Elizabeth. *Raggedy Ann's birthday party book*
Soto, Gary. *Chato and the party animals*
    The old man and his door
Springer, Margaret. *A royal ball*
Spurr, Elizabeth. *The biggest birthday cake in the world*
Stapler, Sarah. *Spruce the moose cuts loose*
Starr, Meg. *Alicia's happy day*
Steptoe, Javaka. *The Jones family express*
Stickland, Paul. *Bears*
Stock, Catherine. *The birthday present*
Stott, Rowena. *The hedgehog feast*
Suen, Anastasia. *Willie's birthday*
Tafuri, Nancy. *The barn party*
Tegen, Katherine Brown. *Dracula and Frankenstein are friends*
Thompson, Kay. *Kay Thompson's Eloise takes a bawth [sic]*
Trimble, Patti. *What day is it?*
Tryon, Leslie. *Albert's birthday*
Tudor, Tasha. *The doll's Christmas*
Uff, Caroline. *Happy birthday, Lulu*
Vincent, Gabrielle. *Merry Christmas, Ernest and Celestine*
Waldron, Jan L. *John Pig's Halloween*
Wallace, John. *Tiny Rabbit goes to a birthday party*
Wallace, Nancy Elizabeth. *Tell-a-bunny*
Wardlaw, Lee. *Bow-wow birthday*
Wegen, Ron. *The Halloween costume party*
Wells, Rosemary. *Bunny party*

Weninger, Brigitte. *Happy birthday, Davy*
West, Colin. *Go tell it to the toucan*
Willard, Nancy. *The mouse, the cat and Grandmother's hat*
Wilson, Sarah. *Uncle Albert's flying birthday*
Wiseman, Bernard. *Morris has a birthday party!*
Wojtowycz, David. *Dudley's birthday party*
Worth, Bonnie. *Peter Cottontail's surprise*
Yolen, Jane. *Piggins*
Zalben, Jane Breskin. *Saturday night at the Beastro*
Zimmer, Dirk. *The trick-or-treat trap*
Zion, Gene. *Jeffie's party*

Passover *see* Holidays – Passover

Patience *see* Character traits – patience

Patterns *see* Concepts – patterns

Pawnee Indians *see* Indians of North America – Pawnee

Peacocks, peahens *see* Birds – peacocks, peahens

Peddlers *see* Careers – peddlers

Pegasus *see* Mythical creatures – Pegasus

Pelicans *see* Birds – pelicans

Pen pals

Calmenson, Stephanie. *Wanted*
Caple, Kathy. *Harry's smile*
Holub, Joan. *Pen pals*

Penguins *see* Birds – penguins

Penobscot Indians *see* Indians of North America – Penobscot

Perfectionism *see* Character traits – perfectionism

Perseverance *see* Character traits – perseverance

Persia *see* Foreign lands – Persia

Persistence *see* Character traits – persistence

Perspective *see* Concepts – perspective

Peru *see* Foreign lands – Peru

Petroglyphs

Taylor, Harriet Peck. *Secrets of the stone*
Webb, Denise. *The same sun was in the sky*

Petroleum *see* Oil

Pets

Abercrombie, Barbara. *Bad dog, Dodger*
    Charlie Anderson
Abley, Mark. *Ghost cat*
Adoff, Arnold. *Daring Dog and Captain Cat*
    The return of Rex and Ethel
Ahlberg, Allan. *The pet shop*
Aiken, Joan. *Arabel and Mortimer*
Ajmera, Maya. *Animal friends*
    A kid's best friend
Alexander, Martha G. *No ducks in our bathtub*
Allard, Harry. *It's so nice to have a wolf around the house*
Allen, Jonathan. *My cat*
    My dog

Allen, Marjorie N. *One, two, three – ah-choo!*
Allen, Pamela. *My cat Maisie*
Ambrus, Victor G. *Count, Dracula*
Anholt, Laurence. *The new puppy*
Ardizzone, Edward. *Diana and her rhinoceros*
Asch, Frank. *The last puppy*
Atwood, Margaret. *Anna's pet*
Baehr, Patricia. *Mouse in the house*
Baldner, Gaby. *Joba and the wild boar = Joba und das wildschwein*
Balian, Lorna. *Amelia's nine lives*
Barasch, Marc Ian. *No plain pets!*
Bare, Colleen Stanley. *Guinea pigs don't read books*
   To love a cat
   To love a dog
Bartoletti, Susan Campbell. *Nobody's nosier than a cat*
Barton, Byron. *Jack and Fred*
Barwin, Gary. *The racing worm brothers*
Bastin, Marjolein. *A little dog for Vera*
Baylor, Byrd. *Amigo*
Beatty, Hetty Burlingame. *Moorland pony*
Belpré, Pura. *Santiago*
Benchley, Peter. *Jonathan visits the White House*
Bennett, Kelly. *Not Norman*
Berenstain, Stan. *The Berenstain bears' trouble with pets*
The best cat in the world
Bibbel, Mark. *Oh, Harry!*
Bishop, Claire Huchet. *The truffle pig*
Blackwood, Gladys Rourke. *Whistle for Cindy*
Blance, Ellen. *Monster buys a pet*
Blegvad, Lenore. *The great hamster hunt*
Bliss, Corinne Demas. *That dog Melly!*
Boegehold, Betty. *Pawpaw's run*
Borovsky, Paul. *The fish that wasn't*
Breeze, Lynn. *Baby's animals*
   Baby's clothes
Brenner, Barbara A. *The five pennies*
Brett, Jan. *Annie and the wild animals*
   The first dog
Brice, Tony. *The bashful goldfish*
Brock, Emma Lillian. *A pet for Barbie*
Bröger, Achim. *Bruno takes a trip*
   Francie's paper puppy
Brothers, Aileen. *Jiffy, Miss Boo and Mr. Roo*
Brown, Marc Tolon. *Arthur's new puppy*
   Arthur's new puppy [board book]
   Arthur's pet business
   Arthur's TV trouble
Brown, Margaret Wise. *The days before now*
   The good little bad little pig
Brown, Ruth. *Our puppy's vacation*
Brunhoff, Laurent de. *Babar and the Wully-Wully*
Brutschy, Jennifer. *Celeste and Crabapple Sam*
Bryant, Donna. *My rabbit Roberta*
Burningham, John. *The rabbit*
Burns, Theresa. *You're not my cat*
Burton, Jane. *Ginger the kitten*
   Gipper the guinea pig
   Hoppy the toad
   Jack the puppy
Bushey, Jeanne. *A sled dog for Moshi*
Calder, S. J. *If you were a cat*
Calders, Pere. *Brush*
Calhoun, Mary. *High-wire Henry*
   Tonio's cat
Calmenson, Stephanie. *My dog's the best*
   Shaggy, waggy dogs (and others)
Capucilli, Alyssa Satin. *Bathtime for Biscuit*
   Biscuit wins a prize
   Happy birthday, Biscuit!
Carlson, Natalie Savage. *Spooky night*
Carlstrom, Nancy White. *Who gets the sun out of bed?*
Carr, Jan. *The nature of the beast*
Carrick, Carol. *The accident*
   A clearing in the forest
   The foundling
   Lost in the storm
Carroll, Ruth. *Pet tale*

Carter, Noelle. *My pet*
Caseley, Judith. *Mr. Green Peas*
Casey, Patricia. *My cat Jack*
Chalmers, Mary. *Six dogs, twenty-three cats, forty-five mice, and one*
   hundred sixteen spiders
Chapouton, Anne-Marie. *Ben finds a friend*
Chase, Jan Brinckerhoff. *The golden song*
Chataway, Carol. *The perfect pet*
Chenery, Janet. *Pickles and Jake*
Child, Lauren. *I want a pet*
   That pesky rat
Childress, Mark. *Joshua and Bigtooth*
Chittum, Ida. *The cat's pajamas*
Christian, Mary Blount. *Devin and Goliath*
Chwast, Seymour. *Mr. Merlin and the turtle*
Clements, Andrew. *Dolores and the big fire*
   Tara and Tiree, fearless friends
Cleveland-Peck, Patricia. *City cat, country cat*
Coerr, Eleanor. *The Josefina story quilt*
Coffelt, Nancy. *Good night, Sigmund*
Coffey, Maria. *A cat in a kayak*
Cohen, Miriam. *Jim's dog Muffins*
Cole, Babette. *Princess Smartypants*
Cole, Joanna. *Big Goof and Little Goof*
Collicott, Sharleen. *Toestomper and the bad butterflies*
Collington, Peter. *My darling kitten*
Collins, Pat Lowery. *Tumble, tumble, tumbleweed*
Cooney, Nancy Evans. *Go away monsters, lickety split!*
Cooper, Elizabeth K. *The fish from Japan*
Cooper, Melrose. *Pets!*
Copeland, Eric. *Milton, my father's dog*
Corrin, Ruth. *Mister cat*
Cousins, Lucy. *Pet animals*
Cowley, Joy. *Agapanthus Hum and Major Bark*
Cowley, Stewart. *What's that sound?*
Crane, Donn. *Flippy and Skippy*
Crawford, Ron. *Pet?*
Crisp, Marty. *Black and white*
Crowell, Maryalicia. *A horse in the house*
Cummings, Betty Sue. *Turtle*
Cuyler, Margery. *Freckles and Jane*
Dale, Penny. *Wake up, Mr. B.!*
Daly, Kathleen N. *Strawberry Shortcake and pets on parade*
Daly, Niki. *Just like Archie*
   What's cooking, Jamela?
Darling, Kathy (Mary Kathleen). *ABC cats*
   ABC dogs
Davenier, Christine. *Leon and Albertine*
Davies, Andrew. *Poonam's pets*
Davis, Patricia Anne. *Brian's bird*
Day, Alexandra. *Darby, the special-order pup*
   Special deliveries
Day, Betsy. *Stefan and Olga*
De Hamel, Joan. *Hemi's pet*
Delton, Judy. *I'll never love anything ever again*
   A pet for Duck and Bear
Dennard, Deborah. *Do cats have nine lives?*
De Paola, Tomie (Thomas Anthony). *Little Grunt and the big egg*
DiSalvo-Ryan, DyAnne. *A dog like Jack*
Dodds, Dayle Ann. *Pet wash*
Doyle, Malachy. *Sleepy Pendoodle*
Dubois, Claude K. *Looking for Ginny*
Dubowski, Cathy East. *A cake for Jake*
Dunn, Judy. *The little goat*
   The little puppy
   The little rabbit
Elsdale, Bob. *Mac side up*
Elson, Raymond. *Pets*
Enell, Trinka. *Roll over, Rosie*
Ernst, Lisa Campbell. *Walter's tail*
Evans, Mark. *Guinea pigs*
   Kitten
   Puppy
   Rabbit
Falwell, Cathryn. *P.J. & Puppy*
Farish, Terry. *The cat who liked potato soup*
Faulkner, Keith. *My pets*

Mazer, Anne. *The salamander room*
Miles, Miska. *The rice bowl pet*
    Somebody's dog
Miller, Margaret. *My best friends*
Miller, Michaela. *Guinea pigs*
Miller, Virginia. *Be gentle!*
Monks, Lydia. *Aaaarrgghh! spider!*
Moore, Inga. *Six dinner Sid*
Moran, Alex. *Come here, tiger*
Morehead, Debby. *A special place for Charlee*
Morgan, Allen. *Molly and Mr. Maloney*
Morgan, Michaela. *Edward gets a pet*
Morozumi, Atsuko. *My friend gorilla*
Most, Bernard. *My very own octopus*
    Pets in trumpets and other word-play riddles
Mott, Evelyn Clarke. *Hot dog*
Mozelle, Shirley. *The pig is in the pantry, the cat is on the shelf*
Nelson, Robin. *Pet fish*
    Pet frog
    Pet guinea pig
    Pet hamster
    Pet hermit crab
Newberry, Clare Turlay. *April's kittens*
    Barkis
    Herbert the lion
    Percy, Polly and Pete
Newfield, Marcia. *Iggy*
Noble, Trinka Hakes. *Jimmy's boa and the big splash birthday bash*
Numeroff, Laura Joffe. *Laura Numeroff's 10-step guide to living with your monster*
O'Connor, Jane. *The perfect puppy for me*
O'Donnell, Elizabeth Lee. *I can't get my turtle to move*
O'Hagan, Caroline. *It's easy to have a caterpillar visit you*
    It's easy to have a snail visit you
    It's easy to have a worm visit you
Ohi, Ruth. *Pants off first*
Oram, Hiawyn. *A boy wants a dinosaur*
Orbach, Ruth. *Please send a panda*
Ormerod, Jan. *Kitten day*
Ostheeren, Ingrid. *The blue monster*
    The new dog
Owen, Ann (1953–). *Caring for your pet*
Oxenbury, Helen. *Our dog*
Palatini, Margie. *The perfect pet*
Parish, Peggy. *No more monsters for me!*
    Scruffy
Patchett, Fiona. *Rabbits*
Pearce, Philippa. *Emily's own elephant*
Pershall, Mary K. *Hello, Barney!*
A pet for me
Petersen-Fleming, Judy. *Kitten training and critters, too!*
    Puppy training and critters, too!
Pets
Petty, Kate. *Gerbils*
    Hamsters
    Rabbits
Pfeffer, Wendy. *What's it like to be a fish?*
Phillips, Betty Lou. *Emily goes wild*
Phillips, Joan. *My new boy*
Pitcher, Caroline. *Nico's octopus*
Pittman, Helena Clare. *A dinosaur for Gerald*
Polacco, Patricia. *Mrs. Katz and Tush*
Politi, Leo. *Lito and the clown*
Pollock, Penny. *Emily's tiger*
Pomerantz, Charlotte. *The birthday letters*
Primavera, Elise. *Plantpet*
Pringle, Laurence P. *Naming the cat*
Provensen, Alice. *An owl and three pussycats*
Pursell, Margaret Sanford. *Polly the guinea pig*
    Shelley the sea gull
Quackenbush, Robert M. *No mouse for me*
Rand, Gloria. *Little Flower*
Rathmann, Peggy. *10 minutes till bedtime*
Rayner, Mary. *Marathon and Steve*
Reiser, Lynn. *Any kind of dog*
Remkiewicz, Frank. *The last time I saw Harris*
Reynolds, Marilynn. *A present for Mrs. Kazinski*

Ridlon, Marcia. *Kittens and more kittens*
Rockwell, Anne F. *I love my pets*
    My pet hamster
Roffey, Maureen. *Here, kitty kitty!*
    Quick, catch Dan!
Rogers, Fred. *When a pet dies*
Rosen, Michael J. (1954–). *Bonesy and Isabel*
Rosen, Winifred. *Henrietta and the day of the iguana*
Ross, George Maxim. *When Lucy went away*
Ross, Tony. *I want a cat*
Rotner, Shelley. *Pick a pet*
Rouillard, Wendy. *Barnaby's bunny*
Sadler, Judy Ann. *Sandwiches for Duke*
Sandberg, Inger. *Nicholas' favorite pet*
San Souci, Robert D. *The silver charm*
Scamell, Ragnhild. *The wish come true cat*
Schaffer, Marion. *I love my cat*
Schick, Alice. *Just this once*
Schlein, Miriam. *That's not Goldie!*
Schmeltz, Susan Alton. *Pets I wouldn't pick*
Schneider, Howie. *Chewy Louie*
Schwartz, Henry. *Albert goes Hollywood*
    How I captured a dinosaur
Scruton, Clive. *Mary's pets*
Seabrooke, Brenda. *The best burglar alarm*
Seeber, Dorothea P. *A pup just for me . . . A boy just for me*
Seignobosc, Françoise. *The story of Colette*
Sendak, Maurice. *Some swell pup*
Seymour, Tres. *I love my buzzard*
Sharmat, Marjorie Weinman. *I'm the best*
    Nate the Great and the fishy prize
Shea, Kitty. *Out and about at the vet clinic*
Sierra, Judy. *There's a zoo in room 22*
Simon, Norma. *Cats do, dogs don't*
    Mama cat's year
    Oh, that cat!
Simon, Seymour. *Cats*
    Dogs
Skorpen, Liesel Moak. *All the Lassies*
Smath, Jerry. *But no elephants*
Smith, Lane. *The big pets*
Smith, Maggie (Margaret C.). *Desser, the best ever cat*
Smyth, Gwenda. *A pet for Mrs. Arbuckle*
Sneed, Brad. *Lucky Russell*
Snow, Pegeen. *A pet for Pat*
Spier, Peter. *The pet store*
Spooner, J. B. *The story of the little Black Dog*
Springer, Margaret. *A royal ball*
Spurr, Elizabeth. *A pig named Perrier*
Stanley, Mandy. *In the park*
    Perfect pets
Stanton, Karen. *Mr. K and Yudi*
Starke, Katherine. *Dogs and puppies*
Steiner, Charlotte. *Polka Dot*
Stevenson, James. *Mr. Hacker*
    Will you please feed our cat?
Stevenson, Suçie. *Jessica the blue streak*
Stoddard, Sandol. *My very own special particular private and personal cat*
    Turtle time
Suen, Anastasia. *Willie's birthday*
Szilagyi, Mary. *Thunderstorm*
Tabler, Judith. *The new puppy*
Tallon, Robert. *Latouse my moose*
Teague, Mark. *Dear Mrs. LaRue*
Thaler, Mike. *My puppy*
Thomas, Jane Resh. *Scaredy dog*
Tidd, Louise Vitellaro. *The best pet yet*
Tracqui, Valérie. *The dog*
Trapani, Iza. *How much is that doggie in the window?*
    Row, row, row your boat
Turner, Pamela S. *Hachiko*
Tusa, Tricia. *Chicken*
Udry, Janice May. *"Oh no, cat!"*
    What Mary Jo wanted
Uff, Caroline. *Hello, Lulu*
Vaës, Alain. *The wild hamster*

Varga, Judy. *Miss Lollipop's lion*
Vaughan, Marcia Kapok. *Whistling Dixie*
Viorst, Judith. *The tenth good thing about Barney*
Vreeken, Elizabeth. *Henry*
Vries, Anke de. *My elephant can do almost anything*
Wahl, Jan. *Dracula's cat and Frankenstein's dog*
   My cat Ginger
Wahl, Mats. *Grandfather's laika*
Wallace-Brodeur, Ruth. *Goodbye, Mitch*
Ward, Lynd. *The biggest bear*
Waring, Richard (Richard M. N.). *Alberto the dancing alligator*
Wayland, April Halprin. *To Rabbittown*
Weird pet poems
Wells, Rosemary. *Lucy comes to stay*
Whatley, Bruce. *That magnetic dog*
Wilcox, Cathy. *Enzo the Wonderfish*
Wilhelm, Hans. *I'll always love you*
Williams, Sue. *Let's go visiting*
Wilson, Budge. *The fear of Angelina Domino*
Wirth, Beverly. *Margie and me*
Wisbeski, Dorothy Gross. *Picaro, a pet otter*
Wittbold, Maureen. *Mending Peter's heart*
Wolf, Jake. *Daddy, could I have an elephant?*
Wolski, Slawomir. *Tiger cat*
Wong, Herbert H. *My goldfish*
Wright, Dare. *The lonely doll learns a lesson*
Yaccarino, Dan. *New pet*
   An octopus followed me home
   Oswald
Ziefert, Harriet. *Murphy meets the treadmill*
Zimelman, Nathan. *Positively no pets allowed*
Zimmerman, Andrea Griffing. *My dog Toby*
Zinnemann-Hope, Pam. *Find your coat, Ned*
Zolotow, Charlotte (Shapiro). *The old dog*
   The poodle who barked at the wind
Zweifel, Frances W. *Bony*

Pharaohs *see* Royalty – pharaohs

Philippines *see* Foreign lands – Philippines

Phoenix *see* Mythical creatures – phoenix

Photographers *see* Careers – photographers

Photography *see* Activities – photographing

Physical handicaps *see* Handicaps – physical handicaps

Physicians *see* Careers – doctors

Pianos *see* Musical instruments – pianos

Picnics *see* Activities – picnicking

Picture puzzles

Alarcón, Francisco X. *Iguanas in the snow and other winter poems / poemas = Iguanas en la nieve y otros poemas de invierno / poemas*
Anno, Mitsumasa. *Anno's alphabet*
   Anno's animals
   Anno's counting book
   Anno's counting house
   Anno's flea market
   Anno's Italy
   Anno's journey
   Anno's magical ABC
   Dr. Anno's magical midnight circus
Barber, Patti. *First number book*
Blyler, Allison. *Finding foxes*
Carter, David A. *Who's under that hat?*
Cauley, Lorinda Bryan. *What do you know!*
Cressy, Judith. *Can you find it?*
   Can you find it, too?
Dahl, Michael. *Downhill fun*

Eggs and legs
Footprints in the snow
From the garden
Hands down
One big building
Davis, Kate (1951–). *Barnyard babies*
Davis, Lee. *P. B. Bear's birthday party*
Day, Shirley. *Waldo's back yard*
Ehlert, Lois. *In my world*
Ellwand, David. *Alfred's party*
Faulkner, Keith. *A trick or a treat?*
Garland, Michael. *Christmas City*
Geisert, Arthur. *Mystery*
Grimm, Jacob. *The elves and the shoemaker*, ill. by Doug Cushman
Gukova, Julia. *All mixed-up!*
Handford, Martin. *Find Waldo now*
   The great Waldo search
   Where's Waldo?
Horenstein, Henry. *A is for – ?*
Jenkins, Steve. *I see a kookaburra*
King, Dave. *Counting book*
Laidlaw, Ken. *The amazing I spy ABC*
MacDonald, Suse. *Look whooo's counting*
   Peck, slither and slide
McGrath, Barbara Barbieri. *Kellogg's froot loops color fun book*
McGuire, Richard. *What's wrong with this book?*
McLean-Carr, Carol. *Fairy dreams*
McMillan, Bruce. *Mouse views*
Maisner, Heather. *Save Brave Ted*
Marsh, T. J. *Way out in the desert*
Marzollo, Jean. *I spy little animals*
   I spy little book
   I spy little bunnies
   I spy little Christmas
   I spy little letters
   I spy little numbers
   I spy little wheels
   I spy, mystery
   I spy, year-round challenger!
Munro, Roxie. *Mazescapes*
Nims, Bonnie Larkin. *Where is the bear at school?*
O'Malley, Kevin. *Who killed Cock Robin?*
Palazzo, Tony (Anthony D.). *Waldo the woodchuck*
Ringgold, Faith. *Cassie's word quilt*
Rogers, Paul (Patrick). *What can you see?*
Rotner, Shelley. *Parts*
Schwartz, David M. *If you hopped like a frog*
Steiner, Joan (Joan Catherine). *Look-alikes*
   Look-alikes, Jr.
Teddyland
The three little pigs. *The three little pigs*, ill. by Doug Cushman
Tildes, Phyllis Limbacher. *Animals in camouflage*
Toft, Kim Michelle. *Neptune's nursery*
   One less fish
Turner, Ann Warren. *Angel hide and seek*
Twinem, Neecy. *In the air*
Wallner, John C. *Look and find*
Wallwork, Amanda. *Find the fish that looks like this*
Weitzman, Jacqueline Preiss. *You can't take a balloon into the National Gallery*
Wick, Walter. *Can you see what I see? Cool collections*
   Can you see what I see? Dream machine
   Can you see what I see? picture puzzles to search and solve
   Can you see what I see? Seymour and the juice box boat
   Can you see what I see? Seymour makes new friends
   Can you see what I see? The night before Christmas
   I spy a book of picture riddles
   I spy Christmas
   I spy extreme challenger!
   I spy fantasy
   I spy gold challenger!
   I spy school days
   I spy spooky night
   I spy super challenger!
   I spy treasure hunt
   I spy ultimate challenger!
Wiesmüller, Dieter. *In the blink of an eye*

Wright, Rachel. *Plundering pirates*
Wynne-Jones, Tim. *On Tumbledown Hill*

Pigeons *see* Birds – pigeons

Pigs *see* Animals – pigs

Pilgrims

Behrens, June. *The feast of Thanksgiving*
Bruchac, Joseph. *Squanto's journey*
Bunting, Eve (Anne Evelyn). *How many days to America?*
Dalgliesh, Alice. *The Thanksgiving story*
DeLage, Ida. *Pilgrim children on the Mayflower*
George, Jean Craighead. *The first Thanksgiving*
Gibbons, Gail. *Thanksgiving Day*
Greene, Rhonda Gowler. *The very first Thanksgiving Day*
Harness, Cheryl. *Three young pilgrims*
Hennessy, B. G. (Barbara G.). *One little, two little, three little pilgrims*
Kroll, Steven. *One tough turkey*
Lowitz, Sadyebeth. *The pilgrims' party*
Metaxas, Eric. *Squanto and the miracle of Thanksgiving*
Peacock, Carol Antoinette. *Pilgrim cat*
Szekeres, Cyndy. *Long ago*
Van Leeuwen, Jean. *Across the wide dark sea*

Pilots *see* Careers – airplane pilots

Pima Indians *see* Indians of North America – Pima

Pioneer life *see* U.S. history – frontier & pioneer life

Pirates

Ahlberg, Allan. *Skeleton crew*
Ahlberg, Janet. *It was a dark and stormy night*
Allen, Pamela. *I wish I had a pirate suit*
Arro, Lena. *By geezers and galoshes!*
Baum, Louis. *JuJu and the pirate*
Bunting, Eve (Anne Evelyn). *Little Badger, terror of the seven seas*
Burningham, John. *Come away from the water, Shirley*
Carryl, Charles E. (Charles Edward). *A capital ship*
    The walloping window-blind, ill. by Jim LaMarche
    The walloping window blind, ill. by Ted Rand
Clibbon, Meg. *Imagine you're a pirate!*
Cole, Babette. *The trouble with Uncle*
Collington, Peter. *The angel and the soldier boy*
Day, Jan. *The pirate, Pink*
    Pirate Pink and treasures of the reef
DeLage, Ida. *ABC pirate adventure*
Devlin, Harry. *The walloping window blind*, ill. by author
Dewey, Ariane. *Laffite, the pirate*
Dyke, John. *Pigwig and the pirates*
Farber, Erica. *Ooey gooey*
Faulkner, Matt. *The amazing voyage of Jackie Grace*
Fox, Mem. *Tough Boris*
Ginsburg, Mirra. *Four brave sailors*
Gliori, Debi. *The princess and the pirate king*
Graham, Mary Stuart (Campbell). *The pirates' bridge*
Haseley, Dennis. *The pirate who tried to capture the moon*
Hayes, Geoffrey. *The mystery of the pirate ghost*
Helquist, Brett. *Roger, the jolly pirate*
Hutchins, Pat. *One-eyed Jake*
Impey, Rose. *Who's a bright girl?*
Isadora, Rachel. *The pirates of Bedford Street*
Joslin, Sesyle. *Señor Baby Elephant, the pirate*
Keats, Ezra Jack. *Maggie and the pirate*
Kessler, Leonard P. *The pirates' adventure on Spooky Island*
Kimmel, Eric A. *The Erie Canal pirates*
    Robin Hook, pirate hunter!
Kroll, Steven. *Are you pirates?*
    The pigrates clean up
Krosoczka, Jarrett J. *Bubble bath pirates*
Lamm, C. Drew. *Pirates*
Leonard, Marcia. *Violet and the pirates*
Lichtenheld, Tom. *Everything I know about pirates*

Lloyd, David. *Grandma and the pirate*
Löfgren, Ulf. *Alvin the pirate*
McAllister, Angela. *The babies of Cockle Bay*
McCully, Emily Arnold. *The pirate queen*
McFarland, Lyn Rossiter. *The pirate's parrot*
MacGill-Callahan, Sheila. *To capture the wind*
McNaughton, Colin. *Captain Abdul's pirate school*
    Jolly Roger and the pirates of Captain Abdul
McNeil, Florence. *Sail away*
McPhail, David M. *Edward and the pirates*
Mahy, Margaret. *The horrendous hullabaloo*
    The man whose mother was a pirate
    Sailor Jack and the twenty orphans
Marston, Elsa. *Cynthia and the runaway gazebo*
Morgan, Allen. *Matthew and the midnight pirates*
My first Raggedy Ann, Raggedy Ann and Andy and the camel with the wrinkled knees
Nash, Ogden. *Custard the dragon*
Peppé, Rodney. *The kettleship pirates*
Perkins, Al. *Tubby and the lantern*
Priest, Robert H. *The pirate's eye*
Richardson, Bill. *Sally Dog Little*
Roberts, Thom. *Pirates in the park*
Ross, Dave (David). *Gorp and the space pirates*
Ross, Tony. *Treasure of Cozy Cove*
Scarry, Richard. *Pie rats ahoy!*
Schotter, Roni. *Captain Bob sets sail*
Sharratt, Nick. *Ahoy, Pirate Pete*
    Mrs. Pirate
Thompson, Brenda. *Pirates*
Tucker, Kathy. *Do pirates take baths?*
Walker, Barbara K. (Barbara Kerlin). *Pigs and pirates*
Ward, Helen. *The moonrat and the white turtle*
Weiss, Ellen. *The pirates of Tarnoonga*
Wick, Walter. *I spy treasure hunt*
Woychuk, Denis. *Pirates*
Wright, Rachel. *Plundering pirates*
Young, James. *Penelope and the pirates*

Pixies *see* Mythical creatures – pixies

Planes *see* Airplanes, airports

Planets

Barlowe, Sy. *A child's book of stars*
Barner, Bob. *Stars, stars, stars*
Branley, Franklyn M. (Mansfield). *The planets in our solar system*
Cecil, Laura. *Noah and the space ark*
Gibbons, Gail. *The planets*
Glyman, Caroline A. *What's above the sky?*
Pinkney, J. Brian. *Cosmo and the robot*
Rau, Dana Meachen. *Mars*
Rockwell, Anne F. *Pur stars*
Simon, Seymour. *Destination, Mars*
Theodorou, Rod. *Across the solar system*
Wethered, Peggy. *Touchdown Mars!*
Yaccarino, Dan. *First day on a strange new planet*
    New pet
Yorinks, Arthur. *Company's going*

Plants

Adelson, Leone. *Please pass the grass*
Agran, Rick. *Pumpkin shivaree*
Alexander, Cecil Frances. *All things bright and beautiful*, ill. by Anna Vojtech
Aliki. *Corn is maize*
    My visit to the aquarium
Appelt, Kathi. *Watermelon day*
Arnold, Caroline. *A walk by the seashore*
    A walk in the desert
    A walk in the woods
    A walk on the Great Barrier Reef
    A walk up the mountain
Arnold, Katya. *Let's find it!*

Atnip, Linda. *Miranda's magic garden*
Ayer, Jacqueline. *The paper-flower tree*
Azarian, Mary. *A gardener's alphabet*
Back, Christine. *Bean and plant*
Baker, Jeannie. *The hidden forest*
    The story of rosy dock
Baker, Jeffrey J. W. *Patterns of nature*
Bardill, Linard. *The great golden thing*
Bash, Barbara. *Desert giant*
Berenstain, Stan. *The Berenstain bears and the prize pumpkin*
    The Berenstain bears' that stump must go!
Bernhard, Durga. *Earth, sky, wet, dry*
Berson, Harold. *Pop! goes the turnip*
Bishop, Gavin. *Mrs. McGinty and the bizarre plant*
Blackmore, Vivien. *Why corn is golden*
Brown, Marc Tolon. *Your first garden book*
Brownell, Barbara. *Spin's really wild U.S.A. tour*
Bruce, Lisa. *Fran's flower*
Bryant-Mole, Karen. *Moving*
Bulla, Clyde Robert. *A tree is a plant*
Busch, Phyllis S. *Cactus in the desert*
    Lions in the grass
Butterworth, Nick. *Jasper's beanstalk*
Cannon, Janell. *Little Yau*
Carle, Eric. *The tiny seed*
Cash, Megan Montague. *What makes the seasons?*
Cave, Kathryn. *One child, one seed*
Chapman, Carol. *Barney Bipple's magic dandelions*
Christian, Mary Blount. *The green thumb thief*
Cohn, Janice I. *Molly's rosebush*
Cole, Henry. *Jack's garden*
Cole, Joanna. *Evolution*
    Plants in winter
Cotten, Cynthia. *At the edge of the woods*
Craig, M. Jean. *Spring is like the morning*
Credle, Ellis. *Down, down the mountain*
Cristini, Ermanno. *In the pond*
Cross, Diana Harding. *Some plants have funny names*
Cross, Genevieve. *A trip to the yard*
Darby, Gene. *What is a plant?*
Davis, Aubrey. *The enormous potato*
Day, Trevor. *Youch! it bites!*
Delaney, A. *Pearl's first prize plant*
Dietl, Ulla. *The plant-and-grow project book*
Dobson, David. *Can we save them?*
Domanska, Janina. *The turnip*
Dunphy, Madeleine. *Here is the tropical rain forest*
Ehlert, Lois. *Leaf man*
Ellentuck, Shan. *A sunflower as big as the sun*
Euvremer, Teryl. *The thieves of Peck's pocket*
Fisher, Aileen Lucia. *And a sunflower grew*
    As the leaves fall down
    Mysteries in the garden
    Now that spring is here
    Plant magic
    Prize performance
    Seeds on the go
    Swords and daggers
    We went looking
Five little pumpkins
Flanagan, Alice K. *Soil*
Fleischman, Paul. *Weslandia*
Fleming, Denise. *Where once there was a wood*
Ford, Miela. *Sunflower*
Fowler, Allan. *Corn . . . on and off the cob*
Gage, Wilson. *Anna's garden songs*
    Anna's summer songs
Geis, Jacqueline. *Where the buffalo roam*
Gibbons, Gail. *The berry book*
    From seed to plant
    Nature's green umbrella
Ginsburg, Mirra. *Mushroom in the rain*
The green grass grows all around
Greenberg, Polly. *Oh, Lord, I wish I was a buzzard*
Grey, Mini. *The very smart pea and the princess-to-be*
Guiberson, Brenda Z. *Cactus hotel*
Hall, Zoe. *It's pumpkin time!*

Hammersmith, Craig. *Watch it grow*
Harris, Jim. *Jack and the giant*
Hayward, Linda. *What homework?*
Heller, Ruth. *Plants that never ever bloom*
Henderson, Douglas. *Dinosaur tree*
Hewett, Anita. *The tale of the turnip*
Hillert, Margaret. *The magic beans*
Himmelman, John. *A dandelion's life*
Hines, Anna Grossnickle. *Miss Emma's wild garden*
Hogan, Paula Z. *The dandelion*
Holmes, Anita. *The 100-year-old cactus*
Holub, Joan. *The garden that we grew*
Horn, Sandra Ann. *The dandelion wish*
Hubbell, Will. *Pumpkin Jack*
Hutchins, Pat. *Titch*
Inches, Alison. *Corduroy's garden*
Ipcar, Dahlov (Zorach). *Hard scrabble harvest*
Jack and the beanstalk. *The history of Mother Twaddle and the mar-*
    velous achievements of her son Jack
    Jack and the beanstalk, ill. by Val Biro
    Jack and the beanstalk, ill. by Aljoscha Blau
    Jack and the beanstalk, ill. by Lorinda Bryan Cauley
    Jack and the beanstalk, ill. by Steve Cox
    Jack and the beanstalk, ill. by Lydia Halverson
    Jack and the beanstalk, ill. by Julek Heller
    Jack and the beanstalk, ill. by John Howe
    Jack and the beanstalk, ill. by Steven Kellogg
    Jack and the beanstalk, ill. by Al Lorenz
    Jack and the beanstalk, ill. by Ed Parker
    Jack and the beanstalk, ill. by Tony Ross
    Jack and the beanstalk, ill. by Niamh Sharkey
    Jack and the beanstalk, ill. by Gennady Spirin
    Jack and the beanstalk, ill. by William Stobbs
    Jack and the beanstalk, ill. by James Warhola
    Jack and the beanstalk, ill. by Anne Wilsdorf
    Jack and the beanstalk = Juan y los frijoles magicos, ill. by Arnal
        Ballester
    Jack the giant killer, ill. by Anne Wilsdorf
    Jack the giantkiller, ill. by Tony Ross
Jenkins, Martin. *Fly traps!*
Johnson, Janice (Janice Kay). *Rosamund*
Johnston, Tony. *Big red apple*
Jordan, Helene J. (Helene Jamieson). *Seeds of wind and water*
Keats, Ezra Jack. *Clementina's cactus*
Kepes, Juliet. *The seed that peacock planted*
Ketteman, Helen. *The year of no more corn*
Kimmel, Eric A. *Pumpkinhead*
Kirk, David. *Nova's ark*
Kirkpatrick, Rena K. *Leaves*
    Seeds and weeds
Kite, L. Patricia. *Dandelion adventures*
Klingel, Cynthia Fitterer. *Forests*
    Oceans
Kottke, Jan. *From seed to pumpkin*
Kranking, Kathy. *The ocean is . . .*
Krauss, Ruth. *The carrot seed*
Krings, Antoon. *Oliver's strawberry patch*
Kuchalla, Susan. *All about seeds*
Lember, Barbara Hirsch. *A book of fruit*
Le Tord, Bijou. *Picking and weaving*
Lewis, Naomi. *Leaves*
The little red hen. *The cock, the mouse and the little red hen*, ill. by
    Lorinda Bryan Cauley
    The cock, the mouse and the little red hen, ill. by Graham Percy
    The little red hen, ill. by Byron Barton
    The little red hen, ill. by Emily Bolam
    The little red hen, ill. by Janina Domanska
    The little red hen, ill. by Paul Galdone
    The little red hen, ill. by Dennis Hockerman
    Little red hen, ill. by Norman Messenger
    The little red hen, ill. by Mel Pekarsky
    The little red hen, ill. by William Stobbs
    The little red hen, ill. by Annie West
    The little red hen, ill. by Margot Zemach
    The little red hen and the ear of wheat, ill. by Elisabeth Bell
    The Little Red Hen makes a pizza
Little, Lessie Jones. *I can do it by myself*

Plasterers *see* Careers – plasterers

Playing *see* Activities – playing

Plays *see* Theater

Plovers *see* Birds – plovers

Plumbers *see* Careers – plumbers

Pockets *see* Clothing

Poetry

What does the sky say?
Who said boo?
Carroll, Lewis. *Jabberwocky*, ill. by Graeme Base
  Jabberwocky, ill. from Disney archives
  Jabberwocky, ill. by Jane Breskin Zalben
  The walrus and the carpenter, ill. by Julian Doyle
  The walrus and the carpenter, ill. by Jane Breskin Zalben
Carryl, Charles E. (Charles Edward). *The camel's lament*
  The walloping window-blind, ill. by Jim LaMarche
  The walloping window blind, ill. by Ted Rand
Carton, Lonnie Caming. *Mommies*
Cassedy, Sylvia. *Red dragonfly on my shoulder*
Caudill, Rebecca. *Wind, sand and sky*
Cazet, Denys. *Minnie and Moo: will you be my Valentine?*
  Night lights
Cendrars, Blaise. *Shadow*
Chaikin, Miriam. *Don't step on the sky*
Charles, Donald. *Shaggy dog's animal alphabet*
Charles, R. H. (Robert Henry). *The roundabout turn*
Chase, Edith Newlin. *Secret dawn*
A child's calendar
Chin, Charlie. *China's bravest girl*
Chorao, Kay. *The baby's bedtime book*
  The baby's good morning book
Christelow, Eileen. *Five little monkeys jumping on the bed*
Christmas in the stable, ill. by Beverly K. Duncan
Christmas presents
Chukovskii, Kornei Ivanovich. *Telephone*, ill. by Vladimir Radunsky
Ciardi, John. *John J. Plenty and Fiddler Dan*
  The monster den
Clark, Leonard. *Drums and trumpets*
Clavel, Bernard. *Castle of books*
Clifford, Eth. *Red is never a mouse*
Clifton, Lucille. *Everett Anderson's Christmas coming*
  Some of the days of Everett Anderson
Cline-Ransome, Lesa. *Quilt alphabet*
Clise, Michele Durkson. *Ophelia's bedtime book*
Clithero, Sally. *Beginning-to-read poetry*
Coatsworth, Elizabeth. *A peaceable kingdom, and other poems*
  Song of the camels
Cole, William. *I went to the animal fair*
  A zooful of animals
Coleridge, Sara. *January brings the snow*
Conrad, Pam. *Animal lullabies*
Cooper, Floyd. *Coming home*
Cox, Palmer. *The Brownies*
Coyne, Rachel. *Daughter, have I told you?*
Craft, Ruth. *The day of the rainbow*
Cuetara, Mittie. *Baby business*
Cummings, E. E. (Edward Estlin). *Hist whist*
  In just-spring
  Little tree, ill. by Deborah Kogan Ray
  Little tree, ill. by Mary C. Smith
Cushman, Doug. *Giants*
Cutlip, Kimbra L. *Firefighter's night before Christmas*
Dahl, Roald. *Dirty beasts*
Dalmais, Anne-Marie. *In my garden*
Days like this
De Gerez, Toni. *My song is a piece of jade*
Delacre, Lulu. *Arroz con leche*
  Las Navidades
Dennis, Suzanne E. *Answer me that*
De Regniers, Beatrice Schenk. *A bunch of poems and verses*
  Cats cats cats
  It does not say meow!
The dog writes on the window with his nose, and other poems
Don't tell the scarecrow
Dotlich, Rebecca Kai. *A family like yours*
  In the spin of things
  Lemonade sun
Dowers, Patrick. *One day scene through a leaf*
Dragon poems
Dragonwagon, Crescent. *Alligators and others all year long!*
Driz, Ovsei. *The boy and the tree*
The drowsy hours
Dubanevich, Arlene. *Tom's tail*

Duncan, Lois. *Songs from dreamland*
Dunphy, Madeleine. *Here is the southwestern desert*
Eastwick, Ivy O. *Cherry stones! Garden swings!*
  Rainbow over all
  Some folks like cats, and other poems
Edwards, Richard. *Moon frog*
Elias, Joyce. *Whose toes are those?*
Eliot, T. S. (Thomas Stearns). *Mr. Mistoffelees with Mungojerrie and Rumpelteazer*
Elliott, David. *An alphabet of rotten kids!*
Elves, fairies and gnomes
Emberley, Barbara. *Drummer Hoff*
  Night's nice
  One wide river to cross
Esbensen, Barbara Juster. *Dance with me*
  Echoes for the eye
  The night rainbow
  Who shrank my grandmother's house?
Ets, Marie Hall. *Beasts and nonsense*
Evans, Lezlie. *Rain song*
Evans, Mel. *The tiniest sound*
Facklam, Margery. *Only a star*
Fairies, trolls and goblins galore
Fairy poems for the very young
Farber, Norma. *As I was crossing Boston Common*
  How the hibernators came to Bethlehem
  How the left-behind beasts built Ararat
  How to ride a tiger
  Never say ugh to a bug
  Small wonders
  There goes feathertop!
  There once was a woman who married a man
  Up the down elevator
  When it snowed that night
  Where's Gomer?
Farjeon, Eleanor. *Around the seasons*
  Between the earth and sun
  Cats
  Cats sleep anywhere, ill. by Mary Price Jenkins
  Cats sleep anywhere, ill. by Anne Mortimer
Feldman, Jacqueline. *The lavender box*
Field, Edward. *Magic words*
Field, Eugene. *The gingham dog and the calico cat*, ill. by Janet Street
  The gingham dog and the calico cat, ill. by Johanna Westerman
  Wynken, Blynken and Nod, ill. by Barbara Cooney
  Wynken, Blynken and Nod, ill. by Susan Jeffers
  Wynken, Blynken and Nod, ill. by Holly Johnson
  Wynken, Blynken and Nod, ill. by Johanna Westerman
Field, Rachel Lyman. *General store*, ill. by Giles Laroche
  General store, ill. by Nancy Winslow Parker
  If once you have slept on an island
Finfer, Celentha. *Grandmother dear*
First graces
First prayers, ill. by Anna Maria Magagna
First prayers, ill. by Tasha Tudor
Fisher, Aileen Lucia. *Best little house*
  Do bears have mothers too?
  The house of a mouse
  I like weather
  I wonder how, I wonder why
  In one door and out the other
  In the middle of the night
  Like nothing at all
  Listen, rabbit
  My first Hanukkah book
  My mother and I
  Mysteries in the garden
  Rabbits, rabbits
  Sing of the earth and sky
  Skip around the year
  We went looking
  When it comes to bugs
  Where does everyone go?
Fitch, Sheree. *No two snowflakes*
Flanders, Michael. *Creatures great and small*
Fletcher, Ralph J. *Grandpa never lies*

See my lovely poison ivy, and other verses about witches, ghosts and things
Mora, Pat. *Confetti*
   Delicious hullabaloo = Pachanga deliciosa
   Listen to the desert = Oye al desierto
   The desert is my mother = El desierto es mi madre
   This big sky
Morgenstern, Christian. *Lullabies, lyrics and gallows songs*
Morice, Dave. *Dot town*
   A visit from St. Alphabet
Morrison, Bill. *Squeeze a sneeze*
Morrison, Sean. *Is that a happy hippopotamus?*
Morse, Samuel French. *Sea sums*
Moss, Jeffrey. *The songs of Sesame Street in poems and pictures*
Moss, Jenny Jackson. *Cajun night after Christmas*
Most, Bernard. *Four and twenty dinosaurs*
Mother Goose. *Arnold Lobel book of Mother Goose*
Mullins, Edward S. *Animal limericks*
Munsterberg, Peggy. *Beastly banquet*
Murphy, Elspeth Campbell. *Do you see me God?*
   Happy Easter, God
Myers, Tim (Tim Brian). *Basho and the fox*
Myers, Walter Dean. *Brown angels*
   Glorious angels
   Harlem
Namm, Diane. *Little bear*
Nash, Ogden. *The adventures of Isabel*, ill. by Walter Lorraine
   The adventures of Isabel, ill. by James Marshall
   The animal garden
   A boy is a boy
   Custard the dragon
   Custard the dragon and the wicked knight, ill. by Lynn Munsinger
   Custard the dragon and the wicked knight, ill. by Linell Nash
Nave, Yolanda. *Goosebumps and butterflies*
Neidigh, Sherry. *Creatures at my feet*
Newsome, Effie Lee. *Wonders*
Nichol, Barbara. *Biscuits in the cupboard*
Nicholls, Judith. *Someone I like*
Nichols, Grace. *Asana and the animals*
Nidey, Kelli. *When autumn falls*
Nikola-Lisa, W. *America: my land, your land, our land*
   Bein' with you this way
Nims, Bonnie Larkin. *Just beyond reach and other riddle poems*
Noda, Takayo. *Dear world*
Norman, Charles. *The hornbean tree and other poems*
Northey, Lawrence. *I'm a hop hop hoppity frog*
Noyes, Alfred. *The highwayman*
Numeroff, Laura Joffe. *Sometimes I wonder if poodles like noodles*
Nye, Naomi Shihab. *Benito's dream bottle*
   Come with me
O'Donnell, Elizabeth Lee. *Sing me a window*
   The twelve days of summer
Ogburn, Jacqueline K. *The reptile ball*
O Huigin, Sean. *King of the birds*
O'Keefe, Susan Heyboer. *One hungry monster*
Olaleye, Isaac. *The distant talking drum*
Oppenheim, Joanne. *Have you seen roads?*
   Have you seen trees?, ill. by Irwin Rosenhouse
   Have you seen trees?, ill. by Jean and Mou-Sien Tseng
Orgel, Doris. *Merry merry FIBruary*
Otten, Charlotte F. *January rides the wind*
Otto, Carolyn. *Dinosaur chase*
   Ducks, ducks, ducks
Oxenbury, Helen. *Tiny Tim*
Pace, David. *Shouting Sharon*
Pack, Robert. *How to catch a crocodile*
   Then what did you do?
The palm of my heart
Paolilli, Paul. *Silver seeds*
Paraskevas, Betty. *Gracie Graves and the kids from room 402*
   Junior Kroll and Company
   A very Kroll Christmas
Paré, Roger. *Animal capers*
   Circus days
   Play time
   Summer days
Paterson, A. B. (Andrew Barton). *The man from Ironbark*

Mulga Bill's bicycle
Patz, Nancy. *Moses supposes his toeses are roses and 7 other silly old rhymes*
   Sarah Bear and Sweet Sidney
Paxton, Tom. *Jennifer's rabbit*
Peaceable kingdom
Pearson, Debora. *Leo's tree*
Pearson, Tracey Campbell. *A apple pie*
Penner, Fred. *Proud*
Peppé, Rodney. *Cat and mouse*
Perdorno, Willie. *Visiting Langston*
Perkins, Al. *The digging-est dog*
Perry, Andrea. *Here's what you do when you can't find your shoe*
A pet for me
Peterson, Sue H. *Swim with me*
Pfister, Marcus. *I see the moon*
Piatti, Celestino. *Celestino Piatti's animal ABC*
Pickering, Jimmy. *It's fall*
   It's winter
Plath, Sylvia. *The bed book*
Please, Mr. Crocodile!
Plotz, Helen. *A week of lullabies*
Plourde, Lynn. *Pigs in the mud in the middle of the rud*
A pocketful of stars
Poems for the very young
Poems go clang!
Polisar, Barry Louis. *Insect soup*
   A little less noise
Pollock, Penny. *When the moon is full*
Pomerantz, Charlotte. *All asleep*
   If I had a Paka
   The tamarindo puppy and other poems
Powell, Consie. *Amazing apples*
Prelutsky, Jack. *Awful Ogre's awful day*
   The baby uggs are hatching
   Beneath a blue umbrella
   Circus
   The frogs wore red suspenders
   Halloween countdown
   Monday's troll
   The pack rat's day and other poems
   The queen of Eene
   Rainy rainy Saturday
   The Random House book of poetry for children
   Read-aloud rhymes for the very young
   Ride a purple pelican
   The snopp on the sidewalk and other poems
   Tyrannosaurus was a beast
Prince, Pamela. *The secret world of teddy bears*
Ra, Carol F. *Trot, trot to Boston*
Radley, Gail. *Rainy day rhymes*
Ray, Mary Lyn. *Mud*
Reader's Digest children's book of poetry
Reeves, James. *Ragged Robin*
Rhyme time around the day
Rice, Eve. *City night*
Richards, Laura Elizabeth Howe. *Jiggle joggle jee*
Rigby, Rodney. *There's a building on Sixth Avenue*
Riley, James Whitcomb. *Little Orphan Annie*
Robb, Laura. *Snuffles and snouts*
Robertson, Joanne. *Sea witches*
Roche, P. K. (Patrick K.). *Jump all the morning*
Rosales, Melodye Benson. *'Twas the night b'fore Christmas*
Roscoe, William. *The butterfly's ball and the grasshopper's feast*
Rose, Deborah Lee. *The twelve days of kindergarten*
Rosen, Michael (1946–). *How the animals got their colors*
   Smelly jelly smelly fish
   Under the bed
   You can't catch me!
Rossetti, Christina Georgina. *Color*
   Fly away, fly away over the sea
   What is pink?
Rovetch, Lissa. *Ook the book*
   Sweet dreams, little one
Russo, Susan. *The ice cream ocean and other delectable poems of the sea*
Rutherford, Meg. *Animal poems*
Ruurs, Margriet. *Animal alphabet*

Willard, Nancy. *The Moon & Riddles Diner and the Sunnyside Café*
  Pish posh, said Hieronymous Bosch
  A visit to William Blake's inn
  The voyage of the Ludgate Hill
Williams, Barbara. *Donna Jean's disaster*
Wilson, Anna. *Over in the grasslands*
Wilson, Sarah. *June is a tune that jumps on a stair*
Windham, Sophie. *Down in the marvelous deep*
Winnick, Karen B. *A year goes round*
Winters, Kay. *Did you see what I saw?*
Wise, William. *Dinosaurs forever*
Witch poems
Wolfe, Frances. *Where I live*
Wolman, Bernice. *Taking turns*
Wood, Douglas. *Northwoods cradle song*
Woolaver, Lance. *Christmas with the rural mail*
  From Ben Loman to the sea
Worth, Valerie. *At Christmastime*
Wright, Josephine Lord. *Cotton Cat and Martha Mouse*
Yeoman, John. *Our village*
Yerxa, Leo. *Last leaf first snowflake to fall*
Yolen, Jane. *Bird watch*
  Child of faerie, child of earth
  How beastly!
  Nocturne
  Ring of earth
  Snow, snow
  The three bears holiday rhyme book
  The three bears rhyme book
  Welcome to the sea of sand
You and me
Yummy! eating through a day
Ziner, Feenie. *Counting carnival*
Zolotow, Charlotte (Shapiro). *River winding*
  Some things go together

Poland *see* Foreign lands – Poland

Polar bears *see* Animals – polar bears

Police officers *see* Careers – police officers

Polio *see* Illness – poliomyelitis

Polish Americans *see* Ethnic groups in the U.S. – Polish Americans

Poltergeists *see* Ghosts

Ponds *see* Lakes, ponds

Ponies *see* Animals – horses, ponies

Pooka spirit *see* Mythical creatures – pooka spirit

Poor *see* Homeless; Poverty

Pop-up books *see* Format, unusual – toy & movable books

Porcupines *see* Animals – porcupines

Porpoises *see* Animals – dolphins

Portugal *see* Foreign lands – Portugal

Possums *see* Animals – possums

Post office

Ahlberg, Janet. *The jolly Christmas postman*
  The jolly pocket postman
  The jolly postman
Barkan, Joanne. *Whiskerville post office*

Beim, Jerrold. *Country mailman*
Bell, Norman. *Linda's airmail letter*
Bergel, Colin. *Mail by the pail*
Brandt, Betty. *Special delivery*
Buchheimer, Naomi. *Let's go to a post office*
Carter, Don. *Send it!*
Gibbons, Gail. *The post office book*
Gliori, Debi. *Penguin post*
Haley, Gail E. *The post office cat*
Hedderwick, Mairi. *Katie Morag delivers the mail*
Henri, Adrian. *The postman's palace*
Horning, Sandra. *The giant hug*
Kightley, Rosalinda. *The postman*
Koscielniak, Bruce. *Euclid Bunny delivers the mail*
Landström, Olof. *Will goes to the post office*
Marshak, S. (Samuil). *Hail to mail*
Maury, Inez. *My mother the mail carrier = Mi mama la cartera*
Rylant, Cynthia. *Mr. Griggs' work*
Scarry, Richard. *Richard Scarry's Postman Pig and his busy neighbors*
Schneider, Howie. *Fast 'n Snappy*
Scott, Ann Herbert. *Hi!*
Shea, Kitty. *Out and about at the post office*
Skurzynski, Gloria. *Here comes the mail*

Postal workers *see* Careers – postal workers

Potawatomi Indians *see* Indians of North America – Potawatomi

Potty training *see* Toilet training

Pourquoi tales *see* Folk & fairy tales – pourquoi tales

Poverty

Alexander, Lloyd. *The king's fountain*
Ambrus, Victor G. *The three poor tailors*
Andersen, H. C. (Hans Christian). *The little match girl*, ill. by Rachel Isadora
  The little match girl, ill. by Blair Lent
  The little match girl, ill. by Jerry Pinkney
Balet, Jan B. *The fence*
Bartoletti, Susan Campbell. *The Christmas promise*
Bates, Artie Ann. *Ragsale*
Belton, Sandra. *May'naise sandwiches and sunshine tea*
Bettina (Bettina Ehrlich). *Pantaloni*
Brand, Oscar. *When I first came to this land*
Burnett, Frances Hodgson. *A little princess*
Carey, Valerie Scho. *Maggie Mab and the bogey beast*
Coltman, Paul. *Tinker Jim*
Cooper, Susan. *Danny and the Kings*
Czernecki, Stefan. *The sleeping bread*
De Paola, Tomie (Thomas Anthony). *Helga's dowry*
De Veaux, Alexis. *Na-ni*
Diller, Harriett. *The waiting day*
Friedrich, Elizabeth. *Leah's pony*
Garay, Luis. *Pedrito's day*
Goodman, Louise. *Ida's doll*
Greene, Jacqueline Dembar. *What his father did*
Haggerty, Mary Elizabeth. *A crack in the wall*
Harshman, Marc. *Uncle James*
Hazen, Barbara Shook. *Tight times*
Hoban, Lillian. *Stick-in-the-mud turtle*
Hutchins, H. J. (Hazel J.). *Tess*
Keeping, Charles. *Joseph's yard*
Kudler, David. *The Seven Gods of Luck*
Levine, Abby. *Too much mush!*
Lindgren, Astrid. *My nightingale is singing*
Littlesugar, Amy. *Tree of hope*
McCrea, James. *The king's procession*
Maiorano, Robert. *Francisco*
Mills, Lauren A. *The rag coat*
Namioka, Lensey. *The loyal cat*
Nickens, Bessie. *Walking the log*
Nolan, Madeena Spray. *My daddy don't go to work*
Park, Frances. *The royal bee*

Parton, Dolly. *Coat of many colors*
Powell, E. Sandy. *A chance to grow*
Provensen, Alice. *Shaker Lane*
Quattlebaum, Mary. *The shine man*
Rose, Anne K. *How does a czar eat potatoes?*
Sawyer, Ruth. *Journey cake, ho!*
Schermbrucker, Reviva. *Charlie's house*
Seabrooke, Brenda. *The swan's gift*
Shiefman, Vicky. *Sunday potatoes, Monday potatoes*
Sonneborn, Ruth A. *Friday night is papa night*
    Seven in a bed
Steptoe, John. *Uptown*
Thomas, Jane Resh. *Lights on the river*
Turner, Ann Warren. *Dust for dinner*
Vainio, Pirkko. *The Christmas angel*
Wells, Ruth. *The farmer and the poor god*
Wilde, Oscar. *The happy prince*
Ziefert, Harriet. *When I first came to this land*

Pow-wows

Bouchard, Dave. *The song within my heart*

Power failures

Baisch, Cris. *When the lights went out*
Cölle, Gisela. *The star tree*
Freeman, Don. *The night the lights went out*
Grejniec, Michael. *Who is my neighbor?*
Leavy, Una. *Harry's stormy night*
Quackenbush, Robert M. *Funny bunnies on the run*
Rockwell, Anne F. *Blackout*
Rodriguez, Bobbie. *Sarah's sleepover*

Powhatan Indians *see* Indians of North America –
    Powhatan

Practicality *see* Character traits – practicality

Prairie dogs *see* Animals – prairie dogs

Prairie wolves *see* Animals – coyotes

Prayers *see* Religion

Praying mantis *see* Insects – praying mantis

Preachers *see* Careers – clergy

Pregnancy *see* Birth

Prehistoric man *see* Cavemen

Prehistory

Ahlberg, Allan. *Dinosaur dreams*
Aliki. *Digging up dinosaurs*
    Dinosaur bones
    Dinosaurs are different
    My visit to the dinosaurs
Arnold, Caroline. *Giant shark*
Barber, Antonia. *Satchelmouse and the dinosaurs*
Barner, Bob. *Too many dinosaurs*
Barton, Byron. *Bones, bones, dinosaur bones*
    Dinosaurs, dinosaurs
Baylor, Byrd. *If you are a hunter of fossils*
Berenstain, Stan. *After the dinosaurs*
    The Berenstain bears and the missing dinosaur bone
    The day of the dinosaur
Berger, Melvin. *Prehistoric mammals*
    Why did the dinosaurs disappear?
Bilgrami, Shaheen. *Amazing dinosaur discovery*
Bishop, Roma. *My first pop-up book of dinosaurs*
    My first pop-up book of prehistoric animals
Blackwood, Mary. *Derek the knitting dinosaur*

Boynton, Sandra. *Dinosaur's binkit*
    Oh my oh my oh dinosaurs!
Brasch, Kate. *Prehistoric monsters*
Brenner, Barbara A. *Dinosaurium*
Brimner, Larry Dane. *Dinosaurs dance*
Brown, Laurie Krasny. *Dinosaurs alive and well*
    Dinosaurs divorce
    Dinosaurs to the rescue
    Dinosaurs travel
    When dinosaurs die
Brown, Marc Tolon. *Dinosaurs, beware!*
Camp, Lindsay. *Dinosaurs at the supermarket*
Carrick, Carol. *Patrick's dinosaurs*
    Patrick's dinosaurs on the Internet
    What happened to Patrick's dinosaurs?
Cohen, Daniel. *Dinosaurs*
Cole, Joanna. *The magic school bus in the time of the dinosaurs*
Craig, M. Jean. *Dinosaurs and more dinosaurs*
    Curious George and the dinosaur
Cutts, David. *More about dinosaurs*
Daly, Kathleen N. *Dinosaurs*
Damjan, Mischa. *How do dinosaurs say goodnight?*
Davis, Reda. *Martin's dinosaur*
Demi. *Find Demi's dinosaurs*
    Dinosaurs and monsters
Donnelly, Liza. *Dinosaur beach*
    Dinosaur garden
    Dinosaurs' Halloween
Eastman, David. *The story of dinosaurs*
Emberley, Michael. *More dinosaurs!*
Faulkner, Keith. *David dreaming of dinosaurs*
Gay, Tenner Ottley. *Dinosaurs and their relatives in action*
Gibbons, Gail. *Dinosaurs*
    Prehistoric animals
Goode, Diane. *The dinosaur's new clothes*
Gorbaty, Norman. *Get up and go, little dinosaur!*
Gordon, Sharon. *Dinosaurs in trouble*
Granowsky, Alvin. *The dinosaurs' last days*
    Meat-eating dinosaurs
Harrison, Carol. *Dinosaurs everywhere!*
Hartmann, Wendy. *The dinosaurs are back and it's all your fault, Edward!*
Haynes, Max. *Dinosaur island*
Hearn, Diane Dawson. *Dad's dinosaur day*
Henderson, Douglas. *Dinosaur tree*
Hennessy, B. G. (Barbara G.). *Busy Dinah Dinosaur*
    The dinosaur who lived in my backyard
    Meet Dinah Dinosaur
Heyer, Carol. *Dinosaurs!*
Hodgetts, Blake Christopher. *Dream of the dinosaurs*
Hoff, Syd. *Danny and the dinosaur go to camp*
    Happy birthday, Danny and the dinosaur!
Hooks, William H. *Mr. Dinosaur*
Hopkins, Lee Bennett. *Dinosaurs*
Hurd, Edith Thacher. *Dinosaur, my darling*
Inkpen, Mick. *The very good dinosaur*
Joyce, William. *Dinosaur Bob*
Kellogg, Steven (Stephen). *Prehistoric Pinkerton*
Knight, David C. *Dinosaur days*
Koontz, Robin Michal. *Dinosaur dream*
Kurokawa, Mitsuhiro. *Dinosaur valley*
Maccarone, Grace. *Dinosaurs*
McGuire, Leslie. *Who will play with Little Dinosaur?*
McMullan, Kate (Hall). *Dinosaur riddles*
McNaughton, Colin. *If dinosaurs were cats and dogs*
Manning, Linda. *Dinosaur days*
Mansell, Dom. *If dinosaurs came to town*
Martin, Linda. *When dinosaurs go to school*
Mayhew, James. *Katie and the dinosaurs*
Milton, Joyce. *Dinosaur days*
Moseley, Keith. *Dinosaurs*
Mosley, Francis. *The dinosaur eggs*
Most, Bernard. *Dinosaur cousins?*
    A dinosaur named after me
    Dinosaur questions
    Four and twenty dinosaurs
    How big were the dinosaurs?

If the dinosaurs came back
The littlest dinosaurs
Whatever happened to the dinosaurs?
Where to look for a dinosaur
Mullins, Patricia. *Dinosaur encore*
Murphy, Jim. *Dinosaur for a day*
Nolan, Dennis. *Dinosaur dream*
Oram, Hiawyn. *A boy wants a dinosaur*
Otto, Carolyn. *Dinosaur chase*
Palazzo-Craig, Janet. *Little Danny Dinosaur*
Parish, Peggy. *Dinosaur time*
Penner, Lucille Recht. *Dinosaur babies*
Petersen, David. *Dinosaur National Monument*
Petty, Kate. *Dinosaurs*
Pfister, Marcus. *Dazzle the dinosaur*
Pittman, Helena Clare. *A dinosaur for Gerald*
Polhamus, Jean Burt. *Dinosaur do's and don'ts*
    Doctor Dinosaur
Pulver, Robin. *Mrs. Toggle and the dinosaur*
Ripley, Catherine. *Two dozen dinosaurs*
Royston, Angela. *Dinosaurs*
Sant, Laurent Sauveur. *Dinosaurs*
Schwartz, Henry. *How I captured a dinosaur*
See the dinosaurs
Selsam, Millicent E. *A first look at dinosaurs*
Seymour, Peter S. *What's in the prehistoric forest?*
Shields, Carol Diggory. *Saturday night at the dinosaur stomp*
Silverman, Maida. *Dinosaur babies*
Simon, Seymour. *The largest dinosaurs*
    The smallest dinosaurs
Sirois, Allen. *Dinosaur dress up*
Sis, Peter. *Dinosaur!*
Stevenson, James. *The most amazing dinosaur*
Stewart, Frances Todd. *Dinosaurs and other creatures of long ago*
Stickland, Paul. *Dinosaur roar!*
    Dinosaur stomp!
    Ten terrible dinosaurs
Sundgaard, Arnold. *Jethro's difficult dinosaur*
Talbott, Hudson. *Going Hollywood! A dinosaur's dream*
Taylor, Scott. *Dinosaur James*
Thayer, Jane. *Quiet on account of dinosaur*
Wahl, Jan. *The field mouse and the dinosaur named Sue*
    I met a dinosaur
Watson, John. *We're the noisy dinosaurs!*
Wild, Margaret. *My dearest dinosaur*
Wilkes, Angela. *The big book of dinosaurs*
Zallinger, Peter. *Dinosaurs*

Prejudice

Ada, Alma Flor. *The malachite palace*
Anders, Rebecca. *A look at prejudice and understanding*
Boedoe, Geefwee. *Arrowville*
Brophy, Nannette. *The color of my fur*
Brown, Ken (Ken James). *What's the time, Grandma Wolf?*
Carlson, Nancy L. *Loudmouth George and the new neighbors*
Coleman, Evelyn. *White socks only*
Coles, Robert. *The story of Ruby Bridges*
Couric, Katie. *The brand new kid*
Crowther, Kitty. *Jack and Jim*
Egan, Tim. *Metropolitan cow*
Escudie, René. *Paul and Sebastian*
Fries, Claudia. *A pig is moving in*
Fuchshuber, Annegert. *Carly*
Glen, Maggie. *Ruby*
Hoffman, Eric. *Play Lady = La Señora Juguetona*
Ikeda, Daisaku. *Over the deep blue sea*
Klingel, Cynthia Fitterer. *Rosa Parks*
Le Guin, Ursula K. *Fish soup*
Let's talk about race
Littlesugar, Amy. *Jonkonnu*
Lorbiecki, Marybeth. *Sister Anne's hands*
McCourt, Lisa. *Chicken soup for little souls: Della Splatnuk birthday girl*
McKissack, Patricia C. *Goin' someplace special*
Medearis, Michael. *Daisy and the doll*
Miller, M. L. *Those Bottles!*

Miller, William. *The bus ride*
    Night golf
Mitchell, Margaree King. *Susie Mae*
Morris, Ann. *Grandma Lois remembers*
Mostacchi, Massimo. *The beast and the boy*
Pfister, Marcus. *Milo and the mysterious island*
Polacco, Patricia. *Mr. Lincoln's way*
Ringgold, Faith. *If a bus could talk*
Rosen, Michael (1946–). *This is our house*
Rubinetti, Donald. *Cappy the lonely camel*
Schami, Rafik. *Albert and Lila*
Shange, Ntozake. *Whitewash*
Smalls, Irene. *Don't say ain't*
Tarpley, Natasha Anastasia. *Joe-Joe's first flight*
Ungerer, Tomi. *Flix*
Valentine, Johnny. *One dad, two dads, brown dad, blue dads*
Van Allsburg, Chris. *The widow's broom*
Wells, Rosemary. *Yoko*
Wiles, Debbie. *Freedom summer*
Woodson, Jacqueline. *The other side*
Yezerski, Thomas F. *Together in Pinecone Patch*
Yin. *Coolies*

Preschool *see* School – nursery

Pride *see* Character traits – pride

Priests *see* Careers – clergy

Princes *see* Royalty – princes

Princesses *see* Royalty princesses

Printers *see* Careers – printers

Prisons

Butterworth, Oliver. *A visit to the big house*
Dupasquier, Philippe. *The great escape*
Hickman, Martha Whitmore. *When Andy's father went to prison*
McKee, David. *123456789 Benn*
Solotareff, Grégoire. *Don't call me little bunny*

Problem solving

Adler, David A. *The children of Chelm*
Æsop. *The crow and the pitcher*
Alexander, Martha G. *I'll protect you from the jungle beasts*
    Move over, Twerp
    Out! Out! Out!
    We never get to do anything
    We're in big trouble, Blackboard Bear
Allington, Richard L. *Thinking*
Ames, Mildred. *The wonderful box*
Armitage, Ronda. *Ice creams for Rosie*
    The lighthouse keeper's catastrophe
    The lighthouse keeper's lunch
Armstrong-Ellis, Carey. *Prudy's problem and how she solved it*
Arnosky, Jim. *Mud time and more*
Asch, Frank. *Mr. Maxwell's mouse*
Ashley, Bernard. *Dinner ladies don't count*
Bakken, Harold. *The special string*
Balet, Jan B. *The fence*
Barklem, Jill. *The secret staircase*
Barrett, Judi. *What's left?*
Barry, Katharina. *A bug to hug*
Beim, Lorraine. *Two is a team*
Benarde, Anita. *The pumpkin smasher*
Berg, Jean Horton. *The O'Learys and friends*
Bester, Roger. *Guess what?*
Blaine, Marge (Margery Kay). *The terrible thing that happened at our house*
Booth, Eugene. *At the circus*
    At the fair
    In the air
    In the garden

In the jungle
 Under the ocean
Brillhart, Julie. *Story hour – starring Megan!*
Brodmann, Aliana. *Such a noise!*
Bröger, Achim. *Little Harry*
Brown, Jeff. *Flat Stanley*
Brown, Margaret Wise. *They all saw it*
Browne, Anthony. *Bear hunt*
Buchanan, Heather S. *George and Matilda Mouse and the floating school*
 George Mouse's first summer
Bulette, Sara. *The splendid belt of Mr. Big*
Burton, Marilee Robin. *Tail toes eyes ears nose*
Butterworth, Nick. *Jingle bells*
 The secret path
Calhoun, Mary. *Audubon cat*
Carlson, Nancy L. *Harriet and the garden*
Carrick, Carol. *Ben and the porcupine*
Chaffin, Lillie D. *Tommy's big problem*
Chapman, Carol. *Herbie's troubles*
Christensen, Gardell Dano. *Mrs. Mouse needs a house*
Cleary, Beverly. *The real hole*
Clymer, Ted. *The horse and the bad morning*
Cole, Babette. *Princess Smartypants*
Cole, Joanna. *It's too noisy*
Cooney, Nancy Evans. *The blanket that had to go*
 Donald says thumbs down
Cooper, Jacqueline. *Angus and the Mona Lisa*
Corbalis, Judy. *The cuckoo bird*
Cressey, James. *Fourteen rats and a rat-catcher*
Cummings, Pat. *Jimmy Lee did it*
Davis, Aubrey. *The enormous potato*
Deedy, Carmen Agra. *Agatha's feather bed*
Demarest, Chris L. *Kitman and Willy at sea*
De Paola, Tomie (Thomas Anthony). *Charlie needs a cloak*
Dewey, Ariane. *The fish Peri*
Dickinson, Mary. *Alex's bed*
Domanska, Janina. *The turnip*
Economakis, Olga. *Oasis of the stars*
Elkin, Benjamin. *Such is the way of the world*
Emberley, Ed (Edward Randolph). *Rosebud*
Farber, Norma. *How the left-behind beasts built Ararat*
Fassler, Joan. *Boy with a problem*
Feder, Paula Kurzband. *Where does the teacher live?*
Gardella, Tricia. *Blackberry booties*
George, Lindsay Barrett. *In the woods*
Gerstein, Mordicai. *Stop those pants!*
Gordon, Margaret. *The supermarket mice*
Greene, Carol. *The golden locket*
Grindley, Sally. *Who is it?*
Hancock, Sibyl. *Freaky Francie*
Harber, Frances. *My king has donkey ears*
Heitler, Susan M. (Susan McCrensky). *David decides, no more thumb-sucking*
Henwood, Simon. *The troubled village*
Hewett, Anita. *The tale of the turnip*
Hines, Anna Grossnickle. *Maybe a band-aid will help*
Hoban, Lillian. *Arthur's funny money*
Horvath, Betty F. *The cheerful quiet*
Houston, John A. *The bright yellow rope*
 A mouse in my house
Hughes, Shirley. *An evening at Alfie's*
Hulse, Gillian. *Morris, where are you?*
Ives, Penny. *Mrs. Santa Claus*
Johnson, Paul Brett. *Mr. Persnickety and Cat Lady*
Jonas, Ann. *Holes and peeks*
Joyce, William. *Big time Olie*
Keats, Ezra Jack. *Goggles*
 Whistle for Willie
Keenen, George. *The preposterous week*
Klimowicz, Barbara. *The strawberry thumb*
Kroll, Steven. *Looking for Daniela*
Lebentritt, Julia. *The Kooken*
Leonard, Marcia. *Birthday in a bathtub*
 Little owl leaves the nest
Levitin, Sonia. *Who owns the moon?*
Lexau, Joan M. *Benjie*

Benjie on his own
Lobel, Arnold. *On the day Peter Stuyvesant sailed into town*
London, Sara. *Firehorse Max*
Low, Joseph. *What if . . . ?*
Lyon, David. *The brave little computer*
McCloskey, Robert. *Lentil*
Maestro, Betsy. *The guessing game*
Maiorano, Robert. *Francisco*
Manson, Christopher. *Here begins the tale of the marvellous blue mouse*
Marie, Geraldine. *The magic box*
Maris, Ron. *Hold tight, bear!*
Marshall, James. *Four little troubles*
Marshall, Margaret. *Mike*
Martinez, Ruth. *Mrs. McDockerty's knitting*
Masini, Beatrice. *A brave little princess*
Mayer, Mercer. *Just big enough*
 What do you do with a kangaroo?
Merriam, Eve. *The birthday door*
Milhous, Katherine. *The turnip*
Munsch, Robert N. *Jonathan cleaned up – then he heard a sound*
Murphy, Stuart J. *The best vacation ever*
 Treasure map
Myers, Walter Dean. *The golden serpent*
Myrick, Jean Lockwood. *Ninety-nine pockets*
Nakagawa, Rieko. *Guri and Gura*
Ness, Evaline. *Do you have the time, Lydia?*
Oakley, Graham. *The church mice in action*
Obrist, Jürg. *They do things right in Albern*
Olaleye, Isaac. *Bitter bananas*
Parkinson, Kathy. *The enormous turnip*
Partridge, Jenny. *Hopfellow*
 Mr. Squint
 Peterkin Pollensnuff
Payne, Emmy. *Katy no-pocket*
Poydar, Nancy. *The perfectly horrible Halloween*
Rice, Eve. *Peter's pockets*
Robb, Brian. *My grandmother's djinn*
Robison, Deborah. *Bye-bye, old buddy*
 No elephants allowed
Root, Phyllis. *Rattletrap car*
 Rattletrap car [board book]
Rose, Anne K. *The talking turnip*
Salat, Cristina. *Peanut's emergency*
SanAngelo, Ryan. *Eddie spaghetti*
Schermer, Judith. *Mouse in house*
Schurr, Cathleen. *The long and the short of it*
Segal, Lore Groszmann. *The story of old Mrs. Brubeck and how she looked for trouble and where she found him*
Seuss, Dr. *Did I ever tell you how lucky you are?*
 Hunches in bunches
Sharmat, Marjorie Weinman. *The pizza monster*
Singh, Jacquelin. *Fat Gopal*
Smith, Donald. *Who's wearing my baseball cap?*
 Who's wearing my bow tie?
 Who's wearing my sneakers?
 Who's wearing my sunglasses?
Smith, Jim. *The frog band and the onion seller*
Sondheimer, Ilse. *The magic of Pomme*
Spinelli, Eileen. *Wanda's monster*
Steel, Danielle. *Max and the baby sitter*
Stevenson, James. *Quick! Turn the page!*
Stihler, Chérie B. *The giant cabbage turnip*
Talbot, John. *Pins and needles*
Thayer, Jane. *What's a ghost going to do?*
Thomas, Patricia. *"There are rocks in my socks!" said the ox to the fox*
Thompson, Vivian Laubach. *Camp-in-the-yard*
Titus, Eve. *Anatole and the cat*
 Anatole and the pied piper
 Anatole and the poodle
 Anatole and the robot
 Anatole and the thirty thieves
 Anatole and the toyshop
 Anatole in Italy
Tolstoy, Aleksey Nikolayevich. *The enormous turnip*
 The gigantic turnip, ill. by Niamh Sharkey
 The great big enormous turnip

Türk, Hanne. *Max versus the cube*
  A surprise for Max
Tusa, Tricia. *Camilla's new hairdo*
Twinem, Neecy. *Changing colors*
  High in the trees
Uhlberg, Myron. *Mad Dog McGraw*
Vagin, Vladimir Vasilévich. *The enormous carrot*
Van Horn, William. *Twitchtoe, the beastfinder*
Van Kampen, Vlasta. *It couldn't be worse*
Wallen, Ila. *The moon in my room*
Wilhelm, Hans. *I lost my tooth!*
Williams, Karen Lynn. *Painted dreams*
Winthrop, Elizabeth. *Maggie and the monster*
Wiseman, Bernard. *Doctor Duck and Nurse Swan*
Wold, Jo Anne. *Tell them my name is Amanda*
Wynne-Jones, Tim. *Builder of the moon*
Wyse, Lois. *Two guppies, a turtle and Aunt Edna*
Yagelski, Robert. *The day the lifting bridge stuck*
Yektai, Niki. *What's missing?*
Yolen, Jane. *Piggins*
Yorinks, Arthur. *Bravo, Minski*
Zemach, Margot. *It could always be worse*
Ziefert, Harriet. *The turnip*
  You can't buy a dinosaur with a dime

Progress

Barton, Byron. *Wheels*
Burton, Virginia Lee. *The little house*
Duvoisin, Roger Antoine. *Lonely Veronica*
Fife, Dale. *Empty lot*
  The little park
Goodall, John S. *The story of an English village*
Greene, Graham. *The little fire engine*
Harrison, David Lee. *Little turtle's big adventure*
Heine, Helme. *Prince Bear*
Hoban, Russell. *Arthur's new power*
Ipcar, Dahlov (Zorach). *One horse farm*
MacGill-Callahan, Sheila. *And still the turtle watched*
Murschetz, Luis. *Mister Mole*
Peet, Bill (William Bartlett). *Countdown to Christmas*
  Farewell to Shady Glade
  The wump world
Ray, Mary Lyn. *Pumpkins*
Shecter, Ben. *Emily, girl witch of New York*
Steiner, Jörg. *The bear who wanted to be a bear*
Tusa, Tricia. *Sherman and Pearl*

Promptness *see* Behavior – promptness

Proverbs

Kneen, Maggie. *"Too many cooks . . ."*
Swann, Brian. *A basket full of white eggs*

Ptarmigans *see* Birds – ptarmigans

Pueblo Indians *see* Indians of North America – Pueblo

Puerto Rico *see* Foreign lands – Puerto Rico

Puffins *see* Birds – puffins

Pumas *see* Animals – cougars

Punchball *see* Sports – punchball

Punctuality *see* Behavior – promptness

Puppeteers *see* Careers – puppeteers

Puppets

Anastasio, Dina. *Baby Piggy and giant bubble*
Atene, Ann (Anna). *The golden guitar*

Blau, Judith. *Bunny Mitten's book*
Brandenberg, Franz. *Aunt Nina's visit*
Brennan, Joseph Killorin. *Gobo and the river*
Bruce, Sheilah B. *The radish day jubilee*
Cahill, Chris. *Bear magic*
  Bunny magic
  Spider magic
  Turtle magic
Calmenson, Stephanie. *ABC*
Chernoff, Goldie Taub. *Puppet party*
Children's Television Workshop. *Muppets in my neighborhood*
Cleaver, Elizabeth. *The enchanted caribou*
Collodi, Carlo. *The adventures of Pinocchio*
  Pinocchio
Eaton, Su. *Punch and Judy in the rain*
Elliott, Dan. *Ernie's little lie*
  A visit to the Sesame Street firehouse
Findlay, Lisa. *What's in Oscar's trashcan?*
Fitzpatrick, Marie-Louise. *Lizzy and Skunk*
Freeman, Don. *The paper party*
Freudberg, Judy. *Susan and Gordon adopt a baby*
Gikow, Louise. *Baby Kermit's Christmas*
  Boober Fraggle's ghosts
  Bye-bye, pacifier
  Count with me
  Follow that Fraggle!
  For every child, a better world
  I am Kermit
  Jim Henson's Muppets in Rowlf's big test
  Jim Henson's Muppets in What's fair is fair
  Sprocket's Christmas tale
Gilmour, H. B. *Why Wembley Fraggle couldn't sleep*
Greaves, Margaret. *Petrushka*
Hautzig, Deborah. *Big Bird at the beach*
  Ernie and Bert's new kitten
  Grover's bad dream
  It's not fair!
  A visit to the Sesame Street hospital
  A visit to the Sesame Street library
Hayward, Linda. *Baker, baker, cookie maker*
  The biggest cookie in the world
  The case of the missing Duckie
  A day in the life of Oscar the Grouch
  Elmo goes to day camp
  Ernie and Bert's summer project
  Grover's summer vacation
  I can count to ten and back again
Heymans, Margriet. *Pippin and Robber Grumblecroak's big baby*
Howe, James. *The case of the missing mother*
Kates, Bobbi Jane. *We're different, we're the same*
Keats, Ezra Jack. *Louie*
Klimowicz, Barbara. *The strawberry thumb*
Lerner, Sharon. *Big Bird's copycat day*
  Follow the monsters!
Lewis, Shari. *Baby Lamb Chop loves animals*
  Baby Lamb Chop loves numbers
  Baby Lamb Chop loves nursery school
  Baby Lamb Chop loves the beach
  Baby Lamb Chop loves words
Little, Mary E. *Ricardo and the puppets*
Masks and puppets
Moss, Jeffrey. *The Sesame Street ABC storybook*
  The songs of Sesame Street in poems and pictures
Mother Goose. *The Sesame Street players present Mother Goose*
Muntean, Michaela. *Kermit and Robin's scary story*
  Mokey and the festival of the bells
  Muppet babies through the year
The Muppet Show book
One rubber duckie
Parsons, Virginia. *Pinocchio and Gepetto*
  Pinocchio and the money tree
  Pinocchio goes on the stage
  Pinocchio plays truant
Peters, Sharon. *Puppet show*
Pfister, Marcus. *Rainbow fish board book and finger puppet*
Poskanzer, Susan Cornell. *Puppeteer*
Potter, Giselle. *The year I didn't go to school*

Provensen, Alice. *Punch in New York*
Roberts, Sarah. *Bert and the missing mop mix-up*
  Ernie's big mess
  I want to go home!
Ross, Anna. *I did it!*
  I have to go
  Naptime
  Say the magic word, please
Ryder, Joanne. *Hello, first grade*
Sesame Street. *Ernie and Bert can . . . can you?*
  Sesame Street sign language fun
  Sesame Street word book
Smith, Lane. *Pinocchio, the boy*
Steiner, Charlotte. *Pete's puppets*
Stevenson, Jocelyn. *Jim Henson's Muppets at sea*
  Red and the pumpkins
Stiles, Norman. *I'll miss you, Mr. Hooper*
Stone, Jon. *Big Bird in China*
Tettelbaum, Michael. *The cave of the lost Fraggle*
The Timbertoes 1 2 3 counting book
The Timbertoes ABC alphabet book
Tornborg, Pat. *The Sesame Street cookbook*
Trimble, Marcia. *Peppy's shadow*
Weare, Tim. *Hide-and-seek with Leo*
  I'm a little giraffe
  I'm a little penguin
  I'm a little puppy
Weiss, Ellen. *Mokey's birthday present*
  Pigs in space
  You are the star of a Muppet adventure
Weiss, George (George David). *What a wonderful world*
Who took the cookie?
Wilson, Sarah. *Elmo says, achoo!*
Young, Ed (Edward). *The rooster's horns*

Purim *see* Holidays – Purim

Purses *see* Clothing – handbags, purses

Puzzles *see also* Picture puzzles; Rebuses; Riddles & jokes

Birchman, David Francis. *Jigsaw Jackson*
Boatfield, Jonny. *The twilight book*
Bourke, Linda. *Eye count*
Capucilli, Karen. *The jelly bean fun book*
Demi. *Find Demi's baby animals*
  Find Demi's dinosaurs
  Find Demi's sea creatures
Geisert, Arthur. *Pigs from 1 to 10*
Kneen, Maggie. *When you're not looking*
Owen, Annie. *From snowflakes to sandcastles*
Pfister, Marcus. *The rainbow fish floor puzzle book*
Simmons, Jane. *Splish splash Daisy*
Waber, Bernard. *Do you see a mouse?*

Quail *see* Birds – quail

Quechua Indians *see* Indians of South America – Quechua

Queens *see* Royalty – queens

Questioning *see* Character traits – questioning

Quicksand *see* Sand

Quilts

Bateson-Hill, Margaret. *Shota and the star quilt*
Bourgeois, Paulette. *Oma's quilt*
Brenner, Barbara A. *The flying patchwork quilt*
Brown, Margaret Wise. *Bunny's noisy book*
  Bunny's noisy book [board book]
Chorao, Kay. *Kate's quilt*
Cline-Ransome, Lesa. *Quilt alphabet*
  Quilt counting
Coerr, Eleanor. *The Josefina story quilt*
Cole, Barbara Hancock. *Texas star*
Dwyer, Mindy. *Quilt of dreams*
Ernst, Lisa Campbell. *Sam Johnson and the blue ribbon quilt*
Fleisher, Robbin. *Quilts in the attic*
Flournoy, Valerie. *The patchwork quilt*
Gibbons, Gail. *The quilting bee*
Guback, Georgia. *Luka's quilt*
Hermes, Patricia. *When snow lay soft on the mountain*
Hesse, Karen. *Lavender*
Hines, Anna Grossnickle. *Pieces, a year in poems and quilts*
Howard, Ellen. *The log cabin quilt*
Ipcar, Dahlov (Zorach). *The calico jungle*
Johnston, Tony. *The quilt story*
  That summer
Jonas, Ann. *The quilt*
Koralek, Jenny. *The boy and the cloth of dreams*
Kuskin, Karla. *Patchwork island*
Leedahl, Shelley A. (Shelley Ann). *The bone talker*
Martin, Jacqueline Briggs. *Bizzy Bones and the lost quilt*
Min, Willemien. *Peter's patchwork dream*
Moss, P. Buckley (Pat Buckley). *Reuben and the quilt*
Paul, Ann Whitford. *Eight hands round*
  The seasons sewn
Polacco, Patricia. *The keeping quilt*
Radley, Gail. *The spinner's gift*
Ransom, Candice F. *The promise quilt*
Ringgold, Faith. *Cassie's word quilt*
  Tar Beach
Root, Phyllis. *The name quilt*
Smucker, Barbara Claasen. *Selina and the bear paw quilt*
Steiner, Charlotte. *The sleepy quilt*
Stevens, Kathleen. *Aunt Skilly and the stranger*
Stroud, Bettye. *The patchwork path*
Torres, Leyla. *Liliana's grandmothers*
Vincent, Gabrielle. *Ernest and Celestine's patchwork quilt*
Warner, Sunny. *The moon quilt*
Whelan, Gloria. *Bringing the farmhouse home*
Whittington, Mary K. *The patchwork lady*
Willard, Nancy. *The mountains of quilt*
Yolen, Jane. *Old Dame Counterpane*
Yorinks, Arthur. *Quack!*
Zagwÿn, Deborah Turney. *The pumpkin blanket*
Ziefert, Harriet. *Before I was born*

Rabbis *see* Careers – clergy

Rabbits *see* Animals – rabbits

Raccoons *see* Animals – raccoons

Race car drivers *see* Careers – race car drivers

Race relations *see* Prejudice

Racing *see* Sports – racing

Radios

Barasch, Lynne. *Radio rescue*
Dorros, Arthur. *Radio Man = Don Radio*
Schneider, Christine M. *Saxophone Sam and his snazzy jazz band*

Railroad engineers *see* Careers – railroad engineers

Railroads *see* Trains

Rain *see* Weather – rain

Rainbows *see* Weather – rainbows

Rajahs *see* Royalty – rajahs

Ramadan *see* Holidays – Ramadan

Ranchers *see* Careers – ranchers

Rangers *see* Careers – park rangers

Rats *see* Animals – rats

Ravens *see* Birds – ravens

Reading *see* Books, reading

Rebuses

Adler, David A. *Bunny rabbit rebus*
Asbjørnsen, P. C. (Peter Christen). *The three billy goats Gruff*, ill. by Heidi Petach
Banks, Kate (Katherine A.). *The bird, the monkey, and the snake in the jungle*
Capucilli, Alyssa Satin. *Inside a barn in the country*
  Inside a house that is haunted
  Inside a zoo in the city
Cole, Joanna. *Monster and Muffin*
Coletta, Irene. *From A to Z*
Davis, Lee. *P. B. Bear's birthday party*
Dodds, Siobhan. *Words and pictures*
Doolittle, Eileen. *The ark in the attic*
Downie, Jill. *Alphabet puzzle*
Dubowski, Cathy East. *Picky Nicky*
Gilman, Rita Golden. *Mole in a hole*
Grimm, Jacob. *Sleeping Beauty*, ill. by John Wallner
Hayward, Linda. *D is for doll*
Herman, Gail. *Otto the cat*
Heuck, Sigrid. *Pony and Bear are friends*
  Who stole the apples?
Hill, Eric. *Spot's walk in the woods*
Hooks, William H. *The Gruff brothers*
  Read-a-rebus
The house that Jack built. *The house that Jack built*, ill. by Jeanette Winter
Lewison, Wendy Cheyette. *Don't wake the baby!*
Marzollo, Jean. *I love you*
  I see a star
  The rebus treasury
Mitter, Matt. *Once upon a rhyme*
Morris, Ann. *The Cinderella rebus book*
  The Little Red Riding Hood rebus book
Mother Goose. *Mother Goose in hieroglyphics*
Neitzel, Shirley. *The bag I'm taking to Grandma's*
  The dress I'll wear to the party
  The house I'll build for the wrens
  I'm not feeling well today
  I'm taking a trip on my train
  We're making breakfast for mother
O'Connor, Jane. *Benny's big bubble*
Partch, Virgil Franklin. *The Christmas cookie sprinkle snitcher*
Pizer, Abigail. *It's a perfect day*
Reit, Seymour. *Rebus bears*

The three bears. *Goldilocks and the three bears*, ill. by Madelaine Gill Linden
The three little pigs. *The three little pigs*, ill. by Madelaine Gill
Weil, Lisl. *Mother Goose picture riddles*
Wyllie, Stephen. *The great race*

Reindeer *see* Animals – reindeer

Religion

Adler, David A. *A picture book of Hanukkah*
  A picture book of Israel
Æsop. *Androcles and the lion*, ill. by Janusz Grabianski
  Androcles and the lion, ill. by Janet Stevens
Aichinger, Helga. *The shepherd*
Alborghetti, Marci. *Miracle of the myrrh*
Aleichem, Sholem. *Hanukah money*
Alexander, Cecil Frances. *All things bright and beautiful*, ill. by Leo Politi
  All things bright and beautiful, ill. by Bruce Whatley
Aliki. *Mummies made in Egypt*
All night, all day
Amazing graces
Ammon, Richard. *An Amish Christmas*
Anderson, Debby. *Let's talk about Heaven*
Angeletti, Roberta. *Nefertari, princess of Egypt*
Anglund, Joan Walsh. *A book of good tidings from the Bible*
Aoki, Hisako. *Santa's favorite story*
Araten, Harry. *Two by two*
Aronow, Sara. *Seven days of creation*
Baker, Betty. *And me, coyote!*
Baker, Sanna Anderson. *Who's a friend of the water-spurting whale*
Balet, Jan B. *The gift*
Baring-Gould, S. (Sabine). *Now the day is over*
Barker, Peggy. *What happened when grandma died*
Barton, Bob. *Paul Gallico's The small miracle*
Bawden, Nina. *St. Francis of Assisi*
Bayar, Steven. *Rachel and Mischa*
Baylor, Byrd. *The way to start a day*
Baynes, Pauline. *Let there be light*
  Thanks be to God
Bea, Holly. *Bless your heart*
  My spiritual alphabet book
  Where does God live?
Bedard, Michael. *The wolf of Gubbio*
Behrens, June. *Hanukkah*
  Passover
Berger, Barbara Helen. *Animalia*
  The donkey's dream
Bernhard, Emery. *The tree that rains*
Bible. *Best-loved Bible verses for children*
Bible. New Testament. *The Lord's prayer*, Catholic version, ill. by Ingri and Edgar Parin d'Aulaire
  The Lord's prayer, Protestant version, ill. by Ingri and Edgar Parin d'Aulaire
  The Lord's prayer, ill. by George Kraus
  The Lord's prayer, ill. by Tim Ladwig
Bible. New Testament. Corinthians, 1st, XIII. *Love is*
Bible. New Testament. Gospels. *Easter*, ill. by Fiona French
Bible. Old Testament. Daniel. *Shadrach, Meshach, and Abednego*
Bible. Old Testament. Ecclesiastes. *To every thing there is a season*
Bible. Old Testament. Genesis. *Genesis*
  The story of the creation
Bible. Old Testament. Jonah. *Jonah and the great fish*, ill. by Jim Cummins
Bible. Old Testament. Joseph. *Joseph and his brothers*
Bible. Old Testament. Psalms. *The Lord is my shepherd*, ill. by George Kraus
  The Lord is my shepherd, ill. by Tasha Tudor
  Psalm twenty-three
  The twenty-third Psalm
Bless the beasts
Bolden, Tonya. *Rock of ages*
Boling, Ruth L. *Come worship with me*
Borchard, Therese Johnson. *Taste and see the goodness of the Lord*
Boroson, Martin. *Becoming me*
Bratton, Heidi. *Imagine*

Yes, I can!
Brin, Ruth F. *The story of Esther*
Briscoe, D. Stuart. *Where is God?*
Briscoe, Jill. *The innkeeper's daughter*
Brokering, Herbert F. *Earth and all stars*
Brown, Katherine. *The Small One*
Brown, Margaret Wise. *On Christmas eve*, ill. by Nancy Edwards
    Calder
    On Christmas eve, ill. by Beni Montresor
Bruna, Dick. *Christmas*
Buckley, Helen Elizabeth. *Moonlight kite*
Buckley, Ray. *God's love is like . . .*
Burdekin, Harold. *A child's grace*
Burningham, John. *Whaddayamean*
Butterworth, Nick. *The house on the rock*
    The lost sheep
    The precious pearl
    The two sons
Carlson, Lori Marie. *Hurray for Three Kings' Day*
Carlson, Melody. *The Easterville miracle*
Carlstrom, Nancy White. *Does God know how to tie shoes?*
    What does the sky say?
Caswell, Helen Rayburn. *God must like to laugh*
    Parable of the good Samaritan
Chaikin, Miriam. *Exodus*
Chanover, Hyman. *Happy Hanukah everybody*
Chapman, Jean. *Moon-Eyes*
Chase, Catherine. *The miracles at Cana*
Children go where I send thee
Children's prayers from around the world
A child's book of prayers
Christian, Mary Blount. *Anna and the strangers*
    Grandfathers, God's gift to children
    Grandmothers, God's gift to children
Coatsworth, Elizabeth. *Song of the camels*
Cohen, Barbara. *The binding of Isaac*
    The donkey's story
    First fast
    Here come the Purim players!, ill. by Shoshana Mekibel
Cohen, Deborah Bodin. *The seventh day*
Cole, Joanna. *A gift from Saint Francis*
Cooner, Donna D. (Donna Danell). *The world God made*
Cooney, Barbara. *A little prayer*
Daly, Kathleen N. *Jesus our friend*
Davidson, Alice J. *The story of creation*
Davis, Aubrey. *Bagels from Benny*
Dellinger, Annetta. *You are special to Jesus*
De Paola, Tomie (Thomas Anthony). *Christopher*
    The clown of God
    The Lady of Guadalupe
    The legend of Old Befana
    My first Chanukah
    The night of Las Posadas
    The parables of Jesus
    Patrick
Din dan don, it's Christmas
Douglas, Robert W. *John Paul II*
Downes, Belinda. *Every little angel's handbook*
Downey, Lynn. *This is the earth that God made*
Drucker, Malka. *Grandma's latkes*
    A Jewish holiday ABC
Easwaran, Eknath. *The monkey and the mango*
Ehrlich, Amy. *The story of Hannukah*
Eisenberg, Ann. *Bible heroes I can be*
    I can celebrate
Emerman, Ellen. *Is it Shabbos yet?*
Farber, Norma. *How the hibernators came to Bethlehem*
    When it snowed that night
Fass, David E. *The shofar that lost its voice*
Feder, Harriet K. *Not yet, Elijah!*
Field, Rachel Lyman. *Prayer for a child*
Fienberg, Anna. *Joseph*
Figley, Marty Rhodes. *The story of Zacchaeus*
Filleul, Liz. *Tumbler*
First graces
First prayers, ill. by Anna Maria Magagna
First prayers, ill. by Tasha Tudor

Fisher, Aileen Lucia. *The story of Easter*
Fisher, Leonard Everett. *The seven days of creation*
Fishman, Cathy Goldberg. *On Hanukkah*
    On Passover
    On Rosh Hashanah and Yom Kippur
    On Shabbat
Fitch, Florence Mary. *A book about God*
Foreman, Juli. *Great beginnings*
Foreman, Michael. *Cat in the manger*
Forrester, Victoria. *Poor Gabriella*
Frank, Penny. *In the beginning*
Fraser, James Howard. *Los Posadas*
The friendly beasts
The friendly beasts and a partridge in a pear tree, ill. by Virginia Pear-
    sons
Galdone, Paul. *The first seven days*
Gauch, Patricia Lee. *The little friar who flew*
Geisert, Arthur. *After the flood*
Gellman, Marc. *Where does God live?*
Gerstein, Mordicai. *Queen Esther the morning star*
Ghazi, Suhaib Hamid. *Ramadan*
Giuliano, Katie. *All the way to God*
Gleeson, Brian. *The Savior is born*
Goddard, Carrie Lou. *Isn't it a wonder!*
Godwin, Laura. *Barnyard prayers*
Goldin, Barbara Diamond. *Cakes and miracles*
    A mountain of blintzes
Gold-Vukson, Marji E. *The colors of my Jewish Year*
    Grandpa and me on Tu B'Shevat
Good, Merle. *Amos and Susie*
Graham, Lorenz B. *David he no fear*
    Hongry catch the foolish boy
    A road down in the sea
Gramatky, Hardie. *Nikos and the sea god*
Greene, Carol. *God's good creation*
Griessman, Annette. *Jenny's prayer*
Grimes, Nikki. *At break of day*
    Come Sunday
    From a child's heart
    When Daddy prays
Groner, Judyth Saypol. *All about Hanukkah*
    All about Sukkot
    Thank you, God!
Haas, Dorothy. *My first communion*
Hallinan, P. K. (Patrick K.). *The small town children's Easter*
Hamil, Thomas Arthur. *Brother Alonzo*
Hanukkah lights
Harber, Frances. *The brothers' promise*
Harmer, Juliet. *Prayers for children*
Hartman, Bob. *The birthday of a king*
    The morning of the world
    A night the stars danced for joy
    Who brought the bread?
    Who wrecked the roof?
Hawxhurst, Joan C. *Bubbe and Gram, my two grandmothers*
Heck, Elisabeth. *The black sheep*
Heine, Helme. *One day in paradise*
Helldorfer, M. C. (Mary Claire). *Clap clap!*
Hennessy, B. G. (Barbara G.). *The first night*
Hest, Amy. *The Friday nights of Nana*
Higgs, Liz Curtis. *Go away, dark night*
Hillman, Priscilla. *The Merry-Mouse book of prayers and graces*
Hirsh, Marilyn. *I love Passover*
    Joseph who loved the Sabbath
    Potato pancakes all around
Hodges, Margaret. *The golden deer*
    The legend of Saint Christopher
    Saint Christopher
    St. Jerome and the lion
Hoffman, Mary. *Miracles*
    Parables, stories Jesus told
Holland, Cheri. *Maccabee jamboree*
Hopkins, Lee Bennett. *All God's children*
    And God bless me
Houselander, Caryll. *Petook*
How much does God love me?
Howard, Ellen. *The log cabin church*

Hughes, Shirley. *Lucy and Tom's Christmas*
Hunt, Angela Elwell. *The tale of three trees*
Hutton, Warwick. *Adam and Eve*
    Persephone
    Theseus and the Minotaur
I imagine angels
I've seen the promised land
Ife, Elaine. *The childhood of Jesus*
    Stories Jesus told
Jaffe, Nina. *Tales for the seventh day*
Jendresen, Erik. *Hanuman*
Johnson, Dinah. *Sunday week*
Johnson, Grace. *The candle in the window*
Johnson, James Weldon. *The Creation*
Jones, Jessie Mae Orton. *A little child*
    Small rain
Jüchen, Aurel von. *The Holy Night*
Kahn, Katherine Janus. *The shofar calls to us*
Kajpust, Melissa. *A dozen silk diapers*
Karlinsky, Ruth Schild. *My first book of Mitzvos*
Karon, Jan. *Miss Fannie's hat*
Kassirer, Sue. *Joseph and his coat of many colors*
Keats, Ezra Jack. *God is in the mountain*
Kennedy, X. J. *The beasts of Bethlehem*
Kimmel, Eric A. *The Chanukkah guest*
    The Chanukkah tree
    Gershon's monster
    Hershel and the Hanukkah goblins
    One winter night
    Ten suns
    Why the snake crawls on its belly
Kimmelman, Leslie. *Dance, sing, remember*
    Hanukkah lights, Hanukkah nights
    Hooray! it's Passover!
    The runaway latkes
    Sound the shofar!
Kipling, Rudyard. *The miracle of the mountain*
Knapp, John, II. *A pillar of pepper and other Bible nursery rhymes*
Knowlton, Laurie Lazzaro. *God be in my heart*
Koralek, Jenny. *Hanukkah*
Kress, Camille. *Purim*
Krishnaswami, Uma. *Holi*
Kropf, Latifa Berry. *It's Hanukkah time!*
    It's seder time!
Krulik, Nancy E. *Is it Hanukkah yet?*
Krull, Kathleen. *Songs of praise*
Kushner, Lawrence. *Because Nothing Looks Like God*
Kuskin, Karla. *A great miracle happened there*
    Jerusalem, shining still
Lamstein, Sarah Marwil. *Annie's Shabbat*
Lattimore, Deborah Nourse. *The sailor who captured the sea*
Lee, Jeanne M. *I once was a monkey*
Leeton, Will C. *The Tower of Babel*
Lehman-Wilzig, Tami. *Keeping the promise*
Lepon, Shoshana. *Hillel builds a house*
LeSourd, Nancy. *Christy, Christmastime at Cutter Gap*
Lester, Julius. *What a truly cool world*
    Why heaven is far away
Let there be light
Le Tord, Bijou. *The deep blue sea*
    God's little seeds
    The river and the rain
    Sing a new song
Levine, Arthur A. *All the lights in the night*
    The boy who drew cats
Lewis, Jacqueline Janette. *You are so wonderful*
Lexau, Joan M. *More beautiful than flowers*
Libney, Varda. *What I like about Passover*
Lindbergh, Reeve. *The circle of days*
    On morning wings
Lines, Kathleen. *Once in royal David's city*
Lister, Clare. *My first Passover [board book]*
Little book of prayers
London, Jonathan. *Into this night we are rising*
Long, Kathy. *Hallelujah the clown*
Lucado, Max. *Small gifts in God's hands*
Lundy, Charlotte. *Thank you, Esther*

Thank you, Ruth and Naomi
Maccarone, Grace. *A child's good night prayer*
McDermott, Gerald. *The voyage of Osiris*
McDonough, Yona Zeldis. *Eve and her sisters*
McGee, Marni. *The colt and the king*
McKissack, Patricia C. *My Bible ABC book*
McLerran, Alice. *The ghost dance*
Madonna. *Yakov and the seven thieves*
Manushkin, Fran. *Hooray for Hanukkah!*
    Latkes and applesauce
    The matzah that Papa brought home
    Miriam's cup
    Starlight and candles
Mark, Jan. *The tale of Tobias*
Marshall, Lyn. *Yoga for your children*
Martin, Ann M. *Leo the Magnificat*
Martin, Bill (William Ivan). *Adam, Adam, what do you see?*
Marx, David F. *Ramadan*
Marzollo, Jean. *Miriam and her brother Moses*
Matthews, Caitlin. *The blessing seed*
Mayer, Marianna. *Perseus*
Medina, Tony. *Christmas makes me think*
Melcher, Mary. *Mommy, who does God love?*
Metaxas, Eric. *Bible ABC*
    David and Goliath
Michael, Emory H. *Androcles and the lion*
Mitchell, Cynthia. *Here a little child I stand*
Miyoshi, Sekiya. *Singing David*
Modesitt, Jeanne. *It's Hanukkah!*
    Songs of Chanukah
Moorman, Margaret. *Light the lights!*
Moss, Marissa. *The ugly menorah*
Murphy, Elspeth Campbell. *Do you see me God?*
    Happy Easter, God
Myra, Harold Lawrence. *Thanksgiving*
Namioka, Lensey. *The loyal cat*
Nayer, Judy. *The eight nights of Hanukka*
Nerlove, Miriam. *Easter*
    Hanukkah
    Passover
    Purim
    Shabbat
    The Ten Commandments for Jewish children
Nettleton, Pamela Hill. *Martin Luther King, Jr.*
Newman, Lesléa. *Matzo ball moon*
Noah, build your boat
Nobisso, Josephine. *The weight of a Mass*
Nomura, Noriko S. *I am Shinto*
Norris, Kathleen. *The holy twins: Benedict and Scholastica*
Oberman, Sheldon. *King Solomon, Sheba, and the hoopoe bird*
    Sound of the shofar
O'Keefe, Susan Heyboer. *Angel prayers*
    Good night, God bless
Oppenheim, Shulamith Levey. *The hundredth name*
    Iblis
Orgel, Doris. *The flower of Sheba*
Otto, Carolyn. *Pioneer church*
Parton, Dolly. *Coat of many colors*
Pieńkowski, Jan. *Easter*
Podwal, Mark H. *The menorah story*
    A sweet year
Polacco, Patricia. *Chicken Sunday*
Poole, Josephine. *Joan of Arc*
Price, Christine. *One is God*
Quattlebaum, Mary. *In the beginning*
Quintero-Spongberg, Emily. *Hannibal and the king*
Rael, Elsa Okon. *When Zaydeh danced on Eldridge Street*
Ragz, M. M. *Lost little angel*
Ransom, Candice F. *Mother Teresa*
Ray, Mary Lyn. *Shaker boy*
Reed, Allison. *Genesis*
Renberg, Dalia Hardof. *King Solomon and the bee*
Rich, Scharlotte. *Who made the wild woods?*
Rock, Lois. *God bless me, God bless you*
    I wonder why?
    Learning about prayer
    The Lord's prayer

Rosen, Michael J. (1954–). *Chanukah lights everywhere*
Rosenblum, Richard. *The old synagogue*
Rosenfeld, Dina Herman. *How in the world does bread come from the earth?*
Rothenberg, Joan Keller. *Inside-out grandma*
Rouss, Sylvia A. *Sammy Spider's first Passover*
    Sammy Spider's first Shabbat
Rylant, Cynthia. *Bless us all*
    Give me grace
Sabuda, Robert James. *St. Valentine*
San Souci, Robert D. *Little gold star*
Santangelo, Colony Elliott. *Brother Wolf of Gubbio*
Sasso, Sandy Eisenberg. *Cain and Abel*
    For heaven's sake
    God's paintbrush
    In God's name
Sattgast, L. J. *Look what God made*
Schaefer, Lola M. *Hanukkah*
Schanzer, Rosalyn. *In the synagogue*
Schlessinger, Laura. *Dr. Laura Schlessinger's Where's God?*
Scholey, Arthur. *Baboushka*
Schotter, Roni. *Hanukkah!*
    Passover magic
    Purim play
Schrier, Jeffrey. *On the wings of eagles*
Schur, Maxine Rose. *Day of delight*
Schwartz, Amy. *Mrs. Moskowitz and the Sabbath candlesticks*
Schwartz, Lynne Sharon. *The four questions*
Schweiger-Dmi'el, Itzhak. *Hanna's Sabbath dress*
Scott, Lesbia. *I sing a song of the saints of God*
Seignobosc, Françoise. *The thank-you book*
Shollar, Leah. *A thread of kindness*
Shulevitz, Uri. *The magician*
Silverman, Erica. *Gittel's hands*
Silverman, Maida. *My first book of Jewish holidays*
Simon, Norma. *The story of Hanukkah*
    The story of Passover
Singer, Marilyn. *Minnie's Yom Kippur birthday*
Slate, Joseph. *Who is coming to our house?*
A small treasury of Easter poems and prayers
The song of the Three Holy Children
Sper, Emily. *Hanukkah*
    The Passover seder
Springer, Sally. *Let's make latkes*
Stan-Padilla, Viento. *Dream Feather*
Stevens, Jan Romero. *Twelve lizards leaping*
Stillerman, Marci. *Nine spoons*
Stohs, Anita. *An Easter alleluia*
Stortz, Diane M. *Barnaby Mouse, detective, and the mystery of the big book*
Swain, Gwenyth. *I wonder as I wander*
Swamp, Jake. *Giving thanks*
Swartz, Nancy Sohn. *In our image*
Tada, Joni Eareckson. *The incredible discovery of Lindsey Renee*
Tangvald, Christine Harder. *The best thing about Easter*
Tarbescu, Edith. *Annushka's voyage*
Taylor, Mark. *"Lamb," said the lion, "I am here."*
Taylor, Shirley. *The cross in the egg*
Thomas, Kathy. *The angel's quest*
Thompson, Lauren. *Love one another*
Thorne, Jenny. *Adam and Eve*
    The walls of Jericho
Titherington, Jeanne. *A child's prayer*
Tolstoy, Aleksey Nikolayevich. *Shoemaker Martin*
Tompert, Ann. *The pied piper of Peru*
    Saint Nicholas
    Saint Patrick
Topek, Susan Remick. *Shalom, Shabbat*
Trist, Glenda. *A child's book of prayers*
Trottier, Maxine. *Little dog Moon*
    The walking stick
Tudor, Tasha. *More prayers*
Tulloch, Shirley. *Who made me?*
Turner, Ann Warren. *Angel hide and seek*
    Shaker hearts
Ungar, Richard. *Rachel's gift*
Van der Meer, Ron. *Oh Lord!*

Van Leeuwen, Jean. *Across the wide dark sea*
Vasiliu, Mircea. *Everything is somewhere*
Vidrine, Beverly Barras. *Easter Day alphabet*
Volkmer, Jane Anne. *Song of Chirimia = La Musica de la Chirimia*
Vorst, Rochel Groner. *The sukkah that I built*
Waldman, Sarah. *Light*
Walters, Julie. *God is like . . .*
Wangerin, Walter. *Angels and all children*
    Water come down
Webber, Christopher. *Praise the Lord, my soul*
Wedeven, Carol. *The Easter cave*
Weilerstein, Sadie Rose. *K'tonton's Yom Kippur kitten*
Weiss, Bernard P. *I am Jewish*
Weitzman, Elizabeth. *I am Jewish American*
What a morning!
Wheeler, Opal. *Sing in praise*
Wiesner, William. *The Tower of Babel*
Wildsmith, Brian. *The Easter story*
    Joseph
    Mary
    The true cross
Wilkinson, Bruce. *The prayer of Jabez for young hearts*
Wilkon, Józef. *Lullaby for a newborn king*
Wilkowski, Susan. *Baby's Bris*
Williams, Marcia. *Joseph and his magnificent coat of many colors*
Winthrop, Elizabeth. *He is risen*
Wohl, Lauren L. *Matzoh mouse*
Wojciechowski, Susan. *The Christmas miracle of Jonathan Toomey*
Wood, Douglas. *Old Turtle*
Woodtor, Dee. *Big meeting*
Wright, Christine. *Bedtime prayers*
Wright, Lesley. *A child's book of values*
Yenne, Bill. *Joshua and the battle of Jericho*
Young, Ed (Edward). *What about me?*
Zagwÿn, Deborah Turney. *Papa's latkes*
Zalben, Jane Breskin. *Happy Passover, Rosie*
    Leo and Blossom's Sukkah
    Pearl's eight days of Chanukah
Ziefert, Harriet. *Animals of the Bible*
    First He made the sun
    People of the Bible

Religion – Buddhism

Quinn, Daniel P. *I am Buddhist*

Religion – Daniel

Bible. Old Testament. Daniel. *Daniel in the lions' den*, ill. by Leon Baxter
    Daniel in the lions' den, ill. by Jim Cummins
    Daniel in the lions' den, ill. by Diana Mayo
Goldsboro, Bobby. *Jonah and the whale; and, Daniel in the lion's den*
McCarthy, Michael. *The story of Daniel in the lions' den*
Marzollo, Jean. *Daniel in the lion's den*

Religion – David

Auld, Mary. *David and Goliath*
Bible. Old Testament. David. *David and Goliath*
    David and the giant
Brin, Ruth F. *David and Goliath*
De Regniers, Beatrice Schenk. *David and Goliath*, ill. by Scott Cameron
    David and Goliath, ill. by Richard M. Powers
Fisher, Leonard Everett. *David and Goliath*
Goldsboro, Bobby. *Noah and the ark; and, David and Goliath*

Religion – Hinduism

Gilmore, Rachna. *Lights for Gita*
Pandya, Meenal. *Here comes Diwali*
Verma, Jatinder Nath. *The story of Divaali*

Religion – Islam

Oppenheim, Shulamith Levey. *And the earth trembled*

Religion – Jonah

Auld, Mary. *The story of Jonah*
Baumann, Kurt. *The story of Jonah*
Bible. Old Testament. Jonah. *The Book of Jonah*
  Jonah, ill. by Kurt Mitchell
  Jonah and the great fish, ill. by Leon Baxter
Bulla, Clyde Robert. *Jonah and the great fish*
Gerstein, Mordicai. *Jonah and the two great fish*
Goldsboro, Bobby. *Jonah and the whale; and, Daniel in the lion's den*
Haiz, Danah. *Jonah's journey*
Hutton, Warwick. *Jonah and the great fish*
MacBeth, George. *Jonah and the Lord*
McDermott, Beverly Brodsky. *Jonah*
Patterson, Geoffrey. *Jonah and the whale*
Thorne, Jenny. *Jonah and the whale*
Williams, Marcia. *Jonah and the whale*

Religion – Moses

Auld, Mary. *Exodus from Egypt*
Gerstein, Mordicai. *The shadow of a flying bird*
Hayward, Linda. *Baby Moses*
Hodges, Margaret. *Moses*
Hutton, Warwick. *Moses in the bulrushes*
Ife, Elaine. *Moses in the bulrushes*
Kessler, Brad. *Moses in Egypt*
Marzollo, Jean. *Miriam and her brother Moses*
Paterson, Katherine. *The angel and the donkey*
Topek, Susan Remick. *Ten good rules*

Religion – Nativity

Adams, Georgie. *The first Christmas*
Allan, Nicholas. *Jesus' Christmas party*
Arnold, Mary. *The fussy angel*
Berry, James. *Celebration song*
Bible. New Testament. Gospels. *Bethlehem*
  Christmas
  The Christmas story, ill. by James Bernardin
  The first Christmas
  The Nativity
  The story of Christmas, ill. by Jane Ray
Blaich, Ute. *The star*
Bolognese, Don. *A new day*
Brown, Margaret Wise. *A child is born*
  Christmas in the barn
Buck, Nola. *Christmas in the manger*
Bunting, Eve (Anne Evelyn). *We were there*
  Who was born this special day?
Butterfield, Moira. *The Christmas story*
Butterworth, Nick. *The Nativity play*
Byrd, Robert. *Saint Francis and the Christmas donkey*
Calhoun, Mary. *A shepherd's gift*
Cardillo-Young, Donatella. *The yellow coat*
Carlson, Melody. *King of the stable*
  What Nick and Holly found in grandpa's attic
Carlstrom, Nancy White. *I am Christmas*
Chalmers, Mary. *A Christmas story*
Chorao, Kay. *The Christmas story*
Christmas in the stable, ill. by Beverly K. Duncan
The Christmas story, paintings from the Metropolitan Museum of Art
Clements, Andrew. *Bright Christmas*
Cooney, Barbara. *The story of Christmas*
Crawford, Sheryl Ann. *The baby who changed the world*
Crossley-Holland, Kevin. *How many miles to Bethlehem?*
Daffis-Felicelli, Christine. *The little star of Bethlehem*
Damjan, Mischa. *The little seahorse and the Christmas pearl*
DeBoer, Jesslyn. *Getting ready for Christmas*
De Paola, Tomie (Thomas Anthony). *The Christmas pageant*
  The story of the three wise kings
DeVajay, Szabolcs. *The animals' gift*
Dowley, Tim. *The shepherds' tale*
  The wise men's tale
Farber, Norma. *All those mothers at the manger*
Fleetwood, Jenni. *While shepherds watched*

Foote, Dan. *The cobbler, the princess, and the newborn King*
Gambill, Henrietta D. *Little Christmas animals*
Ganeri, Anita. *The story of Christmas*
Ginolfi, Arthur. *The tiny star*
Gliori, Debi. *What can I give him?*
Goffin, Josse. *The Christmas story*
  Silent Christmas
Graham, Lorenz B. *Every man heart lay down*
Greene, Rhonda Gowler. *The stable where Jesus was born*
Hartman, Bob. *Granny Mae's Christmas play*
Hautzig, Deborah. *The Christmas story*
Hayes, Sarah. *Away in a manger*
Hayles, Marsha. *The feathered crown*
Helldorfer, M. C. (Mary Claire). *Daniel's gift*
Hickman, Martha Whitmore. *A baby born in Bethlehem*
Hoffman, Mary. *Three wise women*
Hoffmann, Felix. *The story of Christmas*
Hofmeyr, Dianne. *The stone*
Hogrogian, Nonny. *The first Christmas*
Holcomb, Nan. *Leah's night of wonder*
Holder, Mig. *The fourth wise man*
Hooks, William H. *The legend of the Christmas rose*
Horn, Sandra Ann. *Babushka*
Huffaker, Alice. *That first Christmas day*
Hughes, Langston. *Carol of the brown king*
Jewell, Nancy. *Christmas lullaby*
Keats, Ezra Jack. *The little drummer boy*
Ketcham, Sallie. *The Christmas bird*
Knowlton, Laurie Lazzaro. *The Nativity*
Kramlich, Carolyn Walz. *Mary's treasure box*
Kroll, Virginia L. *The Christmas cow*
Laurence, Margaret. *The Christmas birthday story*
Lewandowski, Frrich. *It's Christmas again*
Lewis, J. Patrick. *Long was the winter road they traveled*
Lindgren, Astrid. *Christmas in the stable*
Lucado, Max. *Jacob's gift*
Lussert, Anneliese. *The Christmas visitor*
Maccarone, Grace. *A child was born*
McCaughrean, Geraldine. *The story of the Nativity*
McDermott, Gerald. *The light of the world*
MacDonald, Alan. *The not-so-wise man*
McGinley-Nally, Sharon. *The friendly beasts*
Mackall, Dandi Daley. *Off to Bethlehem!*
Maier, Paul L. *The very first Christmas*
Mayper, Monica. *Come and see*
Milligan, Bryce. *Brigid's cloak*
Mills, Claudia. *One small lost sheep*
Moore, Karen Ann. *The baby king*
Moret, Brigitte Frey. *The bear's Christmas*
Nappa, Mike. *Do you see the star?*
Nikola-Lisa, W. *Hallelujah!*
  To hear the angels sing
Nussbaumer, Mares. *Away in a manger*
O'Connor, Francine M. *The ABC's of Christmas*
Oppenheim, Joanne. *The Christmas witch*
Pfister, Marcus. *The Christmas star*
Phifer, Martha Nelson. *The colors of Christmas*
Pingry, Patricia. *Joseph's story*
Quattrocki, Carolyn. *The little drummer boy*
Rabe, Berniece. *The first Christmas candy cane*
Rodanas, Kristina. *The little drummer boy*
Root, Phyllis. *All for the newborn baby*
Safran, Sheri. *The musical cherub*
Sahagun, Bernardino de. *Spirit child*
Schmid, Eleonore. *Hare's Christmas gift*
A small treasury of Christmas poems and prayers
Smith, Kathryn. *Little Donkey's Christmas story*
  Little Lamb's Christmas story
Spang, Günter. *The ox and the Donkey*
Speirs, John. *The little boy's Christmas gift*
Summers, Susan. *The fourth wise man*
Tafuri, Nancy. *The donkey's Christmas song*
Tangvald, Christine Harder. *The best thing about Christmas*
  Hey, Mr. Angel!
  The Rinky Dinky Donkey
Tazewell, Charles. *The littlest angel*, ill. by Deborah Lanino
  The littlest angel, ill. by Paul Micich

The littlest angel, ill. by Rebecca Thornburgh
They followed a bright star
Thury, Frederick. *The last straw*
Tolan, Stephanie S. *Bartholomew's blessing*
Trent, Robbie. *The first Christmas*
VanderKlipp, Michael A. *Joy to the world!*
Walburg, Lori. *The legend of the candy cane*
Walker, Joni. *Tell me the Christmas story*
Wangerin, Walter. *Probity Jones and the Fear Not Angel*
Watts, Bernadette. *The Christmas bird*
Wells, Joel. *The manger mouse*
Wijngaard, Juan. *The Nativity*
Wildsmith, Brian. *A Christmas story*
Williams, Marcia. *The first Christmas*
Winthrop, Elizabeth. *A child is born*
Wright, Sue (Sue M.). *The Christmas path*

Religion – Noah

Alberts, Nancy Markham. *No toys on Sunday*
Allan, Nicholas. *The bird*
Allen, Jonathan. *Two by two by two*
Auld, Mary. *Noah's ark*
Bible. Old Testament. Noah. *Noah and the ark*, ill. by Pauline Baynes
 Noah and the ark, ill. by Jim Cummins
Bolliger, Max. *Noah and the rainbow*
Brent, Isabelle. *Noah's ark*
Brown, Rick. *Who built the ark?*
Chase, Catherine. *Noah's ark*
Cousins, Lucy. *Noah's ark*
 Noah's ark [board book]
Cullen, Lynn. *Little Scraggly Hair*
Delessert, Etienne. *The endless party*
De Paola, Tomie (Thomas Anthony). *Noah and the ark*
Duvoisin, Roger Antoine. *A for the ark*
Elborn, Andrew. *Noah and the ark and the animals*
Emberley, Barbara. *One wide river to cross*
Farber, Norma. *How the left-behind beasts built Ararat*
 Where's Gomer?
Figley, Marty Rhodes. *Noah's wife*
Fischetto, Laura. *Inside Noah's ark*
French, Fiona. *Rise and shine*
Fussenegger, Gertrud. *Noah's ark*
Gauch, Patricia Lee. *Noah*
Geisert, Arthur. *The ark*
Gerstein, Mordicai. *Noah and the great flood*
Goffstein, M. B. (Marilyn Brooke). *My Noah's ark*
Goldsboro, Bobby. *Noah and the ark; and, David and Goliath*
Goodhart, Pippa. *Noah makes a boat*
Graham, Lorenz B. *God wash the world and start again*
Greenfield, Karen R. *Sister Yessa's story*
Haley, Gail E. *Noah's ark*
Harker, Lesley. *Annie's ark*
Haubensak-Tellenbach, Margrit. *The story of Noah's ark*
Hayward, Linda. *Noah's ark*
Henrioud, Charles. *Mr. Noah and the animals*
Hewitt, Kathryn. *Two by two*
Hogrogian, Nonny. *Noah's ark*
Hutton, Warwick. *Noah and the great flood*
Ife, Elaine. *Noah and the ark*
Janisch, Heinz. *Noah's ark*
Jonas, Ann. *Aardvarks, disembark!*
Kuskin, Karla. *The animals and the ark*
Lenski, Lois. *Mr. and Mrs. Noah*
Le Tord, Bijou. *Noah's trees*
Lewis, J. Patrick. *The boat of many rooms*
Ludwig, Warren. *Old Noah's elephants*
MacBeth, George. *Noah's journey*
McCarthy, Michael. *The story of Noah and the ark*
McCaughrean, Geraldine. *The story of Noah and the ark*
 Unicorns! Unicorns!
McKié, Roy. *Noah's ark*
Martin, Charles E. *Noah's ark*
Mee, Charles L. *Noah*
Olson, Arielle North. *Noah's cats and the devil's fire*
Palazzo, Tony (Anthony D.). *Noah's ark*

Paley, Joan. *One more river*
Philip, Neil. *Noah and the devil*
Pinkney, Jerry. *Noah's ark*
Rose, Gerald. *Trouble in the ark*
Rounds, Glen. *Washday on Noah's ark*
Rouss, Sylvia A. *The littlest pair*
Santore, Charles. *A stowaway on Noah's Ark*
Sasso, Sandy Eisenberg. *Naamah, Noah's wife*
 A prayer for the earth
Singer, Isaac Bashevis. *Why Noah chose the dove*
Smith, Elmer Boyd. *The story of Noah's ark*
Smith, Roger. *How the animals saved the ark and put two and two together*
Spier, Peter. *Noah's ark*
Sting (Musician). *Rock steady*
Thorne, Jenny. *Noah's ark*
Turnbull, Ann. *Too tired*
Walton, Rick. *Noah's square dance*
Webb, Clifford. *The story of Noah*
Wiesner, William. *Noah's ark*
Wilson, Anne. *Noah's ark*
Windham, Sophie. *Noah's ark*

Remembering *see* Memories, memory

Repetitive stories *see* Cumulative tales

Reptiles

Barrett, Judi. *Snake is totally tail*
Colby, C. B. (Carroll Burleigh). *Who went there?*
Cortesi, Wendy W. *Explore a spooky swamp*
Cristini, Ermanno. *In the pond*
Florian, Douglas. *Lizards, frogs, and polliwogs*
Green, Jen. *Reptiles*
Harris, Susan. *Reptiles*
Heller, Ruth. *How to hide a crocodile and other reptiles*
Hunter, Anne. *What's in the pond*
Kuchalla, Susan. *What is a reptile?*
McDonald, Megan. *Reptiles are my life*
Nayer, Judy. *Reptiles*
Ogburn, Jacqueline K. *The reptile ball*
Pluckrose, Henry Arthur. *Reptiles*
Sill, Cathryn P. *About amphibians*
Vyner, Sue. *The stolen egg*

Reptiles – alligators, crocodiles

Aliki. *Keep your mouth closed, dear*
 Use your head, dear
Aruego, José. *A crocodile's tale*
 Rockabye crocodile
Baker, Keith. *Meet Mr. and Mrs. Green*
Balzola, Asun. *Munia and the orange crocodile*
Bare, Colleen Stanley. *Never kiss an alligator*
Becker, Bonny. *The Christmas crocodile*
Bedard, Michael. *Sitting ducks*
Bradman, Tony. *See you later, alligator*
Brown, Jo. *Where's my mommy?*
Brown, Ruth. *Crazy Charlie*
Calmenson, Stephanie. *Get well, gators!*
Campbell, M. Rudolph. *The talking crocodile*
Carrick, Carol. *The crocodiles still wait*
 Norman fools the tooth fairy
Cazet, Denys. *The duck with squeaky feet*
Chen, Chih-Yuan. *Guji Guji*
Childress, Mark. *Joshua and Bigtooth*
Christelow, Eileen. *Five little monkeys sitting in a tree*
 Five little monkeys wash the car
 Jerome and the Witchcraft kids
 Jerome camps out
 Jerome the babysitter
Cousins, Lucy. *Maisy cleans up*
 Maisy goes shopping
Cushman, Doug. *Nasty Kyle the crocodile*
Dahl, Roald. *The enormous crocodile*

Daly, Niki. *Mary Malloy and the baby who wouldn't sleep*
De Groat, Diane. *Alligator's toothache*
De Paola, Tomie (Thomas Anthony). *Bill and Pete*
　　Bill and Pete go down the Nile
　　Bill and Pete to the rescue
Dorros, Arthur. *Alligator shoes*
Dragonwagon, Crescent. *Alligator arrived with apples*
Dumbleton, Mike. *Dial-a-croc*
Duvoisin, Roger Antoine. *The crocodile in the tree*
　　Crocus
Eastman, P. D. (Philip D.). *Flap your wings*
Eduar, Gilles. *Jooka saves the day*
Engel, Diana. *Josephina hates her name*
Fleming, Candace. *Gator gumbo*
Freedman, Claire. *Where's your smile, crocodile?*
Galdone, Paul. *The monkey and the crocodile*
Gantos, Jack (John, Jr.). *Swampy alligator*
Garrett, Ann. *Keeper of the swamp*
Gerrard, Roy. *Croco'nile*
Gomi, Taro. *The crocodile and the dentist*
Gralley, Jean. *Very boring alligator*
Gross, Ruth Belov. *Alligators and other crocodilians*
Guiberson, Brenda Z. *Spoonbill swamp*
Guy, Rosa. *Mother crocodile*
Hartelius, Margaret A. *The chicken's child*
Heller, Ruth. *How to hide a crocodile and other reptiles*
Hill, Eric. *Spot's baby sister*
Hirschi, Ron. *Who lives in . . . Alligator Swamp?*
Hoban, Russell. *Arthur's new power*
　　Dinner at Alberta's
Hodeir, André. *Warwick's 3 bottles*
Holland, Isabelle. *Kevin's hat*
Hurd, Thacher. *Mama don't allow*
Inkpen, Mick. *Crocodile!*
Jaquith, Priscilla. *Bo Rabbit smart for true*
Keeshan, Robert. *Alligator in the basement*
Keven, Elisa. *Ernest*
Kinnell, Galway. *How the alligator missed breakfast*
Kipling, Rudyard. *The elephant's child*, ill. by John A. Rowe
Kirn, Ann. *The tale of a crocodile*
Kleven, Elisa. *Ernst*
　　The puddle pail
Klingel, Cynthia Fitterer. *Crocodiles*
Knüppel, Helga. *The adventures of Christabel Crocodile*
　　Christabel Crocodile's birthday egg
Kraus, Robert. *Good morning, Miss Gator*
Kunhardt, Edith. *Danny and the Easter egg*
　　Danny's birthday
　　Danny's Christmas star
　　Danny's mystery Valentine
　　Trick or treat, Danny!
Lexau, Joan M. *Crocodile and hen*
Lionni, Leo. *Cornelius*
　　An extraordinary egg
Llewellyn, Claire. *Crocodile*
McCarthy, Bobette. *See you later, alligator*
McPhail, David M. *Alligators are awful (and they have terrible manners, too)*
Malkin, Michele. *Pinky's sweet tooth*
Marcellino, Fred. *I, crocodile*
Markle, Sandra. *Outside and inside alligators*
Mayer, Marianna. *Alley oop!*
Mayer, Mercer. *There's an alligator under my bed*
Minarik, Else Holmelund. *No fighting, no biting!*
Mollel, Tololwa M. (Tololwa Marti). *Shadow dance*
Montanari, Eva. *The crocodile's true colors*
Moon, Nicola. *Alligator tails and crocodile cakes*
Moss, Jenny Jackson. *Cajun night after Christmas*
Muntean, Michaela. *Alligator's garden*
Nobisso, Josephine. *For the sake of a cake*
Noonan, Diana. *The crocodile*
Novak, Matt. *Gertie and Gumbo*
Offen, Hilda. *Elephant pie*
Olson, Mary. *An alligator ate my brother*
Pack, Robert. *How to catch a crocodile*
Parker, Nancy Winslow. *The crocodile under Louis Finneberg's bed*
Paye, Won-Ldy. *Mrs. Chicken and the hungry crocodile*

Peterson, Esther Allen. *Frederick's alligator*
Pickett, Carla. *Calvin Crocodile and the terrible noise*
Postgate, Daniel. *The richest crocodile in the world*
Reneaux, J. J. *Why Alligator hates Dog*
Rice, James. *Gaston goes to Texas*
Richards, Jean. *How the elephant got his trunk*
Robinson, Claire. *Crocodiles*
Rubel, Nicole. *It came from the swamp*
Sadler, Marilyn. *Elizabeth, Larry, and Ed*
Schneider, Howie. *Fast 'n Snappy*
Schubert, Ingrid. *There's a crocodile under my bed!*
Sendak, Maurice. *Alligators all around*
Shaw, Evelyn S. *Alligator*
Shipton, Jonathan. *No biting, horrible crocodile!*
Sierra, Judy. *Counting crocodiles*
　　The gift of the crocodile
Smath, Jerry. *A hat so simple*
Stapler, Sarah. *Cordellia, dance!*
Stevenson, James. *Monty*
　　No need for Monty
Stone, Kazuko G. *Goodnight Twinklegator*
Thomassie, Tynia. *Feliciana Feydra LeRoux*
Trosclair. *Cajun night before Christmas*
Vaughan, Marcia Kapok. *Snap!*
Velthuijs, Max. *Crocodile's masterpiece*
Venable, Alan. *The checker players*
Vrombaut, An. *Clarabella's teeth*
Waber, Bernard. *Funny, funny Lyle*
　　Lovable Lyle
　　Lyle and the birthday party
　　Lyle at Christmas
　　Lyle at the office
　　Lyle finds his mother
　　Lyle, Lyle Crocodile
Walsh, Ellen Stoll. *For Pete's sake*
Waring, Richard (Richard M. N.). *Alberto the dancing alligator*
Wasmuth, Eleanor. *An alligator day*
　　The picnic basket
Watts, Marjorie-Ann. *Crocodile medicine*
　　Crocodile plaster
Weiss, Ellen. *Millicent Maybe*
West, Colin. *Have you seen the crocodile?*
Whitehouse, Patricia. *Alligator*
Willis, Jeanne. *The boy who lost his bellybutton*
Ziefert, Harriet. *Egad, alligator!*

Reptiles – chameleons

Benevelli, Alberto. *The colors of the chameleon*
Laden, Nina. *Private I. Guana, the case of the missing chameleon*
Watt, Mélanie. *Leon the chameleon*

Reptiles – crocodiles *see* Reptiles – alligators, crocodiles

Reptiles – iguanas

Alarcón, Francisco X. *Iguanas in the snow and other winter poems / poemas = Iguanas en la nieve y otros poemas de invierno / poemas*
Caseley, Judith. *Mr. Green Peas*
Jango-Cohen, Judith. *Desert iguanas*
Johnston, Tony. *The iguana brothers, a perfect day*
Laden, Nina. *Private I. Guana, the case of the missing chameleon*
McDonald, Megan. *The night Iguana left home*
Newfield, Marcia. *Iggy*
Rosen, Winifred. *Henrietta and the day of the iguana*
Senisi, Ellen B. *All kinds of friends, even green*

Reptiles – Komodo dragons

Myers, Christopher A. *Turnip soup*

Reptiles – lizards

Ada, Alma Flor. *Daniel's mystery egg*
Anderson, Lonzo. *Izzard*
Carle, Eric. *The mixed-up chameleon*
Conklin, Gladys. *I caught a lizard*

Cummings, Pat. *Ananse and the lizard*
Du Quette, Keith. *Hotel Animal*
Hightower, Susan. *Twelve snails to one lizard*
Himmelman, John. *Talester the lizard*
Hooks, William H. *Mr. Dinosaur*
Jenkins, Martin. *Chameleons are cool*
Laden, Nina. *Private I. Guana, the case of the missing chameleon*
Lionni, Leo. *A color of his own*
London, Jonathan. *What Newt could do for Turtle*
Lopshire, Robert. *I am better than you*
McNeely, Jeannette. *Where's Izzy?*
Mora, Pat. *Delicious hullabaloo = Pachanga deliciosa*
Myers, Christopher A. *Turnip soup*
Ryder, Joanne. *Lizard in the sun*
Shannon, George. *Lizard's home*
   Lizard's song
Strete, Craig Kee. *They thought they saw him*
Tews, Susan. *Lizard sees the world*
Wood, Audrey. *Jubal's wish*

Reptiles – monitor lizards

Kennaway, Adrienne. *Bushbaby*

Reptiles – salamanders

Bernhard, Emery. *Salamanders*
Mazer, Anne. *The salamander room*
Walsh, Ellen Stoll. *Pip's magic*

Reptiles – snakes

Aardema, Verna. *What's so funny, Ketu?*
Allard, Harry. *The cactus flower bakery*
Anaya, Rudolfo A. *Roadrunner's dance*
Appleby, Leonard G. *Snakes*
Arnosky, Jim. *Crinkleroot's visit to Crinkle Cove*
   Rattlesnake dance
Baker, Keith. *Hide and snake*
Banchek, Linda. *Snake in, snake out*
Banks, Kate (Katherine A.). *The bird, the monkey, and the snake in the jungle*
Berman, Ruth. *Buzzing rattlesnakes*
Berson, Harold. *Joseph and the snake*
Birchmore, Daniel A. *Harry, the happy snake of Happy Hollow*
Bodsworth, Nan. *A nice walk in the jungle*
Bower, Tamara. *The shipwrecked sailor*
Buckley, Richard. *The greedy python*
Cannon, Janell. *Verdi*
Carlson, Natalie Savage. *Marie Louise and Christophe at the carnival*
Creighton, Jill. *One day there was nothing to do*
Czernecki, Stefan. *The singing snake*
Davol, Marguerite W. *How snake got his hiss*
   The snake's tales
Demi. *The hallowed horse*
Demuth, Patricia Brennan. *Snakes*
Durant, Alan. *Snake supper*
Faulkner, Keith. *The snake's mistake*
Forrester, Victoria. *Oddward*
Freschet, Berniece. *The watersnake*
Gray, Libba Moore. *Small green snake*
Hoff, Syd. *Slithers*
Jaquith, Priscilla. *Bo Rabbit smart for true*
Johnson, Angela. *The girl who wore snakes*
Johnston, Tony. *Slither McCreep and his brother, Joe*
Jonell, Lynne. *I need a snake*
Kastner, Jill. *Snake hunt*
Kimmel, Eric A. *Why the snake crawls on its belly*
Kipling, Rudyard. *Rikki-tikki-tavi*, ill. by Lambert Davis
   Rikki-tikki-tavi, ill. by Jerry Pinkney
Kudrna, C. Imbior. *To bathe a boa*
Lauber, Patricia. *Snakes are hunters*
Le Guin, Ursula K. *Solomon Leviathan's nine hundred and thirty-first trip around the world*
Lemerise, Bruce. *Sheldon's lunch*
Lesikin, Joan. *Down the road*
Lester, Julius. *Why heaven is far away*

Lionni, Leo. *In the rabbitgarden*
MacGill-Callahan, Sheila. *The last snake in Ireland*
McMullan, Kate (Hall). *Snakey riddles*
Marshall, James. *Snake, his story*
Mason, Adrienne. *Snakes*
Newton, Patricia Montgomery. *The frog who drank the waters of the world*
Noble, Trinka Hakes. *The day Jimmy's boa ate the wash*
   Jimmy's boa and the big splash birthday bash
   Jimmy's boa bounces back
Nygaard, Elizabeth. *Snake alley band*
Olaleye, Isaac. *Lake of the Big Snake*
Oppenheim, Joanne. *Mrs. Peloki's snake*
Parsons, Alexandra. *Amazing snakes*
Patent, Dorothy Hinshaw. *Slinky, scaly, slithery snakes*
Patton, Don. *Pythons*
Pilkey, Dav. *A friend for Dragon*
Prather, Ray. *The ostrich girl*
Pringle, Laurence P. *Snakes*
Reinl, Edda. *The little snake*
Shannon, George. *Lizard's home*
Smith, Mavis. *A snake mistake*
Spohn, Kate. *Turtle and Snake and the Christmas tree*
   Turtle and Snake go camping
   Turtle and Snake's Valentine's Day
Strete, Craig Kee. *The lost boy and the monster*
Stroud, Bettye. *Dance y'all*, ill. by Cornelious Van Wright & Ying-Hwa Hu
Tseng, Grace. *White tiger, blue serpent*
Ungerer, Tomi. *Crictor*
Waber, Bernard. *The snake*
Walsh, Ellen Stoll. *Mouse count*
Welling, Peter J. *Shawn O'Hisser, the last snake in Ireland*
Wildsmith, Brian. *Python's party*
Willis, Jeanne. *Be gentle, Python!*

Reptiles – turtles, tortoises

Abisch, Roz. *The clever turtle*
Æsop. *The hare and the tortoise*, ill. by Paul Galdone
   The hare and the tortoise, ill. by Carol Jones
   The hare and the tortoise, ill. by Gerald Rose
   The hare and the tortoise, ill. by Helen Ward
   The hare and the tortoise, ill. by Peter Weevers
   The tortoise and the hare, ill. by Sara Rojo
   The tortoise and the hare, adapt. & ill. by Janet Stevens
Arnosky, Jim. *Turtle in the sea*
Asch, Frank. *Turtle tale*
Augarde, Steve (Stephen). *Barnaby Shrew, Black Dan and . . . the mighty wedgwood*
   Barnaby Shrew goes to sea
Bauer, Marion Dane. *Frog's best friend*
Baumann, Hans. *The hare's race*
Berger, Melvin. *Look out for turtles!*
Bourgeois, Paulette. *Franklin and Harriet*
   Franklin and the thunderstorm
   Franklin in the dark
   Franklin rides a bike
   Franklin says "I love you"
   Franklin's baby sister
   Franklin's Christmas gift
   Franklin's class trip
   Franklin's new friend
   Franklin's secret club
Bryan, Ashley. *Turtle knows your name*
Buckley, Richard. *The foolish tortoise*
Cahill, Chris. *Turtle magic*
Casin, Sheridan. *Little Turtle and the song of the sea*
Chottin, Ariane. *A home for Little Turtle*
Christian, Mary Blount. *Devin and Goliath*
Chwast, Seymour. *Mr. Merlin and the turtle*
Collins, Pat Lowery. *Tomorrow, up and away!*
Coste, Marion. *Honu*
Coursen, Valerie. *Mordant's wish*
Cousteau Society. *Turtles*
Creighton, Jill. *One day there was nothing to do*
Cromie, William J. *Steven and the green turtle*

Cummings, Betty Sue. *Turtle*
Cuyler, Margery. *Road signs*
Darby, Gene. *What is a turtle?*
Davies, Nicola. *One tiny turtle*
Davis, Alice Vaught. *Timothy Turtle*
DeSpain, Pleasant. *The dancing turtle*
Dodd, Lynley. *The smallest turtle*
Domanska, Janina. *Look, there is a turtle flying*
   The tortoise and the tree
Du Bois, William Pène. *The hare and the tortoise and the tortoise and the hare = La liebre y la tortuga and La tortuga y la liebre*
Elks, Wendy. *Charles B. Wombat and the very strange thing*
Emberley, Ed (Edward Randolph). *Rosebud*
Falwell, Cathryn. *Turtle splash!*
Florian, Douglas. *Turtle day*
Floyd, Lucy. *Rabbit and turtle go to school*
Freeman, Don. *The turtle and the dove*
Freschet, Berniece. *Turtle pond*
George, William T. *Box turtle at Long Pond*
Goldsmith, Howard. *Shy little turtle*
   Toto the timid turtle
Gorbachev, Valeri. *Whose hat is it?*
Graham, Al. *Timothy Turtle*
Guiberson, Brenda Z. *Into the sea*
Harris, Dorothy Joan. *Four seasons for Toby*
Harrison, David Lee. *Little turtle's big adventure*
Hoban, Lillian. *Stick-in-the-mud turtle*
   Turtle spring
Horn, Peter. *The best father of all*
   When I grow up . . .
Jacobs, Francine. *Lonesome George, the giant tortoise*
Jeffery, Graham. *Thomas the tortoise*
Jeffrey, Sean. *Franklin's big search-and-solve flap book*
Jennings, Linda M. *Franklin's neighborhood*
Jennings, Sharon. *Franklin and the contest*
   Franklin and the magic show
   Franklin and the scooter
   Franklin forgives
   Franklin goes to the hospital
   Franklin makes a deal
   Franklin stays up
   Franklin wants a badge
   Franklin's music lessons
   Franklin's reading lesson
   Franklin's surprise
   Franklin's Thanksgiving
   Franklin's trading cards
Joyce, William. *Bently and egg*
Katz, Avner. *Tortoise solves a problem*
Kimmel, Eric A. *Anansi goes fishing*
Korman, Susan. *Box turtle at Silver Pond Lane*
Kraus, Robert. *Wise Old Owl's canoe trip adventure*
Kulling, Monica. *Waiting for Amos*
La Fontaine, Jean de. *The hare and the tortoise*
Leedy, Loreen. *Tracks in the sand*
Lesikin, Joan. *Down the road*
Lillegard, Dee. *Tortoise brings the mail*
London, Jonathan. *What Newt could do for Turtle*
Lowell, Susan. *The tortoise and the jackrabbit*
Lubell, Winifred. *Rosalie, the bird market turtle*
McDermott, Gerald. *Jabutí the tortoise*
MacGill-Callahan, Sheila. *And still the turtle watched*
MacGregor, Ellen. *Theodor Turtle*
McGuire-Turcotte, Casey A. *How Honu the turtle got his shell*
McLenighan, Valjean. *Turtle and rabbit*
Maestro, Giulio. *The tortoise's tug of war*
Maris, Ron. *I wish I could fly*
Marshall, James. *Eugene*
   Four little troubles
   Sing out, Irene
   Yummers too
Martin, Francesca. *Clever Tortoise*
Matsutani, Miyoko. *The fisherman under the sea*
Métral, Yvette. *The turtle*
Mollel, Tololwa M. (Tololwa Marti). *Ananse's feast*
   The flying tortoise
   The king and the tortoise

Moore, Eva. *Franklin and the baby*
Murdocca, Sal (Salvatore). *Tuttle's shell*
O'Donnell, Elizabeth Lee. *I can't get my turtle to move*
Ó Flatharta, Antoine. *Hurry and the monarch*
Palazzo-Craig, Janet. *Turtles*
Parry, Marian. *King of the fish*
Patton, Don. *Sea turtles*
Repchuk, Caroline. *The race*
Ross, Gayle. *How Turtle's back was cracked*
St. Pierre, Wendy. *Henry finds a home*
Sanfield, Steve. *The great turtle drive*
San Souci, Daniel. *The rabbit and the dragon king*
Sayre, April Pulley. *Turtle, turtle, watch out!*
Shearer, Marilyn J. *The crown of fools*
Spohn, Kate. *Turtle and Snake and the Christmas tree*
   Turtle and Snake go camping
   Turtle and Snake's Valentine's Day
Spooner, Michael. *Old Meshikee and the little crabs*
Stoddard, Sandol. *Turtle time*
Thayer, Jane. *Mr. Turtle's magic glasses*
Thayer, Mike. *In the middle of the puddle*
Troughton, Joanna. *Tortoise's dream*
Turner, Charles. *The turtle and the moon*
Van Woerkom, Dorothy. *Harry and Shelburt*
Vogel, Amos. *How little Lori visited Times Square*
Vozar, David. *M. C. Turtle and the hip hop hare*
Ward, Helen. *The moonrat and the white turtle*
Wiese, Kurt. *The cunning turtle*
Williams, Barbara. *Albert's toothache*
Wilson, Barbara Ker. *The turtle and the island*
Wolf, Ann. *The rabbit and the turtle*
Wolfson, Margaret. *Turtle songs*
Wyse, Lois. *Two guppies, a turtle and Aunt Edna*
Yashima, Taro. *Seashore story*
Zagwÿn, Deborah Turney. *Turtle spring*
Ziefert, Harriet. *Where's the turtle?*

Resourcefulness *see* Behavior – resourcefulness; Character traits – resourcefulness

Responsibility *see* Character traits – responsibility

Rest *see* Sleep

Restaurants

Adinolfi, JoAnn. *Tina's diner*
Anderson, Peggy Perry. *Out to lunch*
Christelow, Eileen. *The robbery at the diamond dog diner*
Coombs, Patricia. *Mouse Café*
Davis, Maggie S. *The rinky-dink café*
Dorros, Arthur. *When the pigs took over*
Egan, Tim. *Friday night at Hodges' café*
Herman, Gail. *Pizza cats*
Impey, Rose. *Joe's café*
Kirk, Daniel. *Breakfast at the Liberty Diner*
Krementz, Jill. *Benjy goes to a restaurant*
Lewin, Ted. *Big Jimmy's Kum Kau Chinese take out*
Lin, Grace. *Dim sum for everyone*
London, Jonathan. *Froggy eats out*
Loomis, Christine. *In the diner*
Moss, Marissa. *Mel's diner*
Pearson, Tracey Campbell. *Where does Joe go?*
Perry, Robert. *Down at the Seaweed Café*
Pittman, Helena Clare. *Uncle Phil's diner*
Polacco, Patricia. *In Enzo's splendid gardens*
Radabaugh, Melinda Beth. *Going to a restaurant*
Stadler, John. *Animal café*
Waber, Bernard. *Fast food! gulp! gulp!*
Willard, Nancy. *The Moon & Riddles Diner and the Sunnyside Café*
Yee, Wong Herbert. *Hamburger Heaven*

Rhinoceros *see* Animals – rhinoceros

Rhyming text

Aardema, Verna. *Bringing the rain to Kapiti Plain*
  The riddle of the drum
ABC school riddles
Ackerman, Karen. *The banshee*
  Flannery Row
  This old house
Ada, Alma Flor. *The Christmas tree = El Arbol de Navidad*
Adler, David A. *You think it's fun to be a clown!*
Adlerman, Daniel. *Africa calling*
Adoff, Arnold. *Black is brown is tan*
  Greens
Adorjan, Carol Madden. *I can! Can you?*
Æsop. *Androcles and the lion*, ill. by Robert Rayevsky
  Once in a wood
Agard, John. *No hickory no dickory no dock*
Agell, Charlotte. *To the island*
Ahlberg, Allan. *Cops and robbers*
  Monkey do!
Ahlberg, Janet. *Each peach pear plum*
  The jolly Christmas postman
  The jolly pocket postman
  The jolly postman
  Peek-a-boo!
Aiken, Conrad Potter. *Tom, Sue and the clock*
Alarcón, Karen Beaumont. *Louella Mae, she's run away!*
Alborough, Jez. *Bare bear*
  Captain Duck
  Duck in the truck
  Esther's trunk
  Fix-It Duck
  Ice cream bear
  It's the bear
  There's something at the mail slot
  Where's my teddy?
Alda, Arlene. *Pig, horse, or cow, don't wake me now*
  Sheep, sheep, sheep, help me fall asleep
Alderson, Sue Ann. *Bonnie McSmithers is at it again!*
Alexander, Anne (Anna Barbara Cooke). *I want to whistle*
Alexander, Sue. *Who goes out on Halloween?*
All year round
Allard, Harry. *The hummingbirds' day*
Allen, Jeffrey. *Up the steps, down the slide*
Allen, Jonathan. *Big owl, little towel*
  One with a bun
  Purple sock, pink sock
Allen, Judy. *What is a wall, after all?*
Allen, Marjorie N. *Changes*
Allen, Pamela. *Mr. McGee*
  Who sank the boat?
Allen, Robert. *Ten little babies eat*
Allison, Diane Worfolk. *In window eight, the moon is late*
Ambler, C. Gifford (Christopher Gifford). *Ten little foxhounds*
Anastas, Margaret. *A hug for you*
  Mommy's best kisses
Anastasio, Dina. *Baby Piggy and giant bubble*
  Pass the peas, please
Anawalt, Paula Bonnier. *The crystal palace*
Anderson, Lena. *Tick-tock*
Anderson, Peggy Perry. *Out to lunch*
Anderson, Stephen Axel. *I know the moon*
Andreae, Giles. *Giraffes can't dance*
  Love is a handful of honey
  Pants
  The pop-up Rumble in the jungle
  Rumble in the jungle
  There's a house inside my mommy
Andrews, Sylvia. *Dancing in my bones*
Andrews-Goebel, Nancy. *The pot that Juan built*
Anglund, Joan Walsh. *A child's year*
  Christmas is here
  How many days has Baby to play?
Anholt, Catherine. *Bear and baby*
  Kids
  One, two, three, count with me
  Toddlers

What I like
What makes me happy?
Appelt, Kathi. *The Alley Cat's Meow*
  Bats around the clock
  Bats on parade
  Cowboy dreams
  Incredible me!
  Oh my baby, little one
  Rain dance
  A red wagon year
  Someone's come to our house
Apperley, Dawn. *Good night, sleep tight, little bunnies*
  Santa Claus will come tonight
Aragon, Jane Chelsea. *Salt hands*
  Winter harvest
Archambault, John. *A beautiful feast for a big king cat*
  Counting sheep
Armour, Richard Willard. *The adventures of Egbert the Easter egg*
  Animals on the ceiling
  Sea full of whales
  The year Santa went modern
Arnold, Katya. *Knock, knock, teremok!*
Arnold, Tedd. *Five ugly monsters*
  Green Wilma
  More parts
  Ollie forgot
  Parts
Arnosky, Jim. *A manatee morning*
Aronow, Sara. *Seven days of creation*
Arquette, Kerry. *What did you do today?*
Artell, Mike. *Petite Rouge*
Asch, Frank. *The alphabet zoo*
  Baby in the box
Ashman, Linda. *Babies on the go*
  Castles, caves, and honeycombs
  How to make a night
  Just another morning
  Maxwell's magic mix-up
Ashton, Elizabeth Allen. *An old-fashioned ABC book*
  An old-fashioned one two three book
Attenberger, Walburga. *The little man in winter*
  Who knows the little man?
Atwood, Ann. *The little circle*
Auerbach, Julie Jaslow. *Everything's changing – It's pesach!*
Aylesworth, Jim. *The folks in the valley*
  Mary's mirror
  Mr. McGill goes to town
  My sister's rusty bike
  Old Black Fly
  One crow
  Wake up, little children
Ayres, Pam. *Guess what?*
  Guess who?
  When dad cuts down the chestnut tree
  When dad fills in the garden pond
Babson, Jane F. *Babson's bestiary*
Bach, Othello. *Lilly, Willy and the mail-order witch*
Backx, Patsy. *Skippy and Jack*
Baer, Edith. *This is the way we go to school*
  Words are like faces
Baicker, Karen. *Pea pod babies*
Bailey, Mary Bryant. *Jeoffry's Christmas*
Baillie, Marilyn. *Nose to toes*
Baker, Keith. *Cat tricks*
  Hide and snake
  Little Green
  Who is the beast?
Baker, Liza. *I love you because you're you*
Baker, Sanna Anderson. *Who's a friend of the water-spurting whale*
Ballart, Elisabet. *Let's count*
Bang, Molly. *Ten, nine, eight*
Banigan, Sharon Stearns. *Circus magic*
Barack, Marcy. *Season song*
Baranski, Joan Sullivan. *Round is a pancake*
Barasch, Marc Ian. *No plain pets!*
Barner, Bob. *Dinosaur bones*
  Stars, stars, stars

Barracca, Debra. *Maxi, the hero*
  Maxi, the star
  A taxi dog Christmas
Barracca, Sal. *The adventures of taxi dog*
Barrett, Judi. *Pickles have pimples*
  Which witch is which?
Barrett, Mary Brigid. *Day care days*
Barry, Robert E. *Mr. Willowby's Christmas tree*
Bartalos, Michael. *Shadowville*
Bartoletti, Susan Campbell. *Nobody's nosier than a cat*
Base, Graeme. *My grandma lived in Gooligulch*
Baskin, Leonard. *Hosie's zoo*
Baskwill, Jane. *Somewhere*
Bateman, Teresa. *April foolishness*
  Farm flu
  Hunting the daddyosaurus
  A plump and perky turkey
  The princesses have a ball
Bauer, Marion Dane. *My mother is mine*
Bauer, Steven. *The strange and wonderful tale of Robert McDoodle*
Baylor, Byrd. *Amigo*
  The desert is theirs
  Desert voices
  Everybody needs a rock
  One small blue bead
Bea, Holly. *Bless your heart*
  My spiritual alphabet book
Beaumont, Karen. *Duck, duck, goose!*
Beck, Ian. *Five little ducks*
Becker, Bonny. *Tickly prickly*
Beil, Karen Magnuson. *A cake all for me!*
Beisner, Monika. *Catch that cat!*
  Topsy turvy: the world of upside down
Bemelmans, Ludwig. *Madeline*
  Madeline and the bad hat
  Madeline and the gypsies
  Madeline in London
  Madeline's Christmas
  Madeline's rescue
  Welcome home!
Benjamin, Alan. *A change of plans*
  Rat-a-tat, pitter pat
  Ribtickle Town
Bentley, Dawn. *Fuzzy bear*
  Fuzzy Bear's potty book
Berends, Polly Berrien. *I heard said the bird*
Berenstain, Stan. *The bear detectives*
  The Berenstain bears and the missing dinosaur bone
  The Berenstain bears and the spooky old tree
  The Berenstain bears' Christmas tree
  The Berenstain bears' that stump must go!
  He bear, she bear
Berg, Jean Horton. *The wee little man*
Berger, Judith. *Butterflies and rainbows*
Berkes, Marianne Collins. *Marsh music*
Bernardoni, Robert. *Christmas all over*
Berridge, Celia. *Hannah's temper*
Bertram, Debbie. *The best place to read*
Beskow, Elsa Maartman. *Children of the forest*
  Peter in Blueberry Land
  Peter's adventures in Blueberry Land
Betz, Betty. *Manners for moppets*
Birchman, David Francis. *Brother Billy Bronto's bygone blues band*
Birchmore, Daniel A. *Pilly, Polly, and Wee*
Bird, E. J. *How do bears sleep?*
Black, Irma (Simonton). *Is this my dinner?*
Black, Sonia. *Hanging out with Mom*
Blackstone, Stella. *Baby high, baby low*
  Bear at home
  Bear in sunshine
  Bear's busy family
  How big is a pig?
  An island in the sun
  Secret seahorse
  Secret seahorse [board book]
  Who are you?
Blackwood, Mary. *Derek the knitting dinosaur*

Blake, Quentin. *Fantastic Daisy Artichoke*
  Mister Magnolia
  Quentin Blake's ABC
  Simpkin
Blazek, Sarah Kirwan. *An Irish Hallowe'en*
Blegvad, Lenore. *First friends*
  One is for the sun
  This is me
Blocksma, Mary. *Where's that duck?*
Blomgren, Jennifer. *Where do I sleep?*
Bloom, Suzanne. *We keep a pig in the parlor*
Blos, Joan W. *Old Henry*
Blumenthal, Nancy. *Count-a-saurus*
Blyler, Allison. *Finding foxes*
Bodwell, Gaile. *The long day of the giants*
Boedoe, Geefwee. *Arrowville*
Boegehold, Betty. *The fight*
  Pawpaw's run
Boesky, Amy. *Planet Was*
Bond, Felicia. *Tumble bumble*
Bono, Mary. *Ugh! a bug*
Boon, Debbie. *My gran*
Bornstein, Ruth Lercher. *The seedling child*
Borten, Helen. *Do you go where I go?*
  Do you hear what I hear?
  Do you know what I know?
Bos, Claire. *Maurice the hippo*
  Webster's wardrobe
Bottner, Barbara. *There was nobody there*
Bowie, C. W. *Busy fingers*
  Busy toes
Boyd, Lizi. *Lulu Crow's garden*
  Mouse in a house
Boynton, Sandra. *Birthday monsters!*
  But not the hippopotamus
  Dinosaur's binkit
  The going to bed book
  Good night, good night
  Hippos go berserk
  Moo, baa, la la la!
  Oh my oh my oh dinosaurs!
  One, two, three!
  Yay, you! : moving out, moving up, moving on
Bradby, Marie. *Once upon a farm*
Bradman, Tony. *The bad babies' book of colors*
  The bad babies' counting book
  A bad week for the three bears
  This little baby
Braun, Kathy. *Kangaroo and kangaroo*
Breeze, Lynn. *Baby's animals*
  Baby's clothes
  Baby's food
  Baby's toys
  This little baby goes out
  This little baby's bedtime
  This little baby's morning
Brennan, Linda Crotta. *Marshmallow kisses*
Brenner, Barbara A. *The color wizard*
  Good morning, garden
Brenner, Emily. *On the first day of grade school*
Brent, Isabelle. *Cameo cats*
Bridgman, Elizabeth. *All the little bunnies*
Bridwell, Norman. *Clifford's neighborhood*
Briggs, Kelly Paul. *Lighthouse lullaby*
Bright, Robert. *My hopping bunny*
Brillhart, Julie. *When daddy came to school*
  When Daddy took us camping
Brimner, Larry Dane. *Cowboy up!*
  Nana's hog
  What good is a tree?
Brink, Carol Ryrie. *Goody O'Grumpity*
Bronson, Linda. *The circus alphabet*
Brooke, L. Leslie (Leonard Leslie). *Johnny Crow's garden*
  Johnny Crow's new garden
Brooks, Bruce. *Each a piece*
The brothers gruesome
Brouillard, Anne. *The bathtub prima donna*

Brown, Calef. *Tippintown*
Brown, Judith Gwyn. *Alphabet dreams*
Brown, Ken (Ken James). *What's the time, Grandma Wolf?*
Brown, Marc Tolon. *Monster's lunchbox*
  Pickle things
  The silly tail book
  Teddy bear, teddy bear
  There's no place like home
  Wings on things
  Witches four
Brown, Margaret Wise. *Another important book*
  Big red barn, ill. by Felicia Bond
  Big red barn, ill. by Rosella Hartman
  A child is born
  Christmas in the barn
  The diggers
  My world of color
  Sailor boy jig
  Sleepy ABC
  Two little trains
  Where have you been?, ill. by Leo and Diane Dillon
  Whistle for the train
Brown, Ruth. *Mad summer night's dream*
  Toad
Browne, Philippa-Alys. *A gaggle of geese*
Brownlow, Michael. *The big white book with almost nothing in it*
  Way out West – with a baby!
Bruce, Lisa. *Engines, engines*
Bruna, Dick. *Christmas*
  The happy apple
  Kitten Nell
  Little bird tweet
  The orchestra
  Poppy Pig goes to market
  Tilly and Tess
Bryan, Ashley. *Beat the story-drum, pum-pum*
  The cat's purr
Buchanan, Sue. *Mud Pie Annie*
Buck, Nola. *Christmas in the manger*
  Gotcha!
  Halloween parade
  How a baby grows
  The littlest witch
  Oh, cats!
Buckley, Helen Elizabeth. *Josie and the snow*
  Josie's Buttercup
  Where did Josie go?
Buckley, Richard. *The foolish tortoise*
  The greedy python
Bucknall, Caroline. *One bear all alone*
  One bear in the hospital
  One bear in the picture
Buehner, Caralyn. *Snowmen at night*
  Snowmen at night [board book]
Buff, Mary (Marsh). *Hurry, Skurry and Flurry*
Bullard, Lisa. *Not enough beds!*
Buller, Jon. *Toad on the road*
Bullock, Kathleen. *It chanced to rain*
Bunting, Eve (Anne Evelyn). *The bones of Fred Mcfee*
  Butterfly house
  Flower garden
  Happy birthday, dear duck
  My backpack
  The pumpkin fair
  Red fox running
  Scary, scary Halloween
  Sunflower house
Burdett, Lois. *Hamlet for kids*
  A midsummer night's dream for kids
  Romeo and Juliet for kids
  The tempest for kids
Burleigh, Robert. *I love going through this book*
  It's funny where Ben's train takes him
  Messenger, messenger
Burnside, Julian. *Matilda and the dragon*
Burnstein, John. *Slim Goodbody*
Burroway, Janet. *The truck on the track*

Burton, Katherine. *One gray mouse*
Bus-a-saurus bop
Bush, John. *The cross-with-us rhinoceros*
  The fish who could wish
  The giraffe who got in a knot
Butler, Dorothy. *Higgledy, piggledy, hobbledy hoy*
Butler, John. *Hush, little ones*
Butterworth, Nick. *All together now!*
Bynum, Janie. *Altoona Baboona*
Cabrera, Jane. *Panda Big and Panda Small*
Caffey, Donna. *Yikes-lice!*
Cain, Janan. *The way I feel*
Calmenson, Stephanie. *Dinner at the Panda Palace*
  Engine, engine, number nine
  It begins with an A
  One little monkey
  Roller skates!
  Shaggy, waggy dogs (and others)
  Ten furry monsters
  Where will the animals stay?
Cameron, C. C. *One for me, one for you*
Cameron, John. *If mice could fly*
Cappetta, Cynthia. *Chairs, chairs, chairs!*
Capucilli, Alyssa Satin. *Bear hugs*
  Inside a barn in the country
  Inside a house that is haunted
  Inside a zoo in the city
  Mrs. McTats and her houseful of cats
  Peekaboo bunny
  What kind of kiss?
Carlson, Melody. *The Easterville miracle*
  Farmer Brown's field trip
  When the creepy things come out
Carlson, Nancy L. *Take time to relax*
Carlstrom, Nancy White. *Better not get wet, Jesse Bear*
  Goodbye geese
  Guess who's coming, Jesse Bear
  Happy birthday, Jesse Bear!
  How do you say it today, Jesse Bear?
  It's about time, Jesse Bear
  Jesse Bear's tra-la tub
  Jesse Bear's tum-tum tickle
  Jesse Bear's wiggle-jiggle jump-up
  Jesse Bear's yum-yum crumble
  Kiss your sister, Rose Marie
  Let's count it out, Jesse Bear
  The moon came too
  No nap for Benjamin Badger
  Northern lullaby
  Rise and shine!
  Ten Christmas sheep
  What a scare, Jesse Bear!
  What would you do if you lived at the zoo?
  Where is Christmas, Jesse Bear?
  Wild wild sunflower child Anna
Carmack, Lisa Jobe. *Philippe in Monet's garden*
Carney, Margaret (Margaret Rose). *Where does a tiger-heron spend the night?*
Carr, Jan. *Dappled apples*
  Splish, splash, spring
Carroll, Kathleen Sullivan. *One red rooster*
Carter, David A. *Flapdoodle dinosaurs*
Carter, Noelle. *My house*
  My pet
Casanova, Mary. *One-dog canoe*
Cash, Megan Montague. *I saw the sea and the sea saw me*
Cassidy, Dianne. *Circus animals*
  Circus people
Caswell, Helen Rayburn. *God must like to laugh*
Cate, Rikki. *A cat's tale*
Cauley, Lorinda Bryan. *Treasure hunt*
Causley, Charles. *"Quack!" said the billy-goat*
Cave, Kathryn. *Out for the count*
Cazet, Denys. *Nothing at all*
Chaconas, Don. *On a wintry morning*
Chandra, Deborah. *A is for Amos*
  Miss Mabel's table

Chapman, Cheryl. *Pass the fritters, critters*
Chapman, Nancy Kapp. *Doggie dreams*
Chardiet, Bernice. *C is for circus*
Charles, Donald. *Calico Cat at school*
   Calico Cat at the zoo
   Calico Cat meets bookworm
   Calico Cat's exercise book
   Calico Cat's year
   Time to rhyme with Calico Cat
Charles, Faustin. *A Caribbean counting book*
Charlip, Remy. *Baby hearts and baby flowers*
   "Mother, mother I feel sick"
   Sleepytime rhyme
Cherry, Lynne. *The armadillo from Amarillo*
   Who's sick today?
Chesworth, Michael. *Archibald Frisby*
Chetkowski, Emily. *Pumpkin smile*
Chitwood, Suzanne Tanner. *Wake up, big barn!*
Chönz, Selina. *A bell for Ursli*
   Florina and the wild bird
   The snowstorm
Chorao, Kay. *Carousel round and round*
   Knock at the door and other baby action rhymes
   Number one number fun
   Peekaboo! Was it you?
Christelow, Eileen. *Five little monkeys sitting in a tree*
   Five little monkeys wash the car
Chukovskii, Kornei Ivanovich. *The telephone*, ill. by Blair Lent
Churchill, Vicki. *Sometimes I like to curl up in a ball*
Cibula, Matt S. *The contrary kid*
   Slumgullion, the executive pig
Civardi, Anne. *The wacky book of witches*
Clarke, Gus. *Ten green monsters*
Cleary, Beverly. *The hullabaloo ABC*, ill. by Ted Rand
   The hullabaloo ABC, ill. by Earl Thollander
Clifton, Lucille. *Everett Anderson's friend*
   Everett Anderson's goodbye
   Everett Anderson's nine months long
   Everett Anderson's 1-2-3
   Everett Anderson's year
   One of the problems of Everett Anderson
Cline-Ransome, Lesa. *Quilt alphabet*
   Quilt counting
Coats, Laura Jane. *Ten little animals*
Coats, Lucy. *One hungry baby*
Coatsworth, Elizabeth. *The children come running*
   The giant golden book of cat stories
Cobb, Annie. *Wheels!*
Cocca-Leffler, Maryann. *Jungle Halloween*
Cohen, Caron Lee. *Whiffle Squeek*
Cohen, Nora. *From apple to zipper*
Colandro, Lucille. *There was a cold lady who swallowed some snow!*
Colborn, Mary Palenick. *Rainy day slug*
Cole, Babette. *Babette Cole's beastly birthday book*
   Babette Cole's brother
   Babette Cole's ponies
   The bad good manners book
   Dad
   The hairy book
   Mum
   The silly book
   The slimy book
   The smelly book
Cole, Joanna. *Animal sleepyheads*
   Fun on wheels, ill. by Whitney Darrow
   Fun on wheels, ill. by Don Gauthier
Cole, William. *Frances face-maker*
   Have I got dogs!
   That pest Jonathan
   What's good for a four-year-old?
   What's good for a six-year-old?
   What's good for a three-year-old?
Coleman, Michael. *One, two, three, oops!*
Coletta, Irene. *From A to Z*
Coltman, Paul. *Tinker Jim*
Conover, Chris. *Six little ducks*
Cooner, Donna D. (Donna Danell). *The world God made*

Cooney, Barbara. *A garland of games and other diversions*
Cooper, Melrose. *I got a family*
   Pets!
Copp, James (Andrew James). *Martha Matilda O'Toole*
Corey, Shana. *Boats!*
Cotten, Cynthia. *At the edge of the woods*
   Count in the dark with Glo Worm
   Count me in
Couric, Katie. *The brand new kid*
Couture, Susan Arkin. *The biggest horse I ever did see*
   The block book
Cowen-Fletcher, Jane. *Baby angels*
Cowley, Stewart. *Five little kittens*
   Hide-and-seek puppies
   Little bunny
   Little chick
   Little lost rabbit
   The naughty ducklings
   "Tweet, tweet, tweet"
Cox, Phil Roxbee. *Fox on a box*
   Goose on the loose
   Shark in the park
   Ted in a red bed
Craft, Ruth. *The winter bear*
Crebbin, June. *Cows in the kitchen*
   Into the castle
Crisp, Marty. *Totally polar*
Cronin, Doreen. *Wiggle*
Crowley, Arthur. *Bonzo Beaver*
   The wagon man
Crum, Shutta. *All on a sleepy night*
   The bravest of the brave
Cuetara, Mittie. *The crazy crawler crane and other very short truck stories*
   Terrible Teresa and other very short stories
Cullen, Catherine Ann. *The magical, mystical, marvelous coat*
   Thirsty baby
Cummings, Pat. *Angel baby*
   Clean your room, Harvey Moon!
   Jimmy Lee did it
   My aunt came back
Cummings, Phil. *Goodness gracious!*
Cuneo, Mary Louise. *What can a giant do?*
Curtis, Jamie Lee. *I'm gonna like me*
   It's hard to be five
   Today I feel silly and other moods that make my day
   Where do balloons go?
Curtiss, A. B. *In the company of bears*
Cushman, Doug. *The ABC mystery*
   Once upon a pig
Cusimano, Maryann K. *You are my I love you*
Daly, Niki. *The boy on the beach*
Daniels, Teri. *Just enough*
Davidson, Rebecca Piatt. *All the world's a stage*
Davis, David (David R.). *Jazz cats*
Davis, Lee. *The lifesize animal opposites book*
Davis, Maggie S. *The rinky-dink café*
Davol, Marguerite W. *The heart of the wood*
Dayton, Laura. *LeRoy's birthday circus*
Deady, Kathleen W. *All year long*
   It's time!
Dealey, Erin. *Goldie Locks has chicken pox*
DeFelice, Cynthia C. *Clever crow*
Degen, Bruce. *Jamberry*
   Sailaway home
   Teddy bear towers
Delaunay, Sonia. *Sonia Delaunay's alphabet*
Demarest, Chris L. *Bus*
   Fall
   Farmer Nat
   Firefighters A to Z
   Hotshots!
   Plane
   Ship
   Spring
   Summer
   Train

Fitzpatrick, Marie-Louise. *I'm a tiger, too!*
Five little pumpkins
Flather, Lisa. *Ten silly dogs*
Fleischman, Paul. *Rondo in C*
Fleming, Candace. *Who invited you?*
Fleming, Denise. *Barnyard banter*
   In the small, small pond
Florian, Douglas. *A pig is big*
   A potter
   Vegetable garden
   A winter day
Flynn, Kitson. *Carrot in my pocket*
Foord, Jo. *The book of babies*
Fowler, Richard. *Cat's story*
Fox, Mem. *Boo to a goose*
   The magic hat
   Shoes from grandpa
   Sleepy bears
   Time for bed
   Where is the green sheep?
   Zoo-looking
Fox, Perla. *The Wooodles*
Frampton, David. *The whole night through*
Freeman, Don. *The day is waiting*
   Mop Top
Freymann, Saxton. *Dr. Pompo's nose*
   One lonely seahorse
Frith, Michael K. *I'll teach my dog 100 words*
Fuge, Charles. *I know a rhino*
Fujikawa, Gyo. *Ten little babies*
Gág, Wanda. *ABC bunny*
Gage, Wilson. *Down in the boondocks*
Galdone, Joanna. *Gertrude, the goose who forgot*
Gardner, Beau. *Whooo's a fright on Halloween night?*
Garelick, May. *Look at the moon*, ill. by Barbara Garrison
   Look at the moon, ill. by Leonard Weisgard
   Where does the butterfly go when it rains?, ill. by Leonard Weisgard
   Where does the butterfly go when it rains?, ill. by Nicholas Wilton
Garland, Michael. *Christmas City*
   Last night at the zoo
   The mouse before Christmas
Garne, S. T. *By a blazing blue sea*
Garrett, Ann. *What's for lunch?*
Garriel, Barbara S. *I know a shy fellow who swallowed a cello*
Gay, Marie-Louise. *Moonbeam on a cat's ear*
   Rainy day magic
Gelbard, Jane. *My bye-bye bottle book*
   My dressing book
   My eating book
   My sharing book
Gelman, Rita Golden. *Hey, kid*
Gelsanliter, Wendy. *Dancin' in the kitchen*
Geras, Adèle. *Sleep tight, Ginger Kitten*
Geringer, Laura. *The cow is mooing anyhow*
Gerrard, Roy. *Croco'nile*
   The Favershams
   Jocasta Carr, movie star
   Mik's mammoth
   The Roman twins
   Rosie and the rustlers
   Sir Cedric
   Sir Cedric rides again
Gershator, Phillis. *When it starts to snow*
Gerstein, Mordicai. *Daisy's garden*
Gewing, Lisa. *Mama, daddy, baby and me*
Ghigna, Charles. *The alphabet parade*
   Mice are nice
Gilchrist, Theo E. *Halfway up the mountain*
Gile, John. *Oh, how I wished I could read!*
Gilman, Rita Golden. *Mole in a hole*
The gingerbread boy. *The gingerbread boy*, ill. by Paul Galdone
   Whiff, sniff, nibble and chew
Ginsburg, Mirra. *Four brave sailors*
   Kitten from one to ten
   The sun's asleep behind the hill
Glass, Julie. *A dollar for Penny*
Gliori, Debi. *Mr. Bear says, "Are you there, Baby Bear?"*

   No matter what
   Polar Bolero
   What can I give him?
Godwin, Laura. *Central Park serenade*
   Little white dog
   What the baby hears
Goldblatt, Eli. *Leo loves round*
Golding, Kim. *Alphababies*
Goldstone, Bruce. *The beastly feast*
Gold-Vukson, Marji E. *Grandpa and me on Tu B'Shevat*
Gollub, Matthew. *Ten oni drummers*
Gomi, Taro. *Toot!*
Good, Merle. *Amos and Susie*
   Dan's pants
Goode, Molly. *Mama loves*
Goodspeed, Peter. *A rhinoceros wakes me up in the morning*
Gordon, Jeffie Ross. *Two badd babies*
Graham Barber, Lynda. *Spy hops and belly flops*
Graham, Lorenz B. *Song of the boat*
Grahame, Kenneth. *Duck song*
Graham-Yooll, Liz. *Timothy Tib*
Gralley, Jean. *Very boring alligator*
Gravdahl, John. *Curious catwalk*
Graves, Keith. *Frank was a monster who wanted to dance*
   Pet boy
Gray, Libba Moore. *Is there room on the feather bed?*
   Small green snake
Gray, Nigel. *Fly*
   The grocer's daughter
Greaves, Margaret. *The mice of Nibbling Village*
Greeley, Valerie. *The acorn's story*
   White is the moon
Greenberg, Dan. *The bed who ran away from home*
Greenberg, David (David T.). *Bugs!*
   Skunks
   Slugs
Greene, Carol. *The world's biggest birthday cake*
Greene, Rhonda Gowler. *At grandma's*
   Barnyard song
   Eek! Creak! Snicker, sneak
   Jamboree day
   The stable where Jesus was born
   The very first Thanksgiving Day
Greenfield, Eloise. *Kia Tanisha*
   On my horse
   Water, water
Greenwood, Ann. *A pack of dreams*
Grimes, Nikki. *Baby's bedtime*
   C is for city
   Wild, wild hair
Grimm, Jacob. *The traveling musicians of Bremen*
Grossman, Bill. *The banging book*
   The bear whose bones were Jezebel Jones
   Cowboy Ed
   Donna O'Neeshuck was chased by some cows
   The guy who was five minutes late
   My little sister ate one hare
   My little sister hugged an ape
   Tommy at the grocery store
Grossman, Virginia. *Ten little rabbits*
Gryspeerdt, Rebecca. *Counting friends*
Guarino, Deborah. *Is your mama a llama?*
Guenther, James. *Turnagain, Ptarmigan, where did you go?*
Gugler, Laurel Dee. *Facing the day*
   Muddle cuddle
Gulbis, Stephen. *Cowgirl Rosie and her five baby bison*
Gundersheimer, Karen. *Find cat, wear hat*
   Happy winter
   Splish splash bang crash!
Guthrie, Arlo. *Mooses come walking*
Haas, Irene. *The Maggie B*
Hague, Kathleen. *Alphabears*
   Calendarbears
   Out of the nursery, into the night
   Ten little bears
Hallinan, P. K. (Patrick K.). *I know I belong*

Hoopes, Lyn Littlefield. *Mommy, daddy, me*
Horowitz, Dave. *A monkey among us*
Horsbrugh, Wilma. *The train to Glasgow*
Houk, Randy. *Chessie, the travelin' man*
    Rico's hawk
    Ruffle, Coo and Hoo Doo
Houston, John A. *The bright yellow rope*
Howard, Reginald. *The big, big wall*
Howells, Mildred. *The woman who lived in Holland*
Hru, Dakari. *Tickle, tickle*
Hubbard, Patricia. *My crayons talk*
    Trick or treat countdown
Hubbell, Patricia. *Pots and pans*
    Rabbit moon
    Sea, sand, me!
    Sidewalk trip
    Wrapping paper romp
Huck, Charlotte S. *A creepy countdown*
Hudson, Cheryl Willis. *Animal sounds for baby*
    Good morning baby
    Good night baby
    Let's count, baby
Huffaker, Alice. *That first Christmas day*
Hughes, Shirley. *All shapes and sizes*
    Bathwater's hot
    Colors
    Noisy
    Out and about
    Rhymes for Annie Rose
    Two shoes, new shoes
    When we went to the park
Hull, Rod. *Mr. Betts and Mr. Potts*
Hulme, Joy N. *Bubble trouble*
    Sea squares
    Sea sums
Hunt, Jonathan. *One is a mouse*
Hunter, Jana Novotny. *Little ones do*
Hurd, Edith Thacher. *Caboose*
    Come and have fun
Hurd, Thacher. *Cat's pajamas*
Huss, Sally. *I love you with all my hearts*
Hutchins, H. J. (Hazel J.). *Beneath the bridge*
Hutchins, Pat. *The tale of Thomas Mead*
    Ten red apples
    Which witch is which?
    The wind blew
Imbody, Amy. *Snug as a bug?*
Inkpen, Mick. *Anything cuddly will do!*
    Crocodile!
    This troll, that troll
    The very good dinosaur
    Where, oh where, is Kipper's bear?
Intrater, Roberta Grobel. *Two eyes, a nose, and a mouth*
Inwald, Robin. *Cap it off with a smile*
Ipcar, Dahlov (Zorach). *Black and white*
    The cat came back
    Hard scrabble harvest
    My wonderful Christmas tree
Irwin, Michael. *Bears in my bed*
Isaacs, Gwynne L. *Baby face*
Isadora, Rachel. *Bring on that beat*
    Not just tutus
Jabar, Cynthia. *Bored blue? Think what you can do!*
Jack and the beanstalk. *The history of Mother Twaddle and the marvelous achievements of her son Jack*
    Jack and the beanstalk, ill. by Anne Wilsdorf
    Jack the giant killer, ill. by Anne Wilsdorf
Jackson, Alison. *The ballad of Valentine*
    I know an old lady who swallowed a pie
    If the shoe fits
Jacobs, Kate. *A sister's wish*
Jakob, Donna. *My bike*
Jam, Teddy. *Night cars*
Jane, Pamela. *Monster countdown*
    Monster mischief
Janosch. *Tonight at nine*
Janovitz, Marilyn. *Bowl patrol!*

    Can I help?
    Is it time?
    What could be keeping Santa?
Jefferds, Vincent. *Disney's elegant book of manners*
Jenkin-Pearce, Susie. *The seashell song*
Jennings, Linda M. *Hide and seek birthday treat*
Jensen, Patricia. *The mess*
Jewell, Nancy. *ABC cat*
    Christmas lullaby
    Five little kittens
Johnson, Angela. *Mama bird, baby birds*
Johnson, B. J. *A hat like that*
    My blanket Burt
Johnson, Gillian. *My sister Gracie*
Johnston, Tony. *Desert dog*
    Little bear sleeping
Jones, Bill T. *Dance*
Jorgensen, Gail. *Crocodile Beat*
Jorgensen, Richard. *Reading with Dad*
Joyce, Susan. *ABC animal riddles*
    ABC nature riddles
    Alphabet riddles
Joyce, William. *Rolie Polie Olie*
    Sleepy time Olie
Jukes, Mavis. *You're a bear*
Kahl, Virginia. *The Baron's booty*
    The Duchess bakes a cake
    How do you hide a monster?
    The perfect pancake
    Plum pudding for Christmas
Kahn, Joan. *Hi, Jock, run around the block*
Kaiser Johnson, Lee. *If I ran the family*
Kalan, Robert. *Moving day*
Kamen, Gloria. *"Paddle," said the swan*
Karas, G. Brian. *Skidamarink*
Karlin, Nurit. *The fat cat sat on the mat*
    Ten little bunnies
Kates, Bobbi Jane. *We're different, we're the same*
Katz, Karen. *Twelve hats for Lena*
Kavanagh, Peter. *I love my mama*
Kavanaugh, James J. *The crooked angel*
Kay, Verla. *Covered wagons, bumpy trails*
    Gold fever
    Iron horses
    Orphan train
Keillor, Garrison. *Cat, you better come home*
    The old man who loved cheese
Keith, Adrienne. *Fairies from A to Z*
Keller, Holly. *What I see*
Kelley, Marty. *The rules*
    Summer stinks
Kemp, Moira. *I'm a little teapot*
    Knock at the door
    Round and round the garden
Kesselman, Wendy Ann. *Sand in my shoes*
Kessler, Ethel. *Do baby bears sit in chairs?*
Ketteman, Helen. *Grandma's cat*
Khalsa, Dayal Kaur. *Green cat*
Kharms, Daniil. *The story of a boy named Will, who went sledding down the hill*
Killion, Bette. *Just think!*
Kimmel, Eric A. *The Erie Canal pirates*
Kimmelman, Leslie. *Round the turkey*
Kinerk, Robert. *Clorinda*
    Slim and Miss Prim
King, Christopher L. *The vegetables go to bed*
King, Larry L. *Because of Lozo Brown*
King, Stephen Michael. *Emily loves to bounce*
Kingman, Lee. *Catch the baby!*
Kirk, Daniel. *Bus stop, bus go*
    Moondogs
    The snow family
    Trash trucks!
Kirk, David. *Little bird, Biddle bird*
    Little bunny, Biddle bunny
    Little Miss Spider
    Little Miss Spider at Sunny Patch School

The wild baby gets a puppy
Lipkind, William. *Sleepyhead*
Lithgow, John. *Carnival of the animals*
　I'm a manatee
　Marsupial Sue
　Micawber
　The remarkable Farkle McBride
Little old lady who swallowed a fly. *I know an old lady*, ill. by G.
　Brian Karas
　There was an old lady who swallowed a fly, ill. by Simms Taback
Little, Mimi Otey. *Blue moon soup spoon*
Livingston, Irene. *Finklehopper Frog*
　Finklehopper Frog cheers
Livingston, Myra Cohn. *Higgledy-Piggledy*
Lloyd, Megan. *Chicken tricks*
Lobe, Mira. *Valerie and the good-night swing*
Lobel, Arnold. *Martha, the movie mouse*
　On Market Street
　On the day Peter Stuyvesant sailed into town
　The rose in my garden
Lodge, Bernard. *Cloud Cuckoo Land (and other odd spots)*
　Rhyming Nell
London, Jonathan. *Candystore man*
　Fireflies, fireflies, light my way
　I see the moon and the moon sees me
　Little Red Monkey
　Park beat
　What do you love?
　What do you love? [board book]
　Who bop
Longfellow, Layne. *Imaginary menagerie*
Loomans, Diane. *The lovables in the kingdom of self-esteem*
Loomis, Christine. *Astro Bunnies*
　At the laundromat
　At the library
　The cleanup surprise
　Cowboy bunnies
　The Hippo Hop
　One cow coughs
　Rush hour
　Scuba bunnies
Lopshire, Robert. *I want to be somebody new!*
　New tricks I can do!
　Put me in the zoo
Lorbiecki, Marybeth. *Sister Anne's hands*
Lord, John Vernon. *Mr. Mead and his garden*
Lorenz, Lee. *Pig and duck buy a truck*
Losordo, Stephen. *Cow moo me*
Lotz, Karen E. *Snowsong whistling*
Low, Alice. *Aunt Lucy went to buy a hat*
　Witch's holiday
Lukasewich, Lori. *The night fire*
Lund, Deb. *Dinosailors*
Lund, Doris Herold. *The paint-box sea*
Lundell, Margo. *The furry bedtime book*
Lundgren, Mary Beth. *Seven scary monsters*
Lunn, Carolyn. *A buzz is part of a bee*
Lyne, Alice. *A, my name is . . .*
Lyon, George Ella. *A day at damp camp*
　Mama is a miner
　The outside inn
McAfee, Annalena. *Kirsty knows best*
McAllister, Angela. *Sleepy Ella*
MacBeth, George. *Noah's journey*
McBratney, Sam. *The caterpillow fight*
McCall, Francis X. *A huge hog is a big pig*
Maccarone, Grace. *Cars! Cars! Cars!*
　A child was born
　The class trip
　The classroom pet
　I have a cold
　I shop with my daddy
　Itchy, itchy chicken pox
　Oink! moo! how do you do?
　Pizza party
　Sharing time troubles
McCarthy, Bobette. *Dreaming*

See you later, alligator
　Ten little hippos
McCarthy, Michael. *The story of Daniel in the lions' den*
　The story of Noah and the ark
McCurdy, Michael. *The old man and the fiddle*
MacDonald, Amy. *Cousin Ruth's tooth*
　Quentin Fenton Herter three
　Rachel Fister's blister
MacDonald, Elizabeth. *Miss Poppy and the honey cake*
McDonald, Megan. *Bedbugs*
MacDonald, Suse. *Elephants on board*
McGee, Marni. *Sleepy me*
　Wake up, me!
McGinley, Phyllis. *All around the town*
　How Mrs. Santa Claus saved Christmas
　Lucy McLockett
　Wonderful time
McGinty, Alice B. *Ten little lambs*
McGough, Roger. *Counting by numbers*
　What on earth can it be?
McGovern, Ann. *Eggs on your nose*
McGrath, Barbara Barbieri. *Kellogg's froot loops color fun book*
　Kellogg's froot loops counting fun book
McGuire, Richard. *What's wrong with this book?*
McHenry, E. B. *Poodlena*
Mackall, Dandi Daley. *Off to Bethlehem!*
McKelvey, Douglas Kaine. *Locust pocus*
McKié, Roy. *Snow*
McKinney, Barbara Shaw. *Pass the energy, please*
McKissack, Patricia C. *Messy Bessey and the birthday overnight*
　Messy Bessey's closet
　Messy Bessey's holidays
McLaren, Chesley. *Zat cat*
McLean, Janet. *Dog tales*
McLean-Carr, Carol. *Fairy dreams*
MacLeod, Elizabeth. *I heard a little baa*
McLerran, Alice. *Hugs*
　Kisses
McMillan, Bruce. *Puffins climb, penguins rhyme*
McMullan, Kate (Hall). *Rock-a-baby band*
McNaughton, Colin. *If dinosaurs were cats and dogs*
Maconie, Robin. *Alice and her fabulous teeth*
McPartland, Suzy. *Good morning, sun*
　Sleepy-time moon
　Toy-shop surprise
　Zoom, car, zoom
McPhail, David M. *Big brown bear*
　Pigs ahoy
　Pigs aplenty, pigs galore!
　Those can-do pigs
Maestro, Marco. *Geese find the missing piece*
Maguire, Arlene H. *Special people, special ways*
Maguire, Gregory. *Crabby Cratchitt*
　Lucas Fishbone
Mahy, Margaret. *The Christmas tree tangle*
　17 kings and 42 elephants
　A summery Saturday morning
　When the king rides by
Maloney, Peter (1955–). *Belly button boy*
　The magic hockey stick
　Redbird at Rockefeller Center
Mandel, Peter. *Say hey*
Manning, Linda. *Animal hours*
Manning, Maurie J. *The aunts go marching*
Manushkin, Fran. *Let's go riding in our strollers*
Many, Paul. *The great pancake escape*
Marciano, John Bemelmans. *Madeline says merci*
Marcin, Marietta. *A zoo in her bed*
Margalith, Joan. *The babies are landing*
Mark, Jan. *Fun with Mrs. Thumb*
Markes, Julie. *Thanks for Thanksgiving*
Marsh, T. J. *Way out in the desert*
Marshak, S. (Samuil). *The absentminded fellow*
　The Month-Brothers
　The pup grew up!
Marshall, James. *Hey, diddle, daddle*
Marshall, Janet Perry. *Ohmygosh, my pocket*

Martin, Bill (William Ivan). *Adam, Adam, what do you see?*
  Barn dance!
  Brown bear, brown bear, what do you see?
  Chicka chicka boom boom
  Chicka chicka boom boom [board book]
  Chicka chicka sticka sticka
  The happy hippopotami
  Here are my hands
  Listen to the rain
  Little granny quarterback
  Maestro plays
  The magic pumpkin
  Polar bear, polar bear, what do you hear?
  The turning of the year
  The wizard
Martin, David. *Lizzie and her dolly*
  Lizzie and her friend
  Lizzie and her kitty
  Lizzie and her puppy
  We've all got bellybuttons
Martin, Jerome. *Carrot/parrot*
  Mitten/kitten
Martin, Linda. *When dinosaurs go to school*
Martin, Mary Jane. *From Anne to Zach*
Marzollo, Jean. *Christmas cats*
  Do you know new?
  Home sweet home
  I spy little animals
  I spy little book
  I spy little bunnies
  I spy little Christmas
  I spy little letters
  I spy little numbers
  I spy little wheels
  I spy, mystery
  I spy, year-round challenger!
  Mama, Mama
  Papa, papa
  Pretend you're a cat
  Shanna's ballerina show
  Shanna's teacher show
  Sun song
  Ten cats have hats
  Ten little eggs
  Thanksgiving cats
  Uproar on Hollercat Hill
  Valentine cats
  Welcome to the Shanna show
  What's the matter with Mother Goose?
Masurel, Claire. *Ten dogs in the window*
Mathews, Judith. *Nathaniel Willy, scared silly*
Mathews, Louise. *Bunches and bunches of bunnies*
Mathis, Melissa Bay. *Animal house*
Maxner, Joyce. *Lady Bugatti*
  Nicholas Cricket
May, Robert Lewis. *Rudolph the red-nosed reindeer,* ill. by David Wenzel
Maynard, Bill. *Incredible Ned*
  Quiet, Wyatt!
  Santa's time off
Mayo, Margaret. *Dig dig digging*
  Emergency!
  Wiggle waggle fun
Mayper, Monica. *Oh snow*
Mazzola, Frank. *Counting is for the birds*
Meade, Holly. *A place to sleep*
Medearis, Angela Shelf. *Best friends in the snow*
  Bye-bye, babies!
  Dancing with the Indians
  The ghost of Sifty-Sifty Sam
  Here comes the snow
  The 100th day of school
  Rum-a-tum-tum
  Seeds grow
  We play on a rainy day
Meggendorfer, Lothar. *The genius of Lothar Meggendorfer*
Meister, Cari. *Busy, busy city street*

Mellage, Nanette. *See me grow, head to toe*
Mellings, Joan. *It's fun to go to school*
Melmed, Laura Krauss. *Capital! Washington D.C. from A to Z*
  Fright night flight
  A hug goes around
  I love you as much . . .
  Jumbo's lullaby
  The Marvelous Market on Mermaid
Mendoza, George. *Traffic jam*
  Were you a wild duck, where would you go?
Merberg, Julie. *In the garden with Van Gogh*
  A magical day with Matisse
Merriam, Eve. *Low song*
  On my street
  Ten rosy roses
  Train leaves the station
  What in the world?
  Where's that cat?
Merski, P. K. *Roaring, boring, Alice*
Metaxas, Eric. *Bible ABC*
  The birthday ABC
  Uncle Mugsy and the terrible twins of Christmas
Meyers, Susan. *Everywhere babies*
Michels, Tilde. *Who's that knocking at my door?*
Michelson, Richard. *Did you say ghosts?*
  Ten times better
Miles, Miska. *Apricot ABC*
Milgrim, David. *Cows can't fly*
  Here in space
  Why Benny barks
Milios, Rita. *Sneaky Pete*
Millen, C. M. *Blue bowl down*
Miller, Edna. *Mousekin's ABC*
Miller, J. Philip. *We all sing with the same voice*
Miller, Moira. *The proverbial mouse*
Miller, Ruth. *The bear on the bed*
  I went to the farm
Minters, Frances. *Cinder-Elly*
  Princess Fishtail
  Sleepless Beauty
  Too big, too small, just right
Miranda, Anne. *Beep! beep!*
  Counting
  Does a mouse have a house?
  The elephant at the Waldorf
  Monster math
Mitchell, Adrian. *Twice my size*
Mitter, Matt. *ABC: alphabet rhymes*
  Once upon a rhyme
  1, 2, 3, counting rhymes
Mitton, Tony. *Dinosaurumpus*
  Down by the cool of the pool
  Flashing fire engines
Mockford, Caroline. *Cleo and Caspar*
  Cleo in the snow
  Cleo on the move
  Cleo the cat
  Cleo's alphabet book
  Cleo's counting book
  Come here, Cleo
Moffatt, Judith. *The pumpkin man*
  Trick-or-treat faces
  Who stole the cookies?
Moncure, Jane Belk. *Happy healthkins*
  The healthkin food train
  Healthkins exercise!
  Healthkins help
Monfried, Lucia. *Dishes all done*
Monks, Lydia. *The cat barked?*
Montgomery, Michael G. *'Night, America*
Moore, Dessie. *Let's pretend*
Moore, Elaine. *Roly-poly puppies*
Moore, Julia. *While you sleep*
Mora, Emma. *Gideon, the little bear cub*
Mora, Jo (Joseph Jacinto). *Budgee Budgee Cottontail*
Mora, Pat. *One, two, three = Uno, dos, tres*
Moreillon, Judi. *Sing down the rain*

Morgan, Mary. *My good night book*
Morgan, Michaela. *Brave, brave mouse*
Morgan-Vanroyen, Mary. *Guess who I love?*
Morgenstern, Constance. *Good night, feet*
Morris, Ann. *Shoes, shoes, shoes*
Morrow, Tara Jaye. *Mommy loves her baby; Daddy loves his baby*
Moss, Lloyd. *Our marching band*
    Zin! zin! zin! A violin
Mother Goose. *Hickory, dickory, dock*, ill. by Suzanne Duranceau
Mott, Evelyn Clarke. *Cool cat*
    Hot dog
Muntean, Michaela. *Bicycle bear*
    Bicycle Bear rides again
Murphy, Mary. *My puffer train*
Murphy, Stuart J. *Animals on board*
    The best vacation ever
    Circus shapes
    Elevator magic
    Every buddy counts
    Get up and go!
    Rabbit's pajama party
Murray, Marjorie Dennis. *The stars are waiting*
Namm, Diane. *Bunny's bedtime*
Nappa, Mike. *Do you see the star?*
Neitzel, Shirley. *The bag I'm taking to Grandma's*
    The dress I'll wear to the party
    The house I'll build for the wrens
    I'm not feeling well today
    I'm taking a trip on my train
    The jacket I wear in the snow
    We're making breakfast for mother
Nerlove, Miriam. *Christmas*
    Easter
    Halloween
    Hanukkah
    I made a mistake
    I meant to clean my room today
    If all the world were paper
    Just one tooth
    Passover
    Thanksgiving
    Valentine's Day
Newberry, Clare Turlay. *The kittens' ABC*
Newcome, Zita. *Animal fun*
    Pop-up toddlerobics
    Toddlerobics
Newell, Peter. *The slant book*
Newman, Lesléa. *Cats, cats, cats*
    Dogs, dogs, dogs
    Pigs, pigs, pigs
    Runaway dreidel
Newton-John, Olivia. *A pig tale*
Nichol, B. P. *On the merry-go-round*
Nichol, Barbara. *Trunks all aboard*
Nichols, Grace. *Asana and the animals*
Nightingale, Sandy. *A giraffe on the moon*
Nikola-Lisa, W. *No babies asleep*
    Shake dem Halloween bones
    Summer sun risin'
    Tangletalk
    To hear the angels sing
    Wheels go round
Nims, Bonnie Larkin. *Where is the bear?*
    Where is the bear at school?
    Where is the bear in the city?
Nobisso, Josephine. *For the sake of a cake*
    Hot-cha-cha!
Nolan, Dennis. *Wizard McBean and his flying machine*
Noll, Sally. *Off and counting*
Noonan, Julia. *Bath day*
    Breakfast time
    Mouse by mouse
Northey, Lawrence. *I'm a hop hop hoppity frog*
Novak, Matt. *The Pillow War*
Numeroff, Laura Joffe. *Chimps don't wear glasses*
    Monster munchies
O'Book, Irene. *Maybe my baby*

O'Brien, John (1953–). *Mother Hubbard's Christmas*
Ochiltree, Dianne. *Pillow pup*
O'Connor, Francine M. *The ABC's of Christmas*
O'Donnell, Elizabeth Lee. *Winter visitors*
Offen, Hilda. *As quiet as a mouse*
    A fox got my socks
    The sheep made a leap
O'Keefe, Susan Heyboer. *Angel prayers*
    Good night, God bless
    Love me, love you
Olsen, Ib Spang. *The grown-up trap*
O'Malley, Kevin. *Carl caught a flying fish*
    Who killed Cock Robin?
Once I was . . .
One, two, skip a few!
O'Neill, Mary. *Big red hen*
Oppenheim, Joanne. *Do you like cats?*
    Donkey's tale
    Have you seen bugs?
    The story book prince
    You can't catch me!
Orbach, Ruth. *Apple pigs*
Orgel, Doris. *Two crows counting*
Ormerod, Jan. *If you're happy and you know it!*
    Ms. MacDonald has a class
    Rock-a-baby
Osborne, Valerie. *One big yo to go*
Over in the meadow, ill. by Ezra Jack Keats
Owens, Mary Beth. *A caribou alphabet*
Oxenbury, Helen. *Pig tale*
Pacilio, V. J. *Ling Cho and his three friends*
Packard, Mary. *Bubble trouble*
    The kite
    Same and different
    We are monsters
Pacovská, Kveta. *One, five, many*
Paraskevas, Betty. *Cecil Bunions and the midnight train*
    The ferocious beast with the polka-dot hide
Parker, Victoria. *Bearum scarum*
Parr, Letitia. *A man and his hat*
Partch, Virgil Franklin. *The Christmas cookie sprinkle snitcher*
Partridge, Elizabeth. *Moon glowing*
Paschkis, Julie. *Play all day*
Patrick, Jean L. S. *If I had a snowplow*
Patron, Susan. *Dark cloud strong breeze*
Patterson, Elizabeth Burman. *Whose eyes are these?*
Paul, Ann Whitford. *Everything to spend the night . . . from A to Z*
Paulsen, Gary. *Worksong*
Pavey, Peter. *One dragon's dream*
Paxton, Tom. *The marvelous toy*
Pearson, Tracey Campbell. *Where does Joe go?*
Peck, Robert Newton. *Hamilton*
Peek, Merle. *The balancing act*
Peet, Bill (William Bartlett). *Ella*
    Hubert's hair-raising adventures
    Huge Harold
    Kermit the hermit
    The kweeks of Kookatumdee
    The luckiest one of all
    No such things
    The pinkish, purplish, bluish egg
    Randy's dandy lions
    Smokey
    Zella, Zack, and Zodiac
Pelham, David. *Sam's pizza*
    Sam's sandwich
Pendziwol, Jean. *No dragons for tea*
    A treasure at sea for dragon and me
Perkins, Al. *The ear book*
    Hand, hand, fingers, thumb
    The nose book
Perkins, Charles. *Swinging on a rainbow*
Perry, Robert. *Down at the Seaweed Café*
Peters, Lisa Westberg. *October smiled back*
Petie, Haris. *Billions of bugs*
    The seed the squirrel dropped
Peyo. *What do smurfs do all day?*

Phifer, Martha Nelson. *The colors of Christmas*
Phillips, Joan. *Peek-a-boo! I see you!*
Phillips, Louis. *The upside down riddle book*
Pickering, Jimmy. *It's fall*
Pike, Carol. *The nutty queen*
Pilkey, Dav. *The Moonglow Roll-O-Rama*
   'Twas the night before Thanksgiving
Pinczes, Elinor J. *Arctic fives arrive*
   Inchworm and a half
   My full moon is square
   A remainder of one
Pittman, Helena Clare. *Sunrise*
Piven, Hanokh. *The perfect purple feather*
Plourde, Lynn. *Spring's sprung*
   Wild child
   Winter waits
Plummer, David. *Counting kittens*
Polisar, Barry Louis. *The haunted house party*
Pollard, Nik. *The river*
Pomerantz, Charlotte. *The ballad of the long-tailed rat*
   Flap your wings and try
   Here comes Henny
   How many trucks can a tow truck tow?
   The mousery
   The piggy in the puddle
Poppy Bear
Posada, Mia. *Ladybugs*
   Robins
Poskanzer, Susan Cornell. *Riddles about Hannukah*
Poydar, Nancy. *Rhyme time Valentine*
Prater, John. *"No!" said Joe*
   Once upon a picnic
   Once upon a time
Prelutsky, Jack. *The mean old mean hyena*
   The terrible tiger
   Wild witches' ball
Preston, Edna Mitchell. *Pop Corn and Ma Goodness*
Price, Hope Lynne. *These hands*
Provensen, Alice. *Karen's opposites*
Pumphrey, Jerome. *Creepy things are scaring me*
Puner, Helen Walker. *Daddys, what they do all day*
   The sitter who didn't sit
Puppies and kittens
Raczka, Bob. *Art is . . .*
Rader, Laura. *Tea for me, tea for you*
Randall, Ronne. *The Hanukkah mice*
Raphael, Elaine. *Turnabout*
Rash, Andy. *Agent A to Agent Z*
Raskin, Ellen. *Ghost in a four-room apartment*
   Who, said Sue, said whoo?
Rau, Dana Meachen. *Chilly Charlie*
   Clown around
   I'll make you a card
   Rubber duck
   Shoo crow, shoo!
Ray, Karen. *Sleep song*
Reasoner, Charles. *Ants, ants, ants*
Reddix, Valerie. *Millie and the mudhole*
Reeves, Howard W. *There was an old witch*
Reeves, Mona Rabun. *I had a cat*
   The spooky eerie night noise
Regan, Dana. *Monkey see, monkey do*
Regan, Dian Curtis. *Daddies*
Reid, Barbara. *The party*
Reid, Rob. *Wave goodbye*
Reiss, Mike. *How Murray saved Christmas*
   Late for school
   Santa claustrophobia
Reitman, Andrea. *Mouse in the house*
Repchuk, Caroline. *The race*
Rey, H. A. (Hans Augusto). *Elizabite*
   Elizabite, adventures of a carnivorous plant
   Feed the animals
   See the circus
   Where's my baby?
Rice, James. *Gaston goes to Texas*
Richardson, Bill. *But if they do*

Rinder, Lenore. *A big mistake*
Ring, Elizabeth. *Some stuff*
Rink, Cindy. *Where does the wind blow?*
Rives. *If I were a polar bear*
Robbins, Ruth. *Baboushka and the three kings*
Roberts, Bethany. *Birthday mice*
   Camel caravan
   Christmas mice
   Easter mice
   Fourth of July mice
   Valentine mice!
Roberts, Cliff. *Start with a dot*
Robertson, Patrisha Grainger. *Cirque du Soleil*
Robinson, Fay. *Where did all the dragons go?*
Robinson, Tim. *Tobias, the quig, and the rumplenut tree*
Rock, Lois. *God bless me, God bless you*
   I wish tonight
   I wonder why?
Rodda, Emily. *Where do you hide two elephants?*
Rogers, Paul (Patrick). *From me to you*
   Ruby's dinnertime
   Ruby's potty
   Sheepchase
   What will the weather be like today?
Rollings, Susan. *New shoes, red shoes*
Roosa, Karen. *Beach day*
Root, Phyllis. *One duck stuck*
   One duck stuck [board book]
   Rattletrap car
   Rattletrap car [board book]
   Ten sleepy sheep
Rose, Anne K. *How does a czar eat potatoes?*
Rose, Deborah Lee. *Birthday zoo*
   Meredith's mother takes the train
Rosen, Michael J. (1954–). *Avalanche*
Rosenberg, Liz. *Eli's night-light*
   Window, mirror, moon
Rosenfeld, Dina Herman. *How in the world does bread come from the earth?*
Rosselson, Leon. *Where's my mom?*
Roth, Carol. *The little school bus*
Roth, Susan L. *Night-time numbers*
Rothstein, Gloria. *Sheep asleep*
Rotner, Shelley. *Citybook*
   Parts
Rovetch, Lissa. *Crocs in shirts, hippos in skirts*
   TLC grow with me
Rowan, Paula S. *Rick and Rocky*
Rowinski, Kate. *Cats in the dark*
Rubin, C. M. *Eleanor, Ellatony, Ellencake, and me*
Russell, Sandra Joanne. *A farmer's dozen*
Ruurs, Margriet. *A Pacific alphabet*
Ryan, Pam Muñoz. *Armadillos sleep in dugouts*
   The crayon counting book
   Hello, Ocean!
   Hello ocean = Hola mar
   Mud is cake
   One hundred is a family
   A pinky is a baby mouse, and other baby animal names
Ryder, Joanne. *Big bear ball*
   Chipmunk song
   Each living thing
   A fawn in the grass
   Hello, tree!
   A house by the sea
Rylant, Cynthia. *Bear day*
   Bless us all
   Bunny bungalow
   Give me grace
Sabuda, Robert James. *The mummy's tomb*
Sage, Angie. *Monkeys in the jungle*
Sage, Michael. *Dippy dos and don'ts*
Saltzman, David. *The jester has lost his jingle*
Samton, Sheila White. *Beside the bay*
   Frogs in clogs
   Ten tiny monsters
   The world from my window

Sanfield, Steve. *Snow*
Sanger, Amy Wilson. *First book of sushi*
San Souci, Robert D. *Cinderella Skeleton*
    The Hobyahs
Sardegna, Jill. *The roly-poly spider*
Saul, Carol P. *Barn cat*
Sava, Donna Lynn. *Teddy bear dreams*
Sayre, April Pulley. *It's my city*
    Trout, trout, trout
Sazer, Nina. *What do you think I saw?*
Scanlon, Elizabeth Garton. *A sock is a pocket for your toes*
Schaefer, Lola M. *Loose tooth*
    This is the sunflower
Schafer, Milton. *That crazy Barb'ra*
Scharer, Niko. *Emily's house*
Schertle, Alice. *The skeleton in the closet*
Schindel, John. *Busy penguins*
Schmeltz, Susan Alton. *Pets I wouldn't pick*
Schneider, Christine M. *Picky Mrs. Pickle*
    Saxophone Sam and his snazzy jazz band
Schnitzlein, Danny. *The monster who ate my peas*
Schnur, Steven. *Night lights*
Schotter, Richard. *There's a dragon about*
Schroeder, Binette. *Laura*
Schumaker, Ward. *Dance!*
The scrubbly-bubbly car wash
Scruggs, Afi. *Jump rope magic*
Scruton, Clive. *Mary's pets*
Seeber, Dorothea P. *A pup just for me*
Seibold, J. Otto. *Penguin dreams*
Sellers, Ronnie. *My first day at school*
Sendak, Maurice. *Pierre*
    Seven little monsters
Sensel, Joni. *Bears barge in*
Serfozo, Mary. *Dirty Kurt*
    A head is for hats
    There's a square
    Who wants one?
Serraillier, Ian. *Suppose you met a witch*
Seuling, Barbara. *Spring song*
Seuss, Dr. *And to think that I saw it on Mulberry Street*
    The butter battle book
    The cat in the hat
    The cat in the hat comes back!
    The cat's quizzer
    Come over to my house
    Did I ever tell you how lucky you are?
    Dr. Seuss's ABC
    Dr. Seuss's sleep book
    The eye book
    The foot book
    Fox in socks
    Gerald McBoing Boing
    Gerald McBoing Boing sound book
    A great day for up
    Green eggs and ham
    Happy birthday to you!
    Hooper Humperdink . . . ? Not him!
    Hop on Pop
    Horton hatches the egg
    Horton hears a Who!
    How the Grinch stole Christmas
    Hunches in bunches
    I am not going to get up today!
    I can lick 30 tigers today and other stories
    I can read with my eyes shut
    I can write!
    I had trouble getting to Solla Sollew
    I wish that I had duck feet
    If I ran the circus
    If I ran the zoo
    In a people house
    The king's stilts
    McElligot's pool
    Marvin K. Mooney, will you please go now!
    Mr. Brown can moo! Can you?
    Oh say can you say?

    Oh, the thinks you can think!
    On beyond zebra
    One fish, two fish, red fish, blue fish
    Please try to remember the first of Octember!
    Scrambled eggs super!
    The shape of me and other stuff
    The Sneetches, and other stories
    There's a wocket in my pocket
    Thidwick, the big-hearted moose
    The tooth book
    Wacky Wednesday
Seven spunky monkeys
Sewall, Marcia. *Ridin' that strawberry roan*
Sexton, Gwain. *There once was a king*
Seymour, Tres. *I love my buzzard*
    Too quiet for these old bones
Shahan, Sherry. *The jazzy alphabet*
Shannon, Terry Miller. *Tub toys*
Shapiro, Arnold L. *Who says that?*
Sharratt, Nick. *Monday run-day*
    Mrs. Pirate
    Shark in the park
    Snazzy aunties
Shaw, Nancy (Nancy E.). *Raccoon tune*
    Sheep in a jeep
    Sheep in a shop
    Sheep on a ship
    Sheep out to eat
    Sheep take a hike
    Sheep trick or treat
Shea, Pegi Deitz. *I see me!*
Sheppard, Jeff. *Splash, splash*
Sherman, Nancy. *Gwendolyn and the weathercock*
    Gwendolyn the miracle hen
Shields, Carol Diggory. *Colors*
    Day by day a week goes round
    Martian rock
    Month by month a year goes round
    Saturday night at the dinosaur stomp
Shortall, Leonard W. *One way*
Shulevitz, Uri. *Rain rain rivers*
Shute, Linda. *Halloween party*
Siddals, Mary McKenna. *Millions of snowflakes*
    Tell me a season
Siebert, Diane. *Cave*
    Plane song
    Train song
    Truck song
Sierra, Judy. *The house that Drac built*
    There's a zoo in room 22
    'Twas the fright before Christmas
    Wild about books
Silverman, Erica. *Follow the leader*
    The Halloween house
    On the morn of Mayfest
Silverstein, Shel. *A giraffe and a half*
    The giving tree
Simmons, Jane. *Daisy's favorite things*
Simon, Charnan. *Mud!*
Simon, Francesca. *But what does the hippopotamus say?*
    Calling all toddlers
Simon, Mina Lewiton. *Is anyone here?*
Singer, Marilyn. *Boo hoo boo-boo*
    Fred's bed
    Solomon sneezes
Singh, Jacquelin. *Fat Gopal*
Siomades, Lorianne. *Cuckoo can't find you*
    Kangaroo and cricket
    A place to bloom
Skwarek, Skip. *The horrors of Howling Hall*
Slate, Joseph. *The great big wagon that rang*
    Miss Bindergarten celebrates the 100th day of kindergarten
    Miss Bindergarten stays home from kindergarten
    Miss Bindergarten takes a field trip with kindergarten
    Who is coming to our house?
Slepian, Jan. *The hungry thing returns*
Sloat, Teri. *Farmer Brown goes round and round*

Farmer Brown shears his sheep
Patty's pumpkin patch
Pieces of Christmas
There was an old lady who swallowed a trout
The thing that bothered Farmer Brown
Slobodkin, Louis. *Clear the track for Michael's magic train*
  Friendly animals
  Millions and millions and millions
  One is good, but two are better
  The seaweed hat
  Up high and down low
Small, David. *George Washington's cows*
Smalls-Hector, Irene. *Kevin and his dad*
Smath, Jerry. *A hat so simple*
Smith, Linda. *Mrs. Biddlebox*
  When Moon fell down
Smith, Mavis. *Fred, is that you?*
  'Twas the day after Thanksgiving
Smith-Moore, J. J. *Sally Small*
Snell, Gordon. *'Twas the day after Christmas*
Snow, Alan. *The monster book of ABC sounds*
Snow, Pegeen. *A pet for Pat*
Southwell, Jandelyn. *The little country town*
Speed, Toby. *Two cool cows*
Spence, Robert, III. *Clickety clack*
Spier, Peter. *Noah's ark*
Spilka, Arnold. *A lion I can do without*
  Little birds don't cry
Spinelli, Eileen. *The best time of day*
  Here comes the year
  I know it's autumn
  Rise the moon
  A safe place called home
  What do angels wear?
  When Mama comes home tonight
Spohn, Kate. *Snow play*
  The wet dry book
Spurr, Elizabeth. *Two bears beneath the stairs*
Stadler, John. *Cat is back at bat*
Steiner, Joan (Joan Catherine). *Look-alikes*
  Look-alikes, Jr.
Stern, Ellen. *I saw a bullfrog*
Stevenson, Drew. *The ballad of Penelope Lou . . . and me*
Stewart, Sarah. *The library*
Stickland, Paul. *Bears*
  Dinosaur roar!
  Dinosaur stomp!
  Ten terrible dinosaurs
Sting (Musician). *Rock steady*
Stobbs, William. *This little piggy*
Stoddard, Sandol. *Bedtime for bear*
  Bedtime mouse
  My very own special particular private and personal cat
  Turtle time
Stohs, Anita. *An Easter alleluia*
Stone, Phoebe. *What night do the angels wander?*
Stone, Rosetta. *Because a little bug went ka-choo!*
Stonem, Tanya Lee. *D is for dreidel*
Stover, Jo Ann. *If everybody did*
Struges, Philemon. *I love school*
  I love trains
Stuart, Chad. *The Ballymara flood*
Sturges, Philemon. *I love bugs*
  I love trucks!
  Ten flashing fireflies
Stutson, Caroline. *By the light of the Halloween moon*
  Cowpokes
  Night train
  Prairie primer A to Z
Suen, Anastasia. *Baby born*
  Baby born [board book]
  Delivery
  Raise the roof
  Red light, green light
  Subway
  Window music
Sullivan, Charles. *Numbers at play*

Sundgaard, Arnold. *Jethro's difficult dinosaur*
Supraner, Robyn. *Would you rather be a tiger?*
Sutherland, Marc. *The waiting place*
Sutton, Eve. *My cat likes to hide in boxes*
Svendsen, Carol. *Hulda*
Sweeney, Jacqueline. *Katie and the night noises*
Sweetland, Nancy Rose. *God's quiet things*
Szekeres, Cyndy. *Cyndy Szekeres' learn to count, funny bunnies*
  Toby's please and thank you
Tafuri, Nancy. *Snowy flowy blowy*
Tang, Greg. *Math appeal*
Tangvald, Christine Harder. *Hey, Mr. Angel!*
Taylor, Scott. *Dinosaur James*
Temple, Charles A. *Train*
Tether, Graham. *The hair book*
Thomas, Patricia. *The one and only, super-duper, golly-whopper, jim-dandy, really-handy clock-tock-stopper*
  "Stand back," said the elephant, "I'm going to sneeze!"
  "There are rocks in my socks!" said the ox to the fox
Thomas, Shelley Moore. *Putting the world to sleep*
Thompson, Carol. *Baby days*
Thompson, Richard. *The follower*
Thomson, Ruth. *My bear: I can . . . can you?*
  My bear: I like . . . do you?
The three little pigs. *The three little pigs*, ill. by Erik Blegvad
  The three little pigs, ill. by Caroline Bucknall
  The three little pigs, ill. by William Pène Du Bois
  The three little pigs and the big bad wolf
Tippett, James Sterling. *Counting the days*
Todd, Mark. *Monster trucks*
  What will you be for Halloween?
Toft, Kim Michelle. *Neptune's nursery*
  One less fish
Trapani, Iza. *Row, row, row your boat*
  What am I?
Trent, Robbie. *The first Christmas*
Tresselt, Alvin R. *Follow the wind*
Trimble, Marcia. *Moonbeams for Santa*
Tripp, Valerie. *Happy, happy Mother's Day*
  Sillyhen's big surprise
Tryon, Leslie. *Albert's Christmas*
  Albert's play
Tucker, Kathy. *Do cowboys ride bikes?*
  Do knights take naps?
  Do pirates take baths?
Turner, Ann Warren. *Angel hide and seek*
  Shaker hearts
Turner, Gwenda. *Over on the farm*
Two little eyes and other action rhymes
Tyrrell, Anne. *Elizabeth Jane gets dressed*
  Mary Ann always can
Van der Beek, Deborah. *Superbabe!*
VanderKlipp, Michael A. *Joy to the world!*
Van Dusen, Chris. *Down to the sea with Mr. Magee*
Van Laan, Nancy. *Little baby Bobby*
  Little Fish lost
  Mama rocks, Papa sings
  A mouse in my house
  People, people, everywhere
  Possum come a-knocking
  Round and round again
  So say the little monkeys
  This is the hat
  A tree for me
Van Rynbach, Iris. *Five little pumpkins*
Vaughan, Marcia Kapok. *The dancing dragon*
  We're going on a ghost hunt
VerDorn, Bethea. *Moon glows*
Vogel, Ilse-Margret. *The don't be scared book*
Von Königslöw, Andrea Wayne. *Would you love me?*
Vozar, David. *M. C. Turtle and the hip hop hare*
  Yo, hungry wolf!
Vulliamy, Clara. *Bang and shout*
  Blue hat, red coat
  Boo baby boo!
  Good night, baby
  Wide awake

Yum yum
Waber, Bernard. *Fast food! gulp! gulp!*
   Gina
   The mouse that snored
Waddell, Martin. *My great grandpa*
   The park in the dark
Wahl, Jan. *Elf night*
   Follow me cried Bee
   I met a dinosaur
   Rabbits on roller skates!
   The sleepytime book
Waite, Judy. *Mouse, look out!*
Wakefield, Joyce. *Ask a silly question*
   From where you are
Waldron, Jan L. *Angel Pig and the hidden Christmas*
   John Pig's Halloween
Wallace, Nancy Elizabeth. *Rabbit's bedtime*
Wallen, Ila. *The moon in my room*
Walters, Virginia. *Are we there yet, Daddy?*
Walton, Rick. *The bear came over to my house*
   How can you dance?
   Little dogs say "Rough!"
   Noah's square dance
   So many bunnies
Ward, Heather Patricia. *I promise I'll find you*
Ward, Jennifer. *Over in the garden*
   Somewhere in the ocean
Wardlaw, Lee. *The chair where bear sits*
Warner, Sunny. *Madison finds a line*
Watson, Clyde. *Applebet*
   Hickory stick rag
Wax, Wendy. *A very mice Christmas*
Waysman, Dvora. *My Jewish days of the week*
Weatherford, Carole Boston. *Jazz baby*
Weeks, Sarah. *Baa-choo!*
   Bite me, I'm a shape
   Bite me, I'm a book
   Drip, drop
   Mrs. McNosh and the great big squash
   My somebody special
   Oh my gosh, Mrs. McNosh!
   Splish splash
Weigel, Jeff. *Atomic Ace (he's just my dad)*
Weiss, Nicki. *Sun sand sea sail*
   The world turns round and round
Welber, Robert. *Goodbye, hello*
Welch, Willy. *Dancing with Daddy*
   Grumpy Bunnies
Wells, Philip. *Daddy Island*
Wells, Rosemary. *Don't spill it again, James*
   First tomato
   Moss pillows
   My kindergarten
   Noisy Nora
   Read to your bunny
   Shy Charles
Weninger, Brigitte. *The elf's hat*
West, Colin. *The king's toothache*
West, Kipling. *A rattle of bones*
Westcott, Nadine Bernard. *Peanut butter and jelly*
Weston, Martha. *Jack and Jill and Big Dog Bill*
   Space guys!
What will we do with the baby-o?
Whatley, Bruce. *That magnetic dog*
Wheeler, Lisa. *Jazz baby*
   Sixteen cows
Whitman, Candace. *The night is like an animal*
Whittaker, Nicola. *Feet*
   Hair
Whybrow, Ian. *Parcel for Stanley*
   Quacky quack-quack!
Wick, Walter. *Can you see what I see? Cool collections*
   Can you see what I see? Dream machine
   Can you see what I see? picture puzzles to search and solve
   Can you see what I see? Seymour and the juice box boat
   Can you see what I see? Seymour makes new friends
   I spy a book of picture riddles

I spy Christmas
I spy extreme challenger!
I spy fantasy
I spy gold challenger!
I spy school days
I spy spooky night
I spy super challenger!
I spy treasure hunt
I spy ultimate challenger!
Wild, Robin. *Little Pig and the big bad wolf*
Wildsmith, Brian. *Animal tricks*
Wilkinson, Bruce. *The prayer of Jabez for young hearts*
Willard, Nancy. *The mouse, the cat and Grandmother's hat*
   Night story
Willey, Margaret. *Thanksgiving with me*
Williams, Jay. *I wish I had another name*
Williams, Jenny (Jennifer). *Playtime 1 2 3*
Williams, Linda. *Horse in the pigpen*
Williams, Rozanne Lanczak. *The coin counting book*
   The purple snerd
Williams, Sue. *Dinnertime*
   I went walking
   I went walking [board book]
   Let's go visiting
Williams, Suzanne. *Old MacDonald in the city*
Williams, Terry Tempest. *Between cattails*
Willis, Jeanne. *Do little mermaids wet their beds*
   The monster bed
   The monster storm
   Sloth's shoes
   Susan laughs
Wilner, Isabel. *A garden alphabet*
Wilson, Karma. *Bear stays up for Christmas*
Wilson, Sarah. *Elmo says, achoo!*
   Good zap, little grog
   Love and kisses
Wing, Natasha. *The night before the night before Christmas*
Winters, Kay. *Wolf watch*
Winthrop, Elizabeth. *Halloween hats*
   Shoes
   Sledding
Wiseman, Bernard. *Little new kangaroo*
Wishinsky, Frieda. *Jennifer Jones won't leave me alone*
Witte, Anna. *The parrot Tico Tango*
Wittels, Harriet. *Things I hate!*
Wolf, Sallie. *Peter's trucks*
Wolff, Ferida. *On Halloween night*
Wong, Janet S. *Grump*
Wood, Audrey. *The napping house*
   The napping house wakes up
   Silly Sally
   Ten little fish
Wood, Jakki. *One bear with bees in his hair*
Wright, Betty Ren. *Pet detectives!*
Wynne-Jones, Tim. *On Tumbledown Hill*
Yaccarino, Dan. *Five little ducks*
   Zoom! Zoom! Zoom! I'm off to the moon!
Yates, Philip. *Ten little mummies*
Yee, Wong Herbert. *Big black bear*
   A drop of rain
   Eek! There's a mouse in the house
   Fireman Small
   Fireman Small, fire down below
   Fireman Small to the rescue
   Mrs. Brown went to town
   The Officers' Ball
   A small Christmas
Yektai, Niki. *Bears in pairs*
   Hi bears, bye bears
Yeoman, John. *Old Mother Hubbard's dog dresses up*
   Old Mother Hubbard's dog learns to play
   Old Mother Hubbard's dog needs a doctor
   Old Mother Hubbard's dog takes up sport
Yep, Laurence. *Tiger woman*
Yolen, Jane. *Beneath the ghost moon*
   Harvest home
   How do dinosaurs clean their rooms?

Riddles & jokes

Trick or eeek!
Maestro, Giulio. *Halloween howls*
   A raft of riddles
   Riddle romp
Maestro, Marco. *Geese find the missing piece*
   What do you hear when cows sing?
Marzollo, Jean. *I spy, mystery*
   I spy, year-round challenger!
McMullan, Kate (Hall). *Back-to-school belly busters*
   Hanukkah ha-has
   Ho ho ho, ha ha ha
   Ribbit riddles
Medearis, Angela Shelf. *The freedom riddle*
Mitton, Tony. *Riddledy piggledy*
Modell, Frank. *Look out, it's April Fools' Day*
Moncure, Jane Belk. *Riddle me a riddle*
Mooser, Stephen. *Funnyman's first case*
Most, Bernard. *Pets in trumpets and other word-play riddles*
   Zoodles
Nims, Bonnie Larkin. *Just beyond reach and other riddle poems*
Peppé, Rodney. *Hey, riddle, diddle*
Peterson, Scott K. *What's your name?*
Phillips, Louis. *The upside down riddle book*
Poskanzer, Susan Cornell. *Riddles about Hannukah*
Potter, Beatrix. *The tale of Squirrel Nutkin*
Regan, Dian Curtis. *How do you know it's Halloween?*
Romanoli, Robert. *What's so funny?!!*
Roop, Peter. *Going buggy!*
   Holiday howlers
   Let's celebrate!
   Stick out your tongue!
Rosenbloom, Joseph. *The funniest joke book ever!*
Schultz, Sam. *Animal antics: the beast jokes ever*
   Monster mayhem
Selberg, Ingrid. *Nature's hidden world*
Seuss, Dr. *The cat's quizzer*
Shields, Carol Diggory. *Colors*
   Homes
   On the go
   Patterns
Sloat, Teri. *Rib-ticklers*
Speed, Toby. *Watervoices*
Swann, Brian. *A basket full of white eggs*
   The house with no door
Swanson, June. *Punny places*
   Summit up
Thaler, Mike. *The yellow brick toad*
Thompson, Lauren. *One riddle, one answer*
Türk, Hanne. *Max versus the cube*
Wakefield, Joyce. *Ask a silly question*
Walton, Rick. *Dumb clucks!*
   How many?
   Something's fishy!
Warrick, Karen Clemens. *If I had a tail*
   Who needs that nose?
Wick, Walter. *I spy Christmas*
   I spy extreme challenger!
   I spy fantasy
   I spy gold challenger!
   I spy school days
   I spy spooky night
   I spy super challenger!
   I spy treasure hunt
   I spy ultimate challenger!
Wolff, Patricia Rae. *The toll-bridge troll*
Woodworth, Viki. *Fairy tale jokes*
Young, Ed (Edward). *High on a hill*
Young, Ruth. *Who says moo?*
Ziefert, Harriet. *Math riddles*
Zwetchkenbaum, G. *The Peanuts shape circus puzzle book*
   The Peanuts sleepy time puzzle book
   The Snoopy farm puzzle book
   Snoopy safari puzzle book

Right & left *see* Concepts – left & right

Riots

Bunting, Eve (Anne Evelyn). *Smoky night*

Rivers

Ashforth, Camilla. *Willow on the river*
Atwell, Debby. *River*
Baker, Sanna Anderson. *Mississippi going north*
Bandes, Hanna. *Sleepy river*
Brennan, Joseph Killorin. *Gobo and the river*
Brook, Judy. *Tim mouse goes down the stream*
Burke, Timothy. *Tugboats in action*
Bush, Timothy. *Three at sea*
Bushey, Jerry. *The barge book*
Cameron, Eileen. *Canyon*
Carlstrom, Nancy White. *Raven and river*
Carrick, Carol. *The brook*
Cherry, Lynne. *A river ran wild*
   The shaman's apprentice
Craighead, Charles. *The eagle and the river*
Crampton, Gertrude. *Scuffy the tugboat*
Cunningham, David. *A crow's journey*
Dabcovich, Lydia. *Follow the river*
Day, Alexandra. *River parade*
Drake, John. *The beginning of the river*
Drawson, Blair. *All along the river*
Flack, Marjorie. *The boats on the river*
George, Jean Craighead. *Everglades*
Gerrard, Roy. *Croco'nile*
Gilliland, Judith Heide. *River*
Gorog, Judith. *Zilla Sasparilla and the mud baby*
Grahame, Kenneth. *The wind in the willows: the river bank:*
Gramatky, Hardie. *Little Toot on the Mississippi*
Grasshopper to the rescue
Greene, Carol. *Reading about the river otter*
   Sunflower Island
Grifalconi, Ann. *Flyaway girl*
Halpern, Shari. *My river*
Harness, Cheryl. *Mark Twain and the queens of the Mississippi*
Harrison, David Lee. *Rivers*
Holling, Holling C. (Holling Clancy). *Paddle-to-the-sea*
Hooper, Meredith. *River story*
Keeping, Charles. *Alfie finds the other side of the world*
Kellogg, Steven (Stephen). *Mike Fink*
Kovacs, Deborah. *Moonlight on the river*
Kurtz, Jane. *River friendly, river wild*
LaMarche, Jim. *The raft*
Lewin, Ted. *Amazon boy*
Lillegard, Dee. *The hee-haw river*
Locker, Thomas. *Where the river begins*
London, Jonathan. *White water*
MacDonald, Elizabeth. *Dilly-Dally and the nine secrets*
Magdanz, James S. *Go home, river*
Michl, Reinhard. *A day on the river*
Miller, Debbie S. *River of life*
Murphy, Shirley Rousseau. *Tattie's river journey*
Mwenye Hadithi. *Hot hippo*
Oakley, Graham. *The church mice adrift*
Peters, Lisa Westberg. *Good morning, river!*
Pfeffer, Wendy. *The big flood*
Pollard, Nik. *The river*
Reynolds, Jan. *Amazon*
Russell, Naomi. *The stream*
Sanders, Scott R. (Scott Russell). *Crawdad Creek*
Schmid, Eleonore. *The water's journey*
Schofield, Jennifer. *Animal babies in ponds and rivers*
Tennyson, Alfred, Baron. *The brook*
Walsh, Ellen Stoll. *Dot and Jabber and the mystery of the missing*
   stream
Wilson, Sarah. *Big day on the river*

Roads

Bate, Norman. *Who built the highway?*
Field, Rachel Lyman. *A road might lead to anywhere*
Goodall, John S. *The story of a main street*

Hennessy, B. G. (Barbara G.). *Road builders*
Hindley, Judy. *The big red bus*
Johnston, Tony. *Amber on the mountain*
Kehoe, Michael. *Road closed*
Kilby, Don. *On the road*
Kroninger, Stephen. *If I crossed the road*
Lyon, George Ella. *Who came down that road?*
Morris, Dewi. *Sandy's street*
Nikola-Lisa, W. *One hole in the road*
Plourde, Lynn. *Pigs in the mud in the middle of the rud*
Pringle, Laurence P. *Jesse builds a road*
Roennfeldt, Robert. *A day on the avenue*
Royston, Angela. *Monster road builders*
Tusa, Tricia. *Sherman and Pearl*

Robbers *see* Crime

Robins *see* Birds – robins

Robots

Barner, Bob. *Space race*
Bradford, Ann. *The mystery of the square footsteps*
Bunting, Eve (Anne Evelyn). *The robot birthday*
Bush, Timothy. *Benjamin McFadden and the robot babysitter*
Cole, Babette. *The trouble with Dad*
Cushman, Doug. *Space cat*
Dewan, Ted. *The sorcerer's apprentice*
Dupasquier, Philippe. *A robot named chip*
Greene, Carol. *Robots*
Hoban, Lillian. *The laziest robot in zone one*
James, Brian. *Supertwins meet the dangerous dino-robots*
Johnson, Stephen T. *My little blue robot*
Joyce, William. *Rolie Polie Olie*
　　Rolie Polie Olie, how many howdys?
　　Sleepy time Olie
　　Snowie Rolie
Kirk, David. *Nova's ark*
Kiser, Kevin. *Buzzy Widget*
Krahn, Fernando. *Robot-bot-bot*
Kroll, Steven. *Otto*
Lauber, Patricia. *Get ready for robots!*
Loomis, Christine. *The cleanup surprise*
Marshall, Edward. *Space case*
Marzollo, Jean. *Jed and the space bandits*
　　Jed's junior space patrol
Novak, Matt. *The Robobots*
Paul, Sherry. *2-B and the rock 'n roll band*
　　2-B and the space visitor
Pinkney, J. Brian. *Cosmo and the robot*
Schwab, Eva. *Robert and the Robot*
Titus, Eve. *Anatole and the robot*
Whybrow, Ian. *Sammy and the robots*
Yaccarino, Dan. *If I had a robot*

Rock climbing *see* Sports – rock climbing

Rockets *see* Space & space ships

Rocking chairs *see* Furniture – chairs

Rocking horses *see* Toys – rocking horses

Rocks

Baylor, Byrd. *Everybody needs a rock*
Chetwin, Grace. *Mr. Meredith and the truly remarkable stone*
Christian, Peggy. *If you find a rock*
Cole, Joanna. *The magic school bus inside the earth*
Flanagan, Alice K. *Rocks*
Gammell, Stephen. *Twigboy*
Gans, Roma. *Let's go rock collecting*
　　Rock collecting
Goble, Paul. *Iktomi and the boulder*
Harshman, Marc. *Rocks in my pocket*
Hurst, Carol Otis. *Rocks in his head*

Kaufman, Jeff. *Milk rock*
Kehoe, Michael. *The rock quarry book*
Lee, Jeanne M. *Legend of the Li River*
Lesynski, Loris. *Rocksy*
Lionni, Leo. *On my beach there are many pebbles*
McKee, David. *The hill and the rock*
Marston, Elsa. *A griffin in the garden*
Mills, Judith Christine. *The stonehook schooner*
Parnall, Peter. *The rock*
Pellant, Chris. *The best book of fossils, rocks, and minerals*
Peters, Lisa Westberg. *Meg and dad discover treasure in the air*
Polacco, Patricia. *My ol' man*
Selsam, Millicent E. *A first look at rocks*
Stuve-Bodeen, Stephanie. *Elizabeti's doll*
Trimble, Marcia. *Malinda Martha and her stepping stones*
Walker, Alice. *Finding the green stone*
Weller, Frances Ward. *Matthew Wheelock's wall*

Rodeos

Gibbons, Gail. *Yippee-yay!*
Harper, Jo. *Ollie Jolly, rodeo clown*

Roller skating *see* Sports – roller skating

Romania *see* Foreign lands – Romania

Roosters *see* Birds – chickens

Rosh Hashanah *see* Holidays – Rosh Hashanah

Royalty

Aardema, Verna. *The riddle of the drum*
Abrons, Mary. *For Alice a palace*
Adinolfi, JoAnn. *The Egyptian polar bear*
Aitken, Amy. *Ruby, the red knight*
Allen, Pamela. *Bertie and the bear*
　　A lion in the night
Andersen, H. C. (Hans Christian). *The swineherd*, ill. by Dorothée Duntze
Anderson, Lonzo. *Two hundred rabbits*
Asher, Sandy. *Princess Bee and the royal good-night story*
Babbitt, Natalie. *Bub, or, The very best thing*
Babbitt, Samuel F. *The forty-ninth magician*
Bang, Betsy. *Tuntuni the tailor bird*
Bang, Molly. *Tye May and the magic brush*
Baring, Maurice. *The blue rose*
Barry, David. *The Rajah's rice*
Basile, Giambattista. *Petrosinella*
Berenzy, Alix. *A frog prince*
Beresford, Elisabeth. *Jack and the magic stove*
Berson, Harold. *The thief who hugged a moonbeam*
Bohdal, Susi. *The magic honey jar*
Bolliger, Max. *The most beautiful song*
Bond, Michael. *Paddington at the palace*
Bowden, Joan Chase. *A new home for Snow Ball*
Brierley, Louise. *King Lion and his cooks*
Browne, Caroline. *Mrs. Christie's farmhouse*
Burningham, John. *Time to get out of the bath, Shirley*
Carle, Eric. *Walter the baker*
Chapman, Gaynor. *The luck child*
Climo, Shirley. *The Egyptian Cinderella*
　　King of the birds
　　The Korean Cinderella
Company González, Mercé. *Killian and the dragons*
Coombs, Patricia. *Tilabel*
Cooney, Barbara. *Little brother and little sister*
Cretien, Paul D. *Sir Henry and the dragon*
Day, David. *The swan children*
De La Mare, Walter (Walter John). *Molly Whuppie*
Delessert, Etienne. *The seven dwarfs*
De Regniers, Beatrice Schenk. *May I bring a friend?*
Dewey, Ariane. *Dorin and the dragon*
Domanska, Janina. *Look, there is a turtle flying*
Dos Santos, Joyce Audy. *The diviner*

Duke, Kate. *Aunt Isabel tells a good one*
Elkin, Benjamin. *Gillespie and the guards*
 The wisest man in the world
Espenscheid, Gertrude E. *The oh ball*
Fisher, Leonard Everett. *Theseus and the Minotaur*
Fleischman, Sid. *Longbeard the wizard*
Foreman, Michael. *War and peas*
Freeman, Don. *Forever laughter*
Galdone, Paul. *The amazing pig*
 The monster and the tailor
Gay, Michel. *Bibi's birthday surprise*
Geras, Adèle. *The nutcracker*
Gianni, Peg. *Alex, the amazing juggler*
Gill, Janet. *Basket Weaver and Catches Many Mice*
Glass, Andrew. *Chickpea and the talking cow*
The golden goose, ill. by William Stobbs
Grimm, Jacob. *The earth gnome*
 The goose girl, ill. by Sabine Bruntjen
 The goose girl, ill. by Robert Sauber
 King Grisly-Beard
 Rumpelstiltskin, ill. by Jacqueline Ayer
 Rumpelstiltskin, ill. by Donna Diamond
 Rumpelstiltskin, ill. by Paul Galdone
 Rumpelstiltskin, ill. by Jonathan Langley
 Rumpelstiltskin, ill. by David Shaw
 Rumpelstiltskin, ill. by Gennady Spirin
 Rumpelstiltskin, ill. by John Wallner
 Rumpelstiltskin, ill. by Bernadette Watts
 Rumpelstiltskin, ill. by Paul O. Zelinsky
Hague, Michael. *The nutcracker*
Hayes, Sarah. *Bad egg*
Heine, Helme. *The most wonderful egg in the world*
Helldorfer, M. C. (Mary Claire). *Cabbage Rose*
Helmer, Marilyn. *Three royal tales*
Hilton, Nette. *Prince Lachlan*
Hoffmann, E. T. A. *The nutcracker*, ill. by Francesca Crespi
 The nutcracker, ill. by Renée Graef
 The nutcracker, ill. by Rachel Isadora
 The nutcracker, ill. by Joanna Isles
 The nutcracker, ill. by Maurice Sendak
 The nutcracker, ill. by Lisbeth Zwerger
 The nutcracker ballet, ill. by Carolyn Ewing
 The nutcracker ballet, ill. by Vladimir Vasilévich Vagin
Kahl, Virginia. *The Baron's booty*
 The Duchess bakes a cake
 Plum pudding for Christmas
Kennedy, Richard. *The lost kingdom of Karnica*
Kimmel, Eric A. *The four gallant sisters*
Kroll, Steven. *Fat magic*
Kurtz, Jane. *Miro in the kingdom of the sun*
Langner, Nola. *By the light of the silvery moon*
Langton, Jane. *The hedgehog boy*
 The queen's necklace
Lasker, David. *The boy who loved music*
Laskowski, Jerzy. *Master of the royal cats*
Lee, Jeanne M. *Toad is the uncle of heaven*
Littledale, Freya. *The magic plum tree*
Lobel, Anita. *Sven's bridge*
Locker, Thomas. *The young artist*
Lorenz, Lee. *The feathered ogre*
McCrea, James. *The magic tree*
McDermott, Gerald. *The voyage of Osiris*
McLenighan, Valjean. *What you see is what you get*
 You are what you are
McNaughton, Colin. *The rat race*
Mahood, Kenneth. *The laughing dragon*
Marlowe, Pete. *One Arabian morning*
Martin, Bill (William Ivan). *Rock it, sock it, number line*
Matsutani, Miyoko. *The fisherman under the sea*
Mayer, Marianna. *Baba Yaga and Vasilisa the Brave*
 The black horse
 The spirit of the blue light
Miller, M. L. *Dizzy from fools*
Montresor, Beni. *The witches of Venice*
Mother Goose. *The golden goose book*, ill. by L. Leslie Brooke
 Sing a song of sixpence, ill. by Leonard Lubin
Moxley, Susan. *Abdul's treasure*

Muller, Robin. *The sorcerer's apprentice*
Myers, Walter Dean. *The golden serpent*
Myller, Rolf. *Rolling round*
Nesbit, Edith. *The last of the dragons*
Nishikawa, Osamu. *Alexander and the blue ghost*
Oram, Hiawyn. *Skittlewonder and the wizard*
Orgel, Doris. *The flower of Sheba*
Pittman, Helena Clare. *A grain of rice*
Price, Leontyne. *Aïda*
Pushkin, Aleksandr Sergeevich. *The tale of Tsar Saltan*
Radley, Gail. *The spinner's gift*
Rappaport, Doreen. *The new king*
Richter, Mischa. *To bed, to bed!*
Rogasky, Barbara. *The water of life*
Rose, Gerald. *The bird garden*
Ross, Tony. *Towser and the terrible thing*
Saddler, Allen. *The Archery contest*
San Souci, Robert D. *The white cat*
Schiller, Barbara. *The white rat's tale*
Scholey, Arthur. *Baboushka*
Schwartz, Amy. *Her Majesty, Aunt Essie*
Scott, Sally. *The magic horse*
Seuss, Dr. *Bartholomew and the Oobleck*
Shulevitz, Uri. *One Monday morning*
Steig, William. *Roland, the minstrel pig*
Stephenson, Dorothy. *The night it rained toys*
Thomas, Shelley Moore. *Good night, Good Knight*
Tompert, Ann. *The Tzar's bird*
Torre, Betty L. *The luminous pearl*
Trez, Denise. *Maila and the flying carpet*
 The royal hiccups
Vernon, Adele. *The riddle*
Wahl, Jan. *Cabbage moon*
Wiesner, David. *The loathsome dragon*
Williams, Jay. *School for sillies*
Winthrop, Elizabeth. *Vasilissa the beautiful*
Wisniewski, David. *The warrior and the wise man*
Yen, Clara. *Why rat comes first*
Yolen, Jane. *The seeing stick*
Young, Miriam Burt. *The sugar mouse cake*
Zemach, Harve. *The tricks of Master Dabble*

Royalty – emperors

Æsop. *The ant and the grasshopper*
Andersen, H. C. (Hans Christian). *The emperor's new clothes*, ill. by Angela Barrett
 The emperor's new clothes, ill. by Erik Blegvad
 The emperor's new clothes, ill. by Virginia Lee Burton
 The emperor's new clothes, ill. by Robert Byrd
 The emperor's new clothes, ill. by Charlene DeLage
 The emperor's new clothes, ill. by Jack and Irene Delano
 The emperor's new clothes, ill. by Demi
 The emperor's new clothes, ill. by Hélène Desputeaux
 The emperor's new clothes, ill. by Birte Dietz
 The emperor's new clothes, ill. by Dorothée Duntze
 The emperor's new clothes, ill. by Pamela Baldwin Ford
 The emperor's new clothes, ill. by Jack Kent
 The emperor's new clothes, ill. by Monika Laimgruber
 The emperor's new clothes, ill. by Anne F. Rockwell
 The emperor's new clothes, ill. by Janet Stevens
 The emperor's new clothes, ill. by Eve Tharlet
 The emperor's new clothes, ill. by Robert Van Nutt
 The emperor's new clothes, ill. by Nadine Bernard Westcott
 The emperor's nightingale, ill. from the Disney archives
 The emperor's nightingale, ill. by Georges Lemoine
 The nightingale, ill. by Harold Berson
 The nightingale, ill. by Nancy Ekholm Burkert
 The nightingale, ill. by Demi
 The nightingale, ill. by Beni Montresor
 The nightingale, ill. by Regolo Ricci
 The nightingale, ill. by Christopher Santoro
 The nightingale, ill. by Lisbeth Zwerger
Asch, Frank. *The flower faerie*
Bauld, Jane Scoggins. *Journey of the third seed*
Brighton, Catherine. *My Napoleon*
Chang, Margaret Scrogin. *The cricket warrior*

Demi. *The empty pot*
Goode, Diane. *The dinosaur's new clothes*
Hughes, Peter. *The emperor's oblong pancake*
Johnson, Crockett. *The emperor's gifts*
Lasky, Kathryn. *The emperor's old clothes*
Manson, Christopher. *Here begins the tale of the marvellous blue mouse*
Marcellino, Fred. *I, crocodile*
Mayer, Mercer. *Shibumi and the kitemaker*
Morris, Winifred. *The future of Yen-Tzu*
Nikly, Michelle. *The emperor's plum tree*
Perlman, Janet. *The Emperor Penguin's new clothes*
Shulevitz, Uri. *What is a wise bird like you doing in a silly tale like this?*
Tompert, Ann. *The jade horse, the cricket, and the peach stone*
Wolff, Ferida. *The emperor's garden*
Yacowitz, Caryn. *The jade stone*
Yolen, Jane. *The emperor and the kite*
Young, Ed (Edward). *Cat and Rat*

Royalty – khans

Yep, Laurence. *The Khan's daughter*

Royalty – kings

Alexander, Lloyd. *The king's fountain*
Alexander, Sue. *World famous Muriel and the scary dragon*
Aliki. *The king's day*
Anno, Mitsumasa. *The king's flower*
Armstrong, Jennifer. *Little Salt Lick and the Sun King*
Arnold, Tedd. *The twin princes*
Aroner, Miriam. *The kingdom of singing birds*
Aruego, José. *The king and his friends*
Auerbach, Marjorie. *King Lavra and the barber*
Balet, Jan B. *The king and the broom maker*
Balouch, Kristen. *The king and the three thieves*
Baranski, Joan Sullivan. *Round is a pancake*
Biers-Ariel, Matt. *Solomon and the trees*
Birch, David. *The king's chessboard*
Black, Charles C. *The royal nap*
Borchers, Elisabeth. *There comes a time*
Bosca, Francesca. *The apple king*
Boswell, Stephen. *King Gorboduc's fabulous zoo*
Brown, Ruth. *The grizzly revenge*
Brunhoff, Jean de. *Babar the king*
    Babar the king, facsimile ed
Brunhoff, Laurent de. *Babar's visit to Bird Island*
Brusca, María Cristina. *The cook and the king*
Buffett, Jimmy. *The jolly mon*
Bunting, Eve (Anne Evelyn). *Demetrius and the golden goblet*
Burdett, Lois. *Macbeth for kids*
Chwast, Seymour. *Bushy bride*
Cole, Babette. *King Change-A-Lot*
Cole, Brock. *The king at the door*
Collier, Mary Jo. *The king's giraffe*
Crabtree, Judith. *The sparrow's story at the king's command*
Cunliffe, John. *The king's birthday cake*
Curry, Jane Louise. *The Christmas knight*
Cushman, Doug. *The mystery of King Karfu*
Day, David. *King of the woods*
Deedy, Carmen Agra. *The yellow star*
Degen, Bruce. *Teddy bear towers*
DeLuise, Dom. *King Bob's new clothes*
De Paola, Tomie (Thomas Anthony). *The legend of the persian carpet*
Derby, Sally. *King Kenrick's splinter*
Diakité, Baba Wagué. *The magic gourd*
Dieterlé, Nathalie. *I am the king!*
Domanska, Janina. *King Krakus and the dragon*
Eisner, Will. *Sundiata*
Elkin, Benjamin. *The king who could not sleep*
    The king's wish and other stories
Evans, Richard Paul. *The spyglass*
Farley, Carol J. *The king's secret*
Fern, Eugene. *The king who was too busy*
French, Fiona. *King of another country*

Friedman, Aileen. *The king's commissioners*
Froese, Deborah L. *The wise washerman*
Gackenbach, Dick. *Harvey, the foolish pig*
    King Wacky
Gershator, Phillis. *Only one cowry*
Gibert, Bruno. *The king is naked!*
Gifaldi, David. *The boy who spoke colors*
Ginsburg, Mirra. *The king who tried to fry an egg on his head*
Gregory, Valiska. *Through the mickle woods*
Grimm, Jacob. *The golden bird*, ill. by Isabelle Brent
    The golden bird, ill. by Sandro Nardini
    Iron Hans
    Iron John, ill. by Trina Schart Hyman
    Iron John, ill. by Winslow Pels
Harber, Frances. *My king has donkey ears*
Harness, Cheryl. *The queen with bees in her hair*
Haywood, Carolyn. *The king's monster*
Heine, Helme. *King Bounce the 1st*
Hewitt, Kathryn. *King Midas and the golden touch*
Hughes, Peter. *The king who loved candy*
Huling, Jan. *Puss in cowboy boots*
Hutchins, Pat. *King Henry's palace*
Jackson, Ellen B. *The impossible riddle*
Karlin, Nurit. *A train for the king*
Kessler, Leonard P. *Soup for the king*
Kherdian, David. *The golden bracelet*
Kimmel, Eric A. *Squash it!*
    Three sacks of truth
Kraus, Robert. *The king's trousers*
Krudop, Walter Lyon. *The man who caught fish*
Lang, Andrew. *The flying ship*
Leonard, Marcia. *King Lionheart's castle*
Love, Ann. *Ice cream at the castle*
    The prince who wrote a letter
Luttrell, Ida. *The star counters*
McCrea, James. *The king's procession*
MacDonald, Alan. *The not-so-wise man*
MacGill-Callahan, Sheila. *The children of Lir*
    When Solomon was king
McKee, David. *King Rollo and the birthday*
    King Rollo and the bread
    King Rollo and the new shoes
McKissack, Patricia C. *King Midas and his gold*
    The king's new clothes
McMullen, Eunice. *Dragon for breakfast*
Mahy, Margaret. *17 kings and 42 elephants*
    When the king rides by
Manson, Christopher. *A gift for the king*
Mark, Jan. *The Midas touch*
Martin, C. L. G. *The dragon nanny*
Martin, Rafe. *The monkey bridge*
    The Shark God
Mayer, Marianna. *Marcel the pastry chef*
    The prince and the pauper
Medearis, Angela Shelf. *Too much talk*
Metaxas, Eric. *David and Goliath*
    Puss in boots
Miller, M. L. *The enormous snore*
Milton, Nancy. *The giraffe that walked to Paris*
Mitchell, Adrian. *Nobody rides the unicorn*
Mollel, Tololwa M. (Tololwa Marti). *Dume's roar*
    The king and the tortoise
Muller, Robin. *The magic paintbrush*
Myller, Rolf. *How big is a foot?*
Nobisso, Josephine. *The weight of a Mass*
Noble, Trinka Hakes. *The king's tea*
Noyes, Alfred. *The highwayman*
Oberman, Sheldon. *King Solomon, Sheba, and the hoopoe bird*
    The wisdom bird
Ørdal, Stina Langlo. *Princess Aasta*
Osborne, Mary Pope. *The brave little seamstress*
Paterson, Katherine. *The angel and the donkey*
Peet, Bill (William Bartlett). *How Droofus the dragon lost his head*
Perkins, Al. *King Midas and the golden touch*
Perrault, Charles. *Puss in boots*, ill. by Marcia Brown
    Puss in boots, ill. by Lorinda Bryan Cauley
    Puss in boots, ill. by Jean Claverie

Puss in boots, ill. by Andrea Da Rif
Puss in boots, ill. by Stasys Eidrigevicius
Puss in boots, ill. by Hans Fischer
Puss in boots, ill. by Paul Galdone
Puss in boots, retold and ill. by John S. Goodall
Puss in boots, retold and ill. by Gail E. Haley
Puss in boots, ill. by Steve Light
Puss in boots, ill. by Giuliano Lunelli
Puss in boots, ill. by Fred Marcellino [pub. by Farrar, 1990]
Puss in boots, ill. by Fred Marcellino [pub. by Farrar, 1998]
Puss in boots, ill. by Julia Noonan
Puss in boots, ill. by Tony Ross
Puss in boots, ill. by William Stobbs
Puss in boots, ill. by Yan Thomas
Puss in boots, ill. by Alain Vaës
Puss in boots, ill. by Barry Wilkinson
Peters, Andrew. *Salt is sweeter than gold*
Peterson, Julienne. *Caterina, the clever farm girl*
Pevear, Richard. *Our king has horns!*
Pfister, Marcus. *How Leo learned to be king*
Pieńkowski, Jan. *Pizza!*
Postgate, Oliver. *Noggin and the whale*
　Noggin the king
Pullman, Philip. *Puss in boots*, ill. by Ian Beck
Reit, Seymour. *The king who learned to smile*
Robison, Nancy. *Ten tall soldiers*
Saddler, Allen. *The king gets fit*
San Souci, Robert D. *A weave of words*
Santore, Charles. *William the Curious*
Sawyer, Ruth. *The remarkable Christmas of the cobbler's sons*
Seuss, Dr. *The king's stilts*
Sexton, Gwain. *There once was a king*
Siekkinen, Raija. *Mister King*
Sierra, Judy. *The beautiful butterfly*
Skipper, Mervyn. *The fooling of King Alexander*
Slate, Joseph. *The secret stars*
Souhami, Jessica. *Rama and the demon king*
Steptoe, John. *Mufaro's beautiful daughters*
Stewig, John Warren. *King Midas*
Storr, Catherine (Cole). *King Midas*
Tchana, Katrin. *Sense Pass King*
Thomson, Peggy. *The king has horse's ears*
Tom Thumb. *The adventures of Tom Thumb*, ill. by Kinuko Y. Craft
Va, Leong. *A letter to the king*
Van Laan, Nancy. *The legend of El Dorado*
Ward, Helen. *The king of the birds*
Wersba, Barbara. *Do tigers ever bite kings?*
West, Colin. *The king of Kennelwick castle*
　The king's toothache
Wilde, Oscar. *The happy prince*
Wilkes, Larry. *The king's egg dance*
Wisniewski, David. *Sundiata*
Wolkstein, Diane. *Bouki dances the Kokioko*
Wood, Audrey. *King Bidgood's in the bathtub*
Yep, Laurence. *The shell woman and the king*
Yolen, Jane. *King Long Shanks*
　The sea king

Royalty – pharaohs

Mike, Jan M. *Gift of the Nile*
Sabuda, Robert James. *Tutankhamen's gift*

Royalty – princes

Allchin, Rosalind. *The frog princess*
Allen, Jonathan. *Wake up, Sleeping Beauty*
Arnold, Tedd. *The twin princes*
Aulaire, Ingri Mortenson d'. *East of the sun and west of the moon*
Baum, Arline. *Opt*
Baumann, Kurt. *The prince and the lute*
Behan, Brendan. *The king of Ireland's son*
Berenzy, Alix. *Rapunzel*
Birrer, Cynthia. *The lady and the unicorn*
Bliss, Corinne Demas. *The magic apple*
Boesky, Amy. *Planet Was*
Brenner, Barbara A. *The prince and the pink blanket*

Bruna, Dick. *Dick Bruna's Cinderella*
Burdett, Lois. *Hamlet for kids*
Canfield, Jane White. *The frog prince*
Cecil, Laura. *The frog princess*
Cinderella
Clayton, Elaine. *The yeoman's daring daughter and the princes in the tower*
Climo, Shirley. *The Persian Cinderella*
Coburn, Jewell Reinhart. *Angkat*
　Jouanah
Cole, Babette. *King Change-A-Lot*
　Prince Cinders
Daly, Jude. *Fair, Brown & Trembling*
Damjan, Mischa. *The little prince and the tiger cat*
Dasent, George W. *East o' the sun, west o' the moon*
Debecker, Benoît. *The naughty prince*
The firebird. *The firebird*, ill. by Reg Cartwright
　The firebird, ill. by Francesca Crespi
　The firebird, ill. by Demi
　The firebird, adapt. and ill. by Rachel Isadora
　The firebird, ill. by Moira Kemp
　The firebird, ill. by Kris Waldherr
　The firebird, ill. by Boris Zvorykin
　The tale of the firebird, ill. by Gennady Spirin
Gál, László. *The parrot*
Geras, Adèle. *Sleeping beauty*
　Swan Lake
Gray, Nigel. *The frog prince*
Greene, Ellin. *Billy Beg and his bull*
Grimm, Jacob. *Cinderella*, ill. by Nonny Hogrogian
　Cinderella, ill. by Svend Otto S
　The donkey prince
　The frog prince, ill. by Paul Galdone
　The frog prince, ill. by Todd Ouren
　The frog prince, ill. by Binette Schroeder
　The golden bird, ill. by Isabelle Brent
　The golden bird, ill. by Sandro Nardini
　Iron Hans
　Iron John, ill. by Trina Schart Hyman
　Iron John, ill. by Winslow Pels
　The princess and the frog, ill. by Rachel Isadora
　The princess and the frog, ill. by Will Eisner
　Rapunzel, ill. by Jutta Ash
　Rapunzel, ill. by Sheilah Beckett
　Rapunzel, ill. by Bert Dodson
　Rapunzel, ill. by Maja Dusíkova
　Rapunzel, ill. by Michael Hague
　Rapunzel, ill. by Trina Schart Hyman
　Rapunzel, ill. by Kris Waldherr
　Rapunzel, ill. by Bernadette Watts
　Rapunzel, ill. by Paul O. Zelinsky
　Rose Red and the bear prince
　The sleeping beauty, ill. by Warwick Hutton
　The sleeping beauty, ill. by Trina Schart Hyman
　The sleeping beauty, ill. by Monika Laimgruber
　The sleeping beauty, ill. by Mercer Mayer
　Sleeping Beauty, ill. by Fina Rifa
　The sleeping beauty, ill. by Ruth Sanderson
　Sleeping Beauty, ill. by John Wallner
Hague, Kathleen. *East of the sun and west of the moon*
Han, Oki S. *Kongi and Potgi*
Hastings, Selina. *The singing ringing tree*
Haugaard, Erik Christian. *Prince Boghole*
Heine, Helme. *Prince Bear*
Helldorfer, M. C. (Mary Claire). *The mapmaker's daughter*
Helmer, Marilyn. *Three prince charming tales*
Hilton, Nette. *Prince Lachlan*
Hopkins, Lee Bennett. *The horned toad prince*
Ikeda, Daisaku. *The snow country prince*
Jackson, Ellen B. *Cinder Edna*
Jacobs, Joseph. *Tattercoats*
Jennings, Linda M. *The sleeping beauty*
Johnson, Crockett. *The frowning prince*
Kimmel, Eric A. *One Eye, Two Eyes, Three Eyes*
　The three princes
Knight, Hilary. *Hilary Knight's Cinderella*
Kvasnosky, Laura McGee. *What shall I dream?*

Lattimore, Deborah Nourse. *Cinderhazel*
  The prince and the golden ax
Lester, Helen. *Princess Penelope's parrot*
Lobel, Arnold. *Prince Bertram the bad*
Love, Ann. *Ice cream at the castle*
Lunge-Larsen, Lise. *The race of the Birkebeiners*
McCaughrean, Geraldine. *Beauty and the beast*
MacDonald, George. *Little Daylight*
McKee, David. *Prince Peter and the teddy bear*
McKissack, Patricia C. *Cinderella*, ill. by Tom Dunnington
Mann, Pamela. *The frog princess?*
Manson, Christopher. *The crab prince*
Martin, Rafe. *The storytelling princess*
Metaxas, Eric. *The white cat*
Mike, Jan M. *The bird maiden*
Milligan, Bryce. *The prince of Ireland and the three magic stallions*
Mills, Lauren A. *The dog prince*
  Fairy wings
Milne, A. A. (Alan Alexander). *Prince Rabbit*
Minters, Frances. *Cinder-Elly*
Morris, Ann. *The Cinderella rebus book*
Murphy, Shirley Rousseau. *Wind child*
Nones, Eric Jon. *Canary prince*
Oppenheim, Joanne. *The story book prince*
Osborne, Mary Pope. *Molly and the prince*
Patz, Nancy. *Gina Farina and the Prince of Mintz*
Perrault, Charles. *Cinderella*, ill. by Sheilah Beckett
  Cinderella, ill. by Marcia Brown
  Cinderella, ill. by Paul Galdone
  Cinderella, ill. by Diane Goode
  Cinderella, ill. by Susan Jeffers
  Cinderella, ill. by Loek Koopmans
  Cinderella, ill. by Emanuele Luzzati
  Cinderella, ill. by James Marshall
  Cinderella, ill. by Phil Smith
  Cinderella = Cenicienta
  The sleeping beauty, ill. by David Walker
Piumini, Roberto. *Doctor Me Di Cin*
Priestley, Alice. *Someone is reading this book*
The prince who knew his fate
Pyle, Howard. *The Swan Maiden*
Richardson, Jean. *The sleeping beauty*
Roberts, Lynn (Lynn M.). *Cinderella, an Art Deco love story*
Rogers, Paul (Patrick). *Tumbledown*
Sanderson, Ruth. *Cinderella*
  The enchanted wood
  Papa Gatto
San Souci, Robert D. *Cinderella Skeleton*
Scieszka, Jon. *The frog prince, continued*
Sherman, Josepha. *Vassilisa the wise*
Souhami, Jessica. *Rama and the demon king*
Sperberg, Roger. *The story of the sleeping beauty, whose name was Briar Rose*
Springer, Margaret. *A royal ball*
Stanley, Fay. *The last princess*
Tooinsky, Izzi. *The turkey prince*
Verma, Jatinder Nath. *The story of Divaali*
Wade, Barrie. *Cinderella*
Wells, Rosemary. *The little lame prince*
Yolen, Jane. *The firebird*
  The sea king
  Wings

Royalty – princesses

Ada, Alma Flor. *The malachite palace*
Afanas'ev, Aleksandr N. *Salt*
Allchin, Rosalind. *The frog princess*
Allen, Jonathan. *Wake up, Sleeping Beauty*
Allen, Linda. *The mouse bride*
Andersen, H. C. (Hans Christian). *The princess and the pea*, ill. by Emily Bolam
  The princess and the pea, ill. by Charlene Delage
  The princess and the pea, ill. by Dorothée Duntze
  The princess and the pea, ill. by Dick Gackenbach
  The princess and the pea, ill. by Paul Galdone
  The princess and the pea, ill. by Camille Semelet

The princess and the pea, ill. by Janet Stevens
The princess and the pea, ill. by Suçie Stevenson
The princess and the pea, ill. by Eve Tharlet
Angeletti, Roberta. *Nefertari, princess of Egypt*
Auch, Mary Jane. *The princess and the pizza*
Bateman, Teresa. *The princesses have a ball*
Bawden, Nina. *Princess Alice*
Bazilian, Barbara. *Princess Lily*
Cecil, Laura. *The frog princess*
Cole, Babette. *Princess Smartypants*
Cooper, Susan. *Tam Lin*
Costa, Nicoletta. *The mischievous princess*
DeChristopher, Marlowe. *Greencoat and the swanboy*
DeFelice, Cynthia C. *The real, true Dulcie Campbell*
  Three perfect peaches
Flot, Jeannette B. *Princess Kalina and the hedgehog*
French, Vivian. *The thistle princess*
Gál, László. *The parrot*
Gekiere, Madeleine. *The frilly lily and the princess*
Gliori, Debi. *The princess and the pirate king*
Goodhart, Pippa. *Arthur's tractor*
Grambling, Lois G. *The witch who wanted to be a princess*
Gray, Nigel. *The frog prince*
Greaves, Margaret. *Kate Crackernuts*
  Sarah's lion
Greene, Ellin. *Billy Beg and his bull*
Grey, Mini. *The very smart pea and the princess-to-be*
Grimm, Jacob. *The frog prince*, ill. by Paul Galdone
  The frog prince, ill. by Todd Ouren
  The frog prince, ill. by Binette Schroeder
  The golden goose, ill. by Dorothée Duntze
  The golden goose, ill. by Dennis McDermott
  The golden goose, ill. by Isadore Seltzer
  The golden goose, ill. by Martin Ursell
  The princess and the frog, ill. by Rachel Isadora
  The princess and the frog, ill. by Will Eisner
  The six servants
  The sleeping beauty, ill. by Warwick Hutton
  The sleeping beauty, ill. by Trina Schart Hyman
  The sleeping beauty, ill. by Monika Laimgruber
  The sleeping beauty, ill. by Mercer Mayer
  Sleeping Beauty, ill. by Fina Rifa
  The sleeping beauty, ill. by Ruth Sanderson
  Sleeping Beauty, ill. by John Wallner
  The twelve dancing princesses, ill. by Kinuko Y. Craft
  The twelve dancing princesses, ill. by Anne Dalton
  The twelve dancing princesses, ill. by Dennis Hockerman
  The twelve dancing princesses, ill. by Errol Le Cain
  The twelve dancing princesses, ill. by Gerald McDermott
  The twelve dancing princesses, ill. by Jane Ray
  The twelve dancing princesses, ill. by Uri Shulevitz
  The twelve dancing princesses, ill. by Suçie Stevenson
  The twelve princesses, ill. by Gordon Fitchett
Gwynne, Fred. *Pondlarker*
Hastings, Selina. *The singing ringing tree*
Haugaard, Erik Christian. *Princess Horrid*
Heine, Helme. *The boxer and the princess*
  Prince Bear
Hindley, Judy. *Princess Rosa's winter*
Hooks, William H. *The monster from the sea*
Huck, Charlotte S. *Princess Furball*
Inkpen, Mick. *Lullabyhullaballoo!*
Isele, Elizabeth. *The frog princess*
Jennings, Linda M. *The sleeping beauty*
Keller, Emily Snowell. *Sleeping Bunny*
Kimmel, Eric A. *Rimonah of the Flashing Sword*
  The three princes
Kleven, Elisa. *The paper princess*
Kroll, Steven. *Princess Abigail and the wonderful hat*
Lang, Andrew. *The flying ship*
Laroche, Michel. *The snow rose*
Lester, Helen. *Princess Penelope's parrot*
Lewis, J. Patrick. *The frog princess*
  The night of the goat children
Lewison, Wendy Cheyette. *The princess and the potty*
  Princess Buttercup
Lobel, Anita. *A birthday for the princess*

Love, Ann. *The prince who wrote a letter*
Lum, Kate. *Princesses are not quitters!*
McCourt, Lisa. *Good night, Princess Pruney Toes*
MacDonald, George. *The light princess*, ill. by Katie Thamer Treherne
    Little Daylight
Mack, Todd. *Princess Penelope*
McNaughton, Janet. *Brave Jack and the unicorn*
Manna, Anthony L. *Mr. Semolina-Semolinus*
Martin, Claire. *Boots and the glass mountain*, ill. by Gennady Spirin
    The race of the golden apples
Martin, Rafe. *The storytelling princess*
Marzollo, Jean. *Welcome to the Shanna show*
Masini, Beatrice. *A brave little princess*
Maugham, W. Somerset (William Somerset). *Princess September and the nightingale*
Mayer, Mercer. *Shibumi and the kitemaker*
Meeker, Clare Hodgson. *A tale of two rice birds*
Metaxas, Eric. *Princess Scargo and the birthday pumpkin*
Mike, Jan M. *The bird maiden*
    Clever Karlis
    Juan Bobo and the horse of seven colors
Miller, M. L. *Dizzy from fools*
Mills, Lauren A. *Tatterhood and the hobgoblins*
Milne, A. A. (Alan Alexander). *The magic hill*
Milord, Susan. *Willa the wonderful*
Mollel, Tololwa M. (Tololwa Marti). *The princess who lost her hair*
Nesbit, Edith. *Melisande*
Ness, Evaline. *Pavo and the princess*
Nikly, Michelle. *The princess on the nut*
Nones, Eric Jon. *Canary prince*
Oram, Hiawyn. *Princess Chamomile gets her way*
    The second princess
Ørdal, Stina Langlo. *Princess Aasta*
Pancheri, Jan. *The twelve poodle princess*
Perlman, Janet. *The penguin and the pea*
Perrault, Charles. *The sleeping beauty*, ill. by David Walker
Peters, Andrew. *Salt is sweeter than gold*
Priceman, Marjorie. *Princess Picky*
Reesink, Marijke. *The princess who always ran away*
Richardson, Jean. *The sleeping beauty*
Ringgold, Faith. *The invisible princesses*
Scieszka, Jon. *The frog prince, continued*
Scrimger, Richard. *Princess Bun Bun*
The secret princess handbook; or, How to be a little princess
Shannon, Margaret. *The red wolf*
Sharratt, Nick. *Once upon a time . . .*
Shearer, Marilyn J. *The Nubian princess*
Shepard, Aaron. *The princess mouse*
Shields, Carol Diggory. *I am really a princess*
Slobodkin, Louis. *Colette and the princess*
Sperberg, Roger. *The story of the sleeping beauty, whose name was Briar Rose*
Springer, Margaret. *A royal ball*
Stanley, Fay. *The last princess*
Thompson, Lauren. *One riddle, one answer*
Thurber, James. *Many moons*, ill. by Marc Simont
    Many moons, ill. by Louis Slobodkin
Turnbull, Ann. *The tapestry cats*
Vaës, Alain. *The princess and the pea*
Vesey, A. *The princess and the frog*
Waddell, Martin. *The tough princess*
Walsh, Ellen Stoll. *Jack's tale*
Williams, Jay. *The practical princess*
Wolfson, Margaret. *Turtle songs*
Zakhoder, Boris Vladimirovich. *The good stepmother*

Royalty – queens

Bell, Anthea. *The wise queen*
Bowden, Joan Chase. *A hat for the queen*
Brown, Ruth. *The grizzly revenge*
Burdett, Lois. *Macbeth for kids*
Engelbreit, Mary. *Queen of the class*
Evans, Nate. *The mixed-up zoo of professor Yahoo*
Garrett, Jennifer. *The queen who stole the sky*
Greaves, Margaret. *Kate Crackernuts*

Grimm, Jacob. *The six servants*
Harness, Cheryl. *The queen with bees in her hair*
Hennessy, B. G. (Barbara G.). *The missing tarts*
Hiatt, Fred. *If I were queen of the world*
Lewis, J. Patrick. *Isabella Abnormella and the very, very finicky Queen of Trouble*
Lobato, Arcadio. *The greatest treasure*
McGrory, Anik. *Mouton's impossible dream*
Mahy, Margaret. *The queen's goat*
Manna, Anthony L. *Mr. Semolina-Semolinus*
Masini, Beatrice. *A brave little princess*
Mayer, Mercer. *The queen always wanted to dance*
Mills, Lauren A. *Fin and the imp*
Myers, Bernice. *The flying shoes*
Nobisso, Josephine. *The weight of a Mass*
Oberman, Sheldon. *The wisdom bird*
Osborne, Mary Pope. *The brave little seamstress*
Oxenbury, Helen. *The queen and Rosie Randall*
Paterson, John (John Barstow). *Blueberries for the queen*
Paxton, Tom. *Engelbert the elephant*
Pike, Carol. *The nutty queen*
San Souci, Robert D. *A weave of words*
Sharratt, Nick. *The green queen*
Silverman, Maida. *The magic well*
Turnbull, Ann. *The tapestry cats*
Van Woerkom, Dorothy. *The queen who couldn't bake gingerbread*
Wild, Margaret. *The queen's holiday*

Royalty – rajahs

Demi. *One grain of rice*
Rumford, James. *Nine animals and the well*

Royalty – sultans

Ambrus, Victor G. *The Sultan's bath*
Kimmel, Eric A. *The valiant red rooster*
Lottridge, Celia Barker. *The little rooster and the diamond button*

Royalty – tsars

Gorbachev, Valeri. *The fool of the world and the flying ship*
Hoffman, Mary. *Clever Katya*
Lottridge, Celia Barker. *Music for the Tsar of the Sea*
Metaxas, Eric. *The fool and the flying ship*
Ogburn, Jacqueline K. *The magic nesting doll*
Ransome, Arthur. *The fool of the world and the flying ship*
Rose, Anne K. *How does a czar eat potatoes?*
Sanderson, Ruth. *The golden mare, the firebird, and the magic ring*
San Souci, Robert D. *Peter and the blue witch baby*
Winthrop, Elizabeth. *The little humpbacked horse*

Rummage sales *see* Garage sales, rummage sales

Running *see* Activities – running; Sports – racing

Running away *see* Behavior – running away

Russia *see* Foreign lands – Russia

Russian Americans *see* Ethnic groups in the U.S. – Russian Americans

Rwanda *see* Foreign lands – Rwanda

Sadness *see* Emotions – sadness

Safety

Arnold, Caroline. *Who keeps us safe?*
Bahr, Amy C. *It's ok to say no*
  Sometimes it's ok to tell secrets
  What should you do when . . . ?
  Your body is your own
Baker, Eugene H. *Bicycles*
  Fire
  Home
  Outdoors
  School
  Water
Berenstain, Stan. *The Berenstain bears learn about strangers*
Brill, Marlene Targ. *Margaret Knight, girl inventor*
Brown, Marc Tolon. *Dinosaurs, beware!*
Brown, Margaret Wise. *Red light, green light*
Chlad, Dorothy. *Bicycles are fun to ride*
  Matches, lighters, and firecrackers are not toys
  Poisons make you sick
Cleary, Beverly. *Lucky Chuck*
Cuyler, Margery. *Stop drop and roll*
Emecheta, Buchi. *Nowhere to play*
Ethan, Eric. *Helicopters*
Girard, Linda Walvoord. *My body is private*
  Who is a stranger, and what should I do?
Gordon, Sharon. *Bruises*
Hoban, Lillian. *Arthur's back to school day*
Joyce, Irma. *Never talk to strangers*
Kaczman, James. *A bird and his worm*
Kevi. *Don't talk to strangers*
Lakin, Pat (Patricia). *Aware and alert*
Leaf, Munro. *Safety can be fun*
Levete, Sarah. *Looking after myself*
Lindgren, Barbro. *Sam's lamp*
Loewen, Nancy. *Bicycle safety*
  Emergencies
  School safety
  Traffic safety
McKissack, Patricia C. *Who is coming?*
McLeod, Emilie Warren. *The bear's bicycle*
Maestro, Betsy. *Bike trip*
Mattern, Joanne. *Safety at school*
  Safety in public places
  Safety in the water
Mayo, Margaret. *Emergency!*
Meyer, Linda D. *Safety zone*
Moss, Elaine. *Polar*
Myller, Lois. *No! No!*
Pendziwol, Jean. *No dragons for tea*
  A treasure at sea for dragon and me
Petty, Kate. *Being careful with strangers*
Pfister, Marcus. *Hang on, Hopper!*
Rand, Gloria. *Willie takes a hike*
Rex, Michael. *My fire engine*
Roche, Denis (Denis M.). *Little Pig is capable*
Royston, Angela. *Fire fighters*
Russell, Pamela. *Do you have a secret?*
Salat, Cristina. *Peanut's emergency*
Schulson, Rachel Ellenberg. *Guns . . . what you should know*
Shortall, Leonard W. *One way*
Smaridge, Norah. *Watch out!*
Spelman, Cornelia Maude. *Your body belongs to you*
Spinelli, Eileen. *A safe place called home*
Trottier, Maxine. *A safe place*
Viorst, Judith. *Try it again, Sam*
Vogel, Carole Garbuny. *The dangers of strangers*
Yamashita, Haruo. *Mice at the beach*
Ziefert, Harriet. *No, no, Nicky!*

Sahara Desert *see* Foreign lands – Sahara Desert

Sailing *see* Sports – sailing

Sailors

Agell, Charlotte. *The sailor's book*
Ahlberg, Allan. *Master Salt the sailor's son*
Anderson, Lena. *Stina's visit*
Brown, Margaret Wise. *Sailor boy jig*
Bruna, Dick. *The sailor*
Calhoun, Mary. *Henry the sailor cat*
Conrad, Pam. *The lost sailor*
Crews, Donald. *Sail away*
Denton, Terry. *Home is the sailor*
Flanagan, Alice K. *Riding the ferry with Captain Cruz*
Friedman, Ina R. *How my parents learned to eat*
Ginsburg, Mirra. *Four brave sailors*
Helldorfer, M. C. (Mary Claire). *Sailing to the sea*
Hest, Amy. *A sort-of sailor*
Jewell, Nancy. *Sailor song*
Kimmel, Eric A. *Billy Lazroe and the King of the Sea*
Lattimore, Deborah Nourse. *The sailor who captured the sea*
Lenski, Lois. *The little sailboat*
Locker, Thomas. *Sailing with the wind*
Lund, Deb. *Dinosailors*
Maass, Robert. *Tugboats*
McCurdy, Michael. *The sailor's alphabet*
McKinley, Robin. *My father is in the Navy*
Mahy, Margaret. *Sailor Jack and the twenty orphans*
Manning, Mick. *What a Viking!*
Metaxas, Eric. *Stormalong, the legendary sea captain*
Mills, Judith Christine. *The stonehook schooner*
O'Neill, Alexis. *Loud Emily*
Rand, Gloria. *Sailing home*
Slawski, Wolfgang. *Captain Jonathan sails the sea*
Stevenson, Drew. *The ballad of Penelope Lou . . . and me*
Van Allsburg, Chris. *The wreck of the Zephyr*
Waddell, Martin. *Sailor Bear*
Waters, Tony. *Sailor's bride*
Whittle, Emily. *Sailor cats*
Winter, Jeanette. *Follow the drinking gourd*
Yezerski, Thomas F. *A full hand*
Zeman, Ludmila. *Sindbad*

Saint Patrick's Day *see* Holidays – St. Patrick's Day

Salamanders *see* Reptiles – salamanders

Salesmen *see* Careers – salesmen

Sand *see also* Sea & seashore – beaches

Apperley, Dawn. *In the sand*
Bason, Lillian. *Castles and mirrors and cities of sand*
Garland, Sherry. *Summer sands*
Inkpen, Mick. *Sandcastle*
Jones, Rebecca C. *Down at the bottom of the deep dark sea*
Krementz, Jill. *Jack goes to the beach*
Lies, Brian. *Hamlet and the magnificent sandcastle*
Lloyd, David. *Grandma and the pirate*
MacDonald, Maryann. *Ben at the beach*
Nolan, Dennis. *The castle builder*
Ormondroyd, Edward. *Johnny Castleseed*
Roach, Marilynne K. *Dune fox*
Robbins, Ken. *Beach days*
Robertson, M. P. *The sandcastle*
Roddie, Shen. *Sandbear*
Turnbull, Ann. *The sand horse*
Vasiliu, Mircea. *A day at the beach*
Watanabe, Shigeo. *I'm the king of the castle!*
Webb, Angela. *Talkabout sand*
Yee, Brenda Shannon. *Sand castle*

Sandcastles *see* Sand

Sandman *see* Mythical creatures – sandman

Sandpipers *see* Birds – sandpipers

Sandstorms *see* Weather – sandstorms

Sanitation workers *see* Careers – sanitation workers

Santa Claus

Ambrus, Victor G. *Santa Claus takes off*
Amoss, Berthe. *What did you lose, Santa?*
Aoki, Hisako. *Santa's favorite story*
Apperley, Dawn. *Santa Claus will come tonight*
Ardizzone, Aingelda. *The night ride*
Armour, Richard Willard. *The year Santa went modern*
Arnold, Katya. *The adventures of Snowwoman*
Augustin, Barbara. *Antonella and her Santa Claus*
Autry, Gene. *Here comes Santa Claus*
Bailey, Mary Bryant. *Jeoffry's Christmas*
Bernardoni, Robert. *Christmas all over*
Bishop, Roma. *Santa pays a visit*
Brett, Jan. *The wild Christmas reindeer*
Briggs, Raymond. *Father Christmas*
　　Father Christmas goes on holiday
Bröger, Achim. *The Santa Clauses*
Brown, Marc Tolon. *Arthur's Christmas*
Burningham, John. *Harvey Slumfenburger's Christmas present*
Catalano, Dominic. *Santa and the three bears*
Catalanotto, Peter. *Christmas always . . .*
Chalmers, Mary. *Merry Christmas, Harry*
Clark, Elizabeth. *Father Christmas and the donkey*
Clements, Andrew. *Santa's secret helper*
Collington, Peter. *On Christmas eve*
Compton, Kenn. *Happy Christmas to all!*
Conrad, Pam. *The Tub People's Christmas*
Crespi, Francesca. *Santa Claus is coming!*
Currey, Anna. *Truffle's Christmas*
Cuyler, Margery. *Fat Santa*
Darling, Kathy (Mary Kathleen). *The mystery in Santa's toyshop*
David, Lawrence. *Peter Claus and the naughty list*
DeLage, Ida. *ABC Santa Claus*
Delamare, David. *The Christmas secret*
Demi. *The legend of Saint Nicholas*
Denton, Kady MacDonald. *Christmas boot*
De Paola, Tomie (Thomas Anthony). *Get dressed, Santa!*
Drescher, Henrik. *Looking for Santa Claus*
Dubowski, Cathy East. *The Christmas Santa almost missed*
Duquennoy, Jacques. *North Pole, South Pole*
Duvoisin, Roger Antoine. *The Christmas whale*
　　One thousand Christmas beards
Edens, Cooper. *Nicholi*
Ehrlich, Amy. *Bunnies at Christmastime*
Ephron, Delia. *Santa and Alex*
Faulkner, Keith. *Charlie Chimp's Christmas*
Fearnley, Jan. *Little Robin's Christmas*
Foreman, Michael. *The perfect present*
Frazee, Marla. *Santa Claus, the world's number one toy expert*
French, Vivian. *Christmas kitten*
Gaffington, Urslan Judith. *Silver berries and Christmas magic*
Gammell, Stephen. *Wake up, bear . . . It's Christmas!*
Gomi, Taro. *Santa through the window*
Hayes, Sarah. *A bad start for Santa*
Hayward, Linda. *The runaway Christmas toy*
Haywood, Carolyn. *A Christmas fantasy*
　　How the reindeer saved Santa
　　Santa Claus forever!
Hazen, Barbara Shook. *Santa clues*
　　The story of Santa Claus
High, Linda Oatman. *The last chimney of Christmas eve*
Hill, Eric. *Spot's magical Christmas*
Hoff, Syd. *Santa's moose*
　　Where's Prancer?
Holmquist, Delano. *SantaSaurus*
Hurd, Thacher. *Santa Mouse and the ratdeer*
Ives, Penny. *Mrs. Santa Claus*
Janovitz, Marilyn. *What could be keeping Santa?*
Johnson, Crockett. *Harold at the North Pole*
Johnson, Russell. *Trouble at Christmas*
Johnston, Tony. *A Kenya Christmas*
Joyce, William. *Santa calls*
Kellogg, Steven (Stephen). *Santa Claus is comin' to town*
Kessler, Leonard P. *That's not Santa!*

Kimpton, Diana. *The bear Santa Claus forgot*
Knight, Hilary. *Angels and berries and candy canes*
Krahn, Fernando. *How Santa Claus had a long and difficult journey delivering his presents*
Krensky, Stephen. *How Santa got his job*
　　How Santa lost his job
Kroll, Steven. *Santa's crash-bang Christmas*
Kunnas, Mauri. *Santa Claus and his elves*
　　Twelve gifts for Santa Claus
Landa, Norbert. *Little Bear's Christmas*
Lee, Quinlan B. *Crazy Christmas chaos*
Lee, Stan. *Stan Lee's superhero Christmas*
Lewis, J. Patrick. *The Christmas of the reddle moon*
Lubin, Leonard B. *Christmas gift-bringers*
McCaughrean, Geraldine. *How the reindeer got their antlers*
McGinley, Phyllis. *How Mrs. Santa Claus saved Christmas*
McPhail, David M. *Mistletoe*
　　Santa's book of names
Maloney, Peter (1955–). *Redbird at Rockefeller Center*
May, Robert Lewis. *Rudolph the red-nosed reindeer*, ill. by Diana Magnuson
　　Rudolph the red-nosed reindeer, ill. by David Wenzel
Maynard, Bill. *Santa's time off*
Miles, Calvin. *Calvin's Christmas wish*
Mogensen, Jan. *Teddy's Christmas gift*
Moore, Clement Clarke. *The night before Christmas*, ill. by Jan Brett
　　The night before Christmas, ill. by Tomie de Paola
　　The night before Christmas, comp. by Cooper Edens and Harold Darling; ill. by various nineteenth- and twentieth-century artists
　　The night before Christmas, ill. by Mary Engelbreit
　　The night before Christmas, ill. by Michael Foreman
　　The night before Christmas, ill. by Gyo Fujikawa
　　The night before Christmas, ill. by Scott Gustafson
　　The night before Christmas, ill. by Cheryl Harness
　　The night before Christmas, ill. by Raquel Jaramillo
　　The night before Christmas, ill. by Loretta Krupinski
　　The night before Christmas, ill. by Anita Lobel
　　The night before Christmas, ill. by James Marshall
　　The night before Christmas, ill. by Ted Rand
　　The night before Christmas, ill. by Jacqueline Rogers
　　The night before Christmas, ill. by Ruth Sanderson
　　The night before Christmas, ill. by Robert Sebuda
　　The night before Christmas, ill. by Robin Spowart
　　The night before Christmas, ill. by Gustaf Tenggren
　　The night before Christmas, ill. by Tasha Tudor
　　The night before Christmas, ill. by Wendy Watson
　　The night before Christmas, ill. by Bruce Whatley
　　The night before Christmas, ill. by Jody Wheeler
　　The night before Christmas in signed English
　　The teddy bears' night before Christmas
　　'Twas the night before Christmas, ill. by Matt Tavares
　　A visit from St. Nicholas
Morrissey, Dean. *The Christmas ship*
Moss, Jenny Jackson. *Cajun night after Christmas*
Murdocca, Sal (Salvatore). *Christmas bear*
Neugebauer, Charise. *Santa's gift*
Nixon, Joan Lowery. *That's the spirit, Claude*
Novak, Matt. *The last Christmas present*
Ostheeren, Ingrid. *I'm the real Santa Claus!*
Paxton, Tom. *The story of Santa Claus*
Pearson, Tracey Campbell. *Where does Joe go?*
Peet, Bill (William Bartlett). *Countdown to Christmas*
Pfister, Marcus. *Wake up, Santa Claus!*
Polacco, Patricia. *Welcome Comfort*
Primavera, Elise. *Auntie Claus*
　　Auntie Claus and the key to Christmas
Prøysen, Alf. *Christmas eve at Santa's*
Pulver, Robin. *Christmas for a kitten*
Reiss, Mike. *How Murray saved Christmas*
　　Santa claustrophobia
Rosales, Melodye Benson. *'Twas the night b'fore Christmas*
Rosenberg, Liz. *On Christmas eve*
Rylant, Cynthia. *Little Whistle's Christmas*
Santa Claus is coming to town
Santa's little library of Christmas stories
Schrecker, Judie. *Santa's new reindeer*

Sharmat, Marjorie Weinman. *I'm Santa Claus and I'm famous*
Sierra, Judy. *'Twas the fright before Christmas*
Sloat, Teri. *Pieces of Christmas*
Solheim, James. *Santa's secrets revealed*
Stainton, Sue. *Santa's snow cat*
Steven, Kenneth C. *The bearer of gifts*
Sykes, Julie. *Careful, Santa*
  Hurry, Santa!
Taylor, Jane. *Twinkle, twinkle little star*, ill. by Julia Noonan
Thompson, Lauren. *Mouse's first Christmas*
  Mouse's first Christmas [board book]
Tompert, Ann. *Saint Nicholas*
Trimble, Marcia. *Moonbeams for Santa*
Trosclair. *Cajun night before Christmas*
Tryon, Leslie. *Albert's Christmas*
Turner, Sandy. *Silent night*
Tutt, Kay Cunningham. *And now we call him Santa Claus*
Van Allsburg, Chris. *The polar express*
Wallace, Ivy. *Pookie believes in Santa Claus*
Watson, Wendy. *Holly's Christmas eve*
Weil, Lisl. *Santa Claus around the world*
Weinberg, Larry (Lawrence). *The Forgetful Bears help Santa*
Wells, Rosemary. *McDuff's new friend*
  Max's Christmas
Weninger, Brigitte. *A letter to Santa Claus*
Wick, Walter. *Can you see what I see? The night before Christmas*
Wilder, Laura Ingalls. *Santa comes to little house*
Wilhelm, Hans. *Schnitzel's first Christmas*
Willey, Margaret. *Clever Beatrice Christmas*
Wolff, Patricia Rae. *A new, improved Santa*
Wood, Audrey. *The Christmas adventure of Space Elf Sam*
Wright, Cliff. *Santa's ark*
Yee, Wong Herbert. *A small Christmas*
Yin. *Dear Santa, please come to the 19th floor*
Yorinks, Arthur. *Christmas in July*
Ziefert, Harriet. *Presents for Santa*

Saving things *see* Behavior – saving things

Saxophones *see* Musical instruments – saxophones

Scandinavia *see* Foreign lands – Scandinavia

Scarecrows

Bolliger, Max. *The wooden man*
Brown, Ken (Ken James). *The scarecrow's hat*
Brown, Margaret Wise. *The little scarecrow boy*
Cazet, Denys. *Nothing at all*
Dillon, Jana. *Jeb Scarecrow's pumpkin patch*
Farber, Norma. *There goes feathertop!*
Fleischman, Sid. *The scarebird*
Gordon, Sharon. *Sam the scarecrow*
Hart, Jeanne McGahey. *Scareboy*
Lewis, Rob. *Hello, Mr. Scarecrow*
Lifton, Betty Jean. *Joji and the Amanojaku*
  Joji and the dragon
  Joji and the fog
Maris, Ron. *Ducks quack*
Martin, Bill (William Ivan). *Barn dance!*
Miller, Edna. *Pebbles, a pack rat*
Oana, Kay D. *Robbie and the raggedy scarecrow*
Rau, Dana Meachen. *Shoo crow, shoo!*
Rylant, Cynthia. *Scarecrow*
San Souci, Robert D. *Feathertop*
Schaefer, Carole Lexa. *Under the midsummer sky*
Schertle, Alice. *Witch Hazel*
Tripp, Paul. *The strawman who smiled by mistake*
Watts, Bernadette. *Tattercoats*
Williams, Linda. *The little old lady who was not afraid of anything*

School

Adelson, Leone. *All ready for school*
Ahlberg, Allan. *The Cinderella show*
  Me and my friend

Ajmera, Maya. *Back to school*
Alexander, Martha G. *Move over, Twerp*
Aliki. *Marianthe's story one: painted words; Marianthe's story two: spoken memories*
Allard, Harry. *Miss Nelson is back*
  Miss Nelson is missing!
Ambrus, Victor G. *Son of Dracula*
Amper, Thomas. *Booker T. Washington*
Ancona, George. *Ricardo's day*
Annett, Cora. *The dog who thought he was a boy*
Arkin, David. *Black and white*
Arnold, Caroline. *Where do you go to school?*
Arnold, Katrin. *Anna joins in*
Arnold, Tedd. *Green Wilma*
Aseltine, Lorraine. *First grade can wait*
Ashley, Bernard. *Dinner ladies don't count*
Aulaire, Ingri Mortenson d'. *Children of the northlights*
  Nils
Babbitt, Lorraine. *Pink like the geranium*
Baehr, Patricia. *School isn't fair*
Baer, Edith. *This is the way we go to school*
Baird, Anne. *The guppies of Hilly Dale House*
Baker, Eugene H. *School*
Ballard, Robin. *My day, your day*
Ballart, Elisabet. *Let's count*
Bare, Colleen Stanley. *Critter, the class cat*
Barkan, Joanne. *Whiskerville school*
Bateman, Teresa. *The Bully Blockers Club*
Behrens, June. *Who am I?*
Beim, Jerrold. *The taming of Toby*
Bercaw, Edna Coe. *Halmoni's day*
Berenstain, Stan. *The Berenstain bears' report card trouble*
  The Berenstain bears' trouble at school
Berquist, Grace. *Speckles goes to school*
Binnamin, Vivian. *The case of the anteater's missing lunch*
  The case of the mysterious mermaid
Bird, Malcolm. *The school in Murky Wood*
Biro, Val. *Gumdrop goes to school*
Blance, Ellen. *Monster at school*
  Monster goes to school
Blaustein, Muriel. *Jim chimp's story*
Bloom, Suzanne. *Piggy Monday*
Blue, Rose. *How many blocks is the world?*
Bluthenthal, Diana Cain. *Matilda the moocher*
Boegehold, Betty. *The fight*
Boelts, Maribeth. *Little Bunny's cool tool set*
  Summer's end
Bogart, Jo Ellen. *Jeremiah learns to read*
Bognomo, Joel Eboueme. *Madoulina*
Bond, Felicia. *The Halloween performance*
  The Halloween play
Boon, Emilie. *1 2 3 how many animals can you see?*
Borden, Louise. *The day Eddie met the author*
  Good luck, Mrs. K!
Bourgeois, Paulette. *Too many chickens*
Boyd, Selma. *I met a polar bear*
Bradman, Tony. *It came from outer space*
  Michael
Brandenberg, Franz. *No school today!*
Brenner, Emily. *On the first day of grade school*
Bridges, Shirin Yim. *Ruby's wish*
Brillhart, Julie. *Anna's goodbye apron*
  When daddy came to school
Brooks, Ron. *Timothy and Gramps*
Brown, Janet Allison. *A little princess*
Brown, Kathryn. *Muledred*
Brown, Laurie Krasny. *Rex and Lilly school time*
Brown, Marc Tolon. *Arthur and the true Francine*
  Arthur goes to school
  Arthur's teacher moves in
  Arthur's teacher trouble
  Arthur's underwear
  Arthur's Valentine
  The true Francine
Brown, Ruth. *The shy little angel*
Brown, Tricia. *Hello, amigos!*
Bruna, Dick. *The school*

Lindbergh, Reeve. *The awful aardvarks go to school*
Lindgren, Astrid. *I want to go to school, too*
Littlesugar, Amy. *Freedom school, yes!*
Loewen, Nancy. *School safety*
London, Jonathan. *Froggy's first kiss*
   Shawn and Keeper: show-and-tell
Loomis, Christine. *The cleanup surprise*
Lorbiecki, Marybeth. *Sister Anne's hands*
Lucas, Barbara (Barbara M.). *Snowed in*
Lundy, Charlotte. *Thank you, Esther*
McAllister, Angela. *Nesta, the little witch*
McBratney, Sam. *I'm sorry*
McCain, Becky R. (Becky Ray). *Nobody knew what to do*
Maccarone, Grace. *The classroom pet*
   The lunch box surprise
   Sharing time troubles
McCourt, Lisa. *Chicken soup for little souls: The Goodness Gorillas*
   Chicken soup for little souls: The new kid and the cookie thief
   It's time for school, Stinky Face
McCully, Emily Arnold. *School*
McDonald, Megan. *Insects are my life*
   Reptiles are my life
McGeorge, Constance W. *Boomer goes to school*
McKissack, Robert L. *Try your best*
MacLachlan, Patricia. *Three names*
McLenighan, Valjean. *I know you cheated*
McMillan, Bruce. *Mouse views*
McNaughton, Colin. *Captain Abdul's pirate school*
McPhail, David M. *A bug, a bear, and a boy go to school*
Maestro, Betsy. *Harriet at school*
Maestro, Marco. *Geese find the missing piece*
Magorian, Michelle. *Who's going to take care of me?*
Malloy, Judy. *Bad Thad*
Marokvia, Merelle. *A French school for Paul*
Marshall, Edward. *Fox at school*
Marshall, James. *The Cut-Ups crack up*
   The Cut-Ups cut loose
Marshall, Janet Perry. *Ohmygosh, my pocket*
Martin, Ann M. *Rachel Parker, kindergarten show-off*
Martin, Charles E. *For rent*
Martin, Linda. *When dinosaurs go to school*
Mattern, Joanne. *Safety at school*
Matthias, Catherine. *Out the door*
Mayer, Mercer. *Little Monster at school*
Mayne, William. *Barnabas walks*
McMullan, Kate (Hall). *Back-to-school belly busters*
Medearis, Angela Shelf. *The 100th day of school*
Medearis, Michael. *Daisy and the doll*
Mellings, Joan. *It's fun to go to school*
Meshover, Leonard. *The guinea pigs that went to school*
   The monkey that went to school
Miles, Miska. *Show and tell . . .*
Miller, Margaret. *Now I'm big*
Mills, Claudia. *Gus and Grandpa and show-and-tell*
Milord, Susan. *Willa the wonderful*
Mitchell, Margaree King. *Susie Mae*
Montanari, Eva. *The crocodile's true colors*
Moon, Nicola. *Something special*
Mora, Pat. *The rainbow tulip*
Moremen, Grace E. *No, no, Natalie*
Morris, Ann. *I am six*
Morrison, Bill. *Louis James hates school*
Moss, Marissa. *But not Kate*
   Regina's big mistake
Moss, Miriam. *Wibble wobble*
Mueller, Virginia. *Monster goes to school*
Munsch, Robert N. *From far away*
   Get out of bed!
   Mmm, cookies!
   Show-and-tell
   Stephanie's ponytail
   Thomas' snowsuit
   We share everything!
Murphy, Stuart J. *Get up and go!*
   100 days of cool
   The penny pot
Naylor, Phyllis Reynolds. *Jennifer Jean, the Cross-Eyed Queen*

Neitzel, Shirley. *I'm not feeling well today*
Neuschwander, Cindy. *Amanda Bean's amazing dream*
Nichols, Paul. *Big Paul's school bus*
Nims, Bonnie Larkin. *Where is the bear at school?*
Norac, Carl. *Hello, sweetie pie*
Numeroff, Laura Joffe. *If you take a mouse to school*
O'Donnell, Peter. *Carnegie's excuse*
O'Malley, Kevin. *Carl caught a flying fish*
   Straight to the pole
O'Neill, Alexis. *The Recess Queen*
Oppenheim, Joanne. *Mrs. Peloki's class play*
   Mrs. Peloki's snake
   Mrs. Peloki's substitute
Ormerod, Jan. *Ms. MacDonald has a class*
Ormsby, Virginia H. *Twenty-one children plus ten*
Paek, Min. *Aekyung's dream*
Palacios, Argentina. *A Christmas surprise for Chabelita*
Palatini, Margie. *Bedhead*
Panek, Dennis. *Ba ba sheep wouldn't go to sleep*
Paraskevas, Betty. *Gracie Graves and the kids from room 402*
Parish, Peggy. *Jumper goes to school*
Park, Frances. *The royal bee*
Passen, Lisa. *Attack of the 50-foot teacher*
   The incredible shrinking teacher
Paterson, Katherine. *Marvin one too many*
Pattou, Edith. *Mrs. Spitzer's garden*
Payne, Sherry Neuwirth. *A contest*
Pearson, Susan. *Everybody knows that!*
Pillar, Marjorie. *Join the band!*
Plourde, Lynn. *School picture day*
Polacco, Patricia. *Mr. Lincoln's way*
   Thank you, Mr. Falker
   Welcome Comfort
Polisar, Barry Louis. *The trouble with Ben*
Pomeranc, Marion Hess. *The can-do Thanksgiving*
Porte, Barbara Ann. *Harry's mom*
Porto, Tony. *Blue aliens*
   Get red
Poulin, Stéphane. *Can you catch Josephine?*
Powers, Mary E. *Our teacher's in a wheelchair*
Poydar, Nancy. *Busy Bea*
   The perfectly horrible Halloween
   Rhyme time Valentine
   Snip, snip . . . snow!
Price, Michelle. *Mean Melissa*
Priceman, Marjorie. *Emeline at the circus*
Pringle, Laurence P. *One room school*
Pulver, Robin. *Axle Annie*
   Mrs. Toggle and the dinosaur
   Mrs. Toggle's beautiful blue shoe
   Mrs. Toggle's zipper
   Nobody's mother is in second grade
Rabe, Berniece. *The balancing girl*
Rathmann, Peggy. *Officer Buckle and Gloria*
   Ruby the copycat
Rayner, Mary. *Crocodarling*
Reiser, Lynn. *Earthdance*
Rice, David L. *Because Brian hugged his mother*
Rickert, Janet Elizabeth. *Russ and the almost perfect day*
Rider, Joanne. *First grade valentines*
Robb, Diane Burton. *The alphabet war*
Roche, Denis (Denis M.). *The best class picture ever*
   Mim, gym, and June
Rockwell, Anne F. *Becoming butterflies*
   Career day
   Father's Day
   Halloween Day
   Mother's Day
   100 school days
   Show and tell day
   Thanksgiving Day
   Valentine's Day, ill. by Lizzy Rockwell
   When Hugo went to school
Rogers, Jacqueline. *Kindergarten ABC*
   Tiptoe into kindergarten
Rose, Deborah Lee. *The twelve days of kindergarten*
Rosenberg, Maxine B. *My friend Leslie*

Ross, Pat. *Molly and the slow teeth*
Roth, Carol. *The little school bus*
Rouillard, Wendy. *Barnaby's bunny*
Rowe, Jeanne A. *A trip through a school*
Rowe, John A. *Tommy DoLittle*
Ruurs, Margriet. *Ms. Bee's magical bookcase*
Ryder, Eileen. *Winklet goes to school*
Ryder, Joanne. *First grade ladybugs*
   Hello, first grade
Rylant, Cynthia. *The ticky-tacky doll*
Sadler, Marilyn. *Alistair's time machine*
Saltzberg, Barney. *Crazy hair day*
   Phoebe and the spelling bee
Schafer, Milton. *That crazy Barb'ra*
Schertle, Alice. *Jeremy Bean's St. Patrick's Day*
Schick, Eleanor. *The little school at Cottonwood Corners*
Schomp, Virginia. *If you were a . . . teacher*
Schreck, Karen Halvorsen. *Lucy's family tree*
Schwartz, Amy. *Things I learned in second grade*
Scieszka, Jon. *Baloney, Henry P.*
Selsam, Millicent E. *More potatoes!*
Senisi, Ellen B. *All kinds of friends, even green*
   Just kids
   Kindergarten kids
Shannon, David. *David goes to school*
Sheldon, Dyan. *Unicorn dreams*
Shields, Carol Diggory. *Lunch money and other poems about school*
Shipton, Jonathan. *No biting, horrible crocodile!*
Sierra, Judy. *There's a zoo in room 22*
Simms, Laura. *Rotten teeth*
Simon, Charnan. *Show-and-tell Sam*
Simon, Francesca. *Spider school*
Simon, Norma. *All families are special*
   I'm busy, too
   What do I do?
   What do I say?
Singer, Marilyn. *All we needed to say*
Slate, Joseph. *Miss Bindergarten celebrates the 100th day of kindergarten*
   Miss Bindergarten stays home from kindergarten
   Miss Bindergarten takes a field trip with kindergarten
Smalls, Irene. *Don't say ain't*
Smath, Jerry. *Elephant goes to school*
Solomon, Chuck. *Moving up from kindergarten to first grade*
Spier, Peter. *My school*
Spirin, Gennady. *Philipok*
Spirn, Michele. *I am the turkey*
Spurr, Elizabeth. *Mrs. Minetta's car pool*
Stadler, Alexander. *Beverly Billingsly takes a bow*
Stanley, Diane. *The good-luck pencil*
Staunton, Ted. *Taking care of Crumley*
Steptoe, John. *Creativity*
   Jeffrey Bear cleans up his act
Stevens, Carla. *Pig and the blue flag*
Stoeke, Janet Morgan. *Minerva Louise at school*
Suen, Anastasia. *Hamster chase*
Sundvall, Viveca. *Mimi and the biscuit factory*
Surat, Michele Maria. *Angel child, dragon child*
Sutherland, Colleen. *Jason goes to show-and-tell*
Tagg, Christine. *Who will you meet on Scary Street?*
Teague, Mark. *The Lost and found*
   The secret shortcut
Teyssèdre, Fabienne. *Joseph wants to read*
Thayer, Jane. *Gus was a real dumb ghost*
Tidd, Louise Vitellaro. *I'll do it later*
Topek, Susan Remick. *A costume for Noah*
Tryon, Leslie. *Albert's alphabet*
   Patsy says
Turner, Gwenda. *Playbook*
Tyler, Linda Wagner. *Waiting for mom*
Udry, Janice May. *What Mary Jo shared*
Vande Velde, Vivian. *Troll teacher*
Vigna, Judith. *Anyhow, I'm glad I tried*
Waber, Bernard. *Evie & Margie*
Watson, Clyde. *Hickory stick rag*
Weiss, Leatie. *My teacher sleeps in school*
Welch, Willy. *Grumpy Bunnies*

Wells, Rosemary. *First tomato*
   The germ busters
   The Halloween parade
   Letters and sounds
   McDuff goes to school
   Mama, don't go!
   My kindergarten
   The school play
   Yoko
Whitcomb, Mary E. *Odd Velvet*
White, Florence Meiman. *How to lose your lunch money*
White, Paul. *Janet at school*
Whitehead, Jenny. *Lunch box mail and other poems*
Whitney, Alma Marshak. *Just awful*
Wick, Walter. *I spy school days*
Wiesner, David. *Sector 7*
Williams, Barbara. *Donna Jean's disaster*
Willis, Jeanne. *The long blue blazer*
Willis, Val. *The mystery in the bottle*
   The secret in the matchbox
Wing, Natasha. *Jalapeño bagels*
Winters, Kay. *Did you see what I saw?*
   The teeny tiny ghost and the monster
Winthrop, Elizabeth. *Tough Eddie*
Wiseman, Bernard. *Tails are not for painting*
Wishinsky, Frieda. *Give Maggie a chance*
   Jennifer Jones won't leave me alone
Wittman, Sally. *The boy who hated Valentine's Day*
   The wonderful Mrs. Trumbly
Wolff, Patricia Rae. *The toll-bridge troll*
Wood, Douglas. *What teachers can't do*
Woodruff, Elvira. *Show and tell*
Wright, Betty Ren. *The blizzard*
Yaccarino, Dan. *First day on a strange new planet*
Yashima, Taro. *Crow boy*
Zimelman, Nathan. *How the second grade got $8,205.50 to visit the Statue of Liberty*
Zimmett, Debbie. *Eddie enough*

School – field trips

Alberti, Theresa Jarosz. *Out and about at the planetarium*
Allard, Harry. *Miss Nelson has a field day*
Bemelmans, Ludwig. *Madeline*
Bourgeois, Paulette. *Franklin's class trip*
Butterworth, Nick. *Field day*
   The school trip
Caseley, Judith. *Field Day Friday*
Cohen, Miriam. *Lost in the museum*
Cole, Joanna. *The magic school bus and the electric field trip*
   The magic school bus at the waterworks
   The magic school bus in the time of the dinosaurs
   The magic school bus inside a beehive
   The magic school bus inside a hurricane
   The magic school bus inside the human body
   The magic school bus lost in the solar system
   The magic school bus on the ocean floor
   The magic school bus shows and tells
Deady, Kathleen W. *Out and about at the zoo*
Dubois, Muriel L. *Out and about at the fire station*
Ericsson, Jennifer A. *Out and about at the bakery*
Kallen, Stuart A. *The airport*
   The farm
   The fire station
   The museum
   The police station
   The zoo
Katz, Susan. *Mrs. Brown on exhibit*
Kirk, David. *Nova's ark*
Lithgow, John. *Carnival of the animals*
Maccarone, Grace. *The class trip*
Mayr, Diane. *Out and about at the apple orchard*
Millman, Isaac. *Moses goes to a concert*
Murphy, Andy. *Out and about at the dairy farm*
Noble, Trinka Hakes. *The day Jimmy's boa ate the wash*
Rechner, Amy. *Out and about at the aquarium*
Shea, Kitty. *Out and about at the post office*

Out and about at the science center
Out and about at the supermarket
Out and about at the vet clinic
Slate, Joseph. *Miss Bindergarten takes a field trip with kindergarten*

School – first day

Ahlberg, Janet. *Starting school*
Alexander, Martha G. *Sabrina*
Anholt, Laurence. *Billy and the big new school*
Begaye, Lisa Shook. *Building a bridge*
Berenstain, Stan. *The Berenstain bears go to school*
Black, Harley. *Amazing magic school*
Bloom, Suzanne. *The bus for us*
Blue, Rose. *I am here = Yo estoy aqui*
Boelts, Maribeth. *Little Bunny's preschool countdown*
Bram, Elizabeth. *I don't want to go to school*
Brandenberg, Franz. *Six new students*
Breinburg, Petronella. *Shawn goes to school*
Brillhart, Julie. *Molly rides the school bus*
Bruna, Dick. *Miffy goes to school*
Calmenson, Stephanie. *The kindergarten book*
Carlson, Nancy L. *Look out kindergarten, here I come!*
Cazet, Denys. *Born in the gravy*
  Never spit on your shoes
Charlton, Nancy Lee. *Derek's dog days*
Child, Lauren. *I am too absolutely small for school*
Chorao, Kay. *Molly's lies*
Clarke, Gus. *Eddie and Teddy*
Cohen, Miriam. *Will I have a friend?*
Coles, Alison. *Michael's first day*
Cooney, Nancy Evans. *The blanket that had to go*
Coontz, Otto. *A real class clown*
Corey, Shana. *First graders from Mars: Horus's horrible day*
Cork, Barbara Taylor. *Sam starts school*
D'Amico, Carmela. *Ella, the elegant elephant*
Danneberg, Julie. *First day jitters*
Danziger, Paula. *Get ready for second grade, Amber Brown*
Delton, Judy. *My mom made me go to school*
  The new girl at school
De Paola, Tomie (Thomas Anthony). *Meet the Barkers*
Edwards, Becky. *My first day at nursery school*
Edwards, Julie Andrews. *Dumpy at school*
Falwell, Cathryn. *David's drawing*
Flood, Bo. *I'll go to school if . . .*
Forward, Toby. *What did you do today?*
Gantos, Jack (John, Jr.). *Back to school for Rotten Ralph*
Goodall, John S. *Naughty Nancy goes to school*
Goodman, Joan Elizabeth. *Bernard goes to school*
Gorbachev, Valeri. *Chicken chickens go to school*
Greenfield, Eloise. *Me and Neesie*, ill. by Moneta Barnett
  Me and Neesie, ill. by Jan Spivey Gilchrist
Hains, Harriet. *My new school*
Hamilton-Merritt, Jane. *My first days of school*
Harris, Robie H. *I am not going to school today*
Hautzig, Deborah. *Little Witch goes to school*
Henkes, Kevin. *Jessica*
  Wimberly worried
Hest, Amy. *Off to school, Baby Duck*
Hill, Eric. *Spot goes to school*
Hillman, Priscilla. *The Merry-Mouse schoolhouse*
Howe, James. *When you go to kindergarten*
Jagtenberg, Yvonne. *Jack the wolf*
Jenkin-Pearce, Susie. *Bad Boris goes to school*
Johnston, Tony. *Sparky and Eddie, the first day of school*
Kantrowitz, Mildred. *Willy Bear*
Kaufmann, Nancy. *Bye, Bye*
Keller, Holly. *Harry and Tuck*
Kirk, David. *Little Miss Spider at Sunny Patch School*
Krementz, Jill. *Katharine goes to nursery school*
Langreuter, Jutta. *Little Bear goes to kindergarten*
Lasker, Joe. *Nick joins in*
Lasky, Kathryn. *Lunch bunnies*
Leonard, Marcia. *Hannah the hamster hunter*
Léonard, Marie. *Tibili, the little boy who didn't want to go to school*
Lester, Mike. *A is for salad*
Levitin, Sonia. *When Kangaroo goes to school*

London, Jonathan. *Froggy goes to school*
MacDonald, Maryann. *Little Hippo starts school*
McGhee, Alison. *Countdown to kindergarten*
McMahon, Patricia. *Listen for the bus*
McQuade, Jacqueline. *At preschool with Teddy Bear*
Marshall, James. *Eugene*
  Sing out, Irene
Meredith, Carol. *Jamie Anderson wouldn't . . .*
Millman, Isaac. *Moses goes to school*
Musgrave, Susan. *Dreams are more real than bathtubs*
Novak, Matt. *Jazzbo goes to school*
Oxenbury, Helen. *First day of school*
Pak, Soyung. *Sumi's first day of school ever*
Pennypacker, Sara. *Stuart's cape*
Pérez, L. King. *First day in grapes*
Poydar, Nancy. *First day, hooray!*
Quackenbush, Robert M. *First grade jitters*
Radabaugh, Melinda Beth. *Going to school*
Rankin, Joan. *First day*
Recorvits, Helen. *My name is Yoon*
Riddell, Edwina. *My first day at preschool*
Robbins, Beth. *Tom's first day at school*
Rockwell, Anne F. *Welcome to kindergarten*
Rosenberry, Vera. *Vera's first day of school*
Rusackas, Francesca. *I love you all day long*
Schaefer, Charles E. *Cat's got your tongue?*
Schwartz, Amy. *Annabelle Swift, kindergartner*
Schweninger, Ann. *Off to school!*
Sellers, Ronnie. *My first day at school*
Sharmat, Mitchell. *Sherman is a slowpoke*
Slate, Joseph. *Miss Bindergarten gets ready for kindergarten*
Smalls-Hector, Irene. *Beginning school*
Steel, Danielle. *Martha's new school*
Stein, Sara Bonnett. *A child goes to school*
Stevenson, James. *That dreadful day*
Stuve-Bodeen, Stephanie. *Elizabeti's school*
Tanner, Suzy-Jane. *Tinyflock Nursery School*
Taulbert, Clifton L. *Little Cliff's first day of school*
Tompert, Ann. *Will you come back for me?*
Turner, Ethel. *Walking to school*
Uegaki, Chieri. *Suki's kimono*
Veldkamp, Tjibbe. *The school trip*
Ward, Nick. *Don't eat the teacher*
Warren, Cathy. *Fred's first day*
Watts, Marjorie-Ann. *Zebra goes to school*
Weiss, Nicki. *Barney is big*
Wells, Rosemary. *Emily's first 100 days of school*
  How many? How much?
  Timothy goes to school
Wild, Margaret. *Tom goes to kindergarten*
Willis, Jeanne. *Be gentle, Python!*
  Be quiet, Parrot!
  No biting, Puma!
  Take turns, Penguin!
Wolde, Gunilla. *Betsy's first day at nursery school*
Wolf, Bernard. *Adam Smith goes to school*

School – nursery

Antoine, Héloïse. *Curious kids go to preschool*
Barrett, Mary Brigid. *Day care days*
Boelts, Maribeth. *Little Bunny's preschool countdown*
Brandt, Amy. *Benjamin comes back = Benjamin regresa*
  When Katie was our teacher = Cuando Katie era muestra maestra
Budney, Blossom. *N is for nursery school*
Coker, Gylbert. *Naptime*
Cole, Joanna. *When Mommy and Daddy go to work*
Day, Alexandra. *Carl goes to daycare*
Demuth, Patricia Brennan. *Busy at day care head to toe*
Edvall, Lilian. *The rabbit who longed for home*
Edwards, Becky. *My first day at nursery school*
Elliott, David. *Hunter's best friend at school*
Henkes, Kevin. *Wimberly worried*
Krementz, Jill. *Katharine goes to nursery school*
Kuklin, Susan. *Going to my nursery school*
Lenski, Lois. *Debbie goes to nursery school*
Lewis, Shari. *Baby Lamb Chop loves nursery school*

Lindgren, Barbro. *Rosa goes to daycare*
McNaughton, Colin. *At playschool*
McQuade, Jacqueline. *At preschool with Teddy Bear*
Murkoff, Heidi Eisenberg. *What to expect at preschool*
O'Brien, Anne Sibley. *Come play with us*
Phillips, Tamara. *Day care ABC*
Rankin, Joan. *First day*
Riddell, Edwina. *My first day at preschool*
Rockwell, Harlow. *My nursery school*
Rogers, Fred. *Going to day care*
Roth, Harold. *Nursery school*
Rubel, Nicole. *Goldie's nap*
Schaefer, Carole Lexa. *Someone says*
Schwartz, Amy. *The boys teams*
Senisi, Ellen B. *Hurray for pre-K!*
Sierra, Judy. *Preschool to the rescue*
Struges, Philemon. *I love school*
Tanner, Suzy-Jane. *Tinyflock Nursery School*
Tompert, Ann. *Will you come back for me?*
Valens, Amy. *Jesse's day care*
Weeks, Sarah. *My somebody special*
Wolde, Gunilla. *Betsy's first day at nursery school*

School principals *see* Careers – school principals

School teachers *see* Careers – teachers

Science

Abisch, Roz. *Let's find out about butterflies*
Addy, Sharon Hart. *Right here on this spot*
Adler, David A. *Redwoods are the tallest trees in the world*
Alberti, Theresa Jarosz. *Out and about at the planetarium*
Aliki. *Corn is maize*
  Digging up dinosaurs
  Dinosaurs are different
  Fossils tell of long ago
  The long lost coelacanth and other living fossils
  My feet
  My hands
  My visit to the dinosaurs
  A weed is a flower
  Wild and woolly mammoths
Allen, Gertrude E. *Everyday animals*
Allen, Judy. *Are you a butterfly?*
  Are you a grasshopper?
  Are you a ladybug?
  Are you a snail?
  Are you an ant?
Allen, Martha Dickson. *Real life monsters*
Allen, Pamela. *Mr. Archimedes' bath*
  Who sank the boat?
Allington, Richard L. *Science*
  Talking
Anderson, Lucia Z. *The smallest life around us*
Anderson, Stephen Axel. *I know the moon*
Andry, Andrew C. *How babies are made*
Annixter, Jane. *Brown rats, black rats*
Applebaum, Stan. *Going my way?*
Appleby, Leonard G. *Snakes*
Arnold, Caroline. *The biggest living thing*
  Five nests
  Sun fun
Arnosky, Jim. *All about deer*
  Crinkleroot's guide to knowing butterflies and moths
Aruego, José. *Symbiosis*
Arvetis, Chris. *Why does it fly?*
  Why is it dark?
Asch, Frank. *The sun is my favorite star*
Asimov, Isaac. *The best new thing*
  The moon
Atkins, Jeannine. *Mary Anning and the sea dragon*
 Baby animals
Back, Christine. *Bean and plant*
  Chicken and egg
  Spider's web

  Tadpole and frog
Bailey, Jill. *The life cycle of a spider*
Baker, Gayle. *Special delivery*
Baker, Jeannie. *One hungry spider*
Baker, Jeffrey J. W. *Patterns of nature*
Balestrino, Philip. *Hot as an ice cube*
  The skeleton inside you
Balian, Lorna. *Where in the world is Henry?*
Bancroft, Henrietta. *Animals in winter*
Baran, Tancy. *Bees*
Barlowe, Sy. *A child's book of stars*
Barner, Bob. *Elephant facts*
  Stars, stars, stars
Barrett, Norman S. *Spiders*
Bartlett, Margaret Farrington. *The clean brook*
  Down the mountain
  Where the brook begins
Bason, Lillian. *Castles and mirrors and cities of sand*
  Spiders
Batherman, Muriel. *Animals live here*
Baylor, Byrd. *If you are a hunter of fossils*
Behrens, June. *Whales of the world*
  Whalewatch!
Bendick, Jeanne. *All around you*
  What made you you?
  Why can't I?
Berenstain, Stan. *The Berenstain bears' science fair*
Berger, Melvin. *Brrr! a book about polar animals*
  Buzz! a book about insects
  Dive! a book of deep sea creatures
  Early humans
  Germs make me sick!
  How do airplanes fly?
  How's the weather?
  Look out for turtles!
  Oil spill!
  Spinning spiders
  Switch on, switch off
  Why I sneeze, shiver, hiccup, and yawn
Bernhard, Emery. *Dragonfly*
  Eagles
  Ladybug
  Reindeer
  Salamanders
Boegehold, Betty. *Bear underground*
Bonners, Susan. *Hunter in the snow*
Brady, Irene. *Wild mouse*
Branley, Franklyn M. (Mansfield). *Air is all around you*
  Comets
  Down comes the rain
  Earthquakes
  Eclipse
  Flash, crash, rumble, and roll
  Floating and sinking
  Floating in space
  Gravity is a mystery
  High sounds, low sounds
  Hurricane watch
  Is there life in outer space?
  Journey into a black hole
  Light and darkness
  The moon seems to change
  North, south, east and west
  The planets in our solar system
  Rain and hail
  The sky is full of stars
  Snow is falling
  The sun, our nearest star
  Sunshine makes the seasons
  Tornado alert
  Volcanoes
  What makes a magnet?
  What makes day and night
  What the moon is like
Brasch, Kate. *Prehistoric monsters*
Brenner, Barbara A. *The tremendous tree book*
  Where's that cat?

Brighton, Catherine. *Five secrets in a box*
   The fossil girl
   Galileo's treasure box
Brooks, Robert B. *So that's how I was born*
Brouillette, Jeanne S. *Moths*
Brown, Don. *Rare treasure*
Bryant-Mole, Karen. *Magnets*
   Moving
Budbill, David. *Christmas tree farm*
Bundey, Nikki. *In the park*
   In the snow
   In the water
   On a bike
Burt, Olive (Woolley). *Let's find out about bread*
Burton, Jane. *Chick*
Busch, Phyllis S. *Cactus in the desert*
   City lots
   Lions in the grass
   Once there was a tree
   Puddles and ponds
Butler, Daphne. *What happens when food cooks?*
Carrick, Carol. *The blue lobster*
   The crocodiles still wait
   Octopus
   Patrick's dinosaurs
   Two coyotes
Cash, Megan Montague. *What makes the seasons?*
Challoner, Jack. *The science book of numbers*
Charosh, Mannis. *The ellipse*
Chenery, Janet. *The toad hunt*
Chesworth, Michael. *Archibald Frisby*
Christenson, Larry. *The wonderful way that babies are made*
Clark, Harry. *The first story of the whale*
Clay, Pat. *Ants*
   Beetles
Cobb, Vicki. *I fall down*
   I get wet
   I see myself
   Lots of rot
   Open your eyes
Coffelt, Nancy. *Dogs in space*
Colby, C. B. (Carroll Burleigh). *Who lives there?*
   Who went there?
Coldrey, Jennifer. *The world of chickens*
   The world of crabs
   The world of frogs
   The world of rabbits
   The world of squirrels
Cole, Babette. *Mommy laid an egg!*
Cole, Joanna. *A calf is born*
   A chick hatches
   Evolution
   Find the hidden insect
   A fish hatches
   How you were born
   Hungry, hungry sharks
   The magic school bus in the time of the dinosaurs
   The magic school bus inside a beehive
   The magic school bus inside a hurricane
   The magic school bus inside the earth
   The magic school bus inside the human body
   The magic school bus lost in the solar system
   The magic school bus on the ocean floor
   The magic school bus shows and tells
   My puppy is born
   Plants in winter
   You can't smell a flower with your ear
   Your insides
Conklin, Gladys. *Cheetahs, the swift hunters*
   I caught a lizard
   I like beetles
   I like butterflies
   I like caterpillars
   I watch flies
   If I were a bird
   Journey of the gray whales
   Little apes

   Lucky ladybugs
   Praying mantis
   We like bugs
   When insects are babies
Conrad, Pam. *Call me Ahnighito*
Cooke, Ann. *Giraffes at home*
Cosgrove, Margaret. *Wintertime for animals*
Craig, M. Jean. *Dinosaurs and more dinosaurs*
Cromie, William J. *Steven and the green turtle*
Crozat, François. *I am a little caterpillar*
Cushman, Doug. *Mouse and Mole and the Christmas walk*
Cutts, David. *I can read about creatures of the night*
   Look . . . a butterfly
Dabcovich, Lydia. *Busy beavers*
Dalton, Cindy Devine. *Sound*
Daly, Kathleen N. *Today's biggest animals*
   Unusual animals
Daniel, Doris Temple. *Pauline and the peacock*
Darby, Gene. *What is a bird?*
   What is a butterfly?
   What is a fish?
   What is a plant?
   What is a turtle?
David, Eugene. *Crystal magic*
Davies, Jacqueline. *The boy who drew birds*
Davies, Kay. *My apple*
   My balloon
   My drum
   My mirror
Day, Marie. *Dragon in the rocks*
DeLuise, Dom. *Charlie the caterpillar*
Dennard, Deborah. *Lemur landing*
Dewey, Ariane. *Small Cloud*
Dietl, Ulla. *The plant-and-grow project book*
Diffily, Deborah. *Jurassic shark*
Dobson, David. *Can we save them?*
Dodd, Lynley. *The smallest turtle*
Dorros, Arthur. *Ant cities*
   Follow the water from brook to ocean
   The fungus that ate my school
Eastman, David. *What is a fish?*
Eastman, Patricia. *Sometimes things change*
Egan, Tim. *The experiments of Doctor Vermin*
Engdahl, Sylvia. *Our world is earth*
Engelbrektson, Sune. *Gravity at work and play*
   The sun is a star
Esbensen, Barbara Juster. *The night rainbow*
Fischer, Vera Kistiakowsky. *One way is down*
Fischer-Nagel, Heiderose. *A kitten is born*
   A puppy is born
Fisher, Aileen Lucia. *And a sunflower grew*
   As the leaves fall down
   Like nothing at all
   Mysteries in the garden
   Now that spring is here
   Petals yellow and petals red
   Plant magic
   Prize performance
   Seeds on the go
   Swords and daggers
Flanagan, Alice K. *Rocks*
   Sunshine
   Water
   Weather
   Wind
Florian, Douglas. *A bird can fly*
Flower, Phyllis. *Barn owl*
Fowler, Allan. *Cubs and colts and calves and kittens*
   So that's how the moon changes shape!
   Spiders are not insects
   What do you see in a cloud?
Freedman, Russell. *Hanging on*
   Tooth and claw
   When winter comes
Freeman, Mae Blacker. *The sun, the moon and the stars*
Freschet, Berniece. *Bear mouse*
   The little woodcock

Moose baby
Wood duck baby
Friskey, Margaret (Margaret Richards). *Birds we know*
Frith, Michael K. *Some of us walk, some fly, some swim*
Gans, Roma. *Rock collecting*
When birds change their feathers
Gelman, Rita Golden. *A koala grows up*
George, Jean Craighead. *All upon a stone*
Gibbons, Gail. *Exploring the deep, dark sea*
From seed to plant
Monarch butterfly
Prehistoric animals
Sharks
Soaring with the wind
Sun up, sun down
Girard, Linda Walvoord. *You were born on your very first birthday*
Glaser, Linda. *Magnificent monarchs*
Wonderful worms
Goldin, Augusta. *Ducks don't get wet*
Salt
The shape of water
Spider silk
Straight hair, curly hair
Where does your garden grow?
Gore, Sheila. *My shadow*
Graeber, Jean B. *Bantie and her chicks*
Granowsky, Alvin. *The dinosaurs' last days*
Meat-eating dinosaurs
Greenwood, Rosie. *I wonder why volcanoes blow their tops*
Gross, Ruth Belov. *Alligators and other crocodilians*
Grosvenor, Donna. *Pandas*
Haines, Gail Kay. *Fire*
Hamberger, John. *The day the sun disappeared*
Hariton, Anca. *Butterfly story*
Harris, Louise Dyer. *Flash, the life of a firefly*
Harris, Susan. *Creatures that look alike*
Reptiles
Harrison, David Lee. *Caves*
Earthquakes
Hartley, Karen. *Ant*
Bee
Cockroach
Ladybug
Snail
Harvey, Bev. *The bear family*
The cat family
The dog family
The hawk family
The horse family
Hawcock, David. *Dinosaur hunt*
Hawes, Judy. *Fireflies in the night*
Ladybug, ladybug, fly away home
Shrimps
Spring peepers
Watch honeybees with me
Why frogs are wet
Hawkinson, Lucy (Ozone). *Birds in the sky*
Heiligman, Deborah. *From caterpillar to butterfly*
Heller, Ruth. *Chickens aren't the only ones*
Hickling, Meg. *Boys, girls and body science*
Hirschi, Ron. *What is a bird?*
Where do birds live?
Who lives in . . . Alligator Swamp?
Hirst, Robin. *My place in space*
Hodge, Deborah. *Ants*
Bears
Bees
Eagles
Salmon
Hoffman, Mary. *Animals in the wild: elephant*
Animals in the wild: monkey
Animals in the wild: panda
Animals in the wild: tiger
Hogan, Paula Z. *The black swan*
The butterfly
The dandelion
The frog

The honeybee
The oak tree
The penguin
The salmon
Holderness, Jackie. *What is a shadow?*
Hollenbeck, Kathleen M. *Islands of ice*
Holmes, Anita. *The 100-year-old cactus*
House mouse, photos by David Thompson
Howell, Ruth. *Splash and flow*
Hurd, Edith Thacher. *Look for a bird*
The mother kangaroo
Sandpipers
Starfish
Isenbart, Hans-Heinrich. *A duckling is born*
Jackson, Jacqueline. *Chicken ten thousand*
Jenkins, Priscilla Belz. *A nest full of eggs*
Johnston, Johanna. *Penguin's way*
Whale's way
Johnston, Tony. *Sparky and Eddie, trouble with bugs*
Sparky and Eddie, trouble with rats
Jolivet, Joëlle. *Zoo-ology*
Jolliffe, Anne. *From pots to plastics*
Water, wind and wheels
Jones, Brian. *Space*
Jordan, Helene J. (Helene Jamieson). *How a seed grows*
Justice, Jennifer. *The tiger*
Kaizuki, Kiyonori. *A calf is born*
Kalas, Sybille. *The beaver family book*
Kalz, Jill. *Northern lights*
Kane, Henry B. *Wings, legs, or fins*
Karas, G. Brian. *Atlantic*
Kaufmann, John. *Birds are flying*
Flying giants of long ago
Kelly, Irene. *Ebbie and Flo*
Kirkpatrick, Rena K. *Leaves*
Look at flowers
Magnets
Pond life
Rainbow colors
Seeds and weeds
Trees
Weather
Klingel, Cynthia Fitterer. *Deserts*
Knight, David C. *Dinosaur days*
Komori, Atsushi. *Animal mothers*
Krupinski, Loretta. *Into the woods*
Krupp, E. C. (Edwin C.). *The comet and you*
Kuchalla, Susan. *All about seeds*
Kumin, Maxine W. *Eggs of things*
Landshoff, Ursula. *Cats are good company*
Lane, Margaret. *The frog*
The squirrel
Lasky, Kathryn. *Science fair bunnies*
Lauber, Patricia. *Be a friend to trees*
How we learned the earth is round
Snakes are hunters
What's hatching out of that egg?
Who eats what?
Leach, Michael. *Rabbits*
Legg, Gerald. *From egg to chicken*
From seed to sunflower
Lehn, Barbara. *What is a scientist?*
Leutscher, Alfred. *Earth*
Water
Lewis, Naomi. *Swan*
Lilly, Kenneth. *Animal builders*
Animal climbers
Animal jumpers
Animal runners
Animal swimmers
Llewellyn, Claire. *The best book of bugs*
The best book of sharks
Lloyd, David. *Air*
Lobb, Janice. *Color and noise! Let's play with toys!*
Counting sheep! How do we sleep?
Dig and sow! How do plants grow?
Listen and see! What's on TV?

Locker, Thomas. *Sky tree*
Loewen, Nancy. *Busy buzzers*
Mabey, Richard. *Oak and company*
McCauley, Jane R. *Baby birds and how they grow*
McClung, Robert. *How animals hide*
　　Sphinx
McCurry, Kristen. *Safari babies*
McKeever, Katherine. *A family for Minerva*
McMillan, Bruce. *Counting wildflowers*
McNulty, Faith. *Woodchuck*
McQuade, Jacqueline. *Small babies*
Madgwick, Wendy. *Up in the air*
　　Water play
Maestro, Betsy. *How do apples grow?*
　　Why do leaves change color?
Mainwaring, Jane. *My feather*
Markle, Sandra. *Creepy, crawly baby bugs*
　　Outside and inside dinosaurs
Marzollo, Jean. *I'm a caterpillar*
Mason, Adrienne. *Lu and Clancy sound off*
　　Snakes
May, Charles Paul. *High-noon rocket*
Merrill, Jean. *The girl who loved caterpillars*
Meshover, Leonard. *The guinea pigs that went to school*
　　The monkey that went to school
Meyers, Susan. *The truth about gorillas*
Michels, Tilde. *At the frog pond*
Milgrom, Harry. *Egg-ventures*
Miller, Edna. *Jumping bean*
Miller, Judith Ransom. *Nabob and the geranium*
Millhouse, Nicholas. *Blue-footed booby*
Mitgutsch, Ali. *From gold to money*
　　From graphite to pencil
　　From sea to salt
　　From swamp to coal
Moché, Dinah L. *The astronauts*
Moseley, Keith. *Dinosaurs*
Most, Bernard. *Where to look for a dinosaur*
Nagda, Anne Whitehead. *World above the clouds*
Newton, James R. *A forest is reborn*
　　Forest log
Oleson, Jens. *Snail*
Oxford Scientific Films. *Grey squirrel*
　　The spider's web
Palazzo-Craig, Janet. *Our friend the sun*
　　Turtles
Parish, Peggy. *Dinosaur time*
Parker, Nancy Winslow. *Bugs*
Parsons, Alexandra. *Amazing birds*
　　Amazing mammals
　　Amazing snakes
　　Amazing spiders
Pascoe, Gwen. *Deep in a rainforest*
Patterson, Elizabeth Burman. *Whose eyes are these?*
Penner, Lucille Recht. *Dinosaur babies*
　　Monster bugs
Penrose, Gordon. *More science surprises from Dr. Zed*
Peters, Lisa Westberg. *The sun, the wind and the rain*
　　Water's way
Pfeffer, Wendy. *From tadpole to frog*
　　Wiggling worms at work
Pipe, Jim. *What makes it swing?*
Pluckrose, Henry Arthur. *Ants*
　　Bears
　　Bees and wasps
　　Butterflies and moths
　　Elephants
　　Floating and sinking
　　Horses
　　Hot and cold
　　Reptiles
　　Whales
Polacco, Patricia. *Meteor!*
Posada, Mia. *Dandelions, stars in the grass*
Pouyanne, Rési. *What I see hidden by the pond*
Powzyk, Joyce Ann. *Tasmania*
Pringle, Laurence P. *Crows*

　　Snakes
Pursell, Margaret Sanford. *A look at birth*
　　Polly the guinea pig
　　Shelley the sea gull
　　Sprig the tree frog
Rabinowitz, Sandy. *What's happening to Daisy?*
Rau, Dana Meachen. *Mars*
Relf, Patricia. *The magic school bus plants seeds*
Richards, Jane. *A horse grows up*
Riley, Joelle. *Quiet owls*
Robinson, Claire. *Crocodiles*
　　Penguins
Robinson, Fay. *Fantastic frog*
Rockwell, Anne F. *One bean*
Rotter, Charles. *Seals*
　　Walruses
Royston, Angela. *Heavy and light*
　　Levers
　　Life cycle of a guinea pig
　　Life cycle of a mushroom
　　Life cycle of a salmon
　　Life cycle of an oak tree
　　Smooth and rough
　　Strange plants
Russell, Solveig Paulson. *What good is a tail?*
Ryan, Pam Muñoz. *How do you raise a raisin?*
Ryder, Joanne. *Fireflies*
　　Rainbow wings
　　Snail in the woods
　　The spiders dance
　　Where butterflies grow
Sadler, Marilyn. *Alistair's time machine*
St. Pierre, Stephanie. *Cheetahs*
　　Jaguars
　　Leopards
　　Lynx
　　Siberian tigers
Samson, Suzanne M. *Fairy dusters and blazing stars*
Sandeman, Anna. *Skin, teeth, and hair*
Sayre, April Pulley. *Army ant parade*
　　Dig, wait, listen
　　The hungry hummingbird
Schanzer, Rosalyn. *How Ben Franklin stole the lightning*
Schilling, Betty. *Two kittens are born*
Schlein, Miriam. *Lucky porcupine!*
　　What's wrong with being a skunk?
Schmid, Eleonore. *The water's journey*
Schneider, Herman. *Follow the sunset*
Schoberle, Ceile. *Beyond the Milky Way*
Schulz, Charles M. *Snoopy's facts and fun book about nature*
Schwartz, David M. *If you hopped like a frog*
Selberg, Ingrid. *Nature's hidden world*
Selsam, Millicent E. *All kinds of babies*
　　Egg to chick
　　A first look at bird nests
　　A first look at caterpillars
　　A first look at cats
　　A first look at flowers
　　A first look at kangaroos, koalas and other animals with pouches
　　A first look at monkeys
　　A first look at owls, eagles and other hunters of the sky
　　A first look at rocks
　　A first look at seashells
　　A first look at sharks
　　A first look at spiders
　　A first look at the world of plants
　　A first look at whales
　　How kittens grow
　　How puppies grow
　　Is this a baby dinosaur?
　　More potatoes!
　　Seeds and more seeds
　　Where do they go?
Seuling, Barbara. *Flick a switch*
　　From head to toe
Seymour, Peter S. *How the weather works*
　　What's in the deep blue sea?

What's in the prehistoric forest?
Shapp, Martha. *Let's find out about babies*
Shaw, Evelyn S. *Alligator*
   Fish out of school
   Nest of wood ducks
   Octopus
   Sea otters
Shea, Kitty. *Out and about at the science center*
Sheehan, Angela. *The beaver*
   The duck
   The otter
   The penguin
Sheffield, Margaret. *Before you were born*
   Where do babies come from?
Showers, Paul. *Before you were a baby*
   A drop of blood
   Ears are for hearing
   Hear your heart
   Look at your eyes
   No measles, no mumps for me
   Sleep is for everyone
   Where does the garbage go?
   You can't make a move without your muscles
Silverman, Maida. *Dinosaur babies*
Simon, Seymour. *Beneath your feet*
   Icebergs and glaciers
   Let's try it out in the air
   Let's try it out in the water
   Wild bears
Singer, Marilyn. *Tough beginnings*
Sklansky, Amy E. *Where do chicks come from?*
Stecher, Miriam B. *Max, the music-maker*
Steig, William. *The toy brother*
Stein, Sara Bonnett. *Cat*
   Mouse
Strange, Florence. *Rock-a-bye whale*
Sugita, Yutaka. *The flower family*
Sykes, Julie. *Little Rocket's special star*
Tagholm, Sally. *The frog*
Thompson, Susan L. *Diary of a monarch butterfly*
Toft, Kim Michelle. *Neptune's nursery*
Tomecek, Steve. *Dirt*
Townsend, Anita. *The kangaroo*
Tracqui, Valérie. *The ladybug*
Tresselt, Alvin R. *How far is far?*
   Rain drop splash
Van Woerkom, Dorothy. *Hidden messages*
Vasiliu, Mircea. *A day at the beach*
Vern, Alex. *Where do frogs come from?*
Vyner, Sue. *The stolen egg*
Walker, Sally M. *Levers*
Wandelmaier, Roy. *Stars*
Watts, Barrie. *Apple tree*
   Bird's nest
   Butterfly and caterpillar
   Dandelion
   Hamster
   Ladybug
   Mushrooms
   Rabbit
   Tomato
Waxman, Laura Hamilton. *Diving dolphins*
Webb, Angela. *Talkabout air*
   Talkabout light
   Talkabout reflections
   Talkabout sand
   Talkabout soil
   Talkabout sound
   Talkabout water
Wexler, Jerome (LeRoy). *Flowers, fruits, seeds*
   Wonderful pussy willows
Wilkes, Angela. *Me and my body*
Williams, Gweneira Maureen. *Timid Timothy, the kitten who learned to be brave*
Wilson, Ron. *Mice*
Wilson-Max, Ken. *Max loves sunflowers*
Wong, Herbert H. *My goldfish*

My ladybug
My plant
Our caterpillars
Our earthworms
Our tree
Wright, Rachel. *My amazing body*
Wyler, Rose. *Puddles and ponds*
   Raindrops and rainbows
   The starry sky
Yabuuchi, Masayuki. *Animals sleeping*
Yolen, Jane. *Welcome to the icehouse*
Ziefert, Harriet. *Getting ready for new baby*
Zoehfeld, Kathleen Weidner. *How mountains are made*
   What lives in a shell?
   What's alive?
Zoll, Max Alfred. *A flamingo is born*

Scientists *see* Careers – scientists

Scotland *see* Foreign lands – Scotland

Scuba diving *see* Sports – skin diving

Sculptors *see* Careers – sculptors

Sea & seashore

Agell, Charlotte. *The sailor's book*
Albert, Burton. *Where does the trail lead?*
Alexander, Sally Hobart. *Sarah's surprise*
Aliki. *Those summers*
Allen, Laura Jean. *Ottie and the star*
Allen, Pamela. *Hidden treasure*
Amoss, Berthe. *Old Hannibal and the hurricane*
Anderson, Lena. *Stina*
Andreae, Giles. *Commotion in the ocean*
Andrews, Jan. *Very last first time*
Anrooy, Frans van. *The sea horse*
Appelt, Kathi. *I see the moon*
Apperley, Dawn. *In the sand*
Ardizzone, Edward. *Little Tim and the brave sea captain*
   Peter the wanderer
   Ship's cook Ginger
   Tim all alone
   Tim and Charlotte
   Tim and Ginger
   Tim and Lucy go to sea
   Tim in danger
   Tim to the rescue
   Tim's friend Towser
   Tim's last voyage
Arnold, Caroline. *Giant shark*
   A walk by the seashore
   A walk on the Great Barrier Reef
Arnosky, Jim. *Turtle in the sea*
Asch, Frank. *Sand cake*
   Starbaby
Ashforth, Camilla. *Willow by the sea*
Axelrod, Amy. *Pigs on a blanket*
Baker, Jeannie. *The hidden forest*
Bang, Molly. *Yellow ball*
Barber, Antonia. *The mousehole cat*
Barclay, Jane. *Going on a journey to the sea*
Barklem, Jill. *Sea story*
Bat-Ami, Miriam. *Sea, salt, and air*
Bate, Norman. *What a wonderful machine is a submarine*
Bennett, Rainey. *The secret hiding place*
Bentley, Anne. *The Groggs have a wonderful summer*
Berger, Melvin. *Dive! a book of deep sea creatures*
   Oil spill!
Berkes, Marianne Collins. *Seashells by the seashore*
Bernhard, Emery. *The way of the willow branch*
Biro, Maureen Boyd. *Walking with Maga*
Biro, Val. *Gumdrop floats away*
Bishop, Gavin. *Little Rabbit and the sea*
Blackstone, Stella. *An island in the sun*

Secret seahorse
Secret seahorse [board book]
Blake, Quentin. *Mrs. Armitage and the big wave*
Blake, Robert J. *Spray*
Blathwayt, Benedict. *The runaway train*
Bliss, Corinne Demas. *The boy who was generous with salt*
Bond, Michael. *Paddington at the seaside*
Bonsall, Crosby Newell. *Mine's the best*
Booth, Eugene. *Under the ocean*
Bornstein, Ruth Lercher. *A beautiful seashell*
Boyle, Doe. *Otter on his own*
Brady, Kimberley Smith. *Keeper for the sea*
Brenner, Barbara A. *One small place by the sea*
Bright, Robert. *Georgie and the noisy ghost*
Brown, Marc Tolon. *D. W. all wet*
Brown, Margaret Wise. *The seashore noisy book*
    Sneakers
    Sneakers, the seaside cat
Bruna, Dick. *Miffy at the seaside*
Brutschy, Jennifer. *Celeste and Crabapple Sam*
Buchanan, Heather S. *George Mouse's covered wagon*
Bundey, Nikki. *In the water*
Bunting, Eve (Anne Evelyn). *Demetrius and the golden goblet*
    Ducky
Burdett, Lois. *Twelfth night*
Burnard, Damon. *I spy in the ocean*
Burningham, John. *Come away from the water, Shirley*
Bush, Timothy. *Three at sea*
Butler, Andrea. *Mr. Sun and Mr. Sea*
Buzzeo, Toni. *The sea chest*
Calhoun, Mary. *Henry the sailor cat*
Calmenson, Stephanie. *Hotter than a hot dog!*
Carle, Eric. *A house for Hermit Crab*
    10 little rubber ducks
Carlstrom, Nancy White. *Swim the silver sea, Joshie Otter*
Carter, Debby L. *Clipper*
Casin, Sheridan. *Little Turtle and the song of the sea*
Coffey, Maria. *A cat adrift*
Cohen, Caron Lee. *Whiffle Squeek*
Cohen, Miriam. *See you in second grade!*
Cole, Babette. *The trouble with Uncle*
Cole, Joanna. *The magic school bus on the ocean floor*
Cole, Sheila. *When the tide is low*
Coles, Alison. *Michael and the sea*
Collicott, Sharleen. *Seeing stars*
Condra, Estelle. *See the ocean*
Conrad, Pam. *The lost sailor*
Cooney, Barbara. *Hattie and the wild waves*
Coplans, Peta. *Cat and dog*
Corney, Estelle. *Pa's top hat*
Cote, Nancy. *Flip-flops*
Cottle, Joan. *Miles away from home*
Cousins, Lucy. *Za-Za's baby brother*
Cousteau Society. *Albatross*
    Dolphins
    Manatees
    Otters
    Penguins
    Seals
    Turtles
    Whales
Cowan, Catherine. *My life with the wave*
Cowell, Cressida. *Hiccup the seasick Viking*
Craig, Helen. *Charlie and Tyler at the seashore*
Crane, Alan. *Pepita bonita*
Dahl, Michael. *One giant splash*
    Starry arms
Daly, Niki. *Why the sun and moon live in the sky*
Damjan, Mischa. *The little sea horse*
Darling, Kathy (Mary Kathleen). *Seashore babies*
Davidson, Amanda. *Teddy at the seashore*
Davies, Nicola. *Big blue whale*
    Oceans and seas
    One tiny turtle
Day, Jan. *The pirate, Pink*
    Pirate Pink and treasures of the reef
Decker, Dorothy W. *Stripe and the merbear*

Demarest, Chris L. *My blue boat*
    Summer
Denton, Terry. *Home is the sailor*
DeRubertis, Barbara. *Columbus Day*
DeSaix, Frank. *The girl who danced with dolphins*
Dexter, Alison. *Grandma*
Dickson, Louise. *The vanishing cat*
Dodd, Anne Westcott. *The story of the sea glass*
Dodd, Lynley. *The smallest turtle*
Domanska, Janina. *If all the seas were one sea*
Dos Santos, Joyce Audy. *Sand dollar, sand dollar*
Doubilet, Anne. *Under the sea from A to Z*
Drummond, Allan. *Moby Dick*
Dunbar, Joyce. *The sand children*
Dunphy, Madeleine. *Here is the coral reef*
Dupasquier, Philippe. *Dear Daddy . . .*
    Jack at sea
Dyke, John. *Pigwig and the pirates*
Ehrlich, H. M. *Gotcha, Louie!*
    Louie's goose
Enderle, Judith (Ann) Ross. *Six sandy sheep*
Engels-Fietzek, Petra. *Sophie and the seagull*
Esbensen, Barbara Juster. *Sponges are skeletons*
Farber, Norma. *I swim an ocean in my sleep*
Faulkner, Keith. *Sam at the seaside*
Field, Eugene. *Wynken, Blynken and Nod*, ill. by Barbara Cooney
    Wynken, Blynken and Nod, ill. by Susan Jeffers
    Wynken, Blynken and Nod, ill. by Holly Johnson
    Wynken, Blynken and Nod, ill. by Johanna Westerman
Fisher, Leonard Everett. *Sky, sea, the jetty, and me*
Fitzpatrick, Marie-Louise. *You, me and the big blue sea*
Florian, Douglas. *In the swim*
Foreman, Michael. *Jack's fantastic voyage*
    One world
    Seal surfer
Fowler, Allan. *The biggest animal ever*
    Friendly dolphins
Francia, Silvia. *Roberta's vacation*
Frasier, Debra. *Out of the ocean*
Freeman, Don. *Come again, pelican*
French, Vivian. *Whale journey*
    Why the sea is salt
Freymann, Saxton. *One lonely seahorse*
Galloway, Ruth. *Fidgety fish*
Garland, Sherry. *Summer sands*
Gay, Marie-Louise. *Stella, star of the sea*
Gay, Michel. *Little auto*
Gebert, Warren. *The old ball and the sea*
Gedin, Birgitta. *The little house from the sea*
George, Jean Craighead. *The wentletrap trap*
Gerrard, Jean. *Matilda Jane*
Gerrard, Roy. *Sir Francis Drake*
Gibbons, Gail. *Exploring the deep, dark sea*
Ginsburg, Mirra. *Four brave sailors*
Goodall, John S. *Paddy under water*
Gordon, Sharon. *Dolphins and porpoises*
Goudey, Alice E. *Houses from the sea*
Grassby, Donna. *A seaside alphabet*
Gretz, Susanna. *Teddy bears at the seaside*
Grindley, Sally. *A flag for Grandma*
    Peter's place
Guiberson, Brenda Z. *Into the sea*
    Lobster boat
Gutman, Anne. *Gaspard at the seashore*
Haas, Irene. *The Maggie B*
Halak, Glenn. *A grandmother's story*
Haley, Gail E. *Sea tale*
Hallinan, P. K. (Patrick K.). *Three freckles past a hair*
Hamilton, K. R. (Kersten R). *This is the ocean*
Hanze. *Yann and the whale*
Harris, Trudy. *Pattern fish*
Harrison, Troon. *Don't dig so deep, Nicholas!*
Hayashi, Leslie Ann. *Fables from the sea*
Hayles, Karen. *What is stuck*
Helldorfer, M. C. (Mary Claire). *Harmonica night*
Hellen, Nancy. *Creatures of the ocean*
Heller, Nicholas. *An adventure at sea*

Henderson, Kathy. *The little boat*
  The storm
Henley, Claire. *In the ocean*
  Sunny day
Heyduck-Huth, Hilde. *The starfish*
Hill, Eric. *Spot goes on holiday*
Hines, Anna Grossnickle. *Gramma's walk*
Hirschi, Ron. *Ocean*
Hoff, Syd. *Albert the albatross*
Hofstrand, Mary. *By the sea*
Hopkins, Lee Bennett. *The sea is calling me*
Hopkinson, Deborah. *Birdie's lighthouse*
Horowitz, Ruth. *Crab moon*
Hort, Lenny. *We're going on a treasure hunt*
How big is the ocean?
Hulme, Joy N. *Sea squares*
  Sea sums
Hunt, Jonathan. *Leif's saga*
Hunter, Anne. *What's in the tide pool?*
Hurd, Edith Thacher. *Starfish*
Inkpen, Mick. *Sandcastle*
Iwasaki, Chihiro. *What's fun without a friend?*
Jackson, Shelley. *The old woman and the wave*
James, Simon. *Sally and the limpet*
Jango-Cohen, Judith. *Clinging sea horses*
Jenkin-Pearce, Susie. *The seashell song*
Jessup, Harley. *Grandma summer*
Johnson, Angela. *Joshua by the sea*
Johnson, Pamela. *A mouse's tale*
Jones, Rebecca C. *Down at the bottom of the deep dark sea*
Joseph, Lynn. *Jasmine's parlour day*
Joslin, Sesyle. *Baby elephant goes to China*
Karas, G. Brian. *Atlantic*
Kesselman, Wendy Ann. *Sand in my shoes*
Kimmel, Eric A. *Billy Lazroe and the King of the Sea*
Kimura, Yasuko. *Fergus and the sea monster*
Kipling, Rudyard. *The crab that played with the sea*
Kitamura, Satoshi. *Captain Toby*
Kite, L. Patricia. *Down in the sea. The jellyfish*
  Down in the sea. The octopus
Klingel, Cynthia Fitterer. *Oceans*
Koch, Michelle. *By the sea*
Komaiko, Leah. *Just my dad and me*
Kranking, Kathy. *The ocean is . . .*
Kraus, Robert. *Herman the helper*
Kuskin, Karla. *City dog*
  I am me
  Sand and snow
Lacome, Julie. *Seashore*
Lakin, Pat (Patricia). *Dad and me in the morning*
Landström, Olof. *Boo and Baa at sea*
Leedy, Loreen. *Tracks in the sand*
Leonard, Marcia. *Swimming in the sand*
Le Tord, Bijou. *Joseph and Nellie*
Levine, Evan. *Not the piano, Mrs. Medley!*
Lewis, Paul Owen. *Storm boy*
Lilly, Kenneth. *Animals of the ocean*
Lionni, Leo. *Swimmy*
Llewellyn, Claire. *The best book of sharks*
Lloyd, David. *Grandma and the pirate*
Lobato, Arcadio. *The greatest treasure*
Lobel, Arnold. *Uncle Elephant*
Loomis, Christine. *Scuba bunnies*
Lottridge, Celia Barker. *Music for the Tsar of the Sea*
Lund, Doris Herold. *The paint-box sea*
McAfee, Annalena. *The visitors who came to stay*
McCarthy, Meghan. *The adventures of Patty and the big red bus*
McCarty, Peter. *Hondo and Fabian*
McCloskey, Robert. *Bert Dow, deep-water man*
  One morning in Maine
  Time of wonder
McClure, Gillian. *Selkie*
McCurdy, Michael. *The sailor's alphabet*
McCurry, Kristen. *Ocean babies*
McDonald, Megan. *Is this a house for Hermit Crab?*
MacDonald, Suse. *Sea shapes*
McKee, David. *The day the tide went out and out and out*

McKenna, Virginia. *Back to the blue*
MacKinnon, Debbie. *Sarah's shovel*
McMillan, Bruce. *One sun*
McNaughton, Colin. *Oomph!*
Maddern, Eric. *Curious clownfish*
Mahy, Margaret. *The man whose mother was a pirate*
  Sailor Jack and the twenty orphans
  A summery Saturday morning
Mallory, Kenneth. *Families of the deep blue sea*
Marshall, James. *Hey, diddle, daddle*
Marshall, Janet Perry. *Banana moon*
Marston, Elsa. *Cynthia and the runaway gazebo*
Martin, Antoinette Truglio. *Famous seaweed soup*
Matsutani, Miyoko. *The fisherman under the sea*
Mendoza, George. *The scribbler*
Metaxas, Eric. *Stormalong, the legendary sea captain*
Miller, Margaret. *At the shore*
Miller, Ruth. *I went to the bay*
Mills, Patricia. *On an island in the bay*
Modarressi, Mitra. *The parent thief*
Modesitt, Jeanne. *Lunch with Milly*
Mogensen, Jan. *Teddy in the undersea kingdom*
Morgan, Allen. *Nicole's boat*
Morse, Samuel French. *Sea sums*
Mudd-Ruth, Maria. *The ultimate ocean book*
Munsch, Robert N. *A promise is a promise*
Muzik, Katharine. *At home in the coral reef*
Nakatani, Chiyoko. *Fumio and the dolphins*
Nakawatari, Harutaka. *The sea and I*
Napoli, Guillier. *Adventure at Mont-Saint-Michel*
Nayer, Judy. *Sea creatures*
Naylor, Phyllis Reynolds. *The picnic*
Nelson, Robert Lyn. *Ocean friends*
Newton, Jill. *Cat-fish*
Nicoll, Helen. *Meg at sea*
Nobisso, Josephine. *Shh! the whale is smiling*
Nolan, Dennis. *The castle builder*
O'Donnell, Elizabeth Lee. *The twelve days of summer*
Olujic, Grozdana. *Rose of Mother-of-Pearl*
Orgel, Doris. *On the sand dune*
Ormondroyd, Edward. *Johnny Castleseed*
Ostheeren, Ingrid. *Fabian Youngpig sails the world*
Palazzo-Craig, Janet. *What's under the ocean?*
Pallotta, Jerry. *The dory story*
  Going lobstering
  Underwater counting
Patkau, Karen. *In the sea*
Peet, Bill (William Bartlett). *Cyrus the unsinkable sea serpent*
  Kermit the hermit
Perrow, Angeli. *Captain's castaway*
Peters, Lisa Westberg. *The sun, the wind and the rain*
Pfister, Marcus. *Milo and the mysterious island*
  Rainbow fish ABC
  Rainbow fish and the sea monsters' cave
Pollard, Nik. *The tide*
Poulin, Stéphane. *Travels for two*
Prater, John. *The perfect day*
Pratt, Kristin Joy. *A swim through the sea*
Pryor, Bonnie. *Lottie's dream*
Quinlan, Patricia. *Emma's sea journey*
Raff, Courtney Granet. *Giant of the sea*
Rand, Gloria. *Aloha, Salty!*
  Sailing home
  Salty sails north
Ray, Deborah Kogan. *Fog drift morning*
Reiser, Lynn. *Little clam*
Richardson, Judith Benét. *The way home*
Riddell, Chris. *Platypus*
Roberts, Sarah. *I want to go home!*
Rockwell, Anne F. *Ferryboat ride!*
  The storm
Rodgers, Richard. *A real nice clambake*
Roffey, Maureen. *I spy on vacation*
Root, Phyllis. *Sam, who was swallowed by a shark*
Rose, Deborah Lee. *Into the A, B, sea*
Round, Graham. *Hangdog*
Rowinski, Kate. *L. L. Bear's island adventure*

Royston, Angela. *Sea animals*
   Shells
Russ, Lavinia. *Alec's sand castle*
Russo, Susan. *The ice cream ocean and other delectable poems of the sea*
Ryder, Joanne. *A house by the sea*
   A wet and sandy day
Rylant, Cynthia. *The whales*
Samton, Sheila White. *Beside the bay*
San Souci, Daniel. *The rabbit and the dragon king*
San Souci, Robert D. *Brave Margaret*
   Nicholas Pipe
Schlein, Miriam. *The sun, the wind, the sea and the rain*
Schulz, Charles M. *Snoopy's facts and fun book about seashores*
Schumacher, Claire. *Alto and Tango*
Schweninger, Ann. *Summertime*
The Sea World alphabet book
Seaside poems
Selsam, Millicent E. *A first look at seashells*
   Sea monsters of long ago
Seymour, Peter S. *What lives in the sea?*
   What's in the deep blue sea?
Sharratt, Nick. *Look what I found!*
   Mrs. Pirate
Shaw, Alison. *Until I saw the sea*
Shaw, Evelyn S. *Fish out of school*
   Octopus
Shea, Pegi Deitz. *Bungalow fungalow*
Shepard, Aaron. *The sea king's daughter*
Simmons, Jane. *Ebb and Flo and the greedy gulls*
Simon, Mina Lewiton. *Is anyone here?*
Sis, Peter. *An ocean world*
   Ship ahoy!
Slawski, Wolfgang. *Captain Jonathan sails the sea*
Slobodkin, Louis. *The seaweed hat*
Smith, Raymond Kenneth. *The long dive*
Smith, Theresa Kalab. *The fog is secret*
Spooner, J. B. *The story of the little Black Dog*
Stadler, John. *One seal*
Stafford, Kim Robert. *We got here together*
Steiner, Barbara (Annette). *The whale brother*
Steiner, Charlotte. *Listen to my seashell*
Stevenson, James. *Clams can't sing*
   July
   Which one is Whitney?
Stevenson, Jocelyn. *Jim Henson's Muppets at sea*
Stevenson, Robert Louis. *Block city*
Stock, Catherine. *Sophie's bucket*
Stone, Lynn M. *Getting around*
   Life of the kelp forest
Strahl, Rudi. *Sandman in the lighthouse*
Straker, Joan Ann. *Animals that live in the sea*
Strauss, Susan. *When woman became the sea*
Sutherland, Marc. *MacMurtrey's wall*
Tamar, Erika. *Donnatalee*
Tate, Suzanne. *Crabby's water wish*
Taylor, Mark. *The bold fisherman*
Thaxter, Celia. *Celia's island journal*
Thompson, Brenda. *The winds that blow*
Thompson, Richard. *Gurgle, bubble, splash*
Titherington, Jeanne. *Baby's boat*
   Baby's boat [board book]
Toft, Kim Michelle. *Neptune's nursery*
Tokuda, Wendy. *Humphrey the lost whale*
Tomlinson, Theresa. *Little stowaway*
Townsend, Emily Rose. *Seals*
Tresselt, Alvin R. *Hide and seek fog*
   I saw the sea come in
Trimble, Marcia. *Malinda Martha and her stepping stones*
Tucker, Kathy. *Do pirates take baths?*
Turbak, Gary. *Ocean animals in danger*
Turkle, Brinton. *Do not open*
   Obadiah the Bold
   The sky dog
Turnbull, Ann. *The sand horse*
Ungerer, Tomi. *The Mellops go diving for treasure*
Van Dusen, Chris. *Down to the sea with Mr. Magee*
Vaughan, Marcia Kapok. *Abbie against the storm*

Vernon, Tannis. *Little Pig and the blue-green sea*
Vinson, Pauline. *Willie goes to the seashore*
Waber, Bernard. *I was all thumbs*
Waddell, Martin. *The big big sea*
   Sailor Bear
Wahl, Jan. *The adventures of Underwater Dog*
Walker, Sally M. *Seahorse reef*
Ward, Helen. *Old shell, new shell*
Ward, Jennifer. *Somewhere in the ocean*
Waters, Tony. *Sailor's bride*
Watson, Nancy Dingman. *When is tomorrow?*
The weekend
Wegen, Ron. *Sand castle*
Weiss, Nicki. *Sun sand sea sail*
Weller, Frances Ward. *Madaket Millie*
   Riptide
Whittle, Emily. *Sailor cats*
Wild, Margaret. *The queen's holiday*
Willard, Nancy. *The voyage of the Ludgate Hill*
Williams, Garth. *Benjamin's treasure*
Windham, Sophie. *Down in the marvelous deep*
Winkelman, Barbara Gaines. *Puffer's surprise*
Winton, Tim. *The deep*
Wolfe, Frances. *One wish*
   Where I live
Wolfson, Margaret. *Turtle songs*
Wolkstein, Diane. *The day Ocean came to visit*
Wood, Jakki. *Across the big blue sea*
Wood, John Norris. *Oceans*
Woolaver, Lance. *From Ben Loman to the sea*
Yashima, Taro. *Seashore story*
Yee, Brenda Shannon. *Sand castle*
Yee, Paul. *The jade necklace*
Yolen, Jane. *The sea king*
Young, Ruth. *Daisy's taxi*
Zeman, Ludmila. *Sindbad*
Ziefert, Harriet. *A dozen dogs*
   Good night, Jessie!
Zoehfeld, Kathleen Weidner. *Great white shark, ruler of the sea*
   What lives in a shell?
Zolotow, Charlotte (Shapiro). *The seashore book*
Zuchora-Walske, Christine. *Spiny sea stars*

Sea & seashore – beaches

Bare, Colleen Stanley. *Elephants on the beach*
Baum, Susan. *The beach*
Beardshaw, Rosalind. *Grandma's beach*
Blance, Ellen. *Monster goes to the beach*
Bruna, Dick. *Miffy at the beach*
Buchanan, Heather S. *Emily Mouse's beach house*
Carmichael, Clay. *Bear at the beach*
Carrick, Carol. *Beach bird*
Cash, Megan Montague. *I saw the sea and the sea saw me*
Daly, Niki. *The boy on the beach*
De Paola, Tomie (Thomas Anthony). *Katie and Kit at the beach*
Dickens, Lucy. *At the beach*
Donnelly, Liza. *Dinosaur beach*
Florian, Douglas. *Beach day*
Garelick, May. *Down to the beach*
Graham, Bob. *Greetings from Sandy Beach*
Greenberg, Melanie Hope. *At the beach*
Hänel, Wolfram. *Mary and the mystery dog*
   Mia the beach cat
Hautzig, Deborah. *Big Bird at the beach*
Hill, Eric. *Spot goes to the beach*
Hubbell, Patricia. *Sea, sand, me!*
Huneck, Stephen. *Sally goes to the beach*
Imoto, Yoko. *Skipper at the beach*
Inkpen, Mick. *Kipper's sunny day*
Johnson, Jane. *Bertie on the beach*
Knutson, Kimberley. *Beach babble*
Koch, Dorothy Clarke. *I play at the beach*
Krementz, Jill. *Jack goes to the beach*
Kumin, Maxine W. *The beach before breakfast*
Landström, Olof. *Will goes to the beach*
Lester, Alison. *Magic beach*

Lewis, Shari. *Baby Lamb Chop loves the beach*
Lionni, Leo. *On my beach there are many pebbles*
MacDonald, Maryann. *Ben at the beach*
Mathers, Petra. *Lottie's new beach towel*
Murphy, Patti Beling. *Elinor and Violet*
Naylor, Phyllis Reynolds. *Please do feed the bears*
Oxenbury, Helen. *Beach day*
   Tom and Pippo on the beach
Paraskevas, Betty. *Hoppy and Joe*
   Monster Beach
Pendziwol, Jean. *A treasure at sea for dragon and me*
Perry, Robert. *Down at the Seaweed Café*
Pirani, Felix. *Abigail at the beach*
Rau, Dana Meachen. *Stroll by the sea*
Robbins, Ken. *Beach days*
Robertson, M. P. *The sandcastle*
Rockwell, Anne F. *At the beach*
Roosa, Karen. *Beach day*
Ryan, Pam Muñoz. *Hello, Ocean!*
   Hello ocean = Hola mar
Ryder, Joanne. *Beach party*
Selby, Jennifer. *Beach bunny*
Seymour, Peter S. *What's at the beach?*
Sis, Peter. *Beach ball*
Stevenson, James. *The worst person in the world at Crab Beach*
Stojic, Manya. *Wet pebbles under our feet*
Tobias, Tobi. *At the beach*
Vasiliu, Mircea. *A day at the beach*
Vullo, Vera. *About things you find at the beach*
Walsh, Ellen Stoll. *Hamsters to the rescue*
Waugh, Peter. *The great cannon beach mouse caper*
Yamashita, Haruo. *Mice at the beach*
Yektai, Niki. *Bears at the beach*
Ziefert, Harriet. *Keeping daddy awake on the way home from the beach*

Sea lions *see* Animals – sea lions

Sea serpents *see* Monsters; Mythical creatures

Seagulls *see* Birds – seagulls

Seahorses *see* Crustaceans – seahorses

Seals *see* Animals – seals

Seamstresses *see* Careers – seamstresses

Seashore *see* Sand; Sea & seashore – beaches

Seasons

Adoff, Arnold. *In for winter, out for spring*
Alexander, Cecil Frances. *All things bright and beautiful*, ill. by
   Anna Vojtech
All year round
Ammon, Richard. *An Amish year*
Anholt, Catherine. *Sun, snow, stars, sky*
Anno, Mitsumasa. *Anno's counting book*
Appelt, Kathi. *A red wagon year*
Arnosky, Jim. *Outdoors on foot*
Austin, Heather. *Visiting Aunt Sylvia's*
Barack, Marcy. *Season song*
Barker, Cicely Mary. *Flower fairies of the seasons*
Bartels, Alice L. *The beast*
Beskow, Elsa Maartman. *Children of the forest*
Birnbaum, Abe. *Green eyes*
Blegvad, Erik. *Burnie's hill*
Blocksma, Mary. *Apple tree! Apple tree!*
Borden, Louise. *Caps, hats, socks and mittens*
   The watching game
Bowen, Betsy. *Antler, bear, canoe*
Boyle, Doe. *Summer coat, winter coat*
Branley, Franklyn M. (Mansfield). *Sunshine makes the seasons*
Brown, Kerry. *Tupag the dreamer*
Brown, Margaret Wise. *The little island*

   Love songs of the little bear
Browne, Anthony. *Voices in the park*
Bruchac, Joseph. *Thirteen moons on turtle's back*
Brunhoff, Laurent de. *Meet Babar and his family*
Bunting, Eve (Anne Evelyn). *Moonstick*
Burningham, John. *Seasons*
Burrowes, Adjoa J. *Grandma's purple flowers*
Calmenson, Stephanie. *My book of the seasons*
Carle, Eric. *The tiny seed*
Carlstrom, Nancy White. *How does the wind walk?*
   Midnight dance of the snowshoe hare
Carrick, Carol. *The old barn*
Cash, Megan Montague. *What makes the seasons?*
Charles, Donald. *Calico Cat's year*
Chorao, Kay. *Little farm by the sea*
Clifton, Lucille. *Everett Anderson's year*
Cole, Joanna. *Big Goof and Little Goof*
Coleridge, Sara. *January brings the snow*
Curti, Anna. *Seasons*
Dahl, Michael. *From the garden*
Deady, Kathleen W. *All year long*
De Paola, Tomie (Thomas Anthony). *Four stories for four seasons*
Derby, Sally. *My steps*
Desimini, Lisa. *My house*
Domanska, Janina. *Spring is*
Don't tell the scarecrow
Dow, Katharine. *My time of year*
Dragonwagon, Crescent. *Jemima remembers*
Drawson, Blair. *Mary Margaret's tree*
Dupasquier, Philippe. *Our house on the hill*
Duvoisin, Roger Antoine. *The house of four seasons*
Edens, Cooper. *A present for Rose*
Edwards, Richard. *Copy me, Copycub*
Ehlert, Lois. *Red leaf, yellow leaf*
Ewart, Claire. *The giant*
Farjeon, Eleanor. *Around the seasons*
Fisher, Aileen Lucia. *As the leaves fall down*
   Going barefoot
   Like nothing at all
Fleming, Denise. *In the small, small pond*
Florian, Douglas. *A year in the country*
Foster, Doris Van Liew. *A pocketful of seasons*
Fowler, Susi Gregg. *When summer ends*
Fox, Charles Philip. *Mr. Stripes the gopher*
Gackenbach, Dick. *Ida Fanfanny*
Geisert, Bonnie. *Mountain town*
   Prairie town
George, Jean Craighead. *Dear Rebecca, winter is here*
   Look to the north
George, Kristine O'Connell. *Old Elm speaks*
Gerstein, Mordicai. *Daisy's garden*
   The story of May
Gibbons, Gail. *Farming*
   The reasons for seasons
   The seasons of Arnold's apple tree
Ginsburg, Mirra. *The old man and his birds*
Goennel, Heidi. *Seasons*
Gomi, Taro. *Spring is here*
Good, Merle. *Amos and Susie*
Gray, Libba Moore. *My mama had a dancing heart*
Greenstein, Elaine. *As big as you*
Greydanus, Rose. *Changing seasons*
Grohmann, Susan. *The dust under Mrs. Merriweather's bed*
Guenther, James. *Turnagain, Ptarmigan, where did you go?*
Haley, Gail E. *Go away, stay away*
   The green man
Hall, Donald. *The ox-cart man*
Hall, Fergus. *Groundsel*
Hall, Zoe. *The apple pie tree*
Harris, Dorothy Joan. *Four seasons for Toby*
Hawkes, Kevin. *His Royal Buckliness*
Helldorfer, M. C. (Mary Claire). *Gather up, gather in*
Henderson, Kathy. *A year in the city*
Hewitt, Sally. *All year round*
   Woods and meadows
Heyduck-Huth, Hilde. *The strawflower*
Hines, Anna Grossnickle. *Pieces, a year in poems and quilts*

Hirschi, Ron. *Seya's song*
Hoberman, Mary Ann. *Right outside my window*
Hopkins, Lee Bennett. *Ring out, wild bells*
Horton, Barbara Savadge. *What comes in spring?*
Howell, Ruth. *Everything changes*
Howell, Will C. *I call it sky*
Hunter, Anne. *Possum's harvest moon*
Hurd, Edith Thacher. *The day the sun danced*
Hutton, Warwick. *Persephone*
Ichikawa, Satomi. *A child's book of seasons*
Iverson, Diane. *Discover the seasons*
Jacobs, Leland B. (Leland Blair). *Just around the corner*
Jauck, Andrea. *Assateague*
Johnson, Amy Crane. *Cinnamon and the April shower = Canela y el aguacero de abril*
Johnston, Tony. *Once in the country*
  Yonder
Jordan, Sandra. *Christmas tree farm*
Kandoian, Ellen. *Molly's seasons*
Kelley, Marty. *Fall is not easy*
Kespert, Deborah. *Rain and shine*
King-Smith, Dick. *Cuckoobush farm*
Kinsey-Warnock, Natalie. *From dawn till dusk*
Kirk, David. *Little bunny, Biddle bunny*
Kroll, Virginia L. *The seasons and someone*
Krull, Kathleen. *Songs of praise*
Krupp, Robin Rector. *Let's go traveling in Mexico*
Kwitz, Mary DeBall. *Mouse at home*
Lasky, Kathryn. *Mommy's hands*
Leonard, Marcia. *Bear's busy year*
Lesser, Carolyn. *Great crystal bear*
  What a wonderful day to be a cow
Lewis, J. Patrick. *July is a mad mosquito*
Lewis, Naomi. *Leaves*
Lionni, Leo. *A busy year*
  Mouse days
  When?
Lister, Mary. *The Winter King and the Summer Queen*
Littlewood, Valerie. *The season clock*
Llewellyn, Claire. *My first book of time*
Lobel, Arnold. *Frog and Toad all year*
Locker, Thomas. *Sky tree*
London, Jonathan. *Park beat*
  What Newt could do for Turtle
Lotz, Karen E. *Can't sit still*
McDermott, Gerald. *Daughter of earth*
MacKinnon, Debbie. *The seasons*
Maestro, Betsy. *Through the year with Harriet*
Mangin, Marie-France. *Suzette and Nicholas and the seasons clock*
Manushkin, Fran. *The best toy of all*
Marshak, S. (Samuil). *The Month-Brothers*
Martin, Bill (William Ivan). *The turning of the year*
Marzollo, Jean. *Once upon a springtime*
Miller, Edna. *Mousekin's fables*
Miller, Jane. *Seasons on the farm*
Miller, Moira. *The search for spring*
Moore, Christopher J. *Ishtar and Tammuz*
Mora, Emma. *Gideon, the little bear cub*
Muller, Gerda. *Around the oak*
  Circle of seasons
Muntean, Michaela. *Muppet babies through the year*
Murphy, Mary. *Here comes spring, and summer and fall and winter*
Nightingale, Sandy. *The witch's spell*
Nikola-Lisa, W. *The year with Grandma Moses*
Oliver, Stephen. *Seasons*
Oppenheim, Joanne. *Have you seen trees?*, ill. by Irwin Rosenhouse
  Have you seen trees?, ill. by Jean and Mou-Sien Tseng
Owen, Roy. *The ibis and the egret*
Paul, Ann Whitford. *The seasons sewn*
Pearson, Susan. *My favorite time of year*
Peters, Lisa Westberg. *Good morning, river!*
Pizer, Abigail. *Charlie the puppy*
  Hattie the goat
  Penelope pig
  Percy the duck
Pollock, Penny. *When the moon is full*
Provensen, Alice. *A book of seasons*

  The year at Maple Hill Farm
Rau, Dana Meachen. *In the yard*
Roach, Marilynne K. *Dune fox*
Rockwell, Anne F. *Ducklings and pollywogs*
  First comes spring
Rosenberry, Vera. *Run, jump, whiz, splash*
Ross, Michael Elsohn. *Earth cycles*
Rucki, Ani. *When the Earth wakes*
Ryder, Joanne. *Under your feet*
Schulman, Janet. *A bunny for all seasons*
Schulz, Charles M. *Snoopy's facts and fun book about seasons*
Shields, Carol Diggory. *Month by month a year goes round*
Siddals, Mary McKenna. *Tell me a season*
Silverman, Erica. *Warm in winter*
Simon, Norma. *Mama cat's year*
Smith, William Jay (1918–). *The sun is up*
Spinelli, Eileen. *Summerbath, winterbath*
Spohn, David. *Nate's treasure*
Stewart, Sarah. *The money tree*
Tafuri, Nancy. *Snowy flowy blowy*
Takabayashi, Mari. *I live in Brooklyn*
Taylor, Theodore. *Hello, Arctic!*
Tresselt, Alvin R. *It's time now!*
  Johnny Maple-Leaf
Trimble, Marcia. *Flower Green*
Tudor, Tasha. *Around the year*
Udry, Janice May. *A tree is nice*
Verdet, Andre. *All about time*
Watts, Bernadette. *Tattercoats*
Weiss, Nicki. *On a hot, hot day*
Welber, Robert. *Song of the seasons*
Wellington, Anne. *Apple pie*
Wells, Rosemary. *Night sounds, morning colors*
Whitehouse, Patricia. *Seasons ABC*
  Seasons 1 2 3
Wick, Walter. *Can you see what I see? Cool collections*
Wildsmith, Brian. *Seasons*
Wolff, Ashley. *A year of birds*
Wood, Joyce. *Grandmother Lucy in her garden*
Yolen, Jane. *Ring of earth*
  Welcome to the icehouse
Zagwÿn, Deborah Turney. *Turtle spring*
Zeman, Ludmila. *The first red maple leaf*
Ziefert, Harriet. *Bear all year*
Zimmermann, H. Werner (Heinz Werner). *Alphonse knows . . . twelve months make a year*
Zolotow, Charlotte (Shapiro). *In my garden*
  The song

Seasons – fall

Adelson, Leone. *All ready for school*
Æsop. *The ant and the grasshopper*, ill. by Amy Lowry Poole
  The ant and the grasshopper, ill. by Sara Rojo
Allington, Richard L. *Autumn*
Arnosky, Jim. *Every autumn comes the bear*
Barklem, Jill. *Autumn story*
  The high hills
Blades, Ann. *Fall*
Bliss, Corinne Demas. *Matthew's meadow*
Brode, Robyn. *November*
  October
  September
Bunting, Eve (Anne Evelyn). *Peepers*
  The pumpkin fair
Burg, Ann. *Autumn walk*
Carr, Jan. *Dappled apples*
Cavagnaro, David. *The pumpkin people*
Cohen, Peter Zachary. *Authorized autumn charts of the Upper Red Canoe River country*
Demarest, Chris L. *Fall*
Denslow, Sharon Phillips. *At Taylor's place*
Dutton, Sandra. *The cinnamon hen's autumn day*
Frank, John. *A chill in the air*
Fregosi, Claudia. *The happy horse*
Freschet, Berniece. *Owl in the garden*
George, Lindsay Barrett. *In the woods*

Gibbons, Gail. *The pumpkin book*
Glaser, Linda. *It's fall*
Godwin, Laura. *The best fall of all*
    Happy and Honey
Griffith, Helen V. *Alex remembers*
Hall, Zoe. *Fall leaves fall*
Harshman, Marc. *Red are the apples*
Hirschi, Ron. *Fall*
Hoban, Julia. *Amy loves the wind*
Hopkins, Lee Bennett. *Merrily comes our harvest in*
Iwamura, Kazuo. *The fourteen forest mice and the harvest moon watch*
Jackson, Ellen B. *The autumn equinox*
    November
    October
    September
Knutson, Kimberley. *Ska-tat!*
Koller, Jackie French. *Nickommoh!*
Kumin, Maxine W. *Follow the fall*
Lapp, Eleanor. *The mice came in early this year*
Leaf by leaf
Lenski, Lois. *Now it's fall*
London, Jonathan. *Fall rap*
Lotz, Karen E. *Snowsong whistling*
Maass, Robert. *When autumn comes*
McNaughton, Colin. *Autumn*
Maestro, Betsy. *Why do leaves change color?*
Moncure, Jane Belk. *Word Bird's fall words*
Moore, Elaine. *Grandma's smile*
Nidey, Kelli. *When autumn falls*
Ott, John. *Peter Pumpkin*
Pickering, Jimmy. *It's fall*
Plourde, Lynn. *Wild child*
Potter, Beatrix. *The tale of Squirrel Nutkin*
Potter, Tessa. *Digger, the story of a mole in the fall*
Robbins, Ken. *Autumn leaves*
Roth, Harold. *Autumn days*
Rylant, Cynthia. *In November*
Schnur, Steven. *Autumn*
Schweninger, Ann. *Autumn days*
Shapiro, Jody Fickes. *Up, up, up! It's apple-picking time*
Spetter, Jung-Hee. *Lily and Trooper's fall*
Spinelli, Eileen. *I know it's autumn*
Taylor, Mark. *Henry explores the mountains*
Tejima, Keizaburo. *The bears' autumn*
Thayer, Tanya. *Fall*
Tresselt, Alvin R. *Autumn harvest*
    Johnny Maple-Leaf
Udry, Janice May. *Emily's autumn*
Updike, David. *An autumn tale*
Van Allsburg, Chris. *The stranger*
Wheeler, Cindy. *Marmalade's yellow leaf*
Whitehouse, Patricia. *Fall*
Yerxa, Leo. *Last leaf first snowflake to fall*
Zoehfeld, Kathleen Weidner. *Apples, apples*
Zolotow, Charlotte (Shapiro). *Say it!*

Seasons – spring

Agell, Charlotte. *Mud makes me dance in the spring*
Alexander, Sue. *There's more . . . much more*
Allington, Richard L. *Spring*
Anglund, Joan Walsh. *Spring is a new beginning*
Arden, Carolyn. *Goose moon*
Barker, Cicely Mary. *Flower fairies of the spring*
Barklem, Jill. *Spring story*
Barrett, John M. *The Easter bear*
Baum, Arline. *One bright Monday morning*
Beck, Andrea. *Elliot gets stuck*
Beer, Kathleen Costello. *What happens in the spring*
Belting, Natalia Maree. *Summer's coming in*
Berenstain, Stan. *The Berenstain bears and the real Easter eggs*
Blades, Ann. *Spring*
Boon, Emilie. *It's spring, Peterkin*
Bornstein, Ruth Lercher. *Rabbit's good news*
Bourgeois, Paulette. *Franklin's baby sister*
Brode, Robyn. *April*
    March

May
Brown, Craig McFarland. *In the spring*
Carlstrom, Nancy White. *Raven and river*
Carr, Jan. *Splish, splash, spring*
Chall, Marsha Wilson. *Sugarbush spring*
Chönz, Selina. *A bell for Ursli*
Clifton, Lucille. *The boy who didn't believe in spring*
Cohen, Carol L. *Wake up, groundhog!*
Craig, M. Jean. *Spring is like the morning*
Cummings, E. E. (Edward Estlin). *In just-spring*
Dabcovich, Lydia. *Sleepy bear*
Delton, Judy. *Three friends find spring*
Demarest, Chris L. *Spring*
Demi. *Demi's basket of books*
    Little baby lamb
De Posadas Mane, Carmen. *Mister North Wind*
Dewey, Ariane. *The tea squall*
Dodd, Lynley. *Wake up, bear*
Dragonwagon, Crescent. *Strawberry dress escape*
Emberley, Michael. *Welcome back, Sun*
Ernst, Lisa Campbell. *Wake up, it's Spring!*
Fish, Helen Dean. *When the root children wake up*, published by Lippincott, 1930
    When the root children wake up, published by Green Tiger Pr., 1988
Fisher, Aileen Lucia. *My mother and I*
    Now that spring is here
    The story of Easter
Fontes, Justine Korman. *Signs of spring*
Forrester, Victoria. *The touch said hello*
Glaser, Linda. *It's spring*
Harness, Cheryl. *The queen with bees in her hair*
Hest, Amy. *Ruby's storm*
Hirschi, Ron. *Spring*
Hoban, Lillian. *The sugar snow spring*
    Turtle spring
Hopkins, Lee Bennett. *Easter buds are springing*
Hunter, Anne. *Possum and the peeper*
Hurd, Edith Thacher. *The day the sun danced*
Hurd, Thacher. *Blackberry ramble*
Ichikawa, Satomi. *Sun through small leaves*
Iwamura, Kazuo. *The fourteen forest mice and the spring meadow picnic*
Jackson, Ellen B. *April*
    March
    May
    The spring equinox
Janice. *Little Bear's pancake party*
Johnson, Crockett. *Time for spring*
    Will spring be early or will spring be late?
Kesselman, Wendy Ann. *Time for Jody*
Kinsey-Warnock, Natalie. *When spring comes*
Kite, L. Patricia. *Dandelion adventures*
Koscielniak, Bruce. *Geoffrey Groundhog predicts the weather*
Kraus, Robert. *The first robin*
    Springfellow's parade
Krauss, Ruth. *The happy day*
Kroll, Steven. *I love spring!*
Kroll, Virginia L. *Naomi knows it's springtime*
Larry, Charles. *Peboan and Seegwun*
Lenski, Lois. *Spring is here*
Lerner, Carol. *Flowers of a woodland spring*
Levens, George. *Kippy the koala*
Lewison, Wendy Cheyette. *Princess Buttercup*
Lindbergh, Reeve. *North country spring*
Lucht, Irmgard. *In this night*
Maass, Robert. *When spring comes*
McNaughton, Colin. *Spring*
Martin, Charles E. *Island rescue*
Miller, Edna. *Mousekin's Easter basket*
Minarik, Else Holmelund. *It's spring!*
Moncure, Jane Belk. *Word Bird's spring words*
Moore, Elaine. *Grandma's garden*
Morgan-Vanroyen, Mary. *Night ride*
Nordqvist, Sven. *Festus and Mercury: ruckus in the garden*
Oppenheim, Joanne. *Could it be?*
Patz, Nancy. *Sarah Bear and Sweet Sidney*

Peters, Lisa Westberg. *Cold little duck, duck, duck*
Pfister, Marcus. *Hopper*
   Hopper hunts for spring
Pitcher, Caroline. *Are you spring?*
Plourde, Lynn. *Spring's sprung*
Poppy Bear
Ray, Mary Lyn. *Mud*
Richardson, Judith Benét. *Old winter*
Rockwell, Anne F. *My spring robin*
Schlein, Miriam. *Little Red Nose*
Schnur, Steven. *Spring*
   Spring thaw
Schulman, Janet. *Countdown to spring*
Seignobosc, Françoise. *Springtime for Jeanne-Marie*
Selkowe, Valrie M. *Spring green*
Seuling, Barbara. *Spring song*
Sewall, Marcia. *The Green Mist*
Shannon, George. *Spring*
Silverman, Erica. *On the morn of Mayfest*
Skofield, James. *Crow moon, worm moon*
Spetter, Jung-Hee. *Lily and Trooper's spring*
Stafford, William. *The animal that drank up sound*
Taylor, Harriet Peck. *Two days in May*
Taylor, Judy. *Dudley and the monster*
Taylor, Mark. *Henry the castaway*
Thayer, Tanya. *Spring*
Tresselt, Alvin R. *Hi, Mister Robin*
Wallace, Nancy Elizabeth. *Paperwhite*
Walters, Catherine. *When will it be spring?*
Warren, Cathy. *Springtime bears*
Waterton, Betty. *Pettranella*
Weedn, Flavia. *The giant's garden*
Wells, Rosemary. *Forest of dreams*
   Max's chocolate chicken
Whitehouse, Patricia. *Spring*
Whittington, Mary K. *Winter's child*
Wilde, Oscar. *Fairy tales of Oscar Wilde*
   The selfish giant, ill. by S. Saelig Gallagher
   The selfish giant, ill. by Dom Mansell
   The selfish giant, ill. by Fabian Negrin
   The selfish giant, ill. by Lisbeth Zwerger
Wolkstein, Diane. *The magic wings*
Wood, Audrey. *When the root children wake up*
Wood, Joyce. *Grandmother Lucy in her garden*
Woolaver, Lance. *From Ben Loman to the sea*
Worth, Bonnie. *Peter Cottontail's surprise*
Zimmermann, H. Werner (Heinz Werner). *Alphonse knows . . . the colour of spring*
Zion, Gene. *Really spring*

Seasons – summer

Ackerman, Karen. *In the park with dad*
Adelson, Leone. *All ready for summer*
Alarcón, Francisco X. *From the bellybutton of the moon and other summer poems / poemas = Del ombligo de la luna y otros poemas de verano / poemas*
Aliki. *Those summers*
Allington, Richard L. *Summer*
Appelt, Kathi. *Watermelon day*
Barker, Cicely Mary. *Flower fairies of the summer*
Barklem, Jill. *Summer story*
Bat-Ami, Miriam. *Sea, salt, and air*
Beim, Jerrold. *The swimming hole*
Belting, Natalia Maree. *Summer's coming in*
Bentley, Anne. *The Groggs have a wonderful summer*
Berenstain, Stan. *The Berenstain bears go to camp*
Blades, Ann. *Back to the cabin*
   Summer
Boelts, Maribeth. *Little Bunny's preschool countdown*
   Summer's end
Bowden, Joan Chase. *Emilio's summer day*
Brennan, Linda Crotta. *Marshmallow kisses*
Brode, Robyn. *August*
   July
   June
Brown, Margaret Wise. *The summer noisy book*

Buchanan, Heather S. *George Mouse's first summer*
Bunting, Eve (Anne Evelyn). *Sunflower house*
Burgunder, Rose. *From summer to summer*
Burke, Jennifer S. *Hot days*
Burn, Doris. *The summerfolk*
Calmenson, Stephanie. *Hotter than a hot dog!*
Carmichael, Clay. *Bear at the beach*
Cavagnaro, David. *The pumpkin people*
Chönz, Selina. *Florina and the wild bird*
Chwast, Seymour. *Still another children's book*
Craft, Ruth. *The day of the rainbow*
Crews, Nina. *One hot summer day*
Crisp, Marty. *Totally polar*
Demarest, Chris L. *Summer*
Denslow, Sharon Phillips. *Night owls*
Dotlich, Rebecca Kai. *Lemonade sun*
Dragonwagon, Crescent. *The itch book*
English, Karen. *Hot day on Abbott Avenue*
Factor, Jane. *Summer*
Farjeon, Eleanor. *Mr. Garden*
Florian, Douglas. *Summersaults*
Gage, Wilson. *Anna's summer songs*
Gans, Roma. *Hummingbirds in the garden*
Garelick, May. *Down to the beach*
George, Lindsay Barrett. *Around the pond*
Gershwin, George. *Summertime from Porgy and Bess*
Gerstein, Mordicai. *The seal mother*
Glaser, Linda. *It's summer*
Godwin, Laura. *Central Park serenade*
Goodall, John S. *An Edwardian summer*
Griese, Arnold A. *Anna's Athabaskan summer*
Griffith, Helen V. *Georgia music*
Haas, Irene. *A summertime song*
Hall, Donald. *Lucy's summer*
Hayward, Linda. *Ernie and Bert's summer project*
Haywood, Carolyn. *Hello, star*
Hedderwick, Mairi. *P. D. Pebbles' summer or winter book*
Helldorfer, M. C. (Mary Claire). *Silver Rain Brown*
Henkes, Kevin. *Grandpa and Bo*
Henley, Claire. *Sunny day*
Hesse, Karen. *Come on, rain*
Hirschi, Ron. *Summer*
Inkpen, Mick. *Hissss!*
Iwamura, Kazuo. *The fourteen forest mice and the summer laundry day*
Jackson, Ellen B. *August*
   July
   June
   The summer solstice
Jessup, Harley. *Grandma summer*
Johnson, Neil. *Jack Creek cowboy*
Kelley, Marty. *Summer stinks*
Kesselman, Wendy Ann. *Sand in my shoes*
Knotts, Howard. *The summer cat*
Komoda, Beverly. *The too hot day*
Kuskin, Karla. *Sand and snow*
Lasky, Kathryn. *My island grandma*, ill. by Emily Arnold McCully
   My island grandma, ill. by Amy Schwartz
Layton, Neal. *Hot, hot, hot*
Lemberg, Stephen H. *Scaredy dog*
Lenski, Lois. *On a summer day*
Lewis, Kim. *One summer day*
Lister, Mary. *The Winter King and the Summer Queen*
London, Jonathan. *Sun dance, water dance*
Lund, Doris Herold. *The paint-box sea*
Maass, Robert. *When summer comes*
McCloskey, Robert. *Time of wonder*
McNaughton, Colin. *Summer*
Mahy, Margaret. *A summery Saturday morning*
Martin, Charles E. *For rent*
   Sam saves the day
Michels, Tilde. *What a beautiful day!*
Moncure, Jane Belk. *Word Bird's summer words*
Moore, Elaine. *Grandma's house*
Njeng, Pierre Yves. *Vacation in the village*
O'Donnell, Elizabeth Lee. *The twelve days of summer*
Paraskevas, Betty. *Hoppy and Joe*
Paulsen, Gary. *Canoe days*

Peters, Lisa Westberg. *The hayloft*
Polacco, Patricia. *Mrs. Mack*
Posey, Lee. *Night rabbits*
Poydar, Nancy. *Cool Ali*
Robins, Joan. *Addie runs away*
Ryder, Joanne. *Bears out there*
Scheer, Julian. *By the light of the captured moon*
Schick, Eleanor. *One summer night*
Schnur, Steven. *Summer*
Schweninger, Ann. *Summertime*
Spetter, Jung-Hee. *Lily and Trooper's summer*
Stevenson, Harvey. *Grandpa's house*
Stevenson, James. *July*
Stobbs, William. *There's a hole in my bucket*
Stock, Catherine. *An island summer*
Stroud, Bettye. *Down home at Miss Dessa's*
Tamar, Erika. *Donnatalee*
Taylor, Mark. *Henry explores the jungle*
Thayer, Tanya. *Summer*
Thomas, Ianthe. *Lordy, Aunt Hattie*
Toye, William. *How summer came to Canada*
Van Leeuwen, Jean. *Touch the sky summer*
Wagner, Jenny. *Amy's monster*
Waters, Jennifer. *Summer fun*
Whitehouse, Patricia. *Summer*
Woodson, Jacqueline. *The other side*
Woodtor, Dee. *Big meeting*
Yashima, Taro. *The village tree*
Yolen, Jane. *Before the storm*
  Milkweed days
Zagwÿn, Deborah Turney. *The sea house*
Zion, Gene. *The summer snowman*
Zolotow, Charlotte (Shapiro). *Summer is . . .*

Seasons – winter

Adelson, Leone. *All ready for winter*
Æsop. *The ant and the grasshopper*, ill. by Amy Lowry Poole
  The ant and the grasshopper, ill. by Sara Rojo
Alarcón, Francisco X. *Iguanas in the snow and other winter poems /*
  poemas = Iguanas en la nieve y otros poemas de invierno / poemas
Allington, Richard L. *Winter*
Anholt, Laurence. *Summerhouse*
Aragon, Jane Chelsea. *Winter harvest*
Arnosky, Jim. *Every autumn comes the bear*
Asch, Frank. *Good night, Baby Bear*
  Mooncake
Attenberger, Walburga. *The little man in winter*
Auch, Mary Jane. *Bird dogs can't fly*
Aulaire, Ingri Mortenson d'. *Children of the northlights*
Baird, Audrey B. *A cold snap!*
Bancroft, Henrietta. *Animals in winter*
Barasch, Lynne. *A winter walk*
Barklem, Jill. *The secret staircase*
  Winter story
Barnhart, Peter. *The wounded duck*
Bartoli, Jennifer. *In a meadow, two hares hide*
  Snow on bear's nose
Bassett, Lisa. *Beany and Scamp*
Bauer, Caroline Feller. *Midnight snowman*
Blades, Ann. *Mary of mile 18*
  Winter
Blumenthal, Deborah. *Ice palace*
Bodecker, N. M. (Nils Mogens). *Hurry, hurry, Mary dear!*
Briggs, Raymond. *The bear*
Brode, Robyn. *December*
  February
  January
Brown, Margaret Wise. *The winter noisy book*
Bruna, Dick. *Miffy in the snow*
Brutschy, Jennifer. *The winter fox*
Buckley, Helen Elizabeth. *Josie and the snow*
Bundey, Nikki. *In the snow*
Bunting, Eve (Anne Evelyn). *Red fox running*
  Winter's coming
Burke, Jennifer S. *Cold days*
Burton, Virginia Lee. *Katy and the big snow*

Campbell, Rod. *Buster keeps warm*
Caple, Kathy. *Hillary to the rescue*
Carlson, Natalie Savage. *Surprise in the mountains*
Carlstrom, Nancy White. *Goodbye geese*
  The snow speaks
Carr, Jan. *Frozen noses*
Carrick, Carol. *The polar bears are hungry*
  Two coyotes
Cartwright, Ann. *The winter hedgehog*
Cech, John. *First snow, magic snow*
Chaconas, Don. *On a wintry morning*
Chaffin, Lillie D. *We be warm till springtime comes*
Chapman, Cheryl. *Snow on snow on snow*
Chönz, Selina. *The snowstorm*
Christelow, Eileen. *The five-dog night*
Christiana, David. *The first snow*
  White nineteens
Christiansen, Candace. *The ice horse*
Cole, Joanna. *Plants in winter*
Cosgrove, Margaret. *Wintertime for animals*
Cote, Nancy. *It feels like snow*
Cotten, Cynthia. *Snow ponies*
Coutant, Helen. *First snow*
Coxe, Molly. *Whose footprints?*
Craft, Ruth. *The winter bear*
Craighead, Charles. *The eagle and the river*
Crews, Nina. *Snowball*
Cuyler, Margery. *The biggest, best snowman*
Dabcovich, Lydia. *Sleepy bear*
Dahl, Michael. *Downhill fun*
  Footprints in the snow
De Beer, Hans. *Bernard Bear's amazing adventure*
Delton, Judy. *My mom hates me in January*
  Three friends find spring
Demarest, Chris L. *Winter*
Deprisco, Dorothea. *Snowbear's winter day*
Dewey, Jennifer Owings. *Once I knew a spider*
Dionetti, Michelle V. *The day Eli went looking for bear*
Dixon, Ann. *Winter is . . .*
Dobson, Clive. *Fred's TV*
Dunphy, Madeleine. *Here is the Arctic winter*
Easterling, Bill. *Prize in the snow*
Ehlert, Lois. *Snowballs*
Fisher, Aileen Lucia. *Where does everyone go?*
Flack, Marjorie. *Angus lost*
Fleming, Denise. *Time to sleep*
Florian, Douglas. *A winter day*
Ford, Christine. *Snow!*
Frank, John. *A chill in the air*
Fredericks, Anthony D. *In one tidepool*
Freedman, Russell. *When winter comes*
Freeman, Don. *The night the lights went out*
Frost, Robert. *Stopping by woods on a snowy evening*
Fujikawa, Gyo. *That's not fair!*
Funakoshi, Canna. *One evening*
Gammell, Stephen. *Is that you, winter?*
George, Jean Craighead. *Dear Rebecca, winter is here*
George, William T. *Christmas at Long Pond*
Gershator, Phillis. *When it starts to snow*
Gipson, Morrell. *Whose tracks are these?*
Glaser, Linda. *It's winter*
Grindley, Sally. *What will I do without you?*
Gundersheimer, Karen. *Happy winter*
Harshman, Marc. *A little excitement*
Hartley, Deborah. *Up north in the winter*
Harvey, Amanda. *Stormy weather*
Hasler, Eveline. *Winter magic*
Hedderwick, Mairi. *P. D. Pebbles' summer or winter book*
Henderson, Kathy. *Disney's Bambi: the winter trail*
Henkes, Kevin. *Oh!*
Hertz, Ole. *Tobias goes ice fishing*
Hill, Susan. *Beware, beware*
Hindley, Judy. *Princess Rosa's winter*
Hirschi, Ron. *Winter*
Hoban, Russell. *Some snow said hello*
Hoff, Syd. *When will it snow?*
Hoffman, Alice. *Fireflies*

Hol, Coby. *Lisa and the snowman*
Honda, Tetsuya. *Wild horse winter*
Hoopes, Lyn Littlefield. *When I was little*
Howard, Kim. *In wintertime*
Iwamura, Kazuo. *The fourteen forest mice and the winter sledding day*
Jackson, Ellen B. *December*
　　February
　　January
　　The winter solstice
Janosch. *Dear snowman*
Johnston, Tony. *The last snow of winter*
　　Mole and Troll trim the tree
Jones, Jennifer Berry. *Who lives in the snow?*
Keats, Ezra Jack. *The snowy day*
　　The snowy day [board book]
King, Deborah. *The flight of the snow geese*
Kinsey-Warnock, Natalie. *The wild horses of Sweetbriar*
Knotts, Howard. *The winter cat*
Komoda, Beverly. *The winter day*
Kovalski, Maryann. *Jingle bells*
Krauss, Ruth. *The happy day*
Krementz, Jill. *A very young skier*
Kumin, Maxine W. *A winter friend*
Kuskin, Karla. *In the flaky frosty morning*
　　Sand and snow
　　Under my hood I have a hat
Lapp, Eleanor. *The mice came in early this year*
Larry, Charles. *Peboan and Seegwun*
Lathrop, Dorothy Pulis. *Who goes there?*
Lawson, Julie. *Midnight in the mountains*
Lenski, Lois. *I like winter*
Linch, Elizabeth Johanna. *Samson*
Lindgren, Astrid. *The tomten*
　　The tomten and the fox
Lister, Mary. *The Winter King and the Summer Queen*
Littledale, Freya. *The snow child*
London, Jonathan. *Froggy gets dressed*
Lotz, Karen E. *Snowsong whistling*
Lucas, Barbara (Barbara M.). *Snowed in*
Maass, Robert. *When winter comes*
McCully, Emily Arnold. *First snow*
McLaughlin, Lissa. *Why won't winter go?*
McNaughton, Colin. *Winter*
Mamin-Sibiryak, D. N. *Grey Neck*
Manuel, Lynn. *The night the moon blew kisses*
Martchenko, Michael. *Bird feeder banquet*
Martin, Charles E. *Island winter*
Michels, Tilde. *Who's that knocking at my door?*
Miller, Edna. *Mousekin's golden house*
Moffatt, Judith. *Snow shapes*
Moncure, Jane Belk. *Word Bird's winter words*
Moore, Elaine. *Grandma's promise*
Morgan, Allen. *Sadie and the snowman*
Morpurgo, Michael. *The silver swan*
Munsch, Robert N. *Thomas' snowsuit*
Nelson, Robin. *A snowy day*
O'Donnell, Elizabeth Lee. *Winter visitors*
Odoyevsky, Vladimir. *Old Father Frost*
Parnall, Peter. *Alfalfa Hill*
　　Winter barn
Partridge, Elizabeth. *Moon glowing*
Patz, Nancy. *Sarah Bear and Sweet Sidney*
Paul, Korky. *Winnie in winter*
Pearson, Tracey Campbell. *Where does Joe go?*
Pfister, Marcus. *Hopper*
Pickering, Jimmy. *It's winter*
Pittman, Helena Clare. *Uncle Phil's diner*
Plourde, Lynn. *Winter waits*
Porter, Sue. *Parsnip*
Poydar, Nancy. *Snip, snip . . . snow!*
Prusski, Jeffrey. *Bring back the deer*
Quinlan, Patricia. *Anna's red sled*
Radin, Ruth Yaffe. *A winter place*
Reiser, Lynn. *My dog Truffle*
Retan, Walter. *The snowplow that tried to go south*
Richardson, Judith Benét. *Old winter*
Roberts, Bethany. *Waiting-for-spring stories*

Rockwell, Anne F. *The first snowfall*
Root, Phyllis. *Grandmother Winter*
Roth, Harold. *Winter days*
Rowinski, Kate. *L. L. Bear's island adventure*
Ruurs, Margriet. *Emma's cold day*
Ryder, Joanne. *Winter whale*
Schick, Eleanor. *City in the winter*
Schindler, Regina. *The bear's cave*
Schlein, Miriam. *Deer in the snow*
　　Go with the sun
Schnur, Steven. *Winter*
Schweninger, Ann. *Wintertime*
Selsam, Millicent E. *Keep looking!*
　　Where do they go?
Seuling, Barbara. *Winter lullaby*
Silverman, Erica. *Warm in winter*
Simon, Francesca. *Camels don't ski*
Spetter, Jung-Hee. *Lily and Trooper's winter*
Spohn, David. *Winter wood*
Stafford, William. *The animal that drank up sound*
Steig, William. *Brave Irene*
Stevenson, James. *Brr!*
Stewart, Paul. *A little bit of winter*
Stojic, Manya. *Snow*
Sutherland, Colleen. *Jason goes to show-and-tell*
Szekeres, Cyndy. *The mouse that Jack built*
Takao, Yuko. *A winter concert*
Taylor, Mark. *Henry the explorer*
Tejima, Keizaburo. *Fox's dream*
Thayer, Tanya. *Winter*
Toye, William. *How summer came to Canada*
Tudor, Tasha. *Snow before Christmas*
Turkle, Brinton. *Thy friend, Obadiah*
Udry, Janice May. *Mary Jo's grandmother*
Valgardson, W. D. *Winter rescue*
Van Laan, Nancy. *Shingebiss*
　　When winter comes
Van Vorst, M. L. *A Norse lullaby*
Vigna, Judith. *Boot weather*
Wabbes, Marie. *It's snowing, Little Rabbit*
Waber, Bernard. *Bearsie Bear and the surprise sleepover party*
Wallace, Ivy. *Pookie puts the world right*
Wallace, Karen. *A bed for winter*
Walters, Catherine. *When will it be spring?*
Ward, Andrew. *Baby bear and the long sleep*
Watanabe, Shigeo. *Ice cream is falling!*
Watson, Wendy. *Has winter come?*
　　Tales for a winter's eve
Weiss, Ellen. *Clara the fortune-telling chicken*
Wellington, Monica. *Bunny's first snowflake*
Wells, Rosemary. *Forest of dreams*
Whitehouse, Patricia. *Winter*
Whittington, Mary K. *Winter's child*
Whybrow, Ian. *Harry and the snow king*
Winch, Madeleine. *Come by chance*
Yerxa, Leo. *Last leaf first snowflake to fall*
Yolen, Jane. *Snow, snow*

Secret codes

Balian, Lorna. *Humbug potion*

Secrets *see* Behavior – secrets

Seeds

Alda, Arlene. *Morning glory Monday*
Anno, Mitsumasa. *Anno's magic seeds*
Back, Christine. *Bean and plant*
Bauld, Jane Scoggins. *Journey of the third seed*
Carle, Eric. *The tiny seed*
Cave, Kathryn. *One child, one seed*
Edwards, Nancy. *Glenna's seeds*
Gibbons, Gail. *From seed to plant*
Greeley, Valerie. *The acorn's story*
Hall, Zoe. *The surprise garden*
Himmelman, John. *A dandelion's life*

Holub, Joan. *The garden that we grew*
Howard, Ellen. *The big seed*
Hubbell, Will. *Pumpkin Jack*
Jordan, Helene J. (Helene Jamieson). *How a seed grows*
Karon, Jan. *The trellis and the seed*
King, Elizabeth. *Backyard sunflower*
Kite, L. Patricia. *Dandelion adventures*
Kottke, Jan. *From seed to pumpkin*
Kuchalla, Susan. *All about seeds*
Legg, Gerald. *From seed to sunflower*
Lerner, Harriet Goldhor. *What's so terrible about swallowing an apple seed?*
Le Tord, Bijou. *God's little seeds*
    Sing a new song
Martin, Jacqueline Briggs. *Button, bucket, sky*
Marzollo, Jean. *I'm a seed*
Medearis, Angela Shelf. *Seeds grow*
Mockford, Caroline. *What's this?*
Pak, Soyung. *A place to grow*
Petie, Haris. *The seed the squirrel dropped*
Pin, Isabel. *The seed*
Ramirez, Melissa Bourbon. *The flight of the sunflower*
Relf, Patricia. *The magic school bus plants seeds*
Robbins, Ken. *Seeds*
Rockwell, Anne F. *One bean*
Santucci, Barbara. *Anna's corn*
Sasso, Sandy Eisenberg. *Naamah, Noah's wife*
Schaefer, Lola M. *This is the sunflower*
Selsam, Millicent E. *Seeds and more seeds*
Shecter, Ben. *Partouche plants a seed*
Takihara, Koji. *Rolli*
Walsh, Ellen Stoll. *Dot and Jabber and the great acorn mystery*
Watson, Mary. *The butterfly seeds*

Seeing *see* Anatomy – eyes; Glasses; Handicaps – blindness; Senses – sight

Seeing eye dogs *see* Animals – service animals

Seeking better things *see* Behavior – seeking better things

Self-concept

Ackerman, Karen. *Bean's big day*
Ahlberg, Janet. *The bear nobody wanted*
Alborough, Jez. *Beaky*
Alden, Joan. *A boy's best friend*
Aliki. *All by myself!*
Anderson, Wayne. *Dragon*
Appell, Clara. *Now I have a daddy haircut*
Appelt, Kathi. *Incredible me!*
Bach, Alice. *Warren Weasel's worse than measles*
Backker, Vera de. *Coco the koala*
Bahr, Amy C. *It's ok to say no*
    Sometimes it's ok to tell secrets
    What should you do when . . . ?
    Your body is your own
Bannatyne-Cugnet, Jo. *Estelle and the self-esteem machines*
Barbero, Maria. *The bravest mouse*
Barnes, Laura T. *Ernest and the big itch*
    Teeny tiny Ernest
Barnwell, Ysaye M. *No mirrors in my Nana's house*
Bea, Holly. *My spiritual alphabet book*
Behrens, June. *Who am I?*
Belton, Sandra. *Pictures for Miss Josie*
Benjamin, A. H. *A duck so small*
Bentley, Nancy. *I've got your nose!*
Berger, Terry. *I have feelings*
Berliner, Franz. *Miserable Marabou*
Bertrand, Cécile. *Mr. and Mrs. Smith have only one child, but what a child!*
Bishop, Brett. *Clayton's path*
Blegvad, Lenore. *This is me*
Blume, Judy. *The one in the middle is a green kangaroo*
Bolliger, Max. *The rabbit with the sky blue ears*
Borden, Louise. *A. Lincoln and me*

Bowman, Pete. *I wish I were big*
Boyce, Katie. *Hector the hermit crab*
Brandenberg, Alexa. *I am me!*
Brown, Ruth. *Crazy Charlie*
Browne, Anthony. *Willy the wimp*
Buchanan, Sue. *Mud Pie Annie*
Buehner, Caralyn. *Superdog, the heart of a hero*
Caple, Kathy. *Harry's smile*
    Starring Hillary
Carle, Eric. *The mixed-up chameleon*
Carlson, Nancy L. *ABC, I like me!*
    I like me
Carmichael, Clay. *Used-up Bear*
Casler, Leigh. *The boy who dreamed of an acorn*
Catalanotto, Peter. *Matthew A.B.C.*
Charles, Donald. *Ugly bug*
Charlip, Remy. *Hooray for me!*
Charlot, Martin. *Felisa and the magic tikling bird*
Cheng, Andrea. *Anna the bookbinder*
Chetkowski, Emily. *Pumpkin smile*
Chottin, Ariane. *A home for Little Turtle*
    Little Goat's new horns
Cibula, Matt S. *Slumgullion, the executive pig*
Clark, Sue. *Bodies*
    Clothes
    Faces
    Feelings
Climo, Shirley. *The little red ant and the great big crumb*
Cohen, Miriam. *No good in art*
    So what?
Corey, Shana. *First graders from Mars: Nergal and the Great Space Race*
    First graders from Mars: The problem with Pelly
Curtis, Jamie Lee. *I'm gonna like me*
Cuyler, Margery. *From here to there*
Damjan, Mischa. *The fake flamingos*
Daniels, Teri. *Just enough*
De Groat, Diane. *Liar, liar, pants on fire*
DeLage, Ida. *Am I a bunny?*
De Regniers, Beatrice Schenk. *Everyone is good for something*
De Veaux, Alexis. *An enchanted hair tale*
Dorfman, Craig. *I knew you could!*
Drachman, Eric. *Leo the lightning bug*
Edwards, Julie Andrews. *Simeon's gift*
Edwards, Pamela Duncan. *Gigi and Lulu's gigantic fight*
Elster, Jean Alicia. *Just call me Joe Joe*
English, Karen. *Nadia's hands*
Ernst, Lisa Campbell. *Bubba and Trixie*
Faulkner, Keith. *The puzzled penguin*
Fierstein, Harvey. *The sissy duckling*
Fitzhugh, Louise. *I am five*
    I am three
Foreman, Michael. *Panda's puzzle, and his voyage of discovery*
Fox, Mem. *The straight line wonder*
Fujikawa, Gyo. *See what I can be!*
Gauch, Patricia Lee. *Presenting Tanya, the Ugly Duckling*
Geraghty, Paul. *The hoppameleon*
Gibson, Kari Smalley. *Mooki's secret*
Gifford, Kathie Lee. *Moochie's surprise*
Girard, Linda Walvoord. *My body is private*
Glen, Maggie. *Ruby to the rescue*
Goldin, Barbara Diamond. *Cakes and miracles*
Gordon, David. *The ugly truckling*
Gordon, Gaelyn. *Duckat*
Grambling, Lois G. *The witch who wanted to be a princess*
Grant, Rose Marie. *Andiamo, Weasel*
Graves, Keith. *Loretta, ace Pinky Scout*
Green, Stephanie. *Not just another moose*
Green-Armytage, Stephen. *Dudley, the little terrier that could*
Greenburg, Dan. *Through the medicine cabinet*
Gregorowski, Christopher. *Fly, eagle, fly!*
Gregory, Valiska. *A Valentine for Norman Noggs*
Grimes, Nikki. *My man Blue*
Gwynne, Fred. *Pondlarker*
Hallinan, P. K. (Patrick K.). *I know I belong*
    I know who I am
    I'm glad to be me

Where's Michael?
Harsh, Fred. *Alfie*
Hartman, Bob. *The one and only Delgado Cheese*
Harvey, Amanda. *Dog-eared*
Hasler, Eveline. *The giantess*
Havill, Juanita. *Jamaica and the substitute teacher*
Hayles, Marsha. *A pet of a pet*
Heide, Florence Parry. *The bigness contest*
Hellings, Colette. *Too little, too big*
Hellman, Gary. *The karate way*
Henderson, Alicia Terry. *Call me black, call me beautiful*
Hest, Amy. *You're the boss, Baby Duck*
Hines, Anna Grossnickle. *All by myself*
Hoban, Russell. *A near thing for Captain Najork*
Hodge, Deborah. *Emma's story*
Hoffman, Mary. *Amazing Grace*
Holman, Sandy Lynne. *Grandpa, is everything black bad?*
Howard, Arthur. *Cosmo zooms*
Hubbard, Woodleigh Marx. *All that you are*
Inkpen, Mick. *Nothing*
Irbinskas, Heather. *How Jackrabbit got his very long ears*
Jagtenberg, Yvonne. *Jack the wolf*
Jennings, Linda M. *Tom's tail*
Johnston, Deborah. *Mathew Michael's beastly day*
Joly, Fanny. *Mr. Fine, porcupine*
Joslin, Mary. *The shore beyond*
Kaiser Johnson, Lee. *If I ran the family*
Karlin, Nurit. *Little big mouse*
    A train for the king
Keats, Ezra Jack. *Peter's chair*
    Whistle for Willie
Keller, Holly. *Horace*
King-Smith, Dick. *The spotty pig*
Kirk, Daniel. *Bigger*
Kirk, David. *Little bird, Biddle bird*
Koski, Mary. *Impatient Pamela asks, "Why are my feet so huge?"*
    Impatient Pamela wants a bigger family
Krauss, Ruth. *The carrot seed*
Kroll, Virginia L. *Boy, you're amazing!*
    The Christmas cow
Kuskin, Karla. *What did you bring me?*
Lane, Megan Halsey. *Something to crow about*
Lawrence, Michael (Michael C.). *The caterpillar that roared*
Leaf, Munro. *Noodle*
Lewis, Jacqueline Janette. *You are so wonderful*
Lewis, Paul Owen. *Grasper*
Lionni, Leo. *Mr. McMouse*
    Pezzettino
Lipkind, William. *The little tiny rooster*
Lipson, Beth Weiner. *Benjamin's perfect solution*
Lithgow, John. *Marsupial Sue*
Lobel, Gillian. *Does anybody love me?*
Loomans, Diane. *The lovables in the kingdom of self-esteem*
Lovell, Patty. *Stand tall, Molly Lou Melon*
Lozoff, Bo. *The wonderful life of a fly who couldn't fly*
Lucado, Max. *You are mine*
Lundy, Charlotte. *Thank you, Esther*
McAllister, Angela. *The enchanted flute*
McCaughrean, Geraldine. *How the reindeer got their antlers*
MacDonald, Allan. *The pig in a wig*
McKee, David. *Elmer and the kangaroo*
McKissack, Robert L. *Try your best*
Maloney, Peter (1955–). *His mother's nose*
Mangan, Anne. *Browny, the smallest bear of all*
Manson, Ainslie. *Ballerinas don't wear glasses*
Markes, Julie. *Good thing you're not an octopus!*
Martín Larrañaga, Ana. *The big wide-mouthed frog*
May, Kara. *Joe Lion's big boots*
Medearis, Angela Shelf. *Annie's gifts*
Medearis, Michael. *Daisy and the doll*
Milios, Rita. *Yo soy = I am*
Mills, Joyce C. *Little Tree*
Milway, Katie Smith. *Cappuccina goes to town*
Minarik, Else Holmelund. *Am I beautiful?*
Monks, Lydia. *The cat barked?*
Monnier, Miriam. *Just right*
Moss, Marissa. *But not Kate*

Regina's big mistake
Mueller, Doris L. *Small One's adventure*
Munsch, Robert N. *Makeup mess*
Murphy, Jill. *A piece of cake*
Nishimura, Kae. *Dinah*
Nolan, Lucy A. *Jack Quack*
O'Donnell, Elizabeth Lee. *Patrick's day*
Oram, Hiawyn. *Just Dog*
    The wrong overcoat
Palmer, Mary Babcock. *No-sort-of-animal*
Parr, Todd. *The okay book*
Pearson, Susan. *Lenore's big break*
Peet, Bill (William Bartlett). *Pamela Camel*
Petty, Dini. *The queen, the bear and the bumblebee*
Pfister, Marcus. *Just the way you are*
Polisar, Barry Louis. *The trouble with Ben*
Prater, John. *The greatest show on earth*
Purdy, Carol. *Least of all*
Raschka, Christopher. *Arlene sardine*
    Waffle
Richardson, Jean. *Tall inside*
Richardson, John. *Grunt*
Robertson, Janet. *Oscar's spots*
Roe, Eileen. *All I am*
Rotner, Shelley. *What can you do?*
Rubin, C. M. *Eleanor, Ellatony, Ellencake, and me*
Rühmann, Karl. *Filbert flies*
Sadler, Marilyn. *It's not easy being a bunny*
Savageau, Cheryl. *Muskrat will be swimming*
Scamell, Ragnhild. *Who likes Wolfie?*
Schneider, Christine M. *Picky Mrs. Pickle*
Schreck, Karen Halvorsen. *Lucy's family tree*
Schroeder, Binette. *Laura*
Schwarz, Viviane. *The adventures of a nose*
Serfozo, Mary. *A head is for hats*
Seuss, Dr. *Oh, the places you'll go!*
Sharmat, Marjorie Weinman. *I'm terrific*
    Taking care of Melvin
    The 329th friend
Shields, Carol Diggory. *I am really a princess*
Shipton, Jonathan. *What if?*
Shott, Steve (Stephen). *Look at me*
Simon, Norma. *All kinds of children*
    Why am I different?
Skulavik, Mary Alys. *Bert*
Slobodkin, Louis. *Magic Michael*
Smalls-Hector, Irene. *Louise's gift*
Smith, Lane. *Pinocchio, the boy*
Stadler, John. *Ready, set, go!*
Steers, Billy. *Tractor Mac*
Stockton, Frank Richard. *The bee-man of Orn*
Stren, Patti. *Mountain Rose*
Supraner, Robyn. *Would you rather be a tiger?*
Swanson, Susan Marie. *The first thing my mama told me*
Talbott, Hudson. *Going Hollywood! A dinosaur's dream*
Talley, Carol. *Clarissa*
Terry, Michael. *Rhino's horns*
Thompson, Kay. *Kay Thompson's Eloise's what I absolutely love love love*
Titherington, Jeanne. *Big world, small world*
Tobias, Tobi. *Jane wishing*
Tooinsky, Izzi. *The turkey prince*
Turnage, Sheila. *Trout the magnificent*
Turner, Sandy. *Otto's trunk*
Tusa, Tricia. *Chicken*
    Libby's new glasses
Udry, Janice May. *How I faded away*
Vries, Anke de. *Grey mouse*
Waber, Bernard. *"You look ridiculous," said the rhinoceros to the hippopotamus*
Wagner, Karen. *Silly Fred*
Wallace, John. *The twins*
Weedn, Flavia. *The enchanted tree*
Weigelt, Udo. *Old Beaver*
White, Amanda. *Rip and Rap*
Williams, Barbara. *Donna Jean's disaster*
Wilson, Gina. *Ignis*

Oxenbury, Helen. *I see*
Pluckrose, Henry Arthur. *Seeing*
  Things we see
Quigley, Lillian Fox. *The blind men and the elephant*
Raskin, Ellen. *Spectacles*
Rauzon, Mark J. *Eyes and ears*
Reuter, Margaret. *My mother is blind*
Sargent, Susan. *My favorite place*
Saxe, John Godfrey. *The blind men and the elephant*
Shecter, Ben. *The stocking child*
Showers, Paul. *Look at your eyes*
Smith, Lane. *Glasses . . . who needs 'em?*
Thayer, Jane. *Mr. Turtle's magic glasses*
Thomson, Ruth. *Eyes*
Tusa, Tricia. *Libby's new glasses*
Wright, Lillian. *Seeing*
Yolen, Jane. *The seeing stick*
Young, Ed (Edward). *Seven blind mice*

Senses – smell

Aliki. *My five senses*
Allen, Jonathan. *Mucky moose*
Allington, Richard L. *Smelling*
Borten, Helen. *Do you know what I know?*
Brenner, Barbara A. *Faces, faces, faces*
Cole, Babette. *The smelly book*
Doughtie, Charles. *Gabriel Wrinkles, the bloodhound who couldn't smell*
Fair, David. *The fabulous four skunks*
Fowler, Allan. *Smelling things*
Gackenbach, Dick. *Barker's crime*
Gordon, Sharon. *Smelling*
Hartley, Karen. *Smelling in living things*
Jaynes, Ruth M. *Melinda's Christmas stocking*
Kajikawa, Kimiko. *Yoshi's feast*
Keillor, Garrison. *The old man who loved cheese*
Knutson, Kimberley. *Ska-tat!*
Lionni, Leo. *What?*
Moncure, Jane Belk. *What your nose knows!*
Nelson, Robin. *Smelling*
Nikly, Michelle. *The perfume of memory*
Perkins, Al. *The nose book*
Pluckrose, Henry Arthur. *Smelling*
Posthuma, Sieb. *Benny*
Rose, Gerald. *Scruff*
Saunders, Susan. *A sniff in time*
Southwell, Jandelyn. *The little country town*
Wright, Lillian. *Smelling and tasting*

Senses – taste

Aliki. *My five senses*
Allington, Richard L. *Tasting*
Bonsignore, Joan. *Stick out your tongue*
Borten, Helen. *Do you know what I know?*
Brenner, Barbara A. *Faces, faces, faces*
Fowler, Allan. *Tasting things*
Hartley, Karen. *Tasting in living things*
Jaynes, Ruth M. *Melinda's Christmas stocking*
Lionni, Leo. *What?*
Moncure, Jane Belk. *A tasting party*
Nelson, Robin. *Tasting*
Pluckrose, Henry Arthur. *Tasting*
Wright, Lillian. *Smelling and tasting*

Senses – touch

Adoff, Arnold. *Touch the poem*
Aliki. *My five senses*
Allington, Richard L. *Touching*
Becker, Bonny. *Tickly prickly*
Borten, Helen. *Do you know what I know?*
Brenner, Barbara A. *Faces, faces, faces*
Brown, Marcia. *Touch will tell*
Carle, Eric. *My very first book of touch*
Fowler, Allan. *Feeling things*

Gibson, Myra Tomback. *What is your favorite thing to touch?*
Hartley, Karen. *Touching in living things*
Isadora, Rachel. *I touch*
Jaynes, Ruth M. *Melinda's Christmas stocking*
Lionni, Leo. *What?*
Moncure, Jane Belk. *The touch book*
Nelson, Robin. *Touching*
Oliver, Stephen. *Touch*
Otto, Carolyn. *I can tell by touching*
Oxenbury, Helen. *I touch*
Pluckrose, Henry Arthur. *Things we touch*
  Touching
Sherman, Joanne. *Because it's my body*
Wright, Lillian. *Touching*
Yates, Irene. *All about touch*

Serbia *see* Foreign lands – Serbia

Service animals *see* Animals – service animals

Sewing *see* Activities – sewing

Sex instruction

Allan, Nicholas. *Where Willy went*
Brown, Laurie Krasny. *What's the big secret?*
Collard, Sneed B. *Making animal babies*

Sex roles *see* Gender roles

Sextuplets *see* Multiple births – sextuplets

Shadows

Anno, Mitsumasa. *Anno's sundial*
  In shadowland
Asch, Frank. *Bear shadow*
Bartalos, Michael. *Shadowville*
Berger, Barbara Helen. *The jewel heart*
Bond, Felicia. *Wake up, Vladimir*
Bulla, Clyde Robert. *What makes a shadow?*
Calmenson, Stephanie. *Kinderkittens, show-and-tell*
Cendrars, Blaise. *Shadow*
Chorao, Kay. *Shadow night*
Christelow, Eileen. *Henry and the dragon*
De Regniers, Beatrice Schenk. *The shadow book*
Dodd, Anne Westcott. *Footprints and shadows*
Dorros, Arthur. *Me and my shadow*
Farber, Norma. *Return of the shadows*
Freeman, Don. *Gregory's Shadow*
Gackenbach, Dick. *Barker's crime*
  Mr. Wink and his shadow, Ned
Goor, Ron. *Shadows*
Gore, Sheila. *My shadow*
Haseley, Dennis. *Ghost catcher*
Hoban, Tana. *Shadows and reflections*
Holderness, Jackie. *What is a shadow?*
Kent, Jack. *The biggest shadow in the zoo*
Lewin, Betsy. *Groundhog day*
MacDonald, Amy. *Quentin Fenton Herter three*
McHargue, Georgess. *Private zoo*
Mahy, Margaret. *The boy with two shadows*
Marol, Jean-Claude. *Vagabul and his shadow*
Michaels, William. *Clare and her shadow*
Narahashi, Keiko. *I have a friend*
Olofsdotter, Marie. *Sofia and the Heartmender*
Robison, Nancy. *Ten tall soldiers*
Rosenberg, Liz. *Grandmother and the runaway shadow*
Severn, Jeffrey. *George and his giant shadow*
Simon, Seymour. *Shadow magic*
Swinburne, Stephen R. *Guess whose shadow?*
Tompert, Ann. *Nothing sticks like a shadow*
Van Nutt, Julia. *The monster in the shadows*
Walter, Mildred Pitts. *Darkness*
Welling, Peter J. *Andrew McGroundhog and his shady shadow*
Willard, Nancy. *Shadow story*

Winter, Susan. *My shadow*
Zemke, Deborah. *The shadow of Matilda Hunt*

Shakers *see* Ethnic groups in the U.S. – Shakers

Shakespeare

Freeman, Don. *Will's quill*

Shape *see* Concepts – shape

Shaped books *see* Format, unusual

Sharing *see* Behavior – sharing

Sharks *see* Fish – sharks

Shavuot *see* Holidays – Shavuot

Shawnee Indians *see* Indians of North America – Shawnee

Sheep *see* Animals – sheep

Shells *see* Sea & seashore

Shepherds *see* Careers – shepherds

Sheriffs *see* Careers – sheriffs

Ships *see* Boats, ships

Shirts *see* Clothing – shirts

Shopping

Allard, Harry. *I will not go to market today*
Anholt, Catherine. *Truffles in trouble*
Ardizzone, Edward. *The little girl and the tiny doll*
Armitage, Ronda. *Harry hates shopping!*
Arnold, Caroline. *What will we buy?*
Baggette, Susan K. *Jonathan goes to the grocery store*
Bates, Artie Ann. *Ragsale*
Baugh, Dolores M. *Supermarket*
Bertrand, Cécile. *Let's pretend!*
Birchall, Mark. *Hen goes shopping*
Birdseye, Tom. *Soap! Soap! Don't forget the soap!*
Black, Irma (Simonton). *The little old man who could not read*
Bond, Michael. *Paddington's lucky day*
Bradman, Tony. *Dilly speaks up*
    Wait and see
Brenner, Barbara A. *Somebody's slippers, somebody's shoes*
Bulion, Leslie. *Fatuma's new cloth*
Bunting, Eve (Anne Evelyn). *Market day*
Burningham, John. *The shopping basket*
Butterworth, Nick. *Just like Jasper*
    When we go shopping
Calmenson, Stephanie. *The birthday hat*
Cass, Joan E. *The cats go to market*
Chase, Catherine. *Baby mouse goes shopping*
Chen, Chih-Yuan. *On my way to buy eggs*
Chorao, Kay. *Molly's Moe*
Claverie, Jean. *Shopping*
Cocca-Leffler, Maryann. *Bus route to Boston*
Cousins, Lucy. *Maisy goes shopping*
Daly, Niki. *Mama, papa and baby Joe*
    Not so fast Songololo
Day, Alexandra. *Carl goes shopping*
Dodds, Dayle Ann. *The Kettles get new clothes*
Edens, Cooper. *The Animal Mall*
Edwards, Linda Strauss. *The downtown day*
Enderle, Judith (Ann) Ross. *What would Mama do?*
Faulkner, Keith. *Sam helps out*
Flanagan, Alice K. *A busy day at Mr. Kang's grocery store*
Fyleman, Rose. *A fairy went a-marketing*

Garland, Sarah. *Going shopping*
Gershator, Phillis. *Sweet, sweet fig banana*
Gill, Shelley. *The big buck adventure*
Gretz, Susanna. *Teddy bears go shopping*
Greydanus, Rose. *Susie goes shopping*
Grossman, Bill. *Tommy at the grocery store*
Grossman, Patricia. *Saturday market*
Guzzo, Sandra E. *Fox and Heggie*
Hamm, Diane Johnston. *Laney's lost momma*
Hastings, Evelyn Beilhart. *The department store*
Hines, Anna Grossnickle. *Don't worry, I'll find you*
Hutchins, Pat. *Don't forget the bacon!*
Ichikawa, Satomi. *Suzanne and Nicholas at the market*
Johnson, Marion. *Caillou, new shoes*
Kilroy, Sally. *Market day*
Leblanc, Anne. *Shopping with Benjamin*
Leonard, Marcia. *No new pants!*
    Shopping for snowflakes
Lindbergh, Reeve. *The awful aardvarks shop for school*
Lobel, Arnold. *On Market Street*
London, Jonathan. *Ali, child of the desert*
Loomis, Christine. *At the mall*
Maccarone, Grace. *I shop with my daddy*
McPhail, David M. *The cereal box*
Martin, David. *Five little piggies*
Maschler, Fay. *T. G. and Moonie go shopping*
Mother Goose. *To market! To market!*, ill. by Emma Lillian Brock
Munsch, Robert N. *Something good*
    Where is Gah-Ning?
Murphy, Stuart J. *Just enough carrots*
Nethery, Mary. *Orange cat goes to market*
Newcome, Zita. *Rosie goes shopping*
Oliver, Stephen. *Shopping*
Oxenbury, Helen. *The shopping trip*
    Tom and Pippo go shopping
Patz, Nancy. *Pumpernickel tickle and mean green cheese*
Potter, Beatrix. *The tale of Little Pig Robinson*
Prater, John. *"No!" said Joe*
Pratt, Pierre. *Shopping*
Rader, Laura. *Santa's new suit*
Rice, Eve. *New blue shoes*
Rockwell, Anne F. *The supermarket*
Ross, Christine. *Lily and the present*
Rubel, Nicole. *Goldie*
Russell, Betty. *Big store, funny door*
Russo, Marisabina. *Mama talks too much*
Shaw, Nancy (Nancy E.). *Sheep in a shop*
Shohet, Marti. *Market days*
Shopping
Smith, Barry. *Tom and Annie go shopping*
Solomon, Joan. *A present for Mum*
Spier, Peter. *Food market*
Thayer, Tanya. *Spending money*
Winn, Chris. *My day*
Wood, Don. *Merry Christmas, big hungry bear*
Yardley, Thompson. *Buy now, pay later*
Ziefert, Harriet. *Bear goes shopping*
Zinnemann-Hope, Pam. *Let's go shopping, Ned*

Shops *see* Stores

Shoshone Indians *see* Indians of North America – Shoshone

Shows *see* Theater

Shrews *see* Animals – shrews

Shrimp *see* Crustaceans – shrimp

Shyness *see* Character traits – shyness

Siam *see* Foreign lands – Thailand

Siberia *see* Foreign lands – Siberia

Sibling rivalry

Adoff, Arnold. *Hard to be six*
Aitken, Amy. *Wanda's circus*
Alexander, Martha G. *I'll be the horse if you'll play with me*
  Marty McGee's space lab, no girls allowed
  Nobody asked me if I wanted a baby sister
  When the new baby comes, I'm moving out
Allen, Pamela. *Hidden treasure*
Alter, Anna. *Estelle and Lucy*
Amoss, Berthe. *It's not your birthday*
  Tom in the middle
Anholt, Catherine. *Aren't you lucky!*
Armitage, Ronda. *The bossing of Josie*
Arnstein, Helene S. *Billy and our new baby*
Bach, Alice. *The smartest bear and his brother Oliver*
Baker, Betty. *My sister says*
Baker, Charlotte. *Little brother*
Bassett, Lisa. *Koala Christmas*
Bedford, David. *Ella's games*
Beecroft, John. *What? Another cat!*
Benson, Ellen. *Philip's little sister*
Berenstain, Stan. *The Berenstain bears and the double dare*
  The Berenstain bears get in a fight
Bernhard, Emery. *Spotted Eagle and Black Crow*
Bider, Djemma. *A drop of honey*
Blume, Judy. *The Pain and The Great One*
Blumenthal, Deborah. *Don't let the peas touch!*
Bond, Felicia. *Poinsettia and her family*
Bottner, Barbara. *Big boss! Little boss!*
  Jungle day
Bourgeois, Paulette. *Franklin and Harriet*
Boyd, Lizi. *Sam is my half brother*
Bradman, Tony. *Dilly speaks up*
  Brothers and sisters are like that!
Brown, Marc Tolon. *D. W. all wet*
Bruna, Dick. *Dick Bruna's Cinderella*
Buchanan, Heather S. *Emily Mouse's garden*
Bulla, Clyde Robert. *Keep running, Allen!*
Bullock, Kathleen. *A surprise for Mitzi Mouse*
Byrne, David. *Stay up late*
Caines, Jeannette. *Abby*
Carlson, Nancy L. *Harriet and Walt*
  Louanne Pig in the perfect family
Carlstrom, Nancy White. *Kiss your sister, Rose Marie*
Caseley, Judith. *Silly baby*
Castiglia, Julie. *Jill the pill*
Chalmers, Audrey. *Fancy be good*
Chenery, Janet. *Wolfie*
Chorao, Kay. *George told Kate*
Cinderella
Clarke, Gus. *Along came Eric*
Cleary, Beverly. *Janet's thingamajigs*
Clifton, Lucille. *My brother fine with me*
Climo, Shirley. *The Egyptian Cinderella*
  The Korean Cinderella
  The Persian Cinderella
Coburn, Jewell Reinhart. *Angkat*
  Jouanah
Cole, Joanna. *The new baby at your house*
Conaway, Judith. *I'll get even*
Conta, Marcia Maher. *Feelings between brothers and sisters*
Cooke, Trish. *When I grow bigger*
Cooper, Helen (Helen F.). *Little monster did it!*
Corey, Dorothy. *Will there be a lap for me?*
Cottringer, Anne. *Ella and the naughty lion*
Cousins, Lucy. *Za-Za's baby brother*
Croft, Priscilla. *Dealing with jealousy*
Crowley, Arthur. *Bonzo Beaver*
Cutler, Jane. *Darcy and Gran don't like babies*
Daly, Jude. *Fair, Brown & Trembling*
Daly, Niki. *Look at me!*
Davies, Gill. *Wilbur waited*
De Hamel, Joan. *Hemi's pet*
Delaney, Molly. *My sister*
De Lynam, Alicia Garcia. *It's mine!*
Dewan, Ted. *Crispin and the 3 little piglets*

Dragonwagon, Crescent. *I hate my brother Harry*
  I hate my sister Maggie
Drescher, Joan E. *The birth-order blues*
  The marvelous mess
Dubanevich, Arlene. *Pig William*
Dubois, Claude K. *He's my jumbo!*
Duncan, Lois. *Giving away Suzanne*
Edelman, Elaine. *I love my baby sister (most of the time)*
Ehrlich, Amy. *Bunnies at Christmastime*
  Bunnies on their own
Engel, Diana. *Josephina, the great collector*
Etherington, Frank. *The spaghetti word race*
Fair, Sylvia. *The bedspread*
Fife, Dale. *Rosa's special garden*
Fisher, Iris L. *Katie-Bo*
Franklin, Jonathan. *Don't wake the baby*
Galbraith, Kathryn Osebold. *Katie did!*
  Roommates
Gauch, Patricia Lee. *Christina Katerina and the time she quit the family*
Geras, Adèle. *Sleeping beauty*
Gewing, Lisa. *Mama, daddy, baby and me*
Gili, Phillida. *Fanny and Charles*
Ginsburg, Mirra. *Two greedy bears*
Graham, Richard. *Jack and the monster*
Greene, Carol. *Hinny Winny Bunco*
Greenfield, Eloise. *She come bringing me that little baby girl*
Grimm, Jacob. *Cinderella*, ill. by Nonny Hogrogian
  Cinderella, ill. by Svend Otto S
Hamilton, Morse. *Big sisters are bad witches*
  Little sister for sale
  My name is Emily
Hänel, Wolfram. *Little elephant runs away*
Harper, Anita. *It's not fair!*
Hazen, Barbara Shook. *If it weren't for Benjamin (I'd always get to lick the icing spoon)*
  Why couldn't I be an only kid like you, Wigger?
Heckman, Philip. *Waking upside down*
Hedderwick, Mairi. *Katie Morag and the tiresome Ted*
Heide, Florence Parry. *Oh, grow up!*
Heller, Nicholas. *An adventure at sea*
Helmering, Doris Wild. *We're going to have a baby*
Henkes, Kevin. *Julius, the baby of the world*
Henriod, Lorraine. *Grandma's wheelchair*
Hines, Anna Grossnickle. *They really like me!*
Hoban, Lillian. *Arthur's pen pal*
Hoban, Russell. *A baby sister for Frances*
  The battle of Zormla
  The great gum drop robbery
  Some snow said hello
  They came from Aargh!
Holabird, Katharine. *Angelina's baby sister*
Hooker, Ruth. *Sara loves her big brother*
Hoopes, Lyn Littlefield. *When I was little*
Hurwitz, Johanna. *Russell's secret*
Hutchins, H. J. (Hazel J.). *Katie's babbling brother*
Hutchins, Pat. *The very worst monster*
Itaya, Satoshi. *Buttons and Bo*
Jacobs, Kate. *A sister's wish*
Johnston, Tony. *I'm gonna tell mama I want an iguana*
  Slither McCreep and his brother, Joe
Jonell, Lynne. *It's my birthday, too!*
Joosse, Barbara M. *I love you the purplest*
Joyce, William. *Santa calls*
Kassirer, Sue. *Joseph and his coat of many colors*
Keller, Holly. *Geraldine first*
  Geraldine's baby brother
  Too big
Kiser, SuAnn. *The catspring somersault flying one-handed flip-flop*
Knight, Hilary. *Hilary Knight's Cinderella*
Knight, Joan. *Opal in the closet*
Knox-Wagner, Elaine. *The oldest kid*
Koller, Jackie French. *Baby for sale*
Kroll, Steven. *The squirrels' Thanksgiving*
Lacoe, Addie. *Just not the same*
Lakin, Pat (Patricia). *Don't touch my room*
  Oh, brother!

Siblings *see* Family life – brothers; Family life – brothers & sisters; Family life – sisters; Family life – stepfamilies

Sickness *see* Health & fitness; Illness

Sight *see* Anatomy – eyes; Glasses; Handicaps – blindness; Senses – sight

Sign language

Acredolo, Linda P. *My first baby signs*
Baker, Pamela J. *My first book of sign*
Bove, Linda. *Sign language ABC with Linda Bove*
Chaplin, Susan Gibbons. *I can sign my ABCs*
Greenberg, Judith E. *What is the sign for friend?*
Millman, Isaac. *Moses goes to a concert*
Moore, Clement Clarke. *The night before Christmas in signed English*
Mother Goose. *Nursery rhymes from Mother Goose in signed English*
Uhlberg, Myron. *The printer*
Sesame Street. *Sesame Street sign language fun*
Waller, Curt. *Baby's first signs*
    More baby's first signs
Wheeler, Cindy. *More simple signs*
    Simple signs
Winnie-the-Pooh's ABC

Sign painters *see* Careers – sign painters

Signs & signboards

Slawson, Michele Benoit. *Signs for sale*

Siksika Indians *see* Indians of North America – Siksika

Singers *see* Careers – opera singers; Careers – singers

Singing *see* Activities – singing

Single-parent families *see* Family life – single-parent families

Sioux Indians *see* Indians of North America – Cheyenne (Sioux); Indians of North America – Dakota (Sioux); Indians of North America – Sioux

Sisters *see* Family life; Family life – brothers; Family life – brothers & sisters; Family life – sisters; Sibling rivalry

Size *see* Concepts – size

Skateboarding *see* Sports – skateboarding

Skating *see* Sports – ice skating; Sports – hockey; Sports – roller skating

Skeletons *see* Anatomy – skeletons

Skiing *see* Sports – skiing

Skin *see* Anatomy – skin

Skin diving *see* Sports – skin diving

Skunks *see* Animals – skunks

Sky

Asch, Frank. *Starbaby*
Belting, Natalia Maree. *The sun is a golden earring*
Birdseye, Tom. *A song of stars*
Branley, Franklyn M. (Mansfield). *Comets*
    The sky is full of stars

Carle, Eric. *Little cloud*
    Little cloud [board book]
Carlstrom, Nancy White. *What does the sky say?*
Conway, Diana Cohen. *Northern lights*
Dalton, Anne. *Prince Starr*
Dayrell, Elphinstone. *Why the sun and the moon live in the sky*
Dayton, Mona. *Earth and sky*
Dee, Ruby. *Tower to heaven*
Dewey, Ariane. *The sky*
Gerson, Mary-Joan. *Why the sky is far away*
Glyman, Caroline A. *What's above the sky?*
Hines, Anna Grossnickle. *Sky all around*
Hopkinson, Deborah. *Maria's comet*
Ichikawa, Satomi. *Nora's stars*
Jacobson, Jennifer Richard. *A net of stars*
London, Jonathan. *Let the lynx come in*
Moroney, Lynn. *Elinda who danced in the sky*
Osborne, Mary Pope. *Moonhorse*, ill. by David McPhail
    Moonhorse, ill. by S. M. Saelig
Otto, Carolyn. *That sky, that rain*
Oughton, Jerrie. *How the stars fell into the sky*
Pinczes, Elinor J. *Arctic fives arrive*
Rosen, Sidney. *Where's the big dipper?*
Sabuda, Robert James. *The Blizzard's robe*
Schoberle, Ceile. *Beyond the Milky Way*
Shaw, Charles Green. *It looked like spilt milk*
Spier, Peter. *Dreams*
Standiford, Natalie. *Dollhouse mouse*
Stone, Kazuko G. *Goodnight Twinklegator*
Taylor, Harriet Peck. *Ulaq and the northern lights*
Taylor, Jane. *Twinkle, twinkle little star*, ill. by Heather Collins
    Twinkle, twinkle, little star, ill. by Michael Hague
    Twinkle, twinkle little star, ill. by Julia Noonan
Waboose, Jan Bourdeau. *SkySisters*
Wyler, Rose. *The starry sky*

Slavery

Altman, Linda Jacobs. *The legend of Freedom Hill*
Benjamin, Anne. *Young Harriet Tubman*
Bible. Old Testament. Joseph. *Joseph and his brothers*
Coleman, Evelyn. *To be a drum*
Dupré, Rick. *Agassu*
Edwards, Pamela Duncan. *Barefoot*
Gerrard, Roy. *The Roman twins*
Grifalconi, Ann. *The village that vanished*
Hathorn, Libby (Elizabeth). *Sky sash so blue*
Hopkinson, Deborah. *Sweet Clara and the freedom quilt*
Johnson, D. B. (Donald B.). *Henry climbs a mountain*
Johnson, Dolores. *Now let me fly*
    Seminole diary
Johnson, James Weldon. *Lift ev'ry voice and sing*
Johnston, Tony. *The wagon*
Lilly, Melinda. *From slavery to freedom*
McGhee, Alison. *In the hollow of your hand*
McGill, Alice. *Molly Bannaky*
Medearis, Angela Shelf. *The freedom riddle*
Miller, Robert H. (Robert Henry). *The story of Nat Love*
Miller, William. *Frederick Douglass*
Monjo, F. N. *The drinking gourd*
Nelson, Vaunda Micheaux. *Almost to freedom*
Nolen, Jerdine. *Big Jabe*
Pinkney, Andrea Davis. *Dear Benjamin Banneker*
Riggio, Anita. *Secret signs*
Ringgold, Faith. *The invisible princesses*
Rochelle, Belinda. *Jewels*
Sanders, Scott R. (Scott Russell). *A place called Freedom*
Siegelson, Kim L. *In the time of the drums*
Smalls-Hector, Irene. *Irene Jennie and the Christmas masquerade*
    Jenny Reen and the Jack Muh Lantern
Stroud, Bettye. *The leaving*
    The patchwork path
Uchida, Yoshiko. *The bracelet*
Weatherford, Carole Boston. *Juneteenth jamboree*
Winter, Jeanette. *Follow the drinking gourd*
Wright, Courtni Crump. *Journey to freedom*
    Jumping the broom

Sledding *see* Sports – sledding

Sleep

Alexander, Martha G. *I'll protect you from the jungle beasts*
Allen, Jonathan. *Wake up, Sleeping Beauty*
Andersen, H. C. (Hans Christian). *The princess and the pea*, ill. by Emily Bolam
  The princess and the pea, ill. by Charlene Delage
  The princess and the pea, ill. by Dorothée Duntze
  The princess and the pea, ill. by Dick Gackenbach
  The princess and the pea, ill. by Paul Galdone
  The princess and the pea, ill. by Camille Semelet
  The princess and the pea, ill. by Janet Stevens
  The princess and the pea, ill. by Suçie Stevenson
  The princess and the pea, ill. by Eve Tharlet
Apperley, Dawn. *Don't wake the baby*
Arnold, Caroline. *Sleepytime for zoo animals*
Arnold, Tedd. *Five ugly monsters*
Asch, Frank. *Good night, Baby Bear*
Asher, Sandy. *Princess Bee and the royal good-night story*
Aylesworth, Jim. *The bad dream*
  Tonight's the night
Bach, Alice. *The smartest bear and his brother Oliver*
Banks, Kate (Katherine A.). *Close your eyes*
Bauer, Marion Dane. *Sleep, little one, sleep*
Baum, Louis. *I want to see the moon*
Beckman, Kaj. *Lisa cannot sleep*
Bergen, Lara Rice. *Washington Irving's Rip Van Winkle*
Bergman, Mara. *Musical beds*
Bertrand, Lynne. *Dragon naps*
Bilezikian, Gary. *While I slept*
Black, Charles C. *The royal nap*
Blomgren, Jennifer. *Where do I sleep?*
Bottner, Barbara. *There was nobody there*
Brande, Marlie. *Sleepy Nicholas*
Branford, Henrietta. *Little Pig Figwort can't get to sleep*
Bright, Robert. *Me and the bears*
Brown, Margaret Wise. *A child's good night book*
  The Golden sleepy book
  Sheep don't count sheep
  Sleepy ABC
  The sleepy little lion
  The sleepy men
Brown, Myra Berry. *First night away from home*
Bunting, Eve (Anne Evelyn). *No nap*
Burstein, Fred. *Rebecca's nap*
Burton, Jane. *Animals at rest*
Butler, John. *Hush, little ones*
  While you were sleeping
Calhoun, Mary. *While I sleep*
Camp, Lindsay. *The biggest bed in the world*
Carlstrom, Nancy White. *No nap for Benjamin Badger*
Carman, William. *What's that noise?*
Carpenter, Mary-Chapin. *Dreamland*
Caseley, Judith. *Slumber party!*
  Sophie and Sammy's library sleepover
Cazet, Denys. *I'm not sleepy*
  Mother night
Chalmers, Mary. *Take a nap, Harry*
Child, Lauren. *My dream bed*
Chislett, Gail. *Whump*
Chorao, Kay. *Lester's overnight*
Ciardi, John. *Scrappy, the pup*
Clise, Michele Durkson. *Ophelia's bedtime book*
Coker, Gylbert. *Naptime*
Collard, Sneed B. *Animals asleep*
Collington, Peter. *Little pickle*
Crossley-Holland, Kevin. *Sleeping Nanna*
Dale, Penny. *Ten out of bed*
Daly, Niki. *Mary Malloy and the baby who wouldn't sleep*
De Paola, Tomie (Thomas Anthony). *Fight the night*
  When everyone was fast asleep
De Vries, Maggie. *How sleep found Tabitha*
Dodd, Lynley. *Wake up, bear*
Dowling, Paul. *Are you sleepy, Puff?*
Downey, Lynn. *The flea's sneeze*

  The drowsy hours
Dupasquier, Philippe. *I can't sleep*
Edwards, Patricia Kier. *Chester and Uncle Willoughby*
Edwards, Richard. *Good night, Copycub*
Edwards, Roberta. *Anna Bear's first winter*
Elkin, Benjamin. *The king who could not sleep*
Esbensen, Barbara Juster. *The dream mouse*
Evans, Eva Knox. *Sleepy time*
Facklam, Margery. *I go to sleep*
Farber, Werner. *Night lion*
Feldman, Eve B. *Animals don't wear pajamas*
Fernandes, Eugenie. *Sleepy little mouse*
Field, Eugene. *Wynken, Blynken and Nod*, ill. by Barbara Cooney
  Wynken, Blynken and Nod, ill. by Susan Jeffers
  Wynken, Blynken and Nod, ill. by Holly Johnson
  Wynken, Blynken and Nod, ill. by Johanna Westerman
Foreman, Michael. *Dad! I can't sleep*
Fox, Mem. *Night noises*
  Sleepy bears
Frampton, David. *The whole night through*
Gamble, Isobel. *Who's that?*
Geras, Adèle. *Sleep tight, Ginger Kitten*
Gerber, Carole. *Arctic dreams*
Gilmour, H. B. *Why Wembley Fraggle couldn't sleep*
Goodman, Joan Elizabeth. *Bernard's nap*
Grambling, Lois G. *Night sounds*
Grejniec, Michael. *Albert's nap*
Gretz, Susanna. *I'm not sleepy*
Grey, Mini. *The very smart pea and the princess-to-be*
Grimm, Jacob. *The sleeping beauty*, ill. by Warwick Hutton
  The sleeping beauty, ill. by Trina Schart Hyman
  The sleeping beauty, ill. by Monika Laimgruber
  The sleeping beauty, ill. by Mercer Mayer
  Sleeping Beauty, ill. by Fina Rifa
  The sleeping beauty, ill. by Ruth Sanderson
  Sleeping Beauty, ill. by John Wallner
Hamm, Diane Johnston. *Rock-a-bye farm*
Harshman, Marc. *All the way to morning*
Harshman, Terry Webb. *Porcupine's pajama party*
Hazelaar, Cor. *Zoo dreams*
Hazen, Barbara Shook. *Where do bears sleep?*, ill. by Mary Morgan-Vanroyen
  Where do bears sleep?, ill. by Ian E. Staunton
Heine, Helme. *King Bounce the 1st*
  The marvelous journey through the night
Henkes, Kevin. *Shhhh*
Hennessy, B. G. (Barbara G.). *Sleep tight*
Hertz, Grete Janus. *Olie's bedtime walk*
Hindley, Judy. *The sleepy book*
Hirschi, Ron. *A time for sleeping*
Hooper, Patricia. *Where do you sleep, little one?*
Hopkins, Lee Bennett. *Still as a star*
Howard, Jane R. *When I'm sleepy*
Hutchins, Pat. *Good night owl*
Inkpen, Mick. *Kipper*
Irving, Washington. *Rip Van Winkle*, ill. by John Howe
  Rip Van Winkle, ill. by Thomas Locker
  Rip Van Winkle, ill. by Peter Wingham
James, Betsy. *The dream stair*
Janovitz, Marilyn. *Is it time?*
Jeffers, Susan. *All the pretty horses*
Jennings, Linda M. *The sleeping beauty*
Jensen, Patricia. *Go to sleep, little groundhog*
Johnston, Tony. *The Chizzywink and the Alamagoozlum*
  Little Rabbit goes to sleep
Jonovitz, Marilyn. *Maybe, my baby*
Joosse, Barbara M. *A houseful of Christmas*
Kajikawa, Kimiko. *Sweet dreams*
Kamish, Daniel. *The night scary beasties popped out of my head*
Kantrowitz, Mildred. *Willy Bear*
Karlin, Nurit. *The dream factory*
Katz, Avner. *The little pickpocket*
Keats, Ezra Jack. *Dreams*
Kemp, Moira. *Lift-the-flap kitten*
Khalsa, Dayal Kaur. *Sleepers*
Khan, Rukhsana. *Bedtime ba-a-a-lk*
Koralek, Jenny. *The boy and the cloth of dreams*

Kotzwinkle, William. *The nap master*
Krahn, Fernando. *Sleep tight, Alex Pumpernickel*
Kraus, Robert. *Good night little one*
    Good night Richard Rabbit
    Milton the early riser
    See the moon
Laimgruber, Monika. *Susannah and the Sandman*
Lewis, J. Patrick. *Isabella Abnormella and the very, very finicky Queen of Trouble*
Lewis, Kim. *Good night, Harry*
Lewison, Wendy Cheyette. *Going to sleep on the farm*
Lively, Penelope. *Good night, sleep tight*
Lobb, Janice. *Counting sheep! How do we sleep?*
Lucas, Barbara (Barbara M.). *Sleeping over*
McCarthy, Bobette. *Dreaming*
McCauley, Jane R. *The way animals sleep*
McGhee, Alison. *In the hollow of your hand*
McGinty, Alice B. *Ten little lambs*
McMullan, Kate (Hall). *Good night, Stella*
    The noisy giant's tea party
    Papa's song
McPartland, Suzy. *Sleepy-time moon*
McPhail, David M. *The dream child*
Mallat, Kathy. *Seven stars, more!*
Marino, Dorothy. *Edward and the boxes*
Martin, Jacqueline Briggs. *Grandmother Bryant's pocket*
Massie, Diane Redfield. *The baby beebee bird*
Meade, Holly. *A place to sleep*
Merriam, Eve. *Goodnight to Annie*, ill. by Carol Schwartz
Moon, Nicola. *Tick-tock, drip-drop*
Moore, Julia. *While you sleep*
Most, Bernard. *Z-Z-Zoink!*
Mueller, Virginia. *Monster can't sleep*
Munsch, Robert N. *Get out of bed!*
Murphy, Jill. *Peace at last*
Mwalimu. *Awful aardvark*
Nichol, B. P. *Once, a lullaby*
Nobisso, Josephine. *The moon's lullaby*
    The yawn
Novak, Matt. *The Pillow War*
    While the shepherd slept
O'Brien, Mary. *Counting sheep to sleep*
Oppenheim, Joanne. *The story book prince*
Ormerod, Jan. *Moonlight*
    Sleeping
Owen, Roy. *My night forest*
Oxenbury, Helen. *Say goodnight*
Packard, Mary. *Don't make a sound*
Panek, Dennis. *Ba ba sheep wouldn't go to sleep*
Perlman, Janet. *The penguin and the pea*
Perrault, Charles. *The sleeping beauty*, ill. by David Walker
Pfister, Marcus. *The sleepy owl*
Plath, Sylvia. *The bed book*
Preston, Edna Mitchell. *Monkey in the jungle*
Purmell, Ann. *Where wild babies sleep*
Reidel, Marlene. *Jacob and the robbers*
Reiser, Lynn. *Night thunder and the Queen of the Wild Horses*
Richardson, Jean. *The sleeping beauty*
Richardson, Judith Benét. *Old winter*
Riddell, Chris. *The wish factory*
Riggio, Anita. *Wake up, William!*
Robbins, Maria Polushkin. *Mother, Mother, I want another*
    Mother, Mother I want another
Root, Phyllis. *Ten sleepy sheep*
Rosenberg, Liz. *Adelaide and the night train*
Ross, Anna. *Naptime*
Roth, Carol. *Little Bunny's sleepless night*
Rowand, Phyllis. *It is night*
Rubel, Nicole. *Goldie's nap*
Sage, Chris. *Sleepy baby*
Sage, James. *To sleep*
Saleh, Harold J. *Even tiny ants must sleep*
Schneider, Nina. *While Susie sleeps*
Schubert, Leda. *Winnie all day long*
Scotton, Rob. *Russell the sheep*
Seuss, Dr. *Dr. Seuss's sleep book*
    I am not going to get up today!

Shepperson, Rob. *The sandman*
Showers, Paul. *Sleep is for everyone*
Simmons, Jane. *The dreamtime fairies*
    Go to sleep, Daisy
Simon, Norma. *Where does my cat sleep?*
Slingsby, Janet. *Hush-a-bye babies*
Sloat, Teri. *The thing that bothered Farmer Brown*
Slobodkin, Louis. *Wide-awake owl*
Somary, Wolfgang. *Night and the candlemaker*
Sonneborn, Ruth A. *Seven in a bed*
Sperberg, Roger. *The story of the sleeping beauty, whose name was Briar Rose*
Spinelli, Eileen. *Where is the night train going?*
Stanley, Diane. *Birdsong lullaby*
Steel, Danielle. *Freddie's first night away*
Stevenson, James. *We can't sleep*
Stockdale, Susan. *Some sleep standing up*
Sugita, Yutaka. *Good night 1, 2, 3*
Swain, Ruth Freeman. *Bedtime!*
Szekeres, Cyndy. *Good night, Sammy*
Tafuri, Nancy. *Where we sleep*
Takamado no Miya Hisako. *Katie and the dream-eater*
Tobias, Tobi. *Chasing the goblins away*
Trez, Denise. *Good night, Veronica*
Tucker, Kathy. *Do knights take naps?*
Twining, Edith. *Sandman*
Uribe, Verónica. *Buzz buzz buzz*
Vaës, Alain. *The princess and the pea*
Van Laan, Nancy. *Sleep, sleep, sleep*
Van Vorst, M. L. *A Norse lullaby*
Vulliamy, Clara. *Good night, baby*
Waber, Bernard. *Ira sleeps over*
Waddell, Martin. *Can't you sleep, Little Bear?*
Wahl, Jan. *The sleepytime book*
    Sylvester Bear overslept
    The toy circus
Wallwork, Amanda. *Sleep songs*
Walton, Rick. *So many bunnies*
Weigelt, Udo. *The Sandman*
Weir, Alison. *Peter, good night*
Weisgard, Leonard. *Who dreams of cheese?*
Weiss, Nicki. *Where does the brown bear go?*
    Where does the brown bear go? [board book]
Wersba, Barbara. *Amanda dreaming*
Whatley, Bruce. *Captain Pajamas*
Wheeler, Cindy. *Marmalade's nap*
Whiteside, Karen. *Lullaby of the wind*
Wolcott, Patty. *Eeeeeek!*
Wolfe, Frances. *It is the wind*
Wong, Janet S. *Grump*
Wood, Audrey. *Moonflute*
    The napping house
    The napping house wakes up
Woolf, Virginia. *Nurse Lugton's curtain*
Yabuuchi, Masayuki. *Animals sleeping*
Yolen, Jane. *Dragon night and other lullabies*
    Time for naps
Yulya. *Bears are sleeping*
Zagone, Theresa. *No nap for me*
Ziefert, Harriet. *Cow in the house*
    Good night everyone!
    I want to sleep in your bed!
    Say good night!
    Sleepy dog
    What do ducks dream?
Zolotow, Charlotte (Shapiro). *The sleepy book*, ill. by Vladimir Bobri
    The sleepy book, ill. by Ilse Plume
Zwetchkenbaum, G. *The Peanuts sleepy time puzzle book*

Sleep – snoring

Binnamin, Vivian. *The case of the snoring stegosaurus*
DeLage, Ida. *The old witch and the snores*
Haseley, Dennis. *The cave of snores*
Kraus, Robert. *Ludwig the dog who snored symphonies*
Long, Melinda. *When Papa snores*

Miller, M. L. *The enormous snore*
Waber, Bernard. *The mouse that snored*

Sleepovers

Berenstain, Stan. *The Berenstain bears and the slumber party*
Bottner, Barbara. *Two messy friends*
Brown, Marc Tolon. *Arthur's first sleepover*
Caseley, Judith. *Slumber party!*
Dale, Penny. *Daisy Rabbit's tree house*
Giglio, Judy. *The tapping tale*
Greene, Rhonda Gowler. *At grandma's*
Harshman, Terry Webb. *Porcupine's pajama party*
Hill, Eric. *Spot sleeps over*
Jackson, Isaac. *Somebody's new pajamas*
Jennings, Sharon. *Franklin wants a badge*
Lipniacka, Ewa. *To bed . . . or else!*
Lucas, Barbara (Barbara M.). *Sleeping over*
McKissack, Patricia C. *Messy Bessey and the birthday overnight*
Murphy, Stuart J. *Rabbit's pajama party*
Radabaugh, Melinda Beth. *Sleeping over*
Rodriguez, Bobbie. *Sarah's sleepover*
Ruelle, Karen Gray. *Easy as apple pie*
Steel, Danielle. *Freddie's first night away*
Vulliamy, Clara. *Small*
Waber, Bernard. *Bearsie Bear and the surprise sleepover party*

Slight-of-hand *see* Magic

Sloths *see* Animals – sloths

Slugs *see* Animals – slugs

Smallness *see* Character traits – smallness

Smell *see* Anatomy – noses; Senses – smell

Smiles, smiling *see* Anatomy – faces

Snails *see* Animals – snails

Snakes *see* Reptiles – snakes

Snoring *see* Noise, sounds; Sleep – snoring

Snow *see* Weather – blizzards; Weather – snow

Snow plows *see* Machines

Snowmen

Arnold, Katya. *The adventures of Snowwoman*
Bauer, Caroline Feller. *Midnight snowman*
Briggs, Raymond. *Building the snowman*
    Dressing up
    The party
    The snowman
    The snowman [a lift-the-flap board book]
    The snowman storybook
    The snowman tell-the-time book
    Walking in the air
Buehner, Caralyn. *Snowmen at night*
    Snowmen at night [board book]
Carlson, Nancy L. *Snowden*
Chorao, Kay. *Kate's snowman*
Colandro, Lucille. *There was a cold lady who swallowed some snow!*
Cuyler, Margery. *The biggest, best snowman*
Ehlert, Lois. *Snowballs*
Erskine, Jim. *The snowman*
Garland, Michael. *Christmas magic*
Goffstein, M. B. (Marilyn Brooke). *Our snowman*
Gordon, Sharon. *Friendly snowman*
Hoban, Julia. *Amy loves the snow*
Hol, Coby. *Lisa and the snowman*

Holl, Adelaide. *The runaway giant*
Hughes, Shirley. *The snow lady*
Inkpen, Mick. *Penguin small*
Janosch. *Dear snowman*
Johnson, Crockett. *Time for spring*
Joos, Françoise. *The golden snowflake*
Joyce, William. *Snowie Rolie*
Kellogg, Steven (Stephen). *The mystery of the missing red mitten*
Kirk, Daniel. *The snow family*
Komoda, Beverly. *The winter day*
Kuskin, Karla. *In the flaky frosty morning*
Leonard, Marcia. *The best snowman ever*
Lobe, Mira. *The snowman who went for a walk*
Loretan, Sylvia. *Bob the snowman*
Mack, Gail. *Yesterday's snowman*
McKee, David. *Snow woman*
Miller, Edna. *Mousekin's frosty friend*
Morgan, Allen. *Sadie and the snowman*
Parillo, Tony. *Michelangelo's surprise*
Peddle, Daniel. *Snow day*
Pittman, Helena Clare. *The snowman's path*
Schaefer, Carole Lexa. *Snow pumpkin*
Weedn, Flavia. *The little snow bear*
Whybrow, Ian. *Harry and the snow king*
    Wish, change, friend
Yee, Patrick. *Winter rabbit*
Ziefert, Harriet. *The snow child*
Zion, Gene. *The summer snowman*

Soccer *see* Sports – soccer

Society Islands *see* Foreign lands – South Sea Islands

Socks *see* Clothing – socks

Sofas *see* Furniture – couches, sofas

Soldiers *see* Careers – military

Soldiers, toy *see* Toys – soldiers

Solitude *see* Behavior – solitude

Songs

Abisch, Roz. *Sweet Betsy from Pike*
Adams, Pam. *This old man*
Alexander, Cecil Frances. *All things bright and beautiful*, ill. by Leo Politi
    All things bright and beautiful, ill. by Bruce Whatley
Alger, Leclaire Gowans. *All in the morning early*
    Kellyburn Braes
All night, all day
Alley, R. W. (Robert W.). *There once was a witch*
Arkin, David. *Black and white*
Ash, Jutta. *Wedding birds*
Autry, Gene. *Here comes Santa Claus*
B-52's (Musical group). *Wig!*
Bangs, Edward. *Yankee Doodle*
Baring-Gould, S. (Sabine). *Now the day is over*
Barner, Bob. *Dem bones*
Bates, Katharine Lee. *America the beautiful*, ill. by Chris Gall
    America the beautiful, ill. by Wendell Minor
    America the beautiful, ill. by Neil Waldman
Beall, Pamela Conon. *Wee Sing if you're happy and you know it*
The bear
Belafonte, Harry. *Island in the sun*
Berlin, Irving. *Easter parade*
    God bless America
Billy Boy (folk-song). *Billy Boy*
Birdseye, Tom. *She'll be comin' round the mountain*
Bliss, Corinne Demas. *Nina's waltz*
Boesel, Ann Sterling. *Sing and sing again*
    Singing with Peter and Patsy
Botwin, Esther. *A treasury of songs for little children*

Bowman, Pete. *The Christmas songbook*
Boynton, Sandra. *Good night, good night*
Brand, Oscar. *When I first came to this land*
Bratton, John. *The teddy bears' picnic*, ill. by Renate Kozikowski
Briggs, Raymond. *The white land*
Bring a torch, Jeannette, Isabella
Brokering, Herbert F. *Earth and all stars*
Brown, Marc Tolon. *Play rhymes*
Bryan, Ashley. *I'm going to sing*
   Lion and the ostrich chicks
Buffett, Jimmy. *The jolly mon*
Burgie, Irving. *Caribbean carnival*
Burke, Bobby. *Daddy's little girl*
Butler, Geoff. *Ode to Newfoundland*
Byrne, David. *Stay up late*
Canyon, Christopher. *John Denver's Sunshine on my shoulders*
Carle, Eric. *Today is Monday*
Carpenter, Mary-Chapin. *Halley came to Jackson*
Carryl, Charles E. (Charles Edward). *A capital ship*
Carter, David A. *If you're happy and you know it, clap your hands*
   Old MacDonald had a farm
Caseley, Judith. *Molly Pink*
Cazet, Denys. *Dancing*
Chalk, Gary. *Yankee Doodle*
Child, Lydia Maria. *Over the river and through the wood*
Christmas carols
Cohen, Miriam. *Down in the subway*
Collins, Billy. *Daddy's little boy*
Conover, Chris. *Six little ducks*
Cooner, Donna D. (Donna Danell). *I know an old Texan who swallowed a fly*
Count me in
Craver, Mike. *Beaver ball at the bug club*
Crum, Shutta. *My mountain song*
Cutler, Ivor. *Doris*
Daily, Don. *The twelve days of Christmas cats*
Dalton, Alene. *My new picture book of songs*
Dann, Penny. *Eensy weensy spider*
Delacre, Lulu. *Arroz con leche*
   Las Navidades
Delaney, A. *The gunnywolf*
Delessert, Etienne. *A long long song*
Denslow, W. W. *Denslow's picture book treasury*
Denver, John. *The children and the flowers*
De Regniers, Beatrice Schenk. *Was it a good trade?*
Devlin, Harry. *The walloping window blind*, ill. by author
Din dan don, it's Christmas
Domanska, Janina. *Busy Monday morning*
Donovan, Mary Lee. *Won't you come and play with me?*
Duncan, Lois. *Songs from dreamland*
Durell, Ann. *The Diane Goode book of American folk tales and songs*
Duvoisin, Roger Antoine. *Petunia and the song*
Ellwand, David. *Ten in the bed*
Emberley, Barbara. *One wide river to cross*
   Simon's song
Emerson, Sally. *The Kingfisher nursery rhyme songbook*
Farjeon, Eleanor. *Morning has broken*
The farmer in the dell. *The farmer in the dell*, ill. by John O'Brien
   The farmer in the dell, ill. by Kathy Parkinson
   The farmer in the dell, ill. by Mary Maki Rae
   The farmer in the dell, ill. by Diane Stanley
   The farmer in the dell, ill. by Alexandra Wallner
Fern, Eugene. *Birthday presents*
Findon, Joanne. *Auld lang syne*
Fine, Howard. *A piggie Christmas*
Fitzgerald, Ella. *A-tisket, a-tasket*
Flanders, Michael. *The hippopotamus song*
Fleming, Candace. *Gabriella's song*
The fox went out on a chilly night
French, Fiona. *Rise and shine*
The friendly beasts and a partridge in a pear tree, ill. by Virginia Pearsons
A frog he would a-wooing go (folk-song). *Frog went a-courtin'*, ill. by Feodor Rojankovsky
   Frog went a-courting, retold & ill. by Dominic Catalano
   Froggie went a-courting, ill. by Chris Conover
   Froggie went a courting, ill. by Marjorie Priceman

   Mr. Frog went a-courting
   Wendy Watson's frog went a-courting
Garcia, Jerry. *The teddy bears' picnic*
Gershator, David. *Moon rooster*
Gershwin, George. *Summertime from Porgy and Bess*
Gilbert, Yvonne. *Baby's book of lullabies and cradle songs*
Go tell Aunt Rhody. *Go tell Aunt Rhody*, ill. by Aliki
   Go tell Aunt Rhody, ill. by Robert M. Quackenbush
Goode, Diane. *Diane Goode's book of silly stories & songs*
Goodhart, Pippa. *Row, row, row your boat*
Graham, Steve. *Dear old Donegal*
Granfield, Linda. *Silent night*
The green grass grows all around
Greene, Carol. *A computer went a-courting*
   Hinny Winny Bunco
   The thirteen days of Halloween
Guthrie, Woody. *Bling blang*
   My dolly
   This land is your land
   Woody's 20 grow big songs
Hale, Sarah Josepha Buell. *Mary had a little lamb*, ill. by Iza Trapani
   Mary had a little lamb [board book], ill. by Iza Trapani
Hallworth, Grace. *Down by the river*
   Sing me a story
Halpern, Shari. *What shall we do when we all go out?*
Harris, Leon A. *The great diamond robbery*
Harrison, David Lee. *The animals' song*
Hillenbrand, Will. *Down by the station*
Hirsh, Marilyn. *One little goat*
Hoban, Brom. *Skunk Lane*
Hoban, Lillian. *Harry's song*
Hoberman, Mary Ann. *Bill Grogan's goat*
   Mary had a little lamb, ill. by Nadine Bernard Westcott
Hobzek, Mildred. *We came a-marching . . . 1, 2, 3*
Hodges, Margaret. *Silent night*
Hogrogian, Nonny. *The cat who loved to sing*
Homme, Bob. *The friendly giant's birthday*
Hooper, Maureen Brett. *Silent night*
Hoose, Philip M. *Hey little ant*
Hot cross buns, and other old street cries
Houston, John A. *The bright yellow rope*
   A mouse in my house
   A room full of animals
Hush songs
Ipcar, Dahlov (Zorach). *The cat came back*
   The song of the day birds and the night birds
I've been working on the railroad
Ivimey, John William. *The complete story of the three blind mice*, ill. by Paul Galdone
   The complete version of ye three blind mice, ill. by Walton Corbould
   Three blind mice, ill. by Lorinda Bryan Cauley
   Three blind mice, ill. by Victoria Chess
Johnson, James Weldon. *Lift ev'ry voice and sing*
Johnson, Paul Brett. *Little Bunny Foo Foo*
Johnston, Mary Anne. *Sing me a song*
Johnston, Tony. *Grandpa's song*
Jonas, Ann. *Bird talk*
Jones, Carol. *This old man*
Judd, Naomi. *Naomi Judd's guardian angels*
Kapp, Paul. *Cock-a-doodle-doo! Cock-a-doodle-dandy!*
Keats, Ezra Jack. *The little drummer boy*
Kellogg, Steven (Stephen). *A-hunting we will go!*
   Give the dog a bone
   I was born about 10,000 years ago
   Santa Claus is comin' to town
   Yankee Doodle
Kemp, Moira. *I'm a little teapot*
Kennedy, Jimmy. *The teddy bears' picnic*, ill. by Michael Hague
Key, Francis Scott. *The Star Spangled Banner*, ill. by Ingri & Edgar Parin D'Aulaire
   The Star-Spangled Banner, ill. by Paul Galdone
   The Star-Spangled Banner, ill. by Dana Regan
   The Star-Spangled Banner, ill. by Peter Spier
Kimmel, Eric A. *Why worry?*
King, Bob. *Sitting on the farm*
Kirk, Daniel. *Go!*

Knight, Hilary. *A firefly in a fir tree*
Koontz, Robin Michal. *This old man*
Kovalski, Maryann. *Jingle bells*
    The wheels on the bus
Kroll, Steven. *By the dawn's early light*
Krull, Kathleen. *Songs of praise*
Kuskin, Karla. *Paul*
Lambert, Paulette Livers. *Evening*
Langstaff, John M. *Oh, a-hunting we will go*
    Ol' Dan Tucker
    On Christmas day in the morning
    Over in the meadow
    Soldier, soldier, won't you marry me?
    The swapping boy
    The two magicians
Lansky, Bruce. *Sweet dreams*
Lear, Edward. *The pelican chorus*, ill. by Harold Berson
    The pelican chorus and the quangle wangle's hat, ill. by Kevin W.
        Maddison
Lenski, Lois. *At our house*
    Davy and his dog
    Davy goes places
    Debbie and her grandma
    A dog came to school
    I like winter
    I went for a walk
    The life I live
Lester, Alison. *Isabella's bed*
Let me call you sweetheart
Leventhal, Debra. *What is your language?*
Lippman, Sidney. *A you're adorable*
Lishak, Anthony. *Row your boat*
Lithgow, John. *Marsupial Sue*
Little old lady who swallowed a fly. *Fancy that!*
    Golly Gump swallowed a fly
    I know an old lady, ill. by Abner Graboff
    I know an old lady, ill. by G. Brian Karas
    I know an old lady, ill. by Steve McInturff
    I know an old lady, ill. by Albert Miller
    I know an old lady who swallowed a fly, ill. by Stephen Gulbis
    I know an old lady who swallowed a fly, ill. by Glen Rounds
    I know an old lady who swallowed a fly, ill. by William Stobbs
    I know an old lady who swallowed a fly, ill. by Nadine Bernard
        Westcott
    There was an old lady, ill. by Nick Bantock
    There was an old lady who swallowed a fly, ill. by Pam Adams
    There was an old lady who swallowed a fly, ill. by Colin Hawkins
    There was an old lady who swallowed a fly, ill. by Simms Taback
    There was an old woman, ill. by Steven Kellogg
Long, Sylvia. *Deck the hall*
Lord, Beman. *The days of the week*
Lubach, Peter. *Harry and the singing fish*
Lullaby and goodnight
McCarthy, Bobette. *Buffalo girls*
McCutcheon, John. *Happy adoption day!*
McGee, Shelagh. *I'm a little teapot*
McGinley-Nally, Sharon. *The friendly beasts*
Mack, Stanley (Stan). *Ten bears in my bed*
McLerran, Alice. *Dreamsong*
McNally, Darcie. *In a cabin in a wood*
Mallett, David. *Inch by inch*
Manson, Christopher. *A farmyard song*
    The tree in the wood
Margolin, H. Ellen. *Goin' to Boston*
Maril, Lee. *Mr. Bunny paints the eggs*
Mayo, Margaret. *Wiggle waggle fun*
Medearis, Angela Shelf. *The zebra-riding cowboy*
Melmed, Laura Krauss. *The first song ever sung*
Miller, J. Philip. *We all sing with the same voice*
Mills, Alan. *The hungry goat*
Modesitt, Jeanne. *Songs of Chanukah*
Mohr, Joseph. *Silent night*
Moon, Dolly M. *My very first book of cowboy songs*
Morgenstern, Christian. *Lullabies, lyrics and gallows songs*
Morley, Carol. *Farmyard song*
Moses, Will. *Silent night*
Moss, Jeffrey. *The songs of Sesame Street in poems and pictures*

Moss, Marissa. *Knick knack paddywack*
Most, Bernard. *Row, row, row your goat*
Mother Goose. *London Bridge is falling down*, ill. by Ed Emberley
    London Bridge is falling down, ill. by Peter Spier
    The Mother Goose songbook
    Mother Goose's melodies
    Thirty old-time nursery songs
Munsch, Robert N. *Mortimer*
My first songs
Neale, J. M. (John Mason). *Good King Wenceslas*
Nelson, Esther L. *The funny songbook*
    Holiday singing and dancing games
    The silly songbook
Newbolt, Henry John, Sir. *Rilloby-rill*
Newland, Mary Reed. *Good King Wenceslas*
Niland, Kilmeny. *A bellbird in a flame tree*
Norworth, Jack. *Take me out to the ballgame*
O Christmas tree
Old MacDonald had a farm. *E I E I O*
    Old MacDonald, ill. by Rosemary Wells
    Old MacDonald had a farm, ill. by Holly Berry
    Old MacDonald had a farm, ill. by Lorinda Bryan Cauley
    Old MacDonald had a farm, ill. by Mel Crawford
    Old MacDonald had a farm, ill. by Tracey English
    Old MacDonald had a farm, ill. by David Frankland
    Old MacDonald had a farm, ill. by Abner Graboff
    Old MacDonald had a farm, ill. by Nancy Hellen
    Old MacDonald had a farm, ill. by Carol Jones
    Old MacDonald had a farm, ill. by Tracey Campbell Pearson
    Old MacDonald had a farm, ill. by Robert M. Quackenbush
    Old MacDonald had a farm, ill. by Glen Rounds
    Old McDonald had a farm, ill. by Iain Smith
    Old MacDonald had a farm, ill. by Jessica Souhami
    Old MacDonald had a farm, ill. by William Stobbs
    Old MacDonald had a farm, ill. by Prue Theobalds
On the little hearth
Oppenheim, Joanne. *The eency weency spider*
Ormerod, Jan. *Ms. MacDonald has a class*
Over in the meadow, ill. by Ezra Jack Keats
Paley, Joan. *One more river*
A paper of pins
Parton, Dolly. *Coat of many colors*
Paterson, A. B. (Andrew Barton). *Waltzing Matilda*
Paxton, Tom. *Going to the zoo*
    The marvelous toy
Peek, Merle. *The balancing act*
    Mary wore her red dress and Henry wore his green sneakers
Pfister, Marcus. *I see the moon*
Philpot, Lorna. *Amazing Anthony Ant*
Pierpont, James. *Jingle bells*
Poston, Elizabeth. *Baby's song book*
Preston, Edna Mitchell. *Pop Corn and Ma Goodness*
Price, Christine. *One is God*
Quackenbush, Robert M. *Clementine*
    The man on the flying trapeze
    Pop! goes the weasel and Yankee Doodle
    She'll be comin' 'round the mountain
    Skip to my Lou
    There'll be a hot time in the old town tonight
Quattrocki, Carolyn. *The little drummer boy*
Raebeck, Lois. *Who am I?*
Raffi. *Baby beluga*
    Down by the bay
    Everything grows
    Like me and you
    One light, one sun
    Rise and shine
    Shake my sillies out
    Wheels on the bus
Raposo, Joe. *The Sesame Street song book*
Ray, Mary Lyn. *Shaker boy*
Rayner, Mary. *One by one*
    Ten pink piglets
Rey, H. A. (Hans Augusto). *Humpty Dumpty and other Mother Goose
    songs*
Richardson, Jean. *Stephen's feast*
Robbins, Ruth. *Baboushka and the three kings*

Rodanas, Kristina. *The little drummer boy*
Rodgers, Richard. *My favorite things*
    A real nice clambake
Peek, Merle. *Roll over!*
Root, Phyllis. *Soup for supper*
Ross, Tony. *This old man*
Rounds, Glen. *The boll weevil*
    Casey Jones
    The strawberry roan
    Sweet Betsy from Pike
Sanfield, Steve. *The girl who wanted a song*
Santa Claus is coming to town
Schackburg, Richard. *Yankee Doodle*
Schanzer, Rosalyn. *The Old Chisholm Trail*
Scott, Lesbia. *I sing a song of the saints of God*
Seeger, Pete. *The foolish frog*
Seskin, Steve. *Don't laugh at me*
Sewall, Marcia. *Animal song*
Shannon, George. *Lizard's song*
    Oh, I love!
Shepard, Aaron. *The princess mouse*
Simmons, Jane. *Daisy says, "Here we go round the mulberry bush"*
    Daisy says, "If you're happy and you know it"
Simon, Paul. *At the zoo*
Simple gifts
Singer, Marilyn. *The maiden on the moor*
    Will you take me to town on strawberry day?
Slavin, Bill. *The cat came back*
Sloat, Teri. *Hark! The aardvark angels sing*
Slobodkin, Louis. *Wide-awake owl*
Smith, Charles R. *I'll be there*
    My gal
Smith, Will (1968–). *Just the two of us*
Snell, Gordon. *Twelve days, a Christmas countdown*
The song of the Three Holy Children
Spier, Peter. *The Erie Canal*
Staines, Bill. *All God's critters got a place in the choir*
Stern, Elsie-Jean. *Wee Robin's Christmas song*
Stevens, Jan Romero. *Twelve lizards leaping*
Stobbs, William. *There's a hole in my bucket*
Stohs, Anita. *An Easter alleluia*
Swain, Gwenyth. *I wonder as I wander*
Sweet, Melissa. *Fiddle-i-fee*
Taylor, Jane. *Twinkle, twinkle little star*, ill. by Heather Collins
    Twinkle, twinkle, little star, ill. by Michael Hague
    Twinkle, twinkle little star, ill. by Julia Noonan
Taylor, Mark. *The bold fisherman*
    Old Blue, you good dog you
Tompert, Ann. *A carol for Christmas*
Trapani, Iza. *How much is that doggie in the window?*
    I'm a little teapot
    The itsy bitsy spider
    Shoo fly!
Trivas, Irene. *Emma's Christmas*
The twelve days of Christmas. English folk song. *Brian Wildsmith's The twelve days of Christmas*
    Jack Kent's twelve days of Christmas
    The twelve days of Christmas, ill. by Jan Brett
    The twelve days of Christmas, ill. by Rachel Griffin
    The twelve days of Christmas, ill. by Ilonka Karasz
    The twelve days of Christmas, ill. by Ilse Plume
    The twelve days of Christmas, ill. by Erika Schneider
    The twelve days of Christmas, ill. by Vladimir Vagin
    The twelve days of Christmas, ill. by Sophie Windham
    The twelve days of Christmas [board book], ill. by Jan Brett
Vaughan, Marcia Kapok. *Wombat stew*
Wallace, Nancy Elizabeth. *Apples, apples, apples*
Wallner, John C. *Old MacDonald had a farm*
Ward, Jennifer. *Over in the garden*
We wish you a merry Christmas
Weeks, Sarah. *Crocodile smile*
Weiss, George (George David). *What a wonderful world*
Weiss, Nicki. *If you're happy and you know it*
Welch, Willy. *Playing right field*
Wells, Rosemary. *The bear went over the mountain*
    Bingo
    The itsy-bitsy spider

Wenning, Elisabeth. *The Christmas mouse*
Westcott, Nadine Bernard. *Skip to my Lou*
    There's a hole in the bucket
What a morning!
What will we do with the baby-o?
Wheeler, Opal. *Sing in praise*
    Sing Mother Goose
Whippo, Walt. *Little white duck*
Widdecombe Fair
Wilder, Laura Ingalls. *My little house songbook*
Williams, Suzanne. *The witch casts a spell*
Wolff, Ashley. *The bells of London*
Wood, Audrey. *Birdsong*
    When the root children wake up
Yaccarino, Dan. *Five little ducks*
Yolen, Jane. *Jane Yolen's Old MacDonald songbook*
    The lap-time song and play book
Young, Russell. *Dragonsong*
Yulya. *Bears are sleeping*
Zelinsky, Paul O. *The wheels on the bus*
Zemach, Harve. *Mommy, buy me a China doll*
Zemach, Margot. *Some from the moon, some from the sun*
Ziefert, Harriet. *When I first came to this land*
Zolotow, Charlotte (Shapiro). *The song*

Sons *see* Family life – sons

Sorcerers *see* Wizards

Sounds *see* Noise, sounds

South Africa *see* Foreign lands – South Africa

South America *see* Foreign lands – South America

South Pole *see* Foreign lands – Antarctic

South Sea Islands *see* Foreign lands – South Sea Islands

Southwest Indians *see* Indians of North America – Southwest

Soviet Union *see* Foreign lands – Soviet Union

Space & space ships

Agee, Jon. *Dmitri the astronaut*
Alexander, Martha G. *Marty McGee's space lab, no girls allowed*
    You're a genius, Blackboard Bear
Anderson, Joan. *Richie's rocket*
Asimov, Isaac. *The best new thing*
Axelrod, Amy. *They'll believe me when I'm gone*
Barden, Rosalind. *TV monster*
Barner, Bob. *Space race*
Barton, Byron. *I want to be an astronaut*
Bartram, Simon. *Man on the moon*
Behrens, June. *I can be an astronaut*
Berenstain, Stan. *The Berenstain bears on the moon*
Blocksma, Mary. *Easy-to-make spaceships that really fly*
Bradman, Tony. *It came from outer space*
    Michael
Branley, Franklyn M. (Mansfield). *Floating in space*
    The International Space Station
    Is there life in outer space?
    Journey into a black hole
    The planets in our solar system
Bredeson, Carmen. *Getting ready for space*
    Liftoff!
    Living on a space shuttle
Brewster, Patience. *Ellsworth and the cats from Mars*
Brunhoff, Laurent de. *Babar visits another planet*
Butterworth, Nick. *QPootle 5*
Carey, Valerie Scho. *Harriet and William and the terrible creature*
Carrick, Carol. *Patrick's dinosaurs on the Internet*
Catalanotto, Peter. *Dad and me*

Cecil, Laura. *Noah and the space ark*
Chambers, Roland. *Rooftop rocket party*
Coffelt, Nancy. *Dogs in space*
Cole, Babette. *The trouble with Gran*
Cole, Joanna. *The magic school bus lost in the solar system*
Collicott, Sharleen. *Seeing stars*
Corey, Shana. *First graders from Mars: Horus's horrible day*
  First graders from Mars: Nergal and the Great Space Race
  First graders from Mars: Tera, star student
  First graders from Mars: The problem with Pelly
Counsel, June. *But Martin!*
Cox, Judy. *The West Texas chili monster*
Cushman, Doug. *Space cat*
Debecker, Benoît. *The naughty prince*
Delaney, Ned. *Cosmic chickens*
Demarest, Chris L. *The lunatic adventure of Kitman and Willy*
Dillon, Jana. *Lucky O'Leprechaun in school*
DiTerlizzi, Tony. *Jimmy Zangwow's out-of-this-world, moon pie adventure*
Eco, Umberto. *The three astronauts*
Elliott, David. *Hazel Nutt, Alien Hunter*
Fisher, Aileen Lucia. *Sing of the earth and sky*
Freeman, Don. *Space witch*
Freeman, Mae Blacker. *You will go to the moon*
Fuchs, Erich. *Journey to the moon*
Glass, Andrew. *My brother tries to make me laugh*
Graham, Ian. *The best book of spaceships*
Greene, Carol. *Astronauts work in space*
Greydanus, Rose. *Trouble in space*
Haddon, Mark. *The Sea of Tranquillity*
Hergé. *Explorers on the moon*
Hillert, Margaret. *Up, up and away*
Hirst, Robin. *My place in space*
Holland, Simon. *Space*
Hopkins, Lee Bennett. *Blast off!*
Hurd, Thacher. *Moo Cow Kaboom!*
Johnson, Crockett. *Harold's trip to the sky*
Jones, Brian. *Space*
Keats, Ezra Jack. *Regards to the man in the moon*
Kirk, Daniel. *Moondogs*
Kirk, David. *Nova's ark*
Kroll, Steven. *The magic rocket*
Kuskin, Karla. *A space story*
Lauber, Patricia. *You're aboard spaceship Earth*
Leedy, Loreen. *Blast off to Earth!*
  How humans make friends
  Postcards from Pluto
Loomis, Christine. *Astro Bunnies*
Lorenz, Lee. *Hugo and the spacedog*
McCarthy, Meghan. *The adventures of Patty and the big red bus*
MacDonald, Suse. *Space spinners*
McMullan, Kate (Hall). *Spacey riddles*
McNaughton, Colin. *Here come the aliens!*
McPhail, David M. *Tinker and Tom and the Star Baby*
Maisner, Heather. *Planet monster*
Marshall, Edward. *Space case*
Marshall, James. *Merry Christmas, space case*
Marzollo, Jean. *Jed and the space bandits*
  Jed's junior space patrol
May, Charles Paul. *High-noon rocket*
Mayer, Mercer. *Astronaut critter*
Mayers, Florence Cassen. *The National Air and Space Museum*
Moché, Dinah L. *The astronauts*
Mooser, Stephen. *Funnyman meets the monster from outer space*
Moss, Marissa. *Knick knack paddywack*
Murphy, Jill. *What next, baby bear!*
Osborne, Mary Pope. *Moonhorse*, ill. by S. M. Saelig
Ostrow, Vivian. *My brother is from outer space*
Ottley, Matt. *What Faust saw*
Oxenbury, Helen. *Tom and Pippo see the moon*
Pallotta, Jerry. *Twizzlers percentages book*
Paul, Sherry. *2-B and the space visitor*
Peet, Bill (William Bartlett). *The wump world*
Petty, Dini. *The queen, the bear and the bumblebee*
Pinkney, J. Brian. *Cosmo and the robot*
Pinkwater, Daniel Manus. *Guys from space*

  Wallpaper from space
Podendorf, Illa. *Space*
Pryor, Bonnie. *Mr. Munday and the space creatures*
Rau, Dana Meachen. *Neil Armstrong*
Rey, H. A. (Hans Augusto). *Curious George gets a medal*
Robison, Nancy. *UFO kidnap*
Rockwell, Anne F. *Space vehicles*
Root, Phyllis. *The hungry monster*
Rosen, Michael (1946–). *Mission Ziffoid*
Rosen, Sidney. *How far is a star?*
  Where does the moon go?
Ross, Dave (David). *Gorp and the space pirates*
  Space monster
  Space Monster Gorp and the runaway computer
Ross, Tony. *I'm coming to get you!*
Sadler, Marilyn. *Alistair in outer space*
  Alistair's time machine
Schoberle, Ceile. *Beyond the Milky Way*
Schomp, Virginia. *If you were an . . . astronaut*
Scieszka, Jon. *Baloney, Henry P.*
Sharratt, Nick. *Rocket countdown*
Shields, Carol Diggory. *Martian rock*
Sis, Peter. *Starry messenger*
Snow, Alan. *The truth about cats*
Steadman, Ralph. *The little red computer*
Suen, Anastasia. *Man on the moon*
Theodorou, Rod. *Across the solar system*
Thomas, Frances. *One day, Daddy*
Thompson, Richard. *Sky full of babies*
Ungerer, Tomi. *Moon man*
Van Allsburg, Chris. *Zathura*
Vaughn, Jenny. *On the moon*
Wallace, Karen. *Rockets and spaceships*
Weiss, Ellen. *Pigs in space*
Weston, Martha. *Space guys!*
Wethered, Peggy. *Touchdown Mars!*
Wildsmith, Brian. *Professor Noah's spaceship*
Willis, Jeanne. *Earth mobiles as explained by Professor Xargle*
  Earth tigerlets as explained by Professor Xargle
  Earthlets as explained by Professor Xargle
  The long blue blazer
Wood, Audrey. *The Christmas adventure of Space Elf Sam*
Wynne-Jones, Tim. *Builder of the moon*
Yaccarino, Dan. *First day on a strange new planet*
  New pet
  Zoom! Zoom! Zoom! I'm off to the moon!
Yolen, Jane. *Moon ball*
Yorinks, Arthur. *Company's coming*
  Company's going
  Quack!
Young, Ruth. *A trip to Mars*
Zaffo, George J. *The giant book of things in space*
Ziegler, Ursina. *Squaps the moonling*

Spain *see* Foreign lands – Spain

Sparrows *see* Birds – sparrows

Special Olympics *see* Sports – Special Olympics

Spectacles *see* Glasses

Speech *see* Handicaps – stuttering; Language

Speed *see* Concepts – speed

Spelunking *see* Caves

Spiders

Aardema, Verna. *Anansi does the impossible!*
  Anansi finds a fool
  The vingananee and the tree toad
Adelson, Leone. *Please pass the grass*
Back, Christine. *Spider's web*

Bailey, Jill. *The life cycle of a spider*
Baker, Jeannie. *One hungry spider*
Banks, Kate (Katherine A.). *Spider, spider*
Barrett, Norman S. *Spiders*
Bason, Lillian. *Spiders*
Berger, Melvin. *Spinning spiders*
Berman, Ruth. *Spinning spiders*
Berry, James. *First palm trees*
Bodkin, Odds. *The Christmas cobwebs*
Brandenberg, Franz. *Fresh cider and apple pie*
Bryan, Ashley. *The dancing granny*
Cahill, Chris. *Spider magic*
Carle, Eric. *The very busy spider*
Chenery, Janet. *Wolfie*
Climo, Shirley. *The cobweb Christmas*
Collins, Heather. *Eensy weensy spider*
Conklin, Gladys. *I caught a lizard*
Crothers, Samuel McChord. *Miss Muffet's Christmas party*
Dann, Penny. *Eensy weensy spider*
Dewey, Jennifer Owings. *Once I knew a spider*
Fisher, Aileen Lucia. *When it comes to bugs*
Fowler, Allan. *Spiders are not insects*
French, Vivian. *Spider watching*
Freschet, Berniece. *The web in the grass*
Galdone, Joanna. *Honeybee's party*
George, Jean Craighead. *All upon a stone*
Gibbons, Gail. *Spiders*
Glaser, Linda. *Spectacular spiders*
Gleeson, Brian. *Anansi*
Goldin, Augusta. *Spider silk*
Graham, Margaret Bloy. *Be nice to spiders*
Hawcock, David. *Spider*
Hawes, Judy. *My daddy longlegs*
Hawkins, Colin. *Incy wincy spider*
Heinrichs, Ann. *Spiders*
Himmelman, John. *A house spider's life*
Howitt, Mary Botham. *Mary Howitt's The spider and the fly*
Joosse, Barbara M. *Spiders in the fruit cellar*
Kajpust, Melissa. *A dozen silk diapers*
Keens-Douglas, Richardo. *Anancy and the haunted house*
Ketteman, Helen. *Armadilly chili*
Kimmel, Eric A. *Anansi and the magic stick*
   Anansi and the moss-covered rock
   Anansi and the talking melon
   Anansi goes fishing
Kirk, David. *Little Miss Spider*
   Little Miss Spider at Sunny Patch School
   Miss Spider's ABC
   Miss Spider's new car
   Miss Spider's tea party
Koralek, Jenny. *The cobweb curtain*
Kraus, Robert. *Dance, Spider, dance!*
   How Spider saved Easter
   How Spider saved Halloween
   How Spider saved Turkey
   How Spider saved Valentine's Day
   The trouble with spider
Lake, Mary Dixon. *The royal drum*
Lasky, Kathryn. *Show and tell bunnies*
Lewis, J. Patrick. *The little buggers*
Llewellyn, Claire. *The best book of bugs*
   Some bugs glow in the dark
   Spiders have fangs
London, Jonathan. *Dream weaver*
McDermott, Gerald. *Anansi the spider*
MacDonald, Amy. *The spider who created the world*
MacDonald, Suse. *Space spinners*
McNulty, Faith. *The lady and the spider*
Mead, Katherine. *How spiders got eight legs*
Mollel, Tololwa M. (Tololwa Marti). *Ananse's feast*
Monks, Lydia. *Aaaarrgghh! spider!*
Morley, Carol. *A spider and a pig*
Murawski, Darlyne A. *Bug faces*
Musgrove, Margaret. *The spider weaver*
O'Neil, Amanda. *I wonder why spiders spin webs*
Oppenheim, Joanne. *The eency weency spider*
   Have you seen bugs?

Oxford Scientific Films. *The spider's web*
Parsons, Alexandra. *Amazing spiders*
Penner, Lucille Recht. *Monster bugs*
Pieńkowski, Jan. *Pizza!*
Policoff, Stephen Phillip. *Cesar's amazing journey*
Rose, Anne K. *Spider in the sky*
Rouss, Sylvia A. *Sammy Spider's first Passover*
   Sammy Spider's first Shabbat
Ryder, Joanne. *The spiders dance*
Sammy Spider's first Tu B'Shevat
Sardegna, Jill. *The roly-poly spider*
Selsam, Millicent E. *A first look at spiders*
Shields, Carol Diggory. *The bugliest bug*
Simon, Francesca. *Spider school*
Siomades, Lorianne. *The itsy bitsy spider*
Spinelli, Eileen. *Sophie's masterpiece*
Temple, Frances. *Tiger soup*
Trapani, Iza. *The itsy bitsy spider*
Wagner, Jenny. *Aranea*
Wells, Rosemary. *The itsy-bitsy spider*
Wishinsky, Frieda. *Nothing scares us*
Wood, David. *Silly spider!*
Yolen, Jane. *Spider Jane*

Split page books *see* Format, unusual

Sponges *see* Animals – sponges

Spooks *see* Ghosts; Mythical creatures – goblins

Spoonbills *see* Birds – spoonbills

Sports

Axelrod, Amy. *Pigs on the ball*
Berenstain, Stan. *The Berenstain bears go out for the team*
   The Berenstain bears' report card trouble
Blaustein, Muriel. *Play ball, Zachary!*
Blumenthal, Deborah. *Ice palace*
Bundey, Nikki. *In the park*
   In the snow
   In the water
Bush, Timothy. *Three at sea*
Butterworth, Nick. *Field day*
Carlson, Nancy L. *Bunnies and their sports*
Carr, Jan. *Frozen noses*
Carrick, Carol. *The climb*
Caseley, Judith. *Molly Pink goes hiking*
Cole, Babette. *Three cheers for Errol!*
Cole, Joanna. *Riding Silver Star*
Dadey, Debbie. *Shooting star: Annie Oakley, the legend*
Dubois, Muriel L. *I like sports: what can I be?*
Hayden, Kate. *Horse show*
Hoberman, Mary Ann. *Mr. and Mrs. Muddle*
Johnston, Tony. *Sparky and Eddie, wild, wild rodeo!*
Lehn, Barbara. *What is an athlete?*
Liatsos, Sandra Olson. *Bicycle riding and other poems*
London, Jonathan. *White water*
McKissack, Robert L. *Try your best*
Martin, Bill (William Ivan). *White Dynamite and Curly Kidd*
Millen, C. M. *The low-down laundry line blues*
Miller, Margaret. *Here we go!*
   Water play
Ormerod, Jan. *Bend and stretch*
Pendziwol, Jean. *A treasure at sea for dragon and me*
Peterson, Esther Allen. *Penelope gets wheels*
Rayner, Mary. *Marathon and Steve*
Riddle, Tohby. *Careful with that ball, Eugene!*
Rotenberg, Lisa. *Rodeo pup*
Saddler, Allen. *The Archery contest*
Schomp, Virginia. *If you were a . . . ballplayer*
Sports! sports! sports!
Tinkelman, Murray. *Cowgirl*
Yeoman, John. *Old Mother Hubbard's dog takes up sport*

Sports – archery

Fisher, Leonard Everett. *William Tell*

Sports – baseball

Baseball ABC
Baseball 1-2-3
Bildner, Phil. *Shoeless Joe and Black Betsy*
Blackstone, Margaret. *This is baseball*
Bottner, Barbara. *Nana Hannah's piano*
Burleigh, Robert. *Home run*
Carrier, Roch. *The longest home run*
Christian, Mary Blount. *The sand lot*
Cohen, Ron. *My dad's baseball*
Cooper, Elisha. *Ballpark*
Cristaldi, Kathryn. *Baseball ballerina*
  Baseball ballerina strikes out
Curtis, Gavin. *The bat boy and his violin*
Day, Alexandra. *Frank and Ernest play ball*
Delaney, Ned. *Two strikes, four eyes*
Downing, Joan. *Baseball is our game*
Eaton, Deborah. *The rainy day grump*
Elster, Jean Alicia. *Just call me Joe Joe*
Fauchald, Nick. *Batter up!*
  Nice hit!
Giff, Patricia Reilly. *Ronald Morgan goes to bat*
Golenbock, Peter. *Hank Aaron*
Gordon, Sharon. *Play ball, Kate!*
Greene, Carol. *I can be a baseball player*
Herman, Gail. *Double-header*
Hernandez, Keith. *First-base hero*
Hillert, Margaret. *Play ball*
Hoff, Syd. *The littlest leaguer*
  Slugger Sal's slump
Hooks, William H. *Mr. Baseball*
Hopkinson, Deborah. *Girl wonder*
Isadora, Rachel. *Max*
  Nick plays baseball
Joyce, William. *Baseball Bob*
Ketteman, Helen. *I remember papa*
Kovalski, Maryann. *Take me out to the ball game*
Kraus, Robert. *Mort the sport*
Latimer, Jim. *The fox under first base*
Lexau, Joan M. *I'll tell on you*
Little, Jean. *Bats about baseball*
McConnachie, Brian. *Elmer and the chickens vs. the big league*
McCully, Emily Arnold. *Mouse practice*
Mandel, Peter. *Say hey*
Mara, Wil. *Jackie Robinson*
Marzollo, Jean. *Baseball brothers*
Mellage, Nanette. *Coming home*
Mochizuki, Ken. *Baseball saved us*
Morgan, Allen. *Matthew and the midnight ball game*
Motomora, Mitchell. *Specs*
Norworth, Jack. *Take me out to the ballgame*
Paxton, Tom. *The jungle baseball game*
Perkins, Al. *Don and Donna go to bat*
Portnoy, Mindy Avra. *Matzah ball*
Prager, Annabelle. *The baseball birthday party*
Rappaport, Doreen. *Dirt on their skirts*
Rubin, Jeff. *Baseball brothers*
Sachs, Marilyn. *Fleet-footed Florence*
  Matt's mitt
Schulman, Janet. *Camp Kee Wee's secret weapon*
Stadler, John. *Hooray for snail!*
Tavares, Matt. *Mudball*
  Oliver's game
  Zachary's ball
Thayer, Ernest Lawrence. *Casey at the bat*, ill. by Christopher Bing
  Casey at the bat, ill. by Gerald Fitzgerald
  Casey at the bat, ill. by Patricia Polacco
Van Nutt, Julia. *Skyrockets and snickerdoodles*
Waber, Bernard. *Gina*
Welch, Willy. *Playing right field*
Yolen, Jane. *Moon ball*
Zagwÿn, Deborah Turney. *Apple batter*

Sports – basketball

Barber, Barbara E. *Allie's basketball dream*
Bateman, Teresa. *The princesses have a ball*
Fauchald, Nick. *Jump ball!*
Henderson, Kathy. *I can be a basketball player*
Jordan, Roslyn M. *Salt in his shoes*
Martin, Bill (William Ivan). *Swish!*
Porte, Barbara Ann. *Harry's visit*
Suen, Anastasia. *Loose tooth*

Sports – bicycling

Andersen, Karen Born. *What's the matter, Sylvie, can't you ride?*
Aylesworth, Jim. *My sister's rusty bike*
Baker, Eugene H. *Bicycles*
Bang, Molly. *Delphine*
Barbot, Daniel. *A bicycle for Rosaura*
Baugh, Dolores M. *Bikes*
Beardshaw, Rosalind. *Grandpa's surprise*
  Grandpa's surprise
Bentley, Anne. *The Groggs' day out*
Blackstone, Stella. *Bear on a bike*
Blake, Quentin. *Mrs. Armitage on wheels*
Blance, Ellen. *Monster, Lady Monster and the bike ride*
Bourgeois, Paulette. *Franklin rides a bike*
Breinburg, Petronella. *Shawn's red bike*
Brown, Marc Tolon. *D. W. rides again!*
Bruna, Dick. *Miffy's bicycle*
Bundey, Nikki. *On a bike*
Bunting, Eve (Anne Evelyn). *Summer wheels*
Burleigh, Robert. *Messenger, messenger*
Cabban, Vanessa. *Bertie and Small and the fast bike ride*
Chlad, Dorothy. *Bicycles are fun to ride*
Crews, Donald. *Bicycle race*
Crowley, Michael. *Shack and back*
De Paola, Tomie (Thomas Anthony). *Kit and Kat*
Dowling, Paul. *You can do it, Rabbit*
Dragonwagon, Crescent. *Annie flies the birthday bike*
Eckart, Edana. *I can ride a bike*
Glass, Andrew. *Charles T. McBiddle*
Goldin, David. *Go-Go-Go!*
Harder, Dan (Dan Wymbs). *Colliding with Chris*
Heine, Helme. *Friends*
Holabird, Katharine. *Angelina's birthday surprise*
Hughes, Shirley. *Wheels*
Jakob, Donna. *My bike*
Johnston, Tony. *Three little bikers*
Krings, Antoon. *Oliver's bicycle*
Liebler, John. *Frog counts to ten*
Loewen, Nancy. *Bicycle safety*
London, Jonathan. *Let's go, Froggy!*
McLeod, Emilie Warren. *The bear's bicycle*
Maestro, Betsy. *Bike trip*
Mason, Jane B. *Hello, two-wheeler!*
Mollel, Tololwa M. (Tololwa Marti). *My rows and piles of coins*
Montanari, Eva. *Dino bikes*
Morgan-Vanroyen, Mary. *Night ride*
Muntean, Michaela. *Bicycle bear*
  Bicycle Bear rides again
Myers, Bernice. *Herman and the bears and the giants*
Olaleye, Isaac. *Bikes for rent!*
Paterson, A. B. (Andrew Barton). *Mulga Bill's bicycle*
Rey, H. A. (Hans Augusto). *Curious George rides a bike*
Rockwell, Anne F. *Bikes*
Say, Allen. *The bicycle man*
Schwartz, David M. *Sugargrandpa*
Shannon, David. *Duck on a bike*
Stott, Dorothy. *Little Duck's bicycle ride*
Strub, Susanne. *Lulu on her bike*
Sueyoshi, Akiko. *Ladybird on a bicycle*
Thomas, Jane Resh. *Wheels*
Wormell, Christopher. *Blue Rabbit and the runaway wheel*
Yorinks, Arthur. *Ugh*
Zullo, Germano. *Marta and the bicycle*

Sports – bowling

Eckart, Edana. *I can bowl*
Egan, Tim. *The blunder of the Rogues*

Sports – boxing

Ahlberg, Allan. *Mr. Biff the boxer*

Sports – camping *see* Camps, camping

Sports – fishing

Aldridge, Josephine Haskell. *Fisherman's luck*
　A penny and a periwinkle
Alexander, Sally Hobart. *Maggie's whopper*
Anderson, Lena. *Bunny fun*
Bettina (Bettina Ehrlich). *Pantaloni*
Bodnar, Judit Z. *Tale of a tail*
　A wagonload of fish
Bradman, Tony. *That's not a fish*
Brady, Kimberley Smith. *Keeper for the sea*
Carlstrom, Nancy White. *Wishing at dawn in summer*
Carney, Margaret (Margaret Rose). *The biggest fish in the lake*
Cech, John. *The southernmost cat*
Cook, Bernadine. *The little fish that got away*
Creech, Sharon. *Fishing in the air*
Delacre, Lulu. *Nathan's fishing trip*
Delton, Judy. *Duck goes fishing*
Demarest, Chris L. *Orville's odyssey*
Dewey, Ariane. *Splash!*
Elkin, Benjamin. *Six foolish fishermen*
Emmons, Chip. *Sammy wakes his dad*
Engel, Diana. *Fishing*
Farish, Terry. *The cat who liked potato soup*
Franklin, Kristine L. *The gift*
Gentle, Victor. *Killer sharks, killer people*
George, William T. *Fishing at Long Pond*
Gibbons, Gail. *Surrounded by sea*
Goffstein, M. B. (Marilyn Brooke). *Fish for supper*
Gray, Catherine. *Tammy and the gigantic fish*
Gréban, Quentin. *Nestor*
Griffith, Helen V. *Grandaddy's place*
Hall, Bill. *Fish tale*
Hann, Jacquie. *Up day, down day*
Hanze. *Yann and the whale*
Hertz, Ole. *Tobias catches trout*
　Tobias goes ice fishing
Hest, Amy. *Rosie's fishing trip*
Igus, Toyomi. *When I was little*
Ipcar, Dahlov (Zorach). *The biggest fish in the sea*
Johnston, Tony. *Fishing Sunday*
Joosse, Barbara M. *I love you the purplest*
Kidd, Nina. *June Mountain secret*
Koller, Jackie French. *Fish fry tonight*
Kovacs, Deborah. *Moonlight on the river*
Krudop, Walter Lyon. *Blue claws*
　The man who caught fish
Lapp, Eleanor. *In the morning mist*
Lawson, Julie. *A morning to polish and keep*
London, Jonathan. *Old salt, young salt*
　Where the big fish are
Long, Earlene. *Gone fishing*
Luenn, Nancy. *Nessa's fish*
McKissack, Patricia C. *A million fish . . . more or less*
Maris, Ron. *Bernard's boring day*
Martin, David. *Piggy and Dad go fishing*
Marzollo, Jean. *Amy goes fishing*
Mayer, Mercer. *A boy, a dog, a frog and a friend*
　A boy, a dog and a frog
Miles, Miska. *No, no, Rosina*
Moore, Elaine. *Deep river*
Munsch, Robert N. *Get me another one!*
Ness, Evaline. *Sam, Bangs, and moonshine*
Nicolai, Margaret. *Kitaq goes ice fishing*
Noll, Sally. *Lucky morning*
Nordqvist, Sven. *Festus and Mercury wishing to go fishing*

Oppel, Kenneth. *Peg and the whale*
Parker, Dorothy D. *Liam's catch*
Partridge, Elizabeth. *Oranges on Golden Mountain*
Paterson, Brian. *Zigby dives in*
Pope, Geraldine. *The empty creel*
Potter, Beatrix. *The tale of Mr. Jeremy Fisher*, ill. by author
　The tale of Mr. Jeremy Fisher, ill. by David Jorgensen
Rey, Margret (Margret Elisabeth Waldstein). *Curious George flies a kite*
Roth, Roger. *Fishing for Methuselah*
San Souci, Robert D. *Six foolish fishermen*
Say, Allen. *A river dream*
Sharp, N. L. *Today I'm going fishing with my dad*
Stevenson, Robert Louis. *The moon*
Surany, Anico. *Ride the cold wind*
Taylor, Mark. *The bold fisherman*
Thorne, Jenny. *My uncle*
Valgardson, W. D. *Winter rescue*
Wahl, Jan. *The fishermen*
Waldron, Kathleen Cook. *Loon Lake fishing derby*
Ward, Sally G. *Punky goes fishing*
Waterton, Betty. *A salmon for Simon*
Watson, Nancy Dingman. *Tommy's mommy's fish*, ill. by Aldren Auld Watson
　Tommy's mommy's fish, ill. by Thomas Aldren Dingman Watson
Wildsmith, Brian. *Pelican*
Williams, Garth. *Benjamin's treasure*
Wilson, Bob. *Stanley Bagshaw and the twenty-two ton whale*
Yerxa, Leo. *A fish tale, or, The little one that got away*

Sports – football

Barber, Tiki. *By my brother's side*
Carlson, Nancy L. *Louanne Pig in making the team*
Esiason, Boomer. *A boy named Boomer*
Fauchald, Nick. *Touchdown!*
Gifford, Kathie Lee. *Giff's big game*
Kuskin, Karla. *The Dallas Titans get ready for bed*
Martin, Bill (William Ivan). *Little granny quarterback*
Myers, Bernice. *Sidney Rella and the glass sneaker*
Stadler, John. *Snail saves the day*
Temple, Bob. *Randy Moss*

Sports – golf

Fauchald, Nick. *Tee off!*
Miller, William. *Night golf*
Waldron, Kathleen Cook. *Rough day at Loon Lake*

Sports – gymnastics

Brown, Marc Tolon. *D. W. flips!*
Hoban, Lillian. *Arthur's birthday party*
Kuklin, Susan. *Going to my gymnastics class*
Newcome, Zita. *Pop-up toddlerobics*
　Toddlerobics
Roche, Denis (Denis M.). *Mim, gym, and June*
Stevens, Carla. *Pig and the blue flag*
Taylor, Sean. *Boing!*
Wood, Tim. *Gymnastics*

Sports – hiking

Curious George goes hiking
Johnson, D. B. (Donald B.). *Henry hikes to Fitchburg*
Katschke, Judy. *Take a hike, Snoopy*
Lester, Helen. *Lin's backpack*
London, Jonathan. *The waterfall*
Rand, Gloria. *Willie takes a hike*
Shaw, Nancy (Nancy E.). *Sheep take a hike*

Sports – hockey

Brownridge, William Roy. *The moccasin goalie*
Carter, Anne Laurel. *The F team*
Fauchald, Nick. *Face off!*
Jam, Teddy. *The kid line*

Kidd, Bruce. *Hockey showdown*
Maloney, Peter (1955–). *The magic hockey stick*
Napier, Matt. *Z is for zamboni*
Shaw, Mary. *Brady Brady and the big mistake*
    Brady Brady and the great rink
    Brady Brady and the runaway goalie
    Brady Brady and the Twirlin' Torpedo goalie
Stevenson, James. *Sam the Zamboni man*

Sports – hunting

Allen, Judy. *Tiger*
Backovsky, Jan. *Trouble in Paradise*
Baker, Betty. *Sonny-Boy Sim*
Bemelmans, Ludwig. *Parsley*
Bernhard, Emery. *The girl who wanted to hunt*
Browne, Anthony. *Bear hunt*
Burch, Robert. *The hunting trip*
Burningham, John. *Harquin*
Calhoun, Mary. *Houn' dog*
Carrick, Donald. *The deer in the pasture*
    Harold and the great stag
Cowcher, Helen. *Jaguar*
De Paola, Tomie (Thomas Anthony). *The hunter and the animals*
De Regniers, Beatrice Schenk. *Catch a little fox*
Dionetti, Michelle V. *The day Eli went looking for bear*
Drummond, Allan. *Moby Dick*
Duvoisin, Roger Antoine. *The happy hunter*
Gage, Wilson. *Cully Cully and the bear*
Geraghty, Paul. *The hunter*
Hader, Berta Hoerner. *The mighty hunter*
Heinz, Brian J. *Nanuk, lord of the ice*
Hertz, Ole. *Tobias goes seal hunting*
Hoban, Russell. *The dancing tigers*
Hodges, Margaret. *The golden deer*
Jones, Maurice. *I'm going on a dragon hunt*
Judes, Marie-Odile. *Max, the stubborn little wolf*
Kahl, Virginia. *How do you hide a monster?*
Kamen, Gloria. *The ringdoves*
Kastner, Jill. *Snake hunt*
Kellogg, Steven (Stephen). *Tallyho, Pinkerton!*
Kilroy, Sally. *The baron's hunting party*
Krause, Ute. *Nora and the great bear*
Kroll, Steven. *One tough turkey*
Lacapa, Michael. *Antelope Woman*
Langstaff, John M. *Oh, a-hunting we will go*
Livermore, Elaine. *Looking for Henry*
MacDonald, Suse. *Nanta's lion*
Mari, Iela. *Eat and be eaten*
Mendoza, George. *The hunter I might have been*
Michels, Tilde. *Who's that knocking at my door?*
Parish, Peggy. *Good hunting, Blue Sky*
    Ootah's lucky day
Peet, Bill (William Bartlett). *Buford the little bighorn*
    The gnats of knotty pine
Prusski, Jeffrey. *Bring back the deer*
Rohmer, Harriet. *The invisible hunters*
Roop, Peter. *The buffalo jump*
Rosen, Michael (1946–). *We're going on a bear hunt*
Steiner, Charlotte. *Pete and Peter*
Turnbull, Ann. *Rob goes a-hunting*
Wahl, Jan. *Tiger watch*
Wildsmith, Brian. *Hunter and his dog*
Withers, Carl. *The wild ducks and the goose*
Wolcott, Patty. *Eeeeeek!*

Sports – ice skating

Bailey, Linda. *The best figure skater in the whole wide world*
Blackstone, Margaret. *This is figure skating*
Carlson, Nancy L. *Snowden*
DiVito, Anna. *Elephants on ice*
Hoban, Lillian. *Mr. Pig and Sonny too*
Holabird, Katharine. *Angelina ice skates*
Isadora, Rachel. *Sophie skates*
Karas, G. Brian. *Skidamarink*
Khalsa, Dayal Kaur. *The snow cat*

Lindman, Maj. *Snipp, Snapp, Snurr and the yellow sled*
Medearis, Angela Shelf. *Poppa's itchy Christmas*
Morris, Ann. *Little skaters*
O'Connor, Jane. *Kate skates*
Radin, Ruth Yaffe. *A winter place*
Rambeck, Richard. *Kristi Yamaguchi*
Stadler, John. *Ready, set, go!*
Stevenson, James. *Sam the Zamboni man*
Van Stockum, Hilda. *A day on skates*
Wallace-Brodeur, Ruth. *Home by five*
Weiss, Nicki. *Dog boy cap skate*

Sports – jumping rope

Brown, Marc Tolon. *Teddy bear, teddy bear*
English, Karen. *Hot day on Abbott Avenue*
Hru, Dakari. *The magic moonberry jump ropes*

Sports – karate

Hellman, Gary. *The karate way*
Morris, Ann. *Karate boy*
Rockwell, Anne F. *Chip and the karate kick*

Sports – mountain climbing

George, Jean Craighead. *Cliff hanger*
George, Jean Craighead. *To climb a waterfall*
Haswell, Peter. *Pog climbs Mount Everest*

Sports – Olympics

Emerson, Carl. *Marion Jones*
Hennessy, B. G. (Barbara G.). *Olympics!*
Mariotti, Mario. *Hand games*
Richards, Jean. *The first Olympic games*
Schulz, Charles M. *You're the greatest, Charlie Brown*

Sports – punchball

Best, Cari. *Last licks*

Sports – racing

Aarle, Thomas Van. *Don't put your cart before the horse race*
Adams, Adrienne. *The great Valentine's Day balloon race*
Æsop. *The hare and the tortoise*, ill. by Paul Galdone
    The hare and the tortoise, ill. by Carol Jones
    The hare and the tortoise, ill. by Gerald Rose
    The hare and the tortoise, ill. by Helen Ward
    The hare and the tortoise, ill. by Peter Weevers
    The tortoise and the hare, ill. by Sara Rojo
    The tortoise and the hare, adapt. & ill. by Janet Stevens
Alborough, Jez. *Running Bear*
Anderson, Laurie Halse. *Ndito runs*
Anderson, Peggy Perry. *We go in a circle*
Ashforth, Camilla. *Calamity*
Bacon, Ethel. *To see the moon*
Baumann, Hans. *The hare's race*
Baynton, Martin. *Fifty and the great race*
Benchley, Nathaniel. *Walter the homing pigeon*
Berenstain, Stan. *The Berenstain bears and the big road race*
Biro, Val. *Gumdrop on the Brighton run*
    Gumdrop races a train
Blake, Robert J. *Akiak*
Bullard, Lisa. *Powerboats*
    Stock cars
Calloway, Northern J. *Northern J. Calloway presents Super-vroomer!*
Caseley, Judith. *Field Day Friday*
Crews, Donald. *Bicycle race*
Crowley, Michael. *Shack and back*
Cuyler, Margery. *Road signs*
Dahl, Michael. *One checkered flag*
Dickens, Frank. *Boffo*
Dodds, Dayle Ann. *The Great Divide*
Floyd, Lucy. *Rabbit and turtle go to school*
Goldin, David. *Go-Go-Go!*

Hall, Derek. *Tiger runs*
Heine, Helme. *Three little friends: the racing cart*
Hurd, Edith Thacher. *Last one home is a green pig*
Isenberg, Barbara. *The adventures of Albert, the running bear*
  Albert the running bear gets the jitters
Kessler, Leonard P. *The big mile race*
Kolar, Bob. *Racer dogs*
Kurtz, Jane. *Only a pigeon*
La Fontaine, Jean de. *The hare and the tortoise*
Leedy, Loreen. *The race*
Libby, Barbara. *I rode the red horse*
Lowell, Susan. *The tortoise and the jackrabbit*
McLenighan, Valjean. *Turtle and rabbit*
McNaughton, Colin. *The rat race*
McPhail, David M. *The great race*
Marshall, Edward. *Fox on wheels*
Miranda, Anne. *Vroom, chugga, vroom-vroom*
Moore, John. *Granny Stickleback*
Mora, Pat. *The race of toad and deer*
Nelson, Kristin L. *Monster trucks*
Neuhaus, David. *His finest hour*
Otsuka, Yuzo. *Suho and the white horse*
Piehl, Janet. *Formula One race cars*
Reimold, Mary Gallagher. *My mom is a runner*
Repchuk, Caroline. *The race*
Rex, Michael. *My race car*
Schwartz, David M. *Sugargrandpa*
Seibert, Patricia. *Mush!*
Shearer, Marilyn J. *The crown of fools*
Todd, Mark. *Start your engines*
Van Woerkom, Dorothy. *Harry and Shelburt*
Vozar, David. *M. C. Turtle and the hip hop hare*
Wilkinson, Sylvia. *I can be a race car driver*
Wood, Tim. *Motor racing*
  Motorcycling
Wyllie, Stephen. *The great race*
Zullo, Germano. *Marta and the bicycle*

Sports – rock climbing

London, Jonathan. *The waterfall*

Sports – roller skating

Calmenson, Stephanie. *Roller skates!*
Crary, Elizabeth. *I'm frustrated*
Gifford, Kathie Lee. *Giff the scaredy bear*
Johnson, Mildred D. *Wait, skates!*
Kemp, Moira. *Round and round the garden*
Pilkey, Dav. *The Moonglow Roll-O-Rama*
Saltzberg, Barney. *Hip, hip, hooray day!*
Wahl, Jan. *Rabbits on roller skates!*
Witt, Alexa. *It's great to skate*

Sports – sailing

Agell, Charlotte. *To the island*
Ahlberg, Allan. *Skeleton crew*
Beck, Andrea. *Elliot's shipwreck*
Blackstone, Stella. *An island in the sun*
Crews, Donald. *Sail away*
Greydanus, Rose. *Climb aboard*
Lund, Deb. *Dinosailors*
McNeil, Florence. *Sail away*
Marshall, Janet Perry. *Banana moon*
Schubert, Ingrid. *There's always room for one more*
Simon, Charnan. *Click and the kids go sailing*
Uhlberg, Myron. *Lemuel, the fool*
Van Dusen, Chris. *Down to the sea with Mr. Magee*
Whittle, Emily. *Sailor cats*
Wilson, Sarah. *Big day on the river*

Sports – skateboarding

Brimner, Larry Dane. *Cat on wheels*
Carlson, Nancy L. *Arnie and the skateboard gang*
Havill, Juanita. *Embarcadero upset*

Howard, Arthur. *Cosmo zooms*
Mammano, Julie. *Rhinos who skateboard*
Ziefert, Harriet. *April Fool*

Sports – skiing

Calhoun, Mary. *Cross-country cat*
Dahl, Michael. *Downhill fun*
Freeman, Don. *Ski pup*
Hutchins, H. J. (Hazel J.). *Ben's snow song*
Krementz, Jill. *A very young skier*
Lindman, Maj. *Snipp, Snapp, Snurr and the red shoes*
Marol, Jean-Claude. *Vagabul goes skiing*
Moran, George. *Imagine me on a sit-ski!*
Peet, Bill (William Bartlett). *Buford the little bighorn*
Simon, Francesca. *Camels don't ski*

Sports – skin diving

Baker, Jeannie. *The hidden forest*
Carrick, Carol. *Dark and full of secrets*
Loomis, Christine. *Scuba bunnies*
Ungerer, Tomi. *The Mellops go diving for treasure*

Sports – sledding

Bacon, Ethel. *To see the moon*
Chaconas, Don. *On a wintry morning*
Curious George goes sledding
Fearnley, Jan. *A perfect day for it*
Iwamura, Kazuo. *The fourteen forest mice and the winter sledding day*
Kharms, Daniil. *The story of a boy named Will, who went sledding down the hill*
Seibert, Patricia. *Mush!*
Weston, Martha. *Jack and Jill and Big Dog Bill*
Winthrop, Elizabeth. *Sledding*

Sports – snowboarding

Mammano, Julie. *Rhinos who snowboard*

Sports – soccer

Browne, Anthony. *Willy the wizard*
Brownridge, William Roy. *The final game*
Burleigh, Robert. *Goal*
Catalanotto, Peter. *Dylan's day out*
Eckart, Edana. *I can play soccer*
Farndon, John. *It's just a game*
Fauchald, Nick. *Score!*
Finchler, Judy. *You're a good sport, Miss Malarkey*
Flanagan, Alice K. *Coach John and his soccer team*
Hamm, Mia. *Winners never quit*
Klingel, Cynthia Fitterer. *Soccer*
Lakin, Pat (Patricia). *A good sport*
Lester, Helen. *Hurty feelings*
London, Jonathan. *Froggy plays soccer*
McNaughton, Colin. *Preston's goal!*
Mammano, Julie. *Rhinos who play soccer*
Murphy, Stuart J. *Game time*
Rockwell, Anne F. *Morgan plays soccer*
Saltzberg, Barney. *Soccer mom from outer space*
Vyner, Tim. *World team*

Sports – Special Olympics

Pulver, Robin. *Way to go, Alex!*

Sports – surfing

Blake, Quentin. *Mrs. Armitage and the big wave*
Bundey, Nikki. *In the water*
Minters, Frances. *Princess Fishtail*
Ormondroyd, Edward. *Broderick*
Raglus, Jeff. *Schnorky the wave puncher*

Sports – swimming

Alexander, Martha G. *We never get to do anything*
Anderson, Lena. *Bunny fun*
Atkins, Jeannine. *Get set! Swim!*
Barclay, Jane. *Going on a journey to the sea*
Beatty, Hetty Burlingame. *Droopy*
Beim, Jerrold. *The swimming hole*
Berridge, Celia. *Going swimming*
Borden, Louise. *Albie the lifeguard*
Brown, M. K. (Mary K.). *Let's go swimming with Mr. Sillypants*
Bundey, Nikki. *In the water*
Cohn, Norma. *Brother and sister*
Coles, Alison. *Michael and the sea*
Cooper, Susan. *Frog*
Cousins, Lucy. *Maisy goes swimming*
    Maisy's pool
Day, Alexandra. *River parade*
Eckart, Edana. *I can swim*
George, Lindsay Barrett. *William and Boomer*
Ginsburg, Mirra. *The chick and the duckling*
Gutman, Anne. *Gaspard at the seashore*
Hall, Derek. *Otter swims*
Heiligman, Deborah. *Mike Swan, sink or swim*
Henley, Claire. *Joe's pool*
Herman, Gail. *The littlest duckling*
Hest, Amy. *Make the team, Baby Duck*
Jay, Betsy. *Swimming lessons*
Keeshan, Robert. *Itty Bitty Kitty makes a big splash*
Khalsa, Dayal Kaur. *The snow cat*
Kliphuis, Christine. *Robbie and Ronnie*
Krings, Antoon. *Oliver's pool*
Lasky, Kathryn. *Sea swan*
London, Jonathan. *Froggy learns to swim*
Mattern, Joanne. *Safety in the water*
Moore, Inga. *Aktil's big swim*
Newman, Jeff. *Reginald*
Ormerod, Jan. *Ben goes swimming*
Peterson, Sue H. *Swim with me*
Pfister, Marcus. *Hang on, Hopper!*
Rice, Eve. *Swim!*
Riley, Linda Capus. *Elephants swim*
Rockwell, Anne F. *Katie Catz makes a splash*
Schuurmans, Hilde. *Sydney won't swim*
Schwartz, Roslyn. *The mole sisters and the rainy day*
Shortall, Leonard W. *Tony's first dive*
Stanley, Mandy. *At the pool*
Stevens, Carla. *Hooray for pig!*
Stott, Dorothy. *Too much*
Strub, Susanne. *Lulu goes swimming*
Umansky, Kay. *You can swim, Jim*
Van Leeuwen, Jean. *Too hot for ice cream*
Volkmann, Roy. *Curious kittens*
Waddell, Martin. *The pig in the pond*
Ward, Nick. *Come on Baby Duck*
Watanabe, Shigeo. *Let's go swimming*
Weston, Martha. *Tuck in the pool*
Winton, Tim. *The deep*

Sports – T-ball

Bunting, Eve (Anne Evelyn). *Trouble on the T-ball team*
Gemme, Leila Boyle. *T-ball is our game*

Sports – Tae Kwon Do

Pinkney, J. Brian. *Jojo's flying side kick*

Sports – volleyball

Fauchald, Nick. *Bump! set! spike!*

Sports – wrestling

Boelts, Maribeth. *Big Daddy, frog wrestler*
Morgan, Allen. *Matthew and the midnight wrestlers*
Novak, Matt. *Gertie and Gumbo*

Ogburn, Jacqueline K. *The Masked Maverick*
Stren, Patti. *Mountain Rose*

Sportsmanship

Farndon, John. *It's just a game*
Finchler, Judy. *You're a good sport, Miss Malarkey*
Flanagan, Alice K. *Coach John and his soccer team*
Gifford, Kathie Lee. *Giff's big game*
Hamm, Mia. *Winners never quit*
Krosoczka, Jarrett J. *Max for president*

Spring *see* Seasons – spring

Squirrels *see* Animals – squirrels

Stage *see* Theater

Starfish *see* Crustaceans – starfish

Stars

Ada, Alma Flor. *Jordi's star*
Allen, Laura Jean. *Ottie and the star*
Asch, Frank. *Starbaby*
Barlowe, Sy. *A child's book of stars*
Barner, Bob. *Stars, stars, stars*
Baumgart, Klaus. *Laura's Christmas star*
    Laura's secret
    Laura's star
Benjamin, A. H. *Mouse, mole and the falling star*
Birdseye, Tom. *A song of stars*
Boon, Emilie. *Peterkin meets a star*
Branley, Franklyn M. (Mansfield). *Journey into a black hole*
    The sky is full of stars
Carpenter, Mary-Chapin. *Halley came to Jackson*
Clément, Claude. *The man who lit the stars*
Coatsworth, Elizabeth. *Good night*
Cölle, Gisela. *The star tree*
Daffis-Felicelli, Christine. *The little star of Bethlehem*
Davis, Karen. *Star light, star bright*
DeBoer, Jesslyn. *Follow the star*
De Montaño, Martha Kreipe. *Coyote in love with a star*
Doherty, Berlie. *The midnight man*
Dussling, Jennifer. *Stars*
Elschner, Géraldine. *Moonchild, star of the sea*
Elzbieta. *Dikou and the baby star*
Facklam, Margery. *Only a star*
Field, Susan. *The sun, the moon, and the silver baboon*
Fisher, Aileen Lucia. *Sing of the earth and sky*
Freeman, Mae Blacker. *The sun, the moon and the stars*
Gibbons, Gail. *Stargazers*
Ginolfi, Arthur. *The tiny star*
Glyman, Caroline A. *What's above the sky?*
Goble, Paul. *The lost children*
Hansen, Felicity. *The first bear*
Hillman, Elizabeth. *Min-Yo and the moon dragon*
Hines, Anna Grossnickle. *Sky all around*
Hoffman, Mary. *Three wise women*
Horácek, Petr. *When the moon smiled*
Hort, Lenny. *How many stars in the sky*
Ichikawa, Satomi. *Nora's stars*
Kuskin, Karla. *A space story*
Langley, Karen. *Shine*
Lee, Jeanne M. *The legend of the milky way*
London, Jonathan. *Liplap's wish*
Luttrell, Ida. *The star counters*
McDonald, Megan. *My house has stars*
Mallat, Kathy. *Seven stars, more!*
Marzollo, Jean. *I see a star*
Matze, Claire Sidhom. *The stars in my Geddoh's sky*
Mitton, Jacqueline. *Zoo in the sky*
Mobley, Jane. *The star husband*
Modesitt, Jeanne. *The night call*
Nappa, Mike. *Do you see the star?*
Nelson, S. D. *The Star People*

Newman, Lesléa. *Too far away to touch*
Oughton, Jerrie. *How the stars fell into the sky*
Pfister, Marcus. *The Christmas star*
Puttock, Simon. *A ladder to the stars*
Radley, Gail. *The night Stella hid the stars*
Ray, Deborah Kogan. *Stargazing sky*
Reynolds, Peter H. *Sydney's star*
Robbins, Sandra. *The firefly star*
Rockwell, Anne F. *Pur stars*
Rosen, Sidney. *How far is a star?*
     Where's the big dipper?
Sis, Peter. *Starry messenger*
Slate, Joseph. *The secret stars*
     The star rocker
Stone, Kazuko G. *Goodnight Twinklegator*
The sun, the moon, and the stars
Sykes, Julie. *Little Rocket's special star*
Taylor, Jane. *Twinkle, twinkle little star*, ill. by Heather Collins
     Twinkle, twinkle, little star, ill. by Michael Hague
     Twinkle, twinkle little star, ill. by Julia Noonan
Tazewell, Charles. *The littlest angel*, ill. by Deborah Lanino
     The littlest angel, ill. by Paul Micich
     The littlest angel, ill. by Rebecca Thornburgh
They followed a bright star
Tibo, Gilles. *Simon and the snowflakes*
Tomecek, Steve. *Stars*
Wandelmaier, Roy. *Stars*
Weedn, Flavia. *The star gift*
Widman, Christine. *The star grazers*
Wilson-Max, Ken. *Max's starry night*
Winter, Jeanette. *Follow the drinking gourd*
Wyler, Rose. *The starry sky*
Yeomans, Thomas. *For every child a star*
Zimelman, Nathan. *The star of Melvin*

Stealing *see* Behavior – stealing; Crime

Steam shovels *see* Machines

Steamrollers *see* Machines

Stepchildren *see* Divorce; Family life – stepfamilies

Stepfamilies *see* Divorce; Family life – stepfamilies

Stepparents *see* Divorce; Family life – stepfamilies

Stones *see* Rocks

Storekeepers *see* Careers – storekeepers

Stores

Alakija, Polly. *Catch that goat!*
Alexander, Liza. *Ernie gets lost*
Anholt, Catherine. *Truffles in trouble*
Arkin, Alan. *One present from Flekman's*
Baggette, Susan K. *Jonathan goes to the grocery store*
Baugh, Dolores M. *Let's go*
     Supermarket
Bograd, Larry. *Lost in the store*
Bond, Michael. *Paddington Bear and the Christmas surprise*
Carling, Amelia Lau. *Mama and Papa have a store*
     Mama and Papa have a store
Carlstrom, Nancy White. *Baby-O*
Christian, Mary Blount. *The bookstore mouse*
Cooper, Letice Ulpha. *The bear who was too big*
Corey, Shana. *Milly and the Macy's Parade*
Cowley, Joy. *The video shop sparrow*
Cowley, Stewart. *What's that sound?*
Curious George visits a toy store
Day, Alexandra. *Carl goes shopping*
DeLage, Ida. *ABC pigs go to market*
Dematons, Charlotte. *Let's go*
DiSalvo-Ryan, DyAnne. *Grandpa's corner store*

Ehlert, Lois. *Market day*
Field, Rachel Lyman. *General store*, ill. by Giles Laroche
     General store, ill. by Nancy Winslow Parker
Flanagan, Alice K. *A busy day at Mr. Kang's grocery store*
     Buying a pet from Ms. Chavez
Fleming, Candace. *The hatmaker's sign*
Freeman, Don. *Corduroy*
Gibbons, Gail. *Department store*
Gomi, Taro. *I lost my dad*
Gordon, Margaret. *The supermarket mice*
Graham, Amanda. *Who wants Arthur?*
Grossman, Bill. *Tommy at the grocery store*
Hale, Kathleen. *Orlando, the frisky housewife*
Hamm, Diane Johnston. *Laney's lost momma*
Harris, Leon A. *The great diamond robbery*
Haseley, Dennis. *The thieves' market*
Hastings, Evelyn Beilhart. *The department store*
Hoff, Syd. *Merry Christmas, Henrietta!*
Houston, Gloria. *But no candy*
Jackson, Jean. *Mrs. Piccolo's easy chair*
Johnson, Angela. *The Rolling Store*
Johnson, Paul Brett. *Farmers' market*
Krull, Kathleen. *Supermarket*
Lewin, Ted. *Big Jimmy's Kum Kau Chinese take out*
     Market!
Lippman, Peter. *The Know-It-Alls mind the store*
Lobel, Arnold. *On Market Street*
London, Jonathan. *Candystore man*
Loomis, Christine. *At the mall*
Loupy, Christophe. *Don't worry, Wags*
McNaughton, Colin. *At the stores*
McPartland, Suzy. *Toy-shop surprise*
Maitland, Barbara. *The bookstore burglar*
     The bookstore ghost
     The bookstore valentine
Maschler, Fay. *T. G. and Moonie go shopping*
Masters, Anthony. *Ricky's rat gang*
Meddaugh, Susan. *The witches' supermarket*
Melmed, Laura Krauss. *The Marvelous Market on Mermaid*
Miller, Alice P. *The little store on the corner*
Miranda, Anne. *To market, to market*
Modarressi, Mitra. *Yard sale*
Munsch, Robert N. *Something good*
Murphy, Stuart J. *Just enough carrots*
Naylor, Phyllis Reynolds. *Sweet strawberries*
Oliver, Stephen. *Shopping*
O'Neill, Alexis. *Estela's swap*
Paraskevas, Betty. *The tangerine bear*
Parks, Carmen. *Farmers market*
Pearson, Tracey Campbell. *The storekeeper*
Pieńkowski, Jan. *Bel and Bub and the black hole*
Potter, Beatrix. *Ginger and Pickles*
Rockwell, Anne F. *The supermarket*
Rubel, Nicole. *Goldie*
Rylant, Cynthia. *Little Whistle*
     Little Whistle's Christmas
     Little Whistle's dinner party
     Little Whistle's medicine
Sawyer, Jean. *Our village shop*
Scarry, Richard. *Richard Scarry's great big mystery book*
Schaefer, Lola M. *Supermarket*
Shea, Kitty. *Out and about at the supermarket*
Shelby, Anne. *We keep a store*
Skolsky, Mindy Warshaw. *Hannah and the whistling tea kettle*
Solomon, Joan. *A present for Mum*
Spier, Peter. *Food market*
     The pet store
     The toy shop
Steiner, Jörg. *The bear who wanted to be a bear*
Wellington, Monica. *Apple farmer Annie*
Wells, Rosemary. *Max's dragon shirt*
Williams, Barbara. *I know a salesperson*
Williams, Karen Lynn. *Tap-tap*
Young, Ed (Edward). *Donkey trouble*

Stories in rhyme *see* Rhyming text

Storks *see* Birds – storks

Storms *see* Weather – storms

Storytelling *see* Activities – storytelling

Strangers *see* Behavior – talking to strangers

Streams *see* Rivers

Streets *see* Roads

String

Bakken, Harold. *The special string*
Calhoun, Mary. *The traveling ball of string*
Fleischman, Paul. *Lost!*
Geisert, Arthur. *The giant ball of string*
Hindley, Judy. *A piece of string is a wonderful thing*

Stubbornness *see* Character traits – stubbornness

Stuttering *see* Handicaps – stuttering

Submarines *see* Boats, ships

Suits *see* Clothing – suits

Sukkot *see* Holidays – Sukkot

Sullivan Islands *see* Foreign lands – South Sea Islands

Sultans *see* Royalty – sultans

Summer *see* Seasons – summer

Sun

Alda, Arlene. *Hurry Granny Annie*
Anno, Mitsumasa. *Anno's sundial*
    In shadowland
Arnold, Caroline. *Sun fun*
Asch, Frank. *The sun is my favorite star*
Barlowe, Sy. *A child's book of stars*
Baylor, Byrd. *The way to start a day*
Bernstein, Margery. *How the sun made a promise and kept it*
Bishop, Gavin. *Maui and the sun*
Branley, Franklyn M. (Mansfield). *Eclipse*
    The planets in our solar system
    The sun, our nearest star
    Sunshine makes the seasons
Butler, Andrea. *Mr. Sun and Mr. Sea*
Canyon, Christopher. *John Denver's Sunshine on my shoulders*
Carlstrom, Nancy White. *Who gets the sun out of bed?*
Chall, Marsha Wilson. *Rupa raises the sun*
Daly, Niki. *Why the sun and moon live in the sky*
Day, Alexandra. *Helping the sun*
Dayrell, Elphinstone. *Why the sun and the moon live in the sky*
De Gerez, Toni. *Louhi, witch of North Farm*
Derby, Sally. *The mouse who owned the sun*
De Regniers, Beatrice Schenk. *Who likes the sun?*
Desimini, Lisa. *Sun and moon*
Elkin, Benjamin. *Why the sun was late*
Ellwand, David. *Midas Mouse*
Emberley, Michael. *Welcome back, Sun*
Engelbrektson, Sune. *The sun is a star*
Euvremer, Teryl. *Sun's up*
Field, Susan. *The sun, the moon, and the silver baboon*
Fisher, Aileen Lucia. *Sing of the earth and sky*
Flanagan, Alice K. *Sunshine*
Freeman, Mae Blacker. *The sun, the moon and the stars*
Gantschev, Ivan. *Good morning, good night*
Gerstein, Mordicai. *The sun's day*
Gibbons, Gail. *Sun up, sun down*

Ginsburg, Mirra. *How the sun was brought back to the sky*
    Where does the sun go at night?
Goudey, Alice E. *The day we saw the sun come up*
Greene, Carol. *Shine, sun!*
Gregory, Valiska. *When stories fell like shooting stars*
Hamberger, John. *The day the sun disappeared*
Harrison, David Lee. *Wake up, sun!*
Hendra, Sue. *Oliver's wood*
Henley, Claire. *Sunny day*
Hines, Anna Grossnickle. *What can you do in the sun?*
Hurd, Edith Thacher. *The day the sun danced*
Huth, Holly Young. *The son of the sun and the daughter of the moon*
Ivory, Lesley Anne. *Cats in the sun*
Kandoian, Ellen. *Under the sun*
Kinney, Jean. *What does the sun do?*
Kleven, Elisa. *Sun bread*
Kramsky, Jerry. *The cranky sun*
La Fontaine, Jean de. *The north wind and the sun*
Lindbergh, Reeve. *What is the sun?*
London, Jonathan. *Like butter on pancakes*
McDermott, Gerald. *Musicians of the sun*
McPartland, Suzy. *Good morning, sun*
Markoe, Merrill. *The day my dogs became guys*
Marzollo, Jean. *Sun song*
Meeker, Clare Hodgson. *Who wakes rooster?*
Mollel, Tololwa M. (Tololwa Marti). *A promise to the sun*
Nelson, Robin. *A sunny day*
Novak, Matt. *Claude and Sun*
Obrist, Jürg. *The miser who wanted the sun*
Oliviero, Jamie. *The fish skin*
Ormerod, Jan. *Sunshine*
Palazzo-Craig, Janet. *Our friend the sun*
Peet, Bill (William Bartlett). *Cock-a-doodle Dudley*
Polacco, Patricia. *I can hear the sun*
Ringi, Kjell (Arne Sorensen). *The sun and the cloud*
Roche, Hannah. *Sandra's sun hat*
Roth, Susan L. *The story of light*
San Souci, Robert D. *Peter and the blue witch baby*
Schlein, Miriam. *The sun looks down*
    The sun, the wind, the sea and the rain
Schneider, Herman. *Follow the sunset*
Sherman, Pat. *The sun's daughter*
Shulevitz, Uri. *Dawn*
Slate, Joseph. *Story time for Little Porcupine*
Storm, Theodor. *Little Hobbin*
The sun, the moon, and the stars
Tafuri, Nancy. *What the sun sees / What the moon sees*
Theodorou, Rod. *Across the solar system*
Tresselt, Alvin R. *Sun up*, ill. by author
    Sun up, ill. by Henri Sorensen
Troughton, Joanna. *Who will be the sun?*
Whitethorne, Baje. *Sunpainters*
Wildsmith, Brian. *What the moon saw*
Williams, Laura E. *Torch fishing with the sun*
Wolkstein, Diane. *The day Ocean came to visit*

Superstition

Chall, Marsha Wilson. *Rupa raises the sun*
DeFelice, Cynthia C. *Willy's silly grandma*
Hassett, John. *Father Sun, Mother Moon*
Jenkins, Steve. *Duck's breath and mouse pie*
McNaughton, Colin. *Don't step on the crack!*
Sewall, Marcia. *The Green Mist*

Surfing *see* Sports – surfing

Suriname *see* Foreign lands – Suriname

Swallows *see* Birds – swallows

Swamps

Appelt, Kathi. *Where, where is Swamp Bear?*
Arnosky, Jim. *Raccoon on his own*
    Wild and swampy

Berkes, Marianne Collins. *Marsh music*
Dennard, Deborah. *Bullfrog at Magnolia Circle*
Fleming, Candace. *Who invited you?*
Garrett, Ann. *Keeper of the swamp*
LeBox, Annette. *Wild bog tea*
London, Jonathan. *What Newt could do for Turtle*
San Souci, Robert D. *Little Pierre*
Talley, Linda. *Jackson's plan*
Thomas, Joyce Carol. *The gospel Cinderella*
Vaughan, Marcia Kapok. *Whistling Dixie*
Yolen, Jane. *Welcome to the river of grass*

Swans *see* Birds – swans

Swapping *see* Activities – trading

Sweaters *see* Clothing – sweaters

Sweden *see* Foreign lands – Sweden

Swimming *see* Sports – swimming

Swinging *see* Activities – swinging

Switzerland *see* Foreign lands – Switzerland

Symbiosis

Stone, Lynn M. *Partners*

T-ball *see* Sports – T-ball

Tables *see* Furniture – tables

Tae Kwon Do *see* Sports – Tae Kwon Do

Tailors *see* Careers – tailors

Tails *see* Anatomy – tails

Taiwan *see* Foreign lands – Taiwan

Talking *see* Activities – talking

Talking to strangers *see* Behavior – talking to strangers

Tall tales

Adams, Ken. *When I was your age*
Aliki. *The story of Johnny Appleseed*
Anderson, Laurie Halse. *The big cheese of Third Street*
Aylesworth, Jim. *My sister's rusty bike*
Balcziak, Bill. *John Henry*
    Paul Bunyan
    Pecos Bill
Bang, Betsy. *The cucumber stem*
Calhoun, Mary. *Jack and the whoopee wind*
Cohen, Caron Lee. *Renata, Whizbrain and the ghost*
    Sally Ann Thunder Ann Whirlwind Crockett
Cole, Brock. *Buttons*
Darling, Kathy (Mary Kathleen). *Pecos Bill finds a horse*
Davol, Marguerite W. *The loudest, fastest, best drummer in Kansas*
Day, Edward C. *John Tabor's ride*
Dewey, Ariane. *Febold Feboldson*
    Pecos Bill
    The tea squall

Domanska, Janina. *What happens next?*
Drummond, Allan. *Casey Jones*
Emberley, Barbara. *The story of Paul Bunyan*
Felton, Harold W. *Pecos Bill and the mustang*
Gleeson, Brian. *Finn McCoul*
    Paul Bunyan
Gorbachev, Valeri. *Where is the apple pie?*
Graves, Keith. *Uncle Blubbafink's seriously ridiculous stories*
Griffin, Kitty. *The foot-stomping adventures of Clementine Sweet*
Helldorfer, M. C. (Mary Claire). *Jack, Skinny Bones, and the golden pancakes*
Isaacs, Anne. *Swamp Angel*
Keats, Ezra Jack. *John Henry*
Kellogg, Steven (Stephen). *I was born about 10,000 years ago*
    Johnny Appleseed
    Mike Fink
    Paul Bunyan
    Pecos Bill
    Sally Ann Thunder Ann Whirlwind Crockett
Ketteman, Helen. *Heat wave*
    Shoeshine Whittaker
Kimmel, Eric A. *The Erie Canal pirates*
Koren, Edward. *Very hairy Harry*
Lent, Blair. *John Tabor's ride*
Lester, Julius. *John Henry*
Lindbergh, Reeve. *Johnny Appleseed*
Lobel, Arnold. *Mouse tales*
McAllister, Angela. *The clever cowboy*
McGill, Alice. *Sure as sunrise*
MacGill-Callahan, Sheila. *The last snake in Ireland*
McKissack, Patricia C. *A million fish . . . more or less*
Metaxas, Eric. *Stormalong, the legendary sea captain*
Nolen, Jerdine. *Big Jabe*
    Harvey Potter's balloon farm
    Thunder Rose
Oppel, Kenneth. *Peg and the whale*
Root, Phyllis. *Kiss the cow*
    Rosie's fiddle
Roth, Roger. *Fishing for Methuselah*
Roth, Susan L. *The biggest frog in Australia*
Rounds, Glen. *Washday on Noah's ark*
Rubel, Nicole. *A cowboy named Ernestine*
Schanzer, Rosalyn. *How Ben Franklin stole the lightning*
Schnitzler, Pattie L. *Widdermaker*
Shepard, Aaron. *Master man*
Shulevitz, Uri. *What is a wise bird like you doing in a silly tale like this?*
Sis, Peter. *A small tall tale from the far Far North*
Smith, Janice Lee. *Jess and the stinky cowboys*
Spurr, Elizabeth. *The long, long letter*
Swain, Gwenyth. *Johnny Appleseed*
Wahl, Jan. *The singing geese*
White, Linda Arms. *Comes a wind*
Willey, Margaret. *Clever Beatrice, an Upper Peninsula conte*
Williams, Suzanne. *Library Lil*
Wood, Audrey. *The Bunyans*
Wooldridge, Connie Nordhielm. *The legend of Strap Buckner*
Wright, Catherine (Catherine E.). *Steamboat Annie and the thousand-pound catfish*
Zeman, Ludmila. *Sindbad in the land of giants*

Tanzania *see* Foreign lands – Tanzania

Tapirs *see* Animals – tapirs

Tarascan Indians *see* Indians of North America – Tarascan

Tardiness *see* Behavior – promptness, tardiness

Taste *see* Senses – taste

Taxi drivers *see* Careers – taxi drivers

Taxis

Barracca, Debra. *A taxi dog Christmas*
Barracca, Sal. *The adventures of taxi dog*
Best, Cari. *Taxi! Taxi!*
Maestro, Betsy. *Taxi*
Mitchell, Lucy Sprague. *The taxi that hurried*
Moore, Lilian. *Papa Albert*
Nordqvist, Sven. *Porker's taxi*
Ross, Jessica. *Ms. Klondike*

Teachers *see* Careers – teachers

Teasing *see* Behavior – bullying

Teddy bears *see* Toys – bears

Teeth

Alper, Ann Fitzgerald. *Harry McNairy, Tooth Fairy*
Balzola, Asun. *Munia and the orange crocodile*
Barnett, Naomi. *I know a dentist*
Bate, Lucy. *Little rabbit's loose tooth*
Beeler, Selby B. *Throw your tooth on the roof*
Berridge, Celia. *Hannah's temper*
Birdseye, Tom. *Airmail to the moon*
Bouchard, Dave. *Fairy*
Brown, Marc Tolon. *Arthur's tooth*
Brown, Ruth. *Crazy Charlie*
Bunting, Eve (Anne Evelyn). *Trouble on the T-ball team*
Carrick, Carol. *Norman fools the tooth fairy*
Carson, Jo. *Pulling my leg*
Catalanotto, Peter. *Christmas always . . .*
Chandra, Deborah. *George Washington's teeth*
Chardiet, Bernice. *Martin and the tooth fairy*
Chetkowski, Emily. *Pumpkin smile*
Clement, Rod. *Grandpa's teeth*
Cole, Joanna. *The missing tooth*
Collington, Peter. *The tooth fairy*
Cooney, Nancy Evans. *The wobbly tooth*
Curious George goes to the dentist
Davis, Katie (Katie I.). *Mabel the Tooth Fairy and how she got her job*
De Groat, Diane. *Alligator's toothache*
Dinan, Carolyn. *Say cheese!*
Durant, Alan. *Dear tooth fairy*
Duvoisin, Roger Antoine. *Crocus*
Edwards, Pamela Duncan. *Dear Tooth Fairy*
Eriksson, Eva. *The tooth trip*
Falwell, Cathryn. *Dragon tooth*
Farber, Erica. *Ooey gooey*
Flanagan, Alice K. *Dr. Kanner, dentist with a smile*
Gillerlain, Gayle. *Reverend Thomas's false teeth*
Gomi, Taro. *The crocodile and the dentist*
Grambling, Lois G. *This whole Tooth Fairy thing's nothing but a big rip-off!*
Gunther, Louise. *A tooth for the tooth fairy*
Hallinan, P. K. (Patrick K.). *My dentist, my friend*
Heller, Nicholas. *The tooth tree*
Hooks, William H. *The mystery of the missing tooth*
James, Brian. *The Supertwins and tooth trouble*
Jay, Betsy. *Jane vs. the Tooth Fairy*
Jenkin-Pearce, Susie. *Boris's big ache*
Johnson, Arden. *The Lost Tooth Club*
Kaye, Marilyn. *The real tooth fairy*
Keller, Laurie. *Open wide: tooth school inside*
Krensky, Stephen. *My loose tooth*
Kroll, Steven. *Loose tooth*
Laminack, Lester L. *Trevor's wiggly-wobbly tooth*
Luttrell, Ida. *Milo's toothache*
Maccarone, Grace. *My tooth is about to fall out*
McCloskey, Robert. *One morning in Maine*
MacDonald, Amy. *Cousin Ruth's tooth*
MacDonald, Maryann. *Rosie's baby tooth*
McGinley, Phyllis. *Lucy McLockett*
Maconie, Robin. *Alice and her fabulous teeth*
McPhail, David M. *The bear's toothache*

Mellor, Corinne. *Clark the toothless shark*
Miles, Elizabeth J. *Mouths and teeth*
Mitra, Annie. *Tusk! Tusk!*
Moss, Miriam. *Wibble wobble*
Munsch, Robert N. *Andrew's loose tooth*
Murkoff, Heidi Eisenberg. *What to expect when you go to the dentist*
Nerlove, Miriam. *Just one tooth*
Noll, Sally. *I have a loose tooth*
O'Brien, Patrick. *Megatooth*
Olson, Mary. *Nice try, Tooth Fairy*
Paxton, Tom. *The story of the Tooth Fairy*
Pomerantz, Charlotte. *The mango tooth*
Quin-Harkin, Janet. *Helpful Hattie*
Richter, Alice Numeroff. *You can't put braces on spaces*
Ricketts, Michael. *Teeth*
Rockwell, Harlow. *My dentist*
Rosenberry, Vera. *Vera goes to the dentist*
Ross, Pat. *Molly and the slow teeth*
Sandeman, Anna. *Skin, teeth, and hair*
Scamell, Ragnhild. *Who likes Wolfie?*
Schaefer, Lola M. *Dental office*
    Loose tooth
Seuss, Dr. *The tooth book*
Silverman, Martin. *My tooth is loose*
Simms, Laura. *Rotten teeth*
Sis, Peter. *Madlenka*
Suen, Anastasia. *Loose tooth*
Sundvall, Viveca. *Mimi and the biscuit factory*
Swanson, Diane. *The dentist and you*
Vrombaut, An. *Clarabella's teeth*
Wells, Rosemary. *The school play*
West, Colin. *The king's toothache*
Wilhelm, Hans. *I lost my tooth!*
Williams, Barbara. *Albert's toothache*
Wolf, Bernard. *Michael and the dentist*
Zalben, Jane Breskin. *Buster gets braces*

Telephone

Allen, Jeffrey. *Mary Alice, operator number 9*
    Mary Alice returns
Chukovskii, Kornei Ivanovich. *Telephone*, ill. by Vladimir Radunsky
Dodds, Siobhan. *Ting-a-ling!*
Jackson, Jean. *Big lips and hairy arms*
King, Bob. *Sitting on the farm*
Koski, Mary. *Impatient Pamela calls 9-1-1*
Raschka, Christopher. *Ring! Yo?*
Telephones
Weiss, Ellen. *Telephone time*
Wyse, Lois. *Two guppies, a turtle and Aunt Edna*

Telephone operators *see* Careers – telephone operators

Television

Barden, Rosalind. *TV monster*
Barracca, Debra. *Maxi, the star*
Berenstain, Stan. *The Berenstain bears and too much TV*
Bergen, Lara Rice. *Blue's world of words*
Brown, Marc Tolon. *The bionic bunny show*
Davis, Gary. *Working at a TV station*
Dobson, Clive. *Fred's TV*
Heilbroner, Joan. *Tom the TV cat*
Krauss, Ronnie. *Take a look, it's in a book*
Lobb, Janice. *Listen and see! What's on TV?*
McCully, Emily Arnold. *Zaza's big break*
McPhail, David M. *Fix-it*
Nickle, John. *TV Rex*
Novak, Matt. *Mouse TV*
Polacco, Patricia. *Aunt Chip and the great Triple Creek dam affair*
Rodda, Emily. *Power and glory*

Telling stories *see* Activities – storytelling

Telling time *see* Clocks, watches; Time

Temper tantrums *see* Emotions – anger

Texas

Cole, Barbara Hancock. *Texas star*
Cox, Judy. *The West Texas chili monster*
Du Bois, William Pène. *Otto in Texas*
Munro, Roxie. *The inside-outside book of Texas*
Rice, James. *Gaston goes to Texas*

Textless *see* Wordless

Thailand *see* Foreign lands – Thailand

Thanksgiving *see* Holidays – Thanksgiving

Theater

Ackerman, Karen. *Bean's big day*
Agee, Jon. *Milo's hat trick*
Ahlberg, Allan. *The Cinderella show*
Alexander, Sue. *Seymour the prince*
    Small plays for special days
    Small plays for you and a friend
Avi. *Silent movie*
Beeke, Jemma. *The Rickety Barn show*
Behrens, June. *Christmas-magic wagon*
    The feast of Thanksgiving
Berenstain, Stan. *The Berenstain bears get stage fright*
Bond, Felicia. *The Halloween play*
Boyd, Lizi. *Princess, cowboy, pirate, elf*
Brighton, Catherine. *Hope's gift*
Brown, Don. *Mack made movies*
Brown, Marc Tolon. *Arthur's Thanksgiving*
Brown, Ruth. *The shy little angel*
Butterworth, Nick. *The Nativity play*
Calhoun, Mary. *Henry the Christmas cat*
Calmenson, Stephanie. *No stage fright for me!*
Caple, Kathy. *Starring Hillary*
Carlson, Nancy L. *The talent show*
Cartlidge, Michelle. *Mouse theater*
Caseley, Judith. *Mickey's class play*
Cazet, Denys. *The duck with squeaky feet*
Cohen, Miriam. *Starring first grade*
Curious George goes to a movie
Daly, Kathleen N. *Strawberry Shortcake and pets on parade*
Daly, Niki. *Bravo, Zan Angelo!*
Davidson, Rebecca Piatt. *All the world's a stage*
De Groat, Diane. *Liar, liar, pants on fire*
De Paola, Tomie (Thomas Anthony). *Stagestruck*
    The Christmas pageant
    The night of Las Posadas
    Sing, Pierrot, sing
De Regniers, Beatrice Schenk. *Picture book theater*
Dunrea, Olivier. *Appearing tonight! Mary Heather Elizabeth Livingstone*
Edwards, Pamela Duncan. *Bravo, Livingstone Mouse!*
Engelbreit, Mary. *Queen of the class*
Ernst, Lisa Campbell. *When Bluebell sang*
Ets, Marie Hall. *Another day*
Ford, Miela. *My day in the garden*
Fox, Mem. *Wombat divine*
Freeman, Don. *Hattie the backstage bat*
    Will's quill
Freeman, Lydia. *Pet of the Met*
French, Vivian. *A Christmas star called Hannah*
A frog he would a-wooing go (folk-song). *Frog went a-courting*, retold & ill. by Dominic Catalano
Frye, Dean. *Days of sunshine, days of rain*
Gallwey, Kay. *Dancing Daisy*
Gauch, Patricia Lee. *Tanya and the magic wardrobe*
Gershwin, George. *Summertime from Porgy and Bess*
Giff, Patricia Reilly. *The almost awful play*
Goffstein, M. B. (Marilyn Brooke). *An actor*
Goodall, John S. *Paddy's evening out*
Grimm, Jacob. *King Grisly-Beard*

Hartman, Bob. *Granny Mae's Christmas play*
    The one and only Delgado Cheese
Hodges, Margaret. *Comus*
Hoffman, Mary. *Amazing Grace*
Hoffmann, E. T. A. *The nutcracker*, ill. by Maurice Sendak
Holabird, Katharine. *Angelina ice skates*
    Angelina on stage
Hughes, Shirley. *Angel Mae*
Isadora, Rachel. *Jesse and Abe*
    Lili on stage
    Opening night
Isherwood, Shirley. *Flora the frog*
Jane, Pamela. *Milo and the greatest trick ever*
Jennings, Sharon. *Franklin and the magic show*
Johnson, Dolores. *The best bug to be*
Komaiko, Leah. *Aunt Elaine does the dance from Spain*
Krauss, Ronnie. *Take a look, it's in a book*
Krementz, Jill. *A very young actress*
Krensky, Stephen. *Shooting for the moon*
Lakin, Pat (Patricia). *The palace of stars*
Langley, Karen. *Shine*
Lawlor, Laurie. *The biggest pest on Eighth Avenue*
Lawson, Julie. *Arizona Charlie and the Klondike Kid*
Layton, Aviva. *The squeakers*
Leedy, Loreen. *The bunny play*
Lester, Helen. *Tackylocks and the three bears*
Levine, Arthur A. *Sheep dreams*
Lewison, Wendy Cheyette. *Shy Vi*
Lithgow, John. *Marsupial Sue presents "The Runaway Pancake"*
Littlesugar, Amy. *Tree of hope*
Lobel, Arnold. *Martha, the movie mouse*
Lubach, Peter. *Harry and the singing fish*
McClintock, Barbara. *The battle of Luke and Longnose*
McCully, Emily Arnold. *The evil spell*
    My real family
    Speak up, Blanche!
    Zaza's big break
McDonald, Megan. *Penguin and Little Blue*
Maiorano, Robert. *Backstage*
Marshall, James. *Swine lake*
Martin, Judith. *The tree angel*
Mills, Elaine. *Marinetta at the ballet*
Novak, Matt. *While the shepherd slept*
Oppenheim, Joanne. *Mrs. Peloki's class play*
Ormerod, Jan. *Ms. MacDonald has a class*
Paraskevas, Betty. *Marvin, the tap-dancing horse*
Patz, Nancy. *Gina Farina and the Prince of Mintz*
Pearson, Susan. *Lenore's big break*
Philpot, Graham. *Fabulous fairy tale follies*
Potter, Giselle. *The year I didn't go to school*
Rockwell, Anne F. *Thanksgiving Day*
Rose, Mitchell. *Norman*
Sage, James. *The boy and the dove*
Schotter, Roni. *Purim play*
Schwartz, Henry. *Albert goes Hollywood*
Sendak, Maurice. *Maurice Sendak's Really Rosie*
Spinelli, Eileen. *Six hogs on a scooter*
Spirn, Michele. *I am the turkey*
Stadler, Alexander. *Beverly Billingsly takes a bow*
Steiner, Charlotte. *Kiki is an actress*
Tangvald, Christine Harder. *Hey, Mr. Angel!*
Trimble, Marcia. *Peppy's shadow*
Tryon, Leslie. *Albert's play*
Vail, Rachel. *Over the moon*
Waber, Bernard. *Evie & Margie*
Wells, Rosemary. *The school play*
Wharton, Thomas. *Hildegard sings*
Whippo, Walt. *Little white duck*
Yeoman, John. *The young performing horse*

Thieves *see* Crime

Thumb sucking

Cooney, Nancy Evans. *Donald says thumbs down*
Dionne, Wanda. *Little Thumb*
Ernst, Kathryn F. *Danny and his thumb*

Heitler, Susan M. (Susan McCrensky). *David decides, no more thumb-sucking*
Inkpen, Mick. *Arnold*
Klimowicz, Barbara. *The strawberry thumb*
Sonnenschein, Harriet. *Harold's hideaway thumb*
Tobias, Tobi. *The quitting deal*
Tufts, Mary L. *The wee kitten who sucked her thumb*

Thunder *see* Weather – lightning, thunder; Weather – storms

Tibet *see* Foreign lands – Tibet

Tigers *see* Animals – tigers

Time

Aiken, Conrad Potter. *Tom, Sue and the clock*
Aldag, Kurt. *Some things never change*
Allancé, Mireille d'. *How long?*
Allen, Jeffrey. *Mary Alice, operator number 9*
Allington, Richard L. *Time*
Ambrus, Victor G. *What's the time, Dracula?*
Ancona, George. *Handtalk zoo*
Anderson, Lena. *Tick-tock*
Anno, Mitsumasa. *Anno's sundial*
Appelt, Kathi. *Bats around the clock*
Axelrod, Amy. *Pigs on a blanket*
Aylesworth, Jim. *The completed hickory dickory dock*
Becker, Bonny. *Just a minute*
Bloom, Becky. *Mr. Cuckoo*
Bodwell, Gaile. *The long day of the giants*
Bragdon, Lillian J. *Tell me the time, please*
Brown, Ken (Ken James). *What's the time, Grandma Wolf?*
Carle, Eric. *The grouchy ladybug*
Cartlidge, Michelle. *Mouse time*
Charlip, Remy. *Why I will never ever ever ever have enough time to read this book*
Colman, Hila. *Watch that watch*
Cousins, Lucy. *Maisy's first clock*
Dale, Elizabeth. *How long?*
Dunbar, James. *Tick-tock*
Fleischman, Paul. *Time train*
Gerstein, Mordicai. *The sun's day*
Gibbons, Gail. *Clocks and how they go*
Gordon, Sharon. *Tick tock clock*
Gregory, Nan. *Amber waiting*
Grunwald, Lisa. *Now, soon, later*
Handford, Martin. *Find Waldo now*
    Where's Waldo now
Harper, Dan. *Telling time with Big Mama Cat*
Hawkins, Colin. *What time is it, Mr. Wolf?*
Hay, Dean. *Now I can count*
Henderson, Douglas. *Dinosaur tree*
Henwood, Simon. *The clock shop*
Hoff, Syd. *Henrietta, the early bird*
Hopkins, Lee Bennett. *It's about time*
Hutchins, Pat. *Clocks and more clocks*
Jakob, Donna. *My bike*
Jones, Carol. *What's the time, Mr. Wolf?*
Katz, Bobbi. *Tick-tock, let's read the clock*
Killingback, Julia. *What time is it, Mrs. Bear?*
Krasilovsky, Phyllis. *The man who tried to save time*
Krensky, Stephen. *The big time bears*
Littlewood, Valerie. *The season clock*
Llewellyn, Claire. *My first book of time*
Lyon, George Ella. *Father Time and the day boxes*
McCaughrean, Geraldine. *My grandmother's clock*
McGinley, Phyllis. *Wonderful time*
McGuire, Richard. *Night becomes day*
McKee, David. *The school bus comes at eight o'clock*
McMillan, Bruce. *Time to . . .*
Maestro, Betsy. *Around the clock with Harriet*
Manning, Linda. *Animal hours*
May, Charles Paul. *High-noon rocket*
Merriam, Eve. *Train leaves the station*

Mother Goose. *The real Mother Goose clock book*
Mueller, Virginia. *Monster goes to school*
Murphy, Stuart J. *Game time*
    Get up and go!
Ness, Evaline. *Do you have the time, Lydia?*
Nobens, C. A. *Montgomery's time zone*
Older, Jules. *Telling time*
Pieńkowski, Jan. *Time*
Plourde, Lynn. *Winter waits*
Pluckrose, Henry Arthur. *Time*
Richards, Kitty. *It's about time, Max!*
Rockwell, Anne F. *Bear Child's book of hours*
Rohmann, Eric. *Time flies*
Rosa-Mendoza, Gladys. *What time is it? = Qué hora es?*
Sadler, Marilyn. *Alistair's time machine*
Schlein, Miriam. *It's about time*
Schuett, Stacey. *Somewhere in the world right now*
Scott, Janine. *Time to tell*
Seignobosc, Françoise. *What time is it, Jeanne-Marie?*
Sharratt, Nick. *The time it took Tom*
Singer, Marilyn. *Nine o'clock lullaby*
Skutina, Vladimir. *Nobody has time for me*
Slobodkin, Louis. *The late cuckoo*
Stanley, Diane. *Joining the Boston Tea Party*
Steinmetz, Leon. *Clocks in the woods*
Sweeney, Joan. *Me counting time*
Thompson, Carol. *Time*
Turner, Gwenda. *Once upon a time*
Verdet, Andre. *All about time*
Vyner, Tim. *World team*
Watson, Nancy Dingman. *When is tomorrow?*
Wilson-Max, Ken. *Wake up; Sleep tight*
Ziner, Feenie. *The true book of time*
Zolotow, Charlotte (Shapiro). *Over and over*

Tin soldiers *see* Toys – soldiers

Tlingit Indians *see* Indians of North America – Tlingit

Toads *see* Frogs & toads

Toes *see* Anatomy – toes

Toilet training

Allison, Alida. *The toddler's potty book*
Bentley, Dawn. *Fuzzy Bear's potty book*
Caseley, Judith. *Annie's potty*
Civardi, Anne. *Potty time*
Cole, Joanna. *My big boy potty*
    My big girl potty
    Your new potty
Falwell, Cathryn. *P.J. & Puppy*
Freeman, Mylo. *Potty*
Gomi, Taro. *Everyone poops*
Lewison, Wendy Cheyette. *The princess and the potty*
Lindgren, Barbro. *Sam's potty*
Miller, Virginia. *On your potty!*
Morgan, Richard. *Zoo poo*
My potty book for boys
My potty book for girls
Patrick, Denise Lewis. *No diapers for baby!*
Piggy and Bear in their underwear
Reichmeier, Betty. *Potty time!*
Rogers, Fred. *Going to the potty*
Rogers, Paul (Patrick). *Ruby's potty*
Ross, Tony. *I want my potty*
Sears, William, M.D. *You can go to the potty*
Willems, Mo. *Time to pee*
Young, Ruth. *My potty chair*

Tongue twisters

Bodecker, N. M. (Nils Mogens). *Snowman Sniffles and other verse*
Brown, Marcia. *Peter Piper's alphabet*
Buck, Nola. *Creepy crawly critters and other Halloween tongue twisters*

Santa's short suit shrunk and other Christmas tongue twisters
Bunting, Eve (Anne Evelyn). *Say it fast*
Gordon, Jeffie Ross. *Six sleepy sheep*
Johnson, Odette. *One prickly porcupine*
Keller, Charles. *Tongue twisters*
Mahy, Margaret. *Simply delicious!*
Monster poems
Obligado, Lilian. *Faint frogs feeling feverish and other terrifically tantalizing tongue twisters*
Patz, Nancy. *Pumpernickel tickle and mean green cheese*
Pomerantz, Charlotte. *The piggy in the puddle*
Radunsky, Eugenia. *Yucka Drucka Droni*
Rovetch, Lissa. *Ook the book*
Smith, Robert Paul. *Jack Mack*

Tongues *see* Anatomy – tongues

Tonsillectomy *see* Illness – tonsillectomy

Tools

Araki, Mie. *The magic toolbox*
Barton, Byron. *Tools*
Beim, Jerrold. *Tim and the tool chest*
Boelts, Maribeth. *Little Bunny's cool tool set*
Carle, Eric. *My very first book of tools*
Clements, Andrew. *Workshop*
Connor, Leslie. *Miss Bridie chose a shovel*
DeSantis, Kenny. *A doctor's tools*
Gibbons, Gail. *The art box*
   Tool book
Kelley, True. *Hammers and mops, pencils and pots*
Kesselman, Judi R. *I can use tools*
Lerner, Marguerite Rush. *Doctors' tools*
Miller, Margaret. *Who uses this?*
Morris, Ann. *Tools*
Neitzel, Shirley. *The house I'll build for the wrens*
Pluckrose, Henry Arthur. *Things we cut*
Rockwell, Anne F. *The toolbox*
Snyder, Inez. *Building tools*
   Gardening tools
Wallace, John. *Building a house with Mr. Bumble*
Zaffo, George J. *The giant nursery book of things that work*

Tooth fairy *see* Fairies; Teeth

Tornadoes *see* Weather – tornadoes

Tortoises *see* Reptiles – turtles, tortoises

Toucans *see* Birds – toucans

Touch *see* Senses – touch

Towns *see* Cities, towns

Toy & movable books *see* Format, unusual – toy & movable books

Toy makers *see* Careers – toy makers

Toys

Abolafia, Yossi. *Yanosh's Island*
Adlerman, Daniel. *Africa calling*
Alden, Joan. *A boy's best friend*
Alexander, Martha G. *Good night, Lily*
   Lily and Willy
   The story grandmother told
   Where's Willy?
   Willy's boot
Anderson, Lena. *Bunny box*
Ardizzone, Aingelda. *The night ride*
Arkin, Alan. *One present from Flekman's*
Asch, Frank. *Baby in the box*

Ashforth, Camilla. *Calamity*
   Horatio's bed
   Monkey tricks
Atwell, Debby. *Humphrey Thud*
Ayer, Jacqueline. *Nu Dang and his kite*
Ayers, Rebecca Hickox. *Per and the Dala horse*
Bailey, Debbie. *Toys*
Bambi
Bang, Molly. *One fall day*
Beck, Andrea. *Elliot bakes a cake*
   Elliot bakes a cake
   Elliot digs for treasure
   Elliot gets stuck
   Elliot's bath
   Elliot's Christmas surprise
   Elliot's emergency
   Elliot's noisy night
   Elliot's shipwreck
Beckman, Kaj. *Lisa cannot sleep*
Bianco, Margery Williams. *The velveteen rabbit*, ill. by Allen Atkinson
   The velveteen rabbit, ill. by Monique Félix
   The velveteen rabbit, ill. by Michael Green
   The velveteen rabbit, ill. by Michael Hague
   The velveteen rabbit, ill. by Estella Hickman
   The velveteen rabbit, ill. by Steve Johnson & Lou Fancher
   The velveteen rabbit, ill. by David Jorgensen
   The velveteen rabbit, ill. by Thea Kliros
   The velveteen rabbit, ill. by Elizabeth Miles
   The velveteen rabbit, ill. by William Nicholson
   The velveteen rabbit, ill. by Robyn Officer
   The velveteen rabbit, ill. by Ilse Plume
   The velveteen rabbit, ill. by S. D. Schindler
   The velveteen rabbit, ill. by Tien
Billam, Rosemary. *Fuzzy rabbit*
Binzen, Bill. *Alfred goes house hunting*
Birchall, Mark. *Rabbit's birthday surprise*
   Rabbit's wooly sweater
Bishop, Roma. *Toys*
Blake, Quentin. *Clown*
Boegehold, Betty. *Hurray for Pippa!*
Bohdal, Susi. *Harry the hare*
Bornstein, Ruth Lercher. *Annabelle*
Bourgeois, Paulette. *Franklin and Harriet*
   Franklin's class trip
Bowman, Pete. *I wish I were big*
Brandenberg, Franz. *Aunt Nina and her nephews and nieces*
Breese, Gillian. *The amazing adventures of Teddy Tum Tum*
Breeze, Lynn. *Baby's toys*
Brisson, Pat. *Hobbledy-clop*
Brown, Ruth. *I don't like it!*
Browne, Anthony. *Gorilla*
Bruna, Dick. *My toys*
Bryant, Dean. *See the bear*
Buchanan, Heather S. *George and Matilda Mouse and the floating school*
Bunting, Eve (Anne Evelyn). *Ducky*
Burdick, Margaret. *Bobby Otter and the blue boat*
Burns, Maurice. *Go ducks, go!*
Butterworth, Nick. *Albert the bear*
   All together now!
   Just like Jasper
   When it's time for bed
   When there's work to do
   When we go shopping
   When we play together
Cabban, Vanessa. *Bertie and Small and the brave sea journey*
   Bertie and Small and the fast bike ride
Cader, Lisa Lebowitz. *When I wear my crown*
   When I wear my tiara
Campbell, Rod. *Buster's morning*
Capucilli, Alyssa Satin. *Biscuit visits the pumpkin patch*
Carle, Eric. *10 little rubber ducks*
Carlstrom, Nancy White. *Barney is best*
Cartlidge, Michelle. *Good night, Teddy*
Chichester Clark, Emma. *I love you, Blue Kangaroo!*
   Where are you, Blue Kangaroo?

Chorao, Kay. *Carousel round and round*
   Kate's car
   Molly's Moe
Cocca-Leffler, Maryann. *Missing: one stuffed rabbit*
Collington, Peter. *The midnight circus*
Conrad, Pam. *Doll Face has a party!*
   The Tub grandfather
   The Tub People
   The Tub People's Christmas
Coombs, Patricia. *The lost playground*
Cooper, Helen (Helen F.). *Tatty-Ratty*
Corbett, Grahame. *Guess who?*
   Who is hiding?
   Who is inside?
   Who is next?
Couture, Susan Arkin. *The block book*
Cowen-Fletcher, Jane. *Farmer Will*
Craig, M. Jean. *Boxes*
Crampton, Gertrude. *Scuffy the tugboat*
Cuneo, Mary Louise. *Mail for Husher Town*
Curious George visits a toy store
Dale, Penny. *Ten out of bed*
   Ten play hide-and-seek
Daly, Niki. *Old Bob's brown bear*
   Vim, the rag mouse
Davenport, Zoë. *Toys*
Dedieu, Thierry. *The little Christmas soldier*
De Lynam, Alicia Garcia. *It's mine!*
Demarest, Chris L. *My blue boat*
   My little red car
Demi. *The magic boat*
De Vries, Maggie. *How sleep found Tabitha*
Dewan, Ted. *Baby gets the zapper*
DiFiori, Lawrence. *My toys*
Dobrin, Arnold Jack. *Josephine's 'magination*
Dodds, Siobhan. *Grandpa Bud*
   Ting-a-ling!
Dowling, Paul. *Meg and Jack's new friends*
Drescher, Henrik. *Look-alikes*
Drummond, Violet H. *Phewtus the squirrel*
Dugan, Barbara. *Loop the loop*
Dunbar, Joyce. *Lollopy*
Egielski, Richard. *Slim and Jim*
Ehrlich, H. M. *Louie's goose*
Elson, Raymond. *Toys*
Emberley, Rebecca. *My toys = Mi juguetes*
Ernst, Lisa Campbell. *The letters are lost!*
   The rescue of Aunt Pansy
Falconer, Ian. *Olivia – and the missing toy*
Farber, Werner. *Night lion*
Faulkner, Keith. *The monster in my toybox*
Feiffer, Jules. *I lost my bear*
Field, Eugene. *The gingham dog and the calico cat*, ill. by Janet
   Street
   The gingham dog and the calico cat, ill. by Johanna Westerman
Fox, Christyan. *What color is that, PiggyWiggy?*
Fox, Mem. *A bedtime story*
Francis, Anna B. *Pleasant dreams*
Frankel, Ben. *Tertius and Pliny*
Frazee, Marla. *Santa Claus, the world's number one toy expert*
Freedman, Claire. *Night-night, Emily*
Gackenbach, Dick. *Poppy the panda*
Galbraith, Kathryn Osebold. *Laura Charlotte*
Garay, Luis. *Pedrito's day*
Gay, Michel. *Bibi's birthday surprise*
Geras, Adèle. *The nutcracker*
Gerstein, Mordicai. *Bedtime, everybody!*
Ginsburg, Mirra. *Four brave sailors*
Gomi, Taro. *Guess who?*
Goodhart, Pippa. *Row, row, row your boat*
Greenfield, Eloise. *Kia Tanisha drives her car*
Greenleaf, Ann. *No room for Sarah*
Grey, Mini. *Traction Man is here*
Grifalconi, Ann. *The toy trumpet*
Grimes, Nikki. *Someone's baby-sitting*
   Someone's fighting
Gugler, Laurel Dee. *Muddle cuddle*

Gundersheimer, Karen. *Shapes to show*
Hague, Michael. *The nutcracker*
Hale, Irina. *Chocolate mouse and sugar pig*
   The lost toys
Haus, Felice. *Beep! Beep! I'm a jeep*
Hayashi, Akiko. *Aki and the fox*
Hayes, Sarah. *Lucy Anna and the Finders*
   This is the bear and the bad little girl
Hayward, Linda. *The runaway Christmas toy*
Heap, Sue. *Cowboy Baby*
Henderson, Kathy. *Baby knows best*
   The little boat
Herman, Gail. *There is a town*
Hill, Eric. *Spot's toy box*
Hillert, Margaret. *The birthday car*
Hillman, Priscilla. *The Merry-Mouse book of toys*
Hindley, Judy. *Rosy's visitors*
Hippely, Hilary Horder. *Adventure on Klickitat Island*
Hissey, Jane. *Hoot*
   Jolly snow
   Jolly Tall
   Little Bear lost
   Old Bear
   Old Bear [board book]
   Old Bear, a pop-up book
   Ruff
Hoban, Russell. *La corona and the tin frog*
Hoffman, Eric. *No fair to tigers = No es justo para los tigres*
Hoffmann, E. T. A. *The nutcracker*, ill. by Francesca Crespi
   The nutcracker, ill. by Renée Graef
   The nutcracker, ill. by Rachel Isadora
   The nutcracker, ill. by Joanna Isles
   The nutcracker, ill. by Lisbeth Zwerger
   The nutcracker ballet, ill. by Carolyn Ewing
   The nutcracker ballet, ill. by Vladimir Vasilévich Vagin
Hollyn, Lynn. *Lynn Hollyn's Christmas toyland*
Hooks, William H. *Mr. Monster*
Hoopes, Lyn Littlefield. *Wing-a-ding*
Howell, Lynn. *Winifred's new bed*
Hughes, Richard. *Gertrude's child*
Hughes, Shirley. *David and dog*
   Dogger
Hutchins, Pat. *Tidy Titch*
Ichikawa, Satomi. *La La Rose*
   Nora's castle
   Nora's stars
Inkpen, Mick. *Kipper's bathtime*
   Kipper's snowy day
   Kipper's toybox
   Nothing
   Thing
Inns, Christopher. *Next! please*
Isherwood, Shirley. *Something for James*
Ivory, Lesley Anne. *The birthday cat*
Jahn-Clough, Lisa. *My friend and I*
Jocelyn, Marthe. *A day with Nellie*
Johnson, Crockett. *The blue ribbon puppies*
   Ellen's lion
Johnson, Jane. *Sybil and the blue rabbit*
Jonas, Ann. *Now we can go*
Jones, Harold. *There and back again*
Joyce, William. *The Leaf Men and the brave good bugs*
Kahn, Joan. *Seesaw*
Kastner, Jill. *Merry Christmas, Princess Dinosaur*
   Princess Dinosaur
Kennedy, Marge M. *The book of boo!*
Kent, Jack. *Piggy Bank Gonzalez*
Kerins, Tony (Anthony). *The brave ones*
   Tat Rabbit's treasure
Kerr, Judith. *Mog and bunny*
Kraus, Robert. *The tree that stayed up until next Christmas*
Kroll, Steven. *The magic rocket*
Leonard, Alain. *Barnaby and the big gorilla*
Leonard, Marcia. *My pal Al*
Leslie, Amanda. *Hidden toys*
Lewis, Kim. *Good night, Harry*
   Here we go Harry

Jamie's tiger
The toy circus
Ward, Nick. *Giant*
Weber, Linda Kay. *Louie Larkey and the bad dream patrol*
Weiss, Nicki. *Where does the brown bear go?*
Where does the brown bear go? [board book]
Wells, Rosemary. *Bunny party*
Max's bedtime
Max's birthday
Max's toys
Weninger, Brigitte. *What's the matter, Davy?*
Westcott, Nadine Bernard. *Going to bed*
Whybrow, Ian. *Harry and the bucketful of dinosaurs*
Harry and the dinosaurs say "Raahh"
Sammy and the robots
Wild, Margaret. *Let the celebrations begin!*
Williams, Karen Lynn. *Galimoto*
Winthrop, Elizabeth. *Bear and Roly-Poly*
Wisniewski, David. *Sumo Mouse*
Yolen, Jane. *Time for naps*
Yorinks, Arthur. *Harry and Lulu*
Ziefert, Harriet. *Baby Ben's go-go book*
Come out, Jessie!
Good night everyone!

Toys – balloons

Augustin, Barbara. *Antonella and her Santa Claus*
Baker, Alan. *Benjamin's balloon*
Brown Rabbit's shape book
Barrows, Marjorie Wescott. *Muggins' big balloon*
Bonsall, Crosby Newell. *Mine's the best*
Boon, Emilie. *Belinda's balloon*
Bright, Robert. *Georgie and the runaway balloon*
Brock, Emma Lillian. *Surprise balloon*
Bullock, Kathleen. *Rabbits are coming*
Carrick, Carol. *The highest balloon on the common*
Chase, Catherine. *My balloon*
Coxe, Molly. *Louella and the yellow balloon*
Curtis, Jamie Lee. *Where do balloons go?*
Davies, Kay. *My balloon*
Faulkner, Keith. *Pop! went another balloon!*
Fenton, Edward. *The big yellow balloon*
Glennon, Karen M. *Miss Eva and the red balloon*
Goodsell, Jane. *Toby's toe*
Gray, Nigel. *A balloon for grandad*
Inkpen, Mick. *The blue balloon*
Kotzwinkle, William. *Walter, the farting dog: trouble at the yard sale*
Mari, Iela. *The magic balloon*
Matthias, Catherine. *Too many balloons*
Too many balloons = Demasiados globos
Munsch, Robert N. *Where is Gah-Ning?*
Nolen, Jerdine. *Harvey Potter's balloon farm*
Rau, Dana Meachen. *Lots of balloons*
Robledo, Honorio. *Nico visits the moon*
Ross, Christine. *Lily and the present*
Sharmat, Marjorie Weinman. *I don't care*
Taylor, Alastair. *Swollobog*
Watanabe, Yuichi. *Wally the whale who loved balloons*
Weitzman, Jacqueline Preiss. *You can't take a balloon into the Metropolitan Museum*
You can't take a balloon into the National Gallery
Willard, Nancy. *The well-mannered balloon*

Toys – balls

Bang, Molly. *Yellow ball*
Baron, Alan. *Little Pig's bouncy ball*
Egielski, Richard. *Three magic balls*
Espenscheid, Gertrude E. *The oh ball*
Hamberger, John. *The lazy dog*
Holl, Adelaide. *The remarkable egg*
Hooks, William H. *Where's Lulu?*
Kellogg, Steven (Stephen). *The mystery of the magic green ball*
Krahn, Fernando. *The biggest Christmas tree on earth*
Lillegard, Dee. *My yellow ball*
Lindgren, Barbro. *Sam's ball*

McClintock, Marshall. *Stop that ball*
McMillan, Bruce. *Beach ball – left, right*
Maley, Anne. *Have you seen my mother?*
Schubert, Leda. *Winnie plays ball*
Tafuri, Nancy. *The ball bounced*
Yardley, Joanna. *The red ball*

Toys – bears

Alborough, Jez. *My friend bear*
Where's my teddy?
Aldis, Dorothy (Keeley). *Hiding*
Alexander, Martha G. *I'll protect you from the jungle beasts*
Allison, Catherine. *Brown paper bear*
Anglund, Joan Walsh. *How many days has Baby to play?*
Teddy bear tales
Anholt, Catherine. *Bear and baby*
Appiah, Sonia. *Amoko and Efua Bear*
Ardizzone, Aingelda. *The night ride*
Arnold, Tedd. *My first drawing book*
Asch, Frank. *In the eye of the teddy*
Ashforth, Camilla. *Horatio's bed*
Monkey tricks
Willow at Christmas
Willow by the sea
Willow on the river
Atwell, Debby. *Humphrey Thud*
Aylesworth, Jim. *Teddy bear tears*
Bansemer, Roger. *Rachael's splendifilous adventure*
Barker, Inga-Lil. *Why teddy bears are brown*
Beck, Ian. *Home before dark*
Teddy's snowy day
Behrens, June. *The manners book*
Bohdal, Susi. *Bobby the bear*
Bond, Michael. *Paddington Bear goes to the hospital*
Paddington Bear in the garden
Bowman, Pete. *Goodnight, teddy bear*
Boyle, Constance. *The story of Little Owl*
Breese, Gillian. *The amazing adventures of Teddy Tum Tum*
Brown, Myra Berry. *First night away from home*
Buchholz, Quint. *Sleep well, little bear*
Bucknall, Caroline. *One bear all alone*
One bear in the hospital
One bear in the picture
Bush, Timothy. *Teddy bear, teddy bear*
Butler, Dorothy. *My brown bear Barney*
My brown bear Barney at the party
My brown bear Barney in trouble
Butterworth, Nick. *Albert the bear*
Carmichael, Clay. *Lonesome bear*
Used-up Bear
Cartlidge, Michelle. *Good night, Teddy*
Teddy's cat
Teddy's Christmas
Teddy's friends
Castle, Caroline. *Grandpa Baxter and the photographs*
Clarke, Gus. *Eddie and Teddy*
Clise, Michele Durkson. *Ophelia's bedtime book*
Cooper, Letice Ulpha. *The bear who was too big*
Cousins, Lucy. *Maisy's bedtime*
Cox, Phil Roxbee. *Ted in a red bed*
Craft, Ruth. *The winter bear*
Cusimano, Maryann K. *You are my I love you*
Daly, Niki. *Old Bob's brown bear*
Teddy's ear
Darling, Abigail. *Teddy bears' picnic cookbook*
Davidson, Amanda. *Teddy at the seashore*
Teddy goes outside
Teddy in the garden
Teddy's birthday
Teddy's first Christmas
Davis, Douglas F. *There's an elephant in the garage*
Davis, Lee. *P. B. Bear's birthday party*
Decker, Dorothy W. *Stripe and the merbear*
Stripe visits New York
Degen, Bruce. *Teddy bear towers*
Douglass, Barbara. *Good as new*

Ellwand, David. *Ten in the bed*
Feiffer, Jules. *I lost my bear*
Ferguson, Don. *Winnie the Pooh's A to Zzzz*
Flora, James. *Sherwood walks home*
Fox, Christyan. *What shape is that, PiggyWiggy?*
Freedman, Claire. *Night-night, Emily*
Freeman, Don. *Beady Bear*
    Corduroy
    Corduroy's busy street and Corduroy goes to the doctor
    A pocket for Corduroy
Freeman, Lydia. *Corduroy's day*
Galbraith, Richard. *Reuben runs away*
Gallaz, Christophe. *Threadbear*
Gantschev, Ivan. *The Christmas teddy bear*
Garcia, Jerry. *The teddy bears' picnic*
Gauch, Patricia Lee. *Bravo, Tanya*
    Christina Katerina and the great bear train
    Dance, Tanya
Glen, Maggie. *Ruby*
Greene, Carol. *Margarete Steiff, toy maker*
Gretz, Susanna. *Hide-and-seek*
    I'm not sleepy
    Teddy bears ABC
    Teddy bears at the seaside
    Teddy bears cure a cold
    Teddy bears go shopping
    Teddy bears' moving day
    Teddy bears 1 – 10
    Teddy bears stay indoors
    Teddy bears take the train
    Teddybears cookbook
    Too dark!
Greydanus, Rose. *Trouble in space*
Grindley, Sally. *Knock, knock! Who's there?*
    Too big bear
Hague, Kathleen. *Alphabears*
    Bear hugs
    Numbears
    Out of the nursery, into the night
Hague, Michael. *Teddy bear, teddy bear*
Haldane, Suzanne. *Teddies and machines*
    Teddies and trucks
Hale, Irina. *Brown bear in a brown chair*
    How I found a friend
Hansen, Felicity. *The first bear*
Harris, Trudy. *Up bear, down bear*
Harrison, Joanna. *Dear bear*
Hawkins, Colin. *Dip, dip, dip*
    One finger, one thumb
    Oops-a-Daisy
    Where's bear?
Hayes, Geoffrey. *Bear by himself*
Hayes, Sarah. *This is the bear*
    This is the bear and the picnic lunch
    This is the bear and the scary night
Hegg, Tom. *Peef and his best friend*
Henderson, Kathy. *Disney's Pooh's grand adventure: the search for Christopher Robin*
Hennessy, B. G. (Barbara G.). *Corduroy at the zoo*
    Corduroy's birthday
    Corduroy's Christmas
    Corduroy's Easter
    Corduroy's Halloween
Herman, Gail. *Teddy bear for sale*
Hines, Anna Grossnickle. *I'll tell you what they say*
Hissey, Jane. *Jolly snow*
    Jolly Tall
    Little Bear lost
    Little bear's bedtime
    Little Bear's day
    Little Bear's trousers
    Old Bear
    Old Bear [board book]
    Old Bear, a pop-up book
Horse, Harry. *A friend for Little Bear*
Howe, Caroline Walton. *Teddy Bear's bird and beast band*
Hutchins, H. J. (Hazel J.). *It's raining, Yancy and Bear*

Ichikawa, Satomi. *Fickle Barbara*
    The first bear in Africa!
Inches, Alison. *Corduroy writes a letter*
    Corduroy's garden
    Corduroy's hike
Ingpen, Robert. *The idle bear*
Inkpen, Mick. *One bear at bedtime*
    Threadbear
    Where, oh where, is Kipper's bear?
James, J. Alison. *The bears' Christmas surprise*
Joerns, Consuelo. *The forgotten bear*
Johnston, Tony. *My best friend Bear*
Kantrowitz, Mildred. *Willy Bear*
Keller, Holly. *A bear for Christmas*
Kelley, True. *Day-care teddy bear*
Kemp, Moira. *Round and round the garden*
Kennedy, Jimmy. *The teddy bears' Christmas*
    The teddy bears' picnic, ill. by Alexandra Day
    The teddy bears' picnic, ill. by Michael Hague
    The teddy bears' picnic, ill. by Prue Theobalds
Kennedy, Marge M. *The book of boo!*
Kimpton, Diana. *The bear Santa Claus forgot*
Kocí, Marta. *Sarah's bear*
Lawson, Carol. *Teddy bear, teddy bear*
Leblanc, Anne. *Benjamin finds a friend*
    Shopping with Benjamin
Lester, Robin. *Wuzzy takes off*
Le-Tan, Pierre. *Visit to the North Pole*
Lewis, Kim. *First snow*
Lewis, Naomi. *Once upon a rainbow*
Lewison, Wendy Cheyette. *Where's my teddy?*
Lillie, Patricia. *Floppy teddy bear*
Lindgren, Barbro. *Sam's teddy bear*
Lindsay, Elizabeth. *A letter for Maria*
Little, Jean. *Jess was the brave one*
Lundell, Margo. *Teddy bear's birthday*
McCue, Lisa. *Corduroy's best Halloween ever!*
    Corduroy's party
    Corduroy's toys
MacDonald, Maryann. *Sam's worries*
McFarland, Lyn Rossiter. *The pirate's parrot*
McKay, Hilary. *Where's bear?*
McKee, David. *Elmer and the lost teddy*
    The monster and the teddy bear
    Prince Peter and the teddy bear
MacLeod, Elizabeth. *I heard a little baa*
McLeod, Emilie Warren. *The bear's bicycle*
McPhail, David M. *The dream child*
    First flight
    The teddy bear
McQuade, Jacqueline. *At preschool with Teddy Bear*
    At the petting zoo with Teddy Bear
    Christmas with Teddy Bear
    Good times with Teddy Bear
Magnus, Erica. *My secret place*
Maisner, Heather. *Save Brave Ted*
Maitland, Barbara. *My bear and me*
Mansell, Dom. *My old teddy*
Marcus, Susan. *The missing button adventure*
Maris, Ron. *Are you there, bear?*
Marzollo, Jean. *Jed's junior space patrol*
    The teddy bear book
Matje, Martin. *Celeste*
Milne, A. A. (Alan Alexander). *Eeyore loses a tail*
    House at Pooh corner [a pop-up book]
    Pooh and some bees
    Pooh goes visiting
    Pooh's alphabet book
    Pooh's counting book
    Pooh's quiz book
    Tigger tales
    Winnie-the-Pooh: a pop-up book
Mogensen, Jan. *Lost and found Teddy*
    Teddy and the Chinese dragon
    Teddy in the undersea kingdom
    Teddy runs away
    Teddy's birthday bugle

Teddy's Christmas gift
When Teddy woke early
Moore, Clement Clarke. *The teddy bears' night before Christmas*
Moss, Elaine. *Polar*
Murphy, Mary. *Some things change*
Naylor, Phyllis Reynolds. *The picnic*
Please do feed the bears
Nims, Bonnie Larkin. *Where is the bear?*
Where is the bear at school?
Novak, Matt. *Jazzbo and Googy*
O'Donnell, Elizabeth Lee. *Sing me a window*
O'Donnell, Peter. *Moonlit journey*
O'Malley, Kevin. *The box*
Ormondroyd, Edward. *Theodore*
Theodore's rival
Paraskevas, Betty. *The tangerine bear*
Pearson, Susan. *Baby and the bear*
Phillips, Joan. *Lucky bear*
Pike, Carol. *The nutty queen*
Prince, Pamela. *The secret world of teddy bears*
Rascal. *Orson*
Ratnett, Michael. *Jenny's bear*
Reynolds, Adrian. *Pete and Polo's farmyard adventure*
Richardson, Jean. *The bear who went to the ballet*
Romanek, Enid Warner. *Teddy*
Root, Phyllis. *Contrary bear*
Sava, Donna Lynn. *Teddy bear dreams*
Schroeder, Binette. *Laura*
Sheldon, Dyan. *Love, your bear, Pete*
Siewert, Margaret. *Bear hunt*
Skorpen, Liesel Moak. *Charles*
Stadler, John. *Catilda*
Steger, Hans-Ulrich. *Traveling to Tripiti*
Straight, Susan. *Bear E. Bear*
Sutherland, Colleen. *Jason goes to show-and-tell*
Teddyland
Thomson, Ruth. *My bear: I can . . . can you?*
My bear: I like . . . do you?
Tibo, Gilles. *The grand journey of Mr. Man*
Tildes, Phyllis Limbacher. *Billy's big-boy bed*
Tobias, Tobi. *Moving day*
Tyger, Rory. *Newton*
Van Laan, Nancy. *Little baby Bobby*
Waber, Bernard. *Ira sleeps over*
Waddell, Martin. *Night night Cuddly Bear*
Sailor Bear
Small Bear lost
When the teddy bears came
Wahl, Jan. *Humphrey's bear*
Weber, Linda Kay. *Louie Larkey and the bad dream patrol*
Weninger, Brigitte. *Good-bye, daddy!*
Weston, Martha. *Bea's four bears*
Wickstrom, Sylvie (Sylvie Kantrovitz). *I love you, Mister Bear*
Wilhelm, Hans. *A cool kid – like me!*
Worthington, Phoebe. *Teddy bear baker*
Teddy bear coalman
Teddy bear farmer
Wright, Dare. *The doll and the kitten*
Edith and Midnight
Edith and Mr. Bear
Edith and the duckling
A gift from the lonely doll
The lonely doll
The lonely doll learns a lesson
Yektai, Niki. *Hi bears, bye bears*
Young, Ruth. *Golden Bear*
Zalben, Jane Breskin. *A perfect nose for Ralph*
Ziefert, Harriet. *Clara Ann Cookie go to bed!*

Toys – blocks

Hutchins, Pat. *Changes, changes*
Mayers, Patrick. *Just one more block*
Winthrop, Elizabeth. *That's mine*
Wynne-Jones, Tim. *Builder of the moon*

Toys – dolls

Ackerman, Karen. *Moveable Mabeline*
Ainsworth, Ruth. *The mysterious Baba and her magic caravan*
Albert, Shirley. *Doll party*
Alberts, Nancy Markham. *No toys on Sunday*
Ardizzone, Aingelda. *The night ride*
Ardizzone, Edward. *The little girl and the tiny doll*
Ayer, Jacqueline. *Little Silk*
Ayres, Becky Hickox. *Matreshka*
Bannon, Laura. *Manuela's birthday*
Barber, Antonia. *Satchelmouse and the doll's house*
Bartels, Alice L. *The grandmother doll*
Beck, Andrea. *Elliot's emergency*
Bernhard, Josephine Butkowska. *Nine cry-baby dolls*
Bertrand, Diane Gonzales. *The last doll = La última muñeca*
Blegvad, Lenore. *Rainy day Kate*
Bliss, Corinne Demas. *The littlest matryoshka*
Bonners, Susan. *The wooden doll*
Bright, Robert. *The travels of Ching*
Brown, Margaret Wise. *Dr. Squash the doll doctor*
Brown, Ruth. *I don't like it!*
Buffett, Jimmy. *Trouble dolls*
Conrad, Pam. *Doll Face has a party!*
Dahlbäck-Lutteman, Helena. *My sister Lotta and me*
Dalmais, Anne-Marie. *Betsy the bunny*
Dodge, Mary Mapes. *Mary Anne*
Dreifus, Miriam W. *Brave Betsy*
English, Karen. *Big wind coming!*
Fonteyn, Margot, Dame. *Coppélia*
Francis, Frank. *Natasha's new doll*
Garelick, May. *Just my size*
Goffstein, M. B. (Marilyn Brooke). *Me and my captain*
Our prairie home
Goodman, Louise. *Ida's doll*
Greenfield, Eloise. *My doll, Keshia*
Guthrie, Woody. *My dolly*
Hall, Patricia. *Hooray for reading!*
Hammerschlag, Carl A. *The go away doll*
Hermes, Patricia. *When snow lay soft on the mountain*
Hines, Anna Grossnickle. *Don't worry, I'll find you*
Keep your old hat
Maybe a band-aid will help
Moompa, Toby, and Bomp
Hoban, Russell. *The stone doll of Sister Brute*
How Raggedy Ann got her candy heart
Huff, Vivian. *Let's make paper dolls*
James, Betsy. *The mud family*
Jaques, Faith. *Tilly's house*
Tilly's rescue
Jennings, Linda M. *Coppelia*
Johnston, Johanna. *Sugarplum*
Karas, Jacqueline. *The doll house*
Keller, Holly. *Geraldine's blanket*
Kroll, Steven. *The hand-me-down doll*
Krupinski, Loretta. *Best friends*
Kuklin, Susan. *From head to toe*
Kunhardt, Dorothy. *Kitty's new doll*
Lamm, C. Drew. *Anniranni and Mollymishi, the wild-haired doll*
Lasky, Kathryn. *Sophie and Rose*
Lenski, Lois. *Debbie and her dolls*
Let's play house
Lewison, Wendy Cheyette. *My favorite doll*
Lexau, Joan M. *The rooftop mystery*
McClintock, Barbara. *Dahlia*
McGinley, Phyllis. *The most wonderful doll in the world*
McGuire, Richard. *What goes around comes around*
McKissack, Patricia C. *Nettie Jo's friends*
McMillan, Bruce. *Ghost doll*
Mariana. *The journey of Bangwell Putt*
Maris, Ron. *Hold tight, bear!*
Mark, Jan. *Fun with Mrs. Thumb*
Martin, David. *Lizzie and her dolly*
Mayer, Marianna. *Baba Yaga and Vasilisa the Brave*
Medearis, Michael. *Daisy and the doll*
Mills, Elaine. *Marinetta at the ballet*

My first Raggedy Ann, Raggedy Ann and Andy and the camel with the wrinkled knees
My first Raggedy Ann, Raggedy Ann and Andy and the nice police officer
My first Raggedy Ann, Raggedy Ann's wishing pebble
Nelson, Vaunda Micheaux. *Almost to freedom*
Newsome, Jill. *Dream dancer*
Nivola, Claire A. *Elisabeth*
Norling, Beth. *The stone baby*
Ogburn, Jacqueline K. *The magic nesting doll*
Oram, Hiawyn. *Baba Yaga and the wise doll*
Ormerod, Jan. *Making friends*
   Miss Mouse takes off
Pattison, Darcy. *The journey of Oliver K. Woodman*
Pellowski, Anne. *The nine crying dolls*
Peters, Stephanie True. *Raggedy Ann and Andy and the magic potion*
Pincus, Harriet. *Minna and Pippin*
Polacco, Patricia. *Babushka's doll*
   Betty Doll
Politi, Leo. *Rosa*
Pomerantz, Charlotte. *The chalk doll*
Pryor, Ainslie. *The baby blue cat and the smiley worm doll*
   The baby blue cat and the whole batch of cookies
Ransom, Candice F. *The Christmas dolls*
Rosenberg, Liz. *The scrap doll*
Russo, Marisabina. *The trouble with baby*
Sandburg, Carl (Charles August). *The wedding procession of the rag doll and the broom handle and who was in it*
Schulman, Janet. *The big hello*
   The great big dummy
Shecter, Ben. *The stocking child*
Silbaugh, Elizabeth. *Raggedy Ann's birthday party book*
Skorpen, Liesel Moak. *Elizabeth*
Smith, Maggie (Margaret C.). *Noly Poly Rabbit Tail and me*
Steig, William. *Yellow and pink*
Stuve-Bodeen, Stephanie. *Elizabeti's doll*
Tada, Joni Eareckson. *Forever friends*
Tudor, Tasha. *The doll's Christmas*
Turner, Ann Warren. *Secrets from the dollhouse*
Udry, Janice May. *Emily's autumn*
   Thump and Plunk, ill. by Geoffrey Hayes
   Thump and Plunk, ill. by Ann Schweninger
Waddell, Martin. *The hidden house*
   The toymaker
Wahl, Jan. *The Muffletumps*
   The Muffletumps' Christmas party
   The Muffletumps' Halloween scare
Wells, Rosemary. *Peabody*
Wilson, Julia. *Becky*
Winthrop, Elizabeth. *Katharine's doll*
   Vasilissa the beautiful
Wiseman, Bernard. *Oscar is a mama*
Wright, Dare. *The doll and the kitten*
   Edith and Midnight
   Edith and Mr. Bear
   Edith and the duckling
   A gift from the lonely doll
   The lonely doll
   The lonely doll learns a lesson
Yaroshevskaya, Kim. *Little Kim's doll*
Zemach, Harve. *Mommy, buy me a China doll*
Zolotow, Charlotte (Shapiro). *William's doll*

Toys – hobby horses *see* Toys – rocking horses

Toys – pandas *see* Toys – bears

Toys – rocking horses

Chandra, Deborah. *A is for Amos*
Donaldson, Lois. *Karl's wooden horse*
Lindman, Maj. *Snipp, Snapp, Snurr and the magic horse*
Mayer, Mercer. *The rocking horse angel*
Roberts, Thom. *Pirates in the park*
Robertson, Lilian. *Runaway rocking horse*
Sokol, Edward. *Meet Stinky Magee*

Toys – soldiers

Andersen, H. C. (Hans Christian). *The steadfast tin soldier*, ill. by Charlene DeLage
   The steadfast tin soldier, ill. by Thomas di Grazia
   The steadfast tin soldier, ill. by Paul Galdone
   The steadfast tin soldier, ill. by Rachel Isadora
   The steadfast tin soldier, ill. by David Jorgensen
   The steadfast tin soldier, ill. by Monika Laimgruber
   The steadfast tin soldier, ill. by P. J. Lynch
   The steadfast tin soldier, ill. by Fred Marcellino
   The steadfast tin soldier, ill. by Alain Vaës
Brown, Margaret Wise. *Dr. Squash the doll doctor*
Collington, Peter. *The angel and the soldier boy*
Nicholson, William, Sir. *Clever Bill*
Rylant, Cynthia. *Little Whistle's medicine*
Sowden, Henry. *The grand old Duke of York*

Toys – teddy bears *see* Toys – bears

Toys – tin soldiers *see* Toys – soldiers

Toys – trains

Fujita, Miho. *The little choo-choo*
Heller, Nicholas. *Peas*
Hindley, Judy. *The little train*
Hooks, William H. *The mighty Santa Fe*
Kroll, Steven. *Toot! Toot!*
Lewis, Kevin. *Chugga-chugga choo-choo*
McPhail, David M. *The train*
Mallat, Kathy. *Trouble on the tracks*
Merriam, Eve. *Train leaves the station*
Richards, Laura Elizabeth Howe. *Jiggle joggle jee*

Toys – wagons

Appelt, Kathi. *A red wagon year*
Behrens, June. *Christmas-magic wagon*
Dodd, Lynley. *A dragon in a wagon*
Lindgren, Barbro. *Sam's wagon*
Powell, Alma. *My little wagon [board book]*

Tractors

Baynton, Martin. *Fifty and the fox*
   Fifty and the great race
   Fifty gets the picture
   Fifty saves his friend
Big noisy trucks and diggers
Blum, Mark. *Big trucks and diggers in 3-D*
Cowley, Joy. *The rusty, trusty tractor*
Goodhart, Pippa. *Arthur's tractor*
Israel, Marion Louise. *The tractor on the farm*
Kilby, Don. *In the country*
Laird, Elizabeth. *The day Patch stood guard*
   The day Sidney ran off
   The day the ducks went skating
   The day Veronica was nosy
Lewis, Kim. *One summer day*
Mayo, Margaret. *Dig dig digging*
Nelson, Kristin L. *Farm tractors*
Nilsén, Anna. *Drive your tractor*
Porter, Sue. *Parsnip and the runaway tractor*
Rickard, Graham. *Let's look at tractors*
Steers, Billy. *Tractor Mac*
Stille, Darlene R. *Tractors*
Young, Miriam Burt. *If I drove a tractor*

Trading *see* Activities – trading

Traffic, traffic signs

Arnold, Tedd. *The signmaker's assistant*
Bank Street College of Education. *Green light, go*
Baugh, Dolores M. *Bikes*
Bell, Babs. *The bridge is up!*

Brown, Margaret Wise. *Red light, green light*
Chwast, Seymour. *Traffic jam*
Cuyler, Margery. *Road signs*
Krahn, Fernando. *Mr. Top*
Kulman, Andrew. *Red light stop, green light go*
Loewen, Nancy. *Traffic safety*
Maestro, Betsy. *Traffic*
Meister, Cari. *Busy, busy city street*
Mendoza, George. *Traffic jam*
Mitchell, Lucy Sprague. *The taxi that hurried*
Pearson, Debora. *Alphabeep*
Robbins, Ken. *Trucks, giants of the highway*
Shortall, Leonard W. *One way*
Suen, Anastasia. *Red light, green light*
Thayer, Jane. *Andy and the runaway horse*
Yagelski, Robert. *The day the lifting bridge stuck*

Train engineers *see* Careers – railroad engineers

Trains

Ahlberg, Allan. *The ghost train*
Ammon, Richard. *Trains at work*
Ardizzone, Edward. *Nicholas and the fast-moving diesel*
Awdry, W. *Happy birthday, Thomas!*
Ayars, James Sterling. *Caboose on the roof*
Aylesworth, Jim. *Country crossing*
Ayres, Pam. *Piggo has a train ride*
Balgassi, Haemi. *Peacebound trains*
Barkan, Joanne. *Boxcar*
    Caboose
    Locomotive
    Passenger car
Barton, Byron. *Trains*
Beim, Jerrold. *Country train*
Bemelmans, Ludwig. *Quito express*
Big book of trains
Biro, Val. *Gumdrop races a train*
Blathwayt, Benedict. *The runaway train*
Bontemps, Arna Wendell. *The fast sooner hound*
Booth, Philip E. *Crossing*
Brandenberg, Franz. *Everyone ready?*
Broekel, Ray. *Trains*
Bröger, Achim. *Bruno takes a trip*
Brown, Margaret Wise. *The train to Timbuctoo*
    Two little trains
    Whistle for the train
Bunce, William. *Freight trains*
Bunting, Eve (Anne Evelyn). *Train to somewhere*
Burleigh, Robert. *It's funny where Ben's train takes him*
Burningham, John. *Hey! Get off our train*
Burton, Virginia Lee. *Choo choo*
Calmenson, Stephanie. *Engine, engine, number nine*
Chall, Marsha Wilson. *Prairie train*
Cohen, Miriam. *Down in the subway*
Collicutt, Paul. *This train*
Corney, Estelle. *Pa's top hat*
Crews, Donald. *Freight train*
    Inside freight train
    Shortcut
Curious George takes a train
Cushman, Jerome. *Marvella's hobby*
Cyrus, Kurt. *Slow train to Oxmox*
Demarest, Chris L. *Train*
Dorfman, Craig. *I knew you could!*
Drummond, Allan. *Casey Jones*
Ehrlich, Amy. *The everyday train*
Emberley, Ed (Edward Randolph). *Ed Emberley's drawing book of trucks and trains*
Emmett, Fredrick Rowland. *New world for Nellie*
Fleischman, Paul. *Time train*
Gantschev, Ivan. *The Christmas train*
    The train to Grandma's
Gibbons, Faye. *Full steam ahead*
Gibbons, Gail. *Trains*
Goble, Paul. *Death of the iron horse*
Gramatky, Hardie. *Homer and the circus train*

Greene, Graham. *The little train*
Gretz, Susanna. *Teddy bears take the train*
Gurney, John. *Dinosaur train*
Hathorn, Libby (Elizabeth). *The tram to Bondi beach*
Hawkins, Colin. *Come for a ride on the ghost train*
Hayashi, Akiko. *Aki and the fox*
Hayward, Linda. *The runaway Christmas toy*
Highet, Alistair. *The yellow train*
Hill, Lee Sullivan. *Trains*
Hines, Gary. *A ride in the crummy*
Hoberman, Mary Ann. *Bill Grogan's goat*
Horsbrugh, Wilma. *The train to Glasgow*
Howard, Elizabeth Fitzgerald. *Mac and Marie and the train toss surprise*
Hurd, Edith Thacher. *Caboose*
    Engine, engine no. 9
Hurd, Thacher. *Hobo dog*
I've been working on the railroad
Johnson, Angela. *Casey Jones*
    I dream of trains
Johnston, Tony. *How many miles to Jacksonville?*
Kalman, Maira. *Next stop, Grand Central*
Kay, Verla. *Iron horses*
    Orphan train
Kelly, Mij. *William and the night train*
Kirby, David K. *Cows are going to Paris*
Kirk, Daniel. *Breakfast at the Liberty Diner*
Koscielniak, Bruce. *Hector and Prudence – all aboard!*
Kroll, Steven. *Toot! Toot!*
Lakin, Pat (Patricia). *Subway sonata*
Lawson, Julie. *Bear on the train*
    Emma and the silk train
Le Guin, Ursula K. *Tom Mouse*
Lenski, Lois. *The little train*
Lewis, Kim. *The last train*
London, Jonathan. *The owl who became the moon*
Loomis, Christine. *We're going on a trip*
Lyon, George Ella. *A regular rolling Noah*
McAllister, Angela. *Jessie's journey*
Macaulay, David. *Black and white*
McCully, Emily Arnold. *An outlaw Thanksgiving*
MacKinnon, Debbie. *Tom's train*
McPhail, David M. *Moony B. Finch, fastest draw in the West*
    The train
Maestro, Betsy. *All aboard overnight*
Magee, Doug. *All aboard ABC*
Marshak, S. (Samuil). *The pup grew up!*
Marshall, Ray. *The train*
Martin, Bill (William Ivan). *Smoky Poky*
Martin, C. L. G. *The blueberry train*
Meeks, Esther K. *One is the engine*, ill. by Ernie King
    One is the engine, ill. by Joe Rogers
Mills, Claudia. *Gus and Grandpa ride the train*
Mogensen, Jan. *Lost and found Teddy*
Moss, Marissa. *True heart*
Mott, Evelyn Clarke. *Steam train ride*
Munsch, Robert N. *Jonathan cleaned up – then he heard a sound*
Murphy, Mary. *My puffer train*
Neitzel, Shirley. *I'm taking a trip on my train*
Nickl, Peter. *Ra ta ta tam*
Nobisso, Josephine. *John Blair and the great Hinckley fire*
O'Brien, Patrick. *Steam, smoke, and steel*
Ó Flatharta, Antoine. *The prairie train*
Oram, Hiawyn. *Going to Grandpa's*
Paraskevas, Betty. *Cecil Bunions and the midnight train*
Peet, Bill (William Bartlett). *The caboose who got loose*
    Smokey
Pierce, Jack. *The freight train book*
Pinkney, Gloria Jean. *The Sunday outing*
Piper, Watty. *The little engine that could*
Quattlebaum, Mary. *Underground train*
Ray, Mary Lyn. *All aboard*
Rex, Michael. *My freight train*
Richards, Jon. *Trains*
Rockwell, Anne F. *Trains*
Rodgers, Frank. *Who's afraid of the ghost train?*
Rogers, Hal. *Trains*

Rosenberg, Liz. *Adelaide and the night train*
Ross, Diana. *The story of the little red engine*
Rounds, Glen. *Casey Jones*
Rush, Ken. *Friday's journey*
Rylant, Cynthia. *Silver packages*
Sasaki, Isao. *Snow*
Sattler, Helen Roney. *Train whistles*
Scarry, Huck. *Huck Scarry's steam train journey*
Shine, Deborah. *The little engine that could pudgy word book*
Siebert, Diane. *Train song*
Simon, Seymour. *Seymour Simon's book of trains*
Slobodkin, Louis. *Clear the track for Michael's magic train*
Smith, Joseph A. (Joseph Anthony). *Circus train*
Spence, Robert, III. *Clickety clack*
Stevenson, James. *All aboard!*
Stinson, Kathy. *Teddy Rabbit*
Struges, Philemon. *I love trains*
Stutson, Caroline. *Night train*
Suen, Anastasia. *Subway*
    Window music
Temple, Charles A. *Train*
Thayer, Jane. *I like trains*
Thomas's big railway pop-up book
Thompson, Richard. *Jesse on the night train*
Trains
Tunnell, Michael O. *Mailing May*
Van Allsburg, Chris. *The polar express*
Voake, Charlotte. *Here comes the train*
Weelen, Guy. *The little red train*
Wells, Rosemary. *Don't spill it again, James*
Wetterer, Margaret. *Kate Shelley and the midnight express*
Wilson-Max, Ken. *Big blue engine*
Wondriska, William. *Puff*
Wormell, Christopher. *Puff, puff, chugga-chugga*
Wyllie, Stephen. *Ghost train*
Yin. *Coolies*
Yolen, Jane. *Animal train*
Young, Miriam Burt. *If I drove a train*
Ziefert, Harriet. *Train song*

Trains, toy *see* Toys – trains

Transportation

Ardizzone, Edward. *Nicholas and the fast-moving diesel*
Arnold, Caroline. *How do we travel?*
Baer, Edith. *This is the way we go to school*
Bagwell, Richard. *This is an airport*
Barkan, Joanne. *Boxcar*
    Caboose
    Locomotive
    Passenger car
Barner, Bob. *Elevator escalator book*
Barton, Byron. *Airport*
Baugh, Dolores M. *Trucks and cars to ride*
Bell, Babs. *The bridge is up!*
Billout, Guy. *By camel or by car*
Broekel, Ray. *Trains*
    Trucks
Burton, Virginia Lee. *Maybelle, the cable car*
Calmenson, Stephanie. *Zip, whiz, zoom!*
Campbell, Rod. *Look inside! Land, sea, air*
Cars and trucks
Cars and trucks and other vehicles
Cave, Ron. *Airplanes*
    Automobiles
    Motorcycles
Chancellor, Deborah. *Traveling on land*
Cleary, Beverly. *Lucky Chuck*
Collicutt, Paul. *This train*
Crews, Donald. *School bus*
    School bus [board book]
    Truck
Dalmais, Anne-Marie. *The Elephant's airplane and other machines*
Davis, Caroline. *My little rowboat*
Demarest, Chris L. *Lindbergh*
    My little red car

Emberley, Ed (Edward Randolph). *Cars, boats, and planes*
Fecher, Sarah. *On the move*
Flanagan, Alice K. *Riding the ferry with Captain Cruz*
    Riding the school bus with Mrs. Kramer
Gay, Michel. *Little truck*
Gibbons, Gail. *New road!*
Gomi, Taro. *Bus stop*
Gramatky, Hardie. *Sparky*
Haas, Jessie. *Getting ready to drive a horse and cart*
Hellen, Nancy. *Bus stop*
Hill, Lee Sullivan. *Trains*
Hoberman, Mary Ann. *How do I go?*
Ingoglia, Gina. *The big book of real airplanes*
Kalman, Maira. *Next stop, Grand Central*
Kimmel, Eric A. *Charlie drives the stage*
Kirk, Daniel. *Go!*
Koren, Edward. *Behind the wheel*
Lawson, Julie. *Emma and the silk train*
Lenski, Lois. *Davy goes places*
    Lois Lenski's big book of Mr. Small
Levinson, Riki. *I go with my family to Grandma's*
Lishak, Anthony. *Row your boat*
Loomis, Christine. *Rush hour*
Maass, Robert. *Tugboats*
McAllister, Angela. *Jessie's journey*
McCourt, Lisa. *I miss you, Stinky Face*
MacDonald, Suse. *Elephants on board*
McNaught, Harry. *The truck book*
McNaughton, Colin. *Walk rabbit walk*
Mahy, Margaret. *A busy day for a good grandmother*
Mantegazza, Giovanna. *Look inside a car*
    Look inside an airplane
Marston, Hope Irvin. *Big rigs*
Martin, C. L. G. *The blueberry train*
Mayo, Margaret. *Choo choo clickety-clack*
Mills, Claudia. *Gus and Grandpa ride the train*
Miranda, Anne. *Vroom, chugga, vroom-vroom*
Morris, Ann. *On the go*
Munari, Bruno. *The birthday present*
Nikola-Lisa, W. *Wheels go round*
Nobles, Kristen M. *Drive this book*
Old MacDonald had a farm. Old MacDonald had a farm, ill. by Jessica Souhami
Oliver, Stephen. *Things that go*
Olschewski, Alfred. *The wheel rolls over*
100 words about transportation
Oppenheim, Joanne. *Have you seen roads?*
Pluckrose, Henry Arthur. *On the move*
Quattlebaum, Mary. *Underground train*
Rau, Dana Meachen. *Ways to go*
Reasoner, Charles. *Who drives this?*
Relf, Patricia. *Tonka trucks night and day*
Rey, H. A. (Hans Augusto). *How do you get there?*
Richards, Jon. *Jetliners*
    Trains
Ringgold, Faith. *If a bus could talk*
Robbins, Ken. *Trucks, giants of the highway*
Rockwell, Anne F. *Ferryboat ride!*
    Planes
    Things that go
    Trains
Rogers, Hal. *Airplanes*
    Buses
    Cars
    Trains
Rotner, Shelley. *Boats afloat*
Rylant, Cynthia. *Silver packages*
Scarry, Richard. *Richard Scarry's hop aboard! Here we go!*
Schomp, Virginia. *If you were a . . . pilot*
Seibold, J. Otto. *Mr. Lunch takes a plane ride*
Simon, Seymour. *Seymour Simon's book of trains*
    Seymour Simon's book of trucks
Spinelli, Eileen. *Six hogs on a scooter*
Stanley, Mandy. *On the move*
Stevenson, James. *No need for Monty*
Stickland, Paul. *Truck jam*
Stille, Darlene R. *Police cars*

Jaspersohn, William. *Timber!*
Johnston, Tony. *Big red apple*
　　Isabel's house of butterflies
　　Mole and Troll trim the tree
Jordan, Sandra. *Christmas tree farm*
Joslin, Mary. *The tale of the heaven tree*
Karpin, Florence Baker. *Tree spirits*
Keister, Douglas. *Fernando's gift = El regalo de Fernando*
Kelley, Marty. *Fall is not easy*
Kellogg, Steven (Stephen). *Johnny Appleseed*
Kessler, Cristina. *My great-grandmother's gourd*
King, B. A. *The very best Christmas tree*
Kirk, Barbara. *Grandpa, me and our house in the tree*
Kirkpatrick, Rena K. *Trees*
Krahn, Fernando. *The biggest Christmas tree on earth*
Kraus, Robert. *The tree that stayed up until next Christmas*
Krupinski, Loretta. *Christmas in the city*
Lakin, Pat (Patricia). *Oh, brother!*
Lauber, Patricia. *Be a friend to trees*
Lavies, Bianca. *Lily pad pond*
　　Tree trunk traffic
Le Tord, Bijou. *Noah's trees*
Levine, Arthur A. *Pearl Moscowitz's last stand*
Lewis, Naomi. *Leaves*
Lindbergh, Reeve. *Johnny Appleseed*
Lindgren, Astrid. *Lotta's Christmas surprise*
　　Of course Polly can do almost everything
Lionni, Leo. *A busy year*
Llewellyn, Claire. *Tree*
Lloyd, David. *Hello, goodbye*
Locker, Thomas. *Sky tree*
Löfgren, Ulf. *The wonderful tree*
London, Jonathan. *The sugaring-off party*
Lyon, George Ella. *A B Cedar*
Mabey, Richard. *Oak and company*
McCord, David. *Every time I climb a tree*
McPhail, David M. *Henry Bear's Christmas*
Maestro, Betsy. *How do apples grow?*
　　Why do leaves change color?
Mahy, Margaret. *The Christmas tree tangle*
Maloney, Peter (1955–). *Redbird at Rockefeller Center*
Mamchur, Carolyn Marie. *The popcorn tree*
Manson, Christopher. *The tree in the wood*
Margolis, Richard J. *Big bear, spare that tree*
Marshall, James. *Three up a tree*
Martin, Bill (William Ivan). *Chicka chicka boom boom*
　　Chicka chicka boom boom [board book]
　　Chicka chicka sticka sticka
Martin, Jacqueline Briggs. *Button, bucket, sky*
Mathis, Melissa Bay. *Animal house*
Maynard, Joyce. *New house*
Mayr, Diane. *Out and about at the apple orchard*
Miles, Miska. *Apricot ABC*
Miller, Debbie S. *Are trees alive?*
Mills, Joyce C. *Gentle Willow*
　　Little Tree
Moss, Miriam. *This is the tree*
Muller, Gerda. *Around the oak*
Munsch, Robert N. *Up, up, down!*
Myers, Bernice. *Charlie's birthday present*
Neville, Mary. *The Christmas tree ride*
Newton, James R. *Forest log*
Nightingale, Sandy. *Cider apples*
Nikly, Michelle. *The emperor's plum tree*
Noble, Trinka Hakes. *Apple tree Christmas*
O Christmas tree
Oana, Kay D. *Robbie and the raggedy scarecrow*
Oppenheim, Joanne. *Have you seen trees?*, ill. by Irwin Rosenhouse
　　Have you seen trees?, ill. by Jean and Mou-Sien Tseng
Orbach, Ruth. *Apple pigs*
Pearson, Debora. *Leo's tree*
Peet, Bill (William Bartlett). *Merle the high flying squirrel*
Petie, Haris. *The seed the squirrel dropped*
Pfister, Marcus. *Hopper's treetop adventure*
Pike, Norman. *The peach tree*
Pittman, Helena Clare. *The angel tree*
Pomerantz, Charlotte. *Mangaboom*

Powell, Consie. *Amazing apples*
　　Old dog Cora and the Christmas tree
Pyle, Howard. *The Swan Maiden*
Quindlen, Anna. *The tree that came to stay*
Rayevsky, Inna. *The talking tree*
Recknagel, Friedrich. *Sarah's willow*
Reed-Jones, Carol. *The tree in the ancient forest*
Reiser, Lynn. *Christmas counting*
Robbins, Ken. *Apples*
　　Autumn leaves
Robinson, Tim. *Tobias, the quig, and the rumplenut tree*
Rogow, Zak. *Oranges*
Romain, Trevor. *Jemma's journey*
Royston, Angela. *Life cycle of an oak tree*
Ruelle, Karen Gray. *The crunchy, munchy Christmas tree*
Russell, Naomi. *The tree*
Ryder, Joanne. *Hello, tree!*
Sammy Spider's first Tu B'Shevat
Sato, Satoru. *I wish I had a big, big tree*
Schertle, Alice. *In my treehouse*
Schmid, Eleonore. *The squirrel and the moon*
Schotter, Roni. *In the piney woods*
Silverstein, Shel. *The giving tree*
Spalding, Andrea. *Solomon's tree*
Speirs, John. *The little boy's Christmas gift*
Spilsbury, Louise. *Oranges*
Spohn, Kate. *Turtle and Snake and the Christmas tree*
Spurr, Elizabeth. *The gumdrop tree*
Stemp, Robin. *Guy and the flowering plum tree*
Stewart, Sarah. *The money tree*
Stone, Marti. *The singing fir tree*
Swain, Gwenyth. *Johnny Appleseed*
Thelen, Gerda. *The toy maker*
Thornhill, Jan. *A tree in a forest*
Torres, Melissa A. *The great Christmas tree celebration*
Tresselt, Alvin R. *The dead tree*
　　The gift of the tree
　　Johnny Maple-Leaf
Trottier, Maxine. *Prairie willow*
Tudor, Bethany. *Samuel's tree house*
Udry, Janice May. *A tree is nice*
Van Laan, Nancy. *A tree for me*
Van Leeuwen, Jean. *Nothing here but trees*
Vieira, Linda. *The ever-living tree*
Waldman, Neil. *The never-ending greenness*
Walsh, Ellen Stoll. *Dot and Jabber and the great acorn mystery*
Ward, Helen. *The tin forest*
Watts, Barrie. *Apple tree*
Weedn, Flavia. *The enchanted tree*
Welch, Willy. *Dancing with Daddy*
Weninger, Brigitte. *Little apple*
Williams, Sam. *Angel's Christmas cookies*
Winter, Jeanette. *The Christmas tree ship*
Wong, Herbert H. *Our tree*
Yashima, Taro. *The village tree*
Young, Ed (Edward). *Up a tree*
Zagwÿn, Deborah Turney. *Apple batter*
Zalben, Jane Breskin. *Pearl plants a tree*
Zoehfeld, Kathleen Weidner. *Apples, apples*
Zolotow, Charlotte (Shapiro). *The beautiful Christmas tree*

Trickery *see* Behavior – trickery

Tricks *see* Magic

Trinidad *see* Foreign lands – Trinidad

Trolleys *see* Cable cars, trolleys

Trolls *see* Mythical creatures – trolls

Trombones *see* Musical instruments – trombones

Truck drivers *see* Careers – truck drivers

Trucks

Tsars *see* Royalty – tsars

Tsimshian Indians *see* Indians of North America – Tsimshian

Tsunamis

Hodges, Margaret. *The wave*

Tu B'Shevat *see* Holidays – Tu B'Shevat

Turkey *see* Foreign lands – Turkey

Turkeys *see* Birds – turkeys

Turtles *see* Reptiles – turtles, tortoises

TV *see* Television

Twa Indians *see* Indians of North America – Twa

Twilight

Berger, Barbara Helen. *Grandfather Twilight*
Fletcher, Ralph J. *Twilight comes twice*
Huth, Holly Young. *Twilight*
Major, Beverly. *Playing sardines*
Udry, Janice May. *The moon jumpers*

Twins *see* Multiple births – twins

Tyrol *see* Foreign lands – Tyrol

U.S. history

Abisch, Roz. *The Pumpkin Heads*
Accorsi, William. *My name is Pocahontas*
Ackerman, Karen. *The tin heart*
Addy, Sharon Hart. *Right here on this spot*
Adler, David A. *A picture book of Abraham Lincoln*
    A picture book of Benjamin Franklin
    A picture book of Eleanor Roosevelt
    A picture book of George Washington
    A picture book of John F. Kennedy
    A picture book of Martin Luther King, Jr.
    A picture book of Thomas Jefferson
Aliki. *George and the cherry tree*
    The many lives of Benjamin Franklin
    The story of William Penn
    A weed is a flower
Altman, Susan. *Followers of the north star*
Andersen, H. C. (Hans Christian). *The tinderbox*, ill. by Barry Moser
Anderson, Laurie Halse. *Thank you, Sarah*
Appelbaum, Diana Karter. *Cocoa ice*
Armentrout, David. *John Muir*
Atwell, Debby. *Pearl*
Aulaire, Ingri Mortenson d'. *Abraham Lincoln*
    Pocahontas
Balgassi, Haemi. *Peacebound trains*
Bangs, Edward. *Yankee Doodle*
Barner, Bob. *Which way to the Revolution?*
Bartlett, Robert Merrill. *The story of Thanksgiving*
Bartoletti, Susan Campbell. *The Christmas promise*
    The flag maker
Bates, Katharine Lee. *America the beautiful*, ill. by Chris Gall
    America the beautiful, ill. by Wendell Minor

America the beautiful, ill. by Neil Waldman
Battle-Lavert, Gwendolyn. *Papa's mark*
Benchley, Peter. *Jonathan visits the White House*
Benjamin, Anne. *Young Pocahontas*
Berlin, Irving. *God bless America*
Bethell, Jean. *Three cheers for Mother Jones!*
Bildner, Phil. *Shoeless Joe and Black Betsy*
Binns, Tristan Boyer. *The Liberty Bell*
Bliss, Corinne Demas. *Hurricane!*
Blumberg, Rhoda. *Bloomers!*
Borden, Louise. *A. Lincoln and me*
    America is . . .
    Goodbye, Charles Lindbergh
Bredeson, Carmen. *George W. Bush, the 43rd president*
Brill, Marlene Targ. *Bronco Charlie and the Pony Express*
    Margaret Knight, girl inventor
Brink, Carol Ryrie. *Goody O'Grumpity*
Brown, Don. *A voice from the wilderness*
Brownell, Barbara. *Spin's really wild U.S.A. tour*
Bruchac, Joseph. *Squanto's journey*
Bulla, Clyde Robert. *Washington's birthday*
Bunting, Eve (Anne Evelyn). *The blue and the gray*
    A picnic in October
    Train to somewhere
Burke, Rick. *George Washington*
Calhoun, Mary. *Flood!*
Carlson, Laurie M. *Boss of the plains*
Carrier, Lark. *A tree's tale*
Chalk, Gary. *Yankee Doodle*
Chandra, Deborah. *George Washington's teeth*
Chenault, Nell. *Parsifal the Poddley*
Cherry, Lynne. *A river ran wild*
Chial, Debra. *M is for Minnesota*
Christensen, Bonnie. *Woody Guthrie, poet of the people*
Coleman, Evelyn. *To be a drum*
    White socks only
Cooney, Barbara. *Eleanor*
Corey, Shana. *You forgot your skirt, Amelia Bloomer*
Dadey, Debbie. *Shooting star: Annie Oakley, the legend*
    Will Rogers: larger than life
Dalgliesh, Alice. *The Thanksgiving story*
DeLage, Ida. *Pilgrim children on the Mayflower*
Demarest, Chris L. *Lindbergh*
De Paola, Tomie (Thomas Anthony). *An early American Christmas*
    My first Thanksgiving
DeRubertis, Barbara. *Columbus Day*
Dewey, Ariane. *Laffite, the pirate*
Drummond, Allan. *Liberty*
Dunlap, Julie. *Louisa May and Mr. Thoreau's flute*
Dupré, Rick. *The wishing chair*
Edwards, Pamela Duncan. *Barefoot*
    Boston Tea Party
Everett, Gwen. *Li'l Sis and Uncle Willie*
Figley, Marty Rhodes. *The schoolchildren's blizzard*
Fischetto, Laura. *All pigs on deck*
Fisher, Leonard Everett. *Stars and stripes*
Fisher, Mary M. *Rosita's bridge*
Fleming, Candace. *A big cheese for the White House*
    The hatmaker's sign
Friedrich, Elizabeth. *Leah's pony*
Garland, Michael. *The President and Mom's apple pie*
George, Jean Craighead. *The first Thanksgiving*
Gerrard, Roy. *Wagons west!*
Gibbons, Gail. *Apples*
Giblin, James Cross. *George Washington*
Gleiter, Jan. *Paul Revere*
    Sacagawea
Gorsline, Marie. *North American Indians*
Green, Stephanie. *Betsy Ross and the silver thimble*
Greene, Rhonda Gowler. *The very first Thanksgiving Day*
Greenfield, Eloise. *Easter parade*
Greeson, Janet. *An American army of two*
Griest, Lisa. *Lost at the White House*
Haley, Gail E. *Jack Jouett's ride*
Hall, Donald. *Lucy's Christmas*
    Lucy's summer
Harness, Cheryl. *Mark Twain and the queens of the Mississippi*

Small, David. *George Washington's cows*
Smalls-Hector, Irene. *Jenny Reen and the Jack Muh Lantern*
Smith, Barry. *The first voyage of Christopher Columbus*
Smucker, Barbara Claasen. *Selina and the bear paw quilt*
Sneve, Virginia Driving Hawk. *The Cherokees*
    The Nez Perce
Spier, Peter. *The Erie Canal*
    The legend of New Amsterdam
    We the people
Stanley, Diane. *Joining the Boston Tea Party*
    Thanksgiving on Plymouth Plantation
Stanley, Fay. *The last princess*
Stevenson, Harvey. *Looking at liberty*
Stewart, Sarah. *The gardener*
Stier, Catherine. *If I were president*
Suen, Anastasia. *Man on the moon*
Swain, Gwenyth. *I wonder as I wander*
Szekeres, Cyndy. *Long ago*
Temple, Bob. *Ellis Island*
This place I know
Thomas, Mark. *Clothes in Colonial America*
    Fun and games in Colonial America
    Work in Colonial America
Thomson, Sarah L. *Stars and stripes*
Trottier, Maxine. *Flags*
Tunnell, Michael O. *Mailing May*
Turkle, Brinton. *The adventures of Obadiah*
    Obadiah the Bold
    Thy friend, Obadiah
Turner, Ann Warren. *Abe Lincoln remembers*
    Dust for dinner
    Shaker hearts
    When Mr. Jefferson came to Philadelphia
Uchida, Yoshiko. *The bracelet*
Uhlberg, Myron. *Flying over Brooklyn*
Valzania, Kim. *Tennessee*
Van Leeuwen, Jean. *Across the wide dark sea*
Vaughan, Marcia Kapok. *Abbie against the storm*
Vaughn, Jenny. *On the moon*
Vieira, Linda. *The ever-living tree*
Waldman, Neil. *They came from the Bronx*
Wallner, Alexandra. *Betsy Ross*
    The first air voyage in the United States
Washington, Donna L. *The story of Kwanzaa*
Weatherford, Carole Boston. *Juneteenth jamboree*
Weller, Frances Ward. *Madaket Millie*
Wells, Rosemary. *The house in the mail*
Wetterer, Margaret. *Kate Shelley and the midnight express*
Wetterer, Margaret K. *The snow walker*
Whittier, John Greenleaf. *Barbara Frietchie*
Winnick, Karen B. *Sybil's night ride*
Winter, Jeanette. *The Christmas tree ship*
    Follow the drinking gourd
Winters, Kay. *Abe Lincoln, the boy who loved books*
Woodson, Jacqueline. *Coming on home soon*
Wooldridge, Connie Nordhielm. *When Esther Morris headed west*
Wright, Courtni Crump. *Journey to freedom*
    Jumping the broom
Yezerski, Thomas F. *A full hand*
Yin. *Coolies*
Yolen, Jane. *Letting Swift River go*
    My brothers' flying machine

U.S. history – frontier & pioneer life

Abisch, Roz. *Sweet Betsy from Pike*
Ackerman, Karen. *Araminta's paint box*
Adams, Jean Ekman. *Clarence and the great surprise*
Aliki. *The story of Johnny Appleseed*
Altman, Linda Jacobs. *The legend of Freedom Hill*
Amsden, Janet. *Grizzly Pete and the ghosts*
Anderson, Leone Castell. *Surprise at Muddy Creek*
Aston, Claire. *Wild West*
Balcziak, Bill. *Paul Bunyan*
    Pecos Bill
Belting, Natalia Maree. *Verity Mullens and the Indian*
Bishop, Ann. *Wild Bill Hiccup's riddle book*

Brandt, Betty. *Special delivery*
Brownlow, Michael. *Way out West – with a baby!*
Chandler, Edna Walker. *Cattle drive*
    Pony rider
    Secret tunnel
Clement-Davies, David. *Spirit: stallion of the Cimarron*
Cohen, Caron Lee. *Bronco dogs*
Darling, Kathy (Mary Kathleen). *Pecos Bill finds a horse*
Davis, Kenneth C. *Don't know much about the pioneers*
Dewey, Ariane. *Pecos Bill*
Doughtie, Charles. *High Henry . . . the cowboy who was too tall to ride*
    a horse
Emberley, Barbara. *The story of Paul Bunyan*
Enderle, Judith (Ann) Ross. *Nell Nugget and the cow caper*
Erdrich, Louise. *The range eternal*
Everett, Percival L. *The one that got away*
A farmer boy birthday
Felton, Harold W. *Pecos Bill and the mustang*
Fleming, Candace. *Westward ho, Carlotta!*
Frank, John. *The toughest cowboy, Or, How the Wild West was tamed*
Gerrard, Roy. *Rosie and the rustlers*
    Wagons west!
Gibbons, Gail. *Yippee-yay!*
Glass, Andrew. *Bewildered for three days*
    The sweetwater run
Glasscock, Sarah. *My prairie summer*
Gleeson, Brian. *Paul Bunyan*
Griffin, Kitty. *Cowboy Sam and those confounded secrets*
Grossman, Bill. *Cowboy Ed*
Hancock, Sibyl. *Old Blue*
Harper, Jo. *Jalapeno Hal*
    Prairie dog pioneers
Harvey, Brett. *Cassie's journey*
    My prairie year
Helldorfer, M. C. (Mary Claire). *Hog music*
Holub, Joan. *Cinderdog and the wicked stepcat*
Hooker, Ruth. *Matthew the cowboy*
Howard, Ellen. *The log cabin Christmas*
    The log cabin church
    The log cabin quilt
Isaacs, Anne. *Swamp Angel*
Jakes, John. *Susanna of the Alamo*
Johnston, Tony. *The cowboy and the black-eyed pea*
    Sunsets of the West
Joosse, Barbara M. *Lewis and papa*
Karim, Roberta. *Kindle me a riddle*
Kay, Verla. *Gold fever*
Kellogg, Steven (Stephen). *Johnny Appleseed*
    Paul Bunyan
    Pecos Bill
    Sally Ann Thunder Ann Whirlwind Crockett
Kennedy, Richard. *The contests at Cowlick*
Ketteman, Helen. *Shoeshine Whittaker*
Kimmel, Eric A. *Charlie drives the stage*
    Four dollars and fifty cents
Kinsey-Warnock, Natalie. *The bear that heard crying*
Kramer, Sydelle. *Wagon train*
Kunstler, James Howard. *Annie Oakley*
Lawson, Robert. *They were strong and good*
Levitin, Sonia. *Boom town*
    Nine for California
    Taking charge
Lindbergh, Reeve. *Johnny Appleseed*
Lowell, Susan. *The bootmaker and the elves*
    Cindy Ellen
    Dusty Locks and the three bears
Lyndon, Kerry Raines. *A birthday for Blue*
MacLachlan, Patricia. *What you know first*
McLerran, Alice. *The year of the ranch*
Mara, Wil. *Laura Ingalls Wilder*
Medearis, Angela Shelf. *The zebra-riding cowboy*
Miller, Robert H. (Robert Henry). *The story of Nat Love*
Nixon, Joan Lowery. *If you say so, Claude*
    That's the spirit, Claude
    You bet your britches, Claude
Nolen, Jerdine. *Thunder Rose*
Ó Flatharta, Antoine. *The prairie train*

Paul, Ann Whitford. *The seasons sewn*
Pryor, Bonnie. *Lottie's dream*
Quackenbush, Robert M. *Pete Pack Rat*
Reynolds, Marilynn. *The new land*
    The prairie fire
Rounds, Glen. *Cowboys*
    Sod houses on the Great Plains
Sanders, Scott R. (Scott Russell). *A place called Freedom*
    Warm as wool
Schnitzler, Pattie L. *Widdermaker*
Scott, Ann Herbert. *Big Cowboy Western*
Sewall, Marcia. *Ridin' that strawberry roan*
Smith, Janice Lee. *Jess and the stinky cowboys*
Sorensen, Henri. *New Hope*
Stadler, John. *The ballad of Wilbur and the moose*
Stilz, Carol Curtis. *Grandma Buffalo, May, and me*
Strand, Keith. *Grandfather's Christmas tree*
Stutson, Caroline. *Prairie primer A to Z*
    Sugar snow
Swain, Gwenyth. *Johnny Appleseed*
Tracqui, Valérie. *The horse*
Turner, Ann Warren. *Dakota dugout*
    Red flower goes West
Van Leeuwen, Jean. *Going west*
    Nothing here but trees
Van Woerkom, Dorothy. *Becky and the bear*
Walton, Rick. *Dance, pioneer, dance!*
Whiteley, Opal Stanley. *Only Opal*
Wilder, Laura Ingalls. *Going to town*
    My little house songbook
    Santa comes to little house
Winter, Jeanette. *Cowboy Charlie*
Wittmann, Patricia. *Buffalo Thunder*
Wood, Audrey. *The Bunyans*
Wright, Courtni Crump. *Wagon train*
Yorinks, Arthur. *Whitefish Will rides again*

Ukraine *see* Foreign lands – Ukraine

Umbrellas

Biro, Val. *Miranda's umbrella*
Blance, Ellen. *Monster and the magic umbrella*
Bright, Robert. *My red umbrella*
Chesworth, Michael. *Rainy day dream*
Ching. *The baboon's umbrella*
Chorao, Kay. *Maudie's umbrella*
Cole, William. *Aunt Bella's umbrella*
Demi. *The leaky umbrella*
Drescher, Henrik. *The yellow umbrella*
Feczko, Kathy. *Umbrella parade*
Levine, Rhoda. *Harrison loved his umbrella*
Lipkind, William. *Professor Bull's umbrella*
Liu, Jae Soo. *Yellow umbrella*
Pinkwater, Daniel Manus. *Roger's umbrella*
Sáenz, Benjamin Alire. *Grandma Fina and her wonderful umbrellas =*
    La abuelita Fina y sus sombrillas maravillosas
Smath, Jerry. *Mr. Digby's bad day*
Todd, Barbara. *The rainmaker*
Yashima, Taro. *Umbrella*

Uncles *see* Family life – aunts, uncles

Unhappiness *see* Emotions – happiness; Emotions –
    sadness

UNICEF

Castle, Caroline. *For every child*
Coatsworth, Elizabeth. *The children come running*

Unicorns *see* Mythical creatures – unicorns

Unnoticed *see* Behavior – unnoticed, unseen

Unusual format *see* Format, unusual

Up & down *see* Concepts – up & down

Ute Indians *see* Indians of North America – Ute

Uzbekistan *see* Foreign lands – Uzbekistan

Vacationing *see* Activities – vacationing

Vacuum cleaners *see* Machines – vacuum cleaners

Valentine's Day *see* Holidays – Valentine's Day

Values

Mahy, Margaret. *Pillycock's shop*
Schlein, Miriam. *The pile of junk*

Vampires *see* Monsters – vampires

Vanity *see* Character traits – vanity

Vatican City *see* Foreign lands – Vatican City

Venezuela *see* Foreign lands – Venezuela

Veterinarians *see* Careers – veterinarians

Vietnam *see* Foreign lands – Vietnam

Vietnamese Americans *see* Ethnic groups in the U.S. –
    Vietnamese Americans

Vikings

Cowell, Cressida. *Hiccup the seasick Viking*
Manning, Mick. *What a Viking!*
Schachner, Judith Byron. *Yo, Vikings*

Violence, nonviolence

Charters, Janet. *The general*
Cohn, Janice I. *"Why did it happen?"*
Duvoisin, Roger Antoine. *The happy hunter*
Fitzhugh, Louise. *Bang, bang, you're dead*
Foreman, Michael. *Moose*
Hader, Berta Hoerner. *Mister Billy's gun*
Leaf, Munro. *The story of Ferdinand the bull*
Lobel, Anita. *Potatoes, potatoes*
Peet, Bill (William Bartlett). *The pinkish, purplish, bluish egg*
Sharmat, Marjorie Weinman. *Walter the wolf*
Wiesner, William. *Tops*
Wondriska, William. *The tomato patch*

Violins *see* Musical instruments – violins

Volcanoes

Branley, Franklyn M. (Mansfield). *Volcanoes*
George, Jean Craighead. *Dear Katie, the volcano is a girl*
Greenwood, Rosie. *I wonder why volcanoes blow their tops*
Grifalconi, Ann. *The village of round and square houses*
Kimmel, Eric A. *The two mountains*
Lewis, Paul Owen. *Frog girl*
Lewis, Thomas P. *Hill of fire*

Simon, Seymour. *Danger! volcanoes*

Vultures *see* Birds – vultures

Wagons *see* Toys – wagons

Waiters *see* Careers – waiters, waitresses

Waitresses *see* Careers – waiters, waitresses

Wales *see* Foreign lands – Wales

Walking *see* Activities – walking

Walruses *see* Animals – walruses

Wampanoag Indians *see* Indians of North America – Wampanoag

War

Ackerman, Karen. *The tin heart*
   When mama retires
Adler, David A. *The number on my grandfather's arm*
Ambrus, Victor G. *Brave soldier Janosch*
Armstrong, Jennifer. *King crow*
Aulaire, Ingri Mortenson d'. *Wings for Per*
Baillie, Allan. *Rebel!*
Balgassi, Haemi. *Peacebound trains*
Bartoletti, Susan Campbell. *The flag maker*
Baumann, Kurt. *The prince and the lute*
Breckler, Rosemary K. *Sweet dried apples*
Briggs, Raymond. *The tin-pot foreign general and the old iron woman*
Brunhoff, Laurent de. *Babar's battle*
Bunting, Eve (Anne Evelyn). *The blue and the gray*
   Gleam and Glow
   One candle
   So far from the sea
   The wall
Chiang, Wei. *The legend of Mu Lan = La heroina Hua Mulan*
Coerr, Eleanor. *Sadako*
Cutler, Jane. *The cello of Mr. O*
Deedy, Carmen Agra. *The yellow star*
De Paola, Tomie (Thomas Anthony). *The mysterious giant of Barletta*
Dupasquier, Philippe. *Jack at sea*
Eco, Umberto. *The bomb and the general*
Elzbieta. *Jon-Jon and Annette*
Fitzhugh, Louise. *Bang, bang, you're dead*
Fleming, Candace. *Boxes for Katje*
Foreman, Michael. *War and peas*
Fox, Mem. *Feathers and fools*
Garland, Sherry. *The lotus seed*
Gauch, Patricia Lee. *Once upon a Dinkelsbühl*
Gleiter, Jan. *Paul Revere*
Goble, Paul. *Death of the iron horse*
Gold, Julie. *From a distance*
Greenfield, Eloise. *Easter parade*
Greeson, Janet. *An American army of two*
Grimm, Wilhelm. *Dear Mili*
Haseley, Dennis. *Horses with wings*
Hearne, Betsy Gould. *Seven brave women*
Heide, Florence Parry. *Sami and the time of the troubles*
Hest, Amy. *The ring and the window seat*
Hodges, Margaret. *The hero of Bremen*
Hoestlandt, Jo. *Star of fear, star of hope*
Holbrook, Stewart. *America's Ethan Allen*

Houston, Gloria. *But no candy*
Howard, Elizabeth Fitzgerald. *Papa tells Chita a story*
Hughes, Peter. *The king who loved candy*
Hutton, Warwick. *The Trojan horse*
Ikeda, Daisaku. *The cherry tree*
James, J. Alison. *The drums of Noto Hanto*
Jones, Rebecca C. *The biggest (and best) flag that ever flew*
Keefer, Janice Kulyk. *Anna's goat*
Key, Francis Scott. *The Star Spangled Banner*, ill. by Ingri & Edgar Parin D'Aulaire
   The Star Spangled Banner, ill. by Dana Regan
Khan, Rukhsana. *The roses in my carpets*
Klingel, Cynthia Fitterer. *Paul Revere's ride*
Lee, Milly. *Nim and the war effort*
Littlesugar, Amy. *Lisette's angel*
Longfellow, Henry Wadsworth. *Paul Revere's ride*, ill. by Paul Galdone
   Paul Revere's ride, ill. by Nancy Winslow Parker
   Paul Revere's ride, ill. by Charles Santore
Lyon, George Ella. *Cecil's story*
McAllister, Angela. *The battle of Sir Cob and Sir Filbert*
McKee, David. *Tusk tusk*
Mattingley, Christobel. *The angel with a mouth-organ*
Miller, Edward. *Frederick Ferdinand Fox*
Mochizuki, Ken. *Baseball saved us*
   Heroes
Morimoto, Junko. *My Hiroshima*
Munsch, Robert N. *From far away*
Myers, Edward. *Forri the baker*
Nerlove, Miriam. *Flowers on the wall*
Nivola, Claire A. *Elisabeth*
Norman, Philip Ross. *The carrot war*
Oberman, Sheldon. *By the Hanukkah light*
Oppenheim, Shulamith Levey. *The lily cupboard*
Paterson, John (John Barstow). *Blueberries for the queen*
Phillips, Louis. *The brothers Wrong and Wrong Again*
Pin, Isabel. *The seed*
Poffenberger, Nancy M. *September 11, 2001*
Polacco, Patricia. *The butterfly*
Poole, Josephine. *Joan of Arc*
Popov, Nikolai. *Why?*
Pringle, Laurence P. *One room school*
Radunsky, Vladimir. *Manneken pis*
Raven, Margot Theis. *Mercedes and the chocolate pilot*
Rupprecht, Siegfried P. *The tale of the vanishing rainbow*
Sandman, Rochel. *Perfect porridge*
Santella, Andrew. *George Washington*
Seuss, Dr. *The butter battle book*
Seymour, Tres. *We played marbles*
Shea, Pegi Deitz. *The whispering cloth*
Smucker, Barbara Claasen. *Selina and the bear paw quilt*
Stillerman, Marci. *Nine spoons*
Stone, Bernard. *The charge of the mouse brigade*
Tibo, Gilles. *The grand journey of Mr. Man*
Trottier, Maxine. *Flags*
Turner, Ann Warren. *When Mr. Jefferson came to Philadelphia*
Vigna, Judith. *Nobody wants a nuclear war*
Wade, Mary Dodson. *Cinco de Mayo*
Wells, Rosemary. *The language of doves*
Whittier, John Greenleaf. *Barbara Frietchie*
Wild, Margaret. *Let the celebrations begin!*
Winnick, Karen B. *Sybil's night ride*
Woodson, Jacqueline. *Coming on home soon*
Yenne, Bill. *Joshua and the battle of Jericho*
Yolen, Jane. *All those secrets of the world*
Zhang, Song Nan. *The ballad of Mulan*
Ziefert, Harriet. *A new coat for Anna*

Warthogs *see* Animals – warthogs

Washboards *see* Musical instruments – washboards

Washing machines *see* Machines

Washington's Birthday *see* Holidays – Washington's Birthday

Wasps *see* Insects – wasps

Watches *see* Clocks, watches

Water

Asch, Frank. *Water*
Atwell, Debby. *River*
Base, Graeme. *The water hole*
Cobb, Vicki. *I get wet*
Cole, Joanna. *The magic school bus at the waterworks*
Cullen, Catherine Ann. *Thirsty baby*
Cunningham, David. *A crow's journey*
Dorros, Arthur. *Follow the water from brook to ocean*
Doyle, Malachy. *Splash, Joshua, splash!*
Duvall, Jill. *Who keeps the water clean? Ms. Schindler!*
Flanagan, Alice K. *Water*
Frost, Helen. *Drinking water*
George, Jean Craighead. *To climb a waterfall*
Glaser, Omri. *Round the garden*
Graham, Joan Bransfield. *Splish splash*
Greenfield, Eloise. *Water, water*
Grindley, Sally. *Peter's place*
Grobler, Piet. *Hey, frog!*
Guthrie, Donna. *Nobiah's well*
Hamilton, K. R. (Kersten R). *This is the ocean*
Hathorn, Libby (Elizabeth). *The wonder thing*
Jackson, Ellen B. *The precious gift*
Jackson, Shelley. *The old woman and the wave*
Jolliffe, Anne. *Water, wind and wheels*
Kalz, Jill. *Water*
Keams, Geri. *Snail girl brings water*
Kerley, Barbara. *A cool drink of water*
Kessler, Cristina. *My great-grandmother's gourd*
Koch, Michelle. *World water watch*
Leutscher, Alfred. *Water*
Lobb, Janice. *Splish! Splosh! Why do we wash?*
Locker, Thomas. *Water dance*
Lucado, Max. *All you ever need*
McDonnell, Flora. *Splash!*
Madgwick, Wendy. *Water play*
Martin, David. *Lizzie and her friend*
Mattern, Joanne. *Safety in the water*
Miller, Margaret. *Water play*
Paterson, Katherine. *Celia and the sweet, sweet water*
Peters, Lisa Westberg. *Water's way*
Pitcher, Caroline. *The snow whale*
Pollock, Penny. *Water is wet*
Rauzon, Mark J. *Water, water everywhere*
Riley, Linda Capus. *Elephants swim*
Russell, Naomi. *The stream*
Ryder, Joanne. *The waterfall's gift*
Schmid, Eleonore. *The water's journey*
Seuling, Barbara. *Drip! drop!*
Sheppard, Jeff. *Splash, splash*
Simon, Seymour. *Let's try it out in the water*
Southey, Robert. *The cataract of Lodore*
Speed, Toby. *Watervoices*
Stafford, Kim Robert. *We got here together*
Verboven, Agnes. *Ducks like to swim*
Weninger, Brigitte. *Precious water*
Wyler, Rose. *Puddles and ponds*
Yolen, Jane. *Letting Swift River go*

Water buffaloes *see* Animals – water buffaloes

Weapons

Bolliger, Max. *The wooden man*
Duvoisin, Roger Antoine. *The happy hunter*
Emberley, Barbara. *Drummer Hoff*
Fitzhugh, Louise. *Bang, bang, you're dead*
Hader, Berta Hoerner. *Mister Billy's gun*
Krensky, Stephen. *Shooting for the moon*
Schulson, Rachel Ellenberg. *Guns . . . what you should know*
Wondriska, William. *The tomato patch*

Weasels *see* Animals – weasels

Weather

Allington, Richard L. *Autumn*
  Spring
  Summer
  Winter
Anholt, Catherine. *Sun, snow, stars, sky*
Ardizzone, Edward. *Tim to the rescue*
Asch, Frank. *Country pie*
Baird, Audrey B. *A cold snap!*
Barrett, Judi. *Cloudy with a chance of meatballs*
  Pickles to Pittsburgh
Baum, Arline. *One bright Monday morning*
Bell, Norman. *Linda's airmail letter*
Berger, Melvin. *How's the weather?*
Blackstone, Stella. *Bear in sunshine*
Bolliger, Max. *The wooden man*
Branley, Franklyn M. (Mansfield). *Down comes the rain*
  Rain and hail
Brenner, Barbara A. *The snow parade*
Brown, Margaret Wise. *The little island*
Burgert, Hans-Joachim. *Samulo and the giant*
Burke, Jennifer S. *Cold days*
  Hot days
Calmenson, Stephanie. *Hotter than a hot dog!*
Canyon, Christopher. *John Denver's Sunshine on my shoulders*
Carlstrom, Nancy White. *What does the sky say?*
Chambers, Catherine. *Heat wave*
Crews, Donald. *Cloudy day/sunny day*
Davidson, Amanda. *Teddy goes outside*
Denega, Danielle. *Rain or shine*
Dewey, Ariane. *Febold Feboldson*
DeWitt, Lyndia. *What will the weather be?*
Dunphy, Madeleine. *Here is the tropical rain forest*
Fisher, Aileen Lucia. *I like weather*
Flanagan, Alice K. *Weather*
Fowler, Allan. *What's the weather today?*
Frye, Dean. *Days of sunshine, days of rain*
Gackenbach, Dick. *Ida Fanfanny*
Gibbons, Gail. *Weather words and what they mean*
Ginsburg, Mirra. *Four brave sailors*
Gliori, Debi. *Willie Bear and the Wish Fish*
Gould, Deborah. *Camping in the Temple of the Sun*
Greenberg, Barbara. *The bravest babysitter*
Grohmann, Susan. *The dust under Mrs. Merriweather's bed*
Havill, Juanita. *Treasure nap*
Hayden, Lea. *Sunny day – rainy day*
Hayward, Linda. *Sunny Day Bunny*
Hill, Eric. *Spot looks at weather*
Hines, Anna Grossnickle. *What can you do in the sun?*
Howell, Will C. *I call it sky*
Inkpen, Mick. *Kipper's book of weather*
Jackson, Ellen B. *April*
  August
  December
  February
  January
  July
  June
  March
  May
  November
  October
  September
A January fog will freeze a hog
Jaynes, Ruth M. *Benny's four hats*
Kespert, Deborah. *Rain and shine*
Ketteman, Helen. *Heat wave*
Kirkpatrick, Rena K. *Weather*
Koscielniak, Bruce. *Geoffrey Groundhog predicts the weather*
Let's count the raindrops
Lewin, Betsy. *Hip, hippo, hooray!*
Livinson, Nancy Smiler. *North Pole, South Pole*
Locker, Thomas. *Water dance*
Lotz, Karen E. *Can't sit still*

McCloskey, Robert. *Time of wonder*
McKee, David. *Elmer's weather*
Maestro, Betsy. *Temperature and you*
　　Through the year with Harriet
Marshak, S. (Samuil). *The Month-Brothers*
Mollel, Tololwa M. (Tololwa Marti). *A promise to the sun*
Moore, Elaine. *Grandma's garden*
Nelson, Robin. *A sunny day*
O'Mara, Carmel. *Sunny day*
Palazzo-Craig, Janet. *What makes the weather*
Peters, Lisa Westberg. *The sun, the wind and the rain*
　　Water's way
Pieńkowski, Jan. *Weather*
Roche, Hannah. *Sandra's sun hat*
Rockwell, Anne F. *Blackout*
Rogers, Paul (Patrick). *What will the weather be like today?*
Schlein, Miriam. *The sun, the wind, the sea and the rain*
Schweninger, Ann. *Summertime*
Seymour, Peter S. *How the weather works*
Sherrow, Victoria. *Wilbur waits*
Singer, Marilyn. *On the same day in March*
Stevenson, James. *Heat wave at Mud Flat*
Tresselt, Alvin R. *Sun up*, ill. by author
　　Sun up, ill. by Henri Sorensen
Vance, Eleanor Graham. *Jonathan*
Van Leeuwen, Jean. *Too hot for ice cream*
Vigna, Judith. *Boot weather*
Watts, Bernadette. *Tattercoats*
Zolotow, Charlotte (Shapiro). *The storm book*

Weather – blizzards

Figley, Marty Rhodes. *The schoolchildren's blizzard*
Hobbie, Holly. *Toot and Puddle, I'll be home for Christmas*
Joosse, Barbara M. *A houseful of Christmas*
Spinelli, Eileen. *Coming through the blizzard*
Trottier, Maxine. *Storm at Batoche*
Wetterer, Margaret K. *The snow walker*
Wright, Betty Ren. *The blizzard*

Weather – clouds

Arqués, Isabel M. *Ken's cloud*
Burke, Jennifer S. *Cloudy days*
　　Sunny days
Burningham, John. *Cloudland*
Carle, Eric. *Little cloud*
　　Little cloud [board book]
Coursen, Valerie. *Mordant's wish*
Cummings, Pat. *C.L.O.U.D.S.*
De Paola, Tomie (Thomas Anthony). *The cloud book*
Dewey, Ariane. *Small Cloud*
Fowler, Allan. *What do you see in a cloud?*
Greenblat, Rodney Alan. *Thunder Bunny*
Greene, Carol. *Hi, clouds*
Locker, Thomas. *Cloud dance*
Lustig, Michael. *Willy Whyner, cloud designer*
McFall, Gardner. *Jonathan's cloud*
Manushkin, Fran. *Swinging and swinging*
Marol, Jean-Claude. *Vagabul in the clouds*
Nelson, Robin. *A cloudy day*
Oliviero, Jamie. *The fish skin*
Ray, Deborah Kogan. *The cloud*
Rayner, Mary. *The rain cloud*
Renberg, Dalia Hardof. *Hello, clouds!*
Ringi, Kjell (Arne Sorensen). *The sun and the cloud*
Shaw, Charles Green. *It looked like spilt milk*
Spier, Peter. *Dreams*
Turkle, Brinton. *The sky dog*
Wandelmaier, Roy. *Clouds*
Wegen, Ron. *Sky dragon*
Wiesner, David. *Sector 7*
Williams, Leslie. *A bear in the air*

Weather – cold

Baker, Susan. *First look at keeping warm*

Chambers, Catherine. *Big freeze*
Faulkner, Keith. *The puzzled penguin*
Hoban, Lillian. *The sugar snow spring*
Ruurs, Margriet. *Emma's cold day*

Weather – droughts

Aardema, Verna. *Bringing the rain to Kapiti Plain*
Booth, David. *The dust bowl*
Burke, Katie. *Lightning bug thunder*
Cowley, Joy. *Singing down the rain*
Czernecki, Stefan. *The hummingbird's gift*
Fleming, Candace. *Professor Fergus Fahrenheit and his wonderful weather machine*
Frascino, Edward. *Nanny Noony and the dust queen*
Friedrich, Elizabeth. *Leah's pony*
Guthrie, Donna. *Nobiah's well*
Hamilton, Virginia. *Drylongso*
Harper, Jo. *Jalapeno Hal*
James, Betsy. *The mud family*
Kessler, Cristina. *My great-grandmother's gourd*
Lind, Michael. *Bluebonnet girl*
Malotki, Ekkehart. *The magic hummingbird*
Metaxas, Eric. *Princess Scargo and the birthday pumpkin*
Oliviero, Jamie. *The fish skin*
Peterson, Jeanne Whitehouse. *Don't forget Winona*
Rappaport, Doreen. *The long-haired girl*
Yep, Laurence. *The junior thunder lord*

Weather – floods

Alexander, Ellen. *Llama and the great flood*
Arenson, Roberta. *Manu and the talking fish*
Auld, Mary. *Noah's ark*
Bernhard, Emery. *The tree that rains*
Bible. Old Testament. Noah. *Noah and the ark*, ill. by Pauline Baynes
　　Noah and the ark, ill. by Jim Cummins
Bolliger, Max. *Noah and the rainbow*
Brent, Isabelle. *Noah's ark*
Brown, Rick. *Who built the ark?*
Calhoun, Mary. *Flood!*
Carson, Jo. *The great shaking*
Cartwright, Ann. *Norah's ark*
Cech, John. *Django*
Chase, Catherine. *Noah's ark*
Cousins, Lucy. *Noah's ark*
　　Noah's ark [board book]
Cullen, Lynn. *Little Scraggly Hair*
Delessert, Etienne. *The endless party*
De Paola, Tomie (Thomas Anthony). *Noah and the ark*
Duvoisin, Roger Antoine. *A for the ark*
Elborn, Andrew. *Noah and the ark and the animals*
Emberley, Barbara. *One wide river to cross*
Farber, Norma. *How the left-behind beasts built Ararat*
　　Where's Gomer?
Figley, Marty Rhodes. *Noah's wife*
Fischetto, Laura. *Inside Noah's ark*
French, Fiona. *Rise and shine*
Fussenegger, Gertrud. *Noah's ark*
Gauch, Patricia Lee. *Noah*
Geisert, Arthur. *The ark*
Gerstein, Mordicai. *Noah and the great flood*
Goble, Paul. *Remaking the earth*
Goffstein, M. B. (Marilyn Brooke). *My Noah's ark*
Goldsboro, Bobby. *Noah and the ark; and, David and Goliath*
Goodhart, Pippa. *Noah makes a boat*
Graham, Lorenz B. *God wash the world and start again*
Haley, Gail E. *Noah's ark*
Harker, Lesley. *Annie's ark*
Harrison, Troon. *The floating orchard*
Haubensak-Tellenbach, Margrit. *The story of Noah's ark*
Hayward, Linda. *Noah's ark*
Hendrick, Mary Jean. *If anything ever goes wrong at the zoo*
Henrioud, Charles. *Mr. Noah and the animals*
Hewitt, Kathryn. *Two by two*
Hogrogian, Nonny. *Noah's ark*

Hutton, Warwick. *Noah and the great flood*
Ife, Elaine. *Noah and the ark*
Ipcar, Dahlov (Zorach). *A flood of creatures*
James, Betsy. *The mud family*
Janisch, Heinz. *Noah's ark*
Jonas, Ann. *Aardvarks, disembark!*
Ketteman, Helen. *The year of no more corn*
Kishida, Eriko. *The hippo boat*
Kurtz, Jane. *River friendly, river wild*
Kuskin, Karla. *The animals and the ark*
Lenski, Lois. *Mr. and Mrs. Noah*
Le Tord, Bijou. *Noah's trees*
Lewis, J. Patrick. *The boat of many rooms*
Ludwig, Warren. *Old Noah's elephants*
Lyon, George Ella. *Come a tide*
MacBeth, George. *Noah's journey*
McCarthy, Michael. *The story of Noah and the ark*
McCaughrean, Geraldine. *The story of Noah and the ark*
McKié, Roy. *Noah's ark*
Maggi, María Elena. *The great canoe*
Martin, Charles E. *Noah's ark*
Mee, Charles L. *Noah*
Miller, M. L. *Those Bottles!*
Morgan, Allen. *Matthew and the midnight flood*
Morpurgo, Michael. *Jo-Jo the melon donkey*
Olson, Arielle North. *Noah's cats and the devil's fire*
Palazzo, Tony (Anthony D.). *Noah's ark*
Paley, Joan. *One more river*
Pfeffer, Wendy. *The big flood*
Pinkney, Jerry. *Noah's ark*
Rose, Gerald. *Trouble in the ark*
Rosen, Michael J. (1954–). *The dog who walked with God*
Rounds, Glen. *Washday on Noah's ark*
Sasso, Sandy Eisenberg. *A prayer for the earth*
Singer, Isaac Bashevis. *Why Noah chose the dove*
Smith, Elmer Boyd. *The story of Noah's ark*
Smith, Roger. *How the animals saved the ark and put two and two together*
Spier, Peter. *Noah's ark*
Stewart, Paul. *Rabbit's wish*
Sting (Musician). *Rock steady*
Stuart, Chad. *The Ballymara flood*
Tapio, Pat Decker. *The lady who saw the good side of everything*
Thorne, Jenny. *Noah's ark*
Turnbull, Ann. *Too tired*
Velthuijs, Max. *Frog is a hero*
Walton, Rick. *Noah's square dance*
Webb, Clifford. *The story of Noah*
Wiesner, William. *Noah's ark*
Wilson, Anne. *Noah's ark*
Windham, Sophie. *Noah's ark*
Woelfle, Gretchen. *Katje the windmill cat*

Weather – fog

Bacheller, Irving. *Lost in the fog*
Fowler, Susi Gregg. *Fog*
Fry, Christopher. *The boat that mooed*
Keeping, Charles. *Alfie finds the other side of the world*
Lifton, Betty Jean. *Joji and the fog*
May, Robert Lewis. *Rudolph the red-nosed reindeer*, ill. by Diana Magnuson
    Rudolph the red-nosed reindeer, ill. by David Wenzel
Morse, Samuel French. *Sea sums*
Munari, Bruno. *The circus in the mist*
Pearson, Susan. *Silver morning*
Ryder, Joanne. *Fog in the meadow*
Schroder, William. *Pea soup and serpents*
Smith, Theresa Kalab. *The fog is secret*
Tresselt, Alvin R. *Hide and seek fog*

Weather – hurricanes

Bliss, Corinne Demas. *Hurricane!*
Cole, Joanna. *The magic school bus inside a hurricane*
Egan, Tim. *Distant Feathers*
Lakin, Pat (Patricia). *Hurricane!*

London, Jonathan. *Hurricane!*
Wallner, Alexandra. *Sergio and the hurricane*

Weather – lightning, thunder

Armentrout, Patricia. *Lights in the sky*
Arvetis, Chris. *Why does it thunder and lightning?*
Bourgeois, Paulette. *Franklin and the thunderstorm*
Branley, Franklyn M. (Mansfield). *Flash, crash, rumble, and roll*
Bryan, Ashley. *The story of lightning and thunder*
Burke, Katie. *Lightning bug thunder*
Cazet, Denys. *Minnie and Moo meet Frankenswine*
Climo, Shirley. *Stolen thunder*
Crowe, Robert L. *Tyler Toad and the thunder*
Flanagan, Alice K. *Thunder and lightning*
Henley, Claire. *Stormy day*
Hines, Anna Grossnickle. *Rumble thumble boom!*
Hobbie, Holly. *Toot and Puddle, you are my sunshine*
Hutchins, H. J. (Hazel J.). *One dark night*
Marino, Dorothy. *Good-bye thunderstorm*
Martin, David. *Little Chicken Chicken*
Nikola-Lisa, W. *Storm*
Novak, Matt. *Rolling*
Polacco, Patricia. *Thunder cake*
Reiser, Lynn. *Night thunder and the Queen of the Wild Horses*
Shepard, Aaron. *Master man*
Sussman, Susan. *Hippo thunder*
Szilagyi, Mary. *Thunderstorm*

Weather – mist *see* Weather – fog

Weather – rain

Aardema, Verna. *Bringing the rain to Kapiti Plain*
Appelt, Kathi. *Rain dance*
Arnosky, Jim. *Rabbits and raindrops*
Arqués, Isabel M. *Ken's cloud*
Auld, Mary. *Noah's ark*
Baird, Audrey B. *Storm coming!*
Baker, Jill. *Basil of Bywater Hollow*
Base, Graeme. *The water hole*
Bassett, Preston R. *Raindrop stories*
Bentley, Dawn. *Fuzzy bear*
Bergere, Thea. *Paris in the rain with Jean and Jacqueline*
Bible. Old Testament. Noah. *Noah and the ark*, ill. by Pauline Baynes
    Noah and the ark, ill. by Jim Cummins
Blegvad, Lenore. *Rainy day Kate*
Bolliger, Max. *Noah and the rainbow*
Bonnici, Peter. *The first rains*
Boon, Emilie. *Peterkin's wet walk*
Bourgeois, Paulette. *Big Sarah's little boots*
Branley, Franklyn M. (Mansfield). *Down comes the rain*
    Rain and hail
Brent, Isabelle. *Noah's ark*
Bright, Robert. *My red umbrella*
Brouillard, Anne. *The bathtub prima donna*
Brown, Rick. *Who built the ark?*
Buchanan, Ken. *It rained on the desert today*
Bullock, Kathleen. *It chanced to rain*
Burke, Jennifer S. *Rainy days*
Burningham, John. *Mr. Gumpy's motor car*
Calhoun, Mary. *Euphonia and the flood*
Carle, Eric. *Little cloud*
    Little cloud [board book]
Carlson, Nancy L. *What if it never stops raining?*
Carlstrom, Nancy White. *What does the rain play?*
Carrick, Carol. *Sleep out*
    The washout
Cartwright, Ann. *Norah's ark*
Cazet, Denys. *You make the angels cry*
Charlip, Remy. *Where is everybody?*
Chase, Catherine. *Noah's ark*
Claverie, Jean. *The picnic*
Colborn, Mary Palenick. *Rainy day slug*
Cole, Sheila. *When the rain stops*
Cole, William. *Aunt Bella's umbrella*

Conover, Chris. *Sam Panda and Thunder Dragon*
Cousins, Lucy. *Noah's ark*
   Noah's ark [board book]
Cowley, Joy. *Singing down the rain*
Crary, Elizabeth. *I'm mad*
Crews, Nina. *You are here*
Crimi, Carolyn. *Tessa's tip-tapping toes*
Cullen, Lynn. *Little Scraggly Hair*
Dawavendewa, Gerald. *The butterfly dance*
Delessert, Etienne. *The endless party*
De Paola, Tomie (Thomas Anthony). *Katie and Kit at the beach*
   Noah and the ark
Dewey, Ariane. *Small Cloud*
Dragonwagon, Crescent. *Rainy day together*
Drury, Tim. *When I'm big*
Dubanevich, Arlene. *Pig William*
Duvoisin, Roger Antoine. *A for the ark*
Eaton, Deborah. *The rainy day grump*
Edwards, Dorothy. *A wet Monday*
Edwards, Pamela Duncan. *Warthogs paint*
Elborn, Andrew. *Noah and the ark and the animals*
Emberley, Barbara. *One wide river to cross*
Evans, Lezlie. *Rain song*
Farber, Norma. *How the left-behind beasts built Ararat*
   Where's Gomer?
Ferro, Beatriz. *Caught in the rain*
Figley, Marty Rhodes. *Noah's wife*
Fischetto, Laura. *Inside Noah's ark*
Flanagan, Alice K. *Rain*
Fleming, Candace. *Professor Fergus Fahrenheit and his wonderful weather machine*
Ford, Miela. *My day in the garden*
Freeman, Don. *Dandelion*
French, Fiona. *Rise and shine*
Fussenegger, Gertrud. *Noah's ark*
Garelick, May. *Where does the butterfly go when it rains?*, ill. by Leonard Weisgard
   Where does the butterfly go when it rains?, ill. by Nicholas Wilton
Gauch, Patricia Lee. *Noah*
Gay, Marie-Louise. *Rainy day magic*
Geisert, Arthur. *The ark*
Germein, Katrina. *Big rain coming*
Gerstein, Mordicai. *Noah and the great flood*
Ginsburg, Mirra. *Mushroom in the rain*
Glaser, Omri. *Round the garden*
Goffstein, M. B. (Marilyn Brooke). *My Noah's ark*
Goldsboro, Bobby. *Noah and the ark; and, David and Goliath*
Goodhart, Pippa. *Noah makes a boat*
Gorbachev, Valeri. *Nicky and the rainy day*
   One rainy day
Goudey, Alice E. *The good rain*
Graham, Lorenz B. *God wash the world and start again*
Greene, Carol. *Rain! Rain!*
Greenfield, Karen R. *Sister Yessa's story*
Gutman, Anne. *Gaspard and Lisa's rainy day*
Hafner, Marylin. *Molly and Emmett's camping adventure*
Haley, Gail E. *Noah's ark*
Harker, Lesley. *Annie's ark*
Harper, Jo. *Jalapeno Hal*
Harrison, Troon. *The floating orchard*
Haubensak-Tellenbach, Margrit. *The story of Noah's ark*
Hayden, Lea. *Sunny day – rainy day*
Hayward, Linda. *Noah's ark*
Helldorfer, M. C. (Mary Claire). *Silver Rain Brown*
Henrioud, Charles. *Mr. Noah and the animals*
Hershenhorn, Esther. *There goes Lowell's party!*
Hesse, Karen. *Come on, rain*
Hest, Amy. *In the rain with Baby Duck*
Hewitt, Kathryn. *Two by two*
Hines, Anna Grossnickle. *The greatest picnic in the world*
   Taste the raindrops
   What can you do in the rain?
Hoban, Julia. *Amy loves the rain*
Hoban, Russell. *The rain door*
Hogrogian, Nonny. *Noah's ark*
Holl, Adelaide. *The rain puddle*
Hurd, Edith Thacher. *Johnny Lion's rubber boots*

Hutchins, H. J. (Hazel J.). *It's raining, Yancy and Bear*
Hutton, Warwick. *Noah and the great flood*
Ife, Elaine. *Noah and the ark*
Inkpen, Mick. *Kipper's rainy day*
   Splosh!
Iwasaki, Chihiro. *Staying home alone on a rainy day*
James, Betsy. *The mud family*
Janisch, Heinz. *Noah's ark*
Johanasen, Heather. *About the rain forest*
Johnson, Angela. *Rain feet*
Johnson, D. B. (Donald B.). *Henry works*
Jonas, Ann. *Aardvarks, disembark!*
Jones, Elizabeth. *Sunshine and Storm*
Kalan, Robert. *Rain*
Keats, Ezra Jack. *A letter to Amy*
Keith, Eros. *Nancy's backyard*
Keller, Holly. *Will it rain?*
Kennedy, Kim. *Napoleon*
Kishida, Eriko. *The hippo boat*
Knutson, Kimberley. *Jungle jamboree*
   Muddigush
Krings, Antoon. *Oliver's bicycle*
Kroll, Steven. *Doctor on an elephant*
Kurtz, Jane. *Rain romp*
Kuskin, Karla. *The animals and the ark*
   James and the rain
Kwitz, Mary DeBall. *When it rains*
Laser, Michael. *The rain*
Lee, Jeanne M. *Toad is the uncle of heaven*
Lenski, Lois. *Mr. and Mrs. Noah*
Le Tord, Bijou. *Noah's trees*
Lewis, J. Patrick. *The boat of many rooms*
Lewison, Wendy Cheyette. *Raindrop, plop*
   So many boots
Lindbergh, Reeve. *What is the sun?*
Liu, Jae Soo. *Yellow umbrella*
Lloyd, David. *Hello, goodbye*
London, Jonathan. *Puddles*
   What the animals were waiting for
Ludwig, Warren. *Old Noah's elephants*
Lukesová, Milena. *The little girl and the rain*
MacBeth, George. *Noah's journey*
McCarthy, Michael. *The story of Noah and the ark*
McCaughrean, Geraldine. *The story of Noah and the ark*
McKié, Roy. *Noah's ark*
McPhail, David M. *The puddle*
Maggi, María Elena. *The great canoe*
Manning, Maurie J. *The aunts go marching*
Marino, Dorothy. *Good-bye thunderstorm*
Martin, Bill (William Ivan). *Listen to the rain*
Martin, Charles E. *Noah's ark*
Medearis, Angela Shelf. *We play on a rainy day*
Mee, Charles L. *Noah*
Mitchell, Marianne. *Gullywasher gulch*
Munsch, Robert N. *Mud puddle*
Murphy, Shirley Rousseau. *Tattie's river journey*
Nakabayashi, Ei. *The rainy day puddle*
Nelson, Robin. *A rainy day*
Olaleye, Isaac. *In the Rainfield*
Oliviero, Jamie. *The fish skin*
Olson, Arielle North. *Noah's cats and the devil's fire*
O'Mara, Carmel. *Rainy day*
Otto, Carolyn. *That sky, that rain*
Palazzo, Tony (Anthony D.). *Noah's ark*
Paley, Joan. *One more river*
Patron, Susan. *Dark cloud strong breeze*
Pinkney, Jerry. *Noah's ark*
Pinkwater, Daniel Manus. *Rainy morning*
Plourde, Lynn. *Pigs in the mud in the middle of the rud*
Potter, Tessa. *Digger, the story of a mole in the fall*
Prelutsky, Jack. *Rainy rainy Saturday*
Preston, Edna Mitchell. *Pop Corn and Ma Goodness*
Radley, Gail. *Rainy day rhymes*
Raschka, Christopher. *John Coltrane's giant steps*
Raskin, Ellen. *And it rained*
Ray, Mary Lyn. *Red rubber boot day*
Rayner, Mary. *One by one*

Ricketts, Michael. *Rain*
Robbins, Ruth. *How the first rainbow was made*
Roche, Harriet. *Pete's puddles*
Rose, Gerald. *Trouble in the ark*
Rounds, Glen. *Washday on Noah's ark*
Ryder, Joanne. *A wet and sandy day*
Sasso, Sandy Eisenberg. *A prayer for the earth*
Scheer, Julian. *Rain makes applesauce*
Scheffler, Ursel. *A walk in the rain*
Schlein, Miriam. *The sun, the wind, the sea and the rain*
Schwartz, Roslyn. *The mole sisters and the rainy day*
Seignobosc, Françoise. *The big rain*
Serfozo, Mary. *Rain talk*
Shannon, David. *The rain came down*
Shannon, George. *April showers*
Sherman, Nancy. *Gwendolyn and the weathercock*
Shulevitz, Uri. *Rain rain rivers*
Simmie, Lois. *Mister got to go*
Simms, Laura. *The bone man*
Simon, Norma. *The wet world*, ill. by Jane Miller
   The wet world, ill. by Alexi Natchev
Singer, Isaac Bashevis. *Why Noah chose the dove*
Skofield, James. *All wet! All wet!*
Smath, Jerry. *Mr. Digby's bad day*
Smith, Elmer Boyd. *The story of Noah's ark*
Smith, Roger. *How the animals saved the ark and put two and two together*
Soya, Kiyoshi. *A house of leaves*
Spalding, Andrea. *It's raining, it's pouring*
Spetter, Jung-Hee. *Lily and Trooper's winter*
Spier, Peter. *Noah's ark*
   Peter Spier's rain
Stanley, Sanna. *The rains are coming*
Stevenson, James. *Heat wave at Mud Flat*
Sting (Musician). *Rock steady*
Stock, Catherine. *Gugu's house*
Stojic, Manya. *Rain*
Sykes, Julie. *Smudge*
Tapio, Pat Decker. *The lady who saw the good side of everything*
Taylor, Mark. *Henry the castaway*
Thayer, Mike. *In the middle of the puddle*
Thorne, Jenny. *Noah's ark*
Todd, Barbara. *The rainmaker*
Tresselt, Alvin R. *Rain drop splash*
Türk, Hanne. *Rainy day Max*
Turnbull, Ann. *Too tired*
Velthuijs, Max. *Little Man finds a home*
Verboven, Agnes. *Ducks like to swim*
Vincent, Gabrielle. *Ernest and Celestine's picnic*
Wagner, Jenny. *Aranea*
Wahl, Jan. *Follow me cried Bee*
Walton, Rick. *Noah's square dance*
Wandelmaier, Roy. *Clouds*
Webb, Clifford. *The story of Noah*
Weeks, Sarah. *Drip, drop*
Wellington, Monica. *Bunny's rainbow day*
Wells, Rosemary. *Don't spill it again, James*
Wiesner, William. *Noah's ark*
Wilson, Anne. *Noah's ark*
Windham, Sophie. *Noah's ark*
Wyler, Rose. *Raindrops and rainbows*
Yashima, Taro. *Umbrella*
Yee, Wong Herbert. *A drop of rain*
Yep, Laurence. *The junior thunder lord*
Yim, Natasha. *Otto's rainy day*
Zinnemann-Hope, Pam. *Find your coat, Ned*
Zolotow, Charlotte (Shapiro). *The quarreling book*
   The storm book

Weather – rainbows

Anglund, Joan Walsh. *Rainbow love*
Armentrout, Patricia. *Lights in the sky*
Asch, Frank. *Skyfire*
Auld, Mary. *Noah's ark*
Barry, Frances. *Duckie's rainbow*

Bible. Old Testament. Noah. *Noah and the ark*, ill. by Pauline Baynes
Bolliger, Max. *Noah and the rainbow*
Brent, Isabelle. *Noah's ark*
Chase, Catherine. *Noah's ark*
Cousins, Lucy. *Noah's ark*
   Noah's ark [board book]
Craft, Ruth. *The day of the rainbow*
Cullen, Lynn. *Little Scraggly Hair*
De Paola, Tomie (Thomas Anthony). *Noah and the ark*
Elborn, Andrew. *Noah and the ark and the animals*
Fischetto, Laura. *Inside Noah's ark*
Freeman, Don. *A rainbow of my own*
Fussenegger, Gertrud. *Noah's ark*
Gauch, Patricia Lee. *Noah*
Geisert, Arthur. *After the flood*
Goodhart, Pippa. *Noah makes a boat*
Haley, Gail E. *Noah's ark*
Haubensak-Tellenbach, Margrit. *The story of Noah's ark*
Haynes, Max. *Sparky's rainbow repair*
Henrioud, Charles. *Mr. Noah and the animals*
Hewitt, Kathryn. *Two by two*
Hines, Anna Grossnickle. *What can you do in the sun?*
Hogrogian, Nonny. *Noah's ark*
Hooper, Patricia. *How the sky's housekeeper wore her scarves*
Hutton, Warwick. *Noah and the great flood*
Ife, Elaine. *Noah and the ark*
Janisch, Heinz. *Noah's ark*
Kirkpatrick, Rena K. *Rainbow colors*
Krupp, E. C. (Edwin C.). *The rainbow and you*
Kunhardt, Edith. *Red day, green day*
Kwitz, Mary DeBall. *When it rains*
Lenski, Lois. *Mr. and Mrs. Noah*
Ludwig, Warren. *Old Noah's elephants*
MacBeth, George. *Noah's journey*
McCaughrean, Geraldine. *The story of Noah and the ark*
McKié, Roy. *Noah's ark*
Marino, Dorothy. *Buzzy Bear and the rainbow*
Martin, Charles E. *Noah's ark*
Mee, Charles L. *Noah*
Palazzo, Tony (Anthony D.). *Noah's ark*
Paley, Joan. *One more river*
Pinkney, Jerry. *Noah's ark*
Pinkney, Sandra L. *A rainbow all around me*
Robbins, Ruth. *How the first rainbow was made*
Rupprecht, Siegfried P. *The tale of the vanishing rainbow*
Shannon, David. *The rain came down*
Singer, Isaac Bashevis. *Why Noah chose the dove*
Smith, Elmer Boyd. *The story of Noah's ark*
Sting (Musician). *Rock steady*
Thorne, Jenny. *Noah's ark*
Walsh, Melanie. *Ned's rainbow*
Webb, Clifford. *The story of Noah*
Wellington, Monica. *Bunny's rainbow day*
Weston, Martha. *Peony's rainbow*
Williams, Leslie. *A bear in the air*
Wilson, Anne. *Noah's ark*
Wyler, Rose. *Raindrops and rainbows*
Zolotow, Charlotte (Shapiro). *The storm book*

Weather – sandstorms

London, Jonathan. *Ali, child of the desert*

Weather – snow

Alarcón, Francisco X. *Iguanas in the snow and other winter poems / poemas = Iguanas en la nieve y otros poemas de invierno / poemas*
Alborough, Jez. *Ice cream bear*
Arqués, Isabel M. *Ken's cloud*
Bahr, Mary. *My brother loved snowflakes*
Bahr, Robert. *Blizzard at the zoo*
Barklem, Jill. *Winter story*
Bartoli, Jennifer. *Snow on bear's nose*
Bauer, Caroline Feller. *Midnight snowman*
Beck, Ian. *Teddy's snowy day*
Blades, Ann. *Winter*

Bogacki, Tomasz. *Cat and mouse in the snow*
Bradby, Marie. *The longest wait*
Branley, Franklyn M. (Mansfield). *Snow is falling*
Briggs, Raymond. *The snowman tell-the-time book*
Brown, Margaret Wise. *The winter noisy book*
Bruna, Dick. *Another story to tell*
   Miffy in the snow
Buckley, Helen Elizabeth. *Josie and the snow*
Bundey, Nikki. *In the snow*
Burningham, John. *The snow*
   Trubloff
Burns, Kate. *In the snow*
Burton, Virginia Lee. *Katy and the big snow*
Bushey, Jeanne. *A sled dog for Moshi*
Butterworth, Nick. *One snowy night*
Bynum, Janie. *Altoona up north*
Carle, Eric. *Dream snow*
Carlson, Nancy L. *Take time to relax*
Carlstrom, Nancy White. *The snow speaks*
Cech, John. *First snow, magic snow*
Chapman, Cheryl. *Snow on snow on snow*
Chönz, Selina. *The snowstorm*
Christiana, David. *The first snow*
Claverie, Jean. *Working*
Cocca-Leffler, Maryann. *Ice-cold birthday*
Colandro, Lucille. *There was a cold lady who swallowed some snow!*
Cote, Nancy. *It feels like snow*
Cotten, Cynthia. *Snow ponies*
Crews, Nina. *Snowball*
Crisp, Marty. *Totally polar*
Croll, Carolyn. *The little snowgirl*
Cunningham, David. *A crow's journey*
Curious George in the snow
Cuyler, Margery. *The biggest, best snowman*
da Costa, Deborah. *Snow in Jerusalem*
Dahl, Michael. *Footprints in the snow*
De Groat, Diane. *Jingle bells, homework smells*
Delaney, A. *Monster tracks?*
Delton, Judy. *Brimhall turns detective*
   A walk on a snowy night
Deprisco, Dorothea. *Snowbear's winter day*
Diviny, Sean. *Snow inside the house*
Dooley, Norah. *Everybody serves soup*
Dorian, Marguerite. *When the snow is blue*
Dowling, Paul. *Jimmy's snowy book*
Duncan, Jane. *Brave Janet Reachfar*
Dunrea, Olivier. *It's snowing*
Enderle, Judith (Ann) Ross. *Six snowy sheep*
Fain, Moira. *Snow day*
Fearnley, Jan. *A perfect day for it*
Figueredo, D. H. *When this world was new*
Fitch, Sheree. *No two snowflakes*
Flanagan, Alice K. *Snow*
Fleischman, Paul. *Lost!*
Ford, Christine. *Snow!*
Frost, Robert. *The runaway*
Funakoshi, Canna. *One evening*
Galbraith, Kathryn Osebold. *Look! Snow!*
Gammell, Stephen. *Is that you, winter?*
Gantschev, Ivan. *The Christmas teddy bear*
Gay, Marie-Louise. *Stella, queen of the snow*
George, Jean Craighead. *Snow bear*
Gershator, Phillis. *When it starts to snow*
Gipson, Morrell. *Whose tracks are these?*
Gliori, Debi. *The snow lambs*
   The snowchild
Greene, Carol. *Snow Joe*
Gunther, Louise. *Anna's snow day*
Hader, Berta Hoerner. *The big snow*
Halpern, Julie. *Toby and the snowflakes*
Harshman, Marc. *Snow company*
Henderson, Kathy. *Disney's Bambi: the winter trail*
Henkes, Kevin. *Oh!*
Hidaka, Masako. *Girl from the snow country*
Himmelman, John. *The day-off machine*
Hines, Anna Grossnickle. *What can you do in the snow?*
Hissey, Jane. *Jolly snow*

Hoban, Julia. *Amy loves the snow*
Hoban, Lillian. *Silly Tilly's Valentine*
   The sugar snow spring
Hoban, Russell. *Some snow said hello*
Hobbie, Holly. *Toot and Puddle, I'll be home for Christmas*
Hoff, Syd. *When will it snow?*
Honda, Tetsuya. *Wild horse winter*
Hughes, Shirley. *The snow lady*
Hutchins, H. J. (Hazel J.). *Ben's snow song*
   Norman's snowball
Inkpen, Mick. *Kipper's snowy day*
Ives, Penny. *The snow angel*
Iwasaki, Chihiro. *The birthday wish*
Janosch. *Dear snowman*
Johnston, Tony. *The last snow of winter*
Joos, Françoise. *The golden snowflake*
Joosse, Barbara M. *Snow day!*
Joyce, William. *Snowie Rolie*
Keats, Ezra Jack. *The snowy day*
   The snowy day [board book]
Keller, Holly. *Geraldine's big snow*
Keown, Elizabeth. *Emily's snowball*
Kharms, Daniil. *The story of a boy named Will, who went sledding down the hill*
Kneen, Maggie. *The Christmas surprise*
Kovalski, Maryann. *Jingle bells*
Krauss, Ruth. *The happy day*
Kuskin, Karla. *In the flaky frosty morning*
Lachner, Dorothea. *The gift from Saint Nicholas*
Lakin, Pat (Patricia). *Snow day!*
Landa, Norbert. *Little Bear's Christmas*
Landry, Leo. *The snow ghosts*
Landström, Olof. *Boo and Baa in windy weather*
Lasky, Kathryn. *Lucille's snowsuit*
Leblanc, Anne. *Benjamin in the snow*
Lewis, Kim. *First snow*
Lewison, Wendy Cheyette. *Hello, snow!*
London, Jonathan. *Froggy gets dressed*
Loretan, Sylvia. *Bob the snowman*
Lucas, Barbara (Barbara M.). *Snowed in*
Ludwig, Warren. *Good morning, Granny Rose*
McAllister, Angela. *The snow angel*
McCully, Emily Arnold. *First snow*
   An outlaw Thanksgiving
McCutcheon, Marc. *Grandfather's Christmas camp*
McGuirk, Leslie. *Tucker flips!*
McKee, David. *Elmer in the snow*
McKié, Roy. *Snow*
McPhail, David M. *Snow lion*
McQuade, Jacqueline. *Snow babies*
Manuel, Lynn. *The night the moon blew kisses*
Martin, Jacqueline Briggs. *Snowflake Bentley*
Marzollo, Jean. *Snow angel*
Mayper, Monica. *Oh snow*
Medearis, Angela Shelf. *Best friends in the snow*
   Here comes the snow
Meister, Cari. *Tiny the snow dog*
Mercer, Lynn. *Schubert's snowflakes*
Mockford, Caroline. *Cleo in the snow*
Munsch, Robert N. *Thomas' snowsuit*
Nelson, Robin. *A snowy day*
Norman, Philip Ross. *A mammoth imagination*
O'Malley, Kevin. *Straight to the pole*
Parillo, Tony. *Michelangelo's surprise*
Parnall, Peter. *Alfalfa Hill*
Peddle, Daniel. *Snow day*
Pfister, Marcus. *Penguin Pete and Little Tim*
Pickering, Jimmy. *It's winter*
Pitcher, Caroline. *The snow whale*
Poydar, Nancy. *Snip, snip . . . snow!*
Pulver, Robin. *Axle Annie*
Raphael, Elaine. *Donkey, it's snowing*
Raschka, Christopher. *John Coltrane's giant steps*
Retan, Walter. *The snowplow that tried to go south*
Rockwell, Anne F. *The first snowfall*
Root, Phyllis. *Grandmother Winter*
Rosen, Michael J. (1954–). *Avalanche*

Rosenberg, Liz. *On Christmas eve*
Ruelle, Karen Gray. *The crunchy, munchy Christmas tree*
    Snow Valentines
Sanfield, Steve. *Snow*
Sasaki, Isao. *Snow*
Sauer, Julia Lina. *Mike's house*
Saunders, Dave. *Snowtime*
Schaefer, Carole Lexa. *Snow pumpkin*
Schick, Eleanor. *City in the winter*
Schlein, Miriam. *Deer in the snow*
Schmid, Eleonore. *The water's journey*
Schroeder, Binette. *Tuffa and the snow*
Shulevitz, Uri. *Snow*
Siddals, Mary McKenna. *Millions of snowflakes*
Simmonds, Posy. *Lulu and the flying babies*
Simmons, Jane. *Little Fern's first winter*
Skofield, James. *Snow country*
Spetter, Jung-Hee. *Lily and Trooper's winter*
Spohn, Kate. *Snow play*
Stafford, Liliana. *The snow bear*
Steig, William. *Brave Irene*
Stojic, Manya. *Snow*
Tibo, Gilles. *Simon and the snowflakes*
Todd, Kathleen. *Snow*
Tresselt, Alvin R. *White snow, bright snow*
Tudor, Tasha. *Snow before Christmas*
Udry, Janice May. *Mary Jo's grandmother*
Uhlberg, Myron. *Flying over Brooklyn*
Updike, David. *A winter's journey*
Van Laan, Nancy. *Moose tales*
Wabbes, Marie. *It's snowing, Little Rabbit*
Waddell, Martin. *Snow bears*
Wallace, Nancy Elizabeth. *Snow*
Watanabe, Shigeo. *Ice cream is falling!*
Watson, Nancy Dingman. *Sugar on snow*
Weller, Frances Ward. *The angel of Mill Street*
Wellington, Monica. *Bunny's first snowflake*
Wheeler, Cindy. *Marmalade's snowy day*
Whybrow, Ian. *Harry and the snow king*
Williams, Sam. *Snowy magic*
Yerxa, Leo. *Last leaf first snowflake to fall*
Yolen, Jane. *Snow, snow*
Zion, Gene. *The summer snowman*
Zolotow, Charlotte (Shapiro). *Hold my hand*
    Something is going to happen

Weather – storms

Adoff, Arnold. *Make a circle, keep us in*
    Tornado!
Aldridge, Josephine Haskell. *Fisherman's luck*
Amoss, Berthe. *Old Hannibal and the hurricane*
Anderson, Lena. *Stina*
Anderson, Lonzo. *The day the hurricane happened*
Anholt, Catherine. *Chimp and Zee and the big storm*
Arvetis, Chris. *Why does it thunder and lightning?*
Asare, Meshack. *Sosu's call*
Bahr, Robert. *Blizzard at the zoo*
Baird, Audrey B. *Storm coming!*
Barber, Antonia. *The mousehole cat*
Bearcub and Mama
Beard, Darleen Bailey. *Twister*
Bourgeois, Paulette. *Franklin and the thunderstorm*
Bradby, Marie. *The longest wait*
Branley, Franklyn M. (Mansfield). *Hurricane watch*
    Tornado alert
Brown, Alan. *Hoot and Holler*
Brown, Ruth. *One stormy night*
Bryan, Ashley. *The story of lightning and thunder*
Buchanan, Ken. *It rained on the desert today*
Burdett, Lois. *The tempest for kids*
Burstein, Fred. *Anna's rain*
Bushey, Jeanne. *A sled dog for Moshi*
Butterworth, Nick. *One blowy night*
Carrick, Carol. *Lost in the storm*
Chesworth, Michael. *Rainy day dream*
Chönz, Selina. *The snowstorm*

Cocca-Leffler, Maryann. *Ice-cold birthday*
Crews, Donald. *Sail away*
Davol, Marguerite W. *Why butterflies go by on silent wings*
Delamare, David. *The Christmas secret*
Delton, Judy. *A walk on a snowy night*
Dennis, Morgan. *The sea dog*
Dodds, Dayle Ann. *Sing, Sophie!*
Doyle, Malachy. *Storm cats*
Duncan, Jane. *Brave Janet Reachfar*
English, Karen. *Big wind coming!*
Faulkner, Matt. *The amazing voyage of Jackie Grace*
Fisher, Leonard Everett. *Sky, sea, the jetty, and me*
Flanagan, Alice K. *Thunder and lightning*
Foreman, Michael. *Jack's fantastic voyage*
Gantschev, Ivan. *The Christmas teddy bear*
Gedin, Birgitta. *The little house from the sea*
George, Jean Craighead. *Cliff hanger*
Gliori, Debi. *Mr. Bear to the rescue*
    The snow lambs
Graham, Georgia. *The strongest man this side of Cremona*
Gray, Libba Moore. *Is there room on the feather bed?*
Greenfield, Karen R. *Sister Yessa's story*
Harshman, Marc. *Snow company*
    The storm
Harvey, Brett. *My prairie Christmas*
Haughton, Emma. *Rainy day*
Henderson, Kathy. *The storm*
Henley, Claire. *Stormy day*
Hershenhorn, Esther. *There goes Lowell's party!*
Hest, Amy. *Ruby's storm*
Hines, Anna Grossnickle. *Rumble thumble boom!*
Hippely, Hilary Horder. *Adventure on Klickitat Island*
Hobbie, Holly. *Toot and Puddle, I'll be home for Christmas*
    Toot and Puddle, you are my sunshine
Hopkinson, Deborah. *Birdie's lighthouse*
Hutchins, H. J. (Hazel J.). *One dark night*
Johnson, Amy Crane. *Cinnamon and the April shower = Canela y el*
    aguacero de abril
Keats, Ezra Jack. *Clementina's cactus*
Keller, Holly. *Will it rain?*
Kimura, Yuichi. *One stormy night . . .*
Kitamura, Satoshi. *Captain Toby*
Kovacs, Deborah. *Moonlight on the river*
Kuiper, Nannie. *Bravo, brave beavers*
Landström, Olof. *Boo and Baa get wet*
    Boo and Baa in windy weather
Leavy, Una. *Harry's stormy night*
Lee, Jeanne M. *Ba-Nam*
Leeson, Christine. *Molly and the storm*
Lewis, Paul Owen. *Storm boy*
McBratney, Sam. *Just you and me*
Marino, Dorothy. *Good-bye thunderstorm*
Martin, David. *Little Chicken Chicken*
Mayer, Mercer. *The rocking horse angel*
Miller, William. *A house by the river*
Morley, Carol. *A spider and a pig*
Nikola-Lisa, W. *Storm*
Noble, Trinka Hakes. *Apple tree Christmas*
Olson, Arielle North. *The lighthouse keeper's daughter*
Perrow, Angeli. *Lighthouse dog to the rescue*
Polacco, Patricia. *Thunder cake*
Quackenbush, Robert M. *Batbaby*
Raglus, Jeff. *Schnorky the wave puncher*
Rand, Gloria. *Aloha, Salty!*
Rettich, Margret. *The voyage of the jolly boat*
Reynolds, Peter H. *Sydney's star*
Rockwell, Anne F. *The storm*
Rosenberg, Liz. *On Christmas eve*
Rowinski, Kate. *L. L. Bear's island adventure*
Sadler, Judy Ann. *Sandwiches for Duke*
Sampson, Michael R. *Caddie, the golf dog*
Simmie, Lois. *Mister got to go*
Stainton, Sue. *The lighthouse cat*
Steig, William. *Brave Irene*
Stolz, Mary (Mary Slattery). *Storm in the night*
Stone, Phoebe. *When the Wind Bears go dancing*
Sutherland, Marc. *MacMurtrey's wall*

Szilagyi, Mary. *Thunderstorm*
Tafuri, Nancy. *Will you be my friend?*
Taylor, Judy. *Sophie and Jack help out*
Trapani, Iza. *Row, row, row your boat*
Vainio, Pirkko. *The dream house*
Van Allsburg, Chris. *The wreck of the Zephyr*
Van Nutt, Julia. *Pumpkins from the sky?*
Wellington, Monica. *Bunny's rainbow day*
    Night rabbits
Wiesner, David. *Hurricane*
Willard, Nancy. *The voyage of the Ludgate Hill*
Williams, Garth. *Benjamin's treasure*
Willis, Jeanne. *The monster storm*
Wilson, Sarah. *Beware the dragons!*
Wondriska, William. *The stop*
Yolen, Jane. *Before the storm*
Young, Ed (Edward). *The lost horse*

Weather – thunder *see* Weather – lightning, thunder

Weather – tornadoes

Arnold, Marsha Diane. *The bravest of us all*
Beard, Darleen Bailey. *Twister*
Chambers, Catherine. *Tornado*
Fisher, Carolyn. *A twisted tale*
Griffin, Kitty. *The foot-stomping adventures of Clementine Sweet*
Lyon, George Ella. *One lucky girl*
Prigger, Mary Skillings. *Aunt Minnie and the twister*
Sloat, Teri. *Farmer Brown goes round and round*

Weather – wind

Ardizzone, Edward. *Tim's last voyage*
Asch, Frank. *Like a windy day*
Barrett, Judi. *The wind thief*
Birchmore, Daniel A. *The white curtain*
Boegehold, Betty. *What the wind told*
Brown, Margaret Wise. *When the wind blew*
Burgess, Thornton. *Old Mother West Wind*
Burke, Jennifer S. *Windy days*
Butterworth, Nick. *One blowy night*
Calhoun, Mary. *Jack and the whoopee wind*
Carlstrom, Nancy White. *How does the wind walk?*
Cartwright, Ann. *The winter hedgehog*
Climo, Shirley. *The match between the winds*
De Posadas Mane, Carmen. *Mister North Wind*
DiPucchio, Kelly S. *What's the magic word?*
Dorros, Arthur. *Feel the wind*
Ehlert, Lois. *Leaf man*
Ets, Marie Hall. *Gilberto and the wind*
Flanagan, Alice K. *Wind*
Garrison, Christian. *Little pieces of the west wind*
Greene, Carol. *Please, wind?*
Hamilton, Virginia. *Drylongso*
Henderson, Kathy. *The storm*
Hines, Anna Grossnickle. *What can you do in the wind?*
Hoban, Julia. *Amy loves the wind*
Huntington, Amy. *One Monday*
Hutchins, Pat. *The wind blew*
Karas, G. Brian. *The windy day*
Keats, Ezra Jack. *A letter to Amy*
Ketteman, Helen. *The year of no more corn*
La Fontaine, Jean de. *The north wind and the sun*
Lasky, Kathryn. *The Gates of the Wind*
Leemis, Ralph. *Mister Momboo's hat*
Lexau, Joan M. *Who took the farmer's hat?*
Lindbergh, Reeve. *What is the sun?*
Lipson, Michael. *How the wind plays*
Littledale, Freya. *Peter and the north wind*
Lobel, Arnold. *The turnaround wind*
McAllister, Angela. *The wind garden*
MacDonald, Elizabeth. *The very windy day*
McKay, Louise. *Marny's ride with the wind*
McKee, David. *Elmer and the wind*
    Elmer takes off
McPhail, David M. *The day the dog said, "Cock-a-doodle doo!"*

Martin, Bill (William Ivan). *Old devil wind*
Mitchell, Robin. *Windy*
Moore, Lilian. *While you were chasing a hat*
Munsch, Robert N. *Millicent and the wind*
Murphy, Shirley Rousseau. *Wind child*
Nelson, Robin. *A windy day*
Olaleye, Isaac. *In the Rainfield*
Patron, Susan. *Dark cloud strong breeze*
Poydar, Nancy. *Rhyme time Valentine*
Purdy, Carol. *Iva Dunnit and the big wind*
Ramirez, Melissa Bourbon. *The flight of the sunflower*
Rice, Inez. *The March wind*
Rink, Cindy. *Where does the wind blow?*
Roberts, Bethany. *The wind's garden*
Roche, Hannah. *Corey's kite*
Root, Phyllis. *One windy Wednesday*
Saltzberg, Barney. *It must have been the wind*
Schick, Eleanor. *City in the winter*
Schlein, Miriam. *The sun, the wind, the sea and the rain*
Stone, Phoebe. *When the Wind Bears go dancing*
Thompson, Brenda. *The winds that blow*
Tresselt, Alvin R. *Follow the wind*
    The wind and Peter
Ungerer, Tomi. *The hat*
Uttley, Alison. *Sam Pig and the wind*
Vaughan, Marcia Kapok. *The Sea-Breeze Hotel*
White, Linda Arms. *Comes a wind*
Whiteside, Karen. *Lullaby of the wind*
Widman, Christine. *Housekeeper of the wind*
Wilhelm, Hans. *It's too windy!*
Yolen, Jane. *The girl who loved the wind*
Zolotow, Charlotte (Shapiro). *When the wind stops*

Weather reporters *see* Careers – meteorologists

Weavers *see* Careers – weavers

Weaving *see* Activities – weaving

Weddings

Ambrus, Victor G. *Country wedding*
Ammon, Richard. *An Amish wedding*
Ash, Jutta. *Wedding birds*
Balian, Lorna. *A sweetheart for Valentine*
Barasch, Lynne. *The reluctant flower girl*
Barklem, Jill. *Summer story*
Beck, Martine. *The wedding of Brown Bear and White Bear*
Benjamin, Amanda. *Two's company*
Brown, Marc Tolon. *D. W. thinks big [board book]*
Caseley, Judith. *My sister Celia*
Claret, Maria. *Melissa Mouse*
Cock Robin. *The courtship, merry marriage, and feast of Cock Robin and Jenny Wren*
Coombs, Patricia. *Mouse Café*
Cox, Judy. *Now we can have a wedding!*
De Paola, Tomie (Thomas Anthony). *Helga's dowry*
Drescher, Joan E. *My mother's getting married*
Edwards, Pamela Duncan. *The wacky wedding*
English, Karen. *Nadia's hands*
Euvremer, Teryl. *Triple whammy*
Friedman, Laurie B. *A style all her own*
A frog he would a-wooing go (folk-song). *Frog went a-courting*, retold & ill. by Dominic Catalano
    Froggie went a-courting, ill. by Chris Conover
    Froggie went a courting, ill. by Marjorie Priceman
    Mr. Frog went a-courting
    Wendy Watson's frog went a-courting
Furgang, Kathy. *Flower girl*
Ganly, Helen. *Jyoti's journey*
Gantos, Jack (John, Jr.). *Wedding bells for Rotten Ralph*
Gibbons, Faye. *Mountain wedding*
Goodall, John S. *Naughty Nancy*
Greene, Ellin. *Ling-li and the phoenix fairy*
Gregory, Valiska. *Babysitting for Benjamin*
Grimm, Jacob. *The goose girl*, ill. by Sabine Bruntjen

The goose girl, ill. by Robert Sauber
Mrs. Fox's wedding
Rumpelstiltskin, ill. by Jacqueline Ayer
Rumpelstiltskin, ill. by Donna Diamond
Rumpelstiltskin, ill. by Paul Galdone
Rumpelstiltskin, ill. by Jonathan Langley
Rumpelstiltskin, ill. by David Shaw
Rumpelstiltskin, ill. by Gennady Spirin
Rumpelstiltskin, ill. by John Wallner
Rumpelstiltskin, ill. by Bernadette Watts
Rumpelstiltskin, ill. by Paul O. Zelinsky
Snow White, ill. by Claudia Wolf
Snow White and Rose Red, ill. by Adrienne Adams
Snow White and Rose Red, ill. by John Wallner
Snow White and Rose Red, ill. by Bernadette Watts
Snow White and the seven dwarfs, ill. by Wanda Gág
Gross, Ruth Belov. *The girl who wouldn't get married*
Heine, Helme. *The pigs' wedding*
Hennessy, B. G. (Barbara G.). *Jake baked the cake*
Herman, Gail. *Flower girl*
Hest, Amy. *Fancy Aunt Jess*
 The go-between
Hoban, Lillian. *Mr. Pig and Sonny too*
Hogrogian, Nonny. *Carrot cake*
Hürlimann, Ruth. *The mouse with the daisy hat*
Jaffe, Nina. *The way meat loves salt*
Johnson, Angela. *The wedding*
Johnston, Tony. *The cowboy and the black-eyed pea*
Karlins, Mark. *Music over Manhattan*
Kimmel, Eric A. *The greatest of all*
Kroll, Steven. *The pigrates clean up*
Langton, Jane. *The hedgehog boy*
LaTeef, Nelda. *The hunter and the ebony tree*
Lewin, Hugh. *Jafta and the wedding*
Lewison, Wendy Cheyette. *I am a flower girl*
Lillegard, Dee. *The day the daisies danced*
Little, Mimi Otey. *Yoshiko and the foreigner*
Marshall, Janet Perry. *A honey of a day*
Mathers, Petra. *Dodo gets married*
Mayer, Marianna. *Marcel the pastry chef*
Morris, Ann. *Weddings*
Munsch, Robert N. *Ribbon rescue*
Naylor, Phyllis Reynolds. *"I can't take you anywhere!"*
Nobisso, Josephine. *The weight of a Mass*
Patterson, José. *Mazal-Tov*
Pilkey, Dav. *The Silly Gooses*
Prose, Francine. *Dybbuk*
Quin-Harkin, Janet. *Peter Penny's dance*
Ross, Lillian Hammer. *The little old man and his dreams*
Rylant, Cynthia. *The bookshop dog*
Samuels, Vyanne. *Carry go bring come*
Sandburg, Carl (Charles August). *The wedding procession of the rag doll and the broom handle and who was in it*
Seguin-Fontes, Marthe. *A wedding book*
Sierra, Judy. *The beautiful butterfly*
Simmonds, Posy. *The chocolate wedding*
Smith, Barry. *Minnie and Ginger*
Soto, Gary. *Snapshots from the wedding*
Speed, Toby. *Hattie baked a wedding cake*
The squire's bride
Stadler, John. *The cats of Mrs. Calamari*
Suhl, Yuri. *Simon Boom gives a wedding*
Summers, Kate. *Milly's wedding*
Trivas, Irene. *Emma's Christmas*
Van Laan, Nancy. *La boda*
Varga, Judy. *Janko's wish*
West, Colin. *I brought my love a tabby cat*
Williams, Barbara. *Whatever happened to Beverly Bigler's birthday?*
Williams, Garth. *The rabbits' wedding*
Wittman, Sally. *The wonderful Mrs. Trumbly*
Wright, Courtni Crump. *Jumping the broom*
Yep, Laurence. *The Khan's daughter*
Yezerski, Thomas F. *Together in Pinecone Patch*
Yorinks, Arthur. *Company's going*
Young, Ed (Edward). *Mouse match*
Young, James. *Everyone loves the moon*
Zalben, Jane Breskin. *Beni's first wedding*

Weekdays *see* Days of the week, months of the year

Weight *see* Concepts – weight

Welders *see* Careers – welders

Werewolves *see* Mythical creatures – werewolves

West *see* U.S. history – frontier & pioneer life

West Indies *see* Foreign lands – West Indies

Whalers *see* Careers – whalers

Whales *see* Animals – whales

Wheelchairs *see* Handicaps – physical handicaps

Wheels

Barton, Byron. *Wheels*
Berenstain, Stan. *Bears on wheels*
Cobb, Annie. *Wheels!*
Cole, Joanna. *Fun on wheels*, ill. by Whitney Darrow
 Fun on wheels, ill. by Don Gauthier
Dubowski, Cathy East. *Cave boy*
Hindley, Judy. *The wheeling and whirling-around book*
Lynn, Sara. *Wheels*
Miller, Margaret. *Wheels go 'round*
Myller, Rolf. *Rolling round*
Nikola-Lisa, W. *Wheels go round*
Olschewski, Alfred. *The wheel rolls over*
Rotner, Shelley. *Wheels around*
Snoopy on wheels

Whistles

Adelson, Leone. *Who blew that whistle?*
Bason, Lillian. *Pick a raincoat, pick a whistle*
Brown, Margaret Wise. *Whistle for the train*
Egielski, Richard. *Three magic balls*
Sattler, Helen Roney. *Train whistles*
Schaefer, Carole Lexa. *The little French whistle*
Tompert, Ann. *The silver whistle*
Watts, Bernadette. *The Christmas bird*

Whistling *see* Activities – whistling

Wildebeests *see* Animals – wildebeests

Willfulness *see* Character traits – willfulness

Wind *see* Weather – wind

Windigos Indians *see* Indians of North America – Windigos

Windmills

Yeoman, John. *Mouse trouble*

Window cleaners *see* Careers – window cleaners

Wings *see* Anatomy – wings

Winter *see* Seasons – winter

Wisdom *see* Character traits – wisdom

Wishing *see* Behavior – wishing

Witches

Adams, Adrienne. *A Halloween happening*
   A woggle of witches
Adler, David A. *I know I'm a witch*
Alexander, Sue. *More Witch, Goblin, and Ghost stories*
   Who goes out on Halloween?
   Witch, Goblin and Ghost are back
   Witch, Goblin, and Ghost in the haunted woods
   Witch, Goblin and sometimes Ghost
Allen, Jonathan. *Wake up, Sleeping Beauty*
Alley, R. W. (Robert W.). *There once was a witch*
Andersen, H. C. (Hans Christian). *The tinderbox*, ill. by Warwick Hutton
   The tinderbox, ill. by Barry Moser
Anderson, Robin. *Sinabouda Lily*
Anglund, Joan Walsh. *Nibble nibble mousekin*
Armitage, Ronda. *The bossing of Josie*
Arnold, Katya. *Baba Yaga and the little girl*
Aulaire, Ingri Mortenson d'. *East of the sun and west of the moon*
Ayres, Becky Hickox. *Matreshka*
Bach, Othello. *Hector McSnector and the mail-order Christmas witch*
   Lilly, Willy and the mail-order witch
Baden, Robert. *And Sunday makes seven*
Balian, Lorna. *Humbug potion*
   Humbug witch
Barrett, Judi. *Which witch is which?*
Basile, Giambattista. *Petrosinella*
Bateson-Hill, Margaret. *Masha and the firebird*
Benarde, Anita. *The pumpkin smasher*
Bender, Robert. *A little witch magic*
Bentley, Nancy. *I've got your nose!*
Berenzy, Alix. *Rapunzel*
Berridge, Celia. *Grandmother's tales*
Berson, Harold. *Charles and Claudine*
Biro, Val. *Miranda's umbrella*
Bridwell, Norman. *The witch grows up*
   The witch next door
Brown, Marc Tolon. *Spooky riddles*
   Witches four
Bruna, Dick. *Dick Bruna's Snow-White and the seven dwarfs*
Buck, Nola. *The littlest witch*
Buckley, Paul. *Amy Belligera and the fireflies*
Buehner, Caralyn. *A job for Wittilda*
Burch, Robert. *The jolly witch*
Calhoun, Mary. *The witch of Hissing Hill*
   The witch who lost her shadow
   The witch's pig
   Wobble the witch cat
Calmenson, Stephanie. *The little witch sisters*
Campbell, Ann-Jeanette. *Dora's box*
Carlson, Nancy L. *Witch lady*
Carlson, Natalie Savage. *Spooky and the bad luck raven*
   Spooky and the witch's goat
   Spooky and the wizard's bats
   Spooky night
Christelow, Eileen. *Glenda Feathers casts a spell*
Christian, Mary Blount. *Scarabee, the witch's cat*
Civardi, Anne. *The wacky book of witches*
Cole, Babette. *Don't go out tonight*
   The trouble with Mom
Cole, Joanna. *Bony-legs*
Comissiong, Lynette. *Mind me good now!*
Coombs, Patricia. *Dorrie and the haunted schoolhouse*
Cooney, Barbara. *Little brother and little sister*
Coppinger, Tom. *Curse in reverse*
Coville, Bruce. *Sarah and the dragon*
   Sarah's unicorn
Cretien, Paul D. *Sir Henry and the dragon*
Dasent, George W. *East o' the sun, west o' the moon*
Davis, Katie (Katie I.). *Scared stiff*
Davis, Maggie S. *Rickety witch*
Degen, Bruce. *The little witch and the riddle*
De Gerez, Toni. *Louhi, witch of North Farm*
DeLage, Ida. *ABC Halloween witch*
   Beware! Beware! A witch won't share
   The old witch and her magic basket
   The old witch and the crows

The old witch and the dragon
The old witch and the ghost parade
The old witch and the snores
The old witch and the wizard
The old witch finds a new house
The old witch gets a surprise
The old witch goes to the ball
The old witch's party
Weeny witch
What does a witch need?
The witchy broom
De Paola, Tomie (Thomas Anthony). *Big Anthony, his story*
   Merry Christmas, Strega Nona
   Strega Nona
   Strega Nona meets her match
   Strega Nona takes a vacation
   Strega Nona's magic lessons
De Regniers, Beatrice Schenk. *Willy O'Dwyer jumped in the fire*
Desmoinaux, Christel. *"Hallo-what?"*
Devlin, Wende. *Old Black Witch!*
   Old Witch and the polka-dot ribbon
   Old Witch rescues Halloween
Donaldson, Julia. *Room on the broom*
Edmund and the White Witch
Embry, Margaret. *The blue-nosed witch*
Euvremer, Teryl. *Triple whammy*
Five little pumpkins
Flora, James. *Grandpa's ghost stories*
Fox, Mem. *Guess what?*
Francis, Frank. *Natasha's new doll*
Frascino, Edward. *Nanny Noony and the dust queen*
   Nanny Noony and the magic spell
Freeman, Don. *Space witch*
   Tilly Witch
Gabler, Mirko. *The alphabet soup*
Giannini, Enzo. *Little Parsley*
Ginsburg, Mirra. *Pampalche of the silver teeth*
Glassman, Peter. *My working mom*
Gordon, Lynn. *The witch's revenge*
Gordon, Sharon. *Three little witches storybook*
Grambling, Lois G. *The witch who wanted to be a princess*
Greaves, Margaret. *Kate Crackernuts*
   Mother Cuspen
   The witch cat
   The witch's servant
Greene, Carol. *The thirteen days of Halloween*
Greeson, Janet. *The stingy baker*
Grimm, Jacob. *Hansel and Gretel*, ill. by Adrienne Adams
   Hansel and Gretel, ill. by Anthony Browne
   Hansel and Gretel, ill. by Susan Jeffers
   Hansel and Gretel, ill. by Winslow P. Pels
   Hansel and Gretel, ill. by Jane Ray
   Hansel and Gretel, ill. by Conxita Rodriguez
   Hansel and Gretel, ill. by Christopher Santoro
   Hansel and Gretel, ill. by John Wallner
   Hansel and Gretel, ill. by Claudia Wolf
   Hansel and Gretel, ill. by Paul O. Zelinsky
   Hansel and Gretel, ill. by Lisbeth Zwerger
   Jorinda and Joringel, ill. by Adrienne Adams
   Jorinda and Joringel, ill. by Jutta Ash
   Jorinda and Joringel, ill. by Margot Tomes
   Rapunzel, ill. by Jutta Ash
   Rapunzel, ill. by Sheilah Beckett
   Rapunzel, ill. by Bert Dodson
   Rapunzel, ill. by Maja Dusíková
   Rapunzel, ill. by Michael Hague
   Rapunzel, ill. by Trina Schart Hyman
   Rapunzel, ill. by Kris Waldherr
   Rapunzel, ill. by Bernadette Watts
   Rapunzel, ill. by Paul O. Zelinsky
   The sleeping beauty, ill. by Warwick Hutton
   The sleeping beauty, ill. by Trina Schart Hyman
   The sleeping beauty, ill. by Monika Laimgruber
   The sleeping beauty, ill. by Mercer Mayer
   Sleeping Beauty, ill. by Fina Rifa
   The sleeping beauty, ill. by Ruth Sanderson
   Sleeping Beauty, ill. by John Wallner
   Snow White, ill. by Trina Schart Hyman

Yuck!
Tagg, Christine. *Who will you meet on Scary Street?*
Tatcheva, Eva. *Witch Zelda's birthday cake*
Thompson, Harwood. *The witch's cat*
Thompson, Richard. *The follower*
Tunnell, Michael O. *Halloween pie*
Utton, Peter. *The witch's hand*
Van Allsburg, Chris. *The widow's broom*
Wahl, Jan. *Little Johnny Buttermilk*
Walker, Barbara K. (Barbara Kerlin). *Teeny-Tiny and the witch-woman*
Walt Disney Productions. *Walt Disney's Snow White and the seven dwarfs*
Walton, Rick. *Pig, Pigger, Piggest*
Watson, Jane Werner. *Which is the witch?*
Weil, Lisl. *The candy egg bunny*
Whitcher, Susan. *The key to the cupboard*
White, Carolyn. *Whuppity Stoorie*
Williams, Jay. *The city witch and the country witch*
Williams, Suzanne. *The witch casts a spell*
Winthrop, Elizabeth. *Vasilissa the beautiful*
Witch poems
Wolff, Ferida. *On Halloween night*
Wood, Audrey. *Heckedy Peg*
Yolen, Jane. *The flying witch*
   The girl in the golden bower
Ziefert, Harriet. *Two little witches*
Zimmer, Dirk. *The trick-or-treat trap*

Wizards

Barber, Antonia. *The enchanter's daughter*
Bazilian, Barbara. *Princess Lily*
Bradfield, Roger (Jolly Roger). *Giants come in different sizes*
Brenner, Barbara A. *The color wizard*
Brunhoff, Laurent de. *Babar and the succotash bird*
Carlson, Natalie Savage. *Spooky and the wizard's bats*
Clibbon, Meg. *Imagine you're a wizard!*
Conover, Chris. *The wizard's daughter*
DeLage, Ida. *The old witch and the wizard*
De Regniers, Beatrice Schenk. *Picture book theater*
Dewan, Ted. *The sorcerer's apprentice*
Dines, Glen. *Pitadoe, the color maker*
Fleischman, Sid. *Longbeard the wizard*
Fox, Mem. *The magic hat*
Glassman, Peter. *The wizard next door*
Grimm, Jacob. *The donkey prince*
Haseley, Dennis. *The cave of snores*
Kherdian, David. *The golden bracelet*
Kimmel, Margaret Mary. *Magic in the mist*
Leichman, Seymour. *The wicked wizard and the wicked witch*
Lester, Helen. *The wizard, the fairy and the magic chicken*
Lobel, Arnold. *The great blueness and other predicaments*
McCrea, James. *The story of Olaf*
Madden, Don. *The Wartville wizard*
Martin, Bill (William Ivan). *The wizard*
Mayer, Mercer. *Mrs. Beggs and the wizard*
Nolan, Dennis. *Wizard McBean and his flying machine*
O'Brien, John (1953–). *Poof!*
Oksner, Robert M. *The incompetent wizard*
Oram, Hiawyn. *Skittlewonder and the wizard*
Saunders, Susan. *A sniff in time*
Scott, Sally. *The magic horse*
Service, Pamela F. *The wizard of wind and rock*
Smith, Janice Lee. *Wizard and Wart in trouble*
Snyder, Zilpha Keatley. *The changing maze*
Stockton, Frank Richard. *The bee-man of Orn*
Tom Thumb. *The adventures of Tom Thumb*, ill. by Kinuko Y. Craft
Walsh, Ellen Stoll. *Mouse magic*
Whitcher, Susan. *The key to the cupboard*
Yolen, Jane. *The firebird*
Zijlstra, Tjerk. *Benny and his geese*
Zimmermann, H. Werner (Heinz Werner). *Alphonse knows . . . a circle is not a Valentine*
   Alphonse knows . . . the colour of spring
   Alphonse knows . . . twelve months make a year
   Alphonse knows . . . zero is not enough

Wolves *see* Animals – wolves

Wombats *see* Animals – wombats

Wood-hoopoe *see* Birds – wood-hoopoes

Woodcarvers *see* Careers – woodcarvers

Woodchucks *see* Animals – groundhogs

Woodpeckers *see* Birds – woodpeckers

Woods *see* Forest, woods

Word games *see* Language

Wordless

Alexander, Martha G. *Bobo's dream*
   Out! Out! Out!
   3 magic flip books
Aliki. *Tabby*
Andersen, H. C. (Hans Christian). *The ugly duckling*, ill. by Maria Ruis
Anderson, Lena. *Bunny bath*
   Bunny box
   Bunny fun
   Bunny party
   Bunny story
   Bunny surprise
Anno, Mitsumasa. *Anno's animals*
   Anno's Britain
   Anno's counting book
   Anno's counting house
   Anno's flea market
   Anno's Italy
   Anno's journey
   Anno's peekaboo
   Anno's U.S.A.
   Dr. Anno's magical midnight circus
   Topsy turvies: more pictures to stretch the imagination
   Topsy turvies: pictures to stretch the imagination
Arnosky, Jim. *Mouse letters*
   Mouse numbers and letters
   Mouse writing
   Mud time and more
Asch, Frank. *In the eye of the teddy*
Asch, George. *Linda*
Baker, Jeannie. *Window*
Bakken, Harold. *The special string*
Bambi
Banchek, Linda. *Snake in, snake out*
Bang, Molly. *The grey lady and the strawberry snatcher*
Barton, Byron. *Where's Al?*
Baum, Willi. *Birds of a feather*
Blades, Ann. *Fall*
   Spring
   Summer
   Winter
Blake, Quentin. *Clown*
Bonners, Susan. *Just in passing*
Briggs, Raymond. *Building the snowman*
   Dressing up
   Father Christmas
   Father Christmas goes on holiday
   The party
   The snowman
   Walking in the air
Brown, Craig McFarland. *Patchwork farmer*
Bruna, Dick. *Another story to tell*
   A story to tell
Bullock, Kathleen. *Rabbits are coming*
Bunting, Eve (Anne Evelyn). *We need a bigger zoo!*
Burlson, Joe. *Space colony*
Burton, Marilee Robin. *The elephant's nest*
Butterworth, Nick. *Amanda's butterfly*

The mystery of the giant footprints
Robot-bot-bot
Sebastian and the mushroom
The secret in the dungeon
Sleep tight, Alex Pumpernickel
Who's seen the scissors?
Lehman, Barbara. *The red book*
Lemke, Horst. *Places and faces*
Lewis, Stephen (Stephen Paul). *Zoo city*
Lilly, Kenneth. *Animals in the country*
Lionni, Leo. *What?*
　　When?
　　Where?
　　Who?
Lisker, Sonia O. *Lost*
Liu, Jae Soo. *Yellow umbrella*
Lubach, Peter. *Harry and the singing fish*
McCue, Lisa. *Corduroy's party*
　　Corduroy's toys
McCully, Emily Arnold. *The Christmas gift*
　　First snow
　　Four hungry kittens
　　New baby
　　Picnic
　　School
MacGregor, Marilyn. *Baby takes a trip*
　　On top
Maizlish, Lisa. *The ring*
Mari, Iela. *Eat and be eaten*
　　The magic balloon
Maris, Ron. *Hold tight, bear!*
Marol, Jean-Claude. *Vagabul and his shadow*
　　Vagabul escapes
　　Vagabul goes skiing
　　Vagabul in the clouds
Mayer, Mercer. *Ah-choo*
　　A boy, a dog, a frog and a friend
　　A boy, a dog and a frog
　　Bubble bubble
　　Frog goes to dinner
　　Frog on his own
　　Frog, where are you?
　　The great cat chase
　　Hiccup
　　One frog too many
　　Oops
　　Two moral tales
Mogensen, Jan. *The forty-six little men*
My body
Nygren, Tord. *The red thread*
Oakley, Graham. *Graham Oakley's magical changes*
Ogle, Lucille. *I spy*
O'Malley, Kevin. *The box*
Ormerod, Jan. *Moonlight*
　　Sunshine
Oxenbury, Helen. *Beach day*
　　Good night, good morning
　　Monkey see, monkey do
　　Mother's helper
　　The shopping trip
Panek, Dennis. *Catastrophe Cat at the zoo*
Peddle, Daniel. *Snow day*
Perrault, Charles. *Puss in boots*, retold and ill. by John S. Goodall
Pitcher, Caroline. *Animals*
　　Cars and boats
Ponti, Claude. *Adele's album*
Popov, Nikolai. *Why?*
Prater, John. *The gift*
Raney, Ken. *Stick horse*
Rappus, Gerhard. *When the sun was shining*
Reasoner, Charles. *The big busy building*
Richter, Mischa. *Quack?*
Ringi, Kjell (Arne Sorensen). *The winner*
Rockhill, Dennis. *Polar slumber = Sueño polar*
Roennfeldt, Robert. *A day on the avenue*
Rohmann, Eric. *Time flies*
Rojankovsky, Feodor. *Animals on the farm*
Saltzberg, Barney. *The yawn*

Sara. *Across town*
　　The rabbit, the fox, and the wolf
Sasaki, Isao. *Snow*
Schick, Eleanor. *The little school at Cottonwood Corners*
　　Making friends
Schories, Pat. *Mouse around*
Schubert, Dieter. *Where's my monkey?*
Selig, Sylvie. *Kangaroo*
Shimin, Symeon. *A special birthday*
Shopping
Sis, Peter. *Dinosaur!*
　　An ocean world
　　Ship ahoy!
Smith, Lane. *Flying Jake*
Sneed, Brad. *Picture a letter*
Spier, Peter. *Dreams*
　　Noah's ark
　　Peter Spier's rain
Stevenson, James. *Grandpa's great city tour*
Stobbs, William. *Animal pictures*
Struppi
Sugita, Yutaka. *My friend Little John and me*
Tafuri, Nancy. *Do not disturb*
　　Early morning in the barn
　　Junglewalk
　　Rabbit's morning
Tanaka, Hideyuki. *The happy dog*
Tildes, Phyllis Limbacher. *Baby animals black and white*
Türk, Hanne. *Goodnight Max*
　　Happy birthday Max
　　Max packs
　　Max the artlover
　　Max versus the cube
　　Merry Christmas Max
　　Rainy day Max
　　Raking leaves with Max
　　The rope skips Max
　　Snapshot Max
　　A surprise for Max
Turkle, Brinton. *Deep in the forest*
Ueno, Noriko. *Elephant buttons*
Ungerer, Tomi. *One, two, where's my shoe?*
　　Snail, where are you?
Vincent, Gabrielle. *Breakfast time, Ernest and Celestine*
　　A day, a dog
　　Ernest and Celestine's patchwork quilt
A visit to a pond
Ward, Lynd. *The silver pony*
Wegen, Ron. *The balloon trip*
Weitzman, Jacqueline Preiss. *You can't take a balloon into the Metropolitan Museum*
　　You can't take a balloon into the National Gallery
Wezel, Peter. *The good bird*
　　The naughty bird
Wiesner, David. *Free fall*
　　Sector 7
Wilson, April. *April Wilson's magpie magic*
Winter, Paula. *The bear and the fly*
　　Sir Andrew
Wood, A. J. *Look! The ultimate spot-the-difference book*
Wouters, Anne. *This book is for us*
　　This book is too small
Young animals in the zoo
Young domestic animals
Young, Ed (Edward). *Up a tree*
Zager, Karen. *Bubbles*
Zoo animals

Working *see* Activities – working; Careers

World

Anno, Mitsumasa. *All in a day*
Banks, Kate (Katherine A.). *Baboon*
Bendick, Jeanne. *All around you*
Branley, Franklyn M. (Mansfield). *The planets in our solar system*
Brann, Esther. *'Round the world*
Brown, Margaret Wise. *Four fur feet*

Delessert, Etienne. *How the mouse was hit on the head by a stone and so discovered the world*
Derby, Sally. *The mouse who owned the sun*
Domanska, Janina. *What do you see?*
Douglas, Michael. *Round, round world*
Ekker, Ernest A. *What is beyond the hill?*
Gikow, Louise. *For every child, a better world*
Goffstein, M. B. (Marilyn Brooke). *School of names*
Johnson, Crockett. *Upside down*
Lakin, Pat (Patricia). *Family*
    Grandparents
Nesbit, Edith. *The ice dragon*
Peet, Bill (William Bartlett). *Chester the worldly pig*
Pow, Tom. *Who is the world for?*
Quin-Harkin, Janet. *Peter Penny's dance*
Schimmel, Schim. *The family of earth*
Schlein, Miriam. *Herman McGregor's world*
Schneider, Herman. *Follow the sunset*
Schuett, Stacey. *Somewhere in the world right now*
Singer, Marilyn. *On the same day in March*
Snow, Alan. *My first atlas*
Spier, Peter. *People*
Weiss, Nicki. *The world turns round and round*
Wood, Douglas. *Making the world*

Worms *see* Animals – worms

Worrying *see* Behavior – worrying

Wrecking machines *see* Machines

Wrens *see* Birds – wrens

Wrestling *see* Sports – wrestling

Writers *see* Careers – writers; Children as authors

Writing *see* Activities – writing

Writing letters *see* Letters, cards

Yaks *see* Animals – yaks

Yana Indians *see* Indians of North America – Yana

Yanomamo Indians *see* Indians of South America – Yanomamo

Yom Kippur *see* Holidays – Yom Kippur

Yukon Territory *see* Foreign lands – Yukon Territory

Yupik Indians *see* Indians of North America – Yupik

Zaire *see* Foreign lands – Zaire

Zanzibar *see* Foreign lands – Zanzibar

Zapotec Indians *see* Indians of North America – Zapotec

Zebras *see* Animals – zebras

Zodiac

Demi. *The dragon's tale and other animal fables of the Chinese zodiac*
Fisher, Leonard Everett. *Star signs*
Kimmel, Eric A. *The rooster's antlers*
Van Woerkom, Dorothy. *The rat, the ox and the zodiac*
Yen, Clara. *Why rat comes first*
Young, Ed (Edward). *Cat and Rat*

Zookeepers *see* Careers – zookeepers

Zoos

Ahlberg, Allan. *Monkey do!*
Aitken, Amy. *Kate and Mona in the jungle*
Aliki. *My visit to the zoo*
Allamand, Pascale. *The camel who left the zoo*
Allen, Robert. *The zoo book*
Amery, H. *At the zoo*
    The zoo picture book
Ancona, George. *Handtalk zoo*
Argent, Kerry. *Animal capers*
Arnold, Caroline. *Mealtime for zoo animals*
    Mother and baby zoo animals
    Noisytime for zoo animals
    Playtime for zoo animals
    Sleepytime for zoo animals
    Splashtime for zoo animals
Arthur, Catherine. *My sister's silent world*
Ashabranner, Brent. *I'm in the zoo, too*
Bahr, Robert. *Blizzard at the zoo*
Barry, Robert E. *Next please*
Barton, Byron. *Zoo animals*
Baskin, Leonard. *Hosie's zoo*
Bauer, Helen. *Good times at the park*
Belloc, Hilaire. *Jim, who ran away from his nurse, and was eaten by a lion*
Biro, Val. *Gumdrop at the zoo*
Bishop, Bonnie. *Ralph rides away*
Blance, Ellen. *Monster goes to the zoo*
Blue, Rose. *Black, black, beautiful black*
Blumberg, Rhoda. *Jumbo*
Bodsworth, Nan. *Monkey business*
Bolliger, Max. *Sandy at the children's zoo*
Bond, Michael. *Paddington at the zoo*
Boswell, Stephen. *King Gorboduc's fabulous zoo*
Bottner, Barbara. *Zoo song*
Brennan, John. *Zoo day*
Bridges, William. *Lion Island*
Bright, Robert. *Me and the bears*
Brown, Margaret Wise. *The big fur secret*
    Don't frighten the lion
Browne, Anthony. *Gorilla*
    Zoo
Bruna, Dick. *Miffy at the zoo*
Buehner, Caralyn. *The escape of Marvin the ape*
Bunting, Eve (Anne Evelyn). *We need a bigger zoo!*
Calmenson, Stephanie. *Where will the animals stay?*
Campbell, Rod. *Dear zoo*
Canning, Kate. *A painted tale*
Capucilli, Alyssa Satin. *Inside a zoo in the city*
Carle, Eric. *1, 2, 3 to the zoo*
Carlstrom, Nancy White. *What would you do if you lived at the zoo?*
Carrick, Carol. *Patrick's dinosaurs*
Chalmers, Audrey. *Hundreds and hundreds of pancakes*
Charles, Donald. *Calico Cat at the zoo*
Chichester Clark, Emma. *The story of Horrible Hilda and Henry*
Cohen, Caron Lee. *Pigeon, pigeon*
Colonius, Lillian. *At the zoo*
Curious George visits the zoo
Cutler, Ivor. *The animal house*
Cuyler, Margery. *That's good! that's bad!*
Deady, Kathleen W. *Out and about at the zoo*

DeLage, Ida. *ABC triplets at the zoo*
Denim, Sue. *The Dumb Bunnies go to the zoo*
De Vicq de Cumptich, Roberto. *Bembo's zoo*
Drescher, Henrik. *The yellow umbrella*
Dyer, Heather. *Tina and the penguin*
Edwards, Frank B. *New at the zoo*
Elliott, George. *The boy who loved bananas*
Evans, Nate. *The mixed-up zoo of professor Yahoo*
Fatio, Louise. *The happy lion*
　The happy lion and the bear
　The happy lion in Africa
　The happy lion roars
　The happy lion's rabbits
　The happy lion's treasure
　Hector and Christina
　The three happy lions
Fay, Hermann. *My zoo*
Flora, James. *Leopold, the see-through crumbpicker*
Florian, Douglas. *At the zoo*
Ford, Miela. *Watch us play*
Fox, Mem. *Zoo-looking*
Garland, Michael. *Last night at the zoo*
Gibbons, Gail. *Zoo*
Goodman, Susan E. *What do you do – at the zoo?*
Gordon, Shirley. *Grandma zoo*
Graham, Margaret Bloy. *Be nice to spiders*
Greeley, Valerie. *Zoo animals*
Greydanus, Rose. *Animals at the zoo*
Groening, Maggie. *Maggie Simpson's book of animals*
Grossman, Bill. *The bear whose bones were Jezebel Jones*
Grosvenor, Donna. *Zoo babies*
Hader, Berta Hoerner. *Lost in the zoo*
Hanlon, Emily. *What if a lion eats me and I fall into a hippopotamus' mud hole?*
Hanna, Jack. *The petting zoo*
Harrison, David Lee. *Detective Bob and the great ape escape*
Hart, Christopher. *Merwin, master of disguise*
Hathon, Elizabeth. *We go to the zoo*
Hazelaar, Cor. *Zoo dreams*
Hellen, Nancy. *Circle zoo*
　A visit to the zoo
Hendrick, Mary Jean. *If anything ever goes wrong at the zoo*
Henley, Claire. *At the zoo*
Hennessy, B. G. (Barbara G.). *Corduroy at the zoo*
Hewett, Joan. *Tiger, tiger, growing up*
Hillenbrand, Will. *Down by the station*
Hoban, Tana. *A children's zoo*
Hoff, Syd. *Sammy the seal*
Hopkins, Lee Bennett. *To the zoo*
Howe, James. *The day the teacher went bananas*
Hubbell, Patricia. *Bouncing time*
Irvine, Georgeanne. *Bo the orangutan*
　Elmer the elephant
　Georgie the giraffe
　Lindi the leopard
　The nursery babies
　Sasha the cheetah
　Sydney the koala
　Tully the tree kangaroo
Isenberg, Barbara. *The adventures of Albert, the running bear*
Jeram, Anita. *Bill's belly button*
Johnson, Louise. *Malunda*
Kallen, Stuart A. *The zoo*
Kilroy, Sally. *Babies' zoo*
Kishida, Eriko. *The hippo boat*
Knight, Bertram T. *Working at a zoo*
Knight, Hilary. *Where's Wallace?*
Knowles, Sheena. *Edward the emu*
Lewis, Stephen (Stephen Paul). *Zoo city*
Lilly, Kenneth. *Animals at the zoo*
Lippman, Peter. *New at the zoo*
Lisker, Sonia O. *Lost*
Lobel, Arnold. *A holiday for Mister Muster*
　A zoo for Mister Muster
Löfgren, Ulf. *Alvin the zookeeper*

London, Jonathan. *A koala for Katie*
Lööf, Jan. *Uncle Louie's fantastic sea voyage*
Maccarone, Grace. *The class trip*
McCarthy, Ruth. *Katie and the smallest bear*
McGovern, Ann. *Zoo, where are you?*
Machotka, Hana. *What do you do at a petting zoo?*
McKean, Thomas. *Hooray for Grandma Jo!*
McQuade, Jacqueline. *At the petting zoo with Teddy Bear*
Marshall, Janet Perry. *My camera*
Martin, Bill (William Ivan). *Polar bear, polar bear, what do you hear?*
Matthias, Catherine. *Too many balloons*
Mead, Alice. *Billy and Emma*
Meeks, Esther K. *Something new at the zoo*
Miklowitz, Gloria D. *The zoo that moved*
Morgan, Richard. *Zoo poo*
Morozumi, Atsuko. *My friend gorilla*
Moses, Amy. *At the zoo*
Munari, Bruno. *Bruno Munari's zoo*
Munsch, Robert N. *Alligator baby*
Noble, Kate. *The blue elephant*
Ormerod, Jan. *When we went to the zoo*
Oxenbury, Helen. *Monkey see, monkey do*
Panek, Dennis. *Catastrophe Cat at the zoo*
Parker, Nancy Winslow. *Working frog*
Paxton, Tom. *Going to the zoo*
Phillips, Betty Lou. *Emily goes wild*
Pieńkowski, Jan. *Zoo*
Pinkwater, Daniel Manus. *Bad bears in the big city*
　Irving and Muktuk
Policoff, Stephen Phillip. *Cesar's amazing journey*
Propp, James. *Tuscanini*
Rathmann, Peggy. *Good night, Gorilla*
Ray, Deborah Kogan. *Sunday morning we went to the zoo*
Reitveld, Jane Klatt. *Monkey island*
Rey, H. A. (Hans Augusto). *Curious George takes a job*
　Feed the animals
Rice, Eve. *Sam who never forgets*
Riddle, Tohby. *The great escape from City Zoo*
Roffey, Maureen. *I spy at the zoo*
Rojankovsky, Feodor. *Animals in the zoo*
Roosevelt, Michelle Chopin. *Zoo animals*
Rose, Deborah Lee. *Birthday zoo*
Ross, Christine. *Lily and the bears*
Rovetch, Lissa. *Crocs in shirts, hippos in skirts*
Rowan, James P. *I can be a zoo keeper*
Ryder, Joanne. *Little panda*
San Diego Zoological Society. *Families*
　A visit to the zoo
Schneider, Antonie. *Luke the Lionhearted*
Schumacher, Claire. *King of the zoo*
Seuss, Dr. *If I ran the zoo*
Sierra, Judy. *Wild about books*
Simon, Paul. *At the zoo*
Snyder, Dick. *One day at the zoo*
　Talk to me tiger
Tensen, Ruth M. *Come to the zoo!*
Tester, Sylvia Root. *A visit to the zoo*
Tokuda, Wendy. *Samson the hot tub bear*
Unwin, Pippa. *The great zoo hunt!*
Waber, Bernard. *A lion named Shirley Williamson*
Waldman, Neil. *They came from the Bronx*
Whitehouse, Patricia. *Alligator*
　Elephants
　Flamingo
　Hippopotamus
　Ostrich
　Sea lion
　Tiger
Woodruff, Elvira. *Mrs. McCloskey's monkeys*
Ylla. *Look who's talking*
Young, Miriam Burt. *Please don't feed Horace*
Ziefert, Harriet. *On our way to the zoo*

Zuni Indians *see* Indians of North America – Zuni

Bibliographic Guide

Arranged alphabetically by author's name in boldface (or by title, if author is unknown), each entry includes title, illustrator, publisher, publication date, and subjects. Joint authors and their titles appear as short entries, with the main author name (in parentheses after the title) citing where the complete entry will be found. Where only an author and title are given, complete information is listed under the title as the main entry. ISBNs are included for titles that have been added since the second edition.

A is for alphabet by Cathy, Marly & Wendy; ill. by George Suyeoka. Scott, 1968. Subj: ABC books.

Aardema, Verna. *Anansi does the impossible! an Ashanti tale* ill. by Lisa Desimini. Atheneum, 1997. ISBN 0-689-81092-X Subj: Folk & fairy tales. Foreign lands – Africa. Spiders.

Anansi finds a fool: an Ashanti tale ill. by Bryna Waldman. Dial, 1992. ISBN 0-8037-1165-4 Subj: Behavior – trickery. Folk & fairy tales. Mythical creatures. Spiders.

Bimwili and the Zimwi ill. by Susan Meddaugh. Dial, 1985. ISBN 0-8037-0213-2 Subj: Folk & fairy tales. Foreign lands – Africa. Foreign lands – Zanzibar. Mythical creatures – trolls.

Borreguita and the coyote ill. by Petra Mathers. Knopf, 1991. ISBN 0-679-90921-4 Subj: Animals – coyotes. Animals – sheep. Behavior – trickery. Folk & fairy tales. Foreign lands – Mexico.

Bringing the rain to Kapiti Plain: a Nandi tale ill. by Beatriz A. Vidal. Dial, 1981. ISBN 0-8037-0807-6 Subj: Cumulative tales. Folk & fairy tales. Foreign lands – Africa. Rhyming text. Weather – droughts. Weather – rain.

Half-a-ball-of-kenki: an Ashanti tale retold by Verna Aardema; ill. by Diane Stanley Zuromskis. Warne, 1979. ISBN 0-7232-6158-X Subj: Animals – leopards. Folk & fairy tales. Foreign lands – Africa. Insects – flies.

Jackal's flying lesson: a Khoikhoi tale ill. by Dale Gottlieb. Knopf, 1995. ISBN 0-679-95813-4 Subj: Activities – flying. Animals – jackals. Behavior – trickery. Birds. Folk & fairy tales. Foreign lands – Africa. Foreign lands – Namibia.

Ji-nongo-nongo means riddles ill. by Jerry Pinkney. Four Winds, 1978. ISBN 0-590-07474-1 Subj: Folk & fairy tales. Foreign lands – Africa. Riddles & jokes.

Koi and the kola nuts ill. by Joe Cepeda. Atheneum, 1999. ISBN 0-689-81760-6 Subj: Character traits – kindness to animals. Folk & fairy tales. Foreign lands – Liberia.

The lonely lioness and the ostrich chicks: a Masai tale ill. by Yumi Heo. Owen, 1992. ISBN 0-679-96934-9 Subj: Animals – lions. Animals – mongooses. Behavior – needing someone. Birds – ostriches. Emotions – loneliness. Folk & fairy tales. Foreign lands – Africa.

Misoso ill. by Reynold Ruffins. Knopf, 1994. ISBN 0-679-93430-8 Subj: Folk & fairy tales. Foreign lands – Africa.

Oh, Kojo! How could you! an Ashanti tale ill. by Marc Brown. Dial, 1984. ISBN 0-8037-0007-5 Subj: Folk & fairy tales. Foreign lands – Africa. Humorous stories.

Pedro and the padre ill. by Friso Henstra. Dial, 1991. ISBN 0-8037-0523-9 Subj: Character traits – honesty. Folk & fairy tales. Foreign lands – Mexico.

Princess Gorilla and a new kind of water ill. by Victoria Chess. Dial, 1988. ISBN 0-8037-0413-5 Subj: Animals. Animals – gorillas. Folk & fairy tales. Foreign lands – Africa.

Rabbit makes a monkey of lion ill. by Jerry Pinkney. Dial, 1988. ISBN 0-8037-0298-1 Subj: Animals. Behavior – trickery. Foreign lands – Africa. Jungle.

The riddle of the drum: a tale from Tizapan, Mexico ill. by Tony Chen. Four Winds, 1978. ISBN 0-590-07489-X Subj: Cumulative tales. Folk & fairy tales. Foreign lands – Mexico. Rhyming text. Royalty.

Sebgugugu the glutton: a Bantu tale from Rwanda ill. by Nancy L. Clouse. Eerdmans, 1993. ISBN 0-8028-5073-1 Subj: Behavior – greed. Character traits – foolishness. Folk & fairy tales. Foreign lands – Africa. Foreign lands – Rwanda.

Traveling to Tondo: a tale of the Nkundo of Zaire ill. by Will Hillenbrand. Knopf, 1991. ISBN 0-679-90081-0 Subj: Activities – traveling. Animals. Folk & fairy tales. Foreign lands – Congo (Democratic Republic). Foreign lands – Zaire.

The vingananee and the tree toad ill. by Ellen Weiss. Warne, 1983. ISBN 0-7232-6217-9 Subj: Animals. Folk & fairy tales. Foreign lands – Africa. Foreign lands – Liberia. Spiders.

What's so funny, Ketu? a Nuer tale ill. by Marc Brown. Dial, 1982. ISBN 0-8037-9370-7 Subj: Animals. Behavior – secrets. Foreign lands – Africa. Foreign lands – Sudan. Humorous stories. Reptiles – snakes.

Who's in Rabbit's house? ill. by Leo & Diane Dillon. Dial, 1977. ISBN 0-8037-9551-3 Subj: Animals. Folk & fairy tales. Foreign lands – Africa. Humorous stories. Insects – butterflies, caterpillars.

Why mosquitoes buzz in people's ears: a West African tale ill. by Leo & Diane Dillon. Dial, 1975. ISBN 0-8037-6087-6 Subj: Animals. Caldecott award books. Folk & fairy tales. Foreign lands – Africa. Insects – mosquitoes.

Aarle, Thomas Van. *Don't put your cart before the horse race* ill. by Bob Barner. Houghton Mifflin, 1980. ISBN 0-395-29095-3 Subj: Animals – horses, ponies. Sports – racing.

Aaron, Jane. *When I'm afraid* ill. by author. St. Martin's, 1998. ISBN 0-307-44057-5 Subj: Emotions – fear. Family life.

Abbot, Sara. *see* Zolotow, Charlotte (Shapiro)

ABC school riddles comp. & ed. by Susan Joyce; ill. by Freddie Levin. Peel Productions, 2001. ISBN 0-939217-54-6 Subj: ABC books. Rhyming text. Riddles & jokes.

ABCDEFGHIJKLMNOPQRSTUVWXYZ in English and Spanish ill. by Robert Tallon. Lion, 1981. ISBN 0-874-60359-5 Subj: ABC books. Foreign languages.

Abel, Laurie. *Bisnipian blast-off: an action counting book* (Arnold, Tedd)

Abel, Ray. *The new sitter* (Abel, Ruth)

Abel, Ruth. *The new sitter* by Ruth & Ray Abel; ill. by Ray Abel. Oxford Univ. Pr., 1950. Subj: Activities – babysitting.

Abel, Simone. *Follow that chicken!* ill. by Simone Abel; written by Angela. Sterling, 2000. ISBN 0-8069-0310-4 Subj: Birds – chickens. Concepts – opposites. Format, unusual – board books. Format, unusual – toy & movable books. Language.

How now, cow? ill. by Simone Abel; witten by Angela Chambers. Sterling, 2000. ISBN 0-8069-0275-2 Subj: Animals – bulls, cows. Format, unusual – board books. Format, unusual – toy & movable books.

Aber, Linda Williams. *Carrie measures up!* ill. by Joy Allen. Kane/Miller, 2001. ISBN 1-57565-100-9 Subj: Activities – knitting. Concepts – measurement. Family life – grandmothers.

Abercrombie, Barbara. *Bad dog, Dodger* ill. by Adam Gustavson. McElderry, 2002. ISBN 0-689-83782-8 Subj: Animals – babies. Animals – dogs. Pets.

Charlie Anderson ill. by Mark Graham. Macmillan, 1990. ISBN 0-689-50486-1 Subj: Animals – cats. Family life. Pets.

Michael and the cats ill. by Mark Graham. McElderry, 1993. ISBN 0-689-50543-4 Subj: Animals – cats. Family life – aunts, uncles.

Abisch, Roslyn Kroop. *see* Abisch, Roz

Abisch, Roz. *The clever turtle* ill. by Boche Kaplan. Prentice-Hall, 1969. Subj: Animals. Folk & fairy tales. Foreign lands – Africa. Reptiles – turtles, tortoises.

Let's find out about butterflies ill. by Boche Kaplan. Watts, 1972. ISBN 0-531-00077-X Subj: Insects – butterflies, caterpillars. Metamorphosis. Science.

Mai-Ling and the mirror: a Chinese folktale ill. by Boche Kaplan. Prentice-Hall, 1969. Subj: Emotions – envy, jealousy. Folk & fairy tales. Foreign lands – China.

Open your eyes ill. by Boche Kaplan. Parents' Magazine Pr., 1964. Subj: Concepts – color. Imagination.

The Pumpkin Heads ill. by Boche Kaplan. Prentice-Hall, 1968. Based on an anecdote from general history of Connecticut, by Reverend Samuel Peters. Subj: Hair. U.S. history.

Sweet Betsy from Pike by Roz Abisch & Boche Kaplan; ill. by Boche Kaplan. McCall, 1970. ISBN 0-8415-2006-2 Subj: Character traits – perseverance. Folk & fairy tales. Music. Songs. U.S. history – frontier & pioneer life.

'Twas in the moon of wintertime: the first American Christmas carol adapt. by Roz Abisch; ill. by Boche Kaplan. Prentice-Hall, 1969. ISBN 0-1393-3358-4 Subj: Holidays – Christmas. Indians of North America – Huron. Music.

Abley, Mark. *Ghost cat* ill. by Karen Reczuch. Douglas & McIntyre, 2001. ISBN 0-88899-433-8 Subj: Animals – cats. Death. Emotions – loneliness. Emotions – sadness. Pets.

Aboff, Marcie. *The giant jelly bean jar* ill. by Paige Billin-Frye. Dutton, 2004. ISBN 0-613-89801-X Subj: Character traits – shyness. Contests. Riddles & jokes.

Abolafia, Yossi. *A fish for Mrs. Gardenia* ill. by author. Greenwillow, 1988. ISBN 0-688-07468-5 Subj: Activities – baking, cooking. Behavior – lost & found possessions.

Fox tale ill. by author. Greenwillow, 1991. ISBN 0-688-09542-9 Subj: Animals. Animals – foxes. Behavior – trickery.

My three uncles ill. by author. Greenwillow, 1984. ISBN 0-688-04025-X Subj: Character traits – individuality. Family life – aunts, uncles. Multiple births – triplets.

Yanosh's Island ill. by author. Greenwillow, 1987. ISBN 0-688-06817-0 Subj: Activities – flying. Behavior – seeking better things. Islands. Toys.

Abrams, Pam. *Now I eat my ABC's* ill. by Bruce Wolf. Scholastic, 2004. ISBN 0-439-64942-0 Subj: ABC books. Food. Format, unusual – board books.

Abrons, Mary. *For Alice a palace* ill. by Gertrude Barrer-Russell. W. R. Scott, 1966. Subj: ABC books. Birthdays. Poetry. Royalty.

Absolutely angels: poems for children and other believers sel. by Mary Lou Carney; ill. by Viqui Maggio. Wordsong, 1998. ISBN 1-56397-708-7 Subj: Angels. Poetry.

Accorsi, William. *My name is Pocahontas* ill. by author. Holiday, 1992. ISBN 0-8234-0932-5 Subj: Indians of North America – Powhatan. U.S. history.

Rachel Carson ill. by author. Holiday, 1993. ISBN 0-8234-0994-5 Subj: Careers – scientists. Ecology.

Short short short stories ill. by author. Greenwillow, 1991. ISBN 0-688-10181-X Subj: Activities. Humorous stories.

Ackerman, Diane. *Monk seal hideaway* photos by Bill Curtsinger. Crown, 1995. ISBN 0-517-59674-1 Subj: Animals – endangered animals. Animals – seals. Islands.

Ackerman, Karen. *Araminta's paint box* ill. by Betsy Lewin. Macmillan, 1990. ISBN 0-689-31462-0 Subj: Behavior – lost & found possessions. U.S. history – frontier & pioneer life.

The banshee ill. by David Ray. Putnam, 1990. ISBN 0-399-21924-2 Subj: Night. Rhyming text.

Bean's big day ill. by Paul Mombourquette. Kids Can, 2004. ISBN 1-55337-444-4 Subj: Careers – actors. Cities, towns. Self-concept. Theater.

Bingleman's midway ill. by Barry Moser. Boyds Mills, 1995. ISBN 1-563-97366-9 Subj: Behavior – running away. Careers – farmers. Fairs, festivals.

By the dawn's early light ill. by Catherine Stock. Atheneum, 1994. ISBN 0-689-31788-3 Subj: Activities – working. Ethnic groups in the U.S. – African Americans. Family life – grandmothers. Family life – mothers.

Flannery Row ill. by Karen Ann Weinhaus. Little, 1986. ISBN 0-87113-054-8 Subj: ABC books. Names. Rhyming text.

I know a place ill. by Deborah Kogan Ray. Houghton Mifflin, 1992. ISBN 0-395-53932-3 Subj: Family life. Homes, houses.

In the park with dad: a story for kids whose parents don't live together ill. by Linda Crockett-Blassingame. St. Paul Books & Media, 1996. ISBN 0-8198-3669-9 Subj: Divorce. Family life. Family life – fathers. Parks. Seasons – summer.

Just like Max ill. by George Schmidt. Knopf, 1990. ISBN 0-394-90176-2 Subj: Careers – tailors. Family life. Old age.

Moveable Mabeline ill. by Linda Allen. Putnam, 1990. ISBN 0-399-21580-8 Subj: Family life – sisters. Toys – dolls.

The sleeping porch ill. by Elizabeth Sayles. Morrow, 1995. ISBN 0-688-12823-8 Subj: Family life. Homes, houses. Moving.

Song and dance man ill. by Stephen Gammell. Knopf, 1988. ISBN 0-394-99330-6 Subj: Activities – dancing. Caldecott award books. Family life – grandfathers.

This old house ill. by Sylvie Wickstrom. Atheneum, 1992. ISBN 0-689-31741-7 Subj: Animals. Homes, houses. Rhyming text.

The tin heart ill. by Michael Hays. Macmillan, 1990. ISBN 0-689-31461-2 Subj: U.S. history. War.

Walking with Clara Belle ill. by Debbie Mason. St. Paul Books & Media, 1993. ISBN 0-8198-8243-7 Subj: Activities – walking. Memories, memory. Old age.

When mama retires ill. by Alexa Grace. Knopf, 1992. ISBN 0-679-90289-9 Subj: Activities – working. Family life – mothers. War.

Ackley, Edith Flack. *Please* ill. by Telka Ackley. Stokes, 1941. Subj: Etiquette.

Thank you ill. by Telka Ackley. Stokes, 1942. Subj: Etiquette.

Acredolo, Linda P. *My first baby signs* by Linda Acredolo & Susan Goodwyn; photos by Penny Gentieu. HarperFestival, 2002. ISBN 0-06-009074-X Subj: Communication. Format, unusual – board books. Handicaps – deafness. Sign language.

Ada, Alma Flor. *The Christmas tree = El Arbol de Navidad* ill. by Terry Ybáñez. Hyperion, 1997. ISBN 0-7868-0151-4 Subj: Cumulative tales. Foreign languages. Holidays – Christmas. Rhyming text. Trees.

Daniel's mystery egg ill. by G. Brian Karas. Harcourt, 2000. ISBN 0-15-216231-3 Subj: Eggs. Imagination. Reptiles – lizards.

Dear Peter Rabbit ill. by Leslie Tryon. Atheneum, 1994. ISBN 0-689-31850-2 Subj: Animals. Folk & fairy tales. Letters, cards.

Friend frog ill. by Lori Lohstoeter. Harcourt, 2000. ISBN 0-15-201522-1 Subj: Animals – mice. Friendship. Frogs & toads.

Gathering the sun: an alphabet in Spanish and English ill. by Simon Silva. Lothrop, 1997. ISBN 0-688-13904-3 Subj: ABC books. Foreign languages. Poetry.

The gold coin ill. by Neil Waldman. Macmillan, 1991. ISBN 0-689-31633-X Subj: Behavior – stealing. Circular tales. Crime. Cumulative tales. Foreign lands – Central America.

I love Saturdays y domingos ill. by Elivia Savadier. Atheneum, 2002. ISBN 0-689-31819-7 Subj: Ethnic groups in the U.S. – Mexican Americans. Family life – grandparents. Language.

Jordi's star ill. by Susan Gaber. Atheneum, 1994. ISBN 0-399-22832-2 Subj: Animals – goats. Careers – shepherds. Friendship. Stars.

The malachite palace ill. by Leonid Gore. Atheneum, 1998. ISBN 0-689-31972-X Subj: Birds. Folk & fairy tales. Prejudice. Royalty – princesses.

Pio peep! (Pio peep!)

The rooster who went to his uncle's wedding ill. by Kathleen Kuchera. Atheneum, 1993. ISBN 0-399-22412-2 Subj: Birds – chickens. Cumulative tales. Folk & fairy tales. Foreign lands.

The unicorn of the west ill. by Abigail Pizer. Atheneum, 1994. ISBN 0-689-31778-6 Subj: Animals. Forest, woods. Friendship. Mythical creatures – unicorns.

With love, Little Red Hen ill. by Leslie Tryon. Atheneum, 2001. ISBN 0-689-82581-1 Subj: Ethnic groups in the U.S. – Cuban Americans. Letters, cards.

Adam, Barbara. *The big, big box* ill. by author. Doubleday, 1960. Subj: Activities – playing. Animals – cats. Imagination.

Adams, Adrienne. *The Christmas party* ill. by author. Scribners, 1978. ISBN 0-684-15930-9 Subj: Animals – rabbits. Holidays – Christmas. Parties.

The Easter egg artists ill. by author. Scribners, 1976. ISBN 0-684-14652-5 Subj: Activities – painting. Activities – vacationing. Animals – rabbits. Holidays – Easter.

The great Valentine's Day balloon race ill. by author. Scribners, 1980. ISBN 0-684-16640-2 Subj: Activities – ballooning. Animals –

rabbits. Careers – artists. Holidays – Valentine's Day. Sports – racing.

A Halloween happening ill. by author. Scribners, 1981. ISBN 0-684-17166-X Subj: Holidays – Halloween. Parties. Witches.

Two hundred rabbits (Anderson, Lonzo)

A woggle of witches ill. by author. Scribners, 1971. ISBN 0-684-12506-4 Subj: Holidays – Halloween. Witches.

Adams, Eric J. *On the day his daddy left* by Eric J. Adams & Kathleen Adams; ill. by Layne Johnson. A. Whitman, 2000. ISBN 0-8075-6072-3 Subj: Divorce. Family life.

Adams, Georgie. *The first Christmas* ill. by Anna C. Leplar. Broadman & Holman, 1997. ISBN 0-8054-0175-X Subj: Holidays – Christmas. Religion – Nativity.

Fish fish fish ill. by Brigitte Willgoss. Dial, 1993. ISBN 0-8037-1208-1 Subj: Fish.

Adams, Jean Ekman. *Clarence and the great surprise* ill. by author. Rising Moon, 2001. ISBN 0-87358-795-2 Subj: Animals – dogs. Animals – horses, ponies. Animals – pigs. Handicaps – deafness. U.S. history – frontier & pioneer life.

Clarence and the purple horse bounce into town ill. by author. Rising Moon, 2003. ISBN 0-87358-826-6 Subj: Animals – horses, ponies. Animals – pigs. Cities, towns. Country. Food. Friendship.

Adams, Jeanie. *Going for oysters* ill. by author. A. Whitman, 1994. ISBN 0-8075-2978-8 Subj: Careers – fishermen. Family life. Foreign lands – Australia.

Adams, Kathleen (Kathleen Marion). *On the day his daddy left* (Adams, Eric J.)

Adams, Ken. *When I was your age* ill. by Bal Biro. Barron's, 1991. ISBN 0-8120-6249-3 Subj: Family life – grandfathers. Tall tales.

Adams, Lisa K. *Dealing with teasing* ill. with photos. Rosen, 1997. ISBN 0-8239-5070-0 Subj: Behavior – misbehavior.

Adams, Pam. *There was an old lady who swallowed a fly* (Little old lady who swallowed a fly)

This old man ill. by author. Child's Play, 1990. ISBN 0-85953-026-4 Subj: Counting, numbers. Farms. Format, unusual. Songs.

Adams, Richard (Richard Newbold). *The tyger voyage* ill. by Nicola Bayley. Knopf, 1976. ISBN 0-394-40796-2 Subj: Animals – tigers. Humorous stories. Poetry.

Adamson, Deb. *Monkey see, monkey do: an animal exercise book for you!* (Holsonback, Anita)

Adamson, Gareth. *Old man up a tree* ill. by author. Abelard-Schuman, 1963. Subj: Character traits – curiosity. Crime. Humorous stories.

Adamson, Joy. *Elsa: the true story of a lioness* photos by author. Pantheon, 1961. Subj: Animals – lions. Foreign lands – Africa.

Elsa and her cubs photos by author. Harcourt, 1965. Subj: Animals – lions. Foreign lands – Africa.

Pippa the cheetah and her cubs photos by author. Harcourt, 1971. ISBN 0-15-262125-3 Subj: Animals – cheetahs. Foreign lands – Africa.

Addy, Sharon Hart. *Right here on this spot* ill. by John Clapp. Houghton Mifflin, 1999. ISBN 0-395-73091-0 Subj: Careers – archaeologists. Farms. Fossils. Science. U.S. history.

A visit with great-grandma ill. by author. A. Whitman, 1988. ISBN 0-8075-8497-5 Subj: Family life – grandmothers.

When wishes were horses ill. by Brad Sneed. Houghton, 2002. ISBN 0-618-13166-3 Subj: Animals – horses, ponies. Behavior – wishing.

Adedjouma, Davida. *The palm of my heart: poetry by African American children* (The palm of my heart)

Adelberg, Doris. *see* Orgel, Doris

Adelborg, Ottilia. *Clean Peter and the children of Grubbylea* trans. by Ada Wallas; ill. by author. Platt, 1968. Subj: Character traits – cleanliness. Poetry.

Adelson, Leone. *All ready for school* ill. by Kathleen Elgin. McKay, 1957. Subj: School. Seasons – fall.

All ready for summer ill. by Kathleen Elgin. McKay, 1955. Subj: Seasons – summer.

All ready for winter ill. by Kathleen Elgin. McKay, 1952. Subj: Seasons – winter.

The mystery bear: a Purim story ill. by Naomi Howland. Clarion, 2004. ISBN 0-618-33725-3 Subj: Animals – bears. Behavior – misunderstanding. Holidays – Purim. Jewish culture.

Please pass the grass ill. by Roger Antoine Duvoisin. McKay, 1960. Subj: Insects. Plants. Poetry. Spiders.

Who blew that whistle? ill. by Oscar Fabrès. W. R. Scott, 1946. Subj: Careers – police officers. Character traits – helpfulness. Whistles.

Adinolfi, JoAnn. *The Egyptian polar bear* ill. by author. Houghton Mifflin, 1994. ISBN 0-395-68074-3 Subj: Animals – polar bears. Foreign lands – Egypt. Friendship. Humorous stories. Royalty.

Tina's diner ill. by author. S&S, 1997. ISBN 0-689-80634-5 Subj: Activities – baking, cooking. Careers – plumbers. Cities, towns. Restaurants.

Adkins, Jan. *Heavy equipment* ill. by author. Scribners, 1980. ISBN 0-684-16641-0 Subj: Machines. Trucks.

Adler, David A. *Base five* ill. by Larry Ross. Crowell, 1975. ISBN 0-690-00669-1 Subj: Counting, numbers.

Bunny rabbit rebus ill. by Madelaine Gill Linden. Crowell, 1983. ISBN 0-690-04197-7 Subj: Animals – rabbits. Food. Rebuses.

The carsick zebra and other riddles ill. by Tomie de Paola. Holiday, 1983. ISBN 0-8234-0479-X Subj: Animals. Riddles & jokes.

The children of Chelm ill. by Arthur Friedman. Bonim Books, 1980. ISBN 0-88482-773-9 Subj: Foreign lands – Poland. Humorous stories. Jewish culture. Problem solving.

The children's book of Jewish holidays ill. by David Sears. Mesorah, 1987. ISBN 0-89906-810-3 Subj: Holidays. Jewish culture.

Helen Keller ill. by John Wallner. Holiday, 2003. ISBN 0-8234-1606-2 Subj: Character traits – persistence. Handicaps – blindness. Handicaps – deafness.

Hiding from the Nazis ill. by Karen Ritz. Holiday, 1997. ISBN 0-8234-1288-1 Subj: Behavior – hiding. Family life. Holocaust. Jewish culture.

The house on the roof: a Sukkot story ill. by Marilyn Hirsh. Bonim Books, 1976. ISBN 0-8848-2905-7 Subj: Homes, houses. Jewish culture.

How tall, how short, how far away ill. by Nancy Tobin. Holiday, 1999. ISBN 0-8234-1375-6 Subj: Concepts – measurement.

I know I'm a witch ill. by Suçie Stevenson. Holt, 1988. ISBN 0-8050-0427-0 Subj: Imagination. Witches.

A little at a time ill. by author. Random House, 1976. ISBN 0-394-92533-5 Subj: Character traits – questioning. Family life – grandfathers.

The number on my grandfather's arm ill. by Rose Eichenbaum. UAHC Pr., 1987. ISBN 0-8074-0328-8 Subj: Jewish culture. War.

A picture book of Abraham Lincoln ill. by John & Alexandra Wallner. Holiday, 1989. ISBN 0-8234-0731-4 Subj: U.S. history.

A picture book of Amelia Earhart ill. by Jeff Fisher. Holiday, 1998. ISBN 0-8234-1315-2 Subj: Careers – airplane pilots.

A picture book of Benjamin Franklin ill. by John & Alexandra Wallner. Holiday, 1990. ISBN 0-8234-0792-6 Subj: U.S. history.

A picture book of Eleanor Roosevelt ill. by Robert Casilla. Holiday, 1991. ISBN 0-8234-0856-6 Subj: U.S. history.

A picture book of George Washington ill. by John & Alexandra Wallner. Holiday, 1989. ISBN 0-8234-0732-2 Subj: U.S. history.

A picture book of Hanukkah ill. by Linda Heller. Holiday, 1982. ISBN 0-8234-0458-7 Subj: Holidays – Hanukkah. Jewish culture. Religion.

A picture book of Israel ill. with photos. Holiday, 1984. ISBN 0-8234-0513-3 Subj: Foreign lands – Israel. Jewish culture. Religion.

A picture book of Jewish holidays ill. by Linda Heller. Holiday, 1981. ISBN 0-8234-0396-3 Subj: Holidays. Holidays – Hanukkah. Holidays – Passover. Jewish culture.

A picture book of John F. Kennedy ill. by Robert Casilla. Holiday, 1991. ISBN 0-8234-0884-1 Subj: U.S. history.

A picture book of Martin Luther King, Jr. ill. by Robert Casilla. Holiday, 1989. ISBN 0-8234-0770-5 Subj: Ethnic groups in the U.S. – African Americans. U.S. history.

A picture book of Passover ill. by Linda Heller. Holiday, 1982. ISBN 0-8234-0439-0 Subj: Holidays – Passover. Jewish culture.

A picture book of Thomas Jefferson ill. by John & Alexandra Wallner. Holiday, 1990. ISBN 0-8234-0791-8 Subj: U.S. history.

Redwoods are the tallest trees in the world ill. by Kazue Mizumura. Crowell, 1978. ISBN 0-690-01368-X Subj: Forest, woods. Science. Trees.

3D, 2D, 1D ill. by Harvey Weiss. Crowell, 1975. ISBN 0-690-00543-1 Subj: Concepts – measurement. Concepts – perspective. Concepts – shape.

You think it's fun to be a clown! ill. by Ray Cruz. Doubleday, 1980. ISBN 0-385-14460-1 Subj: Circus. Clowns, jesters. Rhyming text.

Adler, Irene. *see* Storr, Catherine (Cole)

Adlerman, Daniel. *Africa calling: nightime falling* ill. by Kimberly Adlerman. Whispering Coyote, 1996. ISBN 1-879085-98-4 Subj: Animals. Dreams. Foreign lands – Africa. Imagination. Night. Rhyming text. Toys.

Adoff, Arnold. *Big sister tells me that I'm black* ill. by Lorenzo Lynch. Holt, 1976. ISBN 0-03-014546-5 Subj: Ethnic groups in the U.S. – African Americans. Family life. Poetry.

Birds ill. by Troy Howell. Lippincott, 1982. ISBN 0-397-31974-6 Subj: Birds. Poetry.

Black is brown is tan ill. by Emily Arnold McCully. HarperCollins, 2002. ISBN 0-06-028777-2 Subj: Family life. Marriage, interracial. Rhyming text.

The cabbages are chasing the rabbits ill. by Janet Stevens. Harcourt, 1985. ISBN 0-15-213875-7 Subj: Cumulative tales. Poetry.

Daring Dog and Captain Cat ill. by Joe Cepeda. S&S, 2001. ISBN 0-689-82599-4 Subj: Animals – cats. Animals – dogs. Night. Pets.

Flamboyan ill. by Karen Barbour. Harcourt, 1988. ISBN 0-15-228404-4 Subj: Activities – flying. Dreams. Islands. Trees.

Greens ill. by Betsy Lewin. Lothrop, 1988. ISBN 0-688-04277-5 Subj: Concepts – color. Rhyming text.

Hard to be six ill. by Cheryl Hanna. Lothrop, 1990. ISBN 0-688-09579-8 Subj: Family life – sisters. Sibling rivalry.

I am the running girl ill. by Ronald Himler. Harper, 1979. ISBN 0-06-020095-2 Subj: Activities – running. Ethnic groups in the U.S. – African Americans. Poetry.

In for winter, out for spring ill. by Jerry Pinkney. Harcourt, 1991. ISBN 0-15-238637-8 Subj: Ethnic groups in the U.S. – African Americans. Family life. Poetry. Seasons.

Love letters ill. by Lisa Desimini. Blue Sky, 1997. ISBN 0-590-48478-8 Subj: Emotions – love. Letters, cards. Poetry.

Ma nDa La ill. by Emily Arnold McCully. HarperCollins, 1971. ISBN 0-06-020085-5 Subj: Family life. Foreign lands – Africa.

Make a circle, keep us in: poems for a good day ill. by Ronald Himler. Delacorte, 1975. ISBN 0-440-05909-7 Subj: Family life. Night. Poetry. Weather – storms.

OUTside INside Poems ill. by John Steptoe. Lothrop, 1981. ISBN 0-688-51942-3 Subj: Poetry.

The return of Rex and Ethel ill. by Catherine Deeter. Harcourt, 1996. ISBN 0-15266-367-3 Subj: Animals – dogs. Death. Emotions – grief. Pets.

Street music: city poems ill. by Karen Barbour. HarperCollins, 1994. ISBN 0-06-021523-2 Subj: Cities, towns. Poetry.

Today we are brother and sister ill. by Glo Coalson. Lothrop, 1981. ISBN 0-688-51973-3 Subj: Family life – brothers & sisters. Poetry.

Tornado! poems ill. by Ronald Himler. Delacorte, 1977. ISBN 0-440-08965-4 Subj: Poetry. Weather – storms.

Touch the poem ill. by Bill Creevy. Scholastic, 1996. ISBN 0-590-47970-9 Subj: Poetry. Senses – touch.

Where wild Willie? ill. by Emily Arnold McCully. HarperCollins, 1978. ISBN 0-06-020093-6 Subj: Behavior – running away. Cities, towns. Ethnic groups in the U.S. – African Americans. Poetry.

Adorjan, Carol Madden. *I can! Can you?* ill. by Miriam Nerlove. Rev. ed. A. Whitman, 1990. Orignal title: Someone I know. ISBN 0-8075-3491-9 Subj: Activities – playing. Family life – sisters. Rhyming text.

Adshead, Gladys L. *Brownies – hush!* ill. by Elizabeth Orton Jones. Oxford Univ. Pr., 1938. Subj: Character traits – helpfulness. Folk & fairy tales. Mythical creatures – elves.

Brownies – it's Christmas ill. by Velma Ilsley. Oxford Univ. Pr., 1955. Subj: Holidays – Christmas. Mythical creatures – elves.

Brownies – they're moving ill. by Richard Lebenson. Walck, 1970. ISBN 0-8098-1163-4 Subj: Character traits – helpfulness. Moving. Mythical creatures – elves.

Æsop. *Æsop* sel. & ill. by Gaynor Chapman. Atheneum, 1972. ISBN 0-689-30024-7 Subj: Folk & fairy tales.

Æsop's fables retold by Werner Thuswaldner; trans. by Anthea Bell; ill. by Giselda Dürr. North-South, 1994. ISBN 1-55858-340-8 Subj: Folk & fairy tales. Format, unusual – toy & movable books.

Æsop's fables sel. & ill. by Michael Hague. Holt, 1985. ISBN 0-03-002038-7 Subj: Folk & fairy tales.

Æsop's fables sel. & ill. by Heidi Holder. Viking, 1981. ISBN 0-670-10643-7 Subj: Folk & fairy tales.

Æsop's fables: a pull-the-tab-pop-up-book ill. by Claire Littlejohn. Dial, 1988. ISBN 0-8037-0487-9 Subj: Folk & fairy tales. Format, unusual – toy & movable books.

Æsop's fables ill. by Jerry Pinkney. SeaStar, 2000. ISBN 1-587-17003-5 Subj: Folk & fairy tales.

Æsop's fables retold by Carol Watson; ill. by Nick Price. Usborne, 1982. ISBN 0-86020-667-X Subj: Folk & fairy tales.

Æsop's fables ill. by Lisbeth Zwerger. Picture Book Studio, 1991. ISBN 0-88708-108-8 Subj: Folk & fairy tales.

Androcles and the lion ill. by Janusz Grabianski. Watts, 1970. ISBN 0-531-01856-3 Subj: Animals – lions. Character traits – helpfulness. Character traits – kindness to animals. Folk & fairy tales. Foreign lands – Italy. Religion.

Androcles and the lion retold & ill. by Dennis Nolan. Harcourt, 1997. ISBN 0-15-203355-6 Subj: Animals – lions. Character traits – helpfulness. Character traits – kindness to animals. Folk & fairy tales. Foreign lands – Italy.

Androcles and the lion: and other Æsop fables adapt. by Tom Paxton; ill. by Robert Rayevsky. Morrow, 1991. ISBN 0-688-09683-2 Subj: Animals – lions. Character traits – helpfulness. Character traits – kindness to animals. Folk & fairy tales. Foreign lands – Italy. Rhyming text.

Androcles and the lion adapt. & ill. by Janet Stevens. Holiday, 1989. ISBN 0-8234-0768-3 Subj: Animals – lions. Character traits – helpfulness. Character traits – kindness to animals. Folk & fairy tales. Foreign lands – Italy. Religion.

Animal fables from Æsop adapt. & ill. by Barbara McClintock. Godine, 2000. ISBN 1-56792-144-2 Subj: Animals. Folk & fairy tales.

Anno's Æsop: a book of fables by Æsop and Mr. Fox (Anno, Mitsumasa)

The ant and the dove retold by Mary Lewis Wang; ill. by Ching. Childrens Pr., 1989. ISBN 0-516-02367-5 Subj: Birds – doves. Character traits – helpfulness. Folk & fairy tales. Friendship. Insects – ants.

The ant and the grasshopper retold by Mark White; ill. by Sara Rojo. Picture Window, 2004. ISBN 1-4048-0217-7 Subj: Activities – working. Folk & fairy tales. Insects – ants. Insects – grasshoppers. Seasons – fall. Seasons – winter.

The ant and the grasshopper retold & ill. by Amy Lowry Poole. Holiday, 2000. ISBN 0-8234-1477-9 Subj: Activities – working. Folk & fairy tales. Foreign lands – China. Insects – ants. Insects – grasshoppers. Royalty – emperors. Seasons – fall. Seasons – winter.

Belling the cat retold by Eric Blair; ill. by Diane Silverman. Picture Window, 2004. ISBN 1-4048-0321-1 Subj: Animals – cats. Animals – mice. Folk & fairy tales.

Belling the cat and other Æsop fables (Paxton, Tom)

The best of Æsop's fables retold by Margaret Clark; ill. by Charlotte Voake. Little, 1990. ISBN 0-316-14499-1 Subj: Folk & fairy tales.

The boy who cried wolf retold by Eric Blair; ill. by Dianne Silverman. Picture Window, 2004. ISBN 1-4048-0319-X Subj: Animals – wolves. Behavior – lying. Behavior – trickery. Folk & fairy tales.

The children's Æsop retold by Stephanie Calmenson; ill. by Robert Byrd. Doubleday, 1988. ISBN 1-56397-041-4 Subj: Folk & fairy tales. Format, unusual – toy & movable books.

The country mouse and the city mouse ill. by Laura Lydecker. Knopf, 1987. ISBN 0-394-99027-7 Subj: Animals – mice. Cities, towns. Country. Folk & fairy tales.

The country mouse and the city mouse retold by Eric Blair; ill. by Diane Silverman. Picture Window, 2004. ISBN 1-4048-0318-1 Subj: Animals – mice. Cities, towns. Country. Folk & fairy tales.

The crow and the pitcher retold by Eric Blair; ill. by Diane Silverman. Picture Window, 2004. ISBN 1-4048-0322-X Subj: Birds – crows. Character traits – cleverness. Folk & fairy tales. Problem solving.

The dancin' fox (Nikola-Lisa, W.)

Doctor Coyote: a Native American Æsop's fables (Bierhorst, John)

The dog and the wolf retold by Eric Blair; ill. by Diane Silverman. Picture Window, 2004. ISBN 1-4048-0323-8 Subj: Animals – dogs. Animals – wolves. Character traits – freedom. Folk & fairy tales.

The donkey in the lion's skin retold by Eric Blair; ill. by Diane Silverman. Picture Window, 2004. ISBN 1-4048-0320-3 Subj: Animals. Animals – donkeys. Animals – foxes. Behavior – trickery. Clothing. Disguises.

The donkey ride (Showalter, Jean B.)

Fables from Æsop adapt. & ill. by Tom Lynch. Viking, 2000. ISBN 0-670-88948-2 Subj: Folk & fairy tales.

The fables of Æsop ed. by Ruth Spriggs; ill. by Frank Baber. Rand McNally, 1975. ISBN 0-528-82070-2 Subj: Folk & fairy tales.

Feed me! an Æsop fable (Hooks, William H.)

The fox and the grapes retold by Mark White; ill. by Sara Rojo. Picture Window, 2004. ISBN 1-4048-0218-5 Subj: Animals – foxes. Folk & fairy tales. Food.

The goose that laid the golden egg retold by Mark White; ill. by Sara Rojo. Picture Window, 2004. ISBN 1-4048-0219-3 Subj: Behavior – greed. Birds – geese. Careers – farmers. Eggs. Folk & fairy tales.

The hare and the frogs adapt. & ill. by William Stobbs. Merrimack, 1979. ISBN 0-370-30098-X Subj: Animals – rabbits. Folk & fairy tales. Frogs & toads.

The hare and the tortoise ill. by Paul Galdone. Whittlesey House, 1962. Subj: Animals – rabbits. Folk & fairy tales. Reptiles – turtles, tortoises. Sports – racing.

The hare and the tortoise retold & ill. by Carol Jones. Houghton Mifflin, 1996. ISBN 0-395-81368-9 Subj: Animals – rabbits. Folk & fairy tales. Format, unusual – toy & movable books. Reptiles – turtles, tortoises. Sports – racing.

The tortoise and the hare retold by Mark White; ill. by Sara Rojo. Picture Window, 2004. ISBN 1-4048-0215-0 Subj: Animals – rabbits. Folk & fairy tales. Reptiles – turtles, tortoises. Sports – racing.

The hare and the tortoise adapt. & ill. by Gerald Rose. Macmillan, 1988. ISBN 0-689-71197-2 Subj: Animals – rabbits. Folk & fairy tales. Reptiles – turtles, tortoises. Sports – racing.

The tortoise and the hare: an Æsop fable adapt. & ill. by Janet Stevens. Holiday, 1984. ISBN 0-8234-0510-9 Subj: Animals – rabbits. Folk & fairy tales. Reptiles – turtles, tortoises. Sports – racing.

The hare and the tortoise retold & ill. by Helen Ward. Millbrook, 1999. ISBN 0-7613-1318-4 Subj: Animals – rabbits. Folk & fairy tales. Reptiles – turtles, tortoises. Sports – racing.

The hare and the tortoise adapt. by Caroline Castle; ill. by Peter Weevers. Dial, 1985. ISBN 0-8037-0138-1 Subj: Animals – rabbits. Folk & fairy tales. Reptiles – turtles, tortoises. Sports – racing.

The lion and the mouse adapt. & ill. by Carol Jones. Random House, 1998. ISBN 0-395-86956-0 Subj: Animals – lions. Animals – mice. Character traits – helpfulness. Folk & fairy tales.

The lion and the mouse by Gail Herman; ill. by Lisa McCue. Random House, 1998. ISBN 0-679-98674-X Subj: Animals – lions. Animals – mice. Character traits – helpfulness. Folk & fairy tales.

The lion and the mouse retold by Mark White; ill. by Sara Rojo. Picture Window, 2004. ISBN 1-4048-0216-9 Subj: Animals – lions. Animals – mice. Character traits – helpfulness. Character traits – kindness. Folk & fairy tales.

The lion and the mouse adapt. & ill. by Gerald Rose. Macmillan, 1988. ISBN 0-689-71196-4 Subj: Animals – lions. Animals – mice. Character traits – helpfulness. Folk & fairy tales.

The lion and the mouse retold & ill. by Bernadette Watts. North-South, 2000. ISBN 0-7358-1221-7 Subj: Animals – lions. Animals – mice. Character traits – helpfulness. Folk & fairy tales.

The lion and the mouse: an Æsop fable ill. by Ed Young. Doubleday, 1980. ISBN 0-385-15463-1 Subj: Animals – lions. Animals – mice. Character traits – helpfulness. Folk & fairy tales.

The miller, his son and their donkey ill. by Roger Antoine Duvoisin. McGraw-Hill, 1962. Subj: Animals – donkeys. Character traits – perseverance. Folk & fairy tales. Humorous stories.

The miller, his son and their donkey ill. by Eugen Sopko. Holt, 1985. ISBN 0-8050-0475-0 Subj: Animals – donkeys. Character traits – perseverance. Folk & fairy tales.

Milly and Tilly: the story of a town mouse and a country mouse (Summers, Kate)

Once in a wood: ten tales from Æsop adapt. & ill. by Eve Rice. Greenwillow, 1980. ISBN 0-688-84191-0 Subj: Folk & fairy tales. Rhyming text.

The race (Repchuk, Caroline)

The raven and the fox adapt. & ill. by Gerald Rose. Macmillan, 1988. ISBN 0-689-71194-8 Subj: Animals – foxes. Birds – ravens. Folk & fairy tales.

Road signs: a harey race with a tortoise (Cuyler, Margery)

Seven fables from Æsop retold & ill. by R. W. Alley. Dodd, 1986. ISBN 0-396-08820-1 Subj: Animals. Folk & fairy tales.

Smog, the city dog (Meserve, Adria)

Tales from Æsop retold & ill. by Harold Jones. Watts, 1982. ISBN 0-531-04074-7 Subj: Folk & fairy tales.

The lion and the mouse and other Æsop fables retold by Doris Orgel; ill. by Bert Kitchen. DK, 2000. ISBN 0-7894-2665-X Subj: Animals. Folk & fairy tales.

Three Æsop fox fables ill. by Paul Galdone. Seabury Pr., 1971. ISBN 0-395-28810-X Subj: Animals – foxes. Behavior – trickery. Character traits – flattery. Folk & fairy tales.

The town mouse and the country mouse ill. by Lorinda Bryan Cauley. Putnam, 1984. ISBN 0-399-21123-3 Subj: Animals – mice. Cities, towns. Country. Folk & fairy tales.

The town mouse and the country mouse retold & ill. by Helen Craig. Candlewick, 1992. ISBN 1-56402-102-5 Subj: Animals – mice. Cities, towns. Country. Folk & fairy tales.

The town mouse and the country mouse ill. by Paul Galdone. McGraw-Hill, 1971. ISBN 0-07-022694-6 Subj: Animals – mice. Cities, towns. Country. Folk & fairy tales.

The town mouse and the country mouse ill. by Tom Garcia. Troll, 1979. ISBN 0-89375-109-X Subj: Animals – mice. Cities, towns. Country. Folk & fairy tales.

The town mouse and the country mouse adapt. & ill. by Janet Stevens. Holiday, 1987. ISBN 0-8234-0633-4 Subj: Animals – mice. Cities, towns. Country. Folk & fairy tales.

The town mouse and the country mouse: an Æsop fable retold & ill. by Bernadette Watts. North-South, 1998. ISBN 1-55858-988-0 Subj: Animals – mice. Cities, towns. Country. Folk & fairy tales.

Town mouse, country mouse retold & ill. by Jan Brett. Putnam, 1994. ISBN 0-399-22622-2 Subj: Animals – cats. Animals – mice. Birds – owls. Cities, towns. Country. Folk & fairy tales.

Town mouse, country mouse retold & ill. by Carol Jones. Houghton Mifflin, 1995. ISBN 0-395-71129-0 Subj: Animals – mice. Cities, towns. Country. Folk & fairy tales.

Twelve tales from Æsop (Carle, Eric)

The wolf in sheep's clothing retold by Mark White; ill. by Sara Rojo. Picture Window, 2004. ISBN 1-4048-0220-7 Subj: Animals –

sheep. Animals – wolves. Behavior – trickery. Clothing. Disguises.

Wolf! Wolf! adapt. & ill. by Gerald Rose. Macmillan, 1988. ISBN 0-689-71195-6 Subj: Behavior – lying. Behavior – trickery. Folk & fairy tales.

Afanas'ev, Aleksandr N. *Russian folk tales* trans. by Robert Chandler; ill. by Ivan I. Bilibin. Random House, 1980. ISBN 0-87773-195-0 Subj: Folk & fairy tales. Foreign lands – Russia.

Salt: from a Russian folktale adapt. by Jane Langton; trans. by Alice Plume; ill. by Ilse Plume. Walt Disney, 1992. ISBN 1-56282-179-2 Subj: Behavior – greed. Family life – brothers. Folk & fairy tales. Foreign lands – Russia. Royalty – princesses.

Agard, John. *Dig away two-hole Tim* ill. by Jennifer Northway. Bodley Head, 1982. ISBN 0-370-30421-7 Subj: Activities – digging. Behavior – misbehavior. Foreign lands – Guyana.

No hickory no dickory no dock: Caribbean nursery rhymes by John Agard & Grace Nichols; ill. by Cynthia Jabar. Candlewick, 1995. ISBN 1-56402-156-4 Subj: Foreign lands – Caribbean Islands. Nursery rhymes. Rhyming text.

Agee, Joel. *The crow in the snow and other bedtime stories* (Moser, Erwin)

Agee, Jon. *Dmitri the astronaut* ill. by author. HarperCollins, 1996. ISBN 0-06-205075-3 Subj: Animals. Careers – astronauts. Moon. Space & space ships.

Ellsworth ill. by author. Pantheon, 1983. ISBN 0-394-95995-7 Subj: Activities – playing. Animals – dogs. Imagination.

The incredible painting of Felix Clousseau ill. by author. Farrar, 1988. ISBN 0-374-33633-4 Subj: Activities – painting. Art. Imagination.

Milo's hat trick ill. by author. Hyperion, 2001. ISBN 0-7868-0902-7 Subj: Animals – bears. Careers – magicians. Magic. Theater.

Z goes home ill. by author. Hyperion, 2003. ISBN 0-7868-1987-1 Subj: ABC books.

Agell, Charlotte. *Mud makes me dance in the spring* ill. by author. Tilbury House, 1994. ISBN 0-88448-112-3 Subj: Family life. Imagination. Seasons – spring.

The sailor's book ill. by author. Firefly, 1991. ISBN 0-920668-90-9 Subj: Boats, ships. Dragons. Sailors. Sea & seashore.

To the island ill. by author. DK, 1998. ISBN 0-7894-2505-X Subj: Animals. Islands. Rhyming text. Sports – sailing.

Aggs, Patrice. *The visitor* ill. by author. Orchard, 1999. ISBN 0-531-33059-1 Subj: Animals – cats. Animals – giraffes. Character traits – being different.

Agostinelli, Maria Enrica. *I know something you don't know* ill. by author. Watts, 1970. Translation of Ich weiss etwas, was du nicht weisst. ISBN 0-531-01920-9 Subj: Games. Participation.

On wings of love: the United Nations declaration of the rights of the child ill. by author. Collins-World, 1979. ISBN 0-529-05529-5 Subj: Birds – doves. Emotions – love.

Agran, Rick. *Pumpkin shivaree* ill. by Sara Anderson. Handprint, 2003. ISBN 1-59354-006-X Subj: Holidays – Halloween. Plants.

Ahlberg, Allan. *The adventures of Bert* by Allan Ahlberg & Raymond Briggs; ill. by Raymond Briggs. Farrar, 2001. ISBN 0-374-30092-5 Subj: Humorous stories.

The baby's catalogue (Ahlberg, Janet)

The bear nobody wanted (Ahlberg, Janet)

Big bad pig by Allan Ahlberg & Colin McNaughton; ill. by Colin McNaughton. Random House, 1985. ISBN 0-394-87194-4 Subj: Animals. Concepts. Concepts – opposites. Language.

A bit more Bert by Allan Ahlbert & Raymond Briggs; ill. by Raymond Briggs. Farrar, 2002. ISBN 0-374-32489-1 Subj: Humorous stories.

The black cat ill. by André Amstutz. Greenwillow, 1990. ISBN 0-688-09904-1 Subj: Anatomy – skeletons. Animals – cats.

Bravest ever bear ill. by Paul Howard. Candlewick, 1999. ISBN 0-7636-0783-5 Subj: Animals – bears. Folk & fairy tales. Humorous stories.

Burglar Bill (Ahlberg, Janet)

Bye-bye, baby: a sad story with a happy ending (Ahlberg, Janet)

The Cinderella show by Allan & Janet Ahlberg; ill. by authors. Viking, 1987. ISBN 0-670-81037-1 Subj: Folk & fairy tales. School. Theater.

Cops and robbers ill. by Janet Ahlberg. Greenwillow, 1979. ISBN 0-688-84178-3 Subj: Careers – police officers. Crime. Foreign lands – England. Holidays – Christmas. Rhyming text.

Crash, bang, wallop! ill. by Colin McNaughton. Random House, 1986. ISBN 0-394-87198-7 Subj: Noise, sounds.

Dinosaur dreams ill. by André Amstutz. Greenwillow, 1991. ISBN 0-688-09956-4 Subj: Anatomy – skeletons. Dinosaurs. Dreams. Prehistory.

Each peach pear plum: an "I spy" story (Ahlberg, Janet)

Fee fi fo fum by Allan Ahlberg & Colin McNaughton; ill. by Colin McNaughton. Random House, 1985. ISBN 0-394-97193-0 Subj: Concepts. Concepts – opposites. Counting, numbers. Language.

Funnybones (Ahlberg, Janet)

The ghost train ill. by André Amstutz. Greenwillow, 1992. ISBN 0-688-11435-0 Subj: Anatomy – skeletons. Humorous stories. Monsters. Trains.

Half a pig ill. by Jessica Ahlberg. Candlewick, 2004. ISBN 0-7636-2373-3 Subj: Animals – pigs. Humorous stories.

Happy worm by Allan Ahlberg & Colin McNaughton; ill. by Colin McNaughton. Random House, 1985. ISBN 0-394-97196-5 Subj: Concepts. Concepts – opposites. Language.

Help! by Allan Ahlberg & Colin McNaughton; ill. by Colin McNaughton. Random House, 1985. ISBN 0-394-97190-6 Subj: Concepts. Language.

It was a dark and stormy night (Ahlberg, Janet)

Jeremiah in the dark wood (Ahlberg, Janet)

The jolly Christmas postman (Ahlberg, Janet)

The jolly pocket postman (Ahlberg, Janet)

The jolly postman (Ahlberg, Janet)

The little worm book (Ahlberg, Janet)

Master Salt the sailor's son ill. by André Amstutz. Golden Pr., 1982, c1980. ISBN 0-307-61708-4 Subj: Behavior – hiding. Family life. Islands. Sailors.

Me and my friend ill. by Colin McNaughton. Random House, 1986. ISBN 0-394-87199-5 Subj: Activities. Activities – playing. Dictionaries. Monsters. School.

Miss Brick, the builder's baby ill. by Colin McNaughton. Golden Pr., 1982. ISBN 0-307-61702-5 Subj: Activities – making things. Babies. Family life.

Mr. and Mrs. Hay the horse ill. by Colin McNaughton. Golden Pr., 1982. ISBN 0-307-61704-1 Subj: Careers – entertainers. Circus. Family life.

Mr. Biff the boxer ill. by Janet Ahlberg. Western, 1982. ISBN 0-307-61701-7 Subj: Family life. Sports – boxing.

Mr. Buzz the beeman ill. by Faith Jaques. Golden Pr., 1982. ISBN 0-307-61703-3 Subj: Communities, neighborhoods. Family life. Insects – bees.

Mockingbird ill. by Paul Howard. Candlewick, 1998. ISBN 0-7636-0439-9 Subj: Babies. Family life. Lullabies.

Monkey do! ill. by André Amstutz. Candlewick, 1998. ISBN 0-7636-0466-6 Subj: Animals – monkeys. Behavior – misbehavior. Behavior – running away. Rhyming text. Zoos.

Mrs. Plug the plumber ill. by Joe Wright. Golden Pr., 1982. ISBN 0-307-61706-8 Subj: Careers – plumbers. Family life.

Mrs. Wobble the waitress ill. by Janet Ahlberg. Golden Bks., 1982. ISBN 0-307-61707-6 Subj: Activities – working. Careers – waiters, waitresses. Family life.

Mrs. Lather's laundry ill. by André Amstutz. Golden Pr., 1982. ISBN 0-307-61705-X Subj: Character traits – cleanliness. Family life. Laundry.

Mystery tour ill. by André Amstutz. Greenwillow, 1991. ISBN 0-688-09958-0 Subj: Anatomy – skeletons. Behavior – lost & found possessions. Humorous stories. Night.

Peek-a-boo! (Ahlberg, Janet)

The pet shop ill. by André Amstutz. Greenwillow, 1990. ISBN 0-688-09906-8 Subj: Anatomy – skeletons. Pets.

Playmates (Ahlberg, Janet)

Skeleton crew ill. by André Amstutz. Greenwillow, 1992. ISBN 0-688-11436-9 Subj: Activities – vacationing. Anatomy – skeletons. Boats, ships. Pirates. Sports – sailing.

The snail house ill. by Gillian Tyler. Candlewick, 2000. ISBN 0-7636-0711-8 Subj: Activities – storytelling. Animals – snails. Concepts – size. Family life – grandmothers.

Starting school (Ahlberg, Janet)

Yum yum (Ahlberg, Janet)

Ahlberg, Janet. *The baby's catalogue* by Janet & Allan Ahlberg; ill. by authors. Little, 1983. ISBN 0-316-02037-0 Subj: Babies. Family life.

The bear nobody wanted by Janet & Allan Ahlberg; ill. by authors. Viking, 1992. ISBN 0-670-83982-5 Subj: Format, unusual – toy & movable books. Self-concept.

Burglar Bill by Janet & Allan Ahlberg; ill. by authors. Greenwillow, 1977. ISBN 0-688-84078-7 Subj: Crime.

Bye-bye, baby: a sad story with a happy ending by Janet & Allan Ahlberg; ill. by Janet Ahlberg. Little, 1989. ISBN 0-316-02034-6 Subj: Babies. Behavior – needing someone. Family life.

The Cinderella show (Ahlberg, Allan)

Each peach pear plum: an "I spy" story by Janet & Allan Ahlberg; ill. by authors. Viking, 1978. ISBN 0-670-28705-9 Subj: Games. Rhyming text.

Funnybones by Janet & Allan Ahlberg; ill. by authors. Greenwillow, 1981. ISBN 0-688-84238-0 Subj: Activities – playing. Anatomy – skeletons. Ghosts. Night.

It was a dark and stormy night by Janet & Allan Ahlberg; ill. by Janet Ahlberg. Viking, 1993. ISBN 0-670-84620-1 Subj: Activities – storytelling. Character traits – cleverness. Crime. Pirates.

Jeremiah in the dark wood by Janet & Allan Ahlberg; ill. by Janet Ahlberg. Viking, 1987. ISBN 0-670-40637-6 Subj: Behavior – stealing. Forest, woods. Mythical creatures.

The jolly Christmas postman by Janet & Allan Ahlberg; ill. by authors. Little, 1991. ISBN 0-316-02033-8 Subj: Careers – postal workers. Format, unusual. Holidays – Christmas. Nursery rhymes. Post office. Rhyming text.

The jolly pocket postman by Janet & Allan Ahlberg; ill. by authors. Little, 1995. ISBN 0-316-60202-7 Subj: Careers – postal workers. Format, unusual – toy & movable books. Post office. Rhyming text.

The jolly postman by Janet & Allan Ahlberg; ill. by authors. Little, 1986. ISBN 0-316-02036-2 Subj: Careers – postal workers. Format, unusual – toy & movable books. Post office. Rhyming text.

The little worm book by Janet & Allan Ahlberg; ill. by authors. Viking, 1980. ISBN 0-670-43438-8 Subj: Animals – worms. Humorous stories.

Peek-a-boo! by Janet & Allan Ahlberg; ill. by authors. Viking, 1981. ISBN 0-670-54598-8 Subj: Babies. Family life. Format, unusual – toy & movable books. Games. Rhyming text.

Playmates by Janet & Allan Ahlberg; ill. by authors. Viking, 1985. ISBN 0-670-55988-1 Subj: Activities – playing. Format, unusual – toy & movable books.

Starting school by Janet & Allan Ahlberg; ill. by authors. Viking, 1988. ISBN 0-670-82175-6 Subj: School – first day.

Yum yum by Janet & Allan Ahlberg; ill. by authors. Viking, 1985. ISBN 0-670-79620-4 Subj: Food. Format, unusual – toy & movable books.

Aichinger, Helga. *The shepherd* ill. by author. Crowell, 1967. Subj: Angels. Careers – shepherds. Dreams. Holidays – Christmas. Religion.

Aiello, Susan. *A hat like that* (Johnson, B. J.)

My blanket Burt (Johnson, B. J.)

Aigner-Clark, Julie. *Language nursery* cover ill. by Nadeem Zaidi. Hyperion, 2001. ISBN 0-7868-0810-1 Subj: Foreign languages. Format, unusual – board books.

Aiken, Conrad Potter. *Tom, Sue and the clock* ill. by Julie Maas. Macmillan, 1966. Subj: Clocks, watches. Rhyming text. Time.

Aiken, Joan. *Arabel and Mortimer* ill. by Quentin Blake. Doubleday, 1981. ISBN 0-385-15643-X Subj: Birds – ravens. Imagination. Pets.

The shoemaker's boy ill. by Victor G. Ambrus. S&S, 1994. ISBN 0-671-86647-8 Subj: Careers – shoemakers. Folk & fairy tales. Middle Ages.

Ainsworth, Ruth. *The mysterious Baba and her magic caravan* ill. by Joan Hickson. André Deutsch, 1980. ISBN 0-233-97200-5 Subj: Character traits – generosity. Toys – dolls.

Aitken, Amy. *Kate and Mona in the jungle* ill. by author. Bradbury, 1981. ISBN 0-878-88167-0 Subj: Animals. Imagination. Jungle. Zoos.

Ruby! ill. by author. Bradbury, 1979. ISBN 0-878-88144-1 Subj: Careers. Imagination.

Ruby, the red knight ill. by author. Bradbury, 1983. ISBN 0-02-700340-X Subj: Character traits – bravery. Imagination. Royalty.

Wanda's circus ill. by author. Bradbury, 1985. ISBN 0-02-700370-1 Subj: Animals. Circus. Family life. Sibling rivalry.

Ajmera, Maya. *Animal friends: a global celebration of children and their animals* by Maya Ajmera & John D. Ivanko; ill. with photos. Charlesbridge, 2002. ISBN 1-57091-502-4 Subj: Animals. Format, unusual – board books. Pets.

Back to school by Maya Ajmera & John D. Ivanko; ill. with photos. Charlesbridge, 2001. ISBN 1-57091-383-8 Subj: Foreign lands. School.

Come out and play by Maya Ajmera & John Ivanko. Charlesbridge, 2001. ISBN 1-57091-385-4 Subj: Activities – playing. Foreign lands.

A kid's best friend Maya Ajmera & Alex Fisher; ill. with photos. Charlesbridge, 2002. ISBN 1-57091-513-X Subj: Animals – dogs. Pets.

To be a kid Maya Ajmera & John D. Ivanko; ill. with photos. Charlesbridge, 1999. ISBN 0-88106-841-1 Subj: Activities. Family life. Foreign lands.

Akass, Susan. *Number nine duckling* ill. by Alex Ayliffe. Boyds Mills, 1993. ISBN 1-56397-224-7 Subj: Activities – jumping. Animals. Birds – ducks. Emotions – fear. Farms.

Akens, Floyd. *see* Baum, L. Frank (Lyman Frank)

Akers, Floyd. *see* Baum, L. Frank (Lyman Frank)

Aksakov, Sergei. *The scarlet flower* trans. by Isadora Levin; ill. by Boris Diodorov. Harcourt, 1989. ISBN 0-15-270487-6 Subj: Activities – traveling. Family life – fathers. Flowers. Foreign lands – Russia.

Alakija, Polly. *Catch that goat!* ill. by author. Barefoot, 2002. ISBN 1-84148-908-5 Subj: Animals – goats. Counting, numbers. Foreign lands – Africa. Stores.

Alan, Sandy. *The plaid peacock* ill. by Kelly Oechsli. Pantheon, 1965. Subj: Birds – peacocks, peahens. Foreign lands – India.

Alarcón, Francisco X. *From the bellybutton of the moon and other summer poems / poems = Del ombligo de la luna y otros poemas de verano / poemas* ill. by Maya Christina Gonzalez. Childrens Pr., 1998. ISBN 0-89239-153-7 Subj: Foreign lands – Mexico. Foreign languages. Nature. Poetry. Seasons – summer.

Iguanas in the snow and other winter poems / poemas = Iguanas en la nieve y otros poemas de invierno / poemas ill. by Maya Christina Gonzalez. Childrens Pr., 2001. ISBN 0-89239-168-5 Subj: Foreign languages. Picture puzzles. Poetry. Reptiles – iguanas. Seasons – winter. Weather – snow.

Alarcón, Karen Beaumont. *Louella Mae, she's run away!* ill. by Rosanne Litzinger. Holt, 1997. ISBN 0-8050-3532-X Subj: Animals – pigs. Behavior – lost & found possessions. Farms. Rhyming text.

Alavedra, Joan. *They followed a bright star* (They followed a bright star)

Albert, Burton. *Mine, yours, ours* ill. by Lois Axeman. A. Whitman, 1977. ISBN 0-807-55148-1 Subj: Behavior – sharing. Concepts.

Where does the trail lead? ill. by J. Brian Pinkney. S&S, 1991. ISBN 0-671-73409-1 Subj: Islands. Sea & seashore.

Albert, Richard E. *Alejandro's gift* ill. by Sylvia Long. Chronicle, 1994. ISBN 0-8118-0436-4 Subj: Animals. Character traits – kindness to animals. Desert. Gifts.

Albert, Shirley. *Doll party* ill. by Amy Flynn. Grosset, 1994. ISBN 0-448-40183-5 Subj: Animals – mice. Character traits – willfulness. Family life – mothers. Parties. Toys – dolls.

Albert, Toni. *I heard the willow weep* ill. by Margaret Brandt. Trickle Creek, 2000. ISBN 1-929432-00-3 Subj: Ecology. Poetry.

Alberti, Theresa Jarosz. *Out and about at the planetarium* ill. by Becky Shipe. Picture Window, 2004. ISBN 1-4048-0299-1 Subj: Astronomy. School – field trips. Science.

Alberts, Nancy Markham. *No toys on Sunday* ill. by Erin McGonigle Brammer. Morehouse, 1998. ISBN 0-8192-1740-9 Subj: Activities – playing. Character traits – cleverness. Days of the week, months of the year. Religion – Noah. Toys – dolls.

Alborghetti, Marci. *Miracle of the myrrh* ill. by Hervé Blondon. Winslow, 2000. ISBN 1-8908-1716-3 Subj: Character traits – generosity. Handicaps. Religion.

Alborough, Jez. *Bare bear* ill. by author. Knopf, 1984. ISBN 0-394-96808-5 Subj: Activities – bathing. Animals – polar bears. Rhyming text.

Beaky ill. by author. Houghton Mifflin, 1990. ISBN 0-395-53348-1 Subj: Animals. Birds. Self-concept.

Can you jump like a kangaroo? ill. by author. Candlewick, 1996. ISBN 1-56402-880-1 Subj: Activities. Animals. Format, unusual – toy & movable books.

Can you peck like a hen? ill. by author. Candlewick, 1996. ISBN 1-56402-881-X Subj: Animals. Format, unusual – toy & movable books.

Captain Duck ill. by author. HarperCollins, 2003. ISBN 0-06-052123-9 Subj: Animals. Birds – ducks. Boats, ships. Rhyming text.

Clothesline ill. by author. Candlewick, 1993. ISBN 1-56402-243-9 Subj: Animals. Clothing. Format, unusual – toy & movable books.

Cuddly Dudley ill. by author. Candlewick, 1993. ISBN 1-56402-095-9 Subj: Behavior – solitude. Birds – penguins. Character traits – being different. Family life – brothers & sisters.

Duck in the truck ill. by author. HarperCollins, 2000. ISBN 0-06-028685-7 Subj: Animals. Birds – ducks. Rhyming text. Trucks.

Esther's trunk ill. by author. Warner, 1988. ISBN 1-55782-007-4 Subj: Animals – elephants. Rhyming text.

Fix-It Duck ill. by author. HarperCollins, 2002. ISBN 0-06-000699-4 Subj: Animals. Birds – ducks. Rhyming text.

The grass is always greener ill. by author. Dial, 1987. ISBN 0-8037-0468-2 Subj: Animals – sheep. Behavior – seeking better things. Farms.

Hide and seek ill. by author. Candlewick, 1994. ISBN 1-56402-369-9 Subj: Activities – playing. Animals. Behavior – hiding. Format, unusual – toy & movable books.

Hug ill. by author. Candlewick, 2000. ISBN 0-7636-1287-1 Subj: Animals. Animals – chimpanzees. Behavior – lost. Behavior – needing someone. Family life – mothers.

Ice cream bear ill. by author. Candlewick, 1997. ISBN 0-7636-0293-0 Subj: Animals – bears. Dreams. Food. Rhyming text. Weather – snow.

It's the bear ill. by author. Candlewick, 1994. ISBN 1-56402-486-5 Subj: Activities – picnicking. Animals – bears. Behavior – stealing. Emotions – fear. Family life – mothers. Food. Rhyming text.

My friend bear ill. by author. Candlewick, 1998. ISBN 0-7636-0583-2 Subj: Animals – bears. Emotions – loneliness. Friendship. Toys – bears.

Running Bear ill. by author. Knopf, 1985. ISBN 0-394-97963-X Subj: Animals – polar bears. Behavior – bad day. Sports – racing.

There's something at the mail slot ill. by author. Candlewick, 1995. ISBN 1-56402-523-3 Subj: Animals. Character traits – bravery. Rhyming text.

Watch out! Big Bro's coming! ill. by author. Candlewick, 1997. ISBN 0-7636-0130-6 Subj: Animals. Animals – mice. Concepts – size. Emotions – fear. Family life – brothers & sisters.

Where's my teddy? ill. by author. Candlewick, 1992. ISBN 1-56402-048-7 Subj: Animals – bears. Forest, woods. Rhyming text. Toys – bears.

Alcantara, Ricardo. *Dog and cat* ill. by Gusti; trans. by Elizabeth Uhlig. Millbrook, 1999. ISBN 0-7613-1420-2 Subj: Animals – cats. Animals – dogs. Emotions – fear. Friendship.

Alcott, Louisa May. *Little women* (Brown, Janet Allison)

An old-fashioned Thanksgiving ill. by Jody Wheeler. Ideals, 1993. ISBN 0-8249-8630-X Subj: Family life. Family life – grandmothers. Food. Holidays – Thanksgiving.

Alda, Arlene. *Arlene Alda's ABC* photos by author. Tricycle, 1993. ISBN 1-883672-01-5 Subj: ABC books.

Arlene Alda's 1 2 3: what do you see? photos by author. Tricycle, 1998. ISBN 1-883672-71-6 Subj: Counting, numbers.

Hurry Granny Annie ill. by Eve Aldridge. Tricycle, 1999. ISBN 1-883672-72-4 Subj: Behavior – hurrying. Family life – grandmothers. Sun.

Matthew and his dad photos by author. S&S, 1983. ISBN 0-671-45158-8 Subj: Clothing. Family life – fathers.

Morning glory Monday ill. by Maryann Kovalski. Tundra, 2003. ISBN 0-88776-620-X Subj: Communities, neighborhoods. Ethnic groups in the U.S. – Italian Americans. Family life – mothers. Flowers. Seeds.

Pig, horse, or cow, don't wake me now photos by author. Doubleday, 1994. ISBN 0-385-32032-9 Subj: Animals. Cumulative tales. Morning. Noise, sounds. Rhyming text.

Sheep, sheep, sheep, help me fall asleep photos by author. Delacorte, 1992. ISBN 0-385-30791-8 Subj: Animals. Animals – sheep. Bedtime. Rhyming text.

Sonya's mommy works photos by author. Messner, 1982. ISBN 0-671-46167-2 Subj: Activities – working. Family life – mothers.

Aldag, Kurt. *Some things never change* ill. by Ken Rush. Macmillan, 1992. ISBN 0-02-700205-5 Subj: Automobiles. Careers – mechanics. Time.

Alden, Joan. *A boy's best friend* ill. by Catherine Hopkins. Wonderland, 1992. ISBN 1-55583-203-2 Subj: Animals – dogs. Behavior – bullying. Self-concept. Toys.

Alden, Laura. *Saying I'm sorry* ill. by Dan Siculan. Child's World, 1983. ISBN 0-89565-247-1 Subj: Etiquette.

When? ill. by Lois Axeman. Childrens Pr., 1983. ISBN 0-516-06592-0 Subj: Character traits – curiosity. Character traits – questioning.

Alderson, Brian W. *Cakes and custard: children's rhymes* (Cakes and custard)

The Helen Oxenbury nursery rhyme book (The Helen Oxenbury nursery rhyme book)

Alderson, Sue Ann. *Bonnie McSmithers is at it again!* ill. by Fiona Garrick. Tree Frog Pr., 1980. ISBN 0-88967-028-5 Subj: Activities. Character traits – individuality. Rhyming text.

Ida and the wool smugglers ill. by Ann Blades. Macmillan, 1987. ISBN 0-689-50440-3 Subj: Character traits – cleverness. Crime. Islands.

Wherever bears be: a story for two voices ill. by Arden Johnson. Tricycle, 1999. ISBN 1-883672-77-5 Subj: Animals – bears. Emotions – fear. Food.

Aldis, Dorothy (Keeley). *All together: a child's treasury of verse* ill. by Helen D. Jameson, Marjorie Flack, & Margaret Freeman. Putnam, 1952. ISBN 0-399-20006-1 Subj: Poetry.

Before things happen ill. by Margaret Freeman. Putnam, 1939. Subj: Poetry.

Hello day ill. by Susan Elson. Putnam, 1959. Subj: Poetry.

Hiding ill. by Heather Collins. Viking, 1994. ISBN 0-670-85410-7 Subj: Behavior – hiding. Family life. Poetry. Toys – bears.

Quick as a wink ill. by Peggy Westphal. Putnam, 1960. Subj: Insects. Poetry.

Aldridge, Josephine Haskell. *The best of friends* ill. by Betty Peterson. Parnassus, 1963. Subj: Animals. Friendship.

Fisherman's luck ill. by Ruth Robbins. Parnassus, 1966. Subj: Careers – fishermen. Character traits – luck. Sports – fishing. Weather – storms.

A penny and a periwinkle ill. by Ruth Robbins. Parnassus, 1961. Subj: Sports – fishing.

A possible tree ill. by Daniel San Souci. Macmillan, 1993. ISBN 0-02-700407-4 Subj: Animals. Ecology. Holidays – Christmas. Trees.

Aleichem, Sholem. *Hanukah money* ill. by Uri Shulevitz. Greenwillow, 1978. ISBN 0-688-84120-1 Subj: Folk & fairy tales. Foreign lands. Holidays – Hanukkah. Jewish culture. Religion.

Alemany, Norah E. *My mother the mail carrier = Mi mama la cartera* (Maury, Inez)

Alexander, Anne (Anna Barbara Cooke). *ABC of cars and trucks* ill. by Ninon. Doubleday, 1956. Subj: ABC books. Automobiles. Poetry. Trucks.

Boats and ships from A to Z ill. by Will Huntington. Rand McNally, 1961. Subj: Boats, ships.

I want to whistle ill. by Abner Graboff. Abelard-Schuman, 1958. Subj: Activities – whistling. Rhyming text.

My daddy and I ill. by Cyril Satorsky. Abelard-Schuman, 1961. Subj: Counting, numbers. Family life – fathers. Poetry.

Noise in the night ill. by Abner Graboff. Rand McNally, 1960. Subj: Emotions – fear. Night. Noise, sounds.

Alexander, Cecil Frances. *All things bright and beautiful: a hymn* ill. by Leo Politi. Scribners, 1962. Subj: Creation. Music. Nature. Poetry. Religion. Songs.

All things bright and beautiful ill. by Anna Vojtech. North-South, 2004. ISBN 0-7358-1892-4 Subj: Animals. Country. Nature. Plants. Poetry. Seasons.

All things bright and beautiful ill. by Bruce Whatley. HarperCollins, 2001. ISBN 0-06-026618-X Subj: Creation. Music. Nature. Poetry. Religion. Songs.

Alexander, Ellen. *Chaska and the golden doll* ill. by author. Arcade, 1994. ISBN 1-55970-241-9 Subj: Foreign lands – Peru. Foreign lands – South America. Indians of South America.

Llama and the great flood ill. by author. HarperCollins, 1989. ISBN 0-690-04729-0 Subj: Animals – llamas. Folk & fairy tales. Foreign lands – Peru. Weather – floods.

Alexander, Liza. *Ernie gets lost* ill. by Tom Cooke. Childrens Pr., 1985. ISBN 0-307-62115-4 Subj: Behavior – lost. Stores.

A visit to the Sesame Street Museum ill. by Joe Mathieu. Random House, 1987. ISBN 0-394-98715-2 Subj: Museums.

Alexander, Lloyd. *Fortune tellers* ill. by Trina Schart Hyman. Dutton, 1992. ISBN 0-525-44849-7 Subj: Careers – fortune tellers. Cumulative tales. Foreign lands – Africa. Foreign lands – Cameroon.

The house Gobbaleen ill. by Diane Goode. Dutton, 1995. ISBN 0-525-45289-3 Subj: Animals – cats. Behavior – trickery. Character traits – foolishness. Character traits – luck. Monsters. Mythical creatures – goblins.

How the cat swallowed thunder ill. by Judith Byron Schachner. Dutton, 2000. ISBN 0-525-46449-2 Subj: Animals – cats. Behavior – misbehavior. Folk & fairy tales – pourquoi tales.

The king's fountain ill. by Ezra Jack Keats. Dutton, 1971. ISBN 0-525-33240-5 Subj: Folk & fairy tales. Poverty. Royalty – kings.

The truthful harp ill. by Evaline Ness. Holt, 1967. Subj: Character traits – honesty. Folk & fairy tales. Music. Musical instruments – harps.

Alexander, Martha G. *And my mean old mother will be sorry, Blackboard Bear* ill. by author. Candlewick, 2000. ISBN 0-7636-0668-5 Subj: Animals – bears. Behavior – running away. Emotions – anger. Imagination – imaginary friends.

Blackboard Bear ill. by author. 2nd ed. Candlewick, 1999. ISBN 0-7636-0667-7 Subj: Activities – playing. Animals – bears. Concepts – size. Imagination – imaginary friends.

Bobo's dream ill. by author. Dial, 1970. Subj: Animals – dogs. Dreams. Ethnic groups in the U.S. – African Americans. Imagination. Wordless.

Even that moose won't listen to me ill. by author. Dial, 1988. ISBN 0-8037-0188-8 Subj: Animals – moose. Behavior – disbelief. Family life.

Good night, Lily ill. by author. Candlewick, 1993. ISBN 1-56402-164-5 Subj: Activities – playing. Bedtime. Family life – brothers & sisters. Format, unusual – board books. Toys.

How my library grew by Dinah ill. by author. H. W. Wilson, 1982. ISBN 0-8242-0670-3 Subj: Libraries.

I sure am glad to see you, Blackboard Bear ill. by author. Candlewick, 2001. First published by Dial, 1976. ISBN 0-7636-0669-3 Subj: Animals – bears. Behavior – bullying. Imagination – imaginary friends.

I'll be the horse if you'll play with me ill. by author. Dial, 1975. ISBN 0-8037-5511-2 Subj: Activities – playing. Behavior – fighting, arguing. Family life. Sibling rivalry.

I'll never share you, Blackboard Bear ill. by author. Candlewick, 2003. ISBN 0-7636-1590-0 Subj: Activities – drawing. Animals – bears. Behavior – sharing.

I'll protect you from the jungle beasts ill. by author. Dial, 1973. ISBN 0-8037-4309-2 Subj: Emotions – fear. Imagination – imaginary friends. Problem solving. Sleep. Toys – bears.

Lily and Willy ill. by author. Candlewick, 1993. ISBN 1-56402-163-7 Subj: Activities – playing. Family life – brothers & sisters. Format, unusual – board books. Toys.

Maggie's moon ill. by author. Dial, 1982. ISBN 0-8037-5721-2 Subj: Animals – dogs. Moon. Night.

Marty McGee's space lab, no girls allowed ill. by author. Dial, 1981. ISBN 0-8037-5156-7 Subj: Family life. Gender roles. Imagination. Sibling rivalry. Space & space ships.

Maybe a monster ill. by author. Dial, 1968. ISBN 0-8037-5508-2 Subj: Emotions – fear. Monsters.

Move over, Twerp ill. by author. Dial, 1981. ISBN 0-8037-6140-6 Subj: Behavior – bullying. Character traits – perseverance. Humorous stories. Problem solving. School.

My outrageous friend Charlie ill. by author. Dial, 1989. ISBN 0-8037-0588-3 Subj: Character traits – confidence. Friendship. Humorous stories. Magic.

No ducks in our bathtub ill. by author. Dial, 1973. ISBN 0-8037-6217-8 Subj: Frogs & toads. Pets.

Nobody asked me if I wanted a baby sister ill. by author. Dial, 1971. ISBN 0-8037-6402-2 Subj: Babies. Emotions – envy, jealousy. Family life – new sibling. Family life – sisters. Sibling rivalry.

Out! Out! Out! ill. by author. Dial, 1968. ISBN 0-685-01457-6 Subj: Birds. Problem solving. Wordless.

Pigs say oink: a first book of sounds ill. by author. Random House, [1981] c1978. ISBN 0-394-93838-0 Subj: Animals. Noise, sounds.

Sabrina ill. by author. Dial, 1971. ISBN 0-8037-7547-4 Subj: Emotions – embarrassment. Names. School – first day.

The story grandmother told ill. by author. Dial, 1969. Subj: Ethnic groups in the U.S. – African Americans. Family life – grandmothers. Toys.

3 magic flip books: The magic hat; The magic box; The magic picture ill. by author. Dial, 1984. ISBN 0-8037-0051-2 Subj: Format, unusual – toy & movable books. Magic. Wordless.

We never get to do anything ill. by author. Dial, 1970. ISBN 0-8037-9416-9 Subj: Behavior – boredom. Character traits – perseverance. Games. Problem solving. Sports – swimming.

We're in big trouble, Blackboard Bear ill. by author. Dial, 1980. ISBN 0-8037-9742-7 Subj: Animals – bears. Behavior – misbehavior. Imagination – imaginary friends. Night. Problem solving.

When the new baby comes, I'm moving out ill. by author. Dial, 1979. ISBN 0-8037-9558-0 Subj: Animals – babies. Emotions – envy, jealousy. Family life – new sibling. Sibling rivalry.

Where does the sky end, Grandpa? ill. by author. Harcourt, 1992. ISBN 0-15-295603-4 Subj: Activities – walking. Character traits – questioning. Family life – grandfathers. Nature.

Where's Willy? ill. by author. Candlewick, 1993. ISBN 1-56402-161-0 Subj: Activities – playing. Family life – brothers & sisters. Format, unusual – board books. Games. Toys.

Willy's boot ill. by author. Candlewick, 1993. ISBN 1-56402-162-9 Subj: Activities – playing. Family life – brothers & sisters. Format, unusual – board books. Toys.

You're a genius, Blackboard Bear ill. by author. Candlewick, 1995. ISBN 1-56402-238-2 Subj: Animals – bears. Dreams. Imagination – imaginary friends. Night. Space & space ships.

Alexander, Sally Hobart. *Maggie's whopper* ill. by Deborah Kogan Ray. Macmillan, 1992. ISBN 0-02-700201-2 Subj: Animals – bears. Family life – aunts, uncles. Sports – fishing.

Sarah's surprise ill. by Jill Kastner. Macmillan, 1990. ISBN 0-02-700391-4 Subj: Emotions – fear. Sea & seashore.

Alexander, Sue. *Behold the trees* ill. by Leonid Gore. Levine, 2001. ISBN 0-590-76211-7 Subj: Ecology. Foreign lands – Israel. Trees.

Dear Phoebe ill. by Eileen Christelow. Little, 1984. ISBN 0-316-03123-1 Subj: Animals – dormice. Behavior – growing up. Emotions – loneliness. Emotions – love. Family life.

Ellsworth and Millicent ill. by David Scott Meier. Picture Book Studio, 1992. ISBN 0-88708-247-5 Subj: Animals – hippopotamuses. Behavior – dissatisfaction. Friendship.

Marc the Magnificent ill. by Tomie de Paola. Pantheon, 1978. ISBN 0-394-93728-7 Subj: Character traits – optimism. Magic.

More Witch, Goblin, and Ghost stories ill. by Jeanette Winter. Pantheon, 1978. ISBN 0-394-93933-6 Subj: Ghosts. Mythical creatures – goblins. Witches.

Nadia the willful ill. by Lloyd Bloom. Pantheon, 1983. ISBN 0-394-95265-0 Subj: Character traits – willfulness. Emotions – love. Emotions – sadness. Family life. Foreign lands – Arabia.

One more time, Mama ill. by David Soman. Cavendish, 1999. ISBN 0-7614-5051-3 Subj: Birth. Family life – mothers. Nature.

Peacocks are very special ill. by Victoria Chess. Doubleday, 1976. ISBN 0-385-02169-0 Subj: Animals – jackals. Birds – peacocks, peahens. Character traits – cleverness.

Seymour the prince ill. by Lillian Hoban. Pantheon, 1979. ISBN 0-394-94141-1 Subj: Clubs, gangs. Theater.

Small plays for special days ill. by Tom Huffman. Seabury Pr., 1977. ISBN 0-8164-3184-1 Subj: Holidays. Theater.

Small plays for you and a friend ill. by Olivia Cole. Houghton Mifflin, 1974. ISBN 0-8164-3125-6 Subj: Friendship. Theater.

There's more . . . much more ill. by Patience Brewster. Harcourt, 1987. ISBN 0-15-200605-2 Subj: Animals – squirrels. Seasons – spring.

What's wrong now, Millicent? ill. by David Scott Meier. S&S, 1996. ISBN 0-689-80680-9 Subj: Animals – hippopotamuses. Behavior – dissatisfaction. Friendship.

Who goes out on Halloween? ill. by G. Brian Karas. Bantam, 1990. ISBN 0-553-05891-6 Subj: Holidays – Halloween. Monsters. Mythical creatures – goblins. Rhyming text. Witches.

Witch, Goblin and Ghost are back ill. by Jeanette Winter. Pantheon, 1985. ISBN 0-394-96296-6 Subj: Ghosts. Mythical creatures – goblins. Witches.

Witch, Goblin, and Ghost in the haunted woods ill. by Jeanette Winter. Pantheon, 1981. ISBN 0-394-94443-7 Subj: Ghosts. Mythical creatures – goblins. Witches.

Witch, Goblin and sometimes Ghost ill. by Jeanette Winter. Pantheon, 1976. ISBN 0-394-93216-1 Subj: Behavior – forgetfulness. Emotions – fear. Friendship. Ghosts. Mythical creatures – goblins. Witches.

World famous Muriel ill. by Chris L. Demarest. Little, 1984. ISBN 0-316-03131-3 Subj: Birthdays. Humorous stories. Mystery stories.

World famous Muriel and the magic mystery ill. by Marla Frazee. HarperCollins, 1990. ISBN 0-690-04789-4 Subj: Libraries. Magic. Mystery stories.

World famous Muriel and the scary dragon ill. by Chris L. Demarest. Little, 1985. ISBN 0-316-03134-8 Subj: Dragons. Royalty – kings.

Alger, Leclaire Gowans. *All in the morning early* ill. by Evaline Ness. Holt, 1963. Subj: Caldecott award honor books. Folk & fairy tales. Foreign lands – Scotland. Poetry. Songs.

Always room for one more ill. by Nonny Hogrogian. Holt, 1965. Children's story based on the Scottish ballad of the same title. ISBN 0-8050-0331-2 Subj: Caldecott award books. Cumulative tales. Folk & fairy tales. Foreign lands – Scotland. Homes, houses. Music.

Kellyburn Braes ill. by Evaline Ness. Harcourt, 1968. Subj: Devil. Foreign lands – Scotland. Foreign languages. Music. Poetry. Songs.

Aliki. *Ah, music!* ill. by author. HarperCollins, 2003. ISBN 0-06-028727-6 Subj: Music.

All by myself! ill. by author. HarperCollins, 2000. ISBN 0-06-028930-9 Subj: Activities. Character traits – confidence. Character traits – individuality. Self-concept.

At Mary Bloom's ill. by author. Greenwillow, 1976. ISBN 0-688-84048-8 Subj: Animals – babies. Animals – mice.

Best friends together again ill. by author. Greenwillow, 1995. ISBN 0-688-13754-7 Subj: Friendship. Moving.

Christmas tree memories ill. by author. HarperCollins, 1991. ISBN 0-06-020008-1 Subj: Family life. Holidays – Christmas. Memories, memory. Trees.

Communication ill. by author. Greenwillow, 1993. ISBN 0-688-11248-X Subj: Activities – writing. Language.

Corn is maize: the gift of the Indians ill. by author. Crowell, 1976. ISBN 0-690-00976-3 Subj: Gardens, gardening. Indians of North America. Plants. Science.

Digging up dinosaurs ill. by author. Rev. ed. Crowell, 1988. ISBN 0-690-04716-9 Subj: Activities – digging. Dinosaurs. Humorous stories. Prehistory. Science.

Dinosaur bones ill. by author. HarperCollins, 1988. ISBN 0-690-04550-6 Subj: Dinosaurs. Prehistory.

Dinosaurs are different ill. by author. Crowell, 1985. ISBN 0-690-04458-5 Subj: Dinosaurs. Prehistory. Science.

Diogenes: the story of the Greek philosopher ill. by author. Prentice-Hall, 1969. Subj: Character traits – honesty. Folk & fairy tales. Foreign lands – Greece.

The eggs: a Greek folk tale ill. by adapt. Pantheon, 1969. ISBN 0-06-443385-4 Subj: Behavior – greed. Character traits – cleverness. Folk & fairy tales. Foreign lands – Greece. Humorous stories.

Feelings ill. by author. Greenwillow, 1984. ISBN 0-688-03832-8 Subj: Emotions. Friendship.

Fossils tell of long ago ill. by author. Rev. ed. Crowell, 1990. ISBN 0-690-31379-9 Subj: Dinosaurs. Fossils. Science.

George and the cherry tree ill. by author. Dial, 1964. Subj: Character traits – bravery. Folk & fairy tales. U.S. history.

Hello! Good-bye! ill. by author. Greenwillow, 1996. ISBN 0-688-14334-2 Subj: Language.

How a book is made ill. by author. HarperCollins, 1986. ISBN 0-690-04498-4 Subj: Books, reading. Libraries.

I'm growing! ill. by author. HarperCollins, 1992. ISBN 0-06-020245-9 Subj: Behavior – growing up.

Jack and Jake ill. by author. Greenwillow, 1986. ISBN 0-688-06100-1 Subj: Behavior – mistakes. Character traits – individuality. Family life. Multiple births – twins.

June 7! ill. by author. Macmillan, 1972. Subj: Birthdays. Cumulative tales. Family life.

Keep your mouth closed, dear ill. by author. Dial, 1966. ISBN 0-8037-4418-8 Subj: Behavior – carelessness. Family life. Reptiles – alligators, crocodiles.

The king's day ill. by author. HarperCollins, 1989. ISBN 0-690-04590-5 Subj: Foreign lands – France. Royalty – kings.

The long lost coelacanth and other living fossils ill. by author. Crowell, 1973. ISBN 0-690-50478-0 Subj: Fish. Fossils. Science.

Manners ill. by author. Greenwillow, 1990. ISBN 0-688-09199-7 Subj: Etiquette.

The many lives of Benjamin Franklin ill. by author. S&S, 1988. ISBN 0-671-66119-1 Subj: U.S. history.

Marianthe's story one: painted words; Marianthe's story two: spoken memories ill. by author. Greenwillow, 1998. ISBN 0-688-15662-2 Subj: Family life. Foreign lands. Format, unusual. School.

Milk from cow to carton ill. by author. HarperCollins, 1992. ISBN 0-06-020435-4 Subj: Animals – bulls, cows. Careers – farmers. Food.

Mummies made in Egypt ill. by author. Crowell, 1979. ISBN 0-690-03859-3 Subj: Death. Foreign lands – Egypt. Religion.

My feet ill. by author. HarperCollins, 1990. ISBN 0-690-04815-7 Subj: Anatomy – feet. Science.

My five senses ill. by author. Rev. ed. HarperCollins, 1989. ISBN 0-690-04794-0 Subj: Senses – hearing. Senses – sight. Senses – smell. Senses – taste. Senses – touch.

My hands ill. by author. Rev. ed. Harper, 1992. ISBN 0-06-445096-1 Subj: Anatomy – hands. Science.

My visit to the aquarium ill. by author. HarperCollins, 1993. ISBN 0-06-021459-7 Subj: Animals. Aquariums. Fish. Plants.

My visit to the dinosaurs ill. by author. Rev. ed. Crowell, 1985. ISBN 0-690-04423-2 Subj: Dinosaurs. Museums. Prehistory. Science.

My visit to the zoo ill. by author. HarperCollins, 1997. ISBN 0-06-024943-9 Subj: Animals. Animals – endangered animals. Birds. Ecology. Zoos.

Overnight at Mary Bloom's ill. by author. Greenwillow, 1987. ISBN 0-688-06765-4 Subj: Activities. Activities – playing. Friendship. Night.

The story of Johnny Appleseed ill. by author. S&S, 1988. Reprint. Originally published: Englewood Cliffs, N.J.: Prentice-Hall, c1963. ISBN 0-671-66298-8 Subj: Character traits – generosity. Gardens, gardening. Tall tales. Trees. U.S. history – frontier & pioneer life.

The story of William Penn ill. by author. S&S, 1994. ISBN 0-671-88558-8 Subj: Character traits – kindness. U.S. history.

Tabby ill. by author. HarperCollins, 1995. ISBN 0-06-024916-1 Subj: Animals – cats. Ethnic groups in the U.S. – Hispanic Americans. Wordless.

Those summers ill. by author. HarperCollins, 1996. ISBN 0-06-024938-2 Subj: Family life. Sea & seashore. Seasons – summer.

Three gold pieces: a Greek folk tale ill. by author. Pantheon, 1967. ISBN 0-394-91737-5 Subj: Character traits – luck. Folk & fairy tales. Foreign lands – Greece.

The twelve months ill. by adapt. Greenwillow, 1978. ISBN 0-688-84164-3 Subj: Behavior – dissatisfaction. Character traits – optimism. Folk & fairy tales. Foreign lands – Greece.

The two of them ill. by author. Greenwillow, 1979. ISBN 0-688-84225-9 Subj: Character traits – helpfulness. Character traits – loyalty. Family life – grandfathers.

Use your head, dear ill. by author. Greenwillow, 1983. ISBN 0-688-01812-2 Subj: Behavior – forgetfulness. Birthdays. Reptiles – alligators, crocodiles.

We are best friends ill. by author. Greenwillow, 1982. ISBN 0-688-00823-2 Subj: Emotions – anger. Emotions – loneliness. Friendship. Moving.

A weed is a flower: the life of George Washington Carver ill. by author. S&S, 1988. ISBN 0-671-66118-3 Subj: Character traits – perseverance. Ethnic groups in the U.S. – African Americans. Science. U.S. history.

Welcome, little baby ill. by author. Greenwillow, 1987. ISBN 0-688-06811-1 Subj: Babies. Family life.

Wild and woolly mammoths ill. by author. HarperCollins, 1996. ISBN 0-06-026277-X Subj: Animals. Science.

The wish workers ill. by author. Dial, 1962. Subj: Behavior – dissatisfaction. Behavior – wishing. Birds. Magic.

The all-amazing ha ha book ill. by Max Dann. Oxford Univ. Pr., 1987. ISBN 0-19-554581-8 Subj: Folk & fairy tales. Foreign lands – Australia. Humorous stories. Language.

All night, all day: *a child's first book of African-American spirituals* selected and ill. by Ashley Bryan. Macmillan, 1991. ISBN 0-689-31662-3 Subj: Ethnic groups in the U.S. – African Americans. Music. Musical instruments – guitars. Musical instruments – pianos. Religion. Songs.

All the pretty little horses ill. by Linda Saport. Clarion, 1999. ISBN 0-395-93097-9 Subj: Animals – horses, ponies. Ethnic groups in the U.S. – African Americans. Family life – mothers. Lullabies.

All year round: *a book to benefit children in need* by Lisa Desimini . . . [et al.]; ill. by Lisa Desimini. Scholastic, 1997. Written and illustrated in conjunction with the Robin Hood Foundation to benefit a Women in Need (WIN) shelter for homeless women and children in New York. ISBN 0-590-36097-3 Subj: Poetry. Rhyming text. Seasons.

Allamand, Pascale. *The animals who changed their colors* ill. by Elizabeth Watson Taylor. Morrow, 1979. ISBN 0-688-51900-8 Subj: Animals. Behavior – imitation. Character traits – individuality. Concepts – color. Humorous stories.

The camel who left the zoo ill. by author; English version by Michael Bullock. Scribners, 1976. ISBN 0-684-14824-2 Subj: Animals. Behavior – running away. Zoos.

Cocoa beans and daisies: how Swiss chocolate is made photos by author. Warne, 1978. ISBN 0-7232-6156-3 Subj: Food. Foreign lands – Switzerland.

The little goat in the mountains trans. by Michael Bullock; ill. by author. Warne, 1978. ISBN 0-7232-6149-0 Subj: Animals – goats.

The pop rooster ill. by author; English version by Michael Bullock. Scribners, 1975. ISBN 0-224-01113-8 Subj: Activities – singing. Birds – chickens. Cities, towns.

Allan, Nicholas. *The bird* ill. by author. Doubleday, 1998. ISBN 0-385-32573-8 Subj: Behavior – sharing. Birds – pigeons. Emotions – loneliness. Islands. Religion – Noah.

Jesus' Christmas party ill. by author. Random House, 1991. ISBN 0-679-82688-2 Subj: Holidays – Christmas. Religion – Nativity.

The thing that ate Aunt Julia ill. by author. Dial, 1991. ISBN 0-8037-0872-6 Subj: Family life – aunts, uncles. Imagination.

Where Willy went ill. by author. Knopf, 2005. ISBN 0-375-93030-2 Subj: Sex instruction.

Allancé, Mireille d'. *How long?* ill. by Alan Marks. Orchard, 1998. ISBN 0-689-83826-3 Subj: Animals – dormice. Emotions – love. Family life – mothers. Time.

Allard, Harry. *Bumps in the night* ill. by James Marshall. Doubleday, 1979. ISBN 0-385-12943-2 Subj: Animals. Ghosts. Noise, sounds.

The cactus flower bakery ill. by Ned Delaney. HarperCollins, 1991. ISBN 0-06-020047-2 Subj: Animals – armadillos. Careers – bakers. Food. Friendship. Reptiles – snakes.

Crash helmet ill. by Jean-Claude Suarès. Prentice-Hall, 1977. ISBN 0-13-188961-3 Subj: Birds – vultures. Emotions – loneliness. Mummies.

The hummingbirds' day ill. by Betsy Lewin. Houghton Mifflin, 1991. ISBN 0-395-55029-7 Subj: Birds – humming birds. Rhyming text.

I will not go to market today ill. by James Marshall. Dial, 1979. ISBN 0-8037-4020-4 Subj: Birds – chickens. Shopping.

It's so nice to have a wolf around the house ill. by James Marshall. Doubleday, 1977. ISBN 0-385-11301-3 Subj: Crime. Old age. Pets.

May I stay? ill. by F. A. Fitzgerald. Prentice-Hall, 1977. ISBN 0-13-566323-7 Subj: Character traits – questioning. Folk & fairy tales. Foreign lands – Germany. Foreign lands – Norway.

Miss Nelson has a field day ill. by James Marshall. Houghton Mifflin, 1985. ISBN 0-395-36690-9 Subj: Behavior – secrets. Humorous stories. School – field trips.

Miss Nelson is back by Harry Allard & James Marshall; ill. by James Marshall. Houghton Mifflin, 1982. ISBN 0-395-32956-6 Subj: Behavior – misbehavior. Careers – teachers. Humorous stories. School.

Miss Nelson is missing! by Harry Allard & James Marshall; ill. by James Marshall. Houghton Mifflin, 1977. ISBN 0-395-25296-2 Subj: Behavior – misbehavior. Careers – teachers. Humorous stories. School.

The Stupids die ill. by James Marshall. Houghton Mifflin, 1981. ISBN 0-395-30347-8 Subj: Behavior – misunderstanding. Humorous stories.

The Stupids have a ball by Harry Allard & James Marshall; ill. by James Marshall. Houghton Mifflin, 1978. ISBN 0-395-26497-9 Subj: Family life. Humorous stories. Parties.

The Stupids step out ill. by James Marshall. Houghton Mifflin, 1974. ISBN 0-395-18513-0 Subj: Activities. Family life. Humorous stories.

The Stupids take off by Harry Allard & James Marshall; ill. by James Marshall. Houghton Mifflin, 1989. ISBN 0-395-50068-0 Subj: Activities – flying. Family life. Humorous stories.

There's a party at Mona's tonight ill. by James Marshall. Double-day, 1981. ISBN 0-385-15186-1 Subj: Animals – pigs. Behavior – trickery. Humorous stories. Parties.

Three is company (Waechter, Friedrich Karl)

Allbright, Viv. *Ten go hopping* ill. by author. Faber, 1985. ISBN 0-571-13473-4 Subj: Counting, numbers. Cumulative tales.

Allchin, Rosalind. *The frog princess* ill. by author. Kids Can, 2001. ISBN 1-55337-000-7 Subj: Frogs & toads. Royalty – princes. Royalty – princesses.

Allen, Alex B. *see* Heide, Florence Parry

Allen, Allyn. *see* Eberle, Irmengarde

Allen, Debbie. *Brothers of the knight* ill. by Kadir Nelson. Dial, 1999. ISBN 0-8037-2488-8 Subj: Activities – dancing. Family life – brothers. Folk & fairy tales. Foreign lands – Germany.

Dancing in the wings ill. by Kadir Nelson. Dial, 2000. ISBN 0-8037-2501-9 Subj: Activities – dancing. Ballet. Ethnic groups in the U.S. – African Americans.

Allen, Frances Charlotte. *Little hippo* ill. by Laura Jean Allen. Putnam, 1971. Subj: Animals – hippopotamuses. Emotions – sadness.

Allen, Gertrude E. *Everyday animals* ill. by author. Houghton Mifflin, 1961. Subj: Animals. Forest, woods. Science.

Allen, Jeffrey. *Bonzini! the tattooed man* ill. by James Marshall. Little, 1976. ISBN 0-316-03427-4 Subj: Circus. Clowns, jesters.

Mary Alice, operator number 9 ill. by James Marshall. Little, 1975. ISBN 0-316-03425-8 Subj: Activities – working. Animals. Birds – ducks. Careers – telephone operators. Telephone. Time.

Mary Alice returns ill. by James Marshall. Little, 1986. ISBN 0-316-03429-0 Subj: Birds – ducks. Careers – telephone operators. Telephone.

Nosey Mrs. Rat ill. by James Marshall. Viking, 1985. ISBN 0-670-80880-6 Subj: Animals. Behavior – gossip. Character traits – curiosity.

The secret life of Mr. Weird ill. by Ned Delaney. Little, 1982. ISBN 0-316-03428-2 Subj: Animals – dogs. Behavior – dissatisfaction. Behavior – seeking better things. Games. Imagination.

Up the steps, down the slide ill. by author. Tambourine, 1992. ISBN 0-688-11784-8 Subj: Animals – cats. Concepts – opposites. Rhyming text.

Allen, Jonathan. *A bad case of animal nonsense* ill. by author. Godine, 1997. ISBN 1-567-92083-7 Subj: Animals. Humorous stories. Poetry.

Big owl, little towel ill. by author. Tambourine, 1992. ISBN 0-688-11783-X Subj: Concepts – size. Format, unusual – board books. Rhyming text.

Mucky moose ill. by author. Macmillan, 1991. ISBN 0-02-700251-9 Subj: Animals – moose. Animals – wolves. Character traits – cleanliness. Senses – smell.

My cat ill. by author. Dial, 1986. ISBN 0-8037-0292-2 Subj: Animals – cats. Pets.

My dog ill. by author. G. Stevens, 1989. ISBN 0-8368-0095-8 Subj: Animals – dogs. Pets.

One with a bun ill. by author. Tambourine, 1992. ISBN 0-688-11781-3 Subj: Counting, numbers. Format, unusual – board books. Rhyming text.

Purple sock, pink sock ill. by author. Tambourine, 1992. ISBN 0-688-11782-1 Subj: Animals – cats. Clothing. Concepts – color. Format, unusual – board books. Rhyming text.

Two by two by two ill. by author. Dial, 1995. ISBN 0-8037-1838-1 Subj: Animals. Behavior – sharing. Boats, ships. Religion – Noah.

Wake up, Sleeping Beauty ill. by author. Dial, 1997. ISBN 0-8037-2212-5 Subj: Fairies. Folk & fairy tales. Royalty – princes. Royalty – princesses. Sleep. Witches.

Who's at the door? (The three little pigs)

Allen, Judy. *Are you a butterfly?* by Judy Allen & Tudor Humphries; ill. by Tudor Humphries. Kingfisher, 2000. ISBN 0-75345-240-5 Subj: Insects – butterflies, caterpillars. Science.

Are you a grasshopper? by Judy Allen & Tudor Humphries; ill. by Tudor Humphries. Kingfisher, 2002. ISBN 0-75345-366-5 Subj: Insects – grasshoppers. Science.

Are you a ladybug? by Judy Allen & Tudor Humphries; ill. by Tudor Humphries. Kingfisher, 2000. ISBN 0-75345-241-3 Subj: Insects – ladybugs. Science.

Are you a snail? by Judy Allen & Tudor Humphries; ill. by Tudor Humphries. Kingfisher, 2000. ISBN 0-75345-242-1 Subj: Animals – snails. Science.

Are you an ant? by Judy Allen & Tudor Humphries; ill. by Tudor Humphries. Kingfisher, 2002. ISBN 0-75345-365-7 Subj: Insects – ants. Science.

Eagle ill. by Tudor Humphries. Candlewick, 1994. ISBN 1-56402-143-2 Subj: Animals – endangered animals. Birds – eagles. Foreign lands – Philippines. Jungle.

Elephant ill. by Tudor Humphries. Candlewick, 1993. ISBN 1-56402-069-X Subj: Animals – elephants. Animals – endangered animals. Foreign lands – Africa.

Panda ill. by Tudor Humphries. Candlewick, 1993. ISBN 1-56402-142-4 Subj: Animals – endangered animals. Animals – pandas. Foreign lands – China.

Seal ill. by Tudor Humphries. Candlewick, 1994. ISBN 1-56402-145-9 Subj: Animals – endangered animals. Animals – seals. Ecology. Foreign lands – Greece.

Tiger ill. by Tudor Humphries. Candlewick, 1992. ISBN 1-56402-083-5 Subj: Animals – endangered animals. Animals – tigers. Foreign lands – China. Sports – hunting.

Whale ill. by Tudor Humphries. Candlewick, 1993. ISBN 1-56402-160-2 Subj: Animals – endangered animals. Animals – whales. Ecology.

What is a wall, after all? ill. by Alan Baron. Candlewick, 1995. ISBN 1-56402-248-8 Subj: Concepts. Rhyming text.

Allen, Laura Jean. *Ottie and the star* ill. by author. HarperCollins, 1979. ISBN 0-06-020108-8 Subj: Animals – otters. Family life. Sea & seashore. Stars.

Rollo and Tweedy and the case of the missing cheese ill. by author. HarperCollins, 1983. ISBN 0-06-020097-9 Subj: Animals – mice. Careers – detectives. Food. Foreign lands – France. Mystery stories.

Rollo and Tweedy and the ghost of Dougal Castle ill. by author. HarperCollins, 1992. ISBN 0-06-020107-X Subj: Careers – detectives. Castles. Ghosts. Mystery stories.

Where is Freddy? ill. by author. HarperCollins, 1986. ISBN 0-06-020099-5 Subj: Activities – flying. Behavior – lost. Careers – detectives. Mystery stories.

Allen, Linda. *The giant who had no heart* ill. by author. Philomel, 1988. ISBN 0-399-21446-1 Subj: Folk & fairy tales. Foreign lands – Norway. Giants.

Mr. Simkin's grandma ill. by Loretta Lustig. Morrow, 1979. ISBN 0-688-32191-7 Subj: Family life – grandmothers. Family life – grandparents. Humorous stories.

The mouse bride ill. by author. Putnam, 1992. ISBN 0-399-22136-0 Subj: Animals – mice. Folk & fairy tales. Foreign lands – Finland. Royalty – princesses.

Mrs. Simkin's bed ill. by Loretta Lustig. Morrow, 1980. ISBN 0-688-32233-6 Subj: Animals. Furniture – beds. Humorous stories.

Allen, Marjorie N. *Changes* by Marjorie N. Allen & Shelley Rotner; photos by Shelley Rotner. Macmillan, 1991. ISBN 0-02-700252-7 Subj: Nature. Rhyming text.

One, two, three – ah-choo! ill. by Dick Gackenbach. Coward, 1980. ISBN 0-698-30718-6 Subj: Animals. Humorous stories. Pets.

Allen, Martha Dickson. *Real life monsters* ill. by author. Prentice-Hall, 1979. ISBN 0-13-766568-7 Subj: Animals. Monsters. Science.

Allen, Pamela. *Belinda* ill. by author. Viking, 1992. ISBN 0-670-84372-5 Subj: Animals – bulls, cows. Careers – farmers.

Bertie and the bear ill. by author. Coward, 1984. ISBN 0-698-20600-2 Subj: Activities – dancing. Animals – bears. Animals – dogs. Noise, sounds. Royalty.

Fancy that! ill. by author. Orchard, 1988. ISBN 0-531-08363-2 Subj: Birds – chickens. Farms.

Hidden treasure ill. by author. Putnam, 1987. Orig. published as Herbert and Harry. ISBN 0-399-21427-5 Subj: Behavior – greed. Behavior – hiding things. Sea & seashore. Sibling rivalry.

I wish I had a pirate suit ill. by author. Viking, 1990. ISBN 0-670-82475-5 Subj: Activities – playing. Behavior – wishing. Imagination. Pirates.

A lion in the night ill. by author. Putnam, 1986. ISBN 0-399-21203-5 Subj: Animals – lions. Babies. Behavior – wishing. Imagination. Royalty.

Mr. Archimedes' bath ill. by author. Lothrop, 1980. ISBN 0-688-51919-9 Subj: Activities – bathing. Animals. Humorous stories. Science.

Mr. McGee ill. by author. Nelson, 1987. ISBN 0-17-006908-7 Subj: Humorous stories. Rhyming text.

My cat Maisie ill. by author. Viking, 1991. ISBN 0-670-83251-0 Subj: Animals – cats. Friendship. Pets.

Who sank the boat? ill. by author. Coward, 1983. ISBN 0-698-20576-6 Subj: Animals. Boats, ships. Rhyming text. Science.

Allen, Robert. *Numbers: a first counting book* photos by Mottke Weissman. Platt, 1968. Subj: Counting, numbers.

Round and square ill. by Philippe Thomas. Platt, 1965. Subj: Concepts – shape.

Ten little babies count by Janet Martin [pseud.]; photos by Michael Watson. St. Martin's, 1986. ISBN 0-312-79112-7 Subj: Babies. Clothing. Counting, numbers. Family life – new sibling. Format, unusual – board books.

Ten little babies dress by Janet Martin [pseud.]; photos by Michael Watson. St. Martin's, 1986. ISBN 0-312-79113-5 Subj: Babies. Clothing. Counting, numbers. Format, unusual – board books.

Ten little babies eat by Janet Martin [pseud.]; photos by Michael Watson. St. Martin's, 1986. ISBN 0-312-79114-3 Subj: Anatomy. Babies. Counting, numbers. Food. Format, unusual – board books. Rhyming text.

Ten little babies play: a book of colors by Janet Martin [pseud.]; photos by Michael Watson. St. Martin's, 1986. ISBN 0-312-79115-1 Subj: Activities – playing. Babies. Concepts – color. Counting, numbers. Format, unusual – board books.

The zoo book: a child's world of animals photos by Peter Sahula. Platt, 1968. Subj: Animals. Zoos.

Allen, Susan. *Read anything good lately?* by Susan Allen & Jane Lindaman; ill. by Vicky Enright. Millbrook, 2003. ISBN 0-7613-2322-8 Subj: ABC books. Books, reading. Language.

Allen, Thomas B. (Thomas Burt). *On grandaddy's farm* ill. by author. Knopf, 1989. ISBN 0-394-99613-5 Subj: Family life. Farms.

Where children live ill. by author. Prentice-Hall, 1980. ISBN 0-13-957126-4 Subj: Foreign lands.

Allende, Ricardo. *Princesa and Friskie* (Johnson, Diana F.)

Aller, Susan B. *Emma and the night dogs* ill. by Marni Backer. A. Whitman, 1997. ISBN 0-8075-1993-6 Subj: Animals – dogs. Behavior – lost. Character traits – helpfulness.

Alley, R. W. (Robert W.). *Seven fables from Æsop* (Æsop)

There once was a witch ill. by author. HarperFestival, 2003. ISBN 0-06-000795-8 Subj: Format, unusual – board books. Holidays – Halloween. Music. Songs. Witches.

Alleyne, Ellen. *see* Rossetti, Christina Georgina

Allingham, William. *The fairies* ill. by Michael Hague. Holt, 1989. ISBN 0-8050-1003-3 Subj: Fairies. Poetry.

Allington, Richard L. *Autumn* by Richard L. Allington & Kathleen Krull; ill. by Bruce Bond. Raintree, 1985. ISBN 0-8172-1343-0 Subj: Seasons – fall. Weather.

Colors ill. by Noel Spangler. Raintree, 1985. ISBN 0-8172-1280-9 Subj: Concepts – color.

Feelings by Richard L. Allington & Kathleen Cowles; ill. by Brian Cody. Raintree, 1985. ISBN 0-8172-1295-7 Subj: Activities. Emotions.

Hearing by Richard L. Allington & Kathleen Cowles; ill. by Wayne Dober. Raintree, 1985. ISBN 0-8172-1291-4 Subj: Activities. Senses – hearing.

Letters ill. by Tom Garcia. Raintree, 1985. ISBN 0-8172-1384-8 Subj: ABC books. Games. Language.

Looking by Richard L. Allington & Kathleen Cowles; ill. by Bill Bober. Raintree, 1981. ISBN 0-8172-1290-6 Subj: Activities. Senses – sight.

Measuring by Richard L. Allington & Kathleen Krull; ill. by Noel Spangler. Raintree, 1985. ISBN 0-8172-1389-9 Subj: Concepts – measurement.

Numbers ill. by Tom Garcia. Raintree, 1985. ISBN 0-8172-1278-7 Subj: Counting, numbers.

Opposites ill. by Eulala Conner. Raintree, 1985. ISBN 0-8172-1279-5 Subj: Concepts – opposites.

Reading by Richard L. Allington & Kathleen Krull; ill. by Joel Naprstek. Raintree, 1985. ISBN 0-8172-1322-8 Subj: Books, reading.

Science by Richard L. Allington & Kathleen Krull; ill. by James Teason. Raintree, 1985. ISBN 0-8172-1387-2 Subj: Science.

Shapes ill. by Lois Ehlert. Raintree, 1985. ISBN 0-8172-1277-9 Subj: Concepts – shape. Concepts – size.

Smelling by Richard L. Allington & Kathleen Cowles; ill. by Rick Thrun. Raintree, 1981. ISBN 0-8172-1293-0 Subj: Activities. Senses – smell.

Spring by Richard L. Allington & Kathleen Krull; ill. by Lynn Uhde. Raintree, 1981. ISBN 0-8172-1342-2 Subj: Seasons – spring. Weather.

Summer by Richard L. Allington & Kathleen Krull; ill. by Dennis Hockerman. Raintree, 1985. ISBN 0-8172-1341-4 Subj: Seasons – summer. Weather.

Talking by Richard L. Allington & Kathleen Krull; ill. by Rick Thrun. Raintree, 1985. ISBN 0-8172-2492-0 Subj: Communication. Language. Science.

Tasting by Richard L. Allington & Kathleen Cowles; ill. by Noel Spangler. Raintree, 1985. ISBN 0-8172-1292-2 Subj: Activities. Senses – taste.

Thinking by Richard L. Allington & Kathleen Krull; ill. by Tom Garcia. Raintree, 1985. ISBN 0-8172-1319-8 Subj: Problem solving.

Time by Richard L. Allington & Kathleen Krull; ill. by Yoshi Miyake. Raintree, 1985. ISBN 0-8172-1388-0 Subj: Time.

Touching by Richard L. Allington & Kathleen Cowles; ill. by Yoshi Miyake. Raintree, 1985. ISBN 0-8172-1294-9 Subj: Activities. Senses – touch.

Winter by Richard L. Allington & Kathleen Krull; ill. by John Wallner. Raintree, 1985. ISBN 0-8172-1340-6 Subj: Seasons – winter. Weather.

Words by Richard L. Allington & Kathleen Krull; ill. by Ray Cruz. Raintree, 1982. ISBN 0-8172-1385-6 Subj: Communication. Language.

Writing by Richard L. Allington & Kathleen Krull; ill. by Yoshi Miyake. Raintree, 1985. ISBN 0-8175-1321-X Subj: Activities – writing.

Allinson, Beverley. *Effie* ill. by Barbara Reid. Scholastic, 1991. ISBN 0-590-44045-4 Subj: Animals – elephants. Character traits – being different. Friendship. Insects – ants.

Allison, Alida. *The toddler's potty book* by Alida Allison & Paula Sapphire. Price Stern Sloan, 1981, 1979. ISBN 0-8431-0673-5 Subj: Behavior – growing up. Toilet training.

Allison, Catherine. *Brown paper bear* ill. by Neil Reed. Scholastic, 2004. ISBN 0-439-63900-X Subj: Toys – bears.

Allison, Diane Worfolk. *In window eight, the moon is late* ill. by author. Little, 1988. ISBN 0-316-03435-5 Subj: Bedtime. Dreams. Rhyming text.

This is the key to the kingdom ill. by reteller. Little, 1992. ISBN 0-316-03432-0 Subj: Ethnic groups in the U.S. – African Americans. Flowers. Nursery rhymes.

Allred, Mary. *Grandmother Poppy and the children's tea party* ill. by Paul Behrens. Broadman & Holman, 1984. ISBN 0-8054-4292-8 Subj: Family life – grandmothers. Parties.

Grandmother Poppy and the funny-looking bird ill. by Paul Behrens. Broadman & Holman, 1981. ISBN 0-8054-4269-3 Subj: Birds. Character traits – kindness to animals. Family life – grandmothers.

Alper, Ann Fitzerald. *Harry McNairy, Tooth Fairy* ill. by Bridget Starr Taylor. A. Whitman, 1998. ISBN 0-8075-3166-9 Subj: Fairies. Teeth.

Alphabestiary: animal poems from A to Z sel. by Jane Yolen; ill. by Allen Eitzen. Boyds Mills, 1995. ISBN 1-56397-222-0 Subj: Animals. Poetry.

Alphaus, N. Y. *see* Rubin, Cynthia Elyce

Alphin, Elaine Marie. *Dinosaur hunter* ill. by Don Bolognese. HarperCollins, 2003. ISBN 0-06-028304-1 Subj: Dinosaurs. Fossils.

Alrawi, Karim. *The girl who lost her smile* ill. by Czernecki, Stefan. Winslow, 2000. ISBN 1-890817-17-1 Subj: Emotions. Foreign lands – Iraq.

Alter, Anna. *Estelle and Lucy* ill. by author. Greenwillow, 2001. ISBN 0-688-17883-9 Subj: Animals – cats. Animals – mice. Concepts – size. Family life – sisters. Sibling rivalry.

Althea. *Castle life* ill. by Maureen Galvani. Merrimack, 1980. Subj: Middle Ages.

Jeremy Mouse and cat ill. by author. Merrimack, 1980. ISBN 0-8659-2562-3 Subj: Animals – cats. Animals – mice. Behavior – trickery.

Altman, Linda Jacobs. *Amelia's road* ill. by Enrique O. Sánchez. Lee & Low, 1993. ISBN 1-880000-04-0 Subj: Activities – working. Behavior – seeking better things. Careers – migrant workers. Family life. Homes, houses. Trees.

The legend of Freedom Hill ill. by Cornelius Van Wright & Ying-Hwa Hu. Lee & Low, 2000. ISBN 1-58430-003-5 Subj: Ethnic groups in the U.S. – African Americans. Slavery. U.S. history – frontier & pioneer life.

Singing with Momma Lou ill. by author. Lee & Low, 2002. ISBN 1-58430-040-X Subj: Ethnic groups in the U.S. – African Americans. Family life – grandmothers. Illness – Alzheimer's. Old age.

Altman, Susan. *Followers of the north star: rhymes about African American heroes, heroines, and historical times* by Susan Altman & Susan Lechner; ill. by Byron Wooden. Childrens Pr., 1993. ISBN 0-516-05151-2 Subj: Ethnic groups in the U.S. – African Americans. Poetry. U.S. history.

Alvarez, Julia. *The secret footprints* ill. by Fabian Negrin. Knopf, 2000. ISBN 0-679-99309-6 Subj: Folk & fairy tales. Foreign lands – Dominican Republic. Indians of Central America – Taino.

Amado, Elisa. *Trees are hanging from the sky* (Argueta, Jorge)

Amazing graces: prayers and poems for children comp. by June Cotner; ill. by Jan Palmer. HarperCollins, 2001. ISBN 0-688-15567-7 Subj: Poetry. Religion.

Ambler, C. Gifford (Christopher Gifford). *Ten little foxhounds* ill. by author. Childrens Pr., 1968. Subj: Animals – dogs. Counting, numbers. Foreign lands – England. Rhyming text.

Ambrus, Gyozo Laszlo. *see* Ambrus, Victor G.

Ambrus, Victor G. *Brave soldier Janosch* ill. by author. Harcourt, 1967. Subj: Careers – military. Foreign lands – Hungary. War.

Count, Dracula ill. by author. Crown, 1992. ISBN 0-517-58969-9 Subj: Counting, numbers. Monsters. Pets.

Country wedding ill. by author. Addison-Wesley, 1975. ISBN 0-20-100197-7 Subj: Animals – foxes. Animals – wolves. Food. Weddings.

Grandma, Felix, and Mustapha Biscuit ill. by author. Morrow, 1982. ISBN 0-688-01287-6 Subj: Animals – cats. Animals – hamsters. Family life – grandmothers. Humorous stories.

The little cockerel ill. by author. Harcourt, 1968. Subj: Birds – chickens. Character traits – perseverance. Folk & fairy tales.

Mishka ill. by author. Warne, 1978. ISBN 0-7232-6150-4 Subj: Animals – elephants. Character traits – perseverance. Circus. Music. Musical instruments – violins.

Never laugh at bears: a Transylvanian folk tale ill. by author. Peter Bedrick, 1992. ISBN 0-8722-6465-3 Subj: Animals – bears. Careers – farmers. Folk & fairy tales.

Santa Claus takes off ill. by Glenys Ambrus. Oxford Univ. Pr., 1991. ISBN 0-19-279878-2 Subj: Holidays – Christmas. Santa Claus.

The seven skinny goats ill. by author. Harcourt, 1969. Subj: Activities – dancing. Animals – goats. Folk & fairy tales. Music.

Son of Dracula ill. by author. Oxford Univ. Pr., 1990. ISBN 0-19-279813-8 Subj: Family life – sons. Monsters. School.

The Sultan's bath ill. by author. Oxford Univ. Pr., 1971. ISBN 0-1927-9677-1 Subj: Activities – bathing. Folk & fairy tales. Foreign lands – India. Royalty – sultans.

The three poor tailors ill. by author. Harcourt, 1966. Subj: Activities – whistling. Animals – goats. Careers – tailors. Folk & fairy tales. Foreign lands – Hungary. Poverty.

What's the time, Dracula? ill. by author. Crown, 1992. ISBN 0-517-58970-2 Subj: Careers – dentists. Clocks, watches. Monsters. Time.

Amenta, Charles A. (Charles Anthony). *Russell is extra special: a book about autism for children* written & ill. by Charles A. Amenta III. Magination Pr., 1992. ISBN 0-94535-443-6 Subj: Handicaps – autism.

Amery, H. *At the zoo* ill. by author. Educational Development, 1984. ISBN 0-86020-854-0 Subj: Animals. Zoos.

The farm picture book ill. by author. Educational Development, 1988. ISBN 0-7460-0128-2 Subj: Animals. Farms.

Going to the fair ill. by author. Educational Development, 1987. ISBN 0-88110-262-8 Subj: Fairs, festivals.

Goldilocks and the three bears (The three bears)

The three little pigs (The three little pigs)

The zoo picture book ill. by author. Educational Development, 1988. ISBN 0-7460-0127-4 Subj: Animals. Format, unusual. Zoos.

Ames, Mildred. *The wonderful box* ill. by Richard Cuffari. Dutton, 1978. ISBN 0-525-43200-0 Subj: Character traits – curiosity. Problem solving.

Ames, Rose. *see* Wyler, Rose

Ammon, Richard. *An Amish Christmas* ill. by Pamela Patrick. Atheneum, 1996. ISBN 0-689-80377-X Subj: Ethnic groups in the U.S. – Amish. Holidays – Christmas. Religion.

Amish horses ill. by Pamela Patrick. Atheneum, 2001. ISBN 0-689-82623-0 Subj: Animals – horses, ponies. Ethnic groups in the U.S. – Amish. Farms.

An Amish wedding ill. by Pamela Patrick. Atheneum, 1998. ISBN 0-689-81677-4 Subj: Ethnic groups in the U.S. – Amish. Weddings.

An Amish year ill. by Pamela Patrick. Atheneum, 2000. ISBN 0-689-82622-2 Subj: Ethnic groups in the U.S. – Amish. Seasons.

Trains at work photos by Darrell Peterson & Richard Ammon. Atheneum, 1993. ISBN 0-689-31740-9 Subj: Trains.

Amoit, Pierre. *Bijou, the little bear* ill. by author. Coward, 1950. Subj: Animals – bears. Circus. Clowns, jesters.

Amoore, Susannah. *Motley the cat* ill. by Mary Fedden. Viking, 1997. ISBN 0-670-87730-1 Subj: Animals – cats. Mystery stories.

Amoss, Berthe. *It's not your birthday* ill. by author. HarperCollins, 1966. Subj: Birthdays. Sibling rivalry.

Old Hannibal and the hurricane ill. by author. Walt Disney, 1991. ISBN 1-56282-098-2 Subj: Boats, ships. Sea & seashore. Weather – storms.

Tom in the middle ill. by author. HarperCollins, 1988. ISBN 0-06-020064-2 Subj: Family life – brothers. Sibling rivalry.

What did you lose, Santa? ill. by author. HarperCollins, 1987. ISBN 0-694-00197-X Subj: Behavior – lost & found possessions. Holidays – Christmas. Santa Claus.

Amper, Thomas. *Booker T. Washington* ill. by Jeni Reeves. Carolrhoda, 1998. ISBN 1-57505-094-3 Subj: Careers – teachers. Ethnic groups in the U.S. – African Americans. School.

Amsden, Janet. *Grizzly Pete and the ghosts* ill. by John Beder. Annick, 2002. ISBN 1-55037-719-1 Subj: Careers – miners. Ghosts. U.S. history – frontier & pioneer life.

Amusing moments in the wild: animals and their friends ill. with photos. Moonstone, 2001. ISBN 0-9707768-3-7 Subj: Animals.

Anastas, Margaret. *A hug for you* ill. by Susan Winter. HarperCollins, 2005. ISBN 0-06-623614-2 Subj: Animals. Birds – ducks. Emotions – love. Family life – parents. Friendship. Insects. Rhyming text.

Mommy's best kisses ill. by Susan Winter. HarperCollins, 2003. ISBN 0-06-623606-1 Subj: Animals. Emotions – love. Family life – mothers. Rhyming text.

Anastasio, Dina. *Baby Piggy and giant bubble* ill. by Tom Cooke. Muppet Pr., 1986. ISBN 0-8713-5096-3 Subj: Bubbles. Imagination. Puppets. Rhyming text.

Pass the peas, please: a book of manners ill. by Katy Keck Arnsteen. Warner, 1988. ISBN 1-55782-021-X Subj: Etiquette. Rhyming text.

Anawalt, Paula Bonnier. *The crystal palace* ill. by author. Abongold, 1997. ISBN 0-9668414-0-9 Subj: Behavior – wishing. Bubbles. Castles. Northern lights. Rhyming text.

Anaya, Rudolfo A. *Farolitos for Abuelo* ill. by Edward Gonzales. Hyperion, 1998. ISBN 0-7868-2186-8 Subj: Death. Ethnic groups in the U.S. – Mexican Americans. Family life – grandfathers. Holidays – Christmas.

Maya's children: the story of La Llorona ill. by Maria Baca. Hyperion, 1997. ISBN 0-7868-2124-8 Subj: Folk & fairy tales. Foreign lands – Central America. Foreign lands – Mexico.

Roadrunner's dance ill. by David Diaz. Hyperion, 2000. ISBN 0-7868-2209-0 Subj: Animals. Behavior – bullying. Birds – roadrunners. Creation. Desert. Reptiles – snakes.

Anchondo, Mary. *How we came to the fifth world: a creation story from Ancient Mexico* (Rohmer, Harriet)

Ancona, George. *Barrio: José's neighborhood* ill. by author. Harcourt, 1998. ISBN 0-15-201049-1 Subj: Communities, neighborhoods. Ethnic groups in the U.S. – Hispanic Americans.

Dancing is ill. by author. Dutton, 1981. ISBN 0-525-28490-7 Subj: Activities – dancing.

Handtalk: an ABC of finger spelling and sign language (Charlip, Remy)

Handtalk zoo by George & Mary Beth Ancona; photos by George Ancona. Macmillan, 1989. ISBN 0-02-700801-0 Subj: Animals. Communication. Handicaps – deafness. Language. Senses – hearing. Time. Zoos.

Helping out photos by author. Clarion, 1985. ISBN 0-89919-278-5 Subj: Character traits – helpfulness.

I feel: a picture book of emotions ill. by author. Dutton, 1977. ISBN 0-525-32525-5 Subj: Emotions.

It's a baby! ill. by author. Dutton, 1979. ISBN 0-525-32598-0 Subj: Babies.

Let's dance! ill. by author. Morrow, 1998. ISBN 0-688-16212-6 Subj: Activities – dancing.

Pablo remembers: the fiesta of the Day of the Dead ill. by author. Lothrop, 1993. ISBN 0-688-11250-1 Subj: Fairs, festivals. Foreign lands – Mexico. Holidays – Day of the Dead.

Ricardo's day photos by author. Scholastic, 1995. ISBN 0-590-29257-9 Subj: School.

Ancona, Mary Beth. *Handtalk: an ABC of finger spelling and sign language* (Charlip, Remy)

Handtalk zoo (Ancona, George)

Anders, Rebecca. *A look at death* photos by Maria S. Forrai; foreword by Robert C. Slater. Lerner, 1978. ISBN 0-822-51308-0 Subj: Death.

A look at prejudice and understanding ill. by Maria S. Forrai. Lerner, 1976. ISBN 0-8225-1306-4 Subj: Prejudice.

Andersen, H. C. (Hans Christian). *The dinosaur's new clothes* (Goode, Diane)

The emperor and the nightingale retold & ill. by Meilo So. Bradbury, 1992. ISBN 0-02-786045-0 Subj: Birds – nightingales. Character traits – freedom. Folk & fairy tales. Foreign lands – China.

The emperor and the nightingale ill. by James Watling. Troll, 1979. ISBN 0-89375-112-X Subj: Birds – nightingales. Character traits – freedom. Folk & fairy tales. Foreign lands – China.

The emperor's new clothes ill. by Angela Barrett. Candlewick, 1997. ISBN 0-7636-0119-5 Subj: Character traits – pride. Character traits – vanity. Clothing. Folk & fairy tales. Imagination. Royalty – emperors.

The emperor's new clothes ill. by Erik Blegvad. Harcourt, 1959. Translation of Kejserens nye klæder by Erik Blegvad. Subj: Character traits – pride. Character traits – vanity. Clothing. Folk & fairy tales. Humorous stories. Imagination. Royalty – emperors.

The emperor's new clothes ill. by Virginia Lee Burton. Houghton Mifflin, 2004, 1949. Translation of Kejserens nye klæder. ISBN 0-618-34420-9 Subj: Character traits – pride. Character traits – vanity. Clothing. Folk & fairy tales. Humorous stories. Imagination. Royalty – emperors.

The emperor's new clothes retold by Riki Levinson; ill. by Robert Byrd. Dutton, 1991. ISBN 0-525-44611-7 Subj: Animals. Character traits – pride. Character traits – vanity. Clothing. Folk & fairy tales. Humorous stories. Imagination. Royalty – emperors.

The emperor's new clothes adapt. by Susan Blackaby; ill. by Charlene DeLage. Picture Window, 2004. ISBN 1-4048-0224-X Subj: Character traits – pride. Character traits – vanity. Clothing. Folk & fairy tales. Humorous stories. Imagination. Royalty – emperors.

The emperor's new clothes adapt. by Jean Van Leeuwen; ill. by Jack & Irene Delano. Random House, 1971. Translation of Kejserens nye klæder. Text adapted from Hans Christian Andersen and other sources by Jean Van Leeuwen. ISBN 0-394-82105-4 Subj: Character traits – pride. Character traits – vanity. Clothing. Folk & fairy tales. Humorous stories. Imagination. Royalty – emperors.

The emperor's new clothes: a tale set in China retold & ill. by Demi. McElderry, 2000. ISBN 0-689-83068-8 Subj: Character traits – pride. Character traits – vanity. Clothing. Folk & fairy tales. Foreign lands – China. Humorous stories. Royalty – emperors.

The emperor's new clothes ill. by Hélène Desputeaux. Gallery Books, 1984. ISBN 0-8317-2736-5 Subj: Character traits – pride. Character traits – vanity. Clothing. Folk & fairy tales. Humorous stories. Imagination. Royalty – emperors.

The emperor's new clothes ill. by Birte Dietz; trans. by M. R. James; adapt. by Jean Van Leeuwen. Van Nostrand, 1972. Translation of Kejserens nye klæder. Subj: Character traits – pride. Character traits – vanity. Clothing. Folk & fairy tales. Humorous stories. Imagination. Royalty – emperors.

The emperor's new clothes adapt. by Anthea Bell; ill. by Dorothée Duntze. Holt, 1986. ISBN 0-8050-0010-0 Subj: Character traits – pride. Character traits – vanity. Clothing. Folk & fairy tales. Humorous stories. Imagination. Royalty – emperors.

The emperor's new clothes ill. by Dorothée Duntze. North-South, 1997. ISBN 1-55858-689-X Subj: Character traits – pride. Character traits – vanity. Clothing. Folk & fairy tales. Imagination. Royalty – emperors.

The emperor's new clothes ill. by Pamela Baldwin Ford. Troll, 1979. Translation of Kejserens nye klæder. ISBN 0-8937-5132-4 Subj: Character traits – pride. Character traits – vanity. Clothing. Folk & fairy tales. Humorous stories. Imagination. Royalty – emperors.

The emperor's new clothes a new English version by Ruth Belov Gross; ill. by Jack Kent. Four Winds, 1977. Adapt. of Kejserens nye klæder by Ruth Belov Gross. ISBN 0-590-07502-0 Subj: Character traits – pride. Character traits – vanity. Clothing. Folk & fairy tales. Humorous stories. Imagination. Royalty – emperors.

The emperor's new clothes ill. by Monika Laimgruber. Addison-Wesley, 1973. Translation of Kejserens nye klæder. Subj: Character traits – pride. Character traits – vanity. Clothing. Folk & fairy tales. Humorous stories. Imagination. Royalty – emperors.

The emperor's new clothes ill. by Anne F. Rockwell. Crowell, 1982. Translation of Kejserens nye klæder by H. W. Dulcken. ISBN 0-690-04149-7 Subj: Character traits – pride. Character traits – vanity. Clothing. Folk & fairy tales. Humorous stories. Imagination. Royalty – emperors.

The emperor's new clothes adapt. & ill. by Janet Stevens. Holiday, 1985. ISBN 0-8234-0566-4 Subj: Character traits – pride. Character traits – vanity. Clothing. Folk & fairy tales. Humorous stories. Imagination. Royalty – emperors.

The emperor's new clothes adapt. & ill. by Eve Tharlet; trans. by Rosemary Lanning. North-South, 2000. ISBN 0-7358-1341-8 Subj: Character traits – pride. Character traits – vanity. Clothing. Folk & fairy tales. Foreign lands – China. Humorous stories. Royalty – emperors.

The emperor's new clothes adapt. by Eric Metaxas; ill. by Robert Van Nutt. Minibook ed. S&S, 1995. ISBN 0-689-80058-4 Subj: Character traits – pride. Character traits – vanity. Clothing. Folk & fairy tales. Format, unusual. Imagination. Royalty – emperors.

The emperor's new clothes ill. by Nadine Bernard Westcott. Little, 1984. Subj: Character traits – pride. Character traits – vanity. Clothing. Folk & fairy tales. Humorous stories. Imagination. Royalty – emperors.

The emperor's nightingale retold by Teddy Slater; ill. from the Disney archives. Walt Disney, 1992. ISBN 1-56282-134-2 Subj: Birds – nightingales. Character traits – freedom. Folk & fairy tales. Foreign lands – China. Royalty – emperors.

The emperor's nightingale trans. by Erik Haugaard; ill. by Georges Lemoine. Schocken, 1981. ISBN 0-8052-3780-1 Subj: Birds – nightingales. Character traits – freedom. Folk & fairy tales. Foreign lands – China. Royalty – emperors.

The fir tree ill. by Stephanie Britt. HarperCollins, 1988. ISBN 0-60-020078-2 Subj: Folk & fairy tales. Holidays – Christmas. Trees.

The fir tree trans. by H. W. Dulcken; ill. by Nancy Ekholm Burkert. HarperCollins, 1970. Tr. of Grantræet. ISBN 0-8249-8389-0 Subj: Folk & fairy tales. Holidays – Christmas. Trees.

The fir tree adapt. & ill. by Diane Goode. Random House, 1988. ISBN 0-394-81941-1 Subj: Folk & fairy tales. Holidays – Christmas. Trees.

The fir tree adapt. by Marcel Imsand; ill. by Rita Marshall. Creative Ed., 1983. ISBN 0-87191-949-4 Subj: Folk & fairy tales. Holidays – Christmas. Trees.

The fir tree adapt. & ill. by Bernadette Watts. North-South, 1990. ISBN 1-55858-093-X Subj: Folk & fairy tales. Holidays – Christmas. Trees.

It's perfectly true! adapt. & ill. by Janet Stevens. Holiday, 1987. ISBN 0-8234-0672-5 Subj: Behavior – gossip. Character traits – vanity. Death. Folk & fairy tales.

Little Ida's flowers ill. by Linda Allen. Putnam, 1990. ISBN 0-399-21571-9 Subj: Flowers. Folk & fairy tales.

The little match girl ill. by Rachel Isadora. Putnam, 1987. Translation of Den lille pige med svovlstikkerne. ISBN 0-399-21336-8

Subj: Death. Folk & fairy tales. Holidays – New Year's. Homeless. Poverty.

The little match girl ill. by Blair Lent. Houghton Mifflin, 1968. Translation of Den lille pige med svovlstikkerne. ISBN 1-56397-470-3 Subj: Death. Folk & fairy tales. Holidays – New Year's. Homeless. Poverty.

The little match girl ill. by Jerry Pinkney. Fogelman, 1999. ISBN 0-8037-2314-8 Subj: Death. Folk & fairy tales. Holidays – New Year's. Homeless. Poverty.

The little mermaid adapt. by Susan Blackaby; ill. by Charlene Delage. Picture Window, 2004. ISBN 1-4048-0221-5 Subj: Folk & fairy tales. Mythical creatures – mermaids, mermen.

The little mermaid trans. by Eva Le Gallienne; ill. by Edward Frascino. HarperCollins, 1971. ISBN 0-06-023783-X Subj: Folk & fairy tales. Mythical creatures – mermaids, mermen.

The little mermaid ill. by Michael Hague. Holt, 1993. ISBN 0-8050-1010-6 Subj: Folk & fairy tales. Mythical creatures – mermaids, mermen.

The little mermaid retold & ill. by Rachel Isadora. Putnam, 1998. ISBN 0-399-22813-6 Subj: Folk & fairy tales. Mythical creatures – mermaids, mermen.

The little mermaid adapt. by Anthea Bell; ill. by Chihiro Iwasaki. Alphabet Pr., 1984. Adapt. of Den lille havfrue. ISBN 0-907234-59-3 Subj: Folk & fairy tales. Mythical creatures – mermaids, mermen.

The little mermaid ill. by Dorothy Pulis Lathrop. Macmillan, 1939. Subj: Folk & fairy tales. Mythical creatures – mermaids, mermen.

The little mermaid retold by Deborah Hautzig; ill. by Darcy May. Random House, 2003. ISBN 0-679-92241-5 Subj: Folk & fairy tales. Mythical creatures – mermaids, mermen.

The little mermaid ill. by Josef Palecek. Faber, 1981. Translation of Den lille havfrue by M. R. James. ISBN 0-571-11847-X Subj: Folk & fairy tales. Mythical creatures – mermaids, mermen.

The little mermaid adapt. by Freya Littledale; ill. by Daniel San Souci. Scholastic, 1986. ISBN 0-590-33590-1 Subj: Folk & fairy tales. Mythical creatures – mermaids, mermen.

The little mermaid retold & ill. by Katie Thamer Treherne. Harcourt, 1989. ISBN 0-15-246320-8 Subj: Folk & fairy tales. Mythical creatures – mermaids, mermen.

The nightingale ill. by Harold Berson. Lippincott, 1962. Subj: Birds – nightingales. Character traits – freedom. Folk & fairy tales. Foreign lands – China. Royalty – emperors.

The nightingale trans. by Eva Le Gallienne; ill. by Nancy Ekholm Burkert. HarperCollins, 1965. Subj: Birds – nightingales. Character traits – freedom. Folk & fairy tales. Foreign lands – China. Royalty – emperors.

The nightingale ill. by Alison Claire Darke. Doubleday, 1989. ISBN 0-385-26082-2 Subj: Birds – nightingales. Character traits – freedom. Folk & fairy tales. Foreign lands – China.

The nightingale adapt. by Anna Bier; ill. by Demi. Harcourt, 1985. Adapt. of Nattergalen. ISBN 0-15-257427-1 Subj: Birds – nightingales. Character traits – freedom. Folk & fairy tales. Foreign lands – China. Royalty – emperors.

The nightingale adapt. by Alan Benjamin; ill. by Beni Montresor. Crown, 1985. Adapt. of Nattergalen. ISBN 0-517-55211-6 Subj: Birds – nightingales. Character traits – freedom. Folk & fairy tales. Foreign lands – China. Royalty – emperors.

The nightingale trans. by Naomi Lewis; ill. by Josef Palecek. North-South, 1990. ISBN 1-55858-090-5 Subj: Birds – nightingales. Character traits – freedom. Folk & fairy tales. Foreign lands – China.

The nightingale retold by Michael Bedard; ill. by Regolo Ricci. Houghton Mifflin, 1992. ISBN 0-395-60735-3 Subj: Birds –

nightingales. Character traits – freedom. Folk & fairy tales. Foreign lands – China. Royalty – emperors.

The nightingale retold by Dom DeLuise; ill. by Christopher Santoro. S&S, 1998. ISBN 0-689-81749-5 Subj: Activities – baking, cooking. Birds – nightingales. Character traits – freedom. Folk & fairy tales. Food. Foreign lands – China. Royalty – emperors.

The nightingale ill. by Lisbeth Zwerger; trans. from Danish by Anthea Bell. North-South, 1999. Adapt. of Nattergalen. ISBN 0-7358-1118-0 Subj: Birds – nightingales. Character traits – freedom. Folk & fairy tales. Foreign lands – China. Royalty – emperors.

The old man is always right ill. by Feodor Rojankovsky. HarperCollins, 1940. Subj: Activities – trading. Folk & fairy tales. Humorous stories.

The penguin and the pea (Perlman, Janet)

The princess and the pea (Vaës, Alain)

The princess and the pea retold by Harriet Ziefert; ill. by Emily Bolam. Viking, 1996. ISBN 0-670-86054-9 Subj: Folk & fairy tales. Royalty – princesses. Sleep.

The princess and the pea adapt. by Susan Blackaby; ill. by Charlene Delage. Picture Window, 2004. ISBN 1-4048-0223-1 Subj: Folk & fairy tales. Royalty – princesses. Sleep.

The princess and the pea ill. by Dorothée Duntze. Holt, 1985. ISBN 0-8050-0170-0 Subj: Folk & fairy tales. Royalty – princesses. Sleep.

The princess and the pea ill. by Dick Gackenbach. Macmillan, 1983. ISBN 0-02-735800-3 Subj: Folk & fairy tales. Royalty – princesses. Sleep.

The princess and the pea ill. by Paul Galdone. Seabury Pr., 1978. Translation of Den prindsessen paa aerten. ISBN 0-8164-3202-3 Subj: Folk & fairy tales. Royalty – princesses. Sleep.

The princess and the pea ill. by Camille Semelet. Abbeville, 1999. ISBN 0-7892-0515-7 Subj: Folk & fairy tales. Royalty – princesses. Sleep.

The princess and the pea adapt. & ill. by Janet Stevens. Holiday, 1982. ISBN 0-8234-0442-0 Subj: Folk & fairy tales. Royalty – princesses. Sleep.

The princess and the pea retold & ill. by Suçie Stevenson. Doubleday, 1992. ISBN 0-385-41376-9 Subj: Folk & fairy tales. Royalty – princesses. Sleep.

The princess and the pea trans. by Anthea Bell; ill. by Eve Tharlet. Picture Book Studio, 1987. ISBN 0-88708-052-9 Subj: Folk & fairy tales. Royalty – princesses. Sleep.

The red shoes trans. from Danish by Anthea Bell; ill. by Chihiro Iwasaki. Alphabet Pr., 1983. ISBN 0-907234-26-7 Subj: Activities – dancing. Angels. Character traits – pride. Clothing – shoes.

The snow queen trans. by Naomi Lewis; ill. by Angela Barrett. Candlewick, 1993. ISBN 1-56402-215-3 Subj: Character traits – bravery. Emotions – love. Folk & fairy tales.

The snow queen ill. by Toma Bogdanovic. Scroll Pr., n.d. An adapt. of Sneedronningen by Naomi Lewis. Subj: Character traits – bravery. Emotions – love. Folk & fairy tales. Foreign lands – Denmark.

The snow queen ill. by June Atkin Corwin. Atheneum, 1968. ISBN 0-689-30018-2 Subj: Character traits – bravery. Emotions – love. Folk & fairy tales.

The snow queen sel. & ed. by Neil Philip; ill. by Sally Holmes. Lothrop, 1989. ISBN 0-688-09048-6 Subj: Character traits – bravery. Emotions – love. Folk & fairy tales.

The snow queen adapt. by Amy Ehrlich; ill. by Susan Jeffers. Dial, 1982. ISBN 0-8037-8029-X Subj: Character traits – bravery. Emotions – love. Folk & fairy tales.

The snow queen adapt. by Naomi Lewis; ill. by Errol Le Cain. Viking, 1979. ISBN 0-670-65378-0 Subj: Character traits – bravery. Emotions – love. Folk & fairy tales.

The snow queen: a fairy tale adapt. by Anthea Bell; ill. by Bernadette Watts. Holt, 1987. First pub. in Sweden under the title Die Schneekönigin. ISBN 0-8050-0485-8 Subj: Character traits – bravery. Emotions. Folk & fairy tales.

The snow queen trans. by Eva Le Gallienne; ill. by Arieh Zeldich. HarperCollins, 1985. ISBN 0-06-023695-7 Subj: Character traits – bravery. Emotions – love. Folk & fairy tales.

The snow queen and other stories from Hans Andersen ill. by Edmund Dulac. Doubleday, 1976. ISBN 0-385-11678-0 Subj: Folk & fairy tales.

The steadfast tin soldier adapt. by Susan Blackaby; ill. by Charlene Delage. Picture Window, 2004. ISBN 1-4048-0226-6 Subj: Folk & fairy tales. Toys – soldiers.

The steadfast tin soldier ill. by Thomas di Grazia. Prentice-Hall, 1981. ISBN 0-13-846295-X Subj: Folk & fairy tales. Toys – soldiers.

The steadfast tin soldier ill. by Paul Galdone. Houghton Mifflin, 1979. Translation of Den standhaftige tinsoldat. ISBN 0-395-28964-5 Subj: Folk & fairy tales. Toys – soldiers.

The steadfast tin soldier retold & ill. by Rachel Isadora. Putnam, 1996. ISBN 0-399-22676-1 Subj: Folk & fairy tales. Toys – soldiers.

The steadfast tin soldier adapt. by Joel Tuber; ill. by David Jorgensen. Knopf, 1986. ISBN 0-394-88402-7 Subj: Folk & fairy tales. Toys – soldiers.

The steadfast tin soldier ill. by Monika Laimgruber. Atheneum, 1971. Translation of Den standhaftige tinsoldat. Subj: Folk & fairy tales. Toys – soldiers.

The steadfast tin soldier trans. from Danish by Naomi Lewis; ill. by P. J. Lynch. Harcourt, 1992. ISBN 0-15-200599-4 Subj: Folk & fairy tales. Toys – soldiers.

The steadfast tin soldier retold by Tor Seidler; ill. by Fred Marcellino. HarperCollins, 1992. ISBN 0-06-205001-X Subj: Folk & fairy tales. Toys – soldiers.

The steadfast tin soldier ill. by Alain Vaës. Little, 1983. Translation of Den standhaftige tinsoldat. ISBN 0-316-03949-7 Subj: Folk & fairy tales. Toys – soldiers.

The swineherd ill. by Erik Blegvad. Harcourt, 1958. Translation of Den svinedrengen by Erik Blegvad. Subj: Character traits – cleverness. Character traits – selfishness. Folk & fairy tales.

The swineherd ill. by Dorothée Duntze. Holt, 1987. Translation of Den svinedrengen by Naomi Lewis. ISBN 0-8050-0232-4 Subj: Character traits – cleverness. Character traits – selfishness. Folk & fairy tales. Royalty.

The swineherd adapt. & ill. by Deborah Hahn. Lothrop, 1991. ISBN 0-688-10053-8 Subj: Character traits – cleverness. Character traits – selfishness. Folk & fairy tales.

The swineherd trans. from Danish by Anthea Bell; ill. by Lisbeth Zwerger. Morrow, 1982. Tr. of Den svinedrengen. ISBN 0-688-00930-1 Subj: Character traits – cleverness. Character traits – selfishness. Folk & fairy tales.

Thumbelina trans. by R. P. Keigwin; ill. by Adrienne Adams. Scribners, 1961. Tr. of Tommelise. Subj: Character traits – smallness. Folk & fairy tales.

Thumbelina retold by James Riordan; ill. by Wayne Anderson. Putnam, 1991. ISBN 0-399-21756-8 Subj: Character traits – smallness. Folk & fairy tales.

Thumbelina retold by Jane Falloon; ill. by Emma Chichester Clark. McElderry, 1996. ISBN 0-689-81181-0 Subj: Character traits – smallness. Folk & fairy tales.

Thumbelina ill. by Alison Claire Darke. Doubleday, 1991. ISBN 0-385-41404-8 Subj: Character traits – smallness. Folk & fairy tales.

Thumbelina adapt. by Susan Blackaby; ill. by Charlene Delage. Picture Window, 2004. ISBN 1-4048-0225-8 Subj: Character traits – smallness. Folk & fairy tales.

Thumbelina ill. by Demi. Putnam, 1987. ISBN 0-396-09241-1 Subj: Character traits – smallness. Folk & fairy tales.

Thumbelina trans. by Erik Haugaard; ill. by Arlene Graston. Delacorte, 1997. ISBN 0-385-32251-8 Subj: Character traits – smallness. Folk & fairy tales.

Thumbelina ill. by Susan Jeffers; retold by Amy Ehrlich. Dial, 1979. Translation of Tommelise. ISBN 0-8037-8815-0 Subj: Character traits – smallness. Folk & fairy tales.

Thumbelina retold by Deborah Hautzig; ill. by Kaarina Kaila. Knopf, 1990. ISBN 0-679-90667-3 Subj: Character traits – smallness. Folk & fairy tales.

Thumbelina ill. by Christine Willis Nigognossian. Troll, 1979. Translation of Tommelise. ISBN 0-89375-141-3 Subj: Character traits – smallness. Folk & fairy tales.

Thumbelina ill. by Gustaf Tenggren. S&S, 1953. Translation of Tommelise. Subj: Character traits – smallness. Folk & fairy tales.

Thumbelina trans. by Richard & Clara Winston; ill. by Lisbeth Zwerger. Morrow, 1980. Tr. of Tommelise. ISBN 0-688-32235-2 Subj: Character traits – smallness. Folk & fairy tales.

Thumbeline trans. by Anthea Bell; ill. by Lisbeth Zwerger. Picture Book Studio, 1985. ISBN 0-88708-006-5 Subj: Character traits – smallness. Folk & fairy tales.

The tinderbox ill. by Warwick Hutton. Macmillan, 1988. ISBN 0-689-50458-6 Subj: Folk & fairy tales. Magic. Witches.

The tinderbox ill. by Barry Moser. Little, 1990. ISBN 0-316-03938-1 Subj: Folk & fairy tales. Magic. U.S. history. Witches.

The ugly duckling ill. by Adrienne Adams. Scribners, 1965. Translation of Den grimme ælling by R. P. Keigwin. Subj: Birds – ducks. Birds – swans. Character traits – appearance. Character traits – being different. Folk & fairy tales.

The ugly duckling ill. by Lorinda Bryan Cauley. Harcourt, 1979. ISBN 0-15-292435-3 Subj: Birds – ducks. Birds – swans. Character traits – appearance. Character traits – being different. Folk & fairy tales.

The ugly duckling adapt. by Susan Blackaby; ill. by Charlene Delage. Picture Window, 2004. ISBN 1-4048-0222-3 Subj: Birds – ducks. Birds – swans. Character traits – appearance. Character traits – being different. Folk & fairy tales.

The ugly duckling retold & ill. by Troy Howell. Putnam, 1990. ISBN 0-399-22158-1 Subj: Birds – ducks. Birds – swans. Character traits – appearance. Character traits – being different. Folk & fairy tales.

The ugly duckling trans. by Phyllis Palecek; ill. by Tadasu Izawa & Shigemi Hijikata. Grosset, 1971. Tr. of Den grimme ælling. ISBN 0-4480-4235-5 Subj: Birds – ducks. Birds – swans. Character traits – appearance. Character traits – being different. Folk & fairy tales.

The ugly duckling trans. by Anne Stewart; ill. by Monika Laimgruber. Greenwillow, 1985. ISBN 0-688-04951-6 Subj: Birds – ducks. Birds – swans. Character traits – appearance. Character traits – being different. Folk & fairy tales.

The ugly duckling trans. by R. P. Keigwin; ill. by Johannes Larsen. Ward, 1956. Tr. of Den grimme ælling. Subj: Birds – ducks. Birds – swans. Character traits – appearance. Character traits – being different. Folk & fairy tales.

The ugly duckling adapt. by Marianna Mayer; ill. by Thomas Locker. Macmillan, 1987. ISBN 0-02-765130-4 Subj: Birds – ducks. Birds – swans. Character traits – appearance. Character traits – being different. Folk & fairy tales.

The ugly duckling trans. by Anthea Bell; ill. by Alan Marks. Picture Book Studio, 1990. ISBN 0-88708-116-9 Subj: Birds – ducks. Birds – swans. Character traits – appearance. Character traits – being different. Folk & fairy tales.

The ugly duckling adapt. by Phyllis Hoffman; ill. by Josef Palecek. Abelard-Schuman, 1972. ISBN 0-200-71739-1 Subj: Birds – ducks. Birds – swans. Character traits – appearance. Character traits – being different. Folk & fairy tales.

The ugly duckling adapt. & ill. by Jerry Pinkney. Morrow, 1999. ISBN 0-688-15933-8 Subj: Birds – ducks. Birds – swans. Caldecott award honor books. Character traits – appearance. Character traits – being different. Folk & fairy tales.

The ugly duckling retold by M. Eulalia Valeri; trans. from Spanish by Leland Northam; ill. by Maria Ruis. Silver Burdett, 1985. ISBN 0-382-09071-3 Subj: Birds – ducks. Birds – swans. Character traits – appearance. Character traits – being different. Folk & fairy tales. Wordless.

The ugly duckling adapt. by Lilian Moore; ill. by Daniel San Souci. Scholastic, 1987. ISBN 0-590-40957-3 Subj: Birds – ducks. Birds – swans. Character traits – appearance. Character traits – being different. Folk & fairy tales.

The ugly duckling retold by Kevin Crossley-Holland; ill. by Meilo So. Knopf, 2001. ISBN 0-375-91319-X Subj: Birds – ducks. Birds – swans. Character traits – appearance. Character traits – being different. Folk & fairy tales.

The ugly duckling adapt. by Joel Tuber & Clara Stites; ill. by Robert Van Nutt. Knopf, 1986. ISBN 0-394-88403-5 Subj: Birds – ducks. Birds – swans. Character traits – appearance. Character traits – being different. Folk & fairy tales.

The ugly duckling retold & ill. by Bernadette Watts. North-South, 2000. Subj: Birds – ducks. Birds – swans. Character traits – appearance. Character traits – being different. Folk & fairy tales.

The ugly little duck adapt. by Patricia C. & Fredrick McKissack; ill. by Peggy Perry Anderson. Childrens Pr., 1986. Prepared under the direction of Robert Hillerick. ISBN 0-516-03982-2 Subj: Birds – ducks. Birds – swans. Character traits – appearance. Character traits – being different. Folk & fairy tales.

The wild swans trans. from Danish by Naomi Lewis; ill. by Angela Barrett. HarperCollins, 1984. ISBN 0-911745-36-X Subj: Birds – swans. Folk & fairy tales. Magic.

The wild swans retold by Amy Ehrlich; ill. by Susan Jeffers. Dial, 1981. ISBN 0-8037-9391-X Subj: Birds – Folk & fairy tales. Magic.

The woman with the eggs adapt. by Jan Wahl; ill. by Ray Cruz. Crown, 1974. An adaptation of a poem by H. C. Andersen pub. in Den danske bondeve+L:n, 1836. ISBN 0-517-51587-3 Subj: Behavior – greed. Eggs. Folk & fairy tales.

Andersen, Karen Born. *An alphabet in five acts* ill. by Flint Born. Dial, 1993. ISBN 0-8037-1441-6 Subj: ABC books.

What's the matter, Sylvie, can't you ride? ill. by author. Dial, 1981. ISBN 0-8037-9621-8 Subj: Emotions. Sports – bicycling.

Anderson, Adrienne Adams. *see* Adams, Adrienne

Anderson, C. W. (Clarence Williams). *Billy and Blaze* ill. by author. Aladdin, 1992. ISBN 0-689-71608-7 Subj: Animals – horses, ponies. Birthdays. Family life.

Blaze and the forest fire ill. by author. Macmillan, 1938. ISBN 0-02-702080-0 Subj: Animals – horses, ponies. Fire.

Blaze and the gray spotted pony ill. by author. Macmillan, 1968. ISBN 0-02-701150-X Subj: Animals – horses, ponies.

Blaze and the gypsies ill. by author. Macmillan, 1937. Subj: Animals – horses, ponies. Crime. Gypsies.

Blaze and the Indian cave ill. by author. Macmillan, 1964. ISBN 0-02-702470-9 Subj: Animals – horses, ponies. Cowboys, cowgirls.

Blaze and the lost quarry ill. by author. Macmillan, 1966. ISBN 0-606-05758-7 Subj: Animals – horses, ponies. Cowboys, cowgirls.

Blaze and the mountain lion ill. by author. Macmillan, 1959. Subj: Animals – cougars. Animals – horses, ponies. Cowboys, cowgirls.

Blaze and Thunderbolt ill. by author. Macmillan, 1955. ISBN 0-689-71712-1 Subj: Animals – horses, ponies. Cowboys, cowgirls.

Blaze finds forgotten roads ill. by author. Macmillan, 1970. ISBN 0-02-701340-5 Subj: Animals – horses, ponies. Behavior – lost. Cowboys, cowgirls.

Blaze finds the trail ill. by author. Macmillan, 1950. ISBN 0-02-041450-1 Subj: Animals – horses, ponies. Behavior – lost. Cowboys, cowgirls.

Blaze shows the way ill. by author. Macmillan, 1969. ISBN 0-606-05759-5 Subj: Animals – horses, ponies.

The crooked colt ill. by author. Macmillan, 1954. Subj: Animals – horses, ponies.

Linda and the Indians ill. by author. Macmillan, 1952. Subj: Animals – horses, ponies. Imagination. Indians of North America.

Lonesome little colt ill. by author. Macmillan, 1961. ISBN 0-02-041490-0 Subj: Animals – horses, ponies. Character traits – kindness to animals.

A pony for Linda ill. by author. Macmillan, 1951. Subj: Animals – horses, ponies.

A pony for three ill. by author. Macmillan, 1958. Subj: Animals – horses, ponies.

The rumble seat pony ill. by author. Macmillan, 1971. Subj: Animals – horses, ponies. Character traits – kindness to animals. Parades.

Anderson, Debby. *Let's talk about Heaven* ill. by author. Chariot Books, 1991. ISBN 1-55513-531-5 Subj: Religion.

Anderson, Douglas. *Let's draw a story* ill. by author. Sterling, 1959. Subj: Animals – cats. Animals – dogs. Art. Family life. Games.

Anderson, James. *A letter to the king* (Va, Leong)

Anderson, Janet S. *Sunflower Sal* ill. by Elizabeth Johns. A. Whitman, 1997. ISBN 0-8075-7662-X Subj: Careers – farmers. Concepts – shape. Concepts – size. Country. Flowers.

Anderson, Joan. *Harry's helicopter* ill. by George Ancona. Morrow, 1990. ISBN 0-688-09187-3 Subj: Activities – flying. Helicopters. Imagination.

Richie's rocket photos by George Ancona. Morrow, 1993. ISBN 0-688-11305-2 Subj: Careers – astronauts. Space & space ships.

Sally's submarine photos by George Ancona. Morrow, 1995. ISBN 0-688-12691-X Subj: Boats, ships. Family life – fathers. Imagination.

Anderson, John L. *see* Anderson, Lonzo

Anderson, Laurie Halse. *The big cheese of Third Street* ill. by David Gordon. S&S, 2002. ISBN 0-689-82464-5 Subj: Behavior – bullying. Character traits – persistence. Concepts – size. Tall tales.

Ndito runs ill. by Anita Van der Merwe. Holt, 1996. ISBN 0-8050-3265-7 Subj: Animals. Foreign lands – Kenya. Sports – racing.

No time for Mother's Day ill. by Dorothy Donohue. A. Whitman, 1999. ISBN 0-8075-4955-X Subj: Family life – mothers. Gifts. Holidays – Mother's Day.

Thank you, Sarah: the woman who saved Thanksgiving ill. by Matt Faulkner. S&S, 2002. ISBN 0-689-84787-4 Subj: Holidays – Thanksgiving. U.S. history.

Turkey pox ill. by Dorothy Donohue. A. Whitman, 1996. ISBN 0-8075-8127-5 Subj: Family life. Family life – grandmothers. Holidays – Thanksgiving. Illness – chicken pox.

Anderson, Lena. *Bunny bath* ill. by author. Farrar, 1991. ISBN 91-29-59652-1 Subj: Activities – bathing. Animals – rabbits. Format, unusual – board books. Wordless.

Bunny box ill. by author. Farrar, 1991. ISBN 91-29-59858-3 Subj: Animals – rabbits. Bedtime. Family life – mothers. Format, unusual – board books. Toys. Wordless.

Bunny fun ill. by author. Farrar, 1991. ISBN 91-29-59860-5 Subj: Animals – rabbits. Format, unusual – board books. Sports – fishing. Sports – swimming. Wordless.

Bunny party ill. by author. Farrar, 1991. ISBN 91-29-59134-1 Subj: Animals – rabbits. Format, unusual – board books. Parties. Wordless.

Bunny story ill. by author. Farrar, 1991. ISBN 91-29-59132-5 Subj: Animals. Animals – rabbits. Bedtime. Format, unusual – board books. Wordless.

Bunny surprise ill. by author. Farrar, 1991. ISBN 91-29-59654-8 Subj: Animals – rabbits. Format, unusual – board books. Wordless.

Stina ill. by author. Greenwillow, 1989. ISBN 0-688-08881-3 Subj: Family life – grandfathers. Sea & seashore. Weather – storms.

Stina's visit ill. by author. Greenwillow, 1991. ISBN 0-688-09666-2 Subj: Birthdays. Family life – grandfathers. Friendship. Old age. Sailors.

Tick-tock ill. by author. Doubleday, 1998. ISBN 0-385-32554-1 Subj: Animals. Clocks, watches. Family life – aunts, uncles. Rhyming text. Time.

Anderson, Leone Castell. *It's O.K. to cry* ill. by Richard Wahl. Child's World, 1979. ISBN 0-8956-5094-0 Subj: Death. Family life – aunts, uncles.

My friend next door ill. by Pat Karch. Dandelion, 1983. ISBN 0-8969-3212-5 Subj: Friendship.

Surprise at Muddy Creek ill. by Helen Endres. Dandelion, 1984. ISBN 0-8969-3222-2 Subj: Indians of North America. U.S. history – frontier & pioneer life.

The wonderful shrinking shirt ill. by Irene Trivas. A. Whitman, 1983. ISBN 0-8075-9171-8 Subj: Clothing – shirts. Humorous stories.

Anderson, Lonzo. *Arion and the dolphins* ill. by Adrienne Adams. Scribners, 1978. Based on an ancient Greek legend. ISBN 0-684-15128-6 Subj: Animals – dolphins. Boats, ships. Folk & fairy tales. Foreign lands – Greece.

The day the hurricane happened ill. by Ann Grifalconi. Scribners, 1974. ISBN 0-684-13495-0 Subj: Family life. Foreign lands – Caribbean Islands. Weather – storms.

The haganinny ill. by Susan Harris Andersen. Ginn, 1973. ISBN 0-663-25493-0 Subj: Imagination.

The Halloween party ill. by Adrienne Adams. Scribners, 1974. ISBN 0-684-14002-0 Subj: Holidays – Halloween. Parties.

Izzard ill. by Adrienne Adams. Scribners, 1973. ISBN 0-684-13247-8 Subj: Foreign lands – Caribbean Islands. Reptiles – lizards.

Mr. Biddle and the birds ill. by Adrienne Adams. Scribners, 1971. ISBN 0-684-12315-0 Subj: Activities – flying. Birds.

Two hundred rabbits by Lonzo Anderson & Adrienne Adams; ill. by Adrienne Adams. Viking, 1968. Subj: Animals – rabbits. Fairies. Magic. Royalty.

Anderson, Lucia Z. *The smallest life around us* ill. by Leigh Grant. Crown, 1978. ISBN 0-517-53227-1 Subj: Science.

Anderson, M. T. *Strange Mr. Satie* ill. by Petra Mathers. Viking, 2003. ISBN 0-670-03637-4 Subj: Careers – composers. Foreign lands – France.

Anderson, Neil. *see* Beim, Jerrold

Anderson, Paul S. *Red fox and the hungry tiger* ill. by Robert Kraus. Addison-Wesley, 1962. Subj: Animals – foxes. Animals – tigers. Character traits – cleverness. Friendship.

Anderson, Peggy Perry. *Out to lunch* ill. by author. Houghton Mifflin, 1998. ISBN 0-395-89826-9 Subj: Behavior – misbehavior. Etiquette. Family life. Frogs & toads. Restaurants. Rhyming text.

Time for bed, the babysitter said ill. by author. Houghton Mifflin, 1987. ISBN 0-395-41851-8 Subj: Activities – babysitting. Bedtime. Frogs & toads.

To the tub ill. by author. Houghton Mifflin, 1996. ISBN 0-395-77614-7 Subj: Activities – bathing. Family life – fathers. Frogs & toads.

We go in a circle ill. by author. Houghton, 2004. ISBN 0-618-44756-3 Subj: Animals – horses, ponies. Handicaps. Sports – racing.

Anderson, Robin. *Sinabouda Lily: a folk tale from Papua New Guinea* ill. by Jennifer Allen. Oxford Univ. Pr., 1979. ISBN 0-19-554201-0 Subj: Activities – swinging. Folk & fairy tales. Foreign lands – New Guinea. Magic. Witches.

Anderson, Scoular. *MacPelican's American adventure* ill. by author. Candlewick, 1998. ISBN 0-7636-0443-7 Subj: Activities – traveling. Behavior – lost.

Anderson, Stephen Axel. *I know the moon* ill. by Greg Couch. Philomel, 2001. ISBN 0-399-23425-X Subj: Animals. Emotions. Moon. Rhyming text. Science.

Anderson, Wayne. *Dragon* ill. by author. S&S, 1992. ISBN 0-671-78397-1 Subj: Dragons. Imagination. Self-concept.

Andre, Evelyn M. *Places I like to be* photos by author. Abingdon, 1980. ISBN 0-687-31540-9 Subj: Activities. Poetry.

Andreae, Giles. *Cock-a-doodle-doo!* ill. by David Wojtowycz. Tiger Tales, 2002. ISBN 1-58925-020-6 Subj: Animals. Poetry.

Commotion in the ocean ill. by David Wojtowycz. Little Tiger, 1998. ISBN 1-888444-39-8 Subj: Poetry. Sea & seashore.

Giraffes can't dance ill. by Guy Parker-Rees. Orchard, 2001. ISBN 0-439-28719-7 Subj: Activities – dancing. Animals – giraffes. Character traits – individuality. Rhyming text.

Love is a handful of honey ill. by Vanessa Cabban. Little Tiger, 1999. ISBN 1-888444-58-4 Subj: Animals – bears. Rhyming text.

Pants by Giles Andreae & Nick Sharratt; ill. by Nick Sharratt. Fickling, 2003. ISBN 0-385-75014-5 Subj: Clothing – pants. Humorous stories. Rhyming text.

The pop-up Rumble in the jungle ill. by David Wojtowycz. Tiger Tales, 2001. ISBN 1-58925-658-1 Subj: Animals. Format, unusual – toy & movable books. Insects – ants. Jungle. Rhyming text.

Rumble in the jungle ill. by David Wojtowycz. Little Tiger, 1997. ISBN 1-888444-08-8 Subj: Animals. Insects – ants. Jungle. Rhyming text.

There's a house inside my mommy ill. by Vanessa Cabban. A. Whitman, 2002. ISBN 0-8075-7853-3 Subj: Babies. Birth. Family life – brothers. Family life – mothers. Rhyming text.

Andreasen, Dan. *Rose Red and the bear prince* (Grimm, Jacob)

Andrews, F. Emerson (Frank Emerson). *Nobody comes to dinner* ill. by Lydia Dabcovich. Little, 1977. ISBN 0-316-04221-8 Subj: Behavior – bad day. Emotions – anger. Imagination – imaginary friends.

Andrews, Jan. *The auction* ill. by Karen Reczuch. Macmillan, 1991. ISBN 0-02-705535-3 Subj: Emotions – anger. Emotions – sadness. Family life – grandfathers. Farms.

Very last first time ill. by Ian Wallace. Atheneum, 1986. ISBN 0-689-50388-1 Subj: Eskimos. Food. Foreign lands – Canada. Sea & seashore.

Andrews, Sylvia. *Dancing in my bones* ill. by Ellen Mueller. Harper-Festival, 2001. ISBN 0-694-01316-1 Subj: Activities – dancing. Anatomy. Rhyming text.

Andrews, Wayne. *Snow White and Rose Red* (Grimm, Jacob)

Andrews-Goebel, Nancy. *The pot that Juan built* ill. by David Diaz. Lee & Low, 2002. ISBN 1-58430-038-8 Subj: Art. Careers – potters. Rhyming text.

Andry, Andrew C. *Hi, new baby: a book to help your child learn about the new baby* by Andrew C. Andry & Suzanne C. Kratka; ill. by Thomas di Grazia. S&S, 1979, c1968. ISBN 0-671-65132-3 Subj: Babies. Birth. Family life – brothers & sisters. Family life – new sibling.

How babies are made by Andrew C. Andry & Steven Schepp; ill. by Blake Hampton. Rev. ed. Time-Life, 1979. ISBN 0-316-04227-7 Subj: Babies. Birth. Science.

Andújar, Gloria. *Cuckoo, a Mexican folktale = Cucú: un cuento folklórico mexicano* (Ehlert, Lois)

Angeletti, Roberta. *Nefertari, princess of Egypt* ill. by author. Oxford Univ. Pr., 1998. ISBN 0-19-521507-9 Subj: Foreign lands – Egypt. Imagination. Religion. Royalty – princesses.

Angeli, Marguerite De. *see* De Angeli, Marguerite

Angelis, Nancy de. *see* Angelo, Nancy Carolyn Harrison

Angelo, Nancy Carolyn Harrison. *Camembert* ill. by author. Houghton Mifflin, 1958. Subj: Animals – mice. Art. Careers – artists. Foreign lands – France.

Angelo, Valenti. *The acorn tree* ill. by author. Viking, 1958. Subj: Animals – chipmunks. Animals – squirrels. Birds – bluejays. Character traits – selfishness. Trees.

The candy basket ill. by author. Viking, 1960. Subj: Animals – mice. Behavior – greed.

Angelou, Maya. *Angelina of Italy* ill. by Lizzy Rockwell. Random House, 2004. ISBN 0-375-92832-4 Subj: Food. Foreign lands – Italy.

Kofi and his magic photos by Margaret Courtney-Clarke; designed by Alexander Isley Design. Potter, 1996. ISBN 0-375-92566-X Subj: Foreign lands – Ghana.

My painted house, my friendly chicken, and me photos by Margaret Courtney-Clarke. Random House, 2003. ISBN 0-375-92567-8 Subj: Art. Foreign lands – South Africa. Homes, houses. Poetry.

Anglund, Joan Walsh. *A is for always: an ABC book* ill. by author. Harcourt, 1968. ISBN 0-15-200670-2 Subj: ABC books.

The Adam book ill. by author. Random House, 1979. ISBN 0-394-94227-2 Subj: Language.

Baby brother ill. by author. Random House, 1985. ISBN 0-394-96837-9 Subj: Babies. Family life – brothers & sisters.

A book of good tidings from the Bible ill. by author. Harcourt, 1965. Subj: Religion.

The brave cowboy ill. by author. McMeel, 2000, 1959. ISBN 0-7407-0649-7 Subj: Activities – playing. Character traits – bravery. Cowboys, cowgirls. Games. Imagination.

A child's year ill. by author. Golden Bks., 1992. ISBN 0-307-00141-5 Subj: Days of the week, months of the year. Rhyming text.

Christmas is a time of giving ill. by author. Harcourt, 1961. ISBN 0-15-217863-5 Subj: Character traits – generosity. Holidays – Christmas.

Christmas is here ill. by author. Random House, 1986. ISBN 0-694-88404-3 Subj: Format, unusual – board books. Holidays – Christmas. Rhyming text.

Christmas is love ill. by author. Harcourt, 1988. ISBN 0-15-200425-4 Subj: Emotions – love. Holidays – Christmas. Poetry.

Cowboy and his friend ill. by author. Harcourt, 1961. ISBN 0-15-220369-9 Subj: Animals – bears. Cowboys, cowgirls. Friendship. Imagination – imaginary friends.

The cowboy's Christmas ill. by author. Atheneum, 1972. ISBN 0-689-30301-7 Subj: Animals – bears. Cowboys, cowgirls. Holidays – Christmas. Imagination – imaginary friends.

Cowboy's secret life ill. by author. Harcourt, 1963. ISBN 0-15-223565-9 Subj: Cowboys, cowgirls. Games. Imagination.

Emily and Adam book of opposites ill. by author. Random House, 1979. ISBN 0-394-94230-2 Subj: Concepts – opposites. Language.

The Emily book ill. by author. Random House, 1979. ISBN 0-394-94237-X Subj: Clothing. Language.

A friend is someone who likes you ill. by author. Harcourt, 1958. ISBN 0-15-229678-6 Subj: Friendship.

How many days has Baby to play? ill. by author. Harcourt, 1988. ISBN 0-15-200460-2 Subj: Babies. Days of the week, months of the year. Rhyming text. Toys – bears.

Look out the window ill. by author. Random House, 1978. Subj: Character traits – individuality.

Love is a baby ill. by author. Harcourt, 1992. ISBN 0-15-200517-X Subj: Babies. Emotions – love. Poetry.

Love is a special way of feeling ill. by author. Harcourt, 1960. ISBN 0-15-249724-2 Subj: Emotions – love.

Love one another ill. by author. Determined Prod., 1981. ISBN 0-915696-45-2 Subj: Foreign lands. Foreign languages.

Morning is a little child: poems ill. by author. Harcourt, 1969. ISBN 0-15-255652-4 Subj: Morning. Poetry.

Nibble nibble mousekin: a tale of Hansel and Gretel ill. by author. Harcourt, 1962. ISBN 0-15-257400-X Subj: Folk & fairy tales. Forest, woods. Witches.

Poems of childhood ill. by author. Harcourt, 1996. ISBN 0-15-262961-0 Subj: Poetry.

Rainbow love ill. by author. Determined Prod., 1982. ISBN 0-915696-51-7 Subj: Character traits – optimism. Weather – rainbows.

Spring is a new beginning ill. by author. Harcourt, 1963. ISBN 0-15-278161-7 Subj: Seasons – spring.

Teddy bear tales ill. by author. Random House, 1985. ISBN 0-394-97171-X Subj: Holidays – Christmas. Toys – bears.

Anholt, Catherine. *All about you* by Catherine & Laurence Anholt; ill. by authors. Viking, 1992. ISBN 0-670-84488-8 Subj: Character traits – questioning. Language.

Aren't you lucky! ill. by author. Little, 1991. ISBN 0-316-04264-1 Subj: Babies. Family life – new sibling. Family life – sisters. Sibling rivalry.

Bear and baby written & ill. by Catherine & Laurence Anholt. Candlewick, 1993. ISBN 1-56402-235-8 Subj: Rhyming text. Toys – bears.

Catherine and Laurence Anholt's big book of families by Catherine & Laurence Anholt; ill. by authors. Candlewick, 1998. ISBN 0-7636-0323-6 Subj: Family life.

Chaos at Cold Custard Farm ill. by author. Oxford Univ. Pr., 1988. ISBN 0-19-520645-2 Subj: Animals. Farms.

Chimp and Zee and the big storm written & ill. by Catherine & Laurence Anholt. Fogelman, 2002. ISBN 0-8037-2700-3 Subj: Animals – chimpanzees. Behavior – lost. Weather – storms.

Chimp and Zee's noisy book written & ill. by Catherine & Laurence Anholt. Fogelman, 2002. ISBN 0-8037-2772-0 Subj: Animals. Animals – chimpanzees. Format, unusual – board books. Noise, sounds.

Come back, Jack! written & ill. by Catherine & Laurence Anholt. Candlewick, 1994. ISBN 1-56402-313-3 Subj: Behavior – boredom. Books, reading. Nursery rhymes.

First words and pictures by Catherine & Laurence Anholt; ill. by authors. Candlewick, 1996. ISBN 0-763-60041-5 Subj: Language.

Good days, bad days ill. by author. Putnam, 1991. ISBN 0-399-22283-9 Subj: Concepts – opposites. Family life.

Here come the babies written & ill. by Catherine & Laurence Anholt. Candlewick, 1995. ISBN 1-56402-209-9 Subj: Babies. Family life – new sibling. Poetry.

Kids written & ill. by Catherine & Laurence Anholt. Candlewick, 1992. ISBN 1-56402-097-5 Subj: Character traits – individuality. Rhyming text.

A kiss like this by Catherine & Laurence Anholt; ill. by authors. Barron's, 1997. ISBN 0-7641-5068-5 Subj: Animals. Animals – lions.

Monkey around with Chimp and Zee [board book] by Catherine & Laurence Anholt; ill. by authors. Fogelman, 2002. ISBN 0-8037-2773-9 Subj: Animals – chimpanzees. Format, unusual – board books.

One, two, three, count with me written & ill. by Catherine & Laurence Anholt. Viking, 1994. ISBN 0-670-85261-9 Subj: Anatomy. Concepts. Counting, numbers. Days of the week, months of the year. Rhyming text.

Snow fairy and the spaceman ill. by author. Delacorte, 1991. ISBN 0-385-30422-6 Subj: Birthdays. Friendship. Parties.

Sophie and the new baby (Anholt, Laurence)

Sun, snow, stars, sky by Catherine & Laurence Anholt; ill. by authors. Viking, 1995. ISBN 0-670-86196-0 Subj: Seasons. Weather.

Toddlers written & ill. by Catherine & Laurence Anholt. Candlewick, 1993. ISBN 1-56402-242-0 Subj: Babies. Rhyming text.

Tom's rainbow walk ill. by author. Little, 1990. ISBN 0-316-04261-7 Subj: Activities – knitting. Concepts – color. Family life – grandmothers.

Truffles in trouble ill. by author. Little, 1987. ISBN 0-316-04260-9 Subj: Animals – pigs. Shopping. Stores.

Truffles is sick ill. by author. Little, 1987. ISBN 0-316-04259-5 Subj: Animals – pigs. Illness.

Twins, two by two by Catherine & Laurence Anholt; ill. by authors. Candlewick, 1992. ISBN 1-56402-041-X Subj: Animals. Bedtime. Multiple births – twins.

What I like by Catherine & Laurence Anholt; ill. by Catherine Anholt. Putnam, 1991. ISBN 0-399-21863-7 Subj: Character traits – individuality. Emotions. Rhyming text.

What makes me happy? written & ill. by Catherine & Laurence Anholt. Candlewick, 1995. ISBN 1-56402-482-2 Subj: Babies. Emotions. Rhyming text.

When I was a baby ill. by author. Little, 1989. ISBN 0-316-04262-5 Subj: Babies. Behavior – growing up. Family life.

Anholt, Laurence. *All about you* (Anholt, Catherine)

Bear and baby (Anholt, Catherine)

Billy and the big new school ill. by Catherine Anholt. A. Whitman, 1999. ISBN 0-8075-0743-1 Subj: Behavior – growing up. Birds. School – first day.

Camille and the sunflowers: a story about Vincent Van Gogh ill. by author. Barron's, 1994. ISBN 0-8120-6409-7 Subj: Art. Careers – artists. Foreign lands – Holland. Friendship.

Catherine and Laurence Anholt's big book of families (Anholt, Catherine)

Chimp and Zee's noisy book (Anholt, Catherine)

Come back, Jack! (Anholt, Catherine)

First words and pictures (Anholt, Catherine)

The forgotten forest ill. by author. Sierra Club, 1992. ISBN 0-87156-569-2 Subj: Ecology. Forest, woods.

Here come the babies (Anholt, Catherine)

Jack and the dreamsack ill. by Ross Collins. Bloomsbury, 2003. ISBN 1-58234-786-7 Subj: Dreams. Night.

Kids (Anholt, Catherine)

A kiss like this (Anholt, Catherine)

Monkey around with Chimp and Zee [board book] (Anholt, Catherine)

The new puppy ill. by Catherine Anholt. Artists & Writers Guild, 1995. ISBN 0-307-17516-2 Subj: Animals – dogs. Pets.

One, two, three, count with me (Anholt, Catherine)

Sophie and the new baby ill. by author; story by Catherine Anholt. A. Whitman, 2000. ISBN 0-8075-7550-X Subj: Babies. Birth. Family life – new sibling.

Summerhouse ill. by Lynne Russell. DK, 1999. ISBN 0-7894-4377-5 Subj: Family life – grandmothers. Imagination. Seasons – winter.

Sun, snow, stars, sky (Anholt, Catherine)

Toddlers (Anholt, Catherine)

Twins, two by two (Anholt, Catherine)

What I like (Anholt, Catherine)

What makes me happy? (Anholt, Catherine)

Animal nursery rhymes sel. by Angela Wilkes; ill. with photos. DK, 1992. ISBN 1-56458-122-5 Subj: Animals. Nursery rhymes.

Animal 123's ill. with photos. Cedco, 1998. World Wildlife Fund: Saving life on earth. ISBN 0-7683-2033-X Subj: Animals. Counting, numbers.

Annett, Cora. *The dog who thought he was a boy* ill. by Walter Lorraine. Houghton Mifflin, 1965. ISBN 0-395-18471-1 Subj: Animals – dogs. Birthdays. School.

When the porcupine moved in ill. by Peter Parnall. Watts, 1971. ISBN 0-531-01987-X Subj: Animals – porcupines. Animals – rabbits. Behavior – trickery.

Annixter, Jane. *Brown rats, black rats* by Jane & Paul Annixter; ill. by Gilbert Riswold. Prentice-Hall, 1977. ISBN 0-13-084400-4 Subj: Animals – rats. Science.

Annixter, Paul. *Brown rats, black rats* (Annixter, Jane)

Anno, Masaichiro. *Anno's magical ABC: an anamorphic alphabet* (Anno, Mitsumasa)

Anno, Mitsumasa. *All in a day* by Mitsumasa Anno & others; ill. by Mitsumasa Anno. Putnam, 1986. ISBN 0-399-21311-2 Subj: Activities. Foreign lands. World.

Anno's Æsop: a book of fables by Æsop and Mr. Fox adapt. & ill. by author. Watts, 1989. ISBN 0-531-08374-8 Subj: Animals – foxes. Folk & fairy tales.

Anno's alphabet: an adventure in imagination ill. by author. Crowell, 1975. ISBN 0-690-00546-5 Subj: ABC books. Imagination. Optical illusions. Picture puzzles.

Anno's animals ill. by author. Collins-World, 1979. ISBN 0-529-05546-5 Subj: Animals. Games. Imagination. Picture puzzles. Wordless.

Anno's Britain ill. by author. Philomel, 1982. ISBN 0-399-20861-5 Subj: Foreign lands – England. Games. Imagination. Wordless.

Anno's counting book ill. by author. Crowell, 1975. ISBN 0-690-01288-8 Subj: Counting, numbers. Imagination. Optical illusions. Picture puzzles. Seasons. Wordless.

Anno's counting house ill. by author. Philomel, 1982. Translation of 10-nin no yukai na hikkoshi. ISBN 0-399-20896-8 Subj: Counting, numbers. Games. Imagination. Optical illusions. Picture puzzles. Wordless.

Anno's faces ill. by author. Putnam, 1989. ISBN 0-399-21711-8 Subj: Anatomy – faces. Concepts – shape. Format, unusual.

Anno's flea market ill. by author. Philomel, 1984. Translation of Nomi no ichi. ISBN 0-399-21033-8 Subj: Games. Imagination. Optical illusions. Picture puzzles. Wordless.

Anno's hat tricks ill. by author. Putnam, 1985. ISBN 0-399-21212-4 Subj: Counting, numbers. Magic.

Anno's Italy ill. by author. Collins-World, 1980. Japanese ed. entitled My journey II, a translation of Tabi no ehon, II. ISBN 0-529-05560-0 Subj: Foreign lands – Italy. Games. Imagination. Optical illusions. Picture puzzles. Wordless.

Anno's journey ill. by author. Putnam, 1981. Pub. in 1977 under title: My journey, a translation of Tabi no ehon. ISBN 0-529-05419-1 Subj: Games. Imagination. Optical illusions. Picture puzzles. Wordless.

Anno's magic seeds ill. by author. Philomel, 1995. ISBN 0-399-22538-2 Subj: Counting, numbers. Gardens, gardening. Seeds.

Anno's magical ABC: an anamorphic alphabet by Mitsumasa & Masaichiro Anno; ill. by authors. Putnam, 1981. ISBN 0-399-20788-0 Subj: ABC books. Format, unusual – toy & movable books. Games. Imagination. Optical illusions. Picture puzzles.

Anno's masks ill. by author. Philomel, 1990. ISBN 0-399-21860-2 Subj: Animals. Format, unusual – toy & movable books. Masks.

Anno's math games ill. by author. Philomel, 1987. ISBN 0-399-21151-9 Subj: Concepts. Counting, numbers. Riddles & jokes.

Anno's math games II ill. by author. Putnam, 1989. ISBN 0-399-21615-4 Subj: Concepts. Counting, numbers. Riddles & jokes.

Anno's math games III ill. by author. Putnam, 1991. ISBN 0-399-22274-X Subj: Concepts. Counting, numbers. Riddles & jokes.

Anno's peekaboo ill. by author. Putnam, 1988. ISBN 0-399-21520-4 Subj: Format, unusual. Wordless.

Anno's sundial ill. by author. Philomel, 1987. ISBN 0-399-21374-0 Subj: Earth. Format, unusual – toy & movable books. Shadows. Sun. Time.

Anno's U.S.A. ill. by author. Philomel, 1983. Translation of Tabi no ehon, IV. ISBN 0-399-20974-3 Subj: Games. Imagination. Wordless.

Dr. Anno's magical midnight circus ill. by author. Weatherhill, 1972. ISBN 0-8348-2011-0 Subj: Circus. Clowns, jesters. Imagination. Optical illusions. Picture puzzles. Wordless.

In shadowland ill. by author. Watts, 1988. ISBN 0-531-08341-1 Subj: Folk & fairy tales. Shadows. Sun.

The king's flower ill. by author. Collins-World, 1979. ISBN 0-529-05459-0 Subj: Concepts – size. Flowers. Imagination. Royalty – kings.

Topsy turvies: more pictures to stretch the imagination ill. by author. Putnam, 1989. ISBN 0-399-21557-3 Subj: Games. Imagination. Optical illusions. Wordless.

Topsy turvies: pictures to stretch the imagination ill. by author. Weatherhill, 1970. Subj: Games. Imagination. Optical illusions. Wordless.

Upside-downers: more pictures to stretch the imagination adapt. into English by Meredith Weatherby & Susan Trumbull; ill. by author. Weatherhill, 1971. ISBN 0-8348-2005-6 Subj: Games. Imagination. Optical illusions.

Anrooy, Frans van. *The sea horse* ill. by Jaap Tol. Harcourt, 1968, c1967. Originally pub. in Holland under the title of Het Zeepaardje. Subj: Dreams. Emotions – fear. Night. Sea & seashore.

Antle, Nancy. *Sam's Wild West Show* ill. by Simms Taback. Dial, 1995. ISBN 0-8037-1533-1 Subj: Cowboys, cowgirls. Crime.

Antoine, Héloïse. *Curious kids go to preschool* ill. by Ingrid Godon. Peachtree, 1996. ISBN 1-56145-129-0 Subj: Language. School – nursery.

Anzaldúa, Gloria. *Prietita and the ghost woman = Prietita y la llorona* ill. by Maya Christina Gonzalez. Children's Book Pr., 1995. ISBN 0-89239-136-7 Subj: Ethnic groups in the U.S. – Mexican Americans. Foreign languages. Ghosts. Illness.

Aoki, Elaine M. *The White Swan express* (Okimoto, Jean Davies)

Aoki, Hisako. *Santa's favorite story* by Hisako Aoki & Ivan Gantschev; ill. by authors. Neugebauer, 1982. ISBN 0-90-723416-X Subj: Animals. Holidays – Christmas. Religion. Santa Claus.

Appelbaum, Diana Karter. *Cocoa ice* ill. by Holly Meade. Orchard, 1997. ISBN 0-531-33040-0 Subj: Foreign lands – Caribbean Islands. U.S. history.

Appelbaum, Neil. *Is there a hole in your head?* ill. by author. Ivan Obolensky, 1963. ISBN 0-8392-3012-5 Subj: Animals – whales. Games.

Appell, Clara. *Now I have a daddy haircut* by Clara & Morey Appell; photos by authors. Dodd, 1960. Subj: Behavior – growing up. Careers – barbers. Hair. Self-concept.

Appell, Morey. *Now I have a daddy haircut* (Appell, Clara)

Appelt, Kathi. *The Alley Cat's Meow* ill. by Jon Goodell. Harcourt, 2002. ISBN 0-15-201980-4 Subj: Activities – dancing. Animals – cats. Rhyming text.

Bats around the clock ill. by Melissa Sweet. HarperCollins, 2000. ISBN 0-68816-470-6 Subj: Activities – dancing. Animals – bats. Clocks, watches. Music. Rhyming text. Time.

Bats on parade ill. by Melissa Sweet. Morrow, 1999. ISBN 0-688-15666-5 Subj: Animals – bats. Counting, numbers. Music. Musical instruments – bands. Parades. Rhyming text.

Bayou lullaby ill. by Neil Waldman. Morrow, 1995. ISBN 0-688-12856-4 Subj: Bedtime. Ethnic groups in the U.S. Lullabies. Night.

Cowboy dreams ill. by Barry Root. HarperCollins, 1999. ISBN 0-06-027764-5 Subj: Bedtime. Cowboys, cowgirls. Dreams. Night. Rhyming text.

Elephants aloft ill. by Keith Baker. Harcourt, 1993. ISBN 0-15-225384-X Subj: Activities – ballooning. Animals – elephants. Foreign lands – Africa. Foreign lands – India.

I see the moon ill. by Debra Reid Jenkins. Eerdmans, 1997. ISBN 0-8028-5118-5 Subj: Lullabies. Moon. Sea & seashore.

Incredible me! ill. by G. Brian Karas. HarperCollins, 2003. ISBN 0-06-028623-7 Subj: Character traits – individuality. Rhyming text. Self-concept.

Oh my baby, little one ill. by Jane Dyer. Harcourt, 2000. ISBN 0-15-200041-0 Subj: Emotions – love. Family life – mothers. Rhyming text.

Rain dance ill. by Emilie Chollat. HarperFestival, 2001. ISBN 0-694-01291-2 Subj: Counting, numbers. Rhyming text. Weather – rain.

A red wagon year ill. by Laura McGee Kvasnosky. Harcourt, 1996. ISBN 0-15-277991-4 Subj: Communities, neighborhoods. Days of the week, months of the year. Rhyming text. Seasons. Toys – wagons.

Someone's come to our house ill. by Nancy Carpenter. Eerdmans, 1999. ISBN 0-8028-5144-4 Subj: Babies. Family life. Rhyming text.

Watermelon day ill. by Dale Gottlieb. Holt, 1996. ISBN 0-8050-2304-6 Subj: Character traits – patience. Family life. Food. Plants. Seasons – summer.

Where, where is Swamp Bear? ill. by Megan Halsey. HarperCollins, 2002. ISBN 0-688-17103-6 Subj: Animals – bears. Family life – grandfathers. Swamps.

Apperley, Dawn. *Blossom and Boo: a story about best friends* ill. by author. Little, 2000. ISBN 0-316-04963-8 Subj: Animals – bears. Animals – rabbits. Friendship.

Blossom and Boo stay up late: a story about bedtime ill. by author. Little, 2002. ISBN 0-316-05312-0 Subj: Animals – bears. Animals – rabbits. Bedtime. Night.

Don't wake the baby ill. by author. Bloomsbury, 2001. ISBN 0-7475-5003-4 Subj: Animals – squirrels. Babies. Family life – new sibling. Humorous stories. Senses. Sleep.

Flip and Flop ill. by author. Orchard, 2001. ISBN 0-439-28892-4 Subj: Activities – playing. Birds – penguins. Family life – brothers.

Good night, sleep tight, little bunnies ill. by author. Scholastic, 2002. ISBN 0-439-22525-6 Subj: Animals. Bedtime. Birds. Night. Rhyming text.

How does your garden grow? (Burns, Kate)

In the jungle by Dawn Apperley & Kate Burns; ill. by Dawn Apperley. Little, 1996. ISBN 0-316-11821-4 Subj: Animals. Behavior – hiding. Format, unusual – toy & movable books. Jungle.

In the sand ill. by Kate Burns. Little, 1996. ISBN 0-316-11822-2 Subj: Desert. Format, unusual – toy & movable books. Sand. Sea & seashore.

Santa Claus will come tonight ill. by author. Scholastic, 2002. ISBN 0-439-40449-5 Subj: Animals. Holidays – Christmas. Rhyming text. Santa Claus.

Appiah, Sonia. *Amoko and Efua Bear* ill. by Carol Easmon. Macmillan, 1989. ISBN 0-02-705591-4 Subj: Foreign lands – Ghana. Toys – bears.

Apple, Margot. *Blanket* ill. by author. Houghton Mifflin, 1990. ISBN 0-395-51522-X Subj: Animals. Bedtime. Clothing.

Brave Martha ill. by author. Houghton Mifflin, 1999. ISBN 0-395-59422-7 Subj: Animals – cats. Bedtime. Emotions – fear. Monsters. Night.

Applebaum, Stan. *Going my way?* by Stan Applebaum & Victoria Cox; ill. by Leonard W. Shortall. Harcourt, 1976. ISBN 0-15-231125-4 Subj: Animals. Science.

Appleby, Leonard G. *Snakes* photos by author. A & C Black, 1983. ISBN 0-7136-2350-0 Subj: Reptiles – snakes. Science.

Arabian Nights. *The first book of tales of ancient Araby* comp. by Charles Mozley. Watts, 1960. Subj: Folk & fairy tales. Foreign lands – Arabia.

The flying carpet ill. by Marcia Brown. Scribners, 1956. Subj: Activities – flying. Folk & fairy tales. Magic.

The magic horse (Scott, Sally)

The tale of Aladdin and the wonderful lamp: a story from the Arabian Nights adapt. by Eric A. Kimmel; ill. by Ju-Hong Chen. Holiday, 1992. ISBN 0-8234-0938-4 Subj: Folk & fairy tales. Magic. Mythical creatures.

The tale of Ali Baba and the forty thieves: a story from the Arabian nights (Kimmel, Eric A.)

Aragon, Jane Chelsea. *Lullaby* ill. by Kandy Radzinski. Chronicle, 1989. ISBN 0-87701-576-7 Subj: Lullabies.

The major and the mousehole mice ill. by John O'Brien. S&S, 1990. ISBN 0-671-68853-7 Subj: Animals – mice. Careers – military. Homes, houses.

Salt hands ill. by Ted Rand. Dutton, 1989. ISBN 0-525-44489-0 Subj: Animals – deer. Nature. Night. Rhyming text.

Winter harvest ill. by Leslie A. Baker. Little, 1989. ISBN 0-316-04937-9 Subj: Animals – deer. Character traits – kindness to animals. Night. Rhyming text. Seasons – winter.

Araki, Mie. *The magic toolbox: starring Fred and Lulu* ill. by author. Chronicle, 2003. ISBN 0-8118-3564-2 Subj: Animals – rabbits. Animals – rhinoceros. Magic. Tools.

Aralan, Haydé. *Milton* ill. by author. Chronicle, 2000. ISBN 0-8118-2762-3 Subj: Animals – cats.

Milton's Christmas ill. by author. Chronicle, 2000. ISBN 0-8118-2842-5 Subj: Animals – cats. Behavior – misbehavior. Holidays – Christmas.

Araten, Harry. *Two by two* ill. by author. Kar-Ben Copies, 1991. ISBN 0-929371-53-4 Subj: Religion.

Arbeit, Eleanor Werner. *Mrs. Cat hides something* ill. by author. Gibbs Smith, 1985. ISBN 0-87905-205-8 Subj: Animals – babies. Animals – cats. Family life.

Arcellana, Francisco. *The mats* ill. by Hermès Alègrè. Kane/Miller, 1999. ISBN 0-916291-86-3 Subj: Family life. Foreign lands – Philippines.

Archambault, John. *A beautiful feast for a big king cat* by John Archambault & Bill Martin, Jr.; ill. by Bruce Degen. HarperCollins, 1994. ISBN 0-06-022904-7 Subj: Animals – cats. Animals – mice. Behavior – misbehavior. Rhyming text.

The birth of a whale ill. by Janet Skiles. Silver Burdett, 1996. ISBN 0-382-39566-2 Subj: Animals – whales. Birth. Poetry.

Chicka chicka boom boom (Martin, Bill [William Ivan])

Chicka chicka boom boom [board book] (Martin, Bill [William Ivan])

Chicka chicka sticka sticka: an ABC sticker book (Martin, Bill [William Ivan])

Counting kittens (Plummer, David)

Counting sheep ill. by John Rombola. Holt, 1989. ISBN 0-8050-1135-8 Subj: Animals. Bedtime. Counting, numbers. Rhyming text.

Here are my hands (Martin, Bill [William Ivan])

Knots on a counting rope (Martin, Bill [William Ivan])

Listen to the rain (Martin, Bill [William Ivan])

The magic pumpkin (Martin, Bill [William Ivan])

Up and down on the merry-go-round (Martin, Bill [William Ivan])

White Dynamite and Curly Kidd (Martin, Bill [William Ivan])

Words (Martin, Bill [William Ivan])

Archbold, Rick. *Safari* (Bateman, Robert)

Arden, Carolyn. *Goose moon* ill. by Jim Postier. Boyds Mills, 2004. ISBN 0-613-79879-1 Subj: Moon. Seasons – spring.

Ardizzone, Aingelda. *The night ride* ill. by Edward Ardizzone. Windmill, 1975. ISBN 0-5256-1535-0 Subj: Holidays – Christmas. Night. Santa Claus. Toys. Toys – bears. Toys – dolls.

Ardizzone, Edward. *Diana and her rhinoceros* ill. by author. Oxford Univ. Pr., [1979] c1964. Reprint of the ed. published by Bodley Head, London. ISBN 0-19-520172-8 Subj: Animals – rhinoceros. Pets.

Johnny the clockmaker ill. by author. Walck, 1960. Subj: Careers – clockmakers. Clocks, watches.

The little girl and the tiny doll ill. by author. Delacorte, 1967. Subj: Behavior – lost & found possessions. Shopping. Toys – dolls.

Little Tim and the brave sea captain ill. by author. Walck, 1955. Subj: Boats, ships. Character traits – bravery. Sea & seashore.

Lucy Brown and Mr. Grimes ill. by author. Walck, 1970. A new version of a story published in 1937. ISBN 0-8098-1179-0 Subj: Emotions – loneliness. Foreign lands – England. Old age. Orphans.

Nicholas and the fast-moving diesel ill. by author. Eyre & Spottiswoode, 1980. ISBN 0-19-520230-9 Subj: Trains. Transportation.

Paul, the hero of the fire ill. by author. Walck, 1963. A new version of a story published in 1949. Subj: Activities – working. Behavior – growing up. Character traits – bravery. Merry-go-rounds.

Peter the wanderer ill. by author. Walck, 1963. Subj: Character traits – bravery. Character traits – cleverness. Character traits – honesty. Sea & seashore.

Ship's cook Ginger ill. by author. Macmillan, 1978, c1977. First published in London by Bodley Head, 1977. ISBN 0-02-705680-5 Subj: Boats, ships. Sea & seashore.

Tim all alone ill. by author. Oxford Univ. Pr., 1957. ISBN 0-19-272125-9 Subj: Boats, ships. Sea & seashore.

Tim and Charlotte ill. by author. Oxford Univ. Pr., 1979. ISBN 0-19-279562-7 Subj: Boats, ships. Character traits – bravery. Sea & seashore.

Tim and Ginger ill. by author. Walck, 1965. ISBN 0-19-272113-5 Subj: Boats, ships. Sea & seashore.

Tim and Lucy go to sea ill. by author. Walck, 1958. Subj: Boats, ships. Friendship. Sea & seashore.

Tim in danger ill. by author. Walck, 1953. ISBN 0-19-272106-2 Subj: Boats, ships. Sea & seashore.

Tim to the rescue ill. by author. Walck, 1949. Subj: Boats, ships. Character traits – bravery. Character traits – loyalty. Sea & seashore. Weather.

Tim's friend Towser ill. by author. Walck, 1962. ISBN 0-19-272112-7 Subj: Animals – dogs. Boats, ships. Sea & seashore.

Tim's last voyage ill. by author. Walck, 1972. ISBN 0-8098-1200-2 Subj: Boats, ships. Sea & seashore. Weather – wind.

Arenson, Roberta. *Manu and the talking fish* ill. by author. Barefoot, 2000. ISBN 1-84148-032-0 Subj: Fish. Folk & fairy tales. Foreign lands – India. Weather – floods.

Argent, Kerry. *Animal capers* ill. by author. Dial, 1990. ISBN 0-8037-0752-5 Subj: ABC books. Animals. Foreign lands – Australia. Zoos.

Happy birthday wombat! ill. by author. Little, 1991. ISBN 0-316-05097-0 Subj: Animals – wombats. Birthdays. Format, unusual – toy & movable books.

One woolly wombat (Trinca, Rod)

Wombat and Bandicoot: best friends ill. by author. Little, 1990. ISBN 0-316-05096-2 Subj: Animals – bandicoots. Animals – wombats. Foreign lands – Australia. Friendship.

Argueta, Jorge. *Trees are hanging from the sky* ill. by Rafael Yockteng, trans. by Elisa Amado. Groundwood, 2003. ISBN 0-88899-509-1 Subj: Dreams. Foreign lands – El Salvador. Poetry.

Argueta, Manlio. *The magic dogs of the volcanoes* trans. from Spanish by Stacey Ross; ill. by Elly Simmons. Children's Book Pr., 1990. ISBN 0-89239-064-6 Subj: Animals – dogs. Foreign lands – El Salvador. Magic.

Arkin, Alan. *One present from Flekman's* ill. by Richard Egielski. HarperCollins, 1999. ISBN 0-06-024531-X Subj: Family life – grandfathers. Stores. Toys.

Tony's hard work day ill. by James Stevenson. HarperCollins, 1972. ISBN 0-06-020138-X Subj: Activities – working. Family life. Homes, houses.

Arkin, David. *Black and white* music by Earl Robinson; ill. by author. Golden Pr., 1966. Subj: Foreign lands – Africa. Music. School. Songs.

Armalyte, Olimpija. *How the cock wrecked the manor* (How the cock wrecked the manor)

Armentrout, David. *John Muir* by David & Patricia Armentrout; ill. with photos. Rourke, 2002. ISBN 1-58952-055-6 Subj: Ecology. U.S. history.

Armentrout, Patricia. *Lights in the sky* ill. by author. Rourke, 1996. ISBN 1-57103-155-3 Subj: Northern lights. Weather – lightning, thunder. Weather – rainbows.

Armer, Laura Adams. *The forest pool* ill. by author. Longman, 1938. Subj: Caldecott award honor books. Forest, woods.

Armitage, David. *Harry hates shopping!* (Armitage, Ronda)

Ice creams for Rosie (Armitage, Ronda)

The lighthouse keeper's catastrophe (Armitage, Ronda)

My brother Sammy (Edwards, Becky)

One moonlit night (Armitage, Ronda)

Armitage, Marcia. *Lupatelli's favorite nursery tales* ill. by Anthony Lupatelli. Grosset, 1977. ISBN 0-488-13065-3 Subj: Folk & fairy tales.

Armitage, Ronda. *The bossing of Josie* ill. by David Armitage. Elsevier-Dutton, 1980. ISBN 0-233-97231-5 Subj: Birthdays. Family life. Magic. Sibling rivalry. Witches.

Don't forget, Matilda ill. by David Armitage. Elsevier-Dutton, 1979. ISBN 0-233-97075-4 Subj: Family life. Foreign lands – England.

Harry hates shopping! by Ronda & David Armitage; ill. by David Armitage. Scholastic, 1992. ISBN 0-590-45886-8 Subj: Animals – koalas. Behavior. Family life – brothers & sisters. Shopping.

Ice creams for Rosie by Ronda & David Armitage; ill. by David Armitage. Elsevier-Dutton, 1981. ISBN 0-233-97361-3 Subj: Food. Islands. Problem solving.

The lighthouse keeper's catastrophe by Ronda & David Armitage; ill. by David Armitage. Dutton, 1986. ISBN 0-233-97891-7 Subj: Animals – cats. Behavior – lost & found possessions. Lighthouses. Problem solving.

The lighthouse keeper's lunch ill. by David Armitage. Elsevier-Dutton, 1979. ISBN 0-233-96869-7 Subj: Birds – seagulls. Food. Lighthouses. Problem solving.

The lighthouse keeper's rescue ill. by David Armitage. Dutton, 1989. ISBN 0-233-98428-3 Subj: Animals – whales. Lighthouses. Old age.

One moonlit night by Ronda & David Armitage; ill. by David Armitage. Dutton, 1983. ISBN 0-233-97540-3 Subj: Camps, camping. Family life. Night.

Armour, Richard Willard. *The adventures of Egbert the Easter egg* ill. by Paul Galdone. McGraw-Hill, 1965. Subj: Holidays – Easter. Rhyming text.

Animals on the ceiling ill. by Paul Galdone. McGraw-Hill, 1966. Subj: Animals. Humorous stories. Imagination. Rhyming text.

Have you ever wished you were something else? ill. by Scott Gustafson. Childrens Pr., 1983. ISBN 0-516-03475-8 Subj: Animals. Poetry.

Sea full of whales ill. by Paul Galdone. McGraw-Hill, 1974. ISBN 0-07-002280-1 Subj: Animals – whales. Rhyming text.

The year Santa went modern ill. by Paul Galdone. McGraw-Hill, 1964. Subj: Holidays – Christmas. Rhyming text. Santa Claus.

Armstrong, Jennifer. *Chin Yu Min and the ginger cat* ill. by Mary GrandPré. Crown, 1993. ISBN 0-517-58657-6 Subj: Animals – cats. Character traits – pride. Character traits – vanity. Foreign lands – China.

King crow ill. by Eric Rohmann. Crown, 1995. ISBN 0-517-59635-0 Subj: Birds – crows. Character traits – kindness to animals. Emotions – envy, jealousy. Handicaps – blindness. War.

Little Salt Lick and the Sun King ill. by Jon Goodell. Crown, 1994. ISBN 0-517-59621-0 Subj: Activities – baking, cooking. Animals – dogs. Royalty – kings.

Pierre's dream ill. by Susan Gaber. Dial, 1999. ISBN 0-8037-2460-8 Subj: Character traits – laziness. Circus. Dreams.

Pockets ill. by Mary GrandPré. Crown, 1998. ISBN 0-517-70927-9 Subj: Activities – sewing. Careers – tailors. Clothing – pockets. Imagination.

Armstrong-Ellis, Carey. *Prudy's problem and how she solved it: ill. by author.* Abrams, 2002. ISBN 0-8109-0569-8 Subj: Behavior – collecting things. Humorous stories. Museums. Problem solving.

Arneson, D. J. *Secret places* ill. by Peter Arnold. Holt, 1971. ISBN 0-0308-6225-6 Subj: Ecology. Forest, woods.

Arnold, Caroline. *Australian animals* ill. with photos. HarperCollins, 2000. ISBN 0-688-16767-5 Subj: Animals. Foreign lands – Australia.

The biggest living thing ill. by author. Carolrhoda, 1983. ISBN 0-87614-245-5 Subj: Science. Trees.

Everybody has a birthday ill. by Anthony Accardo. Watts, 1987. ISBN 0-531-10094-4 Subj: Birthdays.

Five nests ill. by Ruth Sanderson. Dutton, 1980. Includes index. ISBN 0-525-29760-X Subj: Animals. Birds. Science.

Giant shark: megalodon, prehistoric super predator ill. by Laurie Caple. Clarion, 2000. ISBN 0-395-91419-1 Subj: Fish – sharks. Prehistory. Sea & seashore.

How do we communicate? photos by Ginger Giles. Watts, 1983. ISBN 0-531-04505-6 Subj: Communication.

How do we have fun? photos by Ginger Giles. Watts, 1983. ISBN 0-531-04506-4 Subj: Activities. Activities – playing.

How do we travel? photos by Ginger Giles. Watts, 1983. ISBN 0-531-04507-2 Subj: Activities – traveling. Transportation.

Mealtime for zoo animals photos by Richard Hewett. Carolrhoda, 1999. ISBN 1-57505-389-6 Subj: Animals. Food. Zoos.

Mother and baby zoo animals photos by Richard Hewett. Carolrhoda, 1999. ISBN 1-57505-285-7 Subj: Animals. Animals – babies. Zoos.

My friend from outer space ill. by Carol Nicklaus. Watts, 1981. ISBN 0-531-04192-1 Subj: Friendship. Imagination.

Noisytime for zoo animals photos by Richard Hewett. Carolrhoda, 1999. ISBN 1-57505-289-X Subj: Animals. Noise, sounds. Zoos.

Playtime for zoo animals photos by Richard Hewett. Carolrhoda, 1999. ISBN 1-57505-287-3 Subj: Activities – playing. Animals. Zoos.

Sleepytime for zoo animals photos by Richard Hewett. Carolrhoda, 1999. ISBN 1-57505-290-3 Subj: Animals. Sleep. Zoos.

Splashtime for zoo animals photos by Richard Hewett. Carolrhoda, 1999. ISBN 1-57505-288-1 Subj: Activities – playing. Animals. Zoos.

Sun fun ill. by author. Watts, 1981. ISBN 0-531-04312-6 Subj: Science. Sun.

The terrible Hodag ill. by Lambert Davis. Harcourt, 1989. ISBN 0-15-284750-2 Subj: Behavior – greed. Folk & fairy tales. Forest, woods. Monsters.

A walk by the seashore ill. by Freya Tanz. Silver Burdett, 1990. ISBN 0-671-68662-3 Subj: Animals. Ecology. Plants. Sea & seashore.

A walk in the desert ill. by Freya Tanz. Silver Burdett, 1990. ISBN 0-671-68664-X Subj: Animals. Desert. Ecology. Plants.

A walk in the woods ill. by Freya Tanz. Silver Burdett, 1990. ISBN 0-671-68665-8 Subj: Animals. Ecology. Forest, woods. Plants.

A walk on the Great Barrier Reef ill. with photos by Arthur Arnold & Marty Snyderman. Silver Burdett, 1988. ISBN 0-87614-285-4 Subj: Animals. Ecology. Foreign lands – Australia. Plants. Sea & seashore.

A walk up the mountain ill. by Freya Tanz. Silver Burdett, 1990. ISBN 0-671-68663-1 Subj: Animals. Ecology. Mountains. Plants.

What is a community? ill. by Carole Bertole. Watts, 1982. ISBN 0-531-04444-0 Subj: Careers. Communities, neighborhoods.

What we do when someone dies ill. by Helen K. Davie. Watts, 1987. ISBN 0-531-10095-2 Subj: Death. Emotions – grief.

What will we buy? photos by Ginger Giles. Watts, 1983. ISBN 0-531-04508-0 Subj: Money. Shopping.

Where do you go to school? ill. by Carole Bertole. Watts, 1982. Includes index. ISBN 0-531-04442-4 Subj: Careers – teachers. Communities, neighborhoods. School.

Who keeps us healthy? ill. by Carole Bertole. Watts, 1982. ISBN 0-531-04440-8 Subj: Careers – doctors. Careers – nurses. Health & fitness.

Who keeps us safe? photos by Carole Bertole. Watts, 1983. ISBN 0-531-04441-6 Subj: Careers. Safety.

Who works here? ill. by Carole Bertole. Watts, 1982. ISBN 0-531-04443-2 Subj: Careers. Communities, neighborhoods.

Arnold, Katrin. *Anna joins in* ill. by Renate Seelig. Abingdon, 1983. ISBN 0-687-01530-8 Subj: Handicaps. Illness. School.

Arnold, Katya. *The adventures of Snowwoman* retold & ill. by Katya Arnold. Holiday, 1998. Based on a story by V. Suteev. ISBN 0-8234-1390-X Subj: Animals. Holidays – Christmas. Santa Claus. Snowmen.

Baba Yaga and the little girl ill. by reteller. North-South, 1994. ISBN 1-55858-288-6 Subj: Character traits – cleverness. Family life – stepfamilies. Folk & fairy tales. Foreign lands – Russia. Witches.

Knock, knock, teremok! ill. by adapt. North-South, 1994. ISBN 1-55858-330-0 Subj: Cumulative tales. Folk & fairy tales. Foreign lands – Russia. Homes, houses. Rhyming text.

Let's find it! my first nature guide ill. by author. Holiday, 2002. ISBN 0-8234-1539-2 Subj: Animals. Nature. Plants.

Meow! retold & ill. by Katya Arnold. Holiday, 1998. Based on a story by V. Suteev. ISBN 0-8234-1361-6 Subj: Animals. Animals – cats. Animals – dogs. Noise, sounds.

That apple is mine! ill. by reteller. Holiday, 2000. based on a story by V. Suteev. ISBN 0-8234-1629-1 Subj: Behavior – sharing. Folk & fairy tales. Foreign lands – Russia.

Arnold, Lynda. *My Mommy has AIDS* ill. by Ellen M. Monahan & students of Rosemont School of the Holy Child. Dream Pub., 1998. ISBN 1-892073-01-3 Subj: Children as illustrators. Family life – mothers. Illness – AIDS.

Arnold, Marsha Diane. *The bravest of us all* ill. by Brad Sneed. Dial, 2000. ISBN 0-8037-2409-8 Subj: Character traits – bravery. Emotions – fear. Family life – sisters. Weather – tornadoes.

The chicken salad club ill. by Julie Downing. Dial, 1998. ISBN 0-8037-1916-7 Subj: Family life. Family life – great-grandparents. Old age.

Metro cat ill. by Jack E. Davis. Golden Bks., 2001. ISBN 0-307-10213-0 Subj: Animals – cats. Foreign lands – France.

Arnold, Mary. *The fussy angel* ill. by Patsy Nealon. Bethlehem Books, 1995. ISBN 1-883937-10-8 Subj: Angels. Holidays – Christmas. Religion – Nativity.

Arnold, Tedd. *Actions* ill. by author. Little Simon, 1985. ISBN 0-671-55492-1 Subj: Format, unusual – board books. Nursery rhymes.

Bisnipian blast-off: an action counting book ill. by Tedd Arnold; written by Laurie Abel; designed & paper engineered by Vincent Morales. Discovery Toys, 1990. ISBN 0-9399-7927-6 Subj: Counting, numbers. Format, unusual – toy & movable books. Mythical creatures.

Colors ill. by author. Little Simon, 1985. ISBN 0-671-55493-X Subj: Concepts – color. Format, unusual – board books. Nursery rhymes.

Five ugly monsters ill. by author. Scholastic, 1995. ISBN 0-590-22226-0 Subj: Counting, numbers. Monsters. Rhyming text. Sleep.

Green Wilma ill. by author. Dial, 1993. ISBN 0-8037-1314-2 Subj: Character traits – being different. Dreams. Frogs & toads. Rhyming text. School.

Huggly gets dressed ill. by author. Scholastic, 1997. ISBN 0-590-11759-9 Subj: Clothing. Monsters. Night.

Huggly takes a bath ill. by author. Scholastic, 1998. ISBN 0-590-91820-6 Subj: Behavior – misbehavior. Monsters. Night.

More parts ill. by author. Dial, 2001. ISBN 0-8037-1417-3 Subj: Anatomy. Language. Rhyming text.

Mother Goose's words of wit and wisdom: a book of months ill. by author. Dial, 1990. ISBN 0-8037-0826-2 Subj: Behavior. Days of the week, months of the year. Nursery rhymes.

My first drawing book ill. by author. Workman, 1986. ISBN 0-89480-350-6 Subj: Format, unusual – board books. Format, unusual – toy & movable books. Toys – bears.

No jumping on the bed! ill. by author. Dial, 1987. ISBN 0-8037-0038-5 Subj: Bedtime. Behavior – misbehavior. Dreams. Furniture – beds. Imagination.

No more water in the tub! ill. by author. Dial, 1995. ISBN 0-8037-1583-8 Subj: Activities – bathing. Cumulative tales. Imagination.

Ollie forgot ill. by author. Dial, 1988. ISBN 0-8037-0488-7 Subj: Behavior – forgetfulness. Circular tales. Middle Ages. Rhyming text.

Opposites ill. by author. Little Simon, 1985. ISBN 0-671-55494-8 Subj: Concepts – opposites. Format, unusual – board books. Nursery rhymes.

Parts ill. by author. Dial, 1997. ISBN 0-8037-2041-6 Subj: Anatomy. Rhyming text.

The signmaker's assistant ill. by author. Dial, 1992. ISBN 0-8037-1011-9 Subj: Behavior – misbehavior. Traffic, traffic signs.

The simple people ill. by Andrew Shachat. Dial, 1992. ISBN 0-8037-1013-5 Subj: Activities – making things. Communities, neighborhoods.

Sounds ill. by author. Little Simon, 1985. ISBN 0-671-77826-9 Subj: Animals. Format, unusual – board books. Noise, sounds. Nursery rhymes.

The twin princes ill. by author. Dial, 1998. ISBN 0-8037-1418-1 Subj: Family life – brothers. Royalty – kings. Royalty – princes.

Arnold, Tim. *The three billy goats Gruff* (Asbjørnsen, P. C. [Peter Christen])

Arnosky, Jim. *All about deer* ill. by author. Scholastic, 1996. ISBN 0-590-46792-1 Subj: Animals – deer. Science.

All about frogs ill. by author. Scholastic, 2002. ISBN 0-590-48164-9 Subj: Frogs & toads.

All about turkeys ill. by author. Scholastic, 1998. ISBN 0-590-48147-9 Subj: Birds – turkeys.

All night near the water ill. by author. Putnam, 1994. ISBN 0-399-22629-X Subj: Birds – ducks. Night.

Armadillo's orange ill. by author. Putnam, 2003. ISBN 0-399-23412-8 Subj: Animals – armadillos. Behavior – lost. Friendship. Homes, houses.

Beaver pond, moose pond ill. by author. National Geographic, 2000. ISBN 0-7922-7692-2 Subj: Animals – beavers. Animals – moose. Lakes, ponds.

Come out, muskrats ill. by author. Lothrop, 1989. ISBN 0-688-05458-7 Subj: Animals – muskrats. Nature.

Crinkleroot's guide to knowing animal habitats ill. by author. S&S, 1997. ISBN 0-689-80583-7 Subj: Animals. Nature.

Crinkleroot's guide to knowing butterflies and moths ill. by author. S&S, 1996. ISBN 0-689-80587-X Subj: Insects – butterflies, caterpillars. Insects – moths. Science.

Crinkleroot's guide to knowing the trees ill. by author. Macmillan, 1992. ISBN 0-02-705855-7 Subj: Forest, woods. Nature. Trees.

Crinkleroot's guide to walking in wild places ill. by author. Bradbury, 1990. ISBN 0-02-705842-5 Subj: Activities – walking. Nature.

Crinkleroot's 25 birds every child should know ill. by author. Bradbury, 1993. ISBN 0-02-705859-X Subj: Birds. Nature.

Crinkleroot's 25 fish every child should know ill. by author. Bradbury, 1993. ISBN 0-02-705844-1 Subj: Fish. Nature.

Crinkleroot's 25 mammals every child should know ill. by author. Bradbury, 1994. ISBN 0-02-705845-X Subj: Animals. Nature.

Crinkleroot's visit to Crinkle Cove ill. by author. S&S, 1998. ISBN 0-689-81602-2 Subj: Ecology. Nature. Reptiles – snakes.

Deer at the brook ill. by author. Lothrop, 1986. ISBN 0-688-04100-0 Subj: Animals – deer.

Every autumn comes the bear ill. by author. Putnam, 1993. ISBN 0-399-22508-0 Subj: Animals. Animals – bears. Hibernation. Seasons – fall. Seasons – winter.

I see animals hiding ill. by author. Scholastic, 1995. ISBN 0-590-48143-6 Subj: Animals. Behavior – hiding. Nature.

A manatee morning ill. by author. S&S, 2000. ISBN 0-689-81604-9 Subj: Animals – manatees. Rhyming text.

Mouse letters: a very first alphabet book ill. by author. Clarion, 1999. ISBN 0-039-55538-6 Subj: ABC books. Animals – mice. Wordless.

Mouse numbers and letters ill. by author. Harcourt, 1982. ISBN 0-15-256022-X Subj: ABC books. Animals – mice. Counting, numbers. Wordless.

Mouse writing ill. by author. Harcourt, 1983. ISBN 0-15-256028-9 Subj: ABC books. Activities – writing. Animals – mice. Birds. Wordless.

Mud time and more: Nathaniel stories ill. by author. Addison-Wesley, 1979. ISBN 0-20-100173-X Subj: Problem solving. Wordless.

Outdoors on foot ill. by author. Coward, 1978. ISBN 0-698-30684-8 Subj: Activities – walking. Humorous stories. Seasons.

Rabbits and raindrops ill. by author. Putnam, 1997. ISBN 0-399-22635-4 Subj: Animals – rabbits. Weather – rain.

Raccoon on his own ill. by author. Putnam, 2001. ISBN 0-399-22756-3 Subj: Animals – raccoons. Character traits – curiosity. Swamps.

Raccoons and ripe corn ill. by author. Lothrop, 1987. ISBN 0-688-05456-0 Subj: Animals – raccoons. Farms. Food. Night.

Rattlesnake dance ill. by author. Putnam, 2000. ISBN 0-399-22755-5 Subj: Activities – dancing. Reptiles – snakes.

Turtle in the sea ill. by author. Putnam, 2002. ISBN 0-399-22757-1 Subj: Reptiles – turtles, tortoises. Sea & seashore.

Watching foxes ill. by author. Lothrop, 1985. ISBN 0-688-04260-0 Subj: Activities – playing. Animals – foxes.

Wild and swampy ill. by author. HarperCollins, 2000. ISBN 0-688-17120-6 Subj: Animals. Format, unusual – toy & movable books. Swamps.

Arnott, Kathleen. *Spiders, crabs and creepy crawlers: two African folktales* ill. by Bette Davis. Garrard, 1978. ISBN 0-8116-4412-X Subj: Folk & fairy tales. Foreign lands – Africa.

Arnsteen, Katy Keck. *Mrs. Gigglebelly is coming for tea* (Guthrie, Donna)

Arnstein, Helene S. *Billy and our new baby* ill. by M. Jane Smyth. Human Sciences Pr., 1973. ISBN 0-8770-5093-7 Subj: Babies. Family life – new sibling. Sibling rivalry.

Aroner, Miriam. *The kingdom of singing birds* ill. by Shelly O. Haas. Kar-Ben Copies, 1993. ISBN 0-929371-43-7 Subj: Activities – singing. Birds. Folk & fairy tales. Royalty – kings.

Aronin, Ben. *The secret of the Sabbath fish* ill. by Shay Rieger. Jewish Publication Society, 1979. ISBN 0-8276-0110-7 Subj: Folk & fairy tales. Food. Format, unusual – board books. Jewish culture.

Aronow, Sara. *Seven days of creation* ill. by Lynne Cassouto. Sepher-Hermon Pr., 1985. ISBN 0-87203-119-5 Subj: Creation. Religion. Rhyming text.

Arqués, Isabel M. *Ken's cloud* ill. by Angela Pelaez. North-South, 2001. ISBN 0-7358-1526-7 Subj: Behavior – boredom. Weather – clouds. Weather – rain. Weather – snow.

Arquette, Kerry. *What did you do today?* ill. by Nancy Hayashi. Harcourt, 2002. ISBN 0-15-201414-4 Subj: Activities. Animals. Rhyming text.

Arquette, Lois S. *see* Duncan, Lois

Arrhenius, Peter. *The Penguin Quartet* ill. by Ingela Peterson. Carolrhoda, 1998. ISBN 1-57505-252-0 Subj: Birds – penguins. Careers – musicians.

Arro, Lena. *By geezers and galoshes!* ill. by Catarina Kruusval. R&S Books, 2001. ISBN 91-29-65348-7 Subj: Boats, ships. Family life – aunts, uncles. Old age. Pirates.

Artell, Mike. *Legs: a who's-under-the-flap book* ill. by author. Little Simon, 1996. ISBN 0-689-80621-3 Subj: Anatomy. Animals. Format, unusual – toy & movable books.

Petite Rouge: a Cajun Red Riding Hood ill. by Jim Harris. Dial, 2003. ISBN 0-8037-2514-0 Subj: Animals. Folk & fairy tales. Rhyming text.

Arthur, Catherine. *My sister's silent world* ill. by Nathan Talbot. Childrens Pr., 1979. ISBN 0-516-02022-6 Subj: Birthdays. Family life. Handicaps – deafness. Senses – hearing. Zoos.

Arthur, Malcolm. *Puss in boots* (Perrault, Charles)

Puss in boots (Perrault, Charles)

Artis, Vicki Kimmel. *Pajama walking* ill. by Emily Arnold McCully. Houghton Mifflin, 1981. ISBN 0-395-30343-5 Subj: Activities – playing. Friendship. Night.

Artzybasheff, Boris. *Seven Simeons* ill. by author. Viking, 1937. Subj: Caldecott award honor books.

Aruego, Ariane. *see* Dewey, Ariane

Aruego, José. *A crocodile's tale: a Philippine folk story* by José Aruego & Ariane Dewey; ill. by authors. Scribners, 1972. ISBN 0-684-12806-3 Subj: Folk & fairy tales. Foreign lands – Philippines. Reptiles – alligators, crocodiles.

The king and his friends ill. by author. Scribners, 1969. Subj: Dragons. Friendship. Mythical creatures. Royalty – kings.

Look what I can do ill. by author. Aladdin, 1988, c1971. ISBN 0-689-71205-7 Subj: Animals. Behavior – imitation. Folk & fairy tales. Foreign lands – Philippines. Games.

Pilyo the piranha ill. by author. Macmillan, 1971. Subj: Fish. Foreign lands – South America.

Rockabye crocodile: a folktale from the Philippines by José Aruego & Ariane Dewey; ill. by authors. Mulberry, 1993. ISBN 0-688-06739-5 Subj: Animals – pigs. Folk & fairy tales. Foreign lands – Philippines. Reptiles – alligators, crocodiles.

Splash! (Dewey, Ariane)

Symbiosis: a book of unusual friendships ill. by author. Scribners, 1970. Subj: Science.

We hide, you seek by José Aruego & Ariane Dewey; ill. by authors. Greenwillow, 1979. ISBN 0-688-84201-1 Subj: Animals. Behavior – hiding. Foreign lands – Africa. Games.

Weird friends: unlikely allies in the animal kingdom by José Aruego & Ariane Dewey; ill. by authors. Harcourt, 2002. ISBN 0-15-202128-0 Subj: Animals. Behavior – needing someone. Fish.

Arundel, Anne. *see* Arundel, Jocelyn

Arundel, Jocelyn. *Shoes for Punch* ill. by Wesley Dennis. McGraw-Hill, 1964. Subj: Animals – horses, ponies.

Arvetis, Chris. *Why does it fly?* by Chris Arvetis & Carole Palmer; ill. by James Buckley. Rand McNally, 1984. ISBN 0-528-82074-5 Subj: Activities – flying. Animals. Science.

Why does it thunder and lightning? by Chris Arvetis & Carole Palmer; ill. by James Buckley. Macmillan, 1985. ISBN 0-528-82671-9 Subj: Weather – lightning, thunder. Weather – storms.

Why is it dark? by Chris Arvetis & Carole Palmer; ill. by James Buckley. Rand McNally, 1984. ISBN 0-528-82075-3 Subj: Animals. Concepts. Science.

Asare, Meshack. *Cat . . . in search of a friend* ill. by author. Kane/Miller, 1986. ISBN 0-916291-07-3 Subj: Animals – cats. Behavior – needing someone. Friendship.

Sosu's call ill. by author. Kane/Miller, 2002. ISBN 1-929132-21-2 Subj: Animals – dogs. Character traits – bravery. Foreign lands – Africa. Handicaps. Weather – storms.

Asbjørnsen, P. C. (Peter Christen). *Billy goats Gruff* retold by Stephen Cosgrove; ill. by Wendy Edelson. Ideals Children's Books, 1988. ISBN 0-8249-8271-1 Subj: Animals – goats. Character traits – cleverness. Cumulative tales. Folk & fairy tales. Mythical creatures – trolls.

Billy goats Gruff retold & ill. by Susan Hellard. Putnam, 1986. ISBN 0-399-21291-4 Subj: Animals – goats. Character traits – cleverness. Cumulative tales. Folk & fairy tales. Mythical creatures – trolls.

The man who kept house by P. C. Asbjørnsen & J. E. Moe; ill. by Svend Otto S. Macmillan, 1992. ISBN 0-689-50560-4 Subj: Animals. Family life. Folk & fairy tales. Foreign lands – Norway.

The squire's bride: a Norwegian folk tale (The squire's bride)

The three billy goats Gruff adapt. & ill. by Tim Arnold. McElderry, 1993. ISBN 0-689-50575-2 Subj: Animals – goats. Character traits – cleverness. Folk & fairy tales. Mythical creatures – trolls.

The three billy goats Gruff adapt. & ill. by Robert Bender. Holt, 1993. ISBN 0-8050-2529-4 Subj: Animals – goats. Character traits – cleverness. Cumulative tales. Folk & fairy tales. Mythical creatures – trolls.

The three billy goats Gruff ill. by Marcia Brown. Harcourt, 1957. Subj: Animals – goats. Character traits – cleverness. Cumulative tales. Folk & fairy tales. Mythical creatures – trolls.

The three billy goats Gruff retold & ill. by Stephen Carpenter. HarperCollins, 1998. ISBN 0-694-01033-2 Subj: Animals – goats. Character traits – cleverness. Folk & fairy tales. Mythical creatures – trolls.

Three billy goats Gruff adapt. by Patricia C. & Fredrick McKissack; ill. by Tom Dunnington. Childrens Pr., 1987. ISBN 0-516-02366-7 Subj: Animals – goats. Character traits – cleverness. Cumulative tales. Folk & fairy tales. Mythical creatures – trolls.

The three billy goats Gruff ill. by Paul Galdone. Seabury Pr., 1973. Translation of De tre bukkene Bruse. ISBN 0-8164-3080-2 Subj: Animals – goats. Character traits – cleverness. Cumulative tales. Folk & fairy tales. Mythical creatures – trolls.

The three billy goats Gruff retold by Tom Roberts; ill. by David Jorgensen. S&S, 1995. ISBN 0-689-80060-6 Subj: Animals – goats. Character traits – cleverness. Cumulative tales. Folk & fairy tales. Mythical creatures – trolls.

The three billy goats Gruff retold & ill. by Dennis Kendrick. Random House, 1979. ISBN 0-394-62044-5 Subj: Animals – goats. Character traits – cleverness. Cumulative tales. Folk & fairy tales. Mythical creatures – trolls.

The three billygoats Gruff adapted by Lucy Kincaid; ill. by Eric Kincaid. Rourke, 1983. ISBN 0-8659-2184-9 Subj: Animals – goats. Character traits – cleverness. Cumulative tales. Folk & fairy tales. Mythical creatures – trolls.

Three billy goats Gruff ill. by Thea Kliros. HarperFestival, 2003. ISBN 0-06-008237-2 Subj: Animals – goats. Character traits – cleverness. Cumulative tales. Folk & fairy tales. Mythical creatures – trolls.

The three billy goats Gruff retold & ill. by Jonathan Langley. HarperCollins, 1998. ISBN 0-06-021474-0 Subj: Animals – goats. Character traits – cleverness. Cumulative tales. Folk & fairy tales. Mythical creatures – trolls.

The three billy goats Gruff retold by Jennifer Greenway; ill. by Loretta Lustig. Andrews & McMeel, 1991. Adapt. of Peter Christen Asbjørnsen's Tre bukkene Bruse. ISBN 0-8362-4913-5 Subj: Animals – goats. Character traits – cleverness. Cumulative tales. Folk & fairy tales. Mythical creatures – trolls.

The three billy goats Gruff retold by Alvin Granowsky; ill. by Thomas Newbury. Steck-Vaughn, 1996. ISBN 0-8114-7128-4 Subj: Animals – goats. Character traits – cleverness. Folk & fairy tales. Format, unusual – toy & movable books. Mythical creatures – trolls.

The three billy goats Gruff retold by Ellen Rudin; ill. by Lilian Obligado. Golden Pr., 1982. ISBN 0-307-68117-3 Subj: Animals – goats. Character traits – cleverness. Cumulative tales. Folk & fairy tales. Mythical creatures – trolls.

The three billy goats Gruff ill. by Ed Parker. Troll, 1979. ISBN 0-89375-121-9 Subj: Animals – goats. Character traits – cleverness. Cumulative tales. Folk & fairy tales. Mythical creatures – trolls.

The three billy goats Gruff retold by Lisa Meltzer; ill. by Heidi Petach. Checkerboard, 1989. ISBN 0-02-898242-8 Subj: Animals – goats. Character traits – cleverness. Cumulative tales. Folk & fairy tales. Mythical creatures – trolls. Rebuses.

The three billy goats Gruff retold by Harriet Ziefert; ill. by Laura Rader. Tambourine, 1994. ISBN 0-688-13259-6 Subj: Animals – goats. Character traits – cleverness. Cumulative tales. Folk & fairy tales. Format, unusual – toy & movable books. Mythical creatures – trolls.

The three billy goats Gruff retold & ill. by Glenn Rounds. Holiday, 1993. ISBN 0-8234-1015-3 Subj: Animals – goats. Character traits – cleverness. Cumulative tales. Folk & fairy tales. Mythical creatures – trolls.

The three billy goats Gruff adapt. & ill. by Janet Stevens. Harcourt, 1987. ISBN 0-15-286396-6 Subj: Animals – goats. Character traits – cleverness. Cumulative tales. Folk & fairy tales. Mythical creatures – trolls.

The three billy goats Gruff ill. by William Stobbs. McGraw-Hill, 1967. Subj: Animals – goats. Character traits – cleverness. Cumulative tales. Folk & fairy tales. Mythical creatures – trolls.

The three billy goats Gruff adapt. & ill. by Svend Otto S. D. C. Heath, 1989. ISBN 0-669-13287-X Subj: Animals – goats. Character traits – cleverness. Cumulative tales. Folk & fairy tales. Mythical creatures – trolls.

The truth about three billy goats Gruff as told to Steven Otfinoski; pictures by Rowan Barnes-Murphy. WhistleStop, 1994. ISBN 0-8167-3013-X Subj: Animals – goats. Character traits – cleverness. Cumulative tales. Folk & fairy tales. Mythical creatures – trolls.

Who's that tripping over my bridge? (Salley, Coleen)

The three billy goats gruff (Wade, Barrie)

The three Billygoats Gruff and Mean Calypso Joe (Youngquist, Cathrene Valente)

Asch, Devin. *Baby Duck's new friend* (Asch, Frank)

Like a windy day (Asch, Frank)

Asch, Frank. *The alphabet zoo* ill. by Lee Lee Brazeal. Scott Foresman, 1989. ISBN 0-673-74984-3 Subj: ABC books. Activities. Rhyming text.

Baby Bird's first nest ill. by author. Harcourt, 1999. ISBN 0-15-201726-7 Subj: Animals – babies. Birds. Character traits – helpfulness. Frogs & toads.

Baby Duck's new friend by Frank Asch & Devin Asch; ill. by authors. Harcourt, 2001. ISBN 0-15-202257-0 Subj: Birds – ducks. Character traits – confidence.

Baby in the box ill. by author. Holiday, 1989. ISBN 0-8234-0725-X Subj: Babies. Rhyming text. Toys.

Barnyard lullaby ill. by author. S&S, 1998. ISBN 0-689-81363-5 Subj: Animals. Careers – farmers. Lullabies. Music. Noise, sounds.

Bear shadow ill. by author. Prentice-Hall, 1985. ISBN 0-13-071580-8 Subj: Animals – bears. Shadows.

Bear's bargain ill. by author. Prentice-Hall, 1985. ISBN 0-13-071606-5 Subj: Animals – bears. Birds. Emotions – envy, jealousy.

Bread and honey ill. by author. Parents' Magazine Pr., 1981. Adapt. from the author's Monkey face. ISBN 0-8193-1078-6 Subj: Activities – painting. Animals. Animals – bears. Family life – mothers.

Cactus poems photos by Ted Levin. Harcourt, 1998. ISBN 0-15-200676-1 Subj: Desert. Ecology. Poetry.

City sandwich ill. by author. Greenwillow, 1978. ISBN 0-688-84156-2 Subj: Cities, towns. Imagination. Poetry.

Country pie ill. by author. Greenwillow, 1979. ISBN 0-688-84188-0 Subj: Country. Poetry. Weather.

Dear brother by Frank Asch & Vladimir Vagin; ill. by authors. Scholastic, 1992. ISBN 0-590-43107-2 Subj: Animals – mice. Books, reading. Cities, towns. Country. Family life. Family life – brothers. Letters, cards.

The earth and I ill. by author. Gulliver, 1994. ISBN 0-15-200443-2 Subj: Earth. Nature.

The flower faerie by Frank Asch & Vladimir Vagin; ill. by Frank Asch. Scholastic, 1993. ISBN 0-590-45493-5 Subj: Fairies. Folk & fairy tales. Royalty – emperors.

George's store ill. by author. Parents' Magazine Pr., 1983. ISBN 0-8368-0877-0 Subj: Birds – parakeets, parrots. Careers – storekeepers.

Gia and the one hundred dollars worth of bubblegum based on a story by Cresent Giasullo; ill. by author with a little help from Russell Alan Bush & Linda & Pat Galle. McGraw-Hill, 1974. ISBN 0-07-002418-9 Subj: Activities.

Good lemonade ill. by author. Watts, 1976. ISBN 0-531-01093-7 Subj: Activities – working. Food.

Good night, Baby Bear ill. by author. Harcourt, 1998. ISBN 0-15-200836-5 Subj: Animals – bears. Bedtime. Family life. Seasons – winter. Sleep.

Goodbye house ill. by author. Prentice-Hall, 1986. ISBN 0-13-360272-9 Subj: Animals – bears. Family life. Moving.

Goodnight horsey ill. by author. Prentice-Hall, 1981. ISBN 0-13-360461-6 Subj: Animals – horses, ponies. Bedtime. Family life – fathers. Games. Imagination.

Happy birthday, moon! ill. by author. Prentice-Hall, 1982. ISBN 0-13-383687-8 Subj: Animals – bears. Birthdays. Moon.

Here comes the cat (Vagin, Vladimir Vasilévich)

I can blink ill. by author. Crown, 1986. ISBN 0-517-56119-0 Subj: Animals. Character traits – appearance. Format, unusual – toy & movable books.

I can roar ill. by author. Crown, 1986. ISBN 1-55074-382-1 Subj: Animals. Format, unusual – toy & movable books. Noise, sounds.

In the eye of the teddy ill. by author. Harper, 1973. ISBN 0-06-020152-5 Subj: Toys – bears. Wordless.

Insects from outer space by Frank Asch & Vladimir Vagin; ill. by Vladimir Vagin. Scholastic, 1994. ISBN 0-590-45489-7 Subj: Insects. Parties.

Just like daddy ill. by author. Prentice-Hall, 1981. ISBN 0-1351-4042-0 Subj: Animals – bears. Behavior – imitation. Family life – fathers.

The last puppy ill. by author. Prentice-Hall, 1980. ISBN 0-1352-4058-1 Subj: Animals – dogs. Pets.

Like a windy day by Frank Asch & Devin Asch; ill. by authors. Harcourt, 2002. ISBN 0-15-216376-X Subj: Activities. Weather – wind.

Little Devil's ABC ill. by author. Scribners, 1979. ISBN 0-684-16096-X Subj: ABC books. Devil.

Little Devil's 123 ill. by author. Scribners, 1979. ISBN 0-684-16294-6 Subj: Counting, numbers. Devil.

MacGooses's grocery ill. by James Marshall. Dial, 1978. ISBN 0-8037-5231-8 Subj: Birds – geese. Eggs.

Milk and cookies ill. by author. Parents' Magazine Pr., 1992. ISBN 0-8368-0878-9 Subj: Animals – bears. Bedtime. Dragons. Dreams.

Mr. Maxwell's mouse ill. by Devin Asch. Kids Can, 2004. ISBN 1-55337-486-X Subj: Animals – cats. Animals – mice. Problem solving.

Monkey face ill. by author. Parents' Magazine Pr., 1977. ISBN 0-819-30863-3 Subj: Activities – drawing. Animals. Behavior – dissatisfaction.

Monsieur Saguette and his baguette ill. by author. Kids Can, 2004. ISBN 1-55337-461-4 Subj: Character traits – helpfulness. Food.

Moonbear ill. by author. Little Simon, 1993. ISBN 0-671-86743-1 Subj: Animals – bears. Birds. Food. Moon. Night.

Moonbear's books ill. by author. Little Simon, 1993. ISBN 0-671-86744-X Subj: Animals – bears. Books, reading. Format, unusual – board books.

Moonbear's canoe ill. by author. Little Simon, 1993. ISBN 0-671-86745-8 Subj: Animals – bears. Canoes & canoeing. Format, unusual – board books.

Moonbear's dream ill. by author. S&S, 1999. ISBN 0-689-82244-8 Subj: Animals. Animals – bears. Behavior – misbehavior. Birds. Dreams.

Moonbear's friend ill. by author. Little Simon, 1993. ISBN 0-671-86746-6 Subj: Animals – bears. Friendship.

Moonbear's pet ill. by author. S&S, 1997. ISBN 0-689-80794-5 Subj: Animals – bears. Birds. Fish. Friendship. Frogs & toads.

Mooncake ill. by author. Prentice-Hall, 1983. ISBN 0-1360-1013-X Subj: Animals – bears. Birds. Moon. Seasons – winter.

Moondance ill. by author. Scholastic, 1993. ISBN 0-590-45487-0 Subj: Activities – dancing. Animals – bears. Moon.

Moongame ill. by author. Prentice-Hall, 1984. ISBN 0-13-600503-9 Subj: Activities – dancing. Animals – bears. Behavior – hiding. Moon.

Oats and wild apples ill. by author. Holiday, 1988. ISBN 0-8234-0677-6 Subj: Animals – bulls, cows. Animals – deer. Friendship.

Popcorn ill. by author. Parents' Magazine Pr., 1979. ISBN 0-819-31002-6 Subj: Animals – bears. Food. Holidays – Halloween. Parties.

Rebecka ill. by author. HarperCollins, 1972. ISBN 0-06-020149-5 Subj: Activities – playing. Animals – dogs. Imagination.

Sand cake ill. by author. Parents' Magazine Pr., 1979. ISBN 0-8193-0986-9 Subj: Activities – picnicking. Animals – bears. Humorous stories. Sea & seashore.

Short train, long train ill. by author. Scholastic, 1992. ISBN 0-590-44493-X Subj: Concepts – opposites. Format, unusual – toy & movable books. Language.

Skyfire ill. by author. S&S, 1988. ISBN 0-671-66692-4 Subj: Animals – bears. Weather – rainbows.

Starbaby ill. by author. Scribners, 1980. ISBN 0-684-16490-6 Subj: Babies. Sea & seashore. Sky. Stars.

The sun is my favorite star ill. by author. Harcourt, 2000. ISBN 0-15-202127-2 Subj: Astronomy. Science. Sun.

Turtle tale ill. by author. Dial, 1978. ISBN 0-8037-8783-9 Subj: Humorous stories. Reptiles – turtles, tortoises.

Water ill. by author. Harcourt, 1995. ISBN 0-15-200189-1 Subj: Nature. Water.

Yellow, yellow ill. by Mark Alan Stamaty. McGraw-Hill, 1971. Subj: Clothing. Concepts – color.

Ziggy Piggy and the three little pigs ill. by author. Kids Can, 1998. ISBN 1-55074-515-8 Subj: Animals – pigs. Animals – wolves. Character traits – cleverness. Folk & fairy tales.

Asch, George. *Linda* ill. by author. McGraw-Hill, 1969. Subj: Cities, towns. Emotions – happiness. Wordless.

Aseltine, Lorraine. *First grade can wait* ill. by Virginia Wright-Frierson. A. Whitman, 1988. ISBN 0-8075-2451-4 Subj: Behavior – growing up. School.

I'm deaf and it's okay by Lorraine Aseltine, Evelyn Mueller & Nancy Tait; ill. by Helen Cogancherry. A. Whitman, 1986. ISBN 0-8075-3472-2 Subj: Emotions – anger. Emotions – fear. Handicaps – deafness. Senses – hearing.

Ash, Jutta. *Rapunzel* (Grimm, Jacob)

Wedding birds ill. by author. Little, 1987. ISBN 0-87113-122-6 Subj: Birds. Music. Songs. Weddings.

Ashabranner, Brent. *I'm in the zoo, too* ill. by Janet Stevens. Dutton, 1989. ISBN 0-525-65002-4 Subj: Animals. Animals – squirrels. Zoos.

Asher, Sandy. *Princess Bee and the royal good-night story* ill. by Cat Bowman Smith. A. Whitman, 1989. ISBN 0-8075-6624-1 Subj: Bedtime. Behavior – needing someone. Family life. Royalty. Sleep.

Stella's dancing days ill. by Kathryn Brown. Harcourt, 2001. ISBN 0-15-201613-9 Subj: Activities – dancing. Animals – cats.

Ashey, Bella. *see* Breinburg, Petronella

Ashforth, Camilla. *Calamity* ill. by author. Candlewick, 1993. ISBN 1-56402-252-8 Subj: Animals. Sports – racing. Toys.

Horatio's bed ill. by author. Candlewick, 1992. ISBN 1-56402-057-6 Subj: Bedtime. Toys. Toys – bears.

Monkey tricks ill. by author. Candlewick, 1992. ISBN 1-56402-170-X Subj: Behavior – misbehavior. Toys. Toys – bears.

Willow at Christmas ill. by author. Candlewick, 2002. ISBN 0-7636-1850-0 Subj: Farms. Holidays – Christmas. Toys – bears.

Willow by the sea ill. by author. Candlewick, 2002. ISBN 0-7636-1401-7 Subj: Animals. Sea & seashore. Toys – bears.

Willow on the river ill. by author. Candlewick, 2002. ISBN 0-7636-1088-7 Subj: Activities – picnicking. Rivers. Toys – bears.

Ashley, Bernard. *Dinner ladies don't count* ill. by Janet Duchesne. Watts, 1981. ISBN 0-531-04281-2 Subj: Behavior – misbehavior. Birthdays. Problem solving. School.

Ashley, Jill. *Riddles about Christmas* photos by Rob Gray. Silver Pr., 1990. ISBN 0-671-70552-0 Subj: Holidays – Christmas. Poetry. Riddles & jokes.

Ashley Bryan's abc of African American poetry ill. by Ashley Bryan. Atheneum, 1997. ISBN 0-689-81209-4 Subj: ABC books. Ethnic groups in the U.S. – African Americans. Poetry.

Ashman, Linda. *Babies on the go* ill. by Jane Dyer. Harcourt, 2003. ISBN 0-15-201894-8 Subj: Animals – babies. Rhyming text.

Castles, caves, and honeycombs ill. by Lauren Stringer. Harcourt, 2001. ISBN 0-15-202211-2 Subj: Animals. Homes, houses. Rhyming text.

The essential worldwide monster guide ill. by David Small. S&S, 2003. ISBN 0-689-82640-0 Subj: Monsters. Mythical creatures. Poetry.

How to make a night ill. by Tricia Tusa. HarperCollins, 2004. ISBN 0-06-029014-5 Subj: Bedtime. Night. Rhyming text.

Just another morning ill. by Claudio Muñoz. HarperCollins, 2004. ISBN 0-06-029054-4 Subj: Day. Imagination. Rhyming text.

Maxwell's magic mix-up ill. by Regan Dunnick. S&S, 2001. ISBN 0-689-83178-1 Subj: Birthdays. Careers – magicians. Parties. Rhyming text.

The tale of Wagmore Gently ill. by John Bendall-Brunello. Dutton, 2002. ISBN 0-525-46916-8 Subj: Anatomy – tails. Animals – dogs.

Ashton, Elizabeth Allen. *An old-fashioned ABC book* ill. by Jessie Willcox Smith. Viking, 1990. ISBN 0-670-83048-8 Subj: ABC books. Rhyming text.

An old-fashioned one two three book ill. by Jessie Willcox Smith. Viking, 1991. ISBN 0-670-83499-8 Subj: Counting, numbers. Rhyming text.

Asimov, Isaac. *Animals of the Bible* ill. by Howard Berelson. Doubleday, 1978. ISBN 0-385-07215-5 Subj: Animals.

The best new thing ill. by Symeon Shimin. Collins-World, 1971. Subj: Earth. Science. Space & space ships.

The moon ill. by Alex Ebel. Follett, 1967. Subj: Moon. Science.

Askar, Saoussan. *From far away* (Munsch, Robert N.)

Astley, Judy. *When one cat woke up* ill. by author. Dial, 1990. ISBN 0-8037-0782-7 Subj: Animals – cats. Counting, numbers.

Aston, Claire. *Wild West* ill. by Mark Stacey. Barron's, 2001. ISBN 0-7641-5312-9 Subj: U.S. history – frontier & pioneer life.

Aston, Dianna Hutts. *Loony Little* ill. by Kelly Murphy. Candlewick, 2003. ISBN 0-7636-1682-6 Subj: Animals. Behavior – gossip. Birds – loons. Cumulative tales. Foreign lands – Arctic.

At the farm ill. by Roser Capdevila. Firefly, 1985. ISBN 0-920303-08-0 Subj: Farms. Format, unusual – board books.

Ata, Te. *Baby Rattlesnake* adapt. by Lynn Moroney; ill. by Veg Reisberg. Children's Book Pr., 1989. ISBN 0-89239-049-2 Subj: Folk & fairy tales. Indians of North America – Chickasaw.

Atene, Ann (Anna). *The golden guitar* ill. by author. Little, 1967. Subj: Foreign lands – Italy. Music. Musical instruments – guitars. Puppets.

Atkins, Jeannine. *Aani and the tree huggers* ill. by Venantius Pinto. Lee & Low, 1995. ISBN 1-880000-24-5 Subj: Ecology. Foreign lands – India. Trees.

Get set! Swim! ill. by Hector Viveros Lee. Lee & Low, 1998. ISBN 1-880000-66-0 Subj: Character traits – pride. Ethnic groups in the U.S. – Puerto Rican Americans. Sports – swimming.

Mary Anning and the sea dragon ill. by Michael Dooling. Farrar, 1999. ISBN 0-374-34840-5 Subj: Careers – paleontologists. Dinosaurs. Dragons. Foreign lands – England. Fossils. Science.

Robin's home ill. by Candace Whitman. Farrar, 2001. ISBN 0-374-36337-4 Subj: Behavior – growing up. Birds – robins.

Atnip, Linda. *Miranda's magic garden* ill. by Ann Rothan. Bluestar, 1997. ISBN 1-885394-21-7 Subj: Bedtime. Dreams. Gardens, gardening. Plants.

Attenberger, Walburga. *The little man in winter* ill. by author. Random House, 1972. Translation of Het mannetje in de winter. ISBN 0-394-92428-2 Subj: Foreign lands – Germany. Rhyming text. Seasons – winter.

Who knows the little man? ill. by author. Random House, 1972. Translation of Wie kent dat kleine mannetje? ISBN 0-394-92427-4 Subj: Foreign lands – Germany. Rhyming text.

Attenborough, Elizabeth. *Walk rabbit walk* (McNaughton, Colin)

Atwell, Debby. *Barn* ill. by author. Houghton Mifflin, 1996. ISBN 0-395-78568-5 Subj: Barns.

Humphrey Thud ill. by author. Candlewick, 1995. ISBN 1-56402-538-1 Subj: Animals. Magic. Toys. Toys – bears.

Pearl ill. by author. Houghton, 2001. ISBN 0-395-88416-0 Subj: Family life. U.S. history.

River ill. by author. Houghton Mifflin, 1999. ISBN 0-395-93546-6 Subj: Ecology. Rivers. Water.

The Thanksgiving door ill. by author. Houghton, 2003. ISBN 0-618-24036-5 Subj: Holidays – Thanksgiving. Immigrants.

Atwood, Ann. *The little circle* ill. by author. Scribners, 1967. Subj: Concepts – shape. Rhyming text.

Atwood, Margaret. *Anna's pet* by Margaret Atwood & Joyce Barkhouse; ill. by Ann Blades. Lorimer, 1980. ISBN 0-88862-249-X Subj: Animals. Character traits – optimism. Country. Pets.

Auch, Herm. *Poultrygeist* (Auch, Mary Jane)

The princess and the pizza (Auch, Mary Jane)

Souperchicken (Auch, Mary Jane)

Auch, Mary Jane. *Bantam of the opera* ill. by author. Holiday, 1997. ISBN 0-8234-1312-8 Subj: Activities – singing. Birds – chickens. Humorous stories.

Bird dogs can't fly ill. by author. Holiday, 1993. ISBN 0-8234-1050-1 Subj: Animals – dogs. Birds – geese. Friendship. Seasons – winter.

The Easter egg farm ill. by author. Holiday, 1992. ISBN 0-8234-0917-1 Subj: Birds – chickens. Eggs. Holidays – Easter.

Eggs mark the spot ill. by author. Holiday, 1996. ISBN 0-8234-1242-3 Subj: Art. Birds – chickens. Crime. Eggs.

Hen lake ill. by author. Holiday, 1995. ISBN 0-8234-1188-5 Subj: Activities – dancing. Ballet. Birds – chickens. Birds – peacocks, peahens.

Monster brother ill. by author. Holiday, 1994. ISBN 0-8234-1095-1 Subj: Babies. Bedtime. Emotions – fear. Family life – brothers. Family life – new sibling. Monsters.

The nutquacker ill. by author. Holiday, 1999. ISBN 0-8234-1524-4 Subj: Animals. Birds – ducks. Farms. Holidays – Christmas.

Peeping Beauty ill. by author. Holiday, 1993. ISBN 0-8234-1001-3 Subj: Activities – dancing. Animals – foxes. Ballet. Birds – chickens.

Poultrygeist by Mary Jane & Herm Auch; ill. by authors. Holiday, 2003. ISBN 0-8234-1756-5 Subj: Animals. Behavior. Birds – chickens. Ghosts. Holidays – Halloween.

The princess and the pizza by Mary Jane & Herm Auch; ill. by Herm Auch. Holiday, 2002. ISBN 0-8234-1683-6 Subj: Activities – baking, cooking. Folk & fairy tales. Food. Humorous stories. Royalty – princesses.

Souperchicken by Mary Jane & Herm Auch; ill. by authors. Holiday, 2003. ISBN 0-8234-1704-2 Subj: Animals. Birds – chickens. Books, reading.

Auer, Martin. *Now, now Markus* by Martin Auer & Simone Klages; ill. by authors. Greenwillow, 1989. ISBN 0-688-08975-5 Subj: Behavior – misbehavior. Birds – swans. Giants.

Auerbach, Julie Jaslow. *Everything's changing – It's pesach!* ill. by Chari Radin. Kar-Ben Copies, 1986. ISBN 0-930494-53-9 Subj: Holidays – Passover. Jewish culture. Rhyming text.

Auerbach, Marjorie. *King Lavra and the barber* ill. by author. Knopf, 1964. Subj: Behavior – secrets. Careers – barbers. Folk & fairy tales. Royalty – kings.

Augarde, Steve (Stephen). *Barnaby Shrew, Black Dan and . . . the mighty wedgwood* ill. by author. Elsevier-Dutton, 1980. ISBN 0-233-97104-1 Subj: Animals – mice. Animals – rats. Animals – shrews. Behavior – boasting. Birds – parakeets, parrots. Reptiles – turtles, tortoises.

Barnaby Shrew goes to sea ill. by author. Elsevier-Dutton, 1979. ISBN 0-233-96957-8 Subj: Animals – rats. Animals – shrews. Boats, ships. Reptiles – turtles, tortoises.

Garage: a pop-up book ill. by author. Charlesbridge, 2002. ISBN 1-57091-507-5 Subj: Careers – mechanics. Format, unusual – toy & movable books.

Humpty Dumpty (Mother Goose)

Pig ill. by author. Bradbury, 1977. ISBN 0-87888-099-2 Subj: Animals – pigs. Farms. Fire.

Augustin, Barbara. *Antonella and her Santa Claus* ill. by Gerhard Lahr. Kane/Miller, 2001. ISBN 1-929132-13-1 Subj: Letters, cards. Santa Claus. Toys – balloons.

Aulaire, Edgar Parin d'. *Abraham Lincoln* (Aulaire, Ingri Mortenson d')

Animals everywhere (Aulaire, Ingri Mortenson d')

Children of the northlights (Aulaire, Ingri Mortenson d')

Don't count your chicks (Aulaire, Ingri Mortenson d')

East of the sun and west of the moon (Aulaire, Ingri Mortenson d')

Foxie, the singing dog (Aulaire, Ingri Mortenson d')

Nils (Aulaire, Ingri Mortenson d')

Ola (Aulaire, Ingri Mortenson d')

Pocahontas (Aulaire, Ingri Mortenson d')

The terrible troll-bird (Aulaire, Ingri Mortenson d')

Too big (Aulaire, Ingri Mortenson d')

The two cars (Aulaire, Ingri Mortenson d')

Wings for Per (Aulaire, Ingri Mortenson d')

Aulaire, Ingri Mortenson d'. *Abraham Lincoln* by Ingri & Edgar Parin d'Aulaire; ill. by authors. Rev. ed. Doubleday, 1957. ISBN 0-385-07674-6 Subj: Caldecott award books. U.S. history.

Animals everywhere by Ingri & Edgar Parin d'Aulaire; ill. by authors. Doubleday, 1940. Subj: Animals.

Children of the northlights by Ingri & Edgar Parin d'Aulaire; ill. by authors. Viking, 1962. Subj: Activities – bathing. Activities – playing. Animals. Family life. Folk & fairy tales. Foreign lands – Lapland. School. Seasons – winter.

Don't count your chicks by Ingri & Edgar Parin d'Aulaire; ill. by authors. Doubleday, 1943. ISBN 0-440-40771-0 Subj: Behavior – greed. Birds – chickens. Folk & fairy tales. Humorous stories.

East of the sun and west of the moon ed. by Ingri & Edgar Parin d'Aulaire; ill. by eds. Viking, 1938. ISBN 0-670-28748-2 Subj: Animals – polar bears. Folk & fairy tales. Foreign lands – Norway. Royalty – princes. Witches.

Foxie, the singing dog by Ingri & Edgar Parin d'Aulaire; ill. by authors. Doubleday, 1949. Subj: Animals – cats. Animals – dogs. Birds – chickens.

Nils by Ingri & Edgar Parin d'Aulaire; ill. by authors. Doubleday, 1948. Subj: Character traits – being different. Cowboys, cowgirls. Family life. School.

Ola by Ingri & Edgar Parin d'Aulaire; ill. by authors. Doubleday, 1932. Subj: Foreign lands – Norway.

Pocahontas by Ingri & Edgar Parin d'Aulaire; ill. by authors. Doubleday, [1985] c1946. ISBN 0-385-07454-9 Subj: Indians of North America – Powhatan. U.S. history.

The terrible troll-bird by Ingri & Edgar Parin d'Aulaire; ill. by authors. Doubleday, 1976. ISBN 0-385-03475-X Subj: Foreign lands – Norway. Mythical creatures – trolls.

Too big by Ingri & Edgar Parin d'Aulaire; ill. by authors. Doubleday, 1945. Subj: Behavior – growing up. Concepts – size.

The two cars by Ingri & Edgar Parin d'Aulaire; ill. by authors. Doubleday, 1955. Subj: Automobiles.

Wings for Per by Ingri & Edgar Parin d'Aulaire; ill. by authors. Doubleday, 1944. Subj: Activities – flying. Character traits – bravery. Farms. War.

Auld, Mary. *Daniel in the lions' den* (Bible Old Testament Daniel)

David and Goliath ill. by Diana Mayo. Watts, 2000. ISBN 0-531-14522-0 Subj: Foreign lands – Israel. Giants. Religion – David.

Exodus from Egypt ill. by Diana Mayo. Watts, 2000. ISBN 0-531-14585-9 Subj: Foreign lands – Egypt. Religion – Moses.

My aunt and uncle ill. with photos. G. Stevens, 2004. ISBN 0-8368-3923-4 Subj: Family life. Family life – aunts, uncles.

My brother ill. with photos. G. Stevens, 2004. ISBN 0-8368-3924-2 Subj: Family life. Family life – brothers.

My dad ill. with photos. G. Stevens, 2004. ISBN 0-8368-3925-0 Subj: Family life. Family life – fathers.

My grandparents ill. with photos. G. Stevens, 2004. ISBN 0-8368-3926-9 Subj: Family life. Family life – grandparents.

My mom ill. with photos. G. Stevens, 2004. ISBN 0-8368-3927-7 Subj: Family life. Family life – mothers.

My sister ill. with photos. G. Stevens, 2004. ISBN 0-8368-3928-5 Subj: Family life. Family life – sisters.

Noah's ark ill. by Diana Mayo. Watts, 2000. ISBN 0-531-14523-9 Subj: Animals. Boats, ships. Religion – Noah. Weather – floods. Weather – rain. Weather – rainbows.

The story of Jonah ill. by Diana Mayo. Watts, 1999. ISBN 0-531-14517-4 Subj: Animals – whales. Religion – Jonah.

Austin, Heather. *Visiting Aunt Sylvia's: a Maine adventure* ill. by author. Down East, 2002. ISBN 0-8927-2523-0 Subj: Family life – aunts, uncles. Seasons.

Austin, Margot. *Barney's adventure* ill. by author. Dutton, 1941. Subj: Circus. Clowns, jesters.

A friend for Growl Bear ill. by David McPhail. HarperCollins, 1999. ISBN 0-06-027802-1 Subj: Animals. Animals – bears. Behavior – needing someone.

Austin, Patricia. *The cat who loved Mozart* ill. by Henri Sorensen. Holiday, 2001. ISBN 0-8234-1535-X Subj: Animals – cats. Music. Musical instruments – pianos.

Austin, Virginia. *Say please* ill. by author. Candlewick, 1995. ISBN 1-56402-496-2 Subj: Animals. Books, reading. Etiquette.

Autry, Gene. *Here comes Santa Claus* words & music by Gene Autry & Oakley Haldeman; ill. by Bruce Whatley. HarperCollins, 2002. ISBN 0-06-028269-X Subj: Animals – dogs. Holidays – Christmas. Music. Santa Claus. Songs.

Auzary-Luton, Sylvie. *1, 2, 3, music!* ill. by author. Orchard, 1999. ISBN 0-531-30188-5 Subj: Family life. Family life – grandfathers. Music.

Averill, Esther. *The fire cat* ill. by author. HarperCollins, 1960. ISBN 0-06-020196-7 Subj: Animals – cats. Careers – firefighters.

Avi. *Silent movie* ill. by C. B. Mordan. Atheneum, 2003. ISBN 0-689-84145-0 Subj: Immigrants. Theater.

Awdry, W. *Happy birthday, Thomas!* ill. by Owain Bell. Random House, 2003. Based on The Railway Series. ISBN 0-679-90809-9 Subj: Birthdays. Parties. Trains.

Axelrod, Amy. *Pigs in the corner: fun with math and dance* ill. by Sharon McGinley-Nally. S&S, 2001. ISBN 0-689-82470-X Subj: Activities – dancing. Animals – pigs.

Pigs in the pantry: fun with math and cooking ill. by Sharon McGinley-Nally. S&S, 1997. ISBN 0-689-80665-5 Subj: Activities – baking, cooking. Animals – pigs. Counting, numbers. Food.

Pigs on a blanket ill. by Sharon McGinley-Nally. S&S, 1996. ISBN 0-689-80505-5 Subj: Animals – pigs. Behavior – promptness, tardiness. Clocks, watches. Sea & seashore. Time.

Pigs on the ball: fun with math and sports ill. by Sharon McGinley-Nally. S&S, 1998. ISBN 0-689-81565-4 Subj: Animals – pigs. Concepts – shape. Counting, numbers. Family life. Sports.

Pigs on the move: fun with math and travel ill. by Sharon McGinley-Nally. S&S, 1999. ISBN 0-689-81070-9 Subj: Activities – traveling. Animals – pigs. Concepts – distance. Concepts – measurement. Holidays – Christmas.

Pigs will be pigs ill. by Sharon McGinley-Nally. Four Winds, 1994. ISBN 0-02-765415-X Subj: Animals – pigs. Family life. Food. Money.

They'll believe me when I'm gone ill. by Jack E. Davis. Dutton, 2003. ISBN 0-525-46660-6 Subj: Family life. Humorous stories. Space & space ships.

Axworthy, Anni. *Along came Toto* ill. by author. Candlewick, 1993. ISBN 1-56402-172-6 Subj: Animals – cats. Animals – dogs. Behavior – needing someone.

Ben's Wednesday ill. by author. David & Charles, 1986. ISBN 0-340-33289-1 Subj: Dreams. Monsters. Night.

Guess what I am ill. by author. Candlewick, 1998. ISBN 0-7636-0625-1 Subj: Animals. Format, unusual.

Guess what I'll be ill. by author. Candlewick, 1998. ISBN 0-7636-0626-X Subj: Animals. Format, unusual.

Ayal, Ora. *The adventures of Chester the chest* by Ora Ayal & Naomi Löw Nakao; ill. by Ora Ayal. HarperCollins, 1982. ISBN 0-06-020306-4 Subj: Activities – flying. Behavior – boredom. Imagination.

Ugbu trans. by Naomi Löw Nakao; ill. by author. HarperCollins, 1979. ISBN 0-06-020308-0 Subj: Activities – playing. Imagination.

Ayars, James Sterling. *Caboose on the roof* ill. by Bob Hodgell. Abelard-Schuman, 1956. Subj: Homes, houses. Humorous stories. Trains.

Contrary Jenkins (Caudill, Rebecca)

Aye, Nila. *When I'm big* (Drury, Tim)

Ayer, Jacqueline. *Little Silk* ill. by author. Harcourt, 1970. ISBN 0-15-247450-1 Subj: Behavior – lost. Toys – dolls.

Nu Dang and his kite ill. by author. Harcourt, 1959. Subj: Behavior – lost & found possessions. Foreign lands – Thailand. Kites. Toys.

The paper-flower tree: a tale from Thailand ill. by author. Harcourt, 1962. Subj: Character traits – optimism. Foreign lands – Thailand. Plants.

A wish for little sister ill. by author. Harcourt, 1962. Subj: Behavior – wishing. Birds. Birthdays. Family life. Foreign lands – Thailand.

Ayers, Rebecca Hickox. *Per and the Dala horse* ill. by Yvonne Gilbert. Doubleday, 1993. ISBN 0-385-32075-2 Subj: Animals – horses, ponies. Family life – brothers. Farms. Folk & fairy tales. Foreign lands – Sweden. Magic. Mythical creatures – trolls. Toys.

Zorro and Quwi: tales of a trickster pig ill. by Kim Howard. Doubleday, 1997. ISBN 0-385-32122-8 Subj: Animals – foxes. Animals – guinea pigs. Folk & fairy tales. Foreign lands – Peru.

Aylesworth, Jim. *The bad dream* ill. by Judith Friedman. A. Whitman, 1985. ISBN 0-8075-0506-4 Subj: Animals – dogs. Dreams. Family life. Sleep.

The burger and the hot dog ill. by Stephen Gammell. Atheneum, 2001. ISBN 0-689-83897-2 Subj: Food. Poetry.

The cat and the fiddle and more ill. by Richard Hull. Atheneum, 1992. ISBN 0-689-31715-8 Subj: Nursery rhymes. Poetry.

The completed hickory dickory dock ill. by Eileen Christelow. Macmillan, 1990. ISBN 0-689-31606-2 Subj: Animals – mice. Clocks, watches. Counting, numbers. Nursery rhymes. Time.

Country crossing ill. by Ted Rand. Macmillan, 1991. ISBN 0-689-31580-5 Subj: Noise, sounds. Trains.

The folks in the valley ill. by Stefano Vitale. HarperCollins, 1992. ISBN 0-06-021929-7 Subj: ABC books. Rhyming text.

The full belly bowl ill. by Wendy Halperin. Atheneum, 1998. ISBN 0-689-81033-4 Subj: Folk & fairy tales. Magic.

The gingerbread man (The gingerbread boy)

The good-night kiss ill. by Walter Lyon Krudop. Atheneum, 1993. ISBN 0-689-31515-5 Subj: Animals. Bedtime. Night.

Hanna's hog ill. by Glen Rounds. Atheneum, 1988. ISBN 0-689-31367-5 Subj: Animals – pigs. Behavior – stealing. Behavior – trickery.

Hush up! ill. by Glen Rounds. Holt, 1980. ISBN 0-03-054841-1 Subj: Character traits – laziness. Humorous stories. Noise, sounds.

McGraw's Emporium ill. by Mavis Smith. Holt, 1995. ISBN 0-8050-3192-8 Subj: Animals – cats. Friendship. Illness.

Mary's mirror ill. by Richard Egielski. Holt, 1982. ISBN 0-03-060392-7 Subj: Behavior – greed. Emotions – envy, jealousy. Rhyming text.

Mr. McGill goes to town ill. by Thomas Graham. Holt, 1989. ISBN 0-8050-0772-5 Subj: Character traits – helpfulness. Cumulative tales. Fairs, festivals. Friendship. Rhyming text.

Mother Halverson's new cat ill. by Toni Goffe. Macmillan, 1989. ISBN 0-689-31465-5 Subj: Animals – cats. Character traits – practicality.

My sister's rusty bike ill. by Richard Hull. Atheneum, 1996. ISBN 0-689-31798-0 Subj: Activities – traveling. Rhyming text. Sports – bicycling. Tall tales.

My son John woodcuts by David Frampton. Holt, 1994. ISBN 0-8050-1725-9 Subj: Careers – farmers. Farms. Nursery rhymes.

Old Black Fly ill. by Stephen Gammell. Holt, 1992. ISBN 0-8050-1401-2 Subj: ABC books. Insects – flies. Rhyming text.

One crow: a counting rhyme ill. by Ruth Young. HarperCollins, 1988. ISBN 0-397-32175-9 Subj: Animals. Counting, numbers. Farms. Rhyming text.

Shenandoah Noah ill. by Glen Rounds. Holt, 1985. ISBN 0-03-003749-2 Subj: Activities – working. Emotions – embarrassment. Humorous stories.

Siren in the night ill. by Tom Centola. A. Whitman, 1983. ISBN 0-8075-7374-4 Subj: Activities – walking. Emotions – fear. Family life. Noise, sounds.

Teddy bear tears ill. by Jo Ellen McAllister-Stammen. Atheneum, 1997. ISBN 0-689-31776-X Subj: Bedtime. Emotions – fear. Toys – bears.

Through the night ill. by Pamela Patrick. S&S, 1998. ISBN 0-689-80642-6 Subj: Activities – driving. Family life – fathers. Night.

Tonight's the night ill. by John Wallner. A. Whitman, 1981. ISBN 0-8075-8020-1 Subj: Bedtime. Dreams. Night. Sleep.

Two terrible frights ill. by Eileen Christelow. Atheneum, 1987. ISBN 0-689-31327-6 Subj: Animals – mice. Emotions – fear. Night.

Wake up, little children: a rise-and-shine rhyme ill. by Walter Lyon Krudop. Atheneum, 1996. ISBN 0-689-31857-X Subj: Activities. Country. Morning. Rhyming text.

Ayres, Becky Hickox. *Matreshka* ill. by Alexi Natchev. Doubleday, 1992. ISBN 0-385-30657-1 Subj: Folk & fairy tales. Foreign lands – Russia. Toys – dolls. Witches.

Victoria flies high ill. by Robin Michal Koontz. Dutton, 1990. ISBN 0-525-65014-8 Subj: Activities – flying. Animals – pigs. Magic.

Ayres, Pam. *Guess what?* ill. by Julie Lacome. Knopf, 1988. ISBN 0-394-99287-3 Subj: Rhyming text.

Guess who? ill. by Julie Lacome. Knopf, 1988. ISBN 0-394-99288-1 Subj: Rhyming text.

Piggo and the nosebag ill. by Andy Ellis. Parkwest, 1991. ISBN 0-563-20922-4 Subj: Animals – pigs.

Piggo has a train ride ill. by Andy Ellis. Parkwest, 1992. ISBN 0-563-20921-6 Subj: Animals – pigs. Trains.

When dad cuts down the chestnut tree ill. by Percy Graham. Knopf, 1988. ISBN 0-394-90435-4 Subj: Family life – fathers. Nature. Rhyming text. Trees.

When dad fills in the garden pond ill. by Percy Graham. Knopf, 1988. ISBN 0-394-90441-4 Subj: Activities – digging. Family life – fathers. Nature. Rhyming text.

Azaad, Meyer (Mahmud). *Half for you* ill. by Nahid Haqiqat. Carolrhoda, 1971. ISBN 0-87614-016-9 Subj: Behavior – sharing. Birds. Careers. Clothing.

Azarian, Mary. *A farmer's alphabet* ill. by author. Godine, 1981. ISBN 0-87923-394-X Subj: ABC books. Activities. Farms.

A gardener's alphabet ill. by author. Houghton, 2000. ISBN 0-618-03380-7 Subj: ABC books. Gardens, gardening. Language. Plants.

The tale of John Barleycorn or, From barley to beer: a traditional English ballad ill. by author. Godine, 1983. ISBN 0-87923-446-6 Subj: Folk & fairy tales. Food. Foreign lands – England. Middle Ages. Music. Poetry.

Azore, Barbara. *Wanda and the wild hair* ill. by Georgia Graham. Tundra, 2005. ISBN 0-88776-717-6 Subj: Animals. Character traits – individuality. Cumulative tales. Hair.

B. B. Blacksheep and Company: a collection of favorite nursery rhymes ill. by Nick Butterworth. Grosset, 1982. ISBN 0-448-16577-5 Subj: Animals. Nursery rhymes.

B-52's (Musical group). *Wig!* ill. by Laura Levine. Hyperion, 1995. ISBN 0-7868-2064-0 Subj: Hair. Songs.

Baba, Noboru. *Eleven cats and a pig* ill. by author. Carolrhoda, 1988. ISBN 0-87614-338-9 Subj: Animals – cats. Behavior – misbehavior. Character traits – selfishness.

Eleven cats and albatrosses ill. by author. Carolrhoda, 1988. ISBN 0-87614-335-4 Subj: Animals – cats. Behavior – misbehavior. Character traits – selfishness.

Eleven cats in a bag ill. by author. Carolrhoda, 1988. ISBN 0-87614-336-2 Subj: Animals – cats. Behavior – misbehavior. Character traits – selfishness.

Eleven hungry cats ill. by author. Carolrhoda, 1988. ISBN 0-87614-337-0 Subj: Animals – cats. Behavior – misbehavior. Character traits – selfishness.

Babbitt, Lorraine. *Pink like the geranium* ill. by author. Childrens Pr., 1973. ISBN 0-516-08841-6 Subj: Behavior. Clothing. Family life. School.

Babbitt, Natalie. *Bub, or, The very best thing* ill. by author. Harper-Collins, 1994. ISBN 0-06-205045-1 Subj: Emotions – love. Family life. Middle Ages. Royalty.

Nellie, a cat on her own ill. by author. Farrar, 1989. ISBN 0-374-35506-1 Subj: Activities – dancing. Animals – cats. Character traits – freedom.

Ouch! a tale from Grimm retold by Natalie Babbitt; ill. by Fred Marcellino. HarperCollins, 1998. ISBN 0-06-205067-2 Subj: Folk & fairy tales. Foreign lands – Germany.

The something ill. by author. Farrar, 1970. ISBN 0-374-37137-7 Subj: Emotions – fear. Monsters. Night.

Babbitt, Samuel F. *The forty-ninth magician* ill. by Natalie Babbitt. Pantheon, 1966. Subj: Magic. Royalty.

Babcock, Chris. *No moon, no milk!* ill. by Mark Teague. Crown, 1993. ISBN 0-517-58780-7 Subj: Animals – bulls, cows. Moon.

The babes in the woods. *The old ballad of the babes in the woods* ed. by Kathleen Lines; ill. by Edward Ardizzone. Walck, 1972. Derived from a Chapbook ed. published in 1640. ISBN 0-8098-1197-9 Subj: Folk & fairy tales. Orphans. Poetry.

Babson, Jane F. *Babson's bestiary* ill. by author. Winstead Pr., 1991. ISBN 0-940787-02-4 Subj: ABC books. Animals. Rhyming text.

Baby animals ill. with photos. DK, 2003. ISBN 0-7894-9750-6 Subj: Animals – babies. Format, unusual – toy & movable books. Science.

Baby's first book of colors ill. by Nina Barbaresi. Platt, 1986. ISBN 0-448-10827-5 Subj: Animals – rabbits. Concepts – color. Format, unusual – board books.

Baby's words photos sel. by Debby Slier. Macmillan, 1988. ISBN 0-02-688751-7 Subj: Babies. Format, unusual – board books. Language.

Bach, Alice. *The day after Christmas* ill. by Mary Chalmers. Harper-Collins, 1975. ISBN 0-06-020314-5 Subj: Emotions. Holidays – Christmas.

Millicent the magnificent ill. by Steven Kellogg. HarperCollins, 1978. ISBN 0-06-020312-9 Subj: Animals – bears. Circus. Emotions – envy, jealousy. Family life.

The smartest bear and his brother Oliver ill. by Steven Kellogg. HarperCollins, 1975. ISBN 0-06-020335-8 Subj: Animals – bears. Family life. Food. Sibling rivalry. Sleep.

Warren Weasel's worse than measles ill. by Hilary Knight. Harper-Collins, 1980. ISBN 0-06-020327-7 Subj: Animals – bears. Animals – weasels. Self-concept.

Bach, Othello. *Hector McSnector and the mail-order Christmas witch* ill. by Timothy Hildebrandt. Caedmon, 1984. ISBN 0-89845-342-9 Subj: Holidays – Christmas. Magic. Witches.

Lilly, Willy and the mail-order witch ill. by Timothy Hildebrandt. Caedmon, 1983. ISBN 0-89845-048-9 Subj: Activities – working. Imagination. Magic. Music. Rhyming text. Witches.

Bacheller, Irving. *Lost in the fog* adapt. & ill. by Loretta Krupinski. Little, 1990. ISBN 0-316-07462-4 Subj: Behavior – lost. Birds – geese. Weather – fog.

Back, Christine. *Bean and plant* photos by Barrie Watts. Silver Burdett, 1986. ISBN 0-382-09286-4 Subj: Plants. Science. Seeds.

Chicken and egg photos by Bo Jarner. Silver Burdett, 1986. ISBN 0-382-09284-8 Subj: Birds – chickens. Eggs. Science.

Spider's web photos by Barrie Watts. Silver Burdett, 1986. ISBN 0-382-09288-8 Subj: Science. Spiders.

Tadpole and frog photos by Barrie Watts. Silver Burdett, 1986. ISBN 0-382-09285-6 Subj: Frogs & toads. Science.

Back, Rachel Tzvia. *The perfect purple feather* (Piven, Hanokh)

Backhouse, Joy. *The voyage of the jolly boat* (Rettich, Margret)

Backker, Vera de. *Coco the koala* ill. by author. G. Stevens, 2000. ISBN 0-8368-2729-5 Subj: Animals – koalas. Self-concept.

Backovsky, Jan. *Trouble in Paradise* ill. by author. Tambourine, 1992. ISBN 0-688-11858-5 Subj: Animals. Islands. Sports – hunting.

Backstein, Karen. *The blind men and the elephant* ill. by Annie Mitra. Scholastic, 1992. ISBN 0-590-45813-2 Subj: Animals – elephants. Folk & fairy tales. Foreign lands – India. Handicaps – blindness. Senses – sight.

Backx, Patsy. *Josie and Mr. Fernandez* ill. by author. G. Stevens, 2002. ISBN 0-8368-3079-2 Subj: Animals – dogs. Behavior – sharing. Food.

Skippy and Jack ill. by author. G. Stevens, 2002. ISBN 0-8368-3080-6 Subj: Activities – dancing. Animals – dogs. Rhyming text.

Bacon, Ethel. *To see the moon* ill. by David Ray. BridgeWater, 1996. ISBN 0-8167-3822-X Subj: Animals – dogs. Moon. Sports – racing. Sports – sledding.

Bacon, Joan Chase. *see* Bowden, Joan Chase

Baden, Robert. *And Sunday makes seven* ill. by Michelle Edwards. A. Whitman, 1990. ISBN 0-8075-0356-8 Subj: Days of the week, months of the year. Folk & fairy tales. Foreign lands – Costa Rica. Foreign languages. Witches.

Baehr, Patricia. *Mouse in the house* ill. by Laura Lydecker. Holiday, 1994. ISBN 0-8234-1102-8 Subj: Animals – mice. Cumulative tales. Pets.

School isn't fair ill. by R. W. Alley. Macmillan, 1992. ISBN 0-689-71544-7 Subj: School.

Baer, Edith. *This is the way we go to school* ill. by Steve Björkman. Scholastic, 1990. ISBN 0-590-43161-7 Subj: Rhyming text. School. Transportation.

The wonder of hands photos by Tana Hoban. Macmillan, 1992. ISBN 0-02-708138-9 Subj: Anatomy – hands.

Words are like faces ill. by Karen Gundersheimer. Pantheon, 1980. ISBN 0-394-94028-8 Subj: Language. Rhyming text.

Baer, Gene. *Thump thump rat-a-tat-tat* ill. by Lois Ehlert. Harper-Collins, 1989. ISBN 0-06-020362-5 Subj: Music. Musical instruments – bands. Parades.

Bagert, Brod. *Chicken socks and other contagious poems* ill. by Tim Ellis. Boyds Mills, 1993. ISBN 1-56397-292-1 Subj: Poetry.

Giant children ill. by Tedd Arnold. Dial, 2002. ISBN 0-8037-2556-6 Subj: Poetry.

The gooch machine: a collection of humorous poems to perform ill. by Tim Ellis. Boyds Mills, 1997. ISBN 1-56397-294-8 Subj: Poetry.

Baggette, Susan K. *Jonathan goes to the doctor* photos by William J. Moriarty. Brookfield, 1998. ISBN 0-9660172-1-8 Subj: Careers – doctors. Format, unusual – board books. Illness.

Jonathan goes to the grocery store photos by William J. Moriarty. Brookfield, 1998. ISBN 0-9660172-2-6 Subj: Communities, neighborhoods. Family life – grandparents. Format, unusual – board books. Handicaps – physical handicaps. Shopping. Stores.

Jonathan goes to the library photos by William J. Moriarty. Brookfield, 1998. ISBN 0-9660172-3-4 Subj: Books, reading. Careers – librarians. Communities, neighborhoods. Family life – grandparents. Libraries. Monsters.

Bagwell, Elizabeth. *This is an airport* (Bagwell, Richard)

Bagwell, Richard. *This is an airport* by Richard & Elizabeth Bagwell; photos by Lee Balterman. Follett, 1967. Subj: Airplanes, airports. Transportation.

Bahous, Sally. *Sitti and the cats* ill. by Nancy Malick. Bookmakers Guild, 1993. ISBN 1-879373-61-0 Subj: Animals – cats. Character traits – selfishness. Folk & fairy tales. Foreign lands – Palestine. Middle Ages.

Bahr, Amy C. *It's ok to say no: a book for parents and children to read together* ill. by Frederick Bennett Green. Grosset, 1986. ISBN 0-448-15328-9 Subj: Behavior – talking to strangers. Safety. Self-concept.

Sometimes it's ok to tell secrets: a book for parents and children to read together ill. by Frederick Bennett Green. Grosset, 1986. ISBN 0-448-15325-4 Subj: Behavior – secrets. Safety. Self-concept.

What should you do when . . . ? a book for parents and children to read together ill. by Frederick Bennett Green. Grosset, 1986. ISBN 0-448-15327-0 Subj: Safety. Self-concept.

Your body is your own: a book for parents and children to read together ill. by Frederick Bennett Green. Grosset, 1986. ISBN 0-448-15326-2 Subj: Safety. Self-concept.

Bahr, Mary. *The memory box* ill. by David Cunningham. A. Whitman, 1992. ISBN 0-8075-5052-3 Subj: Family life – grandfathers. Illness – Alzheimer's. Memories, memory.

My brother loved snowflakes ill. by Laura Jacobsen. Boyds Mills, 2002. ISBN 1-56397-689-7 Subj: Careers – meteorologists. Careers – photographers. Weather – snow.

Bahr, Robert. *Blizzard at the zoo* ill. by Consuelo Joerns. Lothrop, 1982. ISBN 0-688-00424-5 Subj: Animals. Weather – snow. Weather – storms. Zoos.

Baicker, Karen. *Pea pod babies* ill. by Sam Williams. Handprint, 2003. ISBN 1-59354-003-5 Subj: Babies. Character traits – individuality. Gardens, gardening. Rhyming text.

Bailey, Debbie. *Clothes* photos by Susan Huszar. Firefly, 1991. ISBN 1-55037-167-3 Subj: Clothing. Format, unusual – board books.

Grandma photos by Susan Huszar. Firefly, 1994. ISBN 1-55037-966-6 Subj: Ethnic groups in the U.S. Family life – grandmothers. Format, unusual – board books.

Grandpa photos by Susan Huszar. Firefly, 1994. ISBN 1-55037-967-4 Subj: Ethnic groups in the U.S. Family life – grandfathers. Format, unusual – board books.

Hats photos by Susan Huszar. Firefly, 1991. ISBN 1-55037-159-2 Subj: Clothing – hats. Format, unusual – board books.

My dad photos by Susan Huszar. Firefly, 1991. ISBN 1-55037-164-9 Subj: Family life – fathers. Format, unusual – board books.

My family photos by Susan Huszar. Annick, 1998. ISBN 1-55037-510-5 Subj: Family life. Format, unusual – board books.

My mom photos by Susan Huszar. Firefly, 1991. ISBN 1-55037-163-0 Subj: Family life – mothers. Format, unusual – board books.

The playground photos by Susan Huszar. Annick, 1998. ISBN 1-55037-511-3 Subj: Activities – playing. Communities, neighborhoods. Family life. Format, unusual – board books.

Shoes photos by Susan Huszar. Firefly, 1991. ISBN 1-55037-161-4 Subj: Clothing – shoes. Format, unusual – board books.

Toys photos by Susan Huszar. Firefly, 1991. ISBN 1-55037-165-7 Subj: Format, unusual – board books. Toys.

Bailey, Donna. *Camels* ill. with photos. Steck-Vaughn, 1991. ISBN 0-8114-2644-0 Subj: Animals – camels.

Dolphins ill. with photos. Steck-Vaughn, 1991. ISBN 0-8114-2647-5 Subj: Animals – dolphins.

Giraffes ill. with photos. Steck-Vaughn, 1991. ISBN 0-8114-2646-7 Subj: Animals – giraffes.

Bailey, Jill. *Eyes* photos by Jim Bailey. Putnam, 1984. ISBN 0-399-21026-1 Subj: Anatomy – eyes. Animals. Birds. Format, unusual – board books.

Feet photos by Jim Bailey. Putnam, 1984. ISBN 0-399-21029-6 Subj: Anatomy – feet. Animals. Birds. Format, unusual – board books.

The life cycle of a spider ill. by Jackie Harland. Bookwright, 1989. ISBN 0-531-18288-6 Subj: Nature. Science. Spiders.

Mouths photos by Jim Bailey. Putnam, 1984. ISBN 0-399-21028-8 Subj: Anatomy – mouths. Animals. Birds. Format, unusual – board books.

Noses photos by Jim Bailey. Putnam, 1984. ISBN 0-399-21027-X Subj: Anatomy – noses. Animals. Format, unusual – board books.

Worm ill. by author. Heinemann, 1998. ISBN 1-57572-665-3 Subj: Animals – worms.

Bailey, Linda. *The best figure skater in the whole wide world* ill. by Alan Daniel & Lea Daniel. Kids Can, 2001. ISBN 1-55074-879-3 Subj: Sports – ice skating.

Gordon Loggins and the three bears ill. by Tracy Walker. Kids Can, 1997. ISBN 1-55074-362-7 Subj: Animals – bears. Folk & fairy tales.

Stanley's party ill. by Bill Slavin. Kids Can, 2003. ISBN 1-55337-382-0 Subj: Animals – dogs. Parties.

When Addie was scared ill. by Wendy Bailey. Kids Can, 1999. ISBN 1-55074-431-3 Subj: Character traits – bravery. Emotions – fear. Family life – grandmothers. Farms.

Bailey, Mary Bryant. *Jeoffry's Christmas* ill. by Elizabeth Sayles. Farrar, 2002. ISBN 0-374-33676-8 Subj: Animals – cats. Holidays – Christmas. Rhyming text. Santa Claus. Trees.

Bailey, Philip H. *What shall we do when we all go out?* (Halpern, Shari)

Baillie, Allan. *Drac and the gremlin* ill. by Jane Tanner. Dial, 1989. ISBN 0-8037-0628-6 Subj: Activities – playing. Games. Imagination.

Rebel! ill. by Di Wu. Ticknor & Fields, 1994. ISBN 0-395-63250-4 Subj: Character traits – bravery. Foreign lands – Burma. War.

Baillie, Marilyn. *More science surprises from Dr. Zed* (Penrose, Gordon)

Nose to toes ill. by Marisol Sarrazin. Boyds Mills, 2001. ISBN 1-56397-319-7 Subj: Activities – playing. Animals. Imagination. Rhyming text.

Side by side: animals who help each other ill. by Romi Caron. Firefly, 1997. ISBN 1-895688-56-6 Subj: Animals. Character traits – helpfulness.

Bains, Rae. *Hiccups, hiccups* ill. by Otto Coontz. Troll, 1981. ISBN 0-89375-537-0 Subj: Hiccups.

Baird, Anne. *Baby socks* ill. by author. Morrow, 1984. ISBN 0-688-02436-X Subj: Babies. Clothing – socks. Format, unusual – board books.

The Christmas lamb ill. by author. Morrow, 1989. ISBN 0-688-07775-7 Subj: Animals – sheep. Holidays – Christmas.

The guppies of Hilly Dale House ill. by Mary Morgan. S&S, 1991. ISBN 0-671-69201-1 Subj: Activities. School.

Kiss, kiss ill. by author. Morrow, 1984. ISBN 0-688-02493-9 Subj: Babies. Family life. Format, unusual – board books.

Little tree ill. by author. Morrow, 1984. ISBN 0-688-02421-9 Subj: Format, unusual – board books. Trees.

No sheep ill. by author. Morrow, 1984. ISBN 0-688-02377-0 Subj: Bedtime. Format, unusual – board books.

Baird, Audrey B. *A cold snap! frosty poems* ill. by Patrick O'Brien. Wordsong, 2002. ISBN 1-56397-633-1 Subj: Poetry. Seasons – winter. Weather.

Storm coming! ill. by Patrick O'Brien. Wordsong, 2001. ISBN 1-56397-887-3 Subj: Poetry. Weather – rain. Weather – storms.

Baisch, Cris. *When the lights went out* ill. by Ulises Wensell. Putnam, 1987. ISBN 0-399-21415-1 Subj: Family life. Light, lights. Power failures.

Baker, Alan. *Benjamin and the box* ill. by author. Lippincott, 1978. ISBN 0-397-31774-3 Subj: Animals – hamsters. Friendship. Humorous stories.

Benjamin bounces back ill. by author. Lippincott, 1978. ISBN 0-397-31809-X Subj: Animals – hamsters. Humorous stories. Imagination.

Benjamin's balloon ill. by author. Lothrop, 1990. ISBN 0-688-09744-8 Subj: Animals – hamsters. Humorous stories. Toys – balloons.

Benjamin's book ill. by author. Lothrop, 1983. ISBN 0-688-01697-9 Subj: Animals – hamsters. Behavior – misbehavior. Humorous stories.

Benjamin's dreadful dream ill. by author. Lippincott, 1980. ISBN 0-397-31903-7 Subj: Animals – hamsters. Behavior – misbehavior. Humorous stories.

Benjamin's portrait ill. by author. Lothrop, 1987. ISBN 0-688-06878-2 Subj: Activities – painting. Animals – hamsters. Behavior – bad day. Careers – artists. Concepts – color. Humorous stories.

Black and White Rabbit's ABC ill. by author. Kingfisher, 1994. ISBN 1-85697-851-2 Subj: ABC books. Activities – painting. Animals – rabbits. Cumulative tales.

Brown Rabbit's shape book ill. by author. Kingfisher, 1994. ISBN 1-85697-950-4 Subj: Animals – rabbits. Concepts – shape. Toys – balloons.

Gray Rabbit's one, two, three ill. by author. Kingfisher, 1994. ISBN 1-85697-952-0 Subj: Animals. Animals – rabbits. Counting, numbers.

Little Rabbit's first number book ill. by author. Kingfisher, 1998. ISBN 0-7534-5167-0 Subj: Animals – rabbits. Counting, numbers.

Little Rabbit's first word book ill. by author. Kingfisher, 1996. ISBN 0-7534-5020-8 Subj: Animals – rabbits. Language.

Two tiny mice ill. by author. Dial, 1991. ISBN 0-8037-0973-0 Subj: Animals. Animals – mice. Nature.

Where's mouse? ill. by author. Kingfisher, 1992. ISBN 1-85697-821-4 Subj: Animals. Animals – mice. Behavior – lost & found possessions. Family life – mothers. Format, unusual – toy & movable books.

White Rabbit's color book ill. by author. Kingfisher, 1994. ISBN 1-85697-953-9 Subj: Activities – painting. Animals – rabbits. Concepts – color.

Baker, Barbara. *Digby and Kate* ill. by Marsha Winborn. Dutton, 1988. ISBN 0-525-44370-3 Subj: Animals – cats. Animals – dogs. Friendship.

Digby and Kate again ill. by Marsha Winborn. Dutton, 1989. ISBN 0-525-44477-7 Subj: Animals – cats. Animals – dogs. Friendship.

Digby and Kate and the beautiful day ill. by Marsha Winborn. Dutton, 1998. ISBN 0-525-45855-7 Subj: Animals – cats. Animals – dogs. Friendship.

Baker, Betty. *And me, coyote!* ill. by Maria Horvath. Macmillan, 1982. ISBN 0-02-708280-6 Subj: Animals – coyotes. Character traits – cleverness. Creation. Folk & fairy tales. Indians of North America. Religion.

My sister says ill. by Tricia Taggart. Macmillan, 1984. ISBN 0-02-708160-5 Subj: Behavior – wishing. Boats, ships. Family life – fathers. Imagination. Sibling rivalry.

Partners ill. by Emily Arnold McCully. Greenwillow, 1978. ISBN 0-688-84151-1 Subj: Animals – badgers. Animals – coyotes. Character traits – cleverness. Character traits – helpfulness. Character traits – laziness. Farms. Friendship.

Rat is dead and ant is sad: based on a Pueblo Indian tale ill. by Mamoru Funai. HarperCollins, 1981. ISBN 0-06-020347-1 Subj: Cumulative tales. Death. Emotions – grief. Emotions – sadness. Folk & fairy tales. Indians of North America – Pueblo.

Sonny-Boy Sim ill. by Susanne Suba. Rand McNally, 1948. Subj: Animals. Family life. Humorous stories. Sports – hunting.

Three fools and a horse ill. by Glen Rounds. Macmillan, 1975. ISBN 0-02-708250-4 Subj: Animals – horses, ponies. Humorous stories. Indians of North America – Apache.

Worthington Botts and the steam machine ill. by Sal Murdocca. Macmillan, 1981. ISBN 0-02-708190-7 Subj: Books, reading. Humorous stories. Machines.

Baker, Bonnie Jeanne. *A pear by itself* ill. by author. Childrens Pr., 1982. ISBN 0-516-02032-3 Subj: Counting, numbers.

Baker, Charlotte. *Little brother* ill. by author. McKay, 1959. Subj: Animals – dogs. Babies. Emotions – envy, jealousy. Family life – new sibling. Sibling rivalry.

Baker, Donna. *I want to be a librarian* ill. by Richard Wahl. Childrens Pr., 1978. ISBN 0-516-01715-2 Subj: Careers – librarians. Libraries.

I want to be a pilot ill. by Richard Wahl. Childrens Pr., 1978. ISBN 0-516-01720-9 Subj: Airplanes, airports. Careers – airplane pilots.

I want to be a police officer ill. by Richard Wahl. Childrens Pr., 1978. ISBN 0-516-01721-7 Subj: Careers – police officers.

Baker, Eugene H. *Bicycles* ill. by Tom Dunnington. Creative Ed., 1980. ISBN 0-87191-738-6 Subj: Animals. Safety. Sports – bicycling.

Fire ill. by Tom Dunnington. Creative Ed., 1980. ISBN 0-87191-735-1 Subj: Animals. Fire. Safety.

Home ill. by Tom Dunnington. Creative Ed., 1980. ISBN 0-87191-739-4 Subj: Animals. Safety.

I want to be a computer operator ill. by Tom Dunnington. Childrens Pr., 1973. ISBN 0-516-01741-1 Subj: Careers. Computers.

Outdoors ill. by Tom Dunnington. Creative Ed., 1980. ISBN 0-87191-736-X Subj: Animals. Safety.

School ill. by Tom Dunnington. Creative Ed., 1980. ISBN 0-87191-737-8 Subj: Animals. Safety. School.

Water ill. by Tom Dunnington. Creative Ed., 1980. ISBN 0-87191-740-8 Subj: Animals. Safety.

Baker, Gayle. *Special delivery: a book for kids about cesarean and vaginal birth* ill. by Debra Hillyer. Chas. Franklin Pr., 1981. ISBN 0-9603516-2-0 Subj: Babies. Birth. Family life – mothers. Hospitals. Science.

Baker, Jeannie. *Grandmother* ill. by author. Elsevier-Dutton, 1979. ISBN 0-233-96975-6 Subj: Art. Family life – grandmothers.

The hidden forest ill. by author. Greenwillow, 2000. ISBN 0-688-15760-2 Subj: Foreign lands – Tasmania. Plants. Sea & seashore. Sports – skin diving.

Home in the sky ill. by author. Greenwillow, 1984. ISBN 0-688-03842-5 Subj: Animals – dogs. Birds – pigeons. Character traits – kindness to animals. Cities, towns.

Millicent ill. by author. Elsevier-Dutton, 1980. ISBN 0-233-97201-3 Subj: Birds – pigeons. Character traits – individuality. Cities, towns.

One hungry spider ill. by author. Elsevier-Dutton, 1983. ISBN 0-233-97429-6 Subj: Counting, numbers. Science. Spiders.

The story of rosy dock ill. by author. Greenwillow, 1995. ISBN 0-688-11493-8 Subj: Ecology. Foreign lands – Australia. Plants.

Where the forest meets the sea ill. by author. Greenwillow, 1988. ISBN 0-688-06364-0 Subj: Ecology. Foreign lands – Australia. Forest, woods.

Window ill. by author. Greenwillow, 1991. ISBN 0-688-08918-6 Subj: Ecology. Foreign lands – Australia. Wordless.

Baker, Jeffrey J. W. *Patterns of nature* photos by Jaroslav Salek. Doubleday, 1967. Subj: Animals. Birds. Flowers. Plants. Science. Trees.

Baker, Jill. *Basil of Bywater Hollow* ill. by Lynn Bywaters Ferris. Holt, 1987. ISBN 0-8050-0268-5 Subj: Animals – bears. Fairs, festivals. Weather – rain.

Baker, Karen Lee. *Seneca* ill. by author. Greenwillow, 1997. ISBN 0-688-14030-0 Subj: Animals – horses, ponies.

Baker, Keith. *Cat tricks* ill. by author. Harcourt, 1997. ISBN 0-15-292857-X Subj: Animals – cats. Format, unusual – toy & movable books. Rhyming text.

The dove's letter ill. by author. Harcourt, 1988. ISBN 0-15-224133-7 Subj: Birds – doves. Emotions – love. Letters, cards.

Hide and snake ill. by author. Harcourt, 1991. ISBN 0-15-233986-8 Subj: Games. Reptiles – snakes. Rhyming text.

Little Green ill. by author. Harcourt, 2001. ISBN 0-15-292859-6 Subj: Activities – painting. Birds – humming birds. Rhyming text.

The magic fan ill. by author. Harcourt, 1989. ISBN 0-15-250750-7 Subj: Careers – carpenters. Foreign lands – Japan. Imagination.

Meet Mr. and Mrs. Green ill. by author. Harcourt, 2002. ISBN 0-613-71636-1 Subj: Camps, camping. Fairs, festivals. Reptiles – alligators, crocodiles.

Who is the beast? ill. by author. Harcourt, 1990. ISBN 0-15-296057-0 Subj: Animals – tigers. Rhyming text.

Baker, Ken. *Brave little monster* ill. by Geoffrey Hayes. HarperCollins, 2001. ISBN 0-06-028699-7 Subj: Bedtime. Emotions – fear. Monsters. Night.

Baker, Laura Nelson. *The friendly beasts* ill. by Nicolas Sidjakov. Parnassus, 1958. Adapt. from an old English Christmas carol of the same title. Subj: Animals. Holidays – Christmas. Music.

O children of the wind and pines ill. by Inez Storer. Lippincott, 1967. Subj: Holidays – Christmas. Indians of North America. Music.

Baker, Leslie A. *The antique store cat* ill. by author. Little, 1992. ISBN 0-316-07837-9 Subj: Animals – cats. Behavior – running away.

Paris cat ill. by author. Little, 1999. ISBN 0-316-07309-1 Subj: Animals – cats. Behavior – lost. Behavior – lost & found possessions. Foreign lands – France.

The third-story cat ill. by author. Little, 1987. ISBN 0-316-07832-8 Subj: Animals – cats. Behavior – running away.

You bad dog! ill. by author. Dutton, 2003. ISBN 0-525-47127-8 Subj: Activities – playing. Animals – dogs. Behavior – misbehavior.

Baker, Liza. *Dinosaur days* ill. by Andy Chiang; color by Sharon Matsumoto. HarperFestival, 2003. Based on a teleplay by Don Gillies. ISBN 0-06-000541-6 Subj: Activities – drawing. Dinosaurs. Jungle.

I love you because you're you ill. by David McPhail. Scholastic, 2001. ISBN 0-439-20638-3 Subj: Animals – foxes. Emotions – love. Family life – mothers. Rhyming text.

Baker, Margaret. *A puppy called Spinach* by Margaret & Mary Baker; ill. by Mary Baker. Dodd, 1939. Subj: Animals – dogs. Behavior – misbehavior.

Baker, Mary. *A puppy called Spinach* (Baker, Margaret)

Baker, Olaf. *Where the buffaloes begin* ill. by Stephen Gammell. Warne, 1981. ISBN 0-670-82760-6 Subj: Animals – buffaloes. Caldecott award honor books. Folk & fairy tales. Indians of North America.

Baker, Pamela J. *My first book of sign* ill. by Patricia Bellan Gillen. Gallaudet Univ. Pr., 1986. ISBN 0-930323-20-3 Subj: Handicaps – deafness. Senses – hearing. Sign language.

Baker, Roberta. *No ordinary Olive* ill. by Debbie Tilley. Little, 2002. ISBN 0-316-07336-9 Subj: Character traits – individuality. Family life – daughters. Family life – parents. Imagination.

Baker, Sanna Anderson. *Mississippi going north* ill. by Bill Farnsworth. A. Whitman, 1996. ISBN 0-8075-5164-3 Subj: Canoes & canoeing. Family life. Nature. Rivers.

Who's a friend of the water-spurting whale handlettered & ill. by Tomie de Paola. David C. Cook, 1987. ISBN 0-89191-587-7 Subj: Religion. Rhyming text.

Baker, Susan. *First look at keeping warm* ill. by author. G. Stevens, 1991. ISBN 0-8368-0704-9 Subj: Weather – cold.

Baker, Taftt. *The hokey pokey* (La Prise, Larry)

Bakken, Harold. *The special string* ill. by Mischa Richter. Prentice-Hall, 1981. ISBN 0-13-826370-1 Subj: Character traits – helpfulness. Humorous stories. Problem solving. String. Wordless.

Balan, Bruce. *Pie in the sky* ill. by Clare Skilbeck. Viking, 1993. ISBN 0-670-85150-7 Subj: Birthdays. Food.

Balcziak, Bill. *John Henry* ill. by Drew Rose. Compass Pt., 2003. ISBN 0-7565-0457-0 Subj: Character traits – perseverance. Character traits – pride. Ethnic groups in the U.S. – African Americans. Folk & fairy tales. Tall tales.

Paul Bunyan ill. by Patrick Girouard. Compass Pt., 2003. ISBN 0-7565-0459-7 Subj: Animals – oxen. Careers – lumberjacks. Tall tales. U.S. history – frontier & pioneer life.

Pecos Bill ill. by Roberta Collier-Morales. Compass Pt., 2003. ISBN 0-7565-0460-0 Subj: Cowboys, cowgirls. Tall tales. U.S. history – frontier & pioneer life.

Baldner, Gaby. *Joba and the wild boar = Joba und das wildschwein* ill. by Gerhard Oberländer. Hastings House, 1961. Text in English and German. Subj: Animals – pigs. Character traits – bravery. Foreign languages. Pets.

Balducci, Rita. *Little Bear's timeless tales* ill. by Amy Flynn. Reader's Digest, 2003. ISBN 0-7944-0215-1 Subj: Folk & fairy tales.

Balestra, Alejandra. *The last doll = La última muñeca* (Bertrand, Diane Gonzales)

Pepita takes time = Pepita, siempre tarde (Lachtman, Ofelia Dumas)

Balestrino, Philip. *Fat and skinny* ill. by Pam Makie. Crowell, 1975. ISBN 0-690-00665-9 Subj: Character traits – appearance.

Hot as an ice cube ill. by Tomie de Paola. Crowell, 1971. ISBN 0-690-40415-8 Subj: Concepts. Science.

The skeleton inside you ill. by True Kelley. Rev. ed. HarperCollins, 1989. ISBN 0-690-04733-9 Subj: Anatomy – skeletons. Science.

Balet, Jan B. *Amos and the moon* ill. by author. Oxford Univ. Pr., 1948. Subj: Moon.

The fence: a Mexican tale ill. by author. Delacorte, 1969. Translation of Der Zaun. ISBN 0-356-02847-X Subj: Family life. Folk & fairy tales. Foreign lands – Mexico. Poverty. Problem solving.

Five Rollatinis ill. by author. Lippincott, 1959. Subj: Animals – horses, ponies. Circus. Family life.

The gift: a Portuguese Christmas tale ill. by author. Delacorte, 1967. Subj: Foreign lands – Portugal. Gifts. Holidays – Christmas. Religion.

Joanjo: a Portuguese tale ill. by author. Delacorte, 1967. Subj: Character traits – ambition. Dreams. Fish. Foreign lands – Portugal.

The king and the broom maker ill. by author. Delacorte, 1968. Translation of König und der Besenbinder. Subj: Behavior – dissatisfaction. Royalty – kings.

Ned and Ed and the lion ill. by author. Oxford Univ. Pr., 1949. Subj: Animals – lions. Imagination. Multiple births – twins.

Balgassi, Haemi. *Peacebound trains* ill. by Chris K. Soentpiet. Houghton Mifflin, 1996. ISBN 0-395-72093-1 Subj: Family life – daughters. Family life – grandmothers. Family life – mothers. Foreign lands – Korea. Trains. U.S. history. War.

Balian, Lorna. *Amelia's nine lives* ill. by author. Abingdon, 1986. ISBN 0-687-01250-3 Subj: Animals – cats. Behavior – lost. Pets.

Bah! Humbug? ill. by author. Abingdon, 1977. ISBN 0-687-02345-9 Subj: Holidays – Christmas.

Elephant? ill. by adapt. Abingdon, 1964. Adapt. [by Lorna Balian] from a poem by John Godfrey Saxe. Subj: Animals – elephants. Handicaps – blindness. Senses – sight.

A garden for a groundhog ill. by author. Abingdon, 1985. ISBN 0-687-14009-9 Subj: Animals – groundhogs. Farms. Gardens, gardening. Holidays – Groundhog Day.

Humbug potion: an A B Cipher ill. by author. Abingdon, 1984. ISBN 0-687-18021-X Subj: ABC books. Magic. Secret codes. Witches.

Humbug rabbit ill. by author. Star Bright, 2004. Originally pub. by Abingdon, 1974. ISBN 1-932065-40-7 Subj: Animals – rabbits. Eggs. Family life – grandmothers. Holidays – Easter.

Humbug witch ill. by author. Abingdon, 1965. ISBN 1-881772-24-1 Subj: Holidays – Halloween. Witches.

Leprechauns never lie ill. by author. Abingdon, 1980. ISBN 0-687-21371-1 Subj: Animals – cats. Folk & fairy tales. Foreign lands – Ireland. Humorous stories. Mythical creatures – leprechauns.

Mother's Mother's Day ill. by author. Abingdon, 1982. ISBN 0-685-57645-0 Subj: Animals – mice. Family life – mothers. Holidays – Mother's Day.

The socksnatchers ill. by author. Abingdon, 1988. ISBN 0-687-39047-8 Subj: Clothing – socks. Mystery stories.

Sometimes it's turkey ill. by author. Abingdon, 1973. ISBN 0-687-39074-5 Subj: Birds – turkeys. Holidays – Thanksgiving.

A sweetheart for Valentine ill. by author. Abingdon, 1987. ISBN 0-687-40771-0 Subj: Giants. Holidays – Valentine's Day. Weddings.

Where in the world is Henry? ill. by author. Bradbury, 1972. ISBN 1-881772-27-6 Subj: Concepts – size. Science.

Wilbur's space machine ill. by author. Holiday, 1990. ISBN 0-8234-0836-1 Subj: Activities – flying. Ecology. Friendship.

Ball, Duncan. *Jeremy's tail* ill. by Donna Rawlins. Orchard, 1991. ISBN 0-531-08551-1 Subj: Activities – traveling. Games.

Ballard, Robin. *Carnival* ill. by author. Greenwillow, 1995. ISBN 0-688-13237-5 Subj: Fairs, festivals. Friendship. Parades.

Cat and Alex and the magic flying carpet ill. by author. HarperCollins, 1991. ISBN 0-06-020390-0 Subj: Animals – cats. Magic.

Good-bye, house ill. by author. Greenwillow, 1994. ISBN 0-688-12526-3 Subj: Family life. Homes, houses. Moving.

Gracie ill. by author. Greenwillow, 1993. ISBN 0-688-11807-0 Subj: Divorce. Family life.

Granny and me ill. by author. Greenwillow, 1992. ISBN 0-688-10549-1 Subj: Family life. Family life – grandmothers.

I used to be the baby ill. by author. Greenwillow, 2002. ISBN 0-06-029586-4 Subj: Babies. Family life – brothers.

My day, your day ill. by author. Greenwillow, 2001. ISBN 0-688-17796-4 Subj: Activities – working. Day. Family life – parents. School.

My father is far away ill. by author. Greenwillow, 1992. ISBN 0-688-10954-3 Subj: Emotions – loneliness. Family life – fathers.

Tonight and tomorrow ill. by author. Greenwillow, 2000. ISBN 0-688-16790-X Subj: Bedtime. Night.

When I am a sister ill. by author. Greenwillow, 1998. ISBN 0-688-15398-4 Subj: Babies. Family life – fathers. Family life – stepfamilies.

When we get home ill. by author. Greenwillow, 1999. ISBN 0-688-16168-5 Subj: Activities – traveling. Bedtime. Family life.

Ballart, Elisabet. *Let's count* ill. by Roser Capdevila. Thomasson-Grant, 1992. ISBN 1-56566-011-0 Subj: Animals. Animals – sheep. Counting, numbers. Rhyming text. School.

Balmer, Helen. *Jungle adventure* ill. by author. S&S, 1993. ISBN 0-671-86768-7 Subj: Animals. Family life – grandfathers. Format, unusual – toy & movable books. Jungle.

Balog, James. *James Balog's animals A to Z* ill. by author. Chronicle, 1996. ISBN 0-8118-1339-8 Subj: ABC books. Animals. Animals – endangered animals.

Balouch, Kristen. *The king and the three thieves* ill. by reteller. Viking, 2000. ISBN 0-670-88059-0 Subj: Crime. Folk & fairy tales. Foreign lands – Iran. Royalty – kings.

Balterman, Lee. *Girders and cranes* photos by author. A. Whitman, 1990. ISBN 0-8075-2923-0 Subj: Activities – making things. Buildings. Machines.

Balzano, Jeanne. *The wee moose* ill. by Enrico Arno. Parents' Magazine Pr., 1964. Subj: Animals – mice. Farms.

Balzola, Asun. *Munia and the day things went wrong* ill. by author. Cambridge Univ. Pr., 1988. ISBN 0-521-35643-1 Subj: Behavior – bad day. Family life.

Munia and the moon ill. by author. Cambridge Univ. Pr., 1989. ISBN 0-521-37143-0 Subj: Moon. Night.

Munia and the orange crocodile ill. by author. Cambridge Univ. Pr., 1988. ISBN 0-521-35642-3 Subj: Dreams. Reptiles – alligators, crocodiles. Teeth.

Munia and the red shoes ill. by author. Cambridge Univ. Pr., 1989. ISBN 0-521-37142-2 Subj: Behavior – growing up. Clothing – shoes.

Bambi ill. by Christa Stephan. Imported Pubs., 1983. ISBN 0-8285-2584-6 Subj: Format, unusual – board books. Toys. Wordless.

Banbery, Fred. *Paddington at the circus* (Bond, Michael)

Banchek, Linda. *Snake in, snake out* ill. by Elaine Arnold. Crowell, 1978. ISBN 0-690-03853-4 Subj: Birds – parakeets, parrots. Concepts – in & out. Concepts – opposites. Reptiles – snakes. Wordless.

Bancroft, Catherine. *Felix's hat* by Catherine Bancroft & Hannah Coale Gruenberg; ill. by Hannah Coal Gruenberg. Four Winds, 1993. ISBN 0-02-708325-X Subj: Clothing – hats. Dreams. Frogs & toads.

Bancroft, Henrietta. *Animals in winter* by Henrietta Bancroft & Richard G. Van Gelder; ill. by Helen K. Davie. HarperCollins, 1997. ISBN 0-06-445165-8 Subj: Animals. Birds. Science. Seasons – winter.

Bancroft, Laura. *see* Baum, L. Frank (Lyman Frank)

Bandes, Hanna. *Sleepy river* ill. by Jeanette Winter. Putnam/Philomel, 1993. ISBN 0-399-22349-5 Subj: Animals. Indians of North America. Night. Rivers.

Bang, Betsy. *The cucumber stem* ill. by Tony Chen. Greenwillow, 1980. Adapt. from a Bengali folk tale. ISBN 0-688-84213-5 Subj: Character traits – smallness. Foreign lands – India. Tall tales.

The old woman and the red pumpkin ill. by Molly Bang. Macmillan, 1975. Adapt. and tr. from a Bengali folk tale by Betsy Bang. ISBN 0-02-708360-8 Subj: Animals. Character traits – cleverness. Folk & fairy tales. Foreign lands – India.

The old woman and the rice thief ill. by Molly Bang. Greenwillow, 1978. Adapt. and tr. from a Bengali folk tale by Betsy Bang. ISBN 0-688-84098-1 Subj: Animals. Character traits – cleverness. Folk & fairy tales. Foreign lands – India.

Tuntuni the tailor bird ill. by Molly Bang. Greenwillow, 1978. Adapt. and tr. from a Bengali folk tale by Betsy Bang. ISBN 0-688-84167-8 Subj: Birds. Folk & fairy tales. Foreign lands – India. Royalty.

Bang, Molly. *Dawn* ill. by author. Morrow, 1983. An adaptation of the Japanese folk tale known as The Crane Wife. ISBN 0-688-02404-1 Subj: Activities – weaving. Behavior – secrets. Birds – cranes. Character traits – curiosity. Folk & fairy tales. Foreign lands – Japan.

Delphine ill. by author. Morrow, 1988. ISBN 0-688-05637-7 Subj: Animals. Sports – bicycling.

The goblins giggle and other stories ill. by author. Peter Smith, 1988. ISBN 0-8446-6360-3 Subj: Mythical creatures – goblins.

Goose ill. by author. Blue Sky, 1996. ISBN 0-590-89005-0 Subj: Activities – flying. Animals – groundhogs. Birds – geese.

The grey lady and the strawberry snatcher ill. by author. Four Winds, 1980. ISBN 0-590-07547-0 Subj: Caldecott award honor books. Imagination. Wordless.

One fall day ill. by author. Greenwillow, 1994. ISBN 0-688-07016-7 Subj: Activities – playing. Bedtime. Toys.

The paper crane ill. by author. Greenwillow, 1985. ISBN 0-688-04109-4 Subj: Birds – cranes. Character traits – kindness. Folk & fairy tales.

Ten, nine, eight ill. by author. Greenwillow, 1983. ISBN 0-688-00907-7 Subj: Bedtime. Caldecott award honor books. Counting, numbers. Ethnic groups in the U.S. – African Americans. Lullabies. Rhyming text.

Tye May and the magic brush ill. by author. Greenwillow, 1981. ISBN 0-688-84290-9 Subj: Activities – painting. Royalty.

When Sophie gets angry – really, really angry . . . ill. by author. Blue Sky, 1999. ISBN 0-590-18979-4 Subj: Caldecott award honor books. Emotions – anger. Family life – sisters.

Wiley and the hairy man ill. by adapt. Macmillan, 1976. ISBN 0-02-708370-5 Subj: Bedtime. Character traits – cleverness. Ethnic groups in the U.S. – African Americans. Folk & fairy tales. Monsters.

Yellow ball ill. by author. Morrow, 1991. ISBN 0-688-06315-2 Subj: Activities – playing. Sea & seashore. Toys – balls.

Bangs, Edward. *Yankee Doodle* ill. by Steven Kellogg. Parents' Magazine Pr., 1976. ISBN 0-819-30834-X Subj: Songs. U.S. history.

Bania, Michael. *Kumak's house* ill. by author. Alaska Northwest Bks., 2002. ISBN 0-8824-0540-3 Subj: Alaska. Eskimos. Indians of North America – Inuit.

Banigan, Sharon Stearns. *Circus magic* ill. by Katharina Maillard. Dutton, 1958. Subj: Circus. Magic. Rhyming text.

Banish, Roslyn. *A forever family* ill. by author with Jennifer Jordan-Wong. HarperCollins, 1992. ISBN 0-06-021674-3 Subj: Adoption. Ethnic groups in the U.S. Family life.

Let me tell you about my baby photos by author. HarperCollins, 1988. Previously published as: I want to tell you about my baby,

HarperCollins 1982. ISBN 0-06-020383-8 Subj: Babies. Birth. Family life – new sibling.

Bank Street College of Education. *Around the city* ill. by Aurelius Battaglia & others. Rev. ed. Macmillan, 1972. Subj: Cities, towns.

Green light, go ill. by Jack Endewelt & others. Rev. ed. Macmillan, 1972. Subj: Cities, towns. Traffic, traffic signs.

In the city ill. by Dan Dickas. Rev. ed. Macmillan, 1972. ISBN 0-02-258930-9 Subj: Cities, towns.

My city ill. by Ron Becker & others. Macmillan, 1965. Subj: Cities, towns.

People read ill. by Dan Dickas. Rev. ed. Macmillan, 1972. ISBN 0-02-258940-6 Subj: Books, reading. Careers.

Uptown, downtown ill. by Ron Becker & others. Macmillan, 1965. Subj: Cities, towns.

Banks, Kate (Katherine A.). *Alphabet soup* ill. by Peter Sis. Knopf, 1988. ISBN 0-394-99151-6 Subj: Family life. Food. Imagination.

And if the moon could talk ill. by Georg Hallensleben. Farrar, 1998. ISBN 0-374-30299-5 Subj: Bedtime. Dreams. Moon. Night.

Baboon ill. by Georg Hallensleben. Farrar, 1997. ISBN 0-374-30474-2 Subj: Animals – baboons. Family life – mothers. World.

The bird, the monkey, and the snake in the jungle ill. by Tomasz Bogacki. Farrar, 1999. ISBN 0-374-30729-6 Subj: Animals – monkeys. Behavior – sharing. Birds. Rebuses. Reptiles – snakes.

Close your eyes ill. by Georg Hallensleben. Farrar, 2002. ISBN 0-374-31382-2 Subj: Animals – tigers. Dreams. Family life – mothers. Sleep.

Mama's coming home ill. by Tomasz Bogacki. Farrar, 2003. ISBN 0-374-34747-6 Subj: Activities – working. Family life. Family life – mothers. Gender roles.

The night worker ill. by Georg Hallensleben. Farrar, 2000. ISBN 0-374-35520-7 Subj: Activities – working. Careers – construction workers. Family life – fathers.

Peter and the talking shoes ill. by Marc Rosenthal. Knopf, 1994. ISBN 0-394-92723-0 Subj: Behavior – lost & found possessions. Clothing – shoes. Cumulative tales.

Spider, spider ill. by Georg Hallensleben. Farrar, 1996. ISBN 0-374-37151-2 Subj: Family life – mothers. Imagination. Spiders.

Banks, Merry. *Animals of the night* ill. by Ronald Himler. Macmillan, 1990. ISBN 0-684-19093-1 Subj: Animals. Nature. Night.

Bannatyne-Cugnet, Jo. *Estelle and the self-esteem machines* ill. by Leslie Bell. Red Deer Pr., 1993. ISBN 0-889950-97-0 Subj: Self-concept.

A prairie alphabet ill. by Yvette Moore. Tundra, 1992. ISBN 0-88776-282-1 Subj: ABC books. Foreign lands – Canada.

Bannerman, Helen. *Little Black Sambo* ill. by author. Platt, 1933. Subj: Animals – tigers. Character traits – cleverness. Family life. Foreign lands – India.

Little Black Sambo ill. by Nina R. Jordan. Whitman, 1934. Subj: Animals – tigers. Character traits – cleverness. Family life – India.

Little Black Sambo ill. by Gladys Turkey Mitchell. Whitman, 1953. Subj: Animals – tigers. Character traits – cleverness. Family life. Foreign lands – India.

Little Black Sambo ill. by Robert Moore. Grosset, 1942. Subj: Animals – tigers. Character traits – cleverness. Family life. Foreign lands – India.

Little Black Sambo ill. by Fern Bisel Peat. Saalfield, 1932. Subj: Animals – tigers. Character traits – cleverness. Foreign lands – India.

Little Black Sambo ill. by Mary LaFetra Russell. Sam'l Gabriel Sons, 1948. Subj: Animals – tigers. Character traits – cleverness. Family life. Foreign lands – India.

Little Black Sambo ill. by Cobb X. Shinn. A. Whitman, 1925. Subj: Animals – tigers. Character traits – cleverness. Family life. Foreign lands – India.

Little Black Sambo ill. by Terry & Mary Smith. Whitman, 1930. Subj: Animals – tigers. Character traits – cleverness. Family life. Foreign lands – India.

Little Black Sambo ill. by Suzanne. Whitman, 1950. Subj: Animals – tigers. Character traits – cleverness. Family life. Foreign lands – India.

Little Black Sambo ill. by Gustaf Tenggren. S&S, 1948. Subj: Animals – tigers. Character traits – cleverness. Family life. Foreign lands – India.

Little Black Sambo ill. by Keith Ward. A. Whitman, 1935. Subj: Animals – tigers. Character traits – cleverness. Family life. Foreign lands – India.

Little Black Sambo ill. by Julian Wehr. Duenewald, 1949. Subj: Animals – tigers. Character traits – cleverness. Family life. Foreign lands – India.

The Little Black Sambo story book by Helen Bannerman & Frank Ver Beck; ill. by Helen Bannerman. Altemus, 1930. Subj: Animals – tigers. Character traits – cleverness. Family life. Foreign lands – India.

Sam and the tigers: a new telling of Little Black Sambo (Lester, Julius)

Sambo and the twins ill. by author. Stokes, 1936. Subj: Folk & fairy tales. Foreign lands – India.

The story of Little Babaji ill. by Fred Marcellino. HarperCollins, 1996. ISBN 0-06-205065-6 Subj: Animals – tigers. Character traits – cleverness. Family life. Foreign lands – India.

The story of Little Black Sambo ill. by author. Reilly, 1905. Introduction by L. Frank Baum. Subj: Animals – tigers. Character traits – cleverness. Family life. Foreign lands – India.

The story of Little Black Sambo ill. by author. Lippincott, 1915. Subj: Animals – tigers. Character traits – cleverness. Family life. Foreign lands – India.

The story of Little Black Sambo ill. by author. Stokes, 1923. Subj: Animals – tigers. Character traits – cleverness. Family life. Foreign lands – India.

The story of Little Black Sambo ill. by author. Altemus, 1931. Subj: Animals – tigers. Character traits – cleverness. Family life. Foreign lands – India.

The story of Little Black Sambo ill. by author. Lippincott, 1943. First published in the U.S. by Stokes in 1900. Subj: Animals – tigers. Character traits – cleverness. Family life. Foreign lands – India.

The story of Little Black Sambo ill. by author. Greenhouse, 1986. ISBN 0-9616844-1-0 Subj: Animals – tigers. Character traits – cleverness. Family life. Foreign lands – India.

The story of Little Black Sambo ill. by author. HarperCollins, 1990. ISBN 0-397-30006-9 Subj: Animals – tigers. Character traits – cleverness. Family life. Foreign lands – India.

The story of little black Sambo ill. by author. Applewood, 1996. ISBN 1-55709-414-4 Subj: Animals – tigers. Character traits – cleverness. Family life. Foreign lands – India.

The story of Little Black Sambo ill. by Christopher Bing. Handprint, 2003. ISBN 1-92976-655-6 Subj: Animals – tigers. Character traits – cleverness. Family life. Foreign lands – India.

The story of Little Black Sambo "pop-up" picture by C. Carey Cloud. Blue Ribbon, 1934. Subj: Animals – tigers. Character traits – cleverness. Family life. Foreign lands – India. Format, unusual – toy & movable books.

The story of Little Black Sambo ill. by Judith Russell. Cherokee, 1995. ISBN 0-87797-265-6 Subj: Animals – tigers. Character traits – cleverness. Family life. Foreign lands – India.

The story of the teasing monkey ill. by author. Lippincott, 1907. Subj: Animals – lions. Animals – monkeys.

Bannon, Laura. *The best house in the world* ill. by author. Houghton Mifflin, 1952. Subj: Animals. Homes, houses. Imagination.

Hat for a hero: a Tarasean boy of Mexico ill. by author. A. Whitman, 1954. Subj: Character traits – bravery. Clothing – hats. Foreign lands – Mexico.

Little people of the night ill. by author. Houghton Mifflin, 1963. Subj: Animals. Emotions – fear. Night.

Manuela's birthday ill. by author. A. Whitman, 1972. Orig. pub. in 1939. ISBN 0-8075-4973-8 Subj: Birthdays. Foreign lands – Mexico. Toys – dolls.

Red mittens ill. by author. Houghton Mifflin, 1946. ISBN 0-395-19863-1 Subj: Animals. Behavior – lost & found possessions. Clothing – gloves, mittens.

The scary thing ill. by author. Houghton Mifflin, 1956. Subj: Animals. Emotions – fear.

Bansemer, Roger. *Rachael's splendifilous adventure* by Roger Bansemer & Daryl May; ill. by Roger Bansemer. Windswept House, 1991. ISBN 0-932433-83-9 Subj: Activities – ballooning. Activities – traveling. Toys – bears.

Bantock, Nick. *Runners, sliders, bouncers, climbers* by Nick Bantock & Stacie Strong; designed by Nick Bantock & Doug Bergstreser; paper engineering by Rodger Smith; ill. by Nick Bantock. Hyperion, 1992. ISBN 1-56282-219-5 Subj: Activities. Animals. Format, unusual – toy & movable books.

There was an old lady (Little old lady who swallowed a fly)

Barack, Marcy. *Season song* ill. by Thierry Courtin. HarperFestival, 2002. ISBN 0-694-01567-9 Subj: Format, unusual – board books. Rhyming text. Seasons.

Baran, Tancy. *Bees* ill. by author. Grosset, 1971. Subj: Insects – bees. Science.

Baranski, Joan Sullivan. *Round is a pancake* ill. by Yu-Mei Han. Dutton, 2001. ISBN 0-525-46173-6 Subj: Concepts – shape. Food. Rhyming text. Royalty – kings.

Barasch, Lynne. *Old friends* ill. by author. Farrar, 1998. ISBN 0-374-35611-4 Subj: Animals – dogs. Dreams. Family life. Friendship. Old age.

Radio rescue ill. by author. Farrar, 2000. ISBN 0-374-36166-5 Subj: Activities. Radios.

The reluctant flower girl ill. by author. HarperCollins, 2001. ISBN 0-06-028810-8 Subj: Family life – sisters. Friendship. Weddings.

Rodney's inside story ill. by author. Watts, 1992. ISBN 0-531-08593-7 Subj: Animals – rabbits. Bedtime. Books, reading. Food.

A winter walk ill. by author. Ticknor & Fields, 1993. ISBN 0-395-65937-X Subj: Concepts – color. Seasons – winter.

Barasch, Marc Ian. *No plain pets!* ill. by Henrik Drescher. HarperCollins, 1991. ISBN 0-06-022473-8 Subj: Animals. Pets. Rhyming text.

Barbaresi, Nina. *Firemouse* ill. by author. Crown, 1987. ISBN 0-517-56337-1 Subj: Animals – cats. Animals – mice. Careers – firefighters.

Barbato, Juli. *From bed to bus* ill. by Brian Schatell. Macmillan, 1985. ISBN 0-02-708380-2 Subj: Family life. Morning.

Mom's night out ill. by Brian Schatell. Macmillan, 1985. ISBN 0-02-708480-9 Subj: Family life – fathers. Food.

Barbe, Walter B. *Some folks like cats, and other poems* (Eastwick, Ivy O.)

Barber, Antonia. *Catkin* ill. by P. J. Lynch. Candlewick, 1994. ISBN 1-56402-485-7 Subj: Animals – cats. Fairies. Little people. Riddles & jokes.

The enchanter's daughter ill. by Errol Le Cain. Farrar, 1988. ISBN 0-374-32170-1 Subj: Birds. Magic. Wizards.

Gemma and the baby chick ill. by Karin Littlewood. Scholastic, 1993. ISBN 0-590-45479-X Subj: Birds – chickens. Eggs. Family life – mothers. Farms.

The mousehole cat ill. by Nicola Bayley. Macmillan, 1990. ISBN 0-02-708331-4 Subj: Animals – cats. Foreign lands – England. Sea & seashore. Weather – storms.

Satchelmouse and the dinosaurs ill. by Claudio Muñoz. Barron's, 1988. ISBN 0-8120-5872-0 Subj: Dinosaurs. Imagination. Magic. Prehistory.

Satchelmouse and the doll's house ill. by Claudio Muñoz. Barron's, 1988. ISBN 0-8120-5873-9 Subj: Character traits – kindness. Toys – dolls.

Barber, Barbara E. *Allie's basketball dream* ill. by Darryl Ligasan. Lee & Low, 1996. ISBN 1-880000-38-5 Subj: Character traits – perseverance. Ethnic groups in the U.S. – African Americans. Sports – basketball.

Saturday at the new you ill. by Anna Rich. Lee & Low, 1994. ISBN 1-880000-06-7 Subj: Activities – working. Beauty shops. Careers. Communities, neighborhoods. Ethnic groups in the U.S. – African Americans. Family life – mothers.

Barber, Patti. *First number book* ill. by Mandy Stanley. Kingfisher, 2001. ISBN 0-7534-5338-X Subj: Counting, numbers. Picture puzzles.

Barber, Ronde. *By my brother's side* (Barber, Tiki)

Barber, Tiki. *By my brother's side* by Tiki & Ronde Barber with Robert Burleigh; ill. by Barry Root. S&S, 2004. ISBN 0-689-86559-7 Subj: Ethnic groups in the U.S. – African Americans. Family life – brothers. Multiple births – twins. Sports – football.

Barbero, Maria. *The bravest mouse* ill. by author; trans. by Sibylle Kazeroid. North-South, 2002. ISBN 0-7358-1709-X Subj: Animals – cats. Animals – mice. Character traits – bravery. Self-concept.

Barbosa, Rogério Andrade. *African animal tales* adapt. by Feliz Guthrie; ill. by Cica Fittipaldi. Volcano Pr., 1993. ISBN 0-912078-96-0 Subj: Animals. Character traits – cleverness. Character traits – patience. Folk & fairy tales. Foreign lands – Africa.

Barbot, Daniel. *A bicycle for Rosaura* ill. by Morella Fuenmayor. Kane/Miller, 1991. ISBN 0-916291-34-0 Subj: Animals. Birds – chickens. Birthdays. Foreign lands – Venezuela. Sports – bicycling.

Barbour, Karen. *Little Nino's pizzeria* ill. by author. Harcourt, 1987. ISBN 0-15-247650-4 Subj: Family life. Food.

Mr. Bow Tie ill. by author. Harcourt, 1991. ISBN 0-15-256165-X Subj: Character traits – kindness. Family life. Homeless.

Nancy ill. by author. Harcourt, 1989. ISBN 0-15-256675-9 Subj: Friendship. Moving. Parties.

Barchilon, Jacques. *The authentic Mother Goose fairy tales and nursery rhymes* ed. by Jacques Barchilon & Henry Pettit. Alan Swallow, 1960. Subj: Nursery rhymes.

Barclay, Jane. *Going on a journey to the sea* ill. by Elizabeth Mikau. Lobster, 2002. ISBN 1-894222-34-2 Subj: Activities – playing. Sea & seashore. Sports – swimming.

Barclay, William. *The cobweb curtain: a Christmas story* (Koralek, Jenny)

Barden, Rosalind. *TV monster* ill. by author. Crown, 1989. ISBN 0-517-56934-5 Subj: Monsters. Space & space ships. Television.

Bardill, Linard. *The great golden thing* ill. by Miriam Monnier; trans. by J. Alison James. North-South, 2002. ISBN 0-7358-1594-1 Subj: Animals – bears. Animals – rabbits. Careers – magicians. Flowers. Plants.

Bare, Colleen Stanley. *Busy, busy squirrels* photos by author. Dutton, 1991. ISBN 0-525-65063-6 Subj: Animals – squirrels.

Critter, the class cat photos by author. Putnam, 1989. ISBN 0-399-21710-X Subj: Animals – cats. School.

Elephants on the beach photos by author. Dutton, 1990. ISBN 0-525-65018-0 Subj: Animals – seals. Sea & seashore – beaches.

Guinea pigs don't read books photos by author. Dodd, 1985. ISBN 0-396-08538-5 Subj: Animals – guinea pigs. Pets.

Never grab a deer by the ear photos by author. Cobblehill, 1993. ISBN 0-525-65112-8 Subj: Animals – deer. Nature.

Never kiss an alligator photos by author. Dutton, 1989. ISBN 0-525-65003-2 Subj: Reptiles – alligators, crocodiles.

Sammy, dog detective photos by author. Dutton, 1998. ISBN 0-525-65253-1 Subj: Animals – dogs. Careers – police officers.

To love a cat photos by author. Dodd, 1986. ISBN 0-396-08834-1 Subj: Animals – cats. Pets.

To love a dog photos by author. Dodd, 1987. ISBN 0-396-09057-5 Subj: Animals – dogs. Pets.

Tree squirrels photos by author. Dodd, 1983. ISBN 0-396-08208-4 Subj: Animals – squirrels.

Who comes to the water hole? photos by author. Dutton, 1991. ISBN 0-525-65073-3 Subj: Animals. Foreign lands – Africa. Jungle.

Baring, Maurice. *The blue rose* ill. by Anne Dalton. Heinemann, 1987. ISBN 0-7182-2100-1 Subj: Folk & fairy tales. Royalty.

Baring-Gould, Ceil. *The annotated Mother Goose* (Mother Goose)

Baring-Gould, S. (Sabine). *Now the day is over* ill. by Preston McDaniels. Morehouse, 2001. ISBN 0-8192-1868-5 Subj: Bedtime. Religion. Songs.

Baring-Gould, William S. *The annotated Mother Goose* (Mother Goose)

Barish, Wendy. *Trains* (Trains)

Barkan, Joanne. *Boxcar* ill. by Richard Walz. Macmillan, 1992. ISBN 0-689-71573-0 Subj: Format, unusual – board books. Trains. Transportation.

Caboose ill. by Richard Walz. Macmillan, 1992. ISBN 0-689-71574-9 Subj: Format, unusual – board books. Trains. Transportation.

Locomotive ill. by Richard Walz. Macmillan, 1992. ISBN 0-689-71576-5 Subj: Format, unusual – board books. Trains. Transportation.

Passenger car ill. by Richard Walz. Macmillan, 1992. ISBN 0-689-71575-7 Subj: Format, unusual – board books. Trains. Transportation.

Whiskerville bake shop ill. by Karen Lee Schmidt. Putnam, 1990. ISBN 0-448-19467-8 Subj: Animals – mice. Buildings. Careers – bakers. Format, unusual – board books.

Whiskerville firehouse ill. by Karen Lee Schmidt. Putnam, 1990. ISBN 0-448-19468-6 Subj: Animals – mice. Buildings. Careers – firefighters. Format, unusual – board books.

Whiskerville post office ill. by Karen Lee Schmidt. Putnam, 1990. ISBN 0-448-19466-X Subj: Animals – mice. Buildings. Careers – postal workers. Format, unusual – board books. Post office.

Whiskerville school ill. by Karen Lee Schmidt. Putnam, 1990. ISBN 0-448-19465-1 Subj: Animals – mice. Buildings. Careers – teachers. Format, unusual – board books. School.

Barker, Carol. *Achilles and Diana* (Bates, H. E. [Herbert Ernest])

Achilles the donkey (Bates, H. E. [Herbert Ernest])

Barker, Cicely Mary. *Berry flower fairies* ill. by author. Putnam, 1981. Vol. [2] of a set of 4 v. issued in a case with title: Flower fairies miniature library. ISBN 0-399-20823-2 Subj: Fairies. Flowers. Format, unusual. Poetry.

Blossom flower fairies ill. by author. Putnam, 1981. Vol. [1] of a set of 4 v. issued in a case with title: Flower fairies miniature library. ISBN 0-399-20823-2 Subj: Fairies. Flowers. Format, unusual. Poetry.

Flower fairies of the garden ill. by author. Viking, 1991. ISBN 0-7232-3758-1 Subj: Fairies. Flowers. Gardens, gardening. Poetry.

Flower fairies of the seasons ill. by author. HarperCollins, 1984. First published in 1923. ISBN 0-911745-48-3 Subj: Fairies. Flowers. Poetry. Seasons. Trees.

Flower fairies of the spring ill. by author. Warne, 1991. ISBN 0-7232-4433-2 Subj: Fairies. Flowers. Poetry. Seasons – spring.

Flower fairies of the summer ill. by author. Warne, 1991. ISBN 0-7232-3754-9 Subj: Fairies. Flowers. Poetry. Seasons – summer.

Flower fairies of the trees ill. by author. Viking, 1991. ISBN 0-872-26022-4 Subj: Fairies. Flowers. Poetry. Trees.

Flower fairies postcard book ill. by author. Warne, 1991. ISBN 0-7232-3710-7 Subj: Fairies. Flowers. Poetry.

Spring flower fairies ill. by author. Putnam, 1981. Vol. [3] of a set of 4 v. issued in a case with title: Flower fairies miniature library. ISBN 0-399-20823-2 Subj: Fairies. Flowers. Format, unusual. Poetry.

Summer flower fairies ill. by author. Putnam, 1981. Vol. [4] of a set of 4 v. issued in a case with title: Flower fairies miniature library. ISBN 0-399-20823-2 Subj: Fairies. Flowers. Format, unusual. Poetry.

Barker, George. *Why teddy bears are brown* (Barker, Inga-Lil)

Barker, Inga-Lil. *Why teddy bears are brown* by Inga-Lil & George Barker; ill. by authors. Crowell, 1946. Subj: Behavior – greed. Toys – bears.

Barker, Melvern J. *Country fair* ill. by author. Oxford Univ. Pr., 1955. Subj: Animals – bulls, cows. Fairs, festivals.

Little island star ill. by author. Oxford Univ. Pr., 1954. Subj: Lighthouses.

Barker, Peggy. *What happened when grandma died* ill. by Patricia Mattozzi. Concordia, 1984. ISBN 0-570-04090-6 Subj: Death. Emotions – grief. Family life – grandmothers. Religion.

Barkhouse, Joyce. *Anna's pet* (Atwood, Margaret)

Barklem, Jill. *Autumn story* ill. by author. Atheneum, 1999. ISBN 0-689-83054-8 Subj: Animals – mice. Behavior – lost. Seasons – fall.

The big book of Brambly Hedge ill. by author. Putnam, 1981. ISBN 0-399-20833-X Subj: Animals – mice. Country.

The high hills ill. by author. Atheneum, 1999. ISBN 0-689-83091-2 Subj: Activities – traveling. Animals – mice. Seasons – fall.

Sea story ill. by author. Putnam, 1991. ISBN 0-399-21844-0 Subj: Sea & seashore.

The secret staircase ill. by author. Putnam, 1983. ISBN 0-689-83090-4 Subj: Animals – mice. Behavior – secrets. Food. Problem solving. Seasons – winter.

Spring story ill. by author. Putnam, 1980. Subj: Animals – mice. Birthdays. Seasons – spring.

Summer story ill. by author. Putnam, 1980. ISBN 0-399-61157-6 Subj: Animals – mice. Seasons – summer. Weddings.

Winter story ill. by author. Putnam, 1980. ISBN 0-689-83057-2 Subj: Animals – mice. Seasons – winter. Weather – snow.

Barlowe, Sy. *A child's book of stars* ill. with photos. Maxton, 1953. Subj: Astronomy. Moon. Northern lights. Planets. Science. Stars. Sun.

Barnard, A. M. *see* Alcott, Louisa May

Barner, Bob. *Dem bones* ill. by author. Chronicle, 1996. ISBN 0-8118-0827-0 Subj: Anatomy. Ethnic groups in the U.S. – African Americans. Songs.

Dinosaur bones ill. by author. Chronicle, 2001. ISBN 0-8118-3158-2 Subj: Careers – paleontologists. Dinosaurs. Fossils. Rhyming text.

Elephant facts ill. by author. Dutton, 1979. ISBN 0-525-29200-4 Subj: Animals – elephants. Science.

Elevator escalator book ill. by author. Doubleday, 1990. ISBN 0-385-26667-7 Subj: Animals – dogs. Elevators, escalators. Transportation.

Space race ill. by author. Bantam, 1995. ISBN 0-553-37567-9 Subj: Concepts – shape. Counting, numbers. Robots. Space & space ships.

Stars, stars, stars ill. by author. Chronicle, 2002. ISBN 0-8118-3159-0 Subj: Astronomy. Planets. Rhyming text. Science. Stars.

Too many dinosaurs ill. by author. Bantam, 1995. ISBN 0-553-37566-0 Subj: Counting, numbers. Dinosaurs. Prehistory.

Which way to the Revolution? ill. by author. Holiday, 1998. ISBN 0-8234-1352-7 Subj: Animals – mice. Maps. U.S. history.

Barnes, Laura T. *Ernest and the big itch* ill. by Carol A. Camburn. Barnsyard, 2002. ISBN 0-9674681-2-4 Subj: Animals – donkeys. Birds. Friendship. Self-concept.

Ernest's special Christmas ill. by Carol A. Camburn. Barnsyard, 2003. ISBN 0-9674681-3-2 Subj: Animals. Animals – donkeys. Character traits – helpfulness. Friendship.

Teeny tiny Ernest ill. by Carol A. Camburn. Barnsyard, 2000. ISBN 0-9674681-1-6 Subj: Animals – donkeys. Concepts – size. Self-concept.

Twist and Ernest ill. by Carol A. Camburn. Barnsyard, 1999. ISBN 0-9674681-0-8 Subj: Animals – donkeys. Animals – horses, ponies. Friendship.

Barnes-Murphy, Rowan. *Numbers* ill. by author. Ideals, 1992. ISBN 0-8249-8531-1 Subj: Animals – cats. Animals – mice. Circus. Counting, numbers. Format, unusual – toy & movable books.

One, two, buckle my shoe (One, two, buckle my shoe)

Barnett, Naomi. *I know a dentist* ill. by Linda Boehm. Putnam, 1977. ISBN 0-399-61097-9 Subj: Careers – dentists. Teeth.

Barnhart, Peter. *The wounded duck* ill. by Adrienne Adams. Scribners, 1979. ISBN 0-684-16255-5 Subj: Birds – ducks. Character traits – kindness to animals. Death. Seasons – winter.

Barnwell, Ysaye M. *No mirrors in my Nana's house* ill. by Synthia Saint James. Harcourt, 1999. ISBN 0-15-201825-5 Subj: Ethnic groups in the U.S. – African Americans. Family life – grandmothers. Self-concept.

Baron, Alan. *Little Pig's bouncy ball* ill. by author. Candlewick, 1996. ISBN 1-56402-805-4 Subj: Activities – playing. Animals. Animals – dogs. Animals – pigs. Behavior – misunderstanding. Cumulative tales. Toys – balls.

Red Fox dances ill. by author. Candlewick, 1996. ISBN 1-56402-803-8 Subj: Activities – dancing. Animals. Animals – foxes. Behavior – trickery. Cumulative tales.

Barr, Cathrine. *A horse for Sherry* ill. by author. Walck, 1963. Subj: Animals – horses, ponies. Farms.

Hound dog's bone ill. by author. Walck, 1961. Subj: Animals – dogs. Animals – foxes. Behavior – stealing. Humorous stories.

Little Ben ill. by author. Walck, 1960. Subj: Animals – beavers. Character traits – bravery.

Sammy seal ov the sircus ill. by author. [1st initial teaching alphabet ed.]. Walck, 1955, 1964. Subj: Animals – seals. Circus. Clowns, jesters.

Barr, Jene. *Fire snorkel number 7* ill. by Joe Rogers. A. Whitman, 1965. Subj: Careers – firefighters. Fire. Trucks.

Barracca, Debra. *The adventures of taxi dog* (Barracca, Sal)

Maxi, the hero by Debra & Sal Barracca; ill. by Mark Buehner. Dial, 1991. ISBN 0-8037-0940-4 Subj: Animals – dogs. Cities, towns. Crime. Rhyming text.

Maxi, the star by Debra & Sal Barracca; ill. by Alan Ayers. Dial, 1993. ISBN 0-8037-1349-5 Subj: Activities – traveling. Animals – dogs. Rhyming text. Television.

A taxi dog Christmas by Debra & Sal Barracca; ill. by Alan Ayers. Dial, 1994. ISBN 0-8037-1368-1 Subj: Animals – dogs. Cities, towns. Holidays – Christmas. Rhyming text. Taxis.

Barracca, Sal. *The adventures of taxi dog* by Sal & Debra Barracca; ill. by Mark Buehner. Dial, 1990. ISBN 0-8037-0672-3 Subj: Animals – dogs. Cities, towns. Rhyming text. Taxis.

Maxi, the hero (Barracca, Debra)

Maxi, the star (Barracca, Debra)

A taxi dog Christmas (Barracca, Debra)

Barraclough, Sue. *Rain and shine* (Kespert, Deborah)

Barrett, John M. *The bear who slept through Christmas* ill. by Rick Reinert Productions. Ideals, 1980. ISBN 0-8249-7175-2 Subj: Animals – bears. Hibernation. Holidays – Christmas. Humorous stories.

The Easter bear ill. by Rick Reinert Productions. Childrens Pr., 1981. ISBN 0-516-09190-5 Subj: Animals – bears. Animals – rabbits. Holidays – Easter. Seasons – spring.

Oscar the selfish octopus ill. by Joe Servello. Human Sciences Pr., 1978. ISBN 0-87705-355-9 Subj: Character traits – selfishness. Octopuses.

Barrett, Joyce Durham. *Willie's not the hugging kind* ill. by Pat Cummings. HarperCollins, 1989. ISBN 0-06-020417-6 Subj: Character traits – confidence. Emotions – love. Ethnic groups in the U.S. Family life. Friendship.

Barrett, Judi. *Animals should definitely not act like people* ill. by Ron Barrett. Atheneum, 1980. ISBN 0-689-30768-3 Subj: Animals. Behavior – imitation.

Animals should definitely not wear clothing ill. by Ron Barrett. Atheneum, 1970. ISBN 0-689-20592-9 Subj: Animals. Behavior – imitation. Clothing.

An apple a day ill. by Tim Lewis. Atheneum, 1973. ISBN 0-689-30105-7 Subj: Food. Illness.

Benjamin's 365 birthdays ill. by Ron Barrett. Atheneum, 1974. ISBN 0-689-30130-8 Subj: Birthdays.

Cloudy with a chance of meatballs ill. by Ron Barrett. Atheneum, 1978. ISBN 0-689-30647-4 Subj: Family life – grandfathers. Food. Imagination. Weather.

I hate to go to bed ill. by Ray Cruz. Four Winds, 1977. ISBN 0-590-07472-5 Subj: Bedtime. Imagination.

I hate to take a bath ill. by Charles B. Slackman. Atheneum, 1981. ISBN 0-590-07429-6 Subj: Behavior – growing up. Concepts – size.

I'm too small, you're too big ill. by David S. Rose. Atheneum, 1981. ISBN 0-689-30800-0 Subj: Behavior – growing up. Concepts – opposites. Family life – fathers.

Old MacDonald had an apartment house ill. by Ron Barrett. Atheneum, 1969. ISBN 0-689-81757-6 Subj: Cities, towns. Farms. Gardens, gardening.

Peter's pocket ill. by Julia Noonan. Atheneum, 1974. ISBN 0-689-30403-X Subj: Clothing.

Pickles have pimples ill. by Lonni Sue Johnson. Atheneum, 1986. ISBN 0-689-31187-7 Subj: Rhyming text.

Pickles to Pittsburgh: the sequel to Cloudy with a chance of meatballs written & colored by Judi Barrett; drawn by Ron Barrett. Atheneum, 1997. ISBN 0-689-80104-1 Subj: Family life – grandparents. Food. Weather.

Snake is totally tail ill. by L. S. Johnson. Atheneum, 1983. ISBN 0-689-30979-1 Subj: Animals. Insects. Reptiles.

The things that are most in the world ill. by John Nickle. Atheneum, 1998. ISBN 0-689-81333-3 Subj: Language.

What's left? ill. by author. Atheneum, 1983. ISBN 0-689-30874-4 Subj: Participation. Problem solving.

Which witch is which? ill. by Sharleen Collicott. Atheneum, 2001. ISBN 0-689-82940-X Subj: Rhyming text. Witches.

The wind thief Ill. by Diane Dawson Hearn. Atheneum, 1977. ISBN 0-689-30564-8 Subj: Clothing – hats. Weather – wind.

Barrett, Lawrence Louis. *Twinkle, the baby colt* ill. by author. Knopf, 1945. Subj: Animals – horses, ponies. Behavior – running away.

Barrett, Mary Brigid. *Day care days* ill. by Patti Beling Murphy. Little, 1999. ISBN 0-316-08456-5 Subj: Family life. Rhyming text. School – nursery.

The man of the house at Huffington Row: a Christmas story ill. by author. Harcourt, 1998. ISBN 0-15-201580-9 Subj: Character traits – kindness. Family life – brothers & sisters. Holidays – Christmas.

Barrett, Norman S. *Spiders* ill. by author. Watts, 1989. ISBN 0-531-10702-7 Subj: Science. Spiders.

Barrie, J. M. (James M.). *Peter Pan* ill. by Diane Goode. Random House, 1983. ISBN 0-394-95717-2 Subj: Folk & fairy tales. Mythical creatures – pixies.

Barringer, William. *Gregory and Alexander* ill. by Kim LaFave. Orca, 2003. ISBN 1-55143-252-8 Subj: Animals – mice. Friendship. Insects – butterflies, caterpillars. Metamorphosis.

Barron, Rex. *Fed up! a feast of frazzled foods* ill. by author. Putnam, 2000. ISBN 0-399-23450-0 Subj: ABC books. Food.

Barron, T. A. *Where is Grandpa?* ill. by Chris K. Soentpiet. Philomel, 2000. ISBN 0-399-23037-8 Subj: Death. Emotions – grief. Family life – grandfathers.

Barrows, Marjorie Wescott. *Fraidy cat* ill. by Barbara Maynard. Rand McNally, 1942. Subj: Animals – cats. Character traits – bravery. Format, unusual.

The funny hat ill. by Norv Mink. Rand McNally, 1943. Subj: Behavior – lost & found possessions. Clothing – hats. Format, unusual.

Muggins' big balloon ill. by Anne Sellers Leaf. Rand McNally, 1967. ISBN 0-8382-0557-7 Subj: Animals – mice. Toys – balloons.

Muggins Mouse ill. by Anne Sellers Leaf. Rand McNally, 1965, c1964. Subj: Animals – mice.

Muggins takes off ill. by Anne Sellers Leaf. Rand McNally, 1964. ISBN 0-8382-0559-3 Subj: Animals – mice.

The Rand McNally book of favorite Muggins Mouse stories ill. by Anne Sellers Leaf. Rand McNally, 1965. Subj: Animals – mice.

Timothy Tiger ill. by Keith Ward. Rand McNally, 1943. Subj: Animals – tigers.

Barry, David. *The Rajah's rice* ill. by Donna Perrone. Scientific American, 1994. ISBN 0-7167-6568-3 Subj: Animals – elephants. Character traits – cleverness. Counting, numbers. Folk & fairy tales. Foreign lands – India. Royalty.

Barry, Frances. *Duckie's rainbow* ill. by author. Candlewick, 2003. ISBN 0-7636-2066-1 Subj: Birds – ducks. Concepts – color. Format, unusual – toy & movable books. Weather – rainbows.

Barry, Katharina. *A is for anything* ill. by author. Harcourt, 1961. Subj: ABC books. Poetry.

A bug to hug ill. by author. Harcourt, 1964. Subj: Imagination. Poetry. Problem solving.

Barry, Robert E. *Animals around the world* ill. by author. McGraw-Hill, 1967. Subj: ABC books. Animals. Poetry.

Mr. Willowby's Christmas tree ill. by Paul Galdone. McGraw-Hill, 1963. ISBN 0-89966-935-2 Subj: Holidays – Christmas. Rhyming text. Trees.

Next please ill. by author. Houghton Mifflin, 1961. Subj: Careers – barbers. Zoos.

Bartalos, Michael. *Shadowville* ill. by author. Viking, 1995. ISBN 0-67086-161-8 Subj: Holidays – Groundhog Day. Rhyming text. Shadows.

Bartels, Alice L. *The beast* ill. by Gilles Tibo. Firefly, 1990. ISBN 1-55037-101-0 Subj: Folk & fairy tales. Monsters. Night. Seasons.

The grandmother doll ill. by Dušan Petricic. Firefly, 2001. ISBN 1-55037-667-5 Subj: Activities – making things. Illness. Imagination. Toys – dolls.

Barth, Dominic. *George paints his house* (Bassède, Francine)

Barthelme, Donald. *The slightly irregular fire engine: or, The hithering thithering djinn* ill. by author. Farrar, 1971. Collage ill. made from nineteenth-century engravings. ISBN 0-374-37038-9 Subj: Imagination.

Bartlett, Margaret Farrington. *The clean brook* ill. by Aldren Auld Watson. McGraw-Hill, 1960. ISBN 0-690-19556-7 Subj: Science.

Down the mountain: a book about the ever-changing soil ill. by Rhys Caparn. Addison-Wesley, 1963. Subj: Science.

Raindrop stories (Bassett, Preston R.)

Where the brook begins ill. by Aldren Auld Watson. Crowell, 1961. Subj: Science.

Bartlett, Robert Merrill. *Jack Horner and song of sixpence* ill. by Emily Newton Barto. Longman, 1943. Subj: Nursery rhymes.

The story of Thanksgiving ill. by Sally Wern Comport. Harper-Collins, 2001. ISBN 0-06-028779-9 Subj: Holidays – Thanksgiving. Indians of North America – Wampanoag. U.S. history.

Bartlett, Susan. *Libraries* ill. by Gioia Fiammenghi. Holt, 1964. Subj: Libraries.

Barto, Emily Newton. *Chubby bear* ill. by author. Longman, 1941. Subj: Animals – bears. Poetry.

Bartoletti, Susan Campbell. *The Christmas promise* ill. by David Christiana. Blue Sky, 2001. ISBN 0-590-98451-9 Subj: Family life – daughters. Family life – fathers. Holidays – Christmas. Homeless. Poverty. U.S. history.

The flag maker ill. by Claire A. Nivola. Houghton, 2004. ISBN 0-618-26757-3 Subj: Flags. U.S. history. War.

Nobody's nosier than a cat ill. by Beppe Giacobbe. Hyperion, 2003. ISBN 0-7868-1614-7 Subj: Animals – cats. Pets. Rhyming text.

Silver at night ill. by David Ray. Crown, 1994. ISBN 0-517-59427-7 Subj: Activities – working. Careers – miners. Emotions – love. Ethnic groups in the U.S. – Italian Americans.

Bartoli, Jennifer. *In a meadow, two hares hide* ill. by Takeo Ishida; ed. by Kathy Pacini. A. Whitman, 1978. Subj: Animals – rabbits. Seasons – winter.

Nonna ill. by Joan E. Drescher. Harvey House, 1975. ISBN 0-8178-5212-3 Subj: Death. Emotions – grief. Family life. Family life – grandmothers.

Snow on bear's nose: a story of a Japanese moon bear cub ed. by Caroline Rubin; ill. by Takeo Ishida. A. Whitman, 1972. ISBN 0-8075-7520-8 Subj: Animals – bears. Behavior – lost. Foreign lands – Japan. Hibernation. Seasons – winter. Weather – snow.

Barton, Bob. *Paul Gallico's The small miracle* retold by Bob Barton; ill. by Carolyn Croll. Holt, 2003. ISBN 0-8050-6745-0 Subj: Animals – donkeys. Foreign lands – Italy. Religion.

Barton, Byron. *Airplanes* ill. by author. Crowell, 1986. ISBN 0-690-04532-8 Subj: Airplanes, airports.

Airport ill. by author. Crowell, 1982. ISBN 0-690-04169-1 Subj: Airplanes, airports. Careers – airplane pilots. Transportation.

Boats ill. by author. Crowell, 1986. ISBN 0-690-04563-0 Subj: Boats, ships.

Bones, bones, dinosaur bones ill. by author. HarperCollins, 1990. ISBN 0-690-04827-0 Subj: Dinosaurs. Prehistory.

Building a house ill. by author. Greenwillow, 1981. ISBN 0-688-84291-7 Subj: Homes, houses.

Buzz, buzz, buzz ill. by author. Macmillan, 1973. ISBN 0-02-708450-7 Subj: Cumulative tales. Insects – bees.

Dinosaurs, dinosaurs ill. by author. HarperCollins, 1989. ISBN 0-690-04768-1 Subj: Dinosaurs. Prehistory.

Harry is a scaredy-cat ill. by author. Macmillan, 1974. ISBN 0-02-708440-X Subj: Circus. Emotions – fear.

Hester ill. by author. Greenwillow, 1975. ISBN 0-688-84009-4 Subj: Character traits – patience.

I want to be an astronaut ill. by author. Crowell, 1988. ISBN 0-690-04744-4 Subj: Careers – astronauts. Character traits – ambition. Space & space ships.

Jack and Fred ill. by author. Macmillan, 1974. ISBN 0-02-708400-0 Subj: Animals – dogs. Animals – rabbits. Pets.

The little red hen (The little red hen)

Machines at work ill. by author. HarperCollins, 1987. ISBN 0-690-04573-5 Subj: Activities – working. Machines.

My car ill. by author. Greenwillow, 2001. ISBN 0-06-029625-9 Subj: Automobiles.

The three bears (The three bears)

Tools ill. by author. HarperFestival, 1995. ISBN 0-694-00623-8 Subj: Language. Tools.

Trains ill. by author. Crowell, 1986. ISBN 0-690-04534-4 Subj: Trains.

Trucks ill. by author. Crowell, 1986. ISBN 0-690-04530-1 Subj: Trucks.

The wee little woman ill. by author. HarperCollins, 1995. ISBN 0-06-023388-5 Subj: Animals – cats. Behavior – running away. Behavior – stealing.

Wheels ill. by author. Crowell, 1979. ISBN 0-690-03952-2 Subj: Progress. Wheels.

Where's Al? ill. by author. Seabury Pr., 1972. Subj: Animals – dogs. Behavior – lost. Wordless.

Zoo animals ill. by author. HarperFestival, 1995. ISBN 0-694-00620-3 Subj: Animals. Zoos.

Barton, Julia. *Are you asleep, rabbit?* (Campbell, Alison)

Barton, Pat. *A week is a long time* ill. by Jutta Ash. Academy Chicago, 1980. ISBN 0-200-72464-9 Subj: Clothing. Country.

Bartone, Elisa. *American, too* ill. by Ted Lewin. Lothrop, 1996. ISBN 0-688-13279-0 Subj: Communities, neighborhoods. Ethnic groups in the U.S. – Italian Americans.

Peppe the lamplighter ill. by Ted Lewin. Lothrop, 1993. ISBN 0-688-10269-7 Subj: Caldecott award honor books. Cities, towns. Ethnic groups in the U.S. – Italian Americans. Family life – brothers & sisters. Family life – fathers.

Bartos-Hoppner, Barbara. *The pied piper of Hamelin* trans. by Anthea Bell; ill. by Annegert Fuchshuber. Lippincott, 1987. Adapt. of the poem The pied piper of Hamelin by Robert Browning. ISBN 0-397-32240-2 Subj: Animals – rats. Behavior – trickery. Folk & fairy tales. Foreign lands – Germany.

Bartram, Simon. *Man on the moon: a day in the life of Bob* ill. by author. Candlewick, 2002. ISBN 0-7636-1897-7 Subj: Careers – astronauts. Moon. Mythical creatures. Space & space ships.

Baruch, Dorothy. *I would like to be a pony and other wishes* ill. by Mary Chalmers. HarperCollins, 1959. Subj: Behavior – wishing. Poetry.

Kappa's tug-of-war with the big brown horse: the story of a Japanese water imp ill. by Sanryo Sakai. Tuttle, 1962. Subj: Animals. Farms. Folk & fairy tales. Foreign lands – Japan. Mythical creatures – imps.

Barwin, Gary. *The racing worm brothers* ill. by Kitty Macaulay. Annick, 1998. ISBN 1-55037-541-5 Subj: Animals – worms. Pets.

Bascom, Joe. *Malcolm Softpaws* ill. by author. Lippincott, 1958. Subj: Animals – cats. Behavior – greed. Character traits – selfishness.

Malcolm's job ill. by author. Lippincott, 1959. Subj: Animals – cats. Family life. Music.

Base, Graeme. *Animalia* ill. by author. Abrams, 1987. ISBN 0-8109-1868-4 Subj: ABC books. Animals.

Jungle drums ill. by author. Abrams, 2004. ISBN 0-8109-5044-8 Subj: Animals. Animals – warthogs. Behavior – wishing. Foreign lands – Africa. Jungle. Magic. Musical instruments – drums.

My grandma lived in Gooligulch ill. by author. Australian Book Source, 1988, 1983. ISBN 0-944176-01-1 Subj: Animals. Family life – grandmothers. Foreign lands – Australia. Rhyming text.

The water hole ill. by author. Abrams, 2001. ISBN 0-8109-4568-1 Subj: Animals. Counting, numbers. Water. Weather – rain.

Baseball ABC ill. with photos. DK, 2001. "Published in partnership with & licensed by Major League Baseball Properties." ISBN 0-7894-7338-0 Subj: ABC books. Format, unusual – board books. Sports – baseball.

Baseball 1-2-3 ill. with photos. DK, 2001. "Published in partnership with & licensed by Major League Baseball Properties." ISBN 0-7894-7339-9 Subj: Counting, numbers. Format, unusual – board books. Sports – baseball.

Bash, Barbara. *Desert giant: the world of the Saguaro cactus* ill. by author. Little, 1988. ISBN 0-316-08301-1 Subj: Desert. Plants.

Urban roosts ill. by author. Little, 1990. ISBN 0-316-08306-2 Subj: Birds. Cities, towns. Nature.

Bashevis, Isaac. *see* Singer, Isaac Bashevis

Basile, Giambattista. *Petrosinella: a Neapolitan Rapunzel* adapt. by John Edward Taylor; ill. by Diane Stanley. Warne, 1981. ISBN 0-7232-6196-2 Subj: Folk & fairy tales. Foreign lands – Italy. Royalty. Witches.

Baskin, Leonard. *Hosie's alphabet* ill. by author; words by Hosea, Tobias & Lisa Baskin. Viking, 1972. ISBN 0-670-37958-1 Subj: ABC books. Caldecott award honor books. Children as authors.

Hosie's aviary ill. by author; words mostly by Tobias Baskin & others. Viking, 1979. ISBN 0-670-37965-4 Subj: Birds. Children as authors.

Hosie's zoo ill. by author; words by Tobias Baskin & others. Viking, 1981. ISBN 0-670-37968-9 Subj: Animals. Rhyming text. Zoos.

Baskin, Tobias. *Hosie's aviary* (Baskin, Leonard)

Hosie's zoo (Baskin, Leonard)

Baskwill, Jane. *Somewhere* ill. by Trish Hill. Mondo, 1996. ISBN 1-57255-132-1 Subj: Nature. Rhyming text.

Bason, Lillian. *Castles and mirrors and cities of sand* ill. by Allan Eitzen. Lothrop, 1968. Subj: Animals. Sand. Science.

Pick a raincoat, pick a whistle ill. by Allan Eitzen. Lothrop, 1966. Subj: Activities – whistling. Trees. Whistles.

Spiders ill. with photos. National Geographic, 1974. ISBN 0-870-44156-6 Subj: Science. Spiders.

Those foolish Molboes! ill. by Margot Tomes. Coward, 1977. ISBN 0-698-30642-2 Subj: Behavior – hiding things. Character traits – cleverness. Character traits – foolishness. Folk & fairy tales. Foreign lands – Denmark.

Bass, Jules. *Herb, the vegetarian dragon* ill. by Debbie Harter. Barefoot, 1999. ISBN 1-902283-36-8 Subj: Character traits – individuality. Dragons. Food.

Bassède, Francine. *A day with the Bellyflops* ill. by author. Orchard, 2000. ISBN 0-531-33242-X Subj: Animals – pigs. Family life – brothers & sisters. Family life – mothers.

George paints his house ill. by author; trans. by Dominic Barth. Orchard, 1999. ISBN 0-531-33150-4 Subj: Activities – painting. Animals – cats. Birds – ducks. Concepts – color. Homes, houses.

George's store at the shore ill. by author. Orchard, 1998. ISBN 0-531-33083-4 Subj: Counting, numbers.

Bassett, Jeni. *The chicks' trick* ill. by author. Cobblehill, 1995. ISBN 0-525-65152-7 Subj: Behavior – fighting, arguing. Birds – chickens. Family life.

Bassett, Lisa. *Beany and Scamp* ill. by Jeni Bassett. Dodd, 1987. ISBN 0-396-08822-8 Subj: Animals – bears. Animals – squirrels.

Behavior – lost. Behavior – lost & found possessions. Seasons – winter.

Beany wakes up for Christmas ill. by Jeni Bassett. Putnam, 1988. ISBN 0-399-21668-5 Subj: Animals – bears. Animals – squirrels. Friendship. Hibernation. Holidays – Christmas.

A clock for Beany ill. by Jeni Bassett. Dodd, 1985. ISBN 0-396-08484-2 Subj: Animals. Animals – bears. Birthdays. Clocks, watches.

Koala Christmas ill. by Jeni Bassett. Dutton, 1991. ISBN 0-525-65065-2 Subj: Animals – koalas. Foreign lands – Australia. Holidays – Christmas. Sibling rivalry.

Bassett, Preston R. *Raindrop stories* by Preston R. Bassett & Margaret Farrington Bartlett; ill. by Jim Arnosky. Four Winds, 1981. ISBN 0-590-07628-0 Subj: Noise, sounds. Weather – rain.

Basso, Bill. *The top of the pizzas* ill. by author. Dodd, 1977. ISBN 0-396-07463-4 Subj: Activities – working. Food. Monsters.

Bastin, Marjolein. *A little dog for Vera* ill. by author. Stewart, Tabori & Chang, 1991. ISBN 0-55670-208-6 Subj: Animals – dogs. Animals – mice. Pets.

My name is Vera ill. by author. Barron's, 1985. ISBN 0-8120-5690-6 Subj: Animals – mice. Friendship.

Vera and her friends ill. by author. Barron's, 1985. ISBN 0-8120-5689-2 Subj: Animals – mice. Friendship.

Vera dresses up ill. by author. Barron's, 1985. ISBN 0-8120-5691-4 Subj: Animals – mice. Clothing.

Vera in the kitchen ill. by author. Barron's, 1988. ISBN 0-8120-6087-3 Subj: Activities – baking, cooking. Animals – mice.

Vera the mouse ill. by author. Barron's, 1986. ISBN 0-8120-7391-6 Subj: Animals – mice.

Vera's special hobbies ill. by author. Barron's, 1985. ISBN 0-8120-5692-2 Subj: Animals – mice. Nature.

Bat-Ami, Miriam. *Sea, salt, and air* ill. by Mary O'Keefe Young. S&S, 1993. ISBN 0-02-708495-7 Subj: Behavior – growing up. Family life – grandparents. Sea & seashore. Seasons – summer.

Batchelor, Louise. *Whoops!* ill. by author. Zero to Ten, 1998. ISBN 1-8408-9024-X Subj: Activities – playing. Friendship.

Batchelor, Mary. *Children's prayers from around the world* (Children's prayers from around the world)

Bate, Lucy. *How Georgina drove the car very carefully from Boston to New York* ill. by Tamar Taylor. Crown, 1989. ISBN 0-517-57142-0 Subj: Activities – traveling. Family life – grandparents. Imagination.

Little rabbit's loose tooth ill. by Diane de Groat. Crown, 1975. ISBN 0-517-52240-3 Subj: Animals – rabbits. Fairies. Teeth.

Bate, Norman. *Vulcan* ill. by author. Scribners, 1960. Subj: Machines.

What a wonderful machine is a submarine ill. by author. Scribners, 1961. Subj: Boats, ships. Sea & seashore.

Who built the bridge? ill. by author. Crown, 1975. ISBN 0-684-13449-7 Subj: Machines.

Who built the highway? ill. by author. Scribners, 1953. Subj: Machines. Roads.

Bateman, Robert. *Safari* by Robert Bateman & Rick Archbold; ill. by authors. Little, 1998. ISBN 0-316-08265-1 Subj: Animals. Foreign lands – Africa.

Bateman, Teresa. *April foolishness* ill. by Nadine Bernard Westcott. A. Whitman, 2004. ISBN 0-8075-0404-1 Subj: Family life – grandparents. Farms. Holidays – April Fools' Day. Rhyming text.

The Bully Blockers Club ill. by Jackie Urbanovic. A. Whitman, 2004. ISBN 0-8075-0918-3 Subj: Behavior – bullying. Clubs, gangs. School.

Farm flu ill. by Nadine Bernard Westcott. A. Whitman, 2001. ISBN 0-8075-2274-0 Subj: Animals. Farms. Illness – influenza. Rhyming text.

Harp o' gold ill. by Jill Weber. Holiday, 2001. ISBN 0-8234-1523-6 Subj: Folk & fairy tales. Music.

Hunting the daddyosaurus ill. by Benrei Huang. A. Whitman, 2002. ISBN 0-8075-1433-0 Subj: Dinosaurs. Family life – brothers. Family life – fathers. Rhyming text.

Leprechaun gold ill. by Rosanne Litzinger. Holiday, 1998. ISBN 0-8234-1344-6 Subj: Folk & fairy tales. Mythical creatures – leprechauns.

The merbaby ill. by Patience Brewster. Holiday, 2001. ISBN 0-8234-1531-7 Subj: Careers – fishermen. Family life – brothers. Mythical creatures – mermaids, mermen.

A plump and perky turkey ill. by Jeff Shelly. Cavendish, 2004. ISBN 0-7714-5188-9 Subj: Birds – turkeys. Holidays – Thanksgiving. Rhyming text.

The princesses have a ball ill. by Lynne Cravath. A. Whitman, 2002. ISBN 0-8075-6626-8 Subj: Folk & fairy tales. Rhyming text. Royalty – princesses. Sports – basketball.

Bates, Artie Ann. *Ragsale* ill. by Jeff Chapman-Crane. Houghton Mifflin, 1995. ISBN 0-395-70030-2 Subj: Family life. Poverty. Shopping.

Bates, H. E. (Herbert Ernest). *Achilles and Diana* by H. E. Bates & Carol Barker; ill. by Carol Barker. Dobson, 1963. Subj: Animals – donkeys.

Achilles the donkey by H. E. Bates & Carol Barker; ill. by Carol Barker. Watts, 1963. Subj: Animals – donkeys. Behavior – running away.

Bates, Ivan. *All by myself* ill. by author. HarperCollins, 2000. ISBN 0-06-028585-0 Subj: Animals. Animals – elephants. Character traits – individuality.

Bates, Katharine Lee. *America the beautiful* ill. by Chris Gall. Little, 2004. ISBN 0-316-73743-7 Subj: Music. Poetry. Songs. U.S. history.

America the beautiful ill. by Wendell Minor. Putnam, 2003. ISBN 0-399-23885-9 Subj: Music. Poetry. Songs. U.S. history.

America the beautiful ill. by Neil Waldman. Atheneum, 1993. ISBN 0-689-31861-8 Subj: Music. Poetry. Songs. U.S. history.

Bateson-Hill, Margaret. *Lao Lao of Dragon Mountain* ill. by Francesca Pelizzoli; Chinese text by Manyee Wan; paper cuts by Shaliu Qu. Zero to Ten, 1996. ISBN 1-899883-64-9 Subj: Folk & fairy tales. Foreign lands – China. Foreign languages. Paper.

Masha and the firebird by Margaret Bateson-Hill & Anne Wilson; ill. by Anne Wilson. Zero to Ten, 2000. ISBN 1-84089-134-3 Subj: Eggs. Folk & fairy tales. Foreign lands – Russia. Witches.

Shota and the star quilt ill. by Christine Fowler; Lakota text by Philomine Lakota. Zero to Ten, 2001, 1998. ISBN 1-8408-9021-5 Subj: Indians of North America – Lakota (Sioux). Quilts.

Batherman, Muriel. *Animals live here* ill. by author. Greenwillow, 1979. ISBN 0-688-84206-2 Subj: Animals. Science.

Some things you should know about my dog ill. by author. Prentice-Hall, 1976. ISBN 0-13-822544-3 Subj: Animals – dogs.

Batt, Tanya Robyn. *The faerie's gift* ill. by Nicoletta Ceccoli. Barefoot, 2003. ISBN 1-84148-998-0 Subj: Activities – working. Fairies. Folk & fairy tales.

Batten, Mary. *Who has a belly button?* ill. by Higgins Bond. Peachtree, 2004. ISBN 1-56145-235-1 Subj: Anatomy – navels. Animals. Birth.

Battle-Lavert, Gwendolyn. *The barber's cutting edge* ill. by Raymond Holbert. Children's Book Pr., 1994. ISBN 0-8923-9127-8 Subj: Careers – barbers. Ethnic groups in the U.S. – African Americans. Hair. Language.

The music in Derrick's heart ill. by Colin Bootman. Holiday, 2000. ISBN 0-8234-1353-5 Subj: Careers – musicians. Ethnic groups in the U.S. – African Americans. Musical instruments – harmonicas.

Papa's mark ill. by Colin Bootman. Holiday, 2003. ISBN 0-8234-1650-X Subj: Activities – writing. Books, reading. Ethnic groups in the U.S. – African Americans. Family life – fathers. U.S. history.

The shaking bag ill. by Aminah Brenda Lynn Robinson. A. Whitman, 2000. ISBN 0-8075-7328-0 Subj: Birds – ravens. Character traits – generosity. Ethnic groups in the U.S. – African Americans.

Battles, Edith. *One to teeter-totter* ill. by Rosalind Fry. A. Whitman, 1973. ISBN 0-8075-6103-7 Subj: Emotions – loneliness. Family life. Friendship. Games.

The terrible terrier ill. by Tom Funk. Addison-Wesley, 1972. ISBN 0-20-109366-9 Subj: Animals – dogs. Behavior – greed.

The terrible trick or treat ill. by Tom Funk. Addison-Wesley, 1970. Subj: Behavior – greed. Holidays – Halloween.

What does the rooster say, Yoshio? ill. by Toni Hormann. A. Whitman, 1978. ISBN 0-8075-3628-8 Subj: Animals. Foreign lands – Japan. Language.

Bauer, Caroline Feller. *Midnight snowman* ill. by Catherine Stock. Atheneum, 1987. ISBN 0-689-31294-6 Subj: Seasons – winter. Snowmen. Weather – snow.

My mom travels a lot ill. by Nancy Winslow Parker. Warne, 1981. ISBN 0-7232-6203-9 Subj: Careers. Family life – mothers.

Too many books! ill. by Diane Paterson. Viking, 1986. ISBN 0-670-81130-0 Subj: Behavior – collecting things. Books, reading. Libraries.

Bauer, Helen. *Good times at the park* photos by Hubert A. Lowman. Melmont, 1954. Subj: Activities – playing. Birthdays. Parks. Zoos.

Bauer, Marion Dane. *Frog's best friend* ill. by Diane Dawson Hearn. Holiday, 2002. ISBN 0-8234-1501-5 Subj: Animals. Friendship. Frogs & toads. Reptiles – turtles, tortoises.

Grandmother's song ill. by Pamela Rossi. S&S, 2000. ISBN 0-689-82272-3 Subj: Babies. Birth. Family life – grandmothers. Family life – mothers.

If you had a nose like an elephant's trunk ill. by Susan Winter. Holiday, 2001. ISBN 0-8234-1589-9 Subj: Anatomy. Animals.

If you were born a kitten ill. by Jo Ellen McAllister Stammen. S&S, 1997. ISBN 0-689-80111-4 Subj: Animals. Animals – babies.

Jason's bears ill. by Kevin Hawkes. Hyperion, 2000. ISBN 0-7868-2303-8 Subj: Animals – bears. Emotions – fear. Family life – brothers.

My mother is mine ill. by Peter Elwell. S&S, 2001. ISBN 0-689-82267-7 Subj: Animals. Family life – mothers. Holidays – Mother's Day. Letters, cards. Rhyming text.

Sleep, little one, sleep ill. by author. S&S, 1999. ISBN 0-689-82250-2 Subj: Animals. Bedtime. Family life – fathers. Sleep.

Toes, ears, and nose! a lift-the-flap book ill. by Karen Katz. Little Simon, 2003. ISBN 0-689-84712-2 Subj: Anatomy. Format, unusual – toy & movable books.

Uh-oh! a lift-the-flap story ill. by Valeria Petrone. Little Simon, 2002. ISBN 0-689-84711-4 Subj: Accidents. Format, unusual – toy & movable books.

When I go camping with Grandma ill. by Allen Garns. BridgeWater, 1995. ISBN 0-8167-3448-8 Subj: Camps, camping. Family life – grandmothers.

Why do kittens purr? ill. by Henry Cole. S&S, 2003. ISBN 0-689-84179-5 Subj: Animals. Behavior.

Bauer, Steven. *The strange and wonderful tale of Robert McDoodle* ill. by Brad Sneed. S&S, 1999. ISBN 0-689-80619-1 Subj: Animals – dogs. Behavior – dissatisfaction. Behavior – running away. Birthdays. Rhyming text.

Baugh, Dolores M. *Bikes* by Dolores M. Baugh & Marjorie P. Pulsifer; ill. by Eve Hoffmann. Rev. ed. Chandler, 1965. Subj: Sports – bicycling. Traffic, traffic signs.

Let's go by Dolores M. Baugh & Marjorie P. Pulsifer; ill. by Eve Hoffmann. Noble, 1970. Subj: Stores.

Let's see the animals by Dolores M. Baugh & Marjorie P. Pulsifer; ill. by Eve Hoffmann. Chandler, 1965. Subj: Animals.

Let's take a trip by Dolores M. Baugh & Marjorie P. Pulsifer; ill. by Richard Szumski & others. Chandler, 1965. Subj: Libraries. Machines.

Slides by Dolores M. Baugh & Marjorie P. Pulsifer; ill. by Eve Hoffmann. Noble, 1970. Subj: Activities – playing.

Supermarket by Dolores M. Baugh & Marjorie P. Pulsifer; ill. by Eve Hoffmann. Noble, 1970. Subj: Food. Shopping. Stores.

Swings by Dolores M. Baugh & Marjorie P. Pulsifer; ill. by Eve Hoffmann. Noble, 1970. Subj: Activities – playing. Activities – swinging.

Trucks and cars to ride by Dolores M. Baugh & Marjorie P. Pulsifer; ill. by Eve Hoffmann. Noble, 1970. Subj: Automobiles. Transportation. Trucks.

Bauld, Jane Scoggins. *Journey of the third seed* ill. by Cynthia G. Darr. Eakin, 2000. ISBN 1-57168-428-X Subj: Foreign lands – Japan. Gardens, gardening. Royalty – emperors. Seeds.

Baum, Arline. *One bright Monday morning* by Arline & Joseph Baum; ill. by Joseph Baum. Random House, 1973, c1962. ISBN 0-394-82650-7 Subj: Counting, numbers. Seasons – spring. Weather.

Opt: an illusionary tale by Arline & Joseph Baum; ill. by authors. Viking, 1987. ISBN 0-670-80870-9 Subj: Birthdays. Optical illusions. Royalty – princes.

Baum, Joseph. *One bright Monday morning* (Baum, Arline)

Opt: an illusionary tale (Baum, Arline)

Baum, L. Frank (Lyman Frank). *Mother Goose in prose* ill. by Maxfield Parrish. Bounty Books, 1986, c1901. ISBN 0-685-16878-6 Subj: Nursery rhymes.

Baum, Louis. *After dark* ill. by Susan Varley. Overlook Pr., 1990. ISBN 0-87951-382-9 Subj: Family life – mothers.

I want to see the moon ill. by Niki Daly. Overlook Pr., 1989. ISBN 0-87951-367-5 Subj: Bedtime. Moon. Sleep.

JuJu and the pirate ill. by Philippe Matter. HarperCollins, 1984. ISBN 0-911745-14-9 Subj: Activities – traveling. Birds – parakeets, parrots. Pirates.

One more time ill. by Paddy Bouma. Morrow, 1986. ISBN 0-688-06587-2 Subj: Divorce. Family life – fathers.

Baum, Susan. *The beach* ill. by author. HarperCollins, 1991. ISBN 0-06-107416-0 Subj: Sea & seashore – beaches.

City shapes ill. by author. HarperCollins, 1991. ISBN 0-06-107417-9 Subj: Cities, towns. Concepts – shape.

Baum, Willi. *Birds of a feather* ill. by author. Addison-Wesley, 1969. Subj: Birds. Wordless.

Bauman, A. F. *Guess where you're going, guess what you'll do* ill. by True Kelley. Houghton Mifflin, 1989. ISBN 0-395-50211-X Subj: Concepts. Games. Participation.

Bauman, Amy. *I know an old lady* (Little old lady who swallowed a fly)

Baumann, Hans. *Chip has many brothers* ill. by Eric Carle. Philomel, 1985. ISBN 0-399-21283-3 Subj: Animals. Character traits – kindness to animals. Folk & fairy tales. Magic.

The hare's race ill. by Antoni Boratynski; trans. from German by Elizabeth D. Crawford. Morrow, 1976. ISBN 0-688-32067-8 Subj: Animals – rabbits. Folk & fairy tales. Reptiles – turtles, tortoises. Sports – racing.

Mischa and his brothers trans. from German by Peter F. Neumeyer; ill. by Reinhard Michl. Green Tiger Pr., 1985. ISBN 0-88138-051-2 Subj: Character traits – being different. Family life – brothers. Forest, woods.

Baumann, Kurt. *The paper airplane* ill. by Fulvio Testa. Little, 1982. ISBN 0-316-08389-5 Subj: Airplanes, airports. Imagination.

Piro and the fire brigade ill. by Jiri Bernard. Faber, 1981. Translation of: Piro und die Feuerwehr. ISBN 0-571-11843-7 Subj: Animals – dogs. Careers – firefighters. Character traits – bravery. Fire. Foreign lands – Switzerland.

The prince and the lute ill. by Jean Claverie. North-South, 1986. First pub. in Switzerland under the title Der Prinz und die Laute. ISBN 0-03-008018-5 Subj: Character traits – kindness. Folk & fairy tales. Royalty – princes. War.

Puss in boots (Perrault, Charles)

The story of Jonah trans. from German by Jock J. Curle; ill. by Allison Reed. Holt, 1987. ISBN 0-8050-0233-2 Subj: Animals – whales. Behavior – misbehavior. Religion – Jonah.

Baumgardner, Mary Alice. *Alexandra, keeper of dreams* ill. by author. Rocky River, 1993. ISBN 0-944576-08-7 Subj: Activities – dancing. Ballet. Birds – ducks. Character traits – perseverance.

Baumgart, Klaus. *Anna and the little green dragon* ill. by author. Walt Disney, 1992. ISBN 1-56282-167-9 Subj: Behavior – misbehavior. Dragons.

Don't be afraid, Tommy ill. by author. Little Tiger, 1998. ISBN 1-888444-32-0 Subj: Animals – dogs. Behavior – growing up. Emotions – fear.

Laura's Christmas star ill. by author. Little Tiger, 1999. ISBN 1-888444-59-2 Subj: Holidays – Christmas. Magic. Stars. Trees.

Laura's secret ill. by author; English text by Judy Waite. Tiger Tales, 2003. ISBN 1-58925-031-1 Subj: Behavior – wishing. Family life – brothers & sisters. Kites. Magic. Stars.

Laura's star ill. by author. Tiger Tales, 2002. ISBN 1-58925-374-4 Subj: Friendship. Stars.

The little green dragon steps out ill. by author. Hyperion, 1992. ISBN 1-56282-255-1 Subj: Books, reading. Dragons. Dreams. Night.

Bawden, Juliet. *One year old* photos by Helen Pask. Holt, 1990. ISBN 0-8050-1257-5 Subj: Counting, numbers.

Bawden, Nina. *Princess Alice* ill. by Phillida Gili. Dutton, 1986. ISBN 0-233-97746-5 Subj: Adoption. Family life. Royalty – princesses.

St. Francis of Assisi ill. by Pascale Allamand. Lothrop, 1983. ISBN 0-688-01653-7 Subj: Character traits – generosity. Religion.

William Tell ill. by Pascale Allamand. Lothrop, 1981. ISBN 0-688-51985-7 Subj: Character traits – bravery. Folk & fairy tales. Foreign lands – Switzerland.

Bax, Martin. *Edmond went far away* ill. by Michael Foreman. Harcourt, 1989. ISBN 0-15-225105-7 Subj: Activities – walking. Animals. Farms.

Bayar, Ilene. *Rachel and Mischa* (Bayar, Steven)

Bayar, Steven. *Rachel and Mischa* by Steven & Ilene Bayar; ill. by Marlene Lobell Ruthen; photos by Joanne Strauss. Kar-Ben Copies, 1988. ISBN 0-930-49477-6 Subj: Character traits – freedom. Jewish culture. Religion.

Bayer, Jane. *A my name is Alice* ill. by Steven Kellogg. Dial, 1984. ISBN 0-8037-0124-1 Subj: ABC books. Animals. Names.

Bayley, Nicola. *Crab cat* ill. by author. Knopf, 1984. ISBN 0-394-86499-0 Subj: Animals – cats. Imagination.

Elephant cat ill. by author. Knopf, 1984. ISBN 0-394-86497-2 Subj: Animals – cats. Imagination.

Nicola Bayley's book of nursery rhymes ill. by author. Knopf, 1975. ISBN 0-394-83561-1 Subj: Nursery rhymes.

One old Oxford ox ill. by author. Atheneum, 1977. ISBN 0-689-30608-3 Subj: Animals. Counting, numbers.

Parrot cat ill. by author. Knopf, 1984. ISBN 0-394-86496-4 Subj: Animals – cats. Imagination.

Polar bear cat ill. by author. Knopf, 1984. ISBN 0-394-86501-4 Subj: Animals – cats. Imagination.

Spider cat ill. by author. Knopf, 1984. ISBN 0-394-86500-6 Subj: Animals – cats. Imagination.

Baylor, Byrd. *Amigo* ill. by Garth Williams. Macmillan, 1963. ISBN 0-606-03982-1 Subj: Animals – prairie dogs. Pets. Rhyming text.

The best town in the world ill. by Ronald Himler. Scribners, 1983. ISBN 0-684-18035-9 Subj: Cities, towns.

Coyote cry ill. by Symeon Shimin. Lothrop, 1972. Subj: Animals – coyotes. Animals – dogs.

The desert is theirs ill. by Peter Parnall. Scribners, 1975. ISBN 0-684-14266-X Subj: Caldecott award honor books. Desert. Ecology. Folk & fairy tales. Indians of North America – Papago. Rhyming text.

Desert voices ill. by Peter Parnall. Scribners, 1981. ISBN 0-684-16712-3 Subj: Animals. Desert. Rhyming text.

Everybody needs a rock ill. by Peter Parnall. Scribners, 1974. ISBN 0-684-13899-9 Subj: Rhyming text. Rocks.

A God on every mountain top: stories of southwest Indian sacred mountains ill. by Carol Brown. Scribners, 1981. ISBN 0-684-16758-1 Subj: Folk & fairy tales. Indians of North America.

Guess who my favorite person is ill. by Robert Andrew Parker. Scribners, 1977. ISBN 0-684-15197-9 Subj: Friendship. Games.

Hawk, I'm your brother ill. by Peter Parnall. Scribners, 1976. ISBN 0-684-14571-5 Subj: Birds – hawks. Caldecott award honor books. Character traits – freedom. Indians of North America.

If you are a hunter of fossils ill. by Peter Parnall. Macmillan, 1980. ISBN 0-684-16419-1 Subj: Fossils. Prehistory. Science.

I'm in charge of celebrations ill. by Peter Parnall. Scribners, 1986. ISBN 0-684-18579-2 Subj: Desert. Nature.

Moon song ill. by Ronald Himler. Scribners, 1982. ISBN 0-684-17463-4 Subj: Animals – coyotes. Folk & fairy tales. Indians of North America. Moon.

One small blue bead ill. by Ronald Himler. Scribners, 1992. ISBN 0-684-19334-5 Subj: Cavemen. Rhyming text.

The other way to listen ill. by Peter Parnall. Scribners, 1978. ISBN 0-684-16017-X Subj: Nature. Poetry.

The table where rich people sit ill. by Peter Parnall. Scribners, 1994. ISBN 0-684-19653-0 Subj: Family life. Money. Nature.

The way to start a day ill. by Peter Parnall. Aladdin, 1986, c1978. ISBN 0-684-15651-2 Subj: Caldecott award honor books. Folk & fairy tales. Foreign lands. Religion. Sun.

We walk in sandy places ill. by Marilyn Schweitzer. Scribners, 1976. ISBN 0-684-14526-X Subj: Animals. Desert.

When clay sings ill. by Tom Bahti. Scribners, 1972. ISBN 0-684-12807-1 Subj: Art. Caldecott award honor books. Indians of North America.

Your own best secret place ill. by Peter Parnall. Scribners, 1979. ISBN 0-684-16111-7 Subj: Behavior – hiding things. Behavior – secrets.

Baynes, Pauline. *How dog began* ill. by author. Holt, 1987. ISBN 0-8050-0011-9 Subj: Animals – dogs. Animals – wolves. Caves.

Let there be light ill. by author. Macmillan, 1991. ISBN 0-02-708542-2 Subj: Religion.

Noah and the ark (Bible Old Testament Noah)

Thanks be to God ill. by author. Macmillan, 1990. ISBN 0-02-708541-4 Subj: Religion.

Baynton, Martin. *Fifty and the fox* ill. by author. Crown, 1986. ISBN 0-517-56069-0 Subj: Animals – foxes. Farms. Tractors.

Fifty and the great race ill. by author. Crown, 1987. ISBN 0-517-56354-1 Subj: Fairs, festivals. Farms. Sports – racing. Tractors.

Fifty gets the picture ill. by author. Crown, 1987. ISBN 0-517-56355-X Subj: Activities – digging. Careers – artists. Farms. Tractors.

Fifty saves his friend ill. by author. Crown, 1986. ISBN 0-517-56022-4 Subj: Animals – rats. Farms. Friendship. Tractors.

Why do you love me? ill. by author. Greenwillow, 1990. ISBN 0-688-09157-1 Subj: Character traits – questioning. Emotions – love. Family life – fathers.

Bazilian, Barbara. *Princess Lily* by Barbara Bazilian & Judith Fine; ill. by Barbara Bazilian. Whispering Coyote, 1998. ISBN 1-58089-006-7 Subj: Folk & fairy tales. Royalty – princesses. Wizards.

The red shoes ill. by reteller. Whispering Coyote, 1997. ISBN 1-879085-56-9 Subj: Activities – dancing. Behavior – wishing. Character traits – pride. Clothing – shoes. Folk & fairy tales.

Bea, Holly. *Bless your heart* ill. by Kim Howard. Kramer, 2001. ISBN 0-915811-94-4 Subj: Bedtime. Religion. Rhyming text.

My spiritual alphabet book ill. by Kim Howard. Kramer, 2000. ISBN 0-915811-83-9 Subj: ABC books. Religion. Rhyming text. Self-concept.

Where does God live? ill. by Kim Howard. Starseed Pr., 1997. ISBN 0-915811-73-1 Subj: Family life – grandmothers. Religion.

Beach, Stewart. *Good morning, sun's up!* ill. by Yutaka Sugita. Scroll Pr., 1970. German ed. has title: Guten Morgen, liebe Sonne! Subj: Animals. Games. Morning.

Beall, Pamela Conon. *Wee Sing if you're happy and you know it* by Pamela Conn Beall and Susan Hagen Nipp; ill. by Hala Wittwer. Price Stern Sloan, 2002. ISBN 0-8431-7759-4 Subj: Format, unusual – board books. Insects. Songs.

Beames, Margaret. *Night cat* ill. by Sue Hitchcock. Scholastic, 2003. ISBN 0-439-38576-8 Subj: Animals. Animals – cats. Gardens, gardening. Night.

The bear: an American folk song ill. by Kenneth Spengler. Mondo, 2002. ISBN 1-59034-190-2 Subj: Animals – bears. Birds – eagles. Camps, camping. Music. Songs.

Bearcub and Mama ill. by Mélanie Watt. Kids Can, 2005. ISBN 1-55337-566-1 Subj: Animals – bears. Family life – mothers. Family life – sons. Weather – storms.

Beard, Darleen Bailey. *Twister* ill. by Nancy Carpenter. Farrar, 1999. ISBN 0-374-37977-7 Subj: Character traits – helpfulness. Family life. Weather – storms. Weather – tornadoes.

Beardshaw, Rosalind. *Grandma's beach* ill. by author. Bloomsbury, 2004. ISBN 1-58234-935-5 Subj: Family life – grandmothers. Sea & seashore – beaches.

Grandpa's surprise ill. by author. Bloomsbury, 2004. ISBN 1-58234-934-7 Subj: Family life – grandfathers. Foreign lands – England. Sports – bicycling.

Beaton, Clare. *At home = A la maison* ill. by author. Barron's, 2001. ISBN 0-7641-1693-2 Subj: Foreign languages. Homes, houses.

How loud is a lion? ill. by author. Barefoot, 2002. ISBN 1-84148-896-8 Subj: Animals. Jungle. Noise, sounds.

One moose, twenty mice ill. by author. Barefoot, 1999. ISBN 1-902283-37-6 Subj: Animals. Animals – cats. Counting, numbers.

One moose, twenty mice [board book] ill. by author. Barefoot, 1999. ISBN 1-841482-85-4 Subj: Animals. Animals – cats. Counting, numbers. Format, unusual – board books.

Zoë and her zebra ill. by author. Barefoot, 1999. ISBN 1-902283-75-9 Subj: ABC books. Language.

Beatty, Hetty Burlingame. *Bucking horse* ill. by author. Houghton Mifflin, 1957. Subj: Animals – horses, ponies. Cowboys, cowgirls.

Droopy ill. by author. Houghton Mifflin, 1954. Subj: Animals – mules. Character traits – stubbornness. Sports – swimming.

Little Owl Indian ill. by author. Houghton Mifflin, 1951. Subj: Animals – horses, ponies. Fire. Indians of North America.

Moorland pony ill. by author. Houghton Mifflin, 1961. Subj: Activities – traveling. Animals – horses, ponies. Character traits – kindness to animals. Family life. Foreign lands – England. Pets.

Beaumont, Karen. *Duck, duck, goose! a coyote's on the loose!* ill. by José Aruego & Ariane Dewey. HarperCollins, 2004. ISBN 0-06-050804-3 Subj: Animals. Animals – coyotes. Farms. Rhyming text.

Beautiful moments in the wild: animals and their colors ill. with photos. Moonstone, 2002. ISBN 0-9707768-7-X Subj: Animals. Concepts – color.

Bechstein, Ludwig. *The rabbit catcher and other fairy tales* trans. & intro. by Randall Jarrell; ill. by Ugo Fontana. Macmillan, 1962. Subj: Folk & fairy tales. Foreign lands – Germany.

Bechtold, Lisze. *Edna's tale* ill. by author. Houghton, 2001. ISBN 0-618-09164-5 Subj: Anatomy – tails. Animals – cats.

Beck, Andrea. *Elliot bakes a cake* ill. by author. Kids Can, 1999. ISBN 1-55074-443-7 Subj: Activities – baking, cooking. Animals – moose. Birthdays. Toys.

Elliot digs for treasure ill. by author. Kids Can, 2001. ISBN 1-55074-806-8 Subj: Animals. Animals – moose. Behavior – hiding things. Gardens, gardening. Maps. Toys.

Elliot gets stuck ill. by author. Kids Can, 2002. ISBN 1-55337-014-7 Subj: Animals. Animals – moose. Seasons – spring. Toys.

Elliot's bath ill. by author. Kids Can, 2001. ISBN 1-55074-802-5 Subj: Activities – bathing. Animals – moose. Toys.

Elliot's Christmas surprise ill. by author. Kids Can, 2003. ISBN 1-55337-474-6 Subj: Animals. Animals – moose. Friendship. Gifts. Holidays – Christmas. Toys.

Elliot's emergency ill. by author. Kids Can, 1998. ISBN 1-55074-441-0 Subj: Activities – sewing. Animals. Animals – moose. Friendship. Toys – dolls.

Elliot's great big lift-the-flap book ill. by author. Kids Can, 2003. ISBN 1-55337-373-1 Subj: Animals – moose. Concepts – color. Concepts – shape. Counting, numbers. Format, unusual – toy & movable books.

Elliot's noisy night ill. by author. Kids Can, 2002. ISBN 1-55337-011-2 Subj: Animals – moose. Bedtime. Night. Noise, sounds. Toys.

Elliot's shipwreck ill. by author. Kids Can, 2000. ISBN 1-55074-698-7 Subj: Activities – playing. Animals. Animals – moose. Boats, ships. Friendship. Sports – sailing. Toys.

Beck, Ian. *Emily and the golden acorn* ill. by author. S&S, 1992. ISBN 0-671-75979-5 Subj: Boats, ships. Family life – brothers & sisters. Imagination. Trees.

Five little ducks ill. by author. Holt, 1993. ISBN 0-8050-2525-1 Subj: Animals – foxes. Birds – ducks. Counting, numbers. Rhyming text.

Home before dark ill. by author. Scholastic, 2001. ISBN 0-439-17522-4 Subj: Behavior – lost. Toys – bears.

Teddy's snowy day ill. by author. Scholastic, 2002. ISBN 0-439-17520-8 Subj: Behavior – lost. Toys – bears. Weather – snow.

Beck, Martine. *Rescue of Brown Bear and White Bear* ill. by Marie H. Henry. Little, 1991. ISBN 0-316-08654-1 Subj: Animals – bears.

The wedding of Brown Bear and White Bear trans. from French by Aliyah Morgenstern; ill. by Marie H. Henry. Little, 1990. ISBN 0-316-08652-5 Subj: Animals – bears. Weddings.

Beck, Scott. *A mud pie for mother* ill. by author. Dutton, 2003. ISBN 0-525-47040-9 Subj: Animals – pigs. Birthdays. Character traits – generosity. Family life – mothers. Gifts.

Pepito the brave ill. by author. Dutton, 2001. ISBN 0-525-46524-3 Subj: Birds. Character traits – bravery. Emotions – fear.

Becker, Bonny. *An ant's day off* ill. by Nina Laden. S&S, 2003. ISBN 0-689-82274-X Subj: Animals. Insects – ants.

The Christmas crocodile ill. by David Small. S&S, 1997. ISBN 0-689-81503-4 Subj: Behavior – mistakes. Holidays – Christmas. Reptiles – alligators, crocodiles.

Just a minute ill. by Jack E. Davis. S&S, 2003. ISBN 0-689-83374-1 Subj: Time.

Tickly prickly ill. by Shari Halpern. HarperFestival, 1999. ISBN 0-694-01239-4 Subj: Animals. Rhyming text. Senses – touch.

Becker, Edna. *Nine hundred buckets of paint* ill. by Margaret Bradfield. Abingdon, 1945. Subj: Activities – painting. Homes, houses. Moving.

Becker, Helaine. *Mama likes to mambo* ill. by John Beder. Stoddart, 2001. ISBN 0-7737-3316-7 Subj: Animals. Foreign lands – Canada. Poetry.

Becker, John Leonard. *Seven little rabbits* ill. by Barbara Cooney. Walker, 1973. ISBN 0-8027-6130-5 Subj: Animals – rabbits. Counting, numbers.

Becker, May Lamberton. *The rainbow Mother Goose* (Mother Goose)

Beckett, Hilary. *The rooster's horns: a Chinese puppet play to make and perform* (Young, Ed [Edward])

Beckman, Beatrice. *I can be a teacher* ill. with photos. Childrens Pr., 1985. ISBN 0-516-01843-4 Subj: Careers – teachers.

Beckman, Kaj. *Lisa cannot sleep* ill. by Per Beckman. Watts, 1970. ISBN 0-531-01931-4 Subj: Bedtime. Family life. Sleep. Toys.

Bedard, Michael. *The nightingale* (Andersen, H. C. [Hans Christian])

Sitting ducks ill. by author. Putnam, 1998. ISBN 0-399-22847-0 Subj: Birds – ducks. Friendship. Reptiles – alligators, crocodiles.

The wolf of Gubbio ill. by Murray Kimber. Stoddart, 2000. ISBN 0-7737-3250-0 Subj: Animals – wolves. Folk & fairy tales. Religion.

Bedford, A. N. (Annie North). *see* Watson, Jane Werner

Bedford, David. *Big bears can!* ill. by Gaby Hansen. Tiger Tales, 2001. ISBN 1-58925-006-0 Subj: Animals – bears. Concepts – size. Family life – brothers.

Ella's games ill. by Peter Kavanagh. Barron's, 2002. ISBN 0-7641-5583-0 Subj: Animals – mice. Family life – brothers & sisters. Sibling rivalry.

Shaggy Dog and the terrible itch ill. by Gwyneth Williamson. Barron's, 2001. ISBN 0-7641-5391-9 Subj: Activities – bathing. Animals – dogs. Illness.

Touch the sky, my little bear by David Bedford & Jane Chapman; ill. by Jane Chapman. Handprint, 2001. ISBN 1-929766-20-3 Subj: Animals – polar bears. Behavior – growing up. Family life – mothers.

Bedtime ed. by Mary Lee Donovan. Candlewick, 1999. ISBN 0-7636-0932-3 Subj: Bedtime. Format, unusual – board books.

The bedtime book: a collection of fairy tales ill. by Daniel San Souci. Messner, 1985. ISBN 0-671-60505-4 Subj: Folk & fairy tales.

Beech, Caroline. *Peas again for lunch* ill. by Gina Calleja. Annick, 1981. Subj: Behavior – misbehavior. Imagination.

Beecroft, John. *What? Another cat!* ill. by Kurt Wiese. Dodd, 1960. Subj: Animals – cats. Sibling rivalry.

Beeke, Jemma. *The Rickety Barn show* ill. by Lynne Chapman. Doubleday, 2001. ISBN 0-385-32795-1 Subj: Animals. Farms. Theater.

Beeke, Tiphanie. *Roar like a lion!* ill. by author. Gullane, 2001. ISBN 1-86233-143-X Subj: Animals. Animals – endangered animals. Communication. Noise, sounds.

Beeler, Selby B. *How many Elephants?* ill. by Barney Saltzberg. Candlewick, 2004. ISBN 0-7636-1583-8 Subj: Animals – elephants. Counting, numbers. Format, unusual – toy & movable books.

Throw your tooth on the roof: tooth traditions from around the world ill. by G. Brian Karas. Houghton Mifflin, 1998. ISBN 0-395-89108-6 Subj: Folk & fairy tales. Teeth.

Beer, Kathleen Costello. *What happens in the spring* ill. with photos. National Geographic, 1977. ISBN 0-8704-4242-2 Subj: Seasons – spring.

Bees created by Gallimard Jeunesse, Ute Fuhr & Raoul Sautai; ill. by Ute Fuhr & Raoul Sautai. Scholastic, 1997. ISBN 0-590-93780-4 Subj: Format, unusual – toy & movable books. Insects – bees.

Begaye, Lisa Shook. *Building a bridge* ill. by Libba Tracy. Northland, 1993. ISBN 0-87358-557-7 Subj: Friendship. Indians of North America – Navajo. School – first day.

Behan, Brendan. *The king of Ireland's son* ill. by P. J. Lynch. Orchard, 1997. ISBN 0-531-09549-5 Subj: Folk & fairy tales. Foreign lands – Ireland. Royalty – princes.

Behn, Harry. *Crickets and bullfrogs and whispers of thunder* sel. by Lee Bennett Hopkins; ill. by author. Harcourt, 1984. ISBN 0-15-220885-2 Subj: Poetry.

Trees ill. by James R. Endicott. Holt, 1992. ISBN 0-8050-1926-X Subj: Poetry. Trees.

What a beautiful noise ill. by Harold Berson. Collins-World, 1970. Subj: Humorous stories. Music. Musical instruments. Noise, sounds.

Behrens, June. *Can you walk the plank?* ill. by Michele & Tom Grimm. Childrens Pr., 1976. ISBN 0-516-03673-4 Subj: Activities. Games. Imagination.

Christmas-magic wagon ill. by Marjorie Burgeson. Childrens Pr., 1975. ISBN 0-516-08880-7 Subj: Character traits – generosity. Holidays – Christmas. Magic. Theater. Toys – wagons.

The feast of Thanksgiving ill. by Anne Siberell. Childrens Pr., 1974. ISBN 0-516-08725-8 Subj: Holidays – Thanksgiving. Pilgrims. Theater.

Fiesta! ill. by Scott Taylor. Childrens Pr., 1978. ISBN 0-516-08815-7 Subj: Ethnic groups in the U.S. – Mexican Americans. Holidays – Cinco de Mayo.

Hanukkah ill. by Terry Behrens. Childrens Pr., 1983. ISBN 0-516-02386-1 Subj: Holidays – Hanukkah. Jewish culture. Religion.

I can be a nurse ill. with photos. Childrens Pr., 1986. ISBN 0-516-01893-0 Subj: Careers – nurses.

I can be a pilot ill. with photos. Childrens Pr., 1985. ISBN 0-516-01888-4 Subj: Careers – airplane pilots.

I can be a truck driver ill. with photos. Childrens Pr., 1985. ISBN 0-516-01848-5 Subj: Careers – truck drivers.

I can be an astronaut ill. with photos. Childrens Pr., 1984. ISBN 0-516-01837-X Subj: Careers – astronauts. Space & space ships.

The manners book: what's right, Ned? ill. by Michele & Tom Grimm. Childrens Pr., 1980. ISBN 0-516-08750-9 Subj: Etiquette. Toys – bears.

Passover photos by Terry Behrens. Childrens Pr., 1987. ISBN 0-516-02389-6 Subj: Holidays – Passover. Jewish culture. Religion.

Powwow photos comp. by Terry Behrens. Childrens Pr., 1983. ISBN 0-516-02387-X Subj: Indians of North America.

Soo Ling finds a way ill. by Taro Yashima. Childrens Pr., 1965. Subj: Ethnic groups in the U.S. – Chinese Americans. Family life – grandfathers. Foreign lands – China. Laundry.

Whales of the world ill. with photos. Childrens Pr., 1987. ISBN 0-516-08877-7 Subj: Animals – dolphins. Animals – whales. Science.

Whalewatch! ill. by John Olguin. Childrens Pr., 1978. Photographs collected by John Olguin. ISBN 0-516-08873-4 Subj: Animals – whales. Science.

Who am I? photos by Ray Ambraziunas. Elk Grove Pr., 1968. Subj: School. Self-concept.

Beifuss, John. *Armadillo Ray* ill. by Peggy Turley. Chronicle, 1995. ISBN 0-8118-2277-X Subj: Animals. Animals – armadillos. Birds – owls. Imagination. Moon.

Beil, Karen Magnuson. *A cake all for me!* ill. by Paul Meisel. Holiday, 1998. ISBN 0-8234-1368-3 Subj: Activities – baking, cooking. Animals. Animals – pigs. Food. Rhyming text.

Beim, Jerrold. *Country mailman* ill. by Leonard W. Shortall. Morrow, 1958. Subj: Careers – postal workers. Character traits – helpfulness. Emotions – envy, jealousy. Post office.

Country train ill. by Leonard W. Shortall. Morrow, 1950. Subj: Character traits – individuality. Trains.

Eric on the desert ill. by Louis Darling. Morrow, 1953. Subj: Animals. Character traits – bravery. Desert.

Freckle face ill. by Barbara Cooney. Crowell, 1957. Subj: Character traits – appearance. Character traits – being different. Character traits – individuality.

Jay's big job ill. by Tracy Sugarman. Morrow, 1957. Subj: Activities – painting. Activities – working. Family life.

The little igloo (Beim, Lorraine)

Lucky Pierre (Beim, Lorraine)

Sasha and the samovar (Beim, Lorraine)

Sir Halloween ill. by Tracy Sugarman. Morrow, 1959. Subj: Holidays – Halloween.

The smallest boy in the class ill. by Meg Wohlberg. Morrow, 1949. ISBN 0-688-31442-2 Subj: Behavior – sharing. Character traits – smallness. Names.

The swimming hole ill. by Louis Darling. Morrow, 1950. Subj: Behavior. Ethnic groups in the U.S. – African Americans. Friendship. Seasons – summer. Sports – swimming.

The taming of Toby ill. by Tracy Sugarman. Morrow, 1953. Subj: Behavior – misbehavior. Imagination. School.

Tim and the tool chest ill. by Tracy Sugarman. Morrow, 1951. Subj: Tools.

Two is a team (Beim, Lorraine)

With dad alone ill. by Don Sibley. Harcourt, 1954. Subj: Death. Family life – fathers.

Beim, Lorraine. *The little igloo* by Lorraine & Jerrold Beim; ill. by Howard Simon. Harcourt, 1941. Subj: Animals – dogs. Eskimos.

Lucky Pierre by Lorraine & Jerrold Beim; ill. by Howard Simon. Harcourt, 1940. Subj: Behavior – collecting things. Careers – fishermen. Character traits – luck. Family life.

Sasha and the samovar by Lorraine & Jerrold Beim; ill. by Rafaello Busoni. Harcourt, 1944. Subj: Fairies. Foreign lands – Russia.

Two is a team by Lorraine & Jerrold Beim; ill. by Ernest Crichlow. Harcourt, 1945. Subj: Behavior – fighting, arguing. Ethnic groups in the U.S. – African Americans. Friendship. Problem solving.

Beisert, Heide Helene. *Poor fish* trans. from German by Marion Koenig; ill. by author. HarperCollins, 1982. ISBN 0-571-12514-X Subj: Birds. Ecology. Fish.

Beisner, Monika. *Catch that cat!* ill. by author. Farrar, 1990. ISBN 0-374-31226-5 Subj: Animals – cats. Rhyming text. Riddles & jokes.

Monika Beisner's book of riddles ill. by author. Farrar, 1983. ISBN 0-374-30866-7 Subj: Humorous stories. Riddles & jokes.

Secret spells and curious charms ill. by author. Farrar, 1986. ISBN 0-374-36692-6 Subj: Behavior – secrets. Magic.

Topsy turvy: the world of upside down ill. by author. Farrar, 1987. ISBN 0-374-37679-4 Subj: Concepts. Rhyming text.

Belafonte, Harry. *Island in the sun* by Harry Belafonte and Lord Burgess; ill. by Alex Ayliffe. Dial, 1999. ISBN 0-8037-2387-3 Subj: Foreign lands – Jamaica. Music. Songs.

Bell, Anthea. *Æsop's fables* (Æsop)

Albert and Lila (Schami, Rafik)

Billy the brave (Chapouton, Anne-Marie)

The brave little tailor (Grimm, Jacob)

Bremen town musicians (Grimm, Jacob)

The Bremen town musicians (Grimm, Jacob)

The Christmas angel (Vainio, Pirkko)

Cinderella (Perrault, Charles)

The clown said no (Damjan, Mischa)

The crow who stood on his beak (Schami, Rafik)

The emperor's new clothes (Andersen, H. C. [Hans Christian])

The fake flamingos (Damjan, Mischa)

The farmer and the moon (Lussert, Anneliese)

Fatima and the dream thief (Schami, Rafik)

The fisherman and his wife (Grimm, Jacob)

The five fingers and the moon (Kurt, Kemal)

Frog in love (Velthuijs, Max)

The gold at the end of the rainbow (Hänel, Wolfram)

The golden goose (Grimm, Jacob)

Goodbye little bird (Damjan, Mischa)

The goose girl (Grimm, Jacob)

Grimm Tom Thumb (Tom Thumb)

Jack and the beanstalk (Jack and the beanstalk)

Jack in luck (Grimm, Jacob)

Little brother and little sister (Grimm, Jacob)

Little Hobbin (Storm, Theodor)

The little mermaid (Andersen, H. C. [Hans Christian])

Lullabies, lyrics and gallows songs (Morgenstern, Christian)

Lumina: a story for the dark time of the year (Weninger, Brigitte)

The magic honey jar (Bohdal, Susi)

The merry pranks of Till Eulenspiegel (Janisch, Heinz)

Mumble bear (Ruck-Pauquèt, Gina)

Nick Ribbeck of Ribbeck of Havelland (Fontane, Theodor)

The nightingale (Andersen, H. C. [Hans Christian])

Noah's ark (Fussenegger, Gertrud)

The nutcracker (Hoffmann, E. T. A.)

Peter and the wolf (Prokofiev, Sergei Sergeievitch)

The pied piper of Hamelin (Bartos-Hoppner, Barbara)

The princess and the pea (Andersen, H. C. [Hans Christian])

The proud white cat (Hürlimann, Ruth)

Puss in boots (Perrault, Charles)

The red shoes (Andersen, H. C. [Hans Christian])

Rumpelstiltskin (Grimm, Jacob)

Sandman in the lighthouse (Strahl, Rudi)

Sarah's willow (Recknagel, Friedrich)

The six servants (Grimm, Jacob)

The six swans (Grimm, Jacob)

The sleeping beauty (Grimm, Jacob)

The snow queen: a fairy tale (Andersen, H. C. [Hans Christian])

Snow White and the seven dwarves (Grimm, Jacob)

The strange child (Hoffmann, E. T. A.)

Swan Lake: a traditional folktale ill. by Chihiro Iwasaki. Picture Book Studio, 1986. Adapt. of Tchaikovsky's Lebedinoe ozero.

ISBN 0-88708-028-6 Subj: Activities – dancing. Ballet. Birds – swans. Folk & fairy tales. Magic.

The swineherd (Andersen, H. C. [Hans Christian])

Thumbeline (Andersen, H. C. [Hans Christian])

The trip to Panama (Janosch)

The ugly duckling (Andersen, H. C. [Hans Christian])

The wise queen ill. by Chihiro Iwasaki. Picture Book Studio, 1986. ISBN 0-88708-014-6 Subj: Character traits – cleverness. Character traits – wisdom. Folk & fairy tales. Riddles & jokes. Royalty – queens.

The wishing table (Grimm, Jacob)

Bell, Babs. *The bridge is up!* ill. by Rob Hefferan. HarperCollins, 2004. ISBN 0-06-053794-9 Subj: Automobiles. Bridges. Cumulative tales. Traffic, traffic signs. Transportation.

Bell, Janet. *see* Clymer, Eleanor Lowenton

Bell, Norman. *Linda's airmail letter* ill. by Patricia Villemain. Follett, 1964. Subj: Birthdays. Friendship. Letters, cards. Post office. Weather.

Bellamy, David. *How green are you?* ill. by Penny Dann. Crown, 1991. ISBN 0-517-58447-6 Subj: Animals – whales. Ecology.

The roadside ill. by Jill Dow. Crown, 1988. ISBN 0-517-56976-0 Subj: Ecology.

The rock pool ill. by Jill Dow. Crown, 1988. ISBN 0-517-56977-9 Subj: Ecology.

Beller, Janet. *A-B-C-ing: an action alphabet* ill. with photos. Crown, 1984. ISBN 0-517-55208-6 Subj: ABC books. Activities.

Belling the cat and other stories retold by Leland B. Jacobs; ill. by Harold Berson. Golden Pr., 1960. Subj: Animals. Folk & fairy tales.

Belloc, Hilaire. *The bad child's book of beasts* ill. by Basil T. Blackwood [B.A.T.]. Knopf, 1965. Originally published in 1896. Subj: Animals. Behavior. Humorous stories.

The bad child's book of beasts, and more beasts for worse children ill. by Harold Berson. Grosset, 1966. Subj: Animals. Humorous stories. Poetry.

The bad child's pop-up book of beasts ill. by Wallace Tripp. Putnam, 1987. ISBN 0-399-21431-3 Subj: Animals. Format, unusual – toy & movable books. Poetry.

Jim, who ran away from his nurse, and was eaten by a lion ill. by Victoria Chess. Little, 1987. ISBN 0-316-13815-0 Subj: Animals – lions. Behavior – misbehavior. Behavior – running away. Zoos.

Matilda who told lies and was burned to death ill. by Steven Kellogg. Dial, 1970. Subj: Behavior – lying. Behavior – misbehavior. Fire. Poetry.

More beasts for worse children ill. by Basil T. Blackwood [B.A.T.]. Knopf, 1966. Subj: Animals. Poetry.

Bellows, Cathy. *Four fat rats* ill. by author. Macmillan, 1987. ISBN 0-02-708830-8 Subj: Animals – rats. Behavior – greed. Character traits – meanness.

The Grizzly sisters ill. by author. Macmillan, 1991. ISBN 0-02-709032-9 Subj: Animals – bears. Behavior – misbehavior.

The royal raccoon ill. by author. Macmillan, 1989. ISBN 0-02-709031-0 Subj: Animals – raccoons. Character traits – conceit.

Bellville, Cheryl Walsh. *Large animal veterinarians* (Bellville, Rod)

Bellville, Rod. *Large animal veterinarians* by Rod & Cheryl Walsh Bellville; photos by authors. Carolrhoda, 1983. ISBN 0-87614-211-0 Subj: Animals. Careers – veterinarians.

Belpré, Pura. *Dance of the animals: a Puerto Rican folk tale* ill. by Paul Galdone. Warne, 1972. ISBN 0-7232-6039-7 Subj: Animals. Folk & fairy tales. Foreign lands – Puerto Rico.

Pérez and Martina: a Portorican folk tale ill. by Carlos Sanchez. Rev. ed. Warne, 1961. Originally pub. in 1960. ISBN 0-7232-6017-6 Subj: Animals – mice. Folk & fairy tales. Foreign lands – Puerto Rico. Insects.

Santiago ill. by Symeon Shimin. Warne, 1969. Subj: Birds – chickens. Ethnic groups in the U.S. Ethnic groups in the U.S. – Puerto Rican Americans. Pets.

Belting, Natalia Maree. *Christmas folk* ill. by Barbara Cooney. Holt, 1969. ISBN 0-03-072375-2 Subj: Foreign lands – England. Holidays – Christmas. Poetry.

Summer's coming in ill. by Adrienne Adams. Holt, 1970. ISBN 0-03-084250-6 Subj: Foreign lands – England. Holidays. Poetry. Seasons – spring. Seasons – summer.

The sun is a golden earring ill. by Bernarda Bryson. Holt, 1962. Subj: Caldecott award honor books. Folk & fairy tales. Sky.

Verity Mullens and the Indian ill. by Leonard Everett Fisher. Holt, 1960. Subj: Animals – dogs. Behavior – lost. Indians of North America. U.S. history – frontier & pioneer life.

Belton, Sandra. *May'naise sandwiches and sunshine tea* ill. by Gail Gordon Carter. Four Winds, 1994. ISBN 0-02-709035-3 Subj: Family life – grandmothers. Friendship. Poverty.

Pictures for Miss Josie ill. by Benny Andrews. Greenwillow, 2003. ISBN 0-688-17481-7 Subj: Careers – artists. Ethnic groups in the U.S. – African Americans. Friendship. Self-concept.

Bemelmans, Ludwig. *Hansi* ill. by author. Viking, 1934. Subj: Activities – vacationing. Foreign lands – Tyrol. Holidays – Christmas.

Madeline ill. by author. Viking, 1939. Subj: Caldecott award honor books. Foreign lands – France. Hospitals. Orphans. Rhyming text. School – field trips.

Madeline [pop-up book] ill. by author. Viking, 1987. ISBN 0-670-81667-1 Subj: Foreign lands – France. Format, unusual – toy & movable books. Hospitals. Orphans.

Madeline and the bad hat ill. by author. Viking, 1956. Subj: Behavior – animals, dislike of. Behavior – misbehavior. Foreign lands – France. Orphans. Rhyming text.

Madeline and the gypsies ill. by author. Viking, 1959. ISBN 0-670-44682-3 Subj: Behavior – lost. Foreign lands – France. Gypsies. Orphans. Rhyming text.

Madeline in London ill. by author. Viking, 1978, c1961. ISBN 0-14-050199-1 Subj: Animals – horses, ponies. Birthdays. Foreign lands – England. Orphans. Rhyming text.

Madeline's Christmas ill. by author. Viking, 1985. ISBN 0-670-80666-8 Subj: Foreign lands – France. Holidays – Christmas. Illness. Magic. Orphans. Rhyming text.

Madeline's rescue ill. by author. Viking, 1978, c1953. ISBN 0-14-050207-6 Subj: Animals – dogs. Caldecott award books. Foreign lands – France. Orphans. Rhyming text.

Parsley ill. by author. HarperCollins, 1955. ISBN 0-06-020455-9 Subj: Animals – deer. Sports – hunting. Trees.

Quito express ill. by author. Viking, 1938. Subj: Activities – traveling. Family life. Foreign lands – Ecuador. Trains.

Rosebud ill. by author. Random House, 1993, c1942. ISBN 0-679-94913-5 Subj: Animals. Character traits – pride. Folk & fairy tales. Foreign lands – Africa. Humorous stories.

Sunshine ill. by author. S&S, 1950. Subj: Cities, towns. Family life. Homes, houses. Humorous stories.

Welcome home! ill. by author. HarperCollins, 1970. Based on a poem by Beverley Bogert. Subj: Animals – foxes. Character traits – cleverness. Rhyming text.

Benarde, Anita. *The pumpkin smasher* ill. by author. Walker, 1972. ISBN 0-8027-6109-7 Subj: Holidays – Halloween. Problem solving. Witches.

Benchley, Nathaniel. *The deep dives of Stanley Whale* ill. by Mischa Richter. HarperCollins, 1973. ISBN 0-06-020464-8 Subj: Animals – whales. Character traits – bravery.

The flying lessons of Gerald Pelican ill. by Mamoru Funai. Harper-Collins, 1970. ISBN 0-06-020482-6 Subj: Activities – flying. Birds – pelicans.

Walter the homing pigeon ill. by Whitney Darrow, Jr. Harper-Collins, 1981. ISBN 0-06-020508-3 Subj: Birds – pigeons. Food. Humorous stories. Sports – racing.

Benchley, Peter. *Jonathan visits the White House* ill. by Richard Bergere. McGraw-Hill, 1964. Subj: Animals – dogs. Birthdays. Pets. U.S. history.

Bender, Robert. *The A to Z beastly jamboree* ill. by author. Lodestar, 1996. ISBN 0-525-67520-5 Subj: ABC books. Activities. Animals. Language.

A little witch magic ill. by author. Holt, 1992. ISBN 0-8050-2126-4 Subj: Friendship. Holidays – Halloween. Witches.

The three billy goats Gruff (Asbjørnsen, P. C. [Peter Christen])

Bendick, Jeanne. *All around you: a first look at the world* foreword by Glenn O. Blough; ill. by author. McGraw-Hill, 1951. ISBN 0-07-004464-3 Subj: Nature. Science. World.

What made you you? ill. by author. McGraw-Hill, 1971. ISBN 0-07-004502-X Subj: Babies. Science.

Why can't I? ill. by author. McGraw-Hill, 1969. ISBN 0-07-004491-0 Subj: Animals. Behavior – imitation. Participation. Science.

Benedek, Elissa P. *The secret worry* ill. by Patricia Rosamilia. Human Sciences Pr., 1984. ISBN 0-89885-133-5 Subj: Behavior – worrying. Emotions – fear.

Benedictus, Roger. *Fifty million sausages* ill. by Kenneth Mahood. Elsevier-Dutton, 1979. ISBN 0-233-96692-7 Subj: Food. Humorous stories. Imagination. Machines.

Beneduce, Ann Keay. *Jack and the beanstalk* (Jack and the beanstalk)

Philipok (Spirin, Gennady)

Benét, William Rose. *Mother Goose* (Mother Goose)

Timothy's angels ill. by Constantin Alajalov. Crowell, 1947. Subj: Activities – playing. Angels. Poetry.

Benevelli, Alberto. *The colors of the chameleon* ill. by Loretta Serofil-loi. G. Stevens, 2002. ISBN 0-8368-3042-3 Subj: Animals. Concepts – color. Reptiles – chameleons.

Ben-'Ezer, Ehud. *Hosni the dreamer: an Arabian tale* ill. by Uri Shulevitz. Farrar, 1997. ISBN 0-374-33340-8 Subj: Careers – shepherds. Folk & fairy tales.

Beni, Ruth. *Sir Baldergog the great* ill. by author. Dutton, 1985. ISBN 0-233-97628-0 Subj: Activities. Behavior – lost. Islands.

Benjamin, A. H. *A duck so small* ill. by Elisabeth Holstien. Little Tiger, 1998. ISBN 1-888444-30-4 Subj: Birds – ducks. Character traits – smallness. Self-concept.

It could have been worse ill. by Tim Warnes. Little Tiger, 1998. ISBN 1-888444-26-6 Subj: Animals – mice. Character traits – luck.

Mouse, mole and the falling star ill. by John Bendall-Brunello. Dutton, 2002. ISBN 0-525-46880-3 Subj: Animals – mice. Animals – moles. Behavior – sharing. Friendship. Stars.

Benjamin, Alan. *Busy bunnies* ill. by Christopher Santoro. S&S, 1988. ISBN 0-671-64807-1 Subj: Activities. Animals – rabbits.

A change of plans ill. by Steven Kellogg. Four Winds, 1982. ISBN 0-590-07730-9 Subj: Activities – picnicking. Boats, ships. Family life. Rhyming text.

A nickel buys a rhyme ill. by Karen Lee Schmidt. Morrow, 1993. ISBN 0-688-06699-2 Subj: Poetry.

The nightingale (Andersen, H. C. [Hans Christian])

1000 monsters ill. by Sal Murdocca. Four Winds, 1979. ISBN 0-590-07636-1 Subj: Format, unusual – toy & movable books. Humorous stories. Monsters.

Rat-a-tat, pitter pat ill. by Margaret Miller. HarperCollins, 1987. ISBN 0-690-04611-1 Subj: Language. Noise, sounds. Rhyming text.

Ribtickle Town ill. by Ann Schweninger. Four Winds, 1983. ISBN 0-590-07880-3 Subj: Behavior – lost. Food. Giants. Imagination. Rhyming text.

Benjamin, Amanda. *Two's company* ill. by author. Viking, 1995. ISBN 0-670-84876-X Subj: Family life – mothers. Family life – stepfamilies. Weddings.

Benjamin, Anne. *Young Harriet Tubman: freedom fighter* ill. by Ellen Beier. Troll, 1992. ISBN 0-8167-2538-1 Subj: Character traits – freedom. Ethnic groups in the U.S. – African Americans. Slavery.

Young Pocahontas: Indian princess ill. by Christine Powers. Troll, 1997. ISBN 0-8167-2534-9 Subj: Character traits – bravery. Indians of North America. U.S. history.

Benjamin, Floella. *Skip across the ocean: nursery rhymes from around the world* ill. by Sheila Moxley. Orchard, 1995. ISBN 0-531-09455-3 Subj: Foreign lands. Lullabies. Nursery rhymes.

Bennett, Barbara. *Lion's precious gift* ill. by Amanda Hall. Barron's, 2002. ISBN 0-7641-5533-4 Subj: Animals – lions. Babies.

Bennett, David. *One cow moo moo* ill. by Andy Cooke. Holt, 1990. ISBN 0-8050-1416-0 Subj: Animals. Counting, numbers. Cumulative tales. Noise, sounds.

Bennett, Jill. *Animal fair* ill. by Susie Jenkin-Pearce. Viking, 1990. ISBN 0-670-82691-X Subj: Animals. Poetry.

A cup of starshine ill. by Graham Percy. Harcourt, 1992. ISBN 0-15-220982-4 Subj: Poetry.

Days are where we live and other poems ill. by Maureen Roffey. Lothrop, 1982. ISBN 0-688-00852-6 Subj: Activities. Poetry.

Machine poems by Jill Bennett & Nick Sharratt; ill. by Nick Sharratt. Oxford Univ. Pr., 1991. ISBN 0-19-276094-7 Subj: Machines. Poetry.

Noisy poems ill. by Nick Sharratt. Oxford Univ. Pr., 1990. ISBN 0-19-276063-7 Subj: Noise, sounds. Poetry.

People poems ill. by Nick Sharratt. Oxford Univ. Pr., 1991. ISBN 0-19-276086-6 Subj: Poetry.

Roger was a razor fish and other poems ill. by Maureen Roffey. Lothrop, 1981. ISBN 0-688-51986-5 Subj: Humorous stories. Poetry.

Seaside poems (Seaside poems)

Spooky poems coll. by Jill Bennett; ill. by Mary Rees. Little, 1989. ISBN 0-316-08987-7 Subj: Monsters. Poetry.

Teeny tiny ill. by Tomie de Paola. Putnam, 1986. ISBN 0-399-21293-0 Subj: Folk & fairy tales. Foreign lands – England. Ghosts.

Tiny Tim: verses for children (Oxenbury, Helen)

Bennett, Kelly. *Not Norman* ill. by Noah Jones. Candlewick, 2005. ISBN 0-7636-2384-9 Subj: Ethnic groups in the U.S. – African Americans. Fish. Friendship. Pets.

Bennett, Olivia. *A Turkish afternoon* photos by Christopher Cormack. David & Charles, 1984. Subj: Family life. Foreign lands – England. Foreign lands – Turkey.

Bennett, Rainey. *After the sun goes down* ill. by author. Collins-World, 1961. Subj: Birds – owls. Night.

The secret hiding place ill. by author. Collins-World, 1960. Subj: Animals – hippopotamuses. Behavior – solitude. Poetry. Sea & seashore.

Bennett, Rowena. *The day is dancing and other poems* ill. by Rainey Bennett. Follett, 1968. Subj: Imagination. Poetry.

Songs from around a toadstool table ill. by Betty Fraser. Follett, 1967. Subj: Fairies. Imagination. Nature. Poetry.

Benson, Ellen. *Philip's little sister* ill. by Rachael Davis. Childrens Pr., 1979. ISBN 0-516-02023-4 Subj: Family life. Sibling rivalry.

Benson, Kathleen. *Count your way through Brazil* (Haskins, Jim [James])

Benson, Laura Lee. *This is our earth* ill. by John Carrozza. Charlesbridge, 1994. ISBN 0-88106-445-9 Subj: Earth. Ecology. Nature.

Benson, Patrick. *Little penguin* ill. by author. Putnam, 1991. ISBN 0-399-21757-6 Subj: Birds – penguins. Concepts – size. Foreign lands – Antarctic.

Bentley, Anne. *The Groggs' day out* ill. by Roy Bentley. Elsevier-Dutton, 1981. ISBN 0-233-97348-6 Subj: Foreign lands – England. Sports – bicycling.

The Groggs have a wonderful summer by Anne & Roy Bentley; ill. by Roy Bentley. Elsevier-Dutton, 1980. ISBN 0-233-97199-8 Subj: Foreign lands – England. Sea & seashore. Seasons – summer.

Bentley, Dawn. *Busy little beaver* ill. by Beth Stover. Soundprints, 2003. ISBN 1-59249-011-5 Subj: Animals – beavers. Family life.

Fuzzy bear: a getting dressed book designed by Willabel L. Tong; ill. by Krisztina Nagy; paper-engineered by Renée Jablow & Dennis Meyer. Piggy Toes, 1998. Subj: Animals – bears. Clothing. Format, unusual – toy & movable books. Rhyming text. Weather – rain.

Fuzzy Bear's potty book designed by Melanie Random; ill. by Krisztina Nagy; paper-engineered by Dennis Meyer. Piggy Toes, 2001. ISBN 1-58117-161-7 Subj: Animals – bears. Behavior – growing up. Format, unusual – toy & movable books. Rhyming text. Toilet training.

Welcome back, Puffin ill. by Beth Stover. Soundprints, 2003. ISBN 1-59249-009-3 Subj: Birds – puffins. Family life.

Bentley, Nancy. *I've got your nose!* ill. by Don Madden. Doubleday, 1991. ISBN 0-385-41296-7 Subj: Anatomy – noses. Behavior – dissatisfaction. Behavior – wishing. Magic. Self-concept. Witches.

Bentley, Roy. *The Groggs have a wonderful summer* (Bentley, Anne)

Benton, Robert. *Don't ever wish for a 7-foot bear* ill. by Sally Benton. Knopf, 1972. ISBN 0-394-92399-5 Subj: Animals – bears. Behavior – wishing. Humorous stories.

Little brother, no more ill. by author. Knopf, 1960. Subj: Family life. Names.

Bercaw, Edna Coe. *Halmoni's day* ill. by Robert Hunt. Dial, 2000. ISBN 0-8037-2445-4 Subj: Ethnic groups in the U.S. – Korean Americans. Family life – grandmothers. School.

Berends, Polly Berrien. *I heard said the bird* ill. by Brad Sneed. Dial, 1995. ISBN 0-14-056426-8 Subj: Animals. Babies. Birds. Farms. Rhyming text.

Ladybug and dog and the night walk ill. by Cyndy Szekeres. Random House, 1980. ISBN 0-394-93398-2 Subj: Animals – dogs. Friendship. Insects – fireflies. Insects – ladybugs. Night.

Berenstain, Jan. *After the dinosaurs* (Berenstain, Stan)

The bear detectives: the case of the missing pumpkin (Berenstain, Stan)

Bears in the night (Berenstain, Stan)

Bears on wheels (Berenstain, Stan)

The Berenstain bears and mama's new job (Berenstain, Stan)

The Berenstain bears and the bad dream (Berenstain, Stan)

The Berenstain bears and the bad habit (Berenstain, Stan)

The Berenstain bears and the big road race (Berenstain, Stan)

The Berenstain bears and the double dare (Berenstain, Stan)

The Berenstain bears and the ghost of the forest (Berenstain, Stan)

The Berenstain bears and the messy room (Berenstain, Stan)

The Berenstain bears and the missing dinosaur bone (Berenstain, Stan)

The Berenstain bears and the missing honey (Berenstain, Stan)

The Berenstain bears and the prize pumpkin (Berenstain, Stan)

The Berenstain bears and the real Easter eggs (Berenstain, Stan)

The Berenstain bears and the sitter (Berenstain, Stan)

The Berenstain bears and the slumber party (Berenstain, Stan)

The Berenstain bears and the spooky old tree (Berenstain, Stan)

The Berenstain bears and the trouble with friends (Berenstain, Stan)

The Berenstain bears and the truth (Berenstain, Stan)

The Berenstain bears and the week at grandma's (Berenstain, Stan)

The Berenstain bears and the wild, wild honey (Berenstain, Stan)

The Berenstain bears and too much birthday (Berenstain, Stan)

The Berenstain bears and too much junk food (Berenstain, Stan)

The Berenstain bears and too much TV (Berenstain, Stan)

The Berenstain bears and too much vacation (Berenstain, Stan)

The Berenstain bears blaze a trail (Berenstain, Stan)

The Berenstain bears' Christmas tree (Berenstain, Stan)

The Berenstain bears' counting book (Berenstain, Stan)

The Berenstain bears don't pollute anymore (Berenstain, Stan)

The Berenstain bears forget their manners (Berenstain, Stan)

The Berenstain bears get in a fight (Berenstain, Stan)

The Berenstain bears get stage fright (Berenstain, Stan)

The Berenstain bears get the gimmies (Berenstain, Stan)

The Berenstain bears go out for the team (Berenstain, Stan)

The Berenstain bears go to camp (Berenstain, Stan)

The Berenstain bears go to school (Berenstain, Stan)

The Berenstain bears go to the doctor (Berenstain, Stan)

The Berenstain bears in the dark (Berenstain, Stan)

The Berenstain bears learn about strangers (Berenstain, Stan)

The Berenstain bears meet Santa Bear (Berenstain, Stan)

The Berenstain bears' moving day (Berenstain, Stan)

The Berenstain bears no girls allowed (Berenstain, Stan)

The Berenstain bears on the moon (Berenstain, Stan)

The Berenstain bears ready, set, go! (Berenstain, Stan)

The Berenstain bears' report card trouble (Berenstain, Stan)

The Berenstain bears' science fair (Berenstain, Stan)

The Berenstain bears' that stump must go! (Berenstain, Stan)

The Berenstain bears trick or treat (Berenstain, Stan)

The Berenstain bears' trouble at school (Berenstain, Stan)

The Berenstain bears' trouble with money (Berenstain, Stan)

The Berenstain bears' trouble with pets (Berenstain, Stan)

The Berenstain bears visit the dentist (Berenstain, Stan)

The Berenstains' B book (Berenstain, Stan)

The day of the dinosaur (Berenstain, Stan)

He bear, she bear (Berenstain, Stan)

Inside outside upside down (Berenstain, Stan)

Old hat, new hat (Berenstain, Stan)

Berenstain, Michael. *The dwarks: book 1* ill. by author. Bantam, 1983. ISBN 0-553-15341-2 Subj: Family life. Mythical creatures.

Peat Moss and Ivy and the birthday present ill. by author. Random House, 1986. ISBN 0-394-97605-3 Subj: Animals – chipmunks. Birthdays.

Peat Moss and Ivy's backyard adventure ill. by author. Random House, 1986. ISBN 0-394-97604-5 Subj: Animals – chipmunks.

The ship book ill. by author. McKay, 1978. ISBN 0-679-20449-0 Subj: Boats, ships.

The troll book ill. by author. Random House, 1980. ISBN 0-394-94295-7 Subj: Folk & fairy tales. Mythical creatures – trolls.

Berenstain, Stan. *After the dinosaurs* by Stan & Jan Berenstain; ill. by authors. Random House, 1988. ISBN 0-394-90518-0 Subj: Animals – bears. Dinosaurs. Prehistory.

The bear detectives: the case of the missing pumpkin by Stan & Jan Berenstain; ill. by authors. Random House, 1975. ISBN 0-394-93127-0 Subj: Animals – bears. Careers – detectives. Mystery stories. Rhyming text.

Bears in the night by Stan & Jan Berenstain; ill. by authors. Random House, 1971. ISBN 0-394-92286-7 Subj: Animals – bears. Bedtime. Night. Noise, sounds.

Bears on wheels by Stan & Jan Berenstain; ill. by authors. Random House, 1969. ISBN 0-394-90967-4 Subj: Animals – bears. Counting, numbers. Wheels.

The Berenstain bears and mama's new job by Stan & Jan Berenstain; ill. by authors. Random House, 1984. ISBN 0-394-96881-6 Subj: Animals – bears. Careers.

The Berenstain bears and the bad dream by Stan & Jan Berenstain; ill. by authors. Random House, 1988. ISBN 0-394-97341-0 Subj: Animals – bears. Dreams.

The Berenstain bears and the bad habit by Stan & Jan Berenstain; ill. by authors. Random House, 1987. ISBN 0-394-97340-2 Subj: Animals – bears.

The Berenstain bears and the big road race by Stan & Jan Berenstain; ill. by authors. Random House, 1987. ISBN 0-394-99134-6 Subj: Animals – bears. Sports – racing.

The Berenstain bears and the double dare by Stan & Jan Berenstain; ill. by authors. Random House, 1988. ISBN 0-394-99748-4 Subj: Animals – bears. Sibling rivalry.

The Berenstain bears and the ghost of the forest by Stan & Jan Berenstain; ill. by authors. Random House, 1988. ISBN 0-394-90565-2 Subj: Animals – bears. Forest, woods. Ghosts.

The Berenstain bears and the messy room by Stan & Jan Berenstain; ill. by authors. Random House, 1983. ISBN 0-394-95639-7 Subj: Animals – bears. Mystery stories.

The Berenstain bears and the missing dinosaur bone by Stan & Jan Berenstain; ill. by authors. Random House, 1980. ISBN 0-394-94447-X Subj: Animals – bears. Museums. Mystery stories. Prehistory. Rhyming text.

The Berenstain bears and the missing honey by Stan & Jan Berenstain; ill. by authors. Random House, 1987. ISBN 0-394-99133-8 Subj: Animals – bears. Mystery stories.

The Berenstain bears and the prize pumpkin by Stan & Jan Berenstain; ill. by authors. Random House, 1990. ISBN 0-679-90847-1 Subj: Animals – bears. Holidays – Thanksgiving. Plants.

The Berenstain bears and the real Easter eggs by Stan & Jan Berenstain; ill. by authors. Random House, 2002. ISBN 0-375-91133-2 Subj: Animals – bears. Eggs. Holidays – Easter. Seasons – spring.

The Berenstain bears and the sitter by Stan & Jan Berenstain; ill. by authors. Random House, 1981. ISBN 0-394-94837-8 Subj: Activities – babysitting. Animals – bears. Magic.

The Berenstain bears and the slumber party by Stan & Jan Berenstain; ill. by authors. McKay, 1990. ISBN 0-679-90419-0 Subj: Animals – bears. Bedtime. Parties. Sleepovers.

The Berenstain bears and the spooky old tree by Stan & Jan Berenstain; ill. by authors. Random House, 1978. ISBN 0-394-93910-7 Subj: Animals – bears. Rhyming text. Trees.

The Berenstain bears and the trouble with friends by Stan & Jan Berenstain; ill. by authors. Random House, 1987. ISBN 0-394-97339-9 Subj: Animals – bears. Friendship.

The Berenstain bears and the truth by Stan & Jan Berenstain; ill. by authors. Random House, 1983. ISBN 0-394-95640-0 Subj: Animals – bears. Behavior – lying. Behavior – misbehavior. Family life.

The Berenstain bears and the week at grandma's by Stan & Jan Berenstain; ill. by authors. Random House, 1986. ISBN 0-394-97335-6 Subj: Animals – bears. Family life – grandmothers.

The Berenstain bears and the wild, wild honey by Stan & Jan Berenstain; ill. by authors. Random House, 1983. ISBN 0-394-85924-3 Subj: Animals – bears. Nature.

The Berenstain bears and too much birthday by Stan & Jan Berenstain; ill. by authors. Random House, 1986. ISBN 0-394-97332-1 Subj: Animals – bears. Birthdays.

The Berenstain bears and too much junk food by Stan & Jan Berenstain; ill. by authors. Random House, 1985. ISBN 0-394-97217-1 Subj: Animals – bears. Food.

The Berenstain bears and too much TV by Stan & Jan Berenstain; ill. by authors. Random House, 1984. ISBN 0-394-96570-1 Subj: Animals – bears. Family life. Television.

The Berenstain bears and too much vacation by Stan & Jan Berenstain; ill. by authors. Random House, 1989. ISBN 0-394-93014-2 Subj: Activities – vacationing. Animals – bears.

The Berenstain bears blaze a trail by Stan & Jan Berenstain; ill. by authors. Random House, 1987. ISBN 0-394-99132-X Subj: Animals – bears.

The Berenstain bears' Christmas tree by Stan & Jan Berenstain; ill. by authors. Random House, 1980. ISBN 0-394-94566-2 Subj: Animals – bears. Family life. Holidays – Christmas. Rhyming text. Trees.

The Berenstain bears' counting book by Stan & Jan Berenstain; ill. by authors. Random House, 1976. ISBN 0-394-83246-9 Subj: Animals – bears. Counting, numbers.

The Berenstain bears don't pollute anymore by Stan & Jan Berenstain; ill. by authors. Random House, 1991. ISBN 0-679-92351-9 Subj: Animals – bears. Ecology.

The Berenstain bears forget their manners by Stan & Jan Berenstain; ill. by authors. Random House, 1985. ISBN 0-394-97333-X Subj: Animals – bears. Etiquette. Family life.

The Berenstain bears get in a fight by Stan & Jan Berenstain; ill. by authors. Random House, 1982. ISBN 0-394-95132-8 Subj: Animals – bears. Behavior – bad day. Sibling rivalry.

The Berenstain bears get stage fright by Stan & Jan Berenstain; ill. by authors. Random House, 1986. ISBN 0-394-97337-2 Subj: Animals – bears. Emotions – fear. Theater.

The Berenstain bears get the gimmies by Stan & Jan Berenstain; ill. by authors. Random House, 1988. ISBN 0-394-90566-0 Subj: Animals – bears. Behavior – greed.

The Berenstain bears go out for the team by Stan & Jan Berenstain; ill. by authors. Random House, 1987. ISBN 0-394-97338-0 Subj: Animals – bears. Sports.

The Berenstain bears go to camp by Stan & Jan Berenstain; ill. by authors. Random House, 1982. ISBN 0-394-95131-X Subj: Animals – bears. Camps, camping. Seasons – summer.

The Berenstain bears go to school by Stan & Jan Berenstain; ill. by authors. Random House, 1978. ISBN 0-394-93736-8 Subj: Animals – bears. School – first day.

The Berenstain bears go to the doctor by Stan & Jan Berenstain; ill. by authors. Random House, 1981. ISBN 0-394-94835-1 Subj: Animals – bears. Careers – doctors.

The Berenstain bears in the dark by Stan & Jan Berenstain; ill. by authors. Random House, 1982. Subj: Animals – bears. Family life. Imagination. Night.

The Berenstain bears learn about strangers by Stan & Jan Berenstain; ill. by authors. Random House, 1985. ISBN 0-394-87334-3 Subj: Animals – bears. Behavior – talking to strangers. Emotions – fear. Family life. Safety.

The Berenstain bears meet Santa Bear by Stan & Jan Berenstain; ill. by authors. Random House, 1988. ISBN 0-394-89797-8 Subj: Animals – bears. Holidays – Christmas.

The Berenstain bears' moving day by Stan & Jan Berenstain; ill. by authors. Random House, 1981. Subj: Animals – bears. Family life. Friendship. Moving.

The Berenstain bears no girls allowed by Stan & Jan Berenstain; ill. by authors. Random House, 1986. ISBN 0-394-97331-3 Subj: Animals – bears. Clubs, gangs. Family life – brothers & sisters.

The Berenstain bears on the moon by Stan & Jan Berenstain; ill. by authors. Random House, 1985. ISBN 0-394-97180-9 Subj: Animals – bears. Animals – dogs. Moon. Space & space ships.

The Berenstain bears ready, set, go! by Stan & Jan Berenstain; ill. by authors. Random House, 1988. ISBN 0-394-90564-4 Subj: Animals – bears.

The Berenstain bears' report card trouble by Stan & Jan Berenstain; ill. by authors. Random House, 2000. ISBN 0-375-91127-8 Subj: Animals – bears. Family life. School. Sports.

The Berenstain bears' science fair by Stan & Jan Berenstain; ill. by authors. Random House, 1977. Subj: Animals – bears. Science.

The Berenstain bears' that stump must go! by Stan & Jan Berenstain; ill. by authors. Random House, 2000. ISBN 0-679-98963-3 Subj: Animals – bears. Plants. Rhyming text. Trees.

The Berenstain bears trick or treat by Stan & Jan Berenstain; ill. by authors. Random House, 1989. ISBN 0-679-90091-8 Subj: Animals – bears. Holidays – Halloween.

The Berenstain bears' trouble at school by Stan & Jan Berenstain; ill. by authors. Random House, 1987. ISBN 0-394-97336-4 Subj: Animals – bears. Behavior. School.

The Berenstain bears' trouble with money by Stan & Jan Berenstain; ill. by authors. Random House, 1983. Subj: Animals – bears. Money.

The Berenstain bears' trouble with pets by Stan & Jan Berenstain; ill. by authors. Random House, 1990. ISBN 0-679-90848-X Subj: Animals – bears. Pets.

The Berenstain bears visit the dentist by Stan & Jan Berenstain; ill. by authors. Random House, 1981. Subj: Animals – bears. Careers – dentists.

The Berenstains' B book by Stan & Jan Berenstain; ill. by authors. Random House, 1971. Subj: ABC books. Animals – bears.

The day of the dinosaur by Stan & Jan Berenstain; ill. by Michael Berenstain. Random House, 1987. ISBN 0-394-99130-3 Subj: Dinosaurs. Prehistory.

He bear, she bear by Stan & Jan Berenstain; ill. by authors. Random House, 1974. Subj: Animals – bears. Rhyming text.

Inside outside upside down by Stan & Jan Berenstain; ill. by authors. Random House, 1968. Subj: Animals – bears. Concepts.

Old hat, new hat by Stan & Jan Berenstain; ill. by authors. Random House, 1970. Subj: Animals – bears. Concepts – shape. Concepts – size.

Berenzy, Alix. *A frog prince* ill. by author. Holt, 1989. ISBN 0-8050-0426-2 Subj: Folk & fairy tales. Frogs & toads. Kissing. Royalty.

Rapunzel retold & ill. by Alix Berenzy. Holt, 1995. ISBN 0-8050-1283-4 Subj: Folk & fairy tales. Royalty – princes. Witches.

Beresford, Elisabeth. *Jack and the magic stove* ill. by Rita van Bilsen. Hutchinson, 1984. Subj: Behavior – wishing. Folk & fairy tales. Royalty.

Snuffle to the rescue ill. by Gunvor Edwards. Penguin, 1975. Subj: Animals – dogs.

Berg, Charles Ramírez. *The gift of the poinsettia = El regalo de la flor de nochebuena* (Mora, Pat)

Berg, Jean Horton. *The little red hen* (The little red hen)

The noisy clock shop ill. by Art Seiden. Grosset, 1950. Subj: Clocks, watches. Noise, sounds.

The O'Learys and friends ill. by Mary Stevens. Follett, 1961. Subj: Animals – cats. Behavior – misunderstanding. Moving. Problem solving.

The wee little man ill. by Charles Geer. Follett, 1963. Subj: Animals – cats. Little people. Night. Noise, sounds. Rhyming text.

Berg, Leila. *Folk tales for reading and telling* ill. by George Him. Collins-World, 1966. Subj: Folk & fairy tales. Foreign lands.

Bergel, Colin. *Mail by the pail* ill. by Mark Koenig. Wayne State Univ., 2000. ISBN 0-8143-2890-3 Subj: Birthdays. Boats, ships. Family life – fathers. Post office.

Bergen, Lara Rice. *Blue's world of words* ill. by Victoria Miller. Simon Spotlight, 2002. ISBN 0-689-84741-6 Subj: Animals – dogs. Dictionaries. Language. Television.

Washington Irving's Rip Van Winkle ill. by Donald Cook. Grosset, 1997. ISBN 0-448-41733-2 Subj: Behavior – lost. Folk & fairy tales. Mythical creatures – elves. Sleep.

Berger, Barbara Helen. *All the way to Lhasa* ill. by reteller. Philomel, 2002. ISBN 0-399-23387-3 Subj: Animals – yaks. Folk & fairy tales. Foreign lands – Tibet.

Angels on a pin ill. by author. Philomel, 2000. ISBN 0-399-23247-8 Subj: Cities, towns. Concepts – size.

Animalia ill. by author. Tricycle, 1999. ISBN 1-58246-012-4 Subj: Animals. Folk & fairy tales. Foreign lands. Religion.

The donkey's dream ill. by author. Philomel, 1986. ISBN 0-399-21233-7 Subj: Animals – donkeys. Dreams. Holidays – Christmas. Religion.

Grandfather Twilight ill. by author. Putnam, 1986. ISBN 0-399-20996-4 Subj: Folk & fairy tales. Moon. Twilight.

The jewel heart ill. by author. Philomel, 1994. ISBN 0-399-22681-8 Subj: Activities – dancing. Ballet. Emotions – love. Music. Musical instruments – violins. Shadows.

A lot of otters ill. by author. Philomel, 1997. ISBN 0-399-22910-8 Subj: Animals – otters. Behavior – lost. Moon.

When the sun rose ill. by author. Philomel, 1986. ISBN 0-399-21360-0 Subj: Friendship. Imagination – imaginary friends.

Berger, Gilda. *How do airplanes fly?* (Berger, Melvin)

How's the weather? (Berger, Melvin)

Why did the dinosaurs disappear? the great dinosaur mystery (Berger, Melvin)

Berger, Judith. *Butterflies and rainbows* by Judith Berger & Terry Landau; ill. by Carmen Lowhar. Bande House, 1982. Subj: Concepts – color. Rhyming text.

Berger, Melvin. *Brrr! a book about polar animals* ill. with photos. Scholastic, 2000. ISBN 0-439-20165-9 Subj: Animals. Foreign lands – Arctic. Science.

Buzz! a book about insects ill. with photos. Scholastic, 2000. ISBN 0-439-08748-1 Subj: Insects. Science.

Dive! a book of deep sea creatures ill. with photos. Scholastic, 2000. ISBN 0-439-08747-3 Subj: Animals. Boats, ships. Fish. Science. Sea & seashore.

Early humans: a pop-up book ill. by Michael Welply. Putnam, 1988. ISBN 0-399-21476-3 Subj: Format, unusual – toy & movable books. Science.

Germs make me sick! ill. by Marylin Hafner. Crowell, 1985. ISBN 0-690-04429-1 Subj: Illness. Science.

How do airplanes fly? by Melvin & Gilda Berger; ill. by Paul Babb. Ideals, 1996. ISBN 1-57102-058-6 Subj: Activities – flying. Airplanes, airports. Science.

How's the weather? by Melvin & Gilda Berger; ill. by John Emil Cymerman. Ideals, 1996. ISBN 0-8249-8641-5 Subj: Science. Weather.

Look out for turtles! ill. by Megan Lloyd. HarperCollins, 1992. ISBN 0-06-022540-8 Subj: Nature. Reptiles – turtles, tortoises. Science.

Oil spill! ill. by Paul Mirocha. HarperCollins, 1994. ISBN 0-06-022912-8 Subj: Ecology. Oil. Science. Sea & seashore.

Ouch! a book about cuts, scratches and scrapes ill. by Pat Stewart. Dutton, 1991. ISBN 0-525-67323-7 Subj: Health & fitness. Illness.

Prehistoric mammals devised & designed by Keith Moseley; ill. by Robert Cremins. Putnam, 1986. ISBN 0-399-21312-0 Subj: Animals. Format, unusual – toy & movable books. Prehistory.

Spinning spiders ill. by S. D. Schindler. HarperCollins, 2003. ISBN 0-06-028697-0 Subj: Science. Spiders.

Switch on, switch off ill. by Carolyn Croll. HarperCollins, 1992. ISBN 0-690-04786-X Subj: Light, lights. Science.

Why did the dinosaurs disappear? the great dinosaur mystery by Melvin & Gilda Berger; ill. by Susan Harrison. Ideals, 1995. ISBN 1-57102-033-0 Subj: Dinosaurs. Prehistory.

Why I sneeze, shiver, hiccup, and yawn ill. by Paul Meisel. Rev. ed. of: Why I cough, sneeze, shiver, hiccup, & yawn. Crowell, c1983. HarperCollins, 2000. ISBN 0-06-028143-X Subj: Hiccups. Illness – allergies. Illness – asthma. Science.

Berger, Terry. *Ben's ABC day* photos by Alice Kandell. Lothrop, 1982. Subj: ABC books.

Friends photos by Alice Kandell. Messner, 1981. Subj: Friendship.

How does it feel when your parents get divorced? photos by Miriam Shapiro. Messner, 1977. Subj: Divorce. Emotions. Family life.

I have feelings ill. by Howard Spivak. Behavioral, 1971. Subj: Emotions. Self-concept.

I have feelings too photos by Michael E. Ach. Human Sciences Pr., 1979. Subj: Emotions.

The turtles' picnic and other nonsense stories ill. by Erkki Alanen. Crown, 1977. Subj: Activities – picnicking. Animals.

Bergere, Thea. *Paris in the rain with Jean and Jacqueline* ill. by Richard Bergere. McGraw-Hill, 1963. Subj: Cities, towns. Foreign lands – France. Weather – rain.

Bergman, David. *The turtle and the two ducks: animal fables* (Plante, Patricia)

Bergman, Donna. *City fox* ill. by Peter E. Hanson. Atheneum, 1992. ISBN 0-689-31687-9 Subj: Animals – foxes. Character traits – kindness to animals. Cities, towns. Friendship. Old age.

Timmy Green's blue lake ill. by Ib Ohlsson. Tambourine, 1992. ISBN 0-688-10748-6 Subj: Activities – playing. Ecology. Imagination.

Bergman, Mara. *Musical beds* ill. by Marjolein Pottie. McElderry, 2002. ISBN 0-689-84463-8 Subj: Bedtime. Family life. Sleep.

Bergman, Tamar. *Where is?* ill. by Rutu Modan. Houghton, 2002. ISBN 0-618-09539-X Subj: Animals – cats. Family life – grandparents. Family life – mothers.

Bergstreser, Doug. *Runners, sliders, bouncers, climbers* (Bantock, Nick)

Bergstrom, Corinne. *Losing your best friend* ill. by Patricia Rosamilia. Human Sciences Pr., 1980. Subj: Friendship.

Bergström, Gunilla. *Is that a monster, Alfie Atkins?* ill. by Robert Swindells. Farrar, 1989. ISBN 9-12-959136-8 Subj: Animals – rabbits. Monsters.

Who's scaring Alfie Atkins? trans. by Joan Sandin; ill. by author. Farrar, 1987. ISBN 91-29-58318-7 Subj: Emotions – fear. Family life – fathers. Ghosts.

You have a girlfriend, Alfie Atkins? ill. by Joan Sandin. Farrar, 1988. ISBN 9-12-959062-0 Subj: Emotions – love.

Beris, Sandra. *The cat's surprise* (Seguin-Fontes, Marthe)

A wedding book (Seguin-Fontes, Marthe)

Berkes, Marianne Collins. *Marsh music* ill. by Robert Noreika. Millbrook, 2000. ISBN 0-7613-1850-X Subj: Animals. Birds. Frogs & toads. Noise, sounds. Rhyming text. Swamps.

Seashells by the seashore ill. by Robert Noreika. Dawn, 2002. ISBN 1-58469-035-6 Subj: Counting, numbers. Sea & seashore.

Berkley, Ethel S. *Ups and down: a first book of space* ill. by Kathleen Elgin. Addison-Wesley, 1951. Subj: Concepts. Concepts – up & down.

Berkowitz, Linda. *Alfonse, where are you?* ill. by author. Crown, 1996. ISBN 0-517-70046-8 Subj: Activities – playing. Animals. Birds – chickens. Birds – geese. Farms. Games.

Berlan, Kathryn Hook. *Andrew's amazing monsters* ill. by Maxie Chambliss. Atheneum, 1993. ISBN 0-689-31739-5 Subj: Activities – drawing. Monsters. Night. Parties.

Berlin, Irving. *Easter parade* ill. by Lisa McCue. HarperCollins, 2003. ISBN 0-06-029126-5 Subj: Animals – rabbits. Holidays – Easter. Music. Songs.

God bless America ill. by Lynn Munsinger. HarperCollins, 2002. ISBN 0-06-009789-2 Subj: Music. Songs. U.S. history.

Berliner, Franz. *Miserable Marabou* ill. by Irene Hedlund. G. Stevens, 1989. ISBN 0-8368-0094-X Subj: Birds. Birds – storks. Self-concept.

Wildebeest ill. by Lilian Brogger. Ideals, 1991. ISBN 0-8249-8488-9 Subj: Animals – wildebeests. Behavior – sharing. Character traits – individuality.

Berman, Linda. *The goodbye painting* ill. by Mark Hannon. Human Sciences Pr., 1983. Subj: Activities – babysitting.

Berman, Ruth. *Buzzing rattlesnakes* photos by David T. Roberts & David M. Schleser. Lerner, 1998. ISBN 0-8225-3603-X Subj: Reptiles – snakes.

Climbing tree frogs photos by John Netherton. Lerner, 1998. ISBN 0-8225-3605-6 Subj: Frogs & toads.

Fishing bears photos by Lynn M. Stone. Lerner, 1998. ISBN 0-8225-3601-3 Subj: Animals – bears.

Spinning spiders photos by David T. Roberts & David M. Schleser. Lerner, 1998. ISBN 0-8225-3604-8 Subj: Spiders.

Squeaking bats ill. with photos. Lerner, 1998. ISBN 0-8225-3602-1 Subj: Animals – bats.

Watchful wolves photos by William Muñoz. Lerner, 1998. ISBN 0-8225-3600-5 Subj: Animals – wolves.

Bernadette. *see* Watts, Bernadette

Bernard, Fred. *The yellow train* (Highet, Alistair)

Bernard, Robin. *Juma and the honey-guild* ill. by Nneka Bennett. Silver Burdett, 1996. ISBN 0-382-39162-4 Subj: Behavior – sharing. Birds. Family life – fathers. Foreign lands – Africa. Foreign languages.

Bernardoni, Robert. *Christmas all over* ill. by Ruth Hunter McAnespy. Pelican, 1996. ISBN 1-56554-205-3 Subj: Holidays – Christmas. Mythical creatures – elves. Rhyming text. Santa Claus.

Bernhard, Durga. *Alphabeasts: a hide and seek alphabet book* ill. by author. Holiday, 1993. ISBN 0-8234-0993-7 Subj: ABC books. Animals. Behavior – hiding. Nature.

Earth, sky, wet, dry: a book of nature opposites ill. by author. Orchard, 2000. ISBN 0-531-33213-6 Subj: Animals. Concepts – opposites. Nature. Plants.

To and fro, fast and slow ill. by author. Walker, 2001. ISBN 0-8027-8783-5 Subj: Cities, towns. Concepts – opposites. Country. Divorce. Family life.

What's Maggie up to? ill. by author. Holiday, 1992. ISBN 0-8234-0969-4 Subj: Animals – cats. Birds. Family life.

Bernhard, Emery. *Dragonfly* ill. by Durga Bernhard. Holiday, 1993. ISBN 0-8234-1033-1 Subj: Insects – dragonflies. Nature. Science.

Eagles: lions of the sky ill. by Durga Bernhard. Holiday, 1994. ISBN 0-8234-1105-2 Subj: Birds – eagles. Nature. Science.

The girl who wanted to hunt ill. by Durga Bernhard. Holiday, 1994. ISBN 0-8234-1125-7 Subj: Birds – owls. Folk & fairy tales. Foreign lands – Russia. Foreign lands – Siberia. Sports – hunting.

How Snowshoe Hare rescued the sun: a tale from the Arctic ill. by Durga Bernhard. Holiday, 1993. ISBN 0-8234-1043-9 Subj: Animals. Eskimos. Folk & fairy tales – pourquoi tales. Foreign lands – Russia. Foreign lands – Siberia.

Ladybug ill. by Durga Bernhard. Holiday, 1992. ISBN 0-8234-0986-4 Subj: Insects – ladybugs. Nature. Science.

Reindeer ill. by Durga Bernhard. Holiday, 1994. ISBN 0-8234-1097-8 Subj: Animals – reindeer. Science.

Salamanders ill. by Durga Bernhard. Holiday, 1995. ISBN 0-8234-1148-6 Subj: Reptiles – salamanders. Science.

Spotted Eagle and Black Crow: a Lakota legend ill. by Durga Bernhard. Holiday, 1993. ISBN 0-8234-1007-2 Subj: Birds – eagles. Folk & fairy tales. Indians of North America – Lakota (Sioux). Sibling rivalry.

The tree that rains: the flood myth of the Huichol Indians of Mexico ill. by Durga Bernhard. Holiday, 1994. ISBN 0-8234-1108-7 Subj: Folk & fairy tales. Foreign lands – Mexico. Indians of North America – Huichol. Religion. Trees. Weather – floods.

The way of the willow branch ill. by Durga Bernhard. Harcourt, 1996. ISBN 0-15-200844-6 Subj: Nature. Sea & seashore. Trees.

Bernhard, Josephine Butkowska. *Lullaby: why the pussy-cat washes himself so often; a folk-tale adapted from the Polish* ill. by Irena Lorentowicz. Roy Pub., 1944. Subj: Animals – cats. Folk & fairy tales. Foreign lands – Poland. Lullabies.

Nine cry-baby dolls ill. by Irena Lorentowicz. Roy Pub., 1945. Subj: Folk & fairy tales. Foreign lands – Poland. Toys – dolls.

Bernheim, Evelyne. *In Africa* (Bernheim, Marc)

A week in Aya's world: the Ivory Coast (Bernheim, Marc)

Bernheim, Marc. *In Africa* by Marc & Evelyne Bernheim; photos by authors. Atheneum, 1973. ISBN 0-689-30315-7 Subj: Family life. Foreign lands – Africa.

A week in Aya's world: the Ivory Coast by Marc & Evelyne Bernheim; photos by authors. Macmillan, 1970. Subj: Foreign lands – Africa.

Bernstein, Alan. *Regal the golden eagle* (Klinting, Lars)

Bernstein, Joanne E. *Creepy crawly critter riddles* by Joanne E. Bernstein & Paul Cohen; ill. by Rosekrans Hoffman. A. Whitman, 1986. ISBN 0-8075-1345-8 Subj: Animals. Insects. Riddles & jokes.

What was the wicked witch's real name? and other character riddles by Joanne E. Bernstein & Paul Cohen; ill. by Ann Iosa. A. Whitman, 1986. ISBN 0-8075-8854-7 Subj: Riddles & jokes.

When people die by Joanne E. Bernstein & Steven V. Gullo; photos by Rosmarie Hausherr. Dutton, 1977. ISBN 0-525-42545-4 Subj: Death. Emotions – grief.

Bernstein, Margery. *Coyote goes hunting for fire: a California Indian myth* by Margery Bernstein & Janet Kobrin; ill. by Ed Heffernan. Scribners, 1974. ISBN 0-684-13768-2 Subj: Animals. Animals – coyotes. Fire. Folk & fairy tales. Indians of North America – Yana.

Earth namer: a California Indian myth by Margery Bernstein & Janet Kobrin; ill. by Ed Heffernan. Scribners, 1974. ISBN 0-684-

13769-0 Subj: Creation. Earth. Folk & fairy tales. Indians of North America – Maidu.

The first morning: an African myth by Margery Bernstein & Janet Kobrin; ill. by Enid Warner Romanek. Scribners, 1976. ISBN 0-684-14533-2 Subj: Animals. Folk & fairy tales. Foreign lands – Africa.

How the sun made a promise and kept it: a Canadian Indian myth retold by Margery Bernstein & Janet Kobrin; ill. by Ed Heffernan. Scribners, 1974. ISBN 0-684-13770-4 Subj: Animals – beavers. Folk & fairy tales. Indians of North America – Bungee. Indians of North America – Ojibwa. Sun.

Bernstein, Robin. *Terrible, terrible!* ill. by Shauna Mooney Kawasaki. Kar-Ben Copies, 1998. ISBN 1-58013-016-X Subj: Folk & fairy tales. Jewish culture.

Berquist, Grace. *The boy who couldn't roar* ill. by Ruth Van Sciver. Abingdon, 1960. Subj: Behavior – bullying. Character traits – selfishness.

Speckles goes to school ill. by Kathleen Elgin. Abingdon, 1952. Subj: Birds – chickens. School.

Berridge, Celia. *At my house* ill. by author. Random House, 1987. ISBN 0-394-99166-4 Subj: Family life. Homes, houses.

Going swimming ill. by author. Random House, 1987. ISBN 0-394-99165-6 Subj: Sports – swimming.

Grandmother's tales ill. by author. Elsevier-Dutton, 1981. ISBN 0-233-97357-5 Subj: Bedtime. Family life – grandmothers. Witches.

Hannah's new boots ill. by author. Scholastic, 1993. ISBN 0-590-45888-4 Subj: Clothing – shoes.

Hannah's temper ill. by author. Scholastic, 1992. ISBN 0-590-45887-6 Subj: Behavior – misbehavior. Emotions – anger. Rhyming text. Teeth.

On my street ill. by author. Random House, 1987. ISBN 0-394-88163-X Subj: Communities, neighborhoods.

Berry, Christine. *Mama went walking* ill. by María Cristina Brusca. Holt, 1990. ISBN 0-8050-1261-3 Subj: Activities – walking. Emotions – fear. Family life – mothers. Imagination.

Berry, Holly. *Busy Lizzie* ill. by author. North-South, 1994. ISBN 1-55858-324-6 Subj: Activities – playing. Bedtime. Participation.

Berry, James. *Celebration song* ill. by Louise Brierley. S&S, 1994. ISBN 0-671-89446-3 Subj: Birth. Holidays – Christmas. Poetry. Religion – Nativity.

Don't leave an elephant to go and chase a bird ill. by Ann Grifalconi. S&S, 1996. ISBN 0-689-80464-4 Subj: Animals – elephants. Behavior – trickery. Folk & fairy tales. Foreign lands – Ghana.

First palm trees: an Anancy Spiderman story ill. by Greg Couch. S&S, 1997. ISBN 0-689-81060-1 Subj: Folk & fairy tales. Foreign lands – Caribbean Islands. Spiders.

Berry, Joy Wilt. *Being destructive* ill. by John Costanza. Rev. ed. Childrens Pr., 1984. ISBN 0-516-02681-X Subj: Behavior – misbehavior.

Being selfish ill. by John Costanza. Rev. ed. Childrens Pr., 1984. ISBN 0-516-02682-8 Subj: Behavior – misbehavior. Character traits – selfishness.

Disobeying ill. by John Costanza. Rev. ed. Childrens Pr., 1984. ISBN 0-516-02683-6 Subj: Behavior – misbehavior.

Fighting ill. by John Costanza. Rev. ed. Childrens Pr., 1984. ISBN 0-516-02684-4 Subj: Behavior – fighting, arguing. Behavior – misbehavior.

Throwing tantrums ill. by John Costanza. Rev. ed. Childrens Pr., 1984. ISBN 0-516-02685-2 Subj: Behavior – misbehavior.

Whining ill. by John Costanza. Rev. ed. Childrens Pr., 1984. ISBN 0-516-02686-0 Subj: Behavior – misbehavior.

Berson, Harold. *Balarin's goat* ill. by author. Crown, 1972. ISBN 0-517-50105-8 Subj: Animals – goats. Folk & fairy tales.

Barrels to the moon ill. by author. Coward, 1982. ISBN 0-698-20551-0 Subj: Folk & fairy tales. Foreign lands – France.

The boy, the baker, the miller and more ill. by author. Crown, 1974. The story is based on a French folk tale called Un Morceau de pain. ISBN 0-517-50326-3 Subj: Cumulative tales. Folk & fairy tales.

Charles and Claudine ill. by adapt. Macmillan, 1980. ISBN 0-02-709230-5 Subj: Folk & fairy tales. Foreign lands – France. Frogs & toads. Magic. Witches.

Henry Possum ill. by author. Crown, 1973. ISBN 0-517-50297-6 Subj: Animals – foxes. Animals – possums. Behavior – lost.

How the devil gets his due ill. by adapt. Crown, 1972. Subj: Character traits – cleverness. Devil. Folk & fairy tales. Foreign lands – France.

I'm bored, Ma! Ill. by author. Crown, 1976. ISBN 0-517-52508-9 Subj: Animals. Behavior – boredom. Imagination.

Joseph and the snake ill. by author. Macmillan, 1979. ISBN 0-02-709200-3 Subj: Animals – foxes. Character traits – cleverness. Character traits – kindness to animals. Folk & fairy tales. Foreign lands – France. Reptiles – snakes.

Kassim's shoes ill. by adapt. Crown, 1977. ISBN 0-517-53063-5 Subj: Behavior – misunderstanding. Folk & fairy tales. Foreign lands – Africa.

Larbi and Leila: a tale of two mice ill. by author. Seabury Pr., 1974. ISBN 0-8164-3113-2 Subj: Behavior – greed. Folk & fairy tales.

A moose is not a mouse ill. by author. Crown, 1975. ISBN 0-517-51869-4 Subj: Animals – mice. Language.

Pop! goes the turnip ill. by author. Grosset, 1966. Subj: Animals – rabbits. Food. Gardens, gardening. Plants.

Raminagrobis and the mice ill. by author. Seabury Pr., 1966. Subj: Animals – cats. Animals – mice. Folk & fairy tales.

The rats who lived in the delicatessen ill. by author. Crown, 1976. ISBN 0-517-52604-2 Subj: Animals – rats. Behavior – greed. Food.

The thief who hugged a moonbeam ill. by author. Seabury Pr., 1972. ISBN 0-395-28767-7 Subj: Behavior – gossip. Crime. Magic. Royalty.

Truffles for lunch ill. by author. Macmillan, 1980. ISBN 0-02-709800-1 Subj: Animals – pigs. Behavior – wishing.

Why the jackal won't speak to the hedgehog: a Tunisian folk tale ill. by adapt. Seabury Pr., 1970. Subj: Animals. Animals – hedgehogs. Character traits – cleverness. Folk & fairy tales. Foreign lands – Africa.

Bertram, Debbie. *The best place to read* by Debbie Bertram & Susan Bloom; ill. by Michael Garland. Random House, 2003. ISBN 0-375-92293-8 Subj: Books, reading. Family life – mothers. Furniture – chairs. Rhyming text.

Bertrand, Cécile. *Let's pretend!* ill. by author. Lothrop, 1993. ISBN 0-688-12378-3 Subj: Animals – dogs. Imagination. Shopping.

Mr. and Mrs. Smith have only one child, but what a child! ill. & trans. from French by author. Lothrop, 1992. ISBN 0-688-11330-3 Subj: Behavior. Family life – only child. Self-concept.

Bertrand, Diane Gonzales. *Family = familia* ill. by Pauline Rodriguez Howard; Spanish trans. by Julia Mercedes Castilla. Piñata, 1999. ISBN 1-55885-269-7 Subj: Ethnic groups in the U.S. – Mexican Americans. Family life. Foreign languages.

The last doll = La última muñeca ill. by Anthony Accardo; Spanish trans. by Alejandra Balestra. Piñata, 2000. ISBN 1-55885-290-5

Subj: Birthdays. Ethnic groups in the U.S. – Mexican Americans. Foreign languages. Toys – dolls.

Uncle Chente's picnic = El picnic de Tío Chente ill. by Pauline Rodriguez Howard; Spanish trans. by Julia Mercedes Castilla. Piñata, 2001. ISBN 1-55885-337-5 Subj: Activities – picnicking. Ethnic groups in the U.S. – Mexican Americans. Family life – aunts, uncles. Foreign languages. Holidays – Fourth of July.

Bertrand, Lynne. *Dragon naps* ill. by Janet Street. Viking, 1996. ISBN 0-670-85403-4 Subj: Bedtime. Counting, numbers. Dragons. Sleep.

One day, two dragons ill. by Janet Street. Potter/Crown, 1992. ISBN 0-517-58413-1 Subj: Careers – doctors. Counting, numbers. Dragons. Illness.

Beskow, Elsa Maartman. *Children of the forest* adapt. from the Swedish by William Jay Smith; ill. by author. Delacorte, 1969. ISBN 0-86315-049-7 Subj: Foreign lands – Sweden. Forest, woods. Rhyming text. Seasons.

Pelle's new suit based on the original by Elsa Beskow; edited by Nova Nestrick; ill. by Bruno Frost. Platt, 1962. ISBN 0-06-020496-6 Subj: Animals – sheep. Clothing. Foreign lands – Sweden.

Peter in Blueberry Land ill. by author. Merrimack, 1984. A new ed. of a 100-year-old picture book. ISBN 0-510-00129-7 Subj: Birthdays. Food. Foreign lands – Sweden. Little people. Magic. Rhyming text.

Peter's adventures in Blueberry Land adapt. by Sheila La Farge; ill. by author. Delacorte, 1975. Pub. in Sweden in 1901. ISBN 0-440-04435-9 Subj: Birthdays. Food. Foreign lands – Sweden. Little people. Magic. Rhyming text.

Bess, Clayton. *The truth about the moon* ill. by Rosekrans Hoffman. Houghton Mifflin, 1983. ISBN 0-395-34551-0 Subj: Folk & fairy tales. Foreign lands – Africa. Moon.

Best, Cari. *Getting used to Harry* ill. by Diane Palmisciano. Orchard, 1996. ISBN 0-531-08794-8 Subj: Family life – stepfamilies.

Last licks: a Spaldeen story ill. by Diane Palmisciano. DK, 1999. ISBN 0-7894-2513-0 Subj: Activities – playing. Sports – punchball.

Montezuma's revenge ill. by Diane Palmisciano. Orchard, 1999. ISBN 0-531-33198-9 Subj: Activities – vacationing. Animals – dogs. Behavior – dissatisfaction.

Taxi! Taxi! ill. by Dale Gottlieb. Little, 1994. ISBN 0-316-09259-2 Subj: Activities – playing. Divorce. Family life – fathers. Taxis.

Three cheers for Catherine the Great! ill. by Giselle Potter. DK, 1999. ISBN 0-7894-2622-6 Subj: Birthdays. Family life – grandmothers. Gifts.

Top banana ill. by Erika Oller. Orchard, 1997. ISBN 0-531-33009-5 Subj: Birds – parakeets, parrots. Character traits – helpfulness. Emotions – envy, jealousy. Flowers.

When Catherine the Great and I were eight! ill. by Giselle Potter. Farrar, 2003. ISBN 0-374-39954-9 Subj: Activities – traveling. Automobiles. Communities, neighborhoods. Concepts – cold & heat. Ethnic groups in the U.S. – Russian Americans. Family life – grandmothers.

The best cat in the world ill. by Ronald Himler. Eerdmans, 2004. ISBN 0-8028-5252-1 Subj: Animals – cats. Death. Emotions – grief. Pets.

The best part of me: children talk about their bodies in pictures & words by Miss Lord's 3,4,5th grade class; photos by Wendy Ewald. Little, 2002. ISBN 0-316-70306-0 Subj: Anatomy. Children as authors. Poetry.

Bester, Roger. *Fireman Jim* photos by author. Crown, 1981. ISBN 0-517-54290-0 Subj: Careers – firefighters. Fire.

Guess what? photos by author. Crown, 1980. ISBN 0-517-54104-1 Subj: Animals. Participation. Problem solving.

Bethell, Jean. *Bathtime.* Holt, 1979. ISBN 0-03-044636-8 Subj: Activities – bathing. Animals.

Hooray for Henry ill. by Sergio Leone. Grosset, 1966. Subj: Character traits – perseverance. Food.

Playmates photos by author. Holt, 1981. ISBN 0-03-053821-1 Subj: Activities – playing. Animals.

Three cheers for Mother Jones! ill. by Kathleen Garry-McCord. Holt, 1980. ISBN 0-03-054831-4 Subj: Activities – working. U.S. history.

Bettina (Bettina Ehrlich). *Cocolo comes to America* ill. by author. HarperCollins, 1949. Subj: Animals – donkeys.

Cocolo's home ill. by author. HarperCollins, 1950. Subj: Animals – donkeys.

Of uncles and aunts ill. by author. Norton, 1964. Subj: Family life – aunts, uncles.

Pantaloni ill. by author. HarperCollins, 1957. Subj: Animals – dogs. Foreign lands – Italy. Poverty. Sports – fishing.

Piccolo ill. by author. HarperCollins, 1954. Subj: Animals – donkeys.

Bettinger, Craig. *Follow me, everybody* ill. by Edward S. Hollander. Doubleday, 1968. Subj: Ethnic groups in the U.S.

Betz, Betty. *Manners for moppets* ill. by author. Grosset, 1962. Subj: Etiquette. Rhyming text.

Bianchi, John. *The lab rats of Doctor Eclair* ill. by author. Firefly, 1997. ISBN 0-921285-49-3 Subj: Animals – rats. Character traits – kindness to animals.

Swine snafu ill. by author. Firefly, 1988. ISBN 0-921285-14-0 Subj: Animals – pigs. Family life. Friendship.

Bianco, Margery Williams. *The hurdy-gurdy man* ill. by Robert Lawson. Gregg, 1979, c1933. Subj: Activities – dancing. Music. Musical instruments – hurdy-gurdies.

The velveteen rabbit: or, How toys became real ill. by Allen Atkinson. Knopf, 1983. ISBN 0-394-53221-X Subj: Animals – rabbits. Emotions – love. Folk & fairy tales. Magic. Toys.

The velveteen rabbit ill. by Monique Félix. Creative Ed., 1994. ISBN 0-8868-2732-9 Subj: Animals – rabbits. Emotions – love. Folk & fairy tales. Magic. Toys.

The velveteen rabbit: or, How toys became real ill. by Michael Green. Running Pr., 1984. ISBN 0-89741-291-8 Subj: Animals – rabbits. Emotions – love. Folk & fairy tales. Magic. Toys.

The velveteen rabbit: or, How toys became real ill. by Michael Hague. Holt, 1983. ISBN 0-03-063517-9 Subj: Animals – rabbits. Emotions – love. Folk & fairy tales. Magic. Toys.

The velveteen rabbit ill. by Estella Hickman. Worthington, 1989. ISBN 0-87406-393-0 Subj: Animals – rabbits. Emotions – love. Folk & fairy tales. Magic. Toys.

The velveteen rabbit: or, How toys became real adapt. by Lou Fancher from the orig. story by Margery Williams; ill. by Steve Johnson & Lou Fancher. Atheneum, 2002. ISBN 0-689-31874-X Subj: Animals – rabbits. Emotions – love. Folk & fairy tales. Magic. Toys.

The velveteen rabbit ill. by David Jorgensen. Knopf, 1985. ISBN 0-394-87711-X Subj: Animals – rabbits. Emotions – love. Folk & fairy tales. Magic. Toys.

The velveteen rabbit retold & ill. by Thea Kliros. HarperFestival, 2003. ISBN 0-06-052746-3 Subj: Animals – rabbits. Emotions – love. Folk & fairy tales. Magic. Toys.

The velveteen rabbit ill. by Elizabeth Miles. Scholastic, 1990. ISBN 0-590-42805-5 Subj: Animals – rabbits. Emotions – love. Folk & fairy tales. Magic. Toys.

The velveteen rabbit: or, How toys became real ill. by William Nicholson. Doubleday, 1991. ISBN 0-385-07748-3 Subj: Animals – rabbits. Emotions – love. Folk & fairy tales. Magic. Toys.

The velveteen rabbit ill. by Robyn Officer. Andrews & McMeel, 1991. ISBN 0-8362-3022-1 Subj: Animals – rabbits. Emotions – love. Folk & fairy tales. Magic. Toys.

The velveteen rabbit: or, How toys became real ill. by Ilse Plume. Godine, 1983. ISBN 0-87923-444-X Subj: Animals – rabbits. Emotions – love. Folk & fairy tales. Magic. Toys.

The velveteen rabbit: or, How toys became real ed. by David Eastman; ill. by S. D. Schindler. Troll, 1987. ISBN 0-8167-1061-9 Subj: Animals – rabbits. Emotions – love. Folk & fairy tales. Magic. Toys.

The velveteen rabbit: or, How toys became real ill. by Tien. S&S, 1983. ISBN 0-671-46784-8 Subj: Animals – rabbits. Emotions – love. Folk & fairy tales. Magic. Toys.

Bibb, Eric. *The dolphin journey* (Orstadius, Brita)

Bibbel, Mark. *Oh, Harry!* ill. by Sarah Massini. Holt, 2003. ISBN 0-8050-6851-1 Subj: Animals – cats. Furniture – beds. Pets.

Bibbons, Faye. *The day the picture man came* ill. by Sherry Meidell. Boyds Mills, 2003. ISBN 1-56397-161-5 Subj: Careers – photographers. Farms.

Bible. *Best-loved Bible verses for children* ill. by Anna Maria Magagna. Grosset, 1983. ISBN 0-448-46626-0 Subj: Religion.

Bible, Charles. *Hamdaani: a traditional tale from Zanzibar* ill. by adapt. Holt, 1977. ISBN 0-03-020846-7 Subj: Animals. Folk & fairy tales. Foreign lands – Africa.

Jennifer's new chair ill. by author. Holt, 1978. ISBN 0-03-022801-8 Subj: Birthdays. Family life. Family life – grandmothers. Fire. Furniture – chairs. Parties.

Bible. New Testament. *The Lord's prayer* ill. by Ingri & Edgar Parin d'Aulaire. Catholic version. Doubleday, 1934. Subj: Religion.

The Lord's prayer ill. by Ingri & Edgar Parin d'Aulaire. Protestant version. Doubleday, 1934. Subj: Religion.

The Lord's prayer ill. by George Kraus. Dutton, 1970. ISBN 0-6716-6524-3 Subj: Religion.

The Lord's prayer ill. by Tim Ladwig. Eerdmans, 1999. ISBN 0-8028-5180-0 Subj: Ethnic groups in the U.S. – African Americans. Religion.

Bible. New Testament. Corinthians, 1st, XIII. *Love is* adapt. from the Bible & ill. by Wendy Anderson Halperin. S&S, 2001. ISBN 0-689-82980-9 Subj: Emotions – love. Religion.

Bible. New Testament. Gospels. *Bethlehem: from the Authorized Version of the King James Bible* ed. & ill. by Fiona French. HarperCollins, 2001. ISBN 0-06-029623-2 Subj: Holidays – Christmas. Religion – Nativity.

Christmas: the King James Version ill. by Jan Pieńkowski. Knopf, 1984. ISBN 0-394-86923-0 Subj: Holidays – Christmas. Religion – Nativity.

The Christmas story: from the Gospel according to St. Luke from the King James Bible ill. by James Bernardin. HarperCollins, 2002. ISBN 0-06-028883-3 Subj: Holidays – Christmas. Religion – Nativity.

Easter: from the King James Bible ed. & ill. by Fiona French. HarperCollins, 2002. ISBN 0-06-623929-X Subj: Holidays – Easter. Religion.

The first Christmas: from the Gospels according to Saint Luke and Saint Matthew ill. by Barbara Neustadt. Crowell, 1960. Subj: Holidays – Christmas. Religion – Nativity.

The Nativity ill. by Julie Vivas. Harcourt, 1988. Text consists of excerpts from the authorized King James version of the Bible. ISBN 0-15-200535-8 Subj: Holidays – Christmas. Religion – Nativity.

The story of Christmas: words from the Gospels of Matthew and Luke ill. by Jane Ray. Dutton, 1991. ISBN 0-525-44768-7 Subj: Holidays – Christmas. Religion – Nativity.

Bible. Old Testament. Daniel. *Daniel in the lions' den* adapt. by Belinda Hollyer; ill. by Leon Baxter. Silver Burdett, 1984. ISBN 0-382-06790-8 Subj: Animals – lions. Religion – Daniel.

Daniel in the lions' den text by Kathleen N. Daly; ill. by Jim Cummins. Rand McNally, 1984. ISBN 0-528-82492-9 Subj: Animals – lions. Format, unusual – board books. Religion – Daniel.

Daniel in the lions' den retold by Mary Auld; ill. by Diana Mayo. S&S, 1999. ISBN 0-531-14514-X Subj: Animals – lions. Religion – Daniel.

Shadrach, Meshach, and Abednego ill. by Paul Galdone. McGraw-Hill, 1965. Subj: Religion.

Bible. Old Testament. David. *David and Goliath* adapt. by Belinda Hollyer; ill. by Leon Baxter. Silver Burdett, 1984. ISBN 0-382-06791-6 Subj: Foreign lands – Israel. Giants. Religion – David.

David and the giant text by Emily Little; ill. by Hans Wilhelm. Random House, 1987. ISBN 0-394-98867-1 Subj: Behavior – bullying. Giants. Religion – David.

Bible. Old Testament. Ecclesiastes. *To every thing there is a season* ill. by Leo & Diane Dillon. Blue Sky, 1998. ISBN 0-590-47887-7 Subj: Religion.

Bible. Old Testament. Genesis. *Genesis* ill. by Ed Young. Geringer, 1997. ISBN 0-06-025356-8 Subj: Creation. Religion.

The story of the creation ill. by Jane Ray. Dutton, 1993. ISBN 0-525-44946-9 Subj: Creation. Religion.

Bible. Old Testament. Jonah. *The Book of Jonah* adapt. & ill. by Peter Spier. Doubleday, 1985. ISBN 0-385-19335-1 Subj: Animals – whales. Religion – Jonah.

Jonah: the complete text of Jonah from the Holy Bible, New International version ill. by Kurt Mitchell. Crossway, 1981. ISBN 0-89107-224-1 Subj: Animals – cats. Animals – mice. Animals – whales. Religion – Jonah.

Jonah and the great fish adapt. by Belinda Hollyer; ill. by Leon Baxter. Silver Burdett, 1984. ISBN 0-382-06792-4 Subj: Animals – whales. Religion – Jonah.

Jonah and the great fish text by Kathleen N. Daly; ill. by Jim Cummins. Rand McNally, 1984. ISBN 0-528-82495-3 Subj: Animals – whales. Format, unusual – board books. Religion.

Bible. Old Testament. Joseph. *Joseph and his brothers* text by Kathleen N. Daly; ill. by Jim Cummins. Rand McNally, 1984. ISBN 0-528-82493-7 Subj: Clothing – coats. Family life – brothers. Foreign lands – Egypt. Format, unusual – board books. Religion. Slavery.

Bible. Old Testament. Noah. *Noah and the ark* adapt. & ill. by Pauline Baynes. Holt, 1988. ISBN 0-8050-0886-1 Subj: Animals. Boats, ships. Religion – Noah. Weather – floods. Weather – rain. Weather – rainbows.

Noah and the ark text by Kathleen N. Daly; ill. by Jim Cummins. Rand McNally, 1984. ISBN 0-528-82490-2 Subj: Animals. Boats, ships. Religion – Noah. Weather – floods. Weather – rain.

Bible. Old Testament. Psalms. *The Lord is my shepherd* ill. by George Kraus. Dutton, 1971. ISBN 0-87807-015-X Subj: Religion.

The Lord is my shepherd: the twenty-third Psalm ill. by Tasha Tudor. Putnam, 1980. ISBN 0-399-20756-2 Subj: Religion.

Psalm twenty-three ill. by Tim Ladwig. African American Family Pr., 1993. ISBN 1-56977-025-5 Subj: Cities, towns. Ethnic groups in the U.S. – African Americans. Religion.

The twenty-third Psalm: from the King James Bible ill. by Michael Hague. Holt, 1997. ISBN 0-8050-3820-5 Subj: Religion.

Bider, Djemma. *The buried treasure* ill. by Debby L. Carter. Dodd, 1982. ISBN 0-396-07991-1 Subj: Folk & fairy tales. Foreign lands – Russia.

A drop of honey ill. by Armen Kojoyian. S&S, 1989. ISBN 0-671-66265-1 Subj: Dreams. Folk & fairy tales. Foreign lands – Armenia. Sibling rivalry.

Bienenfeld, Florence. *My mom and dad are getting a divorce* ill. by Art Scott. EMC, 1980. ISBN 0-88436-753-3 Subj: Divorce. Emotions.

Bier, Anna. *The nightingale* (Andersen, H. C. [Hans Christian])

Bierhorst, John. *Doctor Coyote: a Native American Æsop's fables* ill. by Wendy Watson. Macmillan, 1987. ISBN 0-02-709780-3 Subj: Animals. Animals – coyotes. Folk & fairy tales. Indians of North America – Aztec.

The ring in the prairie: a Shawnee legend trans. by John Bierhorst; ill. by Leo & Diane Dillon. Dial, 1970. ISBN 0-8037-7455-9 Subj: Folk & fairy tales. Indians of North America – Shawnee.

Spirit child: a story of the Nativity (Sahagun, Bernardino de)

The woman who fell from the sky: the Iroquois story of creation ill. by Robert Andrew Parker. Morrow, 1993. ISBN 0-688-10681-1 Subj: Creation. Indians of North America – Iroquois.

Biers-Ariel, Matt. *Solomon and the trees* ill. by Esti Silverberg-Kiss. UAHC Pr., 2001. ISBN 0-8074-0749-6 Subj: Foreign lands – Israel. Holidays. Jewish culture. Royalty – kings.

Big, bad, and a little bit scary: poems that bite back comp. & ill. by Wade Zahares. Viking, 2001. ISBN 0-670-03513-0 Subj: Animals. Poetry.

Big book of trains: National Railway Museum, York, England ill. with photos. DK, 1998. ISBN 0-7894-3436-9 Subj: Trains.

Big noisy trucks and diggers ill. with photos. Chronicle, 2001. ISBN 0-8118-3173-6 Subj: Careers – construction workers. Format, unusual – toy & movable books. Machines. Noise, sounds. Tractors. Trucks.

The big Peter Rabbit book: things to do, games to play, stories, presents to make ill. by Beatrix Potter. Warne, 1986. ISBN 0-7232-3409-4 Subj: Activities – making things. Animals. Games. Riddles & jokes.

Bildner, Phil. *Shoeless Joe and Black Betsy* ill. by C. F. Payne. S&S, 2002. ISBN 0-689-82913-2 Subj: Sports – baseball. U.S. history.

Bileck, Marvin. *Rain makes applesauce* (Scheer, Julian)

Bilezikian, Gary. *While I slept* ill. by author. Orchard, 1990. ISBN 0-531-08475-2 Subj: Night. Noise, sounds. Sleep.

Bilgrami, Shaheen. *Amazing dinosaur discovery: a magic skeleton* ill. by Mike Phillips & Phil Garner; dinosaurs & skeletons ill by Treve Tamblin. Sterling, 2002. ISBN 0-8069-8591-7 Subj: Anatomy. Animals. Dinosaurs. Format, unusual – toy & movable books. Museums. Prehistory.

Farmyard painting party ill. by Patrick Girouard. Sterling, 2002. ISBN 1-4027-0205-1 Subj: Activities – painting. Animals. Concepts – color. Farms. Format, unusual – toy & movable books.

Incredible animal discovery ill. by Mike Phillips & Phil Garner; animals & skeletons ill. by Chris Shields. Sterling, 2002. ISBN 0-8069-8593-3 Subj: Anatomy. Animals. Format, unusual – toy & movable books.

Jungle art show ill. by Patrick Girouard. Sterling, 2002. ISBN 1-4027-0206-X Subj: Activities – painting. Animals. Art. Concepts – color. Format, unusual – toy & movable books. Jungle.

Billam, Rosemary. *Fuzzy rabbit* ill. by Vanessa Julian-Ottie. Random House, 1984. ISBN 0-394-96346-6 Subj: Behavior – needing someone. Birthdays. Emotions – love. Toys.

Billington, Elizabeth T. *The Randolph Caldecott treasury* (Caldecott, Randolph)

Billout, Guy. *By camel or by car: a look at transportation* ill. by author. Prentice-Hall, 1979. ISBN 0-13-109603-6 Subj: Activities – traveling. Transportation.

Billy Boy (folk-song). *Billy Boy* verses sel. by Richard Chase; ill. by Glen Rounds. Childrens Pr., 1966. Subj: Folk & fairy tales. Poetry. Songs.

Binch, Caroline. *Since Dad left* ill. by author. Millbrook, 1998. ISBN 0-7613-0357-X Subj: Divorce. Emotions. Family life.

Bingham, Caroline. *Big book of rescue vehicles* ill. with photos. DK, 2000. ISBN 0-789-45454-8 Subj: Careers – firefighters. Careers – lifeguards. Trucks.

DK big book of airplanes ill. with photos. DK, 2001. ISBN 0-7894-6521-3 Subj: Airplanes, airports.

Bingham, Mindy. *Minou* ill. by Itoko Maeno. Advocacy Pr., 1987. ISBN 0-911655-36-0 Subj: Animals – cats. Behavior – needing someone. Foreign lands – France.

My way Sally by Mindy Bingham & Penelope Colville Paine; ill. by Itoko Maeno. Advocacy Pr., 1988. ISBN 0-911655-27-1 Subj: Animals – dogs. Animals – foxes. Behavior – trickery.

Binnamin, Vivian. *The case of the anteater's missing lunch* ill. by Jeffrey S. Nelsen. Silver Pr., 1990. ISBN 0-671-68816-2 Subj: Activities – picnicking. Animals – anteaters. Mystery stories. School.

The case of the mysterious mermaid ill. by Jeffrey S. Nelsen. Silver Pr., 1990. ISBN 0-671-68817-0 Subj: Aquariums. Mythical creatures – mermaids, mermen. School.

The case of the planetarium puzzle ill. by Jeffrey S. Nelsen. Silver Pr., 1990. ISBN 0-671-68819-7 Subj: Mystery stories.

The case of the snoring stegosaurus ill. by Jeffrey S. Nelsen. Silver Pr., 1990. ISBN 0-671-68818-9 Subj: Dinosaurs. Museums. Mystery stories. Sleep – snoring.

Binns, Tristan Boyer. *The Liberty Bell* ill. with photos. Heinemann, 2001. ISBN 1-58810-119-3 Subj: U.S. history.

Binzen, Bill. *Alfred goes house hunting* ill. by author. Doubleday, 1974. ISBN 0-385-08223-1 Subj: Animals. Homes, houses. Toys.

Carmen photos by author. Coward, 1970. ISBN 0-698-30034-3 Subj: Cities, towns. Friendship.

Birch, David. *The king's chessboard* ill. by Devis Grebu. Dial, 1988. ISBN 0-8037-0367-8 Subj: Character traits – pride. Royalty – kings.

Birchall, Mark. *Hen goes shopping* ill. by author. Dial, 2002. ISBN 0-8037-2690-2 Subj: Activities – shopping. Birds – chickens. Format, unusual – toy & movable books.

Rabbit's birthday surprise ill. by author. Carolrhoda, 2002. ISBN 0-8761-4910-7 Subj: Animals – rabbits. Behavior – lost & found possessions. Parties. Toys.

Rabbit's wooly sweater ill. by author. Carolrhoda, 2001. ISBN 1-57505-465-5 Subj: Animals – rabbits. Behavior. Clothing – sweaters. Toys.

Birchman, David Francis. *Brother Billy Bronto's bygone blues band* ill. by John O'Brien. Lothrop, 1992. ISBN 0-688-10424-X Subj: Dinosaurs. Ghosts. Music. Musical instruments – bands. Rhyming text.

A green horn blowing ill. by Thomas B. Allen. Lothrop, 1997. ISBN 0-688-12389-9 Subj: Careers – musicians. Music. Musical instruments – gourds.

Jigsaw Jackson ill. by Daniel San Souci. Lothrop, 1996. ISBN 0-688-11633-7 Subj: Behavior – misbehavior. Careers – farmers. Farms. Puzzles.

Birchmore, Daniel A. *Harry, the happy snake of Happy Hollow* ill. by Gail E. Lucas. Cucumber Island, 1996. ISBN 1-887813-06-3 Subj: Reptiles – snakes.

Pilly, Polly, and Wee ill. by Gail E. Lucas. Cucumber Island, 1996. ISBN 1-887813-15-2 Subj: Animals. Rhyming text.

The white curtain ill. by Gail E. Lucas. Cucumber Island, 1996. ISBN 1-887813-09-8 Subj: Weather – wind.

Bird, E. J. *How do bears sleep?* ill. by author. Carolrhoda, 1989. ISBN 0-87614-384-2 Subj: Animals – bears. Character traits – curiosity. Character traits – questioning. Hibernation. Rhyming text.

Bird, Malcolm. *The school in Murky Wood* ill. by author. Chronicle, 1993. ISBN 0-8118-0544-1 Subj: Monsters. Night. School.

Birdseye, Debbie Holsclaw. *She'll be comin' round the mountain* (Birdseye, Tom)

Birdseye, Tom. *Airmail to the moon* ill. by Stephen Gammell. Holiday, 1988. ISBN 0-8234-0683-0 Subj: Behavior – lost & found possessions. Character traits – persistence. Teeth.

Look out, Jack! The giant is back ill. by Will Hillenbrand. Holiday, 2001. ISBN 0-8234-1450-7 Subj: Folk & fairy tales. Giants.

Oh yeah! ill. by Ethan Long. Holiday, 2003. ISBN 0-8234-1649-6 Subj: Camps, camping. Character traits – bravery. Night.

A regular flood of mishap ill. by Megan Lloyd. Holiday, 1994. ISBN 0-8234-1070-6 Subj: Behavior – bad day. Country. Family life.

She'll be comin' round the mountain by Tom Birdseye & Debbie Holsclaw Birdseye; ill. by Andrew Glass. Holiday, 1994. ISBN 0-8234-1032-3 Subj: Activities – singing. Country. Friendship. Music. Songs.

Soap! Soap! Don't forget the soap! an Appalachian folktale ill. by Andrew Glass. Holiday, 1993. ISBN 0-8234-1005-6 Subj: Behavior – forgetfulness. Cumulative tales. Folk & fairy tales. Shopping.

A song of stars ill. by Ju-Hong Chen. Holiday, 1990. ISBN 0-8234-0790-X Subj: Emotions – love. Folk & fairy tales. Foreign lands – China. Sky. Stars.

Waiting for baby ill. by Loreen Leedy. Holiday, 1991. ISBN 0-8234-0892-2 Subj: Babies. Family life – new sibling.

Birnbaum, Abe. *Green eyes* ill. by author. Golden Bks., 2001. ISBN 0-307-20203-8 Subj: Animals – cats. Caldecott award honor books. Seasons.

Birney, Betty G. *Tyrannosaurus Tex* ill. by John O'Brien. Houghton Mifflin, 1994. ISBN 0-395-67648-7 Subj: Cowboys, cowgirls. Dinosaurs.

Biro, B. S. *see* Biro, Val

Biro, Maureen Boyd. *Walking with Maga* ill. by Joyce Wheeler. All About Kids, 2002. ISBN 0-9700863-4-2 Subj: Family life – grandmothers. Nature. Old age. Sea & seashore.

Biro, Val. *Gumdrop and the birthday surprise* ill. by author. G. Stevens, 1986. ISBN 1-55532-010-4 Subj: Automobiles. Character traits – helpfulness.

Gumdrop and the farmyard caper ill. by author. G. Stevens, 1985. ISBN 0-918831-11-3 Subj: Animals. Automobiles. Farms.

Gumdrop and the great sausage caper ill. by author. G. Stevens, 1985. ISBN 0-918831-13-X Subj: Animals. Automobiles. Food.

Gumdrop and the secret switches ill. by author. Children's Book Co., 1982. ISBN 0-685-42941-5 Subj: Animals – dogs. Automobiles.

Gumdrop and the steamroller ill. by author. G. Stevens, 1986. ISBN 1-55532-013-9 Subj: Accidents. Automobiles. Machines.

Gumdrop at the zoo ill. by author. G. Stevens, 1985. ISBN 0-918831-10-5 Subj: Automobiles. Zoos.

Gumdrop beats the clock ill. by author. G. Stevens, 1986. First published as Gumdrop in a hurry in the United Kingdom by Hodder & Stoughton Children's Books. ISBN 1-55532-011-2 Subj: Automobiles. Behavior – hurrying. Character traits – helpfulness.

Gumdrop catches a cold ill. by author. G. Stevens, 1985. ISBN 0-918831-14-8 Subj: Automobiles. Illness.

Gumdrop finds a friend ill. by author. Children's Book Co., 1982. ISBN 0-685-42940-7 Subj: Automobiles. Crime.

Gumdrop finds a ghost ill. by author. Children's Book Co., 1982. ISBN 0-685-11061-3 Subj: Automobiles. Ghosts.

Gumdrop floats away ill. by author. G. Stevens, 1985. ISBN 0-918831-09-1 Subj: Automobiles. Sea & seashore.

Gumdrop gets a lift ill. by author. G. Stevens, 1986. ISBN 1-55532-009-0 Subj: Automobiles. Behavior – carelessness. Behavior – needing someone.

Gumdrop gets his wings ill. by author. Children's Book Co., 1982. ISBN 0-685-42939-3 Subj: Automobiles.

Gumdrop goes to school ill. by author. G. Stevens, 1986. ISBN 1-55532-008-2 Subj: Automobiles. Behavior – misbehavior. School.

Gumdrop has a birthday ill. by author. Children's Book Co., 1982. ISBN 0-89813-055-7 Subj: Automobiles. Birthdays.

Gumdrop in double trouble ill. by author. Children's Book Co., 1982. ISBN 0-898130-54-9 Subj: Automobiles. Crime.

Gumdrop is the best ill. by author. G. Stevens, 1985. ISBN 0-918831-12-1 Subj: Automobiles.

Gumdrop on the Brighton run ill. by author. Hodder & Stoughton, 1976. ISBN 0-34020-213-0 Subj: Automobiles. Sports – racing.

Gumdrop races a train ill. by author. G. Stevens, 1986. ISBN 1-55532-012-0 Subj: Automobiles. Sports – racing. Trains.

Gumdrop, the adventures of a vintage car ill. by author. Follett, 1967, c1966. Subj: Automobiles.

Jack and the beanstalk (Jack and the beanstalk)

Miranda's umbrella ill. by author. Peter Bedrick, 1990. ISBN 0-87226-429-7 Subj: Giants. Umbrellas. Witches.

The pied piper of Hamelin ill. by reteller. Silver Burdett, 1985. ISBN 0-382-09014-4 Subj: Animals – rats. Behavior – trickery. Folk & fairy tales. Foreign lands – Germany. Middle Ages.

The three little pigs (The three little pigs)

Tobias and the dragon: a Hungarian folk tale ill. by author. Bedrick/Blackie, 1989. ISBN 0-8722-6427-0 Subj: Dragons. Folk & fairy tales.

The wind in the willows: home sweet home (Grahame, Kenneth)

The wind in the willows: the open road (Grahame, Kenneth)

The wind in the willows: the river bank (Grahame, Kenneth)

The wind in the willows: the wild wood (Grahame, Kenneth)

Birrer, Cynthia. *The lady and the unicorn* by Cynthia & William Birrer; ill. by authors. Lothrop, 1987. ISBN 0-688-04038-1 Subj: Character traits – kindness to animals. Folk & fairy tales. Magic. Mythical creatures – unicorns. Royalty – princes.

Song to Demeter by Cynthia & William Birrer; ill. by authors. Lothrop, 1987. ISBN 0-688-04041-1 Subj: Folk & fairy tales. Foreign lands – Greece.

Birrer, William. *The lady and the unicorn* (Birrer, Cynthia)

Song to Demeter (Birrer, Cynthia)

Bischhoff-Miersch, Andrea. *Do you know the difference?* by Andrea & Michael Bischhoff-Miersch; ill. by Christine Faltermayr. North-South, 1995. Translated by Rosemary Lanning. ISBN 1-55858-372-6 Subj: Animals.

Bischhoff-Miersch, Michael. *Do you know the difference?* (Bischhoff-Miersch, Andrea)

Bishop, Adela. *The Christmas polar bear* ill. by Carole Czapla. DOT Garnet, 1991. ISBN 0-9625620-2-5 Subj: Animals – polar bears. Holidays – Christmas.

The Easter wolf ill. by Carole Czapla. Garnet, 1988. ISBN 0-9625620-1-7 Subj: Animals – rabbits. Animals – wolves. Birds – chickens. Character traits – kindness. Holidays – Easter.

Bishop, Ann. *Chicken riddle* ill. by Jerry Warshaw. A. Whitman, 1972. ISBN 0-8075-1170-4 Subj: Birds – chickens. Humorous stories. Riddles & jokes.

The Ella Fannie elephant riddle book ill. by Jerry Warshaw. A. Whitman, 1974. ISBN 0-8075-1966-9 Subj: Animals – elephants. Humorous stories. Riddles & jokes.

Hey riddle riddle ill. by Jerry Warshaw. A. Whitman, 1968. ISBN 0-8075-3257-6 Subj: Humorous stories. Riddles & jokes.

Merry-go-riddle ill. by Jerry Warshaw. A. Whitman, 1973. ISBN 0-8075-5072-8 Subj: Humorous stories. Riddles & jokes.

Noah riddle? ill. by Jerry Warshaw. A. Whitman, 1970. ISBN 0-8075-5702-1 Subj: Humorous stories. Riddles & jokes.

Oh, riddlesticks! ill. by Jerry Warshaw. A. Whitman, 1976. ISBN 0-8075-5916-4 Subj: Humorous stories. Riddles & jokes.

The riddle ages ill. by Jerry Warshaw. A. Whitman, 1977. ISBN 0-8075-6965-8 Subj: Humorous stories. Middle Ages. Riddles & jokes.

Riddle-iculous rid-alphabet book ill. by Jerry Warshaw. A. Whitman, 1971. ISBN 0-8075-6970-4 Subj: ABC books. Humorous stories. Riddles & jokes.

Wild Bill Hiccup's riddle book ed. by Caroline Rubin; ill. by Jerry Warshaw. A. Whitman, 1969. ISBN 0-8075-9097-5 Subj: Cowboys, cowgirls. Humorous stories. Riddles & jokes. U.S. history – frontier & pioneer life.

Bishop, Bonnie. *No one noticed Ralph* ill. by Jack Kent. Doubleday, 1979. ISBN 0-385-12159-8 Subj: Behavior – unnoticed, unseen. Birds – parakeets, parrots.

Ralph rides away ill. by Jack Kent. Doubleday, 1979. ISBN 0-385-14214-5 Subj: Activities – picnicking. Birds – parakeets, parrots. Zoos.

Bishop, Brett. *Clayton's path* by Brett Bishop & Laura Olson; ill. by Mona Eagle. Apogee, 2001. ISBN 0-9700035-3-6 Subj: Animals – mules. Handicaps – ADD. Self-concept.

Bishop, Claire Huchet. *The five Chinese brothers* by Claire Huchet Bishop & Kurt Wiese; ill. by Kurt Wiese. Coward, 1938. ISBN 0-698-20044-6 Subj: Character traits – cleverness. Family life. Folk & fairy tales. Foreign lands – China.

The man who lost his head ill. by Robert McCloskey. Viking, 1942. ISBN 0-670-45349-8 Subj: Anatomy – heads. Humorous stories.

The truffle pig ill. by Kurt Wiese. Coward, 1971. Subj: Animals – pigs. Foreign lands – France. Pets.

Twenty-two bears ill. by Kurt Wiese. Viking, 1964. Subj: Animals – bears. Counting, numbers. Cumulative tales.

Bishop, Gavin. *Chicken Licken* (Chicken Little)

Little Rabbit and the sea ill. by author. North-South, 1997. ISBN 1-55858-810-8 Subj: Animals – rabbits. Imagination. Sea & seashore.

Maui and the sun: a Maori tale ill. by author. North-South, 1996. ISBN 1-55858-578-8 Subj: Behavior – trickery. Folk & fairy tales. Foreign lands – New Zealand. Sun.

Mrs. McGinty and the bizarre plant ill. by author. Oxford Univ. Pr., 1983. ISBN 0-19-558074-5 Subj: Gardens, gardening. Plants.

The three little pigs (The three little pigs)

Bishop, Roma. *Animals* ill. by author. S&S, 1991. ISBN 0-671-74833-5 Subj: Animals. Format, unusual – board books. Format, unusual – toy & movable books.

Christmas songs ill. by author; paper engineering by Ruth Mawdsley; designed & conceived by Graham Brown. Little Simon, 1994. ISBN 0-671-89516-8 Subj: Format, unusual – toy & movable books. Holidays – Christmas. Music.

Easter counting ill. by author; paper engineering by Ruth Mawdsley. Little Simon, 1996. ISBN 0-689-80612-4 Subj: Counting, numbers. Format, unusual – toy & movable books. Holidays – Easter.

Easter egg hunt ill. by author; paper engineering by Ruth Mawdsley. Little Simon, 1996. ISBN 0-689-80613-2 Subj: Format, unusual – toy & movable books. Holidays – Easter.

Holiday cheer ill. by author; paper engineering by Ruth Mawdsley; designed & conceived by Graham Brown. S&S, 1994. ISBN 0-671-89518-4 Subj: Format, unusual – toy & movable books. Holidays – Christmas.

My first pop-up book of dinosaurs ill. by author; conceived & designed by Graham Brown & Ruth Mawdsley; paper engineering by Ruth Mawdsley; written by Sarah Fabiny. S&S, 1993. ISBN 0-671-86723-7 Subj: Dinosaurs. Format, unusual – toy & movable books. Prehistory.

My first pop-up book of prehistoric animals ill. by author; conceived & designed by Graham Brown & Ruth Mawdsley; paper engineering by Ruth Mawdsley; written by Sarah Hewetson. Little Simon, 1994. ISBN 0-671-89556-7 Subj: Animals. Format, unusual – toy & movable books. Prehistory.

Numbers ill. by author. S&S, 1991. ISBN 0-671-74832-7 Subj: Counting, numbers. Format, unusual – board books. Format, unusual – toy & movable books.

On a safari ill. by author. Little Simon, 1993. ISBN 0-671-88309-7 Subj: Animals. Foreign lands – Africa. Format, unusual – toy & movable books.

Santa pays a visit ill. by author; paper engineering by Ruth Mawdsley; designed & conceived by Graham Brown. S&S, 1994. ISBN 0-671-89519-2 Subj: Format, unusual – toy & movable books. Holidays – Christmas. Santa Claus.

Shapes ill. by author. S&S, 1991. ISBN 0-671-74830-0 Subj: Concepts – shape. Format, unusual – board books. Format, unusual – toy & movable books.

Toys ill. by author. S&S, 1991. ISBN 0-671-74831-9 Subj: Format, unusual – board books. Format, unusual – toy & movable books. Toys.

Bishop, Rudine Sims. *Wonders: the best children's poems of Effie Lee Newsome* (Newsome, Effie Lee)

Bittner, Wolfgang. *Wake up, Grizzly!* ill. by Gustavo Rosemffet; trans. by J. Alison James. North-South, 1996. ISBN 1-55858-519-2 Subj: Animals – bears. Family life. Family life – fathers. Imagination.

Bix, Cynthia Overbeck. *Water, water everywhere* (Rauzon, Mark J.)

Black, Algernon D. *The woman of the wood: a tale from old Russia* ill. by Evaline Ness. Holt, 1973. ISBN 0-03-007436-3 Subj: Folk & fairy tales. Foreign lands – Russia.

Black, Charles C. *The royal nap* ill. by James Stevenson. Viking, 1995. ISBN 0-670-85863-3 Subj: Animals. Hiccups. Middle Ages. Music. Royalty – kings. Sleep.

Black, Floyd. *Alphabet cat* ill. by Carol Nicklaus. Elsevier-Dutton, 1979. ISBN 0-525-69009-3 Subj: ABC books. Animals – cats. Animals – rats.

Black, Harley. *Amazing magic school* ill. by Dana Regan. Sterling, 2000. ISBN 0-8069-1553-6 Subj: Animals. Art. Concepts – color. Format, unusual – toy & movable books. Magic. School – first day.

Magic art class ill. by author. Sterling, 2000. ISBN 0-8069-0600-6 Subj: Activities – painting. Concepts – color. Format, unusual – toy & movable books.

Black, Irma (Simonton). *Big puppy and little puppy* ill. by Theresa Sherman. Holiday, 1960. Subj: Animals – dogs. Concepts – size.

Is this my dinner? ill. by Rosalind Fry. A. Whitman, 1972. ISBN 0-8075-3665-2 Subj: Food. Participation. Rhyming text.

The little old man who could not read ill. by Seymour Fleishman. A. Whitman, 1968. ISBN 0-8075-4621-6 Subj: Books, reading. Shopping.

The taxi that hurried (Mitchell, Lucy Sprague)

Black, Sonia. *Hanging out with Mom* ill. by George Ford. Scholastic, 2000. ISBN 0-590-86636-2 Subj: Family life – mothers. Parks. Rhyming text.

Blackaby, Susan. *The emperor's new clothes* (Andersen, H. C. [Hans Christian])

The little mermaid (Andersen, H. C. [Hans Christian])

The princess and the pea (Andersen, H. C. [Hans Christian])

Rembrandt's hat ill. by Mary Newell DePalma. Houghton, 2002. ISBN 0-618-11452-1 Subj: Animals – bears. Behavior – lost & found possessions. Clothing – hats.

The steadfast tin soldier (Andersen, H. C. [Hans Christian])

Thumbelina (Andersen, H. C. [Hans Christian])

The ugly duckling (Andersen, H. C. [Hans Christian])

Blacker, Terence. *Herbie Hamster, where are you?* ill. by Pippa Unwin. Random House, 1990. ISBN 0-679-80838-8 Subj: Animals – hamsters. Behavior – hiding. Games.

Blackmore, Vivien. *Why corn is golden: stories about plants* ill. by Susana Martínez-Ostos. Little, 1984. ISBN 0-316-54820-0 Subj: Folk & fairy tales. Foreign lands – Mexico. Plants.

Blackstone, Margaret. *This is baseball* ill. by John O'Brien. Holt, 1993. ISBN 0-8050-2390-9 Subj: Sports – baseball.

This is figure skating ill. by John O'Brien. Holt, 1998. ISBN 0-8050-3706-3 Subj: Sports – ice skating.

Blackstone, Stella. *Baby high, baby low* ill. by Denise [Fraifield] & Fernando [Azevedo]. Holiday, 1998. ISBN 0-8234-1345-4 Subj: Babies. Concepts. Concepts – opposites. Rhyming text.

Bear at home ill. by Debbie Harter. Barefoot, 2001. ISBN 1-84148-436-9 Subj: Animals – bears. Homes, houses. Rhyming text.

Bear in a square ill. by Debbie Harter. Barefoot, 1998. ISBN 1-84148-120-3 Subj: Animals – bears. Concepts – shape. Concepts – size. Counting, numbers.

Bear in sunshine ill. by Debbie Harter. Barefoot, 2001. ISBN 1-84148-321-4 Subj: Animals – bears. Rhyming text. Weather.

Bear on a bike ill. by Debbie Harter. Barefoot, 1999. ISBN 1-84148-121-1 Subj: Animals – bears. Ethnic groups in the U.S. – African Americans. Sports – bicycling.

Bear's busy family ill. by Debbie Harter. Barefoot, 1999. ISBN 1-84148-391-5 Subj: Animals – bears. Concepts – color. Rhyming text. Senses.

Cleo and Caspar (Mockford, Caroline)

Cleo in the snow (Mockford, Caroline)

Cleo on the move (Mockford, Caroline)

Cleo the cat (Mockford, Caroline)

Cleo's alphabet book (Mockford, Caroline)

Cleo's counting book (Mockford, Caroline)

How big is a pig? ill. by Clare Beaton. Barefoot, 2000. ISBN 1-84148-077-0 Subj: Activities – storytelling. Animals. Farms. Rhyming text.

An island in the sun ill. by Nicoletta Ceccoli. Barefoot, 2002. ISBN 1-84148-193-9 Subj: Animals – dogs. Cumulative tales. Islands. Rhyming text. Sea & seashore. Sports – sailing.

Making minestrone ill. by Nan Brooks. Barefoot, 2000. ISBN 1-84148-211-0 Subj: Activities – baking, cooking. Food.

Secret seahorse ill. by Clare Beaton. Barefoot, 2004. ISBN 1-84148-704-X Subj: Animals. Fish – seahorses. Foreign lands – South Sea Islands. Rhyming text. Sea & seashore.

Secret seahorse [board book] ill. by Clare Beaton. Barefoot, 2005. ISBN 1-905236-15-8 Subj: Animals. Fish – seahorses. Foreign lands – South Sea Islands. Format, unusual – board books. Rhyming text. Sea & seashore.

Who are you? by Stella Blackstone & Debbie Harter; ill. by Debbie Harter. Abbeville, 1996. ISBN 0-7892-0291-3 Subj: Animals. Format, unusual – board books. Rhyming text.

You and me ill. by Giovanni Manna. Barefoot, 2000. ISBN 1-84148-263-3 Subj: Activities. Concepts – opposites.

Blackwood, Gladys Rourke. *Whistle for Cindy* ill. by author. A. Whitman, 1952. Subj: Activities – whistling. Animals – dogs. Pets.

Blackwood, Mary. *Derek the knitting dinosaur* ill. by Kerry Argent. Carolrhoda, 1990. ISBN 0-87614-400-8 Subj: Activities – knitting. Dinosaurs. Gender roles. Prehistory. Rhyming text.

Blades, Ann. *Back to the cabin* ill. by author. Orca, 1997. ISBN 1-55143-049-5 Subj: Activities – vacationing. Family life. Seasons – summer.

A boy of Taché ill. by author. Tundra, 1995. ISBN 0-8877-6350-2 Subj: Family life – grandfathers. Foreign lands – Canada. Indians of North America – Carrier.

Fall ill. by author. Lothrop, 1990. ISBN 0-688-09232-2 Subj: Format, unusual – board books. Seasons – fall. Wordless.

Mary of mile 18 ill. by author. Tundra, 2001. ISBN 0-88776-581-5 Subj: Animals – dogs. Animals – wolves. Character traits – perseverance. Farms. Foreign lands – Canada. Seasons – winter.

Spring ill. by author. Lothrop, 1990. ISBN 0-688-09230-6 Subj: Format, unusual – board books. Seasons – spring. Wordless.

Summer ill. by author. Lothrop, 1989. ISBN 0-888-99091-X Subj: Family life – brothers. Family life – sisters. Farms. Format, unusual – board books. Seasons – summer. Wordless.

Too small ill. by author. Douglas & McIntyre, 2000. ISBN 0-88899-400-1 Subj: Concepts – size. Family life. Foreign lands – Canada. Moving.

Winter ill. by author. Lothrop, 1990. ISBN 0-888-99093-6 Subj: Family life – brothers. Family life – sisters. Format, unusual – board books. Seasons – winter. Weather – snow. Wordless.

Blaich, Ute. *The star* ill. by Julie Litty. North-South, 2001. ISBN 0-7358-1510-0 Subj: Animals. Birds – owls. Character traits – kindness. Holidays – Christmas. Religion – Nativity.

Blaine, Marge (Margery Kay). *The terrible thing that happened at our house* ill. by John Wallner. Parents' Magazine Pr., 1975. ISBN 0-819-30782-3 Subj: Family life. Family life – mothers. Problem solving.

Blair, Eric. *Belling the cat* (Æsop)

The boy who cried wolf (Æsop)

The brave little tailor (Grimm, Jacob)

The Bremen town musicians (Grimm, Jacob)

The country mouse and the city mouse (Æsop)

The crow and the pitcher (Æsop)

The dog and the wolf (Æsop)

The donkey in the lion's skin (Æsop)

The fisherman and his wife (Grimm, Jacob)

The frog prince (Grimm, Jacob)

Hansel and Gretel (Grimm, Jacob)

Rumpelstiltskin (Grimm, Jacob)

The shoemaker and his elves (Grimm, Jacob)

Snow White (Grimm, Jacob)

Blake, Claire. *The paper chain* by Claire Blake, Eliza Blanchard, Kathy Parkinson; ill. by Kathy Parkinson. Health Pr., 1998. ISBN 0-929173-28-7 Subj: Family life. Family life – mothers. Illness – cancer.

Blake, Jon. *Wriggly Pig* ill. by Susie Jenkin-Pearce. Morrow, 1992. ISBN 0-688-11296-X Subj: Animals – pigs. Behavior. Family life.

You're a hero, Daley B.! ill. by Axel Scheffler. Candlewick, 1994. ISBN 1-56402-367-2 Subj: Animals – rabbits. Animals – weasels.

Blake, Olive. *see* Supraner, Robyn

Blake, Pamela. *Peep-show: a little book of rhymes* ill. by author. Macmillan, 1973. Subj: Nursery rhymes.

Blake, Quentin. *All join in* ill. by author. Little, 1991. ISBN 0-316-09934-1 Subj: Participation. Poetry.

Clown ill. by author. Holt, 1996. ISBN 0-8050-4399-3 Subj: Family life. Friendship. Toys. Wordless.

Cockatoos ill. by author. Little, 1992. ISBN 0-316-09951-1 Subj: Behavior – hiding. Birds – cockatoos. Counting, numbers. Games.

Fantastic Daisy Artichoke ill. by author. Red Fox, 2001. ISBN 0-09-940006-5 Subj: Animals. Friendship. Rhyming text.

Mister Magnolia ill. by author. Jonathan Cape, 1980. ISBN 0-224-10612-1 Subj: Humorous stories. Rhyming text.

Mrs. Armitage and the big wave ill. by author. Harcourt, 1997. ISBN 0-15-201642-2 Subj: Animals – dogs. Sea & seashore. Sports – surfing.

Mrs. Armitage on wheels ill. by author. Knopf, 1988. ISBN 0-394-99498-1 Subj: Humorous stories. Sports – bicycling.

Mrs. Armitage: queen of the road ill. by author. Peachtree, 2003. ISBN 1-56145-287-4 Subj: Animals – dogs. Automobiles. Family life – aunts, uncles. Motorcycles.

Quentin Blake's ABC ill. by author. Knopf, 1989. ISBN 0-394-94149-7 Subj: ABC books. Rhyming text.

Quentin Blake's nursery rhyme book ill. by author. HarperCollins, 1984. ISBN 0-06-020532-6 Subj: Humorous stories. Nursery rhymes.

Simpkin ill. by author. Viking, 1994. ISBN 0-670-85371-2 Subj: Concepts – opposites. Family life – brothers & sisters. Rhyming text.

Snuff ill. by author. Lippincott, 1973. ISBN 0-397-31469-8 Subj: Crime. Knights.

The story of the dancing frog ill. by author. Knopf, 1985. ISBN 0-394-97033-0 Subj: Folk & fairy tales.

Zagazoo ill. by author. Orchard, 1998. ISBN 0-531-30178-8 Subj: Animals. Animals – babies. Behavior – imitation. Monsters.

Blake, Robert J. *Akiak: a tale from the Iditarod* ill. by author. Philomel, 1997. ISBN 0-399-22798-9 Subj: Alaska. Animals – dogs. Sports – racing.

Fledgling ill. by author. Philomel, 2000. ISBN 0-399-23321-0 Subj: Activities – flying. Birds – kestrels. Cities, towns.

The perfect spot ill. by author. Putnam, 1992. ISBN 0-399-22132-8 Subj: Family life – fathers. Forest, woods. Nature.

Spray ill. by author. Philomel, 1996. ISBN 0-399-22770-9 Subj: Boats, ships. Islands. Sea & seashore.

Yudonsi: a tale from the canyons ill. by author. Philomel, 1999. ISBN 0-399-23320-2 Subj: Behavior – misbehavior. Indians of North America.

Blake, William. *The tyger* ill. by Neil Waldman. Harcourt, 1993. ISBN 0-15-292375-6 Subj: Animals – tigers. Creation. Format, unusual. Poetry.

Blakeley, Peggy. *Two little ducks* ill. by Kenzo Kobayashi. Alphabet Pr., 1984. ISBN 0-9072-3407-0 Subj: Communities, neighborhoods.

What shall I be tomorrow? ill. by Helga Aichinger. Alphabet Pr., 1984. ISBN 0-907234-51-8 Subj: Behavior – imitation. Imagination.

Blance, Ellen. *Lady Monster has a plan* by Ellen Blance & Ann Cook; ill. by Quentin Blake. Bowmar, 1977. ISBN 0-8372-2135-8 Subj: Monsters.

Lady Monster helps out by Ellen Blance & Ann Cook; ill. by Quentin Blake. Bowmar, 1977. ISBN 0-8372-2126-9 Subj: Monsters.

Monster and the magic umbrella by Ellen Blance & Ann Cook; ill. by Quentin Blake. Bowmar, 1973. ISBN 0-8372-0835-1 Subj: Magic. Monsters. Umbrellas.

Monster and the mural by Ellen Blance & Ann Cook; ill. by Quentin Blake. Bowmar, 1977. ISBN 0-8372-2124-2 Subj: Monsters.

Monster and the surprise cookie by Ellen Blance & Ann Cook; ill. by Quentin Blake. Bowmar, 1977. ISBN 0-8372-2131-5 Subj: Monsters.

Monster at school by Ellen Blance & Ann Cook; ill. by Quentin Blake. Bowmar, 1973. ISBN 0-8372-0834-3 Subj: Monsters. School.

Monster buys a pet by Ellen Blance & Ann Cook; ill. by Quentin Blake. Bowmar, 1977. ISBN 0-8372-2134-X Subj: Monsters. Pets.

Monster cleans his house by Ellen Blance & Ann Cook; ill. by Quentin Blake. Bowmar, 1973. ISBN 0-8372-0828-9 Subj: Monsters.

Monster comes to the city by Ellen Blance & Ann Cook; ill. by Quentin Blake. Bowmar, 1973. ISBN 0-8372-0826-2 Subj: Cities, towns. Monsters.

Monster gets a job by Ellen Blance & Ann Cook; ill. by Quentin Blake. Bowmar, 1977. ISBN 0-8372-2130-7 Subj: Activities – working. Monsters.

Monster goes around the town by Ellen Blance & Ann Cook; ill. by Quentin Blake. Bowmar, 1977. ISBN 0-8372-2132-3 Subj: Monsters.

Monster goes to school by Ellen Blance & Ann Cook; ill. by Quentin Blake. Bowmar, 1973. ISBN 0-8372-0834-3 Subj: Monsters. School.

Monster goes to the beach by Ellen Blance & Ann Cook; ill. by Quentin Blake. Bowmar, 1977. ISBN 0-8372-2129-3 Subj: Monsters. Sea & seashore – beaches.

Monster goes to the circus by Ellen Blance & Ann Cook; ill. by Quentin Blake. Bowmar, 1977. ISBN 0-8372-2127-7 Subj: Circus. Monsters.

Monster goes to the hospital by Ellen Blance & Ann Cook; ill. by Quentin Blake. Bowmar, 1977. ISBN 0-8372-2128-5 Subj: Hospitals. Monsters.

Monster goes to the museum by Ellen Blance & Ann Cook; ill. by Quentin Blake. Bowmar, 1973. ISBN 0-8372-0832-7 Subj: Monsters. Museums.

Monster goes to the zoo by Ellen Blance & Ann Cook; ill. by Quentin Blake. Bowmar, 1973. ISBN 0-8372-0837-8 Subj: Monsters. Zoos.

Monster has a party by Ellen Blance & Ann Cook; ill. by Quentin Blake. Bowmar, 1973. ISBN 0-8372-0836-X Subj: Monsters. Parties.

Monster, Lady Monster and the bike ride by Ellen Blance & Ann Cook; ill. by Quentin Blake. Bowmar, 1977. ISBN 0-8372-2125-0 Subj: Monsters. Sports – bicycling.

Monster looks for a friend by Ellen Blance & Ann Cook; ill. by Quentin Blake. Bowmar, 1973. ISBN 0-8372-0829-7 Subj: Friendship. Monsters.

Monster looks for a house by Ellen Blance & Ann Cook; ill. by Quentin Blake. Bowmar, 1973. ISBN 0-8372-0827-0 Subj: Monsters.

Monster meets Lady Monster by Ellen Blance & Ann Cook; ill. by Quentin Blake. Bowmar, 1973. ISBN 0-8372-0831-9 Subj: Monsters.

Monster on the bus by Ellen Blance & Ann Cook; ill. by Quentin Blake. Bowmar, 1973. ISBN 0-8372-0830-0 Subj: Buses. Monsters.

Blanchard, Arlene. *The naughty lamb* ill. by Tony Wells. Dial, 1989. ISBN 0-8037-0605-7 Subj: Animals – sheep. Behavior – hiding. Farms. Games.

Sounds my feet make ill. by Vanessa Julian-Ottie. Random House, 1989. ISBN 0-394-89648-3 Subj: Anatomy – feet. Noise, sounds.

Blanchard, Eliza. *The paper chain* (Blake, Claire)

Bland, Fabian. *see* Nesbit, Edith

Blathwayt, Benedict. *Bear's adventure* ill. by author. Knopf, 1988. ISBN 0-394-90568-7 Subj: Animals – bears.

The runaway train ill. by author. Trafalgar Square, 1996. ISBN 1-85681-077-1 Subj: Foreign lands – England. Sea & seashore. Trains.

Tangle and the firesticks ill. by author. Knopf, 1997. ISBN 0-394-98827-2 Subj: Fire. Imagination.

Tangle and the silver bird ill. by author. Knopf, 1989. ISBN 0-394-92780-X Subj: Activities – flying. Animals.

Blau, Judith. *Bunny Mitten's book* ill. by author. Random House, 1991. ISBN 0-679-81315-2 Subj: Animals – rabbits. Puppets.

Blaustein, Muriel. *Baby Mabu and Auntie Moose* ill. by author. Four Winds, 1983. ISBN 0-590-07874-7 Subj: Activities – babysitting. Behavior – misbehavior. Character traits – freedom. Family life – aunts, uncles.

Bedtime, Zachary! ill. by author. HarperCollins, 1987. ISBN 0-06-020537-7 Subj: Animals – tigers. Bedtime. Behavior – misbehavior. Family life.

Jim chimp's story ill. by author. S&S, 1992. ISBN 0-671-74779-7 Subj: Animals – chimpanzees. Character traits – shyness. Imagination. School.

Make friends, Zachary! ill. by author. HarperCollins, 1990. ISBN 0-06-020546-6 Subj: Animals – tigers. Camps, camping. Friendship.

Play ball, Zachary! ill. by author. HarperCollins, 1988. ISBN 0-06-020544-X Subj: Family life – fathers. Sports.

Blazek, Sarah Kirwan. *An Irish Hallowe'en* ill. by James Rice. Pelican, 1999. ISBN 1-56554-413-7 Subj: Foreign lands – Ireland. Holidays – Halloween. Mythical creatures – goblins. Rhyming text.

Blech, Dietlind. *Hello Irina* ill. by author; trans. by Yaak Karsunke. Holt, 1971. Tr. of Allo Irina. ISBN 0-582-16422-2 Subj: Activities – traveling. Animals – horses, ponies.

Blegvad, Erik. *Burnie's hill: a traditional rhyme* ill. by author. Atheneum, 1977. ISBN 0-689-50070-X Subj: Cumulative tales. Foreign lands – Scotland. Nursery rhymes. Seasons.

The emperor's new clothes (Andersen, H. C. [Hans Christian])

One is for the sun (Blegvad, Lenore)

The swineherd (Andersen, H. C. [Hans Christian])

Blegvad, Lenore. *Anna Banana and me* ill. by Erik Blegvad. Atheneum, 1985. ISBN 0-689-50274-5 Subj: Character traits – bravery. Emotions – fear. Imagination.

First friends ill. by Erik Blebgad. HarperFestival, 2000. ISBN 0-694-01273-4 Subj: Behavior – sharing. Friendship. Rhyming text.

The great hamster hunt ill. by Erik Blegvad. Harcourt, 1969. ISBN 0-15-232500-X Subj: Animals – hamsters. Pets.

Hark! Hark! The dogs do bark, and other poems about dogs ill. by Erik Blegvad. Atheneum, 1975. ISBN 0-689-50035-1 Subj: Animals – dogs. Nursery rhymes.

Mr. Jensen and cat ill. by Erik Blegvad. Harcourt, 1965. ISBN 0-15-256214-1 Subj: Animals – cats. Emotions – loneliness. Foreign lands – Denmark.

Mittens for kittens and other rhymes about cats ill. by Erik Blegvad. Atheneum, 1974. ISBN 0-689-50003-3 Subj: Animals – cats. Nursery rhymes.

Once upon a time and Grandma ill. by author. McElderry, 1993. ISBN 0-689-50548-5 Subj: Cities, towns. Family life – grandmothers.

One is for the sun by Lenore & Erik Blegvad; ill. by Erik Blegvad. Harcourt, 1968. Subj: Counting, numbers. Rhyming text.

The parrot in the garret and other rhymes about dwellings ill. by Erik Blegvad. Atheneum, 1982. ISBN 0-689-50217-6 Subj: Birds – parakeets, parrots. Homes, houses. Poetry.

Rainy day Kate ill. by Erik Blegvad. Macmillan, 1988. ISBN 0-689-50442-X Subj: Activities – playing. Imagination. Toys – dolls. Weather – rain.

This is me ill. by Erik Blegvad. Random House, 1986. ISBN 0-394-87816-7 Subj: Anatomy. Format, unusual – board books. Rhyming text. Self-concept.

This little pig-a-wig and other rhymes about pigs ill. by Erik Blegvad. Atheneum, 1978. ISBN 0-689-50110-2 Subj: Animals – pigs. Nursery rhymes.

Bless the beasts: *children's prayers & poems about animals* collected by June Cotner; ill. by Kris Waldherr. SeaStar, 2002. ISBN 1-58717-176-7 Subj: Animals. Poetry. Religion.

Bliss, Austin. *That dog Melly!* (Bliss, Corinne Demas)

Bliss, Corinne Demas. *The boy who was generous with salt* ill. by Michael Hays. Cavendish, 2002. ISBN 0-7614-5099-8 Subj: Birthdays. Careers – chefs, cooks. Careers – fishermen. Sea & seashore.

The disappearing island ill. by Ted Lewin. S&S, 2000. ISBN 0-689-80539-X Subj: Birthdays. Boats, ships. Family life – grandmothers. Islands.

Hurricane! ill. by Lenice Strohmeier. Cavendish, 2000. ISBN 0-7614-5052-1 Subj: U.S. history. Weather – hurricanes.

The littlest matryoshka ill. by Kathryn Brown. Hyperion, 1999. ISBN 0-7868-0153-0 Subj: Behavior – lost. Toys – dolls.

The magic apple ill. by Alexi Natchev. Golden Bks., 2001. ISBN 0-307-46334-6 Subj: Character traits – generosity. Family life – sisters. Folk & fairy tales. Royalty – princes.

Matthew's meadow ill. by Ted Lewin. Harcourt, 1992. ISBN 0-15-200759-8 Subj: Birds – hawks. Nature. Seasons – fall.

Nina's waltz ill. by Deborah Lanino. Orchard, 2000. ISBN 0-531-33281-0 Subj: Contests. Family life – fathers. Music. Songs.

That dog Melly! by Corinne Demas Bliss with Austin Bliss; photos by Corinne Demas Bliss & Jim Judkis. Hastings House, 1981. ISBN 0-8038-7217-8 Subj: Animals – dogs. Friendship. Pets.

Blizzard, Gladys S. *Come look with me: enjoying art with children.* Thomasson-Grant, 1991. ISBN 0-934738-76-9 Subj: Art.

Come look with me: world of play ill. by author. Thomasson-Grant, 1993. ISBN 1-56566-031-5 Subj: Activities – playing. Art. Games.

Block party today ill. by Stéphanie Roth. Knopf, 2004. ISBN 0-375-92216-4 Subj: Communities, neighborhoods. Friendship. Parties.

Blocksma, Dewey. *Easy-to-make spaceships that really fly* (Blocksma, Mary)

Blocksma, Mary. *Apple tree! Apple tree!* ill. by Sandra Cox Kalthoff. Childrens Pr., 1983. ISBN 0-516-01584-2 Subj: Seasons. Trees.

The best dressed bear ill. by Sandra Cox Kalthoff. Childrens Pr., 1984. ISBN 0-516-01585-0 Subj: Activities – dancing. Animals – bears. Clothing.

Did you hear that? ill. by Sandra Cox Kalthoff. Childrens Pr., 1983. ISBN 0-516-01581-8 Subj: Bedtime. Night. Noise, sounds.

Easy-to-make spaceships that really fly by Mary & Dewey Blocksma; ill. by Marisabina Russo. Prentice-Hall, 1983. ISBN 0-13-223180-8 Subj: Activities – making things. Space & space ships.

Grandma Dragon's birthday ill. by Sandra Cox Kalthoff. Childrens Pr., 1983. ISBN 0-516-01582-6 Subj: Birthdays.

The pup went up ill. by Sandra Cox Kalthoff. Childrens Pr., 1983. ISBN 0-516-01583-4 Subj: Animals – dogs. Imagination.

Rub-a-dub-dub: what's in the tub? ill. by Sandra Cox Kalthoff. Childrens Pr., 1984. ISBN 0-516-01586-9 Subj: Activities – bathing. Animals – dogs.

Where's that duck? ill. by Sandra Cox Kalthoff. Childrens Pr., 1985. ISBN 0-516-01587-7 Subj: Birds – ducks. Farms. Rhyming text.

Blomgren, Jennifer. *Where do I sleep?* ill. by Andrea Gabriel. Sasquatch, 2001. ISBN 1-57061-258-7 Subj: Animals – babies. Lullabies. Rhyming text. Sleep.

Blood, Charles L. *The goat in the rug* by Charles L. Blood & Martin A. Link; ill. by Nancy Winslow Parker. Parents' Magazine Pr., 1976. ISBN 0-819-30828-5 Subj: Activities – weaving. Animals – goats. Indians of North America – Navajo.

Bloom, Becky. *Crackers* ill. by Pascal Biet. Orchard, 2001. ISBN 0-531-30326-8 Subj: Activities – working. Animals – cats. Animals – mice. Character traits – kindness.

Mice make trouble ill. by Pascal Biet. Orchard, 2000. ISBN 0-531-33253-5 Subj: Activities – drawing. Animals – mice. Magic.

Mr. Cuckoo ill. by author. Mondo, 1998. ISBN 1-57255-626-9 Subj: Animals. Birds – cuckoos. Clocks, watches. Time.

Wolf ill. by author. Orchard, 1999. ISBN 0-531-33155-5 Subj: Animals. Animals – wolves. Books, reading.

Bloom, Susan (Susan Lynn). *The best place to read* (Bertram, Debbie)

Bloom, Suzanne. *The bus for us* ill. by author. Boyds Mills, 2001. ISBN 1-56397-932-2 Subj: School – first day.

A family for Jamie ill. by author. Crown, 1991. ISBN 0-517-57493-4 Subj: Adoption. Family life.

No place for a pig ill. by author. Boyds Mills, 2003. ISBN 1-59078-047-7 Subj: Animals – pigs. Cities, towns. Homes, houses.

Piggy Monday ill. by author. A. Whitman, 2001. ISBN 0-8075-6529-6 Subj: Animals – pigs. Etiquette. School.

We keep a pig in the parlor ill. by author. Potter/Crown, 1988. ISBN 0-517-56829-2 Subj: Animals – pigs. Farms. Rhyming text.

Bloome, Enid. *The air we breathe!* ill. with photos. Doubleday, 1972. Subj: Ecology.

The water we drink! ill. with photos. Doubleday, 1971. ISBN 0-385-00392-7 Subj: Ecology.

Blos, Joan W. *The days before now: an autobiographical note* (Brown, Margaret Wise)

The grandpa days ill. by Emily Arnold McCully. S&S, 1989. ISBN 0-671-64640-0 Subj: Activities – making things. Family life – grandfathers.

Hello, shoes! ill. by Ann Boyajian. S&S, 1999. ISBN 0-689-81441-0 Subj: Behavior – lost & found possessions. Clothing – shoes. Concepts. Family life – grandfathers.

Martin's hats ill. by Marc Simont. Morrow, 1984. ISBN 0-688-02033-X Subj: Clothing – hats. Imagination.

Old Henry ill. by Stephen Gammell. Morrow, 1987. ISBN 0-688-06400-0 Subj: Behavior – indifference. Character traits – being different. Homes, houses. Rhyming text.

One very best Valentine's Day ill. by Emanuel Schongut. Little Simon, 1989. ISBN 0-671-64639-7 Subj: Holidays – Valentine's Day.

A seed, a flower, a minute, an hour ill. by Hans Poppel. S&S, 1992. ISBN 0-671-73214-5 Subj: Poetry.

Blossom tales ill. by Sarah Dillard. Moon Mt., 2002. ISBN 0-9677929-8-3 Subj: Flowers. Folk & fairy tales. Foreign lands.

Blough, Glenn O. *Christmas trees and how they grow* ill. by Jeanne Bendick. McGraw-Hill, 1961. Subj: Holidays – Christmas. Trees.

Who lives in this meadow? ill. by Jeanne Bendick. McGraw-Hill, 1961. Subj: Animals.

Bloxam, Frances. *Antlers forever!* ill. by Jim Sollers. Down East, 2001. ISBN 0-8927-2512-5 Subj: Animals – moose. Nature.

Blue, Rose. *Black, black, beautiful black* ill. by Emmett Wigglesworth. Watts, 1969. Subj: Ethnic groups in the U.S. – African Americans. Zoos.

How many blocks is the world? ill. by Harold James. Watts, 1970. ISBN 0-531-01836-9 Subj: Cities, towns. Concepts – size. Ethnic groups in the U.S. – African Americans. Family life. School.

I am here = Yo estoy aqui ill. by Moneta Barnett. Watts, 1971. ISBN 0-531-01943-8 Subj: Character traits – being different. Ethnic groups in the U.S. Ethnic groups in the U.S. – Puerto Rican Americans. Foreign languages. School – first day.

Blum, Mark. *Big trucks and diggers in 3-D* ill. by author. Chronicle, 2001. ISBN 0-8118-3172-8 Subj: Format, unusual – toy & movable books. Machines. Tractors. Trucks.

Blumberg, Rhoda. *Bloomers!* ill. by Mary Morgan-Vanroyen. Bradbury, 1993. ISBN 0-02-711684-0 Subj: Clothing. U.S. history.

Jumbo ill. by Jonathan Hunt. Macmillan, 1992. ISBN 0-02-711683-2 Subj: Animals – elephants. Circus. Zoos.

Blume, Judy. *The one in the middle is a green kangaroo* ill. by Irene Trivas. Macmillan, 1991. ISBN 0-02-711055-9 Subj: Family life. Self-concept.

The Pain and The Great One ill. by Irene Trivas. Bradbury, 1984. Orig. pub. in Free to be . . . you and me, McGraw-Hill, 1974. ISBN 0-02-711100-8 Subj: Family life. Sibling rivalry.

Blume, Karin. *Circus* written & ill. by Karin Blume & Brigitte Blume. Abbeville, 1996. ISBN 0-7892-0179-8 Subj: Circus. Format, unusual – board books.

My new friends written & ill. by Karin Blume & Brigitte Blume. Abbeville, 1996. ISBN 0-7892-0180-1 Subj: Anatomy – hands. Format, unusual – board books.

Blumenthal, Deborah. *Aunt Claire's yellow beehive hair* ill. by Mary GrandPré. Dial, 2001. ISBN 0-8037-2509-4 Subj: Behavior – collecting things. Family life. Memories, memory.

Don't let the peas touch! ill. by Timothy Basil Ering. Levine, 2004. ISBN 0-439-29732-X Subj: Family life – sisters. Sibling rivalry.

Ice palace ill. by Ted Rand. Clarion, 2003. ISBN 0-618-15960-6 Subj: Fairs, festivals. Seasons – winter. Sports.

Blumenthal, Nancy. *Count-a-saurus* ill. by Robert Jay Kaufman. Macmillan, 1989. ISBN 0-02-749391-1 Subj: Counting, numbers. Dinosaurs. Rhyming text.

Blundell, Tony. *Beware of boys* ill. by author. Greenwillow, 1992. ISBN 0-688-10925-X Subj: Activities – baking, cooking. Animals – wolves. Character traits – cleverness.

Joe on Sunday ill. by author. Dial, 1987. ISBN 0-8037-0446-1 Subj: Behavior. Imagination.

Bluthenthal, Diana Cain. *I'm not invited?* ill. by author. Atheneum, 2003. ISBN 0-689-84141-8 Subj: Emotions. Friendship. Parties.

Matilda the moocher ill. by author. Orchard, 1997. ISBN 0-531-33003-6 Subj: Behavior. Friendship. School.

Blutig, Eduard. *see* Gorey, Edward (St. John)

Blyler, Allison. *Finding foxes* ill. by Robert J. Blake. Putnam, 1991. ISBN 0-399-22264-2 Subj: Animals – foxes. Nature. Picture puzzles. Rhyming text.

Blyth, Alan. *Cinderella: the story of Rossini's opera* (Perrault, Charles)

Boada, Francesc. *Cinderella = Cenicienta* (Perrault, Charles)

Board, Kjersti. *Bridget and the gray wolves* (Lindbergh, Reeve)

The little jester (Olofsson, Helena)

Boase, Susan. *Lucky boy* ill. by author. Houghton, 2002. ISBN 0-618-13175-2 Subj: Animals – dogs. Behavior – needing someone. Emotions – grief.

Boatfield, Jonny. *The twilight book* ill. by author. Bloomsbury, 2000. ISBN 0-7475-5083-2 Subj: Books, reading. Games. Mystery stories. Puzzles.

Bober, Suzanne. *In the garden with Van Gogh* (Merberg, Julie)

A magical day with Matisse (Merberg, Julie)

Bock, Lee. *Oh, crumps! = Ay, caramba!* ill. by Morgan Midgett; trans. by Eida de la Vega. Raven Tree, 2003. ISBN 0-9720192-4-3 Subj: Animals. Careers – farmers. Farms. Foreign languages. Noise, sounds.

Bodecker, N. M. (Nils Mogens). *Good night little one* (Kraus, Robert)

Good night Richard Rabbit (Kraus, Robert)

Hurry, hurry, Mary dear! ill. by Erik Blegvad. McElderry, 1998. ISBN 0-689-81770-3 Subj: Poetry. Seasons – winter.

"It's raining," said John Twaining: Danish nursery rhymes ill. by author. Atheneum, 1973. ISBN 0-689-30316-5 Subj: Foreign lands – Denmark. Humorous stories. Nursery rhymes.

"Let's marry" said the cherry, and other nonsense poems ill. by author. Atheneum, 1974. ISBN 0-689-50004-1 Subj: Humorous stories. Poetry.

Miss Jaster's garden ill. by author. Golden Bks., 1972. ISBN 0-307-41181-8 Subj: Animals – hedgehogs. Gardens, gardening.

Snowman Sniffles and other verse ill. by author. Atheneum, 1983. ISBN 0-689-50263-X Subj: Humorous stories. Poetry. Tongue twisters.

Bodger, Joan. *Belinda's ball* ill. by Mark Thurman. Atheneum, 1981. ISBN 0-689-30836-1 Subj: Concepts.

Bodkin, Odds. *The Christmas cobwebs* ill. by Terry Widener. Harcourt, 2001. ISBN 0-15-201459-4 Subj: Ethnic groups in the U.S. – German Americans. Family life. Holidays – Christmas. Spiders.

The crane wife ill. by Gennady Spirin. Harcourt, 1998. ISBN 0-15-201407-1 Subj: Activities – weaving. Birds – cranes. Character traits – kindness to animals. Folk & fairy tales. Foreign lands – Japan.

Bodnar, Judit Z. *Tale of a tail* ill. by John Sandford. Lothrop, 1998. ISBN 0-688-12175-6 Subj: Animals – bears. Animals – foxes. Sports – fishing.

A wagonload of fish trans. & adapt. by Judit Z. Bodnar; ill. by Alexi Natchev. Lothrop, 1996. ISBN 0-688-12173-X Subj: Animals – foxes. Character traits – cleverness. Folk & fairy tales. Foreign lands – Hungary. Sports – fishing.

Bodsworth, Nan. *Monkey business* ill. by author. Dial, 1987. ISBN 0-8037-0393-7 Subj: Animals. Behavior – wishing. Imagination. Zoos.

A nice walk in the jungle ill. by author. Viking, 1990. ISBN 0-670-82476-3 Subj: Activities – walking. Foreign lands – Australia. Jungle. Reptiles – snakes.

Bodwell, Gaile. *The long day of the giants* ill. by Leon Steinmetz. McGraw-Hill, 1975. Subj: Giants. Rhyming text. Time.

Boedoe, Geefwee. *Arrowville* ill. by author. Geringer, 2004. ISBN 0-06-055599-8 Subj: Prejudice. Rhyming text.

Boegehold, Betty. *Bear underground* ill. by Jim Arnosky. Doubleday, 1980. ISBN 0-385-15063-6 Subj: Animals – bears. Insects. Science.

Daddy doesn't live here anymore: a book about divorce ill. by Deborah Borgo. Childrens Pr., 1985. ISBN 0-307-62480-3 Subj: Divorce. Emotions – anger. Family life.

The fight ill. by Robin Oz. Bantam, 1991. ISBN 0-553-07086-X Subj: Behavior – fighting, arguing. Rhyming text. School.

A horse called Starfire ill. by Neil Waldman. G. Stevens, 1998. ISBN 0-8368-1763-X Subj: Animals – horses, ponies. Indians of North America.

Hurray for Pippa! ill. by Cyndy Szekeres. Knopf, 1980. ISBN 0-394-94067-9 Subj: Behavior – talking to strangers. Imagination. Toys.

In the castle of cats ill. by Jan Brett. Dutton, 1981. ISBN 0-525-32541-7 Subj: Animals – cats. Imagination.

Pawpaw's run ill. by Christine Price. Dutton, 1968. Subj: Animals – cats. Behavior – lost. Character traits – cleverness. Emotions – love. Pets. Rhyming text.

Pippa Mouse ill. by Cyndy Szekeres. Knopf, 1973. ISBN 0-394-92671-4 Subj: Animals – mice.

Pippa pops out! ill. by Cyndy Szekeres. Knopf, 1979. ISBN 0-394-94057-1 Subj: Animals – mice.

The rainbow ribbon (Hooks, William H.)

Read-a-rebus (Hooks, William H.)

Small Deer's magic tricks ill. by Jacqueline Chwast. Coward, 1977. ISBN 0-698-30659-7 Subj: Animals – deer. Behavior – trickery.

Three to get ready ill. by Mary Chalmers. HarperCollins, 1965. ISBN 0-06-020551-2 Subj: Animals – cats. Behavior.

What the wind told ill. by Emanuel Schongut. Parents' Magazine Pr., 1974. ISBN 0-8193-0757-2 Subj: Weather – wind.

You are much too small ill. by Valérie Michaut. Bantam, 1990. ISBN 0-553-05895-9 Subj: Animals – pigs. Family life.

Boehm, Arlene P. *Jack in search of Art* ill. by author. Roberts Rinehart, 1998. ISBN 1-57098-244-9 Subj: Animals – bears. Art. Behavior – mistakes. Museums.

Boelts, Maribeth. *Big Daddy, frog wrestler* ill. by Benrei Huang. A. Whitman, 2000. ISBN 0-8075-0717-2 Subj: Family life – fathers. Frogs & toads. Sports – wrestling.

Grace and Joe ill. by Martine Gourbault. A. Whitman, 1994. ISBN 0-8075-3019-0 Subj: Careers – postal workers. Friendship.

Little Bunny's cool tool set ill. by Kathy Parkinson. A. Whitman, 1997. ISBN 0-8075-4584-8 Subj: Animals – rabbits. Behavior – sharing. Friendship. School. Tools.

Little Bunny's pacifier plan ill. by Kathy Parkinson. A. Whitman, 1999. ISBN 0-8075-4581-3 Subj: Animals – rabbits. Behavior – growing up.

Little Bunny's preschool countdown ill. by Kathy Parkinson. A. Whitman, 1996. ISBN 0-8075-4582-1 Subj: Animals – rabbits. Behavior – worrying. School – first day. School – nursery. Seasons – summer.

Looking for Sleepy ill. by Bernadette Pons. A. Whitman, 2004. ISBN 0-8075-0447-5 Subj: Animals – bears. Bedtime. Family life – fathers. Family life – sons.

Summer's end ill. by Ellen Kandoian. Houghton Mifflin, 1995. ISBN 0-395-70559-2 Subj: School. Seasons – summer.

You're a brother, Little Bunny! ill. by Kathy Parkinson. A. Whitman, 2001. ISBN 0-8075-9446-6 Subj: Animals – rabbits. Babies. Family life – brothers. Family life – brothers & sisters. Family life – new sibling.

Boesel, Ann Sterling. *Sing and sing again* ill. by Louise Costello. Oxford Univ. Pr., 1938. Subj: Music. Songs.

Singing with Peter and Patsy ill. by Pelagie Doane. Oxford Univ. Pr., 1944. Subj: Music. Songs.

Boesky, Amy. *Planet Was* ill. by Nadine Bernard Westcott. Little, 1990. ISBN 0-316-10084-6 Subj: Rhyming text. Royalty – princes.

Bofill, Francesc. *Jack and the beanstalk = Juan y los frijoles magicos* (Jack and the beanstalk)

Bogacki, Tomasz. *Cat and mouse in the night* ill. by author. Farrar, 1998. ISBN 0-374-31190-0 Subj: Animals – cats. Animals – mice. Night.

Cat and mouse in the snow ill. by author. Farrar, 1999. ISBN 0-374-31192-7 Subj: Activities – playing. Animals – cats. Animals – mice. Weather – snow.

Circus girl ill. by author. Farrar, 2001. ISBN 0-374-31291-5 Subj: Character traits – helpfulness. Circus. Friendship.

I hate you! I like you! ill. by author. Farrar, 1997. ISBN 0-374-33544-3 Subj: Animals. Emotions.

My first garden ill. by author. Farrar, 2000. ISBN 0-374-32518-9 Subj: Gardens, gardening.

Bogan, Paulette. *Goodnight Lulu* ill. by author. Bloomsbury, 2003. ISBN 1-58234-803-0 Subj: Bedtime. Birds – chickens. Family life – mothers.

Momma's magical purse ill. by author. Bloomsbury, 2004. ISBN 1-58234-842-1 Subj: Animals – cats. Animals – dogs. Clothing – handbags, purses. Family life – mothers. Magic.

Spike in the city ill. by author. Putnam, 2000. ISBN 0-399-23442-X Subj: Animals – dogs. Behavior – lost & found possessions. Cities, towns.

Bogart, Jo Ellen. *Daniel's dog* ill. by Janet Wilson. Scholastic, 1990. ISBN 0-590-43402-0 Subj: Babies. Ethnic groups in the U.S. – African Americans. Family life – brothers & sisters. Family life – new sibling. Imagination – imaginary friends.

Jeremiah learns to read ill. by Laura Fernandez & Rick Jacobson. Orchard, 1999. ISBN 0-531-33190-3 Subj: Books, reading. Family life. Old age. School.

Boggiss, Lisa. *Maisy at the farm* (Cousins, Lucy)

Bognomo, Joel Eboueme. *Madoulina* ill. by author. Boyds Mills, 1999. ISBN 1-56397-769-9 Subj: Careers – teachers. Foreign lands – Cameroon. School.

Bogot, Howard. *I'm growing* by Howard Bogot & Daniel B. Syme; ill. by Janet Compere. UAHC Pr., 1982. ISBN 0-8074-0167-6 Subj: Behavior – growing up. Jewish culture.

Bograd, Larry. *Egon* ill. by Dirk Zimmer. Macmillan, 1980. ISBN 0-02-710970-4 Subj: Animals. Character traits – curiosity.

Felix in the attic ill. by Dirk Zimmer. Harvey House, 1978. ISBN 0-8178-5917-9 Subj: Family life.

Lost in the store ill. by Victoria Chess. Macmillan, 1981. ISBN 0-02-710980-1 Subj: Behavior – lost. Stores.

Bohanon, Paul. *Golden Kate* ill. by Gertrude Howe. Oxford Univ. Pr., 1943. Subj: Character traits – generosity. Farms.

Bohdal, Susi. *Bobby the bear* ill. by author. Holt, 1986. ISBN 0-03-008028-2 Subj: Format, unusual – board books. Friendship. Toys – bears.

Harry the hare ill. by author. Holt, 1986. ISBN 0-03-008029-0 Subj: Format, unusual – board books. Toys.

The magic honey jar trans. by Anthea Bell; ill. by author. North-South, 1987. ISBN 0-8050-0491-2 Subj: Behavior – greed. Dreams. Royalty.

1, 2, 3, what do you see? an animal counting book ill. by author. North-South, 1997. ISBN 1-55858-647-4 Subj: Animals. Counting, numbers. Gifts.

Tiger baby ill. by author; trans. by J. Alison James. North-South, 2001. ISBN 0-7358-1433-3 Subj: Animals – tigers. Character traits – curiosity. Jungle.

Tom cat ill. by author. Doubleday, 1977. ISBN 0-385-13612-9 Subj: Animals. Animals – cats. Communication.

Bohman, Nils Axel Erik. *Jim, Jock and Jumbo* ill. by Einar Norelius. Dutton, 1946. Subj: Animals – elephants. Animals – hippopotamuses. Animals – lions. Humorous stories.

Boholm-Olsson, Eva. *Tuan* trans. by Dianne Jonasson; ill. by Pham van Don. Farrar, 1988. ISBN 91-29-58766-2 Subj: Family life. Foreign lands – Vietnam.

Bois, Ivy Du. *see* DuBois, Ivy

Bois, William Pène Du. *see* Du Bois, William Pène

Boland, Janice. *Annabel* ill. by Megan Halsey. Dial, 1993. ISBN 0-8037-1255-3 Subj: Animals – pigs. Character traits – individuality.

Annabel again ill. by Megan Halsey. Dial, 1995. ISBN 0-8037-1757-1 Subj: Animals – pigs. Homes, houses.

A dog named Sam ill. by G. Brian Karas. Dial, 1996. ISBN 0-8037-1531-5 Subj: Animals – dogs. Behavior – misbehavior.

Bolden, Tonya. *Rock of ages: a tribute to the Black church* ill. by Gregory Christie. Knopf, 2001. ISBN 0-679-99485-8 Subj: Ethnic groups in the U.S. – African Americans. Poetry. Religion.

Boling, Katharine. *New year be coming! a Gullah year* ill. by Daniel Minter. A. Whitman, 2002. ISBN 0-8075-5590-8 Subj: Days of the week, months of the year. Poetry.

Boling, Ruth L. *Come worship with me* ill. by Tracey Dahle Carrier. Geneva, 2001. ISBN 0-664-50045-5 Subj: Days of the week, months of the year. Religion.

Bolliger, Max. *The fireflies* trans. & adapt. by Roseanna Hoover; ill. by Jiri Trnka. Atheneum, 1970. Subj: Family life. Folk & fairy tales. Foreign lands – Czechoslovakia. Insects – fireflies. Night.

The giants' feast ill. by Monica Laimgruber. Addison-Wesley, 1976. Translation of Das Reisenfest; English version by Barbara Willard. ISBN 0-241-89255-4 Subj: Food. Giants.

The golden apple ill. by Celestino Piatti; trans. by Roseanna Hoover. Atheneum, 1970. Subj: Behavior – greed. Family life. Food.

The lonely prince ill. by Jürg Obrist. Atheneum, 1982. ISBN 0-689-50215-X Subj: Emotions – loneliness. Friendship.

The magic bird ill. by Jan Lenica. David & Charles, 1988. ISBN 0-86264-146-2 Subj: Behavior – growing up. Character traits – kindness to animals. Giants.

The most beautiful song ill. by Jindra Capek. Little, 1981. ISBN 0-316-10117-6 Subj: Music. Musical instruments – flutes. Royalty.

Noah and the rainbow: an ancient story trans. by Clyde Robert Bulla; ill. by Helga Aichinger. Crowell, 1972. ISBN 0-698-58449-0 Subj: Animals. Boats, ships. Religion – Noah. Weather – floods. Weather – rain. Weather – rainbows.

The rabbit with the sky blue ears ill. by Jürg Obrist. David & Charles, 1989. ISBN 0-86241-204-8 Subj: Anatomy – ears. Animals – rabbits. Self-concept.

Sandy at the children's zoo trans. from German by Elisabeth Gemming; ill. by Klaus Brunner. Crowell, 1967. ISBN 0-690-71956-6 Subj: Behavior – lost. Zoos.

The wooden man ill. by Fred Bauer. Seabury Pr., 1974. Translation of Der Mann aus Holz. ISBN 0-816-43129-9 Subj: Scarecrows. Weapons. Weather.

Bolognese, Don. *Donkey and Carlo* (Raphael, Elaine)

Donkey, it's snowing (Raphael, Elaine)

A new day ill. by author. Delacorte, 1970. Subj: Activities – traveling. Babies. Ethnic groups in the U.S. – Mexican Americans. Family life. Holidays – Christmas. Religion – Nativity.

The sleepy watchdog (Bolognese, Elaine)

Turnabout (Raphael, Elaine)

Bolognese, Elaine. *The sleepy watchdog* by Elaine & Don Bolognese; ill. by Don Bolognese. Lothrop, 1964. Subj: Animals – dogs. Character traits – laziness.

Bolton, Evelyn. *see* Bunting, Eve (Anne Evelyn)

Boltz, Dan. *Dan's pants* (Good, Merle)

Bond, Felicia. *Christmas in the chicken coop* ill. by author. Crowell, 1983. ISBN 0-690-04333-3 Subj: Birds – chickens. Holidays – Christmas. Trees.

Four Valentines in a rainstorm ill. by author. Crowell, 1983. ISBN 0-690-04307-4 Subj: Friendship. Holidays – Valentine's Day.

The Halloween performance ill. by author. Crowell, 1983. ISBN 0-690-04309-0 Subj: Animals – mice. Holidays – Halloween. School.

The Halloween play ill. by author. HarperCollins, 1999. ISBN 0-06-028684-9 Subj: Animals – mice. Holidays – Halloween. School. Theater.

Mary Betty Lizzie McNutt's birthday ill. by author. Crowell, 1983. ISBN 0-690-04256-6 Subj: Animals – pigs. Birthdays.

Poinsettia and her family ill. by author. HarperCollins, 1981. ISBN 0-690-04145-4 Subj: Animals – pigs. Behavior. Family life. Moving. Sibling rivalry.

Poinsettia and the firefighters ill. by author. Crowell, 1984. ISBN 0-690-04400-3 Subj: Animals – pigs. Bedtime. Night. Noise, sounds.

Tumble bumble ill. by author. Front St., 1996. ISBN 1-886910-15-4 Subj: Animals. Counting, numbers. Insects. Rhyming text.

Wake up, Vladimir ill. by author. Crowell, 1987. ISBN 0-690-04453-4 Subj: Animals – groundhogs. Behavior – running away. Dreams. Shadows.

Bond, Jean Carey. *A is for Africa* ill. by author. Watts, 1969. Subj: ABC books. Foreign lands – Africa.

Bond, Michael. *Paddington and the knickerbocker rainbow* ill. by David McKee. Putnam, 1985. ISBN 0-399-21202-7 Subj: Animals – bears. Food. Foreign lands – England. Language.

Paddington at the circus by Michael Bond & Fred Banbery; ill. by Fred Banbery. Random House, 1973. ISBN 0-394-92918-7 Subj: Animals – bears. Circus. Foreign lands – England.

Paddington at the fair ill. by David McKee. Putnam, 1986. ISBN 0-399-21271-X Subj: Animals – bears. Fairs, festivals. Foreign lands – England.

Paddington at the palace ill. by David McKee. Putnam, 1986. ISBN 0-399-21340-6 Subj: Animals – bears. Foreign lands – England. Royalty.

Paddington at the seaside ill. by Fred Banbery. Random House, 1975. ISBN 0-394-93801-1 Subj: Activities – vacationing. Animals – bears. Foreign lands – England. Sea & seashore.

Paddington at the tower ill. by Fred Banbery. Random House, 1975. ISBN 0-394-93802-X Subj: Animals – bears. Foreign lands – England.

Paddington at the zoo ill. by David McKee. Putnam, 1985. ISBN 0-399-21201-9 Subj: Animals – bears. Behavior – lost & found possessions. Foreign lands – England. Zoos.

Paddington Bear ill. by R. W. Alley. HarperCollins, 1998. ISBN 0-06-027854-4 Subj: Animals – bears.

Paddington Bear ill. by John Lobban. HarperCollins, 1992. ISBN 0-694-00394-8 Subj: Animals – bears. Family life. Foreign lands – England.

Paddington Bear and the Busy Bee Carnival ill. by R. W. Alley. HarperCollins, 1998. ISBN 0-06-027765-3 Subj: Animals – bears. Contests. Fairs, festivals.

Paddington Bear and the Christmas surprise ill. by R. W. Alley. HarperCollins, 1997. ISBN 0-694-00897-4 Subj: Animals – bears. Careers. Holidays – Christmas. Stores.

Paddington Bear goes to the hospital by Michael Bond and Karen Jankel; ill. by R. W. Alley. HarperCollins, 2001. ISBN 0-694-01563-6 Subj: Accidents. Hospitals. Toys – bears.

Paddington Bear in the garden ill. by R. W. Alley. HarperCollins, 2002. ISBN 0-06-029696-8 Subj: Gardens, gardening. Toys – bears.

Paddington cleans up ill. by David McKee. Putnam, 1986. ISBN 0-399-21339-2 Subj: Activities – working. Animals – bears. Foreign lands – England.

Paddington's ABC ill. by John Lobban. Viking, 1991. ISBN 0-670-84104-8 Subj: ABC books. Animals – bears.

Paddington's art exhibit ill. by David McKee. Putnam, 1986. ISBN 0-399-21270-1 Subj: Activities – painting. Animals – bears. Art. Foreign lands – England.

Paddington's colors ill. by John Lobban. Viking, 1991. ISBN 0-670-84102-1 Subj: Animals – bears. Concepts – color.

Paddington's garden ill. by Fred Banbery. Random House, 1973. ISBN 0-394-92643-9 Subj: Animals – bears. Family life. Foreign lands – England. Gardens, gardening.

Paddington's lucky day ill. by Fred Banbery. Random House, 1974, c1973. ISBN 0-394-92919-5 Subj: Animals – bears. Character traits – luck. Foreign lands – England. Shopping.

Paddington's 1 2 3 ill. by John Lobban. Viking, 1991. ISBN 0-670-84103-X Subj: Animals – bears. Counting, numbers.

Paddington's opposites ill. by John Lobban. Viking, 1991. ISBN 0-670-84105-6 Subj: Animals – bears. Concepts – opposites.

Bond, Rebecca. *Bravo, Maurice!* ill. by author. Little, 2000. ISBN 0-316-10545-7 Subj: Careers. Family life. Noise, sounds.

Just like a baby ill. by author. Little, 1999. ISBN 0-316-10416-7 Subj: Babies. Cumulative tales. Family life. Furniture – cradles.

Bond, Ruskin. *Cherry tree* ill. by Allan Eitzen. Boyds Mills, 1991. ISBN 1-878093-21-5 Subj: Family life – grandfathers. Foreign lands – India. Trees.

Flames in the forest ill. by Valerie Littlewood. Watts, 1981. ISBN 0-531-04282-0 Subj: Fire. Foreign lands – India. Forest, woods.

Bonfils, Bolette. *Peter joins the circus* ill. by Jan Mogensen. Crocodile, 1994. ISBN 1-56656-154-X Subj: Animals. Animals – rabbits. Circus. Format, unusual – toy & movable books.

Bonino, Louise. *The cozy little farm* ill. by Angelia Straeter. Random House, 1946. Subj: Animals. Farms.

Bonne, Rose. *I know an old lady* (Little old lady who swallowed a fly)

I know an old lady who swallowed a fly (Little old lady who swallowed a fly)

Bonners, Susan. *Hunter in the snow: the lynx* ill. by author. Little, 1994. ISBN 0-316-10201-6 Subj: Animals – lynx. Science.

Just in passing ill. by author. Lothrop, 1989. ISBN 0-688-07712-9 Subj: Circular tales. Wordless.

Why does the cat do that? ill. by author. Holt, 1998. ISBN 0-8050-4377-2 Subj: Animals – cats. Behavior.

The wooden doll ill. by author. Lothrop, 1991. ISBN 0-688-08282-3 Subj: Family life – grandparents. Toys – dolls.

Bonnett-Rampersaud, Louise. *Polly Hopper's pouch* ill. by Lina Chesak-Librace. Dutton, 2001. ISBN 0-525-46525-1 Subj: Animals – kangaroos. Character traits – curiosity. Foreign lands – Australia.

Bonnici, Peter. *The festival* ill. by Lisa Kopper. Carolrhoda, 1985. ISBN 0-87614-229-3 Subj: Behavior – growing up. Foreign lands – India. Holidays.

The first rains ill. by Lisa Kopper. Carolrhoda, 1985. ISBN 0-87614-228-5 Subj: Weather – rain.

Bonning, Tony. *Another fine mess* ill. by Sally Hobson. Little Tiger, 1998. ISBN 1-888444-43-6 Subj: Animals. Animals – foxes. Character traits – cleanliness. Circular tales.

Fox tale soup ill. by Sally Hobson. S&S, 2002. Originally published under title: Stone soup. Great Britain : Gullane, 2001. ISBN 0-689-84900-1 Subj: Animals – foxes. Character traits – cleverness. Farms. Folk & fairy tales. Food.

Bono, Mary. *Ugh! a bug* ill. by author. Walker, 2002. ISBN 0-8027-8800-9 Subj: Insects – ladybugs. Rhyming text.

Bonsall, Crosby Newell. *The amazing the incredible super dog* ill. by author. HarperCollins, 1986. ISBN 0-06-020591-1 Subj: Animals – cats. Animals – dogs. Behavior – boasting.

And I mean it, Stanley ill. by author. HarperCollins, 1974. ISBN 0-06-020568-7 Subj: Activities – playing. Animals – dogs.

The day I had to play with my sister ill. by author. HarperCollins, 1972. ISBN 0-06-020576-8 Subj: Family life. Games.

I'll show you cats (Ylla)

It's mine! A greedy book ill. by author. HarperCollins, 1964. ISBN 0-06-020586-5 Subj: Behavior – greed. Friendship.

Listen, listen! by Crosby Newell Bonsall & Ylla; photos by Ylla. HarperCollins, 1961. Subj: Animals – cats. Animals – dogs. Character traits – appearance.

Look who's talking (Ylla)

Mine's the best ill. by author. HarperCollins, 1973. ISBN 0-06-020578-4 Subj: Behavior – boasting. Sea & seashore. Toys – balloons.

Polar bear brothers (Ylla)

Who's afraid of the dark? ill. by author. HarperCollins, 1980. ISBN 0-06-020598-9 Subj: Animals – dogs. Emotions – fear. Night.

Bonsignore, Joan. *Stick out your tongue: fantastic facts, features, and functions of animal and human tongues* ill. by John Ward. Peachtree, 2001. ISBN 1-56145-230-0 Subj: Anatomy – tongues. Senses – taste.

Bontemps, Arna Wendell. *The fast sooner hound* by Arna Wendell Bontemps & Jack Conroy; ill. by Virginia Lee Burton. Houghton Mifflin, 1942. ISBN 0-395-18657-9 Subj: Animals – dogs. Trains.

The book of Pooh: Biglet adapt. by Marge Kennedy; based on the screenplay by Andy Yerkes; photos by John E. Barrett. Disney Pr., 2002. ISBN 0-7868-3363-7 Subj: Animals – pigs. Concepts – size. Dreams.

Bookman, Charlotte. *see* Zolotow, Charlotte (Shapiro)

Boon, Debbie. *My gran* ill. by author. Millbrook, 1998. ISBN 0-7613-0312-X Subj: Family life – grandmothers. Rhyming text.

Boon, Emilie. *Belinda's balloon* ill. by author. Knopf, 1985. ISBN 0-394-97342-9 Subj: Animals – bears. Family life. Toys – balloons.

It's spring, Peterkin ill. by author. Random House, 1986. ISBN 0-394-87997-X Subj: Character traits – kindness to animals. Format, unusual – board books. Seasons – spring.

1 2 3 how many animals can you see? ill. by author. Random House, 1987. ISBN 0-531-08301-2 Subj: Animals. Counting, numbers. School.

Peterkin meets a star ill. by author. Random House, 1984. ISBN 0-394-96284-2 Subj: Imagination. Stars.

Peterkin's very own garden ill. by author. Random House, 1987. ISBN 0-394-88666-6 Subj: Animals. Format, unusual – board books. Gardens, gardening.

Peterkin's wet walk ill. by author. Random House, 1984. ISBN 0-394-96285-0 Subj: Animals. Imagination. Weather – rain.

Booth, David. *The dust bowl* ill. by author. Kids Can, 1997. ISBN 1-55074-295-7 Subj: Careers – farmers. Family life. Foreign lands – Canada. Weather – droughts.

Booth, Eugene. *At the circus* ill. by Derek Collard. Raintree, 1977. ISBN 0-8393-0112-X Subj: Circus. Concepts. Games. Participation. Problem solving.

At the fair ill. by Derek Collard. Raintree, 1977. ISBN 0-8393-0114-6 Subj: Concepts. Fairs, festivals. Games. Participation. Problem solving.

In the air ill. by Derek Collard. Raintree, 1977. ISBN 0-8393-0105-7 Subj: Concepts. Games. Participation. Problem solving.

In the garden ill. by Derek Collard. Raintree, 1977. ISBN 0-8393-0115-4 Subj: Concepts. Games. Participation. Problem solving.

In the jungle ill. by Derek Collard. Raintree, 1977. ISBN 0-8393-0104-9 Subj: Concepts. Games. Jungle. Participation. Problem solving.

Under the ocean ill. by Derek Collard. Raintree, 1977. ISBN 0-8393-0108-1 Subj: Concepts. Games. Participation. Problem solving. Sea & seashore.

Booth, Philip E. *Crossing* ill. by Bagram Ibatoulline. Candlewick, 2001. ISBN 0-7636-1420-3 Subj: Poetry. Trains.

Borack, Barbara. *Grandpa* ill. by Ben Shecter. HarperCollins, 1967. Subj: Family life – grandfathers.

Borchard, Therese Johnson. *Taste and see the goodness of the Lord* ill. by Phyllis V. Saroff. Paulist Pr., 2000. ISBN 0-8091-6665-8 Subj: Religion.

Borchers, Elisabeth. *Dear Sarah* trans. & adapt. from German by Elizabeth Shub; ill. by Wilhelm Schlote. Greenwillow, 1980. ISBN 0-688-84277-1 Subj: Activities – traveling. Communication. Foreign lands.

There comes a time trans. by Babette Deutsch; ill. by Dietlind Blech. Doubleday, 1969. Subj: Days of the week, months of the year. Poetry. Royalty – kings.

Borden, Beatrice Brown. *Wild animals of Africa* photos by author. Random House, 1982. ISBN 0-394-95306-1 Subj: Animals. Birds. Foreign lands – Africa.

Borden, Louise. *A. Lincoln and me* ill. by Ted Lewin. Scholastic, 2000. ISBN 0-590-45714-4 Subj: Birthdays. Self-concept. U.S. history.

Albie the lifeguard ill. by Elizabeth Sayles. Scholastic, 1993. ISBN 0-590-44585-5 Subj: Behavior – growing up. Careers – lifeguards. Sports – swimming.

America is . . . ill. by Stacey Schuett. McElderry, 2002. ISBN 0-689-83900-6 Subj: Poetry. U.S. history.

Caps, hats, socks and mittens ill. by Lillian Hoban. Scholastic, 1989. ISBN 0-590-41257-4 Subj: Clothing. Seasons.

The day Eddie met the author ill. by Adam Gustavson. McElderry, 2001. ISBN 0-689-83405-5 Subj: Books, reading. Careers – authors. School.

Good luck, Mrs. K! ill. by Adam Gustavson. McElderry, 1999. ISBN 0-689-82147-6 Subj: Careers – teachers. Illness – cancer. School.

Goodbye, Charles Lindbergh: based on a true story ill. by Thomas B. Allen. McElderry, 1998. ISBN 0-689-81536-0 Subj: Activities – flying. Careers – airplane pilots. U.S. history.

Thanksgiving is . . . ill. by Steve Björkman. Scholastic, 1997. ISBN 0-590-33128-0 Subj: Holidays – Thanksgiving.

The watching game ill. by Teri Weidner. Scholastic, 1991. ISBN 0-590-43600-7 Subj: Country. Family life – grandmothers. Seasons.

Borg, Inga. *Plupp builds a house* ill. by author. Warne, 1961. Subj: Animals. Foreign lands – Lapland. Homes, houses.

Borlenghi, Patricia. *From albatross to zoo* ill. by Piers Harper. Scholastic, 1992. ISBN 0-590-45483-8 Subj: ABC books. Animals. Foreign languages.

Bornstein, Ruth Lercher. *Annabelle* ill. by author. Crowell, 1978. ISBN 0-690-03810-0 Subj: Behavior – lost. Toys.

A beautiful seashell ill. by author. HarperCollins, 1990. ISBN 0-06-020595-4 Subj: Family life – great-grandparents. Sea & seashore.

The dancing man ill. by author. Seabury Pr., 1978. ISBN 0-8164-3214-7 Subj: Activities – dancing. Foreign lands – Europe.

I'll draw a meadow ill. by author. HarperCollins, 1979. ISBN 0-06-020613-6 Subj: Activities – vacationing. Animals – dogs.

Indian bunny ill. by author. Childrens Pr., 1973. ISBN 0-516-08723-1 Subj: Animals – rabbits. Indians of North America.

Jim ill. by author. Seabury Pr., 1978. ISBN 0-8164-3204-X Subj: Animals – dogs. Behavior – lost. Character traits – bravery.

Of course a goat ill. by author. HarperCollins, 1980. ISBN 0-06-020609-8 Subj: Animals – goats. Family life.

Rabbit's good news ill. by author. Clarion, 1995. ISBN 0-395-68700-4 Subj: Animals – rabbits. Nature. Seasons – spring.

The seedling child ill. by author. Harcourt, 1987. ISBN 0-15-272459-1 Subj: Friendship. Imagination – imaginary friends. Rhyming text.

That's how it is when we draw ill. by author. Clarion, 1997. ISBN 0-395-82509-1 Subj: Activities – drawing. Art. Poetry.

Boroson, Martin. *Becoming me: a story of creation* ill. by Christopher Gilvan-Cartwright. Skylight Paths, 2000. ISBN 1-893361-11-X Subj: Creation. Religion.

Borovsky, Paul. *The fish that wasn't* ill. by author. Hyperion, 1994. ISBN 1-56282-582-8 Subj: Animals – whales. Birthdays. Fish. Pets.

Nico ill. by author. Hyperion, 1993. ISBN 0-517-58855-2 Subj: Animals – monkeys. Behavior – greed. Character traits – helpfulness.

Borten, Helen. *Do you go where I go?* ill. by author. Abelard-Schuman, 1972. Subj: Humorous stories. Rhyming text.

Do you hear what I hear? ill. by author. Abelard-Schuman, 1960. Subj: Noise, sounds. Rhyming text. Senses – hearing.

Do you know what I know? ill. by author. Abelard-Schuman, 1970. ISBN 0-20-071695-6 Subj: Rhyming text. Senses – hearing. Senses – sight. Senses – smell. Senses – taste. Senses – touch.

Do you move as I do? ill. by author. Abelard-Schuman, 1963. Subj: Emotions. Health & fitness.

Do you see what I see? ill. by author. Abelard-Schuman, 1959. Subj: Art. Concepts. Senses – sight.

Halloween ill. by author. Crowell, 1965. ISBN 0-690-36314-1 Subj: Holidays – Halloween.

A picture has a special look ill. by author. Abelard-Schuman, 1961. Subj: Art.

Borton, Lady. *Fat chance!* ill. by Deborah Kogan Ray. Putnam, 1993. ISBN 0-399-21963-3 Subj: Animals – cats. Farms. Illness.

Junk pile! ill. by Kimberly Bulcken Root. Philomel, 1997. ISBN 0-399-22728-8 Subj: Friendship. Handicaps.

Bos, Burny. *Alexander the great* ill. by Hans de Beer; trans. by J. Alison James. North-South, 2000. ISBN 0-7358-1344-2 Subj: Animals – bears. Animals – cats. Animals – mice. Clothing – costumes.

Fun with the Molesons ill. by Hans de Beer; trans. by J. Alison James. North-South, 2000. ISBN 0-7358-1353-1 Subj: Animals – moles. Family life.

Meet the Molesons ill. by Hans de Beer; trans. by J. Alison James. North-South, 1994. ISBN 1-55858-258-4 Subj: Animals – moles. Family life. Multiple births – twins.

Ollie the elephant ill. by Hans de Beer. North-South, 1989. ISBN 1-55858-012-3 Subj: Animals – elephants. Behavior – wishing. Family life.

Prince Valentino ill. by Hans de Beer. North-South, 1990. ISBN 1-55858-089-1 Subj: Birds – storks. Friendship. Frogs & toads.

Bos, Claire. *Maurice the hippo* by Claire & Maarten Bos; ill. by authors. Orchard, 1998. ISBN 0-531-30098-6 Subj: Animals – hippopotamuses. Format, unusual – board books. Rhyming text.

Webster's wardrobe by Claire & Maarten Bos; ill. by authors. Orchard, 1998. ISBN 0-531-30097-8 Subj: Animals – seals. Clothing. Format, unusual – board books. Rhyming text.

Bos, Maarten. *Maurice the hippo* (Bos, Claire)

Webster's wardrobe (Bos, Claire)

Bosak, Susan V. *Something to remember me by* ill. by author. Communication Project, 1999. ISBN 1-896232-01-9 Subj: Family life – grandparents. Old age.

Bosca, Francesca. *The apple king* ill. by Giuliano Ferri; trans. by J. Alison James. North-South, 2001. ISBN 0-7358-1397-3 Subj: Animals. Behavior – sharing. Royalty – kings. Trees.

Bossom, Naomi. *A scale full of fish and other turnabouts* ill. by author. Greenwillow, 1979. ISBN 0-688-84203-8 Subj: Humorous stories. Language.

Boston. Children's Hospital Medical Center. *Curious George goes to the hospital* (Rey, Margret [Margret Elisabeth Waldstein])

Boswell, Stephen. *King Gorboduc's fabulous zoo* ill. by Beverley Gooding. Dutton, 1986. ISBN 0-525-44267-7 Subj: Dragons. Royalty – kings. Zoos.

Botel, Morton. *Sad Mrs. Sam Sack* (Brothers, Aileen)

Bothwell, Jean. *Paddy and Sam* ill. by Margaret Ayer. Abelard-Schuman, 1952. Subj: Behavior – lost. Birds – ducks.

Bottner, Barbara. *Big boss! Little boss!* ill. by author. Pantheon, 1978. ISBN 0-394-93939-5 Subj: Behavior – lost & found possessions. Sibling rivalry.

Bootsie Barker bites ill. by Peggy Rathmann. Putnam, 1992. ISBN 0-399-22125-5 Subj: Activities – playing. Behavior – bullying.

Horrible Hannah ill. by Joan E. Drescher. Crown, 1980. ISBN 0-517-53973-X Subj: Animals – dogs. Friendship. Moving.

Jungle day: or, How I learned to love my nosey little brother ill. by author. Delacorte, 1978. ISBN 0-440-04384-0 Subj: Sibling rivalry.

Mean Maxine ill. by author. Pantheon, 1980. ISBN 0-394-94219-1 Subj: Character traits – meanness. Friendship. Imagination.

Messy ill. by author. Delacorte, 1979. ISBN 0-440-05493-1 Subj: Activities – dancing. Behavior – carelessness.

Myra ill. by author. Macmillan, 1979. ISBN 0-02-711740-5 Subj: Activities – dancing. Imagination.

Nana Hannah's piano ill. by Diana Cain Bluthenthal. Putnam, 1996. ISBN 0-399-22656-7 Subj: Family life – grandmothers. Music. Musical instruments – pianos. Sports – baseball.

Pish and Posh by Barbara Bottner & Gerald Kruglik; ill. by Barbara Bottner. Tegen, 2004. ISBN 0-06-051417-5 Subj: Behavior – lost & found possessions. Fairies. Magic.

Rosa's room ill. by Beth Spiegel. Peachtree, 2004. ISBN 1-56145-302-1 Subj: Family life – mothers. Friendship. Furniture – beds. Moving.

There was nobody there ill. by author. Macmillan, 1978. ISBN 0-02-711000-1 Subj: Bedtime. Imagination. Rhyming text. Sleep.

Two messy friends ill. by author. Scholastic, 1998. ISBN 0-613-16867-4 Subj: Character traits – cleanliness. Character traits – orderliness. Friendship. Hygiene. Sleepovers.

Wallace's lists by Barbara Bottner & Gerald Kruglik; ill. by Olof Landström. Tegen, 2004. ISBN 0-06-000225-5 Subj: Animals – mice. Character traits – orderliness. Friendship.

Zoo song ill. by Lynn Munsinger. Scholastic, 1987. ISBN 0-590-41005-9 Subj: Animals. Music. Musical instruments – violins. Zoos.

Botwin, Esther. *A treasury of songs for little children* ill. by Evelyn Urbanowich. Hart, 1954. Subj: Music. Songs.

Bouchard, Dave. *Fairy* ill. by Dean Griffiths. Orca, 2001. ISBN 1-55143-212-9 Subj: Fairies. Teeth.

Prairie born ill. by Peter Shostak. Orca, 1997. ISBN 1-55143-092-4 Subj: Foreign lands – Canada. Poetry.

The song within my heart ill. by Allen Sapp. Raincoast, 2002. ISBN 1-55192-559-1 Subj: Activities – storytelling. Indians of North America. Pow-wows.

Boucher, Jerry. *Fire truck nuts and bolts* photos by author. Carolrhoda, 1993. ISBN 0-87614-783-X Subj: Activities – making things. Careers – firefighters. Trucks.

Bouhuys, Mies. *The lady of Stavoren: a story from Holland* ill. by Francien Van Westering. Penguin, 1979. ISBN 0-14-030802-4 Subj: Folk & fairy tales. Foreign lands – Holland.

Boujon, Claude. *The fairy with the long nose* ill. by author. Macmillan, 1987. ISBN 0-689-50424-1 Subj: Anatomy – noses. Fairies. Magic.

Boulton, Jane. *Only Opal: the diary of a young girl* (Whiteley, Opal Stanley)

Bour, Danièle. *The house from morning to night* ill. by author. Kane/Miller, 1985. ISBN 0-916291-01-4 Subj: Homes, houses.

Bourgeois, Paulette. *Big Sarah's little boots* ill. by Brenda Clark. Scholastic, 1987. ISBN 0-590-42622-2 Subj: Behavior – growing up. Clothing – shoes. Family life. Weather – rain.

Fire fighters ill. by Kim LaFave. Kids Can, 1998. ISBN 1-55074-438-0 Subj: Careers – firefighters. Communities, neighborhoods. Fire.

Franklin and Harriet ill. by Brenda Clark. Scholastic, 2001. ISBN 0-439-26424-3 Subj: Animals. Character traits – helpfulness. Family life – brothers & sisters. Reptiles – turtles, tortoises. Sibling rivalry. Toys.

Franklin and the baby (Moore, Eva)

Franklin and the thunderstorm ill. by Brenda Clark. Scholastic, 1998. ISBN 0-590-02635-6 Subj: Animals. Emotions – fear. Reptiles – turtles, tortoises. Weather – lightning, thunder. Weather – storms.

Franklin goes to the hospital (Jennings, Sharon)

Franklin in the dark ill. by Brenda Clark. Kids Can, 1986. ISBN 0-919964-93-1 Subj: Emotions – fear. Night. Reptiles – turtles, tortoises.

Franklin rides a bike ill. by Brenda Clark. Kids Can, 1997. ISBN 1-55074-414-3 Subj: Animals. Reptiles – turtles, tortoises. Sports – bicycling.

Franklin says "I love you" ill. by Brenda Clark. Scholastic, 2002. ISBN 1-55337-035-X Subj: Behavior – worrying. Birthdays. Family life – mothers. Gifts. Reptiles – turtles, tortoises.

Franklin's baby sister ill. by Brenda Clark. Scholastic, 2000. ISBN 1-55074-794-0 Subj: Babies. Family life – brothers & sisters. Reptiles – turtles, tortoises. Seasons – spring.

Franklin's Christmas gift ill. by Brenda Clark. Kids Can, 1998. ISBN 1-55074-466-6 Subj: Gifts. Holidays – Christmas. Reptiles – turtles, tortoises.

Franklin's class trip by Paulette Bourgeois & Sharon Jennings; ill. by Brenda Clark. Scholastic, 1999. ISBN 0-590-13002-1 Subj: Animals. Dinosaurs. Museums. Reptiles – turtles, tortoises. School – field trips. Toys.

Franklin's new friend ill. by Brenda Clark. Scholastic, 1997. ISBN 0-590-02592-9 Subj: Animals – moose. Friendship. Reptiles – turtles, tortoises.

Franklin's secret club ill. by Brenda Clark. Kids Can, 1998. ISBN 0-59013-000-5 Subj: Animals. Clubs, gangs. Friendship. Reptiles – turtles, tortoises.

Franklin's Thanksgiving (Jennings, Sharon)

Garbage collectors ill. by Kim LaFave. Kids Can, 1998. ISBN 1-55074-440-2 Subj: Careers – sanitation workers. Communities, neighborhoods.

Oma's quilt ill. by Stephane Jorisch. Kids Can, 2001. ISBN 1-55074-777-0 Subj: Family life – grandmothers. Quilts.

Police officers ill. by Kim LaFave. Kids Can, 1999. ISBN 1-55074-502-6 Subj: Careers – police officers. Communities, neighborhoods.

Postal workers ill. by Kim LaFave. Kids Can, 1998. ISBN 1-55074-504-2 Subj: Birthdays. Careers – postal workers. Communities, neighborhoods.

Too many chickens ill. by Bill Slavin. Little, 1991. ISBN 0-316-10358-6 Subj: Animals. Birds – chickens. School.

Bourguignon, Laurence. *A friend for Tiger* ill. by Laurence Henno. BridgeWater, 1994. ISBN 0-8167-3907-2 Subj: Animals – rabbits. Animals – tigers. Circus. Friendship.

Bourke, Linda. *Ethel's exceptional egg* ill. by author. Harvey House, 1977. ISBN 0-817-85622-6 Subj: Birds – chickens. Eggs. Fairs, festivals.

Eye count: a book of counting puzzles ill. by author. Chronicle, 1995. ISBN 0-8118-0732-0 Subj: ABC books. Counting, numbers. Language. Puzzles.

Boutell, Clarence Burley. *The fat baron* ill. by Frank Lieberman. Houghton Mifflin, 1946. Subj: Food. Imagination. Knights.

Bouton, Josephine. *Favorite poems for the children's hour* ill. by Bonnie & Bill Rutherford. Platt, 1967. Subj: Poetry.

Boutwell, Edna. *Red rooster* ill. by Bernard Garbutt. Atheneum, 1950. Subj: Birds – chickens. Cumulative tales. Folk & fairy tales.

Bove, Linda. *Sign language ABC with Linda Bove* ill. by Tom Cooke. Random House, 1985. ISBN 0-394-97516-2 Subj: ABC books. Handicaps – deafness. Senses – hearing. Sign language.

Bowden, Joan Chase. *The bear's surprise party* ill. by Jerry Scott. Golden Pr., 1975. ISBN 0-307-60809-3 Subj: Animals – bears. Parties.

Boo and the flying flews ill. by Don Leake. Western, 1974. Subj: Animals – dogs. Circus.

The bouncy baby bunny ill. by Patience Brewster. Golden Bks., 1999. ISBN 0-307-10217-3 Subj: Animals – rabbits. Family life.

Bouncy baby bunny finds his bed ill. by Christine Westerberg. Western, 1977. ISBN 0-307-60029-7 Subj: Animals – rabbits. Bedtime.

Emilio's summer day ill. by Ben Shecter. HarperCollins, 1966. Subj: Cities, towns. Ethnic groups in the U.S. – Puerto Rican Americans. Seasons – summer.

The Ginghams and the backward picnic ill. by Joane Koenig. Western, 1979. ISBN 0-307-60148-X Subj: Activities – picnicking.

A hat for the queen ill. by Olindo Giacomini. Golden Pr., 1974. Subj: Clothing – hats. Royalty – queens.

Little grey rabbit ill. by Lorinda Bryan Cauley. Western, 1979. ISBN 0-307-68651-5 Subj: Animals – rabbits.

A new home for Snow Ball ill. by Jan Pyk. Western, 1979. ISBN 0-307-60800-X Subj: Animals – horses, ponies. Royalty.

Strong John ill. by Sal Murdocca. Macmillan, 1980. ISBN 0-02-711790-1 Subj: Behavior – trickery. Folk & fairy tales.

Who took the top hat trick? ill. by Jim Cummins. Golden Pr., 1974. Subj: Behavior – lost & found possessions. Magic.

Bowden, Miriam. *The adventure of Paz in the land of numbers* ill. by Anna-Maria Crum. Humanics, 1992. ISBN 0-89334-450-9 Subj: Animals. Animals – koalas. Counting, numbers. Foreign languages.

Bowdish, Lynea. *The carousel ride* ill. by Patrick Girouard. Childrens Pr., 1998. ISBN 0-516-20967-1 Subj: Imagination. Merry-go-rounds.

Bowen, Anne. *I loved you before you were born* ill. by Greg Shed. HarperCollins, 2001. ISBN 0-06-028721-7 Subj: Babies. Family life – grandmothers. Memories, memory.

When you visit Grandma and Grandpa ill. by Tomasz Bogacki. Lerner, 2004. ISBN 1-57505-610-0 Subj: Babies. Family life – brothers & sisters. Family life – grandparents.

Bowen, Betsy. *Antler, bear, canoe* ill. by author. Little, 1991. ISBN 0-316-10376-4 Subj: ABC books. Forest, woods. Nature. Seasons.

Tracks in the wild ill. by author. Houghton Mifflin, 1998. ISBN 0-316-10377-2 Subj: Animals. Forest, woods. Nature.

Bowen, Keith. *Katy's gift* ill. by author; words by Dan Gutman. Courage Books, 1998. ISBN 0-7624-0169-9 Subj: Character traits – generosity. Character traits – individuality. Ethnic groups in the U.S. – Amish. Family life – brothers & sisters. Friendship.

Bowen, Vernon. *The lazy beaver* ill. by Jim Davis. McKay, 1948. Subj: Animals – beavers. Character traits – laziness.

Bower, Gary. *Ivy's icicle* ill. by Jan Bower. Tyndale, 2002. ISBN 0-8423-7417-5 Subj: Behavior – forgiving. Family life – brothers & sisters. Family life – grandmothers.

Bower, Tamara. *The shipwrecked sailor: an Egyptian tale with hieroglyphs* ill. by reteller. Atheneum, 2000. ISBN 0-689-83046-7 Subj: Folk & fairy tales. Foreign lands – Egypt. Hieroglyphics. Magic. Reptiles – snakes.

Bowers, Kathleen Rice. *At this very minute* ill. by Linda Shute. Little, 1983. ISBN 0-316-10400-0 Subj: Bedtime. Imagination.

Bowers, Tim. *A new home* ill. by author. Harcourt, 2002. ISBN 0-15-216564-9 Subj: Animals – squirrels. Friendship. Moving.

Bowie, C. W. *Busy fingers* ill. by Fred Willingham. Whispering Coyote, 2003. ISBN 1-58089-036-9 Subj: Anatomy – fingers. Rhyming text.

Busy toes ill. by Fred Willingham. Whispering Coyote, 1998. ISBN 1-879085-72-0 Subj: Activities. Anatomy – toes. Rhyming text.

Bowles, Brad. *Grandma's band* ill. by Anthony Chan. Stemmer House, 1989. ISBN 0-88045-112-2 Subj: Family life – grandmothers. Music. Musical instruments – bands. Musical instruments – washboards.

Bowling, David Louis. *Dirty Dingy Daryl* ill. by Patricia Hendy Bowling. Inka Dinka Ink, 1981. ISBN 0-939700-00-X Subj: Character traits – cleanliness.

Bowman, Pete. *The Christmas songbook* ill. by author. Putnam, 1990. ISBN 0-399-21918-8 Subj: Format, unusual – toy & movable books. Holidays – Christmas. Music. Songs.

Goodnight, teddy bear ill. by author. Kingfisher, 1995. ISBN 1-85697-552-5 Subj: Bedtime. Format, unusual – board books. Night. Nursery rhymes. Poetry. Toys – bears.

I wish I were big ill. by author. Hutchinson, 1997. ISBN 0-09-176588-9 Subj: Animals. Behavior – wishing. Concepts – size. Self-concept. Toys.

Boxall, Ed. *Francis the scaredy cat* ill. by author. Candlewick, 2002. ISBN 0-7636-1767-9 Subj: Animals – cats. Emotions – fear. Monsters.

Boxer, Devorah. *26 ways to be somebody else* ill. by author. Pantheon, 1960. Subj: ABC books. Careers.

A boy went out to gather pears: an old verse ill. by Felix Hoffmann. Harcourt, 1966. Subj: Cumulative tales. Poetry.

Boyce, Katie. *Hector the hermit crab* ill. by author. Bloomsbury, 2003. ISBN 1-58234-800-6 Subj: Character traits – confidence. Crustaceans – crabs. Friendship. Self-concept.

Boyd, Lizi. *Baby play* ill. by author. Workman, 1992. ISBN 1-56305-310-1 Subj: Animals – cats. Babies. Format, unusual – board books. Format, unusual – toy & movable books.

Baby's journal ill. by author. Chronicle, 1995. ISBN 0-8118-0780-0 Subj: Babies.

Bailey the big bully ill. by author. Viking, 1989. ISBN 0-670-82719-3 Subj: Behavior – bullying.

Black dog red house ill. by author. Little, 1993. ISBN 0-316-10443-4 Subj: Animals – dogs. Concepts – color. Friendship.

Bunny hop ill. by author. Workman, 1992. ISBN 1-56305-308-X Subj: Animals – rabbits. Format, unusual – board books. Format, unusual – toy & movable books.

Half wild and half child ill. by author. Viking, 1988. ISBN 0-670-82072-5 Subj: Behavior – misbehavior. Character traits – willfulness.

I love Daddy ill. by author. Candlewick, 2004. ISBN 0-7636-2217-6 Subj: Activities. Family life – fathers. Family life – sons. Frogs & toads.

I love Mommy ill. by author. Candlewick, 2004. ISBN 0-7636-2216-8 Subj: Activities. Family life – mothers. Family life – sons. Frogs & toads.

Lulu Crow's garden ill. by author. Little, 1998. ISBN 0-316-10419-1 Subj: Animals. Birds – crows. Gardens, gardening. Rhyming text.

Mouse in a house ill. by author. Little, 1993. ISBN 0-316-10444-2 Subj: Animals – mice. Format, unusual. Homes, houses. Rhyming text.

The not-so-wicked stepmother ill. by author. Viking, 1987. ISBN 0-670-81589-6 Subj: Activities. Behavior – misunderstanding. Birds – ducks. Family life – stepfamilies.

Princess, cowboy, pirate, elf ill. by author. Hyperion, 1995. ISBN 0-7868-1059-9 Subj: Clothing – hats. Imagination. Theater.

Sam is my half brother ill. by author. Viking, 1990. ISBN 0-670-83046-1 Subj: Babies. Family life – new sibling. Family life – stepfamilies. Sibling rivalry.

Sweet dreams, Willy ill. by author. Viking, 1992. ISBN 0-670-84382-2 Subj: Bedtime. Dreams. Imagination. Night.

Willy and the cardboard boxes ill. by author. Viking, 1991. ISBN 0-670-83636-2 Subj: Activities – playing. Imagination.

Boyd, Pauline. *The how: making the best of a mistake* (Boyd, Selma)

I met a polar bear (Boyd, Selma)

Boyd, Selma. *The how: making the best of a mistake* by Selma & Pauline Boyd; ill. by Peggy Luks. Human Sciences Pr., 1981. ISBN 0-87705-076-3 Subj: Behavior – mistakes. Emotions – embarrassment. Friendship.

I met a polar bear by Selma & Pauline Boyd; ill. by Patience Brewster. Lothrop, 1983. ISBN 0-688-01885-8 Subj: Animals. Behavior – promptness, tardiness. Imagination. School.

Boyden, Linda. *The blue roses* ill. by Amy Córdova. Lee & Low, 2002. ISBN 1-58430-037-X Subj: Death. Emotions. Family life – grandfathers. Gardens, gardening. Indians of North America.

Boyle, Constance. *Little Owl and the weed* ill. by author. Barron's, 1985. ISBN 0-8120-5639-6 Subj: Birds. Gardens, gardening.

The story of Little Owl ill. by author. Barron's, 1985. ISBN 0-8120-5638-8 Subj: Behavior – lost & found possessions. Birds – owls. Toys – bears.

Boyle, Doe. *Gray wolf pup* ill. by Jeff Domm. Soundprints, 1993. ISBN 1-56899-010-3 Subj: Alaska. Animals – wolves.

Otter on his own ill. by Lisa Bonforte. Soundprints, 1995. ISBN 1-56899-129-0 Subj: Animals – otters. Sea & seashore.

Summer coat, winter coat: the story of a snowshoe hare ill. by Allen Davis. Soundprints, 1993. ISBN 1-56899-015-4 Subj: Animals – rabbits. Nature. Seasons.

Boyle, Vere. *Beauty and the beast* ill. by author. Barron's, 1988. ISBN 0-8120-5902-6 Subj: Character traits – appearance. Character traits – loyalty. Emotions – love. Folk & fairy tales. Magic.

Boynton, Sandra. *A is for angry* ill. by author. Workman, 1983. ISBN 0-89480-453-7 Subj: ABC books. Animals.

Barnyard dance! ill. by author. Workman, 1993. ISBN 1-56305-442-6 Subj: Activities – dancing. Animals. Farms. Format, unusual – board books.

Birthday monsters! ill. by author. Workman, 1993. ISBN 1-56305-443-4 Subj: Birthdays. Format, unusual – board books. Monsters. Rhyming text.

But not the hippopotamus ill. by author. S&S, 1982. ISBN 0-671-44904-4 Subj: Animals – hippopotamuses. Format, unusual – board books. Rhyming text.

Chloë and Maude ill. by author. Little, 1985. ISBN 0-316-10492-2 Subj: Animals – cats. Friendship.

Dinosaur's binkit ill. by author. Little Simon, 1998. ISBN 0-689-82203-0 Subj: Bedtime. Dinosaurs. Format, unusual – board books. Format, unusual – toy & movable books. Prehistory. Rhyming text.

Doggies ill. by author. S&S, 1984. ISBN 0-671-49318-3 Subj: Animals – dogs. Format, unusual – board books.

The going to bed book ill. by author. S&S, 1982. ISBN 0-671-44902-8 Subj: Animals. Bedtime. Format, unusual – board books. Rhyming text.

Good night, good night ill. by author. Random House, 1985. ISBN 0-394-97285-6 Subj: Animals. Bedtime. Music. Rhyming text. Songs.

Hester in the wild ill. by author. HarperCollins, 1979. ISBN 0-06-020654-3 Subj: Animals – hippopotamuses. Animals – pigs. Camps, camping.

Hippos go berserk ill. by author. Little, 1979. ISBN 0-316-16488-4 Subj: Animals – hippopotamuses. Counting, numbers. Rhyming text.

Horns to toes and in between ill. by author. S&S, 1984. ISBN 0-671-49319-1 Subj: Anatomy. Format, unusual – board books.

If at first . . . ill. by author. Little, 1980. ISBN 0-316-10487-6 Subj: Animals – elephants. Animals – mice. Character traits – perseverance. Humorous stories.

Moo, baa, la la la! ill. by author. Newly rev. ed. Little Simon, 1995. ISBN 0-671-44901-X Subj: Animals. Format, unusual – board books. Noise, sounds. Rhyming text.

Oh my oh my oh dinosaurs! ill. by author. Workman, 1993. ISBN 1-56305-441-8 Subj: Dinosaurs. Format, unusual – board books. Prehistory. Rhyming text.

One, two, three! ill. by author. Workman, 1993. ISBN 1-56305-444-2 Subj: Counting, numbers. Format, unusual – board books. Rhyming text.

Opposites ill. by author. S&S, 1982. ISBN 0-671-44903-6 Subj: Concepts – opposites. Format, unusual – board books.

Yay, you! : moving out, moving up, moving on ill. by author. S&S, 2001. ISBN 0-689-84283-X Subj: Character traits – individuality. Rhyming text.

Bozylinsky, Hannah Heritage. *Lala Salama* ill. by author. Putnam, 1993. ISBN 0-399-22022-4 Subj: Animals. Bedtime. Foreign lands – Africa. Foreign languages. Lullabies.

Bozzo, Maxine Zohn. *Toby in the country, Toby in the city* ill. by Frank Modell. Greenwillow, 1982. ISBN 0-688-00917-4 Subj: Cities, towns. Country.

Bradbury, Ray. *Switch on the night* ill. by Leo & Diane Dillon. Knopf, 2000, 1993. ISBN 0-375-80608-3 Subj: Emotions – fear. Friendship. Night.

Switch on the night ill. by Madeleine Gekiere. Pantheon, 1955. Subj: Emotions – fear. Friendship. Night.

Bradby, Marie. *The longest wait* ill. by Peter Catalanotto. Orchard, 1998. ISBN 0-531-08721-2 Subj: Careers – postal workers. Weather – snow. Weather – storms.

Momma, where are you from? ill. by Chris K. Soentpiet. Orchard, 2000. ISBN 0-531-33105-9 Subj: Cities, towns. Ethnic groups in the U.S. – African Americans. Family life – mothers.

More than anything else ill. by Chris K. Soentpiet. Orchard, 1995. ISBN 0-531-08764-6 Subj: Behavior – seeking better things. Books, reading. Ethnic groups in the U.S. – African Americans.

Once upon a farm ill. by Ted Rand. Orchard, 2002. ISBN 0-439-31766-5 Subj: Ethnic groups in the U.S. – African Americans. Farms. Rhyming text.

Bradfield, Roger (Jolly Roger). *The flying hockey stick* ill. by author. Rand McNally, 1966. Subj: Activities – flying. Humorous stories. Machines.

Giants come in different sizes ill. by author. Rand McNally, 1966. Subj: Giants. Wizards.

A good night for dragons ill. by author. Addison-Wesley, 1967. ISBN 0-201-09201-8 Subj: Dragons. Knights.

Bradford, Ann. *The mystery at Misty Falls* by Ann Bradford & Kal Gezi; ill. by Mina Gow McLean. Childrens Pr., 1980. ISBN 0-516-06491-6 Subj: Animals – raccoons. Clubs, gangs. Mystery stories.

The mystery in the secret club house by Ann Bradford & Kal Gezi; ill. by Mina Gow McLean. Childrens Pr., 1978. ISBN 0-89565-027-4 Subj: Clubs, gangs. Crime. Mystery stories.

The mystery of the blind writer by Ann Bradford & Kal Gezi; ill. by Mina Gow McLean. Childrens Pr., 1980. ISBN 0-516-06493-2 Subj: Animals – dogs. Clubs, gangs. Crime. Handicaps – blindness. Mystery stories.

The mystery of the live ghosts by Ann Bradford & Kal Gezi; ill. by Mina Gow McLean. Childrens Pr., 1978. ISBN 0-89565-026-6 Subj: Holidays – Halloween. Mystery stories.

The mystery of the midget clown by Ann Bradford & Kal Gezi; ill. by Mina Gow McLean. Childrens Pr., 1980. ISBN 0-516-06495-9 Subj: Clowns, jesters. Clubs, gangs. Mystery stories.

The mystery of the missing dogs by Ann Bradford & Kal Gezi; ill. by Mina Gow McLean. Childrens Pr., 1980. ISBN 0-516-06492-4 Subj: Animals – dogs. Clubs, gangs. Handicaps. Mystery stories.

The mystery of the missing raccoon by Ann Bradford & Kal Gezi; ill. by Mina Gow McLean. Childrens Pr., 1978. ISBN 0-89565-025-8 Subj: Animals – raccoons. Character traits – freedom. Mystery stories.

The mystery of the square footsteps by Ann Bradford & Kal Gezi; ill. by Mina Gow McLean. Childrens Pr., 1980. ISBN 0-516-06496-7 Subj: Clubs, gangs. Mystery stories. Robots.

The mystery of the tree house by Ann Bradford & Kal Gezi; ill. by Mina Gow McLean. Childrens Pr., 1980. ISBN 0-516-06494-0 Subj: Birds – parakeets, parrots. Clubs, gangs. Crime. Mystery stories.

Bradford, Karleen. *You can't rush a cat* by Karleen Bradford & Leslie Elizabeth Watts; ill. by Leslie Elizabeth Watts. Orca, 2004. ISBN 1-55143-247-1 Subj: Animals – cats. Family life – grandfathers.

Bradley, Kimberly Brubaker. *Favorite things* ill. by Laura Huliska-Beith. Dial, 2003. ISBN 0-8037-2597-3 Subj: Bedtime. Day. Family life – mothers. Imagination.

Pop! a book about bubbles photos by Margaret Miller. HarperCollins, 2001. ISBN 0-06-028701-2 Subj: Bubbles.

Bradman, Tony. *The bad babies' book of colors* ill. by Deborah Van der Beek. Knopf, 1987. ISBN 0-394-99046-3 Subj: Behavior – misbehavior. Birthdays. Concepts – color. Rhyming text.

The bad babies' counting book ill. by Deborah Van der Beek. Knopf, 1986. ISBN 0-394-98352-1 Subj: Behavior – misbehavior. Counting, numbers. Rhyming text.

A bad week for the three bears ill. by Jenny Williams. Random House, 1993. ISBN 0-679-83379-X Subj: Animals – bears. Behavior – misbehavior. Family life. Rhyming text.

Billy and the baby ill. by Jan Lewis. Barron's, 1992. ISBN 0-8120-6328-7 Subj: Babies. Family life – brothers. Family life – new sibling.

Daddy's lullaby ill. by Jason Cockcroft. McElderry, 2002. ISBN 0-689-84295-3 Subj: Family life – fathers. Lullabies.

Dilly speaks up ill. by Susan Hellard. Viking, 1991. ISBN 0-670-83680-X Subj: Dinosaurs. Shopping. Sibling rivalry.

A goodnight kind of feeling ill. by Clive Scruton. Holiday, 1998. ISBN 0-8234-1351-9 Subj: Animals – cats. Family life.

It came from outer space ill. by Carol Wright. Dial, 1992. ISBN 0-8037-1098-4 Subj: School. Space & space ships.

Look out, he's behind you ill. by Margaret Chamberlain. Putnam, 1988. ISBN 0-399-21485-2 Subj: Animals – wolves. Behavior – talking to strangers. Forest, woods. Format, unusual – toy & movable books.

Michael ill. by Tony Ross. Macmillan, 1991. ISBN 0-02-711850-9 Subj: Behavior – misbehavior. Character traits – individuality. School. Space & space ships.

Not like this, like that ill. by Joanna Burroughes. Oxford Univ. Pr., 1988. ISBN 0-19-520712-2 Subj: Character traits – foolishness. Counting, numbers. Family life – fathers.

See you later, alligator ill. by Colin Hawkins. Dial, 1986. ISBN 0-8037-0267-1 Subj: Animals. Format, unusual – toy & movable books. Reptiles – alligators, crocodiles.

That's not a fish ill. by Susie Jenkin-Pearce. Trafalgar Square, 1993. ISBN 0-460-88121-3 Subj: Family life. Sports – fishing.

This little baby ill. by Jenny Williams. Putnam, 1990. ISBN 0-399-22202-2 Subj: Babies. Rhyming text.

Through my window ill. by Eileen Browne. Silver Burdett, 1986. ISBN 0-382-09258-9 Subj: Family life. Illness.

Wait and see ill. by Eileen Browne. Oxford Univ. Pr., 1988. ISBN 0-19-520644-4 Subj: Family life. Shopping.

Brady, Irene. *Wild mouse* ill. by author. Scribners, 1976. ISBN 0-684-14664-9 Subj: Animals – mice. Science.

Brady, Kimberley Smith. *Keeper for the sea* ill. by Peter M. Fiore. S&S, 1995. ISBN 0-689-80472-5 Subj: Family life – grandfathers. Sea & seashore. Sports – fishing.

Brady, Susan. *Find my blanket* ill. by author. HarperCollins, 1988. ISBN 0-397-32248-8 Subj: Animals – mice. Behavior – hiding things. Family life.

Bragdon, Lillian J. *Tell me the time, please* ill. by Frank & Margaret Phares. Lippincott, 1937. Subj: Clocks, watches. Time.

Braithwaite, Jill. *Police cars* ill. by author. Lerner, 2004. ISBN 0-8225-0770-6 Subj: Automobiles. Careers – police officers.

Bram, Elizabeth. *I don't want to go to school* ill. by author. Greenwillow, 1977. ISBN 0-688-84095-7 Subj: School – first day.

One day I closed my eyes and the world disappeared ill. by author. Dial, 1978. ISBN 0-8037-6613-0 Subj: Senses – sight.

Saturday morning lasts forever ill. by author. Dial, 1978. ISBN 0-8037-7628-4 Subj: Activities – playing.

There is someone standing on my head ill. by author. Dial, 1979. ISBN 0-8037-8649-2 Subj: Imagination – imaginary friends.

Woodruff and the clocks ill. by author. Dial, 1980. ISBN 0-8037-9633-1 Subj: Behavior – collecting things. Clocks, watches.

Brami, Elisabeth. *Mommy time* by Elisabeth Brami & Anne-Sophie Tschiegg; ill. by Anne-Sophie Tschiegg. Kane/Miller, 2002. ISBN 1-929132-22-0 Subj: Family life – mothers. Imagination.

Branagh, Kenneth. *Hamlet for kids* (Burdett, Lois)

Brand, Millen. *This little pig named Curly* ill. by John Hamberger. Crown, 1968. Subj: Animals – pigs. Farms.

Brand, Oscar. *When I first came to this land* ill. by Doris Burn. Putnam, 1974. ISBN 0-399-60906-7 Subj: Cumulative tales. Folk & fairy tales. Poverty. Songs.

Brande, Marlie. *Sleepy Nicholas* adapt. by Noel Streatfield; ill. by author. Follett, 1970. ISBN 0-695-40071-3 Subj: Foreign lands – Denmark. Sleep.

Brandenberg, Alexa. *Ballerina flying* ill. by author. HarperCollins, 2002. ISBN 0-06-029550-3 Subj: Activities – dancing. Ballet.

I am me! ill. by author. Harcourt, 1996. ISBN 0-15-200974-4 Subj: Careers. Self-concept.

Brandenberg, Aliki. *see* Aliki

Brandenberg, Franz. *Aunt Nina and her nephews and nieces* ill. by Aliki. Greenwillow, 1983. ISBN 0-688-01870-X Subj: Animals. Animals – babies. Animals – cats. Birthdays. Family life – aunts, uncles. Toys.

Aunt Nina, good night ill. by Aliki. Greenwillow, 1989. ISBN 0-688-07464-2 Subj: Bedtime. Family life – aunts, uncles.

Aunt Nina's visit ill. by Aliki. Greenwillow, 1984. ISBN 0-688-01766-5 Subj: Animals – cats. Family life – aunts, uncles. Puppets.

Cock-a-doodle-doo ill. by Aliki. Greenwillow, 1986. ISBN 0-688-06104-4 Subj: Animals. Farms. Noise, sounds.

Everyone ready? ill. by Aliki. Greenwillow, 1979. ISBN 0-688-84198-8 Subj: Activities – traveling. Animals – mice. Family life. Trains.

Fresh cider and apple pie ill. by Aliki. Macmillan, 1973. ISBN 0-02-711910-6 Subj: Food. Insects – flies. Spiders.

A fun weekend ill. by Alexa Brandenberg. Greenwillow, 1991. ISBN 0-688-09721-9 Subj: Activities – vacationing. Animals – bears. Family life.

The hit of the party ill. by Aliki. Greenwillow, 1985. ISBN 0-688-04241-4 Subj: Animals – hamsters. Parties.

I wish I was sick, too! ill. by Aliki. Greenwillow, 1976. ISBN 0-688-84047-7 Subj: Behavior – wishing. Illness.

No school today! ill. by Aliki. Macmillan, 1975. ISBN 0-02-711930-0 Subj: Animals – cats. Behavior – mistakes. School.

Otto is different ill. by James Stevenson. Greenwillow, 1985. ISBN 0-688-04254-6 Subj: Activities. Character traits – being different. Octopuses.

A robber! A robber! ill. by Aliki. Greenwillow, 1975. ISBN 0-688-84027-2 Subj: Animals – cats. Crime. Night. Noise, sounds.

A secret for grandmother's birthday ill. by Aliki. Greenwillow, 1975. ISBN 0-688-84012-4 Subj: Behavior – secrets. Birthdays. Family life – grandmothers.

Six new students ill. by Aliki. Greenwillow, 1978. ISBN 0-688-84124-4 Subj: Animals – mice. School – first day.

What's wrong with a van? ill. by Aliki. Greenwillow, 1987. ISBN 0-688-06775-1 Subj: Animals – cats. Automobiles. Behavior – seeking better things. Family life.

Brandenburg, Jim. *Scruffy: a wolf finds his place in the pack* photos by author; ed. by JoAnn Bren Guernsey. Walker, 1996. ISBN 0-8027-8446-1 Subj: Animals – wolves. Foreign lands – Arctic.

Brandle, Bine. *Flusi, the sock monster* ill. by author. Kane/Miller, 2004. ISBN 1-929132-69-7 Subj: Behavior – lost & found possessions. Clothing – socks. Monsters.

Brandon, Siobhán. *The bird's story* ill. by Caroline Jayne Church. Zero to Ten, 1999. ISBN 1-84089-120-3 Subj: Animals – buffaloes. Behavior. Birds – herons. Format, unusual.

Brandt, Amy. *Benjamin comes back = Benjamin regresa* ill. by Janice Lee Porter. Redleaf, 2000. ISBN 1-884834-79-5 Subj: Family life – mothers. Foreign languages. School – nursery.

When Katie was our teacher = Cuando Katie era muestra maestra ill. by Janice Lee Porter. Redleaf, 2000. ISBN 1-884834-78-7 Subj: Careers – teachers. Foreign languages. School – nursery.

Brandt, Betty. *Special delivery* ill. by Kathy Haubrich. Carolrhoda, 1988. ISBN 0-87614-312-5 Subj: Careers – postal workers. Letters, cards. Post office. U.S. history – frontier & pioneer life.

Branford, Henrietta. *Little Pig Figwort can't get to sleep* ill. by Claudio Muñoz. Clarion, 2000. ISBN 0-618-15968-1 Subj: Animals – pigs. Bedtime. Sleep.

Branley, Franklyn M. (Mansfield). *Air is all around you* ill. by Holly Keller. Rev. ed. Crowell, 1986. ISBN 0-690-04503-4 Subj: Science.

Comets ill. by Giulio Maestro. Crowell, 1984. Subj: Science. Sky.

Down comes the rain ill. by James Graham Hale. HarperCollins, 1997. ISBN 0-06-025338-X Subj: Science. Weather. Weather – rain.

Earthquakes ill. by Richard Rosenblum. HarperCollins, 1990. ISBN 0-690-04663-4 Subj: Earth. Science.

Eclipse: darkness in daytime ill. by Donald Crews. Rev. ed. HarperCollins, 1988. ISBN 0-690-04619-7 Subj: Science. Sun.

Flash, crash, rumble, and roll ill. by Barbara & Ed Emberley. Rev. ed. Crowell, 1985. ISBN 0-690-04425-9 Subj: Science. Weather – lightning, thunder.

Floating and sinking ill. by Robert Galster. Crowell, 1967. ISBN 0-690-30918-X Subj: Science.

Floating in space ill. by True Kelley. HarperCollins, 1998. ISBN 0-06-025433-5 Subj: Careers – astronauts. Science. Space & space ships.

Gravity is a mystery ill. by Don Madden. Rev. ed. Crowell, 1986. ISBN 0-690-04527-1 Subj: Science.

High sounds, low sounds ill. by Paul Galdone. Crowell, 1967. ISBN 0-690-38018-6 Subj: Noise, sounds. Science.

How little and how much: a book about scales ill. by Byron Barton. Crowell, 1976. ISBN 0-690-01058-3 Subj: Concepts – measurement.

Hurricane watch ill. by Giulio Maestro. Crowell, 1985. ISBN 0-690-04471-2 Subj: Science. Weather – storms.

The International Space Station ill. by True Kelley. HarperCollins, 2000. ISBN 0-06-028703-9 Subj: Space & space ships.

Is there life in outer space? ill. by Don Madden. Crowell, 1984. ISBN 0-690-04375-9 Subj: Science. Space & space ships.

Journey into a black hole ill. by Marc Simont. Crowell, 1986. ISBN 0-690-04544-1 Subj: Science. Space & space ships. Stars.

Light and darkness ill. by Stacey Schuett. Rev. ed. HarperCollins, 1998. ISBN 0-06-027295-3 Subj: Science.

The moon seems to change ill. by Barbara & Ed Emberley. Crowell, 1987. ISBN 0-690-04585-9 Subj: Moon. Science.

North, south, east and west ill. by Robert Galster. Crowell, 1966. ISBN 0-690-58609-4 Subj: Science.

The planets in our solar system ill. by Don Madden. Crowell, 1981. ISBN 0-690-04026-1 Subj: Planets. Science. Space & space ships. Sun. World.

Rain and hail ill. by Harriett Barton. Rev. ed. Crowell, 1983. ISBN 0-690-04353-8 Subj: Science. Weather. Weather – rain.

The sky is full of stars ill. by Felicia Bond. Crowell, 1981. ISBN 0-690-04123-3 Subj: Science. Sky. Stars.

Snow is falling ill. by Holly Keller. Rev. ed. Crowell, 1986. ISBN 0-690-04548-4 Subj: Science. Weather – snow.

The sun, our nearest star ill. by Edward Miller. Rev. & newly ill. ed. HarperCollins, 2002. ISBN 0-06-028535-4 Subj: Earth. Science. Sun.

Sunshine makes the seasons ill. by Giulio Maestro. Rev. ed. Crowell, 1985. ISBN 0-690-04482-8 Subj: Science. Seasons. Sun.

Tornado alert ill. by Giulio Maestro. Crowell, 1988. ISBN 0-690-04688-X Subj: Science. Weather – storms.

Volcanoes ill. by Marc Simont. Crowell, 1985. ISBN 0-690-04431-3 Subj: Science. Volcanoes.

What makes a magnet? ill. by True Kelley. HarperCollins, 1996. ISBN 0-06-026442-X Subj: Science.

What makes day and night ill. by Arthur Dorros. Rev. ed. Crowell, 1986. ISBN 0-690-04524-7 Subj: Earth. Science.

What the moon is like ill. by True Kelley. Rev. ed. Crowell, 1986. ISBN 0-690-04512-3 Subj: Moon. Science.

Brann, Esther. *A book for baby* ill. by author. Macmillan, 1945. Subj: Activities. Babies. Family life.

'Round the world ill. by author. Macmillan, 1935. Subj: Activities – traveling. Foreign lands. World.

Brannen, Ann. *E. H. Grieg's Peer Gynt* (Grieg, E. H. [Edvard Hagerup])

The sorcerer's apprentice (Dukas, P. [Paul Abraham])

Brasch, Kate. *Prehistoric monsters* photos by Jean-Philippe Varin. Merrimack, 1985. ISBN 0-88162-098-X Subj: Animals. Dinosaurs. Prehistory. Science.

Bratton, Heidi. *Imagine: a story about the beginning* ill. by author. Paulist Pr., 1997. ISBN 0-8091-6642-9 Subj: Creation. Format, unusual – board books. Religion.

Yes, I can! ill. by author. Paulist Pr., 1997. ISBN 0-8091-6639-9 Subj: Format, unusual – board books. Religion.

Bratton, John. *The teddy bears' picnic* ill. by Renate Kozikowski. Macmillan, 1990. ISBN 0-690-04703-7 Subj: Activities – picnicking. Format, unusual. Music. Songs.

Braun, Kathy. *Kangaroo and kangaroo* ill. by Jim McMullan. Doubleday, 1965. Subj: Animals – kangaroos. Behavior – collecting things. Rhyming text.

Braun, Sebastien. *I love my daddy* ill. by author. HarperCollins, 2004. ISBN 0-06-054311-6 Subj: Animals – bears. Day. Family life – fathers. Family life – sons.

I love my mommy ill. by author. HarperCollins, 2004. ISBN 0-06-054310-8 Subj: Animals – squirrels. Family life – mothers.

Braun, Trudi. *My goose Betsy* ill. by John Bendall-Brunello. Candlewick, 1998. ISBN 0-7636-0449-6 Subj: Birds – geese. Farms.

Braybrooks, Ann. *Plenty of pockets* ill. by Scott Menchin. Harcourt, 2000. ISBN 0-15-202173-6 Subj: Character traits – orderliness. Clothing – pockets.

Breathed, Berke (Berkeley). *Edward Fudwupper fibbed big: explained by Fannie Fudwupper* ill. by author. Little, 2000. ISBN 0-316-10675-5 Subj: Aliens. Character traits – honesty. Family life – brothers & sisters.

A wish for wings that work ill. by author. Little, 1991. ISBN 0-316-10758-1 Subj: Activities – flying. Behavior – wishing. Birds – penguins. Holidays – Christmas.

Brébeuf, Jean de, Saint. *The Huron carol* ill. by Frances Tyrrell. Dutton, 1992. ISBN 0-525-44909-4 Subj: Foreign lands – Canada. Holidays – Christmas. Indians of North America – Huron. Music.

Brecht, Bertolt. *Uncle Eddie's moustache* ill. by Ursula Kirchberg; trans. by Muriel Rukeyser. Pantheon, 1974. Tr. of Onkel Ede hat einen Schnurrbart. ISBN 0-394-92819-9 Subj: Family life – aunts, uncles. Humorous stories. Poetry.

Breckler, Rosemary K. *Hoang breaks the lucky teapot* ill. by Adrian Frankel. Houghton Mifflin, 1992. ISBN 0-395-57031-X Subj: Character traits – luck. Ethnic groups in the U.S. – Vietnamese Americans. Family life. Foreign languages.

Sweet dried apples: a Vietnamese wartime childhood ill. by Deborah Kogan Ray. Houghton Mifflin, 1996. ISBN 0-395-73570-X Subj: Careers – doctors. Death. Foreign lands – Vietnam. War.

Breda, Tjalmar. *see* DeJong, David Cornel

Bredeson, Carmen. *George W. Bush, the 43rd president* ill. with period reproductions, photos & maps. Enslow, 2002. ISBN 0-7660-2100-9 Subj: U.S. history.

Getting ready for space ill. with photos. Childrens Pr., 2003. ISBN 0-516-22498-0 Subj: Careers – astronauts. Space & space ships.

Liftoff! ill. with photos. Childrens Pr., 2003. ISBN 0-516-22499-9 Subj: Careers – astronauts. Space & space ships.

Living on a space shuttle ill. with photos. Childrens Pr., 2003. ISBN 0-516-22528-6 Subj: Careers – astronauts. Space & space ships.

Looking at maps and globes ill. with photos. Childrens Pr., 2001. ISBN 0-516-22351-8 Subj: Maps.

Breebaart, Joeri. *When I die, will I get better?* by Joeri & Piet Breebaart; ill. by Piet Breebaart. Peter Bedrick, 1993. ISBN 0-87226-375-4 Subj: Animals. Death. Family life – brothers.

Breebaart, Piet. *When I die, will I get better?* (Breebaart, Joeri)

Breese, Gillian. *The amazing adventures of Teddy Tum Tum* by Gillian Breese & Tony Langham; ill. by Patrick Lowry. Arcade, 1992. ISBN 1-55970-185-4 Subj: Toys. Toys – bears.

Breeze, Lynn. *Baby's animals* ill. by author. Barron's, 1994. ISBN 0-812-06411-9 Subj: Animals. Babies. Format, unusual – board books. Noise, sounds. Pets. Rhyming text.

Baby's clothes ill. by author. Barron's, 1994. ISBN 0-812-06410-0 Subj: Babies. Clothing. Format, unusual – board books. Noise, sounds. Pets. Rhyming text.

Baby's food ill. by author. Barron's, 1994. ISBN 0-812-06413-5 Subj: Babies. Counting, numbers. Food. Format, unusual – board books. Rhyming text.

Baby's toys ill. by author. Barron's, 1994. ISBN 0-812-06412-7 Subj: Babies. Format, unusual – board books. Rhyming text. Toys.

This little baby goes out by Lynn Breeze & Ann Morris; ill. by Lynn Breeze. Little, 1993. ISBN 0-316-10854-5 Subj: Babies. Family life – mothers. Format, unusual – board books. Rhyming text.

This little baby's bedtime by Lynn Breeze & Ann Morris; ill. by Lynn Breeze. Little, 1993. ISBN 0-316-58419-3 Subj: Babies. Bedtime. Family life. Format, unusual – board books. Rhyming text.

This little baby's morning by Lynn Breeze & Ann Morris; ill. by Lynn Breeze. Barron's, 1993. ISBN 0-316-10855-3 Subj: Activities – playing. Babies. Family life – mothers. Format, unusual – board books. Rhyming text.

Breinburg, Petronella. *Doctor Shawn* ill. by Errol Lloyd. Crowell, 1975. ISBN 0-690-00722-1 Subj: Activities – playing. Careers – doctors. Ethnic groups in the U.S. – African Americans.

Shawn goes to school ill. by Errol Lloyd. Crowell, 1973. ISBN 0-690-00277-7 Subj: Ethnic groups in the U.S. – African Americans. Friendship. School – first day.

Shawn's red bike ill. by Errol Lloyd. Crowell, 1976. ISBN 0-690-01115-6 Subj: Ethnic groups in the U.S. – African Americans. Sports – bicycling.

Brennan, Herbie. *Frankenstella and the video store monster* ill. by Cathy Gale. Bloomsbury, 2002. ISBN 1-58234-752-2 Subj: Monsters.

Brennan, Jan. *Born two-gether* photos by Leo Brennan. J & L Books, 1984. ISBN 0-9613536-1-9 Subj: Family life. Multiple births – twins.

Brennan, John. *Zoo day* by John Brennan & Leonie Keaney; ill. with photos. Carolrhoda, 1989. ISBN 0-87614-358-3 Subj: Animals. Zoos.

Brennan, Joseph Killorin. *Gobo and the river* ill. by Diane Dawson Hearn. Holt, 1985. ISBN 0-03-004552-5 Subj: Character traits – perseverance. Puppets. Rivers.

Brennan, Linda Crotta. *Marshmallow kisses* ill. by Mari Takabayashi. Houghton, 2000. ISBN 0-395-73872-5 Subj: Rhyming text. Seasons – summer.

Brennan, Patricia D. *Hitchety hatchety up I go!* ill. by Robert Rayevsky. Macmillan, 1985. ISBN 0-02-712300-6 Subj: Behavior – stealing. Folk & fairy tales. Little people.

Brenner, Anita. *I want to fly* ill. by Lucienne Bloch. Addison-Wesley, 1943. Subj: Airplanes, airports. Imagination.

Brenner, Barbara A. *Beef stew* ill. by Catherine Siracusa. Random House, 2004, c1990. ISBN 0-394-95046-1 Subj: Family life – grandmothers. Food. Friendship.

The boy who loved to draw: Benjamin West ill. by Olivier Dunrea. Houghton, 1999. ISBN 0-395-85080-0 Subj: Art. Careers – artists.

The color wizard ill. by Leo & Diane Dillon. Bantam, 1989. ISBN 0-553-05825-8 Subj: Concepts – color. Rhyming text. Wizards.

Dinosaurium ill. by Donna Bragenitz. Bantam, 1993. ISBN 0-553-07614-0 Subj: Dinosaurs. Imagination. Museums. Prehistory.

A dog I know ill. by Fred Brenner. HarperCollins, 1983. ISBN 0-06-020685-3 Subj: Animals – dogs. Humorous stories.

Faces, faces, faces photos by George Ancona. Dutton, 1970. ISBN 0-525-29518-6 Subj: Anatomy – faces. Emotions. Ethnic groups in the U.S. Senses – hearing. Senses – sight. Senses – smell. Senses – taste. Senses – touch.

The five pennies ill. by Erik Blegvad. Knopf, 1964. Subj: Money. Pets.

The flying patchwork quilt ill. by Fred Brenner. Addison-Wesley, 1965. Subj: Activities – flying. Magic. Quilts.

Good morning, garden ill. by Denise Ortakales. NorthWord, 2004. ISBN 1-55971-888-9 Subj: Gardens, gardening. Morning. Rhyming text.

Good news ill. by Kate Duke. Bantam, 1991. ISBN 0-553-07091-6 Subj: Behavior – gossip. Birds – geese. Cumulative tales.

How do you make a bubble? (Hooks, William H.)

Lion and Lamb by Barbara A. Brenner & William H. Hooks; ill. by Bruce Degen. G. Stevens, 1998, c1990. ISBN 0-553-05829-0 Subj: Animals – lions. Animals – sheep. Friendship.

Mr. Tall and Mr. Small ill. by Tomi Ungerer. Addison-Wesley, 1966. ISBN 0-8050-2757-2 Subj: Animals – giraffes. Animals – mice. Character traits – conceit. Fire.

No way, Slippery Slick! a child's first book about drugs (Oppenheim, Joanne)

One small place by the sea ill. by Tom Leonard. HarperCollins, 2004. ISBN 0-688-17183-4 Subj: Animals. Ecology. Sea & seashore.

Ostrich feathers ill. by Vera B. Williams & Evelyn Armstrong. Parents' Magazine Pr., 1979. ISBN 0-8193-0922-2 Subj: Animals. Behavior – greed.

The prince and the pink blanket ill. by Nola Langner. Four Winds, 1980. ISBN 0-590-07614-0 Subj: Family life. Royalty – princes.

Rosa and Marco and the three wishes ill. by Megan Halsey. Bradbury, 1992. ISBN 0-02-712315-4 Subj: Behavior – wishing. Character traits – foolishness. Family life – brothers & sisters. Fish.

The snow parade ill. by Mary Tara O'Keefe. Crown, 1984. ISBN 0-571-55210-8 Subj: Counting, numbers. Parades. Weather.

Somebody's slippers, somebody's shoes ill. by Leslie Jacobs. Addison-Wesley, 1957. Subj: Clothing – shoes. Shopping.

The tremendous tree book by Barbara Brenner & May Garelick; ill. by Fred Brenner. Caroline House, 1992, c1979. ISBN 1-8780-9356-8 Subj: Science. Trees.

Two orphan cubs by Barbara Brenner & May Garelick; ill. by Erika Kors. Walker, 1989. ISBN 0-8027-6869-5 Subj: Animals – bears. Character traits – kindness to animals. Nature.

What the elephant told ill. by Akemi Gutierrez. Holt, 2003. ISBN 0-8050-6442-7 Subj: Animals – babies. Animals – elephants. Babies.

Where's that cat? ill. by Carol Schwartz. Scholastic, 1995. ISBN 0-590-45216-9 Subj: Animals – cats. Science.

Brenner, Emily. *On the first day of grade school* ill. by Bruce Whatley. HarperCollins, 2004. ISBN 0-06-051041-2 Subj: Animals. Careers – teachers. Cumulative tales. Rhyming text. School.

Brent, Isabelle. *Cameo cats* ill. by sel. Little, 1992. ISBN 0-316-10836-7 Subj: Animals – cats. Art. Rhyming text.

Noah's ark ill. by author. Little, 1992. ISBN 0-316-10837-5 Subj: Animals. Boats, ships. Religion – Noah. Weather – floods. Weather – rain. Weather – rainbows.

Brentano, Clemens. *Schoolmaster Whackwell's wonderful sons* ill. by Maurice Sendak. Random House, 1962. Subj: Behavior – growing up. Careers. Folk & fairy tales.

Bresnick-Perry, Roslyn. *Leaving for America* ill. by Mira Reisberg. Childrens Pr., 1992. ISBN 0-89239-105-7 Subj: Family life. Foreign lands – Russia. Jewish culture. Moving.

Brett, Jan. *Annie and the wild animals* ill. by author. Houghton Mifflin, 1985. ISBN 0-395-37800-1 Subj: Animals. Animals – cats. Emotions – loneliness. Pets.

Armadillo rodeo ill. by author. Putnam, 1995. ISBN 0-399-22803-9 Subj: Animals. Animals – armadillos. Behavior – mistakes. Family life.

Berlioz the bear ill. by author. Putnam, 1991. ISBN 0-399-22248-0 Subj: Animals. Animals – bears. Cumulative tales. Music. Musical instruments – bands.

Christmas trolls ill. by author. Putnam, 1993. ISBN 0-399-22507-2 Subj: Animals – hedgehogs. Behavior – sharing. Behavior – stealing. Holidays – Christmas. Mythical creatures – trolls.

Comet's nine lives ill. by author. Putnam, 1996. ISBN 0-399-22931-0 Subj: Animals – cats. Animals – dogs. Behavior – carelessness. Lighthouses.

Daisy comes home ill. by author. Putnam, 2002. ISBN 0-399-23618-X Subj: Behavior – lost. Birds – chickens. Foreign lands – China.

The first dog ill. by author. Harcourt, 1988. ISBN 0-15-227650-5 Subj: Animals – dogs. Animals – wolves. Art. Caves. Pets.

Fritz and the beautiful horses ill. by author. Houghton Mifflin, 1981. ISBN 0-395-30850-X Subj: Animals – horses, ponies. Behavior – wishing. Character traits – cleverness. Folk & fairy tales.

Gingerbread baby (The gingerbread boy)

Goldilocks and the three bears (The three bears)

The hat ill. by author. Putnam, 1997. ISBN 0-399-23101-3 Subj: Animals. Animals – hedgehogs. Clothing.

Hedgie's surprise ill. by author. Putnam, 2000. ISBN 0-399-23477-2 Subj: Animals – hedgehogs. Birds – chickens. Character traits – cleverness. Eggs. Food. Mythical creatures – trolls.

The mitten ill. by author. Putnam, 1990. ISBN 0-399-23109-9 Subj: Behavior – lost & found possessions. Folk & fairy tales. Foreign lands – Ukraine. Format, unusual – board books.

Town mouse, country mouse (Æsop)

The trouble with trolls ill. by author. Putnam, 1992. ISBN 0-399-22336-3 Subj: Animals – dogs. Character traits – cleverness. Clothing. Mythical creatures – trolls.

Who's that knocking on Christmas eve? ill. by author. Putnam, 2002. ISBN 0-399-23873-5 Subj: Foreign lands – Norway. Holidays – Christmas. Mythical creatures – trolls.

The wild Christmas reindeer ill. by author. Putnam, 1990. ISBN 0-399-22192-1 Subj: Animals – reindeer. Holidays – Christmas. Santa Claus.

Brett, Jessica. *Animals on the go* ill. by Richard Cowdrey. Harcourt, 2000. ISBN 0-15-202584-7 Subj: Animals.

Breverton, David. *Here comes bulldozer* ill. by Brian Bartle. Grosset, 1992. ISBN 0-448-40590-1 Subj: Format, unusual – toy & movable books. Machines. Trucks.

Here comes fire truck ill. by Brian Bartle. Grosset, 1992. ISBN 0-448-40592-X Subj: Format, unusual – toy & movable books. Trucks.

Here comes the dump truck ill. by Brian Bartle. Grosset, 1992. ISBN 0-448-40591-1 Subj: Format, unusual – toy & movable books. Trucks.

Here comes the tow truck ill. by Brian Bartle. Grosset, 1992. ISBN 0-448-40593-8 Subj: Format, unusual – toy & movable books. Trucks.

Brewer, Dan. *Silver seeds* (Paolilli, Paul)

Brewster, Patience. *Ellsworth and the cats from Mars* ill. by author. Houghton Mifflin, 1981. ISBN 0-395-29612-9 Subj: Animals – cats. Behavior – lost. Space & space ships.

Nobody ill. by author. Houghton Mifflin, 1982. ISBN 0-89919-110-X Subj: Behavior – dissatisfaction. Imagination – imaginary friends.

Rabbit Inn ill. by author. Little, 1991. ISBN 0-316-10747-6 Subj: Animals – rabbits. Hotels.

Two bushy badgers ill. by author. Little, 1995. ISBN 0-316-10862-6 Subj: Animals – badgers. Friendship.

Brian, Janeen. *Where does Thursday go?* ill. by Stephen Michael King. Clarion, 2001. ISBN 0-618-21264-7 Subj: Animals – bears. Birds. Days of the week, months of the year.

Brice, Tony. *Baby animals* ill. by author. Rand McNally, 1945. Subj: Animals. Babies.

The bashful goldfish ill. by author. Rand McNally, 1942. Subj: Character traits – shyness. Fish. Pets.

Bridge, Chris. *Andrew's story: a book about a boy who beat cancer* photos by author. Lerner, 2002. ISBN 0-8225-2587-9 Subj: Health & fitness. Illness – cancer.

Bridges, Margaret Park. *Am I big or little?* ill. by Tracy Dockray. SeaStar, 2000. ISBN 1-58717-020-5 Subj: Concepts – size. Family life – mothers.

Edna elephant ill. by Janie Bynum. Candlewick, 2002. ISBN 0-7636-1555-2 Subj: Activities. Animals – elephants.

If I were your father ill. by Kady MacDonald Denton. Morrow, 1999. ISBN 0-688-15193-0 Subj: Family life – fathers. Imagination.

Will you take care of me? ill. by Melissa Sweet. Morrow, 1998. ISBN 0-688-15195-7 Subj: Animals – kangaroos. Family life – mothers.

Bridges, Shirin Yim. *Ruby's wish* ill. by Sophie Blackall. Chronicle, 2002. ISBN 0-8118-3490-5 Subj: Foreign lands – China. Gender roles. School.

Bridges, William. *Lion Island* photos by Emmy Haas & Sam Dunton. Morrow, 1965. ISBN 0-688-31519-4 Subj: Animals – lions. Zoos.

Ookie, the walrus who likes people photos by Emmy Haas & Sam Dunton. Morrow, 1962. Subj: Animals – walruses.

Bridgman, Elizabeth. *All the little bunnies: a counting book* ill. by author. Atheneum, 1977. ISBN 0-689-50068-7 Subj: Counting, numbers. Rhyming text.

How to travel with grownups ill. by Eleanor Hazard. Crowell, 1980. ISBN 0-690-04010-5 Subj: Activities – traveling. Foreign lands.

Nanny bear's cruise ill. by author. HarperCollins, 1981. ISBN 0-06-020689-6 Subj: Activities – traveling. Animals – bears. Boats, ships.

A new dog next door ill. by author. HarperCollins, 1978. ISBN 0-06-020673-X Subj: Animals – dogs.

Bridle, Martin. *Punch and Judy in the rain* (Eaton, Su)

Bridwell, Norman. *Clifford counts bubbles* ill. by author. Scholastic, 1992. ISBN 0-590-45872-8 Subj: Animals – dogs. Bubbles. Counting, numbers.

Clifford goes to Hollywood ill. by author. Scholastic, 1981. ISBN 0-606-03090-5 Subj: Animals – dogs. Character traits – loyalty.

Clifford's ABC ill. by author. Scholastic, 1984. ISBN 0-590-48694-2 Subj: ABC books. Animals – dogs.

Clifford's good deeds ill. by author. Four Winds, 1975. ISBN 0-590-07439-3 Subj: Animals – dogs. Automobiles. Behavior – mistakes. Careers – firefighters. Character traits – helpfulness.

Clifford's Halloween ill. by author. Four Winds, 1967. ISBN 0-590-66159-0 Subj: Animals – dogs. Holidays – Halloween.

Clifford's neighborhood ill. by Carolyn Bracken & Ken Edwards. Scholastic, 2002. ISBN 0-439-33242-7 Subj: Animals – dogs. Format, unusual – toy & movable books. Rhyming text.

Glow-in-the-dark Halloween ill. by Thompson Bros. Scholastic, 2001. ISBN 0-439-30566-7 Subj: Animals – dogs. Format, unusual. Holidays – Halloween.

The witch grows up ill. by author. Scholastic, 1980. ISBN 0-590-30045-8 Subj: Humorous stories. Magic. Witches.

The witch next door ill. by author. Four Winds, 1966. ISBN 0-590-40433-4 Subj: Witches.

Brierley, Louise. *King Lion and his cooks* ill. by author. Holt, 1982. ISBN 0-03-061218-7 Subj: Animals. Food. Royalty.

Briggs, Kelly Paul. *Lighthouse lullaby* ill. by author. Down East, 2000. ISBN 0-8927-2486-2 Subj: Bedtime. Lighthouses. Rhyming text.

Briggs, Raymond. *The adventures of Bert* (Ahlberg, Allan)

The bear ill. by author. Random House, 1994. ISBN 0-679-96944-6 Subj: Animals – polar bears. Imagination. Seasons – winter.

A bit more Bert (Ahlberg, Allan)

Building the snowman ill. by author. Little, 1985. ISBN 0-316-10813-8 Subj: Snowmen. Wordless.

Dressing up ill. by author. Little, 1985. ISBN 0-316-10814-6 Subj: Clothing. Snowmen. Wordless.

Father Christmas ill. by author. Random House, 1997. ISBN 0-679-88776-8 Subj: Holidays – Christmas. Santa Claus. Wordless.

Father Christmas goes on holiday ill. by author. Coward, 1975. ISBN 0-14-050187-8 Subj: Activities – vacationing. Holidays – Christmas. Santa Claus. Wordless.

Fee fi fo fum ill. by author. Coward, 1964. Subj: Nursery rhymes.

Jim and the beanstalk ill. by author. Coward, 1970. ISBN 0-698-11577-5 Subj: Folk & fairy tales. Giants. Humorous stories. Old age.

The man ill. by author. Random House, 1995. ISBN 0-679-87643-X Subj: Fairies.

The party ill. by author. Little, 1985. ISBN 0-316-10816-2 Subj: Parties. Snowmen. Wordless.

Ring-a-ring o' roses ill. by author. Coward, 1962. Subj: Nursery rhymes.

The snowman ill. by author. Random House, 1978. ISBN 0-394-93973-5 Subj: Friendship. Snowmen. Wordless.

The snowman [a lift-the-flap board book] ill. by author. Random House, 1998. ISBN 0-679-88896-9 Subj: Concepts – color. Counting, numbers. Format, unusual – toy & movable books. Snowmen.

The snowman storybook ill. by author. Random House, 1997. ISBN 0-679-98343-0 Subj: Snowmen.

The snowman tell-the-time book ill. by author. H. Hamilton, 1991. ISBN 0-241-13112-X Subj: Clocks, watches. Format, unusual – toy & movable books. Snowmen. Weather – snow.

The tin-pot foreign general and the old iron woman ill. by author. H. Hamilton, 1984. ISBN 0-241-11362-8 Subj: War.

Walking in the air ill. by author. Little, 1985. ISBN 0-316-10815-4 Subj: Imagination. Snowmen. Wordless.

The white land: a picture book of traditional rhymes and verses comp. & ill. by Raymond Briggs. Coward, 1963. Subj: Nursery rhymes. Songs.

Bright, Paul. *Quiet!* ill. by Guy Parker-Rees. Scholastic, 2003. ISBN 0-439-54512-9 Subj: Animals. Animals – lions. Jungle. Noise, sounds.

Bright, Robert. *Georgie* ill. by author. Doubleday, 1944. ISBN 0-385-07307-0 Subj: Family life. Farms. Ghosts.

Georgie and the baby birds ill. by author. Doubleday, 1983. ISBN 0-385-17246-X Subj: Birds. Character traits – helpfulness. Ghosts.

Georgie and the ball of yarn ill. by author. Doubleday, 1983. ISBN 0-385-17244-3 Subj: Character traits – helpfulness. Ghosts.

Georgie and the buried treasure ill. by author. Doubleday, 1979. ISBN 0-385-14626-4 Subj: Ghosts.

Georgie and the little dog ill. by author. Doubleday, 1983. ISBN 0-385-17247-8 Subj: Animals – dogs. Character traits – helpfulness. Ghosts.

Georgie and the magician ill. by author. Doubleday, 1966. ISBN 0-385-01021-4 Subj: Ghosts. Magic.

Georgie and the noisy ghost ill. by author. Doubleday, 1971. ISBN 0-590-20614-1 Subj: Activities – vacationing. Ghosts. Noise, sounds. Sea & seashore.

Georgie and the robbers ill. by author. Doubleday, 1963. ISBN 0-389-01470-8 Subj: Crime. Ghosts.

Georgie and the runaway balloon ill. by author. Doubleday, 1983. ISBN 0-385-17245-1 Subj: Animals – mice. Character traits – helpfulness. Ghosts. Toys – balloons.

Georgie goes west ill. by author. Doubleday, 1973. ISBN 0-385-05277-4 Subj: Cowboys, cowgirls. Ghosts.

Georgie to the rescue ill. by author. Doubleday, 1956. Subj: Birds – owls. Cities, towns. Ghosts.

Georgie's Christmas carol ill. by author. Doubleday, 1975. ISBN 0-385-02410-X Subj: Ghosts. Holidays – Christmas.

Georgie's Halloween ill. by author. Doubleday, 1958. Subj: Ghosts. Holidays – Halloween.

Gregory, the noisiest and strongest boy in Grangers Grove ill. by author. Doubleday, 1969. Subj: Character traits – laziness. Food. Noise, sounds.

I like red ill. by author. Doubleday, 1955. Subj: Concepts – color. Hair.

Me and the bears ill. by author. Doubleday, 1951. Subj: Animals – bears. Behavior – wishing. Friendship. Sleep. Zoos.

Miss Pattie ill. by author. Doubleday, 1954. Subj: Animals – cats.

My hopping bunny ill. by author. Doubleday, 1971. Subj: Activities – jumping. Animals – rabbits. Rhyming text.

My red umbrella ill. by author. Morrow, 1959. ISBN 0-688-31619-0 Subj: Counting, numbers. Umbrellas. Weather – rain.

The travels of Ching ill. by author. Addison-Wesley, 1943. Subj: Foreign lands – China. Toys – dolls.

Which is Willy? ill. by author. Doubleday, 1962. Subj: Birds – penguins. Character traits – individuality.

Bright star shining: *poems for Christmas* sel. by Michael Harrison & Christopher Stuart-Clark. Eerdmans, 1998. ISBN 0-8028-5177-0 Subj: Holidays – Christmas. Poetry.

Brightman, Alan. *Like me* ill. by author. Little, 1976. ISBN 0-316-10808-1 Subj: Character traits – being different. Handicaps – mental handicaps.

Brighton, Catherine. *Five secrets in a box* ill. by author. Dutton, 1987. ISBN 0-525-44318-5 Subj: Behavior – secrets. Foreign lands – Italy. Science.

The fossil girl: Mary Anning's dinosaur discovery ill. by author. Millbrook, 1999. ISBN 0-7613-1468-7 Subj: Careers – archaeologists. Dinosaurs. Foreign lands – England. Fossils. Science.

Galileo's treasure box ill. by author. Walker, 2001. ISBN 0-8027-8768-1 Subj: Science.

Hope's gift ill. by author. Doubleday, 1988. ISBN 0-385-24598-X Subj: Character traits – kindness to animals. Gifts. Theater.

Mozart ill. by author. Doubleday, 1990. ISBN 0-385-41538-9 Subj: Careers – composers. Careers – musicians.

My hands, my world ill. by author. Macmillan, 1984. ISBN 0-02-712900-4 Subj: Handicaps – blindness. Imagination – imaginary friends. Senses – sight.

My Napoleon ill. by author. Millbrook, 1997. ISBN 0-7613-0106-2 Subj: Foreign lands – France. Royalty – emperors.

Nijinsky ill. by author. Doubleday, 1989. ISBN 0-385-24926-8 Subj: Activities – dancing. Ballet. Foreign lands – Russia.

Brill, Marlene Targ. *Bronco Charlie and the Pony Express* ill. by Craig Orback. Carolrhoda, 2004. ISBN 1-57505-587-2 Subj: Animals – horses, ponies. Careers – postal workers. U.S. history.

Margaret Knight, girl inventor ill. by Joanne Friar. Millbrook, 2001. ISBN 0-7613-1756-2 Subj: Activities – weaving. Careers – inventors. Children as inventors. Safety. U.S. history.

Brillhart, Julie. *Anna's goodbye apron* ill. by author. A. Whitman, 1990. ISBN 0-8075-0375-4 Subj: Careers – teachers. Clothing – aprons. School.

The dino expert ill. by author. A. Whitman, 1993. ISBN 0-8075-1597-3 Subj: Birds. Dinosaurs.

Molly rides the school bus ill. by author. A. Whitman, 2002. ISBN 0-8075-5210-0 Subj: Buses. School – first day.

Story hour – starring Megan! ill. by author. A. Whitman, 1992. ISBN 0-8075-7628-X Subj: Activities – storytelling. Books, reading. Careers – librarians. Family life – mothers. Libraries. Problem solving.

When daddy came to school ill. by author. A. Whitman, 1995. ISBN 0-8075-8878-4 Subj: Birthdays. Family life – fathers. Rhyming text. School.

When Daddy took us camping ill. by author. A. Whitman, 1997. ISBN 0-8075-8879-2 Subj: Camps, camping. Family life – fathers. Rhyming text.

Brimner, Larry Dane. *Aggie and Will* ill. by Rebecca McKillip Thornburgh. Childrens Pr., 1998. ISBN 0-516-20754-7 Subj: Books, reading. Friendship. Libraries.

The big, beautiful, brown box ill. by Christine Tripp. Childrens Pr., 2001. ISBN 0-516-22160-4 Subj: Activities – playing. Character traits – cooperation.

Cat on wheels ill. by Mary Peterson. Boyds Mills, 2000. ISBN 1-56397-747-8 Subj: Animals – cats. Behavior – carelessness. Imagination. Sports – skateboarding.

Country Bear's good neighbor ill. by Ruth Tietjen Councell. Watts, 1988. ISBN 0-531-08308-X Subj: Animals – bears. Food.

Country Bear's surprise ill. by Ruth Tietjen Councell. Orchard, 1991. ISBN 0-531-08411-6 Subj: Animals – bears. Birthdays. Parties.

Cowboy up! ill. by Susan Miller. Childrens Pr., 1999. ISBN 0-516-21199-4 Subj: Animals – horses, ponies. Cowboys, cowgirls. Rhyming text.

Dinosaurs dance ill. by Patrick Girouard. Childrens Pr., 1998. ISBN 0-516-20752-0 Subj: Animals. Animals – dogs. Friendship. Prehistory.

Elliot Fry's good-bye ill. by Eugenie Fernandes. Boyds Mills, 1994. ISBN 1-56397-113-5 Subj: Behavior – running away. Family life.

If dogs had wings ill. by Chris L. Demarest. Boyds Mills, 1996. ISBN 1-56397-146-1 Subj: Activities – flying. Animals – dogs.

The littlest wolf ill. by José Aruego & Ariane Dewey. HarperCollins, 2002. ISBN 0-06-029040-4 Subj: Animals – wolves. Behavior – growing up.

Max and Felix ill. by Les Gray. Boyds Mills, 1993. ISBN 1-56397-010-4 Subj: Activities – photographing. Friendship. Frogs & toads.

Nana's hog ill. by Susan Miller. Childrens Pr., 1998. ISBN 0-516-20755-5 Subj: Animals – pigs. Character traits – individuality. Family life – grandmothers. Rhyming text.

What good is a tree? ill. by Leo Landry. Childrens Pr., 1998. ISBN 0-516-20953-1 Subj: Rhyming text. Trees.

Brin, Ruth F. *David and Goliath* ill. by H. Hechtkopf. Lerner, 1977. ISBN 0-8225-0365-4 Subj: Foreign lands – Israel. Giants. Religion – David.

The story of Esther ill. by H. Hechtkopf. Lerner, 1976. ISBN 0-8225-0364-6 Subj: Foreign lands – Israel. Religion.

Brinckloe, Julie. *Fireflies!* ill. by author. Macmillan, 1985. ISBN 0-02-713310-9 Subj: Behavior – growing up. Insects – fireflies.

Gordon's house ill. by author. Doubleday, 1976. ISBN 0-385-06905-7 Subj: Animals – bears.

Playing marbles ill. by author. Morrow, 1988. ISBN 0-688-07144-9 Subj: Activities – playing. Games.

Bring a torch, Jeannette, Isabella ill. by Adrienne Adams. Scribners, 1963. A provincial carol attributed to Nicholas Saboly, seventeenth century. Subj: Foreign lands – France. Holidays – Christmas. Music. Songs.

Brink, Carol Ryrie. *Goody O'Grumpity* ill. by Ashley Wolff. North-South, 1994. ISBN 1-55858-328-9 Subj: Activities – baking, cooking. Rhyming text. U.S. history.

Brion, David. *Space vehicles* (Rockwell, Anne F.)

Briscoe, D. Stuart. *Where is God?* ill. by Sally Marinin. Baker Bks., 1993. ISBN 0-8010-1038-1 Subj: Religion.

Briscoe, Jill. *The innkeeper's daughter* ill. by Dennis Hockerman. Childrens Pr., 1984. ISBN 0-516-09484-X Subj: Handicaps. Holidays – Christmas. Religion.

Brisson, Pat. *Hobbledy-clop* ill. by Maxie Chambliss. Boyds Mills, 2003. ISBN 1-56397-888-1 Subj: Animals. Cumulative tales. Family life – grandmothers. Toys.

Kate on the coast ill. by Rick Brown. Bradbury, 1992. ISBN 0-02-714341-4 Subj: Activities – traveling. Activities – vacationing. Letters, cards.

Magic carpet ill. by Amy Schwartz. Macmillan, 1991. ISBN 0-02-714340-6 Subj: Activities – traveling. Family life – aunts, uncles. Imagination.

Star blanket ill. by Erica Magnus. Boyds Mills, 2003. ISBN 1-56397-889-X Subj: Bedtime. Family life – fathers. Memories, memory.

Wanda's roses ill. by Maryann Cocca-Leffler. Boyds Mills, 1994. ISBN 1-56397-136-4 Subj: Behavior – disbelief. Character traits – optimism. Communities, neighborhoods. Flowers. Gardens, gardening.

Your best friend, Kate ill. by Rick Brown. Bradbury, 1989. ISBN 0-02-714350-3 Subj: Activities – traveling. Activities – vacationing. Family life. Letters, cards.

Bro, Marguerite (Harmon). *The animal friends of Peng-u* ill. by Seong Moy. Doubleday, 1965. Subj: Animals. Folk & fairy tales. Foreign lands – China.

Brock, Emma Lillian. *The birds' Christmas tree* ill. by author. Knopf, 1946. Subj: Birds. Character traits – kindness to animals. Holidays – Christmas.

Mr. Wren's house ill. by author. Knopf, 1944. Subj: Birds – wrens. Family life. Humorous stories.

Nobody's mouse ill. by author. Knopf, 1938. Subj: Animals. Cities, towns. Humorous stories.

One little Indian boy ill. by author. Hale, 1932. Subj: Indians of North America.

A pet for Barbie ill. by author. Knopf, 1947. Subj: Family life. Pets.

Pig with a front porch ill. by author. Knopf, 1937. Subj: Animals – pigs. Behavior – dissatisfaction.

A present for Auntie ill. by author. Knopf, 1939. Subj: Family life – aunts, uncles.

Skipping Island ill. by author. Knopf, 1958. Subj: Humorous stories. Islands.

Surprise balloon ill. by author. Knopf, 1949. Subj: Activities – flying. Animals. Toys – balloons.

Brocket, Ray. *Even the devil is afraid of a shrew: a folktale of Lapland* (Stalder, Valerie)

Brode, Robyn. *April* ill. with photos. Weekly Reader, 2003. ISBN 0-8368-3579-4 Subj: Days of the week, months of the year. Holidays. Seasons – spring.

August ill. with photos. Weekly Reader, 2003. ISBN 0-8368-3583-2 Subj: Activities – vacationing. Days of the week, months of the year. Holidays. Seasons – summer.

December ill. with photos. Weekly Reader, 2003. ISBN 0-8368-3587-5 Subj: Days of the week, months of the year. Holidays. Seasons – winter.

February ill. with photos. Weekly Reader, 2003. ISBN 0-8368-3577-8 Subj: Days of the week, months of the year. Holidays. Seasons – winter.

January ill. with photos. Weekly Reader, 2003. ISBN 0-8368-3576-X Subj: Days of the week, months of the year. Holidays. Seasons – winter.

July ill. with photos. Weekly Reader, 2003. ISBN 0-8368-3582-4 Subj: Days of the week, months of the year. Holidays. Seasons – summer.

June ill. with photos. Weekly Reader, 2003. ISBN 0-8368-3581-6 Subj: Days of the week, months of the year. Holidays. Seasons – summer.

March ill. with photos. Weekly Reader, 2003. ISBN 0-8368-3578-6 Subj: Days of the week, months of the year. Holidays. Seasons – spring.

May ill. with photos. Weekly Reader, 2003. ISBN 0-8368-3580-8 Subj: Days of the week, months of the year. Holidays. Seasons – spring.

November ill. with photos. Weekly Reader, 2003. ISBN 0-8368-3586-7 Subj: Days of the week, months of the year. Holidays. Seasons – fall.

October ill. with photos. Weekly Reader, 2003. ISBN 0-8368-3585-9 Subj: Days of the week, months of the year. Holidays. Seasons – fall.

September ill. with photos. Weekly Reader, 2003. ISBN 0-8368-3584-0 Subj: Days of the week, months of the year. Holidays. Seasons – fall.

Brodmann, Aliana. *Such a noise!* trans. from German by Aliana Brodmann & David Fillingham; ill. by Hans Poppel. Kane/Miller, 1989. Translation of: Ein Wunderlicher Rat. ISBN 0-916291-25-1 Subj: Folk & fairy tales. Humorous stories. Jewish culture. Noise, sounds. Problem solving.

Brodsky, Beverly. *see* McDermott, Beverly Brodsky

Brodzinsky, Anne Braff. *The mulberry bird* ill. by Diana L. Stanley. Rev. ed. Perspectives Pr., 1996. ISBN 0-944934-15-3 Subj: Adoption. Birds. Family life – stepfamilies.

Broekel, Ray. *Dangerous fish* ill. with photos. Childrens Pr., 1982. ISBN 0-516-01635-0 Subj: Fish.

I can be an author ill. by author. Childrens Pr., 1986. ISBN 0-516-01891-4 Subj: Careers – writers.

I can be an auto mechanic. Childrens Pr., 1985. ISBN 0-516-01885-X Subj: Automobiles. Careers – mechanics.

The painter and the bird (Velthuijs, Max)

Trains ill. with photos. Childrens Pr., 1981. ISBN 0-516-01652-0 Subj: Trains. Transportation.

Trucks ill. with photos. Childrens Pr., 1983. ISBN 0-516-01688-1 Subj: Transportation. Trucks.

Brogan, Peggy. *Sounds around the clock* (Martin, Bill [William Ivan])

Sounds I remember (Martin, Bill [William Ivan])

Sounds of home (Martin, Bill [William Ivan])

Sounds of laughter (Martin, Bill [William Ivan])

Sounds of numbers (Martin, Bill [William Ivan])

Bröger, Achim. *Bruno takes a trip* trans. from German by Caroline Gueritz; ill. by Gisela Kalow. Morrow, 1978. ISBN 0-688-32138-0 Subj: Activities – traveling. Pets. Trains.

Francie's paper puppy ill. by Michele Sambin. Alphabet Pr., 1984. Translation of: Wollen wir Freunde sein? ISBN 0-907234-56-9 Subj: Animals – dogs. Art. Country. Emotions – loneliness. Imagination. Pets.

Little Harry trans. from German by Elizabeth D. Crawford; ill. by Judy Morgan. Morrow, 1979. ISBN 0-688-32185-2 Subj: Humorous stories. Imagination. Problem solving.

The Santa Clauses ill. by Ute Krause. Dial, 1986. ISBN 0-8037-0266-3 Subj: Holidays – Christmas. Humorous stories. Santa Claus.

Brokering, Herbert F. *Earth and all stars: hyms and songs for young and old* ill. by author. Augsburg Fortress, 2003. ISBN 0-8006-5929-5 Subj: Music. Religion. Songs.

Bromhall, Winifred. *Bridget's growing day* ill. by author. Knopf, 1957. Subj: Behavior – growing up. Character traits – smallness. Foreign lands – Ireland.

Johanna arrives ill. by author. Knopf, 1941. Subj: Activities – traveling. Foreign lands – Holland.

Mary Ann's first picture ill. by author. Knopf, 1947. Subj: Activities – painting. Art. Birthdays.

Middle Matilda ill. by author. Knopf, 1962. Subj: Behavior – lost & found possessions. Clothing. Family life.

Bronson, Linda. *The circus alphabet* ill. by author. Holt, 2001. ISBN 0-8050-6294-7 Subj: ABC books. Circus. Rhyming text.

Hey, diddle, diddle (Mother Goose)

Sleigh bells and snowflakes (Sleigh bells and snowflakes)

Brook, Judy. *Hector and Harriet the night hamsters: two adventures* ill. by author. Dutton, 1985. ISBN 0-233-97625-6 Subj: Animals – hamsters.

Tim mouse goes down the stream ill. by author. Lothrop, 1975. ISBN 0-688-51698-X Subj: Animals – hedgehogs. Animals – mice. Character traits – bravery. Rivers.

Tim mouse visits the farm ill. by author. Lothrop, 1977. ISBN 0-688-51796-X Subj: Animals – hedgehogs. Animals – mice. Farms.

Brooke, L. Leslie (Leonard Leslie). *The golden goose book* (Mother Goose)

Johnny Crow's garden ill. by author. Warne, 1903. ISBN 0-7232-3429-9 Subj: Animals. Rhyming text.

Johnny Crow's new garden ill. by author. Warne, 1935. ISBN 0-7232-0568-X Subj: Animals. Rhyming text.

Johnny Crow's party ill. by author. Warne, 1907. ISBN 0-7232-0566-3 Subj: Animals. Parties.

Oranges and lemons ill. by author. Warne, 1913. Subj: Nursery rhymes.

Ring o' roses ill. by author. Houghton Mifflin, 1992. ISBN 0-395-61304-3 Subj: Nursery rhymes.

This little pig went to market (Mother Goose)

Brooks, Alan. *Frogs jump* ill. by Steven Kellogg. Scholastic, 1996. ISBN 0-590-45528-1 Subj: Animals. Counting, numbers.

Brooks, Andrea. *The guinea pigs' adventure* ill. by author. Little, 1980. ISBN 0-316-10961-4 Subj: Animals – guinea pigs.

Brooks, Ben. *Lemonade parade* ill. by Bill Slavin. A. Whitman, 1992. ISBN 0-8075-4432-9 Subj: Activities – working. Family life – fathers. Money.

Brooks, Bruce. *Each a piece* ill. by Elena Pavlov. HarperCollins, 1998. ISBN 0-06-023595-0 Subj: Format, unusual – toy & movable books. Rhyming text.

Brooks, Erik. *The practically perfect pajamas* ill. by author. Winslow, 2000. ISBN 1-890817-22-8 Subj: Animals – polar bears. Behavior – teasing. Clothing – pajamas.

Brooks, Gregory. *Monroe's island* ill. by author. Bradbury, 1979. ISBN 0-87888-140-9 Subj: Imagination.

Brooks, Gwendolyn. *Bronzeville boys and girls* ill. by Ronni Solbert. HarperCollins, 1956. ISBN 0-06-020651-9 Subj: Poetry.

Brooks, Nigel. *Country mouse cottage: how we lived one hundred years ago* by Nigel Brooks & Abigail Homer; ill. by authors. Walker, 2000. ISBN 0-8027-8752-5 Subj: Animals – mice. Country. Foreign lands – England.

Town mouse house: how we lived one hundred years ago by Nigel Brooks & Abigail Homer; ill. by authors. Walker, 2000. ISBN 0-8027-8732-0 Subj: Animals – mice. Cities, towns. Foreign lands – England.

Brooks, Robert B. *So that's how I was born* ill. by Susan Perl. S&S, 1983. ISBN 0-671-44501-4 Subj: Babies. Birth. Family life. Science.

Brooks, Ron. *Timothy and Gramps* ill. by author. Bradbury, 1978. ISBN 0-8788-8139-5 Subj: Family life – grandfathers. School.

Broome, Errol. *The smallest koala* ill. by Gwen Mason. Australian Book Source, 1988. ISBN 0-949447-65-X Subj: Animals – koalas. Character traits – curiosity. Food.

Brophy, Nannette. *The color of my fur* ill. by author. Winston-Derek, 1992. ISBN 1-55523-456-9 Subj: Animals – rabbits. Concepts – color. Friendship. Prejudice.

Brothers, Aileen. *Jiffy, Miss Boo and Mr. Roo* ill. by Audean Johnson. Follett, 1966. Subj: Birds – chickens. Pets.

Sad Mrs. Sam Sack by Aileen Brothers & Morton Botel; ill. by Muriel & Jim Collins. Follett, 1963. Subj: Behavior – dissatisfaction. Family life. Humorous stories.

Brothers and sisters are like that! Sel. by the Child Study Association of America; ill. by Michael Hampshire. Crowell, 1971. ISBN 0-690-16042-9 Subj: Family life. Sibling rivalry.

The brothers gruesome ill. by Drahos Zak. Houghton, 2000. ISBN 0-618-00515-3 Subj: Behavior – greed. Monsters. Rhyming text.

Brott, Ardyth. *Jeremy's decision* ill. by Michael Martchenko. Kane/Miller, 1990. ISBN 0-916291-31-6 Subj: Careers. Music.

Brouillard, Anne. *The bathtub prima donna* ill. by author. Abrams, 1999. ISBN 0-8109-4093-0 Subj: Activities – bathing. Activities – singing. Rhyming text. Weather – rain.

Brouillette, Jeanne S. *Moths* ill. by Bill Barss. Follett, 1966. Subj: Insects. Science.

Brown, Abbie Farwell. *The Christmas angel* ill. by Reginald Birch. Houghton Mifflin, 1910. Subj: Angels. Holidays – Christmas.

Brown, Alan. *Hoot and Holler* ill. by Rimantas Rolia. Knopf, 2001. ISBN 0-375-91417-X Subj: Birds – owls. Emotions. Friendship. Weather – storms.

Brown, Andrew. *Armored animals* ill. by author. Crabtree, 1997. ISBN 0-8650-5558-0 Subj: Animals.

Baby animals ill. by author. Crabtree, 1997. ISBN 0-8650-5559-9 Subj: Animals – babies.

Dangerous animals ill. by author. Crabtree, 1997. ISBN 0-8650-5560-2 Subj: Animals.

Brown, Beatrice Curtis. *Jonathan Bing* ill. by Judith Gwyn Brown. Lothrop, 1968. Subj: Poetry.

Jonathan Bing ill. by Pelagie Doane. Oxford Univ. Pr., 1937. Subj: Poetry.

Brown, Calef. *Tippintown* ill. by autnhor. Houghton, 2003. ISBN 0-618-14972-4 Subj: Imagination. Rhyming text.

Brown, Craig McFarland. *City sounds* ill. by author. Greenwillow, 1992. ISBN 0-688-10029-5 Subj: Careers – farmers. Cities, towns. Noise, sounds.

In the spring ill. by author. Greenwillow, 1994. ISBN 0-688-10984-5 Subj: Animals – babies. Babies. Birth. Seasons – spring.

My barn ill. by author. Greenwillow, 1991. ISBN 0-688-08786-8 Subj: Animals. Barns. Farms.

Patchwork farmer ill. by author. Greenwillow, 1989. ISBN 0-688-07736-6 Subj: Activities – sewing. Careers – farmers. Clothing. Farms. Wordless.

Brown, Daphne Faunce. *see* FaunceBrown, Daphne

Brown, David. *Someone always needs a policeman* ill. by author. S&S, 1972. ISBN 0-671-65168-4 Subj: Careers – police officers.

Brown, Don. *Alice Ramsey's grand adventure* ill. by author. Houghton Mifflin, 1997. ISBN 0-395-70127-9 Subj: Activities – traveling. Automobiles.

Mack made movies ill. by author. Roaring Brook, 2003. ISBN 0-7613-2504-2 Subj: Careers – motion picture producers. Theater.

Odd boy out: young Albert Einstein ill. by author. Houghton, 2004. ISBN 0-618-49298-4 Subj: Behavior – misunderstanding. Careers – scientists. Character traits – individuality.

One giant leap: the story of Neil Armstrong ill. by author. Houghton Mifflin, 1998. ISBN 0-395-88401-2 Subj: Careers – astronauts.

Rare treasure: Mary Anning and her remarkable discoveries ill. by author. Houghton, 1999. ISBN 0-395-92286-0 Subj: Careers – paleontologists. Foreign lands – England. Fossils. Gender roles. Science.

Ruth Law thrills a nation ill. by author. Ticknor & Fields, 1993. ISBN 0-395-66404-7 Subj: Airplanes, airports. Careers – airplane pilots.

Uncommon traveler: Mary Kingsley in Africa ill. by author. Houghton, 2000. ISBN 0-618-00273-1 Subj: Careers – explorers. Foreign lands – Africa. Foreign lands – England.

A voice from the wilderness: the story of Anna Howard ill. by author. Houghton, 2001. ISBN 0-618-08362-6 Subj: U.S. history.

Brown, Elinor. *The little story book* ill. by author. Oxford Univ. Pr., 1940. Subj: Activities.

Brown, Graham. *Christmas songs* (Bishop, Roma)

Holiday cheer (Bishop, Roma)

My first pop-up book of dinosaurs (Bishop, Roma)

My first pop-up book of prehistoric animals (Bishop, Roma)

Santa pays a visit (Bishop, Roma)

Brown, Jane Clark. *Whonk, and whonk again* ill. by author. Houghton Mifflin, 1989. ISBN 0-395-49211-4 Subj: Behavior – lost. Boats, ships. Cities, towns. Noise, sounds.

Brown, Janet Allison. *A little princess* by Frances Hodgson Burnett; retold by Janet Allison Brown; ill. by Graham Rust. Viking, 2001. ISBN 0-670-89913-5 Subj: Foreign lands – England. Orphans. School.

Little women by Louisa May Alcott; retold by Janet Allison Brown; ill. by Dinah Dryhurst. Viking, 2001. ISBN 0-670-89912-7 Subj: Family life – sisters.

The secret garden by Frances Hodgson Burnett; retold by Janet Allison Brown; ill. by Graham Rus. Viking, 2001. ISBN 0-670-89911-9 Subj: Foreign lands – England. Gardens, gardening. Handicaps – physical handicaps.

The wind in the willows (Grahame, Kenneth)

Brown, Jeff. *Flat Stanley* ill. by Tomi Ungerer. HarperCollins, 1961. ISBN 0-06-020681-0 Subj: Family life. Humorous stories. Problem solving.

Brown, Jo. *Where's my mommy?* ill. by author. Tiger Tales, 2002. ISBN 1-58925-015-X Subj: Animals. Birds – chickens. Family life – mothers. Reptiles – alligators, crocodiles.

Brown, Judith Gwyn. *Alphabet dreams* ill. by author. Prentice-Hall, 1976. ISBN 0-13-022806-0 Subj: ABC books. Rhyming text.

The happy voyage ill. by author. Macmillan, 1965. Subj: Boats, ships.

Max and the truffle pig ill. by author. Abingdon, 1963. Subj: Animals – pigs. Behavior – lost. Food. Foreign lands – France.

Brown, Katherine. *The Small One: a good Samaritan* ill. by author. Disney Pr., 1998. ISBN 0-7868-0481-5 Subj: Animals – donkeys. Character traits – kindness to animals. Religion.

Brown, Kathryn. *Muledred* ill. by author. Harcourt, 1990. ISBN 0-15-256265-6 Subj: Animals – mules. Clocks, watches. Family life – grandfathers. School.

Brown, Ken (Ken James). *Mucky Pup* ill. by author. Dutton, 1997. ISBN 0-525-45886-7 Subj: Animals. Animals – dogs. Farms.

Mucky Pup's Christmas ill. by author. Dutton, 1999. ISBN 0-525-46141-8 Subj: Animals – dogs. Animals – pigs. Behavior – misbehavior. Farms. Holidays – Christmas.

Nellie's knot ill. by author. Four Winds, 1993. ISBN 0-02-714930-7 Subj: Animals – elephants. Behavior – forgetfulness.

The scarecrow's hat ill. by author. Peachtree, 2001. ISBN 1-56145-240-8 Subj: Birds – chickens. Books, reading. Clothing – hats. Scarecrows.

What's the time, Grandma Wolf? ill. by author. Peachtree, 2001. ISBN 1-56145-250-5 Subj: Animals. Animals – wolves. Family life – grandmothers. Prejudice. Rhyming text. Time.

Brown, Kerry. *Tupag the dreamer* ill. by Linda Saport. Cavendish, 2001. ISBN 0-7614-5076-9 Subj: Creation. Eskimos. Foreign lands – Arctic. Seasons.

Brown, Laurie Krasny. *The bionic bunny show* (Brown, Marc Tolon)

Dinosaurs alive and well by Laurie Krasny Brown & Marc Tolon Brown; ill. by authors. Little, 1990. ISBN 0-316-10998-3 Subj: Dinosaurs. Health & fitness. Prehistory.

Dinosaurs divorce by Laurene Krasny Brown & Marc Brown; ill. by Marc Brown. Atlantic Monthly, 1986. ISBN 0-8711-3089-0 Subj: Dinosaurs. Divorce. Prehistory.

Dinosaurs to the rescue by Laurie Krasny Brown & Marc Tolon Brown; ill. by Marc Tolon Brown. Little, 1992. ISBN 0-316-11087-6 Subj: Dinosaurs. Ecology. Prehistory.

Dinosaurs travel by Laurie Krasny Brown & Marc Brown; ill. by Marc Brown. Little, 1988. ISBN 0-316-11076-0 Subj: Activities – traveling. Dinosaurs. Prehistory.

How to be a friend: a guide to making friends and keeping them by Laurie Krasny Brown & Marc Brown; ill. by Marc Brown. Little, 1998. ISBN 0-316-10913-4 Subj: Dinosaurs. Friendship.

Rex and Lilly school time by Laurie Krasny Brown & Marc Brown; ill. by Marc Brown. Little, 1997. ISBN 0-316-10920-7 Subj: Dinosaurs. Family life – brothers & sisters. School.

Visiting the art museum by Laurene Krasny Brown & Marc Brown; ill. by authors. Dutton, 1986. ISBN 0-525-44233-2 Subj: Art. Museums.

What's the big secret? talking about sex with girls and boys by Laurie Krasny Brown & Marc Brown; ill. by Marc Brown. Little, 1997. ISBN 0-316-10915-0 Subj: Anatomy. Family life. Sex instruction.

When dinosaurs die: a guide to understanding death by Laurie Krasny Brown & Marc Tolon Brown; ill. by Marc Tolon Brown. Little, 1996. ISBN 0-316-10917-7 Subj: Death. Dinosaurs. Emotions. Family life. Prehistory.

Brown, M. K. (Mary K.). *Let's go swimming with Mr. Sillypants* ill. by author. Crown, 1986. ISBN 0-517-56185-9 Subj: Dreams. Sports – swimming.

Brown, Marc Tolon. *Arthur and the true Francine* ill. by author. Little, 1996. ISBN 0-316-11136-8 Subj: Animals. Behavior – lying. School.

Arthur babysits ill. by author. Little, 1992. ISBN 0-316-11293-3 Subj: Activities – babysitting. Animals – aardvarks. Multiple births – twins.

Arthur goes to camp ill. by author. Little, 1982. ISBN 0-316-11218-6 Subj: Animals. Camps, camping.

Arthur goes to school ill. by author. Random House, 1995. ISBN 0-679-86734-1 Subj: Animals – aardvarks. Format, unusual – board books. Format, unusual – toy & movable books. School.

Arthur lost and found ill. by author. Little, 1998. ISBN 0-316-10912-6 Subj: Animals – aardvarks. Behavior – lost. Buses. Careers – bus drivers.

Arthur meets the president ill. by author. Little, 1991. ISBN 0-316-11265-8 Subj: Activities – traveling. Animals – aardvarks. Family life – sisters.

Arthur tricks the tooth fairy ill. by author. Random House, 1997. ISBN 0-679-98464-X Subj: Animals – aardvarks. Behavior – trickery. Fairies. Family life – brothers & sisters.

Arthur writes a story ill. by author. Little, 1996. ISBN 0-316-10916-9 Subj: Activities – writing. Animals – aardvarks.

Arthur's animal adventure ill. by author. Random House, 2002. ISBN 0-375-80699-7 Subj: ABC books. Animals. Animals – aardvarks. Foreign lands – Australia. Format, unusual – board books.

Arthur's April fool ill. by author. Little, 1983. ISBN 0-316-11196-1 Subj: Animals. Holidays – April Fools' Day.

Arthur's baby ill. by author. Little, 1987. ISBN 0-316-11123-6 Subj: Animals – aardvarks. Babies. Family life – new sibling.

Arthur's birthday ill. by author. Little, 1989. ISBN 0-316-11073-6 Subj: Animals – aardvarks. Birthdays. Friendship. Parties.

Arthur's chicken pox ill. by author. Little, 1994. ISBN 0-316-11384-0 Subj: Animals – aardvarks. Circus. Family life. Illness – chicken pox.

Arthur's Christmas ill. by author. Little, 1984. ISBN 0-316-11180-5 Subj: Animals. Gifts. Holidays – Christmas. Santa Claus.

Arthur's computer disaster ill. by author. Little, 1997. ISBN 0-316-11016-7 Subj: Animals – aardvarks. Behavior – misbehavior. Computers.

Arthur's eyes ill. by author. Little, 1979. ISBN 0-316-11063-9 Subj: Animals. Glasses. Senses – sight.

Arthur's family vacation ill. by author. Little, 1993. ISBN 0-316-11312-3 Subj: Activities – vacationing. Animals – aardvarks. Family life.

Arthur's first sleepover ill. by author. Little, 1994. ISBN 0-316-11445-6 Subj: Animals – aardvarks. Behavior – misbehavior. Camps, camping. Family life – brothers & sisters. Monsters. Sleepovers.

Arthur's Halloween ill. by author. Little, 1982. ISBN 0-316-11116-3 Subj: Animals. Holidays – Halloween.

Arthur's neighborhood ill. by author. Random House, 1996. ISBN 0-679-86737-6 Subj: Animals – aardvarks. Communities, neighborhoods. Format, unusual – toy & movable books.

Arthur's new puppy ill. by author. Little, 1993. ISBN 0-316-11355-7 Subj: Animals – aardvarks. Animals – dogs. Pets.

Arthur's new puppy [board book] ill. by author. 1st board book ed. Little, 1997. ISBN 0-316-11133-3 Subj: Animals – aardvarks. Animals – dogs. Format, unusual – board books. Pets.

Arthur's nose ill. by author. Little, 2001, 1976. ISBN 0-316-11884-2 Subj: Anatomy – noses. Animals – aardvarks.

Arthur's perfect Christmas ill. by author. Little, 2000. ISBN 0-316-11968-7 Subj: Animals. Animals – aardvarks. Holidays – Christmas.

Arthur's pet business ill. by author. Little, 1990. ISBN 0-316-11262-3 Subj: Animals – aardvarks. Animals – dogs. Pets.

Arthur's really helpful word book ill. by author. Random House, 1997. ISBN 0-679-98735-5 Subj: Animals – aardvarks. Books, reading. Language.

Arthur's spookiest Halloween ill. by author. Random House, 2003. ISBN 0-375-81004-8 Subj: Animals – aardvarks. Format, unusual – toy & movable books. Holidays – Halloween.

Arthur's teacher moves in ill. by author. Little, 2000. ISBN 0-316-11979-2 Subj: Animals. Animals – aardvarks. Careers – teachers. School.

Arthur's teacher trouble ill. by author. Little, 1986. ISBN 0-87113-091-2 Subj: Animals. School.

Arthur's Thanksgiving ill. by author. Little, 1983. ISBN 0-316-11060-4 Subj: Animals. Holidays – Thanksgiving. Theater.

Arthur's tooth ill. by author. Little, 1985. ISBN 0-87113-006-8 Subj: Animals. Teeth.

Arthur's TV trouble ill. by author. Little, 1995. ISBN 0-316-10919-3 Subj: Animals – aardvarks. Money. Pets.

Arthur's underwear ill. by author. Little, 1999. ISBN 0-316-11012-4 Subj: Animals. Animals – aardvarks. Behavior – worrying. Clothing. Emotions – embarrassment. School.

Arthur's Valentine ill. by author. Little, 1980. ISBN 0-316-11062-0 Subj: Animals. Holidays – Valentine's Day. School.

The bionic bunny show by Marc Brown & Laurene Krasny Brown; ill. by Marc Brown. Little, 1984. ISBN 0-316-11120-1 Subj: Animals. Animals – rabbits. Television.

Can you jump like a frog? ill. by author. Dutton, 1989. ISBN 0-525-44463-7 Subj: Format, unusual – toy & movable books. Frogs & toads. Nursery rhymes.

The cloud over Clarence ill. by author. Dutton, 1979. ISBN 0-525-28013-8 Subj: Animals – cats. Behavior – carelessness. Friendship.

Count to ten ill. by author. Western, 1982. ISBN 0-307-10627-6 Subj: Counting, numbers. Format, unusual – board books.

D. W. all wet ill. by author. Little, 1988. ISBN 0-316-11077-9 Subj: Animals – anteaters. Sea & seashore. Sibling rivalry.

D. W. flips! ill. by author. Little, 1987. ISBN 0-316-11239-9 Subj: Animals – anteaters. Sports – gymnastics.

D. W., go to your room! ill. by author. Little, 1999. ISBN 0-316-10905-3 Subj: Animals – aardvarks. Character traits – meanness. Family life – sisters.

D. W. rides again! ill. by author. Little, 1998. ISBN 0-316-11128-7 Subj: Animals – aardvarks. Family life – brothers & sisters. Sports – bicycling.

D. W. thinks big [board book] ill. by author. Little, 1998. ISBN 0-316-11112-0 Subj: Accidents. Animals – aardvarks. Family life – brothers & sisters. Format, unusual – board books. Weddings.

D. W.'s library card ill. by authnor. Little, 2001. ISBN 0-316-11013-2 Subj: Animals – aardvarks. Books, reading. Family life – brothers & sisters.

D. W.'s lost blankie ill. by author. Little, 1998. ISBN 0-316-10914-2 Subj: Animals – aardvarks. Behavior – lost & found possessions. Family life.

D. W., the picky eater ill. by author. Little, 1995. ISBN 0-316-10957-6 Subj: Animals – aardvarks. Family life. Food.

Dinosaurs alive and well (Brown, Laurie Krasny)

Dinosaurs, beware! a safety guide by Marc Brown & Stephen Krensky; ill. by authors. Little, 1982. ISBN 0-316-11228-3 Subj: Dinosaurs. Prehistory. Safety.

Dinosaurs divorce (Brown, Laurie Krasny)

Dinosaurs to the rescue (Brown, Laurie Krasny)

Dinosaurs travel (Brown, Laurie Krasny)

Finger rhymes ill. by author. Dutton, 1980. ISBN 0-525-29732-4 Subj: Games. Nursery rhymes. Participation.

Glasses for D. W. ill. by author. Random House, 1995. ISBN 0-679-98043-1 Subj: Animals – aardvarks. Family life – brothers & sisters. Glasses.

Hand rhymes ill. by sel. Dutton, 1985. ISBN 0-525-44201-4 Subj: Games. Nursery rhymes.

How to be a friend: a guide to making friends and keeping them (Brown, Laurie Krasny)

Lenny and Lola ill. by author. Dutton, 1978. ISBN 0-525-33465-3 Subj: Circus.

Marc Brown's Boat book ill. by author. Golden Pr., 1982. ISBN 0-307-12262-X Subj: Animals – aardvarks. Boats, ships. Format, unusual – board books.

Marc Brown's full house ill. by author. Addison-Wesley, 1977. ISBN 0-201-00341-4 Subj: Monsters.

Monster's lunchbox ill. by author. Little, 1995. ISBN 0-316-11313-1 Subj: Format, unusual – toy & movable books. Monsters. Rhyming text.

Moose and goose ill. by author. Dutton, 1978. ISBN 0-525-35175-2 Subj: Animals – moose. Birds – geese.

One, two buckle my shoe ill. by author. Dutton, 1989. ISBN 0-525-44462-9 Subj: Animals – rabbits. Format, unusual – toy & movable books. Games. Nursery rhymes.

Perfect pigs: an introduction to manners by Marc Brown & Stephen Krensky; ill. by authors. Little, 1983. ISBN 0-316-11079-5 Subj: Animals – pigs. Etiquette.

Pickle things ill. by author. Parents' Magazine Pr., 1980. ISBN 0-8193-1028-X Subj: Food. Rhyming text.

Play rhymes ill. by author. Dutton, 1987. ISBN 0-525-44336-3 Subj: Games. Music. Nursery rhymes. Songs.

Rex and Lilly school time (Brown, Laurie Krasny)

The silly tail book ill. by author. Parents' Magazine Pr., 1983. ISBN 0-8193-1109-X Subj: Animals. Rhyming text.

Spooky riddles ill. by author. Random House, 1983. ISBN 0-394-96093-9 Subj: Ghosts. Humorous stories. Monsters. Riddles & jokes. Witches.

Teddy bear, teddy bear ill. by author. Dutton, 1989. ISBN 0-525-44531-5 Subj: Format, unusual – toy & movable books. Rhyming text. Sports – jumping rope.

There's no place like home ill. by author. Parents' Magazine Pr., 1984. ISBN 0-8193-1125-1 Subj: Homes, houses. Rhyming text.

The true Francine ill. by author. Little, 1987. ISBN 0-316-11212-7 Subj: Animals – aardvarks. Behavior. Friendship. School.

Two little monkeys ill. by author. Dutton, 1989. ISBN 0-525-44533-1 Subj: Format, unusual – toy & movable books. Nursery rhymes.

Visiting the art museum (Brown, Laurie Krasny)

What do you call a dumb bunny? and other rabbit riddles, games, jokes and cartoons ill. by author. Little, 1983. ISBN 0-316-11117-1 Subj: Animals – rabbits. Format, unusual – toy & movable books. Games. Humorous stories. Riddles & jokes.

What's the big secret? talking about sex with girls and boys (Brown, Laurie Krasny)

When dinosaurs die: a guide to understanding death (Brown, Laurie Krasny)

Wings on things ill. by author. Random House, 1982. ISBN 0-394-95130-1 Subj: Activities – flying. Rhyming text.

Witches four ill. by author. Parents' Magazine Pr., 1993. ISBN 0-8368-0893-2 Subj: Rhyming text. Witches.

Your first garden book ill. by author. Little, 1981. ISBN 0-316-11217-8 Subj: Gardens, gardening. Plants.

Brown, Marcia. *All butterflies: an ABC* ill. by author. Scribners, 1974. ISBN 0-684-13771-2 Subj: ABC books.

The blue jackal ill. by author. Scribners, 1977. ISBN 0-684-14905-2 Subj: Animals. Behavior – trickery. Folk & fairy tales. Foreign lands – India.

The bun: a tale from Russia ill. by author. Harcourt, 1972. ISBN 0-152-13450-6 Subj: Animals. Behavior – greed. Character traits – cleverness. Cumulative tales. Folk & fairy tales.

Dick Whittington and his cat (Dick Whittington and his cat)

Felice ill. by author. Scribners, 1958. Subj: Animals – cats. Foreign lands – Italy.

Henry fisherman ill. by author. Scribners, 1949. Subj: Caldecott award honor books. Careers – fishermen.

How, hippo! ill. by author. Scribners, 1969. Subj: Animals – hippopotamuses.

Listen to a shape photos by author. Watts, 1979. ISBN 0-531-02930-1 Subj: Concepts – shape.

The little carousel ill. by author. Scribners, 1946. Subj: Cities, towns. Emotions – loneliness. Kites. Merry-go-rounds. Money.

The neighbors ill. by author. Scribners, 1967. Text adapted from Afanas'yev. Subj: Animals – foxes. Animals – rabbits. Cumulative tales. Foreign lands – Russia. Homes, houses.

Once a mouse . . . adapt. & ill. by author. Scribners, 1961. ISBN 0-684-12662-1 Subj: Animals. Caldecott award books. Character traits – vanity. Concepts – size. Folk & fairy tales. Foreign lands – India. Magic.

Peter Piper's alphabet ill. by author. Scribners, 1959. Subj: ABC books. Nursery rhymes. Tongue twisters.

Shadow (Cendrars, Blaise)

Skipper John's cook ill. by author. Scribners, 1951. Subj: Activities – baking, cooking. Boats, ships. Caldecott award honor books.

Stone soup ill. by author. Scribners, 1947. ISBN 0-684-92296-7 Subj: Caldecott award honor books. Careers – military. Character traits – cleverness. Folk & fairy tales. Food. Foreign lands – Russia.

Tamarindo! ill. by author. Scribners, 1960. Subj: Animals – donkeys. Behavior – lost. Foreign lands – Greece.

Touch will tell photos by author. Watts, 1979. ISBN 0-531-02931-X Subj: Concepts. Senses – touch.

Walk with your eyes photos by author. Watts, 1979. ISBN 0-531-02925-5 Subj: Concepts. Senses – sight.

Brown, Margaret Wise. *Afro-Bets book of colors* ill. by Culverson Blair. Just Us Books, 1991. ISBN 0-940975-29-7 Subj: Concepts – color. Ethnic groups in the U.S. – African Americans.

Afro-Bets book of shapes ill. by Culverson Blair. Just Us Books, 1991. ISBN 0-940975-28-9 Subj: Concepts – shape. Ethnic groups in the U.S. – African Americans.

Another important book ill. by Christopher Raschka. HarperCollins, 1999. ISBN 0-06-026283-4 Subj: Behavior – growing up. Rhyming text.

Baby animals ill. by Mary Cameron. Random House, 1941. Subj: Animals.

Baby animals ill. by Susan Jeffers. Rev. ed. Random House, 1989. ISBN 0-394-92040-6 Subj: Animals.

Big dog, little dog ill. by Leonard Weisgard. Doubleday, 1943. Subj: Animals – dogs. Concepts – size.

The big fur secret ill. by Robert De Veyrac. HarperCollins, 1944. Subj: Animals. Communication. Zoos.

Big red barn ill. by Felicia Bond. HarperCollins, 1989. ISBN 0-06-020749-3 Subj: Animals. Barns. Farms. Rhyming text.

Big red barn ill. by Rosella Hartman. Addison-Wesley, 1956. ISBN 0-201-09114-1 Subj: Animals. Barns. Farms. Rhyming text.

Bumble bee ill. by Victoria Raymond. HarperCollins, 1999. ISBN 0-694-01749-3 Subj: Format, unusual – board books. Insects – bees. Poetry.

Bumble bugs and elephants ill. by Clement Hurd. W. R. Scott, 1938. Subj: Concepts – size.

Bunny's noisy book ill. by Lisa McCue. Hyperion, 2000. ISBN 0-7868-2428-X Subj: Animals – rabbits. Careers – seamstresses. Noise, sounds. Quilts.

Bunny's noisy book [board book] ill. by Lisa McCue. Hyperion, 2001. ISBN 0-7868-0744-X Subj: Animals – rabbits. Careers – seamstresses. Format, unusual – board books. Noise, sounds. Quilts.

A child is born ill. by Floyd Cooper. Hyperion, 2000. ISBN 0-7868-2564-2 Subj: Holidays – Christmas. Religion – Nativity. Rhyming text.

A child's good morning book ill. by Jean Charlot. HarperCollins, 1995. Previously published as: A child's good morning. 1952. ISBN 0-06-024539-5 Subj: Animals. Morning.

A child's good night book ill. by Jean Charlot. Addison-Wesley, 1950. ISBN 0-06-020752-3 Subj: Bedtime. Caldecott award honor books. Night. Sleep.

Christmas in the barn ill. by Barbara Cooney. Crowell, 1952. ISBN 0-690-19272-X Subj: Holidays – Christmas.

Christmas in the barn ill. by Diane Goode. HarperCollins, 2004. ISBN 0-06-052635-1 Subj: Farms. Holidays – Christmas. Religion – Nativity. Rhyming text.

The country noisy book ill. by Leonard Weisgard. HarperCollins, 1994. ISBN 0-06-020811-2 Subj: Animals – dogs. Country. Noise, sounds. Participation.

The days before now: an autobiographical note adapt. by Joan W. Blos; ill. by Thomas B. Allen. S&S, 1994. ISBN 0-671-79628-3 Subj: Animals. Careers – writers. Pets.

The dead bird ill. by Remy Charlip. W. R. Scott, 1958. ISBN 0-06-020758-2 Subj: Death. Emotions – grief.

The diggers ill. by Daniel Kirk. Hyperion, 1995. ISBN 0-7868-2001-2 Subj: Activities – digging. Animals. Machines. Poetry. Rhyming text.

The dirty little boy ill. by Steven Salerno. Winslow, 2001. ISBN 1-890817-52-X Subj: Activities – bathing. Animals. Character traits – cleanliness.

Dr. Squash the doll doctor ill. by J. P. Miller. S&S, 1952. Subj: Character traits – kindness. Toys – dolls. Toys – soldiers.

Don't frighten the lion ill. by H. A. Rey. HarperCollins, 1942. ISBN 0-06-443262-9 Subj: Animals. Animals – dogs. Character traits – cleverness. Zoos.

Dream book ill. by Richard Flöethe. Random House, 1950. ISBN 1-56282-211-X Subj: Dreams.

The duck photos by Ylla. HarperCollins, 1953. Subj: Animals. Birds – ducks. Character traits – vanity.

The fierce yellow pumpkin ill. by Richard Egielski. HarperCollins, 2003. ISBN 0-06-024481-X Subj: Behavior – wishing. Holidays – Halloween.

Five little firemen by Margaret Wise Brown & Edith Thacher Hurd; ill. by Tibor Gergely. S&S, 1948. Subj: Careers – firefighters. Noise, sounds.

Four fur feet ill. by Remy Charlip. W. R. Scott, 1961. ISBN 0-7868-2000-4 Subj: Activities – walking. Poetry. World.

Fox eyes ill. by Garth Williams. Pantheon, 1977, 1951. ISBN 0-394-93116-5 Subj: Animals. Animals – foxes.

The friendly book ill. by Garth Williams. Random House, 2003. ISBN 0-307-10643-8 Subj: Animals. Poetry.

Give yourself to the rain ill. by Teri L. Weidner. McElderry, 2002. ISBN 0-689-83344-X Subj: Poetry.

The golden birthday book ill. by Leonard Weisgard. Western, 1989. ISBN 0-307-12096-1 Subj: Animals. Birthdays.

The golden egg book ill. by Leonard Weisgard. S&S, 1947. ISBN 0-685-05367-9 Subj: Animals – rabbits. Birds – ducks. Eggs. Holidays – Easter.

The Golden sleepy book ill. by Garth Williams. Random House, 2004. ISBN 0-375-92779-4 Subj: Animals. Poetry. Sleep.

The good little bad little pig ill. by Dan Yaccarino. Hyperion, 2002. ISBN 0-7868-2514-6 Subj: Animals – pigs. Pets.

Goodnight moon ill. by Clement Hurd. HarperCollins, 1934. ISBN 0-590-73302-8 Subj: Animals – rabbits. Bedtime. Moon.

House of a hundred windows Cat & architecture by Robert de Veyrac; ill. by Henri Rousseau & others. HarperCollins, 1945. Subj: Animals – cats. Homes, houses.

The indoor noisy book ill. by Leonard Weisgard. HarperCollins, 1942. ISBN 0-06-020821-X Subj: Animals – dogs. Games. Noise, sounds. Participation.

The little brass band ill. by Clement Hurd. HarperCollins, 1948. Subj: Cumulative tales. Music. Musical instruments – bands.

Little chicken ill. by Leonard Weisgard. HarperCollins, 1943. ISBN 0-06-020740-X Subj: Animals – rabbits. Birds – chickens.

Little Donkey close your eyes ill. by Ashley Wolff. HarperCollins, 1995. ISBN 0-06-024483-6 Subj: Animals – donkeys. Bedtime. Night. Poetry.

The little farmer ill. by Esphyr Slobodkina. Addison-Wesley, 1948. Subj: Dreams. Farms.

The little fir tree ill. by Barbara Cooney. Crowell, 1954. ISBN 0-06-028190-1 Subj: Holidays – Christmas. Trees.

The little fireman ill. by Esphyr Slobodkina. HarperCollins, 1993. ISBN 0-06-021476-7 Subj: Careers – firefighters. Concepts – shape. Concepts – size. Fire.

The little fisherman ill. by Dahlov Ipcar. Addison-Wesley, 1945. Subj: Careers – fishermen. Fish.

The little fur family ill. by Garth Williams. HarperCollins, 1946. ISBN 0-06-020746-9 Subj: Activities. Animals. Format, unusual.

The little island ill. by Leonard Weisgard. Doubleday, 1946. Subj: Caldecott award books. Islands. Seasons. Weather.

Little lost lamb ill. by Leonard Weisgard. Doubleday, 1945. ISBN 0-7868-2322-4 Subj: Animals – sheep. Behavior – lost. Caldecott award honor books.

The little scarecrow boy ill. by David Diaz. HarperCollins, 1998. ISBN 0-06-026290-7 Subj: Family life. Scarecrows.

Love songs of the little bear ill. by Susan Jeffers. Hyperion, 2001. ISBN 0-7868-2445-X Subj: Animals – bears. Poetry. Seasons.

My world ill. by Clement Hurd. HarperFestival, 2002. ISBN 0-694-00862-1 Subj: Animals – rabbits. Family life.

My world of color ill. by Loretta Krupinski. Hyperion, 2002. ISBN 0-7868-2519-7 Subj: Concepts – color. Rhyming text.

Nibble nibble ill. by Leonard Weisgard. Addison-Wesley, 1959. ISBN 0-201-09291-3 Subj: Poetry.

Night and day ill. by Leonard Weisgard. HarperCollins, 1942. Subj: Animals – cats. Emotions – fear. Night.

Noisy book ill. by Leonard Weisgard. HarperCollins, 1939. ISBN 0-06-020831-7 Subj: Noise, sounds. Participation.

On Christmas eve ill. by Nancy Edwards Calder. HarperCollins, 1996. ISBN 0-06-023649-3 Subj: Family life. Holidays – Christmas. Night. Religion.

On Christmas eve ill. by Beni Montresor. Harper, 1985, c1961. ISBN 0-201-09297-2 Subj: Family life. Holidays – Christmas. Night. Religion.

Once upon a time in pigpen and three other stories ill. by Ann Strugnell. Addison-Wesley, 1980. ISBN 0-201-00343-0 Subj: Animals. Humorous stories.

A pussycat's Christmas ill. by Anne Mortimer. HarperCollins, 1994. ISBN 0-06-023533-0 Subj: Animals – cats. Holidays – Christmas.

Pussycat's Christmas ill. by Helen Stone. HarperCollins, 1949. ISBN 0-690-65993-8 Subj: Animals – cats. Holidays – Christmas.

The quiet noisy book ill. by Leonard Weisgard. HarperCollins, 1950. ISBN 0-06-021220-9 Subj: Animals – dogs. Morning. Noise, sounds. Participation.

Red light, green light ill. by Leonard Weisgard. Scholastic, 1992. ISBN 0-590-44558-8 Subj: Concepts – color. Safety. Traffic, traffic signs.

Robin's room ill. by Steve Johnson & Lou Fancher. Hyperion, 2002. ISBN 0-7868-2516-2 Subj: Character traits – being different. Family life. Homes, houses.

The runaway bunny ill. by Clement Hurd. Harper, 1972, c1942. ISBN 0-06-020766-3 Subj: Animals – rabbits. Behavior – running away. Family life – mothers. Holidays – Easter.

The runaway bunny [board book] ill. by Clement Hurd. HarperFestival, 2001. ISBN 0-694-01671-3 Subj: Animals – rabbits. Behavior – running away. Family life – mothers. Format, unusual – board books.

Sailor boy jig ill. by Dan Andreasen. McElderry, 2002. ISBN 0-689-83348-2 Subj: Activities – dancing. Animals – dogs. Concepts. Rhyming text. Sailors.

The seashore noisy book ill. by Leonard Weisgard. HarperCollins, 1993, c1941. ISBN 0-06-020841-4 Subj: Animals – dogs. Noise, sounds. Participation. Sea & seashore.

Sheep don't count sheep ill. by Benrei Huang. McElderry, 2003. ISBN 0-689-83346-6 Subj: Animals – sheep. Sleep.

SHHhhh . . . . Bang: a whispering book ill. by Robert De Veyrac. HarperCollins, 1943. Subj: Noise, sounds.

Sleepy ABC ill. by Esphyr Slobodkina. HarperCollins, 1994. ISBN 0-06-024285-X Subj: ABC books. Bedtime. Rhyming text. Sleep.

The sleepy little lion ill. by Ylla. HarperCollins, 1947. ISBN 0-06-020771-X Subj: Animals – lions. Sleep.

The sleepy men ill. by Robert Rayevsky. Hyperion, 1996. ISBN 0-7868-0154-9 Subj: Bedtime. Moon. Sleep.

Sneakers ill. by Jean Charlot. Addison-Wesley, 1979, 1955. Reissue of 1955 ed. published by W. R. Scott under title Seven stories about a cat named Sneakers. ISBN 0-2010-0625-1 Subj: Animals – cats. Behavior – misbehavior. Sea & seashore.

Sneakers, the seaside cat ill. by Anne Mortimer. HarperCollins, 2003. ISBN 0-06-028693-8 Subj: Animals – cats. Behavior – misbehavior. Sea & seashore.

The steamroller: a fantasy ill. by Evaline Ness. Walker, 1974. Published in 1938 in the author's collection, The fish with the deep sea smile. ISBN 0-8027-6192-5 Subj: Holidays – Christmas. Machines.

Streamlined pig ill. by Kurt Wiese. HarperCollins, 1938. Subj: Activities – flying. Airplanes, airports. Animals. Character traits – bravery.

The summer noisy book ill. by Leonard Weisgard. HarperCollins, 1993, c1951. ISBN 0-06-020856-2 Subj: Animals – dogs. Farms. Noise, sounds. Participation. Seasons – summer.

They all saw it photos by Ylla. HarperCollins, 1944. Subj: Animals. Problem solving.

Three little animals ill. by Garth Williams. HarperCollins, 1956. Subj: Activities – traveling. Animals. Behavior – lost. Cities, towns.

The train to Timbuctoo ill. by Art Seiden. Golden Bks., 1999. ISBN 0-307-10215-7 Subj: Trains.

Two little miners ill. by Edith Thacher Hurd. S&S, 1949. Subj: Careers – miners.

Two little trains ill. by Jean Charlot. Addison-Wesley, 1949. ISBN 0-201-09381-2 Subj: Rhyming text. Trains.

Under the sun and the moon and other poems ill. by Tom Leonard. Hyperion, 1993. ISBN 1-56282-355-8 Subj: Poetry.

Wait till the moon is full ill. by Garth Williams. HarperCollins, 1948. ISBN 0-06-020801-5 Subj: Animals. Animals – raccoons. Character traits – questioning. Moon. Night.

Wheel on the chimney by Margaret Wise Brown & Tibor Gergely; ill. by Tibor Gergely. Lippincott, 1954. ISBN 0-397-30296-7 Subj: Birds – storks. Caldecott award honor books. Character traits – luck. Foreign lands – Hungary.

When the wind blew ill. by Geoffrey Hayes. HarperCollins, 1977, 1937. ISBN 0-06-020868-6 Subj: Animals – cats. Illness. Weather – wind.

Where have you been? ill. by Barbara Cooney. Reissue of Crowell, 1952 ed. Hastings House, 1981. ISBN 0-8038-8018-9 Subj: Animals. Poetry.

Where have you been? ill. by Leo and Diane Dillon. HarperCollins, 2004. ISBN 0-06-028379-3 Subj: Animals. Rhyming text.

The whispering rabbit ill. by Cyndy Szekeres. Western, 1992. ISBN 0-307-00138-5 Subj: Animals – rabbits. Insects – bees.

Whistle for the train ill. by Leonard Weisgard. Doubleday, 1956. Subj: Rhyming text. Trains. Whistles.

The winter noisy book ill. by Charles Green Shaw. HarperCollins, 1994. ISBN 0-06-020866-X Subj: Animals – dogs. Noise, sounds. Participation. Seasons – winter. Weather – snow.

The wonderful house ill. by J. P. Miller. S&S, 1950. ISBN 0-307-20313-1 Subj: Homes, houses.

The wonderful story book ill. by J. P. Miller. S&S, 1948. Subj: Poetry.

Young kangaroo ill. by Symeon Shimin. Addison-Wesley, 1955. ISBN 1-56282-410-4 Subj: Animals – kangaroos.

Brown, Myra Berry. *Benjy's blanket* ill. by Dorothy Marino. Watts, 1962. Subj: Animals – cats. Behavior – growing up.

Best friends ill. by Don Freeman. Golden Gate, 1967. Subj: Friendship. Poetry.

Company's coming for dinner ill. by Dorothy Marino. Watts, 1960. Subj: Character traits – helpfulness. Etiquette. Parties.

First night away from home ill. by Dorothy Marino. Watts, 1960. Subj: Activities – playing. Friendship. Sleep. Toys – bears.

Pip camps out ill. by Phyllis Graham. Golden Gate, 1966. Subj: Camps, camping. Family life. Night.

Brown, Palmer. *Something for Christmas* ill. by author. Harper-Collins, 1958. Subj: Animals – mice. Character traits – generosity. Emotions – love. Holidays – Christmas.

Brown, Richard Eric. *One hundred words about animals* ill. by author. Harcourt, 1987. ISBN 0-15-200550-1 Subj: Animals.

Brown, Rick. *Who built the ark?* ill. by author. Viking, 1994. ISBN 0-670-85160-4 Subj: Animals. Boats, ships. Counting, numbers. Format, unusual. Religion – Noah. Weather – floods. Weather – rain.

Brown, Ruth. *Alphabet times four* ill. by author. Dutton, 1991. ISBN 0-525-44831-4 Subj: ABC books. Foreign languages.

The big sneeze ill. by author. Lothrop, 1985. ISBN 0-688-04666-5 Subj: Farms. Humorous stories.

Copycat ill. by author. Dutton, 1994. ISBN 0-525-45326-1 Subj: Animals. Animals – cats. Behavior.

Crazy Charlie ill. by author. Rourke, 1982. ISBN 0-86592-124-5 Subj: Reptiles – alligators, crocodiles. Self-concept. Teeth.

Cry baby ill. by author. Dutton, 1997. ISBN 0-525-45902-2 Subj: Family life – sisters.

A dark, dark tale ill. by author. Dial, 1981. ISBN 0-8037-1673-7 Subj: Cumulative tales. Foreign lands – England.

The ghost of Greyfriar's Bobby ill. by author. Dutton, 1996. ISBN 0-525-45581-7 Subj: Animals – dogs. Character traits – persistence. Foreign lands – Scotland.

The grizzly revenge ill. by author. Andersen, 1983. ISBN 0-8626-4024-5 Subj: Animals. Character traits – kindness to animals. Royalty – kings. Royalty – queens.

Holly, the true story of a cat ill. by author. Holt, 2000. ISBN 0-8050-6500-8 Subj: Animals – cats. Holidays – Christmas.

I don't like it! ill. by author. Dutton, 1990. ISBN 0-525-44559-5 Subj: Animals – dogs. Emotions – envy, jealousy. Toys. Toys – dolls.

If at first you do not see ill. by author. Holt, 1983. ISBN 0-03-063521-7 Subj: Format, unusual – toy & movable books. Insects – butterflies, caterpillars.

Ladybug, ladybug ill. by author. Dutton, 1988. ISBN 0-525-44423-8 Subj: Insects – ladybugs. Nursery rhymes.

Mad summer night's dream ill. by author. Dutton, 1999. ISBN 0-525-46010-1 Subj: Dreams. Rhyming text.

One stormy night ill. by author. Dutton, 1993. ISBN 0-525-45091-2 Subj: Animals. Ghosts. Night. Weather – storms.

Our cat Flossie ill. by author. Dutton, 1986. ISBN 0-525-44256-1 Subj: Activities. Animals – cats.

Our puppy's vacation ill. by author. Dutton, 1987. ISBN 0-525-44326-6 Subj: Activities – playing. Activities – vacationing. Animals – dogs. Pets.

The picnic ill. by author. Dutton, 1992. ISBN 0-525-45012-2 Subj: Activities – picnicking. Animals.

The shy little angel ill. by author. Dutton, 1998. ISBN 0-525-46079-9 Subj: Angels. School. Theater.

Toad ill. by author. Dutton, 1997. ISBN 0-525-45757-7 Subj: Frogs & toads. Rhyming text.

The world that Jack built ill. by author. Dutton, 1991. ISBN 0-525-44635-4 Subj: Cumulative tales. Ecology.

Brown, Tricia. *The city by the bay: a magical journey around San Francisco* by Tricia Brown & the Junior League of San Francisco; ill. by Elisa Kleven. Chronicle, 1993. ISBN 0-811-80233-7 Subj: Activities – traveling. Cities, towns.

Hello, amigos! photos by Fran Ortiz. Holt, 1986. ISBN 0-8050-0090-9 Subj: Birthdays. Ethnic groups in the U.S. – Mexican Americans. Family life. School.

Someone special, just like you photos by Fran Ortiz. Holt, 1984. ISBN 0-03-069706-9 Subj: Emotions. Handicaps.

Browne, Anthony. *Animal fair* ill. by author. Candlewick, 2002. ISBN 0-7636-1831-4 Subj: Animals. Animals – monkeys. Fairs, festivals. Format, unusual – toy & movable books.

Bear goes to town ill. by author. Doubleday, 1989. ISBN 0-385-26524-7 Subj: Animals. Animals – bears. Art. Imagination.

Bear hunt ill. by author. Atheneum, 1980. ISBN 0-689-30733-0 Subj: Animals – bears. Art. Problem solving. Sports – hunting.

The big baby ill. by author. Knopf, 1994. ISBN 0-679-84737-5 Subj: Babies. Character traits – vanity. Family life – fathers.

Changes ill. by author. Julia MacRae Books, 1991. ISBN 0-679-91029-8 Subj: Babies. Family life. Imagination.

Gorilla ill. by author. Candlewick, 2002, 1983. "First published by Julia MacRae Books" ISBN 0-7636-1813-6 Subj: Animals – gorillas. Birthdays. Family life – fathers. Imagination. Toys. Zoos.

I like books ill. by author. Knopf, 1989. ISBN 0-394-84186-7 Subj: Animals – chimpanzees. Books, reading.

I like books [board book] ill. by author. Candlewick, 2004. ISBN 0-7636-2162-5 Subj: Animals – chimpanzees. Books, reading. Format, unusual – board books.

The little bear book ill. by author. Doubleday, 1989. ISBN 0-385-26006-7 Subj: Animals. Animals – bears. Art. Imagination.

Look what I've got! ill. by author. Watts, 1980. ISBN 0-394-99860-X Subj: Behavior – boasting. Imagination.

My dad ill. by author. DK, 2000. ISBN 0-7894-2681-1 Subj: Family life – fathers.

Piggybook ill. by author. Knopf, 1986. ISBN 0-394-98416-1 Subj: Animals – pigs. Family life – mothers.

The shape game ill. by author. Farrar, 2003. ISBN 0-374-36764-7 Subj: Art. Careers – authors. Careers – illustrators. Foreign lands – Great Britain. Museums.

Things I like ill. by author. Knopf, 1989. ISBN 0-394-94192-6 Subj: Activities – playing. Animals – chimpanzees.

Through the magic mirror ill. by author. Greenwillow, 1992. ISBN 0-688-10725-7 Subj: Imagination. Magic.

The tunnel ill. by author. Knopf, 1989. ISBN 0-3949-4582-4 Subj: Family life – brothers & sisters.

Voices in the park ill. by author. DK, 1998. ISBN 0-7894-2522-X Subj: Animals – dogs. Animals – gorillas. Parks. Seasons.

Willy and Hugh ill. by author. Knopf, 1991. ISBN 0-679-91446-3 Subj: Animals – chimpanzees. Animals – gorillas. Friendship.

Willy the champ ill. by author. Knopf, 1986. ISBN 0-394-97907-9 Subj: Animals – chimpanzees. Animals – gorillas. Behavior – bullying.

Willy the dreamer ill. by author. Candlewick, 1998. ISBN 0-7636-0378-3 Subj: Animals – chimpanzees. Dreams.

Willy the wimp ill. by author. Knopf, 1985. ISBN 0-394-97061-6 Subj: Animals – chimpanzees. Animals – gorillas. Self-concept.

Willy the wizard ill. by author. Knopf, 1995. ISBN 0-679-97644-2 Subj: Animals – chimpanzees. Clothing – shoes. Sports – soccer.

Willy's pictures ill. by author. Candlewick, 2000. ISBN 0-7636-0962-5 Subj: Animals – chimpanzees. Art. Careers – artists.

Zoo ill. by author. Knopf, 1992. ISBN 0-679-93946-6 Subj: Animals. Family life. Zoos.

Browne, Caroline. *Mrs. Christie's farmhouse* ill. by author. Doubleday, 1977. ISBN 0-385-13275-1 Subj: Country. Farms. Gardens, gardening. Humorous stories. Royalty.

Browne, Eileen. *No problem* ill. by David Parkins. Candlewick, 1993. ISBN 1-56402-200-5 Subj: Airplanes, airports. Animals. Birthdays. Books, reading.

Tick-tock ill. by David Parkins. Candlewick, 1994. ISBN 1-56402-300-1 Subj: Animals – squirrels. Behavior – misbehavior. Clocks, watches.

Where's that bus? ill. by author. S&S, 1991. ISBN 0-671-73810-0 Subj: Activities – picnicking. Animals – moles. Animals – rabbits. Animals – squirrels. Buses. Friendship.

Browne, Gerard. *The aircraft lift-the-flap book* ill. by author. Lodestar, 1992. ISBN 0-525-67351-2 Subj: Airplanes, airports. Format, unusual – toy & movable books.

Browne, Philippa-Alys. *A gaggle of geese: the collective names of the animal kingdom* ill. by author. Atheneum, 1996. ISBN 0-689-80761-9 Subj: Animals. Birds. Concepts. Rhyming text.

Browne, Vee. *Monster birds: a Navajo folktale* ill. by Baje Whitethorne. Northland, 1993. ISBN 0-87359-558-5 Subj: Birds. Folk & fairy tales. Indians of North America – Navajo. Monsters. Multiple births – twins.

Brownell, Barbara. *Spin's really wild U.S.A. tour* ill. by Barbara Gibson. National Geographic, 1996. ISBN 0-7922-3422-7 Subj: Animals. Nature. Plants. U.S. history.

Browner, Richard. *Everyone has a name* ill. by Emma Landau. Walck, 1961. Subj: Animals. Names. Poetry.

Look again! ill. by Emma Landau. Atheneum, 1962. Subj: Concepts.

Browning, Robert. *The pied piper of Hamelin* (Bartos-Hoppner, Barbara)

The pied piper of Hamelin (Mayer, Mercer)

The pied piper of Hamelin adapt. by Sharon Chmielarz; ill. by Pat & Robin DeWitt. Stemmer House, 1990. ISBN 0-88045-115-7 Subj: Animals – rats. Behavior – trickery. Folk & fairy tales. Foreign lands – Germany. Poetry.

The pied piper of Hamelin ill. by Kate Greenaway. Warne, [1910]. ISBN 0-688-03810-7 Subj: Animals – rats. Behavior – trickery. Folk & fairy tales. Foreign lands – Germany. Poetry.

The pied piper of Hamelin ill. by Anatoly Ivanov. Lothrop, 1986. ISBN 0-688-03810-1 Subj: Animals – rats. Behavior – trickery. Folk & fairy tales. Foreign lands – Germany. Poetry.

The pied piper of Hamelin adapt. by Sara & Stephen Corrin; ill. by Errol Le Cain. Harcourt, 1989. ISBN 0-15-261596-2 Subj: Animals – rats. Behavior – trickery. Folk & fairy tales. Foreign lands – Germany. Poetry.

The pied piper of Hamelin retold by Robert Holden; ill. by Drahos Zak. Houghton Mifflin, 1998. ISBN 0-395-89918-4 Subj: Animals – rats. Behavior – trickery. Folk & fairy tales. Foreign lands – Germany. Poetry.

Brownlow, Michael. *The big white book with almost nothing in it* ill. by author. Ragged Bears, 2001. ISBN 1-929927-24-X Subj: Format, unusual – toy & movable books. Rhyming text.

Way out West – with a baby! ill. by author. Ragged Bears, 2000. ISBN 1-929927-04-5 Subj: Babies. Cowboys, cowgirls. Rhyming text. U.S. history – frontier & pioneer life.

Brownridge, William Roy. *The final game: the further adventures of the moccasin goalie* ill. by author. Orca, 1997. ISBN 1-55143-100-9 Subj: Behavior – sharing. Sports – soccer.

The moccasin goalie ill. by author. Orca, 1996. ISBN 1-55143-042-8 Subj: Emotions. Handicaps. Indians of North America. Sports – hockey.

Broyles, Anne. *Shy Mama's Halloween* ill. by Leane Morin. Tilbury, 2000. ISBN 0-88448-218-9 Subj: Ethnic groups in the U.S. – Russian Americans. Family life. Holidays – Halloween. Immigrants.

Bruandet, Jerome. *Baby clown* (Dedieu, Thierry)

Bruce, Lisa. *Engines, engines* by Lisa Bruce & Stephen Waterhouse; ill. by Stephenh Waterhouse. Bloomsbury, 2000. ISBN 0-7475-5013-1 Subj: Counting, numbers. Foreign lands – India. Rhyming text.

Fran's flower ill. by Rosalind Beardshaw. HarperCollins, 2000. ISBN 0-06-028621-0 Subj: Flowers. Gardens, gardening. Plants.

Fran's friend ill. by Rosalind Beardshaw. Bloomsbury, 2003. ISBN 1-58234-777-8 Subj: Animals – dogs. Friendship. Gifts.

Oliver's alphabets ill. by Debi Gliori. Bradbury, 1993. ISBN 0-02-735996-4 Subj: ABC books. Language.

Bruce, Sheilah B. *The radish day jubilee* ill. by Lawrence DiFiori. Holt, 1983. ISBN 0-03-068678-4 Subj: Imagination. Poetry. Puppets.

Bruchac, James. *How Chipmunk got his stripes: a tale of bragging and teasing* (Bruchac, Joseph)

Bruchac, Joseph. *A boy called Slow: the true story of Sitting Bull* ill. by Rocco Baviera. Philomel, 1994. ISBN 0-399-22692-3 Subj: Behavior – growing up. Indians of North America – Dakota (Sioux).

The circle of thanks: native American poems and songs of Thanksgiving ill. by Murv Jacob. BridgeWater, 1996. ISBN 0-8167-4012-7 Subj: Folk & fairy tales. Indians of North America. Nature. Poetry.

Crazy horse's vision ill. by S. D. Nelson. Lee & Low, 2000. ISBN 1-880000-94-6 Subj: Indians of North America – Lakota (Sioux).

The first strawberries: a Cherokee story ill. by Anna Vojtech. Dial, 1993. ISBN 0-8037-1332-0 Subj: Folk & fairy tales. Indians of North America – Cherokee.

Gluskabe and the four wishes ill. by Christine Nyburg Shrader. Cobblehill, 1995. ISBN 0-525-65164-0 Subj: Behavior – wishing. Folk & fairy tales. Indians of North America – Abnaki.

The great ball game: a Muskogee story ill. by Susan L. Roth. Dial, 1994. ISBN 0-8037-1540-4 Subj: Animals. Behavior – fighting, arguing. Birds. Folk & fairy tales. Indians of North America – Creek. Indians of North America – Muskogee.

How Chipmunk got his stripes: a tale of bragging and teasing by Joseph Burchac & James Bruchac; ill. by José Aruego & Ariane Dewey. Dial, 2001. ISBN 0-8037-2404-7 Subj: Animals – chipmunks. Folk & fairy tales – pourquoi tales. Indians of North America.

Many nations: an alphabet of Native America ill. by Robert F. Goetzl. BridgeWater, 1997. ISBN 0-8167-4389-4 Subj: ABC books. Indians of North America.

Squanto's journey ill. by Greg Shed. Silver Whistle, 2000. ISBN 0-15-201817-4 Subj: Holidays – Thanksgiving. Indians of North America – Wampanoag. Pilgrims. U.S. history.

Thirteen moons on turtle's back by Joseph Bruchac & Jonathan London; ill. by Thomas Locker. Putnam, 1992. ISBN 0-399-22141-7 Subj: Folk & fairy tales. Indians of North America. Poetry. Seasons.

Brumbeau, Jeff. *Miss Hunnicutt's hat* ill. by Gail de Marcken. Orchard, 2003. ISBN 0-439-31895-5 Subj: Character traits – individuality. Clothing – hats.

Bruna, Dick. *Another story to tell* ill. by author. Methuen, 1978. ISBN 0-458-92680-9 Subj: Weather – snow. Wordless.

B is for bear: an A-B-C ill. by author. Methuen, 1971. ISBN 0-416-93100-6 Subj: ABC books.

Christmas ill. by author; trans. & English verse by Eve Merriam. Doubleday, 1969. Tr. of Kerstmis. Subj: Holidays – Christmas. Religion. Rhyming text.

The Christmas book ill. by author. Methuen, 1964. Subj: Holidays – Christmas.

Dick Bruna's Cinderella ill. by author. Follett, 1966. Subj: Family life – stepfamilies. Folk & fairy tales. Royalty – princes. Sibling rivalry.

Dick Bruna's Little Red Riding Hood by Jacob & Wilhelm Grimm; ill. by Dick Bruna. Follett, 1966. Subj: Animals – wolves. Behavior – talking to strangers. Family life – grandmothers. Folk & fairy tales.

Dick Bruna's picture word book ill. by author. Random House, 1989. ISBN 0-517-05662-3 Subj: Concepts. Dictionaries.

Dick Bruna's Snow-White and the seven dwarfs ill. by author. Follett, 1966. Subj: Dwarfs, midgets. Emotions – envy, jealousy. Folk & fairy tales. Magic. Witches.

Dick Bruna's Tom Thumb ill. by author. Follett, 1966. Subj: Dwarfs, midgets. Folk & fairy tales.

Farmer John ill. by author. Price Stern Sloan, 1984. ISBN 0-8431-1526-2 Subj: Farms.

The fish ill. by author. Follett, 1963. English verse tr. from the Dutch by Sandra Greifenstein. ISBN 0-416-30341-2 Subj: Fish. Food. Poetry.

The happy apple by Dick Bruna & Judith Klugmann; ill. by Dick Bruna. Hart, 1959. Subj: Activities – flying. Behavior – wishing. Rhyming text.

I can count ill. by author. Two Continents, 1975. ISBN 0-8467-0082-4 Subj: Counting, numbers.

I can count more ill. by author. Two Continents, 1976. ISBN 0-8467-0168-5 Subj: Counting, numbers.

I can dress myself ill. by author. Methuen, 1977. ISBN 0-458-93270-1 Subj: Behavior – growing up. Clothing.

I can read ill. by author. Two Continents, 1975. ISBN 0-8467-0086-7 Subj: Books, reading.

I can read difficult words ill. by author. Methuen, 1978. ISBN 0-458-92690-6 Subj: Books, reading.

I can read more ill. by author. Two Continents, 1976. ISBN 0-8431-1539-4 Subj: Books, reading.

I know more about numbers ill. by author. Methuen, 1981. ISBN 0-416-20870-3 Subj: Counting, numbers.

Kitten Nell ill. by author. Follett, 1963. Subj: Animals – cats. Humorous stories. Rhyming text.

Lisa and Lynn ill. by author. Two Continents, 1975. ISBN 0-8431-1537-8 Subj: Multiple births – twins.

The little bird ill. by author. Two Continents, 1975. ISBN 0-8431-1541-6 Subj: Birds.

Little bird tweet ill. by author. Follett, 1963. Subj: Birds. Farms. Rhyming text.

Miffy ill. by author. Follett, 1970. Translation of Nijntje. ISBN 0-695-80117-1 Subj: Animals – rabbits. Family life.

Miffy at the beach ill. by author. Methuen, 1980. ISBN 0-416-30151-7 Subj: Animals – rabbits. Sea & seashore – beaches.

Miffy at the playground ill. by author. Methuen, 1980. ISBN 0-416-30161-4 Subj: Activities – playing. Animals – rabbits.

Miffy at the seaside ill. by author. Follett, 1970. Translation of Nijntje aan zee. ISBN 0-695-80118-X Subj: Animals – rabbits. Sea & seashore.

Miffy at the zoo ill. by author. Follett, 1970. Translation of Nijntje in de dierentuin. ISBN 0-695-80121-X Subj: Animals – rabbits. Zoos.

Miffy goes flying ill. by author. Two Continents, 1976. ISBN 0-8431-1535-1 Subj: Activities – flying. Animals – rabbits.

Miffy goes to school ill. by author. Price Stern Sloan, 1984. ISBN 0-8431-1530-0 Subj: Animals – rabbits. School – first day.

Miffy in the hospital ill. by author. Methuen, 1978. ISBN 0-458-92700-7 Subj: Animals – rabbits. Hospitals. Illness.

Miffy in the snow ill. by author. Follett, 1970. Translation of Nijntje in de sneeuw. ISBN 0-695-80119-8 Subj: Animals – rabbits. Seasons – winter. Weather – snow.

Miffy loves New York City! ill. by author. Big Tent, 2003. ISBN 1-59226-179-5 Subj: Animals – rabbits. Cities, towns. Format, unusual – board books.

Miffy the ghost ill. by author. Big Tent, 2003. ISBN 1-59226-063-2 Subj: Animals – rabbits. Format, unusual – board books. Ghosts.

Miffy's bicycle ill. by author. Price Stern Sloan, 1984. ISBN 0-8431-1527-0 Subj: Animals – rabbits. Sports – bicycling.

Miffy's birthday ill. by author. Two Continents, 1976. ISBN 0-8431-1545-9 Subj: Animals – rabbits. Birthdays. Family life.

Miffy's dream ill. by author. Methuen, 1980. ISBN 0-416-88650-7 Subj: Activities – playing. Animals – rabbits. Dreams.

My shirt is white ill. by author. Two Continents, 1975. ISBN 0-416-30291-2 Subj: Clothing. Concepts – color.

My toys ill. by author. Methuen, 1980. ISBN 0-416-30761-2 Subj: Format, unusual – toy & movable books. Toys.

The orchestra ill. by author. Price Stern Sloan, 1984. ISBN 0-8431-1529-7 Subj: Music. Musical instruments – orchestras. Rhyming text.

Poppy Pig goes to market ill. by author. Methuen, 1981. ISBN 0-416-20890-8 Subj: Animals – pigs. Counting, numbers. Rhyming text.

The sailor ill. by author. Methuen, 1980. ISBN 0-416-30171-1 Subj: Activities – traveling. Boats, ships. Sailors.

The school ill. by author. Methuen, 1980. ISBN 0-416-30181-9 Subj: School.

Snuffy ill. by author. Two Continents, 1975. ISBN 0-8431-1548-3 Subj: Animals – dogs. Behavior – lost.

Snuffy and the fire ill. by author. Two Continents, 1975. ISBN 0-8431-1549-1 Subj: Animals – dogs. Fire.

A story to tell ill. by author. Two Continents, 1975. ISBN 0-8431-1576-9 Subj: Friendship. Wordless.

Tilly and Tess ill. by author. Follett, 1963. Subj: Birthdays. Multiple births – twins. Rhyming text.

Brunhoff, Jean de. *Babar and Father Christmas* trans. by Merle Haas; ill. by author. Random House, 1940. Translation of Babar et le Père Nöel. ISBN 0-394-89265-8 Subj: Animals – elephants. Holidays – Christmas.

Babar and his children trans. by Merle Haas; ill. by author. Random House, 1938. ISBN 0-394-90577-6 Subj: Animals – elephants. Multiple births – triplets.

Babar and Zephir trans. from French by Merle Haas; ill. by author. Reprint of 1937 ed. Random House, 1942. Subj: Animals – elephants. Animals – monkeys.

Babar the king trans. by Merle Haas; ill. by author. Random House, 1935. ISBN 0-394-90580-6 Subj: Animals – elephants. Royalty – kings.

Babar the king trans. by Merle Haas; ill. by author. Facsimile ed. Random House, 1986. ISBN 0-394-88245-8 Subj: Animals – elephants. Royalty – kings.

The story of Babar, the little elephant trans. by Merle Haas; ill. by author. Random House, 1984, c1933. ISBN 0-394-86823-4 Subj: Animals – elephants. Behavior – running away. Foreign lands – France.

The travels of Babar trans. by Merle Haas; ill. by author. Random House, 1934, 1961. ISBN 0-394-90576-8 Subj: Activities – traveling. Animals – elephants.

Brunhoff, Laurent de. *Babar and the ghost* ill. by author. Abrams, 2001, 1981. ISBN 0-8109-4398-0 Subj: Animals – elephants. Castles. Ghosts.

Babar and the ghost ill. by author. Easy-to-read ed. Random House, 1986. ISBN 0-394-97908-7 Subj: Animals – elephants. Ghosts.

Babar and the succotash bird ill. by author. Abrams, 2000. ISBN 0-8109-5700-0 Subj: Animals – elephants. Birds. Wizards.

Babar and the Wully-Wully ill. by author. Abrams, 2001, 1975. ISBN 0-8109-4397-2 Subj: Animals – elephants. Pets.

Babar comes to America trans. by M. Jean Craig; ill. by author. Random House, 1965. Translation of Babar en Amérique. Subj: Animals – elephants.

Babar learns to cook ill. by author. Random House, 1979. ISBN 0-394-94108-X Subj: Activities – baking, cooking. Animals – elephants.

Babar the magician ill. by author. Random House, 1980. ISBN 0-394-84360-6 Subj: Animals – elephants. Animals – monkeys. Magic.

Babar visits another planet trans. by Merle Haas; ill. by author. Random House, 1972. Translation of Babar sur la planète molle. ISBN 0-394-92429-0 Subj: Animals – elephants. Space & space ships.

Babar's ABC ill. by author. Abrams, 2001, 1983. ISBN 0-8109-5705-8 Subj: ABC books. Animals – elephants.

Babar's battle ill. by author. Random House, 1992. ISBN 0-679-91068-9 Subj: Animals – elephants. Animals – rhinoceros. War.

Babar's birthday surprise ill. by author. Random House, 1970. Translation of Anniversaire de Babar. ISBN 0-394-90591-1 Subj: Animals – elephants. Birthdays.

Babar's book of color ill. by author. Random House, 1984. ISBN 0-394-86896-X Subj: Animals – elephants. Concepts – color.

Babar's castle trans. by Merle Haas; ill. by author. Random House, 1962. ISBN 0-394-90586-5 Subj: Animals – elephants.

Babar's counting book ill. by author. Random House, 1986. ISBN 0-394-97517-0 Subj: Animals. Animals – elephants. Counting, numbers.

Babar's cousin, that rascal Arthur trans. by Merle Haas; ill. by author. Random House, 1948. Translation of Babar et ce coquin d'Arthur. A continuation of the Babar stories of Jean de Brunhoff. ISBN 0-394-90581-4 Subj: Activities – vacationing. Animals – elephants. Behavior – misbehavior.

Babar's fair will be opened next Sunday trans. by Merle Haas; ill. by author. Random House, 1954. Translation of La fête de Célesteville. ISBN 0-394-90584-9 Subj: Animals – elephants. Fairs, festivals.

Babar's little circus star ill. by author. Random House, 1988. ISBN 0-394-98959-7 Subj: Animals. Animals – elephants. Circus.

Babar's little girl ill. by author. Abrams, 2001, 1987. ISBN 0-8109-5703-5 Subj: Animals – elephants. Behavior – carelessness. Behavior – lost. Character traits – kindness to animals.

Babar's Museum of Art: (closed Mondays) ill. by author. Abrams, 2003. ISBN 0-8109-4597-5 Subj: Animals – elephants. Art. Museums.

Babar's mystery ill. by author. Random House, 1978. ISBN 0-394-93920-4 Subj: Activities – vacationing. Animals – elephants. Crime.

Babar's picnic ill. by author. Random House, 1991. ISBN 0-679-81245-8 Subj: Activities – picnicking. Animals – elephants.

Babar's visit to Bird Island ill. by author. Random House, 1952. Subj: Animals – elephants. Birds. Islands. Royalty – kings.

Meet Babar and his family ill. by author. Abrams, 2002. ISBN 0-8109-0555-8 Subj: Animals – elephants. Family life. Seasons.

The rescue of Babar ill. by author. Random House, 1993. ISBN 0-679-93897-4 Subj: Animals. Animals – elephants. Crime.

Serafina the giraffe ill. by author. Collins-World, 1961. Subj: Animals – giraffes. Birthdays. Humorous stories.

Brusca, María Cristina. *The cook and the king* by María Cristina Brusca & Toña Wilson; ill. by María Cristina Brusca. Holt, 1993. ISBN 0-8050-2355-0 Subj: Folk & fairy tales. Foreign lands – South America. Royalty – kings.

When jaguars ate the moon: and other stories about animals and plants of the Americas by María Cristina Brusca & Toña Wilson; ill. by María Cristina Brusca. Holt, 1995. ISBN 0-8050-2797-1 Subj: ABC books. Animals. Animals – jaguars. Folk & fairy tales. Foreign lands – South America.

Bruss, Deborah. *Book! book! book!* ill. by Tiphanie Beeke. Levine, 2001. ISBN 0-439-13525-7 Subj: Animals. Books, reading. Libraries. Noise, sounds.

Brustlein, Janice Tworkov. *see* Janice

Brutschy, Jennifer. *Celeste and Crabapple Sam* ill. by Eileen Christelow. Lodestar, 1994. ISBN 0-525-67416-0 Subj: Animals. Behavior – hiding. Character traits – persistence. Friendship. Pets. Sea & seashore.

Just one more story ill. by Cat Bowman Smith. Orchard, 2001. ISBN 0-531-33296-9 Subj: Activities – storytelling. Activities – traveling. Family life – fathers.

The winter fox ill. by Allen Garns. Knopf, 1993. ISBN 0-679-91524-9 Subj: Animals – foxes. Animals – rabbits. Character traits – kindness to animals. Family life. Seasons – winter.

Bruzzone, Catherine. *Puppy finds a friend = Cachorrito encuentra un amigo* ill. by John Bendall-Brunello; Spanish trans. by Thessa Judkins. Barron's, 2000. ISBN 0-7641-5283-1 Subj: Activities – playing. Animals – babies. Animals – dogs. Foreign languages. Friendship.

Puppy finds a friend = Le petit chien se trouve un ami ill. by John Bendall-Brunello; French trans. by Christophe Dillinger. Barron's, 2000. ISBN 0-7641-5285-8 Subj: Activities – playing. Animals – babies. Animals – dogs. Foreign languages. Friendship.

Bryan, Ashley. *All night, all day: a child's first book of African-American spirituals* (All night, all day)

Beat the story-drum, pum-pum ill. by adapt. Atheneum, 1980. ISBN 0-689-30769-1 Subj: Cumulative tales. Folk & fairy tales. Foreign lands – Africa. Rhyming text.

Beautiful blackbird ill. by author. Atheneum, 2003. ISBN 0-689-84731-9 Subj: Birds – blackbirds. Folk & fairy tales. Foreign lands – Zambia.

The cat's purr ill. by author. Atheneum, 1985. ISBN 0-689-31086-2 Subj: Animals – cats. Animals – rats. Folk & fairy tales. Rhyming text.

The dancing granny retold & ill. by Ashley Bryan. Aladdin, 1987. ISBN 0-689-71149-2 Subj: Folk & fairy tales. Gardens, gardening. Mythical creatures. Spiders.

I'm going to sing: Black American spirituals, Vol. II ill. by author. Atheneum, 1982. ISBN 0-689-30915-5 Subj: Ethnic groups in the U.S. – African Americans. Songs.

Lion and the ostrich chicks: and other African tales ill. by author. Atheneum, 1986. ISBN 0-689-31311-X Subj: Folk & fairy tales. Foreign lands – Africa. Songs.

Sh-ko and his eight wicked brothers ill. by Fumio Yoshimura. Atheneum, 1988. ISBN 0-689-31446-9 Subj: Character traits – kindness to animals. Folk & fairy tales. Foreign lands – Japan.

Sing to the sun ill. by author. HarperCollins, 1992. ISBN 0-06-020833-3 Subj: Foreign lands – Caribbean Islands. Nature. Poetry.

The story of lightning and thunder ill. by author. Atheneum, 1993. ISBN 0-689-31836-7 Subj: Folk & fairy tales. Foreign lands – Africa. Weather – lightning, thunder. Weather – storms.

Turtle knows your name ill. by author. Macmillan, 1989. ISBN 0-689-31578-3 Subj: Family life – grandmothers. Folk & fairy tales. Names. Reptiles – turtles, tortoises.

Bryan, Dorothy. *Friendly little Jonathan* by Dorothy & Marguerite Bryan; ill. by Marguerite Bryan. Dodd, 1939. Subj: Animals – dogs. Friendship.

Just Tammie! by Dorothy & Marguerite Bryan; ill. by Marguerite Bryan. Dodd, 1951. Subj: Animals – dogs.

Bryan, Marguerite. *Friendly little Jonathan* (Bryan, Dorothy)

Just Tammie! (Bryan, Dorothy)

Bryant, Bernice. *Follow the leader* ill. by author. Houghton Mifflin, 1950. Subj: Behavior – bullying. Behavior – growing up. Character traits – selfishness.

Bryant, Dean. *Here am I* ill. by author. Rand McNally, 1947. Subj: Activities.

See the bear ill. by author. Rand McNally, 1947. Subj: Toys.

Bryant, Donna. *My rabbit Roberta* ill. by Jakki Wood. Barron's, 1991. ISBN 0-8120-6210-8 Subj: Animals – rabbits. Pets.

Bryant, Michael. *The story of Nat Love* (Miller, Robert H. [Robert Henry])

Bryant, Sara Cone. *Epaminondas* (Merriam, Eve)

Epaminondas and his auntie ill. by Inez Hogan. Houghton Mifflin, 1938. Subj: Behavior – misunderstanding. Family life – aunts, uncles. Folk & fairy tales. Humorous stories.

Bryant-Mole, Karen. *Magnets* ill. with photos. Heinemann, 1998. ISBN 1-57572-629-7 Subj: Science.

Moving ill. by author. Heinemann Interactive, 1998. ISBN 1-57572-630-0 Subj: Animals. Plants. Science.

Bryson, Bernarda. *The twenty miracles of Saint Nicolas* ill. by author. Atlantic Monthly, 1960. Subj: Folk & fairy tales. Foreign lands. Holidays – Christmas.

Buchanan, Debby. *It rained on the desert today* (Buchanan, Ken)

Buchanan, Heather S. *Emily Mouse saves the day* ill. by author. Dial, 1985. ISBN 0-8037-0175-6 Subj: Animals – mice. Character traits – helpfulness. Family life.

Emily Mouse's beach house ill. by author. Dial, 1987. ISBN 0-8037-0263-9 Subj: Animals – mice. Sea & seashore – beaches.

Emily Mouse's first adventure ill. by author. Dial, 1985. ISBN 0-8037-0174-8 Subj: Animals – mice. Character traits – kindness to animals.

Emily Mouse's garden ill. by author. Dial, 1987. ISBN 0-8037-0261-2 Subj: Animals – mice. Gardens, gardening. Sibling rivalry.

George and Matilda Mouse and the floating school ill. by author. S&S, 1990. ISBN 0-671-70613-6 Subj: Animals – mice. Problem solving. School. Toys.

George and Matilda Mouse and the moon rocket ill. by author. S&S, 1992. ISBN 0-671-75864-0 Subj: Animals – mice. Holidays – Guy Fawkes Day. Moon.

George Mouse learns to fly ill. by author. Dial, 1985. ISBN 0-8037-0172-1 Subj: Activities – flying. Airplanes, airports. Animals – mice.

George Mouse's covered wagon ill. by author. Dial, 1987. ISBN 0-8037-0258-2 Subj: Activities – traveling. Activities – vacationing. Animals – mice. Sea & seashore.

George Mouse's first summer ill. by author. Dial, 1985. ISBN 0-8037-0173-X Subj: Animals – mice. Character traits – cleverness. Problem solving. Seasons – summer.

George Mouse's riverboat band ill. by author. Dial, 1987. ISBN 0-8037-0260-4 Subj: Animals – mice. Boats, ships.

Buchanan, Joan. *It's a good thing* ill. by Barbara Di Lella. Firefly, 1984. ISBN 0-920236-72-3 Subj: Activities – walking. Behavior – carelessness. Humorous stories.

Buchanan, Ken. *It rained on the desert today* by Ken & Debby Buchanan; ill. by Libba Tracy. Northland, 1994. ISBN 0-87358-575-5 Subj: Desert. Poetry. Weather – rain. Weather – storms.

This house is made of mud ill. by Libba Tracy. Northland, 1991. ISBN 0-87358-518-6 Subj: Desert. Homes, houses.

Buchanan, Sue. *Mud Pie Annie: God's recipe for doing your best* by Sue Buchanan & Dana Shafer; ill. by Joy Allen. Zonderkidz, 2001. ISBN 0-613-71694-9 Subj: Character traits – cleverness. Rhyming text. Self-concept.

Buchheimer, Naomi. *Let's go to a post office* ill. by Ruth Van Sciver. Putnam, 1957. Subj: Careers – postal workers. Communication. Post office.

Let's go to a school ill. by Ruth Van Sciver. Putnam, 1957. Subj: School.

Buchholz, Quint. *Sleep well, little bear* ill. by author; tr. by Peter F. Neumeyer. Farrar, 1994. ISBN 0-374-37026-5 Subj: Bedtime. Night. Toys – bears.

Buck, Frank. *Jungle animals* by Frank Buck; text by Ferrin Fraser; ill. by Roger Vernam. Random House, 1945. Subj: Animals.

Buck, Nola. *The basement stairs* ill. by Jonathan Lambert. Harper-Collins, 1993. ISBN 0-694-00649-1 Subj: Emotions – fear. Format, unusual – toy & movable books.

Christmas in the manger ill. by Felicia Bond. HarperFestival, 1994. ISBN 0-694-00605-X Subj: Format, unusual – toy & movable books. Holidays – Christmas. Religion – Nativity. Rhyming text.

Creepy crawly critters and other Halloween tongue twisters ill. by Sue Truesdell. HarperCollins, 1995. ISBN 0-06-024809-2 Subj: Animals. Holidays – Halloween. Insects. Language. Tongue twisters.

Gotcha! ill. by Jonathan Lambert. HarperCollins, 1994. ISBN 0-694-00648-3 Subj: Format, unusual – toy & movable books. Ghosts. Holidays – Halloween. Rhyming text.

Halloween parade ill. by Jonathan Lambert. HarperCollins, 1994. ISBN 0-694-00646-7 Subj: Format, unusual – toy & movable books. Holidays – Halloween. Rhyming text.

Hey, little baby! ill. by R. W. Alley. HarperFestival, 1999. ISBN 0-694-01200-9 Subj: Babies. Behavior – growing up. Family life – brothers & sisters.

How a baby grows ill. by Pamela Paparone. HarperFestival, 1998. ISBN 0-694-00873-7 Subj: Babies. Format, unusual – board books. Rhyming text.

The littlest witch ill. by Jonathan Lambert. HarperCollins, 1994. ISBN 0-694-00647-5 Subj: Format, unusual – toy & movable books. Holidays – Halloween. Rhyming text. Witches.

Oh, cats! ill. by Nadine Bernard Westcott. HarperCollins, 1997. ISBN 0-06-025374-6 Subj: Activities – playing. Animals – cats. Language. Rhyming text.

Santa's short suit shrunk and other Christmas tongue twisters ill. by Sue Truesdell. HarperCollins, 1997. ISBN 0-06-026663-5 Subj: Games. Holidays – Christmas. Language. Tongue twisters.

Sid and Sam ill. by G. Brian Karas. HarperCollins, 1996. ISBN 0-06-025372-X Subj: Activities – playing. Activities – singing. Language.

Buck, Pearl S. (Pearl Sydenstricker). *The Chinese story teller* ill. by Regina Shekerjian. John Day, 1971. Subj: Animals – cats. Animals – dogs. Emotions – envy, jealousy. Folk & fairy tales. Foreign lands – China.

The little fox in the middle ill. by Robert Jones. Collier, 1966. Subj: Animals – foxes. Emotions – loneliness. Family life. Friendship.

Buckaway, C. M. *Alfred, the dragon who lost his flame* ill. by Sarie Jenkins. Firefly, 1982. Subj: Dragons. Imagination. Magic.

Buckingham, Simon. *Alec and his flying bed* ill. by author. Lothrop, 1991. ISBN 0-688-10556-4 Subj: Activities – flying. Furniture – beds. Imagination.

Buckley, Helen Elizabeth. *Grandfather and I* ill. by Paul Galdone. Lothrop, 1959. ISBN 0-688-12534-4 Subj: Activities – walking. Family life – grandfathers.

Grandmother and I ill. by Paul Galdone. Lothrop, 1961. ISBN 0-688-12532-8 Subj: Emotions – love. Family life – grandmothers.

Josie and the snow ill. by Evaline Ness. Lothrop, 1964. Subj: Rhyming text. Seasons – winter. Weather – snow.

Josie's Buttercup ill. by Evaline Ness. Lothrop, 1967. Subj: Animals – dogs. Rhyming text.

The leftover bridge ill. by Oki S. Han. Lothrop, 1999. ISBN 0-688-13485-8 Subj: Bridges.

Moonlight kite ill. by Elise Primavera. Lothrop, 1997. ISBN 0-688-10932-2 Subj: Behavior – sharing. Emotions – loneliness. Kites. Religion.

Someday with my father ill. by Ellen Eagle. HarperCollins, 1985. ISBN 0-06-020877-5 Subj: Dreams. Family life – fathers. Illness.

"Take care of things," Edward said ill. by Katherine Coville. Lothrop, 1991. ISBN 0-688-07732-3 Subj: Activities – playing. Family life – brothers.

Where did Josie go? ill. by Jan Ormerod. Lothrop, 1999. ISBN 0-688-16507-9 Subj: Family life. Games. Rhyming text.

Buckley, Kate. *Love notes* ill. by author. A. Whitman, 1988. ISBN 0-8075-4780-8 Subj: Behavior – growing up. Holidays – Valentine's Day. Poetry. School.

Buckley, Paul. *Amy Belligera and the fireflies* ill. by Kate Buckley. A. Whitman, 1987. ISBN 0-8075-0324-X Subj: Insects – fireflies. Magic. Night. Witches.

Buckley, Ray. *God's love is like . . .* ill. by author. Abingdon, 1998. ISBN 0-687-05626-8 Subj: Jewish culture. Religion.

Buckley, Richard. *The foolish tortoise* ill. by Eric Carle. Picture Book Studio, 1985. ISBN 0-88708-002-2 Subj: Behavior – seeking better things. Folk & fairy tales. Reptiles – turtles, tortoises. Rhyming text.

The greedy python ill. by Eric Carle. Picture Book Studio, 1985. ISBN 0-88708-001-4 Subj: Behavior – greed. Folk & fairy tales. Reptiles – snakes. Rhyming text.

Buckmaster, Henrietta. *Lucy and Loki* ill. by Barbara Cooney. Scribners, 1958. Subj: Animals – cats. Animals – dogs. Behavior – imitation.

Bucknall, Caroline. *One bear all alone* ill. by author. Dial, 1986. ISBN 0-8037-0238-8 Subj: Counting, numbers. Rhyming text. Toys – bears.

One bear in the hospital ill. by author. Dial, 1991. ISBN 0-8037-0847-5 Subj: Hospitals. Illness. Rhyming text. Toys – bears.

One bear in the picture ill. by author. Dial, 1988. ISBN 0-8037-0463-1 Subj: Character traits – cleanliness. Rhyming text. Toys – bears.

The three little pigs (The three little pigs)

Budbill, David. *Christmas tree farm* ill. by Donald Carrick. Macmillan, 1974. ISBN 0-02-715330-4 Subj: Farms. Holidays – Christmas. Science. Trees.

Budd, E. S. *Military helicopters* ill. with photos. Child's World, 2002. ISBN 1-56766-981-6 Subj: Helicopters.

Military trucks ill. with photos. Child's World, 2002. ISBN 1-56766-982-4 Subj: Trucks.

Budd, Lillian. *The people on Long Ago Street* ill. by Marilyn Miller. Rand McNally, 1964. Subj: Family life – great-grandparents. Imagination.

The pie wagon ill. by Marilyn Miller. Lothrop, 1960. Subj: ABC books. Food.

Budney, Blossom. *After dark* ill. by Tony Chen. Lothrop, 1975. ISBN 0-688-51703-X Subj: Night.

A kiss is round ill. by Vladimir Bobri. Lothrop, 1954. ISBN 0-688-51177-5 Subj: Concepts – shape. Poetry.

N is for nursery school ill. by Vladimir Bobri. Lothrop, 1956. Subj: ABC books. School – nursery.

Buehner, Caralyn. *The escape of Marvin the ape* by Caralyn & Mark Buehner; ill. by Mark Buehner. Dial, 1992. ISBN 0-8037-1124-7

Subj: Animals – gorillas. Character traits – freedom. Cities, towns. Zoos.

Fanny's dream ill. by Mark Buehner. Dial, 1996. ISBN 0-8037-1497-1 Subj: Behavior – wishing. Careers – farmers. Farms. Folk & fairy tales.

I did it, I'm sorry ill. by Mark Buehner. Dial, 1998. ISBN 0-8037-2011-4 Subj: Animals. Behavior. Character traits.

It's a spoon, not a shovel ill. by Mark Buehner. Dial, 1998. ISBN 0-8037-1495-5 Subj: Etiquette. Humorous stories.

A job for Wittilda by Caralyn & Mark Buehner; ill. by Mark Buehner. Dial, 1993. ISBN 0-8037-1150-6 Subj: Activities – working. Food. Witches.

Snowmen at night ill. by Mark Buehner. Fogelman, 2002. ISBN 0-8037-2550-7 Subj: Night. Rhyming text. Snowmen.

Snowmen at night [board book] ill. by Mark Buehner. Dial, 2004. ISBN 0-8037-3041-1 Subj: Format, unusual – board books. Night. Rhyming text. Snowmen.

Superdog, the heart of a hero ill. by Mark Buehner. HarperCollins, 2004. ISBN 0-06-623621-5 Subj: Animals – dogs. Concepts – size. Self-concept.

Buehner, Mark. *The escape of Marvin the ape* (Buehner, Caralyn)

A job for Wittilda (Buehner, Caralyn)

Buell, Ellen Lewis. *Read me a poem: children's favorite poetry* ill. by Anna Maria Magagna. Grosset, 1965. Subj: Poetry.

Buff, Conrad. *Dash and Dart* (Buff, Mary [Marsh])

Forest folk (Buff, Mary [Marsh])

Hurry, Skurry and Flurry (Buff, Mary [Marsh])

Buff, Mary (Marsh). *Dash and Dart* by Mary & Conrad Buff; ill. by authors. Viking, 1942. Subj: Animals – deer. Caldecott award honor books. Forest, woods.

Forest folk by Mary & Conrad Buff; ill. by authors. Viking, 1962. Subj: Animals. Animals – deer. Forest, woods.

Hurry, Skurry and Flurry by Mary & Conrad Buff; ill. by authors. Viking, 1954. Subj: Animals – squirrels. Rhyming text.

Buffett, Jimmy. *The jolly mon* by Jimmy & Savannah Jane Buffett; ill. by Lambert Davis. Harcourt, 1988. ISBN 0-15-240530-5 Subj: Activities – traveling. Foreign lands – Caribbean Islands. Music. Musical instruments – guitars. Royalty – kings. Songs.

Trouble dolls by Jimmy & Savannah Jane Buffet; ill. by Lambert Davis. Harcourt, 1991. ISBN 0-15-290790-4 Subj: Behavior – lost. Magic. Toys – dolls.

Buffett, Savannah Jane. *The jolly mon* (Buffett, Jimmy)

Trouble dolls (Buffett, Jimmy)

Bugni, Alice. *Moose racks, bear tracks and other Alaska kidsnacks* ill. by Shannon Cartwright. Sasquatch, 1999. ISBN 1-57061-214-5 Subj: Activities – baking, cooking. Food.

Bugs ill. with photos. Cedco, 1998. ISBN 0-7683-2032-1 Subj: Insects.

Bulette, Sara. *The elf in the singing tree* ill. by Tom Dunnington. Follett, 1964. Reading consultant: Morton Botel. Subj: Imagination. Mythical creatures – elves.

The splendid belt of Mr. Big ill. by Lou Myers. Follett, 1964. Reading consultant: Morton Botel. Subj: Animals – monkeys. Clothing. Concepts – size. Problem solving.

Bulion, Leslie. *Fatuma's new cloth* ill. by Nicole Tadgell. Moon Mt., 2002. ISBN 0-9677929-7-5 Subj: Family life – mothers. Foreign lands – Africa. Shopping.

Bulla, Clyde Robert. *Dandelion Hill* ill. by Bruce Degen. Dutton, 1982. ISBN 0-525-45101-3 Subj: Animals – bulls, cows. Behavior – growing up. Farms.

Daniel's duck ill. by Joan Sandin. HarperCollins, 1979. ISBN 0-06-020909-7 Subj: Activities. Art. Emotions – embarrassment.

Jonah and the great fish ill. by Helga Aichinger. Crowell, 1970. Subj: Animals – whales. Religion – Jonah.

Keep running, Allen! ill. by Satomi Ichikawa. Crowell, 1978. ISBN 0-690-01375-2 Subj: Behavior – solitude. Sibling rivalry.

Noah and the rainbow: an ancient story (Bolliger, Max)

Poor boy, rich boy ill. by Marcia Sewall. HarperCollins, 1982. ISBN 0-06-020897-X Subj: Orphans.

The story of Valentine's Day ill. by Susan Estelle Kwas. HarperCollins, 1999. ISBN 0-06-027884-6 Subj: Holidays – Valentine's Day.

The stubborn old woman ill. by Anne F. Rockwell. Crowell, 1980. ISBN 0-690-03946-8 Subj: Behavior – needing someone. Character traits – persistence. Character traits – stubbornness.

A tree is a plant ill. by Lois Lignell. Crowell, 1960. Subj: Plants. Trees.

Valentine cat ill. by Leonard Weisgard. Crowell, 1959. ISBN 0-690-85730-6 Subj: Animals – cats. Holidays – Valentine's Day.

Washington's birthday ill. by Don Bolognese. Crowell, 1967. ISBN 0-690-86796-4 Subj: Holidays – Washington's Birthday. U.S. history.

What makes a shadow? ill. by June Otani. HarperCollins, 1994. ISBN 0-06-022915-2 Subj: Shadows.

Bullard, Lisa. *Not enough beds! a Christmas alphabet book* ill. by Joni Oeltjenbruns. Carolrhoda, 1999. ISBN 1-57505-356-X Subj: ABC books. Bedtime. Furniture – beds. Holidays – Christmas. Rhyming text.

Powerboats ill. with photos. Lerner, 2004. ISBN 0-8225-0744-7 Subj: Boats, ships. Sports – racing.

Stock cars ill. with photos. Lerner, 2004. ISBN 0-8225-0694-7 Subj: Automobiles. Sports – racing.

Trick-or-treat on Milton Street ill. by Joni Oeltjenbruns. Carolrhoda, 2001. ISBN 1-57505-158-3 Subj: Family life – stepfamilies. Holidays – Halloween. Moving.

Buller, Jon. *Toad on the road* by Jon Buller & Susan Schade; ill. by authors. Random House, 1992. ISBN 0-679-92689-5 Subj: Animals. Automobiles. Frogs & toads. Rhyming text.

Bulloch, Ivan. *Patterns* consultants, Wendy & David Clemson; ill. with photos. World Book, 1997. ISBN 0-7166-4903-9 Subj: Concepts. Concepts – shape.

Bullock, Kathleen. *It chanced to rain* ill. by author. S&S, 1992. ISBN 0-671-66005-5 Subj: Activities – walking. Animals. Rhyming text. Weather – rain.

Rabbits are coming ill. by author. S&S, 1991. ISBN 0-671-72963-2 Subj: Animals – rabbits. Toys – balloons. Wordless.

A surprise for Mitzi Mouse ill. by author. S&S, 1989. ISBN 0-671-67331-9 Subj: Animals – mice. Emotions – envy, jealousy. Family life – sisters. Sibling rivalry.

Bullock, Michael. *The camel who left the zoo* (Allamand, Pascale)

The pop rooster (Allamand, Pascale)

Bunce, William. *Freight trains* ill. by Lemuel B. Line. Putnam, 1954. Subj: Trains.

Bundey, Nikki. *In the park* ill. by Virginia Gray. Carolrhoda, 1998. ISBN 1-57505-277-6 Subj: Activities. Science. Sports.

In the snow ill. by Virginia Gray. Carolrhoda, 1998. ISBN 1-57505-086-2 Subj: Activities. Science. Seasons – winter. Sports. Weather – snow.

In the water ill. by Virginia Gray. Carolrhoda, 1998. ISBN 1-57505-085-4 Subj: Activities. Science. Sea & seashore. Sports. Sports – surfing. Sports – swimming.

On a bike ill. by Virginia Gray. Carolrhoda, 1998. ISBN 1-57505-278-4 Subj: Science. Sports – bicycling.

Bundt, Nancy. *The fire station book* text by Jeff Linzer; photos by Nancy Bundt. Carolrhoda, 1981. ISBN 0-87614-126-2 Subj: Careers – firefighters.

Bunin, Catherine. *Is that your sister? a true story of adoption* by Catherine Bunin & Sherry Bunin; ill. with photos. Pantheon, 1976. ISBN 0-394-93230-7 Subj: Adoption. Family life.

Bunin, Sherry. *Is that your sister? a true story of adoption* (Bunin, Catherine)

Buntain, Ruth Jaeger. *The birthday story* ill. by Eloise Wilkin. Holiday, 1953. Subj: Birthdays. Emotions – loneliness. Friendship.

Bunting, Eve (Anne Evelyn). *Anna's table* ill. by Taia Morley. NorthWord, 2003. ISBN 1-55971-841-2 Subj: Behavior – collecting things. Nature. Poetry.

Barney the Beard ill. by Imero Gobbato. Parents' Magazine Pr., 1975. ISBN 0-8193-0729-7 Subj: Activities – baking, cooking. Careers – bakers.

The big cheese ill. by Sal Murdocca. Macmillan, 1977. ISBN 0-02-715370-3 Subj: Cumulative tales. Emotions – loneliness. Humorous stories. Old age.

The big red barn ill. by Howard Knotts. Harcourt, 1979. ISBN 0-15-207145-8 Subj: Death. Family life.

The blue and the gray ill. by Ned Bittinger. Scholastic, 1996. ISBN 0-590-60197-0 Subj: Ethnic groups in the U.S. – African Americans. Friendship. U.S. history. War.

The bones of Fred Mcfee ill. by Kurt Cyrus. Harcourt, 2002. ISBN 0-15-202004-7 Subj: Anatomy – skeletons. Holidays – Halloween. Rhyming text.

Box, fox, ox, and the peacock ill. by Leslie H. Morrill. Ginn, 1974. ISBN 0-663-25470-1 Subj: Animals – foxes. Animals – oxen. Behavior – fighting, arguing. Birds – peacocks, peahens.

Butterfly house ill. by Greg Shed. Scholastic, 1999. ISBN 0-590-84884-4 Subj: Family life – grandfathers. Insects – butterflies, caterpillars. Metamorphosis. Rhyming text.

Can you do this, Old Badger? ill. by LeUyen Pham. Harcourt, 1999. ISBN 0-15-201654-6 Subj: Animals – badgers. Old age.

Cheyenne again ill. by Irving Toddy. Clarion, 1995. ISBN 0-395-70364-6 Subj: Indians of North America – Cheyenne (Sioux). Indians of North America – Great Plains. School.

Christmas cricket ill. by Timothy Bush. Clarion, 2002. ISBN 0-618-06554-7 Subj: Holidays – Christmas. Insects – crickets.

Clancy's coat ill. by Lorinda Bryan Cauley. Warne, 1984. ISBN 0-7232-6252-7 Subj: Foreign lands – Ireland. Friendship.

The day before Christmas ill. by Beth Peck. Clarion, 1992. ISBN 0-89919-866-X Subj: Activities – dancing. Death. Family life – grandfathers. Family life – mothers. Holidays – Christmas.

The days of summer ill. by William Low. Harcourt, 2001. ISBN 0-15-201840-9 Subj: Divorce. Family life – grandparents. Family life – sisters.

A day's work ill. by Ronald Himler. Clarion, 1994. ISBN 0-395-67321-6 Subj: Activities – working. Character traits – honesty. Ethnic groups in the U.S. – Mexican Americans. Family life – grandfathers. Gardens, gardening.

December ill. by David Diaz. Harcourt, 1997. ISBN 0-15-201434-9 Subj: Character traits – helpfulness. Holidays – Christmas. Homeless.

Demetrius and the golden goblet ill. by Michael Hague. Harcourt, 1980. ISBN 0-15-223186-2 Subj: Royalty – kings. Sea & seashore.

Ducky ill. by David Wisniewski. Clarion, 1997. ISBN 0-395-75185-3 Subj: Activities – traveling. Sea & seashore. Toys.

Flower garden ill. by Kathryn Hewitt. Harcourt, 1994. ISBN 0-15-228776-0 Subj: Birthdays. Family life – mothers. Flowers. Gardens, gardening. Rhyming text.

Fly away home ill. by Ronald Himler. Houghton Mifflin, 1991. ISBN 0-395-55962-6 Subj: Airplanes, airports. Family life – fathers. Homeless.

Ghost's hour, spook's hour ill. by author. Clarion, 1987. ISBN 0-89919-484-2 Subj: Animals – dogs. Emotions – fear. Family life. Night.

Girls A to Z ill. by Suzanne Bloom. Boyds Mills, 2002. ISBN 1-56397-147-X Subj: Careers. Names.

Gleam and Glow ill. by Peter Sylvada. Harcourt, 2001. ISBN 0-15-202596-0 Subj: Fish. Foreign lands – Bosnia-Herzegovina. War.

Going home ill. by David Diaz. HarperCollins, 1996. ISBN 0-06-026296-6 Subj: Ethnic groups in the U.S. – Mexican Americans. Family life. Foreign lands – Mexico. Holidays – Christmas.

Goose dinner ill. by Howard Knotts. Harcourt, 1981. ISBN 0-05-232224-8 Subj: Birds – geese. Farms.

Happy birthday, dear duck ill. by Jan Brett. Clarion, 1988. ISBN 0-89919-541-5 Subj: Animals. Birds – ducks. Birthdays. Rhyming text.

The happy funeral ill. by Vo-Dinh Mai. HarperCollins, 1982. ISBN 0-06-020894-5 Subj: Death. Ethnic groups in the U.S. – Chinese Americans. Family life – grandfathers.

How many days to America? a Thanksgiving story ill. by Beth Peck. Clarion, 1988. ISBN 0-89919-521-0 Subj: Character traits – freedom. Holidays – Thanksgiving. Pilgrims.

I don't want to go to camp ill. by Maryann Cocca-Leffler. Boyds Mills, 1996. ISBN 1-56397-393-6 Subj: Camps, camping. Emotions. Family life – mothers.

I have an olive tree ill. by Karen Barbour. HarperCollins, 1999. ISBN 0-06-027574-X Subj: Ethnic groups in the U.S. – Greek Americans. Family life. Foreign lands – Greece. Trees.

In the haunted house ill. by Susan Meddaugh. Houghton Mifflin, 1990. ISBN 0-395-51589-0 Subj: Ghosts. Holidays – Halloween. Homes, houses.

Jane Martin, dog detective ill. by Amy Schwartz. Harcourt, 1984. ISBN 0-15-239586-5 Subj: Animals – dogs. Behavior – lost. Careers – detectives. Mystery stories.

Jin Woo ill. by Chris K. Soentpiet. Clarion, 2001. ISBN 0-395-93872-4 Subj: Adoption. Ethnic groups in the U.S. – Korean Americans. Family life – brothers.

Little Badger, terror of the seven seas ill. by LeUyen Pham. Harcourt, 2001. ISBN 0-15-202395-X Subj: Animals – badgers. Imagination. Pirates.

Little Badger's just-about birthday ill. by LeUyen Pham. Harcourt, 2002. Subj: Animals. Animals – badgers. Birthdays. Parties.

Magic and the night river ill. by Allen Say. HarperCollins, 1978. ISBN 0-06-020913-5 Subj: Birds – cormorants. Careers – fishermen. Family life – grandfathers. Foreign lands – Japan.

The man who could call down owls ill. by Charles Mikolaycak. Macmillan, 1984. ISBN 0-02-715380-0 Subj: Behavior – greed. Birds – owls. Magic.

Market day ill. by Holly Berry. HarperCollins, 1996. ISBN 0-06-025368-1 Subj: Fairs, festivals. Foreign lands – Ireland. Shopping.

The memory string ill. by Ted Rand. Clarion, 2000. ISBN 0-395-86146-2 Subj: Emotions – grief. Family life – stepfamilies. Memories, memory.

Monkey in the middle ill. by Lynn Munsinger. Harcourt, 1984. ISBN 0-15-255316-9 Subj: Animals – monkeys. Emotions – envy, jealousy. Friendship.

Moonstick: the seasons of the Sioux ill. by John Sandford. HarperCollins, 1997. ISBN 0-06-024805-X Subj: Indians of North America – Dakota (Sioux). Moon. Nature. Seasons.

The Mother's Day mice ill. by Jan Brett. Clarion, 1986. ISBN 0-89919-387-0 Subj: Animals – mice. Holidays – Mother's Day.

My backpack ill. by Maryann Cocca-Leffler. Boyds Mills, 1997. ISBN 1-56397-433-9 Subj: Behavior. Family life. Rhyming text.

My special day at third street school ill. by Suzanne Bloom. Boyds Mills, 2004. ISBN 0-613-79887-2 Subj: Careers – authors. School.

Night of the gargoyles ill. by David Wiesner. Clarion, 1994. ISBN 0-395-66553-1 Subj: Buildings. Monsters. Museums. Mythical creatures.

Night tree ill. by Ted Rand. Harcourt, 1991. ISBN 0-15-257425-5 Subj: Animals. Character traits – kindness to animals. Family life. Holidays – Christmas. Trees.

No nap ill. by Susan Meddaugh. Houghton Mifflin, 1989. ISBN 0-89919-813-9 Subj: Bedtime. Sleep.

On Call Back Mountain ill. by Barry Moser. Blue Sky, 1997. ISBN 0-590-25929-6 Subj: Animals – wolves. Careers – firefighters. Careers – park rangers. Death. Friendship.

One candle ill. by Wendy Popp. Cotler, 2002. ISBN 0-06-028116-2 Subj: Holidays – Hanukkah. War.

Our teacher's having a baby ill. by Diane de Groat. Clarion, 1992. ISBN 0-395-60470-2 Subj: Babies. Careers – teachers. School.

Peepers ill. by James Ransome. Harcourt, 2000. ISBN 0-15-260297-6 Subj: Activities – traveling. Nature. Seasons – fall.

A perfect Father's Day ill. by Susan Meddaugh. Houghton Mifflin, 1991. ISBN 0-395-52590-X Subj: Family life – fathers. Holidays – Father's Day.

A picnic in October ill. by Nancy Carpenter. Harcourt, 1999. ISBN 0-15-201656-2 Subj: Activities – picnicking. Birthdays. Emotions – embarrassment. Ethnic groups in the U.S. – Italian Americans. Family life – grandmothers. Immigrants. U.S. history.

The pumpkin fair ill. by Eileen Christelow. Clarion, 1997. ISBN 0-395-70060-4 Subj: Fairs, festivals. Rhyming text. Seasons – fall.

Red fox running ill. by Wendell Minor. Clarion, 1993. ISBN 0-395-58919-3 Subj: Animals – foxes. Rhyming text. Seasons – winter.

Riding the tiger ill. with woodcuts by David Frampton. Clarion, 2001. ISBN 0-395-93872-4 Subj: Animals – tigers. Cities, towns. Clubs, gangs.

The robot birthday ill. by Marie DeJohn. Dutton, 1980. ISBN 0-525-38542-8 Subj: Birthdays. Robots.

Rudi's pond ill. by Ronald Himler. Clarion, 1999. ISBN 0-395-89067-5 Subj: Death. Emotions – grief. Friendship.

St. Patrick's Day in the morning ill. by Jan Brett. Houghton Mifflin, 1980. ISBN 0-395-29098-8 Subj: Holidays – St. Patrick's Day.

Say it fast ill. by True Kelley. Ginn, 1974. ISBN 0-663-25467-1 Subj: Language. Tongue twisters.

Scary, scary Halloween ill. by Jan Brett. Houghton Mifflin, 1986. ISBN 0-89919-414-1 Subj: Holidays – Halloween. Monsters. Mythical creatures – goblins. Rhyming text.

Secret place ill. by Ted Rand. Clarion, 1996. ISBN 0-395-64367-8 Subj: Cities, towns. Nature.

Sing a song of piglets: a calendar in verse ill. by Emily Arnold McCully. Clarion, 2002. ISBN 0-618-01137-4 Subj: Animals – babies. Animals – pigs. Days of the week, months of the year. Poetry.

Smoky night ill. by David Diaz. Harcourt, 1994. ISBN 0-15-269954-6 Subj: Caldecott award books. Cities, towns. Communities, neighborhoods. Emotions – anger. Ethnic groups in the U.S. Riots.

So far from the sea ill. by Chris Soentpiet. Clarion, 1998. ISBN 0-395-72095-8 Subj: Ethnic groups in the U.S. – Japanese Americans. Family life – grandfathers. War.

Someday a tree ill. by Ronald Himler. Clarion, 1993. ISBN 0-395-61309-4 Subj: Activities – picnicking. Ecology. Family life – mothers. Trees.

Summer wheels ill. by Thomas B. Allen. Harcourt, 1992. ISBN 0-15-207000-1 Subj: Friendship. Sports – bicycling.

Sunflower house ill. by Kathryn Hewitt. Harcourt, 1996. ISBN 0-15-200483-1 Subj: Flowers. Gardens, gardening. Rhyming text. Seasons – summer.

Sunshine home ill. by Diane de Groat. Clarion, 1994. ISBN 0-395-63309-5 Subj: Emotions. Family life – grandmothers. Old age.

Swan in love ill. by Jo Ellen McAllister-Stammen. Atheneum, 2000. ISBN 0-689-82080-1 Subj: Animals. Birds – swans. Boats, ships. Emotions – love.

Terrible things ill. by Stephen Gammell. HarperCollins, 1980. ISBN 0-06-020904-6 Subj: Animals. Emotions – fear.

Train to somewhere ill. by Ronald Himler. Clarion, 1996. ISBN 0-395-71325-0 Subj: Emotions. Family life – stepfamilies. Orphans. Trains. U.S. history.

The traveling men of Ballycoo ill. by Kaethe Zemach. Harcourt, 1983. ISBN 0-15-289792-5 Subj: Activities – traveling. Music.

Trouble on the T-ball team ill. by Irene Trivas. Clarion, 1997. ISBN 0-395-66060-2 Subj: Sports – T-ball. Teeth.

A turkey for Thanksgiving ill. by Diane de Groat. Ticknor & Fields, 1991. ISBN 0-89919-793-0 Subj: Animals – moose. Birds – turkeys. Holidays – Thanksgiving.

Twinnies ill. by Nancy Carpenter. Harcourt, 1997. ISBN 0-15-291592-3 Subj: Babies. Family life – sisters. Multiple births – twins.

The Valentine bears ill. by Jan Brett. Seabury Pr., 1983. ISBN 0-89919-138-X Subj: Animals – bears. Holidays – Valentine's Day.

The wall ill. by Ronald Himler. Clarion, 1990. ISBN 0-395-51588-2 Subj: Careers – military. Family life. War.

We need a bigger zoo! ill. by Bob Barner. Ginn, 1974. ISBN 0-663-25446-9 Subj: Animals. Wordless. Zoos.

We were there: a Nativity story ill. by Wendell Minor. Clarion, 2001. ISBN 0-395-82265-3 Subj: Animals. Holidays – Christmas. Religion – Nativity.

The Wednesday surprise ill. by Donald Garrick. Ticknor & Fields, 1989. ISBN 0-89919-721-3 Subj: Birthdays. Books, reading. Family life. Family life – grandmothers.

Who was born this special day? by Eve Bunting & Leonid Gore; ill. by Leonid Gore. Atheneum, 2001. ISBN 0-689-82302-9 Subj: Holidays – Christmas. Poetry. Religion – Nativity.

Winter's coming ill. by Howard Knotts. Harcourt, 1977. ISBN 0-15-298036-9 Subj: Family life – grandparents. Farms. Seasons – winter.

Bunting, Jane. *The children's visual dictionary* ill. by David Hopkins. DK, 1995. ISBN 1-56458-881-5 Subj: Dictionaries. Language.

My first ABC ill. by author. DK, 1993. ISBN 1-56458-403-8 Subj: ABC books. Language.

My first word book ill. by author. DK, 1996. ISBN 0-7894-0463-X Subj: Activities. Dictionaries. Language.

Burch, Robert. *The hunting trip* ill. by Susanne Suba. Scribners, 1971. ISBN 0-684-12495-5 Subj: Character traits – kindness to animals. Family life. Food. Sports – hunting.

Joey's cat ill. by Don Freeman. Viking, 1969. ISBN 0-670-40789-5 Subj: Animals – cats. Animals – possums. Ethnic groups in the U.S. – African Americans. Family life.

The jolly witch ill. by Leigh Grant. Dutton, 1975. ISBN 0-525-32797-5 Subj: Character traits – cleanliness. Witches.

Burchard, Peter. *The Carol Moran* ill. by author. Macmillan, 1958. Subj: Boats, ships.

Burdekin, Harold. *A child's grace* by Harold Burdekin & Ernest Claxton; the grace by Mrs. E. Rutter Leatham; photos by Harold Burdekin. Dutton, 1938. Subj: Activities. Poetry. Religion.

Burden-Patmon, Denise. *Carnival* by Denise Burden-Patmon with Kathryn D. Jones; ill. by Reynold Ruffins. Modern Curriculum, 1992. ISBN 0-8136-2275-1 Subj: Ethnic groups in the U.S. – African Americans. Fairs, festivals. Music.

Imani's gift at Kwanzaa ill. by Floyd Cooper. Modern Curriculum, 1992. ISBN 0-8136-2244-1 Subj: Ethnic groups in the U.S. – African Americans. Family life. Gifts. Holidays – Kwanzaa.

Burdett, Lois. *Hamlet for kids* intro. by Kenneth Branagh; written & ill. by children. Firefly, 2000. ISBN 1-55209-522-3 Subj: Children as authors. Children as illustrators. Crime. Foreign lands – Denmark. Rhyming text. Royalty – princes.

Macbeth for kids written & ill. by children. Black Moss, 1996. ISBN 0-8875-3287-X Subj: Behavior – fighting, arguing. Children as authors. Children as illustrators. Crime. Foreign lands – Scotland. Royalty – kings. Royalty – queens.

A midsummer night's dream for kids written & ill. by children. Firefly, 1997. ISBN 1-55209-130-9 Subj: Children as authors. Children as illustrators. Dreams. Rhyming text.

Romeo and Juliet for kids written & ill. by children. Firefly, 1998. ISBN 1-55209-244-5 Subj: Behavior – fighting, arguing. Children as authors. Children as illustrators. Emotions – love. Family life. Rhyming text.

The tempest for kids written & ill. by children. Firefly, 1999. ISBN 1-55209-355-7 Subj: Children as authors. Children as illustrators. Emotions. Islands. Magic. Rhyming text. Weather – storms.

Twelfth night written & ill. by children. Firefly, 1997. ISBN 0-8875-3233-0 Subj: Behavior – mistakes. Behavior – trickery. Boats, ships. Character traits. Children as authors. Children as illustrators. Sea & seashore.

Burdick, Margaret. *Bobby Otter and the blue boat* ill. by author. Little, 1987. ISBN 0-316-11616-5 Subj: Activities – trading. Animals. Animals – otters. Toys.

Sara Raccoon and the secret place ill. by author. Little, 1992. ISBN 0-316-11617-3 Subj: Animals. Animals – raccoons. Behavior – solitude. Friendship.

Burg, Ann. *Autumn walk* ill. by Kelly Asbury. HarperFestival, 2003. ISBN 0-06-009741-8 Subj: Format, unusual – board books. Seasons – fall.

Burgert, Hans-Joachim. *Samulo and the giant* ill. by author. Holt, 1970. ISBN 0-03081-493-6 Subj: Character traits – bravery. Weather.

Burgess, Anthony. *The land where the ice cream grows* (Testa, Fulvio)

Burgess, Gelett. *The little father* ill. by Richard Egielski. Farrar, 1985. ISBN 0-374-34596-1 Subj: Character traits – smallness. Family life – fathers. Poetry.

Burgess, Thornton. *Old Mother West Wind* ill. by Michael Hague. Holt, 1990. ISBN 0-8050-1005-X Subj: Animals. Weather – wind.

Burgie, Irving. *Caribbean carnival: songs of the West Indies* ill. by Frané Lessac; afterword by Rosa Guy. Tambourine, 1992. ISBN 0-688-10780-X Subj: Foreign lands – West Indies. Music. Songs.

Island in the sun (Belafonte, Harry)

Burgunder, Rose. *From summer to summer* ill. by author. Viking, 1965. Subj: Poetry. Seasons – summer.

Burke, Bobby. *Daddy's little girl* words & music by Bobby Burke & Horace Gerlach; ill. by Maggie Kneen. HarperCollins, 2004. ISBN 0-06-028722-5 Subj: Animals – rabbits. Family life – daughters. Family life – fathers. Music. Songs.

Burke, Jennifer S. *Cloudy days* ill. with photos. Childrens Pr., 2000. ISBN 0-516-23117-0 Subj: Activities. Weather – clouds.

Cold days ill. with photos. Childrens Pr., 2000. ISBN 0-516-23118-9 Subj: Cities, towns. Concepts – cold & heat. Seasons – winter. Weather.

Hot days ill. with photos. Childrens Pr., 2000. ISBN 0-516-23119-7 Subj: Cities, towns. Concepts – cold & heat. Seasons – summer. Weather.

Ovals ill. with photos. Childrens Pr., 2000. ISBN 0-516-23076-X Subj: Activities. Cities, towns. Concepts – shape.

Rainy days ill. with photos. Childrens Pr., 2000. ISBN 0-516-23120-0 Subj: Activities. Cities, towns. Weather – rain.

Rectangles ill. with photos. Childrens Pr., 2000. ISBN 0-516-23077-8 Subj: Cities, towns. Concepts – shape.

Squares ill. with photos. Childrens Pr., 2000. ISBN 0-516-23078-6 Subj: Cities, towns. Concepts – shape.

Stars ill. with photos. Childrens Pr., 2000. ISBN 0-516-23079-4 Subj: Cities, towns. Concepts – shape.

Sunny days ill. with photos. Childrens Pr., 2000. ISBN 0-516-23121-9 Subj: Activities. Weather – clouds.

Triangles ill. with photos. Childrens Pr., 2000. ISBN 0-516-23080-8 Subj: Cities, towns. Concepts – shape.

Windy days ill. with photos. Childrens Pr., 2000. ISBN 0-516-23122-7 Subj: Cities, towns. Weather – wind.

Burke, Katie. *Lightning bug thunder* ill. by Sheila McGraw. Firefly, 1998. ISBN 1-55209-271-2 Subj: Imagination. Insects – fireflies. Nature. Weather – droughts. Weather – lightning, thunder.

Burke, Rick. *George Washington* ill. with photos, maps, & illus,. Heinemann, 2003. ISBN 1-4034-0158-6 Subj: U.S. history.

Burke, Timothy. *Tugboats in action* photos by author. A. Whitman, 1993. ISBN 0-8075-8112-7 Subj: Activities – working. Boats, ships. Rivers.

Burke-Weiner, Kimberly. *The maybe garden* ill. by Fredrika Spillman. Beyond Words, 1992. ISBN 0-941831-56-6 Subj: Character traits – individuality. Family life – mothers. Gardens, gardening. Imagination.

Burland, Brian. *St. Nicholas and the tub* ill. by Joseph Low. Holiday, 1964. Subj: Folk & fairy tales. Holidays – Christmas.

Burleigh, Robert. *By my brother's side* (Barber, Tiki)

Goal ill. by Stephen T. Johnson. Harcourt, 2001. ISBN 0-15-201789-5 Subj: Poetry. Sports – soccer.

Home run: the story of Babe Ruth ill. by Mike Wimmer. Silver Whistle, 1998. ISBN 0-15-200970-1 Subj: Sports – baseball.

I love going through this book ill. by Dan Yaccarino. Cotler, 2001. ISBN 0-06-028806-X Subj: Books, reading. Rhyming text.

It's funny where Ben's train takes him ill. by Joanna Yardley. Orchard, 1999. ISBN 0-531-33106-7 Subj: Bedtime. Imagination. Rhyming text. Trains.

Langston's train ride ill. by Leonard Jenkins. Orchard, 2004. ISBN 0-439-35239-8 Subj: Careers – poets. Ethnic groups in the U.S. – African Americans.

Lookin' for Bird in the big city ill. by Marek Los. Harcourt, 2000. ISBN 0-15-202031-4 Subj: Careers – musicians. Cities, towns. Ethnic groups in the U.S. – African Americans. Music. Musical instruments – trumpets.

Messenger, messenger ill. by Barry Root. Atheneum, 2000. ISBN 0-689-82103-4 Subj: Careers – messengers. Cities, towns. Rhyming text. Sports – bicycling.

Burlingham, Mary. *The climbing book* (Steiner, Charlotte)

Burlson, Joe. *Space colony* ill. by author. Putnam, 1984. ISBN 0-399-21058-X Subj: Format, unusual. Wordless.

Burn, Doris. *The summerfolk* ill. by author. Coward, 1968. Subj: Seasons – summer.

Burnard, Damon. *The amazing adventures of Soupy Boy* ill. by author. Houghton, 1998. ISBN 0-395-91225-3 Subj: Food. Humorous stories. Imagination.

Dave's haircut ill. by author. Dutton, 2003. ISBN 0-525-46967-2 Subj: Careers – barbers. Hair. School.

I spy in the jungle ill. by Julia Cairns. Chronicle, 2001. ISBN 0-8118-2987-1 Subj: Animals. Format, unusual – board books. Games. Jungle.

I spy in the ocean ill. by Julia Cairns. Chronicle, 2001. ISBN 0-8118-2988-X Subj: ABC books. Animals. Format, unusual – board books. Sea & seashore.

Burnett, Frances Hodgson. *A little princess* adapt. & ill. by Barbara McClintock. HarperCollins, 2000. ISBN 0-06-029010-2 Subj: Foreign lands – England. Orphans. Poverty. School.

A little princess (Brown, Janet Allison)

The secret garden (Brown, Janet Allison)

Burningham, Helen Oxenbury. *see* Oxenbury, Helen

Burningham, John. *Aldo* ill. by author. Crown, 1992. ISBN 0-517-58699-1 Subj: Emotions – loneliness. Friendship. Imagination – imaginary friends.

Avocado baby ill. by author. Crowell, 1982. ISBN 0-690-04244-2 Subj: Babies. Family life. Food.

The baby ill. by author. Candlewick, 1994. ISBN 1-56402-334-6 Subj: Babies. Emotions. Family life – brothers & sisters.

The blanket ill. by author. Crowell, 1976, 1975. ISBN 0-690-01270-5 Subj: Behavior – lost & found possessions. Night.

Borka: the adventures of a goose with no feathers ill. by author. Random House, 1963. ISBN 0-394-90727-2 Subj: Birds – geese. Character traits – being different. Character traits – meanness. Foreign lands – England.

Cannonball Simp ill. by author. Bobbs-Merrill, 1966. ISBN 1-56402-338-9 Subj: Animals – dogs. Circus. Clowns, jesters.

Cloudland ill. by author. Crown, 1996. ISBN 0-051-70929-5 Subj: Imagination. Weather – clouds.

Cluck baa ill. by author. Viking, 1985. ISBN 0-670-22580-0 Subj: Animals. Noise, sounds.

Come away from the water, Shirley ill. by author. Crowell, 1977. ISBN 0-690-01361-2 Subj: Imagination. Pirates. Sea & seashore.

Count up: learning sets ill. by author. Viking, 1983. ISBN 0-670-24410-4 Subj: Counting, numbers. Format, unusual – board books.

Courtney ill. by author. Crown, 1994. ISBN 0-517-59884-1 Subj: Animals – dogs. Family life.

The cupboard ill. by author. Crowell, 1977. ISBN 0-224-01134-0 Subj: Food.

The dog ill. by author. Crowell, 1975. ISBN 0-690-01272-1 Subj: Animals – dogs. Format, unusual – board books.

First steps: letters, numbers, colors, opposites ill. by author. Candlewick, 1994. ISBN 1-56402-205-6 Subj: ABC books. Concepts. Concepts – color. Concepts – opposites. Counting, numbers.

Five down: numbers as signs ill. by author. Viking, 1983. ISBN 0-670-31698-9 Subj: Counting, numbers. Format, unusual – board books.

The friend ill. by author. Crowell, 1975. ISBN 0-690-01274-8 Subj: Friendship.

Grandpa ill. by author. Crown, 1985. ISBN 0-517-55643-X Subj: Death. Emotions – grief. Family life – grandfathers.

Harquin: the fox who went down to the valley ill. by author. Bobbs-Merrill, 1968. Subj: Animals – foxes. Character traits – cleverness. Sports – hunting.

Harvey Slumfenburger's Christmas present ill. by author. Candlewick, 1993. ISBN 1-56402-246-3 Subj: Character traits – helpfulness. Holidays – Christmas. Santa Claus.

Hey! Get off our train ill. by author. Crown, 1990. ISBN 0-517-57643-0 Subj: Animals. Dreams. Trains.

Humbert, Mister Firkin and the Lord Mayor of London ill. by author. Bobbs-Merrill, 1967. ISBN 0-517-57312-1 Subj: Animals – horses, ponies. Character traits – pride. Emotions – envy, jealousy.

Jangle twang ill. by author. Viking, 1985. ISBN 0-670-40570-5 Subj: Music. Musical instruments. Noise, sounds.

John Burningham's ABC ill. by author. Crown, 1993. ISBN 0-517-59504-4 Subj: ABC books.

John Burningham's colors ill. by author. Crown, 1986. ISBN 0-517-55961-7 Subj: Concepts – color.

John Burningham's 1 2 3 ill. by author. Crown, 1985. ISBN 0-517-55962-5 Subj: Counting, numbers.

John Patrick Norman McHennessy – the boy who was always late ill. by author. Crown, 1987. ISBN 0-517-56805-5 Subj: Behavior – promptness, tardiness. Imagination. School.

Just cats: learning groups ill. by author. Viking, 1983. ISBN 0-670-41094-2 Subj: Counting, numbers. Format, unusual – board books.

The magic bed ill. by author. Knopf, 2003. ISBN 0-375-92423-X Subj: Dreams. Furniture – beds. Magic.

Mr. Gumpy's motor car ill. by author. Macmillan, 1975, 1973. ISBN 0-02-716200-1 Subj: Automobiles. Weather – rain.

Mr. Gumpy's outing ill. by author. Macmillan, 1971. ISBN 0-03-086613-8 Subj: Animals. Behavior – fighting, arguing. Boats, ships. Cumulative tales.

Pigs plus: learning addition ill. by author. Viking, 1983. ISBN 0-670-55508-8 Subj: Counting, numbers. Format, unusual – board books.

The rabbit ill. by author. Crowell, 1975. ISBN 0-690-00907-0 Subj: Animals – rabbits. Pets.

Read one: numbers as words ill. by author. Viking, 1983. ISBN 0-670-58986-1 Subj: Counting, numbers. Format, unusual – board books.

Ride off: learning subtraction ill. by author. Viking, 1983. ISBN 0-670-59798-8 Subj: Counting, numbers. Format, unusual – board books.

The school ill. by author. Crowell, 1975. ISBN 0-690-00903-8 Subj: Activities. School.

Seasons ill. by author. Bobbs-Merrill, 1970. Subj: Seasons.

The shopping basket ill. by author. Candlewick, 1996. ISBN 1-56402-688-4 Subj: Animals. Character traits – cleverness. Humorous stories. Shopping.

Skip trip ill. by author. Viking, 1984. ISBN 0-670-65016-1 Subj: Activities. Noise, sounds.

Slam bang ill. by author. Viking, 1985. ISBN 0-670-65076-5 Subj: Automobiles. Noise, sounds.

Sniff shout ill. by author. Viking, 1984. ISBN 0-670-65349-7 Subj: Activities. Noise, sounds.

The snow ill. by author. Crowell, 1975. ISBN 0-690-00905-4 Subj: Family life. Weather – snow.

Time to get out of the bath, Shirley ill. by author. Crowell, 1978. ISBN 0-690-01379-5 Subj: Activities – bathing. Imagination. Royalty.

Trubloff: the mouse who wanted to play the balalaika ill. by author. Random House, 1965. ISBN 0-394-97316-X Subj: Animals – mice. Music. Musical instruments – balalaikas. Weather – snow.

Whaddayamean ill. by author. Crown, 1999. ISBN 0-517-80067-5 Subj: Earth. Ecology. Religion.

Where's Julius? ill. by author. Crown, 1986. ISBN 0-517-56511-0 Subj: Activities – playing. Family life. Food. Imagination.

Wobble pop ill. by author. Viking, 1984. Subj: Activities. Noise, sounds.

Would you rather . . . ill. by author. Crowell, 1978. ISBN 0-690-03918-2 Subj: Imagination.

Burns, Diane L. *Arbor Day* ill. by Kathy Rogers. Carolrhoda, 1988. ISBN 0-87614-346-X Subj: Trees.

Backyard beasties by Diane L. Burns & Peter & Connie Roop; ill. by Brian Gable. Carolrhoda, 2004. ISBN 1-57505-646-1 Subj: Animals. Riddles & jokes.

Elephants never forget! ill. by Joan Hanson. Lerner, 1987. ISBN 0-8225-0992-X Subj: Animals – elephants. Riddles & jokes.

Burns, Kate. *How does your garden grow?* by Kate Burns & Dawn Apperley. Levinson Books, 1997. ISBN 1-899607-51-X Subj: Format, unusual – toy & movable books. Gardens, gardening.

In the jungle (Apperley, Dawn)

In the snow ill. by author. Little, 1996. ISBN 0-316-11820-6 Subj: Animals. Behavior – hiding. Format, unusual – toy & movable books. Weather – snow.

Burns, Marilyn. *Amanda Bean's amazing dream* (Neuschwander, Cindy)

The 512 ants on Sullivan Street (Losi, Carol A.)

Burns, Maurice. *Go ducks, go!* ill. by Ron Brooks. Scholastic, 1988. ISBN 0-590-41167-5 Subj: Activities – playing. Country. Family life. Toys.

Burns, Theresa. *You're not my cat* ill. by author. HarperCollins, 1989. ISBN 0-397-32341-7 Subj: Animals – cats. Pets.

Burnside, Julian. *Matilda and the dragon* ill. by Bettina Guthridge. Allen & Unwin, 1993. ISBN 1-86373-127-X Subj: Dragons. Dreams. Night. Rhyming text.

Burnstein, Chaya M. *The Jewish kids' Hebrew-English wordbook* ill. by author. Jewish Publication Society, 1993. ISBN 0-8276-0381-9 Subj: ABC books. Dictionaries. Jewish culture. Language.

Burnstein, John. *Slim Goodbody: what can go wrong and how to be strong* ill. with photos & drawings. McGraw-Hill, 1978. ISBN 0-07-009242-7 Subj: Health & fitness. Rhyming text.

Burroway, Janet. *The truck on the track* ill. by John Vernon Lord. Bobbs-Merrill, 1970. ISBN 0-224-61807-5 Subj: Humorous stories. Rhyming text. Trucks.

Burrowes, Adjoa J. *Grandma's purple flowers* ill. by author. Lee & Low, 2000. ISBN 1-880000-73-3 Subj: Death. Emotions. Family life – grandmothers. Seasons.

Bursik, Rose. *Amelia's fantastic flight* ill. by author. Holt, 1992. ISBN 0-8050-1872-7 Subj: Activities – traveling. Airplanes, airports. Imagination.

Burstein, Chaya M. *Joseph and Anna's time capsule* ill. by Nancy Edwards Calder. S&S, 1984. ISBN 0-671-50712-5 Subj: Jewish culture.

Burstein, Fred. *Anna's rain* ill. by Harvey Stevenson. Orchard, 1990. ISBN 0-531-08427-2 Subj: Birds. Family life – fathers. Weather – storms.

The dancer ill. by Joan Auclair. Bradbury, 1993. ISBN 0-02-715625-7 Subj: Activities – dancing. Ballet. Cities, towns. Family life – fathers.

Rebecca's nap ill. by Helen Cogancherry. Bradbury, 1988. ISBN 0-02-715620-6 Subj: Family life. Sleep.

Whispering in the park ill. by Helen Cogancherry. Macmillan, 1992. ISBN 0-02-715621-4 Subj: Activities – playing. Fish. Parks.

Burt, Olive (Woolley). *Let's find out about bread* ill. by Mimi Korach. Watts, 1966. Subj: Food. Science.

Burton, Jane. *ABC* photos by author. Snapshot, 1994. ISBN 1-56458-533-6 Subj: ABC books. Format, unusual.

Animals at home ill. with photos. Newington, 1991. ISBN 1-878137-12-3 Subj: Animals. Nature.

Animals at night ill. with photos. Newington, 1991. ISBN 1-878137-13-1 Subj: Animals. Nature. Night.

Animals at rest ill. with photos. Newington, 1991. ISBN 1-878137-14-X Subj: Animals. Nature. Sleep.

Animals at work ill. with photos. Newington, 1991. ISBN 1-878137-15-8 Subj: Animals. Nature.

Animals eating ill. with photos. Newington, 1991. ISBN 1-878137-00-X Subj: Animals. Food. Nature.

Animals fighting ill. with photos. Newington, 1991. ISBN 1-878137-03-4 Subj: Animals. Behavior – fighting, arguing. Nature.

Animals keeping clean ill. with photos. Random House, 1989. ISBN 0-394-92261-1 Subj: Animals. Nature.

Animals keeping cool ill. with photos. Random House, 1989. ISBN 0-394-92260-3 Subj: Animals. Nature.

Animals keeping safe ill. with photos. Random House, 1989. ISBN 0-394-92263-8 Subj: Animals. Nature.

Animals keeping warm ill. with photos. Random House, 1989. ISBN 0-394-92262-X Subj: Animals. Nature.

Animals learning ill. with photos. Newington, 1991. ISBN 1-878137-01-8 Subj: Animals. Nature.

Animals talking ill. with photos. Newington, 1991. ISBN 1-878137-02-6 Subj: Animals. Nature. Noise, sounds.

Buffy the barn owl photos by Jane Burton & Kim Taylor. G. Stevens, 1989. ISBN 0-8368-0202-0 Subj: Birds – owls.

Caper the kid photos by author. G. Stevens, 1989. ISBN 0-8368-0203-9 Subj: Animals – babies. Animals – goats. Behavior – growing up.

Chester the chick photos by Jane Burton & Kim Taylor. G. Stevens, 1989. ISBN 0-8368-0204-7 Subj: Birds – chickens.

Chick [written & ed. by Angela Royston] ill. by Rowan Clifford; photos by author. Dutton, 1992. ISBN 0-525-67355-5 Subj: Birds – chickens. Birth. Format, unusual. Science.

Dabble the duckling photos by Jane Burton & Kim Taylor. G. Stevens, 1989. ISBN 0-8368-0205-5 Subj: Birds – ducks.

Dazy the guinea pig photos by Jane Burton & Kim Taylor. G. Stevens, 1989. ISBN 0-8368-0206-3 Subj: Animals – guinea pigs.

Dizzie the pony photos by author. G. Stevens, 1989. ISBN 0-8368-0207-1 Subj: Animals – babies. Animals – horses, ponies. Behavior – growing up.

Fancy the fox photos by author. Random House, 1988. ISBN 0-394-99963-0 Subj: Animals – babies. Animals – foxes. Behavior – growing up. Orphans.

Freckles the rabbit photos by Jane Burton & Kim Taylor. G. Stevens, 1989. ISBN 0-8368-0208-X Subj: Animals – rabbits.

Ginger the kitten photos by Jane Burton & Kim Taylor. G. Stevens, 1989. ISBN 0-8368-0213-6 Subj: Animals – babies. Animals – cats. Behavior – growing up. Pets.

Gipper the guinea pig photos by author. Random House, 1988. ISBN 0-394-99961-4 Subj: Animals – babies. Animals – guinea pigs. Behavior – growing up. Pets.

Hoppy the toad photos by author. Random House, 1989. ISBN 0-394-92270-0 Subj: Animals – babies. Behavior – growing up. Frogs & toads. Pets.

Jack the puppy photos by author. Random House, 1988. ISBN 0-394-99641-0 Subj: Animals – babies. Animals – dogs. Behavior – growing up. Pets.

Kitten [written & ed. by Angela Royston] photos by author. Dutton, 1991. ISBN 0-525-67343-1 Subj: Animals – cats. Birth. Format, unusual – board books.

Pacer, the pony photos by author. Random House, 1989. ISBN 0-394-92271-9 Subj: Animals – babies. Animals – horses, ponies. Behavior – growing up.

Puppy [written & ed. by Angela Royston] photos by author. Dutton, 1991. ISBN 0-525-67342-3 Subj: Animals – dogs. Birth. Format, unusual – board books.

Rabbit (Watson, Carol)

Snowy, the barn owl photos by author. Random House, 1989. ISBN 0-394-92268-9 Subj: Behavior – growing up. Birds – owls.

Surfer the seal photos by author. Random House, 1989. ISBN 0-394-92269-7 Subj: Animals – babies. Animals – seals. Behavior – growing up.

Taddy the toad photos by author. G. Stevens, 1989. ISBN 0-8368-0211-X Subj: Behavior – growing up. Frogs & toads.

Trill the fox cub photos by Jane Burton & Kim Taylor. G. Stevens, 1989. ISBN 0-8368-0212-8 Subj: Animals – foxes.

Burton, Katherine. *One gray mouse* by Katherine Burton & Kim Fernandes; ill. by Kim Fernandes. Kids Can, 1997. ISBN 1-55074-225-6 Subj: Animals. Animals – mice. Concepts – color. Counting, numbers. Rhyming text.

Burton, Marilee Robin. *Aaron awoke: an alphabet story* ill. by author. HarperCollins, 1982. ISBN 0-06-020892-9 Subj: ABC books. Farms.

The elephant's nest ill. by author. HarperCollins, 1979. ISBN 0-06-020906-2 Subj: Animals. Humorous stories. Wordless.

Oliver's birthday ill. by author. HarperCollins, 1986. ISBN 0-06-020880-5 Subj: Birds – ostriches. Birthdays.

Tail toes eyes ears nose ill. by author. HarperCollins, 1988. ISBN 0-06-020874-0 Subj: Animals. Problem solving. Riddles & jokes.

Burton, Martin Nelson. *The whale comedian* ill. by Charles Jordan. London Town, 1999. ISBN 0-9666490-8-7 Subj: Animals – whales. Careers – comedians.

Burton, Robert. *The egg* photos by Jan Burton & Kim Taylor. DK, 1994. ISBN 1-56458-460-7 Subj: Birds. Eggs.

Burton, Virginia Lee. *Choo choo: the story of a little engine who ran away* ill. by author. Houghton Mifflin, 1937. ISBN 0-395-17684-0 Subj: Behavior – running away. Trains.

Katy and the big snow ill. by author. Houghton Mifflin, 1943. ISBN 0-606-03726-8 Subj: Cities, towns. Cumulative tales. Machines. Seasons – winter. Weather – snow.

The little house ill. by author. Houghton Mifflin, 1939. ISBN 0-606-01531-0 Subj: Caldecott award books. Cities, towns. Country. Ecology. Homes, houses. Progress.

Maybelle, the cable car ill. by author. Houghton Mifflin, 1939. ISBN 0-395-24905-8 Subj: Cable cars, trolleys. Cities, towns. Transportation.

Mike Mulligan and his steam shovel ill. by author. Houghton Mifflin, 1967. ISBN 0-395-16961-5 Subj: Activities – working. Machines.

Bus-a-saurus bop ill. by David Clark. Bloomsbury, 2003. ISBN 1-58234-850-2 Subj: Buses. Rhyming text. School.

Busch, Phyllis S. *Cactus in the desert* ill. by Harriett Barton. Crowell, 1979. ISBN 0-690-01336-1 Subj: Desert. Plants. Science.

City lots: living things in vacant spots photos by Arline Strong. Collins-World, 1970. Subj: Cities, towns. Science.

Lions in the grass: the story of the dandelion, a green plant photos by Arline Strong. Collins-World, 1968. Subj: Plants. Science.

Once there was a tree: the story of the tree, a changing home for plants and animals photos by Arline Strong. Collins-World, 1968. Subj: Science. Trees.

Puddles and ponds: living things in watery places photos by Arline Strong. Collins-World, 1969. Subj: Ecology. Science.

Bush, Barbara. *In the heart of the village: the world of the Indian Banyan tree* photos by author. Sierra Club, 1996. ISBN 0-87156-575-7 Subj: Foreign lands – India. Nature. Trees.

Bush, John. *The cross-with-us rhinoceros* ill. by Paul Geraghty. Dutton, 1988. ISBN 0-525-44411-4 Subj: Animals – rhinoceros. Behavior – misunderstanding. Rhyming text.

The fish who could wish ill. by Korky Paul. Kane/Miller, 1991. ISBN 0-916291-35-9 Subj: Behavior – wishing. Fish. Rhyming text.

The giraffe who got in a knot by John Bush & Paul Geraghty; ill. by Paul Geraghty. Price Stern Sloan, 1987. ISBN 0-8431-1993-4 Subj: Animals. Animals – giraffes. Jungle. Rhyming text.

Bush, Timothy. *Benjamin McFadden and the robot babysitter* ill. by author. Crown, 1998. ISBN 0-517-79985-5 Subj: Activities – babysitting. Behavior – wishing. Robots.

Ferocious girls, steamroller boys, and other poems in between ill. by author. Orchard, 2000. ISBN 0-531-33250-0 Subj: Poetry.

James in the house of Aunt Prudence ill. by author. Crown, 1993. ISBN 0-517-58882-X Subj: Family life – aunts, uncles. Imagination.

Teddy bear, teddy bear ill. by author. Greenwillow, 2005. ISBN 0-06-057836-X Subj: Activities. Behavior – lost. Nursery rhymes. Toys – bears.

Three at sea ill. by author. Crown, 1994. ISBN 0-517-59300-9 Subj: Animals. Rivers. Sea & seashore. Sports.

Bushey, Jeanne. *The polar bear's gift* ill. by Vladyana Langer Krykorka. Red Deer Pr., 2000. ISBN 0-88995-220-5 Subj: Animals – polar bears. Character traits – helpfulness. Foreign lands – Canada. Friendship. Indians of North America – Inuit.

A sled dog for Moshi ill. by Germaine Arnaktauyok. Hyperion, 1994. ISBN 1-56282-632-8 Subj: Animals – dogs. Eskimos. Indians of North America – Inuit. Pets. Weather – snow. Weather – storms.

Bushey, Jerry. *The barge book* photos by author. Carolrhoda, 1984. ISBN 0-87614-205-6 Subj: Activities – trading. Boats, ships. Rivers.

Building a fire truck photos by author. Carolrhoda, 1981. ISBN 0-87614-170-X Subj: Careers – firefighters. Trucks.

Busy baby photos sel. by Debby Slier. Macmillan, 1988. ISBN 0-02-688753-3 Subj: Babies. Format, unusual – board books.

Butcher, Julia. *The sheep and the rowan tree* ill. by author. Holt, 1984. ISBN 0-03-071602-0 Subj: Behavior – wishing. Trees.

Butler, Andrea. *Mr. Sun and Mr. Sea* ill. by Lily Toy Hong. Scott Foresman, 1994. ISBN 0-673-36198-5 Subj: Folk & fairy tales. Foreign lands – Africa. Format, unusual – toy & movable books. Sea & seashore. Sun.

Butler, Daphne. *What happens when food cooks?* ill. with photos. Raintree, 1996. ISBN 0-8172-4155-8 Subj: Activities – baking, cooking. Food. Science.

Butler, Dorothy. *Another happy tale* ill. by John Hurford. Interlink, 1991. ISBN 0-940793-88-1 Subj: Character traits – luck. Family life. Farms.

A happy tale ill. by John Hurford. Interlink, 1990. ISBN 0-940793-61-X Subj: Activities – traveling. Airplanes, airports. Character traits – luck.

Higgledy, piggledy, hobbledy hoy ill. by Lyn Kriegerd. Greenwillow, 1991. ISBN 0-688-08661-6 Subj: Activities – picnicking. Animals. Parades. Rhyming text.

My brown bear Barney ill. by Elizabeth Fuller. Greenwillow, 1989. ISBN 0-688-08568-7 Subj: Activities – traveling. School. Toys – bears.

My brown bear Barney at the party ill. by Elizabeth Fuller. Greenwillow, 2000. ISBN 0-688-17549-X Subj: Birthdays. Parties. Toys – bears.

My brown bear Barney in trouble ill. by Elizabeth Fuller. Greenwillow, 1993. ISBN 0-688-10522-X Subj: Friendship. Toys – bears.

Butler, Geoff. *The hangashore* ill. by author. Tundra, 1998. ISBN 0-8877-6444-4 Subj: Behavior. Foreign lands – Canada. Handicaps – Down syndrome.

Ode to Newfoundland ill. by author; lyrics by Sir Cavendish Boyle. Tundra, 2003. ISBN 0-88776-631-5 Subj: Foreign lands – Canada. Music. Songs.

Butler, John. *Hush, little ones* ill. by author. Peachtree, 2003. ISBN 1-56145-269-6 Subj: Animals – babies. Night. Rhyming text. Sleep.

Pi-shu, the little panda ill. by author. Peachtree, 2001. ISBN 1-56145-242-4 Subj: Animals – babies. Animals – endangered animals. Animals – pandas.

While you were sleeping ill. by author. Peachtree, 1999. ISBN 1-56145-211-4 Subj: Animals. Bedtime. Counting, numbers. Night. Sleep.

Whose baby am I? ill. by authro. Viking, 2001. ISBN 0-670-89683-7 Subj: Animals – babies.

Butler, Kristi T. *Rip's secret spot* ill. by Joe Cepeda. Harcourt, 2000. ISBN 0-15-202640-1 Subj: Animals – dogs. Behavior – lost & found possessions.

Butler, M. Christina. *One snowy night* ill. by Tina Macnaughton. Good Bks., 2004. ISBN 1-56148-452-0 Subj: Animals. Character traits – generosity. Clothing – hats. Format, unusual – toy & movable books. Gifts. Holidays – Christmas.

Butler, Stephen. *Henny Penny* (Chicken Little)

The mouse and the apple ill. by author. Tambourine, 1994. ISBN 0-688-12811-4 Subj: Animals. Animals – mice. Character traits – patience.

Butterfield, Moira. *Brown, fierce, and furry* ill. by Wayne Ford. Raintree, 1997. ISBN 0-8172-4586-3 Subj: Animals – bears.

The Christmas story ill. with soft sculptures by Christine Potter; designs & concept by Rachael O'Neill. Gold Key Book, 1994. ISBN 0-307-16176-5 Subj: Holidays – Christmas. Religion – Nativity.

Fast, strong, and striped ill. by Wayne Ford. Raintree, 1997. ISBN 0-8172-4583-9 Subj: Animals – tigers.

Magic world of learning created by Jay Young; written by Moira Butterfield; ill. by Sian Tucker. Sterling, 2001. ISBN 0-8069-5587-2 Subj: Format, unusual – toy & movable books. Games.

Butterfield-Campbell, Jill. *The queen and Rosie Randall* (Oxenbury, Helen)

Butterworth, Nick. *Albert the bear* ill. by author. HarperCollins, 2002. ISBN 0-06-053688-8 Subj: Friendship. Toys. Toys – bears.

All together now! ill. by author. Little, 1995. ISBN 0-316-11932-6 Subj: Activities – picnicking. Format, unusual – toy & movable books. Rhyming text. Toys.

Amanda's butterfly ill. by author. Delacorte, 1991. ISBN 0-385-30434-X Subj: Character traits – kindness. Fairies. Insects – butterflies, caterpillars. Wordless.

Busy people ill. by author. Candlewick, 1992. ISBN 1-56402-056-8 Subj: Careers.

Field day by Nick Butterworth & Mick Inkpen; ill. by Mick Inkpen. Delacorte, 1991. ISBN 0-385-30328-9 Subj: School – field trips. Sports.

The house on the rock by Nick Butterworth & Mick Inkpen; ill. by Mick Inkpen. Multnomah, 1986. ISBN 0-8807-0146-3 Subj: Character traits – foolishness. Homes, houses. Religion.

Jasper's beanstalk by Nick Butterworth & Mick Inkpen; ill. by Mick Inkpen. Bradbury, 1993. ISBN 0-02-716231-1 Subj: Animals – cats. Behavior – dissatisfaction. Days of the week, months of the year. Plants.

Jingle bells ill. by author. Orchard, 1998. ISBN 0-531-30124-9 Subj: Animals – cats. Animals – mice. Holidays – Christmas. Problem solving.

Just like Jasper ill. by Mick Inkpen. Little, 1989. ISBN 0-316-11917-2 Subj: Animals – cats. Shopping. Toys.

The lost sheep ill. by Mick Inkpen. Multnomah, 1986. ISBN 0-88-070147-1 Subj: Animals – sheep. Behavior – lost. Religion.

Making faces ill. by author. Candlewick, 1993. ISBN 1-56402-212-9 Subj: Anatomy – faces. Character traits – appearance. Emotions. Format, unusual – toy & movable books.

My dad is awesome ill. by author. Candlewick, 1992. ISBN 1-56402-033-9 Subj: Behavior – boasting. Family life – fathers. Holidays – Father's Day.

My grandma is wonderful ill. by author. Candlewick, 1991. ISBN 1-56402-100-9 Subj: Family life – grandmothers.

My grandpa is amazing ill. by author. Candlewick, 1992. ISBN 1-56402-099-1 Subj: Behavior – boasting. Family life – grandfathers.

My mom is excellent ill. by author. Candlewick, 1994. ISBN 1-56402-289-7 Subj: Family life – mothers.

The Nativity play by Nick Butterworth & Mick Inkpen; ill. by authors. Little, 1985. ISBN 0-316-11903-2 Subj: Holidays – Christmas. Religion – Nativity. School. Theater.

Nice or nasty by Nick Butterworth & Mick Inkpen; ill. by authors. Little, 1987. ISBN 0-316-11915-6 Subj: Concepts – opposites.

Nick Butterworth's book of nursery rhymes ill. by sel. Viking, 1991. ISBN 0-670-83551-X Subj: Nursery rhymes.

One blowy night ill. by author. Little, 1992. ISBN 0-316-11919-9 Subj: Animals. Character traits – kindness to animals. Character traits – optimism. Weather – storms. Weather – wind.

One snowy night ill. by author. Little, 1990. ISBN 0-316-11918-0 Subj: Animals. Character traits – kindness to animals. Night. Weather – snow.

The precious pearl ill. by Mick Inkpen. Multnomah, 1986. ISBN 0-88-070145-5 Subj: Religion.

QPootle 5 ill. by author. Atheneum, 2001. ISBN 0-689-84243-0 Subj: Aliens. Space & space ships.

The rescue party ill. by author. Little, 1993. ISBN 0-316-11923-7 Subj: Activities – picnicking. Animals. Careers – park rangers. Format, unusual – toy & movable books.

The school trip by Nick Butterworth & Mick Inkpen; ill. by Mick Inkpen. Delacorte, 1990. ISBN 0-385-30243-6 Subj: Museums. School – field trips.

The secret path ill. by author. Little, 1994. ISBN 0-316-11914-8 Subj: Animals. Careers – park rangers. Gardens, gardening. Problem solving.

The two sons ill. by Mick Inkpen. Multnomah, 1986. ISBN 0-88-070148-X Subj: Character traits – helpfulness. Family life – brothers. Family life – fathers. Religion.

When it's time for bed ill. by author. Little, 1994. ISBN 0-316-11902-4 Subj: Bedtime. Format, unusual – toy & movable books. Toys.

When there's work to do ill. by author. Little, 1994. ISBN 0-316-11906-7 Subj: Activities – working. Format, unusual – board books. Toys.

When we go shopping ill. by author. Little, 1994. ISBN 0-316-11900-8 Subj: Format, unusual – board books. Shopping. Toys.

When we play together ill. by author. Little, 1994. ISBN 0-316-11901-6 Subj: Activities – playing. Format, unusual – board books. Toys.

Butterworth, Oliver. *A visit to the big house* ill. by Susan Avishai. Houghton Mifflin, 1993. ISBN 0-395-52805-4 Subj: Family life – fathers. Prisons.

Buxbaum, Susan Kovacs. *Splash! all about baths* by Susan Kovacs Buxbaum & Rita Golden Gelman; ill. by Maryann Cocca-Leffler. Little, 1987. ISBN 0-316-30726-2 Subj: Activities – bathing.

Buzzeo, Toni. *The sea chest* ill. by Mary GrandPré. Dial, 2002. ISBN 0-8037-2703-8 Subj: Islands. Lighthouses. Sea & seashore.

Byars, Betsy Cromer. *Ant plays bear* ill. by Marc Simont. Viking, 1997. ISBN 0-670-86776-4 Subj: Family life – brothers. Friendship.

Go and hush the baby ill. by Emily Arnold McCully. Puffin, 1982, 1971. ISBN 0-14-050396-X Subj: Babies. Family life – new sibling. Games.

The groober ill. by author. Harper, 1967. Subj: Animals. Behavior – dissatisfaction.

The lace snail ill. by author. Viking, 1975. ISBN 0-670-41614-2 Subj: Animals. Animals – snails. Gifts.

My brother, Ant ill. by Marc Simont. Viking, 1996. ISBN 0-670-86664-4 Subj: Family life – brothers. Insects – ants.

Byers, Rinda M. *Mycca's baby* ill. by David Tamura. Orchard, 1990. ISBN 0-531-08428-0 Subj: Babies. Family life.

Byfield, Barbara Ninde. *The haunted churchbell* ill. by author. Doubleday, 1971. Subj: Character traits – cleverness. Emotions – fear. Humorous stories.

Bynum, Janie. *Altoona Baboona* ill. by author. Harcourt, 1999. ISBN 0-15-201860-3 Subj: Activities – ballooning. Animals. Islands. Rhyming text.

Altoona up north ill. by author. Harcourt, 2001. ISBN 0-15-202313-5 Subj: Animals – baboons. Concepts – cold & heat. Family life – aunts, uncles. Weather – snow.

Otis ill. by author. Harcourt, 2000. ISBN 0-15-202153-1 Subj: Animals – pigs. Character traits – cleanliness. Character traits – individuality. Friendship. Frogs & toads.

Byrd, Robert. *Marcella was bored* ill. by author. Dutton, 1985. ISBN 0-525-44156-5 Subj: Animals – cats. Behavior – running away. Family life.

Saint Francis and the Christmas donkey ill. by author. Dutton, 2000. ISBN 0-525-46480-8 Subj: Animals – donkeys. Holidays – Christmas. Religion – Nativity.

Byrne, David. *Stay up late* ill. by Maira Kalman. Viking, 1987. ISBN 0-670-81895-X Subj: Babies. Family life. Sibling rivalry. Songs.

Cabban, Vanessa. *Bertie and Small and the brave sea journey* ill. by author. Candlewick, 1999. ISBN 0-7636-0878-5 Subj: Activities – traveling. Imagination. Toys.

Bertie and Small and the fast bike ride ill. by author. Candlewick, 1999. ISBN 0-7636-0879-3 Subj: Activities – playing. Sports – bicycling. Toys.

Cabrera, Jane. *Bear's good night* ill. by author. Candlewick, 2002. ISBN 0-7636-1796-2 Subj: Animals – bears. Bedtime. Format, unusual – toy & movable books.

Monkey's play time ill. by author. Candlewick, 2002. ISBN 0-7636-1795-4 Subj: Activities – playing. Animals. Animals – monkeys. Format, unusual – board books.

Old Mother Hubbard (Martin, Sarah Catherine)

Panda Big and Panda Small ill. by author. DK, 1998. ISBN 0-7894-3485-7 Subj: Animals – pandas. Format, unusual – board books. Friendship. Rhyming text.

Rory and the lion ill. by author. DK, 1999. ISBN 0-7894-4843-2 Subj: Animals – lions. Noise, sounds.

Cader, Lisa Lebowitz. *When I wear my crown* ill. by Laura Huliska-Beith. Chronicle, 2002. ISBN 0-8118-3484-0 Subj: Activities – playing. Imagination. Toys.

When I wear my tiara ill. by Laura Huliska-Beith. Chronicle, 2002. ISBN 0-8118-3485-9 Subj: Activities – playing. Imagination. Toys.

Cadnum, Michael. *The lost and found house* ill. by Steve Johnson & Lou Fancher. Viking, 1997. ISBN 0-670-84884-0 Subj: Emotions. Family life. Moving.

Caen, Herb. *The cable car and the dragon* ill. by Barbara Ninde Byfield. Chronicle, 1972. ISBN 0-87701-390-X Subj: Cable cars, trolleys.

Caffey, Donna. *Yikes-lice!* ill. by Patrick Girouard. A. Whitman, 1998. ISBN 0-8075-9374-5 Subj: Family life. Insects – lice. Rhyming text.

Cahill, Chris. *Bear magic* ill. by Mitchell Rose & Ruth Young. Schneider Educational, 1990. ISBN 1-877779-00-8 Subj: Animals – bears. Format, unusual – board books. Poetry. Puppets.

Bunny magic ill. by Mitchell Rose & Ruth Young. Schneider Educational, 1990. ISBN 1-877779-02-4 Subj: Animals – rabbits. Format, unusual – board books. Poetry. Puppets.

Spider magic ill. by Mitchell Rose & Ruth Young. Schneider Educational, 1990. ISBN 1-877779-03-2 Subj: Format, unusual. Format, unusual – board books. Puppets. Spiders.

Turtle magic ill. by Mitchell Rose & Ruth Young. Schneider Educational, 1990. ISBN 1-877779-01-6 Subj: Format, unusual. Format, unusual – board books. Puppets. Reptiles – turtles, tortoises.

Cain, Janan. *The way I feel* ill. by author. Parenting Pr., 2000. ISBN 1-8847-3471-5 Subj: Emotions. Rhyming text.

Cain, Sheridan. *Look out for the big bad fish!* ill. by Tanya Linch. Little Tiger, 1998. ISBN 1-888444-27-4 Subj: Activities – jumping. Fish. Frogs & toads.

Why so sad, Brown Rabbit? ill. by Jo Kelly. Dutton, 1998. ISBN 0-525-45963-4 Subj: Animals – rabbits. Behavior – needing someone. Birds – ducks. Family life – mothers.

Caines, Jeannette. *Abby* ill. by Steven Kellogg. HarperCollins, 1973. ISBN 0-06-020922-4 Subj: Adoption. Ethnic groups in the U.S. – African Americans. Family life. Sibling rivalry.

Chilly stomach ill. by Pat Cummings. HarperCollins, 1986. ISBN 0-06-020977-1 Subj: Child abuse. Emotions – fear. Family life.

Daddy ill. by Ronald Himler. HarperCollins, 1977. ISBN 0-06-020924-0 Subj: Divorce. Ethnic groups in the U.S. – African Americans. Family life – fathers.

I need a lunch box ill. by Pat Cummings. HarperCollins, 1988. ISBN 0-06-020985-2 Subj: Emotions – envy, jealousy. Family life.

Just us women ill. by Pat Cummings. HarperCollins, 1982. ISBN 0-06-020942-9 Subj: Activities – traveling. Automobiles. Ethnic groups in the U.S. – African Americans.

Window wishing ill. by Kevin Brooks. HarperCollins, 1980. ISBN 0-06-020934-8 Subj: Family life – grandmothers.

Cairo, Jasmine. *Our brother has Down's syndrome: an introduction for children* (Cairo, Shelley)

Cairo, Shelley. *Our brother has Down's syndrome: an introduction for children* by Shelley, Jasmine & Tara Cairo; photos by Irene McNeil; designed by Helmut W. Weyerstrahs. Firefly, 1985. ISBN 0-920303-30-7 Subj: Family life. Handicaps.

Cairo, Tara. *Our brother has Down's syndrome: an introduction for children* (Cairo, Shelley)

Cakes and custard: children's rhymes comp. by Brian W. Alderson; ill. by Helen Oxenbury. Morrow, 1975, 1974. ISBN 0-688-32050-3 Subj: Nursery rhymes.

Calcagnino, Steve. *The body book* (Rotner, Shelley)

Caldecott, Randolph. *Panjandrum picture book* ill. by author. Warne, 1885. Subj: Nursery rhymes.

The Queen of Hearts ill. by author. Warne, 1881. Subj: Nursery rhymes.

The Randolph Caldecott treasury sel. & ed. by Elizabeth T. Billington; ill. by author. Warne, 1978. ISBN 0-7232-6139-3 Subj: Folk & fairy tales.

Randolph Caldecott's favorite nursery rhymes ill. by author. Castle Books, 1980. Subj: Nursery rhymes.

Randolph Caldecott's John Gilpin and other stories ill. by author. Warne, 1977. The diverting history of John Gilpin.—The house that Jack built.—The frog he would a-wooing go.—The milkmaid. Subj: Nursery rhymes.

Randolph Caldecott's picture book, no. 1 ill. by author. Warne, 1879. Subj: Nursery rhymes.

Randolph Caldecott's picture book, no. 2 ill. by author. Warne, 1879. Subj: Nursery rhymes.

Sing a song of sixpence (Mother Goose)

The three jovial huntsmen ill. by author. Warne, 1880. Subj: Nursery rhymes.

Calder, Lyn. *Walt Disney's Alice's tea party* ill. by Jesse Clay. Walt Disney, 1992. ISBN 1-56282-199-7 Subj: Activities – making things. Parties.

Calder, S. J. *If you were a bird* ill. by Cornelius Van Wright. Silver Pr., 1989. ISBN 0-671-68595-3 Subj: Birds – robins.

If you were a cat ill. by Cornelius Van Wright. Silver Pr., 1989. ISBN 0-671-68598-8 Subj: Animals – cats. Pets.

If you were a fish ill. by Cornelius Van Wright. Silver Pr., 1989. ISBN 0-671-68596-1 Subj: Aquariums. Fish.

If you were an ant ill. by Cornelius Van Wright. Silver Pr., 1989. ISBN 0-671-68597-X Subj: Insects – ants.

Calders, Pere. *Brush* trans. from Spanish by Marguerite Feitlowitz; ill. by Carme Solé Vendrell. Kane/Miller, 1986. ISBN 0-916291-05-7 Subj: Crime. Family life. Imagination. Pets.

Caldwell, Mary. *Morning, rabbit, morning* ill. by Ann Schweninger. HarperCollins, 1982. ISBN 0-06-020940-2 Subj: Animals – rabbits. Morning.

Calhoun, Mary. *Audubon cat* ill. by Susan Bonners. Morrow, 1981. ISBN 0-688-32253-0 Subj: Animals – cats. Food. Problem solving.

Big Sixteen ill. by Trina Schart Hyman. Morrow, 1983. ISBN 0-688-02351-7 Subj: Ethnic groups in the U.S. – African Americans. Folk & fairy tales.

Blue-ribbon Henry ill. by Erick Ingraham. Morrow, 1998. ISBN 0-688-14675-9 Subj: Animals – cats. Character traits – helpfulness. Fairs, festivals.

Cross-country cat ill. by Erick Ingraham. Morrow, 1979. ISBN 0-688-32186-0 Subj: Animals – cats. Character traits – cleverness. Sports – skiing.

Euphonia and the flood ill. by Simms Taback. Parents' Magazine Pr., 1976. ISBN 0-819-30837-4 Subj: Animals. Boats, ships. Character traits – helpfulness. Weather – rain.

Flood! ill. by Erick Ingraham. Morrow, 1997. ISBN 0-688-13920-5 Subj: Family life. U.S. history. Weather – floods.

The goblin under the stairs ill. by Janet McCaffery. Morrow, 1968. Subj: Behavior – misbehavior. Folk & fairy tales. Mythical creatures – goblins.

Henry the Christmas cat ill. by Erick Ingraham. HarperCollins, 2002. ISBN 0-688-16561-3 Subj: Animals – cats. Animals – sheep. Holidays – Christmas. Theater.

Henry the sailor cat ill. by Erick Ingraham. Morrow, 1994. ISBN 0-688-10841-5 Subj: Animals – cats. Boats, ships. Sailors. Sea & seashore.

High-wire Henry ill. by Erick Ingraham. Morrow, 1991. ISBN 0-688-08984-4 Subj: Animals – cats. Animals – dogs. Emotions – envy, jealousy. Pets.

Hot-air Henry ill. by Erick Ingraham. Morrow, 1981. ISBN 0-688-00502-0 Subj: Activities – ballooning. Animals – cats.

Houn' dog ill. by Roger Antoine Duvoisin. Morrow, 1959. Subj: Animals – dogs. Animals – foxes. Sports – hunting.

The hungry leprechaun ill. by Roger Antoine Duvoisin. Harber, 1962. Subj: Food. Foreign lands – Ireland. Holidays – St. Patrick's Day. Mythical creatures – leprechauns.

Jack and the whoopee wind ill. by Dick Gackenbach. Morrow, 1987. ISBN 0-688-06138-9 Subj: Character traits – cleverness. Machines. Tall tales. Weather – wind.

Jack the wise and the Cornish cuckoos ill. by Tasha Tudor. Morrow, 1978. ISBN 0-688-32132-1 Subj: Character traits – helpfulness. Character traits – wisdom. Folk & fairy tales.

Mrs. Dog's own house ill. by Janet McCaffery. Morrow, 1972. Subj: Animals – dogs. Homes, houses.

The nine lives of Homer C. Cat ill. by Roger Antoine Duvoisin. Morrow, 1961. Subj: Animals – cats. Behavior – imitation. Humorous stories.

Old man Whickutt's donkey ill. by Tomie de Paola. Parents' Magazine Pr., 1975. ISBN 0-819-30788-2 Subj: Animals – donkeys. Character traits – perseverance. Folk & fairy tales. Humorous stories.

The pixy and the lazy housewife ill. by Janet McCaffery. Morrow, 1969. Subj: Behavior – trickery. Folk & fairy tales. Foreign lands – England. Mythical creatures – pixies.

The runaway brownie ill. by Janet McCaffery. Morrow, 1967. Subj: Character traits – pride. Folk & fairy tales. Foreign lands – Scotland. Mythical creatures – elves.

A shepherd's gift ill. by Raúl Colón. HarperCollins, 2001. ISBN 0-688-15177-9 Subj: Careers – shepherds. Gifts. Holidays – Christmas. Orphans. Religion – Nativity.

The thieving dwarfs ill. by Janet McCaffery. Morrow, 1967. Subj: Character traits – kindness. Dwarfs, midgets. Folk & fairy tales. Foreign lands – Germany.

Tonio's cat ill. by Ed Martinez. Morrow, 1996. ISBN 0-688-13315-0 Subj: Animals – cats. Ethnic groups in the U.S. – Mexican Americans. Friendship. Pets.

The traveling ball of string ill. by Janet McCaffery. Morrow, 1969. Subj: Behavior – saving things. Humorous stories. String.

While I sleep ill. by Ed Young. Morrow, 1992. ISBN 0-688-08201-7 Subj: Bedtime. Sleep.

The witch of Hissing Hill ill. by Janet McCaffery. Morrow, 1964. ISBN 0-688-31762-6 Subj: Animals – cats. Holidays – Halloween. Witches.

The witch who lost her shadow ill. by Trinka Hakes Noble. HarperCollins, 1979. ISBN 0-06-020947-X Subj: Animals – cats. Character traits – loyalty. Emotions. Friendship. Witches.

The witch's pig: a Cornish folktale ill. by Tasha Tudor. Morrow, 1977. ISBN 0-688-32092-9 Subj: Animals – pigs. Folk & fairy tales. Foreign lands – England. Witches.

Wobble the witch cat ill. by Roger Antoine Duvoisin. Morrow, 1958. ISBN 0-688-31621-2 Subj: Animals – cats. Holidays – Halloween. Witches.

Callan, Elizabeth Koda. *Good luck pony* ill. by author. Workman, 1990. ISBN 0-89480-859-1 Subj: Animals – horses, ponies. Character traits – confidence. Character traits – luck. Emotions – fear.

Callan, Lyndall. *Dirt on their skirts* (Rappaport, Doreen)

Callen, Larry. *Dashiel and the night* ill. by Leslie Holt Morrill. Dutton, 1981. ISBN 0-525-28540-7 Subj: Bedtime. Dreams. Imagination. Insects – fireflies. Night.

Calloway, Northern J. *Northern J. Calloway presents Super-vroomer!* Written by Carol Hall; ill. by Sammis McLean; conceived by Northern J. Calloway. Doubleday, 1978. Written by Carol Hall; conceived by Northern J. Calloway. ISBN 0-385-14178-5 Subj: Ethnic groups in the U.S. – African Americans. Sports – racing.

Calmenson, Stephanie. *ABC: featuring Jim Henson's Sesame Street Muppets* ill. by John Nez. Western, in conjunction with Children's Television Workshop, 1986. At head of title: CTW Sesame Street. "Featuring Jim Henson's Sesame Street Muppets." ISBN 0-307-07016-6 Subj: ABC books. Puppets.

The after school book ill. by Beth Weiner Lipson. Grosset, 1984. ISBN 0-448-11227-2 Subj: Animals. School.

All aboard the goodnight train ill. by Normand Chartier. Grosset, 1984. ISBN 0-448-11226-4 Subj: Animals. Bedtime. Lullabies.

The birthday hat ill. by Susan Gantner. Grosset, 1983. ISBN 0-448-21705-8 Subj: Animals – hippopotamuses. Birthdays. Shopping.

The children's Æsop (Æsop)

Come to my party ill. by Beth Weiner Lipson. Parents' Magazine Pr., 1991. ISBN 0-8193-1195-2 Subj: Animals – raccoons. Birthdays. Counting, numbers.

Dinner at the Panda Palace ill. by Nadine Bernard Westcott. HarperCollins, 1991. ISBN 0-06-021011-7 Subj: Animals. Animals – pandas. Counting, numbers. Food. Rhyming text.

Engine, engine, number nine ill. by Paul Meisel. Hyperion, 1996. ISBN 0-7868-2127-2 Subj: Rhyming text. Trains.

Fido ill. by Maxie Chambliss. Scholastic, 1987. ISBN 0-590-40410-5 Subj: Animals – dogs. Careers.

The frog principal ill. by Denise Brunkus. Scholastic, 2001. ISBN 0-590-37070-0 Subj: Careers – school principals. Frogs & toads. Magic. School.

Get well, gators! by Stephanie Calmenson & Joanna Cole; ill. by Lynn Munsinger. Morrow, 1998. Subj: Fairs, festivals. Illness. Reptiles – alligators, crocodiles.

Good for you! toddler rhymes for toddler times ill. by Melissa Sweet. HarperCollins, 2001. ISBN 0-688-17737-9 Subj: Babies. Poetry.

Hotter than a hot dog! ill. by Elivia Savadier. Little, 1994. ISBN 0-316-12479-6 Subj: Cities, towns. Family life – grandmothers. Sea & seashore. Seasons – summer. Weather.

It begins with an A ill. by Marisabina Russo. Hyperion, 1993. ISBN 1-56282-123-7 Subj: ABC books. Rhyming text. Riddles & jokes.

The kindergarten book ill. by Beth Weiner Lipson. Grosset, 1983. ISBN 0-448-14499-9 Subj: Activities. Animals. Emotions – fear. School. School – first day.

Kinderkittens, show-and-tell ill. by Diane de Groat. Scholastic, 1994. ISBN 0-590-46349-7 Subj: Anatomy – hands. Animals – cats. School. Shadows.

Kinderkittens, who took the cookie from the cookie jar? ill. by Diane de Groat. Scholastic, 1995. ISBN 0-590-46350-0 Subj: Animals – babies. Animals – cats. Food. School.

The little witch sisters ill. by R. W. Alley. Parents' Magazine Pr., 1993. ISBN 0-8368-0970-X Subj: Character traits – helpfulness. Family life – sisters. Magic. Witches.

Meet Penny ill. by Carolyn Bracken. Marvel, 1986. ISBN 0-8713-5152-8 Subj: Activities. Format, unusual – board books.

Meet Timmy ill. by Carolyn Bracken. Marvel, 1986. ISBN 0-8713-5151-X Subj: Activities. Format, unusual – board books.

My book of the seasons ill. by Eugenie. Golden Bks., 1999. ISBN 0-307-68122-X Subj: Seasons. Senses.

My dog's the best ill. by Marcy Dunn Ramsey. Scholastic, 1997. ISBN 0-59033-072-1 Subj: Animals – dogs. Pets.

Never take a pig to lunch and other funny poems about animals ill. by Hilary Knight. Doubleday, 1982. ISBN 0-385-15593-X Subj: Animals – pigs. Poetry.

No stage fright for me! ill. by Rose Mary Berlin. Western, 1988. ISBN 0-307-10284-X Subj: Emotions – fear. Theater.

One little monkey ill. by Ellen Appleby. Parents' Magazine Pr., 1994. ISBN 0-8368-0988-2 Subj: Animals. Animals – monkeys. Counting, numbers. Jungle. Rhyming text.

One red shoe (the other's blue!) ill. by Lisa McCue Karsten. Golden Bks., 1987. ISBN 0-307-60908-1 Subj: Animals – rabbits. Clothing – shoes.

Pat-a-cake and other play rhymes (Cole, Joanna)

Perfect puppy ill. by Thomas F. Yezerski. Clarion, 2001. ISBN 0-618-01139-0 Subj: Animals – babies. Animals – dogs. Emotions – love.

Pin the tail on the donkey and other party games (Cole, Joanna)

The principal's new clothes ill. by Denise Brunkus. Scholastic, 1989. ISBN 0-590-41822-X Subj: Careers – school principals. Careers – tailors. Character traits – pride. Character traits – vanity. Clothing. Folk & fairy tales. School.

Roller skates! ill. by True Kelley. Scholastic, 1992. ISBN 0-590-45716-0 Subj: Rhyming text. Sports – roller skating.

Rosie, a visiting dog's story ill. by Justin Sutcliffe. Clarion, 1994. ISBN 0-395-65477-7 Subj: Animals – dogs. Illness. Old age.

Shaggy, waggy dogs (and others) photos by Justin Sutcliffe. Clarion, 1998. ISBN 0-395-77605-8 Subj: Animals – dogs. Pets. Rhyming text.

The teeny tiny teacher ill. by Denis Roche. Scholastic, 1998. ISBN 0-590-37123-1 Subj: Careers – teachers. Folk & fairy tales. Ghosts. School.

Ten furry monsters ill. by Maxie Chambliss. G. Stevens, 1994. ISBN 0-8368-0989-0 Subj: Counting, numbers. Monsters. Rhyming text.

Wanted: warm, furry friend ill. by Amy Schwartz. Macmillan, 1990. ISBN 0-02-716390-3 Subj: Animals – rabbits. Friendship. Pen pals.

Welcome, baby! ill. by Melissa Sweet. HarperCollins, 2002. ISBN 0-06-000492-4 Subj: Babies. Poetry.

What am I? ill. by Karen Gundersheimer. HarperCollins, 1989. ISBN 0-06-020998-4 Subj: Riddles & jokes.

Where is Grandma Potamus? ill. by Susan Gantner. Grosset, 1983. ISBN 0-448-21706-6 Subj: Animals – hippopotamuses. Behavior – lost.

Where will the animals stay? ill. by Ellen Appleby. Parents' Magazine Pr., 1983. ISBN 0-819-31119-7 Subj: Animals. Homes, houses. Rhyming text. Zoos.

Why did the chicken cross the road? and other riddles, old and new (Cole, Joanna)

Zip, whiz, zoom! ill. by Dorothy Stott. Little, 1992. ISBN 0-316-12478-8 Subj: Activities – traveling. Birthdays. Family life – grandmothers. Transportation.

Calvert, Elinor H. *see* Lasell, Fen

Cameron, Alice. *The cat sat on the mat* ill. by Carol Jones. Houghton Mifflin, 1994. ISBN 0-395-68392-0 Subj: Animals – cats. Animals – mice. Format, unusual.

Cameron, Ann. *Harry (the monster)* ill. by Jeanette Winter. Pantheon, 1980. ISBN 0-394-94162-4 Subj: Bedtime. Character traits – bravery. Emotions – fear. Monsters.

Cameron, C. C. *One for me, one for you* ill. by Grace Lin. Roaring Brook, 2003. ISBN 0-7613-2807-6 Subj: Behavior – sharing. Counting, numbers. Rhyming text.

Cameron, Eileen. *Canyon* photos by Michael Collier. Mikaya, 2002. ISBN 1-931414-03-3 Subj: Canyons. Earth. Poetry. Rivers.

Cameron, Elizabeth Jane. *see* Duncan, Jane

Cameron, John. *If mice could fly* ill. by author. Atheneum, 1979. ISBN 0-689-30731-4 Subj: Animals – cats. Animals – mice. Character traits – cleverness. Rhyming text.

Cameron, Polly. *The cat who thought he was a tiger* ill. by author. Coward, 1956. Subj: Animals – cats. Circus.

A child's book of nonsense ill. by author. Coward, 1960. Subj: Humorous stories. Poetry.

"I can't," said the ant: a second book of nonsense ill. by author. Coward, 1961. Subj: Family life. Insects – ants. Participation. Poetry.

Camp, Lindsay. *The biggest bed in the world* ill. by Jonathan Langley. HarperCollins, 2000. ISBN 0-06-028687-3 Subj: Bedtime. Family life. Furniture – beds. Sleep.

Dinosaurs at the supermarket ill. by Clare Skilbeck. Viking, 1993. ISBN 0-670-84802-6 Subj: Dinosaurs. Imagination. Prehistory.

Keeping up with Cheetah ill. by Jill Newton. Lothrop, 1993. ISBN 0-688-12655-3 Subj: Animals – cheetahs. Animals – hippopotamuses. Friendship.

Why? ill. by Tony Ross. Putnam, 1998. ISBN 0-399-23396-2 Subj: Aliens. Character traits – questioning. Family life – fathers.

Campbell, Alison. *Are you asleep, rabbit?* by Alison Campbell & Julia Barton; ill. by Gill Scriven. Lothrop, 1990. ISBN 0-688-09491-0 Subj: Animals – rabbits. Bedtime.

Campbell, Ann-Jeanette. *Dora's box* ill. by Fabian Negrin. Knopf, 1998. ISBN 0-679-97642-6 Subj: Emotions. Folk & fairy tales. Mythical creatures. Witches.

Let's find out about boats ill. by author. Watts, 1967. Subj: Boats, ships.

Let's find out about color ill. by author. Watts, 1966. Subj: Concepts – color.

Queenie Farmer had fifteen daughters ill. by Holly Meade. Silver Whistle, 2002. ISBN 0-15-201933-2 Subj: Family life – daughters. Family life – mothers.

Campbell, M. Rudolph. *The talking crocodile* ill. by Judy Piussi-Campbell. Atheneum, 1968. Adapt. from Krokodil by Fyodor Dostoyevsky. Subj: Foreign lands – Russia. Reptiles – alligators, crocodiles.

Campbell, Rod. *Buster gets dressed* ill. by author. Barron's, 1988. ISBN 0-8120-5922-0 Subj: Clothing. Format, unusual – toy & movable books.

Buster keeps warm ill. by author. Barron's, 1988. ISBN 0-8120-5923-9 Subj: Clothing. Format, unusual – toy & movable books. Seasons – winter.

Buster's afternoon ill. by author. HarperCollins, 1984. ISBN 0-911745-74-2 Subj: Character traits – curiosity. Flowers. Format, unusual – toy & movable books. Nature.

Buster's morning ill. by author. HarperCollins, 1984. ISBN 0-911745-73-4 Subj: Character traits – curiosity. Format, unusual – toy & movable books. Homes, houses. Toys.

Dear zoo ill. by author. Four Winds, 1984. ISBN 0-02-716440-3 Subj: Animals. Format, unusual – toy & movable books. Zoos.

Funwheels with moving parts! ill. by author. S&S, 1985. ISBN 0-671-54707-0 Subj: Automobiles. Format, unusual – toy & movable books.

Henry's busy day ill. by author. Viking, 1984. ISBN 0-670-80024-4 Subj: Animals – dogs. Behavior – misbehavior. Format, unusual.

It's mine ill. by author. Barron's, 1988. ISBN 0-8120-5921-2 Subj: Anatomy. Animals. Format, unusual – toy & movable books.

Look inside! All kinds of places ill. by author. HarperCollins, 1983. ISBN 0-911745-72-6 Subj: Format, unusual – board books. Wordless.

Look inside! Land, sea, air ill. by author. HarperCollins, 1983. ISBN 0-911745-71-8 Subj: Format, unusual – board books. Transportation. Wordless.

Misty's mischief ill. by author. Viking, 1985. ISBN 0-670-80149-6 Subj: Animals – cats. Behavior – misbehavior. Format, unusual.

My pop-up garden friends ill. by author. Aladdin, 1993. ISBN 0-689-71643-5 Subj: Animals. Format, unusual – toy & movable books. Gardens, gardening.

Oh dear! ill. by author. Four Winds, 1986. ISBN 0-590-07944-1 Subj: Eggs. Farms. Format, unusual – toy & movable books.

Playwheels with moving parts! ill. by author. S&S, 1985. ISBN 0-671-54706-2 Subj: Format, unusual – toy & movable books. Trucks.

Campbell, Wayne. *What a catastrophe!* ill. by Eileen Christelow. Bradbury, 1987. ISBN 0-02-716420-9 Subj: Family life. Frogs & toads.

Campoy, F. Isabel. *Pio peep!* (Pio peep!)

Rosa Raposa ill. by José Aruego & Ariane Dewey. Harcourt, 2002. ISBN 0-15-202161-2 Subj: Animals – foxes. Animals – jaguars. Behavior – trickery. Foreign lands – South America. Jungle.

Can you see the red balloon? ill. by Debbie Harter. Orchard, 1998. ISBN 0-531-30077-3 Subj: Concepts – color.

Canetti, Yanitzia. *Hello ocean = Hola mar* (Ryan, Pam Muñoz)

Canfield, Jack. *Chicken soup for little souls: Della Splatnuk birthday girl* (McCourt, Lisa)

Chicken soup for little souls: The best night out with Dad (McCourt, Lisa)

Chicken soup for little souls: The Goodness Gorillas (McCourt, Lisa)

Chicken soup for little souls: The never-forgotten doll (McCourt, Lisa)

Chicken soup for little souls: The new kid and the cookie thief (McCourt, Lisa)

Canfield, Jane White. *The frog prince: a true story* ill. by Winn Smith. HarperCollins, 1970. Subj: Frogs & toads. Royalty – princes.

Swan cove ill. by Jo Polseno. HarperCollins, 1978. ISBN 0-06-020949-6 Subj: Birds – swans.

Canning, Kate. *A painted tale* ill. by author. Barron's, 1979. ISBN 0-8120-5358-3 Subj: Animals – tigers. Art. Behavior – imitation. Zoos.

Cannon, Annie. *The bat in the boot* ill. by author. Orchard, 1996. ISBN 0-531-08795-6 Subj: Animals – bats. Character traits – kindness to animals.

Cannon, Janell. *Crickwing* ill. by author. Harcourt, 2000. ISBN 0-15-201790-9 Subj: Character traits – helpfulness. Insects – ants. Insects – cockroaches.

Little Yau ill. by author. Harcourt, 2002. ISBN 0-15-201791-7 Subj: Disguises. Illness. Plants.

Stellaluna ill. by author. Harcourt, 1993. ISBN 0-15-280217-7 Subj: Animals – bats. Birds. Character traits – being different. Family life – mothers. Friendship.

Stellaluna: a pop-up book and mobile ill. by author. Harcourt, 1997. ISBN 0-15-201530-2 Subj: Animals – bats. Birds. Character traits – being different. Family life – mothers. Format, unusual – toy & movable books. Friendship.

Trupp: a fuzzhead tale ill. by author. Harcourt, 1995. ISBN 0-15-200130-1 Subj: Cities, towns. Homeless. Mythical creatures.

Verdi ill. by author. Harcourt, 1997. ISBN 0-15-201028-9 Subj: Behavior – growing up. Jungle. Reptiles – snakes.

Cantieni, Benita. *Little Elephant and Big Mouse* trans. by Oliver Gadsby; ill. by Fred Gächter. Alphabet Pr., 1981. Orig. title: Der Kleine Elefant und die Grosse Maus. ISBN 0-907234-09-7 Subj: Animals – elephants. Animals – mice. Concepts – size.

Canyon, Christopher. *John Denver's Ancient rhymes: a dolphin lullaby* ill. by adapt. Dawn, 2004. ISBN 1-58469-064-X Subj: Animals – dolphins. Lullabies. Music.

John Denver's Sunshine on my shoulders ill. by adapt. Dawn, 2003. ISBN 0-613-68518-0 Subj: Music. Songs. Sun. Weather.

Caple, Kathy. *The biggest nose* ill. by author. Houghton Mifflin, 1985. ISBN 0-395-36894-4 Subj: Anatomy – noses. Animals – elephants. Character traits – being different. School.

The coolest place in town ill. by author. Houghton Mifflin, 1990. ISBN 0-395-51523-8 Subj: Animals – hippopotamuses. Family life – brothers & sisters.

Fox and bear ill. by author. Houghton Mifflin, 1992. ISBN 0-395-55634-1 Subj: Animals – bears. Animals – foxes. Friendship.

Harry's smile ill. by author. Houghton Mifflin, 1987. ISBN 0-395-43417-3 Subj: Friendship. Pen pals. Self-concept.

Hillary to the rescue ill. by author. Carolrhoda, 2000. ISBN 1-57505-420-5 Subj: Animals – cats. Seasons – winter.

Inspector Aardvark and the perfect cake ill. by author. Windmill, 1980. ISBN 0-671-96108-X Subj: Animals – aardvarks. Careers – bakers.

The purse ill. by author. Houghton Mifflin, 1986. ISBN 0-395-41852-6 Subj: Activities – working. Clothing – handbags, purses. Family life. Money.

Starring Hillary ill. by author. Carolrhoda, 1999. ISBN 1-57505-261-X Subj: Animals – cats. Self-concept. Theater.

The wimp ill. by author. Houghton Mifflin, 1994. ISBN 0-395-63115-7 Subj: Animals – pigs. Behavior – bullying. Family life – brothers & sisters.

Worm gets a job ill. by author. Candlewick, 2004. ISBN 0-7636-1694-X Subj: Activities – painting. Animals. Animals – worms. Contests. Money.

Cappetta, Cynthia. *Chairs, chairs, chairs!* ill. by Rick Stromoski. Childrens Pr., 1999. ISBN 0-516-21542-6 Subj: Furniture – chairs. Rhyming text.

Caprio, Annie De. *see* DeCaprio, Annie

Captain Kangaroo. *see* Keeshan, Robert

Capucilli, Alyssa Satin. *Bathtime for Biscuit* ill. by Pat Schories. HarperCollins, 1998. ISBN 0-06-027938-9 Subj: Activities – bathing. Animals – dogs. Pets.

Bear hugs ill. by Jim Ishi. Golden Bks., 2000. ISBN 0-307-26113-1 Subj: Animals – bears. Emotions – love. Family life. Rhyming text.

Biscuit ill. by Pat Schories. HarperCollins, 1996. ISBN 0-06-026198-6 Subj: Animals – dogs. Bedtime.

Biscuit finds a friend ill. by Pat Schories. HarperCollins, 1997. ISBN 0-06-027413-1 Subj: Animals – dogs. Birds – ducks. Friendship.

Biscuit gives a gift ill. by Pat Schories. HarperFestival, 2004. ISBN 0-06-009467-2 Subj: Animals – dogs. Format, unusual – board books. Holidays.

Biscuit goes to school ill. by Pat Schories. HarperCollins, 2002. ISBN 0-060-28683-0 Subj: Animals – dogs. School.

Biscuit loves school ill. by Pat Schories. HarperFestival, 2003. ISBN 0-06-009454-0 Subj: Animals – dogs. Format, unusual – toy & movable books. School.

Biscuit visits the pumpkin patch ill. by Pat Schories. HarperFestival, 2004. ISBN 0-06-009466-4 Subj: Activities – bathing. Animals. Animals – moose. Toys.

Biscuit wants to play ill. by Pat Schories. HarperCollins, 2001. ISBN 0-06-028070-0 Subj: Activities – playing. Animals – babies. Animals – cats. Animals – dogs.

Biscuit wins a prize ill. by Pat Schories. HarperCollins, 2004. ISBN 0-06-009457-5 Subj: Animals – dogs. Pets.

Biscuit's big friend ill. by Pat Schories. HarperCollins, 2003. ISBN 0-06-029168-0 Subj: Animals – dogs. Friendship.

Biscuit's new trick ill. by Pat Schories. HarperCollins, 2000. ISBN 0-06-028068-9 Subj: Animals – babies. Animals – dogs.

Biscuit's picnic ill. by Pat Schories. HarperCollins, 1998. ISBN 0-06-028072-7 Subj: Activities – picnicking. Animals – dogs.

Biscuit's Valentine's Day ill. by Pat Schories. HarperFestival, 2001. ISBN 0-694-01222-X Subj: Animals – babies. Animals – dogs. Format, unusual – toy & movable books. Holidays – Valentine's Day.

Good morning, pond ill. by Cynthia Jabar. Hyperion, 1994. ISBN 1-56282-675-1 Subj: Cumulative tales. Lakes, ponds. Morning. Nature.

Happy birthday, Biscuit! ill. by Pat Schories. HarperCollins, 1999. ISBN 0-06-028361-0 Subj: Animals – cats. Animals – dogs. Birthdays. Pets.

Happy Hanukkah, Biscuit ill. by Pat Schories. HarperFestival, 2002. ISBN 0-694-01525-3 Subj: Animals – dogs. Format, unusual – toy & movable books. Gifts. Holidays – Hanukkah. Jewish culture.

Hello, Biscuit! ill. by Pat Schories. HarperCollins, 1998. ISBN 0-06-028071-9 Subj: Animals – dogs. Names.

Inside a barn in the country: a rebus read-along story ill. by Tedd Arnold. Scholastic, 1993. ISBN 0-590-46999-1 Subj: Animals. Cumulative tales. Noise, sounds. Rebuses. Rhyming text.

Inside a house that is haunted: a rebus read-along story ill. by Tedd Arnold. Scholastic, 1998. ISBN 0-590-99716-5 Subj: Animals. Cumulative tales. Ghosts. Rebuses. Rhyming text.

Inside a zoo in the city ill. by Tedd Arnold. Scholastic, 2000. ISBN 0-590-99715-7 Subj: Animals. Cumulative tales. Rebuses. Rhyming text. Zoos.

Merry Christmas, from Biscuit ill. by Pat Schories. HarperFestival, 2001. ISBN 0-694-01522-9 Subj: Animals – dogs. Holidays – Christmas.

Mrs. McTats and her houseful of cats ill. by Joan Rankini. McElderry, 2001. ISBN 0-689-83185-4 Subj: ABC books. Animals – cats. Counting, numbers. Rhyming text.

Only my dad and me ill. by Tiphanie Beeke. HarperFestival, 2003. ISBN 0-694-52584-7 Subj: Animals – rabbits. Family life – fathers. Format, unusual – toy & movable books.

Only my mom and me ill. by Tiphanie Beeke. HarperFestival, 2003. ISBN 0-694-52585-5 Subj: Animals – cats. Family life – mothers. Format, unusual – toy & movable books.

Peekaboo bunny ill. by Mary Melcher. Scholastic, 1994. ISBN 0-590-46754-9 Subj: Animals – rabbits. Format, unusual – toy & movable books. Games. Rhyming text.

What kind of kiss? ill. by Hiroe Nakata. HarperFestival, 2002. ISBN 0-694-01573-3 Subj: Animals – bears. Family life – mothers. Kissing. Rhyming text.

Capucilli, Karen. *The jelly bean fun book* ill. with photos. Little Simon, 2001. ISBN 0-689-84071-3 Subj: Food. Puzzles.

Caputo, Robert. *More than just pets: why people study animals* photos by author. Coward, 1980. ISBN 0-698-20460-3 Subj: Anatomy. Ecology.

Carabine, Sue. *A firefighter's night before Christmas* ill. by Shauna Mooney Kawasaki. Gibbs Smith, 2003. ISBN 1-58685-269-8 Subj: Careers – firefighters. Holidays – Christmas. Poetry.

Cardillo-Young, Donatella. *The yellow coat* ill. by Geoffrey Brittingham. Scythe, 1996. ISBN 1-55523-729-0 Subj: Holidays – Christmas. Religion – Nativity.

Cardoza, Lois S. *see* Duncan, Lois

Carey, Bonnie. *Grasshopper to the rescue: a Georgian story* (Grasshopper to the rescue)

Carey, Helen H. *Adopted* (Greenberg, Judith E.)

Carey, Mary. *The owl who loved sunshine* ill. by Joe Giordano. Golden Pr., 1977. ISBN 0-307-13433-4 Subj: Birds – owls. Character traits – individuality. Character traits – kindness to animals.

Carey, Valerie Scho. *The devil and mother Crump* ill. by Arnold Lobel. HarperCollins, 1987. ISBN 0-06-020983-6 Subj: Behavior – trickery. Character traits – meanness. Devil. Folk & fairy tales.

Harriet and William and the terrible creature ill. by Lynne Cherry. Dutton, 1985. ISBN 0-525-44154-9 Subj: Animals – squirrels. Character traits – helpfulness. Monsters. Space & space ships.

Maggie Mab and the bogey beast ill. by Johanna Westerman. Arcade, 1992. ISBN 1-55970-155-2 Subj: Character traits – optimism. Folk & fairy tales. Poverty.

Quail song: a Pueblo Indian tale ill. by Ivan Barnett. Putnam, 1990. ISBN 0-399-21936-6 Subj: Animals – coyotes. Behavior – trickery. Birds – quail. Folk & fairy tales. Indians of North America – Pueblo.

Tsugele's broom ill. by Dirk Zimmer. HarperCollins, 1993. ISBN 0-06-020987-9 Subj: Character traits – individuality. Folk & fairy tales. Foreign lands – Poland.

Carigiet, Alois. *Anton the goatherd* ill. by author. Walck, 1966. Subj: Animals – goats. Behavior – lost.

The pear tree, the birch tree and the barberry bush ill. by author. Walck, 1967. Subj: Foreign lands – Switzerland. Trees.

Carle, Eric. *Do you want to be my friend?* ill. by author. Crowell, 1971. ISBN 0-690-24276-X Subj: Animals – mice. Friendship. Wordless.

Does a kangaroo have a mother, too? ill. by author. HarperCollins, 2000. ISBN 0-06-028767-5 Subj: Animals. Family life – mothers.

Dragons dragons and other creatures that never were ill. by author. Philomel, 1991. ISBN 0-399-22105-0 Subj: Dragons. Mythical creatures. Poetry.

Draw me a star ill. by author. Philomel, 1992. ISBN 0-399-21877-7 Subj: Activities – drawing. Circular tales.

Dream snow ill. by author. Philomel, 2000. ISBN 0-399-23579-5 Subj: Farms. Format, unusual – toy & movable books. Holidays – Christmas. Weather – snow.

From head to toe ill. by author. HarperCollins, 1997. ISBN 0-06-023516-0 Subj: Activities. Anatomy. Animals. Format, unusual – board books.

The grouchy ladybug ill. by author. Crowell, 1977. English title: The bad-tempered ladybird. ISBN 0-690-01392-2 Subj: Behavior. Insects – ladybugs. Time.

Have you seen my cat? ill. by author. Watts, 1973. ISBN 0-531-02552-7 Subj: Animals – cats. Behavior – lost.

Hello, red fox ill. by author. S&S, 1998. ISBN 0-689-81775-4 Subj: Animals. Art. Birthdays. Concepts – color. Frogs & toads. Holidays.

A house for Hermit Crab ill. by author. Little Simon, 2004. ISBN 0-689-87064-7 Subj: Crustaceans – crabs. Homes, houses. Sea & seashore.

I see a song ill. by author. Crowell, 1973. ISBN 0-690-43307-7 Subj: Music. Musical instruments – violins. Wordless.

Little cloud ill. by author. Philomel, 1996. ISBN 0-399-23034-3 Subj: Concepts – shape. Imagination. Sky. Weather – clouds. Weather – rain.

Little cloud [board book] ill. by author. 1st board book ed. Philomel, 1998. ISBN 0-399-23191-9 Subj: Concepts – shape. Format, unusual – board books. Imagination. Sky. Weather – clouds. Weather – rain.

The mixed-up chameleon ill. by author. Crowell, 1975; rev. ed. 1984. ISBN 0-690-00924-0 Subj: Character traits – being different. Concepts – color. Reptiles – lizards. Self-concept.

My apron: a story from my childhood ill. by author. Philomel, 1994. ISBN 0-399-22824-1 Subj: Careers – plasterers. Clothing – aprons. Family life – aunts, uncles.

My very first book of colors ill. by author. HarperCollins, 1985. ISBN 0-694-00011-6 Subj: Concepts – color. Format, unusual.

My very first book of food ill. by author. Crowell, 1986. ISBN 0-694-00130-9 Subj: Food. Format, unusual – toy & movable books.

My very first book of growth ill. by author. Crowell, 1986. ISBN 0-694-00094-9 Subj: Behavior – growing up. Format, unusual.

My very first book of heads and tails ill. by author. Crowell, 1986. ISBN 0-694-00128-7 Subj: Anatomy. Format, unusual – toy & movable books.

My very first book of homes ill. by author. Crowell, 1986. ISBN 0-694-00092-2 Subj: Format, unusual. Homes, houses.

My very first book of motion ill. by author. Crowell, 1986. ISBN 0-694-00093-0 Subj: Concepts. Format, unusual.

My very first book of numbers ill. by author. HarperCollins, 1985. ISBN 0-694-00012-4 Subj: Counting, numbers. Format, unusual.

My very first book of shapes ill. by author. HarperCollins, 1985. ISBN 0-694-00013-2 Subj: Concepts – shape. Format, unusual.

My very first book of sounds ill. by author. Crowell, 1986. ISBN 0-694-00131-7 Subj: Format, unusual – toy & movable books. Noise, sounds.

My very first book of tools ill. by author. Crowell, 1986. ISBN 0-694-00129-5 Subj: Format, unusual – toy & movable books. Tools.

My very first book of touch ill. by author. Crowell, 1986. ISBN 0-694-00095-7 Subj: Format, unusual. Senses – touch.

My very first book of words ill. by author. HarperCollins, 1985. ISBN 0-694-00014-0 Subj: Format, unusual. Language.

1, 2, 3 to the zoo: a counting book ill. by author. Philomel, 1996. ISBN 0-399-23013-0 Subj: Animals. Counting, numbers. Zoos.

Pancakes, pancakes ill. by author. Knopf, 1970. ISBN 0-394-90490-7 Subj: Cumulative tales. Food.

Papa, please get the moon for me ill. by author. Alphabet Pr., 1986. ISBN 0-88708-026-X Subj: Format, unusual – toy & movable books. Moon.

The rooster who set out to see the world ill. by author. S&S, 1991. ISBN 0-8870-8178-9 Subj: Activities – traveling. Birds – chickens. Counting, numbers.

Rooster's off to see the world ill. by author. Picture Book Studio, 1987. ISBN 0-88708-042-1 Subj: Activities – traveling. Birds – chickens. Counting, numbers.

The secret birthday message ill. by author. Crowell, 1972. ISBN 0-690-72348-2 Subj: Birthdays. Format, unusual – toy & movable books.

"Slowly, slowly, slowly," said the sloth ill. by author. Philomel, 2002. ISBN 0-399-23954-5 Subj: Animals. Animals – sloths. Jungle.

10 little rubber ducks ill. by author. HarperCollins, 2005. ISBN 0-06-074076-0 Subj: Animals. Birds – ducks. Counting, numbers. Format, unusual. Sea & seashore. Toys.

The tiny seed ill. by author. Rev. ed. Picture Book Studio, 1987. ISBN 0-88708-015-4 Subj: Plants. Seasons. Seeds.

Today is Monday ill. by author. Philomel, 1993. ISBN 0-399-21966-8 Subj: Animals. Days of the week, months of the year. Food. Songs.

Twelve tales from Æsop ill. by adapt. Putnam, 1980. ISBN 0-399-61163-0 Subj: Folk & fairy tales.

The very busy spider ill. by author. Philomel, 1985. ISBN 0-399-21166-7 Subj: Animals. Spiders.

The very clumsy click beetle ill. by author. Philomel, 1999. ISBN 0-399-23201-X Subj: Character traits – perseverance. Insects – beetles.

The very hungry caterpillar ill. by author. Collins-World, 1979. ISBN 0-529-00776-2 Subj: Days of the week, months of the year. Format, unusual. Insects – butterflies, caterpillars. Metamorphosis.

The very lonely firefly ill. by author. Philomel, 1995. ISBN 0-399-22774-1 Subj: Format, unusual – toy & movable books. Insects – fireflies.

The very quiet cricket ill. by author. Putnam, 1990. ISBN 0-399-21885-8 Subj: Format, unusual. Insects – crickets. Noise, sounds.

Walter the baker ill. by author. S&S, 1995. ISBN 0-689-80078-9 Subj: Activities – working. Careers – bakers. Food. Royalty.

Watch out! A giant! ill. by author. Collins-World, 1978. ISBN 0-529-05456-6 Subj: Format, unusual – toy & movable books. Giants.

Carlesimo, Cheryl. *The Saturday kid* (Sorel, Edward)

Carleton, Barbee Oliver. *Benny and the bear* ill. by Dagmar Wilson. Follett, 1960. Subj: Animals – bears. Character traits – bravery.

Carling, Amelia Lau. *Mama and Papa have a store* ill. by author. Dial, 1998. ISBN 0-8037-2045-9 Subj: Careers – storekeepers. Family life. Foreign lands – Guatemala. Immigrants. Stores.

Mama and Papa have a store ill. by author. Groundwood, 2003. Tr. of: La tienda de Mamá y Papá. ISBN 0-88899-538-5 Subj: Family life. Foreign lands – Guatemala. Immigrants. Stores.

Carlisle, Clark. *see* Holding, James

Carlisle, Madelyn. *Bridges* (Carlisle, Norman)

Carlisle, Norman. *Bridges* by Norman & Madelyn Carlisle; ill. with photos. Childrens Pr., 1983. ISBN 0-516-01677-6 Subj: Bridges.

Carlson, Laurie M. *Boss of the plains: the hat that won the West* ill. by Holly Meade. DK, 1998. ISBN 0-7894-2479-7 Subj: Clothing – hats. U.S. history.

Carlson, Lori Marie. *Hurray for Three Kings' Day* ill. by Ed Martinez. Morrow, 1998. ISBN 0-688-16240-1 Subj: Ethnic groups in the U.S. – Hispanic Americans. Holidays. Religion.

Carlson, Maria. *Peter and the wolf* (Prokofiev, Sergei Sergeievitch)

Carlson, Melody. *The day the circus came to town* ill. by Ned Butterfield. Crossway, 2000. ISBN 1-58134-158-X Subj: Circus.

The Easterville miracle ill. by Susan Reagan. Broadman & Holman, 2004. ISBN 0-8054-2680-9 Subj: Holidays – Easter. Religion. Rhyming text.

Farmer Brown's field trip ill. by Steve Björkman. Crossway, 2000. ISBN 1-58134-142-3 Subj: Careers – farmers. Glasses. Rhyming text.

Forever friends (Tada, Joni Eareckson)

King of the stable ill. by Chris Ellison. Crossway, 1998. ISBN 1-58134-032-X Subj: Holidays – Christmas. Religion – Nativity.

What Nick and Holly found in grandpa's attic ill. by Jose Miralles. Gold'n'Honey, 1998. ISBN 1-57673-372-6 Subj: Family life – grandfathers. Holidays – Christmas. Religion – Nativity.

When the creepy things come out ill. by Susan Reagan. Broadman & Holman, 2003. ISBN 0-8054-2687-6 Subj: Emotions – fear. Holidays – Halloween. Night. Rhyming text.

Carlson, Nancy L. *ABC, I like me!* ill. by author. Viking, 1997. ISBN 0-670-87458-2 Subj: ABC books. Language. Self-concept.

Arnie and the new kid ill. by author. Viking, 1990. ISBN 0-670-82499-2 Subj: Accidents. Animals. Friendship. Handicaps – physical handicaps. School.

Arnie and the skateboard gang ill. by author. Viking, 1995. ISBN 0-670-85722-X Subj: Animals. Animals – cats. Character traits – bravery. Character traits – foolishness. Sports – skateboarding.

Arnie and the stolen markers ill. by author. Puffin, 1989. ISBN 0-14-050707-8 Subj: Animals. Behavior – stealing. Crime.

Arnie goes to camp ill. by author. Viking, 1988. ISBN 0-670-81549-7 Subj: Activities. Animals. Animals – cats.

Bunnies and their hobbies ill. by author. Carolrhoda, 1984. ISBN 0-87614-257-9 Subj: Activities. Animals – rabbits.

Bunnies and their sports ill. by author. Viking, 1987. ISBN 0-670-81109-2 Subj: Animals – rabbits. Sports.

Harriet and George's Christmas treat ill. by author. Carolrhoda, 2001. ISBN 1-57505-506-6 Subj: Animals – dogs. Animals – rabbits. Food. Holidays – Christmas.

Harriet and the garden ill. by author. Carolrhoda, 1982. ISBN 0-87614-184-X Subj: Animals – dogs. Problem solving.

Harriet and the roller coaster ill. by author. Carolrhoda, 1982. ISBN 0-87614-183-1 Subj: Animals – dogs. Character traits – bravery.

Harriet and Walt ill. by author. Carolrhoda, 1982. ISBN 0-87614-185-8 Subj: Animals – dogs. Sibling rivalry.

Harriet's Halloween candy ill. by author. Carolrhoda, 1982. ISBN 0-87614-182-3 Subj: Animals – dogs. Behavior – greed.

Harriet's recital ill. by author. Carolrhoda, 1982. ISBN 0-87614-181-5 Subj: Animals – dogs. Emotions – fear.

Hooray for Grandparent's Day! ill. by author. Viking, 2000. ISBN 0-670-88876-1 Subj: Family life – grandparents. Friendship. School.

How about a hug? ill. by author. Viking, 2001. ISBN 0-670-03506-8 Subj: Animals. Animals – pigs.

How to lose all your friends ill. by author. Viking, 1994. ISBN 0-670-84906-5 Subj: Behavior – misbehavior. Character traits – meanness. Character traits – selfishness. Etiquette. Friendship.

I like me ill. by author. Viking, 1988. ISBN 0-670-82062-8 Subj: Character traits – individuality. Self-concept.

It's going to be perfect ill. by author. Viking, 1998. ISBN 0-670-87802-2 Subj: Dreams. Family life.

Life is fun ill. by author. Viking, 1993. ISBN 0-670-84206-0 Subj: Behavior. Emotions – happiness.

Look out kindergarten, here I come! ill. by author. Viking, 1999. ISBN 0-670-88378-6 Subj: Activities. Animals – mice. School – first day.

Louanne Pig in making the team ill. by author. Carolrhoda, 1985. ISBN 0-87614-281-1 Subj: Animals. Animals – pigs. Cheerleading. Friendship. School. Sports – football.

Louanne Pig in the mysterious Valentine ill. by author. Carolrhoda, 1985. ISBN 0-87614-282-X Subj: Animals – pigs. Holidays – Valentine's Day.

Louanne Pig in the perfect family ill. by author. Carolrhoda, 1985. ISBN 0-87614-280-3 Subj: Animals – pigs. Family life. Sibling rivalry.

Loudmouth George and the big race ill. by author. Carolrhoda, 1983. ISBN 0-87614-215-3 Subj: Animals – rabbits. Behavior – boasting. Emotions – embarrassment.

Loudmouth George and the cornet ill. by author. Carolrhoda, 1983. ISBN 0-87614-214-5 Subj: Animals – rabbits. Behavior – boasting.

Loudmouth George and the fishing trip ill. by author. Carolrhoda, 1983. ISBN 0-87614-213-7 Subj: Animals – rabbits. Behavior – boasting.

Loudmouth George and the new neighbors ill. by author. Carolrhoda, 1983. ISBN 0-87614-216-1 Subj: Animals – rabbits. Behavior – boasting. Prejudice.

Loudmouth George and the sixth-grade bully ill. by author. Carolrhoda, 1983. ISBN 0-87614-217-X Subj: Animals – rabbits. Behavior – boasting. Behavior – bullying. Behavior – stealing.

My best friend moved away ill. by author. Viking, 2001. ISBN 0-670-89498-2 Subj: Friendship. Moving.

Poor Carl ill. by author. Viking, 1989. ISBN 0-670-81774-0 Subj: Animals – dogs. Babies. Emotions – envy, jealousy.

Sit still! ill. by author. Viking, 1996. ISBN 0-670-85721-1 Subj: Behavior – fidgeting. School.

Smile a lot! ill. by author. Carolrhoda, 2002. ISBN 0-87614-869-0 Subj: Character traits – optimism. Frogs & toads.

Snowden ill. by author. Viking, 1997. ISBN 0-670-88078-7 Subj: Friendship. Snowmen. Sports – ice skating.

Take time to relax ill. by author. Viking, 1991. ISBN 0-670-83287-1 Subj: Animals – beavers. Family life. Rhyming text. Weather – snow.

The talent show ill. by author. Carolrhoda, 1985. ISBN 0-87614-284-6 Subj: Animals. Theater.

There's a big, beautiful world out there! ill. by author. Viking, 2002. ISBN 0-670-03580-7 Subj: Emotions – fear.

A visit to grandma's ill. by author. Viking, 1991. ISBN 0-670-83288-X Subj: Animals – beavers. Family life – grandmothers. Holidays – Thanksgiving.

What if it never stops raining? ill. by author. Viking, 1992. ISBN 0-670-81775-9 Subj: Behavior – worrying. Weather – rain.

Witch lady ill. by author. Carolrhoda, 1985. ISBN 0-87614-283-8 Subj: Animals – pigs. Emotions – fear. Witches.

Carlson, Natalie Savage. *Marie Louise and Christophe at the carnival* ill. by José Aruego & Ariane Dewey. Scribners, 1981. ISBN 0-684-17014-0 Subj: Animals – mongooses. Reptiles – snakes.

Marie Louise's heyday ill. by José Aruego & Ariane Dewey. Scribners, 1975. ISBN 0-684-14360-7 Subj: Activities – babysitting. Animals – mongooses. Animals – possums.

Runaway Marie Louise ill. by José Aruego & Ariane Dewey. Scribners, 1977. ISBN 0-684-15045-X Subj: Animals – mongooses. Behavior – running away.

Spooky and the bad luck raven ill. by Andrew Glass. Lothrop, 1988. ISBN 0-688-07651-3 Subj: Animals – cats. Witches.

Spooky and the ghost cat ill. by Andrew Glass. Lothrop, 1985. ISBN 0-688-04317-8 Subj: Animals – cats. Holidays – Halloween. Magic.

Spooky and the witch's goat ill. by Andrew Glass. Lothrop, 1989. ISBN 0-688-08541-5 Subj: Animals – cats. Animals – goats. Magic. Witches.

Spooky and the wizard's bats ill. by Andrew Glass. Lothrop, 1986. ISBN 0-688-06281-4 Subj: Animals – bats. Animals – cats. Holidays – Halloween. Magic. Witches. Wizards.

Spooky night ill. by Andrew Glass. Lothrop, 1982. ISBN 0-688-00935-2 Subj: Animals – cats. Holidays – Halloween. Pets. Witches.

Surprise in the mountains ill. by Elise Primavera. HarperCollins, 1983. ISBN 0-06-021009-5 Subj: Animals. Holidays – Christmas. Seasons – winter.

Time for the white egret ill. by Charles Robinson. Scribners, 1978. ISBN 0-684-15990-2 Subj: Animals – bulls, cows. Birds – egrets. Farms.

Carlstrom, Nancy White. *Baby-O* ill. by Suçie Stevenson. Little, 1992. ISBN 0-316-12851-1 Subj: Cumulative tales. Family life. Foreign lands – Caribbean Islands. Stores.

Barney is best ill. by James Graham Hale. HarperCollins, 1994. ISBN 0-06-022876-8 Subj: Ethnic groups in the U.S. – Hispanic Americans. Family life. Hospitals. Illness – tonsillectomy. Toys.

Before you were born ill. by Linda Saport. Eerdmans, 2002. ISBN 0-8028-5185-1 Subj: Babies. Birth. Family life. Family life – parents. Poetry.

Better not get wet, Jesse Bear ill. by Bruce Degen. Macmillan, 1988. ISBN 0-02-717280-5 Subj: Animals – bears. Rhyming text.

Blow me a kiss, Miss Lilly ill. by Amy Schwartz. HarperCollins, 1990. ISBN 0-06-021013-3 Subj: Death. Emotions – grief. Friendship. Old age.

Does God know how to tie shoes? ill. by Lori McElrath-Eslick. Eerdmans, 1993. ISBN 0-8028-5074-X Subj: Religion.

Fish and flamingo ill. by Lisa Desimini. Little, 1993. ISBN 0-316-12859-7 Subj: Birds – flamingos. Fish. Friendship.

Glory ill. by Debra Reid Jenkins. Eerdmans, 2001. ISBN 0-8028-5143-6 Subj: Creation. Poetry.

Goodbye geese ill. by Ed Young. Putnam, 1991. ISBN 0-399-21832-7 Subj: Character traits – questioning. Family life – fathers. Rhyming text. Seasons – winter.

Graham cracker animals 1-2-3 ill. by John Sandford. Macmillan, 1989. ISBN 0-02-717270-8 Subj: Counting, numbers. Poetry.

Grandpappy ill. by Laurel Molk. Little, 1990. ISBN 0-316-12855-4 Subj: Family life – grandfathers.

Guess who's coming, Jesse Bear ill. by Bruce Degen. S&S, 1998. ISBN 0-689-80702-3 Subj: Animals – bears. Family life – cousins. Rhyming text.

Happy birthday, Jesse Bear! ill. by Bruce Degen. Macmillan, 1994. ISBN 0-02-717277-5 Subj: Animals – bears. Birthdays. Parties. Rhyming text.

Heather hiding ill. by Dennis Nolan. Macmillan, 1990. ISBN 0-02-717370-4 Subj: Activities – playing. Family life.

How do you say it today, Jesse Bear? ill. by Bruce Degen. Macmillan, 1992. ISBN 0-02-717276-7 Subj: Animals – bears. Days of the week, months of the year. Rhyming text.

How does the wind walk? ill. by Deborah Kogan Ray. Macmillan, 1993. ISBN 0-02-717275-9 Subj: Seasons. Weather – wind.

I am Christmas ill. by Lori McElrath-Eslick. Eerdmans, 1995. ISBN 0-8028-5075-8 Subj: Foreign lands – Israel. Holidays – Christmas. Religion – Nativity.

I'm not moving, mama! ill. by Thor Wickstrom. Macmillan, 1990. ISBN 0-02-717286-4 Subj: Animals – mice. Moving.

It's about time, Jesse Bear ill. by Bruce Degen. Macmillan, 1990. ISBN 0-02-717351-8 Subj: Animals – bears. Rhyming text.

Jesse Bear, what will you wear? ill. by Bruce Degen. Macmillan, 1986. ISBN 0-02-717350-X Subj: Animals – bears. Clothing. Family life.

Jesse Bear's tra-la tub ill. by Bruce Degen. Aladdin, 1994. ISBN 0-689-71715-6 Subj: Activities – bathing. Animals – bears. Format, unusual – board books. Rhyming text.

Jesse Bear's tum-tum tickle ill. by Bruce Degen. Aladdin, 1994. ISBN 0-689-71716-4 Subj: Animals – bears. Format, unusual – board books. Rhyming text.

Jesse Bear's wiggle-jiggle jump-up ill. by Bruce Degen. Aladdin, 1994. ISBN 0-689-71717-2 Subj: Animals – bears. Clothing. Format, unusual – board books. Rhyming text.

Jesse Bear's yum-yum crumble ill. by Bruce Degen. Aladdin, 1994. ISBN 0-689-71718-0 Subj: Animals – bears. Character traits – cleanliness. Format, unusual – board books. Rhyming text.

Kiss your sister, Rose Marie ill. by Thor Wickstrom. Macmillan, 1992. ISBN 0-02-717271-6 Subj: Animals – rabbits. Babies. Family life – new sibling. Family life – sisters. Rhyming text. Sibling rivalry.

Let's count it out, Jesse Bear ill. by Bruce Degen. S&S, 1996. ISBN 0-689-80478-4 Subj: Animals – bears. Counting, numbers. Rhyming text.

Midnight dance of the snowshoe hare: poems of Alaska ill. by Ken Kuroi. Philomel, 1998. ISBN 0-399-22746-6 Subj: Alaska. Animals. Animals – rabbits. Poetry. Seasons.

The moon came too ill. by Stella Ormai. Macmillan, 1987. ISBN 0-02-717380-1 Subj: Activities – vacationing. Behavior – collecting things. Family life – grandmothers. Rhyming text.

Moose in the garden ill. by Lisa Desimini. HarperCollins, 1990. ISBN 0-06-021014-1 Subj: Animals – moose. Food. Gardens, gardening.

No nap for Benjamin Badger ill. by Dennis Nolan. Macmillan, 1991. ISBN 0-02-717285-6 Subj: Animals – badgers. Rhyming text. Sleep.

Northern lullaby ill. by Leo & Diane Dillon. Putnam, 1992. ISBN 0-399-21806-8 Subj: Bedtime. Eskimos. Lullabies. Nature. Rhyming text.

Raven and river ill. by Jon Van Zyle. Little, 1997. ISBN 0-316-12894-5 Subj: Alaska. Animals. Birds – ravens. Rivers. Seasons – spring.

Rise and shine! ill. by Dominic Catalano. HarperCollins, 1993. ISBN 0-06-021452-X Subj: Animals. Farms. Rhyming text.

The snow speaks ill. by Jane Dyer. Little, 1992. ISBN 0-316-12861-9 Subj: Country. Seasons – winter. Weather – snow.

Swim the silver sea, Joshie Otter ill. by Ken Kuroi. Philomel, 1993. ISBN 0-399-21872-6 Subj: Animals – otters. Bedtime. Foreign lands – Arctic. Sea & seashore.

Ten Christmas sheep ill. by Cynthia Fisher. Eerdmans, 1996. ISBN 0-8028-5137-1 Subj: Animals – sheep. Format, unusual – toy & movable books. Holidays – Christmas. Rhyming text.

Thanksgiving Day at our house ill. by R. W. Alley. S&S, 1999. ISBN 0-689-80360-5 Subj: Family life. Holidays – Thanksgiving. Poetry.

The way to Wyatt's house ill. by Mary Morgan. Walker, 2000. ISBN 0-8027-8742-8 Subj: Animals. Farms. Friendship.

What a scare, Jesse Bear! ill. by Bruce Degen. S&S, 1999. ISBN 0-689-81961-7 Subj: Animals – bears. Holidays – Halloween. Rhyming text.

What does the rain play? ill. by Henri Sorensen. Macmillan, 1993. ISBN 0-02-717273-2 Subj: Animals – cats. Family life. Weather – rain.

What does the sky say? ill. by Tim Ladwig. Eerdmans, 2001. ISBN 0-8028-5208-4 Subj: Nature. Poetry. Religion. Sky. Weather.

What would you do if you lived at the zoo? ill. by Lizi Boyd. Little, 1994. ISBN 0-316-12867-8 Subj: Animals. Format, unusual – toy & movable books. Rhyming text. Zoos.

Where is Christmas, Jesse Bear? ill. by Bruce Degen. S&S, 2000. ISBN 0-689-81962-5 Subj: Animals – bears. Holidays – Christmas. Rhyming text.

Who gets the sun out of bed? ill. by David McPhail. Little, 1992. ISBN 0-316-12862-7 Subj: Animals – rabbits. Moon. Morning. Pets. Sun.

Who said boo? Halloween poems for the very young ill. by R. W. Alley. S&S, 1995. ISBN 0-689-80308-7 Subj: Holidays – Halloween. Poetry.

Wild wild sunflower child Anna ill. by Jerry Pinkney. Macmillan, 1987. ISBN 0-02-717360-7 Subj: Ethnic groups in the U.S. – African Americans. Rhyming text.

Wishing at dawn in summer ill. by Diane Worfolk Allison. Little, 1993. ISBN 0-316-12854-6 Subj: Behavior – wishing. Family life – brothers & sisters. Sports – fishing.

Carmack, Lisa Jobe. *Philippe in Monet's garden* ill. by Lisa Canney Chesaux. Museum of Fine Arts, 1998. ISBN 0-8784-6456-5 Subj: Art. Frogs & toads. Museums. Rhyming text.

Carman, William. *What's that noise?* ill. by author. Random House, 2002. ISBN 0-375-91052-2 Subj: Emotions – fear. Imagination. Night. Noise, sounds. Sleep.

Carmi, Giora. *see* Karmi, Giora

Carmichael, Clay. *Bear at the beach* ill. by author. North-South, 1996. ISBN 1-558585-70-2 Subj: Animals – bears. Behavior – seeking better things. Friendship. Sea & seashore – beaches. Seasons – summer.

Lonesome bear ill. by author. North-South, 2001. ISBN 1-55858-968-6 Subj: Behavior – lost & found possessions. Toys – bears.

Used-up Bear ill. by author. North-South, 1998. ISBN 1-55858-902-3 Subj: Emotions – love. Self-concept. Toys – bears.

Carney, Margaret (Margaret Rose). *At Grandpa's sugar bush* ill. by Janet Wilson. Kids Can, 1998. ISBN 1-55074-341-4 Subj: Careers – farmers. Food. Foreign lands – Canada. Trees.

The biggest fish in the lake ill. by Janet Wilson. Kids Can, 2001. ISBN 1-55074-720-7 Subj: Family life – grandfathers. Sports – fishing.

Where does a tiger-heron spend the night? ill. by Mélanie Watt. Kids Can, 2002. ISBN 1-55337-022-8 Subj: Birds. Format, unusual – toy & movable books. Rhyming text.

Carney, Mary Lou. *Absolutely angels: poems for children and other believers* (Absolutely angels)

Carpenter, Mary-Chapin. *Dreamland: a lullaby* ill. by Julia Noonan. HarperCollins, 1996. ISBN 0-06-025403-3 Subj: Bedtime. Dreams. Lullabies. Sleep.

Halley came to Jackson ill. by Dan Andreasen. HarperCollins, 1998. ISBN 0-06-025400-1 Subj: Astronomy. Songs. Stars.

Carpenter, Stephen. *The three billy goats Gruff* (Asbjørnsen, P. C. [Peter Christen])

Carr, Jan. *Big Truck and Little Truck* ill. by Ivan Bates. Scholastic, 2000. ISBN 0-439-07177-1 Subj: Farms. Trucks.

Dappled apples ill. by Dorothy Donohue. Holiday, 2001. ISBN 0-8234-1583-X Subj: Rhyming text. Seasons – fall.

Dark day, light night ill. by James Ransome. Hyperion, 1995. ISBN 0-7868-2014-4 Subj: Character traits – meanness. Emotions – anger. Family life – aunts, uncles.

Frozen noses ill. by Dorothy Donohue. Holiday, 1999. ISBN 0-8234-1462-0 Subj: Activities. Friendship. Seasons – winter. Sports.

The nature of the beast ill. by G. Brian Karas. Tambourine, 1996. ISBN 0-688-13597-8 Subj: Behavior – misbehavior. Monsters. Pets.

Splish, splash, spring ill. by Dorothy Donohue. Holiday, 2001. ISBN 0-8234-1578-3 Subj: Rhyming text. Seasons – spring.

Sweet hearts ill. by Dorothy Donohue. Holiday, 2003. ISBN 0-8234-1732-8 Subj: Animals – pandas. Holidays – Valentine's Day.

Carrick, Carol. *The accident* ill. by Donald Carrick. Seabury Pr., 1976. ISBN 0-8164-3172-8 Subj: Accidents. Animals – dogs. Death. Emotions – grief. Pets.

Banana beer ill. by Margot Apple. A. Whitman, 1995. ISBN 0-8075-0568-4 Subj: Animals – orangutans. Family life. Illness – alcoholism.

Beach bird by Carol & Donald Carrick; ill. by Donald Carrick. Dial, 1973. Subj: Birds – seagulls. Sea & seashore – beaches.

Ben and the porcupine ill. by Donald Carrick. Houghton Mifflin, 1981. ISBN 0-395-30171-8 Subj: Animals – dogs. Animals – porcupines. Problem solving.

Big old bones: a dinosaur tale ill. by Donald Carrick. Houghton Mifflin, 1992. ISBN 0-395-61582-8 Subj: Dinosaurs.

The blue lobster: a life cycle by Carol & Donald Carrick; ill. by Donald Carrick. Dial, 1975. ISBN 0-8037-4483-8 Subj: Crustaceans – lobsters. Science.

The brook by Carol & Donald Carrick; ill. by Donald Carrick. Macmillan, 1967. Subj: Rivers.

A clearing in the forest by Carol & Donald Carrick; ill. by Donald Carrick. Dial, 1970. Subj: Ecology. Forest, woods. Pets.

The climb ill. by Donald Carrick. Houghton Mifflin, 1980. ISBN 0-395-29431-2 Subj: Activities – babysitting. Sports.

The crocodiles still wait ill. by Donald Carrick. Houghton Mifflin, 1980. ISBN 0-395-29102-X Subj: Dinosaurs. Reptiles – alligators, crocodiles. Science.

Dark and full of secrets ill. by Donald Carrick. Houghton Mifflin, 1984. ISBN 0-89919-271-8 Subj: Emotions – fear. Sports – skin diving.

The foundling ill. by Donald Carrick. Seabury Pr., 1977. ISBN 0-816-43199-X Subj: Animals – dogs. Pets.

The highest balloon on the common by Carol & Donald Carrick; ill. by Donald Carrick. Greenwillow, 1977. ISBN 0-688-84100-7 Subj: Behavior – lost. Fairs, festivals. Toys – balloons.

In the moonlight, waiting ill. by Donald Carrick. Clarion, 1990. ISBN 0-89919-867-8 Subj: Animals. Birth. Farms.

Left behind ill. by Donald Carrick. Clarion, 1988. ISBN 0-89919-535-0 Subj: Behavior – lost. Cities, towns. School.

Lost in the storm ill. by Donald Carrick. Greenwillow, 1981. ISBN 0-8164-3124-8 Subj: Animals – dogs. Islands. Pets. Weather – storms.

Melanie ill. by Alisher Dianov. Clarion, 1996. ISBN 0-395-66555-8 Subj: Birds – seagulls. Family life – grandfathers. Folk & fairy tales. Handicaps – blindness. Mythical creatures – trolls.

Norman fools the tooth fairy ill. by Lisa McCue. Scholastic, 1992. ISBN 0-590-42240-5 Subj: Behavior – trickery. Fairies. Monsters. Reptiles – alligators, crocodiles. Teeth.

Octopus ill. by Donald Carrick. Seabury Pr., 1978. ISBN 0-395-28777-4 Subj: Octopuses. Science.

The old barn ill. by Donald Carrick. Bobbs-Merrill, 1966. Subj: Barns. Seasons.

Old Mother Witch ill. by Donald Carrick. Seabury Pr., 1975. ISBN 0-816-43148-5 Subj: Behavior – misunderstanding. Character traits – meanness. Holidays – Halloween. Illness.

Patrick's dinosaurs ill. by Donald Carrick. Houghton Mifflin, 1983. ISBN 0-89919-189-4 Subj: Animals. Dinosaurs. Imagination. Prehistory. Science. Zoos.

Patrick's dinosaurs on the Internet ill. by David Milgrim. Clarion, 1999. ISBN 0-395-50949-1 Subj: Computers. Dinosaurs. Imagination. Prehistory. School. Space & space ships.

Paul's Christmas birthday ill. by Donald Carrick. Greenwillow, 1978. ISBN 0-688-84159-7 Subj: Birthdays. Holidays – Christmas.

The polar bears are hungry ill. by Paul Carrick. Clarion, 2002. ISBN 0-618-15962-2 Subj: Animals – bears. Animals – polar bears. Seasons – winter.

A rabbit for Easter ill. by Donald Carrick. Greenwillow, 1979. ISBN 0-688-84195-3 Subj: Animals – rabbits. Behavior – carelessness. Holidays – Easter.

Sleep out ill. by Donald Carrick. Seabury Pr., 1973. ISBN 0-816-43094-2 Subj: Behavior – solitude. Camps, camping. Weather – rain.

Two coyotes ill. by Donald Carrick. Houghton Mifflin, 1982. ISBN 0-89919-078-2 Subj: Animals – coyotes. Science. Seasons – winter.

Two very little sisters ill. by Erika Weihs. Clarion, 1993. ISBN 0-395-60927-5 Subj: Character traits – being different. Circus. Little people.

Valentine ill. by Paddy Bouma. Clarion, 1995. ISBN 0-395-66554-X Subj: Animals – sheep. Family life – grandmothers. Family life – mothers. Holidays – Valentine's Day.

The washout ill. by Donald Carrick. Seabury Pr., 1978. ISBN 0-1864-3217-1 Subj: Activities – vacationing. Boats, ships. Weather – rain.

What happened to Patrick's dinosaurs? ill. by Donald Carrick. Houghton Mifflin, 1986. ISBN 0-89919-406-0 Subj: Dinosaurs. Imagination. Prehistory.

Carrick, Donald. *Beach bird* (Carrick, Carol)

The blue lobster: a life cycle (Carrick, Carol)

The brook (Carrick, Carol)

A clearing in the forest (Carrick, Carol)

The deer in the pasture ill. by author. Greenwillow, 1976. ISBN 0-688-84023-X Subj: Animals – bulls, cows. Animals – deer. Farms. Sports – hunting.

Harold and the giant knight ill. by author. Houghton Mifflin, 1982. ISBN 0-89919-060-X Subj: Farms. Humorous stories. Knights.

Harold and the great stag ill. by author. Clarion, 1988. ISBN 0-89919-514-8 Subj: Animals – deer. Foreign lands – England. Forest, woods. Humorous stories. Middle Ages. Sports – hunting.

The highest balloon on the common (Carrick, Carol)

Milk ill. by author. Greenwillow, 1985. ISBN 0-688-04823-4 Subj: Animals – bulls, cows. Farms. Food.

Morgan and the artist ill. by author. Clarion, 1985. ISBN 0-89919-300-5 Subj: Activities – painting. Art. Careers – artists.

Carrick, Malcolm. *The extraordinary hatmaker* ill. by author. Grosset, 1977. ISBN 0-448-13001-7 Subj: Clothing – hats.

I can squash elephants! a Masai tale about monsters ill. by author. Viking, 1978. ISBN 0-670-38983-8 Subj: Animals. Folk & fairy tales. Foreign lands – Africa. Insects – butterflies, caterpillars. Monsters.

Carrier, Lark. *A Christmas promise* ill. by author. Picture Book Studio, 1986. ISBN 0-88708-032-4 Subj: Animals. Friendship. Holidays – Christmas. Trees.

Scout and Cody ill. by author. Picture Book Studio, 1987. ISBN 0-88708-013-8 Subj: Activities – playing. Animals – dogs. Behavior – growing up. Imagination.

There was a hill . . . ill. by author. Picture Book Studio, 1985. ISBN 0-907234-70-4 Subj: Format, unusual. Imagination.

A tree's tale ill. by author. Dial, 1996. ISBN 0-8037-1203-0 Subj: Forest, woods. Trees. U.S. history.

Carrier, Roch. *The longest home run* ill. by Sheldon Cohen; trans. by Sheila Fischman. Tundra, 1993. ISBN 0-88776-312-X Subj: Foreign lands – Canada. Magic. Sports – baseball.

Carroll, Kathleen Sullivan. *One red rooster* ill. by Suzette Barbier. Houghton Mifflin, 1992. ISBN 0-395-60195-9 Subj: Animals. Concepts – color. Counting, numbers. Rhyming text.

Carroll, Latrobe. *Pet tale* (Carroll, Ruth)

Carroll, Lewis. *Jabberwocky* ill. by Graeme Base. Abrams, 1989. ISBN 0-8109-1150-7 Subj: Humorous stories. Mythical creatures. Poetry.

Jabberwocky ill. from Disney archives. Walt Disney, 1992. ISBN 1-56282-246-2 Subj: Humorous stories. Mythical creatures. Poetry.

Jabberwocky ill. by Jane Breskin Zalben. Warne, 1977. ISBN 0-723-26145-8 Subj: Humorous stories. Mythical creatures. Poetry.

The nursery "Alice" intro. by Martin Gardner; ill. by Sir John Tenniel. McGraw-Hill, 1966. A facsimile of the 2d ed. (1890) of Carroll's adapt. of Alice's Adventures in Wonderland. Subj: Dreams. Imagination.

The walrus and the carpenter ill. by Julian Doyle. Merrimack, 1986. ISBN 0-88162-218-4 Subj: Humorous stories. Poetry.

The walrus and the carpenter ill. by Jane Breskin Zalben. Holt, 1986. ISBN 0-8050-0071-2 Subj: Humorous stories. Poetry.

Carroll, Ruth. *Old Mrs. Billups and the black cats* ill. by author. Walck, 1961. Subj: Animals – cats. Humorous stories.

Pet tale by Ruth & Latrobe Carroll; ill. by Ruth Carroll. Oxford Univ. Pr., 1949. Subj: Pets.

What Whiskers did ill. by author. Walck, 1965. Subj: Animals – dogs. Animals – foxes. Animals – rabbits. Behavior – running away. Wordless.

Where's the bunny? ill. by author. Walck, 1950. Subj: Activities – playing. Animals – dogs. Animals – rabbits. Games. Participation. Wordless.

Carryl, Charles E. (Charles Edward). *The camel's lament* ill. by Charles Santore. Random House, 2004. ISBN 0-375-91426-9 Subj: Animals. Animals – camels. Poetry.

A capital ship: or, The walloping window-blind ill. by Paul Galdone. McGraw-Hill, 1963. Subj: Boats, ships. Music. Pirates. Songs.

The walloping window-blind adapt. & ill. by Jim LaMarche. Lothrop, 1994. ISBN 0-688-12518-2 Subj: Boats, ships. Pirates. Poetry.

The walloping window blind ill. by Ted Rand. Arcade, 1992. ISBN 1-55970-154-4 Subj: Boats, ships. Pirates. Poetry.

Cars and trucks ill. by Daisuke Yokoi. S&S, 1984. ISBN 0-671-49879-7 Subj: Automobiles. Format, unusual – board books. Transportation. Trucks.

Cars and trucks and other vehicles created by Gallimard Jeunesse & Claude Delafosse; ill. by Sophie Kniffke. Scholastic, 1996. ISBN 0-590-62371-0 Subj: Automobiles. Format, unusual. Transportation. Trucks.

Carson, Jo. *The great shaking: an account of the earthquakes of 1811 and 1812* ill. by Robert Andrew Parker. Orchard, 1994. ISBN 0-531-08659-3 Subj: Animals – bears. Earth. Earthquakes. Weather – floods.

Pulling my leg ill. by Julie Downing. Orchard, 1990. ISBN 0-531-08417-5 Subj: Family life – aunts, uncles. Teeth.

You hold me and I'll hold you ill. by Annie Cannon. Orchard, 1992. ISBN 0-531-08495-7 Subj: Death. Emotions – grief. Family life.

Carter, Alden R. *Big brother Dustin* photos by Dan Young with Carol Carter. A. Whitman, 1998. ISBN 0-8075-0715-6 Subj: Babies. Family life – brothers & sisters. Handicaps – Down syndrome. Names.

I'm tougher than asthma! by Alden R. Carter & Siri M. Carter; photos by Dan Young. A. Whitman, 1996. ISBN 0-8075-3474-9 Subj: Illness – asthma.

I'm tougher than diabetes! photos by Carol Shadis Carter. A. Whitman, 2001. ISBN 0-8075-1572-8 Subj: Illness – diabetes.

Seeing things my way photos by Carol S. Carter. A. Whitman, 1998. ISBN 0-8075-7296-9 Subj: Handicaps. Illness.

Carter, Angela. *The sleeping beauty and other favourite fairy tales* ill. by Michael Foreman. Schocken, 1984. ISBN 0-8052-3921-9 Subj: Fairies. Folk & fairy tales.

Carter, Anne. *The twelve dancing princesses* (Grimm, Jacob)

Carter, Anne (1953–). *My home bay* ill. by Alan & Lea Daniel. Red Deer Pr., 2004. ISBN 0-88995-284-1 Subj: Foreign lands – Canada. Friendship.

Carter, Anne Laurel. *Beauty and the beast* ill. by Binette Schroeder. Potter/Crown, 1986. A retelling of Belle et la bête by Madame Leprince de Beaumont. ISBN 0-517-56173-5 Subj: Character traits – appearance. Character traits – loyalty. Emotions – love. Folk & fairy tales. Magic.

Bella's secret garden ill. by John Butler. Crown, 1987. ISBN 0-517-56308-8 Subj: Animals – cats. Animals – rabbits. Behavior – greed. Character traits – kindness to animals.

Circus play ill. by Joanne Fitzgerald. Orca, 2002. ISBN 1-55143-225-0 Subj: Circus. Imagination.

The F team Ill. by Rose Cowles. Orca, 2003. ISBN 1-55143-241-2 Subj: Behavior – bullying. Character traits – perseverance. Sports – hockey.

The fisherwoman ill. by Louise Brierley. Lothrop, 1991. ISBN 0-688-09873-8 Subj: Behavior – seeking better things. Magic.

Molly in danger ill. by John Butler. Crown, 1987. ISBN 0-517-56534-X Subj: Animals – moles. Moving. Nature.

Ruff leaves home ill. by John Butler. Crown, 1986. ISBN 0-517-56068-2 Subj: Animals – foxes. Behavior – lost.

Scurry's treasure ill. by John Butler. Crown, 1987. ISBN 0-517-56535-8 Subj: Animals – squirrels. Nature.

Tall in the saddle ill. by David McPhail. Orca, 1999. ISBN 1-55143-154-8 Subj: Cowboys, cowgirls. Family life – fathers. Imagination.

Under a prairie sky ill. by Alan & Lea Daniel. Orca, 2002. ISBN 1-55143-226-9 Subj: Careers – police officers. Foreign lands – Canada.

Carter, David A. *Chanukah bugs: a pop-up celebration* ill. by author. Little Simon, 2002. ISBN 0-689-81860-2 Subj: Format, unusual – toy & movable books. Holidays – Hanukkah. Insects.

Easter bugs: a springtime pop-up ill. by author. Little Simon, 2001. ISBN 0-689-81862-9 Subj: Eggs. Format, unusual – toy & movable books. Holidays – Easter. Insects.

Flapdoodle dinosaurs: a colorful pop-up book ill. by author. Little Simon, 2001. ISBN 0-689-84643-6 Subj: Dinosaurs. Format, unusual – toy & movable books. Rhyming text.

How many bugs in a box? ill. by author. S&S, 1988. ISBN 0-671-64965-5 Subj: Format, unusual – toy & movable books. Insects.

If you're happy and you know it, clap your hands ill. by author. Scholastic, 1997. ISBN 0-590-93828-2 Subj: Emotions. Format, unusual. Music. Songs.

I'm a little mouse (Carter, Noelle)

In a dark, dark wood: an old tale with a new twist ill. by author. Little Simon, 2002. ISBN 0-689-85280-0 Subj: Format, unusual – toy & movable books. Ghosts. Homes, houses.

Old MacDonald had a farm: a pop-up book ill. by author. Scholastic, 2001. ISBN 0-439-26468-5 Subj: Animals. Careers – farmers. Cumulative tales. Farms. Format, unusual – toy & movable books. Music. Noise, sounds. Songs.

Peekaboo bugs: a hide-and-seek book ill. by author. Little Simon, 2002. ISBN 0-689-85035-2 Subj: Format, unusual – toy & movable books. Games. Insects.

Who's under that hat? ill. & paper engineering by author; text by Sarah Weeks. Harcourt, 2005. ISBN 0-15-205467-7 Subj: Clothing. Format, unusual – toy & movable books. Picture puzzles.

Carter, Debby L. *Clipper* ill. by author. HarperCollins, 1981. ISBN 0-06-021128-8 Subj: Animals – dogs. Sea & seashore.

Carter, Don. *Get to work, trucks!* ill. by author. Roaring Brook, 2002. ISBN 0-7613-2518-2 Subj: Machines. Trucks.

Heaven's all-star jazz band ill. by author. Knopf, 2002. ISBN 0-375-91571-0 Subj: Careers – musicians. Ethnic groups in the U.S. – African Americans. Family life – grandfathers. Music. Musical instruments – bands.

Send it! ill. by author. Roaring Brook, 2003. ISBN 0-7613-2573-5 Subj: Careers – postal workers. Post office.

Carter, Donna Renee. *Music in the family* ill. by Cortrell J. Harris. Lindsey Pub., 1996. ISBN 1-885242-01-8 Subj: Family life. Foreign lands – Jamaica. Music.

Carter, Dorothy (Dorothy A.). *Wilhe'mina Miles after the stork night* ill. by Harvey Stevenson. Farrar, 1999. ISBN 0-374-33551-6 Subj: Behavior – growing up. Birth. Family life – mothers.

Carter, James. *see* Mayne, William

Carter, Katharine. *Houses* ill. with photos. Childrens Pr., 1982. ISBN 0-516-01672-5 Subj: Homes, houses.

Ships and seaports ill. with photos. Childrens Pr., 1982. ISBN 0-516-01656-3 Subj: Boats, ships.

Carter, Noelle. *I'm a little mouse* by Noelle & David A. Carter; ill. by David A. Carter. Holt, 1991. ISBN 0-8050-1420-9 Subj: Animals. Animals – mice. Behavior – lost. Format, unusual.

My house ill. by author. Viking, 1991. ISBN 0-670-83922-1 Subj: Animals. Format, unusual – toy & movable books. Homes, houses. Rhyming text.

My pet ill. by author. Viking, 1991. ISBN 0-670-83923-X Subj: Animals. Format, unusual – toy & movable books. Pets. Rhyming text.

Where's my squishy ball? ill. by author. Scholastic, 1993. ISBN 0-590-47385-9 Subj: Animals – cats. Animals – mice. Behavior – lost & found possessions. Format, unusual – toy & movable books.

Carter, Penny. *A new house for the Morrisons* ill. by author. Viking, 1993. ISBN 0-670-84567-1 Subj: Behavior – seeking better things. Family life. Homes, houses. Moving.

Carter, Peter. *My old grandad* (Harranth, Wolf)

The snowman who went for a walk (Lobe, Mira)

Valerie and the good-night swing (Lobe, Mira)

Carter, Phyllis Ann. *see* Eberle, Irmengarde

Carter, Siri M. *I'm tougher than asthma!* (Carter, Alden R.)

Cartier, Wesley. *Marco's run* ill. by Reynold Ruffins. Harcourt, 2001. ISBN 0-15-216243-7 Subj: Activities – running. Concepts – speed. Imagination.

Cartlidge, Michelle. *Baby mice at home* ill. by author. Dutton, 1992. ISBN 0-525-44840-3 Subj: Animals – babies. Animals – mice. Format, unusual – board books.

Bear in the forest ill. by author. Dutton, 1991. ISBN 0-525-44674-5 Subj: Animals. Animals – bears. Forest, woods. Format, unusual – board books.

The bear's bazaar: a storycraft book ill. by author. Lothrop, 1980. ISBN 0-688-51922-9 Subj: Activities. Animals – bears.

Bears on the go ill. by author. Dutton, 1992. ISBN 0-525-44841-1 Subj: Animals – bears. Automobiles. Format, unusual – board books.

Bunny's birthday ill. by author. Dutton, 1992. ISBN 0-525-44843-8 Subj: Animals – rabbits. Birthdays. Format, unusual – board books. Parties.

Doggy days ill. by author. Dutton, 1992. ISBN 0-525-44844-6 Subj: Animals – dogs. Format, unusual – board books.

Duck in the pond ill. by author. Dutton, 1991. ISBN 0-525-44675-3 Subj: Animals. Birds – ducks. Format, unusual – board books. Lakes, ponds.

Elephant in the jungle ill. by author. Dutton, 1991. ISBN 0-525-44676-1 Subj: Animals. Animals – elephants. Format, unusual – board books. Jungle.

Fairy letters ill. by author. Campbell Books, 1993. ISBN 1-8529-2142-0 Subj: Animals – mice. Fairies. Format, unusual – toy & movable books. Letters, cards.

Good night, Teddy ill. by author. Candlewick, 1992. ISBN 1-56402-076-2 Subj: Activities – bathing. Bedtime. Toys. Toys – bears.

A house for Lily Mouse ill. by author. Prentice-Hall, 1986. ISBN 0-13-395849-3 Subj: Animals – mice. Homes, houses. Moving.

Michelle Cartlidge's book of words ill. by author. Dutton, 1994. ISBN 0-525-45254-0 Subj: Animals – mice. Dictionaries. Language.

Mouse birthday ill. by author. Dutton, 1994. ISBN 0-525-45237-0 Subj: Animals – mice. Birthdays. Format, unusual – toy & movable books.

Mouse Christmas ill. by author. Dutton, 1996. ISBN 0-525-45684-8 Subj: Animals – mice. Format, unusual – toy & movable books. Holidays – Christmas.

Mouse in the house ill. by author. Dutton, 1991. ISBN 0-525-44678-8 Subj: Animals – mice. Format, unusual – board books. Homes, houses.

Mouse letters ill. by author. Dutton, 1993. ISBN 0-525-45089-0 Subj: Animals – mice. Format, unusual – toy & movable books. Letters, cards.

Mouse theater ill. by author. Dutton, 1992. ISBN 0-525-44980-9 Subj: Animals – mice. Format, unusual – toy & movable books. Theater.

Mouse time ill. by author. Dutton, 1991. ISBN 0-525-44766-0 Subj: Animals – mice. Format, unusual – toy & movable books. Time.

A mouse's diary ill. by author. Lothrop, 1982. ISBN 0-688-51987-3 Subj: Activities. Animals – mice.

Mouse's scrapbook ill. by author. Dutton, 1995. ISBN 0-525-45423-3 Subj: Animals – mice. Format, unusual – toy & movable books.

Pippin and Pod ill. by author. Pantheon, 1978. ISBN 0-394-93845-3 Subj: Activities – playing. Animals – mice. Behavior – lost. Behavior – misbehavior.

Teddy trucks ill. by author. Lothrop, 1982. ISBN 0-688-00905-0 Subj: Animals – bears. Careers – truck drivers. Trucks.

Teddy's cat ill. by author. Candlewick, 1996. ISBN 1-56402-944-1 Subj: Animals – cats. Toys – bears.

Teddy's Christmas ill. by author. Walker, 1986. ISBN 0-671-62912-3 Subj: Holidays – Christmas. Toys – bears.

Teddy's friends ill. by author. Candlewick, 1992. ISBN 1-56402-077-0 Subj: Activities – playing. Friendship. Toys – bears.

Carton, Lonnie Caming. *Mommies* ill. by Leslie Jacobs. Random House, 1960. Subj: Activities. Family life – mothers. Poetry.

Cartwright, Ann. *Norah's ark* ill. by Reg Cartwright. S&S, 1984. ISBN 0-671-52540-9 Subj: Animals. Farms. Weather – floods. Weather – rain.

The winter hedgehog ill. by Reg Cartwright. Macmillan, 1990. ISBN 0-02-717775-0 Subj: Animals – hedgehogs. Helicopters. Seasons – winter. Weather – wind.

Cartwright, Reg. *The band over the hill* (Isherwood, Shirley)

Casalis, Anna. *Dinosaurs [board book]* concept by Andrea Dami; text by Anna Casalis; ill. by Franco Tempesta. Little Simon, 2001. ISBN 0-689-85130-8 Subj: Dinosaurs. Format, unusual – board books.

Casanova, Mary. *The hunter* ill. by Ed Young. Atheneum, 2000. ISBN 0-689-82906-X Subj: Folk & fairy tales. Foreign lands – China.

One-dog canoe ill. by Ard Hoyt. Kroupa, 2003. ISBN 0-374-35638-6 Subj: Animals. Canoes & canoeing. Rhyming text.

Caseley, Judith. *Ada potato* ill. by author. Greenwillow, 1988. ISBN 0-688-07843-9 Subj: Character traits – cleverness. Music. Musical instruments – violins. School.

Annie's potty ill. by author. Greenwillow, 1990. ISBN 0-688-09066-4 Subj: Behavior – growing up. Toilet training.

Apple pie and onions ill. by author. Greenwillow, 1987. ISBN 0-688-06763-8 Subj: Ethnic groups in the U.S. Family life – grandmothers.

Bully ill. by author. Greenwillow, 2001. ISBN 0-688-17868-5 Subj: Behavior – bullying. School.

Cousins ill. by author. Greenwillow, 1990. ISBN 0-688-08434-6 Subj: Character traits – individuality. Family life – cousins.

Dear Annie ill. by author. Greenwillow, 1991. ISBN 0-688-10011-2 Subj: Activities – writing. Emotions – love. Family life – grandfathers. Letters, cards.

Field Day Friday ill. by author. Greenwillow, 2000. ISBN 0-688-16762-4 Subj: Friendship. School – field trips. Sports – racing.

Grandpa's garden lunch ill. by author. Greenwillow, 1990. ISBN 0-688-08817-1 Subj: Family life – grandparents. Food. Gardens, gardening.

Harry and Willy and Carrothead ill. by author. Greenwillow, 1991. ISBN 0-688-09493-7 Subj: Character traits – confidence. Friendship. Handicaps – physical handicaps.

Mama, coming and going ill. by author. Greenwillow, 1994. ISBN 0-688-11442-3 Subj: Babies. Family life – mothers. Family life – new sibling.

Mickey's class play ill. by author. Greenwillow, 1998. ISBN 0-688-15406-9 Subj: Animals. Birds – ducks. School. Theater.

Mr. Green Peas ill. by author. Greenwillow, 1995. ISBN 0-688-12860-2 Subj: Pets. Reptiles – iguanas. School.

Molly Pink ill. by author. Greenwillow, 1985. ISBN 0-688-04005-5 Subj: Emotions – embarrassment. School. Songs.

Molly Pink goes hiking ill. by author. Greenwillow, 1985. ISBN 0-688-05700-4 Subj: Character traits – appearance. Sports.

My sister Celia ill. by author. Greenwillow, 1986. ISBN 0-688-06484-1 Subj: Family life – sisters. Weddings.

The noisemakers ill. by author. Greenwillow, 1992. ISBN 0-688-09395-7 Subj: Activities – playing. Behavior. Libraries. Noise, sounds.

On the town ill. by auithor. Greenwillow, 2002. ISBN 0-06-029585-6 Subj: Communities, neighborhoods.

Silly baby ill. by author. Greenwillow, 1988. ISBN 0-688-07356-5 Subj: Babies. Family life – new sibling. Sibling rivalry.

Slumber party! ill. by author. Greenwillow, 1996. ISBN 0-688-14016-5 Subj: Bedtime. Birthdays. Parties. Sleep. Sleepovers.

Sophie and Sammy's library sleepover ill. by author. Greenwillow, 1993. ISBN 0-688-10616-1 Subj: Books, reading. Family life – brothers & sisters. Libraries. Sleep.

Three happy birthdays ill. by author. Greenwillow, 1989. ISBN 0-688-08180-0 Subj: Birthdays.

When Grandpa came to stay ill. by author. Greenwillow, 1986. ISBN 0-688-06129-X Subj: Death. Emotions – grief. Family life – grandfathers. Jewish culture.

Witch mama ill. by author. Greenwillow, 1996. ISBN 0-688-14458-6 Subj: Family life. Holidays – Halloween.

Casey, Denise. *The friendly prairie dog* photos by Tim W. Clark & others. Dodd, 1987. ISBN 0-396-08901-1 Subj: Animals – prairie dogs.

Casey, Patricia. *Beep! Beep! Oink! Oink! animals in the city* ill. by author. Candlewick, 1997. ISBN 0-7636-0306-6 Subj: Animals. Cities, towns. Noise, sounds.

Cluck cluck ill. by author. Lothrop, 1988. ISBN 0-688-07768-4 Subj: Animals. Birds – chickens. Farms. Noise, sounds.

My cat Jack ill. by author. Candlewick, 1994. ISBN 1-56402-410-5 Subj: Animals – cats. Pets.

One day at Wood Green Animal Shelter ill. by author. Candlewick, 2001. ISBN 0-7636-1210-3 Subj: Animals.

Quack quack ill. by author. Lothrop, 1988. ISBN 0-688-07765-X Subj: Birds – chickens. Birds – ducks. Eggs.

Casey, Tina. *The runaway Valentine* ill. by Theresa Smythe. A. Whitman, 2001. ISBN 0-8075-7178-4 Subj: Holidays – Valentine's Day.

Cash, Megan Montague. *I saw the sea and the sea saw me* ill. by author. Viking, 2001. ISBN 0-670-89966-6 Subj: Animals. Rhyming text. Sea & seashore – beaches. Senses.

What makes the seasons? ill. by author. Viking, 2003. ISBN 0-670-03598-X Subj: Animals – cats. Ethnic groups in the U.S. – African Americans. Plants. Science. Seasons.

Cash, Rosanne. *Penelope Jane: a fairy's tale* ill. by G. Brian Karas. Cotler, 2000. ISBN 0-06-027544-8 Subj: Fairies. Fire. School.

Casin, Sheridan. *Little Turtle and the song of the sea* ill. by Norma Burgin. Crocodile, 2000. ISBN 1-56656-355-0 Subj: Reptiles – turtles, tortoises. Sea & seashore.

Casler, Leigh. *The boy who dreamed of an acorn* ill. by Shonto Begay. Philomel, 1994. ISBN 0-399-22547-1 Subj: Dreams. Indians of North America – Chinook. Self-concept. Trees.

Cass, Joan E. *The cat thief* ill. by William Stobbs. Abelard-Schuman, 1961. Subj: Animals – cats. Behavior – stealing. Crime. Night.

The cats go to market ill. by William Stobbs. Abelard-Schuman, 1969. ISBN 0-2007-1581-X Subj: Animals – cats. Shopping.

Cassedy, Sylvia. *The best cat suit of all* ill. by Rosekrans Hoffman. Dial, 1991. ISBN 0-8037-0517-4 Subj: Animals – cats. Friendship. Holidays – Halloween. Illness. Moving.

Moon-uncle, moon-uncle: rhymes from India sel. & trans. by Sylvia Cassedy & Parvathi Thampi; ill. by Susanne Suba. Doubleday, 1973. Subj: Foreign lands – India. Nursery rhymes.

Red dragonfly on my shoulder trans. by Sylvia Cassedy & Kunihiro Suetake; ill. by Molly Bang. HarperCollins, 1992. ISBN 0-06-022625-0 Subj: Animals. Foreign lands – Japan. Poetry.

Cassidy, Dianne. *Circus animals* ill. by author. Little, 1985. ISBN 0-316-13241-1 Subj: Animals. Circus. Format, unusual – board books. Format, unusual – toy & movable books. Rhyming text.

Circus people ill. by author. Little, 1985. ISBN 0-316-13243-8 Subj: Circus. Format, unusual – board books. Format, unusual – toy & movable books. Rhyming text.

Cassidy, Sheila. *The creation: the story of how God created the world* ill. by Emma Hunk. Crossroad, 1996. ISBN 0-8245-1506-4 Subj: Creation.

Cassie, Brian. *Say it again* ill. by David Mooney. Charlesbridge, 2000. ISBN 0-88106-341-X Subj: Animals. Language.

Castaneda, Omar S. *Abuela's weave* ill. by Enrique O. Sánchez. Lee & Low, 1993. ISBN 1-880000-00-8 Subj: Activities – weaving. Fairs, festivals. Family life – grandmothers. Foreign lands – Guatemala.

Casterline, L. C. (Linda C.). *The sounds of music* ill. by Lane Yerkes. G. Stevens, 2004. ISBN 0-8368-4100-X Subj: Music. Musical instruments.

Castiglia, Julie. *Jill the pill* ill. by Steven Kellogg. Atheneum, 1979. ISBN 0-689-50105-6 Subj: Family life. Sibling rivalry.

Castilla, Julia Mercedes. *Dancing Miranda = Baila, Miranda, baila* (De Anda, Diane)

Family = familia (Bertrand, Diane Gonzales)

Magda's tortillas = Las tortillas de Magada (Chavarría-Cháirez, Becky)

Uncle Chente's picnic = El picnic de Tío Chente (Bertrand, Diane Gonzales)

Castillo, Violetta. *Animal babies* (Zoll, Max Alfred)

Castle, Caroline. *For every child: the UN Convention on the Rights of the Child in words & pictures.* Fogelman/UNICEF, 2001. ISBN 0-8037-2650-3 Subj: UNICEF.

Grandpa Baxter and the photographs ill. by Pete Bowman. Orchard, 1993. ISBN 0-531-08637-2 Subj: Activities – photographing. Family life. Family life – grandfathers. Toys – bears.

The hare and the tortoise (Æsop)

Herbert Binns and the flying tricycle ill. by Peter Weevers. Dial, 1987. ISBN 0-8037-0041-5 Subj: Animals. Animals – mice. Character traits – cleverness. Emotions – envy, jealousy.

Naughty! by Caroline Castle & Sam Childs; ill. by Sam Childs. Knopf, 2001. ISBN 0-375-91359-9 Subj: Activities – playing. Animals – babies. Animals – hippopotamuses. Animals – zebras. Bedtime. Humorous stories.

Castle, Sue. *Face talk, hand talk, body talk* ill. by Frances McLaughlin-Gill. Doubleday, 1977. ISBN 0-385-11019-7 Subj: Anatomy. Emotions.

Caswell, Helen Rayburn. *God must like to laugh* ill. by author. Abingdon, 1987. ISBN 0-687-01869-2 Subj: Creation. Religion. Rhyming text.

Parable of the good Samaritan ill. by author. Abingdon, 1992. ISBN 0-687-30023-1 Subj: Character traits – kindness. Religion.

Catalano, Dominic. *Frog went a-courting: a musical play in six acts* (A frog he would a-wooing go [folk-song])

The frog went a-courting: a musical play in six acts (A frog he would a-wooing go [folk-song])

Mr. Bassett plays ill. by author. Boyds Mills, 2003. ISBN 1-590-78007-8 Subj: Animals – dogs. Friendship.

Santa and the three bears ill. by author. Boyds Mills, 2000. ISBN 1-56397-864-4 Subj: Animals – bears. Holidays – Christmas. Santa Claus.

Catalanotto, Peter. *Christmas always . . .* ill. by author. Orchard, 1991. ISBN 0-531-08546-5 Subj: Bedtime. Holidays – Christmas. Santa Claus. Teeth.

Dad and me ill. by author. DK, 1999. ISBN 0-7894-2584-X Subj: Careers – astronauts. Family life – fathers. Imagination. Space & space ships.

Dylan's day out ill. by author. Orchard, 1989. ISBN 0-531-08429-9 Subj: Animals – dogs. Sports – soccer.

Emily's art. Atheneum, 2001. ISBN 0-689-83831-X Subj: Careers – artists. Contests.

Matthew A.B.C. ill. by author. Atheneum, 2002. ISBN 0-689-84582-0 Subj: ABC books. Names. School. Self-concept.

Mr. Mumble ill. by author. Orchard, 1990. ISBN 0-531-08480-9 Subj: Animals. Behavior – misunderstanding.

The painter ill. by author. Orchard, 1996. ISBN 0-531-08765-4 Subj: Activities – painting. Art. Family life – fathers.

Catchpole, Clive. *Deserts* ill. by Brian McIntyre. Dial, 1984. ISBN 0-8037-0035-0 Subj: Animals. Desert.

Grasslands ill. by Peter Snowball. Dial, 1984. ISBN 0-8037-0082-2 Subj: Animals.

Jungles ill. by Denise Finney. Dial, 1984. ISBN 0-8037-0034-2 Subj: Animals. Jungle.

Mountains ill. by Brian McIntyre. Dial, 1984. ISBN 0-8037-0086-5 Subj: Animals.

Cate, Rikki. *A cat's tale* ill. by Shirley Hughes. Harcourt, 1982. ISBN 0-15-215538-4 Subj: Animals – cats. Behavior – stealing. Foreign lands – Scotland. Rhyming text.

The caterpillar who turned into a butterfly. S&S, 1980. ISBN 0-671-41347-3 Subj: Format, unusual – board books. Insects – butterflies, caterpillars. Metamorphosis.

Cathon, Laura E. *Tot Botot and his little flute* ill. by Arnold Lobel. Macmillan, 1970. Subj: Animals. Caldecott award honor books. Foreign lands – India. Music. Musical instruments – flutes.

Caudill, Rebecca. *Contrary Jenkins* by Rebecca Caudill & James Sterling Ayars; ill. by Glen Rounds. Holt, 1969. ISBN 0-03-076295-2 Subj: Behavior. Country. Humorous stories.

A pocketful of cricket ill. by Evaline Ness. Holt, 1964. Subj: Behavior – sharing. Caldecott award honor books. Farms. Insects – crickets. School.

Wind, sand and sky ill. by Donald Carrick. Dutton, 1976. ISBN 0-525-42899-2 Subj: Desert. Poetry.

Cauley, Lorinda Bryan. *The animal kids* ill. by author. Putnam, 1979. ISBN 0-399-20677-9 Subj: Animals. Behavior – imitation.

The bake-off ill. by author. Putnam, 1978. ISBN 0-399-61086-3 Subj: Activities – baking, cooking. Animals.

Clap your hands ill. by author. Putnam, 1992. ISBN 0-399-22118-2 Subj: Activities. Activities – playing. Games. Nursery rhymes.

The cock, the mouse and the little red hen (The little red hen)

Goldilocks and the three bears (The three bears)

The goose and the golden coins ill. by adapt. Harcourt, 1981. ISBN 0-15-232206-X Subj: Birds – geese. Folk & fairy tales. Foreign lands – Italy. Humorous stories.

Jack and the beanstalk (Jack and the beanstalk)

The pancake boy (The gingerbread boy)

Pease porridge hot: a Mother Goose cookbook ill. by author. Putnam, 1977. ISBN 0-399-20591-8 Subj: Activities – baking, cooking. Food. Nursery rhymes.

Puss in boots (Perrault, Charles)

Treasure hunt ill. by author. Putnam, 1994. ISBN 0-399-22447-5 Subj: Activities – picnicking. Animals – bears. Rhyming text.

The trouble with Tyrannosaurus Rex ill. by author. Harcourt, 1988. ISBN 0-15-290880-3 Subj: Behavior – bullying. Character traits – cleverness. Dinosaurs.

What do you know! ill. by author. Putnam, 2001. ISBN 0-399-23573-6 Subj: Picture puzzles.

Causley, Charles. *Dick Whittington: a story from England* (Dick Whittington and his cat)

Early in the morning ill. by Michael Foreman. Viking, 1987. ISBN 0-670-80810-5 Subj: Music. Nursery rhymes.

"Quack!" said the billy-goat ill. by Barbara Firth. Lippincott, 1986. ISBN 0-397-32192-9 Subj: Animals. Humorous stories. Noise, sounds. Rhyming text.

Cavagnaro, David. *The pumpkin people* by David Cavagnaro & Maggie Cavagnaro; ill. with photos. Scribners, 1979. ISBN 0-684-16109-5 Subj: Gardens, gardening. Holidays – Halloween. Seasons – fall. Seasons – summer.

Cavagnaro, Maggie. *The pumpkin people* (Cavagnaro, David)

Cave, Joyce. *Airplanes* (Cave, Ron)

Automobiles (Cave, Ron)

Motorcycles (Cave, Ron)

Cave, Kathryn. *The boy who became an eagle* ill. by Nick Maland. DK, 2000. ISBN 0-7894-2666-8 Subj: Activities – flying. Fairs, festivals.

Henry's song ill. by Sue Hendra. Eerdmans, 2000. ISBN 0-8028-5198-3 Subj: Activities – singing. Animals. Character traits – individuality.

One child, one seed: a South African counting book photos by Gisèle Wulfsohn. Holt, 2003. ISBN 0-8050-7204-7 Subj: Counting, numbers. Foreign lands – Nkandla. Foreign lands – South Africa. Plants. Seeds.

Out for the count ill. by Chris Riddell. S&S, 1992. ISBN 0-671-75591-9 Subj: Animals. Bedtime. Counting, numbers. Cumulative tales. Rhyming text.

You've got dragons ill. by Nick Maland. Peachtree, 2003. ISBN 1-56145-284-X Subj: Dragons. Emotions – fear.

Cave, Ron. *Airplanes* by Ron & Joyce Cave; ill. by David West & others. Watts, 1982. ISBN 0-531-04418-1 Subj: Airplanes, airports. Transportation.

Automobiles by Ron & Joyce Cave; ill. by David West & others. Watts, 1982. ISBN 0-531-04419-X Subj: Automobiles. Transportation.

Motorcycles by Ron & Joyce Cave; ill. by David West & others. Watts, 1982. ISBN 0-531-04420-3 Subj: Motorcycles. Transportation.

Cazet, Denys. *Are there any questions?* ill. by author. Orchard, 1992. ISBN 0-531-08601-1 Subj: Animals. Animals – cats. School.

Big shoe, little shoe ill. by author. Bradbury, 1984. ISBN 0-02-717820-X Subj: Activities – babysitting. Animals – rabbits. Family life – grandparents.

Born in the gravy ill. by author. Orchard, 1993. ISBN 0-531-08638-0 Subj: Ethnic groups in the U.S. – Mexican Americans. Family life. School – first day.

Christmas moon ill. by author. Bradbury, 1984. ISBN 0-02-717810-2 Subj: Animals – rabbits. Family life – grandfathers. Holidays – Christmas. Moon.

Dancing ill. by Craig Bond. Orchard, 1995. ISBN 0-531-08766-2 Subj: Activities – dancing. Activities – singing. Babies. Family life – fathers. Noise, sounds. Songs.

Daydreams ill. by author. Orchard, 1990. ISBN 0-531-08481-7 Subj: Dreams. Imagination. School.

December 24th ill. by author. Bradbury, 1986. ISBN 0-02-717950-8 Subj: Animals – rabbits. Birthdays. Family life – grandfathers. Holidays.

The duck with squeaky feet ill. by author. Bradbury, 1980. ISBN 0-87888-171-9 Subj: Animals. Birds – ducks. Reptiles – alligators, crocodiles. Theater.

Elvis the rooster almost goes to heaven ill. by author. HarperCollins, 2003. ISBN 0-06-000501-7 Subj: Birds – chickens. Humorous stories.

A fish in his pocket ill. by author. Watts, 1987. ISBN 0-531-08313-6 Subj: Birthdays. Character traits – kindness. Death. School.

Frosted glass ill. by author. Bradbury, 1987. ISBN 0-02-717960-5 Subj: Animals. Animals – dogs. Art. School.

Good morning, Maxine! ill. by author. Bradbury, 1989. ISBN 0-02-717940-0 Subj: Animals – cats.

Great-Uncle Felix ill. by author. Watts, 1988. ISBN 0-531-08350-0 Subj: Animals – rhinoceros. Emotions – embarrassment. Family life – aunts, uncles.

I'm not sleepy ill. by author. Orchard, 1992. ISBN 0-531-08498-1 Subj: Bedtime. Family life – fathers. Sleep.

Lucky me ill. by author. Bradbury, 1983. ISBN 0-87888-192-1 Subj: Animals. Birds – chickens. Character traits – luck. Food.

Minnie and Moo and the musk of Zorro ill. by author. DK, 2000. ISBN 0-7894-2652-8 Subj: Animals – bulls, cows. Birds – chickens. Disguises.

Minnie and Moo and the potato from Planet X ill. by author. HarperCollins, 2002. ISBN 0-06-623751-3 Subj: Aliens. Animals – bulls, cows.

Minnie and Moo and the Thanksgiving tree ill. by author. DK, 2000. ISBN 0-7894-2654-4 Subj: Animals – bulls, cows. Holidays – Thanksgiving.

Minnie and Moo go to Paris ill. by author. DK, 1999. ISBN 0-7894-2595-5 Subj: Animals. Animals – bulls, cows. Buses. Foreign lands – France. Humorous stories.

Minnie and Moo meet Frankenswine ill. by author. HarperCollins, 2001. ISBN 0-06-623749-1 Subj: Animals – bulls, cows. Emotions – fear. Humorous stories. Monsters. Weather – lightning, thunder.

Minnie and Moo save the earth ill. by author. DK, 1999. ISBN 0-7894-2594-7 Subj: Aliens. Animals – bulls, cows. Humorous stories.

Minnie and Moo: the night before Christmas ill. by author. HarperCollins, 2002. ISBN 0-06-623753-X Subj: Animals – bulls, cows. Birds – chickens. Holidays – Christmas. Humorous stories.

Minnie and Moo: the night of the living bed ill. by author. HarperCollins, 2003. ISBN 0-06-000504-1 Subj: Animals. Animals – bulls, cows. Dreams. Holidays – Halloween. Humorous stories.

Minnie and Moo: will you be my Valentine? ill. by author. HarperCollins, 2003. ISBN 0-06-623755-6 Subj: Animals. Animals – bulls, cows. Emotions – love. Farms. Holidays – Valentine's Day. Poetry.

Minnie and Moo: the attack of the Easter bunnies ill. by author. HarperCollins, 2004. ISBN 0-06-000507-6 Subj: Animals. Animals – bulls, cows. Farms. Holidays – Easter.

Mother night ill. by author. Orchard, 1989. ISBN 0-531-08430-2 Subj: Animals. Bedtime. Night. Sleep.

Mud baths for everyone ill. by author. Bradbury, 1981. ISBN 0-8788-8178-6 Subj: Animals – pigs. Behavior – bullying. Emotions – fear.

Never poke a squid ill. by author. Orchard, 2000. ISBN 0-531-33279-9 Subj: Animals. Friendship. Holidays – Halloween. School.

Never spit on your shoes ill. by author. Orchard, 1990. ISBN 0-531-08447-7 Subj: Animals. Animals – cats. School – first day.

Night lights: 24 poems to sleep on ill. by author. Orchard, 1997. ISBN 0-531-33010-9 Subj: Bedtime. Poetry.

Nothing at all ill. by author. Orchard, 1994. ISBN 0-531-08672-0 Subj: Animals. Cumulative tales. Farms. Noise, sounds. Rhyming text. Scarecrows.

The octopus ill. by author. HarperCollins, 2005. ISBN 0-06-051089-7 Subj: Activities – storytelling. Animals – dogs. Family life – grandparents. Illness – chicken pox. Octopuses.

Saturday ill. by author. Bradbury, 1985. ISBN 0-02-717800-5 Subj: Animals – dogs. Family life – grandparents.

Sunday ill. by author. Bradbury, 1988. ISBN 0-02-717970-2 Subj: Animals. Family life.

You make the angels cry ill. by author. Bradbury, 1982. ISBN 0-02-717830-7 Subj: Animals – rabbits. Weather – rain.

Cazzola, Gus. *The bells of Santa Lucia* ill. by Pierr Morgan. Putnam, 1991. ISBN 0-399-21804-1 Subj: Animals – sheep. Death. Family life – grandmothers. Foreign lands – Italy.

Cech, John. *Django* ill. by Sharon McGinley-Nally. Macmillan, 1994. ISBN 0-02-765705-1 Subj: Animals. Folk & fairy tales. Music. Musical instruments – violins. Weather – floods.

First snow, magic snow ill. by Sharon McGinley-Nally. Four Winds, 1992. ISBN 0-02-717971-0 Subj: Folk & fairy tales. Foreign lands – Russia. Seasons – winter. Weather – snow.

My grandmother's journey ill. by Sharon McGinley-Nally. Macmillan, 1991. ISBN 0-02-718135-9 Subj: Activities – traveling. Family life – grandmothers. Friendship.

The southernmost cat ill. by Kathy Osborn. S&S, 1996. ISBN 0-689-80510-1 Subj: Activities – writing. Animals – cats. Animals – whales. Sports – fishing.

Cecil, Ivon. *Kirby Kelvin and the not laughing lessons* ill. by Judy Love. Whispering Coyote, 1998. ISBN 1-8790-8595-X Subj: Behavior. School.

Cecil, Laura. *The frog princess* ill. by Emma Chichester Clark. Greenwillow, 1995. ISBN 0-688-13506-4 Subj: Folk & fairy tales. Foreign lands – Italy. Frogs & toads. Magic. Middle Ages. Royalty – princes. Royalty – princesses.

Noah and the space ark ill. by Emma Chichester Clark. Carolrhoda, 1998. ISBN 1-57505-255-5 Subj: Animals. Ecology. Planets. Space & space ships.

Cecil, Mirabel. *Lottie's cats* ill. by Francesca Martin. Crown, 1990. ISBN 0-517-57707-0 Subj: Animals – cats. Holidays – Halloween.

Celenza, Anna Harwell. *The farewell symphony* ill. by JoAnn E. Kitchel. Talewinds, 2000. ISBN 1-57091-406-0 Subj: Careers – composers. Music.

Cendrars, Blaise. *Shadow* trans. & ill. by Marcia Brown. Scribners, 1982. ISBN 0-684-17226-7 Subj: Caldecott award books. Folk & fairy tales. Foreign lands – Africa. Poetry. Shadows.

Cerf, Bennett Alfred. *Bennett Cerf's book of animal riddles* ill. by Roy McKié. Random House, 1964. ISBN 0-394-80034-6 Subj: Humorous stories. Riddles & jokes.

Bennett Cerf's book of laughs ill. by Carl Rose. Random House, 1959. ISBN 0-394-90011-1 Subj: Humorous stories. Riddles & jokes.

Bennett Cerf's book of riddles ill. by Roy McKié. Random House, 1960. ISBN 0-394-90015-4 Subj: Humorous stories. Riddles & jokes.

More riddles ill. by Roy McKié. Random House, 1961. Subj: Humorous stories. Riddles & jokes.

Chacon, Michelle Netten. *How the Indians bought the farm* (Strete, Craig Kee)

Chaconas, Don. *On a wintry morning* ill. by Stephen T. Johnson. Viking, 2000. ISBN 0-670-89245-9 Subj: Family life – fathers. Rhyming text. Seasons – winter. Sports – sledding.

Chadwick, Tim. *Cabbage moon* ill. by Piers Harper. Orchard, 1994. ISBN 0-531-06827-7 Subj: Animals – rabbits. Food. Moon.

Chafetz, Henry. *The legend of Befana* ill. by Ronni Solbert. Houghton Mifflin, 1958. Subj: Folk & fairy tales. Foreign lands – Italy. Holidays – Christmas.

Chaffin, Lillie D. *Tommy's big problem* ill. by Haris Petie. Lantern Pr., 1965. ISBN 0-8313-0016-7 Subj: Babies. Behavior – growing up. Family life. Problem solving.

We be warm till springtime comes ill. by Lloyd Bloom. Macmillan, 1980. ISBN 0-02-717910-9 Subj: Character traits – bravery. Seasons – winter.

Chaikin, Miriam. *Don't step on the sky: a handful of haiku* ill. by Hiroe Nakata. Holt, 2002. ISBN 0-8050-6474-5 Subj: Nature. Poetry.

Esther ill. by Vera Rosenberry. Jewish Publication Society, 1987. ISBN 0-8276-0272-3 Subj: Foreign lands – Persia. Holidays. Jewish culture.

Exodus ill. by Charles Mikolaycak. Holiday, 1987. ISBN 0-8234-0607-5 Subj: Jewish culture. Religion.

Hanukkah ill. by Ellen Weiss. Holiday, 1990. ISBN 0-8234-0816-7 Subj: Holidays – Hanukkah. Jewish culture.

On the little hearth (On the little hearth)

Chalk, Gary. *Mr. Frog went a-courting: discover the secret story* (A frog he would a-wooing go [folk-song])

Yankee Doodle ill. by author. DK, 1993. ISBN 1-56458-202-7 Subj: Music. Songs. U.S. history.

Chall, Marsha Wilson. *Bonaparte* ill. by Wendy Anderson Halperin. DK, 2000. ISBN 0-7894-2617-X Subj: Animals – dogs. Foreign lands – France. School.

Happy Birthday, America! ill. by Guy Porfirio. Lothrop, 2000. ISBN 0-688-13052-6 Subj: Family life. Holidays – Fourth of July.

Mattie ill. by Barbara Lehman. Lothrop, 1992. ISBN 0-688-09730-8 Subj: Family life – brothers & sisters.

Prairie train ill. by John Thompson. HarperCollins, 2003. ISBN 0-688-13434-3 Subj: Cities, towns. Country. Family life – grandmothers. Trains.

Rupa raises the sun ill. by Rosanne Litzinger. DK, 1998. ISBN 0-7894-2496-7 Subj: Humorous stories. Morning. Sun. Superstition.

Sugarbush spring ill. by Jim Daly. Lothrop, 2000. ISBN 0-688-14908-1 Subj: Family life. Food. Seasons – spring.

Up north at the cabin ill. by Steve Johnson. Lothrop, 1992. ISBN 0-688-09733-2 Subj: Activities – vacationing. Forest, woods. Nature.

Challoner, Jack. *The science book of numbers* ill. with photos. Harcourt, 1992. ISBN 0-15-200623-0 Subj: Counting, numbers. Science.

Chalmers, Audrey. *Fancy be good* ill. by author. Viking, 1941. Subj: Animals – cats. Behavior – misbehavior. Sibling rivalry.

Hector and Mr. Murfit ill. by author. Viking, 1953. Subj: Animals – dogs. Concepts – size.

Hundreds and hundreds of pancakes ill. by author. Viking, 1942. Subj: Animals. Food. Humorous stories. Zoos.

Chalmers, Mary. *Be good, Harry* ill. by author. HarperCollins, 1967. ISBN 0-06-443027-8 Subj: Activities – babysitting. Animals – cats.

Boots finds a house ill. by author. HarperCollins, 1958. Subj: Animals – cats. Boats, ships.

The cat who liked to pretend ill. by author. HarperCollins, 1959. Subj: Animals – cats. Imagination.

A Christmas story ill. by author. Rev. ed. HarperCollins, 1987, 1956. ISBN 0-06-021191-1 Subj: Animals. Holidays – Christmas. Religion – Nativity. Trees.

Come for a walk with me ill. by author. HarperCollins, 1955. Subj: Animals – rabbits.

Come to the doctor, Harry ill. by author. HarperCollins, 1981. ISBN 0-06-021179-2 Subj: Animals – cats. Illness.

Easter parade ill. by author. HarperCollins, 1988. ISBN 0-06-021233-0 Subj: Animals. Holidays – Easter. Parades.

George Appleton ill. by author. HarperCollins, 1957. Subj: Animals – cats. Dragons.

A hat for Amy Jean ill. by author. HarperCollins, 1956. Subj: Birthdays. Character traits – generosity. Clothing – hats.

Here comes the trolley ill. by author. HarperCollins, 1955. Subj: Activities – picnicking. Activities – traveling. Cable cars, trolleys.

Kevin ill. by author. HarperCollins, 1957. Subj: Animals – rabbits. Cities, towns.

Merry Christmas, Harry ill. by author. HarperCollins, 1977. ISBN 0-06-021183-0 Subj: Animals – cats. Holidays – Christmas. Santa Claus.

Mr. Cat's wonderful surprise ill. by author. HarperCollins, 1961. Subj: Activities – picnicking. Animals – cats. Family life.

Six dogs, twenty-three cats, forty-five mice, and one hundred sixteen spiders ill. by author. HarperCollins, 1986. ISBN 0-06-021189-X Subj: Humorous stories. Parties. Pets.

Take a nap, Harry ill. by author. HarperCollins, 1964. ISBN 0-06-021244-6 Subj: Animals – cats. Family life. Sleep.

Throw a kiss, Harry ill. by author. HarperCollins, 1990. ISBN 0-06-021245-4 Subj: Animals – cats. Careers – firefighters.

Chamberlain, Margaret. *You can swim, Jim* (Umansky, Kay)

Chamberlin-Calamar, Pat. *Alaska's twelve days of summer* ill. by Shannon Cartwright. Sasquatch, 2003. ISBN 1-57061-341-9 Subj: Alaska. Animals. Counting, numbers.

Chambers, Catherine. *Big freeze* ill. with photos. Heinemann, 2002. ISBN 1-58810-658-6 Subj: Weather – cold.

Christmas ill. by author. Raintree, 1997. ISBN 0-8172-4608-8 Subj: Holidays – Christmas.

Heat wave ill. with photos. Heinemann, 2002. ISBN 1-58810-657-8 Subj: Concepts – cold & heat. Weather.

Tornado ill. with photos. Heinemann, 2002. ISBN 1-58810-652-7 Subj: Weather – tornadoes.

Chambers, Roland. *Rooftop rocket party* ill. by author. Roaring Brook, 2003. ISBN 0-7613-2744-4 Subj: Careers – scientists. Moon. Parties. Space & space ships.

Chambless, Jane. *Tucker and the bear* ill. by author. S&S, 1989. ISBN 0-671-67357-2 Subj: Animals – bears. Friendship.

Chan, Arlene. *Awakening the dragon: the dragon boat festival* ill. by Song Nan Zhang. Tundra, 2004. ISBN 0-88776-656-0 Subj: Boats, ships. Fairs, festivals. Foreign lands – China.

Chan, Chin-Yi. *Good luck horse* ill. by Plao Chan. Whittlesey House, 1943. Subj: Animals – horses, ponies. Caldecott award honor books.

Chancellor, Deborah. *Holidays!* ill. with photos. DK, 2000. ISBN 0-7894-5710-5 Subj: Holidays.

Maps and mapping ill. with photos. Kingfisher, 2004. ISBN 0-7534-5759-8 Subj: Careers – cartographers. Maps.

Traveling on land ill. with photos. Two-Can, 2001. ISBN 0-915741-80-6 Subj: Activities – traveling. Transportation.

Chandler, Edna Walker. *Cattle drive* ill. by Jack Merryweather. Benefic Pr., 1966. Subj: Cowboys, cowgirls. U.S. history – frontier & pioneer life.

Cowboy Andy ill. by Raymond Kinstler. Random House, 1959. Subj: Cowboys, cowgirls.

Pony rider ill. by Jack Merryweather. Benefic Pr., 1966. Subj: Animals – horses, ponies. Cowboys, cowgirls. U.S. history – frontier & pioneer life.

Secret tunnel ill. by Jack Merryweather. Benefic Pr., 1967. Subj: Cowboys, cowgirls. U.S. history – frontier & pioneer life.

Chandler, Robert. *Russian folk tales* (Afanas'ev, Aleksandr N.)

Chandoha, Walter. *A baby bunny for you* ill. by author. Collins, 1968. Subj: Animals – rabbits.

A baby goat for you ill. by author. Collins, 1968. Subj: Animals – goats.

A baby goose for you ill. by author. Collins, 1968. Subj: Birds – geese.

Chandra, Deborah. *A is for Amos* ill. by Keiko Narahashi. Farrar, 1999. ISBN 0-374-30001-1 Subj: ABC books. Animals – horses, ponies. Farms. Rhyming text. Toys – rocking horses.

George Washington's teeth ill. by Brock Cole. Farrar, 2003. ISBN 0-374-32534-0 Subj: Teeth. U.S. history.

Miss Mabel's table ill. by Max Grover. Harcourt, 1994. ISBN 0-15-276712-6 Subj: Activities – baking, cooking. Counting, numbers. Cumulative tales. Rhyming text.

Chang, Margaret Scrogin. *The beggar's magic* ill. by David Johnson. McElderry, 1997. ISBN 0-689-81340-6 Subj: Character traits – selfishness. Folk & fairy tales. Foreign lands – China. Magic.

The cricket warrior by Margaret & Raymond Chang; ill. by Warwick Hutton. McElderry, 1994. ISBN 0-689-50605-8 Subj: Folk & fairy tales. Foreign lands – China. Insects – crickets. Royalty – emperors.

Chang, Raymond. *The cricket warrior* (Chang, Margaret Scrogin)

Chanin, Michael. *Chief's blanket* ill. by Kim Howard. H. J. Kramer, 1997. ISBN 0-915811-78-2 Subj: Activities – weaving. Family life – grandmothers. Illness. Indians of North America – Navajo.

Chanover, Alice. *Happy Hanukah everybody* (Chanover, Hyman)

Chanover, Hyman. *Happy Hanukah everybody* by Hyman & Alice Chanover; ill. by Maurice Sendak. United Synagogue Books, 1954. ISBN 0-8381-0712-5 Subj: Holidays – Hanukkah. Jewish culture. Music. Religion.

Chapin, Cynthia. *Squad car 55* ill. by Dale Fleming. A. Whitman, 1966. Educational consultant: Jene Barr. Subj: Careers – police officers.

Chaplin, Susan Gibbons. *I can sign my ABCs* ill. by Laura McCaul. Gallaudet Univ. Pr., 1986. ISBN 0-930323-19-X Subj: ABC books. Handicaps – deafness. Senses – hearing. Sign language.

Chapman, Carol. *Barney Bipple's magic dandelions* ill. by Steven Kellogg. Dutton, 1988, 1977. ISBN 0-525-44449-1 Subj: Behavior – wishing. Flowers. Magic. Plants.

Herbie's troubles ill. by Kelly Oechsli. Dutton, 1981. ISBN 0-525-31645-0 Subj: Behavior – bullying. Behavior – misbehavior. Problem solving.

The tale of Meshka the Kvetch ill. by Arnold Lobel. Dutton, 1980. ISBN 0-525-40745-6 Subj: Behavior – dissatisfaction. Folk & fairy tales. Jewish culture.

Chapman, Cheryl. *Pass the fritters, critters* ill. by Susan L. Roth. Bradbury, 1993. ISBN 0-02-717975-3 Subj: Animals. Etiquette. Rhyming text.

Snow on snow on snow ill. by Synthia Saint James. Dial, 1994. ISBN 0-8037-1457-2 Subj: Animals – dogs. Ethnic groups in the U.S. – African Americans. Family life. Language. Seasons – winter. Weather – snow.

Chapman, Elizabeth. *Suzy* ill. by Margery Gill. Salem House, 1987. ISBN 0-370-30375-X Subj: Character traits – being different. Handicaps – blindness. Senses – sight.

Chapman, Gaynor. *Æsop* (Æsop)

The luck child ill. by author. Atheneum, 1968. Based on a story of the Brothers Grimm. Subj: Folk & fairy tales. Royalty.

Chapman, Jane. *Touch the sky, my little bear* (Bedford, David)

Chapman, Jean. *Moon-Eyes* ill. by Astra Lacis. McGraw-Hill, 1980. ISBN 0-07-010648-7 Subj: Animals – cats. Folk & fairy tales. Foreign lands – Italy. Holidays – Christmas. Religion.

Chapman, Nancy Kapp. *Doggie dreams* ill. by Lee Chapman. Putnam, 2000. ISBN 0-399-23443-8 Subj: Animals – dogs. Dreams. Rhyming text.

Chapman, Noralee. *The story of Barbara* ill. by Helen S. Hull. John Knox, 1963. Subj: Adoption.

Chapouton, Anne-Marie. *Ben finds a friend* trans. by Andrea Mernan; ill. by Ulises Wensell. Putnam, 1986. ISBN 0-399-21268-X Subj: Cities, towns. Friendship. Pets.

Billy the brave trans. from French by Anthea Bell; ill. by Jean Claverie. Holt, 1986. ISBN 0-03-008019-3 Subj: Character traits – bravery. Monsters. Night.

Sebastian is always late ill. by Chantal van der Berghe. Holt, 1987. ISBN 0-8050-0487-4 Subj: Imagination. School.

Chapra, Mimi. *Amelia's show-and-tell fiesta = Amelia y la fiesta de "muestra y cuenta"* ill. by Martha Avilés Junco. HarperCollins, 2004. ISBN 0-06-050256-8 Subj: Ethnic groups in the U.S. – Cuban Americans. Foreign languages. School.

Charbonnet, Gabrielle. *Boodil, my dog* (Lindenbaum, Pija)

Chardiet, Bernice. *C is for circus* ill. by Brinton Turkle. Walker, 1971. ISBN 0-8027-6083-X Subj: ABC books. Circus. Rhyming text.

Martin and the tooth fairy by Bernice Chardiet & Grace Maccarone; ill. by G. Brian Karas. Scholastic, 1991. ISBN 0-590-44396-8 Subj: Fairies. Money. School. Teeth.

Charles, Donald. *Calico Cat at school* ill. by author. Childrens Pr., 1981. ISBN 0-516-03445-6 Subj: Animals – cats. Rhyming text. School.

Calico Cat at the zoo ill. by author. Childrens Pr., 1981. ISBN 0-516-03443-X Subj: Animals. Animals – cats. Rhyming text. Zoos.

Calico Cat meets bookworm ill. by author. Childrens Pr., 1978. ISBN 0-516-03441-3 Subj: Animals – cats. Libraries. Rhyming text.

Calico Cat's exercise book ill. by author. Childrens Pr., 1982. ISBN 0-516-03457-X Subj: Animals – cats. Animals – mice. Health & fitness – exercise. Rhyming text.

Calico Cat's year ill. by author. Childrens Pr., 1984. ISBN 0-516-03461-8 Subj: Animals – cats. Days of the week, months of the year. Rhyming text. Seasons.

Chancay and the secret of fire ill. by author. Putnam, 1990. ISBN 0-399-22129-8 Subj: Fire. Folk & fairy tales. Foreign lands – Peru.

Shaggy dog's animal alphabet ill. by author. Childrens Pr., 1979. ISBN 0-516-03674-2 Subj: ABC books. Animals. Poetry.

Shaggy dog's birthday ill. by author. Childrens Pr., 1986. ISBN 0-516-03576-2 Subj: Animals – dogs. Birthdays. Etiquette.

Shaggy dog's Halloween ill. by author. Childrens Pr., 1984. ISBN 0-516-03575-4 Subj: Animals – dogs. Character traits – appearance. Holidays – Halloween.

Shaggy dog's tall tale ill. by author. Childrens Pr., 1980. ISBN 0-516-03616-5 Subj: Animals – dogs.

Time to rhyme with Calico Cat ill. by author. Childrens Pr., 1978. ISBN 0-516-03629-7 Subj: Animals – cats. Animals – dogs. Rhyming text.

Ugly bug ill. by author. Dial, 1994. ISBN 0-8037-1205-7 Subj: Character traits – appearance. Insects. Self-concept.

Charles, Faustin. *A Caribbean counting book* ill. by Roberta Arenson. Houghton Mifflin, 1996. ISBN 0-395-77944-8 Subj: Counting, numbers. Foreign lands – Caribbean Islands. Rhyming text.

Charles, N. N. *What am I? Looking through shapes at apples and grapes* ill. by Diane & Leo Dillon. Scholastic, 1994. ISBN 0-590-47891-5 Subj: Concepts – color. Concepts – shape. Format, unusual – toy & movable books. Riddles & jokes.

Charles, Nicholas. *see* Kuskin, Karla

Charles, R. H. (Robert Henry). *The roundabout turn* ill. by L. Leslie Brooke. Warne, 1930. Subj: Frogs & toads. Merry-go-rounds. Poetry.

Charles, Veronika Martenova. *The crane girl* ill. by author. Orchard, 1993. ISBN 0-531-05485-3 Subj: Behavior – running away. Birds – cranes. Family life. Folk & fairy tales. Foreign lands – Japan.

The maiden of the mist ill. by author. Stoddart, 2001. ISBN 0-7737-3297-7 Subj: Folk & fairy tales. Indians of North America – Seneca.

Charlip, Remy. *Arm in arm* ill. by author. Tricycle, 1997. ISBN 1-883672-50-3 Subj: Games. Humorous stories.

Baby hearts and baby flowers ill. by author. Greenwillow, 2002. ISBN 0-06-029591-0 Subj: Babies. Bedtime. Rhyming text.

Fortunately ill. by author. Parents' Magazine Pr., 1964. Subj: Humorous stories. Participation.

Handtalk: an ABC of finger spelling and sign language by Remy Charlip, Mary Beth & George Ancona; ill. by George Ancona. Parents' Magazine Pr., 1974. ISBN 0-8193-0706-8 Subj: ABC books. Communication. Handicaps – deafness. Language. Senses – hearing.

Handtalk birthday: a number and story book in sign language photos by George Ancona. Four Winds, 1987. ISBN 0-02-718080-8 Subj: Birthdays. Handicaps – deafness. Language. Senses – hearing.

Harlequin and the gift of many colors by Remy Charlip & Burton Supree; ill. by Remy Charlip. Parents' Magazine Pr., 1973. ISBN 0-819-30495-6 Subj: Concepts – color. Folk & fairy tales. Foreign lands – France. Gifts.

Hooray for me! by Remy Charlip & Lilian Moore; ill. by Vera B. Williams. Rev. ed. Harcourt, 1995. ISBN 1-883672-43-0 Subj: Character traits – individuality. Family life. Self-concept.

"Mother, mother I feel sick" by Remy Charlip & Burton Supree; ill. by Remy Charlip. Tricycle, 2001. Orig. published by Parents' Magazine Pr., 1966. ISBN 1-58246-043-4 Subj: Careers – doctors. Humorous stories. Illness. Rhyming text.

Peanut butter party ill. by author. Tricycle, 1999. ISBN 1-883672-69-4 Subj: Activities – baking, cooking. Food. Parties.

Sleepytime rhyme ill. by author. Greenwillow, 1999. ISBN 0-688-16272-X Subj: Babies. Family life – mothers. Nursery rhymes. Rhyming text.

Thirteen by Remy Charlip & Jerry Joyner; ill. by Remy Charlip. Parents' Magazine Pr., 1975. ISBN 0-819-30808-0 Subj: Counting, numbers. Humorous stories.

The tree angel (Martin, Judith)

Where is everybody? ill. by author. Addison-Wesley, 1957. Subj: Games. Weather – rain.

Why I will never ever ever ever have enough time to read this book ill. by Jon J. Muth. Tricycle, 2000. ISBN 1-58246-018-3 Subj: Books, reading. Day. Time.

Charlot, Martin. *Felisa and the magic tikling bird* ill. by Martin Charlot from a story by Jodi Parry Belknap. Island Heritage, 1973. ISBN 0-8348-3015-9 Subj: Activities – dancing. Folk & fairy tales. Foreign lands – Philippines. Handicaps. Self-concept.

Sunnyside up ill. by author. Weatherhill, 1972. ISBN 0-8348-3000-0 Subj: Wordless.

Charlton, Elizabeth. *Jeremy and the ghost* ill. by Celia Reisman. Dandelion, 1979. ISBN 0-89799-118-4 Subj: Character traits – bravery. Ghosts. Holidays – Halloween.

Terrible tyrannosaurus ill. by Andrew Glass. Elsevier-Nelson, 1981. ISBN 0-525-66724-5 Subj: Behavior – bullying. Behavior – imitation. Dinosaurs.

Charlton, Nancy Lee. *Derek's dog days* ill. by Chris L. Demarest. Harcourt, 1996. ISBN 0-15-223219-2 Subj: Animals – dogs. Imagination. School – first day.

Charmatz, Bill. *The Troy St. bus* ill. by author. Macmillan, 1977. ISBN 0-02-718160-X Subj: Animals – horses, ponies. School.

Charosh, Mannis. *The ellipse* ill. by Leonard P. Kessler. Crowell, 1972. ISBN 0-690-25856-9 Subj: Concepts – shape. Science.

Number ideas through pictures ill. by Giulio Maestro. Crowell, 1975. ISBN 0-690-00156-8 Subj: Concepts. Counting, numbers.

Charters, Janet. *The general* by Janet Charters & Michael Foreman; ill. by Michael Foreman. Dutton, 1961. Subj: Violence, nonviolence.

Chase, Alice. *see* McHargue, Georgess

Chase, Catherine. *An alphabet book* ill. by June Goldsborough. Dandelion, 1979. ISBN 0-89799-087-0 Subj: ABC books.

Baby mouse goes shopping ill. by Jill Elgin. Elsevier-Nelson, 1981. ISBN 0-525-66742-3 Subj: Animals – mice. Shopping.

Baby mouse learns his ABC's ill. by Jill Elgin. Dandelion, 1979. ISBN 0-89799-089-7 Subj: ABC books. Animals – mice.

Feet ill. by Susan Reiss. Dandelion, 1979. ISBN 0-89799-104-4 Subj: Anatomy – feet. Concepts – left & right.

Hot and cold ill. by Gail Gibbons. Dandelion, 1979. ISBN 0-89799-110-9 Subj: Concepts.

The miracles at Cana ill. by Wayne Atkinson. Dandelion, 1979. ISBN 0-89799-124-9 Subj: Religion.

The mouse in my house ill. by Gail Gibbons. Dandelion, 1979. ISBN 0-89799-126-5 Subj: Animals – mice. Homes, houses.

My balloon ill. by Gail Gibbons. Dandelion, 1979. ISBN 0-89799-127-3 Subj: Toys – balloons.

The nightingale and the fool ill. by Judith Cheng. Dandelion, 1979. ISBN 0-89799-129-X Subj: Birds – nightingales. Folk & fairy tales. Foreign lands – India.

Noah's ark ill. by Elliot Ivenbaum. Dandelion, 1979. ISBN 0-89799-130-3 Subj: Animals. Boats, ships. Religion – Noah. Weather – floods. Weather – rain. Weather – rainbows.

Pete, the wet pet ill. by Gail Gibbons. Elsevier-Nelson, 1981. ISBN 0-525-66746-6 Subj: Animals – dogs. Family life.

Chase, Edith Newlin. *Secret dawn* ill. by Yolaine Lefebvre. Firefly, 1996. ISBN 1-55209-028-0 Subj: Morning. Poetry. Trees.

Chase, Jan Brinckerhoff. *The golden song* ill. by author. J.N. Townsend, 1993. ISBN 1-880158-01-9 Subj: Birds – canaries. Character traits – kindness to animals. Friendship. Pets.

Chase, Mary. *The wicked, wicked ladies in the haunted house* ill. by Peter Sis. Knopf, 2003. ISBN 0-375-92572-4 Subj: Ghosts. Magic. Mythical creatures – leprechauns.

Chase, Richard. *Billy Boy* (Billy Boy [folk-song])

Jack and the three sillies ill. by Joshua Tolford. Houghton Mifflin, 1950. Subj: Folk & fairy tales.

Chasek, Judith. *Have you seen Wilhelmina Krumpf?* ill. by Sal Murdocca. Lothrop, 1973. ISBN 0-688-51523-1 Subj: Foreign lands – Holland.

Chataway, Carol. *The perfect pet* ill. by Greg Holfeld. Kids Can, 2001. ISBN 1-55337-178-X Subj: Animals – pigs. Pets.

Chaucer, Geoffrey. *Chanticleer and the fox* adapt. & ill. by Barbara Cooney. Crowell, 1958. Adapt. of the "Nun's priest's tale" from the Canterbury tales. ISBN 0-690-18562-6 Subj: Animals – foxes. Birds – chickens. Caldecott award books. Character traits – flattery. Farms. Folk & fairy tales.

Chausse, Sylvie. *The egg and I* ill. by François Crozat. Silver Pr., 1997. ISBN 0-382-39286-8 Subj: Character traits – luck. Dinosaurs. Eggs. Family life – cousins.

Chavarría-Cháirez, Becky. *Magda's piñata magic = Magda y la piñata mágica* ill. by Anne Vega; Spanish trans. by Gabriela Baeza Ventura. Piñata, 2001. ISBN 1-55885-320-0 Subj: Birthdays. Family life – brothers & sisters. Foreign languages. Parties.

Magda's tortillas = Las tortillas de Magada ill. by Anne Vega; Spanish trans. by Mercedes Castilla. Piñata, 2000. ISBN 1-55885-286-7 Subj: Activities – baking, cooking. Birthdays. Concepts – shape. Food. Foreign languages.

Chen, Chih-Yuan. *Guji Guji* ill. by author. Kane/Miller, 2004. ISBN 1-929132-67-0 Subj: Birds – ducks. Reptiles – alligators, crocodiles.

On my way to buy eggs ill. by author. Kane/Miller, 2003. ISBN 1-929132-49-2 Subj: Activities – shopping. Food. Foreign lands – Taiwan. Imagination.

Chen, Kerstin. *Lord of the cranes* ill. by Jian Jiang Chen; trans. by J. Alison James. North-South, 2000. ISBN 0-7358-1193-8 Subj: Birds – cranes. Folk & fairy tales. Foreign lands – China.

Chen, Tony. *Animals showing off* ill. by Tony Chen; written by Jane R. McCauley. National Geographic, 1989. ISBN 0-87044-724-6 Subj: Animals. Format, unusual – toy & movable books.

Chenault, Nell. *Parsifal the Poddley* ill. by Vee Guthrie. Little, 1960. Subj: Emotions – loneliness. Mythical creatures. U.S. history.

Chenery, Janet. *Pickles and Jake* ill. by Lilian Obligado. Viking, 1975. ISBN 0-670-55335-2 Subj: Animals – cats. Animals – dogs. Pets.

The toad hunt ill. by Ben Shecter. HarperCollins, 1967. ISBN 0-06-021263-2 Subj: Frogs & toads. Science.

Wolfie ill. by Marc Simont. HarperCollins, 1969. ISBN 0-440-40496-7 Subj: Sibling rivalry. Spiders.

Cheng, Andrea. *Anna the bookbinder* ill. by Ted Rand. Walker, 2003. ISBN 0-8027-8831-9 Subj: Books, reading. Careers – bookbinders. Family life. Family life – fathers. Self-concept.

Grandfather counts ill. by Ange Zhang. Lee & Low, 2000. ISBN 1-58430-010-8 Subj: Communication. Ethnic groups in the U.S. – Chinese Americans. Family life – grandfathers. Language.

Cheng, Hou-Tien. *The Chinese New Year* ill. by author. Holt, 1976. ISBN 0-03-017511-9 Subj: Foreign lands – China. Holidays – Chinese New Year.

Chermayeff, Ivan. *Tomato and other colors* ill. by author. Prentice-Hall, 1981. ISBN 0-13-924753-X Subj: Concepts – color.

Chernoff, Goldie Taub. *Clay-dough, play-dough* ill. & photos by Margaret A. Hartelius. Walker, 1974. ISBN 0-8027-6178-X Subj: Activities.

Just a box? ill. by Margaret A. Hartelius. Walker, 1973. ISBN 0-8027-6138-0 Subj: Activities.

Pebbles and pods: a book of nature crafts ill. by Margaret A. Hartelius. Walker, 1973. ISBN 0-8027-6137-2 Subj: Activities.

Puppet party ill. by Margaret A. Hartelius. Walker, 1972. ISBN 0-8027-6100-3 Subj: Activities. Puppets.

Cherry, Lynne. *Archie, follow me* ill. by author. Dutton, 1990. ISBN 0-525-44647-8 Subj: Animals – cats. Forest, woods.

The armadillo from Amarillo ill. by author. Harcourt, 1994. ISBN 0-15-200359-2 Subj: Activities – flying. Animals – armadillos. Rhyming text.

The dragon and the unicorn ill. by author. Harcourt, 1995. ISBN 0-15-224193-0 Subj: Dragons. Ecology. Monsters. Mythical creatures – unicorns.

The great kapok tree: a tale of the Amazon rain forest ill. by author. Harcourt, 1990. ISBN 0-15-200520-X Subj: Animals. Ecology. Foreign lands – Brazil. Jungle. Trees.

Grizzly bear text & ed. by Lucia Monfried; ill. by author. Dutton, 1998. ISBN 0-525-45793-3 Subj: Animals – bears. Format, unusual – board books.

How Groundhog's garden grew ill. by author. Blue Sky, 2003. ISBN 0-439-32371-1 Subj: Animals – groundhogs. Animals – squirrels. Food. Gardens, gardening.

Orangutan text & ed. by Lucia Monfried; ill. by author. Dutton, 1998. ISBN 0-525-45794-1 Subj: Animals – orangutans. Format, unusual – board books.

A river ran wild ill. by author. Harcourt, 1992. ISBN 0-15-200542-0 Subj: Ecology. Nature. Rivers. U.S. history.

Seal text & ed. by Lucia Monfried; ill. by author. Dutton, 1998. ISBN 0-525-45796-8 Subj: Animals – seals. Format, unusual – board books.

The shaman's apprentice by Lynne Cherry & Mark Plotkin; ill. by Lynne Cherry. Harcourt, 1998. ISBN 0-15-201281-8 Subj: Foreign lands – South America. Forest, woods. Rivers.

Snow leopard text & ed. by Lucia Monfried; ill. by author. Dutton, 1998. ISBN 0-525-45797-6 Subj: Animals – leopards. Format, unusual – board books.

Who's sick today? ill. by author. Dutton, 1988. ISBN 0-525-44380-0 Subj: Animals. Illness. Rhyming text.

Cheshire, Marc. *Here comes Eloise!* ill. by Carolyn Bracken. Little Simon, 2005. Based on Kay Thompson's Eloise; & the art of Hilary Knight. ISBN 0-689-87154-6 Subj: Format, unusual – toy & movable books. Hotels.

Love & kisses, Eloise ill. by Ted Enik. Little Simon, 2005. Based on Kay Thompson's Eloise; & the art of Hilary Knight. ISBN 0-689-87156-2 Subj: Emotions – love. Holidays – Valentine's Day.

Chess, Victoria. *Alfred's alphabet walk* ill. by author. Greenwillow, 1979. ISBN 0-688-84223-2 Subj: ABC books. Behavior – misbehavior.

Poor Esmé ill. by author. Holiday, 1982. ISBN 0-8234-0455-2 Subj: Babies. Behavior – wishing. Emotions – loneliness. Family life – new sibling.

Chester, Jonathan. *Busy penguins* (Schindel, John)

Splash! a penguin counting book by Jonathan Chester & Kirsty Melville; ill. with photos. Tricycle, 1997. ISBN 1-883672-56-2 Subj: Birds – penguins. Counting, numbers. Foreign lands – Antarctic. Nature.

Chesworth, Michael. *Archibald Frisby* ill. by author. Farrar, 1994. ISBN 0-374-30392-4 Subj: Camps, camping. Rhyming text. Science.

Rainy day dream ill. by author. Farrar, 1992. ISBN 0-374-36177-0 Subj: Dreams. Umbrellas. Weather – storms. Wordless.

Chetkowski, Emily. *Pumpkin smile* ill. by Dawn Peterson. Seven Coin, 2001. ISBN 0-9700974-2-5 Subj: Holidays – Halloween. Rhyming text. Self-concept. Teeth.

Chetwin, Grace. *Box and Cox* ill. by David Small. Bradbury, 1990. ISBN 0-02-718314-9 Subj: Careers – hatters. Careers – printers. Humorous stories.

Mr. Meredith and the truly remarkable stone ill. by Catherine Stock. Bradbury, 1989. ISBN 0-02-718313-0 Subj: Rocks.

Chevalier, Christa. *The little bear who forgot* ed. by Kathleen Tucker; ill. by author. A. Whitman, 1984. ISBN 0-8075-4571-6 Subj: Animals – bears. Family life.

Spence and the sleepytime monster ill. by author. A. Whitman, 1984. ISBN 0-8075-7574-7 Subj: Bedtime. Imagination. Monsters.

Spence is small ill. by author. A. Whitman, 1987. ISBN 0-8075-7567-4 Subj: Character traits – helpfulness. Character traits – smallness.

Spence isn't Spence anymore ill. by author. A. Whitman, 1985. ISBN 0-8075-7565-8 Subj: Character traits – appearance.

Spence makes circles ill. by author. A. Whitman, 1982. ISBN 0-8075-7570-4 Subj: Behavior – mistakes. Humorous stories.

Chevalier, Joan. *Suzette and Nicholas and the seasons clock* (Mangin, Marie-France)

Chevance, Audrey. *Tutu* ill. by author. Dutton, 1991. ISBN 0-525-44769-5 Subj: Activities – dancing. Ballet. Careers – seamstresses.

Cheyette, Wendy. *see* Lewison, Wendy Cheyette

Chial, Debra. *M is for Minnesota* ed. by Helene Anderson & Julie Bach; ill. by author. Voyageur Pr., 1994. ISBN 0-8965-8234-5 Subj: ABC books. U.S. history.

Chiang, Ch'eng-an. *The legend of Mu Lan = La heroina Hua Mulan* (Chiang, Wei)

Chiang, Wei. *The legend of Mu Lan = La heroina Hua Mulan* written & ill. by Jiang, Wei & Gen, Xing. Victory, 1992. ISBN 1-878217-01-1 Subj: Folk & fairy tales. Foreign lands – China. Foreign languages. War.

Clark, Emma Chichester. *see* Chichester Clark, Emma

Chichester Clark, Emma. *Follow the leader!* ill. by author. McElderry, 2003. ISBN 0-689-84296-1 Subj: Animals. Animals – tigers. Games.

I love you, Blue Kangaroo! ill. by author. Doubleday, 1999. ISBN 0-385-32638-6 Subj: Behavior – needing someone. Toys.

Little Miss Muffet's count-along surprise ill. by author. Bantam, 1997. ISBN 0-385-32517-7 Subj: Animals. Birthdays. Counting, numbers. Nursery rhymes. Parties.

Lunch with Aunt Augusta ill. by author. Dial, 1992. ISBN 0-8037-1104-2 Subj: Animals – lemurs. Family life – aunts, uncles. Food. Jungle.

More! ill. by author. Doubleday, 1999. ISBN 0-385-32630-0 Subj: Activities – playing. Behavior – greed. Behavior – seeking better things. Family life – mothers. Family life – sons. Imagination.

The story of Horrible Hilda and Henry ill. by author. Little, 1989. ISBN 0-316-14498-3 Subj: Animals – lions. Behavior – misbehavior. Zoos.

Where are you, Blue Kangaroo? ill. by author. Random House, 2001. ISBN 0-385-32797-8 Subj: Animals – kangaroos. Toys.

Chicken Little. *Chicken Licken* text by Kenneth McLeish; ill. by Jutta Ash. Bradbury, 1973. ISBN 0-582-16469-9 Subj: Animals. Behavior – gossip. Behavior – trickery. Birds – chickens. Cumulative tales. Folk & fairy tales.

Chicken Licken adapt. & ill. by Gavin Bishop. Oxford Univ. Pr., 1985. ISBN 0-19-558108-3 Subj: Animals. Behavior – gossip. Behavior – trickery. Birds – chickens. Cumulative tales. Folk & fairy tales.

Chicken Little ill. by Sally Hobson. S&S, 1994. ISBN 0-671-89548-6 Subj: Animals. Behavior – gossip. Behavior – trickery. Birds – chickens. Cumulative tales. Folk & fairy tales.

Henny Penny retold by Harriet Ziefert; ill. by Emily Bolam. Viking, 1997. ISBN 0-670-86810-8 Subj: Animals. Behavior – gossip. Behavior – trickery. Birds – chickens. Cumulative tales. Folk & fairy tales.

Henny Penny ill. by Stephen Butler. Morrow, 1991. ISBN 0-688-09922-X Subj: Animals. Behavior – gossip. Behavior – trickery. Birds – chickens. Cumulative tales. Folk & fairy tales.

Henny Penny ill. by Paul Galdone. Seabury Pr., 1968. Subj: Animals. Behavior – gossip. Behavior – trickery. Birds – chickens. Cumulative tales. Folk & fairy tales.

Henny Penny ill. by William Stobbs. Follett, 1968. ISBN 0-3700-0780-8 Subj: Animals. Behavior – gossip. Behavior – trickery. Birds – chickens. Cumulative tales. Folk & fairy tales.

Henny-Penny retold & ill. by Jane Wattenberg. Scholastic, 2000. ISBN 0-439-07817-2 Subj: Animals. Behavior – gossip. Behavior – trickery. Birds – chickens. Cumulative tales. Folk & fairy tales.

The sky is falling Betty Miles; ill. by Cynthia Fisher. S&S, 1998. ISBN 0-689-81790-8 Subj: Animals. Behavior – gossip. Behavior – trickery. Birds – chickens. Cumulative tales. Folk & fairy tales.

The story of Chicken Licken adapt. & ill. by Jan Ormerod. Lothrop, 1986. ISBN 0-688-06058-7 Subj: Animals. Behavior – gossip. Behavior – trickery. Birds – chickens. Cumulative tales. Folk & fairy tales.

Chiefari, Janet. *Kids are baby goats* ill. with photos. Dodd, 1984. ISBN 0-396-08316-1 Subj: Animals – goats. Fairs, festivals.

Chiemruom, Sothea. *Dara's Cambodian New Year* ill. by Dam Nang Pin. Modern Curriculum, 1992. ISBN 0-813-62256-5 Subj: Ethnic groups in the U.S. – Cambodian Americans. Holidays – New Year's.

Child, Lauren. *Beware of the storybook wolves* ill. by author. Levine, 2001. ISBN 0-439-20500-X Subj: Animals – wolves. Folk & fairy tales. Mythical creatures.

Clarice Bean, guess who's babysitting? ill. by author. Candlewick, 2001. ISBN 0-7636-1373-8 Subj: Activities – babysitting. Careers – firefighters. Family life – aunts, uncles.

Clarice Bean, that's me ill. by author. Candlewick, 1999. ISBN 0-7636-0961-7 Subj: Family life.

I am not sleepy and I will not go to bed ill. by author. Candlewick, 2001. ISBN 0-7636-1570-6 Subj: Animals. Bedtime.

I am too absolutely small for school ill. by author. Candlewick, 2004. ISBN 0-7636-2403-9 Subj: Family life – brothers & sisters. School – first day.

I want a pet ill. by author. Tricycle, 1999. ISBN 1-883672-82-1 Subj: Pets.

I will never not ever eat a tomato ill. by author. Candlewick, 2000. ISBN 0-7636-1188-3 Subj: Food. Imagination.

My dream bed ill. by author. Scholastic, 2002. ISBN 0-439-30912-3 Subj: Format, unusual – toy & movable books. Furniture – beds. Sleep.

That pesky rat ill. by author. Candlewick, 2002. ISBN 0-7636-1873-X Subj: Animals – rats. Names. Pets.

What planet are you from Clarice Bean? ill. by author. Candlewick, 2002. ISBN 0-7636-1696-6 Subj: Ecology. Family life. Humorous stories. Trees.

Child, Lydia Maria. *Over the river and through the wood* ill. by Brinton Turkle. Coward, 1974. First published in 1844 as The boy's Thanksgiving Day in the 2d vol. of the author's Flowers for children. ISBN 0-698-30553-1 Subj: Family life – grandparents. Farms. Holidays – Thanksgiving. Songs.

Child Study Association of America. *Brothers and sisters are like that!* (Brothers and sisters are like that!)

Children go where I send thee: an American spiritual ill. by Kathryn E. Shoemaker. Winston, 1980. ISBN 0-03-056673-8 Subj: Ethnic groups in the U.S. – African Americans. Music. Religion.

Children's prayers from around the world comp. by Mary Batchelor. Sadlier, 1981. Subj: Children as authors. Religion.

Children's Television Workshop. *ABC: featuring Jim Henson's Sesame Street Muppets* (Calmenson, Stephanie)

Muppets in my neighborhood ill. by Harry McNaught. Random House, 1977. ISBN 0-394-83593-X Subj: Format, unusual – board books. Puppets.

The Sesame Street book of letters (Sesame Street)

The Sesame Street book of numbers (Sesame Street)

The Sesame Street book of opposites with Zero Mostel (Mendoza, George)

The Sesame Street book of people and things (Sesame Street)

The Sesame Street book of shapes (Sesame Street)

The Sesame Street players present Mother Goose: featuring Jim Henson's Sesame Street Muppets (Mother Goose)

The Sesame Street song book (Raposo, Joe)

A visit to the Sesame Street firehouse: featuring Jim Henson's Sesame Street Muppets (Elliott, Dan)

Childress, Mark. *Joshua and Bigtooth* ill. by Rick Meyerowitz. Little, 1992. ISBN 0-316-14011-2 Subj: Activities – dancing. Parties. Pets. Reptiles – alligators, crocodiles.

Joshua and the big bad blue crabs ill. by Mary Barrett Brown. Little, 1996. ISBN 0-316-14118-6 Subj: Behavior – misbehavior. Crustaceans – crabs. Food.

Childs, Sam. *Naughty!* (Castle, Caroline)

A child's book of prayers ill. by Michael Hague. Holt, 1985. ISBN 0-03-001412-3 Subj: Religion.

A child's calendar ill. by Trina Schart Hyman. Holiday, 1999. ISBN 0-8234-1445-0 Subj: Caldecott award honor books. Calendars. Days of the week, months of the year. Poetry.

A child's picture English-Hebrew dictionary ill. by Ita Meshi. Adama, 1985. ISBN 0-915361-07-8 Subj: ABC books. Dictionaries. Foreign languages. Jewish culture.

A child's treasury of nursery rhymes ill. by Kady MacDonald Denton. Kingfisher, 1998. ISBN 0-7534-5109-3 Subj: Nursery rhymes.

Chimaera. *see* Farjeon, Eleanor

Chin, Charlie. *China's bravest girl: the legend of Hua Mu Lan* ill. by Tomie Arai; trans. from Chinese by Wang Xing Chu. Children's Book Pr., 1993. ISBN 0-89239-120-0 Subj: Careers – military. Folk & fairy tales. Foreign lands – China. Poetry.

Chin, Steven A. *Dragon Parade: a Chinese New Year story* ill. by Mou-Sien Tseng. Raintree, 1993. ISBN 0-8114-7215-9 Subj: Ethnic groups in the U.S. – Chinese Americans. Holidays – Chinese New Year.

Chinery, Michael. *Desert animals* ill. by Eric Robson & David Wright. Random House, 1992. ISBN 0-679-92048-X Subj: Animals. Desert.

Grassland animals ill. by John Butler & Brian McIntyre. Random House, 1992. ISBN 0-679-92045-5 Subj: Animals.

Ching. *The baboon's umbrella* ill. by author. Childrens Pr., 1991. ISBN 0-516-05131-8 Subj: Animals – baboons. Folk & fairy tales. Foreign lands – Africa. Umbrellas.

Ching, Simon. *The cricket's cage: a Chinese folktale* (Czernecki, Stefan)

Chin-Lee, Cynthia. *A is for Asia* ill. by Yumi Heo. Orchard, 1997. ISBN 0-531-33011-7 Subj: ABC books. Foreign lands – Asia.

Chinn, Karen. *Sam and the lucky money* ill. by Cornelius Van Wright & Ying-Hwa Hu. Lee & Low, 1995. ISBN 1-880000-13-X Subj: Character traits – generosity. Ethnic groups in the U.S. – Chinese Americans. Holidays – Chinese New Year. Homeless.

Chislett, Gail. *Melinda's no's cold* ill. by Hélène Desputeaux. Firefly, 1991. ISBN 1-55037-196-7 Subj: Careers – doctors. Illness. Language.

The rude visitors ill. by Barbara Di Lella. Firefly, 1984. Subj: Behavior – carelessness. Imagination.

Whump ill. by Vladyana Krykorka. Firefly, 1989. ISBN 1-55037-041-3 Subj: Bedtime. Family life. Sleep.

Chittum, Ida. *The cat's pajamas* ill. by Art Cumings. Parents' Magazine Pr., 1980. ISBN 0-8193-1030-1 Subj: Animals – cats. Pets.

Chitwood, Suzanne Tanner. *Wake up, big barn!* ill. by author. Scholastic, 2002. ISBN 0-439-26627-0 Subj: Animals. Farms. Rhyming text.

Chlad, Dorothy. *Bicycles are fun to ride* ill. by Lydia Halverson. Childrens Pr., 1984. ISBN 0-516-01975-9 Subj: Safety. Sports – bicycling.

Matches, lighters, and firecrackers are not toys ill. by Lydia Halverson. Childrens Pr., 1982. ISBN 0-516-01982-1 Subj: Safety.

Poisons make you sick ill. by Lydia Halverson. Childrens Pr., 1984. ISBN 0-516-01976-1 Subj: Safety.

Strangers ill. by Lydia Halverson. Childrens Pr., 1982. ISBN 0-516-01984-8 Subj: Behavior – talking to strangers.

Chmielarz, Sharon. *Down at Angel's* ill. by Jill Kastner. Ticknor & Fields, 1994. ISBN 0-395-65993-0 Subj: Character traits – kindness. Friendship. Holidays – Christmas.

The pied piper of Hamelin (Browning, Robert)

Cho, Shinta. *The gas we pass: the story of farts* ill. by author; trans. by Amanda Mayer Stinchecum. Kane/Miller, 1994. ISBN 0-916291-52-9 Subj: Anatomy. Animals. Etiquette.

Chocolate, Deborah M. Newton. *Imani in the belly* ill. by Alex Boies. BridgeWater, 1994. ISBN 0-8167-3466-6 Subj: Animals. Character traits – bravery. Folk & fairy tales. Foreign lands – Africa.

Kente colors ill. by John Ward. Walker, 1996. ISBN 0-8027-8389-9 Subj: Clothing. Concepts – color. Foreign lands – Africa. Holidays – Kwanzaa.

Kwanzaa ill. by Melodye Rosales. Childrens Pr., 1990. ISBN 0-516-03991-1 Subj: Ethnic groups in the U.S. – African Americans. Family life. Holidays – Kwanzaa.

The piano man ill. by Eric Velasquez. Walker, 1998. ISBN 0-8027-8647-2 Subj: Careers – musicians. Ethnic groups in the U.S. – African Americans. Family life – grandparents. Music. Musical instruments – pianos.

Chodos-Irvine, Margaret. *Ella Sarah gets dressed* ill. by author. Harcourt, 2003. ISBN 0-15-216413-8 Subj: Caldecott award honor books. Character traits – individuality. Clothing. Family life. Friendship. Parties.

Choi, Sook Nyul. *Halmoni and the picnic* ill. by Karen Dugan. Houghton Mifflin, 1993. ISBN 0-395-61626-3 Subj: Ethnic groups in the U.S. – Korean Americans. Family life – grandmothers.

Yunmi and Halmoni's trip ill. by Karen Dugan. Houghton Mifflin, 1997. ISBN 0-395-81180-5 Subj: Ethnic groups in the U.S. – Korean Americans. Family life. Family life – grandmothers. Foreign lands – Korea.

Choi, Yangsook. *The name jar* ill. by author. Knopf, 2001. ISBN 0-375-90613-4 Subj: Ethnic groups in the U.S. – Korean Americans. Names. School.

New cat ill. by author. Farrar, 1999. ISBN 0-374-35512-6 Subj: Animals – cats. Animals – mice.

The sun girl and the moon boy retold & ill. by Yangsook Choi. Knopf, 1997. ISBN 0-679-98386-4 Subj: Animals – tigers. Behavior – talking to strangers. Folk & fairy tales. Foreign lands – Korea.

Choldenko, Gennifer. *Moonstruck: the true story of the cow that jumped over the moon* ill. by Paul Yalowitz. Hyperion, 1997. ISBN 0-7868-2130-2 Subj: Animals – bulls, cows. Animals – horses, ponies. Character traits – perseverance. Moon. Nursery rhymes.

Chönz, Selina. *A bell for Ursli* ill. by Alois Carigiet. Walck, 1950. Subj: Foreign lands – Switzerland. Rhyming text. Seasons – spring.

Florina and the wild bird trans. by Anne & Ian Serraillier; ill. by Alois Carigiet. Walck, 1966. Translation of Flurina und das Wildvöglein. Subj: Birds. Foreign lands – Switzerland. Rhyming text. Seasons – summer.

The snowstorm ill. by Alois Carigiet. Walck, 1958. Translated from the German. Subj: Foreign lands – Switzerland. Rhyming text. Seasons – winter. Weather – snow. Weather – storms.

Chorao, Kay. *Annie and cousin Precious* ill. by author. Dutton, 1994. ISBN 0-525-45238-9 Subj: Activities – playing. Animals – dogs. Family life – cousins.

The baby's bedtime book comp. & ill. by Kay Chorao. Dutton, 1984. ISBN 0-525-44149-2 Subj: Nursery rhymes. Poetry.

Baby's Christmas treasury ill. by author. Random House, 1991. ISBN 0-679-90198-1 Subj: Babies. Holidays – Christmas.

The baby's good morning book ill. by adapt. Dutton, 1986. ISBN 0-525-44257-X Subj: Babies. Morning. Poetry.

Carousel round and round ill. by author. Clarion, 1995. ISBN 0-395-63632-9 Subj: Animals. Merry-go-rounds. Rhyming text. Toys.

Cathedral mouse ill. by author. Dutton, 1988. ISBN 0-525-44400-9 Subj: Animals – mice. Homes, houses.

The cherry pie baby ill. by author. Dutton, 1989. ISBN 0-525-44435-1 Subj: Activities – trading. Animals – dogs. Babies.

The child's story book ill. by adapt. Dutton, 1987. ISBN 0-525-44328-2 Subj: Folk & fairy tales.

The Christmas story ill. by adapt. Holiday, 1996. ISBN 0-8234-1251-2 Subj: Holidays – Christmas. Religion – Nativity.

George told Kate ill. by author. Dutton, 1987. ISBN 0-525-44293-6 Subj: Animals – elephants. Sibling rivalry.

Ida and Betty and the secret eggs ill. by author. Houghton Mifflin, 1991. ISBN 0-395-52591-8 Subj: Animals – cats. Country. Eggs. Friendship.

Kate's box ill. by author. Dutton, 1982. ISBN 0-525-44010-0 Subj: Animals – elephants. Behavior – hiding.

Kate's car ill. by author. Dutton, 1982. ISBN 0-525-44011-9 Subj: Animals – elephants. Toys.

Kate's quilt ill. by author. Dutton, 1982. ISBN 0-525-44012-7 Subj: Animals – elephants. Quilts.

Kate's snowman ill. by author. Dutton, 1982. ISBN 0-525-44013-5 Subj: Animals – elephants. Snowmen.

Knock at the door and other baby action rhymes ill. by author. Dutton, 1999. ISBN 0-525-45969-3 Subj: Animals – cats. Babies. Nursery rhymes. Rhyming text.

Lemon moon ill. by author. Holiday, 1983. ISBN 0-8234-0490-0 Subj: Animals. Bedtime. Dreams. Family life – grandmothers.

Lester's overnight ill. by author. Dutton, 1977. ISBN 0-525-33480-7 Subj: Emotions – fear. Family life. Imagination. Sleep.

Little farm by the sea ill. by author. Holt, 1998. ISBN 0-8050-5053-1 Subj: Careers – farmers. Family life. Farms. Seasons.

Maudie's umbrella ill. by author. Dutton, 1975. ISBN 0-525-34770-4 Subj: Behavior – lost & found possessions. Umbrellas.

Molly's lies ill. by author. Seabury Pr., 1979. ISBN 0-816-43225-2 Subj: Behavior – lost & found possessions. Behavior – lying. Friendship. School – first day.

Molly's Moe ill. by author. Seabury Pr., 1976. ISBN 0-816-43171-X Subj: Behavior – lost & found possessions. Shopping. Toys.

Mother Goose magic ill. by author. Dutton, 1994. ISBN 0-525-45064-5 Subj: Nursery rhymes.

Number one number fun ill. by author. Holiday, 1995. ISBN 0-8234-1142-7 Subj: Animals. Circus. Counting, numbers. Rhyming text.

Peekaboo! Was it you? ill. by author. Random House, 1994. ISBN 0-679-84629-8 Subj: Activities. Format, unusual – board books. Games. Rhyming text.

Pig and Crow ill. by author. Holt, 2000. ISBN 0-8050-5863-X Subj: Activities – trading. Animals – pigs. Behavior. Birds – crows.

Rock, rock, my baby ill. by author. Random House, 1993. ISBN 0-679-84333-7 Subj: Format, unusual – board books. Lullabies.

Shadow night ill. by author. Dutton, 2001. ISBN 0-525-46685-1 Subj: Emotions – fear. Family life. Shadows.

Chottin, Ariane. *Beaver gets lost* ill. by Marcelle Geneste; adapt. by Deborah Kovacs. Reader's Digest, 1992. ISBN 0-89577-419-4 Subj: Animals – beavers. Animals – squirrels. Behavior – lost. Character traits – ambition.

The curious little dolphin adapt. by Patricia Jensen; ill. by Olivier Raquois. Reader's Digest, 1992. ISBN 0-8957-7425-9 Subj: Animals – dolphins. Character traits – curiosity.

A home for Little Turtle ill. by Pascale Wirth; adapt. by Deborah Kovacs. Reader's Digest, 1992. ISBN 0-89577-420-8 Subj: Animals. Emotions – envy, jealousy. Reptiles – turtles, tortoises. Self-concept.

Little Goat's new horns adapt. by Patricia Jensen; ill. by Pascale Wirth. Reader's Digest, 1993. ISBN 0-8957-7544-1 Subj: Animals – goats. Emotions – envy, jealousy. Self-concept.

Little Kangaroo finds his way adapt. by Patricia Jensen; ill. by Catherine Fichaux. Reader's Digest, 1993. ISBN 0-8957-7543-3 Subj: Animals – kangaroos. Character traits – confidence.

Little Mouse's rescue adapt. by Patricia Jensen; ill. by Malgorzata Dzierzawska. Reader's Digest, 1993. ISBN 0-8957-7505-0 Subj: Animals – cats. Animals – mice. Friendship.

Chouinard, Mariko. *The amazing animal alphabet book* (Chouinard, Roger)

One magic box (Chouinard, Roger)

Chouinard, Roger. *The amazing animal alphabet book* by Roger & Mariko Chouinard; ill. by Roger Chouinard. Doubleday, 1988. ISBN 0-385-24029-5 Subj: ABC books. Animals.

One magic box by Roger & Mariko Chouinard; ill. by authors. Doubleday, 1989. ISBN 0-385-26204-3 Subj: Animals. Counting, numbers. Magic.

Chow, Octavio. *The invisible hunters* (Rohmer, Harriet)

Christelow, Eileen. *Don't wake up Mama! another five little monkeys story* ill. by author. Clarion, 1992. ISBN 0-395-60176-2 Subj: Activities – baking, cooking. Animals – monkeys. Birthdays. Family life – mothers. Food.

Five little monkeys jumping on the bed ill. by author. Houghton Mifflin, 1991. ISBN 0-395-55701-1 Subj: Animals – monkeys. Bedtime. Behavior – misbehavior. Counting, numbers. Nursery rhymes. Poetry.

Five little monkeys sitting in a tree ill. by author. Houghton Mifflin, 1991. ISBN 0-395-54434-3 Subj: Activities – picnicking. Animals – monkeys. Behavior – misbehavior. Counting, numbers. Reptiles – alligators, crocodiles. Rhyming text.

Five little monkeys wash the car ill. by author. Clarion, 2000. ISBN 0-395-92566-5 Subj: Animals – monkeys. Automobiles. Reptiles – alligators, crocodiles. Rhyming text.

Five little monkeys with nothing to do ill. by author. Clarion, 1996. ISBN 0-395-75830-0 Subj: Animals – monkeys. Behavior – boredom. Family life.

The five-dog night ill. by author. Clarion, 1993. ISBN 0-395-62399-5 Subj: Animals – dogs. Seasons – winter.

Gertrude, the bulldog detective ill. by author. Houghton Mifflin, 1992. ISBN 0-395-58701-8 Subj: Animals – dogs. Careers – detectives. Mystery stories.

Glenda Feathers casts a spell ill. by author. Houghton Mifflin, 1990. ISBN 0-395-51122-4 Subj: Animals. Witches.

The great pig escape ill. by author. Clarion, 1994. ISBN 0-395-66973-1 Subj: Animals – pigs. Behavior – running away. Careers – farmers.

The great pig search ill. by author. Clarion, 2001. ISBN 0-618-04910-X Subj: Animals – pigs. Behavior – running away.

Henry and the dragon ill. by author. Houghton Mifflin, 1984. ISBN 0-89919-220-3 Subj: Animals – rabbits. Bedtime. Dragons. Shadows.

Henry and the red stripes ill. by author. Houghton Mifflin, 1982. ISBN 0-89919-118-5 Subj: Animals – foxes. Animals – rabbits. Illness.

Jerome and the Witchcraft kids ill. by author. Clarion, 1988. ISBN 0-8991-9742-6 Subj: Activities – babysitting. Behavior – misbehavior. Holidays – Halloween. Reptiles – alligators, crocodiles.

Jerome camps out ill. by author. Clarion, 1998. ISBN 0-395-75831-9 Subj: Behavior – bullying. Camps, camping. Reptiles – alligators, crocodiles.

Jerome the babysitter ill. by author. Houghton Mifflin, 1985. ISBN 0-89919-331-5 Subj: Activities – babysitting. Behavior – trickery. Character traits – cleverness. Reptiles – alligators, crocodiles.

Mr. Murphy's marvelous invention ill. by author. Clarion, 1983. ISBN 0-89919-141-X Subj: Animals – pigs. Inventions.

Not until Christmas, Walter! ill. by author. Clarion, 1997. ISBN 0-395-82273-4 Subj: Animals – dogs. Holidays – Christmas.

Olive and the magic hat ill. by author. Clarion, 1987. ISBN 0-89919-513-X Subj: Animals. Behavior – trickery. Clothing – hats. Magic.

The robbery at the diamond dog diner ill. by author. Clarion, 1986. ISBN 0-89919-425-7 Subj: Animals. Behavior – secrets. Behavior – trickery. Birds. Crime. Restaurants.

What do authors do? ill. by author. Clarion, 1995. ISBN 0-395-71124-X Subj: Careers – artists. Careers – writers.

Where's the big bad wolf? ill. by author. Clarion, 2002. ISBN 0-618-18194-6 Subj: Animals. Animals – wolves. Careers – detectives. Humorous stories. Mystery stories.

Christensen, Bonnie. *Woody Guthrie, poet of the people* ill. by author. Knopf, 2001. ISBN 0-375-91113-8 Subj: Careers – musicians. Music. U.S. history.

Christensen, Gardell Dano. *Mrs. Mouse needs a house* ill. by author. Holt, 1958. Subj: Animals. Animals – mice. Homes, houses. Problem solving.

Christensen, Jack. *The forgotten rainbow* by Jack & Lee Christensen; ill. by authors. Morrow, 1960. Subj: Behavior – wishing. Folk & fairy tales.

Christensen, Lee. *The forgotten rainbow* (Christensen, Jack)

Christenson, Larry. *The wonderful way that babies are made* ill. by Dwight Walles. Bethany House, 1982. ISBN 0-87123-627-3 Subj: Babies. Birth. Family life. Science.

Christian, Frank P. *Dancin' in the kitchen* (Gelsanliter, Wendy)

Christian, Mary Blount. *Anna and the strangers* ill. by Charles T. Cox. Abingdon, 1981. ISBN 0-687-01529-4 Subj: Holidays – Christmas. Religion.

April fool ill. by Diane Dawson. Macmillan, 1982. ISBN 0-02-718280-0 Subj: Folk & fairy tales. Foreign lands – England. Holidays – April Fools' Day.

The bookstore mouse ill. by Gary A. Lippincott. Harcourt, 1995. ISBN 0-15-200203-0 Subj: Animals – mice. Books, reading. Dragons. Stores.

Christmas reflections ill. by Arch Kirchhoff. Concordia, 1980. ISBN 0-570-03494-9 Subj: Cities, towns. Country. Family life. Holidays – Christmas.

The devil take you, Barnabas Beane! ill. by Anne Burgess. Crowell, 1980. ISBN 0-690-03998-0 Subj: Behavior – greed. Character traits – generosity. Character traits – selfishness.

Devin and Goliath ill. by Normand Chartier. Addison-Wesley, 1974. ISBN 0-2010-1026-7 Subj: Pets. Reptiles – turtles, tortoises.

The doggone mystery ill. by Irene Trivas. A. Whitman, 1980. ISBN 0-8075-1656-2 Subj: Behavior – stealing. Crime. Mystery stories.

Go west, swamp monsters ill. by Marc Brown. Dial, 1985. ISBN 0-8037-0144-6 Subj: Activities – picnicking. Behavior – misbehavior. Behavior – running away. Monsters.

Grandfathers, God's gift to children ill. by Susan Morris. Concordia, 1982. ISBN 0-570-04069-8 Subj: Family life – grandfathers. Religion.

Grandmothers, God's gift to children ill. by Susan Morris. Concordia, 1982. ISBN 0-570-04068-X Subj: Family life – grandmothers. Religion.

The green thumb thief ill. by Don Madden. A. Whitman, 1982. ISBN 0-8075-3040-9 Subj: Animals – dogs. Behavior – stealing. Clubs, gangs. Plants.

No dogs allowed, Jonathan! ill. by Don Madden. Addison-Wesley, 1973. ISBN 0-2010-1028-3 Subj: Animals – dogs.

Nothing much happened today ill. by Don Madden. Addison-Wesley, 1973. ISBN 0-2010-1024-0 Subj: Cumulative tales. Humorous stories.

The sand lot ill. by Dennis Kendrick. Harvey House, 1978. ISBN 0-8178-5827-X Subj: Activities – playing. Behavior – fighting, arguing. Sports – baseball.

Scarabee, the witch's cat ill. by Sybil McEntire. Steck-Vaughn, 1973. ISBN 0-8114-7750-9 Subj: Animals – cats. Witches.

Christian, Peggy. *Chocolate, a glacier grizzly* ill. by Carol Cottone-Kolthoff. Benefactory, 1997. ISBN 1-882728-63-7 Subj: Animals – bears. Careers – park rangers.

If you find a rock photos by Barbara Hirsch Lember. Harcourt, 2000. ISBN 0-15-239339-0 Subj: Rocks.

Christiana, David. *The first snow* ill. by author. Scholastic, 1996. ISBN 0-590-22855-2 Subj: Seasons – winter. Weather – snow.

A Tooth Fairy's tale ill. by author. Farrar, 1994. ISBN 0-374-37677-8 Subj: Fairies. Giants. Mythical creatures – sandman.

White nineteens ill. by author. Farrar, 1992. ISBN 0-374-38390-1 Subj: Animals. Fairies. Forest, woods. Seasons – winter.

Christiansen, C. B. *Mara in the morning* ill. by Catherine Stock. Macmillan, 1991. ISBN 0-689-31616-X Subj: Morning. Noise, sounds.

My mother's house, my father's house ill. by Irene Trivas. Macmillan, 1989. ISBN 0-689-31394-2 Subj: Divorce. Emotions. Family life.

Christiansen, Candace. *The ice horse* ill. by Thomas Locker. Dial, 1993. ISBN 0-8037-1401-7 Subj: Animals – horses, ponies. Family life – aunts, uncles. Seasons – winter.

A Christmas book trans. from Danish by Joan Tate; ill. by Svend Otto S. Larousse, 1982. ISBN 0-88332-286-2 Subj: Foreign lands – Denmark. Holidays – Christmas.

Christmas carols ill. by Diane Goode. Random House, 1983. ISBN 0-394-85723-2 Subj: Holidays – Christmas. Songs.

Christmas in the stable poems sel. & ill. by Beverly K. Duncan. Harcourt, 1990. ISBN 0-15-217758-2 Subj: Animals. Holidays – Christmas. Poetry. Religion – Nativity.

Christmas presents: holiday poetry sel. by Lee Bennett Hopkins; ill. by Melanie W. Hall. HarperCollins, 2004. ISBN 0-06-008055-8 Subj: Holidays – Christmas. Poetry.

The Christmas story told through paintings from the Metropolitan Museum of Art with commentary by Richard Mühlberger. Harcourt, 1990. ISBN 0-15-200426-2 Subj: Art. Holidays – Christmas. Museums. Religion – Nativity.

Chrustowski, Rick. *Bright beetle* ill. by author. Holt, 2000. ISBN 0-8050-6058-8 Subj: Insects – ladybugs.

Hop frog ill. by author. Holt, 2003. ISBN 0-8050-6688-8 Subj: Frogs & toads.

Chukovskii, Kornei Ivanovich. *Good morning, chick* adapt. by Mirra Ginsburg; ill. by Byron Barton. Greenwillow, 1980. ISBN 0-688-84284-4 Subj: Birds – chickens. Noise, sounds.

The telephone adapt. from Russian by William Jay Smith in collaboration with Max Hayward; ill. by Blair Lent. Delacorte, 1977. ISBN 0-440-06040-0 Subj: Communication. Humorous stories. Rhyming text.

Telephone ill. by Vladimir Radunsky; trans. & adapt. by Jamey Gambrell. North-South, 1996. ISBN 1-55858-481-1 Subj: Animals. Poetry. Telephone.

Church, Kristine. *My brother John* ill. by Kilmeny Niland. Morrow, 1991. ISBN 0-688-10801-6 Subj: Character traits – bravery. Emotions – fear. Family life – brothers & sisters. Monsters.

Churchill, Vicki. *Sometimes I like to curl up in a ball* ill. by Charles Fuge. Sterling, 2001. ISBN 0-8069-7943-7 Subj: Animals – wombats. Rhyming text.

Chute, Beatrice Joy. *Journey to Christmas* ill. by Erik Blegvad. Dutton, 1958. Subj: Character traits – generosity. Holidays – Christmas.

Chwast, Seymour. *Alphabet parade* ill. by author. Harcourt, 1991. ISBN 0-15-200351-7 Subj: ABC books. Parades. Wordless.

Bushy bride: a Norwegian fairy tale ill. by reteller. Creative Ed., 1983. ISBN 0-87191-952-4 Subj: Emotions – envy, jealousy. Family life – stepfamilies. Folk & fairy tales. Foreign lands – Norway. Royalty – kings.

Harry, I need you! ill. by author. Houghton, 2002. ISBN 0-618-17917-8 Subj: Animals – babies. Animals – cats. Imagination.

Mr. Merlin and the turtle ill. by author. Greenwillow, 1996. ISBN 0-688-14632-5 Subj: Animals. Format, unusual – toy & movable books. Magic. Pets. Reptiles – turtles, tortoises.

Moonride (Ziefert, Harriet)

Still another alphabet book by Seymour Chwast & Martin Stephen Moskof; ill. by authors. McGraw-Hill, 1969. Subj: ABC books. Wordless.

Still another children's book by Seymour Chwast & Martin Stephen Moskof; ill. by authors. McGraw-Hill, 1972. Subj: Dreams. Seasons – summer.

Still another number book by Seymour Chwast & Martin Stephen Moskof; ill. by authors. McGraw-Hill, 1971. Subj: Counting, numbers.

Tall city, wide country: a book to read forward and backward ill. by author. Viking, 1983. ISBN 0-670-69236-0 Subj: Activities – traveling. Cities, towns. Country. Format, unusual.

Traffic jam ill. by author. Houghton Mifflin, 1999. ISBN 0-395-97495-X Subj: Animals – babies. Animals – cats. Careers – police officers. Cities, towns. Format, unusual – toy & movable books. Traffic, traffic signs.

The twelve circus rings ill. by author. Harcourt, 1993. ISBN 0-15-200627-3 Subj: Animals. Circus. Counting, numbers.

Ciardi, John. *John J. Plenty and Fiddler Dan: a new fable of the grasshopper and the ant* ill. by Madeleine Gekiere. Lippincott, 1963. Subj: Behavior – saving things. Insects – ants. Insects – grasshoppers. Poetry.

The monster den: or, Look what happened at my house — and to it ill. by Edward Gorey. Lippincott, 1966. ISBN 1-878093-35-5 Subj: Monsters. Poetry.

Scrappy, the pup ill. by Jane Miller. Lippincott, 1960. Subj: Animals – dogs. Behavior – growing up. Sleep.

Cibula, Matt S. *The contrary kid* ill. by Brian Strassburg. Zino Pr., 1995. ISBN 1-55933-177-1 Subj: Character traits – being different. Rhyming text.

Slumgullion, the executive pig: a tale told in rhyme of a swine in his prime ill. by Tamara L. Boudreau. Zino Pr., 1994. ISBN 1-55933-149-6 Subj: Animals – pigs. Rhyming text. Self-concept.

What's up with you, Taquandra Fu? ill. by Brian Strassburg. Zino Pr., 1997. ISBN 1-55933-212-3 Subj: Behavior. Character traits – individuality. Humorous stories. School.

Ciliotta, Claire. *"Why am I going to the hospital?"* by Claire Ciliotta & Carole Livingston; ill. by Dick Wilson. Lyle Stuart, 1982. ISBN 0-8184-0316-0 Subj: Hospitals. Illness.

Cimarusti, Marie Torres. *Peek-a-moo* ill. by Stephanie Peterson. Dutton, 1998. ISBN 0-525-46083-7 Subj: Activities – playing. Animals. Farms. Format, unusual – toy & movable books.

Cimino, Maria. *Who's there? Open the door* (Munari, Bruno)

Cinderella ill. by K. Y. Craft. SeaStar, 2000. ISBN 1-5871-7005-1 Subj: Family life – stepfamilies. Folk & fairy tales. Royalty – princes. Sibling rivalry.

Cisneros, Sandra. *Hairs = Pelitos* trans. & ill. by Terry Ybáñez. Knopf, 1994. ISBN 0-679-96171-2 Subj: Ethnic groups in the U.S. – Hispanic Americans. Family life. Foreign languages. Hair.

City ill. by Roser Capdevila. Firefly, 1986. ISBN 0-920303-45-5 Subj: Cities, towns. Format, unusual – board books. Wordless.

Civardi, Anne. *Potty time* ill. by Jonathan Langley. S&S, 1988. ISBN 0-671-65896-4 Subj: Behavior – growing up. Toilet training.

Things people do ill. by Stephen Cartwright; designed by Roger Priddy. Usborne, 1985. ISBN 0-86020-864-8 Subj: Activities – working. Careers. Games. Islands.

The wacky book of witches ill. by Graham Philpot. Cartwheel, 1991. ISBN 0-590-45094-8 Subj: Rhyming text. Witches.

Claret, Maria. *The chocolate rabbit* ill. by author. Barron's, 1985. ISBN 0-416-48260-0 Subj: Animals – rabbits. Behavior – carelessness. Eggs. Holidays – Easter.

Melissa Mouse ill. by author. Barron's, 1985. ISBN 0-8120-5623-X Subj: Animals – mice. Weddings.

Clark, Ann Nolan. *In my mother's house* ill. by Velino Herrera. Viking, 1941. Subj: Caldecott award honor books. Family life. Indians of North America – Tewa.

The little Indian basket maker ill. by Harrison Begay. Melmont, 1955. Subj: Activities – working. Indians of North America – Papago.

The little Indian pottery maker ill. by Don Perceval. Melmont, 1955. Subj: Activities – working. Indians of North America – Pueblo.

Tia Maria's garden ill. by Ezra Jack Keats. Viking, 1963. Subj: Desert.

Clark, Brenda. *Franklin and the baby* (Moore, Eva)

Franklin's Thanksgiving (Jennings, Sharon)

Clark, Elizabeth. *Father Christmas and the donkey* ill. by Jan Ormerod. Viking, 1993. ISBN 0-670-84811-5 Subj: Animals – donkeys. Character traits – kindness to animals. Holidays – Christmas. Santa Claus.

Clark, Garel. *see* Garlick, May

Clark, Harry. *The first story of the whale* ill. by author. Houghton Mifflin, 1938. Subj: Animals – whales. Games. Science.

Clark, Leonard. *Drums and trumpets: poetry for the youngest* ill. by Heather Copley. Bodley Head, 1979. ISBN 0-370-01010-X Subj: Nursery rhymes. Poetry.

Clark, Margaret. *The best of Æsop's fables* (Æsop)

Clark, Roberta. *Why?* ill. by Lois Axeman. Childrens Pr., 1983. ISBN 0-516-06594-7 Subj: Character traits – curiosity. Character traits – questioning.

Clark, Sue. *Bodies* ill. by author. Hyperion, 1994. ISBN 0-7868-0035-6 (set) Subj: Anatomy. Format, unusual – board books. Self-concept.

Clothes ill. by author. Hyperion, 1994. ISBN 0-7868-0035-6 (set) Subj: Clothing. Format, unusual – board books. Self-concept.

Faces ill. by author. Hyperion, 1994. ISBN 0-7868-0035-6 (set) Subj: Anatomy – faces. Format, unusual – board books. Self-concept.

Feelings ill. by author. Hyperion, 1994. ISBN 0-7868-0035-6 (set) Subj: Emotions. Format, unusual – board books. Self-concept.

Clarke, Ginjer L. *Platypus!* ill. by Paul Mirocha. Random House, 2004. ISBN 0-375-92417-5 Subj: Animals – platypuses.

Sharks! ill. by Steven James Petruccio. Grosset, 2001. ISBN 0-448-42588-2 Subj: Fish – sharks.

Clarke, Gus. *Along came Eric* ill. by author. Lothrop, 1991. ISBN 0-688-10301-4 Subj: Babies. Family life – brothers. Family life – new sibling. Sibling rivalry.

Eddie and Teddy ill. by author. Lothrop, 1991. ISBN 0-688-10039-2 Subj: Friendship. School – first day. Toys – bears.

How many days to my birthday? ill. by author. Lothrop, 1992. ISBN 0-688-11237-4 Subj: Birthdays. Character traits – patience. Character traits – questioning. Days of the week, months of the year.

Ten green monsters ill. by author. Western, 1994. ISBN 0-307-17605-3 Subj: Counting, numbers. Format, unusual – toy & movable books. Monsters. Rhyming text.

Claude-Lafontaine, Pascale. *Monsieur Bussy, the celebrated hamster* ill. by Annick Delhumeau. McGraw-Hill, 1968. Subj: Animals – hamsters. Character traits – ambition.

Clavel, Bernard. *Castle of books* ill. by Yan Nascimbene. Chronicle, 2001. ISBN 0-8118-3501-4 Subj: Castles. Family life. Poetry.

Claverie, Jean. *The party* ill. by author. Crown, 1986. ISBN 0-517-56026-7 Subj: Behavior – misbehavior. Parties.

The picnic ill. by author. Crown, 1986. ISBN 0-517-56025-9 Subj: Activities – picnicking. Weather – rain.

Shopping ill. by author. Crown, 1986. ISBN 0-517-56024-0 Subj: Family life. Shopping.

Working ill. by author. Crown, 1986. ISBN 0-517-56021-6 Subj: Activities – working. Family life – fathers. Weather – snow.

Claxton, Ernest. *A child's grace* (Burdekin, Harold)

Clay, Helen. *Ants* (Clay, Pat)

Beetles (Clay, Pat)

Clay, Pat. *Ants* by Pat & Helen Clay; ill. with photos. Global Lib. Mktg. Serv., 1984. ISBN 0-7136-2386-1 Subj: Insects – ants. Nature. Science.

Beetles by Pat & Helen Clay; photos by authors. A & C Black, 1983. Subj: Insects – beetles. Science.

Claybourne, Anna. *Insects* ill. with photos. Copper Beech, 2000. ISBN 0-7613-1215-3 Subj: Insects.

Clayton, Elaine. *Ella's trip to the museum* ill. by author. Crown, 1996. ISBN 0-517-70081-6 Subj: Activities – dancing. Art. Magic. Museums.

Pup in school ill. by author. Crown, 1993. ISBN 0-517-59086-7 Subj: Animals – dogs. Behavior – bullying. Character traits – meanness. Friendship. School.

The yeoman's daring daughter and the princes in the tower ill. by author. Crown, 1999. ISBN 0-517-70985-6 Subj: Behavior – running away. Foreign lands – England. Royalty – princes.

Clayton, Gordon. *Lamb* Written by Angela Royston; ill. by Jane Cradock-Watson; photos by Gordon Clayton. Lodestar, 1992. ISBN 0-525-67359-8 Subj: Animals – sheep. Behavior – growing up. Birth.

Clearman, Deborah. *The goose's tale* ill. by author. Whispering Coyote, 1996. ISBN 1-879085-85-2 Subj: Activities – flying. Birds – geese.

Cleary, Beverly. *The growing-up feet* ill. by DyAnne DiSalvo-Ryan. Morrow, 1987. ISBN 0-688-06620-8 Subj: Behavior – growing up. Family life. Multiple births – twins.

The hullabaloo ABC ill. by Ted Rand. Rev. ed. Morrow, 1998. ISBN 0-688-15183-3 Subj: ABC books. Farms. Noise, sounds. Rhyming text.

The hullabaloo ABC ill. by Earl Thollander. Parnassus, 1960. ISBN 0-8746-6048-3 Subj: ABC books. Farms. Noise, sounds. Rhyming text.

Janet's thingamajigs ill. by DyAnne DiSalvo-Ryan. Morrow, 1987. ISBN 0-688-06618-6 Subj: Behavior – collecting things. Behavior – growing up. Family life. Sibling rivalry.

Lucky Chuck ill. by J. Winslow Higginbottom. Morrow, 1984. ISBN 0-688-02738-5 Subj: Behavior – carelessness. Motorcycles. Safety. Transportation.

Petey's bedtime story ill. by David Small. Morrow, 1993. ISBN 0-688-10661-7 Subj: Bedtime. Family life.

The real hole ill. by DyAnne DiSalvo-Ryan. Morrow, 1986. ISBN 0-688-05851-5 Subj: Activities – digging. Multiple births – twins. Problem solving. Trees.

Two dog biscuits ill. by DyAnne DiSalvo-Ryan. Morrow, 1986. ISBN 0-688-05848-5 Subj: Animals – cats. Animals – dogs. Multiple births – twins.

Cleaver, Elizabeth. *ABC* ill. by author. Atheneum, 1985. ISBN 0-689-31072-2 Subj: ABC books.

The enchanted caribou ill. by author. Atheneum, 1985. ISBN 0-689-31170-2 Subj: Animals – reindeer. Folk & fairy tales. Foreign lands – Canada. Indians of North America – Inuit. Magic. Puppets.

Clem, Tricia. *Great beginnings: the story of God's creation* (Foreman, Juli)

Clemens, Samuel. *see* Twain, Mark

Clément, Claude. *Be careful, Little Antelope* (Jensen, Patricia)

Be patient, Little Chick (Jensen, Patricia)

Gentle Little Lion (Jensen, Patricia)

Go to sleep, little groundhog (Jensen, Patricia)

The hungry duckling ill. by Marcelle Geneste. Reader's Digest, 1992. ISBN 0-89577-418-6 Subj: Animals. Birds – ducks. Character traits – being different. Food.

Kitty's special job (Jensen, Patricia)

Little Donkey learns to help (Jensen, Patricia)

Little Squirrel's special nest (Jensen, Patricia)

The man who lit the stars ill. by John Howe. Little, 1992. ISBN 0-316-14741-9 Subj: Homeless. Stars.

The painter and the wild swans ill. by Frédéric Clément. Dial, 1986. ISBN 0-8037-0268-X Subj: Birds – swans. Folk & fairy tales.

The voice of the wood ill. by Frédéric Clément. Dial, 1989. ISBN 0-8037-0635-9 Subj: Music. Musical instruments – cellos. Trees.

Clement, Gary. *Just stay put: a Chelm story* ill. by author. Firefly, 1996. ISBN 0-88899-239-4 Subj: Folk & fairy tales. Foreign lands – Poland. Jewish culture.

Clement, Rod. *Frank's great museum adventure* ill. by author. HarperCollins, 1999. ISBN 0-06-027674-6 Subj: Animals – dogs. Museums.

Grandpa's teeth ill. by author. HarperCollins, 1998. ISBN 0-06-027671-1 Subj: Family life – grandfathers. Mystery stories. Teeth.

Just another ordinary day ill. by author. HarperCollins, 1997. ISBN 0-06-027666-5 Subj: Animals. Humorous stories. School.

Clement-Davies, David. *Spirit: stallion of the Cimarron* ill. by William Maughan. Dutton, 2002. ISBN 0-525-46735-1 Subj: Animals – horses, ponies. Indians of North America. U.S. history – frontier & pioneer life.

Clements, Andrew. *The beast and the boy* (Mostacchi, Massimo)

Big Al and Shrimpy ill. by Yoshi. S&S, 2002. ISBN 0-689-84247-3 Subj: Concepts – size. Fish. Friendship.

Brave as a tiger (Palecek, Libuse)

Brave Norman ill. by Ellen Beier. S&S, 2001. ISBN 0-689-82914-0 Subj: Animals – dogs. Handicaps – blindness.

Bright Christmas: an angel remembers ill. by Kate Kiesler. Clarion, 1996. ISBN 0-395-72096-6 Subj: Angels. Holidays – Christmas. Religion – Nativity.

The Christmas teddy bear (Gantschev, Ivan)

Circus family dog ill. by Sue Truesdell. Clarion, 2000. ISBN 0-395-78648-7 Subj: Animals – dogs. Circus.

A dog's best friend (Mostacchi, Massimo)

Dolores and the big fire ill. by Ellen Beier. S&S, 2002. ISBN 0-689-82916-7 Subj: Animals – cats. Pets.

Double trouble in Walla Walla ill. by Sal Murdocca. Millbrook, 1997. ISBN 0-7613-0275-1 Subj: Humorous stories. Language. School.

Good morning, good night (Gantschev, Ivan)

Little pig, big trouble (Tharlet, Eve)

Mother Earth's counting book ill. by Lonni Sue Johnson. Picture Book Studio, 1990. ISBN 0-88708-138-X Subj: Counting, numbers. Earth.

Santa's secret helper ill. by Debrah Santini. Picture Book Studio, 1990. ISBN 0-88708-136-3 Subj: Character traits – helpfulness. Holidays – Christmas. Santa Claus.

Slippers at home ill. by Janie Bynum. Dutton, 2004. ISBN 0-525-47138-3 Subj: Animals – babies. Animals – dogs. Homes, houses.

Tara and Tiree, fearless friends ill. by Ellen Beier. S&S, 2002. ISBN 0-689-82917-5 Subj: Animals – dogs. Foreign lands – Canada. Pets.

Temple cat ill. by Kate Kiesler. Clarion, 1996. ISBN 0-395-69842-1 Subj: Animals – cats. Behavior – running away. Foreign lands – Egypt.

Temple cat ill. by Alan Marks. Picture Book Studio, 1991. ISBN 0-88708-184-3 Subj: Animals – cats. Behavior – running away. Foreign lands – Egypt.

Where is Mr. Mole? (Gantschev, Ivan)

Workshop ill. by David Wisniewski. Clarion, 1998. ISBN 0-395-85579-9 Subj: Merry-go-rounds. Tools.

Clemesha, David. *My dog Toby* (Zimmerman, Andrea Griffing)

Trashy town (Zimmerman, Andrea Griffing)

Clemson, David. *Patterns* (Bulloch, Ivan)

Clemson, Wendy. *Patterns* (Bulloch, Ivan)

Cleveland, David. *The April rabbits* ill. by Nurit Karlin. Coward, 1978. ISBN 0-698-20463-8 Subj: Animals – rabbits. Counting, numbers.

Cleveland-Peck, Patricia. *City cat, country cat* ill. by Gilly Marklew. Morrow, 1992. ISBN 0-688-11645-0 Subj: Animals – cats. Behavior – sharing. Cities, towns. Country. Pets.

Clewes, Dorothy. *Happiest day* ill. by Sofia. Coward, 1959. Subj: Emotions – loneliness. School.

Henry Hare's boxing match ill. by Patricia W. Turner. Coward, 1950. Subj: Animals. Behavior – imitation.

Hide and seek ill. by Sofia. Coward, 1960. Subj: Farms.

The wild wood ill. by Irene Hawkins. Coward, 1948. Subj: Animals. Character traits – kindness to animals.

Clibbon, Lucy. *Imagine you're a fairy!* (Clibbon, Meg)

Imagine you're a mermaid! (Clibbon, Meg)

Imagine you're a pirate! (Clibbon, Meg)

Imagine you're a wizard! (Clibbon, Meg)

Clibbon, Meg. *Imagine you're a fairy!* by Meg Clibbon & Lucy Clibbon; ill. by Lucy Clibbon. Annick, 2002. ISBN 1-55037-743-4 Subj: Fairies. Imagination.

Imagine you're a mermaid! by Meg Clibbon & Lucy Clibbon; ill. by Lucy Clibbon. Annick, 2002. ISBN 1-55037-791-4 Subj: Imagination. Mythical creatures – mermaids, mermen.

Imagine you're a pirate! by Meg Clibbon & Lucy Clibbon; ill. by Lucy Clibbon. Annick, 2002. ISBN 1-55037-741-8 Subj: Imagination. Pirates.

Imagine you're a wizard! by Meg Clibbon & Lucy Clibbon; ill. by Lucy Clibbon. Annick, 2002. ISBN 1-55037-793-0 Subj: Imagination. Wizards.

Clifford, David. *Your face is a picture* (Clifford, Eth)

Clifford, Eth. *A bear before breakfast* ill. by Kelly Oechsli. Putnam, 1962. Subj: Communication. Language.

Red is never a mouse ill. by Bill Heckler. Bobbs-Merrill, 1960. Subj: Concepts – color. Poetry.

Your face is a picture by Eth & David Clifford; photos by David Clifford; ed. consultant: Leo Fay. E. C. Seale, 1963. Subj: Emotions. Ethnic groups in the U.S.

Clifton, Lucille. *All us come cross the water* ill. by John Steptoe. Holt, 1973. ISBN 0-03-091976-2 Subj: Character traits – pride. Ethnic groups in the U.S. – African Americans. School.

Amifika ill. by Thomas di Grazia. Dutton, 1977. ISBN 0-525-25548-6 Subj: Emotions – fear. Ethnic groups in the U.S. – African Americans. Family life. Family life – fathers.

The boy who didn't believe in spring ill. by Brinton Turkle. Dutton, 1973. ISBN 0-525-27145-7 Subj: Cities, towns. Ethnic groups in the U.S. – African Americans. Seasons – spring.

Don't you remember? ill. by Evaline Ness. Dutton, 1973. ISBN 0-525-28840-6 Subj: Birthdays. Ethnic groups in the U.S. – African Americans. Family life. Memories, memory.

Everett Anderson's Christmas coming ill. by Evaline Ness. Holt, 1971. ISBN 0-03-080219-9 Subj: Cities, towns. Ethnic groups in the U.S. – African Americans. Holidays – Christmas. Poetry.

Everett Anderson's friend ill. by Ann Grifalconi. Holt, 1992. ISBN 0-8050-2246-5 Subj: Ethnic groups in the U.S. – African Americans. Friendship. Rhyming text.

Everett Anderson's goodbye ill. by Ann Grifalconi. Holt, 1988, 1983. ISBN 0-8050-0800-4 Subj: Death. Emotions – grief. Emotions – love. Ethnic groups in the U.S. – African Americans. Family life. Rhyming text.

Everett Anderson's nine months long ill. by Ann Grifalconi. Holt, 1987, 1970. ISBN 0-03-043536-6 Subj: Babies. Ethnic groups in the U.S. – African Americans. Family life – new sibling. Rhyming text.

Everett Anderson's 1-2-3 ill. by Ann Grifalconi. Holt, 1977. ISBN 0-03-017441-4 Subj: Ethnic groups in the U.S. – African Americans. Family life. Rhyming text.

Everett Anderson's year ill. by Ann Grifalconi. Holt, 1992. ISBN 0-8050-2310-0 Subj: Ethnic groups in the U.S. – African Americans. Rhyming text. Seasons.

Good, says Jerome ill. by Stephanie Douglas. Dutton, 1973. ISBN 0-525-30865-2 Subj: Emotions – fear. Ethnic groups in the U.S. – African Americans. Family life. Moving.

My brother fine with me ill. by Moneta Barnett. Holt, 1975. ISBN 0-03-014171-0 Subj: Behavior – running away. Ethnic groups in the U.S. – African Americans. Family life. Sibling rivalry.

My friend Jacob ill. by Thomas di Grazia. Dutton, 1980. ISBN 0-525-35487-5 Subj: Character traits – helpfulness. Ethnic groups in the U.S. – African Americans. Friendship. Handicaps.

One of the problems of Everett Anderson ill. by Ann Grifalconi. Holt, 2001. ISBN 0-8050-5201-1 Subj: Child abuse. Ethnic groups in the U.S. – African Americans. Rhyming text.

Some of the days of Everett Anderson ill. by Evaline Ness. Holt, 1987, 1970. ISBN 0-03-084404-5 Subj: Days of the week, months of the year. Ethnic groups in the U.S. – African Americans. Family life. Poetry.

Three wishes ill. by Stephanie Douglas. Viking, 1976. ISBN 0-670-71063-6 Subj: Behavior – wishing. Ethnic groups in the U.S. – African Americans. Friendship.

Three wishes ill. by Michael Hays. Doubleday, 1992. ISBN 0-385-30497-8 Subj: Behavior – wishing. Ethnic groups in the U.S. – African Americans. Friendship.

Climo, Lindee. *Chester's barn* ill. by author. Tundra, 1982. ISBN 0-88776-132-1 Subj: Barns. Farms. Foreign lands – Canada.

Clyde ill. by author. Tundra, 1986. ISBN 0-88776-185-2 Subj: Animals – horses, ponies. Behavior – seeking better things. Machines.

Climo, Shirley. *The adventure of Walter* ill. by Ingrid Fetz. Atheneum, 1965. Subj: Animals – whales. Character traits – curiosity.

The cobweb Christmas ill. by Joe Lasker. Crowell, 1982. ISBN 0-690-04216-7 Subj: Animals. Holidays – Christmas. Magic. Spiders.

The Egyptian Cinderella ill. by Ruth Heller. HarperCollins, 1989. ISBN 0-690-04824-6 Subj: Family life – stepfamilies. Folk & fairy tales. Foreign lands – Egypt. Royalty. Sibling rivalry.

The Irish Cinderlad ill. by Loretta Krupinski. HarperCollins, 1996. ISBN 0-06-024397-X Subj: Animals – bulls, cows. Folk & fairy tales. Foreign lands – Ireland.

King of the birds ill. by Ruth Heller. HarperCollins, 1988. ISBN 0-690-04623-5 Subj: Birds. Character traits – cleverness. Royalty.

The Korean Cinderella ill. by Ruth Heller. HarperCollins, 1993. ISBN 0-06-020433-8 Subj: Family life – stepfamilies. Folk & fairy tales. Foreign lands – Korea. Royalty. Sibling rivalry.

The little red ant and the great big crumb: a Mexican fable ill. by Francisco X. Mora. Clarion, 1995. ISBN 0-395-70732-3 Subj: Animals. Foreign lands – Mexico. Insects – ants. Self-concept.

The match between the winds ill. by Roni Shepherd. Macmillan, 1991. ISBN 0-02-719035-8 Subj: Folk & fairy tales. Foreign lands – Borneo. Weather – wind.

The Persian Cinderella ill. by Robert Florczak. HarperCollins, 1999. ISBN 0-06-026765-8 Subj: Fairies. Family life – stepfamilies. Folk & fairy tales. Foreign lands – Persia. Royalty – princes. Sibling rivalry.

Stolen thunder: a Norse myth ill. by Alexander Koshkin. Clarion, 1994. ISBN 0-395-64368-6 Subj: Folk & fairy tales. Foreign lands. Mythical creatures. Weather – lightning, thunder.

Cline-Ransome, Lesa. *Quilt alphabet* ill. by James E. Ransome. Holiday, 2001. ISBN 0-8234-1453-1 Subj: ABC books. Country. Poetry. Quilts. Rhyming text.

Quilt counting ill. by James E. Ransome. SeaStar, 2002. ISBN 1-58717-178-3 Subj: Counting, numbers. Country. Quilts. Rhyming text.

Clinton, Susan. *I can be an architect.* Childrens Pr., 1986. ISBN 0-516-01890-6 Subj: Careers – architects.

Clise, Michele Durkson. *Ophelia's bedtime book* photos by Marsha Burns. Viking, 1994. ISBN 0-670-85310-0 Subj: Bedtime. Night. Poetry. Sleep. Toys – bears.

Clithero, Myrtle E. *see* Clithero, Sally

Clithero, Sally. *Beginning-to-read poetry* ill. by Erik Blegvad. Follett, 1967. Subj: Poetry.

Clymer, Eleanor Lowenton. *The tiny little house* ill. by Ingrid Fetz. Atheneum, 1964. Subj: Homes, houses.

A yard for John ill. by Mildred Boyle. McBride, 1943. Subj: Moving.

Clymer, Ted. *The horse and the bad morning* by Ted Clymer & Miska Miles; ill. by Leslie Holt Morrill. Dutton, 1982. ISBN 0-525-45103-X Subj: Animals. Behavior – dissatisfaction. Problem solving.

Cneut, Carll. *The amazing love story of Mr. Morf* ill. by author. Clarion, 2003. ISBN 0-618-33170-0 Subj: Animals. Animals – dogs. Circus. Friendship. Insects – fleas.

Coats, Laura Jane. *Alphabet garden* ill. by author. Macmillan, 1993. ISBN 0-02-719042-0 Subj: ABC books. Gardens, gardening.

City cat ill. by author. Macmillan, 1987. ISBN 0-02-719051-X Subj: Animals – cats. Cities, towns.

Marcella and the moon ill. by author. Macmillan, 1986. ISBN 0-02-719050-1 Subj: Activities – painting. Birds – ducks. Moon.

Mr. Jordan in the park ill. by author. Macmillan, 1988. ISBN 0-02-719053-6 Subj: Behavior – growing up. Old age. Parks.

The oak tree ill. by author. Macmillan, 1987. ISBN 0-02-719052-8 Subj: Trees.

Ten little animals ill. by author. Macmillan, 1990. ISBN 0-02-719054-4 Subj: Animals. Counting, numbers. Rhyming text.

Coats, Lucy. *Bedtime for Rosie Rabbit* (Yee, Patrick)

Neil's numberless world ill. by Neal Layton. DK, 2000. ISBN 0-7894-6354-7 Subj: Birthdays. Clocks, watches. Counting, numbers. Magic.

One hungry baby: a bedtime counting rhyme ill. by Sue Hellard. Crown, 1994. ISBN 0-517-59887-6 Subj: Animals – babies. Babies. Bedtime. Counting, numbers. Rhyming text.

Coatsworth, Elizabeth. *The children come running: UNICEF greeting cards.* Golden Pr., 1961. The illustrations [by Roger Duvoisin and others] . . . first appeared as UNICEF greeting cards. Subj: Holidays – Christmas. Rhyming text. UNICEF.

The giant golden book of cat stories ill. by Feodor Rojankovsky. S&S, 1953. Subj: Animals – cats. Folk & fairy tales. Rhyming text.

Good night ill. by José Aruego. Macmillan, 1972. Subj: Bedtime. Stars.

Lonely Maria ill. by Evaline Ness. Pantheon, 1960. Subj: Emotions – loneliness. Family life – grandfathers. Islands.

A peaceable kingdom, and other poems ill. by Fritz Eichenberg. Pantheon, 1958. Subj: Animals. Poetry.

Pika and the roses ill. by Kurt Wiese. Pantheon, 1959. Subj: Animals – rabbits. Character traits – cleverness.

Song of the camels: a Christmas poem ill. by Anna Vojtech. North-South, 1997. ISBN 1-55858-812-4 Subj: Animals – camels. Holidays – Christmas. Poetry. Religion.

Under the green willow ill. by Janina Domanska. Macmillan, 1971. ISBN 0-688-03846-8 Subj: Birds. Fish. Food.

Cobb, Abigail Jane. *Meet my grandmother. She's a children's book author* (McElroy, Lisa Tucker)

Cobb, Annie. *The long wait* ill. by Liza Woodruff. Kane Pr., 2000. ISBN 1-57565-094-0 Subj: Counting, numbers. Parks – amusement.

Wheels! ill. by Davy Jones. Random House, 1996. ISBN 0-679-96445-2 Subj: Rhyming text. Wheels.

Cobb, Vicki. *Feeding yourself* ill. by Marylin Hafner. HarperCollins, 1989. ISBN 0-397-32325-5 Subj: Behavior – growing up.

Getting dressed ill. by Marylin Hafner. HarperCollins, 1989. ISBN 0-397-32143-0 Subj: Behavior – growing up. Clothing.

How the doctor knows you're fine ill. by Anthony Ravielli. Lippincott, 1973. ISBN 0-397-31240-7 Subj: Careers – doctors. Health & fitness.

I fall down ill. by Julia Gorton. HarperCollins, 2004. ISBN 0-688-17843-X Subj: Concepts – weight. Science.

I get wet ill. by Julia Gorton. HarperCollins, 2002. ISBN 0-688-17839-1 Subj: Science. Water.

I see myself ill. by Julia Gorton. HarperCollins, 2002. ISBN 0-688-17837-5 Subj: Mirrors. Science.

Keeping clean ill. by Marylin Hafner. HarperCollins, 1989. ISBN 0-397-32313-1 Subj: Character traits – cleanliness.

Lots of rot ill. by Brian Schatell. Lippincott, 1981. ISBN 0-397-31939-8 Subj: Science.

Open your eyes ill. by Cynthia C. Lewis. Millbrook, 2002. ISBN 0-7613-1705-8 Subj: Anatomy – eyes. Science. Senses – sight.

Writing it down ill. by Marylin Hafner. HarperCollins, 1989. ISBN 0-397-32327-1 Subj: Activities – writing.

Cobbett, Richard. *see* Pluckrose, Henry Arthur

Cober, Alan E. *Cober's choice* ill. by author. Dutton, 1979. ISBN 0-525-28065-0 Subj: Animals. Art.

Coburn, Jewell Reinhart. *Angkat: the Cambodian Cinderella* ill. by Eddie Flotte. Shen's Bks., 1998. ISBN 1-885008-09-0 Subj: Family life – stepfamilies. Folk & fairy tales. Foreign lands – Cambodia. Royalty – princes. Sibling rivalry.

Jouanah: a Hmong Cinderella adapt. by Jewell Reinhart Coburn with Tzexa Cherta Lee; ill. by Anne Sibley O'Brien. Shen's Bks., 1996. ISBN 1-885008-01-5 Subj: Family life – stepfamilies. Folk & fairy tales. Foreign lands. Royalty – princes. Sibling rivalry.

Cocagnac, A. M. (Augustin Maurice). *The three trees of the Samurai* adapt. from a Japanese no play; ill. by Alain Le Foll. Dial, 1970. ISBN 0-8252-0043-1 Subj: Folk & fairy tales. Foreign lands – Japan.

Cocca-Leffler, Maryann. *Bravery soup* ill. by author. A. Whitman, 2002. ISBN 0-8075-0870-5 Subj: Animals – bears. Animals – foxes. Animals – raccoons. Emotions – fear.

Bus route to Boston ill. by author. Boyds Mills, 2000. ISBN 1-56397-723-0 Subj: Activities – traveling. Buses. Cities, towns. Shopping.

Ice-cold birthday ill. by author. Grosset, 1992. ISBN 0-448-40381-1 Subj: Birthdays. Character traits – luck. Parties. Weather – snow. Weather – storms.

Jungle Halloween ill. by author. A. Whitman, 2000. ISBN 0-8075-4056-0 Subj: Animals. Holidays – Halloween. Rhyming text.

Missing: one stuffed rabbit ill. by author. A. Whitman, 1998. ISBN 0-8075-5161-9 Subj: Animals – rabbits. Behavior – lost. School. Toys.

Mr. Tanen's ties ill. by author. A. Whitman, 1999. ISBN 0-8075-5301-8 Subj: Careers – school principals. Clothing – neckties. School.

Wednesday is spaghetti day ill. by author. Scholastic, 1990. ISBN 0-590-42894-2 Subj: Activities – baking, cooking. Animals – cats. Days of the week, months of the year. Food.

Cock Robin. *The courtship, merry marriage, and feast of Cock Robin and Jenny Wren: to which is added the doleful death of Cock Robin* ill. by Barbara Cooney. Scribners, 1965. Subj: Animals. Birds – robins. Birds – wrens. Death. Nursery rhymes. Weddings.

Who killed Cock Robin? ill. by William Stobbs. Oxford Univ. Pr., 1990. ISBN 0-19-279862-6 Subj: Animals. Birds – robins. Birds – wrens. Death. Format, unusual – board books. Nursery rhymes.

Coco, Eugene Bradley. *The fiddler's son* ill. by Robert James Sabuda. Green Tiger Pr., 1988. ISBN 0-88138-111-X Subj: Music.

The wishing well ill. by Robert James Sabuda. Green Tiger Pr., 1988. ISBN 0-88138-112-8 Subj: Behavior – greed. Behavior – wishing. Circular tales. Magic.

Coe, Lloyd. *Charcoal* ill. by author. Crowell, 1946. Subj: Animals – sheep.

Coerr, Eleanor. *The big balloon race* ill. by Carolyn Croll. Harper-Collins, 1992. ISBN 0-06-021353-1 Subj: Activities – ballooning.

Chang's paper pony ill. by Deborah Kogan Ray. HarperCollins, 1988. ISBN 0-06-021329-9 Subj: Animals – horses, ponies. Ethnic groups in the U.S. – Chinese Americans.

The Josefina story quilt ill. by Bruce Degen. HarperCollins, 1986. ISBN 0-06-021349-3 Subj: Activities – traveling. Birds – chickens. Pets. Quilts.

Sadako ill. by Ed Young. Putnam, 1993. ISBN 0-399-21771-1 Subj: Birds – cranes. Death. Foreign lands – Japan. Illness. War.

Coffelt, Nancy. *The dog who cried woof* ill. by author. Harcourt, 1995. ISBN 0-15-200201-4 Subj: Animals – cats. Animals – dogs. Noise, sounds.

Dogs in space ill. by author. Harcourt, 1993. ISBN 0-15-200440-8 Subj: Animals – dogs. Science. Space & space ships.

Good night, Sigmund ill. by author. Harcourt, 1992. ISBN 0-15-200464-5 Subj: Activities – playing. Animals – cats. Pets.

Coffey, Maria. *A cat adrift* ill. by Eugenie Fernandes. Annick, 2002. ISBN 1-55037-727-2 Subj: Animals – cats. Animals – rats. Sea & seashore.

A cat in a kayak ill. by Eugenie Fernandes. Annick, 1998. ISBN 1-55037-509-1 Subj: Animals. Animals – cats. Behavior – dissatisfaction. Pets.

A seal in the family ill. by Eugenie Fernandes. Annick, 1999. ISBN 1-55037-581-4 Subj: Animals – cats. Animals – seals. Careers – veterinarians. Character traits – kindness to animals.

Cohen, Barbara. *The binding of Isaac* ill. by Charles Mikolaycak. Lothrop, 1978. ISBN 0-688-51830-3 Subj: Religion.

The chocolate wolf ill. by David Ray. Philomel, 1996. ISBN 0-399-21961-7 Subj: Animals – rats. Animals – wolves. Behavior – running away.

The demon who would not die ill. by Anatoly Ivanov. Atheneum, 1982. ISBN 0-689-30917-1 Subj: Folk & fairy tales. Foreign lands – Russia. Monsters.

The donkey's story ill. by Susan Jeanne Cohen. Lothrop, 1988. ISBN 0-688-04105-1 Subj: Animals – donkeys. Religion.

Even higher ill. by Anatoly Ivanov. Lothrop, 1987. ISBN 0-688-06453-1 Subj: Character traits – generosity. Holidays. Jewish culture.

First fast ill. by Martin Lemelman. UAHC Pr., 1987. ISBN 0-8074-0354-7 Subj: Holidays – Yom Kippur. Jewish culture. Religion.

Gooseberries to oranges ill. by Beverly Brodsky McDermott. Lothrop, 1982. ISBN 0-688-00691-4 Subj: Jewish culture. Moving.

Here come the Purim players! ill. by Beverly Brodsky McDermott. Lothrop, 1984. ISBN 0-688-02108-5 Subj: Folk & fairy tales. Holidays – Purim. Jewish culture. Middle Ages.

Here come the Purim players! ill. by Shoshana Mekibel. UAHC Pr., 1998. ISBN 0-8074-0645-7 Subj: Foreign lands – Czechoslovakia. Holidays – Purim. Jewish culture. Religion.

Make a wish, Molly ill. by Jan Naimo Jones. Doubleday, 1994. ISBN 0-385-31079-X Subj: Behavior – misunderstanding. Birthdays. Ethnic groups in the U.S. – Russian Americans. Friendship. Jewish culture. Parties.

Cohen, Burton. *Nelson makes a face* ill. by William Schroder. Lothrop, 1978. ISBN 0-688-51850-8 Subj: Character traits – appearance.

Cohen, Carol L. *Wake up, groundhog!* ill. by author. Crown, 1975. ISBN 0-517-51693-4 Subj: Animals – groundhogs. Clocks, watches. Hibernation. Holidays – Groundhog Day. Seasons – spring.

Cohen, Caron Lee. *Bronco dogs* ill. by Roni Shepherd. Dutton, 1991. ISBN 0-525-44721-0 Subj: Animals – dogs. Cowboys, cowgirls. Crime. Ghosts. U.S. history – frontier & pioneer life.

Digger Pig and the turnip ill. by Christopher Denise. Harcourt, 2000. ISBN 0-15-202524-3 Subj: Animals. Behavior – sharing. Character traits – laziness. Cumulative tales. Folk & fairy tales.

Happy to you! ill. by Rosanne Litzinger. Clarion, 2001. ISBN 0-689-82421-1 Subj: Babies. Emotions – happiness. Family life – mothers.

Martin and the giant lions ill. by Elizabeth Sayles. Clarion, 2002. ISBN 0-618-04908-8 Subj: Animals – lions. Dreams. Imagination. Night. Parks.

The mud pony: a traditional Skidi Pawnee tale ill. by Shonto Begay. Scholastic, 1988. ISBN 0-590-41525-5 Subj: Animals – horses, ponies. Folk & fairy tales. Indians of North America – Pawnee.

Pigeon, pigeon ill. by G. Brian Karas. Dutton, 1992. ISBN 0-525-44866-7 Subj: Animals. Concepts – perspective. Zoos.

Renata, Whizbrain and the ghost ill. by Blanche Sims. Atheneum, 1987. ISBN 0-689-31271-1 Subj: Character traits – cleverness. Ghosts. Tall tales.

Sally Ann Thunder Ann Whirlwind Crockett ill. by Ariane Dewey. Greenwillow, 1985. ISBN 0-688-04007-1 Subj: Behavior – trickery. Tall tales.

Three yellow dogs ill. by Peter Sis. Greenwillow, 1986. ISBN 0-688-06231-8 Subj: Animals – dogs. Language.

Where's the fly? ill. by Nancy Barnet. Greenwillow, 1996. ISBN 0-688-14045-9 Subj: Concepts – perspective.

Whiffle Squeek ill. by Ted Rand. Dodd, 1987. ISBN 0-396-08999-2 Subj: Animals – cats. Monsters. Rhyming text. Sea & seashore.

Cohen, Daniel. *America's very own monsters* ill. by Tom Huffman. Dodd, 1982. ISBN 0-396-08069-3 Subj: Monsters.

Apatosaurus ill. with photos. Bridgestone, 2001. ISBN 0-7368-0616-4 Subj: Dinosaurs. Fossils.

Dinosaurs ill. by Jean Zallinger. Doubleday, 1987. ISBN 0-385-23415-5 Subj: Dinosaurs. Prehistory.

Pteranodon ill. with photos. Bridgestone, 2001. ISBN 0-7368-0612-2 Subj: Dinosaurs. Fossils.

Stegosaurus ill. with photos. Bridgestone, 2001. ISBN 0-7368-0618-0 Subj: Dinosaurs. Fossils.

Triceratops ill. with photos. Bridgestone, 2001. ISBN 0-7368-0619-9 Subj: Dinosaurs. Fossils.

Tyrannosaurus rex ill. with photos. Bridgestone, 2001. ISBN 0-7368-0620-2 Subj: Dinosaurs. Fossils.

Velociraptor ill. with photos. Bridgestone, 2001. ISBN 0-7368-0621-0 Subj: Dinosaurs. Fossils.

Cohen, Deborah Bodin. *The seventh day* ill. by Melanie Hall. Kar-Ben Copies, 2005. ISBN 0-929371-24-0 Subj: Creation. Religion.

Cohen, Miriam. *Bee my Valentine!* ill. by Lillian Hoban. Greenwillow, 1978. ISBN 0-688-84129-5 Subj: Holidays – Valentine's Day. School.

Best friends ill. by Lillian Hoban. Aladdin, 1989, c1971. ISBN 0-689-71334-7 Subj: Friendship. School.

Don't eat too much turkey! ill. by Lillian Hoban. Greenwillow, 1987. ISBN 0-688-07142-2 Subj: Behavior – sharing. School.

Down in the subway ill. by Melanie Hope Greenberg. DK, 1998. ISBN 0-7894-2510-6 Subj: Cities, towns. Foreign lands – Caribbean Islands. Imagination. Songs. Trains.

Eddy's dream photos by Adam Cohen. Star Bright, 2000. ISBN 1-887734-57-0 Subj: Behavior. Dreams. Imagination. School.

First grade takes a test ill. by Lillian Hoban. Greenwillow, 1980. ISBN 0-688-84265-8 Subj: Friendship. School.

It's George! ill. by Lillian Hoban. Greenwillow, 1988. ISBN 0-688-06813-8 Subj: Character traits – being different. School.

Jim meets the thing ill. by Lillian Hoban. Greenwillow, 1981. ISBN 0-688-00617-5 Subj: Behavior – growing up. Emotions – fear. Monsters. School.

Jim's dog Muffins ill. by Lillian Hoban. Greenwillow, 1984. ISBN 0-688-02565-X Subj: Animals – dogs. Death. Emotions – grief. Pets.

Liar, liar, pants on fire! ill. by Lillian Hoban. Greenwillow, 1985. ISBN 0-688-04245-7 Subj: Behavior – lying. Character traits – generosity. Friendship. School.

Lost in the museum ill. by Lillian Hoban. Greenwillow, 1979. ISBN 0-688-84187-2 Subj: Behavior – lost. Museums. School – field trips.

Mimmy and Sophie ill. by Thomas F. Yezerski. Farrar, 1998. ISBN 0-374-34988-6 Subj: Ethnic groups in the U.S. – Russian Americans. Family life. Family life – sisters. Immigrants.

The new teacher ill. by Lillian Hoban. Macmillan, 1972. ISBN 0-02-042390-X Subj: School.

No good in art ill. by Lillian Hoban. Greenwillow, 1980. ISBN 0-688-80234-6 Subj: Art. School. Self-concept.

The real-skin rubber monster mask ill. by Lillian Hoban. Greenwillow, 1990. ISBN 0-688-09123-7 Subj: Emotions – fear. Holidays – Halloween. Masks. School.

See you in second grade! ill. by Lillian Hoban. Greenwillow, 1989. ISBN 0-688-07139-2 Subj: Friendship. School. Sea & seashore.

See you tomorrow ill. by Lillian Hoban. Greenwillow, 1983. ISBN 0-688-01805-X Subj: Handicaps – blindness. School. Senses – sight.

So what? ill. by Lillian Hoban. Greenwillow, 1982. ISBN 0-688-01203-5 Subj: School. Self-concept.

Starring first grade ill. by Lillian Hoban. Greenwillow, 1985. ISBN 0-688-04030-6 Subj: Behavior – misbehavior. School. Theater.

Tough Jim ill. by Lillian Hoban. Macmillan, 1974. ISBN 0-02-722760-X Subj: Behavior – bullying. Parties. School.

When will I read? ill. by Lillian Hoban. Greenwillow, 1977. ISBN 0-688-84073-6 Subj: Books, reading. School.

Will I have a friend? ill. by Lillian Hoban. Macmillan, 1967. ISBN 0-689-71333-9 Subj: Ethnic groups in the U.S. Friendship. School – first day.

Cohen, Nora. *From apple to zipper* ill. by Donna Kern. Aladdin, 1993. ISBN 0-689-71708-3 Subj: ABC books. Rhyming text.

Cohen, Paul. *Creepy crawly critter riddles* (Bernstein, Joanne E.)

What was the wicked witch's real name? and other character riddles (Bernstein, Joanne E.)

Cohen, Peter Zachary. *Authorized autumn charts of the Upper Red Canoe River country* ill. by Tomie de Paola. Atheneum, 1972. Subj: ABC books. Boats, ships. Games. Seasons – fall.

Boris's glasses ill. by Olof Landström; tr. by Joan Sandin. Farrar, 2003. ISBN 91-29-65942-6 Subj: Animals. Animals – hamsters. Glasses.

Olson's meat pies trans. by Richard E. Fisher, ill. by Olof Landström. Farrar, 1989. ISBN 9-129-59180-5 Subj: Behavior – mistakes. Food.

Cohen, Ron. *My dad's baseball* ill. by author. Lothrop, 1994. ISBN 0-688-12391-0 Subj: Family life – fathers. Sports – baseball.

Cohn, Diana. *Dream carver* ill. by Amy Córdova. Chronicle, 2002. ISBN 0-8118-1244-8 Subj: Animals. Art. Careers – woodcarvers. Foreign lands – Mexico.

Cohn, Janice I. *I had a friend named Peter: talking to children about the death of a friend* ill. by Gail Owens. Morrow, 1987. ISBN 0-688-06686-0 Subj: Death. Emotions – grief. Friendship.

Molly's rosebush ill. by Gail Owens. A. Whitman, 1994. ISBN 0-8075-5213-5 Subj: Babies. Death. Emotions – grief. Family life. Plants.

"Why did it happen?" helping young children cope in a violent world ill. by Gail Owens. Morrow, 1994. ISBN 0-688-12313-9 Subj: Behavior – stealing. Crime. Emotions – anger. Violence, nonviolence.

Cohn, Norma. *Brother and sister* ill. by author. Oxford Univ. Pr., 1942. Subj: Animals – cats. Sports – swimming.

Coker, Gylbert. *Naptime* ill. by author. Delacorte, 1978. ISBN 0-440-06304-3 Subj: School – nursery. Sleep.

Colandro, Lucille. *There was a cold lady who swallowed some snow!* ill. by Jared Lee. Scholastic, 2003. ISBN 0-439-47109-5 Subj: Cumulative tales. Rhyming text. Snowmen. Weather – snow.

Colborn, Mary Palenick. *Rainy day slug* ill. by Lorie Ann Grover. Sasquatch, 2000. ISBN 1-57061-238-2 Subj: Animals – slugs. Rhyming text. Weather – rain.

Colby, C. B. (Carroll Burleigh). *Who lives there?* ill. by author. Atheneum, 1953. Subj: Animals. Birds. Homes, houses. Insects. Science.

Who went there? ill. by author. Atheneum, 1953. Subj: Animals. Birds. Reptiles. Science.

Coldrey, Jennifer. *Danger colors* (Oxford Scientific Films)

Hide and seek (Oxford Scientific Films)

Penguins photos by Douglas Allan & others. André Deutsch, 1983. ISBN 0-233-97524-1 Subj: Birds – penguins.

The world of chickens ill. with photos. G. Stevens, 1987. ISBN 1-55532-071-6 Subj: Birds – chickens. Science.

The world of crabs photos by Oxford Scientific Films. G. Stevens, 1986. ISBN 1-55532-063-5 Subj: Crustaceans – crabs. Science.

The world of frogs photos by Oxford Scientific Films. G. Stevens, 1986. ISBN 1-55532-024-4 Subj: Frogs & toads. Science.

The world of rabbits photos by Oxford Scientific Films. G. Stevens, 1986. ISBN 1-55532-064-3 Subj: Animals – rabbits. Science.

The world of squirrels photos by Oxford Scientific Films. G. Stevens, 1986. ISBN 1-55532-065-1 Subj: Animals – squirrels. Science.

Cole, Annette. *see* Steiner, Barbara (Annette)

Cole, Babette. *Babette Cole's beastly birthday book* by Babette Cole with Ron Van der Meer; ill. by Babette Cole. Doubleday, 1991. ISBN 0-385-41679-2 Subj: Birthdays. Format, unusual – toy & movable books. Rhyming text.

Babette Cole's brother ill. by author; paper engineered by Raphael Rangel. WH Books, 1997. ISBN 0-4348-0101-1 Subj: Family life – brothers. Format, unusual – toy & movable books. Rhyming text.

Babette Cole's ponies ill. by author; paper engineered by Bruce Reifel. Warner, 1995. ISBN 0-4469-1071-6 Subj: Animals – horses, ponies. Format, unusual – toy & movable books. Rhyming text.

The bad good manners book ill. by author. Dial, 1996. ISBN 0-8037-2006-8 Subj: Etiquette. Rhyming text.

Bad habits! or, The taming of Lucretzia Crum ill. by author. Dial, 1999. ISBN 0-8037-2432-2 Subj: Behavior – misbehavior. School.

Cupid ill. by author. Putnam, 1990. ISBN 0-399-22215-4 Subj: Emotions – love. Mythical creatures.

Dad ill. by author; paper engineered by Bruce Reifel. WH Books, 1997. ISBN 0-4348-0100-3 Subj: Family life – fathers. Format, unusual – toy & movable books. Rhyming text.

Dr. Dog ill. by author. Knopf, 1997. ISBN 0-679-86720-1 Subj: Animals – dogs. Character traits – cleanliness. Health & fitness. Hygiene.

Don't go out tonight ill. by author. Doubleday, 1982. Folding book; 31 x 127 cm. full size, folded to 31 cm. ISBN 0-385-18090-X Subj: Format, unusual – toy & movable books. Illness – measles. Witches.

The hairy book ill. by author. Random House, 1985. ISBN 0-394-97026-8 Subj: Hair. Rhyming text.

Hurray for Ethelyn ill. by author. Little, 1991. ISBN 0-316-15189-0 Subj: Animals – rats. Behavior – bullying. Emotions – envy, jealousy.

King Change-A-Lot ill. by author. Putnam, 1989. ISBN 0-399-21670-7 Subj: Behavior – dissatisfaction. Royalty – kings. Royalty – princes.

Lady Lupin's book of etiquette ill. by author. Peachtree, 2001. ISBN 1-56145-257-2 Subj: Animals – babies. Animals – dogs. Etiquette.

Mommy laid an egg! or where do babies come from? ill. by author. Chronicle, 1993. ISBN 0-8118-0350-3 Subj: Babies. Birth. Family life. Science.

Mum ill. by author; paper engineered by Renée Jablow. WH Books, 1997. ISBN 0-4348-0099-6 Subj: Family life – mothers. Format, unusual – toy & movable books. Rhyming text.

Nungu and the elephant ill. by author. McGraw-Hill, 1980. ISBN 0-07-011696-2 Subj: Animals – elephants. Foreign lands – Africa. Magic.

Nungu and the hippopotamus ill. by author. McGraw-Hill, 1979. ISBN 0-07-011695-4 Subj: Animals – hippopotamuses. Foreign lands – Africa.

Prince Cinders ill. by author. Putnam, 1988. ISBN 0-399-21502-6 Subj: Folk & fairy tales. Magic. Royalty – princes.

Princess Smartypants ill. by author. Putnam, 1987. ISBN 0-399-21409-7 Subj: Pets. Problem solving. Royalty – princesses.

The silly book ill. by author. Doubleday, 1990. ISBN 0-385-41238-X Subj: Friendship. Rhyming text.

The slimy book ill. by author. Random House, 1986. ISBN 0-394-98166-9 Subj: Dreams. Rhyming text.

The smelly book ill. by author. S&S, 1988. ISBN 0-671-65670-8 Subj: Rhyming text. Senses – smell.

Supermoo! ill. by author. Putnam, 1993. ISBN 0-399-22422-X Subj: Animals – bulls, cows. Ecology. Nature.

Tarzanna! ill. by author. Putnam, 1992. ISBN 0-399-21837-8 Subj: Animals. Behavior – misbehavior. Jungle. Language.

Three cheers for Errol! ill. by author. Putnam, 1989. ISBN 0-399-21671-5 Subj: Animals – rats. Sports.

The trouble with Dad ill. by author. Putnam, 1986. ISBN 0-399-21206-X Subj: Activities – working. Family life – fathers. Robots.

The trouble with Gran ill. by author. Putnam, 1987. ISBN 0-399-21428-3 Subj: Family life – grandmothers. Space & space ships.

The trouble with Grandad ill. by author. Putnam, 1988. ISBN 0-399-21545-X Subj: Concepts – size. Family life – grandfathers. Gardens, gardening.

The trouble with Mom ill. by author. Coward, 1984. ISBN 0-698-20597-9 Subj: Family life – mothers. School. Witches.

The trouble with Uncle ill. by author. Little, 1992. ISBN 0-316-15190-4 Subj: Family life – aunts, uncles. Imagination. Pirates. Sea & seashore.

Truelove ill. by author. Dial, 2002. ISBN 0-8037-2717-8 Subj: Animals – dogs. Babies. Emotions – love. Humorous stories.

The un-wedding ill. by author. Knopf, 1997. ISBN 0-679-88898-5 Subj: Divorce. Family life.

Winni Allfours ill. by author. BridgeWater, 1993. ISBN 0-8167-3307-4 Subj: Animals – horses, ponies. Family life.

Cole, Barbara Hancock. *Texas star* ill. by Barbara Minton. Orchard, 1990. ISBN 0-531-08420-5 Subj: Family life. Quilts. Texas.

Cole, Brock. *Buttons* ill. by author. Farrar, 2000. ISBN 0-374-31001-7 Subj: Clothing. Family life – daughters. Family life – fathers. Humorous stories. Tall tales.

The giant's toe ill. by author. Farrar, 1986. ISBN 0-374-32559-6 Subj: Anatomy. Folk & fairy tales. Giants.

The king at the door ill. by author. Doubleday, 1979. ISBN 0-385-14719-8 Subj: Behavior – disbelief. Character traits – kindness. Foreign lands – England. Royalty – kings.

Larky Mavis ill. by author. Farrar, 2001. ISBN 0-374-34365-9 Subj: Angels. Babies.

Nothing but a pig ill. by author. Doubleday, 1981. ISBN 0-385-17064-5 Subj: Animals – pigs. Behavior – imitation. Behavior – seeking better things. Friendship.

Cole, Davis. *see* Elting, Mary

Cole, Henry. *I took a walk* ill. by author. Greenwillow, 1998. ISBN 0-688-15116-7 Subj: Format, unusual – toy & movable books. Nature.

Jack's garden ill. by author. Greenwillow, 1995. ISBN 0-688-13501-3 Subj: Cumulative tales. Gardens, gardening. Plants.

Cole, Joanna. *Animal sleepyheads: one to ten* ill. by Jeni Bassett. Scholastic, 1988. ISBN 0-590-40919-0 Subj: Animals. Counting, numbers. Rhyming text.

Aren't you forgetting something, Fiona? ill. by Ned Delaney. Parents' Magazine Pr., 1984. ISBN 0-8193-1121-9 Subj: Animals – elephants. Behavior – forgetfulness.

Big Goof and Little Goof by Joanna & Philip Cole; ill. by M. K. Brown. Scholastic, 1989. ISBN 0-590-41591-3 Subj: Concepts – size. Pets. Seasons.

Bony-legs ill. by Dirk Zimmer. Four Winds, 1983. ISBN 0-590-07882-8 Subj: Folk & fairy tales. Foreign lands – Russia. Magic. Witches.

Bully trouble ill. by Marylin Hafner. Random House, 2003. ISBN 0-394-94949-8 Subj: Behavior – bullying.

A calf is born photos by Jerome Wexler. Morrow, 1975. ISBN 0-688-32036-8 Subj: Animals – babies. Animals – bulls, cows. Birth. Science.

A chick hatches photos by Jerome Wexler. Morrow, 1976. ISBN 0-688-32087-2 Subj: Birds – chickens. Science.

The Clown-Arounds ill. by Jerry Smath. G. Stevens, 1994. ISBN 0-8368-0995-5 Subj: Clowns, jesters. Contests. Family life. Humorous stories.

The Clown-Arounds go on vacation ill. by Jerry Smath. Parents' Magazine Pr., 1993. ISBN 0-8368-0966-1 Subj: Activities – vacationing. Behavior – lost. Clowns, jesters. Humorous stories. Riddles & jokes.

The Clown-Arounds have a party ill. by Jerry Smath. Parents' Magazine Pr., 1995. ISBN 0-8368-0999-8 Subj: Clowns, jesters. Emotions – sadness. Family life.

Doctor Change ill. by Donald Carrick. Morrow, 1986. ISBN 0-688-06136-2 Subj: Character traits – cleverness. Folk & fairy tales.

Don't call me names! just right for 4's and 5's ill. by Lynn Munsinger. McKay, 1990. ISBN 0-679-90258-9 Subj: Behavior – bullying. Friendship. Frogs & toads.

Don't tell the whole world ill. by Kate Duke. HarperCollins, 1990. ISBN 0-690-04811-4 Subj: Behavior. Behavior – secrets. Folk & fairy tales. Money.

Evolution ill. by Aliki. Crowell, 1987. ISBN 0-690-04598-0 Subj: Animals. Plants. Science.

Find the hidden insect by Joanna Cole & Jerome Wexler; photos by Jerome Wexler. Morrow, 1979. ISBN 0-688-32203-4 Subj: Insects. Science.

A fish hatches photos by Jerome Wexler. Morrow, 1978. ISBN 0-688-32153-4 Subj: Fish. Science.

Fun on wheels ill. by Whitney Darrow, Jr. Morrow, 1977. ISBN 0-688-32102-X Subj: Activities. Rhyming text. Wheels.

Fun on wheels ill. by Don Gauthier. Delmar, 1990. ISBN 0-8273-4141-5 Subj: Activities. Rhyming text. Wheels.

Get well, Clown-Arounds! ill. by Jerry Smath. Parents' Magazine Pr., 1983. ISBN 0-8193-1096-4 Subj: Clowns, jesters. Humorous stories. Illness. Riddles & jokes.

Get well, gators! (Calmenson, Stephanie)

A gift from Saint Francis: the first crèche ill. by Michèle Lemieux. Morrow, 1989. ISBN 0-688-06503-1 Subj: Character traits – kindness. Religion.

Golly Gump swallowed a fly (Little old lady who swallowed a fly)

How I was adopted: Samantha's story ill. by Maxie Chambliss. Morrow, 1995. ISBN 0-688-11930-1 Subj: Adoption. Family life.

How you were born photos by Margaret Miller. Rev. and expanded ed. Morrow, 1993. ISBN 0-688-12059-8 Subj: Babies. Birth. Family life. Science.

Hungry, hungry sharks ill. by Patricia Wynne. Random House, 1986. ISBN 0-394-97471-9 Subj: Fish – sharks. Science.

I'm a big brother ill. by Maxie Chambliss. Morrow, 1997. ISBN 0-688-14507-8 Subj: Babies. Family life – brothers.

I'm a big sister ill. by Maxie Chambliss. Morrow, 1997. ISBN 0-688-14509-4 Subj: Babies. Family life – sisters.

It's too noisy ill. by Kate Duke. HarperCollins, 1989. ISBN 0-690-04737-1 Subj: Animals. Folk & fairy tales. Humorous stories. Jewish culture. Noise, sounds. Problem solving.

Large as life daytime animals ill. by Kenneth Lilly. Knopf, 1985. ISBN 0-394-97188-4 Subj: Animals.

Large as life nighttime animals ill. by Kenneth Lilly. Knopf, 1985. ISBN 0-394-97189-2 Subj: Animals. Night.

The magic school bus and the electric field trip ill. by Bruce Degen. Scholastic, 1997. ISBN 0-590-44682-7 Subj: Careers – electricians. School – field trips.

The magic school bus at the waterworks ill. by Bruce Degen. Scholastic, 1986. ISBN 0-590-40361-3 Subj: School – field trips. Water.

The magic school bus explores the senses ill. by Bruce Degen. Scholastic, 1999. ISBN 0-590-44697-5 Subj: School. Senses.

The magic school bus in the time of the dinosaurs ill. by Bruce Degen. Scholastic, 1994. ISBN 0-590-44688-6 Subj: Buses. Careers – teachers. Dinosaurs. Magic. Prehistory. School – field trips. Science.

The magic school bus inside a beehive ill. by Bruce Degen. Scholastic, 1990. ISBN 0-590-44684-3 Subj: Buses. Careers – teachers. Insects – bees. Magic. School – field trips. Science.

The magic school bus inside a hurricane ill. by Bruce Degen. Scholastic, 1995. ISBN 0-590-44686-X Subj: School – field trips. Science. Weather – hurricanes.

The magic school bus inside the earth ill. by Bruce Degen. Scholastic, 1987. ISBN 0-590-40759-7 Subj: Careers – geologists. Earth. Rocks. Science.

The magic school bus inside the human body ill. by Bruce Degen. Scholastic, 1989. ISBN 0-590-41426-7 Subj: Anatomy. School – field trips. Science.

The magic school bus lost in the solar system ill. by Bruce Degen. Scholastic, 1990. ISBN 0-590-41428-3 Subj: Buses. Careers – teachers. Magic. School – field trips. Science. Space & space ships.

The magic school bus on the ocean floor ill. by Bruce Degen. Scholastic, 1992. ISBN 0-590-41430-5 Subj: Buses. Careers – teachers. Magic. School – field trips. Science. Sea & seashore.

The magic school bus plants seeds: a book about how living things grow (Relf, Patricia)

The magic school bus shows and tells ill. by Bruce Degen. Scholastic, 1997. ISBN 0-590-92242-4 Subj: Careers – archaeologists. Fossils. School – field trips. Science.

The missing tooth ill. by Marylin Hafner. Random House, 1988. ISBN 0-394-99279-2 Subj: Friendship. Teeth.

Mixed-up magic ill. by True Kelley. Hastings House, 1987. ISBN 0-8038-9298-5 Subj: Behavior – wishing. Magic. Mythical creatures – elves.

Monster and Muffin ill. by Karen Lee Schmidt. Grosset, 1996. ISBN 0-448-41146-6 Subj: Animals – dogs. Friendship. Rebuses.

Monster manners ill. by Jared D. Lee. Scholastic, 1995. ISBN 0-590-40926-3 Subj: Etiquette. Monsters.

My big boy potty ill. by Maxie Chambliss. HarperCollins, 2000. ISBN 0-688-17042-0 Subj: Behavior – growing up. Toilet training.

My big girl potty ill. by Maxie Chambliss. HarperCollins, 2000. ISBN 0-688-17041-2 Subj: Behavior – growing up. Toilet training.

My new kitten photos by Margaret Miller. Morrow, 1995. ISBN 0-688-12902-1 Subj: Animals – cats. Friendship.

My puppy is born photos by Margaret Miller. Morrow, 1991. ISBN 0-688-09771-5 Subj: Animals – dogs. Birth. Science.

The new baby at your house photos by Hella Hammid. Morrow, 1998. ISBN 0-688-05807-8 Subj: Babies. Emotions – envy, jealousy. Family life – new sibling. Sibling rivalry.

Norma Jean, jumping bean ill. by Lynn Munsinger. Random House, 1987. ISBN 0-394-98668-7 Subj: Activities – jumping. Animals – kangaroos. School.

Pat-a-cake and other play rhymes comp. by Joanna Cole & Stephanie Calmenson; ill. by Alan Tiegreen. Morrow, 1992. ISBN 0-688-11039-8 Subj: Nursery rhymes.

Pin the tail on the donkey and other party games comp. by Joanna Cole & Stephanie Calmenson; ill. by Alan Tiegreen. Morrow, 1993. ISBN 0-688-11892-5 Subj: Games. Parties.

Plants in winter ill. by Kazue Mizumura. Crowell, 1973. ISBN 0-690-62886-2 Subj: Plants. Science. Seasons – winter. Trees.

Riding Silver Star photos by Margaret Miller. Morrow, 1996. ISBN 0-688-13896-9 Subj: Animals – horses, ponies. Sports.

The secret box ill. by Joan Sandin. Morrow, 1971. Subj: Behavior – stealing.

Sharing is fun ill. by Maxie Chambliss. HarperCollins, 2004. ISBN 0-06-050499-4 Subj: Activities – playing. Behavior – sharing. Format, unusual – board books.

Sweet dreams, Clown-Arounds! ill. by Jerry Smath. G. Stevens, 1993. ISBN 0-8193-0976-9 Subj: Bedtime. Clowns, jesters. Family life.

When Mommy and Daddy go to work ill. by Maxie Chambliss. HarperCollins, 2001. ISBN 0-688-17044-7 Subj: Family life – parents. School – nursery.

When you were inside mommy ill. by Maxie Chambliss. HarperCollins, 2001. ISBN 0-688-17043-9 Subj: Babies. Birth. Family life – mothers.

Why did the chicken cross the road? and other riddles, old and new comp. by Joanna Cole & Stephanie Calmenson; ill. by Alan Tiegreen. Morrow, 1994. ISBN 0-688-12203-5 Subj: Riddles & jokes.

You can't smell a flower with your ear: all about your 5 senses ill. by Mavis Smith. Grosset, 1994. ISBN 0-448-40469-9 Subj: Science. Senses.

Your insides ill. by Paul Meisel. Putnam, 1992. ISBN 0-399-22123-9 Subj: Anatomy. Science.

Your new potty ill. by Margaret Miller. Morrow, 1989. ISBN 0-688-06106-0 Subj: Behavior – growing up. Toilet training.

Cole, Julia. *My parents' divorce* ill. by Christopher O'Neill. Copper Beech, 1998. ISBN 0-7613-0869-5 Subj: Divorce. Family life.

Cole, Kenneth, Dr. *No bad news* photos by John Ruebartsch. A. Whitman, 2001. ISBN 0-8075-4743-3 Subj: Careers – barbers. Cities, towns. Communities, neighborhoods. Ethnic groups in the U.S. – African Americans.

Cole, Michael. *Head in the sand* ill. by Rowan Clifford. Carolrhoda, 1990. ISBN 0-87614-435-0 Subj: Animals. Behavior – hiding. Birds.

Cole, Philip (Philip A.). *Big Goof and Little Goof* (Cole, Joanna)

Cole, Sheila. *The hen that crowed* ill. by Barbara Rogoff. Lothrop, 1993. ISBN 0-688-10113-5 Subj: Animals. Birds – chickens.

When the rain stops ill. by Henri Sorensen. Lothrop, 1991. ISBN 0-688-07655-6 Subj: Country. Family life – fathers. Weather – rain.

When the tide is low ill. by Virginia Wright-Frierson. Lothrop, 1985. ISBN 0-688-04067-5 Subj: Animals. Sea & seashore.

Cole, William. *Aunt Bella's umbrella* ill. by Jacqueline Chwast. Doubleday, 1970. Subj: Character traits – helpfulness. Family life – aunts, uncles. Umbrellas. Weather – rain.

Frances face-maker ill. by Tomi Ungerer. Collins-World, 1963. Subj: Bedtime. Emotions. Family life. Participation. Rhyming text.

Have I got dogs! ill. by Margot Apple. Viking, 1993. ISBN 0-670-83070-4 Subj: Animals – dogs. Rhyming text.

I went to the animal fair ill. by Colette Rosselli. Collins-World, 1959. ISBN 0-529-03530-8 Subj: Animals. Poetry.

That pest Jonathan ill. by Tomi Ungerer. HarperCollins, 1970. Subj: Behavior – misbehavior. Family life. Rhyming text.

What's good for a four-year-old? ill. by Tomi Ungerer. Holt, 1967. Subj: Activities – playing. Rhyming text.

What's good for a six-year-old? ill. by Ingrid Fetz. Holt, 1965. Subj: Activities – playing. Rhyming text.

What's good for a three-year-old? ill. by Lillian Hoban. Holt, 1974. ISBN 0-03-007441-X Subj: Activities – babysitting. Birthdays. Rhyming text.

A zooful of animals ill. by Lynn Munsinger. Houghton Mifflin, 1992. ISBN 0-395-52278-1 Subj: Animals. Poetry.

Coleman, Evelyn. *The glass bottle tree* ill. by Gail Gordon Carter. Orchard, 1995. ISBN 0-531-08767-0 Subj: Communication. Ethnic groups in the U.S. – African Americans. Family life – grandmothers. Trees.

To be a drum ill. by Aminah Brenda Lynn Robinson. A. Whitman, 1998. ISBN 0-8075-8006-6 Subj: Ethnic groups in the U.S. – African Americans. Foreign lands – Africa. Slavery. U.S. history.

White socks only ill. by Tyrone Geter. A. Whitman, 1996. ISBN 0-8075-8955-1 Subj: Ethnic groups in the U.S. – African Americans. Prejudice. U.S. history.

Coleman, Michael. *Lazy Ozzie* ill. by Gwyneth Williamson. Little Tiger, 1996. ISBN 1-888444-02-9 Subj: Animals. Birds – owls. Character traits – laziness. Family life.

One, two, three, oops! ill. by Gwyneth Williamson. Little Tiger, 1998. ISBN 1-888444-45-2 Subj: Counting, numbers. Rhyming text.

Coleridge, Sara. *January brings the snow: a book of months* ill. by Jenni Oliver. Dial, 1986. ISBN 0-8037-0314-7 Subj: Days of the week, months of the year. Poetry. Seasons.

Coles, Alison. *Michael and the sea* ill. by Michael Charlton. E D C, 1985. ISBN 0-88110-268-7 Subj: Emotions – fear. Sea & seashore. Sports – swimming.

Michael in the dark ill. by Michael Charlton. E D C, 1985. ISBN 0-88110-267-9 Subj: Emotions – fear. Night.

Michael's first day ill. by Michael Charlton. E D C, 1985. ISBN 0-88110-266-0 Subj: Emotions – fear. School – first day.

Coles, Robert. *The story of Ruby Bridges* ill. by George Ford. Scholastic, 1995. ISBN 0-590-43967-7 Subj: Character traits – bravery. Ethnic groups in the U.S. – African Americans. Prejudice. School.

Coletta, Hallie. *From A to Z* (Coletta, Irene)

Coletta, Irene. *From A to Z* by Irene & Hallie Coletta; ill. by Hallie Coletta. Prentice-Hall, 1979. ISBN 0-13-331678-5 Subj: ABC books. Rebuses. Rhyming text.

Colette, Sidonie Gabrielle. *The boy and the magic* trans. by Christopher Fry; ill. by Gerard Hoffnung. Putnam, 1965. Subj: Behavior – misbehavior. Magic. Music.

Collard, Sneed B. *Animal dads* ill. by Jenkins. Houghton, 1997. ISBN 0-395-83621-2 Subj: Animals. Behavior. Family life – fathers. Gender roles.

Animals asleep ill. by Anik McGrory. Houghton, 2004. ISBN 0-618-27697-1 Subj: Animals. Sleep.

Beaks! ill. by Robin Brickman. Charlesbridge, 2002. ISBN 1-57091-387-0 Subj: Anatomy. Birds.

Creepy creatures ill. by Kristin Kest. Rev. ed. of Do they scare you, 1992. Charlesbridge, 1997. ISBN 0-88106-837-3 Subj: Animals.

Leaving home ill. by Joan Dunning. Houghton, 2002. ISBN 0-618-11454-8 Subj: Animals – babies. Behavior. Behavior – growing up.

Making animal babies ill. by Steve Jenkins. Houghton, 2000. ISBN 0-395-95317-0 Subj: Animals. Sex instruction.

Cölle, Gisela. *The star tree* ill. by author; trans. by Rosemary Lanning. North-South, 1997. ISBN 1-55858-742-X Subj: Holidays – Christmas. Power failures. Stars.

Collicott, Sharleen. *Mildred and Sam* ill. by author. Geringer, 2003. ISBN 0-06-026682-1 Subj: Animals – mice. Babies. Family life. Homes, houses.

Seeing stars ill. by author. Dial, 1996. ISBN 0-8037-1523-4 Subj: Activities – flying. Animals. Sea & seashore. Space & space ships.

Toestomper and the bad butterflies ill. by author. Houghton, 2003. ISBN 0-618-14092-1 Subj: Behavior. Insects – butterflies, caterpillars. Metamorphosis. Pets.

Toestomper and the caterpillars ill. by author. Houghton Mifflin, 1999. ISBN 0-395-91168-0 Subj: Animals. Behavior – bullying. Character traits – kindness to animals. Clubs, gangs. Insects – butterflies, caterpillars.

Collicutt, Paul. *This car* ill. by author. Farrar, 2002. ISBN 0-374-39965-4 Subj: Automobiles.

This train ill. by author. Farrar, 1999. ISBN 0-374-37493-7 Subj: Trains. Transportation.

Collier, Bryan. *Uptown* ill. by author. Holt, 2000. ISBN 0-805-05721-0 Subj: Cities, towns. Ethnic groups in the U.S. – African Americans.

Collier, Ethel. *I know a farm* ill. by Honoré Guilbeau. Addison-Wesley, 1960. Subj: Farms.

Who goes there in my garden? ill. by Honoré Guilbeau. Abelard-Schuman, 1963. Subj: Character traits – helpfulness. Gardens, gardening.

Collier, James Lincoln. *Danny goes to the hospital* ill. by Yale Joel. Norton, 1970. Subj: Hospitals.

Collier, John. *The backyard* ill. by author. Viking, 1993. ISBN 0-670-83609-5 Subj: Imagination.

Collier, Mary Jo. *The king's giraffe* by Mary Jo Collier & Peter Collier; ill. by Stéphane Poulin. S&S, 1996. ISBN 0-671-88133-7 Subj: Animals – giraffes. Foreign lands – France. Royalty – kings.

Collier, Peter. *The king's giraffe* (Collier, Mary Jo)

Collington, Peter. *The angel and the soldier boy* ill. by author. Knopf, 1987. ISBN 0-394-98626-1 Subj: Angels. Behavior – stealing. Pirates. Toys – soldiers. Wordless.

Clever cat ill. by author. Random House, 2000. ISBN 0-375-90477-8 Subj: Animals – cats. Character traits – cleverness. Character traits – individuality. Humorous stories.

Little pickle ill. by author. Dutton, 1986. ISBN 0-525-44230-8 Subj: Behavior – misbehavior. Dreams. Sleep. Wordless.

The midnight circus ill. by author. Knopf, 1992. ISBN 0-679-93262-3 Subj: Animals – horses, ponies. Circus. Dreams. Toys. Wordless.

My darling kitten ill. by author. Knopf, 1988. ISBN 0-394-89924-5 Subj: Animals – cats. Pets.

On Christmas eve ill. by author. Knopf, 1990. ISBN 0-679-90830-7 Subj: Fairies. Holidays – Christmas. Santa Claus. Wordless.

A small miracle ill. by author. Random House, 1997. ISBN 0-679-88725-3 Subj: Character traits – helpfulness. Holidays – Christmas. Old age. Wordless.

The tooth fairy ill. by author. Random House, 1995. ISBN 0-679-97168-8 Subj: Fairies. Teeth. Wordless.

Collins, Billy. *Daddy's little boy* music by author; ill. by Maggie Kneen. HarperCollins, 2004. ISBN 0-06-029003-X Subj: Animals – bears. Family life – fathers. Family life – sons. Music. Songs.

Collins, Bonnie. *Rocks in my pocket* (Harshman, Marc)

Collins, Heather. *Eensy weensy spider* ill. by author. Kids Can, 1997. ISBN 1-55074-406-2 Subj: Format, unusual – board books. Nursery rhymes. Spiders.

Hey, diddle, diddle (Mother Goose)

Jack and Jill (Mother Goose)

Little Miss Muffet (Mother Goose)

Collins, Judith Graham. *Josh's scary dad* ill. by Diane Paterson. Abingdon, 1983. ISBN 0-687-20546-8 Subj: Character traits – appearance. Humorous stories.

Collins, Pat Lowery. *Don't tease the guppies* ill. by Marylin Hafner. Putnam, 1994. ISBN 0-399-22530-7 Subj: Aquariums. Books, reading. Family life – brothers.

I am an artist ill. by Robin Brickman. Millbrook, 1992. ISBN 1-56294-082-1 Subj: Art. Careers – artists.

My friend Andrew ill. by Howard Berelson. Prentice-Hall, 1981. ISBN 0-13-608844-9 Subj: Behavior – boasting. Imagination.

Taking care of Tucker ill. by Maxie Chambliss. Putnam, 1989. ISBN 0-399-21586-7 Subj: Behavior – misbehavior. Behavior – needing someone. Family life.

Tomorrow, up and away! ill. by Lynn Munsinger. Houghton Mifflin, 1990. ISBN 0-395-51524-6 Subj: Activities – flying. Animals. Animals – squirrels. Reptiles – turtles, tortoises.

Tumble, tumble, tumbleweed ill. by Charles Robinson. A. Whitman, 1982. ISBN 0-8075-8122-4 Subj: Friendship. Pets.

Waiting for baby Joe ill. by Joan Whinham Dunn. A. Whitman, 1990. ISBN 0-8075-8625-0 Subj: Babies. Family life – brothers & sisters. Family life – new sibling.

Collins, Ross. *Alvie eats soup* ill. by author. Levine, 2002. ISBN 0-439-27265-3 Subj: Family life – grandmothers. Food.

What if? (Thomas, Frances)

Collins, Sheila Hebert. *'T Pousette et 't Poulette: a Cajun Hansel and Gretel* ill. by Patrick Soper. Pelican, 2001. ISBN 1-56554-764-0 Subj: Ethnic groups in the U.S. – Cajuns. Folk & fairy tales.

Collodi, Carlo. *The adventures of Pinocchio* adapt. by Stephanie Spinner; ill. by Diane Goode. Random House, 1983. ISBN 0-394-95910-8 Subj: Behavior – lying. Behavior – misbehavior. Character traits – loyalty. Folk & fairy tales. Puppets.

Pinocchio adapt. by Eric Metaxas; ill. by Brian Ajhar. Rabbit Ears, 1996. ISBN 0-689-80230-7 Subj: Behavior – lying. Behavior – misbehavior. Character traits – loyalty. Folk & fairy tales. Puppets.

Colman, Hila. *Peter's brownstone house* ill. by Leonard Weisgard. Morrow, 1963. Subj: Cities, towns. Homes, houses.

Watch that watch ill. by Leonard Weisgard. Morrow, 1962. Subj: Animals. Clocks, watches. Time.

Colonius, Lillian. *At the zoo* by Lillian Colonius & Glen W. Schroeder; ill. by Glen W. Schroeder. Melmont, 1954. Subj: Zoos.

Coltman, Paul. *Tinker Jim* ill. by Gillian McClure. Farrar, 1992. ISBN 0-374-37611-5 Subj: Crime. Food. Foreign lands – England. Homeless. Poverty. Rhyming text.

Coman, Carolyn. *Losing things at Mr. Mudd's* ill. by Lance Hidy. Farrar, 1992. ISBN 0-374-34657-7 Subj: Behavior – lost & found possessions.

Combs, Kathy. *Cowboy Sam and those confounded secrets* (Griffin, Kitty)

The foot-stomping adventures of Clementine Sweet (Griffin, Kitty)

Come out to play ill. by Jeanette Winter. Knopf, 1986. ISBN 0-394-97742-4 Subj: Cities, towns. Moon. Nursery rhymes.

Come to the circus. S&S, 1980. ISBN 0-671-41479-8 Subj: Circus. Format, unusual – board books.

Comissiong, Lynette. *Mind me good now!* ill. by Marie Lafrance. Firefly, 1997. ISBN 1-55037-483-4 Subj: Folk & fairy tales. Foreign lands – Caribbean Islands. Witches.

Company González, Mercé. *Killian and the dragons* adapt. by Paula Franklin; ill. by Agustí Asensio Sauri. Silver Burdett, 1986. ISBN 0-382-09180-9 Subj: Dragons. Emotions – fear. Royalty.

Compestine, Ying Chang. *The runaway rice cake* ill. by Tungwai Chau. S&S, 2001. ISBN 0-689-82972-8 Subj: Character traits – generosity. Food. Foreign lands – China. Holidays – Chinese New Year.

The story of chopsticks ill. by YongSheng Xuan. Holiday, 2001. ISBN 0-8234-1526-0 Subj: Food. Foreign lands – China.

The story of noodles ill. by YongSheng Xuan. Holiday, 2002. ISBN 0-8234-1600-3 Subj: Activities – baking, cooking. Food. Foreign lands – China.

The story of paper ill. by YongSheng Xuan. Holiday, 2003. ISBN 0-8234-1705-0 Subj: Foreign lands – China. Paper. School.

Compos, Tito. *Muffler man = El hombre mofle* Lamberto & Beto Alvarez; trans. by Evangelina Vigil-Piñón. Piñata, 2001. ISBN 1-55885-318-9 Subj: Art. Ethnic groups in the U.S. – Mexican Americans. Family life – fathers. Family life – sons. Foreign languages.

Compton, Joanne. *Ashpet: an Appalachian tale* ill. by Kenn Compton. Holiday, 1994. ISBN 0-8234-1106-0 Subj: Character traits – kindness. Folk & fairy tales.

Granny Greenteeth and the noise in the night (Compton, Kenn)

Jack the giant chaser: an Appalachian tale (Compton, Kenn)

Little Rabbit's Easter surprise ill. by Kenn Compton. Holiday, 1992. ISBN 0-8234-0920-1 Subj: Animals – rabbits. Holidays – Easter.

Sody Sallyratus ill. by Kenn Compton. Holiday, 1995. ISBN 0-8234-1165-6 Subj: Animals – bears. Folk & fairy tales.

Compton, Kenn. *Granny Greenteeth and the noise in the night* by Kenn & Joanne Compton; ill. by Kenn Compton. Holiday, 1993. ISBN 0-8234-1051-X Subj: Bedtime. Cumulative tales. Emotions – fear. Folk & fairy tales. Noise, sounds.

Happy Christmas to all! ill. by author. Holiday, 1991. ISBN 0-8234-0890-6 Subj: Behavior – secrets. Holidays – Christmas. Mythical creatures – elves. Santa Claus.

Jack the giant chaser: an Appalachian tale by Kenn & Joanne Compton; ill. by Kenn Compton. Holiday, 1993. ISBN 0-8234-

0998-8 Subj: Character traits – cleverness. Folk & fairy tales. Giants.

Conaway, Judith. *I'll get even* ill. by Mark Gubin. Raintree, 1977. ISBN 0-817-20964-6 Subj: Emotions – loneliness. Sibling rivalry.

Condra, Estelle. *See the ocean* ill. by Linda Crockett-Blassingame. Ideals, 1994. ISBN 1-57102-005-5 Subj: Family life. Handicaps – blindness. Sea & seashore.

Cone, Molly. *Squishy, misty, damp & muddy: the in-between world of wetlands* ill. by Molly Cone. Sierra Club, 1996. ISBN 0-87156-480-7 Subj: Animals. Ecology.

Conford, Ellen. *Eugene the brave* ill. by John M. Larrecq. Little, 1978. ISBN 0-316-15292-7 Subj: Animals – possums. Character traits – bravery. Emotions – fear. Night.

Impossible, possum ill. by Rosemary Wells. Little, 1971. Subj: Animals – possums. Character traits – individuality.

Just the thing for Geraldine ill. by John M. Larrecq. Little, 1974. ISBN 0-316-15304-4 Subj: Animals – possums. Character traits – perseverance.

Why can't I be William? ill. by Philip Wende. Little, 1972. Subj: Emotions – envy, jealousy. Family life. Family life – only child. Friendship.

Conger, Lesley. *Tops and bottoms* ill. by Imero Gobbato. Four Winds, 1970. Subj: Folk & fairy tales. Foreign lands – England. Monsters.

Conger, Marion. *The chipmunk that went to church* ill. by author. S&S, 1952. Subj: Animals – chipmunks. Emotions – loneliness.

The little golden holiday book ill. by author. S&S, 1951. Subj: Holidays.

Conklin, Gladys. *Cheetahs, the swift hunters* ill. by Charles Robinson. Holiday, 1976. ISBN 0-8234-0280-0 Subj: Animals – cheetahs. Science.

I caught a lizard ill. by Artur Marokvia. Holiday, 1967. Subj: Animals. Insects. Reptiles – lizards. Science. Spiders.

I like beetles ill. by Jean Zallinger. Holiday, 1975. ISBN 0-8234-0262-2 Subj: Insects – beetles. Science.

I like butterflies ill. by Barbara Latham. Holiday, 1960. Subj: Insects – butterflies, caterpillars. Science.

I like caterpillars ill. by Barbara Latham. Holiday, 1958. Subj: Insects – butterflies, caterpillars. Science.

I watch flies ill. by Jean Zallinger. Holiday, 1977. ISBN 0-8234-0290-8 Subj: Insects – flies. Science.

If I were a bird ill. by Artur Marokvia. Holiday, 1965. Subj: Birds. Science.

Journey of the gray whales ill. by Leonard Everett Fisher. Holiday, 1974. ISBN 0-8234-0244-4 Subj: Animals – whales. Science.

Little apes ill. by Joseph Cellini. Holiday, 1970. Subj: Animals – gorillas. Science.

Lucky ladybugs ill. by Glen Rounds. Holiday, 1968. Subj: Insects – ladybugs. Science.

Praying mantis: the garden dinosaur ill. by Glen Rounds. Holiday, 1978. ISBN 0-8234-0323-8 Subj: Insects – praying mantis. Science.

We like bugs ill. by Artur Marokvia. Holiday, 1962. Subj: Insects. Science.

When insects are babies ill. by Artur Marokvia. Holiday, 1969. Subj: Insects. Science.

Connelly, Gwen. *Holiday howlers* (Roop, Peter)

Connor, Leslie. *Miss Bridie chose a shovel* ill. by Mary Azarian. Houghton, 2004. ISBN 0-618-30564-5 Subj: Ethnic groups in the U.S. – Irish Americans. Immigrants. Tools.

Conover, Chris. *Froggie went a-courting* (A frog he would a-wooing go [folk-song])

The lion's share ill. by author. Farrar, 2000. ISBN 0-374-34532-5 Subj: Activities – flying. Animals. Animals – lions. Books, reading. Mythical creatures.

Mother Goose and the sly fox ill. by author. Farrar, 1991. ISBN 0-374-35072-8 Subj: Animals – foxes. Behavior – talking to strangers. Birds – geese. Folk & fairy tales.

Sam Panda and Thunder Dragon ill. by author. Farrar, 1992. ISBN 0-374-36393-5 Subj: Animals – pandas. Dragons. Weather – rain.

Six little ducks ill. by author. Crowell, 1976. ISBN 0-690-01037-0 Subj: Birds – ducks. Counting, numbers. Music. Rhyming text. Songs.

The wizard's daughter: a Viking legend ill. by author. Little, 1984. ISBN 0-316-15314-1 Subj: Folk & fairy tales. Foreign lands – Denmark. Wizards.

Conrad, Donna. *See you soon, Moon* ill. by Don Carter. Random House, 2001. ISBN 0-375-90656-8 Subj: Activities – traveling. Family life – grandmothers. Moon. Night.

Conrad, Pam. *Animal lingo* ill. by Barbara Bustetter Falk. HarperCollins, 1995. ISBN 0-06-023402-4 Subj: Animals. Foreign languages. Noise, sounds.

Animal lullabies ill. by Richard Cowdrey. Geringer, 1997. ISBN 0-06-024719-3 Subj: Animals. Lullabies. Poetry.

Call me Ahnighito ill. by Richard Egielski. HarperCollins, 1995. ISBN 0-06-023323-0 Subj: Careers – explorers. Foreign lands – Greenland. Science.

Doll Face has a party! ill. by Brian Selznick. HarperCollins, 1994. ISBN 0-06-024263-9 Subj: Parties. Toys. Toys – dolls.

The lost sailor ill. by Richard Egielski. HarperCollins, 1992. ISBN 0-06-021696-4 Subj: Boats, ships. Careers – military. Character traits – luck. Sailors. Sea & seashore.

Molly and the strawberry day ill. by Mary Szilagyi. HarperCollins, 1993. ISBN 0-06-021370-1 Subj: Family life. Food.

The rooster's gift ill. by Eric Beddows. HarperCollins, 1996. ISBN 0-06-023604-3 Subj: Birds – chickens. Character traits – pride. Gifts. Morning.

This mess ill. by Elizabeth Sayles. Hyperion, 1998. ISBN 0-7868-2131-0 Subj: Character traits – cleanliness. Family life.

The Tub grandfather ill. by Richard Egielski. HarperCollins, 1993. ISBN 0-06-022896-2 Subj: Family life – grandfathers. Toys.

The Tub People ill. by Richard Egielski. HarperCollins, 1989. ISBN 0-06-021341-8 Subj: Activities – bathing. Toys.

The Tub People's Christmas ill. by Richard Egielski. Geringer, 1999. ISBN 0-06-026029-7 Subj: Holidays – Christmas. Santa Claus. Toys. Trees.

Conran, Sebastian. *My first ABC book* ill. by author. Macmillan, 1988. ISBN 0-689-71198-0 Subj: ABC books.

Conroy, Jack. *The fast sooner hound* (Bontemps, Arna Wendell)

Conta, Marcia Maher. *Feelings between brothers and sisters* by Marcia Maher Conta & Maureen Reardon; photos by Jules M. Rosenthal. Raintree, 1974. ISBN 0-817-20039-8 Subj: Emotions. Family life. Sibling rivalry.

Feelings between friends by Marcia Maher Conta & Maureen Reardon; photos by Jules M. Rosenthal. Raintree, 1974. ISBN 0-817-20041-X Subj: Emotions. Friendship.

Feelings between kids and grownups by Marcia Maher Conta & Maureen Reardon; photos by Jules M. Rosenthal. Raintree, 1974. ISBN 0-817-20043-6 Subj: Emotions.

Feelings between kids and parents by Marcia Maher Conta & Maureen Reardon; photos by Jules M. Rosenthal. Raintree, 1974. ISBN 0-516-03002-7 Subj: Emotions. Family life.

Contos, Alexander. *Tanya and the tobo man = Tanya y el hombre tobo* (Koplow, Lesley)

Conway, Celeste. *Where is Papa now?* ill. by author. Boyds Mills, 1994. ISBN 1-56397-130-5 Subj: Activities – traveling. Boats, ships. Family life – fathers.

Conway, Diana Cohen. *Northern lights* ill. by Shelly O. Haas. Kar-Ben Copies, 1994. ISBN 0-929371-79-8 Subj: Eskimos. Holidays – Hanukkah. Jewish culture. Northern lights. Sky.

Cony, Frances. *Old McDonald had a farm* (Old MacDonald had a farm)

Cook, Ann. *Lady Monster has a plan* (Blance, Ellen)

Lady Monster helps out (Blance, Ellen)

Monster and the magic umbrella (Blance, Ellen)

Monster and the mural (Blance, Ellen)

Monster and the surprise cookie (Blance, Ellen)

Monster at school (Blance, Ellen)

Monster buys a pet (Blance, Ellen)

Monster cleans his house (Blance, Ellen)

Monster comes to the city (Blance, Ellen)

Monster gets a job (Blance, Ellen)

Monster goes around the town (Blance, Ellen)

Monster goes to school (Blance, Ellen)

Monster goes to the beach (Blance, Ellen)

Monster goes to the circus (Blance, Ellen)

Monster goes to the hospital (Blance, Ellen)

Monster goes to the museum (Blance, Ellen)

Monster goes to the zoo (Blance, Ellen)

Monster has a party (Blance, Ellen)

Monster, Lady Monster and the bike ride (Blance, Ellen)

Monster looks for a friend (Blance, Ellen)

Monster looks for a house (Blance, Ellen)

Monster meets Lady Monster (Blance, Ellen)

Monster on the bus (Blance, Ellen)

Cook, Bernadine. *The little fish that got away* ill. by Crockett Johnson. HarperCollins, 2005. ISBN 0-06-055714-1 Subj: Fish. Sports – fishing.

Looking for Susie ill. by Judith Shahn. Addison-Wesley, 1959. ISBN 0-206-02241-4 Subj: Animals – cats. Family life. Farms.

Cook, Grace. *Two little eyes and other action rhymes* (Two little eyes and other action rhymes)

Cook, Joel. *The rat's daughter* ill. by author. Boyds Mills, 1993. ISBN 1-56397-140-2 Subj: Animals – rats. Folk & fairy tales. Foreign lands – Japan.

Cook, Marion B. *Waggles and the dog catcher* ill. by Louis Darling. Morrow, 1951. Subj: Animals – dogs.

Cook, Scott. *The gingerbread boy* (The gingerbread boy)

Mother Goose (Mother Goose)

Cooke, Ann. *Giraffes at home* ill. by Robert M. Quackenbush. HarperCollins, 1972. ISBN 0-690-33083-9 Subj: Animals – giraffes. Science.

Cooke, Barbara. *see* Alexander, Anne (Anna Barbara Cooke)

Cooke, Trish. *The grandad tree* ill. by Sharon Wilson. Candlewick, 2000. ISBN 0-7636-0815-7 Subj: Death. Emotions – grief. Family life – grandfathers. Memories, memory. Nature. Trees.

Mr. Pam Pam and the Hullabazoo ill. by Patrice Aggs. Candlewick, 1994. ISBN 1-56402-411-3 Subj: Ethnic groups in the U.S. – African Americans. Humorous stories.

So much ill. by Helen Oxenbury. Candlewick, 1994. ISBN 1-56402-344-3 Subj: Babies. Birthdays. Cumulative tales. Family life.

When I grow bigger ill. by John Bendall-Brunello. Candlewick, 1994. ISBN 1-56402-430-X Subj: Behavior – growing up. Concepts – size. Family life. Sibling rivalry.

Coombs, Patricia. *Dorrie and the haunted schoolhouse* ill. by author. Clarion, 1992. ISBN 0-395-60116-9 Subj: School. Witches.

Lisa and the grompet ill. by author. Lothrop, 1970. Subj: Behavior – running away. Fairies. Family life.

The lost playground ill. by author. Lothrop, 1963. Subj: Behavior – lost & found possessions. Character traits – being different. Toys.

The magic pot ill. by author. Lothrop, 1977. ISBN 0-688-51792-7 Subj: Devil. Folk & fairy tales. Foreign lands – Denmark. Magic.

The magician and McTree ill. by author. Lothrop, 1984. ISBN 0-688-02111-5 Subj: Animals – cats. Behavior – secrets. Magic. Middle Ages.

Molly Mullett ill. by author. Lothrop, 1975. ISBN 0-688-51692-0 Subj: Character traits – bravery. Monsters.

Mouse Café ill. by author. Lothrop, 1972. Subj: Animals – mice. Character traits – selfishness. Restaurants. Weddings.

Tilabel ill. by author. Lothrop, 1978. ISBN 0-688-51831-1 Subj: Activities – weaving. Animals – groundhogs. Folk & fairy tales. Foreign lands – Germany. Royalty.

Cooner, Donna D. (Donna Danell). *I know an old Texan who swallowed a fly* ill. by Ann Hollis Rife. Hendrick-Long, 1996. ISBN 1-885777-14-0 Subj: Cumulative tales. Folk & fairy tales. Insects – flies. Songs.

The world God made ill. by Kim Simons. Word, 1994. ISBN 0-8499-1162-1 Subj: Creation. Cumulative tales. Nature. Religion. Rhyming text.

Cooney, Barbara. *Chanticleer and the fox* (Chaucer, Geoffrey)

Eleanor ill. by author. Viking, 1996. ISBN 0-670-86159-6 Subj: Family life. U.S. history.

A garland of games and other diversions: an alphabet book initial letters by Suzanne R. Morse; ill. by author. Holt, 1969. ISBN 0-03-081016-7 Subj: ABC books. Rhyming text.

Hattie and the wild waves ill. by author. Viking, 1990. ISBN 0-670-83056-9 Subj: Family life. Sea & seashore.

Island boy ill. by author. Viking, 1988. ISBN 0-670-81749-X Subj: Death. Emotions – grief. Family life. Islands.

Little brother and little sister ill. by author. Doubleday, 1982. ISBN 0-685-14583-7 Subj: Character traits – loyalty. Folk & fairy tales. Foreign lands – Germany. Royalty. Witches.

The little juggler ill. by author. Hastings House, 1982. Reprint of 1961 ed. ISBN 0-8038-4239-2 Subj: Holidays – Christmas.

A little prayer ill. by author. Hastings House, 1967. Subj: Religion.

Miss Rumphius ill. by author. Viking, 1982. ISBN 0-670-47958-6 Subj: Activities – traveling. Flowers.

Snow-White and Rose-Red (Grimm, Jacob)

The story of Christmas ill. by Loretta Krupinski. HarperCollins, 1995. ISBN 0-06-023434-2 Subj: Holidays. Holidays – Christmas. Religion – Nativity.

Cooney, Nancy Evans. *The blanket that had to go* ill. by Diane Dawson. Putnam, 1981. ISBN 0-399-20716-3 Subj: Behavior – growing up. Problem solving. School – first day.

Chatter-box Jamie ill. by Marylin Hafner. Putnam, 1993. ISBN 0-399-22208-1 Subj: Activities – playing. Character traits – shyness. School.

Donald says thumbs down ill. by Maxie Chambliss. Putnam, 1987. ISBN 0-399-21373-2 Subj: Behavior – growing up. Emotions – embarrassment. Problem solving. Thumb sucking.

Go away monsters, lickety split! ill. by Maxie Chambliss. Putnam, 1990. ISBN 0-399-21935-8 Subj: Emotions – fear. Monsters. Pets.

The wobbly tooth ill. by Marylin Hafner. Putnam, 1978. ISBN 0-399-20615-9 Subj: Teeth.

Coontz, Otto. *The quiet house* ill. by author. Little, 1978. ISBN 0-316-15533-0 Subj: Animals – dogs. Eggs. Emotions – loneliness. Friendship.

A real class clown ill. by author. Little, 1979. ISBN 0-316-15534-9 Subj: Circus. Clowns, jesters. School – first day.

Starring Rosa ill. by author. Little, 1980. ISBN 0-316-15535-7 Subj: Animals – pigs. Food. Humorous stories.

Cooper, Ann (Ann C.). *In the forest* ill. by Dorothy Emerling. Denver Museum of Natural History Pr., 1996. ISBN 0-916278-71-9 Subj: Animals. Forest, woods. Nature.

Cooper, Elisha. *Ballpark* ill. by author. Greenwillow, 1998. ISBN 0-688-15755-6 Subj: Sports – baseball.

Building ill. by author. Greenwillow, 1999. ISBN 0-688-16494-3 Subj: Buildings. Careers – architects.

Country fair ill. by author. Greenwillow, 1997. ISBN 0-688-15531-6 Subj: Country. Fairs, festivals.

Ice cream ill. by author. Greenwillow, 2002. ISBN 0-06-001424-5 Subj: Food.

Magic thinks big ill. by author. Greenwillow, 2004. ISBN 0-06-058165-4 Subj: Animals – cats. Behavior – indecision.

Cooper, Elizabeth K. *The fish from Japan* ill. by Beth & Joe Krush. Harcourt, 1969. Subj: Fish. Imagination. Kites. Pets.

Cooper, Floyd. *Coming home: from the life of Langston Hughes* ill. by author. Philomel, 1994. ISBN 0-399-22682-6 Subj: Ethnic groups in the U.S. – African Americans. Family life. Poetry.

Cooper, Helen (Helen F.). *The bear under the stairs* ill. by author. Dial, 1993. ISBN 0-8037-1279-0 Subj: Animals – bears. Emotions – fear. Imagination.

Little monster did it! ill. by author. Dial, 1996. ISBN 0-8037-1993-0 Subj: Babies. Behavior – misbehavior. Emotions – envy, jealousy. Family life. Sibling rivalry.

Pumpkin soup ill. by author. Farrar, 1999. ISBN 0-374-36164-9 Subj: Activities – baking, cooking. Animals. Animals – cats. Animals – squirrels. Birds – ducks. Friendship.

Tatty-Ratty ill. by author. Farrar, 2002. ISBN 0-374-37386-8 Subj: Animals – rabbits. Behavior – lost & found possessions. Imagination. Toys.

Cooper, Jacqueline. *Angus and the Mona Lisa* ill. by author. Lothrop, 1981. ISBN 0-688-41972-0 Subj: Animals – cats. Behavior – stealing. Problem solving.

Cooper, Letice Ulpha. *The bear who was too big* ill. by Ruth Ives. Follett, 1963. Subj: Stores. Toys – bears.

Cooper, Melrose. *Gettin' through Thursday* ill. by Nneka Bennett. Lee & Low, 1998. ISBN 1-880000-67-9 Subj: Ethnic groups in the U.S. – African Americans. Family life – single-parent families. School.

I got a family ill. by Dale Gottlieb. Holt, 1993. ISBN 0-8050-1965-0 Subj: Family life. Rhyming text.

Pets! ill. by Yumi Heo. Holt, 1998. ISBN 0-8050-3893-0 Subj: Animals. Circus. Pets. Rhyming text.

Cooper, Patrick. *Never trust a squirrel* ill. by Catherine Walters. Dutton, 1999. ISBN 0-525-46009-8 Subj: Animals – guinea pigs. Animals – squirrels. Character traits – curiosity.

Cooper, Paulette. *Let's find out about Halloween* ill. by Errol Le Cain. Watts, 1972. ISBN 0-531-00075-3 Subj: Holidays – Halloween.

Cooper, Susan. *Danny and the Kings* ill. by Jos. A. Smith. McElderry, 1993. ISBN 0-689-50577-9 Subj: Character traits – helpfulness. Holidays – Christmas. Poverty. Trees.

Frog ill. by Jane Browne. McElderry, 2002. ISBN 0-689-84302-X Subj: Frogs & toads. Sports – swimming.

Giff the scaredy bear (Gifford, Kathie Lee)

Giff's big game (Gifford, Kathie Lee)

Jethro and the jumbie ill. by Ashley Bryan. Atheneum, 1979. ISBN 0-689-50140-4 Subj: Emotions – anger. Foreign lands – Caribbean Islands. Mythical creatures.

Matthew's dragon ill. by Jos. A. Smith. Macmillan, 1991. ISBN 0-689-50512-4 Subj: Animals. Dragons. Dreams.

Moochie's surprise (Gifford, Kathie Lee)

The Selkie girl ill. by Warwick Hutton. Aladdin, 1991. ISBN 0-689-71467-X Subj: Animals – seals. Folk & fairy tales. Foreign lands – Ireland. Foreign lands – Scotland. Mythical creatures – selkies.

The silver cow: a Welsh tale ill. by Warwick Hutton. Atheneum, 1983. ISBN 0-689-50236-2 Subj: Behavior – greed. Character traits – smallness. Folk & fairy tales. Foreign lands – England.

Tam Lin ill. by Warwick Hutton. Macmillan, 1991. ISBN 0-689-50505-1 Subj: Folk & fairy tales. Foreign lands – Scotland. Mythical creatures – elves. Royalty – princesses.

Coopersmith, Jerome. *A Chanukah fable for Christmas* ill. by Syd Hoff. Putnam, 1969. Subj: Behavior – wishing. Holidays – Hanukkah. Jewish culture.

Cope, Dawn. *Humpty Dumpty's favorite nursery rhymes* comp. by Dawn & Peter Cope; ill. by Jessie M. King, Randolph Caldecott & others. Holt, 1981. ISBN 0-03-059907-5 Subj: Nursery rhymes.

Cope, Peter. *Humpty Dumpty's favorite nursery rhymes* (Cope, Dawn)

Copeland, Cynthia L. *What are you waiting for?* ill. by Mike Gordon. Millbrook, 2003. ISBN 0-7613-2804-1 Subj: Careers – construction workers. Machines.

Copeland, Eric. *Milton, my father's dog* ill. by author. Tundra, 1994. ISBN 0-88776-339-1 Subj: Animals – dogs. Family life. Pets.

Copeland, Helen. *Meet Miki Takino* ill. by Kurt Werth. Lothrop, 1963. Subj: Ethnic groups in the U.S. – Japanese Americans. Family life – grandparents.

Coplans, Peta. *Cat and dog* ill. by author. Viking, 1996. ISBN 0-670-86766-7 Subj: Animals – cats. Animals – dogs. Counting, numbers. Sea & seashore.

Spaghetti for Suzy ill. by author. Houghton Mifflin, 1993. ISBN 0-395-65232-4 Subj: Animals. Character traits – stubbornness. Food.

Copp, Andrew James. *see* Copp, James (Andrew James)

Copp, James (Andrew James). *Martha Matilda O'Toole* ill. by Steven Kellogg. Bradbury, 1969. Originally appeared as a song in the author's phonorecord: Jim Copp tales. Subj: Behavior – forgetfulness. Humorous stories. Rhyming text. School.

Copp, Jim. *see* Copp, James (Andrew James)

Coppinger, Tom. *Curse in reverse* ill. by Dirk Zimmer. Atheneum, 2003. ISBN 0-689-83096-3 Subj: Folk & fairy tales. Witches.

Corbalis, Judy. *The cuckoo bird* ill. by David Armitage. HarperCollins, 1991. ISBN 0-06-021698-0 Subj: Behavior – greed. Birds – cuckoos. Family life – grandmothers. Problem solving.

Porcellus, the flying pig ill. by Helen Craig. Dial, 1988. ISBN 0-8037-0486-0 Subj: Activities – flying. Animals – pigs. Character traits – being different.

Corbett, Grahame. *Guess who?* ill. by author. Dial, 1982. ISBN 0-8037-3036-5 Subj: Format, unusual – board books. Participation. Toys.

What number now? ill. by author. Dial, 1982. ISBN 0-8037-9735-4 Subj: Counting, numbers. Format, unusual – board books. Participation.

Who is hiding? ill. by author. Dial, 1982. ISBN 0-8037-9748-6 Subj: Format, unusual – board books. Participation. Toys.

Who is inside? ill. by author. Dial, 1982. ISBN 0-8037-9726-5 Subj: Format, unusual – board books. Participation. Toys.

Who is next? ill. by author. Dial, 1982. ISBN 0-8037-9759-1 Subj: Format, unusual – board books. Participation. Toys.

Corcos, Lucille. *The city book* ill. by author. Golden Pr., 1972. Subj: Cities, towns.

Corddry, Thomas I. *Kibby's big feat* ill. by Quentin Blake. Follett, 1971. ISBN 0-695-80146-5 Subj: Bedtime. Behavior – lost. Jungle.

Córdova, Amy. *Abuelita's heart* ill. by author. S&S, 1997. ISBN 0-689-80181-5 Subj: Desert. Ethnic groups in the U.S. Foreign languages.

Corey, Dorothy. *Everybody takes turns* ill. by Lois Axeman. A. Whitman, 1979. Subj: Behavior – sharing.

A shot for baby bear ill. by Doug Cushman. A. Whitman, 1988. ISBN 0-8075-7348-5 Subj: Animals. Careers – doctors.

Tomorrow you can ill. by Lois Axeman. A. Whitman, 1977. ISBN 0-8075-8015-5 Subj: Behavior – growing up.

We all share ill. by Rondi Colette. A. Whitman, 1980. ISBN 0-8075-8696-X Subj: Behavior – sharing.

Will it ever be my birthday? ill. by Eileen Christelow. A. Whitman, 1986. ISBN 0-8075-9106-8 Subj: Animals. Birthdays. Emotions – envy, jealousy. Holidays – Halloween. Parties.

Will there be a lap for me? ill. by Nancy Poydar. A. Whitman, 1992. ISBN 0-8075-9109-2 Subj: Babies. Behavior – needing someone. Family life. Family life – new sibling. Sibling rivalry.

You go away ill. by Lois Axeman. A. Whitman, 1976. ISBN 0-8075-9441-5 Subj: Behavior – needing someone. Concepts. Emotions – fear.

Corey, Shana. *Ballerina bear* ill. by Pamela Paparone. Random House, 2002. ISBN 0-375-91416-1 Subj: Activities – dancing. Animals – bears. Ballet. Character traits – confidence.

Boats! ill. by Mike Reed. Random House, 2003. ISBN 0-375-90221-X Subj: Boats, ships. Rhyming text.

First graders from Mars: Horus's horrible day ill. by Mark Teague. Scholastic, 2001. ISBN 0-439-26220-8 Subj: Aliens. Behavior – bad day. Humorous stories. School – first day. Space & space ships.

First graders from Mars: Nergal and the Great Space Race ill. by Mark Teague. Scholastic, 2002. ISBN 0-439-26633-5 Subj: Aliens. Health & fitness. Humorous stories. School. Self-concept. Space & space ships.

First graders from Mars: Tera, star student ill. by Mark Teague. Scholastic, 2002. ISBN 0-439-26634-3 Subj: Aliens. Behavior. Humorous stories. School. Space & space ships.

First graders from Mars: The problem with Pelly ill. by Mark Teague. Scholastic, 2002. ISBN 0-439-26632-7 Subj: Aliens. Character traits – individuality. Humorous stories. Self-concept. Space & space ships.

Milly and the Macy's Parade ill. by Brett Helquist. Scholastic, 2002. ISBN 0-439-29754-0 Subj: Cities, towns. Holidays – Christmas. Holidays – Thanksgiving. Immigrants. Parades. Stores.

You forgot your skirt, Amelia Bloomer ill. by Chesley McLaren. Scholastic, 2000. ISBN 0-439-07819-9 Subj: Clothing. Gender roles. U.S. history.

Cork, Barbara Taylor. *Katie goes to the hospital* ill. by Siobhan Dodds. McGraw-Hill, 2002. ISBN 1-57768-986-0 Subj: Hospitals. Illness.

Sam starts school ill. by Nicola Smee. McGraw-Hill, 2002. ISBN 1-57768-989-5 Subj: School – first day.

Cormack, M. Grant. *Animal tales from Ireland* ill. by Vana Earle. John Day, 1955. First published in England, 1954. Subj: Animals. Folk & fairy tales. Foreign lands – Ireland.

Cornelia. *see* Hale, Sara Josepha Buel

Cornette. *Purple coyote* ill. by Rochette. Doubleday, 1999. ISBN 0-385-32664-5 Subj: Animals – coyotes. Character traits – curiosity.

Corney, Estelle. *Pa's top hat* ill. by Hilary Abrahams. Elsevier-Dutton, 1981. ISBN 0-233-97255-2 Subj: Sea & seashore. Trains.

Cornish, Sam. *Grandmother's pictures* ill. by Jeanne Johns. Bradbury, 1974. ISBN 0-912-84604-6 Subj: Family life. Family life – grandmothers.

Corpi, Lucha. *Where fireflies dance = Ahí, donde bailan las luciérnagas* ill. by Mira Reisberg. Children's Book Pr., 1997. ISBN 0-89239-145-6 Subj: Careers – writers. Family life. Family life – brothers & sisters. Foreign lands – Mexico. Foreign languages.

Corrigan, Kathy. *Emily Umily* ill. by Vlasta van Kampen. Firefly, 1984. ISBN 0-920236-96-0 Subj: Emotions – embarrassment. Handicaps. School.

Corrin, Ruth. *Mister cat* ill. by John Hurford. Interlink, 1991. ISBN 0-940793-89-X Subj: Animals – cats. Birth. Pets.

Corrin, Sara. *Mrs. Fox's wedding* (Grimm, Jacob)

The pied piper of Hamelin (Browning, Robert)

Corrin, Stephen. *Mrs. Fox's wedding* (Grimm, Jacob)

The pied piper of Hamelin (Browning, Robert)

Corry, Frances. *Here comes Pontus* (Jeppson, Ann-Sofie)

You're growing up, Pontus (Jeppson, Ann-Sofie)

Cort, Ben. *Pigs can't fly!* ill. by author. Barron's, 2002. ISBN 0-7641-5532-6 Subj: Animals – pigs. Behavior – imitation. Emotions – loneliness.

Cortesi, Wendy W. *Explore a spooky swamp* ill. by Joseph H. Bailey. National Geographic, 1979. ISBN 0-8704-4263-5 Subj: Animals. Birds. Frogs & toads. Reptiles.

Cosgrove, Margaret. *Wintertime for animals* ill. by author. Dodd, 1975. ISBN 0-396-07177-5 Subj: Animals. Science. Seasons – winter.

Cosgrove, Stephen (Edward). *Billy goats Gruff* (Asbjørnsen, P. C. [Peter Christen])

Sleepy time bunny by Stephen Cosgrove & Charles Reasoner. Price Stern Sloan, 1984. ISBN 0-8431-0997-1 Subj: Animals – rabbits. Bedtime. Format, unusual – board books. Night.

Cossi, Olga. *Gus the bus* ill. by Howie Schneider. Scholastic, 1989. ISBN 0-590-41616-2 Subj: Buses.

Costa, Nicoletta. *The birthday party [board book]* ill. by author. Grosset, 1984. Subj: Animals – cats. Birthdays. Family life. Format, unusual – board books. Parties.

The clever dog ill. by author. Macmillan, 1985. ISBN 0-02-724670-1 Subj: Animals – dogs. Character traits – cleverness.

Dressing up ill. by author. Grosset, 1984. ISBN 0-448-23401-7 Subj: Animals – cats. Format, unusual – board books.

A friend comes to play ill. by author. Grosset, 1984. ISBN 0-448-23403-3 Subj: Animals – cats. Format, unusual – board books. Friendship.

The grown-up dog ill. by author. Macmillan, 1985. ISBN 0-02-724680-9 Subj: Activities. Animals – dogs.

The mischievous princess ill. by author. Silver Burdett, 1986. ISBN 0-382-09179-5 Subj: Folk & fairy tales. Royalty – princesses.

The missing cat ill. by author. Grosset, 1984. ISBN 0-448-23402-5 Subj: Animals – cats. Format, unusual – board books.

Molly and Tom, the birthday party ill. by author. Grosset, 1984. ISBN 0-448-23404-1 Subj: Animals – cats. Birthdays. Family life. Parties.

The naughty puppy ill. by author. Macmillan, 1985. ISBN 0-02-724660-4 Subj: Animals – dogs. Behavior – misbehavior.

The new puppy ill. by author. Macmillan, 1985. ISBN 0-02-724650-7 Subj: Animals – dogs. Behavior – misbehavior.

Coste, Marion. *Honu* ill. by Cissy Gray. Univ. of Hawaii Pr., 1993. ISBN 0-8248-1507-6 Subj: Hawaii. Reptiles – turtles, tortoises.

Costello, Emily. *Realm of the panther* ill. by Wes Siegrist. Soundprints, 2000. ISBN 1-56899-847-3 Subj: Animals – babies. Animals – cougars. Forest, woods.

Cote, Nancy. *Flip-flops* ill. by author. A. Whitman, 1998. ISBN 0-8075-2504-9 Subj: Activities. Clothing – shoes. Sea & seashore.

It feels like snow ill. by author. Boyds Mills, 2003. ISBN 1-59078-054-X Subj: Behavior – sharing. Seasons – winter. Weather – snow.

Cotler, Joanna. *Sky above earth below* ill. by author. HarperCollins, 1990. ISBN 0-06-021366-3 Subj: Airplanes, airports.

Cotner, June. *Amazing graces: prayers and poems for children* (Amazing graces)

Bless the beasts: children's prayers & poems about animals (Bless the beasts)

Cotret, Ghislaine R. de. *North Pole, South Pole* (Duquennoy, Jacques)

Cotten, Cynthia. *At the edge of the woods* ill. by Reg Cartwright. Holt, 2002. ISBN 0-8050-6354-4 Subj: Animals. Counting, numbers. Forest, woods. Plants. Rhyming text.

Snow ponies ill. by Jason Cockcroft. Holt, 2001. ISBN 0-8050-6063-4 Subj: Animals – horses, ponies. Seasons – winter. Weather – snow.

Cottle, Joan. *Emily's shoes* ill. by author. Childrens Pr., 1999. ISBN 0-516-21585-X Subj: Activities – bathing. Clothing – shoes.

Miles away from home ill. by author. Harcourt, 2001. ISBN 0-15-202212-0 Subj: Activities – vacationing. Animals – dogs. Behavior – misunderstanding. Sea & seashore.

Cotton, Jacqueline S. *Polar bears* ill. by author. Lerner, 2004. ISBN 0-8225-3776-1 Subj: Animals – polar bears.

Cottringer, Anne. *Ella and the naughty lion* ill. by Russell Ayto. Houghton Mifflin, 1996. ISBN 0-395-79753-5 Subj: Animals – lions. Babies. Emotions – envy, jealousy. Family life – new sibling. Imagination – imaginary friends. Sibling rivalry.

Coulter, Hope Norman. *Uncle Chuck's truck* ill. by Rick Brown. Bradbury, 1993. ISBN 0-02-724825-9 Subj: Animals – bulls, cows. Family life – aunts, uncles. Farms. Trucks.

Counsel, June. *But Martin!* ill. by Carolyn Dinan. Faber, 1984. ISBN 0-571-13349-5 Subj: Character traits – being different. Space & space ships.

Count in the dark with Glo Worm ill. by Denise Fleming. Random House, 1985. ISBN 0-394-87273-8 Subj: Bedtime. Counting, numbers. Format, unusual. Rhyming text.

Count me in: 44 songs and rhymes about numbers. Sterling, 1985. ISBN 0-7136-2622-4 Subj: Counting, numbers. Music. Rhyming text. Songs.

Counting rhymes ill. by Corinne Malvern. S&S, 1946. Subj: Counting, numbers. Nursery rhymes.

Couric, Katie. *The brand new kid* ill. by Marjorie Priceman. Doubleday, 2000. ISBN 0-385-50030-0 Subj: Behavior – bullying. Ethnic groups in the U.S. – Hungarian Americans. Prejudice. Rhyming text. School.

Coursen, Valerie. *Mordant's wish* ill. by author. Holt, 1997. ISBN 0-8050-4374-8 Subj: Animals – moles. Behavior – wishing. Friendship. Reptiles – turtles, tortoises. Weather – clouds.

Court, Rob. *Color.* Child's World, 2003. ISBN 1-56766-069-X Subj: Art. Concepts – color.

Cousins, Lucy. *Count with Maisy* ill. by author. Candlewick, 1999. ISBN 0-7636-0234-5 Subj: Animals – mice. Counting, numbers. Format, unusual – board books.

Country animals ill. by author. Morrow, 1991. ISBN 0-688-10070-8 Subj: Animals. Country. Format, unusual – board books.

Doctor Maisy ill. by author. Candlewick, 2001. ISBN 0-7636-1612-5 Subj: Activities – playing. Animals. Animals – mice. Birds.

Farm animals ill. by author. Morrow, 1991. ISBN 0-688-10071-6 Subj: Animals. Farms. Format, unusual – board books.

Flower in the garden ill. by author. Candlewick, 1992. ISBN 1-56402-029-0 Subj: Flowers. Format, unusual. Wordless.

Garden animals ill. by author. Morrow, 1991. ISBN 0-688-10072-4 Subj: Animals. Format, unusual – board books.

Happy birthday, Maisy ill. by author; paper engineering by Lisa Boggiss. Candlewick, 1998. ISBN 0-7636-0577-8 Subj: Animals. Animals – mice. Birthdays. Format, unusual – toy & movable books.

Hen on the farm ill. by author. Candlewick, 1992. ISBN 1-56402-032-0 Subj: Birds – chickens. Farms. Format, unusual. Wordless.

Humpty Dumpty and other nursery rhymes ill. by author. Dutton, 1996. ISBN 0-525-45675-9 Subj: Format, unusual – board books. Nursery rhymes.

Jack and Jill: and other nursery rhymes ill. by selector. Dutton, 1996, c1989. ISBN 0-525-45676-7 Subj: Format, unusual – board books. Nursery rhymes.

Jazzy in the jungle ill. by author. Candlewick, 2002. ISBN 0-7636-1903-5 Subj: Animals. Animals – lemurs. Behavior – lost. Family life – mothers. Format, unusual – toy & movable books. Jungle.

Katy Cat and Beaky Boo ill. by author. Candlewick, 1996. ISBN 1-56402-884-4 Subj: Animals. Animals – cats. Concepts. Format, unusual – toy & movable books.

Kite in the park ill. by author. Candlewick, 1992. ISBN 1-56402-031-0 Subj: Format, unusual. Kites. Parks. Wordless.

Little Miss Muffet: and other nursery rhymes ill. by selector. Dutton, 1997. ISBN 0-525-45749-6 Subj: Format, unusual – board books. Nursery rhymes.

Maisy at the fair ill. by augthor. Candlewick, 2001. ISBN 0-7636-1500-5 Subj: Animals. Animals – mice. Fairs, festivals.

Maisy at the farm ill. by author; paper engineering by Lisa Boggiss. Candlewick, 1998. ISBN 0-7636-0576-X Subj: Animals – mice. Farms. Format, unusual – toy & movable books.

Maisy cleans up ill. by author. Candlewick, 2002. ISBN 0-7636-1711-3 Subj: Animals – mice. Friendship. Reptiles – alligators, crocodiles.

Maisy dresses up ill. by author. Candlewick, 1999. ISBN 0-7636-0885-8 Subj: Animals. Animals – mice. Clothing – costumes. Parties.

Maisy goes shopping ill. by author. Candlewick, 2001. ISBN 0-7636-1501-3 Subj: Animals – mice. Reptiles – alligators, crocodiles. Shopping.

Maisy goes swimming ill. by author. Little, 1990. ISBN 0-316-15834-8 Subj: Animals – mice. Format, unusual – toy & movable books. Sports – swimming.

Maisy goes to bed ill. by author. Little, 1990. ISBN 0-316-15832-1 Subj: Animals – mice. Bedtime. Format, unusual – toy & movable books.

Maisy goes to school ill. by author. Candlewick, 1992. ISBN 1-56402-085-1 Subj: Animals – mice. Format, unusual – toy & movable books. School.

Maisy goes to the playground ill. by author. Candlewick, 1992. ISBN 1-56402-084-3 Subj: Activities – playing. Animals – mice. Format, unusual – toy & movable books.

Maisy makes gingerbread ill. by author. Candlewick, 1999. ISBN 0-7636-0887-4 Subj: Activities – baking, cooking. Animals – mice. Food.

Maisy makes lemonade ill. by author. Candlewick, 2002. ISBN 0-7636-1728-8 Subj: Animals – elephants. Animals – mice. Behavior – sharing. Character traits – helpfulness.

Maisy's ABC ill. by author. Candlewick, 1995. ISBN 1-56402-419-9 Subj: ABC books. Animals – mice. Format, unusual – toy & movable books.

Maisy's bedtime ill. by author. Candlewick, 1999. ISBN 0-7636-0884-X Subj: Animals. Animals – mice. Bedtime. Dreams. Toys – bears.

Maisy's big flap book ill. by author. Candlewick, 2001. ISBN 0-7636-1189-1 Subj: Animals. Animals – mice. Format, unusual – toy & movable books.

Maisy's colors ill. by author. Candlewick, 1997. ISBN 0-7636-0159-4 Subj: Animals – mice. Concepts – color.

Maisy's farm ill. by author. Candlewick, 2001. ISBN 0-7636-1294-4 Subj: Animals. Animals – mice. Farms. Format, unusual – toy & movable books.

Maisy's first clock ill. by author. Candlewick, 2002. ISBN 0-7636-1788-1 Subj: Animals – mice. Format, unusual – toy & movable books. Time.

Maisy's halloween ill. by author. Candlewick, 2004. ISBN 0-7636-2579-5 Subj: Animals. Animals – mice. Format, unusual – board books. Holidays – Halloween.

Maisy's morning on the farm ill. by author. Candlewick, 2001. ISBN 0-7636-1610-9 Subj: Animals. Animals – mice. Farms.

Maisy's noisy day ill. by author. Candlewick, 2002. ISBN 0-7636-1917-5 Subj: Animals. Animals – mice. Format, unusual – board books. Noise, sounds.

Maisy's pirate treasure hunt ill. by author. Candlewick, 2004. ISBN 0-7636-2469-1 Subj: Animals – mice. Format, unusual – toy & movable books.

Maisy's pool ill. by author. Candlewick, 1999. ISBN 0-7636-0886-6 Subj: Animals. Animals – mice. Sports – swimming.

Maisy's pop-up playhouse ill. by author. Candlewick, 1995. ISBN 1-56402-635-3 Subj: Animals – mice. Format, unusual – toy & movable books. Homes, houses.

Maisy's rainbow dream ill. by author. Candlewick, 2003. ISBN 0-7636-2195-1 Subj: Animals – mice. Concepts – color. Dreams.

Maisy's twinkly, crinkly counting book ill. by author. Candlewick, 2004. ISBN 0-7636-2273-7 Subj: Animals – mice. Counting, numbers. Format, unusual – toy & movable books.

Noah's ark ill. by author. Candlewick, 1993. ISBN 1-56402-213-7 Subj: Animals. Boats, ships. Religion – Noah. Weather – floods. Weather – rain. Weather – rainbows.

Noah's ark [board book] ill. by author. Candlewick, 2004. ISBN 0-7636-2446-2 Subj: Animals. Boats, ships. Format, unusual – board books. Religion – Noah. Weather – floods. Weather – rain. Weather – rainbows.

Pet animals ill. by author. Morrow, 1991. ISBN 0-688-10073-2 Subj: Animals. Format, unusual – board books. Pets.

Portly's hat ill. by author. Dutton, 1989. ISBN 0-525-44457-2 Subj: Birds. Birds – penguins. Clothing – hats.

Teddy in the house ill. by author. Candlewick, 1992. ISBN 1-56402-030-4 Subj: Format, unusual. Wordless.

Wee Willie Winkie and other nursery rhymes ill. by selector. Dutton, 1997. ISBN 0-525-45751-8 Subj: Format, unusual – board books. Nursery rhymes.

What can Pinky hear? ill. by author. Candlewick, 1997, c1991. ISBN 0-7636-0109-8 Subj: Animals – rabbits. Format, unusual – toy & movable books. Noise, sounds. Senses – hearing.

What can Pinky see? ill. by author. Candlewick, 1997, c1991. ISBN 0-7636-0110-1 Subj: Animals – rabbits. Format, unusual – toy & movable books. Senses – sight.

What can rabbit hear? ill. by author. Morrow, 1991. ISBN 0-688-10455-X Subj: Animals. Animals – rabbits. Format, unusual – toy & movable books. Noise, sounds. Senses – hearing.

What can rabbit see? ill. by author. Morrow, 1991. ISBN 0-688-10454-1 Subj: Animals. Animals – rabbits. Format, unusual – toy & movable books. Glasses. Senses – sight.

Za-Za's baby brother ill. by author. Candlewick, 1995. ISBN 1-56402-582-9 Subj: Animals – zebras. Family life. Nature. Sea & seashore. Sibling rivalry.

Cousteau Society. *Albatross* ill. with photos. Little Simon, 1993. ISBN 0-671-86565-X Subj: Birds – albatrosses. Nature. Sea & seashore.

Dolphins ill. with photos. Little Simon, 1992. ISBN 0-671-77062-4 Subj: Animals – dolphins. Nature. Sea & seashore.

Manatees ill. with photos. Little Simon, 1993. ISBN 0-671-86566-8 Subj: Animals – manatees. Nature. Sea & seashore.

Otters ill. with photos. Little Simon, 1993. ISBN 0-671-86567-6 Subj: Animals – otters. Nature. Sea & seashore.

Penguins ill. with photos. Little Simon, 1991. ISBN 0-671-77058-6 Subj: Birds – penguins. Nature. Sea & seashore.

Seals ill. with photos. Little Simon, 1992. ISBN 0-671-77061-6 Subj: Animals – seals. Nature. Sea & seashore.

Turtles ill. with photos. Little Simon, 1992. ISBN 0-671-77059-4 Subj: Nature. Reptiles – turtles, tortoises. Sea & seashore.

Whales ill. with photos. Little Simon, 1993. ISBN 0-671-86564-1 Subj: Animals – whales. Nature. Sea & seashore.

Coutant, Helen. *First snow* ill. by Vo-Dinh Mai. Knopf, 1974. ISBN 0-394-92831-8 Subj: Death. Emotions – grief. Family life – grandmothers. Seasons – winter.

Couture, Susan Arkin. *The biggest horse I ever did see* ill. by Claire Ewart. Geringer, 1997. ISBN 0-06-023468-7 Subj: Animals – horses, ponies. Imagination. Rhyming text.

The block book ill. by Petra Mathers. HarperCollins, 1990. ISBN 0-06-020524-5 Subj: Behavior – collecting things. Rhyming text. Toys.

Melanie Jane ill. by Isabelle Dervaux. HarperCollins, 1996. ISBN 0-06-023392-3 Subj: Behavior – misbehavior. Emotions – anger.

Couvillon, Alice W. *Mimi and Jean-Paul's Cajun Mardi Gras* (Moore, Elizabeth)

Covault, Ruth M. *Pablo and Pimienta* ill. by Francisco Mora; trans. by Patricia Hinton Davison. Northland, 1994. ISBN 0-87358-588-7 Subj: Animals – coyotes. Careers – migrant workers. Ethnic groups in the U.S. – Mexican Americans. Foreign languages.

Coville, Bruce. *The foolish giant* by Bruce & Katherine Coville; ill. by Katherine Coville. Lippincott, 1978. ISBN 0-397-31800-6 Subj: Character traits – bravery. Character traits – kindness. Friendship. Giants. Magic.

My grandfather's house ill. by Henri Sorensen. BridgeWater, 1996. ISBN 0-816-73804-1 Subj: Death. Emotions – grief. Family life – grandfathers.

The prince of butterflies ill. by John Clapp. Harcourt, 2002. ISBN 0-15-201454-3 Subj: Animals – endangered animals. Insects – butterflies, caterpillars.

Sarah and the dragon ill. by Beth Peck. Lippincott, 1984. ISBN 0-397-32070-1 Subj: Character traits – kindness. Dragons. Folk & fairy tales. Magic. Mythical creatures. Witches.

Sarah's unicorn by Bruce & Katherine Coville; ill. by authors. Lippincott, 1979. ISBN 0-397-31873-1 Subj: Animals. Character traits – meanness. Mythical creatures – unicorns. Witches.

Coville, Katherine. *The foolish giant* (Coville, Bruce)

Sarah's unicorn (Coville, Bruce)

Cowan, Catherine. *My friend the piano* ill. by Kevin Hawkes. Lothrop, 1998. ISBN 0-688-13240-5 Subj: Family life – mothers. Music. Musical instruments – pianos.

My life with the wave based on the story by Octavio Paz; trans. & adapt. for children by Catherine Cowan; ill. by Mark Buehner. Lothrop, 1997. ISBN 0-688-12661-8 Subj: Character traits – individuality. Sea & seashore.

Cowcher, Helen. *Jaguar* ill. by author. Scholastic, 1997. ISBN 0-590-29937-9 Subj: Animals – jaguars. Foreign lands – Venezuela. Sports – hunting.

Rain forest ill. by author. Farrar, 1988. ISBN 0-374-36167-3 Subj: Animals. Foreign lands – South America. Forest, woods. Machines.

Tigress ill. by author. Farrar, 1991. ISBN 0-374-37567-4 Subj: Animals – endangered animals. Animals – tigers. Character traits – kindness to animals.

Cowell, Cressida. *Don't do that, Kitty Kilroy* ill. by authnor. Orchard, 1999. ISBN 0-531-30209-1 Subj: Behavior – misbehavior. Family life – daughters. Family life – mothers.

Hiccup the seasick Viking ill. by author. Orchard, 2000. ISBN 0-531-30278-4 Subj: Character traits – bravery. Emotions – fear. Illness. Sea & seashore. Vikings.

What shall we do with the Boo-Hoo Baby? ill. by author. Scholastic, 2003. ISBN 0-439-44266-4 Subj: Animals. Babies. Behavior. Emotions.

Cowen-Fletcher, Jane. *Baby angels* ill. by author. Candlewick, 1996. ISBN 1-56402-666-3 Subj: Angels. Babies. Rhyming text.

Farmer Will ill. by author. Candlewick, 2001. ISBN 0-7636-0988-9 Subj: Animals. Imagination. Toys.

Mama zooms ill. by author. Scholastic, 1993. ISBN 0-590-45774-8 Subj: Family life – mothers. Handicaps – physical handicaps.

Cowles, Kathleen. *Feelings* (Allington, Richard L.)

Hearing (Allington, Richard L.)

Looking (Allington, Richard L.)

Smelling (Allington, Richard L.)

Tasting (Allington, Richard L.)

Touching (Allington, Richard L.)

Cowley, Joy. *Agapanthus Hum and Major Bark* ill. by Jennifer Plecas. Philomel, 2001. ISBN 0-399-23322-9 Subj: Animals – dogs. Pets.

Big moon tortilla ill. by Dyanne Strongbow. Boyds Mills, 1998. ISBN 1-56397-601-3 Subj: Behavior – mistakes. Family life – grandmothers. Food. Indians of North America – Tohono O'Odham.

Gracias, the Thanksgiving turkey ill. by Joe Cepeda. Scholastic, 1996. ISBN 0-590-46976-2 Subj: Birds – turkeys. Careers – truck drivers. Ethnic groups in the U.S. – Puerto Rican Americans. Family life – fathers. Holidays – Thanksgiving.

Mrs. Goodstory ill. by Erica Dornbusch. Boyds Mills, 2001. ISBN 1-56397-774-5 Subj: Books, reading. Imagination.

The rusty, trusty tractor ill. by Olivier Dunrea. Boyds Mills, 1999. ISBN 1-56397-565-3 Subj: Careers – farmers. Family life – grandfathers. Tractors.

Singing down the rain ill. by Jan Spivey Gilchrist. HarperCollins, 1997. ISBN 0-06-027603-7 Subj: Activities – singing. Ethnic groups in the U.S. – African Americans. Weather – droughts. Weather – rain.

The video shop sparrow ill. by author. Boyds Mills, 1999. ISBN 1-56397-826-1 Subj: Birds – sparrows. Character traits – kindness to animals. Stores.

Where horses run free ill. by Layne Johnson. Boyds Mills, 2003. ISBN 1-59078-062-0 Subj: Animals – horses, ponies. Cowboys, cowgirls.

Cowley, Stewart. *Down Ladybug Lane* ill. by Susi Adams. Reader's Digest, 1993. ISBN 0-89577-481-X Subj: Animals. Counting, numbers. Format, unusual – board books.

Five little kittens ill. by Kate Davies. Reader's Digest, 1992. ISBN 0-89577-454-2 Subj: Animals – cats. Counting, numbers. Format, unusual – board books. Format, unusual – toy & movable books. Rhyming text.

From my window ill. by Caroline Jayne Church. Reader's Digest, 1994. ISBN 0-89577-595-6 Subj: Format, unusual – toy & movable books. Gardens, gardening.

Hide-and-seek puppies ill. by Kate Davies. Reader's Digest, 1991. ISBN 0-89577-455-0 Subj: Animals – dogs. Counting, numbers. Format, unusual – board books. Format, unusual – toy & movable books. Games. Rhyming text.

In dragonfly forest ill. by Elizabeth Gatt. Reader's Digest, 1993. ISBN 0-89577-479-8 Subj: Animals. Counting, numbers. Format, unusual – board books.

In songbird jungle ill. by Cindy Rosenheim. Reader's Digest, 1993. ISBN 0-89577-480-1 Subj: Animals. Counting, numbers. Format, unusual – board books.

Little bunny ill. by Susi Adams. Reader's Digest, 1996. ISBN 1-57584-006-5 Subj: Animals – rabbits. Format, unusual – board books. Rhyming text.

Little chick ill. by Susi Adams. Reader's Digest, 1996. ISBN 1-57584-007-3 Subj: Birds – chickens. Counting, numbers. Format, unusual – board books. Rhyming text.

Little lost rabbit ill. by Susi Adams. Reader's Digest, 1992. ISBN 0-89577-445-3 Subj: Animals – rabbits. Behavior – lost. Counting, numbers. Format, unusual – board books. Format, unusual – toy & movable books. Rhyming text.

The naughty ducklings ill. by Susi Adams. Reader's Digest, 1991. ISBN 0-89577-444-5 Subj: Behavior – misbehavior. Birds – ducks. Counting, numbers. Format, unusual – board books. Format, unusual – toy & movable books. Rhyming text.

On Butterfly Farm ill. by Elizabeth Gatt. Reader's Digest, 1993. ISBN 0-89577-478-X Subj: Animals. Counting, numbers. Format, unusual – board books. Insects – butterflies, caterpillars.

"Tweet, tweet, tweet" ill. by Susan Nethery. Western, 1994. ISBN 0-307-17350-X Subj: Birds. Format, unusual – board books. Noise, sounds. Rhyming text.

What's that sound? ill. by Caroline Church. Reader's Digest, 1994. ISBN 0-89577-596-4 Subj: Animals. Format, unusual – board books. Noise, sounds. Pets. Stores.

Cox, David. *Ayu and the perfect moon* ill. by author. Bodley Head, 1984. ISBN 0-370-30533-7 Subj: Activities – dancing. Foreign lands – Bali.

Bossyboots ill. by author. Crown, 1987. ISBN 0-517-56491-2 Subj: Character traits – willfulness. Crime. Foreign lands – Australia.

Tin Lizzie and Little Nell ill. by author. Merrimack, 1984. ISBN 0-370-30922-7 Subj: Animals – horses, ponies. Foreign lands – Australia. Machines.

Cox, Judy. *Go to sleep, Groundhog* ill. by Paul Meisel. Holiday, 2004. ISBN 0-8234-1645-3 Subj: Animals – groundhogs. Hibernation. Holidays – Groundhog Day.

My family plays music ill. by Elbrite Brown. Holiday, 2003. ISBN 0-8234-1591-0 Subj: Careers – musicians. Family life. Musical instruments.

Now we can have a wedding! ill. by DyAnne DiSalvo-Ryan. Holiday, 1998. ISBN 0-8234-1342-X Subj: Ethnic groups in the U.S. Food. Weddings.

Rabbit pirates: a tale of the Spinach Main ill. by Emily Arnold McCully. Harcourt, 1999. ISBN 0-15-201832-8 Subj: Animals – foxes. Animals – rabbits. Behavior – trickery. Food. Foreign lands – France. Friendship.

The West Texas chili monster ill. by John O'Brien. BridgeWater, 1998. ISBN 0-8167-4546-3 Subj: Food. Space & space ships. Texas.

Cox, Lynn. *Crazy alphabet* ill. by Rodney McRae. Orchard, 1992. ISBN 0-531-08566-X Subj: ABC books. Cumulative tales.

Cox, Palmer. *Another Brownie book* ill. by author. McGraw-Hill, 1967. Re-publication of the orig. 1890 ed. Subj: Mythical creatures – elves.

The Brownies: their book ill. by author. McGraw-Hill, 1967. Republication of the orig. 1887 ed. Subj: Mythical creatures – elves. Poetry.

Cox, Paul. *The case of the botched book* ill. by author. Green Tiger Pr., 1992. ISBN 0-671-77586-3 Subj: Animals – badgers. Animals – koalas. Careers – detectives. Mystery stories.

The great eucalyptus mystery ill. by author. Green Tiger Pr., 1992. ISBN 0-671-77574-X Subj: Animals – badgers. Animals – koalas. Careers – detectives. Mystery stories.

The riddle of the floating island ill. by author. Green Tiger Pr., 1992. ISBN 0-671-77579-0 Subj: Animals – badgers. Animals – koalas. Careers – detectives. Mystery stories.

Cox, Phil Roxbee. *Fox on a box* ill. by Stephen Cartwright. Scholastic, 2004. ISBN 0-7945-0443-4 Subj: Animals – foxes. Format, unusual – toy & movable books. Language. Rhyming text.

Goose on the loose ill. by Stephen Cartwright. Scholastic, 2001. ISBN 0-613-75091-8 Subj: Birds – geese. Format, unusual – toy & movable books. Language. Rhyming text.

Shark in the park ill. by Stephen Cartwright. Scholastic, 2002. ISBN 0-439-52876-3 Subj: Fish – sharks. Format, unusual – toy & movable books. Language. Rhyming text.

Ted in a red bed ill. by Stephen Cartwright. EDC, 1999. ISBN 0-7460-3023-1 Subj: Birds – ducks. Concepts – color. Format, unusual – toy & movable books. Furniture – beds. Games. Language. Rhyming text. Toys – bears.

Cox, Victoria. *Going my way?* (Applebaum, Stan)

Coxe, Molly. *Big egg* ill. by author. Random House, 1997. ISBN 0-679-98126-8 Subj: Animals – babies. Birds – chickens. Birds – ostriches. Humorous stories.

Bunny and the beast ill. by Pamela Silin-Palmer. Random House, 2001. ISBN 0-375-80468-4 Subj: Animals. Folk & fairy tales. Foreign lands – France.

Louella and the yellow balloon ill. by Crowell, 1988. ISBN 0-690-04748-7 Subj: Circus. Toys – balloons.

6 sticks ill. by author. Random House, 1999. ISBN 0-679-98689-8 Subj: Animals – mice. Concepts – shape. Counting, numbers.

Whose footprints? ill. by author. HarperCollins, 1990. ISBN 0-690-04837-8 Subj: Animals. Family life. Farms. Seasons – winter.

Coxon, Michèle. *The cat who lost his purr* ill. by author. Peter Bedrick, 1991. ISBN 0-87226-453-X Subj: Animals – cats. Behavior – needing someone.

Coy, John. *Night driving* ill. by Peter McCarty. Holt, 1996. ISBN 0-805-02931-1 Subj: Activities – traveling. Automobiles. Family life – fathers. Night.

Two old potatoes and me ill. by Carolyn Fisher. Knopf, 2003. ISBN 0-375-92180-X Subj: Divorce. Family life – daughters. Family life – fathers. Food.

Vroomaloom zoom ill. by Joe Cepeda. Crown, 2000. ISBN 0-517-80010-1 Subj: Activities – traveling. Automobiles. Bedtime. Imagination. Noise, sounds.

Coyne, Rachel. *Daughter, have I told you?* ill. by Virginia Halstead. Holt, 1998. ISBN 0-8050-5301-8 Subj: Family life – daughters. Family life – mothers. Poetry.

Crabtree, Judith. *The sparrow's story at the king's command* ill. by author. Oxford Univ. Pr., 1983. ISBN 0-19-554359-9 Subj: Birds – sparrows. Royalty – kings.

Craft, Ruth. *Carrie Hepple's garden* ill. by Irene Haas. Atheneum, 1979. ISBN 0-689-50099-8 Subj: Animals – cats. Character traits – bravery. Gardens, gardening.

The day of the rainbow ill. by Niki Daly. Viking, 1989. ISBN 0-670-82456-9 Subj: Behavior – lost & found possessions. Cities, towns. Emotions – anger. Poetry. Seasons – summer. Weather – rainbows.

The winter bear ill. by Erik Blegvad. Atheneum, 1974. ISBN 0-00-195869-0 Subj: Rhyming text. Seasons – winter. Toys – bears.

Craig, Helen. *Angelina's ballet class* (Holabird, Katharine)

Angelina's Halloween (Holabird, Katharine)

Charlie and Tyler at the seashore ill. by author. Candlewick, 1995. ISBN 1-56402-573-X Subj: Animals – mice. Family life – cousins. Sea & seashore.

I see the moon, and the moon sees me: Helen Craig's book of nursery rhymes ill. by author. HarperCollins, 1993. ISBN 0-06-021454-6 Subj: Nursery rhymes.

The night of the paper bag monsters ill. by author. Knopf, 1985. ISBN 0-394-97307-0 Subj: Animals – pigs. Friendship. Monsters.

The Random House book of nursery stories ill. by reteller. Random House, 1999. ISBN 0-375-90586-3 Subj: Folk & fairy tales.

Susie and Alfred in a busy day in town ill. by author. Candlewick, 1994. ISBN 1-56402-380-X Subj: Animals – pigs. Cities, towns. Family life – brothers & sisters.

Susie and Alfred in the knight, the princess and the dragon ill. by author. Knopf, 1985. ISBN 0-394-87212-6 Subj: Animals – pigs. Art. Imagination.

The town mouse and the country mouse (Æsop)

A welcome for Annie ill. by author. Knopf, 1994. ISBN 0-394-97954-0 Subj: Animals – pigs. Behavior – misbehavior. Behavior – trickery. Friendship.

Craig, Janet. *see* Palazzo-Craig, Janet

Craig, M. Jean. *Babar comes to America* (Brunhoff, Laurent de)

Boxes ill. by Joe Lasker. Norton, 1964. Subj: Concepts – shape. Concepts – size. Games. Participation. Toys.

Dinosaurs and more dinosaurs ill. by George Solonevich. Four Winds, 1968. Subj: Dinosaurs. Prehistory. Science.

The donkey prince (Grimm, Jacob)

The dragon in the clock box ill. by Kelly Oechsli. Norton, 1962. Subj: Dragons. Family life. Imagination.

The man whose name was not Thomas ill. by Diane Stanley. Doubleday, 1981. ISBN 0-385-15064-4 Subj: Careers – bakers. Humorous stories.

Spring is like the morning ill. by Don Almquist. Putnam, 1965. Subj: Animals. Morning. Plants. Seasons – spring.

What did you dream? ill. by Margery Gill. Abelard-Schuman, 1964. Subj: Dreams. Morning.

Craighead, Charles. *The eagle and the river* photos by Tom Mangelsen. Macmillan, 1994. ISBN 0-02-762265-7 Subj: Animals. Birds – eagles. Ecology. Rivers. Seasons – winter.

Crampton, Gertrude. *Scuffy the tugboat* ill. by Tibor Gergely. Random House, 2003. ISBN 0-307-10547-4 Subj: Activities – traveling. Boats, ships. Rivers. Toys.

Crampton, Patricia. *The beaver family book* (Kalas, Sybille)

The dragon with red eyes (Lindgren, Astrid)

The goose family book (Kalas, Sybille)

My nightingale is singing (Lindgren, Astrid)

The penguin family book (Somme, Lauritz)

Peter and the wolf (Prokofiev, Sergei Sergeievitch)

Crane, Alan. *Pepita bonita* ill. by author. Nelson, 1942. Subj: Birds – pelicans. Foreign lands – Mexico. Sea & seashore.

Crane, Donn. *Flippy and Skippy: the two flying squirrels* ill. by author. Winston, 1940. Subj: Animals – squirrels. Pets.

Crane, Lucy. *The frog prince* (Grimm, Jacob)

Crary, Elizabeth. *I'm frustrated* ill. by Jean Whitney. Parenting Pr., 1992. ISBN 0-943990-64-5 Subj: Emotions. Sports – roller skating.

I'm mad ill. by Jean Whitney. Parenting Pr., 1992. ISBN 0-943990-62-9 Subj: Emotions – anger. Weather – rain.

I'm proud ill. by Jean Whitney. Parenting Pr., 1992. ISBN 0-943990-66-1 Subj: Character traits – pride.

When you're mad and you know it by Elizabeth Crary & Shari Steelsmith; ill. by Mits Katayama. Parenting Pr., 1996. ISBN 1-884734-10-3 Subj: Emotions – anger. Format, unusual – board books.

Craven, Carolyn. *What the mailman brought* ill. by Tomie de Paola. Putnam, 1987. ISBN 0-399-21290-6 Subj: Activities – painting. Careers – postal workers. Emotions – loneliness. Illness. Imagination.

Craver, Mike. *Beaver ball at the bug club* ill. by Joan Kaghan. Farrar, 1992. ISBN 0-374-30662-1 Subj: Animals. Music. Parties. Songs.

Crawford, Elizabeth D. *Baby animals on the farm* (Isenbart, Hans-Heinrich)

Barry: the story of a brave St. Bernard (Hürlimann, Bettina)

Blackie and Marie (Kocí, Marta)

Hansel and Gretel (Grimm, Jacob)

The hare's race (Baumann, Hans)

Little Harry (Bröger, Achim)

Little red cap (Grimm, Jacob)

The seven ravens (Grimm, Jacob)

The three little pigs (The three little pigs)

Tiger cat (Wolski, Slawomir)

Traveling to Tripiti (Steger, Hans-Ulrich)

Crawford, Phyllis. *The blot: little city cat* ill. by Holling C. Holling. Jonathan Cape, 1930. Subj: Animals – cats.

Crawford, Ron. *Pet?* ill. by author. Green Tiger Pr., 1993. ISBN 0-671-79675-5 Subj: Animals. Pets.

Crawford, Sheryl Ann. *The baby who changed the world* ill. by Sonya Wilson. Faith Kids, 2000. ISBN 0-7814-3431-9 Subj: Animals. Animals – donkeys. Religion – Nativity.

Crayder, Teresa. *see* Colman, Hila

Crebbin, June. *Cows in the kitchen* ill. by Katharine McEwen. Candlewick, 1998. ISBN 0-7636-0645-6 Subj: Animals. Behavior – misbehavior. Careers – farmers. Rhyming text.

Fly by night ill. by Stephen Lambert. Candlewick, 1993. ISBN 1-56402-149-1 Subj: Activities – flying. Birds – owls. Night.

Into the castle ill. by John Bendall-Brunello. Candlewick, 1996. ISBN 1-56402-822-4 Subj: Castles. Monsters. Rhyming text.

Credle, Ellis. *Big fraid, little fraid: a folktale* ill. by author. Macmillan, 1964. Subj: Emotions – fear. Folk & fairy tales. Night.

Down, down the mountain ill. by author. Nelson, 1961, c1934. Subj: Clothing. Family life. Plants.

Creech, Sharon. *A fine, fine school* ill. by Harry Bliss. Harper-Collins, 2001. ISBN 0-06-027737-8 Subj: Careers – school principals. School.

Fishing in the air ill. by Chris Raschka. HarperCollins, 2000. ISBN 0-06-028112-X Subj: Family life – fathers. Family life – sons. Imagination. Sports – fishing.

Creighton, Jill. *Maybe a monster* ill. by Ruth Ohi. Firefly, 1989. ISBN 1-55037-037-5 Subj: Activities – playing. Imagination.

One day there was nothing to do ill. by Ruth Ohi. Firefly, 1990. ISBN 1-55037-091-X Subj: Activities. Animals. Behavior – boredom. Imagination. Reptiles – snakes. Reptiles – turtles, tortoises.

Cremins, Robert. *My animal ABC* ill. by author. Crown, 1983. Subj: ABC books. Animals. Format, unusual – toy & movable books.

My animal Mother Goose ill. by author. Crown, 1983. Subj: Animals. Format, unusual – toy & movable books. Nursery rhymes.

Pop up baby brontosaurus ill. by author; paper engineering by Dick Dudley. Dial, 1989. ISBN 0-8037-0726-6 Subj: Dinosaurs. Format, unusual – toy & movable books.

Pop up baby coelophysis ill. by author; paper engineering by Dick Dudley. Dial, 1989. ISBN 0-8037-0735-5 Subj: Dinosaurs. Format, unusual – toy & movable books.

Pop up baby pteranodon ill. by author; paper engineering by Dick Dudley. Dial, 1989. ISBN 0-8037-0732-0 Subj: Dinosaurs. Format, unusual – toy & movable books.

Pop up baby stegosaurus ill. by author; paper engineering by Dick Dudley. Dial, 1989. ISBN 0-8037-0733-9 Subj: Dinosaurs. Format, unusual – toy & movable books.

Pop up baby triceratops ill. by author; paper engineering by Dick Dudley. Dial, 1989. ISBN 0-8037-0734-7 Subj: Dinosaurs. Format, unusual – toy & movable books.

Pop up baby tyrannosaurus rex ill. by author; paper engineering by Dick Dudley. Dial, 1989. ISBN 0-8037-0731-2 Subj: Dinosaurs. Format, unusual – toy & movable books.

Crespi, Francesca. *Little Bear and the oompah-pah* ill. by author. Dial, 1987. ISBN 0-8037-0394-5 Subj: Animals – bears. Holidays. Music. Musical instruments – bands.

Make a joyful noise: a pop-up book of Christmas carols ill. by author. Little Simon, 1997. ISBN 0-689-81526-3 Subj: Format, unusual – toy & movable books. Holidays – Christmas. Music.

Santa Claus is coming! ill. by author. Holt, 1987. ISBN 0-8050-0472-6 Subj: Format, unusual – toy & movable books. Holidays – Christmas. Santa Claus.

Silent night ill. by author. Holt, 1987. ISBN 0-8050-0471-8 Subj: Format, unusual – toy & movable books. Holidays – Christmas.

Crespo, George. *How the sea began: a Taino myth* ill. by Pané, Ramón, d. Clarion, 1993. ISBN 0-395-63033-9 Subj: Creation. Folk & fairy tales – pourquoi tales. Foreign lands – Puerto Rico. Indians of North America – Taino.

Cressey, James. *The dragon and George* ill. by Tamasin Cole. Prentice-Hall, 1979. ISBN 0-13-219154-7 Subj: Dragons. Foreign lands – England. Knights. Middle Ages.

Fourteen rats and a rat-catcher ill. by Tamasin Cole. Prentice-Hall, 1978. ISBN 0-13-329920-1 Subj: Animals – rats. Family life. Problem solving.

Max the mouse ill. by Tamasin Cole. Prentice-Hall, 1979. ISBN 0-13-566299-0 Subj: Animals – mice. Crime.

Pet parrot ill. by Tamasin Cole. Prentice-Hall, 1979. ISBN 0-13-661793-X Subj: Birds – parakeets, parrots. Crime.

Cresswell, Helen. *Two hoots and the king* ill. by Martine Blanc. Crown, 1978. ISBN 0-517-53494-0 Subj: Behavior – mistakes. Birds – owls.

Two hoots in the snow ill. by Martine Blanc. Crown, 1978. ISBN 0-517-53495-9 Subj: Behavior – mistakes. Birds – owls.

Cressy, Judith. *Can you find it?* ill. with paintings. Abrams, 2002. ISBN 0-8109-3279-2 Subj: Art. Museums. Picture puzzles.

Can you find it, too? ill. with paintings. Abrams, 2004. ISBN 0-8109-5046-4 Subj: Art. Museums. Picture puzzles.

Cretan, Gladys Yessayan. *Lobo and Brewster* ill. by Patricia Coombs. Lothrop, 1971. Subj: Animals – cats. Animals – dogs. Emotions – envy, jealousy.

Ten brothers with camels ill. by Piero Ventura. Golden Pr., 1975. ISBN 0-307-15690-7 Subj: Counting, numbers. Desert.

Cretien, Paul D. *Sir Henry and the dragon* ill. by author. Follett, 1958. Subj: Animals – horses, ponies. Dragons. Knights. Royalty. Witches.

Crew, Gary. *Bright star* ill. by Anne Spudvilas. Kane/Miller, 1997. Originally published in Australia in 1996 by Thomas C. Lothian Pty. Ltd., Port Melbourne, Victoria, Australia. ISBN 0-916291-75-8 Subj: Astronomy. Careers – astronomers. Character traits – freedom. Dreams. Family life. Foreign lands – Australia.

Crewe, Sabrina. *The bear* ill. by Robert Morton. Raintree, 1997. ISBN 0-817-24367-4 Subj: Animals – bears. Nature.

The bee ill. with photos & illustrations. Raintree, 1997. ISBN 0-817-24362-3 Subj: Insects – bees. Nature.

Crews, Donald. *Bicycle race* ill. by author. Greenwillow, 1985. ISBN 0-688-05172-3 Subj: Counting, numbers. Sports – bicycling. Sports – racing.

Carousel ill. by author. Greenwillow, 1982. ISBN 0-688-00909-3 Subj: Merry-go-rounds.

Cloudy day/sunny day ill. by author. Harcourt, 1999. ISBN 0-15-201997-9 Subj: Activities – playing. Ethnic groups in the U.S. – African Americans. Weather.

Flying ill. by author. Greenwillow, 1986. ISBN 0-688-04319-4 Subj: Activities – flying. Airplanes, airports.

Freight train ill. by author. Greenwillow, 1978. ISBN 0-688-80165-X Subj: Caldecott award honor books. Trains.

Harbor ill. by author. Greenwillow, 1982. ISBN 0-688-00862-3 Subj: Boats, ships.

Inside freight train ill. by author. HarperFestival, 2001. ISBN 0-688-17087-0 Subj: Format, unusual – toy & movable books. Trains.

Light ill. by author. Greenwillow, 1981. ISBN 0-688-00310-9 Subj: Concepts. Light, lights.

Night at the fair ill. by author. Greenwillow, 1998. ISBN 0-688-11484-9 Subj: Fairs, festivals. Night.

Parade ill. by author. Greenwillow, 1983. ISBN 0-688-01996-X Subj: Cities, towns. Parades.

Sail away ill. by author. Greenwillow, 1995. ISBN 0-688-11054-1 Subj: Boats, ships. Family life. Sailors. Sports – sailing. Weather – storms.

School bus ill. by author. Greenwillow, 1984. ISBN 0-688-02808-X Subj: Buses. School. Transportation.

School bus [board book] ill. by author. Greenwillow, 2002. ISBN 0-694-01690-X Subj: Buses. Format, unusual – board books. School. Transportation.

Shortcut ill. by author. Greenwillow, 1992. ISBN 0-688-06436-1 Subj: Ethnic groups in the U.S. – African Americans. Trains.

Ten black dots ill. by author. Rev. ed. Greenwillow, 1986. ISBN 0-688-06068-4 Subj: Concepts – shape. Counting, numbers.

Truck ill. by author. Greenwillow, 1980. ISBN 0-688-84244-5 Subj: Caldecott award honor books. Transportation. Trucks. Wordless.

We read: A to Z ill. by author. Harper, 1984, c1967. Reprint. Originally published: New York: Harper & Row, [1967]. ISBN 0-688-03844-1 Subj: ABC books. Concepts.

Crews, Nina. *A ghost story* ill. by author. Greenwillow, 2001. ISBN 0-688-17674-7 Subj: Ethnic groups in the U.S. – African Americans. Family life. Family life – aunts, uncles. Ghosts.

A high, low, near, far, loud, quiet story ill. by author. Greenwillow, 1999. ISBN 0-688-16795-0 Subj: Activities. Concepts – opposites. Family life – brothers & sisters.

I'll catch the moon ill. by author. Greenwillow, 1996. ISBN 0-688-14135-8 Subj: Imagination. Moon. Night.

One hot summer day ill. by author. Greenwillow, 1995. ISBN 0-688-13394-0 Subj: Cities, towns. Ethnic groups in the U.S. – African Americans. Seasons – summer.

Snowball ill. by author. Greenwillow, 1997. ISBN 0-688-14929-4 Subj: Activities – playing. Seasons – winter. Weather – snow.

You are here ill. by author. Greenwillow, 1998. ISBN 0-688-15753-X Subj: Ethnic groups in the U.S. – African Americans. Family life. Imagination. Weather – rain.

Crichton, Michael. *see* Douglas, Michael

Crimi, Carolyn. *Don't need friends* ill. by Lynn Munsinger. Doubleday, 1999. ISBN 0-385-32643-2 Subj: Animals. Animals – dogs. Animals – rats. Behavior – needing someone. Friendship.

Tessa's tip-tapping toes ill. by Marsha Gray Carrington. Scholastic, 2002. ISBN 0-439-31768-1 Subj: Activities – dancing. Activities – singing. Animals – cats. Animals – mice. Weather – rain.

Crisp, Marty. *Black and white* ill. by Sherry Neidigh. Rising Moon, 2000. ISBN 0-8735-8756-1 Subj: Animals. Animals – dogs. Farms. Pets.

Totally polar ill. by Viv Eisner. Rising Moon, 2001. ISBN 0-8735-8789-8 Subj: Humorous stories. Imagination. Rhyming text. Seasons – summer. Weather – snow.

Cristaldi, Kathryn. *Baseball ballerina* ill. by Abby Carter. Random House, 2003. ISBN 0-679-91734-9 Subj: Activities – dancing. Ballet. Gender roles. Sports – baseball.

Baseball ballerina strikes out ill. by Abby Carter. Random House, 2000. ISBN 0-679-99132-8 Subj: Activities – dancing. Ballet. Behavior – bullying. Sports – baseball.

Cristini, Ermanno. *In my garden* by Ermanno Cristini & Luigi Puricelli; ill. by authors. Alphabet Pr., [1985] c1981. Orig title: Falter, Blumen, Tierre und Ich. ISBN 0-907234-05-4 Subj: Gardens, gardening. Wordless.

In the pond by Ermanno Cristini & Luigi Puricelli; ill. by authors. Alphabet Pr., 1984. ISBN 0-907234-43-7 Subj: Animals. Insects. Plants. Reptiles.

In the woods by Ermanno Cristini & Luigi Puricelli; ill. by authors. Alphabet Pr., 1983. ISBN 0-907234-31-3 Subj: Animals. Birds. Forest, woods. Wordless.

Croft, Priscilla. *Dealing with jealousy* ill. by author. PowerKids, 1996. ISBN 0-8239-2326-6 Subj: Emotions – envy, jealousy. Sibling rivalry.

Croll, Carolyn. *The little snowgirl* ill. by author. Putnam, 1989. ISBN 0-399-21691-X Subj: Folk & fairy tales. Foreign lands – Russia. Holidays – Christmas. Weather – snow.

The three brothers ill. by author. Putnam, 1991. ISBN 0-399-22195-6 Subj: Family life – brothers. Family life – fathers. Farms. Folk & fairy tales. Foreign lands – Germany.

Too many babas ill. by author. HarperCollins, 1979. ISBN 0-06-021384-1 Subj: Behavior – sharing. Food.

Cromie, William J. *Steven and the green turtle* ill. by Tom Eaton. HarperCollins, 1970. ISBN 0-590-30904-8 Subj: Animals – endangered animals. Reptiles – turtles, tortoises. Science.

Crompton, Anne Eliot. *The lifting stone* ill. by Marcia Sewall. Holiday, 1978. ISBN 0-8234-0325-4 Subj: Character traits – cleverness. Folk & fairy tales.

The winter wife: an Abnaki folktale ill. by Robert Andrew Parker. Little, 1975. ISBN 0-316-16143-8 Subj: Character traits – loyalty. Folk & fairy tales. Indians of North America – Abnaki.

Crompton, Margaret. *The house where Jack lives* ill. by Margery Gill. Merrimack, 1980. ISBN 0-370-30027-0 Subj: Family life. Foreign lands – England. Homes, houses.

Cronin, Doreen. *Click, clack, moo* ill. by Betsy Lewin. S&S, 2000. ISBN 0-689-83213-3 Subj: Activities – writing. Animals – bulls, cows. Behavior – dissatisfaction. Birds. Caldecott award honor books. Careers – farmers. Farms.

Diary of a worm ill. by Harry Bliss. Cotler, 2003. ISBN 0-06-000151-8 Subj: Activities – writing. Animals – worms.

Giggle, giggle, quack ill. by Betsy Lewin. S&S, 2002. ISBN 0-689-84506-5 Subj: Animals. Birds – ducks. Farms.

Wiggle ill. by Scott Menchin. Atheneum, 2005. ISBN 0-689-86375-6 Subj: Activities. Animals – dogs. Participation. Rhyming text.

Crook, Connie Brummel. *Maple moon* ill. by Scott Cameron. Stoddart, 1997. ISBN 0-7737-3017-6 Subj: Food. Foreign lands – Canada. Indians of North America – Missisauga.

Crosby-Jones, Michael. *Goodbye Rune* (Kaldhol, Marit)

Cross, Diana Harding. *Some birds have funny names* ill. by Jan Brett. Crown, 1981. ISBN 0-517-54005-3 Subj: Birds. Names.

Some plants have funny names ill. by Jan Brett. Crown, 1983. ISBN 0-517-54840-2 Subj: Names. Plants.

Cross, Genevieve. *My bunny book* ill. by Charles Clement. Doubleday, 1952. Subj: Animals – rabbits. Holidays – Easter.

A trip to the yard ill. by Marjorie Hartwell & Rachel Dixon. Doubleday, 1952. Subj: Animals. Birds. Plants.

Cross, Verda. *Great-grandma tells of threshing day* ill. by Gail Owens. A. Whitman, 1992. ISBN 0-8075-3042-5 Subj: Family life – great-grandparents. Farms.

Crossley-Holland, Kevin. *The green children* ill. by Margaret Gordon. Seabury Pr., 1968. Subj: Character traits – being different. Folk & fairy tales. Foreign lands – England.

How many miles to Bethlehem? ill. by Peter Malone. Levine, 2004. ISBN 0-439-67642-8 Subj: Holidays – Christmas. Religion – Nativity.

The pedlar of Swaffham ill. by Margaret Gordon. Seabury Pr., 1971. ISBN 0-395-28786-3 Subj: Careers – peddlers. Folk & fairy tales.

Sleeping Nanna ill. by Peter Melnyczuk. Ideals, 1990. ISBN 0-8249-8458-7 Subj: Dreams. Islands. Senses. Sleep.

The ugly duckling (Andersen, H. C. [Hans Christian])

Croswell, Volney. *How to hide a hippopotamus* ill. by author. Dodd, 1958. Subj: Animals – hippopotamuses. Behavior – hiding things. Concepts – size.

Crothers, Samuel McChord. *Miss Muffet's Christmas party* ill. by Olive M. Long. Houghton Mifflin, 1929. Subj: Parties. Spiders.

Crowe, Robert L. *Clyde monster* ill. by Kay Chorao. Dutton, 1976. ISBN 0-525-28025-1 Subj: Emotions – fear. Monsters. Night.

Tyler Toad and the thunder ill. by Kay Chorao. Dutton, 1980. ISBN 0-525-41795-8 Subj: Animals. Noise, sounds. Weather – lightning, thunder.

Crowell, Maryalicia. *A horse in the house* ill. by Leonard P. Kessler. Addison-Wesley, 1957. Subj: Cities, towns. Pets.

Crowley, Arthur. *Bonzo Beaver* ill. by Annie Gusman. Houghton Mifflin, 1980. ISBN 0-395-29081-3 Subj: Activities – babysitting. Animals – beavers. Rhyming text. Sibling rivalry.

The boogey man ill. by Annie Gusman. Houghton Mifflin, 1978. ISBN 0-395-26458-8 Subj: Behavior – dissatisfaction. Behavior – misbehavior. Family life. Monsters.

The ugly book ill. by Annie Gusman. Houghton Mifflin, 1982. ISBN 0-395-31858-0 Subj: Character traits – appearance.

The wagon man ill. by Annie Gusman. Houghton Mifflin, 1981. ISBN 0-395-30346-X Subj: Dreams. Rhyming text. Riddles & jokes.

Crowley, Michael. *New kid on Spurwick Ave.* ill. by Abby Carter. Little, 1992. ISBN 0-316-16230-2 Subj: Activities – making things. Clubs, gangs. Communities, neighborhoods. Friendship. Imagination.

Shack and back ill. by Abby Carter. Little, 1993. ISBN 0-316-16231-0 Subj: Clubs, gangs. Sports – bicycling. Sports – racing.

Crowther, Kitty. *Jack and Jim* ill. by author. Hyperion, 2000. ISBN 0-7868-2527-8 Subj: Birds. Friendship. Prejudice.

Crowther, Robert. *All the fun of the fair* ill. by author. Candlewick, 1992. ISBN 1-56402-001-0 Subj: Fairs, festivals. Format, unusual – toy & movable books.

Animal rap! ill. by author. Candlewick, 1993. ISBN 1-56402-207-2 Subj: Animals. Format, unusual – toy & movable books. Noise, sounds.

Animal snap! ill. by author. Candlewick, 1993. ISBN 1-56402-208-0 Subj: Animals. Format, unusual – toy & movable books.

Colors ill. by author. Candlewick, 2001. ISBN 0-7636-1404-1 Subj: Concepts – color. Format, unusual – toy & movable books.

Dump trucks and diggers ill. by author. Candlewick, 1996. ISBN 0-7636-0008-3 Subj: Activities – digging. Format, unusual – toy & movable books. Machines. Trucks.

Hide and seek counting book ill. by author. Viking, 1981. ISBN 0-670-48997-2 Subj: Counting, numbers. Format, unusual – toy & movable books.

The most amazing hide-and-seek alphabet book ill. by author. Viking, 1978. Subj: ABC books. Format, unusual – toy & movable books.

The most amazing hide-and-seek opposites book ill. by author. Viking, 1985. ISBN 0-670-80121-6 Subj: Concepts – opposites. Format, unusual – toy & movable books.

My pop-up surprise ABC ill. by author. Orchard, 1996. ISBN 0-531-30038-2 Subj: ABC books. Format, unusual – toy & movable books.

My pop-up surprise 1 2 3 ill. by author. Orchard, 1997. ISBN 0-531-30039-0 Subj: Counting, numbers. Format, unusual – toy & movable books.

Pop goes the weasel! 25 pop-up nursery rhymes comp. & ill. by Robert Crowther. Viking, 1987. ISBN 0-670-81815-1 Subj: Format, unusual – toy & movable books. Nursery rhymes.

Shapes ill. by author. Candlewick, 2002. ISBN 0-7636-1889-6 Subj: Concepts – shape. Format, unusual – toy & movable books.

Who lives in the country? ill. by author. Candlewick, 1992. ISBN 1-56402-090-8 Subj: Animals. Country. Format, unusual – toy & movable books.

Who lives in the garden? ill. by author. Candlewick, 1992. ISBN 1-56402-091-6 Subj: Animals. Format, unusual – toy & movable books. Gardens, gardening.

Who lives on the farm? ill. by author. Walker, 1989. ISBN 0-744-51504-1 Subj: Farms. Format, unusual – toy & movable books.

Croxford, Vera. *All kinds of animals* ill. by author. Grosset, 1972, c1968. Orig. title: All sorts of animals (Hamlyn Pub. Group, 1968). ISBN 0-448-03786-6 Subj: Animals.

Crozat, François. *I am a little cat* ill. by author. Barron's, 1992. ISBN 0-8120-6277-9 Subj: Animals – cats. Format, unusual – board books.

I am a little caterpillar ill. by author. Barron's, 1995. ISBN 0-8120-6485-2 Subj: Format, unusual – board books. Insects – butterflies, caterpillars. Metamorphosis. Science.

I am a little dog ill. by author. Barron's, 1992. ISBN 0-8120-6276-0 Subj: Animals – dogs. Format, unusual – board books.

Cruickshank, Margrit. *We're going to feed the ducks* ill. by Rosie Reeve. G. Stevens, 2004. ISBN 0-8368-4027-5 Subj: Animals. Birds. Birds – ducks. Food.

Crum, Shutta. *All on a sleepy night* ill. by Sylvie Daigneault. Stoddart, 2001. ISBN 0-7737-3315-9 Subj: Bedtime. Family life – grandparents. Rhyming text.

The bravest of the brave ill. by Tim Bowers. Knopf, 2005. ISBN 0-375-92637-2 Subj: Animals. Animals – skunks. Character traits – bravery. Counting, numbers. Emotions – fear. Forest, woods. Rhyming text.

Fox and Fluff ill. by John Bendall-Brunello. A. Whitman, 2002. ISBN 0-8075-2544-8 Subj: Animals – foxes. Birds – chickens. Family life – fathers.

My mountain song ill. by Ted Rand. Clarion, 2004. ISBN 0-618-15970-3 Subj: Family life – cousins. Family life – grandparents. Farms. Songs.

Who took my hairy toe? ill. by Katya Krénina. A. Whitman, 2001. ISBN 0-8075-5972-5 Subj: Anatomy – toes. Folk & fairy tales. Holidays – Halloween. Monsters.

Crume, Marion W. *Let me see you try* ill. by Jacques Rupp. Bowmar, 1968. Subj: Activities. Participation.

Listen! photos by Cliff Rowe & Judy Houston. Bowmar, 1968. Subj: Activities. Ethnic groups in the U.S. Participation.

What do you say? photos by Harvey Mandlin. Bowmar, 1967. Subj: Activities. Participation.

Crummel, Susan Stevens. *And the dish ran away with the spoon* (Stevens, Janet)

Cook-a-doodle-doo! (Stevens, Janet)

My big dog (Stevens, Janet)

Tumbleweed stew ill. by Janet Stevens. Harcourt, 2000. ISBN 0-15-202628-2 Subj: Animals – rabbits. Behavior – trickery.

Crump, Donald J. *Creatures small and furry* ill. with photos. National Geographic, 1983. ISBN 0-87044-491-3 Subj: Animals.

Crunk, Tony. *Big Mama* ill. by Margot Apple. Farrar, 2000. ISBN 0-374-30688-5 Subj: Family life – grandmothers. Orphans.

Grandpa's overalls ill. by Scott Nash. Orchard, 2001. ISBN 0-531-33321-3 Subj: Animals – dogs. Careers – farmers. Clothing – pants. Family life – grandfathers. Farms.

Cuetara, Mittie. *Baby business* ill. by author. Dutton, 2003. ISBN 0-525-47026-3 Subj: Babies. Poetry.

The crazy crawler crane and other very short truck stories ill. by author. Dutton, 1998. ISBN 0-525-45951-0 Subj: Rhyming text. Trucks.

Terrible Teresa and other very short stories ill. by author. Dutton, 1997. ISBN 0-525-45768-2 Subj: Behavior. Rhyming text.

Cullen, Catherine Ann. *The magical, mystical, marvelous coat* ill. by David Christiana. Little, 2001. ISBN 0-316-16334-1 Subj: Clothing. Magic. Rhyming text.

Thirsty baby ill. by David McPhail. Little, 2003. ISBN 0-316-16357-0 Subj: Babies. Folk & fairy tales. Rhyming text. Water.

Cullen, Lynn. *Little Scraggly Hair: a dog on Noah's Ark* ill. by Jacqueline Rogers. Holiday, 2003. ISBN 0-8234-1772-7 Subj: Anatomy – noses. Animals. Animals – dogs. Boats, ships. Religion – Noah. Weather – floods. Weather – rain. Weather – rainbows.

The mightiest heart ill. by Laurel Long. Dial, 1998. ISBN 0-8037-2293-1 Subj: Animals – dogs. Character traits – loyalty. Folk & fairy tales. Foreign lands – Wales.

Cummings, Betty Sue. *Turtle* ill. by Susan Dodge. Atheneum, 1981. ISBN 0-689-30805-1 Subj: Behavior – lost. Pets. Reptiles – turtles, tortoises.

Cummings, E. E. (Edward Estlin). *Fairy tales* ill. by John Eaton. Harcourt, [1975] c1965. ISBN 0-15-629895-3 Subj: Folk & fairy tales. Imagination.

Fairy tales ill. by Meilo So. Liveright, 2004. ISBN 0-8714-0658-6 Subj: Folk & fairy tales.

Hist whist ill. by Deborah Kogan Ray. Crown, 1989. ISBN 0-517-57258-3 Subj: Holidays – Halloween. Poetry.

In just-spring ill. by Heidi Goennel. Little, 1988. ISBN 0-316-16390-2 Subj: Poetry. Seasons – spring.

Little tree ill. by Deborah Kogan Ray. Crown, 1987. ISBN 0-517-56598-6 Subj: Holidays – Christmas. Poetry. Trees.

Little tree ill. by Mary C. Smith. Element Children's, 1999. ISBN 1-902618-55-6 Subj: Holidays – Christmas. Poetry. Trees.

Cummings, Pat. *Ananse and the lizard* ill. by author. Holt, 2002. ISBN 0-8050-6476-1 Subj: Animals. Folk & fairy tales – pourquoi tales. Foreign lands – Ghana. Reptiles – lizards.

Angel baby ill. by author. Lothrop, 2000. ISBN 0-688-14822-0 Subj: Babies. Ethnic groups in the U.S. – African Americans. Family life – brothers & sisters. Rhyming text.

C is for city (Grimes, Nikki)

Carousel ill. by author. Bradbury, 1994. ISBN 0-02-725512-3 Subj: Animals. Birthdays. Emotions – anger. Ethnic groups in the U.S. – African Americans. Family life. Merry-go-rounds.

Clean your room, Harvey Moon! ill. by author. Bradbury, 1991. ISBN 0-02-725511-5 Subj: Character traits – cleanliness. Ethnic groups in the U.S. – African Americans. Rhyming text.

C.L.O.U.D.S. ill. by author. Lothrop, 1986. ISBN 0-688-04683-5 Subj: Weather – clouds.

Jimmy Lee did it ill. by author. Lothrop, 1985. ISBN 0-688-04633-9 Subj: Ethnic groups in the U.S. – African Americans. Family life – brothers. Imagination – imaginary friends. Problem solving. Rhyming text.

My aunt came back ill. by author. HarperCollins, 1998. ISBN 0-694-01059-6 Subj: Activities – traveling. Ethnic groups in the U.S. – African Americans. Family life – aunts, uncles. Rhyming text.

Petey Moroni's Camp Runamok diary ill. by author. Bradbury, 1992. ISBN 0-02-725513-1 Subj: Animals – raccoons. Camps, camping. Ethnic groups in the U.S.

Cummings, Phil. *Goodness gracious!* ill. by Craig Smith. Watts, 1992. ISBN 0-531-08567-8 Subj: Anatomy. Rhyming text.

Cummings, W. T. (Walter Thies). *The kid* ill. by author. McGraw-Hill, 1960. Subj: Animals – horses, ponies. Behavior – seeking better things. Emotions – loneliness. Music.

Miss Esta Maude's secret ill. by author. McGraw-Hill, 1961. Subj: Automobiles. Behavior – secrets. Careers – teachers.

Wickford of Beacon Hill ill. by author. McGraw-Hill, 1962. Subj: Birds – cockatoos.

Cummins, Julie. *Country kid, city kid* ill. by Ted Rand. Holt, 2002. ISBN 0-8050-6467-2 Subj: Camps, camping. Cities, towns. Country. Farms.

The inside-outside book of libraries (Munro, Roxie)

Cuneo, Diane. *Mary Louise loses her manners* ill. by Jack E. Davis. Doubleday, 1999. ISBN 0-385-32538-X Subj: Behavior. Etiquette.

Cuneo, Mary Louise. *How to grow a picket fence* ill. by Nadine Bernard Westcott. HarperCollins, 1993. ISBN 0-06-020864-3 Subj: Gardens, gardening. Imagination.

Inside a sandcastle and other secrets ill. by Jan Brett. Houghton Mifflin, 1979. ISBN 0-395-27805-8 Subj: Character traits – smallness.

Mail for Husher Town ill. by Pam Paparone. Greenwillow, 2000. ISBN 0-688-16525-7 Subj: Activities – playing. Careers – postal workers. Letters, cards. Toys.

What can a giant do? ill. by Benrei Huang. HarperCollins, 1994. ISBN 0-06-021217-9 Subj: Concepts – size. Giants. Imagination – imaginary friends. Rhyming text.

Cunliffe, John. *The king's birthday cake* ill. by Faith Jaques. Elsevier-Dutton, 1979. ISBN 0-233-96453-3 Subj: Activities – baking, cooking. Birthdays. Cumulative tales. Royalty – kings.

Sara's giant and the upside down house ill. by Hilary Abrahams. Elsevier-Dutton, 1980. ISBN 0-233-97202-1 Subj: Giants.

Cunningham, David. *A crow's journey* ill. by author. A. Whitman, 1996. ISBN 0-8075-1356-3 Subj: Birds – crows. Rivers. Water. Weather – snow.

Cunningham, Julia. *A mouse called Junction* ill. by Michael Hague. Pantheon, 1980. ISBN 0-394-94112-8 Subj: Animals – mice. Animals – rats. Emotions. Emotions – fear. Friendship.

The vision of François the fox ill. by Nicholas Angelo. Pantheon, 1969. Subj: Animals – foxes.

Curious George and the dinosaur ed. by Margret Rey & Alan J. Shalleck. Houghton Mifflin, 1989. ISBN 0-395-51942-X Subj: Animals – monkeys. Dinosaurs. Prehistory.

Curious George and the dump truck ill. from the Curious George film series. Houghton Mifflin, 1984. ISBN 0-395-36635-6 Subj: Animals – monkeys. Character traits – curiosity. Trucks.

Curious George and the dump truck ill. in the style of H. A. Rey by Vipah Interactive. Houghton Mifflin, 1999. The 1984 ed. of this title has a different story line. ISBN 0-395-97832-7 Subj: Animals – monkeys. Birds – ducks. Parks. Trucks.

Curious George and the hot air balloon ill. in the style of H. A. Rey by Vipah Interactive. Houghton Mifflin, 1998. ISBN 0-395-92338-7 Subj: Activities – ballooning. Animals – monkeys. Behavior.

Curious George and the pizza ill. from the Curious George film series. Houghton Mifflin, 1985. ISBN 0-395-39039-7 Subj: Animals – monkeys. Character traits – curiosity. Food.

Curious George and the puppies ill. in the style of H. A. Rey by Vipah Interactive. Houghton, 1998. ISBN 0-395-92334-4 Subj:

Animals – dogs. Animals – monkeys. Behavior – misbehavior. Money.

Curious George at the fire station ill. from the Curious George film series. Houghton Mifflin, 1985. ISBN 0-395-39037-0 Subj: Animals – monkeys. Careers – firefighters. Character traits – curiosity.

Curious George goes camping ill. in the style of H. A. Rey by Vipah Interactive. Houghton Mifflin, 1999. ISBN 0-395-97831-9 Subj: Animals – monkeys. Camps, camping.

Curious George goes hiking ill. from the Curious George film series. Houghton Mifflin, 1985. ISBN 0-395-39038-9 Subj: Animals – monkeys. Character traits – curiosity. Sports – hiking.

Curious George goes sledding ill. from the Curious George film series. Houghton Mifflin, 1984. ISBN 0-395-36637-2 Subj: Animals – monkeys. Character traits – curiosity. Sports – sledding.

Curious George goes to a chocolate factory: based on the original character by Margret and H. A. Rey ill. in the style of H. A. Rey by Vipah Interactive. Houghton Mifflin, 1998. ISBN 0-395-91216-4 Subj: Animals – monkeys. Behavior – misbehavior. Food.

Curious George goes to a movie: based on the original character by Margret and H. A. Rey ill. in the style of H. A. Rey by Vipah Interactive. Houghton Mifflin, 1998. ISBN 0-395-91901-0 Subj: Animals – monkeys. Behavior – misbehavior. Theater.

Curious George goes to an ice cream shop ed. by Margret Rey & Alan J. Shalleck. Houghton Mifflin, 1989. ISBN 0-395-51943-8 Subj: Animals – monkeys. Food.

Curious George goes to school ed. by Margret Rey & Alan J. Shalleck. Houghton Mifflin, 1989. ISBN 0-395-51944-6 Subj: Animals – monkeys. School.

Curious George goes to the aquarium ill. from the Curious George film series. Houghton Mifflin, 1984. ISBN 0-395-36634-8 Subj: Animals – monkeys. Aquariums. Character traits – curiosity. Fish.

Curious George goes to the circus ill. from the Curious George film series. Houghton Mifflin, 1984. ISBN 0-395-36636-4 Subj: Animals – monkeys. Character traits – curiosity. Circus.

Curious George goes to the dentist ed. by Margret Rey & Alan J. Shalleck. Houghton Mifflin, 1989. ISBN 0-395-51941-1 Subj: Animals – monkeys. Careers – dentists. Teeth.

Curious George in the big city ill. in the style of H. A. Rey by Martha Weston. Houghton, 2001. ISBN 0-618-15252-0 Subj: Animals – monkeys. Character traits – curiosity. Cities, towns.

Curious George in the snow: based on the original character by Margret and H. A. Rey ill. in the style of H. A. Rey by Vipah Interactive. Houghton Mifflin, 1998. ISBN 0-395-91902-9 Subj: Animals – monkeys. Behavior – misbehavior. Weather – snow.

Curious George makes pancakes ill. in the style of H. A. Rey by Vipah Interactive. Houghton, 1998. ISBN 0-395-92337-9 Subj: Animals – monkeys. Food. Hospitals.

Curious George takes a train ill. in the style of H. A. Rey by Martha Weston. Houghton, 2002. ISBN 0-618-06566-0 Subj: Animals – monkeys. Character traits – curiosity. Trains.

Curious George visits a toy store ill. in the style of H. A. Rey by Martha Weston. Houghton, 2002. ISBN 0-618-06398-6 Subj: Animals – monkeys. Character traits – curiosity. Stores. Toys.

Curious George visits the zoo ill. from the Curious George film series. Houghton Mifflin, 1985. ISBN 0-395-39036-2 Subj: Animals – monkeys. Character traits – curiosity. Zoos.

Curious George's 1 to 10 and back again ill. by H. A. Rey. Houghton, 2001. ISBN 0-618-12074-2 Subj: Animals – monkeys. Counting, numbers. Format, unusual – board books.

Curle, Jock J. *The four good friends* ill. by Bernadette Watts. Holt, 1987. ISBN 0-8050-0231-6 Subj: Animals. Character traits – helpfulness. Character traits – kindness to animals.

Lucky Hans (Grimm, Jacob)

The sleepy owl (Pfister, Marcus)

The story of Jonah (Baumann, Kurt)

Currey, Anna. *Tickling tigers* ill. by author. Barron's, 1996. ISBN 0-8120-6594-8 Subj: Animals – mice. Animals – tigers. Behavior – boasting.

Truffle's Christmas ill. by author. Orchard, 2000. ISBN 0-531-30289-X Subj: Animals – mice. Holidays – Christmas. Santa Claus.

Curry, Jane Louise. *The Christmas knight* ill. by DyAnne DiSalvo-Ryan. McElderry, 1993. ISBN 0-689-50572-8 Subj: Behavior – sharing. Character traits – kindness. Holidays – Christmas. Knights. Middle Ages. Royalty – kings.

Little, little sister ill. by Erik Blegvad. Macmillan, 1989. ISBN 0-689-50459-4 Subj: Character traits – smallness. Family life. Family life – sisters. Farms.

Curry, Nancy. *The littlest house* ill. by Jacques Rupp. Bowmar, 1968. Subj: Family life. Homes, houses.

Curry, Peter. *Animals* ill. by author. Price Stern Sloan, 1984. ISBN 0-8431-0924-6 Subj: Animals.

Curti, Anna. *At home* ill. by author. Little, 1991. ISBN 0-316-16538-7 Subj: Family life.

Seasons ill. by author. Little, 1991. ISBN 0-316-16539-5 Subj: Animals – wolves. Format, unusual – board books. Seasons.

Curtis, Gavin. *The bat boy and his violin* ill. by E. B. Lewis. S&S, 1998. ISBN 0-689-80099-1 Subj: Ethnic groups in the U.S. – African Americans. Music. Musical instruments – violins. Sports – baseball.

Grandma's baseball ill. by author. Crown, 1990. ISBN 0-517-57390-3 Subj: Emotions. Ethnic groups in the U.S. – African Americans. Family life – grandparents.

Curtis, Jamie Lee. *I'm gonna like me* ill. by Laura Cornell. Cotler, 2002. ISBN 0-06-028762-4 Subj: Behavior. Rhyming text. Self-concept.

It's hard to be five: learning how to work my control panel ill. by Laura Cornell. Cotler, 2004. ISBN 0-06-008096-5 Subj: Behavior – growing up. Rhyming text.

Tell me again about the night I was born ill. by Laura Cornell. HarperCollins, 1996. ISBN 0-06-024529-8 Subj: Adoption. Babies. Family life.

Today I feel silly and other moods that make my day ill. by Laura Cornell. HarperCollins, 1998. ISBN 0-06-024561-1 Subj: Emotions. Family life. Format, unusual – toy & movable books. Rhyming text.

When I was little: a four-year-old's memoir of her youth ill. by Laura Cornell. HarperCollins, 1993. ISBN 0-06-021079-6 Subj: Babies. Behavior – growing up.

Where do balloons go? ill. by Laura Cornell. HarperCollins, 2000. ISBN 0-06-027981-8 Subj: Rhyming text. Toys – balloons.

Curtis, Neil. *How paper is made* ill. by Peter Greenland. Lerner, 1992. ISBN 0-8225-2376-0 Subj: Activities – making things. Paper.

Curtis Brown, Beatrice. *see* Brown, Beatrice Curtis

Curtiss, A. B. *In the company of bears* ill. by Barbara Stone. Oldcastle, 1994. ISBN 0-932529-72-0 Subj: Activities. Animals – polar bears. Rhyming text.

Cushman, Doug. *The ABC mystery* ill. by author. HarperCollins, 1993. ISBN 0-06-021227-6 Subj: ABC books. Animals. Careers – detectives. Mystery stories. Rhyming text.

Giants comp. & ill. by Doug Cushman. Platt, 1980. ISBN 0-448-13623-6 Subj: Giants. Poetry.

Mouse and Mole and the Christmas walk ill. by author. Scientific American, 1994. ISBN 0-7167-6560-8 Subj: Animals – mice. Animals – moles. Ecology. Holidays – Christmas. Science. Trees.

The mystery of King Karfu ill. by author. HarperCollins, 1996. ISBN 0-06-024797-5 Subj: Animals – wombats. Careers – detectives. Foreign lands – Egypt. Mystery stories. Royalty – kings.

The mystery of the monkey's maze ill. by author. HarperCollins, 1999. ISBN 0-06-027720-3 Subj: Animals. Careers – detectives. Foreign lands – Borneo. Mystery stories.

Nasty Kyle the crocodile ill. by author. Grosset, 1983. ISBN 0-448-16592-9 Subj: Behavior – dissatisfaction. Concepts. Reptiles – alligators, crocodiles.

Once upon a pig comp. & ill. by Doug Cushman. Grosset, 1982. ISBN 0-448-47492-1 Subj: Animals – pigs. Rhyming text.

Possum stew ill. by author. Dutton, 1990. ISBN 0-525-44566-8 Subj: Animals – possums. Behavior – trickery. Food.

Space cat ill. by author. HarperCollins, 2004. ISBN 0-06-008966-0 Subj: Animals – cats. Robots. Space & space ships.

Cushman, Jerome. *Marvella's hobby* ill. by Prue Theobalds. Abelard-Schuman, 1962. Subj: Animals – bulls, cows. Trains.

Cusimano, Maryann K. *You are my I love you* ill. by Satomi Ichikawa. Philomel, 2001. ISBN 0-399-23392-X Subj: Family life – parents. Rhyming text. Toys – bears.

Cutler, Ebbitt. *Paulino* (Simons, Traute)

Cutler, Ivor. *The animal house* ill. by Helen Oxenbury. Morrow, 1977, 1976. ISBN 0-688-32110-0 Subj: Animals. Homes, houses. Zoos.

Doris ill. by Claudio Muñoz. Morrow, 1992. ISBN 0-688-11939-5 Subj: Birds. Songs.

Herbert: five stories ill. by Patrick Benson. Lothrop, 1988. ISBN 0-688-08148-7 Subj: Animals. Imagination.

Cutler, Jane. *The cello of Mr. O* ill. by Greg Couch. Dutton, 1999. ISBN 0-525-46119-1 Subj: Careers – musicians. Character traits – bravery. Musical instruments – cellos. War.

Darcy and Gran don't like babies ill. by Susannah Ryan. Scholastic, 1993. ISBN 0-590-44587-1 Subj: Babies. Emotions – envy, jealousy. Family life – grandmothers. Family life – new sibling. Sibling rivalry.

Mr. Carey's garden ill. by G. Brian Karas. Houghton Mifflin, 1996. ISBN 0-395-68191-X Subj: Animals – snails. Friendship. Gardens, gardening.

Cutlip, Kimbra L. *Firefighter's night before Christmas* ill. by James Rice. Pelican, 2002. ISBN 1-58980-054-0 Subj: Careers – firefighters. Holidays – Christmas. Poetry.

Cutts, David. *The gingerbread boy* (The gingerbread boy)

I can read about creatures of the night ill. by Janice Kinnealy; consultant, Kathy Carlstead. Troll, 1998. ISBN 0-8167-4345-2 Subj: Ghosts. Monsters. Night. Science.

Look . . . a butterfly ill. by Eulala Conner. Troll, 1982. ISBN 0-89375-662-8 Subj: Insects – butterflies, caterpillars. Metamorphosis. Science.

More about dinosaurs ill. by Gregory C. Wenzel. Troll, 1982. ISBN 0-89375-668-7 Subj: Dinosaurs. Prehistory.

Cuyler, Margery. *Baby Dot* ill. by Ellen Weiss. Houghton Mifflin, 1990. ISBN 0-395-51934-9 Subj: Dinosaurs. School.

The biggest, best snowman ill. by Will Hillenbrand. Scholastic, 1998. ISBN 0-590-13922-3 Subj: Animals. Concepts – size. Seasons – winter. Snowmen. Weather – snow.

Fat Santa ill. by Marsha Winborn. Holt, 1987. ISBN 0-8050-0423-8 Subj: Character traits – helpfulness. Dreams. Holidays – Christmas. Santa Claus.

Freckles and Jane ill. by Leslie Holt Morrill. Holt, 1989. ISBN 0-8050-0643-5 Subj: Animals – dogs. Friendship. Pets.

Freckles and Willie ill. by Marsha Winborn. Holt, 1986. ISBN 0-03-003772-7 Subj: Animals – dogs. Friendship.

From here to there ill. by Yu Cha Pak. Holt, 1999. ISBN 0-8050-3191-X Subj: Ethnic groups in the U.S. – Mexican Americans. Geography. Self-concept.

100th day worries ill. by Arthur Howard. S&S, 2000. ISBN 0-689-82979-5 Subj: Counting, numbers. School.

Road signs: a harey race with a tortoise ill. by Steve Haskamp. Winslow, 2000. ISBN 1-890817-236 Subj: Animals. Animals – rabbits. Reptiles – turtles, tortoises. Sports – racing. Traffic, traffic signs.

Shadow's baby ill. by Ellen Weiss. Houghton Mifflin, 1989. ISBN 0-89919-831-7 Subj: Animals – dogs. Babies. Family life.

Sir William and the pumpkin monster ill. by Marsha Winborn. Holt, 1984. ISBN 0-03-064032-6 Subj: Ghosts. Holidays – Halloween.

Stop drop and roll ill. by Arthur Howard. S&S, 2001. ISBN 0-689-84355-0 Subj: Behavior – worrying. Emotions – fear. Fire. Safety. School.

That's good! that's bad! ill. by David Catrow. Holt, 1991. ISBN 0-8050-1535-3 Subj: Animals. Zoos.

Cyrus, Kurt. *Slow train to Oxmox* ill. by author. Farrar, 1998. ISBN 0-374-37047-8 Subj: Behavior. Character traits – patience. Trains.

Czarnecki, Lois R. *The six wrinkled Woos* ill. by Laura Almada. Ohana Pr., 1992. ISBN 0-9627275-0-4 Subj: Animals – dogs.

Czech, Jan M. *An American face* ill. by Frances Clancy. Child & Family Pr., 2000. ISBN 0-8786-8718-1 Subj: Adoption. Ethnic groups in the U.S. – Korean Americans.

Czernecki, Stefan. *The cricket's cage: a Chinese folktale* trans. by Simon Ching; ill. by author. Hyperion, 1997. ISBN 0-7868-2234-1 Subj: Buildings. Folk & fairy tales. Foreign lands – China. Insects – crickets.

Huevos rancheros ill. by author. Crocodile, 2002. ISBN 1-56656-428-X Subj: Animals – coyotes. Birds – chickens. Character traits – cleverness.

The hummingbird's gift by Stefan Czernecki & Timothy Rhodes; ill. by Stefan Czernecki; weavings by Juliana Reyes de Silva & Juan Hilario Silva. Hyperion, 1994. ISBN 1-56282-605-0 Subj: Birds – humming birds. Foreign lands – Mexico. Gifts. Holidays – Day of the Dead. Indians of North America – Tarascan. Weather – droughts.

Pancho's piñata by Stefan Czernecki & Timothy Rhodes; ill. by Stefan Czernecki. Walt Disney, 1992. ISBN 1-56282-278-0 Subj: Emotions – happiness. Folk & fairy tales. Foreign lands – Mexico. Holidays – Christmas.

Paper lanterns ill. by author. Talewinds, 2000. ISBN 1-57091-410-9 Subj: Character traits – persistence. Foreign lands – China. Paper.

The singing snake by Stefan Czernecki & Timothy Rhodes; ill. by Stefan Czernecki. Hyperion, 1993. ISBN 1-56282-400-7 Subj:

Activities – singing. Animals. Birds – larks. Folk & fairy tales. Foreign lands – Australia. Reptiles – snakes.

The sleeping bread by Stefan Czernecki & Timothy Rhodes; ill. by Stefan Czernecki. Hyperion, 1992. ISBN 1-56282-183-0 Subj: Activities – baking, cooking. Food. Foreign lands – Guatemala. Poverty.

Zorah's magic carpet ill. by author. Hyperion, 1995. ISBN 0-7868-2066-7 Subj: Activities – traveling. Activities – weaving. Folk & fairy tales. Foreign lands – Morocco. Magic.

Dabcovich, Lydia. *Busy beavers* ill. by author. Dutton, 1988. ISBN 0-525-44384-3 Subj: Animals – beavers. Science.

Ducks fly ill. by author. Dutton, 1990. ISBN 0-525-44586-2 Subj: Activities – flying. Birds – ducks.

Follow the river ill. by author. Dutton, 1980. ISBN 0-525-30015-5 Subj: Rivers.

The keys to my kingdom ill. by author. Lothrop, 1992. ISBN 0-688-09775-8 Subj: Foreign languages. Nursery rhymes.

Mrs. Huggins and her hen Hannah ill. by author. Dutton, 1985. ISBN 0-525-44203-0 Subj: Birds – chickens. Death. Emotions – grief. Friendship.

The polar bear son: an Inuit tale ill. by reteller. Clarion, 1997. ISBN 0-395-72766-9 Subj: Animals – polar bears. Eskimos. Folk & fairy tales. Foreign lands – Arctic.

Sleepy bear ill. by author. Dutton, 1982. ISBN 0-525-39465-6 Subj: Animals – bears. Seasons – spring. Seasons – winter.

da Costa, Deborah. *Snow in Jerusalem* ill. by Cornelius Van Wright & Ying-Hwa Hu. A. Whitman, 2001. ISBN 0-8075-7521-6 Subj: Animals – cats. Foreign lands – Israel. Weather – snow.

Dadey, Debbie. *Shooting star: Annie Oakley, the legend* ill. by Scott Goto. Walker, 1997. ISBN 0-8027-8485-2 Subj: Folk & fairy tales. Sports. U.S. history.

Will Rogers: larger than life ill. by Scott Goto. Walker, 1999. ISBN 0-8027-8682-0 Subj: Folk & fairy tales. U.S. history.

Daffis-Felicelli, Christine. *The little star of Bethlehem* ill. by author. Roman, 1993. ISBN 0-937739-20-0 Subj: Holidays – Christmas. Religion – Nativity. Stars.

Daghlian, Suzanne. *Babies help out* (Leonard, Marcia)

Favorite colors (Leonard, Marcia)

Dahl, Michael. *Downhill fun* ill. by Todd Ouren. Picture Window, 2004. ISBN 1-4048-0579-6 Subj: Counting, numbers. Picture puzzles. Seasons – winter. Sports – skiing.

Eggs and legs ill. by Todd Ouren. Picture Window, 2005. ISBN 1-4048-0945-7 Subj: Counting, numbers. Eggs. Picture puzzles.

Footprints in the snow ill. by Todd Ouren. Picture Window, 2004. ISBN 1-4048-0946-5 Subj: Counting, numbers. Picture puzzles. Seasons – winter. Weather – snow.

From the garden ill. by Todd Ouren. Picture Window, 2004. ISBN 1-4048-0578-8 Subj: Counting, numbers. Food. Gardens, gardening. Picture puzzles. Seasons.

Hands down ill. by Todd Ouren. Picture Window, 2004. ISBN 1-4048-0948-1 Subj: Counting, numbers. Picture puzzles.

Lots of ladybugs! ill. by Todd Ouren. Picture Window, 2005. ISBN 1-4048-0944-9 Subj: Counting, numbers. Insects – ladybugs.

On the launch pad ill. by Todd Ouren. Picture Window, 2004. ISBN 1-4048-0581-8 Subj: Counting, numbers. Space & space ships.

One big building ill. by Todd Ouren. Picture Window, 2004. ISBN 1-4048-0580-X Subj: Counting, numbers. Machines. Picture puzzles.

One checkered flag ill. by Todd Ouren. Picture Window, 2004. ISBN 1-4048-0576-1 Subj: Automobiles. Counting, numbers. Sports – racing.

One giant splash ill. by Todd Ouren. Picture Window, 2004. ISBN 1-4048-0577-X Subj: Animals. Counting, numbers. Fish. Sea & seashore.

Pie for piglets ill. by Todd Ouren. Picture Window, 2005. ISBN 1-4048-0943-0 Subj: Animals – pigs. Counting, numbers.

Starry arms ill. by Todd Ouren. Picture Window, 2004. ISBN 1-4048-0947-3 Subj: Animals. Counting, numbers. Sea & seashore.

Dahl, Roald. *Dirty beasts* ill. by Rosemary Fawcett. Farrar, 1983. ISBN 0-374-31790-9 Subj: Bedtime. Dreams. Monsters. Poetry.

The enormous crocodile ill. by Quentin Blake. Knopf, 1978. ISBN 0-394-93594-2 Subj: Animals. Reptiles – alligators, crocodiles.

The giraffe and the pelly and me ill. by Quentin Blake. Farrar, 1985. ISBN 0-374-32602-9 Subj: Activities – working. Animals. Careers – window cleaners. Crime.

Dahl, Tessa. *Babies, babies, babies* ill. by Siobhan Dodds. Viking, 1991. ISBN 0-670-83921-3 Subj: Babies. Birth. Family life.

The same but different ill. by Arthur Robins. Viking, 1989. ISBN 0-670-82572-7 Subj: Activities. Family life.

Dahlbäck-Lutteman, Helena. *My sister Lotta and me* retold by Rika Lesser; ill. by Charlotte Ramel. Holt, 1993. ISBN 0-8050-2558-8 Subj: Activities – playing. Family life – sisters. Toys – dolls.

Dahlie, Elizabeth. *Bernelly & Harriet: the country mouse & the city mouse* ill. by author. Little, 2002. ISBN 0-316-60811-4 Subj: Animals – mice. Cities, towns. Country. Family life – cousins. Folk & fairy tales.

Daily, Don. *The twelve days of Christmas cats* ill. by author. Courage Books, 1998. ISBN 0-7624-0384-5 Subj: Animals – cats. Counting, numbers. Holidays – Christmas. Songs.

Dakos, Kalli. *Our principal promised to kiss a pig* by Kalli Dakos & Alicia DesMarteau; ill. by Carl DiRocco. A. Whitman, 2004. ISBN 0-8075-6629-2 Subj: Animals – pigs. Books, reading. Careers – school principals. School.

Dale, Elizabeth. *How long?* ill. by Alan Marks. Orchard, 1998. ISBN 0-531-30101-X Subj: Animals – dormice. Family life – mothers. Time.

Dale, Penny. *All about Alice* ill. by author. Candlewick, 1992. ISBN 1-56402-171-8 Subj: Activities – playing. Family life – sisters.

Bet you can't ill. by author. Lippincott, 1987. ISBN 0-397-32256-9 Subj: Bedtime. Character traits – orderliness. Ethnic groups in the U.S. – African Americans. Family life – brothers & sisters.

Big Brother, Little Brother ill. by author. Courage Books, 1997. ISBN 0-7636-0146-2 Subj: Family life – brothers.

Daisy Rabbit's tree house ill. by author. Candlewick, 1995. ISBN 1-56402-641-8 Subj: Animals. Animals – rabbits. Homes, houses. Night. Sleepovers. Trees.

The elephant tree ill. by author. Putnam, 1991. ISBN 0-399-22282-0 Subj: Animals. Animals – elephants. Jungle. Trees.

Ten out of bed ill. by author. Candlewick, 1994. ISBN 1-56402-322-2 Subj: Bedtime. Counting, numbers. Sleep. Toys.

Ten play hide-and-seek ill. by author. Candlewick, 1998. ISBN 0-7636-0654-5 Subj: Bedtime. Behavior – hiding. Toys.

Wake up, Mr. B.! ill. by author. Candlewick, 1992. ISBN 1-56402-104-1 Subj: Animals – dogs. Family life. Imagination. Morning. Pets.

Dale, Ruth Bluestone. *Benjamin . . . and Sylvester also* ill. by J. B. Handelsman. McGraw-Hill, 1960. Subj: Animals – dogs. Behavior – dissatisfaction. Country.

Daleo, Morgan Simone. *A spirited alphabet: from A to Z* ill. by Frank Riccio. Hampton Roads, 1999. ISBN 1-57174-148-8 Subj: ABC books.

Dalgleish, Sharon. *Working dogs* ill. with photos. Chelsea, 2005. ISBN 0-7910-8275-X Subj: Animals – dogs. Animals – service animals. Farms.

Dalgliesh, Alice. *The little wooden farmer* ill. by Anita Lobel. Macmillan, 1988, c1930. ISBN 0-02-725590-5 Subj: Farms.

The Thanksgiving story ill. by Helen Moore Sewell. Scribners, [1987] c1954. ISBN 0-684-18999-2 Subj: Caldecott award honor books. Holidays – Thanksgiving. Pilgrims. U.S. history.

The turnip (Milhous, Katherine)

D'Allancé, Mireille. *see* Allancé, Mireille d'

Dallas-Conte, Juliet. *Cock-a-moo-moo* ill. by Alison Bartlett. Little, 2001. ISBN 0-316-60505-0 Subj: Animals. Birds – chickens. Farms. Noise, sounds.

Dallas-Smith, Peter. *Trumpets in Grumpetland* ill. by Peter Cross. Random House, 1985. ISBN 0-394-97028-4 Subj: Music. Musical instruments – trumpets. Mythical creatures.

Dalmais, Anne-Marie. *And may the best animal win!* ill. by Doris Susan Smith. Golden Bks., 1986. ISBN 0-307-15841-1 Subj: Activities – making things. Animals. Contests.

The Best bedtime stories of Mother Bear ill. by Violayne Hulné; English trans. by Diane Cohen. Derrydale Books, 1988, c1987. ISBN 0-517-66273-6 Subj: Animals – bears. Bedtime.

Best bedtime stories of Mother Cat ill. by Violayne Hulné; English trans. by Diane Cohen. Derrydale Books, 1988. ISBN 0-517-66272-8 Subj: Animals – cats. Bedtime.

Best bedtime stories of Mother Hen ill. by Violayne Hulné; English trans. by Diane Cohen. Derrydale Books, 1987. ISBN 0-517-65493-8 Subj: Bedtime. Birds – chickens.

Best bedtime stories of Mother Mouse ill. by Violayne Hulné; English trans. by Diane Cohen. Derrydale Books, 1987. ISBN 0-517-65492-X Subj: Animals – mice. Bedtime.

Best bedtime stories of Mother Pig ill. by Violayne Hulné; English trans. by Diane Cohen. Derrydale Books, 1988. ISBN 0-517-66276-0 Subj: Animals – pigs. Bedtime.

Best bedtime stories of Mother Sheep ill. by Violayne Hulné; English trans. by Diane Cohen. Derrydale Books, 1988, c1987. ISBN 0-517-66274-4 Subj: Animals – sheep. Bedtime.

Betsy the bunny ill. by Annie Bonhomme; English trans. by Diane Cohen. Derrydale Books, 1987. ISBN 0-517-65308-7 Subj: Animals – rabbits. Behavior – lost. Toys – dolls.

The butterfly book of birds ill. by Guy Michel. Two Continents, 1977. ISBN 0-8467-0226-6 Subj: Birds.

Danny the duck ill. by Annie Bonhomme; English trans. by Diane Cohen. Derrydale Books, 1987. ISBN 0-517-65309-5 Subj: Behavior – promptness, tardiness. Birds – ducks.

The Elephant's airplane and other machines ill. by Doris Susan Smith. Golden Bks., 1984. ISBN 0-307-65579-2 Subj: Animals. Transportation.

Henry the hedgehog ill. by Annie Bonhomme; English trans. by Diane Cohen. Derrydale Books, 1987. ISBN 0-517-65310-9 Subj: Activities – vacationing. Animals – hedgehogs. Family life – grandparents.

In my garden: learning to count ill. by Genji. Two Continents, 1977. ISBN 0-8467-0219-3 Subj: Counting, numbers. Poetry.

Kelly the kitten ill. by Annie Bonhomme; English trans. by Diane Cohen. Derrydale Books, 1987. ISBN 0-517-65311-7 Subj: Animals – cats. Friendship. School.

Molly and Mimi the mouse twins ill. by Annie Bonhomme; English trans. by Diane Cohen. Derrydale Books, 1987. ISBN 0-517-65312-5 Subj: Animals – mice. Birthdays. Multiple births – twins.

Petey the puppy ill. by Annie Bonhomme; English trans. by Diane Cohen. Derrydale Books, 1987. ISBN 0-517-65313-3 Subj: Activities – making things. Animals – dogs. Homes, houses.

Dalton, Alene. *My new picture book of songs* scores by Reah Allen; ill. by Gini Bunnell. Osmond Pub., 1979. ISBN 0-89888-002-5 Subj: Music. Songs.

Dalton, Anne. *Prince Starr* ill. by author. Kaye & Ward, 1985. ISBN 0-7182-2101-X Subj: Folk & fairy tales. Sky.

This is the way ill. by author. Scholastic, 1992. ISBN 0-590-45892-2 Subj: Family life. Nursery rhymes.

Dalton, Cindy Devine. *Sound* ill. by Kathleen Carreiro. Rourke, 2001. ISBN 1-58952-015-7 Subj: Noise, sounds. Science.

Daly, Catherine. *Whiskers* ill. by Tom Leonard. Golden Bks., 2000. ISBN 0-307-46214-5 Subj: Animals. Hair.

Daly, Jude. *Fair, Brown & Trembling: an Irish Cinderella story* ill. by author. Farrar, 2000. ISBN 0-374-32247-3 Subj: Family life – stepfamilies. Folk & fairy tales. Foreign lands – Ireland. Royalty – princes. Sibling rivalry.

Daly, Kathleen N. *Daniel in the lions' den* (Bible Old Testament Daniel)

Dinosaurs ill. by Tim & Greg Hildebrandt. Golden Pr., 1977. ISBN 0-307-11835-5 Subj: Dinosaurs. Prehistory.

The Giant little Golden Book of dogs ill. by Tibor Gergely. S&S, 1957. Subj: Animals – dogs.

Jesus our friend ill. by Jim Cummins. Rand McNally, 1984. ISBN 0-528-82494-5 Subj: Format, unusual – board books. Religion.

Jonah and the great fish (Bible Old Testament Jonah)

Joseph and his brothers (Bible Old Testament Joseph)

The Macmillan picture wordbook ill. by John Wallner. Macmillan, 1982. ISBN 0-02-725600-6 Subj: Dictionaries.

Making friends ill. by Maryann Cocca-Leffler. Parker Brothers, 1984. ISBN 0-910-31327-X Subj: Friendship.

Noah and the ark (Bible Old Testament Noah)

Strawberry Shortcake and pets on parade ill. by Pat Sustendal. Parker Brothers, 1983. ISBN 0-910-31306-7 Subj: Pets. Theater.

The three bears (The three bears)

Today's biggest animals ill. by Tim & Greg Hildebrandt. Golden Pr., 1977. ISBN 0-307-61836-6 Subj: Animals. Science.

Unusual animals ill. by Tim & Greg Hildebrandt. Golden Pr., 1977. ISBN 0-307-61834-7 Subj: Animals. Science.

Daly, Maureen. *Patrick visits the library* ill. by Paul Lantz. Dodd, 1961. Subj: Animals – dogs. Birthdays. Libraries.

Daly, Niki. *Ben's gingerbread man* ill. by author. Viking, 1985. ISBN 0-670-80806-7 Subj: Family life – mothers. Food.

The boy on the beach ill. by author. McElderry, 1999. ISBN 0-689-82175-1 Subj: Behavior – lost. Family life. Foreign lands – South Africa. Rhyming text. Sea & seashore – beaches.

Bravo, Zan Angelo! a commedia dell'arte tale ill. by author. Farrar, 1998. ISBN 0-374-30953-1 Subj: Clowns, jesters. Fairs, festivals. Family life. Foreign lands – Italy. Theater.

The dinosaurs are back and it's all your fault, Edward! (Hartmann, Wendy)

Jamela's dress ill. by author. Farrar, 1999. ISBN 0-374-33667-9 Subj: Clothing – dresses. Foreign lands – South Africa.

Joseph's other red sock ill. by author. Atheneum, 1982. ISBN 0-689-50216-8 Subj: Clothing – socks.

Just like Archie ill. by author. Viking, 1986. ISBN 0-670-81253-6 Subj: Pets.

Look at me! ill. by author. Viking, 1986. ISBN 0-670-81252-8 Subj: Sibling rivalry.

Mama, papa and baby Joe ill. by author. Viking, 1991. ISBN 0-670-84161-7 Subj: Shopping.

Mary Malloy and the baby who wouldn't sleep ill. by author. Western, 1993. ISBN 0-307-17501-4 Subj: Foreign lands – Egypt. Moon. Reptiles – alligators, crocodiles. Sleep.

Monsters are like that ill. by author. Viking, 1985. ISBN 0-670-80807-5 Subj: Family life – brothers & sisters. Monsters.

My dad ill. by author. McElderry, 1995. ISBN 0-689-50620-1 Subj: Family life – fathers. Illness.

Not so fast Songololo ill. by author. Atheneum, 1986. ISBN 0-689-50367-9 Subj: Cities, towns. Family life – grandmothers. Foreign lands – Africa. Foreign lands – South Africa. Shopping.

Old Bob's brown bear ill. by author. Farrar, 2002. ISBN 0-374-35612-2 Subj: Family life – grandfathers. Toys. Toys – bears.

Once upon a time ill. by author. Farrar, 2003. ISBN 0-374-35633-5 Subj: Books, reading. Foreign lands – South Africa. Friendship. School.

Papa Lucky's shadow ill. by author. McElderry, 1992. ISBN 0-689-50541-8 Subj: Activities – dancing. Family life – grandfathers.

Somewhere in Africa (Mennen, Ingrid)

Teddy's ear ill. by author. Viking, 1985. ISBN 0-670-80808-3 Subj: Family life – mothers. Toys – bears.

Thank you Henrietta ill. by author. Viking, 1986. ISBN 0-670-81254-4 Subj: Character traits – helpfulness.

Vim, the rag mouse ill. by author. Atheneum, 1979. ISBN 0-689-50141-2 Subj: Crime. Toys.

What's cooking, Jamela? ill. by author. Farrar, 2001. ISBN 0-374-35602-5 Subj: Birds – chickens. Emotions. Foreign lands – South Africa. Holidays – Christmas. Pets.

Why the sun and moon live in the sky ill. by author. Lothrop, 1995. ISBN 0-688-13332-0 Subj: Folk & fairy tales. Foreign lands – Nigeria. Moon. Sea & seashore. Sun.

Dame Wiggins of Lee and her seven wonderful cats ed. by John Ruskin; ill. by Robert Broomfield. McGraw-Hill, 1963. Ascribed to Richard Scrafton Sharpe and Mrs. Pearson. Endpapers: reproduction of Kate Greenaway drawings. Subj: Nursery rhymes.

Dami, Andrea. *Dinosaurs [board book]* (Casalis, Anna)

D'Amico, Carmela. *Ella, the elegant elephant* by Carmela & Steven D'Amico; ill. by Steven D'Amico. Levine, 2004. ISBN 0-439-62792-3 Subj: Animals – elephants. Behavior – bullying. Clothing – hats. Moving. School – first day.

D'Amico, Steven. *Ella, the elegant elephant* (D'Amico, Carmela)

Damjan, Mischa. *Atuk* ill. by Józef Wilkon. North-South, 1989. ISBN 1-55858-091-3 Subj: Animals – dogs. Animals – wolves. Eskimos. Foreign lands – Arctic.

The big squirrel and the little rhinoceros ill. by Hans de Beer; trans. by Lenny Hort. North-South, 1991. ISBN 1-55858-117-0 Subj: Animals. Behavior – wishing. Concepts – size.

The clown said no ill. by Józef Wilkon; trans. by Anthea Bell. North-South, 1986. ISBN 0-8050-0055-0 Subj: Behavior – seeking better things. Circus. Clowns, jesters.

December's travels ill. by Dusan Kállay. Dial, 1986. ISBN 0-8037-0257-4 Subj: Days of the week, months of the year. Holidays – Christmas.

The fake flamingos ill. by Józef Wilkon; trans. by Anthea Bell. North-South, 1987. ISBN 0-8050-0490-4 Subj: Birds – flamingos. Birds – storks. Self-concept.

Goodbye little bird trans. from German by Anthea Bell; ill. by Dorothée Duntze. Faber, 1983. ISBN 0-571-12520-4 Subj: Birds. Friendship.

How do dinosaurs say goodnight? ill. by Mark Teague. Blue Sky, 2000. ISBN 0-590-31681-8 Subj: Bedtime. Dinosaurs. Family life – mothers. Prehistory.

The little prince and the tiger cat ill. by Ralph Steadman. McGraw-Hill, 1967. Subj: Animals – cats. Foreign lands – Japan. Royalty – princes.

The little sea horse ill. by Riccardo Bellettati. Faber, 1983. ISBN 0-571-12519-0 Subj: Fish. Imagination. Sea & seashore.

The little seahorse and the Christmas pearl ill. by Alexander Reichstein; tr. by Marianne Martens. North-South, 2001. ISBN 0-7358-1506-2 Subj: Fish – seahorses. Holidays – Christmas. Religion – Nativity.

The wolf and the kid ill. by Max Velthuijs. McGraw-Hill, 1967. Subj: Animals – goats. Animals – wolves. Character traits – cleverness.

Damrell, Liz. *With the wind* ill. by Stephen Marchesi. Watts, 1991. ISBN 0-531-08482-5 Subj: Animals – horses, ponies. Handicaps – physical handicaps.

D'Andrea, Annette Cole. *see* Steiner, Barbara (Annette)

Daniel, Anne. *see* Steiner, Barbara (Annette)

Daniel, Doris Temple. *Pauline and the peacock* ill. by Barbara Brown Schoenewolf. E. C. Temple, 1980. ISBN 0-936650-00-1 Subj: Birds – peacocks, peahens. Family life. Farms. Science.

Daniel, Kira. *Teacher* ill. by Diane Paterson. Troll, 1989. ISBN 0-8167-1430-4 Subj: Careers – teachers.

Daniels, Guy. *The peasant's pea patch* (The peasant's pea patch)

The Tsar's riddles: or, the wise little girl ill. by Paul Galdone. McGraw-Hill, 1967. Subj: Character traits – cleverness. Folk & fairy tales. Foreign lands – Russia. Riddles & jokes.

Daniels, Teri. *G-Rex* ill. by Tracey Campbell Pearson. Orchard, 2000. ISBN 0-531-33243-8 Subj: Dinosaurs. Family life – brothers.

Just enough ill. by Harley Jessup. Viking, 2000. ISBN 0-670-88873-7 Subj: Rhyming text. Self-concept.

Math man ill. by Timothy Bush. Orchard, 2001. ISBN 0-439-29308-1 Subj: Counting, numbers. School.

Dann, Penny. *Eensy weensy spider* ill. by author. Barron's, 2003. ISBN 0-7641-5662-4 Subj: Format, unusual – board books. Games. Nursery rhymes. Songs. Spiders.

Danneberg, Julie. *First day jitters* ill. by Judy Love. Charlesbridge, 2000. ISBN 1-58089-054-7 Subj: Careers – teachers. School – first day.

First year letters ill. by Judy Love. Charlesbridge, 2003. ISBN 1-58089-084-9 Subj: Careers – teachers. Letters, cards. School.

D'Antonio, Nancy. *Our baby from China* ill. by author. A. Whitman, 1997. ISBN 0-8075-6162-2 Subj: Adoption. Ethnic groups in the U.S. – Chinese Americans. Family life. Foreign lands – China.

Dantzer-Rosenthal, Marya. *Some things are different, some things are the same* ill. by Miriam Nerlove. A. Whitman, 1986. ISBN 0-8075-7535-6 Subj: Concepts.

Danziger, Paula. *Get ready for second grade, Amber Brown* ill. by Tony Ross. Putnam, 2002. ISBN 0-399-23607-4 Subj: School – first day.

Darby, Gene. *What is a bird?* ill. by Lucy & John Hawkinson. Benefic Pr., 1959. Subj: Birds. Science.

What is a butterfly? ill. by Lucy & John Hawkinson. Benefic Pr., 1958. Subj: Insects – butterflies, caterpillars. Metamorphosis. Science.

What is a fish? ill. by Lucy & John Hawkinson. Benefic Pr., 1958. Subj: Fish. Science.

What is a plant? ill. by Lucy & John Hawkinson. Benefic Pr., 1959. Subj: Plants. Science.

What is a turtle? ill. by Lucy & John Hawkinson. Benefic Pr., 1959. Subj: Reptiles – turtles, tortoises. Science.

D'Arc, Karen Scourby. *My grandmother is a singing Yaya* ill. by Diane Palmisciano. Orchard, 2001. ISBN 0-531-33323-X Subj: Activities – singing. Ethnic groups in the U.S. – Greek Americans. Family life – grandmothers.

Da Rif, Andrea. *The blueberry cake that little fox baked* ill. by author. Atheneum, 1984. ISBN 0-689-50307-5 Subj: Activities – baking, cooking. Birthdays.

Darling, Abigail. *Teddy bears' picnic cookbook* ill. by Alexandra Day. Viking, 1991. ISBN 0-670-82947-1 Subj: Activities – baking, cooking. Activities – picnicking. Food. Toys – bears.

Darling, Benjamin. *Valerie and the silver pear* ill. by Daniel Lane. Four Winds, 1992. ISBN 0-02-726100-X Subj: Activities – baking, cooking. Family life – grandfathers.

Darling, Christina. *Mirror* (Day, Alexandra)

Darling, Harold. *The night before Christmas* (Moore, Clement Clark)

Darling, Kathy (Mary Kathleen). *ABC cats* photos by Tara Darling. Walker, 1998. ISBN 0-8027-8667-7 Subj: ABC books. Animals – cats. Pets.

ABC dogs photos by Tara Darling. Walker, 1997. ISBN 0-8027-8635-9 Subj: ABC books. Animals – dogs. Pets.

Amazon A B C photos by Tara Darling. Lothrop, 1996. ISBN 0-688-13779-2 Subj: ABC books. Animals. Foreign lands – Amazon.

Arctic babies photos by Tara Darling. Walker, 1996. ISBN 0-8027-8414-3 Subj: Animals. Birds. Foreign lands – Arctic.

Bug circus ill. by Buck Brown. Garrard, 1976. ISBN 0-8116-4301-8 Subj: Circus. Insects.

Desert babies photos by Tara Darling. Walker, 1997. ISBN 0-8027-8480-1 Subj: Animals. Animals – babies. Desert.

The Easter bunny's secret ill. by Kelly Oechsli. Garrard, 1978. Subj: Animals – rabbits. Holidays – Easter.

The mystery in Santa's toyshop ill. by Lori Pierson. Garrard, 1978. Subj: Holidays – Christmas. Mystery stories. Santa Claus.

Pecos Bill finds a horse ill. by Lou Cunette. Garrard, 1979. ISBN 0-8116-4047-7 Subj: Animals. Animals – horses, ponies. Cowboys, cowgirls. Mythical creatures. Tall tales. U.S. history – frontier & pioneer life.

Rain forest babies photos by Tara Darling. Walker, 1996. ISBN 0-8027-8412-7 Subj: Animals. Foreign lands. Forest, woods.

Seashore babies photos by Tara Darling. Walker, 1997. ISBN 0-8027-8477-1 Subj: Animals. Sea & seashore.

Darling, Mary Kathleen. *see* Darling, Kathy (Mary Kathleen)

Darrow, Sharon. *Old Thunder and Miss Raney* ill. by Kathryn Brown. DK, 2000. ISBN 0-7894-2619-6 Subj: Animals – horses, ponies. Contests. Fairs, festivals. Food.

Dasent, George W. *The cat on the Dovrefell: a Christmas tale* (De Paola, Tomie [Thomas Anthony])

East o' the sun, west o' the moon trans. by George W. Dasent; ill. by Gillian Barlow. Putnam, 1988. ISBN 0-399-21570-0 Subj: Animals – polar bears. Folk & fairy tales. Foreign lands – Norway. Royalty – princes. Witches.

Daudet, Alphonse. *The brave little goat of Monsieur Séguin: a picture story from Provence* ill. by Chiyoko Nakatani. Collins-World, 1968. Translation and adaptation of La chèvre de M. Séguin. Subj: Animals – goats. Animals – wolves. Foreign lands – France.

Dauer, Rosamond. *Bullfrog builds a house* ill. by Byron Barton. Greenwillow, 1977. ISBN 0-688-84090-6 Subj: Friendship. Frogs & toads. Homes, houses.

Bullfrog grows up ill. by Byron Barton. Greenwillow, 1976. ISBN 0-688-84020-5 Subj: Animals – mice. Behavior – growing up. Frogs & toads.

My friend, Jasper Jones ill. by Jerry Joyner. Parents' Magazine Pr., 1977. ISBN 0-8193-0888-9 Subj: Behavior – misbehavior. Imagination – imaginary friends.

The 300 pound cat ill. by Skip Morrow. Holt, 1981. ISBN 0-03-049111-2 Subj: Animals – cats. Behavior – greed.

Daugherty, Charles Michael. *Wisher* ill. by James Henry Daugherty. Viking, 1960. Subj: Animals – cats. Behavior – wishing. Dreams.

Daugherty, James Henry. *Andy and the lion* ill. by author. Viking, 1938. ISBN 0-670-12433-8 Subj: Animals – lions. Caldecott award honor books. Character traits – kindness to animals. Humorous stories. Libraries.

The picnic: a frolic in two colors and three parts ill. by author. Viking, 1958. Subj: Activities – picnicking. Animals – lions. Animals – mice.

Daugherty, Sonia (Medvedeva). *Vanka's donkey* ill. by James Henry Daugherty. Stokes, 1940. Subj: Animals – donkeys. Folk & fairy tales. Foreign lands – Russia.

Daughtry, Duanne. *What's inside?* photos by author. Knopf, 1984. ISBN 0-394-96249-4 Subj: Concepts – in & out. Wordless.

D'Aulaire, Edgar Parin. *see* Aulaire, Edgar Parin d'

D'Aulaire, Ingri Mortenson. *see* Aulaire, Ingri Mortenson d'

Dauphin, Francine Legrand. *A French A. B. C.* ill. by author. Coward, 1947. Subj: ABC books. Foreign lands – France. Foreign languages.

Davenier, Christine. *Leon and Albertine* ill. by author; trans. by Dominic Barth. Orchard, 1998. ISBN 0-531-30072-2 Subj: Animals. Animals – pigs. Birds – chickens. Emotions – love. Pets.

Davenport, Zoë. *Toys* ill. by author. Ticknor & Fields, 1995. ISBN 0-395-71539-3 Subj: Toys.

David, Eugene. *Crystal magic* ill. by Abner Graboff. Prentice-Hall, 1965. Subj: Science.

David, Lawrence. *Full moon* (Wilcox, Brian)

The good little girl ill. by Clément Oubrerie. Doubleday, 1998. ISBN 0-385-32614-9 Subj: Behavior – misbehavior. Behavior – needing someone. Character traits – meanness. Family life.

The land of the hungry armadillos ill. by Frédérique Bertrand. Doubleday, 2000. ISBN 0-385-32698-X Subj: Animals – armadillos. Behavior – greed. Family life – brothers & sisters. Monsters.

Peter Claus and the naughty list ill. by Delphine Durand. Doubleday, 2001. ISBN 0-385-32654-8 Subj: Behavior. Holidays – Christmas. Santa Claus.

Superhero Max ill. by Tara Calahan King. Doubleday, 2002. ISBN 0-385-32746-3 Subj: Clothing – costumes. Holidays – Halloween.

Davidson, Alice J. *The story of creation* ill. by Victoria Marshall. C.R. Gibson, 1984. ISBN 0-8378-5066-5 Subj: Creation. Religion.

Davidson, Amanda. *Teddy at the seashore* ill. by author. Holt, 1984. Originally published under title: Teddy at the seaside. ISBN 0-03-071026-X Subj: Foreign lands – England. Sea & seashore. Toys – bears.

Teddy goes outside ill. by author. Holt, 1985. ISBN 0-03-005004-9 Subj: Format, unusual – board books. Toys – bears. Weather.

Teddy in the garden ill. by author. Holt, 1986. ISBN 0-03-008502-0 Subj: Behavior – lost & found possessions. Gardens, gardening. Toys – bears.

Teddy's birthday ill. by author. Holt, 1985. ISBN 0-03-002887-6 Subj: Birthdays. Toys – bears.

Teddy's first Christmas ill. by author. Holt, 1982. ISBN 0-03-062616-1 Subj: Holidays – Christmas. Toys – bears.

Davidson, Jill A. *And that's what happened to little Lucy* ill. by Paul Meisel. Random House, 1989. ISBN 0-394-99945-2 Subj: Activities – trading. Activities – walking. Animals. Forest, woods.

Davidson, Rebecca Piatt. *All the world's a stage* ill. by Anita Lobel. Greenwillow, 2003. ISBN 0-06-029627-5 Subj: Careers – writers. Cumulative tales. Rhyming text. Theater.

Davies, Andrew. *Poonam's pets* ill. by Paul Dowling. Viking, 1990. ISBN 0-670-83321-5 Subj: Animals – lions. Pets. School.

Davies, Gill. *Can't, don't, won't* by Gill Davies & Rachael O'Neill; ill. by Rachael O'Neill. Sterling, 2001. ISBN 0-8069-7841-4 Subj: Behavior – misbehavior. Behavior – running away. Birds – penguins. Character traits – laziness.

Tiny's big wish by Gill Davies & Rachael O'Neill; ill. by Rachael O'Neill. Sterling, 2001. ISBN 0-8069-7839-2 Subj: Animals – elephants. Behavior – growing up.

Wilbur waited by Gill Davies & Rachael O'Neill; ill. by Rachael O'Neill. Sterling, 2001. ISBN 0-8069-7843-0 Subj: Animals – tigers. Babies. Family life – brothers & sisters. Family life – new sibling. Sibling rivalry.

Davies, Jacqueline. *The boy who drew birds: a story of John James Audubon* ill. by Melissa Sweet. Houghton, 2004. ISBN 0-618-24343-7 Subj: Birds. Careers – artists. Careers – ornithologists. Science.

Davies, Kay. *My apple* by Kay Davies & Wendy Oldfield; photos by Fiona Pragoff. G. Stevens, 1994. ISBN 0-8368-1114-3 Subj: Food. Nature. Science.

My balloon by Kay Davies & Wendy Oldfield; photos by Fiona Pragoff. Doubleday, 1990. ISBN 0-385-41199-5 Subj: Activities. Concepts – perspective. Science. Toys – balloons.

My drum by Kay Davies & Wendy Oldfield; photos by Fiona Pragoff. G. Stevens, 1991. ISBN 0-8368-1116-X Subj: Music. Musical instruments – drums. Science.

My mirror by Kay Davies & Wendy Oldfield; photos by Fiona Pragoff. Doubleday, 1990. ISBN 0-385-41196-0 Subj: Activities. Concepts – perspective. Science.

Davies, Nicola. *Bat loves the night* ill. by Sarah Fox-Davies. Candlewick, 2001. ISBN 0-7636-1202-2 Subj: Animals – bats. Night.

Big blue whale ill. by Nick Maland. Candlewick, 1997. ISBN 1-56402-895-X Subj: Animals – whales. Sea & seashore.

Oceans and seas ill. with photos. Kingfisher, 2004. ISBN 0-7534-5758-X Subj: Ecology. Sea & seashore.

One tiny turtle ill. by Jane Chapman. Candlewick, 2001. ISBN 0-7636-1549-8 Subj: Reptiles – turtles, tortoises. Sea & seashore.

Davies, Sally. *When William went away* ill. by author. Carolrhoda, 1999. ISBN 1-57505-303-9 Subj: Friendship. Moving.

Davies, Sumiko. *see* Sumiko

Davis, Alice Vaught. *Timothy Turtle* ill. by Guy Brown Wiser. Harcourt, 1940. Subj: Character traits – helpfulness. Reptiles – turtles, tortoises.

Davis, Aubrey. *Bagels from Benny* ill. by Dušan Petricic. Kids Can, 2003. ISBN 1-55337-417-7 Subj: Family life – grandfathers. Folk & fairy tales. Food. Foreign lands – Spain. Jewish culture. Religion.

Bone button borscht ill. by Dušan Petricic. Kids Can, 1997. ISBN 1-55074-224-8 Subj: Character traits – generosity. Folk & fairy tales. Food. Homeless. Jewish culture.

The enormous potato ill. by Dušan Petricic. Kids Can, 1998. ISBN 1-55074-386-4 Subj: Behavior – sharing. Cumulative tales. Farms. Folk & fairy tales. Food. Plants. Problem solving.

Sody salleratus ill. by Alan & Lea Daniel. Kids Can, 1998. ISBN 1-55074-281-7 Subj: Animals – bears. Folk & fairy tales. Food.

Davis, Caroline. *My little rocking horse lullabies* ill. by author. Little Simon, 2002. ISBN 0-689-84687-8 Subj: Format, unusual – board books. Lullabies.

My little rowboat ill. by author. Little Simon, 2002. ISBN 0-689-84686-X Subj: Format, unusual – board books. Nursery rhymes. Transportation.

Davis, Charles E. *Creatures at my feet* (Neidigh, Sherry)

Davis, David (David R.). *Jazz cats* ill. by Chuck Galey. Pelican, 2001. ISBN 1-56554-859-0 Subj: Animals – cats. Music. Rhyming text.

Davis, Douglas F. *The lion's tail* ill. by Ronald Himler. Atheneum, 1980. ISBN 0-689-50153-6 Subj: Animals – lions. Folk & fairy tales. Foreign lands – Africa.

There's an elephant in the garage ill. by Steven Kellogg. Dutton, 1979. ISBN 0-525-41050-3 Subj: Animals. Animals – cats. Imagination. Toys – bears.

Davis, Gary. *Working at a TV station* ill. with photos. Childrens Pr., 1998. ISBN 0-516-20750-4 Subj: Careers. Television.

Davis, Gibbs. *Katy's first haircut* ill. by Linda Shute. Houghton Mifflin, 1985. ISBN 0-395-38942-9 Subj: Emotions – embarrassment. Hair.

The other Emily ill. by Linda Shute. Houghton Mifflin, 1984. ISBN 0-395-35482-X Subj: Behavior – sharing. Names.

Davis, Hubert J. *A January fog will freeze a hog: and other weather folklore* (A January fog will freeze a hog)

Davis, Jennifer. *Before you were born* ill. by Laura Cornell. Workman, 1997. ISBN 0-7611-1200-6 Subj: Babies. Birth. Family life. Format, unusual – toy & movable books.

Davis, Karen. *Star light, star bright* ill. by author. Green Tiger Pr., 1993. ISBN 0-671-79455-8 Subj: Behavior – wishing. Stars.

Davis, Kate (1951–). *Barnyard babies* ill. by C. D. Hullinger. Innovative KIDS, 2001. ISBN 1-58476-061-3 Subj: Animals – babies. Format, unusual – toy & movable books. Picture puzzles.

Davis, Katie (Katie I.). *I hate to go to bed!* ill. by author. Harcourt, 1999. ISBN 0-15-201920-0 Subj: Bedtime. Dreams. Family life. Parties.

Mabel the Tooth Fairy and how she got her job ill. by author. Harcourt, 2003. ISBN 0-15-216307-7 Subj: Careers – dentists. Fairies. Humorous stories. Teeth.

Scared stiff ill. by author. Harcourt, 2001. ISBN 0-15-202305-4 Subj: Emotions – fear. Witches.

Who hoots? ill. by author. Harcourt, 2002. ISBN 0-15-216616-5 Subj: Animals. Noise, sounds.

Who hops? ill. by author. Harcourt, 1998. ISBN 0-15-201839-5 Subj: Animals.

Davis, Kenneth C. *Don't know much about the pioneers* ill. by Renée Andriani. HarperCollins, 2003. ISBN 0-06-028618-0 Subj: Activities – traveling. U.S. history – frontier & pioneer life.

Davis, Lavinia (Riker). *Roger and the fox* ill. by Hildegard Woodward. Doubleday, 1947. Subj: Animals – foxes. Caldecott award honor books.

The wild birthday cake ill. by Hildegard Woodward. Doubleday, 1949. Subj: Birthdays. Caldecott award honor books.

Davis, Lee. *Feeding time* photos by author. DK, 2001. ISBN 0-7894-7358-5 Subj: Animals. Food.

The lifesize animal opposites book ill. with photos. DK, 1994. ISBN 1-56458-720-7 Subj: Animals. Concepts – opposites. Concepts – size. Format, unusual – toy & movable books. Rhyming text.

P. B. Bear's birthday party photos by author. DK, 1994. ISBN 1-56458-380-5 Subj: Birthdays. Parties. Picture puzzles. Rebuses. Toys – bears.

Davis, Maggie S. *The best way to Ripton* ill. by Stephen Gammell. Holiday, 1982. ISBN 0-8234-0459-5 Subj: Activities – traveling. Humorous stories.

A garden of whales ill. by Jennifer Barrett O'Connell. Camden House, 1993. ISBN 0-944475-36-1 Subj: Animals – endangered animals. Animals – whales. Dreams. Gardens, gardening.

Grandma's secret letter ill. by John Wallner. Holiday, 1982. ISBN 0-8234-0382-3 Subj: Behavior – secrets. Character traits – kindness. Mythical creatures – elves.

Rickety witch ill. by Kay Chorao. Holiday, 1984. ISBN 0-8234-0521-4 Subj: Holidays – Halloween. Witches.

The rinky-dink café ill. by John Sandford. S&S, 1988. ISBN 0-671-66408-5 Subj: Animals – pigs. Food. Restaurants. Rhyming text.

Something magic ill. by Mary O'Keefe Young. S&S, 1991. ISBN 0-671-69627-0 Subj: Family life.

Davis, Patricia Anne. *Brian's bird* ill. by Layne Johnson. A. Whitman, 2000. ISBN 0-8075-0881-0 Subj: Birds – parakeets, parrots. Family life – brothers. Handicaps – blindness. Pets.

Davis, Reda. *Martin's dinosaur* ill. by Louis Slobodkin. Crowell, 1959. Subj: Dragons. Foreign lands – England. Prehistory.

Davison, Martine. *Kevin and the school nurse* ill. by Marylin Hafner. Random House, 1992. ISBN 0-679-91821-3 Subj: Careers – nurses. Food. School.

Maggie and the emergency room ill. by Marylin Hafner. Random House, 1992. ISBN 0-679-91818-3 Subj: Hospitals. Illness.

Rita goes to the hospital ill. by John Jones. Random House, 1992. ISBN 0-679-91820-5 Subj: Hospitals. Illness – tonsillectomy.

Robby visits the doctor ill. by Nancy Stevenson. Random House, 1992. ISBN 0-679-91819-1 Subj: Anatomy – ears. Careers – doctors. Illness.

Davison, Patricia Hinton. *Pablo and Pimienta* (Covault, Ruth M.)

Davol, Marguerite W. *Batwings and the curtain of night* ill. by Mary GrandPré. Orchard, 1997. ISBN 0-531-33005-2 Subj: Animals. Animals – bats. Bedtime. Creation. Dreams. Folk & fairy tales. Night.

Black, white, just right ill. by Irene Trivas. A. Whitman, 1993. ISBN 0-8075-0785-7 Subj: Ethnic groups in the U.S. Family life. Marriage, interracial.

The heart of the wood ill. by Sheila Hamanaka. S&S, 1992. ISBN 0-671-74778-9 Subj: Cumulative tales. Music. Musical instruments – violins. Rhyming text.

How snake got his hiss: an original tale ill. by Mercedes McDonald. Orchard, 1996. ISBN 0-531-08768-9 Subj: Animals. Cumulative tales. Foreign lands – Africa. Reptiles – snakes.

The loudest, fastest, best drummer in Kansas ill. by Cat Bowman Smith. Orchard, 2000. ISBN 0-531-33191-1 Subj: Musical instruments – drums. Noise, sounds. Tall tales.

The snake's tales ill. by Yumi Heo. Orchard, 2002. ISBN 0-439-31769-X Subj: Activities – storytelling. Reptiles – snakes.

Why butterflies go by on silent wings ill. by Rob Roth. Orchard, 2001. ISBN 0-531-33322-1 Subj: Insects – butterflies, caterpillars. Noise, sounds. Weather – storms.

Davoll, Barbara. *Dusty Mole, private eye* ill. by Dennis Hockerman. Moody, 1992. ISBN 0-8024-2700-6 Subj: Animals. Animals – moles. Behavior – talking to strangers. Mystery stories.

Davy's scary journey ill. by Tim Warnes. Little Tiger, 1997. ISBN 1-888444-10-X Subj: Behavior – running away. Birds – ducks.

Dawavendewa, Gerald. *The butterfly dance* ill. by author. Abbeville, 2001. ISBN 0-7892-0161-5 Subj: Activities – dancing. Indians of North America – Hopi. Weather – rain.

Dawson, Diane. *see* Hearn, Diane Dawson

Dawson, Linda. *Phoebe and the hot water bottles* (Furchgott, Terry)

Dawson, Zöe. *China* ill. with photos. Steck-Vaughn, 1996. ISBN 0-8172-4007-1 Subj: Foreign lands – China.

Japan ill. with photos. Steck-Vaughn, 1996. ISBN 0-81724-011-X Subj: Foreign lands – Japan.

Day, Alexandra. *An ABC of fashionable animals* (Edens, Cooper)

Boswell wide-awake ill. by author. Farrar, 1999. ISBN 0-374-39973-5 Subj: Activities. Animals – bears. Night.

Carl goes shopping ill. by author. Farrar, 1989. ISBN 0-374-31110-2 Subj: Animals – dogs. Shopping. Stores. Wordless.

Carl goes to daycare ill. by author. Farrar, 1993. ISBN 0-374-31093-9 Subj: Activities – playing. Animals – dogs. School – nursery.

Carl makes a scrapbook ill. by author. Farrar, 1994. ISBN 0-374-31129-3 Subj: Activities – babysitting. Activities – making things. Animals – dogs.

Carl pops up ill. by author. S&S, 1994. ISBN 0-671-87105-6 Subj: Activities – babysitting. Animals – dogs. Format, unusual – toy & movable books. Wordless.

Carl's afternoon in the park ill. by author. Farrar, 1991. ISBN 0-374-31109-9 Subj: Activities – babysitting. Animals – dogs. Wordless.

Carl's birthday ill. by author. Farrar, 1995. ISBN 0-374-31144-7 Subj: Activities – babysitting. Animals – dogs. Behavior – misbehavior. Birthdays.

Carl's Christmas ill. by author. Farrar, 1990. ISBN 0-374-31114-5 Subj: Activities – babysitting. Animals – dogs. Holidays – Christmas. Wordless.

Carl's masquerade ill. by author. Farrar, 1992. ISBN 0-374-31094-7 Subj: Animals – dogs. Babies. Parties. Wordless.

The Christmas we moved to the barn by Alexandra Day & Cooper Edens; ill. by Alexandra Day. HarperCollins, 1997. ISBN 0-06-205149-0 Subj: Animals. Family life. Holidays – Christmas. Moving.

Darby, the special-order pup by Alexandra Day & Cooper Edens; ill. by Alexandra Day. Dial, 2000. ISBN 0-8037-2496-9 Subj: Animals – dogs. Pets.

Follow Carl! ill. by author. Farrar, 1998. ISBN 0-374-34380-2 Subj: Activities – babysitting. Activities – playing. Animals – dogs. Parties. Wordless.

Frank and Ernest ill. by author. Scholastic, 1988. ISBN 0-590-41557-3 Subj: Animals – bears. Animals – elephants. Character traits – helpfulness. Language.

Frank and Ernest on the road ill. by author. Scholastic, 1994. ISBN 0-590-45048-4 Subj: Animals – bears. Animals – elephants. Careers – truck drivers. Language. Trucks.

Frank and Ernest play ball ill. by author. Scholastic, 1990. ISBN 0-590-42548-X Subj: Animals – bears. Animals – elephants. Dictionaries. Language. Sports – baseball.

Good dog, Carl ill. by author. Green Tiger Pr., 1985. ISBN 0-8813-8062-8 Subj: Activities – babysitting. Animals – dogs. Wordless.

Helping the animals by Alexandra Day & Cooper Edens; ill. by Alexandra Day. Green Tiger Pr., 1987. ISBN 0-8813-8085-7 Subj: Animals. Character traits – helpfulness. Format, unusual – board books.

Helping the flowers and trees by Alexandra Day & Cooper Edens; ill. by Alexandra Day. Green Tiger Pr., 1987. ISBN 0-8813-8086-5 Subj: Animals. Character traits – helpfulness. Flowers. Format, unusual – board books. Trees.

Helping the night by Alexandra Day & Cooper Edens; ill. by Alexandra Day. Green Tiger Pr., 1987. ISBN 0-8813-8084-9 Subj: Animals. Character traits – helpfulness. Format, unusual – board books. Night.

Helping the sun by Alexandra Day & Cooper Edens; ill. by Alexandra Day. Green Tiger Pr., 1987. ISBN 0-8813-8083-0 Subj: Animals. Character traits – helpfulness. Format, unusual – board books. Sun.

Mirror by Alexandra Day & Christina Darling; ill. by Alexander Day. Farrar, 1997. ISBN 0-374-34720-4 Subj: Imagination. Magic. Mirrors.

Paddy's pay-day ill. by author. Viking, 1989. ISBN 0-670-82598-0 Subj: Animals – dogs. Circus. Country. Money.

River parade ill. by author. Viking, 1990. ISBN 0-670-82946-3 Subj: Boats, ships. Family life – fathers. Rivers. Sports – swimming.

Special deliveries by Alexandra Day & Cooper Edens; ill. by Alexandra Day. HarperCollins, 2001. ISBN 0-06-205152-0 Subj: Animals. Careers – postal workers. Pets.

Day, Betsy. *Stefan and Olga* ill. by author. Dial, 1991. ISBN 0-8037-0817-3 Subj: Birds – geese. Farms. Friendship. Music. Musical instruments – flutes. Pets.

Day, David. *King of the woods* ill. by Ken Brown. Four Winds, 1993. ISBN 0-02-726361-4 Subj: Animals. Birds. Cumulative tales. Forest, woods. Royalty – kings.

The swan children retold by David Day; ill. by Richard Evans. Ideals, 1991. ISBN 0-8249-8461-7 Subj: Birds – swans. Folk & fairy tales. Foreign lands – Ireland. Royalty.

Day, Edward C. *John Tabor's ride* ill. by Dirk Zimmer. Knopf, 1989. ISBN 0-394-98577-X Subj: Activities – traveling. Animals – whales. Humorous stories. Tall tales.

Day, Jan. *The pirate, Pink* ill. by Janeen I. Mason. Pelican, 2001. ISBN 1-56554-879-5 Subj: Family life – daughters. Family life – fathers. Pirates. Sea & seashore.

Pirate Pink and treasures of the reef ill. by Janeen I. Mason. Pelican, 2003. ISBN 1-58980-086-9 Subj: Family life – daughters. Family life – fathers. Pirates. Sea & seashore.

Day, Marie. *Dragon in the rocks* ill. by author. Firefly, 1992. ISBN 0-920775-76-4 Subj: Animals. Careers – paleontologists. Character traits – persistence. Dragons. Fossils. Science.

Edward the "crazy man" ill. by author. Annick, 2002. ISBN 1-55037-721-3 Subj: Friendship. Homeless. Illness – mental illness.

Quennu and the cave bear: a prehistoric tale ill. by author. Owl Books, 1999. ISBN 1-895688-86-8 Subj: Activities – painting. Animals – bears. Caves.

Day, Michael E. *Berry Ripe Moon* ill. by Carol Whitmore. Tide Grass Pr., 1977. Subj: Indians of North America – Penobscot.

Day, Nancy Raines. *A kitten's year* ill. by Anne Mortimer. HarperCollins, 2000. ISBN 0-06-027231-7 Subj: Animals – cats. Days of the week, months of the year.

The lion's whiskers: an Ethiopian folktale ill. by Ann Grifalconi. Scholastic, 1995. ISBN 0-590-45803-5 Subj: Animals – lions. Family life – stepfamilies. Folk & fairy tales. Foreign lands – Ethiopia.

Day, Shirley. *Ruthie's big tree* ill. by author. Firefly, 1982. ISBN 0-920236-35-9 Subj: Character traits – perseverance. Trees.

Waldo's back yard ill. by author. Firefly, 1984. ISBN 0-920236-73-1 Subj: Behavior – dissatisfaction. Character traits – helpfulness. Picture puzzles.

Day, Trevor. *Youch! it bites! real-life monsters up close* ill. with photos. S&S, 2000. ISBN 0-689-83416-0 Subj: Animals. Format, unusual – toy & movable books. Monsters. Plants.

Dayrell, Elphinstone. *Why the sun and the moon live in the sky: an African folktale* ill. by Blair Lent. Houghton Mifflin, 1968. First published in 1914 in the author's Folk stories from southern Nigeria, West Africa. Subj: Caldecott award honor books. Folk & fairy tales. Foreign lands – Africa. Moon. Sky. Sun.

Days like this poems sel. & ill. by Simon James. Candlewick, 1999. ISBN 0-7636-0812-2 Subj: Poetry.

Dayton, Laura. *LeRoy's birthday circus* ill. by Susan Huggins. Nelson, 1981. ISBN 0-525-66744-X Subj: Birthdays. Circus. Counting, numbers. Rhyming text.

Dayton, Mona. *Earth and sky* ill. by Roger Antoine Duvoisin. HarperCollins, 1969. Subj: Behavior – fighting, arguing. Earth. Sky.

Deacon, Alexis. *Slow Loris* ill. by author. Kane/Miller, 2002. ISBN 1-929132-27-1 Subj: Animals. Animals – lorises.

Deady, Kathleen W. *All year long* ill. by Linda Bronson. Carolrhoda, 2004. ISBN 1-57505-537-6 Subj: Rhyming text. Seasons.

It's time! ill. by Jill Newton. HarperFestival, 2002. ISBN 0-694-01565-2 Subj: Animals. Animals – babies. Animals – dogs. Farms. Rhyming text.

Out and about at the zoo ill. by Anne McMullen. Picture Window, 2003. ISBN 1-4048-0041-7 Subj: Animals. School – field trips. Zoos.

Dealey, Erin. *Goldie Locks has chicken pox* ill. by Hanako Wakiyama. Atheneum, 2002. ISBN 0-689-82981-7 Subj: Family life – brothers & sisters. Illness – chicken pox. Rhyming text.

Dean, Leigh. *Two special cards* (Lisker, Sonia O.)

De Anda, Diane. *Dancing Miranda = Baila, Miranda, baila* Lamberto Alvarez; tr. by Julia Mercedes Castilla. Piñata, 2001. ISBN 1-55885-324-3 Subj: Activities – dancing. Ethnic groups in the U.S. – Hispanic Americans. Family life – daughters. Family life – mothers. Foreign languages. Handicaps – physical handicaps. Illness – poliomyelitis.

De Angeli, Marguerite. *The book of nursery and Mother Goose rhymes* comp. & ill. by Marguerite De Angeli. Doubleday, 1954. ISBN 0-385-06246-X Subj: Caldecott award honor books. Nursery rhymes.

Yonie Wondernose: for three little Wondernoses, Nina, David and Kiki ill. by author. Doubleday, 1944. ISBN 0-8361-9083-1 Subj: Caldecott award honor books. Family life. Farms.

DeArmond, Dale. *The seal oil lamp* ill. by author. Little, 1988. ISBN 0-316-17786-5 Subj: Character traits – kindness. Death. Eskimos. Folk & fairy tales. Handicaps – blindness. Senses – sight.

DeBear, Kirsten. *Be quiet, Marina!* photos by Laura Dwight. Star Bright, 2001. ISBN 1-887734-79-1 Subj: Activities – playing. Friendship. Handicaps – cerebral palsy. Handicaps – Down syndrome.

Debecker, Benoît. *The naughty prince* ill. by author. Abrams, 2001. ISBN 0-8109-4304-2 Subj: Behavior – misbehavior. Character traits – meanness. Frogs & toads. Royalty – princes. Space & space ships.

De Beer, Hans. *Ahoy there, little polar bear* ill. by author. Holt, 1988. ISBN 3-85539-006-1 Subj: Animals – polar bears.

Bernard Bear's amazing adventure ill. by author; trans. by Marianne Martens. North-South, 1994. ISBN 1-55858-295-9 Subj: Animals – bears. Animals – dormice. Hibernation. Seasons – winter.

Just like father (Just like father)

Little polar bear ill. by author. Holt, 1987. ISBN 0-8050-0486-6 Subj: Animals – polar bears. Behavior – lost. Friendship.

Little Polar Bear and the big balloon ill. by author. North-South, 2002. ISBN 0-7358-1533-X Subj: Activities – ballooning. Activities – flying. Animals – polar bears. Birds – puffins.

Little polar bear and the brave little hare trans. by J. Alison James; ill. by author. North-South, 1992. ISBN 1-55858-180-4 Subj: Animals – polar bears. Animals – rabbits. Character traits – bravery. Foreign lands – Arctic. Friendship.

Little polar bear and the husky pup ill. by author; trans. by Rosemary Lanning. North-South, 1999. ISBN 0-7358-1155-5 Subj: Animals – dogs. Animals – polar bears. Character traits – kindness to animals.

Little polar bear finds a friend ill. by author. North-South, 1990. ISBN 1-55858-092-1 Subj: Animals – polar bears. Character traits – freedom. Foreign lands – Arctic. Friendship.

Little polar bear, take me home! trans. by J. Alison James; ill. by author. North-South, 1996. ISBN 1-55858-631-8 Subj: Activities – traveling. Animals – polar bears. Animals – tigers. Behavior – lost.

Oh no, Ono! ill. by author. North-South, 2004. ISBN 0-7358-1938-6 Subj: Animals – dogs. Character traits – curiosity. Farms. Humorous stories.

DeBoer, Jesslyn. *Follow the star* ill. by Nancy Munger. Zondervan, 1998. ISBN 0-310-97554-9 Subj: Format, unusual – toy & movable books. Holidays – Christmas. Stars.

Getting ready for Christmas ill. by Nancy Munger. Zondervan, 1998. ISBN 0-310-97561-1 Subj: Animals. Format, unusual – toy & movable books. Holidays – Christmas. Religion – Nativity.

De Brunhoff, Jean. *see* Brunhoff, Jean de

De Brunhoff, Laurent. *see* Brunhoff, Laurent de

De Bruyn, Monica. *Lauren's secret ring* ill. by author. A. Whitman, 1980. ISBN 0-8075-4391-9 Subj: Friendship.

DeCaprio, Annie. *One, two* ill. by Seymour Nydorf. Grosset, 1965. Designed by David Krieger. Subj: Counting, numbers.

DeChristopher, Marlowe. *Greencoat and the swanboy* ill. by reteller. Putnam, 1991. ISBN 0-399-22165-4 Subj: Birds – swans. Folk & fairy tales. Royalty – princesses.

Decker, Dorothy W. *Stripe and the merbear* ill. by author. Dillon, 1986. ISBN 0-87518-329-8 Subj: Mythical creatures. Sea & seashore. Toys – bears.

Stripe visits New York ill. by author. Dillon, 1986. ISBN 0-87518-267-4 Subj: Activities – painting. Art. Cities, towns. Toys – bears.

Dedieu, Thierry. *Baby clown* ill. by author; paper engineering by Jerome Bruandet. Hyperion, 1995. ISBN 0-7868-0075-5 Subj: Babies. Circus. Clowns, jesters. Format, unusual – toy & movable books.

The little Christmas soldier ill. by author; trans. from French by George Wen. Holt, 1993. ISBN 0-8050-2612-6 Subj: Holidays – Christmas. Toys.

Dee, Nicholas. *see* Aiken, Joan

Dee, Rosie. *see* Aiken, Joan

Dee, Ruby. *Tower to heaven* ill. by Jennifer Bent. Holt, 1991. ISBN 0-8050-1460-8 Subj: Folk & fairy tales. Foreign lands – Ghana. Sky.

Two ways to count to ten: a Liberian folktale ill. by Susan Meddaugh. Holt, 1988. ISBN 0-8050-0407-6 Subj: Character traits – cleverness. Folk & fairy tales. Foreign lands – Africa.

Deedy, Carmen Agra. *Agatha's feather bed: not just another wild goose story* ill. by Laura L. Seeley. Peachtree, 1991. ISBN 1-56145-008-1 Subj: Birds – geese. Furniture – beds. Problem solving.

The secret of Old Zeb ill. by Michael P. White. Peachtree, 1997. ISBN 1-56145-115-0 Subj: Boats, ships. Family life.

The yellow star: the legend of King Christian X of Denmark ill. by Henri Sørensen. Peachtree, 2000. ISBN 1-56145-208-4 Subj: Character traits – bravery. Foreign lands – Denmark. Royalty – kings. War.

Deegan, Kim. *My first book of numbers* ill. by author. Bloomsbury, 2002. ISBN 1-58234-755-7 Subj: Counting, numbers. Format, unusual – board books.

My first book of opposites ill. by author. Bloomsbury, 2002. ISBN 1-58234-756-5 Subj: Concepts – opposites. Format, unusual – board books.

Deeter, Catherine. *Seymour Bleu* ill. by author. S&S, 1998. ISBN 0-689-80137-8 Subj: Animals – cats. Art. Careers – artists. Concepts – color. Friendship.

Deetlefs, Rene. *Tabu and the dancing elephants* ill. by Lyn Gilbert. Dutton, 1995. ISBN 0-525-45226-5 Subj: Activities – dancing. Animals – elephants. Behavior – lost. Family life. Folk & fairy tales. Foreign lands – South Africa.

DeFelice, Cynthia C. *Casey in the bath* ill. by Chris L. Demarest. Farrar, 1996. ISBN 0-374-31173-0 Subj: Activities – bathing.

Clever crow ill. by S. D. Schindler. Atheneum, 1998. ISBN 0-689-80671-X Subj: Behavior – trickery. Birds – crows. Character traits – cleverness. Rhyming text.

Cold feet ill. by Robert Andrew Parker. DK, 2000. ISBN 0-7894-2636-6 Subj: Behavior – trickery. Careers – musicians. Clothing – boots. Musical instruments – bagpipes.

The real, true Dulcie Campbell ill. by R. W. Alley. Farrar, 2002. ISBN 0-374-36220-3 Subj: Books, reading. Family life. Royalty – princesses.

Three perfect peaches retold by the Wild Washerwomen Storytellers, Cynthia DeFelice & Mary DeMarsh; ill. by Irene Trivas. Orchard, 1995. ISBN 0-531-08722-0 Subj: Character traits – cleverness. Folk & fairy tales. Foreign lands – France. Royalty – princesses.

When Grampa kissed his elbow ill. by Karl Swanson. Macmillan, 1992. ISBN 0-02-726455-6 Subj: Country. Family life – grandfathers.

Willy's silly grandma ill. by Shelley Jackson. Orchard, 1997. ISBN 0-531-33012-5 Subj: Ethnic groups in the U.S. – African Americans. Family life – grandparents. Ghosts. Superstition.

DeForest, Charlotte B. *The prancing pony: nursery rhymes from Japan* adapt. into English verse for children, with "Kusa-e"; ill. by Keiko Hida. Walker, 1968. Subj: Foreign lands – Japan. Nursery rhymes.

Degen, Bruce. *Aunt Possum and the pumpkin man* ill. by author. HarperCollins, 1977. ISBN 0-06-021413-9 Subj: Animals – cats. Animals – possums. Family life – aunts, uncles. Holidays – Halloween. Wordless.

Goblin walk (Johnston, Tony)

Jamberry ill. by author. HarperCollins, 1983. ISBN 0-06-021417-1 Subj: Animals – bears. Food. Rhyming text.

The little witch and the riddle ill. by author. HarperCollins, 1980. ISBN 0-0602-1414-7 Subj: Friendship. Magic. Riddles & jokes. Witches.

Sailaway home ill. by author. Scholastic, 1996. ISBN 0-590-46443-4 Subj: Animals – pigs. Imagination. Rhyming text.

Teddy bear towers ill. by author. HarperCollins, 1991. ISBN 0-06-021430-9 Subj: Family life – brothers. Imagination. Rhyming text. Royalty – kings. Toys – bears.

De Gerez, Toni. *Louhi, witch of North Farm* ill. by Barbara Cooney. Viking, 1986. A story from Finlands's epic poem The Kalevala. ISBN 0-670-80556-4 Subj: Behavior – stealing. Folk & fairy tales. Foreign lands – Finland. Moon. Sun. Witches.

My song is a piece of jade: poems of ancient Mexico in English and Spanish ill. by William Stark. Little, 1984. ISBN 0-316-81088-6 Subj: Foreign lands – Mexico. Foreign languages. Poetry.

De Groat, Diane. *Alligator's toothache* ill. by author. Crown, 1977. ISBN 0-517-52805-3 Subj: Illness. Reptiles – alligators, crocodiles. Teeth. Wordless.

Good night, sleep tight, don't let the bedbugs bite ill. by author. SeaStar, 2002. ISBN 1-58717-129-5 Subj: Animals – possums. Camps, camping. Ghosts.

Happy birthday to you, you belong in a zoo ill. by author. Morrow, 1999. ISBN 0-688-16545-1 Subj: Animals. Birthdays. Friendship. Gifts. Parties.

Jingle bells, homework smells ill. by author. HarperCollins, 2000. ISBN 0-688-17544-9 Subj: Animals. Animals – possums. Holidays – Christmas. Homework. School. Weather – snow.

Liar, liar, pants on fire ill. by author. SeaStar, 2003. ISBN 1-58717-215-1 Subj: Animals – possums. Behavior – lying. Character traits – honesty. School. Self-concept. Theater.

Lola the elf ill. by author. Night Sky, 2002. ISBN 1-59014-081-8 Subj: Animals – possums. Character traits – helpfulness. Format, unusual – toy & movable books. Holidays – Christmas. Mythical creatures – elves.

Roses are pink, your feet really stink ill. by author. Morrow, 1996. ISBN 0-688-13605-2 Subj: Animals. Behavior – misbehavior. Holidays – Valentine's Day. School.

Trick or treat, smell my feet ill. by author. Morrow, 1998. ISBN 0-688-15767-X Subj: Animals. Clothing – costumes. Family life – brothers & sisters. Holidays – Halloween. School.

DeGross, Monalisa. *Granddaddy's street songs* ill. by Floyd Cooper. Hyperion, 1999. ISBN 0-7868-2132-9 Subj: Activities – working. Careers – peddlers. Ethnic groups in the U.S. – African Americans. Family life – grandfathers.

De Hamel, Joan. *Hemi's pet* ill. by Christine Ross. Houghton Mifflin, 1987. ISBN 0-395-43665-6 Subj: Pets. School. Sibling rivalry.

DeJong, David Cornel. *Looking for Alexander* ill. by Harvey Weiss. Little, 1963. Subj: Animals – cats. Family life – grandmothers.

De Kay, Ormonde. *Rimes de la Mere Oie: Mother Goose rhymes* (Mother Goose)

Delacre, Lulu. *Arroz con leche: popular songs and rhymes from Latin America* ill. by author. Scholastic, 1989. ISBN 0-590-42442-4 Subj: Foreign languages. Games. Music. Poetry. Songs.

Good times with baby ill. by author. Grosset, 1989. ISBN 0-448-21014-2 Subj: Babies.

Nathan and Nicholas Alexander ill. by author. Scholastic, 1986. ISBN 0-590-33956-7 Subj: Animals – elephants. Animals – mice. Behavior – sharing.

Nathan's balloon adventure ill. by author. Scholastic, 1991. ISBN 0-590-44976-1 Subj: Activities – ballooning. Animals – elephants. Animals – mice.

Nathan's fishing trip ill. by author. Scholastic, 1988. ISBN 0-590-41281-7 Subj: Animals – elephants. Animals – mice. Friendship. Sports – fishing.

Las Navidades: popular Christmas songs from Latin America sel. by Lulu Delacre; trans. from Spanish by Elena Paz; arranged by Ana-Maria Rosado; ill. by selector. Scholastic, 1990. ISBN 0-590-43548-5 Subj: Foreign languages. Holidays – Christmas. Music. Poetry. Songs.

Peter Cottontail's Easter book ill. by author. Scholastic, 1991. ISBN 0-590-43338-5 Subj: Animals – rabbits. Holidays – Easter.

Time for school, Nathan! ill. by author. Scholastic, 1989. ISBN 0-590-41942-0 Subj: Animals – elephants. Friendship. School.

De La Fontaine, Jean. *see* La Fontaine, Jean de

Delafosse, Claude. *Cars and trucks and other vehicles* (Cars and trucks and other vehicles)

Houses (Houses)

DeLage, Ida. *ABC Christmas* ill. by Roger Beerworth. Garrard, 1978. ISBN 0-8116-4355-7 Subj: ABC books. Holidays – Christmas.

ABC Easter bunny ill. by Ellen Sloan. Garrard, 1979. ISBN 0-8116-4356-5 Subj: ABC books. Animals – rabbits. Holidays – Easter.

ABC fire dogs ill. by Ellen Sloan. Garrard, 1977. ISBN 0-8116-4351-4 Subj: ABC books. Animals – dogs. Careers – firefighters.

ABC Halloween witch ill. by Lou Cunette. Garrard, 1977. ISBN 0-8116-4353-0 Subj: ABC books. Holidays – Halloween. Witches.

ABC pigs go to market ill. by Kelly Oechsli. Garrard, 1977. ISBN 0-8116-4350-6 Subj: ABC books. Animals – pigs. Stores.

ABC pirate adventure ill. by Buck Brown. Garrard, 1977. ISBN 0-8116-4352-2 Subj: ABC books. Pirates.

ABC Santa Claus ill. by Judith Gwyn Brown. Garrard, 1978. ISBN 0-8116-4354-9 Subj: ABC books. Holidays – Christmas. Santa Claus.

ABC triplets at the zoo ill. by Lori Pierson. Garrard, 1980. ISBN 0-8116-4357-3 Subj: ABC books. Animals. Zoos.

Am I a bunny? ill. by Ellen Sloan. Garrard, 1978. ISBN 0-8116-6072-9 Subj: Animals – rabbits. Self-concept.

Beware! Beware! A witch won't share ill. by Ted Schroeder. Garrard, 1991. ISBN 0-7910-1473-8 Subj: Behavior – sharing. Witches.

A bunny ride ill. by Tracy McVay. Garrard, 1975. ISBN 0-8116-6065-6 Subj: Animals – rabbits. Emotions – envy, jealousy.

Bunny school ill. by Tracy McVay. Garrard, 1976. ISBN 0-8116-6071-0 Subj: Animals – rabbits. School.

Frannie's flower ill. by Ellen Sloan. Garrard, 1979. ISBN 0-8116-6076-1 Subj: Activities – playing. Flowers.

Good morning, lady ill. by Tracy McVay. Garrard, 1974. ISBN 0-8116-6051-6 Subj: Animals. Animals – possums. Careers – peddlers.

The old witch and her magic basket ill. by Ellen Sloan. Garrard, 1978. ISBN 0-8116-4063-9 Subj: Holidays – Halloween. Witches.

The old witch and the crows ill. by Marianne Smith. Garrard, 1983. ISBN 0-8116-4067-1 Subj: Birds – crows. Birds – owls. Night. Witches.

The old witch and the dragon ill. by Unada. Garrard, 1979. ISBN 0-8116-4064-7 Subj: Dragons. Witches.

The old witch and the ghost parade ill. by Jody Taylor. Garrard, 1978. ISBN 0-8116-4062-0 Subj: Ghosts. Witches.

The old witch and the snores ill. by Gil Miret. Chelsea, 1991. ISBN 0-7910-1479-7 Subj: Animals – bears. Caves. Hibernation. Noise, sounds. Sleep – snoring. Witches.

The old witch and the wizard ill. by Mimi Korach. Chelsea, 1991, c1974. ISBN 0-7910-1480-0 Subj: Animals – cats. Witches. Wizards.

The old witch finds a new house ill. by Pat Paris. Garrard, 1979. ISBN 0-7910-1481-9 Subj: Moving. Witches.

The old witch gets a surprise ill. by Ellen Sloan. Chelsea, 1991, c1981. ISBN 0-7910-1482-7 Subj: Activities – ballooning. Witches.

The old witch goes to the ball ill. by Gustave E. Nebel. Chelsea, 1991, c1969. ISBN 0-7910-1483-5 Subj: Clothing – costumes. Holidays – Halloween. Witches.

The old witch's party ill. by Mimi Korach. Chelsea, 1991, c1976. ISBN 0-7910-1484-3 Subj: Holidays – Halloween. Parties. Witches.

Pilgrim children on the Mayflower ill. by Bert Dodson. Garrard, 1980. ISBN 0-8116-4315-8 Subj: Boats, ships. Pilgrims. U.S. history.

The squirrel's tree party ill. by Tracy McVay. Garrard, 1978. ISBN 0-8116-6073-7 Subj: Animals – squirrels. Parties. Trees.

Weeny witch ill. by Kelly Oechsli. Chelsea, 1991, c1968. ISBN 0-7910-1485-1 Subj: Fairies. Night. Witches.

What does a witch need? ill. by Ted Schroeder. Chelsea, 1991, c1971. ISBN 0-7910-1486-X Subj: Animals – dogs. Character traits – helpfulness. Witches.

The witchy broom ill. by Walt Peaver. Chelsea, 1991, c1969. ISBN 0-7910-1487-8 Subj: Magic. Witches.

Delamare, David. *The Christmas secret* ill. by author. S&S, 1991. ISBN 0-671-74822-X Subj: Animals. Friendship. Holidays – Christmas. Santa Claus. Weather – storms.

De La Mare, Walter (Walter John). *Molly Whuppie* ill. by Errol Le Cain. Farrar, 1983. ISBN 0-374-35000-0 Subj: Character traits – bravery. Character traits – cleverness. Giants. Royalty.

Delaney, A. *The butterfly* ill. by author. Crown, 1977. ISBN 0-440-00891-3 Subj: Cumulative tales. Insects – butterflies, caterpillars.

The gunnywolf ill. by author. HarperCollins, 1988. ISBN 0-06-021595-X Subj: Animals – wolves. Behavior – misbehavior. Flowers. Foreign lands – Germany. Songs.

Monster tracks? ill. by author. HarperCollins, 1981. ISBN 0-06-021589-5 Subj: Imagination. Weather – snow.

Pearl's first prize plant ill. by author. HarperCollins, 1997. ISBN 0-06-027357-7 Subj: Fairs, festivals. Gardens, gardening. Plants.

Delaney, M. C. (Michael Clark). *The marigold monster* ill. by Ned Delaney. Dutton, 1983. ISBN 0-525-44023-2 Subj: Humorous stories. Monsters. Riddles & jokes.

Delaney, Molly. *My sister* ill. by author. Atheneum, 1989. ISBN 0-689-31460-4 Subj: Family life – sisters. Sibling rivalry.

Delaney, Ned. *Bad dog!* ill. by author. Morrow, 1987. ISBN 0-688-06596-1 Subj: Animals – dogs. Behavior – lost. Behavior – misbehavior.

Bert and Barney ill. by author. Houghton Mifflin, 1979. ISBN 0-395-28377-9 Subj: Friendship.

Cosmic chickens ill. by author. HarperCollins, 1988. ISBN 0-06-021584-4 Subj: Birds – chickens. Farms. Space & space ships.

One dragon to another ill. by author. Houghton Mifflin, 1976. ISBN 0-395-24209-6 Subj: Character traits – individuality. Dragons. Games. Insects – butterflies, caterpillars. Metamorphosis.

Rufus the doofus ill. by author. Houghton Mifflin, 1978. ISBN 0-395-27153-3 Subj: Behavior – misbehavior. School.

Terrible things could happen ill. by author. Lothrop, 1983. ISBN 0-688-01284-1 Subj: Activities – working. Humorous stories.

Two strikes, four eyes ill. by author. Houghton Mifflin, 1976. ISBN 0-395-24744-6 Subj: Animals – mice. Glasses. Sports – baseball.

A worm for dinner ill. by author. Houghton Mifflin, 1977. ISBN 0-395-25153-2 Subj: Animals – moles. Birds. Friendship.

Delaunay, Sonia. *Sonia Delaunay's alphabet* ill. by author. Crowell, 1972. ISBN 0-690-75228-X Subj: ABC books. Rhyming text.

De la Vega, Eida. *see* Vega, Eida de la

Delessert, Etienne. *The endless party* trans. by Jeffrey Tabberner; ill. by author. Oxford Univ. Pr., 1981. ISBN 0-19-279753-0 Subj: Animals. Boats, ships. Parties. Religion – Noah. Weather – floods. Weather – rain.

How the mouse was hit on the head by a stone and so discovered the world text & ill. by Etienne Delessert in collaboration with Odie Mosimann; foreword by Jean Piaget; trans. by C. Ross Smith. Doubleday, 1971. Subj: Animals – mice. World.

A long long song ill. by author. Farrar, 1988. ISBN 0-374-34638-0 Subj: Imagination. Nursery rhymes. Songs.

The seven dwarfs ill. by author. Creative Ed., 2001. ISBN 0-439-27863-5 Subj: Dwarfs, midgets. Folk & fairy tales. Foreign lands – Germany. Forest, woods. Royalty.

Dellinger, Annetta. *You are special to Jesus* ill. by Jan Brett. Concordia, 1984. ISBN 0-570-04089-2 Subj: Character traits – appearance. Character traits – individuality. Religion.

Del Negro, Janice. *Lucy Dove* ill. by Leonid Gore. DK, 1998. ISBN 0-7894-2514-9 Subj: Folk & fairy tales. Foreign lands – Scotland. Monsters.

Delton, Judy. *Bear and Duck on the run* ill. by Lynn Munsinger. A. Whitman, 1984. ISBN 0-8075-0594-3 Subj: Animals – bears. Birds – ducks.

The best mom in the world by Judy Delton & Elaine Knox-Wagner; ill. by John Faulkner. A. Whitman, 1979. ISBN 0-8075-0665-6 Subj: Behavior – growing up. Family life – mothers.

Brimhall comes to stay ill. by Cyndy Szekeres. Lothrop, 1978. ISBN 0-688-51863-X Subj: Animals – bears. Family life.

Brimhall turns detective ill. by Cherie R. Wyman. Carolrhoda, 1983. ISBN 0-87614-203-X Subj: Animals – bears. Animals – rabbits. Weather – snow.

Brimhall turns to magic ill. by Bruce Degen. Lothrop, 1979. ISBN 0-688-51878-8 Subj: Animals – bears. Animals – rabbits. Magic.

Duck goes fishing ill. by Lynn Munsinger. A. Whitman, 1983. ISBN 0-8075-1722-4 Subj: Animals – foxes. Birds – ducks. Birds – owls. Friendship. Sports – fishing.

The elephant in Duck's garden ill. by Lynn Munsinger. A. Whitman, 1985. ISBN 0-8075-1959-6 Subj: Animals – bears. Animals – elephants. Behavior – worrying. Birds – ducks.

Groundhog's Day at the doctor ill. by Giulio Maestro. Parents' Magazine Pr., 1981. ISBN 0-8193-1042-5 Subj: Animals – groundhogs. Holidays – Groundhog Day. Illness.

Hired help for Rabbit ill. by Lisa McCue. Aladdin, 1992. ISBN 0-689-71522-6 Subj: Activities – working. Animals – rabbits.

I never win! ill. by Cathy Gilchrist. Carolrhoda, 1981. ISBN 0-87614-139-4 Subj: Character traits – luck. Games.

I'll never love anything ever again ill. by Rodney Pate. A. Whitman, 1985. ISBN 0-8075-3521-4 Subj: Animals – dogs. Emotions – sadness. Pets.

I'm telling you now ill. by Lillian Hoban. Dutton, 1983. ISBN 0-525-44037-2 Subj: Activities. Behavior. Character traits – individuality.

It happened on Thursday ill. by June Goldsborough. A. Whitman, 1978. ISBN 0-8075-3669-5 Subj: Character traits – luck. Family life. Illness.

Lee Henry's best friend ill. by John Faulkner. A. Whitman, 1980. ISBN 0-8075-4417-5 Subj: Emotions – loneliness. Friendship. Moving.

My grandma's in a nursing home ill. by Charles Robinson. A. Whitman, 1986. ISBN 0-8075-5333-6 Subj: Emotions – loneliness. Family life – grandmothers. Old age.

My mom hates me in January ill. by John Faulkner. A. Whitman, 1977. ISBN 0-8075-5365-5 Subj: Behavior – boredom. Seasons – winter.

My mom made me go to camp ill. by Lisa McCue. Delacorte, 1990. ISBN 0-385-30040-9 Subj: Camps, camping. Family life – mothers.

My mom made me go to school ill. by Lisa McCue. Delacorte, 1991. ISBN 0-385-30330-0 Subj: Family life – mothers. School – first day.

My mom made me take piano lessons ill. by Lisa McCue. Doubleday, 1993. ISBN 0-385-31091-9 Subj: Family life – mothers. Music. Musical instruments – pianos.

My mother lost her job today ill. by Irene Trivas. A. Whitman, 1980. ISBN 0-8075-5359-X Subj: Activities – working. Character traits – optimism. Family life – mothers.

My Uncle Nikos ill. by Marc Simont. Crowell, 1983. ISBN 0-690-04165-9 Subj: Family life – aunts, uncles. Foreign lands – Greece.

The new girl at school ill. by Lillian Hoban. Dutton, 1979. ISBN 0-525-35780-7 Subj: School – first day.

No time for Christmas ill. by Anastasia Mitchell. Carolrhoda, 1988. ISBN 0-8761-4327-3 Subj: Animals – bears. Friendship. Gifts. Holidays – Christmas.

On a picnic ill. by Mamoru Funai. Doubleday, 1979. ISBN 0-385-12945-9 Subj: Activities – picnicking. Animals – gorillas. Animals – lions. Behavior – worrying. Birds – geese.

Penny wise, fun foolish ill. by Giulio Maestro. Crown, 1977. ISBN 0-517-52996-3 Subj: Animals – elephants. Behavior – saving things. Birds – ostriches. Character traits – wisdom. Fairs, festivals.

The perfect Christmas gift ill. by Lisa McCue. Macmillan, 1992. ISBN 0-02-728471-9 Subj: Animals. Birds – ducks. Friendship. Gifts. Holidays – Christmas.

A pet for Duck and Bear ill. by Lynn Munsinger. A. Whitman, 1982. ISBN 0-8075-6522-9 Subj: Animals – bears. Birds – ducks. Friendship. Pets.

Rabbit finds a way ill. by Joe Lasker. Crown, 1975. ISBN 0-517-52030-3 Subj: Animals – bears. Animals – rabbits. Food.

Rabbit goes to night school ill. by Lynn Munsinger. A. Whitman, 1986. ISBN 0-8075-6725-6 Subj: Animals – rabbits. Magic. School.

Three friends find spring ill. by Giulio Maestro. Crown, 1977. ISBN 0-517-52888-6 Subj: Animals – rabbits. Birds – ducks. Friendship. Seasons – spring. Seasons – winter.

Two good friends ill. by Giulio Maestro. Crown, 1974. ISBN 0-517-51401-X Subj: Animals – bears. Birds – ducks. Friendship.

A walk on a snowy night ill. by Ruth Rosner. HarperCollins, 1982. ISBN 0-06-021593-3 Subj: Night. Weather – snow. Weather – storms.

DeLuise, Dom. *Charlie the caterpillar* ill. by Christopher Santoro. S&S, 1990. ISBN 0-671-69358-1 Subj: Animals – monkeys. Behavior – growing up. Insects – butterflies, caterpillars. Metamorphosis. Science.

Goldilocks (The three bears)

Hansel and Gretel (Grimm, Jacob)

King Bob's new clothes ill. by Christopher Santoro. S&S, 1996. ISBN 0-671-89727-6 Subj: Character traits – pride. Character traits – vanity. Clothing. Folk & fairy tales. Imagination. Royalty – kings.

The nightingale (Andersen, H. C. [Hans Christian])

Del Vecchio, Ellen. *Big city port* (Maestro, Betsy)

De Lynam, Alicia Garcia. *It's mine!* ill. by author. Dial, 1988. ISBN 0-8037-0509-3 Subj: Behavior – sharing. Sibling rivalry. Toys.

Demarest, Chris L. *Benedict finds a home* ill. by author. Lothrop, 1982. ISBN 0-688-00586-1 Subj: Behavior – seeking better things. Birds.

Bus ill. by author. Harcourt, 1996. ISBN 0-15-200810-1 Subj: Buses. Cities, towns. Format, unusual – board books. Rhyming text.

Clemens' kingdom ill. by author. Lothrop, 1983. ISBN 0-688-01657-X Subj: Animals – lions. Character traits – curiosity. Libraries.

The cowboy ABC ill. by author. Crown, 1976. ISBN 0-7894-2509-2 Subj: ABC books. Cowboys, cowgirls.

Fall ill. by author. Harcourt, 1996. ISBN 0-15-201026-2 Subj: Format, unusual – toy & movable books. Rhyming text. Seasons – fall.

Farmer Nat ill. by author. Harcourt, 1998. ISBN 0-15-200113-1 Subj: Animals. Careers – farmers. Farms. Format, unusual – toy & movable books. Noise, sounds. Rhyming text.

Firefighters A to Z ill. by author. McElderry, 2000. ISBN 0-689-83798-4 Subj: ABC books. Careers – firefighters. Fire. Rhyming text.

Honk! ill. by author. Boyds Mills, 1998. ISBN 1-56397-221-2 Subj: Birds – geese. Family life – mothers. Format, unusual – toy & movable books. Noise, sounds.

Hotshots! ill. by author. McElderry, 2003. ISBN 0-689-84816-1 Subj: Careers – firefighters. Fire. Forest, woods. Rhyming text.

Kitman and Willy at sea ill. by author. S&S, 1991. ISBN 0-671-65696-1 Subj: Animals. Animals – cats. Animals – mice. Problem solving.

Lindbergh ill. by author. Crown, 1993. ISBN 0-517-58719-X Subj: Activities – flying. Airplanes, airports. Transportation. U.S. history.

The lunatic adventure of Kitman and Willy ill. by author. S&S, 1988. ISBN 0-671-65695-3 Subj: Animals – cats. Animals – mice. Moon. Space & space ships.

Morton and Sidney ill. by author. Macmillan, 1987. ISBN 0-02-728450-6 Subj: Behavior – sharing. Monsters.

My blue boat ill. by author. Harcourt, 1995. ISBN 0-15-200177-8 Subj: Activities – bathing. Boats, ships. Imagination. Sea & seashore. Toys.

My little red car ill. by author. Boyds Mills, 1992. ISBN 1-878093-86-X Subj: Activities – traveling. Automobiles. Imagination. Toys. Transportation.

No peas for Nellie ill. by author. Macmillan, 1988. ISBN 0-02-728460-3 Subj: Food. Imagination.

Orville's odyssey ill. by author. Prentice-Hall, 1986. ISBN 0-13-642851-7 Subj: Imagination. Sports – fishing. Wordless.

Plane ill. by author. Harcourt, 1995. ISBN 0-15-200268-5 Subj: Airplanes, airports. Format, unusual – board books. Rhyming text.

Ship ill. by author. Harcourt, 1995. ISBN 0-15-200267-7 Subj: Boats, ships. Rhyming text.

Smokejumpers one to ten ill. by author. McElderry, 2002. ISBN 0-689-84120-5 Subj: Activities – flying. Careers – firefighters. Counting, numbers. Forest, woods.

Spring ill. by author. Harcourt, 1997. ISBN 0-15-201390-3 Subj: Format, unusual – toy & movable books. Rhyming text. Seasons – spring.

Summer ill. by author. Harcourt, 1997. ISBN 0-15-201391-1 Subj: Format, unusual – toy & movable books. Rhyming text. Sea & seashore. Seasons – summer.

Train ill. by author. Harcourt, 1996. ISBN 0-15-200809-8 Subj: Format, unusual – board books. Rhyming text. Trains.

Winter ill. by author. Harcourt, 1996. ISBN 0-15-201027-0 Subj: Format, unusual – toy & movable books. Rhyming text. Seasons – winter.

De Marolles, Chantal. *The lonely wolf* ill. by Eleonore Schmid. Holt, 1986. ISBN 0-8050-0006-2 Subj: Animals – wolves. Character traits – kindness to animals. Foreign lands – Russia.

DeMarsh, Mary. *Three perfect peaches* (DeFelice, Cynthia C.)

Demas, Corinne. *see* Bliss, Corinne Demas

Dematons, Charlotte. *Let's go* ill. by author. Front St., 2001. ISBN 1-886910-65-0 Subj: Imagination. Stores.

De Mejo, Oscar. *La Bella Magellona and the little cavalier* ill. by author. Putnam, 1992. ISBN 0-399-22138-7 Subj: Concepts – shape. Concepts – size. Emotions – love. Folk & fairy tales.

Oscar de Mejo's ABC ill. by author. HarperCollins, 1992. ISBN 0-06-020517-2 Subj: ABC books. Art.

Demers, Dominique. *Old Thomas and the little fairy* ill. by Stéphane Poulin; English text by Sheila Fischman. Dominique & Friends, 2000. Tr. of: Vieux Thomas et la petite fée. ISBN 1-894363-45-0 Subj: Animals – dogs. Careers – fishermen. Emotions – anger. Fairies.

Demi. *The adventures of Marco Polo* ill. by author. Holt, 1982. ISBN 0-03-061263-2 Subj: Activities – traveling. Foreign lands – China.

The artist and the architect ill. by author. Holt, 1991. ISBN 0-8050-1685-6 Subj: Careers – architects. Careers – artists. Emotions – envy, jealousy. Folk & fairy tales. Foreign lands – China.

Chen Ping and his magic axe ill. by author. Dodd, 1987. ISBN 0-396-08907-0 Subj: Character traits – honesty. Folk & fairy tales. Foreign lands – China. Magic.

A Chinese zoo: fables and proverbs ill. by adapt. Harcourt, 1987. ISBN 0-15-217510-5 Subj: Animals. Folk & fairy tales. Foreign lands – China.

Cuddly chick ill. by author. Grosset, 1988. ISBN 0-448-19154-7 Subj: Birds – chickens. Format, unusual – board books. Format, unusual – toy & movable books.

Demi's basket of books ill. by author. Grosset, 1989. ISBN 0-448-14975-3 Subj: Animals. Holidays – Easter. Seasons – spring.

Demi's Christmas surprise ill. by author. Grosset, 1990. ISBN 0-448-19167-9 Subj: Animals. Format, unusual – board books. Holidays – Christmas.

Demi's count the animals 1-2-3 ill. by author. Grosset, 1986. ISBN 0-448-18980-1 Subj: Animals. Counting, numbers. Rhyming text.

Demi's dragons and fantastic creatures ill. by author. Holt, 1993. ISBN 0-8050-2564-2 Subj: Animals. Dragons. Format, unusual – toy & movable books. Rhyming text.

Demi's find the animals A B C: an alphabet-game book ill. by author. Grosset, 1985. ISBN 0-448-18970-4 Subj: ABC books. Animals. Behavior – hiding things.

Demi's opposites: an animal game book ill. by author. Grosset, 1987. ISBN 0-448-18995-X Subj: Animals. Concepts – opposites. Games.

Demi's reflective fables ill. by author. Grosset, 1988. ISBN 0-448-09281-6 Subj: Folk & fairy tales. Foreign lands – China.

Downy duckling ill. by author. Grosset, 1988. ISBN 0-448-19153-9 Subj: Birds – ducks. Format, unusual – board books. Format, unusual – toy & movable books.

Dragon kites and dragonflies: a collection of Chinese nursery rhymes ill. by adapt. Harcourt, 1986. ISBN 0-15-224199-X Subj: Dragons. Foreign lands – China. Nursery rhymes.

The dragon's tale and other animal fables of the Chinese zodiac retold & ill. by Demi. Holt, 1996. ISBN 0-8050-3446-3 Subj: Dragons. Folk & fairy tales. Foreign lands – China. Zodiac.

The emperor's new clothes: a tale set in China (Andersen, H. C. [Hans Christian])

The empty pot ill. by author. Holt, 1990. ISBN 0-8050-1217-6 Subj: Character traits – honesty. Folk & fairy tales. Foreign lands – China. Gardens, gardening. Royalty – emperors.

Find Demi's baby animals ill. by author. Grosset, 1990. ISBN 0-448-19169-5 Subj: Animals. Puzzles.

Find Demi's dinosaurs: an animal game book ill. by author. Grosset, 1989. ISBN 0-448-19020-6 Subj: Dinosaurs. Prehistory. Puzzles.

Find Demi's sea creatures: an animal game book ill. by author. Putnam, 1991. ISBN 0-399-22112-3 Subj: Animals. Fish. Puzzles.

The firebird (The firebird)

Fleecy bunny ill. by author. Grosset, 1987. ISBN 0-448-19151-2 Subj: Animals – rabbits. Format, unusual – board books.

Fleecy lamb ill. by author. Grosset, 1987. ISBN 0-448-19152-0 Subj: Animals – sheep. Format, unusual – board books.

Follow the line ill. by author. Holt, 1981. ISBN 0-03-059112-0 Subj: Wordless.

Fuzzy wuzzy puppy ill. by author. Grosset, 1986. ISBN 0-448-18985-2 Subj: Animals – dogs. Format, unusual – board books. Format, unusual – toy & movable books.

The greatest treasure ill. by author. Scholastic, 1998. ISBN 0-590-31339-8 Subj: Folk & fairy tales. Foreign lands – China.

The hallowed horse ill. by adapt. Dodd, 1987. ISBN 0-396-08908-9 Subj: Animals – horses, ponies. Folk & fairy tales. Foreign lands – India. Reptiles – snakes.

Happy, happy Chinese New Year ill. by author. Crown, 1997. ISBN 0-375-82642-4 Subj: Foreign lands – China. Holidays – Chinese New Year.

The leaky umbrella ill. by author. Prentice-Hall, 1980. ISBN 0-13-526962-8 Subj: Behavior – mistakes. Foreign lands – Japan. Umbrellas.

The legend of Saint Nicholas ill. by author. McElderry, 2003. ISBN 0-689-84681-9 Subj: Holidays – Christmas. Santa Claus.

Liang and the magic paintbrush ill. by author. Holt, 1988. ISBN 0-8050-0801-2 Subj: Activities – painting. Foreign lands – China. Magic.

Little baby lamb ill. by author. Putnam, 1993. ISBN 0-448-40580-6 Subj: Animals – sheep. Format, unusual – board books. Seasons – spring.

Little bitty bunny ill. by author. Grosset, 1992. ISBN 0-448-41089-3 Subj: Animals – rabbits. Clothing – hats. Format, unusual – board books. Format, unusual – toy & movable books. Holidays – Easter.

Little chick chick ill. by author. Grosset, 1992. ISBN 0-448-41090-7 Subj: Birds – chickens. Eggs. Format, unusual – board books. Format, unusual – toy & movable books. Holidays – Easter.

Little lucky ducky ill. by author. Putnam, 1993. ISBN 0-448-40581-4 Subj: Birds – ducks. Format, unusual – board books.

The magic boat ill. by author. Holt, 1990. ISBN 0-8050-1141-2 Subj: Boats, ships. Folk & fairy tales. Foreign lands – China. Magic. Toys.

The magic tapestry ill. by adapt. Holt, 1994. ISBN 0-8050-2810-2 Subj: Folk & fairy tales. Foreign lands – China. Magic.

One grain of rice: a mathematical folktale ill. by author. Scholastic, 1997. ISBN 0-5909-3998-X Subj: Character traits – cleverness. Character traits – selfishness. Counting, numbers. Folk & fairy tales. Royalty – rajahs.

The peek-a-boo ABC ill. by author. Random House, 1982. ISBN 0-394-85418-7 Subj: ABC books. Format, unusual – toy & movable books.

So soft kitty ill. by author. Grosset, 1986. ISBN 0-448-18986-0 Subj: Animals – cats. Format, unusual – board books. Format, unusual – toy & movable books.

The stonecutter ill. by author. Crown, 1995. ISBN 0-517-59865-5 Subj: Behavior – wishing. Folk & fairy tales. Foreign lands – China.

Three little elephants ill. by author. Random House, 1981. ISBN 0-394-84760-1 Subj: Animals. Animals – elephants. Format, unusual – toy & movable books. Jungle.

Under the shade of the mulberry tree ill. by author. Prentice-Hall, 1979. ISBN 0-13-936476-5 Subj: Character traits – cleverness. Folk & fairy tales. Foreign lands – China.

Where is it? ill. by author. Doubleday, 1979. ISBN 0-385-14847-X Subj: Riddles & jokes.

Where is Willie Worm? ill. by author. Random House, 1981. ISBN 0-394-84759-8 Subj: Animals – worms. Format, unusual – toy & movable books.

De Montaño, Martha Kreipe. *Coyote in love with a star* ill. by Tom Coffin. National Museum of the American Indian, 1998. ISBN 0-7892-0162-3 Subj: Animals – coyotes. Folk & fairy tales. Indians of North America – Potawatomi. Stars.

DeMunn, Michael. *The earth is good: a chant in praise of nature* ill. by Jim McMullan. Scholastic, 1999. ISBN 0-590-35010-2 Subj: Earth. Nature.

Demuth, Patricia Brennan. *Achoo! all about colds* ill. by Maggie Smith. Grosset, 1997. ISBN 0-448-41348-5 Subj: Illness.

Busy at day care head to toe photos by Jack Demuth. Dutton, 1996. ISBN 0-525-45603-1 Subj: Rhyming text. School – nursery.

Max, the bad-talking parrot ill. by Bo Zaunders. Dodd, 1986. ISBN 0-396-08767-1 Subj: Behavior – misunderstanding. Birds – parakeets, parrots. Etiquette. Rhyming text.

Ornery morning ill. by Craig McFarland Brown. Dutton, 1991. ISBN 0-525-44688-5 Subj: Animals. Behavior – bad day. Careers – farmers. Cumulative tales. Farms.

Snakes ill. by Judith Moffatt. Grosset, 1993. ISBN 0-448-40514-8 Subj: Reptiles – snakes.

Denchfield, Nick. *Desmond the dog* by Nick Denchfield & Ant Parker; ill. by Ant Parker. Harcourt, 1997. ISBN 0-15-201340-7 Subj: Animals – dogs. Behavior – misbehavior. Family life – brothers & sisters.

Desmond the dog, a wag-the-tail pop-up book by Nick Denchfield & Ant Parker; ill. by Ant Parker. Macmillan, 1997. ISBN 0-33367-954-7 Subj: Animals – dogs. Behavior – misbehavior. Family life – brothers & sisters. Format, unusual – toy & movable books.

Denega, Danielle. *Numbers* ill. by Donald Grant. Scholastic, 2001. ISBN 0-439-29728-1 Subj: Counting, numbers. Format, unusual – toy & movable books.

Rain or shine ill. by Pierre-Marie Valat. Scholastic, 2001. ISBN 0-439-29730-3 Subj: Format, unusual – toy & movable books. Weather.

Denim, Sue. *The Dumb Bunnies* ill. by Dav Pilkey. Blue Sky, 1994. ISBN 0-590-47798-0 Subj: Animals – rabbits. Family life.

The Dumb Bunnies' Easter ill. by Dav Pilkey. Blue Sky, 1995. ISBN 0-590-20241-3 Subj: Animals – rabbits. Family life. Holidays – Christmas. Holidays – Easter.

The Dumb Bunnies go to the zoo ill. by Dav Pilkey. Blue Sky, 1997. ISBN 0-590-84735-X Subj: Animals. Animals – rabbits. Family life. Zoos.

Make way for Dumb Bunnies ill. by Dav Pilkey. Blue Sky, 1996. ISBN 0-590-58286-0 Subj: Activities. Animals – rabbits. Family life.

Denison, Carol. *A part-time dog for Nick* ill. by Jane Miller. Dodd, 1959. Subj: Animals – dogs. Family life.

Dennard, Deborah. *Bullfrog at Magnolia Circle* ill. by Kristin Kest. Soundprints, 2002. ISBN 1-931465-04-5 Subj: Animals. Frogs & toads. Insects. Swamps.

Do cats have nine lives? the strange things people say about animals around the house ill. by Jackie Urbanovic. Carolrhoda, 1993. ISBN 0-87614-720-1 Subj: Animals. Pets.

Hedgehog haven ill. by Robert Hynes. Soundprints, 2001. ISBN 1-56899-987-9 Subj: Animals – hedgehogs. Country. Ecology. Foreign lands – England. Format, unusual.

Koala country ill. by James McKinnon. Soundprints, 2000. ISBN 1-56899-887-2 Subj: Animals. Animals – koalas. Foreign lands – Australia. Forest, woods.

Lemur landing ill. by Kristin Kest. Soundprints, 2001. ISBN 1-56899-978-X Subj: Animals – lemurs. Foreign lands – Madagascar. Forest, woods. Science.

Travis and the better mousetrap ill. by Theresa Burns. Cobblehill, 1996. ISBN 0-525-65178-0 Subj: Animals. Animals – mice. Family life – aunts, uncles. Inventions.

Dennis, Lynne. *Raymond Rabbit's early morning* ill. by author. Dutton, 1987. ISBN 0-525-44316-9 Subj: Animals – rabbits. Family life. Morning.

Dennis, Morgan. *Burlap* ill. by author. Viking, 1945. Subj: Animals – bears. Animals – dogs.

The pup himself ill. by author. Viking, 1943. Subj: Animals – dogs.

The sea dog ill. by author. Viking, 1958. Subj: Animals – dogs. Boats, ships. Weather – storms.

Skit and Skat ill. by author. Viking, 1952. Subj: Animals – cats. Animals – dogs.

Dennis, Suzanne E. *Answer me that* ill. by Owen Wood. Bobbs-Merrill, 1969. Subj: Animals. Humorous stories. Poetry.

Dennis, Wesley. *Flip* ill. by author. Viking, 1941. ISBN 0-670-31876-0 Subj: Animals. Dreams. Farms.

Flip and the cows ill. by author. Viking, 1942. ISBN 0-208-02240-6 Subj: Animals – bulls, cows. Animals – horses, ponies. Farms.

Flip and the morning ill. by author. Viking, 1977, c1951. ISBN 0-670-31934-1 Subj: Animals – horses, ponies. Morning.

Tumble, the story of a mustang ill. by author. Hastings House, 1966. Subj: Animals – horses, ponies. Character traits – freedom.

DeNoble, Augustine. *Brother Joseph* ill. by Judith Brown. Ignatius, 2000. ISBN 1-883937-40-X Subj: Careers – artists. Careers – clergy.

Denslow, Sharon Phillips. *At Taylor's place* ill. by Nancy Carpenter. Bradbury, 1990. ISBN 0-02-728685-1 Subj: Careers – carpenters. Farms. Seasons – fall.

Bus riders ill. by Nancy Carpenter. Macmillan, 1993. ISBN 0-02-728682-7 Subj: Buses. Careers – bus drivers. Illness.

Hazel's circle ill. by Sharon McGinley-Nally. Four Winds, 1992. ISBN 0-02-728683-5 Subj: Birds – chickens. Communities, neighborhoods.

Night owls ill. by Jill Kastner. Bradbury, 1990. ISBN 0-02-728681-9 Subj: Activities. Night. Seasons – summer.

On the trail with Miss Pace ill. by G. Brian Karas. S&S, 1995. ISBN 0-02-728688-6 Subj: Careers – teachers. Cowboys, cowgirls. Multiple births – twins.

Radio boy ill. by Alec Gillman. S&S, 1994. ISBN 0-02-728684-3 Subj: Careers – inventors.

Riding with Aunt Lucy ill. by Nancy Carpenter. Bradbury, 1991. ISBN 0-02-728686-X Subj: Activities – traveling. Animals – pigs. Family life – aunts, uncles.

Woollybear good-bye ill. by Nancy Cote. Four Winds, 1994. ISBN 0-02-728687-8 Subj: Insects – butterflies, caterpillars. Moving. School.

Denslow, W. W. *Denslow's picture book treasury* ill. by author. Arcade, 1990. ISBN 1-55970-071-8 Subj: Nursery rhymes. Songs.

Denton, Kady MacDonald. *Christmas boot* ill. by author. Little, 1990. ISBN 0-316-18091-2 Subj: Clothing – shoes. Holidays – Christmas. Santa Claus.

Granny is a darling ill. by author. Macmillan, 1988. ISBN 0-689-50452-7 Subj: Bedtime. Family life – grandmothers. Monsters. Night.

The picnic ill. by author. Dutton, 1988. ISBN 0-525-44376-2 Subj: Activities – picnicking. Family life.

Denton, Terry. *Home is the sailor* ill. by author. Houghton Mifflin, 1989. ISBN 0-395-51525-4 Subj: Activities – traveling. Animals. Boats, ships. Sailors. Sea & seashore.

The school for laughter ill. by author. Houghton Mifflin, 1990. ISBN 0-395-53353-8 Subj: Behavior – lost & found possessions. School.

Denver, John. *The children and the flowers* ill. by Randi Gullerud. Green Tiger Pr., 1979. Subj: Flowers. Songs.

John Denver's Ancient rhymes: a dolphin lullaby (Canyon, Christopher)

DePalma, Mary Newell. *The strange egg* ill. by author. Houghton, 2001. ISBN 0-618-09507-1 Subj: Animals – monkeys. Birds. Eggs. Friendship.

De Paola, Paula. *Rosie and the yellow ribbon* ill. by Janet Wolf. Little, 1992. ISBN 0-316-18100-5 Subj: Birthdays. Cities, towns. Concepts – color. Friendship.

De Paola, Tomie (Thomas Anthony). *Stagestruck* ill. by author. Putnam, 2005. ISBN 0-399-24338-0 Subj: Behavior – misbehavior. School. Theater.

Andy (that's my name) ill. by author. Prentice-Hall, 1973. ISBN 0-13-036731-1 Subj: Behavior – greed. Character traits – smallness. Friendship. Games. Names.

The art lesson ill. by author. Putnam, 1989. ISBN 0-399-21688-X Subj: Art. Family life. School.

The baby sister ill. by author. Putnam, 1996. ISBN 0-399-22908-6 Subj: Babies. Family life – grandmothers. Family life – new sibling. Family life – sisters.

Baby's first Christmas ill. by author. Putnam, 1988. ISBN 0-399-21591-3 Subj: Babies. Holidays – Christmas.

Big Anthony and the magic ring ill. by author. Harcourt, 1979. ISBN 0-15-207124-5 Subj: Character traits – appearance. Magic.

Big Anthony, his story ill. by author. Putnam, 1998. ISBN 0-399-23189-7 Subj: Folk & fairy tales. Foreign lands – Italy. Witches.

Bill and Pete ill. by author. Putnam, 1978. ISBN 0-399-20646-9 Subj: Birds – plovers. Foreign lands – Africa. Humorous stories. Reptiles – alligators, crocodiles. School.

Bill and Pete go down the Nile ill. by author. Putnam, 1987. ISBN 0-399-21395-3 Subj: Behavior – stealing. Birds – plovers. Foreign lands – Egypt. Museums. Reptiles – alligators, crocodiles. School.

Bill and Pete to the rescue ill. by author. Putnam, 1998. ISBN 0-399-23208-7 Subj: Animals. Birds – plovers. Reptiles – alligators, crocodiles.

Bonjour, Mister Satie ill. by author. Putnam, 1991. ISBN 0-399-21782-7 Subj: Animals – cats. Art. Family life – aunts, uncles. Foreign lands – France.

Boss for a day ill. by author. Grosset, 2002. ISBN 0-448-42618-8 Subj: Activities – working. Animals – dogs. Behavior – bossy. Family life – brothers & sisters. Multiple births – twins.

The bubble factory ill. by author. Grosset, 1996. ISBN 0-448-41349-3 Subj: Bubbles. Family life – brothers & sisters. Family life – grandfathers. Multiple births – twins.

The cat on the Dovrefell: a Christmas tale trans. by George W. Dasent; ill. by author. Putnam, 1979. ISBN 0-399-20680-9 Subj: Holidays – Christmas. Mythical creatures – trolls.

Charlie needs a cloak ill. by author. Prentice-Hall, 1973. ISBN 0-13-128355-3 Subj: Animals – mice. Animals – sheep. Clothing – coats. Problem solving.

The Christmas pageant ill. by author. Winston, 1978. ISBN 0-03-046356-4 Subj: Holidays – Christmas. Religion – Nativity. Theater.

Christopher: the holy giant ill. by author. Holiday, 1994. ISBN 0-8234-0862-0 Subj: Religion.

The cloud book ill. by author. Holiday, 1975. ISBN 0-8234-0531-1 Subj: Weather – clouds.

The clown of God: an old story ill. by author. Harcourt, 1978. ISBN 0-15-219175-5 Subj: Foreign lands – Italy. Holidays – Christmas. Religion.

Country farm ill. by author. Putnam, 1984. ISBN 0-399-21056-3 Subj: Animals. Farms. Format, unusual. Wordless.

Criss-cross applesauce photos by B. A. King; ill. by the B. A. King children. Addison-Wesley, 1979. ISBN 0-89169-023-9 Subj: Children as illustrators.

An early American Christmas ill. by author. Holiday, 1987. ISBN 0-8234-0617-2 Subj: Holidays – Christmas. U.S. history.

The family Christmas tree book ill. by author. Holiday, 1980. ISBN 0-8234-0416-1 Subj: Family life. Holidays – Christmas. Trees.

Favorite nursery tales ill. by adapt. Putnam, 1986. ISBN 0-399-21319-8 Subj: Folk & fairy tales. Nursery rhymes.

Fight the night ill. by author. Lippincott, 1968. Subj: Bedtime. Sleep.

Fin M'Coul: the giant of Knockmany Hill ill. by author. Holiday, 1981. ISBN 0-8234-0384-X Subj: Folk & fairy tales. Foreign lands – Ireland. Giants.

Flicks ill. by author. Harcourt, 1979. ISBN 0-15-228487-7 Subj: Humorous stories. Wordless.

Four stories for four seasons ill. by author. Prentice-Hall, 1977. ISBN 0-13-330175-3 Subj: Boats, ships. Gardens, gardening. Hibernation. Seasons.

Get dressed, Santa! ill. by author. Grosset, 1996. ISBN 0-448-41258-6 Subj: Format, unusual – board books. Holidays – Christmas. Rhyming text. Santa Claus.

Haircuts for the Woolseys ill. by author. Putnam, 1989. ISBN 0-399-21662-6 Subj: Animals – sheep. Family life – grandmothers.

Helga's dowry ill. by author. Harcourt, 1977. ISBN 0-15-233701-6 Subj: Emotions – love. Mythical creatures – trolls. Poverty. Weddings.

Hide-and-seek all week ill. by author. Grosset, 2001. ISBN 0-448-42545-9 Subj: Animals – dogs. Games. Multiple births – twins. School.

The hunter and the animals ill. by author. Holiday, 1981. ISBN 0-8234-0397-1 Subj: Animals. Sports – hunting. Wordless.

Jamie O'Rourke and the big potato ill. by author. Putnam, 1992. ISBN 0-399-22257-X Subj: Character traits – laziness. Folk & fairy tales. Foreign lands – Ireland. Mythical creatures – leprechauns. Mythical creatures – pooka spirit.

Jamie O'Rourke and the pooka ill. by author. Putnam, 2000. ISBN 0-399-23467-5 Subj: Character traits – laziness. Foreign lands – Ireland. Mythical creatures – goblins.

Jingle, the Christmas clown ill. by author. Putnam, 1992. ISBN 0-399-22338-X Subj: Animals. Circus. Clowns, jesters. Foreign lands – Italy. Holidays – Christmas.

Katie and Kit at the beach ill. by author. Little, 1987. ISBN 0-671-61722-2 Subj: Format, unusual – board books. Sea & seashore – beaches. Weather – rain.

Katie, Kit and cousin Tom ill. by author. Little, 1987. ISBN 0-671-61724-9 Subj: Activities – playing. Animals – cats. Behavior – bullying. Family life. Format, unusual – board books.

Katie's good idea ill. by author. Little, 1987. ISBN 0-671-61725-7 Subj: Behavior – growing up. Format, unusual – board books.

Kit and Kat ill. by author. Grosset, 1994. ISBN 0-448-40749-3 Subj: Animals – cats. Behavior – bullying. Clothing – pajamas. Family life – grandfathers. Sports – bicycling.

The knight and the dragon ill. by author. Putnam, 1980. ISBN 0-606-03327-0 Subj: Dragons. Knights. Libraries.

The Lady of Guadalupe ill. by author. Holiday, 1980. ISBN 0-8234-0373-4 Subj: Foreign lands – Mexico. Religion.

The legend of Old Befana ill. by author. Harcourt, 1980. ISBN 0-15-243816-5 Subj: Folk & fairy tales. Foreign lands – Italy. Religion.

The legend of the bluebonnet ill. by author. Putnam, 1983. ISBN 0-399-20937-9 Subj: Flowers. Folk & fairy tales. Indians of North America – Comanche.

The legend of the Indian paintbrush ill. by author. Putnam, 1987. ISBN 0-399-21534-4 Subj: Activities – painting. Flowers. Folk & fairy tales. Indians of North America – Great Plains.

The legend of the persian carpet ill. by Claire Ewart. Putnam, 1993. ISBN 0-399-22415-7 Subj: Folk & fairy tales. Foreign lands – Persia. Royalty – kings.

Little Grunt and the big egg: a prehistoric fairy tale ill. by author. Holiday, 1990. ISBN 0-8234-0730-6 Subj: Dinosaurs. Folk & fairy tales. Pets.

Marcos: red, yellow, blue ill. by author. Putnam, 2003. ISBN 0-399-24010-1 Subj: Concepts – color. Family life – brothers & sisters. Foreign languages. Format, unusual – board books. Multiple births – twins.

Marianna May and Nursey ill. by author. Holiday, 1983. ISBN 0-8234-0473-0 Subj: Character traits – cleanliness.

Meet the Barkers: Morgan and Moffat go to school ill. by author. Putnam, 2001. ISBN 0-399-23708-9 Subj: Animals – dogs. Family life – brothers & sisters. Multiple births – twins. School – first day.

Merry Christmas, Strega Nona ill. by author. Harcourt, 1986. ISBN 0-15-253183-1 Subj: Foreign lands – Italy. Holidays – Christmas. Humorous stories. Magic. Witches.

Michael Bird-Boy ill. by author. Prentice-Hall, 1975. ISBN 0-13-580803-0 Subj: Ecology.

My first Chanukah ill. by author. Putnam, 1989. ISBN 0-399-21780-0 Subj: Format, unusual – board books. Holidays – Hanukkah. Jewish culture. Religion.

My first Thanksgiving ill. by author. Putnam, 1992. ISBN 0-399-22327-4 Subj: Friendship. Holidays – Thanksgiving. U.S. history.

The mysterious giant of Barletta: an Italian folktale ill. by author. Harcourt, 1984. ISBN 0-15-256347-4 Subj: Folk & fairy tales. Foreign lands – Italy. Giants. War.

Nana Upstairs and Nana Downstairs ill. by author. Putnam, 1973. ISBN 0-399-60787-0 Subj: Death. Emotions – grief. Family life – grandmothers. Family life – great-grandparents. Old age.

Nana Upstairs and Nana Downstairs ill. by author. New ill. by author. Putnam, 1998. ISBN 0-399-23108-0 Subj: Death. Emotions – grief. Family life – grandmothers. Family life – great-grandparents. Old age.

A new Barker in the house ill. by author. Putnam, 2002. ISBN 0-399-23865-4 Subj: Adoption. Animals – dogs. Ethnic groups in the U.S. – Hispanic Americans. Family life – brothers & sisters. Multiple births – twins.

The night of Las Posadas ill. by author. Putnam, 1999. ISBN 0-399-23400-4 Subj: Holidays – Christmas. Religion. Theater.

Noah and the ark ill. by author. Winston, 1983. ISBN 0-86683-819-8 Subj: Animals. Boats, ships. Religion – Noah. Weather – floods. Weather – rain. Weather – rainbows.

Now one foot, now the other ill. by author. Putnam, 1981. ISBN 0-399-20774-0 Subj: Family life – grandfathers. Illness.

Oliver Button is a sissy ill. by author. Harcourt, 1979. ISBN 0-15-257852-8 Subj: Activities – dancing. Ballet. Character traits – individuality.

Pajamas for Kit ill. by author. Little, 1987. ISBN 0-671-61723-0 Subj: Bedtime. Clothing. Family life – grandparents. Format, unusual – board books.

Pancakes for breakfast ill. by author. Harcourt, 1978. ISBN 0-15-259455-8 Subj: Activities – baking, cooking. Food. Wordless.

The parables of Jesus ill. by author. Holiday, 1987. ISBN 0-8234-0636-9 Subj: Religion.

Patrick: patron saint of Ireland ill. by author. Holiday, 1992. ISBN 0-8234-0924-4 Subj: Foreign lands – Ireland. Religion.

The popcorn book ill. by author. Holiday, 1978. ISBN 0-8234-0314-9 Subj: Activities – baking, cooking. Food.

The Prince of the Dolomites ill. by author. Harcourt, 1980. ISBN 0-15-263528-9 Subj: Activities – storytelling. Folk & fairy tales. Foreign lands – Italy. Moon. Mythical creatures.

The quicksand book ill. by author. Holiday, 1977. ISBN 0-8234-0291-6 Subj: Behavior – carelessness.

Sing, Pierrot, sing: a picture book in mime ill. by author. Harcourt, 1983. ISBN 0-15-274988-8 Subj: Clowns, jesters. Theater. Wordless.

Songs of the fog maiden ill. by author. Holiday, 1979. ISBN 0-8234-0341-6 Subj: Rhyming text.

The story of the three wise kings ill. by author. Putnam, 1983. ISBN 0-399-20998-0 Subj: Holidays – Christmas. Religion – Nativity.

Strega Nona: an old tale ill. by author. Prentice-Hall, 1975. ISBN 0-13-851600-6 Subj: Behavior – forgetfulness. Caldecott award honor books. Humorous stories. Magic. Witches.

Strega Nona meets her match ill. by author. Putnam, 1993. ISBN 0-399-22421-1 Subj: Folk & fairy tales. Humorous stories. Magic. Witches.

Strega Nona takes a vacation ill. by author. Putnam, 2000. ISBN 0-399-23562-0 Subj: Activities – vacationing. Bubbles. Witches.

Strega Nona's magic lessons ill. by author. Harcourt, 1982. ISBN 0-15-281785-9 Subj: Behavior – carelessness. Humorous stories. Magic. Witches.

Things to make and do for Valentine's Day ill. by author. Watts, 1976. ISBN 0-531-01187-9 Subj: Activities – baking, cooking. Activities – making things. Games. Holidays – Valentine's Day.

Tom ill. by author. Putnam, 1993. ISBN 0-399-22417-3 Subj: Family life – grandfathers. Friendship. Names.

Tomie de Paola's Mother Goose ill. by sel. Putnam, 1985. ISBN 0-399-21258-2 Subj: Nursery rhymes.

Tony's bread ill. by author. Putnam, 1989. ISBN 0-399-21693-6 Subj: Careers – bakers. Folk & fairy tales. Food. Foreign lands – Italy.

Too many Hopkins ill. by author. Putnam, 1989. ISBN 0-399-21661-8 Subj: Animals – rabbits. Family life. Gardens, gardening.

The unicorn and the moon ill. by author. Silver Pr., 1995. ISBN 0-382-24659-4 Subj: Behavior – trickery. Moon. Mythical creatures – unicorns.

When everyone was fast asleep ill. by author. Holiday, 1976. ISBN 0-8234-0278-9 Subj: Sleep.

De Posadas Mane, Carmen. *Mister North Wind* adapt. by Joanne Fink; trans. from Spanish by Candido A. Valderrama; ill. by Alfonso Ruano. Silver Burdett, 1986. ISBN 0-382-09191-4 Subj: Animals. Character traits – bravery. Seasons – spring. Weather – wind.

Deprisco, Dorothea. *Snowbear's winter day* ill. by Dagmar Fehlau. Piggy Toes, 2002. ISBN 1-58117-133-1 Subj: Activities – playing.

Animals. Animals – bears. Forest, woods. Format, unusual – toy & movable books. Seasons – winter. Weather – snow.

What will I become? (Lunsford, Annie)

Who lives here? (Lunsford, Annie)

Derby, Sally. *King Kenrick's splinter* ill. by Leonid Gore. Walker, 1994. ISBN 0-8027-8323-6 Subj: Character traits – bravery. Parades. Royalty – kings.

The mouse who owned the sun ill. by Friso Henstra. Four Winds, 1993. ISBN 0-02-766965-3 Subj: Activities – traveling. Animals – mice. Sun. World.

My steps ill. by Adjoa J. Burrowes. Lee & Low, 1996. ISBN 1-880000-40-7 Subj: Activities – playing. Ethnic groups in the U.S. – African Americans. Seasons.

Two fools and a horse ill. by Robert Rayevsky. Cavendish, 2002. ISBN 0-7614-5119-6 Subj: Behavior – lost & found possessions. Careers – peddlers. Crime.

De Regniers, Beatrice Schenk. *A bunch of poems and verses* ill. by Mary Jane Dunton. Seabury Pr., 1977. ISBN 0-8164-3185-X Subj: Poetry.

Catch a little fox: variations on a folk rhyme ill. by Brinton Turkle. Seabury Pr., 1979. ISBN 0-395-28821-5 Subj: Character traits – cleverness. Nursery rhymes. Sports – hunting.

Cats cats cats ill. by Bill Sokol. Pantheon, 1958. Subj: Animals – cats. Poetry.

Circus photos by Al Giese. Viking, 1966. Subj: Circus.

David and Goliath ill. by Scott Cameron. Orchard, 1996. ISBN 0-531-08796-4 Subj: Foreign lands – Israel. Giants. Religion – David.

David and Goliath ill. by Richard M. Powers. Viking, 1965. Subj: Foreign lands – Israel. Giants. Religion – David.

Everyone is good for something ill. by Margot Tomes. Houghton Mifflin, 1980. ISBN 0-395-28967-X Subj: Animals – cats. Folk & fairy tales. Foreign lands – Russia. Self-concept.

The giant story ill. by Maurice Sendak. HarperCollins, 1953. Subj: Family life. Giants.

Going for a walk ill. by Robert Knox. HarperCollins, 1993. Orig. title: The little book. ISBN 0-06-022957-8 Subj: Activities – walking. Animals. Farms. Friendship.

How Joe the bear and Sam the mouse got together ill. by Bernice Myers. Lothrop, 1990. ISBN 0-688-09080-X Subj: Animals – bears. Animals – mice. Friendship.

It does not say meow! ill. by Paul Galdone. Seabury Pr., 1972. ISBN 0-8164-3086-1 Subj: Animals. Participation. Poetry. Riddles & jokes.

Jack and the beanstalk (Jack and the beanstalk)

Jack the giant killer: Jack's first and finest adventure retold in verse as well as other useful information about giants including how to shake hands with a giant (Jack and the beanstalk)

Laura's story ill. by Jack Kent. Atheneum, 1979. ISBN 0-689-30677-6 Subj: Imagination.

A little house of your own ill. by Irene Haas. Harcourt, 1987, c1982. ISBN 0-15-245787-9 Subj: Family life. Homes, houses. Imagination.

Little Sister and the Month Brothers ill. by Margot Tomes. Lothrop, 1994. Orig. published by Seabury Pr., 1976. ISBN 0-688-05293-2 Subj: Days of the week, months of the year. Folk & fairy tales. Foreign lands.

May I bring a friend? ill. by Beni Montresor. Atheneum, 1964. ISBN 0-689-20615-1 Subj: Animals. Caldecott award books. Friendship. Humorous stories. Rhyming text. Royalty.

Picture book theater: the mysterious stranger and the magic spell ill. by William Lahey Cummings. Seabury Pr., 1982. ISBN 0-89919-061-8 Subj: Animals – cats. Animals – mice. Theater. Wizards.

Red Riding Hood ill. by Edward Gorey. Atheneum, 1972. Retold in verse for boys and girls to read themselves. Subj: Animals – wolves. Behavior – talking to strangers. Folk & fairy tales. Rhyming text.

Sam and the impossible thing story by Tamara Kitt; ill. by Brinton Turkle. Norton, 1967. Subj: Activities – baking, cooking. Food. Monsters. Rhyming text.

The shadow book ill. by Isabel Gordon. Harcourt, 1960. Subj: Shadows.

So many cats! ill. by Ellen Weiss. Clarion, 1985. ISBN 0-89919-322-6 Subj: Animals – cats. Counting, numbers. Rhyming text.

Something special ill. by Irene Haas. Harcourt, 1958. Subj: Rhyming text.

A special birthday party for someone very special ill. by Brinton Turkle. Norton, 1966. Subj: Animals – skunks. Birthdays.

Waiting for mama ill. by Victoria de Larrea. Clarion, 1984. ISBN 0-89919-222-X Subj: Imagination.

Was it a good trade? ill. by Irene Haas. Harcourt, 1956. Subj: Activities – trading. Rhyming text. Songs.

What can you do with a shoe? ill. by Maurice Sendak. Harper-Collins, 1955. ISBN 0-06-024850-5 Subj: Games. Imagination.

What did you put in your pocket? ill. by Michael Grejniec. Harper-Collins, 2003. ISBN 0-06-029029-3 Subj: Animals. Clothing. Cumulative tales. Days of the week, months of the year. Food.

Who likes the sun? ill. by Leona Pierce. Harcourt, 1961. Subj: Sun.

Willy O'Dwyer jumped in the fire: variations on a folk rhyme ill. by Beni Montresor. Atheneum, 1968. Subj: Fire. Moon. Nursery rhymes. Witches.

DeRubertis, Barbara. *Columbus Day: let's meet Christopher Columbus* ill. by Thomas Sperling. Phoenix Learning Resources, 1992. ISBN 0-7915-1904-X Subj: Boats, ships. Careers – explorers. Sea & seashore. U.S. history.

Janey Crane ill. by Eva Vágréti Cockrille. Kane/Miller, 1997. ISBN 1-57565-022-3 Subj: Language. Noise, sounds. Rhyming text.

Joey Goat ill. by Jan Pyk. Kane/Miller, 1997. ISBN 1-57565-025-8 Subj: Language. Noise, sounds. Rhyming text.

Lulu's lemonade ill. by Paige Billin-Frye. Kane Pr., 2000. ISBN 1-57565-093-2 Subj: Activities – baking, cooking. Concepts – measurement. Food.

Suzy Mule ill. by Eva Vágréti Cockrille. Kane/Miller, 1997. ISBN 1-57565-026-6 Subj: Language. Noise, sounds. Rhyming text.

Tiny Tiger ill. by Eva Vágréti Cockrille. Kane/Miller, 1997. ISBN 1-57565-024-X Subj: Language. Noise, sounds. Rhyming text.

Zeely Zebra ill. by Eva Vágréti Cockrille. Kane/Miller, 1997. ISBN 1-57565-023-1 Subj: Language. Noise, sounds. Rhyming text.

DeSaix, Deborah Durland. *In the back seat* ill. by author. Farrar, 1993. ISBN 0-374-33639-3 Subj: Activities – traveling. Automobiles. Family life. Imagination.

DeSaix, Frank. *The girl who danced with dolphins* ill. by Debbi Durland DeSaix. Farrar, 1991. ISBN 0-374-32626-6 Subj: Animals – dolphins. Dreams. Sea & seashore.

DeSantis, Kenny. *A doctor's tools* photos by Patricia Agre. Dodd, 1985. ISBN 0-396-08516-4 Subj: Careers – doctors. Tools.

Deschamps, Nicola. *Duckling* (Duckling)

Emergency! (Emergency!)

Desimini, Lisa. *All year round: a book to benefit children in need* (All year round)

Dot the Firedog ill. by author. Blue Sky, 2001. ISBN 0-439-23322-4 Subj: Animals – dogs. Careers – firefighters.

I am running away today ill. by author. Walt Disney, 1992. ISBN 1-56282-121-0 Subj: Animals – cats. Behavior – running away.

Moon soup ill. by author. Hyperion, 1993. ISBN 1-56282-464-3 Subj: Food. Imagination. Moon.

My house ill. by author. Holt, 1994. ISBN 0-8050-3144-8 Subj: Homes, houses. Seasons.

Sun and moon: a giant love story ill. by author. Blue Sky, 1999. ISBN 0-590-18720-1 Subj: Friendship. Giants. Moon. Sun.

DesMarteau, Alicia. *Our principal promised to kiss a pig* (Dakos, Kalli)

Desmoinaux, Christel. *"Hallo-what?"* ill. by author. McElderry, 2003. ISBN 0-689-84795-5 Subj: Holidays – Halloween. Witches.

Mrs. Hen's big surprise ill. by author. McElderry, 2000. ISBN 0-689-83403-9 Subj: Animals. Birds – chickens. Dinosaurs. Eggs.

DeSpain, Pleasant. *The dancing turtle: a folktale from Brazil* ill. by David Boston. August House, 1998. ISBN 0-87483-502-X Subj: Behavior – trickery. Folk & fairy tales. Foreign lands – Brazil. Reptiles – turtles, tortoises.

Deutch, Glen. *Blue aliens* (Porto, Tony)

Get red (Porto, Tony)

Deutsch, Babette. *There comes a time* (Borchers, Elisabeth)

DeVajay, Szabolcs. *The animals' gift* ill. by Lilian Obligado. S&S, 1994. ISBN 0-671-72962-4 Subj: Animals – donkeys. Animals – oxen. Holidays – Christmas. Religion – Nativity.

De Veaux, Alexis. *An enchanted hair tale* ill. by Cheryl Hanna. HarperCollins, 1987. ISBN 0-06-021624-7 Subj: Character traits – being different. Ethnic groups in the U.S. – African Americans. Hair. Imagination. Self-concept.

Na-ni ill. by author. HarperCollins, 1973. ISBN 0-06-021628-X Subj: Character traits – questioning. Cities, towns. Emotions – sadness. Poverty.

De Vicq de Cumptich, Roberto. *Bembo's zoo* ill. by author. Holt, 2000. ISBN 0-8050-6382-X Subj: ABC books. Animals. Zoos.

Devine, Monica. *Carry me, Mama* ill. by Pauline Paquin. Stoddart, 2001. ISBN 0-7737-3317-5 Subj: Activities – walking. Behavior – growing up. Family life.

Devlin, Harry. *Aunt Agatha, there's a lion under the couch!* (Devlin, Wende)

Cranberry autumn (Devlin, Wende)

Cranberry Christmas (Devlin, Wende)

Cranberry Easter (Devlin, Wende)

Cranberry summer (Devlin, Wende)

Cranberry Thanksgiving (Devlin, Wende)

Cranberry Valentine (Devlin, Wende)

Old Black Witch! (Devlin, Wende)

Old Witch and the polka-dot ribbon (Devlin, Wende)

Old Witch rescues Halloween (Devlin, Wende)

The walloping window blind: an old nautical tale ill. by author. Van Nostrand, 1968. Adapt. from an old sea tune. Subj: Boats, ships. Pirates. Songs.

Devlin, Wende. *Aunt Agatha, there's a lion under the couch!* by Wende & Harry Devlin; ill. by authors. Van Nostrand, 1968. Subj: Animals – lions. Emotions – fear. Family life – aunts, uncles. Furniture. Imagination.

Cranberry autumn by Wende & Harry Devlin; ill. by Hary Devlin. Four Winds, 1993. ISBN 0-02-729936-8 Subj: Character traits – helpfulness. Family life – grandmothers. Garage sales, rummage sales.

Cranberry Christmas by Wende & Harry Devlin; ill. by authors. Parents' Magazine Pr., 1976. ISBN 0-819-30845-5 Subj: Behavior – sharing. Character traits – helpfulness. Holidays – Christmas.

Cranberry Easter by Wende & Harry Devlin; ill. by Harry Devlin. Four Winds, 1990. ISBN 0-02-729935-X Subj: Behavior – worrying. Holidays – Easter.

Cranberry Halloween ill. by Harry Devlin. Four Winds, 1982. ISBN 0-590-07854-2 Subj: Behavior – stealing. Holidays – Halloween.

Cranberry summer by Wende & Harry Devlin; ill. by Harry Devlin. Four Winds, 1992. ISBN 0-02-729181-2 Subj: Animals – donkeys. Character traits – kindness to animals. Holidays – Fourth of July.

Cranberry Thanksgiving by Wende & Harry Devlin; ill. by Harry Devlin. Parents' Magazine Pr., 1971. ISBN 0-819-30499-9 Subj: Holidays – Thanksgiving.

Cranberry Valentine by Wende & Harry Devlin; ill. by authors. Four Winds, 1986. ISBN 0-02-729200-2 Subj: Character traits – shyness. Holidays – Valentine's Day.

Old Black Witch! by Wende & Harry Devlin; ill. by Harry Devlin. Four Winds, 1992. Orig. published by Encyclopaedia Brit., 1963. ISBN 0-02-729185-5 Subj: Activities – baking, cooking. Witches.

Old Witch and the polka-dot ribbon by Wende & Harry Devlin; ill. by Harry Devlin. Parents' Magazine Pr., 1970. ISBN 0-819-30418-2 Subj: Activities – baking, cooking. Fairs, festivals. Food. Witches.

Old Witch rescues Halloween by Wende & Harry Devlin; ill. by Harry Devlin. Parents' Magazine Pr., 1972. ISBN 0-819-30609-6 Subj: Activities – baking, cooking. Holidays – Halloween. Witches.

De Vries, Maggie. *How sleep found Tabitha* ill. by Sheena Lott. Orca, 2002. ISBN 1-55143-193-9 Subj: Bedtime. Imagination. Sleep. Toys.

Once upon a golden apple (Little, Jean)

Dewan, Ted. *Baby gets the zapper* ill. by author. Random House, 2002. ISBN 0-385-74618-0 Subj: Activities – playing. Babies. Imagination. Toys.

Crispin and the 3 little piglets ill. by author. Doubleday, 2003. ISBN 0-385-74633-4 Subj: Animals – pigs. Babies. Family life – brothers & sisters. Family life – new sibling. Sibling rivalry.

Crispin, the pig who had it all ill. by authnor. Doubleday, 2000. ISBN 0-385-32540-1 Subj: Activities – playing. Animals – pigs. Holidays – Christmas.

The sorcerer's apprentice ill. by author. Doubleday, 1998. ISBN 0-385-32537-1 Subj: Folk & fairy tales. Magic. Robots. Wizards.

Dewey, Ariane. *A crocodile's tale: a Philippine folk story* (Aruego, José)

Dorin and the dragon ill. by author. Greenwillow, 1982. ISBN 0-688-00911-5 Subj: Dragons. Dreams. Magic. Royalty.

Febold Feboldson ill. by author. Greenwillow, 1984. ISBN 0-688-02534-X Subj: Farms. Tall tales. Weather.

The fish Peri ill. by author. Macmillan, 1979. ISBN 0-02-730100-1 Subj: Folk & fairy tales. Foreign lands – Turkey. Magic. Problem solving.

Laffite, the pirate ill. by author. Greenwillow, 1985. ISBN 0-688-04230-9 Subj: Folk & fairy tales. Pirates. U.S. history.

Pecos Bill ill. by author. Greenwillow, 1983. ISBN 0-688-01412-7 Subj: Cowboys, cowgirls. Tall tales. U.S. history – frontier & pioneer life.

Rockabye crocodile: a folktale from the Philippines (Aruego, José)

The sky ill. by author. Green Tiger Pr., 1993. ISBN 0-671-77835-8 Subj: Sky.

Small Cloud ill. by Annie Gusman. Walker, 1994. ISBN 0-8027-7488-1 Subj: Folk & fairy tales. Science. Weather – clouds. Weather – rain.

Splash! by José Aruego & Ariane Dewey; ill. by authors. Harcourt, 2001. ISBN 0-15-216256-9 Subj: Animals – bears. Character traits – clumsiness. Sports – fishing.

The tea squall ill. by author. Greenwillow, 1988. ISBN 0-688-07493-6 Subj: Parties. Seasons – spring. Tall tales.

The thunder god's son: a Peruvian folktale ill. by author. Greenwillow, 1981. ISBN 0-688-84295-X Subj: Folk & fairy tales. Foreign lands – Peru. Magic.

We hide, you seek (Aruego, José)

Weird friends: unlikely allies in the animal kingdom (Aruego, José)

Dewey, Jennifer Owings. *Once I knew a spider* ill. by Jean Cassels. Walker, 2002. ISBN 0-8027-8700-2 Subj: Family life. Seasons – winter. Spiders.

Poison dart frogs ill. by author. Boyds Mills, 1998. ISBN 1-56397-655-2 Subj: Frogs & toads.

Stories on stone: rock art, images from the ancient ones ill. by author. Little, 1996. ISBN 0-316-18211-7 Subj: Activities – writing. Art. Communication. Indians of North America – Pueblo.

DeWitt, Jamie. *Jamie's turn* ill. by Julie Brinckloe. Raintree, 1984. ISBN 0-940742-37-3 Subj: Farms. Illness.

DeWitt, Lyndia. *What will the weather be?* ill. by Carolyn Croll. HarperCollins, 1991. ISBN 0-06-021597-6 Subj: Weather.

Dexter, Alison. *Grandma* ill. by author. HarperCollins, 1993. ISBN 0-06-021144-X Subj: Family life – grandmothers. Sea & seashore.

De Zutter, Hank. *Who says a dog goes bow-wow?* ill. by Suse MacDonald. Doubleday, 1993. ISBN 0-385-30659-8 Subj: Animals. Foreign languages. Noise, sounds.

Diakité, Baba Wagué. *The hunterman and the crocodiles* ill. by author. Scholastic, 1997. ISBN 0-590-89828-0 Subj: Behavior – lying. Folk & fairy tales. Foreign lands – Africa.

The magic gourd ill. by author. Scholastic, 2003. ISBN 0-439-43960-4 Subj: Animals – rabbits. Behavior – greed. Folk & fairy tales. Foreign lands – Mali. Royalty – kings.

Diamond, Donna. *The Bremen town musicians* (Grimm, Jacob)

Rumpelstiltskin (Grimm, Jacob)

Díaz, Katacha. *Carolina's gift* ill. by Gredna Landolt. Soundprints, 2002. ISBN 1-56899-695-0 Subj: Birthdays. Family life – grandmothers. Foreign lands – Peru. Gifts.

Dick Whittington and his cat. *Dick Whittington* retold by Kathleen Lines; ill. by Edward Ardizzone. Walck, 1970. ISBN 0-8098-1172-3 Subj: Activities – trading. Animals – cats. Folk & fairy tales. Foreign lands – England. Middle Ages.

Dick Whittington: a story from England retold by Charles Causley; ill. by Antony Maitland. Penguin, 1979. Subj: Activities – trading. Animals – cats. Folk & fairy tales. Foreign lands – England. Middle Ages.

Dick Whittington and his cat retold & ill. by Marcia Brown. Scribners, 1950. Subj: Activities – trading. Animals – cats. Caldecott award honor books. Folk & fairy tales. Foreign lands – England. Middle Ages.

Dick Whittington and his cat retold by Eva Moore; ill. by Kurt Werth. Seabury Pr., 1974. ISBN 0-8164-3126-4 Subj: Activities – trading. Animals – cats. Folk & fairy tales. Foreign lands – England. Middle Ages.

Dickens, Charles. *The animals' Christmas carol* (Smath, Jerry)

Dickens, Frank. *Boffo: the great motorcycle race* ill. by author. Parents' Magazine Pr., 1978. ISBN 0-8193-0957-5 Subj: Character traits – cleverness. Motorcycles. Sports – racing.

Dickens, Lucy. *At the beach* ill. by author. Viking, 1991. ISBN 0-670-83927-2 Subj: Activities – playing. Family life. Format, unusual – board books. Sea & seashore – beaches.

Dancing class ill. by author. Viking, 1992. ISBN 0-670-84484-5 Subj: Activities – dancing. Ethnic groups in the U.S.

Dirty Henry ill. by author. Viking, 1991. ISBN 0-670-83578-1 Subj: Activities – bathing. Animals – dogs.

Go fish ill. by author. Viking, 1991. ISBN 0-670-84164-1 Subj: Animals – polar bears. Emotions – fear.

Our day ill. by author. Viking, 1991. ISBN 0-670-83929-9 Subj: Activities – playing. Family life. Format, unusual – board books.

Outside ill. by author. Viking, 1991. ISBN 0-670-83928-0 Subj: Activities – playing. Family life. Format, unusual – board books.

Playtime ill. by author. Viking, 1991. ISBN 0-670-83926-4 Subj: Activities – playing. Family life. Format, unusual – board books.

Dickinson, Mary. *Alex and Roy* ill. by Charlotte Firmin. Elsevier-Dutton, 1981. ISBN 0-233-97347-8 Subj: Friendship. Imagination.

Alex's bed ill. by Charlotte Firmin. Elsevier-Dutton, 1980. ISBN 0-233-97207-2 Subj: Character traits – cleanliness. Furniture – beds. Problem solving.

Alex's outing ill. by Charlotte Firmin. Dutton, 1983. ISBN 0-233-97558-6 Subj: Activities – picnicking. Behavior – nagging. Country.

Dickinson, Mike. *My dad doesn't even notice* ill. by author. Elsevier-Dutton, 1982. ISBN 0-233-97385-0 Subj: Behavior – misunderstanding. Imagination.

Dickson, Louise. *The vanishing cat* ill. by Pat Cupples. Kids Can, 2001. ISBN 1-55337-026-0 Subj: Activities – traveling. Animals – cats. Animals – dogs. Boats, ships. Careers – detectives. Magic. Sea & seashore.

Did dinosaurs have feathers? ill. by Lucia Washburn. HarperCollins, 2004. ISBN 0-06-029027-7 Subj: Birds. Dinosaurs.

Dierssen, Andreas. *Timid Timmy* ill. by Felix Scheinberger; tr. by Marianne Martens. North-South, 2003. ISBN 0-7358-1812-6 Subj: Animals – rabbits. Character traits – bravery. Character traits – honesty.

Timmy's new friend ill. by Felix Scheinberger. North-South, 2004. ISBN 0-7358-1921-1 Subj: Animals – bears. Animals – rabbits. Behavior – forgiving. Friendship.

Dieterlé, Nathalie. *I am the king!* ill. by author. Orchard, 2001. ISBN 0-531-30324-1 Subj: Animals – rabbits. Behavior – misbehavior. Family life. Royalty – kings.

Dietl, Ulla. *The plant-and-grow project book* ill. by author. Sterling, 1993. ISBN 0-806-90456-9 Subj: Gardens, gardening. Plants. Science.

Diffily, Deborah. *Jurassic shark* ill. by Karen Carr. HarperCollins, 2004. ISBN 0-06-008250-X Subj: Fish – sharks. Fossils. Science.

DiFiori, Lawrence. *Baby animals* ill. by author. Macmillan, 1983. ISBN 0-02-730620-8 Subj: Animals. Format, unusual – board books.

The farm ill. by author. Macmillan, 1983. ISBN 0-02-730630-5 Subj: Farms. Format, unusual – board books.

If I had a little car ill. by author. Golden Pr., 1985. ISBN 0-307-12305-7 Subj: Automobiles. Format, unusual – board books. Imagination.

My first book ill. by author. Macmillan, 1983. ISBN 0-02-730610-0 Subj: Books, reading. Format, unusual – board books.

My toys ill. by author. Macmillan, 1983. ISBN 0-02-730600-3 Subj: Format, unusual – board books. Toys.

D'Ignazio, Fred. *Katie and the computer* ill. by Stan Gilliam. Creative Computing, 1980. ISBN 0-916688-11-9 Subj: Computers. Imagination.

Dijs, Carla. *Are you my daddy?* ill. by author. S&S, 1990. ISBN 0-671-70227-0 Subj: Animals. Format, unusual – toy & movable books.

Are you my mommy? ill. by author. S&S, 1990. ISBN 0-671-70226-2 Subj: Animals. Format, unusual – toy & movable books.

Big and small ill. by author. Grosset, 1989. ISBN 0-448-09075-9 Subj: Concepts – opposites. Format, unusual – toy & movable books.

How many? ill. by author. Grosset, 1989. ISBN 0-448-09076-7 Subj: Counting, numbers. Format, unusual – toy & movable books.

Mommy, what if—? ill. by author. Little Simon, 2002. ISBN 0-689-84692-4 Subj: Animals. Animals – elephants. Family life – mothers. Format, unusual – toy & movable books.

Mommy, would you love me if . . . ? ill. by author. S&S, 1996. ISBN 0-689-80813-5 Subj: Animals. Family life – mothers. Format, unusual – toy & movable books.

Pretend you're a hippo ill. by author. S&S, 1992. ISBN 0-671-76057-2 Subj: Animals – hippopotamuses. Format, unusual – toy & movable books. Imagination. Jungle. Rhyming text.

Diller, Harriett. *Big band sound* ill. by Andrea Shine. Boyds Mills, 1996. ISBN 1-56397-129-1 Subj: Music. Musical instruments – bands. Noise, sounds.

The faraway drawer ill. by Andrea Shine. Boyds Mills, 1996. ISBN 1-56397-190-9 Subj: Clothing – sweaters. Family life – great-grandparents. Imagination.

Grandaddy's highway ill. by Henri Sorensen. Caroline House, 1993. ISBN 1-878093-63-0 Subj: Activities – traveling. Family life – grandfathers. Trucks.

The waiting day ill. by Chi Chung. Green Tiger Pr., 1994. ISBN 0-671-86579-X Subj: Boats, ships. Folk & fairy tales. Foreign lands – China. Poverty.

Dilley, Becki. *Sixty fingers, sixty toes: see how the Dilley sextuplets grow!* by Becki & Keith Dilley; photos by E. Anthony Valainis. Walker, 1998. ISBN 0-8027-8614-6 Subj: Babies. Family life – brothers & sisters. Multiple births – sextuplets.

Dilley, Keith. *Sixty fingers, sixty toes: see how the Dilley sextuplets grow!* (Dilley, Becki)

Dillinger, Christophe. *Hurry up, Molly = Dépêche-toi, Molly* (Morton, Lone)

Puppy finds a friend = Le petit chien se trouve un ami (Bruzzone, Catherine)

Dillon, Barbara. *The beast in the bed* ill. by Chris Conover. Morrow, 1981. ISBN 0-688-22254-4 Subj: Furniture – beds. Imagination – imaginary friends. Monsters.

Dillon, Eilis. *The cats' opera* ill. by Kveta Vanecek. Bobbs-Merrill, 1963. Subj: Animals – cats. Music.

Dillon, Jana. *Jeb Scarecrow's pumpkin patch* ill. by author. Houghton Mifflin, 1992. ISBN 0-395-57578-8 Subj: Birds – crows. Holidays – Halloween. Scarecrows.

Lucky O'Leprechaun ill. by author. Pelican, 1998. ISBN 1-56554-333-5 Subj: Character traits – luck. Family life – aunts, uncles. Holidays – St. Patrick's Day. Mythical creatures – leprechauns.

Lucky O'Leprechaun comes to America ill. by author. Pelican, 2000. Gretna, LA. ISBN 1-56554-816-7 Subj: Ethnic groups in the U.S. – Irish Americans. Family life – aunts, uncles. Humorous stories. Mythical creatures – leprechauns.

Lucky O'Leprechaun in school ill. by author. Pelican, 2003. ISBN 1-58980-035-4 Subj: Moon. Mythical creatures – leprechauns. School. Space & space ships.

Din, Anne Bar. *The story of colors = La historia de los colores* (Marcos, subcomandante)

Din dan don, it's Christmas ill. by Janina Domanska. Greenwillow, 1975. Text is a rendition of an anonymous Polish Christmas carol. ISBN 0-688-84003-5 Subj: Foreign lands – Poland. Holidays – Christmas. Religion. Songs.

Dinan, Carolyn. *The lunch box monster* ill. by author. Faber, 1983. ISBN 0-571-13153-0 Subj: Imagination – imaginary friends. Monsters.

Say cheese! ill. by author. Viking, 1986. ISBN 0-670-80954-3 Subj: Character traits – being different. School. Teeth.

Dinardo, Jeffrey. *Timothy and the night noises* ill. by author. Prentice-Hall, 1986. ISBN 0-13-922048-8 Subj: Emotions – fear. Frogs & toads. Night. Noise, sounds.

The wolf who cried boy ill. by author. Grosset, 1989. ISBN 0-448-09314-6 Subj: Animals – wolves. Behavior – lying. Behavior – trickery. Folk & fairy tales.

Dineen, Jacqueline. *Frédéric Chopin* ill. by author. Carolrhoda, 1996. ISBN 1-57505-248-2 Subj: Careers – composers. Music. Musical instruments – pianos.

Lions ill. with photos. Smart Apple Media, 2004. ISBN 1-58340-230-6 Subj: Animals – lions.

Dines, Glen. *Gilly and the wicharoo* ill. by author. Lothrop, 1968. Subj: Behavior – trickery. Character traits – cleverness. Foreign lands – England.

Pitadoe, the color maker ill. by author. Macmillan, 1959. Subj: Concepts – color. Wizards.

A tiger in the cherry tree ill. by author. Macmillan, 1958. Subj: Animals – tigers. Behavior – forgetfulness. Character traits – shyness. Foreign lands – Japan. Magic.

Dinosaurs and monsters ill. by Louise Nevett. Watts, 1984. ISBN 0-531-04770-9 Subj: Activities. Dinosaurs. Monsters. Prehistory.

Dionetti, Michelle V. *Coal mine peaches* ill. by Anita Riggio. Watts, 1991. ISBN 0-531-08548-1 Subj: Character traits – optimism. Ethnic groups in the U.S. – Italian Americans. Family life – grandfathers.

The day Eli went looking for bear ill. by Joyce Audy Dos Santos. Addison-Wesley, 1980. ISBN 0-201-02663-5 Subj: Animals. Family life – mothers. Seasons – winter. Sports – hunting.

Painting the wind ill. by Kevin Hawkes. Little, 1996. ISBN 0-316-18602-3 Subj: Activities – painting. Art.

Thalia Brown and the blue bug ill. by James Calvin. Addison-Wesley, 1979. ISBN 0-201-01399-1 Subj: Art. Character traits – pride. Ethnic groups in the U.S. – African Americans.

Dionne, Wanda. *Little Thumb* ill. by Jana Dillon. Pelican, 2000. ISBN 1-56554-754-3 Subj: Rhyming text. Thumb sucking.

Diot, Alain. *Better, best, bestest* ill. by Joel Naprstek. Dial, 1977. ISBN 0-8252-0478-X Subj: Behavior – boasting. Family life – fathers.

Diouf, Sylviane A, (Sylviane Anna). *Bintou's braids* ill. by Shane W. Evans. Chronicle, 2001. ISBN 0-8118-2514-0 Subj: Foreign lands – Africa. Hair.

DiPucchio, Kelly S. *What's the magic word?* ill. by Marsha Winborn. HarperCollins, 2005. ISBN 0-06-000579-3 Subj: Animals. Birds. Weather – wind.

DiSalvo-Ryan, DyAnne. *A castle on Viola Street* ill. by author. HarperCollins, 2001. ISBN 0-688-17691-7 Subj: Character traits – generosity. Homes, houses.

City green ill. by author. Morrow, 1994. ISBN 0-688-12787-8 Subj: Cities, towns. Communities, neighborhoods. Gardens, gardening.

A dog like Jack ill. by author. Holiday, 1999. ISBN 0-8234-1369-1 Subj: Animals – dogs. Death. Emotions – grief. Pets.

Grandpa's corner store ill. by author. HarperCollins, 2000. ISBN 0-688-16717-9 Subj: Communities, neighborhoods. Family life – grandfathers. Stores.

Disher, Garry. *Switch cat* ill. by Andrew McLean. Ticknor & Fields, 1995. ISBN 0-395-71643-8 Subj: Animals – cats. Moving. Rhyming text.

Diska, Pat. *Andy says . . . Bonjour!* ill. by Chris Jenkyns. Vanguard, 1954. Subj: Animals – cats. Foreign lands – France. Foreign languages.

DiTerlizzi, Tony. *Jimmy Zangwow's out-of-this-world, moon pie adventure* ill. by author. S&S, 2000. ISBN 0-689-80076-2 Subj: Food. Imagination. Moon. Space & space ships.

Ted ill. by author. S&S, 2001. ISBN 0-689-83235-4 Subj: Family life – fathers. Imagination – imaginary friends.

Diviny, Sean. *Halloween Motel* ill. by Joe Rocco. HarperCollins, 2000. ISBN 0-06-028816-7 Subj: Ghosts. Holidays – Halloween. Hotels. Monsters. Rhyming text.

Snow inside the house ill. by Joe Rocco. HarperCollins, 1998. ISBN 0-06-027354-2 Subj: Imagination. Nature. Rhyming text. Weather – snow.

DiVito, Anna. *Elephants on ice* ill. by author. Dial, 1991. ISBN 0-8037-0798-3 Subj: Animals – elephants. Sports – ice skating.

Dixon, Amy Jackson. *Cajun night after Christmas* (Moss, Jenny Jackson)

Dixon, Ann. *The blueberry shoe* ill. by Evon Zerbetz. Alaska Northwest Bks., 1999. ISBN 0-88240-518-7 Subj: Alaska. Animals. Behavior – lost & found possessions. Clothing – shoes. Cumulative tales. Family life. Food.

How raven brought light to people ill. by James Watts. Macmillan, 1992. ISBN 0-689-50536-1 Subj: Birds – ravens. Folk & fairy tales – pourquoi tales. Indians of North America – Tlingit.

Waiting for Noël ill. by Mark Graham. Eerdmans, 2000. ISBN 0-8028-5192-4 Subj: Babies. Birth. Birthdays. Family life. Holidays – Christmas.

Winter is . . . ill. by Mindy Dwyer. Alaska Northwest Bks., 2002. ISBN 0-8824-0543-8 Subj: Family life – brothers & sisters. Rhyming text. Seasons – winter.

Dixon, Chuck. *Batman: the joker's apprentice* ill. by John Calmette & Todd Winter. Little, 1996. ISBN 0-316-17798-9 Subj: Crime.

Dobbs, Rose. *More once-upon-a-time stories* ill. by Flavia Gág. Random House, 1961. Subj: Folk & fairy tales.

Once-upon-a-time story book ill. by Walter Hodges. Random House, 1958. Subj: Folk & fairy tales.

Dobkin, Bonnie. *Everybody says* ill. by Keith Neely. Childrens Pr., 1993. ISBN 0-516-02019-6 Subj: Character traits – individuality. Ethnic groups in the U.S. – African Americans. Friendship.

Dobrin, Arnold Jack. *Josephine's 'magination* ill. by author. Four Winds, 1973. ISBN 0-590-43494-2 Subj: Foreign lands – Caribbean Islands. Imagination. Toys.

Dobson, Clive. *Fred's TV* ill. by author. Firefly, 1989. ISBN 0-920668-60-7 Subj: Birds. Character traits – kindness to animals. Seasons – winter. Television.

Dobson, David. *Can we save them? endangered species of North America* ill. by James M. Needham. Charlesbridge, 1997. ISBN 0-88106-824-1 Subj: Animals – endangered animals. Ecology. Plants. Science.

Dodd, Anne Westcott. *Footprints and shadows* ill. by Henri Sorensen. S&S, 1992. ISBN 0-671-78716-0 Subj: Shadows.

The story of the sea glass ill. by Mary Beth Owens. Down East, 1999. ISBN 0-8927-2416-1 Subj: Family life – grandmothers. Sea & seashore.

Dodd, Emma. *Dog's ABC* ill. by author. Dutton, 2000. ISBN 0-525-46837-4 Subj: ABC books. Animals – dogs.

Dog's colorful day ill. by author. Dutton, 2001. ISBN 0-525-46528-6 Subj: Animals – dogs. Concepts – color. Counting, numbers.

Dog's noisy day ill. by author. Dutton, 2003. ISBN 0-525-47015-8 Subj: Animals. Animals – dogs. Farms. Noise, sounds.

Dodd, Lynley. *The apple tree* ill. by author. G. Stevens, 1985. ISBN 0-918831-08-3 Subj: Animals – possums. Behavior – stealing. Food. Trees.

A dragon in a wagon ill. by author. G. Stevens, 2000. ISBN 0-8368-2687-6 Subj: Animals – dogs. Imagination. Rhyming text. Toys – wagons.

Find me a tiger ill. by author. G. Stevens, 2001. ISBN 0-8368-2781-3 Subj: Animals. Behavior – hiding. Rhyming text.

Hairy Maclary from Donaldson's dairy ill. by author. G. Stevens, 1985. ISBN 0-918831-05-9 Subj: Animals – cats. Animals – dogs. Cumulative tales. Emotions – fear. Rhyming text.

Hairy Maclary, Scattercat ill. by author. G. Stevens, 1988. ISBN 1-555-32123-2 Subj: Animals – cats. Animals – dogs. Behavior – bullying. Rhyming text.

Hairy Maclary, sit ill. by author. G. Stevens, 1998. ISBN 0-8368-2093-2 Subj: Animals – dogs. Rhyming text.

Hairy Maclary's bone ill. by author. G. Stevens, 1985. ISBN 0-918331-06-7 Subj: Animals – dogs. Character traits – cleverness. Cumulative tales. Rhyming text.

Hairy Maclary's caterwaul caper ill. by author. G. Stevens, 2000. ISBN 0-8368-2690-6 Subj: Animals – cats. Animals – dogs. Rhyming text. Trees.

Hairy Maclary's rumpus at the vet ill. by author. G. Stevens, 2000. ISBN 0-8368-2691-4 Subj: Animals – dogs. Behavior – misbehavior. Careers – veterinarians. Rhyming text.

Hairy Maclary's showbusiness ill. by author. G. Stevens, 1992. ISBN 0-8368-0763-4 Subj: Animals – cats. Animals – dogs. Rhyming text.

The minister's cat: ABC ill. by author. G. Stevens, 1994. ISBN 0-8368-1073-2 Subj: ABC books. Animals – cats.

The nickle nackle tree ill. by author. Macmillan, 1976. ISBN 0-241-89330-5 Subj: Counting, numbers. Rhyming text.

Schnitzel von Krumm forget-me-not ill. by author. G. Stevens, 1998. ISBN 0-8368-2094-0 Subj: Activities – vacationing. Animals – dogs. Behavior – forgetfulness. Rhyming text.

Schnitzel von Krumm's basketwork ill. by author. G. Stevens, 2001. ISBN 0-8368-2783-X Subj: Animals – dogs. Emotions – happiness. Rhyming text.

Slinky Malinki ill. by author. G. Stevens, 2001. ISBN 0-8368-2784-8 Subj: Animals – cats. Crime. Rhyming text.

Slinky Malinki catflaps ill. by author. G. Stevens, 1999. ISBN 0-8368-2249-8 Subj: Animals – cats. Rhyming text.

Slinky Malinki, open the door ill. by author. G. Stevens, 2001. ISBN 0-8368-2785-6 Subj: Animals – cats. Behavior – misbehavior. Birds. Rhyming text.

The smallest turtle ill. by author. G. Stevens, 1985. ISBN 0-918831-07-5 Subj: Reptiles – turtles, tortoises. Science. Sea & seashore.

Wake up, bear ill. by author. G. Stevens, 1988. ISBN 1-555-32124-0 Subj: Animals. Animals – bears. Seasons – spring. Sleep.

Dodds, Dayle Ann. *The color box* ill. by Giles Laroche. Little, 1992. ISBN 0-316-18820-4 Subj: Animals – monkeys. Concepts – color. Format, unusual – toy & movable books.

Do bunnies talk? ill. by Arlene Dubanevich. HarperCollins, 1992. ISBN 0-06-020249-1 Subj: Animals. Animals – rabbits. Language. Noise, sounds. Rhyming text.

The Great Divide ill. by Tracy Mitchell. Candlewick, 1999. ISBN 0-7636-0442-9 Subj: Counting, numbers. Rhyming text. Sports – racing.

The Kettles get new clothes ill. by Jill McElmurry. Candlewick, 2002. ISBN 0-7636-1091-7 Subj: Animals – dogs. Clothing. Shopping.

Pet wash ill. by Tor Freeman. Candlewick, 2001. ISBN 0-7636-0989-7 Subj: Activities – bathing. Animals. Pets. Rhyming text.

The shape of things ill. by Julie Lacome. Candlewick, 1994. ISBN 1-56402-224-2 Subj: Concepts – shape.

Sing, Sophie! ill. by Rosanne Litzinger. Candlewick, 1997. ISBN 0-7636-0131-4 Subj: Activities – singing. Family life. Rhyming text. Weather – storms.

Wheel away! ill. by Thacher Hurd. HarperCollins, 1991. ISBN 0-06-021689-1 Subj: Circular tales. Format, unusual. Rhyming text.

Where's Pup? ill. by Pierre Pratt. Dial, 2003. ISBN 0-8037-2744-5 Subj: Animals – dogs. Circus. Clowns, jesters. Format, unusual – toy & movable books. Rhyming text.

Dodds, Siobhan. *Charles Tiger* ill. by author. Little, 1988. ISBN 0-316-18817-4 Subj: Animals. Animals – tigers. Behavior – lost & found possessions.

Elizabeth Hen ill. by author. Little, 1988. ISBN 0-316-18818-2 Subj: Animals. Birds – chickens. Counting, numbers. Eggs. Farms.

Grandpa Bud ill. by author. Candlewick, 1993. ISBN 1-56402-175-0 Subj: Activities – baking, cooking. Cumulative tales. Family life – grandfathers. Toys.

Ting-a-ling! ill. by author. DK, 1999. ISBN 0-7894-4841-6 Subj: Activities – bathing. Family life – mothers. Telephone. Toys.

Words and pictures ill. by author. Candlewick, 1992. ISBN 1-56402-042-8 Subj: Activities. Dictionaries. Rebuses.

Dodge, Mary Mapes. *Mary Anne* ill. by June Amos Grammer. Lothrop, 1983. ISBN 0-688-02089-5 Subj: Rhyming text. Toys – dolls.

Dodgson, Charles Lutwidge. *see* Carroll, Lewis

Doepker, David. *Animal babies* ill. with photos. Sterling, 2004. ISBN 1-4027-1717-2 Subj: Animals – babies. Format, unusual – board books.

Farm babies ill. with photos. Sterling, 2004. ISBN 1-4027-1714-8 Subj: Animals – babies. Farms. Format, unusual – board books. Noise, sounds.

The dog writes on the window with his nose, and other poems coll. by David Kherdian; ill. by Nonny Hogrogian. Four Winds, 1977. ISBN 0-590-07448-2 Subj: Poetry.

Doherty, Berlie. *The midnight man* ill. by Ian Andrew. Candlewick, 1998. ISBN 0-7636-0700-2 Subj: Dreams. Moon. Night. Stars.

Paddiwak and cozy ill. by Alison Bartlett. Orchard, 1991. ISBN 0-531-30180-X Subj: Animals – cats. Emotions – envy, jealousy.

Paddiwak and cozy ill. by Teresa O'Brien. Dial, 1989. ISBN 0-8037-0483-6 Subj: Animals – cats. Emotions – envy, jealousy.

Snowy ill. by Keith Bowen. Dial, 1993. ISBN 0-8037-1343-6 Subj: Animals – horses, ponies. Boats, ships. Family life. School.

Dollinger, Renate. *The rabbi who flew* ill. by author. Booksmythe, 2001. ISBN 0-945585-20-9 Subj: Activities – flying. Careers – clergy. Careers – shoemakers. Jewish culture.

Domanska, Janina. *A was an angler* ill. by author. Greenwillow, 1991. ISBN 0-688-06991-6 Subj: ABC books. Nursery rhymes.

The best of the bargain ill. by author. Greenwillow, 1977. ISBN 0-688-84062-0 Subj: Animals – foxes. Animals – hedgehogs. Behavior – trickery. Character traits – cleverness. Folk & fairy tales. Foreign lands – Poland. Gardens, gardening.

Busy Monday morning ill. by author. Greenwillow, 1985. ISBN 0-688-03834-4 Subj: Folk & fairy tales. Foreign lands – Poland. Music. Songs.

I saw a ship a-sailing ill. by author. Macmillan, 1972. Subj: Boats, ships. Holidays – Christmas. Nursery rhymes.

If all the seas were one sea ill. by author. Macmillan, 1971. ISBN 0-02-732540-7 Subj: Caldecott award honor books. Nursery rhymes. Sea & seashore.

King Krakus and the dragon ill. by author. Greenwillow, 1979. ISBN 0-688-84189-9 Subj: Character traits – cleverness. Dragons. Folk & fairy tales. Foreign lands – Poland. Royalty – kings.

Look, there is a turtle flying ill. by author. Macmillan, 1968. Subj: Folk & fairy tales. Foreign lands – Poland. Reptiles – turtles, tortoises. Royalty.

Marek, the little fool ill. by author. Greenwillow, 1982. ISBN 0-688-00913-1 Subj: Folk & fairy tales. Foreign lands.

Palmiero and the ogre ill. by author. Macmillan, 1967. Subj: Behavior – forgetfulness. Folk & fairy tales. Magic. Mythical creatures – ogres.

A scythe, a rooster and a cat ill. by author. Greenwillow, 1981. ISBN 0-688-84308-5 Subj: Folk & fairy tales. Foreign lands – Russia.

Spring is ill. by author. Greenwillow, 1976. ISBN 0-688-84026-4 Subj: Animals – dogs. Character traits – curiosity. Seasons.

The tortoise and the tree ill. by author. Greenwillow, 1978. ISBN 0-688-84132-5 Subj: Folk & fairy tales. Foreign lands – Africa. Reptiles – turtles, tortoises.

The turnip ill. by author. Macmillan, 1969. Subj: Character traits – cooperation. Cumulative tales. Farms. Folk & fairy tales. Foreign lands – Russia. Plants. Problem solving.

What do you see? ill. by author. Macmillan, 1974. ISBN 0-02-732830-9 Subj: Animals. Rhyming text. World.

What happens next? ill. by author. Greenwillow, 1983. ISBN 0-688-01749-5 Subj: Tall tales.

Why so much noise? ill. by author. HarperCollins, 1965. Adapt. of the tale entitled 'The elephant has a bet with the tiger,' [as recorded] by Walter William Skeat. Subj: Animals – elephants. Animals – tigers. Character traits – cleverness. Folk & fairy tales. Foreign lands – India. Noise, sounds.

Domestic animals ill. with photos. Imported Pubs., 1983. ISBN 0-8285-2429-7 Subj: Animals. Format, unusual – board books. Wordless.

Dominguez, Angel. *Diary of a Victorian mouse* ill. by author. Arcade, 1991. ISBN 1-55970-121-8 Subj: Animals – mice. Foreign lands – England.

Donahue, Shari Faden. *The zebra-striped whale with the polka-dot tail* ill. by author. Arimax, 2001. ISBN 0-9634287-3-X Subj: Animals. Imagination. Rhyming text.

Donaldson, Joan. *The real pretend* ill. by Tasha Tudor. Checkerboard, 1992. ISBN 1-56288-158-2 Subj: Activities – playing. Behavior – misunderstanding. Family life – brothers.

Donaldson, Julia. *The gruffalo* ill. by Axel Scheffler. Dial, 1999. ISBN 0-8037-2386-5 Subj: Animals. Animals – mice. Monsters. Rhyming text.

Room on the broom ill. by Axel Scheffler. Dial, 2001. ISBN 0-8037-2657-0 Subj: Animals. Behavior – lost & found possessions. Dragons. Rhyming text. Witches.

Donaldson, Lois. *Karl's wooden horse* ill. by Annie Bergmann. A. Whitman, 1970. ISBN 0-8075-4107-9 Subj: Dreams. Holidays – Christmas. Night. Toys – rocking horses.

Donnelly, Jennifer. *Humble pie* ill. by Stephen Gammell. Atheneum, 2002. ISBN 0-689-84435-2 Subj: Behavior. Behavior – greed. Folk & fairy tales. Food.

Donnelly, Liza. *Dinosaur beach* ill. by author. Scholastic, 1991. ISBN 0-590-42175-1 Subj: Cities, towns. Dinosaurs. Prehistory. Sea & seashore – beaches.

Dinosaur garden ill. by author. Scholastic, 1991. ISBN 0-590-43172-2 Subj: Cities, towns. Dinosaurs. Gardens, gardening. Prehistory.

Dinosaurs' Halloween ill. by author. Scholastic, 1987. ISBN 0-590-41025-3 Subj: Cities, towns. Dinosaurs. Holidays – Halloween. Prehistory.

Donohue, Dorothy. *Big and little on the farm* ill. by author. Golden Bks., 1999. ISBN 0-307-10225-4 Subj: Animals. Animals – babies. Concepts – size. Farms.

Veggie soup ill. by author. Winslow, 2000. ISBN 1-890817-21-X Subj: Activities – baking, cooking. Animals. Animals – rabbits. Food. Friendship.

Donovan, Gail. *The copycat fish* ill. by David Austin Clar Studio. Night Sky, 2001. ISBN 1-59014-018-4 Subj: Fish. Format, unusual. School.

A fishy story ill. by David Austin Clar Studio. Night Sky, 2001. ISBN 1-59014-019-2 Subj: Character traits – honesty. Fish. Format, unusual. School.

Hidden treasures ill. by David Austin Clar Studio. Night Sky, 2001. ISBN 1-59014-021-4 Subj: Fish. School.

Lost at sea ill. by David Austin Clar Studio. Night Sky, 2001. ISBN 1-59014-020-6 Subj: Behavior – lost. Fish. Format, unusual. School.

Donovan, Mary Lee. *Bedtime* (Bedtime)

Won't you come and play with me? ill. by Cynthia Jabar. Houghton Mifflin, 1998. ISBN 0-395-84630-7 Subj: Activities – playing. Music. Nursery rhymes. Songs.

Don't tell the scarecrow: and other Japanese poems by Issa, Yayu, Kikaku & other Japanese poets; ill. by Talivaldis Stubis. Four Winds, 1970. Subj: Foreign lands – Japan. Poetry. Seasons.

Dooley, Norah. *Everybody bakes bread* ill. by Peter J. Thornton. Carolrhoda, 1996. ISBN 0-87614-864-X Subj: Activities – baking, cooking. Communities, neighborhoods. Ethnic groups in the U.S. Food.

Everybody brings noodles ill. by Peter J. Thornton. Carolrhoda, 2002. ISBN 0-8761-4455-5 Subj: Communities, neighborhoods. Ethnic groups in the U.S. Food. Foreign lands. Parties.

Everybody cooks rice ill. by Peter J. Thornton. Carolrhoda, 1991. ISBN 0-87614-412-1 Subj: Ethnic groups in the U.S. Family life. Food.

Everybody serves soup ill. by Peter J. Thornton. Carolrhoda, 2000. ISBN 1-57505-422-1 Subj: Activities – baking, cooking. Ethnic groups in the U.S. Food. Gifts. Weather – snow.

Dooley, Virginia. *Tubes in my ears: my trip to the hospital* ill. by Miriam Katin. Mondo, 1996. ISBN 1-57255-118-6 Subj: Hospitals. Illness.

Doolittle, Bev. *The forest has eyes* ill. by Elise Maclay. Greenwich Workshop, 1998. ISBN 0-86713-055-5 Subj: Indians of North America. Nature.

Reading the wild ill. by Elise Maclay. Greenwich Workshop, 2001. ISBN 0-86713-061-X Subj: Animals. Birds. Nature.

Doolittle, Eileen. *The ark in the attic: an alphabet adventure* photos by Starr Ockenga. Godine, 1987. ISBN 0-87923-648-1 Subj: ABC books. Rebuses. Riddles & jokes.

World of wonders: a trip through numbers photos by Starr Ockenga; ill. by author. Houghton Mifflin, 1988. ISBN 0-325-48726-9 Subj: Counting, numbers. Imagination. Rhyming text.

Doray, Malika. *One more Wednesday* ill. by author; tr. by Suzanne Freeman. Greenwillow, 2001. ISBN 0-06-029590-2 Subj: Animals. Death. Emotions – grief. Family life – grandmothers. Memories, memory.

Dorfman, Craig. *I knew you could!* ill. by Christina Ong. Platt, 2003. ISBN 0-448-43148-3 Subj: Rhyming text. Self-concept. Trains.

Dorian, Marguerite. *When the snow is blue* ill. by author. Lothrop, 1960. Subj: Animals – bears. Imagination. Weather – snow.

Dornbusch, Erica. *Finding Kate's shoes* ill. by author. Firefly, 2001. ISBN 1-55037-671-3 Subj: Behavior – lost & found possessions. Clothing – shoes. Family life – mothers. Imagination. Wordless.

Doro, Ann. *Twin pickle* ill. by Clare Mackie. Holt, 1996. ISBN 0-8050-3802-7 Subj: Multiple births – twins. Rhyming text.

Dörrie, Doris. *Lottie's princess dress* ill. by Julia Kaergel. Dial, 1999. ISBN 0-8037-2388-1 Subj: Clothing – dresses. Family life – daughters. Family life – mothers.

Dorros, Arthur. *Abuela* ill. by Elisa Kleven. Dutton, 1991. ISBN 0-525-44750-4 Subj: Activities – flying. Cities, towns. Ethnic groups in the U.S. Family life – grandmothers. Foreign languages.

Alligator shoes ill. by author. Dutton, 1982. ISBN 0-525-44001-1 Subj: Reptiles – alligators, crocodiles.

Ant cities ill. by author. Crowell, 1987. ISBN 0-690-04570-0 Subj: Insects – ants. Science.

City chicken ill. by Henry Cole. HarperCollins, 2003. ISBN 0-06-028483-8 Subj: Animals. Birds – chickens. Cities, towns. Country. Humorous stories.

Feel the wind ill. by author. HarperCollins, 1989. ISBN 0-690-04741-X Subj: Weather – wind.

Follow the water from brook to ocean ill. by author. HarperCollins, 1991. ISBN 0-06-021599-2 Subj: Science. Water.

The fungus that ate my school ill. by David Catrow. Scholastic, 2000. ISBN 0-590-47704-8 Subj: School. Science.

Julio's magic ill. by Ann Grifalconi. HarperCollins, 2005. ISBN 0-06-029005-6 Subj: Activities – wood carving. Careers – woodcarvers. Contests. Foreign lands – Mexico. Friendship.

Me and my shadow ill. by author. Scholastic, 1990. ISBN 0-590-42772-5 Subj: Shadows.

Pretzels ill. by author. Greenwillow, 1981. ISBN 0-688-00669-8 Subj: Boats, ships. Humorous stories.

Radio Man = Don Radio: a story in English and Spanish trans. by Sandra Dorros. HarperCollins, 1993. Text in English and Spanish. ISBN 0-06-021548-8 Subj: Careers – migrant workers. Communication. Ethnic groups in the U.S. – Mexican Americans. Farms. Radios.

This is my house ill. by author. Scholastic, 1992. ISBN 0-590-45302-5 Subj: Foreign lands. Homes, houses.

Tonight is carnaval ill. with photos of arpilleras sewn by the Club de Madres Virgen del Carmen of Lima, Peru. Dutton, 1991. ISBN 0-525-44641-9 Subj: Fairs, festivals. Farms. Foreign lands – Peru.

When the pigs took over ill. by Diane Greenseid. Dutton, 2002. ISBN 0-525-42030-4 Subj: Animals – pigs. Animals – snails. Ethnic groups in the U.S. – Mexican Americans. Humorous stories. Restaurants.

Dorros, Sandra Marulanda. *Radio Man = Don Radio: a story in English and Spanish* (Dorros, Arthur)

Dorsky, Blanche. *Harry, a true story* ill. by Muriel Batherman. Prentice-Hall, 1977. ISBN 0-13-384198-7 Subj: Animals – rabbits. School.

Dos Santos, Joyce Audy. *The diviner* ill. by author. Lippincott, 1980. ISBN 0-397-31910-X Subj: Character traits – cleverness. Folk & fairy tales. Foreign lands – Canada. Royalty.

Henri and the Loup-Garou ill. by author. Pantheon, 1982. ISBN 0-394-94950-1 Subj: Folk & fairy tales. Foreign lands – Canada. Monsters.

Sand dollar, sand dollar ill. by author. Lippincott, 1980. ISBN 0-397-31894-4 Subj: Sea & seashore.

Dostoyevsky, Fyodor. *The talking crocodile* (Campbell, M. Rudolph)

Dotlich, Rebecca Kai. *A family like yours* ill. by Tammie Lyon. Boyds Mills, 2002. ISBN 1-56397-916-0 Subj: Family life. Poetry.

In the spin of things ill. by Karen Dugan. Boyds Mills, 2003. ISBN 1-56397-145-3 Subj: Concepts – motion. Poetry.

Lemonade sun: and other summer poems ill. by Jan Spivey Gilchrist. Wordsong, 1998. ISBN 1-56397-660-9 Subj: Poetry. Seasons – summer.

Mama loves ill. by Kathryn Brown. HarperCollins, 2004. ISBN 0-06-029408-6 Subj: Animals – pigs. Family life – mothers.

Papa loves ill. by Kathryn Brown. HarperCollins, 2003. ISBN 0-06-029406-X Subj: Animals – pigs. Family life – fathers.

What is a triangle? photos by Maria Ferrari. HarperFestival, 2000. ISBN 0-694-01392-7 Subj: Concepts – shape.

What is round? photos by Maria Ferrari. HarperFestival, 1999. ISBN 0-694-01208-4 Subj: Concepts – shape. Rhyming text.

What is square? photos by Maria Ferrari. HarperFestival, 1999. ISBN 0-694-01207-6 Subj: Concepts – shape. Rhyming text.

Doty, Roy. *Eye fooled you: the big book of optical illusions* ill. by author. Macmillan, 1983. ISBN 0-02-042980-0 Subj: Optical illusions.

Old-one-eye meets his match ill. by author. Lothrop, 1978. ISBN 0-688-51825-7 Subj: Animals – mice. Animals – rats.

Doubilet, Anne. *Under the sea from A to Z* photos by David Doubilet. Crown, 1991. ISBN 0-517-57837-9 Subj: ABC books. Sea & seashore.

Doucet, Sharon Arms. *Why Lapin's ears are long and other stories of the Louisiana bayou* ill. by David Catrow. Orchard, 1997. ISBN 0-531-33041-9 Subj: Animals – rabbits. Folk & fairy tales.

Doughtie, Charles. *Gabriel Wrinkles, the bloodhound who couldn't smell* ill. by Charles D. Saxon. Dodd, 1959. Subj: Animals – dogs. Senses – smell.

High Henry . . . the cowboy who was too tall to ride a horse ill. by Don Gregg. Dodd, 1960. Subj: Animals – giraffes. Cowboys, cowgirls. U.S. history – frontier & pioneer life.

Douglas, Ann. *Baby science: how babies really work!* photos by Hélène Desputeaux. Owl Books, 1998. ISBN 1-895688-83-3 Subj: Babies. Behavior – growing up. Family life.

Before you were born ill. by Eugenie Fernandes. Firefly, 2000. ISBN 1-894379-01-2 Subj: Babies. Birth. Family life. Family life – mothers.

Douglas, Erin. *Get that pest!* ill. by Wong Herbert Yee. Harcourt, 2000. ISBN 0-15-202548-0 Subj: Careers – farmers. Crime. Eggs. Farms.

Douglas, Michael. *Round, round world* ill. by author. Golden Pr., 1960. Subj: Animals – cats. Foreign lands. World.

Douglas, Richardo Keens. *see* Keens-Douglas, Richardo

Douglas, Robert W. *John Paul II: the Pilgrim Pope* ill. with map & photos. Childrens Pr., 1979. ISBN 0-516-03563-0 Subj: Religion.

Douglass, Barbara. *The chocolate chip cookie contest* ill. by Eric Jon Nones. Lothrop, 1985. ISBN 0-688-04044-6 Subj: Activities – baking, cooking. Clowns, jesters.

Good as new ill. by Patiences Brewster. Lothrop, 1982. ISBN 0-688-51983-0 Subj: Behavior – misbehavior. Family life – grandfathers. Toys – bears.

Douzou, Olivier. *Wolf's lunch* ill. by author. Chronicle, 1997. ISBN 0-8118-1806-3 Subj: Animals – wolves. Format, unusual – board books.

Dow, Katharine. *My time of year* ill. by Walter Erhard. Walck, 1961. Subj: Seasons.

Dowdy, Mrs. Regera. *see* Gorey, Edward (St. John)

Dowers, Patrick. *One day scene through a leaf* ill. by author. Green Tiger Pr., 1981. ISBN 0-914676-55-5 Subj: Poetry.

Dowley, Tim. *The shepherds' tale* by Tim Dowley & Peter Wyart; ill. by Martin Pierce. Kregel, 2002. ISBN 0-8254-7257-1 Subj: Format, unusual – toy & movable books. Holidays – Christmas. Religion – Nativity.

The wise men's tale by Tim Dowley & Peter Wyart; ill. by Martin Pierce. Kregel, 2002. ISBN 0-8254-7256-3 Subj: Format, unusual – toy & movable books. Holidays – Christmas. Religion – Nativity.

Dowling, Paul. *Are you sleepy, Puff?* ill. by author. Hyperion, 1993. ISBN 1-56282-393-0 Subj: Animals – cats. Bedtime. Sleep.

Happy birthday, Owl ill. by author. Walt Disney, 1992. ISBN 1-56282-253-5 Subj: Animals. Birds – owls. Birthdays. Parties.

Jimmy's snowy book ill. by author. Bantam, 1994. ISBN 0-553-09649-4 Subj: Animals – dogs. Format, unusual – toy & movable books. Weather – snow.

Meg and Jack are moving ill. by author. Houghton Mifflin, 1990. ISBN 0-395-53514-X Subj: Family life. Moving.

Meg and Jack's new friends ill. by author. Houghton Mifflin, 1990. ISBN 0-395-53513-1 Subj: Behavior – sharing. Friendship. Moving. Toys.

The night journey ill. by author. Delacorte, 1997. ISBN 0-385-32287-9 Subj: Format, unusual – toy & movable books. Night.

Splodger ill. by author. Houghton Mifflin, 1991. ISBN 0-395-57443-9 Subj: Bedtime. Behavior – misbehavior. Imagination.

Where are you going, Jimmy? ill. by author. Thomasson-Grant, 1993. ISBN 1-56566-026-9 Subj: Activities – walking. Animals. Communities, neighborhoods.

You can do it, Rabbit ill. by author. Walt Disney, 1992. ISBN 1-56282-252-7 Subj: Animals – rabbits. Character traits – helpfulness. Sports – bicycling.

You need a bath, Mustard ill. by author. Hyperion, 1993. ISBN 1-56282-392-2 Subj: Activities – bathing. Animals. Animals – bears.

Downes, Belinda. *Every little angel's handbook* words & embroideries by Belinda Downes. Dial, 1997. ISBN 0-8037-2264-8 Subj: Angels. Religion.

Downey, Lynn. *The flea's sneeze* ill. by Karla Firehammer. Holt, 2000. ISBN 0-8050-6103-7 Subj: Animals. Farms. Insects – fleas. Rhyming text. Sleep.

Sing, Henrietta! Sing! ill. by Tony Sansevero. Ideals, 1997. ISBN 1-57102-103-5 Subj: Activities – singing. Food. Friendship. Gardens, gardening.

This is the earth that God made ill. by Benrei Huang. Augsburg Fortress, 2000. ISBN 0-8066-3960-1 Subj: Creation. Cumulative tales. Religion. Rhyming text.

Downie, Jill. *Alphabet puzzle* ill. by author. Lothrop, 1988. ISBN 0-688-08044-8 Subj: ABC books. Rebuses. Riddles & jokes.

Downing, Joan. *Baseball is our game* ill. by Tony Freeman. Childrens Pr., 1982. ISBN 0-516-03402-2 Subj: Sports – baseball.

Downs, Mike. *Pig giggles and rabbit rhymes* ill. by David Sheldon. Chronicle, 2002. ISBN 0-8118-3114-0 Subj: Animals. Humorous stories. Riddles & jokes.

Dowson, Nick. *Tigress* ill. by Jane Chapman. Candlewick, 2004. ISBN 0-7636-2325-3 Subj: Animals – babies. Animals – tigers. Behavior – growing up. Family life – mothers.

Doyle, Charlotte Lackner. *Where's Bunny's mommy?* ill. by Rick Brown. S&S, 1995. ISBN 0-671-88984-8 Subj: Animals – rabbits. Family life – mothers. School.

You can't catch me ill. by Rosanne Litzinger. HarperFestival, 1998. ISBN 0-694-01038-3 Subj: Activities – playing. Rhyming text.

Doyle, Donovan. *see* Boegehold, Betty

Doyle, Malachy. *Baby see, baby do!* ill. by Britta Teckentrup. Putnam, 2002. ISBN 0-399-23728-3 Subj: Animals – babies. Babies. Format, unusual – toy & movable books.

Cow ill. by Angelo Rinaldi. McElderry, 2002. ISBN 0-689-84462-X Subj: Animals – bulls, cows. Farms.

Hungry! Hungry! Hungry! ill. by Paul Hess. Peachtree, 2000. ISBN 1-56145-241-6 Subj: Food. Monsters. Mythical creatures – goblins.

Jody's beans ill. by Judith Allibone. Candlewick, 1999. ISBN 0-7636-0687-1 Subj: Family life – grandfathers. Food. Gardens, gardening.

Sleepy Pendoodle ill. by Julie Vivas. Candlewick, 2002. ISBN 0-7636-1561-7 Subj: Animals – dogs. Pets.

Splash, Joshua, splash! ill. by Ken Wilson-Max. Bloomsbury, 2004. ISBN 1-58234-837-5 Subj: Family life – grandmothers. Water.

Storm cats ill. by Stuart Trotter. McElderry, 2002. ISBN 0-689-84464-6 Subj: Animals – cats. Friendship. Rhyming text. Weather – storms.

Well, a crocodile can! ill. by Britta Teckentrup. Millbrook, 2000. ISBN 0-7613-1032-0 Subj: Activities. Animals. Behavior. Format, unusual – toy & movable books.

Drachman, Eric. *Leo the lightning bug* ill. by James Muscarello. Kidwick, 2001. ISBN 0-9703809-0-9 Subj: Insects – fireflies. Self-concept.

Dragon poems comp. by John Foster & Korky Paul; ill. by Korky Paul. Oxford Univ. Pr., 1992. ISBN 0-19-276096-3 Subj: Dragons. Poetry.

Dragonwagon, Crescent. *Alligator arrived with apples: a potluck alphabet feast* ill. by José Aruego & Ariane Dewey. Macmillan, 1987. ISBN 0-02-733090-7 Subj: ABC books. Animals. Holidays – Thanksgiving. Reptiles – alligators, crocodiles.

Alligators and others all year long! a book of months ill. by José Aruego & Ariane Dewey. Macmillan, 1993. ISBN 0-02-733091-5 Subj: Animals. Days of the week, months of the year. Poetry.

Always, always ill. by Arieh Zeldich. Macmillan, 1984. ISBN 0-02-733080-X Subj: Divorce.

Annie flies the birthday bike ill. by Emily Arnold McCully. Macmillan, 1993. ISBN 0-02-733155-5 Subj: Birthdays. Rhyming text. Sports – bicycling.

Bat in the dining room ill. by S. D. Schindler. Cavendish, 1997. ISBN 0-7614-5007-6 Subj: Animals – bats. Character traits – kindness to animals. Rhyming text.

Coconut ill. by Nancy Tafuri. HarperCollins, 1984. ISBN 0-06-021760-X Subj: Behavior – wishing. Birds – parakeets, parrots.

Diana, maybe ill. by Deborah Kogan Ray. Macmillan, 1987. ISBN 0-02-733180-6 Subj: Behavior – wishing. Family life.

Half a moon and one whole star ill. by Jerry Pinkney. Macmillan, 1986. ISBN 0-02-733120-2 Subj: Dreams. Night. Rhyming text.

Home place ill. by Jerry Pinkney. Macmillan, 1990. ISBN 0-02-733190-3 Subj: Ethnic groups in the U.S. – African Americans. Family life. Homes, houses.

I hate my brother Harry ill. by Dick Gackenbach. HarperCollins, 1983. ISBN 0-06-021758-8 Subj: Sibling rivalry.

I hate my sister Maggie ill. by Leslie Holt Morrill. Macmillan, 1989. ISBN 0-02-733150-4 Subj: Sibling rivalry.

If you call my name ill. by David Palladini. Harper, 1981. ISBN 0-06-021744-8 Subj: Imagination.

The itch book ill. by Joseph Mahler. Macmillan, 1990. ISBN 0-02-733121-0 Subj: Rhyming text. Seasons – summer.

Jemima remembers ill. by Troy Howell. Macmillan, 1984. ISBN 0-02-733070-2 Subj: Farms. Memories, memory. Rhyming text. Seasons.

Katie in the morning ill. by Betsy Day. HarperCollins, 1983. ISBN 0-06-021730-8 Subj: Behavior – solitude. Morning.

Margaret Ziegler is horse-crazy ill. by Peter Elwell. Macmillan, 1988. ISBN 0-02-733230-6 Subj: Animals – horses, ponies.

Rainy day together ill. by Lillian Hoban. HarperCollins, 1971. ISBN 0-06-024688-X Subj: Emotions. Family life. Family life – only child. Weather – rain.

Strawberry dress escape ill. by Lillian Hoban. Scribners, 1975. ISBN 0-684-13912-X Subj: School. Seasons – spring.

The sun begun ill. by Terea Shaffer. Atheneum, 1999. ISBN 0-689-81159-4 Subj: Family life. Family life – fathers. Rhyming text.

This is the bread I baked for Ned ill. by Isadore Seltzer. Macmillan, 1989. ISBN 0-02-733220-9 Subj: Activities – baking, cooking. Cumulative tales. Food. Rhyming text.

When light turns into night ill. by Robert Andrew Parker. HarperCollins, 1975. ISBN 0-06-021740-5 Subj: Behavior – solitude. Night.

Will it be okay? ill. by Ben Shecter. Harper, 1977. ISBN 0-06-021738-3 Subj: Emotions – fear. Family life – mothers.

Wind Rose ill. by Ronald Himler. HarperCollins, 1976. ISBN 0-06-021742-1 Subj: Babies. Emotions – love. Names.

Drake, Jane. *Farming* (Love, Ann)

Fishing (Love, Ann)

Drake, John. *The beginning of the river: Herman's quest* ill. by Kelly Kortekaas. Little Turtle, 1992. ISBN 0-9633574-0-9 Subj: Animals – cats. Rhyming text. Rivers.

Drawson, Blair. *All along the river* ill. by author. Douglas & McIntyre, 2003. ISBN 0-88899-546-6 Subj: Canoes & canoeing. Family life – grandfathers. Imagination. Rivers.

Flying Dimitri ill. by author. Orchard, 1997. ISBN 0-531-30037-4 Subj: Activities – flying. Birthdays. Emotions – loneliness. Family life – fathers. Imagination.

Mary Margaret's tree ill. by author. Orchard, 1996. ISBN 0-531-08871-5 Subj: Imagination. Nature. Seasons. Trees.

Drdek, Richard E. *Horace the friendly octopus* ill. by Joseph Veno. Allyn & Bacon, 1965. Reading consultants: William D. Sheldon and Mary C. Austin. Subj: Friendship. Octopuses.

Dreamer, Sue. *Circus ABC* ill. by author. Little, 1985. ISBN 0-316-19196-5 Subj: ABC books. Circus. Format, unusual – board books.

Circus 1, 2, 3 ill. by author. Little, 1985. ISBN 0-316-19195-7 Subj: Circus. Counting, numbers. Format, unusual – board books.

Dreier, Ted. *Moozie's kind adventure* ill. by Jane Labik. Best Friends Books, 1999. ISBN 0-9662268-1-X Subj: Animals – bulls, cows. Birds – ducks. Farms.

Dreifus, Miriam W. *Brave Betsy* ill. by Sheila Greenwald. Putnam, 1961. Subj: Character traits – bravery. School. Toys – dolls.

Drescher, Henrik. *The boy who ate around* ill. by author. Hyperion, 1994. ISBN 0-7868-2011-X Subj: Food. Monsters.

Klutz ill. by author. Hyperion, 1996. ISBN 0-7868-2182-5 Subj: Circus. Clowns, jesters. Family life.

Look-alikes ill. by author. Lothrop, 1985. ISBN 0-688-05817-5 Subj: Animals – monkeys. Toys.

Looking for Santa Claus ill. by author. Lothrop, 1984. ISBN 0-688-02999-X Subj: Animals – bulls, cows. Holidays – Christmas. Imagination. Santa Claus.

Pat the beastie: a pull-and-poke book ill. by author; paper engineering by Dennis K. Meyer. Hyperion, 1993. ISBN 1-5628-2407-4 Subj: Format, unusual – toy & movable books. Monsters.

Simon's book ill. by author. Lothrop, 1983. ISBN 0-688-02086-0 Subj: Dreams. Monsters.

The strange appearance of Howard Cranebill, Jr. ill. by author. Lothrop, 1982. ISBN 0-688-00962-X Subj: Babies. Birds – storks. Character traits – being different. Family life.

The yellow umbrella ill. by author. Bradbury, 1987. ISBN 0-02-733240-3 Subj: Animals – monkeys. Jungle. Umbrellas. Wordless. Zoos.

Drescher, Joan E. *The birth-order blues* ill. by author. Viking, 1993. ISBN 0-670-83621-4 Subj: Family life. Sibling rivalry.

I'm in charge! ill. by author. Little, 1981. ISBN 0-316-19330-5 Subj: Behavior – growing up. Family life.

The marvelous mess ill. by author. Houghton Mifflin, 1980. ISBN 0-395-28160-7 Subj: Family life. Sibling rivalry.

Max and Rufus ill. by author. Houghton Mifflin, 1982. ISBN 0-395-32435-1 Subj: Animals – dogs. Humorous stories.

My mother's getting married ill. by author. Dial, 1986. ISBN 0-8037-0176-4 Subj: Emotions – envy, jealousy. Family life – mothers. Weddings.

Your family, my family ill. by author. Walker, 1980. ISBN 0-8027-6382-0 Subj: Family life.

Drew, Patricia. *Spotter Puff* ill. by author. Merrimack, 1979. ISBN 0-686-25198-9 Subj: Birds – puffins. Character traits – kindness to animals.

Driscoll, Debbie. *Baby comes home* ill. by Barbara Samuels. S&S, 1993. ISBN 0-671-75540-4 Subj: Babies. Family life – brothers & sisters. Family life – new sibling.

Driscoll, Laura. *The bravest cat! the true story of Scarlett* ill. by DyAnne DiSalvo-Ryan. Grosset, 1997. ISBN 0-448-41720-0 Subj: Animals – cats. Character traits – bravery. Fire.

Driz, Ovsei. *The boy and the tree* trans. by Joachim Neugroschel; ill. by Victor Pivovarov. Prentice-Hall, 1978. ISBN 0-13-080929-2 Subj: Poetry.

**The drowsy hours: *poems for bedtime* sel. by Susan Pearson; ill. by Peter Malone. HarperCollins, 2002. ISBN 0-06-029421-3 Subj: Bedtime. Lullabies. Night. Poetry. Sleep.

Druce, Arden. *Halloween night* ill. by David T. Wenzel. Rising Moon, 2001. ISBN 0-87358-797-9 Subj: Holidays – Halloween. Rhyming text. Riddles & jokes.

Drucker, Malka. *Grandma's latkes* ill. by Eve Chwast. Harcourt, 1992. ISBN 0-15-200468-8 Subj: Family life – grandmothers. Food. Holidays – Hanukkah. Jewish culture. Religion.

A Jewish holiday ABC ill. by Rita Pocock. Harcourt, 1992. ISBN 0-15-200482-3 Subj: ABC books. Holidays. Jewish culture. Religion.

Drummond, Allan. *Casey Jones* ill. by author. Farrar, 2001. ISBN 0-374-31175-7 Subj: Careers – engineers. Rhyming text. Tall tales. Trains.

Liberty ill. by author. Farrar, 2002. ISBN 0-374-34385-3 Subj: Character traits – freedom. U.S. history.

Moby Dick ill. by adapt. Farrar, 1997. ISBN 0-374-34997-5 Subj: Animals – whales. Careers – whalers. Sea & seashore. Sports – hunting.

The willow pattern story ill. by author. North-South, 1992. ISBN 1-55858-172-3 Subj: Emotions – love. Folk & fairy tales. Foreign lands – China.

Drummond, Violet H. *The flying postman* ill. by author. Walck, 1964. Subj: Careers – postal workers. Foreign lands – England. Helicopters.

Phewtus the squirrel ill. by author. Lothrop, 1987. ISBN 0-688-07013-2 Subj: Animals – squirrels. Behavior – lost. Toys.

Drury, Tim. *When I'm big* by Tim Drury & Nila Aye; ill. by Nila Aye. Orchard, 1999. ISBN 0-531-30189-3 Subj: Imagination. Rhyming text. Weather – rain.

Dryden, Emma. *Good morning – good night* ill. by Richard Max Kolding. Random House, 1990. ISBN 0-679-80066-2 Subj: Animals. Format, unusual. Morning. Night.

Dubanevich, Arlene. *Calico cows* ill. by author. Viking, 1993. ISBN 0-670-84436-5 Subj: Animals – bulls, cows. Behavior – lost.

Pig William ill. by author. Bradbury, 1985. ISBN 0-02-733200-4 Subj: Activities – picnicking. Animals – pigs. Behavior – indifference. Sibling rivalry. Weather – rain.

The piggest show on earth ill. by author. Watts, 1989. ISBN 0-531-05789-5 Subj: Animals – pigs. Circus.

Pigs at Christmas ill. by author. Bradbury, 1986. ISBN 0-02-733160-1 Subj: Animals – pigs. Character traits – being different. Holidays – Christmas.

Pigs in hiding ill. by author. Four Winds, 1983. ISBN 0-590-07872-0 Subj: Animals – pigs. Behavior – hiding. Games.

Tom's tail ill. by author. Viking, 1990. ISBN 0-670-83021-6 Subj: Animals – cats. Animals – mice. Poetry. Rhyming text.

Dubar, Joyce. *The very small* ill. by Debi Gliori. Harcourt, 2000. ISBN 0-15-202346-1 Subj: Animals – bears. Behavior – lost. Behavior – sharing. Concepts – size.

Duble, Kathleen Benner. *Pilot mom* ill. by Alan Marks. Charlesbridge, 2003. ISBN 1-57091-555-5 Subj: Careers – airplane pilots. Careers – military. Family life – daughters. Family life – mothers.

Dubois, Claude K. *He's my jumbo!* ill. by author. Viking, 1990. ISBN 0-670-83029-1 Subj: Animals – bears. Behavior – sharing. Sibling rivalry. Wordless.

Looking for Ginny ill. by author. Viking, 1990. ISBN 0-670-83030-5 Subj: Animals – bears. Family life – brothers & sisters. Pets. Wordless.

DuBois, Ivy. *Baby Jumbo* ill. by Elsie Wrigley. Grosset, 1977. ISBN 0-448-14289-9 Subj: Animals – elephants.

Mother fox ill. by Elsie Wrigley. Grosset, 1977. ISBN 0-448-14278-3 Subj: Animals – foxes.

Dubois, Muriel L. *I like animals: what can I be?* ill. with photos. Bridgestone, 2001. ISBN 0-7368-0630-X Subj: Animals. Careers. Careers – veterinarians.

I like computers: what can I be? ill. with photos. Bridgestone, 2001. ISBN 0-7368-0631-8 Subj: Careers. Computers.

I like music: what can I be? ill. with photos. Bridgestone, 2001. ISBN 0-7368-0632-6 Subj: Careers – musicians. Music.

I like sports: what can I be? ill. with photos. Bridgestone, 2001. ISBN 0-7368-0633-4 Subj: Careers. Sports.

Out and about at the fire station ill. by Anne McMullen. Picture Window, 2003. ISBN 1-4048-0039-5 Subj: Careers – firefighters. Fire. School – field trips.

Du Bois, William Pène. *Bear circus* ill. by author. Viking, 1971. ISBN 0-670-15073-8 Subj: Animals. Animals – koalas. Character traits – helpfulness. Circus. Insects – grasshoppers.

Bear party ill. by author. Viking, 1951. ISBN 0-14-050793-0 Subj: Animals. Animals – koalas. Caldecott award honor books. Emotions – anger. Parties.

Elisabeth, the cow ghost ill. by author. Viking, 1964. Subj: Animals – bulls, cows. Ghosts.

Giant Otto ill. by author. Viking, n.d. Subj: Animals – dogs. Giants.

Lazy Tommy pumpkinhead ill. by author. HarperCollins, 1966. Subj: Character traits – laziness. Machines.

Lion ill. by author. Viking, 1957. ISBN 0-670-42950-3 Subj: Animals – lions. Caldecott award honor books.

Otto and the magic potatoes ill. by author. Viking, 1970. ISBN 0-670-52986-9 Subj: Activities – vacationing. Animals – dogs. Fire. Giants.

Otto at sea ill. by author. Viking, 1936. Subj: Animals – dogs. Boats, ships. Giants.

Otto in Africa ill. by author. Viking, 1961. Subj: Animals – dogs. Foreign lands – Africa. Giants.

Otto in Texas ill. by author. Viking, 1959. Subj: Animals – dogs. Giants. Texas.

The hare and the tortoise and the tortoise and the hare = La liebre y la tortuga and La tortuga y la liebre by William Pène Du Bois & Lee Po; ill. by William Pène Du Bois. Doubleday, 1972. Subj: Animals – rabbits. Folk & fairy tales. Foreign languages. Reptiles – turtles, tortoises.

Dubov, Christine Salac. *Aleksandra, where are your toes?* photos by Josef Schneider. St. Martin's, 1986. ISBN 0-312-01717-0 Subj: Anatomy – toes. Format, unusual – board books.

Aleksandra, where is your nose? photos by Josef Schneider. St. Martin's, 1986. ISBN 0-312-01719-7 Subj: Anatomy – noses. Format, unusual – board books.

Ding dong! and other sounds ill. by Elizabeth Hathon. Morrow, 1991. ISBN 0-688-10162-3 Subj: Format, unusual – board books. Noise, sounds.

Knock! and other sounds ill. by Elizabeth Hathon. Morrow, 1991. ISBN 0-688-10161-5 Subj: Format, unusual – board books. Noise, sounds.

Oink! and other sounds ill. by Elizabeth Hathon. Morrow, 1991. ISBN 0-688-10102-X Subj: Animals. Format, unusual – board books. Noise, sounds.

Dubowski, Cathy East. *A cake for Jake* ill. by Mark Dubowski. Checkerboard, 1989. ISBN 0-02-898251-7 Subj: Animals – dogs. Birthdays. Parties. Pets.

Cave boy by Cathy East Dubowski & Mark Dubowski; ill. by Mark Dubowski. Random House, 1988. ISBN 0-394-99571-6 Subj: Birthdays. Gifts. Inventions. Wheels.

The Christmas Santa almost missed ill. by Nan Pollard. McClanahan, 1990. ISBN 1-878624-48-2 Subj: Holidays – Christmas. Mythical creatures – elves. Santa Claus.

Dumpy the dump truck ill. by Mark Samuels. McClanahan, 1990. ISBN 1-878624-32-6 Subj: Trucks.

Fire engine to the rescue ill. by Shirley Beckes. McClanahan, 1990. ISBN 1-878624-37-7 Subj: Careers – firefighters. Fire. Trucks.

Megan's messy room ill. by Mark Dubowski. Star Bright, 1997. ISBN 1-887734-20-1 Subj: Character traits – orderliness. Family life – daughters. Family life – mothers.

Picky Nicky by Cathy East Dubowski & Mark Dubowski; ill. by Mark Dubowski. Grosset, 1996. ISBN 0-448-41295-0 Subj: Food. Rebuses.

Snug Bug by Cathy East Dubowski & Mark Dubowski; ill. by Mark Dubowski. Grosset, 1995. ISBN 0-448-40850-3 Subj: Bedtime. Insects. Rhyming text.

Snug Bug's play day by Cathy East Dubowski & Mark Dubowski; ill. by Mark Dubowski. Grosset, 1997. ISBN 0-448-41642-5 Subj: Activities – playing. Behavior – sharing. Insects. Rhyming text.

Dubowski, Mark. *Cave boy* (Dubowski, Cathy East)

Picky Nicky (Dubowski, Cathy East)

Snug Bug (Dubowski, Cathy East)

Snug Bug's play day (Dubowski, Cathy East)

DuBurke, Randy. *The moon ring* ill. by author. Chronicle, 2002. ISBN 0-8118-3487-5 Subj: Ethnic groups in the U.S. – African Americans. Family life – grandmothers. Magic. Moon.

Duchess of York. *Budgie at Bendick's Point* ill. by John Richardson. S&S, 1989. ISBN 0-671-67684-9 Subj: Airplanes, airports. Helicopters.

Budgie the little helicopter ill. by John Richardson. S&S, 1989. ISBN 0-671-67683-0 Subj: Airplanes, airports. Helicopters.

Duckling ed. by Nicola Deschamps; photos by Jane Burton. DK, 2002. ISBN 0-7894-7856-0 Subj: Birds – ducks. Counting, numbers. Format, unusual – board books.

Dudley, Dick. *Pop up baby brontosaurus* (Cremins, Robert)

Pop up baby coelophysis (Cremins, Robert)

Pop up baby pteranodon (Cremins, Robert)

Pop up baby stegosaurus (Cremins, Robert)

Pop up baby triceratops (Cremins, Robert)

Pop up baby tyrannosaurus rex (Cremins, Robert)

Duerrstein, Richard. *In out, a Disney book of opposites = Dentro fuera, un libro Disney de opuestos* trans. by Daniel Santacruz; ill. by author. Walt Disney, 1993. Text in English and Spanish. ISBN 1-56282-266-7 Subj: Concepts – in & out. Concepts – opposites. Foreign languages.

Mickey is happy: a Disney book of feelings ill. by author. Walt Disney, 1992. ISBN 1-56282-267-5 Subj: Emotions. Format, unusual – board books.

One Mickey Mouse, a Disney book of numbers = Un Ratón Mickey, un libro Disney de números: a Disney book of numbers = Un Ratón Mickey: un libro Disney de números trans. by Daniel Santacruz; ill. by author. Walt Disney, 1993. Text in English and Spanish. ISBN 1-56282-460-0 Subj: Counting, numbers. Foreign languages.

Duff, Maggie (Margaret K.). *Dancing turtle* ill. by Maria Horvath. Macmillan, 1981. ISBN 0-02-733010-9 Subj: Animals. Behavior – trickery. Folk & fairy tales.

The princess and the pumpkin: from a Majorcan tale ill. by Catherine Stock. Macmillan, 1980. ISBN 0-02-783000-1 Subj: Folk & fairy tales. Foreign lands – Spain. Illness.

Rum pum pum ill. by José Aruego & Ariane Dewey. Macmillan, 1978. ISBN 0-02-732950-X Subj: Birds – blackbirds. Folk & fairy tales. Foreign lands – India.

Duffield, Katy. *Farmer McPeepers and his missing milk cows* ill. by Steve Gray. Rising Moon, 2003. ISBN 0-87358-825-8 Subj: Animals – bulls, cows. Careers – farmers. Farms. Glasses. Humorous stories.

Duffy, Dee Dee (Deborah). *Barnyard tracks* ill. by Janet Perry Marshall. Boyds Mills, 1992. ISBN 1-878093-66-5 Subj: Animals. Games.

Dugan, Barbara. *Leaving home with a pickle jar* ill. by Karen Lee Baker. Greenwillow, 1993. ISBN 0-688-10837-7 Subj: Activities – traveling. Friendship. Insects – grasshoppers. Moving.

Loop the loop ill. by James Stevenson. Greenwillow, 1992. ISBN 0-688-09648-4 Subj: Friendship. Illness. Old age. Toys.

Dugin, Andrej. *The brave little tailor* (Grimm, Jacob)

Dukas, P. (Paul Abraham). *The sorcerer's apprentice* adapt. by Makoto Oishi; trans. by Ann Brannen; ill. by Ryohei Yanagihara. Gakken, 1971. Subj: Folk & fairy tales. Magic.

Duke, Kate. *Archaeologists dig for clues* ill. by author. HarperCollins, 1997. ISBN 0-06-027056-X Subj: Activities – digging. Careers – archaeologists.

Aunt Isabel makes trouble ill. by author. Dutton, 1996. ISBN 0-525-45496-9 Subj: Animals – mice. Family life – aunts, uncles.

Aunt Isabel tells a good one ill. by author. Dutton, 1992. ISBN 0-525-44835-7 Subj: Animals. Animals – mice. Bedtime. Family life – aunts, uncles. Royalty.

Bedtime ill. by author. Dutton, 1986. ISBN 0-525-44207-3 Subj: Animals – guinea pigs. Bedtime. Family life. Format, unusual – board books.

Clean-up day ill. by author. Dutton, 1986. ISBN 0-525-44208-1 Subj: Activities – working. Animals – guinea pigs. Family life. Format, unusual – board books.

The guinea pig ABC ill. by author. Dutton, 1983. ISBN 0-525-44058-5 Subj: ABC books. Animals – guinea pigs.

Guinea pigs far and near ill. by author. Dutton, 1984. ISBN 0-525-44112-3 Subj: Animals – guinea pigs. Concepts.

If you walk down this road ill. by author. Dutton, 1993. ISBN 0-525-45072-6 Subj: Animals. Communities, neighborhoods. Family life.

One guinea pig is not enough ill. by author. Dutton, 1998. ISBN 0-525-45918-9 Subj: Activities – playing. Animals – guinea pigs. Counting, numbers.

The playground ill. by author. Dutton, 1986. ISBN 0-525-44206-5 Subj: Activities – playing. Animals – guinea pigs. Family life. Format, unusual – board books.

Seven froggies went to school ill. by author. Dutton, 1985. ISBN 0-525-44160-3 Subj: Frogs & toads. Rhyming text. School.

Twenty is too many ill. by author. Dutton, 2000. ISBN 0-525-42026-6 Subj: Animals – guinea pigs. Boats, ships. Counting, numbers.

What bounces? ill. by author. Dutton, 1986. ISBN 0-525-44209-X Subj: Animals – guinea pigs. Concepts. Family life. Format, unusual – board books.

Dulcken, H. W. *The fir tree* (Andersen, H. C. [Hans Christian])

Dumas, Bianca. *Tia Luisa, the magical cook* ill. by author. Alter-Lingo, 1999. ISBN 0-9669645-4-3 Subj: Activities – baking, cooking. Careers – chefs, cooks. Food. Foreign lands – Mexico. Foreign languages. Magic. Rhyming text.

Dumas, Philippe. *Caesar, cock of the village* ill. by author. Prentice-Hall, 1979. ISBN 0-13-110189-7 Subj: Birds – chickens. Foreign lands – France.

Laura, Alice's new puppy ill. by author. David & Charles, 1979. ISBN 0-575-02568-9 Subj: Animals – dogs.

Laura and the bandits ill. by author. David & Charles, 1980. ISBN 96-86-79851-1 Subj: Animals – dogs. Crime.

Laura loses her head ill. by author. David & Charles, 1982. ISBN 0-575-03016-X Subj: Animals – dogs. Family life – grandfathers. Foreign lands – France.

Laura on the road ill. by author. David & Charles, 1979. ISBN 0-575-02712-6 Subj: Animals – dogs.

Lucy, a tale of a donkey ill. by author. Prentice-Hall, 1977. ISBN 0-13-541169-6 Subj: Animals – donkeys. Behavior – running away.

The story of Edward ill. by author. Parents' Magazine Pr., 1977. ISBN 0-8193-0869-2 Subj: Animals – donkeys. Foreign lands – France.

Dumbleton, Mike. *Dial-a-croc* ill. by Ann James. Watts, 1991. ISBN 0-531-08545-7 Subj: Activities – working. Foreign lands – Australia. Reptiles – alligators, crocodiles.

Dunbar, Fiona. *You'll never guess!* ill. by author. Dial, 1991. ISBN 0-8037-0871-8 Subj: Concepts – shape. Games.

Dunbar, James. *Tick-tock* ill. by author. Carolrhoda, 1998. ISBN 1-57505-251-2 Subj: Clocks, watches. Concepts – measurement. Time.

Dunbar, Joyce. *Baby bird* ill. by Russell Ayto. Candlewick, 1998. ISBN 0-7636-0322-8 Subj: Activities – flying. Animals. Birds. Rhyming text.

A cake for Barney ill. by Emilie Boon. Watts, 1988. ISBN 0-531-08335-7 Subj: Animals – bears. Character traits – assertiveness.

Eggday ill. by Jane Cabrera. Holiday, 1999. ISBN 0-8234-1510-4 Subj: Animals. Birds. Contests. Eggs.

Gander's pond ill. by Helen Craig. Candlewick, 1999. ISBN 0-76360-722-3 Subj: Animals – pandas. Behavior – sharing. Birds – geese.

Indigo and the whale ill. by Geoffrey Patterson. BridgeWater, 1996. ISBN 0-816-73802-5 Subj: Animals – whales. Careers – fishermen. Concepts – color. Family life – fathers. Music.

Lollopy ill. by Susan Varley. Macmillan, 1992. ISBN 0-02-733195-4 Subj: Animals – rabbits. Toys.

The pig who wished ill. by Selina Young. DK, 1999. ISBN 0-7894-3487-3 Subj: Animals – pigs. Behavior – wishing.

The sand children ill. by Mark Edwards. Crocodile, 1999. ISBN 1-56656-309-7 Subj: Dreams. Giants. Sea & seashore.

The secret friend ill. by Helen Craig. Candlewick, 1999. ISBN 0-7636-0720-7 Subj: Animals – pandas. Birds – geese. Friendship. Letters, cards.

Tell me something happy before I go to sleep ill. by Debi Gliori. Harcourt, 1998. ISBN 0-15-201795-X Subj: Animals – rabbits. Bedtime. Dreams. Family life – brothers & sisters.

When I was young ill. by author. Carolrhoda, 1999. ISBN 1-57505-359-4 Subj: Family life. Family life – grandparents. Genealogy.

Why is the sky up? ill. by James Dunbar. Houghton Mifflin, 1991. ISBN 0-395-57580-X Subj: Character traits – questioning. Family life. Nature.

Dunbar, Polly. *Dog Blue* ill. by author. Candlewick, 2004. ISBN 0-7636-2476-4 Subj: Animals – dogs. Concepts – color. Imagination.

Flyaway Katie ill. by author. Candlewick, 2004. ISBN 0-7636-2366-0 Subj: Concepts – color. Emotions. Imagination.

Duncan, Alice Faye. *Miss Viola and Uncle Ed Lee* ill. by Catherine Stock. Atheneum, 1999. ISBN 0-689-80476-8 Subj: Character traits – orderliness. Ethnic groups in the U.S. – African Americans. Friendship. Old age.

Duncan, Beverly K. *Christmas in the stable* (Christmas in the stable)

Duncan, Gregory. *see* McClintock, Marshall

Duncan, Jane. *Brave Janet Reachfar* ill. by Mairi Hedderwick. Seabury Pr., 1975. ISBN 0-8164-3130-2 Subj: Animals – sheep. Character traits – bravery. Weather – snow. Weather – storms.

Janet Reachfar and Chickabird ill. by Mairi Hedderwick. Seabury Pr., 1978. ISBN 0-8164-3203-1 Subj: Behavior – bad day. Farms. Foreign lands – Scotland.

Janet Reachfar and the kelpie ill. by Mairi Hedderwick. Seabury Pr., 1976. ISBN 0-8164-3169-8 Subj: Monsters. Mythical creatures – kelpies.

Duncan, Lois. *Birthday moon* ill. by Susan Davis. Viking, 1989. ISBN 0-670-82238-8 Subj: Birthdays. Moon. Rhyming text.

Giving away Suzanne ill. by Leonard Weisgard. Dodd, 1964. Subj: Sibling rivalry.

Horses of dreamland ill. by Donna Diamond. Little, 1985. ISBN 0-316-19554-5 Subj: Animals – horses, ponies. Dreams. Night.

I walk at night ill. by Steve Johnson & Lou Fancher. Viking, 2000. ISBN 0-670-87513-9 Subj: Activities – walking. Animals – cats. Night. Rhyming text.

The longest hair in the world ill. by Jon McIntosh. Doubleday, 1998. ISBN 0-385-32113-9 Subj: Behavior – wishing. Birthdays. Hair.

The magic of Spider Woman ill. by Shonto Begay. Scholastic, 1996. ISBN 0-590-46155-9 Subj: Activities – weaving. Folk & fairy tales. Indians of North America – Navajo.

Song of the circus ill. by Meg Cundiff. Philomel, 2002. ISBN 0-399-23397-0 Subj: Animals – tigers. Character traits – bravery. Circus. Rhyming text.

Songs from dreamland ill. by Kay Chorao. Knopf, 1989. ISBN 0-394-99904-5 Subj: Lullabies. Music. Poetry. Songs.

Duncan, Riana. *A nutcracker in a tree: a book of riddles* ill. by author. Delacorte, 1981. ISBN 0-385-28733-X Subj: Animals. Riddles & jokes.

When Emily woke up angry ill. by author. Barron's, 1989. ISBN 0-8120-5985-9 Subj: Animals. Emotions – anger.

Dunham, Meredith. *Colors: how do you say it?* ill. by author. Lothrop, 1987. ISBN 0-688-06949-5 Subj: Concepts – color. Foreign languages. Language.

Numbers: how do you say it? ill. by author. Lothrop, 1987. ISBN 0-688-06951-7 Subj: Counting, numbers. Foreign languages. Language.

Picnic: how do you say it? ill. by author. Lothrop, 1987. ISBN 0-688-07097-3 Subj: Activities – picnicking. Foreign languages. Language.

Shapes: how do you say it? ill. by author. Lothrop, 1987. ISBN 0-688-06953-3 Subj: Concepts – shape. Foreign languages. Language.

Dunlap, Julie. *Louisa May and Mr. Thoreau's flute* by Julie Dunlap & Marybeth Lorbiecki; ill. by Mary Azarian. Dial, 2002. ISBN 0-8037-2470-5 Subj: Careers – authors. U.S. history.

Dunn, Judy. *The animals of Buttercup Farm* photos by Phoebe Dunn. Random House, 1981. ISBN 0-394-94798-3 Subj: Animals. Farms.

The little duck ill. by Phoebe Dunn. Random House, 1978. ISBN 0-394-83247-7 Subj: Birds – ducks.

The little goat ill. by Phoebe Dunn. Random House, 1978. ISBN 0-394-93872-0 Subj: Animals – goats. Pets.

The little lamb ill. by Phoebe Dunn. Random House, 1977. ISBN 0-394-83455-0 Subj: Animals – sheep. Character traits – kindness to animals. Farms.

The little puppy photos by Phoebe Dunn. Random House, 1984. ISBN 0-394-96595-7 Subj: Animals – dogs. Pets.

The little rabbit photos by Phoebe Dunn. Random House, 1980. ISBN 0-394-94377-5 Subj: Animals – rabbits. Holidays – Easter. Pets.

Dunn, Phoebe. *Baby's animal friends* photos by author. Random House, 1988. ISBN 0-394-89583-5 Subj: Animals. Babies. Format, unusual – board books.

Busy, busy toddlers photos by author. Random House, 1987. ISBN 0-394-88604-6 Subj: Activities. Babies. Format, unusual – board books.

I'm a baby! photos by author. Random House, 1987. ISBN 0-394-88605-4 Subj: Babies. Format, unusual – board books.

Dunnick, Regan. *Sweet dreams, Douglas* ill. by author. Junior League of Houston, 2002. ISBN 0-9632421-3-X Subj: Animals. Animals – dogs. Bedtime. Dreams. Imagination.

Dunphy, Madeleine. *Here is the Arctic winter* ill. by Alan James Robinson. Hyperion, 1993. ISBN 1-56282-337-X Subj: Animals. Cumulative tales. Foreign lands – Arctic. Rhyming text. Seasons – winter.

Here is the coral reef ill. by Tom Leonard. Hyperion, 1998. ISBN 0-7868-2135-3 Subj: Cumulative tales. Ecology. Sea & seashore.

Here is the southwestern desert ill. by Anne Coe. Hyperion, 1995. ISBN 0-7868-2038-1 Subj: Cumulative tales. Desert. Ecology. Poetry.

Here is the tropical rain forest ill. by Michael Rothman. Hyperion, 1994. ISBN 1-56282-637-9 Subj: Animals. Forest, woods. Plants. Weather.

Dunrea, Olivier. *Appearing tonight! Mary Heather Elizabeth Livingstone* ill. by author. Farrar, 2000. ISBN 0-374-30455-6 Subj: Careers – actors. Theater.

Bear Noel ill. by author. Farrar, 2000. Subj: Animals. Animals – bears. Cumulative tales. Holidays – Christmas.

Deep down underground ill. by author. Macmillan, 1989. ISBN 0-02-732861-9 Subj: Animals. Counting, numbers. Cumulative tales.

Eddy B, pigboy ill. by author. Atheneum, 1983. ISBN 0-689-50277-X Subj: Animals – pigs. Farms.

Fergus and Bridey ill. by author. Holiday, 1985. ISBN 0-8234-0554-0 Subj: Animals – dogs. Boats, ships. Friendship.

It's snowing ill. by author. Farrar, 2002. ISBN 0-374-39992-1 Subj: Babies. Family life – mothers. Weather – snow.

Ollie ill. by author. Houghton, 2003. ISBN 0-618-33928-0 Subj: Birds – geese. Character traits – patience. Eggs. Family life – new sibling.

Ollie the stomper ill. by author. Houghton, 2003. ISBN 0-618-33930-2 Subj: Birds – geese. Clothing – boots.

The painter who loved chickens ill. by Olivier Dunrea. Farrar, 1995. ISBN 0-374-35729-3 Subj: Careers – artists. Character traits – ambition. Cities, towns. Farms.

Peedie ill. by author. Houghton, 2004. ISBN 0-618-35652-5 Subj: Birds – geese. Clothing – hats. Memories, memory.

Ravena ill. by author. Dell, 1992. ISBN 0-8234-0487-0 Subj: Mythical creatures.

The trow-wife's treasure ill. by author. Farrar, 1998. ISBN 0-374-37792-8 Subj: Behavior – lost & found possessions. Careers – farmers. Eggs. Foreign lands – Europe. Mythical creatures – trolls.

Dupasquier, Philippe. *A busy day at the garage* ill. by author. Candlewick, 1996. ISBN 1-56402-590-X Subj: Activities – working. Automobiles. Careers – mechanics. Communities, neighborhoods.

Dear Daddy . . . ill. by author. Bradbury, 1985. ISBN 0-02-733170-9 Subj: Boats, ships. Careers. Family life – fathers. Sea & seashore.

The great escape ill. by author. Houghton Mifflin, 1988. ISBN 0-395-46806-X Subj: Behavior – running away. Prisons. Wordless.

I can't sleep ill. by author. Watts, 1989. ISBN 0-531-08474-4 Subj: Family life. Night. Sleep. Wordless.

Jack at sea ill. by author. Prentice-Hall, 1987. ISBN 0-13-509209-4 Subj: Boats, ships. Sea & seashore. War.

1 2 3, follow me! ill. by author. Candlewick, 2002. ISBN 0-7636-1797-0 Subj: Animals. Counting, numbers. Format, unusual – board books. Wordless.

Our house on the hill ill. by author. Viking, 1988. ISBN 0-670-81971-9 Subj: Seasons. Wordless.

A robot named chip ill. by author. Viking, 1991. ISBN 0-670-83574-9 Subj: Robots.

Duplaix, Georges. *Animal stories* ill. by Feodor Rojankovsky. Western, 1944. Subj: Animals.

The big brown bear ill. by Gustaf Tenggren. Golden Bks., 2001. ISBN 0-307-10209-2 Subj: Animals – bears. Insects – bees.

Dupré, Judith. *The mouse bride* ill. by Fabricio Vandenbroeck. Knopf, 1993. ISBN 0-679-93273-9 Subj: Animals – mice. Folk & fairy tales. Foreign lands – Mexico. Indians of Central America – Maya. Indians of North America – Chol.

Dupre, Kelly. *The raven's gift* ill. by author. Houghton, 2001. ISBN 0-618-01171-4 Subj: Activities – traveling. Birds – ravens. Foreign lands – Greenland.

Dupré, Ramona Dorrel. *Too many dogs* ill. by Howard Baer. Follett, 1960. Subj: Animals – dogs.

Dupré, Rick. *Agassu: legend of the leopard king* ill. by author. Carolrhoda, 1993. ISBN 0-87614-764-3 Subj: Ethnic groups in the U.S. – African Americans. Folk & fairy tales. Foreign lands – Africa. Slavery.

The wishing chair ill. by author. Carolrhoda, 1993. ISBN 0-87614-774-0 Subj: Behavior – wishing. Ethnic groups in the U.S. – African Americans. Family life – grandmothers. U.S. history.

Duquennoy, Jacques. *The ghosts in the cellar* ill. by author. Harcourt, 1998. ISBN 0-15-201775-5 Subj: Castles. Ghosts.

The ghosts' trip to Loch Ness ill. by author; tr. by Kathryn Nanovic. Harcourt, 1996. ISBN 0-15-201440-3 Subj: Foreign lands – Scotland. Ghosts. Monsters.

North Pole, South Pole ill. by author; tr. by Ghislaine R. de Cotret. Raincoast, 2000. ISBN 1-55192-411-0 Subj: Birds – penguins. Foreign lands – Antarctic. Foreign lands – Arctic. Holidays – Christmas. Santa Claus.

Operation ghost ill. by author. Harcourt, 1999. ISBN 0-15-202182-5 Subj: Clocks, watches. Ghosts. Illness. Illness – measles.

Du Quette, Keith. *Hotel Animal* ill. by author. Viking, 1994. ISBN 0-670-85056-X Subj: Animals. Concepts – size. Hotels. Reptiles – lizards.

The house book ill. by author. Putnam, 1999. ISBN 0-399-231838 Subj: Homes, houses. Rhyming text.

Ripping day for a picnic ill. by author. Viking, 1990. ISBN 0-670-08331-8 Subj: Activities – picnicking. Animals. Food.

They call me Woolly: what animal names can tell us ill. by author. Putnam, 2002. ISBN 0-399-23445-4 Subj: Animals. Language. Names.

Duran, Bonté. *The adventures of Arthur and Edmund: a tale of two seals* ill. by Quentin Blake. Atheneum, 1984. ISBN 0-689-50295-8 Subj: Animals – seals.

Durant, Alan. *Big Bad Bunny* ill. by Guy Parker-Rees. Dutton, 2001. ISBN 0-525-46667-3 Subj: Animals – rabbits. Behavior – misbehavior. Crime.

Brown Bear gets in shape ill. by Annabel Hudson. Kingfisher, 2004. ISBN 0-7534-5797-0 Subj: Animals – bears. Animals – chimpanzees. Animals – rabbits.

Dear tooth fairy ill. by Vanessa Cabban. Candlewick, 2003. ISBN 0-7636-2175-7 Subj: Fairies. Format, unusual – toy & movable books. Letters, cards. Teeth.

Mouse party ill. by Sue Heap. Candlewick, 1995. ISBN 1-56402-584-5 Subj: Animals. Animals – elephants. Animals – mice. Homes, houses. Parties.

Snake supper ill. by Ant Parker. Western, 1994. ISBN 0-307-17519-7 Subj: Animals. Food. Format, unusual. Noise, sounds. Reptiles – snakes.

Durell, Ann. *The Diane Goode book of American folk tales and songs* coll. by Ann Durell; ill. by Diane Goode. Dutton, 1989. ISBN 0-525-44458-0 Subj: Folk & fairy tales. Music. Songs.

Dürr, Gisela. *The secret of Trembleton Hall* (Dürr, Ursula)

Dürr, Ursula. *The secret of Trembleton Hall* by Ursula Dürr & Gisela Dürr; ill. by Gisela Dürr. North-South, 1995. ISBN 1-55858-433-1 Subj: Castles. Dreams. Format, unusual. Ghosts. Mythical creatures – elves. School.

Durrell, Julie. *Mouse tails* ill. by author. Crown, 1985. ISBN 0-517-55592-1 Subj: Animals. Animals – mice.

Dussling, Jennifer. *Bugs! bugs! bugs!* ill. with photos. DK, 1998. ISBN 0-7894-3762-7 Subj: Insects.

Stars ill. by Mavis Smith. Grosset, 1996. ISBN 0-448-41149-0 Subj: Astronomy. Stars.

Dutton, Sandra. *The cinnamon hen's autumn day* ill. by author. Atheneum, 1988. ISBN 0-689-31414-0 Subj: Animals – rabbits. Birds – chickens. Seasons – fall.

Duvall, Jill. *Who keeps the water clean? Ms. Schindler!* photos by Lili Duvall. Childrens Pr., 1997. ISBN 0-516-20315-0 Subj: Careers – plumbers. Water.

Duvoisin, Roger Antoine. *A for the ark* ill. by author. Lothrop, 1952. Subj: ABC books. Animals. Boats, ships. Religion – Noah. Weather – floods. Weather – rain.

The Christmas whale ill. by author. Knopf, 1945. Subj: Animals – whales. Holidays – Christmas. Illness. Santa Claus.

The crocodile in the tree ill. by author. Knopf, 1973. ISBN 0-394-92516-5 Subj: Animals. Farms. Friendship. Reptiles – alligators, crocodiles.

Crocus ill. by author. Knopf, 1977. ISBN 0-394-93583-7 Subj: Careers – dentists. Character traits – pride. Farms. Reptiles – alligators, crocodiles. Teeth.

Day and night ill. by author. Knopf, 1960. Subj: Animals – dogs. Birds – owls.

Donkey-donkey ill. by author. Parents' Magazine Pr., 1968. Subj: Animals – donkeys.

Easter treat ill. by author. Knopf, 1954. Subj: Holidays – Easter.

The happy hunter ill. by author. Lothrop, 1961. Subj: Character traits – kindness to animals. Ecology. Sports – hunting. Violence, nonviolence. Weapons.

The house of four seasons ill. by author. Lothrop, 1956. Subj: Activities – painting. Concepts – color. Seasons.

Jasmine ill. by author. Knopf, 1973. ISBN 0-394-92444-4 Subj: Animals. Character traits – individuality. Clothing. Farms.

Lonely Veronica ill. by author. Knopf, 1963. Subj: Animals – hippopotamuses. Cities, towns. Progress.

The missing milkman ill. by author. Knopf, 1967. Subj: Behavior – running away. Dreams. Night.

One thousand Christmas beards ill. by author. Knopf, 1955. Subj: Holidays – Christmas. Santa Claus.

Our Veronica goes to Petunia's farm ill. by author. Knopf, 1962. ISBN 0-394-91469-4 Subj: Animals. Animals – hippopotamuses. Character traits – being different. Farms. Humorous stories.

Periwinkle ill. by author. Knopf, 1976. ISBN 0-394-93298-6 Subj: Animals – giraffes. Emotions – loneliness. Etiquette. Friendship. Frogs & toads.

Petunia ill. by author. 50th anniversary ed. Knopf, 2000, 1977. ISBN 0-394-90865-1 Subj: Animals. Birds – geese. Books, reading. Character traits – pride. Farms. Friendship. Humorous stories.

Petunia and the song ill. by author. Knopf, 1951. Subj: Animals. Birds – geese. Crime. Farms. Friendship. Humorous stories. Noise, sounds. Songs.

Petunia, beware! ill. by author. Knopf, 1958. ISBN 0-394-90867-8 Subj: Animals. Behavior – dissatisfaction. Birds – geese. Farms. Humorous stories.

Petunia, I love you ill. by author. Knopf, 1965. Subj: Animals – raccoons. Behavior – trickery. Birds – geese. Birds – vultures. Farms. Friendship. Humorous stories.

Petunia takes a trip ill. by author. Knopf, 1953. ISBN 0-394-90869-4 Subj: Activities – flying. Activities – vacationing. Animals. Birds – geese. Humorous stories.

Petunia, the silly goose: stories ill. by author. Knopf, 1987. ISBN 0-394-98292-4 Subj: Animals. Birds – geese. Farms. Humorous stories.

Petunia's Christmas ill. by author. Knopf, 1952. ISBN 0-394-90868-6 Subj: Birds – geese. Holidays – Christmas. Humorous stories.

Petunia's treasure ill. by author. Knopf, 1975. Subj: Animals. Birds – geese. Farms. Friendship. Humorous stories.

See what I am ill. by author. Lothrop, 1974. ISBN 0-688-50058-7 Subj: Behavior – boasting. Concepts – color.

Snowy and Woody ill. by author. Knopf, 1979. ISBN 0-394-94241-8 Subj: Animals – bears. Animals – polar bears. Birds – seagulls. Friendship.

Two lonely ducks ill. by author. Knopf, 1955. Subj: Birds – ducks. Counting, numbers. Farms.

Veronica ill. by author. Knopf, 1961. Subj: Animals – hippopotamuses. Character traits – being different. Cities, towns. Farms.

Veronica and the birthday present ill. by author. Knopf, 1971. ISBN 0-394-92282-4 Subj: Animals – cats. Animals – hippopotamuses. Birthdays. Farms.

Veronica's smile ill. by author. Knopf, 1964. Subj: Animals – hippopotamuses. Behavior – boredom.

Dwight, Laura. *We can do it!* ill. with photos. Checkerboard, 1992. ISBN 1-56288-301-1 Subj: Activities. Handicaps.

Dwyer, Mindy. *Aurora, a tale of the Northern Lights* ill. by author. Alaska Northwest Bks., 1997. ISBN 0-8824-0496-2 Subj: Alaska. Animals – reindeer. Behavior – lost. Concepts – color. Folk & fairy tales – pourquoi tales. Foreign lands – Arctic. Northern lights.

Coyote in love ill. by reteller. Alaska Northwest Bks., 1997. ISBN 0-88240-485-7 Subj: Activities – storytelling. Animals – coyotes. Creation. Folk & fairy tales. Indians of North America – Coquelle.

Quilt of dreams ill. by author. Alaska Northwest Bks., 2000. ISBN 0-88240-522-5 Subj: Family life – grandmothers. Family life – mothers. Quilts.

Dyer, Heather. *Tina and the penguin* ill. by Mireille Levert. Kids Can, 2002. ISBN 1-55074-947-1 Subj: Behavior – running away. Birds – penguins. Foreign lands – Antarctic. Zoos.

Dyer, Sarah. *Clementine and Mungo* ill. by author. Bloomsbury, 2004. ISBN 1-58234-883-9 Subj: Animals. Family life – brothers & sisters. Monsters.

Dyjak, Elisabeth. *Bertha's garden* ill. by Janet Wilkins. Houghton Mifflin, 1995. ISBN 0-395-68715-2 Subj: Animals – rabbits. Animals – wolves. Gardens, gardening.

Dyke, John. *Pigwig* ill. by author. Methuen, 1978. ISBN 0-416-87110-0 Subj: Animals – pigs. Behavior – stealing. Character traits – bravery. Emotions – love.

Pigwig and the pirates ill. by author. Methuen, 1979. ISBN 0-416-30121-5 Subj: Animals – pigs. Pirates. Sea & seashore.

Dynely, James. *see* Mayne, William

Dyssegaard, Elisabeth Kallick. *Andrei's search* (Lindgren, Barbro)

Benny's had enough (Lindgren, Barbro)

Do you know Pippi Longstocking? (Lindgren, Astrid)

Heart of mine (Höjer, Dan)

The little house from the sea (Gedin, Birgitta)

Most beloved sister (Lindgren, Astrid)

Will gets a haircut (Landström, Olof)

Will goes to the post office (Landström, Olof)

Eachus, Jennifer. *I'm sorry* (McBratney, Sam)

Eagle, Ellen. *Gypsy's cleaning day* ill. by author. Morrow, 1990. ISBN 0-688-07392-1 Subj: Animals – dogs. Behavior – lost & found possessions. Character traits – cleanliness.

Eagle, Kin. *Rub a dub dub* ill. by Rob Gilbert. Whispering Coyote, 1998. ISBN 1-58089-008-3 Subj: Nursery rhymes.

Earle, Olive L. *Squirrels in the garden* ill. by author. Morrow, 1963. Subj: Animals – squirrels.

Easter babies ill. by Roma Bishop; paper engineering by Ruth Mawdsley. S&S, 1996. ISBN 0-689-80611-6 Subj: Animals. Format, unusual – toy & movable books. Holidays – Easter.

Easterling, Bill. *Prize in the snow* ill. by Mary Beth Owens. Little, 1994. ISBN 0-316-22489-8 Subj: Animals – rabbits. Character traits – kindness to animals. Seasons – winter.

Eastman, David. *The story of dinosaurs* ill. by Joel Snyder. Troll, 1982. ISBN 0-89375-648-2 Subj: Dinosaurs. Prehistory.

The velveteen rabbit: or, How toys became real (Bianco, Margery Williams)

What is a fish? ill. by Lynn Sweat. Troll, 1982. ISBN 0-89375-660-1 Subj: Fish. Science.

Eastman, P. D. (Philip D.). *The alphabet book* ill. by author. Random House, 2000. ISBN 0-375-80603-2 Subj: ABC books.

Are you my mother? ill. by author. Random House, 1960. ISBN 0-394-90018-9 Subj: Behavior – misbehavior. Birds. Family life – mothers.

The cat in the hat dictionary (Seuss, Dr.)

Flap your wings ill. by author. Random House, 1969. ISBN 0-394-90839-2 Subj: Birds. Eggs. Reptiles – alligators, crocodiles.

Go, dog, go! ill. by author. Random House, 1961. ISBN 0-394-90020-0 Subj: Animals – dogs.

Sam and the firefly ill. by author. Random House, 1958. ISBN 0-394-90006-5 Subj: Birds – owls. Insects – fireflies.

Snow (McKie, Roy)

Eastman, Patricia. *Sometimes things change* ill. by Seymour Fleishman. Childrens Pr., 1983. ISBN 0-516-02044-7 Subj: Science.

Easton, Violet. *Elephants never jump* ill. by Carme Solé Vendrell. Little, 1986. ISBN 0-87113-049-1 Subj: Activities – jumping. Animals. Animals – elephants. Humorous stories.

Eastwick, Ivy O. *Cherry stones! Garden swings! poems* ill. by Robert Jones. Abingdon, 1962. Subj: Poetry.

Rainbow over all ill. by Anne Siberell. McKay, 1970. Subj: Poetry.

Some folks like cats, and other poems comp. by Walter B. Barbe; ill. by Mary Kurnick Maass. Boyds Mills, 2002. ISBN 1-56397-450-9 Subj: Poetry.

Easwaran, Eknath. *The monkey and the mango: stories of my granny* ill. by Ilka Jerabek. Nilgiri Press, 1996. ISBN 0-915132-82-6 Subj: Family life – grandmothers. Folk & fairy tales. Foreign lands – India. Religion.

Eaton, Deborah. *The rainy day grump* photos by Dorothy Handelman. Millbrook, 1998. ISBN 0-7613-2018-0 Subj: Activities – playing. Family life – brothers & sisters. Nature. Sports – baseball. Weather – rain.

Eaton, Jason. *The day my runny nose ran away* ill. by Ethan Long. Dutton, 2002. ISBN 0-525-47013-1 Subj: Anatomy – noses. Behavior – running away.

Eaton, Su. *Punch and Judy in the rain* by Su Eaton & Martin Bridle; ill. by authors. Hamish Hamilton, 1985. ISBN 0-241-11222-2 Subj: Puppets.

Eberle, Irmengarde. *Fawn in the woods* photos by Lilo Hess. Crowell, 1962. Subj: Animals – deer.

Eberstadt, Frederick. *What is for my birthday?* (Eberstadt, Isabel [Nash])

Eberstadt, Isabel (Nash). *What is for my birthday?* by Isabel & Frederick Eberstadt; ill. by Leonard Weisgard. Little, 1961. Subj: Birthdays. Illness. Rhyming text.

Eccles, Jane. *Maxwell's birthday* ill. by author. Tambourine, 1991. ISBN 0-688-11037-1 Subj: Birthdays. Family life – mothers. Imagination. Monsters.

Eckart, Edana. *I can bowl* ill. with photos. Childrens Pr., 2002. ISBN 0-516-23972-4 Subj: Family life – fathers. Sports – bowling.

I can play soccer ill. with photos. Childrens Pr., 2002. ISBN 0-516-23969-4 Subj: Sports – soccer.

I can ride a bike ill. with photos. Childrens Pr., 2002. ISBN 0-516-23967-8 Subj: Sports – bicycling.

I can swim ill. with photos. Childrens Pr., 2002. ISBN 0-516-23970-8 Subj: Family life – mothers. Sports – swimming.

Eckert, Horst. *see* Janosch

Eclare, Melanie. *A handful of sunshine* ill. with photos. Ragged Bears, 2000. ISBN 1-929927-14-2 Subj: Flowers. Gardens, gardening.

A harvest of color: growing a vegetable garden ill. with photos. Ragged Bears, 2002. ISBN 1-929927-31-2 Subj: Communities, neighborhoods. Food. Gardens, gardening.

Eco, Umberto. *The bomb and the general* ill. by Eugenio Carmi. Harcourt, 1989. ISBN 0-15-209700-7 Subj: War.

The three astronauts ill. by Eugenio Carmi. Harcourt, 1989. ISBN 0-15-286383-4 Subj: Careers – astronauts. Character traits – appearance. Space & space ships.

Economakis, Olga. *Oasis of the stars* ill. by Blair Lent. Coward, 1965. Subj: Foreign lands – Africa. Problem solving.

Edelman, Elaine. *Boom-de-boom* ill. by Karen Gundersheimer. Pantheon, 1980. ISBN 0-394-94341-4 Subj: Activities – dancing. Old age. Rhyming text.

I love my baby sister (most of the time) ill. by Wendy Watson. Lothrop, 1984. ISBN 0-688-02247-2 Subj: Babies. Family life – sisters. Sibling rivalry.

Edens, Cooper. *An ABC of fashionable animals* by Cooper Edens, Alexandra Day, Welleran Poltarnees. Green Tiger Pr., 1991. ISBN 0-671-75201-4 Subj: ABC books. Animals. Art.

The Animal Mall by Cooper Edens & Daniel Lane; ill. by Edward Miller. Dial, 2000. ISBN 0-8037-1984-1 Subj: Animals. Rhyming text. Shopping.

A child's garden of verses (Stevenson, Robert Louis)

The Christmas we moved to the barn (Day, Alexandra)

Darby, the special-order pup (Day, Alexandra)

The glorious Mother Goose (Mother Goose)

Helping the animals (Day, Alexandra)

Helping the flowers and trees (Day, Alexandra)

Helping the night (Day, Alexandra)

Helping the sun (Day, Alexandra)

Nicholi ill. by A. Scott Banfill. S&S, 1996. ISBN 0-671-50545-9 Subj: Holidays – Christmas. Magic. Santa Claus.

The night before Christmas (Moore, Clement Clark)

A present for Rose ill. by Molly Hashimoto. Sasquatch, 1993. ISBN 0-912365-89-7 Subj: Folk & fairy tales. Foreign lands – Japan. Seasons.

Special deliveries (Day, Alexandra)

Edgett, Ken. *Touchdown Mars! an ABC adventure* (Wethered, Peggy)

Edman, Polly. *Red thread riddles* (Jensen, Virginia Allen)

Edmund and the White Witch adapt. from The chronicles by C. S. Lewis; ill. by Deborah Maze. HarperCollins, 1997. ISBN 0-06-027517-0 Subj: Imagination. Magic. Witches.

Eduar, Gilles. *Dream journey* ill. by author. Orchard, 1999. ISBN 0-531-30202-4 Subj: Animals – camels. Dreams. Rhyming text.

Jooka saves the day ill. by author. Orchard, 1997. ISBN 0-531-30036-6 Subj: Character traits – individuality. Dragons. Reptiles – alligators, crocodiles.

Edvall, Lilian. *The rabbit who longed for home* ill. by Anna-Clara Tidholm; trans. by Elisabeth Kallick. R&S Books, 2001. ISBN 91-29-65391-6 Subj: Animals – rabbits. Emotions. School – nursery.

Edwards, Al. *see* Nourse, Alan Edward

Edwards, Becky. *My brother Sammy* by Becky Edwards & David Armitage; ill. by David Armitage. Millbrook, 1999. ISBN 0-7613-1417-2 Subj: Family life – brothers. Handicaps – autism.

My first day at nursery school ill. by Anthony Flintoft. Bloomsbury, 2002. ISBN 1-58234-761-1 Subj: Emotions. School – first day. School – nursery.

Edwards, Dorothy. *A wet Monday* by Dorothy Edwards & Jenny Williams; ill. by Jenny Williams. Morrow, 1976. ISBN 0-688-32081-3 Subj: Birds – chickens. Character traits – pride. Weather – rain.

Edwards, Frank B. *Is the spaghetti ready?* ill. by John Bianchi. Bungalo, 1998. ISBN 0-921285-67-1 Subj: Activities – baking, cooking. Food.

Melody Mooner stayed up all night ill. by John Bianchi. Firefly, 1991. ISBN 0-921285-03-5 Subj: Animals – pigs. Bedtime. Night.

Mortimer Mooner stopped taking a bath ill. by John Bianchi. Firefly, 1990. ISBN 0-921285-21-3 Subj: Activities – bathing. Animals – pigs. Character traits – cleanliness. Family life.

New at the zoo ill. by John Bianchi. Firefly, 1998. ISBN 0-921285-63-9 Subj: Animals. Zoos.

Troubles with bubbles ill. by John Bianchi. Bungalo, 1998. ISBN 0-921285-63-9 Subj: Activities – bathing. Bubbles.

Edwards, Julie Andrews. *Dumpy at school* by Julie Andrews Edwards & Emma Walton Hamilton; ill. by Tony Walton. Hyperion, 2000. ISBN 0-7868-0610-9 Subj: School – first day. Trucks.

Dumpy the dump truck by Julie Andrews Edwards & Emma Walton Hamilton; ill. by Tony Walton. Hyperion, 2000. ISBN 0-7868-2523-5 Subj: Family life – grandfathers. Farms. Trucks.

Dumpy to the rescue! by Julie Andrews Edwards & Emma Walton Hamilton; ill. by Tony Walton. HarperCollins, 2004. ISBN 0-06-052690-4 Subj: Animals – goats. Behavior – lost & found possessions. Family life. Trucks.

Dumpy's apple shop by Julie Andrews Edwards & Emma Walton Hamilton; ill. by Tony Walton. HarperCollins, 2004. ISBN 0-06-052693-9 Subj: Food. Trucks.

Simeon's gift by Julie Andrews Edwards & Emma Walton Hamilton; ill. by Gennady Spirin. HarperCollins, 2003. ISBN 0-06-008915-6 Subj: Careers – musicians. Self-concept.

Edwards, Linda Strauss. *The downtown day* ill. by author. Pantheon, 1983. ISBN 0-694-95407-6 Subj: Shopping.

Edwards, Lisa. *Disney's Beauty and the beast, a book of manners.* Walt Disney, 1993. ISBN 1-56282-130-X Subj: Character traits – appearance. Character traits – loyalty. Emotions – love. Etiquette. Folk & fairy tales. Magic.

Edwards, Michelle. *Alef-bet: a Hebrew alphabet book* ill. by author. Lothrop, 1992. ISBN 0-688-09725-1 Subj: ABC books. Family life. Foreign languages. Handicaps – physical handicaps. Jewish culture.

A baker's portrait ill. by author. Lothrop, 1991. ISBN 0-688-09713-8 Subj: Careers – artists. Careers – bakers. Family life – aunts, uncles. Jewish culture.

Chicken Man ill. by author. Lothrop, 1991. ISBN 0-688-09709-X Subj: Birds – chickens. Communities, neighborhoods. Foreign lands – Israel.

Dora's book ill. by author. Carolrhoda, 1990. ISBN 0-87614-411-3 Subj: Careers – printers. Careers – writers.

Eve and Smithy: an Iowa tale ill. by author. Lothrop, 1994. ISBN 0-688-11826-7 Subj: Careers – artists. Character traits – helpfulness. Friendship. Gardens, gardening.

Papa's latkes ill. by Stacey Schuett. Candlewick, 2004. ISBN 0-7636-0779-7 Subj: Emotions – grief. Family life – fathers. Family life – single-parent families. Holidays – Hanukkah. Jewish culture.

What's that noise? by Michelle Edwards & Phyllis Root; ill. by Paul Meisel. Candlewick, 2002. ISBN 0-7636-1350-9 Subj: Emotions – fear. Family life – brothers. Night. Noise, sounds.

Edwards, Nancy. *Glenna's seeds* ill. by Sarah K. Hoctor. Child & Family Pr., 2001. ISBN 0-8786-8788-2 Subj: Character traits – kindness. Communities, neighborhoods. Ethnic groups in the U.S. Seeds.

Edwards, Nicola. *Goodnight Baxter* ill. by author. Running Pr., 2004. ISBN 0-7624-1725-0 Subj: Animals – babies. Animals – dogs. Bedtime. Emotions – love. Friendship.

Edwards, Pamela Duncan. *Barefoot: escape on the underground railroad* ill. by Henry Cole. HarperCollins, 1997. ISBN 0-06-027137-X Subj: Behavior – running away. Ethnic groups in the U.S. – African Americans. Slavery. U.S. history.

Boston Tea Party ill. by Henry Cole. Putnam, 2001. ISBN 0-399-23357-1 Subj: U.S. history.

Bravo, Livingstone Mouse! ill. by Henry Cole. Hyperion, 2000. ISBN 0-7868-0307-X Subj: Activities – dancing. Animals. Animals – mice. Insects. Theater.

Clara Caterpillar ill. by Henry Cole. HarperCollins, 2001. ISBN 0-06-028996-1 Subj: Insects – butterflies, caterpillars. Metamorphosis.

Dear Tooth Fairy ill. by Marie-Louise Fitzpatrick. Tegen, 2003. ISBN 0-06-623973-7 Subj: Fairies. Letters, cards. Teeth.

Dinorella: a prehistoric fairy tale ill. by Henry Cole. Hyperion, 1997. ISBN 0-7868-2249-X Subj: Dinosaurs. Folk & fairy tales.

Ed and Fred Flea ill. by Henry Cole. Hyperion, 1999. ISBN 0-7868-2410-7 Subj: Animals – dogs. Behavior – greed. Insects – fleas. Rhyming text.

Four famished foxes and Fosdyke ill. by Henry Cole. HarperCollins, 1995. ISBN 0-06-024926-9 Subj: Activities – baking, cooking. Animals – foxes. Family life – brothers. Food.

Gigi and Lulu's gigantic fight ill. by Henry Cole. Tegen, 2004. ISBN 0-06-050753-5 Subj: Behavior – fighting, arguing. Friendship. School. Self-concept.

The grumpy morning ill. by Darcia Labrosse. Hyperion, 1998. ISBN 0-7868-2279-1 Subj: Animals. Behavior – promptness, tardiness. Farms. Rhyming text.

Honk! ill. by Henry Cole. Hyperion, 1998. ISBN 0-7868-2384-4 Subj: Activities – dancing. Ballet. Birds – swans.

The leprechaun's gold ill. by Henry Cole. Tegen, 2004. ISBN 0-06-623975-3 Subj: Behavior – greed. Careers – harpists. Foreign lands – Ireland. Musical instruments – harps. Mythical creatures – leprechauns.

Livingstone Mouse ill. by Henry Cole. HarperCollins, 1996. ISBN 0-06-025870-5 Subj: Activities – trading. Animals – mice. Careers – explorers.

McGillycuddy could ill. by Sue Porter. Tegen, 2005. ISBN 0-06-029001-3 Subj: Animals. Animals – kangaroos. Farms.

Muldoon ill. by Henry Cole. Hyperion, 2002. ISBN 0-7868-2305-4 Subj: Animals – dogs. Humorous stories.

Roar ill. by Henry Cole. HarperCollins, 2000. ISBN 0-06-028385-8 Subj: Animals. Animals – lions. Counting, numbers. Jungle. Rhyming text.

Rosie's roses ill. by Henry Cole. HarperCollins, 2003. ISBN 0-06-028998-8 Subj: Birthdays. Family life – aunts, uncles. Flowers – roses. Gifts.

Rude mule ill. by Barbara Nascimbeni. Holt, 2002. ISBN 0-8050-7007-9 Subj: Animals – mules. Behavior. Etiquette.

Slop goes the soup ill. by Henry Cole. Hyperion, 2001. ISBN 0-7868-2411-5 Subj: Animals – warthogs. Character traits – clumsiness. Noise, sounds.

Some smug slug ill. by Henry Cole. HarperCollins, 1996. ISBN 0-06-024792-4 Subj: Animals. Animals – slugs.

The wacky wedding: a book of alphabet antics ill. by Henry Cole. Hyperion, 1999. ISBN 0-7868-2248-1 Subj: ABC books. Insects. Insects – ants. Weddings.

Wake-up kisses ill. by Henry Cole. HarperCollins, 2002. ISBN 0-06-623977-X Subj: Animals – babies. Night. Rhyming text.

Warthogs in a box ill. by Henry Cole. Disney Pr., 2002. ISBN 0-7868-0894-2 Subj: Animals – warthogs. Format, unusual – board books. Friendship.

Warthogs in the kitchen: a sloppy counting book ill. by Henry Cole. Hyperion, 1998. ISBN 0-7868-2351-8 Subj: Activities – baking, cooking. Animals – warthogs. Counting, numbers. Rhyming text.

Warthogs paint ill. by Henry Cole. Hyperion, 2001. ISBN 0-7868-2412-3 Subj: Activities – painting. Animals – warthogs. Concepts – color. Rhyming text. Weather – rain.

The worrywarts ill. by Henry Cole. HarperCollins, 1999. ISBN 0-06-028150-2 Subj: Activities – walking. Animals. Behavior – worrying.

The Wright brothers ill. by Henry Cole. Hyperion, 2003. ISBN 0-7868-2682-7 Subj: Activities – flying. Airplanes, airports. Careers – airplane pilots. Cumulative tales.

Edwards, Patricia Kier. *Chester and Uncle Willoughby* ill. by Diane Worfolk Allison. Little, 1987. ISBN 0-316-21173-7 Subj: Family life – aunts, uncles. Imagination. Sleep.

Edwards, Richard. *Always copycub* ill. by Susan Winter. Harper-Collins, 2001. ISBN 0-06-029691-7 Subj: Animals – bears. Behavior – lost. Games.

Copy me, Copycub ill. by Susan Winter. HarperCollins, 1999. ISBN 0-06-028571-0 Subj: Animals – bears. Family life – mothers. Seasons.

Fly with the birds ill. by Satoshi Kitamura. Orchard, 1996. ISBN 0-531-09491-X Subj: Activities. Format, unusual – toy & movable books. Language. Rhyming text.

The forest child ill. by Peter Malone. Orchard, 1995. ISBN 0-531-09463-4 Subj: Animals. Character traits – meanness. Forest, woods.

Good night, Copycub ill. by Susan Winter. HarperCollins, 2004. ISBN 0-06-056671-X Subj: Animals. Animals – bears. Bedtime. Sleep.

Moon frog ill. by Sarah Fox-Davies. Candlewick, 1993. ISBN 1-56402-116-5 Subj: Animals. Poetry.

Ten tall oaktrees ill. by Caroline Crossland. Tambourine, 1993. ISBN 0-688-04621-5 Subj: Counting, numbers. Rhyming text. Trees.

Edwards, Roberta. *Anna Bear's first winter* ill. by Laura Lydecker. Random House, 1986. ISBN 0-394-88199-0 Subj: Animals – bears. Format, unusual – board books. Sleep.

Five silly fishermen ill. by Sylvie Wickstrom. Random House, 1989. ISBN 0-679-90092-6 Subj: Careers – fishermen. Counting, numbers. Folk & fairy tales.

Edwards, Roland. *Tigers* ill. by Judith Riches. Tambourine, 1992. ISBN 0-688-11686-8 Subj: Animals – tigers. Imagination. Night. Rhyming text.

Edwardson, Debby Dahl. *Whale snow* ill. by Annie Patterson. Talewinds, 2003. ISBN 1-57091-393-5 Subj: Animals – whales. Eskimos. Indians of North America – Inuit.

Efron, Marshall. *Gabby the shrew* (Olsen, Alfa-Betty)

Egan, Tim. *The blunder of the Rogues* ill. by author. Houghton Mifflin, 1999. ISBN 0-395-91007-2 Subj: Animals. Crime. Sports – bowling.

Burnt toast on Davenport Street ill. by author. Houghton, 1997. ISBN 0-395-79618-0 Subj: Animals – dogs. Behavior – wishing.

Chestnut Cove ill. by author. Houghton Mifflin, 1995. ISBN 0-395-69823-5 Subj: Character traits – selfishness. Food.

Distant Feathers ill. by author. Houghton Mifflin, 1998. ISBN 0-395-85808-9 Subj: Birds. Humorous stories. Weather – hurricanes.

The experiments of Doctor Vermin ill. by author. Houghton, 2002. ISBN 0-618-13224-4 Subj: Animals – pigs. Animals – wolves. Careers – chefs, cooks. Emotions – fear. Holidays – Halloween. Science.

Friday night at Hodges' café ill. by author. Houghton Mifflin, 1994. ISBN 0-395-68076-X Subj: Animals. Animals – tigers. Birds – ducks. Restaurants.

Metropolitan cow ill. by author. Houghton Mifflin, 1996. ISBN 0-395-73096-1 Subj: Animals. Behavior. Behavior – running away. Friendship. Prejudice.

A mile from Ellington station ill. by author. Houghton, 2001. ISBN 0-618-00393-2 Subj: Animals – bears. Animals – dogs. Emotions – envy, jealousy.

Serious farm ill. by author. Houghton, 2003. ISBN 0-618-22694-X Subj: Animals. Careers – farmers. Farms.

The trial of Cardigan Jones ill. by author. Houghton, 2004. ISBN 0-618-40237-3 Subj: Animals. Animals – moose. Crime. Food.

Egg-napped! ill. by Marsha Winborn. HarperCollins, 2002. ISBN 0-06-028951-1 Subj: Animals. Behavior – lost & found possessions. Birds – geese. Eggs. Rhyming text.

Eggs ill. by Esmé Eve. Grosset, 1971. Subj: Eggs.

Egielski, Richard. *Buz* ill. by author. Geringer, 1995. ISBN 0-06-023567-5 Subj: Health & fitness. Insects.

The gingerbread boy (The gingerbread boy)

Jazper ill. by author. Geringer, 1998. ISBN 0-06-027817-X Subj: Insects. Magic.

Slim and Jim ill. by author. HarperCollins, 2002. ISBN 0-06-028353-X Subj: Animals – cats. Animals – mice. Animals – rats. Toys.

Three magic balls ill. by author. HarperCollins, 2000. ISBN 0-06-026033-5 Subj: Activities – whistling. Magic. Toys – balls. Whistles.

Ehlert, Lois. *Circus* ill. by author. HarperCollins, 1992. ISBN 0-06-020253-X Subj: Circus.

Color farm ill. by author. HarperCollins, 1990. ISBN 0-397-32441-3 Subj: Concepts – color. Concepts – shape. Format, unusual.

Color zoo ill. by author. HarperCollins, 1990. ISBN 0-397-32260-7 Subj: Caldecott award honor books. Concepts – color. Concepts – shape. Format, unusual.

Cuckoo, a Mexican folktale = Cucú: un cuento folklórico mexicano trans. into Spanish by Gloria de Aragón Andujar; ill. by author. Harcourt, 1997. ISBN 0-15-200274-X Subj: Birds. Birds – cuckoos. Character traits – bravery. Fire. Folk & fairy tales. Foreign lands – Mexico. Foreign languages. Indians of Central America – Maya.

Eating the alphabet ill. by author. Harcourt, 1996. ISBN 0-15-201036-X Subj: ABC books. Food.

Feathers for lunch ill. by author. Harcourt, 1990. ISBN 0-15-230550-5 Subj: Animals – cats. Birds. Rhyming text.

Fish eyes: a book you can count on ill. by author. Harcourt, 1990. ISBN 0-15-201618-X Subj: Concepts – color. Counting, numbers. Fish. Rhyming text.

Growing vegetable soup ill. by author. Harcourt, 1987. ISBN 0-15-232575-1 Subj: Food. Gardens, gardening.

Hands ill. by author. Harcourt, 1997. ISBN 0-15-201506-X Subj: Activities – making things. Anatomy – hands. Family life. Format, unusual – toy & movable books.

In my world ill. by author. Harcourt, 2002. ISBN 0-15-216269-0 Subj: Concepts. Format, unusual. Picture puzzles.

Leaf man ill. by author. Harcourt, 2005. ISBN 0-15-205304-2 Subj: Format, unusual. Plants. Weather – wind.

Market day ill. by author. Harcourt, 2000. ISBN 0-15-202158-2 Subj: Farms. Rhyming text. Stores.

Mole's hill: a woodland tale ill. by author. Harcourt, 1994. ISBN 0-15-255116-6 Subj: Animals – foxes. Animals – moles. Folk & fairy tales. Indians of North America – Seneca.

Moon rope = Un lazo a la luna ill. by adapt. Harcourt, 1992. ISBN 0-15-255343-6 Subj: Animals – foxes. Animals – moles. Folk & fairy tales. Foreign lands – Peru. Foreign languages. Moon.

Nuts to you! ill. by author. Harcourt, 1993. ISBN 0-15-257647-9 Subj: Animals – squirrels. Rhyming text.

Planting a rainbow ill. by author. Harcourt, 1988. ISBN 0-15-262609-3 Subj: Flowers. Gardens, gardening.

Red leaf, yellow leaf ill. by author. Harcourt, 1991. ISBN 0-15-266197-2 Subj: Seasons. Trees.

Snowballs ill. by author. Harcourt, 1995. ISBN 0-15-200074-7 Subj: Seasons – winter. Snowmen.

Top cat ill. by author. Harcourt, 1998. ISBN 0-15-201739-9 Subj: Animals – cats. Behavior – sharing. Rhyming text.

Waiting for wings ill. by author. Harcourt, 2001. ISBN 0-15-202608-8 Subj: Format, unusual – toy & movable books. Insects – butterflies, caterpillars. Rhyming text.

Ehrhardt, Reinhold. *Kikeri: or, The proud red rooster* ill. by Bernadette Watts. Collins, 1969. Subj: Birds – chickens. Character traits – pride.

Ehrlich, Amy. *Bunnies all day long* ill. by Marie H. Henry. Dial, 1985. ISBN 0-8037-0185-3 Subj: Activities. Animals – rabbits.

Bunnies and their grandma ill. by Marie H. Henry. Dial, 1985. ISBN 0-8037-0186-1 Subj: Animals – rabbits. Family life – grandmothers.

Bunnies at Christmastime ill. by Marie H. Henry. Dial, 1986. ISBN 0-8037-0321-X Subj: Animals – rabbits. Family life. Family life – aunts, uncles. Holidays – Christmas. Parties. Santa Claus. Sibling rivalry.

Bunnies on their own ill. by Marie H. Henry. Dial, 1986. ISBN 0-8037-0256-6 Subj: Animals – rabbits. Family life. Sibling rivalry.

Cinderella (Perrault, Charles)

Emma's new pony photos by Richard Brown. Random House, 1988. ISBN 0-394-99210-5 Subj: Animals – horses, ponies.

The everyday train ill. by Martha G. Alexander. Dial, 1977. ISBN 0-8037-2192-7 Subj: Behavior – solitude. Trains.

Leo, Zack and Emmie ill. by Steven Kellogg. Dial, 1981. ISBN 0-8037-4761-6 Subj: Friendship. School.

Leo, Zack, and Emmie together again ill. by Steven Kellogg. Dial, 1987. ISBN 0-8037-0382-1 Subj: Friendship. School.

Lucy's winter tale ill. by Troy Howell. Dial, 1992. ISBN 0-8037-0661-8 Subj: Animals. Circus.

Maggie and Silky and Joe ill. by Robert Blake. Viking, 1994. ISBN 0-670-83387-8 Subj: Animals – dogs. Death. Farms.

Parents in the pigpen, pigs in the tub ill. by Steven Kellogg. Dial, 1993. ISBN 0-8037-0928-5 Subj: Animals. Careers – farmers. Farms.

Pome and Peel ill. by László Gál. Dial, 1990. ISBN 0-8037-0288-4 Subj: Folk & fairy tales. Foreign lands – Italy. Magic.

Rapunzel (Grimm, Jacob)

The snow queen (Andersen, H. C. [Hans Christian])

The story of Hannukkah ill. by Ori Sherman. Dial, 1989. ISBN 0-8037-0616-2 Subj: Jewish culture. Religion.

Thumbelina (Andersen, H. C. [Hans Christian])

The wild swans (Andersen, H. C. [Hans Christian])

Zeek Silver Moon ill. by Robert Andrew Parker. Dial, 1972. ISBN 0-8037-9826-1 Subj: Family life. Indians of North America.

Ehrlich, Bettina Bauer. *see* Bettina (Bettina Ehrlich)

Ehrlich, H. M. *Gotcha, Louie!* ill. by Emily Bolam. Houghton, 2002. ISBN 0-618-19549-1 Subj: Activities – playing. Family life – mothers. Sea & seashore.

Louie's goose ill. by Emily Bolam. Houghton Mifflin, 2000. ISBN 0-618-03023-9 Subj: Sea & seashore. Toys.

Eichenberg, Fritz. *Ape in cape* ill. by author. Harcourt, 1952. ISBN 0-15-203722-5 Subj: ABC books. Caldecott award honor books.

Dancing in the moon ill. by author. Harcourt, 1955. ISBN 0-15-221443-7 Subj: Animals. Counting, numbers. Rhyming text.

Eiffers, Joost. *Dr. Pompo's nose* (Freymann, Saxton)

One lonely seahorse (Freymann, Saxton)

Eilenberg, Max. *Cowboy Kid* ill. by Sue Heap. Candlewick, 2000. ISBN 0-7636-1058-5 Subj: Bedtime. Family life – fathers.

Squeak's good idea ill. by Patrick Benson. Candlewick, 2001. ISBN 0-7636-1591-9 Subj: Activities – picnicking. Animals – elephants.

Eisen, Armand. *Goldilocks and the three bears* (The three bears)

Eisenberg, Ann. *Bible heroes I can be* ill. by Rosalyn Schanzer. Kar-Ben Copies, 1990. ISBN 0-929371-09-7 Subj: Religion.

I can celebrate ill. by Rosalyn Schanzer. Kar-Ben Copies, 1989. ISBN 0-930494-93-8 Subj: Format, unusual – board books. Holidays. Jewish culture. Religion.

Eisenberg, Lisa. *Back-to-school belly busters* (McMullan, Kate [Hall])

Batty riddles (McMullan, Kate [Hall])

Bunny riddles (McMullan, Kate [Hall])

Chickie riddles (McMullan, Kate [Hall])

Creepy riddles (McMullan, Kate [Hall])

Dinosaur riddles (McMullan, Kate [Hall])

Fishy riddles (McMullan, Kate [Hall])

Hanukkah ha-has (McMullan, Kate [Hall])

Hearty har har: Valentine riddles you'll love (McMullan, Kate [Hall])

Ho ho ho, ha ha ha (McMullan, Kate [Hall])

Kitty riddles (McMullan, Kate [Hall])

Mummy riddles (McMullan, Kate [Hall])

Puppy riddles (McMullan, Kate [Hall])

Ribbit riddles (McMullan, Kate [Hall])

Sheepish riddles (McMullan, Kate [Hall])

Snakey riddles (McMullan, Kate [Hall])

Spacey riddles (McMullan, Kate [Hall])

Trick or eeek! (McMullan, Kate [Hall])

Eisenberg, Phyllis Rose. *A mitzvah is something special* ill. by Susan Jeschke. HarperCollins, 1978. ISBN 0-06-021808-8 Subj: Family life – grandmothers. Family life – grandparents. Jewish culture.

You're my Nikki ill. by Jill Kastner. Dial, 1992. ISBN 0-8037-1129-8 Subj: Activities – working. Emotions – love. Family life – mothers.

Eisenstein, Marilyn. *Periwinkle isn't Paris* ill. by Rudolf Stüssi. Tundra, 1999. ISBN 0-88776-451-7 Subj: Activities – traveling. Behavior – running away. Emotions. Foreign lands – France. Friendship.

Eisler, Colin. *Cats know best* ill. by Lesley Anne Ivory. Dial, 1988. ISBN 0-8037-0560-3 Subj: Animals – cats.

Eisman, Carol. *I wish I had a big, big tree* (Sato, Satoru)

Eisner, Will. *The princess and the frog* (Grimm, Jacob)

Sundiata ill. by author. NBM, 2003. ISBN 1-56163-332-1 Subj: Folk & fairy tales. Foreign lands – Africa. Foreign lands – Mali. Handicaps. Royalty – kings.

Ekker, Ernest A. *What is beyond the hill?* ill. by Hilde Heyduck-Huth. Lippincott, 1986. ISBN 0-397-32167-8 Subj: Activities – traveling. Imagination. World.

Ekoomiak, Normee. *Arctic memories* ill. by author. Holt, 1990, 1988. ISBN 0-8050-1256-0 Subj: Careers – artists. Eskimos. Indians of North America – Cree. Indians of North America – Inuk. Memories, memory.

Elbling, Peter. *Aria* ill. by Sophy Williams. Viking, 1994. ISBN 0-670-85062-4 Subj: Birds. Character traits – kindness to animals. Communication. Jungle.

Elborn, Andrew. *Big Al* ill. by Yoshi. Picture Book Studio, 1988. ISBN 0-88708-075-8 Subj: Character traits – appearance. Fish. Friendship.

Bird Adalbert ill. by Susi Bohdal. Alphabet Pr., 1983. ISBN 0-907234-45-3 Subj: Behavior – dissatisfaction. Behavior – wishing. Birds. Character traits – appearance. Character traits – vanity. Rhyming text.

Noah and the ark and the animals ill. by Ivan Gantschev. Picture Book Studio, 1984. ISBN 0-907234-58-5 Subj: Animals. Animals – horses, ponies. Boats, ships. Religion – Noah. Weather – floods. Weather – rain. Weather – rainbows.

Elgar, Rebecca. *Tiger and the new baby* (French, Vivian)

Tiger and the temper tantrum (French, Vivian)

Elias, Joyce. *Whose toes are those?* ill. by Cathy Sturm. Barron's, 1992. ISBN 0-8120-6215-9 Subj: Anatomy – toes. Animals. Format, unusual. Poetry. Riddles & jokes.

Eliot, T. S. (Thomas Stearns). *Mr. Mistoffelees with Mungojerrie and Rumpelteazer* ill. by Errol Le Cain. Harcourt, 1991. ISBN 0-15-256230-3 Subj: Animals – cats. Poetry.

Elkin, Benjamin. *Gillespie and the guards* ill. by James Henry Daugherty. Viking, 1956. Subj: Anatomy. Behavior – trickery. Caldecott award honor books. Character traits – cleverness. Royalty.

The king who could not sleep ill. by Victoria Chess. Parents' Magazine Pr., 1975. ISBN 0-819-30776-9 Subj: Cumulative tales. Rhyming text. Royalty – kings. Sleep.

The king's wish and other stories ill. by Leonard W. Shortall. Random House, 1960. Subj: Folk & fairy tales. Royalty – kings.

Lucky and the giant ill. by Katherine Evans. Childrens Pr., 1962. Subj: Character traits – cleverness. Character traits – luck. Character traits – selfishness. Giants.

Six foolish fishermen ill. by Katherine Evans. Childrens Pr., 1957. Based on a folktale in Ashton's Chap-Books of the 18th century. ISBN 0-516-03601-7 Subj: Counting, numbers. Folk & fairy tales. Sports – fishing.

Such is the way of the world ill. by Yoko Mitsuhashi. Parents' Magazine Pr., 1968. Subj: Animals – monkeys. Cumulative tales. Folk & fairy tales. Foreign lands – Africa. Problem solving.

Why the sun was late ill. by James Snyder. Parents' Magazine Pr., 1966. Subj: Animals. Cumulative tales. Insects – flies. Sun.

The wisest man in the world: a legend of ancient Israel retold by Benjamin Elkin; ill. by Anita Lobel. Parents' Magazine Pr., 1968. Subj: Character traits – wisdom. Folk & fairy tales. Foreign lands – Israel. Riddles & jokes. Royalty.

Elks, Wendy. *Charles B. Wombat and the very strange thing* ill. by author. David & Charles, 1989. ISBN 0-09-168910-4 Subj: Animals – wombats. Circus. Reptiles – turtles, tortoises.

Ellen, Barbara. *Phillip the flower-eating phoenix* (Todaro, John)

Ellentuck, Shan. *Did you see what I said?* ill. by author. Doubleday, 1967. Subj: Humorous stories. Language.

A sunflower as big as the sun ill. by author. Doubleday, 1968. Subj: Behavior – boasting. Flowers. Humorous stories. Plants.

Elliott, Dan. *Ernie's little lie* ill. by Joseph Mathieu. Random House, 1983. ISBN 0-394-95440-8 Subj: Art. Behavior – lying. Puppets.

A visit to the Sesame Street firehouse: featuring Jim Henson's Sesame Street Muppets ill. by Joseph Mathieu. Random House, 1983. ISBN 0-394-96029-7 Subj: Careers – firefighters. Fire. Puppets.

Elliott, David. *An alphabet of rotten kids!* ill. by Oscar de Mejo. Putnam, 1991. ISBN 0-399-22260-X Subj: ABC books. Behavior. Poetry.

And here's to you! ill. by Randy Cecil. Candlewick, 2004. ISBN 0-7636-1427-0 Subj: Animals. Birds. Rhyming text.

Hazel Nutt, Alien Hunter Ill. by True Kelley. Holiday, 2004. ISBN 0-8234-1843-X Subj: Humorous stories. Space & space ships.

Hazel Nutt, mad scientist ill. by True Kelley. Holiday, 2003. ISBN 0-8234-1711-5 Subj: Careers – scientists. Humorous stories. Monsters. Music.

Hunter's best friend at school ill. by Lynn Munsinger. HarperCollins, 2002. ISBN 0-06-000231-X Subj: Animals – raccoons. Behavior. Friendship. School – nursery.

Elliott, George. *The boy who loved bananas* ill. by Andrej Krystoforski. Kids Can, 2005. ISBN 1-55337-744-3 Subj: Animals – monkeys. Behavior – imitation. Food. Humorous stories. Zoos.

Elliott, Ingrid Glatz. *Hospital roadmap: a book to help explain the hospital experience to young children* ill. by author. Resources for Children in Hospitals, 1982. ISBN 0-9608150-0-7 Subj: Hospitals. Illness.

Elliott, Robert. *see* Allen, Robert

Ellis, Anne Leo. *Dabble Duck* ill. by Sue Truesdell. HarperCollins, 1984. ISBN 0-06-021818-5 Subj: Birds – ducks. Cities, towns. Emotions – loneliness. Friendship.

Ellis, Sarah. *Big Ben* ill. by Kim Lafave. Fitzhenry & Whiteside, 2001. ISBN 1-55041-679-0 Subj: Family life – brothers & sisters.

Salmon forest (Suzuki, David)

Ellis, Veronica Freeman. *Afro-Bets, first book about Africa* ill. by George Ford. Just Us Books, 1989. ISBN 0-940975-12-2 Subj: Foreign lands – Africa.

Ellwand, David. *Alfred's camera: a collection of picture puzzles* ill. by author. Dutton, 1998. ISBN 0-525-45978-2 Subj: Animals – dogs. Behavior – lost & found possessions.

Alfred's party ill. by author. Dutton, 2000. ISBN 0-525-46385-2 Subj: Animals – dogs. Behavior – lost & found possessions. Birthdays. Picture puzzles.

Cinderlily ill. by author; libretto by Christine Tagg. Candlewick, 2003. ISBN 0-7636-2328-8 Subj: Ballet. Flowers. Folk & fairy tales. Foreign lands – France. Rhyming text.

Midas Mouse photos by author. Lothrop, 2000. ISBN 0-688-16745-4 Subj: Animals – mice. Behavior – wishing. Sun.

Ten in the bed photos by author. Handprint, 2000. ISBN 1-929766-49-1 Subj: Counting, numbers. Format, unusual – board books. Music. Songs. Toys – bears.

Elschner, Géraldine. *Moonchild, star of the sea* ill. by Lieselotte Schwarz; trans. by J. Alison James. North-South, 2002. ISBN 0-7358-1665-4 Subj: Earth. Moon. Stars.

Elsdale, Bob. *Mac side up* ill. by author. Dutton, 2000. ISBN 0-525-46467-0 Subj: Animals – cats. Animals – ferrets. Humorous stories. Pets.

Elsie-Jean. *see* Stern, Elsie-Jean

Elson, Raymond. *Clothes* ill. by Sonia Canals. Larousse, 1996. ISBN 1-85697-660-2 Subj: Clothing. Format, unusual – toy & movable books.

Pets ill. by Sonia Canals. Larousse, 1996. ISBN 1-85697-653-X Subj: Format, unusual – toy & movable books. Pets.

Toys ill. by Sonia Canals. Larousse, 1996. ISBN 1-85697-659-9 Subj: Format, unusual – toy & movable books. Toys.

Elster, Jean Alicia. *Just call me Joe Joe* ill. by Nicole Tadgell. Judson Pr., 2001. ISBN 0-8170-1398-9 Subj: Ethnic groups in the U.S. – African Americans. Self-concept. Sports – baseball.

Elting, Mary. *The big book of real boats and ships* ill. by George J. Zaffo. Grosset, 1951. Subj: Boats, ships.

The Hopi way ill. by Louis Mofsie. Lippincott, 1970. Subj: Indians of North America – Hopi.

Q is for duck: an alphabet guessing game by Mary Elting & Michael Folsom; ill. by Jack Kent. Houghton Mifflin, 1980. ISBN 0-395-29437-1 Subj: ABC books. Animals. Games. Participation.

Elves, fairies and gnomes: poems sel. by Lee Bennett Hopkins; ill. by Rosekrans Hoffman. Knopf, 1980. ISBN 0-394-94351-1 Subj: Fairies. Mythical creatures – elves. Mythical creatures – gnomes. Poetry.

Elwell, Peter. *The king of the pipers* ill. by author. Macmillan, 1984. ISBN 0-02-733460-0 Subj: Devil. Folk & fairy tales.

Ely, Lesley. *Looking after Louis* ill. by Polly Dunbar. A. Whitman, 2004. ISBN 0-8075-4746-8 Subj: Handicaps – autism. School.

Elya, Susan Middleton. *Eight animals bake a cake* ill. by Lee Chapman. Putnam, 2002. ISBN 0-399-23468-3 Subj: Activities – baking, cooking. Animals. Foreign languages. Rhyming text.

Eight animals on the town ill. by Lee Chapman. Putnam, 2000. ISBN 0-399-23437-3 Subj: Animals. Counting, numbers. Foreign languages. Rhyming text.

Say hola to Spanish ill. by Loretta Lopez. Lee & Low, 1996. ISBN 1-880000-29-6 Subj: Foreign languages.

Elzbieta. *Brave Babette and sly Tom* ill. by author. Dial, 1989. ISBN 0-8037-0633-2 Subj: Animals – cats. Animals – mice. Birds. Family life.

Dikou and the baby star ill. by author. Crowell, 1988. ISBN 0-690-04721-5 Subj: Character traits – kindness. Stars.

Dikou and the mysterious moon sheep ill. by author. Crowell, 1988. ISBN 0-690-04694-4 Subj: Behavior – running away. Dreams. Family life. Imagination.

Dikou and the Snivelly Snoak ill. by author. Barron's, 1984. ISBN 0-8120-5622-1 Subj: Behavior – running away. Folk & fairy tales. Foreign lands – France. Monsters.

Dikou the little troon who walks at night ill. by author. Barron's, 1985. ISBN 0-8120-5621-3 Subj: Behavior – lying. Character traits – kindness. Mythical creatures.

Jon-Jon and Annette ill. by author. Holt, 1994. ISBN 0-8050-3299-1 Subj: Animals – rabbits. Emotions – love. War.

Emberley, Barbara. *Drummer Hoff* ill. by Ed Emberley. Prentice-Hall, 1967. Adapt. from a folk verse. ISBN 0-13-220822-9 Subj: Caldecott award books. Careers – military. Cumulative tales. Poetry. Weapons.

Night's nice by Barbara & Ed Emberley; ill. by Ed Emberley. Doubleday, 1963. Subj: Night. Poetry.

One wide river to cross ill. by Ed Emberley. Prentice-Hall, 1966. Includes unacc. melody. Adapt. of the American folk song. ISBN 0-316-23445-1 Subj: Animals. Caldecott award honor books. Folk & fairy tales. Poetry. Religion – Noah. Songs. Weather – floods. Weather – rain.

Simon's song ill. by Ed Emberley. Prentice-Hall, 1969. Includes unacc. melody. Adapt. of the folk song Simple Simon. Subj: Nursery rhymes. Songs.

The story of Paul Bunyan ill. with woodcuts by Ed Emberley. Half Moon, 1994. ISBN 0-671-88557-X Subj: Animals – oxen. Careers – lumberjacks. Tall tales. U.S. history – frontier & pioneer life.

Emberley, Ed (Edward Randolph). *Animals* ill. by author. Little, 1987. ISBN 0-316-23428-1 Subj: Animals. Format, unusual – board books.

Cars, boats, and planes ill. by author. Little, 1987. ISBN 0-316-23430-3 Subj: Airplanes, airports. Automobiles. Boats, ships. Format, unusual – board books. Transportation.

Ed Emberley's ABC ill. by author. Little, 1978. ISBN 0-316-23408-7 Subj: ABC books.

Ed Emberley's amazing look through book ill. by author. Little, 1979. ISBN 0-316-23407-9 Subj: Concepts. Format, unusual. Participation. Riddles & jokes.

Ed Emberley's big green drawing book ill. by author. Little, 1979. ISBN 0-316-23595-4 Subj: Art. Wordless.

Ed Emberley's big orange drawing book ill. by author. Little, 1980. ISBN 0-316-23418-4 Subj: Art.

Ed Emberley's big purple drawing book ill. by author. Little, 1981. ISBN 0-316-23422-2 Subj: Art.

Ed Emberley's crazy mixed-up face game ill. by author. Little, 1981. ISBN 0-316-23420-6 Subj: Anatomy – faces. Art. Games.

Ed Emberley's drawing book: make a world ill. by author. Little, 1972. ISBN 0-316-23598-9 Subj: Art.

Ed Emberley's drawing book of trucks and trains ill. by author. Little, 2002. ISBN 0-316-23898-8 Subj: Activities – drawing. Trains. Trucks.

Ed Emberley's fingerprint drawing book ill. by author. Little, 2000. ISBN 0-316-23638-1 Subj: Activities – drawing. Anatomy – fingers.

Glad monster, sad monster: a book about feelings ill. by author. Little, 1997. ISBN 0-316-57395-7 Subj: Emotions. Format, unusual – toy & movable books. Masks. Monsters.

Go away, big green monster! ill. by author. Little, 1992. ISBN 0-316-23653-5 Subj: Bedtime. Emotions – fear. Format, unusual – toy & movable books. Monsters.

Green says go ill. by author. Little, 1968. ISBN 0-316-23599-7 Subj: Communication. Concepts – color.

Home ill. by author. Little, 1987. ISBN 0-316-23433-8 Subj: Format, unusual – board books. Homes, houses.

Klippity klop ill. by author. Little, 1974. ISBN 0-316-23607-1 Subj: Dragons. Games. Knights. Participation.

Night's nice (Emberley, Barbara)

The parade book ill. by author. Little, 1962. Subj: Parades.

Rosebud ill. by author. Little, 1966. Subj: Character traits – being different. Problem solving. Reptiles – turtles, tortoises.

Sounds ill. by author. Little, 1987. ISBN 0-316-23431-1 Subj: Format, unusual – board books. Noise, sounds.

Thanks, Mom! ill. by author. Little, 2003. ISBN 0-316-24022-2 Subj: Animals. Animals – mice. Circus. Family life – mothers. Food.

The wing on a flea. Little, 2001. ISBN 0-316-23487-7 Subj: Concepts – shape. Rhyming text.

Emberley, Michael. *More dinosaurs! and other prehistoric beasts* ill. by author. Little, 1983. ISBN 0-316-23424-9 Subj: Art. Dinosaurs. Prehistory.

The present ill. by author. Little, 1991. ISBN 0-316-23411-7 Subj: Birthdays. Character traits – generosity.

Ruby ill. by author. Little, 1990. ISBN 0-316-23643-8 Subj: Animals – cats. Animals – mice. Behavior – talking to strangers. Cities, towns.

Welcome back, Sun ill. by author. Little, 1993. ISBN 0-316-23647-0 Subj: Family life. Foreign lands – Norway. Seasons – spring. Sun.

Emberley, Rebecca. *City sounds* ill. by author. Little, 1989. ISBN 0-316-23635-7 Subj: Cities, towns. Noise, sounds.

Drawing with numbers and letters ill. by author. Little, 1981. ISBN 0-316-23406-0 Subj: Art.

Jungle sounds ill. by author. Little, 1989. ISBN 0-316-23636-5 Subj: Jungle. Noise, sounds.

My animals = Mis animales ill. by author. Little, 2002. ISBN 0-316-17343-6 Subj: Animals. Foreign languages. Format, unusual – board books.

My city = Mi cuidad ill. by author. Little, 2005. ISBN 0-316-00051-5 Subj: Cities, towns. Foreign languages. Format, unusual – board books.

My clothes = Mi ropa ill. by author. Little, 2002. ISBN 0-316-17454-8 Subj: Clothing. Foreign languages. Format, unusual – board books.

My colors = Mis colores ill. by author. Little, 2000. ISBN 0-316-23347-1 Subj: Concepts – color. Foreign languages. Format, unusual – board books.

My food = Mi comida ill. by author. Little, 2002. ISBN 0-316-17718-0 Subj: Food. Foreign languages. Format, unusual – board books.

My garden = Mi jardin ill. by author. Little, 2005. ISBN 0-316-00049-3 Subj: Foreign languages. Format, unusual – board books. Gardens, gardening.

My house = Mi casa ill. by author. Little, 1990. ISBN 0-316-23637-3 Subj: Foreign languages. Format, unusual – board books. Homes, houses.

My mother's secret life ill. by author. Little, 1998. ISBN 0-316-23496-6 Subj: Behavior – secrets. Circus. Dreams. Family life – mothers.

My numbers = Mis números ill. by author. Little, 2000. ISBN 0-316-23350-1 Subj: Counting, numbers. Foreign languages. Format, unusual – board books.

My opposites = Mis opuestos ill. by author. Little, 2000. ISBN 0-316-23345-5 Subj: Concepts – opposites. Foreign languages. Format, unusual – board books.

My room = Mi cuarto ill. by author. Little, 2005. ISBN 0-316-00052-3 Subj: Foreign languages. Format, unusual – board books. Homes, houses.

My school = Mi escuela ill. by author. Little, 2005. ISBN 0-316-00050-7 Subj: Foreign languages. Format, unusual – board books. School.

My shapes = Mis formas ill. by author. Little, 2000. ISBN 0-316-23355-2 Subj: Concepts – shape. Foreign languages. Format, unusual – board books.

My toys = Mi juguetes ill. by author. Little, 2002. ISBN 0-316-17494-7 Subj: Foreign languages. Format, unusual – board books. Toys.

Three cool kids ill. by author. Little, 1995. ISBN 0-316-23666-7 Subj: Animals – goats. Animals – rats. Cities, towns. Folk & fairy tales.

Embry, Margaret. *The blue-nosed witch* ill. by Carl Rose. Holiday, 1956. ISBN 0-8234-0011-5 Subj: Holidays – Halloween. Witches.

Emecheta, Buchi. *Nowhere to play* ill. by Peter Archer. Schocken, 1981. ISBN 0-8052-8058-8 Subj: Activities – playing. Foreign lands – England. Safety.

Emergency! ed. by Nicola Deschamps; photos by Richard Leeney & Lynton Gardiner. DK, 2001. ISBN 0-7894-7414-X Subj: Careers – firefighters. Fire. Format, unusual – board books. Trucks.

Emerman, Ellen. *Is it Shabbos yet?* ill. by . Hachai, 2001. ISBN 1-929628-02-1 Subj: Holidays. Jewish culture. Religion.

Just right: the story of a Jewish home ill. by Sarah Kranz. Hachai, 1999. ISBN 0-922613-91-5 Subj: Family life. Homes, houses. Jewish culture.

Emerson, Carl. *Marion Jones* ill. with photos. Child's World, 2001. ISBN 1-56766-970-0 Subj: Activities – running. Ethnic groups in the U.S. – African Americans. Sports – Olympics.

Emerson, Sally. *The Kingfisher nursery rhyme songbook* music arranged by Mary Frank; ill. by Moira & Cohn Maclean. Kingfisher, 1992. ISBN 1-85697-823-0 Subj: Music. Nursery rhymes. Songs.

The nursery treasury ill. by Moira & Colin Maclean. Doubleday, 1988. ISBN 0-385-24650-1 Subj: Nursery rhymes.

Emerson, Scott. *The magic boots* by Scott Emerson & Howard Post; ill. by Howard Post. Gibbs Smith, 1994. ISBN 0-87905-603-7 Subj: Clothing – boots. Imagination.

Emmett, Fredrick Rowland. *New world for Nellie* ill. by author. Harcourt, 1952. Subj: Trains.

Emmett, Jonathan. *Bringing down the moon* ill. by Vanessa Cabban. Candlewick, 2001. ISBN 0-7636-1577-3 Subj: Animals. Animals – moles. Moon.

No place like home ill. by Vanessa Cabban. Candlewick, 2005. ISBN 0-7636-2554-X Subj: Animals. Animals – moles. Homes, houses.

Someone bigger ill. by Adrian Reynolds. Clarion, 2004. ISBN 0-618-44397-5 Subj: Concepts – size. Kites. Rhyming text.

Emmons, Chip. *Sammy wakes his dad* ill. by Shirley Venit Anger. Star Bright, 2002. ISBN 1-887734-87-2 Subj: Family life – fathers. Handicaps – physical handicaps. Sports – fishing.

Emmons, Ramona Ware. *Your world: let's visit the hospital* (Pope, Billy N.)

Empress Michiko of Japan. *The animals* (Mado, Michio)

Encking, Louise F. *The little gardeners* (Morgenstern, Elizabeth)

The toy maker: how a tree becomes a toy village (Thelen, Gerda)

Enderle, Judith (Ann) Ross. *Francis, the earthquake dog* by Judith Ross Enderle & Stephanie Gordon Tessler; ill. by Brooke Scudder. Chronicle, 1996. ISBN 0-8118-0630-8 Subj: Animals – dogs. Earthquakes.

Good junk ill. by Gail Gibbons. Elsevier-Nelson, 1981. ISBN 0-525-66720-2 Subj: Behavior – collecting things.

The good-for-something dragon by Judith Ross Enderle & Stephanie Gordon Tessler; ill. by Les Gray. Caroline House, 1993. ISBN 1-56397-214-X Subj: Dragons.

Nell Nugget and the cow caper by Judith Ross Enderle & Stephanie Gordon Tessler; ill. by Paul Yalowitz. S&S, 1995. ISBN 0-689-80502-0 Subj: Behavior – stealing. Cowboys, cowgirls. U.S. history – frontier & pioneer life.

A pile of pigs by Judith Ross Enderle & Stephanie Gordon Tessler; ill. by Charles Jordan. Bell Books, 1993. ISBN 1-878093-88-6 Subj: Animals. Animals – pigs.

Six creepy sheep by Judith Ross Enderle & Stephanie Gordon Tessler; ill. by John O'Brien. Caroline House, 1992. ISBN 0-56397-092-9 Subj: Animals – sheep. Counting, numbers. Holidays – Halloween. Parties.

Six sandy sheep by Judith Ross Enderle & Stephanie Gordon Tessler; ill. by John O'Brien. Boyds Mills, 1997. ISBN 1-56397-582-3 Subj: Animals – sheep. Counting, numbers. Sea & seashore.

Six snowy sheep by Judith Ross Enderle & Stephanie Gordon Tessler; ill. by John O'Brien. Boyds Mills, 1995. ISBN 1-56397-138-0 Subj: Animals. Counting, numbers. Holidays – Christmas. Weather – snow.

Something's happening on Calabash Street by Judith Ross Enderle & Stephanie Jacob Gordon; ill. by Donna Ingemanson. Chronicle, 2000. ISBN 0-8118-2450-0 Subj: Cities, towns. Communities, neighborhoods. Fairs, festivals. Food. Rhyming text.

Upstairs by Judith Ross Enderle & Stephanie Gordon Tessler; ill. by Kate Salley Palmer. Boyds Mills, 1998. ISBN 1-56397-466-5 Subj: Animals. Cities, towns. Homes, houses.

What would Mama do? by Judith Ross Enderle & Stephanie Gordon Tessler; ill. by Chris L. Demarest. Boyds Mills, 1995. ISBN 1-56397-418-5 Subj: Animals – foxes. Birds – geese. Concepts – measurement. Concepts – weight. Shopping.

Where are you, little Zack? by Judith Ross Enderle & Stephanie Gordon Tessler; ill. by Brian Floca. Houghton Mifflin, 1997. ISBN 0-395-73092-9 Subj: Behavior – lost. Birds – ducks. Cities, towns. Counting, numbers.

Enell, Trinka. *Roll over, Rosie* ill. by Dick Gackenbach. Clarion, 1992. ISBN 0-395-59340-9 Subj: Animals – dogs. Pets.

Engdahl, Sylvia. *Our world is earth* ill. by Don Sibley. Atheneum, 1979. ISBN 0-689-30678-4 Subj: Communication. Earth. Science.

Engel, Diana. *Circle song* ill. by author. Cavendish, 1999. ISBN 0-7614-5040-8 Subj: Bedtime. Concepts – shape. Ethnic groups in the U.S. – African Americans. Family life – fathers. Rhyming text.

Eleanor, Arthur, and Claire ill. by author. Macmillan, 1992. ISBN 0-02-733462-7 Subj: Animals – mice. Death. Family life – grandparents.

Fishing ill. by author. Macmillan, 1993. ISBN 0-02-733463-5 Subj: Ethnic groups in the U.S. – African Americans. Family life – grandfathers. Moving. Sports – fishing.

Gino Badino ill. by author. Morrow, 1991. ISBN 0-688-09503-8 Subj: Animals – mice. Family life. Food.

Josephina hates her name ill. by author. Feminist Pr., 1999. ISBN 1-55861-218-1 Subj: Family life. Names. Reptiles – alligators, crocodiles.

Josephina, the great collector ill. by author. Morrow, 1988. ISBN 0-688-07543-6 Subj: Behavior – collecting things. Sibling rivalry.

The little lump of clay ill. by author. Morrow, 1989. ISBN 0-688-08407-9 Subj: Activities – making things.

The shelf-paper jungle ill. by author. Morrow, 1991. ISBN 0-02-733464-3 Subj: Activities – drawing. Friendship. Jungle. Paper.

Engelbreit, Mary. *Queen of Christmas* ill. by author. HarperCollins, 2003. ISBN 0-06-008176-7 Subj: Gifts. Holidays – Christmas.

Queen of the class ill. by author. HarperCollins, 2004. ISBN 0-06-008179-1 Subj: Royalty – queens. School. Theater.

Engelbrektson, Sune. *Gravity at work and play* ill. by Eric Carle. Holt, 1963. Subj: Science.

The sun is a star ill. by Eric Carle. Holt, 1963. Subj: Science. Sun.

Engels-Fietzek, Petra. *Sophie and the seagull* ill. by Julia Ginsbach. G. Stevens, 2002. ISBN 0-8368-3174-8 Subj: Birds – seagulls. Friendship. Sea & seashore.

England, Linda. *The old cotton blues* ill. by Teresa Flavin. McElderry, 1998. ISBN 0-689-81074-1 Subj: Careers – musicians. Emotions. Ethnic groups in the U.S. – African Americans.

3 kids dreamin' ill. by Dena Schutzer. McElderry, 1997. ISBN 0-689-80866-6 Subj: Careers – musicians. Music. Musical instruments – bands.

Engle, Joanna. *Cap'n kid goes to the South Pole* ill. by Pat Paris. Random House, 1983. ISBN 0-394-85643-0 Subj: Animals – whales.

English, Jennifer. *My mommy's special* ill. with photos. Childrens Pr., 1985. ISBN 0-516-03861-3 Subj: Family life – mothers. Handicaps.

English, Karen. *Big wind coming!* ill. by Cedric Lucas. A. Whitman, 1996. ISBN 0-8075-0726-1 Subj: Ethnic groups in the U.S. – African Americans. Farms. Toys – dolls. Weather – storms.

Hot day on Abbott Avenue ill. by Javaka Steptoe. Clarion, 2004. ISBN 0-395-98527-7 Subj: Ethnic groups in the U.S. – African Americans. Friendship. Seasons – summer. Sports – jumping rope.

Just right stew ill. by Anna Rich. Boyds Mills, 1998. ISBN 1-56397-487-8 Subj: Activities – baking, cooking. Ethnic groups in the U.S. – African Americans. Family life. Food.

Nadia's hands ill. by Jonathan Weiner. Boyds Mills, 1999. ISBN 1-56397-667-6 Subj: Ethnic groups in the U.S. – Pakistani Americans. Family life. Self-concept. Weddings.

Neeny coming, Neeny going ill. by Synthia Saint James. BridgeWater, 1996. ISBN 0-8167-3796-7 Subj: Emotions. Ethnic groups in the U.S. – African Americans. Family life – cousins. Friendship. Islands.

Speak English for us, Marisol ill. by Enrique O. Sánchez. A. Whitman, 2000. ISBN 0-8075-7554-2 Subj: Ethnic groups in the U.S. – Hispanic Americans. Foreign languages.

Engvick, William. *Lullabies and night songs* ed. by William Engvick; music by Alec Wilder; ill. by Maurice Sendak. HarperCollins, 1965. ISBN 0-06-021820-7 Subj: Bedtime. Lullabies. Music.

Enright, Elizabeth. *Zeee* ill. by Susan Gaber. Harcourt, 1993. ISBN 0-15-299958-2 Subj: Behavior – misbehavior. Emotions – anger. Fairies.

Ephron, Delia. *Santa and Alex* ill. by Elise Primavera. Little, 1983. ISBN 0-3162-4300-0 Subj: Holidays – Christmas. Santa Claus.

Erdoes, Richard. *Policemen around the world* ill. by author. McGraw-Hill, 1968. Subj: Careers – police officers.

Erdrich, Liselotte. *Bears make rock soup and other stories* ill. by Lisa Fifield. Children's Book Pr., 2002. ISBN 0-89239-172-3 Subj: Animals. Indians of North America – Great Plains.

Erdrich, Louise. *Grandmother's pigeon* ill. by Jim LaMarche. Hyperion, 1996. ISBN 0-7868-2137-X Subj: Birds – pigeons. Family life – grandmothers.

The range eternal ill. by Steve Johnson and & Fancher. Hyperion, 2002. ISBN 0-7868-0220-0 Subj: Activities – baking, cooking. U.S. history – frontier & pioneer life.

Erickson, Karen. *Do I have to go home?* ill. by Maureen Roffey. Viking, 1989. ISBN 0-670-82673-1 Subj: Behavior.

I like to help ill. by Maureen Roffey. Viking, 1989. ISBN 0-670-82675-8 Subj: Character traits – helpfulness.

I was so mad ill. by Maureen Roffey. Viking, 1987. ISBN 0-670-81573-X Subj: Emotions – anger.

I'll try ill. by Maureen Roffey. Viking, 1987. ISBN 0-670-81572-1 Subj: Character traits – perseverance.

I'm brave! by Karen Erickson & Maureen Roffey; ill. by Maureen Roffey. Viking, 1989. ISBN 0-670-82676-6 Subj: Character traits – bravery.

It's dark – but I'm not scared ill. by Maureen Roffey. Viking, 1987. ISBN 0-670-81571-3 Subj: Emotions – fear. Night.

No one is perfect ill. by Maureen Roffey. Viking, 1987. ISBN 0-670-81570-5 Subj: Behavior – mistakes.

Waiting my turn ill. by Maureen Roffey. Viking, 1989. ISBN 0-670-82674-X Subj: Character traits – patience.

Erickson, Phoebe. *Just follow me* ill. by author. Follett, 1960. Subj: Animals – dogs. Behavior – lost. Homes, houses.

Erickson, Russell E. *Warton and the traders* ill. by Lawrence DiFiori. Lothrop, 1979. ISBN 0-688-51886-9 Subj: Animals – rats. Character traits – cleverness. Character traits – generosity. Frogs & toads.

Warton's Christmas eve adventure ill. by Lawrence DiFiori. Lothrop, 1977. ISBN 0-688-51822-2 Subj: Animals. Frogs & toads. Holidays – Christmas.

Ericsson, Jennifer A. *No milk!* ill. by Ora Eitan. Tambourine, 1993. ISBN 0-688-11306-0 Subj: Animals – bulls, cows. Behavior – misunderstanding.

Out and about at the bakery ill. by Anne McMullen. Picture Window, 2003. ISBN 1-4048-0037-9 Subj: Activities – baking, cooking. Careers – bakers. School – field trips.

She did it! ill. by Nadine Bernard Westcott. Farrar, 2002. ISBN 0-374-36776-0 Subj: Behavior – messy. Family life – sisters. Rhyming text.

Eriksson, Ake. *Joel, Jasper, and Julia* ill. by author. Carolrhoda, 1990. ISBN 0-87614-419-9 Subj: Animals – pigs. Farms.

Eriksson, Eva. *Hocus-pocus* ill. by author; trans. from Swedish by Barbro Eriksson Roehrdanz. Carolrhoda, 1985. ISBN 0-87614-235-8 Subj: Bedtime. Friendship.

Jealousy ill. by author; trans. from Swedish by Barbro Eriksson Roehrdanz. Carolrhoda, 1985. ISBN 0-87614-237-4 Subj: Emotions – envy, jealousy. Friendship. Illness.

Mimi and the biscuit factory (Sundvall, Viveca)

One short week ill. by author; trans. from Swedish by Barbro Eriksson Roehrdanz. Carolrhoda, 1985. ISBN 0-87614-234-X Subj: Behavior – boredom. Birthdays. Friendship.

The tooth trip ill. by author; trans. from Swedish by Barbro Eriksson Roehrdanz. Carolrhoda, 1985. ISBN 0-87614-236-6 Subj: Behavior – lost & found possessions. Friendship. Teeth.

Erlbruch, Wolf. *Leonard* ill. by author. Orchard, 1995. ISBN 0-531-08782-4 Subj: Animals – dogs. Behavior – wishing. Emotions – fear. Fairies.

Mrs. Meyer, the bird adapt. from German by Sabina Magyar & Susan Rich; ill. by author. Orchard, 1997. ISBN 0-531-33017-6 Subj: Activities – flying. Behavior – worrying. Birds.

Ernst, Kathryn F. *Danny and his thumb* ill. by Tomie de Paola. Prentice-Hall, 1973. ISBN 0-13-196725-8 Subj: Behavior – growing up. School. Thumb sucking.

Ernst, Lisa Campbell. *Breakfast time!* (Ziefert, Harriet)

Bubba and Trixie ill. by author. S&S, 1997. ISBN 0-689-81357-0 Subj: Friendship. Insects – butterflies, caterpillars. Insects – ladybugs. Metamorphosis. Self-concept.

Bye-bye, daddy! (Ziefert, Harriet)

A colorful adventure of the bee who left home one Monday morning and what he found along the way ill. by Lee Ernst. Lothrop, 1986. ISBN 0-688-05564-8 Subj: Concepts – color. Insects – bees.

Duke, the Dairy Delight dog ill. by author. S&S, 1996. ISBN 0-689-80750-3 Subj: Animals – dogs. Character traits – cleanliness.

Ginger jumps ill. by author. Bradbury, 1990. ISBN 0-02-733565-8 Subj: Animals – dogs. Circus.

Goldilocks returns ill. by author. S&S, 2000. ISBN 0-689-82537-4 Subj: Animals – bears. Folk & fairy tales. Humorous stories.

Good morning, sun! (Ziefert, Harriet)

Hamilton's art show ill. by author. Lothrop, 1986. ISBN 0-688-04121-3 Subj: Activities – painting. Animals. Art. Gardens, gardening.

Let's get dressed! (Ziefert, Harriet)

The letters are lost! ill. by author. Viking, 1996. ISBN 0-670-86336-X Subj: ABC books. Toys.

Little Red Riding Hood: a newfangled prairie tale ill. by author. S&S, 1995. ISBN 0-689-80145-9 Subj: Activities – baking, cooking. Animals – wolves. Behavior – talking to strangers. Family life – grandmothers. Folk & fairy tales.

Miss Penny and Mr. Grubbs ill. by author. Bradbury, 1991. ISBN 0-02-733563-1 Subj: Animals – rabbits. Emotions – envy, jealousy. Fairs, festivals. Gardens, gardening.

Nattie Parsons' good-luck lamb ill. by author. Viking, 1988. ISBN 0-670-81778-3 Subj: Activities – weaving. Animals – sheep.

The prize pig surprise ill. by author. Lothrop, 1984. ISBN 0-688-03798-4 Subj: Animals – pigs. Behavior – greed. Character traits – cleverness.

The rescue of Aunt Pansy ill. by author. Viking, 1987. ISBN 0-670-81716-3 Subj: Animals – cats. Animals – mice. Family life – aunts, uncles. Format, unusual. Friendship. Toys.

Sam Johnson and the blue ribbon quilt ill. by author. Lothrop, 1983. ISBN 0-688-01517-4 Subj: Activities. Gender roles. Quilts.

Squirrel Park ill. by author. Bradbury, 1993. ISBN 0-02-733562-3 Subj: Animals – squirrels. Ecology. Family life – fathers. Parks. Trees.

Stella Louella's runaway book ill. by author. S&S, 1998. ISBN 0-689-81883-1 Subj: Behavior – lost & found possessions. Careers – librarians. Cumulative tales. Libraries.

The three spinning fairies (Grimm, Jacob)

Up to ten and down again ill. by author. Lothrop, 1986. ISBN 0-688-04542-1 Subj: Activities – picnicking. Counting, numbers.

Wake up, it's Spring! ill. by author. HarperCollins, 2004. ISBN 0-06-008986-5 Subj: Animals. Nature. Seasons – spring.

Walter's tail ill. by author. Bradbury, 1992. ISBN 0-02-733564-X Subj: Animals – dogs. Pets.

When Bluebell sang ill. by author. Bradbury, 1989. ISBN 0-02-733561-5 Subj: Animals – bulls, cows. Theater.

Zinnia and Dot ill. by author. Viking, 1992. ISBN 0-670-83091-7 Subj: Animals – weasels. Behavior – fighting, arguing. Birds – chickens. Eggs.

Erskine, Jim. *Bedtime story* ill. by Ann Schweninger. Crown, 1982. ISBN 0-417-54540-3 Subj: Bedtime. Dreams. Night.

Bert and Susie's messy tale ill. by author. Crown, 1979. ISBN 0-517-53475-4 Subj: Activities. Animals – pigs.

The snowman ill. by author. Crown, 1978. ISBN 0-517-53202-6 Subj: Snowmen.

Esbensen, Barbara Juster. *Dance with me* ill. by Megan Lloyd. HarperCollins, 1995. ISBN 0-06-022823-7 Subj: Activities – dancing. Nature. Poetry.

The dream mouse: a lullaby tale from Old Latvia ill. by Judith Mitchell. Little, 1995. ISBN 0-316-24975-0 Subj: Animals – mice. Dreams. Night. Sleep.

Echoes for the eye: poems to celebrate patterns in nature ill. by Helen K. Davie. HarperCollins, 1996. ISBN 0-06-024399-6 Subj: Concepts – shape. Nature. Poetry.

The great buffalo race: how the buffalo got its hump; a Seneca tale ill. by Helen K. Davie. Little, 1994. ISBN 0-316-24982-3 Subj: Animals – buffaloes. Folk & fairy tales. Indians of North America – Seneca.

Jumping day ill. by Maryann Cocca-Leffler. Boyds Mills, 1999. ISBN 1-56397-709-5 Subj: Activities – jumping. Rhyming text.

Ladder to the sky: how the gift of healing came to the Ojibway nation ill. by Helen K. Davie. Little, 1989. ISBN 0-316-24952-1 Subj: Folk & fairy tales. Indians of North America – Ojibwa. Rhyming text.

The night rainbow ill. by Helen K. Davie. Orchard, 2000. ISBN 0-531-33244-6 Subj: Folk & fairy tales. Indians of North America. Northern lights. Poetry. Science.

Sponges are skeletons ill. by Holly Keller. HarperCollins, 1993. ISBN 0-06-021037-0 Subj: Anatomy – skeletons. Animals – sponges. Sea & seashore.

The star maiden: an Ojibway tale ill. by Helen K. Davie. Little, 1988. ISBN 0-316-24951-3 Subj: Folk & fairy tales. Indians of North America – Ojibwa. Rhyming text.

Who shrank my grandmother's house? ill. by Eric Beddows. HarperCollins, 1992. ISBN 0-06-021828-2 Subj: Behavior – growing up. Poetry.

Eschbacher, Roger. *Nonsense! He yelled* ill. by Adrian Johnson. Dial, 2002. ISBN 0-8037-2582-5 Subj: ABC books. Rhyming text.

Esckelson, Laura. *The copper braid of Shannon O'Shea* ill. by Pam Newton. Dutton, 2003. ISBN 0-525-46138-8 Subj: Foreign lands – Ireland. Hair. Mythical creatures.

Escott, John. *The little red hen* (The little red hen)

Escudie, René. *Paul and Sebastian* trans. by Roderick Townley; ill. by Ulises Wensell. Kane/Miller, 1988. ISBN 0-916291-19-7 Subj: Behavior – lost. Character traits – being different. Family life. Friendship. Prejudice.

Esiason, Boomer. *A boy named Boomer* ill. by Jacqueline Rogers. Scholastic, 1995. ISBN 0-590-52835-1 Subj: Memories, memory. Sports – football.

Espenscheid, Gertrude E. *The oh ball* ill. by author. Crown, 1966. Subj: Royalty. Toys – balls.

Esterl, Arnica. *The fine round cake* trans. from German by Pauline Hejl; ill. by Andrej Dugin & Olga Dugina. Four Winds, 1991. An adaptation of Johnny cake by Joseph Jacobs. ISBN 0-02-733568-2 Subj: Cumulative tales. Folk & fairy tales. Food. Foreign lands – England.

Estes, Kristyn Rehling. *Manuela's gift* ill. by Claire Cotts. Chronicle, 1999. ISBN 0-811-82085-8 Subj: Birthdays. Family life. Foreign lands – Mexico. Gifts.

Ethan, Eric. *Helicopters* ill. with photos. G. Stevens, 2002. ISBN 0-8368-3046-6 Subj: Character traits – helpfulness. Helicopters. Safety.

Etherington, Frank. *The spaghetti word race* ill. by Gina Calleja. Firefly, 1982. ISBN 0-920236-11-1 Subj: Imagination. Sibling rivalry.

Ets, Marie Hall. *Another day* ill. by author. Viking, 1953. Subj: Animals. Forest, woods. Parades. Theater.

Bad boy, good boy ill. by author. Crowell, 1967. Subj: Behavior. Ethnic groups in the U.S. – Mexican Americans. Family life. School.

Beasts and nonsense ill. by author. Viking, 1952. Subj: Animals. Humorous stories. Poetry.

The cow's party ill. by author. Viking, 1958. Subj: Animals – bulls, cows. Behavior – dissatisfaction. Behavior – sharing. Parties.

Elephant in a well ill. by author. Viking, 1972. ISBN 0-670-29169-2 Subj: Animals. Animals – elephants. Character traits – helpfulness. Cumulative tales.

Gilberto and the wind ill. by author. Viking, 1978, c1963. ISBN 0-670-34025-1 Subj: Ethnic groups in the U.S. – Mexican Americans. Weather – wind.

In the forest ill. by author. Viking, 1944. ISBN 0-670-39687-7 Subj: Activities – picnicking. Animals. Caldecott award honor books. Forest, woods. Imagination. Parades.

Just me ill. by author. Viking, 1978, c1965. ISBN 0-670-41109-4 Subj: Animals. Caldecott award honor books. Participation.

Little old automobile ill. by author. Viking, 1948. Subj: Automobiles.

Mister Penny ill. by author. Viking, 1935. Subj: Animals. Caldecott award honor books. Farms.

Mister Penny's circus ill. by author. Viking, 1961. Subj: Animals. Circus.

Mr. Penny's race horse ill. by author. Viking, 1956. Subj: Animals – horses, ponies. Caldecott award honor books. Fairs, festivals. Farms.

Mr. T. W. Anthony Woo ill. by author. Viking, 1951. Subj: Animals – cats. Animals – dogs. Animals – mice. Caldecott award honor books.

Nine days to Christmas ill. by author. Viking, 1959. ISBN 0-670-51350-4 Subj: Caldecott award books. Ethnic groups in the U.S. – Mexican Americans. Foreign lands – Mexico. Holidays – Christmas. Parties.

Play with me ill. by author. Viking, 1955. ISBN 0-670-55977-6 Subj: Activities – playing. Animals. Behavior. Caldecott award honor books.

Talking without words ill. by author. Viking, 1968. ISBN 0-670-69218-2 Subj: Communication. Participation.

Eugenie. *see* Fernandes, Eugenie

Eure, Wesley. *A fish out of water* designed and ill. by Meredith College Art Department. Pelican, 2000. ISBN 1-56554-850-7 Subj: Animals. Birds. Character traits – compromising. Emotions – love. Fish.

Euvremer, Teryl. *After dark* ill. by author. Crown, 1989. ISBN 0-517-57104-8 Subj: Rhyming text.

Sun's up ill. by author. Crown, 1987. ISBN 0-517-56432-7 Subj: Activities – working. Farms. Sun. Wordless.

The thieves of Peck's pocket ill. by author. Crown, 1990. ISBN 0-517-57538-8 Subj: Animals. Behavior – stealing. Crime. Plants.

Triple whammy ill. by author. HarperCollins, 1993. ISBN 0-06-021061-3 Subj: Behavior – trickery. Character traits – meanness. Monsters. Weddings. Witches.

Evans, Dilys. *Fairies, trolls and goblins galore* (Fairies, trolls and goblins galore)

Monster soup and other spooky poems (Monster soup and other spooky poems)

Weird pet poems (Weird pet poems)

Evans, Eva Knox. *Sleepy time* ill. by Reed Champion. Houghton Mifflin, 1962. Subj: Animals. Cumulative tales. Hibernation. Sleep.

That lucky Mrs. Plucky ill. by Jo Ann Stover. McKay, 1961. Subj: Animals – cats. Behavior – collecting things.

Where do you live? ill. by Beatrice Darwin. Golden Pr., 1960. Subj: Animals.

Evans, Katherine. *The boy who cried wolf* ill. by author. A. Whitman, 1960. Subj: Animals – wolves. Behavior – lying. Behavior – trickery. Folk & fairy tales.

A bundle of sticks ill. by author. A. Whitman, 1962. A retelling of an Æsop fable. Subj: Folk & fairy tales.

The maid and her pail of milk ill. by author. A. Whitman, 1959. Subj: Behavior – greed. Folk & fairy tales. Humorous stories.

The man, the boy and the donkey ill. by author. A. Whitman, 1958. Subj: Animals – donkeys. Character traits – practicality. Folk & fairy tales. Humorous stories.

Evans, Katie. *Hunky Dory ate it* ill. by Janet M. Stoeke. Dutton, 1992. ISBN 0-525-44847-0 Subj: Animals – dogs. Food. Rhyming text.

Evans, Lezlie. *Can you count ten toes? count to 10 in 10 different languages* ill. by Denis Roche. Houghton Mifflin, 1999. ISBN 0-395-90499-4 Subj: Counting, numbers. Foreign languages. Rhyming text.

If I were the wind ill. by Victoria Lisi. Ideals, 1997. ISBN 1-57102-096-9 Subj: Family life – mothers. Imagination. Rhyming text.

Rain song ill. by Cynthia Jabar. Houghton Mifflin, 1995. ISBN 0-395-69865-0 Subj: Poetry. Weather – rain.

Evans, Mari. *Singing black* ill. by Ramon Price. Third World Pr., 1978. ISBN 0-940975-80-7 Subj: Ethnic groups in the U.S. – African Americans. Nursery rhymes.

Evans, Mark. *Guinea pigs* ill. with photos. DK, 1992. ISBN 1-56458-125-X Subj: Animals – guinea pigs. Pets.

Kitten ill. with photos. DK, 1992. ISBN 1-56458-126-8 Subj: Animals – cats. Pets.

Puppy ill. with photos. DK, 1992. ISBN 1-56458-127-6 Subj: Animals – dogs. Pets.

Rabbit ill. by author. DK, 1992. ISBN 1-56458-128-4 Subj: Animals – rabbits. Pets.

Evans, Mel. *The tiniest sound* ill. by Ed Young. Doubleday, 1969. Subj: Noise, sounds. Poetry.

Evans, Nate. *The mixed-up zoo of professor Yahoo* ill. by author. Junior League of Kansas City Mo., 1992. ISBN 0-9607076-3-8 Subj: Rhyming text. Royalty – queens. Zoos.

Evans, Richard Paul. *The Christmas candle* ill. by Jacob Collins. S&S, 1998. ISBN 0-689-82319-3 Subj: Character traits – generosity. Holidays – Christmas. Magic.

The dance ill. by Jonathan Linton. S&S, 1999. ISBN 0-689-82351-7 Subj: Activities – dancing. Family life – fathers.

The light of Christmas ill. by Daniel Craig. S&S, 2002. ISBN 0-689-83468-3 Subj: Character traits – kindness. Holidays – Christmas.

The spyglass ill. by Jonathan Linton. S&S, 2001. ISBN 0-689-83466-7 Subj: Character traits – ambition. Royalty – kings.

The tower ill. by Jonathan Linton. S&S, 2001. ISBN 0-689-83467-5 Subj: Character traits – pride. Character traits – vanity.

Everett, Gwen. *Li'l Sis and Uncle Willie: a story based on the life and paintings of William H. Johnson* ill. with photos of paintings by William H. Johnson. Rizzoli, 1992. ISBN 0-8478-1462-9 Subj: Art. Careers – artists. Ethnic groups in the U.S. – African Americans. Family life – aunts, uncles. Museums. U.S. history.

Everett, Percival L. *The one that got away* ill. by Dirk Zimmer. Clarion, 1992. ISBN 0-395-56437-9 Subj: Counting, numbers. Cowboys, cowgirls. Language. U.S. history – frontier & pioneer life.

Everitt, Betsy. *Mean soup* ill. by author. Harcourt, 1992. ISBN 0-15-253146-7 Subj: Activities – baking, cooking. Behavior – bad day. Emotions – anger. Food. School.

Eversole, Robyn Harbert. *The gift stone* ill. by Allen Garns. Knopf, 1998. ISBN 0-679-98684-7 Subj: Careers – miners. Family life – grandparents. Foreign lands – Australia.

The magic house ill. by Peter Palagonia. Orchard, 1992. ISBN 0-531-08524-4 Subj: Activities – dancing. Ballet. Family life – sisters. Imagination.

Red berry wool ill. by Tim Coffey. A. Whitman, 1999. ISBN 0-8075-0654-0 Subj: Animals – sheep. Careers – shepherds.

Everton, Macduff. *Finding the magic circus = El circo magico modelo* ill. by author. Carolrhoda, 1979. ISBN 0-87614-106-8 Subj: Activities – vacationing. Circus. Foreign lands – Mexico. Foreign languages.

Ewart, Claire. *The giant* ill. by author. Walker, 2003. ISBN 0-8027-8837-8 Subj: Emotions – grief. Family life – fathers. Farms. Seasons.

Eyvindson, Peter. *Backward brothers see the light* ill. by Craig Terlson. Red Deer Pr., 1991. ISBN 0-88995-068-7 Subj: Family life – brothers. Folk & fairy tales. Foreign lands – Iceland. Humorous stories.

Ezra, Mark. *The sleepy dormouse* ill. by Gavin Rowe. Crocodile, 1994. ISBN 1-56656-153-1 Subj: Animals – dormice. Animals – mice. Animals – weasels. Gardens, gardening.

Fabiny, Sarah. *My first pop-up book of dinosaurs* (Bishop, Roma)

Facklam, Margery. *The big bug book* ill. by Paul Facklam. Little, 1994. ISBN 0-316-27389-9 Subj: Concepts – size. Insects.

But not like mine ill. by Jeni Bassett. Harcourt, 1988. ISBN 0-15-200419-X Subj: Anatomy. Animals. Format, unusual – toy & movable books.

I eat dinner ill. by Anita Riggio. Little, 1987. ISBN 0-316-27374-0 Subj: Animals. Food.

I go to sleep ill. by Anita Riggio. Little, 1987. ISBN 0-316-27375-9 Subj: Animals. Bedtime. Sleep.

Only a star ill. by Nancy Carpenter. Eerdmans, 1996. ISBN 0-8028-5122-3 Subj: Animals. Holidays – Christmas. Nature. Poetry. Stars.

So can I ill. by Jeni Bassett. Harcourt, 1988. ISBN 0-15-200419-X Subj: Activities. Animals. Format, unusual – toy & movable books.

Factor, Jane. *Summer* ill. by Alison Lester. Viking, 1988. ISBN 0-670-81157-2 Subj: Family life. Foreign lands – Australia. Holidays – Christmas. Rhyming text. Seasons – summer.

Fagan, Cary. *Gogol's coat* ill. by Regolo Ricci. Tundra, 1998. ISBN 0-88776-429-0 Subj: Behavior – stealing. Clothing – coats.

Faglia, Maeto. *Happy birthday, I'm 1* ill. by Luana Rinaldo. Kane/Miller, 2001. ISBN 1-929132-07-7 Subj: Animals – rabbits. Birthdays. Food. Format, unusual – board books.

Happy birthday, I'm 2 ill. by Silvia Vignale. Kane/Miller, 2001. ISBN 1-929132-08-5 Subj: Animals – dogs. Birthdays. Food. Format, unusual – board books.

Happy birthday, I'm 3 ill. by Sophie Fatus. Kane/Miller, 2001. ISBN 1-929132-09-3 Subj: Animals – cats. Birthdays. Food. Format, unusual – board books.

Happy birthday, I'm 4 ill. by Antonella Abbatiello. Kane/Miller, 2001. ISBN 1-929132-10-7 Subj: Animals – bears. Birthdays. Food. Format, unusual – board books.

Fain, James W. *Rodeos* ill. with photos. Childrens Pr., 1983. ISBN 0-516-01685-7 Subj: Animals – horses, ponies. Cowboys, cowgirls.

Fain, Moira. *Snow day* ill. by author. Walker, 1996. ISBN 0-8027-8410-0 Subj: Activities – drawing. Activities – writing. School. Weather – snow.

Fair, David. *The fabulous four skunks* ill. by Bruce Koscielniak. Houghton Mifflin, 1996. ISBN 0-395-73572-6 Subj: Animals – skunks. Music. Senses – smell.

Fair, Sylvia. *The bedspread* ill. by author. Morrow, 1982. ISBN 0-688-00877-1 Subj: Activities. Sibling rivalry.

Fairclough, Chris. *Take a trip to China* photos by author. Watts, 1981. ISBN 0-531-04317-7 Subj: Activities – traveling. Foreign lands – China.

Take a trip to England photos by author. Watts, 1982. ISBN 0-531-04416-5 Subj: Activities – traveling. Foreign lands – England.

Take a trip to Holland photos by author. Watts, 1982. ISBN 0-531-04417-3 Subj: Activities – traveling. Foreign lands – Holland.

Take a trip to Israel photos by author. Watts, 1981. ISBN 0-531-04318-5 Subj: Activities – traveling. Foreign lands – Israel.

Take a trip to Italy photos by author. Watts, 1981. ISBN 0-531-04219-3 Subj: Activities – traveling. Foreign lands – Italy.

Take a trip to West Germany photos by author. Watts, 1981. ISBN 0-531-04320-7 Subj: Activities – traveling. Foreign lands – Germany.

Fairfield, Flora. *see* Alcott, Louisa May

Fairies, trolls and goblins galore comp. by Dilys Evans; ill. by Jacqueline Rogers. S&S, 2000. Subj: Fairies. Mythical creatures. Poetry.

Fairy poems for the very young ill. by Beverlie Manson. Doubleday, 1982. ISBN 0-385-17542-6 Subj: Fairies. Poetry.

Faison, Eleanora. *Becoming* ill. by Cecelia Ercin. Patterson Pr., 1981. ISBN 0-9607432-0-0 Subj: Behavior – growing up.

Falconer, Ian. *Olivia* ill. by author. Atheneum, 2000. ISBN 0-689-82953-1 Subj: Activities. Animals – pigs. Behavior. Caldecott award honor books.

Olivia – and the missing toy ill. by author. Atheneum, 2003. ISBN 0-689-85291-6 Subj: Animals – pigs. Behavior – lost & found possessions. Format, unusual – board books. Toys.

Olivia counts ill. by author. Atheneum, 2002. ISBN 0-689-85087-5 Subj: Animals – babies. Animals – pigs. Counting, numbers. Format, unusual – board books.

Olivia saves the circus ill. by author. Atheneum, 2001. ISBN 0-689-82954-X Subj: Animals – pigs. Circus. School.

Olivia's opposites ill. by author. Atheneum, 2002. ISBN 0-689-85088-3 Subj: Animals – babies. Animals – pigs. Behavior. Concepts – opposites. Format, unusual – board books.

Falda, Dominique. *The treasure chest* trans. by Rosemary Lanning; ill. by author. North-South, 1999. ISBN 0-7358-1050-8 Subj: Animals. Animals – squirrels. Friendship.

Falk, Barbara Bustetter. *Grusha* ill. by author. HarperCollins, 1993. ISBN 0-06-021300-0 Subj: Animals – bears. Character traits – kindness to animals. Circus. Foreign lands – Russia.

Falla, Dominique. *Woodlore* (Miller, Cameron)

Falloon, Jane. *Thumbelina* (Andersen, H. C. [Hans Christian])

Falls, C. B. (Charles Buckles). *ABC book* ill. by author. Morrow, 1998. ISBN 0-688-14712-7 Subj: ABC books.

Falwell, Cathryn. *Christmas for 10* ill. by author. Clarion, 1998. ISBN 0-395-85581-0 Subj: Counting, numbers. Ethnic groups in the U.S. – African Americans. Holidays – Christmas. Rhyming text.

Clowning around ill. by author. Watts, 1991. ISBN 0-531-08552-X Subj: Circus. Concepts – shape. Language.

David's drawing ill. by author. Lee & Low, 2001. ISBN 1-58430-031-0 Subj: Activities – drawing. Ethnic groups in the U.S. – African Americans. Friendship. School – first day.

Dragon tooth ill. by author. Clarion, 1996. ISBN 0-395-56916-8 Subj: Dragons. Family life – fathers. Teeth.

Feast for ten ill. by author. Clarion, 1993. ISBN 0-395-62037-6 Subj: Activities – baking, cooking. Counting, numbers. Ethnic groups in the U.S. – African Americans. Family life. Rhyming text.

Nicky and Alex ill. by author. Houghton Mifflin, 1992. ISBN 0-395-56915-X Subj: Activities – making things. Activities – playing. Babies. Family life – brothers. Format, unusual.

Nicky and grandpa ill. by author. Houghton Mifflin, 1991. ISBN 0-395-56917-6 Subj: Activities – playing. Babies. Family life – grandfathers. Format, unusual.

Nicky loves daddy ill. by author. Houghton Mifflin, 1992. ISBN 0-395-60820-1 Subj: Activities – walking. Babies. Family life – fathers. Format, unusual. Senses.

Nicky, 1-2-3 ill. by author. Houghton Mifflin, 1991. ISBN 0-395-56913-3 Subj: Babies. Counting, numbers. Format, unusual.

Nicky's walk ill. by author. Houghton Mifflin, 1991. ISBN 0-395-56914-1 Subj: Activities – walking. Babies. Concepts – color. Family life – mothers. Format, unusual.

P.J. & Puppy ill. by author. Clarion, 1997. ISBN 0-395-56918-4 Subj: Animals – dogs. Family life – mothers. Pets. Toilet training.

Shape space ill. by author. Clarion, 1992. ISBN 0-395-61305-1 Subj: Concepts – shape. Rhyming text.

Turtle splash! ill. by author. Greenwillow, 2001. ISBN 0-06-029463-9 Subj: Counting, numbers. Reptiles – turtles, tortoises. Rhyming text.

We have a baby ill. by author. Clarion, 1993. ISBN 0-395-62038-4 Subj: Babies. Family life.

Where's Nicky? ill. by author. Houghton Mifflin, 1991. ISBN 0-395-56936-2 Subj: Activities – playing. Babies. Format, unusual. Games.

Word wizard ill. by author. Clarion, 1998. ISBN 0-395-85580-2 Subj: Imagination. Language.

Fancher, Lou. *The quest for the One Big Thing* ill. by Steve Johnson & Lou Fancher. Disney Pr., 1998. ISBN 0-7868-5091-4 Subj: Counting, numbers. Insects – ants.

The velveteen rabbit: or, How toys became real (Bianco, Margery Williams)

Fanelli, Sara. *Button* ill. by author. Little, 1994. ISBN 0-316-27393-7 Subj: Circular tales. Clothing.

The doggy book ill. by author. Running Pr., 1998. ISBN 0-7624-0345-4 Subj: Animals – dogs.

My map book ill. by author. HarperCollins, 1995. ISBN 0-06-026456-X Subj: Format, unusual. Maps.

Fanshawe, Elizabeth. *Rachel* ill. by Michael Charlton. Dutton, 1975. ISBN 0-370-10783-7 Subj: Handicaps. School.

Farber, Erica. *Ooey gooey* by Erica Farber & J. R. Sansevere. Random House, 1998. ISBN 0-679-98991-9 Subj: Food. Pirates. Rhyming text. Teeth.

Farber, Norma. *All those mothers at the manger* ill. by Megan Lloyd. Harper, 1985. ISBN 0-06-021870-3 Subj: Animals. Birth. Family life – mothers. Holidays – Christmas. Religion – Nativity. Rhyming text.

As I was crossing Boston Common ill. by Arnold Lobel. Dutton, 1975. ISBN 0-525-25960-0 Subj: ABC books. Animals. Poetry.

The boy who longed for a lift ill. by Brian Selznick. Geringer, 1997. ISBN 0-06-027109-4 Subj: Behavior – needing someone. Behavior – running away. Family life. Rhyming text.

How does it feel to be old? ill. by Trina Schart Hyman. Dutton, 1988, 1979. ISBN 0-525-44367-3 Subj: Family life – grandparents. Old age.

How the hibernators came to Bethlehem ill. by Barbara Cooney. Walker, 1980. ISBN 0-8027-8313-9 Subj: Animals. Holidays – Christmas. Poetry. Religion.

How the left-behind beasts built Ararat ill. by Antonio Frasconi. Walker, 1978. ISBN 0-8027-6314-6 Subj: Animals. Boats, ships. Poetry. Problem solving. Religion – Noah. Weather – floods. Weather – rain.

How to ride a tiger ill. by Claire Schumacher. Houghton Mifflin, 1983. ISBN 0-395-34553-7 Subj: Animals. Animals – tigers. Poetry.

I swim an ocean in my sleep ill. by Elivia Savadier. Holt, 1997. ISBN 0-8050-3381-5 Subj: Dreams. Rhyming text. Sea & seashore.

Never say ugh to a bug ill. by José Aruego. Greenwillow, 1979. ISBN 0-688-84140-6 Subj: Insects. Poetry.

Return of the shadows ill. by Andrea Baruffi. HarperCollins, 1992. ISBN 0-06-020518-0 Subj: Behavior – running away. Holidays – Groundhog Day. Shadows.

Small wonders ill. by Kazue Mizumura. Coward, 1979. ISBN 0-698-20484-0 Subj: Poetry.

There goes feathertop! ill. by Marc Brown. Unicorn-Dutton, 1979. ISBN 0-525-29667-0 Subj: Behavior – imitation. Poetry. Scarecrows.

There once was a woman who married a man ill. by Lydia Dabcovich. Addison-Wesley, 1978. ISBN 0-20-101947-7 Subj: Humorous stories. Noise, sounds. Poetry.

Up the down elevator ill. by Annie Gusman. Addison-Wesley, 1979. ISBN 0-201-01924-8 Subj: Counting, numbers. Elevators, escalators. Poetry.

When it snowed that night ill. by Petra Mathers. HarperCollins, 1993. ISBN 0-06-021708-1 Subj: Animals. Holidays – Christmas. Poetry. Religion.

Where's Gomer? ill. by William Pène Du Bois. Dutton, 1974. ISBN 0-525-42590-X Subj: Behavior – lost. Boats, ships. Poetry. Religion – Noah. Weather – floods. Weather – rain.

Without wings, mother, how can I fly? ill. by Keiko Narahashi. Holt, 1998. ISBN 0-8050-3380-7 Subj: Animals. Family life – mothers. Rhyming text.

Farber, Werner. *Night lion* trans. from German by Jane Fior; ill. by Barbara Mossman. Houghton Mifflin, 1991. ISBN 0-395-57816-7 Subj: Emotions – fear. Night. Sleep. Toys.

Farge, Phyllis La. *see* La Farge, Phyllis

Farge, Sheila La. *see* La Farge, Sheila

Farish, Terry. *The cat who liked potato soup* ill. by Barry Root. Candlewick, 2003. ISBN 0-7636-0834-3 Subj: Animals – cats. Food. Friendship. Pets. Sports – fishing.

Farjeon, Eleanor. *Around the seasons: poems* ill. by Jane Paton. Walck, 1969. ISBN 0-8098-1143-X Subj: Poetry. Seasons.

Between the earth and sun ill. by Catherine Deeter. HarperCollins, 1996. ISBN 0-06-020796-5 Subj: Nature. Poetry.

Cats ill. by T. Lewis. Contemporary Books, 1989. ISBN 0-8092-4354-7 Subj: Animals – cats. Format, unusual – board books. Poetry.

Cats sleep anywhere ill. by Mary Price Jenkins. Lippincott, 1990. ISBN 0-397-32464-2 Subj: Animals – cats. Poetry.

Cats sleep anywhere ill. by Anne Mortimer. HarperCollins, 1996. ISBN 0-06-027335-6 Subj: Animals – cats. Poetry.

Mr. Garden ill. by Jane Paton. Walck, 1966. Subj: Gardens, gardening. Seasons – summer.

Morning has broken ill. by Tim Ladwig. Eerdmans, 1996. ISBN 0-8028-5127-4 Subj: Family life – grandfathers. Morning. Songs.

Mrs. Malone ill. by Edward Ardizzone. Walck, 1962. Subj: Character traits – generosity. Rhyming text.

Farley, Carol J. *The king's secret* ill. by Robert Jew. HarperCollins, 2001. ISBN 0-688-12777-0 Subj: ABC books. Behavior – secrets. Foreign lands – Korea. Foreign languages. Royalty – kings.

Mr. Pak buys a story Ill. by Benrei Huang. A. Whitman, 1997. ISBN 0-8075-5178-3 Subj: Activities – storytelling. Folk & fairy tales. Foreign lands – Korea.

Farley, Jacqui. *Giant hiccups* ill. by Pamela Venus. G. Stevens, 1998. ISBN 0-8368-2090-8 Subj: Giants. Hiccups.

Farley, Walter. *Black stallion: an easy-to-read adaptation* ill. by Sandy Rabinowitz. Random House, 1986. ISBN 0-394-96876-X Subj: Animals – horses, ponies. Islands.

Farm animals photos by Philip Dowell & others. Macmillan, 1991. ISBN 0-689-71403-3 Subj: Animals. Farms.

Farm animals photos sel. by Debby Slier. Macmillan, 1988. ISBN 0-02-688752-5 Subj: Animals. Format, unusual – board books.

Farm house ill. by Zokeisha; ed. by Kate Klimo. S&S, 1983. ISBN 0-671-46130-3 Subj: Animals. Farms. Format, unusual – board books. Homes, houses.

Farmer, Bonnie. *Isaac's dreamcatcher* ill. by Anouk Perusse-Bell. Lobster, 2001. ISBN 1-894222-46-6 Subj: Dreams. Emotions – fear. Indians of North America.

Farmer, Nancy. *Runnery granary* ill. by Jos. A. Smith. Greenwillow, 1996. ISBN 0-688-14188-3 Subj: Behavior – stealing. Family life – grandmothers. Mythical creatures – gnomes.

Farmer, Patti. *What's he doing now?* ill. by Janet Wilson. Firefly, 1998. ISBN 1-55209-220-8 Subj: Family life – brothers & sisters.

A farmer boy birthday adapt. from the Little house books by Laura Ingalls Wilder; ill. by Jody Wheeler. HarperCollins, 1998. ISBN 0-06-027477-8 Subj: Birthdays. Careers – farmers. U.S. history – frontier & pioneer life.

The farmer in the dell. *The farmer in the dell* ill. by John O'Brien. Boyds Mills, 2000. ISBN 1-56397-775-3 Subj: Careers – farmers. Farms. Games. Music. Songs.

The farmer in the dell ed. by Ann Fay; ill. by Kathy Parkinson. A. Whitman, 1988. ISBN 0-8075-2271-6 Subj: Careers – farmers. Farms. Games. Music. Songs.

The farmer in the dell ill. by Mary Maki Rae. Viking, 1988. ISBN 0-670-81853-4 Subj: Careers – farmers. Farms. Games. Music. Songs.

The farmer in the dell ill. by Diane Stanley. Little, 1978. ISBN 0-316-98889-8 Subj: Careers – farmers. Farms. Games. Music. Songs.

The farmer in the dell ill. by Alexandra Wallner. Holiday, 1998. ISBN 0-8234-1382-9 Subj: Careers – farmers. Farms. Games. Music. Songs.

Farndon, John. *It's just a game* ill. by John Emil Cymerman. Boyds Mills, 1999. ISBN 1-56397-785-0 Subj: Sports – soccer. Sportsmanship.

Farris, Pamela J. *Young Mouse and Elephant* ill. by Valeri Gorbachev. Houghton Mifflin, 1996. ISBN 0-395-73977-2 Subj: Animals. Animals – elephants. Animals – mice. Behavior – boasting. Folk & fairy tales. Foreign lands – Africa.

Fass, David E. *The shofar that lost its voice* ill. by Marlene Lobell Ruthen. UAHC Pr., 1982. ISBN 0-8074-0168-4 Subj: Jewish culture. Religion.

Fassler, David. *What's a virus, anyway? the kids' book about aids* ill. by Kelly McQueen. Waterfront Bks., 1990. ISBN 0-914525-14-X Subj: Health & fitness. Illness.

Fassler, Joan. *All alone with daddy* ill. by Dorothy Lake Gregory. Behavioral, 1969. ISBN 0-87705-009-0 Subj: Family life – fathers.

Boy with a problem ill. by Stuart [i.e. Stewart] Kranz. Behavioral, 1971. ISBN 0-87705-054-6 Subj: Friendship. Problem solving.

Don't worry dear ill. by Stuart [i.e. Stewart] Kranz. Behavioral, 1971. ISBN 0-87705-055-4 Subj: Behavior – growing up. Ethnic groups in the U.S. – African Americans.

Howie helps himself ill. by Joe Lasker. A. Whitman, 1975. ISBN 0-8075-3422-6 Subj: Handicaps.

The man of the house ill. by Peter Landa. Behavioral, 1969. ISBN 0-87705-010-4 Subj: Behavior – growing up. Dragons. Family life – mothers. Monsters.

My grandpa died today ill. by Stuart [i.e. Stewart] Kranz. Behavioral, 1971. ISBN 0-87705-053-8 Subj: Death. Emotions – grief. Family life – grandfathers. Jewish culture. Old age.

One little girl ill. by M. Jane Smyth. Behavioral, 1969. ISBN 0-87705-008-2 Subj: Family life. Handicaps – mental handicaps.

Fast rolling fire trucks ill. by Carolyn Bracken. Grosset, 1984. ISBN 0-448-09876-8 Subj: Careers – firefighters. Format, unusual – board books. Trucks.

Fast rolling work trucks ill. by Alan Singer. Grosset, 1984. ISBN 0-448-09877-6 Subj: Format, unusual – board books. Trucks.

The fat cat ill. by Jack Kent. Parents' Magazine Pr., 1971. Translated from the Danish by Jack Kent. ISBN 0-819-30454-9 Subj: Animals – cats. Cumulative tales.

Fatio, Louise. *Anna, the horse* ill. by Roger Antoine Duvoisin. Atheneum, 1951. Subj: Animals – horses, ponies. Holidays – Christmas.

The happy lion ill. by Roger Antoine Duvoisin. Knopf, 2004. Orig. pub. by McGraw-Hill, 1954. ISBN 0-375-92759-X Subj: Animals – lions. Foreign lands – France. Friendship. Zoos.

The happy lion and the bear ill. by Roger Antoine Duvoisin. McGraw-Hill, 1964. Subj: Animals – bears. Animals – lions. Character traits – appearance. Foreign lands – France. Zoos.

The happy lion in Africa ill. by Roger Antoine Duvoisin. McGraw-Hill, 1955. Subj: Animals – lions. Foreign lands – Africa. Foreign lands – France. Zoos.

The happy lion roars ill. by Roger Antoine Duvoisin. McGraw-Hill, 1957. Subj: Animals – lions. Emotions – loneliness. Foreign lands – France. Zoos.

The happy lion's quest ill. by Roger Antoine Duvoisin. McGraw-Hill, 1961. Subj: Animals – lions. Foreign lands – France.

The happy lion's rabbits ill. by Roger Antoine Duvoisin. McGraw-Hill, 1974. ISBN 0-07-020068-9 Subj: Animals – lions. Animals – rabbits. Character traits – kindness. Foreign lands – France. Zoos.

The happy lion's treasure ill. by Roger Antoine Duvoisin. McGraw-Hill, 1970. Subj: Animals – lions. Emotions – love. Foreign lands – France. Zoos.

The happy lion's vacation ill. by Roger Antoine Duvoisin. McGraw-Hill, 1967. Subj: Activities – vacationing. Animals – lions.

Hector and Christina ill. by Roger Antoine Duvoisin. McGraw-Hill, 1977. ISBN 0-07-020073-4 Subj: Birds – penguins. Character traits – freedom. Friendship. Zoos.

Hector penguin ill. by Roger Antoine Duvoisin. McGraw-Hill, 1973. ISBN 0-07-020066-1 Subj: Birds – penguins. Character traits – individuality.

Marc and Pixie and the walls in Mrs. Jones's garden ill. by Roger Antoine Duvoisin. McGraw-Hill, 1975. ISBN 0-07-020039-4 Subj: Animals – cats. Gardens, gardening.

The red bantam ill. by Roger Antoine Duvoisin. McGraw-Hill, 1963. Subj: Animals – foxes. Birds – chickens. Character traits – bravery. Farms.

The three happy lions ill. by Roger Antoine Duvoisin. McGraw-Hill, 1959. Subj: Animals – lions. Foreign lands – France. Zoos.

Fauchald, Nick. *Batter up! You can play softball* ill. by Ronnie Rooney. Picture Window, 2006. ISBN 1-4048-1152-4 Subj: Sports – baseball.

Bump! set! spike! You can play volleyball ill. by Ronnie Rooney. Picture Window, 2006. ISBN 1-4048-1153-2 Subj: Sports – volleyball.

Face off! You can play hockey ill. by Ronnie Rooney. Picture Window, 2006. ISBN 1-4048-1154-0 Subj: Sports – hockey.

Jump ball! You can play basketball ill. by Bill Dickson. Picture Window, 2004. ISBN 1-4048-0261-4 Subj: Sports – basketball.

Nice hit! You can play baseball ill. by Bill Dickson. Picture Window, 2004. ISBN 1-4048-0259-2 Subj: Sports – baseball.

Score! You can play soccer ill. by Bill Dickson. Picture Window, 2004. ISBN 1-4048-0262-2 Subj: Sports – soccer.

Tee off! You can play golf ill. by Ronnie Rooney. Picture Window, 2006. ISBN 1-4048-1155-9 Subj: Sports – golf.

Touchdown! You can play football ill. by Bill Dickson. Picture Window, 2004. ISBN 1-4048-0260-6 Subj: Sports – football.

Faulkenberry, Lauren. *What do animals do on the weekend?* ill. by author. Novello, 2002. ISBN 0-9708972-4-3 Subj: ABC books. Activities. Animals.

Faulkner, Anne Irvin. *see* Faulkner, Nancy

Faulkner, Keith. *Amble has a dream* ill. by Jonathan Lambert. Price Stern Sloan, 1994. ISBN 0-8431-3653-7 Subj: Dinosaurs. Dreams. Format, unusual – toy & movable books.

Basil Rattlebones ill. by Jonathan Lambert. Barron's, 1997. ISBN 0-8120-6604-9 Subj: Anatomy – skeletons.

Bertie's big blue binoculars ill. by Jo Davies. Barron's, 1996. ISBN 0-8120-6568-9 Subj: Birthdays. Format, unusual – toy & movable books. Senses – sight.

Butterfly ill. by Jonathan Lambert. HarperFestival, 1993. ISBN 0-694-00463-4 Subj: Format, unusual – toy & movable books. Insects – butterflies, caterpillars.

Charlie Chimp's Christmas ill. by Jonathan Lambert. Barron's, 2002. ISBN 0-7641-5556-3 Subj: Animals – chimpanzees. Format, unusual – toy & movable books. Holidays – Christmas. Santa Claus.

David dreaming of dinosaurs ill. by Jonathan Lambert. W. J. Fantasy, 1992. ISBN 1-56021-182-2 Subj: Dinosaurs. Format, unusual – toy & movable books. Museums. Prehistory. Rhyming text.

Do you have my quack? ill. by Rob Hefferan. Scholastic, 2001. ISBN 0-4392-4085-9 Subj: Animals. Birds – ducks. Farms. Format, unusual – toy & movable books. Noise, sounds.

Frog ill. by Jonathan Lambert. HarperFestival, 1993. ISBN 0-694-00464-2 Subj: Format, unusual – toy & movable books. Frogs & toads.

The giraffe who cock-a-doodle-doo'd ill. by Jonathan Lamber. Dial, 2002. ISBN 0-8037-2739-9 Subj: Animals. Format, unusual – toy & movable books. Jungle.

Hector Specter ill. by Jonathan Lambert. Barron's, 1997. ISBN 0-8120-6605-7 Subj: Friendship. Ghosts.

Jumbled jungle ill. by Jonathan Lambert. Scholastic, 2001. ISBN 0-439-30903-4 Subj: Animals. Format, unusual – toy & movable books. Jungle.

The long-nosed pig: a pop-up book ill. by Jonathan Lambert. Dial, 1998. ISBN 0-8037-2296-6 Subj: Anatomy – noses. Animals – pigs. Format, unusual – toy & movable books.

The monster in my bathroom ill. by Jonathan Lambert. Price Stern Sloan, 1993. ISBN 0-8431-3482-8 Subj: Behavior – misbehavior. Family life. Monsters.

The monster in my toybox ill. by Jonathan Lambert. Price Stern Sloan, 1993. ISBN 0-8431-3481-X Subj: Behavior – misbehavior. Family life. Monsters. Toys.

The monster who loved books ill. by Jonathan Lambert. Orchard, 2002. ISBN 0-439-34099-3 Subj: Books, reading. Format, unusual – toy & movable books. Monsters.

Munch looks for lunch ill. by Jonathan Lambert. Price Stern Sloan, 1994. ISBN 0-8431-3652-9 Subj: Dinosaurs. Format, unusual – toy & movable books.

My first one hundred words in French and English ill. by Paul Johnson. S&S, 1993. ISBN 0-671-86447-5 Subj: Foreign languages. Format, unusual – toy & movable books.

My pets ill. by Jonathan Lambert. St. Martin's, 1987. ISBN 0-312-00968-2 Subj: Animals. Format, unusual – toy & movable books. Pets.

Pop! went another balloon! ill. by Rory Tyger. Dutton, 2002. ISBN 0-525-47122-7 Subj: Counting, numbers. Format, unusual – toy & movable books. Toys – balloons.

The puzzled penguin ill. by Jonathan Lambert. Millbrook, 1999. ISBN 0-7613-1042-8 Subj: Birds – penguins. Foreign lands – Antarctic. Format, unusual – toy & movable books. Self-concept. Weather – cold.

Rexerella ill. by Graham Kennedy; paper engineering by Jonathan Lambert. Little Simon, 2002. ISBN 0-689-85355-6 Subj: Dinosaurs. Format, unusual – toy & movable books.

Rumble frightens himself ill. by Jonathan Lambert. Price Stern Sloan, 1994. ISBN 0-8431-3650-2 Subj: Dinosaurs. Format, unusual – toy & movable books.

Sam at the seaside ill. by Jonathan Lambert. Macmillan, 1988. ISBN 0-689-71183-2 Subj: Format, unusual – toy & movable books. Sea & seashore.

Sam helps out ill. by Jonathan Lambert. Macmillan, 1988. ISBN 0-689-71182-4 Subj: Format, unusual – toy & movable books. Shopping.

The scared little bear ill. by Jonathan Lambert. Orchard, 2000. Subj: Bedtime. Emotions – fear. Format, unusual – toy & movable books.

The snake's mistake ill. by Jonathan Lambert. Price Stern Sloan, 1988. ISBN 0-8431-2370-2 Subj: Reptiles – snakes. Rhyming text.

Swoop flies too high ill. by Jonathan Lambert. Price Stern Sloan, 1994. ISBN 0-8431-3651-0 Subj: Dinosaurs. Format, unusual – toy & movable books.

The tallest shortest longest greenest brownest animal in the jungle! ill. by Rory Tyger. Dutton, 2002. ISBN 0-525-46868-4 Subj: Animals. Format, unusual – toy & movable books. Friendship. Jungle.

This is me ill. by Jonathan Lambert. St. Martin's, 1987. ISBN 0-312-00967-4 Subj: Anatomy. Format, unusual – toy & movable books.

A trick or a treat? ill. by Manhar Chauhan. Dutton, 2001. ISBN 0-525-46765-3 Subj: Format, unusual – toy & movable books. Holidays – Halloween. Night. Picture puzzles.

Velma Vampire ill. by Jonathan Lambert. Barron's, 1997. ISBN 0-8120-6606-5 Subj: Monsters.

The wide-mouthed frog ill. by Jonathan Lambert. Dial, 1996. ISBN 0-8037-1875-6 Subj: Animals. Food. Format, unusual – toy & movable books. Frogs & toads.

Faulkner, Matt. *The amazing voyage of Jackie Grace* ill. by author. Scholastic, 1987. ISBN 0-590-40713-9 Subj: Activities – bathing. Boats, ships. Imagination. Pirates. Weather – storms.

Faulkner, Nancy. *Small clown* ill. by Paul Galdone. Doubleday, 1960. Subj: Clowns, jesters.

Faulkner, William J. *Brer Tiger and the big wind* ill. by Roberta Wilson. Morrow, 1995. ISBN 0-688-12986-2 Subj: Behavior – greed. Ethnic groups in the U.S. – African Americans. Folk & fairy tales.

Faunce-Brown, Daphne. *Snuffles' house* ill. by Frances Thatcher. Childrens Pr., 1983. ISBN 0-516-08943-9 Subj: Activities. Animals – cats.

Fauteux, Nicole. *Let's try it out in the air* (Simon, Seymour)

Let's try it out in the water (Simon, Seymour)

Fay, Ann. *Boot weather* (Vigna, Judith)

The farmer in the dell (The farmer in the dell)

I wish my daddy didn't drink so much (Vigna, Judith)

Ooops! (Kline, Suzy)

Fay, Hermann. *My zoo* ill. by author. Hubbard Sci., 1972. ISBN 0-833-10013-8 Subj: Animals. Zoos.

Fayon, Lavinia. *see* Russ, Lavinia

Fazio, Brenda Lena. *Grandfather's story* ill. by author. Sasquatch, 1996. ISBN 1-57061-028-2 Subj: Dreams. Family life – grandfathers. Foreign lands – Japan.

Fazzi, Maura. *The circus of mystery* written & ill. by Maura Fazzi & Peter Kühner; trans. by Rosemary Lanning. North-South, 1999. ISBN 0-7358-1169-5 Subj: Anatomy – noses. Circus. Clowns, jesters. Imagination.

Fearnley, Jan. *Just like you* ill. by author. Candlewick, 2001. ISBN 0-7636-1322-3 Subj: Animals – babies. Animals – mice. Bedtime. Family life – parents.

Little Robin's Christmas ill. by author. Little Tiger, 1998. ISBN 1-888444-40-1 Subj: Animals. Birds – robins. Character traits – generosity. Clothing. Holidays – Christmas. Santa Claus.

Mr. Wolf and the three bears ill. by author. Harcourt, 2002. ISBN 0-15-216423-5 Subj: Activities – baking, cooking. Animals – bears. Animals – wolves. Birthdays.

Mr. Wolf's pancakes ill. by author. Tiger Tales, 2001. ISBN 1-888444-76-2 Subj: Activities – baking, cooking. Animals – wolves. Food.

A perfect day for it ill. by author. Harcourt, 2002. ISBN 0-15-216634-3 Subj: Animals. Animals – bears. Friendship. Sports – sledding. Weather – snow.

A special something ill. by author. Hyperion, 2000. ISBN 0-7868-0589-7 Subj: Babies. Birth. Family life. Family life – new sibling. Imagination.

Watch out! ill. by author. Candlewick, 2004. ISBN 0-7636-2318-0 Subj: Animals – mice. Behavior. Family life – mothers.

Fearrington, Ann. *Who sees the lighthouse?* ill. by Giles Laroche. Putnam, 2002. ISBN 0-399-23703-8 Subj: Counting, numbers. Lighthouses. Rhyming text.

Fecher, Sarah. *On the move* written & ed. by Sarah Fecher & Deborah Kespert; story by Belinda Webster; ill. by Gaëtan Evrard; computer ill. by Jon Stuart. Two-Can, 2000. ISBN 1-58728-605-X Subj: Transportation.

Wild animals written & ed. by Sarah Fecher & Deborah Kespert; story by Belinda Webster; ill. with photos. Two-Can, 1998. ISBN 0-71667-707-5 Subj: Animals. Foreign lands – Africa.

Fechner, Amrei. *I am a little dog* trans. from German by Robert Kimber; ill. by author. Barron's, 1983. ISBN 0-8120-5514-4 Subj: Animals – dogs. Format, unusual – board books.

I am a little elephant ill. by author. Barron's, 1983. ISBN 0-8120-5512-2 Subj: Animals – elephants. Format, unusual – board books.

I am a little lion ill. by author. Barron's, 1983. ISBN 0-8120-5516-0 Subj: Animals – lions. Format, unusual – board books.

Feczko, Kathy. *Halloween party* ill. by Blanche Sims. Troll, 1985. ISBN 0-8167-0354-X Subj: Holidays – Halloween. Parties.

Umbrella parade ill. by Deborah Borgo. Troll, 1985. ISBN 0-8167-0356-6 Subj: Animals. Parades. Umbrellas.

Feder, Harriet K. *Not yet, Elijah!* ill. by Joan Halpern. Kar-Ben Copies, 1989. ISBN 0-930494-95-4 Subj: Holidays – Passover. Jewish culture. Religion. Rhyming text.

What can you do with a bagel? ill. by Sally Springer. Kar-Ben Copies, 1992. ISBN 0-929371-59-3 Subj: Activities – baking, cooking. Food. Jewish culture.

Feder, Jane. *Beany* ill. by Karen Gundersheimer. Pantheon, 1979. ISBN 0-394-93734-1 Subj: Animals – cats.

Table, chair, bear: a book in many languages ill. by author. Ticknor & Fields, 1995. ISBN 0-395-65938-8 Subj: Foreign languages.

Feder, Paula Kurzband. *Where does the teacher live?* ill. by Lillian Hoban. Dutton, 1979. ISBN 0-525-42586-1 Subj: Careers – teachers. Homes, houses. Problem solving. School.

Feelings, Muriel. *Jambo means hello: Swahili alphabet book* ill. by Tom Feelings. Dial, 1974. ISBN 0-8037-4346-7 Subj: ABC books. Caldecott award honor books. Foreign lands – Africa. Foreign languages.

Menjo means one: Swahili counting book ill. by Tom Feelings. Dial, 1972. ISBN 0-8037-5711-5 Subj: Caldecott award honor books. Counting, numbers. Foreign lands – Africa. Foreign languages.

Feelings, Tom. *Something on my mind* (Grimes, Nikki)

Feeney, Stephanie. *Hawaii is a rainbow* photos by Jeff Reese. Kolowalu Books, 1985. ISBN 0-8248-1007-4 Subj: Concepts – color.

Fehlner, Paul. *Dog and cat* ill. by Maxie Chambliss. Childrens Pr., 1990. ISBN 0-516-05353-1 Subj: Animals – cats. Animals – dogs. Rhyming text.

Feiffer, Jules. *Bark, George* ill. by author. HarperCollins, 1999. ISBN 0-06-205185-7 Subj: Animals – dogs. Humorous stories. Noise, sounds.

The daddy mountain ill. by author. Hyperion, 2004. ISBN 0-7868-0912-4 Subj: Family life – daughters. Family life – fathers.

I lost my bear ill. by author. Morrow, 1998. ISBN 0-688-15148-5 Subj: Behavior – lost & found possessions. Family life. Toys. Toys – bears.

Meanwhile . . . ill. by author. HarperCollins, 1997. ISBN 0-06-205155-5 Subj: Books, reading. Imagination.

Feilen, John. *see* May, Julian

Feinberg, Harold S. *Snail in the woods* (Ryder, Joanne)

Feistel, Sally. *The guinea pigs that went to school* (Meshover, Leonard)

The monkey that went to school (Meshover, Leonard)

Feitlowitz, Marguerite. *Brush* (Calders, Pere)

Feldman, Barbara. *Going, going* ill. by author. Firefly, 1989. ISBN 1-55037-045-6 Subj: Activities – traveling. Automobiles. Family life – mothers.

Stephen's frog ill. by author. Firefly, 1991. ISBN 1-55037-200-9 Subj: Family life – grandparents. Farms. Frogs & toads. Pets. Wordless.

Feldman, Eve B. *Animals don't wear pajamas* ill. by Mary Beth Owens. Holt, 1992. ISBN 0-8050-1710-0 Subj: Animals. Bedtime. Ethnic groups in the U.S. Sleep.

Birthdays! celebrating life around the world ill. with children's art provided by Paintbrush Diplomacy. BridgeWater, 1996. ISBN 0-8167-3494-1 Subj: Art. Birthdays. Children as illustrators. Foreign lands.

Feldman, Jacqueline. *The lavender box* ill. by Nannette Hoffman. Ellicott, 1990. ISBN 0-9623903-0-5 Subj: Poetry.

Feldman, Judy. *The alphabet in nature* ill. with photos. Childrens Pr., 1991. ISBN 0-516-05101-6 Subj: ABC books. Nature. Wordless.

Shapes in nature ill. with photos. Childrens Pr., 1991. ISBN 0-516-05102-4 Subj: Concepts – shape. Nature. Wordless.

Feldman, Thea. *Who you callin' chicken?* photos by Stephen Green-Armytage. Abrams, 2003. ISBN 0-8109-4593-2 Subj: Birds – chickens.

Feldmann, Roseann. *Levers* (Walker, Sally M.)

Félix, Monique. *The further adventures of the little mouse trapped in a book* ill. by author. Green Tiger Pr., 1984. ISBN 0-88138-009-1 Subj: Animals – mice. Imagination. Wordless.

The story of a little mouse trapped in a book ill. by author. Green Tiger Pr., 1980. ISBN 0-914676-52-0 Subj: Animals – mice. Imagination. Wordless.

Fellows, Rebecca Nevers. *A lei for Tutu* ill. by Linda Finch. A. Whitman, 1998. ISBN 0-8075-4426-4 Subj: Family life – grandmothers. Flowers. Hawaii.

Felt, Sue. *Hello-goodbye* ill. by author. Doubleday, 1960. Subj: Friendship. Moving.

Rosa-too-little ill. by author. Doubleday, 1950. Subj: Activities – writing. Behavior – growing up. Ethnic groups in the U.S. – Mexican Americans. Family life. Libraries.

Felton, Harold W. *Pecos Bill and the mustang* ill. by Leonard W. Shortall. Prentice-Hall, 1965. ISBN 0-13-655597-7 Subj: Animals – horses, ponies. Cowboys, cowgirls. Tall tales. U.S. history – frontier & pioneer life.

Fender, Kay. *Odette! a bird in Paris* ill. by Philippe Dumas. Prentice-Hall, 1978. ISBN 0-13-630525-3 Subj: Birds. Foreign lands – France. Old age.

Fenner, Carol. *Christmas tree on the mountain* ill. by author. Harcourt, 1966. Subj: Holidays – Christmas. Trees.

Tigers in the cellar ill. by author. Harcourt, 1963. Subj: Animals – tigers. Imagination. Night.

Fenton, Edward. *The big yellow balloon* ill. by Ib Spang Olsen. Doubleday, 1967. Subj: Cumulative tales. Humorous stories. Toys – balloons.

Fierce John ill. by William Pène Du Bois. Doubleday, 1969, c1959. ISBN 0-03-072925-4 Subj: Family life. Imagination.

Fenton, Stephen H. *Who will pick me up when I fall?* (Molnar, Dorothy E.)

Ferguson, Alane. *That new pet!* ill. by Catherine Stock. Lothrop, 1986. ISBN 0-688-05516-8 Subj: Babies. Emotions – envy, jealousy. Pets.

Ferguson, Don. *Winnie the Pooh's A to Zzzz* ill. by Bill Langley & Diana Wakeman. Walt Disney, 1992. ISBN 1-56282-015-X Subj: ABC books. Format, unusual – toy & movable books. Rhyming text. Toys – bears.

Ferguson, Richard. *Bruce the balding moose* (Mellor, Corinne)

Fern, Eugene. *Birthday presents* ill. by author. Farrar, 1967. Includes the song Sing me (2 p.). Subj: Birthdays. Gifts. Songs.

The king who was too busy ill. by author. Ariel, 1966. Subj: Royalty – kings.

The most frightened hero ill. by author. Coward, 1961. Subj: Character traits – bravery. Foreign lands – Scotland.

Pepito's story ill. by author. Ariel, 1960. ISBN 1-878274-04-X Subj: Activities – dancing. Character traits – being different. Illness.

What's he been up to now? ill. by author. Dial, 1961. Subj: Animals – elephants. Friendship.

Fernandes, Eugenie. *Big week for little mouse* ill. by Kim Fernandes. Kids Can, 2004. ISBN 1-55337-665-X Subj: Animals – mice. Birthdays. Concepts – opposites. Days of the week, months of the year. Rhyming text.

Busy Little Mouse ill. by Kim Fernandes; photos by Pat Lacroix. Kids Can, 2002. ISBN 1-55074-776-2 Subj: Animals. Animals – mice. Farms. Noise, sounds. Rhyming text.

A difficult day ill. by author. Kids Can, 1999. ISBN 0-921103-17-4 Subj: Behavior – bad day.

Sleepy little mouse ill. by Kim Fernandes. Kids Can, 2000. ISBN 1-55074-701-0 Subj: Animals – mice. Behavior. Emotions. Sleep.

Fernandes, Kim. *One gray mouse* (Burton, Katherine)

Visiting granny photos by Pat Lacroix; ill. by author. Firefly, 1990. ISBN 1-55037-077-4 Subj: Family life – grandmothers. Food.

Ferns, Ronald. *Osbert and Lucy* ill. by author. HarperCollins, 1989. ISBN 0-06-021836-3 Subj: Animals – dogs. Animals – rabbits. Behavior – running away. Friendship.

Ferraro, Renato. *Alex, the amazing juggler* (Gianni, Peg)

Ferro, Beatriz. *Caught in the rain* ill. by Michele Sambin. Doubleday, 1980. ISBN 0-385-15625-1 Subj: Weather – rain.

Fichter, George S. *Bees, wasps, and ants* ill. by Kristin Kest. Western, 1993. ISBN 0-307-61434-4 Subj: Insects – ants. Insects – bees. Insects – wasps.

Fiday, Beverly. *Time to go* by Beverly & David Fiday; ill. by Thomas B. Allen. Harcourt, 1990. ISBN 0-15-200608-7 Subj: Family life. Farms. Moving.

Fiday, David. *Time to go* (Fiday, Beverly)

Fiddle-i-fee: a traditional American chant ill. by Diane Stanley. Little, 1979. ISBN 0-316-81040-0 Subj: Animals. Cumulative tales. Folk & fairy tales.

Field, Edward. *Magic words: poems* based on songs & stories of the Netsilik Inuit, collected by Knud Rasmussen; ill. by Stefano Vitale. Harcourt, 1998. ISBN 0-15-201498-5 Subj: Creation. Folk & fairy tales. Indians of North America – Inuit. Poetry.

Field, Eugene. *The gingham dog and the calico cat* ill. by Janet Street. Philomel, 1990. ISBN 0-399-22151-4 Subj: Animals – cats. Animals – dogs. Behavior – fighting, arguing. Poetry. Toys.

The gingham dog and the calico cat ill. by Johanna Westerman. North-South, 1994. ISBN 1-55858-292-4 Subj: Animals – cats. Animals – dogs. Behavior – fighting, arguing. Poetry. Toys.

Wynken, Blynken and Nod ill. by Barbara Cooney. Hastings House, 1964. ISBN 0-80388-046-4 Subj: Poetry. Sea & seashore. Sleep.

Wynken, Blynken and Nod ill. by Susan Jeffers. Dutton, 1982. ISBN 0-525-44022-4 Subj: Poetry. Sea & seashore. Sleep.

Wynken, Blynken and Nod ill. by Holly Johnson. Warne, 1973. ISBN 0-723-26100-8 Subj: Poetry. Sea & seashore. Sleep.

Wynken, Blynken and Nod ill. by Johanna Westerman. North-South, 1995. ISBN 1-55858-423-4 Subj: Poetry. Sea & seashore. Sleep.

Field, Rachel Lyman. *General store* ill. by Giles Laroche. Little, 1988. ISBN 0-316-28163-8 Subj: Poetry. Stores.

General store ill. by Nancy Winslow Parker. Greenwillow, 1988. ISBN 0-688-07354-9 Subj: Poetry. Stores.

If once you have slept on an island ill. by Iris Van Rynbach. Boyds Mills, 1993. ISBN 1-56397-106-2 Subj: Islands. Poetry.

Prayer for a child ill. by Elizabeth Orton Jones. Macmillan, 1944. ISBN 0-02-735190-4 Subj: Caldecott award books. Religion.

A road might lead to anywhere ill. by Giles Laroche. Little, 1990. ISBN 0-316-28178-6 Subj: Activities – traveling. Animals – mice. Dreams. Rhyming text. Roads.

Field, Susan. *The sun, the moon, and the silver baboon* ill. by author. HarperCollins, 1993. ISBN 0-06-022991-8 Subj: Animals – baboons. Concepts – color. Night. Stars. Sun.

Fields, Sadie. *Hidden numbers* (Holmes, Stephen)

Fienberg, Anna. *Joseph* ill. by Kim Gamble. Allen & Unwin, 2001. ISBN 1-86448-173-0 Subj: Clothing – coats. Emotions – envy, jealousy. Family life – fathers. Family life – sons. Religion.

Fierstein, Harvey. *The sissy duckling* ill. by Henry Cole. S&S, 2002. ISBN 0-689-83566-3 Subj: Birds – ducks. Gender roles. Self-concept.

Fife, Dale. *Adam's ABC* ill. by Don Robertson. Coward, 1971. Subj: ABC books. Cities, towns. Ethnic groups in the U.S. – African Americans.

Empty lot ill. by Jim Arnosky. Little, 1991. ISBN 0-316-28167-0 Subj: Nature. Progress.

The little park ill. by Janet LaSalle. A. Whitman, 1973. ISBN 0-8075-4634-8 Subj: Animals. Ecology. Parks. Progress.

Rosa's special garden ill. by Marie DeJohn. A. Whitman, 1985. ISBN 0-8075-7115-6 Subj: Ethnic groups in the U.S. – Mexican Americans. Gardens, gardening. Sibling rivalry.

Fifield, Flora. *Pictures for the palace* ill. by Nola Langner. Vanguard, 1957. Subj: Art. Foreign lands – Japan.

Figley, Marty Rhodes. *Noah's wife* ill. by Anita Riggio. Eerdmans, 1998. ISBN 0-8028-5107-X Subj: Boats, ships. Family life. Religion – Noah. Weather – floods. Weather – rain.

The schoolchildren's blizzard ill. by Shelly O. Haas. Carolrhoda, 2004. ISBN 1-57505-586-4 Subj: Careers – teachers. Family life – sisters. U.S. history. Weather – blizzards.

The story of Zacchaeus ill. by Cat Bowman Smith. Eerdmans, 1995. ISBN 0-8028-5092-8 Subj: Foreign lands – Middle East. Religion.

Figueredo, D. H. *When this world was new* ill. by Enrique O. Sánchez. Lee & Low, 1999. ISBN 1-880000-86-5 Subj: Emotions – fear. Ethnic groups in the U.S. – Hispanic Americans. Family life. Immigrants. Moving. Weather – snow.

Filleul, Liz. *Tumbler* ill. by Susan Field. Augsburg Fortress, 2001. ISBN 0-8066-4268-8 Subj: Careers – acrobats. Religion.

Fillingham, David. *Such a noise!* (Brodmann, Aliana)

Finch, Mary. *The little red hen and the ear of wheat* (The little red hen)

Finchler, Judy. *Miss Malarkey won't be in today* ill. by Kevin O'Malley. Walker, 2000. ISBN 0-8027-8653-7 Subj: Careers – teachers. Illness. School.

Testing Miss Malarkey ill. by Kevin O'Malley. Walker, 2000. ISBN 0-8027-8739-8 Subj: Careers – teachers. School.

You're a good sport, Miss Malarkey ill. by Kevin O'Malley. Walker, 2002. ISBN 0-8027-8816-5 Subj: Careers – coaches. Careers – teachers. Sports – soccer. Sportsmanship.

Findlay, Lisa. *What's in Oscar's trashcan?* ill. by Joe Ewers. Random House, 2002. ISBN 0-375-81580-5 Subj: Behavior – lost & found possessions. Format, unusual – toy & movable books. Puppets.

Findon, Joanne. *Auld lang syne* ill. by Ted Nasmith. Stoddart, 1997. ISBN 0-7737-3006-0 Subj: Careers – writers. Songs.

Fine, Anne. *Poor Monty* ill. by Clara Vulliamy. Houghton Mifflin, 1992. ISBN 0-395-60472-9 Subj: Behavior – needing someone. Careers – doctors. Family life – mothers. Gender roles. Illness – chicken pox.

Fine, Edith Hope. *Under the lemon moon* ill. by René King Moreno. Lee & Low, 1999. ISBN 1-880000-69-5 Subj: Behavior – stealing. Character traits – generosity. Foreign lands – Mexico.

Fine, Howard. *A piggie Christmas* ill. by author. Hyperion, 2000. ISBN 0-7868-2505-7 Subj: Animals – pigs. Holidays – Christmas. Music. Songs.

Fine, Judith. *Princess Lily* (Bazilian, Barbara)

Finfer, Celentha. *Grandmother dear* by Celentha Finfer, Esther Wasserberg & Florence Weinberg; ill. by Roy Mathews. Follett, 1968. Subj: Activities – babysitting. Family life – grandmothers. Poetry.

Fink, Dale Borman. *Mr. Silver and Mrs. Gold* ill. by Shirley Chan. Human Sciences Pr., 1980. ISBN 0-87705-447-9 Subj: Friendship. Old age.

Fink, Joanne. *Mister North Wind* (De Posadas Mane, Carmen)

Finn, Isobel. *The very lazy ladybug* ill. by Jack Tickle. Tiger Tales, 2001. ISBN 1-58925-007-9 Subj: Activities – flying. Animals. Character traits – laziness. Insects – ladybugs.

Finsand, Mary Jane. *The town that moved* ill. by Reg Sandland. Carolrhoda, 1983. ISBN 0-87614-200-5 Subj: Cities, towns. Moving.

Finzel, Julia. *Large as life* ill. by author. Lothrop, 1991. ISBN 0-688-10653-6 Subj: Animals. Concepts – size. Games. Insects – ladybugs.

Fior, Jane. *The lazy beaver* (Gallo, Giovanni)

Night lion (Farber, Werner)

Fire ill. by Michael Ricketts. Grosset, 1972. ISBN 0-448-09659-5 Subj: Fire.

The firebird. *The firebird* retold by Selina Hastings; ill. by Reg Cartwright. Holt, 1994. ISBN 1-56402-096-7 Subj: Ballet. Behavior – stealing. Folk & fairy tales. Foreign lands – Russia. Magic. Mythical creatures. Royalty – princes.

The firebird retold by Margaret Greaves; ill. by Francesca Crespi. Dial, 1986. ISBN 0-8037-0265-5 (set) Subj: Ballet. Behavior – stealing. Folk & fairy tales. Foreign lands – Russia. Magic. Mythical creatures. Royalty – princes.

The firebird retold & ill. by Demi. Holt, 1994. ISBN 0-8050-3244-4 Subj: Ballet. Behavior – stealing. Folk & fairy tales. Foreign lands – Russia. Magic. Mythical creatures. Royalty – princes.

The firebird adapt. & ill. by Rachel Isadora. Putnam, 1994. ISBN 0-399-22510-2 Subj: Ballet. Behavior – stealing. Folk & fairy tales. Foreign lands – Russia. Magic. Mythical creatures. Royalty – princes.

The firebird retold & ill. by Moira Kemp. Godine, 1984. ISBN 0-87923-486-5 Subj: Ballet. Behavior – stealing. Folk & fairy tales. Foreign lands – Russia. Magic. Mythical creatures. Royalty – princes.

The firebird adapt. by Robert D. San Souci; ill. by Kris Waldherr. Dial, 1992. ISBN 0-8037-0800-9 Subj: Ballet. Behavior – stealing. Folk & fairy tales. Foreign lands – Russia. Magic. Mythical creatures. Royalty – princes.

The firebird: and other Russian fairy tales ill. by Boris Zvorykin; ed. by Jacqueline Onassis. Viking, 1978. ISBN 0-670-31544-3 Subj: Ballet. Behavior – stealing. Folk & fairy tales. Foreign lands – Russia. Magic. Mythical creatures. Royalty – princes.

The tale of the firebird ill. by Gennady Spirin. Philomel, 2002. ISBN 0-399-23584-1 Subj: Ballet. Behavior – stealing. Folk & fairy tales. Foreign lands – Russia. Magic. Mythical creatures. Royalty – princes.

Firehouse ed. by Kate Klimo; ill. by Zokeisha. S&S, 1983. ISBN 0-671-46128-1 Subj: Careers – firefighters. Fire. Format, unusual – board books. Homes, houses.

Firmin, Josie. *My week* ill. by author. Candlewick, 2001. ISBN 0-7636-1548-X Subj: Days of the week, months of the year. Format, unusual – toy & movable books.

Firmin, Peter. *Basil Brush and the windmills* ill. by author. Prentice-Hall, 1980. ISBN 0-13-066720-X Subj: Animals – foxes. Animals – moles. Ecology.

Chicken stew ill. by author. Merrimack, 1982. ISBN 0-7207-1299-8 Subj: Animals – wolves. Birds – chickens. Gardens, gardening.

Noggin and the whale (Postgate, Oliver)

Noggin the king (Postgate, Oliver)

First graces ill. by Tasha Tudor. Walck, 1989, c1955. ISBN 0-394-94409-7 Subj: Poetry. Religion.

First prayers ill. by Anna Maria Magagna. Macmillan, 1983. ISBN 0-02-762120-0 Subj: Poetry. Religion.

First prayers ill. by Tasha Tudor. Random House, 1989, c1980. ISBN 0-394-84429-1 Subj: Poetry. Religion.

Fischer, Alexandra E. *Look how a baby grows* (Mantegazza, Giovanna)

Look inside a farm (Mantegazza, Giovanna)

Look inside a rainforest (Mantegazza, Giovanna)

Fischer, Hans. *The birthday* ill. by author. Harcourt, 1954. Subj: Animals. Birthdays.

Puss in boots (Perrault, Charles)

Fischer, Vera Kistiakowsky. *One way is down: a book about gravity* ill. by Ward Brackett. Little, 1967. Subj: Concepts – weight. Science.

Fischer-Nagel, Andreas. *A kitten is born* (Fischer-Nagel, Heiderose)

A puppy is born (Fischer-Nagel, Heiderose)

Fischer-Nagel, Heiderose. *A kitten is born* by Heiderose & Andreas Fischer-Nagel; trans. from German by Andrea Mernan; photos by authors. Putnam, 1983. ISBN 0-399-20961-1 Subj: Animals – cats. Birth. Science.

A puppy is born by Heiderose & Andreas Fischer-Nagel; trans. from German by Andrea Mernan; photos by authors. Putnam, 1985. ISBN 0-399-21234-5 Subj: Animals – dogs. Birth. Science.

Fischetto, Laura. *All pigs on deck: Christopher Columbus's second marvelous voyage* ill. by Letizia Galli. Delacorte, 1991. ISBN 0-385-30440-4 Subj: Animals – pigs. Boats, ships. U.S. history.

Inside Noah's ark ill. by Letizia Galli. Viking, 1989. ISBN 0-670-83028-3 Subj: Animals. Boats, ships. Religion – Noah. Weather – floods. Weather – rain. Weather – rainbows.

The jungle is my home ill. by Letizia Galli. Viking, 1991. ISBN 0-670-83550-1 Subj: Animals. Ecology. Foreign lands – South America. Jungle.

Fischman, Sheila. *The longest home run* (Carrier, Roch)

Old Thomas and the little fairy (Demers, Dominique)

Simon's disguise (Tibo, Gilles)

Fischtrom, Harvey. *see* Zemach, Harve

Fish, Hans. *Pitschi, the kitten who always wanted to do something else* ill. by author. North-South, 1996. ISBN 1-55858-645-8 Subj: Animals – cats. Behavior – dissatisfaction.

Fish, Helen Dean. *Four and twenty blackbirds* ill. by Robert Lawson. Stokes, 1937. Subj: Caldecott award honor books. Nursery rhymes.

When the root children wake up ill. by Sibylle Von Olfers. Lippincott, 1930. Retelling of: Etwas von den Wurzelkindern by Sibylle Olfers. ISBN 0-397-30075-1 Subj: Flowers. Insects. Nature. Seasons – spring.

When the root children wake up ill. by Sibylle Von Olfers. Green Tiger Pr., 1988. Retelling of: Etwas von den Wurzelkindern by Sibylle Olfers. ISBN 0-88138-103-9 Subj: Flowers. Insects. Nature. Seasons – spring.

The fish is me sel. by Neil Philip; ill. by Claire Henley. Clarion, 2002. Subj: Activities – bathing. Poetry.

Fisher, Aileen Lucia. *And a sunflower grew* ill. by Trina Schart Hyman; lettering by Paul Taylor. Noble, 1977. ISBN 0-8372-2394-6 Subj: Flowers. Plants. Rhyming text. Science.

Anybody home? ill. by Susan Bonners. Crowell, 1980. ISBN 0-690-04055-5 Subj: Animals. Character traits – curiosity. Rhyming text.

Arbor day ill. by Nonny Hogrogian. Crowell, 1965. Subj: Holidays. Trees.

As the leaves fall down ill. by Barbara Smith. Noble, 1977. ISBN 0-8372-2397-0 Subj: Plants. Science. Seasons. Trees.

Best little house ill. by Arnold Spilka. Crowell, 1966. Subj: Homes, houses. Moving. Poetry.

Do bears have mothers too? ill. by Eric Carle. Crowell, 1973. ISBN 0-690-00167-3 Subj: Animals. Family life – mothers. Poetry.

Going barefoot ill. by Adrienne Adams. Crowell, 1960. Subj: Rhyming text. Seasons.

The house of a mouse ill. by Joan Sandin. HarperCollins, 1988. ISBN 0-06-021849-5 Subj: Animals – mice. Homes, houses. Poetry.

I like weather ill. by Janina Domanska. Crowell, 1963. Subj: Animals – dogs. Poetry. Weather.

I wonder how, I wonder why ill. by Carol Barker. Abelard-Schuman, 1963. Subj: Poetry.

In one door and out the other: a book of poems ill. by Lillian Hoban. Crowell, 1969. Subj: Family life. Poetry.

In the middle of the night ill. by Adrienne Adams. Crowell, 1965. Subj: Night. Poetry.

Like nothing at all ill. by Leonard Weisgard. Crowell, 1962. ISBN 0-690-49379-7 Subj: Nature. Poetry. Science. Seasons.

Listen, rabbit ill. by Symeon Shimin. Crowell, 1964. Subj: Animals – rabbits. Poetry.

My first Hanukkah book ill. by Priscilla Kiedrowski. Childrens Pr., 1985. ISBN 0-516-42905-1 Subj: Holidays – Hanukkah. Jewish culture. Poetry.

My mother and I ill. by Kazue Mizumura. Crowell, 1967. Subj: Family life – mothers. Poetry. Seasons – spring.

Mysteries in the garden ill. by Ati Forberg; lettering by Paul Taylor. Noble, 1977. ISBN 0-8372-2392-0 Subj: Gardens, gardening. Plants. Poetry. Science.

Now that spring is here ill. by Symeon Shimin; lettering by Paul Taylor. Noble, 1977. ISBN 0-8372-2396-2 Subj: Plants. Rhyming text. Science. Seasons – spring.

Petals yellow and petals red ill. by Albert John Pucci; lettering by Paul Taylor. Noble, 1977. ISBN 0-8372-2395-4 Subj: Flowers. Rhyming text. Science.

Plant magic ill. by Barbara Cooney; lettering by Paul Taylor. Noble, 1977. Subj: Plants. Rhyming text. Science.

Prize performance ill. by Margot Tomes. Noble, 1977. ISBN 0-8372-2398-9 Subj: Plants. Rhyming text. Science.

Rabbits, rabbits ill. by Gail Niemann. HarperCollins, 1983. ISBN 0-06-021896-7 Subj: Animals – rabbits. Poetry.

Seeds on the go ill. by Hans Zander; lettering by Paul Taylor. Noble, 1977. ISBN 0-8372-2400-4 Subj: Plants. Rhyming text. Science.

Sing, little mouse ill. by Symeon Shimin. Crowell, 1969. Subj: Animals – mice. Rhyming text.

Sing of the earth and sky ill. by Karmen Thompson. Boyds Mills, 2001. ISBN 1-56397-802-4 Subj: Astronomy. Earth. Moon. Poetry. Space & space ships. Stars. Sun.

Skip around the year ill. by Gioia Fiammenghi. Crowell, 1967. Subj: Holidays. Poetry.

The story of Easter ill. by Stefano Vitale. HarperCollins, 1997. ISBN 0-06-027297-X Subj: Holidays – Easter. Religion. Seasons – spring.

Swords and daggers ill. by James Higa; lettering by Paul Taylor. Noble, 1977. ISBN 0-8372-2393-8 Subj: Plants. Rhyming text. Science.

We went looking ill. by Marie Angel. Crowell, 1968. Subj: Animals. Birds. Insects – ladybugs. Plants. Poetry.

When it comes to bugs ill. by Chris & Bruce Degen. HarperCollins, 1986. ISBN 0-06-021822-3 Subj: Insects. Poetry. Spiders.

Where does everyone go? ill. by Adrienne Adams. Crowell, 1961. Subj: Animals. Hibernation. Poetry. Seasons – winter.

You don't look like your mother ill. by Lilith Jones. Mondo, 2002. ISBN 1-58653-856-X Subj: Animals – babies. Birds – robins. Rhyming text.

Fisher, Alex. *A kid's best friend* (Ajmera, Maya)

Fisher, Carolyn. *A twisted tale* ill. by author. Knopf, 2002. ISBN 0-375-91540-0 Subj: Animals. Farms. Humorous stories. Weather – tornadoes.

Fisher, Iris L. *Katie-Bo: an adoption story* ill. by Miriam Schaer. Watts, 1988. ISBN 0-915361-91-4 Subj: Adoption. Babies. Ethnic groups in the U.S. Family life – new sibling. Sibling rivalry.

Fisher, Leonard Everett. *The ABC exhibit* ill. by author. Macmillan, 1991. ISBN 0-02-735251-X Subj: ABC books.

Boxes! Boxes! ill. by author. Viking, 1984. ISBN 0-670-18334-2 Subj: Concepts. Concepts – color. Counting, numbers. Rhyming text.

Cyclops ill. by author. Holiday, 1991. ISBN 0-8234-0891-4 Subj: Folk & fairy tales. Mythical creatures.

David and Goliath adapt. from the Bible & ill. by Leonard Everett Fisher. Holiday, 1993. ISBN 0-8234-0997-X Subj: Foreign lands – Israel. Giants. Religion – David.

Gutenberg ill. by author. Macmillan, 1993. ISBN 0-02-735238-2 Subj: Careers – printers. Communication. Inventions.

A head full of hats ill. by author. Dial, 1962. Subj: Clothing – hats.

Look around! a book about shapes ill. by author. Viking, 1987. ISBN 0-670-80869-5 Subj: Concepts – shape. Games.

Pumpers, boilers, hooks and ladders: a book of fire engines ill. by author. Dial, 1961. Subj: Careers – firefighters. Trucks.

The seven days of creation ill. by author. Holiday, 1981. Adapt. from the Bible. ISBN 0-8234-0398-X Subj: Creation. Religion.

Sky, sea, the jetty, and me ill. by author. Cavendish, 2001. ISBN 0-7614-5082-3 Subj: Sea & seashore. Weather – storms.

Star signs ill. by author. Holiday, 1983. ISBN 0-8234-0491-9 Subj: Folk & fairy tales. Zodiac.

Stars and stripes: our national flag ill. by author. Holiday, 1993. ISBN 0-8234-1053-6 Subj: U.S. history.

Theseus and the Minotaur ill. by author. Holiday, 1988. ISBN 0-8234-0703-9 Subj: Folk & fairy tales. Mythical creatures. Royalty.

William Tell ill. by author. Farrar, 1996. ISBN 0-374-38436-3 Subj: Folk & fairy tales. Foreign lands – Switzerland. Sports – archery.

Fisher, Mary M. *Rosita's bridge* ill. by Barbara Mathews Whitehead. Maverick, 2001. ISBN 1-893271-18-8 Subj: Careers – singers. Ethnic groups in the U.S. – Mexican Americans. U.S. history.

Fisher, Richard E. *The boy and the dog* (Widerberg, Siv)

Mrs. Pepperpot and the moose (Prøysen, Alf)

Olson's meat pies (Cohen, Peter Zachary)

Shorty takes off (Lindgren, Barbro)

Will's new cap (Landström, Olof)

Fisher, Valorie. *Ellsworth's extraordinary electric ears and other amazing alphabet anecdotes* ill. with photos. Atheneum, 2003. ISBN 0-689-85030-1 Subj: ABC books.

My big brother ill. with photos. Atheneum, 2002. ISBN 0-689-84327-5 Subj: Family life – brothers.

Fishman, Cathy Goldberg. *On Hanukkah* ill. by Melanie W. Hall. Atheneum, 1998. ISBN 0-689-80643-4 Subj: Holidays – Hanukkah. Jewish culture. Religion.

On Passover ill. by Melanie W. Hall. Atheneum, 1997. ISBN 0-689-80528-4 Subj: Holidays – Passover. Jewish culture. Religion.

On Purim ill. by Melanie W. Hall. Atheneum, 2000. ISBN 0-689-82392-4 Subj: Family life. Holidays – Purim. Jewish culture.

On Rosh Hashanah and Yom Kippur ill. by Melanie W. Hall. Atheneum, 1997. ISBN 0-689-80526-8 Subj: Holidays – Rosh Hashanah. Holidays – Yom Kippur. Jewish culture. Religion.

On Shabbat ill. by Melanie W. Hall. Atheneum, 2001. ISBN 0-689-83894-8 Subj: Family life. Holidays. Jewish culture. Religion.

Fitch, Florence Mary. *A book about God* ill. by Henri Sorensen. Lothrop, 1999. ISBN 0-688-16129-4 Subj: Religion.

Fitch, Sheree. *No two snowflakes* ill. by Janet Wilson. Orca, 2001. ISBN 1-55143-206-4 Subj: Poetry. Weather – snow.

Fitchett, Gordon. *The twelve princesses* (Grimm, Jacob)

Fitzgerald, Ella. *A-tisket, a-tasket* by Ella Fitzgerald & Van Alexander; ill by Ora Eitan. Philomel, 2003. ISBN 0-399-23206-0 Subj: Behavior – lost & found possessions. Music. Songs.

Fitzgerald, Joanne. *This is me and where I am* ill. by author. Fitzhenry & Whiteside, 2004. ISBN 1-55041-819-X Subj: Cities, towns. Homes, houses.

Fitz-Gibbon, Sally. *Two shoes, blue shoes, new shoes!* ill. by Farida Zaman. Fitzhenry & Whiteside, 2003. ISBN 1-55041-729-0 Subj: Activities. Clothing – shoes.

Fitzhugh, Louise. *Bang, bang, you're dead* by Louise Fitzhugh & Sandra Scoppettone; ill. by Louise Fitzhugh. HarperCollins, 1969. ISBN 0-06-021914-9 Subj: Activities – playing. Cowboys, cowgirls. Violence, nonviolence. War. Weapons.

I am five ill. by author. Delacorte, 1978. ISBN 0-440-03953-3 Subj: Self-concept.

I am three ill. by Susanna Natti. Delacorte, 1982. ISBN 0-440-04039-6 Subj: Self-concept.

Fitzpatrick, Jean Grasso. *Animals of the forest* (Mora, Emma)

Gideon, the little bear cub (Mora, Emma)

Fitzpatrick, Marie-Louise. *I'm a tiger, too!* ill. by author. Roaring Brook, 2002. ISBN 0-7613-2410-0 Subj: Activities – playing. Animals. Imagination. Rhyming text.

Lizzy and Skunk ill. by author. DK, 2000. ISBN 0-7894-6163-3 Subj: Behavior – lost. Emotions – fear. Puppets.

You, me and the big blue sea ill. by author. Roaring Brook, 2002. ISBN 0-7613-2806-8 Subj: Activities – traveling. Boats, ships. Family life – mothers. Memories, memory. Sea & seashore.

Fitzsimons, Cecilia. *My first birds* ill. by author. HarperCollins, 1985. ISBN 0-06-021892-4 Subj: Birds. Format, unusual – board books.

My first butterflies ill. by author. HarperCollins, 1985. ISBN 0-06-021893-2 Subj: Format, unusual – board books. Insects – butterflies, caterpillars.

Five little pumpkins ill. by Dan Yaccarino. HarperFestival, 1998. ISBN 0-694-01177-0 Subj: Counting, numbers. Format, unusual – board books. Holidays – Halloween. Plants. Rhyming text. Witches.

Flack, Marjorie. *Angus and the cat* ill. by author. Doubleday, [1989], c1931. ISBN 0-685-01488-6 Subj: Animals – cats. Animals – dogs. Character traits – completing things. Character traits – curiosity.

Angus and the ducks ill. by author. Doubleday, 1930. ISBN 0-385-07213-9 Subj: Animals – dogs. Birds – ducks. Character traits – conceit. Character traits – curiosity.

Angus lost ill. by author. Doubleday, [1989], c1932. ISBN 0-385-07214-7 Subj: Animals – dogs. Behavior – lost. Seasons – winter.

Ask Mr. Bear ill. by author. Macmillan, 1932. ISBN 0-02-735390-7 Subj: Animals. Animals – bears. Birthdays. Emotions – love. Family life – mothers.

The boats on the river ill. by author. Viking, 1946. ISBN 0-670-83918-3 Subj: Boats, ships. Caldecott award honor books. Rivers.

The restless robin ill. by author. Houghton Mifflin, 1937. Subj: Birds – robins. Music.

The story about Ping by Marjorie Flack & Kurt Wiese; ill. by Kurt Wiese. Viking, 1933. Subj: Behavior – misbehavior. Birds – ducks. Foreign lands – China.

Tim Tadpole and the great bullfrog ill. by author. Doubleday, 1934. Subj: Frogs & toads.

Wait for William ill. by Marjorie Flack & Richard A. Holberg. Houghton Mifflin, 1934. ISBN 0-395-15484-7 Subj: Circus. Family life. Parades.

William and his kitten ill. by author. Houghton Mifflin, 1938. ISBN 0-395-20212-4 Subj: Animals – cats.

Flanagan, Alice K. *Ask Nurse Pfaff, she'll help you!* photos by Christine Osinski. Childrens Pr., 1997. ISBN 0-516-20495-5 Subj: Careers – nurses. Hospitals.

A busy day at Mr. Kang's grocery store photos by Christine Osinski. Childrens Pr., 1996. ISBN 0-516-20047-X Subj: Careers – storekeepers. Communities, neighborhoods. Ethnic groups in the U.S. – Korean Americans. Shopping. Stores.

Buying a pet from Ms. Chavez photos by Romie Flanagan. Childrens Pr., 1998. ISBN 0-516-20773-3 Subj: Careers – storekeepers. Communities, neighborhoods. Pets. Stores.

Call Mr. Vasquez, he'll fix it! photos by Christine Osinski. Childrens Pr., 1996. ISBN 0-516-20045-3 Subj: Careers – custodians, janitors. Careers – handymen. Homes, houses.

Chinese New Year ill. by Svetlana Zhurkina. Compass Pt., 2004. ISBN 0-7565-0479-1 Subj: Ethnic groups in the U.S. – Chinese Americans. Fairs, festivals. Holidays – Chinese New Year.

Choosing eyeglasses with Mrs. Koutris photos by Romie Flanagan. Childrens Pr., 1998. ISBN 0-516-20775-X Subj: Careers – opticians, optometrists. Careers – storekeepers. Glasses.

Christmas ill. by Viki Woodworth. Compass Pt., 2002. ISBN 0-7565-0085-0 Subj: Holidays – Christmas.

Cinco de Mayo ill. by Patrick Girouard. Compass Pt., 2004. ISBN 0-7565-0480-5 Subj: Ethnic groups in the U.S. – Mexican Americans. Foreign lands – Mexico. Holidays – Cinco de Mayo.

Coach John and his soccer team photos by Christine Osinski. Childrens Pr., 1998. ISBN 0-516-20777-6 Subj: Careers – coaches. Communities, neighborhoods. Sports – soccer. Sportsmanship.

A day in court with Mrs. Trinh photos by Christine Osinski. Childrens Pr., 1997. ISBN 0-516-20008-9 Subj: Careers – judges. Careers – lawyers. Crime.

Dr. Friedman helps animals photos by Christine Osinski. Childrens Pr., 1999. ISBN 0-516-21138-2 Subj: Animals. Careers – veterinarians.

Dr. Kanner, dentist with a smile photos by Christine Osinski. Childrens Pr., 1997. ISBN 0-516-20493-9 Subj: Careers – dentists. Teeth.

Exploring parks with Ranger Dockett photos by Christine Osinski. Childrens Pr., 1997. ISBN 0-516-20496-3 Subj: Careers – park rangers. Parks.

Farmers ill. with photos. Compass Pt., 2003. ISBN 0-7565-0305-1 Subj: Careers – farmers. Farms.

Flying an agricultural plane with Mr. Miller photos by Romie Flanagan. Childrens Pr., 1999. ISBN 0-516-21132-3 Subj: Airplanes, airports. Careers – airplane pilots. Farms.

Halloween ill. by Patrick Girouard. Compass Pt., 2002. ISBN 0-7565-0086-9 Subj: Holidays – Halloween.

Here comes Mr. Eventoff with the mail! photos by Christine Osinski. Childrens Pr., 1998. ISBN 0-516-20776-8 Subj: Careers – postal workers. Communities, neighborhoods. Letters, cards.

Learning about bees from Mr. Krebs photos by Christine Osinski. Childrens Pr., 1999. ISBN 0-516-21136-6 Subj: Careers – beekeepers. Insects – bees.

Learning is fun with Mrs. Perez photos by Romie Flanagan. Childrens Pr., 1998. ISBN 0-516-20774-1 Subj: Careers – teachers. Foreign languages. School.

Letter carriers ill. with photos. Compass Pt., 2000. ISBN 0-7565-0010-9 Subj: Careers – postal workers. Communities, neighborhoods. Letters, cards.

Librarians ill. with photos. Compass Pt., 2001. ISBN 0-7565-0063-X Subj: Books, reading. Careers – librarians. Libraries.

Mayors ill. with photos. Compass Pt., 2001. ISBN 0-7565-0064-8 Subj: Careers – mayors. Cities, towns. Communities, neighborhoods.

Mr. Paul and Mr. Luecke build communities photos by Romie Flanagan. Childrens Pr., 1999. ISBN 0-516-21131-5 Subj: Careers – construction workers. Homes, houses.

Mr. Santizo's tasty treats! photos by Romie Flanagan. Childrens Pr., 1998. ISBN 0-516-20771-7 Subj: Careers – bakers. Ethnic groups in the U.S. – Guatemalan Americans.

Mr. Yee fixes cars photos by Romie Flanagan. Childrens Pr., 1998. ISBN 0-516-20772-5 Subj: Automobiles. Careers – mechanics.

Mrs. Scott's beautiful art photos by Romie Flanagan. Childrens Pr., 1999. ISBN 0-516-21135-8 Subj: Careers – artists. Indians of North America – Cherokee.

Ms. Davison, our librarian photos by Christine Osinski. Childrens Pr., 1996. ISBN 0-516-20009-7 Subj: Books, reading. Careers – librarians. Communities, neighborhoods. Libraries.

Ms. Murphy fights fires photos by Christine Osinski. Childrens Pr., 1997. ISBN 0-516-20494-7 Subj: Careers – firefighters. Communities, neighborhoods. Fire.

Officer Brown keeps neighborhoods safe photos by Christine Osinski. Childrens Pr., 1998. ISBN 0-516-20780-6 Subj: Careers – police officers. Communities, neighborhoods. Crime.

Passover ill. by Ann Koffsky. Compass Pt., 2004. ISBN 0-7565-0481-3 Subj: Holidays – Passover. Jewish culture.

Police officers ill. with photos. Compass Pt., 2000. ISBN 0-7565-0011-7 Subj: Careers – police officers. Communities, neighborhoods. Crime.

Rain ill. with photos. Child's World, 2003. ISBN 1-56766-452-0 Subj: Weather – rain.

Raising cows on the Koebels' farm photos by Romie Flanagan. Childrens Pr., 1999. ISBN 0-516-21133-1 Subj: Animals – bulls, cows. Careers – farmers. Farms.

Riding the ferry with Captain Cruz photos by Christine Osinski. Childrens Pr., 1996. ISBN 0-516-20046-1 Subj: Boats, ships. Sailors. Transportation.

Riding the school bus with Mrs. Kramer photos by Christine Osinski. Childrens Pr., 1998. ISBN 0-516-20779-2 Subj: Careers – bus drivers. Communities, neighborhoods. School. Transportation.

Rocks ill. with photos. Compass Pt., 2001. ISBN 0-7565-0033-8 Subj: Earth. Rocks. Science.

Snow ill. with photos. Child's World, 2003. ISBN 1-56766-453-9 Subj: Weather – snow.

Soil ill. with photos. Compass Pt., 2001. ISBN 0-7565-0035-4 Subj: Animals. Earth. Ecology. Plants.

Sunshine ill. with photos. Child's World, 2003. ISBN 1-56766-454-7 Subj: Science. Sun.

Teachers ill. with photos. Compass Pt., 2001. ISBN 0-7565-0066-4 Subj: Careers – teachers. School.

Thanksgiving ill. by Kathie Kelleher. Compass Pt., 2002. ISBN 0-7565-0087-7 Subj: Holidays – Thanksgiving.

Thunder and lightning ill. with photos. Child's World, 2003. ISBN 1-56766-451-2 Subj: Weather – lightning, thunder. Weather – storms.

Valentine's Day ill. by Shelly Dieterichs. Compass Pt., 2002. ISBN 0-7565-0088-5 Subj: Holidays – Valentine's Day.

A visit to the Gravesens' farm photos by Christine Osinski. Childrens Pr., 1998. ISBN 0-516-20778-4 Subj: Careers – farmers. Communities, neighborhoods. Family life. Farms.

Water ill. with photos. Compass Pt., 2001. ISBN 0-7565-0038-9 Subj: Earth. Science. Water.

Weather ill. with photos. Compass Pt., 2001. ISBN 0-7565-0039-7 Subj: Science. Weather.

The Wilsons, a house-painting team photos by Christine Osinski. Childrens Pr., 1996. ISBN 0-516-20216-2 Subj: Activities – painting. Careers – painters. Homes, houses.

Wind ill. with photos. Child's World, 2003. ISBN 1-56766-455-5 Subj: Science. Weather – wind.

The Zieglers and their apple orchard photos by Romie Flanagan. Childrens Pr., 1999. ISBN 0-516-21134-X Subj: Careers – farmers. Farms. Food. Trees.

Flanders, Michael. *Creatures great and small* ill. by Marcello Minale. Holt, 1965. Subj: Animals. Birds. Poetry.

The hippopotamus song: a muddy love story ill. by Nadine Bernard Westcott; music by Donald Swann & Michael Flanders. Little, 1991. ISBN 0-316-28557-9 Subj: Animals – hippopotamuses. Emotions – love. Music. Songs.

Flather, Lisa. *Ten silly dogs* ill. by author. Orchard, 1999. ISBN 0-531-33192-X Subj: Animals – dogs. Counting, numbers. Rhyming text.

Flatt, Lizann. *My first nature treasury* ill. by Allan Cormack & Deborah Drew-Brook. Sierra Club, 1995. ISBN 0-87156-362-2 Subj: Nature.

Flattinger, Hubert. *Stormy night* ill. by Nathalie Duroussy; trans. by J. Alison James. North-South, 2002. ISBN 0-7358-1667-0 Subj: Bedtime. Emotions – fear. Family life – mothers.

Fleetwood, Jenni. *While shepherds watched* ill. by Peter Melnyczuk. Rev. ed. Broadman & Holman, 1999. ISBN 0-688-11598-5 Subj: Animals – sheep. Birthdays. Holidays – Christmas. Religion – Nativity.

Fleischman, Paul. *The animal hedge* ill. by Lydia Dabcovich. Dutton, 1983. ISBN 0-525-44002-X Subj: Activities – working. Farms. Folk & fairy tales.

The birthday tree ill. by Marcia Sewall. HarperCollins, 1979. ISBN 0-06-021916-5 Subj: Birthdays. Trees.

Lost! a story in string ill. by C. B. Mordan. Holt, 2000. ISBN 0-8050-5583-5 Subj: Behavior – lost. String. Weather – snow.

Rondo in C ill. by Janet Wentworth. HarperCollins, 1988. ISBN 0-06-021857-6 Subj: Imagination. Music. Musical instruments – pianos. Rhyming text.

Sidewalk circus ill. by Kevin Hawkes. Candlewick, 2004. ISBN 0-7636-1107-7 Subj: Circus. Cities, towns. Wordless.

Time train ill. by Claire Ewart. HarperCollins, 1991. ISBN 0-06-021710-3 Subj: Dinosaurs. School. Time. Trains.

Weslandia ill. by Kevin Hawkes. Candlewick, 1999. ISBN 0-7636-0006-7 Subj: Gardens, gardening. Plants.

Fleischman, Sid. *Kate's secret riddle* ill. by Barbara Bottner. Watts, 1977. ISBN 0-531-01334-0 Subj: Illness. Riddles & jokes.

Longbeard the wizard ill. by Charles Bragg. Little, 1970. Subj: Royalty. Wizards.

The scarebird ill. by Peter Sis. Mulberry, 1994. ISBN 0-688-13105-0 Subj: Character traits – kindness. Farms. Friendship. Scarecrows.

Fleisher, Robbin. *Quilts in the attic* ill. by Ati Forberg. Macmillan, 1978. ISBN 0-02-735420-2 Subj: Family life. Games. Quilts.

Fleishman, Seymour. *Too hot in Potzburg* ill. by author. Walker, 1981. ISBN 0-8075-8024-4 Subj: Animals – bears. Machines.

Fleming, Bill. *Kitten training and critters, too!* (Petersen-Fleming, Judy)

Puppy training and critters, too! (Petersen-Fleming, Judy)

Fleming, Candace. *A big cheese for the White House: the true tale of a tremendous cheddar* ill. by S. D. Schindler. DK, 1999. ISBN 0-7894-2573-4 Subj: Food. U.S. history.

Boxes for Katje ill. by Stacey Dressen-McQueen. Farrar, 2003. ISBN 0-374-30922-1 Subj: Character traits – generosity. Foreign lands – Holland. War.

Gabriella's song ill. by Giselle Potter. Atheneum, 1997. ISBN 0-689-80973-5 Subj: Foreign lands – Italy. Music. Songs.

Gator gumbo ill. by Sally Anne Lambert. Farrar, 2004. ISBN 0-374-38050-3 Subj: Animals. Food. Reptiles – alligators, crocodiles.

The hatmaker's sign: a story by Benjamin Franklin retold by Candace Fleming; ill. by Robert Andrew Parker. Orchard, 1998. ISBN 0-531-33075-3 Subj: Careers – storekeepers. Clothing. Stores. U.S. history.

Madame LaGrande and her so high, to the sky, uproarious pompadour ill. by S. D. Schindler. Knopf, 1996. ISBN 0-679-95835-5 Subj: Character traits – vanity. Foreign lands – France. Hair.

Muncha! Muncha! Muncha! ill. by G. Brian Karas. Atheneum, 2002. ISBN 0-689-83152-8 Subj: Animals – rabbits. Gardens, gardening.

Professor Fergus Fahrenheit and his wonderful weather machine ill. by Don Weller. S&S, 1994. ISBN 0-671-87047-5 Subj: Machines. Weather – droughts. Weather – rain.

Westward ho, Carlotta! ill. by David Catrow. Atheneum, 1998. ISBN 0-689-81063-6 Subj: Activities – singing. Careers – opera singers. U.S. history – frontier & pioneer life.

When Agnes caws ill. by Giselle Potter. Atheneum, 1999. ISBN 0-689-81471-2 Subj: Birds. Foreign lands – Himalayas. Noise, sounds.

Who invited you? ill. by George Booth. Atheneum, 2001. ISBN 0-689-83153-6 Subj: Animals. Counting, numbers. Rhyming text. Swamps.

Fleming, Denise. *Alphabet under construction* ill. by author. Holt, 2002. ISBN 0-8050-6848-1 Subj: ABC books. Activities – making things. Animals – mice.

Barnyard banter ill. by author. Holt, 1994. ISBN 0-8050-1957-X Subj: Animals. Farms. Noise, sounds. Rhyming text.

Count! ill. by author. Holt, 1992. ISBN 0-8050-1595-7 Subj: Animals. Counting, numbers.

The everything book ill. by author. Holt, 2000. ISBN 0-8050-6292-0 Subj: Concepts. Nursery rhymes.

The everything book [board book] ill. by author. Holt, 2004. ISBN 0-8050-7709-X Subj: Concepts. Format, unusual – board books. Nursery rhymes.

In the small, small pond ill. by author. Holt, 1993. ISBN 0-8050-2264-3 Subj: Animals. Caldecott award honor books. Frogs & toads. Lakes, ponds. Rhyming text. Seasons.

In the tall, tall grass ill. by author. Holt, 1991. ISBN 0-8050-1635-X Subj: Insects – butterflies, caterpillars. Nature.

Lunch ill. by author. Holt, 1992. ISBN 0-8050-1636-8 Subj: Animals – mice. Concepts – color. Food.

Mama cat has three kittens ill. by author. Holt, 1998. ISBN 0-8050-5745-5 Subj: Animals – babies. Animals – cats. Character traits – being different. Family life – brothers & sisters.

Time to sleep ill. by author. Holt, 1997. ISBN 0-8050-3762-4 Subj: Animals – bears. Hibernation. Seasons – winter.

Where once there was a wood ill. by author. Holt, 1996. ISBN 0-8050-3761-6 Subj: Animals. Nature. Plants.

Fleming, Virginia M. *Be good to Eddie Lee* ill. by Floyd Cooper. Philomel, 1993. ISBN 0-399-21993-5 Subj: Friendship. Handicaps – Down syndrome. Nature.

Fletcher, Claire. *The seashell song* (Jenkin-Pearce, Susie)

Fletcher, Elizabeth. *The little goat* ill. by Deborah & Kilmeny Niland. Grosset, 1977. ISBN 0-448-14287-2 Subj: Animals – goats. Behavior – lost.

What am I? ill. by Deborah & Kilmeny Niland. Grosset, 1977. ISBN 0-448-14280-5 Subj: Animals. Riddles & jokes.

Fletcher, Ralph J. *The circus surprise* ill. by Vladimir Vagin. Clarion, 2001. ISBN 0-395-98029-1 Subj: Behavior – lost. Circus. Clowns, jesters.

Grandpa never lies ill. by Harvey Stevenson. Clarion, 2000. ISBN 0-395-79770-5 Subj: Death. Emotions – grief. Family life – grandfathers. Family life – grandmothers. Poetry.

Hello, harvest moon ill. by Kate Kiesler. Clarion, 2003. ISBN 0-618-16451-0 Subj: Moon. Nature. Night.

Twilight comes twice ill. by Kate Kiesler. Clarion, 1997. ISBN 0-395-84826-1 Subj: Poetry. Twilight.

Flint, Russ. *Let's build a house* ill. by author. Ideals, 1990. ISBN 0-8249-8432-3 Subj: Activities – making things. Homes, houses.

Floca, Brian. *Five trucks* ill. by author. DK, 1999. ISBN 0-7894-2561-0 Subj: Airplanes, airports. Trucks.

The frightful story of Harry Walfish ill. by author. Orchard, 1997. ISBN 0-531-33008-7 Subj: Animals. Behavior – misbehavior. Museums.

Flöethe, Louise Lee. *The Indian and his pueblo* ill. by Richard Flöethe. Scribners, 1960. Subj: Indians of North America.

Flood, Bo. *I'll go to school if . . .* ill. by Ronnie Shipman. Fairview, 1997. ISBN 1-57749-024-X Subj: Emotions – fear. School – first day.

Flora. *Feathers like a rainbow* ill. by author. HarperCollins, 1989. ISBN 0-06-021838-X Subj: Birds. Concepts – color. Folk & fairy tales. Foreign lands – South America. Indians of South America.

Flora, James. *The day the cow sneezed* ill. by author. Harcourt, 1975, c1957. ISBN 0-15-624213-3 Subj: Animals. Cumulative tales. Humorous stories.

Fishing with dad ill. by author. Harcourt, 1967. ISBN 0-15-228100-2 Subj: Boats, ships. Careers – fishermen.

Grandpa's farm: 4 tall tales ill. by author. Harcourt, 1965. Subj: Family life – grandfathers. Farms. Humorous stories.

Grandpa's ghost stories ill. by author. Atheneum, 1978. ISBN 0-689-50112-9 Subj: Family life – grandfathers. Ghosts. Witches.

Leopold, the see-through crumbpicker ill. by author. Harcourt, 1961. Subj: Monsters. Zoos.

My friend Charlie ill. by author. Harcourt, 1964. Subj: Friendship.

Sherwood walks home ill. by author. Harcourt, 1966. Subj: Toys – bears.

Florian, Douglas. *Airplane ride* ill. by author. Crowell, 1984. ISBN 0-690-04365-1 Subj: Activities – flying. Airplanes, airports.

At the zoo ill. by author. Greenwillow, 1992. ISBN 0-688-09629-8 Subj: Animals. Zoos.

An auto mechanic ill. by author. Greenwillow, 1991. ISBN 0-688-10636-6 Subj: Automobiles. Careers – mechanics.

Beach day ill. by author. Greenwillow, 1990. ISBN 0-688-09105-9 Subj: Sea & seashore – beaches.

Beast feast ill. by author. Harcourt, 1994. ISBN 0-15-295178-4 Subj: Animals. Poetry.

A bird can fly ill. by author. Greenwillow, 1980. ISBN 0-688-84266-6 Subj: Animals. Science.

Bow wow meow meow, it's rhyming cats and dogs ill. by author. Harcourt, 2003. ISBN 0-15-216395-6 Subj: Animals – cats. Animals – dogs. Poetry.

A carpenter ill. by author. Greenwillow, 1991. ISBN 0-688-09761-8 Subj: Careers – carpenters.

A chef ill. by author. Greenwillow, 1992. ISBN 0-688-11109-2 Subj: Activities – baking, cooking. Careers – chefs, cooks.

The city ill. by author. Crowell, 1982. ISBN 0-690-04167-5 Subj: Cities, towns. Wordless.

City street ill. by author. Greenwillow, 1990. ISBN 0-688-09544-5 Subj: Cities, towns.

A fisher ill. by author. Greenwillow, 1994. ISBN 0-688-13130-1 Subj: Careers – fishermen.

In the swim ill. by author. Harcourt, 1997. ISBN 0-15-201307-5 Subj: Animals. Poetry. Sea & seashore.

Insectlopedia ill. by author. Harcourt, 1998. ISBN 0-15-201306-7 Subj: Insects. Poetry.

Lizards, frogs, and polliwogs ill. by author. Harcourt, 2001. ISBN 0-15-202591-X Subj: Amphibians. Frogs & toads. Poetry. Reptiles.

Monster Motel ill. by author. Harcourt, 1993. ISBN 0-15-255320-7 Subj: Monsters. Poetry.

Nature walk ill. by author. Greenwillow, 1989. ISBN 0-688-08269-6 Subj: Activities – walking. Nature.

On the wing: bird poems and paintings ill. by author. Harcourt, 1996. ISBN 0-15-200497-1 Subj: Birds. Poetry.

A painter ill. by author. Greenwillow, 1993. ISBN 0-688-11873-9 Subj: Activities – painting. Art. Careers – artists.

People working ill. by author. Crowell, 1983. ISBN 0-690-04264-7 Subj: Activities – working. Careers.

A pig is big ill. by author. Greenwillow, 2000. ISBN 0-688-17126-5 Subj: Concepts – size. Rhyming text.

A potter ill. by author. Greenwillow, 1991. ISBN 0-688-10101-1 Subj: Activities – making things. Activities – working. Art. Rhyming text.

A summer day ill. by author. Greenwillow, 1988. ISBN 0-688-07565-7 Subj: Activities – vacationing. Counting, numbers. Family life.

Summersaults ill. by author. Greenwillow, 2002. ISBN 0-06-029268-7 Subj: Poetry. Seasons – summer.

Turtle day ill. by author. HarperCollins, 1989. ISBN 0-690-04745-2 Subj: Reptiles – turtles, tortoises.

Vegetable garden ill. by author. Harcourt, 1991. ISBN 0-15-293383-2 Subj: Gardens, gardening. Rhyming text.

A winter day ill. by author. Greenwillow, 1987. ISBN 0-688-07352-2 Subj: Family life. Rhyming text. Seasons – winter.

A year in the country ill. by author. Greenwillow, 1989. ISBN 0-688-08187-8 Subj: Country. Farms. Seasons.

Flory, Jane. *The bear on the doorstep* ill. by Carolyn Croll. Houghton Mifflin, 1980. ISBN 0-395-29239-5 Subj: Animals – bears. Animals – rabbits. Homes, houses.

The unexpected grandchildren ill. by Carolyn Croll. Houghton Mifflin, 1977. ISBN 0-395-25797-2 Subj: Behavior – sharing. Family life – grandparents.

We'll have a friend for lunch ill. by Carolyn Croll. Houghton Mifflin, 1974. ISBN 0-395-18448-7 Subj: Animals – cats. Food. Friendship.

Flot, Jeannette B. *Princess Kalina and the hedgehog* adapt. by Frances Marshall; ill. by Dorothée Duntze. Faber, 1981. ISBN 0-571-11844-5 Subj: Animals – hedgehogs. Character traits – cleanliness. Folk & fairy tales. Magic. Royalty – princesses.

Flournoy, Valerie. *The best time of day* ill. by George Ford. Random House, 1979. ISBN 0-394-93799-6 Subj: Activities. Ethnic groups in the U.S. – African Americans. Family life.

The patchwork quilt ill. by Jerry Pinkney. Dial, 1985. ISBN 0-8037-0098-9 Subj: Ethnic groups in the U.S. – African Americans. Family life – grandmothers. Quilts.

Flower, Phyllis. *Barn owl* ill. by Cherryl Pape. HarperCollins, 1978. ISBN 0-06-021921-1 Subj: Birds – owls. Science.

Floyd, Lucy. *Agatha's alphabet, with her very own dictionary* by Lucy Floyd & Kathryn Lasky; ill. by Dora Leder. Rand McNally, 1975. ISBN 0-528-80149-X Subj: ABC books. Dictionaries.

Rabbit and turtle go to school ill. by Christopher Denise. Harcourt, 2000. ISBN 0-15-202679-7 Subj: Animals – rabbits. Folk & fairy tales. Reptiles – turtles, tortoises. School. Sports – racing.

Flugge, Klauss. *Hey Presto! You're a bear!* (Janosch)

Flynn, Kitson. *Carrot in my pocket* ill. by Denise Ortakales. Moon Mt., 2001. ISBN 0-9677929-6-7 Subj: Animals. Behavior – lost & found possessions. Farms. Rhyming text.

Foa, Maryclare. *Songs are thoughts* ill. by author. Orchard, 1995. ISBN 0-531-06893-5 Subj: Foreign lands – Arctic. Indians of North America – Inuit. Poetry.

Foley, Bernice Williams. *The gazelle and the hunter: a folk tale from Persia* ill. by Diana Magnuson. Childrens Pr., 1980. ISBN 0-516-06480-0 Subj: Folk & fairy tales. Foreign lands – Persia.

A walk among clouds: a folk tale from China ill. by Mina Gow McLean. Childrens Pr., 1980. ISBN 0-516-06484-3 Subj: Folk & fairy tales. Foreign lands – China.

Folsom, Marcia. *Easy as pie: a guessing game of sayings* by Marcia & Michael Folsom; ill. by Jack Kent. Houghton Mifflin, 1985. ISBN 0-89919-303-X Subj: Humorous stories. Language.

Folsom, Michael. *Easy as pie: a guessing game of sayings* (Folsom, Marcia)

Q is for duck: an alphabet guessing game (Elting, Mary)

Fontaine, Jan. *The spaghetti tree* ill. by Anne Marshall Runyon. Talespinner, 1980. ISBN 0-934926-00-X Subj: Food. Gardens, gardening. Imagination.

Fontaine, Jean de La. *see* La Fontaine, Jean de

Fontane, Theodor. *Nick Ribbeck of Ribbeck of Havelland* trans. from German by Anthea Bell; ill. by Marta Kocí. Picture Book Studio, 1990. ISBN 0-88708-149-5 Subj: Character traits – generosity. Poetry.

Sir Ribbeck of Ribbeck of Havelland trans. from German by Elizabeth Shub; ill. by Nonny Hogrogian. Macmillan, 1971, c1969. ISBN 0-20-071750-2 Subj: Character traits – generosity. Poetry.

Fontenot, Mary Alice. *Tah-Tye: the last 'possum in the pouch* ill. by Scott R. Blazek. Blue Heron, 1996. ISBN 1-884725-10-4 Subj: Animals – possums. Behavior – growing up. Family life.

Fontes, Justine Korman. *Signs of spring* ill. by Rob Hefferan. Mondo, 2002. ISBN 1-59034-180-5 Subj: Animals – mice. School. Seasons – spring.

Fonteyn, Margot, Dame. *Coppélia* as told by Margot Fonteyn; ill. by Steve Johnson & Lou Fancher. Harcourt, 1998. ISBN 0-15-200428-9 Subj: Activities – dancing. Ballet. Emotions – envy, jealousy. Toys – dolls.

Foord, Jo. *The book of babies* photos by author. Random House, 1991. ISBN 0-679-90955-9 Subj: Activities. Babies. Rhyming text.

Foote, Dan. *The cobbler, the princess, and the newborn King* ill. by author. Chariot Victor, 1999. ISBN 0-7814-3079-8 Subj: Holidays – Christmas. Religion – Nativity.

For laughing out louder: more poems to tickle your funnybone sel. by Jack Prelutsky; ill. by Marjorie Priceman. Knopf, 1995. ISBN 0-679-87063-6 Subj: Poetry.

Ford, Bernette G. *Bright eyes, brown skin* (Hudson, Cheryl Willis)

Ford, Christine. *Snow!* ill. by Candace Whitman. HarperCollins, 1999. ISBN 0-694-01199-1 Subj: Activities – playing. Family life. Seasons – winter. Weather – snow.

Ford, George Cephas. *Walk on!* (Williamson, Mel)

Ford, June. *A child's garden of verses* (Stevenson, Robert Louis)

Ford, Juwanda G. *K is for Kwanzaa: a Kwanzaa alphabet book* ill. by Ken Wilson-Max. Scholastic, 1997. ISBN 0-590-92200-9 Subj: ABC books. Ethnic groups in the U.S. – African Americans. Holidays – Kwanzaa.

Together for Kwanzaa ill. by Shelly Hehenberger. Random House, 2000. ISBN 0-375-90329-1 Subj: Ethnic groups in the U.S. – African Americans. Family life – brothers & sisters. Holidays – Kwanzaa.

Ford, Lauren. *The ageless story* ill. by author. Dodd, 1939. Subj: Caldecott award honor books.

Ford, Miela. *Follow the leader* photos by author. Greenwillow, 1996. ISBN 0-688-14655-4 Subj: Activities – playing. Animals – polar bears.

Mom and me ill. by author. Greenwillow, 1998. ISBN 0-688-15890-0 Subj: Activities – playing. Animals – polar bears. Family life – mothers. Foreign lands – Arctic.

My day in the garden ill. by Anita Lobel. Greenwillow, 1999. ISBN 0-688-15542-1 Subj: Activities – playing. Clothing – costumes. Imagination. Theater. Weather – rain.

Sunflower ill. by Sally Noll. Greenwillow, 1995. ISBN 0-688-13302-9 Subj: Flowers. Gardens, gardening. Nature. Plants.

Watch us play ill. by author. Greenwillow, 1998. ISBN 0-688-15667-X Subj: Activities. Animals – lions. Zoos.

Foreman, Juli. *Great beginnings: the story of God's creation* by Juli Foreman & Tricia Clem; ill. by Kevin Foreman. Thomas More, 1995. ISBN 0-88347-307-0 Subj: Creation. Religion.

Foreman, Michael. *The angel and the wild animal* ill. by author. Atheneum, 1989. ISBN 0-689-31492-2 Subj: Behavior. Family life.

Ben's baby ill. by author. HarperCollins, 1988. ISBN 0-06-021844-4 Subj: Babies. Family life – new sibling.

Cat and canary ill. by author. Dial, 1985. ISBN 0-8037-0137-3 Subj: Animals – cats. Birds – canaries.

Cat in the manger ill. by author. Holt, 2001. ISBN 0-8050-6677-2 Subj: Animals – cats. Holidays – Christmas. Memories, memory. Religion.

Dad! I can't sleep ill. by author. Harcourt, 1995. ISBN 0-15-200307-X Subj: Animals – pandas. Bedtime. Counting, numbers. Family life – fathers. Sleep.

The general (Charters, Janet)

Grandfather's pencil and the room of stories ill. by author. Harcourt, 1994. ISBN 0-15-200061-5 Subj: Activities – storytelling. Activities – writing. Family life – grandfathers.

Jack's fantastic voyage ill. by author. Harcourt, 1992. ISBN 0-15-239496-6 Subj: Boats, ships. Dreams. Family life – grandfathers. Sea & seashore. Weather – storms.

Land of dreams ill. by author. Holt, 1982. ISBN 0-03-062053-8 Subj: Dreams.

The little reindeer ill. by author. Dial, 1997. ISBN 0-8037-2184-6 Subj: Activities – flying. Animals – reindeer. Holidays – Christmas.

Look! Look! ill. by author. Andersen, 1998. ISBN 0-86264-758-4 Subj: Animals. Animals – pandas. Crime.

Moose ill. by author. Pantheon, 1972. Subj: Animals – bears. Animals – moose. Birds – eagles. Violence, nonviolence.

One world ill. by author. Arcade, 1991. ISBN 1-55970-108-0 Subj: Ecology. Sea & seashore.

Panda and the bunyips ill. by author. Schocken, 1987, c1984. ISBN 0-8052-4041-1 Subj: Animals – pandas. Foreign lands – Australia. Mythical creatures.

Panda and the bushfire ill. by author. Prentice-Hall, 1986. ISBN 0-13-648395-X Subj: Animals. Animals – pandas. Fire. Foreign lands – Australia. Mythical creatures.

Panda's puzzle, and his voyage of discovery ill. by author. Bradbury, 1978. ISBN 0-8788-8127-1 Subj: Animals – pandas. Self-concept.

The perfect present ill. by author. Coward McCann, 1967. Subj: Buses. Holidays – Christmas. Santa Claus.

Rock-a-doodle-do! an adaptation of a tale by the Brothers Grimm ill. by adapt. Andersen, 2000. ISBN 0-8626-4951-X Subj: Animals. Careers – musicians. Crime. Folk & fairy tales. Old age.

Seal surfer ill. by author. Harcourt, 1996. ISBN 0-15-201399-7 Subj: Animals – seals. Birth. Family life – grandfathers. Handicaps. Sea & seashore.

Surprise! Surprise! ill. by author. Harcourt, 1995. ISBN 0-15-200038-0 Subj: Animals – pandas. Birthdays. Emotions – fear. Family life – mothers.

The two giants ill. by author. Pantheon, 1967. Subj: Behavior – fighting, arguing. Giants.

War and peas ill. by author. Crowell, 1974. ISBN 0-690-00629-2 Subj: Royalty. War.

Forest, Charlotte B. De. *see* DeForest, Charlotte B.

Forest, Heather. *The baker's dozen* ill. by Susan Graber. Harcourt, 1988. ISBN 0-15-200412-2 Subj: Careers – bakers. Folk & fairy tales.

Stone soup retold by Heather Forest; ill. by Susan Gaber. August House, 1998. ISBN 0-8748-3498-8 Subj: Behavior – sharing. Character traits – cleverness. Folk & fairy tales. Food.

The woman who flummoxed the fairies ill. by Susan Gaber. Harcourt, 1990. ISBN 0-15-299150-6 Subj: Fairies. Folk & fairy tales. Food. Foreign lands – Scotland.

Forrester, Victoria. *The magnificent moo* ill. by author. Atheneum, 1983. ISBN 0-689-30954-6 Subj: Animals – bulls, cows. Animals – cats. Noise, sounds.

Oddward ill. by author. Atheneum, 1982. ISBN 0-689-30912-0 Subj: Holidays. Reptiles – snakes.

Poor Gabriella: a Christmas story ill. by Susan Boulet. Atheneum, 1986. ISBN 0-689-31266-0 Subj: Animals – bulls, cows. Holidays – Christmas. Religion.

The touch said hello ill. by author. Atheneum, 1982. ISBN 0-689-30947-3 Subj: Seasons – spring.

Words to keep against the night ill. by author. Atheneum, 1983. ISBN 0-689-30984-8 Subj: Poetry.

Fort, Patrick. *Redbird* ill. by author. Watts, 1988. ISBN 0-531-05746-1 Subj: Activities – flying. Airplanes, airports. Format, unusual.

Forward, Toby. *Ben's Christmas carol* ill. by Ruth Brown. Dutton, 1996. ISBN 0-525-45593-0 Subj: Animals – mice. Behavior – greed. Behavior – sharing. Holidays – Christmas.

What did you do today? ill. by Carol Thompson. Clarion, 2004. ISBN 0-618-49586-X Subj: School – first day.

Fosberg, John. *Cookie shapes* ill. by author. S&S, 1997. ISBN 0-689-81288-4 Subj: Concepts – shape. Format, unusual – board books.

Ice cream colors ill. by author. Little Simon, 1997. ISBN 0-689-81287-6 Subj: Concepts – color. Format, unusual – board books.

Foster, Doris Van Liew. *A pocketful of seasons* ill. by Talivaldis Stubis. Lothrop, 1961. Subj: Behavior – saving things. Seasons.

Tell me, Mr. Owl ill. by Helen Stone. Lothrop, 1957. Subj: Birds – owls. Holidays – Halloween.

Foster, John. *Dragon poems* (Dragon poems)

Pet poems ill. by Korky Paul. Oxford Univ. Pr., 2000. ISBN 0-19-276191-9 Subj: Animals. Pets. Poetry.

Rhyme time around the day (Rhyme time around the day)

Foster, Karen Sharp. *Good night my little chicks = Buenas noches mis pollitos* adapt. & ill. by Karen Sharp Foster. First Story Pr., 1997. ISBN 1-890326-12-7 Subj: Bedtime. Birds – chickens. Family life. Foreign languages.

Foster, Marian Curtis. *see* Mariana

Foster, Sally. *A pup grows up* photos by author. Dodd, 1984. ISBN 0-396-08314-5 Subj: Animals – dogs. Pets.

Foulds, Elfrida Vipont. *The elephant and the bad baby* ill. by Raymond Briggs. Coward, 1986, 1969. ISBN 0-698-20039-X Subj: Animals – elephants. Babies. Behavior – stealing. Cumulative tales.

Fournier, Catharine. *The coconut thieves* ill. by Janina Domanska. Scribners, 1964. Subj: Animals. Folk & fairy tales. Foreign lands – Africa.

Fowler, Allan. *The biggest animal ever* ill. with photos. Childrens Pr., 1992. ISBN 0-516-06001-5 Subj: Animals – whales. Sea & seashore.

The biggest animal on land ill. with photos. Childrens Pr., 1996. ISBN 0-516-06050-3 Subj: Animals – elephants. Animals – endangered animals.

Corn . . . on and off the cob ill. with photos. Childrens Pr., 1994. ISBN 0-516-06027-9 Subj: Food. Plants.

Cubs and colts and calves and kittens ill. with photos. Childrens Pr., 1991. ISBN 0-516-04913-5 Subj: Animals. Science.

Feeling things ill. with photos. Childrens Pr., 1991. ISBN 0-516-04908-9 Subj: Senses – touch.

Friendly dolphins ill. with photos. Childrens Pr., 1997. ISBN 0-516-20428-9 Subj: Animals – dolphins. Animals – whales. Sea & seashore.

Hard-to-see animals ill. with photos. Childrens Pr., 1997. ISBN 0-516-20548-X Subj: Animals. Concepts – color.

Hearing things ill. with photos. Childrens Pr., 1991. ISBN 0-516-04909-7 Subj: Senses – hearing.

It could still be a bird ill. with photos. Childrens Pr., 1990. ISBN 0-516-04901-1 Subj: Birds.

It could still be endangered ill. with photos. Childrens Pr., 2000. ISBN 0-516-21208-7 Subj: Animals – endangered animals.

Seeing things ill. with photos. Childrens Pr., 1991. ISBN 0-516-04910-0 Subj: Senses – sight.

Simple machines ill. with photos. Childrens Pr., 2001. ISBN 0-516-21680-5 Subj: Machines.

Smelling things ill. with photos. Childrens Pr., 1991. ISBN 0-516-04912-7 Subj: Senses – smell.

So that's how the moon changes shape! ill. with photos. Childrens Pr., 1991. ISBN 0-516-04917-8 Subj: Moon. Science.

Spiders are not insects ill. with photos. Childrens Pr., 1996. ISBN 0-516-06054-6 Subj: Science. Spiders.

Tasting things ill. with photos. Childrens Pr., 1991. ISBN 0-516-04911-9 Subj: Senses – taste.

What do you see in a cloud? ill. with photos. Childrens Pr., 1996. ISBN 0-516-06056-2 Subj: Concepts – shape. Games. Imagination. Participation. Science. Weather – clouds.

What's the weather today? ill. with photos. Childrens Pr., 1991. ISBN 0-516-04918-6 Subj: Weather.

Fowler, Richard. *Cat's cake* ill. by author. Barron's, 1987. ISBN 0-8120-5878-X Subj: Animals. Behavior – dissatisfaction. Food.

Cat's car ill. by author. Barron's, 1988. ISBN 0-81205-920-4 Subj: Animals. Automobiles.

Cat's story ill. by author. Grosset, 1985. ISBN 0-448-07851-1 Subj: Animals – cats. Format, unusual – board books. Rhyming text.

Happy birthday, Mouse! by Richard Fowler & David Wood; ill. by Richard Fowler. Grosset, 1990. ISBN 0-448-19023-0 Subj: Animals. Animals – mice. Birthdays. Counting, numbers. Format, unusual. Parties.

Honeybee's busy day ill. by author. Harcourt, 1994. ISBN 0-15-200055-0 Subj: Format, unusual – toy & movable books. Insects – bees.

Inspector Smart gets the message! ill. by author. Little, 1983. ISBN 0-316-28983-3 Subj: Birthdays. Mystery stories.

Ladybug on the move ill. by author. Harcourt, 1993. ISBN 0-15-200475-0 Subj: Format, unusual – toy & movable books. Insects – ladybugs.

Little Chick's big adventure ill. by author. Harcourt, 1996. ISBN 0-15-201040-8 Subj: Animals. Behavior – lost. Birds – chickens. Format, unusual – toy & movable books.

Mr. Little's noisy car ill. by author. Grosset, 1986. ISBN 0-448-18977-1 Subj: Animals. Automobiles. Format, unusual – toy & movable books. Noise, sounds.

Mr. Little's noisy fire engine ill. by author. Grosset, 1990. ISBN 0-448-40042-1 Subj: Animals. Careers – firefighters. Format, unusual – toy & movable books. Noise, sounds. Trucks.

Mr. Little's noisy truck ill. by author. Grosset, 1989. ISBN 0-448-19021-4 Subj: Animals. Format, unusual – toy & movable books. Noise, sounds. Trucks.

Pop-up trucks ill. by author. Harcourt, 1998. ISBN 0-15-201681-3 Subj: Format, unusual – toy & movable books. Trucks.

Fowler, Susi Gregg. *Beautiful* ill. by Jim Fowler. Greenwillow, 1998. ISBN 0-688-15112-4 Subj: Death. Emotions – love. Family life – aunts, uncles. Gardens, gardening. Illness.

Circle of thanks ill. by Peter Catalanotto. Scholastic, 1998. ISBN 0-590-10066-1 Subj: Alaska. Animals. Character traits – kindness to animals.

Fog ill. by Jim Fowler. Greenwillow, 1992. ISBN 0-688-10594-7 Subj: Activities – singing. Family life. Music. Weather – fog.

I'll see you when the moon is full ill. by Jim Fowler. Greenwillow, 1994. ISBN 0-688-10830-X Subj: Activities – trading. Family life – fathers. Moon.

When Joel comes home ill. by Jim Fowler. Greenwillow, 1993. ISBN 0-688-11065-7 Subj: Adoption. Babies. Friendship.

When summer ends ill. by Marisabina Russo. Greenwillow, 1989. ISBN 0-688-07606-8 Subj: Seasons.

Fowles, John. *Cinderella* (Perrault, Charles)

Fox, Charles Philip. *Come to the circus* photos by author. Reilly & Lee, 1960. Subj: Circus.

A fox in the house photos by author. Reilly & Lee, 1960. Subj: Animals – foxes.

Mr. Stripes the gopher photos by author. Reilly & Lee, 1962. Subj: Animals. Family life. Seasons.

Fox, Christyan. *Astronaut PiggyWiggy* by Christyan & Diane Fox; ill. by Christyan Fox. Handprint, 2002. ISBN 1-929766-41-6 Subj: Animals – pigs. Careers – astronauts. Imagination.

Count to ten, PiggyWiggy! by Christyan & Diane Fox; ill. by Christyan Fox. Handprint, 2001. ISBN 1-929766-18-1 Subj: Activities – baking, cooking. Animals – pigs. Counting, numbers. Food. Format, unusual – board books.

Fire fighter PiggyWiggy by Christyan & Diane Fox; ill. by Christyan Fox. Handprint, 2001. ISBN 1-929766-16-5 Subj: Animals – pigs. Careers – firefighters. Imagination.

What color is that, PiggyWiggy? by Christyan & Diane Fox; ill. by Christyan Fox. Handprint, 2001. ISBN 1-929766-17-3 Subj: Animals – pigs. Clowns, jesters. Concepts – color. Format, unusual – board books. Toys.

What shape is that, PiggyWiggy? by Christyan & Diane Fox; ill. by Christyan Fox. Handprint, 2002. ISBN 1-929766-44-0 Subj: Animals – pigs. Format, unusual – board books. Toys – bears.

Fox, Diane. *Astronaut PiggyWiggy* (Fox, Christyan)

Count to ten, PiggyWiggy! (Fox, Christyan)

Fire fighter PiggyWiggy (Fox, Christyan)

What color is that, PiggyWiggy? (Fox, Christyan)

What shape is that, PiggyWiggy? (Fox, Christyan)

Fox, Dorothea Warren. *Follow me the leader* ill. by author. Parents' Magazine Pr., 1968. Subj: Games. Poetry.

Fox, Louisa. *Every Monday in the mailbox* ill. by Jan Naimo Jones. Eerdmans, 1995. ISBN 0-8028-3792-1 Subj: Death. Emotions – grief. Friendship. Letters, cards. Old age.

Fox, Mem. *Because of the bloomers* ill. by Terry Denton. Harcourt, 1998. ISBN 0-15-200250-2 Subj: Animals – bulls, cows. Clothing. Foreign lands – Australia.

A bedtime story ill. by Elivia Savadier. Mondo, 1996. ISBN 1-57255-136-4 Subj: Bedtime. Books, reading. Family life. Toys.

Boo to a goose ill. by David Miller. Dial, 1998. ISBN 0-8037-2274-5 Subj: Birds – geese. Rhyming text.

Feathers and fools ill. by Nicholas Wilton. Harcourt, 1996. ISBN 0-15-200473-4 Subj: Behavior – sharing. Birds – peacocks, peahens. Birds – swans. War.

Guess what? ill. by Vivienne Goodman. Harcourt, 1990. ISBN 0-15-200452-1 Subj: Witches.

Harriet, you'll drive me wild ill. by Marla Frazee. Harcourt, 2000. ISBN 0-15-201977-4 Subj: Character traits – clumsiness. Emotions – anger. Family life – mothers.

Hattie and the fox ill. by Patricia Mullins. Bradbury, 1987. ISBN 0-02-735470-9 Subj: Animals. Birds – chickens. Cumulative tales. Farms.

Koala Lou ill. by Pamela Lofts. Harcourt, 1989. ISBN 0-15-200502-1 Subj: Animals – koalas. Emotions – love. Family life – mothers.

The magic hat ill. by Tricia Tusa. Harcourt, 2002. ISBN 0-15-201025-4 Subj: Magic. Rhyming text. Wizards.

Night noises ill. by Terry Denton. Harcourt, 1989. ISBN 0-15-200543-9 Subj: Animals – dogs. Birthdays. Night. Noise, sounds. Sleep.

Possum magic ill. by Julie Vivas. Abingdon, 1987. ISBN 0-687-31732-0 Subj: Activities – traveling. Animals – possums. Behavior – wishing. Food. Foreign lands – Australia.

Shoes from grandpa ill. by Patricia Mullins. Watts, 1990. ISBN 0-531-08448-5 Subj: Behavior – growing up. Clothing. Cumulative tales. Family life – grandfathers. Rhyming text.

Sleepy bears ill. by Kerry Argent. Harcourt, 1999. ISBN 0-15-202016-0 Subj: Animals – bears. Lullabies. Rhyming text. Sleep.

Sophie ill. by Aminah Brenda Lynn Robinson. Harcourt, 1994. ISBN 0-15-277160-3 Subj: Birth. Death. Emotions – love. Family life – grandfathers.

The straight line wonder ill. by Marc Rosenthal. Mondo, 1996. ISBN 1-57255-206-9 Subj: Self-concept.

Time for bed ill. by Jane Dyer. Harcourt, 1993. ISBN 0-15-288183-2 Subj: Animals. Bedtime. Family life. Rhyming text.

Tough Boris ill. by Kathryn Brown. Harcourt, 1994. ISBN 0-15-289612-0 Subj: Birds – parakeets, parrots. Pirates.

Where is the green sheep? ill. by Judy Horacek. Harcourt, 2004. ISBN 0-15-204907-X Subj: Animals – sheep. Rhyming text.

Wilfrid Gordon McDonald Partridge ill. by Julie Vivas. Kane/Miller, 1985. ISBN 0-916291-04-9 Subj: Behavior – forgetfulness. Old age.

With love, at Christmas ill. by Gary Lippincott. Abingdon, 1988. ISBN 0-687-45863-3 Subj: Character traits – generosity. Death. Holidays – Christmas.

Wombat divine ill. by Kerry Argent. Harcourt, 1996. ISBN 0-15-201416-0 Subj: Animals. Animals – wombats. Holidays – Christmas. Theater.

Zoo-looking ill. by Candace Whitman. Mondo, 1996. ISBN 1-57255-010-4 Subj: Animals. Rhyming text. Zoos.

Fox, Perla. *The Wooodles: stretching your imagination* by Perla Fox & Deborah Lieberman; ill. by Perla Fox. Full Court, 1996. ISBN 0-9645887-5-7 Subj: Activities – making things. Rhyming text.

Fox, Siv Cedering. *The blue horse and other night poems* ill. by Donald Carrick. Seabury Pr., 1979. ISBN 0-8614-3226-0 Subj: Bedtime. Poetry.

The fox went out on a chilly night ill. by Peter Spier. Doubleday, 1961. ISBN 0-385-00231-9 Subj: Animals – foxes. Caldecott award honor books. Folk & fairy tales. Songs.

Fradon, Dana. *Sir Dana – a knight: as told by his trusty armor* ill. by author. Dutton, 1988. ISBN 0-525-44424-6 Subj: Knights. Middle Ages. Museums.

Fraggalosch, Audrey. *Great grizzly wilderness* ill. by Donald G. Eberhart. Soundprints, 2000. ISBN 1-56899-838-4 Subj: Animals – bears. Family life.

Grizzly bear family ill. by Donald G. Eberhart. Soundprints, 2003. ISBN 1-59249-048-4 Subj: Animals – bears. Behavior – growing up. Family life – mothers. Hibernation.

Trails above the tree line ill. by Higgins Bond. Soundprints, 2002. ISBN 1-56899-941-0 Subj: Animals – babies. Animals – sheep. Family life – mothers.

Frame, Jeron Ashford. *Yesterday I had the blues* ill. by Donald G. Eberhart. Tricycle, 2003. ISBN 1-58246-084-1 Subj: Emotions. Ethnic groups in the U.S. – African Americans. Family life.

Frampton, David. *My beastie book of ABC* ill. by author. HarperCollins, 2002. ISBN 0-06-028823-X Subj: ABC books. Animals. Poetry.

The whole night through ill. by author. HarperCollins, 2002. ISBN 0-06-028826-4 Subj: Animals – leopards. Jungle. Lullabies. Rhyming text. Sleep.

Franceschelli, Christopher. *The bear's cave* (Schindler, Regina)

Francia, Silvia. *Roberta's vacation* ill. by author. Kane/Miller, 1998. ISBN 0-916291-83-9 Subj: Animals – dogs. Friendship. Sea & seashore.

Francis, Anna B. *Pleasant dreams* ill. by author. Holt, 1983. ISBN 0-03-060574-1 Subj: Dreams. Monsters. Toys.

Francis, Frank. *The magic wallpaper* ill. by author. Abelard-Schuman, 1970. ISBN 0-20-071651-4 Subj: Animals. Behavior – lost. Dreams. Imagination.

Natasha's new doll ill. by author. O'Hara, 1971. Subj: Folk & fairy tales. Foreign lands – Russia. Toys – dolls. Witches.

Francis, Panama. *David gets his drum* by David "Panama" Francis & Bob Reiser; ill. by Eric Velasquez. Cavendish, 2002. ISBN 0-7614-5088-2 Subj: Careers – musicians. Family life. Musical instruments – drums.

Franco, Betsy. *Why the frog has big eyes* ill. by Joung Un Kim. Harcourt, 2000. ISBN 0-15-202536-7 Subj: Folk & fairy tales. Frogs & toads.

Françoise. *see* Seignobosc, Françoise

Frank, John. *A chill in the air: nature poems for fall and winter* ill. by Mike Reed. S&S, 2003. ISBN 0-689-83923-5 Subj: Poetry. Seasons – fall. Seasons – winter.

Odds 'n' Ends Alvy ill. by G. Brian Karas. Four Winds, 1993. ISBN 0-02-735675-2 Subj: Inventions. School.

The toughest cowboy, Or, How the Wild West was tamed ill. by Zachary Pullen. S&S, 2004. ISBN 0-689-83462-4 Subj: Animals – dogs. Cowboys, cowgirls. Humorous stories. U.S. history – frontier & pioneer life.

Frank, Josette. *More poems to read to the very young* ill. by Dagmar Wilson. Random House, 1968. Subj: Poetry.

Poems to read to the very young ill. by Dagmar Wilson. Random House, 1988. ISBN 0-394-99768-9 Subj: Poetry.

Frank, Mary. *The Kingfisher nursery rhyme songbook* (Emerson, Sally)

Frank, Penny. *In the beginning* ill. by Tony Morris. Reader's Digest, 1992. ISBN 0-7459-2608-8 Subj: Creation. Religion.

Frankel, Ben. *Tertius and Pliny* ill. by Emma Chichester Clark. Harcourt, 1992. ISBN 0-15-200604-4 Subj: Friendship. Toys.

Frankel, Bernice. *Half-As-Big and the tiger* ill. by Leonard Weisgard. Watts, 1961. Subj: Animals – deer. Animals – tigers. Character traits – cleverness.

Frankenberg, Lloyd. *Wings of rhyme* ill. by Alan Benjamin. Funk & Wagnalls, 1967. Subj: Nursery rhymes. Poetry.

Franklin, Jonathan. *Don't wake the baby* ill. by author. Farrar, 1991. ISBN 0-374-31826-3 Subj: Babies. Family life – brothers & sisters. Family life – new sibling. Imagination. Sibling rivalry.

Franklin, Kristine L. *The gift* ill. by Barbara Lavallee. Chronicle, 1999. ISBN 0-8118-0447-X Subj: Animals – whales. Old age. Sports – fishing.

The old, old man and the very little boy ill. by Terea D. Shaffer. Atheneum, 1992. ISBN 0-689-31735-2 Subj: Foreign lands – Africa. Friendship. Old age.

When the monkeys came back ill. by Robert Roth. Atheneum, 1994. ISBN 0-689-31807-3 Subj: Animals – monkeys. Ecology. Foreign lands – Costa Rica. Forest, woods. Trees.

Franklin, Paula. *Killian and the dragons* (Company González, Mercé)

Franklin, Sheila. *Egyptian art from the Brooklyn Museum: ABC* (Mayers, Florence Cassen)

The Museum of Fine Arts, Boston: ABC (Mayers, Florence Cassen)

The Museum of Modern Art, New York: ABC (Mayers, Florence Cassen)

The National Air and Space Museum: ABC (Mayers, Florence Cassen)

Frantz, Jennifer. *Totem poles* ill. by Allan Eitzen. Grosset, 2001. ISBN 0-448-42476-2 Subj: Indians of North America – Haida.

Frascino, Edward. *My cousin the king* ill. by author. Prentice-Hall, 1985. ISBN 0-13-608423-0 Subj: Animals. Animals – cats. Character traits – cleverness. Character traits – vanity.

Nanny Noony and the dust queen ill. by author. Pippin Pr., 1990. ISBN 0-945912-09-9 Subj: Animals – cats. Farms. Magic. Weather – droughts. Witches.

Nanny Noony and the magic spell ill. by author. Pippin Pr., 1988. ISBN 0-945912-00-5 Subj: Animals – cats. Birds – crows. Farms. Magic. Witches.

Frasconi, Antonio. *See again, say again: a picture book in four languages* ill. by author. Harcourt, 1964. Subj: Foreign languages.

See and say: a picture book in four languages ill. by author. Harcourt, 1955. Subj: Foreign languages.

The snow and the sun = la nieve y el sol: a South American folk rhyme in two languages ill. by author. Harcourt, 1961. ISBN 0-15-276565-4 Subj: Folk & fairy tales. Foreign lands – South America. Foreign languages. Poetry.

Fraser, Ferrin. *Jungle animals* (Buck, Frank)

Fraser, James Howard. *Los Posadas: a Christmas story* ill. by Nick De Grazia. Northland, 1963. Subj: Ethnic groups in the U.S. – Mexican Americans. Foreign lands – Mexico. Holidays – Christmas. Religion.

Fraser, Kathleen. *Adam's world, San Francisco* by Kathleen Fraser & Miriam F. Levy; ill. by Helen D. Hipshman. A. Whitman, 1971. ISBN 0-8075-0174-3 Subj: Cities, towns. Ethnic groups in the U.S. – African Americans. Family life.

Fraser, Mary Ann. *Forest fire!* ill. by author. Fulcrum Kids, 1996. ISBN 1-55591-251-6 Subj: Ecology. Fire. Forest, woods.

How animal babies stay safe ill. by author. HarperCollins, 2002. ISBN 0-06-028804-3 Subj: Animals – babies. Family life – parents.

I.Q. goes to school ill. by author. Walker, 2002. ISBN 0-8027-8813-0 Subj: Animals – mice. Pets. School.

I.Q. goes to the library ill. by author. Walker, 2003. ISBN 0-8027-8877-7 Subj: Animals – mice. Libraries. Pets. School.

Where are the night animals? ill. by author. HarperCollins, 1999. ISBN 0-06-027718-1 Subj: Animals. Night.

Fraser, Phyllis Maurine. *Mother Goose* (Mother Goose)

Mother Goose: or, the old nursery rhymes (Mother Goose)

Frasier, Debra. *On the day you were born* ill. by author. Harcourt, 1991. ISBN 0-15-257995-8 Subj: Babies. Birth. Poetry.

Out of the ocean ill. by author. Harcourt, 1998. ISBN 0-15-258849-3 Subj: Family life – mothers. Sea & seashore.

Fraustino, Lisa Rowe. *The hickory chair* ill. by Benny Andrews. Levine, 2000. ISBN 0-590-52248-5 Subj: Death. Family life – grandmothers. Handicaps – blindness.

Frazee, Marla. *Roller coaster* ill. by author. Harcourt, 2003. ISBN 0-15-204554-6 Subj: Emotions – fear. Parks – amusement.

Santa Claus, the world's number one toy expert ill. by author. Harcourt, 2005. ISBN 0-15-204970-3 Subj: Gifts. Holidays – Christmas. Santa Claus. Toys.

Fredericks, Anthony D. *In one tidepool: crabs, snails, and salty tails* ill. by Jennifer DiRubbio. Dawn, 2002. ISBN 1-58469-039-9 Subj: Animals. Birds – geese. Forest, woods. Seasons – winter.

Freedman, Claire. *Hushabye Lily* ill. by John Bendall-Brunello. Orchard, 2003. ISBN 0-439-47106-0 Subj: Animals – rabbits. Bedtime. Noise, sounds.

Night-night, Emily ill. by Jane Massey. Tiger Tales, 2003. ISBN 1-58925-032-X Subj: Bedtime. Behavior – lost & found possessions. Toys. Toys – bears.

Where's your smile, crocodile? ill. by Sean Julian. Peachtree, 2001. ISBN 1-56145-251-3 Subj: Animals. Emotions. Reptiles – alligators, crocodiles.

Freedman, Florence B. *Brothers: a Hebrew legend* ill. by Robert Andrew Parker. HarperCollins, 1985. ISBN 0-06-021872-X Subj: Emotions – love. Family life – brothers. Folk & fairy tales. Jewish culture.

Freedman, Russell. *Farm babies* photos by author. Holiday, 1981. ISBN 0-8234-0426-9 Subj: Animals. Farms.

Hanging on: how animals carry their young ill. by author. Holiday, 1977. ISBN 0-8234-0292-4 Subj: Animals. Science.

Tooth and claw: a look at animal weapons photos by author. Holiday, 1980. ISBN 0-8234-0406-4 Subj: Animals. Science.

When winter comes ill. by Pamela Johnson. Dutton, 1981. ISBN 0-525-42583-7 Subj: Animals. Science. Seasons – winter.

Freedman, Sally. *Devin's new bed* ill. by Robin Oz. A. Whitman, 1986. ISBN 0-8075-1565-5 Subj: Bedtime. Behavior – growing up. Furniture – beds.

Monster birthday party ill. by Diane Dawson. A. Whitman, 1983. ISBN 0-8075-5259-3 Subj: Birthdays. Monsters. Parties.

Freeman, David. *The nutcracker* (Hoffmann, E. T. A.)

Freeman, Don. *Add-a-line alphabet* ill. by author. Golden Gate, 1968. Subj: ABC books. Animals.

Beady Bear ill. by author. Viking, 1954. ISBN 0-670-15056-8 Subj: Behavior – running away. Toys – bears.

Bearymore ill. by author. Viking, 1976. ISBN 0-670-15174-2 Subj: Animals – bears. Circus. Hibernation.

The chalk box story ill. by author. Lippincott, 1976. ISBN 0-397-31699-2 Subj: Activities – painting. Concepts – color.

Come again, pelican ill. by author. Viking, 1961. Subj: Birds – pelicans. Sea & seashore.

Corduroy ill. by author. Viking, 1968. ISBN 0-670-24133-4 Subj: Clothing. Emotions – love. Ethnic groups in the U.S. – African Americans. Stores. Toys – bears.

Corduroy's best Halloween ever! (McCue, Lisa)

Corduroy's birthday (Hennessy, B. G. [Barbara G.])

Corduroy's busy street and Corduroy goes to the doctor ill. by author. Live Oak Media, 1989. ISBN 0-87499-133-1 Subj: Careers – doctors. Communities, neighborhoods. Format, unusual – board books. Toys – bears.

Corduroy's Christmas (Hennessy, B. G. [Barbara G.])

Corduroy's Easter (Hennessy, B. G. [Barbara G.])

Corduroy's Halloween (Hennessy, B. G. [Barbara G.])

Cyrano the crow ill. by author. Viking, 1960. Subj: Birds – crows.

Dandelion ill. by author. Viking, 1964. ISBN 0-670-25532-7 Subj: Animals – lions. Character traits – appearance. Parties. Weather – rain.

The day is waiting ill. by author; words by Linda Z. Knab. Viking, 1980. ISBN 0-670-71820-3 Subj: Activities. Rhyming text.

Fly high, fly low ill. by author. Viking, 1957. Subj: Birds. Caldecott award honor books. Cities, towns.

Forever laughter ill. by author. Golden Gate, 1970. ISBN 0-8746-4058-X Subj: Clowns, jesters. Humorous stories. Royalty. Wordless.

Gregory's Shadow ill. by author. Viking, 2000. ISBN 0-670-89328-5 Subj: Animals – groundhogs. Holidays – Groundhog Day. Shadows.

The guard mouse ill. by author. Viking, 1967. ISBN 0-670-35639-5 Subj: Animals – mice. Birthdays. Cities, towns. Foreign lands – England.

Hattie the backstage bat ill. by author. Viking, 1970. ISBN 0-670-36253-0 Subj: Animals – bats. Theater.

Mop Top ill. by author. Viking, 1955. Subj: Birthdays. Careers – barbers. Hair. Rhyming text.

The night the lights went out ill. by author. Viking, 1958. Subj: Careers. Night. Power failures. Seasons – winter.

Norman the doorman ill. by author. Viking, 1981, c1959. ISBN 0-14-050588-2 Subj: Animals – mice. Art. Museums.

The paper party ill. by author. Viking, 1974. ISBN 0-670-53804-3 Subj: Imagination. Parties. Puppets.

Pet of the Met (Freeman, Lydia)

A pocket for Corduroy ill. by author. Viking, 1978. ISBN 0-670-56172-X Subj: Clothing. Ethnic groups in the U.S. – African Americans. Laundry. Toys – bears.

Quiet! There's a canary in the library ill. by author. Golden Gate, 1969. ISBN 0-516-08737-1 Subj: Birds – canaries. Emotions – embarrassment. Imagination. Libraries.

A rainbow of my own ill. by author. Viking, 1966. ISBN 0-570-58928-4 Subj: Concepts – color. Weather – rainbows.

The seal and the slick ill. by author. Viking, 1974. ISBN 0-670-62659-7 Subj: Animals – seals. Character traits – kindness to animals. Ecology. Oil.

Ski pup ill. by author. Viking, 1963. Subj: Animals – dogs. Foreign lands – Switzerland. Sports – skiing.

Space witch ill. by author. Viking, 1959. ISBN 0-670-65995-9 Subj: Holidays – Halloween. Space & space ships. Witches.

Tilly Witch ill. by author. Viking, 1969. ISBN 0-670-71303-1 Subj: Character traits – meanness. Holidays – Halloween. Witches.

The turtle and the dove ill. by author. Viking, 1964. Subj: Birds – doves. Reptiles – turtles, tortoises.

Will's quill ill. by author. Viking, 1975. ISBN 0-670-76922-3 Subj: Birds – geese. Foreign lands – England. Shakespeare. Theater.

Freeman, Ira Maximilian. *The sun, the moon and the stars* (Freeman, Mae Blacker)

You will go to the moon (Freeman, Mae Blacker)

Freeman, Jean Todd. *Cynthia and the unicorn* ill. by Leonard Weisgard. Norton, 1967. Subj: Holidays – Christmas. Mythical creatures – unicorns. Poetry.

Freeman, Lydia. *Corduroy's day* ill. by Lisa McCue. Viking, 1985. ISBN 0-670-80521-1 Subj: Counting, numbers. Format, unusual – board books. Toys – bears.

Pet of the Met ill. by Don Freeman. Viking, 1953. ISBN 0-670-54875-8 Subj: Animals – mice. Music. Theater.

Freeman, Mae Blacker. *The sun, the moon and the stars* by Mae & Ira Freeman; ill. by René Martin. Rev. ed. Random House, 1979. ISBN 0-394-90110-X Subj: Moon. Science. Stars. Sun.

You will go to the moon by Mae & Ira Freeman; ill. by Lee J. Ames. Rev. ed. Random House, 1971. ISBN 0-394-92340-5 Subj: Moon. Space & space ships.

Freeman, Martha. *The trouble with babies* ill. by Cat Bowman Smith. Holiday, 2002. ISBN 0-8234-1698-4 Subj: Communities, neighborhoods. Family life – stepfamilies. Moving.

Freeman, Mylo. *Potty* ill. by author. Tricycle, 2002. ISBN 1-58246-070-1 Subj: Animals. Behavior – growing up. Jungle. Toilet training.

Shanti (Padt, Maartje)

Freeman, Suzanne (Suzanne T.). *One more Wednesday* (Doray, Malika)

Freeman, Tor. *Hooray! I'm five today!* ill. by author. Candlewick, 2004. ISBN 0-7636-2452-7 Subj: Animals. Birthdays. Parties.

Fregosi, Claudia. *The happy horse* ill. by author. Greenwillow, 1977. ISBN 0-688-84087-6 Subj: Animals – horses, ponies. Seasons – fall.

The pumpkin sparrow: adapt. from a Korean folktale ill. by author. Morrow, 1977. Subj: Birds – sparrows. Folk & fairy tales. Foreign lands – Korea.

Snow maiden ill. by author. Prentice-Hall, 1979. ISBN 0-13-815340-X Subj: Folk & fairy tales. Foreign lands – Russia.

French, Fiona. *Anancy and Mr. Dry-Bone* ill. by author. Little, 1991. ISBN 0-316-29298-2 Subj: Animals. Clothing. Folk & fairy tales.

Bethlehem: from the Authorized Version of the King James Bible (Bible New Testament Gospels)

The blue bird ill. by author. Walck, 1972. ISBN 0-8098-1194-4 Subj: Birds.

Easter: from the King James Bible (Bible New Testament Gospels)

Hunt the thimble ill. by author. Oxford Univ. Pr., 1978. ISBN 0-19279-719-0 Subj: Games. Participation.

King of another country ill. by author. Scholastic, 1993. ISBN 0-590-46369-1 Subj: Folk & fairy tales. Foreign lands – Africa. Royalty – kings.

Little Inchkin ill. by author. Dial, 1994. ISBN 0-8037-1478-5 Subj: Concepts – size. Folk & fairy tales. Foreign lands – Japan. Little people.

Lord of the animals: a Miwok Indian creation myth ill. by author. Millbrook, 1997. ISBN 0-7613-0112-7 Subj: Animals – coyotes. Creation. Folk & fairy tales. Indians of North America – Miwok.

Rise and shine ill. by adapt. Little, 1989. ISBN 0-316-29299-0 Subj: Boats, ships. Religion – Noah. Songs. Weather – floods. Weather – rain.

Snow White in New York ill. by author. Oxford Univ. Pr., 1987. ISBN 0-19-279808-1 Subj: Cities, towns. Crime. Dwarfs, midgets. Family life – stepfamilies.

French, Jackie. *Diary of a wombat* ill. by Bruce Whatley. Clarion, 2003. ISBN 0-618-38136-8 Subj: Animals – wombats.

French, Paul. *see* Asimov, Isaac

French, Simon. *Guess the baby* ill. by Donna Rawlins. Clarion, 2002. ISBN 0-618-25989-9 Subj: Babies. School.

French, Vivian. *Caterpillar, caterpillar* ill. by Charlotte Voake. Candlewick, 1995. ISBN 1-56402-206-4 Subj: Family life – grandfathers. Insects – butterflies, caterpillars. Metamorphosis.

Christmas kitten ill. by Chris Fisher. Candlewick, 1996. ISBN 0-7636-0046-6 Subj: Animals – cats. Holidays – Christmas. Santa Claus.

A Christmas star called Hannah ill. by Anne Yvonne Gilbert. Candlewick, 1997. ISBN 0-7636-0397-X Subj: Family life – brothers & sisters. Holidays – Christmas. School. Theater.

Growing frogs ill. by Alison Bartlett. Candlewick, 2000. ISBN 0-7636-0317-1 Subj: Animals – babies. Frogs & toads.

It's a go-to-the-park day ill. by Clive Scruton. S&S, 1992. ISBN 0-671-74477-1 Subj: Animals – moles. Behavior – running away.

Lazy Jack ill. by Russell Ayto. Candlewick, 1995. ISBN 1-56402-130-0 Subj: Behavior. Folk & fairy tales.

Little Ghost ill. by John Prater. Candlewick, 1994. ISBN 1-56402-394-X Subj: Activities – flying. Activities – playing. Ghosts.

Little Tiger finds a friend ill. by Andy Cooke. Candlewick, 1996. ISBN 0-7636-0070-9 Subj: Animals – tigers. Friendship. Kites.

Little Tiger goes shopping ill. by Andy Cooke. Candlewick, 1994. ISBN 1-56402-263-3 Subj: Animals. Animals – tigers. Behavior – sharing.

Molly in the middle ill. by Venice Shone. Candlewick, 1996. ISBN 1-56402-945-X Subj: Concepts – size. Family life – brothers & sisters.

Oh no, Anna! ill. by Alex Ayliffe. Peachtree, 1997. ISBN 1-56145-125-8 Subj: Accidents. Concepts – color. Format, unusual – toy & movable books.

Oliver's fruit salad ill. by Alison Bartlett. Orchard, 1998. ISBN 0-531-30087-0 Subj: Family life – grandfathers. Food.

Oliver's vegetables ill. by Alison Bartlett. Orchard, 1995. ISBN 0-531-09462-6 Subj: Family life – grandparents. Food. Gardens, gardening.

Once upon a picnic (Prater, John)

Once upon a time (Prater, John)

One ballerina two ill. by Jan Ormerod. Lothrop, 1991. ISBN 0-688-10334-0 Subj: Activities – dancing. Ballet. Counting, numbers.

A present for mom ill. by Dana Kubick. Candlewick, 2002. ISBN 0-7636-1587-0 Subj: Animals – cats. Gifts. Holidays – Mother's Day.

Red Hen and Sly Fox ill. by Sally Hobson. S&S, 1995. ISBN 0-689-80010-X Subj: Animals – foxes. Birds – chickens. Character traits – cleverness. Folk & fairy tales.

A song for little toad ill. by Barbara Firth. Candlewick, 1998. ISBN 1-56402-614-0 Subj: Family life. Frogs & toads. Lullabies.

Spider watching ill. by Alison Wisenfeld. Candlewick, 1995. ISBN 1-56402-543-8 Subj: Family life – cousins. Spiders.

The thistle princess ill. by Elizabeth Harbour. Candlewick, 1998. ISBN 0-7636-0307-4 Subj: Folk & fairy tales. Royalty – princesses.

Tiger and the new baby by Vivian French & Rebecca Elgar; ill. by Rebecca Elgar. Kingfisher, 1999. ISBN 0-7534-5198-0 Subj: Animals – tigers. Babies. Family life – brothers & sisters.

Tiger and the temper tantrum by Vivian French & Rebecca Elgar; ill. by Rebecca Elgar. Kingfisher, 1999. ISBN 0-7534-5197-2 Subj: Animals – tigers. Behavior. Emotions – anger. Family life.

Whale journey ill. by Lisa Flather. Zero to Ten, 1998. ISBN 1-84089-022-3 Subj: Animals – whales. Sea & seashore.

Why the sea is salt ill. by Patrice Aggs. Candlewick, 1993. ISBN 1-56402-183-1 Subj: Character traits – generosity. Folk & fairy tales. Foreign lands – Norway. Magic. Sea & seashore.

Freschet, Berniece. *The ants go marching* ill. by Stefan Martin. Scribners, 1973. ISBN 0-684-13250-8 Subj: Activities – picnicking. Counting, numbers. Insects – ants. Poetry.

Bear mouse ill. by Donald Carrick. Scribners, 1973. ISBN 0-684-13320-2 Subj: Animals – mice. Science.

Bernard of Scotland Yard ill. by Gina Freschet. Scribners, 1978. ISBN 0-684-15931-7 Subj: Animals – mice. Foreign lands – England. Mystery stories.

Elephant and friends ill. by Glen Rounds. Scribners, 1978. ISBN 0-684-15530-3 Subj: Animals – elephants. Character traits – cleverness.

Five fat raccoons ill. by Irene Brady. Scribners, 1980. ISBN 0-684-16253-9 Subj: Animals – raccoons.

Furlie Cat ill. by Betsy Lewin. Lothrop, 1986. ISBN 0-688-05918-X Subj: Animals – cats. Behavior – bullying. Emotions – fear.

The little woodcock ill. by Leonard Weisgard. Scribners, 1967. Subj: Birds. Science.

Moose baby ill. by Jim Arnosky. Putnam, 1979. ISBN 0-399-61146-0 Subj: Animals – moose. Science.

The old bullfrog ill. by Roger Antoine Duvoisin. Scribners, 1968. ISBN 0-24101-684-3 Subj: Frogs & toads.

Owl in the garden ill. by Carol Newsom. Lothrop, 1985. ISBN 0-688-04048-9 Subj: Animals. Behavior – stealing. Birds. Birds – owls. Seasons – fall.

Possum baby ill. by Jim Arnosky. Putnam, 1978. ISBN 0-399-61105-3 Subj: Animals – possums.

Turtle pond ill. by Donald Carrick. Scribners, 1971. ISBN 0-684-12326-6 Subj: Reptiles – turtles, tortoises.

The watersnake ill. by Susanne Suba. Scribners, 1979. ISBN 0-684-16112-5 Subj: Reptiles – snakes.

The web in the grass ill. by Roger Antoine Duvoisin. Scribners, 1972. ISBN 0-684-12956-6 Subj: Spiders.

Where's Henrietta's hen? ill. by Lorinda Bryan Cauley. Putnam, 1980. ISBN 0-399-20669-8 Subj: Animals. Birds – chickens. Counting, numbers. Farms.

Wood duck baby ill. by Jim Arnosky. Putnam, 1983. ISBN 0-399-61191-6 Subj: Birds – ducks. Science.

Freschet, Gina. *Beto and the bone dance* ill. by author. Farrar, 2001. ISBN 0-374-31720-8 Subj: Ethnic groups in the U.S. – Mexican Americans. Holidays – Day of the Dead.

Naty's parade ill. by author. Farrar, 2000. ISBN 0-374-35500-2 Subj: Behavior – lost. Holidays. Parades.

Freudberg, Judy. *Some, more, most* ill. by Richard Hefter. Larousse, 1976. ISBN 0-8847-0023-2 Subj: Concepts.

Susan and Gordon adopt a baby by Judy Freudberg & Tony Geiss; ill. by Joseph Mathieu. Random House, 1992. ISBN 0-394-98341-6 Subj: Adoption. Family life. Puppets.

Freymann, Saxton. *Dr. Pompo's nose* by Saxton Freymann & Joost Eiffers; ill. by authors. Levine, 2000. ISBN 0-439-11013-0 Subj: Anatomy – noses. Rhyming text.

One lonely seahorse by Saxton Freymann & Joost Eiffers; ill. by authors. Levine, 2000. ISBN 0-439-11014-9 Subj: Counting, numbers. Fish – seahorses. Friendship. Rhyming text. Sea & seashore.

Fribourg, Marjorie G. *Ching-Ting and the ducks* ill. by Artur Marokvia. Sterling, 1957. Subj: Behavior – growing up. Birds – ducks. Foreign lands – China.

Frieden, Sarajo. *The care and feeding of fish* ill. by author. Houghton Mifflin, 1996. ISBN 0-395-71251-3 Subj: Character traits – being different. Fish.

Friedman, Aileen. *The king's commissioners* ill. by Susan Guevara. Scholastic, 1994. ISBN 0-590-48989-5 Subj: Counting, numbers. Royalty – kings.

Friedman, Ina R. *How my parents learned to eat* ill. by Allen Say. Houghton Mifflin, 1984. ISBN 0-395-35379-3 Subj: Family life. Sailors.

Friedman, Laurie B. *A style all her own* ill. by Sharon Watts. Lerner, 2005. ISBN 1-57505-599-6 Subj: Character traits – individuality. Clothing – dresses. Weddings.

Friedman, Mel. *Kitten castle* by Mel Friedman & Ellen Weiss; ill. by Lynn Adams. Kane Pr., 2001. ISBN 1-57565-103-3 Subj: Animals – babies. Animals – cats. Concepts – shape.

Friedrich, Elizabeth. *Leah's pony* ill. by Michael Garland. Boyds Mills, 1996. ISBN 1-56397-189-5 Subj: Careers – farmers. Poverty. U.S. history. Weather – droughts.

Friedrich, Otto. *The Easter bunny that overslept* (Friedrich, Priscilla)

The marshmallow ghosts (Friedrich, Priscilla)

The wishing well in the woods (Friedrich, Priscilla)

Friedrich, Priscilla. *The Easter bunny that overslept* by Priscilla & Otto Friedrich; ill. by Adrienne Adams. Lothrop, 1957. ISBN 0-688-01541-7 Subj: Holidays – Easter.

The marshmallow ghosts by Priscilla & Otto Friedrich; ill. by Louis Slobodkin. Lothrop, 1960. Subj: Ghosts. Holidays – Halloween.

The wishing well in the woods by Priscilla & Otto Friedrich; ill. by Roger Antoine Duvoisin. Lothrop, 1961. Subj: Animals. Behavior – wishing.

Friend, Catherine. *Eddie the raccoon* ill. by Wong Herbert Yee. Candlewick, 2004. ISBN 0-7636-2334-2 Subj: Activities. Animals – raccoons.

Funny Ruby ill. by Rachel Merriman. Candlewick, 2000. ISBN 0-7636-1066-6 Subj: Activities. Animals – sheep.

The friendly beasts ill. by Sarah Chamberlain. Dutton, 1991. ISBN 0-525-44773-3 Subj: Animals. Holidays – Christmas. Music. Religion.

The friendly beasts and a partridge in a pear tree ill. by Virginia Parsons; calligraphy by Sheila Waters. Doubleday, 1966. Subj: Holidays – Christmas. Music. Poetry. Religion. Songs.

Fries, Claudia. *A pig is moving in* ill. by author. Orchard, 2000. ISBN 0-531-33307-8 Subj: Animals. Communities, neighborhoods. Homes, houses. Prejudice.

Friskey, Margaret (Margaret Richards). *Birds we know* ill. with photos. Childrens Pr., 1981. ISBN 0-516-01609-1 Subj: Birds. Science.

Chicken Little, count-to-ten ill. by Katherine Evans. Childrens Pr., 1946. Subj: Counting, numbers.

Indian Two Feet and his eagle feather ill. by John & Lucy Hawkinson. Childrens Pr., 1967. ISBN 0-516-03503-7 Subj: Indians of North America.

Indian Two Feet and his horse ill. by Katherine Evans. Childrens Pr., 1959. ISBN 0-516-03501-0 Subj: Animals – horses, ponies. Indians of North America.

Indian Two Feet and the wolf cubs ill. by John Hawkinson. Childrens Pr., 1971. ISBN 0-516-03506-1 Subj: Animals – wolves. Indians of North America.

Indian Two Feet rides alone ill. by John Hawkinson. Childrens Pr., 1980. ISBN 0-516-03523-1 Subj: Character traits – pride. Indians of North America.

Mystery of the gate sign ill. by Katherine Evans. Childrens Pr., 1958. Subj: Animals – rabbits. Books, reading.

The perky little pumpkin ill. by Tom Dunnington. Childrens Pr., 1990. ISBN 0-516-03564-9 Subj: Holidays – Halloween.

Seven diving ducks ill. by Jean Morey. Childrens Pr., 1965. ISBN 0-516-03605-X Subj: Birds – ducks. Counting, numbers.

Three sides and the round one ill. by Mary Gehr. Childrens Pr., 1973. ISBN 0-516-03627-0 Subj: Concepts – shape.

Frissen. *Yann and the whale* (Hanze)

Frith, Margaret. *Frida Kahlo: the artist who painted herself* ill. by Tomie de Paola. Grosset, 2003. ISBN 0-448-43239-0 Subj: Careers – artists. Foreign lands – Mexico.

Frith, Michael K. *I'll teach my dog 100 words* ill. by P. D. Eastman. Random House, 1973. ISBN 0-394-92692-7 Subj: Animals – dogs. Humorous stories. Rhyming text.

Some of us walk, some fly, some swim ill. by author. Random House, 1971. ISBN 0-394-92325-1 Subj: Animals. Science.

Fritts, Mary Bahr. *If Nathan were here* ill. by Karen A. Jerome. Eerdmans, 2000. ISBN 0-8028-5187-8 Subj: Death. Emotions – grief. Friendship.

Fritz, Jean. *The good giants and the bad Pukwudgies* ill. by Tomie de Paola. Putnam, 1982. ISBN 0-399-20870-4 Subj: Folk & fairy tales. Giants. Indians of North America – Wampanoag.

Froese, Deborah L. *The wise washerman* ill. by Wang Kui. Hyperion, 1996. ISBN 0-7868-2232-5 Subj: Animals – elephants. Character traits – wisdom. Folk & fairy tales. Foreign lands – Burma. Royalty – kings.

A frog he would a-wooing go (folk-song). *Frog went a-courtin'* retold by John Langstaff; ill. by Feodor Rojankovsky. Harcourt, 1955. ISBN 0-15-230214-X Subj: Animals. Caldecott award books. Frogs & toads. Songs.

Frog went a-courting: a musical play in six acts retold & ill. by Dominic Catalano. Boyds Mills, 1998. ISBN 1-56397-637-4 Subj: Animals. Foreign lands – Scotland. Frogs & toads. Music. Songs. Theater. Weddings.

Froggie went a courting adapt. & ill. by Marjorie Priceman. Little, 1999. ISBN 0-316-71227-2 Subj: Animals. Frogs & toads. Songs. Weddings.

Froggie went a-courting retold & ill. by Chris Conover. Farrar, 1986. ISBN 0-374-32466-2 Subj: Animals. Frogs & toads. Music. Songs. Weddings.

Mr. Frog went a-courting: discover the secret story adapt. & ill. by Gary Chalk. DK, 1994. ISBN 1-56458-622-7 Subj: Animals. Foreign lands – England. Frogs & toads. Music. Songs. Weddings.

Wendy Watson's frog went a-courting ill. by Wendy Watson. Lothrop, 1990. ISBN 0-688-06540-6 Subj: Animals. Frogs & toads. Music. Songs. Weddings.

Froissart, Bénédicte. *Uncle Henry's dinner guests* ill. by Pierre Pratt. Firefly, 1990. ISBN 1-55037-141-X Subj: Birds – chickens. Clothing. Family life – aunts, uncles.

From King Boggen's hall to nothing-at-all: *a collection of improbable houses and unusual places found in traditional rhymes and limericks* ill. by Blair Lent. Little, 1967. Subj: Animals. Nursery rhymes.

From morn to midnight sel. by Elaine Moss; ill. by Satomi Ichikawa. Crowell, 1977. ISBN 0-690-01394-9 Subj: Poetry.

Froman, Robert. *Angles are easy as pie* ill. by Byron Barton. Crowell, 1976. ISBN 0-690-00916-X Subj: Concepts.

A game of functions ill. by Enrico Arno. Crowell, 1975. ISBN 0-690-00545-8 Subj: Concepts.

Froment, Eugène. *The story of a round loaf* adapt. & ill. by Kathleen Rebek. Prentice-Hall, 1979. ISBN 0-13-850834-8 Subj: Behavior – misbehavior. Foreign lands – France.

Fromm, Lilo. *Muffel and Plums* ill. by author. Macmillan, 1972. Subj: Animals. Wordless.

Frost, Erica. *see* Supraner, Robyn

Frost, Helen. *Drinking water* ill. with photos. Pebble, 2000. ISBN 0-7368-0534-6 Subj: Water.

Eating right ill. with photos. Pebble, 2000. ISBN 0-7368-0535-4 Subj: Food. Health & fitness.

Feeling angry ill. with photos. Pebble, 2001. ISBN 0-7368-0668-7 Subj: Emotions – anger.

Feeling happy ill. with photos. Pebble, 2001. ISBN 0-7368-0669-5 Subj: Emotions – happiness.

Feeling sad ill. with photos. Pebble, 2001. ISBN 0-7368-0670-9 Subj: Emotions – sadness.

Feeling scared ill. with photos. Pebble, 2001. ISBN 0-7368-0671-7 Subj: Emotions – fear.

The fruit group ill. with photos. Pebble, 2000. ISBN 0-7368-0537-0 Subj: Food. Health & fitness.

The grain group ill. with photos. Pebble, 2000. ISBN 0-7368-0538-9 Subj: Food. Health & fitness.

Martin Luther King, Jr. Day ill. with photos. Pebble, 2000. ISBN 0-7368-0543-5 Subj: Careers – clergy. Ethnic groups in the U.S. – African Americans. Holidays – Martin Luther King, Jr. Day.

Memorial Day ill. with photos. Pebble, 2000. ISBN 0-7368-0544-3 Subj: Holidays – Memorial Day.

Frost, Robert. *Birches* ill. by Ed Young. Holt, 1988. ISBN 0-8050-0570-6 Subj: Poetry. Trees.

The runaway ill. by Glenna Lang. Godine, 1996. ISBN 1-56792-006-3 Subj: Animals – horses, ponies. Emotions – fear. Poetry. Weather – snow.

Stopping by woods on a snowy evening ill. by Susan Jeffers. Dutton, 1978. ISBN 0-525-40115-6 Subj: Forest, woods. Poetry. Seasons – winter.

Fruisen, Catherine Myler. *My mother's pearls* ill. by author. Star Bright, 2005. ISBN 1-595-72005-7 Subj: Family life – daughters. Family life – mothers. Jewelry.

Fry, Christopher. *The boat that mooed* ill. by Leonard Weisgard. Macmillan, 1965. Subj: Boats, ships. Weather – fog.

The boy and the magic (Colette, Sidonie Gabrielle)

Fry, Jenny. *Building numbers* ill. by Jacqueline East. Barron's, 2002. ISBN 0-7641-5499-0 Subj: Counting, numbers. Machines.

Frye, Dean. *Days of sunshine, days of rain* ill. by Roger Antoine Duvoisin. McGraw-Hill, 1965. Subj: Theater. Weather.

Fuchs, Erich. *Journey to the moon* ill. by author. Delacorte, 1969. Translation of Hier Apollo 11. Subj: Moon. Space & space ships. Wordless.

Fuchshuber, Annegert. *Carly* ill. by author; tr. by Florence Howe & Heidi Kirk. Feminist Pr., 1997. ISBN 1-55861-177-0 Subj: Character traits – kindness. Homeless. Prejudice.

Giant story – Mouse tale: a half picture book ill. by author. Carolrhoda, 1988. ISBN 0-87614-319-2 Subj: Animals – dormice. Character traits – bravery. Format, unusual – toy & movable books. Friendship. Giants.

Two peas in a pod ill. by author. Millbrook, 1998. ISBN 0-7613-0410-X Subj: Animals. Animals – babies. Birth. Character traits – individuality. Counting, numbers. Multiple births – twins.

The wishing hat ill. by author. Morrow, 1977. Translation of Korbinian mit dem Wunschhut by Elizabeth D. Crawford. ISBN

0-688-32100-3 Subj: Behavior – wishing. Humorous stories. Magic.

Fuge, Charles. *I know a rhino* ill. by author. Sterling, 2002. ISBN 1-4027-0137-3 Subj: Activities – playing. Animals. Imagination. Rhyming text.

What is stuck (Hayles, Karen)

Yip! Snap! Yap! ill. by author. Tricycle, 2001. ISBN 1-58246-046-9 Subj: Animals – dogs. Noise, sounds.

Fuhr, Ute. *Bees* (Bees)

Native Americans (Native Americans)

Whales (Whales)

Fujikawa, Gyo. *Are you my friend today?* ill. by author. Random House, 1988. ISBN 0-394-99031-5 Subj: Friendship.

Baby Mother Goose ill. by author. Random House, 1989. ISBN 0-394-89032-9 Subj: Nursery rhymes.

Gyo Fujikawa's A to Z picture book ill. by author. Grosset, 1974. ISBN 0-448-13205-2 Subj: ABC books.

Let's grow a garden ill. by author. Grosset, 1978. ISBN 0-448-14613-4 Subj: Format, unusual – board books. Gardens, gardening.

Millie's secret ill. by author. Grosset, 1978. ISBN 0-448-14726-2 Subj: Animals – dogs. Format, unusual – board books. Wordless.

My favorite thing ill. by author. Grosset, 1978. ISBN 0-448-14727-0 Subj: Activities. Format, unusual – board books. Wordless.

Sam's all-wrong day ill. by author. Grosset, 1982. ISBN 0-448-11755-X Subj: Behavior – bad day.

See what I can be! ill. by author. Grosset, 1990. ISBN 0-448-09257-3 Subj: Format, unusual – board books. Imagination. Self-concept.

Shags finds a kitten ill. by author. Grosset, 1983. ISBN 0-448-16465-5 Subj: Animals – cats. Animals – dogs. Emotions – loneliness.

Surprise! Surprise! ill. by author. Grosset, 1978. ISBN 0-448-14557-X Subj: Activities. Format, unusual – board books.

Ten little babies ill. by author. Random House, 1989. ISBN 0-394-89033-7 Subj: Babies. Counting, numbers. Rhyming text.

That's not fair! ill. by author. Grosset, 1983. ISBN 0-448-16466-3 Subj: Activities – playing. Seasons – winter.

Fujita, Miho. *The little choo-choo: sounds, sights and opposites* ill. by author. Doubleday, 1988. ISBN 0-385-24426-6 Subj: Concepts – opposites. Format, unusual – board books. Noise, sounds. Toys – trains.

Fujita, Tamao. *The boy and the bird* trans. from Japanese by Kiyoko Tucker; ill. by Chiyo Ono. HarperCollins, 1972. Subj: Birds. Character traits – freedom. Foreign lands – Japan. Pets.

Fuller, Ted. *Barney the bus* ill. by Pam DeVito. Windswept House, 1989. ISBN 0-932433-49-9 Subj: Buses.

Funai, Mamoru. *Moke and Poki in the rain forest* ill. by author. HarperCollins, 1972. ISBN 0-060-21927-0 Subj: Hawaii. Mythical creatures – menehunes.

Funakoshi, Canna. *One Christmas* ill. by Yohji Izawa. Picture Book Studio, 1990. ISBN 0-88708-140-1 Subj: Holidays – Christmas.

One evening trans. & ill. by Yohji Izawa. Picture Book Studio, 1988. ISBN 0-88708-063-4 Subj: Night. Seasons – winter. Weather – snow.

One morning ill. by Yohji Izawa. Picture Book Studio, 1986. ISBN 0-88707-033-2 Subj: Animals – cats. Morning.

Funazaki, Yasuko. *Baby owl* ill. by Shuji Tateishi. Methuen, 1980. ISBN 0-416-30721-3 Subj: Birds – owls. Emotions – loneliness.

Funk, Tom (Thompson). *I read signs* ill. by author. Holiday, 1962. Subj: Books, reading.

Furchgott, Terry. *Phoebe and the hot water bottles* by Terry Furchgott & Linda Dawson; ill. by Terry Furchgott. Elsevier-Dutton, 1979. ISBN 0-233-96860-1 Subj: Animals – dogs. Character traits – bravery. Pets.

Furgang, Kathy. *Flower girl* ill. by Harley Jessup. Viking, 2002. ISBN 0-670-88950-4 Subj: Weddings.

Furtado, Jo. *Sorry, Miss Folio!* ill. by Frédéric Joos. Kane/Miller, 1988. ISBN 0-916291-18-9 Subj: Books, reading. Imagination. Libraries.

Fussenegger, Gertrud. *Noah's ark* ill. by Annegert Fuchshuber; trans. by Anthea Bell. Lippincott, 1987. Tr. of Die Arche Noah by Anthea Bell. ISBN 0-397-32242-9 Subj: Animals. Boats, ships. Religion – Noah. Weather – floods. Weather – rain. Weather – rainbows.

Futamata, Eigoro. *How not to catch a mouse* ill. by author. Weatherhill, 1972. Translation of Nezumi wa tsukamaru ka. ISBN 0-8348-2007-2 Subj: Animals. Animals – mice.

Fyleman, Rose. *A fairy went a-marketing* ill. by Jamichael Henterly. Dutton, 1986. ISBN 0-525-44258-8 Subj: Character traits – kindness. Fairies. Poetry. Shopping.

Mary Middling and other silly folk sel. by Neil Philip; ill. by Katja Bandlow. Clarion, 2004. ISBN 0-618-38141-4 Subj: Nursery rhymes. Poetry.

Gabel, Susan L. *Where the sun kisses the sea* ill. by Joanne Bowring. Perspectives Pr., 1989. ISBN 0-944934-00-5 Subj: Adoption. Ethnic groups in the U.S. – Asian Americans. Orphans.

Gabler, Mirko. *The alphabet soup* ill. by author. Holt, 1992. ISBN 0-8050-2049-7 Subj: ABC books. Activities – baking, cooking. Food. Multiple births – twins. Witches.

Brakus, Krakus . . . Or the incredible adventure of Mr. Skola's Tourist Club ill. by author. Holt, 1993. ISBN 0-8050-1963-4 Subj: Castles. Ghosts. Magic. School.

Gabriel, Ashala. *Night night toes* ill. by Sue Porter. Little Simon, 2002. ISBN 0-689-85089-1 Subj: Animals – bears. Bedtime. Format, unusual – toy & movable books. Night.

Gackenbach, Dick. *Alice's special room* ill. by author. Houghton Mifflin, 1991. ISBN 0-395-54433-5 Subj: Family life – mothers.

Annie and the mud monster ill. by author. Lothrop, 1982. ISBN 0-688-00792-9 Subj: Parties.

Arabella and Mr. Crack ill. by author. Macmillan, 1982. A retelling of Joseph Jacob's Master of all masters. ISBN 0-02-735770-8 Subj: Behavior – misunderstanding. Folk & fairy tales.

A bag full of pups ill. by author. Houghton Mifflin, 1981. ISBN 0-395-30081-9 Subj: Animals – dogs.

Barker's crime ill. by author. Harcourt, 1996. ISBN 0-15-200628-1 Subj: Animals – dogs. Behavior – greed. Food. Senses – smell. Shadows.

Beauty, brave and beautiful ill. by author. Clarion, 1990. ISBN 0-395-52000-2 Subj: Animals – dogs. Character traits – bravery.

Binky gets a car ill. by author. Houghton Mifflin, 1983. ISBN 0-89919-144-4 Subj: Behavior – carelessness. Birthdays.

Claude and Pepper ill. by author. Coward, 1976. ISBN 0-816-43157-4 Subj: Animals – dogs. Behavior – running away.

Claude has a picnic ill. by author. Clarion, 1993. ISBN 0-395-61161-X Subj: Activities – picnicking. Animals – dogs. Communities, neighborhoods.

Claude the dog ill. by author. Seabury Pr., 1974. ISBN 0-816-43116-7 Subj: Animals – dogs. Behavior – sharing. Holidays – Christmas.

Crackle, Gluck and the sleeping toad ill. by author. Seabury Pr., 1979. ISBN 0-816-43227-9 Subj: Behavior – lying. Farms. Frogs & toads.

The dog and the deep dark woods ill. by author. HarperCollins, 1984. ISBN 0-06-021978-5 Subj: Animals – dogs. Character traits – pride.

Dog for a day ill. by author. Clarion, 1987. ISBN 0-899-19452-4 Subj: Animals – dogs. Machines.

Harry and the terrible whatzit ill. by author. Seabury Pr., 1977. ISBN 0-816-43182-5 Subj: Emotions – fear. Imagination. Monsters.

Harvey, the foolish pig ill. by author. Clarion, 1988. ISBN 0-89919-540-7 Subj: Animals – pigs. Animals – wolves. Character traits – foolishness. Character traits – luck. Royalty – kings.

Hattie be quiet, Hattie be good ill. by author. HarperCollins, 1977. ISBN 0-06-021952-1 Subj: Animals – rabbits. Behavior. Illness.

Hattie rabbit ill. by author. HarperCollins, 1976. ISBN 0-06-021940-8 Subj: Animals – rabbits. Behavior – wishing.

Hurray for Hattie Rabbit! ill. by author. HarperCollins, 1986. ISBN 0-06-021983-1 Subj: Animals – pigs. Animals – rabbits. Family life – mothers.

Ida Fanfanny ill. by author. HarperCollins, 1978. ISBN 0-06-021954-8 Subj: Magic. Seasons. Weather.

King Wacky ill. by author. Crown, 1984. ISBN 0-517-55265-5 Subj: Behavior – misunderstanding. Royalty – kings.

Little bug ill. by author. Houghton Mifflin, 1981. ISBN 0-395-30080-0 Subj: Behavior – seeking better things. Insects.

Mag the magnificent ill. by author. Clarion, 1985. ISBN 0-89919-339-0 Subj: Imagination. Monsters.

Mighty tree ill. by author. Harcourt, 1992. ISBN 0-15-200519-6 Subj: Nature. Trees.

Mr. Wink and his shadow, Ned ill. by author. HarperCollins, 1983. ISBN 0-06-021974-2 Subj: Shadows.

Mother Rabbit's son Tom ill. by author. HarperCollins, 1978. ISBN 0-06-021948-3 Subj: Animals – rabbits. Behavior – dissatisfaction. Food. Pets.

Pepper and all the legs ill. by author. Seabury Pr., 1978. ISBN 0-8164-3221-X Subj: Animals – dogs. Behavior – misbehavior.

The perfect mouse: a Japanese tale ill. by author. Macmillan, 1984. ISBN 0-02-736760-6 Subj: Animals – mice. Folk & fairy tales. Foreign lands – Japan.

The pig who saw everything ill. by author. Seabury Pr., 1978. ISBN 0-816-43205-8 Subj: Animals – pigs. Character traits – curiosity. Farms. Humorous stories.

Poppy the panda ill. by author. Houghton Mifflin, 1984. ISBN 0-89919-276-9 Subj: Bedtime. Clothing. Toys.

Supposes ill. by author. Harcourt, 1989. ISBN 0-15-200594-3 Subj: Animals. Imagination. Riddles & jokes.

Tiny for a day ill. by author. Clarion, 1993. ISBN 0-395-65616-8 Subj: Concepts – size. Inventions.

What's Claude doing? ill. by author. Houghton Mifflin, 1984. ISBN 0-89919-244-6 Subj: Animals – dogs. Illness.

Where are Momma, Poppa, and Sister June? ill. by author. Clarion, 1994. ISBN 0-395-67323-2 Subj: Behavior – worrying. Family life.

With love from Gran ill. by author. Houghton Mifflin, 1989. ISBN 0-89919-842-2 Subj: Activities – traveling. Family life – grandmothers.

Gadsby, Oliver. *Little Elephant and Big Mouse* (Cantieni, Benita)

The moon lake (Gantschev, Ivan)

Gaeddert, LouAnn Bigge. *Noisy Nancy Norris* ill. by Gioia Fiammenghi. Doubleday, 1965. Subj: Behavior. Noise, sounds.

Gaffington, Urslan Judith. *Silver berries and Christmas magic* ill. by Steven Morris. RiverMoon Books, 1996. ISBN 0-9647811-0-7 Subj: Holidays – Christmas. Magic. Santa Claus.

Gaffney, Michael. *Secret forests* ill. by author. Western, 1994. ISBN 0-307-17505-7 Subj: Animals. Forest, woods. Insects.

Gág, Flavia. *Chubby's first year* ill. by author. Holt, 1960. Subj: Animals – cats. Days of the week, months of the year.

Gág, Wanda. *ABC bunny* ill. by author; hand lettered by Howard Gág. Coward, 1978, c1933. ISBN 0-698-20465-4 Subj: ABC books. Animals – rabbits. Rhyming text.

The earth gnome (Grimm, Jacob)

The funny thing ill. by author. Coward, 1929. ISBN 0-698-30087-1 Subj: Dragons. Food. Monsters.

Gone is gone ill. by author. Coward, 1935. ISBN 0-698-30179-X Subj: Activities – working. Behavior – mistakes. Gender roles.

Jorinda and Joringel (Grimm, Jacob)

Millions of cats ill. by author. Coward, 1928. ISBN 0-698-20091-8 Subj: Animals – cats. Character traits – practicality. Cumulative tales.

Nothing at all ill. by author. Coward, 1941. ISBN 0-698-30264-8 Subj: Animals – dogs. Caldecott award honor books. Emotions – loneliness. Magic.

The six swans (Grimm, Jacob)

Snippy and Snappy ill. by author. Coward, 1931. ISBN 0-698-30319-9 Subj: Animals – mice.

The sorcerer's apprentice ill. by Margot Tomes. Coward, 1979. ISBN 0-698-20481-6 Subj: Behavior – misbehavior. Folk & fairy tales. Magic.

Gage, Wilson. *Anna's garden songs* ill. by Lena Castell Anderson. Greenwillow, 1989. ISBN 0-688-08218-1 Subj: Gardens, gardening. Plants. Poetry.

Anna's summer songs ill. by Lena Castell Anderson. Greenwillow, 1988. ISBN 0-688-07181-3 Subj: Plants. Poetry. Seasons – summer.

The crow and Mrs. Gaddy ill. by Marylin Hafner. Greenwillow, 1984. ISBN 0-688-02536-6 Subj: Behavior – trickery. Birds – crows.

Cully Cully and the bear ill. by James Stevenson. Greenwillow, 1983. ISBN 0-688-01769-X Subj: Animals – bears. Sports – hunting.

Down in the boondocks ill. by Glen Rounds. Greenwillow, 1977. ISBN 0-688-84085-X Subj: Crime. Handicaps – deafness. Rhyming text.

Mrs. Gaddy and the ghost ill. by Marylin Hafner. Greenwillow, 1979. ISBN 0-688-84179-1 Subj: Ghosts. Imagination.

Mrs. Gaddy and the fast-growing vine ill. by Marylin Hafner. Greenwillow, 1985. ISBN 0-688-04232-5 Subj: Animals – goats. Behavior – seeking better things. Gardens, gardening.

Gál, László. *The parrot: an Italian folktale* retold & ill. by László & Raffaella Gál. Groundwood, 1997. ISBN 0-88899-287-4 Subj: Birds – parakeets, parrots. Folk & fairy tales. Foreign lands – Italy. Royalty – princes. Royalty – princesses.

Gál, Raffaella. *The parrot: an Italian folktale* (Gál, László)

Galassi, Jonathan. *A boy named Giotto* (Guarnieri, Paolo)

Galbraith, Kathryn Osebold. *Katie did!* ill. by Ted Ramsey. Atheneum, 1982. ISBN 0-689-50237-0 Subj: Behavior – misbehavior. Family life. Sibling rivalry.

Laura Charlotte ill. by Floyd Cooper. Putnam, 1990. ISBN 0-399-21613-8 Subj: Family life – mothers. Toys.

Look! Snow! ill. by Nina Montezinos. McElderry, 1992. ISBN 0-689-50551-5 Subj: Weather – snow.

Roommates ill. by Mark Graham. Macmillan, 1990. ISBN 0-689-50487-X Subj: Babies. Behavior – growing up. Family life – sisters. Sibling rivalry.

Spots are special ill. by Diane Dawson. Atheneum, 1976. ISBN 0-689-50038-6 Subj: Illness. Imagination.

Waiting for Jennifer ill. by Irene Trivas. Macmillan, 1987. ISBN 0-689-50430-6 Subj: Babies. Behavior – secrets. Family life – new sibling. Family life – sisters.

Galbraith, Richard. *Reuben runs away* ill. by author. Watts, 1989. ISBN 0-531-08390-X Subj: Behavior – running away. Toys – bears.

Galchutt, David. *There was magic inside* ill. by author. S&S, 1993. ISBN 0-671-75978-7 Subj: Careers – fishermen. Dragons. Folk & fairy tales. Magic.

Galdone, Joanna. *Amber day* ill. by Paul Galdone. McGraw-Hill, 1978. ISBN 0-07-022686-5 Subj: Devil. Folk & fairy tales.

Gertrude, the goose who forgot ill. by Paul Galdone. Watts, 1975. ISBN 0-531-02735-X Subj: Behavior – forgetfulness. Birds – geese. Rhyming text.

Honeybee's party ill. by Paul Galdone. Watts, 1972. Subj: Insects – bees. Parties. Spiders.

The little girl and the big bear ill. by Paul Galdone. Houghton Mifflin, 1980. ISBN 0-395-29029-5 Subj: Animals – bears. Folk & fairy tales.

The tailypo: a ghost story ill. by Paul Galdone. Seabury Pr., 1977. ISBN 0-8164-3191-4 Subj: Ghosts.

Galdone, Paul. *The amazing pig: an old Hungarian tale* ill. by author. Houghton Mifflin, 1981. ISBN 0-395-29101-1 Subj: Animals – pigs. Folk & fairy tales. Royalty.

Androcles and the lion ill. by author. McGraw-Hill, 1970. Subj: Animals – lions. Character traits – helpfulness. Character traits – kindness to animals. Folk & fairy tales. Foreign lands – Italy.

Cat goes fiddle-i-fee ill. by adapt. Clarion, 1985. ISBN 0-89919-336-6 Subj: Animals. Cumulative tales. Farms. Noise, sounds. Nursery rhymes.

Counting carnival (Ziner, Feenie)

The first seven days ill. by author. Crowell, 1962. Subj: Religion.

The frog prince (Grimm, Jacob)

The greedy old fat man: an American folk tale ill. by author. Houghton Mifflin, 1983. ISBN 0-89919-188-6 Subj: Cumulative tales. Folk & fairy tales.

Hans in luck (Grimm, Jacob)

King of the cats: a ghost story by Joseph Jacobs; ill. by adapt. Houghton Mifflin, 1980. ISBN 0-395-29100-3 Subj: Animals – cats. Folk & fairy tales. Ghosts.

The life of Jack Sprat, his wife and his cat (Jack Sprat)

Little Bo-Peep ill. by author. Ticknor & Fields, 1986. ISBN 0-89919-395-1 Subj: Animals – sheep. Nursery rhymes.

The magic porridge pot ill. by author. Seabury Pr., 1976. ISBN 0-816-43173-6 Subj: Behavior – forgetfulness. Behavior – sharing. Folk & fairy tales. Food. Magic.

The monkey and the crocodile: a Jataka tale from India ill. by author. Seabury Pr., 1969. ISBN 0-395-28806-1 Subj: Animals – monkeys. Character traits – cleverness. Folk & fairy tales. Foreign lands – India. Reptiles – alligators, crocodiles.

The monster and the tailor: a ghost story ill. by author. Houghton Mifflin, 1982. An adaptation of Joseph Jacobs' The sprightly tailor. ISBN 0-89919-116-9 Subj: Careers – tailors. Ghosts. Monsters. Royalty.

Obedient Jack ill. by author. Watts, 1971. ISBN 0-531-01970-5 Subj: Behavior – mistakes. Family life. Folk & fairy tales.

Over in the meadow: an old nursery counting rhyme (Over in the meadow)

Rumpelstiltskin (Grimm, Jacob)

A strange servant: a Russian folktale trans. by Blanche Ross; ill. by author. Knopf, 1977. ISBN 0-394-93453-9 Subj: Animals – rabbits. Behavior – trickery. Folk & fairy tales. Foreign lands – Russia.

The table, the donkey and the stick (Grimm, Jacob)

The teeny-tiny woman: a ghost story ill. by adapt. Clarion, 1984. ISBN 0-89919-270-X Subj: Emotions. Folk & fairy tales. Ghosts.

The three sillies (Jacobs, Joseph)

What's in fox's sack? ill. by author. Houghton Mifflin, 1982. ISBN 0-89919-062-6 Subj: Character traits – cleverness. Folk & fairy tales.

Galea'i Fa'apouli, Sano M. *My days are made of butterflies* (Martin, Bill [William Ivan])

Galindo, Mary Sue. *Icy watermelon = Sandía fría* ill. by Pauline Rodriguez Howard. Piñata, 2001. ISBN 1-55885-306-5 Subj: Ethnic groups in the U.S. – Mexican Americans. Family life – grandparents. Foreign languages.

Galinsky, Ellen. *The baby cardinal* photos by author. Putnam, 1977. ISBN 0-399-20596-9 Subj: Birds – cardinals.

Galko, Francine. *Cave animals* ill. with photos. Heinemann, 2003. ISBN 1-4034-0176-4 Subj: Animals. Caves. Ecology.

Gallant, Kathryn. *The flute player of Beppu* ill. by Kurt Wiese. Coward, 1960. Subj: Character traits – honesty.

Gallaudet Pre-school Signed English Project. *Nursery rhymes from Mother Goose in signed English* (Mother Goose)

Gallaz, Christophe. *Threadbear* ill. by Gabrielle Vincent; trans. by Martin Sokolinsky. Creative Ed., 1993. ISBN 0-88682-630-6 Subj: Careers – toy makers. Emotions. Toys – bears.

Galli, Letizia. *Mona Lisa: the secret of the smile* ill. by author; trans. from Italian by Nicholas B. A. Nicholson. Delacorte, 1996. ISBN 0-385-32108-2 Subj: Art. Careers – artists.

Gallico, Paul. *Paul Gallico's The small miracle* (Barton, Bob)

Gallimard Jeunesse (Publisher). *All about time* (Verdet, Andre)

Bees (Bees)

Cars and trucks and other vehicles (Cars and trucks and other vehicles)

Houses (Houses)

Lions (Lions)

Native Americans (Native Americans)

Trains (Trains)

Whales (Whales)

Gallo, Frank. *Bird calls* ill. by Lori Lohstoeter; sounds recorded by Michael DiGiorgio. Innovative KIDS, 2001. ISBN 1-58476-064-8 Subj: Birds. Format, unusual – toy & movable books. Noise, sounds.

Night sounds ill. by Lori Lohstoeter; sounds recorded by Michael DiGiorgio. Innovative KIDS, 2001. ISBN 1-58476-065-6 Subj: Animals. Format, unusual – toy & movable books. Night. Noise, sounds.

Gallo, Giovanni. *The lazy beaver* ill. by Ermanno Samsa; trans. from Italian by Jane Fior. Putnam, 1983. ISBN 0-399-20965-4 Subj: Activities – working. Animals – beavers.

Galloway, Ruth. *Fidgety fish* ill. by author. Tiger Tales, 2001. ISBN 1-58925-012-5 Subj: Caves. Fish. Sea & seashore.

Gallup, Joan. *Silly animal ABCs* ill. by author. Courage Books, 1999. ISBN 0-7624-0506-6 Subj: ABC books. Animals.

Gallwey, Kay. *Dancing Daisy* ill. by author. Gollancz, 1994. ISBN 0-575-05843-9 Subj: Activities – dancing. Ballet. Theater.

Galouchko, Annouchka. *Shô and the demons of the deep* ill. by author. Annick, 1995. ISBN 1-55037-398-6 Subj: Bedtime. Dreams. Foreign lands – Japan. Kites.

Galvin, Laura Gates. *Bumblebee at Apple Tree Lane* ill. by Kristin Kest. Soundprints, 2000. ISBN 1-56899-820-1 Subj: Insects – bees.

River Otter at Autumn Lane ill. by Christopher Leeper. Soundprints, 2002. ISBN 1-931465-62-2 Subj: Animals – otters. Behavior – growing up. Family life.

Gambill, Henrietta D. *Little Christmas animals* ill. by author. Standard, 1994. ISBN 0-7847-0274-8 Subj: Animals. Holidays – Christmas. Religion – Nativity.

Self-control ill. by Kathryn Hutton. Rev. ed. Childrens Pr., 1982. ISBN 0-516-06528-9 Subj: Behavior. Ethnic groups in the U.S. – African Americans.

Gamble, Isobel. *Who's that?* by Isobel Gamble & Tim Warnes; ill. by Tim Warnes. Barron's, 2001. ISBN 0-7641-5335-8 Subj: Animals. Bedtime. Format, unusual – toy & movable books. Homes, houses. Sleep.

Gambrell, Jamey. *The story of a boy named Will, who went sledding down the hill* (Kharms, Daniil)

Telephone (Chukovskii, Kornei Ivanovich)

Gamgee, John. *Journey through France* ill. by Martin Camm. Troll, 1994. ISBN 0-8167-2759-7 Subj: Foreign lands – France.

Gammell, Stephen. *Git along, old Scudder* ill. by author. Lothrop, 1983. ISBN 0-688-01677-4 Subj: Old age.

How about going for a ride ill. by author. Harcourt, 2001. ISBN 0-15-202682-7 Subj: Activities – traveling. Automobiles. Family life – brothers & sisters.

Is that you, winter? ill. by author. Silver Whistle, 1997. ISBN 0-15-201415-2 Subj: Behavior – bad day. Seasons – winter. Weather – snow.

Once upon MacDonald's farm ill. by author. Four Winds, 1981. ISBN 0-590-07792-9 Subj: Animals. Farms.

The story of Mr. and Mrs. Vinegar ill. by author. Lothrop, 1982. ISBN 0-688-00889-5 Subj: Character traits – foolishness. Folk & fairy tales.

Twigboy ill. by author. Harcourt, 2000. ISBN 0-15-202137-X Subj: Family life – grandmothers. Forest, woods. Insects. Rocks.

Wake up, bear . . . It's Christmas! ill. by author. Morrow, 1990. ISBN 0-688-09934-3 Subj: Animals – bears. Hibernation. Holidays – Christmas. Santa Claus.

Ganeri, Anita. *Animal hideaways* ill. by Halli Verrinder. Little Simon, 1996. ISBN 0-689-80265-X Subj: Animals. Behavior – hiding. Format, unusual – toy & movable books.

The hunt for food ill. by Graham Austin. Millbrook, 1997. ISBN 0-7613-0304-9 Subj: Animals. Food. Nature.

The longest and tallest ill. by Anita Ganeri. Barron's, 1992. ISBN 0-8120-6293-0 Subj: Concepts – measurement.

The story of Christmas ill. by author. DK, 1995. ISBN 0-7894-0146-0 Subj: Holidays – Christmas. Religion – Nativity.

Ganly, Helen. *Jyoti's journey* ill. by author. Dutton, 1986. ISBN 0-233-97899-2 Subj: Family life. Foreign lands – England. Foreign lands – India. Weddings.

Gannett, Ruth Stiles. *Katie and the sad noise* ill. by Ellie Simmons. Random House, 1961. Subj: Animals – dogs. Character traits – kindness. Holidays – Christmas. Noise, sounds.

Gans, Roma. *How do birds find their way?* ill. by Paul Mirocha. HarperCollins, 1996. ISBN 0-06-020225-4 Subj: Activities – traveling. Birds. Nature.

Hummingbirds in the garden ill. by Grambs Miller. Crowell, 1969. Subj: Birds. Gardens, gardening. Seasons – summer.

Let's go rock collecting ill. by Holly Keller. HarperCollins, 1997. ISBN 0-06-027283-X Subj: Behavior – collecting things. Rocks.

Rock collecting ill. by Holly Keller. Crowell, 1984. ISBN 0-690-04266-3 Subj: Behavior – collecting things. Rocks. Science.

When birds change their feathers ill. by Felicia Bond. Crowell, 1980. ISBN 0-690-03948-4 Subj: Birds. Science.

Gant, Elizabeth. *Little Red Riding Hood* (Grimm, Jacob)

Gant, Katherine. *Little Red Riding Hood* (Grimm, Jacob)

Gantos, Jack (John, Jr.). *Aunt Bernice* ill. by Nicole Rubel. Houghton Mifflin, 1978. ISBN 0-395-26461-8 Subj: Behavior – carelessness. Family life – aunts, uncles.

Back to school for Rotten Ralph ill. by Nicole Rubel. HarperCollins, 1998. ISBN 0-06-027532-4 Subj: Animals – cats. Character traits – selfishness. Emotions – envy, jealousy. Emotions – fear. Friendship. School – first day.

Greedy Greeny ill. by Nicole Rubel. Doubleday, 1979. ISBN 0-385-14686-8 Subj: Dreams. Monsters.

Happy birthday, Rotten Ralph ill. by Nicole Rubel. Houghton Mifflin, 1990. ISBN 0-395-53766-5 Subj: Animals – cats. Behavior – misbehavior. Birthdays.

Not so Rotten Ralph ill. by Nicole Rubel. Houghton Mifflin, 1994. ISBN 0-395-62302-2 Subj: Animals – cats. Behavior – misbehavior. School.

The perfect pal ill. by Nicole Rubel. Houghton Mifflin, 1979. ISBN 0-395-28380-9 Subj: Animals. Pets.

Rotten Ralph ill. by Nicole Rubel. Houghton Mifflin, 1976. ISBN 0-395-24276-2 Subj: Animals – cats. Behavior – misbehavior.

Rotten Ralph's Halloween howl ill. by Nicole Rubel. HarperFestival, 1998. ISBN 0-694-00985-7 Subj: Animals – cats. Holidays – Halloween. Monsters.

Rotten Ralph's rotten Christmas ill. by Nicole Rubel. Houghton Mifflin, 1984. ISBN 0-395-35380-7 Subj: Animals – cats. Character traits – meanness. Emotions – envy, jealousy. Holidays – Christmas.

Rotten Ralph's rotten romance ill. by Nicole Rubel. Houghton Mifflin, 1997. ISBN 0-395-73978-0 Subj: Animals – cats. Behavior – misbehavior. Holidays – Valentine's Day. Parties.

Rotten Ralph's show and tell ill. by Nicole Rubel. Houghton Mifflin, 1989. ISBN 0-395-44312-1 Subj: Animals – cats. Character traits – meanness. School.

Rotten Ralph's trick or treat ill. by Nicole Rubel. Houghton Mifflin, 1986. ISBN 0-395-38943-7 Subj: Animals – cats. Character traits – meanness. Holidays – Halloween.

Swampy alligator ill. by Nicole Rubel. Windmill, 1980. ISBN 0-671-96092-X Subj: Birthdays. Character traits – cleanliness. Reptiles – alligators, crocodiles.

Wedding bells for Rotten Ralph ill. by Nicole Rubel. HarperCollins, 1999. ISBN 0-06-027534-0 Subj: Animals – cats. Behavior – misbehavior. Weddings.

The werewolf family ill. by Nicole Rubel. Houghton Mifflin, 1980. ISBN 0-395-28760-X Subj: Monsters.

Worse than Rotten Ralph ill. by Nicole Rubel. Houghton Mifflin, 1978. ISBN 0-395-28106-1 Subj: Animals – cats. Behavior – misbehavior. Character traits – meanness.

Gantschev, Ivan. *The Christmas teddy bear* adapt. by Andrew Clements; ill. by Ivan Gantschev. North-South, 1994. ISBN 1-55858-348-3 Subj: Behavior – lost. Family life – grandfathers. Holidays – Christmas. Toys – bears. Weather – snow. Weather – storms.

The Christmas train ill. by author; trans. from German by Karen M. Klockner. Little, 1984. ISBN 0-316-30346-1 Subj: Character traits – bravery. Holidays – Christmas. Trains.

Good morning, good night ill. by author; adapt. by Andrew Clements. Picture Book Studio, 1991. ISBN 0-88708-183-5 Subj: Friendship. Moon. Sun.

Journey of the storks ill. by author. Alphabet Pr., 1983. ISBN 0-907234-27-5 Subj: Birds – storks.

The moon lake trans. by Oliver Gadsby; ill. by author. Alphabet Pr., 1981. ISBN 0-907234-08-9 Subj: Behavior – greed. Careers – shepherds. Lakes, ponds. Moon.

Otto the bear trans. from German by Karen M. Klockner; ill. by author. Little, 1986. ISBN 0-316-30348-8 Subj: Animals – bears. Character traits – kindness to animals.

RumpRump ill. by author. Alphabet Pr., 1984. ISBN 0-907234-53-4 Subj: Animals – bears. Food. Friendship.

Santa's favorite story (Aoki, Hisako)

The train to Grandma's ill. by author. Picture Book Studio, 1987. ISBN 0-88708-053-7 Subj: Activities – traveling. Family life – grandparents. Format, unusual. Islands. Trains.

Where is Mr. Mole? adapt. by Andrew Clements; ill. by author. Picture Book Studio, 1989. ISBN 0-88708-109-6 Subj: Animals – moles. Behavior – seeking better things. Birds – owls. Format, unusual.

Where the moon lives ill. by author. North-South, 1998. ISBN 1-55858-921-X Subj: Behavior – sharing. Birds – ducks. Birds – swans. Format, unusual – toy & movable books. Moon.

Gantz, David. *Captain Swifty counts to 50* ill. by author. Doubleday, 1982. ISBN 0-385-17527-2 Subj: Counting, numbers.

The genie bear with the light brown hair word book ill. by author. Doubleday, 1982. ISBN 0-385-17528-0 Subj: ABC books. Animals – bears. Animals – mice.

Ganz, Yaffa. *The story of Mimmy and Simmy* ill. by Harvey Klineman. Feldheim, 1985. ISBN 0-87306-385-6 Subj: Behavior – seeking better things. Emotions – envy, jealousy. Jewish culture.

Garaway, Margaret Kahn. *Ashkii and his grandfather* ill. by Harry Warren. Treasure Chest, 1989. ISBN 0-918080-41-X Subj: Careers – shepherds. Family life – grandfathers. Indians of North America – Navajo.

Garay, Luis. *The long road* ill. by author. Tundra, 1997. ISBN 0-88776-408-8 Subj: Activities – traveling. Foreign lands – Canada. Immigrants.

Pedrito's day ill. by author. Orchard, 1997. ISBN 0-531-09522-3 Subj: Foreign lands – Latin America. Poverty. Toys.

Garbutt, Bernard. *Roger, the rosin back* ill. by author. Hastings House, 1961. Subj: Animals – horses, ponies. Circus.

Garcia, Carolyn. *Moonboy* ill. by author. Beyond Words, 1999. ISBN 1-885223-81-1 Subj: Character traits – being different. Friendship. Moon.

Garcia, Jerry. *The teddy bears' picnic* songs arranged & performed by Gerry Garcia & David Grisman; ill. by Bruce Whatley. HarperCollins, 1996. ISBN 0-06-027302-X Subj: Activities – picnicking. Format, unusual. Music. Songs. Toys – bears.

García, Cheo. *Pick a pet* (Rotner, Shelley)

García Lorca, Federico. *The Lieutenant Colonel and the gypsy* trans. & ill. by Marc Simont. Doubleday, 1971. Subj: Foreign lands – Spain. Gypsies. Poetry.

Gardam, Catharine. *The animals' Christmas* ill. by Gavin Rowe. Macmillan, 1990. ISBN 0-689-50502-7 Subj: Animals. Holidays – Christmas.

Gardella, Tricia. *Blackberry booties* ill. by Glo Coalson. Orchard, 2000. ISBN 0-531-33184-9 Subj: Activities – trading. Gifts. Problem solving.

Just like my dad ill. by Margot Apple. HarperCollins, 1993. ISBN 0-06-021938-6 Subj: Cowboys, cowgirls. Family life – fathers.

Gardeski, Christina Mia. *Diwali* ill. with photos. Childrens Pr., 2001. ISBN 0-516-22372-0 Subj: Foreign lands – India. Holidays – Divali.

Gardiner, Lindsey. *Good night, Poppy and Max* ill. by author. Little, 2002. ISBN 0-316-60122-5 Subj: Animals – dogs. Bedtime. Counting, numbers. Format, unusual – board books.

Here come Poppy and Max ill. by author. Little, 2000. ISBN 0-316-60346-5 Subj: Activities – playing. Animals – dogs. Imagination.

If you're happy and you know it! (Ormerod, Jan)

When Poppy and Max grow up ill. by author. Little, 2001. ISBN 0-316-60342-2 Subj: Activities – playing. Animals – dogs. Careers. Imagination.

Gardner, Beau. *Can you imagine . . . ? a counting book* ill. by author. Dodd, 1987. ISBN 0-396-09001-X Subj: Animals. Counting, numbers.

Guess what? ill. by author. Lothrop, 1985. ISBN 0-688-04983-4 Subj: Animals. Concepts – shape. Games.

Have you ever seen . . . ? an ABC book ill. by author. Dodd, 1986. ISBN 0-396-08825-2 Subj: ABC books. Humorous stories.

The look again . . . and again, and again, and again book ill. by author. Lothrop, 1984. ISBN 0-688-03806-9 Subj: Optical illusions.

The turn about, think about, look about book ill. by author. Lothrop, 1980. ISBN 0-688-51969-5 Subj: Optical illusions.

What is it? ill. by author. Putnam, 1989. ISBN 0-399-21664-2 Subj: Concepts – shape. Format, unusual – toy & movable books. Games.

Whooo's a fright on Halloween night? ill. by author. Putnam, 1990. ISBN 0-399-22212-X Subj: Format, unusual – toy & movable books. Holidays – Halloween. Rhyming text.

Gardner, Jane Mylum. *Henry Moore: from bones and stones to sketches and sculptures* ill. by author. Four Winds, 1993. ISBN 0-02-735812-7 Subj: Art. Careers – artists.

Gardner, Martin. *Never make fun of a turtle, my son* ill. by John Alcorn. S&S, 1969. ISBN 0-671-65033-5 Subj: Etiquette. Poetry.

Gardner, Mercedes. *Scooter and the magic star* by Mercedes & Jean Shannon Smith; ill. by Bob Johnson. Atheneum, 1980. ISBN 0-89742-033-0 Subj: Fairies.

Gardner, Sally. *Mama, don't go out tonight* ill. by author. Bloomsbury, 2002. ISBN 1-58234-790-5 Subj: Activities – babysitting. Family life – mothers. Imagination.

Garelick, May. *Down to the beach* ill. by Barbara Cooney. Four Winds, 1973. Subj: Sea & seashore – beaches. Seasons – summer.

Just my size ill. by William Pène du Bois. HarperCollins, 1990. ISBN 0-06-022419-3 Subj: Behavior – growing up. Clothing – coats. Toys – dolls.

Look at the moon ill. by Barbara Garrison. Mondo, 1996. ISBN 1-57255-142-9 Subj: Animals. Moon. Rhyming text.

Look at the moon ill. by Leonard Weisgard. Addison-Wesley, 1969. Subj: Animals. Moon. Rhyming text.

Sounds of a summer night ill. by Beni Montresor. Addison-Wesley, 1963. Subj: Night. Noise, sounds.

The tremendous tree book (Brenner, Barbara A.)

Two orphan cubs (Brenner, Barbara A.)

Where does the butterfly go when it rains? ill. by Leonard Weisgard. Addison-Wesley, 1961. Subj: Insects – butterflies, caterpillars. Rhyming text. Weather – rain.

Where does the butterfly go when it rains? ill. by Nicholas Wilton. Mondo, 1997. ISBN 1-57255-165-8 Subj: Insects – butterflies, caterpillars. Rhyming text. Weather – rain.

Garelli, Cristina. *Farm friends clean up* ill. by Francesca Chessa. Crown, 2000. ISBN 0-517-80082-9 Subj: Animals. Character traits – cleanliness. Farms. Hygiene.

Garfinkel, Bernard. *see* Allen, Robert

Garhan Attebury, Nancy. *Out and about at city hall* ill. by Zachary Trover. Picture Window, 2006. ISBN 1-4048-1146-X Subj: Cities, towns.

Out and about at the bank ill. by Zachary Trover. Picture Window, 2006. ISBN 1-4048-1147-8 Subj: Money.

Out and about at the hospital ill. by Zachary Trover. Picture Window, 2006. ISBN 1-4048-1148-6 Subj: Hospitals. Illness.

Out and about at the United States Mint ill. by Zachary Trover. Picture Window, 2006. ISBN 1-4048-1151-6 Subj: Money.

Garland, Michael. *Angel cat* ill. by author. Boyds Mills, 1998. ISBN 1-56397-726-5 Subj: Angels. Animals – cats. Death. Fire. Pets.

Christmas City ill. by author. Dutton, 2002. ISBN 0-525-46904-4 Subj: Holidays – Christmas. Picture puzzles. Rhyming text.

Christmas magic ill. by author. Dutton, 2001. ISBN 0-525-46797-1 Subj: Holidays – Christmas. Snowmen.

Circus girl ill. by author. Dutton, 1993. ISBN 0-525-45069-6 Subj: Activities – working. Circus. Clowns, jesters. Family life.

Icarus Swinebuckle ill. by autor. A. Whitman, 2000. ISBN 0-8075-3495-1 Subj: Activities – flying. Animals – pigs.

Last night at the zoo ill. by author. Boyds Mills, 2001. ISBN 1-56397-759-1 Subj: Animals. Behavior – running away. Rhyming text. Zoos.

Miss Smith's incredible storybook ill. by author. Dutton, 2003. ISBN 0-525-47133-2 Subj: Books, reading. Careers – teachers. Magic. School.

The mouse before Christmas ill. by author. Dutton, 1997. ISBN 0-525-45578-7 Subj: Animals – mice. Holidays – Christmas. Rhyming text.

My cousin Katie ill. by author. HarperCollins, 1989. ISBN 0-690-04740-1 Subj: Family life. Farms.

The President and Mom's apple pie ill. by author. Dutton, 2003. ISBN 0-525-46887-0 Subj: Food. U.S. history.

Garland, Sarah. *All gone!* ill. by author. Viking, 1990. ISBN 0-670-83074-7 Subj: Babies. Concepts.

Billy and Belle ill. by author. Viking, 1992. ISBN 0-670-84396-2 Subj: Animals. Babies. Family life – new sibling. Family life – sisters. Pets. School.

Going shopping ill. by author. Little, 1985. ISBN 0-87113-001-7 Subj: Family life. Shopping.

Having a picnic ill. by author. Little, 1985. ISBN 0-87113-002-5 Subj: Activities – picnicking. Birds – ducks. Family life.

Oh, no! ill. by author. Viking, 1990. ISBN 0-670-83075-5 Subj: Babies. Behavior – misbehavior.

Polly's puffin ill. by author. Greenwillow, 1989. ISBN 0-688-08749-3 Subj: Babies. Behavior – lost & found possessions. Cities, towns.

Seeing red ill. by Tony Ross. Kane/Miller, 1996. ISBN 0-916291-64-2 Subj: Clothing. Concepts – color. Folk & fairy tales. Foreign lands – England.

Garland, Sherry. *Goodnight, cowboy* ill. by John Kanzler. Scholastic, 1999. ISBN 0-590-98831-X Subj: Bedtime. Cowboys, cowgirls.

The lotus seed ill. by Tatsuro Kiuchi. Harcourt, 1993. ISBN 0-15-249465-0 Subj: Ethnic groups in the U.S. – Vietnamese Americans. Family life – grandmothers. Foreign lands – Vietnam. War.

My father's boat ill. by Ted Rand. Scholastic, 1998. ISBN 0-590-47867-2 Subj: Boats, ships. Careers – fishermen. Ethnic groups in the U.S. – Vietnamese Americans.

Summer sands ill. by Robert J. Lee. Harcourt, 1995. ISBN 0-15-282492-8 Subj: Ecology. Sand. Sea & seashore.

Why ducks sleep on one leg ill. by Jean & Mou-Sien Tseng. Scholastic, 1993. ISBN 0-590-45697-0 Subj: Birds – ducks. Folk & fairy tales. Foreign lands – Vietnam.

Garne, S. T. *By a blazing blue sea* ill. by Lori Lohsteter. Harcourt, 1999. ISBN 0-15-201780-1 Subj: Careers – fishermen. Concepts – color. Foreign lands – Caribbean Islands. Rhyming text.

Garner, Alan. *Little red hen* (The little red hen)

Once upon a time, though it wasn't in your time, and it wasn't in my time, and it wasn't in anybody else's time . . . ill. by Norman Messenger. DK, 1993. ISBN 1-56458-381-3 Subj: Folk & fairy tales.

Garrett, Ann. *Keeper of the swamp* ill. by Karen Chandler. Turtle Books, 1999. ISBN 1-890515-12-4 Subj: Ecology. Family life – grandfathers. Reptiles – alligators, crocodiles. Swamps.

Tales of tails by Ann Garrett & Gene-Michael Higney; ill. by Stephanie Peterson. Dutton, 2000. ISBN 0-525-46491-3 Subj: Anatomy – tails. Animals. Format, unusual – toy & movable books.

What's for lunch? by Ann Garrett & Gene-Michael Higney; ill. by Stephanie Peterson. Dutton, 1999. ISBN 0-525-46251-1 Subj: Animals. Food. Format, unusual – toy & movable books. Rhyming text.

Garrett, Jennifer. *The queen who stole the sky* ill. by Linda Hendry. North Winds, 1986. ISBN 0-590-71524-0 Subj: Character traits – selfishness. Character traits – stubbornness. Royalty – queens.

Garriel, Barbara S. *I know a shy fellow who swallowed a cello* ill. by John O'Brien. Boyds Mills, 2004. ISBN 1-56397-962-4 Subj: Cumulative tales. Humorous stories. Musical instruments – cellos. Rhyming text.

Garrison, Barbara. *Josiah True and the art maker* (Littlesugar, Amy)

Garrison, Christian. *The dream eater* ill. by Diane Goode. Dutton, 1978. ISBN 0-8788-8134-4 Subj: Dragons. Dreams. Foreign lands – Japan.

Little pieces of the west wind ill. by Diane Goode. Dutton, 1975. ISBN 0-8788-8105-0 Subj: Cumulative tales. Weather – wind.

Garten, Jan. *The alphabet tale* ill. by Muriel Batherman. Greenwillow, 1994. ISBN 0-688-12703-7 Subj: ABC books. Animals. Participation. Poetry.

Gascoigne, Bamber. *Why the rope went tight* ill. by Christina Gascoigne. Lothrop, 1981. ISBN 0-688-00590-X Subj: Circus.

Gaston, Susan. *New boots for Salvador* ill. by Lydia Schwartz. Ritchie, 1972. ISBN 0-378-62659-0 Subj: Animals – horses, ponies.

Gates, Frieda. *Owl eyes* ill. by Yoshi Miyake. Lothrop, 1994. ISBN 0-688-12473-9 Subj: Birds – owls. Creation. Folk & fairy tales. Indians of North America – Mohawk.

Gauch, Patricia Lee. *Bravo, Tanya* ill. by Satomi Ichikawa. Putnam, 1992. ISBN 0-399-22145-X Subj: Activities – dancing. Ballet. Toys – bears.

Christina Katerina and Fats and the Great Neighborhood War ill. by Stacey Schuett. Putnam, 1997. ISBN 0-399-22651-6 Subj: Communities, neighborhoods. Friendship.

Christina Katerina and the great bear train ill. by Elise Primavera. Putnam, 1990. ISBN 0-399-21623-5 Subj: Babies. Family life – sisters. Toys – bears.

Christina Katerina and the time she quit the family ill. by Elise Primavera. Putnam, 1987. ISBN 0-399-21408-9 Subj: Behavior – needing someone. Family life. Sibling rivalry.

Dance, Tanya ill. by Satomi Ichikawa. Putnam, 1989. ISBN 0-399-21521-2 Subj: Activities – dancing. Ballet. Behavior – imitation. Toys – bears.

The little friar who flew ill. by Tomie de Paola. Putnam, 1980. ISBN 0-399-20714-7 Subj: Folk & fairy tales. Magic. Religion.

Noah ill. by Jonathan Green. Philomel, 1994. ISBN 0-399-22548-X Subj: Animals. Boats, ships. Religion – Noah. Weather – floods. Weather – rain. Weather – rainbows.

On to Widecombe Fair ill. by Trina Schart Hyman. Putnam, 1978. ISBN 0-399-20563-2 Subj: Fairs, festivals. Folk & fairy tales. Foreign lands – England.

Once upon a Dinkelsbühl ill. by Tomie de Paola. Putnam, 1977. ISBN 0-399-20560-8 Subj: War.

Presenting Tanya, the Ugly Duckling ill. by Satomi Ichikawa. Philomel, 1999. ISBN 0-399-23200-1 Subj: Activities – dancing. Ballet. Self-concept.

Tanya and Emily in a dance for two ill. by Satomi Ichikawa. Philomel, 1994. ISBN 0-399-22688-5 Subj: Activities – dancing. Ballet. Friendship.

Tanya and the magic wardrobe ill. by Satomi Ichikawa. Philomel, 1997. ISBN 0-399-22940-X Subj: Activities – dancing. Ballet. Clothing – costumes. Theater.

Tanya steps out ill. by Satomi Ichikawa. Philomel, 1996. ISBN 0-399-22936-1 Subj: Activities – dancing. Ballet. Format, unusual – toy & movable books.

Uncle Magic ill. by Deborah Kogan Ray. Holiday, 1992. ISBN 0-8234-0937-6 Subj: Family life – aunts, uncles. Magic.

Gauthier, Bertrand. *Animal capers* (Paré, Roger)

Circus days (Paré, Roger)

Play time (Paré, Roger)

Summer days (Paré, Roger)

Gay, Marie-Louise. *Good morning Sam* ill. by author. Douglas & McIntyre, 2003. ISBN 0-88899-528-8 Subj: Clothing. Family life – brothers & sisters. Humorous stories. Morning.

Moonbeam on a cat's ear ill. by author. Silver Burdett, 1986. ISBN 0-385-09162-0 Subj: Animals – cats. Animals – mice. Bedtime. Dreams. Moon. Night. Rhyming text.

On my island ill. by author. Douglas & McIntyre, 2000. ISBN 0-88899-396-X Subj: Animals. Behavior – boredom. Islands.

Rainy day magic ill. by author. A. Whitman, 1989. ISBN 0-8075-6767-1 Subj: Family life. Illness. Imagination. Rhyming text. Weather – rain.

Stella, fairy of the forest ill. by author. Douglas & McIntyre, 2002. ISBN 0-88899-448-6 Subj: Animals. Fairies. Family life – brothers & sisters. Forest, woods.

Stella, queen of the snow ill. by author. Douglas & McIntyre, 2000. ISBN 0-88899-404-4 Subj: Activities – playing. Family life – brothers & sisters. Weather – snow.

Stella, star of the sea ill. by author. Douglas & McIntyre, 1999. ISBN 0-88899-337-4 Subj: Family life – brothers & sisters. Sea & seashore.

Gay, Michel. *Bibi takes flight* ill. by author. Morrow, 1988. ISBN 0-688-06829-4 Subj: Activities – flying. Airplanes, airports. Birds – penguins.

Bibi's birthday surprise ill. by author. Morrow, 1987. ISBN 0-688-06978-9 Subj: Animals. Birds – penguins. Parties. Royalty. Toys.

The Christmas wolf ill. by author. Greenwillow, 1983. ISBN 0-688-02291-X Subj: Animals – wolves. Holidays – Christmas.

Little auto ill. by author. Macmillan, 1986. ISBN 0-02-737900-0 Subj: Automobiles. Sea & seashore.

Little boat ill. by author. Macmillan, 1985. ISBN 0-02-737540-4 Subj: Boats, ships.

Little helicopter ill. by author. Macmillan, 1986. ISBN 0-02-737920-5 Subj: Character traits – smallness. Helicopters.

Little plane ill. by author. Macmillan, 1985. ISBN 0-02-737500-5 Subj: Airplanes, airports.

Little shoe ill. by author. Macmillan, 1986. ISBN 0-02-737890-X Subj: Behavior – lost & found possessions. Clothing – shoes.

Little truck ill. by author. Macmillan, 1985. ISBN 0-02-737520-X Subj: Transportation. Trucks.

Night ride ill. by author. Morrow, 1987. ISBN 0-688-07287-9 Subj: Activities – traveling. Animals. Circus. Family life – fathers. Night.

Rabbit express ill. by author. Morrow, 1985. ISBN 0-688-04648-7 Subj: Animals – cats. Animals – rabbits. Friendship.

Take me for a ride ill. by author. Morrow, 1985. ISBN 0-688-04136-1 Subj: Behavior – lost.

Zee is not scared ill. by author; tr. by Marie Mianowski. Clarion, 2004. ISBN 0-618-43931-5 Subj: Animals – zebras. Bedtime. Emotions – fear. Family life – parents.

Gay, Tenner Ottley. *Dinosaurs and their relatives in action* ill. by Jean Cassels. Macmillan, 1990. ISBN 0-689-71434-3 Subj: Dinosaurs. Format, unusual – toy & movable books. Prehistory.

Sharks in action ill. by Jean Cassels. Macmillan, 1990. ISBN 0-689-71435-1 Subj: Fish – sharks. Format, unusual – toy & movable books.

Gay, Zhenya. *I'm tired of lions* ill. by author. Viking, 1961. Subj: Animals – lions. Behavior – dissatisfaction.

Look! ill. by author. Viking, 1952. Subj: Animals. Libraries. Poetry.

Small one ill. by author. Viking, 1958. Subj: Animals – rabbits. Behavior – lost.

Who's afraid? ill. by author. Viking, 1965. Subj: Emotions – fear.

Gebert, Warren. *The old ball and the sea* ill. by author. Bradbury, 1988. ISBN 0-02-735821-6 Subj: Activities – playing. Sea & seashore.

Geddes, Anne. *Shapes* ill. by author. Cedco, 1997. ISBN 0-7683-2023-2 Subj: Babies. Clothing – costumes. Concepts – shape.

Gedin, Birgitta. *The little house from the sea* trans. by Elisabeth Kallick Dyssegaard; ill. by Petter Pettersson. Farrar, 1988. ISBN 91-29-58770-0 Subj: Boats, ships. Homes, houses. Sea & seashore. Weather – storms.

Geeslin, Campbell. *How Nanita learned to make flan* ill. by Petra Mathers. Atheneum, 1999. ISBN 0-689-81546-8 Subj: Activities – baking, cooking. Clothing – shoes. Food. Foreign lands – Mexico.

Geis, Jacqueline. *Where the buffalo roam* ill. by adapt. Ideals, 1992. ISBN 0-8249-8584-2 Subj: Animals. Desert. Plants. Poetry.

Geisel, Theodor Seuss. *see* Seuss, Dr.

Geisert, Arthur. *After the flood* ill. by author. Houghton Mifflin, 1994. ISBN 0-395-66611-2 Subj: Animals. Boats, ships. Religion. Weather – rainbows.

The ark ill. by author. Houghton Mifflin, 1988. ISBN 0-395-43078-X Subj: Animals. Boats, ships. Religion – Noah. Weather – floods. Weather – rain.

Desert town (Geisert, Bonnie)

The giant ball of string ill. by author. Houghton, 2002. ISBN 0-618-13221-X Subj: Animals – pigs. Behavior – lost & found possessions. Character traits – cooperation. String.

Mountain town (Geisert, Bonnie)

Mystery ill. by author. Houghton, 2003. ISBN 0-618-27293-3 Subj: Animals – pigs. Careers – detectives. Crime. Family life – grandfathers. Museums. Mystery stories. Picture puzzles.

Nursery crimes ill. by author. Houghton, 2001. ISBN 0-618-06487-7 Subj: Animals – pigs. Crime. Farms. Holidays – Thanksgiving. Mystery stories. Trees.

Oink ill. by author. Houghton Mifflin, 1991. ISBN 0-395-55329-6 Subj: Animals – pigs. Behavior – misbehavior. Noise, sounds.

Oink oink ill. by author. Houghton Mifflin, 1993. ISBN 0-395-64048-2 Subj: Animals – pigs. Behavior – misbehavior. Family life – mothers.

Pigaroons ill. by author. Houghton, 2004. ISBN 0-618-41058-9 Subj: Animals – pigs. Crime. Fairs, festivals.

Pigs from 1 to 10 ill. by author. Houghton Mifflin, 1992. ISBN 0-395-58519-8 Subj: Animals – pigs. Counting, numbers. Puzzles.

Prairie town (Geisert, Bonnie)

Geisert, Bonnie. *Desert town* by Bonnie & Arthur Geisert; ill. by Arthur Geisert. Houghton, 2001. ISBN 0-395-95387-1 Subj: Cities, towns. Desert.

Mountain town by Bonnie & Arthur Geisert; ill. by Arthur Geisert. Houghton, 2000. ISBN 0-395-95390-1 Subj: Cities, towns. Mountains. Seasons.

Prairie town by Bonnie & Arthur Geisert; ill. by Arthur Geisert. Houghton Mifflin, 1998. ISBN 0-395-85907-7 Subj: Cities, towns. Communities, neighborhoods. Country. Seasons.

Geiss, Tony. *Susan and Gordon adopt a baby* (Freudberg, Judy)

Gekiere, Madeleine. *The frilly lily and the princess* ill. by author. Lippincott, 1960. Subj: Behavior – fighting, arguing. Royalty – princesses.

Gelbard, Jane. *My bye-bye bottle book* by Jane Gelbard & Betsy Bober Polivy; photos by Arthur J. Klonsky. Grosset, 1989. ISBN 0-448-21526-8 Subj: Babies. Behavior – growing up. Format, unusual – board books. Rhyming text.

My dressing book by Jane Gelbard & Betsy Bober Polivy; photos by Arthur J. Klonsky. Grosset, 1989. ISBN 0-448-21527-6 Subj: Babies. Behavior – growing up. Clothing. Format, unusual – board books. Rhyming text.

My eating book by Jane Gelbard & Betsy Bober Polivy; photos by Arthur J. Klonsky. Grosset, 1989. ISBN 0-448-21528-4 Subj: Babies. Behavior – growing up. Food. Format, unusual – board books. Rhyming text.

My sharing book by Jane Gelbard & Betsy Bober Polivy; photos by Arthur J. Klonsky. Grosset, 1989. ISBN 0-448-21529-2 Subj: Babies. Behavior – growing up. Behavior – sharing. Format, unusual – board books. Rhyming text.

Gellman, Ellie. *It's Chanukah!* ill. by Katherine Janus Kahn. Kar-Ben Copies, 1985. ISBN 0-930494-51-2 Subj: Format, unusual – board books. Holidays – Hanukkah. Jewish culture.

It's Rosh Hashanah! ill. by Katherine Janus Kahn. Kar-Ben Copies, 1985. ISBN 0-930494-50-4 Subj: Format, unusual – board books. Holidays – Rosh Hashanah. Jewish culture.

Shai's Shabbat walk ill. by Chari R. McLean. Kar-Ben Copies, 1985. ISBN 0-930494-49-0 Subj: Format, unusual – board books. Holidays. Jewish culture.

Gellman, Marc. *Where does God live?* ill. by William Zdinak. Triumph, 1991. ISBN 0-8007-3018-6 Subj: Family life – parents. Religion.

Gelman, Amy. *Little big feet* (Schubert, Ingrid)

Gelman, Rita Golden. *Hey, kid* ill. by Carol Nicklaus. Watts, 1977. ISBN 0-531-01333-2 Subj: Humorous stories. Rhyming text.

A koala grows up ill. by Gioia Fiammenghi. Scholastic, 1986. ISBN 0-590-30563-8 Subj: Animals – koalas. Foreign lands – Australia. Science.

Splash! all about baths (Buxbaum, Susan Kovacs)

Gelsanliter, Wendy. *Dancin' in the kitchen* by Wendy Gelsanliter & Frank Christian; ill. by Marjorie Priceman. Putnam, 1988. ISBN 0-399-23035-1 Subj: Activities – baking, cooking. Activities – dancing. Family life. Rhyming text.

Gemme, Leila Boyle. *T-ball is our game* photos by Richard Marshall. Childrens Pr., 1978. ISBN 0-516-03630-0 Subj: Sports – T-ball.

Gemming, Elisabeth. *Sandy at the children's zoo* (Bolliger, Max)

Genechten, Guido Van. *Flop-Ear* ill. by author. Barron's, 2001. ISBN 0-7641-1762-9 Subj: Anatomy – ears. Animals – rabbits. Character traits – individuality.

Gentieu, Penny. *Baby! Talk!* ill. by author. Crown, 1999. ISBN 0-517-80028-4 Subj: Activities. Babies.

Grow! babies! ill. by author. Crown, 2000. ISBN 0-517-80029-2 Subj: Babies. Behavior – growing up.

Gentle, Victor. *Baby sharks* Victor Gentle & Janet Perry; ill. with photos. G. Stevens, 2001. ISBN 0-8368-2824-0 Subj: Animals – babies. Fish – sharks.

Killer sharks, killer people Victor Gentle & Janet Perry; ill. with photos. G. Stevens, 2001. ISBN 0-8368-2826-7 Subj: Fish – sharks. Sports – fishing.

Orcas, killer whales Victor Gentle & Janet Perry; ill. with photos. G. Stevens, 2001. ISBN 0-8368-2883-6 Subj: Animals – whales.

Shark camouflage and armor Victor Gentle & Janet Perry; ill. with photos. G. Stevens, 2001. ISBN 0-8368-2827-5 Subj: Disguises. Fish – sharks.

Very big sharks Victor Gentle & Janet Perry; ill. with photos. G. Stevens, 2001. ISBN 0-8368-2828-3 Subj: Fish – sharks.

The world's strangest shark Victor Gentle & Janet Perry; ill. with photos. G. Stevens, 2001. ISBN 0-8368-2829-1 Subj: Fish – sharks.

Geoghegan, Adrienne. *All your own teeth* ill. by Cathy Gale. Dial, 2001. ISBN 0-8037-2655-4 Subj: Activities – painting. Animals. Jungle.

Dogs don't wear glasses ill. by author. Crocodile, 1996. ISBN 1-56656-208-2 Subj: Animals – dogs. Glasses. Pets. Senses – sight.

There's a wardrobe in my monster! ill. by Adrian Johnson. Carolrhoda, 1999. ISBN 1-57505-414-0 Subj: Behavior – boredom. Monsters. Pets.

George, Jean Craighead. *All upon a stone* ill. by Don Bolognese. Crowell, 1971. ISBN 0-690-05533-1 Subj: Insects. Science. Spiders.

Arctic son ill. by Wendell Minor. Hyperion, 1997. ISBN 0-7868-2255-4 Subj: Eskimos. Foreign lands – Arctic. Indians of North America – Inuit.

Cliff hanger ill. by Wendell Minor. HarperCollins, 2002. ISBN 0-06-000261-1 Subj: Animals – dogs. Family life – fathers. Mountains. Sports – mountain climbing. Weather – storms.

Dear Katie, the volcano is a girl ill. by Daniel Powers. Hyperion, 1998. ISBN 0-7868-2254-6 Subj: Family life – grandmothers. Hawaii. Mythical creatures. Volcanoes.

Dear Rebecca, winter is here ill. by Loretta Krupinski. HarperCollins, 1993. ISBN 0-06-021140-7 Subj: Family life – grandmothers. Nature. Seasons. Seasons – winter.

Everglades ill. by Wendell Minor. HarperCollins, 1995. ISBN 0-06-021229-2 Subj: Ecology. Nature. Rivers.

The first Thanksgiving ill. by Thomas Locker. Philomel, 1993. ISBN 0-399-21991-9 Subj: Holidays – Thanksgiving. Pilgrims. U.S. history.

Frightful's daughter ill. by Daniel San Souci. Dutton, 2002. ISBN 0-525-46907-9 Subj: Birds – falcons.

Giraffe trouble ill. by Anna Vojtech. Disney Pr., 1998. ISBN 0-7868-3167-7 Subj: Animals – giraffes. Animals – lions.

Gorilla gang ill. by Stacey Schuett. Disney Pr., 1998. ISBN 0-7868-3166-9 Subj: Animals – gorillas.

The grizzly bear with the golden ears ill. by Tom Catania. HarperCollins, 1982. ISBN 0-06-021966-1 Subj: Animals – bears.

Little Dog and Duncan poems by Kristine O'Connell George; ill. by June Otani. Clarion, 2002. ISBN 0-618-11758-X Subj: Animals – dogs. Poetry.

Look to the north: a wolf pup diary ill. by Lucia Washburn. HarperCollins, 1997. ISBN 0-06-023640-X Subj: Animals – babies. Animals – wolves. Behavior – growing up. Seasons.

Morning, noon, and night ill. by Wendell Minor. HarperCollins, 1999. ISBN 0-06-023628-0 Subj: Activities. Animals. Day.

Nutik and Amaroq play ball ill. by Ted Rand. HarperCollins, 2001. Subj: Animals – wolves. Eskimos. Foreign lands – Arctic.

Nutik, the wolf pup ill. by Ted Rand. HarperCollins, 2001. ISBN 0-06-028164-2 Subj: Animals – wolves. Eskimos. Family life – brothers & sisters. Foreign lands – Arctic.

Rhino romp ill. by Stacey Schuett. Disney Pr., 1998. ISBN 0-7868-5068-X Subj: Animals – rhinoceros. Behavior – lost.

Snow bear ill. by Wendell Minor. Hyperion, 1999. ISBN 0-7868-0456-4 Subj: Activities – playing. Animals – polar bears. Eskimos. Foreign lands – Arctic. Weather – snow.

To climb a waterfall ill. by Thomas Locker. Philomel, 1995. ISBN 0-399-22673-7 Subj: Sports – mountain climbing. Water.

The wentletrap trap ill. by Symeon Shimin. Dutton, 1978. ISBN 0-525-42310-9 Subj: Ethnic groups in the U.S. – African Americans. Foreign lands – Caribbean Islands. Sea & seashore.

George, Kristine O'Connell. *The great frog race and other poems* ill. by Kate Kiesler. Clarion, 1997. ISBN 0-395-77607-4 Subj: Counting, numbers. Nature. Poetry.

Little Dog and Duncan (George, Jean Craighead)

Old Elm speaks ill. by Kate Kiesler. Clarion, 1998. ISBN 0-395-87611-7 Subj: Poetry. Seasons. Trees.

George, Lindsay Barrett. *Around the pond: who's been here?* ill. by author. Greenwillow, 1996. ISBN 0-688-14377-6 Subj: Animals. Lakes, ponds. Nature. Seasons – summer.

Beaver at Long Pond (George, William T.)

In the woods: who's been here? ill. by author. Greenwillow, 1995. ISBN 0-688-12319-8 Subj: Activities – walking. Animals. Forest, woods. Nature. Problem solving. Seasons – fall.

My bunny and me ill. by author. Greenwillow, 2001. ISBN 0-688-16075-1 Subj: Animals – rabbits. Imagination.

William and Boomer ill. by author. Greenwillow, 1987. ISBN 0-688-06641-0 Subj: Birds – geese. Pets. Sports – swimming.

George, William T. *Beaver at Long Pond* by William T. & Lindsay Barrett George; ill. by Lindsay Barrett George. Greenwillow, 1988. ISBN 0-688-07107-4 Subj: Animals – beavers. Nature. Night.

Box turtle at Long Pond ill. by Lindsay Barrett George. Greenwillow, 1989. ISBN 0-688-08185-1 Subj: Nature. Reptiles – turtles, tortoises.

Christmas at Long Pond ill. by Lindsay Barrett George. Greenwillow, 1992. ISBN 0-688-09215-2 Subj: Animals. Family life – fathers. Forest, woods. Holidays – Christmas. Nature. Seasons – winter. Trees.

Fishing at Long Pond ill. by Lindsay Barrett George. Greenwillow, 1991. ISBN 0-688-09402-3 Subj: Animals. Family life – grandfathers. Sports – fishing.

Georgiady, Nicholas P. *Gertie the duck* ill. by Dagmar Wilson. Follett, 1959. ISBN 0-695-83363-4 Subj: Birds – ducks. Character traits – kindness to animals.

Geraghty, Paul. *The giraffe who got in a knot* (Bush, John)

The great green forest ill. by author. Hutchinson, 1992. ISBN 0-09-176420-3 Subj: Animals. Forest, woods. Noise, sounds.

The hoppameleon ill. by author. Barron's, 2001. ISBN 0-7641-5406-0 Subj: Animals. Friendship. Frogs & toads. Self-concept.

The hunter ill. by author. Crown, 1994. ISBN 0-517-59693-8 Subj: Animals – elephants. Character traits – kindness to animals. Foreign lands – Africa. Sports – hunting.

Look out, Patrick! ill. by author. Macmillan, 1990. ISBN 0-02-735822-4 Subj: Animals – mice. Character traits – luck.

Over the steamy swamp ill. by author. Harcourt, 1989. ISBN 0-15-200561-7 Subj: Animals. Insects. Nature.

Slobcat ill. by author. Macmillan, 1991. ISBN 0-02-735825-9 Subj: Animals – cats. Character traits – laziness.

Solo ill. by author. Crown, 1995. ISBN 0-517-70909-0 Subj: Birds – penguins. Foreign lands – Antarctic.

Stop that noise! ill. by author. Crown, 1992. ISBN 0-517-59158-8 Subj: Animals. Animals – mice. Jungle. Noise, sounds.

Geras, Adèle. *The Cats of Cuckoo Square, Geejay the Hero* ill. by Tony Ross. Dell, 2003. ISBN 0-385-90082-1 Subj: Communities, neighborhoods. Illness – allergies.

Giselle ill. by Emma Chichester Clark. David & Charles, 2000. ISBN 1-86233-226-6 Subj: Activities – dancing. Ballet.

My wishes for you ill. by Cliff Wright. S&S, 2002. ISBN 0-689-85333-5 Subj: Animals. Animals – rabbits. Behavior – wishing. Day. Family life – parents.

The nutcracker ill. by Emma Chichester Clark. David & Charles, 2000. ISBN 1-86233-236-3 Subj: Activities – dancing. Animals – mice. Ballet. Careers – toy makers. Folk & fairy tales. Holidays – Christmas. Imagination. Royalty. Toys.

Rebecca's Passover ill. by Sheila Moxley. Frances Lincoln, 2004. ISBN 1-84507-155-7 Subj: Holidays – Passover. Jewish culture.

Sleep tight, Ginger Kitten ill. by Catherine Walters. Dutton, 2001. ISBN 0-525-46771-8 Subj: Animals – cats. Rhyming text. Sleep.

Sleeping beauty ill. by Emma Chichester Clark. David & Charles, 2000. ISBN 1-86233-246-0 Subj: Activities – dancing. Ballet. Family life – stepfamilies. Folk & fairy tales. Royalty – princes. Sibling rivalry.

Swan Lake ill. by Emma Chichester Clark. David & Charles, 2000. ISBN 1-86233-231-2 Subj: Activities – dancing. Ballet. Birds – swans. Careers – magicians. Folk & fairy tales. Magic. Metamorphosis. Royalty – princes.

Time for ballet ill. by Shelagh McNicholas. Dial, 2004. ISBN 0-8037-2978-2 Subj: Activities – dancing. Ballet.

Geraty, Virginia Mixson. *Gullah night before Christmas* ill. by James Rice. Pelican, 1998. ISBN 1-56554-330-0 Subj: Foreign languages. Holidays – Christmas. Poetry.

Gerber, Carole. *Arctic dreams* ill. by Marty Husted. Whispering Coyote, 1999. ISBN 1-58089-021-0 Subj: Animals. Eskimos. Family life – mothers. Foreign lands – Arctic. Sleep.

Hush! a Gaelic lullaby ill. by Marty Husted. Whispering Coyote, 1997. ISBN 1-879085-57-7 Subj: Foreign lands – Ireland. Foreign languages. Lullabies.

Gerez, Toni De. *see* De Gerez, Toni

Gergely, Tibor. *The great big fire engine book* ill. by author. 1st Random House ed. Golden Bks., 2003. ISBN 0-307-90321-4 Subj: Careers – firefighters. Format, unusual – board books. Trucks.

Wheel on the chimney (Brown, Margaret Wise)

Geringer, Laura. *The cow is mooing anyhow* ill. by Dirk Zimmer. HarperCollins, 1991. ISBN 0-06-021987-4 Subj: ABC books. Animals. Rhyming text.

Look out, look out, it's coming! ill. by Sue Truesdell. HarperCollins, 1992. ISBN 0-06-021712-X Subj: Imagination – imaginary friends. Monsters.

Molly's new washing machine ill. by Petra Mathers. HarperCollins, 1986. ISBN 0-06-022151-8 Subj: Activities – dancing. Animals – rabbits. Behavior – mistakes. Machines.

A three hat day ill. by Arnold Lobel. HarperCollins, 1985. ISBN 0-06-021989-0 Subj: Behavior – collecting things. Clothing – hats.

Yours 'til the ice cracks: a book of Valentines ill. by Andrea Baruffi. HarperCollins, 1992. ISBN 0-06-020399-4 Subj: Holidays – Valentine's Day.

Gerlach, Horace. *Daddy's little girl* (Burke, Bobby)

Germein, Katrina. *Big rain coming* ill. by Bronwyn Bancroft. Clarion, 1999. ISBN 0-618-08344-8 Subj: Australian aborigines. Foreign lands – Australia. Weather – rain.

Gerrard, Jean. *Matilda Jane* ill. by Roy Gerrard. Farrar, 1983. ISBN 0-374-34865-0 Subj: Foreign lands – England. Sea & seashore.

Gerrard, Roy. *Croco'nile* ill. by author. Farrar, 1994. ISBN 0-374-31659-7 Subj: Foreign lands – Egypt. Reptiles – alligators, crocodiles. Rhyming text. Rivers.

The Favershams ill. by author. Farrar, 1983. ISBN 0-374-32292-9 Subj: Rhyming text.

Jocasta Carr, movie star ill. by author. Farrar, 1992. ISBN 0-374-33654-7 Subj: Activities – flying. Activities – traveling. Animals – dogs. Careers – actors. Crime. Foreign lands. Rhyming text.

Mik's mammoth ill. by author. Farrar, 1990. ISBN 0-374-31891-3 Subj: Animals. Character traits – individuality. Rhyming text.

A pocket full of posies ill. by author. Farrar, 1991. ISBN 0-374-36032-4 Subj: Format, unusual – toy & movable books. Nursery rhymes.

The Roman twins ill. by author. Farrar, 1998. ISBN 0-374-36339-0 Subj: Foreign lands – Italy. Multiple births – twins. Rhyming text. Slavery.

Rosie and the rustlers ill. by author. Farrar, 1989. ISBN 0-374-36345-5 Subj: Cowboys, cowgirls. Crime. Rhyming text. U.S. history – frontier & pioneer life.

Sir Cedric ill. by author. Farrar, 1984. ISBN 0-374-36959-3 Subj: Knights. Middle Ages. Rhyming text.

Sir Cedric rides again ill. by author. Farrar, 1987. ISBN 0-374-36961-5 Subj: Knights. Middle Ages. Rhyming text.

Sir Francis Drake: his daring deeds ill. by author. Farrar, 1988. ISBN 0-374-36962-3 Subj: Boats, ships. Foreign lands. Poetry. Sea & seashore.

Wagons west! ill. by author. Farrar, 1996. ISBN 0-374-38249-2 Subj: Activities – traveling. U.S. history. U.S. history – frontier & pioneer life.

Gershator, David. *Moon rooster* by David & Phyllis Gershator; ill. by Megan Halsey. Cavendish, 2001. ISBN 0-7614-5092-0 Subj: Birds – chickens. Moon. Noise, sounds. Songs.

Palampam Day by David & Phillis Gershator; ill. by Enrique O. Sánchez. Cavendish, 1997. ISBN 0-7614-5002-5 Subj: Food. Foreign lands – Caribbean Islands. Foreign languages.

Gershator, Phillis. *Honi and his magic circle* ill. by Shay Rieger. Jewish Publication Society, 1980. ISBN 0-8276-0167-0 Subj: Jewish culture.

Moon rooster (Gershator, David)

Only one cowry: Dahomean tale ill. by David Soman. Orchard, 2000. ISBN 0-531-33288-8 Subj: Folk & fairy tales. Foreign lands – Africa. Royalty – kings.

Palampam Day (Gershator, David)

Sweet, sweet fig banana ill. by Fritz Millvoix. A. Whitman, 1996. ISBN 0-8075-7693-X Subj: Foreign lands – Caribbean Islands. Gardens, gardening. Shopping.

When it starts to snow ill. by Martin Matje. Holt, 1998. ISBN 0-8050-5404-9 Subj: Animals. Rhyming text. Seasons – winter. Weather – snow.

Zzzng! zzzng! zzzng! a Yoruba tale ill. by Theresa Smith. Orchard, 1998. ISBN 0-531-08873-1 Subj: Folk & fairy tales. Foreign lands – Africa. Insects – mosquitoes.

Gershwin, George. *Summertime from Porgy and Bess* ill. by Mike Wimmer. S&S, 1999. ISBN 0-689-80719-8 Subj: Ethnic groups in the U.S. – African Americans. Music. Seasons – summer. Songs. Theater.

Gerson, Corinne. *Good dog, bad dog* ill. by Emily Arnold McCully. Atheneum, 1983. ISBN 0-689-30986-4 Subj: Animals – dogs. Behavior – misbehavior. Pets.

Gerson, Mary-Joan. *Why the sky is far away* ill. by Carla Golembe. Little, 1992. ISBN 0-316-30852-8 Subj: Behavior – greed. Folk & fairy tales. Foreign lands – Nigeria. Sky.

Gerstein, Mordicai. *The absolutely awful alphabet* ill. by author. Harcourt, 1999. ISBN 0-15-201494-2 Subj: ABC books. Animals. Monsters.

Anytime Mapleson and the hungry bears ill. by Susan Yard Harris. HarperCollins, 1990. ISBN 0-06-022415-0 Subj: Animals – bears.

Bedtime, everybody! ill. by author. Hyperion, 1996. ISBN 0-7868-2138-8 Subj: Bedtime. Toys.

Daisy's garden by Mordicai Gerstein & Susan Yard Harris; ill. by authors. Hyperion, 1995. ISBN 0-7868-2080-2 Subj: Animals. Gardens, gardening. Rhyming text. Seasons.

Follow me! ill. by author. Morrow, 1983. ISBN 0-688-01856-4 Subj: Birds – ducks.

The gigantic baby ill. by Arnie Levin. HarperCollins, 1991. ISBN 0-06-022106-2 Subj: Babies. Concepts – shape. Concepts – size. Family life – brothers & sisters.

Guess what? by Mordicai Gerstein & Susan Yard Harris; ill. by Mordicai Gerstein. Crown, 1991. ISBN 0-517-58217-1 Subj: Birthdays. Counting, numbers. Format, unusual – toy & movable books. Gifts.

Jonah and the two great fish ill. by author. S&S, 1997. ISBN 0-689-81373-2 Subj: Animals – whales. Religion – Jonah.

The man who walked between the towers ill. by author. Roaring Brook, 2003. ISBN 0-7613-2868-8 Subj: Activities. Caldecott award books. Careers – aerialists. Format, unusual – toy & movable books.

The mountains of Tibet ill. by author. HarperCollins, 1987. ISBN 0-06-022149-6 Subj: Death. Kites.

The new creatures ill. by author. HarperCollins, 1991. ISBN 0-06-022167-4 Subj: Animals – cats. Animals – dogs. Family life – grandfathers.

Noah and the great flood ill. by author. S&S, 1999. ISBN 0-689-81371-6 Subj: Animals. Boats, ships. Religion – Noah. Weather – floods. Weather – rain.

Prince Sparrow ill. by author. Four Winds, 1984. ISBN 0-590-07907-7 Subj: Birds – sparrows. Emotions – love.

Queen Esther the morning star ill. by author. S&S, 2000. ISBN 0-689-81372-4 Subj: Holidays – Purim. Jewish culture. Religion.

Roll over! ill. by author. Crown, 1984. ISBN 0-517-55209-4 Subj: Counting, numbers. Nursery rhymes.

The room ill. by author. Harper, 1984. ISBN 0-06-021999-8 Subj: Homes, houses.

The seal mother ill. by author. Dial, 1986. ISBN 0-8037-0303-1 Subj: Animals – seals. Folk & fairy tales. Seasons – summer.

The shadow of a flying bird: a legend of the Kurdistani Jews ill. by reteller. Hyperion, 1994. ISBN 0-7868-2012-8 Subj: Death. Folk & fairy tales. Foreign lands – Kurdistan. Jewish culture. Religion – Moses.

Stop those pants! ill. by author. Harcourt, 1998. ISBN 0-15-201495-0 Subj: Behavior – misbehavior. Clothing. Clothing – pants. Problem solving.

The story of May ill. by author. HarperCollins, 1993. ISBN 0-06-022288-3 Subj: Days of the week, months of the year. Seasons.

The sun's day ill. by author. HarperCollins, 1989. ISBN 0-06-022405-3 Subj: Sun. Time.

The wild boy ill. by author. Farrar, 1998. ISBN 0-374-38431-2 Subj: Character traits – kindness. Character traits – patience. Homeless.

William, where are you? ill. by author. Crown, 1985. ISBN 0-517-55644-8 Subj: Animals. Bedtime. Behavior – hiding. Format, unusual – toy & movable books.

Gervais, Bernadette. *Voyage under the stars* by Bernadette Gervais & Francisco Pittau; ill. by Bernadette Gervais. Lothrop, 1992. ISBN 0-688-11329-X Subj: Animals. Behavior – sharing. Birds – geese. Night.

Getz, Arthur. *Humphrey, the dancing pig* ill. by author. Dial, 1980. ISBN 0-8037-4497-8 Subj: Activities – dancing. Animals – pigs. Behavior – dissatisfaction.

Gewing, Lisa. *Mama, daddy, baby and me* ill. by Donna Larimer. Spirit Pr., 1989. ISBN 0-944296-04-1 Subj: Babies. Family life – new sibling. Rhyming text. Sibling rivalry.

Gezi, Kal. *The mystery at Misty Falls* (Bradford, Ann)

The mystery in the secret club house (Bradford, Ann)

The mystery of the blind writer (Bradford, Ann)

The mystery of the live ghosts (Bradford, Ann)

The mystery of the midget clown (Bradford, Ann)

The mystery of the missing dogs (Bradford, Ann)

The mystery of the missing raccoon (Bradford, Ann)

The mystery of the square footsteps (Bradford, Ann)

The mystery of the tree house (Bradford, Ann)

Ghazi, Suhaib Hamid. *Ramadan* ill. by Omar Rayyan. Holiday, 1996. ISBN 0-8234-1254-7 Subj: Holidays – Ramadan. Religion.

Ghigna, Charles. *The alphabet parade* ill. by Patti Woods. River City, 2002. ISBN 1-880216-74-4 Subj: ABC books. Parades. Rhyming text.

Animal trunk ill. by Gabriel. Abrams, 1999. ISBN 0-8109-4200-3 Subj: Animals. Poetry.

Christmas is coming! by Charles Ghigna and Debra Ghigna; ill. by Mary O'Keefe Young. Talewinds, 2000. ISBN 0-88106-113-1 Subj: Holidays – Christmas. Poetry.

Good cats/Bad cats ill. by David Catrow. Walt Disney, 1992. ISBN 1-56282-293-4 Subj: Animals – cats. Behavior – misbehavior. Format, unusual. Poetry.

Good dogs/Bad dogs ill. by David Catrow. Walt Disney, 1992. ISBN 1-56282-291-8 Subj: Animals – dogs. Behavior – misbehavior. Format, unusual. Poetry.

Haiku, the travelers of eternity ill. by Armor Keller. River City, 2001. ISBN 0-913515-15-9 Subj: Nature. Poetry.

Halloween night ill. by Adam McCauley. Running Pr., 2003. ISBN 0-7624-1552-5 Subj: Holidays – Halloween. Poetry.

Mice are nice ill. by Jon Goodell. Random House, 1999. ISBN 0-679-98929-3 Subj: Animals – mice. Pets. Rhyming text.

Ghigna, Debra. *Christmas is coming!* (Ghigna, Charles)

Gianni, Peg. *Alex, the amazing juggler* by Peg Gianni & Renato Ferraro; ill. by Peg Gianni. Holt, 1981. ISBN 0-03-059891-5 Subj: Behavior – running away. Royalty.

Giannini, Enzo. *Little Parsley* ill. by author. S&S, 1990. ISBN 0-671-67197-9 Subj: Folk & fairy tales. Foreign lands – Italy. Witches.

Giasullo, Cresent. *Gia and the one hundred dollars worth of bubblegum* (Asch, Frank)

Gibbie, Mike. *Small Brown Dog's bad remembering day* ill. by Barbara Nascimbeni. Dutton, 2000. ISBN 0-525-46397-6 Subj: Animals – dogs. Cumulative tales. Memories, memory.

Gibbon, David. *Kittens* ill. with photos. Crescent Books, 1979. ISBN 84-499-5052-X Subj: Animals – cats.

Gibbons, Faye. *Emma Jo's song* ill. by Sherry Meidell. Boyds Mills, 2001. ISBN 1-56397-935-7 Subj: Activities – singing. Character traits – confidence. Music.

Full steam ahead ill. by Sherry Meidell. Boyds Mills, 2002. ISBN 1-56397-858-X Subj: Family life – grandfathers. Trains.

Mama and me and the Model-T ill. by Ted Rand. Morrow, 1999. ISBN 0-688-15299-6 Subj: Activities – driving. Automobiles. Family life – mothers. Gender roles.

Mountain wedding ill. by Ted Rand. Morrow, 1996. ISBN 0-688-11349-4 Subj: Country. Family life – stepfamilies. Insects – bees. Weddings.

Gibbons, Gail. *Apples* ill. by author. Holiday, 2000. ISBN 0-8234-1497-3 Subj: Activities – baking, cooking. Food. U.S. history.

The art box ill. by author. Holiday, 1998. ISBN 0-8234-1386-1 Subj: Art. Careers – artists. Tools.

Bats ill. by author. Holiday, 1999. ISBN 0-8234-1457-4 Subj: Animals – bats. Behavior. Night.

The berry book ill. by author. Holiday, 2002. ISBN 0-8234-1697-6 Subj: Activities – baking, cooking. Food. Plants.

Boat book ill. by author. Holiday, 1983. ISBN 0-8234-0478-1 Subj: Boats, ships.

Cats ill. by author. Holiday, 1996. ISBN 0-8234-1253-9 Subj: Animals – cats.

Check it out! the book about libraries ill. by author. Harcourt, 1985. ISBN 0-15-216400-6 Subj: Libraries.

Clocks and how they go ill. by author. Crowell, 1979. ISBN 0-690-03974-3 Subj: Clocks, watches. Time.

County fair ill. by author. Little, 1994. ISBN 0-316-30951-6 Subj: Country. Fairs, festivals.

Deadline! from news to newspaper ill. by author. HarperCollins, 1987. ISBN 0-690-04602-2 Subj: Activities – working. Paper.

Department store ill. by author. Crowell, 1984. ISBN 0-690-04367-8 Subj: Stores.

Dinosaurs ill. by author. Holiday, 1987. ISBN 0-8234-0657-1 Subj: Dinosaurs. Prehistory.

Dogs ill. by author. Holiday, 1996. ISBN 0-8234-1226-1 Subj: Animals – dogs.

Ducks ill. by author. Holiday, 2001. ISBN 0-8234-1567-8 Subj: Birds – ducks.

Easter ill. by author. Holiday, 1989. ISBN 0-8234-0737-3 Subj: Holidays – Easter.

Emergency! ill. by author. Holiday, 1994. ISBN 0-8234-1128-1 Subj: Careers. Character traits – helpfulness. Trucks.

Exploring the deep, dark sea ill. by author. Little, 1999. ISBN 0-316-30945-1 Subj: Boats, ships. Ecology. Science. Sea & seashore.

Farming ill. by author. Holiday, 1988. ISBN 0-8234-0682-2 Subj: Careers. Farms. Seasons.

Fill it up! all about service stations ill. by author. Crowell, 1985. ISBN 0-690-04440-2 Subj: Automobiles. Careers.

Fire! Fire! ill. by author. Crowell, 1984. ISBN 0-690-04416-X Subj: Careers – firefighters.

Flying ill. by author. Holiday, 1986. ISBN 0-8234-0599-0 Subj: Activities – ballooning. Activities – flying. Airplanes, airports.

Frogs ill. by author. Holiday, 1993. ISBN 0-8234-1052-8 Subj: Frogs & toads.

From seed to plant ill. by author. Holiday, 1991. ISBN 0-8234-0872-8 Subj: Plants. Science. Seeds.

Giant pandas ill. by author. Holiday, 2002. ISBN 0-8234-1761-1 Subj: Animals – endangered animals. Animals – pandas. Foreign lands – China.

Grizzly bears ill. by author. Holiday, 2003. Subj: Animals – bears. Animals – endangered animals.

Gulls – gulls – gulls ill. by author. Holiday, 1997. ISBN 0-8234-1323-3 Subj: Birds – seagulls.

Halloween ill. by author. Holiday, 1984. ISBN 0-8234-0524-9 Subj: Holidays – Halloween.

Halloween is . . . ill. by author. Holiday, 2002. ISBN 0-8234-1758-1 Subj: Holidays – Halloween.

Happy birthday! ill. by author. Holiday, 1986. ISBN 0-8234-0614-8 Subj: Birthdays.

The honey makers ill. by author. Morrow, 1997. ISBN 0-688-11387-7 Subj: Food. Insects – bees.

How a house is built ill. by author. Holiday, 1990. ISBN 0-8234-0841-8 Subj: Activities – making things. Homes, houses.

Knights in shining armor ill. by author. Little, 1995. ISBN 0-316-30948-6 Subj: Knights. Middle Ages.

The milk makers ill. by author. Macmillan, 1985. ISBN 0-02-736640-5 Subj: Farms. Food.

The missing maple syrup sap mystery: or, How maple syrup is made ill. by author. Warne, 1979. ISBN 0-7232-6167-9 Subj: Activities. Food. Mystery stories. Trees.

Monarch butterfly ill. by author. Holiday, 1989. ISBN 0-8234-0773-X Subj: Insects – butterflies, caterpillars. Metamorphosis. Science.

Nature's green umbrella: tropical rain forests ill. by author. Morrow, 1994. ISBN 0-688-12353-8 Subj: Animals. Ecology. Forest, woods. Plants.

New road! ill. by author. Crowell, 1983. ISBN 0-690-04343-0 Subj: Transportation.

Paper, paper everywhere ill. by author. Harcourt, 1983. ISBN 0-15-259488-4 Subj: Paper.

Penguins! ill. by author. Holiday, 1998. ISBN 0-8234-1388-8 Subj: Birds – penguins. Foreign lands – Antarctic.

Pigs ill. by author. Holiday, 1999. ISBN 0-8234-1441-8 Subj: Animals – pigs.

The planets ill. by author. Holiday, 1993. ISBN 0-8234-1040-4 Subj: Astronomy. Planets.

Playgrounds ill. by author. Holiday, 1985. ISBN 0-8234-0553-2 Subj: Activities – playing.

Polar bears ill. by author. Holiday, 2001. ISBN 0-8234-1593-7 Subj: Animals – polar bears.

The post office book: mail and how it moves ill. by author. Crowell, 1982. ISBN 0-690-04199-3 Subj: Careers – postal workers. Communication. Post office.

The pottery place ill. by author. Harcourt, 1987. ISBN 0-15-263265-4 Subj: Careers.

Prehistoric animals ill. by author. Holiday, 1988. ISBN 0-8234-0707-1 Subj: Animals. Prehistory. Science.

Puff – flash – bang! a book about signals ill. by author. Morrow, 1993. ISBN 0-688-07378-6 Subj: Communication.

The pumpkin book ill. by author. Holiday, 1999. ISBN 0-8234-1465-5 Subj: Gardens, gardening. Seasons – fall.

The quilting bee ill. by author. HarperCollins, 2004. ISBN 0-688-16398-X Subj: Activities – sewing. Quilts.

The reasons for seasons ill. by author. Holiday, 1995. ISBN 0-8234-1174-5 Subj: Seasons.

Recycle! ill. by author. Little, 1992. ISBN 0-316-30971-0 Subj: Ecology.

Say woof! the day of a country veterinarian ill. by author. Macmillan, 1992. ISBN 0-02-736781-9 Subj: Animals. Careers – veterinarians. Illness.

The seasons of Arnold's apple tree ill. by author. Harcourt, 1988. ISBN 0-15-271246-1 Subj: Food. Seasons. Trees.

Sharks ill. by author. Holiday, 1992. ISBN 0-8234-0960-0 Subj: Fish – sharks. Science.

Soaring with the wind: the bald eagle ill. by author. Morrow, 1998. ISBN 0-688-13731-8 Subj: Birds – eagles. Science.

Spiders ill. by author. Holiday, 1993. ISBN 0-8234-1006-4 Subj: Spiders.

Stargazers ill. by author. Holiday, 1992. ISBN 0-8234-0983-X Subj: Astronomy. Stars.

Sun up, sun down ill. by author. Harcourt, 1983. ISBN 0-15-282781-1 Subj: Science. Sun.

Surrounded by sea ill. by author. Little, 1991. ISBN 0-316-30961-3 Subj: Careers – fishermen. Islands. Sports – fishing.

Tell me, tree ill. by author. Little, 2002. ISBN 0-316-30903-6 Subj: Trees.

Thanksgiving Day ill. by author. Holiday, 1983. ISBN 0-8234-0489-7 Subj: Holidays – Thanksgiving. Pilgrims.

The too-great bread bake book ill. by author. Warne, 1980. ISBN 0-7232-6182-2 Subj: Activities – baking, cooking.

Tool book ill. by author. Holiday, 1982. ISBN 0-8234-0444-7 Subj: Tools.

Trains ill. by author. Holiday, 1987. ISBN 0-8234-0640-7 Subj: Trains.

Trucks ill. by author. Crowell, 1981. ISBN 0-690-04119-5 Subj: Trucks.

Tunnels ill. by author. Holiday, 1984. ISBN 0-8234-0507-9 Subj: Activities – digging.

Up goes the skyscraper! ill. by author. Four Winds, 1986. ISBN 0-02-736780-0 Subj: Buildings. Cities, towns.

Valentine's Day ill. by author. Holiday, 1985. ISBN 0-8234-0572-9 Subj: Holidays – Valentine's Day.

Weather words and what they mean ill. by author. Holiday, 1990. ISBN 0-8234-0805-1 Subj: Language. Weather.

Whales ill. by author. Holiday, 1991. ISBN 0-8234-0900-7 Subj: Animals – whales.

Yippee-yay! a book about cowboys and cowgirls ill. by author. Little, 1998. ISBN 0-316-30944-3 Subj: Animals – bulls, cows. Cowboys, cowgirls. Rodeos. U.S. history – frontier & pioneer life.

Zoo ill. by author. Crowell, 1987. ISBN 0-690-04633-2 Subj: Activities – working. Animals. Zoos.

Gibbs, Lynne. *Don't slurp your soup!* ill. by John Eastwood. McGraw-Hill, 2003. ISBN 1-57768-556-3 Subj: Etiquette.

Gibert, Bruno. *The king is naked!* ill. by author. Clarion, 2004. ISBN 0-618-41067-8 Subj: Animals. Animals – lions. Clothing. Jungle. Royalty – kings.

Giblin, James Cross. *George Washington: a picture book biography* ill. by Michael Dooling. Scholastic, 1992. ISBN 0-59-042550-1 Subj: U.S. history.

Gibson, Betty. *The story of Little Quack* ill. by Kady MacDonald Denton. Little, 1991. ISBN 0-316-30966-4 Subj: Birds – ducks. Farms. Pets.

Gibson, Josephine. *see* Joslin, Sesyle

Gibson, Karen Bush. *Child care workers* ill. with photos. Bridgestone, 2001. ISBN 0-7368-0622-9 Subj: Careers. Communities, neighborhoods.

Emergency medical technicians ill. with photos. Bridgestone, 2001. ISBN 0-7368-0623-7 Subj: Careers. Communities, neighborhoods.

Pharmacists ill. with photos. Bridgestone, 2001. ISBN 0-7368-0624-5 Subj: Careers – pharmacists. Communities, neighborhoods.

Truck drivers ill. with photos. Bridgestone, 2001. ISBN 0-7368-0625-3 Subj: Careers – truck drivers. Communities, neighborhoods.

Gibson, Kari Smalley. *Mooki's secret* by Kari Smalley Gibson with Gary Smalley; ill. by Richard Bernal. Gold'n'Honey, 1998. ISBN 1-57673-266-5 Subj: Animals – beavers. Orphans. Self-concept.

Gibson, Myra Tomback. *What is your favorite thing to touch?* ill. by author. Grosset, 1965. Subj: Poetry. Senses – touch.

Giesen, Rosemary. *Famous planes* (Thompson, Brenda)

Pirates (Thompson, Brenda)

Gifaldi, David. *Ben, king of the river* ill. by Layne Johnson. A. Whitman, 2001. ISBN 0-8075-0635-4 Subj: Camps, camping. Family life – brothers. Handicaps – mental handicaps.

The boy who spoke colors ill. by C. Shana Greger. Houghton Mifflin, 1993. ISBN 0-395-65025-9 Subj: Behavior – greed. Folk & fairy tales. Language. Royalty – kings.

Giff, Patricia Reilly. *The almost awful play* ill. by Susanna Natti. Viking, 1984. ISBN 0-670-11458-8 Subj: Theater.

The beast in Ms. Rooney's room ill. by Blanche Sims. Delacorte, 1986. ISBN 0-385-29492-1 Subj: Books, reading. School.

Good luck, Ronald Morgan ill. by Susanna Natti. Viking, 1996. ISBN 0-670-86303-3 Subj: Animals – cats. Animals – dogs. Pets.

Happy birthday, Ronald Morgan! ill. by Susanna Natti. Viking, 1986. ISBN 0-670-80741-9 Subj: Birthdays. Friendship. School.

I love Saturday ill. by Frank Remkiewicz. Viking, 1989. ISBN 0-670-81409-1 Subj: Behavior – secrets. Cities, towns. Days of the week, months of the year.

Next year I'll be special ill. by Marylin Hafner. Dutton, 1980. ISBN 0-525-35810-2 Subj: Behavior – seeking better things. Dreams. School.

Ronald Morgan goes to bat ill. by Susanna Natti. Viking, 1988. ISBN 0-670-81457-1 Subj: Sports – baseball.

Ronald Morgan goes to camp ill. by Susanna Natti. Viking, 1995. ISBN 0-670-86195-2 Subj: Activities. Camps, camping. Friendship.

Today was a terrible day ill. by Susanna Natti. Viking, 1980. ISBN 0-670-81830-0 Subj: Behavior – bad day. School.

Watch out, Ronald Morgan! ill. by Susanna Natti. Viking, 1985. ISBN 0-670-80433-9 Subj: Glasses. School. Senses – sight.

Giffard, Hannah. *Fast car* ill. by Hannah Giffard. Tambourine, 1993. ISBN 0-688-12444-5 Subj: Automobiles. Concepts – opposites. Format, unusual – board books. Trucks.

Hens say cluck ill. by author. Tambourine, 1993. ISBN 0-688-12442-9 Subj: Animals. Format, unusual – board books. Noise, sounds.

Red bus ill. by author. Tambourine, 1993. ISBN 0-688-12443-7 Subj: Buses. Concepts – color. Format, unusual – board books.

Red Fox ill. by author. Dial, 1991. ISBN 0-8037-0869-6 Subj: Animals – foxes. Food.

Red Fox on the move ill. by author. Dial, 1992. ISBN 0-8037-1057-7 Subj: Animals – foxes. Family life. Moving.

Striped zebra ill. by author. Tambourine, 1993. ISBN 0-688-12441-0 Subj: Animals. Format, unusual – board books.

Gifford, Kathie Lee. *Giff the scaredy bear* by Kathie Lee Gifford, Paul Taublieb, & Susan Cooper; ill. by Debbie Young. Random House, 1997. ISBN 0-679-88504-8 Subj: Animals – bears. Emotions – fear. Sports – roller skating.

Giff's big game by Kathie Lee Gifford, Paul Taublieb, & Susan Cooper; ill. by Debbie Young. Random House, 1997. ISBN 0-679-88495-5 Subj: Animals – bears. Sports – football. Sportsmanship.

Moochie's surprise by Kathie Lee Gifford, Paul Taublieb, & Susan Cooper; ill. by Debbie Young. Random House, 1997. ISBN 0-679-88496-3 Subj: Animals – mice. Friendship. Self-concept.

Giganti, Paul. *Each orange had eight slices* ill. by Donald Crews. Greenwillow, 1992. ISBN 0-688-10429-0 Subj: Counting, numbers.

How many snails? a counting book by Paul Giganti, Jr.; ill. by Donald Crews. Greenwillow, 1988. ISBN 0-688-06370-5 Subj: Counting, numbers.

Giglio, Judy. *The tapping tale* ill. by Joe Cepeda. Harcourt, 2000. ISBN 0-15-202572-3 Subj: Animals – dogs. Noise, sounds. Sleepovers.

Gikow, Louise. *Baby Kermit's Christmas* ill. by Lauren Attinello. Muppet Pr., 1993. ISBN 0-307-13722-8 Subj: Babies. Holidays – Christmas. Puppets.

Boober Fraggle's ghosts ill. by Lawrence DiFiori. Holt, 1985. ISBN 0-03-004549-5 Subj: Emotions – fear. Ghosts. Puppets.

Bye-bye, pacifier ill. by Tom Cooke. Muppet Pr., 1992. ISBN 0-307-12330-8 Subj: Animals – pigs. Babies. Behavior – growing up. Format, unusual – board books. Puppets.

Count with me ill. by David Prebenna. Grolier, 1992. ISBN 0-717-28283-X Subj: Counting, numbers. Puppets.

Follow that Fraggle! ill. by Barbara Lanza. Holt, 1985. ISBN 0-03-004558-4 Subj: Activities – traveling. Animals – dogs. Puppets.

For every child, a better world by Kermit the Frog; in cooperation with the United Nations; as told to Louise Gikow & Ellen Weiss; ill. by Bruce McNally. Western, 1993. ISBN 0-307-65628-4 Subj: Puppets. World.

I am Kermit ill. by Joe Ewers. Muppet Pr., 1993. ISBN 0-307-12170-4 Subj: Format, unusual – board books. Frogs & toads. Puppets.

Jim Henson's Muppets in Rowlf's big test: a book about listening to your conscience ill. by Dave Prebenna. Grolier, 1993. ISBN 0-717-28331-3 Subj: Character traits – honesty. Puppets. School.

Jim Henson's Muppets in What's fair is fair: a book about sharing ill. by Tom Leigh. Grolier, 1992. ISBN 0-717-28269-4 Subj: Behavior – sharing. Fairs, festivals. Friendship. Puppets.

Sprocket's Christmas tale ill. by Lisa McCue. Holt, 1984. ISBN 0-03-000708-9 Subj: Holidays – Christmas. Puppets.

Gilbert, Helen Earle. *Dr. Trotter and his big gold watch* ill. by Margaret Bradfield. Abingdon, 1948. Subj: Careers – doctors. Clocks, watches.

Mr. Plum and the little green tree ill. by Margaret Bradfield. Abingdon, 1946. Subj: Careers – shoemakers. Trees.

Gilbert, Jane. *Indescribably Arabella* ill. by author. Atheneum, 2003. ISBN 0-689-85321-1 Subj: Character traits – individuality.

Gilbert, Lisa Weedn. *The elephant prince* (Weedn, Flavia)

The enchanted tree (Weedn, Flavia)

The giant's garden (Weedn, Flavia)

I feel happy (Weedn, Flavia)

The little snow bear (Weedn, Flavia)

The magic cap (Weedn, Flavia)

The moon maiden (Weedn, Flavia)

The ragged peddler (Weedn, Flavia)

The star gift (Weedn, Flavia)

Gilbert, Suzie. *Hawk Hill* ill. by Sylvia Long. Chronicle, 1996. ISBN 0-8118-0839-4 Subj: Animals. Birds – hawks. Character traits – kindness to animals. Friendship. Illness.

Gilbert, Yvonne. *Baby's book of lullabies and cradle songs* ill. by author. Dial, 1990. ISBN 0-8037-0795-9 Subj: Lullabies. Music. Songs.

Gilchrist, Jan Spivey. *Indigo and moonlight gold* ill. by author. Black Butterfly, 1993. ISBN 0-86316-210-X Subj: Ethnic groups in the U.S. – African Americans. Family life – mothers. Night.

Gilchrist, Theo E. *Halfway up the mountain* ill. by Glen Rounds. Lippincott, 1978. ISBN 0-397-31805-7 Subj: Activities – baking, cooking. Behavior – fighting, arguing. Rhyming text.

Gile, John. *Oh, how I wished I could read!* ill. by Frank Fiorello. John Gile Communications, 1995. ISBN 0-910941-10-6 Subj: Books, reading. Dreams. Rhyming text.

Giles, Almira Astudillo. *Willie wins* ill. by Carl Angel. Lee & Low, 2001. ISBN 1-58430-023-X Subj: Ethnic groups in the U.S. – Filipino Americans. Family life – fathers. School.

Gili, Phillida. *Fanny and Charles: a regency escapade or, The trick that went wrong* ill. by author. Viking, 1983. ISBN 0-670-30697-5 Subj: Activities – vacationing. Animals – mice. Sibling rivalry.

Gilks, Helen. *Bears* ill. by Andrew Bale. Ticknor & Fields, 1993. ISBN 0-395-66899-9 Subj: Animals – bears.

Gill, Bob. *A balloon for a blunderbuss* by Bob Gill & Alastair Reid; ill. by Bob Gill. HarperCollins, 1961. Subj: Activities – trading.

Gill, Janet. *Basket Weaver and Catches Many Mice* ill. by Yangsook Choi. Random House, 1999. ISBN 0-679-98922-6 Subj: Activities – weaving. Animals – cats. Folk & fairy tales. Royalty.

Gill, Joan. *Hush, Jon!* ill. by Tracy Sugarman. Doubleday, 1968. Subj: Babies. Emotions – envy, jealousy. Ethnic groups in the U.S. – African Americans. Family life.

Gill, Madelaine. *The spring hat* ill. by author. S&S, 1993. ISBN 0-671-75664-8 Subj: Animals – rabbits. Clothing – hats. Wordless.

Gill, Shelley. *The big buck adventure* by Shelley Gill & Deborah Tobola; ill. by Grace Lin. Charlesbridge, 2000. ISBN 0-88106-294-4 Subj: Counting, numbers. Money. Shopping.

The egg ill. by Jo-Ellen Bosson. Charlesbridge, 2001. ISBN 1-57091-377-3 Subj: Eggs. Nature.

Gillard, Denise. *Music from the sky* ill. by Stephen Taylor. Douglas & McIntyre, 2001. ISBN 0-88899-311-0 Subj: Family life – grandfathers. Musical instruments – flutes.

Gill-Brown, Vanessa. *Rufferella* ill. by Mandy Stanley. Scholastic, 2001. ISBN 0-439-25617-8 Subj: Animals – dogs. Behavior – imitation.

Gilleo, Alma. *Learning about monsters* ill. by Joe Van Severen. Childrens Pr., 1982. ISBN 0-516-06535-1 Subj: Folk & fairy tales. Monsters. Mythical creatures.

Gillerlain, Gayle. *Reverend Thomas's false teeth* ill. by Dena Schutzer. BridgeWater, 1994. ISBN 0-8167-3303-1 Subj: Behavior – lost & found possessions. Careers – clergy. Teeth.

Gillespi, Haven. *Santa Claus is comin' to town* (Kellogg, Steven [Stephen])

Gillham, Bill. *Can you see it?* photos by Fiona Horne. Putnam, 1986. ISBN 0-399-21323-6 Subj: Games.

The early words picture book photos by Sam Grainger. Coward, 1983. ISBN 0-698-20583-9 Subj: Books, reading.

Let's look for colors by Bill Gillham & Susan Hulme; photos by Jan Siegieda. Putnam, 1984. ISBN 0-698-20612-6 Subj: Concepts – color.

Let's look for numbers by Bill Gillham & Susan Hulme; photos by Jan Siegieda. Putnam, 1984. ISBN 0-698-20613-4 Subj: Counting, numbers.

Let's look for opposites by Bill Gillham & Susan Hulme; photos by Jan Siegieda. Putnam, 1984. ISBN 0-698-20614-2 Subj: Concepts – opposites.

Let's look for shapes by Bill Gillham & Susan Hulme; photos by Jan Siegieda. Putnam, 1984. ISBN 0-698-20615-0 Subj: Concepts – shape.

What can you do? photos by Fiona Horne. Putnam, 1986. ISBN 0-399-21324-4 Subj: Games. Imagination.

What's the difference? photos by Fiona Horne. Putnam, 1986. ISBN 0-399-21321-X Subj: Concepts – opposites. Games.

Where does it go? photos by Fiona Horne. Putnam, 1986. ISBN 0-399-21322-8 Subj: Concepts. Games.

Gillies, Don. *Dinosaur days* (Baker, Liza)

Gilliland, Judith Heide. *The day of Ahmed's secret* (Heide, Florence Parry)

Not in the house, Newton! ill. by Elizabeth Sayles. Clarion, 1995. ISBN 0-395-61195-4 Subj: Activities – drawing. Imagination. Magic.

River ill. by Joyce Powzyk. Houghton Mifflin, 1993. ISBN 0-395-55963-4 Subj: Foreign lands – Amazon. Forest, woods. Rivers.

Sami and the time of the troubles (Heide, Florence Parry)

Gillmor, Don. *The fabulous song* ill. by Marie-Louise Gay. Kane/Miller, 1998. ISBN 0-916291-80-4 Subj: Careers – musicians. Family life.

Yuck, a love story ill. by Marie-Louise Gay. Stoddart, 2000. ISBN 0-7737-3218-7 Subj: Birthdays. Friendship. Moon.

Gilman, Rita Golden. *Mole in a hole* ill. by Holly Hannon. Random House, 2003. ISBN 0-679-99037-2 Subj: Animals. Animals – moles. Rebuses. Rhyming text.

Rice is life ill. by Yangsook Choi. Holt, 2000. ISBN 0-8050-5719-6 Subj: Animals. Food. Foreign lands – Indonesia. Poetry.

Gilmore, Rachna. *Lights for Gita* ill. by Alice Priestley. Tilbury House, 1994. ISBN 0-88448-150-6 Subj: Ethnic groups in the U.S. – East Indian Americans. Holidays – Divali. Moving. Religion – Hinduism.

Gilmour, H. B. *Why Wembley Fraggle couldn't sleep* ill. by Barbara McClintock. Holt, 1985. ISBN 0-03-004557-6 Subj: Puppets. Sleep.

The gingerbread boy. *Gingerbread baby* retold & ill. by Jan Brett. Putnam, 1999. ISBN 0-399-23444-6 Subj: Behavior – running away. Cumulative tales. Folk & fairy tales. Food. Format, unusual – toy & movable books.

The gingerbread boy retold by Harriet Ziefert; ill. by Emily Bolam. Viking, 1995. ISBN 0-670-86052-2 Subj: Behavior – running away. Cumulative tales. Folk & fairy tales.

The gingerbread boy retold & ill. by Scott Cook. Knopf, 1987. ISBN 0-394-98698-9 Subj: Behavior – running away. Cumulative tales. Folk & fairy tales.

The gingerbread boy retold & ill. by Richard Egielski. Geringer, 1997. ISBN 0-06-026031-9 Subj: Behavior – running away. Cumulative tales. Folk & fairy tales. Food.

The gingerbread boy ill. by Paul Galdone. Seabury Pr., 1975. ISBN 0-8164-3132-9 Subj: Behavior – running away. Cumulative tales. Folk & fairy tales. Food. Rhyming text.

The gingerbread boy retold by David Cutts; ill. by Joan Elizabeth Goodman. Troll, 1979. ISBN 0-89375-122-7 Subj: Behavior – running away. Cumulative tales. Folk & fairy tales. Food.

The gingerbread boy ill. by William Curtis Holdsworth. Farrar, 1968. Subj: Behavior – running away. Cumulative tales. Folk & fairy tales. Food.

The gingerbread man retold & ill. by Carol Jones. Houghton, 2002. ISBN 0-618-18822-3 Subj: Behavior – running away. Cumulative tales. Folk & fairy tales. Food.

The gingerbread man retold by Eric A. Kimmel; ill. by Megan Lloyd. Holiday, 1993. ISBN 0-8234-0824-8 Subj: Behavior – running away. Cumulative tales. Folk & fairy tales.

The gingerbread man retold by Jim Aylesworth; ill. by Barbara McClintock. Scholastic, 1998. ISBN 0-590-97219-7 Subj: Behavior – running away. Cumulative tales. Folk & fairy tales. Food.

The gingerbread man retold by Hugh Lupton; ill. by Diana Mayo. Barefoot, 2003. ISBN 1-84148-056-8 Subj: Behavior – running away. Cumulative tales. Folk & fairy tales. Food.

The gingerbread man retold by Barbara Ireson; ill. by Gerald Rose. Norton, 1963. Subj: Behavior – running away. Cumulative tales. Folk & fairy tales. Food.

The gingerbread man retold & ill. by Bonnie & Bill Rutherford. Golden Bks., 2001. ISBN 0-307-10681-0 Subj: Behavior – running away. Cumulative tales. Folk & fairy tales. Food.

The pancake boy adapt. & ill. by Lorinda Bryan Cauley. Putnam, 1988. ISBN 0-399-21505-0 Subj: Behavior – running away. Cumulative tales. Folk & fairy tales. Food.

Whiff, sniff, nibble and chew: The Gingerbread boy retold by Charlotte Pomerantz; ill. by Monica Incisa. Greenwillow, 1984. ISBN 0-688-02552-8 Subj: Behavior – running away. Cumulative tales. Folk & fairy tales. Rhyming text.

Ginolfi, Arthur. *The tiny star: the greatest star the world has ever seen!* ill. by Pat Schories. Tommy Nelson, 1997. ISBN 0-8499-1510-4 Subj: Holidays – Christmas. Religion – Nativity. Stars.

Ginsburg, Mirra. *Across the stream* ill. by Nancy Tafuri. Greenwillow, 1982. ISBN 0-688-01206-X Subj: Animals – foxes. Birds – chickens. Birds – ducks. Dreams.

Asleep, asleep ill. by Nancy Tafuri. Greenwillow, 1992. ISBN 0-688-09154-7 Subj: Bedtime. Lullabies. Night.

The chick and the duckling ill. by José Aruego & Ariane Dewey. Macmillan, 1972. Translation of +G:T+H:Syplenok i utenok by Vladimir Grigorévich Suteyev. ISBN 0-02-735940-9 Subj: Birds – chickens. Birds – ducks. Sports – swimming.

The Chinese mirror ill. by Margot Zemach. Harcourt, 1988. ISBN 0-15-200420-3 Subj: Character traits – appearance. Folk & fairy tales. Foreign lands – Korea.

Clay boy ill. by Jos. A. Smith. Greenwillow, 1997. Adapt. from a Russian folk tale. ISBN 0-688-14410-1 Subj: Activities – making things. Folk & fairy tales. Foreign lands – Russia.

The fisherman's son ill. by Tony Chen. Greenwillow, 1979. ISBN 0-688-84216-X Subj: Character traits – cleverness. Folk & fairy tales. Foreign lands – Russia.

Four brave sailors ill. by Nancy Tafuri. Greenwillow, 1987. ISBN 0-688-06515-5 Subj: Animals – mice. Boats, ships. Dreams. Pirates. Rhyming text. Sailors. Sea & seashore. Toys. Weather.

The fox and the hare ill. by Victor Nolden. Crown, 1969. Subj: Animals. Animals – foxes. Animals – rabbits. Folk & fairy tales. Foreign lands – Russia. Friendship.

Good morning, chick (Chukovskii, Kornei Ivanovich)

How the sun was brought back to the sky adapt. from a Slovenian folk tale; ill. by José Aruego & Ariane Dewey. Macmillan, 1975. ISBN 0-02-735750-3 Subj: Folk & fairy tales. Foreign lands – Czechoslovakia. Sun.

The king who tried to fry an egg on his head ill. by Will Hillenbrand. Macmillan, 1994. ISBN 0-02-736242-6 Subj: Character traits – foolishness. Folk & fairy tales. Foreign lands – Russia. Royalty – kings.

Kitten from one to ten ill. by Giulio Maestro. Crown, 1980. ISBN 0-517-53972-1 Subj: Animals – cats. Counting, numbers. Rhyming text.

Mushroom in the rain ill. by José Aruego & Ariane Dewey. Macmillan, 1988, 1974. Adapt. from the Russian of Vladimir Grigorévich Suteyev. ISBN 0-02-736241-8 Subj: Animals. Animals – foxes. Plants. Weather – rain.

The old man and his birds ill. by Donna Ruff. Greenwillow, 1994. ISBN 0-688-04604-5 Subj: Birds. Days of the week, months of the year. Magic. Seasons.

Ookie-Spooky ill. by Emily Arnold McCully. Crown, 1979. ISBN 0-517-53610-2 Subj: Monsters.

Pampalche of the silver teeth ill. by Rocco Negri. Crown, 1976. ISBN 0-517-52241-1 Subj: Folk & fairy tales. Foreign lands – Russia. Witches.

Striding slippers: an Udmurt tale ill. by Sal Murdocca. Macmillan, 1978. ISBN 0-02-736370-8 Subj: Behavior – stealing. Folk & fairy tales. Magic.

The strongest one of all ill. by José Aruego & Ariane Dewey. Greenwillow, 1977. ISBN 0-688-84081-7 Subj: Animals – sheep. Character traits – bravery. Foreign lands – Russia.

The sun's asleep behind the hill ill. by Paul O. Zelinsky. Greenwillow, 1982. ISBN 0-688-00825-9 Subj: Night. Rhyming text.

Three kittens trans. from the Russian of V. Suteyev; ill. by Lisa McCue. Random House, 1992. ISBN 0-679-93254-2 Subj: Animals – cats. Concepts – color.

Two greedy bears ill. by José Aruego & Ariane Dewey. Macmillan, 1976. ISBN 0-02-736450-X Subj: Animals – bears. Animals – foxes. Behavior – greed. Foreign lands – Hungary. Sibling rivalry.

We adopted you, Benjamin Koo ill. by Linda Shute. A. Whitman, 1985. ISBN 0-8075-8694-3 Subj: Adoption. Ethnic groups in the U.S. – Korean Americans. Family life.

Where does the sun go at night? ill. by José Aruego & Ariane Dewey. Greenwillow, 1980. ISBN 0-688-84245-3 Subj: Night. Sun.

Which is the best place? ill. by Roger Antoine Duvoisin. Macmillan, 1976. Tr. from Gde luchshe by Pyotr Dubochkin. ISBN 0-02-735980-8 Subj: Bedtime. Foreign lands – Russia.

Giovanni, Nikki. *The genie in the jar* ill. by Christopher Raschka. Holt, 1996. ISBN 0-8050-4118-4 Subj: Activities. Ethnic groups in the U.S. – African Americans. Family life – mothers. Mythical creatures – genies. Poetry.

Spin a soft black song ill. by George Martins. Rev. ed. Hill & Wang, 1985. ISBN 0-8090-8796-0 Subj: Ethnic groups in the U.S. – African Americans. Poetry.

The sun is so quiet ill. by Ashley Bryan. Holt, 1996. ISBN 0-8050-4119-2 Subj: Ethnic groups in the U.S. – African Americans. Nature. Poetry.

Gipson, Morrell. *Favorite nursery tales* ill. by S. D. Schindler. Doubleday, 1983. ISBN 0-385-17961-8 Subj: Nursery rhymes.

Hello, Peter ill. by Clement Hurd. Doubleday, 1948. Subj: Activities.

Whose tracks are these? adapt. by Morrell Gipson; story & ill. by Paul Mangold. Garrett Educational Corp., 1990. ISBN 0-944483-93-3 Subj: Animals. Seasons – winter. Weather – snow.

Girard, Linda Walvoord. *Adoption is for always* ill. by Judi Friedman. A. Whitman, 1986. ISBN 0-8075-0185-9 Subj: Adoption. Family life.

At Daddy's on Saturdays ill. by Judith Friedman. A. Whitman, 1987. ISBN 0-8075-0475-0 Subj: Divorce. Emotions – love. Family life.

Jeremy's first haircut ill. by Maryjane Begin. A. Whitman, 1986. ISBN 0-8075-3805-1 Subj: Emotions – fear. Hair.

My body is private ill. by Rodney Pate. A. Whitman, 1984. ISBN 0-8075-5320-4 Subj: Safety. Self-concept.

Who is a stranger, and what should I do? ill. by Helen Cogancherry. A. Whitman, 1985. ISBN 0-8075-9014-2 Subj: Behavior – talking to strangers. Safety.

You were born on your very first birthday ill. by Christa Kieffer. A. Whitman, 1983. ISBN 0-8075-9455-5 Subj: Babies. Birth. Science.

Girion, Barbara. *The boy with the special face* ill. by Heidi Palmer. Abingdon, 1978. ISBN 0-687-03909-6 Subj: Character traits – appearance.

Girnis, Margaret. *ABC for you and me* photos by Shirley Leaman Green. A. Whitman, 2000. ISBN 0-8075-0101-8 Subj: ABC books. Handicaps – Down syndrome.

1, 2, 3 for you and me photos by Shirley Leamon Green. A. Whitman, 2001. ISBN 0-8075-6107-X Subj: Counting, numbers. Handicaps – Down syndrome.

Giuliano, Katie. *All the way to God* by Katie & Michael Giuliano; ill. by the Giuliano children. Golden Bks., 1999. ISBN 0-307-10223-8 Subj: Children as illustrators. Concepts – distance. Emotions – love. Family life – fathers. Religion.

Giuliano, Michael. *All the way to God* (Giuliano, Katie)

Givens, Janet Eaton. *Just two wings* ill. by Susan Dodge. Atheneum, 1984. ISBN 0-689-31001-3 Subj: Birds.

Something wonderful happened ill. by Susan Dodge. Atheneum, 1982. ISBN 0-689-30904-X Subj: Flowers.

Givens, Terryl. *Dragon scales and willow leaves* ill. by Andrew Portwood. Putnam, 1997. ISBN 0-399-22619-2 Subj: Family life – brothers & sisters. Imagination. Multiple births – twins.

Givon, Hannah Gelman. *We shake in a quake* ill. by David Uttal. Tricycle, 1996. ISBN 1-883672-25-2 Subj: Earthquakes.

Glaser, Byron. *Action alphabet* (Neumeier, Marty)

Bonz, inside-out written & ill. by Byron Glaser & Sandra Higashi. Abrams, 2003. ISBN 0-8109-4599-1 Subj: Anatomy – skeletons.

Glaser, Jason. *Pinkeye* ill. with photos. Capstone, 2006. ISBN 0-7368-4292-6 Subj: Anatomy – eyes. Health & fitness. Illness.

Glaser, Linda. *Beautiful bats* ill. by Sharon Lane Holm. Millbrook, 1997. ISBN 0-7613-0254-9 Subj: Animals – bats.

The borrowed Hanukkah latkes ill. by Nancy Cote. A. Whitman, 1997. ISBN 0-8075-0842-X Subj: Behavior – sharing. Friendship. Holidays – Hanukkah. Jewish culture. Old age.

Compost! growing gardens from your garbage ill. by Anca Hariton. Millbrook, 1996. ISBN 1-56294-659-5 Subj: Gardens, gardening. Nature.

It's fall ill. by Susan Swan. Millbrook, 2001. ISBN 0-7613-1758-9 Subj: Nature. Seasons – fall.

It's spring ill. by Susan Swan. Millbrook, 2002. ISBN 0-7613-1760-0 Subj: Nature. Seasons – spring.

It's summer ill. by Susan Swan. Millbrook, 2003. ISBN 0-7613-1757-0 Subj: Nature. Seasons – summer.

It's winter ill. by Susan Swan. Millbrook, 2002. ISBN 0-7613-1759-7 Subj: Nature. Seasons – winter.

Keep your socks on, Albert! ill. by Sally G. Ward. Dutton, 1992. ISBN 0-525-44838-1 Subj: Animals – possums. Clothing – socks. Emotions – fear. Family life – sisters.

Magnificent monarchs ill. by Gay Holland. Millbrook, 2000. ISBN 0-7613-1700-7 Subj: Insects – butterflies, caterpillars. Science.

Mrs. Greenberg's messy Hanukkah ill. by Nancy Cote. A. Whitman, 2004. ISBN 0-8075-5297-6 Subj: Activities – baking, cooking. Character traits – orderliness. Food. Holidays – Hanukkah. Jewish culture.

Our big home ill. by Elisa Kleven. Millbrook, 2000. ISBN 0-7613-1650-7 Subj: Earth. Nature.

Spectacular spiders ill. by Gay W. Holland. Millbrook, 1998. ISBN 0-7613-0353-7 Subj: Gardens, gardening. Spiders.

Stop that garbage truck! ill. by Karen Lee Schmidt. A. Whitman, 1993. ISBN 0-8075-7626-3 Subj: Careers – sanitation workers. Character traits – shyness. Ethnic groups in the U.S. – African Americans.

Wonderful worms ill. by Loretta Krupinski. Millbrook, 1992. ISBN 1-56294-062-7 Subj: Animals – worms. Insects – butterflies, caterpillars. Metamorphosis. Nature. Science.

Glaser, Omri. *Round the garden* ill. by Byron Glaser & Sandra Higashi. Abrams, 1999. ISBN 0-8109-4137-6 Subj: Water. Weather – rain.

Glass, Andrew. *Bewildered for three days: as to why Daniel Boone never wore his coonskin cap* ill. by author. Holiday, 2000. ISBN 0-8234-1446-9 Subj: Animals – bears. Animals – raccoons. U.S. history – frontier & pioneer life.

Charles T. McBiddle ill. by author. Doubleday, 1993. ISBN 0-385-30554-0 Subj: Character traits – persistence. Sports – bicycling.

Chickpea and the talking cow ill. by author. Lothrop, 1987. ISBN 0-688-06175-3 Subj: Animals – bulls, cows. Character traits – smallness. Emotions – love. Family life. Farms. Royalty.

My brother tries to make me laugh ill. by author. Lothrop, 1984. ISBN 0-688-02259-6 Subj: Imagination. Space & space ships.

The sweetwater run: the story of Buffalo Bill Cody and the Pony Express ill. by author. Doubleday, 1996. ISBN 0-385-32220-8 Subj: Animals – horses, ponies. Careers – postal workers. U.S. history – frontier & pioneer life.

The wondrous whirligig: the Wright Brothers' first flying machine ill. by author. Holiday, 2003. ISBN 0-8234-1717-4 Subj: Activities – flying. Careers – inventors. Helicopters.

Glass, Julie. *A dollar for Penny* ill. by Joy Allen. Random House, 2000. ISBN 0-679-98973-0 Subj: Birthdays. Money. Rhyming text.

Glass, Marvin. *What happened today, Freddy Groundhog?* ill. by author. Crown, 1989. ISBN 0-517-57140-4 Subj: Animals – groundhogs. Holidays – Groundhog Day.

Glasscock, Sarah. *My prairie summer* ill. by Ed Martinez. Steck-Vaughn, 1998. ISBN 0-8172-7284-4 Subj: Animals – buffaloes. Farms. U.S. history – frontier & pioneer life.

Glassman, Peter. *My dad's job* ill. by Timothy Bush. S&S, 2003. ISBN 0-689-82890-X Subj: Careers. Family life – fathers. Imagination.

My working mom ill. by Tedd Arnold. Morrow, 1994. ISBN 0-688-12260-4 Subj: Family life – mothers. Magic. Witches.

The wizard next door ill. by Steven Kellogg. Morrow, 1993. ISBN 0-688-10646-3 Subj: Imagination. Magic. Wizards.

Glazer, Lee. *Cookie Becker casts a spell* ill. by Margot Apple. Little, 1980. ISBN 0-316-31582-6 Subj: Character traits – meanness. Magic.

Gleeson, Brian. *Anansi* ill. by Steven Guarnaccia. Picture Book Studio, 1991. ISBN 0-88708-230-0 Subj: Folk & fairy tales. Foreign lands – Jamaica. Spiders.

Finn McCoul ill. by Peter de Sève. Rabbit Ears, 1995. ISBN 0-689-80201-3 Subj: Folk & fairy tales. Foreign lands – Ireland. Giants. Tall tales.

Koi and the kola nuts ill. by Reynold Ruffins. Picture Book Studio, 1992. ISBN 0-88708-281-5 Subj: Character traits – kindness to animals. Folk & fairy tales. Foreign lands – Liberia.

Paul Bunyan ill. by Rick Meyerowitz. Rabbit Ears, 1993. ISBN 0-8870-8302-1 Subj: Animals – oxen. Careers – lumberjacks. Tall tales. U.S. history – frontier & pioneer life.

The Savior is born ill. by Robert Van Nutt. Rabbit Ears, 1992. ISBN 0-88708-283-1 Subj: Holidays – Christmas. Religion.

The tiger and the Brahmin ill. by Kurt Vargo. Rabbit Ears, 1992. ISBN 0-8870-8232-7 Subj: Animals. Animals – tigers. Folk & fairy tales. Foreign lands – India.

Gleeson, Libby. *Cuddle time* ill. by Julie Vivas. Candlewick, 2004. ISBN 0-7636-2320-2 Subj: Family life. Morning.

Gleiter, Jan. *Paul Revere* by Jan Gleiter & Kathleen Thompson; ill. by Francis Balistreri. Raintree, 1995. ISBN 0-8172-2644-3 Subj: Poetry. U.S. history. War.

Sacagawea by Jan Gleiter & Kathleen Thompson; ill. by Yoshi Miyake. Raintree, 1987. ISBN 0-8172-2651-6 Subj: Indians of North America – Shoshone. U.S. history.

Glen, Maggie. *Ruby* ill. by author. Putnam, 1991. ISBN 0-399-22281-2 Subj: Prejudice. Toys – bears.

Ruby to the rescue ill. by author. Putnam, 1992. ISBN 0-399-22149-2 Subj: School. Self-concept.

Glennon, Karen M. *Miss Eva and the red balloon* ill. by Hans Poppel. S&S, 1990. ISBN 0-671-68854-5 Subj: Careers – teachers. Magic. Toys – balloons.

Glicksman, Caroline. *Eric the math bear* ill. by author. Knopf, 2003. ISBN 0-375-92432-9 Subj: Animals – bears. Counting, numbers. Crime.

Gliori, Debi. *Can I have a hug?* ill. by author. Orchard, 2002. ISBN 0-439-27602-0 Subj: Animals – bears. Format, unusual – board books.

Flora's blanket ill. by author. Orchard, 2001. ISBN 0-531-30305-5 Subj: Animals – rabbits. Bedtime. Behavior – lost & found possessions.

Flora's surprise ill. by author. Orchard, 2003. ISBN 0-439-45590-1 Subj: Animals – rabbits. Gardens, gardening. Homes, houses.

A lion at bedtime ill. by author. Barron's, 1994. ISBN 0-8120-6379-1 Subj: Animals – lions. Bedtime. Emotions – fear.

Mr. Bear babysits ill. by author. Golden Bks., 1994. ISBN 0-307-17506-5 Subj: Activities. Activities – babysitting. Animals – bears. Behavior – misbehavior.

Mr. Bear says, "Are you there, Baby Bear?" ill. by author. Orchard, 1999. ISBN 0-531-30182-6 Subj: Animals. Animals – bears. Behavior – lost. Format, unusual – toy & movable books. Rhyming text.

Mr. Bear says peek-a-boo ill. by author. Golden Bks., 1996. ISBN 0-689-81516-6 Subj: Activities – playing. Animals – bears. Format, unusual – board books. Games.

Mr. Bear to the rescue ill. by author. Orchard, 2000. ISBN 0-531-30276-8 Subj: Animals. Animals – bears. Forest, woods. Homes, houses. Weather – storms.

Mr. Bear's new baby ill. by author. Orchard, 1999. ISBN 0-531-30152-4 Subj: Animals – bears. Babies. Family life.

Mr. Bear's picnic ill. by author. Golden Bks., 1995. ISBN 0-615-00266-8 Subj: Activities – picnicking. Animals – bears.

My little brother ill. by author. Candlewick, 1992. ISBN 1-56402-079-7 Subj: Family life – brothers & sisters.

New big house ill. by author. Candlewick, 1992. ISBN 1-56402-036-3 Subj: Activities – making things. Family life. Homes, houses.

New big sister ill. by author. Bradbury, 1991. ISBN 0-02-735995-6 Subj: Babies. Birth. Family life – new sibling. Multiple births – twins.

No matter what ill. by author. Harcourt, 1999. ISBN 0-15-202061-6 Subj: Animals – foxes. Emotions – love. Family life. Rhyming text.

Penguin post ill. by author. Harcourt, 2001. ISBN 0-15-216765-X Subj: Babies. Birds – penguins. Post office.

Polar Bolero ill. by author. Harcourt, 2001. ISBN 0-15-202436-0 Subj: Activities – dancing. Animals – polar bears. Bedtime. Rhyming text.

A present for Big Pig ill. by Kate Simpson. Candlewick, 1995. ISBN 1-56402-460-1 Subj: Animals – pigs. Gifts.

The princess and the pirate king ill. by author. Kingfisher, 1996. ISBN 0-7534-5023-2 Subj: Family life. Pirates. Royalty – princesses.

The snow lambs ill. by author. Scholastic, 1996. ISBN 0-590-20304-5 Subj: Animals – dogs. Animals – sheep. Weather – snow. Weather – storms.

The snowchild ill. by author. Bradbury, 1994. ISBN 0-02-735997-2 Subj: Activities – playing. Emotions – loneliness. Friendship. Weather – snow.

Tickly under there ill. by author. Orchard, 2002. ISBN 0-4392-4404-8 Subj: Animals – bears. Family life – fathers. Format, unusual – board books. Games.

What can I give him? ill. by author. Holiday, 1998. ISBN 0-8234-1392-6 Subj: Gifts. Holidays – Christmas. Religion – Nativity. Rhyming text.

When I'm big ill. by author. Candlewick, 1994. ISBN 1-56402-241-2 Subj: Bedtime. Concepts – size. Imagination.

Willie Bear and the Wish Fish ill. by author. Macmillan, 1995. ISBN 0-02-736021-0 Subj: Animals – bears. Behavior – wishing. Fish. Weather.

Glyman, Caroline A. *Learning your ABC's of nutrition* ill. by Dee Biser. Forest House, 1992. ISBN 1-878363-75-1 Subj: ABC books. Food. Health & fitness.

What's above the sky? a book about the planets ill. by Dee Biser. Forest House, 1992. ISBN 1-878363-76-X Subj: Planets. Sky. Stars.

Go tell Aunt Rhody. *Go tell Aunt Rhody* ill. by Aliki. Macmillan, 1974. ISBN 0-02-700410-4 Subj: Family life – aunts, uncles. Folk & fairy tales. Games. Songs.

Go tell Aunt Rhody: starring the old gray goose, who is a living legend in her own lifetime and the greatest American since the American eagle ill. by Robert M. Quackenbush. Lippincott, 1973. ISBN 0-397-31459-0 Subj: Family life – aunts, uncles. Games. Music. Songs.

Gobhai, Mehlli. *Lakshmi, the water buffalo who wouldn't* ill. by author. Hawthorn, 1969. Subj: Animals – water buffaloes. Foreign lands – India.

Usha, the mouse-maiden ill. by author. Hawthorn, 1969. Subj: Family life. Folk & fairy tales. Foreign lands – India.

Goble, Paul. *Adopted by the eagles: a Plains Indian story of friendship and treachery* ill. by author. Bradbury, 1994. ISBN 0-02-736575-1 Subj: Animals – horses, ponies. Birds – eagles. Folk & fairy tales. Indians of North America – Lakota (Sioux).

Beyond the ridge ill. by author. Bradbury, 1988. ISBN 0-02-736581-6 Subj: Death. Indians of North America – Great Plains.

Buffalo woman ill. by author. Bradbury, 1984. ISBN 0-02-737720-2 Subj: Folk & fairy tales. Indians of North America.

Crow chief: a Plains Indian story ill. by author. Orchard, 1992. ISBN 0-531-08547-3 Subj: Birds – crows. Folk & fairy tales. Indians of North America – Crow.

Death of the iron horse ill. by author. Bradbury, 1987. ISBN 0-02-737830-6 Subj: Indians of North America – Cheyenne (Sioux). Trains. War.

The dream wolf ill. by author. Rev. ed. of The friendly wolf. Bradbury, 1990. ISBN 0-02-736585-9 Subj: Folk & fairy tales. Indians of North America – Great Plains.

The friendly wolf ill. by author. Dutton, 1974. ISBN 0-87888-104-2 Subj: Animals – wolves. Behavior – lost. Indians of North America – Great Plains.

The gift of the sacred dog ill. by author. Bradbury, 1980. ISBN 0-87888-165-4 Subj: Animals – horses, ponies. Folk & fairy tales. Gifts. Indians of North America – Great Plains.

The girl who loved wild horses ill. by author. Dutton, 1978. ISBN 0-87888-121-2 Subj: Animals – horses, ponies. Caldecott award books. Indians of North America.

The great race of the birds and animals ill. by author. Bradbury, 1991. ISBN 0-689-71452-1 Subj: Animals. Birds. Creation. Folk & fairy tales. Indians of North America – Cheyenne (Sioux).

Her seven brothers ill. by author. Bradbury, 1988. ISBN 0-02-737960-4 Subj: Animals – buffaloes. Folk & fairy tales. Indians of North America – Cheyenne (Sioux).

I sing for the animals ill. by author. Bradbury, 1991. ISBN 0-02-737725-3 Subj: Activities – singing. Creation. Nature.

Iktomi and the berries: a Plains Indian story ill. by author. Orchard, 1989. ISBN 0-531-08419-1 Subj: Folk & fairy tales. Indians of North America – Great Plains.

Iktomi and the boulder ed. by Richard Jackson; ill. by author. Watts, 1988. ISBN 0-531-08360-8 Subj: Birthdays. Character traits

– conceit. Folk & fairy tales. Indians of North America – Dakota (Sioux). Indians of North America – Great Plains. Rocks.

Iktomi and the buffalo skull: a Plains Indian story ill. by author. Orchard, 1991. ISBN 0-531-08511-2 Subj: Behavior – trickery. Character traits – conceit. Folk & fairy tales. Indians of North America – Great Plains.

Iktomi and the buzzard ill. by author. Orchard, 1994. ISBN 0-531-08662-3 Subj: Behavior – trickery. Birds – buzzards. Folk & fairy tales. Indians of North America – Dakota (Sioux).

Iktomi and the coyote: a Plains Indian story ill. by author. Orchard, 1998. ISBN 0-531-33108-3 Subj: Behavior – trickery. Folk & fairy tales. Indians of North America – Great Plains. Mythical creatures.

Iktomi and the ducks: a Plains Indian story ill. by author. Orchard, 1990. ISBN 0-531-08483-3 Subj: Animals – coyotes. Behavior – trickery. Birds – ducks. Folk & fairy tales. Indians of North America – Great Plains.

The legend of the White Buffalo Woman ill. by author. National Geographic, 1998. ISBN 0-7922-7074-6 Subj: Folk & fairy tales. Indians of North America – Lakota (Sioux).

The lost children: the boys who were neglected ill. by author. Bradbury, 1993. ISBN 0-02-736555-7 Subj: Character traits – meanness. Folk & fairy tales. Indians of North America – Blackfoot. Indians of North America – Siksika. Orphans. Stars.

Love flute ill. by author. Bradbury, 1992. ISBN 0-02-736261-2 Subj: Character traits – shyness. Emotions – love. Folk & fairy tales. Indians of North America – Dakota (Sioux).

Mystic horse ill. by author. HarperCollins, 2003. ISBN 0-06-029814-6 Subj: Animals – horses, ponies. Folk & fairy tales. Indians of North America – Great Plains. Indians of North America – Pawnee.

Remaking the earth: a creation story from the Great Plains of North America ill. by author. Orchard, 1996. ISBN 0-531-08874-X Subj: Creation. Folk & fairy tales. Indians of North America – Great Plains. Weather – floods.

The return of the buffaloes: a Plains Indian story about famine and renewal of the earth ill. by author. National Geographic, 1996. ISBN 0-7922-2714-X Subj: Animals – buffaloes. Folk & fairy tales. Food. Indians of North America – Lakota (Sioux).

Star boy ill. by author. Bradbury, 1983. ISBN 0-02-722660-3 Subj: Activities – dancing. Character traits – appearance. Folk & fairy tales. Indians of North America – Siksika.

Godard, Alex. *Idora* trans. by Laura McKenna; ill. by author. Kane/Miller, 1999. ISBN 0-916291-89-8 Subj: Animals. Animals – giraffes. Emotions – loneliness.

Mama, across the sea ill. by author; adapt. from the French by George Wen. Holt, 2000. ISBN 0-8050-6161-4 Subj: Behavior – needing someone. Family life – grandmothers. Family life – mothers. Foreign lands – Caribbean Islands.

Goddard, Carrie Lou. *Isn't it a wonder!* ill. by Leigh Grant. Abingdon, 1976. ISBN 0-687-19715-5 Subj: Religion.

Godfrey, Jane. *see* Bowden, Joan Chase

Godkin, Celia. *Sea Otter Inlet* ill. by author. Fitzhenry & Whiteside, 1997. ISBN 1-55041-080-6 Subj: Animals – otters. Ecology.

What about ladybugs? ill. by author. Sierra Club, 1995. ISBN 0-87156-549-8 Subj: Ecology. Gardens, gardening. Insects – ladybugs. Nature.

Godwin, Laura. *Barnyard prayers* ill. by Brian Selznick. Hyperion, 2000. ISBN 0-7868-0355-X Subj: Animals. Poetry. Religion.

The best fall of all ill. by Jane Chapman. McElderry, 2002. ISBN 0-689-84713-0 Subj: Activities – playing. Animals – cats. Animals – dogs. Seasons – fall.

Central Park serenade ill. by Barry Root. HarperCollins, 2002. ISBN 0-06-025892-6 Subj: Cities, towns. Parks. Rhyming text. Seasons – summer.

Happy and Honey ill. by Jane Chapman. McElderry, 2000. ISBN 0-689-83406-3 Subj: Activities – playing. Animals – cats. Animals – dogs. Seasons – fall.

Happy Christmas, Honey ill. by Jane Chapman. McElderry, 2002. ISBN 0-689-84714-9 Subj: Animals – cats. Animals – dogs. Holidays – Christmas.

Honey helps ill. by Jane Chapman. McElderry, 2000. ISBN 0-689-83407-1 Subj: Animals – cats. Animals – dogs. Character traits – helpfulness.

Little white dog ill. by Dan Yaccarino. Hyperion, 1998. ISBN 0-7868-2256-2 Subj: Animals. Concepts – color. Concepts – shape. Imagination. Rhyming text.

What the baby hears ill. by Mary Morgan. Hyperion, 2002. ISBN 0-7868-2484-0 Subj: Animals – babies. Family life – parents. Noise, sounds. Rhyming text.

Goecke, Michael P. *Diplodocus* ill. by author. Abdo, 2002. ISBN 1-57765-633-4 Subj: Dinosaurs.

Goennel, Heidi. *The circus* ill. by author. Morrow, 1992. ISBN 0-688-10884-9 Subj: Circus.

Colors ill. by author. Little, 1990. ISBN 0-316-31843-4 Subj: Concepts – color.

Heidi's zoo: an un-alphabet book ill. by author. Tambourine, 1993. ISBN 0-688-12110-1 Subj: ABC books. Animals.

I pretend ill. by author. Tambourine, 1995. ISBN 0-688-13593-5 Subj: Imagination.

If I were a penguin . . . ill. by author. Little, 1989. ISBN 0-316-31841-8 Subj: Animals. Imagination.

It's my birthday ill. by author. Tambourine, 1992. ISBN 0-688-11422-9 Subj: Birthdays. Parties.

My day ill. by author. Little, 1988. ISBN 0-316-31839-6 Subj: Activities.

My dog ill. by author. Orchard, 1989. ISBN 0-531-08434-5 Subj: Animals – dogs. Pets.

Odds and evens ill. by author. Tambourine, 1994. ISBN 0-688-12919-6 Subj: Counting, numbers.

Seasons ill. by author. Little, 1986. ISBN 0-316-31836-1 Subj: Seasons.

Sometimes I like to be alone ill. by author. Little, 1989. ISBN 0-316-31842-6 Subj: Activities. Behavior – solitude.

When I grow up . . . ill. by author. Little, 1987. ISBN 0-316-31838-8 Subj: Behavior – growing up.

While I am little ill. by author. Tambourine, 1993. ISBN 0-688-12372-4 Subj: Activities. Behavior – growing up.

Goff, Beth. *Where's daddy? the story of a divorce* ill. by Susan Perl. Beacon, 1969. ISBN 0-8070-2388-4 Subj: Divorce.

Goffe, Toni. *The story of creation* ill. by author. Standard, 1997. ISBN 0-7847-0629-9 Subj: Creation.

Toby's animal rescue service ill. by author. David & Charles, 1982. ISBN 0-241-10580-3 Subj: Activities – ballooning. Animals.

Goffin, Josse. *The Christmas story* ill. by author. Ticknor & Fields, 1994. ISBN 0-395-70929-6 Subj: Holidays – Christmas. Religion – Nativity.

Oh! ill. by author. Abrams, 1991. ISBN 0-8109-3660-7 Subj: Format, unusual – toy & movable books. Wordless.

Silent Christmas ill. by author. Boyds Mills, 1991. ISBN 1-878093-08-8 Subj: Holidays – Christmas. Religion – Nativity. Wordless.

Who is the boss? ill. by author. Houghton Mifflin, 1992. ISBN 0-395-61192-X Subj: Behavior – fighting, arguing.

Yes ill. by author. Lothrop, 1993. ISBN 0-688-12376-7 Subj: Animals. Eggs.

Goffstein, M. B. (Marilyn Brooke). *Across the sea* ill. by author. Farrar, 1968. Subj: Foreign lands.

An actor ill. by author. HarperCollins, 1987. ISBN 0-06-022169-0 Subj: Activities – working. Careers. Theater.

An artist ill. by author. Harper, 1980. ISBN 0-06-022013-9 Subj: Art. Careers – artists.

Artists' helpers enjoy the evening ill. by author. HarperCollins, 1987. ISBN 0-06-022182-8 Subj: Art. Concepts – color. Foreign lands – France.

Family scrapbook ill. by author. Farrar, 1978. ISBN 0-374-32269-4 Subj: Family life.

Fish for supper ill. by author. Dial, 1976. ISBN 0-8037-2572-8 Subj: Caldecott award honor books. Family life – grandmothers. Old age. Sports – fishing.

A house, a home photos by author. HarperCollins, 1989. ISBN 0-06-022437-1 Subj: Homes, houses.

Laughing latkes ill. by author. Farrar, 1981. ISBN 0-374-34364-0 Subj: Holidays – Hanukkah. Jewish culture.

A little Schubert ill. by author. HarperCollins, 1972. ISBN 0-87923-540-3 Subj: Music.

Me and my captain ill. by author. Farrar, 1974. ISBN 0-374-34901-0 Subj: Toys – dolls.

My Noah's ark ill. by author. HarperCollins, 1978. ISBN 0-06-022023-6 Subj: Boats, ships. Religion – Noah. Weather – floods. Weather – rain.

Natural history ill. by author. Farrar, 1979. ISBN 0-374-35498-7 Subj: Animals. Character traits – kindness to animals.

Neighbors ill. by author. HarperCollins, 1979. ISBN 0-06-022019-4 Subj: Character traits – shyness. Emotions – loneliness.

Our prairie home: a picture album ill. by author. HarperCollins, 1988. ISBN 0-06-022291-3 Subj: Country. Family life. Toys – dolls.

Our snowman ill. by author. HarperCollins, 1986. ISBN 0-06-022153-4 Subj: Activities – playing. Family life. Snowmen.

School of names ill. by author. HarperCollins, 1986. ISBN 0-06-021985-8 Subj: Names. School. World.

Sleepy people ill. by author. Farrar, 1966. Subj: Bedtime.

A writer ill. by author. HarperCollins, 1984. ISBN 0-06-022143-7 Subj: Activities – working. Careers – writers.

Gold, Julie. *From a distance* ill. by Jane Ray. Dutton, 1998. ISBN 0-525-45872-7 Subj: Activities – singing. War.

Goldblatt, Eli. *Leo loves round* ill. by Wendy Osterweil. Harbinger House, 1990. ISBN 0-943173-49-3 Subj: Concepts – shape. Rhyming text.

The golden goose ill. by William Stobbs. McGraw-Hill, 1967. Subj: Birds – chickens. Cumulative tales. Folk & fairy tales. Humorous stories. Royalty.

Golden tales from long ago: Like Grandpa, Only birds, The three kittens. Delacorte, 1980. Anonymous stories published by Ernest Nister in London near the turn of the century. ISBN 0-440-03015-3 Subj: Format, unusual.

Goldfinger, Jennifer P. *A fish named Spot* ill. by author. Little, 2001. ISBN 0-316-32047-1 Subj: Fish. Pets.

Goldfrank, Helen Colodny Kay. *see* Kay, Helen

Goldhor, Susan Henne. *Franny B. Kranny, there's a bird in your hair* (Lerner, Harriet Goldhor)

What's so terrible about swallowing an apple seed? (Lerner, Harriet Goldhor)

Goldie-Morrison, Karen. *Danger colors* (Oxford Scientific Films)

Hide and seek (Oxford Scientific Films)

Goldin, Augusta. *Ducks don't get wet* ill. by Leonard P. Kessler. Crowell, 1989. ISBN 0-690-04782-7 Subj: Birds – ducks. Science.

Salt ill. by Robert Galster. Crowell, 1966. ISBN 0-690-71815-2 Subj: Science.

The shape of water ill. by Demi. Doubleday, 1979. ISBN 0-385-02385-5 Subj: Science.

Spider silk ill. by Joseph Low. Crowell, 1964. Subj: Science. Spiders.

Straight hair, curly hair ill. by Ed Emberley. Crowell, 1966. ISBN 0-690-77921-6 Subj: Hair. Science.

Where does your garden grow? ill. by Helen Borten. Crowell, 1967. ISBN 0-690-88358-7 Subj: Gardens, gardening. Science.

Goldin, Barbara Diamond. *Cakes and miracles: a Purim tale* ill. by Erika Weihs. Viking, 1991. ISBN 0-670-83047-X Subj: Activities – baking, cooking. Food. Handicaps – blindness. Jewish culture. Religion. Self-concept.

Just enough is plenty: a Hannukkah tale ill. by Seymour Chwast. Viking, 1988. ISBN 0-670-81852-6 Subj: Behavior – sharing. Holidays – Hanukkah. Jewish culture.

A mountain of blintzes ill. by Anik McGrory. Harcourt, 2001. ISBN 0-15-201902-2 Subj: Food. Holidays – Shavuot. Jewish culture. Religion.

Night lights ill. by Laura Sucher. UAHC Pr., 2002. ISBN 0-8074-0803-4 Subj: Emotions – fear. Holidays – Sukkot. Jewish culture.

World's birthday ill. by Jeanette Winter. Harcourt, 1990. ISBN 0-15-299648-6 Subj: Birthdays. Holidays – Rosh Hashanah. Jewish culture.

Goldin, David. *Go-Go-Go!* ill. by author. Abrams, 2000. ISBN 0-8109-4141-4 Subj: Animals. Sports – bicycling. Sports – racing.

Golding, Kim. *Alphababies* ill. by author. DK, 1998. ISBN 0-7894-2529-7 Subj: ABC books. Babies. Rhyming text.

Golding, Theresa Martin. *Memorial Day surprise* ill. by Alexandra Artigas. Boyds Mills, 2004. ISBN 1-59078-048-5 Subj: Ethnic groups in the U.S. Family life – grandfathers. Holidays – Memorial Day.

Goldman, Dara. *There's no such thing!* ill. by author. Putnam, 1990. ISBN 0-399-22193-X Subj: Animals – bears. Behavior – trickery. Character traits – cleverness.

Goldman, Molly Rose. *How to take your grandmother to the museum* (Wyse, Lois)

Goldman, Susan. *Cousins are special* ill. by author. A. Whitman, 1978. ISBN 0-8075-1317-2 Subj: Family life.

Grandma is somebody special ed. by Caroline Rubin; ill. by author. A. Whitman, 1976. ISBN 0-8075-3034-4 Subj: Family life – grandmothers.

Goldner, Kathryn Allen. *The dangers of strangers* (Vogel, Carole Garbuny)

Goldsboro, Bobby. *Jonah and the whale; and, Daniel in the lion's den* ill. by Toni Donelow Stewart. New Canaan, 2003. ISBN 1-889658-

28-6 Subj: Animals – lions. Animals – whales. Religion – Daniel. Religion – Jonah.

Noah and the ark; and, David and Goliath ill. by Toni Donelow Stewart. New Canaan, 2003. ISBN 1-889658-27-8 Subj: Animals – mice. Birds – ducks. Boats, ships. Foreign lands – Israel. Giants. Religion – David. Religion – Noah. Weather – floods. Weather – rain.

Goldsmith, Cathy. *Did I ever tell you how high you can count?* (Hayward, Linda)

I can add upside down! (Hayward, Linda)

Oh, the things you can count from 1-10 (Hayward, Linda)

Wet foot, dry foot, low foot, high foot (Hayward, Linda)

Goldsmith, Howard. *Little lost dog* ill. by Ulises Wensell. Santillana, 1983. ISBN 0-88272-179-8 Subj: Animals – dogs. Behavior – lost. Character traits – honesty. Friendship. Illness.

Shy little turtle ill. by Denny bond. Learning Triangle, 1998. ISBN 0-07-024541-X Subj: Foreign lands – Africa. Reptiles – turtles, tortoises.

Sleepy little owl ill. by Denny Bond. Learning Triangle Pr., 1997. ISBN 0-07-024543-6 Subj: Animals. Bedtime. Birds – owls. Dreams.

Toto the timid turtle ill. by Shirley Chan. Human Sciences Pr., 1981. ISBN 0-87705-525-7 Subj: Reptiles – turtles, tortoises.

Goldstein, Bobbye S. *Bear in mind: a book of bear poems* ill. by William Pène du Bois. Viking, 1989. ISBN 0-670-81907-7 Subj: Animals – bears. Poetry.

Birthday rhymes, special times sel. by Bobbye S. Goldstein; ill. by José Aruego & Ariane Dewey. Delacorte, 1993. ISBN 0-385-30418-8 Subj: Birthdays. Poetry.

Inner chimes: poems on poetry sel. by Bobbye S. Goldstein; ill. by Jane Breskin Zalben. Boyds Mills, 1992. ISBN 1-56397-040-6 Subj: Poetry.

What's on the menu? ill. by Chris L. Demarest. Viking, 1992. ISBN 0-670-83031-3 Subj: Food. Poetry.

Goldstone, Bruce. *The beastly feast* ill. by Blair Lent. Holt, 1998. ISBN 0-8050-3867-1 Subj: Activities – picnicking. Animals. Food. Rhyming text.

Gold-Vukson, Marji E. *The colors of my Jewish Year* ill. by author. Kar-Ben Copies, 1998. ISBN 1-58013-011-9 Subj: Concepts – color. Format, unusual – board books. Jewish culture. Religion.

Grandpa and me on Tu B'Shevat ill. by Leslie Evans. Kar-Ben Copies, 2004. ISBN 1-58013-122-0 Subj: Cumulative tales. Family life – grandfathers. Holidays. Jewish culture. Religion. Rhyming text. Trees.

Golembe, Carla. *Annabelle's big move* ill. by author. Houghton Mifflin, 1999. ISBN 0-395-91543-0 Subj: Animals – dogs. Emotions – loneliness.

Golenbock, Peter. *Hank Aaron* ill. by Paul Lee. Harcourt, 2001. ISBN 0-15-202093-4 Subj: Character traits – bravery. Ethnic groups in the U.S. – African Americans. Sports – baseball.

Gollub, Matthew. *Cool melons – turn to frogs: the life and poems of Issa* story & Haiku trans. by Matthew Gollub; ill. by Kazuko G. Stone; calligraphy by Keiko Smith. Lee & Low, 1998. ISBN 1-880000-71-7 Subj: Careers – poets. Foreign lands – Japan. Poetry.

Gobble, quack, moon ill. by Judy Love. Tortuga, 2002. ISBN 1-889910-20-1 Subj: Activities – dancing. Animals. Animals – bulls, cows. Moon. Music.

Ten oni drummers ill. by Kazuko G. Stone. Lee & Low, 2000. ISBN 1-58430-011-6 Subj: Counting, numbers. Foreign lands – Japan. Foreign languages. Rhyming text.

The twenty-five Mixtec cats ill. by Leovigildo Martinez. Tambourine, 1993. ISBN 0-688-11640-X Subj: Animals – cats. Folk & fairy tales. Foreign lands – Mexico. Magic.

Gomboli, Mario. *Look inside a house* trans. by Denice Patrick; ill. by author. Putnam, 1989. ISBN 0-448-19351-5 Subj: Format, unusual – board books. Homes, houses.

Look inside a ship trans. by Denice Patrick; ill. by author. Putnam, 1989. ISBN 0-448-19352-3 Subj: Boats, ships. Format, unusual – board books.

Gomel, Luc. *The ant, energetic worker* photos by Rémy Amann & Dominique Stoffel. Charlesbridge, 2001. ISBN 1-57091-451-6 Subj: Insects – ants.

Gomi, Taro. *The big book of boxes* ill. by author. Chronicle, 1991. ISBN 0-8118-0067-9 Subj: Concepts – shape.

Bus stop ill. by author. Chronicle, 1988. ISBN 0-87701-551-1 Subj: Activities – traveling. Buses. Transportation.

Coco can't wait! ill. by author. Morrow, 1984. ISBN 0-688-02790-3 Subj: Family life – grandmothers.

The crocodile and the dentist ill. by author. Millbrook, 1994. ISBN 1-56294-555-6 Subj: Careers – dentists. Reptiles – alligators, crocodiles. Teeth.

Everyone poops ill. by author; trans. Amanda Mayer Stinchecum. Kane/Miller, 1993. ISBN 0-916291-45-6 Subj: Nature. Toilet training.

First comes Harry ill. by author. Morrow, 1987. ISBN 0-688-06732-8 Subj: Behavior – hurrying.

Guess what? ill. by author. Chronicle, 1992. ISBN 0-8118-0015-6 Subj: Concepts. Format, unusual – board books.

Guess who? ill. by author. Chronicle, 1991. ISBN 0-8118-0021-0 Subj: Animals. Format, unusual – board books. Games. Toys.

Hi, butterfly! ill. by author. Morrow, 1985. ISBN 0-688-04138-8 Subj: Format, unusual. Insects – butterflies, caterpillars.

I lost my dad ill. by author. Kane/Miller, 2001. ISBN 1-929132-04-2 Subj: Behavior – lost. Family life – fathers. Stores.

My friends ill. by author. Chronicle, 1990. ISBN 0-87701-688-7 Subj: Activities. Animals.

Santa through the window ill. by author. Millbrook, 1995. ISBN 1-56294-454-1 Subj: Animals. Format, unusual – toy & movable books. Gifts. Holidays – Christmas. Santa Claus.

Seeing, saying, doing, playing ill. by author. Chronicle, 1991. ISBN 0-87701-859-6 Subj: Activities. Language.

Spring is here ill. by author. Chronicle, 1989. ISBN 0-87701-626-7 Subj: Animals – bulls, cows. Seasons.

Toot! ill. by author. Morrow, 1986. ISBN 0-688-06421-3 Subj: Illness. Music. Musical instruments – trumpets. Rhyming text.

Where's the fish? ill. by author. Morrow, 1986. ISBN 0-688-06242-3 Subj: Behavior – hiding. Fish.

Who ate it? ill. by author. Millbrook, 1991. ISBN 1-56294-010-4 Subj: Games.

Who hid it? ill. by author. Millbrook, 1991. ISBN 1-56294-011-2 Subj: Games.

Good, Merle. *Amos and Susie: an Amish story* ill. by Cheryl Benner. Good Bks., 1993. ISBN 1-56148-088-6 Subj: Activities. Ethnic groups in the U.S. – Amish. Religion. Rhyming text. Seasons.

Dan's pants Merle Good with Dan & Fran Boltz; ill. by Cheryl Benner. Good Bks., 2000. ISBN 1-56148-307-9 Subj: Clothing – pants. Rhyming text.

Reuben and the fire ill. by P. Buckley Moss. Good Bks., 1993. ISBN 1-56148-091-6 Subj: Ethnic groups in the U.S. – Amish. Family life. Fire.

Good, Phyllis Pellman. *Plain Pig's ABCs: a day on Plain Pig's Amish farm* ill. by Cheryl Benner. Good Bks., 1998. ISBN 1-56148-251-X Subj: ABC books. Animals – pigs. Ethnic groups in the U.S. – Amish. Farms.

The good-hearted youngest brother: *an Hungarian folktale* trans. by Emöke de Papp Severo; ill. by Diane Goode. Bradbury, 1981. ISBN 0-87888-141-7 Subj: Character traits – kindness to animals. Folk & fairy tales. Foreign lands – Hungary. Magic.

Good morning ill. by Summer Durantz. Little Simon, 2002. ISBN 0-689-85099-9 Subj: Format, unusual – board books. Morning.

Goodall, Daphne Machin. *Zebras* ill. with photos. Raintree, 1978. Subj: Animals – zebras.

Goodall, Jane. *Dr. White* ill. by Julie Wintz-Litty. North-South, 1999. ISBN 0-7358-1064-8 Subj: Animals – pigs. Hospitals. Illness.

The eagle and the wren ill. by Alexander Reichstein. North-South, 2000. ISBN 0-7358-1380-9 Subj: Birds. Character traits – cooperation. Folk & fairy tales.

Goodall, John S. *The adventures of Paddy Pork* ill. by author. Harcourt, 1968. ISBN 0-15-201589-2 Subj: Animals – pigs. Behavior – running away. Circus. Format, unusual. Wordless.

The ballooning adventures of Paddy Pork ill. by author. Harcourt, 1969. Subj: Animals – pigs. Format, unusual. Wordless.

Creepy castle ill. by author. Rev. jacket ed. McElderry, 1998. ISBN 0-689-82205-7 Subj: Animals – mice. Format, unusual. Knights. Monsters. Wordless.

An Edwardian Christmas ill. by author. Atheneum, 1978. ISBN 0-689-50106-4 Subj: Foreign lands – England. Format, unusual. Holidays – Christmas. Wordless.

An Edwardian summer ill. by author. Atheneum, 1976. ISBN 0-689-50062-9 Subj: Foreign lands – England. Format, unusual. Seasons – summer. Wordless.

Great days of a country house ill. by author. McElderry, 1992. ISBN 0-689-50545-0 Subj: Foreign lands – England. Homes, houses.

Jacko ill. by author. Harcourt, 1971. ISBN 0-15-239494-X Subj: Animals – monkeys. Boats, ships. Format, unusual. Wordless.

The midnight adventures of Kelly, Dot and Esmeralda ill. by author. McElderry, 1999. ISBN 0-689-82564-1 Subj: Format, unusual. Wordless.

Naughty Nancy ill. by author. Rev. jacket ed. McElderry, 1999. ISBN 0-689-82358-4 Subj: Behavior – misbehavior. Format, unusual. Weddings. Wordless.

Naughty Nancy goes to school ill. by author. McElderry, 1999. ISBN 0-689-82563-3 Subj: Animals – mice. Behavior – misbehavior. Format, unusual. School – first day. Wordless.

Paddy goes traveling ill. by author. Atheneum, 1982. ISBN 0-689-50239-7 Subj: Activities – traveling. Animals – pigs. Format, unusual. Wordless.

Paddy Pork: odd jobs ill. by author. Atheneum, 1983. ISBN 0-689-50293-1 Subj: Activities – working. Animals – pigs. Format, unusual. Wordless.

Paddy Pork's holiday ill. by author. Atheneum, 1976. ISBN 0-689-50043-2 Subj: Activities – vacationing. Animals – pigs. Format, unusual. Wordless.

Paddy to the rescue ill. by author. Atheneum, 1986. ISBN 0-689-50330-X Subj: Animals – pigs. Behavior – stealing. Character traits – bravery. Crime. Wordless.

Paddy under water ill. by author. Atheneum, 1984. ISBN 0-689-50297-4 Subj: Animals – pigs. Format, unusual. Sea & seashore. Wordless.

Paddy's evening out ill. by author. Atheneum, 1973. ISBN 8-689-30412-9 Subj: Animals – pigs. Format, unusual. Theater. Wordless.

Paddy's new hat ill. by author. Atheneum, 1980. ISBN 0-689-50172-2 Subj: Animals – pigs. Careers – police officers. Format, unusual. Wordless.

Puss in boots (Perrault, Charles)

Shrewbettina's birthday ill. by author. Rev. jacket ed. McElderry, 1998. ISBN 0-689-82206-5 Subj: Animals – shrews. Birthdays. Format, unusual. Wordless.

The story of a castle ill. by author. Macmillan, 1986. ISBN 0-689-50405-5 Subj: Foreign lands – England. Format, unusual. Wordless.

The story of a farm ill. by author. Macmillan, 1988. ISBN 0-689-50479-9 Subj: Farms. Foreign lands – England. Format, unusual. Wordless.

The story of a main street ill. by author. Macmillan, 1987. ISBN 0-233-98070-9 Subj: Cities, towns. Format, unusual. Roads. Wordless.

The story of an English village ill. by author. Atheneum, 1979. ISBN 0-689-50125-0 Subj: Cities, towns. Foreign lands – England. Format, unusual. Progress. Wordless.

The surprise picnic ill. by author. Rev. jacket ed. McElderry, 1999. ISBN 0-689-82359-2 Subj: Activities – picnicking. Animals – cats. Food. Format, unusual. Wordless.

Goode, Diane. *Cinderella* (Perrault, Charles)

Diane Goode's book of silly stories & songs ill. by author. Dutton, 1992. ISBN 0-525-44967-1 Subj: Folk & fairy tales. Humorous stories. Music. Songs.

The dinosaur's new clothes ill. by author. Blue Sky, 1999. ISBN 0-590-38360-4 Subj: Character traits – pride. Character traits – vanity. Clothing. Dinosaurs. Folk & fairy tales. Imagination. Prehistory. Royalty – emperors.

The fir tree (Andersen, H. C. [Hans Christian])

I hear a noise ill. by author. Dutton, 1988. ISBN 0-525-44353-3 Subj: Bedtime. Dragons. Emotions – fear. Monsters. Night.

The little book of farm friends ill. by author. Dutton, 1993. ISBN 0-525-45157-9 Subj: Animals. Farms. Nursery rhymes.

Mama's perfect present ill. by author. Dutton, 1996. ISBN 0-525-45493-4 Subj: Animals – dogs. Birthdays. Family life – brothers & sisters. Family life – mothers. Foreign lands – France.

Tiger trouble ill. by author. Blue Sky, 2001. ISBN 0-439-20866-1 Subj: Animals – dogs. Animals – tigers. Cities, towns. Crime. Homes, houses.

Where's our mama? ill. by author. Dutton, 1991. ISBN 0-525-44770-9 Subj: Behavior – lost. Family life – mothers. Foreign lands – France.

Goode, Molly. *Mama loves* ill. by Lisa McCue. Random House, 1999. ISBN 0-679-99462-9 Subj: Animals. Animals – babies. Birds. Family life – mothers. Rhyming text.

Goodenow, Earle. *The last camel* ill. by author. Walck, 1968. Subj: Animals – camels. Foreign lands – Egypt.

The owl who hated the dark ill. by author. Walck, 1969. ISBN 0-8098-1145-6 Subj: Birds – owls. Emotions – fear. Night.

Goodhart, Pippa. *Arthur's tractor: a fairy tale with mechanical parts* ill. by Colin Paine. Bloomsbury, 2003. ISBN 1-58234-847-2 Subj: Careers – farmers. Dragons. Humorous stories. Royalty – princesses. Tractors.

Noah makes a boat ill. by Bernard Lodge. Houghton Mifflin, 1997. ISBN 0-395-86957-9 Subj: Animals. Boats, ships. Religion – Noah. Weather – floods. Weather – rain. Weather – rainbows.

Pudgy, a puppy to love ill. by Caroline Jayne Church. Scholastic, 2003. ISBN 0-439-45699-1 Subj: Animals – babies. Animals – dogs. Behavior – needing someone. Behavior – running away. Friendship.

Row, row, row your boat ill. by Stephen Lambert. Crown, 1997. ISBN 0-517-70970-8 Subj: Animals. Animals – lions. Boats, ships. Dreams. Islands. Music. Songs. Toys.

Goodings, Lennie. *When you grow up* ill. by Jenny Jones. Fogelman, 2001. ISBN 0-8037-2677-5 Subj: Animals – bears. Behavior – growing up. Careers. Family life – mothers.

Goodman, Joan Elizabeth. *Bernard goes to school* ill. by Dominic Catalano. Boyds Mills, 2001. ISBN 1-56397-958-6 Subj: Animals – elephants. School – first day.

Bernard's bath ill. by Dominic Catalano. Boyds Mills, 1996. ISBN 1-56397-323-5 Subj: Activities – bathing. Animals – elephants. Family life.

Bernard's nap ill. by Dominic Catalano. Boyds Mills, 1999. ISBN 1-56397-728-1 Subj: Animals – elephants. Bedtime. Dreams. Sleep.

Goodman, Louise. *Ida's doll* ill. by Debby L. Carter. HarperCollins, 1989. ISBN 0-06-022276-X Subj: Family life – grandmothers. Family life – sisters. Poverty. Toys – dolls.

Goodman, Susan E. *Chopsticks for my noodle soup: Eliza's life in Malaysia* photos by Michael Doolittle. Millbrook, 2000. ISBN 0-7613-1552-7 Subj: Family life. Foreign lands – Malaysia.

What do you do – at the zoo? ill. by Steve Pica. Millbrook, 2002. ISBN 0-7613-2755-X Subj: Animals. Careers – zookeepers. Zoos.

Goodsell, Jane. *Katie's magic glasses* ill. by Barbara Cooney. Houghton Mifflin, 1965. ISBN 0-395-20108-X Subj: Careers – doctors. Glasses. Senses – sight.

Toby's toe ill. by Gioia Fiammenghi. Morrow, 1986. ISBN 0-688-06162-1 Subj: Character traits – kindness. Character traits – meanness. Toys – balloons.

Goodspeed, Peter. *Hugh and Fitzhugh* ill. by Carol Nicklaus. Platt, 1974. ISBN 0-8228-7575-6 Subj: Animals – dogs. Language.

A rhinoceros wakes me up in the morning: a bedtime tale ill. by Dennis Panek. Bradbury, 1982. ISBN 0-87888-201-4 Subj: Animals. Bedtime. Rhyming text.

Goodwyn, Susan. *My first baby signs* (Acredolo, Linda P.)

Goor, Nancy. *All kinds of feet* (Goor, Ron)

In the driver's seat (Goor, Ron)

Shadows: here, there and everywhere (Goor, Ron)

Signs (Goor, Ron)

Goor, Ron. *All kinds of feet* by Ron & Nancy Goor; photos by authors. Crowell, 1984. ISBN 0-690-04385-6 Subj: Anatomy – feet. Animals.

In the driver's seat by Ron & Nancy Goor; photos by authors. Crowell, 1982. ISBN 0-690-04177-2 Subj: Activities. Machines.

Shadows: here, there and everywhere by Ron & Nancy Goor; photos by authors. Crowell, 1981. ISBN 0-690-04133-0 Subj: Shadows.

Signs by Ron & Nancy Goor; photos by authors. Crowell, 1983. ISBN 0-690-04355-4 Subj: Books, reading. Communication.

Gorbachev, Valeri. *Big Little Elephant* ill. by author. Harcourt, 2005. ISBN 0-15-205195-3 Subj: Activities – playing. Animals – elephants. Concepts – size. Emotions – loneliness. Friendship.

Chicken chickens ill. by author. North-South, 2001. ISBN 0-7358-1542-9 Subj: Activities – playing. Animals. Birds – chickens. Character traits – confidence. Parks.

Chicken chickens go to school. North-South, 2003. ISBN 0-7358-1767-7 Subj: Animals. Birds – chickens. Character traits – shyness. Friendship. School – first day.

The fool of the world and the flying ship: a Ukrainian folk tale ill. by adapt. Star Bright, 1998. ISBN 1-887734-19-8 Subj: Activities – flying. Boats, ships. Character traits – cleverness. Folk & fairy tales. Foreign lands – Ukraine. Royalty – tsars.

Goldilocks and the three bears (The three bears)

Nicky and the big, bad wolves ill. by author. North-South, 1998. ISBN 1-55858-918-X Subj: Animals – rabbits. Animals – wolves. Bedtime. Dreams. Emotions – fear.

Nicky and the fantastic birthday gift ill. by author. North-South, 2000. ISBN 0-7358-1379-5 Subj: Animals – rabbits. Birthdays. Family life – mothers.

Nicky and the rainy day ill. by author. North-South, 2002. ISBN 0-7358-1645-X Subj: Animals – rabbits. Family life – brothers & sisters. Weather – rain.

One rainy day ill. by author. Philomel, 2002. ISBN 0-399-23628-7 Subj: Animals. Animals – goats. Animals – pigs. Counting, numbers. Weather – rain.

Where is the apple pie? ill. by author. Philomel, 1999. ISBN 0-399-23385-7 Subj: Animals. Character traits – questioning. Circular tales. Tall tales.

Whose hat is it? ill. by author. HarperCollins, 2004. ISBN 0-06-053435-4 Subj: Animals. Behavior – lost & found possessions. Clothing – hats. Reptiles – turtles, tortoises.

Gorbaty, Norman. *Get up and go, little dinosaur!* ill. by author. Random House, 1990. ISBN 0-679-80693-8 Subj: Dinosaurs. Format, unusual – board books. Prehistory.

Tow truck ill. by author. Grosset, 1993. ISBN 0-448-40597-0 Subj: Format, unusual – toy & movable books. Trucks.

Gordon, David. *The three little rigs* ill. by author. Geringer, 2005. ISBN 0-06-058119-0 Subj: Family life – brothers. Machines. Trucks.

The ugly truckling ill. by author. Geringer, 2004. ISBN 0-06-054601-8 Subj: Airplanes, airports. Family life – brothers & sisters. Self-concept. Trucks.

Gordon, Gaelyn. *Duckat* ill. by Chris Gaskin. Scholastic, 1992. ISBN 0-590-45455-2 Subj: Animals – cats. Birds – ducks. Self-concept.

Gordon, Jeffie Ross. *Six sleepy sheep* ill. by John O'Brien. Boyds Mills, 1991. ISBN 1-878093-06-1 Subj: Animals – sheep. Language. Tongue twisters.

Two badd babies ill. by Chris L. Demarest. Boyds Mills, 1992. ISBN 1-878093-85-1 Subj: Bedtime. Multiple births – twins. Rhyming text.

Gordon, Lynn. *The witch's revenge* ill. by Val Martino. S&S, 1997. ISBN 0-689-81679-0 Subj: Format, unusual – toy & movable books. Holidays – Halloween. Witches.

Gordon, Margaret. *Frogs' holiday* ill. by author. Viking, 1987. ISBN 0-670-80854-7 Subj: Activities – babysitting. Frogs & toads.

The supermarket mice ill. by author. Dutton, 1984. ISBN 0-525-44145-X Subj: Animals – cats. Animals – mice. Problem solving. Stores.

Wilberforce goes on a picnic ill. by author. Morrow, 1982. ISBN 0-688-01481-X Subj: Activities – picnicking. Animals – bears.

Wilberforce goes to a party ill. by author. Viking, 1985. ISBN 0-670-80148-8 Subj: Animals – bears. Behavior – misbehavior. Birthdays. Etiquette. Parties.

Gordon, Ruth. *Feathers* ill. by Lydia Dabcovich. Macmillan, 1993. ISBN 0-02-736511-5 Subj: Character traits – foolishness. Folk & fairy tales. Foreign lands – Poland. Jewish culture.

Gordon, Sharon. *Asthma* ill. with photos. Childrens Pr., 2003. ISBN 0-516-22582-0 Subj: Health & fitness. Illness – asthma.

Bruises ill. with photos. Childrens Pr., 2002. ISBN 0-516-22568-5 Subj: Health & fitness. Safety.

Christmas surprise ill. by John Magine. Troll, 1980. ISBN 0-89375-273-8 Subj: Animals – bears. Holidays – Christmas.

Cuts and scrapes ill. with photos. Childrens Pr., 2002. ISBN 0-516-22566-9 Subj: Health & safety. Illness.

Dinosaurs in trouble ill. by Paul Harvey. Troll, 1980. ISBN 0-89375-274-6 Subj: Dinosaurs. Prehistory.

Dolphins and porpoises ill. by June Goldsborough. Troll, 1985. ISBN 0-8167-0340-X Subj: Animals – dolphins. Sea & seashore.

Easter Bunny's lost egg ill. by John Magine. Troll, 1980. ISBN 0-89375-375-0 Subj: Animals – rabbits. Eggs. Holidays – Easter.

Friendly snowman ill. by John Magine. Troll, 1980. ISBN 0-89375-377-7 Subj: Snowmen.

Pete the parakeet ill. by Paul Harvey. Troll, 1980. ISBN 0-89075-384-X Subj: Birds – parakeets, parrots.

Pinkeye ill. with photos. Childrens Pr., 2003. ISBN 0-516-22583-9 Subj: Anatomy – eyes. Health & fitness. Illness.

Play ball, Kate! ill. by Don Page. Troll, 1981. ISBN 0-89375-525-7 Subj: Sports – baseball.

Sam the scarecrow ill. by Don Silverstein. Troll, 1980. ISBN 0-89375-387-4 Subj: Scarecrows.

Seeing ill. with photos. Childrens Pr., 2001. ISBN 0-516-22291-0 Subj: Anatomy – eyes. Health & fitness. Senses – sight.

Smelling ill. with photos. Childrens Pr., 2001. ISBN 0-516-22292-9 Subj: Anatomy – noses. Health & fitness. Senses – smell.

Three little witches storybook ill. by Deborah Sims. Troll, 1980. ISBN 0-89375-390-4 Subj: Witches.

Tick tock clock ill. by Don Page. Troll, 1982. ISBN 0-89375-676-8 Subj: Clocks, watches. Time.

Trees ill. by Irene Trivas. Troll, 1983. ISBN 0-89375-801-5 Subj: Trees.

What a dog! ill. by Deborah Sims. Troll, 1980. ISBN 0-89375-393-9 Subj: Animals – dogs.

Gordon, Shirley. *Grandma zoo* ill. by Whitney Darrow, Jr. HarperCollins, 1978. ISBN 0-06-022050-3 Subj: Animals. Family life – grandmothers. Zoos.

Gordon, Stephanie Jacob. *Something's happening on Calabash Street* (Enderle, Judith Ross)

Gore, Leonid. *Who was born this special day?* (Bunting, Eve [Anne Evelyn])

Gore, Sheila. *My shadow* photos by Fiona Pragoff. Doubleday, 1990. ISBN 0-385-41198-7 Subj: Activities. Concepts – perspective. Science. Shadows.

Gorey, Edward (St. John). *The tunnel calamity* ill. by author. Putnam, 1984. ISBN 0-399-21055-5 Subj: Format, unusual. Monsters. Wordless.

Gorham, Michael. *see* Elting, Mary

Gorog, Judith. *Zilla Sasparilla and the mud baby* ill. by Amanda Harvey. Candlewick, 1995. ISBN 1-56402-295-1 Subj: Babies. Behavior – worrying. Family life – grandmothers. Family life – mothers. Rivers.

Gorsline, Douglas W. *North American Indians* (Gorsline, Marie)

Gorsline, Marie. *North American Indians* by Marie & Douglas W. Gorsline; ill. by authors. Random House, 1978. ISBN 0-394-93702-3 Subj: Indians of North America. U.S. history.

Nursery rhymes (Mother Goose)

Goss, Linda. *The frog who wanted to be a singer* ill. by Cynthia Jabar. Orchard, 1995. ISBN 0-531-08745-X Subj: Activities – singing. Frogs & toads. Music.

Got, Yves. *Sam loves kisses* ill. by author. Chronicle, 2002. ISBN 0-8118-3505-7 Subj: Emotions. Format, unusual – board books. Kissing.

Sam's big book of words ill. by author. Chronicle, 2001. ISBN 0-8118-3088-8 Subj: Animals – rabbits. Dictionaries. Language.

Sam's little sister ill. by author. Chronicle, 2002. ISBN 0-8118-3504-9 Subj: Animals – rabbits. Family life – brothers & sisters. Format, unusual – board books.

Gottfried, Maya. *Good dog* ill. by Robert Rahway Zakanitch. Knopf, 2005. ISBN 0-375-93049-3 Subj: Animals – dogs. Pets. Poetry.

Last night I dreamed a circus ill. by Robert Rahway Zakanitch. Random House, 2003. ISBN 0-375-92388-8 Subj: Circus. Dreams.

Gottlieb, Dale. *Seeing Eye Willie* ill. by author. Knopf, 1992. ISBN 0-679-92449-3 Subj: Character traits – curiosity. Homeless. Imagination.

Where Jamaica go? ill. by author. Orchard, 1996. ISBN 0-531-08875-8 Subj: Foreign lands – Caribbean Islands. Rhyming text.

Gouck, Maura. *Mountain lions* ill. with photos. Child's World, 2001. ISBN 1-56766-888-7 Subj: Animals – cougars. Nature.

Goudey, Alice E. *The day we saw the sun come up* ill. by Adrienne Adams. Scribners, 1961. Subj: Caldecott award honor books. Family life. Sun.

The good rain ill. by Nora Spicer Unwin. Dutton, 1950. Subj: Weather – rain.

Houses from the sea ill. by Adrienne Adams. Scribners, 1959. Subj: Caldecott award honor books. Sea & seashore.

Red legs ill. by Marie Nonnast. Scribners, 1966. Subj: Insects.

Gould, Deborah. *Aaron's shirt* ill. by Cheryl Harness. Bradbury, 1989. ISBN 0-02-736351-1 Subj: Behavior – growing up. Clothing – shirts.

Brendan's best-timed birthday ill. by Jacqueline Rogers. Bradbury, 1988. ISBN 0-02-737390-8 Subj: Behavior – sharing. Birthdays. Clocks, watches. Parties.

Camping in the Temple of the Sun ill. by Diane Paterson. Bradbury, 1992. ISBN 0-02-736355-4 Subj: Camps, camping. Family life. Weather.

Grandpa's slide show ill. by Cheryl Harness. Lothrop, 1987. ISBN 0-688-06973-8 Subj: Death. Dreams. Emotions – grief. Family life – grandparents.

Goundaud, Karen Jo. *A very mice joke book* ill. by Lynn Munsinger. Houghton Mifflin, 1981. ISBN 0-395-30445-8 Subj: Animals – mice. Riddles & jokes.

Gove, Doris. *My mother talks to trees* ill. by Marilynn H. Mallory. Peachtree, 1999. ISBN 1-56145-166-5 Subj: Activities. Family life – mothers. Trees.

Goyder, Alice. *Holiday in Catland* ill. by author. Crowell, 1979. ISBN 0-690-03932-8 Subj: Activities – vacationing. Animals – cats.

Party in Catland ill. by author. Crowell, 1979. ISBN 0-690-03930-1 Subj: Animals – cats. Parties.

Graber, Janet. *Jacob and the polar bears* ill. by Sandra Salzillo-Shields. Moon Mt., 2002. ISBN 1-931659-00-1 Subj: Animals – polar bears. Clothing – pajamas. Humorous stories. Night.

Grabianski, Janusz. *Cats* ill. by author. Watts, 1966. Subj: Animals – cats.

Grabianski's wild animals ill. by author. Watts, 1969. Translation of Tiere der Wildnis. Subj: Animals.

Horses ill. by author. Watts, 1966. Subj: Animals – horses, ponies.

Grace, Kayla. *Percussion instruments* ill. with photos. Child's World, 2003. ISBN 1-56766-986-7 Subj: Musical instruments – drums.

Graeber, Charlotte Towner. *Nobody's Dog* ill. by Barry Root. Hyperion, 1998. ISBN 0-7868-2093-4 Subj: Animals – dogs. Behavior – needing someone.

Graeber, Jean B. *Bantie and her chicks* ill. by June Hendrickson. Melmont, 1959. Subj: Birds – chickens. School. Science.

Graff, Nancy Price. *In the hush of the evening* ill. by G. Brian Karas. HarperCollins, 1998. ISBN 0-06-022099-6 Subj: Bedtime. Concepts – color. Noise, sounds.

Graham, Al. *Timothy Turtle* ill. by Tony Palazzo. Walck, 1946. Subj: Caldecott award honor books. Character traits – ambition. Character traits – helpfulness. Friendship. Reptiles – turtles, tortoises.

Graham, Amanda. *Picasso, the green tree frog* ill. by John Siow. G. Stevens, 1987. ISBN 1-55532-152-6 Subj: Concepts – color. Frogs & toads.

Who wants Arthur? ill. by Donna Gynell. G. Stevens, 1987. ISBN 1-55532-153-4 Subj: Animals – dogs. Behavior – imitation. Stores.

Graham, Bob. *Benny* ill. by author. Candlewick, 1999. ISBN 0-7636-0813-0 Subj: Animals – dogs. Careers – magicians.

Crusher is coming! ill. by author. Viking, 1987. ISBN 0-670-82081-4 Subj: Babies. Friendship.

First there was Frances ill. by author. Bradbury, 1986. ISBN 0-02-737030-5 Subj: Animals. Family life. Moving.

Greetings from Sandy Beach ill. by author. Kane/Miller, 1992. ISBN 0-916291-40-5 Subj: Activities – vacationing. Camps, camping. Family life. Sea & seashore – beaches.

Has anyone here seen William? ill. by author. Little, 1989. ISBN 0-316-32313-6 Subj: Behavior – misbehavior.

Jethro Byrd, fairy child ill. by author. Candlewick, 2002. ISBN 0-7636-1772-5 Subj: Activities – picnicking. Fairies.

"Let's get a pup!" said Kate ill. by author. Candlewick, 2001. ISBN 0-7636-1452-1 Subj: Animals – dogs. Family life. Pets.

Libby, Oscar and me ill. by author. HarperCollins, 1985. ISBN 0-911745-89-0 Subj: Activities – picnicking. Animals – cats. Animals – dogs.

Max ill. by author. Candlewick, 2000. ISBN 0-7636-1138-7 Subj: Activities – flying. Imagination. Mythical creatures.

Pete and Roland ill. by author. Viking, 1984. ISBN 0-670-54912-6 Subj: Birds – parakeets, parrots. Character traits – kindness to animals.

Queenie, one of the family ill. by author. Candlewick, 1997. ISBN 0-7636-0359-7 Subj: Birds – chickens. Character traits – kindness to animals. Family life.

The red woolen blanket ill. by author. Little, 1988. ISBN 0-316-32310-1 Subj: Behavior – growing up. Concepts – color.

Rose meets Mr. Wintergarten ill. by author. Candlewick, 1992. ISBN 1-56402-039-8 Subj: Friendship. Old age.

Spirit of Hope ill. by author. Mondo, 1996. ISBN 1-57255-202-6 Subj: Family life. Homes, houses. Moving.

The wild ill. by author. HarperCollins, 1987. ISBN 0-87226-139-5 Subj: Family life. Nature. Pets.

Graham, Charlotte. *see* Bowden, Joan Chase

Graham, Georgia. *The strongest man this side of Cremona* ill. by author. Red Deer Pr., 1998. ISBN 0-88995-182-9 Subj: Emotions – love. Family life – fathers. Farms. Weather – storms.

Graham, Ian. *The best book of spaceships* ill. by author. Kingfisher, 1998. ISBN 0-7534-5133-6 Subj: Space & space ships.

Graham, Joan Bransfield. *Flicker flash* ill. by Nancy Davis. Houghton Mifflin, 1999. ISBN 0-395-90501-X Subj: Light, lights. Poetry.

Splish splash ill. by Steven Scott. Houghton, 1994. ISBN 0-395-70128-7 Subj: Poetry. Water.

Graham, John. *A crowd of cows* ill. by Feodor Rojankovsky. Harcourt, 1968. Subj: Animals. Noise, sounds.

I love you, mouse ill. by Tomie de Paola. Harcourt, 1976. ISBN 0-15-238005-1 Subj: Animals. Animals – mice.

Graham, Lorenz B. *David he no fear* ill. by Ann Grifalconi. Crowell, 1971. ISBN 0-690-23265-9 Subj: Religion.

Every man heart lay down ill. by Colleen Browning. Crowell, 1970. ISBN 0-690-27134-4 Subj: Religion – Nativity.

God wash the world and start again ill. by Clare Romano. Crowell, 1971. ISBN 0-690-33295-5 Subj: Boats, ships. Religion – Noah. Weather – floods. Weather – rain.

Hongry catch the foolish boy ill. by James Brown, Jr. Crowell, 1973. Story first appeared in the author's How God fix Jonah, published in 1946. ISBN 0-690-40112-4 Subj: Religion.

A road down in the sea ill. by Gregorio Prestopino. Crowell, 1970. ISBN 0-690-70500-X Subj: Religion.

Song of the boat ill. by Leo & Diane Dillon. Crowell, 1975. ISBN 0-690-75232-6 Subj: Foreign lands – Africa. Rhyming text.

Graham, Margaret Bloy. *Be nice to spiders* ill. by author. HarperCollins, 1967. ISBN 0-06-022073-2 Subj: Spiders. Zoos.

Benjy and his friend Fifi ill. by author. HarperCollins, 1988. ISBN 0-06-022253-0 Subj: Animals – dogs. Character traits – helpfulness. Emotions – fear.

Benjy and the barking bird ill. by author. HarperCollins, 1971. ISBN 0-06-022079-1 Subj: Animals – dogs. Birds – parakeets, parrots. Emotions – envy, jealousy.

Benjy's boat trip ill. by author. HarperCollins, 1977. ISBN 0-06-022093-7 Subj: Animals – dogs. Boats, ships.

Benjy's dog house ill. by author. HarperCollins, 1973. ISBN 0-06-022084-8 Subj: Animals – dogs.

Graham, Mary Stuart (Campbell). *The pirates' bridge* ill. by Winifred Lubell. Lothrop, 1960. Subj: Pirates.

Graham, Richard. *Jack and the monster* ill. by Susan Varley. Houghton Mifflin, 1989. ISBN 0-395-49680-2 Subj: Babies. Emotions – envy, jealousy. Family life – new sibling. Sibling rivalry.

Graham, Steve. *Dear old Donegal* music by author; ill. by John O'Brien. Clarion, 1996. ISBN 0-395-68187-1 Subj: Foreign lands – Ireland. Music. Songs.

Graham, Thomas. *Mr. Bear's boat* ill. by author. Dutton, 1988. ISBN 0-525-44375-4 Subj: Activities – picnicking. Animals – bears. Boats, ships.

Mr. Bear's chair ill. by author. Dutton, 1987. ISBN 0-525-44300-2 Subj: Activities – making things. Animals – bears. Family life. Furniture – chairs.

Graham Barber, Lynda. *Spy hops and belly flops* ill. by Brian Lies. Houghton, 2004. ISBN 0-618-22291-X Subj: Animals. Behavior. Forest, woods. Rhyming text.

Grahame, Kenneth. *Duck song* ill. by Joung Un Kim. HarperFestival, 1998. ISBN 0-694-01163-0 Subj: Birds – ducks. Format, unusual – board books. Rhyming text.

The open road ill. by Beverley Gooding. Scribners, 1980. ISBN 0-684-16471-X Subj: Activities – traveling. Animals.

The reluctant dragon abridged & ill. by Inga Moore. Candlewick, 2004. ISBN 0-7636-2199-4 Subj: Dragons. Knights. Poetry.

The wind in the willows retold by Janet Allison Brown; ill. by Joanne Moss. Viking, 2001. ISBN 0-670-89914-3 Subj: Animals. Animals – badgers. Animals – moles. Animals – rats. Foreign lands – England. Frogs & toads.

A wind in the willows Christmas ill. by Michael Hague. SeaStar, 2000. ISBN 1-587170-07-8 Subj: Animals. Animals – moles. Animals – rats. Holidays – Christmas. Homes, houses.

The wind in the willows: home sweet home ill. by Val Biro. Wanderer, 1987. ISBN 0-671-63629-4 Subj: Animals. Foreign lands – England. Holidays – Christmas. Homes, houses.

The wind in the willows: the open road ill. by Val Biro. Wanderer, 1987. ISBN 0-671-63626-X Subj: Activities – traveling. Animals.

The wind in the willows: the river bank ill. by Val Biro. Wanderer, 1987. ISBN 0-671-63627-8 Subj: Animals. Rivers.

The wind in the willows: the wild wood ill. by Val Biro. Wanderer, 1987. ISBN 0-671-63628-6 Subj: Animals. Forest, woods.

Graham-Yooll, Liz. *Timothy Tib* ill. by author. Ragged Bears, 2001. ISBN 1-929927-25-8 Subj: Animals – cats. Rhyming text.

Gralley, Jean. *Hogula, dread pig of night* ill. by author. Holt, 1999. ISBN 0-8050-5700-5 Subj: Animals – pigs. Friendship. Monsters – vampires.

Very boring alligator ill. by author. Holt, 2001. ISBN 0-8050-6328-5 Subj: Reptiles – alligators, crocodiles. Rhyming text.

Gramatky, Hardie. *Bolivar* ill. by author. Putnam, 1961. Subj: Animals – donkeys. Foreign lands – South America.

Hercules ill. by author. Putnam, 1940. ISBN 0-399-60240-2 Subj: Careers – firefighters. Fire. Museums. Trucks.

Homer and the circus train ill. by author. Putnam, 1957. Subj: Circus. Trains.

Little Toot ill. by author. Putnam, 1939. Subj: Boats, ships. Character traits – ambition.

Little Toot and the Loch Ness monster ill. by Hardie & Dorothea Cooke Gramatky. Putnam, 1989. ISBN 0-399-21684-7 Subj: Boats, ships. Foreign lands – Scotland. Monsters.

Little Toot on the Mississippi ill. by author. Putnam, 1973. Subj: Boats, ships. Rivers.

Little Toot on the Thames ill. by author. Putnam, 1964. Subj: Boats, ships. Foreign lands – England.

Little Toot through the Golden Gate ill. by author. Putnam, 1975. Subj: Boats, ships. Character traits – individuality. Cities, towns.

Loopy ill. by author. Putnam, 1941. Subj: Activities – flying. Airplanes, airports.

Nikos and the sea god ill. by author. Putnam, 1963. Subj: Careers – fishermen. Folk & fairy tales. Mythical creatures. Religion.

Sparky: the story of a little trolley car ill. by author. Putnam, 1952. Subj: Cable cars, trolleys. Transportation.

Grambling, Lois G. *Big Dog* ill. by Andrew L. San Diego. Cavendish, 2001. ISBN 0-7614-5045-9 Subj: Animals – dogs. Dinosaurs. Pets.

Can I have a Stegosaurus, Mom? Can I? Please!? ill. by H. B. Lewis. BridgeWater, 1994. ISBN 0-8167-3386-4 Subj: Dinosaurs. Pets.

Daddy will be there ill. by Walter Gaffney-Kessell. Greenwillow, 1998. ISBN 0-688-14984-7 Subj: Activities. Family life – fathers.

Grandma tells a story ill. by Fred Willingham. Whispering Coyote, 2001. ISBN 1-58089-057-1 Subj: Babies. Birth. Family life – grandparents.

Miss Hildy's missing cape caper ill. by Bridget Starr Taylor. Random House, 2000. ISBN 0-375-90196-5 Subj: Birds – flamingos. Holidays – Halloween. Mystery stories.

Night sounds ill. by Randall R. Ray. Rayve, 1996. ISBN 1-877810-77-0 Subj: Bedtime. Night. Noise, sounds. Sleep.

This whole Tooth Fairy thing's nothing but a big rip-off! ill. by Thomas Payne. Cavendish, 2002. ISBN 0-7614-5104-8 Subj: Animals. Animals – hippopotamuses. Fairies. Teeth.

The witch who wanted to be a princess ill. by Judy Love. Whispering Coyote, 2002. ISBN 1-58089-062-8 Subj: Character traits – honesty. Folk & fairy tales. Royalty – princesses. Self-concept. Witches.

A grand celebration: grandparents in poetry sel. by Carol G. Hittleman & Daniel R. Hittleman; ill. by Kay Life. Boyds Mills, 2002. ISBN 1-56397-901-2 Subj: Family life – grandparents. Poetry.

Granfield, Linda. *The legend of the panda* ill. by Song Nan Zhang. Tundra, 1998. ISBN 0-88776-421-5 Subj: Animals – pandas. Folk & fairy tales. Foreign lands – China.

Silent night: the song from heaven ill. by Nelly & Ernst Hofer. Tundra, 1997. ISBN 0-88776-395-2 Subj: Foreign lands – Austria. Holidays – Christmas. Music. Songs.

Granowsky, Alvin. *At the park* ill. with photos & ill. Copper Beech, 2001. ISBN 0-7613-2167-5 Subj: Animals – dogs. Family life – fathers. Family life – sons. Parks. Pets.

Can I help? ill. by author. Copper Beech, 2001. ISBN 0-7613-2172-1 Subj: Activities – picnicking. Character traits – helpfulness. Parties.

Diggers and cranes ill. by author. Copper Beech, 2000. ISBN 0-7613-1222-6 Subj: Machines.

Dinosaurs ill. by author. Copper Beech, 2000. ISBN 0-7613-1217-X Subj: Dinosaurs.

The dinosaurs' last days ill. by Paul Lopez. Steck-Vaughn, 1992. ISBN 0-8114-3250-5 Subj: Dinosaurs. Prehistory. Science.

Meat-eating dinosaurs ill. by Carol Inouye. Steck-Vaughn, 1992. ISBN 0-8114-3254-8 Subj: Dinosaurs. Prehistory. Science.

The three billy goats Gruff (Asbjørnsen, P. C. [Peter Christen])

Granström, Brita. *Honk! honk!* (Manning, Mick)

My body, your body (Manning, Mick)

Grant, Joan. *The monster that grew small* ill. by Jill K. Schwarz. Lothrop, 1987. ISBN 0-688-06809-X Subj: Character traits – bravery. Character traits – kindness to animals. Emotions – fear. Folk & fairy tales. Foreign lands – Egypt. Monsters.

Grant, Matthew G. *see* May, Julian

Grant, Rose Marie. *Andiamo, Weasel* ill. by Jon Goodell. Knopf, 2002. ISBN 0-375-90607-X Subj: Animals – weasels. Animals – wolves. Birds – crows. Character traits – confidence. Foreign lands – Italy. Self-concept.

Grant, Vernon. *Vernon Grant's Mother Goose* (Mother Goose)

Grassby, Donna. *A seaside alphabet* ill. by Susan Tooke. Tundra, 2000. ISBN 0-88776-516-5 Subj: Foreign lands – Canada. Sea & seashore.

Grasshopper to the rescue: a Georgian story trans. from Russian by Bonnie Carey; ill. by Tasha Tudor. Morrow, 1979. Subj: Character traits – bravery. Cumulative tales. Insects – grasshoppers. Rivers.

Gravdahl, John. *Curious catwalk* ill. by author. Propeller, 2003. ISBN 0-9678577-8-3 Subj: Animals – cats. Character traits – curiosity. Rhyming text.

Graves, Helen. *The brave little kittens* (Wilkon, Piotr)

Graves, Keith. *Frank was a monster who wanted to dance* ill. by author. Chronicle, 1999. ISBN 0-8118-2169-2 Subj: Activities – dancing. Monsters. Rhyming text.

Loretta, ace Pinky Scout ill. by author. Scholastic, 2002. ISBN 0-439-36831-6 Subj: Self-concept.

Pet boy ill. by author. Chronicle, 2000. ISBN 0-8118-2672-4 Subj: Behavior – boredom. Character traits – responsibility. Pets. Rhyming text.

Uncle Blubbafink's seriously ridiculous stories ill. by author. Scholastic, 2001. ISBN 0-439-24083-2 Subj: Tall tales.

Gray, Catherine. *Tammy and the gigantic fish* by Catherine & James Gray; ill. by William Joyce. HarperCollins, 1983. Subj: Family life. Sports – fishing.

Gray, Genevieve. *How far, Felipe?* ill. by Ann Grifalconi. HarperCollins, 1978. Subj: Activities – traveling. Animals – donkeys. Character traits – perseverance.

Send Wendell ill. by Symeon Shimin. McGraw-Hill, 1974. Subj: Character traits – helpfulness. Ethnic groups in the U.S. – African Americans. Family life.

Gray, James. *Tammy and the gigantic fish* (Gray, Catherine)

Gray, Jenny. *see* Gray, Genevieve

Gray, Kes. *Eat your peas* ill. by Nick Sharratt. DK, 2000. ISBN 0-7894-2667-6 Subj: Character traits – persistence. Family life – daughters. Family life – mothers. Food.

The "Get well soon" book ill. by Mary McQuillan. Millbrook, 2000. ISBN 0-7613-1922-0 Subj: Animals. Illness.

Gray, Libba Moore. *Is there room on the feather bed?* ill. by Nadine Bernard Westcott. Orchard, 1997. ISBN 0-531-33013-3 Subj: Animals. Animals – skunks. Cumulative tales. Farms. Rhyming text. Weather – storms.

The little black truck ill. by Elizabeth Sayles. S&S, 1994. ISBN 0-671-78105-7 Subj: Trucks.

Miss Tizzy ill. by Jada Rowland. S&S, 1993. ISBN 0-671-77590-1 Subj: Communities, neighborhoods. Ethnic groups in the U.S. – African Americans. Friendship. Illness.

My mama had a dancing heart ill. by Raúl Colón. Orchard, 1995. ISBN 0-531-08770-0 Subj: Activities – dancing. Ballet. Family life – mothers. Seasons.

Small green snake ill. by Holly Meade. Orchard, 1994. ISBN 0-531-08694-1 Subj: Reptiles – snakes. Rhyming text.

When Uncle took the fiddle ill. by Lloyd Bloom. Orchard, 1999. ISBN 0-531-33137-7 Subj: Family life – aunts, uncles. Music. Musical instruments – violins.

Gray, Nigel. *A balloon for grandad* ill. by Jane Ray. Watts, 1988. ISBN 0-531-08355-1 Subj: Family life – fathers. Family life – grandfathers. Toys – balloons.

A country far away ill. by Philippe Dupasquier. Watts, 1989. ISBN 0-531-08392-6 Subj: Family life. Foreign lands.

The dog show by Nigel Gray & Margaret Wilson; ill. by Margaret Wilson. Cygnet Books, 1996. ISBN 1-875560-63-7 Subj: Animals – cats. Animals – dogs. Contests.

Fly ill. by Craig Smith. Cygnet Books, 1994. ISBN 1-875560-39-4 Subj: Insects – flies. Rhyming text.

The frog prince ill. by Allan Langoulant. Cygnet Books, 1996. ISBN 1-8755-6068-8 Subj: Folk & fairy tales. Frogs & toads. Kissing. Royalty – princes. Royalty – princesses.

The grocer's daughter ill. by David Mackintosh. Univ. of Queensland Pr., 1994. ISBN 0-7022-2703-X Subj: Behavior. Rhyming text.

I'll take you to Mrs. Cole! ill. by Michael Foreman. Kane/Miller, 1992. ISBN 0-916291-39-1 Subj: Behavior – running away. Ethnic groups in the U.S. – African Americans.

It'll all come out in the wash ill. by Edward Frascino. HarperCollins, 1979. Subj: Family life.

Little pig's tale ill. by Mary Rees. Macmillan, 1990. ISBN 0-02-736942-0 Subj: Animals – pigs. Birthdays. Family life.

Pigs can't fly ill. by Carme Solé Vendrell. Andersen, 1990. ISBN 0-8626-4272-8 Subj: Animals – pigs. Concepts – size.

Running away from home ill. by Gregory Rogers. Crown, 1996. ISBN 0-517-70923-6 Subj: Behavior – running away. Family life – fathers.

Gray, Rita. *Nonna's porch* ill. by Terry Widener. Hyperion, 2004. ISBN 0-7868-1613-9 Subj: Country. Family life – grandmothers.

Gray, Samantha. *Birds* by Samantha Gray & Sarah Walker; ill. with photos. DK, 2002. ISBN 0-7894-8550-8 Subj: Birds.

Grayson, Laura. *see* Wilson, Barbara Ker

Grayson, Marion F. *Let's count and count out* (Let's count and count out)

Greaves, Margaret. *The firebird* (The firebird)

Henry's wild morning ill. by Teresa O'Brien. Dial, 1991. ISBN 0-8037-0907-2 Subj: Animals – cats. Character traits – ambition.

Kate Crackernuts ill. by Francesca Crespi. Dial, 1985. ISBN 0-8037-0225-6 (set) Subj: Folk & fairy tales. Foreign lands – England. Magic. Royalty – princesses. Royalty – queens. Witches.

Little Bear and the Papagini circus ill. by Francesca Crespi. Dial, 1986. ISBN 0-8037-0264-7 Subj: Animals – bears. Circus. Family life.

The lucky coin (Underhill, Liz)

The mice of Nibbling Village ill. by Jane Pinkney. Dutton, 1986. ISBN 0-525-44277-4 Subj: Animals – mice. Rhyming text.

Mother Cuspen ill. by Francesca Crespi. Dial, 1985. ISBN 0-8037-0225-6 (set) Subj: Folk & fairy tales. Foreign lands – England. Witches.

The naming ill. by Pauline Baynes. Harcourt, 1993. ISBN 0-15-200534-X Subj: Animals. Mythical creatures – unicorns. Names.

Once there were no pandas ill. by Beverley Gooding. Dutton, 1985. ISBN 0-525-44211-1 Subj: Animals – pandas. Character traits – bravery.

Petrushka ill. by Francesca Crespi. Dial, 1986. ISBN 0-8037-0265-5 (set) Subj: Ballet. Folk & fairy tales. Foreign lands – Russia. Puppets.

Sarah's lion ill. by Honey de Lacey. Barron's, 1992. ISBN 0-8120-6279-5 Subj: Animals – lions. Behavior. Royalty – princesses.

The star horse ill. by Jan Nesbitt. Barron's, 1992. ISBN 0-8120-6294-9 Subj: Animals – horses, ponies. Behavior – wishing. Merry-go-rounds.

The witch cat ill. by Francesca Crespi. Dial, 1985. ISBN 0-8037-0225-6 (set) Subj: Animals – cats. Folk & fairy tales. Foreign lands – England. Witches.

The witch's servant ill. by Francesca Crespi. Dial, 1985. ISBN 0-8037-0225-6 (set) Subj: Folk & fairy tales. Foreign lands – England. Witches.

Gréban, Quentin. *Nestor* ill. by author. Mondo, 2001. ISBN 1-58653-855-1 Subj: Animals – babies. Animals – elephants. Animals – monkeys. Sports – fishing.

Greeley, Valerie. *The acorn's story* ill. by author. Macmillan, 1994. ISBN 0-02-736916-1 Subj: Rhyming text. Seeds. Trees.

Animals ill. by author. Peter Bedrick, 1990. ISBN 0-8722-6435-1 Subj: Animals. Format, unusual – board books.

Farm animals ill. by author. HarperCollins, 1984. Subj: Animals. Farms. Format, unusual – board books. Wordless.

Field animals ill. by author. HarperCollins, 1984. Subj: Animals. Format, unusual – board books. Wordless.

Pets ill. by author. HarperCollins, 1984. Subj: Animals. Format, unusual – board books. Pets. Wordless.

Where's my share? ill. by author. Macmillan, 1990. ISBN 0-02-736761-4 Subj: Animals. Birds. Circular tales. Food. Nursery rhymes.

White is the moon ill. by author. Macmillan, 1991. ISBN 0-02-736915-3 Subj: Animals. Concepts – color. Nature. Rhyming text.

Zoo animals ill. by author. HarperCollins, 1984. Subj: Animals. Format, unusual – board books. Wordless. Zoos.

Green, Adam. *see* Weisgard, Leonard

The funny bunny factory ill. by Leonard Weisgard. Grosset, 1950. Subj: Animals – rabbits. Holidays – Easter.

Green, Donna. *My little artist* ill. by author. Smithmark, 1999. ISBN 0-7651-1742-8 Subj: Careers – artists. Family life – grandmothers.

Green, Jen. *Birds* ill. with photos. Copper Beech, 2000. ISBN 0-7613-1216-1 Subj: Birds.

Our new baby ill. by Christopher O'Neill. Copper Beech, 1998. ISBN 0-7613-0871-7 Subj: Babies. Family life – brothers & sisters.

Reptiles ill. with photos. Copper Beech, 2000. ISBN 0-7613-1214-5 Subj: Reptiles.

Green, Marion. *The magician who lived on the mountain* ill. by John Dyke. Childrens Pr., 1978. Subj: Art. Magic.

Green, Mary McBurney. *Everybody has a house and everybody eats* ill. by Louis Klein. Abelard-Schuman, 1944. Subj: Farms. Homes, houses.

Is it hard? Is it easy? ill. by Lucienne Bloch. Abelard-Schuman, 1948. Subj: Concepts.

Green, Melinda. *Bembelman's bakery* ill. by Barbara Seuling. Parents' Magazine Pr., 1978. ISBN 0-8193-0914-1 Subj: Careers – bakers.

Green, Norma B. *The hole in the dike* ill. by Eric Carle. Crowell, 1974. ISBN 0-690-00676-4 Subj: Character traits – helpfulness. Foreign lands – Holland.

Green, Phyllis. *Bagdad ate it* ill. by Joel Schick. Watts, 1980. ISBN 0-531-02855-0 Subj: Animals – dogs. Behavior – greed.

Uncle Roland, the perfect guest ill. by Marybeth Farrell. Four Winds, 1983. ISBN 0-590-07885-2 Subj: Family life – aunts, uncles.

Green, Stephanie. *Betsy Ross and the silver thimble* ill. by Diana Magnuson. Aladdin, 2002. ISBN 0-689-84967-2 Subj: Activities – sewing. Careers – tailors. Flags. U.S. history.

Not just another moose ill. by Andrea Wallace. Cavendish, 2000. ISBN 0-7614-5061-0 Subj: Animals – moose. Humorous stories. Self-concept.

The green grass grows all around: *a traditional folk song* ill. by Hilde Hoffmann. Macmillan, 1968. Subj: Plants. Poetry. Songs.

Green-Armytage, Stephen. *Dudley, the little terrier that could* ill. by author. Abrams, 1999. ISBN 0-8109-4098-1 Subj: Animals – dogs. Concepts – size. Self-concept.

Greenaway, Kate. *A apple pie* ill. by author. Warne, 1886. ISBN 0-7232-1801-3 Subj: ABC books.

Kate Greenaway's Mother Goose (Mother Goose)

Marigold garden ill. by author. Warne, 1885. Subj: Poetry.

Under the window ill. by author. Warne, 1880?. Subj: Poetry.

Greenaway, Shirley. *Forests* ill. with photos. Newington, 1991. ISBN 1-878137-08-5 Subj: Animals. Forest, woods. Nature.

Jungles ill. with photos. Newington, 1991. ISBN 1-878137-09-3 Subj: Animals. Jungle. Nature.

Greenaway, Theresa. *Centipedes and millipedes* photos by Chris Fairclough; ill. by Dick Twinney & Stefan Chabluk. Raintree, 2000. ISBN 0-7398-1829-5 Subj: Crustaceans – centipedes, millipedes. Pets.

Greenberg, Barbara. *The bravest babysitter* ill. by Diane Paterson. Dial, 1977. ISBN 0-8037-0364-3 Subj: Activities – babysitting. Babies. Emotions – fear. Weather.

Greenberg, Dan. *The bed who ran away from home* ill. by John Wallner. HarperCollins, 1991. ISBN 0-06-022280-8 Subj: Bedtime. Behavior – running away. Furniture – beds. Multiple births – twins. Rhyming text.

Greenberg, David (David T.). *Bugs!* ill. by Lynn Munsinger. Little, 1997. ISBN 0-316-32574-0 Subj: Insects. Rhyming text.

Skunks ill. by Lynn Munsinger. Little, 2001. ISBN 0-316-32606-2 Subj: Animals – skunks. Rhyming text.

Slugs ill. by Victoria Chess. Little, 1983. ISBN 0-316-32658-5 Subj: Animals – snails. Rhyming text.

Greenberg, Judith E. *Adopted* by Judith E. Greenberg & Helen H. Carey; photos by Barbara Kirk. Watts, 1987. ISBN 0-531-10290-4 Subj: Adoption. Babies.

What is the sign for friend? photos by Gayle Rothschild. Watts, 1985. ISBN 0-531-04939-6 Subj: Handicaps – deafness. Senses – hearing. Sign language.

Greenberg, Melanie Hope. *At the beach* ill. by author. Dutton, 1989. ISBN 0-525-44474-2 Subj: Sea & seashore – beaches.

My father's luncheonette ill. by author. Dutton, 1991. ISBN 0-525-44725-3 Subj: Activities – baking, cooking. Careers. Cities, towns. Family life – fathers.

Greenberg, Polly. *Oh, Lord, I wish I was a buzzard* ill. by Aliki. Macmillan, 1968. Subj: Behavior – wishing. Ethnic groups in the U.S. – African Americans. Farms. Plants.

Greenblat, Rodney Alan. *Aunt Ippy's museum of junk* ill. by author. HarperCollins, 1991. ISBN 0-06-022512-2 Subj: Behavior – collecting things. Family life – aunts, uncles.

Thunder Bunny ill. by author. HarperCollins, 1997. ISBN 0-06-026434-9 Subj: Activities – drawing. Activities – traveling. Activities – writing. Animals – rabbits. Imagination. Weather – clouds.

Uncle Wizzmo's new used car ill. by author. HarperCollins, 1990. ISBN 0-06-022098-8 Subj: Automobiles. Family life – aunts, uncles.

Greenburg, Dan. *Great-Grandpa's in the litter box* ill. by Jack E. Davis. Grosset, 1996. ISBN 0-448-41289-6 Subj: Animals – cats. Family life – great-grandparents. Imagination.

Through the medicine cabinet ill. by Jack E. Davis. Grosset, 1996. ISBN 0-448-41291-8 Subj: Imagination. Self-concept.

Greene, Carla. *Doctors and nurses: what do they do?* ill. by Leonard P. Kessler. HarperCollins, 1963. ISBN 0-06-022076-7 Subj: Careers – doctors. Careers – nurses.

I want to be a carpenter ill. by Frances Eckart. Childrens Pr., 1959. Subj: Careers – carpenters.

A motor holiday ill. by Harold L. Van Pelt. Melmont, 1956. Subj: Activities – traveling. Automobiles.

Greene, Carol. *Astronauts work in space* ill. with photos. Child's World, 1998. ISBN 1-56766-406-7 Subj: Careers – astronauts. Space & space ships.

A computer went a-courting: a love song for Valentine's Day ill. by Tom Dunnington. Childrens Pr., 1983. ISBN 0-516-08232-9 Subj: Animals – mice. Computers. Holidays – Valentine's Day. Music. Songs.

God's good creation ill. by Michelle Dorenkamp. Concordia, 1994. ISBN 0-570-09040-7 Subj: Creation. Religion.

The golden locket ill. by Marcia Sewall. Harcourt, 1992. ISBN 0-15-231220-X Subj: Behavior – worrying. Emotions – love. Problem solving.

Hi, clouds ill. by Gene Sharp. Grosset, 1989. ISBN 0-516-02036-6 Subj: Weather – clouds.

Hinny Winny Bunco ill. by Jeanette Winter. HarperCollins, 1982. ISBN 0-06-022129-1 Subj: Music. Musical instruments – violins. Sibling rivalry. Songs.

I can be a baseball player ill. with photos. Childrens Pr., 1985. ISBN 0-516-01845-0 Subj: Careers. Sports – baseball.

I can be a forest ranger ill. with photos. Childrens Pr., 1989. ISBN 0-516-41924-2 Subj: Careers – park rangers. Forest, woods. Nature.

I can be a librarian ill. with photos. Childrens Pr., 1988. ISBN 0-516-01913-9 Subj: Careers – librarians.

I can be a model ill. with photos. Childrens Pr., 1985. ISBN 0-516-01887-6 Subj: Careers – models.

The insignificant elephant ill. by Susan Gantner. Harcourt, 1985. ISBN 0-15-238730-7 Subj: Animals – elephants. Animals – rabbits.

Katherine Dunham: black dancer ill. by author. Childrens Pr., 1992. ISBN 0-516-04252-1 Subj: Activities – dancing. Ethnic groups in the U.S. – African Americans.

Margaret Wise Brown, author of Goodnight moon ill. by author. Childrens Pr., 1993. ISBN 0-516-04254-8 Subj: Activities – writing.

Margarete Steiff, toy maker ill. by author. Childrens Pr., 1993. ISBN 0-516-04257-2 Subj: Toys – bears.

The old ladies who liked cats ill. by Loretta Krupinski. HarperCollins, 1991. ISBN 0-06-022105-4 Subj: Animals – cats. Ecology. Islands. Old age.

Please, wind? ill. by Gene Sharp. Childrens Pr., 1982. ISBN 0-516-02033-1 Subj: Weather – wind.

Rain! Rain! ill. by Larry Frederick. Childrens Pr., 1982. ISBN 0-516-42034-8 Subj: Weather – rain.

Reading about the gray wolf ill. by author. Enslow, 1993. ISBN 0-89490-427-2 Subj: Animals – endangered animals. Animals – wolves.

Reading about the peregrine falcon ill. by author. Enslow, 1993. ISBN 0-89490-422-1 Subj: Animals – endangered animals. Birds – falcons.

Reading about the river otter ill. by author. Enslow, 1993. ISBN 0-89490-425-6 Subj: Animals – endangered animals. Animals – otters. Rivers.

Robots ill. with photos. Childrens Pr., 1983. ISBN 0-516-01684-9 Subj: Robots.

Shine, sun! ill. by Gene Sharp. Childrens Pr., 1983. ISBN 0-516-02038-2 Subj: Sun.

Snow Joe ill. by Paul Sharp. Childrens Pr., 1982. ISBN 0-516-02035-8 Subj: Weather – snow.

Sunflower Island ill. by Leonard Jenkins. HarperCollins, 1999. ISBN 0-06-027327-5 Subj: Boats, ships. Islands. Rivers.

Teachers help us learn photos by Phil Martin. Child's World, 1998. ISBN 1-56766-404-0 Subj: Careers – teachers.

The thirteen days of Halloween ill. by Tom Dunnington. Childrens Pr., 1983. ISBN 0-516-08231-0 Subj: Holidays – Halloween. Music. Songs. Witches.

Where is that cat? ill. by Loretta Krupinski. Hyperion, 1999. ISBN 0-7868-2399-2 Subj: Animals – cats. Behavior – hiding.

The world's biggest birthday cake ill. by Tom Dunnington. Childrens Pr., 1985. ISBN 0-516-08233-7 Subj: Birthdays. Food. Music. Rhyming text.

Greene, Ellin. *Billy Beg and his bull* ill. by Kimberly Bulcken Root. Holiday, 1994. ISBN 0-8234-1100-1 Subj: Animals – bulls, cows. Folk & fairy tales. Foreign lands – Ireland. Magic. Royalty – princes. Royalty – princesses.

The legend of the Christmas rose (Lagerlöf, Selma)

The legend of the cranberry: a Paleo-Indian tale ill. by Brad Sneed. S&S, 1993. ISBN 0-671-75975-2 Subj: Animals. Folk & fairy tales. Indians of North America – Delaware.

Ling-li and the phoenix fairy ill. by Zong-Zhou Wang. Clarion, 1996. ISBN 0-395-71528-8 Subj: Birds. Clothing. Flowers. Folk & fairy tales. Foreign lands – China. Mythical creatures – phoenix. Weddings.

The pumpkin giant ill. by Trina Schart Hyman. Lothrop, 1970. Orig. story by Mary E. Wilkins. Subj: Food. Giants. Holidays – Halloween.

Greene, Graham. *The little fire engine* ill. by Edward Ardizzone. Doubleday, 1973. ISBN 0-385-08908-2 Subj: Fire. Progress.

The little train ill. by Edward Ardizzone. Doubleday, 1973. ISBN 0-385-08907-4 Subj: Behavior – running away. Trains.

Greene, Jacqueline Dembar. *Butchers and bakers, rabbis and kings* ill. by Marilyn Hirsh. Kar-Ben Copies, 1984. ISBN 0-930494-27-X Subj: Foreign lands – Spain. Jewish culture.

What his father did ill. by John O'Brien. Houghton Mifflin, 1992. ISBN 0-395-55042-4 Subj: Folk & fairy tales. Food. Jewish culture. Poverty.

Greene, Joshua. *Hanuman* (Jendresen, Erik)

Greene, Laura. *Change: getting to know about ebb and flow* ill. by Gretchen Will Mayo. Human Sciences Pr., 1981. ISBN 0-898540-10-0 Subj: Concepts.

Help: getting to know about needing and giving ill. by Gretchen Will Mayo. Human Sciences Pr., 1981. ISBN 0-87705-401-0 Subj: Character traits – helpfulness.

Greene, Rhonda Gowler. *At grandma's* ill. by Karla Firehammer. Holt, 2003. ISBN 0-8050-6336-6 Subj: Family life – grandmothers. Rhyming text. Sleepovers.

Barnyard song ill. by Robert Bender. Atheneum, 1997. ISBN 0-689-80758-9 Subj: Animals. Farms. Illness. Noise, sounds. Rhyming text.

The beautiful world that God made ill. by Anne Wilson. Eerdmans, 2002. ISBN 0-8028-5213-0 Subj: Creation. Earth.

Eek! Creak! Snicker, sneak ill. by Jos. A. Smith. Atheneum, 2002. ISBN 0-689-83047-5 Subj: Behavior – trickery. Emotions – fear. Monsters. Rhyming text.

Jamboree day ill. by Jason Wolff. Orchard, 2001. ISBN 0-439-29310-3 Subj: Animals. Jungle. Parties. Rhyming text.

The stable where Jesus was born ill. by Susan Gaber. Atheneum, 1999. ISBN 0-689-81258-2 Subj: Holidays – Christmas. Religion – Nativity. Rhyming text.

The very first Thanksgiving Day ill. by Susan Gaber. Atheneum, 2002. ISBN 0-689-83301-6 Subj: Holidays – Thanksgiving. Pilgrims. Rhyming text. U.S. history.

Greene, Roberta. *Two and me makes three* ill. by Paul Galdone. Coward, 1970. Subj: Ethnic groups in the U.S.

Greene, Shep. *We all sing with the same voice* (Miller, J. Philip)

Greenfield, Eloise. *Africa dream* ill. by Carole M. Byard. John Day, 1977. ISBN 0-381-90061-4 Subj: Dreams. Foreign lands – Africa.

Angels ill. by Jan Spivey Gilchrist. Jump at the Sun, 1998. ISBN 0-7868-0442-4 Subj: Angels. Ethnic groups in the U.S. – African Americans. Poetry.

Big friend, little friend ill. by Jan Spivey Gilchrist. Black Butterfly, 1991. ISBN 0-86316-204-5 Subj: Activities – playing. Ethnic groups in the U.S. – African Americans. Format, unusual – board books. Friendship. Poetry.

Daddy and I ill. by Jan Spivey Gilchrist. Black Butterfly, 1991. ISBN 0-86316-206-1 Subj: Ethnic groups in the U.S. – African Americans. Family life – fathers. Format, unusual – board books. Poetry.

Daydreamers ill. by Tom Feelings. Dial, 1981. ISBN 0-8037-2134-X Subj: Ethnic groups in the U.S. – African Americans. Poetry.

Easter parade ill. by Jan Spivey Gilchrist. Hyperion, 1997. ISBN 0-7868-0326-6 Subj: Ethnic groups in the U.S. – African Americans. Family life – cousins. Holidays – Easter. Parades. U.S. history. War.

First pink light ill. by Moneta Barnett. Crowell, 1976. ISBN 0-690-01087-7 Subj: Ethnic groups in the U.S. – African Americans. Family life – fathers.

Grandpa's face ill. by Floyd Cooper. Putnam, 1988. ISBN 0-399-21525-5 Subj: Character traits – appearance. Family life – grandfathers.

I can do it by myself (Little, Lessie Jones)

I can draw a weeposaur and other dinosaurs ill. by Jan Spivy Gilchrist. Greenwillow, 2001. ISBN 0-688-17635-6 Subj: Dinosaurs. Imagination. Mythical creatures. Poetry.

I make music ill. by Jan Spivey Gilchrist. Black Butterfly, 1991. ISBN 0-86316-205-3 Subj: Ethnic groups in the U.S. – African Americans. Family life. Format, unusual – board books. Music. Poetry.

In the land of words ill. by Jan Spivy Gilchrist. HarperCollins, 2004. ISBN 0-06-028994-5 Subj: Poetry.

Kia Tanisha ill. by Jan Spivey Gilchrist. HarperCollins, 1997. ISBN 0-694-00847-8 Subj: Activities – running. Ethnic groups in the U.S. – African Americans. Rhyming text.

Kia Tanisha drives her car ill. by Jan Spivey Gilchrist. HarperCollins, 1997. ISBN 0-694-00848-6 Subj: Activities – driving. Automobiles. Toys.

Lisa's daddy and daughter day ill. by Jan Spivey Gilchrist. Sundance, 1991. ISBN 0-88741-918-6 Subj: Ethnic groups in the U.S. – African Americans. Family life – daughters. Family life – fathers.

Me and Neesie ill. by Moneta Barnett. Crowell, 1975. ISBN 0-690-00715-9 Subj: Ethnic groups in the U.S. – African Americans. Family life. Imagination – imaginary friends. School – first day.

Me and Neesie ill. by Jan Spivey Gilchrist. HarperCollins, 2005. ISBN 0-06-000702-8 Subj: Ethnic groups in the U.S. – African Americans. Family life. Imagination – imaginary friends. School – first day.

My doll, Keshia ill. by Jan Spivey Gilchrist. Black Butterfly, 1991. ISBN 0-86316-203-7 Subj: Activities – playing. Ethnic groups in the U.S. – African Americans. Format, unusual – board books. Poetry. Toys – dolls.

Nathaniel talking ill. by Jan Spivey Gilchrist. Black Butterfly, 1988. ISBN 0-86316-200-2 Subj: Ethnic groups in the U.S. – African Americans. Poetry.

Night on Neighborhood Street ill. by Jan Spivey Gilchrist. Dial, 1991. ISBN 0-8037-0778-9 Subj: Cities, towns. Communities, neighborhoods. Ethnic groups in the U.S. – African Americans. Night. Poetry.

On my horse ill. by Jan Spivey Gilchrist. HarperFestival, 1995. ISBN 0-694-00583-5 Subj: Animals – horses, ponies. Ethnic groups in the U.S. – African Americans. Imagination. Rhyming text.

She come bringing me that little baby girl ill. by John Steptoe. Lippincott, 1974. ISBN 0-397-31586-4 Subj: Babies. Emotions – envy, jealousy. Ethnic groups in the U.S. – African Americans. Family life – new sibling. Sibling rivalry.

Sweet baby coming ill. by Jan Spivey Gilchrist. HarperCollins, 1994. ISBN 0-694-00578-9 Subj: Babies. Ethnic groups in the U.S. – African Americans. Family life – new sibling. Format, unusual – board books.

Under the Sunday tree ill. by Amos Ferguson. HarperCollins, 1988. ISBN 0-06-022257-3 Subj: Foreign lands – Caribbean Islands. Islands. Poetry.

Water, water ill. by Jan Spivey Gilchrist. HarperFestival, 1999. ISBN 0-694-01247-5 Subj: Ethnic groups in the U.S. – African Americans. Rhyming text. Water.

William and the good old days ill. by Jan Spivey Gilchrist. HarperCollins, 1993. ISBN 0-06-021094-X Subj: Ethnic groups in the U.S. – African Americans. Family life – grandmothers. Illness.

Greenfield, Karen R. *Sister Yessa's story* ill. by Claire Ewart. HarperCollins, 1992. ISBN 0-06-020279-3 Subj: Activities – walking. Animals. Religion – Noah. Weather – rain. Weather – storms.

Greenfield, Monica. *The baby* ill. by Jan Spivey Gilchrist. HarperCollins, 1994. ISBN 0-694-00577-0 Subj: Babies. Ethnic groups in the U.S. – African Americans. Family life. Format, unusual – board books.

Waiting for Christmas ill. by Jan Spivey Gilchrist. Scholastic, 1996. ISBN 0-590-52700-2 Subj: Ethnic groups in the U.S. – African Americans. Family life. Holidays – Christmas.

Greenleaf, Ann. *No room for Sarah* ill. by author. Dodd, 1983. ISBN 0-396-08213-0 Subj: Bedtime. Toys.

Greenlee, Sharon. *When someone dies* ill. by Bill Drath. Peachtree, 1992. ISBN 1-56145-044-8 Subj: Death. Emotions – grief.

Greenstein, Elaine. *As big as you* ill. by author. Knopf, 2002. ISBN 0-375-91353-X Subj: Babies. Behavior – growing up. Family life – mothers. Seasons.

Dreaming: a countdown to sleep ill. by author. Levine, 2000. ISBN 0-439-06302-7 Subj: Bedtime. Counting, numbers.

Emily and the crows ill. by author. Picture Book Studio, 1992. ISBN 0-88708-238-6 Subj: Animals – bulls, cows. Birds – crows. Imagination.

Mrs. Rose's garden ill. by author. S&S, 1996. ISBN 0-88708-264-5 Subj: Fairs, festivals. Gardens, gardening.

Greenway, Jennifer. *The three billy goats Gruff* (Asbjørnsen, P. C. [Peter Christen])

Greenway, Shirley. *Animal homes: burrows* photos by Oxford Scientific Films. Newington, 1991. ISBN 1-87813-711-5 Subj: Animals. Homes, houses.

Can you see me? photos by Oxford Scientific Films. Ideals, 1992. ISBN 0-8249-8575-3 Subj: Animals. Nature.

Color me bright photos by Oxford Scientific Films. Whispering Coyote, 1992. ISBN 1-879085-53-4 Subj: Animals. Concepts – color. Format, unusual – board books. Nature.

Here's ears photos by Oxford Scientific Films. Whispering Coyote, 1992. ISBN 1-879085-50-X Subj: Anatomy – ears. Animals. Format, unusual – board books. Nature.

How big am I? photos by Oxford Scientific Films. Ideals, 1993. ISBN 0-8249-8625-3 Subj: Animals. Concepts – size.

How do I move? photos by Oxford Scientific Films. Ideals, 1992. ISBN 0-8249-8578-8 Subj: Animals. Nature.

Legs and all photos by Oxford Scientific Films. Whispering Coyote, 1992. ISBN 1-879085-52-6 Subj: Anatomy – legs. Animals. Format, unusual – board books. Nature.

A tale of tails photos by Oxford Scientific Films. Whispering Coyote, 1992. ISBN 1-879085-51-8 Subj: Anatomy – tails. Animals. Format, unusual – board books. Nature.

Two's company . . . photos by Oxford Scientific Films. Charlesbridge, 1997. ISBN 0-88106-964-7 Subj: Animals. Concepts.

What do I eat? photos by Oxford Scientific Films. Ideals, 1993. ISBN 0-8249-8627-X Subj: Animals. Food.

Where do I live? photos by Oxford Scientific Films. Ideals, 1992. ISBN 0-8249-8576-1 Subj: Animals. Ecology. Nature.

Whose baby am I? photos by Oxford Scientific Films. Ideals, 1992. ISBN 0-8249-8577-X Subj: Animals. Nature.

Greenwood, Ann. *A pack of dreams* ill. by Bernard Colonna & Mary Elizabeth Gordon. Prentice-Hall, 1979. ISBN 0-13-647784-4 Subj: Dreams. Rhyming text.

Greenwood, Rosie. *I wonder why volcanoes blow their tops* ill. by author. Kingfisher, 2004. ISBN 0-7534-5751-2 Subj: Science. Volcanoes.

Greeson, Janet. *An American army of two* ill. by Patricia Rose Mulvihill. Carolrhoda, 1992. ISBN 0-87614-664-7 Subj: Character traits – cleverness. Family life – sisters. U.S. history. War.

The stingy baker ill. by David LaRochelle. Carolrhoda, 1989. ISBN 0-87614-378-8 Subj: Angels. Careers – bakers. Folk & fairy tales. Magic. Witches.

Gregg, Andy. *Great Rabbit and the long-tailed Wildcat* ill. by Cat Bowman Smith. A. Whitman, 1993. ISBN 0-8075-3047-6 Subj: Anatomy – tails. Animals – cougars. Folk & fairy tales. Indians of North America – Algonquin.

Gregoire, Caroline. *Uglypuss* ill. by author; trans. from French by George Wen. Holt, 1994. ISBN 0-8050-3300-9 Subj: Animals – dogs. Pets.

Gregor, Arthur S. *Animal babies* (Ylla)

The little elephant (Ylla)

1, 2, 3, 4, 5 ill. by Robert Doisneau. Lippincott, 1956. Subj: Counting, numbers.

Gregorich, Barbara. *My friend goes left* ill. by Joyce John; ed. by Joan Hoffman. School Zone Pub., 1984. ISBN 0-88743-008-2 Subj: Poetry. Riddles & jokes.

Gregorowski, Christopher. *Fly, eagle, fly! an African fable* ill. by Niki Daly. McElderry, 2000. ISBN 0-689-82398-3 Subj: Activities – flying. Birds – eagles. Folk & fairy tales. Foreign lands – Africa. Self-concept.

Gregory, Nan. *Amber waiting* ill. by Kady MacDonald Denton. Red Deer Pr., 2003. ISBN 0-88995-258-2 Subj: Behavior – promptness, tardiness. School. Time.

How Smudge came ill. by Ron Lightburn. Walker, 1997. ISBN 0-88995-143-8 Subj: Animals – dogs. Character traits – loyalty. Handicaps – Down syndrome. Pets.

Wild Girl and Gran ill. by Ron Lightburn. Red Deer Pr., 2000. ISBN 0-88995-221-3 Subj: Death. Emotions – grief. Family life – grandmothers. Foreign lands – Canada. Friendship. Imagination.

Gregory, Valiska. *Babysitting for Benjamin* ill. by Lynn Munsinger. Little, 1993. ISBN 0-316-32785-9 Subj: Ethnic groups in the U.S. – Amish. Poetry. Weddings.

Kate's giants ill. by Virginia Austin. Candlewick, 1995. ISBN 1-56402-299-4 Subj: Bedtime. Emotions – fear. Giants. Night.

Looking for angels ill. by Leslie A. Baker. S&S, 1996. ISBN 0-671-50546-7 Subj: Angels.

The oatmeal cookie giant ill. by Jeni Bassett. Four Winds, 1987. ISBN 0-02-738070-X Subj: Animals – dogs. Family life – aunts, uncles. Old age.

Riddle soup ill. by Jeni Bassett. Four Winds, 1987. ISBN 0-02-738090-4 Subj: Activities – baking, cooking. Animals – dogs.

Sunny side up ill. by Jeni Bassett. Four Winds, 1986. ISBN 0-02-738050-5 Subj: Animals – dogs. Character traits – optimism.

Terribly wonderful ill. by Jeni Bassett. Four Winds, 1986. ISBN 0-02-738110-1 Subj: Animals – dogs. Character traits – optimism.

Through the mickle woods ill. by Barry Moser. Little, 1992. ISBN 0-316-32779-4 Subj: Animals – bears. Death. Folk & fairy tales. Forest, woods. Royalty – kings.

A Valentine for Norman Noggs ill. by Martha Winborn. HarperCollins, 1999. ISBN 0-06-027657-6 Subj: Animals – hamsters. Holidays – Valentine's Day. School. Self-concept.

When stories fell like shooting stars ill. by Stefano Vitale. S&S, 1996. ISBN 0-689-80012-6 Subj: Animals. Behavior – greed. Character traits – responsibility. Moon. Sun.

Greifenstein, Sandra. *The fish* (Bruna, Dick)

Greisman, Joan. *Things I hate!* (Wittels, Harriet)

Grejniec, Michael. *Albert's nap* ill. by author. North-South, 1995. ISBN 1-55858-280-0 Subj: Animals – hippopotamuses. Insects – flies. Sleep.

Good morning, good night ill. by author. North-South, 1993. ISBN 1-55858-174-X Subj: Activities. Concepts – opposites. Friendship.

Look ill. by author. North-South, 1993. ISBN 1-55858-213-4 Subj: Communities, neighborhoods. Friendship. Illness.

What do you like? ill. by author. North-South, 1992. ISBN 1-55858-176-6 Subj: Character traits – individuality.

When I open my eyes ill. by author. Holt, 1990. ISBN 0-8050-1417-9 Subj: Animals – sheep. Imagination.

Who is my neighbor? ill. by author. Knopf, 1994. ISBN 0-679-95801-0 Subj: Careers – magicians. Communities, neighborhoods. Power failures.

Grell, Kathryn. *Rufus and Max* (Moers, Hermann)

Gretz, Susanna. *Duck takes off* ill. by author. Four Winds, 1991. ISBN 0-02-737472-6 Subj: Activities – playing. Animals. Birds – ducks. Friendship.

Frog, duck, and rabbit ill. by author. Four Winds, 1992. ISBN 0-02-737327-4 Subj: Animals. Clothing – costumes. Parades.

Frog in the middle ill. by author. Four Winds, 1991. ISBN 0-02-737471-8 Subj: Animals. Behavior – secrets. Birthdays. Emotions – envy, jealousy. Friendship. Frogs & toads.

Hide-and-seek ill. by author. Macmillan, 1986. ISBN 0-02-737400-9 Subj: Bedtime. Behavior – hiding. Emotions – fear. Format, unusual – board books. Games. Night. Toys – bears.

I'm not sleepy ill. by author. Macmillan, 1986. ISBN 0-02-737470-X Subj: Bedtime. Format, unusual – board books. Games. Sleep. Toys – bears.

It's your turn, Roger ill. by author. Dial, 1985. ISBN 0-8037-0198-5 Subj: Animals – pigs. Behavior – sharing. Food.

Rabbit food ill. by author. Candlewick, 1999. ISBN 0-7636-0731-2 Subj: Animals – rabbits. Family life – aunts, uncles. Food.

Rabbit rambles on ill. by author. Four Winds, 1992. ISBN 0-02-737325-8 Subj: Animals. Animals – rabbits. Behavior – boasting. Character traits – honesty. Friendship.

Ready for bed ill. by author. Macmillan, 1986. ISBN 0-02-737460-2 Subj: Bedtime. Format, unusual – board books.

Roger loses his marbles! ill. by author. Dial, 1988. ISBN 0-8037-0565-4 Subj: Animals – pigs. Birthdays. Character traits – practicality.

Roger takes charge! ill. by author. Dial, 1987. ISBN 0-8037-0121-7 Subj: Activities – babysitting. Animals – pigs. Behavior – bullying.

Teddy bears ABC ill. by author. Follett, 1975. ISBN 0-695-40540-3 Subj: ABC books. Counting, numbers. Toys – bears.

Teddy bears at the seaside by Susanna Gretz & Alison Sage; ill. by Susanna Gretz. 1st Four Winds Press ed. Four Winds, 1989. First published in . . . 1972 . . . under title The bears who went to the seaside. ISBN 0-02-738141-2 Subj: Animals – dogs. Sea & seashore. Toys – bears.

Teddy bears cure a cold by Susanna Gretz & Alison Sage; ill. by Susanna Gretz. Four Winds, 1985. ISBN 0-590-07949-2 Subj: Illness. Toys – bears.

Teddy bears go shopping ill. by author. Four Winds, 1982. ISBN 0-590-07861-5 Subj: Shopping. Toys – bears.

Teddy bears' moving day ill. by author. Four Winds, 1981. ISBN 0-590-07819-4 Subj: Moving. Toys – bears.

Teddy bears 1 – 10 ill. by author. Four Winds, 1986, 1969. ISBN 0-02-738140-4 Subj: Counting, numbers. Toys – bears.

Teddy bears stay indoors by Susanna Gretz & Alison Sage; ill. by Susanna Gretz. 2nd American ed. with new text. Four Winds, 1987. Rev. ed. of: The bears who stayed indoors. ISBN 0-02-738150-1 Subj: Activities – playing. Food. Toys – bears.

Teddy bears take the train by Susanna Gretz & Alison Sage; ill. by Susanna Gretz. Four Winds, 1987. ISBN 0-02-738170-6 Subj: Activities – traveling. Toys – bears. Trains.

Teddybears cookbook by Susanna Gretz & Alison Sage; ill. by Susanna Gretz. Doubleday, 1978. ISBN 0-385-14415-6 Subj: Activities – baking, cooking. Toys – bears.

Too dark! ill. by author. Macmillan, 1986. ISBN 0-02-737410-6 Subj: Bedtime. Emotions – fear. Format, unusual – board books. Night. Toys – bears.

Greve, Andreas. *Christopher's dream car* ill. by author. Firefly, 1991. ISBN 1-55037-169-X Subj: Automobiles. Family life – grandparents. Imagination.

Grey, Mini. *Traction Man is here* ill. by author. Knopf, 2005. ISBN 0-375-93191-0 Subj: Clothing – costumes. Family life. Toys.

The very smart pea and the princess-to-be ill. by author. Knopf, 2003. ISBN 0-375-92626-7 Subj: Folk & fairy tales. Plants. Royalty – princesses. Sleep.

Greydanus, Rose. *Animals at the zoo* ill. by Susan Hall. Troll, 1980. ISBN 0-89375-371-8 Subj: Animals. Zoos.

Bedtime story ill. by Doug Cushman. Troll, 1988. ISBN 0-8167-0996-3 Subj: Animals – bears. Bedtime. Family life – fathers.

Big red fire engine ill. by Paul Harvey. Troll, 1980. ISBN 0-89375-372-6 Subj: Careers – firefighters. Trucks.

Changing seasons ill. by Susan Hall. Troll, 1983. ISBN 0-89375-802-3 Subj: Seasons.

Climb aboard ill. by George Ulrich. Troll, 1988. ISBN 0-8167-1099-6 Subj: Animals – bears. Animals – rabbits. Sports – sailing.

Freddie the frog ill. by Tom Garcia. Troll, 1980. ISBN 0-89375-376-9 Subj: Frogs & toads.

Horses ill. by Joel Snyder. Troll, 1983. ISBN 0-89375-900-7 Subj: Animals – horses, ponies.

Let's get a pet ill. by Lynn Sweat. Troll, 1988. ISBN 0-8167-0986-6 Subj: Pets.

Let's pretend ill. by Marsha Winborn. Troll, 1981. ISBN 0-8937-5545-1 Subj: Imagination.

My secret hiding place ill. by Paul Harvey. Troll, 1980. ISBN 0-89375-383-1 Subj: Behavior – hiding.

Someone's baby-sitting ill. by Don Page. Troll, 1981. ISBN 0-8937-5515-X Subj: Holidays – Valentine's Day.

Susie goes shopping ill. by Margot Apple. Troll, 1980. ISBN 0-89375-389-0 Subj: Shopping.

Tree house fun ill. by Chris L. Demarest. Troll, 1980. ISBN 0-89375-391-2 Subj: Homes, houses. Trees.

Trouble in space ill. by Don Page. Troll, 1981. ISBN 0-8937-5517-6 Subj: Space & space ships. Toys – bears.

Willie the slowpoke ill. by Andrea Eberbach. Troll, 1980. ISBN 0-89375-394-7 Subj: Behavior – hurrying.

Grieg, E. H. (Edvard Hagerup). *E. H. Grieg's Peer Gynt* adapt. by Makoto Oishi; trans. by Ann Brannen; ill. by Yoshiharu Suzuki. Gakken, 1971. Subj: Folk & fairy tales. Foreign lands – Norway.

Griese, Arnold A. *Anna's Athabaskan summer* ill. by Charles Ragins. Boyds Mills, 1995. ISBN 1-56397-232-8 Subj: Alaska. Family life. Foreign lands – Arctic. Indians of North America – Athabaskan. Seasons – summer.

Griessman, Annette. *Jenny's prayer* ill. by Mary Anne Lard. Morehouse, 1998. ISBN 0-8192-1746-8 Subj: Animals – cats. Pets. Religion.

Griest, Lisa. *Lost at the White House: a 1909 Easter story* ill. by Andrea Shine. Carolrhoda, 1994. ISBN 0-87614-726-0 Subj: Holidays – Easter. U.S. history.

Griest, Virginia. *In between* ill. by Monica Wellington. Dutton, 1989. ISBN 0-525-44521-8 Subj: Concepts.

Grifalconi, Ann. *The bravest flute: a story of courage in the Mayan tradition* ill. by author. Little, 1994. ISBN 0-316-32878-2 Subj: Foreign lands – Mexico. Holidays – New Year's. Indians of Central America – Maya.

City rhythms ill. by author. Bobbs-Merrill, 1965. Subj: Cities, towns. Ethnic groups in the U.S. – African Americans.

Darkness and the butterfly ill. by author. Little, 1987. ISBN 0-316-32863-4 Subj: Emotions – fear. Foreign lands – Africa. Insects – butterflies, caterpillars. Night.

Electric Yancy ill. by author. Lothrop, 1997. ISBN 0-688-13188-3 Subj: Books, reading. Ethnic groups in the U.S. – African Americans. Imagination.

Flyaway girl ill. by author. Little, 1992. ISBN 0-316-32866-9 Subj: Behavior – growing up. Foreign lands – Africa. Rivers.

Kinda blue ill. by author. Little, 1993. ISBN 0-316-32869-3 Subj: Emotions. Ethnic groups in the U.S. – African Americans. Family life – aunts, uncles. Farms.

Osa's pride ill. by author. Little, 1990. ISBN 0-316-32865-0 Subj: Character traits – pride. Family life – grandmothers. Foreign lands – Africa.

Tiny's hat ill. by author. HarperCollins, 1999. ISBN 0-06-027655-X Subj: Clothing – hats. Emotions – grief. Ethnic groups in the U.S. – African Americans. Family life – fathers.

The toy trumpet ill. by author. Little, 1995. ISBN 0-316-32858-8 Subj: Foreign lands – Mexico. Music. Musical instruments – trumpets. Toys.

The village of round and square houses ill. by author. Little, 1986. ISBN 0-316-32862-6 Subj: Caldecott award honor books. Folk & fairy tales. Foreign lands – Africa. Volcanoes.

The village that vanished ill. by Kadir Nelson. Dial, 2002. ISBN 0-8037-2623-6 Subj: Behavior – hiding. Ethnic groups in the U.S. – African Americans. Foreign lands – Africa. Slavery.

Griff (Andrew Griffin). *Shark-mad Stanley* ill. by author. Hyperion, 2000. ISBN 0-7868-0594-3 Subj: Fish – sharks. Imagination. Pets.

Griffen, Elizabeth. *A dog's book of bugs* ill. by Peter Parnall. Atheneum, 1967. Subj: Insects.

Griffin, Andrew. *see* Griff (Andrew Griffin)

Griffin, Kitty. *Cowboy Sam and those confounded secrets* by Kitty Griffin & Kathy Combs; ill. by Mike Wohnoutka. Clarion, 2001. ISBN 0-618-08854-7 Subj: Behavior – secrets. Humorous stories. U.S. history – frontier & pioneer life.

The foot-stomping adventures of Clementine Sweet by Kitty Griffin & Kathy Combs; ill. by Mike Wohnoutka. Clarion, 2004. ISBN 0-618-24746-7 Subj: Behavior. Humorous stories. Tall tales. Weather – tornadoes.

Griffith, Helen V. *Alex and the cat* ill. by Joseph Low. Greenwillow, 1982. ISBN 0-688-00421-0 Subj: Animals – cats. Animals – dogs.

Alex remembers ill. by Donald Carrick. Greenwillow, 1983. ISBN 0-688-01801-7 Subj: Animals – cats. Animals – dogs. Memories, memory. Moon. Seasons – fall.

Dream meadow ill. by Nancy Barnet. Greenwillow, 1994. ISBN 0-688-12294-9 Subj: Animals – dogs. Death. Old age.

Emily and the enchanted frog ill. by Susan Condie Lamb. Greenwillow, 1989. ISBN 0-688-08484-2 Subj: Behavior – wishing. Crustaceans. Frogs & toads.

Georgia music ill. by James Stevenson. Greenwillow, 1986. ISBN 0-688-06072-2 Subj: Family life – grandfathers. Gardens, gardening. Music. Musical instruments – harmonicas. Nature. Old age. Seasons – summer.

Grandaddy's place ill. by James Stevenson. Greenwillow, 1987. ISBN 0-688-06254-7 Subj: Animals. Country. Family life – grandfathers. Sports – fishing.

Grandaddy's stars ill. by James Stevenson. Greenwillow, 1995. ISBN 0-688-13655-9 Subj: Cities, towns. Family life – grandfathers.

How many candles? ill. by Sonja Lamut. Greenwillow, 1999. ISBN 0-688-16259-2 Subj: Animals. Birthdays. Old age.

Mine will, said John ill. by Muriel Batherman. Greenwillow, 1980. ISBN 0-688-84267-4 Subj: Animals – dogs. Family life. Pets.

More Alex and the cat ill. by Donald Carrick. Greenwillow, 1983. ISBN 0-688-02292-8 Subj: Animals – cats. Animals – dogs.

Nata ill. by Nancy Tafuri. Greenwillow, 1985. ISBN 0-688-04977-X Subj: Behavior – bad day. Fairies.

Pluck's dreams ill. by Susan Condie Lamb. Greenwillow, 1990. ISBN 0-688-08813-9 Subj: Animals – dogs. Dreams.

Grigg, Carol. *The singing snow bear* ill. by author. Houghton Mifflin, 1999. ISBN 0-395-94223-3 Subj: Activities – singing. Animals – polar bears. Animals – whales. Foreign lands – Arctic. Music.

Grimes, Nikki. *At break of day* ill. by Paul Morin. Eerdmans, 1995. ISBN 0-8028-5104-5 Subj: Creation. Religion.

Baby's bedtime ill. by Sylvia Walker. Western, 1995. ISBN 0-307-12872-5 Subj: Babies. Bedtime. Ethnic groups in the U.S. – African Americans. Format, unusual – board books. Rhyming text.

C is for city by Nikki Grimes & Pat Cummings; ill. by Pat Cummings. Lothrop, 1994. ISBN 0-688-11809-7 Subj: ABC books. Cities, towns. Rhyming text.

Come Sunday ill. by Michael Bryant. Eerdmans, 1996. ISBN 0-8028-5108-8 Subj: Ethnic groups in the U.S. – African Americans. Family life. Poetry. Religion.

Danitra Brown leaves town ill. by Floyd Cooper. Lothrop, 1996. ISBN 0-688-13156-5 Subj: Cities, towns. Country. Ethnic groups in the U.S. – African Americans. Friendship. Poetry.

From a child's heart ill. by Brenda Joysmith. Just Us Books, 1993. ISBN 0-940975-44-0 Subj: Ethnic groups in the U.S. – African Americans. Poetry. Religion.

Is it far to Zanzibar? poems about Tanzania ill. by Betsy Lewin. Lothrop, 2000. ISBN 0-688-13158-1 Subj: Foreign lands – Tanzania. Foreign lands – Zanzibar. Poetry.

It's raining laughter photos by Myles C. Pinkney. Dial, 1997. ISBN 0-8037-2004-1 Subj: Behavior – growing up. Ethnic groups in the U.S. – African Americans. Poetry.

Meet Danitra Brown ill. by Floyd Cooper. Lothrop, 1994. ISBN 0-688-12074-1 Subj: Cities, towns. Ethnic groups in the U.S. – African Americans. Family life. Friendship. Poetry.

Minnie's new friend ill. by Peter Emslie & Darren Hunt. Western, 1992. ISBN 0-307-11524-0 Subj: Animals. Friendship.

My man Blue ill. by Jerome Lagarrigue. Dial, 1999. ISBN 0-8037-2326-1 Subj: Ethnic groups in the U.S. – African Americans. Family life – mothers. Friendship. Poetry. Self-concept.

A pocketful of poems ill. by Javaka Steptoe. Clarion, 2001. ISBN 0-395-93868-6 Subj: Cities, towns. Nature. Poetry.

Shoe magic ill. by Terry Widener. Orchard, 2000. ISBN 0-531-33286-1 Subj: Clothing – shoes. Poetry.

Someone's baby-sitting ill. by Sue DiCicco. Golden Bks., 1997. ISBN 0-307-12634-X Subj: Activities – babysitting. Behavior. Toys.

Someone's fighting ill. by Darrell Baker. Golden Bks., 1997. ISBN 0-307-12635-8 Subj: Behavior – fighting, arguing. Friendship. Toys.

Something on my mind by Nikki Grimes & Tom Feelings; ill. by Tom Feelings. Dial, 1978. ISBN 0-8037-8225-X Subj: Behavior – growing up. Emotions. Poetry.

When Daddy prays ill. by Tim Ladwig. Eerdmans, 2002. ISBN 0-8028-5152-5 Subj: Ethnic groups in the U.S. – African Americans. Family life – fathers. Poetry. Religion.

Wild, wild hair ill. by George Ford. Scholastic, 1996. ISBN 0-590-26590-3 Subj: Ethnic groups in the U.S. – African Americans. Hair. Rhyming text.

Grimm, Edward. *The doorman* ill. by Ted Lewin. Orchard, 2000. ISBN 0-531-33280-2 Subj: Careers – doormen. Death. Emotions – grief. Homes, houses.

Grimm, Jacob. *Battle of the beasts: a tale of epic proportions from the brothers Grimm* (Wallis, Diz)

The bear and the kingbird by Jacob & Wilhelm Grimm; trans. by Lore Segal; ill. by Chris Conover. Farrar, 1979. ISBN 0-374-30618-4 Subj: Animals – bears. Birds. Folk & fairy tales.

The bearskinner by Jacob & Wilhelm Grimm; ill. by Felix Hoffmann. Atheneum, 1978. Translation of Der Bärenhuäuter. ISBN 0-689-50123-4 Subj: Devil. Folk & fairy tales.

The brave little seamstress (Osborne, Mary Pope)

The brave little tailor by Jacob & Wilhelm Grimm; ill. by Mark Corcoran. Troll, 1979. ISBN 0-89375-137-5 Subj: Careers – tailors. Character traits – bravery. Folk & fairy tales. Foreign lands – Germany. Giants.

The brave little tailor retold & ill. by Olga Dugina & Andrej Dugin. Abrams, 2000. ISBN 0-8109-4113-9 Subj: Careers – tailors. Character traits – bravery. Folk & fairy tales. Foreign lands – Germany. Giants.

The brave little tailor by Jacob & Wilhelm Grimm; adapt. by Robert D. San Souci; ill. by Daniel San Souci. Doubleday, 1982. ISBN 0-385-17570-1 Subj: Careers – tailors. Character traits – bravery. Folk & fairy tales. Foreign lands – Germany. Giants.

The brave little tailor by Jacob & Wilhelm Grimm; retold by Eric Blair; ill. by David Shaw. Picture Window, 2004. ISBN 1-4048-0315-7 Subj: Careers – tailors. Character traits – bravery. Folk & fairy tales. Foreign lands – Germany. Giants.

The brave little tailor by Jacob & Wilhelm Grimm; trans. by Anthea Bell; ill. by Svend Otto S. Larousse, 1979. ISBN 0-88332-116-5 Subj: Careers – tailors. Character traits – bravery. Folk & fairy tales. Foreign lands – Germany. Giants.

The brave little tailor by Jacob & Wilhelm Grimm; trans. by Anthea Bell; ill. by Eve Tharlet. Picture Book Studio, 1989. ISBN 0-88708-091-X Subj: Careers – tailors. Character traits – bravery. Folk & fairy tales. Foreign lands – Germany. Giants.

The brave little tailor by Jacob & Wilhelm Grimm; retold by Peggy Thomson; ill. by James Warhola. S&S, 1992. ISBN 0-671-73736-8 Subj: Careers – tailors. Character traits – bravery. Folk & fairy tales. Foreign lands – Germany. Giants.

The Bremen town band retold & ill. by Brian Wildsmith. Oxford Univ. Pr., 1999. ISBN 0-19-279034-X Subj: Animals. Careers – musicians. Crime. Folk & fairy tales. Old age.

The Bremen town musicians by Jacob & Wilhelm Grimm; retold & ill. by Donna Diamond. Delacorte, 1981. ISBN 0-440-00827-1 Subj: Animals. Careers – musicians. Crime. Folk & fairy tales. Old age.

The Bremen town musicians by Jacob & Wilhelm Grimm; retold by Eric Blair; ill. by Bill Dickson. Picture Window, 2004. ISBN 1-4048-0310-6 Subj: Animals. Careers – musicians. Crime. Folk & fairy tales. Old age.

The Bremen town musicians by Jacob & Wilhelm Grimm; trans. by Elizabeth Shub; ill. by Janina Domanska. Greenwillow, 1980. ISBN 0-688-84233-X Subj: Animals. Careers – musicians. Crime. Folk & fairy tales. Old age.

The Bremen town musicians by Jacob & Wilhelm Grimm; ill. by Paul Galdone. McGraw-Hill, 1968. Tr. of Der Bremer Stadtmusikanten. Subj: Animals. Careers – musicians. Crime. Folk & fairy tales. Old age.

The Bremen town musicians by Jacob & Wilhelm Grimm; retold & ill. by David Johnson. Macmillan, 1997. ISBN 0-689-80236-6 Subj: Animals. Careers – musicians. Crime. Folk & fairy tales. Old age.

Bremen town musicians by Jacob & Wilhelm Grimm; trans. by Anthea Bell; ill. by Josef Palecek. Picture Book Studio, 1988. ISBN 0-88708-071-5 Subj: Animals. Careers – musicians. Crime. Folk & fairy tales. Old age.

The Bremen town musicians by Jacob & Wilhelm Grimm; retold & ill. by Ilse Plume. Doubleday, 1980. ISBN 0-385-15162-4 Subj: Animals. Careers – musicians. Crime. Folk & fairy tales. Old age.

The Bremen town musicians by Jacob & Wilhelm Grimm; retold & ill. by Janet Stevens. Holiday, 1992. ISBN 0-8234-0939-2 Subj: Animals. Careers – musicians. Crime. Folk & fairy tales. Old age.

The Bremen town musicians by Jacob & Wilhelm Grimm; trans. by Anthea Bell; ill. by Bernadette Watts. North-South, 1992. ISBN 1-55858-148-0 Subj: Animals. Careers – musicians. Crime. Folk & fairy tales. Old age.

Cinderella by Jacob & Wilhelm Grimm; retold & ill. by Nonny Hogrogian. Greenwillow, 1981. ISBN 0-688-84299-2 Subj: Family life – stepfamilies. Folk & fairy tales. Royalty – princes. Sibling rivalry.

Cinderella by Jacob & Wilhelm Grimm; trans. by Anne Rogers; ill. by Svend Otto S. Larousse, 1978. ISBN 0-88332-093-2 Subj: Family life – stepfamilies. Folk & fairy tales. Royalty – princes. Sibling rivalry.

Clever Kate by Jacob & Wilhelm Grimm; adapt. by Elizabeth Shub; ill. by Anita Lobel. Macmillan, 1973. ISBN 0-02-782490-X Subj: Folk & fairy tales. Humorous stories.

The devil with the green hairs by Jacob & Wilhelm Grimm; retold & ill. by Nonny Hogrogian. Knopf, 1983. ISBN 0-394-95560-9 Subj: Devil. Folk & fairy tales.

The diary of Hansel and Gretel (Moerbeek, Kees)

Dick Bruna's Little Red Riding Hood (Bruna, Dick)

Dick Bruna's Snow-White and the seven dwarfs (Bruna, Dick)

The donkey prince by Jacob & Wilhelm Grimm; adapt. by M. Jean Craig; ill. by Barbara Cooney. Doubleday, 1977. ISBN 0-385-11295-5 Subj: Animals – donkeys. Folk & fairy tales. Magic. Royalty – princes. Wizards.

The earth gnome by Jacob & Wilhelm Grimm; trans. by Wanda Gág; ill. by Margot Tomes. Coward, 1985. ISBN 0-698-20618-5 Subj: Folk & fairy tales. Magic. Mythical creatures – gnomes. Royalty.

The elves and the shoemaker by Jacob & Wilhelm Grimm; retold by Marcia Leonard; ill. by Doug Cushman. Silver Pr., 1990. ISBN 0-671-69347-6 Subj: Careers – shoemakers. Character traits – helpfulness. Folk & fairy tales. Foreign lands – Germany. Mythical creatures – elves. Picture puzzles.

The elves and the shoemaker by Jacob & Wilhelm Grimm; ill. by Paul Galdone. Clarion, 1984. Based on Lucy Crane's tr. from the German. Adaption of Wichtelmänner. ISBN 0-89919-226-2 Subj: Careers – shoemakers. Character traits – helpfulness. Folk & fairy tales. Foreign lands – Germany. Mythical creatures – elves.

The elves and the shoemaker by Jacob & Wilhelm Grimm; ill. by Margaret Walty. Barefoot, 1998. ISBN 1-901223-69-8 Subj: Careers – shoemakers. Character traits – helpfulness. Folk & fairy tales. Foreign lands – Germany. Mythical creatures – elves.

The elves and the shoemaker by Jacob & Wilhelm Grimm; adapt. & ill. by Bernadette Watts. North-South, 1997, 1986. ISBN 1-55858-768-3 Subj: Careers – shoemakers. Character traits – helpfulness. Folk & fairy tales. Foreign lands – Germany. Mythical creatures – elves.

The falling stars by Jacob & Wilhelm Grimm; ill. by Eugen Sopko. Holt, 1985. ISBN 0-03-005742-6 Subj: Character traits – generosity. Clothing. Folk & fairy tales.

The fisherman and his wife retold by Rosemary Wells; ill. by Eleanor Hubbard. Dial, 1998. ISBN 0-8037-1851-9 Subj: Animals – cats. Behavior – greed. Folk & fairy tales.

The fisherman and his wife by Jacob & Wilhelm Grimm; trans. by Elizabeth Shub; ill. by Monika Laimgruber. Greenwillow, 1979. ISBN 0-688-86003-6 Subj: Behavior – greed. Folk & fairy tales.

The fisherman and his wife by Jacob & Wilhelm Grimm; trans. from German by Anthea Bell; ill. by Alan Marks. Picture Book Studio, 1989. ISBN 0-88708-072-3 Subj: Behavior – greed. Folk & fairy tales.

The fisherman and his wife by Jacob & Wilhelm Grimm; retold by Eric Blair; ill. by Todd Ouren. Picture Window, 2004. ISBN 1-4048-0317-3 Subj: Behavior – greed. Folk & fairy tales.

The fisherman and his wife by Jacob & Wilhelm Grimm; ill. by Laurinda Spear. Rizzoli, 1992. ISBN 0-8478-1370-3 Subj: Behavior – greed. Folk & fairy tales.

The fisherman and his wife by Jacob & Wilhelm Grimm; adapt. by John Warren Stewig; ill. by Margot Tomes. Holiday, 1988. ISBN 0-8234-0714-4 Subj: Behavior – greed. Folk & fairy tales.

The fisherman and his wife by Jacob & Wilhelm Grimm; trans. by Randall Jarrell; ill. by Margot Zemach. Farrar, 1980. ISBN 0-374-32340-2 Subj: Behavior – greed. Folk & fairy tales.

Fitcher's bird photos by Cindy Sherman. Rizzoli, 1992. ISBN 0-8478-1567-6 Subj: Folk & fairy tales. Magic.

The four clever brothers by Jacob & Wilhelm Grimm; ill. by Felix Hoffmann. Harcourt, 1967. ISBN 0-15-229100-8 Subj: Character traits – cleverness. Dragons. Folk & fairy tales.

The four gallant sisters (Kimmel, Eric A.)

The frog prince trans. by Lucy Crane; adapt. & ill. by Paul Galdone. McGraw-Hill, 1974. An adapt. of the story that appeared in Household stories by the Brothers Grimm, trans. by Lucy Crane. ISBN 0-07-022689-X Subj: Folk & fairy tales. Frogs & toads. Kissing. Royalty – princes. Royalty – princesses.

The frog prince by Jacob & Wilhelm Grimm; retold by Eric Blair; ill. by Todd Ouren. Picture Window, 2004. ISBN 1-4048-0313-0 Subj: Folk & fairy tales. Frogs & toads. Royalty – princes. Royalty – princesses.

The frog prince: or Iron Henry trans. from German by Naomi Lewis; ill. by Binette Schroeder. North-South, 1989. ISBN 1-55858-015-8 Subj: Folk & fairy tales. Frogs & toads. Kissing. Royalty – princes. Royalty – princesses.

The glass mountain adapt. by Diane Wolkstein; ill. by Louisa Bauer. Morrow, 1999. Adapt. from the Grimm Brothers' story Old Rinkrank, also known as The glass mountain. ISBN 0-688-14848-4 Subj: Folk & fairy tales. Mythical creatures – trolls.

The glass mountain by Jacob & Wilhelm Grimm; adapt. & ill. by Nonny Hogrogian. Knopf, 1985. Originally titled The raven. ISBN 0-394-96724-0 Subj: Folk & fairy tales. Giants.

Godfather Cat and Mousie by Jacob & Wilhelm Grimm; adapt. by Doris Orgel; ill. by Ann Schweninger. Macmillan, 1986. ISBN 0-02-768690-6 Subj: Animals – cats. Animals – mice. Folk & fairy tales.

The golden bird by Jacob & Wilhelm Grimm; retold by Neil Philip; ill. by Isabelle Brent. Little, 1995. ISBN 0-316-70522-5 Subj: Animals – foxes. Behavior – greed. Birds. Folk & fairy tales. Royalty – kings. Royalty – princes.

The golden bird: and other fairy tales by Jacob & Wilhelm Grimm; trans. by Randall Jarrell; ill. by Sandro Nardini. Macmillan, 1962. Subj: Animals – foxes. Behavior – greed. Birds. Folk & fairy tales. Royalty – kings. Royalty – princes.

The golden goose by Jacob & Wilhelm Grimm; trans. by Anthea Bell; ill. by Dorothée Duntze. Holt, 1988. ISBN 3-85539-004-5 Subj: Character traits – kindness. Folk & fairy tales. Humorous stories. Royalty – princesses.

The golden goose retold & ill. by Dennis McDermott. Morrow, 2000. ISBN 0-688-11403-2 Subj: Behavior – greed. Birds – geese. Character traits – kindness. Folk & fairy tales. Royalty – princesses.

The golden goose by Jacob & Wilhelm Grimm; adapt. by Susan Saunders; ill. by Isadore Seltzer. Scholastic, 1988. ISBN 0-590-41544-1 Subj: Character traits – kindness. Folk & fairy tales. Humorous stories. Royalty – princesses.

The golden goose by Jacob & Wilhelm Grimm; ill. by Martin Ursell; text by Linda M. Jennings. Silver Burdett, 1985. ISBN 0-382-09147-7 Subj: Character traits – kindness. Folk & fairy tales. Humorous stories. Royalty – princesses.

The goose girl by Jacob & Wilhelm Grimm; trans. by Anthea Bell; ill. by Sabine Bruntjen. Holt, 1988. ISBN 3-85539-003-7 Subj: Folk & fairy tales. Royalty. Weddings.

The goose girl: a story from the Brothers Grimm retold by Eric A. Kimmel; ill. by Robert Sauber. Holiday, 1995. ISBN 0-8234-1074-9 Subj: Folk & fairy tales. Royalty. Weddings.

Grimm Tom Thumb (Tom Thumb)

Hans in luck by Jacob & Wilhelm Grimm; retold & ill. by Paul Galdone. Parents' Magazine Pr., 1979. Translation of Hans in Glück. ISBN 0-8193-1011-5 Subj: Character traits – foolishness. Character traits – luck. Folk & fairy tales.

Hans in luck by Jacob & Wilhelm Grimm; ed. & ill. by Felix Hoffmann. Atheneum, 1975. Translation of Hans in Glück. ISBN 0-689-50020-3 Subj: Character traits – foolishness. Character traits – luck. Folk & fairy tales.

Hansel and Gretel by Jacob & Wilhelm Grimm; trans. by Charles Scribner, Jr.; ill. by Adrienne Adams. Scribners, 1975. ISBN 0-684-14422-X Subj: Behavior – lost. Folk & fairy tales. Forest, woods. Witches.

Hansel and Gretel by Jacob & Wilhelm Grimm; ill. by Anthony Browne. Watts, 1982. ISBN 0-531-04062-3 Subj: Behavior – lost. Folk & fairy tales. Forest, woods. Witches.

Hansel and Gretel by Jacob & Wilhelm Grimm; ill. by Susan Jeffers. Dial, 1980. ISBN 0-8037-3491-3 Subj: Behavior – lost. Folk & fairy tales. Forest, woods. Witches.

Hansel and Gretel by Jacob & Wilhelm Grimm; ill. by Winslow P. Pels. Scholastic, 1988. ISBN 0-590-41793-2 Subj: Behavior – lost. Folk & fairy tales. Forest, woods. Witches.

Hansel and Gretel by Jacob & Wilhelm Grimm; retold & ill. by Jane Ray. Candlewick, 1997. ISBN 0-7636-0358-9 Subj: Behavior – lost. Folk & fairy tales. Forest, woods. Witches.

Hansel and Gretel by Jacob & Wilhelm Grimm; trans. by Leland Northam; adapt. by M. Eulalia Valeri; ill. by Conxita Rodriguez.

Silver Burdett, 1985. ISBN 0-392-09072-1 Subj: Behavior – lost. Folk & fairy tales. Forest, woods. Witches. Wordless.

Hansel and Gretel by Jacob & Wilhelm Grimm; retold by Dom DeLuise; ill. by Christopher Santoro. S&S, 1997. ISBN 0-689-81202-7 Subj: Behavior – lost. Folk & fairy tales. Forest, woods. Witches.

Hansel and Gretel by Jacob & Wilhelm Grimm; ill. by John Wallner. Prentice-Hall, 1985. ISBN 0-13-383654-1 Subj: Behavior – lost. Folk & fairy tales. Forest, woods. Witches.

Hansel and Gretel by Jacob & Wilhelm Grimm; retold by Eric Blair; ill. by Claudia Wolf. Picture Window, 2004. ISBN 1-4048-0316-5 Subj: Behavior – lost. Folk & fairy tales. Forest, woods. Witches.

Hansel and Gretel by Jacob & Wilhelm Grimm; retold by Rika Lesser; ill. by Paul O. Zelinsky. Dodd, 1984. ISBN 0-396-08449-4 Subj: Behavior – lost. Caldecott award honor books. Folk & fairy tales. Forest, woods. Witches.

Hansel and Gretel by Jacob & Wilhelm Grimm; trans. from German by Elizabeth D. Crawford; ill. by Lisbeth Zwerger. Morrow, 1980. ISBN 0-688-32198-4 Subj: Behavior – lost. Folk & fairy tales. Forest, woods. Witches.

The horse, the fox, and the lion by Jacob & Wilhelm Grimm; ill. by Paul Galdone. Seabury Pr., 1968. Adapt. from The fox and the horse [Der Fuchs und das Pferd]. Subj: Animals – dogs. Animals – foxes. Animals – horses, ponies. Animals – lions. Behavior – trickery. Folk & fairy tales. Old age.

Iron Hans by Jacob & Wilhelm Grimm; ill. by Marilee Heyer. Viking, 1993. ISBN 0-670-81741-4 Subj: Folk & fairy tales. Foreign lands – Germany. Royalty – kings. Royalty – princes.

Iron John by Jacob & Wilhelm Grimm; adapt. by Eric A. Kimmel; ill. by Trina Schart Hyman. Holiday, 1994. ISBN 0-8234-1073-0 Subj: Folk & fairy tales. Foreign lands – Germany. Royalty – kings. Royalty – princes.

Iron John by Jacob & Wilhelm Grimm; as told by Marianna Mayer; ill. by Winslow Pels. Morrow, 1998. ISBN 0-688-11555-1 Subj: Folk & fairy tales. Foreign lands – Germany. Royalty – kings. Royalty – princes.

Jack in luck by Jacob & Wilhelm Grimm; trans. & adapt. by Anthea Bell; ill. by Eve Tharlet. Picture Book Studio, 1992. ISBN 0-88708-249-1 Subj: Character traits – foolishness. Folk & fairy tales.

Jorinda and Joringel by Jacob & Wilhelm Grimm; trans. by Elizabeth Shub; ill. by Adrienne Adams. Scribners, 1968. Subj: Folk & fairy tales. Witches.

Jorinda and Joringel by Jacob & Wilhelm Grimm; adapt. by Naomi Lewis; ill. by Jutta Ash. David & Charles, 1987. ISBN 0-86264-064-4 Subj: Folk & fairy tales. Witches.

Jorinda and Joringel by Jacob & Wilhelm Grimm; retold by Wanda Gág; ill. by Margot Tomes. Coward, 1978. ISBN 0-698-20440-9 Subj: Folk & fairy tales. Witches.

King Grisly-Beard by Jacob & Wilhelm Grimm; trans. by Edgar Taylor; ill. by Maurice Sendak. Farrar, 1973. 1823 translation. ISBN 0-374-34134-6 Subj: Character traits – conceit. Folk & fairy tales. Royalty. Theater.

Little brother and little sister by Jacob & Wilhelm Grimm; trans. & adapt. by Anthea Bell; ill. by Bernadette Watts. North-South, 1996. ISBN 1-55858-589-3 Subj: Character traits – loyalty. Family life – stepfamilies. Folk & fairy tales.

Little red cap by Jacob & Wilhelm Grimm; trans. from German by Elizabeth D. Crawford; ill. by Lisbeth Zwerger. Morrow, 1983. ISBN 0-688-01715-0 Subj: Animals – wolves. Behavior – talking to strangers. Folk & fairy tales.

Little Red Riding Hood by Jacob & Wilhelm Grimm; adapt. by Elizabeth & Katherine Gant; ill. by Frank E. Aloise. Abingdon, 1969. Adapt. and music based on retelling of Rotkäppchen.

Incl. melodies with texts, with piano acc. Subj: Animals – wolves. Behavior – talking to strangers. Folk & fairy tales.

Little Red Riding Hood by Jacob & Wilhelm Grimm; adapt. by Margaret Hillert; ill. by Gwen Connelly. Follett, 1982. ISBN 0-695-41543-3 Subj: Animals – wolves. Behavior – talking to strangers. Folk & fairy tales.

Little Red Riding Hood by Jacob & Wilhelm Grimm; ill. by Paul Galdone. McGraw-Hill, 1974. Adapt. from the retelling of Rotkäppchen. ISBN 0-07-022732-2 Subj: Animals – wolves. Behavior – talking to strangers. Folk & fairy tales.

Little Red Riding Hood by Jacob & Wilhelm Grimm; ill. by John S. Goodall. Macmillan, 1988. ISBN 0-689-50457-8 Subj: Animals. Animals – mice. Animals – wolves. Behavior – talking to strangers. Folk & fairy tales. Format, unusual. Wordless.

Little Red Riding Hood by Jacob & Wilhelm Grimm; retold & ill. by Trina Schart Hyman. Holiday, 1983. ISBN 0-8234-0470-6 Subj: Animals – wolves. Behavior – talking to strangers. Caldecott award honor books. Folk & fairy tales.

Little Red Riding Hood by Jacob & Wilhelm Grimm; adapt. & ill. by Mireille Levert. Firefly, 1996. ISBN 0-88899-226-2 Subj: Animals – wolves. Behavior – talking to strangers. Folk & fairy tales.

Little Red Riding Hood by Jacob & Wilhelm Grimm; retold & ill. by David M. McPhail. Scholastic, 1995. ISBN 0-590-48116-9 Subj: Animals – wolves. Behavior – talking to strangers. Folk & fairy tales.

Little Red Riding Hood: a fairy tale by Grimm ill. by Jean-François Martin. Abbeville, 1998. ISBN 0-7892-0421-5 Subj: Animals – wolves. Behavior – talking to strangers. Folk & fairy tales.

Little Red Riding Hood by Jacob & Wilhelm Grimm; ill. by Bernadette Watts. Collins-World, 1969. Subj: Animals – wolves. Behavior – talking to strangers. Folk & fairy tales.

Lucky Hans by Jacob & Wilhelm Grimm; trans. by Jock J. Curle; ill. by Eugen Sopko. Holt, 1986. ISBN 0-8050-0009-7 Subj: Character traits – foolishness. Character traits – luck. Folk & fairy tales.

Mother Holly by Jacob & Wilhelm Grimm; ill. by Bernadette Watts. Crowell, 1972. Based on the Grimm brothers' Frau Holle. ISBN 0-690-56364-7 Subj: Behavior – greed. Character traits – helpfulness. Character traits – laziness. Folk & fairy tales.

Mrs. Fox's wedding by Jacob & Wilhelm Grimm; retold by Sara & Stephen Corrin; ill. by Errol Le Cain. Doubleday, 1980. ISBN 0-385-15762-2 Subj: Animals – foxes. Counting, numbers. Folk & fairy tales. Weddings.

The musicians of Bremen by Jacob & Wilhelm Grimm; retold by Jane Yolen; ill. by John Segal. S&S, 1996. ISBN 0-689-51117-3 Subj: Animals. Careers – musicians. Crime. Folk & fairy tales. Old age.

The musicians of Bremen by Jacob & Wilhelm Grimm; trans. by Anne Rogers; ill. by Svend Otto S. Larousse, 1974. ISBN 0-88332-060-6 Subj: Animals. Careers – musicians. Crime. Folk & fairy tales. Old age.

The musicians of Bremen by Jacob & Wilhelm Grimm; ill. by Martin Ursell; text by Linda M. Jennings. Silver Burdett, 1985. ISBN 0-382-09155-8 Subj: Animals. Careers – musicians. Crime. Folk & fairy tales. Old age.

Nanny goat and the seven little kids by Jacob & Wilhelm Grimm; retold by Eric A. Kimmel; ill. by Janet Stevens. Holiday, 1990. An adaptation of: The wolf and the seven little kids. ISBN 0-8234-0789-6 Subj: Animals – goats. Animals – wolves. Folk & fairy tales.

One gift deserves another by Jacob & Wilhelm Grimm; adapt. by Joanne Oppenheim; ill. by Bo Zaunders. Dutton, 1992. ISBN 0-525-44975-2 Subj: Behavior – greed. Character traits – generosity. Family life – brothers. Gifts.

Ouch! a tale from Grimm (Babbitt, Natalie)

The princess and the frog by Jacob & Wilhelm Grimm; retold & ill. by Rachel Isadora. Greenwillow, 1989. ISBN 0-688-06374-8 Subj: Character traits – willfulness. Folk & fairy tales. Frogs & toads. Royalty – princes. Royalty – princesses.

The princess and the frog by Jacob & Wilhelm Grimm; retold & ill. by Will Eisner. Nantier Beall Minoustchine, 1999. ISBN 1-56163-244-9 Subj: Character traits – willfulness. Folk & fairy tales. Frogs & toads. Royalty – princes. Royalty – princesses.

The rabbit's bride retold & ill. by Holly Meade. Cavendish, 2001. ISBN 0-7614-5081-5 Subj: Animals – rabbits. Character traits – cleverness. Folk & fairy tales. Foreign lands – Germany.

Rapunzel by Jacob & Wilhelm Grimm; retold & ill. by Jutta Ash. Holt, 1982. ISBN 0-03-061219-5 Subj: Folk & fairy tales. Hair. Royalty – princes. Witches.

Rapunzel by Jacob & Wilhelm Grimm; retold by Marianna Mayer; ill. by Sheilah Beckett. Western, 1991. ISBN 0-307-00207-1 Subj: Folk & fairy tales. Hair. Royalty – princes. Witches.

Rapunzel by Jacob & Wilhelm Grimm; ill. by Bert Dodson. Troll, 1979. ISBN 0-89375-135-9 Subj: Folk & fairy tales. Hair. Royalty – princes. Witches.

Rapunzel: a fairy tale by Jacob & Wilhelm Grimm; ill. by Maja Dusíková; trans. by Anthea Bell. North-South, 1997. ISBN 1-55858-685-7 Subj: Folk & fairy tales. Hair. Royalty – princes. Witches.

Rapunzel by Jacob & Wilhelm Grimm; ill. by Michael Hague. Creative Ed., 1984. ISBN 0-87191-936-2 Subj: Folk & fairy tales. Hair. Royalty – princes. Witches.

Rapunzel by Jacob & Wilhelm Grimm; retold by Barbara Rogasky; ill. by Trina Schart Hyman. Holiday, 1982. ISBN 0-8234-0454-4 Subj: Folk & fairy tales. Hair. Royalty – princes. Witches.

Rapunzel by Jacob & Wilhelm Grimm; retold by Amy Ehrlich; ill. by Kris Waldherr. Dial, 1989. ISBN 0-8037-0655-3 Subj: Folk & fairy tales. Hair. Royalty – princes. Witches.

Rapunzel by Jacob & Wilhelm Grimm; adapt. & ill. by Bernadette Watts. HarperCollins, 1975. ISBN 0-690-00980-1 Subj: Folk & fairy tales. Hair. Royalty – princes. Witches.

Rapunzel by Jacob & Wilhelm Grimm; retold & ill. by Paul O. Zelinsky. Dutton, 1997. ISBN 0-525-45607-4 Subj: Caldecott award books. Folk & fairy tales. Hair. Royalty – princes. Witches.

Rock-a-doodle-do! an adaptation of a tale by the Brothers Grimm (Foreman, Michael)

Rose Red and the bear prince by Jacob & Wilhelm Grimm; adapt. & ill. by Dan Andreasen. HarperCollins, 2000. ISBN 0-06-027967-2 Subj: Animals – bears. Dwarfs, midgets. Folk & fairy tales. Magic. Royalty – princes.

Rumpelstiltskin by Jacob & Wilhelm Grimm; ill. by Jacqueline Ayer. Harcourt, 1967. ISBN 0-89375-140-5 Subj: Folk & fairy tales. Magic. Riddles & jokes. Royalty. Weddings.

Rumpelstiltskin by Jacob & Wilhelm Grimm; retold & ill. by Donna Diamond. Holiday, 1983. ISBN 0-8234-0488-9 Subj: Folk & fairy tales. Magic. Riddles & jokes. Royalty. Weddings.

Rumpelstiltskin by Jacob & Wilhelm Grimm; adapt. & ill. by Paul Galdone. Houghton Mifflin, 1985. ISBN 0-89919-266-1 Subj: Folk & fairy tales. Magic. Riddles & jokes. Royalty. Weddings.

Rumpelstiltskin by Jacob & Wilhelm Grimm; retold & ill. by Jonathan Langley. HarperCollins, 1992. ISBN 0-06-020199-1 Subj: Folk & fairy tales. Magic. Riddles & jokes. Royalty. Weddings.

Rumpelstiltskin by Jacob & Wilhelm Grimm; retold by Eric Blair; ill. by David Shaw. Picture Window, 2004. ISBN 1-4048-0311-4 Subj: Folk & fairy tales. Magic. Riddles & jokes. Royalty. Weddings.

Rumpelstiltskin by Jacob & Wilhelm Grimm; retold by Alison Sage; ill. by Gennady Spirin. Dial, 1991. ISBN 0-8037-0908-0 Subj: Folk & fairy tales. Magic. Riddles & jokes. Royalty. Weddings.

Rumpelstiltskin by Jacob & Wilhelm Grimm; ill. by John Wallner. Prentice-Hall, 1984. ISBN 0-13-783747-X Subj: Folk & fairy tales. Magic. Riddles & jokes. Royalty. Weddings.

Rumpelstiltskin by Jacob & Wilhelm Grimm; trans. by Anthea Bell; ill. by Bernadette Watts. North-South, 1993. ISBN 1-55858-189-8 Subj: Folk & fairy tales. Magic. Riddles & jokes. Royalty. Weddings.

Rumpelstiltskin by Jacob & Wilhelm Grimm; adapt. & ill. by Paul O. Zelinsky. Dutton, 1986. ISBN 0-525-44265-0 Subj: Folk & fairy tales. Magic. Riddles & jokes. Royalty. Weddings.

Seven at one blow: a tale from the Brothers Grimm retold by Eric A. Kimmel; ill. by Megan Lloyd. Holiday, 1998. ISBN 0-8234-1383-7 Subj: Careers – tailors. Character traits – bravery. Folk & fairy tales. Foreign lands – Germany. Giants.

The seven ravens by Jacob & Wilhelm Grimm; ill. by Felix Hoffmann. Harcourt, 1963. ISBN 0-06-023552-7 Subj: Birds – ravens. Folk & fairy tales. Magic.

The seven ravens by Jacob & Wilhelm Grimm; trans. from German by Elizabeth D. Crawford; ill. by Lisbeth Zwerger. Morrow, 1981. ISBN 0-688-00372-9 Subj: Birds – ravens. Folk & fairy tales. Magic.

The shoemaker and his elves by Jacob & Wilhelm Grimm; retold by Eric Blair; ill. by Bill Dickson. Picture Window, 2004. ISBN 1-4048-0314-9 Subj: Careers – shoemakers. Character traits – helpfulness. Folk & fairy tales. Foreign lands – Germany. Mythical creatures – elves.

The shoemaker and the elves by Jacob & Wilhelm Grimm; ill. by Adrienne Adams. Macmillan, 1972. ISBN 0-684-12982-5 Subj: Careers – shoemakers. Character traits – helpfulness. Folk & fairy tales. Foreign lands – Germany. Mythical creatures – elves.

The shoemaker and the elves by Jacob & Wilhelm Grimm; ill. by Cynthia & William Birrer. Lothrop, 1983. Adapt. of Wichtelmänner. ISBN 0-688-01989-7 Subj: Careers – shoemakers. Character traits – helpfulness. Folk & fairy tales. Foreign lands – Germany. Mythical creatures – elves.

The shoemaker and the elves by Jacob & Wilhelm Grimm; retold & ill. by Ilse Plume. Harcourt, 1991. ISBN 0-15-274050-3 Subj: Careers – shoemakers. Character traits – helpfulness. Folk & fairy tales. Foreign lands – Germany. Mythical creatures – elves.

Sister night and sister day (Norling, Beth)

The six servants by Jacob & Wilhelm Grimm; ill. by Sergei Goloshapov; trans. by Anthea Bell. North-South, 1996. ISBN 1-55858-476-5 Subj: Folk & fairy tales. Magic. Royalty – princesses. Royalty – queens.

The six swans by Jacob & Wilhelm Grimm; ill. by Dorothée Duntze; trans. by Anthea Bell. North-South, 1998. ISBN 1-55858-983-X Subj: Birds – swans. Folk & fairy tales. Magic.

The six swans by Jacob & Wilhelm Grimm; retold by Robert D. San Souci; ill. by Daniel San Souci. S&S, 1989. ISBN 0-671-65848-4 Subj: Birds – swans. Family life – brothers & sisters. Folk & fairy tales. Magic.

The six swans by Jacob & Wilhelm Grimm; retold by Wanda Gág; ill. by Margot Tomes. Coward, 1982. ISBN 0-689-20552-9 Subj: Birds – swans. Folk & fairy tales. Magic.

The sleeping beauty by Jacob & Wilhelm Grimm; retold & ill. by Warwick Hutton. Atheneum, 1979. ISBN 0-689-50131-5 Subj: Fairies. Folk & fairy tales. Royalty – princes. Royalty – princesses. Sleep. Witches.

The sleeping beauty by Jacob & Wilhelm Grimm; retold & ill. by Trina Schart Hyman. Little, 1977. ISBN 0-316-38702-9 Subj: Fairies. Folk & fairy tales. Royalty – princes. Royalty – princesses. Sleep. Witches.

The sleeping beauty by Jacob & Wilhelm Grimm; ill. by Monika Laimgruber; trans. by Anthea Bell. North-South, 1995. ISBN 1-55858-400-5 Subj: Fairies. Folk & fairy tales. Royalty – princes. Royalty – princesses. Sleep. Witches.

The sleeping beauty by Jacob & Wilhelm Grimm; adapt. & ill. by Mercer Mayer. Macmillan, 1984. ISBN 0-02-765340-4 Subj: Fairies. Folk & fairy tales. Royalty – princes. Royalty – princesses. Sleep. Witches.

Sleeping Beauty by Jacob & Wilhelm Grimm; trans. from Spanish by Leland Northam; adapt. by M. Eulalia Valeri; ill. by Fina Rifa. Silver Burdett, 1985. ISBN 0-382-09068-3 Subj: Fairies. Folk & fairy tales. Royalty – princes. Royalty – princesses. Sleep. Witches. Wordless.

The sleeping beauty by Jacob & Wilhelm Grimm; adapt. by Jane Yolen; ill. by Ruth Sanderson. Knopf, 1986. ISBN 0-394-55431-0 Subj: Fairies. Folk & fairy tales. Royalty – princes. Royalty – princesses. Sleep. Witches.

Sleeping Beauty by Jacob & Wilhelm Grimm; adapt. & ill. by John Wallner. Viking, 1987. ISBN 0-670-81708-2 Subj: Fairies. Folk & fairy tales. Format, unusual – toy & movable books. Rebuses. Royalty – princes. Royalty – princesses. Sleep. Witches.

Snow White by Jacob & Wilhelm Grimm; trans. from German by Paul Heins; ill. by Trina Schart Hyman. Little, 1999, 1974. ISBN 0-316-35450-3 Subj: Dwarfs, midgets. Emotions – envy, jealousy. Folk & fairy tales. Magic. Witches.

Snow White by Jacob & Wilhelm Grimm; ill. by Bernadette Watts. Faber, 1983. ISBN 0-571-12518-2 Subj: Dwarfs, midgets. Emotions – envy, jealousy. Folk & fairy tales. Magic. Witches.

Snow White by Jacob & Wilhelm Grimm; retold by Eric Blair; ill. by Claudia Wolf. Picture Window, 2004. ISBN 1-4048-0312-2 Subj: Dwarfs, midgets. Emotions – envy, jealousy. Folk & fairy tales. Magic. Weddings.

Snow White and Rose Red by Jacob & Wilhelm Grimm; trans. by Wayne Andrews; ill. by Adrienne Adams. Scribners, 1964. Subj: Animals – bears. Dwarfs, midgets. Emotions – envy, jealousy. Folk & fairy tales. Magic. Weddings.

Snow White and Rose Red by Jacob & Wilhelm Grimm; trans. by Andrew Lang; ill. by John Wallner. Prentice-Hall, 1984. ISBN 0-13-815234-9 Subj: Animals – bears. Dwarfs, midgets. Folk & fairy tales. Magic. Weddings.

Snow White and Rose Red by Jacob & Wilhelm Grimm; adapt. & ill. by Bernadette Watts. Holt, 1988. ISBN 0-8050-0738-5 Subj: Animals – bears. Dwarfs, midgets. Folk & fairy tales. Magic. Weddings.

Snow White and the seven dwarfs by Jacob & Wilhelm Grimm; ill. by Wanda Gág. Coward, 1938. Subj: Caldecott award honor books. Dwarfs, midgets. Emotions – envy, jealousy. Folk & fairy tales. Magic. Weddings.

Snow White and the seven dwarfts (Ljungkvist, Laura)

Snow White and the seven dwarves by Jacob & Wilhelm Grimm; adapt. by Anthea Bell; ill. by Chihiro Iwasaki. Picture Book Studio, 1985. ISBN 0-88708-012-X Subj: Dwarfs, midgets. Emotions – envy, jealousy. Folk & fairy tales. Magic. Witches.

Snow-White and Rose-Red adapt. & ill. by Barbara Cooney. Dial, 1966. Subj: Animals – bears. Folk & fairy tales.

The table, the donkey and the stick adapt. & ill. by Paul Galdone. McGraw-Hill, 1976. Adapt. from a retelling of Das tapfere Schneiderlein. ISBN 0-07-022701-2 Subj: Cumulative tales. Folk & fairy tales. Furniture – tables.

Three Grimms' fairy tales: The fox and the geese; The magic porridge pot; The silver pennies by Jacob & Wilhelm Grimm; ill. by Bernadette Watts. Little, 1981. ISBN 0-316-32885-5 Subj: Folk & fairy tales.

The three spinning fairies a tale from the Brothers Grimm; retold & ill. by Lisa Campbell Ernst. Dutton, 2002. ISBN 0-525-46826-9

Subj: Character traits – laziness. Fairies. Folk & fairy tales. Foreign lands – Germany.

Tom Thumb (Tom Thumb)

The traveling musicians of Bremen by Jacob & Wilhelm Grimm; retold by P. K. Page; ill. by Kady MacDonald Denton. Little, 1992. ISBN 0-316-68836-3 Subj: Animals. Careers – musicians. Crime. Folk & fairy tales. Old age. Rhyming text.

The twelve dancing princesses by Jacob & Wilhelm Grimm; retold by Marianna Mayer; ill. by Kinuko Y. Craft. Morrow, 1989. ISBN 0-688-02026-7 Subj: Activities – dancing. Folk & fairy tales. Royalty – princesses.

The twelve dancing princesses by Jacob & Wilhelm Grimm; retold by Anne Carter; ill. by Anne Dalton. HarperCollins, 1989. ISBN 0-397-32373-5 Subj: Activities – dancing. Folk & fairy tales. Royalty – princesses.

The twelve dancing princesses by Jacob & Wilhelm Grimm; ill. by Dennis Hockerman. Troll, 1979. ISBN 0-89375-139-1 Subj: Activities – dancing. Folk & fairy tales. Royalty – princesses.

The twelve dancing princesses by Jacob & Wilhelm Grimm; ill. by Errol Le Cain. Viking, 1978. ISBN 0-670-73358-X Subj: Activities – dancing. Folk & fairy tales. Royalty – princesses.

The twelve dancing princesses by Jacob & Wilhelm Grimm; retold by Marianna Mayer; ill. by Gerald McDermott. Morrow, 1988. Subj: Activities – dancing. Folk & fairy tales. Royalty – princesses.

The twelve dancing princesses by Jacob & Wilhelm Grimm; retold & ill. by Jane Ray. Dutton, 1996. ISBN 0-525-45595-7 Subj: Activities – dancing. Folk & fairy tales. Royalty – princesses.

The twelve dancing princesses by Jacob & Wilhelm Grimm; trans. by Elizabeth Shub; ill. by Uri Shulevitz. Scribners, 1966. Subj: Activities – dancing. Folk & fairy tales. Royalty – princesses.

The twelve dancing princesses by Jacob & Wilhelm Grimm; retold & ill. by Suçie Stevenson. Yearling, 1995. ISBN 0-385-32167-8 Subj: Activities – dancing. Folk & fairy tales. Royalty – princesses.

The twelve princesses by Jacob & Wilhelm Grimm; retold & ill. by Gordon Fitchett. Fogelman, 2000. ISBN 0-8037-2474-8 Subj: Activities – dancing. Birds – ducks. Folk & fairy tales. Royalty – princesses.

The valiant little tailor by Jacob & Wilhelm Grimm; ill. by Victor G. Ambrus. Oxford Univ. Pr., 1980. First pub. in 1971. ISBN 0-19-279727-1 Subj: Careers – tailors. Character traits – bravery. Folk & fairy tales. Giants.

Walt Disney's Snow White and the seven dwarfs (Walt Disney Productions)

The water of life (Rogasky, Barbara)

The wishing table by Jacob & Wilhelm Grimm; trans. by Anthea Bell; ill. by Eve Tharlet. Picture Book Studio, 1988. ISBN 0-88708-064-2 Subj: Cumulative tales. Folk & fairy tales. Furniture – tables.

The wolf and the seven kids by Jacob & Wilhelm Grimm; ill. by Kinuko Y. Craft. Troll, 1979. ISBN 0-89375-138-3 Subj: Animals – goats. Animals – wolves. Folk & fairy tales.

The wolf and the seven little kids by Jacob & Wilhelm Grimm; trans. by Anne Rogers; ill. by Svend Otto S. Larousse, 1977. ISBN 0-88332-080-0 Subj: Animals – goats. Animals – wolves. Folk & fairy tales.

The wolf and the seven little kids by Jacob & Wilhelm Grimm; adapt. by Linda M. Jennings; ill. by Martin Ursell. Silver Burdett, 1986. ISBN 0-382-09306-2 Subj: Animals – goats. Animals – wolves. Folk & fairy tales.

Grimm, Wilhelm. *Battle of the beasts: a tale of epic proportions from the brothers Grimm* (Wallis, Diz)

The bear and the kingbird (Grimm, Jacob)

The bearskinner (Grimm, Jacob)

The brave little seamstress (Osborne, Mary Pope)

The brave little tailor (Grimm, Jacob)

The Bremen town band (Grimm, Jacob)

The Bremen town musicians (Grimm, Jacob)

Cinderella (Grimm, Jacob)

Clever Kate (Grimm, Jacob)

Dear Mili trans. by Ralph Manheim; ill. by Maurice Sendak. Farrar, 1988. ISBN 0-374-31762-3 Subj: Death. Folk & fairy tales. War.

The devil with the green hairs (Grimm, Jacob)

The diary of Hansel and Gretel (Moerbeek, Kees)

Dick Bruna's Little Red Riding Hood (Bruna, Dick)

Dick Bruna's Snow-White and the seven dwarfs (Bruna, Dick)

The donkey prince (Grimm, Jacob)

The earth gnome (Grimm, Jacob)

The elves and the shoemaker (Grimm, Jacob)

The falling stars (Grimm, Jacob)

The fisherman and his wife (Grimm, Jacob)

Fitcher's bird (Grimm, Jacob)

The four clever brothers (Grimm, Jacob)

The four gallant sisters (Kimmel, Eric A.)

The frog prince (Grimm, Jacob)

The frog prince: or Iron Henry (Grimm, Jacob)

The glass mountain (Grimm, Jacob)

Godfather Cat and Mousie (Grimm, Jacob)

The golden bird (Grimm, Jacob)

The golden bird: and other fairy tales (Grimm, Jacob)

The golden goose (Grimm, Jacob)

The goose girl (Grimm, Jacob)

The goose girl: a story from the Brothers Grimm (Grimm, Jacob)

Grimm Tom Thumb (Tom Thumb)

Hans in luck (Grimm, Jacob)

Hansel and Gretel (Grimm, Jacob)

The horse, the fox, and the lion (Grimm, Jacob)

Iron Hans (Grimm, Jacob)

Iron John (Grimm, Jacob)

Jack in luck (Grimm, Jacob)

Jorinda and Joringel (Grimm, Jacob)

King Grisly-Beard (Grimm, Jacob)

Little brother and little sister (Grimm, Jacob)

Little red cap (Grimm, Jacob)

Little Red Riding Hood (Grimm, Jacob)

Little Red Riding Hood: a fairy tale by Grimm (Grimm, Jacob)

Lucky Hans (Grimm, Jacob)

Mother Holly (Grimm, Jacob)

Mrs. Fox's wedding (Grimm, Jacob)

The musicians of Bremen (Grimm, Jacob)

Nanny goat and the seven little kids (Grimm, Jacob)

One gift deserves another (Grimm, Jacob)

Ouch! a tale from Grimm (Babbitt, Natalie)

The princess and the frog (Grimm, Jacob)

The rabbit's bride (Grimm, Jacob)

Rapunzel (Grimm, Jacob)

Rapunzel: a fairy tale (Grimm, Jacob)

Rock-a-doodle-do! an adaptation of a tale by the Brothers Grimm (Foreman, Michael)

Rose Red and the bear prince (Grimm, Jacob)

Rumpelstiltskin (Grimm, Jacob)

Seven at one blow: a tale from the Brothers Grimm (Grimm, Jacob)

The seven ravens (Grimm, Jacob)

The shoemaker and his elves (Grimm, Jacob)

The shoemaker and the elves (Grimm, Jacob)

Sister night and sister day (Norling, Beth)

The six servants (Grimm, Jacob)

The six swans (Grimm, Jacob)

The sleeping beauty (Grimm, Jacob)

Sleeping Beauty (Grimm, Jacob)

Snow White (Grimm, Jacob)

Snow White and Rose Red (Grimm, Jacob)

Snow White and the seven dwarfs (Grimm, Jacob)

Snow White and the seven dwarfts (Ljungkvist, Laura)

Snow White and the seven dwarves (Grimm, Jacob)

Snow-White and Rose-Red (Grimm, Jacob)

The table, the donkey and the stick (Grimm, Jacob)

Three Grimms' fairy tales: The fox and the geese; The magic porridge pot; The silver pennies (Grimm, Jacob)

The three spinning fairies (Grimm, Jacob)

Tom Thumb (Tom Thumb)

The traveling musicians of Bremen (Grimm, Jacob)

The twelve dancing princesses (Grimm, Jacob)

The twelve princesses (Grimm, Jacob)

The ugly duckling (Andersen, H. C. [Hans Christian])

The valiant little tailor (Grimm, Jacob)

Walt Disney's Snow White and the seven dwarfs (Walt Disney Productions)

The water of life (Rogasky, Barbara)

The wishing table (Grimm, Jacob)

The wolf and the seven kids (Grimm, Jacob)

The wolf and the seven little kids (Grimm, Jacob)

Grimsdell, Jeremy. *Kalinzu* ill. by author. Kingfisher, 1993. ISBN 1-85697-886-9 Subj: Animals – buffaloes. Animals – hyenas. Behavior – lost. Foreign lands – Africa.

Grindley, Sally. *Can we play too, Piglittle?* ill. by Andy Ellis. Barron's, 2000. ISBN 0-7641-1582-0 Subj: Activities – playing. Animals – pigs. Behavior – sharing. Character traits – selfishness.

A flag for Grandma ill. by Jason Cockcroft. DK, 1998. ISBN 0-7894-3490-3 Subj: Family life – grandfathers. Family life – grandmothers. Memories, memory. Sea & seashore.

Four black puppies ill. by Clive Scruton. Lothrop, 1987. ISBN 0-688-07266-6 Subj: Animals – dogs. Behavior – misbehavior.

The giant postman ill. by Wendy Smith. Kingfisher, 2000. ISBN 0-7534-5319-3 Subj: Careers – postal workers. Concepts – size. Friendship.

I don't want to! ill. by Carol Thompson. Little, 1990. ISBN 0-316-32893-6 Subj: Behavior. School.

Knock, knock! Who's there? ill. by Anthony Browne. Knopf, 1986. ISBN 0-394-98400-5 Subj: Bedtime. Family life – fathers. Games. Monsters. Toys – bears.

Little Elephant Thunderfoot ill. by John Butler. Peachtree, 1999. ISBN 1-56145-180-0 Subj: Animals – babies. Animals – elephants.

Little Sibu: an orangutan tale ill. by John Butler. Peachtree, 1999. ISBN 1-56145-196-7 Subj: Animals – orangutans. Behavior – growing up. Forest, woods.

Mucky Duck ill. by Neal Layton. Bloomsbury, 2003. ISBN 1-58234-821-9 Subj: Activities. Birds – ducks. Character traits – cleanliness.

A new room for William ill. by Carol Thompson. Candlewick, 2000. ISBN 0-7636-1196-4 Subj: Divorce. Family life. Homes, houses. Moving.

Peter's place ill. by Michael Foreman. Harcourt, 1996. ISBN 0-15-200916-7 Subj: Ecology. Sea & seashore. Water.

Polar Star ill. by John Butler. Peachtree, 1998. ISBN 1-56145-181-9 Subj: Animals – babies. Animals – polar bears. Foreign lands – Arctic.

Shhh! ill. by Peter Utton. Little, 1992. ISBN 0-316-32899-5 Subj: Format, unusual. Giants.

Silly Goose and Dizzy Duck play hide-and-seek ill. by Adrian Reynolds. DK, 1999. ISBN 0-7894-4844-0 Subj: Animals – foxes. Birds – ducks. Birds – geese. Games.

The sorcerer's apprentice ill. by Thomas Taylor. Fogelman, 2002. ISBN 0-8037-2726-7 Subj: Folk & fairy tales. Magic.

The sulky vulture ill. by Michael Terry. Bloomsbury, 2003. ISBN 1-58234-794-8 Subj: Behavior – bad day. Behavior – dissatisfaction. Birds – vultures.

Too big bear ill. by Peter Utton; paper engineering by José R. Seminario. Orchard, 1995. ISBN 1-8521-3931-5 Subj: Concepts – size. Format, unusual – toy & movable books. Toys – bears.

Wake up, dad! ill. by Siobhan Dodds. Doubleday, 1989. ISBN 0-385-26018-0 Subj: Family life. Furniture – beds. Morning.

What are friends for? ill. by Penny Dann. Kingfisher, 1998. ISBN 0-7534-5108-5 Subj: Animals – bears. Animals – foxes. Friendship.

What will I do without you? ill. by Penny Dann. Kingfisher, 1999. ISBN 0-7534-5110-7 Subj: Animals – bears. Animals – foxes. Animals – squirrels. Friendship. Hibernation. Seasons – winter.

Where are my chicks? ill. by Jill Newton. Fogelman, 1999. ISBN 0-8037-2497-7 Subj: Animals. Behavior – lost. Birds – chickens. Counting, numbers.

Who is it? ill. by Rosalind Beardshaw. Peachtree, 2000. ISBN 1-56145-224-6 Subj: Folk & fairy tales. Problem solving. Riddles & jokes.

Why is the sky blue? ill. by Susan Varley. S&S, 1997. ISBN 0-689-81486-0 Subj: Animals – donkeys. Animals – rabbits. Character traits – patience.

Grisman, David. *The teddy bears' picnic* (Garcia, Jerry)

Grist, Julie. *Flying, just plane fun* ill. by author. Spoonbender, 2003. ISBN 0-9725750-0-6 Subj: Activities – flying. Airplanes, airports. Family life – grandfathers.

Groat, Diane. *see* De Groat, Diane

Grobler, Piet. *Hey, frog!* ill. by author. Front St., 2002. ISBN 1-886910-84-7 Subj: Animals. Behavior – greed. Frogs & toads. Water.

Grode, Redway. *see* Gorey, Edward (St. John)

Groening, Maggie. *Maggie Simpson's alphabet book* by Maggie & Matt Groening. HarperCollins, 1991. ISBN 0-06-020236-X Subj: ABC books.

Maggie Simpson's book of animals by Maggie & Matt Groening; ill. by Matt Groening. HarperCollins, 1991. ISBN 0-06-020237-8 Subj: Animals. Zoos.

Maggie Simpson's book of colors and shapes by Maggie & Matt Groening; ill. by Matt Groening. HarperCollins, 1991. ISBN 0-06-020235-1 Subj: Concepts – color. Concepts – shape.

Maggie Simpson's counting book by Maggie & Matt Groening. HarperCollins, 1991. ISBN 0-06-020238-6 Subj: Counting, numbers.

Groening, Matt. *Maggie Simpson's alphabet book* (Groening, Maggie)

Maggie Simpson's book of animals (Groening, Maggie)

Maggie Simpson's book of colors and shapes (Groening, Maggie)

Maggie Simpson's counting book (Groening, Maggie)

Grohmann, Susan. *The dust under Mrs. Merriweather's bed* ill. by author. Whispering Coyote, 1994. ISBN 1-879085-82-8 Subj: Character traits – orderliness. Seasons. Weather.

Groner, Judyth Saypol. *All about Hanukkah* by Judyth Groner & Madeline Wikler; ill. by Rosalyn Schanzer. Kar-Ben Copies, 1988. ISBN 0-930494-81-4 Subj: Holidays – Hanukkah. Jewish culture. Religion.

All about Sukkot by Judyth Groner & Madeline Wikler; ill. by Kinny Kreiswirth. Kar-Ben Copies, 1998. ISBN 1-58013-018-6 Subj: Folk & fairy tales. Holidays – Sukkot. Jewish culture. Religion.

Let's build a Sukkah (Wikler, Madeline)

My first seder (Wikler, Madeline)

My very own Jewish community by Judyth Groner & Madeline Wikler; photos by Madeline Wikler. Kar-Ben Copies, 1984. ISBN 0-930494-32-6 Subj: Communities, neighborhoods. Jewish culture.

The Purim parade (Wikler, Madeline)

Thank you, God! a Jewish child's book of prayers by Judyth Groner & Madeline Wikler; ill. by Shelly O. Haas. Kar-Ben Copies, 1993. ISBN 0-929371-65-8 Subj: Jewish culture. Religion.

Where is the Afikomen? by Judyth Groner & Madeline Wikler; ill. by Chari R. McLean. Kar-Ben Copies, 1985. ISBN 0-930494-52-0 Subj: Format, unusual – board books. Holidays. Jewish culture.

Gross, Alan. *Sometimes I worry . . .* ill. by Mike Venezia. Childrens Pr., 1978. ISBN 0-516-03670-X Subj: Behavior – worrying.

What if the teacher calls on me? ill. by Mike Venezia. Childrens Pr., 1980. ISBN 0-516-03671-8 Subj: Behavior – worrying. School.

Gross, Michael. *The fable of the fig tree* ill. by Mila Lazarevich. Walck, 1975. ISBN 0-8098-1228-2 Subj: Folk & fairy tales. Jewish culture.

Gross, Ruth Belov. *Alligators and other crocodilians* ill. with photos. Four Winds, 1978. ISBN 0-590-07556-X Subj: Reptiles – alligators, crocodiles. Science.

A book about your skeleton ill. by Deborah Robison. Hastings House, 1979. ISBN 0-8038-0794-5 Subj: Anatomy – skeletons. Health & fitness.

The emperor's new clothes (Andersen, H. C. [Hans Christian])

The girl who wouldn't get married ill. by Jack Kent. Four Winds, 1983. ISBN 0-590-07908-5 Subj: Animals – horses, ponies. Folk & fairy tales. Weddings.

What's on my plate? ill. by Isadore Seltzer. Macmillan, 1990. ISBN 0-02-737000-3 Subj: Food.

Grossbart, Francine. *A big city* ill. by author. HarperCollins, 1966. Subj: ABC books. Cities, towns.

Grossblatt, Ruby M. *Who's that sleeping on my sofabed?* ill. by Sara Kranz. Hachai, 1999. ISBN 0-922613-90-7 Subj: Family life. Furniture – beds. Furniture – couches, sofas. Jewish culture.

Grossman, Bill. *The banging book* ill. by Robert Zimmerman. HarperCollins, 1995. ISBN 0-06-024498-4 Subj: Activities – making things. Noise, sounds. Rhyming text.

The bear whose bones were Jezebel Jones ill. by Jonathan Allen. Dial, 1997. ISBN 0-8037-1743-1 Subj: Anatomy – skin. Animals. Animals – bears. Rhyming text. Zoos.

Cowboy Ed ill. by Florence Wint. HarperCollins, 1993. ISBN 0-06-021571-2 Subj: Cowboys, cowgirls. Rhyming text. U.S. history – frontier & pioneer life.

Donna O'Neeshuck was chased by some cows ill. by Sue Truesdell. HarperCollins, 1988. ISBN 0-06-022159-3 Subj: Cumulative tales. Rhyming text.

The guy who was five minutes late ill. by Judy Glasser. HarperCollins, 1990. ISBN 0-06-022269-7 Subj: Behavior – promptness, tardiness. Rhyming text.

My little sister ate one hare ill. by Kevin Hawkes. Crown, 1996. ISBN 0-517-59601-6 Subj: Counting, numbers. Rhyming text.

My little sister hugged an ape ill. by Kevin Hawkes. Knopf, 2004. ISBN 0-517-80018-7 Subj: ABC books. Emotions. Family life – sisters. Rhyming text.

Timothy Tunny swallowed a bunny ill. by Kevin Hawkes. Geringer, 2000. ISBN 0-06-028758-6 Subj: Humorous stories. Poetry.

Tommy at the grocery store ill. by Victoria Chess. HarperCollins, 1989. ISBN 0-06-022409-6 Subj: Animals – pigs. Behavior – lost. Rhyming text. Shopping. Stores.

Grossman, Patricia. *The night ones* ill. by Lydia Dabcovich. Harcourt, 1991. ISBN 0-15-257438-7 Subj: Activities – working. Careers. Night.

Saturday market by Patricia Grossman & Enrique O. Sánchez; ill. by Enrique O. Sánchez. Lothrop, 1994. ISBN 0-688-12177-2 Subj: Foreign lands – Mexico. Indians of North America – Zapotec. Shopping.

Grossman, Virginia. *Ten little rabbits* ill. by Sylvia Long. Chronicle, 1991. ISBN 0-87701-552-X Subj: Animals – rabbits. Counting, numbers. Indians of North America. Rhyming text.

Grosvenor, Donna. *Pandas* photos by author; ill. by George Founds. National Geographic, 1973. ISBN 0-87044-143-4 Subj: Animals – pandas. Science.

Zoo babies ill. by author. National Geographic, 1979. ISBN 0-8704-4262-7 Subj: Animals. Zoos.

Grosz, Peter. *The special gifts* ill. by Giuliano Lunelli; trans. by Rosemary Lanning. North-South, 1998. ISBN 1-55858-962-7 Subj: Behavior – sharing. Gifts. Homes, houses. Old age.

Groundhog at Evergreen Road ill. by Higgins Bond. Soundprints, 2003. ISBN 1-59249-022-0 Subj: Animals – groundhogs. Behavior – growing up. Homes, houses.

Grover, Eulalie Osgood. *Mother Goose* (Mother Goose)

Mother Goose (Mother Goose)

Grover, Max. *The accidental zucchini: an unexpected alphabet* ill. by author. Browndeer, 1993. ISBN 0-15-277695-8 Subj: ABC books. Language.

Groves-Raines, Antony. *The tidy hen* ill. by author. Harcourt, 1961. Subj: Birds – chickens. Character traits – cleanliness.

Gruber, Ruth. *see* Michaels, Ruth

Gruelle, Johnny. *How Raggedy Ann got her candy heart* (How Raggedy Ann got her candy heart)

My first Raggedy Ann, Raggedy Ann and Andy and the camel with the wrinkled knees (My first Raggedy Ann, Raggedy Ann and Andy and the camel with the wrinkled knees)

My first Raggedy Ann, Raggedy Ann and Andy and the nice police officer (My first Raggedy Ann, Raggedy Ann and Andy and the nice police officer)

My first Raggedy Ann, Raggedy Ann's wishing pebble (My first Raggedy Ann, Raggedy Ann's wishing pebble)

Raggedy Ann and Andy and the magic potion (Peters, Stephanie True)

Gruenberg, Hannah Coale. *Felix's hat* (Bancroft, Catherine)

Grunwald, Lisa. *Now, soon, later* ill. by Jane Johnson. Greenwillow, 1995. ISBN 0-688-13946-9 Subj: Character traits – patience. Time.

Grupper, Jonathan. *Destination, rain forest* ill. with photos. National Geographic, 1997. ISBN 0-7922-7018-5 Subj: Ecology. Forest, woods. Nature.

Destination – Rocky Mountains ill. with photos. National Geographic, 2001. ISBN 0-7922-7722-8 Subj: Animals. Ecology. Mountains. Nature.

Gryspeerdt, Rebecca. *Counting friends* ill. by author. Trafalgar Square, 1993. ISBN 1-85681-092-5 Subj: Animals. Counting, numbers. Friendship. Rhyming text.

Guarino, Deborah. *Is your mama a llama?* ill. by Steven Kellogg. Scholastic, 1989. ISBN 0-590-41387-2 Subj: Animals. Animals – llamas. Rhyming text.

Guarnaccia, Steven. *Goldilocks and the three bears* (The three bears)

Guarnieri, Paolo. *A boy named Giotto* ill. by Bimba Landmann; trans. by Jonathan Galassi. Farrar, 1999. ISBN 0-374-30931-0 Subj: Careers – artists. Careers – shepherds. Foreign lands – Italy.

Guback, Georgia. *Luka's quilt* ill. by author. Greenwillow, 1994. ISBN 0-688-12155-1 Subj: Family life – grandmothers. Hawaii. Quilts.

Guenther, James. *Turnagain, Ptarmigan, where did you go?* ill. by Shannon Cartwright. Sasquatch, 2000. ISBN 1-57061-237-4 Subj: Alaska. Birds – ptarmigans. Rhyming text. Seasons.

Gueritz, Caroline. *Bruno takes a trip* (Bröger, Achim)

Guernsey, JoAnn Bren. *Scruffy: a wolf finds his place in the pack* (Brandenburg, Jim)

Guest, C. Z. *Tiny green thumbs* ill. by Loretta Krupinski. Hyperion, 2000. ISBN 0-7868-2533-2 Subj: Animals – mice. Animals – rabbits. Family life – grandmothers. Gardens, gardening.

Guettier, Bénédicte. *The father who had ten children* ill. by author. Dial, 1999. ISBN 0-8037-2446-2 Subj: Counting, numbers. Family life – fathers.

Guggenmos, Josef *Franz, der Drache. Dragon Franz* (Shub, Elizabeth)

Gugler, Laurel Dee. *Facing the day* ill. by Deidre Betteridge. Annick, 1999. ISBN 1-55037-577-6 Subj: Emotions. Family life. Rhyming text.

Monkey tales ill. by Vlasta van Kampen. Annick, 1998. ISBN 1-55037-531-8 Subj: Animals – monkeys. Folk & fairy tales.

Muddle cuddle ill. by Vlasta van Kampen. Annick, 1997. ISBN 1-55037-435-4 Subj: Activities. Family life – fathers. Pets. Rhyming text. Toys.

There's a billy goat in the garden ill. by Clare Beaton. Barefoot, 2003. ISBN 1-84148-089-4 Subj: Animals. Animals – goats. Folk & fairy tales. Foreign lands – Puerto Rico. Insects – bees.

Guiberson, Brenda Z. *Cactus hotel* ill. by Megan Lloyd. Holt, 1991. ISBN 0-8050-1333-4 Subj: Desert. Ecology. Plants.

The emperor lays an egg ill. by Joan Paley. Holt, 2001. ISBN 0-8050-6204-1 Subj: Birds – penguins. Family life.

Into the sea ill. by Alix Berenzy. Holt, 1996. ISBN 0-8050-2263-5 Subj: Nature. Reptiles – turtles, tortoises. Sea & seashore.

Lobster boat ill. by Megan Lloyd. Holt, 1993. ISBN 0-8050-1756-9 Subj: Careers – fishermen. Crustaceans – lobsters. Sea & seashore.

Spoonbill swamp ill. by Megan Lloyd. Holt, 1992. ISBN 0-8050-1583-3 Subj: Birds – spoonbills. Nature. Reptiles – alligators, crocodiles.

Guilfoile, Elizabeth. *Have you seen my brother?* ill. by Mary Stevens. Follett, 1962. Subj: Behavior – lost. Careers – police officers. Cities, towns.

Nobody listens to Andrew ill. by Mary Stevens. Follett, 1957. Subj: Animals – bears. Behavior – needing someone.

Valentine's Day ill. by Gordon Laite. Garrard, 1965. Subj: Holidays – Valentine's Day.

Guitar, Jeremy. *Tidy pig* (McQueen, Lucinda)

Gukova, Julia. *All mixed-up!* ill. by author. North-South, 2000. ISBN 0-7358-1300-0 Subj: Format, unusual – toy & movable books. Picture puzzles. Witches.

Mole's daughter: an adaptation of a Korean folktale ill. by author. Annick, 1998. ISBN 1-55037-525-3 Subj: Animals – moles. Folk & fairy tales. Foreign lands – Korea.

Gulbis, Stephen. *Cowgirl Rosie and her five baby bison* ill. by author. Little, 2001. ISBN 0-316-64712-8 Subj: Animals – babies. Animals – buffaloes. Behavior – lost & found possessions. Cowboys, cowgirls. Rhyming text.

Gullikson, Sandy. *Trouble for breakfast* ill. by author. Dial, 1990. ISBN 0-8037-0776-2 Subj: Animals. Behavior – misbehavior. Food. Illness.

Gullo, Stephen V. *When people die* (Bernstein, Joanne E.)

Gundersheimer, Karen. *A B C, say with me* ill. by author. HarperCollins, 1984. ISBN 0-06-022175-5 Subj: ABC books.

Colors to know ill. by author. HarperCollins, 1986. ISBN 0-06-022196-8 Subj: Animals. Concepts – color.

Find cat, wear hat ill. by author. Scholastic, 1995. ISBN 0-590-48061-8 Subj: Activities – playing. Format, unusual – board books. Noise, sounds. Rhyming text. School.

Happy winter ill. by author. HarperCollins, 1982. ISBN 0-06-022173-9 Subj: Rhyming text. Seasons – winter.

1, 2, 3, play with me ill. by author. HarperCollins, 1984. ISBN 0-06-022177-1 Subj: Animals – mice. Counting, numbers.

Shapes to show ill. by author. HarperCollins, 1986. ISBN 0-06-022197-6 Subj: Animals – mice. Concepts – shape. Toys.

Splish splash bang crash! ill. by author. Scholastic, 1995. ISBN 0-590-48060-X Subj: Activities – playing. Noise, sounds. Rhyming text. School.

Gunning, Monica. *Not a copper penny in me house* ill. by Frané Lessac. Boyds Mills, 1993. ISBN 1-56397-793-1 Subj: Foreign lands – Caribbean Islands. Poetry.

The two Georges = Los dos Jorges ill. by Veronica Mary Miracle. Blaine-Ethridge, 1976. ISBN 0-87917-049-2 Subj: ABC books. Foreign languages.

Gunther, Louise. *Anna's snow day* ill. by Paul Frame. Garrard, 1979. ISBN 0-8116-4310-7 Subj: Weather – snow.

A tooth for the tooth fairy ill. by Jim Cummins. Garrard, 1978. ISBN 0-8116-4308-5 Subj: Fairies. Teeth.

Gunthrop, Karen. *Adam and the wolf* ill. by Attilio Cassinelli. Doubleday, 1967. Translation of Il pulcino e il lupo. Subj: Animals – wolves. Behavior – disbelief. Food.

Rina at the farm ill. by Attilio Cassinelli. Doubleday, 1968. Subj: Farms.

Gunzi, Christiane. *Colors* ill. by author. Two-Can, 2001. ISBN 1-58728-236-4 Subj: Concepts – color.

Numbers ill. by author. Two-Can, 2001. ISBN 1-58728-237-2 Subj: Counting, numbers.

Shapes ill. by author. Two-Can, 2001. ISBN 1-58728-238-0 Subj: Concepts – shape.

Sizes ill. by author. Two-Can, 2001. ISBN 1-58728-239-9 Subj: Concepts – size.

Gurney, John. *Dinosaur train* ill. by author. HarperCollins, 2002. ISBN 0-06-029246-6 Subj: Bedtime. Dinosaurs. Trains.

Guthrie, Arlo. *Mooses come walking* ill. by Alice Brock. Chronicle, 1995. ISBN 0-8118-1051-8 Subj: Animals – moose. Rhyming text.

Guthrie, Donna. *Grandpa doesn't know it's me* ill. by Katy Keck Arnsteen. Human Sciences Pr., 1986. ISBN 0-89885-308-7 Subj: Behavior – forgetfulness. Behavior – lost. Behavior – lost & found possessions. Family life – grandfathers. Illness – Alzheimer's. Old age.

Mrs. Gigglebelly is coming for tea ill. by Katy Keck Arnsteen. S&S, 1989. ISBN 0-671-67937-6 Subj: Family life – mothers. Imagination – imaginary friends. Parties.

Nobiah's well: a modern African folk tale ill. by Robert Roth. Ideals, 1993. ISBN 0-8249-8631-8 Subj: Animals. Folk & fairy tales. Foreign lands – Africa. Water. Weather – droughts.

Not for babies ill. by Katy Keck Arnsteen. S&S, 1993. ISBN 0-671-79362-4 Subj: Night.

One hundred and two steps ill. by Meg Kelleher Aubrey. Cool Kids, 1995. ISBN 1-56790-522-6 Subj: Behavior – secrets. Family life – aunts, uncles. Memories, memory.

A rose for Abby ill. by Dennis Hockerman. Abingdon, 1988. ISBN 0-687-36586-4 Subj: Cities, towns. Ethnic groups in the U.S. – African Americans. Homeless.

The secret admirer ill. by Tony Sansevero. Ideals, 1996. ISBN 1-57102-045-4 Subj: Family life – great-grandparents. Holidays – Valentine's Day. Old age.

This little pig stayed home ill. by Katy Keck Arnsteen. Price Stern Sloan, 1987. ISBN 0-8431-1820-2 Subj: Animals – pigs. Animals – wolves. Careers – chefs, cooks.

The witch has an itch ill. by Katy Keck Arnsteen. Little Simon, 1990. ISBN 0-671-70346-3 Subj: Magic. Witches.

The witch who lives down the hall ill. by Amy Schwartz. Harcourt, 1985. ISBN 0-15-298610-3 Subj: Holidays – Halloween. Magic. Witches.

Guthrie, Feliz. *African animal tales* (Barbosa, Rogério Andrade)

Guthrie, Marjorie Mazia. *Woody's 20 grow big songs* (Guthrie, Woody)

Guthrie, Woody. *Bling blang* ill. by Vladimir Radunsky. Candlewick, 2000. ISBN 0-7636-0769-X Subj: Homes, houses. Music. Songs.

My dolly ill. by Vladimir Radunsky. Candlewick, 2001. ISBN 0-7636-0770-3 Subj: Music. Songs. Toys – dolls.

This land is your land music by author; ill. by Kathy Jakobsen; with a tribute by Pete Seeger. Little, 1998. ISBN 0-316-39215-4 Subj: Music. Songs.

Woody's 20 grow big songs by Woody Guthrie & Marjorie Mazia Guthrie; ill. by Woody Guthrie. HarperCollins, 1992. ISBN 0-06-020283-1 Subj: Music. Songs.

Gutman, Anne. *Gaspard and Lisa, friends forever* by Anne Gutman & Georg Hallensleben, ill. by Georg Hallensleben. Knopf, 2003. ISBN 0-375-82253-4 Subj: Animals – dogs. Friendship. School.

Gaspard and Lisa's Christmas surprise by Anne Gutman & Georg Hallensleben, ill. by Georg Hallensleben. Knopf, 2002. ISBN 0-375-82229-1 Subj: Animals – dogs. Gifts. Holidays – Christmas.

Gaspard and Lisa's rainy day by Anne Gutman & Georg Hallensleben, ill. by Georg Hallensleben. Knopf, 2003. ISBN 0-375-82252-6 Subj: Animals – dogs. Behavior – boredom. Behavior – misbehavior. Friendship. Weather – rain.

Gaspard at the seashore by Anne Gutman & Georg Hallensleben, ill. by Georg Hallensleben. Knopf, 2002. ISBN 0-375-81118-4 Subj: Animals – dogs. Camps, camping. Sea & seashore. Sports – swimming.

Gaspard in the hospital by Anne Gutman & Georg Hallensleben, ill. by Georg Hallensleben. Knopf, 2001. ISBN 0-375-81116-8 Subj: Animals – dogs. Hospitals.

Gaspard on vacation by Anne Gutman & Georg Hallensleben, ill. by Georg Hallensleben. Knopf, 2001. ISBN 0-375-81115-X Subj: Activities – vacationing. Animals – dogs. Boats, ships. Foreign lands – Italy.

Lisa in New York by Anne Gutman & Georg Hallensleben, ill. by Georg Hallensleben. Knopf, 2002. ISBN 0-375-81119-2 Subj: Animals – dogs. Behavior – lost. Family life – aunts, uncles.

Lisa in the jungle by Anne Gutman & Georg Hallensleben, ill. by Georg Hallensleben. Knopf, 2003. ISBN 0-375-82254-2 Subj: Animals – dogs. Character traits – honesty. Jungle. School.

Lisa's airplane trip by Anne Gutman & Georg Hallensleben, ill. by Georg Hallensleben. Knopf, 2001. ISBN 0-375-81114-1 Subj: Activities – traveling. Airplanes, airports. Animals – dogs.

Lisa's baby sister by Anne Gutman & Georg Hallensleben, ill. by Georg Hallensleben. Knopf, 2003. ISBN 0-375-82251-8 Subj: Animals – dogs. Babies. Behavior. Family life – new sibling. Family life – sisters.

Guy, Ginger Foglesong. *Black crow, black crow* ill. by Nancy Winslow Parker. Greenwillow, 1991. ISBN 0-688-08957-7 Subj: Birds – crows. Imagination.

Fiesta ill. by Rene King Moreno. Greenwillow, 1996. ISBN 0-688-14332-6 Subj: Counting, numbers. Fairs, festivals. Foreign lands – Mexico. Foreign languages.

Guy, Rosa. *Billy the Great* ill. by Caroline Binch. Delacorte, 1992. ISBN 0-385-30666-0 Subj: Character traits – individuality. Ethnic groups in the U.S. – African Americans. Family life. Friendship.

Caribbean carnival: songs of the West Indies (Burgie, Irving)

Mother crocodile ill. by John Steptoe. Delacorte, 1981. ISBN 0-440-06406-6 Subj: Animals – monkeys. Folk & fairy tales. Foreign lands – Africa. Reptiles – alligators, crocodiles.

Guy, Suzanne. *The music box: the story of Cristofori* by Suzanne Guy & Donna Lacy; ill. by Donna Lacy. Brunswick, 1998. ISBN 1-55618-172-8 Subj: Foreign lands – Italy. Music. Musical instruments – harpsichords. Musical instruments – pianos.

Guzzo, Sandra E. *Fox and Heggie* ill. by Kathy Parkinson. A. Whitman, 1983. ISBN 0-8075-2546-4 Subj: Animals – foxes. Animals – hedgehogs. Shopping.

Gwynne, Fred. *A chocolate moose for dinner* ill. by author. Messner, 1981. ISBN 0-671-43706-2 Subj: Imagination. Language.

Easy to see why ill. by author. S&S, 1993. ISBN 0-671-79776-X Subj: Animals – dogs. Behavior. Pets.

A little pigeon toad ill. by author. S&S, 1988. ISBN 0-671-66659-2 Subj: Imagination. Language.

Pondlarker ill. by author. S&S, 1992. ISBN 0-671-70846-5 Subj: Frogs & toads. Royalty – princesses. Self-concept.

Haarhoff, Dorian. *Desert December* ill. by Leon Vermeulen. Houghton Mifflin, 1992. Subj: Babies. Desert. Family life – new sibling. Foreign lands – Namibia. Foreign lands – South Africa. Holidays – Christmas.

Haas, Dorothy. *My first communion* photos by William Franklin McMahon. A. Whitman, 1987. ISBN 0-8075-5331-X Subj: Religion.

Haas, Irene. *The Maggie B* ill. by author. Atheneum, 1975. Subj: Behavior – wishing. Boats, ships. Rhyming text. Sea & seashore.

A summertime song ill. by author. McElderry, 1997. ISBN 0-689-50549-3 Subj: Animals. Birthdays. Family life – grandparents. Imagination. Seasons – summer.

Haas, Jessie. *Appaloosa zebra* ill. by Margot Apple. Greenwillow, 2002. ISBN 0-688-17881-2 Subj: ABC books. Animals – horses, ponies.

Busybody Brandy ill. by Yossi Abolafia. Greenwillow, 1994. ISBN 0-688-12793-2 Subj: Animals – dogs. Character traits – responsibility. Farms.

Chipmunk! ill. by Jos. A. Smith. Greenwillow, 1993. ISBN 0-688-11875-5 Subj: Animals – cats. Animals – chipmunks. Behavior – carelessness.

Getting ready to drive a horse and cart ill. by Christine Erickson. Storey Communications, 1995. ISBN 0-88266-381-X Subj: Animals – horses, ponies. Transportation.

Hurry! ill. by Jos. A. Smith. Greenwillow, 2000. ISBN 0-688-16889-2 Subj: Careers – farmers. Family life – grandparents.

Mowing ill. by Jos. A. Smith. Greenwillow, 1994. ISBN 0-688-11681-7 Subj: Character traits – kindness to animals. Family life – grandfathers. Farms.

No foal yet ill. by Jos. A. Smith. Greenwillow, 1995. ISBN 0-688-12926-9 Subj: Animals – horses, ponies. Birth. Family life – grandparents. Farms.

Sugaring ill. by Jos. A. Smith. Greenwillow, 1996. ISBN 0-688-14201-X Subj: Animals – horses, ponies. Family life – grandparents. Food. Trees.

Haas, Merle. *Babar and Father Christmas* (Brunhoff, Jean de)

Babar and his children (Brunhoff, Jean de)

Babar and Zephir (Brunhoff, Jean de)

Babar the king (Brunhoff, Jean de)

Babar visits another planet (Brunhoff, Laurent de)

Babar's castle (Brunhoff, Laurent de)

Babar's cousin, that rascal Arthur (Brunhoff, Laurent de)

Babar's fair will be opened next Sunday (Brunhoff, Laurent de)

The story of Babar, the little elephant (Brunhoff, Jean de)

The travels of Babar (Brunhoff, Jean de)

Haddix, Margaret Peterson. *Say what?* ill. by James Bernardin. S&S, 2004. ISBN 0-689-86255-5 Subj: Behavior. Family life – brothers & sisters. Family life – parents. Language.

Haddon, Mark. *At home* ill. by author. Western, 1994. ISBN 0-307-17575-8 Subj: Activities. Dinosaurs. Format, unusual – board books.

At playgroup ill. by author. Western, 1994. ISBN 0-307-17576-6 Subj: Activities. Dinosaurs. Format, unusual – board books.

Gilbert's gobstopper ill. by author. Dial, 1988. ISBN 0-8037-0506-9 Subj: Behavior – lost & found possessions.

In the garden ill. by author. Western, 1994. ISBN 0-307-17578-2 Subj: Activities. Dinosaurs. Format, unusual – board books. Gardens, gardening.

On vacation ill. by author. Western, 1994. ISBN 0-307-17577-4 Subj: Activities. Activities – vacationing. Dinosaurs. Format, unusual – board books.

The Sea of Tranquillity ill. by Christian Birmingham. Harcourt, 1996. ISBN 0-15-201285-0 Subj: Moon. Space & space ships.

Toni and the tomato soup ill. by author. Harcourt, 1989. ISBN 0-15-200610-9 Subj: Behavior – wishing. Food.

Hader, Berta Hoerner. *The big snow* by Berta & Elmer Hader; ill. by authors. Macmillan, 1948. Subj: Caldecott award books. Weather – snow.

Cock-a-doodle doo: the story of a little red rooster by Berta & Elmer Hader; ill. by authors. Macmillan, 1939. Subj: Birds – chickens. Birds – ducks. Caldecott award honor books. Farms.

Lost in the zoo by Berta & Elmer Hader; ill. by authors. Macmillan, 1951. Subj: Behavior – lost. Zoos.

The mighty hunter by Berta & Elmer Hader; ill. by authors. Macmillan, 1943. Subj: Caldecott award honor books. Ecology. Indians of North America. School. Sports – hunting.

Mister Billy's gun by Berta & Elmer Hader; ill. by authors. Macmillan, 1960. Subj: Birds. Character traits – kindness to animals. Gardens, gardening. Violence, nonviolence. Weapons.

The story of Pancho and the bull with the crooked tail by Berta & Elmer Hader; ill. by authors. Oxford Univ. Pr., 1933. Subj: Animals – bulls, cows. Foreign lands – Mexico.

Hader, Elmer. *The big snow* (Hader, Berta Hoerner)

Cock-a-doodle doo: the story of a little red rooster (Hader, Berta Hoerner)

Lost in the zoo (Hader, Berta Hoerner)

The mighty hunter (Hader, Berta Hoerner)

Mister Billy's gun (Hader, Berta Hoerner)

The story of Pancho and the bull with the crooked tail (Hader, Berta Hoerner)

Hadithi, Mwenye. *see* Mwenye Hadithi

Hafner, Marylin. *Molly and Emmett's camping adventure* ill. by author. McGraw-Hill, 2001. ISBN 1-57768-894-5 Subj: Animals – cats. Camps, camping. Weather – rain.

Molly and Emmett's surprise garden ill. by author. McGraw-Hill, 2000. ISBN 1-57768-895-3 Subj: Animals – cats. Food. Gardens, gardening.

Mommies don't get sick ill. by author. Candlewick, 1995. ISBN 1-56402-287-0 Subj: Family life – mothers. Illness.

A year with Molly and Emmett ill. by author. Candlewick, 1997. ISBN 1-56402-966-2 Subj: Activities. Animals – cats. Friendship. Pets.

Haggerty, Mary Elizabeth. *A crack in the wall* ill. by Rubén De Anda. Lee & Low, 1993. ISBN 1-880000-03-2 Subj: Family life – mothers. Imagination. Poverty.

Hague, Kathleen. *Alphabears: an ABC book* ill. by Michael Hague. Holt, 1984. Subj: ABC books. Rhyming text. Toys – bears.

Bear hugs ill. by Michael Hague. Holt, 1989. ISBN 0-8050-0512-9 Subj: Poetry. Toys – bears.

Calendarbears: a book of months ill. by Michael Hague. Holt, 1997. ISBN 0-8050-3818-3 Subj: Animals – bears. Calendars. Days of the week, months of the year. Rhyming text.

East of the sun and west of the moon retold by Kathleen & Michael Hague; ill. by Michael Hague. Harcourt, 1980. ISBN 0-15-224702-5 Subj: Folk & fairy tales. Foreign lands – Norway. Royalty – princes.

Good night, fairies ill. by Michael Hague. SeaStar, 2002. ISBN 1-58717-134-1 Subj: Bedtime. Fairies. Family life – mothers.

The legend of the Veery bird ill. by Michael Hague. Harcourt, 1985. ISBN 0-15-243824-6 Subj: Birds. Character traits – helpfulness. Folk & fairy tales. Forest, woods.

The man who kept house by Kathleen & Michael Hague; ill. by Michael Hague. Harcourt, 1981. Subj: Family life. Folk & fairy tales. Foreign lands – Norway.

Numbears: a counting book ill. by Michael Hague. Holt, 1986. ISBN 0-03-007194-1 Subj: Counting, numbers. Toys – bears.

Out of the nursery, into the night ill. by Michael Hague. Holt, 1986. ISBN 0-8050-0088-7 Subj: Dreams. Night. Rhyming text. Toys – bears.

Ten little bears: a counting rhyme ill. by Michael Hague. Morrow, 1999. ISBN 0-688-16383-1 Subj: Animals – bears. Counting, numbers. Rhyming text.

Hague, Michael. *Æsop's fables* (Æsop)

Deck the halls ill. by author. Holt, 1991. ISBN 0-8050-1007-6 Subj: Holidays – Christmas. Music.

East of the sun and west of the moon (Hague, Kathleen)

The little mermaid (Andersen, H. C. [Hans Christian])

The man who kept house (Hague, Kathleen)

Michael Hague's world of unicorns ill. by author. Holt, 1986. ISBN 0-8050-0070-4 Subj: Format, unusual. Mythical creatures – unicorns.

Mother Goose (Mother Goose)

The nutcracker ill. by author; text by Sarah L. Thomson. SeaStar, 2003. ISBN 1-58717-255-0 Subj: Activities – dancing. Animals – mice. Ballet. Careers – toy makers. Folk & fairy tales. Holidays – Christmas. Imagination. Royalty. Toys.

The perfect present ill. by author. Morrow, 1996. ISBN 0-688-10880-6 Subj: Animals – kangaroos. Format, unusual – toy & movable books. Gifts. Holidays – Christmas.

Teddy bear, teddy bear ill. by author. Morrow, 1993. ISBN 0-688-12085-7 Subj: Games. Nursery rhymes. Toys – bears.

Hahn, Deborah. *The swineherd* (Andersen, H. C. [Hans Christian])

Hahn, Hannelore. *Take a giant step* ill. by Margot Zemach. Little, 1960. Subj: Games.

Haidle, Elizabeth. *Elmer the grump* ill. by author. Landmark Editions, 1989. ISBN 0-933849-20-6 Subj: Children as authors. Children as illustrators. Friendship. Mythical creatures – elves.

Haines, Gail Kay. *Fire* ill. by Jacqueline Chwast. Morrow, 1975. Subj: Fire. Science.

Haines, Mike. *Countdown to bedtime* ill. by David Melling. Hyperion, 2001. ISBN 0-7868-0741-5 Subj: Animals – porcupines. Animals – raccoons. Bedtime. Format, unusual – toy & movable books.

Hains, Harriet. *My baby brother* ill. by author. DK, 1992. ISBN 1-879431-76-9 Subj: Babies. Family life – brothers & sisters. Family life – new sibling.

My new puppy ill. by author. DK, 1992. ISBN 1-879431-77-7 Subj: Animals – dogs. Pets.

My new school ill. by author. DK, 1992. ISBN 1-56458-116-0 Subj: School – first day.

Our new kitten ill. by author. DK, 1992. ISBN 1-56458-117-9 Subj: Animals – cats. Pets.

Hair ill. by Christine Sharr. Wonder Books, 1971. Subj: Hair.

Haiz, Danah. *Jonah's journey* ill. by H. Hechtkopf. Lerner, 1973. Subj: Animals – whales. Religion – Jonah.

Halak, Glenn. *A grandmother's story* ill. by author. Green Tiger Pr., 1992. ISBN 0-671-74953-6 Subj: Boats, ships. Family life – grandmothers. Sea & seashore.

Haldane, Suzanne. *Teddies and machines* ill. by Maude Salinger. Dutton, 1996. ISBN 0-525-45401-2 Subj: Format, unusual – board books. Machines. Toys – bears.

Teddies and trucks ill. by Maude Salinger. Dutton, 1996. ISBN 0-525-45400-4 Subj: Format, unusual – board books. Machines. Toys – bears.

Haldeman, Oakley. *Here comes Santa Claus* (Autry, Gene)

Hale, Irina. *Boxman* ill. by author. Viking, 1992. ISBN 0-670-84287-7 Subj: Disguises. Family life.

Brown bear in a brown chair ill. by author. Atheneum, 1983. Subj: Character traits – appearance. Furniture – chairs. Toys – bears.

Chocolate mouse and sugar pig ill. by author. Atheneum, 1979. Subj: Animals – mice. Animals – pigs. Behavior – running away. Food. Toys.

Donkey's dreadful day ill. by author. Atheneum, 1982. Subj: Animals – donkeys. Circus. Dreams.

How I found a friend ill. by author. Viking, 1992. ISBN 0-670-84286-9 Subj: Friendship. Toys – bears.

The lost toys ill. by author. Atheneum, 1985. ISBN 0-689-50328-8 Subj: Activities – trading. Behavior – forgetfulness. Toys.

The naughty crow ill. by author. McElderry, 1992. ISBN 0-689-50546-9 Subj: Birds – crows. Foreign lands – Ukraine. Pets.

Small big bad boy ill. by author. Viking, 1991. ISBN 0-670-83818-7 Subj: Behavior – growing up. Behavior – wishing.

Hale, Kathleen. *Orlando and the water cats* ill. by author. Merrimack, 1979. ISBN 0-224-00662-2 Subj: Activities – vacationing. Animals – cats. Family life.

Orlando buys a farm ill. by author. Merrimack, 1980. Subj: Animals – cats. Farms.

Orlando, the frisky housewife ill. by author. Merrimack, 1979. ISBN 0-224-00753-X Subj: Animals – cats. Stores.

Hale, Linda. *The glorious Christmas soup party* ill. by author. Viking, 1962. Subj: Animals – mice. Food. Holidays – Christmas.

Hale, Lucretia. *The lady who put salt in her coffee* adapt. & ill. by Amy Schwartz. Harcourt, 1989. ISBN 0-15-243475-5 Subj: Family life. Humorous stories.

Hale, Michael. *Shoemaker Martin* (Tolstoy, Aleksey Nikolayevich)

Hale, Sarah Josepha Buell. *Mary had a little lamb* ill. by Tomie de Paola. Holiday, 1984. ISBN 0-8234-0509-5 Subj: Animals – sheep. Music. Nursery rhymes. School.

Mary had a little lamb photos by Bruce McMillan. Scholastic, 1990. ISBN 0-590-43773-9 Subj: Animals – sheep. Music. Nursery rhymes. School.

Mary had a little lamb ill. by Salley Mavor. Orchard, 1995. ISBN 0-531-08725-5 Subj: Animals – sheep. Nursery rhymes. School.

Mary had a little lamb ill. by Ann Schweninger. Western, 1992. ISBN 0-307-06139-6 Subj: Animals – sheep. Music. Nursery rhymes. School.

Mary had a little lamb as told & ill. by Iza Trapani. G. Stevens, 1999. ISBN 0-8368-2488-1 Subj: Animals – sheep. Farms. Humorous stories. Music. Nursery rhymes. Songs.

Mary had a little lamb ill. by Suzanne Vasilak. Modern Pub., 1993. ISBN 1-56144-351-4 Subj: Animals – sheep. Music. Nursery rhymes. School.

Mary had a little lamb [board book] ill. by Iza Trapani. Whispering Coyote, 1998. ISBN 1-58089-032-6 Subj: Animals – sheep. Behavior – misbehavior. Format, unusual – board books. Music. Nursery rhymes. Songs.

Haley, Alex. *Young Martin's promise* (Myers, Walter Dean)

Haley, Amanda. *It's a baby's world* ill. by author. Little, 2001. ISBN 0-316-34596-2 Subj: Activities. Babies. Day.

Haley, Gail E. *Birdsong* ill. by author. Crown, 1984. ISBN 0-517-55051-2 Subj: Birds. Character traits – helpfulness. Folk & fairy tales.

Dream peddler ill. by author. Dutton, 1993. ISBN 0-525-45153-6 Subj: Books, reading. Careers – peddlers. Dreams. Foreign lands – England.

Go away, stay away ill. by author. Scribners, 1977. ISBN 0-684-15272-X Subj: Mythical creatures – goblins. Seasons.

The green man ill. by author. Scribners, 1980. ISBN 0-684-16338-1 Subj: Knights. Seasons.

Jack and the bean tree ill. by author. Crown, 1986. ISBN 0-517-55717-7 Subj: Folk & fairy tales. Giants. Magic.

Jack and the fire dragon ill. by author. Crown, 1988. ISBN 0-517-56814-4 Subj: Character traits – bravery. Dragons. Folk & fairy tales.

Jack Jouett's ride ill. by author. Viking, 1973. ISBN 0-670-40466-7 Subj: U.S. history.

Noah's ark ill. by author. Atheneum, 1971. ISBN 0-689-20659-3 Subj: Animals. Boats, ships. Ecology. Religion – Noah. Weather – floods. Weather – rain. Weather – rainbows.

The post office cat ill. by author. Scribners, 1976. ISBN 0-684-14653-3 Subj: Animals – cats. Careers – postal workers. Foreign lands – England. Post office.

Puss in boots (Perrault, Charles)

Sea tale ill. by author. Dutton, 1990. ISBN 0-525-44567-6 Subj: Folk & fairy tales. Mythical creatures – mermaids, mermen. Sea & seashore.

A story, a story ill. by author. Aladdin, 1988, c1970. ISBN 0-689-71201-4 Subj: Caldecott award books. Folk & fairy tales. Foreign lands – Africa.

Two bad boys: a very old Cherokee tale ill. by author. Dutton, 1996. ISBN 0-525-45311-3 Subj: Activities – working. Creation. Indians of North America – Cherokee.

Haley, Patrick. *The little person* ill. by Jonna Kool. East Eagle, 1981. ISBN 0-9605738-0-1 Subj: Activities – traveling.

Hall, Amanda. *The gossipy wife* ill. by author. HarperCollins, 1984. ISBN 0-911745-19-X Subj: Folk & fairy tales. Foreign lands – Russia.

Hall, Bill. *Fish tale* ill. by John E. Johnson. Norton, 1967. Subj: Fish. Sports – fishing.

Hall, Carol. *Northern J. Calloway presents Super-vroomer!* (Calloway, Northern J.)

Hall, Derek. *Baby animals: five stories of endangered species* ill. by John Butler. Candlewick, 1992. ISBN 1-56402-004-5 Subj: Animals – endangered animals.

Elephant bathes ill. by John Butler. Sierra Club, 1985. ISBN 0-394-96529-9 Subj: Activities – bathing. Animals – elephants. Behavior – growing up. Family life.

Gorilla builds ill. by John Butler. Sierra Club, 1985. ISBN 0-394-96530-2 Subj: Animals – gorillas. Behavior – growing up. Family life.

Otter swims ill. by John Butler. Sierra Club, 1984. ISBN 0-394-96503-5 Subj: Animals – otters. Emotions – fear. Sports – swimming.

Panda climbs ill. by John Butler. Sierra Club, 1984. ISBN 0-394-96502-7 Subj: Animals – pandas. Emotions – fear. Trees.

Polar bear leaps ill. by John Butler. Sierra Club, 1985. ISBN 0-394-96531-0 Subj: Animals – polar bears. Behavior – growing up. Family life.

Tiger runs ill. by John Butler. Sierra Club, 1984. ISBN 0-394-96504-3 Subj: Animals – tigers. Emotions – fear. Sports – racing.

Hall, Donald. *Andrew the lion farmer* ill. by Jane Miller. Watts, 1959. Subj: Animals. Humorous stories.

I am the dog, I am the cat ill. by Barry Moser. Dial, 1994. ISBN 0-8037-1505-6 Subj: Animals – cats. Animals – dogs. Pets.

Lucy's Christmas ill. by Michael McCurdy. Harcourt, 1994. ISBN 0-15-276870-X Subj: Activities – making things. Family life. Holidays – Christmas. U.S. history.

Lucy's summer ill. by Michael McCurdy. Harcourt, 1995. ISBN 0-15-276873-4 Subj: Family life. Farms. Seasons – summer. U.S. history.

The man who lived alone ill. by Mary Azarian. Godine, 1984. ISBN 0-87923-538-1 Subj: Behavior – solitude.

The milkman's boy ill. by Greg Shed. Walker, 1997. ISBN 0-8027-8465-8 Subj: Careers – farmers. Food.

The ox-cart man ill. by Barbara Cooney. Viking, 1979. ISBN 0-670-53328-9 Subj: Activities – working. Caldecott award books. Farms. Seasons.

Hall, Fergus. *Groundsel* ill. by author. Merrimack, 1983. ISBN 0-224-01938-4 Subj: Gardens, gardening. Seasons.

Hall, Kathy. *see* McMullan, Kate (Hall)

Hall, Malcolm. *And then the mouse . . .* ill. by Stephen Gammell. Four Winds, 1980. ISBN 0-590-07618-3 Subj: Animals – mice. Folk & fairy tales.

CariCATures ill. by Bruce Degen. Coward, 1978. ISBN 0-698-30685-6 Subj: Animals. Riddles & jokes.

The friends of Charlie Ant Bear ill. by Alexandra Wallner. Coward, 1980. ISBN 0-398-30711-9 Subj: Animals – anteaters. Character traits – optimism.

Hall, Margaret. *Corn* ill. with photos. Heinemann, 2003. ISBN 1-58810-617-9 Subj: Activities – baking, cooking. Farms. Food.

Peanuts ill. with photos. Heinemann, 2003. ISBN 1-58810-619-5 Subj: Activities – baking, cooking. Farms. Food.

Hall, Mikele. *Mommy works, Daddy works* (Pedersen, Marika)

Hall, Pam. *On the edge of the eastern ocean* ill. by author. Silver Burdett, 1982. ISBN 0-88874-055-7 Subj: Birds – puffins. Poetry.

Hall, Patricia. *Hooray for reading!* ill. by Kathryn Mitter. Little Simon, 2002. ISBN 0-689-85206-1 Subj: Books, reading. Toys – dolls.

Hall, Richard. *Humphrey the lost whale* (Tokuda, Wendy)

Hall, Zoe. *The apple pie tree* ill. by Shari Halpern. Scholastic, 1996. ISBN 0-590-62382-6 Subj: Food. Nature. Seasons. Trees.

Fall leaves fall ill. by Shari Halpern. Scholastic, 2000. ISBN 0-590-10079-3 Subj: Seasons – fall. Trees.

It's pumpkin time! ill. by Shari Halpern. Scholastic, 1994. ISBN 0-590-47833-8 Subj: Holidays – Halloween. Plants.

The surprise garden ill. by Shari Halpern. Blue Sky, 1998. ISBN 0-590-10075-0 Subj: Gardens, gardening. Seeds.

Hallensleben, Georg. *Gaspard and Lisa, friends forever* (Gutman, Anne)

Gaspard and Lisa's Christmas surprise (Gutman, Anne)

Gaspard and Lisa's rainy day (Gutman, Anne)

Gaspard at the seashore (Gutman, Anne)

Gaspard in the hospital (Gutman, Anne)

Gaspard on vacation (Gutman, Anne)

Lisa in New York (Gutman, Anne)

Lisa in the jungle (Gutman, Anne)

Lisa's airplane trip (Gutman, Anne)

Lisa's baby sister (Gutman, Anne)

Pauline ill. by author. Farrar, 1999. ISBN 0-374-35758-7 Subj: Animals – elephants. Animals – weasels. Friendship.

Haller, Danita Ross. *Not just any ring* ill. by Deborah Kogan Ray. Knopf, 1982. ISBN 0-394-95082-8 Subj: Magic.

Hallinan, P. K. (Patrick K.). *For the love of our earth* ill. by author. Forest House, 1992. ISBN 1-878363-73-5 Subj: Ecology. Nature.

I know I belong ill. by author. Hazelden, 1991. ISBN 0-89486-782-2 Subj: Rhyming text. Self-concept.

I know who I am ill. by author. Hazelden, 1991. ISBN 0-89486-781-4 Subj: Rhyming text. Self-concept.

I'm glad to be me ill. by author. Childrens Pr., 1977. ISBN 0-516-03509-6 Subj: Activities. Family life – only child. Self-concept.

I'm thankful each day! ill. by author. Childrens Pr., 1981. ISBN 0-8249-8008-5 Subj: Folk & fairy tales.

Just being alone ill. by author. Childrens Pr., 1976. ISBN 0-516-03516-9 Subj: Activities. Behavior – solitude. Family life – only child.

Just open a book ill. by author. Childrens Pr., 1981. ISBN 0-516-03521-5 Subj: Books, reading. Rhyming text.

Let's care about sharing! ill. by author. Ideals, 1997. ISBN 1-57102-105-1 Subj: Behavior – sharing.

Let's learn all we can! ill. by author. Ideals, 1999. ISBN 1-57102-156-6 Subj: Rhyming text. School.

Let's play as a team ill. by author. Ideals, 1996. ISBN 1-57102-099-3 Subj: Activities – playing. Rhyming text.

My dentist, my friend ill. by author. Ideals, 1996. ISBN 1-57102-086-1 Subj: Careers – dentists. Rhyming text. Teeth.

My doctor, my friend ill. by author. Ideals, 1996. ISBN 1-57102-071-3 Subj: Careers – doctors. Illness. Rhyming text.

My teacher's my friend ill. by author. Childrens Pr., 1989. ISBN 0-516-09217-0 Subj: Careers – teachers. Friendship. School.

A rainbow of friends ill. by author. Ideals, 1994. ISBN 0-8249-8657-1 Subj: Character traits – individuality. Friendship. Rhyming text.

The small town children's Easter ill. by author. Ideals, 1988. ISBN 0-8249-8319-X Subj: Holidays – Easter. Religion. Rhyming text.

That's what a friend is ill. by author. Childrens Pr., 1977. ISBN 0-516-03628-9 Subj: Friendship. Rhyming text.

Three freckles past a hair: a grandfather's legacy of love ill. by author. Forest House, 1994. ISBN 1-56674-105-X Subj: Death. Emotions – grief. Family life – grandfathers. Sea & seashore.

Today is Easter! ill. by author. Ideals, 1993. ISBN 1-878363-94-8 Subj: Family life – brothers & sisters. Holidays – Easter. Rhyming text.

Today is Halloween ill. by author. Ideals, 1992. ISBN 1-878363-95-6 Subj: Holidays – Halloween. Rhyming text.

Today is Valentine's Day! ill. by author. Ideals, 1994. ISBN 1-57102-129-9 Subj: Friendship. Holidays – Valentine's Day. Rhyming text. School.

Today is your birthday! ill. by author. Ideals, 1990. ISBN 1-878363-29-8 Subj: Birthdays.

We're very good friends, my aunt and I ill. by author. Childrens Pr., 1989. ISBN 0-516-03655-6 Subj: Family life – aunts, uncles. Friendship. Rhyming text.

When I grow up ill. by author. Ideals, 1995. ISBN 1-57102-061-6 Subj: ABC books. Careers. Rhyming text.

Where's Michael? ill. by author. Childrens Pr., 1978. ISBN 0-516-03668-8 Subj: Behavior – imitation. Self-concept.

Halloweena ill. by Victoria Roberts. Atheneum, 2002. ISBN 0-689-82825-X Subj: Holidays – Halloween. Witches.

Halls, Kelly Milner. *I bought a baby chicken* ill. by Karen Stormer Brooks. Boyds Mills, 2000. ISBN 1-56397-800-8 Subj: Animals – babies. Birds – chickens. Counting, numbers.

Hallworth, Grace. *Down by the river* ill. by Caroline Binch. Scholastic, 1996. ISBN 0-590-69320-4 Subj: Activities – playing. Foreign lands – Caribbean Islands. Poetry. Songs.

Sing me a story ill. by John Clementson. August House, 2002. ISBN 0-87483-672-7 Subj: Activities – dancing. Folk & fairy tales. Foreign lands – Caribbean Islands. Music. Songs.

Halperin, Wendy Anderson. *Love is* (Bible New Testament Corinthians, 1st, XIII)

Once upon a company ill. by author. Orchard, 1998. ISBN 0-531-33089-3 Subj: Activities – making things. Careers.

When chickens grow teeth: a story from the French of Guy de Maupassant retold & ill. by Wendy Anderson Halperin. Orchard, 1996. ISBN 0-531-08876-6 Subj: Birds – chickens. Eggs. Family life. Illness.

Worm gets a job (Caple, Kathy)

Halpern, Julie. *Toby and the snowflakes* ill. by Matthew Cordell. Houghton, 2004. ISBN 0-618-42004-5 Subj: Activities – playing. Emotions – loneliness. Friendship. Weather – snow.

Halpern, Shari. *Hush little baby* (Hush little baby)

I have a pet! ill. by author. Macmillan, 1994. ISBN 0-02-741982-7 Subj: Pets.

Moving from one to ten ill. by author. Macmillan, 1993. ISBN 0-02-741981-9 Subj: Counting, numbers. Moving.

My river ill. by author. Macmillan, 1992. ISBN 0-02-741980-0 Subj: Animals. Ecology. Rivers.

What shall we do when we all go out? text adapt. by Philip H. Bailey; ill. by Shari Halpern. North-South, 1995. ISBN 1-55858-425-0 Subj: Activities – playing. Music. Songs.

Halsey, Megan. *Jump for joy* ill. by author. Bradbury, 1994. ISBN 0-02-742040-X Subj: Days of the week, months of the year.

Halsey, William D. *The magic world of words: a very first dictionary* ed. by William D. Halsey & Christopher G. Morris; ill. by Dora Leder, Angela Adams, & John Hamberger. Macmillan, 1977. ISBN 0-02-578770-5 Subj: Dictionaries.

Hamanaka, Sheila. *I look like a girl* ill. by author. Morrow, 1999. ISBN 0-688-14626-0 Subj: Animals. Imagination. Rhyming text.

Screen of frogs ill. by reteller. Orchard, 1993. ISBN 0-531-08614-3 Subj: Ecology. Folk & fairy tales. Foreign lands – Japan. Frogs & toads.

Hamberger, John. *The day the sun disappeared* ill. by author. Norton, 1964. Subj: Animals. Ecology. Science. Sun.

Hazel was an only pet ill. by author. Norton, 1968. Subj: Animals – dogs. Family life – only child. Pets.

The lazy dog ill. by author. Four Winds, 1971. Subj: Animals – dogs. Toys – balls. Wordless.

The peacock who lost his tail ill. by author. Norton, 1967. Subj: Birds – peacocks, peahens. Character traits – pride.

This is the day ill. by author. Grosset, 1971. ISBN 0-448-21424-5 Subj: Animals – groundhogs. Holidays – Groundhog Day.

Hamil, Thomas Arthur. *Brother Alonzo* ill. by author. Macmillan, 1957. Subj: Religion.

Hamilton, DeWitt. *Sad days, glad days* ill. by Gail Owens. A. Whitman, 1995. ISBN 0-8075-7200-4 Subj: Animals – cats. Family life. Family life – mothers. Illness.

Hamilton, Emily. *My name is Emily* (Hamilton, Morse)

Hamilton, Emma Walton. *Dumpy at school* (Edwards, Julie Andrews)

Dumpy the dump truck (Edwards, Julie Andrews)

Dumpy to the rescue! (Edwards, Julie Andrews)

Dumpy's apple shop (Edwards, Julie Andrews)

Simeon's gift (Edwards, Julie Andrews)

Hamilton, K. R. (Kersten R). *This is the ocean* ill. by Lorianne Siomades. Boyds Mills, 2001. ISBN 1-56397-890-3 Subj: Rhyming text. Sea & seashore. Water.

Hamilton, Morse. *Belching Hill* ill. by Forest Rogers. Greenwillow, 1997. ISBN 0-688-14049-1 Subj: Folk & fairy tales. Foreign lands – Japan. Mythical creatures – ogres.

Big sisters are bad witches ill. by Marylin Hafner. Greenwillow, 1981. ISBN 0-688-84268-2 Subj: Sibling rivalry. Witches.

The black hen, or, The underground inhabitants (Pogorelsky, Antony)

How do you do, Mr. Birdsteps? ill. by Patience Brewster. Avon, 1983. ISBN 0-380-82875-8 Subj: Character traits – shyness.

Little sister for sale ill. by Gioia Fiammenghi. Dutton, 1992. ISBN 0-525-65078-4 Subj: Family life – sisters. Sibling rivalry.

My name is Emily by Morse & Emily Hamilton; ill. by Jenni Oliver. Greenwillow, 1979. ISBN 0-688-84181-3 Subj: Behavior – running away. Sibling rivalry.

Who's afraid of the dark? ill. by Patience Brewster. Avon, 1983. ISBN 0-380-82883-9 Subj: Emotions – fear. Night.

Hamilton, Richard. *Polly's picnic* ill. by Sophy Williams. Bloomsbury, 2003. ISBN 1-58234-819-7 Subj: Activities – picnicking. Animals. Behavior – sharing. Rhyming text.

Hamilton, Virginia. *Drylongso* ill. by Jerry Pinkney. Harcourt, 1992. ISBN 0-15-224241-4 Subj: Ecology. Ethnic groups in the U.S. – African Americans. Farms. Weather – droughts. Weather – wind.

The girl who spun gold ill. by Leo & Diane Dillon. Blue Sky, 2000. ISBN 0-590-47378-6 Subj: Activities – weaving. Behavior – greed. Folk & fairy tales. Foreign lands – West Indies.

Jaguarundi ill. by Floyd Cooper. Blue Sky, 1995. ISBN 0-590-47366-2 Subj: Animals. Animals – endangered animals. Animals – jaguars. Behavior – seeking better things. Ecology.

Hamilton-Merritt, Jane. *My first days of school* photos by author. S&S, 1982. ISBN 0-671-44417-4 Subj: School – first day.

Our new baby photos by author. S&S, 1982. ISBN 0-671-44416-6 Subj: Babies. Family life – new sibling.

Hamley, Dennis. *Tigger and friends* ill. by Meg Rutherford. Lothrop, 1989. ISBN 0-688-08605-5 Subj: Animals – cats. Pets.

Hamm, Diane Johnston. *Grandma drives a motor bed* ill. by Charles Robinson. A. Whitman, 1987. ISBN 0-8075-3025-5 Subj: Family life – grandmothers. Family life – grandparents. Furniture – beds. Handicaps. Illness. Old age.

How many feet in the bed? ill. by Kate Salley Palmer. S&S, 1991. ISBN 0-671-72638-2 Subj: Anatomy – feet. Bedtime. Counting, numbers. Family life.

Laney's lost momma ill. by Sally G. Ward. A. Whitman, 1991. ISBN 0-8075-4340-3 Subj: Behavior – lost. Family life – mothers. Shopping. Stores.

Rock-a-bye farm ill. by Rick Brown. S&S, 1992. ISBN 0-671-74773-8 Subj: Animals. Babies. Bedtime. Careers – farmers. Farms. Night. Sleep.

Hamm, Mia. *Winners never quit* ill. by Carol Thompson. HarperCollins, 2004. ISBN 0-06-074051-5 Subj: Sports – soccer. Sportsmanship.

Hammar, Asa. *Fit for pigs* ill. by Johanna Moller. Checkerboard, 1992. ISBN 1-56288-265-1 Subj: Animals – pigs. Careers – firefighters. Fire. Homes, houses.

Hammarberg, Dyan. *Jessie the chicken* (Pursell, Margaret Sanford)

Polly the guinea pig (Pursell, Margaret Sanford)

Rusty the Irish setter (Overbeck, Cynthia)

Shelley the sea gull (Pursell, Margaret Sanford)

Sprig the tree frog (Pursell, Margaret Sanford)

Hammerschlag, Carl A. *The go away doll* ill. by author. Turtle Island Pr., 1998. ISBN 1-889166-22-7 Subj: Activities – traveling. Friendship. Toys – dolls.

Hammersmith, Craig. *Patterns* ill. with photos. Compass Pt., 2003. ISBN 0-7565-0452-X Subj: Activities – quilting. Concepts.

Watch it grow ill. with photos. Compass Pt., 2002. ISBN 0-7565-0246-2 Subj: Nature. Plants.

What is a family? ill. with photos. Compass Pt., 2003. ISBN 0-7565-0367-1 Subj: Family life.

Hammerstein, Oscar. *My favorite things* (Rodgers, Richard)

A real nice clambake (Rodgers, Richard)

Hammond, Anna. *This home we have made* by Anna Hammond & Joe Matunis; trans. from English by Olga Karman Mendell. Crossroad, 1993. ISBN 0-517-59339-4 Subj: Art. Foreign languages. Homeless.

Hample, Stoo. *Stoo Hample's silly joke book* ill. by author. Delacorte, 1978. ISBN 0-440-08160-2 Subj: Humorous stories. Riddles & jokes.

Yet another big fat funny silly book ill. by author. Delacorte, 1980. ISBN 0-440-09797-5 Subj: Poetry. Riddles & jokes.

Hampshire, Susan. *Rosie's ballet slippers* ill. by Maria Teresa Meloni. HarperCollins, 1996. ISBN 0-06-026504-3 Subj: Activities – dancing. Ballet. Clothing – shoes.

Hamsa, Bobbie. *Animal babies* ill. by Renée Mansfield. Delmar, 1991. ISBN 0-8273-4495-3 Subj: Animals – babies.

Dirty Larry ill. by Paul Sharp. Childrens Pr., 1983. ISBN 0-516-02040-4 Subj: Character traits – cleanliness.

Fast-draw Freddie ill. by Susan Miller. Rev. ed. Childrens Pr., 2000. ISBN 0-516-22153-1 Subj: Activities – drawing. Rhyming text.

Polly wants a cracker ill. by Jerry Warshaw. Childrens Pr., 1986. ISBN 0-516-02071-4 Subj: Birds – parakeets, parrots. Counting, numbers. Rhyming text.

Your pet bear ill. by Tom Dunnington. Childrens Pr., 1980. ISBN 0-516-03351-4 Subj: Animals – bears. Imagination.

Your pet beaver ill. by Tom Dunnington. Childrens Pr., 1980. ISBN 0-516-03352-2 Subj: Animals – beavers. Imagination.

Your pet camel ill. by Tom Dunnington. Childrens Pr., 1980. ISBN 0-516-03362-X Subj: Animals – camels. Imagination.

Your pet elephant ill. by Tom Dunnington. Childrens Pr., 1980. ISBN 0-516-03353-0 Subj: Animals – elephants. Imagination.

Your pet giraffe ill. by Tom Dunnington. Childrens Pr., 1982. ISBN 0-516-03355-7 Subj: Animals – giraffes. Imagination.

Your pet kangaroo ill. by Tom Dunnington. Childrens Pr., 1980. ISBN 0-516-03363-8 Subj: Animals – kangaroos. Imagination.

Your pet penguin ill. by Tom Dunnington. Childrens Pr., 1980. ISBN 0-516-03364-6 Subj: Birds – penguins. Imagination.

Your pet sea lion ill. by Tom Dunnington. Childrens Pr., 1982. ISBN 0-516-03356-5 Subj: Animals – sea lions. Imagination.

Han, Oki S. *Kongi and Potgi: a Cinderella story from Korea* adapt. by Oki S. Han & Stephanie Haboush Plunkett; pictures by Oki S.

Han. Dial, 1994. ISBN 0-8037-1572-2 Subj: Animals. Character traits – helpfulness. Family life – stepfamilies. Folk & fairy tales. Foreign lands – Korea. Royalty – princes.

Sir Whong and the golden pig adapt. by Oki S. Han & Stephanie Haboush Plunkett; pictures by Oki S. Han. Dial, 1993. ISBN 0-8037-1345-2 Subj: Behavior – trickery. Folk & fairy tales. Foreign lands – Korea.

Hancock, Joy Elizabeth. *The loudest little lion* ill. by Eileen Christelow. A. Whitman, 1988. ISBN 0-8075-4773-5 Subj: Animals – lions. Bedtime. Noise, sounds.

Hancock, Sibyl. *Esteban and the ghost* ill. by Dirk Zimmer. Dial, 1983. Adapt. from The tinker and the ghost by Ralph Steele Boggs and Mary Gould Davis. ISBN 0-8037-2411-X Subj: Ghosts.

Freaky Francie ill. by Leonard W. Shortall. Prentice-Hall, 1979. ISBN 0-13-330563-5 Subj: Problem solving.

Old Blue ill. by Erick Ingraham. Putnam, 1980. ISBN 0-399-61141-X Subj: Animals – bulls, cows. Cowboys, cowgirls. U.S. history – frontier & pioneer life.

Handelman, Dorothy. *Babies help out* (Leonard, Marcia)

Peek-a-boo, baby! (Leonard, Marcia)

Handford, Martin. *Find Waldo now* ill. by author. Little, 1994. ISBN 0-316-34232-7 Subj: Activities – traveling. Games. Picture puzzles. Time.

The great Waldo search ill. by author. Little, 1989. ISBN 0-316-34282-3 Subj: Activities – traveling. Games. Picture puzzles.

Plundering pirates: a where's Waldo? fun fact book (Wright, Rachel)

Where's Waldo? ill. by author. Candlewick, 1997. ISBN 0-7636-0310-4 Subj: Activities – traveling. Behavior – lost & found possessions. Foreign lands. Games. Picture puzzles.

Where's Waldo? In Hollywood ill. by author. Candlewick, 1993. ISBN 1-56402-294-3 Subj: Activities – traveling. Games.

Where's Waldo now? ill. by author. Candlewick, 1997. ISBN 0-7636-0308-2 Subj: Activities – traveling. Games. Time.

Where's Waldo? The fantastic journey ill. by author. Candlewick, 1997. ISBN 0-7636-0309-0 Subj: Activities – traveling. Games. Imagination.

Where's Waldo? The wonder book ill. by author. Candlewick, 1997. ISBN 0-7636-0312-0 Subj: Activities – traveling. Behavior – lost & found possessions. Games.

Handforth, Thomas. *Mei Li* ill. by author. Doubleday, 1938. ISBN 0-385-07401-8 Subj: Caldecott award books. Foreign lands – China. Holidays – Chinese New Year.

Handley, Diana. *A brave little princess* (Masini, Beatrice)

Hands, Hargrave. *Bunny sees* ill. by author. Grosset, 1985. ISBN 0-488-10577-2 Subj: Animals – rabbits. Format, unusual – board books. Nature.

Duckling sees ill. by author. Grosset, 1985. ISBN 0-448-10579-9 Subj: Animals. Format, unusual – board books.

Little lamb sees ill. by author. Grosset, 1985. ISBN 0-448-10576-4 Subj: Animals. Format, unusual – board books.

Hänel, Wolfram. *The gold at the end of the rainbow* trans. by Anthea Bell; ill. by Loek Koopmans. North-South, 1997. ISBN 1-55858-693-8 Subj: Character traits – generosity. Family life – grandfathers. Folk & fairy tales. Foreign lands – Ireland. Mythical creatures – leprechauns.

Little elephant runs away ill. by Cristina Kadmon; tr. by J. Alison James. North-South, 2001. ISBN 0-7358-1444-9 Subj: Behavior – lost. Behavior – running away. Family life – brothers & sisters. Sibling rivalry.

Little elephant's song ill. by Cristina Kadmon; tr. by J. Alison James. North-South, 2000. ISBN 0-7358-1298-5 Subj: Animals – elephants. Behavior – growing up. Family life. Noise, sounds.

Mary and the mystery dog ill. by Cristina Kadmon; tr. by J. Alison James. North-South, 1999. ISBN 0-7358-1044-3 Subj: Animals – dogs. Sea & seashore – beaches.

Mia the beach cat ill. by Kirsten Höcker; trans. by J. Alison James. North-South, 1994. ISBN 1-55858-314-9 Subj: Activities – vacationing. Animals – cats. Pets. Sea & seashore – beaches.

Hanhart, Brigitte. *Shoemaker Martin* (Tolstoy, Aleksey Nikolayevich)

Hanklin, Rebecca. *I can be a doctor* ill. with photos. Childrens Pr., 1985. ISBN 0-516-01846-9 Subj: Careers – doctors.

I can be a fire fighter ill. with photos. Childrens Pr., 1985. ISBN 0-516-01847-7 Subj: Careers – firefighters.

Hanlon, Emily. *What if a lion eats me and I fall into a hippopotamus' mud hole?* ill. by Leigh Grant. Delacorte, 1975. ISBN 0-440-05951-8 Subj: Emotions – fear. Imagination. Zoos.

Hanly, Shelia. *Toddler's book of fun things to do* photos by Steve Shott. DK, 1999. ISBN 0-7894-3979-4 Subj: Activities.

Hann, Jacquie. *Crybaby* ill. by author. Four Winds, 1979. ISBN 0-590-07609-4 Subj: Emotions.

Follow the leader ill. by author. Crown, 1982. ISBN 0-517-54603-5 Subj: Activities – playing. Games.

Up day, down day ill. by author. Four Winds, 1978. ISBN 0-590-07519-5 Subj: Character traits – luck. Sports – fishing.

Hanna, Jack. *Jungle Jack Hanna's safari adventure* by Jack Hanna & Rick A. Prebeg; photos by Rick A. Prebeg. Scholastic, 1996. ISBN 0-590-67322-X Subj: Animals. Foreign lands – Africa.

The petting zoo ill. by Neil Brennan. Doubleday, 1992. ISBN 0-385-41694-6 Subj: Animals. Format, unusual – toy & movable books. Zoos.

Hannan, Peter. *The battle of Sillyville: live silly or die!* ill. by author. Knopf, 1991. ISBN 0-679-90286-4 Subj: Behavior. Humorous stories.

Escape from Camp Wannabarf ill. by author. Knopf, 1991. ISBN 0-679-90287-2 Subj: Camps, camping. Humorous stories.

School after dark ill. by author. Knopf, 1991. ISBN 0-679-80288-0 Subj: Humorous stories. Night. School.

Sillyville or bust ill. by author. Knopf, 1991. ISBN 0-679-90285-6 Subj: Activities – traveling. Automobiles. Behavior – boredom. Humorous stories.

Hannant, Judith Stuller. *Doorknob collection of nursery rhymes* ill. by author. Little, 1991. ISBN 0-316-34343-9 Subj: Format, unusual. Format, unusual – board books. Nursery rhymes.

The doorknob collection of pets and pals ill. by author. Little, 1994. ISBN 0-316-34387-0 Subj: Animals. Format, unusual – board books. Nursery rhymes.

Three little kittens ill. by author. Little, 1995. ISBN 0-316-34413-3 Subj: Animals – cats. Behavior – lost & found possessions. Clothing – gloves, mittens. Format, unusual – board books. Nursery rhymes.

Hannert, Todd. *Morning dance* ill. by author. Chronicle, 2001. ISBN 0-8118-2812-3 Subj: Activities – dancing. Morning.

Hanrahan, Barbara. *My sisters love my clothes* ill. by Lise Stork. Perry Heights Pr., 1992. ISBN 0-9630181-0-8 Subj: Clothing. Family life – sisters.

Hansard, Peter. *I like monkeys because . . .* ill. by Patricia Casey. Candlewick, 1993. ISBN 1-56402-196-3 Subj: Animals – monkeys.

Wag, wag, wag ill. by Barbara Firth. Candlewick, 1994. ISBN 1-56402-301-X Subj: Animals – dogs.

Hansen, Biruta Akerbergs. *Parading with piglets* ill. by author. National Geographic, 1996. ISBN 0-7922-2711-5 Subj: ABC books. Animals. Format, unusual – toy & movable books.

Hansen, Carla. *Barnaby Bear builds a boat* by Carla & Vilhelm Hansen; ill. by authors. Random House, 1979. ISBN 0-394-84247-2 Subj: Animals – bears. Boats, ships.

Barnaby Bear visits the farm by Carla & Vilhelm Hansen; ill. by authors. Random House, 1979. ISBN 0-394-84248-0 Subj: Animals – bears. Farms.

Hansen, Felicity. *The first bear* ill. by Anthony Carnabuci. Barefoot, 2000. ISBN 1-84148-012-6 Subj: Animals – bears. Creation. Stars. Toys – bears.

Hansen, Jeff. *Being a fire fighter isn't just squirtin' water* ill. by author. Vantage Pr., 1978. ISBN 0-533-03498-1 Subj: Careers – firefighters.

Hansen, Mark Victor. *Chicken soup for little souls: Della Splatnuk birthday girl* (McCourt, Lisa)

Chicken soup for little souls: The best night out with Dad (McCourt, Lisa)

Chicken soup for little souls: The Goodness Gorillas (McCourt, Lisa)

Chicken soup for little souls: The never-forgotten doll (McCourt, Lisa)

Chicken soup for little souls: The new kid and the cookie thief (McCourt, Lisa)

Hansen, P. (Paul H.). *My granny's purse.* Workman, 2003. ISBN 0-7611-2978-2 Subj: Clothing – handbags, purses. Family life – grandmothers. Format, unusual – toy & movable books.

Hansen, Vilhelm. *Barnaby Bear builds a boat* (Hansen, Carla)

Barnaby Bear visits the farm (Hansen, Carla)

Hanson, Joan. *I don't like Timmy* ill. by author. Carolrhoda, 1972. ISBN 0-8761-4028-2 Subj: Babies. Family life – brothers. Family life – new sibling.

I won't be afraid ill. by author. Carolrhoda, 1974. ISBN 0-8761-4050-9 Subj: Behavior – growing up. Emotions – fear.

I'm going to run away ill. by author. Platt, 1978. ISBN 0-448-46522-1 Subj: Behavior – running away.

Hanson, Mary Elizabeth. *The difference between babies and cookies* ill. by Debbie Tilley. Harcourt, 2002. ISBN 0-15-202406-9 Subj: Babies. Family life – new sibling. Family life – sisters.

The old man and the flea ill. by David Webber Merrell. Rising Moon, 2001. ISBN 0-87358-776-6 Subj: Insects – fleas. Pets.

Snug ill. by Cheryl Munro Taylor. S&S, 1998. ISBN 0-689-81164-0 Subj: Animals – bears. Behavior. Family life – mothers.

Hanson, Regina. *The face at the window* ill. by Linda Saport. Clarion, 1997. ISBN 0-395-78625-8 Subj: Emotions – fear. Foreign lands – Japan. Illness.

A season for mangoes ill. by Eric Velasquez. Clarion, 2004. ISBN 0-618-15972-X Subj: Activities – storytelling. Death. Emotions – grief. Family life – grandmothers. Foreign lands – Jamaica. Memories, memory.

The tangerine tree ill. by Harvey Stevenson. Clarion, 1995. ISBN 0-395-68963-5 Subj: Behavior – worrying. Careers – migrant workers. Emotions – sadness. Family life – fathers. Foreign lands – Jamaica.

Hanukkah lights sel. by Lee Bennett Hopkins; ill. by Melanie Hall. HarperCollins, 2004. ISBN 0-06-008052-3 Subj: Holidays – Hanukkah. Jewish culture. Poetry. Religion.

Hanze. *Yann and the whale* ill. by Hanze; story by Frissen. Kane/Miller, 1997. ISBN 0-916291-71-5 Subj: Animals – whales. Sea & seashore. Sports – fishing.

Hapgood, Miranda. *Martha's mad day* ill. by Emily Arnold McCully. Crown, 1977. ISBN 0-517-52997-1 Subj: Emotions – anger.

Harada, Joyce. *It's the ABC book* ill. by author. Heian Intl., 1982. ISBN 0-89346-157-1 Subj: ABC books.

It's the 0-1-2-3 book ill. by author. Heian Intl., 1985. ISBN 0-89346-252-7 Subj: Counting, numbers.

Harber, Frances. *The brothers' promise* ill. by Thor Wickstrom. A. Whitman, 1998. ISBN 0-8075-0900-0 Subj: Behavior. Family life – brothers. Jewish culture. Religion.

My king has donkey ears ill. by Maryann Kovalski. North Winds, 1986. ISBN 0-590-71522-4 Subj: Folk & fairy tales. Problem solving. Royalty – kings.

Harbour, Elizabeth. *A first picture book of nursery rhymes* ill. by author. Viking, 1995. ISBN 0-670-85030-6 Subj: Nursery rhymes.

Harder, Dan (Dan Wymbs). *Colliding with Chris* ill. by Kevin O'Malley. Hyperion, 1997. ISBN 0-7868-2098-5 Subj: Accidents. Rhyming text. Sports – bicycling.

Hardy, Tad. *Lost cat* ill. by David Goldin. Houghton Mifflin, 1996. ISBN 0-395-73574-2 Subj: Animals – cats. Behavior – lost. Pets. Rhyming text.

Hare, Lorraine. *Who needs her?* ill. by author. Atheneum, 1983. ISBN 0-689-50268-0 Subj: Character traits – cleanliness.

Hare, Norma Q. *Mystery at mouse house* ill. by Stella Ormai. Garrard, 1980. ISBN 0-8116-6412-0 Subj: Behavior – stealing. Mystery stories.

Hargrove, Linda. *Wings across the moon* ill. by Joung Un Kim. HarperFestival, 2001. ISBN 0-694-01280-7 Subj: Animals. Moon. Night. Rhyming text.

Haring, Keith. *Big* ill. by author. Hyperion, 1998. ISBN 0-7868-0390-8 Subj: Clothing. Concepts – color. Concepts – size. Format, unusual – board books.

10 ill. by author. Hyperion, 1998. ISBN 0-7868-0391-6 Subj: Counting, numbers. Foreign languages. Format, unusual – board books.

Hariton, Anca. *Butterfly story* ill. by author. Dutton, 1995. ISBN 0-525-45212-5 Subj: Insects – butterflies, caterpillars. Metamorphosis. Science.

Egg story ill. by author. Dutton, 1992. ISBN 0-525-44861-6 Subj: Birds – chickens. Birth. Eggs.

Harjo, Joy. *The good luck cat* ill. by Paul Lee. Harcourt, 2000. ISBN 0-15-232197-7 Subj: Animals – cats. Character traits – luck. Indians of North America.

Harker, Lesley. *Annie's ark* ill. by author. Scholastic, 2002. ISBN 0-439-36823-5 Subj: Animals. Boats, ships. Religion – Noah. Weather – floods. Weather – rain.

Harley, Bill. *Bear's all-night party* ill. by Melissa Ferreira. August House, 2001. ISBN 0-8748-3572-0 Subj: Animals. Animals – bears. Moon. Parties.

Nothing happened ill. by Ann Miya. Tricycle, 1995. ISBN 1-883672-09-0 Subj: Bedtime. Emotions. Family life. Family life – brothers. Night.

Sarah's story ill. by Eve Aldridge. Tricycle, 1996. ISBN 1-883672-20-1 Subj: Activities – storytelling. Insects – ants. Insects – bees. School.

Harlow, Joan Hiatt. *Shadow bear* ill. by Jim Arnosky. Doubleday, 1981. ISBN 0-385-15067-9 Subj: Animals – polar bears. Emotions – fear. Eskimos.

Harmer, Juliet. *Prayers for children* ill. by author. Viking, 1990. ISBN 0-670-83348-7 Subj: Days of the week, months of the year. Religion.

Harms, D. *The merry starlings* (Marshak, S. [Samuil])

Harms, John, II. *The saving of Sly Manatee* ill. by Robin Lee Makowski. Frederick, 1998. ISBN 0-9653871-3-5 Subj: Animals – manatees.

Harness, Cheryl. *Mark Twain and the queens of the Mississippi* ill. by author. S&S, 1998. ISBN 0-689-81542-5 Subj: Boats, ships. Careers – writers. Rivers. U.S. history.

Midnight in the cemetery: a spooky search-and-find alphabet book ill. by Robin Brickman. S&S, 1999. ISBN 0-689-80873-9 Subj: ABC books. Ghosts. Rhyming text.

Papa's Christmas gift: around the world on the night before Christmas ill. by author. S&S, 1995. ISBN 0-689-80344-3 Subj: Holidays – Christmas. Poetry.

The queen with bees in her hair ill. by author. Holiday, 1993. ISBN 0-8050-1715-1 Subj: Folk & fairy tales. Royalty – kings. Royalty – queens. Seasons – spring.

Three young pilgrims ill. by author. Bradbury, 1992. ISBN 0-02-742643-2 Subj: Pilgrims. U.S. history.

Harold, Jerdine Nolen. *see* Nolen, Jerdine

Harper, Anita. *How we live* ill. by Christine Roche. HarperCollins, 1977. ISBN 0-060-22223-9 Subj: Homes, houses.

How we work ill. by Christine Roche. HarperCollins, 1977. ISBN 0-06-022225-5 Subj: Activities – working. Careers.

It's not fair! ill. by Susan Hellard. Putnam, 1986. ISBN 0-399-21365-1 Subj: Animals – kangaroos. Babies. Family life – new sibling. Sibling rivalry.

Harper, Charise Mericle. *Imaginative inventions* ill. by author. Little, 2001. ISBN 0-316-34725-6 Subj: Inventions.

The Monster Show ill. by author. Houghton, 2004. ISBN 0-618-38797-8 Subj: Monsters.

There was a bold lady who wanted a star ill. by author. Little, 2002. ISBN 0-316-14673-0 Subj: Cumulative tales. Folk & fairy tales. Rhyming text.

The trouble with normal ill. by author. Houghton, 2003. ISBN 0-618-15626-7 Subj: Animals – squirrels. Homes, houses.

When I grow up ill. by author. Chronicle, 2001. ISBN 0-8118-2905-7 Subj: Behavior – growing up.

Harper, Dan. *Sit, Truman* ill. by Barry Moser & Cara Moser. Harcourt, 2001. ISBN 0-15-202616-9 Subj: Activities. Animals – dogs.

Telling time with Big Mama Cat ill. by Barry & Cara Moser. Harcourt, 1998. ISBN 0-15-201738-0 Subj: Animals – cats. Clocks, watches. Format, unusual – toy & movable books. Time.

Harper, Isabelle. *My dog Rosie* ill. by Barry Moser. Blue Sky, 1994. ISBN 0-590-47619-X Subj: Animals – dogs. Children as authors. Family life – grandfathers.

Our new puppy ill. by Barry Moser. Silver Burdett, 1996. ISBN 0-590-56926-0 Subj: Animals – dogs. Family life – grandfathers. Family life – sisters.

Harper, Jamie. *Don't grown-ups ever have fun?* ill. by author. Little, 2003. ISBN 0-316-14664-1 Subj: Behavior. Family life – parents.

Harper, Jessica. *I forgot my shoes* ill. by Kathy Osborn. Putnam, 1999. ISBN 0-399-23149-8 Subj: Clothing – shoes. Memories, memory. Rhyming text.

I'm not going to chase the cat today ill. by Lindsay Harper Dupont. HarperCollins, 2000. ISBN 0-688-17637-2 Subj: Animals – cats. Animals – dogs. Animals – mice. Parties. Rhyming text.

Lizzy's do's and don'ts ill. by Lindsay Harper Dupont. HarperCollins, 2002. ISBN 0-06-623861-7 Subj: Behavior. Family life – mothers. Rhyming text.

Lizzy's ups and downs ill. by Lindsay Harper duPont. HarperCollins, 2004. ISBN 0-06-052064-7 Subj: Emotions. Family life – mothers. Rhyming text. School.

Nora's room ill. by Lindsay Harper duPont. HarperCollins, 2001. ISBN 0-06-029137-0 Subj: Imagination. Noise, sounds. Rhyming text.

Harper, Jo. *Jalapeno Hal* ill. by Jennifer Beck Harris. Four Winds, 1993. ISBN 0-02-742645-9 Subj: Food. U.S. history – frontier & pioneer life. Weather – droughts. Weather – rain.

The legend of Mexicatl ill. by Robert Casilla. Turtle Books, 1998. ISBN 1-890515-05-1 Subj: Folk & fairy tales. Foreign lands – Mexico.

Ollie Jolly, rodeo clown ill. by Amy Meissner. WestWinds, 2002. ISBN 1-55868-552-9 Subj: Clowns, jesters. Cowboys, cowgirls. Rodeos.

Prairie dog pioneers by Jo & Josephine Harper; ill. by Craig Spearing. Turtle Books, 1998. ISBN 1-890515-10-8 Subj: Behavior – misunderstanding. Family life. Family life – daughters. Moving. U.S. history – frontier & pioneer life.

Harper, Josephine. *Prairie dog pioneers* (Harper, Jo)

Harper, Piers. *How the world was saved and other Native American tales* ill. by author. Western, 1994. ISBN 0-307-17507-3 Subj: Creation. Folk & fairy tales. Indians of North America.

If you love a bear ill. by author. Candlewick, 1998. ISBN 0-7636-0371-6 Subj: Activities. Animals – bears.

Harper, Wilhelmina. *The gunniwolf* ill. by William Wiesner. Dutton, 1967. Subj: Animals – wolves. Behavior – misbehavior. Flowers. Foreign lands – Germany.

Harpham, Wendy Schlessel. *The hope tree* (Numeroff, Laura Joffe)

Harranth, Wolf. *The flute concert* ill. by Romulus Candea. Blackbirch, 1998. ISBN 1-56711-803-8 Subj: Behavior – lost & found possessions. Careers – musicians. Music. Musical instruments – flutes.

My old grandad trans. from German by Peter Carter; ill. by Christina Oppermann-Dimow. Merrimack, 1984. ISBN 0-19-279787-5 Subj: Death. Emotions – grief. Emotions – loneliness. Family life – grandfathers. Farms.

Harriott, Ted. *Coming home: a dog's true story* ill. by Lisa Kopper. David & Charles, 1985. ISBN 0-575-03583-8 Subj: Animals – dogs. Character traits – kindness to animals. Death. Emotions – grief.

Harris, Dorothy Joan. *Four seasons for Toby* ill. by Vlasta van Kampen. North Winds, 1987. ISBN 0-590-71677-8 Subj: Reptiles – turtles, tortoises. Seasons.

Goodnight Jeffrey ill. by Nancy Hannans. Warne, 1983. ISBN 0-7232-6224-1 Subj: Bedtime.

Harris, Jim. *Jack and the giant: a story full of beans* ill. by author. Rising Moon, 1997. ISBN 0-87358-680-8 Subj: Folk & fairy tales. Giants. Plants.

Harris, Joel Chandler. *Brer Rabbit and Boss Lion* (Kessler, Brad)

Hello, house! (Hayward, Linda)

Jump! the adventures of Brer Rabbit adapt. by Van Dyke Parks & Malcolm Jones; ill. by Barry Moser. Harcourt, 1986. ISBN 0-15-241350-2 Subj: Animals. Folk & fairy tales.

Jump again! more adventures of Brer Rabbit adapt. by Van Dyke Parks; ill. by Barry Moser. Harcourt, 1987. ISBN 0-15-241352-9 Subj: Animals. Folk & fairy tales.

Harris, John. *A is for artist: a Getty Museum alphabet* (J. Paul Getty Museum)

Harris, Lee. *Never let your cat make lunch for you* ill. by Debbie Tilley. Tricycle, 1999. ISBN 1-883672-80-5 Subj: Activities – baking, cooking. Animals – cats. Food.

Harris, Leon A. *The great diamond robbery* ill. by Joseph Schindelman. Atheneum, 1985. ISBN 0-689-31188-5 Subj: Animals – mice. Character traits – bravery. Crime. Songs. Stores.

The great picture robbery ill. by Joseph Schindelman. Atheneum, 1963. Subj: Animals – mice. Art. Crime. Foreign lands – France.

Harris, Louise Dyer. *Flash, the life of a firefly* by Louise Dyer Harris & Norman Dyer Harris; ill. by Henry B. Kane. Little, 1966. Subj: Insects – fireflies. Science.

Harris, Marian. *Tuesday in Arizona* ill. by Jim Harris. Pelican, 1998. ISBN 1-56554-233-9 Subj: Animals – rats. Careers – miners.

Harris, Nicholas. *Dinosaur* (Scott, Peter David)

Harris, Norman Dyer. *Flash, the life of a firefly* (Harris, Louise Dyer)

Harris, Pamela. *Hot, cold, shy, bold: looking at opposites* photos by author. Kids Can, 1995. ISBN 1-55074-153-5 Subj: Concepts – opposites. Rhyming text.

Harris, Peter. *Perfect Prudence* ill. by Deborah Allwright. Gingham Dog, 2003. ISBN 1-57768-437-0 Subj: Character traits – perfectionism.

Harris, Robie H. *Don't forget to come back* ill. by Harry Bliss. Candlewick, 2004. ISBN 0-7636-1782-2 Subj: Activities – babysitting. Behavior. Family life.

Don't forget to come back ill. by Tony DeLuna. Atheneum, 1963. ISBN 0-394-83849-1 Subj: Activities – babysitting. Behavior. Family life.

Go! Go! Maria! ill. by Michael Emberley. McElderry, 2003. ISBN 0-689-83258-3 Subj: Behavior – growing up. Family life.

Goodbye, Mousie ill. by Jan Ormerod. McElderry, 2001. ISBN 0-689-83217-6 Subj: Animals – mice. Death. Emotions – grief. Pets.

Hi, new baby ill. by Michael Emberley. Candlewick, 2000. ISBN 0-7636-0539-5 Subj: Babies. Family life – brothers & sisters. Family life – new sibling.

Hot Henry ill. by Nicole Hollander. St. Martin's, 1987. ISBN 0-312-01041-9 Subj: Clothing. Family life.

I am not going to school today ill. by Jan Ormerod. McElderry, 2001. ISBN 0-689-83913-8 Subj: School – first day.

I hate kisses ill. by Diane Paterson. Knopf, 1981. ISBN 0-394-94324-4 Subj: Behavior – growing up.

Messy Jessie ill. by Nicole Hollander. St. Martin's, 1987. ISBN 0-312-01067-2 Subj: Behavior – carelessness. Family life.

Harris, Steven Michael. *This is my trunk* ill. by Norma Welliver. Atheneum, 1985. ISBN 0-689-31128-1 Subj: Careers. Circus. Clowns, jesters.

Harris, Susan. *Creatures that look alike* ill. by Don Forrest. Watts, 1980. ISBN 0-531-01375-8 Subj: Animals. Science.

Reptiles ill. by Jim Robins. Watts, 1978. ISBN 0-531-01335-9 Subj: Reptiles. Science.

Harris, Susan Yard. *Daisy's garden* (Gerstein, Mordicai)

Guess what? (Gerstein, Mordicai)

Harris, Trudy. *100 days of school* ill. by Beth Griffis Johnson. Millbrook, 1999. ISBN 0-7613-1271-4 Subj: Counting, numbers. Rhyming text.

Pattern bugs ill. by Anne Canevari Green. Millbrook, 2001. ISBN 0-7613-2107-1 Subj: Concepts – patterns. Insects. Language. Rhyming text.

Pattern fish ill. by Anne Canevari Green. Millbrook, 2000. ISBN 0-7613-1712-0 Subj: Concepts – patterns. Fish. Rhyming text. Sea & seashore.

Up bear, down bear ill. by Ora Eitan. Houghton, 2001. ISBN 0-395-97767-3 Subj: Concepts – up & down. Format, unusual – board books. Toys – bears.

Harrison, Carol. *Dinosaurs everywhere!* ill. by Richard Courtney. Scholastic, 1998. ISBN 0-590-00089-6 Subj: Dinosaurs. Prehistory.

Harrison, David Lee. *The alligator in the closet and other poems around the house* ill. by Jane Kendall. Boyds Mills, 2003. ISBN 1-56397-994-2 Subj: Homes, houses. Poetry.

The animals' song ill. by Chris L. Demarest. Boyds Mills, 1997. ISBN 1-56397-144-5 Subj: Animals. Cumulative tales. Music. Noise, sounds. Rhyming text. Songs.

The book of giant stories ill. by Philippe Fix. Boyds Mills, 2001. ISBN 1-56397-976-4 Subj: Folk & fairy tales. Giants.

The boy who counted stars ill. by Betsy Lewin. Wordsong, 1994. ISBN 1-56397-125-9 Subj: Humorous stories. Poetry.

The case of Og, the missing frog ill. by Jerry Warshaw. Rand McNally, 1972. ISBN 0-528-82635-2 Subj: Frogs & toads. Rhyming text.

Caves ill. by Cheryl Nathan. Boyds Mills, 2001. ISBN 1-56397-915-2 Subj: Caves. Science.

Detective Bob and the great ape escape ill. by Ned Delaney. Parents' Magazine Pr., 1980. ISBN 0-819-31032-8 Subj: Animals – gorillas. Careers – detectives. Mystery stories. Zoos.

Dylan, the eagle-hearted chicken ill. by Karen Stormer Brooks. Boyds Mills, 2002. ISBN 1-56397-982-9 Subj: Behavior – imitation. Birds – chickens. Birds – eagles.

Earthquakes ill. by Cheryl Nathan. Boyds Mills, 2004. ISBN 1-59078-243-7 Subj: Earthquakes. Science.

Farmer's garden ill. by Arden Johnson-Petrov. Boyds Mills, 2000. ISBN 1-56397-776-1 Subj: Animals – dogs. Gardens, gardening. Poetry.

Little boy soup ill. by Toni Goffe. Ladybird, 1990. ISBN 0-7214-5267-1 Subj: Character traits – cleverness. Witches.

Little turtle's big adventure ill. by J. P. Miller. Random House, 1985. c1978. ISBN 0-394-96345-8 Subj: Character traits – kindness to animals. Progress. Reptiles – turtles, tortoises.

Rivers ill. by Cheryl Nathan. Boyds Mills, 2002. ISBN 1-56397-968-3 Subj: Rivers.

A thousand cousins, poems of family life ill. by Betsy Lewin. Wordsong, 1996. ISBN 1-56397-131-3 Subj: Family life. Poetry.

Wake up, sun! ill. by Hans Wilhelm. Random House, 1986. ISBN 0-394-88256-8 Subj: Animals. Morning. Sun.

When cows come home ill. by Chris L. Demarest. Caroline House, 1994. ISBN 1-56397-143-7 Subj: Animals – bulls, cows. Homes, houses. Rhyming text.

Harrison, Joanna. *Dear bear* ill. by author. Carolrhoda, 1994. ISBN 0-87614-839-9 Subj: Activities – writing. Animals – bears. Emotions – fear. Letters, cards. Toys – bears.

Harrison, Michael. *Bright star shining: poems for Christmas* (Bright star shining)

Harrison, Sarah. *In granny's garden* ill. by Mike Wilks. Holt, 1980. ISBN 0-03-050876-2 Subj: Animals. Dinosaurs. Rhyming text.

Harrison, Ted. *A northern alphabet: A is for arctic* ill. by author. Tundra, 1982. ISBN 0-88776-209-3 Subj: ABC books.

O Canada ill. by author. Ticknor & Fields, 1993. ISBN 0-395-66075-0 Subj: Foreign lands – Canada.

Harrison, Troon. *Aaron's awful allergies* ill. by Eugenie Fernandes. Kids Can, 1998. ISBN 1-55074-299-X Subj: Illness – allergies. Pets.

Courage to fly ill. by Zhong-Yang Huang. Red Deer Pr., 2002. ISBN 0-88995-273-6 Subj: Character traits – bravery. Cities, towns. Ethnic groups in the U.S. – African Americans. Friendship. Moving.

Don't dig so deep, Nicholas! ill. by Gary Clement. Owl Books, 1997. ISBN 1-895688-51-5 Subj: Activities – digging. Animals. Foreign lands – Australia. Sea & seashore.

The dream collector ill. by Alan & Lea Daniel. Kids Can, 1999. ISBN 1-55074-437-2 Subj: Animals – dogs. Dreams. Imagination.

The floating orchard ill. by Miranda Jones. Tundra, 2000. ISBN 0-88776-439-8 Subj: Boats, ships. Magic. Trees. Weather – floods. Weather – rain.

Lavender Moon ill. by Eugenie Fernandes. Annick, 1997. ISBN 1-55037-455-9 Subj: Activities – traveling. Careers – bus drivers. Careers – chefs, cooks.

Harrop, Beatrice. *Sing hey, diddle, diddle: 66 nursery rhymes with their traditional tunes* (Mother Goose)

Harsh, Fred. *Alfie* ill. by author. Ideals, 1991. ISBN 0-685-48862-4 Subj: Animals – dogs. Birds – crows. Self-concept.

Harshman, Marc. *All the way to morning* ill. by Felipe Dávalos. Cavendish, 1999. ISBN 0-7614-5042-4 Subj: Bedtime. Night. Noise, sounds. Sleep.

A little excitement ill. by Ted Rand. Cobblehill, 1989. ISBN 0-525-65001-6 Subj: Behavior – wishing. Character traits – bravery. Country. Farms. Fire. Seasons – winter.

Moving days ill. by Wendy Popp. Cobblehill, 1994. ISBN 0-525-65135-7 Subj: Emotions. Family life. Moving.

Only one ill. by Barbara Garrison. Cobblehill, 1993. ISBN 0-525-65116-0 Subj: Counting, numbers. Fairs, festivals.

Red are the apples Marc Harshman & Cheryl Ryan; ill. by Wade Zahares. Gulliver, 2001. ISBN 0-15-201917-0 Subj: Concepts – color. Gardens, gardening. Rhyming text. Seasons – fall.

Roads ill. by Mary Newell DePalma. Cavendish, 2002. ISBN 0-7614-5112-9 Subj: Activities – traveling. Automobiles. Family life – grandparents.

Rocks in my pocket by Marc Harshman & Bonnie Collins; ill. by Toni Goffe. Dutton, 1991. ISBN 0-525-65055-5 Subj: Folk & fairy tales. Rocks.

Snow company ill. by Leslie W. Bowman. Dutton, 1990. ISBN 0-525-65029-6 Subj: Weather – snow. Weather – storms.

The storm ill. by Mark Mohr. Cobblehill, 1995. ISBN 0-525-65150-0 Subj: Emotions – anger. Emotions – fear. Farms. Handicaps – physical handicaps. Weather – storms.

Uncle James ill. by Michael Dooling. Cobblehill, 1993. ISBN 0-525-65110-1 Subj: Behavior – boasting. Death. Family life – aunts, uncles. Farms. Illness. Poverty.

Harshman, Terry Webb. *Porcupine's pajama party* ill. by Doug Cushman. HarperCollins, 1988. ISBN 0-06-022249-2 Subj: Animals – otters. Animals – porcupines. Bedtime. Birds – owls. Monsters. Parties. Sleep. Sleepovers.

Hart, Christopher. *Merwin, master of disguise* ill. by author. Watson-Guptill, 2002. ISBN 0-8230-3049-0 Subj: Animals – elephants. Humorous stories. Zoos.

Hart, Jeanne McGahey. *Scareboy* ill. by Gerhardt Hurt. Parnassus, 1957. ISBN 0-395-27660-8 Subj: Humorous stories. Scarecrows.

Hart, Rebecca. *Tortillas and lullabies = Tortillas y cancioncitas* (Tortillas and lullabies = Tortillas y cancioncitas)

Hartelius, Margaret A. *The chicken's child* ill. by author. Doubleday, 1975. ISBN 0-385-07370-4 Subj: Birds – chickens. Reptiles – alligators, crocodiles. Wordless.

Harter, Debbie. *Walking through the jungle* ill. by author. Orchard, 1997. ISBN 0-531-30035-8 Subj: Animals. Jungle. Rhyming text.

Who are you? (Blackstone, Stella)

Hartley, Deborah. *Up north in the winter* ill. by Lydia Dabcovich. Dutton, 1986. ISBN 0-525-44268-5 Subj: Animals – foxes. Family life – grandfathers. Seasons – winter.

Hartley, Karen. *Ant* by Karen Hartley & Chris Marco; ill. with photos. Heinemann, 1998. ISBN 1-57572-660-2 Subj: Insects – ants. Science.

Bee by Karen Hartley & Chris Marco; ill. with photos. Heinemann, 1998. ISBN 1-57572-661-0 Subj: Insects – bees. Science.

Cockroach by Karen Hartley & Chris Marco; photos by Philip Taylor. Heinemann, 1999. Subj: Insects – cockroaches. Science.

Hearing in living things by Karen Hartley, Chris Macro & Philip Taylor; ill. with photos. Heinemann, 2000. ISBN 1-57572-246-1 Subj: Anatomy – ears. Senses – hearing.

Ladybug by Karen Hartley & Chris Marco; ill. with photos. Heinemann, 1998. ISBN 1-57572-662-9 Subj: Insects – ladybugs. Science.

Seeing in living things by Karen Hartley & Chris Marco; photos by Philip Taylor. Heinemann, 2000. ISBN 1-57572-247-X Subj: Anatomy – eyes. Senses – sight.

The sixth sense and other special senses by Karen Hartley & Chris Marco; photos by Philip Taylor. Heinemann, 2000. ISBN 1-57572-248-8 Subj: Animals. Senses.

Smelling in living things by Karen Hartley & Chris Marco; photos by Philip Taylor. Heinemann, 2000. ISBN 1-57572-249-6 Subj: Anatomy – noses. Senses – smell.

Snail by Karen Hartley & Chris Marco; ill. with photos. Heinemann, 1998. ISBN 1-57572-664-5 Subj: Animals – snails. Science.

Tasting in living things by Karen Hartley & Chris Marco; photos by Philip Taylor. Heinemann, 2000. ISBN 1-57572-250-X Subj: Anatomy – tongues. Senses – taste.

Touching in living things by Karen Hartley & Chris Marco; photos by Philip Taylor. Heinemann, 2000. ISBN 1-57572-251-8 Subj: Senses – touch.

Hartman, Bob. *Aunt Mabel's table* ill. by Richard Max Kolding. Standard, 1994. ISBN 0-7847-0178-4 Subj: Etiquette. Family life – aunts, uncles. Food.

The birthday of a king ill. by Michael McGuire. Victor Books, 1993. ISBN 1-56476-043-X Subj: Birthdays. Holidays – Christmas. Religion.

Granny Mae's Christmas play ill. by Lynne Cravath. Augsburg Fortress, 2001. ISBN 0-8066-4063-4 Subj: Family life. Family life – grandmothers. Holidays – Christmas. Religion – Nativity. Theater.

Lobster for lunch ill. by Jo Ellen McAllister Stammen. Down East, 1992. ISBN 0-89272-302-5 Subj: Crustaceans – lobsters. Family life. Food. Friendship.

The morning of the world ill. by Michael McGuire. Victor Books, 1993. ISBN 1-56476-040-5 Subj: Creation. Religion.

A night the stars danced for joy ill. by Tim Jonke. Lion, 1996. ISBN 0-7459-3684-9 Subj: Holidays – Christmas. Religion.

The one and only Delgado Cheese: a tale of talent, fame and friendship ill. by Donna Kae Nelson. Lion, 1993. ISBN 0-7459-2405-0 Subj: Family life – aunts, uncles. School. Self-concept. Theater.

Who brought the bread? ill. by author. Standard, 1994. ISBN 0-7847-0188-1 Subj: Careers – bakers. Food. Religion.

Who wrecked the roof? ill. by Terri Steiger. Standard, 1994. ISBN 0-7847-0189-X Subj: Family life – fathers. Family life – sons. Religion.

The wolf who cried boy ill. by Tim Raglin. Putnam, 2002. ISBN 0-399-23578-7 Subj: Animals – wolves. Food.

Hartman, Gail. *As the crow flies* ill. by Harvey Stevenson. Bradbury, 1991. ISBN 0-02-743005-7 Subj: Animals. Maps.

As the roadrunner runs: a first book of maps ill. by Cathy Bobak. Bradbury, 1994. ISBN 0-02-743092-8 Subj: Animals. Maps.

For sand castles or seashells ill. by Ellen Weiss. Bradbury, 1990. ISBN 0-02-743091-X Subj: Activities – playing. Concepts.

For strawberry jam or fireflies ill. by Ellen Weiss. Bradbury, 1989. ISBN 0-02-742990-3 Subj: Concepts. Language.

Hartmann, Wendy. *All the magic in the world* ill. by Niki Daly. Dutton, 1993. ISBN 0-525-45092-0 Subj: Careers – sanitation workers. Communities, neighborhoods. Imagination. Magic.

The dinosaurs are back and it's all your fault, Edward! by Wendy Hartmann & Niki Daly; ill. by Niki Daly. McElderry, 1997. ISBN 0-689-81152-7 Subj: Dinosaurs. Eggs. Family life – brothers. Prehistory.

One sun rises: an African wildlife counting book ill. by Nicolaas Maritz. Dutton, 1994. ISBN 0-525-45225-7 Subj: Animals. Counting, numbers. Foreign lands – Africa.

Harvey, Amanda. *Dog days* ill. by author. Random House, 2003. ISBN 0-385-90860-1 Subj: Animals – cats. Animals – dogs. Pets.

Dog gone ill. by author. Random House, 2004. ISBN 0-385-90870-9 Subj: Animals – dogs. Pets.

Dog-eared ill. by author. Doubleday, 2002. ISBN 0-385-72911-1 Subj: Anatomy – ears. Animals – dogs. Pets. Self-concept.

Stormy weather ill. by author. Lothrop, 1992. ISBN 0-688-10608-0 Subj: Behavior – fighting, arguing. Family life. Seasons – winter.

Harvey, Bev. *The bear family* ill. with photos. Chelsea, 2004. ISBN 0-7910-7540-0 Subj: Animals – bears. Science.

The cat family ill. with photos. Chelsea, 2004. ISBN 0-7910-7541-9 Subj: Animals – cats. Science.

The dog family ill. with photos. Chelsea, 2004. ISBN 0-7910-7542-7 Subj: Animals – dogs. Science.

The dolphin family ill. with photos. Chelsea, 2004. ISBN 0-7910-7543-5 Subj: Animals – dolphins.

The hawk family ill. with photos. Chelsea, 2004. ISBN 0-7910-7544-3 Subj: Birds – hawks. Science.

The horse family ill. with photos. Chelsea, 2004. ISBN 0-7910-7545-1 Subj: Animals – horses, ponies. Science.

Harvey, Brett. *Cassie's journey: going West in the 1860s* ill. by Deborah Kogan Ray. Holiday, 1988. ISBN 0-8234-0684-9 Subj: Activities – traveling. Family life. U.S. history – frontier & pioneer life.

Immigrant girl: Becky of Eldridge Street ill. by Deborah Kogan Ray. Holiday, 1987. ISBN 0-8234-0638-5 Subj: Cities, towns. Family life. Jewish culture.

My prairie Christmas ill. by Deborah Kogan Ray. Holiday, 1990. ISBN 0-8234-0827-2 Subj: Holidays – Christmas. Weather – storms.

My prairie year: based on the diary of Elenore Plaisted ill. by Deborah Kogan Ray. Holiday, 1986. ISBN 0-8234-0604-0 Subj: Activities – working. Farms. U.S. history – frontier & pioneer life.

Harvey, Jayne. *Busy bugs* ill. by Bernard Adnet. Grosset, 2003. ISBN 0-448-43234-X Subj: Concepts – patterns. Counting, numbers. Insects. Rhyming text.

Harwick, B. L. *see* Keller, Beverly

Haseley, Dennis. *The cave of snores* ill. by Eric Beddows. HarperCollins, 1987. ISBN 0-06-022215-8 Subj: Animals. Folk & fairy tales. Magic. Sleep – snoring. Wizards.

Crosby ill. by Jonathan Green. Harcourt, 1996. ISBN 0-15-200829-2 Subj: Ethnic groups in the U.S. – African Americans. Friendship. Kites.

Ghost catcher ill. by Lloyd Bloom. HarperCollins, 1991. ISBN 0-06-022247-6 Subj: Death. Emotions – love. Ghosts. Shadows.

Horses with wings ill. by Lynn Curlee. HarperCollins, 1993. ISBN 0-06-022886-5 Subj: Activities – ballooning. Foreign lands – France. War.

Kite flier ill. by David Wiesner. Four Winds, 1986. ISBN 0-02-743110-X Subj: Family life – fathers. Kites.

My father doesn't know about the woods and me ill. by Michael Hays. Atheneum, 1988. ISBN 0-689-31365-9 Subj: Family life – fathers. Forest, woods. Imagination.

The old banjo ill. by Stephen Gammell. Macmillan, 1983. ISBN 0-02-743100-2 Subj: Farms. Music.

The pirate who tried to capture the moon ill. by Sue Truesdell. HarperCollins, 1983. ISBN 0-06-022227-1 Subj: Pirates.

The soap bandit ill. by Jane Chambless. Warne, 1984. ISBN 0-7232-6216-0 Subj: Character traits – cleanliness.

A story for Bear ill. by Jim LaMarche. Harcourt, 2002. ISBN 0-15-200239-1 Subj: Animals – bears. Books, reading.

The thieves' market ill. by Lisa Desimini. HarperCollins, 1991. ISBN 0-06-022493-2 Subj: Crime. Imagination. Night. Stores.

Haskins, Francine. *I remember "121"* ill. by author. Childrens Pr., 1991. ISBN 0-89239-100-6 Subj: Communities, neighborhoods. Ethnic groups in the U.S. – African Americans. Family life. Memories, memory.

Haskins, Ilma. *Color seems* ill. by author. Vanguard, 1973. Subj: Concepts – color.

Haskins, Jim (James). *Count your way through Africa* ill. by Barbara Knutson. Carolrhoda, 1989. ISBN 0-87614-347-8 Subj: Counting, numbers. Foreign lands – Africa. Foreign languages.

Count your way through Brazil by Jim Haskins & Kathleen Benson; ill. by Liz Brenner Dodson. Carolrhoda, 1996. ISBN 0-87614-873-9 Subj: Counting, numbers. Foreign languages.

Count your way through Canada ill. by Steve Michaels. Carolrhoda, 1989. ISBN 0-87614-350-8 Subj: Counting, numbers. Foreign lands – Canada.

Count your way through China ill. by Dennis Hockerman. Carolrhoda, 1987. ISBN 0-87614-302-8 Subj: Counting, numbers. Foreign lands – China.

Count your way through France ill. by Andrea Shine. Carolrhoda, 1996. ISBN 0-87614-874-7 Subj: Counting, numbers. Foreign lands – France. Foreign languages.

Count your way through Germany ill. by Helen Byers. Carolrhoda, 1992. ISBN 0-87614-407-5 Subj: Counting, numbers. Foreign lands – Germany. Foreign languages.

Count your way through Greece ill. by Janice Lee Porter. Carolrhoda, 1996. ISBN 0-87614-875-5 Subj: Counting, numbers. Foreign lands – Greece. Foreign languages.

Count your way through India ill. by Liz Brenner Dodson. Carolrhoda, 1990. ISBN 0-87614-414-8 Subj: Counting, numbers. Foreign lands – India. Foreign languages.

Count your way through Ireland ill. by Beth Wright. Carolrhoda, 1996. ISBN 0-87614-872-0 Subj: Counting, numbers. Foreign lands – Ireland.

Count your way through Israel ill. by Rick Hanson. Carolrhoda, 1990. ISBN 0-87614-415-6 Subj: Counting, numbers. Foreign lands – Israel. Foreign languages.

Count your way through Italy ill. by Beth Wright. Carolrhoda, 1990. ISBN 0-87614-406-7 Subj: Counting, numbers. Foreign lands – Italy. Foreign languages.

Count your way through Japan ill. by Martin Skoro. Carolrhoda, 1987. ISBN 0-87614-301-X Subj: Counting, numbers. Foreign lands – Japan.

Count your way through Korea ill. by Dennis Hockerman. Carolrhoda, 1989. ISBN 0-87614-348-6 Subj: Counting, numbers. Foreign lands – Korea. Foreign languages.

Count your way through Mexico ill. by Helen Byers. Carolrhoda, 1989. ISBN 0-87614-349-4 Subj: Counting, numbers. Foreign lands – Mexico. Foreign languages.

Count your way through Russia ill. by Vera Mednikov. Carolrhoda, 1987. ISBN 0-87614-303-6 Subj: Counting, numbers. Foreign lands – Russia.

Count your way through the Arab world ill. by Dana Gustafson. Carolrhoda, 1987. ISBN 0-87616-304-4 Subj: Counting, numbers. Foreign lands – Arabia.

The Statue of Liberty: America's proud lady ill. with photos. Lerner, 1986. ISBN 0-8225-1706-X Subj: Art. U.S. history.

Hasler, Eveline. *The giantess* ill. by Renate Seelig; trans. by Laura McKenna. Kane/Miller, 1997. ISBN 0-916291-76-6 Subj: Clothing – costumes. Giants. Self-concept.

Martin is our friend ill. by Dorothea Desmarowitz. Abingdon, 1981. ISBN 0-687-23650-9 Subj: Animals – horses, ponies. Character traits – kindness. Handicaps.

Winter magic ill. by Michèle Lemieux. Morrow, 1985. ISBN 0-688-05258-4 Subj: Animals – cats. Night. Seasons – winter.

Hassett, Ann M. *Cat up a tree* (Hassett, John)

Charles of the wild (Hassett, John)

Father Sun, Mother Moon (Hassett, John)

Junior: a little loon tale (Hassett, John)

Mouse in the house (Hassett, John)

The three silly girls Grubb (Hassett, John)

Hassett, John. *Cat up a tree* by John & Ann Hassett; ill. by authors. Houghton, 1998. ISBN 0-395-88415-2 Subj: Animals – cats. Behavior – needing someone. Character traits – helpfulness. Counting, numbers.

Charles of the wild by John & Ann Hassett; ill. by authors. Houghton, 1997. ISBN 0-395-78575-8 Subj: Animals – dogs. Behavior – running away.

Father Sun, Mother Moon by John & Ann Hassett; ill. by authors. Houghton, 2001. ISBN 0-395-97565-4 Subj: Concepts – color. Superstition.

Junior: a little loon tale by John & Ann Hassett; ill. by John Hassett. Down East, 1993. ISBN 0-89272-322-X Subj: Behavior – lost. Behavior – lost & found possessions. Birds – loons. Ecology.

Mouse in the house by John & Ann Hassett; ill. by authors. Houghton, 2004. ISBN 0-618-35317-8 Subj: Animals. Character traits – orderliness. Family life – grandmothers.

The three silly girls Grubb by John & Ann Hassett; ill. by authors. Houghton, 2002. ISBN 0-618-14183-9 Subj: Behavior – bullying. Folk & fairy tales. School.

Hastings, Evelyn Beilhart. *The department store* ill. by Lewis A. Ogan. Melmont, 1956. Subj: Shopping. Stores.

Hastings, Selina. *The firebird* (The firebird)

The man who wanted to live forever ill. by Reg Cartwright. Holt, 1988. ISBN 0-8050-0572-2 Subj: Death. Folk & fairy tales.

Peter and the wolf (Prokofiev, Sergei Sergeievitch)

The singing ringing tree ill. by Louise Brierley. Holt, 1988. ISBN 0-8050-0573-0 Subj: Character traits – kindness. Folk & fairy tales. Magic. Royalty – princes. Royalty – princesses.

Haswell, Peter. *Pog* ill. by author. Watts, 1989. ISBN 0-531-08443-4 Subj: Animals – pigs. Character traits – questioning.

Pog climbs Mount Everest ill. by author. Watts, 1990. ISBN 0-531-08473-6 Subj: Animals – pigs. Sports – mountain climbing.

Hatcher, Charles. *What shape is it?* ill. by Gareth Adamson. Duell, 1966. Subj: Concepts – shape.

Hathon, Elizabeth. *We go to school* photos by author. Random House, 1992. ISBN 0-679-83377-3 Subj: Format, unusual – board books. Format, unusual – toy & movable books. School.

We go to the zoo photos by author. Random House, 1992. ISBN 0-679-83376-5 Subj: Format, unusual – board books. Format, unusual – toy & movable books. Zoos.

Hathorn, Libby (Elizabeth). *Freya's fantastic surprise* ill. by Sharon Thompson. Scholastic, 1989. ISBN 0-86896-381-X Subj: Babies. Character traits – honesty. Emotions – envy, jealousy. Family life – new sibling. Friendship. School.

Sky sash so blue ill. by Benny Andrews. S&S, 1998. ISBN 0-689-81090-3 Subj: Ethnic groups in the U.S. – African Americans. Rhyming text. Slavery.

The tram to Bondi beach ill. by Julie Vivas. Kane/Miller, 1989. ISBN 0-916291-20-0 Subj: Foreign lands – Australia. Trains.

The wonder thing ill. by Peter Gouldthorpe. Houghton Mifflin, 1996. ISBN 0-395-71541-5 Subj: Nature. Riddles & jokes. Water.

Hatkoff, Juliana. *Good-bye tonsils* by Juliana Lee Hatkoff & Craig Hatkoff; ill. by Marilyn Mets. Viking, 2001. ISBN 0-670-89775-2 Subj: Hospitals. Illness – tonsillectomy.

Haubensak-Tellenbach, Margrit. *The story of Noah's ark* ill. by Erna Emhardt. Crown, 1983. ISBN 0-517-55050-4 Subj: Animals. Boats, ships. Religion – Noah. Weather – floods. Weather – rain. Weather – rainbows.

Haugaard, Erik Christian. *The emperor's nightingale* (Andersen, H. C. [Hans Christian])

Prince Boghole ill. by Julie Downing. Macmillan, 1987. ISBN 0-02-743440-0 Subj: Folk & fairy tales. Foreign lands – Ireland. Royalty – princes.

Princess Horrid ill. by Diane Dawson Hearn. Macmillan, 1990. ISBN 0-02-743445-1 Subj: Behavior. Folk & fairy tales. Royalty – princesses. Witches.

Thumbelina (Andersen, H. C. [Hans Christian])

Haugen, Brenda. *Thanksgiving* ill. by Todd Ouren. Picture Window, 2004. ISBN 1-4048-0191-X Subj: Holidays – Thanksgiving. U.S. history.

Haughton, Emma. *Rainy day* ill. by Angelo Rinaldi. Carolrhoda, 2000. ISBN 1-57505-452-3 Subj: Activities – walking. Divorce. Family life – fathers. Weather – storms.

Hauptmann, Tatjana. *A day in the life of Petronella Pig* ill. by author. Holt, 1982. ISBN 0-03-057794-2 Subj: Animals – pigs. Format, unusual. Wordless.

Haus, Felice. *Beep! Beep! I'm a jeep: a toddler's book of "let's pretend"* ill. by Norman Gorbaty. Random House, 1986. ISBN 0-394-88000-5 Subj: Activities – playing. Format, unusual – board books. Imagination. Toys.

Hausherr, Rosmarie. *My first kitten* photos by author. Four Winds, 1985. ISBN 0-02-743420-6 Subj: Animals – cats. Pets.

My first puppy photos by author. Four Winds, 1986. ISBN 0-02-743410-9 Subj: Animals – dogs. Pets.

Hausman, Bonnie. *A to Z, do you ever feel like me?* photos by Sandi Fellman. Dutton, 1999. ISBN 0-525-46216-3 Subj: ABC books. Emotions.

Hausman, Gerald. *Coyote walks on two legs* ill. by Floyd Cooper. Philomel, 1993. ISBN 0-399-22018-6 Subj: Animals – coyotes. Behavior – greed. Behavior – trickery. Character traits – vanity. Folk & fairy tales. Indians of North America – Navajo.

Doctor Bird ill. by Ashley Wolff. Philomel, 1998. ISBN 0-399-22744-X Subj: Birds – humming birds. Folk & fairy tales. Foreign lands – Jamaica.

Eagle boy ill. by Cara & Barry Moser. HarperCollins, 1996. ISBN 0-06-021101-6 Subj: Birds – eagles. Folk & fairy tales. Indians of North America – Navajo.

How Chipmunk got tiny feet ill. by Ashley Wolff. HarperCollins, 1995. ISBN 0-06-022907-1 Subj: Animals. Folk & fairy tales. Indians of North America.

The story of Blue Elk ill. by Kristina Rodanas. Clarion, 1998. ISBN 0-395-84512-2 Subj: Animals – elk. Folk & fairy tales. Indians of North America – Pueblo. Magic.

Turtle Island ABC: a gathering of Native American symbols ill. by Cara & Barry Moser. HarperCollins, 1994. ISBN 0-06-021308-6 Subj: ABC books. Indians of North America.

Hautzig, Deborah. *Beauty and the beast* ill. by Kathy Mitchell. Random House, 1995. ISBN 0-679-95296-9 Subj: Character traits – loyalty. Emotions – love. Folk & fairy tales. Magic.

Big Bird at the beach ill. by Carol Nicklaus; featuring Jim Henson's Sesame Street Muppets. Random House, 1990. ISBN 0-679-80159-6 Subj: Family life – grandmothers. Puppets. Sea & seashore – beaches.

The Christmas story: from the Gospels according to Saint Matthew and Saint Luke ill. by Yoshi Miyake. Random House, 1994. ISBN 0-679-86153-X Subj: Holidays – Christmas. Religion – Nativity.

Ernie and Bert's new kitten ill. by Joe Mathieu; featuring Jim Henson's Sesame Street Muppets. Random House, 1990. ISBN 0-679-90420-4 Subj: Animals – cats. Pets. Puppets.

Get well, Granny Bird ill. by Joseph Mathieu. Random House, 1989. ISBN 0-394-92247-6 Subj: Birds. Family life – grandmothers. Illness.

Grover's bad dream ill. by Joe Mathieu. Random House, 1990. ISBN 0-679-90898-6 Subj: Birthdays. Emotions – envy, jealousy. Parties. Puppets.

It's not fair! ill. by Tom Leigh. Random House, 1986. ISBN 0-394-98151-0 Subj: Activities – working. Behavior – dissatisfaction. Puppets.

The little mermaid (Andersen, H. C. [Hans Christian])

Little Witch goes to school ill. by Sylvie Wickstrom. Random House, 1998. ISBN 0-679-98738-X Subj: School – first day. Witches.

Little Witch's bad dream ill. by Sylvie Wickstrom. Random House, 2000. ISBN 0-679-97342-7 Subj: Behavior. Family life – cousins. Witches.

The nutcracker ballet (Hoffmann, E. T. A.)

Thumbelina (Andersen, H. C. [Hans Christian])

A visit to the Sesame Street hospital ill. by Joseph Mathieu. Random House, 1985. ISBN 0-394-87062-X Subj: Hospitals. Puppets.

A visit to the Sesame Street library: featuring Jim Henson's Sesame Street Muppets ill. by Joe Mathieu. Random House, 1986. ISBN 0-394-97744-0 Subj: Libraries. Puppets.

Why are you so mean to me? ill. by Tom Cooke. Random House, 1986. ISBN 0-394-98060-3 Subj: Emotions – anger.

Hautzig, Esther (Rudomin). *At home: a visit in four languages* ill. by Aliki. Macmillan, 1969. Subj: Family life. Foreign lands – France. Foreign lands – Russia. Foreign lands – Spain. Foreign languages.

In the park: an excursion in four languages ill. by Ezra Jack Keats. Macmillan, 1968. Subj: Foreign lands – France. Foreign lands – Russia. Foreign lands – Spain. Foreign languages. Parks.

Havard, Christian. *The fox, playful prowler* ill. with photos by Viäl Jacana. Charlesbridge, 1995. ISBN 0-88106-434-3 Subj: Animals – foxes.

Haviland, Virginia. *The talking pot* ill. by Melissa Sweet. Little, 1990. ISBN 0-316-35060-5 Subj: Folk & fairy tales. Foreign lands – Denmark.

Havill, Juanita. *Embarcadero upset* ill. by author. Lothrop, 1999. ISBN 0-688-13058-5 Subj: Sports – skateboarding.

I love you more ill. by Amy Aitken. Golden Bks., 1990. ISBN 0-307-10177-0 Subj: Emotions – love.

Jamaica and Brianna ill. by Anne Sibley O'Brien. Houghton Mifflin, 1993. ISBN 0-395-64489-5 Subj: Clothing – boots. Emotions – envy, jealousy. Ethnic groups in the U.S. – African Americans. Ethnic groups in the U.S. – Asian Americans. Friendship.

Jamaica and the substitute teacher ill. by Anne Sibley O'Brien. Houghton Mifflin, 1999. ISBN 0-395-90503-6 Subj: Behavior – cheating. Behavior – misbehavior. Careers – teachers. School. Self-concept.

Jamaica Tag-Along ill. by Anne Sibley O'Brien. Houghton Mifflin, 1989. ISBN 0-395-49602-0 Subj: Activities – playing. Ethnic groups in the U.S. – African Americans. Family life – brothers & sisters. Friendship.

Jamaica's blue marker ill. by Anne Sibley O'Brien. Houghton Mifflin, 1995. ISBN 0-395-72036-2 Subj: Emotions – sadness. Ethnic groups in the U.S. – African Americans. Moving.

Jamaica's find ill. by Anne Sibley O'Brien. Houghton Mifflin, 1986. ISBN 0-395-39376-0 Subj: Behavior – lost & found possessions. Character traits – honesty. Ethnic groups in the U.S. – African Americans.

Kentucky troll ill. by Bert Dodson. Lothrop, 1993. ISBN 0-688-10458-4 Subj: Folk & fairy tales. Mythical creatures – trolls.

Magic fort ill. by Linda Shute. Houghton Mifflin, 1991. ISBN 0-395-50067-2 Subj: Behavior – misbehavior. Family life – brothers. Trees.

Sato and the elephants ill. by Jean & Mou-Sien Tseng. Lothrop, 1993. ISBN 0-688-11156-4 Subj: Animals – elephants. Animals – endangered animals. Careers – artists.

Treasure nap ill. by Elivia Savadier. Houghton Mifflin, 1992. ISBN 0-395-57817-5 Subj: Ethnic groups in the U.S. – Mexican Americans. Family life. Weather.

Hawcock, David. *Ant* by David Hawcock & Lee Montgomery; design & paper engineering by David Hawcock; ill. by Lee Montgomery. Random House, 1994. ISBN 0-679-85469-X Subj: Format, unusual – toy & movable books. Insects – ants.

Bee by David Hawcock & Lee Montgomery; design & paper engineering by David Hawcock; ill. by Lee Montgomery. Random House, 1994. ISBN 0-679-85470-3 Subj: Format, unusual – toy & movable books. Insects – bees.

Beetle by David Hawcock & Lee Montgomery; design & paper engineering by David Hawcock; ill. by Lee Montgomery. Random House, 1996. ISBN 0-679-87566-2 Subj: Format, unusual – toy & movable books. Insects – beetles.

Brontosaurus ill. by author. Holt, 1993. ISBN 0-8050-2361-5 Subj: Dinosaurs. Format, unusual – toy & movable books.

Dinosaur hunt design & paper engineering by David Hawcock; ill. by Philip Hood. Putnam & Grosset, 1995. ISBN 0-399-22777-6 Subj: Careers – paleontologists. Dinosaurs. Format, unusual – toy & movable books. Fossils. Science.

Fly by David Hawcock & Lee Montgomery; design & paper engineering by David Hawcock; ill. by Lee Montgomery. Random House, 1996. ISBN 0-679-87567-0 Subj: Format, unusual – toy & movable books. Insects – flies.

Spider by David Hawcock & Lee Montgomery; design & paper engineering by David Hawcock; ill. by Lee Montgomery. Random House, 1994. ISBN 0-679-85471-1 Subj: Format, unusual – toy & movable books. Spiders.

Stegosaurus ill. by author. Holt, 1993. ISBN 0-8050-2362-3 Subj: Dinosaurs. Format, unusual – toy & movable books.

Triceratops ill. by author. Holt, 1993. ISBN 0-8050-2364-X Subj: Dinosaurs. Format, unusual – toy & movable books.

Tyrannosaurus ill. by author. Holt, 1993. ISBN 0-8050-2363-1 Subj: Dinosaurs. Format, unusual – toy & movable books.

Wasp by David Hawcock & Lee Montgomery; design & paper engineering by David Hawcock; ill. by Lee Montgomery. Random House, 1996. ISBN 0-679-87565-4 Subj: Format, unusual – toy & movable books. Insects – wasps.

Whose coat? ill. by author. Little Simon, 1993. ISBN 0-671-79163-X Subj: Anatomy – skin. Animals. Format, unusual – toy & movable books.

Whose home? ill. by author. Little Simon, 1993. ISBN 0-671-79164-8 Subj: Animals. Format, unusual – toy & movable books. Homes, houses.

Whose nose? ill. by author. Little Simon, 1993. ISBN 0-671-79162-1 Subj: Anatomy – noses. Animals. Format, unusual – toy & movable books.

Hawes, Judy. *Fireflies in the night* ill. by Ellen Alexander. Rev. ed. HarperCollins, 1991. ISBN 0-06-022484-3 Subj: Family life – grandparents. Farms. Insects – fireflies. Night. Science.

Ladybug, ladybug, fly away home ill. by Ed Emberley. Crowell, 1968. Subj: Insects – ladybugs. Science.

My daddy longlegs ill. by Walter Lorraine. Crowell, 1972. ISBN 0-690-56656-5 Subj: Spiders.

Shrimps ill. by Joseph Low. Crowell, 1967. Subj: Fish. Science.

Spring peepers ill. by Graham Booth. Crowell, 1975. ISBN 0-690-00522-9 Subj: Frogs & toads. Science.

Watch honeybees with me ill. by Helen Stone. Crowell, 1964. Subj: Insects – bees. Science.

Why frogs are wet ill. by Don Madden. Crowell, 1968. Subj: Frogs & toads. Science.

Hawkes, Kevin. *His Royal Buckliness* ill. by author. Lothrop, 1992. ISBN 0-688-11063-0 Subj: Giants. Rhyming text. Seasons.

Then the troll heard the squeak ill. by author. Lothrop, 1991. ISBN 0-688-09757-X Subj: Behavior – misbehavior. Mythical creatures – trolls. Rhyming text.

Hawkesworth, Jenny. *The lonely skyscraper* ill. by Emanuel Schongut. Doubleday, 1980. ISBN 0-385-15948-X Subj: Cities, towns. Country.

Hawkins, Colin. *Boo! Who?* by Colin & Jacqui Hawkins; ill. by authors. Holt, 1984. ISBN 0-03-063929-8 Subj: Rhyming text.

Busy ABC by Colin & Jacqui Hawkins; ill. by authors. Viking, 1987. ISBN 0-670-81153-X Subj: ABC books. Activities.

Come for a ride on the ghost train by Colin & Jacqui Hawkins; ill. by Jacqui Hawkins. Candlewick, 1993. ISBN 1-56402-236-6 Subj: Format, unusual – toy & movable books. Ghosts. Monsters. Trains.

Creepy castle Colin & Jacqui Hawkins; ill. by Jacqui Hawkins. Barron's, 2001. ISBN 0-7641-5438-9 Subj: Castles. Format, unusual – toy & movable books. Ghosts. Monsters.

Dip, dip, dip ill. by author. Little, 1986. ISBN 0-87113-087-4 Subj: Activities – playing. Animals – bears. Bedtime. Toys – bears.

The elephant by Colin & Jacqui Hawkins; ill. by authors. Viking, 1986. ISBN 0-670-80314-6 Subj: Animals – elephants. Format, unusual – toy & movable books.

Fairytale news Colin & Jacqui Hawkins; ill. by Jacqui Hawkins. Candlewick, 2004. ISBN 0-7636-2166-8 Subj: Careers – journalists. Folk & fairy tales.

Hey, diddle, diddle by Colin & Jacqui Hawkins; ill. by authors. Candlewick, 1992. ISBN 1-56402-014-2 Subj: Format, unusual – board books. Nursery rhymes.

I'm not sleepy! by Colin & Jacqui Hawkins; ill. by authors. Crown, 1986. ISBN 0-517-55973-0 Subj: Animals – bears. Bedtime.

Incy wincy spider by Colin & Jacqui Hawkins; ill. by authors. Viking, 1986. ISBN 0-670-80317-0 Subj: Format, unusual – toy & movable books. Games. Spiders.

Jen the hen by Colin & Jacqui Hawkins; ill. by Colin Hawkins. Putnam, 1985. ISBN 0-399-21207-8 Subj: Birds – chickens. Birthdays. Format, unusual – toy & movable books. Rhyming text.

Max and the magic word by Colin & Jacqui Hawkins; ill. by authors. Viking, 1986. ISBN 0-670-80853-9 Subj: Animals. Etiquette.

Mig the pig by Colin & Jacqui Hawkins; ill. by Colin Hawkins. Putnam, 1984. ISBN 0-399-21061-X Subj: Animals – pigs. Format, unusual – toy & movable books. Rhyming text.

Old Mother Hubbard (Martin, Sarah Catherine)

One finger, one thumb ill. by author. Little, 1986. ISBN 0-87113-088-2 Subj: Activities – playing. Animals – bears. Bedtime. Toys – bears.

One, two, guess who? Colin & Jacqui Hawkins; ill. by Jacqui Hawkins. Barron's, 2001. ISBN 0-7641-5341-2 Subj: Counting, numbers. Folk & fairy tales. Format, unusual – toy & movable books. Rhyming text.

Oops-a-Daisy ill. by author. Little, 1986. ISBN 0-87113-086-6 Subj: Activities – playing. Animals – bears. Bedtime. Toys – bears.

Pat the cat by Colin & Jacqui Hawkins; ill. by Colin Hawkins. Putnam, 1983. ISBN 0-399-20957-3 Subj: Animals – cats.

Round the garden by Colin & Jacqui Hawkins; ill. by authors. Viking, 1986. ISBN 0-670-80315-4 Subj: Format, unusual – toy & movable books. Games. Gardens, gardening.

Snap! Snap! by Colin & Jacqui Hawkins; ill. by Colin Hawkins. Putnam, 1984. ISBN 0-399-21163-2 Subj: Emotions – fear. Monsters. Night. Rhyming text.

Take away monsters ill. by author. Putnam, 1984. ISBN 0-399-20962-X Subj: Counting, numbers. Format, unusual – toy & movable books. Monsters. Rhyming text.

There was an old lady who swallowed a fly (Little old lady who swallowed a fly)

This little pig by Colin & Jacqui Hawkins; ill. by authors. Viking, 1986. ISBN 0-670-80316-2 Subj: Anatomy – toes. Animals – pigs. Format, unusual – toy & movable books. Games.

Tog the dog by Colin & Jacqui Hawkins; ill. by authors. Putnam, 1986. ISBN 0-399-21338-4 Subj: Animals – dogs. Behavior – lost. Format, unusual – toy & movable books. Language. Rhyming text.

What time is it, Mr. Wolf? ill. by author. Putnam, 1983. ISBN 0-399-20959-X Subj: Animals – wolves. Format, unusual – toy & movable books. Time.

Where's bear? ill. by author. Little, 1986. ISBN 0-87113-090-4 Subj: Activities – playing. Animals – bears. Bedtime. Toys – bears.

Where's my mommy? by Colin & Jacqui Hawkins; ill. by authors. Crown, 1986. ISBN 0-517-55974-9 Subj: Animals. Behavior – needing someone. Family life – mothers.

Hawkins, Jacqui. *Boo! Who?* (Hawkins, Colin)

Busy ABC (Hawkins, Colin)

Come for a ride on the ghost train (Hawkins, Colin)

Creepy castle (Hawkins, Colin)

The elephant (Hawkins, Colin)

Fairytale news (Hawkins, Colin)

Hey, diddle, diddle (Hawkins, Colin)

I'm not sleepy! (Hawkins, Colin)

Incy wincy spider (Hawkins, Colin)

Jen the hen (Hawkins, Colin)

Max and the magic word (Hawkins, Colin)

Mig the pig (Hawkins, Colin)

Old Mother Hubbard (Martin, Sarah Catherine)

One, two, guess who? (Hawkins, Colin)

Pat the cat (Hawkins, Colin)

Round the garden (Hawkins, Colin)

Snap! Snap! (Hawkins, Colin)

This little pig (Hawkins, Colin)

Tog the dog (Hawkins, Colin)

Where's my mommy? (Hawkins, Colin)

Hawkins, Mark. *A lion under her bed* ill. by Jean Vallario. Holt, 1978. ISBN 0-03-040381-2 Subj: Animals – lions. Bedtime. Furniture – beds.

Hawkinson, John. *Birds in the sky* (Hawkinson, Lucy [Ozone])

The old stump ill. by author. A. Whitman, 1965. Subj: Animals – mice. Trees.

Robins and rabbits by John & Lucy Hawkinson; ill. by John Hawkinson. A. Whitman, 1960. Subj: Animals. Birds – robins.

Where the wild apples grow ill. by author. A. Whitman, 1967. Subj: Animals – horses, ponies. Character traits – freedom.

Hawkinson, Lucy (Ozone). *Birds in the sky* by Lucy & John Hawkinson; ill. by authors. Childrens Pr., 1966. Subj: Birds. Science.

Dance, dance, Amy-Chan! ill. by author. A. Whitman, 1964. Subj: Ethnic groups in the U.S. – Japanese Americans.

Robins and rabbits (Hawkinson, John)

Hawthorne, Nathaniel. *The Great Stone Face* (Schmidt, Gary D.)

King Midas and the golden touch (Hewitt, Kathryn)

Hawxhurst, Joan C. *Bubbe and Gram, my two grandmothers* ill. by Jane K. Bynum. Dovetail, 1996. ISBN 0-9661284-2-3 Subj: Family life – grandmothers. Holidays – Christmas. Holidays – Easter. Holidays – Hanukkah. Holidays – Passover. Jewish culture. Religion.

Hay, Dean. *I see a lot of things* ill. by author. Lion, 1966. Subj: Senses – sight.

Now I can count ill. by author. Lion, 1968. Subj: Counting, numbers. Time.

Hay, Timothy. *see* Brown, Margaret Wise

Hayashi, Akiko. *Aki and the fox* ill. by author. Doubleday, 1991. ISBN 0-385-41948-1 Subj: Activities – traveling. Family life – grandmothers. Toys. Trains.

Hayashi, Leslie Ann. *Fables from the sea* ill. by Kathleen Wong Bishop. Univ. of Hawaii Pr., 2000. ISBN 0-8248-2224-2 Subj: Animals. Hawaii. Sea & seashore.

Hayden, Kate. *Baby animals* (Lilly, Kenneth)

Horse show ill. with photos. KD, 2001. ISBN 0-7894-7372-0 Subj: Animals – horses, ponies. Sports.

Hayden, Lea. *Sunny day – rainy day* ill. by Joe Ewers. Random House, 1990. ISBN 0-679-80068-9 Subj: Format, unusual. Weather. Weather – rain.

Hayes, Ann. *Meet the Marching Smithereens* ill. by Karmen Thompson. Harcourt, 1995. ISBN 0-15-253158-0 Subj: Animals. Music. Parades.

Meet the orchestra ill. by Karmen Thompson. Harcourt, 1991. ISBN 0-15-200526-9 Subj: Animals. Music.

Hayes, Geoffrey. *Bear by himself* ill. by author. HarperCollins, 1976. ISBN 0-06-022263-8 Subj: Behavior – solitude. Toys – bears.

Christmas in Puttyville ill. by author. Random House, 1985. ISBN 0-394-97286-4 Subj: Animals – bears. Character traits – generosity. Holidays – Christmas.

Elroy and the witch's child ill. by author. HarperCollins, 1982. ISBN 0-06-022259-X Subj: Animals – cats. Witches.

The mystery of the pirate ghost ill. by author. Random House, 1985. ISBN 0-394-97220-1 Subj: Ghosts. Mystery stories. Pirates.

Patrick and his grandpa ill. by author. Random House, 1986. ISBN 0-394-87287-8 Subj: Animals – bears. Family life – grandfathers. Format, unusual – board books.

Patrick and Ted ill. by author. Four Winds, 1984. ISBN 0-590-07902-6 Subj: Animals – bears. Behavior – growing up.

Patrick at the circus ill. by author. Hyperion, 2002. ISBN 0-7868-2595-2 Subj: Animals – bears. Circus. Clowns, jesters.

The secret inside ill. by author. HarperCollins, 1980. ISBN 0-06-022274-3 Subj: Animals – bears. Dreams.

Hayes, Joe. *Juan Verdades, the man who could not tell a lie* ill. by Joseph Daniel Fiedler. Orchard, 2001. ISBN 0-439-29311-1 Subj: Behavior – lying. Folk & fairy tales. Foreign languages.

Little Gold Star = Estrellita de oro ill. by Gloria Osuna Perez & Lucia Angela Perez. Cinco Puntos, 2000. ISBN 0-938317-49-0 Subj: Birds – hawks. Folk & fairy tales. Foreign languages. Magic.

A spoon for every bite ill. by Rebecca Leer. Orchard, 1996. ISBN 0-531-08799-9 Subj: Behavior – boasting. Ethnic groups in the U.S. – Hispanic Americans. Indians of North America.

Hayes, Sarah. *Away in a manger* ill. by Inga Moore. Little Simon, 1987. ISBN 0-671-64311-8 Subj: Holidays – Christmas. Religion – Nativity.

Bad egg: the true story of Humpty Dumpty ill. by Charlotte Voake. Little, 1987. ISBN 0-316-35184-9 Subj: Behavior – misbehavior. Nursery rhymes. Royalty.

A bad start for Santa ill. by Jamie Charteris. Joy Street, 1986. ISBN 0-316-35183-0 Subj: Behavior – lost & found possessions. Holidays – Christmas. Santa Claus.

The cats of Tiffany Street ill. by author. Candlewick, 1992. ISBN 1-56402-094-0 Subj: Animals – cats.

Clap your hands: finger rhymes ill. by Toni Goffe. Lothrop, 1988. ISBN 0-688-07693-9 Subj: Games. Nursery rhymes.

Eat up, Gemma ill. by Jan Ormerod. Lothrop, 1988. ISBN 0-688-08149-5 Subj: Babies. Ethnic groups in the U.S. – African Americans. Food.

The grumpalump ill. by Barbara Firth. Clarion, 1991. ISBN 0-89919-871-6 Subj: Activities – ballooning. Animals. Rhyming text.

Happy Christmas, Gemma ill. by Jan Ormerod. Lothrop, 1986. ISBN 0-688-06508-2 Subj: Ethnic groups in the U.S. – African Americans. Family life. Family life – grandmothers. Holidays – Christmas.

Lucy Anna and the Finders ill. by author. Candlewick, 2000. ISBN 0-7636-1200-6 Subj: Behavior – lost & found possessions. Behavior – resourcefulness. Mythical creatures. Toys.

Mary Mary ill. by Helen Craig. Macmillan, 1990. ISBN 0-689-50514-0 Subj: Behavior – needing someone. Character traits – being different. Giants.

Nine ducks nine ill. by author. Lothrop, 1990. ISBN 0-688-09535-6 Subj: Animals – foxes. Birds – ducks. Character traits – cleverness. Rhyming text.

This is the bear ill. by Helen Craig. Lippincott, 1986. ISBN 0-397-32171-6 Subj: Behavior – lost. Behavior – secrets. Rhyming text. Toys – bears.

This is the bear and the bad little girl ill. by Helen Craig. Candlewick, 1995. ISBN 1-56402-648-5 Subj: Animals – dogs. Character traits – helpfulness. Toys.

This is the bear and the picnic lunch ill. by Helen Craig. Little, 1989. ISBN 0-316-35248-9 Subj: Activities – picnicking. Animals – dogs. Rhyming text. Toys – bears.

This is the bear and the scary night ill. by Helen Craig. Little, 1992. ISBN 0-316-35250-0 Subj: Character traits – bravery. Night. Rhyming text. Toys – bears.

Hayles, Karen. *What is stuck* by Karen Hayles & Charles Fuge; ill. by Charles Fuge. S&S, 1993. ISBN 0-671-86587-0 Subj: Animals. Animals – whales. Foreign lands – Arctic. Sea & seashore.

Hayles, Marsha. *The feathered crown* ill. by Bernadette Pons. Holt, 2002. ISBN 0-8050-6421-4 Subj: Birds. Gifts. Holidays – Christmas. Religion – Nativity. Rhyming text.

He saves the day ill. by Lynne Cravath. Putnam, 2001. ISBN 0-399-23363-6 Subj: Activities. Imagination. Rhyming text.

A pet of a pet ill. by Scott Nash. Dial, 2001. ISBN 0-8037-2512-4 Subj: Animals. Farms. Pets. Self-concept.

Haynes, Max. *Dinosaur island* ill. by author. Lothrop, 1991. ISBN 0-688-10330-8 Subj: Dinosaurs. Islands. Prehistory.

Grandma's gone to live in the stars ill. by author. A. Whitman, 2000. ISBN 0-8075-3026-3 Subj: Death. Emotions – grief. Family life – grandmothers.

Sparky's rainbow repair photos & ill. by author. Lothrop, 1992. ISBN 0-688-11194-7 Subj: Games. Weather – rainbows.

Ticklemonster and me ill. by author. Doubleday, 1999. ISBN 0-385-32582-7 Subj: Family life – mothers. Games. Monsters.

Haynes, Robert. *The elephant that ga-lumped* (Ward, Nanda Weedon)

Hays, Anna Jane. *The pup speaks up* ill. by Valeria Petrone. Random House, 2003. ISBN 0-375-91232-0 Subj: Animals. Animals – dogs. Noise, sounds. Pets.

Hays, Daniel. *Charley sang a song* (Hays, Hoffman Reynolds)

Hays, Hoffman Reynolds. *Charley sang a song* by Hoffman & Daniel Hays; ill. by Uri Shulevitz. HarperCollins, 1964. Subj: Activities – flying.

Hays, Wilma Pitchford. *Little Yellow Fur* ill. by Richard Cuffari. Coward, 1973. ISBN 0-698-30503-5 Subj: Indians of North America – Dakota (Sioux).

Hayward, Linda. *All stuck up* ill. by Normand Chartier. McKay, 1990. ISBN 0-379-90216-3 Subj: Animals – foxes. Animals – rabbits. Behavior – trickery. Folk & fairy tales.

Alphabet School ill. by Ann Schweninger. Random House, 1989. ISBN 0-394-92226-3 Subj: ABC books. Animals – cats. School.

Baby Moses ill. by Barb Henry. Random House, 1989. ISBN 0-394-99410-8 Subj: Babies. Foreign lands – Egypt. Religion – Moses.

Baker, baker, cookie maker ill. by Tom Brannon. Random House, 1998. ISBN 0-679-98379-1 Subj: Careers – bakers. Puppets. Rhyming text.

The biggest cookie in the world ill. by Joe Ewers. Random House, 1995. ISBN 0-679-97146-7 Subj: Careers – bakers. Puppets.

The case of the missing Duckie ill. by Maggie Swanson. Western, 1992. ISBN 0-307-23124-0 Subj: Behavior – lost & found possessions. Mystery stories. Puppets.

The city worm and the country worm ill. by Carol Nicklaus. Western, 1993. ISBN 0-307-23144-5 Subj: Animals – worms. Cities, towns. Country.

D is for doll ill. by Denise Fleming. Random House, 1988. ISBN 0-394-89635-1 Subj: ABC books. Rebuses. Rhyming text.

A day in the life of a builder ill. with photos. DK, 2001. ISBN 0-7894-7364-X Subj: Careers – construction workers. Homes, houses.

A day in the life of a dancer ill. with photos. DK, 2001. ISBN 0-7894-7370-4 Subj: Activities – dancing. Ballet. Careers – dancers.

A day in the life of a firefighter ill. with photos. DK, 2001. Subj: Careers – firefighters. Fire.

A day in the life of a teacher ill. with photos. DK, 2001. ISBN 0-7894-7368-2 Subj: Careers – teachers. School.

A day in the life of Oscar the Grouch: featuring Jim Henson's Sesame Street Muppets ill. by Bill Davis. Western, 1981. ISBN 0-307-23138-0 Subj: Behavior. Puppets.

Did I ever tell you how high you can count? adapt. by Linda Hayward & Cathy Goldsmith from the works of Dr. Seuss. Random House, 1996. ISBN 0-679-87081-4 Subj: Counting, numbers.

Elmo goes to day camp ill. by Carol Nicklaus. Random House, 1990. ISBN 0-679-80158-8 Subj: Camps, camping. Puppets.

Ernie and Bert's summer project ill. by Carol Nicklaus. Random House, 1991. ISBN 0-679-81051-X Subj: Behavior – collecting things. Museums. Puppets. Seasons – summer.

Goldilocks and the three bears (The three bears)

Grover's summer vacation ill. by Ronald Fritz. Random House, 1989. ISBN 0-394-83969-2 Subj: Activities – vacationing. Puppets.

Hello, house! ill. by Lynn Munsinger. Random House, 1988. Adapt. of: Heyo house by Joel Chandler Harris. ISBN 0-394-98864-7 Subj: Animals – rabbits. Animals – wolves. Behavior – trickery. Ethnic groups in the U.S. – African Americans. Folk & fairy tales. Homes, houses.

I can add upside down! by Linda Hayward & Cathy Goldsmith from the works of Dr. Seuss. Random House, 1995. ISBN 0-679-86754-6 Subj: Counting, numbers.

I can count to ten and back again ill. by Maggie Swanson. Western, 1992. ISBN 0-307-23116-X Subj: Counting, numbers. Puppets.

Noah's ark ill. by Amy Flynn. Random House, 1993. ISBN 0-679-83600-4 Subj: Boats, ships. Religion – Noah. Weather – floods. Weather – rain.

Oh, the things you can count from 1-10 adapt. by Linda Hayward & Cathy Goldsmith from the works of Dr. Seuss. Random House, 1995. ISBN 0-679-86753-8 Subj: Counting, numbers.

Pepe and Papa ill. by Laura Huliska-Beith. Golden Bks., 2001. ISBN 0-307-46114-9 Subj: Folk & fairy tales. Humorous stories.

The runaway Christmas toy ill. by Loretta Krupinski. Random House, 1994. ISBN 0-679-86173-4 Subj: Behavior – running away. Holidays – Christmas. Santa Claus. Toys. Trains.

Sunny Day Bunny ill. by Lucinda McQueen. Grosset, 1986. ISBN 0-448-10452-0 Subj: Animals – rabbits. Family life – grandmothers. Format, unusual – board books. Weather.

The three little pigs (The three little pigs)

Wet foot, dry foot, low foot, high foot by Linda Hayward & Cathy Goldsmith from the works of Dr. Seuss. Random House, 1996. ISBN 0-679-87086-5 Subj: Concepts. Language.

What homework? ill. by Page Eastburn O'Rourke. Kane Pr., 2002. ISBN 1-57565-116-5 Subj: Plants. School.

Hayward, Max. *The telephone* (Chukovskii, Kornei Ivanovich)

Haywood, Carolyn. *A Christmas fantasy* ill. by Glenys & Victor G. Ambrus. Morrow, 1972. ISBN 0-688-30094-4 Subj: Holidays – Christmas. Santa Claus.

Hello, star ill. by Julie Durrell. Morrow, 1987. ISBN 0-688-06651-8 Subj: Animals. Family life – grandparents. Farms. Seasons – summer.

How the reindeer saved Santa ill. by Victor G. Ambrus. Morrow, 1986. ISBN 0-688-05904-X Subj: Animals – reindeer. Character traits – loyalty. Holidays – Christmas. Santa Claus.

The king's monster ill. by Victor G. Ambrus. Morrow, 1980. ISBN 0-688-32214-X Subj: Monsters. Royalty – kings.

Santa Claus forever! ill. by Glenys & Victor G. Ambrus. Morrow, 1983. ISBN 0-688-02345-2 Subj: Behavior – bad day. Holidays – Christmas. Santa Claus.

Hazelaar, Cor. *Dogs everywhere* ill. by author. Knopf, 1995. ISBN 0-679-95439-2 Subj: Animals – dogs. Cities, towns. Pets.

Zoo dreams ill. by author. Farrar, 1997. ISBN 0-374-39730-9 Subj: Animals. Bedtime. Dreams. Sleep. Zoos.

Hazelton, Elizabeth Baldwin. *Sammy, the crow who remembered* ill. by Ann Atwood. Scribners, 1969. Subj: Birds – crows. Family life. Memories, memory.

Hazen, Barbara Shook. *Digby* ill. by Barbara J. Phillips-Duke. HarperCollins, 1997. ISBN 0-06-026254-0 Subj: Animals – dogs. Old age.

Even if I did something awful ill. by Nancy Kincade. Atheneum, 1981. ISBN 0-689-30843-4 Subj: Emotions – love. Family life.

Fang ill. by Leslie Holt Morrill. Atheneum, 1987. ISBN 0-689-31307-1 Subj: Animals – dogs. Character traits – bravery. Emotions – fear.

The Fat Cats, Cousin Scraggs and the monster mice ill. by Lonni Sue Johnson. Atheneum, 1985. ISBN 0-689-31092-7 Subj: Animals – cats. Animals – mice. Behavior – dissatisfaction. Character traits – cleverness.

Good-bye/Hello ill. by Michael Bryant. Atheneum, 1995. ISBN 0-689-31665-8 Subj: Emotions. Moving. Rhyming text.

The gorilla did it! ill. by Ray Cruz. Atheneum, 1974. ISBN 0-689-30138-3 Subj: Animals – gorillas. Imagination – imaginary friends.

Gorilla wants to be the baby ill. by Jacqueline Bardner Smith. Atheneum, 1978. ISBN 0-689-30654-7 Subj: Animals – gorillas. Imagination – imaginary friends.

Happy, sad, silly, mad: a beginning book about emotions ill. by Elizabeth Dauber; ed. consultant: Mary Elting. Grosset, 1971. ISBN 0-448-03622-3 Subj: Emotions.

If it weren't for Benjamin (I'd always get to lick the icing spoon) ill. by Laura Hartman. Human Sciences Pr., 1979. ISBN 0-87705-384-7 Subj: Sibling rivalry.

Katie's wish ill. by Emily Arnold McCully. Dial, 2003. ISBN 0-8037-2478-0 Subj: Ethnic groups in the U.S. – Irish Americans. Family life – fathers. Family life – grandparents. Foreign lands – Ireland.

The knight who was afraid of the dark ill. by Tony Ross. Dial, 1988. ISBN 0-8037-0668-5 Subj: Emotions – fear. Knights. Middle Ages. Night.

The knight who was afraid to fight ill. by Toni Goffe. Dial, 1994. ISBN 0-8037-1592-7 Subj: Emotions – fear. Knights. Middle Ages.

The me I see ill. by Ati Forberg. Abingdon, 1978. ISBN 0-687-23910-9 Subj: Activities – bathing. Anatomy.

Mommy's office ill. by David Soman. Atheneum, 1992. ISBN 0-689-31601-1 Subj: Activities – working. Careers. Family life – mothers.

The new dog ill. by R. W. Alley. Dial, 1996. ISBN 0-8037-1813-6 Subj: Animals – dogs. Behavior. Character traits – bravery.

Santa clues ill. by Simon Galkin. Longmeadow, 1995. ISBN 0-681-00682-X Subj: Character traits – questioning. Holidays – Christmas. Rhyming text. Santa Claus.

The sorcerer's apprentice ill. by Tomi Ungerer. Lancelot Pr., 1969. Subj: Folk & fairy tales. Magic.

Stay, Fang ill. by Leslie Holt Morrill. Atheneum, 1990. ISBN 0-689-31599-6 Subj: Animals – dogs. Pets.

The story of Santa Claus ill. by Carolyn Bracken. Western, 1989. ISBN 0-307-62097-2 Subj: Santa Claus.

Tight times ill. by Trina Schart Hyman. Viking, 1979. ISBN 0-670-71287-6 Subj: Animals – cats. Family life. Family life – only child. Poverty.

Turkey in the straw ill. by Brad Sneed. Dial, 1993. ISBN 0-8037-1299-5 Subj: Activities – dancing. Careers – farmers. Farms.

Two homes to live in ill. by Peggy Luks. Human Sciences Pr., 1978. ISBN 0-8770-5313-8 Subj: Divorce. Emotions.

Wally the worry-warthog ill. by Janet Stevens. Houghton Mifflin, 1990. ISBN 0-89919-896-1 Subj: Animals – warthogs. Behavior – worrying. Emotions – fear.

Where do bears sleep? ill. by Mary Morgan Van Royen. Harper-Collins, 1998. ISBN 0-694-01037-5 Subj: Animals. Rhyming text. Sleep.

Where do bears sleep? ill. by Ian E. Staunton. Addison-Wesley, 1970. Subj: Animals. Rhyming text. Sleep.

Why couldn't I be an only kid like you, Wigger? ill. by Leigh Grant. Atheneum, 1975. ISBN 0-689-30488-9 Subj: Babies. Emotions – envy, jealousy. Family life – only child. Sibling rivalry.

Why did Grandpa die? a book about death ill. by Pat Schories. Childrens Pr., 1985. ISBN 0-307-62484-6 Subj: Death. Emotions – grief. Family life – grandfathers. Old age.

World, world, what can I do? ill. by Margaret Leibold. Morehouse, 1991. ISBN 0-8192-1537-6 Subj: Ecology. Rhyming text.

Head, Judith. *Mud soup* ill. by Susan Guevara. Random House, 2003. ISBN 0-375-91087-5 Subj: Activities – baking, cooking. Ethnic groups in the U.S. – Mexican Americans. Food. Foreign languages.

Heap, Sue. *Cowboy Baby* ill. by author. Candlewick, 1998. ISBN 0-7636-0437-2 Subj: Babies. Bedtime. Cowboys, cowgirls. Family life – fathers. Toys.

Four friends in the garden ill. by author. Candlewick, 2004. ISBN 0-7636-2371-7 Subj: Animals – bears. Animals – rabbits. Animals – sheep. Friendship. Gardens, gardening. Insects – butterflies, caterpillars.

What shall we play? ill. by author. Candlewick, 2002. ISBN 0-7636-1685-0 Subj: Activities – playing. Imagination.

Heard, Georgia. *This place I know* (This place I know)

Hearn, Diane Dawson. *Anna in the garden* ill. by author. Silver Moon, 1994. ISBN 1-881889-57-2 Subj: Flowers. Gardens, gardening.

Bad luck Boswell ill. by author. S&S, 1995. ISBN 0-689-80303-6 Subj: Animals – cats. Character traits – luck. Witches.

Dad's dinosaur day ill. by author. Macmillan, 1993. ISBN 0-02-743485-0 Subj: Dinosaurs. Family life – fathers. Prehistory.

Hearn, Lafcadio. *The funny little woman* (Mosel, Arlene)

Hearn, Michael Patrick. *The porcelain cat* ill. by Leo & Diane Dillon. Little, 1985. ISBN 0-316-35330-2 Subj: Animals – cats. Animals – rats. Cumulative tales. Folk & fairy tales. Magic.

Hearne, Betsy Gould. *Seven brave women* ill. by Bethanne Andersen. Greenwillow, 1997. ISBN 0-688-14503-5 Subj: Character traits – bravery. Family life. Immigrants. U.S. history. War.

Heath, Amy. *Sofie's role* ill. by Sheila Hamanaka. Four Winds, 1992. ISBN 0-02-743505-9 Subj: Activities – baking, cooking. Careers – bakers. Ethnic groups in the U.S. – African Americans. Family life. Holidays – Christmas.

Heatwole, Marsha. *Jambo, watoto!* ill. by author; text by Elizabeth Massie & Barbara Spilman Lawson. Creative Art Pr., 1998. ISBN 0-9642712-3-0 Subj: Animals. Animals – cheetahs. Family life – mothers. Foreign lands – Africa.

Heck, Elisabeth. *The black sheep* trans. by Karen M. Klockner; ill. by Sita Jucker. Little, 1986. ISBN 0-316-35402-3 Subj: Animals – sheep. Behavior – running away. Holidays – Christmas. Religion.

Heckman, Philip. *The moon is following me* ill. by Mary O'Keefe Young. Atheneum, 1991. ISBN 0-689-31565-1 Subj: Activities – traveling. Moon.

Waking upside down ill. by Dwight Been. Atheneum, 1996. ISBN 0-689-31930-4 Subj: Dreams. Family life. Imagination. Sibling rivalry.

Hedderwick, Mairi. *The big Katie Morag storybook* ill. by author. Bodley Head, 1996. ISBN 0-370-32442-0 Subj: Activities – baking, cooking. Family life – grandmothers. Islands.

Katie Morag and the big boy cousins ill. by author. Little, 1987. ISBN 0-316-35403-1 Subj: Behavior – misbehavior. Family life. Family life – grandmothers. Foreign lands – Scotland. Islands.

Katie Morag and the tiresome Ted ill. by author. Little, 1986. ISBN 0-316-35401-5 Subj: Babies. Behavior – misbehavior. Emotions – envy, jealousy. Family life – new sibling. Foreign lands – Scotland. Islands. Sibling rivalry.

Katie Morag and the two grandmothers ill. by author. Little, 1986. ISBN 0-316-35400-7 Subj: Activities – bathing. Animals – sheep. Fairs, festivals. Family life – grandmothers. Foreign lands – Scotland. Islands.

Katie Morag delivers the mail ill. by author. Little, 1987, 1984. ISBN 0-316-35405-8 Subj: Behavior – misbehavior. Careers – postal workers. Family life – grandmothers. Foreign lands – Scotland. Islands. Post office.

P. D. Pebbles' summer or winter book ill. by author. Little, 1989. ISBN 0-316-35406-6 Subj: Family life. Format, unusual. Seasons – summer. Seasons – winter.

Heelan, Jamee Riggio. *Can you hear a rainbow?* ill. by Nicola Simmonds. Peachtree, 2002. ISBN 1-56145-268-8 Subj: Communication. Handicaps – deafness. Language. School.

The making of my special hand, Madison's story ill. by Nicola Simmonds. Peachtree, 1998. ISBN 1-56145-186-X Subj: Handicaps – physical handicaps.

Rolling along, the story of Taylor and his wheelchair ill. by Nicola Simmonds. Peachtree, 2000. ISBN 1-56145-219-X Subj: Handicaps – cerebral palsy. Handicaps – physical handicaps.

Hefter, Richard. *The strawberry book of shapes* ill. by author. Larousse, 1976. ISBN 0-8847-0021-6 Subj: Concepts – shape.

Hegg, Tom. *Peef and his best friend* ill. by Warren Hanson. Waldman, 2001. ISBN 0-931674-49-2 Subj: Friendship. Rhyming text. Toys – bears.

Heidbreder, Robert. *Drumheller dinosaur dance* ill. by Bill Slavin. Kids Can, 2004. ISBN 1-55337-393-6 Subj: Activities – dancing. Dinosaurs.

I wished for a unicorn ill. by Kady MacDonald Denton. Kids Can, 2000. ISBN 1-55074-543-3 Subj: Activities – playing. Behavior – wishing. Imagination. Mythical creatures – unicorns. Rhyming text.

Heide, Florence Parry. *The bigness contest* ill. by Victoria Chess. Joy Street, 1994. ISBN 0-316-35444-9 Subj: Animals – hippopotamuses. Concepts. Self-concept.

The day of Ahmed's secret by Florence Parry Heide & Judith Heide Gilliland; ill. by Ted Lewin. Lothrop, 1990. ISBN 0-688-08895-3 Subj: Activities – working. Activities – writing. Behavior – secrets. Foreign lands – Egypt.

Grim and ghastly goings-on ill. by Victoria Chess. Lothrop, 1992. ISBN 0-688-08322-6 Subj: Monsters. Poetry.

A monster is coming! A monster is coming! by Florence Parry Heide & Roxanne Heide; ill. by Rachi Farrow. Watts, 1980. ISBN 0-531-03449-6 Subj: Monsters.

Oh, grow up! poems to help you survive parents, chores, school, and other afflictions by Florence Parry Heide & Roxanne Heide Pierce; ill. by Nadine Bernard Westcott. Orchard, 1996. ISBN 0-531-08771-9 Subj: Behavior – dissatisfaction. Behavior – growing up. Poetry. Sibling rivalry.

Sami and the time of the troubles by Florence Parry Heide & Judith Heide Gilliland; ill. by Ted Lewin. Clarion, 1992. ISBN 0-395-55964-2 Subj: Family life. Foreign lands – Lebanon. War.

Some things are scary ill. by Jules Feiffer. Candlewick, 2000. ISBN 0-7636-1222-7 Subj: Emotions – fear.

Timothy Twinge by Florence Parry Heide & Roxanne Heide Pierce; ill. by Barbara Lehman. Lothrop, 1993. ISBN 0-688-10763-X Subj: Behavior – worrying. Character traits – bravery. Emotions – fear. Rhyming text.

Heide, Roxanne. *A monster is coming! A monster is coming!* (Heide, Florence Parry)

Heilbroner, Joan. *Robert the rose horse* ill. by Philip Eastman. Random House, 1962. ISBN 0-394-90025-1 Subj: Animals – horses, ponies. Flowers. Humorous stories.

This is the house where Jack lives ill. by Aliki. HarperCollins, 1962. ISBN 0-06-022286-7 Subj: Cumulative tales. Participation.

Tom the TV cat ill. by Sal Murdocca. Random House, 1984. ISBN 0-394-96708-9 Subj: Animals – cats. Behavior – seeking better things. Television.

Heiligman, Deborah. *Babies* ill. by Laura Freeman. National Geographic, 2002. ISBN 0-7922-8205-1 Subj: Babies. Behavior – growing up.

From caterpillar to butterfly ill. by Bari Weissman. HarperCollins, 1996. ISBN 0-06-024268-X Subj: Insects – butterflies, caterpillars. Metamorphosis. Science.

Honeybees ill. by Carla Golembe. National Geographic, 2002. ISBN 0-7922-6678-1 Subj: Insects – bees.

Into the night ill. by Melissa Sweet. HarperCollins, 1990. ISBN 0-06-026382-2 Subj: Bedtime. Family life – mothers. Rhyming text.

Mike Swan, sink or swim ill. by Chris Demarest. First Choice Chapter Book, 1998. ISBN 0-385-32522-3 Subj: Emotions. Family life. Food. Sports – swimming.

On the move ill. by Lizzy Rockwell. HarperCollins, 1996. ISBN 0-06-024742-8 Subj: Activities. Animals.

Pockets ill. by Suzanne Duranceau. Hyperion, 1995. ISBN 0-7868-2141-8 Subj: Clothing – pockets. Family life. Family life – grandfathers.

Heine, Helme. *The boxer and the princess* ill. by author. McElderry, 1998. ISBN 0-689-82195-6 Subj: Animals – rhinoceros. Emotions – love. Royalty – princesses.

Friends ill. by author. Atheneum, 1982. ISBN 0-689-50256-7 Subj: Animals. Friendship. Sports – bicycling.

Friends go adventuring ill. by author. McElderry, 1995. ISBN 0-689-80463-6 Subj: Animals. Friendship.

King Bounce the 1st ill. by author. Alphabet Pr., 1982. ISBN 0-907234-11-9 Subj: Royalty – kings. Sleep.

The marvelous journey through the night trans. by Ralph Manheim; ill. by author. Farrar, 1990. ISBN 0-374-38478-9 Subj: Dreams. Night. Sleep.

Merry-go-round ill. by author. Barron's, 1980. ISBN 0-8120-5393-1 Subj: Activities – working.

Mr. Miller, the dog ill. by author. Atheneum, 1980. ISBN 0-689-50174-9 Subj: Animals – dogs. Behavior – imitation.

Mollywoop trans. by Ralph Manheim; ill. by author. Farrar, 1991. ISBN 0-374-35001-9 Subj: Animals. Birds – chickens. Friendship. Rhyming text.

The most wonderful egg in the world ill. by author. Atheneum, 1983. ISBN 0-689-50280-X Subj: Birds – chickens. Character traits – appearance. Royalty.

One day in paradise ill. by adapt. Atheneum, 1986. ISBN 0-689-50394-6 Subj: Religion.

The pigs' wedding ill. by author. Atheneum, 1979. ISBN 0-689-50127-7 Subj: Animals – pigs. Weddings.

Prince Bear ill. by author. Macmillan, 1989. ISBN 0-689-50484-5 Subj: Animals – bears. Progress. Royalty – princes. Royalty – princesses.

Superhare ill. by author. Barron's, 1979. ISBN 0-8120-5357-5 Subj: Animals – rabbits. Character traits – being different.

Three little friends: the alarm clock ill. by author. Atheneum, 1985. ISBN 0-689-71043-7 Subj: Animals. Birds – chickens. Friendship. Night.

Three little friends: the racing cart ill. by author. Atheneum, 1985. ISBN 0-689-71045-3 Subj: Animals. Birds – chickens. Friendship. Sports – racing.

Three little friends: the visitor ill. by author. Atheneum, 1985. ISBN 0-689-71044-5 Subj: Animals. Birds – chickens. Friendship.

Heinrichs, Ann. *Bats* ill. with photos. Compass Pt., 2004. ISBN 0-7565-0591-7 Subj: Animals – bats.

Grasshoppers ill. with photos. Compass Pt., 2002. ISBN 0-7565-0166-0 Subj: Insects – grasshoppers.

Spiders ill. with photos. Compass Pt., 2004. ISBN 0-7565-0590-9 Subj: Spiders.

Heins, Ethel L. *The cat and the cook and other fables of Krylov* ill. by Anita Lobel. Greenwillow, 1995. ISBN 0-688-12311-2 Subj: Folk & fairy tales. Foreign lands – Russia.

Heins, Paul. *Snow White* (Grimm, Jacob)

Heinst, Marie. *My first number book* photos by author. DK, 1992. ISBN 1-879431-74-2 Subj: Concepts – shape. Counting, numbers. Ethnic groups in the U.S. Games.

Heinz, Brian J. *Butternut Hollow Pond* ill. by Bob Marstall. Millbrook, 2000. ISBN 0-7613-0268-9 Subj: Animals. Ecology. Lakes, ponds.

The monsters' test scary pictures by Sal Murdocca. Millbrook, 1996. ISBN 0-7613-0095-3 Subj: Holidays – Halloween. Monsters. Rhyming text. Witches.

Nanuk, lord of the ice ill. by Gregory Manchess. Dial, 1998. ISBN 0-8037-2195-1 Subj: Animals – polar bears. Eskimos. Foreign lands – Arctic. Indians of North America – Inuit. Sports – hunting.

The wolves ill. by Bernie Fuchs. Dial, 1996. ISBN 0-8037-1736-9 Subj: Animals – endangered animals. Animals – wolves. Nature.

Heitler, Susan M. (Susan McCrensky). *David decides, no more thumb-sucking* photos by Paula Singer. Avon, 1993. Previously published: David decides about thumbsucking. 1st U.S. ed. Denver, CO: Reading Matters, 1985. ISBN 0-380-76852-6 Subj: Behavior – growing up. Problem solving. Thumb sucking.

Hejl, Pauline. *The fine round cake* (Esterl, Arnica)

Helakoski, Leslie. *The smushy bus* ill. by Sal Murdocca. Millbrook, 2002. ISBN 0-7613-1398-2 Subj: Buses. Careers – bus drivers. Counting, numbers. School.

The Helen Oxenbury nursery collection ill. by Helen Oxenbury. Knopf, 2004. ISBN 0-375-92992-4 Subj: Folk & fairy tales. Nursery rhymes. Poetry.

The Helen Oxenbury nursery rhyme book chosen by Brian W. Alderson; ill. by Helen Oxenbury. Morrow, 1987. ISBN 0-688-06899-5 Subj: Nursery rhymes.

Helena, Ann. *The lie* ill. by Ellen Pizer. Raintree, 1977. ISBN 0-8172-0958-1 Subj: Behavior – lying. Emotions. Friendship.

Heling, Kathryn. *Mouse makes magic* by Kathryn Heling & Deborah Hembrook; ill. by Patrick Joseph. Random House, 2003. ISBN 0-375-92184-2 Subj: Animals – mice. Language.

Mouse's hide-and-seek words by Kathryn Heling & Deborah Hembrook; ill. by Patrick Joseph. Random House, 2003. ISBN 0-375-92185-0 Subj: Animals – mice. Language. Rhyming text.

Hellard, Susan. *Baby lemur* ill. by author. Holt, 1999. ISBN 0-8050-6142-8 Subj: Animals – babies. Animals – lemurs. Behavior – growing up. Family life – mothers.

Billy goats Gruff (Asbjørnsen, P. C. [Peter Christen])

Eleanor and the babysitter ill. by author. Little, 1991. ISBN 0-316-35459-7 Subj: Activities – babysitting. Animals – anteaters. Animals – koalas. Monsters.

Froggie goes a-courting ill. by adapt. Putnam, 1988. ISBN 0-399-21508-5 Subj: Frogs & toads.

This little piggy ill. by author. Putnam, 1989. ISBN 0-399-21625-1 Subj: Animals – pigs. Format, unusual. Nursery rhymes.

Time to get up ill. by author. Putnam, 1990. ISBN 0-399-21948-X Subj: Animals. Format, unusual – toy & movable books. Morning. Rhyming text.

Helldorfer, M. C. (Mary Claire). *Cabbage Rose* ill. by Julie Downing. Bradbury, 1993. ISBN 0-02-743513-X Subj: Activities – painting. Folk & fairy tales. Royalty.

Carnival ill. by Dan Yaccarino. Viking, 1996. ISBN 0-670-86687-3 Subj: Activities. Fairs, festivals.

Clap clap! ill. by Sandra Speidel. Viking, 1993. ISBN 0-670-85155-8 Subj: Creation. Religion.

Daniel's gift ill. by Julie Downing. Bradbury, 1987. ISBN 0-02-743511-3 Subj: Animals – sheep. Gifts. Holidays – Christmas. Religion – Nativity.

The darling boys ill. by Megan Halsey. Bradbury, 1992. ISBN 0-02-743516-4 Subj: Behavior – stealing. Careers – bakers. Character traits – cleverness. Family life – brothers & sisters.

Gather up, gather in ill. by Judy Pedersen. Viking, 1994. ISBN 0-670-84752-6 Subj: Seasons.

Harmonica night ill. by Alexi Natchev. Atheneum, 1997. ISBN 0-689-80532-2 Subj: Family life. Family life – grandmothers. Night. Sea & seashore.

Hog music ill. by S. D. Schindler. Viking, 2000. ISBN 0-670-87182-6 Subj: Activities – traveling. Family life – aunts, uncles. Gifts. U.S. history – frontier & pioneer life.

Jack, Skinny Bones, and the golden pancakes ill. by Elise Primavera. Viking, 1996. ISBN 0-670-86006-9 Subj: Behavior – trickery. Character traits – cleverness. Devil. Tall tales.

The mapmaker's daughter ill. by Jonathan Hunt. Bradbury, 1991. ISBN 0-02-743515-6 Subj: Character traits – bravery. Magic. Maps. Royalty – princes. Witches.

Night of the white stag ill. by Yvonne Gilbert. Random House, 1999. ISBN 0-385-32261-5 Subj: Animals – deer. Folk & fairy tales. Forest, woods. Holidays – Christmas. Night.

Sailing to the sea ill. by Loretta Krupinski. Viking, 1991. ISBN 0-670-83520-X Subj: Boats, ships. Family life – aunts, uncles. Sailors.

Silver Rain Brown ill. by Teresa Flavin. Houghton Mifflin, 1999. ISBN 0-395-73093-7 Subj: Birth. Cities, towns. Communities, neighborhoods. Ethnic groups in the U.S. – African Americans. Family life. Seasons – summer. Weather – rain.

Hellen, Nancy. *Animals of the jungle* ill. by author. Peter Bedrick, 1991. ISBN 0-87226-458-0 Subj: Animals. Jungle.

Bus stop ill. by author. Watts, 1988. ISBN 0-531-05765-8 Subj: Buses. Character traits – patience. Format, unusual. Transportation.

Circle farm ill. by author. Bantam, 1994. ISBN 0-553-09635-4 Subj: Animals. Farms. Format, unusual – toy & movable books.

Circle zoo ill. by author. Bantam, 1994. ISBN 0-553-09634-6 Subj: Format, unusual – toy & movable books. Zoos.

Creatures of the ocean ill. by author. Peter Bedrick, 1991. ISBN 0-87226-457-2 Subj: Sea & seashore.

A visit to the farm ill. by author. Peter Bedrick, 1990. ISBN 0-87226-432-7 Subj: Animals. Farms. Format, unusual – toy & movable books.

A visit to the zoo ill. by author. Peter Bedrick, 1990. ISBN 0-87226-431-9 Subj: Animals. Format, unusual – toy & movable books. Zoos.

Heller, George. *Hiroshi's wonderful kite* ill. by Kyuzo Tsugami. Silver Burdett, 1968. Subj: Crime. Foreign lands – Japan. Kites.

Heller, Julek. *Jack and the beanstalk* (Jack and the beanstalk)

Heller, Linda. *Alexis and the golden ring* ill. by author. Macmillan, 1980. ISBN 0-02-743540-7 Subj: Folk & fairy tales. Foreign lands – Russia. Magic.

The castle on Hester Street ill. by author. Jewish Publication Society, 1982. ISBN 0-8276-0206-5 Subj: Family life – grandparents.

Lily at the table ill. by author. Macmillan, 1979. ISBN 0-02-743530-X Subj: Family life. Food. Furniture – tables. Wordless.

Heller, Nicholas. *An adventure at sea* ill. by author. Greenwillow, 1988. ISBN 0-688-07847-8 Subj: Imagination. Sea & seashore. Sibling rivalry.

A book for Woody ill. by author. Greenwillow, 1995. ISBN 0-688-13378-9 Subj: Animals – pigs. Books, reading.

Elwood and the witch ill. by Jos. A. Smith. Greenwillow, 2000. ISBN 0-689-16946-5 Subj: Activities – flying. Animals – pigs. Moon. Witches.

The front hall carpet ill. by author. Greenwillow, 1990. ISBN 0-688-05273-8 Subj: Imagination.

The giant ill. by Jos. A. Smith. Greenwillow, 1997. ISBN 0-688-15225-2 Subj: Careers – artists. Family life – grandfathers. Giants.

Goblins in green ill. by Jos. A. Smith. Greenwillow, 1995. ISBN 0-688-12803-3 Subj: ABC books. Mythical creatures – goblins.

Happy birthday, Moe dog ill. by author. Greenwillow, 1988. ISBN 0-688-07671-8 Subj: Animals – dogs. Birthdays.

Mathilda the dream bear ill. by author. Greenwillow, 1989. ISBN 0-688-08239-4 Subj: Animals. Animals – bears. Dreams.

The monster in the cave ill. by author. Greenwillow, 1987. ISBN 0-688-07314-X Subj: Family life. Holidays – Christmas. Monsters. Parties.

Ogres! ogres! ogres! a feasting frenzy from A to Z ill. by Jos. A. Smith. Greenwillow, 1999. ISBN 0-688-16987-2 Subj: Food. Monsters. Mythical creatures – ogres.

Peas ill. by author. Greenwillow, 1993. ISBN 0-688-12407-0 Subj: Dreams. Food. Toys – trains.

Ten old pails ill. by Yossi Abolafia. Greenwillow, 1994. ISBN 0-688-12420-8 Subj: Behavior – collecting things. Concepts.

This little piggy ill. by Sonja Lamut. Greenwillow, 1997. ISBN 0-688-15175-2 Subj: Bedtime. Family life – grandmothers. Nursery rhymes.

The tooth tree ill. by author. Greenwillow, 1991. ISBN 0-688-09393-0 Subj: Fairies. Teeth. Trees.

A troll story ill. by author. Greenwillow, 1990. ISBN 0-688-08971-2 Subj: Imagination. Mythical creatures – trolls.

Up the wall ill. by author. Greenwillow, 1992. ISBN 0-688-10634-X Subj: Behavior – running away. Family life. Imagination.

Woody ill. by author. Greenwillow, 1994. ISBN 0-688-12805-X Subj: Animals – pigs. Behavior – wishing.

Heller, Ruth. *Animals born alive and well* ill. by author. Grosset, 1982. ISBN 0-448-01822-5 Subj: Animals.

A cache of jewels and other collective nouns ill. by author. Grosset, 1989. ISBN 0-448-19211-X Subj: Language. Rhyming text.

Chickens aren't the only ones ill. by author. Grosset, 1981. ISBN 0-448-01872-1 Subj: Eggs. Science.

Color, color, color, color ill. by author. Putnam & Grosset, 1995. ISBN 0-399-22815-2 Subj: Concepts – color. Rhyming text.

Fantastic! wow! and unreal! a book about interjections and conjunctions ill. by author. Grosset, 1998. ISBN 0-448-41862-2 Subj: Language. Rhyming text.

How to hide a butterfly: and other insects ill. by author. Grosset, 1985. ISBN 0-488-10478-4 Subj: Behavior – hiding. Insects. Insects – butterflies, caterpillars. Rhyming text.

How to hide a crocodile and other reptiles ill. by author. Grosset, 1986. ISBN 0-448-19028-1 Subj: Disguises. Reptiles. Reptiles – alligators, crocodiles. Rhyming text.

How to hide a gray treefrog and other amphibians ill. by author. Grosset, 1986. ISBN 0-448-19026-5 Subj: Animals. Disguises. Frogs & toads. Rhyming text.

How to hide a parakeet and other birds ill. by author. Grosset, 1995. ISBN 0-448-40964-X Subj: Birds. Birds – parakeets, parrots. Disguises. Rhyming text.

How to hide a polar bear: and other mammals ill. by author. Grosset, 1985. ISBN 0-488-10477-6 Subj: Animals. Animals – polar bears. Behavior – hiding. Rhyming text.

How to hide a whip-poor-will and other birds ill. by author. Grosset, 1986. ISBN 0-448-19027-3 Subj: Birds. Disguises. Rhyming text.

How to hide an octopus: and other sea creatures ill. by author. Grosset, 1985. ISBN 0-488-10476-8 Subj: Animals. Crustaceans. Octopuses. Rhyming text.

Kites sail high: a book about verbs ill. by author. Grosset, 1988. ISBN 0-448-10480-6 Subj: Language. Rhyming text.

Many luscious lollipops: a book about adjectives ill. by author. Sandcastle Books, 1992. ISBN 0-448-03151-5 Subj: Language. Rhyming text.

Merry-go-round ill. by author. Sandcastle Books, 1992. ISBN 0-448-40085-5 Subj: Language. Rhyming text.

Mine, all mine: a book about pronouns ill. by author. Grosset, 1997. ISBN 0-448-41606-9 Subj: Language. Rhyming text.

Plants that never ever bloom ill. by author. Grosset, 1984. ISBN 0-448-18964-X Subj: Plants.

The reason for a flower ill. by author. Grosset, 1983. ISBN 0-448-14495-6 Subj: Flowers. Rhyming text.

Heller, Wendy. *Clementine and the cage* ill. by Rex J. Irvine. Kalimát, 1980. ISBN 0-922770-12-X Subj: Behavior – running away. Birds – canaries.

Hellings, Colette. *Too little, too big* ill. by Dominique Maes. Chronicle, 1993. ISBN 0-8118-0530-1 Subj: Animals – mice. Concepts – size. Self-concept.

Hellman, Gary. *The karate way* ill. by author. Doubleday, 2001. ISBN 0-385-32742-0 Subj: Self-concept. Sports – karate.

Hello, baby photos sel. by Debby Slier. Macmillan, 1988. ISBN 0-02-688750-9 Subj: Babies. Format, unusual – board books.

Hellsing, Lennart. *The wonderful pumpkin* ill. by Svend Otto S. Atheneum, 1976, 1975. Translation of Der underbara pumpan. ISBN 0-689-50056-4 Subj: Animals – bears. Food. Holidays – Halloween.

Hellums, Julia Pemberton. *Hold the anchovies!* (Rotner, Shelley)

Helman, Andrea. *Northwest animal babies* (Wolfe, Art)

1, 2, 3 moose (Wolfe, Art)

Helmer, Diana Star. *The cat who came for tacos* ill. by Viví Escrivá. A. Whitman, 2003. ISBN 0-8075-5106-6 Subj: Animals – cats. Etiquette.

Helmer, Marilyn. *Critter riddles* ill. by Eric Parker. Kids Can, 2003. ISBN 1-55337-445-2 Subj: Humorous stories. Riddles & jokes.

Funtime riddles ill. by Jane Kurisu. Kids Can, 2004. ISBN 1-55337-579-3 Subj: Riddles & jokes.

Mr. McGratt and the ornery cat ill. by Martine Gourbault. Kids Can, 1999. ISBN 1-55074-564-6 Subj: Animals – cats. Behavior – misbehavior.

Recess riddles ill. by Jane Kurisu. Kids Can, 2004. ISBN 1-55337-577-7 Subj: Riddles & jokes. School.

Spooky riddles ill. by Eric Parker. Kids Can, 2003. ISBN 1-55337-447-9 Subj: Monsters. Riddles & jokes.

Three barnyard tales ill. by Laura Watson. Kids Can, 2002. ISBN 1-55074-796-7 Subj: Animals. Birds. Folk & fairy tales.

Three cat and mouse tales ill. by Josée Masse. Kids Can, 2004. ISBN 1-55074-943-9 Subj: Animals – cats. Animals – mice. Folk & fairy tales.

Three prince charming tales ill. by Kasia Charko. Kids Can, 2000. ISBN 1-55074-761-4 Subj: Folk & fairy tales. Royalty – princes.

Three royal tales ill. by Dianna Bonder. Kids Can, 2003. ISBN 1-55074-939-0 Subj: Folk & fairy tales. Royalty.

Three tales of enchantment ill. by Kasia Charko. Kids Can, 2001. ISBN 1-55074-843-2 Subj: Folk & fairy tales. Magic.

Three tales of three ill. by Chris Jackson. Kids Can, 2000. ISBN 1-55074-759-2 Subj: Animals. Folk & fairy tales.

Three tales of trickery ill. by Noushin Pajouhesh. Kids Can, 2002. ISBN 1-55074-937-4 Subj: Behavior – trickery. Folk & fairy tales.

Three teeny tiny tales ill. by Veselina Tomova. Kids Can, 2001. ISBN 1-55074-841-6 Subj: Concepts – size. Folk & fairy tales.

Three tuneful tales ill. by Kasia Charko. Kids Can, 2003. ISBN 1-55074-941-2 Subj: Folk & fairy tales. Music.

Yucky riddles ill. by Eric Parker. Kids Can, 2003. ISBN 1-55337-448-7 Subj: Riddles & jokes.

Yummy riddles ill. by Eric Parker. Kids Can, 2003. ISBN 1-55337-446-0 Subj: Food. Riddles & jokes.

Helmering, Doris Wild. *I have two families* ill. by Heidi Palmer. Abingdon, 1981. ISBN 0-687-18507-6 Subj: Family life – stepfamilies.

We're going to have a baby by Doris & John William Helmering; ill. by Robert H. Cassell. Abingdon, 1978. ISBN 0-687-44446-2 Subj: Babies. Family life – new sibling. Sibling rivalry.

Helmering, John William. *We're going to have a baby* (Helmering, Doris Wild)

Helquist, Brett. *Roger, the jolly pirate* ill. by author. HarperCollins, 2004. ISBN 0-06-623806-4 Subj: Humorous stories. Pirates.

Helweg, Hans. *Farm animals* ill. by author. Random House, 1978. ISBN 0-394-93733-3 Subj: Animals. Birds. Farms.

Hembrook, Deborah. *Mouse makes magic* (Heling, Kathryn)

Mouse's hide-and-seek words (Heling, Kathryn)

Hendershot, Judith. *In coal country* ill. by Thomas B. Allen. Knopf, 1987. ISBN 0-394-98190-1 Subj: Family life. Family life – fathers.

Up the tracks to Grandma's ill. by Thomas B. Allen. Knopf, 1993. ISBN 0-679-91964-3 Subj: Country. Family life – grandmothers.

Henderson, Alicia Terry. *Call me black, call me beautiful* ill. by Jennifer C. Kindert. Royal Regal, 2002. ISBN 0-9719490-1-8 Subj: Character traits – individuality. Ethnic groups in the U.S. – African Americans. Self-concept.

Henderson, Douglas. *Dinosaur tree* ill. by author. Bradbury, 1994. ISBN 0-02-743547-4 Subj: Dinosaurs. Plants. Prehistory. Time. Trees.

Henderson, Kathy. *And the good brown earth* ill. by author. Candlewick, 2004. ISBN 0-7636-2301-6 Subj: Family life – grandmothers. Gardens, gardening.

The baby dances ill. by Tony Kerins. Candlewick, 1999. ISBN 0-7636-0374-0 Subj: Babies. Behavior – growing up.

Baby knows best ill. by Brita Granström. Little, 2001. ISBN 0-316-60580-8 Subj: Babies. Rhyming text. Toys.

The baby's book of babies photos by Anthea Sieveking. Dial, 1989. ISBN 0-8037-0634-0 Subj: Babies.

Bounce, bounce, bounce ill. by Carol Thompson. Candlewick, 1994. ISBN 1-56402-311-7 Subj: Activities – playing. Rhyming text.

Bumpety bump ill. by Carol Thompson. Candlewick, 1994. ISBN 1-56402-312-5 Subj: Babies. Family life. Rhyming text.

Counting farm ill. by author. Candlewick, 1996. Cover title: Shaw's counting farm. ISBN 1-56402-758-9 Subj: Animals. Counting, numbers. Farms.

Disney's Bambi: the winter trail penciled by David Pacheco; painted by Valeria Turati. Mouse Works, 1996. ISBN 1-57082-427-4 Subj: Animals – deer. Seasons – winter. Weather – snow.

Disney's Pooh's grand adventure: the search for Christopher Robin adapt. by Kathy Henderson & Victoria Saxon; penciled by Sparky Moore. Mouse Works, 1997. ISBN 1-57082-671-4 Subj: Behavior – lost. Toys – bears.

Don't interrupt! ill. by Susan Hellard. Barron's, 1988. ISBN 0-8120-5785-6 Subj: Family life. Format, unusual – toy & movable books. Rhyming text.

I can be a basketball player ill. by author. Childrens Pr., 1991. ISBN 0-516-01963-5 Subj: Sports – basketball.

I can be a farmer ill. with photos. Childrens Pr., 1989. ISBN 0-516-01923-6 Subj: Careers – farmers. Farms.

I can be a rancher ill. by author. Childrens Pr., 1990. ISBN 0-516-01962-7 Subj: Animals. Careers – ranchers.

In the middle of the night ill. by Jennifer Eachus. Macmillan, 1992. ISBN 0-02-743545-8 Subj: Activities – working. Cities, towns. Night.

The little boat ill. by Patrick Benson. Candlewick, 1995. ISBN 1-56402-420-2 Subj: Boats, ships. Sea & seashore. Toys.

Newborn ill. by Caroline Binch. Dial, 1999. ISBN 0-8037-2434-9 Subj: Babies. Family life.

The storm ill. by author. Candlewick, 1999. ISBN 0-7636-0904-8 Subj: Sea & seashore. Weather – storms. Weather – wind.

A year in the city ill. by Paul Howard. Candlewick, 1996. ISBN 1-56402-872-0 Subj: Cities, towns. Days of the week, months of the year. Seasons.

Hendra, Sue. *Oliver's wood* ill. by author. Candlewick, 1996. ISBN 1-56402-932-8 Subj: Animals. Bedtime. Birds – owls. Sun.

Hendrick, Mary Jean. *If anything ever goes wrong at the zoo* ill. by Jane Dyer. Harcourt, 1993. ISBN 0-15-238007-8 Subj: Animals. Weather – floods. Zoos.

Hendrickson, Karen. *Baby and I can play* ill. by Marina Megale. Parenting Pr., 1986. ISBN 0-943990-13-0 Subj: Activities – playing. Babies. Family life – brothers & sisters.

Fun with toddlers ill. by Marina Megale. Parenting Pr., 1986. ISBN 0-943990-14-9 Subj: Activities – playing. Babies. Family life.

Hendry, Diana. *Back soon!* ill. by Carol Thompson. BridgeWater, 1993. ISBN 0-8167-3487-9 Subj: Animals – cats. Character traits – individuality. Family life.

Dog Donovan ill. by Margaret Chamberlain. Candlewick, 1995. ISBN 1-56402-537-3 Subj: Animals – dogs. Character traits – kindness to animals. Emotions – fear.

Not anywhere house ill. by Thor Wickstrom. Lothrop, 1991. ISBN 0-688-10194-1 Subj: Family life. Moving.

The very noisy night ill. by Jane Chapman. Children's Book Pr., 1999. ISBN 0-525-46261-9 Subj: Animals – mice. Bedtime. Emotions – fear. Night. Noise, sounds.

Henkes, Kevin. *All alone* ill. by author. Greenwillow, 1981. ISBN 0-688-00605-1 Subj: Behavior – solitude.

Bailey goes camping ill. by author. Greenwillow, 1985. ISBN 0-688-05702-0 Subj: Animals – rabbits. Camps, camping. Family life.

The biggest boy ill. by Nancy Tafuri. Greenwillow, 1995. ISBN 0-688-12830-0 Subj: Concepts – shape. Concepts – size.

Chester's way ill. by author. Greenwillow, 1988. ISBN 0-688-07608-4 Subj: Animals – mice. Behavior – bullying.

Chrysanthemum ill. by author. Greenwillow, 1991. ISBN 0-688-09700-6 Subj: Animals. Names. School.

Circle dogs ill. by Dan Yaccarino. Greenwillow, 1998. ISBN 0-688-15447-6 Subj: Animals – dogs. Concepts – shape.

Clean enough ill. by author. Greenwillow, 1982. ISBN 0-688-00829-1 Subj: Activities – bathing.

Good-bye, Curtis ill. by Marisabina Russo. Greenwillow, 1995. ISBN 0-688-12828-9 Subj: Careers – postal workers. Communities, neighborhoods.

Grandpa and Bo ill. by author. Greenwillow, 1986. ISBN 0-688-04957-5 Subj: Family life – grandfathers. Seasons – summer.

Jessica ill. by author. Greenwillow, 1989. ISBN 0-688-07830-3 Subj: Friendship. Imagination – imaginary friends. School – first day.

Julius, the baby of the world ill. by author. Greenwillow, 1990. ISBN 0-688-08944-5 Subj: Family life. Sibling rivalry.

Kitten's first full moon ill. by author. Greenwillow, 2004. ISBN 0-06-058829-2 Subj: Animals – babies. Animals – cats. Behavior – misunderstanding. Caldecott award books. Moon.

Lilly's chocolate heart ill. by author. HarperFestival, 2004. ISBN 0-06-056066-5 Subj: Format, unusual – board books. Holidays – Valentine's Day.

Lilly's purple plastic purse ill. by author. Greenwillow, 1996. ISBN 0-688-12898-X Subj: Animals – mice. Careers – teachers. Clothing – handbags, purses. Emotions – anger. School.

Oh! ill. by Laura Dronzek. Greenwillow, 1999. ISBN 0-688-17054-4 Subj: Activities – playing. Animals. Rhyming text. Seasons – winter. Weather – snow.

Once around the block ill. by Victoria Chess. Greenwillow, 1987. ISBN 0-688-04955-9 Subj: Behavior – boredom. Communities, neighborhoods.

Owen ill. by author. Greenwillow, 1993. ISBN 0-688-11450-4 Subj: Animals – mice. Behavior – growing up. Caldecott award honor books.

Sheila Rae, the brave ill. by author. Greenwillow, 1987. ISBN 0-688-07156-2 Subj: Animals – mice. Behavior – lost. Character traits – bravery. Family life – sisters.

Sheila Rae's peppermint stick ill. by author. HarperFestival, 2001. ISBN 0-06-029451-5 Subj: Animals – mice. Behavior – sharing. Family life – sisters. Food. Format, unusual – board books.

Shhhh ill. by author. Greenwillow, 1989. ISBN 0-688-07986-5 Subj: Family life. Morning. Sleep.

A weekend with Wendell ill. by author. Greenwillow, 1986. ISBN 0-688-06326-8 Subj: Activities – playing. Animals – mice. Behavior – misbehavior. Character traits – selfishness.

Wimberly worried ill. by author. Greenwillow, 2000. ISBN 0-688-17028-5 Subj: Animals – mice. Behavior – worrying. School – first day. School – nursery.

Henkle, Henrietta. *see* Buckmaster, Henrietta

Henley, Claire. *At the zoo* ill. by author. Walt Disney, 1992. ISBN 1-56282-152-0 Subj: Activities. Animals. Zoos.

Dinnertime ill. by author. Grosset, 1994. ISBN 0-448-40826-0 Subj: Animals. Food. Format, unusual – board books.

Farm day ill. by author. Dial, 1991. ISBN 0-8037-0954-4 Subj: Animals. Careers – farmers. Farms.

I'm a baby, too! ill. by author. Grosset, 1994. ISBN 0-448-40825-2 Subj: Animals – babies. Babies. Format, unusual – board books.

In the ocean ill. by author. Walt Disney, 1992. ISBN 1-56282-154-7 Subj: Animals. Fish. Sea & seashore.

Joe's pool ill. by author. Hyperion, 1994. ISBN 1-56282-432-5 Subj: Counting, numbers. Sports – swimming.

Jungle day ill. by author. Dial, 1991. ISBN 0-8037-0959-5 Subj: Animals. Jungle.

Playtime ill. by author. Grosset, 1994. ISBN 0-448-40827-9 Subj: Activities – playing. Animals. Format, unusual – board books.

Quack, quack ill. by author. Grosset, 1994. ISBN 0-448-40828-7 Subj: Animals. Birds. Format, unusual – board books. Noise, sounds.

Stormy day ill. by author. Hyperion, 1993. ISBN 1-56282-343-4 Subj: Weather – lightning, thunder. Weather – storms.

Sunny day ill. by author. Hyperion, 1993. ISBN 1-56282-341-8 Subj: Sea & seashore. Seasons – summer. Sun.

Henley, Karyn. *Hatch!* ill. by Susan Kennedy. Carolrhoda, 1980. ISBN 0-87614-122-X Subj: Animals.

Hennessy, B. G. (Barbara G.). *A, B, C, D, tummy, toes, hands, knee* ill. by Wendy Watson. Viking, 1989. ISBN 0-670-81703-1 Subj: Concepts. Family life. Rhyming text.

Busy Dinah Dinosaur ill. by Ana Martin Larrañaga. Candlewick, 2000. ISBN 0-7636-1140-9 Subj: Activities. Dinosaurs. Prehistory.

Corduroy at the zoo ill. by Lisa McCue. Viking, 2000. Based on the character by Don Freeman. ISBN 0-670-89288-2 Subj: Animals. Format, unusual – toy & movable books. Toys – bears. Zoos.

Corduroy's birthday ill. by Lisa McCue. Viking, 1997. Based on the character by Don Freeman. ISBN 0-670-87065-X Subj: Birthdays. Format, unusual – toy & movable books. Parties. Toys – bears.

Corduroy's Christmas ill. by Lisa McCue. Viking, 1992. Based on the character by Don Freeman. ISBN 0-670-84477-2 Subj: For-

mat, unusual – toy & movable books. Holidays – Christmas. Toys – bears.

Corduroy's Easter ill. by Lisa McCue. Viking, 1998. Based on the character by Don Freeman. ISBN 0-670-88101-5 Subj: Format, unusual – toy & movable books. Holidays – Easter. Toys – bears.

Corduroy's Halloween ill. by Lisa McCue. Viking, 1995. Based on the character by Don Freeman. ISBN 0-670-86193-6 Subj: Clothing – costumes. Format, unusual – toy & movable books. Holidays – Halloween. Toys – bears.

The dinosaur who lived in my backyard ill. by Susan Davis. Viking, 1988. ISBN 0-670-81685-X Subj: Dinosaurs. Imagination. Prehistory.

Eeney, Meeney, Miney, Mo ill. by Letizia Galli. Viking, 1995. ISBN 0-670-82864-5 Subj: Animals. Jungle. Rhyming text.

The first night ill. by Steve Johnson with Lou Fancher. Viking, 1993. ISBN 0-670-83026-7 Subj: Holidays – Christmas. Religion.

Jake baked the cake ill. by Mary Morgan. Viking, 1990. ISBN 0-670-82237-X Subj: Food. Rhyming text. Weddings.

Meet Dinah Dinosaur ill. by Ana Martin Larrañaga. Candlewick, 2000. ISBN 0-7636-1133-6 Subj: Dinosaurs. Prehistory.

Meet Winslow whale ill. by Joyce Howell. Viking, 1994. ISBN 0-670-85632-0 Subj: Animals – whales. Character traits – being different. Friendship.

The missing tarts ill. by Tracey Campbell Pearson. Viking, 1989. ISBN 0-670-82039-3 Subj: Behavior – stealing. Nursery rhymes. Rhyming text. Royalty – queens.

Olympics! ill. by Michael Chesworth. Viking, 1996. ISBN 0-670-86522-2 Subj: Sports – Olympics.

One little, two little, three little pilgrims ill. by Lynne Cravath. Viking, 1999. ISBN 0-670-87779-4 Subj: Counting, numbers. Indians of North America – Wampanoag. Pilgrims.

Road builders ill. by Simms Taback. Viking, 1994. ISBN 0-670-83390-8 Subj: Careers – construction workers. Machines. Roads.

School days ill. by Tracey Campbell Pearson. Viking, 1990. ISBN 0-670-83025-9 Subj: Rhyming text. School.

Sleep tight ill. by Anthony Carnabuci. Viking, 1992. ISBN 0-670-83567-6 Subj: Bedtime. Rhyming text. Sleep.

When you were just a little girl ill. by Jeanne Arnold. Viking, 1991. ISBN 0-670-83998-6 Subj: Family life – grandmothers. Rhyming text.

Henri, Adrian. *The postman's palace* ill. by Simon Henwood. Atheneum, 1990. ISBN 0-689-31667-4 Subj: Buildings. Careers – postal workers. Dreams. Post office.

Henrietta. *A mouse in the house* ill. with photos. DK, 1991. ISBN 1-879431-26-2 Subj: Animals – mice. Birthdays. Games. Rhyming text.

Henriod, Lorraine. *Grandma's wheelchair* ill. by Christa Chevalier. A. Whitman, 1982. ISBN 0-8075-3035-2 Subj: Family life – grandmothers. Handicaps. Sibling rivalry.

Henrioud, Charles. *Mr. Noah and the animals: Monsieur Noé et les animaux* ill. by author. Walck, 1960. Subj: Boats, ships. Religion – Noah. Weather – floods. Weather – rain. Weather – rainbows.

Henry, Lenny. *Charlie and the big chill* ill. by Chris Burke. Trafalgar Square, 1997. ISBN 0-575-05938-9 Subj: Imagination.

Charlie, queen of the desert ill. by Chris Burke. Trafalgar Square, 1997. ISBN 0-575-05939-7 Subj: Foreign lands – Australia. Imagination.

Henry, O. *The gift of the Magi* ill. by Lisbeth Zwerger. Picture Book Studio, 1982. ISBN 0-907234-17-8 Subj: Character traits – generosity. Gifts. Holidays – Christmas.

Henry, Steve. *Nobody asked me!* ill. by author. HarperCollins, 2001. ISBN 0-688-17866-9 Subj: Animals – cats. Family life – brothers. Family life – new sibling.

Henson, Jim. *ABC: featuring Jim Henson's Sesame Street Muppets* (Calmenson, Stephanie)

Baby Piggy and giant bubble (Anastasio, Dina)

Big Bird at the beach (Hautzig, Deborah)

Elmo says, achoo! (Wilson, Sarah)

Ernie and Bert's new kitten (Hautzig, Deborah)

Jim Henson's Muppets in Rowlf's big test: a book about listening to your conscience (Gikow, Louise)

Jim Henson's Muppets in What's fair is fair: a book about sharing (Gikow, Louise)

A visit to the Sesame Street library: featuring Jim Henson's Sesame Street Muppets (Hautzig, Deborah)

Henstra, Friso. *Wait and see* ill. by author. Addison-Wesley, 1978. ISBN 0-201-03077-2 Subj: Machines.

Henterly, Jamichael. *Good night, garden gnome* ill. by autor. Dial, 2001. ISBN 0-8037-2531-0 Subj: Gardens, gardening. Mythical creatures – gnomes.

Henwood, Simon. *The clock shop* ill. by author. Farrar, 1989. ISBN 0-674-31380-6 Subj: Careers – clockmakers. Clocks, watches. Time.

The hidden jungle ill. by author. Farrar, 1992. ISBN 0-374-33070-0 Subj: Cities, towns. Ecology. Trees.

A piece of luck ill. by author. Farrar, 1990. ISBN 0-374-35925-3 Subj: Behavior – greed. Behavior – hiding things. Character traits – luck.

The troubled village ill. by author. Farrar, 1991. ISBN 0-374-37780-4 Subj: Communities, neighborhoods. Problem solving.

The view (Yoaker, Harry)

Heo, Yumi. *Father's rubber shoes* ill. by author. Orchard, 1995. ISBN 0-531-08723-9 Subj: Careers – storekeepers. Clothing – shoes. Ethnic groups in the U.S. – Korean Americans. Family life – fathers.

The green frogs ill. by author. Houghton Mifflin, 1996. ISBN 0-395-68378-5 Subj: Behavior – misbehavior. Folk & fairy tales. Foreign lands – Korea. Frogs & toads.

One afternoon ill. by author. Orchard, 1994. ISBN 0-531-08695-X Subj: Cities, towns. Communities, neighborhoods. Family life – mothers. Noise, sounds.

One Sunday morning ill. by author. Orchard, 1999. ISBN 0-531-33156-3 Subj: Cities, towns. Family life – fathers. Noise, sounds. Parks.

Hepworth, Catherine. *ANTics! an alphabetical anthology* ill. by author. Putnam, 1992. ISBN 0-399-21862-9 Subj: ABC books. Insects – ants.

Bug off! a swarm of insect words ill. by author. Putnam, 1998. ISBN 0-399-22640-0 Subj: Insects. Language.

Heras, Theo. *What will we do with the baby-o?* (What will we do with the baby-o?)

Herford, Oliver. *The most timid in the land* ill. by Sylvia Long. Chronicle, 1992. ISBN 0-87701-862-6 Subj: Animals – rabbits. Middle Ages. Poetry.

Hergé. *Explorers on the moon* ill. by author. Joy Street, 1992. ISBN 0-316-35860-6 Subj: Format, unusual – toy & movable books. Moon. Space & space ships.

Herkert, Barbara. *Birds in your backyard* ill. by author. Dawn, 2001. ISBN 1-58469-026-7 Subj: Activities. Birds.

Herman, Bill. *Jenny's magic wand* by Bill & Helen Herman; photos by Don Perdue. Watts, 1988. ISBN 0-531-10292-0 Subj: Handicaps – blindness. Senses – sight.

Herman, Charlotte. *The memory cupboard* ill. by Ben F. Stahl. A. Whitman, 2003. ISBN 0-8075-5055-8 Subj: Family life. Family life – grandmothers. Holidays – Thanksgiving.

My mother didn't kiss me good-night ill. by Bruce Degen. Dutton, 1980. ISBN 0-525-35495-6 Subj: Behavior – worrying.

Herman, Emily. *Hubknuckles* ill. by Deborah Kogan Ray. Crown, 1985. ISBN 0-517-55646-4 Subj: Ghosts. Holidays – Halloween.

Herman, Gail. *Double-header* ill. by Jerry Smath. Grosset, 1993. ISBN 0-448-40156-8 Subj: Monsters. Sports – baseball.

Fievel's big showdown ill. by Beverly Lazor-Bahr; based on characters created by David Kirschner. Grosset, 1992. ISBN 0-448-40379-X Subj: Animals – cats. Animals – mice. Books, reading. Character traits – bravery.

Flower girl ill. by Paige Billin-Frye. Grosset, 1996. ISBN 0-448-41107-5 Subj: Behavior – dissatisfaction. Family life – sisters. Weddings.

The haunted house ill. by Carol Nicklaus. Random House, 1989. ISBN 0-394-82717-1 Subj: Animals – cats. Ghosts. Homes, houses.

Ice cream soup adapt. by Gail Herman; based on a story by Jack Kent; ill. by R. W. Alley. Random House, 1990. ISBN 0-679-80790-X Subj: Behavior – promptness, tardiness.

Keep your distance ill. by Jerry Smath. Kane Pr., 2001. ISBN 1-57565-107-6 Subj: Concepts – measurement. Family life – sisters.

The lion and the mouse (Æsop)

The littlest duckling ill. by Ann Schweninger. Viking, 1996. ISBN 0-670-85113-2 Subj: Birds – ducks. Family life. Sports – swimming.

Lucky goes to school ill. by Norman Gorbaty. Grosset, 2001. ISBN 0-448-42594-7 Subj: Animals – babies. Animals – dogs. School.

Make way for trucks: big machines on wheels ill. by Christopher Santoro. McKay, 1990. ISBN 0-679-90110-8 Subj: Trucks.

My dog talks ill. by Ron Fritz. Scholastic, 1995. ISBN 0-590-22196-5 Subj: Animals – dogs. Pets.

Otto the cat ill. by Norman Gorbaty. Grosset, 1995. ISBN 0-448-40968-2 Subj: Animals – cats. Animals – dogs. Rebuses.

Pizza cats ill. by Louie del Carmen & James Peters. Simon Spotlight/Nickelodeon, 1999. ISBN 0-689-82391-6 Subj: Animals – cats. Restaurants.

The puppy who went to school ill. by Betina Ogden. Platt, 1992. ISBN 0-448-40481-8 Subj: Animals – dogs. Pets. School.

Teddy bear for sale ill. by Doug Cushman. Scholastic, 1995. ISBN 0-590-25943-1 Subj: Behavior – running away. Toys – bears.

There is a town ill. by Katy Bratun. Random House, 1995. ISBN 0-679-96439-8 Subj: Birthdays. Parties. Toys.

What a hungry puppy! ill. by Norman Gorbaty. Grosset, 1993. ISBN 0-448-40537-7 Subj: Animals – dogs. Behavior – lost & found possessions.

Herman, Helen. *Jenny's magic wand* (Herman, Bill)

Herman, R. A. (Ronnie Ann). *Pal the pony* ill. by Betina Ogden. Grosset, 1996. ISBN 0-448-41257-8 Subj: Animals – horses, ponies. Character traits – ambition. Concepts – size.

Hermes, Patricia. *When snow lay soft on the mountain* ill. by Leslie Baker. Little, 1996. ISBN 0-316-36005-8 Subj: Behavior – wishing.

Family life – aunts, uncles. Family life – fathers. Illness. Quilts. Toys – dolls.

Hern, Lafcadio. *The voice of the great bell* (Hodges, Margaret)

Hernandez, Keith. *First-base hero* ill. by John Manders. Golden Bks., 2002. ISBN 0-307-10626-8 Subj: Format, unusual – toy & movable books. Sports – baseball.

Herold, Ann Bixby. *The helping day* ill. by Victoria de Larrea. Coward, 1980. ISBN 0-698-20492-1 Subj: Character traits – helpfulness.

Herrera, Juan Felipe. *Grandma and Me at the flea = Los meros meros remateros* ill. by Anita de Lucio-Brock. Children's Book Pr., 2002. ISBN 0-89239-171-5 Subj: Communities, neighborhoods. Ethnic groups in the U.S. – Mexican Americans. Family life – grandmothers. Foreign languages.

Herrick, Amy. *Kimbo's marble* ill. by Edward S. Gazsi. HarperCollins, 1993. ISBN 0-06-020374-9 Subj: Family life – brothers & sisters. Folk & fairy tales. Mythical creatures – trolls.

Herring, Ann (King). *Peter and the wolf* (Prokofiev, Sergei Sergeievitch)

Suho and the white horse: a legend of Mongolia (Otsuka, Yuzo)

Herriot, James. *Blossom comes home* ill. by Ruth Brown. St. Martin's, 1988. ISBN 0-312-02169-0 Subj: Animals – bulls, cows. Behavior – needing someone. Farms. Old age.

Bonny's big day ill. by Ruth Brown. St. Martin's, 1987. ISBN 0-312-01000-1 Subj: Animals – horses, ponies. Fairs, festivals. Farms.

Christmas Day kitten ill. by Ruth Brown. St. Martin's, 1986. ISBN 0-312-13407-X Subj: Animals – cats. Character traits – kindness to animals. Holidays – Christmas. Wordless.

Moses the kitten ill. by Peter Barrett. St. Martin's, 1984. ISBN 0-312-54905-9 Subj: Animals – cats. Careers – veterinarians.

Only one woof ill. by Peter Barrett. St. Martin's, 1985. ISBN 0-312-58583-7 Subj: Animals. Animals – dogs. Careers – veterinarians.

Herrmann, Dagmar. *My father always embarrasses me* (Shalev, Meir)

Nobody has time for me (Skutina, Vladimir)

Herrmann, Frank. *The giant Alexander* ill. by George Him. McGraw-Hill, 1965. Subj: Foreign lands – England. Giants.

The giant Alexander and the circus ill. by George Him. McGraw-Hill, 1966. Subj: Circus. Foreign lands – England. Giants.

Hershenhorn, Esther. *Fancy that* ill. by Megan Lloyd. Holiday, 2003. ISBN 0-8234-1605-4 Subj: Careers – artists. Family life – brothers & sisters. Orphans.

There goes Lowell's party! ill. by Jacqueline Rogers. Holiday, 1998. ISBN 0-8234-1313-6 Subj: Birthdays. Family life. Weather – rain. Weather – storms.

Hershey, Kathleen. *Cotton mill town* ill. by Jeanette Winter. Dutton, 1993. ISBN 0-525-44966-3 Subj: Family life – grandmothers. Nature.

Hersom, Donald. *The copycat* (Hersom, Kathleen)

Hersom, Kathleen. *The copycat* by Kathleen & Donald Hersom; ill. by Catherine Stock. Atheneum, 1989. ISBN 0-689-31448-5 Subj: Animals. Behavior – imitation. Noise, sounds. Rhyming text.

Herter, Jonina. *Eighty-eight kisses* ill. with photos. Boss Books, 1978. ISBN 0-932430-02-3 Subj: Babies. Family life – great-grandparents.

Hertz, Grete Janus. *Olie's bedtime walk* tr. from the Danish by Tatin Rose; ill. by Nynke Mare Talsma. Star Bright, 2002. ISBN 1-887734-90-2 Subj: Activities – walking. Activities – working. Night. Sleep.

Hertz, Ole. *Tobias catches trout* trans. from Danish by Tobi Tobias; ill. by author. Carolrhoda, 1984. ISBN 0-87614-263-3 Subj: Foreign lands – Greenland. Sports – fishing.

Tobias goes ice fishing trans. from Danish by Tobi Tobias; ill. by author. Carolrhoda, 1984. ISBN 0-87614-260-9 Subj: Foreign lands – Greenland. Seasons – winter. Sports – fishing.

Tobias goes seal hunting trans. from Danish by Tobi Tobias; ill. by author. Carolrhoda, 1984. ISBN 0-87614-262-5 Subj: Foreign lands – Greenland. Sports – hunting.

Tobias has a birthday trans. from Danish by Tobi Tobias; ill. by author. Carolrhoda, 1984. ISBN 0-87614-261-7 Subj: Birthdays. Foreign lands – Greenland.

Herzig, Alison Cragin. *Bronco busters* ill. by Kimberly Bulcken Root. Putnam, 1998. ISBN 0-399-22917-5 Subj: Animals – horses, ponies. Cowboys, cowgirls.

Hess, Edith. *Peter and Susie find a family* trans. from German by Miriam Moore; ill. by Jacqueline Blass. Abingdon, 1985. ISBN 0-687-30848-8 Subj: Adoption. Family life.

Hess, Paul. *Farmyard animals* ill. by author. De Agostini, 1996. ISBN 1-899883-34-7 Subj: Animals. Farms. Poetry.

Polar animals ill. by author. De Agostini, 1996. ISBN 1-899883-36-3 Subj: Animals. Foreign lands – Arctic. Poetry.

Rainforest animals ill. by author. De Agostini, 1996. ISBN 1-899883-37-1 Subj: Animals. Foreign lands. Forest, woods. Poetry.

Safari animals ill. by author. De Agostini, 1996. ISBN 1-899883-35-5 Subj: Animals. Foreign lands – Africa. Poetry.

Hesse, Karen. *Come on, rain* ill. by Jon J. Muth. Scholastic, 1999. ISBN 0-590-33125-6 Subj: Activities – dancing. Ethnic groups in the U.S. – African Americans. Family life – daughters. Family life – mothers. Seasons – summer. Weather – rain.

Lavender ill. by Andrew Glass. Holt, 1993. ISBN 0-8050-2528-6 Subj: Babies. Family life – aunts, uncles. Family life – cousins. Friendship. Quilts.

Lester's dog ill. by Nancy Carpenter. Crown, 1993. ISBN 0-517-58358-5 Subj: Animals – cats. Animals – dogs. Emotions – fear. Handicaps – deafness.

Poppy's chair ill. by Kay Life. Macmillan, 1993. ISBN 0-02-743705-1 Subj: Death. Emotions – grief. Family life – grandparents.

Hessell, Jenny. *Staying at Sam's* ill. by Jenny Williams. HarperCollins, 1990. ISBN 0-397-32433-2 Subj: Family life.

Hest, Amy. *The babies are coming!* ill. by Chloë Cheese. Crown, 1997. ISBN 0-517-70944-9 Subj: Activities – storytelling. Babies. Libraries.

Baby Duck and the bad eyeglasses ill. by Jill Barton. Candlewick, 1996. ISBN 1-56402-680-9 Subj: Birds – ducks. Family life – grandfathers. Glasses.

Baby Duck and the cozy blanket ill. by Jill Barton. Candlewick, 2002. ISBN 0-7636-1582-X Subj: Birds – ducks. Format, unusual – board books.

Best-ever good-bye party ill. by DyAnne DiSalvo-Ryan. Morrow, 1989. ISBN 0-688-07326-3 Subj: Friendship. Moving.

The crack-of-dawn walkers ill. by Amy Schwartz. Macmillan, 1984. ISBN 0-02-743710-8 Subj: Family life – grandfathers.

Fancy Aunt Jess ill. by Amy Schwartz. Morrow, 1990. ISBN 0-688-08097-9 Subj: Family life – aunts, uncles. Jewish culture. Weddings.

The Friday nights of Nana ill. by Claire A. Nivola. Candlewick, 2001. ISBN 0-7636-0658-8 Subj: Family life – grandmothers. Jewish culture. Religion.

Gabby growing up ill. by Amy Schwartz. S&S, 1998. ISBN 0-689-80573-X Subj: Birthdays. Family life – grandparents. Family life – parents. Hair. Holidays.

The go-between ill. by DyAnne DiSalvo-Ryan. Four Winds, 1992. ISBN 0-02-743632-2 Subj: Emotions – love. Family life – grandmothers. Friendship. Weddings.

Guess who, Baby Duck ill. by Jill Barton. Candlewick, 2004. ISBN 0-7636-1981-7 Subj: Activities – photographing. Birds – ducks. Family life – grandfathers. Illness – cold (disease).

How to get famous in Brooklyn ill. by Linda Dalal Sawaya. S&S, 1993. ISBN 0-02-743655-1 Subj: Activities. Communities, neighborhoods.

In the rain with Baby Duck ill. by Jill Barton. Candlewick, 1995. ISBN 1-56402-532-2 Subj: Babies. Behavior – secrets. Birds – ducks. Family life – grandfathers. Weather – rain.

Jamaica Louise James ill. by Sheila White Samton. Candlewick, 1996. ISBN 1-56402-348-6 Subj: Activities – painting. Birthdays. Ethnic groups in the U.S. – African Americans. Family life – grandmothers.

Kiss good night ill. by Anita Jeram. Candlewick, 2001. ISBN 0-7636-0780-0 Subj: Animals – bears. Bedtime. Family life – mothers. Kissing.

Mabel dancing ill. by Christine Davenier. Candlewick, 2000. ISBN 0-7636-0746-0 Subj: Activities – dancing. Bedtime. Family life – parents. Parties.

Make the team, Baby Duck ill. by Jill Barton. Candlewick, 2002. ISBN 0-7636-1541-2 Subj: Birds – ducks. Character traits – confidence. Family life – grandfathers. Sports – swimming.

The midnight eaters ill. by Karen Gundersheimer. Four Winds, 1989. ISBN 0-02-743630-6 Subj: Family life – grandmothers. Night. Old age.

The mommy exchange ill. by DyAnne DiSalvo-Ryan. Four Winds, 1988. ISBN 0-02-743650-0 Subj: Behavior – dissatisfaction. Family life – mothers.

Nana's birthday party ill. by Amy Schwartz. Morrow, 1993. ISBN 0-688-07498-7 Subj: Birthdays. Careers – artists. Cities, towns. Family life – cousins. Family life – grandmothers.

Nannies for hire ill. by Irene Trivas. Morrow, 1994. ISBN 0-688-12528-X Subj: Activities – babysitting. Babies. Friendship.

Off to school, Baby Duck ill. by Jill Barton. Candlewick, 1999. ISBN 0-7636-0244-2 Subj: Babies. Birds – ducks. Emotions – fear. Family life – grandfathers. School – first day.

The purple coat ill. by Amy Schwartz. Four Winds, 1986. ISBN 0-02-743640-3 Subj: Careers – tailors. Clothing – coats. Concepts – color. Family life. Family life – grandfathers.

The ring and the window seat ill. by Deborah Haeffele. Scholastic, 1990. ISBN 0-590-41350-3 Subj: Careers – carpenters. Family life. War.

Rosie's fishing trip ill. by Paul Howard. Candlewick, 1994. ISBN 1-56402-296-X Subj: Family life – grandfathers. Sports – fishing.

Ruby's storm ill. by Nancy Cote. Four Winds, 1994. ISBN 0-02-743160-6 Subj: Cities, towns. Family life – grandfathers. Seasons – spring. Weather – storms.

A sort-of sailor ill. by Lizzy Rockwell. Four Winds, 1990. ISBN 0-02-743641-1 Subj: Boats, ships. Emotions – fear. Sailors.

Weekend girl ill. by Harvey Stevenson. Morrow, 1993. ISBN 0-688-09690-5 Subj: Activities – photographing. Activities – picnicking. Cities, towns. Family life – grandparents.

You can do it, Sam ill. by Anita Jeram. Candlewick, 2003. ISBN 0-7636-1934-5 Subj: Animals – bears. Character traits – confidence. Family life – mothers. Food.

You're the boss, Baby Duck ill. by Jill Barton. Candlewick, 1997. ISBN 1-56402-667-1 Subj: Babies. Birds – ducks. Emotions – envy, jealousy. Family life – brothers & sisters. Family life – grandfathers. Self-concept.

Hetfield, Jamie. *The Yoruba of West Africa* ill. with photos. Rosen, 1996. ISBN 0-8239-2332-0 Subj: Foreign lands – Africa.

Heuck, Sigrid. *Pony and Bear are friends* ill. by author. Knopf, 1990. ISBN 0-394-92311-1 Subj: Animals – bears. Animals – horses, ponies. Friendship. Rebuses.

Who stole the apples? ill. by author. Knopf, 1986. ISBN 0-394-98371-8 Subj: Activities – traveling. Animals. Behavior – sharing. Rebuses.

Hewetson, Sarah. *My first pop-up book of prehistoric animals* (Bishop, Roma)

Hewett, Anita. *The tale of the turnip* ill. by Margery Gill. McGraw-Hill, 1961. Subj: Character traits – cooperation. Cumulative tales. Farms. Folk & fairy tales. Participation. Plants. Problem solving.

Hewett, Joan. *A flamingo chick grows up* photos by Richard Hewett. Carolrhoda, 2001. ISBN 1-57505-164-8 Subj: Animals – babies. Behavior – growing up. Birds – flamingos.

Fly away free photos by Richard Hewett. Walker, 1981. ISBN 0-8027-6403-7 Subj: Birds – pelicans. Careers – veterinarians. Illness.

A giraffe calf grows up photos by Richard Hewett. Carolrhoda, 2004. ISBN 1-57505-197-4 Subj: Animals – babies. Animals – giraffes. Behavior – growing up.

A harbor seal pup grows up photos by Richard Hewett. Carolrhoda, 2002. ISBN 1-57505-166-4 Subj: Animals – babies. Animals – seals. Behavior – growing up.

A kangaroo joey grows up photos by Richard Hewett. Carolrhoda, 2002. ISBN 1-57505-165-6 Subj: Animals – babies. Animals – kangaroos. Behavior – growing up.

A koala joey grows up photos by Richard Hewett. Carolrhoda, 2004. ISBN 1-57505-198-2 Subj: Animals – babies. Animals – koalas. Behavior – growing up.

A monkey baby grows up photos by Richard Hewett. Carolrhoda, 2004. ISBN 1-57505-199-0 Subj: Animals – babies. Animals – monkeys. Behavior – growing up.

The mouse and the elephant photos by Richard Hewett. Little, 1977. ISBN 0-316-35966-1 Subj: Animals – elephants. Animals – mice.

A penguin chick grows up photos by Richard Hewett. Carolrhoda, 2004. ISBN 1-57505-200-8 Subj: Animals – babies. Behavior – growing up. Birds – penguins.

Rosalie ill. by Donald Carrick. Lothrop, 1987. ISBN 0-688-06229-6 Subj: Animals – dogs. Character traits – kindness to animals. Old age.

A tiger cub grows up photos by Richard Hewett. Carolrhoda, 2002. ISBN 1-57505-163-X Subj: Animals – babies. Animals – tigers. Behavior – growing up.

Tiger, tiger, growing up photos by Richard Hewett. Clarion, 1993. ISBN 0-395-61583-6 Subj: Animals – tigers. Zoos.

Hewitt, Kathryn. *King Midas and the golden touch* by Nathaniel Hawthorne; adapt. & ill. by Kathryn Hewitt. Harcourt, 1987. ISBN 0-15-242800-3 Subj: Behavior – greed. Folk & fairy tales. Royalty – kings.

The three sillies (Jacobs, Joseph)

Two by two: the untold story ill. by author. Harcourt, 1984. ISBN 0-15-291801-9 Subj: Boats, ships. Religion – Noah. Weather – floods. Weather – rain. Weather – rainbows.

Hewitt, Sally. *All year round* ill. by Tony Kenyon & Mike Atkinson. Copper Beech, 2000. ISBN 0-7613-1208-0 Subj: Animals. Ecology. Nature. Seasons.

Animal homes story by Inga Phipps; ill. by Fiametta Dogi. Two-Can, 2000. ISBN 1-58728-600-9 Subj: Animals. Homes, houses.

Face to face safari ill. by Chris Gilvan-Cartwright. Abrams, 2003. ISBN 0-8109-4261-5 Subj: Animals. Format, unusual – toy & movable books. Jungle.

Woods and meadows ill. by Tony Kenyon & Mike Atkinson. Copper Beech, 2000. ISBN 0-7613-1207-2 Subj: Animals. Ecology. Forest, woods. Nature. Seasons.

Heyduck-Huth, Hilde. *The starfish: a treasure chest story* ill. by author. Macmillan, 1987. ISBN 0-689-50434-9 Subj: Animals – starfish. Behavior – collecting things. Sea & seashore.

The strawflower: a treasure chest story ill. by author. Macmillan, 1987. ISBN 0-689-50435-7 Subj: Behavior – collecting things. Flowers. Seasons.

Heyer, Carol. *Dinosaurs! strange and wonderful* ill. by Carol Heyer. Boyds Mills, 1995. ISBN 1-878093-16-9 Subj: Dinosaurs. Prehistory.

Robin Hood ill. by author. Ideals, 1993. ISBN 0-8249-8648-2 Subj: Behavior – greed. Character traits – bravery. Character traits – honesty. Folk & fairy tales.

Heyer, Marilee. *The weaving of a dream: a Chinese folktale* ill. by author. Viking, 1986. ISBN 0-670-80555-6 Subj: Activities – weaving. Folk & fairy tales. Foreign lands – China.

Heymans, Annemie. *The princess in the kitchen garden* written & ill. by Annemie & Margriet Heymans; trans. from Dutch by Johanna H. Prins & Johanna W. Prins. Farrar, 1993. ISBN 0-374-36122-3 Subj: Death. Emotions – grief. Family life. Family life – brothers & sisters.

Heymans, Margriet. *Pippin and Robber Grumblecroak's big baby* ill. by author. Addison-Wesley, 1973. Subj: Crime. Puppets.

The princess in the kitchen garden (Heymans, Annemie)

Heyward, Du Bose. *The country bunny and the little gold shoes* ill. by Marjorie Flack. Houghton Mifflin, 1974, c1939. ISBN 0-395-18557-2 Subj: Animals – rabbits. Character traits – kindness. Holidays – Easter.

Hiatt, Fred. *Baby talk* ill. by Mark Graham. McElderry, 1999. ISBN 0-689-82146-8 Subj: Babies. Family life – brothers. Language.

If I were queen of the world ill. by Mark Graham. McElderry, 1997. ISBN 0-689-80700-7 Subj: Family life – brothers & sisters. Imagination. Royalty – queens.

Hickcox, Ruth. *Great-Grandmother's treasure* ill. by David Soman. Dial, 1998. ISBN 0-8037-1514-5 Subj: Death. Family life – great-grandparents. Memories, memory. Old age.

Hickling, Meg. *Boys, girls and body science* ill. by Kim LaFave. Harbour, 2002. ISBN 1-55017-236-0 Subj: Anatomy. Science.

Hickman, Martha Whitmore. *And God created squash: how the world began* ill. by Giuliano Ferri. A. Whitman, 1993. ISBN 0-8075-0340-1 Subj: Creation.

A baby born in Bethlehem ill. by Giuliano Ferri. A. Whitman, 1999. ISBN 0-8075-5522-3 Subj: Holidays – Christmas. Religion – Nativity.

Eeps creeps, it's my room! ill. by Mary Alice Baer. Abingdon, 1984. ISBN 0-687-11527-2 Subj: Character traits – cleanliness.

My friend William moved away ill. by Bill Myers. Abingdon, 1979. ISBN 0-687-27540-7 Subj: Friendship. Moving.

Robert lives with his grandparents ill. by Tim Hinton. A. Whitman, 1995. ISBN 0-8075-7084-2 Subj: Divorce. Family life – grandparents. School.

When Andy's father went to prison ill. by Larry Raymond. A. Whitman, 1990. Rev. ed. of: When can daddy come home? c1983. ISBN 0-8075-8874-1 Subj: Crime. Family life. Prisons.

Hickox, Rebecca. *see* Ayres, Rebecca Hickox

The golden sandal ill. by Will Hillenbrand. Holiday, 1998. ISBN 0-8234-1331-4 Subj: Clothing. Family life – stepfamilies. Folk & fairy tales. Foreign lands – Iraq.

Hicks, Eleanor B. *see* Coerr, Eleanor

Hidaka, Masako. *Girl from the snow country* trans. from Japanese by Amanda Mayer Stinchecum; ill. by author. Kane/Miller, 1986. ISBN 0-916291-06-5 Subj: Flowers. Folk & fairy tales. Foreign lands – Japan. Weather – snow.

Hide-and-seek bunnies ill. by Judith Moffatt. Grosset, 1996. ISBN 0-448-41283-7 Subj: Animals – rabbits. Format, unusual – toy & movable books. Rhyming text.

Higashi, Sandra. *Bonz, inside-out* (Glaser, Byron)

Higgs, Liz Curtis. *Go away, dark night* ill. by Nancy Munger. WaterBrook, 1998. ISBN 1-57856-129-9 Subj: Emotions – fear. Night. Religion.

The parable of the lily ill. by Nancy Munger. Tommy Nelson, 1997. ISBN 0-7852-7231-3 Subj: Gardens, gardening. Gifts. Holidays – Easter.

High, Linda Oatman. *Barn savers* ill. by Ted Lewin. Boyds Mills, 1999. ISBN 1-56397-403-7 Subj: Barns. Family life – fathers.

Beekeepers ill. by Doug Chayka. Boyds Mills, 1998. ISBN 1-56397-486-X Subj: Family life – grandfathers. Insects – bees.

A Christmas Star ill. by Ronald Himler. Holiday, 1997. ISBN 0-8234-1301-2 Subj: Crime. Gifts. Holidays – Christmas. Trees.

The girl on the high-diving horse ill. by Ted Lewin. Philomel, 2003. ISBN 0-399-23649-X Subj: Animals – horses, ponies. Careers – photographers. Family life – fathers. Parks. U.S. history.

The last chimney of Christmas eve ill. by Kestutis Kasparavicius. Boyds Mills, 2001. ISBN 1-56397-804-0 Subj: Careers. Holidays – Christmas. Santa Claus.

Under New York ill. by Robert Rayevsky. Holiday, 2001. ISBN 0-8234-1551-1 Subj: Cities, towns. Concepts – opposites.

Winter shoes for Shadow Horse ill. by Ted Lewin. Boyds Mills, 2001. ISBN 1-56397-472-X Subj: Animals – horses, ponies. Careers – blacksmiths. Family life – fathers.

Higham, Jon Atlas. *Aardvark's picnic* ill. by author. Little, 1987. ISBN 0-316-36085-6 Subj: Activities – picnicking. Animals. Animals – aardvarks.

Highet, Alistair. *The yellow train* based on a story by Fred Bernard; ill. by François Roca. Creative Ed., 2000. ISBN 1-56846-128-3 Subj: Careers – engineers. Family life – grandfathers. Trains.

Highlights for Children, Inc. *The Timbertoes ABC alphabet book* (The Timbertoes ABC alphabet book)

The Timbertoes 1 2 3 counting book (The Timbertoes 1 2 3 counting book)

Hightower, Susan. *Twelve snails to one lizard: a tale of mischief and measurement* ill. by Matt Novak. S&S, 1997. ISBN 0-689-80452-0 Subj: Animals. Animals – snails. Concepts – measurement. Reptiles – lizards.

Highwater, Jamake. *Moonsong lullaby* photos by Marcia Keegan. Lothrop, 1981. ISBN 0-688-00428-8 Subj: Lullabies. Night. Rhyming text.

Higney, Gene-Michael. *Tales of tails* (Garrett, Ann)

What's for lunch? (Garrett, Ann)

Hill, Donna. *Ms. Glee was waiting* ill. by Diane Dawson. Atheneum, 1978. ISBN 0-689-30618-0 Subj: School.

Hill, Elizabeth Starr. *Evan's corner* ill. by Sandra Speidel. Rev. ed. Viking, 1991. ISBN 0-670-82830-0 Subj: Character traits – helpfulness. Ethnic groups in the U.S. – African Americans. Family life.

Hill, Eric. *At home* ill. by author. Random House, 1983. ISBN 0-394-85638-4 Subj: Animals – bears. Family life. Wordless.

Baby Bear's bedtime ill. by author. Random House, 1984. ISBN 0-394-96572-8 Subj: Animals – bears. Bedtime.

Good morning, baby bear ill. by author. Random House, 1984. ISBN 0-394-96571-X Subj: Animals – bears. Morning.

My pets ill. by author. Random House, 1983. ISBN 0-394-85637-6 Subj: Animals – bears. Pets.

The park ill. by author. Random House, 1983. ISBN 0-394-85636-8 Subj: Activities – walking. Parks. Wordless.

Puppy love ill. by author. Putnam, 1982. ISBN 0-399-20939-5 Subj: Animals – dogs. Emotions – love. Format, unusual – board books.

Spot and friends dress up ill. by author. Putnam, 1996. ISBN 0-399-23031-9 Subj: Animals – dogs. Clothing. Format, unusual – toy & movable books. Friendship.

Spot and friends play ill. by author. Putnam, 1996. ISBN 0-399-23032-7 Subj: Activities – playing. Animals – dogs. Format, unusual – toy & movable books. Friendship.

Spot at home ill. by author. Putnam, 1991. ISBN 0-399-21774-6 Subj: Animals – dogs. Format, unusual – board books.

Spot at play ill. by author. Putnam, 1985. ISBN 0-399-21228-0 Subj: Activities – playing. Animals. Animals – dogs.

Spot at the fair ill. by author. Putnam, 1985. ISBN 0-399-21229-9 Subj: Animals. Animals – dogs. Fairs, festivals. Format, unusual – board books.

Spot bakes a cake ill. by author. Putnam, 1994. ISBN 0-399-22701-6 Subj: Activities – baking, cooking. Animals – dogs. Birthdays. Food. Format, unusual – toy & movable books.

Spot counts from 1 to 10 ill. by author. Putnam, 1989. ISBN 0-399-21672-3 Subj: Animals. Animals – dogs. Counting, numbers. Format, unusual – board books.

Spot goes on holiday ill. by author. Heinemann, 1985. ISBN 0-434-94260-X Subj: Activities – vacationing. Animals – dogs. Format, unusual – toy & movable books. Sea & seashore.

Spot goes to a party ill. by author. Putnam, 1992. ISBN 0-399-22409-2 Subj: Animals – dogs. Cowboys, cowgirls. Format, unusual – toy & movable books. Parties.

Spot goes to school ill. by author. Putnam, 1984. ISBN 0-399-21073-3 Subj: Animals – dogs. Format, unusual – toy & movable books. School – first day.

Spot goes to the beach ill. by author. Putnam, 1985. ISBN 0-399-21247-7 Subj: Activities – playing. Animals – dogs. Family life. Format, unusual – toy & movable books. Sea & seashore – beaches.

Spot goes to the circus ill. by author. Putnam, 1986. ISBN 0-399-21317-1 Subj: Animals – dogs. Circus. Format, unusual – board books.

Spot goes to the farm ill. by author. Putnam, 1987. ISBN 0-399-21434-8 Subj: Animals. Animals – dogs. Farms. Format, unusual – board books. Machines.

Spot goes to the park ill. by author. Putnam, 1991. ISBN 0-399-21833-5 Subj: Activities – playing. Animals – dogs. Format, unusual – toy & movable books. Parks.

Spot in the garden ill. by author. Putnam, 1991. ISBN 0-399-21772-X Subj: Animals – dogs. Format, unusual – board books. Gardens, gardening.

Spot looks at colors ill. by author. Putnam, 1986. ISBN 0-399-21349-X Subj: Animals – dogs. Concepts – color. Format, unusual – board books.

Spot looks at opposites ill. by author. Putnam, 1989. ISBN 0-399-21681-2 Subj: Animals – dogs. Concepts – opposites. Format, unusual – board books.

Spot looks at shapes ill. by author. Putnam, 1986. ISBN 0-399-21350-3 Subj: Animals – dogs. Concepts – shape. Format, unusual – board books.

Spot looks at weather ill. by author. Putnam, 1989. ISBN 0-399-21673-1 Subj: Animals – dogs. Format, unusual – board books. Weather.

Spot on the farm ill. by author. Putnam, 1985. ISBN 0-399-21230-2 Subj: Animals. Animals – dogs. Farms. Format, unusual – board books.

Spot sleeps over ill. by author. Putnam, 1990. ISBN 0-399-21815-7 Subj: Activities – playing. Animals – dogs. Format, unusual – toy & movable books. Friendship. Sleepovers.

Spot visits his grandparents ill. by author. Putnam, 1996. ISBN 0-399-23033-5 Subj: Animals – dogs. Family life – grandparents. Format, unusual – board books.

Spot visits the hospital ill. by author. Putnam, 1987. ISBN 0-399-21397-X Subj: Animals – dogs. Behavior – misbehavior. Hospitals.

Spot's baby sister ill. by author. Putnam, 1989. ISBN 0-399-21640-5 Subj: Animals – dogs. Animals – hippopotamuses. Format, unusual – toy & movable books. Reptiles – alligators, crocodiles.

Spot's big book of colors, shapes and numbers = El libro grande de Spot ill. by author. Putnam, 1994. ISBN 0-399-22782-2 Subj: Animals – dogs. Concepts – color. Concepts – shape. Counting, numbers. Foreign languages.

Spot's big book of colours, shapes, and numbers ill. by author. F. Warne, 1994. ISBN 0-399-22679-6 Subj: Animals – dogs. Concepts – color. Concepts – shape. Counting, numbers.

Spot's big book of words = El libro grande de las palabras de Spot ill. by author. Rev. ed. Putnam, 1989. ISBN 0-399-21689-8 Subj: Animals – dogs. Foreign languages. Language.

Spot's birthday party ill. by author. Putnam, 1982. ISBN 0-399-20903-4 Subj: Birthdays. Folk & fairy tales. Format, unusual – toy & movable books.

Spot's favorite baby animals ill. by author. Putnam, 1997. ISBN 0-399-23157-9 Subj: Animals. Animals – dogs. Format, unusual – board books.

Spot's favorite colors ill. by author. Putnam, 1997. ISBN 0-399-23177-3 Subj: Animals – dogs. Concepts – color. Format, unusual – board books.

Spot's favorite numbers ill. by author. Putnam, 1997. ISBN 0-399-23155-2 Subj: Animals – dogs. Counting, numbers. Format, unusual – board books.

Spot's favorite words ill. by author. Putnam, 1997. ISBN 0-399-23156-0 Subj: Animals – dogs. Format, unusual – board books. Language.

Spot's first Christmas ill. by author. Putnam, 1983. ISBN 0-399-20963-8 Subj: Animals – dogs. Format, unusual – toy & movable books. Holidays – Christmas.

Spot's first Easter ill. by author. Putnam, 1988. ISBN 0-399-21435-6 Subj: Animals – dogs. Eggs. Format, unusual – toy & movable books. Holidays – Easter.

Spot's first 1, 2, 3 frieze ill. by author. F. Warne, 1994. ISBN 0-72324-176-7 Subj: Animals – dogs. Counting, numbers. Format, unusual.

Spot's first picnic ill. by author. Putnam, 1987. ISBN 0-399-21398-8 Subj: Activities – picnicking. Animals – dogs. Behavior – misbehavior.

Spot's first walk ill. by author. Putnam, 1981. ISBN 0-399-20838-0 Subj: Activities – walking. Animals – dogs. Format, unusual – toy & movable books.

Spot's first words ill. by author. Putnam, 1986. ISBN 0-399-21348-1 Subj: Animals – dogs. Format, unusual – board books. Language.

Spot's magical Christmas ill. by author. Putnam, 1995. ISBN 0-399-22912-4 Subj: Animals – dogs. Format, unusual – board books. Holidays – Christmas. Santa Claus.

Spot's toy box ill. by author. Putnam, 1991. ISBN 0-399-21773-8 Subj: Animals – dogs. Format, unusual – board books. Toys.

Spot's walk in the woods ill. by author. Viking, 1993. ISBN 0-670-85080-2 Subj: Activities – playing. Animals – dogs. Forest, woods. Format, unusual – toy & movable books. Rebuses.

Up there ill. by author. Random House, 1983. ISBN 0-394-85635-X Subj: Activities – flying. Animals – bears. Wordless.

Where's Spot? ill. by author. Putnam, 1980. ISBN 0-399-20758-9 Subj: Behavior – lost. Folk & fairy tales. Format, unusual – toy & movable books.

Hill, Frances. *The bug cemetery* ill. by Vera Rosenberry. Holt, 2002. ISBN 0-8050-6370-6 Subj: Death. Emotions – grief. Pets.

Hill, Lee Sullivan. *Earthmovers* ill. with photos. Lerner, 2003. ISBN 0-8225-0689-0 Subj: Careers – construction workers. Machines.

Homes keep us warm ill. with photos. Carolrhoda, 2001. ISBN 1-57505-430-2 Subj: Homes, houses.

Motorcycles ill. with photos. Lerner, 2004. ISBN 0-8225-0695-5 Subj: Motorcycles.

Schools help us learn ill. with photos. Carolrhoda, 1998. ISBN 1-57505-092-7 Subj: School.

Trains photos by Howard Ande. Lerner, 2003. ISBN 0-8225-0692-0 Subj: Trains. Transportation.

Hill, Mary (1977–). *Let's make pizza* ill. with photos. Childrens Pr., 2002. ISBN 0-516-23959-7 Subj: Activities – baking, cooking. Food.

Let's make tacos ill. with photos. Childrens Pr., 2002. ISBN 0-516-23957-0 Subj: Activities – baking, cooking. Food.

Hill, Mary Lou. *My dad's a park ranger* ill. by Tom De Hart. Childrens Pr., 1978. ISBN 0-516-07635-3 Subj: Careers – park rangers. Parks.

My dad's a smokejumper ill. by Don Hendricks. Childrens Pr., 1978. ISBN 0-516-07636-1 Subj: Careers – firefighters. Forest, woods.

Hill, Monica. *see* Watson, Jane Werner

Hill, Susan. *Beware, beware* ill. by Angela Barrett. Candlewick, 1993. ISBN 1-56402-245-5 Subj: Family life – mothers. Imagination. Night. Rhyming text. Seasons – winter.

Can it be true? ill. by Angela Barrett. Viking, 1988. ISBN 0-670-82517-4 Subj: Holidays – Christmas. Rhyming text.

Go away, bad dreams! ill. by Vanessa Julian-Ottie. Random House, 1985. ISBN 0-394-97222-8 Subj: Dreams. Emotions – fear. Family life. Night.

King of kings ill. by John Lawrence. Candlewick, 1993. ISBN 1-56402-210-2 Subj: Babies. Holidays – Christmas. Old age.

Ruby bakes a cake ill. by Margie Moore. HarperCollins, 2004. ISBN 0-06-008976-8 Subj: Activities – baking, cooking. Animals. Animals – raccoons. Food. Friendship.

Simba's A-Z ill. by Doug Hart. Disney Pr., 1998. ISBN 0-7868-3168-5 Subj: ABC books. Animals. Animals – lions. Foreign lands – Africa. Language. Rhyming text.

Stuart at the fun house ill. by Lydia Halverson. HarperCollins, 2001. ISBN 0-06-029635-6 Subj: Animals – mice. Concepts – size. Family life – brothers. Parks – amusement.

Stuart hides out ill. by Lydia Halverson. HarperCollins, 2001. ISBN 0-06-029634-8 Subj: Animals – cats. Animals – mice. Games.

Stuart sets sail ill. by Lydia Halverson. HarperCollins, 2001. ISBN 0-06-029633-X Subj: Activities – picnicking. Animals – mice. Boats, ships. Lakes, ponds.

Hill, Susanna Leonard. *The house that Mack built* ill. by Ken Wilson-Max. Little Simon, 2002. ISBN 0-689-84813-7 Subj: Cumulative tales. Format, unusual – toy & movable books. Homes, houses. Nursery rhymes. Rhyming text.

Hille-Brandts, Lene. *The little black hen* trans. & adapt. by Marion Koenig; ill. by Sigrid Heuck. Childrens Pr., 1968. Translation of Die Henne Gudula. Subj: Behavior – dissatisfaction. Birds – chickens. Folk & fairy tales. Foreign lands – Russia.

Hillenbrand, Will. *Down by the station* ill. by author. Harcourt, 1999. ISBN 0-15-201804-2 Subj: Animals – babies. Cumulative tales. Songs. Zoos.

Fiddle-i-fee ill. by author. Harcourt, 2002. ISBN 0-15-201945-6 Subj: Animals. Babies. Cumulative tales. Farms. Nursery rhymes.

Hiller, Catherine. *Abracatabby* ill. by Victoria De Larrea. Coward, 1981. ISBN 0-698-30727-5 Subj: Animals – cats. Magic.

Argentaybee and the boonie ill. by Cyndy Szekeres. Coward, 1979. ISBN 0-698-20441-7 Subj: Behavior – misbehavior. Imagination – imaginary friends.

Hillerich, Robert L. *Rand McNally picturebook dictionary: a thousand words to see and say* (Rand McNally picturebook dictionary)

Hillert, Margaret. *The birthday car* ill. by Kelly Oechsli. Follett, 1966. ISBN 0-8136-5031-3 Subj: Birthdays. Toys.

The funny baby ill. by Hertha Depper. Follett, 1966. The tale of The Ugly Duckling by H. C. Andersen. ISBN 0-695-83300-6 Subj: Birds – ducks. Birds – swans. Character traits – appearance. Character traits – being different. Folk & fairy tales.

Happy birthday, dear dragon ill. by Carl Kock. Follett, 1977. ISBN 0-695-40743-0 Subj: Birthdays. Dragons.

The little cowboy and the big cowboy ill. by Dan Siculan. Follett, 1980. ISBN 0-695-41453-4 Subj: Cowboys, cowgirls. Family life – fathers.

Little Red Riding Hood (Grimm, Jacob)

The little runaway ill. by Irv Anderson. Follett, 1966. ISBN 0-8136-5052-6 Subj: Animals – cats. Behavior – running away.

The magic beans ill. by Mel Pekarsky. Follett, 1966. The tale of Jack and the beanstalk. ISBN 0-8136-5053-4 Subj: Folk & fairy tales. Giants. Plants.

Merry Christmas, dear dragon ill. by Carl Kock. Follett, 1980. ISBN 0-695-41359-7 Subj: Dragons. Holidays – Christmas.

Play ball ill. by Dick Martin. Follett, 1978. ISBN 0-695-40879-8 Subj: Activities – playing. Games. Sports – baseball.

The three bears ill. by Irma Wilde. Follett, 1963. Subj: Animals – bears. Folk & fairy tales.

The three goats ill. by Mel Pekarsky. Follett, 1963. The tale of The three billy goats Gruff. ISBN 0-695-48720-5 Subj: Animals – goats. Character traits – cleverness. Cumulative tales. Folk & fairy tales. Mythical creatures – trolls.

The three little pigs (The three little pigs)

Tom Thumb (Tom Thumb)

Up, up and away ill. by Robert Masheris. Modern Curriculum, 1981. ISBN 0-8136-5096-8 Subj: Moon. Space & space ships.

What is it? ill. by Kinuko Y. Craft. Follett, 1978. ISBN 0-695-40882-8 Subj: Activities – playing. Animals – dogs. Imagination. Rhyming text.

The yellow boat ill. by Ed Young. Follett, 1966. ISBN 0-8136-5033-X Subj: Boats, ships.

Hillman, Elizabeth. *Min-Yo and the moon dragon* ill. by John Wallner. Harcourt, 1992. ISBN 0-15-254230-2 Subj: Dragons. Folk & fairy tales. Foreign lands – China. Moon. Stars.

Hillman, Priscilla. *A Merry-Mouse book of favorite poems* ill. by author. Doubleday, 1981. ISBN 0-385-17104-8 Subj: Animals – mice. Poetry.

A Merry-Mouse book of months ill. by author. Doubleday, 1980. ISBN 0-385-15595-6 Subj: Animals – mice. Days of the week, months of the year. Format, unusual – toy & movable books. Rhyming text.

A Merry-Mouse book of nursery rhymes comp. & ill. by Priscilla Hillman. Doubleday, 1981. ISBN 0-385-17103-X Subj: Animals – mice. Nursery rhymes.

The Merry-Mouse book of opposites ill. by author. Doubleday, 1983. ISBN 0-385-17918-9 Subj: Animals – mice. Concepts – opposites. Poetry.

The Merry-Mouse book of prayers and graces ill. by author. Doubleday, 1983. ISBN 0-385-18337-2 Subj: Religion. Rhyming text.

The Merry-Mouse book of toys ill. by author. Doubleday, 1983. ISBN 0-385-17916-2 Subj: Animals – mice. Poetry. Toys.

A Merry-Mouse Christmas A B C ill. by author. Doubleday, 1980. ISBN 0-385-15597-2 Subj: ABC books. Animals – mice. Holidays – Christmas. Poetry.

The Merry-Mouse counting and colors book ill. by author. Doubleday, 1983. Subj: Animals – mice. Concepts – color. Counting, numbers.

The Merry-Mouse schoolhouse ill. by author. Doubleday, 1982. ISBN 0-385-17107-2 Subj: Animals – mice. School – first day.

Hilton, Nette. *Andrew Jessup* ill. by Cathy Wilcox. Ticknor & Fields, 1993. ISBN 0-395-66900-6 Subj: Friendship. Moving.

Dirty Dave ill. by Roland Harvey. Watts, 1990. ISBN 0-531-08461-2 Subj: Careers – tailors. Clothing. Crime. Foreign lands – Australia.

The long red scarf ill. by Margaret Power. Carolrhoda, 1990. ISBN 0-87614-399-0 Subj: Activities – knitting. Clothing. Family life – grandfathers. Gender roles.

Prince Lachlan ill. by Ann James. Watts, 1990. ISBN 0-531-08463-9 Subj: Behavior – misbehavior. Royalty. Royalty – princes.

A proper little lady ill. by Cathy Wilcox. Watts, 1990. ISBN 0-531-08460-4 Subj: Clothing.

Himler, Ronald. *The girl on the yellow giraffe* ill. by author. HarperCollins, 1976. ISBN 0-06-022318-9 Subj: Cities, towns. Imagination.

Wake up, Jeremiah ill. by author. HarperCollins, 1979. ISBN 0-06-022324-3 Subj: Morning.

Himmelman, John. *Amanda and the magic garden* ill. by author. Viking, 1987. ISBN 0-670-80823-7 Subj: Animals. Gardens, gardening. Magic. Witches.

Amanda and the witch switch ill. by author. Viking, 1985. ISBN 0-670-11531-2 Subj: Behavior – misbehavior. Behavior – wishing. Character traits – meanness. Frogs & toads. Witches.

The Clover County carrot contest ill. by author. Silver Pr., 1991. ISBN 0-671-69637-8 Subj: Animals – beavers. Careers – inventors. Contests. Family life. Gardens, gardening.

A dandelion's life ill. by author. Childrens Pr., 1998. ISBN 0-516-21177-3 Subj: Flowers. Plants. Seeds.

The day-off machine ill. by author. Silver Pr., 1990. ISBN 0-671-69635-1 Subj: Activities – making things. Animals – beavers. Weather – snow.

Ellen and the goldfish ill. by author. HarperCollins, 1990. ISBN 0-06-022417-7 Subj: Activities – painting. Fish. Friendship.

The great leaf blast-off ill. by author. Silver Pr., 1990. ISBN 0-671-69634-3 Subj: Activities – making things. Animals – beavers. Family life. Trees.

A guest is a guest ill. by author. Dutton, 1991. ISBN 0-525-44720-2 Subj: Animals. Etiquette. Farms.

Honest Tulio ill. by author. BridgeWater, 1997. ISBN 0-8167-3812-2 Subj: Character traits – honesty. Cumulative tales.

A house spider's life ill. by author. Childrens Pr., 1999. ISBN 0-516-21185-4 Subj: Spiders.

Ibis: a true whale story ill. by author. Scholastic, 1990. ISBN 0-590-42848-9 Subj: Animals – whales. Character traits – kindness to animals.

J.J. versus the babysitter ill. by author. BridgeWater, 1996. ISBN 0-8167-3800-9 Subj: Activities – babysitting. Family life – brothers. Multiple births – twins.

Lights out! ill. by author. Troll, 1995. ISBN 0-8167-3450-X Subj: Bedtime. Camps, camping. Emotions – fear. Imagination. Night.

A luna moth's life ill. by author. Childrens Pr., 1998. ISBN 0-516-20821-7 Subj: Insects – moths.

A monarch butterfly's life ill. by author. Childrens Pr., 1999. ISBN 0-516-21147-1 Subj: Insects – butterflies, caterpillars.

Montigue on the high seas ill. by author. Viking, 1988. ISBN 0-670-81861-5 Subj: Animals. Animals – mice. Animals – moles.

A pill bug's life ill. by author. Childrens Pr., 1999. ISBN 0-516-21165-X Subj: Crustaceans.

Simpson Snail sings ill. by author. Dutton, 1992. ISBN 0-525-44978-7 Subj: Activities – singing. Animals – snails. Friendship.

The super camper caper ill. by author. Silver Pr., 1991. ISBN 0-671-69636-X Subj: Animals – beavers. Camps, camping. Careers – inventors.

Talester the lizard ill. by author. Dial, 1982. ISBN 0-8037-8788-X Subj: Reptiles – lizards.

The talking tree: or Don't believe everything you hear ill. by author. Viking, 1986. ISBN 0-670-80775-3 Subj: Animals – dogs. Trees.

Wanted: perfect parents ill. by author. BridgeWater, 1993. ISBN 0-8167-3028-8 Subj: Behavior. Family life.

A wood frog's life ill. by author. Childrens Pr., 1998. ISBN 0-516-21178-1 Subj: Forest, woods. Frogs & toads. Nature.

Hindley, Judy. *The best thing about a puppy* ill. by Pat Casey. Candlewick, 1998. ISBN 0-7636-0596-4 Subj: Animals – babies. Animals – dogs. Pets.

The big red bus ill. by William Benedict. Candlewick, 1995. ISBN 1-56402-639-6 Subj: Accidents. Buses. Format, unusual – toy & movable books. Rhyming text. Roads.

Crazy ABC ill. by Nick Sharratt. Candlewick, 1996. ISBN 1-56402-682-5 Subj: ABC books.

Do like a duck does ill. by Ivan Bates. Candlewick, 2002. ISBN 0-7636-1668-0 Subj: Animals – foxes. Birds – ducks. Rhyming text.

Does a cow say boo? ill. by Brita Granström. Candlewick, 2002. ISBN 0-7636-1718-0 Subj: Animals. Farms. Noise, sounds.

Eyes, nose, fingers and toes ill. by Brita Granström. Candlewick, 1999. ISBN 0-7636-0440-2 Subj: Anatomy. Rhyming text.

Funny walks ill. by Alex Ayliffe. BridgeWater, 1994. ISBN 0-8167-3313-9 Subj: Activities – walking. Animals.

How many twos? ill. by Stephen Bland. Doubleday, 1992. ISBN 0-385-30661-X Subj: Counting, numbers.

Into the jungle ill. by Melanie Epps. Candlewick, 1994. ISBN 1-56402-423-7 Subj: Activities – walking. Animals. Jungle.

Little and big ill. by Nick Sharratt. Candlewick, 1996. ISBN 1-56402-677-9 Subj: Concepts – size. Rhyming text.

The little train ill. by Robert Kendall. Watts, 1990. ISBN 0-531-08450-7 Subj: Activities – making things. Old age. Toys – trains.

Maybe it's a pirate ill. by Selina Young. Thomasson-Grant, 1992. ISBN 1-56566-016-1 Subj: Bedtime. Emotions – fear. Imagination.

Mrs. Mary Malarky's seven cats ill. by Denise Teasdale. Watts, 1990. ISBN 0-531-08422-1 Subj: Activities – babysitting. Animals – cats.

One by one ill. by Nick Sharratt. Candlewick, 1996. ISBN 1-56402-678-7 Subj: Animals. Counting, numbers. Rhyming text.

A piece of string is a wonderful thing ill. by Margaret Chamberlain. Candlewick, 1993. ISBN 1-56402-147-5 Subj: String.

Princess Rosa's winter ill. by Margaret Chamberlain. Kingfisher, 2005. ISBN 0-7534-5859-4 Subj: Middle Ages. Royalty – princesses. Seasons – winter.

Rosy's visitors ill. by Helen Craig. Candlewick, 2002. ISBN 0-7636-1769-5 Subj: Homes, houses. Imagination. Toys.

The sleepy book: a lullaby ill. by Patrice Aggs. Orchard, 1992. ISBN 0-531-08571-6 Subj: Bedtime. Lullabies. Night. Sleep.

Soft and noisy ill. by Patrice Aggs. Walt Disney, 1992. ISBN 1-56282-225-X Subj: Noise, sounds. Senses – hearing.

A song of colors ill. by Mike Bostock. Candlewick, 1998. ISBN 0-7636-0320-1 Subj: Concepts – color. Poetry.

Ten bright eyes ill. by Alison Bartlett. Peachtree, 1998. ISBN 1-56145-173-8 Subj: Animals. Birds. Concepts – shape. Counting, numbers. Format, unusual – toy & movable books.

The tree ill. by Alison Wisenfeld. C.N. Potter, 1990. ISBN 0-517-57630-9 Subj: Trees.

Uncle Harold and the green hat ill. by Peter Utton. Farrar, 1991. ISBN 0-374-38030-9 Subj: Clothing – hats. Family life – aunts, uncles. Humorous stories. Imagination. Magic. Rhyming text.

What's in baby's morning ill. by Jo Burroughes. Candlewick, 2004. ISBN 0-7636-2372-5 Subj: Activities. Babies. Family life.

The wheeling and whirling-around book ill. by Margaret Chamberlain. Candlewick, 1994. ISBN 1-56402-490-3 Subj: Concepts – shape. Wheels.

Hine, Sesyle Joslin. *see* Joslin, Sesyle

Hines, Anna Grossnickle. *All by myself* ill. by author. Clarion, 1985. ISBN 0-89919-293-9 Subj: Behavior – growing up. Self-concept.

Bethany for real ill. by author. Greenwillow, 1985. ISBN 0-688-04009-8 Subj: Activities – playing. Imagination.

Big help ill. by author. Clarion, 1995. ISBN 0-395-68702-0 Subj: Family life – brothers & sisters.

Big like me ill. by author. Greenwillow, 1989. ISBN 0-688-08355-2 Subj: Babies. Behavior – growing up. Family life.

Come to the meadow ill. by author. Houghton Mifflin, 1984. ISBN 0-89919-227-0 Subj: Activities – picnicking. Family life – grandmothers.

Daddy makes the best spaghetti ill. by author. Clarion, 1986. ISBN 0-89919-388-9 Subj: Family life. Family life – fathers. Gender roles.

Don't worry, I'll find you ill. by author. Dutton, 1986. ISBN 0-525-44228-6 Subj: Behavior – lost. Shopping. Toys – dolls.

Even if I spill my milk? ill. by author. Clarion, 1994. ISBN 0-395-65010-0 Subj: Character traits – questioning. Emotions. Family life.

Gramma's walk ill. by author. Greenwillow, 1993. ISBN 0-688-11481-4 Subj: Family life – grandmothers. Handicaps – physical handicaps. Imagination. Nature. Sea & seashore.

Grandma gets grumpy ill. by author. Clarion, 1988. ISBN 0-89919-529-6 Subj: Activities – babysitting. Family life – grandmothers.

The greatest picnic in the world ill. by author. Clarion, 1991. ISBN 0-395-55266-4 Subj: Activities – picnicking. Rhyming text. Weather – rain.

I'll tell you what they say ill. by author. Greenwillow, 1987. ISBN 0-688-06487-6 Subj: Animals. Animals – dogs. Farms. Toys – bears.

It's just me, Emily ill. by author. Clarion, 1987. ISBN 0-89919-487-7 Subj: Activities – playing. Family life – mothers. Rhyming text.

Jackie's lunch box ill. by author. Greenwillow, 1991. ISBN 0-688-09694-8 Subj: Family life – sisters.

Keep your old hat ill. by author. Dutton, 1987. ISBN 0-525-44299-5 Subj: Activities – playing. Toys – dolls.

Maybe a band-aid will help ill. by author. Dutton, 1984. ISBN 0-525-44115-8 Subj: Family life – mothers. Problem solving. Toys – dolls.

Mean old Uncle Jack ill. by author. Clarion, 1990. ISBN 0-395-52137-8 Subj: Behavior. Family life – aunts, uncles. Holidays – Fourth of July.

Miss Emma's wild garden ill. by author. Greenwillow, 1997. ISBN 0-688-14693-7 Subj: Animals. Birds. Flowers. Gardens, gardening. Insects. Plants.

Moompa, Toby, and Bomp ill. by author. Clarion, 1993. ISBN 0-395-61301-9 Subj: Behavior – lost & found possessions. Family life – grandfathers. Toys – dolls.

Moon's wish ill. by author. Houghton Mifflin, 1992. ISBN 0-395-58114-1 Subj: Behavior – wishing. Family life. Moon.

My grandma is coming to town ill. by Melissa Sweet. Candlewick, 2003. ISBN 0-7636-1237-5 Subj: Family life – grandmothers.

My own big bed ill. by Mary Watson. Greenwillow, 1998. ISBN 0-688-15600-2 Subj: Emotions – fear. Furniture – beds.

No, no Jack! ill. by Pierre Pratt. Dial, 2002. ISBN 0-8037-2612-0 Subj: Animals – dogs. Behavior – hiding things. Format, unusual – toy & movable books.

Pieces, a year in poems and quilts ill. by author. Greenwillow, 2001. ISBN 0-688-16964-3 Subj: Nature. Poetry. Quilts. Seasons.

Remember the butterflies ill. by author. Dutton, 1991. ISBN 0-525-44679-6 Subj: Death. Emotions – grief. Family life – grandfathers. Insects – butterflies, caterpillars. Memories, memory.

Rumble thumble boom! ill. by author. Greenwillow, 1992. ISBN 0-688-10912-8 Subj: Bedtime. Emotions – fear. Weather – lightning, thunder. Weather – storms.

The secret keeper ill. by author. Greenwillow, 1990. ISBN 0-688-08946-1 Subj: Behavior – secrets. Family life. Holidays – Christmas.

Sky all around ill. by author. Clarion, 1989. ISBN 0-89919-801-5 Subj: Family life – daughters. Family life – fathers. Night. Sky. Stars.

Taste the raindrops ill. by author. Greenwillow, 1983. ISBN 0-688-01423-2 Subj: Weather – rain.

They really like me! ill. by author. Greenwillow, 1989. ISBN 0-688-07734-X Subj: Activities – playing. Family life. Sibling rivalry.

What can you do in the rain? ill. by Thea Kliros. Greenwillow, 1999. ISBN 0-688-16077-8 Subj: Activities. Format, unusual – board books. Weather – rain.

What can you do in the snow? ill. by Thea Kliros. Greenwillow, 1999. ISBN 0-688-16078-6 Subj: Activities. Format, unusual – board books. Weather – snow.

What can you do in the sun? ill. by Thea Kliros. Greenwillow, 1999. ISBN 0-688-16080-8 Subj: Activities. Format, unusual – board books. Sun. Weather. Weather – rainbows.

What can you do in the wind? ill. by Thea Kliros. Greenwillow, 1999. ISBN 0-688-16079-4 Subj: Activities. Format, unusual – board books. Games. Weather – wind.

What Joe saw ill. by author. Greenwillow, 1994. ISBN 0-688-13124-7 Subj: Behavior – promptness, tardiness. Character traits – individuality.

When the goblins came knocking ill. by author. Greenwillow, 1995. ISBN 0-688-13736-9 Subj: Holidays – Halloween. Memories, memory. Rhyming text.

When we married Gary ill. by author. Greenwillow, 1996. ISBN 0-688-14277-X Subj: Emotions – love. Family life – stepfamilies.

Whose shoes? ill. by LeUyen Pham. Harcourt, 2001. ISBN 0-15-201773-9 Subj: Animals – mice. Clothing – shoes. Family life. Format, unusual – toy & movable books.

Hines, Gary. *A Christmas tree in the White House* ill. by Alexandra Wallner. Holt, 1998. ISBN 0-8050-5076-0 Subj: Ecology. Holidays – Christmas. Trees. U.S. history.

The day of the high climber ill. by Anna Grossnickle Hines. Greenwillow, 1994. ISBN 0-688-11495-4 Subj: Careers – lumberjacks. Family life. Forest, woods. Trees.

A ride in the crummy ill. by Anna Grossnickle Hines. Greenwillow, 1991. ISBN 0-688-09692-1 Subj: Family life – grandfathers. Memories, memory. Trains.

Hines, Stephen W. *Laura Ingalls Wilder's fairy poems* (Wilder, Laura Ingalls)

Hines-Stephens, Sarah. *Bean's games* ill. by Anna Grossnickle Hines. Harcourt, 1998. ISBN 0-15-201606-6 Subj: Activities – playing. Animals – cats.

Hinton, S. E. *Big David, Little David* ill. by Alan Daniel. Doubleday, 1995. ISBN 0-385-31093-5 Subj: Family life – fathers. Names. School.

Hippel, Ursula Von. *see* Von Hippel, Ursula

Hippely, Hilary Horder. *Adventure on Klickitat Island* ill. by Barbara Upton. Dutton, 1998. ISBN 0-525-45293-1 Subj: Animals. Night. Rhyming text. Toys. Weather – storms.

The crimson ribbon ill. by Jo Ellen McAllister Stammen. Putnam, 1994. ISBN 0-399-22542-0 Subj: Behavior – needing someone. Family life.

A song for Lena ill. by Leslie A. Baker. S&S, 1996. ISBN 0-689-80763-5 Subj: Activities – baking, cooking. Family life – grandmothers. Food. Foreign lands – Hungary.

Hippopotamus, Eugene H. *see* Kraus, Robert

The Hippopotamus's birthday and other poems about animals and birds ill. by Roger Hughes; compiled by Linda M. Jennings. Hodder & Stoughton, 1987. ISBN 0-340-38681-9 Subj: Animals. Foreign lands – England. Poetry.

Hirano, Cathy. *The fox's egg* (Isami, Ikuyo)

Mr. Beetle (Tada, Satoshi)

Hirschberg, J. Cotter. *My friend the babysitter* (Watson, Jane Werner)

My friend the dentist (Watson, Jane Werner)

My friend the doctor (Watson, Jane Werner)

Sometimes a family has to move (Watson, Jane Werner)

Sometimes a family has to split up (Watson, Jane Werner)

Sometimes I get angry (Watson, Jane Werner)

Sometimes I'm afraid (Watson, Jane Werner)

Sometimes I'm jealous (Watson, Jane Werner)

Hirschi, Ron. *Faces in the forest* photos by Thomas D. Mangelsen. Cobblehill, 1997. ISBN 0-525-65224-8 Subj: Animals. Birds. Forest, woods.

Fall photos by Thomas D. Mangelsen. Dutton, 1991. ISBN 0-525-65053-9 Subj: Animals. Seasons – fall.

Forest ill. by Barbara Bash. Bantam, 1991. ISBN 0-553-07469-5 Subj: Animals. Ecology. Forest, woods.

Harvest song ill. by Deborah Haeffele. Cobblehill, 1991. ISBN 0-525-65067-9 Subj: Country. Family life – grandmothers. Farms.

Hungry little frog (Kuhn, Dwight)

Loon Lake photos by Daniel J. Cox. Dutton, 1991. ISBN 0-525-65046-6 Subj: Animals. Birds – loons. Nature.

Mountain ill. by Barbara Bash. Bantam, 1992. ISBN 0-553-07998-0 Subj: Animals. Mountains.

Ocean ill. by Barbara Bash. Bantam, 1991. ISBN 0-553-07470-9 Subj: Animals. Fish. Sea & seashore.

Seya's song ill. by Constance R. Bergum. Sasquatch, 1992. ISBN 0-912365-62-5 Subj: Indians of North America – Clallam. Language. Seasons.

Spring photos by Thomas D. Mangelsen. Dutton, 1990. ISBN 0-525-65037-7 Subj: Animals. Seasons – spring.

Summer photos by Thomas D. Mangelsen. Dutton, 1991. ISBN 0-525-65054-7 Subj: Animals. Nature. Seasons – summer.

A time for babies photos by Thomas D. Mangelsen. Cobblehill, 1993. ISBN 0-525-65095-4 Subj: Animals. Animals – babies.

A time for playing photos by Thomas D. Mangelsen. Cobblehill, 1994. ISBN 0-525-65159-4 Subj: Activities – playing. Animals.

A time for singing photos by Thomas D. Mangelsen. Cobblehill, 1994. ISBN 0-525-65096-2 Subj: Activities – singing. Animals. Communication. Noise, sounds.

A time for sleeping photos by Thomas D. Mangelsen. Cobblehill, 1993. ISBN 0-525-65128-4 Subj: Animals. Sleep.

What is a bird? photos by Galen Burrell. Walker, 1987. ISBN 0-8027-6721-4 Subj: Birds. Science.

What is a cat? photos by Linda Quartman Younker. Walker, 1991. ISBN 0-8027-8123-3 Subj: Animals – cats.

What is a horse? photos by Linda Quartman Yonker & author. Walker, 1989. ISBN 0-8027-6877-6 Subj: Animals – horses, ponies.

When morning comes photos by Thomas D. Mangelsen. Boyds Mills, 2000. ISBN 1-56397-766-4 Subj: Animals. Birds. Morning.

When night comes photos by Thomas D. Mangelsen. Boyds Mills, 2000. ISBN 1-56397-766-4 Subj: Animals. Birds. Night.

Where are my bears? photos by Erwin & Peggy Bauer. Bantam, 1992. ISBN 0-553-07805-4 Subj: Animals – bears. Animals – endangered animals.

Where are my prairie dogs and black-footed ferrets? photos by Erwin & Peggy Bauer. Bantam, 1992. ISBN 0-553-07802-X Subj: Animals – endangered animals. Animals – ferrets. Animals – prairie dogs.

Where are my puffins, whales, and seals? photos by Erwin & Peggy Bauer. Bantam, 1992. ISBN 0-553-07803-8 Subj: Animals – endangered animals. Animals – seals. Animals – whales. Birds – puffins.

Where are my swans, whooping cranes, and singing loons? photos by Erwin & Peggy Bauer. Bantam, 1992. ISBN 0-553-07801-1 Subj: Animals – endangered animals. Birds – cranes. Birds – loons. Birds – swans.

Where do birds live? photos by Galen Burrell. Walker, 1987. ISBN 0-8027-6723-0 Subj: Birds. Science.

Where do horses live? photos by Linda Quartman Yonker & author. Walker, 1989. ISBN 0-8027-6879-2 Subj: Animals – horses, ponies.

Who lives in . . . Alligator Swamp? photos by Galen Burrell. Dodd, 1987. ISBN 0-396-09123-7 Subj: Animals. Forest, woods. Reptiles – alligators, crocodiles. Science.

Who lives in . . . the forest? photos by Galen Burrell. Dodd, 1987. ISBN 0-396-09121-0 Subj: Animals. Birds. Forest, woods.

Winter photos by Thomas D. Mangelsen. Dutton, 1990. ISBN 0-525-65026-1 Subj: Animals. Seasons – winter.

Hirschmann, Linda. *In a lick of a flick of a tongue* ill. by Jeni Bassett. Dodd, 1980. ISBN 0-396-07833-8 Subj: Anatomy. Animals.

Hirsh, Marilyn. *Captain Jiri and Rabbi Jacob: from a Jewish folktale* ill. by author. Holiday, 1976. ISBN 0-8234-0279-7 Subj: Folk & fairy tales. Jewish culture.

Could anything be worse? a Yiddish tale ill. by author. Holiday, 1974. ISBN 0-8234-0239-8 Subj: Humorous stories. Jewish culture.

Deborah the dybbuk: a ghost story ill. by author. Holiday, 1978. ISBN 0-8234-0315-7 Subj: Behavior – misbehavior. Character traits – kindness to animals. Ghosts.

I love Hanukkah ill. by author. Holiday, 1984. ISBN 0-8234-0525-7 Subj: Holidays – Hanukkah. Jewish culture.

I love Passover ill. by author. Holiday, 1985. ISBN 0-8234-0549-4 Subj: Holidays – Passover. Jewish culture. Religion.

Joseph who loved the Sabbath ill. by Devis Grebu. Viking, 1986. ISBN 0-670-81194-7 Subj: Folk & fairy tales. Jewish culture. Religion.

Leela and the watermelon by Marilyn Hirsh & Maya Narayan; ill. by Marilyn Hirsh. Crown, 1971. Subj: Babies. Food. Foreign lands – India.

One little goat: a Passover song ill. by author. Holiday, 1979. ISBN 0-8234-0345-9 Subj: Folk & fairy tales. Holidays – Passover. Jewish culture. Songs.

The pink suit ill. by author. Crown, 1970. Subj: Activities – trading. Emotions – embarrassment. Family life. Jewish culture.

Potato pancakes all around: a Hanukkah tale ill. by author. Bonim Books, 1978. ISBN 0-88482-762-3 Subj: Food. Holidays – Hanukkah. Jewish culture. Religion.

The Rabbi and the twenty-nine witches ill. by author. Holiday, 1976. ISBN 0-8234-0270-3 Subj: Careers – clergy. Character traits – cleverness. Jewish culture. Witches.

Where is Yonkela? ill. by author. Crown, 1969. Subj: Babies. Behavior – lost. Jewish culture.

Hirst, Robin. *My place in space* by Robin & Sally Hirst; ill. by Roland Harvey & Joe Levine. Watts, 1990. ISBN 0-531-08459-0 Subj: Astronomy. Buses. Science. Space & space ships.

Hirst, Sally. *My place in space* (Hirst, Robin)

Hiscock, Bruce. *Coyote and badger: desert hunters of the Southwest* ill. by author. Boyds Mills, 2001. ISBN 1-56397-848-2 Subj: Animals. Animals – badgers. Animals – coyotes. Character traits – cooperation. Desert.

Hiser, Berniece T. *The adventure of Charlie and his wheat-straw hat* ill. by Mary Szilagyi. Dodd, 1986. ISBN 0-396-08772-8 Subj: Character traits – bravery. Clothing – hats. Family life – grandmothers. U.S. history.

Hiskey, Iris. *Cassandra who?* ill. by Normand Chartier. S&S, 1992. ISBN 0-671-70574-1 Subj: Animals – cats. Animals – pigs. Clothing. Parties.

I like a snack on an iceberg by Iris Hiskey Arno; ill. by John Sandford. HarperFestival, 1999. ISBN 0-694-01176-2 Subj: Animals. Food. Rhyming text.

The secret of the first one up ill. by Renée Graef. NorthWord, 2003. ISBN 1-55971-867-6 Subj: Animals – groundhogs. Holidays – Groundhog Day.

Hissey, Jane. *Hoot* ill. by author. Random House, 1997. Subj: Bedtime. Birds – owls. Night. Toys.

Jolly snow ill. by author. Putnam, 1991. ISBN 0-399-22131-X Subj: Activities – playing. Toys. Toys – bears. Weather – snow.

Jolly Tall ill. by author. Putnam, 1990. ISBN 0-399-21827-0 Subj: Activities – knitting. Toys. Toys – bears.

Little Bear lost ill. by author. Putnam, 1989. ISBN 0-399-21743-6 Subj: Behavior – lost & found possessions. Games. Toys. Toys – bears.

Little bear's bedtime ill. by author. Random House, 1992. ISBN 0-679-84176-8 Subj: Bedtime. Format, unusual – board books. Rhyming text. Toys – bears.

Little Bear's day ill. by author. Random House, 1993. ISBN 0-679-84175-X Subj: Format, unusual – board books. Rhyming text. Toys – bears.

Little Bear's trousers: an Old Bear story ill. by author. Putnam, 1990. ISBN 0-399-21493-3 Subj: Clothing – pants. Toys – bears.

Old Bear ill. by author. Philomel, 1986. ISBN 0-399-21401-1 Subj: Friendship. Toys. Toys – bears.

Old Bear [board book] ill. by author. 1st American board book ed. Philomel, 1997. ISBN 0-399-23205-2 Subj: Format, unusual – board books. Friendship. Toys. Toys – bears.

Old Bear, a pop-up book ill. by author; paper engineering by Dennis K. Meyer. Hutchinson, 1995. ISBN 0-09-176506-4 Subj: Format, unusual – toy & movable books. Toys. Toys – bears.

Ruff ill. by author. Random House, 1994. ISBN 0-679-86042-8 Subj: Birthdays. Parties. Toys.

Hittleman, Carol G. *A grand celebration: grandparents in poetry* (A grand celebration)

Hitz, Demi. *see* Demi

Ho, Minfong. *Brother Rabbit: a Cambodian tale* ill. by Jennifer Hewitson. Lothrop, 1997. ISBN 0-688-12553-0 Subj: Animals. Animals – rabbits. Folk & fairy tales. Foreign lands – Cambodia.

Hush! a Thai lullaby ill. by Holly Meade. Orchard, 1996. ISBN 0-531-08850-2 Subj: Animals. Caldecott award honor books. Family life – mothers. Foreign lands – Thailand. Lullabies. Noise, sounds.

Maples in the mist: children's poems from the Tang Dynasty ill. by Jean & Mou-Sien Tseng; trans. by Minfong Ho. Lothrop, 1996. ISBN 0-688-12044-X Subj: Foreign lands – China. Poetry.

The two brothers by Minfong Ho & Saphan Ros; ill. by Jean & Mou-Sien Tseng. Lothrop, 1995. ISBN 0-688-12551-4 Subj: Behavior – growing up. Folk & fairy tales. Foreign lands – Cambodia.

Hoban, Brom. *Skunk Lane* ill. by author. HarperCollins, 1983. ISBN 0-06-022348-0 Subj: Animals – skunks. Behavior – growing up. Songs.

Hoban, Julia. *Amy loves the rain* ill. by Lillian Hoban. Harper-Collins, 1989. ISBN 0-06-022358-8 Subj: Family life. Weather – rain.

Amy loves the snow ill. by Lillian Hoban. HarperCollins, 1989. ISBN 0-06-022395-2 Subj: Family life. Snowmen. Weather – snow.

Amy loves the sun ill. by Lillian Hoban. HarperCollins, 1988. ISBN 0-06-022397-9 Subj: Family life. Flowers.

Amy loves the wind ill. by Lillian Hoban. HarperCollins, 1988. ISBN 0-06-022403-7 Subj: Seasons – fall. Weather – wind.

Buzby to the rescue ill. by John Himmelman. HarperCollins, 1993. ISBN 0-06-021024-9 Subj: Activities – working. Animals – cats. Behavior – mistakes. Mystery stories.

Quick chick ill. by Lillian Hoban. Dutton, 1989. ISBN 0-525-44490-4 Subj: Animals. Birds – chickens. Farms. Names.

Hoban, Lillian. *Arthur's back to school day* ill. by author. Harper-Collins, 1996. ISBN 0-06-024956-0 Subj: Animals – chimpanzees. Family life – brothers & sisters. Food. Safety. School.

Arthur's birthday party ill. by author. HarperCollins, 1999. ISBN 0-06-027799-8 Subj: Animals – chimpanzees. Birthdays. Parties. Sports – gymnastics.

Arthur's Christmas cookies ill. by author. HarperCollins, 1972. ISBN 0-06-022368-5 Subj: Activities – baking, cooking. Animals – chimpanzees. Holidays – Christmas.

Arthur's funny money ill. by author. HarperCollins, 1981. ISBN 0-06-022344-8 Subj: Animals – chimpanzees. Money. Problem solving.

Arthur's great big Valentine ill. by author. HarperCollins, 1989. ISBN 0-06-022407-X Subj: Animals – chimpanzees. Emotions – anger. Friendship. Holidays – Valentine's Day.

Arthur's pen pal ill. by author. HarperCollins, 1976. ISBN 0-06-022372-3 Subj: Activities – writing. Animals – chimpanzees. Sibling rivalry.

Arthur's prize reader ill. by author. HarperCollins, 1978. ISBN 0-06-022380-4 Subj: Animals – chimpanzees. Books, reading. Family life.

Big Little Otter ill. by author. HarperCollins, 1997. ISBN 0-694-00850-8 Subj: Animals – otters. Behavior – growing up. Format, unusual – board books.

The case of the two masked robbers ill. by author. HarperCollins, 1986. ISBN 0-06-022299-9 Subj: Animals. Animals – raccoons. Eggs. Masks. Mystery stories.

Harry's song ill. by author. Greenwillow, 1980. ISBN 0-688-84220-8 Subj: Animals – rabbits. Songs.

Here come raccoons ill. by author. Holt, 1977. ISBN 0-03-017781-2 Subj: Animals – raccoons. Multiple births – twins.

It's really Christmas ill. by author. Greenwillow, 1982. ISBN 0-688-00831-3 Subj: Animals – mice. Behavior – wishing. Holidays – Christmas.

The laziest robot in zone one by Lillian & Phoebe Hoban; ill. by Lillian Hoban. HarperCollins, 1983. ISBN 0-06-022352-9 Subj: Animals – dogs. Behavior – lost. Robots.

Mr. Pig and family ill. by author. HarperCollins, 1980. ISBN 0-06-022384-7 Subj: Animals – pigs. Family life.

Mr. Pig and Sonny too ill. by author. HarperCollins, 1977. ISBN 0-06-022341-3 Subj: Animals – pigs. Sports – ice skating. Weddings.

No, no, Sammy Crow ill. by author. Greenwillow, 1981. ISBN 0-688-84297-6 Subj: Birds. Character traits – bravery. Family life – brothers & sisters.

Silly Tilly and the Easter bunny ill. by author. HarperCollins, 1987. ISBN 0-06-022693-6 Subj: Animals – moles. Holidays – Easter. Humorous stories.

Silly Tilly's Valentine ill. by author. HarperCollins, 1998. ISBN 0-06-027401-8 Subj: Animals – moles. Holidays – Valentine's Day. Memories, memory. Weather – snow.

Stick-in-the-mud turtle ill. by author. Greenwillow, 1977. ISBN 0-688-84045-0 Subj: Behavior – dissatisfaction. Poverty. Reptiles – turtles, tortoises.

The sugar snow spring ill. by author. HarperCollins, 1973. ISBN 0-06-022334-0 Subj: Animals – mice. Seasons – spring. Weather – cold. Weather – snow.

Turtle spring ill. by author. Greenwillow, 1978. ISBN 0-688-84136-8 Subj: Reptiles – turtles, tortoises. Seasons – spring.

Hoban, Phoebe. *The laziest robot in zone one* (Hoban, Lillian)

Hoban, Russell. *Ace Dragon Ltd.* ill. by Quentin Blake. Merrimack, 1981. ISBN 0-224-01706-3 Subj: Activities – flying. Dragons.

Arthur's new power ill. by Byron Barton. Crowell, 1978. ISBN 0-690-01371-X Subj: Progress. Reptiles – alligators, crocodiles.

A baby sister for Frances ill. by Lillian Hoban. HarperCollins, 1964. ISBN 0-06-022336-7 Subj: Animals – badgers. Behavior – running away. Emotions – envy, jealousy. Family life. Sibling rivalry.

A bargain for Frances ill. by Lillian Hoban. Harper, 1992. ISBN 0-06-022330-8 Subj: Animals – badgers. Friendship.

The battle of Zormla ill. by Colin McNaughton. Putnam, 1982. ISBN 0-399-61200-9 Subj: Sibling rivalry.

Bedtime for Frances ill. by Garth Williams. HarperCollins, 1995. ISBN 0-06-022351-0 Subj: Animals – badgers. Bedtime. Emotions – fear.

Best friends for Frances ill. by Lillian Hoban. HarperCollins, 1994. ISBN 0-06-022328-6 Subj: Animals – badgers. Family life – brothers. Family life – sisters. Friendship.

Big John Turkle ill. by Martin Baynton. Holt, 1984. ISBN 0-03-069499-X Subj: Character traits – meanness.

A birthday for Frances ill. by Lillian Hoban. HarperCollins, 1995. ISBN 0-06-022339-1 Subj: Animals – badgers. Birthdays. Emotions – envy, jealousy.

Bread and jam for Frances ill. by Lillian Hoban. HarperCollins, 1993. ISBN 0-06-022360-X Subj: Animals – badgers. Food. School.

Charlie Meadows ill. by Martin Baynton. Holt, 1984. ISBN 0-03-069502-3 Subj: Activities – dancing. Animals – mice. Birds – owls.

Charlie the tramp ill. by Lillian Hoban. Four Winds, 1967. Subj: Activities – working. Animals – beavers.

La corona and the tin frog ill. by Nicola Bayley. Merrimack, 1981. ISBN 0-224-01397-1 Subj: Emotions. Toys.

The dancing tigers ill. by David Gentleman. Merrimack, 1981. ISBN 0-224-01374-2 Subj: Activities – dancing. Animals – tigers. Sports – hunting.

Dinner at Alberta's ill. by James Marshall. Crowell, 1975. ISBN 0-690-23993-9 Subj: Behavior. Etiquette. Food. Reptiles – alligators, crocodiles.

Emmet Otter's jug-band Christmas ill. by Lillian Hoban. Parents' Magazine Pr., 1971. ISBN 0-819-30405-0 Subj: Animals – otters. Character traits – generosity. Holidays – Christmas. Music. Musical instruments – bands.

Flat cat ill. by Clive Scruton. Putnam, 1980. ISBN 0-399-61159-2 Subj: Animals – cats. Animals – mice. Animals – rats.

The flight of Bembel Rudzuk ill. by Colin McNaughton. Putnam, 1982. ISBN 0-399-61198-3 Subj: Imagination.

Goodnight ill. by Lillian Hoban. Norton, 1966. Subj: Bedtime. Emotions – fear. Imagination. Poetry.

The great gum drop robbery ill. by Colin McNaughton. Putnam, 1982. ISBN 0-399-61184-3 Subj: Imagination. Sibling rivalry.

Harvey's hideout ill. by Lillian Hoban. Four Winds, 1980, c1969. ISBN 0-590-07767-8 Subj: Animals – muskrats. Behavior – fighting, arguing. Family life – brothers. Family life – sisters.

How Tom beat Captain Najork and his hired sportsmen ill. by Quentin Blake. Atheneum, 1974. ISBN 0-689-30441-2 Subj: Behavior – misbehavior. Games.

Jim Frog ill. by Martin Baynton. Holt, 1984. ISBN 0-03-069501-5 Subj: Frogs & toads. Insects – beetles.

Jim's lion ill. by Ian Andrew. Candlewick, 2001. ISBN 0-7636-1175-1 Subj: Emotions – fear. Hospitals. Illness.

Lavina bat ill. by Martin Baynton. Holt, 1984. ISBN 0-03-069502-1 Subj: Animals – bats.

The little Brute family ill. by Lillian Hoban. Macmillan, 1966. ISBN 0-02-744110-5 Subj: Character traits – meanness. Etiquette.

The marzipan pig ill. by Quentin Blake. Farrar, 1987. ISBN 0-374-34859-6 Subj: Animals. Circular tales. Emotions. Food.

The mole family's Christmas ill. by Lillian Hoban. Four Winds, 1980, c1969. ISBN 0-590-07774-0 Subj: Animals – moles. Character traits – generosity. Holidays – Christmas.

Monsters ill. by Quentin Blake. Scholastic, 1989. ISBN 0-590-43422-5 Subj: Activities – drawing. Imagination. Monsters.

A near thing for Captain Najork ill. by Quentin Blake. Atheneum, 1976. ISBN 0-689-30503-6 Subj: Humorous stories. Self-concept.

Nothing to do ill. by Lillian Hoban. HarperCollins, 1964. Subj: Animals – possums. Behavior – boredom.

The rain door ill. by Quentin Blake. Crowell, 1987. ISBN 0-690-04577-8 Subj: Animals – horses, ponies. Animals – lions. Imagination. Weather – rain.

Some snow said hello ill. by Lillian Hoban. HarperCollins, 1963. Subj: Seasons – winter. Sibling rivalry. Weather – snow.

The sorely trying day ill. by Lillian Hoban. HarperCollins, 1964. Subj: Behavior – bad day. Behavior – fighting, arguing.

The stone doll of Sister Brute ill. by Lillian Hoban. Macmillan, 1968. Subj: Animals – dogs. Emotions. Toys – dolls.

Ten what? a mystery counting book by Russell Hoban & Sylvie Selig; ill. by authors. Scribners, 1974. ISBN 0-684-13400-4 Subj: Counting, numbers.

They came from Aargh! ill. by Colin McNaughton. Putnam, 1981. ISBN 0-399-61182-7 Subj: Family life. Sibling rivalry.

Tom and the two handles ill. by Lillian Hoban. HarperCollins, 1965. ISBN 0-06-022431-2 Subj: Behavior – fighting, arguing.

Trouble on Thunder Mountain ill. by Quentin Blake. Orchard, 2000. ISBN 0-531-30206-7 Subj: Dinosaurs. Mountains. Parks – amusement.

Hoban, Tana. *A B See!* photos by author. Greenwillow, 1982. ISBN 0-688-00833-X Subj: ABC books.

All about where photos by author. Greenwillow, 1991. ISBN 0-688-09698-0 Subj: Concepts. Language.

Big ones, little ones ill. by author. Greenwillow, 1976. ISBN 0-688-84040-X Subj: Animals. Concepts – size. Wordless.

Black on white photos by author. Greenwillow, 1993. ISBN 0-688-11918-2 Subj: Concepts. Wordless.

A children's zoo photos by author. Greenwillow, 1985. ISBN 0-688-05204-5 Subj: Animals. Birds. Zoos.

Circles, triangles, and squares ill. by author. Macmillan, 1974. ISBN 0-02-744830-4 Subj: Concepts – shape. Wordless.

Colors everywhere photos by author. Greenwillow, 1994. ISBN 0-688-12763-0 Subj: Concepts – color. Wordless.

Construction zone ill. by author. Greenwillow, 1997. ISBN 0-688-12285-X Subj: Activities – making things. Machines.

Count and see ill. by author. Macmillan, 1972. ISBN 0-02-744800-2 Subj: Counting, numbers.

Cubes, cones, cylinders and spheres photos by author. Greenwillow, 2000. ISBN 0-688-15326-7 Subj: Concepts – shape.

Dig, drill, dump, fill ill. by author. Greenwillow, 1975. ISBN 0-688-84016-7 Subj: Activities – digging. Machines. Wordless.

Dots, spots, speckles, and stripes photos by author. Greenwillow, 1987. ISBN 0-688-06863-4 Subj: Concepts. Concepts – color. Concepts – shape.

Exactly the opposite photos by author. Greenwillow, 1990. ISBN 0-688-08862-7 Subj: Concepts – opposites. Wordless.

I read signs photos by author. Greenwillow, 1983. ISBN 0-688-02318-5 Subj: Books, reading. Communication.

I read symbols photos by author. Greenwillow, 1983. ISBN 0-688-02332-0 Subj: Books, reading. Communication.

I walk and read photos by author. Greenwillow, 1984. ISBN 0-688-02576-5 Subj: Activities – walking. Books, reading.

Is it larger? Is it smaller? photos by author. Greenwillow, 1985. ISBN 0-688-04028-4 Subj: Concepts – size. Wordless.

Is it red? Is it yellow? Is it blue? photos by author. Greenwillow, 1978. ISBN 0-688-84171-6 Subj: Cities, towns. Concepts – color. Concepts – shape. Concepts – size. Wordless.

Is it rough? Is it smooth? Is it shiny? photos by author. Greenwillow, 1984. ISBN 0-688-03824-7 Subj: Concepts. Wordless.

Just look photos by author. Greenwillow, 1996. ISBN 0-688-14041-6 Subj: Format, unusual – toy & movable books. Wordless.

Let's count photos by author. Greenwillow, 1999. ISBN 0-688-16009-3 Subj: Counting, numbers.

Look again photos by author. Macmillan, 1971. ISBN 0-02-744050-8 Subj: Participation. Senses – sight. Wordless.

Look book photos by author. Greenwillow, 1997. ISBN 0-688-14972-3 Subj: Format, unusual – toy & movable books. Nature. Wordless.

Look! Look! Look! photos by author. Greenwillow, 1988. ISBN 0-688-07240-2 Subj: Concepts. Format, unusual. Wordless.

Look up, look down photos by author. Greenwillow, 1992. ISBN 0-688-10578-5 Subj: Concepts – up & down.

More, fewer, less photos by author. Greenwillow, 1998. ISBN 0-688-15694-0 Subj: Concepts. Counting, numbers. Wordless.

More than one photos by author. Greenwillow, 1981. ISBN 0-688-00597-7 Subj: Language.

Of colors and things photos by author. Greenwillow, 1989. ISBN 0-688-07535-5 Subj: Concepts – color.

One little kitten photos by author. Greenwillow, 1979. ISBN 0-688-80222-2 Subj: Animals – cats. Rhyming text.

1, 2, 3 photos by author. Greenwillow, 1985. ISBN 0-688-02579-X Subj: Counting, numbers. Format, unusual – board books. Wordless.

Over, under and through photos by author. Aladdin, 1987. ISBN 0-689-71111-5 Subj: Concepts.

Panda, panda ill. by author. Greenwillow, 1986. ISBN 0-688-06564-3 Subj: Animals – pandas. Format, unusual – board books.

Push-pull, empty-full: a book of opposites ill. by author. Collier, 1976, c1972. ISBN 0-02-043600-9 Subj: Concepts – opposites.

Red, blue, yellow shoe photos by author. Greenwillow, 1986. ISBN 0-688-06563-5 Subj: Concepts – color. Format, unusual – board books.

Round and round and round photos by author. Greenwillow, 1983. ISBN 0-688-01814-9 Subj: Concepts – shape.

Shadows and reflections photos by author. Greenwillow, 1990. ISBN 0-688-07090-6 Subj: Shadows. Wordless.

Shapes and things ill. by author. Macmillan, 1970. ISBN 0-02-744060-5 Subj: Concepts – shape. Wordless.

Shapes, shapes, shapes photos by author. Greenwillow, 1985. ISBN 0-688-05833-7 Subj: Concepts – shape. Wordless.

So many circles, so many squares photos by author. Greenwillow, 1998. ISBN 0-688-15166-3 Subj: Concepts – shape. Wordless.

Spirals, curves, fanshapes and lines photos by author. Greenwillow, 1992. ISBN 0-688-11229-3 Subj: Concepts – shape. Concepts – size. Wordless.

Take another look photos by author. Greenwillow, 1981. ISBN 0-688-84298-4 Subj: Concepts. Wordless.

26 letters and 99 cents photos by author. Greenwillow, 1987. ISBN 0-688-06362-4 Subj: ABC books. Counting, numbers. Format, unusual.

What is it? photos by author. Greenwillow, 1985. ISBN 0-688-02577-3 Subj: Format, unusual – board books. Wordless.

What is that? photos by author. Greenwillow, 1994. ISBN 0-688-12920-X Subj: Format, unusual – board books. Wordless.

Where is it? ill. by author. Macmillan, 1974. ISBN 0-02-744070-2 Subj: Animals – rabbits. Participation. Rhyming text.

White on black photos by author. Greenwillow, 1993. ISBN 0-688-11919-0 Subj: Concepts. Format, unusual – board books.

Who are they? photos by author. Greenwillow, 1994. ISBN 0-688-12921-8 Subj: Animals. Format, unusual – board books. Wordless.

Hobbie, Holly. *Toot and Puddle* ill. by author. Little, 1997. ISBN 0-316-36552-1 Subj: Activities – traveling. Animals – pigs. Friendship. Letters, cards.

Toot and Puddle, a present for Toot ill. by author. Little, 1998. ISBN 0-316-36556-4 Subj: Animals – pigs. Birthdays. Gifts.

Toot and Puddle, I'll be home for Christmas ill. by author. Little, 2001. ISBN 0-316-36623-4 Subj: Activities – traveling. Animals – pigs. Holidays – Christmas. Weather – blizzards. Weather – snow. Weather – storms.

Toot and Puddle, Puddle's ABC ill. by author. Little, 2000. ISBN 0-316-36593-9 Subj: ABC books. Animals – pigs.

Toot and Puddle, top of the world ill. by author. Little, 2002. ISBN 0-316-36513-0 Subj: Activities – traveling. Animals – pigs. Foreign lands – France. Foreign lands – Nepal. Friendship.

Toot and Puddle, you are my sunshine ill. by author. Little, 1999. ISBN 0-316-36562-9 Subj: Animals – pigs. Emotions. Friendship. Weather – lightning, thunder. Weather – storms.

Hobbs, Will. *Beardream* ill. by Jill Kastner. Atheneum, 1997. ISBN 0-689-31973-8 Subj: Activities – dancing. Animals – bears. Folk & fairy tales. Hibernation. Indians of North America – Ute.

Howling Hill ill. by Jill Kastner. Morrow, 1998. ISBN 0-688-15430-1 Subj: Animals – bears. Animals – wolves. Behavior – growing up. Behavior – lost. Emotions – loneliness.

Hoberman, Mary Ann. *And to think that we thought that we'd never be friends* ill. by Kevin Hawkes. Crown, 1999. ISBN 0-517-80070-5 Subj: Family life – brothers & sisters. Friendship. Rhyming text.

Bill Grogan's goat ill. by Nadine Bernard Westcott. Little, 2002. ISBN 0-316-36232-8 Subj: Animals – goats. Music. Songs. Trains.

The cozy book ill. by Tony Chen. Viking, 1982. ISBN 0-670-24447-3 Subj: Poetry.

Fathers, mothers, sisters, brothers ill. by Marylin Hafner. Little, 1991. ISBN 0-316-36736-2 Subj: Family life. Poetry.

A fine fat pig and other animal poems ill. by Malcah Zeldis. Harper-Collins, 1991. ISBN 0-06-022426-6 Subj: Animals. Poetry.

A house is a house for me ill. by Betty Fraser. Viking, 1978. ISBN 0-670-38016-4 Subj: Homes, houses. Rhyming text.

How do I go? by Mary Ann & Norman Hoberman; ill. by authors. Little, 1958. Subj: Transportation.

I like old clothes ill. by Jacqueline Chwast. Knopf, 1976. ISBN 0-394-93092-4 Subj: Clothing. Rhyming text.

"It's simple," said Simon ill. by Meilo So. Knopf, 2001. ISBN 0-375-91201-0 Subj: Animals. Animals – tigers. Humorous stories.

The looking book ill. by Laura Huliska-Beith. Little, 2002. ISBN 0-316-36328-6 Subj: Animals – cats. Behavior – lost & found possessions. Counting, numbers. Rhyming text.

Marvelous mouse man ill. by Laura Forman. Harcourt, 2002. ISBN 0-15-201715-1 Subj: Animals – mice. Behavior – trickery. Folk & fairy tales. Foreign lands – Germany. Rhyming text.

Mary had a little lamb ill. by Nadine Bernard Westcott. Little, 2003. ISBN 0-316-60687-1 Subj: Animals – sheep. Nursery rhymes. Songs.

Miss Mary Mack ill. by Nadine Bernard Westcott. Little, 1998. ISBN 0-316-93118-7 Subj: Animals – elephants. Nursery rhymes.

Mr. and Mrs. Muddle ill. by Catharine O'Neill. Little, 1988. ISBN 0-316-36735-4 Subj: Animals – horses, ponies. Sports.

Nuts to you and nuts to me: an alphabet of poems ill. by Ronni Solbert. Knopf, 1974. ISBN 0-394-92742-7 Subj: ABC books. Poetry.

One of each ill. by Marjorie Priceman. Little, 1997. ISBN 0-316-36731-1 Subj: Animals – dogs. Behavior – sharing. Friendship. Rhyming text.

Right outside my window ill. by Nicholas Wilton. Mondo, 2002. ISBN 1-59034-194-5 Subj: Rhyming text. Seasons.

The seven silly eaters ill. by Marla Frazee. Harcourt, 1997. ISBN 0-15-200096-8 Subj: Birthdays. Family life – brothers & sisters. Family life – mothers. Food. Rhyming text.

The two sillies ill. by Lynne Cravath. Harcourt, 2000. ISBN 0-15-202221-X Subj: Animals – cats. Animals – mice. Rhyming text.

Hoberman, Norman. *How do I go?* (Hoberman, Mary Ann)

Hobson, Bruce. *see* Mwenye Hadithi

Hobson, Laura Z. *"I'm going to have a baby!"* ill. by May Kirkham. John Day, 1967. Subj: Babies. Birth. Family life – new sibling.

Hobzek, Mildred. *We came a-marching . . . 1, 2, 3* ill. by William Pène Du Bois. Parents' Magazine Pr., 1978. ISBN 0-8193-0975-3 Subj: Folk & fairy tales. Songs.

Hodeir, André. *Warwick's 3 bottles* by André Hodeir & Tomi Ungerer; ill. by Tomi Ungerer. Grove Pr., 1966. Subj: Behavior – misbehavior. Country. Reptiles – alligators, crocodiles.

Hodge, Deborah. *Ants* ill. by Julian Mulock. Kids Can, 2004. ISBN 1-55337-066-X Subj: Insects – ants. Science.

Bears ill. by Pat Stephens. Kids Can, 1997. ISBN 1-55074-269-8 Subj: Animals – bears. Animals – polar bears. Science.

Beavers ill. by Pat Stephens. Kids Can, 1998. ISBN 1-55074-429-1 Subj: Animals – beavers.

Bees ill. by Julian Mulock. Kids Can, 2004. ISBN 1-55337-065-1 Subj: Insects – bees. Science.

Deer, moose, elk and caribou ill. by Pat Stephens. Kids Can, 1998. ISBN 1-55074-435-6 Subj: Animals. Animals – deer. Animals – elk. Animals – moose. Animals – reindeer.

Eagles ill. by Nancy Gray Ogle. Kids Can, 2000. ISBN 1-55074-715-0 Subj: Birds – eagles. Science.

Emma's story ill. by Song Nan Zhang. Tundra, 2003. ISBN 0-88776-632-3 Subj: Adoption. Family life. Foreign lands – Canada. Foreign lands – China. Self-concept.

Salmon ill. by Nancy Gray Ogle. Kids Can, 2002. ISBN 1-55074-961-7 Subj: Fish. Science.

Wild cats: cougars, bobcats and lynx ill. by Nancy Gray Ogle. Kids Can, 1997. ISBN 1-55074-267-1 Subj: Animals – bobcats. Animals – cats. Animals – cougars. Animals – lynx.

Hodges, Margaret. *Buried moon* ill. by Jamichael Henterly. Little, 1990. ISBN 0-316-36793-1 Subj: Folk & fairy tales. Forest, woods. Moon.

Comus adapt. by Margaret Hodges from A masque at Ludlow Castle by John Milton; ill. by Trina Schart Hyman. Holiday, 1996. ISBN 0-8234-1146-X Subj: Careers – magicians. Family life – brothers & sisters. Folk & fairy tales. Forest, woods. Magic. Mythical creatures. Theater.

The fire bringer: a Paiute Indian legend ill. by Peter Parnall. Little, 1972. ISBN 0-316-36783-4 Subj: Folk & fairy tales. Indians of North America – Paiute.

The golden deer ill. by Daniel San Souci. Scribners, 1992. ISBN 0-684-19218-7 Subj: Animals – deer. Character traits – kindness to animals. Foreign lands – India. Religion. Sports – hunting.

The hero of Bremen ill. by Charles Mikolaycak. Holiday, 1993. ISBN 0-8234-0934-1 Subj: Careers – shoemakers. Folk & fairy tales. Foreign lands – Germany. Handicaps – physical handicaps. Knights. War.

Hidden in sand ill. by Paul Birling. Scribners, 1994. ISBN 0-684-19559-3 Subj: Character traits – persistence. Folk & fairy tales. Foreign lands – India.

The kitchen knight ill. by Trina Schart Hyman. Holiday, 1990. ISBN 0-8234-0787-X Subj: Behavior – fighting, arguing. Emotions – love. Folk & fairy tales. Knights. Middle Ages.

The legend of Saint Christopher: from the Golden legend Englished by William Caxton, 1483 ill. by Richard Jesse Watson. Eerdmans, 2002. ISBN 0-8028-5077-4 Subj: Activities – traveling. Religion.

Molly Limbo ill. by Elizabeth J. Miles. Atheneum, 1996. ISBN 0-689-80581-0 Subj: Foreign lands – England. Ghosts. Homes, houses.

Moses ill. by Mike Wimmer. Harcourt, 1999. ISBN 0-15-200946-9 Subj: Religion – Moses.

Saint Christopher ill. by Richard Jesse Watson. Eerdmans, 1997. ISBN 0-8028-5077-4 Subj: Religion.

Saint George and the dragon ill. by Trina Schart Hyman. Little, 1984. ISBN 0-316-36789-3 Subj: Caldecott award books. Dragons. Folk & fairy tales. Foreign lands – England. Middle Ages.

St. Jerome and the lion ill. by Barry Moser. Orchard, 1991. ISBN 0-531-08538-4 Subj: Animals – lions. Character traits – kindness to animals. Folk & fairy tales. Religion.

Saint Patrick and the peddler ill. by Paul Brett Johnson. Orchard, 1993. ISBN 0-531-05489-6 Subj: Character traits – generosity. Character traits – luck. Folk & fairy tales. Foreign lands – Ireland. Ghosts.

Silent night: the song and its story ill. by Tim Ladwig. Eerdmans, 1997. ISBN 0-8028-5138-X Subj: Family life. Holidays – Christmas. Music. Songs.

Up the chimney ill. by Amanda Harvey. Holiday, 1998. ISBN 0-8234-1354-3 Subj: Family life – sisters. Folk & fairy tales. Foreign lands – England. Witches.

The voice of the great bell by Lafcadio Hearn; retold by Margaret Hodges; ill. by Ed Young. Little, 1989. ISBN 0-316-36791-5 Subj: Folk & fairy tales. Foreign lands – China.

The wave ill. by Blair Lent. Houghton Mifflin, 1964. ISBN 0-395-06817-7 Subj: Caldecott award honor books. Folk & fairy tales. Foreign lands – Japan. Tsunamis.

Hodgetts, Blake Christopher. *Dream of the dinosaurs* ill. by Victoria Hodgetts. Doubleday, 1978. ISBN 0-385-12139-3 Subj: Dinosaurs. Dreams. Prehistory.

Hoe, Susan. *Which shoes would you choose?* ill. by Mircea Catusanu. Innovative KIDS, 2002. ISBN 1-58476-102-4 Subj: Clothing – shoes. Format, unusual – board books.

Hoestlandt, Jo. *Star of fear, star of hope* ill. by Johanna Kang; trans. from French by Mark Polizzotti. Walker, 1995. ISBN 0-8027-8374-0 Subj: Foreign lands – France. Friendship. Holocaust. Jewish culture. War.

Hoff, Carol. *The four friends* ill. by Jim Ponter. Follett, 1958. Subj: Animals. Animals – mice.

Hoff, Syd. *Albert the albatross* ill. by author. HarperCollins, 1961. ISBN 0-06-022446-0 Subj: Birds – albatrosses. Sea & seashore.

Arturo's baton ill. by author. Clarion, 1995. ISBN 0-395-71020-0 Subj: Behavior – lost & found possessions. Careers – musicians. Music. Musical instruments – orchestras.

Barkley ill. by author. HarperCollins, 1975. ISBN 0-06-022448-7 Subj: Animals – dogs. Circus. Old age.

Bernard on his own ill. by author. Clarion, 1993. ISBN 0-395-65226-X Subj: Animals – bears. Behavior – lost.

Captain Cat ill. by author. HarperCollins, 1993. ISBN 0-06-020528-8 Subj: Animals – cats. Careers – military.

Chester ill. by author. HarperCollins, 1961. ISBN 0-06-022456-8 Subj: Animals – horses, ponies.

Danny and the dinosaur go to camp ill. by author. HarperCollins, 1996. ISBN 0-06-026440-3 Subj: Camps, camping. Dinosaurs. Prehistory.

Grizzwold ill. by author. HarperCollins, 1963. ISBN 0-06-022481-9 Subj: Animals – bears. Ecology.

Happy birthday, Danny and the dinosaur! ill. by author. HarperCollins, 1995. ISBN 0-06-026438-1 Subj: Birthdays. Dinosaurs. Friendship. Prehistory.

Happy birthday, Henrietta! ill. by author. Garrard, 1983. ISBN 0-8116-4423-5 Subj: Animals – goats. Animals – pigs. Birds – chickens. Birthdays.

Henrietta, circus star ill. by author. Garrard, 1978. ISBN 0-8116-4413-8 Subj: Birds – chickens. Circus.

Henrietta goes to the fair ill. by author. Garrard, 1979. ISBN 0-8116-4416-2 Subj: Birds – chickens. Fairs, festivals.

Henrietta, the early bird ill. by author. Garrard, 1978. ISBN 0-8116-4410-3 Subj: Behavior – mistakes. Birds – chickens. Time.

Henrietta's Halloween ill. by author. Garrard, 1980. ISBN 0-8116-4421-9 Subj: Birds – chickens. Holidays – Halloween. Parties.

The horse in Harry's room ill. by author. HarperCollins, 1970. ISBN 0-06-022483-5 Subj: Animals – horses, ponies. Imagination – imaginary friends.

Julius ill. by author. HarperCollins, 1959. ISBN 0-06-022490-8 Subj: Animals – gorillas.

Lengthy ill. by author. Putnam, 1964. ISBN 0-399-20704-X Subj: Animals – dogs.

The lighthouse children ill. by author. HarperCollins, 1994. ISBN 0-06-022959-4 Subj: Birds – seagulls. Lighthouses.

The littlest leaguer ill. by author. Dutton, 1976. ISBN 0-525-61536-9 Subj: Character traits – smallness. Games. Sports – baseball.

Merry Christmas, Henrietta! ill. by author. Garrard, 1980. ISBN 0-8116-4419-7 Subj: Birds – chickens. Holidays – Christmas. Stores.

Mrs. Brice's mice ill. by author. HarperCollins, 1988. ISBN 0-06-022452-5 Subj: Animals – mice. Character traits – being different. Pets.

My Aunt Rosie ill. by author. HarperCollins, 1972. ISBN 0-06-022503-3 Subj: Family life – aunts, uncles.

Oliver ill. by author. HarperCollins, 1960. ISBN 0-06-022516-5 Subj: Animals – elephants. Character traits – optimism. Circus.

Sammy the seal ill. by author. HarperCollins, 1959. ISBN 0-06-022526-2 Subj: Animals – seals. Zoos.

Santa's moose ill. by author. HarperCollins, 1988, 1979. ISBN 0-06-022506-8 Subj: Animals – moose. Holidays – Christmas. Santa Claus.

Slithers ill. by author. Putnam, 1968. Subj: Reptiles – snakes.

Slugger Sal's slump ill. by author. Dutton, 1979. ISBN 0-525-61590-3 Subj: Character traits – perseverance. Sports – baseball.

Stanley ill. by author. HarperCollins, 1992. ISBN 0-06-022536-X Subj: Cavemen. Character traits – confidence. Homes, houses.

A walk past Ellen's house ill. by author. McGraw-Hill, 1973. ISBN 0-07-029176-4 Subj: Emotions – embarrassment.

Walpole ill. by author. HarperCollins, 1977. ISBN 0-06-022544-0 Subj: Animals – walruses.

When will it snow? ill. by Mary Chalmers. HarperCollins, 1971. ISBN 0-06-022554-8 Subj: Seasons – winter. Weather – snow.

Where's Prancer? ill. by author. HarperCollins, 1997. ISBN 0-06-027601-0 Subj: Animals – reindeer. Holidays – Christmas. Santa Claus.

Who will be my friends? ill. by author. HarperCollins, 1960. ISBN 0-06-022556-4 Subj: Friendship. Moving.

Hoffman, Alice. *Fireflies* ill. by Wayne McLoughlin. Hyperion, 1997. ISBN 0-7868-2180-9 Subj: Animals – wolves. Handicaps. Insects – fireflies. Seasons – winter.

Hoffman, Christine. *Sewing by hand* ill. by Harriett Barton. HarperCollins, 1994. ISBN 0-06-021147-4 Subj: Activities – sewing.

Hoffman, Don. *Billy is a big boy* ill. by Todd Dakins. Popcorn, 2000. ISBN 0-97025-180-7 Subj: Behavior – growing up.

A counting book with Billy and Abigail ill. by Todd Dakins. Dalmation, 2004. ISBN 1-4037-0543-7 Subj: Counting, numbers. Format, unusual – board books. Rhyming text.

Good morning, good night Billy and Abigail ill. by Todd Dakins. Dalmation, 2004. ISBN 1-4037-0542-9 Subj: Family life. Format, unusual – board books. Morning. Night. Rhyming text.

Hoffman, Elizabeth Stokes. *Miss Renée's mice* ill. by Dawn Peterson. Down East, 2001. ISBN 0-89272-505-2 Subj: Animals – mice. Homes, houses.

Miss Renée's mice go to an exhibition ill. by Dawn Peterson. Down East, 2003. ISBN 0-89272-581-8 Subj: Animals – mice. Country. Fairs, festivals.

Hoffman, Eric. *No fair to tigers = No es justo para los tigres* ill. by Janice Lee Porter; trans. by Carmen Sosa-Masso. Redleaf, 1999. ISBN 1-884834-62-0 Subj: Animals – tigers. Foreign languages. Handicaps – physical handicaps. Toys.

Play Lady = La Señora Juguetona ill. by Suzanne Tornquist; trans. by Carmen Sosa-Masso. Redleaf, 1999. ISBN 1-884834-61-2 Subj: Crime. Foreign languages. Gardens, gardening. Prejudice.

Hoffman, Joan. *My friend goes left* (Gregorich, Barbara)

Hoffman, Mary. *Amazing Grace* ill. by Caroline Binch. Dial, 1991. ISBN 0-8037-1040-2 Subj: Ethnic groups in the U.S. – African Americans. School. Self-concept. Theater.

An angel just like me ill. by Cornelius Van Wright & Ying-Hwa Hu. Dial, 1997. ISBN 0-8037-2265-6 Subj: Angels. Ethnic groups in the U.S. – African Americans. Holidays – Christmas.

Animals in the wild: elephant ill. by author. Random House, 1984. ISBN 0-394-86553-7 Subj: Animals – elephants. Science.

Animals in the wild: monkey ill. by author. Random House, 1984. ISBN 0-394-86554-5 Subj: Animals – monkeys. Science.

Animals in the wild: panda ill. by author. Random House, 1984. ISBN 0-394-86555-3 Subj: Animals – pandas. Science.

Animals in the wild: tiger ill. by author. Random House, 1984. ISBN 0-394-86556-1 Subj: Animals – tigers. Science.

Clever Katya ill. by Marie Cameron. Barefoot, 1998. ISBN 1-901223-64-7 Subj: Animals – horses, ponies. Folk & fairy tales. Foreign lands – Russia. Riddles & jokes. Royalty – tsars.

Grace and family ill. by Caroline Binch. Frances Lincoln, 1995. ISBN 0-7112-0868-9 Subj: Ethnic groups in the U.S. – African Americans. Family life. Foreign lands – Gambia.

Henry's baby ill. by Susan Winter. DK, 1993. ISBN 1-56458-196-9 Subj: Babies. Clubs, gangs. Family life – brothers.

Miracles: wonders Jesus worked ill. by Jackie Morris. Fogelman, 2001. ISBN 0-8037-2610-4 Subj: Religion.

Parables, stories Jesus told ill. by Jackie Morris. Fogelman, 2000. ISBN 0-8037-2560-4 Subj: Religion.

Three wise women ill. by Lynne Russell. Fogelman, 1999. ISBN 0-8037-2466-7 Subj: Character traits – wisdom. Holidays – Christmas. Religion – Nativity. Stars.

Hoffman, Phyllis. *Baby's first year* ill. by Sarah Wilson. HarperCollins, 1988. ISBN 0-06-022552-1 Subj: Babies. Behavior – growing up.

Meatball ill. by Emily Arnold McCully. HarperCollins, 1991. ISBN 0-06-022564-5 Subj: Ethnic groups in the U.S. Friendship. School.

Steffie and me ill. by Emily Arnold McCully. HarperCollins, 1970. Subj: Ethnic groups in the U.S. – African Americans. Family life. Friendship. School.

The ugly duckling (Andersen, H. C. [Hans Christian])

We play ill. by Sarah Wilson. HarperCollins, 1990. ISBN 0-06-022558-0 Subj: Activities – playing. Rhyming text. School.

Hoffman, Rosekrans. *Sister Sweet Ella* ill. by author. Morrow, 1981. ISBN 0-688-00866-6 Subj: Babies. Emotions – envy, jealousy. Family life – brothers & sisters. Family life – new sibling. Magic.

Hoffmann, E. T. A. *The nutcracker* retold by Jean Richardson; ill. by Francesca Crespi. Arcade, 1990. ISBN 1-55970-105-6 Subj: Activities – dancing. Animals – mice. Ballet. Careers – toy makers. Folk & fairy tales. Holidays – Christmas. Imagination. Royalty. Toys.

The nutcracker adapt. by Janet Schulman; ill. by Renée Graef. HarperCollins, 1999. ISBN 0-06-027814-5 Subj: Activities – dancing. Animals – mice. Ballet. Careers – toy makers. Folk & fairy tales. Holidays – Christmas. Imagination. Royalty. Toys.

The nutcracker retold & ill. by Rachel Isadora. Macmillan, 1981. Adapt. of Nussknacker und Mausekönig. ISBN 0-02-747470-4 Subj: Activities – dancing. Animals – mice. Ballet. Careers – toy makers. Folk & fairy tales. Holidays – Christmas. Imagination. Royalty. Toys.

The nutcracker retold by David Freeman; ill. by Joanna Isles. Pavilion, 1996. ISBN 1-85793-545-4 Subj: Activities – dancing. Animals – mice. Ballet. Careers – toy makers. Folk & fairy tales. Holidays – Christmas. Imagination. Royalty. Toys.

The nutcracker trans. by Ralph Manheim; ill. by Maurice Sendak. Crown, 1984. ISBN 0-517-55285-X Subj: Activities – dancing. Animals – mice. Ballet. Careers – toy makers. Folk & fairy tales. Holidays – Christmas. Imagination. Royalty. Theater.

The nutcracker retold by Anthea Bell; ill. by Lisbeth Zwerger. Picture Book Studio, 1987. ISBN 0-88708-051-0 Subj: Activities – dancing. Animals – mice. Ballet. Careers – toy makers. Folk & fairy tales. Holidays – Christmas. Imagination. Royalty. Toys.

The nutcracker ballet retold by Deborah Hautzig; ill. by Carolyn Ewing. Random House, 1992. ISBN 0-679-92385-3 Subj: Activities – dancing. Animals – mice. Ballet. Careers – toy makers. Folk & fairy tales. Holidays – Christmas. Imagination. Royalty. Toys.

The nutcracker ballet retold & ill. by Vladimir Vasilévich Vagin. Scholastic, 1995. ISBN 0-590-47220-8 Subj: Activities – dancing. Animals – mice. Ballet. Careers – toy makers. Folk & fairy tales. Holidays – Christmas. Imagination. Royalty. Toys.

The strange child trans. & adapt. by Anthea Bell; ill. by Lisbeth Zwerger. Picture Book Studio, 1984. Adapt. of Das fremde Kind. ISBN 0-907234-60-7 Subj: Death. Emotions – grief. Family life. Folk & fairy tales. Magic.

Hoffmann, Felix. *Hans in luck* (Grimm, Jacob)

The story of Christmas ill. by author. Atheneum, 1975. ISBN 0-689-50031-9 Subj: Holidays – Christmas. Religion – Nativity.

Hofmeyr, Dianne. *The stone: a Persian legend of the Magi* ill. by Jude Daly. Farrar, 1998. ISBN 0-374-37198-9 Subj: Folk & fairy tales. Foreign lands – Iran. Religion – Nativity.

The star-bearer ill. by Jude Daly. Farrar, 2001. ISBN 0-374-37181-4 Subj: Creation. Foreign lands – Egypt.

Hofsepian, Sylvia A. *Why not?* ill. by Friso Henstra. Four Winds, 1991. ISBN 0-02-743980-1 Subj: Animals – cats. Emotions – loneliness.

Hofstrand, Mary. *Albion pig* ill. by author. Knopf, 1984. ISBN 0-394-96255-9 Subj: Animals – pigs. Rhyming text.

By the sea ill. by author. Atheneum, 1989. ISBN 0-689-31421-3 Subj: Animals – pigs. Family life. Rhyming text. Sea & seashore.

Hogan, Bernice. *My grandmother died but I won't forget her* ill. by Nancy Munger. Abingdon, 1983. ISBN 0-687-27548-2 Subj: Death. Emotions – grief. Family life – grandmothers.

Hogan, Inez. *About Nono, the baby elephant* ill. by author. Dutton, 1947. Subj: Animals – elephants. Behavior – misbehavior. Names.

Hogan, Kirk. *The hospital scares me* (Hogan, Paula Z.)

Hogan, Paula Z. *The black swan* ill. by Kinuko Y. Craft. Raintree, 1979. ISBN 0-8172-1254-X Subj: Birds – swans. Science.

The butterfly ill. by Geri K. Strigenz. Raintree, 1979. ISBN 0-8172-1252-3 Subj: Insects – butterflies, caterpillars. Metamorphosis. Science.

The dandelion ill. by Yoshi Miyake. Raintree, 1979. ISBN 0-8172-1250-7 Subj: Plants. Science.

The frog ill. by Geri K. Strigenz. Raintree, 1979. ISBN 0-8172-1253-1 Subj: Frogs & toads. Science.

The honeybee ill. by Geri K. Strigenz. Raintree, 1979. ISBN 0-8172-1256-6 Subj: Insects – bees. Science.

The hospital scares me by Paula Z. Hogan & Kirk Hogan; ill. by Mary Thelen. Raintree, 1980. ISBN 0-8172-1351-1 Subj: Ethnic groups in the U.S. Ethnic groups in the U.S. – African Americans. Hospitals. Illness.

The oak tree ill. by Kinuko Y. Craft. Raintree, 1979. ISBN 0-8172-1251-5 Subj: Science. Trees.

The penguin ill. by Geri K. Strigenz. Raintree, 1979. ISBN 0-8172-1257-4 Subj: Birds – penguins. Science.

The salmon ill. by Yoshi Miyake. Raintree, 1979. ISBN 0-8172-1255-8 Subj: Fish. Science.

Högner, Franz. *From blueprint to house* ill. by author. Carolrhoda, 1986. ISBN 0-87614-295-1 Subj: Homes, houses.

Hogrogian, Nonny. *Carrot cake* ill. by author. Greenwillow, 1977. ISBN 0-688-84061-2 Subj: Animals – rabbits. Behavior. Character traits – compromising. Character traits – shyness. Weddings.

The cat who loved to sing ill. by author. Knopf, 1988. ISBN 0-394-99004-8 Subj: Animals – cats. Cumulative tales. Folk & fairy tales. Songs.

Cinderella (Grimm, Jacob)

The contest ill. by author. Greenwillow, 1976. ISBN 0-688-84042-6 Subj: Caldecott award honor books. Crime. Folk & fairy tales. Foreign lands – Armenia.

The devil with the green hairs (Grimm, Jacob)

The first Christmas ill. by author. Greenwillow, 1995. ISBN 0-688-13580-3 Subj: Holidays – Christmas. Religion – Nativity.

The glass mountain (Grimm, Jacob)

The hermit and Harry and me ill. by author. Little, 1972. Subj: Behavior – indifference. Friendship.

Noah's ark ill. by author. Knopf, 1986. ISBN 0-394-98191-X Subj: Animals. Boats, ships. Religion – Noah. Weather – floods. Weather – rain. Weather – rainbows.

One fine day ill. by Nonny Hogrogian. Macmillan, 1971. ISBN 0-606-01196-X Subj: Animals – foxes. Caldecott award books. Cumulative tales.

Rooster brother ill. by author. Macmillan, 1974. ISBN 0-02-743990-9 Subj: Behavior – stealing. Character traits – cleverness. Crime. Folk & fairy tales.

The tiger of Turkestan ill. by author. Hampton Roads, 2002. ISBN 1-57174-308-1 Subj: Animals – tigers. Character traits – individuality.

Hoguet, Susan Ramsay. *I unpacked my grandmother's trunk: a picture book game* ill. by author. Dutton, 1983. ISBN 0-525-44069-0 Subj: ABC books. Cumulative tales. Games.

Höjer, Dan. *Heart of mine* by Dan Höjer & Lotta Höjer; ill. by authors; tr. by Elisabeth Kallick Dyssegaard. R&S Books, 2001. ISBN 91-29-65301-0 Subj: Adoption. Babies. Family life. Foreign lands.

Höjer, Lotta. *Heart of mine* (Höjer, Dan)

Hoke, Helen L. *The biggest family in the town* ill. by Vance Locke. McKay, 1947. Subj: Family life.

Hol, Coby. *Henrietta saves the show* ill. by author. North-South, 1991. ISBN 1-55858-102-2 Subj: Animals – horses, ponies. Circus.

Lisa and the snowman ill. by author. North-South, 1989. ISBN 1-55858-022-0 Subj: Seasons – winter. Snowmen.

Niki's little donkey ill. by author; trans. by J. Alison James. North-South, 1993. ISBN 1-55858-183-9 Subj: Animals – donkeys. Character traits – kindness to animals. Family life – grandmothers. Foreign lands – Greece.

Tippy Bear and little Sam ill. by author. North-South, 1992. Tr. of: Taps, der Bär, besucht den kleinen Jan. ISBN 1-55858-149-9 Subj: Animals – bears. Babies. Family life.

Tippy Bear goes to a party ill. by author. North-South, 1991. ISBN 1-55858-129-4 Subj: Animals – bears. Parties.

Tippy Bear hunts for honey ill. by author. North-South, 1991. ISBN 1-55858-128-6 Subj: Animals – bears. Character traits – helpfulness.

Tippy Bear's Christmas ill. by author. North-South, 1992. ISBN 1-55858-157-X Subj: Animals. Animals – bears. Holidays – Christmas.

A visit to the farm ill. by author. North-South, 1989. ISBN 1-55858-000-X Subj: Animals. Farms.

Holabird, Katharine. *Alexander and the dragon* ill. by Helen Craig. Potter/Crown, 1988. ISBN 0-517-56996-5 Subj: Bedtime. Behavior – fighting, arguing. Dragons. Friendship.

Alexander and the magic boat ill. by Helen Craig. Crown, 1990. ISBN 0-517-58149-3 Subj: Activities – traveling. Boats, ships. Family life. Imagination.

Angelina and Alice ill. by Helen Craig. Potter/Crown, 1987. ISBN 0-517-56074-7 Subj: Animals – mice. Friendship. School.

Angelina and Henry ill. by Helen Craig. Pleasant, 2002. ISBN 1-58485-523-1 Subj: Animals – mice. Behavior – lost. Camps, camping. Family life – aunts, uncles. Forest, woods.

Angelina and the princess ill. by Helen Craig. Crown, 1984. ISBN 0-517-55273-6 Subj: Activities – dancing. Animals – mice. Ballet.

Angelina at the fair ill. by Helen Craig. Crown, 1985. ISBN 0-517-55744-4 Subj: Animals – mice. Fairs, festivals. Friendship.

Angelina ballerina ill. by Helen Craig. 3rd ed. Pleasant, 2004. ISBN 1-58485-952-0 Subj: Activities – dancing. Animals – mice. Ballet.

Angelina dances ill. by Helen Craig. Random House, 1992. ISBN 0-679-83484-2 Subj: Activities – dancing. Animals – mice. Ballet. Format, unusual – board books.

Angelina ice skates ill. by Helen Craig. 2nd ed. Pleasant, 2001. ISBN 1-58485-146-5 Subj: Animals – mice. Holidays – New Year's. Sports – ice skating. Theater.

Angelina on stage ill. by Helen Craig. Crown, 1986. ISBN 0-517-56073-9 Subj: Activities – dancing. Animals – mice. Ballet. Theater.

Angelina's baby sister ill. by Helen Craig. Pleasant, 2000. ISBN 1-58485-132-5 Subj: Animals – mice. Babies. Family life – new sibling. Family life – sisters. Sibling rivalry.

Angelina's ballet class ill. by Catherine Kanner based on the ill. by Helen Craig. Pleasant, 2001. ISBN 0-613-49711-2 Subj: Activities – dancing. Animals – mice. Ballet.

Angelina's birthday surprise ill. by Helen Craig. Crown, 1989. ISBN 0-517-57325-3 Subj: Animals – mice. Birthdays. Sports – bicycling.

Angelina's Christmas ill. by Helen Craig. Crown, 1986. ISBN 0-517-55823-8 Subj: Animals – mice. Careers – postal workers. Family life – cousins. Holidays – Christmas.

Angelina's Halloween by Katharine Holabird & Helen Craig; ill. by Helen Craig. Pleasant, 2000. ISBN 1-58485-152-X Subj: Animals – mice. Holidays – Halloween.

Christmas with Angelina ill. by Helen Craig. Random House, 1992. ISBN 0-679-83485-0 Subj: Animals – mice. Holidays – Christmas.

The little mouse ABC ill. by Helen Craig. S&S, 1983. ISBN 0-671-47733-1 Subj: ABC books. Animals – mice.

Holbrook, Stewart. *America's Ethan Allen* ill. by Lynd Ward. Houghton Mifflin, 1949. ISBN 0-395-24449-8 Subj: Caldecott award honor books. U.S. history. War.

Holcomb, Nan. *Leah's night of wonder* ill. by Dot Yoder. Jason & Nordic, 1999. ISBN 0-944727-35-2 Subj: Religion – Nativity.

Patrick and Emma Lou ill. by Dot Yoder. Jason & Nordic, 1989. ISBN 0-944727-03-4 Subj: Family life – brothers & sisters. Handicaps – physical handicaps.

Holden, Edith. *The hedgehog feast* ill. by Edith Holden; words by Rowena Stott. Dutton, 1978. ISBN 0-525-61580-2 Subj: Animals – hedgehogs. Food.

Holden, Robert. *The pied piper of Hamelin* (Browning, Robert)

Holder, Heidi. *Æsop's fables* (Æsop)

Carmine the crow ill. by author. Farrar, 1992. ISBN 0-374-31119-6 Subj: Animals. Behavior – sharing. Birds – crows. Forest, woods. Old age.

Crows: an old rhyme ill. by author. Farrar, 1987. ISBN 0-374-31660-0 Subj: Animals – minks. Animals – weasels. Birds – crows. Counting, numbers. Nursery rhymes.

Holder, Mig. *The fourth wise man* ill. by Tony Morris. Augsburg Fortress, 1995. ISBN 0-8066-2713-1 Subj: Holidays – Christmas. Religion – Nativity.

Holderness, Jackie. *What is a shadow?* ill. by author. Copper Beech, 2002. ISBN 0-7613-2821-1 Subj: Light, lights. Science. Shadows.

Holding, James. *The lazy little Zulu* ill. by Aliki. Morrow, 1962. Subj: Character traits – laziness. Foreign lands – Africa.

Holl, Adelaide. *The ABC of cars, trucks and machines* ill. by William Dugan. American Heritage, 1970. ISBN 0-8281-5019-2 Subj: ABC books. Automobiles. Machines. Trucks.

Most-of-the-time Maxie ill. by Hilary Knight. Xerox Family Education Services, 1974. ISBN 0-88375-202-6 Subj: Books, reading. Imagination.

A mouse story: Minnikin, Midgie and Moppet ill. by Priscilla Hillman. Golden Pr., 1977. ISBN 0-307-62362-9 Subj: Animals – mice. Cities, towns. Country.

Mrs. McGarrity's peppermint sweater ill. by Abner Graboff. Lothrop, 1966. Subj: Activities – knitting. Circus. Rhyming text.

My father and I (Ringi, Kjell [Arne Sorensen])

The rain puddle ill. by Roger Antoine Duvoisin. Lothrop, 1965. ISBN 0-688-51096-5 Subj: Animals. Weather – rain.

The remarkable egg ill. by Roger Antoine Duvoisin. Lothrop, 1968. ISBN 0-688-51090-6 Subj: Toys – balls.

The runaway giant ill. by Mamoru Funai. Lothrop, 1967. Subj: Behavior – gossip. Snowmen.

Sir Kevin of Devon ill. by Leonard Weisgard. Lothrop, 1963. Subj: Character traits – bravery. Knights. Rhyming text.

Small Bear builds a playhouse ill. by Cyndy Szekeres. Garrard, 1978. ISBN 0-8116-4454-5 Subj: Animals. Animals – bears. Homes, houses.

Small Bear solves a mystery ill. by Lorinda Bryan Cauley. Garrard, 1979. ISBN 0-8116-4456-1 Subj: Animals – bears. Food. Illness. Mystery stories.

Sylvester, the mouse with the musical ear ill. by N. M. Bodecker. Golden Bks., 2001. ISBN 0-307-20204-6 Subj: Animals – mice. Music.

Holland, Cheri. *Maccabee jamboree: a Hanukkah countdown* ill. by Roz Schanzer. Kar-Ben Copies, 1998. ISBN 1-58013-019-4 Subj: Counting, numbers. Holidays – Hanukkah. Jewish culture. Religion.

Holland, Isabelle. *Kevin's hat* ill. by Leonard B. Lubin. Lothrop, 1984. ISBN 0-688-02360-6 Subj: Clothing – hats. Reptiles – alligators, crocodiles.

Holland, Janice. *You never can tell* ill. by adapt. Scribners, 1963. Adapt. from the tr. by Arthur W. Hummel from the book of Huai-nan tzu, written before 122 B.C. Subj: Character traits – luck. Folk & fairy tales. Foreign lands – China.

Holland, Kevin Crossley. *see* Crossley-Holland, Kevin

Holland, Simon. *Space* ill. with photos. DK, 2001. ISBN 0-7894-8182-0 Subj: Astronomy. Space & space ships.

Holland, Viki. *We are having a baby* ill. by author. Scribners, 1972. ISBN 0-684-12809-8 Subj: Babies. Family life – new sibling.

Hollenbeck, Kathleen M. *Islands of ice* ill. by John Paul Genzo. Soundprints, 2001. ISBN 1-56899-965-8 Subj: Animals – seals. Science.

Holleyman, Sonia. *Mona the vampire* ill. by author. Delacorte, 1991. ISBN 0-385-30299-1 Subj: Books, reading. Imagination. Monsters – vampires.

Holling, Holling C. (Holling Clancy). *Paddle-to-the-sea* ill. by author. Houghton Mifflin, 1941. ISBN 0-395-15082-5 Subj: Caldecott award honor books. Foreign lands – Canada. Rivers.

Hollow, Elizabeth. *In this night* (Lucht, Irmgard)

Hollyer, Belinda. *Daniel in the lions' den* (Bible Old Testament Daniel)

David and Goliath (Bible Old Testament David)

Jonah and the great fish (Bible Old Testament Jonah)

Hollyn, Lynn. *Lynn Hollyn's Christmas toyland* ill. by Lori Anzalone. Knopf, 1985. ISBN 0-394-97631-2 Subj: Fairies. Holidays – Christmas. Toys.

Holm, Mayling Mack. *A forest Christmas* ill. by author. HarperCollins, 1977. ISBN 0-06-022573-4 Subj: Animals. Holidays – Christmas.

Holm, Sharon Lane. *Zoe's hats* ill. by author. Boyds Mills, 2003. ISBN 1-59078-042-6 Subj: Clothing – hats. Concepts – color. Concepts – patterns.

Holman, Felice. *Victoria's castle* ill. by Lillian Hoban. Norton, 1966. Subj: Birds – parakeets, parrots. Humorous stories. Imagination.

Holman, Sandy Lynne. *Grandpa, is everything black bad?* ill. by Lela Kometiani. Culture Coop, 1995. ISBN 0-9644655-0-7 Subj: Ethnic groups in the U.S. – African Americans. Family life – grandfathers. Self-concept.

Holmes, Anita. *Can you find us?* ill. with photos. Benchmark, 2001. ISBN 0-7614-1108-9 Subj: Animals. Disguises.

Flowers and friends ill. with photos. Benchmark, 2001. ISBN 0-7614-1113-5 Subj: Flowers. Friendship. Gardens, gardening.

Insect detector ill. with photos. Benchmark, 2001. ISBN 0-7614-1110-0 Subj: Insects.

The 100-year-old cactus ill. by Carol Lerner. Four Winds, 1983. ISBN 0-590-07634-5 Subj: Desert. Plants. Science.

Where robins fly ill. with photos. Benchmark, 2001. ISBN 0-7614-1109-7 Subj: Birds – robins.

Who dug that hole? ill. with photos. Cavendish, 2001. ISBN 0-7614-1112-7 Subj: Animals. Homes, houses.

Holmes, Efner Tudor. *Amy's goose* ill. by Tasha Tudor. Crowell, 1977. ISBN 0-690-03801-1 Subj: Birds – geese. Character traits – helpfulness. Character traits – kindness to animals.

Carrie's gift ill. by Tasha Tudor. Collins-World, 1978. ISBN 0-529-05429-9 Subj: Animals – dogs. Character traits – kindness to animals. Gifts.

The Christmas cat ill. by Tasha Tudor. Crowell, 1976. ISBN 0-690-01268-3 Subj: Animals – cats. Holidays – Christmas.

Deer in the hollow ill. by Marlowe deChristopher. Philomel, 1993. ISBN 0-399-21735-5 Subj: Animals. Animals – deer. Forest, woods. Holidays – Christmas.

Holmes, Olivia. *The saint and the circus* (Piumini, Roberto)

Holmes, Stephen. *Hidden numbers* text by Sadie Fields; ill. by author. Harcourt, 1990. ISBN 0-15-200469-6 Subj: Counting, numbers. Format, unusual – toy & movable books. Games.

Holmquist, Delano. *SantaSaurus* ill. by Chuck Galey. Pelican, 2002. ISBN 1-56554-933-3 Subj: Character traits – kindness. Dinosaurs. Holidays – Christmas. Santa Claus.

Holsonback, Anita. *Monkey see, monkey do: an animal exercise book for you!* by Anita Holsonback, with rhymes by Deb Adamson; ill. by Leo Timmers. Millbrook, 1997. ISBN 0-7613-0260-3 Subj: Animals. Rhyming text.

Holub, Joan. *Cinderdog and the wicked stepcat* ill. by author. A. Whitman, 2001. ISBN 0-8075-1178-1 Subj: Animals – cats. Animals – dogs. Cowboys, cowgirls. U.S. history – frontier & pioneer life.

The garden that we grew ill. by Hiroe Nakata. Viking, 2001. ISBN 0-670-89799-X Subj: Gardens, gardening. Plants. Rhyming text. Seeds.

Geogra-fleas ill. by Regan Dunnick. A. Whitman, 2004. ISBN 0-8075-2818-8 Subj: Geography. Riddles & jokes.

The Halloween Queen ill. by Theresa Smythe. A. Whitman, 2004. ISBN 0-8075-3138-3 Subj: Holidays – Halloween. Parties. Rhyming text.

Pen pals ill. by author. Grosset, 1997. ISBN 0-448-41613-1 Subj: Letters, cards. Pen pals. School.

The pizza that we made ill. by Lynne Cravath. Viking, 2001. ISBN 0-670-03520-3 Subj: Activities – baking, cooking. Food. Rhyming text.

Scat cats ill. by Rich Davis. Viking, 2001. ISBN 0-670-89279-3 Subj: Animals – cats. Rhyming text.

Turkeys never gobble ill. by Jennifer Beck Harris. HarperFestival, 2002. ISBN 0-06-008091-4 Subj: Animals. Etiquette. Format, unusual – board books. Holidays – Thanksgiving. Rhyming text.

Vincent van Gogh: sunflowers and swirly stars ill. with art reproductions. Grosset, 2001. ISBN 0-448-42612-9 Subj: Art. Careers – artists.

Why do cats meow? ill. by Anna DiVito. Dial, 2001. ISBN 0-8037-2503-5 Subj: Animals – cats. Character traits – questioning.

Why do dogs bark? ill. by Anna DiVito. Dial, 2001. ISBN 0-8037-2504-3 Subj: Animals – dogs. Character traits – questioning.

Holzenthaler, Jean. *My feet do* ill. by George Ancona. Dutton, 1979. ISBN 0-525-35485-9 Subj: Activities. Anatomy – feet.

My hands can ill. by Nancy Tafuri. Dutton, 1978. ISBN 0-525-35490-5 Subj: Activities. Anatomy – hands.

Homel, David. *Animal capers* (Paré, Roger)

Circus days (Paré, Roger)

A friend like you (Paré, Roger)

Play time (Paré, Roger)

Summer days (Paré, Roger)

Homer, Abigail. *Country mouse cottage: how we lived one hundred years ago* (Brooks, Nigel)

Town mouse house: how we lived one hundred years ago (Brooks, Nigel)

Homme, Bob. *The friendly giant's birthday* ill. by Kim LaFave & Carol Snelling. CBC Merchandising, 1982. ISBN 0-88794-099-4 Subj: Birthdays. Giants. Songs.

The friendly giant's book of fire engines ill. by Kim LaFave & Carol Snelling. CBC Merchandising, 1981. ISBN 0-88794-100-1 Subj: Careers – firefighters. Giants. Trucks.

Honda, Tetsuya. *Wild horse winter* ill. by author. Chronicle, 1992. ISBN 0-8118-0251-5 Subj: Animals – horses, ponies. Foreign lands – Japan. Seasons – winter. Weather – snow.

Honey, Elizabeth. *The moon in the man* ill. by author. Allen & Unwin, 2002. ISBN 1-86508-455-7 Subj: Nursery rhymes. Poetry.

Honeycutt, Natalie. *Whistle home* ill. by Annie Cannon. Orchard, 1993. ISBN 0-531-08640-2 Subj: Activities – whistling. Animals – dogs. Emotions – fear. Family life – aunts, uncles.

Hong, Lily Toy. *How the ox star fell from heaven* ill. by author. A. Whitman, 1990. ISBN 0-8075-3428-5 Subj: Animals – oxen. Folk & fairy tales. Food. Foreign lands – China.

Honigsberg, Peter Jan. *Pillow of dreams* ill. by Tony Morse. RDR Books, 1999. ISBN 1-57143-076-8 Subj: Animals – moles. Animals – rabbits. Dreams. Magic.

Hood, Susan. *Look! I can read!* Amy Wummer. Grosset, 2000. ISBN 0-448-42282-4 Subj: Books, reading. Ethnic groups in the U.S. – African Americans. Rhyming text.

Meet Trouble ill. by Kristina Stephenson. Grosset, 2001. ISBN 0-448-42455-X Subj: Animals – cats. Behavior – misbehavior.

The new kid photos by Dorothy Handelman. Millbrook, 1998. ISBN 0-7613-2014-8 Subj: Behavior. Friendship. Rhyming text. School.

Pup and Hound ill. by Linda Hendry. Kids Can, 2004. ISBN 1-55337-674-9 Subj: Animals – dogs. Friendship. Moving.

Pup and Hound move in ill. by Linda Hendry. Kids Can, 2004. ISBN 1-55337-674-9 Subj: Animals – dogs. Friendship.

Hood, Thomas. *Before I go to sleep* ill. by Maryjane Begin-Callanan. Morrow, 1999. ISBN 0-688-12424-0 Subj: Animals. Bedtime. Imagination. Rhyming text.

Hooker, Ruth. *At Grandma and Grandpa's house* ill. by Ruth Rosner. A. Whitman, 1986. ISBN 0-8075-0477-7 Subj: Family life. Family life – grandparents.

Matthew the cowboy ill. by Cat Bowman Smith. A. Whitman, 1990. ISBN 0-8075-4999-1 Subj: Cowboys, cowgirls. Imagination. U.S. history – frontier & pioneer life.

Sara loves her big brother ill. by Margot Apple. A. Whitman, 1987. ISBN 0-8075-7244-6 Subj: Behavior – sharing. Family life – brothers. Family life – new sibling. Sibling rivalry.

Hooks, Bell. *Be boy buzz* ill. by Chris Raschka. Hyperion, 2002. ISBN 0-7868-2633-9 Subj: Activities. Ethnic groups in the U.S. – African Americans. Gender roles.

Happy to be nappy ill. by Chris Raschka. Hyperion, 1999. ISBN 0-7868-2377-1 Subj: Ethnic groups in the U.S. – African Americans. Hair.

Hooks, William H. *A dozen dizzy dogs* ill. by Gary Baseman. G. Stevens, 1997. ISBN 0-8368-1748-6 Subj: Animals – dogs. Counting, numbers. Rhyming text.

Feed me! an Æsop fable ill. by Doug Cushman. G. Stevens, 1996. ISBN 0-8368-1616-1 Subj: Birds. Folk & fairy tales.

The Gruff brothers ill. by Pierre Cornuel. G. Stevens, 1997. ISBN 0-8368-1749-4 Subj: Animals – goats. Character traits – cleverness. Folk & fairy tales. Mythical creatures – trolls. Rebuses.

How do you make a bubble? by William H. Hooks, Joanne Oppenheim, & Barbara A. Brenner; ill. by Doug Cushman. Bantam, 1992. ISBN 0-553-07887-9 Subj: Activities. Bubbles. Rhyming text.

The legend of the Christmas rose ill. by Richard Williams. HarperCollins, 1998. ISBN 0-06-027103-5 Subj: Family life – brothers & sisters. Flowers – roses. Foreign lands – Sweden. Holidays – Christmas. Religion – Nativity.

Lion and Lamb (Brenner, Barbara A.)

The mighty Santa Fe ill. by Angela Trotta Thomas. Macmillan, 1993. ISBN 0-02-744432-5 Subj: Emotions – fear. Family life – great-grandparents. Holidays – Christmas. Toys – trains.

Mr. Baseball ill. by Paul Meisel. G. Stevens, 1998. ISBN 0-8368-1765-6 Subj: Family life – brothers. Sports – baseball.

Mr. Dinosaur ill. by Paul Meisel. G. Stevens, 1997. ISBN 0-8368-1755-9 Subj: Dinosaurs. Eggs. Family life – brothers. Prehistory. Reptiles – lizards.

Mr. Garbage ill. by Kate Duke. G. Stevens, 1997. ISBN 0-8368-1756-7 Subj: Ecology.

Mr. Monster ill. by Paul Meisel. G. Stevens, 1998. ISBN 0-8368-1774-5 Subj: Family life – brothers. Monsters. Toys.

The monster from the sea ill. by Angela Trotta Thomas. G. Stevens, 1997. ISBN 0-8368-1694-3 Subj: Behavior – talking to strangers. Islands. Royalty – princesses.

Moss gown ill. by Donald Carrick. Clarion, 1987. ISBN 0-89919-460-5 Subj: Family life – fathers. Folk & fairy tales. Magic.

The mystery of the missing tooth ill. by Nancy Poydar. G. Stevens, 1998. ISBN 0-8368-1758-3 Subj: Fairies. Teeth.

No way, Slippery Slick! a child's first book about drugs (Oppenheim, Joanne)

Peach boy ill. by June Otani. Bantam, 1992. ISBN 0-553-07621-3 Subj: Behavior – fighting, arguing. Character traits – bravery. Folk & fairy tales. Foreign lands – Japan. Monsters.

The rainbow ribbon by William H. Hooks & Betty Boegehold; ill. by Lynn Munsinger. Viking, 1991. ISBN 0-670-82866-1 Subj: Behavior – running away. Behavior – stealing. Character traits – selfishness.

Read-a-rebus by William H. Hooks, Joanne Oppenheim, Betty D. Boegehold; ill. by Lynn Munsinger. Random House, 1986. ISBN

0-394-95833-0 Subj: Anatomy. Concepts – color. Counting, numbers. Rebuses. Rhyming text.

Rough, tough, Rowdy ill. by Lynn Munsinger. Viking, 1992. ISBN 0-670-82868-8 Subj: Animals. Animals – rabbits. Behavior – bullying. Family life – brothers & sisters.

Snowbear Whittington, an Appalachian Beauty and the Beast ill. by Victoria Lisi. Macmillan, 1994. ISBN 0-02-744355-8 Subj: Animals – bears. Folk & fairy tales. Monsters. Witches.

The three little pigs and the fox (The three little pigs)

Three rounds with rabbit ill. by Lissa McLaughlin. Lothrop, 1984. ISBN 0-688-02364-9 Subj: Animals – rabbits. Character traits – cleverness.

Where's Lulu? ill. by R. W. Alley. Bantam, 1991. ISBN 0-553-07093-2 Subj: Animals – dogs. Ethnic groups in the U.S. – African Americans. Toys – balls.

Hooper, Maureen Brett. *Silent night: a Christmas carol is born* ill. by Kasi Kubiak. Boyds Mills, 2001. ISBN 1-56397-782-6 Subj: Holidays – Christmas. Music. Songs.

Hooper, Meredith. *A cow, a bee, a cookie, and me* ill. by Alison Bartlett. Kingfisher, 1997. ISBN 0-7534-5067-4 Subj: Activities – baking, cooking. Family life – grandparents.

Dogs' Night ill. by Allan Curless & Mark Burgess. Millbrook, 2000. ISBN 0-7613-1824-0 Subj: Animals – dogs. Art. Museums.

River story ill. by Bee Willey. Candlewick, 2000. ISBN 0-7636-0792-4 Subj: Rivers.

Seven eggs ill. by Terry McKenna. HarperCollins, 1985. ISBN 0-06-022586-6 Subj: Counting, numbers. Cumulative tales. Days of the week, months of the year. Eggs. Format, unusual.

Tom's rabbit: a surprise on the way to Antarctica ill. by Bert Kitchen. National Geographic, 1998. ISBN 0-7922-7070-3 Subj: Animals – rabbits. Boats, ships. Foreign lands – Antarctic. Holidays – Christmas.

Hooper, Patricia. *A bundle of beasts* ill. by Mark Steele. Houghton Mifflin, 1987. ISBN 0-395-44259-1 Subj: ABC books. Animals. Language. Poetry.

How the sky's housekeeper wore her scarves ill. by Susan L. Roth. Little, 1995. ISBN 0-316-37255-2 Subj: Weather – rainbows.

Where do you sleep, little one? ill. by John Winch. Holiday, 2001. ISBN 0-8234-1668-2 Subj: Animals. Poetry. Sleep.

Hoopes, Lyn Littlefield. *Daddy's coming home* ill. by Bruce Degen. HarperCollins, 1984. ISBN 0-06-022569-6 Subj: Family life.

Half a button ill. by Trish Parcell Watts. Harper, 1989. ISBN 0-06-024018-0 Subj: Boats, ships. Family life – grandfathers. Gifts. Memories, memory.

Mommy, daddy, me ill. by Ruth Lercher Bornstein. HarperCollins, 1988. ISBN 0-06-022550-5 Subj: Family life. Islands. Nature. Rhyming text.

My own home ill. by Ruth Richardson. HarperCollins, 1991. ISBN 0-06-022571-8 Subj: Animals. Birds – owls. Nature.

Nana ill. by Arieh Zeldich. HarperCollins, 1981. ISBN 0-06-022575-0 Subj: Death. Emotions – grief. Family life – grandmothers.

The unbeatable bread ill. by Brad Sneed. Dial, 1996. ISBN 0-8037-1612-5 Subj: Activities – baking, cooking. Food. Poetry.

When I was little ill. by Marcia Sewall. Dutton, 1983. ISBN 0-525-44053-4 Subj: Emotions – love. Seasons – winter. Sibling rivalry.

Wing-a-ding ill. by Stephen Gammell. Little, 1990. ISBN 0-316-37237-4 Subj: Cumulative tales. Poetry. Toys. Trees.

Hoose, Hannah. *Hey little ant* (Hoose, Philip M.)

Hoose, Philip M. *Hey little ant* by Philip & Hannah Hoose; ill. by Debbie Tilley. Tricycle, 1998. ISBN 1-883672-54-6 Subj: Character traits – kindness to animals. Insects – ants. Music. Songs.

Hoover, Roseanna. *The fireflies* (Bolliger, Max)

The golden apple (Bolliger, Max)

Hopkins, Lee Bennett. *All God's children* ill. by Amanda Schaffer. Harcourt, 1998. ISBN 0-15-201499-3 Subj: Poetry. Religion.

Alphathoughts ill. by Marla Baggetta. Wordsong, 2003. ISBN 1-56397-979-9 Subj: ABC books. Poetry.

And God bless me: prayers, lullabies and dream-poems ill. by Patricia Henderson Lincoln. Knopf, 1982. ISBN 0-394-94624-3 Subj: Lullabies. Poetry. Religion.

Animals from Mother Goose: a question book ill. by Kathryn Hewitt. Harcourt, 1989. ISBN 0-15-200406-8 Subj: Animals. Character traits – questioning. Nursery rhymes.

April, bubbles, chocolate: an ABC of poetry ill. by Barry Root. S&S, 1994. ISBN 0-671-75911-6 Subj: ABC books. Poetry.

Best friends ill. by James Watts. HarperCollins, 1986. ISBN 0-06-022562-9 Subj: Friendship. Poetry.

Blast off! poems about space ill. by Melissa Sweet. HarperCollins, 1995. ISBN 0-06-024261-2 Subj: Poetry. Space & space ships.

Christmas presents: holiday poetry (Christmas presents)

Circus! Circus! ill. by John O'Brien. Knopf, 1982. ISBN 0-394-95342-8 Subj: Circus. Poetry.

Click, rumble, roar: poems about machines photos by Anna Held Audette. Crowell, 1987. ISBN 0-690-04589-1 Subj: Machines. Poetry.

Climb into my lap ill. by Kathryn Brown. S&S, 1998. ISBN 0-689-80715-5 Subj: Poetry.

Creatures ill. by Stella Ormai. Harcourt, 1985. ISBN 0-15-220875-5 Subj: Monsters. Poetry.

Crickets and bullfrogs and whispers of thunder (Behn, Harry)

Dinosaurs ill. by Murray Tinkelman. Harcourt, 1987. ISBN 0-15-223495-0 Subj: Dinosaurs. Poetry. Prehistory.

A dog's life ill. by Linda Rochester Richards. Harcourt, 1983. ISBN 0-05-223937-5 Subj: Animals – dogs. Poetry.

Easter buds are springing ill. by Tomie de Paola. Harcourt, 1979. ISBN 0-15-224705-X Subj: Holidays – Easter. Poetry. Seasons – spring.

Elves, fairies and gnomes: poems (Elves, fairies and gnomes)

Flit, flutter, fly! ill. by Peter Palagonia. Doubleday, 1992. ISBN 0-385-41468-4 Subj: Insects. Poetry.

Go to bed! a book of bedtime poems ill. by Rosekrans Hoffman. Knopf, 1979. ISBN 0-394-93869-0 Subj: Bedtime. Poetry.

Good books, good times ill. by Harvey Stevenson. HarperCollins, 1990. ISBN 0-06-022528-9 Subj: Books, reading. Poetry.

Good rhymes, good times ill. by Frané Lessac. HarperCollins, 1995. ISBN 0-06-023500-4 Subj: Poetry.

Hanukkah lights (Hanukkah lights)

Happy birthday ill. by Hilary Knight. S&S, 1991. ISBN 0-671-70973-9 Subj: Birthdays. Poetry.

The horned toad prince ill. by Michael Austin. Peachtree, 2000. ISBN 1-56145-195-9 Subj: Cowboys, cowgirls. Folk & fairy tales. Frogs & toads. Royalty – princes.

How do you make an elephant float? ill. by Rosekrans Hoffman. A. Whitman, 1983. ISBN 0-8075-3415-3 Subj: Food. Riddles & jokes.

I loved Rose Ann ill. by Ingrid Fetz. Knopf, 1976. ISBN 0-394-93100-0 Subj: Behavior – misunderstanding. Emotions.

I think I saw a snail: young poems for city seasons ill. by Harold James. Crown, 1969. Subj: Cities, towns. Ethnic groups in the U.S. – African Americans. Poetry.

It's about time ill. by Matt Novak. S&S, 1993. ISBN 0-671-78512-5 Subj: Friendship. Poetry. Time.

Merrily comes our harvest in ill. by Ben Shecter. Harcourt, 1978. ISBN 0-15-253179-3 Subj: Holidays – Thanksgiving. Poetry. Seasons – fall.

On the farm ill. by Laurel Molk. Little, 1991. ISBN 0-316-37274-9 Subj: Farms. Poetry.

People from Mother Goose: a question book ill. by Kathryn Hewitt. Harcourt, 1989. ISBN 0-15-200558-7 Subj: Character traits – questioning. Nursery rhymes.

A pet for me (A pet for me)

Questions ill. by Carolyn Croll. HarperCollins, 1992. ISBN 0-06-022413-4 Subj: Character traits – questioning. Poetry.

Ragged shadows: poems of Halloween night ill. by Giles Laroche. Little, 1993. ISBN 0-316-37276-5 Subj: Holidays – Halloween. Poetry.

Ring out, wild bells ill. by Karen Baumann. Harcourt, 1992. ISBN 0-15-267100-5 Subj: Holidays. Poetry. Seasons.

School supplies ill. by Renee Flower. S&S, 1996. ISBN 0-671-51172-6 Subj: Poetry. School.

The sea is calling me ill. by Walter Gaffney-Kessell. Harcourt, 1986. ISBN 0-15-271155-4 Subj: Poetry. Sea & seashore.

The sky is full of song ill. by Dirk Zimmer. HarperCollins, 1983. ISBN 0-06-022583-1 Subj: Poetry.

Song and dance ill. by Cheryl Munro Taylor. S&S, 1997. ISBN 0-689-80159-9 Subj: Poetry.

A song in stone photos by Anna Held Audette. Crowell, 1983. ISBN 0-690-04270-1 Subj: Cities, towns. Poetry.

Sports! sports! sports! (Sports! sports! sports!)

Still as a star ill. by Karen Milone. Little, 1989. ISBN 0-316-37272-2 Subj: Poetry. Sleep.

Through our eyes ill. by Jeffrey Dunn. Little, 1992. ISBN 0-316-19654-1 Subj: Behavior – growing up. Poetry.

To the zoo ill. by John Wallner. Little, 1992. ISBN 0-316-37273-0 Subj: Animals. Poetry. Zoos.

Yummy! eating through a day (Yummy! eating through a day)

Hopkins, Margaret. *Sleepytime for baby mouse* ill. by Karen Lee Schmidt. Platt, 1985. ISBN 0-448-49875-9 Subj: Animals – mice. Bedtime. Family life. Format, unusual – board books.

Hopkins, Marjorie. *Three visitors* ill. by Anne F. Rockwell. Parents' Magazine Pr., 1967. Subj: Eskimos.

Hopkinson, Deborah. *Birdie's lighthouse* ill. by Kimberly Bulcken Root. Atheneum, 1997. ISBN 0-689-81052-0 Subj: Family life – fathers. Lighthouses. Sea & seashore. Weather – storms.

Bluebird summer ill. by Bethanne Andersen. Greenwillow, 2001. ISBN 0-688-17399-3 Subj: Death. Emotions. Family life – grandfathers. Farms. Memories, memory.

Fannie in the kitchen ill. by Nancy Carpenter. Atheneum, 2001. ISBN 0-689-81965-X Subj: Activities – baking, cooking.

Girl wonder ill. by Terry Widener. Atheneum, 2003. ISBN 0-689-83300-8 Subj: Sports – baseball.

Maria's comet ill. by Deborah Lanino. Atheneum, 1999. ISBN 0-689-81501-8 Subj: Careers – astronomers. Family life. Sky.

Sweet Clara and the freedom quilt ill. by author. Knopf, 1993. ISBN 0-679-92311-X Subj: Activities – sewing. Behavior – seeking better things. Slavery.

Hoppe, Matthias. *Mouse and elephant* ill. by Jan Lenica. Little, 1991. ISBN 0-316-37284-6 Subj: Animals. Animals – elephants. Animals – mice. Friendship.

Horace. *Two Roman mice* (Roach, Marilynne K.)

Horácek, Petr. *Flip's day* ill. by author. Candlewick, 2002. ISBN 0-7636-1798-9 Subj: Birds – penguins. Format, unusual – toy & movable books.

Strawberries are red ill. by author. Candlewick, 2001. ISBN 0-7636-1461-0 Subj: Concepts – color. Food. Format, unusual – toy & movable books.

What is black and white? ill. by author. Candlewick, 2001. ISBN 0-7636-1460-2 Subj: Concepts – color.

When the moon smiled ill. by author. Candlewick, 2004. ISBN 0-7636-2209-5 Subj: Animals. Counting, numbers. Moon. Night. Stars.

Horenstein, Henry. *A is for – ? a photographer's alphabet of animals* photos by author. Harcourt, 1999. ISBN 0-15-201582-5 Subj: ABC books. Animals. Picture puzzles.

Arf! beg! catch! dogs from A to Z photos by author. Scholastic, 1999. ISBN 0-590-03380-8 Subj: ABC books. Animals – dogs. Language.

Sam goes trucking photos by author. Houghton Mifflin, 1989. ISBN 0-395-44313-X Subj: Careers – truck drivers. Family life – fathers. Trucks.

Horio, Seishi. *The monkey and the crab* by Saru Kani; retold by Seishi Horio; trans. by D. T. Ooka; ill. by Tsutomu Murakami. Heian Intl., 1985. ISBN 0-89346-246-2 Subj: Animals – monkeys. Crustaceans – crabs. Death.

Horn, Emily. *Excuse me – are you a witch?* ill. by Pawel Pawlak. Whispering Coyote, 2003. ISBN 1-58089-093-8 Subj: Animals – cats. Libraries. School. Witches.

Horn, Peter. *The best father of all* ill. by Cristina Kadmon; trans. by J. Alison James. North-South, 2003. ISBN 0-7358-1680-8 Subj: Animals. Family life – fathers. Reptiles – turtles, tortoises.

When I grow up . . . ill. by Cristina Kadmon; trans. by Rosemary Lanning. North-South, 1999. ISBN 0-7358-1149-0 Subj: Behavior – growing up. Family life – fathers. Reptiles – turtles, tortoises.

Horn, Sandra Ann. *Babushka* ill. by Sophie Fatus. Barefoot, 2002. ISBN 1-84148-353-2 Subj: Folk & fairy tales. Foreign lands – Russia. Holidays – Christmas. Religion – Nativity.

The dandelion wish ill. by Jason Cockcroft. DK, 2000. ISBN 0-7894-6326-1 Subj: Behavior – wishing. Fairs, festivals. Plants.

Horner, Althea J. *Little big girl* ill. by Patricia Rosamilia. Human Sciences Pr., 1983. ISBN 0-89885-098-3 Subj: Behavior – growing up.

Horning, Sandra. *The giant hug* ill. by Valeri Gorbachev. Knopf, 2005. ISBN 0-375-92477-9 Subj: Animals – pigs. Careers – postal workers. Cumulative tales. Family life – grandmothers. Hugging. Post office.

Horowitz, Dave. *A monkey among us* ill. by author. HarperFestival, 2004. ISBN 0-06-054335-3 Subj: Animals – giraffes. Animals – hippopotamuses. Animals – monkeys. Rhyming text.

Horowitz, Ruth. *Bat time* ill. by Susan Avishai. Four Winds, 1991. ISBN 0-02-744541-0 Subj: Animals – bats. Bedtime. Family life – fathers.

Crab moon ill. by Kate Kiesler. Candlewick, 2000. ISBN 0-7636-0709-6 Subj: Animals. Crustaceans – crabs. Sea & seashore.

Mommy's lap ill. by Henri Sorensen. Lothrop, 1993. ISBN 0-688-07236-4 Subj: Babies. Family life – brothers & sisters. Family life – new sibling.

Horsbrugh, Wilma. *The train to Glasgow* ill. by Paul Cox. Clarion, 2004. ISBN 0-618-38143-0 Subj: Cumulative tales. Rhyming text. Trains.

Horse, Harry. *A friend for Little Bear* ill. by author. Candlewick, 1996. ISBN 1-56402-876-3 Subj: Behavior – collecting things. Friendship. Islands. Toys – bears.

Little rabbit lost ill. by author. Peachtree, 2002. ISBN 1-56145-273-4 Subj: Animals – rabbits. Behavior – lost. Parks – amusement.

Hort, Lenny. *The big squirrel and the little rhinoceros* (Damjan, Mischa)

The boy who held back the sea ill. by Thomas Locker. Dial, 1987. Adapt. of Hans Brinker, or The Silver Skates by Mary Mapes Dodge. ISBN 0-8037-0407-0 Subj: Behavior – misbehavior. Character traits – bravery. Folk & fairy tales.

How many stars in the sky ill. by James E. Ransome. Morrow, 1991. ISBN 0-688-10104-6 Subj: Ethnic groups in the U.S. – African Americans. Family life – fathers. Night. Stars.

The tale of the unicorn (Preussler, Otfried)

Tie your socks and clap your feet ill. by Stephen Kroninger. Atheneum, 2000. ISBN 0-689-83195-1 Subj: Humorous stories. Poetry.

We're going on a treasure hunt concept & photos by Tom Arma. Abrams, 2003. ISBN 0-8109-4654-8 Subj: Animals. Babies. Clothing – costumes. Games. Sea & seashore.

We're going on safari concept & photos by Tom Arma. Abrams, 2002. ISBN 0-8109-0574-4 Subj: Animals. Babies. Clothing – costumes.

Horton, Barbara Savadge. *What comes in spring?* ill. by Ed Young. Knopf, 1992. ISBN 0-679-90268-6 Subj: Babies. Birth. Family life. Seasons.

Horvath, Betty F. *Be nice to Josephine* ill. by Pat Grant Porter. Watts, 1970. ISBN 0-531-01939-X Subj: Behavior. Family life.

The cheerful quiet ill. by Jo Ann Stover. Watts, 1969. Subj: Noise, sounds. Problem solving.

Hooray for Jasper ill. by Fermin Rocker. Watts, 1966. Subj: Character traits – smallness. Ethnic groups in the U.S. – African Americans.

Jasper and the hero business ill. by Don Bolognese. Watts, 1977. ISBN 0-531-01317-0 Subj: Character traits – bravery. Ethnic groups in the U.S. – African Americans.

Jasper makes music ill. by Fermin Rocker. Watts, 1967. Subj: Activities – working. Ethnic groups in the U.S. – African Americans. Music.

Will the real Tommy Wilson please stand up? ill. by Charles Robinson. Watts, 1969. Subj: Character traits – individuality. Emotions. Friendship.

Horwitz, Carmel O'Mara. *see* O'Mara, Carmel

Horwitz, Elinor Lander. *Sometimes it happens* ill. by Susan Jeschke. HarperCollins, 1981. ISBN 0-06-022597-1 Subj: Character traits – ambition. Imagination.

When the sky is like lace ill. by Barbara Cooney. Lippincott, 1975. ISBN 0-397-31550-3 Subj: Night.

Horwood, Annie. *Butterfly, butterfly what colors do you see?* ill. by author. Little Simon, 2001. ISBN 0-689-84075-6 Subj: Concepts – color. Format, unusual – toy & movable books. Insects – butterflies, caterpillars.

Hosta, Dar. *I love the night* ill. by author. Brown Dog Bks., 2003. ISBN 0-9721967-0-6 Subj: Animals. Night.

Hot cross buns, and other old street cries sel. by John M. Langstaff; ill. by Nancy Winslow Parker. Atheneum, 1978. ISBN 0-689-50103-X Subj: Music. Poetry. Songs.

Hot potato: mealtime rhymes sel. by Neil Philip; ill. by Claire Henley. Clarion, 2004. ISBN 0-618-31554-3 Subj: Food. Poetry.

Houck, Eric L. *Rabbit surprise* by Eric L. Houck, Jr.; ill. by Dominic Catalano. Crown, 1993. ISBN 0-517-58778-5 Subj: Animals – foxes. Animals – rabbits. Holidays – Fourth of July. Magic.

Houghton, Eric. *The backwards watch* ill. by Simone Abel. Orchard, 1992. ISBN 0-531-08568-6 Subj: Activities – playing. Family life – grandfathers.

The crooked apple tree ill. by Caroline Gold. Barefoot, 1999. ISBN 1-902283-59-7 Subj: Activities – playing. Family life. Games. Trees.

Walter's magic wand ill. by Denise Teasdale. Watts, 1990. ISBN 0-531-08451-5 Subj: Libraries. Magic.

Houk, Randy. *Chessie, the travelin' man* ill. by Paula Bartlett. Benefactory, 1997. ISBN 1-882728-56-4 Subj: Activities – traveling. Animals – manatees. Rhyming text.

Rico's hawk ill. by Nancy Lane. Benefactory, 1998. ISBN 1-58021-029-5 Subj: Birds – hawks. Character traits – kindness to animals. Farms. Illness – mental illness. Rhyming text.

Ruffle, Coo and Hoo Doo ill. by author. Benefactory, 1993. ISBN 1-882728-02-5 Subj: Birds – owls. Birds – parakeets, parrots. Rhyming text.

House mouse photos by David Thompson. Putnam, 1978. ISBN 0-399-20620-5 Subj: Animals – mice. Science.

The house that Jack built. *The house that Jack built* ill. by Randolph Caldecott. G. Routledge, 1878. Subj: Cumulative tales. Nursery rhymes.

The house that Jack built ill. by Seymour Chwast. Random House, 1973. ISBN 0-394-82647-7 Subj: Cumulative tales. Format, unusual – toy & movable books. Nursery rhymes. Participation.

The house that Jack built ill. by Diana Mayo. Barefoot, 2001. ISBN 1-84148-251-X Subj: Cumulative tales. Nursery rhymes.

The house that Jack built ill. by Rodney Peppé. Delacorte, 1970. Subj: Cumulative tales. Nursery rhymes.

The house that Jack built: a Mother Goose nursery rhyme ill. by Janet Stevens. Holiday, 1985. ISBN 0-8234-0548-6 Subj: Circus. Cumulative tales. Nursery rhymes.

The house that Jack built ill. by Jenny Stow. Dial, 1992. ISBN 0-8037-1090-9 Subj: Cumulative tales. Nursery rhymes.

The house that Jack built ill. by Nadine Bernard Westcott. Little, 1991. ISBN 0-316-93138-1 Subj: Cumulative tales. Format, unusual – toy & movable books. Nursery rhymes. Participation.

The house that Jack built retold & ill. by Jeanette Winter. Dial, 2000. ISBN 0-8037-2524-8 Subj: Cumulative tales. Nursery rhymes. Rebuses.

The house that Jack built = la maison que Jacques a batie: la maison que Jacques a batie ill. by Antonio Frasconi. Harcourt, 1958. Subj: Caldecott award honor books. Cumulative tales. Foreign languages. Nursery rhymes.

This is the house that Jack built ill. by Simms Taback. Putnam, 2002. ISBN 0-399-23488-8 Subj: Cumulative tales. Nursery rhymes.

This is the house that Jack built ill. by Liz Underhill. Holt, 1987. ISBN 0-8050-0339-8 Subj: Cumulative tales. Nursery rhymes.

Houselander, Caryll. *Petook: an Easter story* ill. by Tomie de Paola. Holiday, 1988. ISBN 0-8234-0681-4 Subj: Birds – chickens. Holidays – Easter. Religion.

Houses created by Gallimard Jeunesse & Claude Delafosse; ill. by Donald Grant. Scholastic, 1998. ISBN 0-590-38152-0 Subj: Homes, houses.

Houston, Gloria. *But no candy* ill. by Lloyd Bloom. Philomel, 1992. ISBN 0-399-22142-5 Subj: Family life – aunts, uncles. Food. Stores. U.S. history. War.

My Great-Aunt Arizona ill. by Susan Condie Lamb. Harper-Collins, 1992. ISBN 0-06-022607-2 Subj: Careers – teachers. Family life – aunts, uncles.

The year of the perfect Christmas tree: an Appalachian story ill. by Barbara Cooney. Dial, 1988. ISBN 0-8037-0300-7 Subj: Family life. Holidays – Christmas. Trees.

Houston, James. *Kiviok's magic journey: an Eskimo legend* ill. by author. Atheneum, 1973. ISBN 0-689-30419-6 Subj: Birds – geese. Eskimos. Folk & fairy tales.

Houston, John A. *The bright yellow rope* ill. by Winnie Fitch. Addison-Wesley, 1973. ISBN 0-201-02995-2 Subj: Behavior – sharing. Character traits – generosity. Character traits – helpfulness. Problem solving. Rhyming text. Songs.

A mouse in my house ill. by Winnie Fitch. Addison-Wesley, 1973. ISBN 0-201-02989-X Subj: Animals – mice. Cumulative tales. Problem solving. Songs.

A room full of animals ill. by Winnie Fitch. Addison-Wesley, 1973. ISBN 0-201-12997-9 Subj: Animals. Songs.

How big is the ocean? first questions and answers about the beach. Time-Life, 1994. ISBN 0-7835-0897-2 Subj: Sea & seashore.

How much does God love me? ill. by Rory Tyger. Barron's, 2001. ISBN 0-7641-5405-2 Subj: Format, unusual – toy & movable books. Religion.

How Raggedy Ann got her candy heart adapt. from stories by Johnny Gruelle; ill. by Jan Palmer. S&S, 1998. ISBN 0-689-81119-5 Subj: Accidents. Kites. Toys – dolls.

How the cock wrecked the manor trans. from Lithuanian by Olimpija Armalyte; ill. by Albina Makunaite. Imported Pubs., 1982. ISBN 0-8285-2228-6 Subj: Folk & fairy tales. Magic.

Howard, Arthur. *Cosmo zooms* ill. by author. Harcourt, 1999. ISBN 0-15-201788-7 Subj: Animals – dogs. Self-concept. Sports – skateboarding.

Hoodwinked ill. by author. Harcourt, 2001. ISBN 0-15-202656-8 Subj: Pets. Witches.

When I was five ill. by author. Harcourt, 1996. ISBN 0-15-200261-8 Subj: Behavior – growing up. Friendship.

Howard, Elizabeth Fitzgerald. *Aunt Flossie's hats (and crab cakes later)* ill. by James E. Ransome. Houghton Mifflin, 1991. ISBN 0-395-54682-6 Subj: Clothing – hats. Ethnic groups in the U.S. – African Americans. Family life – aunts, uncles.

Chita's Christmas tree ill. by Floyd Cooper. Bradbury, 1989. ISBN 0-02-744621-2 Subj: Ethnic groups in the U.S. – African Americans. Holidays – Christmas.

Mac and Marie and the train toss surprise ill. by Gail Gordon Carter. Four Winds, 1993. ISBN 0-02-744640-9 Subj: Ethnic groups in the U.S. – African Americans. Family life – brothers & sisters. Trains.

Papa tells Chita a story ill. by Floyd Cooper. S&S, 1995. ISBN 0-02-744623-9 Subj: Character traits – bravery. Ethnic groups in the

U.S. – African Americans. Family life – daughters. Family life – fathers. War.

The train to Lulu's ill. by Robert Casilla. Bradbury, 1988. ISBN 0-02-744620-4 Subj: Activities – traveling. Family life – sisters.

Virgie goes to school with us boys ill. by E. B. Lewis. S&S, 1999. ISBN 0-689-80076-2 Subj: Ethnic groups in the U.S. – African Americans. Gender roles. U.S. history.

What's in Aunt Mary's room? ill. by Cedric Lucas. Clarion, 1996. ISBN 0-395-69845-6 Subj: Ethnic groups in the U.S. – African Americans. Family life – aunts, uncles. Family life – sisters.

When will Sarah come? ill. by Nina Crews. Greenwillow, 1999. ISBN 0-688-16181-2 Subj: Ethnic groups in the U.S. – African Americans. Family life – brothers & sisters. Family life – grandmothers. Noise, sounds.

Howard, Ellen. *The big seed* ill. by Lillian Hoban. S&S, 1993. ISBN 0-671-73956-5 Subj: Behavior – growing up. Family life. Family life – stepfamilies. Gardens, gardening. School. Seeds.

The log cabin Christmas ill. by Ronald Himler. Holiday, 2000. ISBN 0-8234-1381-0 Subj: Family life. Holidays – Christmas. U.S. history – frontier & pioneer life.

The log cabin church ill. by Ronald Himler. Holiday, 2002. ISBN 0-8234-1740-8 Subj: Family life. Religion. U.S. history – frontier & pioneer life.

The log cabin quilt ill. by Ronald Himler. Holiday, 1996. ISBN 0-8234-1247-4 Subj: Family life – grandmothers. Quilts. U.S. history – frontier & pioneer life.

Murphy and Kate ill. by Mark Graham. S&S, 1995. ISBN 0-671-79775-1 Subj: Animals – dogs. Death. Emotions – grief.

Howard, Ginger. *William's house* ill. by Larry Day. Millbrook, 2001. ISBN 0-7613-1674-4 Subj: Homes, houses. U.S. history.

Howard, Jane R. *When I'm hungry* ill. by Teri Sloat. Dutton, 1992. ISBN 0-525-44983-3 Subj: Animals. Food.

When I'm sleepy ill. by Lynne Cherry. Dutton, 1985. ISBN 0-525-44204-9 Subj: Imagination. Sleep.

Howard, Jean G. *Of mice and mice* ill. by author. Tidal Pr., 1978. ISBN 0-930954-03-3 Subj: Animals – mice.

Howard, Katherine. *Do you know colors?* (Miller, J. P. [John Parr])

I can count to 100 . . . can you? ill. by Michael J. Smollin. Random House, 1979. ISBN 0-394-84090-9 Subj: Counting, numbers.

My first picture dictionary ill. by Huck Scarry. Random House, 1978. ISBN 0-394-93486-5 Subj: Dictionaries.

Howard, Kim. *In wintertime* ill. by author. Lothrop, 1994. ISBN 0-688-11379-6 Subj: Family life – grandmothers. Foreign lands – Norway. Seasons – winter.

Howard, Reginald. *The big, big wall* ill. by Ariane Dewey & José Aruego. Harcourt, 2000. ISBN 0-15-216504-5 Subj: Eggs. Friendship. Rhyming text.

Howard-Gibbon, Amelia Frances. *An illustrated comic alphabet* ill. by author. Walck, 1967. Subj: ABC books.

Howe, Caroline Walton. *Counting penguins* ill. by author. Harper-Collins, 1983. ISBN 0-06-022619-6 Subj: Birds – penguins. Counting, numbers.

Teddy Bear's bird and beast band ill. by author. Windmill, 1980. ISBN 0-671-96116-0 Subj: Music. Musical instruments – bands. Toys – bears.

Howe, Florence. *Carly* (Fuchshuber, Annegert)

Howe, James. *Bunnicula escapes! a pop-up adventure* ill. by Alan & Lea Daniel; paper engineering by Vicki Teague-Cooper. Morrow, 1995. ISBN 0-688-13212-X Subj: Animals – rabbits. Behavior – running away. Format, unusual – toy & movable books.

The case of the missing mother ill. by William Cleaver. Random House, 1983. ISBN 0-394-85729-1 Subj: Holidays – Mother's Day. Puppets.

Creepy-crawly birthday ill. by Leslie Holt Morrill. Morrow, 1991. ISBN 0-688-09688-3 Subj: Animals – cats. Animals – dogs. Birthdays. Pets.

The day the teacher went bananas ill. by Lillian Hoban. Dutton, 1984. ISBN 0-525-44107-7 Subj: Animals – gorillas. School. Zoos.

Horace and Morris but mostly Dolores ill. by Amy Walrod. Atheneum, 1999. ISBN 0-689-31874-X Subj: Animals – mice. Clubs, gangs. Friendship.

Horace and Morris join the chorus (but what about Dolores?) ill. by Amy Walrod. Atheneum, 2002. ISBN 0-689-83939-1 Subj: Activities – singing. Animals – mice. Character traits – persistence. Emotions – anger. Friendship.

Hot fudge ill. by Leslie Holt Morrill. Morrow, 1990. ISBN 0-688-09701-4 Subj: Animals. Food.

I wish I were a butterfly ill. by Ed Young. Harcourt, 1987. ISBN 0-15-200470-X Subj: Behavior – wishing. Emotions – envy, jealousy.

Pinky and Rex and the just-right pet ill. by Melissa Sweet. Atheneum, 2001. ISBN 0-689-82861-6 Subj: Animals – babies. Animals – cats. Pets.

Rabbit-Cadabra! ill. by Alan Daniel. Morrow, 1993. ISBN 0-688-10403-7 Subj: Animals – cats. Animals – dogs. Animals – rabbits. Careers – magicians.

Scared silly ill. by Leslie Holt Morrill. Morrow, 1989. ISBN 0-688-07667-X Subj: Animals – cats. Animals – dogs. Animals – rabbits. Holidays – Halloween. Witches.

There's a dragon in my sleeping bag ill. by David S. Rose. Atheneum, 1994. ISBN 0-689-31873-1 Subj: Dragons. Family life – brothers. Imagination – imaginary friends.

There's a monster under my bed ill. by David S. Rose. Atheneum, 1986. ISBN 0-689-31178-8 Subj: Emotions – fear. Furniture – beds. Monsters. Night.

When you go to kindergarten photos by Betsy Imershein. Morrow, 1994. ISBN 0-688-12913-7 Subj: School – first day.

Howe, John. *Jack and the beanstalk* (Jack and the beanstalk)

Rip Van Winkle (Irving, Washington)

Howell, Lynn. *Winifred's new bed* by Lynn & Richard Howell; ill. by authors. Knopf, 1985. ISBN 0-394-87772-1 Subj: Animals – cats. Days of the week, months of the year. Format, unusual. Furniture – beds. Toys.

Howell, Richard. *Winifred's new bed* (Howell, Lynn)

Howell, Ruth. *Everything changes* photos by Arline Strong. Atheneum, 1968. Subj: Seasons.

Splash and flow photos by Arline Strong. Atheneum, 1973. ISBN 0-689-30101-4 Subj: Science.

Howell, Troy. *The ugly duckling* (Andersen, H. C. [Hans Christian])

Howell, Will C. *I call it sky* ill. by John Ward. Walker, 1999. ISBN 0-8027-8678-2 Subj: Friendship. Nature. Seasons. Weather.

Zoo flakes ABC ill. by author. Walker, 2002. ISBN 0-8027-8826-2 Subj: ABC books. Activities – making things. Animals. Art. Paper.

Howells, Mildred. *The woman who lived in Holland* ill. by William Curtis Holdsworth. Farrar, 1973. Text originally published in 1898 in St. Nicholas magazine under title: Going too far. ISBN 0-374-38460-6 Subj: Character traits – cleanliness. Foreign lands – Holland. Rhyming text.

Howitt, Mary Botham. *Mary Howitt's The spider and the fly* ill. by Tony DiTerlizzi. S&S, 2002. ISBN 0-689-85289-4 Subj: Caldecott award honor books. Insects – flies. Poetry. Spiders.

Howland, Naomi. *ABCDrive!* ill. by author. Clarion, 1994. ISBN 0-395-66414-4 Subj: ABC books. Activities – traveling. Automobiles.

Latkes, latkes, good to eat: a Chanukah story ill. by author. Clarion, 1999. ISBN 0-395-89903-6 Subj: Folk & fairy tales. Foreign lands – Russia. Holidays – Hanukkah. Jewish culture. Magic.

The matzah man ill. by author. Clarion, 2002. ISBN 0-618-11750-4 Subj: Behavior – running away. Cumulative tales. Food. Holidays – Passover. Jewish culture.

Hoyt-Goldsmith, Diane. *Celebrating Chinese New Year* photos by Lawrence Migdale. Holiday, 1998. ISBN 0-8234-1393-4 Subj: Ethnic groups in the U.S. – Chinese Americans. Holidays – Chinese New Year.

Hru, Dakari. *Joshua's Masai mask* ill. by Anna Rich. Lee & Low, 1993. ISBN 1-880000-02-4 Subj: Behavior – wishing. Ethnic groups in the U.S. – African Americans. Magic. Masks.

The magic moonberry jump ropes ill. by E. B. Lewis. Dial, 1996. ISBN 0-8037-1755-5 Subj: Activities – playing. Family life – sisters. Friendship. Sports – jumping rope.

Tickle, tickle ill. by Ken Wilson-Max. Roaring Brook, 2002. ISBN 0-7613-1537-3 Subj: Activities – playing. Babies. Family life – fathers. Games. Rhyming text.

Hubbard, Patricia. *My crayons talk* ill. by G. Brian Karas. Holt, 1996. ISBN 0-8050-3529-X Subj: Concepts – color. Rhyming text.

Trick or treat countdown ill. by Michael Letzig. Holiday, 1999. ISBN 0-8234-1367-5 Subj: Counting, numbers. Holidays – Halloween. Rhyming text.

Hubbard, Woodleigh Marx. *All that you are* ill. by author. Putnam, 2000. ISBN 0-399-23364-4 Subj: Character traits – optimism. Self-concept.

C is for curious: an ABC of feelings ill. by author. Chronicle, 1990. ISBN 0-8770-1679-8 Subj: ABC books. Emotions.

2 is for dancing: a 1 2 3 of actions ill. by author. Chronicle, 1991. ISBN 0-8770-1895-2 Subj: Activities. Animals. Counting, numbers.

Whoa, jealousy ill. by Madeleine Houston. Putnam, 2002. New York. ISBN 0-399-23435-7 Subj: Behavior. Emotions – envy, jealousy.

Hubbell, Patricia. *Black earth, gold sun* ill. by Mary Newell DePalma. Cavendish, 2001. ISBN 0-7614-5090-4 Subj: Gardens, gardening. Poetry.

Boo! Halloween poems and limericks ill. by Jeff Spackman. Cavendish, 1998. ISBN 0-7614-5023-8 Subj: Holidays – Halloween. Poetry.

Bouncing time ill. by Melissa Sweet. HarperCollins, 2000. ISBN 0-688-17376-4 Subj: Babies. Family life. Poetry. Zoos.

Camel caravan (Roberts, Bethany)

City kids ill. by Teresa Flavin. Cavendish, 2001. ISBN 0-7614-5079-3 Subj: Cities, towns. Poetry.

Earthmates ill. by Jean Cassels. Cavendish, 2000. ISBN 0-7614-5062-9 Subj: Animals. Poetry.

Pots and pans ill. by Diane de Groat. HarperFestival, 1998. ISBN 0-694-01072-3 Subj: Activities – playing. Format, unusual – board books. Noise, sounds. Rhyming text.

Rabbit moon ill. by Wendy Watson. Cavendish, 2002. ISBN 0-7614-5103-X Subj: Animals – rabbits. Days of the week, months of the year. Holidays. Rhyming text.

Sea, sand, me! ill. by Lisa Campbell Ernst. HarperCollins, 2001. ISBN 0-688-17379-9 Subj: Family life – mothers. Rhyming text. Sea & seashore – beaches.

Sidewalk trip ill. by Mari Takabayashi. HarperFestival, 1999. ISBN 0-694-01174-6 Subj: Activities – walking. Cities, towns. Communities, neighborhoods. Family life – mothers. Rhyming text.

Wrapping paper romp ill. by Jennifer Plecas. HarperFestival, 1998. ISBN 0-694-01098-7 Subj: Animals – cats. Babies. Format, unusual – board books. Gifts. Holidays – Halloween. Rhyming text.

Hubbell, Will. *Pumpkin Jack* ill. by author. A. Whitman, 2000. ISBN 0-8075-6665-9 Subj: Holidays – Halloween. Plants. Seeds.

Huck, Charlotte S. *A creepy countdown* ill. by Jos. A. Smith. Greenwillow, 1998. ISBN 0-688-15461-1 Subj: Counting, numbers. Holidays – Halloween. Rhyming text.

Princess Furball ill. by Anita Lobel. Greenwillow, 1989. ISBN 0-688-07838-9 Subj: Character traits – cleverness. Folk & fairy tales. Royalty – princesses.

Secret places poems sel. by Charlotte Huck; ill. by Lindsay Barrett George. Greenwillow, 1993. ISBN 0-688-11670-1 Subj: Behavior – solitude. Poetry.

Hudelhoff, Allen H. *Cats and kids* ill. by Anne Canevari Green. Millbrook, 2002. ISBN 0-7613-2668-5 Subj: Activities – playing. Animals – cats. Character traits – cooperation.

Hudson, Cheryl Willis. *Afro-Bets ABC book* ill. by autor. Just Us Books, 1987. ISBN 0-439-42917-X Subj: ABC books. Ethnic groups in the U.S. – African Americans.

Afro-Bets 123 book ill. by autor. Just Us Books, 1987. ISBN 0-439-42916-1 Subj: Counting, numbers. Ethnic groups in the U.S. – African Americans.

Animal sounds for baby ill. by George Ford. Scholastic, 1995. ISBN 0-590-48029-4 Subj: Animals. Babies. Ethnic groups in the U.S. – African Americans. Format, unusual – board books. Noise, sounds. Rhyming text.

Bright eyes, brown skin by Cheryl Willis Hudson & Bernette G. Ford; ill. by George Ford. Just Us Books, 1990. ISBN 0-940975-10-6 Subj: Ethnic groups in the U.S. – African Americans. Poetry.

Good morning baby ill. by George Ford. Scholastic, 1992. ISBN 0-590-45760-8 Subj: Babies. Ethnic groups in the U.S. – African Americans. Format, unusual – board books. Morning. Rhyming text.

Good night baby ill. by George Ford. Scholastic, 1992. ISBN 0-590-45761-6 Subj: Babies. Bedtime. Ethnic groups in the U.S. – African Americans. Format, unusual – board books. Night. Rhyming text.

Let's count, baby ill. by George Ford. Scholastic, 1995. ISBN 0-590-48028-6 Subj: Counting, numbers. Ethnic groups in the U.S. – African Americans. Format, unusual – board books. Rhyming text.

Hudson, Eleanor. *A whale of a rescue* ill. by Pat Paris. Random House, 1983. ISBN 0-394-85642-2 Subj: Animals – whales.

Hudson, Wade. *Afro-Bets Kids I'm gonna be* ill. by Culverson Blair. Just Us Books, 1992. ISBN 0-940975-40-8 Subj: ABC books. Ethnic groups in the U.S. – African Americans.

I love my family ill. by Cal Massey. Scholastic, 1993. ISBN 0-590-45764-0 Subj: Ethnic groups in the U.S. – African Americans. Family life. Farms.

Jamal's busy day ill. by George Ford. Just Us Books, 1991. ISBN 0-940975-21-1 Subj: Careers – accountants. Careers – architects. Family life – fathers. Family life – mothers. School.

Pass it on: African-American poetry for children ill. by Floyd Cooper. Scholastic, 1993. ISBN 0-590-45770-5 Subj: Ethnic groups in the U.S. – African Americans. Poetry.

Huff, Barbara A. *Once inside the library* ill. by Iris Van Rynbach. Little, 1990. ISBN 0-316-37967-0 Subj: Books, reading. Libraries.

Huff, Vivian. *Let's make paper dolls* photos by author. HarperCollins, 1978. ISBN 0-06-022644-7 Subj: Activities – making things. Paper. Toys – dolls.

Huffaker, Alice. *That first Christmas day* ill. by Keith Neely. Moody, 1989. ISBN 0-8024-2637-9 Subj: Holidays – Christmas. Religion – Nativity. Rhyming text.

Hughes, Langston. *Carol of the brown king: nativity poems* ill. by Ashley Bryan. Atheneum, 1998. ISBN 0-689-81877-7 Subj: Ethnic groups in the U.S. – African Americans. Holidays – Christmas. Poetry. Religion – Nativity.

The sweet and sour animal book ill. by students from the Harlem School of the Arts. Oxford Univ. Pr., 1994. ISBN 0-19-509185-X Subj: ABC books. Animals. Art. Children as illustrators. Poetry.

Hughes, Monica. *A handful of seeds* ill. by Luis Garay. Orchard, 1996. ISBN 0-531-09498-7 Subj: Behavior – sharing. Ethnic groups in the U.S. – Hispanic Americans. Food. Gardens, gardening. Homeless.

Little Fingerling ill. by Brenda Clark. Ideals, 1992. ISBN 0-8249-8553-2 Subj: Character traits – bravery. Character traits – cleverness. Family life. Folk & fairy tales. Foreign lands – Japan. Little people.

Hughes, Peter. *The emperor's oblong pancake* ill. by Gerald Rose. Abelard-Schuman, 1961. Subj: Concepts – shape. Food. Royalty – emperors.

The king who loved candy ill. by Gerald Rose. Abelard-Schuman, 1964. Subj: Food. Royalty – kings. War.

Hughes, Richard. *Gertrude's child* ill. by Rick Schreiter. Crown, 1966. Subj: Behavior – needing someone. Behavior – running away. Toys.

Hughes, Sarah. *Let's play hopscotch* ill. with photos. Childrens Pr., 2000. ISBN 0-516-23112-X Subj: Activities – playing. Games.

Let's play jacks ill. with photos. Childrens Pr., 2000. ISBN 0-516-23113-8 Subj: Activities – playing. Games.

Hughes, Shirley. *Abel's moon* ill. by author. DK, 1999. ISBN 0-7894-4601-4 Subj: Activities – traveling. Activities – writing. Emotions – loneliness. Family life – fathers. Imagination. Moon.

Alfie and the birthday surprise ill. by author. Lothrop, 1998. ISBN 0-688-15187-6 Subj: Animals – cats. Birthdays. Gifts. Parties.

Alfie gets in first ill. by author. Lothrop, 1982. ISBN 0-688-00849-6 Subj: Cumulative tales. Homes, houses.

Alfie gives a hand ill. by author. Lothrop, 1984. ISBN 0-688-02387-8 Subj: Behavior – needing someone. Birthdays. Parties.

Alfie's ABC ill. by author. Lothrop, 1998. ISBN 0-688-16126-X Subj: ABC books. Family life – brothers & sisters.

Alfie's feet ill. by author. Lothrop, 1983. ISBN 0-688-01660-X Subj: Activities – playing.

All shapes and sizes ill. by author. Lothrop, 1986. ISBN 0-688-04205-8 Subj: Concepts – shape. Concepts – size. Rhyming text.

Angel Mae ill. by author. Lothrop, 1989. ISBN 0-688-08539-3 Subj: Babies. Family life – new sibling. Holidays – Christmas. Theater.

Annie Rose is my little sister ill. by author. Candlewick, 2003. ISBN 0-7636-1959-0 Subj: Activities. Family life – brothers & sisters.

Bathwater's hot ill. by author. Lothrop, 1985. ISBN 0-688-04202-3 Subj: Activities – bathing. Concepts – opposites. Family life. Foreign lands – England. Rhyming text.

Being together ill. by author. Candlewick, 1997. ISBN 0-7636-0399-6 Subj: Babies. Family life. Format, unusual – board books.

The big concrete lorry ill. by author. Lothrop, 1990. ISBN 0-688-08535-0 Subj: Activities – making things. Cities, towns. Ethnic groups in the U.S. Homes, houses.

Bouncing ill. by author. Candlewick, 1993. ISBN 1-56402-128-9 Subj: Activities.

Chatting ill. by author. Candlewick, 1994. ISBN 1-56402-340-0 Subj: Communication. Communities, neighborhoods. Family life.

Colors ill. by author. Lothrop, 1986. ISBN 0-688-04206-6 Subj: Concepts – color. Rhyming text.

David and dog ill. by author. Prentice-Hall, 1978. Edition of 1977 published under title: Dogger. ISBN 0-13-197301-0 Subj: Activities – trading. Family life. Toys.

Dogger ill. by author. Lothrop, 1988, 1977. 1978 Prentice-Hall edition published under title David and dog. ISBN 0-688-07981-4 Subj: Activities – trading. Family life. Toys.

An evening at Alfie's ill. by author. Lothrop, 1985. ISBN 0-688-04123-X Subj: Activities – babysitting. Family life. Problem solving.

George the babysitter ill. by author. Prentice-Hall, 1978. ISBN 0-13-352682-8 Subj: Activities – babysitting.

Giving ill. by author. Candlewick, 1993. ISBN 1-56402-129-7 Subj: Character traits – generosity. Family life.

Hiding ill. by author. Candlewick, 1994. ISBN 1-56402-342-7 Subj: Behavior – hiding.

Lucy and Tom's A.B.C. ill. by author. Viking, 1986. ISBN 0-670-81256-0 Subj: ABC books. Family life. Foreign lands – England.

Lucy and Tom's Christmas ill. by author. Viking, 1986. ISBN 0-670-81255-2 Subj: Family life. Foreign lands – England. Holidays – Christmas. Religion.

Lucy and Tom's 1, 2, 3 ill. by author. Viking, 1987. ISBN 0-670-81763-5 Subj: Concepts. Counting, numbers. Family life.

Moving Molly ill. by author. Prentice-Hall, 1979. ISBN 0-13-604587-1 Subj: Emotions – loneliness. Family life. Friendship. Moving.

Noisy ill. by author. Lothrop, 1985. ISBN 0-688-04203-1 Subj: Family life. Foreign lands – England. Noise, sounds. Rhyming text.

Olly and me ill. by author. Candlewick, 2004. ISBN 0-7636-2374-1 Subj: Babies. Family life. Family life – brothers & sisters. Poetry.

Out and about ill. by author. Lothrop, 1988. ISBN 0-688-07691-2 Subj: Family life. Foreign lands – England. Rhyming text.

Playing ill. by author. Candlewick, 1997. ISBN 0-7636-0400-3 Subj: Activities – playing. Format, unusual – board books.

Rhymes for Annie Rose ill. by author. Lothrop, 1995. ISBN 0-688-14220-6 Subj: Family life – brothers & sisters. Rhyming text.

Sally's secret ill. by author. Merrimack, 1980. ISBN 0-370-02010-3 Subj: Behavior – secrets. Homes, houses.

The snow lady ill. by author. Lothrop, 1990. ISBN 0-688-09875-4 Subj: Behavior – misbehavior. Foreign lands – England. Old age. Snowmen. Weather – snow.

Two shoes, new shoes ill. by author. Lothrop, 1986. ISBN 0-688-04207-4 Subj: Clothing – shoes. Rhyming text.

Up and up ill. by author. Lothrop, 1986. First published by Prentice-Hall, 1979. ISBN 0-688-06261-X Subj: Activities – flying. Imagination. Wordless.

Wheels ill. by author. Lothrop, 1991. ISBN 0-688-09880-0 Subj: Birthdays. Friendship. Sports – bicycling.

When we went to the park ill. by author. Lothrop, 1985. ISBN 0-688-04204-X Subj: Counting, numbers. Family life. Family life – grandfathers. Foreign lands – England. Parks. Rhyming text.

Hughes, Vi. *Aziz, the story teller* ill. by Stefan Czernecki. Crocodile, 2001. ISBN 1-56656-456-5 Subj: Activities – storytelling. Family life – fathers.

Hugo, Pierre de. *Lions* (Lions)

Hulbert, Jay. *Armando asked "Why?"* by Jay Hulbert & Sid Kantor; ill. by Pat Hoggan. Raintree, 1990. ISBN 0-8172-3576-0 Subj: Character traits – questioning. Ethnic groups in the U.S. – African Americans. Libraries.

Huling, Jan. *Puss in cowboy boots* ill. by Phil Huling. S&S, 2002. ISBN 0-689-83119-6 Subj: Animals – cats. Character traits – cleverness. Clothing – boots. Folk & fairy tales. Foreign lands – France. Royalty – kings.

Hull, Rod. *Mr. Betts and Mr. Potts* ill. by Jo Davies. Barefoot, 2000. ISBN 1-84148-106-8 Subj: Animals. Careers – veterinarians. Illness. Pets. Rhyming text.

Hulme, Joy N. *Bubble trouble* ill. by Mike Cressy. Childrens Pr., 1999. ISBN 0-516-21584-1 Subj: Activities – playing. Bubbles. Rhyming text.

Eerie feary feeling: a hairy scary pop-up book ill. by Paul Ely. Orchard, 1998. ISBN 0-531-30086-2 Subj: Emotions. Format, unusual – toy & movable books.

Sea squares ill. by Carol Schwartz. Walt Disney, 1991. ISBN 1-56282-080-X Subj: Animals. Counting, numbers. Rhyming text. Sea & seashore.

Sea sums ill. by Carol Schwartz. Hyperion, 1996. ISBN 0-7868-2142-6 Subj: Counting, numbers. Rhyming text. Sea & seashore.

What if? just wondering poems ill. by Valeri Gorbachev. Boyds Mills, 1993. ISBN 1-56397-186-0 Subj: Animals. Poetry.

Hulme, Susan. *Let's look for colors* (Gillham, Bill)

Let's look for numbers (Gillham, Bill)

Let's look for opposites (Gillham, Bill)

Let's look for shapes (Gillham, Bill)

Hulpach, Vladimir. *Ahaiyute and Cloud Eater* ill. by Marek Zawadzki. Harcourt, 1996. ISBN 0-15-201237-0 Subj: Character traits – bravery. Folk & fairy tales. Indians of North America – Zuni. Magic. Monsters.

Hulse, Gillian. *Morris, where are you?* ill. by author. Oxford Univ. Pr., 1988. ISBN 0-19-520646-0 Subj: Animals – cats. Behavior – hiding. Problem solving.

Hume, Stephen Eaton. *Red moon follows truck* ill. by Leslie Elizabeth Watts. Orca, 2001. ISBN 1-55143-218-8 Subj: Activities – traveling. Animals – dogs. Camps, camping. Foreign lands – Canada. Moving.

Humphries, Tudor. *Are you a butterfly?* (Allen, Judy)

Are you a grasshopper? (Allen, Judy)

Are you a ladybug? (Allen, Judy)

Are you a snail? (Allen, Judy)

Are you an ant? (Allen, Judy)

Hiding ill. by author. Orchard, 1997. ISBN 0-5313-0056-0 Subj: Behavior – hiding. Behavior – misbehavior. Family life.

Hundal, Nancy. *Camping* ill. by Brian Deines. Fitzhenry & Whiteside, 2002. ISBN 1-55041-668-5 Subj: Activities – vacationing. Camps, camping. Family life. Poetry.

Number 21 ill. by Brian Deines. Fitzhenry & Whiteside, 2001. ISBN 1-55041-543-3 Subj: Family life – fathers. Trucks.

Twilight fairies ill. by Don Kilby. Fitzhenry & Whiteside, 2002. ISBN 1-55041-645-6 Subj: Fairies.

Hundley, David H. *Bruises* photos by author. Rourke, 1998. ISBN 1-57103-254-1 Subj: Illness.

Huneck, Stephen. *Sally goes to the beach* ill. by author. Abrams, 2000. ISBN 0-8109-4186-4 Subj: Animals – dogs. Sea & seashore – beaches.

Sally goes to the farm ill. by author. Abrams, 2002. ISBN 0-8109-4498-7 Subj: Animals. Animals – dogs. Farms.

Sally goes to the mountains ill. by author. Abrams, 2001. Subj: Animals – dogs. Camps, camping. Mountains.

Hunt, Angela Elwell. *The tale of three trees* ill. by Tim Jonke. Lion, 1999. ISBN 0-7459-4082-X Subj: Folk & fairy tales. Religion. Trees.

Hunt, Bernice Kohn. *Your ant is a which* ill. by Jan Pyk. Harcourt, 1975. ISBN 0-15-299880-2 Subj: Language.

Hunt, Francesca. *see* Holland, Isabelle

Hunt, Jonathan. *Leif's saga* ill. by author. S&S, 1996. ISBN 0-02-745780-X Subj: Boats, ships. Careers – boat builders. Careers – explorers. Family life. Folk & fairy tales. Sea & seashore.

One is a mouse by Jonathan & Lisa Hunt; ill. by authors. Macmillan, 1995. ISBN 0-02-745781-8 Subj: Animals. Counting, numbers. Rhyming text.

Hunt, Joyce. *A first look at bird nests* (Selsam, Millicent E.)

A first look at caterpillars (Selsam, Millicent E.)

A first look at cats (Selsam, Millicent E.)

A first look at dinosaurs (Selsam, Millicent E.)

A first look at dogs (Selsam, Millicent E.)

A first look at flowers (Selsam, Millicent E.)

A first look at kangaroos, koalas and other animals with pouches (Selsam, Millicent E.)

A first look at monkeys (Selsam, Millicent E.)

A first look at owls, eagles and other hunters of the sky (Selsam, Millicent E.)

A first look at rocks (Selsam, Millicent E.)

A first look at seashells (Selsam, Millicent E.)

A first look at sharks (Selsam, Millicent E.)

A first look at spiders (Selsam, Millicent E.)

A first look at the world of plants (Selsam, Millicent E.)

A first look at whales (Selsam, Millicent E.)

Keep looking! (Selsam, Millicent E.)

Hunt, Lisa. *One is a mouse* (Hunt, Jonathan)

Hunt, Nan. *Families are funny* ill. by Deborah Niland. Orchard, 1992. ISBN 0-531-08569-4 Subj: Family life.

Hunter, Anne. *Possum and the peeper* ill. by author. Houghton Mifflin, 1998. ISBN 0-395-84631-5 Subj: Animals. Animals – possums. Frogs & toads. Seasons – spring.

Possum's harvest moon ill. by author. Houghton Mifflin, 1996. ISBN 0-395-73575-0 Subj: Animals. Animals – possums. Moon. Parties. Seasons.

What's in the meadow? ill. by author. Houghton, 2000. ISBN 0-618-01512-4 Subj: Animals. Birds. Insects.

What's in the pond ill. by author. Houghton, 1999. ISBN 0-395-91224-5 Subj: Animals. Insects. Lakes, ponds. Reptiles.

What's in the tide pool? ill. by author. Houghton, 2000. Subj: Animals. Sea & seashore.

Hunter, C. W. *The green gourd* ill. by Tony Griego. Putnam, 1992. ISBN 0-399-22278-2 Subj: Folk & fairy tales. Magic.

Hunter, Dette. *38 ways to entertain your babysitter* ill. by Stephen MacEachern. Annick, 2003. ISBN 1-55037-795-7 Subj: Activities – babysitting. Activities – baking, cooking. Activities – making things. Games.

38 ways to entertain your grandparents ill. by Deirdre Betteridge. Annick, 2002. ISBN 1-55037-749-3 Subj: Activities – baking, cooking. Activities – making things. Family life – grandparents. Games.

Hunter, Jana Novotny. *Little ones do* ill. by Sally Anne Lambert. Dutton, 2001. ISBN 0-525-46690-8 Subj: Dragons. Family life – parents. Rhyming text.

Hunter, Norman. *Professor Branestawn's building bust-up* ill. by Gerald Rose. Merrimack, 1982. ISBN 0-370-30457-8 Subj: Homes, houses. Humorous stories. Machines.

Hunter, Ryan Ann. *Cross a bridge* ill. by Edward Miller. Holiday, 1998. ISBN 0-8234-1340-3 Subj: Bridges.

Into the sky ill. by Edward Miller. Holiday, 1998. ISBN 0-8234-1372-1 Subj: Buildings. Careers – architects.

Hunter, Sally. *Humphrey's bedtime* ill. by author. Holt, 2001. ISBN 0-8050-6903-8 Subj: Animals – elephants. Bedtime. Family life – brothers & sisters.

Humphrey's birthday ill. by author. Holt, 2003. ISBN 0-8050-7421-X Subj: Animals – elephants. Birthdays. Parties.

Humphrey's Christmas ill. by author. Holt, 2002. ISBN 0-8050-7176-8 Subj: Animals – elephants. Family life – brothers & sisters. Holidays – Christmas.

Humphrey's corner ill. by author. Holt, 2001. ISBN 0-8050-6786-8 Subj: Activities – playing. Animals – elephants. Family life – mothers.

Hunter, Tom. *Build it up and knock it down* ill. by James Yang. HarperFestival, 2002. ISBN 0-694-01568-7 Subj: Concepts – opposites. Friendship. Language.

Huntington, Amy. *One Monday* ill. by author. Orchard, 2001. ISBN 0-439-29304-9 Subj: Farms. Weather – wind.

Hurd, Edith Thacher. *The black dog who went into the woods* ill. by Emily Arnold McCully. HarperCollins, 1980. ISBN 0-06-022684-6 Subj: Animals – dogs. Death. Pets.

Caboose ill. by Clement Hurd. Lothrop, 1950. Subj: Rhyming text. Trains.

Christmas eve ill. by Clement Hurd. Harper, 1962. Subj: Animals. Holidays – Christmas.

Come and have fun ill. by Clement Hurd. HarperCollins, 1962. ISBN 0-06-022681-1 Subj: Animals – cats. Animals – mice. Rhyming text.

The day the sun danced ill. by Clement Hurd. HarperCollins, 1965. ISBN 0-06-022692-7 Subj: Seasons. Seasons – spring. Sun.

Dinosaur, my darling ill. by Don Freeman. HarperCollins, 1978. ISBN 0-06-022744-3 Subj: Dinosaurs. Prehistory.

Engine, engine no. 9 ill. by Clement Hurd. Lothrop, 1940. Subj: Trains.

Five little firemen (Brown, Margaret Wise)

Hurry, hurry! ill. by Clement Hurd. HarperCollins, 1960. Subj: Activities – babysitting. Behavior – hurrying.

I dance in my red pajamas ill. by Emily Arnold McCully. Harper-Collins, 1982. ISBN 0-06-022700-1 Subj: Activities – dancing. Family life – grandparents.

Johnny Lion's bad day ill. by Clement Hurd. New ed. Harper-Collins, 2001. ISBN 0-06-029336-5 Subj: Animals – lions. Behavior – bad day. Illness.

Johnny Lion's book ill. by Clement Hurd. New ed. HarperCollins, 2001. ISBN 0-06-029334-9 Subj: Animals – lions. Behavior – lost. Books, reading.

Johnny Lion's rubber boots ill. by Clement Hurd. New ed. Harper-Collins, 2001. ISBN 0-06-029338-1 Subj: Animals – lions. Clothing – boots. Weather – rain.

Last one home is a green pig ill. by Clement Hurd. HarperCollins, 1959. ISBN 0-06-022716-8 Subj: Animals – monkeys. Birds – ducks. Games. Sports – racing.

Little dog, dreaming by Edith Thacher Hurd & Thacher Hurd; ill. by Clement Hurd. HarperCollins, 1967. Subj: Animals – dogs. Dreams.

Look for a bird ill. by Clement Hurd. HarperCollins, 1977. ISBN 0-06-022720-6 Subj: Birds. Nature. Science.

The mother chimpanzee ill. by Clement Hurd. Little, 1978. ISBN 0-316-38327-9 Subj: Animals – chimpanzees. Family life – mothers.

The mother kangaroo ill. by Clement Hurd. Little, 1976. ISBN 0-316-38326-0 Subj: Animals – kangaroos. Family life. Science.

No funny business ill. by Clement Hurd. HarperCollins, 1962. Subj: Activities – picnicking. Animals – cats.

Sandpipers ill. by Lucienne Bloch. Crowell, 1961. Subj: Birds – sandpipers. Science.

The so-so cat ill. by Clement Hurd. HarperCollins, 1964. Subj: Animals – cats. Holidays – Halloween. Witches.

Starfish ill. by Lucienne Bloch. Crowell, 1962. ISBN 0-690-77069-3 Subj: Animals – starfish. Science. Sea & seashore.

Stop, stop ill. by Clement Hurd. HarperCollins, 1961. Subj: Activities – babysitting. Character traits – cleanliness.

Under the lemon tree ill. by Clement Hurd. Little, 1980. ISBN 0-316-38328-7 Subj: Animals – donkeys. Animals – foxes. Character traits – loyalty. Farms.

What whale? Where? ill. by Clement Hurd. HarperCollins, 1966. Subj: Animals – whales. Boats, ships.

The white horse ill. by Tony Chen. HarperCollins, 1970. Subj: Imagination.

Wilson's world ill. by Clement Hurd. HarperCollins, 1971. ISBN 0-06-022750-8 Subj: Art. Ecology.

Hurd, Thacher. *Art dog* ill. by author. HarperCollins, 1996. ISBN 0-06-024425-9 Subj: Activities – painting. Animals – dogs. Art. Museums. Mystery stories.

Axle the freeway cat ill. by author. HarperCollins, 1988. ISBN 0-06-443173-8 Subj: Animals – cats. Friendship.

Blackberry ramble ill. by author. Crown, 1989. ISBN 0-517-57105-6 Subj: Animals – mice. Farms. Seasons – spring.

Cat's pajamas ill. by author. HarperFestival, 2001. ISBN 0-694-01058-8 Subj: Animals – cats. Format, unusual – board books. Language. Rhyming text.

Hobo dog ill. by author. Scholastic, 1980. ISBN 0-590-31283-9 Subj: Activities – traveling. Animals – dogs. Trains.

Little dog, dreaming (Hurd, Edith Thacher)

Little Mouse's big Valentine ill. by author. HarperCollins, 1990. ISBN 0-06-026193-5 Subj: Animals – mice. Holidays – Valentine's Day.

Little Mouse's birthday cake ill. by author. HarperCollins, 1992. ISBN 0-06-020216-5 Subj: Animals – mice. Birthdays.

Mama don't allow ill. by author. HarperCollins, 1984. ISBN 0-06-022690-0 Subj: Animals – possums. Music. Musical instruments – bands. Reptiles – alligators, crocodiles.

Moo Cow Kaboom! ill. by author. HarperCollins, 2003. ISBN 0-06-050502-8 Subj: Animals – bulls, cows. Farms. Space & space ships.

Mystery on the docks ill. by author. HarperCollins, 1983. ISBN 0-06-022702-8 Subj: Animals – rats. Behavior – bad day. Mystery stories.

A night in the swamp: a movable book ill. by author. HarperCollins, 1987. ISBN 0-694-00177-5 Subj: Animals. Format, unusual – toy & movable books. Night.

The pea patch jig ill. by author. Crown, 1986. ISBN 0-517-56307-X Subj: Animals – mice. Gardens, gardening. Music.

The quiet evening ill. by author. Greenwillow, 1978. ISBN 0-688-84166-X Subj: Night.

Santa Mouse and the ratdeer ill. by author. HarperCollins, 1998. ISBN 0-06-027694-0 Subj: Accidents. Animals – mice. Behavior – bad day. Holidays – Christmas. Santa Claus.

Tomato soup ill. by author. Crown, 1992. ISBN 0-517-58238-4 Subj: Animals – cats. Animals – mice. Farms. Illness.

Zoom City ill. by author. HarperCollins, 1998. ISBN 0-694-01057-X Subj: Automobiles. Cities, towns.

Hurford, John. *The dormouse* ill. by author. Associated Booksellers, 1986. ISBN 0-907349-25-0 Subj: Animals. Animals – mice.

Huriet, Genevieve. *Dandelion's vanishing vegetable garden* ill. by Loic Jouannigot. G. Stevens, 1991. ISBN 0-8368-0526-7 Subj: Animals – rabbits. Gardens, gardening.

Hürlimann, Bettina. *Barry: the story of a brave St. Bernard* ill. by Paul Nussbaumer; trans. by Elizabeth D. Crawford. Harcourt, 1968. Subj: Animals – dogs. Character traits – bravery. Character traits – helpfulness.

Hürlimann, Ruth. *The mouse with the daisy hat* ill. by author. White, 1971. ISBN 0-8725-0245-7 Subj: Animals – mice. Clothing – hats. Weddings.

The proud white cat trans. by Anthea Bell; ill. by author. Morrow, 1977. Translation of Der stolze weisse Kater. ISBN 0-688-32095-3 Subj: Animals – cats. Character traits – pride. Folk & fairy tales. Foreign lands – Germany.

Hurst, Brian Seth. *A pig tale* (Newton-John, Olivia)

Hurst, Carol Otis. *Rocks in his head* ill. by James Stevenson. Greenwillow, 2001. ISBN 0-06-029404-3 Subj: Behavior – collecting things. Rocks. U.S. history.

Hurst, Margaret M. *Grannie and the Jumbie* ill. by author. Harper-Collins, 2001. ISBN 0-06-623633-9 Subj: Folk & fairy tales. Foreign lands – Caribbean Islands.

Hurwitz, Johanna. *A dream come true* photos by Michael Craine. R.C. Owen, 1998. ISBN 1-57274-193-7 Subj: Careers – writers.

Ethan out and about ill. by Brian Floca. Candlewick, 2002. ISBN 0-7636-1098-4 Subj: Animals. Family life – fathers. Food.

New shoes for Silvia ill. by Jerry Pinkney. Morrow, 1993. ISBN 0-688-05287-8 Subj: Clothing – shoes. Foreign lands – Latin America.

Russell's secret ill. by Heather Harms Maione. HarperCollins, 2001. ISBN 0-688-17575-9 Subj: Babies. Family life – brothers & sisters. Sibling rivalry.

Hurwitz, Laura. *Safari in South Africa* (Lumry, Amanda)

Hush little baby. *Hush little baby* ill. by Aliki. Prentice-Hall, 1968. ISBN 0-13-448167-4 Subj: Babies. Character traits – generosity. Cumulative tales. Lullabies. Music.

Hush, little baby ill. by Marla Frazee. Browndeer, 1999. ISBN 0-15-201429-2 Subj: Babies. Character traits – generosity. Cumulative tales. Lullabies. Music.

Hush little baby ill. by Shari Halpern. North-South, 1997. ISBN 1-55858-808-6 Subj: Babies. Character traits – generosity. Cumulative tales. Lullabies. Music.

Hush little baby ill. by Jeanette Winter. Pantheon, 1984. ISBN 0-394-96325-3 Subj: Babies. Character traits – generosity. Cumulative tales. Lullabies. Music.

Hush little baby ill. by Margot Zemach. Dutton, 1976. ISBN 0-525-32510-7 Subj: Babies. Character traits – generosity. Cumulative tales. Lullabies. Music.

Hush songs: African American lullabies col., ed., & commentary by Joyce Carol Thomas; ill. by Brenda Joysmith. Jump at the Sun, 2000. ISBN 0-7868-2488-3 Subj: Ethnic groups in the U.S. – African Americans. Lullabies. Music. Songs.

Huss, Sally. *I love you with all my hearts: the many ways a mother loves her daughter* ill. by author. Tommy Nelson, 1998. ISBN 0-8499-5886-5 Subj: Emotions – love. Family life – mothers. Rhyming text.

Hutchings, Tony. *Things that go word book* ill. by author. Rand McNally, 1977. ISBN 0-528-82040-0 Subj: Machines.

Hutchins, H. J. (Hazel J.). *Beneath the bridge* ill. by Ruth Ohi. Annick, 2004. ISBN 1-55037-859-7 Subj: Activities – traveling. Boats, ships. Dreams. Rhyming text.

Ben's snow song ill. by Lisa Smith. Firefly, 1987. ISBN 0-920303-91-9 Subj: Sports – skiing. Weather – snow.

The catfish palace ill. by Ruth Ohi. Firefly, 1993. ISBN 1-55037-316-1 Subj: Character traits – kindness to animals. Fish.

I'd know you anywhere ill. by Ruth Ohi. Annick, 2002. ISBN 1-55037-747-7 Subj: Disguises. Family life – fathers.

It's raining, Yancy and Bear ill. by Ruth Ohi. Firefly, 1998. ISBN 1-55037-529-6 Subj: Toys – bears. Weather – rain.

Katie's babbling brother ill. by Ruth Ohi. Firefly, 1991. ISBN 1-55037-153-3 Subj: Family life. Noise, sounds. Sibling rivalry.

Leanna builds a genie trap ill. by Catharine O'Neill. Firefly, 1986. ISBN 0-920303-54-4 Subj: Behavior – lost & found possessions. Furniture. Mythical creatures – genies.

Nicholas at the library ill. by Ruth Ohi. Firefly, 1990. ISBN 1-55037-134-7 Subj: Books, reading. Imagination. Libraries.

Norman's snowball ill. by Ruth Ohi. Firefly, 1989. ISBN 1-55037-053-7 Subj: Activities – playing. Behavior – lost & found possessions. Family life. Weather – snow.

One dark night ill. by Susan Kathleen Hartung. Viking, 2001. ISBN 0-670-89246-7 Subj: Animals – babies. Animals – cats. Family life – grandparents. Weather – lightning, thunder. Weather – storms.

One duck ill. by Ruth Ohi. Firefly, 1999. ISBN 1-55037-561-X Subj: Birds – ducks. Careers – farmers. Character traits – kindness to animals. Farms.

The sidewalk rescue ill. by Ruth Ohi. Annick, 2004. ISBN 1-55037-831-7 Subj: Activities – drawing. Art.

Tess ill. by Ruth Ohi. Firefly, 1995. ISBN 1-55037-395-1 Subj: Family life. Foreign lands – Canada. Poverty.

Two so small ill. by Ruth Ohi. Firefly, 2000. ISBN 1-55037-651-9 Subj: Babies. Concepts – size. Format, unusual – toy & movable books. Giants.

Hutchins, Pat. *Changes, changes* ill. by author. Macmillan, 1971. ISBN 0-02-745870-9 Subj: Toys – blocks. Wordless.

Clocks and more clocks ill. by author. Macmillan, 1994. ISBN 0-02-745921-7 Subj: Clocks, watches. Humorous stories. Time.

Don't forget the bacon! ill. by author. Greenwillow, 1975. ISBN 0-688-84019-1 Subj: Behavior – forgetfulness. Cumulative tales. Food. Humorous stories. Shopping.

The doorbell rang ill. by author. Greenwillow, 1986. ISBN 0-688-05252-5 Subj: Behavior – sharing. Family life. Friendship.

Good night owl ill. by author. Macmillan, 1991. ISBN 0-689-71541-2 Subj: Birds – owls. Cumulative tales. Noise, sounds. Participation. Sleep.

Happy birthday, Sam ill. by author. Greenwillow, 1978. ISBN 0-688-84160-0 Subj: Birthdays. Family life – grandfathers.

It's my birthday! ill. by author. Greenwillow, 1999. ISBN 0-688-09664-6 Subj: Behavior – sharing. Birthdays. Family life. Gifts. Monsters.

King Henry's palace ill. by author. Greenwillow, 1983. ISBN 0-688-02295-2 Subj: Birthdays. Holidays – Christmas. Royalty – kings.

Little pink pig ill. by author. Greenwillow, 1994. ISBN 0-688-12015-6 Subj: Animals. Animals – pigs. Bedtime. Behavior – promptness, tardiness.

My best friend ill. by author. Greenwillow, 1993. ISBN 0-688-11486-5 Subj: Ethnic groups in the U.S. – African Americans. Friendship.

1 hunter ill. by author. Greenwillow, 1982. ISBN 0-688-00615-9 Subj: Animals. Counting, numbers.

One-eyed Jake ill. by author. Greenwillow, 1979. ISBN 0-688-84183-X Subj: Pirates.

Our baby is best ill. by author. Greenwillow, 1991. Subj: Adoption. Babies. Family life – new sibling. Family life – sisters.

Rosie's walk ill. by author. Macmillan, 1968. ISBN 0-02-745850-4 Subj: Animals – foxes. Birds – chickens. Farms. Humorous stories.

Rosie's walk [board book] ill. by author. 1st Little Simon board book ed. Little Simon, 1998. ISBN 0-689-82231-6 Subj: Animals. Animals – foxes. Birds – chickens. Farms. Format, unusual – board books.

Shrinking mouse ill. by author. Greenwillow, 1997. ISBN 0-688-13962-0 Subj: Animals. Concepts – perspective. Concepts – size.

Silly Billy! ill. by author. Greenwillow, 1992. ISBN 0-688-10818-0 Subj: Family life – brothers & sisters. Monsters.

The silver Christmas tree ill. by author. Macmillan, 1974. ISBN 0-02-745920-7 Subj: Animals. Holidays – Christmas. Trees.

The surprise party ill. by author. Macmillan, 1986, 1969. ISBN 0-02-745930-6 Subj: Animals. Behavior – gossip. Parties.

The tale of Thomas Mead ill. by author. Greenwillow, 1980. ISBN 0-688-84282-8 Subj: Books, reading. Rhyming text.

Ten red apples. Greenwillow, 2000. ISBN 0-688-16798-5 Subj: Animals. Counting, numbers. Food. Noise, sounds. Rhyming text.

Three-star Billy ill. by author. Greenwillow, 1994. ISBN 0-688-13079-8 Subj: Behavior – misbehavior. Monsters. School.

Tidy Titch ill. by author. Greenwillow, 1991. ISBN 0-688-09964-5 Subj: Behavior. Family life. Toys.

Titch ill. by author. Macmillan, 1971. Subj: Concepts – size. Cumulative tales. Family life. Plants.

Titch and Daisy ill. by author. Greenwillow, 1996. ISBN 0-688-13960-4 Subj: Behavior – hiding. Character traits – shyness. Friendship. Parties.

The very worst monster ill. by author. Greenwillow, 1985. ISBN 0-688-04011-X Subj: Monsters. Sibling rivalry.

What game shall we play? ill. by author. Greenwillow, 1990. ISBN 0-688-09197-0 Subj: Animals. Games.

Where's the baby? ill. by author. Greenwillow, 1988. ISBN 0-688-05934-1 Subj: Babies. Behavior – lost. Behavior – misbehavior. Character traits – cleanliness. Monsters.

Which witch is which? ill. by author. Greenwillow, 1989. ISBN 0-688-06358-6 Subj: Games. Holidays – Halloween. Multiple births – twins. Parties. Rhyming text.

The wind blew ill. by author. Macmillan, 1974. ISBN 0-02-745910-1 Subj: Rhyming text. Weather – wind.

You'll soon grow into them, Titch ill. by author. Greenwillow, 1983. ISBN 0-688-01771-1 Subj: Clothing. Family life.

Huth, Holly Young. *Darkfright* ill. by Jenny Stow. Atheneum, 1996. ISBN 0-689-80188-2 Subj: Emotions – fear. Foreign lands – Caribbean Islands. Night.

The son of the sun and the daughter of the moon ill. by Anna Vojtech. Atheneum, 1999. ISBN 0-689-82482-3 Subj: Folk & fairy tales. Foreign lands – Russia. Moon. Sun.

Twilight ill. by David McPhail. Atheneum, 1999. ISBN 0-689-81975-7 Subj: Night. Twilight.

Hutton, Warwick. *Adam and Eve: the Bible story* ill. by adapt. Macmillan, 1987. ISBN 0-689-50433-0 Subj: Religion.

Beauty and the beast retold & ill. by Warwick Hutton. Atheneum, 1985. ISBN 0-689-50316-4 Subj: Character traits – appearance. Character traits – loyalty. Emotions – love. Folk & fairy tales. Magic.

Jonah and the great fish ill. by adapt. Atheneum, 1984. ISBN 0-689-50283-4 Subj: Animals – whales. Religion – Jonah.

Moses in the bulrushes ill. by reteller. Aladdin, 1992. ISBN 0-689-71553-6 Subj: Babies. Foreign lands – Egypt. Jewish culture. Religion – Moses.

Noah and the great flood ill. by author. Atheneum, 1977. ISBN 0-689-50098-X Subj: Animals. Boats, ships. Religion – Noah. Weather – floods. Weather – rain. Weather – rainbows.

The nose tree ill. by adapt. Atheneum, 1981. ISBN 0-689-50166-8 Subj: Anatomy – noses. Character traits – cleverness. Folk & fairy tales. Friendship. Witches.

Persephone ill. by author. McElderry, 1994. ISBN 0-689-50600-7 Subj: Foreign lands – Greece. Mythical creatures. Religion. Seasons.

Perseus ill. by author. McElderry, 1993. ISBN 0-689-50565-5 Subj: Folk & fairy tales. Mythical creatures.

The sleeping beauty (Grimm, Jacob)

Theseus and the Minotaur ill. by author. McElderry, 1989. ISBN 0-689-50473-X Subj: Death. Foreign lands – Greece. Monsters. Mythical creatures. Religion.

The Trojan horse ill. by author. McElderry, 1992. ISBN 0-689-50542-6 Subj: Folk & fairy tales. Foreign lands – Greece. War.

Hyatt, Christine. *Erik and the Christmas horse* (Peterson, Hans)

Erik has a squirrel (Peterson, Hans)

Hyde, Margaret E. *Matisse for kids.* Penguin, 2004. ISBN 1-58980-204-7 Subj: Art. Careers – artists. Format, unusual – board books.

Van Gogh for kids. Penguin, 2004. ISBN 1-58980-207-1 Subj: Art. Careers – artists. Format, unusual – board books.

Hyman, Inge. *Casper and the rainbow bird* (Hyman, Robin)

Hyman, Robin. *Casper and the rainbow bird* by Robin & Inge Hyman; ill. by Yutaka Sugita. Barron's, 1979. ISBN 0-8120-5253-6 Subj: Behavior – running away. Birds – crows. Birds – parakeets, parrots.

Hyman, Trina Schart. *The enchanted forest* ill. by author. Putnam, 1984. ISBN 0-399-21057-1 Subj: Forest, woods. Format, unusual. Wordless.

A little alphabet ill. by author. SeaStar, 2000. Originally pub. Little, Brown, c1980. ISBN 1-58717-008-6 Subj: ABC books. Language.

Little Red Riding Hood (Grimm, Jacob)

The sleeping beauty (Grimm, Jacob)

Hymes, James L. *Oodles of noodles and other rhymes* (Hymes, Lucia)

Hymes, Lucia. *Oodles of noodles and other rhymes* by Lucia & James L. Hymes, Jr.; ill. by authors. Addison-Wesley, 1964. Subj: Poetry.

Hynard, Julia. *Percival's party* ill. by Frances Thatcher. Childrens Pr., 1983. ISBN 0-516-08941-2 Subj: Activities. Parties.

Hynard, Stephen. *Snowy the rabbit* ill. by Frances Thatcher. Childrens Pr., 1983. ISBN 0-516-08942-0 Subj: Activities. Animals – rabbits.

I imagine angels William Lach, ed. Atheneum, 2000. ISBN 0-689-84080-2 Subj: Angels. Art. Religion.

I invited a dragon to dinner ill. by Chris L. Demarest. Philomel, 2002. ISBN 0-399-23567-1 Subj: Humorous stories. Poetry.

I saw Esau ed. by Iona & Peter Opie; ill. by Maurice Sendak. Candlewick, 1992. ISBN 1-56402-046-0 Subj: Poetry. Riddles & jokes.

I want to be a pilot ill. with photos. Firefly, 1999. ISBN 1-55209-449-9 Subj: Airplanes, airports. Careers – airplane pilots.

I've seen the promised land ill. by Leonard Jenkins. HarperCollins, 2004. ISBN 0-06-027704-1 Subj: Careers – clergy. Ethnic groups in the U.S. – African Americans. Religion. U.S. history.

Ichikawa, Satomi. *A child's book of seasons* ill. by author. Parents' Magazine Pr., 1976. Subj: Folk & fairy tales. Seasons.

Fickle Barbara ill. by author. Philomel, 1993. ISBN 0-399-22020-8 Subj: Character traits – loyalty. Friendship. Toys – bears.

The first bear in Africa! ill. by author. Philomel, 2001. ISBN 0-399-23485-3 Subj: Behavior – lost & found possessions. Foreign lands – Africa. Toys – bears.

Isabela's ribbons ill. by author. Philomel, 1995. ISBN 0-399-22772-5 Subj: Activities – playing. Foreign lands – Puerto Rico. Friendship. Imagination. Islands.

La La Rose ill. by author. Philomel, 2004. ISBN 0-399-24029-2 Subj: Animals – rabbits. Behavior – lost. Foreign lands – France. Parks. Toys.

Let's play ill. by author. Philomel, 1981. ISBN 0-399-61186-X Subj: Activities – playing.

Nora's castle ill. by author. Philomel, 1986. ISBN 0-399-21302-3 Subj: Animals. Homes, houses. Parties. Toys.

Nora's duck ill. by author. Putnam, 1991. ISBN 0-399-21805-X Subj: Animals. Birds – ducks. Character traits – kindness to animals.

Nora's roses ill. by author. Philomel, 1993. ISBN 0-399-21968-4 Subj: Behavior – boredom. Flowers. Illness.

Nora's stars ill. by author. Putnam, 1989. ISBN 0-399-21616-2 Subj: Family life – grandmothers. Sky. Stars. Toys.

Nora's surprise ill. by author. Philomel, 1994. ISBN 0-399-22535-8 Subj: Activities – picnicking. Animals – sheep. Birds – geese. Etiquette. Parties.

Sun through small leaves: poems of spring comp. & ill. by Satomi Ichikawa. Collins-World, 1980. ISBN 0-529-05572-4 Subj: Folk & fairy tales. Seasons – spring.

Suzanne and Nicholas at the market ill. by author. Watts, 1977. Translation by Denise Sheldon of Suzette et Nicolas au marché. ISBN 0-85166-669-8 Subj: Family life. Foreign lands – France. Shopping.

Suzanne and Nicholas in the garden ill. by author. St. Martin's, 1978. Translation by Denise Sheldon of Suzette et Nicolas dans leur jardin. ISBN 0-312-77982-8 Subj: Activities – playing. Ecology. Family life. Flowers. Foreign lands – France. Gardens, gardening.

What the little fir tree wore to the Christmas party ill. by author. Philomel, 2001. ISBN 0-399-23746-1 Subj: Holidays – Christmas. Trees.

If dragon flies made honey: *poems* col. by David Kherdian; ill. by José Aruego & Ariane Dewey. Greenwillow, 1977. ISBN 0-688-80101-3 Subj: Poetry.

If you ever meet a whale: *poems* sel. by Myra Cohn Livingston; ill. by Leonard Everett Fisher. Holiday, 1992. ISBN 0-8234-0940-6 Subj: Animals – whales. Poetry.

Ife, Elaine. *The childhood of Jesus* ill. by Eric Rowe. Rourke, 1983. ISBN 0-86625-223-1 Subj: Religion.

Moses in the bulrushes ill. by Eric Rowe. Rourke, 1983. ISBN 0-86625-217-7 Subj: Babies. Foreign lands – Egypt. Jewish culture. Religion – Moses.

Noah and the ark ill. by Russell Lee. Rourke, 1983. ISBN 0-86625-224-X Subj: Animals. Boats, ships. Religion – Noah. Weather – floods. Weather – rain. Weather – rainbows.

Stories Jesus told ill. by Russell Lee. Rourke, 1983. ISBN 0-86625-221-5 Subj: Religion.

Ignatowicz, Nina. *At the frog pond* (Michels, Tilde)

Leo the lion (Wagener, Gerda)

Igus, Toyomi. *Going back home* (Wood, Michele)

Two Mrs. Gibsons ill. by Daryl Wells. Children's Book Pr., 1996. ISBN 0-89239-135-9 Subj: Ethnic groups in the U.S. – African Americans. Ethnic groups in the U.S. – Japanese Americans. Family life – grandmothers. Family life – mothers. Marriage, interracial.

When I was little ill. by Higgins Bond. Just Us Books, 1992. ISBN 0-940975-33-5 Subj: Ethnic groups in the U.S. – African Americans. Family life – grandfathers. Sports – fishing.

Iijima, Geneva Cobb. *The way we do it in Japan* ill. by Paige Billin-Frye. A. Whitman, 2002. ISBN 0-8075-7822-3 Subj: Family life – parents. Foreign lands – Japan. Foreign languages.

Iké, Jane Hori. *A Japanese fairy tale* by Jane Hori Iké & Baruch Zimmerman; ill. by Jane Hori Iké. Warne, 1982. ISBN 0-7232-6208-X Subj: Character traits – appearance. Folk & fairy tales. Foreign lands – Japan.

Ikeda, Daisaku. *The cherry tree* trans. from Japanese by Geraldine McCaughrean; ill. by Brian Wildsmith. Knopf, 1992. ISBN 0-679-92669-0 Subj: Foreign lands – Japan. Hope. Trees. War.

Kanta and the deer ill. by Christina Sun. Weatherhill, 1997. ISBN 0-8348-0406-9 Subj: Animals – deer. Character traits – kindness to animals. Foreign lands – Japan.

Over the deep blue sea ill. by Geraldine McCaughrean. Knopf, 1992. ISBN 0-679-94184-3 Subj: Friendship. Islands. Prejudice.

The princess and the moon ill. by Brian Wildsmith; trans. from Japanese by Geraldine McCaughrean. Knopf, 1992. ISBN 0-679-93620-3 Subj: Animals – rabbits. Behavior. Emotions – anger. Moon.

The snow country prince trans. from Japanese by Geraldine McCaughrean; ill. by Brian Wildsmith. Knopf, 1991. ISBN 0-679-91965-1 Subj: Character traits – kindness to animals. Folk & fairy tales. Foreign lands – Japan. Royalty – princes.

Illyés, Gyula. *Matt the gooseherd: a story from Hungary* ill. by Károly Reich. Penguin, 1979. ISBN 0-14-030803-2 Subj: Birds – geese. Folk & fairy tales. Foreign lands – Hungary.

Ilsley, Velma. *A busy day for Chris* ill. by author. Lippincott, 1957. Subj: ABC books. Poetry.

M is for moving ill. by author. Walck, 1966. Subj: ABC books. Moving.

The pink hat ill. by author. Lippincott, 1956. Subj: Behavior – carelessness. Poetry.

Imagine that! *poems of never-was* sel. by Jack Prelutsky; ill. by Kevin Hawkes. Knopf, 1998. ISBN 0-679-98206-X Subj: Imagination. Poetry.

Imai, Miko. *Lilly's secret* ill. by author. Candlewick, 1994. ISBN 1-56402-232-3 Subj: Animals – cats. Character traits – being different. Friendship.

Little Lumpty ill. by author. Candlewick, 1994. ISBN 1-56402-233-1 Subj: Eggs. Family life – mothers.

Imbody, Amy. *Snug as a bug?* ill. by Mike Gordon. Zonderkidz, 2001. ISBN 0-310-70063-9 Subj: Bedtime. Rhyming text.

Imershein, Betsy. *Finding red, finding yellow* photos by author. Harcourt, 1989. ISBN 0-15-200453-X Subj: Concepts – color. Format, unusual. Wordless.

Trucks photos by author. S&S, 2000. ISBN 0-689-82887-X Subj: Format, unusual – board books. Trucks.

Imoto, Yoko. *Skipper at the beach* ill. by author. Grosset, 1989. ISBN 0-448-09293-X Subj: Animals – cats. Family life. Sea & seashore – beaches.

Skipper is the daddy ill. by author. Grosset, 1989. ISBN 0-448-09294-8 Subj: Animals – cats. Family life.

Impey, Rose. *The ankle grabber* ill. by Moira Kemp. Barron's, 1989. ISBN 0-8120-5973-5 Subj: Emotions – fear. Monsters. Night.

The flat man ill. by Moira Kemp. Barron's, 1988. ISBN 0-8120-5975-1 Subj: Bedtime. Emotions – fear. Monsters. Mythical creatures – goblins. Night.

Joe's café ill. by Sue Porter. Little, 1991. ISBN 0-316-41777-7 Subj: Activities – babysitting. Activities – playing. Family life – brothers & sisters. Restaurants.

Jumble Joan ill. by Moira Kemp. Carolrhoda, 1998. ISBN 1-57505-295-4 Subj: Emotions – fear. Family life – brothers & sisters.

My mom and our dad ill. by Maureen Galvani. Viking, 1991. ISBN 0-670-83663-X Subj: Family life – fathers. Family life – mothers. Multiple births – twins.

Scare yourself to sleep ill. by Moira Kemp. Barron's, 1988. ISBN 0-8120-5974-3 Subj: Emotions – fear. Family life – cousins. Monsters. Night.

Who's a bright girl? ill. by André Amstutz. Barron's, 1989. ISBN 0-8120-6144-6 Subj: Gender roles. Pirates.

Imsand, Marcel. *The fir tree* (Andersen, H. C. [Hans Christian])

In daddy's arms I am tall ill. by Javaka Steptoe. Lee & Low, 1997. ISBN 1-8800003-1-8 Subj: Ethnic groups in the U.S. – African Americans. Family life – fathers. Poetry.

Inches, Alison. *Corduroy writes a letter* ill. by Allan Eitzen. Viking, 2002. Based on the character created by Don Freeman. ISBN 0-670-03548-3 Subj: Activities – writing. Letters, cards. Toys – bears.

Corduroy's garden ill. by Allan Eitzen. Viking, 2002. Based on the character created by Don Freeman. ISBN 0-670-03547-5 Subj: Gardens, gardening. Plants. Toys – bears.

Corduroy's hike ill. by Allan Eitzen. Viking, 2001. Based on the character created by Don Freeman. ISBN 0-670-88945-8 Subj: Activities – walking. Behavior – lost. Toys – bears.

Ingle, Annie. *The big city book* ill. by Tim & Greg Hildebrandt. Platt, 1976. ISBN 0-8228-7616-7 Subj: Cities, towns.

Ingman, Bruce. *Lost property* ill. by author. Houghton Mifflin, 1998. ISBN 0-395-88900-6 Subj: Animals – dogs. Behavior – lost & found possessions. Family life.

A night on the tiles ill. by author. Houghton Mifflin, 1999. ISBN 0-395-93655-1 Subj: Activities. Animals – cats. Foreign lands – France. Night.

Ingoglia, Gina. *The art class* ill. by Ed Rodriguez. Walt Disney, 1992. ISBN 1-56282-227-6 Subj: Art. Character traits – assertiveness. School.

The big book of real airplanes ill. by George Guzzi. Putnam, 1987. ISBN 0-448-19179-2 Subj: Airplanes, airports. Helicopters. Transportation.

Ingpen, Robert. *The idle bear* ill. by author. HarperCollins, 1987. ISBN 0-87226-159-X Subj: Toys – bears.

Inkiow, Dimiter. *Me and Clara and Baldwin the pony* trans. from German by Paula McGuire; ill. by Traudl & Walter Reiner. Pantheon, 1980. ISBN 0-694-94434-8 Subj: Animals – horses, ponies. Behavior – misbehavior.

Me and Clara and Casimir the cat trans. from German by Paula McGuire; ill. by Traudl & Walter Reiner. Pantheon, 1979. ISBN 0-394-94124-1 Subj: Animals – cats.

Me and Clara and Snuffy the dog trans. from German by Paula McGuire; ill. by Traudl & Walter Reiner. Pantheon, 1980. ISBN 0-394-94433-X Subj: Animals – dogs. Behavior – misbehavior.

Me and my sister Clara trans. from German by Paula McGuire; ill. by Traudl & Walter Reiner. Pantheon, 1979. ISBN 0-394-94123-3 Subj: Behavior – misbehavior.

Inkpen, Deborah. *Harriet and the little fat fairy* ill. by author. Barron's, 2002. ISBN 0-7641-5562-8 Subj: Animals – hamsters. Fairies. Holidays – Christmas. Pets.

Inkpen, Mick. *Anything cuddly will do!* ill. by author; paper engineering by Dennis K. Meyer. Orchard, 1993. ISBN 1-8521-3608-1 Subj: Animals. Format, unusual – toy & movable books. Pets. Rhyming text.

Arnold ill. by author. Harcourt, 1998. ISBN 0-15-202289-9 Subj: Animals – dogs. Animals – pigs. Thumb sucking.

Billy's beetle ill. by author. Harcourt, 1992. ISBN 0-15-200427-0 Subj: Animals. Behavior – lost & found possessions. Cumulative tales. Insects – beetles.

The blue balloon ill. by author. Little, 1990. ISBN 0-316-41886-2 Subj: Format, unusual. Imagination. Toys – balloons.

Butterfly ill. by author. Harcourt, 1999. ISBN 0-15-202409-3 Subj: Animals – dogs. Insects – butterflies, caterpillars.

Crocodile! ill. by author. Orchard, 1993. ISBN 1-8521-3609-X Subj: Format, unusual – toy & movable books. Reptiles – alligators, crocodiles. Rhyming text.

Field day (Butterworth, Nick)

The great pet sale ill. by author. Orchard, 1999. ISBN 0-531-30130-3 Subj: Animals. Money. Pets.

Gumboot's chocolatey day ill. by author. Doubleday, 1991. ISBN 0-385-41490-0 Subj: Animals – pigs. Birds – ducks. Food.

Hissss! ill. by author. Harcourt, 2000. ISBN 0-15-204415-8 Subj: Animals – dogs. Seasons – summer.

Honk! ill. by author. Harcourt, 1998. ISBN 0-15-202284-8 Subj: Animals – dogs. Birds – geese. Noise, sounds.

The house on the rock (Butterworth, Nick)

If I had a pig ill. by author. Little, 1988. ISBN 0-316-41887-0 Subj: Animals – pigs. Friendship. Imagination.

If I had a sheep ill. by author. Little, 1988. ISBN 0-316-41888-9 Subj: Animals – sheep. Friendship. Imagination.

Jasper's beanstalk (Butterworth, Nick)

Kipper ill. by author. Little, 1992. ISBN 0-316-41883-8 Subj: Animals – dogs. Behavior – imitation. Sleep.

Kipper and Roly ill. by author. Harcourt, 2001. ISBN 0-15-216344-1 Subj: Animals – dogs. Animals – hamsters. Animals – pigs. Birthdays. Gifts. Pets.

Kipper's A to Z ill. by author. Harcourt, 2000. ISBN 0-15-202594-4 Subj: ABC books. Animals. Animals – dogs. Animals – pigs.

Kipper's bathtime ill. by author. Harcourt, 1999. ISBN 0-15-202694-0 Subj: Activities – bathing. Animals – dogs. Format, unusual – toy & movable books. Toys.

Kipper's bedtime ill. by author. Harcourt, 1999. ISBN 0-15-202403-4 Subj: Animals – dogs. Bedtime. Format, unusual – toy & movable books.

Kipper's birthday ill. by author. Harcourt, 1993. ISBN 0-15-200503-X Subj: Animals – dogs. Behavior – mistakes. Birthdays. Parties.

Kipper's book of colors ill. by author. Harcourt, 1995. ISBN 0-15-200647-8 Subj: Animals – dogs. Concepts – color.

Kipper's book of counting ill. by author. Hodder & Stoughton, 1994. ISBN 0-340-59848-4 Subj: Animals. Animals – dogs. Counting, numbers.

Kipper's book of numbers ill. by author. Harcourt, 1995. ISBN 0-15-200646-X Subj: Animals. Animals – dogs. Counting, numbers.

Kipper's book of opposites ill. by author. Harcourt, 1995. ISBN 0-15-200668-0 Subj: Animals – dogs. Concepts – opposites. Language.

Kipper's book of weather ill. by author. Harcourt, 1995. ISBN 0-15-200644-3 Subj: Animals – dogs. Weather.

Kipper's Christmas eve ill. by author. Harcourt, 1999. ISBN 0-15-202660-6 Subj: Animals – dogs. Format, unusual – toy & movable books. Friendship. Holidays – Christmas.

Kipper's monster ill. by author. Harcourt, 2002. ISBN 0-15-216614-9 Subj: Animals – dogs. Camps, camping. Monsters.

Kipper's playtime ill. by author. Harcourt, 1999. ISBN 0-15-202421-2 Subj: Activities – playing. Animals – dogs. Format, unusual – toy & movable books.

Kipper's rainy day ill. by Stuart Trotter. Harcourt, 2001. Based on the books by Mick Inkpen. ISBN 0-15-216351-4 Subj: Animals – dogs. Format, unusual – toy & movable books. Weather – rain.

Kipper's snacktime ill. by author. Harcourt, 1999. ISBN 0-15-202433-6 Subj: Animals – dogs. Food. Format, unusual – toy & movable books.

Kipper's snowy day ill. by author. Harcourt, 1996. ISBN 0-15-201362-8 Subj: Activities – playing. Animals – dogs. Friendship. Toys. Weather – snow.

Kipper's sunny day ill. by Stuart Trotter. Harcourt, 2002. Based on the books by Mick Inkpen. ISBN 0-15-216357-3 Subj: Animals – dogs. Format, unusual – toy & movable books. Sea & seashore – beaches.

Kipper's toybox ill. by author. Harcourt, 1992. ISBN 0-15-200501-3 Subj: Animals – dogs. Animals – mice. Counting, numbers. Toys.

Lullabyhullaballoo! ill. by author. Artists & Writers Guild, 1994. ISBN 0-307-17509-X Subj: Bedtime. Format, unusual – toy & movable books. Imagination. Noise, sounds. Royalty – princesses.

Meow! ill. by author. Harcourt, 2000. ISBN 0-15-202666-5 Subj: Animals. Animals – cats. Animals – dogs.

The Nativity play (Butterworth, Nick)

Nice or nasty (Butterworth, Nick)

Nothing ill. by author. Orchard, 1998. ISBN 0-531-30076-5 Subj: Names. Self-concept. Toys.

One bear at bedtime ill. by author. Little, 1988. ISBN 0-316-41889-7 Subj: Animals. Bedtime. Counting, numbers. Imagination. Toys – bears.

Penguin small ill. by author. Harcourt, 1993. ISBN 0-15-200567-6 Subj: Activities – trading. Animals – polar bears. Birds – penguins. Emotions – fear. Foreign lands – Antarctic. Foreign lands – Arctic. Format, unusual – toy & movable books. Snowmen.

Picnic ill. by author. Harcourt, 2001. ISBN 0-15-216319-0 Subj: Activities – picnicking. Animals. Animals – dogs.

Sandcastle ill. by author. Harcourt, 1998. ISBN 0-15-202296-1 Subj: Sand. Sea & seashore.

The school trip (Butterworth, Nick)

Splosh! ill. by author. Harcourt, 1998. ISBN 0-15-202299-6 Subj: Animals. Animals – dogs. Weather – rain.

Swing! ill. by author. Harcourt, 2000. ISBN 0-15-202672-X Subj: Activities – playing. Animals – dogs. Friendship.

Thing ill. by author. Harcourt, 2001. ISBN 0-15-216326-3 Subj: Animals – dogs. Bubbles. Toys.

This troll, that troll ill. by author; paper engineering by José R. Seminario. Orchard, 1993. ISBN 1-8521-3607-3 Subj: Format, unusual – toy & movable books. Mythical creatures – trolls. Rhyming text.

Threadbear ill. by author. Little, 1991. ISBN 0-316-41884-6 Subj: Format, unusual. Toys – bears.

The very good dinosaur ill. by author; paper engineering by Rodger Smith. Orchard, 1993. ISBN 1-8521-3610-3 Subj: Dinosaurs. Format, unusual – toy & movable books. Prehistory. Rhyming text.

Where, oh where, is Kipper's bear? a pop-up book with light! ill. by author. Harcourt, 1995. ISBN 0-15-200394-0 Subj: Animals – dogs. Behavior – lost & found possessions. Format, unusual – toy & movable books. Rhyming text. Toys – bears.

Wibbly Pig can dance! ill. by author. Golden Bks., 1995. ISBN 0-307-16626-0 Subj: Activities – dancing. Activities – playing. Animals – pigs. Bedtime.

Wibbly Pig can make a tent ill. by author. Golden Bks., 1995. ISBN 0-307-16628-7 Subj: Activities – making things. Activities – playing. Animals – pigs. Camps, camping. Format, unusual – board books.

Wibbly Pig is upset ill. by author. Golden Bks., 1995. ISBN 0-307-16629-5 Subj: Animals – pigs. Emotions. Format, unusual – board books.

Wibbly Pig likes bananas ill. by author. Golden Bks., 1995. ISBN 0-307-16630-9 Subj: Animals – pigs. Food. Format, unusual – board books.

Wibbly Pig makes pictures ill. by author. Golden Bks., 1995. ISBN 0-307-16625-2 Subj: Activities – drawing. Animals – pigs. Format, unusual – board books.

Wibbly Pig opens his presents ill. by author. Golden Bks., 1995. ISBN 0-307-16627-9 Subj: Animals – pigs. Format, unusual – board books. Gifts.

Inns, Christopher. *Next! please* ill. by author. Tricycle, 2001. ISBN 1-58246-038-8 Subj: Illness. Toys.

Intrater, Roberta Grobel. *Peek-a-boo!* ill. by author. Scholastic, 1997. ISBN 0-590-05896-7 Subj: Babies. Family life. Format, unusual – board books. Games.

Smile! ill. by author. Scholastic, 1997. ISBN 0-590-05899-1 Subj: Babies. Family life. Format, unusual – board books.

Two eyes, a nose, and a mouth ill. by author. Scholastic, 1995. ISBN 0-590-48247-5 Subj: Anatomy – faces. Rhyming text.

Inwald, Robin. *Cap it off with a smile: a guide for making friends* ill. by author. Hilson Press, 1994. ISBN 1-8857-3800-5 Subj: Behavior. Friendship. Rhyming text.

Ipcar, Dahlov (Zorach). *Animal hide and seek* ill. by author. Addison-Wesley, 1947. Subj: Animals.

The biggest fish in the sea ill. by author. Viking, 1972. ISBN 0-670-16541-7 Subj: Concepts – size. Fish. Sports – fishing.

Black and white ill. by author. Knopf, 1963. Subj: Animals – dogs. Dreams. Rhyming text.

Bright barnyard ill. by author. Knopf, 1966. Subj: Animals. Birds. Farms.

Brown cow farm: a counting book ill. by author. Doubleday, 1959. Subj: Animals. Counting, numbers. Farms.

Bug city ill. by author. Holiday, 1975. ISBN 0-8234-0258-4 Subj: Insects.

The calico jungle ill. by author. Knopf, 1965. Subj: Animals. Bedtime. Quilts.

The cat at night ill. by author. Doubleday, 1969. Subj: Animals – cats. Night.

The cat came back ill. by author. Knopf, 1971. ISBN 0-394-82291-9 Subj: Animals – cats. Music. Rhyming text. Songs.

A flood of creatures ill. by author. Holiday, 1973. ISBN 0-8234-0224-X Subj: Animals. Weather – floods.

Hard scrabble harvest ill. by author. Doubleday, 1976. ISBN 0-385-00777-9 Subj: Farms. Holidays – Thanksgiving. Plants. Rhyming text.

I like animals ill. by author. Knopf, 1960. Subj: Animals. Careers.

I love my anteater with an A ill. by author. Knopf, 1964. ISBN 0-394-91267-5 Subj: ABC books. Animals.

The land of flowers ill. by author. Viking, 1974. ISBN 0-670-41754-8 Subj: Animals – sheep. Concepts – size. Flowers. Gardens, gardening.

Lost and found: a hidden animal book ill. by author. Doubleday, 1981. ISBN 0-385-15171-3 Subj: Animals. Participation.

My wonderful Christmas tree ill. by author. Down East, 1999. ISBN 0-89272-475-7 Subj: Animals. Counting, numbers. Holidays – Christmas. Rhyming text.

One horse farm ill. by author. Doubleday, 1950. Subj: Animals – horses, ponies. Farms. Machines. Progress.

Sir Addlepate and the unicorn ill. by author. Doubleday, 1971. Subj: Knights. Mythical creatures – unicorns.

The song of the day birds and the night birds ill. by author. Doubleday, 1967. Subj: Birds. Music. Night. Songs.

Stripes and spots ill. by author. Doubleday, 1953. Subj: Animals – leopards. Animals – tigers.

Ten big farms ill. by author. Knopf, 1958. Subj: Counting, numbers. Farms.

Wild and tame animals ill. by author. Doubleday, 1962. Subj: Animals.

World full of horses ill. by author. Doubleday, 1955. Subj: Animals – horses, ponies.

Irbinskas, Heather. *How Jackrabbit got his very long ears* ill. by Ken Spengler. Northland, 1994. ISBN 0-87358-566-6 Subj: Anatomy – ears. Animals. Animals – rabbits. Behavior. Desert. Folk & fairy tales. Self-concept.

Ireson, Barbara. *The gingerbread man* (The gingerbread boy)

Iribarren, Elena. *Nina Bonita* (Machado, Ana Maria)

Irvine, Georgeanne. *Bo the orangutan* photos by Ron Garrison. Childrens Pr., 1983. ISBN 0-516-09307-X Subj: Animals – monkeys. Zoos.

Elmer the elephant photos by Ron Garrison. Childrens Pr., 1983. ISBN 0-516-09310-X Subj: Animals – elephants. Zoos.

Georgie the giraffe photos by Ron Garrison. Childrens Pr., 1983. ISBN 0-516-09308-8 Subj: Animals – giraffes. Zoos.

Lindi the leopard photos by Ron Garrison. Childrens Pr., 1983. ISBN 0-516-09309-6 Subj: Animals – leopards. Zoos.

The nursery babies photos by Ron Garrison. Childrens Pr., 1983. ISBN 0-516-09311-8 Subj: Animals. Zoos.

Sasha the cheetah photos by Ron Garrison. Childrens Pr., 1982. ISBN 0-516-09303-7 Subj: Animals – cheetahs. Zoos.

Sydney the koala photos by Ron Garrison. Childrens Pr., 1982. ISBN 0-516-09304-5 Subj: Animals – koalas. Zoos.

Tully the tree kangaroo photos by Ron Garrison. Childrens Pr., 1983. ISBN 0-516-09312-6 Subj: Animals. Zoos.

Irving, John. *A sound like someone trying not to make a sound* ill. by Tatjana Hauptmann. Random House, 2004. ISBN 0-385-90910-1 Subj: Animals – mice. Bedtime. Family life – fathers. Monsters. Noise, sounds.

Irving, Washington. *The headless horseman* (Standiford, Natalie)

The legend of Sleepy Hollow (San Souci, Robert D.)

The legend of Sleepy Hollow (Wolkstein, Diane)

Rip Van Winkle adapt. & ill. by John Howe. Little, 1988. ISBN 0-316-37578-0 Subj: Behavior – lost. Folk & fairy tales. Mythical creatures – elves. Sleep.

Rip Van Winkle adapt. & ill. by Thomas Locker. Little, 1988. ISBN 0-8037-0521-2 Subj: Behavior – lost. Folk & fairy tales. Mythical creatures – elves. Sleep.

Rip Van Winkle adapt. by Catherine Storr; ill. by Peter Wingham. Raintree, 1984. ISBN 0-8172-2108-5 Subj: Behavior – lost. Folk & fairy tales. Mythical creatures – elves. Sleep.

Washington Irving's Rip Van Winkle (Bergen, Lara Rice)

Irwin, Michael. *Bears in my bed* ill. by author. Bennett, 2000. ISBN 0-8069-7535-0 Subj: Animals – bears. Imagination. Rhyming text.

Isaacs, Anne. *Cat up a tree* ill. by Stephen Mackey. Dutton, 1998. ISBN 0-525-45994-4 Subj: Animals – cats. Poetry.

Swamp Angel ill. by Paul O. Zelinsky. Dutton, 1994. ISBN 0-525-45271-0 Subj: Caldecott award honor books. Tall tales. U.S. history – frontier & pioneer life.

Isaacs, Gwynne L. *Baby face: a mirror book* ill. by Evelyn Clarke Mott. Random House, 1994. ISBN 0-679-84981-5 Subj: Anatomy – faces. Babies. Format, unusual – toy & movable books. Rhyming text.

Isadora, Rachel. *ABC pop!* ill. by author. Viking, 1999. ISBN 0-670-88329-8 Subj: ABC books. Art.

At the crossroads ill. by author. Greenwillow, 1991. ISBN 0-688-05271-1 Subj: Emotions. Family life. Foreign lands – South Africa.

Babies ill. by author. Greenwillow, 1990. ISBN 0-688-08032-4 Subj: Activities. Babies.

Ben's trumpet ill. by author. Greenwillow, 1979. ISBN 0-688-80194-3 Subj: Caldecott award honor books. Ethnic groups in the U.S. – African Americans. Music. Musical instruments – trumpets.

Bring on that beat ill. by author. Putnam, 2001. ISBN 0-399-23232-X Subj: Ethnic groups in the U.S. – African Americans. Music. Rhyming text.

Caribbean dream ill. by author. Putnam, 1998. ISBN 0-399-23230-3 Subj: Dreams. Foreign lands – Caribbean Islands. Islands.

City seen from A to Z ill. by author. Greenwillow, 1983. ISBN 0-688-01803-3 Subj: ABC books. Cities, towns.

The firebird (The firebird)

Friends ill. by author. Greenwillow, 1990. ISBN 0-688-08265-3 Subj: Activities. Friendship.

I hear ill. by author. Greenwillow, 1985. ISBN 0-688-04062-4 Subj: Babies. Family life. Noise, sounds. Senses – hearing.

I see ill. by author. Greenwillow, 1985. ISBN 0-688-04060-8 Subj: Babies. Family life. Senses – sight.

I touch ill. by author. Greenwillow, 1985. ISBN 0-688-04256-2 Subj: Senses – touch.

Jesse and Abe ill. by author. Greenwillow, 1981. ISBN 0-688-84302-6 Subj: Family life – grandfathers. Theater.

Lili at ballet ill. by author. Putnam, 1993. ISBN 0-399-22423-8 Subj: Activities – dancing. Ballet.

Lili on stage ill. by author. Putnam, 1995. ISBN 0-399-22637-0 Subj: Activities – dancing. Ballet. Careers – dancers. Theater.

Listen to the city ill. by author. Putnam, 2000. ISBN 0-399-23047-5 Subj: Cities, towns. Noise, sounds.

The little mermaid (Andersen, H. C. [Hans Christian])

Max ill. by author. Macmillan, 1976. ISBN 0-02-747450-7 Subj: Activities – dancing. Ballet. Sports – baseball.

My ballet class ill. by author. Greenwillow, 1980. ISBN 0-688-84253-4 Subj: Activities – dancing. Ballet.

My ballet diary ill. by author. Putnam, 1995. ISBN 0-399-22620-6 Subj: Activities – dancing. Ballet.

Nick plays baseball ill. by author. Putnam, 2001. ISBN 0-399-23231-1 Subj: Sports – baseball.

No, Agatha! ill. by author. Greenwillow, 1980. ISBN 0-688-84274-7 Subj: Activities – traveling. Boats, ships.

Not just tutus ill. by author. Putnam, 2003. ISBN 0-399-23603-1 Subj: Activities – dancing. Ballet. Rhyming text.

The nutcracker (Hoffmann, E. T. A.)

123 pop! ill. by author. Viking, 2000. ISBN 0-670-88859-1 Subj: Counting, numbers.

Opening night ill. by author. Greenwillow, 1984. ISBN 0-688-02727-X Subj: Activities – dancing. Theater.

Over the green hills ill. by author. Greenwillow, 1992. ISBN 0-688-10510-6 Subj: Activities – traveling. Communities, neighborhoods. Family life – grandmothers. Foreign lands – South Africa.

Peekaboo morning ill. by author. Putnam, 2002. ISBN 0-399-23602-3 Subj: Ethnic groups in the U.S. – African Americans. Games.

The pirates of Bedford Street ill. by author. Greenwillow, 1988. ISBN 0-688-05208-8 Subj: Imagination. Pirates.

The Potters' kitchen ill. by author. Greenwillow, 1977. ISBN 0-688-84089-2 Subj: Moving.

The princess and the frog (Grimm, Jacob)

Sophie skates ill. by author. Putnam, 1999. ISBN 0-399-23046-7 Subj: Sports – ice skating.

A South African night ill. by author. Greenwillow, 1998. ISBN 0-688-11390-7 Subj: Animals. Foreign lands – Africa. Foreign lands – South Africa. Jungle. Night.

The steadfast tin soldier (Andersen, H. C. [Hans Christian])

Willaby ill. by author. Macmillan, 1977. ISBN 0-02-747746-0 Subj: School.

Isami, Ikuyo. *The fox's egg* trans. from Japanese by Cathy Hirano; ill. by author. Carolrhoda, 1989. ISBN 0-87614-339-7 Subj: Animals – foxes. Birds – chickens. Eggs.

Isele, Elizabeth. *The frog princess: a Russian tale retold* ill. by Michael Hague. HarperCollins, 1984. ISBN 0-690-04218-3 Subj: Folk & fairy tales. Foreign lands – Russia. Frogs & toads. Magic. Royalty – princesses. Witches.

Pooks ill. by Chris L. Demarest. Lippincott, 1983. ISBN 0-397-32045-0 Subj: Activities – traveling. Animals – dogs. Music.

Isenbart, Hans-Heinrich. *Baby animals on the farm* trans. from German by Elizabeth D. Crawford; photos by Ruth Rau. Putnam, 1984. ISBN 0-399-20960-3 Subj: Animals. Farms.

A duckling is born trans. by Catherine Edwards Sadler; photos by Othmar Baumli. Putnam, 1981. ISBN 0-399-20778-3 Subj: Birds – ducks. Birth. Science.

Isenberg, Barbara. *The adventures of Albert, the running bear* by Barbara Isenberg & Susan Wolf; ill. by Dick Gackenbach. Houghton Mifflin, 1982. ISBN 0-89919-113-4 Subj: Animals – bears. Behavior – running away. Sports – racing. Zoos.

Albert the running bear gets the jitters by Barbara Isenberg & Susan Wolf; ill. by Diane de Groat. Clarion, 1987. ISBN 0-89919-532-6 Subj: Animals – bears. Behavior – bullying. Behavior – trickery. Sports – racing.

Albert the running bear's exercise book by Barbara Isenberg & Marjorie Jaffe; ill. by Diane de Groat. Houghton Mifflin, 1984. ISBN 0-89919-294-7 Subj: Animals – bears. Health & fitness – exercise.

Isherwood, Shirley. *The band over the hill* by Shirley Isherwood & Reg Cartwright; ill. by Reg Cartwright. Hutchinson, 1997. ISBN 0-09-176753-9 Subj: Animals – bears. Careers – musicians. Music.

Flora the frog ill. by Anna C. Leplar. Peachtree, 2000. ISBN 1-56145-223-8 Subj: Frogs & toads. School. Theater.

Something for James ill. by Neil Reed. Dial, 1996. ISBN 0-8037-1914-0 Subj: Animals. Mystery stories. Toys.

Ishii, Momoko. *The tongue-cut sparrow* trans. from Japanese by Katherine Paterson; ill. by Suekichi Akaba. Lodestar, 1987. Tr. of Sita-kiri suzume. ISBN 0-525-67199-4 Subj: Behavior – greed. Birds – sparrows. Character traits – kindness to animals. Folk & fairy tales. Foreign lands – Japan.

Isom, Joan Shaddox. *The first starry night* ill. by author. Whispering Coyote, 1997. ISBN 1-8790-8596-8 Subj: Art. Careers – artists.

Israel, Marion Louise. *The tractor on the farm* ill. by Robert Dranko. Melmont, 1958. Subj: Farms. Tractors.

It feels like Christmas! *It feels like Christmas! a book of surprises to touch, see, and sniff* ill. by Denise Fleming. Random House, 1984. ISBN 0-394-86862-5 Subj: Format, unusual – toy & movable books. Holidays – Christmas. Senses.

Itaya, Satoshi. *Buttons and Bo* ill. by author; trans. by Marianne Martens. North-South, 2004. ISBN 0-7358-1883-5 Subj: Animals – bears. Behavior – lost. Family life – brothers. Forest, woods. Sibling rivalry.

Ivanko, John D. (John Duane). *Animal friends: a global celebration of children and their animals* (Ajmera, Maya)

Back to school (Ajmera, Maya)

Come out and play (Ajmera, Maya)

To be a kid (Ajmera, Maya)

Ivanov, Anatoly. *Ol' Jake's lucky day* ill. by author. Lothrop, 1984. ISBN 0-688-02867-5 Subj: Behavior – seeking better things. Character traits – luck. Folk & fairy tales. Foreign lands – Russia. Imagination.

I've been working on the railroad ill. by Nadine Bernard Westcott. Hyperion, 1996. ISBN 0-7868-2041-1 Subj: Folk & fairy tales. Music. Songs. Trains.

Iverson, Diane. *Discover the seasons* ill. by author. Dawn, 1996. ISBN 1-883220-43-2 Subj: Activities. Activities – making things. Nature. Seasons.

Iverson, Genie. *I want to be big* ill. by David McPhail. Dutton, 1979. ISBN 0-525-32539-5 Subj: Behavior – growing up.

Ives, Penny. *The golden angel* ill. by author. Tango, 1995. ISBN 1-8570712-6-3 Subj: Angels. Format, unusual – toy & movable books.

Mrs. Santa Claus ill. by author. Delacorte, 1991. ISBN 0-385-30303-3 Subj: Family life. Gender roles. Holidays – Christmas. Illness. Problem solving. Santa Claus.

On Christmas eve: a three-dimensional celebration ill. by author; paper engineering by David Hawcock. Putnam, 1992. ISBN 0-399-22148-4 Subj: Format, unusual – toy & movable books. Holidays – Christmas.

The snow angel: a pop-up ornament book ill. by author; paper engineering by David Hawcock. Tango, 1995. ISBN 1-8570712-5-5 Subj: Angels. Format, unusual – toy & movable books. Weather – snow.

Ivimey, John William. *The complete story of the three blind mice* ill. by Paul Galdone. Clarion, 1987. ISBN 0-89919-481-8 Subj: Animals – mice. Music. Nursery rhymes. Songs.

The complete version of ye three blind mice ill. by Walton Corbould. Warne, 1909. ISBN 0-7232-2256-8 Subj: Animals – mice. Music. Nursery rhymes. Songs.

Three blind mice ill. by Lorinda Bryan Cauley. Putnam, 1991. ISBN 0-399-21775-4 Subj: Animals – mice. Music. Nursery rhymes. Songs.

Three blind mice ill. by Victoria Chess. Little, 1990. ISBN 0-316-13867-3 Subj: Animals – mice. Music. Nursery rhymes. Songs.

Ivory, Lesley Anne. *The birthday cat* ill. by author. HarperCollins, 1993. ISBN 0-8037-1622-2 Subj: Animals – cats. Animals – rabbits. Behavior – hiding things. Birthdays. Toys.

Cats in the sun ill. by author. Dial, 1991. ISBN 0-8037-0955-2 Subj: Animals – cats. Sun.

A day in London ill. by author. Burke, 1982. ISBN 0-222-00785-0 Subj: Cities, towns. Foreign lands – England.

A day in New York ill. by author. Burke, 1982. ISBN 0-222-00788-5 Subj: Cities, towns.

Meet my cats ill. by author. Dial, 1989. ISBN 0-8037-0602-2 Subj: Animals – cats. Pets.

Iwamatsu, Jun. *see* Yashima, Taro

Iwamura, Kazuo. *The fourteen forest mice and the harvest moon watch* ill. by author. G. Stevens, 1991. ISBN 0-8368-0497-X Subj: Animals – mice. Forest, woods. Moon. Seasons – fall.

The fourteen forest mice and the spring meadow picnic ill. by author. G. Stevens, 1991. ISBN 0-8368-0498-8 Subj: Activities – picnicking. Animals – mice. Forest, woods. Seasons – spring.

The fourteen forest mice and the summer laundry day ill. by author. G. Stevens, 1991. ISBN 0-8368-0576-3 Subj: Animals – mice. Forest, woods. Laundry. Seasons – summer.

The fourteen forest mice and the winter sledding day ill. by author. G. Stevens, 1991. ISBN 0-8368-0499-6 Subj: Animals – mice. Forest, woods. Seasons – winter. Sports – sledding.

Tan Tan's hat ill. by author. Bradbury, 1983. ISBN 0-02-747490-9 Subj: Animals – monkeys. Clothing – hats.

Tan Tan's suspenders ill. by author. Bradbury, 1983. ISBN 0-02-747500-X Subj: Animals – monkeys. Clothing.

Ton and Pon: big and little ill. by author. Bradbury, 1984. ISBN 0-02-747480-1 Subj: Animals – dogs. Concepts – size. Friendship.

Ton and Pon: two good friends ill. by author. Bradbury, 1984. ISBN 0-02-747510-7 Subj: Animals – dogs. Friendship.

Iwasaki, Chihiro. *The birthday wish* ill. by author. McGraw-Hill, 1974, 1972. ISBN 0-07032-073-X Subj: Behavior – wishing. Birthdays. Weather – snow.

Staying home alone on a rainy day ill. by author. McGraw-Hill, 1968. Subj: Family life. Family life – only child. Weather – rain.

What's fun without a friend? ill. by author. McGraw-Hill, 1972. ISBN 0-07-032089-6 Subj: Animals – dogs. Sea & seashore.

Will you be my friend? ill. by author. McGraw-Hill, 1970. ISBN 0-07-032077-2 Subj: Friendship.

Izawa, Yohji. *One evening* (Funakoshi, Canna)

J. Paul Getty Museum. *A is for artist: a Getty Museum alphabet* (John Harris, writer & editor). J. P. Getty Museum, 1997. ISBN 0-89236-377-0 Subj: ABC books. Art. Museums.

Jabar, Cynthia. *Bored blue? Think what you can do!* ill. by author. Little, 1991. ISBN 0-316-43458-2 Subj: Activities. Rhyming text.

Party day! ill. by author. Little, 1987. ISBN 0-316-43456-6 Subj: Animals – rabbits. Birthdays. Counting, numbers.

Shimmy shake earthquake: don't forget to dance poems ed. & ill. by Cynthia Jabar. Little, 1992. ISBN 0-316-43459-0 Subj: Activities – dancing. Poetry.

Jack and the beanstalk. *The history of Mother Twaddle and the marvelous achievements of her son Jack* ill. by Paul Galdone. Seabury Pr., 1974. A verse version of Jack and the beanstalk, written by Basil T. Blackwood [B.A.T.] and pub. in 1807 by J. Harris, London. ISBN 0-8164-3112-4 Subj: Folk & fairy tales. Giants. Plants. Rhyming text.

Jack and the beanstalk retold & ill. by Val Biro. Oxford Univ. Pr., 1990. ISBN 0-19-278008-5 Subj: Folk & fairy tales. Giants. Plants.

Jack and the beanstalk retold by Anthea Bell; ill. by Aljoscha Blau. North-South, 2000. ISBN 0-7358-1375-2 Subj: Folk & fairy tales. Foreign lands – England. Giants. Plants.

Jack and the beanstalk adapt. & ill. by Lorinda Bryan Cauley. Putnam, 1983. ISBN 0-399-20901-8 Subj: Folk & fairy tales. Giants. Plants.

Jack and the beanstalk retold by Maggie Moore; ill. by Steve Cox. Picture Window, 2003. ISBN 1-4048-0059-X Subj: Folk & fairy tales. Giants. Plants.

Jack and the beanstalk adapt. by Sindy McKay; ill. by Lydia Halverson. Treasure Bay, 1997. ISBN 1-891327-00-3 Subj: Folk & fairy tales. Giants. Plants.

Jack and the beanstalk ill. by Julek Heller. Doubleday, 1992. ISBN 0-385-30693-8 Subj: Folk & fairy tales. Giants. Plants.

Jack and the beanstalk retold & ill. by John Howe. Little, 1989. ISBN 0-316-37579-9 Subj: Folk & fairy tales. Giants. Plants.

Jack and the beanstalk retold & ill. by Steven Kellogg. Morrow, 1991. ISBN 0-688-10251-4 Subj: Folk & fairy tales. Giants. Plants.

Jack and the beanstalk retold & ill. by Al Lorenz with Joy Schleh. Abrams, 2002. ISBN 0-8109-1160-4 Subj: Folk & fairy tales. Giants. Plants.

Jack and the beanstalk ill. by Ed Parker. Troll, 1979. ISBN 0-89375-125-1 Subj: Folk & fairy tales. Giants. Plants.

Jack and the beanstalk adapt. & ill. by Tony Ross. Delacorte, 1981. ISBN 0-440-04174-0 Subj: Folk & fairy tales. Giants. Plants.

Jack and the beanstalk retold by Richard Walker; ill. by Niamh Sharkey. Barefoot, 1999. ISBN 1-902283-13-9 Subj: Folk & fairy tales. Giants. Plants.

Jack and the beanstalk retold by Ann Keay Beneduce; ill. by Gennady Spirin. Philomel, 1999. ISBN 0-399-23118-8 Subj: Folk & fairy tales. Giants. Plants.

Jack and the beanstalk ill. by William Stobbs. Dial, 1966. Subj: Folk & fairy tales. Giants. Plants.

Jack and the beanstalk retold by Susan Pearson; ill. by James Warhola. S&S, 1989. ISBN 0-671-67196-0 Subj: Folk & fairy tales. Giants. Plants.

Jack and the beanstalk retold by Beatrice Schenk De Regniers; ill. by Anne Wilsdorf. Atheneum, 1985. ISBN 0-689-31174-5 Subj: Folk & fairy tales. Giants. Plants. Rhyming text.

Jack and the beanstalk = Juan y los frijoles magicos by Francesc Bofill; ill. by Arnal Ballester. Chronicle, 1998. ISBN 0-8118-1843-8 Subj: Folk & fairy tales. Foreign languages. Giants. Plants.

Jack the giant killer: Jack's first and finest adventure retold in verse as well as other useful information about giants including how to shake hands with a giant retold by Beatrice Schenk De Regniers; ill. by Anne Wilsdorf. Atheneum, 1987. ISBN 0-689-31218-0 Subj: Folk & fairy tales. Giants. Plants. Rhyming text.

Jack the giantkiller adapt. & ill. by Tony Ross. David & Charles, 1987. ISBN 0-862-64060-1 Subj: Folk & fairy tales. Giants. Plants.

Jack Sprat. *The life of Jack Sprat, his wife and his cat* retold & ill. by Paul Galdone. McGraw-Hill, 1969. Subj: Animals – cats. Family life. Food. Nursery rhymes.

Jacka, Martin. *Waiting for Billy* ill. by author. Watts, 1991. ISBN 0-531-08533-3 Subj: Animals – dogs. Animals – dolphins. Animals – horses, ponies. Foreign lands – Australia.

Jackson, Aimee. *Ocean babies* (McCurry, Kristen)

Safari babies (McCurry, Kristen)

Jackson, Alison. *The ballad of Valentine* ill. by Tricia Tusa. Dutton, 2002. ISBN 0-525-46720-3 Subj: Holidays – Valentine's Day. Rhyming text.

I know an old lady who swallowed a pie ill. by Judith Byron Schachner. Dutton, 1997. ISBN 0-525-45645-7 Subj: Cumulative tales. Folk & fairy tales. Food. Holidays – Thanksgiving. Humorous stories. Rhyming text.

If the shoe fits ill. by Karla Firehammer. Holt, 2001. ISBN 0-8050-6466-4 Subj: Homes, houses. Nursery rhymes. Rhyming text.

Jackson, Bobby L. *Little Red Ronnika* ill. by Rhonda Mitchell. Multicultural Pub., 1998. ISBN 1-884242-80-4 Subj: Ethnic groups in the U.S. – African Americans. Family life – grandmothers. Folk & fairy tales.

Makimba's animal world ill. by Julienne Jones. Multicultural Pub., 1994. ISBN 0-9634932-9-9 Subj: Animals. Foreign lands – Africa. Language.

Jackson, Byron. *The saggy baggy elephant* (Jackson, Kathryn)

Jackson, Carolyn. *The flying ark* ill. by Graham Bardell. Stoddart, 1995. ISBN 0-7737-5711-2 Subj: Activities – flying. Animals.

Jackson, Chris. *The Gaggle sisters river tour* ill. by author. Lobster, 2002. ISBN 1-894222-58-X Subj: Birds – geese. Character traits – pride. Family life – sisters.

Jackson, Ellen B. *Ants can't dance* ill. by Frank Remkiewicz. Macmillan, 1991. ISBN 0-02-747661-8 Subj: Behavior – disbelief.

April ill. by Kay Life. Charlesbridge, 2002. ISBN 0-88106-908-6 Subj: Days of the week, months of the year. Holidays. Seasons – spring. Weather.

August ill. by Pat DeWitt & Robin DeWitt. Charlesbridge, 2002. ISBN 0-88106-921-3 Subj: Days of the week, months of the year. Holidays. Seasons – summer. Weather.

The autumn equinox ill. by Jan Davey Ellis. Millbrook, 2000. ISBN 0-7613-1354-0 Subj: Fairs, festivals. Holidays. Seasons – fall.

The bear in the bathtub ill. by Margot Apple. Addison-Wesley, 1981. ISBN 0-201-04701-2 Subj: Activities – bathing. Animals – bears. Character traits – cleanliness.

The book of slime ill. by Jan Davey Ellis. Millbrook, 1997. ISBN 0-7613-0042-2 Subj: Anatomy. Nature.

Boris the boring boar ill. by Normand Chartier. Macmillan, 1992. ISBN 0-02-747662-6 Subj: Animals – pigs. Animals – wolves. Emotions – loneliness.

Brown cow, green grass, yellow mellow sun ill. by Victoria Raymond. Hyperion, 1995. ISBN 0-7868-2006-3 Subj: Circular tales. Concepts – color. Farms. Food. Nature.

Cinder Edna ill. by Kevin O'Malley. Lothrop, 1994. ISBN 0-688-12323-6 Subj: Folk & fairy tales. Royalty – princes.

December ill. by Pat DeWitt & Robin DeWitt. Charlesbridge, 2002. ISBN 0-88106-958-2 Subj: Days of the week, months of the year. Holidays. Seasons – winter. Weather.

February ill. by Pat DeWitt & Robin DeWitt. Charlesbridge, 2002. ISBN 0-88106-996-5 Subj: Days of the week, months of the year. Holidays. Seasons – winter. Weather.

The impossible riddle ill. by Alison Winfield. Whispering Coyote, 1995. ISBN 1-879085-93-3 Subj: Character traits – cleverness. Food. Foreign lands – Russia. Riddles & jokes. Royalty – kings.

January ill. by Pat DeWitt & Robin DeWitt. Charlesbridge, 2002. ISBN 0-88106-995-7 Subj: Days of the week, months of the year. Holidays. Seasons – winter. Weather.

July ill. by Pat DeWitt & Robin DeWitt. Charlesbridge, 2002. ISBN 0-88106-920-5 Subj: Days of the week, months of the year. Holidays. Seasons – summer. Weather.

June ill. by Kay Life. Charlesbridge, 2002. ISBN 0-88106-919-1 Subj: Days of the week, months of the year. Holidays. Seasons – summer. Weather.

March ill. by Kay Life. Charlesbridge, 2002. ISBN 0-88106-905-1 Subj: Days of the week, months of the year. Holidays. Seasons – spring. Weather.

May ill. by Kay Life. Charlesbridge, 2002. ISBN 0-88106-918-3 Subj: Days of the week, months of the year. Holidays. Seasons – spring. Weather.

Monsters in my mailbox ill. by Maxie Chambliss. Troll, 1995. ISBN 0-8167-3631-6 Subj: Activities – playing. Clubs, gangs. Monsters.

November ill. by Pat DeWitt & Robin DeWitt. Charlesbridge, 2002. ISBN 0-88106-927-2 Subj: Days of the week, months of the year. Holidays. Seasons – fall. Weather.

October ill. by Pat DeWitt & Robin DeWitt. Charlesbridge, 2002. ISBN 0-88106-923-X Subj: Days of the week, months of the year. Holidays. Seasons – fall. Weather.

The precious gift: a Navaho creation myth ill. by Woodleigh Marx Hubbard. S&S, 1996. ISBN 0-689-80480-6 Subj: Animals. Animals – snails. Creation. Gifts. Indians of North America – Navajo. Water.

September ill. by Pat DeWitt & Robin DeWitt. Charlesbridge, 2002. ISBN 0-88106-922-1 Subj: Days of the week, months of the year. Holidays. Seasons – fall. Weather.

Sometimes bad things happen photos by Shelley Rotner. Millbrook, 2002. ISBN 0-7613-2810-6 Subj: Behavior – bad day. Character traits – helpfulness. Emotions. Emotions – happiness.

The spring equinox ill. by Jan Davey Ellis. Millbrook, 2002. ISBN 0-7613-1955-7 Subj: Holidays. Seasons – spring.

The summer solstice ill. by Jan Davey Ellis. Millbrook, 2001. ISBN 0-7613-1623-X Subj: Holidays. Seasons – summer.

The wacky witch war ill. by Denise Brunkus. WhistleStop, 1996. ISBN 0-8167-3717-7 Subj: School. Witches.

The winter solstice ill. by Jan Davey Ellis. Millbrook, 1994. ISBN 1-56294-400-2 Subj: Holidays. Seasons – winter.

Jackson, Isaac. *Somebody's new pajamas* ill. by David Soman. Dial, 1996. ISBN 0-8037-1549-8 Subj: Clothing – pajamas. Ethnic groups in the U.S. – African Americans. Family life. Friendship. Sleepovers.

Jackson, Jacqueline. *Chicken ten thousand* ill. by Barbara Morrow. Little, 1968. Subj: Birds – chickens. Science.

Jackson, Jean. *Big lips and hairy arms: a monster story* ill. by Vera Rosenberry. DK, 1998. ISBN 0-7894-2521-1 Subj: Emotions – fear. Monsters. Telephone.

Mrs. Piccolo's easy chair ill. by Diane Greenseid. DK, 1999. ISBN 0-7894-2580-7 Subj: Furniture – chairs. Stores.

Thorndike and Nelson ill. by Vera Rosenberry. DK, 1997. ISBN 0-7894-2452-5 Subj: Behavior. Friendship. Monsters.

Jackson, Kathryn. *The golden circus book* ill. by Alice & Martin Provensen. Random House, 2005. ISBN 0-375-83215-7 Subj: Circus. Format, unusual – board books.

The saggy baggy elephant by K. & B. Jackson; ill. by Tenggren. Golden Bks., 2003. ISBN 0-375-92590-2 Subj: Animals – elephants. Behavior – worrying.

Jackson, Richard. *Iktomi and the boulder* (Goble, Paul)

Jackson, Shelley. *The old woman and the wave* ill. by author. DK, 1998. ISBN 0-7894-2484-3 Subj: Character traits – bravery. Emotions – fear. Nature. Sea & seashore. Water.

Jackson, Shirley. *9 magic wishes* ill. by Miles Hyman. Farrar, 2001. ISBN 0-374-35525-8 Subj: Activities – wishing. Magic.

Jackson, Woody. *Counting cows* ill. by author. Harcourt, 1995. ISBN 0-15-220165-3 Subj: Animals – bulls, cows. Counting, numbers. Nature.

Jacobs, Daniel. *What does it do? inventions then and now* ill. with photos. Raintree, 1990. ISBN 0-8172-3586-8 Subj: Machines.

Jacobs, Francine. *Lonesome George, the giant tortoise* ill. by Jean Cassels. Walker, 2003. ISBN 0-8027-8865-3 Subj: Animals – endangered animals. Foreign lands – Galapagos Islands. Reptiles – turtles, tortoises.

Jacobs, Howard. *Cajun night before Christmas* (Trosclair)

Jacobs, Joseph. *The crock of gold: being "The pedlar of Swaffham"* ill. by William Stobbs. Follett, 1971. ISBN 0-695-80213-5 Subj: Careers – peddlers. Dreams. Folk & fairy tales. Foreign lands – England.

Hereafterthis ill. by Paul Galdone. McGraw-Hill, 1973. ISBN 0-07022-691-1 Subj: Animals. Behavior – mistakes. Crime. Farms. Folk & fairy tales.

Hudden and Dudden and Donald O'Neary ill. by Doris Burn. Coward, 1968. Subj: Behavior – greed. Folk & fairy tales. Foreign lands – Ireland.

Johnny-cake ill. by Emma Lillian Brock. Putnam, 1933. Subj: Cumulative tales. Folk & fairy tales. Food.

Johnny-cake ill. by William Stobbs. Viking, 1973, c1972. ISBN 0-670-40826-3 Subj: Cumulative tales. Folk & fairy tales. Food.

King of the cats: a ghost story (Galdone, Paul)

Lazy Jack (Lazy Jack)

Master of all masters ill. by Anne F. Rockwell. Grosset, 1972. ISBN 0-448-26210-X Subj: Folk & fairy tales.

Old Mother Wiggle-Waggle ill. by William Stobbs. Bodley Head, 1980. ISBN 0-370-02048-0 Subj: Folk & fairy tales.

Tattercoats ill. by Margot Tomes. Putnam, 1989. ISBN 0-399-21584-0 Subj: Emotions – love. Family life – grandfathers. Folk & fairy tales. Foreign lands – England. Royalty – princes.

The three sillies retold & ill. by Paul Galdone. Houghton Mifflin, 1981. ISBN 0-395-30172-6 Subj: Folk & fairy tales.

The three sillies retold & ill. by Kathryn Hewitt. Harcourt, 1986. ISBN 0-15-286855-0 Subj: Animals. Animals – pigs. Character traits – foolishness. Folk & fairy tales.

The three sillies adapt. & ill. by Steven Kellogg. Candlewick, 1999. ISBN 0-7636-0811-4 Subj: Animals. Animals – pigs. Character traits – foolishness. Folk & fairy tales.

Jacobs, Kate. *A sister's wish* ill. by Nancy Carpenter. Hyperion, 1996. ISBN 0-7868-2112-4 Subj: Behavior – needing someone. Behavior – wishing. Family life – brothers. Rhyming text. Sibling rivalry.

Jacobs, Laurie A. *So much in common* ill. by Valeri Gorbachev. Caroline House, 1994. ISBN 1-56397-115-1 Subj: Activities – baking, cooking. Animals – goats. Animals – hippopotamuses. Friendship. Gardens, gardening.

Jacobs, Leland B. (Leland Blair). *Belling the cat and other stories* (Belling the cat and other stories)

Is somewhere always far away? ill. by John E. Johnson. Holt, 1967. Subj: Activities – traveling. Character traits – questioning. Poetry.

Is somewhere always far away? poems about places ill. by Jeff Kaufman. Holt, 1995. ISBN 0-8050-2677-0 Subj: Activities – traveling. Character traits – questioning. Poetry.

Just around the corner: poems about the seasons ill. by Jeff Kaufman. Holt, 1993. ISBN 0-8050-2676-2 Subj: Poetry. Seasons.

Jacobs, Paul DuBois. *Abiyoyo returns* (Seeger, Pete)

Jacobs, Shannon K. *The boy who loved morning* ill. by Michael Hays. Little, 1993. ISBN 0-316-45556-3 Subj: Folk & fairy tales. Indians of North America. Morning. Names.

Jacobson, Jennifer Richard. *Moon sandwich mom* ill. by Benrei Huang. A. Whitman, 1999. ISBN 0-8075-4071-4 Subj: Animals. Animals – foxes. Family life – mothers.

A net of stars ill. by Greg Shed. Dial, 1998. ISBN 0-8037-2088-2 Subj: Emotions – fear. Fairs, festivals. Night. Sky.

Jacoby-Nelson, Frank. *In this night* (Lucht, Irmgard)

The red poppy (Lucht, Irmgard)

Jaffe, Marjorie. *Albert the running bear's exercise book* (Isenberg, Barbara)

Jaffe, Nina. *The golden flower: a Taino myth from Puerto Rico* ill. by Enrique O. Sánchez. S&S, 1996. ISBN 0-02-747585-9 Subj: Creation. Folk & fairy tales. Foreign lands – Puerto Rico. Indians of North America – Taino.

In the month of Kislev: a story for Hanukkah ill. by Louise August. Viking, 1992. ISBN 0-670-82863-7 Subj: Folk & fairy tales. Holidays – Hanukkah. Jewish culture.

Older brother, younger brother ill. by Wenhai Ma. Viking, 1995. ISBN 0-670-85645-2 Subj: Family life – brothers. Folk & fairy tales. Foreign lands – Korea.

Tales for the seventh day ill. by Kelly Stribling Sutherland. Scholastic, 2000. ISBN 0-590-12054-9 Subj: Folk & fairy tales. Jewish culture. Religion.

The way meat loves salt: a Cinderella tale from the Jewish tradition ill. by Louise August. Holt, 1998. ISBN 0-8050-4384-5 Subj: Emotions – love. Family life – fathers. Folk & fairy tales. Foreign lands – Europe. Jewish culture. Weddings.

Jaffe, Rona. *Last of the wizards* ill. by Erik Blegvad. S&S, 1961. Subj: Behavior – wishing. Character traits – cleverness.

Jaffrey, Madhur. *Market days* (Shohet, Marti)

Jagendorf, Moritz A. *Kwi-na the eagle: and other Indian tales* ill. by Jack Endewelt; consultant: Carolyn W. Field. Silver Burdett, 1968. Subj: Folk & fairy tales. Indians of North America.

Jagtenberg, Yvonne. *Jack the wolf* ill. by author. Roaring Brook, 2002. ISBN 0-7613-2855-6 Subj: Animals – wolves. Humorous stories. School – first day. Self-concept.

Jack's kite ill. by author. Roaring Brook, 2004. ISBN 0-7613-2940-4 Subj: Camps, camping. Kites.

Jack's rabbit ill. by author. Roaring Brook, 2003. ISBN 0-7613-2916-1 Subj: Activities – drawing. Animals – rabbits. Behavior – running away. Pets.

Jahn-Clough, Lisa. *Alicia's best friends* ill. by author. Houghton, 2003. ISBN 0-618-23951-0 Subj: Friendship.

Missing Molly ill. by author. Houghton, 2000. ISBN 0-618-00980-9 Subj: Behavior – hiding. Friendship. Games.

My friend and I ill. by author. Houghton Mifflin, 1999. ISBN 0-395-93545-8 Subj: Friendship. Toys.

My happy birthday book ill. by author. Houghton Mifflin, 1996. ISBN 0-395-77260-5 Subj: Birthdays. Friendship.

On the hill ill. by author. Houghton, 2004. ISBN 0-618-40741-3 Subj: Animals. Emotions – loneliness. Homes, houses.

1 2 3 yippie ill. by author. Houghton Mifflin, 1998. ISBN 0-395-87003-8 Subj: Animals. Counting, numbers. Parties.

Simon and Molly plus Hester ill. by author. Houghton, 2001. ISBN 0-618-08220-4 Subj: Friendship.

Jain, Laxmi. *Here comes Diwali* (Pandya, Meenal)

Jakes, John. *Susanna of the Alamo* ill. by Paul Bacon. Harcourt, 1986. ISBN 0-15-200595-1 Subj: Character traits – bravery. U.S. history – frontier & pioneer life.

Jakob, Donna. *My bike* ill. by Nelle Davis. Hyperion, 1994. ISBN 1-56282-455-4 Subj: Rhyming text. Sports – bicycling. Time.

My new sandbox ill. by Julia Gorton. Hyperion, 1996. ISBN 0-7868-2144-2 Subj: Activities – playing. Animals. Behavior – sharing.

Tiny toes ill. by Mireille Levert. Hyperion, 1995. ISBN 0-7868-2009-8 Subj: Activities – playing. Anatomy – toes.

Jam, Teddy. *The kid line* ill. by Ange Zhang. Douglas & McIntyre, 2001. ISBN 0-88899-432-X Subj: Family life – fathers. Foreign lands – Canada. Sports – hockey.

Night cars ill. by Eric Beddows. Orchard, 1989. ISBN 0-531-08393-4 Subj: Babies. Cities, towns. Family life – fathers. Night. Rhyming text.

The year of fire ill. by Ian Wallace. McElderry, 1993. ISBN 0-689-50566-3 Subj: Country. Family life – grandfathers. Fire. Foreign lands – Canada. Forest, woods.

James, Betsy. *The dream stair* ill. by Richard Jesse Watson. HarperCollins, 1990. ISBN 0-06-022788-5 Subj: Dreams. Ethnic groups in the U.S. Family life – grandmothers. Sleep.

Flashlight ill. by Stacey Schuett. Knopf, 1997. ISBN 0-679-97970-0 Subj: Emotions – fear. Family life – grandparents. Night.

He wakes me ill. by Helen K. Davie. Watts, 1991. ISBN 0-531-08554-6 Subj: Animals – cats. Pets.

Mary Ann ill. by author. Dutton, 1994. ISBN 0-525-45077-7 Subj: Friendship. Insects – praying mantis. Moving.

The mud family ill. by Paul Morin. Putnam, 1994. ISBN 0-399-22549-8 Subj: Family life. Indians of North America – Anasazi. Toys – dolls. Weather – droughts. Weather – floods. Weather – rain.

Tadpoles ill. by author. Dutton, 1999. ISBN 0-525-46197-3 Subj: Animals – babies. Behavior. Frogs & toads.

James, Brian. *Supertwins and the sneaky, slimy book worms* ill. by Christ Demarest. Scholastic, 2004. ISBN 0-613-72181-0 Subj: Animals – worms. Family life – brothers & sisters. Multiple births – twins. School.

The Supertwins and tooth trouble ill. by Christ Demarest. Scholastic, 2003. ISBN 0-439-46624-5 Subj: Crime. Fairies. Family life – brothers & sisters. Multiple births – twins. Teeth.

The Supertwins meet the bad dogs from space ill. by Christ Demarest. Scholastic, 2003. ISBN 0-439-46623-7 Subj: Animals – dogs. Family life – brothers & sisters. Multiple births – twins. Mythical creatures.

Supertwins meet the dangerous dino-robots ill. by Christ Demarest. Scholastic, 2003. ISBN 0-439-46625-3 Subj: Careers – scientists. Dinosaurs. Family life – brothers & sisters. Multiple births – twins. Robots.

James, Elizabeth. *The little black hen* (Pogorelsky, Antony)

James, Ellen Foley. *Little Bull* ill. with photos. Sterling, 1998. ISBN 0-8069-2095-5 Subj: Animals – elephants. Foreign lands – Africa.

James, J. Alison. *Alexander the great* (Bos, Burny)

The apple king (Bosca, Francesca)

Bailey the bear cub (Kuiper, Nannie)

The bears' Christmas surprise tr. & adapt. by J. Alison James; ill. by Angela Kehlenbeck. North-South, 2000. ISBN 0-7358-1364-7 Subj: Emotions – loneliness. Holidays – Christmas. Toys – bears.

The bears' Christmas surprise (James, J. Alison)

The best father of all (Horn, Peter)

The best of friends (Vainio, Pirkko)

The birthday bear (Schneider, Antonie)

Bravo, brave beavers (Kuiper, Nannie)

The Christmas star (Pfister, Marcus)

Danny, the angry lion (Lachner, Dorothea)

Dazzle the dinosaur (Pfister, Marcus)

Dino bikes (Montanari, Eva)

Don't worry, Wags (Loupy, Christophe)

The dream house (Vainio, Pirkko)

The drums of Noto Hanto ill. by Tsukushi. DK, 1999. ISBN 0-7894-2574-2 Subj: Character traits – bravery. Foreign lands – Japan. Music. Musical instruments – drums. War.

The elf's hat (Weninger, Brigitte)

Eucalyptus wings ill. by Demi. Atheneum, 1995. ISBN 0-689-31886-3 Subj: Activities – flying. Friendship. Magic.

Fabian Youngpig sails the world (Ostheeren, Ingrid)

Finn cooks (Müller, Birte)

Fun with the Molesons (Bos, Burny)

Good-bye, Vivi! (Schneider, Antonie)

The great golden thing (Bardill, Linard)

The happy hedgehog (Pfister, Marcus)

A house is not a home (Liersch, Anne)

How Leo learned to be king (Pfister, Marcus)

It wasn't me (Weigelt, Udo)

Just right (Monnier, Miriam)

Little elephant runs away (Hänel, Wolfram)

Little elephant's song (Hänel, Wolfram)

The little green goose (Sansone, Adele)

Little polar bear and the brave little hare (De Beer, Hans)

Little polar bear, take me home! (De Beer, Hans)

Lord of the cranes (Chen, Kerstin)

Luke the Lionhearted (Schneider, Antonie)

Martin and the Pumpkin Ghost (Ostheeren, Ingrid)

Mary and the mystery dog (Hänel, Wolfram)

Meet the Molesons (Bos, Burny)

Meredith, the witch who wasn't (Lachner, Dorothea)

Meredith's mixed-up magic (Lachner, Dorothea)

Mia the beach cat (Hänel, Wolfram)

The moon man (Scheidl, Gerda Marie)

Moonchild, star of the sea (Elschner, Géraldine)

The new dog (Ostheeren, Ingrid)

Niki's little donkey (Hol, Coby)

Not now, Sara! (Voigt, Hannelore)

Rainbow fish and the big blue whale (Pfister, Marcus)

Rainbow fish and the sea monsters' cave (Pfister, Marcus)

Rainbow fish to the rescue! (Pfister, Marcus)

Special delivery (Weninger, Brigitte)

Stormy night (Flattinger, Hubert)

Tiger baby (Bohdal, Susi)

Wake up, Grizzly! (Bittner, Wolfgang)

Wake up, Santa Claus! (Pfister, Marcus)

Who stole the gold? (Weigelt, Udo)

James, Shirley Kerby. *Going to a horse farm* ill. by Laura Jacques. Charlesbridge, 1992. ISBN 0-88106-477-7 Subj: Animals – horses, ponies. Farms.

James, Simon. *The birdwatchers* ill. by author. Candlewick, 2002. ISBN 0-7636-1676-1 Subj: Birds. Family life – grandfathers.

Days like this (Days like this)

Dear Mr. Blueberry ill. by author. Macmillan, 1991. ISBN 0-689-50529-9 Subj: Animals – whales. Careers – teachers. Imagination. Letters, cards.

Leon and Bob ill. by author. Candlewick, 1997. ISBN 1-56402-991-3 Subj: Foreign lands – England. Friendship. Imagination – imaginary friends.

Little One Step ill. by author. Candlewick, 2003. ISBN 0-7636-2070-X Subj: Birds – ducks. Family life – brothers. Games.

My friend whale ill. by author. Bantam, 1991. ISBN 0-553-07065-7 Subj: Animals – whales.

Sally and the limpet ill. by author. Macmillan, 1991. ISBN 0-689-50528-0 Subj: Crustaceans. Ecology. Sea & seashore.

The wild woods ill. by author. Candlewick, 1993. ISBN 1-56402-219-6 Subj: Animals – squirrels. Family life – grandfathers. Nature.

Jameson, Cynthia. *The house of five bears* ill. by Lorinda Bryan Cauley. Putnam, 1978. ISBN 0-399-61122-3 Subj: Character traits – cleverness. Folk & fairy tales. Foreign lands – Russia.

Jamison, Jocelyn. *Drac's night out* ill. by Bill Basso. Price Stern Sloan, 2001. ISBN 0-8431-4393-2 Subj: Monsters.

Jane, Cabrera. *The lonesome polar bear* ill. by author. Random House, 2002. ISBN 0-375-82410-3 Subj: Animals – polar bears. Behavior – needing someone. Friendship.

Jane, Pamela. *Milo and the fire engine parade* ill. by Meredith Johnson. Mondo, 2002. ISBN 1-59034-192-9 Subj: Animals – dogs. Careers – firefighters. Parades. Trucks.

Milo and the greatest trick ever ill. by Meredith Johnson. Mondo, 2002. ISBN 1-59034-187-2 Subj: Animals – cats. Magic. Theater.

Monster countdown ill. by Nick Zarin-Ackerman. Mondo, 2001. ISBN 1-58653-857-8 Subj: Counting, numbers. Monsters. Rhyming text.

Monster mischief ill. by Vera Rosenberry. Atheneum, 2001. ISBN 0-689-80471-7 Subj: Holidays – Halloween. Monsters. Rhyming text.

Jango-Cohen, Judith. *Chinese New Year* ill. by Jason Chin. Carolrhoda, 2005. ISBN 1-57505-653-4 Subj: Holidays – Chinese New Year.

Clinging sea horses ill. with photos. Lerner, 2001. ISBN 0-8225-3764-8 Subj: Fish – seahorses. Sea & seashore.

Desert iguanas ill. with photos. Lerner, 2001. ISBN 0-8225-3635-8 Subj: Desert. Reptiles – iguanas.

Dump trucks ill. with photos. Lerner, 2003. ISBN 0-8225-0688-2 Subj: Trucks.

Fire trucks ill. with photos. Lerner, 2003. ISBN 0-8225-0077-9 Subj: Careers – firefighters. Trucks.

Flying squirrels ill. with photos. Lerner, 2004. ISBN 0-8225-3772-9 Subj: Animals – squirrels.

Janice. *Angélique* ill. by Roger Antoine Duvoisin. McGraw-Hill, 1960. Subj: Animals – dogs. Behavior – bullying. Birds – ducks.

Little Bear marches in the St. Patrick's Day parade ill. by Mariana. Lothrop, 1967. Subj: Animals – bears. Holidays – St. Patrick's Day. Parades.

Little Bear's Christmas ill. by Mariana. Lothrop, 1964. ISBN 0-688-51076-0 Subj: Animals – bears. Character traits – generosity. Hibernation. Holidays – Christmas.

Little Bear's New Year's party ill. by Mariana. Lothrop, 1973. ISBN 0-688-50002-1 Subj: Animals – bears. Holidays – New Year's. Parties.

Little Bear's pancake party ill. by Mariana. Lothrop, 1960. Subj: Animals – bears. Food. Parties. Seasons – spring.

Little Bear's Sunday breakfast ill. by Mariana. Lothrop, 1958. Subj: Animals – bears. Food.

Little Bear's Thanksgiving ill. by Mariana. Lothrop, 1967. ISBN 0-688-51078-7 Subj: Animals – bears. Holidays – Thanksgiving.

Minette ill. by Alain. McGraw-Hill, 1959. Subj: Animals – cats.

Mr. and Mrs. Button's wonderful watchdogs ill. by Roger Antoine Duvoisin. Lothrop, 1978. ISBN 0-688-51848-6 Subj: Animals – dogs. Crime.

Janisch, Heinz. *The merry pranks of Till Eulenspiegel* ill. by Lisbeth Zwerger; trans. by Anthea Bell. North-South, 2001. ISBN 1-55858-806-X Subj: Behavior – trickery. Folk & fairy tales. Foreign lands – Germany.

Noah's ark ill. by Lisbeth Zwerger. North-South, 1997. ISBN 1-55858-785-3 Subj: Animals. Boats, ships. Religion – Noah. Weather – floods. Weather – rain. Weather – rainbows.

Jankel, Karen. *Paddington Bear goes to the hospital* (Bond, Michael)

Janosch. *Dear snowman* ill. by author. Collins, 1969. Subj: Seasons – winter. Snowmen. Weather – snow.

Hey Presto! You're a bear! trans. by Klauss Flugge; ill. by author. Little, 1980. ISBN 0-316-45765-5 Subj: Imagination.

Joshua and the magic fiddle ill. by author. Collins, 1967. Subj: Magic. Moon. Music. Musical instruments – violins.

Just one apple trans. by Refna Wilkin; ill. by author. Walck, 1966. Subj: Behavior – wishing. Dragons.

The magic auto ill. by author. Crown, 1971. Translation of Das Regenauto. Subj: Automobiles. Magic.

Tonight at nine ill. by author. Walck, 1967. Translation of Heute um neune hinter der Scheune. Subj: Animals. Music. Rhyming text.

The trip to Panama trans. by Anthea Bell; ill. by author. Little, 1978. Translation of Oh, wie schon ist Panama. ISBN 0-316-45766-3 Subj: Activities – traveling. Foreign lands – Panama.

Janovitz, Marilyn. *Baa baa, black sheep* (Mother Goose)

Bowl patrol! ill. by author. North-South, 1996. ISBN 1-55858-637-7 Subj: Animals – dogs. Rhyming text.

Can I help? ill. by author. North-South, 1996. ISBN 1-55858-576-1 Subj: Animals – wolves. Character traits – helpfulness. Family life – fathers. Gardens, gardening. Rhyming text.

Hey, diddle, diddle (Mother Goose)

Hickory dickory dock (Mother Goose)

Is it time? ill. by author. North-South, 1994. ISBN 1-55858-332-7 Subj: Activities – bathing. Animals – wolves. Bedtime. Family life – fathers. Rhyming text. Sleep.

Little Fox ill. by author. North-South, 1999. ISBN 0-7358-1161-X Subj: Animals – foxes.

Look out, bird! ill. by author. North-South, 1994. ISBN 1-55858-250-9 Subj: Animals. Animals – snails. Birds. Circular tales.

Pat-a-cake (Mother Goose)

What could be keeping Santa? ill. by author. North-South, 1997. ISBN 1-55858-820-5 Subj: Animals – reindeer. Holidays – Christmas. Rhyming text. Santa Claus.

Janowitz, Tama. *Hear that?* ill. by Tracy Dockray. SeaStar, 2001. ISBN 1-58717-075-2 Subj: Family life – mothers. Noise, sounds.

A January fog will freeze a hog: and other weather folklore comp. & ed. by Hubert Davis; ill. by John Wallner. Crown, 1977. ISBN 0-517-52811-8 Subj: Folk & fairy tales. Weather.

Jaques, Faith. *Tilly's house* ill. by author. Atheneum, 1979. ISBN 0-689-50138-2 Subj: Homes, houses. Toys – dolls.

Tilly's rescue ill. by author. Atheneum, 1981. ISBN 0-689-50175-7 Subj: Behavior – lost. Character traits – bravery. Friendship. Holidays – Christmas. Toys – dolls.

Jaquith, Priscilla. *Bo Rabbit smart for true: tall tales from the Gullah* ill. by Ed Young. Philomel, 1995. ISBN 0-399-22668-0 Subj: Animals – rabbits. Ethnic groups in the U.S. – African Americans. Folk & fairy tales. Noise, sounds. Reptiles – alligators, crocodiles. Reptiles – snakes.

Jaramillo, Raquel. *Ride, baby, ride!* ill. with photos. Little Simon, 1998. ISBN 0-689-82027-5 Subj: Activities – playing. Babies. Format, unusual – board books.

Jarrell, Mary. *The knee baby* ill. by Symeon Shimin. Farrar, 1973. ISBN 0-374-34246-6 Subj: Babies. Family life. Family life – grandmothers.

Jarrell, Randall. *A bat is born* ill. by John Schoenherr. Doubleday, 1977, c1964. ISBN 0-385-12224-1 Subj: Animals – bats. Birth. Poetry.

The fisherman and his wife (Grimm, Jacob)

The golden bird: and other fairy tales (Grimm, Jacob)

The rabbit catcher and other fairy tales (Bechstein, Ludwig)

Jarrett, Clare. *The best picnic ever* ill. by author. Candlewick, 2004. ISBN 0-7636-2370-9 Subj: Activities – picnicking. Activities – playing. Animals.

Jaspersohn, William. *My hometown library* ill. by author. Houghton Mifflin, 1994. ISBN 0-395-55723-2 Subj: Libraries.

Timber! ill. by author. Little, 1996. ISBN 0-316-45825-2 Subj: Forest, woods. Paper. Trees.

The two brothers ill. by Michael A. Donato. Vermont Folklife Center, 2000. ISBN 0-916718-16-6 Subj: Ethnic groups in the U.S. – German Americans. Family life – brothers. Farms. Immigrants.

Jauck, Andrea. *Assateague: island of the wild ponies* by Andrea Jauck & Larry Points; ill. with photos. Macmillan, 1993. ISBN 0-02-774695-X Subj: Animals – horses, ponies. Islands. Seasons.

Jay, Betsy. *Jane vs. the Tooth Fairy* ill. by Lori Osiecki. Rising Moon, 2000. ISBN 0-87358-739-1 Subj: Fairies. Teeth.

Swimming lessons ill. by Lori Osiecki. Rising Moon, 1998. ISBN 0-8735-8685-9 Subj: Children as authors. Emotions – fear. Sports – swimming.

Jaynes, Ruth M. *Benny's four hats* photos by Harvey Mandlin. Bowmar, 1967. Subj: Clothing – hats. Ethnic groups in the U.S. Participation. Weather.

The biggest house ill. by Jacques Rupp. Bowmar, 1968. Subj: Homes, houses.

Friends! friends! friends! photos by Harvey Mandlin. Bowmar, 1967. Subj: Ethnic groups in the U.S. Friendship. School.

Melinda's Christmas stocking photos by Richard George. Bowmar, 1968. Subj: Ethnic groups in the U.S. – Mexican Americans. Holidays – Christmas. Senses – hearing. Senses – sight. Senses – smell. Senses – taste. Senses – touch.

Tell me please! What's that? photos by Harvey Mandlin. Bowmar, 1968. Subj: Animals. Ethnic groups in the U.S. Ethnic groups in the U.S. – Mexican Americans. Foreign languages.

That's what it is! photos by Harvey Mandlin. Bowmar, 1968. Subj: Ethnic groups in the U.S. Ethnic groups in the U.S. – Mexican Americans. Insects.

Three baby chicks photos by Harvey Mandlin. Bowmar, 1967. Subj: Birds – chickens. School.

What is a birthday child? photos by Harvey Mandlin. Bowmar, 1967. Subj: Birthdays. Character traits – individuality. Ethnic groups in the U.S. Ethnic groups in the U.S. – Mexican Americans.

Jeake, Samuel. *see* Aiken, Conrad Potter

Jefferds, Vincent. *Disney's elegant ABC book.* S&S, 1983. ISBN 0-671-45571-0 Subj: ABC books.

Disney's elegant book of manners. S&S, 1985. ISBN 0-671-60507-0 Subj: Etiquette. Rhyming text.

Jeffers, Susan. *All the pretty horses* ill. by author. Macmillan, 1974. ISBN 0-02-747680-4 Subj: Animals – horses, ponies. Bedtime. Sleep.

Forest of dreams (Wells, Rosemary)

The three jovial huntsmen (Mother Goose)

Wild Robin ill. by author. Dutton, 1976. Based on a tale in Little Prudy's fairy book by R. S. Clarke. ISBN 0-525-42787-2 Subj: Behavior – misbehavior. Foreign lands – Scotland.

Jeffery, Graham. *Thomas the tortoise* ill. by author. Crown, 1988. ISBN 0-517-57043-2 Subj: Character traits – individuality. Character traits – kindness to animals. Reptiles – turtles, tortoises.

Jeffrey, Sean. *Franklin's big search-and-solve flap book* ill. by author. Kids Can, 2005. ISBN 1-55337-522-X Subj: Careers – detectives. Format, unusual – toy & movable books. Reptiles – turtles, tortoises.

Jekyll, Walter. *I have a news: rhymes from the Caribbean* comp. by Walter Jekyll & Neil Philip; ill. by Jacqueline Mair. Lothrop, 1994. ISBN 0-688-13367-3 Subj: Foreign lands – Caribbean Islands. Islands. Nursery rhymes. Poetry.

Jendresen, Erik. *The first story ever told* by Erik Jendresen & Alberto Villoldo; ill. by Yoshi. S&S, 1996. ISBN 0-689-80515-2 Subj: Careers – explorers. Creation. Dreams. Indians of South America – Incas.

Hanuman retold by Erik Jendresen & Joshua M. Greene; ill. by Li Ming. Tricycle, 1998. Based on Valmiki's Ramayana. ISBN 1-883672-78-3 Subj: Animals – monkeys. Foreign lands – India. Mythical creatures. Religion.

Jenkin-Pearce, Susie. *The babies of Cockle Bay* (McAllister, Angela)

Bad Boris and the new kitten ill. by author. Macmillan, 1987. ISBN 0-02-747620-0 Subj: Animals – cats. Animals – elephants. Emotions – envy, jealousy.

Bad Boris goes to school ill. by author. Macmillan, 1989. ISBN 0-02-747621-9 Subj: Animals. Animals – elephants. School – first day.

Boris's big ache ill. by author. Dial, 1989. ISBN 0-8037-0551-4 Subj: Animals – elephants. Behavior – growing up. Teeth.

The enchanted garden ill. by author. Oxford Univ. Pr., 1989. ISBN 0-19-279845-6 Subj: Gardens, gardening. Imagination.

Percy Short and Cuthbert ill. by author. Viking, 1991. ISBN 0-670-82803-3 Subj: Animals – hippopotamuses. Behavior – dissatisfaction. Birds – pelicans. Friendship.

The seashell song by Susie Jenkin-Pearce & Claire Fletcher; ill. by authors. Lothrop, 1992. ISBN 0-688-11726-0 Subj: Rhyming text. Sea & seashore.

Jenkins, Christopher N. H. *The little weaver of Thái-Yên Village* (Trân-Khánh-Tuyê)

Jenkins, Emily. *Five creatures* ill. by Tomasz Bogacki. Frances Foster, 2001. ISBN 0-374-32341-0 Subj: Animals – cats. Family life.

Jenkins, Jessica. *Thinking about colors* ill. by author. Dutton, 1992. ISBN 0-525-44908-6 Subj: Concepts – color. Emotions. Ethnic groups in the U.S.

Jenkins, Jordan. *Learning about love* ill. by Gene Ruggles. Childrens Pr., 1979. ISBN 0-516-02020-X Subj: Emotions – love. Family life – mothers. Illness.

Jenkins, Martin. *Chameleons are cool* ill. by Sue Shields. Candlewick, 1998. ISBN 0-7636-0144-6 Subj: Nature. Reptiles – lizards.

The emperor's egg ill. by Jane Chapman. Candlewick, 1999. ISBN 0-7636-0557-3 Subj: Birds – penguins. Family life – parents.

Fly traps! plants that bite back ill. by David Parkins. Candlewick, 1996. ISBN 1-56402-896-8 Subj: Insects – flies. Plants.

Wings, stings, and wriggly things ill. by author. Candlewick, 1996. ISBN 0-7636-0036-9 Subj: Format, unusual. Insects.

Jenkins, Priscilla Belz. *Falcons nest on skyscrapers* ill. by Megan Lloyd. HarperCollins, 1996. ISBN 0-06-021105-9 Subj: Animals – endangered animals. Birds – falcons. Cities, towns.

A nest full of eggs ill. by Lizzy Rockwell. HarperCollins, 1995. ISBN 0-06-023442-3 Subj: Birds – robins. Eggs. Science.

Jenkins, Steve. *Actual size* ill. by author. Houghton, 2004. ISBN 0-618-37594-5 Subj: Anatomy. Animals. Concepts – size.

Animals in flight by Steve Jenkins & Robin Page; ill. by Steve Jenkins. Houghton, 2001. ISBN 0-618-12351-2 Subj: Activities – flying. Animals. Birds. Dinosaurs. Insects.

Big and little ill. by author. Houghton Mifflin, 1996. ISBN 0-395-72664-6 Subj: Animals. Concepts – size.

Biggest, strongest, fastest ill. by author. Ticknor & Fields, 1995. ISBN 0-395-69701-8 Subj: Animals. Concepts.

Duck's breath and mouse pie: a collection of animal superstitions ill. by author. Ticknor & Fields, 1994. ISBN 0-395-69688-7 Subj: Animals. Folk & fairy tales. Superstition.

Hottest, coldest, highest, deepest ill. by author. Houghton, 1998. ISBN 0-395-89999-0 Subj: Earth. Geography.

I see a kookaburra by Steve Jenkins & Robin Page; ill. by Steve Jenkins. Houghton, 2005. ISBN 0-618-50764-7 Subj: Animals. Ecology. Picture puzzles.

Looking down ill. by author. Houghton, 1995. ISBN 0-395-72665-4 Subj: Concepts – distance.

Slap, squeak, and scatter ill. by author. Houghton, 2001. Subj: Animals. Communication. Noise, sounds.

What do you do when something wants to eat you? ill. by author. Houghton, 1997. ISBN 0-395-82514-8 Subj: Animals.

What do you do with a tail like this? ill. by author. Houghton, 2003. ISBN 0-618-25628-8 Subj: Anatomy. Animals. Caldecott award honor books. Games. Senses.

Jenks, Deneen. *Flowers from Mariko* (Noguchi, Rick)

Jennings, Linda M. *The brave little bunny* ill. by Catherine Walters. Dutton, 1995. ISBN 0-525-45364-4 Subj: Animals – rabbits. Pets.

Coppelia ill. by Krystyna Turska. Silver Burdett, 1984. ISBN 0-382-09241-4 Subj: Activities – dancing. Ballet. Folk & fairy tales. Toys – dolls.

Crispin and the dancing piglet ill. by Krystyna Turska. Silver Burdett, 1986. ISBN 0-382-09242-2 Subj: Activities – dancing. Animals – pigs. Behavior – seeking better things.

Easy peasy! ill. by Tanya Linch. Farrar, 1997. ISBN 0-374-31949-9 Subj: Animals. Animals – cats.

Franklin's neighborhood ill. by Brenda Clark. Kids Can, 1999. ISBN 1-55074-729-0 Subj: Activities – drawing. Animals. Communities, neighborhoods. Reptiles – turtles, tortoises.

The golden goose (Grimm, Jacob)

Hide and seek birthday treat ill. by Joanne Partis. Barron's, 2001. ISBN 0-7641-5336-6 Subj: Animals. Animals – leopards. Behavior – hiding. Birthdays. Games. Jungle. Parties. Rhyming text.

The Hippopotamus's birthday and other poems about animals and birds (The Hippopotamus's birthday and other poems about animals and birds)

The musicians of Bremen (Grimm, Jacob)

The sleeping beauty: the story of the ballet ill. by Francesca Crespi. David & Charles, 1987. ISBN 0-340-33518-1 Subj: Activities – dancing. Ballet. Fairies. Folk & fairy tales. Royalty – princes. Royalty – princesses. Sleep. Witches.

Tom's tail ill. by Tim Warnes. Little, 1995. ISBN 0-316-13341-8 Subj: Animals – pigs. Farms. Self-concept.

The wolf and the seven little kids (Grimm, Jacob)

Jennings, Michael. *The bears who came to breakfix* ill. by Tom Dunnington. Childrens Pr., 1977. ISBN 0-516-03411-1 Subj: Animals – bears. Dreams. Family life – mothers. Moving.

Robin Goodfellow and the giant dwarf ill. by Tomie de Paola. McGraw-Hill, 1981. ISBN 0-07-032451-4 Subj: Behavior – trickery. Dwarfs, midgets. Giants.

Jennings, Sharon. *Franklin and the contest* ill. by Sean Jeffrey . . . et al. Kids Can, 2004. Based on the Franklin books by Paulette Bourgeois & Brenda Clark. ISBN 1-55337-491-6 Subj: Contests. Reptiles – turtles, tortoises.

Franklin and the magic show ill. by Sean Jeffrey . . . et al. Kids Can, 2002. Based on the Franklin books by Paulette Bourgeois & Brenda Clark. ISBN 1-55074-990-0 Subj: Magic. Music. Reptiles – turtles, tortoises. Theater.

Franklin and the scooter ill. by Céleste Gagnon, Alice Sinker & Shelley Southern. Kids Can, 2004. Based on the Franklin books by Paulette Bourgeois & Brenda Clark. ISBN 1-55337-493-2 Subj: Animals – rabbits. Behavior – sharing. Money. Reptiles – turtles, tortoises.

Franklin forgives ill. by Celéste Gagnon, Alice Sinkner & Shelley Southern. Kids Can, 2004. Based on the Franklin books by Paulette Bourgeois & Brenda Clark. ISBN 0-439-62159-3 Subj: Animals. Behavior – forgiving. Reptiles – turtles, tortoises.

Franklin goes to the hospital ill. by Brenda Clark. Kids Can, 2000. Based on the Franklin books by Paulette Bourgeois & Brenda Clark. ISBN 1-55074-732-0 Subj: Hospitals. Illness. Reptiles – turtles, tortoises.

Franklin makes a deal ill. by Sean Jeffrey . . . et al. Kids Can, 2003. Based on the Franklin books by Paulette Bourgeois & Brenda Clark. ISBN 1-55337-469-X Subj: Activities – trading. Animals. Reptiles – turtles, tortoises.

Franklin stays up ill. by Sean Jeffrey . . . et al. Kids Can, 2003. Based on the Franklin books by Paulette Bourgeois & Brenda Clark. ISBN 1-553373-71-5 Subj: Animals. Friendship. Reptiles – turtles, tortoises.

Franklin wants a badge ill. by Sean Jeffrey . . . et al. Kids Can, 2003. Based on the Franklin books by Paulette Bourgeois & Brenda Clark. ISBN 1-553374-67-3 Subj: Animals. Friendship. Reptiles – turtles, tortoises. Sleepovers.

Franklin's class trip (Bourgeois, Paulette)

Franklin's music lessons ill. by Sean Jeffrey . . . et al. Scholastic, 2002. ISBN 0-439-41814-3 Subj: Animals. Musical instruments – pianos. Reptiles – turtles, tortoises. School.

Franklin's reading lesson ill. by Sean Jeffrey . . . et al. Kids Can, 2003. Based on the Franklin books by Paulette Bourgeois & Brenda Clark. ISBN 1-55337-369-3 Subj: Animals. Books, reading. Clubs, gangs. Friendship. Reptiles – turtles, tortoises.

Franklin's surprise ill. by Sean Jeffrey . . . et al. Kids Can, 2003. Based on the Franklin books by Paulette Bourgeois & Brenda Clark. Subj: Animals. Friendship. Parties. Reptiles – turtles, tortoises.

Franklin's Thanksgiving ill. by Brenda Clark. Scholastic, 2001. Based on the Franklin books by Paulette Bourgeois & Brenda Clark. ISBN 1-55074-798-3 Subj: Family life – grandparents. Holidays – Thanksgiving. Reptiles – turtles, tortoises.

Franklin's trading cards ill. by Sean Jeffrey . . . et al. Kids Can, 2003. Based on the Franklin books by Paulette Bourgeois & Brenda Clark. ISBN 1-55337-463-0 Subj: Animals. Behavior – collecting things. Friendship. Reptiles – turtles, tortoises.

No monsters here ill. by Ruth Ohi. Fitzhenry & Whiteside, 2004. ISBN 1-55041-787-8 Subj: Bedtime. Emotions – fear. Family life – fathers.

Priscilla and Rosy ill. by Linda Hendry. Fitzhenry & Whiteside, 2001. ISBN 1-55041-676-6 Subj: Animals – rats. Character traits – loyalty. Friendship.

Priscilla's paw de deux ill. by Linda Hendry. Fitzhenry & Whiteside, 2002. ISBN 1-55041-718-5 Subj: Activities – dancing. Animals – cats. Animals – rats. Ballet. Character traits – cooperation. Emotions – fear.

When Jeremiah found Mrs. Ming ill. by Mireille Levert. Firefly, 1992. ISBN 1-55037-237-8 Subj: Activities. Behavior – boredom.

Jenny, Anne. *The fantastic story of King Brioche the First* ill. by Joycelyne Pache. Lothrop, 1970. Translation by Catherine Barton from La fantastique histoire d roi Brioche Ier. Subj: Activities – flying. Birds.

Jensen, Helen Zane. *When Panda came to our house* ill. by author. Dial, 1985. ISBN 0-8037-0236-1 Subj: Activities. Animals – pandas. Foreign lands – China.

Jensen, Patricia. *Be careful, Little Antelope* by Claude Clément; adapt. by Patricia Jensen; ill. by Pio. Reader's Digest, 1993. Adapt. of: Un petit chamois bien maladroit by Claude Clément. ISBN 0-89577-504-2 Subj: Animals – antelopes. Family life – fathers.

Be patient, Little Chick by Claude Clément; adapt. by Patricia Jensen; ill. by Erost. Reader's Digest, 1993. Adapt. of: Petit poussin pressé by Claude Clément. ISBN 0-8957-7503-4 Subj: Animals – babies. Behavior – growing up. Birds – chickens. Character traits – patience. Concepts – size.

The curious little dolphin (Chottin, Ariane)

Gentle Little Lion by Claude Clément; adapt. by Patricia Jensen; ill. by Marcelle Geneste. Reader's Digest, 1994. Adapt. of: Un Petit Lion si mignon! by Claude Clément. ISBN 0-89577-562-X Subj: Animals – lions. Behavior – growing up. Noise, sounds.

Go to sleep, little groundhog by Claude Clément; adapt. by Patricia Jensen; ill. by Catherine Nouvelle. Reader's Digest, 1992. Adapt. of: Trotte marmotte by Claude Clément. ISBN 0-89577-424-0 Subj: Animals – groundhogs. Sleep.

Kitty's special job by Claude Clément; adapt. by Patricia Jensen; ill. by Olivier Raquois. Reader's Digest, 1992. Adapt. of: Gare à toi, le chat! by Claude Clément. ISBN 0-89577-427-5 Subj: Animals – cats. Animals – mice. Careers. Farms.

Little Donkey learns to help by Claude Clément; adapt. by Patricia Jensen; ill. by Pascal Robin. Reader's Digest, 1993. Adapt. of: Es-tu têtu, Petit Âne? by Claude Clément. ISBN 0-89577-502-6 Subj: Animals – donkeys. Behavior – needing someone. Character traits – helpfulness.

Little Goat's new horns (Chottin, Ariane)

Little Kangaroo finds his way (Chottin, Ariane)

Little Mouse's rescue (Chottin, Ariane)

Little Squirrel's special nest by Claude Clément; adapt. by Patricia Jensen; ill. by Bernadette Pons Fudym. Reader's Digest, 1993. Rev. translation of: Trésor d'Ecureuil by Claude Clément. ISBN 0-89577-542-5 Subj: Animals. Animals – squirrels. Character traits – helpfulness.

The mess ill. by Molly Delaney. Childrens Pr., 1990. ISBN 0-516-05357-4 Subj: Activities – playing. Behavior – messy. Rhyming text.

Jensen, Virginia Allen. *Cat alley* (Olsen, Ib Spang)

Catching: a book for blind and sighted children with pictures to feel as well as to see ill. by author. Putnam, 1984. ISBN 0-399-20997-2 Subj: Concepts – shape. Format, unusual. Handicaps – blindness. Senses – sight.

Red thread riddles by Virginia Allen Jensen & Polly Edman; ill. by authors. Putnam, 1980. ISBN 0-529-05604-6 Subj: Format, unusual. Handicaps – blindness. Riddles & jokes. Senses – sight.

Sara and the door ill. by Ann Strugnell. Addison-Wesley, 1977. ISBN 0-201-03446-8 Subj: Character traits – perseverance. Clothing. Ethnic groups in the U.S. – African Americans.

What's that? ill. by Dorcas Woodbury Haller. Collins-World, 1979. ISBN 0-529-05500-7 Subj: Concepts. Handicaps – blindness. Senses – sight.

Jeppson, Ann-Sofie. *Here comes Pontus* ill. by Catarina Kruusval; Trans. by Frances Corry. R&S Books, 2000. ISBN 91-29-64561-1 Subj: Animals – horses, ponies. Farms.

You're growing up, Pontus ill. by Catarina Kruusval; tr. by Frances Corry. Farrar, 2001. ISBN 91-29-65393-2 Subj: Animals – horses, ponies. Behavior – growing up.

Jeram, Anita. *All together now* ill. by author. Candlewick, 1999. ISBN 0-7636-0846-7 Subj: Animals – mice. Animals – rabbits. Birds – ducks. Orphans.

Bill's belly button ill. by author. Little, 1991. ISBN 0-316-46114-8 Subj: Anatomy – navels. Animals – elephants. Behavior – lost & found possessions. Zoos.

Birthday happy, Contrary Mary ill. by author. Candlewick, 1998. ISBN 0-7636-0448-8 Subj: Animals – mice. Behavior. Birthdays. Parties.

Bunny, my Honey ill. by author. Candlewick, 1999. ISBN 0-7636-0710-X Subj: Animals – mice. Animals – rabbits. Behavior – lost. Birds – ducks. Family life – mothers.

Contrary Mary ill. by author. Candlewick, 1995. ISBN 1-56402-644-2 Subj: Animals – mice. Behavior. Character traits – individuality.

Daisy Dare ill. by author. Candlewick, 1995. ISBN 1-56402-645-0 Subj: Animals – mice. Character traits – being different. Character traits – bravery.

I love my little storybook ill. by author. Candlewick, 2002. ISBN 0-7636-1698-2 Subj: Animals – rabbits. Books, reading. Imagination.

It was Jake ill. by author. Little, 1991. ISBN 0-316-46120-2 Subj: Animals – dogs. Behavior – lying. Behavior – misbehavior. Pets.

Jerome, Judson. *I never saw . . .* ill. by Helga Aichinger. A. Whitman, 1974. ISBN 0-8075-3514-1 Subj: Poetry.

Jeschke, Susan. *Angela and Bear* ill. by author. Holt, 1979. ISBN 0-03-044511-6 Subj: Animals – bears. Imagination – imaginary friends. Magic.

The devil did it ill. by author. Holt, 1979. ISBN 0-03-014506-6 Subj: Animals – bears. Imagination – imaginary friends.

Firerose ill. by author. Holt, 1974. ISBN 0-03-011991-X Subj: Careers – fortune tellers. Dragons. Humorous stories. Magic.

Lucky's choice ill. by author. Scholastic, 1987. ISBN 0-590-40520-9 Subj: Animals – cats. Behavior – needing someone. Behavior – running away. Friendship.

Mia, Grandma and the genie ill. by author. Holt, 1978. ISBN 0-03-028586-0 Subj: Fairies. Family life – grandmothers. Magic. Mythical creatures – genies.

Perfect the pig ill. by author. Holt, 1981. ISBN 0-03-058622-4 Subj: Activities – flying. Animals – pigs.

Rima and Zeppo ill. by author. Dutton, 1976. ISBN 0-525-61524-3 Subj: Magic. Witches.

Tamar and the tiger ill. by author. Holt, 1980. ISBN 0-03-052176-9 Subj: Imagination.

Jessell, Camilla. *The kitten book* ill. by author. Candlewick, 1992. ISBN 1-56402-020-7 Subj: Animals – cats. Birth.

The puppy book ill. by author. Candlewick, 1992. ISBN 1-56402-021-5 Subj: Animals – dogs. Birth.

Jessell, Tim. *Amorak* ill. by author. Creative Ed., 1994. ISBN 0-88682-662-4 Subj: Animals – reindeer. Animals – wolves. Eskimos. Family life – grandfathers. Folk & fairy tales. Foreign lands – Canada.

Jessup, Harley. *Grandma summer* ill. by author. Viking, 1999. ISBN 0-670-88260-7 Subj: Family life – grandmothers. Sea & seashore. Seasons – summer.

Jewell, Nancy. *ABC cat* ill. by Ann Schweninger. HarperCollins, 1983. ISBN 0-06-022848-2 Subj: ABC books. Animals – cats. Rhyming text.

Bus ride ill. by Ronald Himler. HarperCollins, 1978. ISBN 0-06-022842-3 Subj: Buses.

Christmas lullaby ill. by Stefano Vitale. Clarion, 1994. ISBN 0-395-66586-8 Subj: Animals. Religion – Nativity. Rhyming text.

Five little kittens ill. by Elizabeth Sayles. Clarion, 1999. ISBN 0-395-77517-5 Subj: Animals – cats. Rhyming text.

Sailor song ill. by Stefano Vitale. Clarion, 1999. ISBN 0-395-82511-3 Subj: Activities – singing. Careers – military. Sailors.

The snuggle bunny ill. by Mary Chalmers. HarperCollins, 1972. ISBN 0-06-022834-2 Subj: Animals – rabbits. Emotions – love.

Time for Uncle Joe ill. by Joan Sandin. HarperCollins, 1981. ISBN 0-06-022844-X Subj: Death. Emotions – grief. Family life – aunts, uncles.

Try and catch me ill. by Leonard Weisgard. HarperCollins, 1972. ISBN 0-06-022832-6 Subj: Activities – playing. Ecology. Friendship. Imagination.

Jeyaveeran, Ruth. *The road to Mumbai* ill. by author. Houghton, 2004. ISBN 0-618-43419-4 Subj: Animals – monkeys. Foreign lands – India. Imagination.

Jiang, Ji-li. *The magical Monkey King, mischief in heaven* ill. by Hui Hui Su-Kennedy. HarperCollins, 2002. ISBN 0-06-029544-9 Subj: Animals – monkeys. Folk & fairy tales. Foreign lands – China.

Jijii, Hanasaka. *The old man who made the trees bloom* (Shibano, Tamizo)

Jiménez, Francisco. *The Christmas gift = El regalo de Navidad* ill. by Claire B. Cotts. Houghton, 2000. ISBN 0-395-92869-9 Subj: Character traits – kindness. Ethnic groups in the U.S. – Mexican Americans. Foreign languages. Holidays – Christmas. Immigrants.

Jitodai, Hitomi. *I wish I had a big, big tree* (Sato, Satoru)

Jobling, Curtis. *Frankenstein's cat* ill. by author. S&S, 2001. ISBN 0-689-84695-9 Subj: Animals – cats. Animals – dogs. Humorous stories.

Jocelyn, Marthe. *A day with Nellie* ill. by author. Tundra, 2002. ISBN 0-88776-600-5 Subj: Activities – playing. Toys.

Hannah and the seven dresses ill. by author. Dutton, 1999. ISBN 0-525-46113-2 Subj: Birthdays. Clothing – dresses.

Hannah's Collections ill. by author. Dutton, 2000. ISBN 0-525-46442-5 Subj: Behavior – collecting things. School.

Mayfly ill. by author. Tundra, 2004. ISBN 0-88776-676-5 Subj: Activities – vacationing. Cities, towns. Country. Homes, houses.

Joerns, Consuelo. *The foggy rescue* ill. by author. Four Winds, 1980. ISBN 0-590-07744-9 Subj: Animals – mice. Behavior – lost. Boats, ships.

The forgotten bear ill. by author. Four Winds, 1978. ISBN 0-590-07560-8 Subj: Behavior – lost. Toys – bears.

The lost and found house ill. by author. Four Winds, 1979. ISBN 0-590-07627-2 Subj: Animals – mice. Homes, houses.

Oliver's escape ill. by author. Four Winds, 1981. ISBN 0-590-07817-8 Subj: Animals. Animals – dogs. Behavior – running away. Friendship.

Johanasen, Heather. *About the rain forest* by Heather Johanasen & Sindy McKay; ill. with photos. Treasure Bay, 2000. ISBN 1-891327-23-2 Subj: Ecology. Forest, woods. Weather – rain.

Johansen, K. V. (Krista V.). *Pippin and Pudding* ill. by Bernice Lum. Kids Can, 2001. ISBN 1-55074-631-6 Subj: Animals – cats. Animals – dogs. Friendship.

Pippin and the bones ill. by Bernice Lum. Kids Can, 2000. ISBN 1-55074-629-4 Subj: Anatomy – skeletons. Fossils. Museums.

Pippin takes a bath ill. by Bernice Lum. Kids Can, 1999. ISBN 1-55074-627-8 Subj: Activities – bathing. Animals – dogs.

John, Naomi. *Roadrunner* ill. by Peter & Virginia Parnall. Dutton, 1980. ISBN 0-525-38485-5 Subj: Birds. Desert.

Johns, Linda. *Sarah's secret plan* ill. by Denise Brunkus. Troll, 1995. ISBN 0-816-73693-6 Subj: Behavior – promptness, tardiness. Clocks, watches. Family life.

Johnson, Amy Crane. *Cinnamon and the April shower = Canela y el aguacero de abril* ill. by Robb Mommaerts. Raven Tree, 2003. ISBN 0-9720192-2-7 Subj: Animals. Birds – ravens. Foreign languages. Forest, woods. Seasons. Weather – storms.

Mason moves away = Mason se muda ill. by Robb Mommaerts. Raven Tree, 2004. ISBN 0-9720192-3-5 Subj: Animals – beavers. Birds – ravens. Ecology. Foreign languages. Moving.

Johnson, Angela. *The aunt in our house* ill. by David Soman. Orchard, 1996. ISBN 0-531-08852-9 Subj: Emotions – sadness. Ethnic groups in the U.S. Family life – aunts, uncles.

Casey Jones ill. by Loren Long. S&S, 2000. ISBN 0-689-82609-5 Subj: Careers – farmers. Ethnic groups in the U.S. – African Americans. Family life – fathers. Farms. Trains.

Daddy calls me man ill. by Rhonda Mitchell. Orchard, 1997. ISBN 0-531-33042-7 Subj: Careers – artists. Ethnic groups in the U.S. – African Americans. Family life. Poetry.

Do like Kyla ill. by James E. Ransome. Watts, 1990. ISBN 0-531-08452-3 Subj: Ethnic groups in the U.S. – African Americans. Family life – brothers & sisters.

Down the winding road ill. by Shane Evans. DK, 2000. ISBN 0-7894-2596-3 Subj: Country. Ethnic groups in the U.S. – African Americans. Family life. Friendship.

The girl who wore snakes ill. by James E. Ransome. Orchard, 1993. ISBN 0-531-08641-0 Subj: Animals. Ethnic groups in the U.S. – African Americans. Family life – aunts, uncles. Pets. Reptiles – snakes.

I dream of trains ill. by Loren Long. S&S, 2003. ISBN 0-689-82609-5 Subj: Activities – working. Dreams. Family life – fathers. Trains.

Joshua by the sea ill. by Rhonda Mitchell. Orchard, 1994. ISBN 0-531-06846-3 Subj: Ethnic groups in the U.S. – African Americans. Format, unusual – board books. Sea & seashore.

Joshua's night whispers ill. by Rhonda Mitchell. Orchard, 1994. ISBN 0-531-06847-1 Subj: Ethnic groups in the U.S. – African Americans. Family life – fathers. Format, unusual – board books. Night. Noise, sounds.

Julius ill. by Dav Pilkey. Orchard, 1993. ISBN 0-531-08615-1 Subj: Animals – pigs. Ethnic groups in the U.S. – African Americans. Family life – grandfathers. Pets.

The leaving morning ill. by David Soman. Orchard, 1992. ISBN 0-531-08592-9 Subj: Emotions. Ethnic groups in the U.S. – African Americans. Family life. Moving.

Mama bird, baby birds ill. by Rhonda Mitchell. Orchard, 1994. ISBN 0-531-06848-X Subj: Birds. Ethnic groups in the U.S. – African Americans. Format, unusual – board books. Rhyming text.

One of three ill. by David Soman. Watts, 1991. ISBN 0-531-08555-4 Subj: Ethnic groups in the U.S. – African Americans. Family life – sisters.

Rain feet ill. by Rhonda Mitchell. Orchard, 1994. ISBN 0-531-06849-8 Subj: Ethnic groups in the U.S. – African Americans. Format, unusual – board books. Weather – rain.

The Rolling Store ill. by Peter Catalanotto. Orchard, 1997. ISBN 0-531-33015-X Subj: Careers – peddlers. Ethnic groups in the U.S. – African Americans. Family life – grandfathers. Memories, memory. Stores.

Shoes like Miss Alice's ill. by Ken Page. Orchard, 1995. ISBN 0-531-08664-X Subj: Activities – babysitting. Clothing – shoes. Ethnic groups in the U.S. – African Americans.

A sweet smell of roses ill. by Eric Velasquez. S&S, 2005. ISBN 0-689-83252-4 Subj: Ethnic groups in the U.S. – African Americans. Family life – sisters. U.S. history.

Tell me a story, mama ill. by David Soman. Watts, 1989. ISBN 0-531-08394-2 Subj: Family life – mothers.

Those building men ill. by Mike Benny. Blue Sky, 1999. ISBN 0-590-66521-9 Subj: Activities – making things. Careers – construction workers.

Violet's music ill. by Laura Huliska-Beith. Dial, 2004. ISBN 0-8037-2740-2 Subj: Careers – musicians. Music. Musical instruments – bands.

The wedding ill. by David Soman. Orchard, 1999. ISBN 0-531-33139-3 Subj: Ethnic groups in the U.S. – African Americans. Family life – sisters. Weddings.

When I am old with you ill. by David Soman. Watts, 1990. ISBN 0-531-08484-1 Subj: Ethnic groups in the U.S. – African Americans. Family life – grandfathers. Old age.

When mules flew on Magnolia Street ill. by John Ward. Knopf, 2000. ISBN 0-679-99077-1 Subj: Ethnic groups in the U.S. – African Americans. Family life – brothers & sisters. Friendship.

Johnson, Arden. *The Lost Tooth Club* ill. by author. Tricycle, 1998. ISBN 1-883672-55-4 Subj: Clubs, gangs. Teeth.

Johnson, B. J. *A hat like that* by B. J. Johnson & Susan Aiello; ill. by authors. St. Martin's, 1986. ISBN 0-312-36416-4 Subj: Clothing – hats. Format, unusual – toy & movable books. Imagination. Rhyming text.

My blanket Burt by B. J. Johnson & Susan Aiello; ill. by authors. St. Martin's, 1986. ISBN 0-312-55600-4 Subj: Behavior – lost & found possessions. Format, unusual – toy & movable books. Rhyming text.

Johnson, Bruce H. *Apples, alligators, and also alphabets* (Johnson, Odette)

One prickly porcupine (Johnson, Odette)

Johnson, Crockett. *The blue ribbon puppies* ill. by author. HarperCollins, 1958. ISBN 0-590-40626-4 Subj: Animals – dogs. Imagination. Toys.

Ellen's lion ill. by author. HarperCollins, 1959. Subj: Imagination. Toys.

The emperor's gifts ill. by author. Holt, 1965. Subj: Character traits. Character traits – generosity. Gifts. Royalty – emperors.

The frowning prince ill. by author. Harper, 1959. ISBN 0-912846-09-7 Subj: Royalty – princes.

Harold and the purple crayon ill. by author. HarperCollins, 1955. ISBN 0-06-022936-5 Subj: Art. Humorous stories. Imagination.

Harold at the North Pole: a Christmas journey with the purple crayon ill. by author. HarperCollins, 1958. ISBN 0-06-028074-3 Subj: Holidays – Christmas. Humorous stories. Imagination. Santa Claus.

Harold's ABC: another purple crayon adventure ill. by author. HarperCollins, 1963. ISBN 0-606-02127-2 Subj: ABC books. Humorous stories. Imagination.

Harold's circus ill. by author. HarperCollins, 1959. ISBN 0-06-022966-7 Subj: Circus. Humorous stories. Imagination.

Harold's fairy tale: further adventures with the purple crayon ill. by author. HarperCollins, 1956. ISBN 0-06-022976-4 Subj: Folk & fairy tales. Humorous stories. Imagination.

Harold's trip to the sky ill. by author. HarperCollins, 1957. ISBN 0-06-022986-1 Subj: Humorous stories. Imagination. Space & space ships.

A picture for Harold's room ill. by author. HarperCollins, 1960. ISBN 0-06-023006-1 Subj: Art. Humorous stories. Imagination.

Terrible terrifying Toby ill. by author. HarperCollins, 1957. Subj: Animals – dogs.

Time for spring ill. by author. HarperCollins, 1957. Subj: Seasons – spring. Snowmen.

Upside down ill. by author. A. Whitman, 1969. ISBN 0-8075-8345-6 Subj: Animals – kangaroos. Concepts – up & down. World.

We wonder what will Walter be? When he grows up ill. by author. Holt, 1964. Subj: Animals. Behavior – growing up.

Will spring be early or will spring be late? ill. by author. Crowell, 1959. ISBN 0-690-89423-6 Subj: Animals – groundhogs. Holidays – Groundhog Day. Seasons – spring.

Johnson, D. B. (Donald B.). *Henry builds a cabin* ill. by author. Houghton, 2002. ISBN 0-618-13201-5 Subj: Animals – bears. Homes, houses. U.S. history.

Henry climbs a mountain ill. by author. Houghton, 2003. ISBN 0-618-26902-9 Subj: Animals – bears. Character traits – being different. Imagination. Mountains. Slavery.

Henry hikes to Fitchburg ill. by author. Houghton Mifflin, 2000. ISBN 0-395-96867-4 Subj: Activities – walking. Sports – hiking. U.S. history.

Henry works ill. by author. Houghton, 2004. ISBN 0-618-42003-7 Subj: Activities – walking. Activities – working. Activities – writing. Animals – bears. Nature. Weather – rain.

Johnson, David. *The Bremen town musicians* (Grimm, Jacob)

Oh, that Nuzzle! ill. by Tom Brannon. Grosset, 1997. ISBN 0-448-41299-3 Subj: Animals – dogs. Food.

Johnson, Diana F. *Princesa and Friskie* ill. by Ernesto López. Interkids, 1997. Based on Princesa's true story as told by Ricardo Allende. ISBN 0-9657928-0-3 Subj: Animals – cats. Animals – dogs. Foreign languages. Friendship.

Johnson, Dinah. *All around town* photos by Richard Samuel Roberts. Holt, 1998. ISBN 0-8050-5456-1 Subj: Activities – photographing. Careers – photographers. Ethnic groups in the U.S. – African Americans. U.S. history.

Quinnie Blue ill. by James Ransome. Holt, 2000. ISBN 0-8050-4378-0 Subj: Ethnic groups in the U.S. – African Americans. Family life – grandmothers.

Sunday week ill. by Tyrone Geter. Holt, 1999. ISBN 0-8050-4911-8 Subj: Cities, towns. Days of the week, months of the year. Ethnic groups in the U.S. – African Americans. Poetry. Religion.

Johnson, Dolores. *The best bug to be* ill. by author. Macmillan, 1992. ISBN 0-02-747842-4 Subj: Ethnic groups in the U.S. – African Americans. School. Theater.

Grandma's hands ill. by author. Cavendish, 1998. ISBN 0-7614-5025-4 Subj: Emotions – love. Ethnic groups in the U.S. – African Americans. Family life – grandmothers. Farms.

My mom is my show-and-tell ill. by author. Cavendish, 1999. ISBN 0-7614-5041-6 Subj: Ethnic groups in the U.S. – African Americans. Family life – mothers. School.

Now let me fly: the story of a slave family ill. by author. Macmillan, 1993. ISBN 0-02-747699-5 Subj: Ethnic groups in the U.S. – African Americans. Slavery. U.S. history.

Papa's stories ill. by author. Macmillan, 1994. ISBN 0-02-747847-5 Subj: Books, reading. Ethnic groups in the U.S. – African Americans. Family life – fathers.

Seminole diary: remembrances of a slave ill. by author. Macmillan, 1994. ISBN 0-02-747848-3 Subj: Behavior – running away. Ethnic groups in the U.S. – African Americans. Indians of North America – Seminole. Slavery. U.S. history.

What kind of baby-sitter is this? ill. by author. Macmillan, 1991. ISBN 0-02-747846-7 Subj: Activities – babysitting. Ethnic groups in the U.S. – African Americans.

What will mommy do when I'm at school? ill. by author. Macmillan, 1990. ISBN 0-02-747845-9 Subj: Ethnic groups in the U.S. – African Americans. Family life – mothers.

Your dad was just like you ill. by author. Macmillan, 1993. ISBN 0-02-747838-6 Subj: Ethnic groups in the U.S. – African Americans. Family life – fathers. Family life – grandfathers.

Johnson, Donna Kay. *Brighteyes* ill. by author. Holt, 1978. ISBN 0-03-044651-1 Subj: Animals – raccoons. Handicaps – blindness. Senses – sight.

Johnson, Doug. *Never babysit the hippopotamuses!* ill. by Abby Carter. Holt, 1993. ISBN 0-8050-1873-5 Subj: Activities – babysitting. Animals – hippopotamuses.

Substitute teacher plans ill. by Tammy Smith. Holt, 2002. ISBN 0-8050-6520-2 Subj: Activities. Careers – teachers. Humorous stories. School.

Johnson, Elizabeth. *All in free but Janey* ill. by Trina Schart Hyman. Little, 1968. Subj: Games. Imagination.

Johnson, Evelyne. *The cow in the kitchen: a folk tale* ill. by Anthony Rao. S&S, 1983. ISBN 0-671-46004-8 Subj: Behavior – dissatisfaction. Character traits – foolishness.

Johnson, G. Francis. *Has anybody lost a glove?* ill. by Dimitrea Tokunbo. Boyds Mills, 2004. ISBN 1-59078-041-8 Subj: Behavior – lost & found possessions. Clothing – gloves, mittens. Communities, neighborhoods.

Johnson, Gillian. *My sister Gracie* ill. by author. Tundra, 2000. ISBN 0-88776-514-9 Subj: Animals – dogs. Family life – brothers & sisters. Rhyming text.

Johnson, Grace. *The candle in the window* ill. by Mark Elliott. Fleming H. Revell, 2003. ISBN 0-8007-1815-1 Subj: Careers – shoemakers. Character traits – kindness. Foreign lands – Germany. Holidays – Christmas. Religion.

Johnson, James Weldon. *The Creation* ill. by James Ransome. Holiday, 1994. ISBN 0-8234-1069-2 Subj: Creation. Ethnic groups in the U.S. – African Americans. Poetry. Religion.

Lift ev'ry voice and sing ill. by Jan Spivey Gilchrist. Scholastic, 1995. ISBN 0-590-46982-7 Subj: Ethnic groups in the U.S. – African Americans. Slavery. Songs.

Johnson, Jane. *Bertie on the beach* ill. by author. Four Winds, 1981. ISBN 0-590-07822-4 Subj: Circus. Dreams. Sea & seashore – beaches.

My dear Noel: the story of a letter from Beatrix Potter ill. by author. Dial, 1999. ISBN 0-8037-2051-3 Subj: Animals – rabbits. Careers – writers. Letters, cards.

Sybil and the blue rabbit ill. by author. Doubleday, 1980. ISBN 0-385-15758-4 Subj: Imagination. Toys.

Today I thought I'd run away ill. by author. Dutton, 1986. ISBN 0-525-44193-X Subj: Bedtime. Behavior – running away. Monsters.

Johnson, Janet P. *How Mr. Dog got tame: an African-American legend* ill. by Charles Reasoner. Troll, 1998. ISBN 0-8167-4350-9 Subj: Animals – dogs. Animals – wolves. Ethnic groups in the U.S. – African Americans. Folk & fairy tales.

Keelboat Annie: an African-American legend ill. by Charles Reasoner. Troll, 1998. ISBN 0-8167-4347-9 Subj: Ethnic groups in the U.S. – African Americans. Folk & fairy tales.

Johnson, Janice (Janice Kay). *Rosamund* ill. by Deborah Haeffele. S&S, 1994. ISBN 0-671-79329-2 Subj: Names. Plants.

Johnson, Jean. *Teachers A to Z* photos by author. Walker, 1987. ISBN 0-8027-6677-3 Subj: ABC books. Careers – teachers. School.

Johnson, John Emil. *My first book of things* ill. by author. Random House, 1979. ISBN 0-394-84128-X Subj: Format, unusual – board books.

Johnson, Julie. *How do I feel about my stepfamily* ill. by Christopher O'Neill. Copper Beech, 1998. ISBN 0-7613-0868-7 Subj: Emotions. Family life – stepfamilies.

Johnson, Lindsay Lee. *Hurricane Henrietta* ill. by Wally Neibart. Dial, 1998. ISBN 0-8037-1977-9 Subj: Hair. Humorous stories.

Johnson, Louise. *Malunda* ill. by Edward Durose. Carolrhoda, 1982. ISBN 0-87614-177-7 Subj: Animals – rhinoceros. Illness. Zoos.

Johnson, Marion. *Caillou, new shoes* adapt. from the animated series by Marion Johnson; ill., CINAR Animation, adapt. by Éric Sévigny. Chouette, 2002. ISBN 2-89450-327-X Subj: Behavior – growing up. Clothing – shoes. Family life – mothers. Shopping.

Johnson, Mildred D. *Wait, skates!* ill. by Tom Dunnington. Childrens Pr., 1983. ISBN 0-516-02039-0 Subj: Activities – playing. Sports – roller skating.

Johnson, Neil. *Big-top circus* ill. by author. Dial, 1995. ISBN 0-8037-1603-6 Subj: Circus.

Fire and silk: flying in a hot air balloon photos by author. Little, 1991. ISBN 0-316-46959-9 Subj: Activities – ballooning. Activities – flying.

Jack Creek cowboy ill. by author. Dial, 1993. ISBN 0-8037-1229-4 Subj: Cowboys, cowgirls. Friendship. Seasons – summer.

Johnson, Odette. *Apples, alligators, and also alphabets* by Odette & Bruce H. Johnson; ill. by authors. Oxford Univ. Pr., 1991. ISBN 0-19-540757-1 Subj: ABC books.

One prickly porcupine by Odette & Bruce H. Johnson; ill. by authors. Oxford Univ. Pr., 1992. ISBN 0-19-540834-9 Subj: Birthdays. Counting, numbers. Giants. Tongue twisters.

Johnson, Pamela. *A mouse's tale* ill. by author. Harcourt, 1991. ISBN 0-15-256032-7 Subj: Animals – mice. Behavior – collecting things. Boats, ships. Sea & seashore.

Johnson, Paul Brett. *Bearhide and crow* ill. by author. Holiday, 2000. ISBN 0-8234-1470-1 Subj: Activities – trading. Behavior – greed. Birds – crows. Humorous stories.

The cow who wouldn't come down ill. by author. Orchard, 1993. ISBN 0-531-08631-3 Subj: Activities – flying. Animals – bulls, cows. Farms.

Farmers' market ill. by author. Orchard, 1997. ISBN 0-531-33014-1 Subj: Careers – farmers. Farms. Stores.

Frank Fister's hidden talent ill. by author. Orchard, 1994. ISBN 0-531-08663-1 Subj: Crime. Magic.

The goose who went off in a huff ill. by author. Orchard, 2001. Subj: Animals – babies. Animals – elephants. Birds – geese. Family life – mothers. Humorous stories.

Jack outwits the giants ill. by author. McElderry, 2002. ISBN 0-689-83902-2 Subj: Behavior – trickery. Folk & fairy tales. Giants.

Little Bunny Foo Foo: told and sung by the Good Fairy ill. by author. Scholastic, 2004. ISBN 0-439-37301-8 Subj: Animals – rabbits. Behavior – misbehavior. Fairies. Humorous stories. Music. Songs.

Lost ill. by Celeste Lewis. Orchard, 1996. ISBN 0-531-08851-0 Subj: Animals – dogs. Behavior – lost. Camps, camping. Desert. Pets.

Mr. Persnickety and Cat Lady ill. by author. Orchard, 2000. ISBN 0-531-33283-7 Subj: Animals – cats. Animals – mice. Communities, neighborhoods. Problem solving.

Old Dry Fry ill. by author. Scholastic, 1999. ISBN 0-590-37658-6 Subj: Careers – clergy. Folk & fairy tales.

A perfect pork stew ill. by author. Orchard, 1998. ISBN 0-531-33070-2 Subj: Animals – pigs. Behavior – trickery. Witches.

The pig who ran a red light ill. by author. Orchard, 1999. ISBN 0-531-33136-9 Subj: Activities. Animals – pigs. Behavior.

Johnson, Russell. *Trouble at Christmas* ill. by Bernadette Watts. North-South, 1991. ISBN 1-55858-116-2 Subj: Animals. Holidays – Christmas. Santa Claus.

Johnson, Ryerson. *Kenji and the magic geese* ill. by Jean & Mou-Sien Tseng. S&S, 1992. ISBN 0-671-75974-4 Subj: Art. Birds – geese. Foreign lands – Japan.

Let's walk up the wall ill. by Eva Cellini. Holiday, 1967. Subj: Participation.

Upstairs and downstairs ill. by Lisl Weil. Crowell, 1962. Subj: Concepts.

Johnson, Stephen T. *Alphabet city* ill. by author. Viking, 1995. ISBN 0-670-85631-2 Subj: ABC books. Caldecott award honor books. Cities, towns. Concepts.

City by numbers ill. by author. Viking, 1998. ISBN 0-670-87251-2 Subj: Counting, numbers.

My little blue robot ill. by autor. Harcourt, 2002. ISBN 0-15-216524-X Subj: Activities – making things. Format, unusual – toy & movable books. Robots.

Johnson, Suzanne C. *Fribbity ribbit* ill. by Debbie Tilley. Knopf, 2001. ISBN 0-375-91199-5 Subj: Family life. Frogs & toads. Humorous stories.

Johnson, Walter Ryerson. *see* Johnson, Ryerson

Johnston, Deborah. *Mathew Michael's beastly day* ill. by Seymour Chwast. Harcourt, 1992. ISBN 0-15-200521-8 Subj: Animals. Behavior – bad day. Family life. Imagination. Morning. School. Self-concept.

Johnston, Johanna. *Penguin's way* ill. by Leonard Weisgard. Doubleday, 1962. Subj: Birds – penguins. Science.

Sugarplum ill. by Marvin Bileck. Knopf, 1955. Subj: Character traits – smallness. Toys – dolls.

Whale's way ill. by Leonard Weisgard. Doubleday, 1965. Subj: Animals – whales. Science.

Johnston, Marianne. *Dealing with anger* ill. by author. PowerKids, 1996. ISBN 0-8239-2325-8 Subj: Behavior. Emotions – anger.

Dealing with bullying ill. by author. PowerKids, 1996. ISBN 0-8239-2374-6 Subj: Behavior – bullying. Emotions.

Johnston, Mary Anne. *Sing me a song* ill. by John Magine. Childrens Pr., 1977. ISBN 0-913778-81-8 Subj: Animals – rabbits. Songs.

Johnston, Tony. *Alice Nizzy Nazzy, the Witch of Santa Fe* ill. by Tomie de Paola. Putnam, 1995. ISBN 0-399-22788-1 Subj: Behavior – trickery. Folk & fairy tales. Foreign lands – Russia. Witches.

Amber on the mountain ill. by Robert Duncan. Dial, 1994. ISBN 0-8037-1219-7 Subj: Books, reading. Family life. Friendship. Roads.

The badger and the magic fan ill. by Tomie de Paola. Putnam, 1990. ISBN 0-399-21945-5 Subj: Anatomy – noses. Animals – badgers. Behavior – trickery. Folk & fairy tales. Foreign lands – Japan. Magic.

The barn owls ill. by Deborah Kogan Ray. Charlesbridge, 2000. ISBN 0-88106-981-7 Subj: Barns. Birds – owls. Poetry.

Big red apple ill. by Judith Hoffman Corwin. Scholastic, 1999. ISBN 0-439-09860-2 Subj: Circular tales. Plants. Trees.

Bigfoot Cinderrrrella ill. by James Warhola. Putnam, 1998. ISBN 0-399-23021-1 Subj: Folk & fairy tales. Forest, woods. Mythical creatures.

The bull and the fire truck ill. by R. W. Alley. Scholastic, 1996. ISBN 0-590-47597-5 Subj: Animals – bulls, cows. Concepts – color. Trucks.

The Chizzywink and the Alamagoozlum ill. by Robert Bender. Holiday, 1998. ISBN 0-8234-1359-4 Subj: Insects – mosquitoes. Night. Sleep.

The cowboy and the black-eyed pea ill. by Ludwig Warren. Putnam, 1992. ISBN 0-399-22330-4 Subj: Cowboys, cowgirls. Folk & fairy tales. U.S. history – frontier & pioneer life. Weddings.

Day of the Dead ill. by Jeanette Winter. Harcourt, 1997. ISBN 0-15-222863-2 Subj: Foreign lands – Mexico. Holidays – Day of the Dead.

Desert dog ill. by Robert Weatherford. Sierra Club, 2001. ISBN 0-87156-979-5 Subj: Animals – dogs. Animals – goats. Desert. Rhyming text.

Desert song ill. by Ed Young. Sierra Club, 2000. ISBN 0-8715-6491-2 Subj: Animals. Desert. Night.

Farmer Mack measures his pig ill. by Megan Lloyd. HarperCollins, 1986. ISBN 0-06-023018-5 Subj: Animals – pigs. Behavior – boasting. Farms.

Fishing Sunday ill. by Barry Root. Tambourine, 1996. ISBN 0-688-13538-2 Subj: Ethnic groups in the U.S. – Japanese Americans. Family life – grandfathers. Sports – fishing.

Four scary stories ill. by Tomie de Paola. Putnam, 1978. ISBN 0-399-20614-0 Subj: Ghosts. Monsters. Mythical creatures – goblins.

The ghost of Nicholas Greebe ill. by S. D. Schindler. Dial, 1996. ISBN 0-8037-1649-4 Subj: Anatomy – skeletons. Animals – dogs. Ghosts.

Go track a yak ill. by Tim Raglin. S&S, 2003. ISBN 0-689-83789-5 Subj: Animals – yaks. Family life – parents. Folk & fairy tales. Humorous stories. Witches.

Goblin walk by Tony Johnston & Bruce Degen; ill. by Bruce Degen. Putnam, 1991. ISBN 0-399-22238-3 Subj: Animals. Emotions – fear. Family life – grandmothers. Humorous stories. Mythical creatures – goblins.

Grandpa's song ill. by Brad Sneed. Dial, 1991. ISBN 0-8037-0802-5 Subj: Family life – grandfathers. Old age. Songs.

How many miles to Jacksonville? ill. by Bart Forbes. Putnam, 1995. ISBN 0-399-22615-X Subj: Cities, towns. Trains.

The iguana brothers, a perfect day ill. by Mark Teague. Blue Sky, 1995. ISBN 0-590-47468-5 Subj: Family life – brothers. Foreign lands – Mexico. Reptiles – iguanas.

I'm gonna tell mama I want an iguana ill. by Lillian Hoban. Putnam, 1990. ISBN 0-399-21931-X Subj: Family life. Poetry. Sibling rivalry.

Isabel's house of butterflies ill. by Susan Guevara. Sierra Club, 1997. ISBN 0-8715-6409-2 Subj: Foreign lands – Mexico. Insects – butterflies, caterpillars. Trees.

A Kenya Christmas ill. by Leonard Jenkins. Holiday, 2003. ISBN 0-8234-1623-2 Subj: Family life – aunts, uncles. Foreign lands – Kenya. Holidays – Christmas. Santa Claus.

The last snow of winter ill. by Friso Henstra. Tambourine, 1993. ISBN 0-688-10750-8 Subj: Art. Circular tales. Friendship. Seasons – winter. Weather – snow.

Little bear sleeping ill. by Lillian Hoban. Putnam, 1991. ISBN 0-399-22157-3 Subj: Animals – bears. Bedtime. Rhyming text.

Little Rabbit goes to sleep ill. by Harvey Stevenson. HarperCollins, 1994. ISBN 0-06-021241-1 Subj: Animals – rabbits. Bedtime. Emotions – fear. Family life – grandfathers. Night. Sleep.

Little wild parrot ill. by Ora Eitan. Tambourine, 1995. ISBN 0-688-13536-6 Subj: Birds – parakeets, parrots.

Lorenzo the naughty parrot ill. by Leo Politi. Harcourt, 1992. ISBN 0-15-249350-6 Subj: Behavior – misbehavior. Birds – parakeets, parrots. Foreign lands – Mexico. Holidays – Christmas. Parties.

Mole and Troll trim the tree ill. by Wallace Tripp. Putnam, 1974. ISBN 0-399-60909-1 Subj: Animals – moles. Behavior – sharing. Holidays – Christmas. Mythical creatures – trolls. Seasons – winter. Trees.

My best friend Bear ill. by Joy Allen. Rising Moon, 2001. ISBN 0-87358-775-8 Subj: Activities – sewing. Family life – mothers. Toys – bears.

My Mexico = México mío ill. by F. John Sierra. Putnam, 1996. ISBN 0-399-22275-8 Subj: Foreign lands – Mexico. Foreign languages. Poetry.

The old lady and the birds ill. by Stephanie Garcia. Harcourt, 1994. ISBN 0-15-257769-6 Subj: Animals – cats. Birds. Foreign lands – Mexico. Foreign languages. Gardens, gardening.

Once in the country: poems of a farm ill. by Thomas B. Allen. Putnam, 1996. ISBN 0-399-22644-3 Subj: Farms. Nature. Poetry. Seasons.

Pages of music ill. by Tomie de Paola. Putnam, 1988. ISBN 0-399-21436-4 Subj: Activities – painting. Islands. Music.

The promise ill. by Pamela Keavney. Harper, 1992. ISBN 0-06-023020-7 Subj: Animals – bulls, cows. Farms.

The quilt story ill. by Tomie de Paola. Putnam, 1984. ISBN 0-399-21009-1 Subj: Family life. Moving. Quilts.

Slither McCreep and his brother, Joe ill. by Victoria Chess. Harcourt, 1992. ISBN 0-15-276100-4 Subj: Family life – brothers. Reptiles – snakes. Sibling rivalry.

Soup bone ill. by Margot Tomes. Harcourt, 1990. ISBN 0-15-277255-3 Subj: Anatomy – skeletons. Friendship. Holidays – Halloween.

Sparky and Eddie, the first day of school ill. by Susannah Ryan. Scholastic, 1997. ISBN 0-590-47978-4 Subj: Friendship. School – first day.

Sparky and Eddie, trouble with bugs ill. by Susannah Ryan. Scholastic, 1998. Subj: Friendship. Insects. School. Science.

Sparky and Eddie, trouble with rats ill. by Susannah Ryan. Scholastic, 1998. ISBN 0-590-47980-6 Subj: Animals – rats. Friendship. School. Science.

Sparky and Eddie, wild, wild rodeo! ill. by Susannah Ryan. Scholastic, 1998. ISBN 0-590-47984-9 Subj: Cowboys, cowgirls. Friendship. School. Sports.

Sunsets of the West ill. by Ted Lewin. Putnam, 2002. ISBN 0-399-22659-1 Subj: Family life. Moving. U.S. history – frontier & pioneer life.

The tale of Rabbit and Coyote ill. by Tomie de Paola. Putnam, 1994. ISBN 0-399-22258-8 Subj: Animals – coyotes. Animals – rabbits. Folk & fairy tales. Foreign lands – Mexico. Indians of North America – Zapotec.

That summer ill. by Barry Moser. Harcourt, 2002. ISBN 0-15-201585-X Subj: Death. Emotions – grief. Family life. Family life – brothers. Quilts.

Three little bikers ill. by G. Brian Karas. Knopf, 1994. ISBN 0-679-94701-9 Subj: Animals – sheep. Sports – bicycling.

Uncle rain cloud ill. by Fabricio Vandenbroeck. Charlesbridge, 2000. ISBN 0-88106-371-1 Subj: Ethnic groups in the U.S. – Mexican Americans. Family life – aunts, uncles. Language.

The vanishing pumpkin ill. by Tomie de Paola. Putnam, 1983. ISBN 0-3992-0991-3 Subj: Holidays – Halloween. Witches.

The wagon ill. by James E. Ransome. Tambourine, 1996. ISBN 0-688-13537-4 Subj: Ethnic groups in the U.S. – African Americans. Slavery. U.S. history.

We love the dirt ill. by Alexa Brandenberg. Scholastic, 1997. ISBN 0-590-92953-4 Subj: Earth. Farms.

Whale song ill. by Ed Young. Putnam, 1987. ISBN 0-399-21402-X Subj: Animals – whales. Counting, numbers.

The witch's hat ill. by Margot Tomes. Putnam, 1984. ISBN 0-399-21010-5 Subj: Clothing – hats. Magic. Witches.

Yonder ill. by Lloyd Bloom. Dial, 1988. ISBN 0-8037-0278-7 Subj: Cumulative tales. Seasons.

Jolin, Dominique. *It's not fair!* ill. by Dominique Jolin. Crossing Pr., 1996. ISBN 0-89594-780-3 Subj: Behavior – dissatisfaction. Family life – fathers.

Jolivet, Joëlle. *Zoo-ology* ill. by author. Roaring Brook, 2003. ISBN 0-7613-2780-0 Subj: Animals. Science.

Jolley, Mike. *Grunter, a pig with an attitude!* ill. by Deborah Allwright. Millbrook, 1999. ISBN 0-7613-1308-7 Subj: Animals – pigs. Behavior. Birthdays. Format, unusual – toy & movable books.

Jolliffe, Anne. *From pots to plastics* ill. by author. Hawthorn, 1965. Subj: Science.

Water, wind and wheels ill. by author. Hawthorn, 1965. Subj: Science. Water.

Joly, Fanny. *Mr. Fine, porcupine* ill. by Rémi Saillard. Chronicle, 1997. ISBN 0-8118-1842-X Subj: Animals – porcupines. Character traits – appearance. Hair. Self-concept.

Joly-Berbesson, Fanny. *Marceau Bonappetit* ill. by Agnès Mathieu. Carolrhoda, 1989. ISBN 0-87614-369-9 Subj: Animals – mice. Behavior – seeking better things. Food.

Jonas, Ann. *Aardvarks, disembark!* ill. by author. Greenwillow, 1990. ISBN 0-688-07207-0 Subj: ABC books. Animals. Animals – endangered animals. Boats, ships. Religion – Noah. Weather – floods. Weather – rain.

Bird talk ill. by author. Greenwillow, 1999. ISBN 0-688-14173-0 Subj: Birds. Noise, sounds. Songs.

Color dance ill. by author. Greenwillow, 1989. ISBN 0-688-05990-2 Subj: Activities – dancing. Concepts – color.

Holes and peeks ill. by author. Greenwillow, 1984. ISBN 0-688-02538-2 Subj: Caldecott award honor books. Emotions – fear. Problem solving.

Now we can go ill. by author. Greenwillow, 1986. ISBN 0-688-04803-X Subj: Toys.

The quilt ill. by author. Greenwillow, 1984. ISBN 0-688-03826-3 Subj: Bedtime. Dreams. Quilts.

Reflections ill. by author. Greenwillow, 1987. ISBN 0-688-06141-9 Subj: Concepts. Format, unusual.

Round trip ill. by author. Greenwillow, 1983. ISBN 0-688-01781-9 Subj: Activities – traveling. Cities, towns.

Splash! ill. by author. Greenwillow, 1995. ISBN 0-688-11052-5 Subj: Animals. Counting, numbers. Ethnic groups in the U.S. – African Americans. Fish.

The thirteenth clue ill. by author. Greenwillow, 1992. ISBN 0-688-09742-1 Subj: Birthdays. Format, unusual. Mystery stories. Parties.

The trek ill. by author. Greenwillow, 1985. ISBN 0-688-04799-8 Subj: Activities – walking. Animals. Games. Imagination.

Two bear cubs ill. by author. Greenwillow, 1982. ISBN 0-688-01408-9 Subj: Animals – bears. Behavior – lost. Family life – mothers.

Watch William walk ill. by author. Greenwillow, 1997. ISBN 0-688-14175-7 Subj: Activities – walking. Animals – dogs. Birds – ducks. Language.

When you were a baby ill. by author. Greenwillow, 1982. ISBN 0-688-00864-X Subj: Activities. Behavior – growing up.

Where can it be? ill. by author. Greenwillow, 1986. ISBN 0-688-05246-0 Subj: Behavior – lost & found possessions. Format, unusual – toy & movable books.

Jonasson, Dianne. *Tuan* (Boholm-Olsson, Eva)

Jonathan, Langley. *Missing* ill. by author. Cavendish, 2000. ISBN 0-7614-5078-5 Subj: Animals – cats. Behavior – lost.

Jonell, Lynne. *Bravemole* ill. by author. Putnam, 2002. ISBN 0-399-23962-6 Subj: Behavior – needing someone. Family life – mothers.

I need a snake ill. by Petra Mathers. Putnam, 1998. ISBN 0-399-23176-5 Subj: Family life – mothers. Pets. Reptiles – snakes.

It's my birthday, too! ill. by Petra Mathers. Putnam, 1999. ISBN 0-399-23323-7 Subj: Animals – dogs. Birthdays. Family life – brothers. Parties. Sibling rivalry.

Mom pie ill. by Petra Mathers. Putnam, 2001. ISBN 0-399-23422-5 Subj: Behavior – needing someone. Family life – mothers.

Mommy go away! ill. by Petra Mathers. Putnam, 1997. ISBN 0-399-23001-7 Subj: Activities – bathing. Concepts – size. Family life – mothers. Imagination.

When Mommy was mad ill. by Petra Mathers. Putnam, 2002. ISBN 0-399-23433-0 Subj: Animals – moles. Character traits – bravery. Dragons.

Jones, Bill T. *Dance* by Bill T. Jones & Susan Kuklin; photos by Susan Kuklin. Hyperion, 1998. ISBN 0-7868-2307-0 Subj: Activities – dancing. Rhyming text.

Jones, Brian. *Space: a three-dimensional journey* ill. by Richard Clifton-Day. Dial, 1991. ISBN 0-8037-0759-2 Subj: Astronomy. Science. Space & space ships.

Jones, Carol. *The hare and the tortoise* (Æsop)

The lion and the mouse (Æsop)

This old man ill. by author. Houghton Mifflin, 1990. ISBN 0-395-54699-0 Subj: Counting, numbers. Farms. Format, unusual. Music. Songs.

Town mouse, country mouse (Æsop)

What's the time, Mr. Wolf? ill. by author. Houghton Mifflin, 1999. ISBN 0-395-95800-8 Subj: Animals. Animals – wolves. Clocks, watches. Format, unusual – toy & movable books. Time.

Jones, Chuck. *William the backwards skunk* ill. by author. Crown, 1987. ISBN 0-517-56063-1 Subj: Animals – skunks. Behavior – imitation. Forest, woods.

Jones, Diana Wynne. *Yes, dear* ill. by Graham Philpot. Greenwillow, 1992. ISBN 0-688-11195-5 Subj: Behavior – unnoticed, unseen. Family life – grandmothers. Imagination. Magic.

Jones, Elizabeth. *Sunshine and Storm* ill. by James Coplestone. Ragged Bears, 2001. ISBN 1-929927-27-4 Subj: Animals – cats. Animals – dogs. Emotions – anger. Friendship. Weather – rain.

Jones, Harold. *Tales from Æsop* (Æsop)

There and back again ill. by author. Atheneum, 1977. ISBN 0-689-50095-5 Subj: Toys.

Jones, Hettie. *The trees stand shining: poetry of the North American Indians* ill. by Robert Andrew Parker. Dial, 1971. ISBN 0-8037-9084-8 Subj: Indians of North America. Poetry.

Jones, Jennifer Berry. *Heetunka's harvest: a tale of the Plains Indians* ill. by Shannon Keegan. Roberts Rinehart, 1994. ISBN 1-879373-17-3 Subj: Animals – mice. Folk & fairy tales. Indians of North America – Dakota (Sioux).

Who lives in the snow? ill. by Consie Powell. Roberts Rinehart, 1999. ISBN 1-57098-287-2 Subj: Animals. Seasons – winter.

Jones, Jessie Mae Orton. *A little child: the Christmas miracle told in Bible verses* ill. by Elizabeth Orton Jones. Viking, 1946. Subj: Holidays – Christmas. Religion.

Small rain: verses from the Bible ill. by Elizabeth Orton Jones. Viking, 1943. ISBN 0-670-05088-1 Subj: Caldecott award honor books. Poetry. Religion.

Jones, Joy. *Tambourine moon* ill. by Terry Widener. S&S, 1999. ISBN 0-689-80648-5 Subj: Ethnic groups in the U.S. – African Americans. Family life – grandfathers. Moon. Night.

Jones, Kathryn D. *Carnival* (Burden-Patmon, Denise)

Jones, Malcolm. *Jump! the adventures of Brer Rabbit* (Harris, Joel Chandler)

Jones, Maurice. *I'm going on a dragon hunt* ill. by Charlotte Firmin. Four Winds, 1987. ISBN 0-02-748000-3 Subj: Dragons. Sports – hunting.

Jones, Penelope. *I didn't want to be nice* ill. by Rosalie Orlando. Bradbury, 1977. ISBN 0-87888-111-5 Subj: Animals – squirrels. Birthdays. Parties.

I'm not moving! ill. by Amy Aitken. Bradbury, 1980. ISBN 0-87888-156-5 Subj: Family life. Moving.

Jones, Rebecca C. *The biggest (and best) flag that ever flew* ill. by Charles Geer. Cornell Maritime Pr., 1988. ISBN 0-317-67910-4 Subj: U.S. history. War.

The biggest, meanest, ugliest dog in the whole wide world ill. by Wendy Watson. Macmillan, 1982. ISBN 0-02-747800-9 Subj: Animals – dogs. Character traits – meanness. Friendship.

Down at the bottom of the deep dark sea ill. by Virginia Wright-Frierson. Bradbury, 1991. ISBN 0-02-747901-3 Subj: Emotions – fear. Sand. Sea & seashore.

Great Aunt Martha ill. by Shelley Jackson. Dutton, 1995. ISBN 0-525-45257-5 Subj: Family life – aunts, uncles. Old age.

Matthew and Tilly ill. by Beth Peck. Dutton, 1991. ISBN 0-525-44684-2 Subj: Cities, towns. Ethnic groups in the U.S. – African Americans. Friendship.

Jones, Ursula. *The witch's children* ill. by Russell Ayto. Holt, 2003. ISBN 0-8050-7205-5 Subj: Magic. Parks. Witches.

Jong, David Cornel De. *see* DeJong, David Cornel

Jonovitz, Marilyn. *Good morning, Little Fox* ill. by author. North-South, 2001. ISBN 0-7358-1441-4 Subj: Animals – foxes. Family life – fathers. Family life – sons. Food.

Maybe, my baby ill. by autor. North-South, 2003. ISBN 0-7358-1763-4 Subj: Animals – babies. Family life – parents. Sleep.

Three little kittens ill. by author. North-South, 2002. ISBN 0-7358-1643-3 Subj: Animals – cats. Behavior – lost & found possessions. Clothing – gloves, mittens. Nursery rhymes.

Joos, Françoise. *The golden snowflake* ill. by author. Little, 1991. ISBN 0-316-47328-6 Subj: Snowmen. Weather – snow.

Joosse, Barbara M. *Bad dog school* ill. by Jennifer Plecas. Clarion, 2004. ISBN 0-618-13331-3 Subj: Animals – dogs. Pets. School.

Better with two ill. by Catherine Stock. HarperCollins, 1988. ISBN 0-06-023077-0 Subj: Animals – dogs. Death. Pets.

Dinah's mad, bad wishes ill. by Emily Arnold McCully. HarperCollins, 1989. ISBN 0-06-023099-1 Subj: Emotions – anger. Family life – mothers.

Fourth of July ill. by Emily Arnold McCully. Knopf, 1985. ISBN 0-394-95195-6 Subj: Behavior – growing up. Holidays – Fourth of July. Parades.

Ghost wings ill. by Giselle Potter. Chronicle, 2001. ISBN 0-8118-2164-1 Subj: Death. Family life – grandmothers. Foreign lands – Mexico. Holidays – Day of the Dead. Insects – butterflies, caterpillars. Memories, memory.

A houseful of Christmas ill. by Betsy Lewin. Holt, 2001. ISBN 0-8050-6391-9 Subj: Family life. Family life – grandmothers. Holidays – Christmas. Sleep. Weather – blizzards.

I love you the purplest ill. by Mary Whyte. Chronicle, 1996. ISBN 0-8118-0718-5 Subj: Family life – brothers. Family life – mothers. Sibling rivalry. Sports – fishing.

Jam day ill. by Emily Arnold McCully. HarperCollins, 1987. ISBN 0-06-023097-5 Subj: Family life. Family life – grandparents.

Lewis and papa: adventure on the Santa Fe Trail ill. by Jon Van Zyle. Chronicle, 1998. ISBN 0-8118-1959-0 Subj: Activities – traveling. Family life – fathers. Family life – sons. U.S. history – frontier & pioneer life.

Mama, do you love me? ill. by Barbara Lavallee. Chronicle, 1991. ISBN 0-87701-759-X Subj: Emotions – love. Eskimos. Family life – mothers.

The morning chair ill. by Marcia Sewall. Clarion, 1995. ISBN 0-395-62337-5 Subj: Cities, towns. Ethnic groups in the U.S. – Dutch Americans. Furniture – chairs. Immigrants.

Nugget and Darling ill. by Sue Truesdell. Clarion, 1997. ISBN 0-395-64571-9 Subj: Animals – cats. Animals – dogs. Character traits – kindness to animals. Emotions – envy, jealousy.

Snow day! ill. by Jennifer Plecas. Clarion, 1995. ISBN 0-395-66588-4 Subj: Family life. Weather – snow.

Spiders in the fruit cellar ill. by Kay Chorao. Knopf, 1983. ISBN 0-394-95327-4 Subj: Emotions – fear. Spiders.

The thinking place ill. by Kay Chorao. Knopf, 1982. ISBN 0-394-94908-0 Subj: Behavior – misbehavior. Imagination – imaginary friends.

Jordan, Deloris. *Salt in his shoes* (Jordan, Roslyn M.)

Jordan, Helene J. (Helene Jamieson). *How a seed grows* ill. by Loretta Krupinski. Rev. ed. HarperCollins, 1992. ISBN 0-06-020185-1 Subj: Gardens, gardening. Nature. Science. Seeds.

Seeds of wind and water ill. by Nils Hogner. Crowell, 1962. Subj: Plants.

Jordan, Jennifer. *Albert goes to town* ill. by Shannon McNeill. Chronicle, 1997. ISBN 0-8118-0860-2 Subj: Automobiles. Imagination.

Jordan, June. *Kimako's story* ill. by Kay Burford. Houghton Mifflin, 1981. ISBN 0-395-31604-9 Subj: Animals – dogs. Cities, towns. Family life. Pets.

Jordan, Martin. *Amazon alphabet* by Martin & Tanis Jordan; ill. by Tanis Jordan. Kingfisher, 1996. ISBN 1-85697-666-1 Subj: ABC books. Animals. Foreign lands – South America. Jungle.

Jungle days, jungle nights by Martin & Tanis Jordan; ill. by Tanis Jordan. Kingfisher, 1993. ISBN 1-85697-885-0 Subj: Animals. Foreign lands – South America. Jungle.

Jordan, Roslyn M. *Salt in his shoes* by Deloris Jordan with Roslyn M. Jordan; ill. by Kadir A. Nelson. S&S, 2000. ISBN 0-689-83371-7 Subj: Careers. Concepts – size. Family life. Sports – basketball.

Jordan, Sandra. *Christmas tree farm* photos by author. Orchard, 1993. ISBN 0-531-08649-6 Subj: Ecology. Family life. Farms. Holidays – Christmas. Seasons. Trees.

Down on Casey's farm photos by author. Orchard, 1996. ISBN 0-531-08853-7 Subj: Animals. Farms. Imagination. Noise, sounds.

Frog hunt photos by author. Roaring Brook, 2002. ISBN 0-7613-2652-9 Subj: Animals. Frogs & toads. Lakes, ponds.

Jordan, Tanis. *Amazon alphabet* (Jordan, Martin)

Jungle days, jungle nights (Jordan, Martin)

Jorgensen, Gail. *Crocodile Beat* ill. by Patricia Mullins. Bradbury, 1989. ISBN 0-02-748010-0 Subj: Animals. Rhyming text.

Gotcha! ill. by Kerry Argent. Scholastic, 1997. ISBN 0-590-96208-6 Subj: Animals. Animals – bears. Birthdays. Insects – flies.

Jorgensen, Richard. *Reading with Dad* ill. by Warren Hanson. Waldman, 2000. ISBN 0-931674-41-7 Subj: Behavior – growing up. Books, reading. Family life – fathers. Rhyming text.

Joseph, Daniel M. *All dressed up and nowhere to go* by Daniel M. Joseph & Lydia J. Mendel; ill. by Normand Chartier. Houghton Mifflin, 1993. ISBN 0-395-60196-7 Subj: Clothing. Family life – grandparents. Holidays – Christmas.

Joseph, Lynn. *Coconut kind of day* ill. by Sandra Speidel. Lothrop, 1992. ISBN 0-688-09120-2 Subj: Foreign lands – Trinidad. Islands. Poetry.

Fly, Bessie, fly ill. by Yvonne Buchanan. S&S, 1998. ISBN 0-689-81339-2 Subj: Airplanes, airports. Careers – airplane pilots. Ethnic groups in the U.S. – African Americans.

An island Christmas ill. by Catherine Stock. Clarion, 1992. ISBN 0-395-58761-1 Subj: Foreign lands – Trinidad. Holidays – Christmas.

Jasmine's parlour day ill. by Ann Grifalconi. Lothrop, 1994. ISBN 0-688-11488-1 Subj: Activities – working. Family life – mothers. Foreign lands – Trinidad. Islands. Sea & seashore.

Jump up time: a Trinidad Carnival story ill. by Linda Saport. Clarion, 1998. ISBN 0-395-65012-7 Subj: Emotions – envy, jealousy. Fairs, festivals. Family life – sisters. Foreign lands – Trinidad.

Josephs, Rhoda. *The baby bubble book* ill. by Emily Arnold McCully. Grosset, 1988. ISBN 0-448-09256-5 Subj: Activities – bathing. Babies. Bubbles. Format, unusual – board books.

Joslin, Mary. *The goodbye boat* ill. by Claire St. Louis Little. Eerdmans, 1998. ISBN 0-8028-5186-X Subj: Death. Emotions – grief. Family life.

The shore beyond ill. by Alison Jay. Good Bks., 2000. ISBN 1-56148-316-8 Subj: Activities – traveling. Behavior – growing up. Self-concept.

The tale of the heaven tree ill. by Meilo So. Eerdmans, 1999. ISBN 0-8028-5190-8 Subj: Ecology. Gardens, gardening. Trees.

Joslin, Sesyle. *Baby elephant and the secret wishes* ill. by Leonard Weisgard. Harcourt, 1962. Subj: Animals – elephants. Holidays – Christmas.

Baby elephant goes to China ill. by Leonard Weisgard. Harcourt, 1963. Subj: Animals – elephants. Foreign languages. Sea & seashore.

Baby elephant's trunk ill. by Leonard Weisgard. Harcourt, 1961. Subj: Animals – elephants. Foreign lands – France. Foreign languages.

Brave Baby Elephant ill. by Leonard Weisgard. Harcourt, 1960. Subj: Animals – elephants. Bedtime.

Dear dragon: and other useful letter forms for young ladies and gentlemen engaged in everyday correspondence ill. by Irene Haas. Harcourt, 1962. Subj: Activities – writing. Communication. Dragons. Etiquette.

Señor Baby Elephant, the pirate ill. by Leonard Weisgard. Harcourt, 1962. Subj: Animals – elephants. Foreign languages. Pirates.

What do you do, dear? ill. by Maurice Sendak. Addison-Wesley, 1985, c1961. ISBN 0-06-023075-4 Subj: Etiquette. Humorous stories.

What do you say, dear? ill. by Maurice Sendak. Harper, 1986, c1958. ISBN 0-06-023074-6 Subj: Caldecott award honor books. Etiquette. Humorous stories.

Joyce, Irma. *Never talk to strangers* ill. by George Buckett. Western, 1990. ISBN 0-307-12609-9 Subj: Behavior – talking to strangers. Humorous stories. Safety.

Joyce, James. *The cat and the devil* ill. by Richard Erdoes. Dodd, 1965. Subj: Behavior – trickery. Devil.

Joyce, Susan. *ABC animal riddles* ill. by D. C. DuBosque. Peel Productions, 1999. ISBN 0-939217-51-1 Subj: ABC books. Animals. Rhyming text. Riddles & jokes.

ABC nature riddles ill. by Doug DuBosque. Peel Productions, 2000. ISBN 0-9392-1753-8 Subj: ABC books. Language. Nature. Rhyming text. Riddles & jokes.

ABC school riddles (ABC school riddles)

Alphabet riddles ill. by Doug DuBosque. Peel Productions, 1998. ISBN 0-939217-50-3 Subj: ABC books. Rhyming text. Riddles & jokes.

Joyce, William. *Baseball Bob* ill. by author. 1st board book ed. Geringer, 1999. ISBN 0-694-01180-0 Subj: Format, unusual – board books. Sports – baseball.

Bently and egg ill. by author. HarperCollins, 1992. ISBN 0-06-020386-2 Subj: Birds – ducks. Character traits – helpfulness. Eggs. Frogs & toads. Reptiles – turtles, tortoises.

Big time Olie ill. by author. Geringer, 2002. ISBN 0-06-008811-7 Subj: Behavior – growing up. Concepts – size. Family life. Problem solving.

A day with Wilbur Robinson ill. by author. HarperCollins, 1990. ISBN 0-06-022968-3 Subj: Family life.

Dinosaur Bob: and his adventures with the family Lazardo ill. by author. Expanded ed. HarperCollins, 1995. ISBN 0-06-021075-3

Subj: Activities – vacationing. Dinosaurs. Family life. Pets. Prehistory.

George shrinks ill. by author. HarperCollins, 1985. ISBN 0-06-023071-1 Subj: Activities – babysitting. Concepts – size. Family life.

The Leaf Men and the brave good bugs ill. by author. HarperCollins, 1996. ISBN 0-06-027238-4 Subj: Character traits – helpfulness. Gardens, gardening. Insects. Mythical creatures – elves. Old age. Toys.

Life with Bob ill. by author. Geringer, 1998. ISBN 0-694-01181-9 Subj: Dinosaurs. Format, unusual – board books.

Rolie Polie Olie ill. by author. Geringer, 1999. ISBN 0-06-027164-7 Subj: Concepts – shape. Rhyming text. Robots.

Rolie Polie Olie, how many howdys? computer imaging by Nelvana Ltd. Mouse Works, 1999. ISBN 0-7364-0165-2 Subj: Counting, numbers. Format, unusual – board books. Robots.

Santa calls ill. by author. HarperCollins, 1993. ISBN 0-06-021134-2 Subj: Activities – flying. Family life – brothers & sisters. Friendship. Santa Claus. Sibling rivalry.

Sleepy time Olie ill. by author. Geringer, 2001. ISBN 0-06-029614-3 Subj: Bedtime. Inventions. Rhyming text. Robots.

Snowie Rolie ill. by author. Geringer, 2000. ISBN 0-06-029286-5 Subj: Robots. Snowmen. Weather – snow.

Joyner, Jerry. *Thirteen* (Charlip, Remy)

Juan Bobo goes to work ill. by Joe Cepeda. Morrow, 2000. ISBN 0-688-16234-7 Subj: Folk & fairy tales. Foreign lands – Puerto Rico.

Jüchen, Aurel von. *The Holy Night: the story of the first Christmas* trans. from German by Cornelia Schaeffer; ill. by Celestino Piatti. Atheneum, 1968. Subj: Holidays – Christmas. Religion.

Judd, Naomi. *Naomi Judd's guardian angels* ill. by Dan Andreasen. HarperCollins, 2000. ISBN 0-06-027208-2 Subj: Angels. Family life – great-grandparents. Music. Songs.

Judes, Marie-Odile. *Max, the stubborn little wolf* ill. by Martine Bourre; trans. by Joan Robins. HarperCollins, 2001. ISBN 0-06-029417-5 Subj: Animals – wolves. Careers. Family life – fathers. Sports – hunting.

Judkins, Thessa. *Hurry up, Molly = Apúrate, Molly* (Morton, Lone)

Puppy finds a friend = Cachorrito encuentra un amigo (Bruzzone, Catherine)

Jukes, Mavis. *I'll see you in my dreams* ill. by Stacey Schuett. Knopf, 1993. ISBN 0-679-92690-9 Subj: Activities – flying. Death. Family life – aunts, uncles. Illness.

You're a bear ill. by Steve Johnson & Lou Fancher. Knopf, 2003. ISBN 0-375-90267-8 Subj: Animals – bears. Imagination. Night. Rhyming text.

Julian, Alison. *Brave as a bunny can be* ill. by author. Waldman, 2001. ISBN 0-931674-46-8 Subj: Animals – rabbits. Character traits – bravery. Emotions – fear. Family life.

Jung, Minna. *William's ninth life* ill. by Vera Rosenberry. Orchard, 1993. ISBN 05-31-08642-9 Subj: Animals – cats. Old age.

Jungman, Ann. *When the people are away* ill. by Linda Birch. Boyds Mills, 1992. ISBN 1-56397-202-6 Subj: Animals – cats. Parties. Pets.

Just like father ill. by John Huxtable. Sterling, 2003. Based on the books by Hans de Beer. ISBN 1-4027-1289-8 Subj: Animals – polar bears. Family life – fathers. Format, unusual – board books.

Justice, Jennifer. *The tiger* ill. by Graham Allen. Watts, 1979. ISBN 0-531-09154-6 Subj: Animals – tigers. Science.

Kaczman, James. *A bird and his worm* ill. by author. Houghton, 2002. ISBN 0-618-09460-1 Subj: Activities – traveling. Animals – worms. Behavior – talking to strangers. Birds. Character traits – being different. Safety.

Kadono, Eiko. *Grandpa's soup* ill. by Satomi Ichikawa. Eerdmans, 1999. ISBN 0-8028-5195-9 Subj: Behavior – sharing. Emotions – grief. Emotions – loneliness. Family life – grandfathers. Food.

Kahl, Virginia. *Away went Wolfgang* ill. by author. Scribners, 1954. Subj: Animals – dogs. Foreign lands – Austria.

The Baron's booty ill. by author. Scribners, 1963. Subj: Middle Ages. Rhyming text. Royalty.

Droopsi ill. by author. Scribners, 1958. Subj: Foreign lands – Germany. Music.

The Duchess bakes a cake ill. by author. Scribners, 1955. Subj: Activities – baking, cooking. Food. Middle Ages. Rhyming text. Royalty.

Giants, indeed! ill. by author. Scribners, 1974. ISBN 0-684-13659-7 Subj: Giants. Monsters.

How do you hide a monster? ill. by author. Scribners, 1971. ISBN 0-684-12318-5 Subj: Monsters. Rhyming text. Sports – hunting.

Maxie ill. by author. Scribners, 1956. Subj: Animals – dogs. Character traits – perseverance. Foreign lands – Germany. Old age.

The perfect pancake ill. by author. Scribners, 1960. Subj: Character traits – selfishness. Food. Rhyming text.

Plum pudding for Christmas ill. by author. Scribners, 1956. Subj: Food. Holidays – Christmas. Rhyming text. Royalty.

Whose cat is that? ill. by author. Scribners, 1979. ISBN 0-684-16097-8 Subj: Animals – cats. Cumulative tales.

Kahn, Joan. *Hi, Jock, run around the block* ill. by Whitney Darrow, Jr. HarperCollins, 1978. ISBN 0-06-023079-7 Subj: Cities, towns. Rhyming text.

Seesaw ill. by Crosby Newell Bonsall. HarperCollins, 1964. Subj: Games. Toys.

Kahn, Katherine Janus. *The shofar calls to us* ill. by author. Kar-Ben Copies, 1992. ISBN 0-929371-61-5 Subj: Format, unusual – board books. Holidays – Rosh Hashanah. Jewish culture. Religion.

Kahn, Michèle. *My everyday Spanish word book* trans. from French by Michael Mahler & Gwen Marsh; ill. by Benvenuti. Barron's, 1982. ISBN 0-8120-5429-6 Subj: Foreign languages.

Kahn, Rosemary. *Grandma's hat* ill. by Terry Milne. Viking, 1991. ISBN 0-670-84023-8 Subj: Clothing – hats. Family life – grandmothers. Foreign lands – South Africa.

Kahng, Kim. *The loathsome dragon* (Wiesner, David)

Kaiser Johnson, Lee. *If I ran the family* by Lee & Sue Kaiser Johnson; ill. by Roberta Collier-Morales. Free Spirit, 1992. ISBN 0-915793-41-5 Subj: Emotions. Ethnic groups in the U.S. Family life. Rhyming text. Self-concept.

Kaiser Johnson, Sue. *If I ran the family* (Kaiser Johnson, Lee)

Kaizuki, Kiyonori. *A calf is born* ill. by author. Orchard, 1990. ISBN 0-531-08462-0 Subj: Animals – babies. Animals – bulls, cows. Birth. Science.

Kajikawa, Kimiko. *Sweet dreams: how animals sleep* ill. by author. Holt, 1999. ISBN 0-8050-5890-7 Subj: Animals. Sleep.

Yoshi's feast ill. by Yumi Heo. DK, 2000. ISBN 0-7894-2607-2 Subj: Activities – dancing. Folk & fairy tales. Foreign lands – Japan. Friendship. Senses – smell.

Kajpust, Melissa. *A dozen silk diapers* ill. by Veselina Tomova. Hyperion, 1993. ISBN 1-56282-457-0 Subj: Clothing. Holidays – Christmas. Religion. Spiders.

The peacock's pride ill. by Jo'Anne Kelly. Hyperion, 1997. ISBN 0-7868-2233-3 Subj: Behavior – boasting. Birds – peacocks, peahens. Character traits – vanity. Folk & fairy tales. Foreign lands – India.

Kako, Satoshi. *Little Daruma and little Daikoku* ill. by author; trans. by Richard McNamara & Peter Holwett. Tuttle, 2003. ISBN 0-8048-3351-6 Subj: Character traits – cooperation. Foreign lands – Japan. Friendship. Magic.

Little Daruma and little Kaminari ill. by author; trans. by Richard McNamara & Peter Holwett. Tuttle, 2002. ISBN 0-8048-3348-6 Subj: Behavior – lost & found possessions. Foreign lands – Japan. Friendship.

Kalan, Robert. *Blue sea* ill. by Donald Crews. Greenwillow, 1979. ISBN 0-688-84184-8 Subj: Concepts – size. Fish.

Jump, frog, jump! ill. by Byron Barton. Greenwillow, 1981. ISBN 0-688-84271-2 Subj: Cumulative tales. Frogs & toads.

Moving day ill. by Yossi Abolafia. Greenwillow, 1996. ISBN 0-688-13949-3 Subj: Crustaceans – crabs. Cumulative tales. Moving. Rhyming text.

Rain ill. by Donald Crews. Greenwillow, 1978. ISBN 0-688-84139-2 Subj: Weather – rain.

Stop, thief! ill. by Yossi Abolafia. Greenwillow, 1993. ISBN 0-688-11877-1 Subj: Animals. Circular tales.

Kalas, Klaus. *The beaver family book* (Kalas, Sybille)

Kalas, Sybille. *The beaver family book* by Sybille & Klaus Kalas; photos by Sybille Kalas; trans. by Patricia Crampton. Picture Book Studio, 1987. ISBN 0-88708-050-2 Subj: Animals – beavers. Science.

The goose family book trans. by Patricia Crampton; preface by Konrad Lorenz; ill. with photos. Picture Book Studio, 1986. Tr. of Das gänse-kinder-buch. ISBN 0-88708-019-7 Subj: Birds – geese.

The penguin family book (Somme, Lauritz)

Kaldhol, Marit. *Goodbye Rune* trans. by Michael Crosby-Jones; adapt. Catherine Maggs; ill. by Wenche Øyen. Kane/Miller, 1987. Tr. of Farvel, Rune. ISBN 0-916291-11-1 Subj: Death. Emotions – grief. Friendship.

Kallen, Stuart A. *The airport* ill. with photos. Abdo & Daughters, 1997. ISBN 1-56239-711-7 Subj: Airplanes, airports. School – field trips.

Brontosaurus ill. by Kristen Copham. Abdo, 1994. ISBN 1-56239-286-7 Subj: Dinosaurs.

The farm ill. with photos. Abdo & Daughters, 1997. ISBN 1-56239-713-3 Subj: Careers – farmers. Communities, neighborhoods. Farms. School – field trips.

The fire station ill. with photos. Abdo & Daughters, 1997. ISBN 1-56239-710-9 Subj: Careers – firefighters. Communities, neighborhoods. School – field trips.

The museum ill. with photos. Abdo & Daughters, 1997. ISBN 1-56239-709-5 Subj: Communities, neighborhoods. Museums. School – field trips.

The police station ill. with photos. Abdo & Daughters, 1997. ISBN 1-56239-708-7 Subj: Careers – police officers. Communities, neighborhoods. School – field trips.

Stegosaurus ill. by Kristen Copham. Abdo, 1994. ISBN 1-56239-285-9 Subj: Dinosaurs.

Triceratops ill. by Kristen Copham. Abdo, 1994. ISBN 1-56239-288-3 Subj: Dinosaurs.

The zoo ill. with photos. Abdo & Daughters, 1997. ISBN 1-56239-712-5 Subj: Animals. School – field trips. Zoos.

Kallick, Elisabeth. *The rabbit who longed for home* (Edvall, Lilian)

Kallok, Emma. *Gem* ill. by Joel Bower. Tricycle, 2001. ISBN 1-58246-027-2 Subj: Babies. Birth. Children as authors. Ethnic groups in the U.S. Family life – new sibling. Musical instruments – saxophones.

Kalman, Benjamin. *Animals in danger: poems from no man's valley* ill. by Cécile Curtis & Michael Jupp. Random House, 1982. ISBN 0-394-95454-8 Subj: Animals – endangered animals. Ecology. Poetry.

Kalman, Bobbie. *Celebrating the powwow* ill. with photos. Crabtree, 1997. ISBN 0-8650-5640-4 Subj: Fairs, festivals. Indians of North America.

A koala is not a bear! (Sotzek, Hannelore)

Kalman, Maira. *Hey Willy, see the pyramids!* ill. by author. Puffin, 1990, c1988. ISBN 0-14-050840-6 Subj: Bedtime. Family life – sisters. Imagination.

Next stop, Grand Central ill. by author. Putnam, 1999. ISBN 0-399-22926-4 Subj: Trains. Transportation.

Sayonara, Mrs. Kackleman ill. by author. Viking, 1989. ISBN 0-670-82945-5 Subj: Activities – traveling. Foreign lands – Japan.

What Pete ate from A-Z ill. by author. Putnam, 2001. ISBN 0-399-23362-8 Subj: ABC books. Animals – dogs.

Kalz, Jill. *Fruits* ill. with photos. Smart Apple Media, 2003. ISBN 1-58340-299-3 Subj: Food. Health & fitness.

Northern lights ill. with photos. Creative Ed., 2004. ISBN 1-58341-326-X Subj: Northern lights. Science.

Water ill. with photos. Smart Apple Media, 2003. ISBN 1-58340-302-7 Subj: Water.

Kamal, Aleph. *The bird who was an elephant* ill. by Frané Lessac. Lippincott, 1990. ISBN 0-397-32446-4 Subj: Birds. Foreign lands – India.

Kamen, Gloria. *"Paddle," said the swan* ill. by author. Atheneum, 1989. ISBN 0-689-31330-6 Subj: Animals. Bedtime. Rhyming text.

The ringdoves: from the fables of Bidpai ill. by adapt. Atheneum, 1988. ISBN 0-689-31312-8 Subj: Animals. Friendship. Sports – hunting.

Second-hand cat ill. by author. Atheneum, 1992. ISBN 0-689-31631-3 Subj: Animals – cats.

Kamine, Jane. *Mommy's hands* (Lasky, Kathryn)

Kamish, Daniel. *Diggy Dan* by Daniel & David Kamish; ill. by Daniel Kamish. Random House, 2001. ISBN 0-375-90576-6 Subj: Character traits – cleanliness. Character traits – orderliness. Children as illustrators. Imagination.

The night scary beasties popped out of my head by Daniel & David Kamish; ill. by Daniel Kamish. Random House, 1998. ISBN 0-679-

99039-9 Subj: Activities – drawing. Bedtime. Children as illustrators. Dreams. Family life. Monsters. Night. Sleep.

Kamish, David. *The night scary beasties popped out of my head* (Kamish, Daniel)

Kanagy, Ruth A. *The park bench* (Takeshita, Fumiko)

Kanao, Keiko. *Kitten up a tree* ill. by author. Knopf, 1987. ISBN 0-394-88817-0 Subj: Animals – cats. Character traits – curiosity. Family life – mothers.

Kandell, Alice. *Max, the music-maker* (Stecher, Miriam B.)

Kandoian, Ellen. *Is anybody up?* ill. by author. Putnam, 1989. ISBN 0-399-21749-5 Subj: Etiquette. Food.

Maybe she forgot ill. by author. Dutton, 1990. ISBN 0-525-65031-8 Subj: Behavior – growing up. Family life – mothers.

Molly's seasons ill. by author. Dutton, 1992. ISBN 0-525-65076-8 Subj: Seasons.

Under the sun ill. by author. Dodd, 1987. ISBN 0-396-09059-1 Subj: Morning. Night. Sun.

Kane, Henry B. *Wings, legs, or fins* photos & ill. by author. Knopf, 1966. Subj: Animals. Science.

Kangas, Juli. *Fluffy Bunny's friend* ill. by author. Putnam, 1992. ISBN 0-448-40140-1 Subj: Animals – rabbits. Format, unusual – board books. Friendship.

Ginger Kitten's surprise ill. by author. Putnam, 1992. ISBN 0-448-40139-8 Subj: Animals – cats. Format, unusual – board books. Friendship.

Hello, Honey Bear ill. by author. Putnam, 1992. ISBN 0-448-40141-X Subj: Animals – bears. Format, unusual – board books. Friendship.

Kani, Saru. *The monkey and the crab* (Horio, Seishi)

Kannapell, Barbara M. *The night before Christmas in signed English* (Moore, Clement Clark)

Kanome, Kayoko. *Little Mop lost* ill. by author; trans. from Japanese by Prudence Moodie. Carolrhoda, 1992. ISBN 0-87614-738-4 Subj: Animals – dogs. Behavior – lost. Cities, towns.

Kantor, MacKinlay. *The preposterous week* ill. by Kurt Wiese. Putnam, 1942. Subj: Food. Humorous stories.

Kantor, Sid. *Armando asked "Why?"* (Hulbert, Jay)

Kantrowitz, Mildred. *I wonder if Herbie's home yet* ill. by Tony DeLuna. Parents' Magazine Pr., 1971. ISBN 0-819-30466-2 Subj: Friendship.

When Violet died ill. by Emily Arnold McCully. Parents' Magazine Pr., 1973. ISBN 0-719-30691-6 Subj: Birds. Death. Emotions – grief.

Willy Bear ill. by Nancy Winslow Parker. Parents' Magazine Pr., 1976. ISBN 0-819-30884-6 Subj: School – first day. Sleep. Toys – bears.

Kaplan, Boche. *Sweet Betsy from Pike* (Abisch, Roz)

Kaplan, Howard. *Waiting to sing* ill. by Hervé Blondon. DK, 2000. ISBN 0-7894-2615-3 Subj: Death. Emotions – grief. Family life – mothers. Music. Musical instruments – pianos.

Kaplan, John. *Mom and me* photos by author. Scholastic, 1996. ISBN 0-590-47294-1 Subj: Family life – mothers.

Kapp, Paul. *Cock-a-doodle-doo! Cock-a-doodle-dandy!* ill. by Anita Lobel. HarperCollins, 1966. Subj: Music. Songs.

Karas, G. Brian. *Atlantic* ill. by author. Putnam, 2002. ISBN 0-399-23632-5 Subj: Science. Sea & seashore.

Bebe's bad dream ill. by author. Greenwillow, 2000. ISBN 0-688-16183-9 Subj: Aliens. Family life – brothers & sisters. Nightmares.

Home on the bayou ill. by author. S&S, 1996. ISBN 0-689-80516-4 Subj: Behavior – bullying. Cowboys, cowgirls. Family life. Moving.

I know an old lady (Little old lady who swallowed a fly)

Skidamarink ill. by author. HarperFestival, 2002. ISBN 0-694-01595-4 Subj: Animals – polar bears. Birds – penguins. Emotions – love. Format, unusual – toy & movable books. Rhyming text. Sports – ice skating.

The windy day ill. by author. S&S, 1998. ISBN 0-689-81449-6 Subj: Weather – wind.

Karas, Jacqueline. *The doll house* ill. by Judith Riches. Tambourine, 1993. ISBN 0-688-12481-X Subj: Emotions. Friendship. Toys – dolls.

Karim, Roberta. *Kindle me a riddle* ill. by Bethanne Andersen. Greenwillow, 1999. ISBN 0-688-16203-7 Subj: Family life. Riddles & jokes. U.S. history – frontier & pioneer life.

Mandy Sue Day ill. by Karen Ritz. Clarion, 1994. ISBN 0-395-66155-2 Subj: Animals – horses, ponies. Family life. Farms. Handicaps – blindness.

This is a hospital, not a zoo! ill. by Sue Truesdell. Clarion, 1998. ISBN 0-395-72099-0 Subj: Animals. Careers – nurses. Hospitals. Humorous stories. Illness. Imagination.

Kark, Nina Mary. *see* Bawden, Nina

Karkowsky, Nancy. *Grandma's soup* ill. by Shelly O. Haas. Kar-Ben Copies, 1989. ISBN 0-930494-98-9 Subj: Family life – grandmothers. Illness – Alzheimer's. Jewish culture. Old age.

Karlin, Barbara. *Cinderella* (Perrault, Charles)

Karlin, Nurit. *The blue frog* ill. by author. Coward, 1983. ISBN 0-698-20577-4 Subj: Character traits – being different. Frogs & toads.

The dream factory ill. by author. Lippincott, 1988. ISBN 0-397-32212-7 Subj: Dreams. Sleep.

The fat cat sat on the mat ill. by author. HarperCollins, 1996. ISBN 0-06-026674-0 Subj: Animals – cats. Animals – rats. Rhyming text. Witches.

I see, you saw ill. by author. HarperCollins, 1997. ISBN 0-06-026678-3 Subj: Animals. Language.

Little big mouse ill. by author. HarperCollins, 1991. ISBN 0-06-021608-5 Subj: Animals – mice. Concepts – size. Self-concept.

Ten little bunnies ill. by author. S&S, 1994. ISBN 0-671-88026-8 Subj: Animals – rabbits. Counting, numbers. Rhyming text.

The tooth witch ill. by author. Lippincott, 1985. ISBN 0-397-32120-1 Subj: Character traits – kindness. Fairies. Witches.

A train for the king ill. by author. Coward, 1983. ISBN 0-698-20578-2 Subj: Royalty – kings. Self-concept.

Karlins, Mark. *Music over Manhattan* ill. by Jack E. Davis. Doubleday, 1998. ISBN 0-385-32225-9 Subj: Cities, towns. Family life. Music. Musical instruments – trumpets. Weddings.

Karlinsky, Ruth Schild. *My first book of Mitzvos* photos by Isaiah Karlinsky. Feldheim, 1986. ISBN 0-87306-388-0 Subj: Jewish culture. Religion.

Karmi, Giora. *And Shira imagined* ill. by author. Jewish Publication Society, 1988. ISBN 0-8276-0288-X Subj: Activities – traveling. Family life. Foreign lands – Israel. Imagination.

Karn, George. *Circus big and small* ill. by author. Little, 1986. ISBN 0-316-30342-9 Subj: Circus. Concepts – opposites. Format, unusual – board books.

Circus colors ill. by author. Little, 1986. ISBN 0-316-30343-7 Subj: Circus. Concepts – color. Format, unusual – board books.

Karon, Jan. *Miss Fannie's hat* ill. by Toni Goffe. Augsburg Fortress, 1998. ISBN 0-8066-3526-6 Subj: Behavior – sharing. Clothing – hats. Religion.

The trellis and the seed ill. by Robert Gantt Steele. Viking, 2003. ISBN 0-670-89289-0 Subj: Behavior – growing up. Flowers. Seeds.

Karpin, Florence Baker. *Tree spirits* ill. by author. Countryman Pr., 1992. ISBN 0-88150-248-0 Subj: Ecology. Trees.

Karsunke, Yaak. *Hello Irina* (Blech, Dietlind)

Kasparavicius, Kestutis. *The bear family's world tour Christmas* ill. by author. Abrams, 2002. ISBN 0-8109-0573-6 Subj: Activities – traveling. Animals – bears. Holidays – Christmas.

Kasperson, James. *Little brother moose* ill. by Karlyn Holman. Dawn, 1995. ISBN 1-883220-34-3 Subj: Animals – moose. Birds – geese. Senses.

Kassirer, Sue. *Joseph and his coat of many colors* ill. by Danuta Jarecka. S&S, 1997. ISBN 0-689-81227-2 Subj: Clothing – coats. Religion. Sibling rivalry.

Math fair blues ill. by Jerry Smath. Kane Pr., 2001. ISBN 0-613-39339-2 Subj: Concepts – shape. Counting, numbers. Fairs, festivals. Musical instruments – bands.

What's next, Nina? ill. by Page Eastburn O'Rourke. Kane Pr., 2001. ISBN 1-57565-106-8 Subj: Concepts – patterns. Family life – sisters. Jewelry. Parties.

Kastner, Jill. *Barnyard big top* ill. by author. S&S, 1997. ISBN 0-689-80484-9 Subj: Animals. Circus. Family life. Farms.

Merry Christmas, Princess Dinosaur ill. by author. Greenwillow, 2002. ISBN 0-06-000472-X Subj: Dinosaurs. Holidays – Christmas. Toys.

Princess Dinosaur ill. by author. Greenwillow, 2001. ISBN 0-688-17046-3 Subj: Animals – dogs. Dinosaurs. Toys.

Snake hunt ill. by author. Four Winds, 1993. ISBN 0-02-749395-4 Subj: Family life – grandfathers. Reptiles – snakes. Sports – hunting.

Kasza, Keiko. *Don't laugh, Joe* ill. by author. Putnam, 1997. ISBN 0-399-23036-X Subj: Animals – bears. Animals – possums. Behavior.

Dorothy and Mikey ill. by author. Putnam, 2000. ISBN 0-399-23356-3 Subj: Activities – playing. Animals – hippopotamuses. Friendship.

Grandpa Toad's last secret ill. by author. Putnam, 1995. ISBN 0-399-22610-9 Subj: Family life – grandfathers. Frogs & toads. Monsters.

The mightiest ill. by author. Putnam, 2001. ISBN 0-399-23586-8 Subj: Animals – bears. Animals – elephants. Animals – lions. Giants.

A mother for Choco ill. by author. Putnam, 1992. ISBN 0-399-21841-6 Subj: Adoption. Animals. Birds. Emotions – love. Family life – mothers.

The pigs' picnic ill. by author. Putnam, 1988. ISBN 0-399-21543-3 Subj: Activities – picnicking. Animals – pigs. Character traits – appearance.

The rat and the tiger ill. by author. Putnam, 1993. ISBN 0-399-22404-1 Subj: Animals – rats. Animals – tigers. Behavior – bullying. Behavior – sharing. Friendship.

When the elephant walks ill. by author. Putnam, 1990. ISBN 0-399-21755-X Subj: Animals. Cumulative tales. Emotions – fear.

The wolf's chicken stew ill. by author. Putnam, 1987. ISBN 0-399-21400-3 Subj: Animals – wolves. Birds – chickens. Character traits – generosity. Food.

Kates, Bobbi Jane. *We're different, we're the same: featuring Jim Henson's Sesame Street Muppets* ill. by Joe Mathieu. Random House, 1992. ISBN 0-679-83227-0 Subj: Anatomy. Puppets. Rhyming text.

Katschke, Judy. *Take a hike, Snoopy* art adapt. by Nick & Peter LoBianco. Little Simon, 2002. ISBN 0-689-84938-9 Subj: Animals – dogs. Birds. Camps, camping. Sports – hiking.

Katz, Avner. *The little pickpocket* ill. by author. S&S, 1996. ISBN 0-689-80494-6 Subj: Animals – kangaroos. Bedtime. Foreign lands – Australia. Sleep.

Tortoise solves a problem ill. by author. HarperCollins, 1993. ISBN 0-06-020799-X Subj: Homes, houses. Reptiles – turtles, tortoises.

Katz, Bobbi. *The creepy crawly book* ill. by S. D. Schindler. Random House, 1989. ISBN 0-394-82709-0 Subj: Animals. Insects.

Tick-tock, let's read the clock ill. by Carol Nicklaus. Random House, 1988. ISBN 0-394-89399-9 Subj: Clocks, watches. Poetry. Time.

Katz, Karen. *The colors of us* ill. by author. Holt, 1999. ISBN 0-8050-5864-8 Subj: Character traits – individuality. Concepts – color. Ethnic groups in the U.S.

Counting kisses ill. by author. McElderry, 2001. ISBN 0-689-83470-5 Subj: Counting, numbers. Kissing.

Over the moon ill. by author. Holt, 1997. ISBN 0-8050-5013-2 Subj: Adoption. Babies.

Twelve hats for Lena ill. by author. McElderry, 2002. ISBN 0-689-84873-0 Subj: Clothing – hats. Days of the week, months of the year. Rhyming text.

Where is baby's mommy? ill. by author. Little Simon, 2000. ISBN 0-689-83561-2 Subj: Babies. Family life – mothers. Format, unusual – toy & movable books. Games.

Katz, Michael Jay. *Ten potatoes in a pot and other counting rhymes* ill. by June Otani. HarperCollins, 1990. ISBN 0-06-023107-6 Subj: Counting, numbers. Poetry.

Katz, Susan. *Mrs. Brown on exhibit* ill. by R.W. Alley. S&S, 2002. ISBN 0-689-82970-1 Subj: Museums. Poetry. School – field trips.

Kauffman, Lois. *What's that noise?* ill. by Allan Eitzen. Lothrop, 1965. Subj: Family life – fathers. Night. Noise, sounds.

Kaufman, Curt. *Hotel boy* by Curt & Gita Kaufman; photos by Curt Kaufman. Atheneum, 1987. ISBN 0-689-31287-3 Subj: Activities. Cities, towns. Ethnic groups in the U.S. – African Americans. Family life.

Rajesh by Curt & Gita Kaufman; photos by Curt Kaufman. Atheneum, 1985. ISBN 0-689-31074-9 Subj: Handicaps. School.

Kaufman, Gita. *Hotel boy* (Kaufman, Curt)

Rajesh (Kaufman, Curt)

Kaufman, Jeff. *Milk rock* ill. by author. Holt, 1994. ISBN 0-8050-2814-5 Subj: Careers – farmers. Farms. Magic. Rocks.

Kaufmann, John. *Birds are flying* ill. by author. Crowell, 1979. ISBN 0-690-03942-5 Subj: Birds. Science.

Flying giants of long ago ill. by author. Crowell, 1984. ISBN 0-690-04219-1 Subj: Activities – flying. Animals. Birds. Insects. Science.

Kaufmann, Nancy. *Bye, Bye* ill. by Jung-Hee Spetter. Front St., 2003. ISBN 1-886910-95-2 Subj: Animals. Animals – pigs. Family life – fathers. School – first day.

Kaune, Merriman B. *My own little house* ill. by author. Follett, 1957. Subj: Homes, houses.

Kavanagh, Peter. *I love my mama* ill. by Jane Chapman. S&S, 2003. ISBN 0-689-85691-1 Subj: Activities. Animals – elephants. Day. Family life – mothers. Rhyming text.

Kavanaugh, James J. *The crooked angel* ill. by Elaine Havelock. Nash, 1970. ISBN 0-8402-1157-0 Subj: Angels. Rhyming text.

Kawata, Ken. *Animal tails* ill. by Masayuki Yabuuchi. Kane/Miller, 2001. ISBN 1-929132-05-0 Subj: Anatomy – tails. Animals.

Kay, Helen. *An egg is for wishing* ill. by Yaroslava. Abelard-Schuman, 1966. Subj: Behavior – animals, dislike of. Behavior – wishing. Eggs. Foreign lands – Ukraine. Holidays – Easter.

One mitten Lewis ill. by Kurt Werth. Lothrop, 1955. Subj: Behavior – lost & found possessions. Clothing – gloves, mittens.

A stocking for a kitten ill. by Yaroslava. Abelard-Schuman, 1965. Subj: Animals – cats. Family life – grandmothers.

Kay, Ormonde De. *see* De Kay, Ormonde

Kay, Verla. *Broken Feather* ill. by Stephen Alcorn. Putnam, 2002. ISBN 0-399-23550-7 Subj: Indians of North America – Nez Perce. Poetry. U.S. history.

Covered wagons, bumpy trails ill. by S. D. Schindler. Putnam, 2000. ISBN 0-399-22928-0 Subj: Activities – traveling. Homes, houses. Rhyming text. U.S. history.

Gold fever ill. by S.D. Schindler. Putnam, 1999. ISBN 0-399-23027-0 Subj: Careers – miners. Rhyming text. U.S. history – frontier & pioneer life.

Iron horses ill. by Michael McCurdy. Putnam, 1999. ISBN 0-399-23119-6 Subj: Rhyming text. Trains. U.S. history.

Orphan train ill. by Ken Stark. Putnam, 2003. ISBN 0-399-23613-9 Subj: Family life – brothers & sisters. Orphans. Rhyming text. Trains. U.S. history.

Kaye, Buddy. *A you're adorable* (Lippman, Sidney)

Kaye, Geraldine. *The sea monkey: a picture story from Malaysia* ill. by Gay Galsworthy. Collins-World, 1968. ISBN 0-582-16571-1 Subj: Animals – monkeys. Foreign lands – Malaysia.

Kaye, Marilyn. *The real tooth fairy* ill. by Helen Cogancherry. Harcourt, 1990. ISBN 0-15-265780-0 Subj: Fairies. Teeth.

Kazeroid, Sibylle. *The bravest mouse* (Barbero, Maria)

Make a wish, Honey Bear! (Pfister, Marcus)

Meg's wish (Recknagel, Friedrich)

Mole's journey (Weigelt, Udo)

Keams, Geri. *Snail girl brings water: a Navajo story* ill. by Richard Ziehler-Martin. Rising Moon, 1998. ISBN 0-8735-8662-X Subj: Creation. Folk & fairy tales. Indians of North America – Navajo. Water.

Keaney, Leonie. *Zoo day* (Brennan, John)

Keats, Ezra Jack. *Apt. 3* ill. by author. Macmillan, 1971. ISBN 0-689-71059-3 Subj: Cities, towns. Ethnic groups in the U.S. – African Americans. Family life. Handicaps – blindness. Music. Musical instruments – harmonicas. Senses – sight.

Clementina's cactus ill. by author. Viking, 1999. ISBN 0-670-88545-2 Subj: Desert. Plants. Weather – storms. Wordless.

The clubhouse (Suen, Anastasia)

Dreams ill. by author. Macmillan, 1974. ISBN 0-02-749610-4 Subj: Dreams. Ethnic groups in the U.S. – African Americans. Imagination. Night. Sleep.

God is in the mountain ill. by author. Holt, 1994. ISBN 0-8050-3168-5 Subj: Religion.

Goggles ill. by author. Macmillan, 1969. ISBN 0-02-749590-6 Subj: Behavior – bullying. Caldecott award honor books. Cities, towns. Ethnic groups in the U.S. – African Americans. Problem solving.

Hamster chase (Suen, Anastasia)

Hi, cat! ill. by author. Viking, 1999. ISBN 0-670-88546-0 Subj: Animals – cats. Cities, towns. Ethnic groups in the U.S. – African Americans.

Jennie's hat ill. by author. HarperCollins, 1966. ISBN 0-06-023114-9 Subj: Behavior – dissatisfaction. Character traits – kindness to animals. Clothing – hats.

John Henry ill. by author. HarperCollins, 1965. ISBN 0-394-99052-8 Subj: Character traits – perseverance. Character traits – pride. Ethnic groups in the U.S. – African Americans. Folk & fairy tales. Tall tales.

Kitten for a day ill. by author. Watts, 1974. ISBN 0-531-02714-7 Subj: Animals – cats. Animals – dogs. Wordless.

A letter to Amy ill. by author. HarperCollins, 1968. ISBN 0-06-023109-2 Subj: Ethnic groups in the U.S. – African Americans. Friendship. Letters, cards. Parties. Weather – rain. Weather – wind.

The little drummer boy ill. by author. Aladdin, 1987, c1968. Words & music by Katherine Davis, Henry Onorati & Harry Simeonne. ISBN 0-689-71158-1 Subj: Gifts. Holidays – Christmas. Music. Musical instruments – drums. Religion – Nativity. Songs.

Louie ill. by author. Greenwillow, 1975. ISBN 0-688-84002-7 Subj: Character traits – shyness. Ethnic groups in the U.S. – African Americans. Puppets.

Louie's search ill. by author. Four Winds, 1989, c1980. ISBN 0-689-71354-1 Subj: Behavior – needing someone. Family life.

Maggie and the pirate ill. by author. Four Winds, 1979. ISBN 0-590-07602-7 Subj: Death. Pets. Pirates.

My dog is lost! ill. by Ezra Jack Keats. Viking, 1999. ISBN 0-670-88550-9 Subj: Animals – dogs. Behavior – lost. Careers – police officers. Ethnic groups in the U.S. Ethnic groups in the U.S. – Puerto Rican Americans. Foreign languages.

One red sun: a counting book ill. by author. Viking, 1999. ISBN 0-670-88478-2 Subj: Counting, numbers. Format, unusual – board books.

Pet show! ill. by author. Puffin, 2001, c1972. ISBN 0-670-03504-1 Subj: Animals. Cities, towns. Communities, neighborhoods. Ethnic groups in the U.S. – African Americans. Pets.

Peter's chair ill. by author. HarperCollins, 1967. ISBN 0-06-023112-2 Subj: Babies. Behavior – sharing. Ethnic groups in the U.S. – African Americans. Family life – new sibling. Friendship. Furniture – chairs. Self-concept.

Pssst! doggie ill. by author. Watts, 1973. ISBN 0-531-02598-5 Subj: Animals – cats. Animals – dogs. Wordless.

Regards to the man in the moon ill. by author. Four Winds, 1981. ISBN 0-590-07820-8 Subj: Imagination. Space & space ships.

Skates ill. by author. Four Winds, 1981, c1972. ISBN 0-590-07812-7 Subj: Activities – playing. Animals – dogs. Ethnic groups in the U.S. – African Americans. Humorous stories. Wordless.

The snowy day ill. by author. Viking, 1962. Subj: Activities – playing. Caldecott award books. Ethnic groups in the U.S. – African Americans. Seasons – winter. Weather – snow.

The snowy day [board book] ill. by author. Viking, 1996. ISBN 0-670-86733-0 Subj: Activities – playing. Caldecott award books. Ethnic groups in the U.S. – African Americans. Format, unusual – board books. Seasons – winter. Weather – snow.

The trip ill. by author. Greenwillow, 1978. ISBN 0-688-84123-6 Subj: Emotions – loneliness. Ethnic groups in the U.S. – African Americans. Holidays – Halloween. Imagination. Moving.

Whistle for Willie ill. by author. Viking, 1964. Subj: Activities – whistling. Animals – dogs. Ethnic groups in the U.S. – African Americans. Problem solving. Self-concept.

Willie's birthday (Suen, Anastasia)

Keefer, Janice Kulyk. *Anna's goat* ill. by Janet Wilson. Orca, 2000. ISBN 1-55143-153-X Subj: Animals – goats. Family life – sisters. Foreign lands – Europe. War.

Keeler, Patricia A. *A huge hog is a big pig* (McCall, Francis X.)

Keenan, Martha. *The mannerly adventures of Little Mouse* ill. by Meri Shardin. Crown, 1977. ISBN 0-517-52845-2 Subj: Animals – mice. Etiquette.

Keenen, George. *The preposterous week* ill. by Stanley Mack. Dial, 1971. ISBN 0-8037-7072-3 Subj: Behavior – lost & found possessions. Character traits – foolishness. Days of the week, months of the year. Humorous stories. Problem solving.

Keens-Douglas, Richardo. *The nutmeg princess* ill. by Annouchka Galouchko. Firefly, 1992. ISBN 1-55037-239-4 Subj: Character traits – bravery. Character traits – selfishness. Foreign lands – Caribbean Islands. Gardens, gardening.

Anancy and the haunted house ill. by Stéphane Jorisch. Annick, 2002. ISBN 1-55037-737-X Subj: Folk & fairy tales. Holidays – Halloween. Homes, houses. Spiders.

The Miss Meow pageant ill. by Marie Lafrance. Annick, 1998. ISBN 1-55037-537-7 Subj: Animals – cats. Character traits – individuality.

Keep, Linda Lowery. *Day of the Dead* ill. by Barbara Knutson. Carolrhoda, 2004. ISBN 0-87614-914-X Subj: Foreign lands – Mexico. Holidays – Day of the Dead.

Keeping, Charles. *Alfie finds the other side of the world* ill. by author. Watts, 1968. Subj: Cities, towns. Foreign lands – England. Rivers. Weather – fog.

Joseph's yard ill. by author. Watts, 1969. Subj: Gardens, gardening. Poverty.

Molly o' the moors: the story of a pony ill. by author. Collins, 1966. Subj: Animals – horses, ponies. Old age.

Through the window ill. by author. Watts, 1970. ISBN 0-531-01868-7 Subj: Cities, towns. Foreign lands – England.

Willie's fire-engine ill. by author. Oxford Univ. Pr., 1980. ISBN 0-19-279728-X Subj: Activities – playing. Careers – firefighters. Imagination.

Keeshan, Robert. *Alligator in the basement* ill. by Kyle Corkum. Fairview, 1996. ISBN 0-925190-90-X Subj: Animals – monkeys. Family life – grandfathers. Imagination. Reptiles – alligators, crocodiles.

Itty Bitty Kitty ill. by Jane Maday. Fairview, 1997. ISBN 1-57749-017-7 Subj: Animals – cats. Format, unusual – board books.

Itty Bitty Kitty makes a big splash ill. by Jane Maday. Fairview, 1997. ISBN 1-57749-018-5 Subj: Accidents. Animals – cats. Format, unusual – board books. Hotels. Sports – swimming.

She loves me, she loves me not ill. by Maurice Sendak. HarperCollins, 1963. Subj: Games. Holidays – Valentine's Day. Mythical creatures.

Kehoe, Michael. *Road closed* photos by author. Carolrhoda, 1982. ISBN 0-87614-192-0 Subj: Roads.

The rock quarry book photos by author. Carolrhoda, 1981. ISBN 0-87614-142-4 Subj: Rocks.

Keigwin, R. P. *Thumbelina* (Andersen, H. C. [Hans Christian])

The ugly duckling (Andersen, H. C. [Hans Christian])

Keillor, Garrison. *Cat, you better come home* ill. by Steve Johnson & Lou Fancher. Viking, 1995. ISBN 0-670-85112-4 Subj: Animals – cats. Behavior – seeking better things. Rhyming text.

The old man who loved cheese ill. by Anne Wilsdorf. Little, 1996. ISBN 0-316-48615-9 Subj: Food. Rhyming text. Senses – smell.

Keister, Douglas. *Fernando's gift = El regalo de Fernando* ill. with photos. Sierra Club, 1995. ISBN 0-87156-414-9 Subj: Ecology. Family life. Foreign lands – Costa Rica. Foreign languages. Forest, woods. Gifts. Trees.

Keith, Adrienne. *Fairies from A to Z* ill. by Wendy Wallin Malinow. Tricycle, 1994. ISBN 1-883672-10-4 Subj: ABC books. Fairies. Rhyming text.

Keith, Eros. *Bedita's bad day* ill. by author. HarperCollins, 1973. ISBN 0-878-88036-4 Subj: Behavior – bad day. Witches.

Nancy's backyard ill. by author. HarperCollins, 1973. ISBN 0-06-023123-8 Subj: Dreams. Weather – rain.

Rrra-ah ill. by author. Bradbury, 1969. ISBN 0-13-783456-X Subj: Frogs & toads. Pets.

Keller, Beverly. *Fiona's bee* ill. by Diane Paterson. Coward, 1975. ISBN 0-698-30595-7 Subj: Character traits – shyness. Insects – bees.

Pimm's place ill. by Jacqueline Chwast. Coward, 1978. ISBN 0-698-30689-9 Subj: Behavior – solitude. Character traits – bravery. Emotions – fear.

When mother got the flu ill. by Maxie Chambliss. Coward, 1984. ISBN 0-698-30743-7 Subj: Behavior – misbehavior. Family life – mothers. Illness.

Keller, Charles. *School daze* ill. by Sam Q. Weissman. Prentice-Hall, 1979. ISBN 0-13-793620-6 Subj: Humorous stories. Riddles & jokes.

Tongue twisters ill. by Ron Fritz. S&S, 1989. ISBN 0-671-67123-5 Subj: Poetry. Tongue twisters.

Keller, Emily Snowell. *Sleeping Bunny* ill. by Emily Snowell Keller. Random House, 2003. ISBN 0-375-91541-9 Subj: Animals. Animals – rabbits. Folk & fairy tales. Royalty – princesses.

Keller, Holly. *A bear for Christmas* ill. by author. Greenwillow, 1986. ISBN 0-688-05989-9 Subj: Behavior – misbehavior. Family life. Gifts. Holidays – Christmas. Toys – bears.

A bed full of cats ill. by author. Harcourt, 1999. ISBN 0-15-202331-3 Subj: Animals – cats. Behavior – lost & found possessions. Pets.

The best present ill. by author. Greenwillow, 1989. ISBN 0-688-07320-4 Subj: Family life – grandmothers. Hospitals.

Brave Horace ill. by author. Greenwillow, 1998. ISBN 0-688-15408-5 Subj: Animals – leopards. Character traits – bravery. Emotions – fear. Parties.

Cecil's garden ill. by author. Greenwillow, 2002. ISBN 0-06-029594-5 Subj: Animals. Animals – rabbits. Behavior – fighting, arguing.

Cromwell's glasses ill. by author. Greenwillow, 1982. ISBN 0-688-00835-6 Subj: Animals – rabbits. Family life. Glasses. Senses – sight.

Furry ill. by author. Greenwillow, 1992. ISBN 0-688-10520-3 Subj: Animals. Illness. Pets. School.

Geraldine and Mrs. Duffy ill. by author. Greenwillow, 2000. ISBN 0-688-16888-4 Subj: Activities – babysitting. Animals – pigs. Family life – brothers & sisters.

Geraldine first ill. by author. Greenwillow, 1996. ISBN 0-688-14150-1 Subj: Animals – pigs. Family life. Sibling rivalry.

Geraldine's baby brother ill. by author. Greenwillow, 1994. ISBN 0-688-12006-7 Subj: Animals – pigs. Babies. Emotions – envy, jealousy. Family life – new sibling. Sibling rivalry.

Geraldine's big snow ill. by author. Greenwillow, 1988. ISBN 0-688-07514-2 Subj: Animals – pigs. Weather – snow.

Geraldine's blanket ill. by author. Greenwillow, 1984. ISBN 0-688-02540-4 Subj: Animals – pigs. Family life. Toys – dolls.

Goodbye, Max ill. by author. Greenwillow, 1987. ISBN 0-688-06562-7 Subj: Animals – dogs. Death. Emotions – grief. Pets.

Grandfather's dream ill. by author. Greenwillow, 1994. ISBN 0-688-12340-6 Subj: Birds – cranes. Family life – grandfathers. Foreign lands – Vietnam.

Harry and Tuck ill. by author. Greenwillow, 1993. ISBN 0-688-11463-6 Subj: Character traits – individuality. Family life – brothers. Multiple births – twins. School – first day.

Henry's Fourth of July ill. by author. Greenwillow, 1985. ISBN 0-688-04013-6 Subj: Activities – picnicking. Animals – possums. Holidays – Fourth of July.

Henry's happy birthday ill. by author. Greenwillow, 1990. ISBN 0-688-09451-1 Subj: Birthdays. Parties.

Horace ill. by author. Greenwillow, 1991. ISBN 0-688-09832-0 Subj: Adoption. Animals – leopards. Character traits – being different. Self-concept.

Island baby ill. by author. Greenwillow, 1992. ISBN 0-688-10580-7 Subj: Birds – flamingos. Character traits – kindness to animals. Family life – grandfathers. Islands.

Jacob's tree ill. by author. Greenwillow, 1999. ISBN 0-688-15996-6 Subj: Animals – bears. Behavior – growing up. Concepts – size. Family life.

Lizzie's invitation ill. by author. Greenwillow, 1987. ISBN 0-688-06125-7 Subj: Birthdays. Emotions. Friendship.

Maxine in the middle ill. by author. Greenwillow, 1989. ISBN 0-688-08151-7 Subj: Animals – rabbits. Behavior – running away. Family life – brothers & sisters.

Merry Christmas, Geraldine ill. by author. Greenwillow, 1997. ISBN 0-688-14501-9 Subj: Animals – pigs. Character traits – stubbornness. Holidays – Christmas.

The new boy ill. by author. Greenwillow, 1991. ISBN 0-688-09828-2 Subj: Animals – mice. Behavior. School.

Rosata ill. by author. Greenwillow, 1995. ISBN 0-688-05321-1 Subj: Clothing – hats. Friendship.

Ten sleepy sheep ill. by author. Greenwillow, 1983. ISBN 0-688-02307-X Subj: Bedtime.

That's mine, Horace ill. by author. Greenwillow, 2000. ISBN 0-688-17159-1 Subj: Animals. Behavior. Character traits – honesty. School.

Too big ill. by author. Greenwillow, 1983. ISBN 0-688-01999-4 Subj: Animals. Sibling rivalry.

What Alvin wanted ill. by author. Greenwillow, 1990. ISBN 0-688-08934-8 Subj: Activities – babysitting. Babies. Family life – brothers & sisters.

What I see ill. by author. Harcourt, 1999. ISBN 0-15-201996-0 Subj: Rhyming text. Senses – sight.

When Francie was sick ill. by author. Greenwillow, 1985. ISBN 0-688-05434-X Subj: Family life – mothers. Illness.

Will it rain? ill. by author. Greenwillow, 1984. ISBN 0-688-03840-9 Subj: Animals. Weather – rain. Weather – storms.

Keller, Irene. *Benjamin Rabbit and the stranger danger* ill. by Dick Keller. Dodd, 1985. ISBN 0-396-08655-1 Subj: Animals – rabbits. Behavior – talking to strangers. School.

The Thingumajig book of manners ill. by Dick Keller. Ideals, 1981. ISBN 0-8249-8010-7 Subj: Character traits – appearance. Etiquette.

Keller, John G. *Krispin's fair* ill. by Ed Emberley. Little, 1976. ISBN 0-316-48652-3 Subj: Etiquette. Friendship.

Keller, Laurie. *Arnie the doughnut* ill. by author. Holt, 2003. ISBN 0-8050-6283-1 Subj: Food. Humorous stories.

Open wide: tooth school inside ill. by author. Holt, 2000. ISBN 0-8050-6192-4 Subj: Careers – dentists. Health & fitness. Teeth.

The scrambled states of America ill. by author. Holt, 1998. ISBN 0-8050-5802-8 Subj: Maps. U.S. history.

Kelley, Anne. *Daisy's discovery* ill. by Metin Salih. Barron's, 1985. ISBN 0-8120-5676-0 Subj: Animals – dogs. Behavior – lost & found possessions. Birthdays. Family life.

Kelley, Marty. *Fall is not easy* ill. by author. Zino Pr., 1998. ISBN 1-55933-234-4 Subj: Nursery rhymes. Seasons. Trees.

The rules ill. by author. Zino Pr., 2000. ISBN 1-55933-284-0 Subj: Behavior. Rhyming text.

Summer stinks ill. by author. Zino Pr., 2001. ISBN 1-55933-291-3 Subj: ABC books. Rhyming text. Seasons – summer.

Kelley, True. *Blabber Mouse* ill. by author. Dutton, 2001. ISBN 0-525-46742-4 Subj: Animals – mice. Behavior – secrets. School.

Buggly Bear's hiccup cure ill. by author. G. Stevens, 1994. ISBN 0-8368-0982-3 Subj: Animals – bears. Animals – moose. Hiccups.

Claude Monet ill. by author. Grosset, 2001. ISBN 0-448-42613-7 Subj: Activities – painting. Careers – artists. Foreign lands – France.

Day-care teddy bear ill. by author. Random House, 1990. ISBN 0-394-94305-8 Subj: Emotions – fear. Toys – bears.

Hammers and mops, pencils and pots: a first book of tools and gadgets we use around the house ill. by author. Crown, 1994. ISBN 0-517-59626-1 Subj: Dictionaries. Format, unusual – board books. Tools.

I've got chicken pox ill. by author. Dutton, 1994. ISBN 0-525-45185-4 Subj: Illness – chicken pox.

Let's eat ill. by author. Dutton, 1989. ISBN 0-525-44482-3 Subj: Food.

Look again at funny animals ill. by author. Candlewick, 1996. ISBN 1-56402-791-0 Subj: Animals. Senses – sight.

Look again at my funny family ill. by author. Candlewick, 1996. ISBN 1-56402-790-2 Subj: Family life.

Look, baby! Listen, baby! Do, baby! ill. by author. Dutton, 1987. ISBN 0-525-44320-7 Subj: Activities. Anatomy. Babies. Noise, sounds.

A Valentine for Fuzzboom ill. by author. Houghton Mifflin, 1981. ISBN 0-395-30446-6 Subj: Animals – rabbits. Holidays – Valentine's Day.

Kellogg, Steven (Stephen). *A-hunting we will go!* ill. by author. Morrow, 1998. ISBN 0-688-14945-6 Subj: Bedtime. Songs.

Aster Aardvark's alphabet adventures ill. by author. Morrow, 1987. ISBN 0-688-07257-7 Subj: ABC books. Animals. Animals – aardvarks. Birds.

A beasty story (Martin, Bill [William Ivan])

Best friends ill. by author. Dial, 1986. ISBN 0-8037-0101-2 Subj: Animals – dogs. Emotions – envy, jealousy. Friendship.

Can I keep him? ill. by author. Dial, 1971. ISBN 0-8037-0989-7 Subj: Family life. Pets.

Chicken Little ill. by author. Morrow, 1985. ISBN 0-688-05691-1 Subj: Animals. Behavior – trickery. Birds – chickens. Folk & fairy tales.

The Christmas witch ill. by author. Dial, 1992. ISBN 0-8037-1269-3 Subj: Holidays – Christmas. Witches.

Give the dog a bone ill. by author. SeaStar, 2000. ISBN 1-58717-002-7 Subj: Animals – dogs. Counting, numbers. Songs.

I was born about 10,000 years ago: a tall tale ill. by author. Morrow, 1996. ISBN 0-688-13412-2 Subj: Folk & fairy tales. Songs. Tall tales.

The island of the skog ill. by author. Dial, 1973. ISBN 0-8037-3840-4 Subj: Animals – mice. Boats, ships. Islands. Monsters.

Jack and the beanstalk (Jack and the beanstalk)

Johnny Appleseed: a tall tale ill. by author. Morrow, 1988. ISBN 0-688-06418-3 Subj: Activities – traveling. Gardens, gardening. Tall tales. Trees. U.S. history – frontier & pioneer life.

Mike Fink: a tall tale ill. by author. Morrow, 1992. ISBN 0-688-07004-3 Subj: Boats, ships. Rivers. Tall tales. U.S. history.

The mysterious tadpole ill. by author. Dial, 1977. ISBN 0-8037-6246-1 Subj: Frogs & toads. Monsters. Pets.

The mystery of the flying orange pumpkin ill. by author. Dial, 1980. ISBN 0-8037-6116-3 Subj: Holidays – Halloween. Mystery stories.

The mystery of the magic green ball ill. by author. Dial, 1978. ISBN 0-8037-6215-1 Subj: Behavior – lost & found possessions. Gypsies. Mystery stories. Toys – balls.

The mystery of the missing red mitten ill. by author. Dial, 2000. Reworked edition of: The mystery of the missing red mitten. 1974. ISBN 0-8037-2566-3 Subj: Behavior – lost & found possessions. Clothing – gloves, mittens. Mystery stories. Snowmen.

The mystery of the stolen blue paint ill. by author. Dial, 1982. ISBN 0-8037-5659-3 Subj: Mystery stories.

Paul Bunyan: a tall tale ill. by reteller. Morrow, 1984. ISBN 0-688-03850-6 Subj: Animals – oxen. Careers – lumberjacks. Tall tales. U.S. history – frontier & pioneer life.

Pecos Bill ill. by adapt. Morrow, 1986. ISBN 0-688-05872-8 Subj: Cowboys, cowgirls. Tall tales. U.S. history – frontier & pioneer life.

A penguin pup for Pinkerton ill. by author. Dial, 2001. ISBN 0-8037-2536-1 Subj: Animals – dogs. Birds – penguins. Eggs.

Pinkerton, behave! ill. by author. Dial, 1979. ISBN 0-8037-6575-4 Subj: Animals – dogs.

Prehistoric Pinkerton ill. by author. Dial, 1987. ISBN 0-8037-0323-6 Subj: Animals – dogs. Behavior – misbehavior. Dinosaurs. Museums. Prehistory.

Ralph's secret weapon ill. by author. Dial, 1983. ISBN 0-8037-7087-1 Subj: Activities – vacationing. Imagination.

A rose for Pinkerton ill. by author. Dial, 1981. ISBN 0-8037-7503-2 Subj: Animals – cats. Animals – dogs. Behavior – imitation.

Sally Ann Thunder Ann Whirlwind Crockett ill. by author. Morrow, 1995. ISBN 0-688-14043-2 Subj: Tall tales. U.S. history – frontier & pioneer life.

Santa Claus is comin' to town lyrics by Haven Gillespi; ill. by Steven Kellogg. HarperCollins, 2004. ISBN 0-066-23849-8 Subj: Holidays – Christmas. Santa Claus. Songs.

Tallyho, Pinkerton! ill. by author. Dial, 1982. ISBN 0-8037-8743-X Subj: Animals – cats. Animals – dogs. Sports – hunting.

There was an old woman (Little old lady who swallowed a fly)

The three little pigs (The three little pigs)

The three sillies (Jacobs, Joseph)

Yankee Doodle ill. by author. Four Winds, 1980, c1976. ISBN 0-590-07782-1 Subj: Music. Songs. U.S. history.

Kelly, Christie Watts. *Baby on the way* (Sears, William,)

Eat healthy, feel great (Sears, William,)

What baby needs (Sears, William,)

You can go to the potty (Sears, William,)

Kelly, Irene. *Ebbie and Flo* ill. by author. Smith & Kraus, 1997. ISBN 1-57525-115-9 Subj: Fish. Science.

Kelly, Mij. *William and the night train* ill. by Alison Jay. Farrar, 2001. ISBN 0-374-38437-1 Subj: Activities – traveling. Bedtime. Trains.

Kelly, Sheila M. *The A.D.D. book for kids* (Rotner, Shelley)

Feeling thankful (Rotner, Shelley)

Lots of grandparents (Rotner, Shelley)

Lots of moms (Rotner, Shelley)

What can you do? (Rotner, Shelley)

Kemp, Anthea. *Mr. Percy's magic greenhouse* ill. by Penny Metcalfe. David & Charles, 1988. ISBN 0-575-03870-5 Subj: Animals. Gardens, gardening. Jungle. Magic.

Kemp, Moira. *The firebird* (The firebird)

Humpty Dumpty (Mother Goose)

I'm a little teapot ill. by author. Lodestar, 1992. ISBN 0-525-67394-6 Subj: Format, unusual – board books. Rhyming text. Songs.

Knock at the door ill. by author. Lodestar, 1992. ISBN 0-525-67396-2 Subj: Format, unusual – board books. Games. Nursery rhymes. Rhyming text.

Lift-the-flap chick ill. by author. Lodestar, 1998. ISBN 0-525-67565-5 Subj: Animals. Behavior – lost. Birds – chickens. Format, unusual – toy & movable books.

Lift-the-flap kitten ill. by author. Lodestar, 1998. ISBN 0-525-67564-7 Subj: Animals. Animals – cats. Format, unusual – toy & movable books. Sleep.

Lift-the-flap mouse ill. by author. Lodestar, 1998. ISBN 0-525-67563-9 Subj: Animals – mice. Format, unusual – toy & movable books.

Lift-the-flap puppy ill. by author. Lodestar, 1998. ISBN 0-525-67566-3 Subj: Animals – dogs. Format, unusual – toy & movable books.

Round and round the garden ill. by author. Lodestar, 1992. ISBN 0-525-67395-4 Subj: Format, unusual – board books. Gardens, gardening. Rhyming text. Sports – roller skating. Toys – bears.

Kenah, Katharine. *The dream shop* ill. by Peter Catalanotto. HarperCollins, 2002. ISBN 0-688-17901-0 Subj: Dreams. Night.

Predator attack! ill. with photos. McGraw-Hill, 2004. ISBN 0-7696-3176-2 Subj: Animals.

Kendrick, Dennis. *The three billy goats Gruff* (Asbjørnsen, P. C. [Peter Christen])

Kennaway, Adrienne. *Awful aardvark* (Mwalimu)

Bushbaby ill. by author. Little, 1991. ISBN 0-316-48890-9 Subj: Animals – bushbabies. Food. Foreign lands – Africa. Reptiles – monitor lizards.

Little elephant's walk ill. by author. HarperCollins, 1992. ISBN 0-06-020378-1 Subj: Animals. Animals – elephants. Foreign lands – Africa.

Kennedy, Cindy. *The star of Christmas* ill. by Dennis Bredow. Zonderkidz, 2002. ISBN 0-310-70504-5 Subj: Foreign lands – England. Holidays – Christmas.

Kennedy, Jimmy. *The teddy bears' Christmas* adapt. & ill. by Prue Theobalds. Benford, 1999. ISBN 1-56649-241-6 Subj: Holidays – Christmas. Parties. Poetry. Toys – bears.

The teddy bears' picnic ill. by Alexandra Day. Green Tiger Pr., 1983. ISBN 0-88138-010-5 Subj: Activities – picnicking. Toys – bears.

The teddy bears' picnic ill. by Michael Hague. Holt, 1992. ISBN 0-8050-1008-4 Subj: Activities – picnicking. Poetry. Songs. Toys – bears.

The teddy bears' picnic ill. by Prue Theobalds. HarperCollins, 1987. ISBN 0-87226-153-0 Subj: Activities – picnicking. Poetry. Toys – bears.

Kennedy, Joseph. *Lucy goes to the country* ill. by John Canemaker. Alyson Wonderland, 1998. ISBN 1-55583-428-0 Subj: Animals – cats. Country. Homosexuality. Pets.

Kennedy, Kim. *Mr. Bumble* ill. by Doug Kennedy. Hyperion, 1997. ISBN 0-7868-2293-7 Subj: Fairies. Insects – bees.

Napoleon ill. by Kim & Doug Kennedy. Viking, 1995. ISBN 0-670-86404-8 Subj: Activities – playing. Animals – dogs. Weather – rain.

Kennedy, Marge M. *The book of boo!* based on the screenplay by Mitchell Kriegman; photos by John E. Barrett. Disney Pr., 2002. ISBN 0-7868-3364-5 Subj: Animals. Toys. Toys – bears.

The book of Pooh: Biglet (The book of Pooh: Biglet)

Kennedy, Richard. *The contests at Cowlick* ill. by Marc Simont. Little, 1975. Subj: Character traits – cleverness. Cowboys, cowgirls. Humorous stories. U.S. history – frontier & pioneer life.

The leprechaun's story ill. by Marcia Sewall. Dutton, 1979. ISBN 0-525-33472-6 Subj: Foreign lands – Ireland. Mythical creatures – leprechauns.

The lost kingdom of Karnica ill. by Uri Shulevitz. Sierra Club, 1979. ISBN 0-684-16164-8 Subj: Behavior – greed. Royalty.

The porcelain man ill. by Marcia Sewall. Little, 1976. ISBN 0-316-48901-8 Subj: Magic.

Kennedy, X. J. *The beasts of Bethlehem* drawings by Michael McCurdy. McElderry, 1992. ISBN 0-689-50561-2 Subj: Animals. Holidays – Christmas. Poetry. Religion.

Uncle Switch: loony limericks ill. by John O'Brien. McElderry, 1997. ISBN 0-689-80967-0 Subj: Humorous stories. Poetry.

Kenny, Kathryn. *see* Bowden, Joan Chase

Kent, Jack. *The biggest shadow in the zoo* ill. by author. Parents' Magazine Pr., 1992. ISBN 0-8368-0874-6 Subj: Animals – elephants. Shadows.

The caterpillar and the polliwog ill. by author. Prentice-Hall, 1982. ISBN 0-13-120469-6 Subj: Frogs & toads. Insects – butterflies, caterpillars. Metamorphosis.

The Christmas piñata ill. by author. Parents' Magazine Pr., 1975. ISBN 0-8193-0816-1 Subj: Foreign lands – Mexico. Holidays – Christmas.

Clotilda ill. by author. Random House, 1969. ISBN 0-394-93911-5 Subj: Character traits – kindness. Fairies.

The egg book ill. by author. Macmillan, 1975. ISBN 0-02-750200-7 Subj: Eggs. Wordless.

Hoddy doddy ill. by author. Greenwillow, 1979. ISBN 0-688-84192-9 Subj: Foreign lands – Denmark. Humorous stories.

Jack Kent's happy-ever-after book ill. by author. Random House, 1976. ISBN 0-394-93135-1 Subj: Folk & fairy tales.

Jack Kent's hokus pokus bedtime book ill. by author. Random House, 1979. ISBN 0-394-94217-5 Subj: Folk & fairy tales.

Jack Kent's merry Mother Goose (Mother Goose)

Joey ill. by author. Prentice-Hall, 1984. ISBN 0-13-510348-7 Subj: Activities – playing. Animals – kangaroos. Family life – mothers.

Joey runs away ill. by author. Prentice-Hall, 1985. ISBN 0-13-510462-9 Subj: Animals. Animals – kangaroos. Behavior – running away. Behavior – seeking better things. Family life.

Knee-high Nina ill. by author. Doubleday, 1981. ISBN 0-385-15128-4 Subj: Behavior – wishing.

Little Peep ill. by author. Prentice-Hall, 1981. ISBN 0-13-537746-3 Subj: Animals. Birds – chickens. Farms.

Mrs. Mooley ill. by author. Artists & Writers Guild, 1993. ISBN 0-307-17550-2 Subj: Animals – bulls, cows. Character traits – perseverance.

The once-upon-a-time dragon ill. by author. Harcourt, 1982. ISBN 0-15-257885-4 Subj: Bedtime. Behavior – imitation. Dragons.

Piggy Bank Gonzales ill. by author. Parents' Magazine Pr., 1979. ISBN 0-8193-0998-2 Subj: Animals – pigs. Money. Toys.

Round Robin ill. by author. Prentice-Hall, 1982. ISBN 0-13-783332-6 Subj: Birds – robins.

The scribble monster ill. by author. Harcourt, 1981. ISBN 0-15-271031-0 Subj: Behavior – misbehavior.

Silly goose ill. by author. Prentice-Hall, 1983. ISBN 0-13-809947-2 Subj: Animals – foxes. Birds – geese.

Socks for supper ill. by author. Parents' Magazine Pr., 1978. ISBN 0-8193-0965-6 Subj: Friendship.

There's no such thing as a dragon ill. by author. Golden Pr., 1975. ISBN 0-307-12525-4 Subj: Behavior – needing someone. Dragons.

Kent, Lorna. *No, no, Charlie Rascal!* ill. by author. Viking, 1989. ISBN 0-670-82512-3 Subj: Animals – cats. Behavior – misbehavior. Format, unusual.

Kenyon, Tony. *Hyacinth Hop has the hic-hops* ill. by author. Ragged Bears, 2000. ISBN 1-929927-06-1 Subj: Animals – rabbits. Hiccups.

Keo, Ena. *The crane wife* ill. by Cheryl Kirk Noll. Steck-Vaughn, 1998. ISBN 0-817-27258-5 Subj: Activities – weaving. Birds – cranes. Character traits – kindness to animals. Folk & fairy tales. Foreign lands – Japan.

Keown, Elizabeth. *Emily's snowball* ill. by Irene Trivas. Atheneum, 1992. ISBN 0-689-31518-X Subj: Activities – playing. Weather – snow.

Kepes, Juliet. *Cock-a-doodle-doo* ill. by author. Pantheon, 1978. ISBN 0-394-93494-6 Subj: Animals – tigers. Birds – chickens.

Five little monkeys ill. by author. Houghton Mifflin, 1952. Subj: Animals. Animals – monkeys. Caldecott award honor books.

Frogs, merry ill. by author. Pantheon, 1961. Subj: Frogs & toads. Hibernation.

Lady bird, quickly ill. by author. Little, 1964. Subj: Insects – ladybugs. Nursery rhymes.

Run little monkeys, run, run, run ill. by author. Pantheon, 1974. ISBN 0-394-92795-8 Subj: Animals – leopards. Animals – monkeys. Participation.

The seed that peacock planted ill. by author. Little, 1967. Subj: Birds – peacocks, peahens. Magic. Music. Plants.

The story of a bragging duck ill. by author. Houghton Mifflin, 1983. ISBN 0-395-32863-2 Subj: Behavior – boasting. Birds – ducks. Character traits – vanity.

Ker Wilson, Barbara. *see* Wilson, Barbara Ker

Kerins, Tony (Anthony). *The brave ones* ill. by author. Candlewick, 1996. ISBN 1-56402-812-7 Subj: Animals. Character traits – bravery. Forest, woods. Noise, sounds. Toys.

Tat Rabbit's treasure ill. by author. McElderry, 1993. ISBN 0-689-50553-1 Subj: Clothing. Toys.

Kerley, Barbara. *A cool drink of water* ill. by author. National Geographic, 2002. ISBN 0-7922-6723-0 Subj: Water.

Kerlin, Barbara K. *see* Walker, Barbara K. (Barbara Kerlin)

Kern, Noris. *I love you with all my heart* ill. by author. Chronicle, 1998. ISBN 0-8118-2031-9 Subj: Animals – polar bears. Emotions – love. Family life – mothers.

Kerr, Judith. *Mog and bunny* ill. by author. Knopf, 1989. ISBN 0-394-92249-2 Subj: Animals – cats. Family life. Pets. Toys.

Mog, the forgetful cat ill. by author. Collins, 2000. ISBN 0-00-195507-1 Subj: Animals – cats. Behavior – forgetfulness.

Mog's bad thing ill. by author. Collins, 2000. ISBN 0-00-198385-7 Subj: Animals – cats. Contests.

Mog's Christmas ill. by author. Collins-World, 1976. ISBN 0-529-05376-4 Subj: Animals – cats. Holidays – Christmas.

The other goose ill. by author. HarperCollins, 2002. ISBN 0-06-008583-5 Subj: Birds – geese. Emotions – loneliness.

The tiger who came to tea ill. by author. HarperCollins, 2002. ISBN 0-06-051781-6 Subj: Animals – tigers. Food.

Kerr, Phyllis Forbes. *I tricked you* ill. by author. S&S, 1990. ISBN 0-671-69408-1 Subj: Animals – mice. Behavior. School.

Kerrigan, Anthony. *Mother Goose in Spanish: Poesias de la Madre Oca* (Mother Goose)

Kerry, Lois. *see* Duncan, Lois

Kershen, L. Michael (Lloyd Michael). *Why buffalo roam* ill. by Monica Hansen. Stemmer House, 1993. ISBN 0-88-045043-6 Subj: Animals – buffaloes. Children as authors. Indians of North America – Comanche.

Keselman, Gabriela. *The gift* ill. by Pep Montserrat; trans. by Laura McKenna. Kane/Miller, 1999. ISBN 0-916291-91-X Subj: Birthdays. Family life. Gifts.

Kespert, Deborah. *On the move* (Fecher, Sarah)

Rain and shine story by Sue Barraclough; ed. by Sarah Levete; main ill. by Fran Jordan. Two-Can, 2000. ISBN 1-58728-609-2 Subj: Careers – meteorologists. Seasons. Weather.

Wild animals (Fecher, Sarah)

Kesselman, Judi R. *I can use tools* by Judi R. Kesselman & Franklynn Peterson; ill. by Tomás Gonzales. Elsevier-Nelson, 1981. ISBN 0-525-66725-3 Subj: Tools.

Kesselman, Wendy Ann. *Angelita* ill. by Norma Holt. Hill & Wang, 1970. ISBN 0-8090-2662-7 Subj: Cities, towns. Emotions – loneliness. Ethnic groups in the U.S. Ethnic groups in the U.S. – Puerto Rican Americans.

Emma ill. by Barbara Cooney. Doubleday, 1980. ISBN 0-385-13462-2 Subj: Art. Emotions – loneliness.

Sand in my shoes ill. by Ronald Himler. Hyperion, 1995. ISBN 0-7868-2045-4 Subj: Rhyming text. Sea & seashore. Seasons – summer.

There's a train going by my window ill. by Tony Chen. Doubleday, 1982. ISBN 0-385-15670-7 Subj: Activities – traveling.

Time for Jody ill. by Gerald Dumas. HarperCollins, 1975. ISBN 0-06-023139-4 Subj: Animals – groundhogs. Hibernation. Holidays – Groundhog Day. Seasons – spring.

Kessler, Brad. *Brer Rabbit and Boss Lion* coll. by Joel Chandler Harris; written by Brad Kessler; ill. by Bill Mayer. Rabbit Ears, 1996. ISBN 0-88708-273-4 Subj: Animals. Ethnic groups in the U.S. – African Americans. Folk & fairy tales.

Moses in Egypt ill. by Phil Huling. S&S, 1997. ISBN 0-689-80226-9 Subj: Jewish culture. Religion – Moses.

Kessler, Cristina. *Jubela* ill. by JoEllen McAllister Stammen. S&S, 2001. ISBN 0-689-81895-5 Subj: Animals – babies. Animals – rhinoceros. Foreign lands – Africa. Orphans.

My great-grandmother's gourd ill. by Walter Lyon Krudop. Orchard, 2000. ISBN 0-531-33284-5 Subj: Family life – grandmothers. Foreign lands – Sudan. Trees. Water. Weather – droughts.

One night: a story from the desert ill. by Ian Schoenherr. Philomel, 1995. ISBN 0-399-22726-1 Subj: Animals – goats. Behavior – growing up. Desert. Foreign lands – Africa. Night.

Kessler, Ethel. *Are there hippos on the farm?* by Ethel & Len Kessler; ill. by authors. S&S, 1987. ISBN 0-671-62066-5 Subj: Animals. Farms. Format, unusual – board books.

Are there seals in the sandbox? by Ethel & Len Kessler; ill. by Leonard P. Kessler. S&S, 1990. ISBN 0-671-70539-3 Subj: Animals – seals. Format, unusual – board books. Parks.

Do baby bears sit in chairs? by Ethel & Leonard P. Kessler; ill. by authors. Doubleday, 1961. Subj: Animals. Furniture – chairs. Rhyming text.

Is there a gorilla in the band? by Ethel & Len Kessler; ill. by Leonard P. Kessler. S&S, 1994. ISBN 0-671-88303-8 Subj: Animals – gorillas. Format, unusual – board books. Music. Musical instruments – bands.

Is there a horse in your house? by Ethel & Len Kessler; ill. by Leonard P. Kessler. Little Simon, 1990. ISBN 0-671-70540-7 Subj: Animals – horses, ponies. Format, unusual – board books.

Is there a penguin at your party? by Ethel & Len Kessler; ill. by Leonard P. Kessler. S&S, 1994. ISBN 0-671-88302-X Subj: Birds – penguins. Birthdays. Format, unusual – board books. Parties.

Is there an elephant in your kitchen? by Ethel & Len Kessler; ill. by authors. S&S, 1987. ISBN 0-671-62065-7 Subj: Animals. Format, unusual – board books. Homes, houses.

Two, four, six, eight: a book about legs by Ethel & Leonard P. Kessler; ill. by Leonard P. Kessler. Dodd, 1980. ISBN 0-396-07842-7 Subj: Counting, numbers.

Kessler, Jascha. *Rose of Mother-of-Pearl* (Olujic, Grozdana)

Kessler, Leonard P. *Are there hippos on the farm?* (Kessler, Ethel)

Are there seals in the sandbox? (Kessler, Ethel)

Are we lost, daddy? ill. by author. Grosset, 1967. Subj: Activities – vacationing. Behavior – lost. Family life. Family life – fathers.

The big mile race ill. by author. Greenwillow, 1983. ISBN 0-688-01421-6 Subj: Animals. Sports – racing.

Do baby bears sit in chairs? (Kessler, Ethel)

Do you have any carrots? ill. by Lori Pierson. Garrard, 1979. ISBN 0-8116-6074-5 Subj: Animals. Food.

Hey, diddle, diddle (Mother Goose)

Hickory dickory dock (Mother Goose)

Is there a gorilla in the band? (Kessler, Ethel)

Is there a horse in your house? (Kessler, Ethel)

Is there a penguin at your party? (Kessler, Ethel)

Is there an elephant in your kitchen? (Kessler, Ethel)

Mr. Pine's mixed-up signs ill. by author. Grosset, 1961. Subj: Glasses. Senses – sight.

Mr. Pine's purple house ill. by author. Grosset, 1965. Subj: Activities – painting. Concepts – color.

Mrs. Pine takes a trip ill. by author. Grosset, 1966. Subj: Activities – traveling.

The pirates' adventure on Spooky Island ill. by author. Garrard, 1979. ISBN 0-8116-4414-6 Subj: Islands. Pirates.

The silly Mother Goose ill. by author. Garrard, 1980. ISBN 0-8116-7401-0 Subj: Nursery rhymes.

Soup for the king ill. by author. Grosset, 1969. Subj: Careers – bakers. Food. Royalty – kings.

That's not Santa! ill. by author. Scholastic, 1994. ISBN 0-590-48140-1 Subj: Clothing – costumes. Holidays – Christmas. Santa Claus.

Two, four, six, eight: a book about legs (Kessler, Ethel)

Ketcham, Sallie. *Bach's big adventure* ill. by Timothy Bush. Orchard, 1999. ISBN 0-531-33140-7 Subj: Careers – organists. Music. Musical instruments – organs.

The Christmas bird ill. by Stacey Schuett. Augsburg Fortress, 2000. ISBN 0-8066-3871-0 Subj: Birds – robins. Folk & fairy tales. Foreign lands – England. Holidays – Christmas. Religion – Nativity.

Ketner, Mary Grace. *Ganzy remembers* ill. by Barbara Sparks. Atheneum, 1991. ISBN 0-689-31610-0 Subj: Family life – grandmothers. Family life – great-grandparents. Hospitals. Memories, memory. Old age.

Ketteman, Helen. *Armadillo tattletale* ill. by Keith Graves. Scholastic, 2000. ISBN 0-590-99723-8 Subj: Animals – armadillos. Behavior – gossip.

Armadilly chili ill. by Will Terry. A. Whitman, 2004. ISBN 0-8075-0457-2 Subj: Animals – armadillos. Behavior – sharing. Birds – bluebirds. Character traits – laziness. Food. Friendship. Frogs & toads. Spiders.

Aunt Hilarity's bustle ill. by James Warhola. S&S, 1992. ISBN 0-671-73958-1 Subj: Clothing. Family life – aunts, uncles.

Bubba the cowboy prince: a fractured Texas tale ill. by James Warhola. Scholastic, 1997. ISBN 0-590-25506-1 Subj: Animals – bulls, cows. Cowboys, cowgirls. Folk & fairy tales. Humorous stories. Parties.

Grandma's cat ill. by Marsha Lynn Winborn. Houghton Mifflin, 1996. ISBN 0-395-73094-5 Subj: Animals – cats. Family life – grandmothers. Rhyming text.

Heat wave ill. by Scott Goto. Walker, 1998. ISBN 0-8027-8645-6 Subj: Farms. Tall tales. Weather.

I remember papa ill. by Greg Shed. Dial, 1998. ISBN 0-8037-1849-7 Subj: Behavior – lost & found possessions. Careers – farmers. Family life – fathers. Sports – baseball.

Not yet, Yvette ill. by Irene Trivas. A. Whitman, 1992. ISBN 0-8075-5771-4 Subj: Birthdays. Character traits – patience. Ethnic

groups in the U.S. – African Americans. Family life – fathers. Family life – mothers.

Shoeshine Whittaker ill. by Scott Goto. Walker, 1999. ISBN 0-8027-8715-0 Subj: Careers. Tall tales. U.S. history – frontier & pioneer life.

The year of no more corn ill. by Robert Andrew Parker. Orchard, 1993. ISBN 0-531-08550-3 Subj: Farms. Plants. Weather – floods. Weather – wind.

Kettner, Christine. *An ordinary cat* ill. by author. HarperCollins, 1991. ISBN 0-06-023173-4 Subj: Animals – cats. Behavior. Pets.

Keven, Elisa. *Ernest* ill. by author. Dutton, 1989. ISBN 0-525-44515-3 Subj: Character traits – questioning. Reptiles – alligators, crocodiles.

Kevi. *Don't talk to strangers* ill. by JibJab Media. Scholastic, 2003. ISBN 0-439-31385-6 Subj: Behavior – talking to strangers. Safety.

Key, Francis Scott. *The Star Spangled Banner* ill. by Ingri & Edgar Parin D'Aulaire. Applewood, 1999. ISBN 1-55709-390-3 Subj: Songs. U.S. history. War.

The Star-Spangled Banner ill. by Paul Galdone. Crowell, 1966. ISBN 0-690-77281-5 Subj: Songs. U.S. history.

The Star Spangled Banner ill. by Dana Regan. Random House, 2002. ISBN 0-375-91596-6 Subj: Songs. U.S. history. War.

The Star-Spangled Banner ill. by Peter Spier. Doubleday, 1973. ISBN 0-385-07746-7 Subj: Songs. U.S. history.

Keyser, Marcia. *Roger on his own* ill. by Diane Dawson. Crown, 1982. ISBN 0-517-54476-8 Subj: Animals – dogs. Behavior – solitude.

Keyts, Ezra Jack. *Loose tooth* (Suen, Anastasia)

Keyworth, C. L. *New day* ill. by Carolyn Bracken. Morrow, 1986. ISBN 0-688-05922-8 Subj: Moving.

Khalsa, Dayal Kaur. *Green cat* ill. by author. Tundra, 2002. ISBN 0-88776-586-6 Subj: Animals – cats. Rhyming text.

How pizza came to Queens ill. by author. Tundra, 1989. ISBN 0-88776-231-X Subj: Emotions – loneliness. Food.

I want a dog ill. by author. Crown, 1987. ISBN 0-517-56532-3 Subj: Animals – dogs. Behavior – growing up. Family life.

My family vacation ill. by author. Potter/Crown, 1988. ISBN 0-517-56697-4 Subj: Activities – vacationing. Family life.

Sleepers ill. by author. Crown, 1988. ISBN 0-517-56917-5 Subj: Bedtime. Sleep.

The snow cat ill. by author. Potter/Crown, 1992. ISBN 0-517-59183-9 Subj: Animals – cats. Imagination – imaginary friends. Sports – ice skating. Sports – swimming.

Tales of a gambling grandma ill. by author. Crown, 1986. ISBN 0-517-56137-9 Subj: Family life – grandmothers. Games.

Khan, Rukhsana. *Bedtime ba-a-a-lk* ill. by Kristi Frost. Stoddart, 1998. ISBN 0-7737-3068-0 Subj: Bedtime. Dreams. Lullabies. Sleep.

The roses in my carpets ill. by Ronald Himler. Holiday, 1998. ISBN 0-8234-1399-3 Subj: Activities – weaving. Foreign lands – Afghanistan. Homeless. War.

Kharms, Daniil. *First, second* ill. by Marc Rosenthal; trans. from Russian by Richard Pevear. Farrar, 1996. ISBN 0-374-32339-9 Subj: Counting, numbers. Cumulative tales.

The story of a boy named Will, who went sledding down the hill ill. by Vladimir Radunsky; trans. by Jamey Gambrell. North-South, 1993. ISBN 1-55858-215-0 Subj: Animals. Cumulative tales. Rhyming text. Sports – sledding. Weather – snow.

Khdir, Kate. *Little ghost* ill. by Caroline Church. Barron's, 1991. ISBN 0-8120-6203-5 Subj: Ghosts. Holidays – Halloween. School.

Kherdian, David. *The animal* ill. by Nonny Hogrogian. Knopf, 1984. ISBN 0-394-95597-8 Subj: Animals.

By myself ill. by Nonny Hogrogian. Holt, 1993. ISBN 0-8050-2386-0 Subj: Imagination – imaginary friends. Nature. School.

The cat's midsummer jamboree ill. by Nonny Hogrogian. Putnam, 1990. ISBN 0-399-22222-7 Subj: Animals. Animals – cats. Music. Musical instruments – mandolins.

Country cat, city cat ill. by Nonny Hogrogian. Four Winds, 1978. ISBN 0-590-07482-2 Subj: Animals – cats. Poetry.

The dog writes on the window with his nose, and other poems (The dog writes on the window with his nose, and other poems)

The golden bracelet ill. by Nonny Hogrogian. Holiday, 1998. ISBN 0-8234-1362-4 Subj: Activities – weaving. Careers. Folk & fairy tales. Foreign lands – Armenia. Royalty – kings. Wizards.

If dragon flies made honey: poems (If dragon flies made honey)

Lullaby for Emily ill. by Nonny Hogrogian. Holt, 1995. ISBN 0-8050-2957-5 Subj: Lullabies.

Right now ill. by Nonny Hogrogian. Knopf, 1983. ISBN 0-394-95596-X Subj: Emotions.

Kibbey, Marsha. *My grammy* ill. by Karen Ritz. Carolrhoda, 1988. ISBN 0-87614-328-1 Subj: Character traits – patience. Family life – grandmothers. Illness. Old age.

Kidd, Bruce. *Hockey showdown* ill. by Leoung O'Young. Lorimer, 1980. ISBN 0-88862-525-X Subj: Character traits – meanness. Sports – hockey.

Kidd, Nina. *June Mountain secret* ill. by author. HarperCollins, 1991. ISBN 0-06-023168-8 Subj: Family life – fathers. Sports – fishing.

Kidd, Richard. *Almost famous Daisy!* ill. by author. S&S, 1996. ISBN 0-689-80390-7 Subj: Activities – painting. Activities – traveling. Art.

Monsieur Thermidor: a fantastic fishy tale ill. by Lindsey Kidd. Blackbirch, 1998. ISBN 1-56711-800-3 Subj: Activities – baking, cooking. Animals. Careers – chefs, cooks. Crustaceans – lobsters.

Kightley, Rosalinda. *ABC* ill. by author. Little, 1986. ISBN 0-316-49930-7 Subj: ABC books.

The farmer ill. by author. Macmillan, 1988. ISBN 0-02-750290-2 Subj: Careers – farmers. Farms.

Opposites ill. by author. Little, 1986. ISBN 0-316-49931-5 Subj: Concepts – opposites.

The postman ill. by author. Macmillan, 1988. ISBN 0-02-750270-8 Subj: Careers – postal workers. Cities, towns. Post office.

Shapes ill. by author. Little, 1986. ISBN 0-316-54005-6 Subj: Concepts – shape.

Kilborne, Sarah S. *Peach and Blue* ill. by Steve Johnson & Lou Fancher. Knopf, 1994. ISBN 0-679-93929-6 Subj: Food. Friendship. Frogs & toads.

Kilburn, Greta. *The Christmas carp* (Tornqvist, Rita)

Kilby, Don. *At a construction site* ill. by author. Kids Can, 2003. ISBN 1-55337-378-2 Subj: Careers – construction workers. Machines. Trucks.

In the city ill. by author. Kids Can, 2004. ISBN 1-55337-471-1 Subj: Cities, towns. Machines. Trucks.

In the country ill. by author. Kids Can, 2004. ISBN 1-55337-472-X Subj: Country. Machines. Tractors. Trucks.

On the road ill. by author. Kids Can, 2003. ISBN 1-55337-379-0 Subj: Roads. Trucks.

Killilea, Marie (Marie Lyons). *Newf* ill. by Ian Schoenherr. Philomel, 1992. ISBN 0-399-21875-0 Subj: Animals – cats. Animals – dogs. Friendship.

Killingback, Julia. *Busy Bears at the fire station* ill. by author. Oxford Univ. Pr., 1988. ISBN 0-19-520653-3 Subj: Animals – bears. Careers – firefighters.

Busy Bears' picnic ill. by author. Oxford Univ. Pr., 1988. ISBN 0-19-520654-1 Subj: Activities – picnicking. Animals – bears.

Monday is washing day ill. by author. Morrow, 1985. ISBN 0-688-04077-2 Subj: Activities – working. Animals – bears. Family life.

What time is it, Mrs. Bear? ill. by author. Morrow, 1985. ISBN 0-688-04076-4 Subj: Animals – bears. Family life. Time.

Killion, Bette. *Just think!* ill. by Linda Bronson. HarperFestival, 2001. ISBN 0-694-01315-3 Subj: Concepts. Family life – mothers. Rhyming text.

Kilreon, Beth. *see* Walker, Barbara K. (Barbara Kerlin)

Kilroy, Sally. *Animal noises* ill. by author. Four Winds, 1983. ISBN 0-590-07915-8 Subj: Animals. Format, unusual – board books. Noise, sounds. Wordless.

Babies' bodies ill. by author. Scholastic, 1983. ISBN 0-590-07914-X Subj: Anatomy. Babies. Format, unusual – board books.

Babies' homes ill. by author. Scholastic, 1984. ISBN 0-590-07945-X Subj: Format, unusual – board books. Homes, houses.

Babies' outings ill. by author. Scholastic, 1984. ISBN 0-590-07946-8 Subj: Format, unusual – board books.

Babies' zoo ill. by author. Scholastic, 1984. ISBN 0-590-07947-6 Subj: Animals. Format, unusual – board books. Zoos.

Baby colors ill. by author. Four Winds, 1983. ISBN 0-590-07917-4 Subj: Babies. Concepts – color. Format, unusual – board books.

The baron's hunting party ill. by author. Viking, 1987. ISBN 0-670-81313-3 Subj: Sports – hunting.

Busy babies ill. by author. Scholastic, 1984. ISBN 0-590-07948-4 Subj: Activities. Babies. Format, unusual – board books.

Copycat drawing book ill. by author. Dial, 1981. ISBN 0-8037-1116-6 Subj: Art.

Grandpa's garden ill. by author. Viking, 1986. ISBN 0-670-80338-3 Subj: Family life – grandparents. Gardens, gardening.

Market day ill. by author. Viking, 1986. ISBN 0-670-80339-1 Subj: Family life – fathers. Shopping.

Noisy homes ill. by author. Scholastic, 1983. ISBN 0-590-07916-6 Subj: Format, unusual – board books. Noise, sounds.

On the road ill. by author. Viking, 1986. ISBN 0-670-80337-5 Subj: Activities – traveling. Buses. Family life – mothers.

What a week! ill. by author. Viking, 1986. ISBN 0-670-80336-7 Subj: Family life.

Kimber, Robert. *I am a little cat* (Spanner, Helmut)

I am a little dog (Fechner, Amrei)

Kimmel, Elizabeth Cody. *My penguin Osbert* ill. by author. Candlewick, 2004. ISBN 0-7636-1699-0 Subj: Birds – penguins. Gifts. Holidays – Christmas. Humorous stories.

Kimmel, Eric A. *Anansi and the magic stick* ill. by Janet Stevens. Holiday, 2001. ISBN 0-8234-1443-4 Subj: Animals – hyenas. Folk & fairy tales. Foreign lands – Africa. Magic. Spiders.

Anansi and the moss-covered rock ill. by Janet Stevens. Holiday, 1990. ISBN 0-8234-0689-X Subj: Animals. Behavior – trickery. Folk & fairy tales. Spiders.

Anansi and the talking melon ill. by Janet Stevens. Holiday, 1994. ISBN 0-8234-1104-4 Subj: Animals. Animals – elephants. Behavior – trickery. Folk & fairy tales. Foreign lands – Africa. Spiders.

Anansi goes fishing ill. by Janet Stevens. Holiday, 1992. ISBN 0-8234-0918-X Subj: Behavior – trickery. Folk & fairy tales. Foreign lands – Africa. Reptiles – turtles, tortoises. Spiders.

Asher and the capmakers ill. by Will Hillenbrand. Holiday, 1993. ISBN 0-8234-1031-5 Subj: Fairies. Folk & fairy tales. Holidays – Hanukkah. Jewish culture.

Baba Yaga ill. by Megan Lloyd. Holiday, 1991. ISBN 0-8234-0854-X Subj: Behavior – trickery. Folk & fairy tales. Foreign lands – Russia. Witches.

Bearhead ill. by Charles Mikolaycak. Holiday, 1991. ISBN 0-8234-0902-3 Subj: Animals – bears. Folk & fairy tales. Foreign lands – Russia. Witches.

Bernal and Florinda ill. by Robert Rayevsky. Holiday, 1994. ISBN 0-8234-1089-7 Subj: Folk & fairy tales. Foreign lands – Spain.

Billy Lazroe and the King of the Sea: a tale of the Northwest ill. by Michael Steirnagle. Browndeer, 1996. ISBN 0-15-200108-5 Subj: Careers – military. Folk & fairy tales. Mythical creatures. Sailors. Sea & seashore.

The birds' gift: a Ukrainian Easter story ill. by Katya Krenina. Holiday, 1999. ISBN 0-8234-1384-5 Subj: Birds. Character traits – kindness to animals. Eggs. Folk & fairy tales. Foreign lands – Ukraine. Holidays – Easter.

Boots and his brothers ill. by Kimberly Bulcken Root. Holiday, 1992. ISBN 0-8234-0886-8 Subj: Folk & fairy tales. Foreign lands – Norway. Magic.

The Chanukkah guest ill. by Giyora Karmi. Holiday, 1990. ISBN 0-8234-0788-8 Subj: Holidays – Hanukkah. Jewish culture. Religion.

The Chanukkah tree ill. by Giyora Karmi. Holiday, 1988. ISBN 0-8234-0705-5 Subj: Folk & fairy tales. Holidays – Hanukkah. Jewish culture. Religion.

Charlie drives the stage ill. by Glen Rounds. Holiday, 1989. ISBN 0-8234-0738-1 Subj: Transportation. U.S. history – frontier & pioneer life.

Count Silvernose ill. by Omar Rayyan. Holiday, 1996. ISBN 0-8234-1216-4 Subj: Character traits – cleverness. Folk & fairy tales. Foreign lands – Italy.

Easy work! an old tale ill. by Andrew Glass. Holiday, 1998. ISBN 0-8234-1349-7 Subj: Folk & fairy tales. Foreign lands – Norway.

The Erie Canal pirates ill. by Andrew Glass. Holiday, 2002. ISBN 0-8234-1657-7 Subj: Boats, ships. Folk & fairy tales. Music. Pirates. Rhyming text. Tall tales.

Four dollars and fifty cents ill. by Glen Rounds. Holiday, 1990. ISBN 0-8234-0817-5 Subj: Cowboys, cowgirls. Crime. Humorous stories. Money. U.S. history – frontier & pioneer life.

The four gallant sisters adapt. from the Brothers Grimm; ill. by Tatyana Yuditskaya. Holt, 1992. ISBN 0-8050-1901-4 Subj: Character traits – bravery. Dragons. Folk & fairy tales. Foreign lands – Germany. Royalty.

Gershon's monster: a story for the Jewish New Year ill. by Jon J. Muth. Scholastic, 2000. ISBN 0-439-10839-X Subj: Folk & fairy tales. Holidays – Rosh Hashanah. Jewish culture. Religion.

The gingerbread man (The gingerbread boy)

The goose girl: a story from the Brothers Grimm (Grimm, Jacob)

The greatest of all ill. by Giyora Karmi. Holiday, 1991. ISBN 0-8234-0885-X Subj: Animals – mice. Folk & fairy tales. Foreign lands – Japan. Weddings.

Grizz! ill. by Andrew Glass. Holiday, 2000. ISBN 0-8234-1469-8 Subj: Cowboys, cowgirls. Devil. Folk & fairy tales.

Hershel and the Hanukkah goblins ill. by Trina Schart Hyman. Holiday, 1989. ISBN 0-8234-0769-1 Subj: Caldecott award honor books. Holidays – Hanukkah. Jewish culture. Mythical creatures – goblins. Religion.

I took my frog to the library ill. by Blanche Sims. Viking, 1990. ISBN 0-670-82418-6 Subj: Animals. Libraries. Pets.

Iron John (Grimm, Jacob)

The magic dreidels ill. by Katya Krénina. Holiday, 1996. ISBN 0-8234-1256-3 Subj: Folk & fairy tales. Holidays – Hanukkah. Jewish culture.

Nanny goat and the seven little kids (Grimm, Jacob)

The old woman and her pig (The old woman and her pig)

One Eye, Two Eyes, Three Eyes: a Hutzul tale ill. by Dirk Zimmer. Holiday, 1996. ISBN 0-8234-1183-4 Subj: Animals – goats. Folk & fairy tales. Foreign lands – Ukraine. Royalty – princes. Witches.

One winter night ill. by Jon Goodell. Doubleday, 2000. ISBN 0-385-32652-1 Subj: Holidays – Hanukkah. Jewish culture. Religion.

Onions and garlic ill. by Katya Arnold. Holiday, 1996. ISBN 0-8234-1222-9 Subj: Activities – trading. Behavior – greed. Folk & fairy tales. Jewish culture.

Pumpkinhead ill. by Steve Haskamp. Winslow, 2001. ISBN 1-890817-33-3 Subj: Activities – traveling. Anatomy – heads. Animals – squirrels. Plants.

Rimonah of the Flashing Sword ill. by Omar Rayyan. Holiday, 1995. ISBN 0-8234-1093-5 Subj: Emotions – envy, jealousy. Folk & fairy tales. Foreign lands – Egypt. Royalty – princesses.

Robin Hook, pirate hunter! ill. by Michael Dooling. Scholastic, 2001. ISBN 0-590-68199-0 Subj: Pirates.

The rooster's antlers: a story of the Chinese zodiac ill. by YongSheng Xuan. Holiday, 1999. ISBN 0-8234-1385-3 Subj: Animals. Birds – chickens. Creation. Dragons. Zodiac.

The runaway tortilla ill. by Randy Cecil. Winslow, 2000. ISBN 1-890817-18-X Subj: Behavior – running away. Cumulative tales. Folk & fairy tales.

Seven at one blow: a tale from the Brothers Grimm (Grimm, Jacob)

Sirko and the wolf: a Ukrainian tale ill. by Robert Sauber. Holiday, 1997. ISBN 0-8234-1257-1 Subj: Animals – dogs. Animals – wolves. Folk & fairy tales. Foreign lands – Ukraine.

Squash it! a true and ridiculous tale ill. by Robert Rayevsky. Holiday, 1997. ISBN 0-8234-1299-7 Subj: Folk & fairy tales. Foreign lands – Spain. Insects – fleas. Royalty – kings.

The tale of Aladdin and the wonderful lamp: a story from the Arabian Nights (Arabian Nights)

The tale of Ali Baba and the forty thieves: a story from the Arabian nights retold by Eric A. Kimmel; ill. by Will Hillenbrand. Holiday, 1996. ISBN 0-8234-1258-X Subj: Behavior – stealing. Folk & fairy tales. Foreign lands – Middle East.

Ten suns: a Chinese legend ill. by YongSheng Xuan. Holiday, 1998. ISBN 0-8234-1317-9 Subj: Animals – cats. Concepts – shape. Concepts – size. Holidays – Hanukkah. Jewish culture. Religion.

The three princes ill. by Leonard Everett Fisher. Holiday, 1994. ISBN 0-8234-1115-X Subj: Folk & fairy tales. Foreign lands – Arabia. Royalty – princes. Royalty – princesses.

Three sacks of truth ill. by Robert Rayevsky. Holiday, 1993. ISBN 0-8234-0921-X Subj: Folk & fairy tales. Foreign lands – France. Royalty – kings.

The two mountains: an Aztec legend ill. by Leonard Everett Fisher. Holiday, 2000. ISBN 0-8234-1504-X Subj: Folk & fairy tales. Foreign lands – Mexico. Indians of North America – Aztec. Mountains. Volcanoes.

The valiant red rooster: a story from Hungary ill. by Katya Arnold. Holt, 1994. ISBN 0-8050-2781-5 Subj: Birds – chickens. Folk & fairy tales. Foreign lands – Hungary. Royalty – sultans.

Why the snake crawls on its belly ill. by Allen Davis. Pitspopany, 2001. ISBN 1-930143-20-6 Subj: Folk & fairy tales – pourquoi tales. Religion. Reptiles – snakes.

Why worry? ill. by Beth Cannon. Pantheon, 1979. ISBN 0-394-94010-5 Subj: Insects – crickets. Insects – grasshoppers. Music. Songs.

The witch's face: a Mexican tale ill. by Fabricio Vandenbroeck. Holiday, 1993. ISBN 0-8234-1038-2 Subj: Folk & fairy tales. Foreign lands – Mexico. Witches.

Zigazak! ill. by Jon Goodell. Doubleday, 2001. ISBN 0-385-32652-1 Subj: Careers – clergy. Holidays – Hanukkah. Jewish culture.

Kimmel, Haven. *Orville, a dog story* ill. by Robert Andrew Parker. Clarion, 2003. ISBN 0-618-15955-X Subj: Animals – dogs. Emotions. Farms.

Kimmel, Margaret Mary. *Magic in the mist* ill. by Trina Schart Hyman. Atheneum, 1975. ISBN 0-689-50026-2 Subj: Dragons. Magic. Wizards.

Kimmelman, Leslie. *Dance, sing, remember* ill. by Ora Eitan. HarperCollins, 2000. ISBN 0-06-027726-2 Subj: Holidays. Jewish culture. Religion.

Frannie's fruits ill. by Petra Mathers. HarperCollins, 1989. ISBN 0-06-023143-2 Subj: Animals – dogs. Careers – storekeepers. Family life.

Hanukkah lights, Hanukkah nights ill. by John Himmelman. HarperCollins, 1992. ISBN 0-06-020369-2 Subj: Family life. Holidays – Hanukkah. Jewish culture. Religion.

Hooray! it's Passover! ill. by John Himmelman. HarperCollins, 1996. ISBN 0-06-024674-X Subj: Family life. Holidays – Passover. Jewish culture. Religion.

Me and Nana ill. by Marilee Robin Burton. HarperCollins, 1990. ISBN 0-06-023163-7 Subj: Family life – grandmothers. Friendship.

Round the turkey ill. by Nancy Cote. A. Whitman, 2002. ISBN 0-8075-7131-8 Subj: Family life. Holidays – Thanksgiving. Rhyming text.

The runaway latkes ill. by Paul Yalowitz. A. Whitman, 2000. ISBN 0-8075-7176-8 Subj: Behavior – running away. Holidays – Hanukkah. Jewish culture. Religion.

Sound the shofar! a story for Rosh Hashanah and Yom Kippur ill. by John Himmelman. HarperCollins, 1998. ISBN 0-06-027498-0 Subj: Family life – aunts, uncles. Holidays – Rosh Hashanah. Holidays – Yom Kippur. Jewish culture. Religion.

Kimpton, Diana. *The bear Santa Claus forgot* ill. by Anna Kiernan. Scholastic, 1994. ISBN 0-590-26564-4 Subj: Holidays – Christmas. Santa Claus. Toys – bears.

Kimura, Yasuko. *Fergus and the sea monster* ill. by author. McGraw-Hill, 1978. ISBN 0-07-034559-7 Subj: Animals – dogs. Friendship. Monsters. Sea & seashore.

Kimura, Yuichi. *One stormy night . . .* ill. by Hiroshi Abe. Kodansha, 2003. ISBN 4-7700-2970-5 Subj: Animals – goats. Animals – wolves. Emotions – fear. Foreign lands – Japan. Friendship. Weather – storms.

One sunny day . . . ill. by Hiroshi Abe. Kodansha, 2003. ISBN 4-7700-2971-3 Subj: Animals – goats. Animals – wolves. Emotions – fear. Foreign lands – Japan. Friendship. Nature.

Kincaid, Lucy. *The three billygoats Gruff* (Asbjørnsen, P. C. [Peter Christen])

Kinerk, Robert. *Clorinda* ill. by Steven Kellogg. S&S, 2003. ISBN 0-689-86449-3 Subj: Activities – dancing. Animals – bulls, cows. Ballet. Character traits – perseverance. Rhyming text.

Slim and Miss Prim ill. by Jim Harris. Rising Moon, 1998. ISBN 0-8735-8689-1 Subj: Cowboys, cowgirls. Crime. Emotions – love. Rhyming text.

Kines, Pat Decker. *see* Tapio, Pat Decker

King, B. A. *The very best Christmas tree* ill. by Michael McCurdy. Godine, 1984. ISBN 0-87923-539-X Subj: Holidays – Christmas. Trees.

King, Bob. *Sitting on the farm* ill. by Bill Slavin. Orchard, 1992. ISBN 0-531-08585-6 Subj: Activities – picnicking. Animals. Cumulative tales. Music. Songs. Telephone.

King, Christopher L. *The boy who ate the moon* ill. by John Wallner. Putnam, 1988. ISBN 0-399-21459-3 Subj: Activities – flying. Moon.

The vegetables go to bed ill. by Mary GrandPré. Crown, 1994. ISBN 0-517-59126-X Subj: Bedtime. Food. Rhyming text.

King, Dave. *Counting book* photos by author. DK, 1998. ISBN 0-7894-3448-2 Subj: Counting, numbers. Picture puzzles.

King, Deborah. *Cloudy* ill. by author. Putnam, 1990. ISBN 0-399-22242-1 Subj: Animals – cats.

Custer: the true story of a horse ill. by author. Putnam, 1992. ISBN 0-399-22147-6 Subj: Animals – horses, ponies. Friendship.

The flight of the snow geese ill. by author. Orchard, 1998. ISBN 0-531-30088-9 Subj: Birds – geese. Seasons – winter.

Sirius and Saba ill. by author. David & Charles, 1982. ISBN 0-241-10599-4 Subj: Animals – dogs. Islands.

King, Elizabeth. *Backyard sunflower* photos by author. Dutton, 1993. ISBN 0-525-45082-3 Subj: Flowers. Gardens, gardening. Seeds.

Pumpkin patch photos by author. Dutton, 1990. ISBN 0-525-44640-0 Subj: Gardens, gardening. Holidays – Halloween.

King, Larry L. *Because of Lozo Brown* ill. by Amy Schwartz. Viking, 1988. ISBN 0-670-81031-2 Subj: Friendship. Imagination. Rhyming text.

King, Patricia. *Mable the whale* ill. by Katherine Evans. Follett, 1958. ISBN 0-695-35443-4 Subj: Animals – whales.

King, Stephen Michael. *Emily loves to bounce* ill. by author. Philomel, 2003. ISBN 0-399-23886-7 Subj: Activities – jumping. Activities – playing. Rhyming text.

Henry and Amy (right-way-round and upside down) ill. by author. Walker, 1998. ISBN 0-8027-8687-1 Subj: Character traits – individuality. Concepts – opposites. Friendship.

King, Thomas. *Coyote sings to the moon* ill. by Johnny Wales. West-Winds, 2001. ISBN 1-55868-642-8 Subj: Animals. Animals – coyotes. Creation. Folk & fairy tales. Moon.

Kingman, Lee. *Catch the baby!* ill. by Susanna Natti. Viking, 1989. ISBN 0-670-81751-1 Subj: Family life. Rhyming text.

Peter's long walk ill. by Barbara Cooney. Doubleday, 1953. Subj: Activities – walking. Animals. Country. Friendship.

Pierre Pigeon ill. by Arnold Edwin Bare. Houghton Mifflin, 1943. Subj: Birds – pigeons. Caldecott award honor books.

Kingsland, Robin. *Bus stop bop* ill. by Alex Ayliffe. Viking, 1991. ISBN 0-670-83919-1 Subj: Activities – dancing. Buses. Music. Musical instruments – guitars.

King-Smith, Dick. *All pigs are beautiful* ill. by Anita Jeram. Candlewick, 1993. ISBN 1-56402-148-3 Subj: Animals – pigs.

Cuckoobush farm ill. by Kazuko. Greenwillow, 1988. ISBN 0-688-07681-5 Subj: Farms. Multiple births – twins. Seasons.

Dick King-Smith's Alphabeasts ill. by Quentin Blake. Macmillan, 1992. ISBN 0-02-750720-3 Subj: ABC books. Language. Poetry.

Farmer Bungle forgets ill. by Martin Honeysett. Atheneum, 1987. ISBN 0-689-31370-5 Subj: Behavior – forgetfulness. Farms. Humorous stories.

I love guinea pigs ill. by Anita Jeram. Candlewick, 1995. ISBN 1-56402-389-3 Subj: Animals – guinea pigs. Pets.

Puppy love ill. by Anita Jeram. Candlewick, 1997. ISBN 0-7636-0116-0 Subj: Animals – dogs. Emotions – love. Pets.

The spotty pig ill. by Mary Wormell. Farrar, 1997. ISBN 0-374-37154-7 Subj: Animals – pigs. Self-concept.

Kinnell, Galway. *How the alligator missed breakfast* ill. by Lynn Munsinger. Houghton Mifflin, 1982. ISBN 0-395-32436-X Subj: Reptiles – alligators, crocodiles.

Kinney, Jean. *What does the sun do?* ill. by Cle Kinney. W. R. Scott, 1967. Subj: Sun.

Kinsey, Elizabeth. *see* Clymer, Eleanor Lowenton

Kinsey, Helen. *The bear that heard crying* (Kinsey-Warnock, Natalie)

Kinsey-Warnock, Natalie. *The bear that heard crying* by Natalie Kinsey-Warnock & Helen Kinsey; ill. by Ted Rand. Cobblehill, 1993. ISBN 0-525-65103-9 Subj: Animals – bears. Behavior – lost. U.S. history – frontier & pioneer life.

A Christmas like Helen's ill. by Mary Azarian. Houghton, 2004. ISBN 0-618-23137-4 Subj: Family life. Farms. Holidays – Christmas.

A farm of her own ill. by Kathleen Kolb. Dutton, 2001. ISBN 0-525-46507-3 Subj: Family life – aunts, uncles. Family life – cousins. Farms.

The fiddler of the Northern Lights ill. by Leslie W. Bowman. Cobblehill, 1996. ISBN 0-525-65143-8 Subj: Family life – grandfathers. Folk & fairy tales. Foreign lands – Canada. Music. Musical instruments – violins. Northern lights.

From dawn till dusk ill. by Mary Azarian. Houghton, 2002. ISBN 0-618-18655-7 Subj: Family life. Farms. Seasons.

On a starry night ill. by David McPhail. Orchard, 1994. ISBN 0-531-08670-4 Subj: Emotions – fear. Family life. Nature. Night.

The summer of Stanley ill. by Donald Gates. Cobblehill, 1997. ISBN 0-525-65177-2 Subj: Animals – goats. Birthdays. Family life – brothers & sisters. Farms.

When spring comes ill. by Stacey Schuett. Dutton, 1993. ISBN 0-525-45008-4 Subj: Family life – fathers. Farms. Seasons – spring.

The wild horses of Sweetbriar ill. by Ted Rand. Dutton, 1990. ISBN 0-525-65015-6 Subj: Animals – horses, ponies. Islands. Seasons – winter.

Wilderness cat ill. by Mark Graham. Cobblehill, 1992. ISBN 0-525-65068-7 Subj: Animals – cats. Foreign lands – Canada. Moving.

Kinter, Judith. *King of magic, man of glass* ill. by Dirk Zimmer. Clarion, 1998. ISBN 0-395-79730-6 Subj: Behavior – greed. Folk & fairy tales. Foreign lands – Germany.

Kipling, Rudyard. *The beginning of the armadillos* ill. by Lorinda Bryan Cauley. Harcourt, 1985. ISBN 0-15-206380-3 Subj: Animals – armadillos.

The beginning of the armadillos ill. by Charles Keeping. HarperCollins, 1983. ISBN 0-911745-03-3 Subj: Animals – armadillos.

The crab that played with the sea ill. by Michael Foreman. HarperCollins, 1983. ISBN 0-911745-06-8 Subj: Crustaceans – crabs. Sea & seashore.

The elephant's child ill. by Louise Brierley. HarperCollins, 1985. ISBN 0-87226-030-5 Subj: Animals. Animals – elephants. Character traits – curiosity. Foreign lands – Africa.

The elephant's child ill. by Lorinda Bryan Cauley. Harcourt, 1983. ISBN 0-15-225385-8 Subj: Animals. Animals – elephants. Character traits – curiosity. Foreign lands – Africa.

The elephant's child ill. by Tim Raglin. Knopf, 1986. ISBN 0-394-88401-9 Subj: Animals. Animals – elephants. Character traits – curiosity. Foreign lands – Africa.

The elephant's child ill. by John A. Rowe. North-South, 1995. ISBN 1-55858-370-X Subj: Animals. Animals – elephants. Character traits – curiosity. Foreign lands – Africa. Reptiles – alligators, crocodiles.

How the camel got his hump ill. by Quentin Blake. HarperCollins, 1985. ISBN 0-87226-029-1 Subj: Animals. Animals – camels. Behavior – misbehavior. Folk & fairy tales – pourquoi tales. Foreign lands – Africa.

How the camel got his hump ill. by Tim Raglin. Rabbit Ears, 1989. ISBN 0-88708-096-0 Subj: Animals. Animals – camels. Behavior – misbehavior. Folk & fairy tales – pourquoi tales. Foreign lands – Africa.

How the camel got his hump ill. by Lisbeth Zwerger. North-South, 2001. ISBN 0-7358-1483-X Subj: Animals. Animals – camels. Behavior – misbehavior. Folk & fairy tales – pourquoi tales. Foreign lands – Africa.

How the elephant got his trunk (Richards, Jean)

How the leopard got his spots ill. by Caroline Ebborn. HarperCollins, 1986. ISBN 0-87226-072-0 Subj: Animals – leopards. Folk & fairy tales – pourquoi tales.

How the leopard got his spots ill. by Lori Lohstoeter. Picture Book Studio, 1989. ISBN 0-88708-112-6 Subj: Animals – leopards. Folk & fairy tales – pourquoi tales.

How the rhinoceros got his skin ill. by Leonard Weisgard. Walker, 1974. ISBN 0-8027-6150-X Subj: Anatomy – skin. Animals – rhinoceros. Folk & fairy tales – pourquoi tales.

The miracle of the mountain adapt. by Aroline Arnett Beecher Leach; ill. by Willi Baum. Addison-Wesley, 1969. Adapt. from The Miracle of Purun Bhagat, by Rudyard Kipling. Subj: Animals. Foreign lands – India. Religion.

Rikki-tikki-tavi ill. by Lambert Davis. Harcourt, 1992. ISBN 0-15-267015-7 Subj: Animals – mongooses. Character traits – bravery. Character traits – cleverness. Foreign lands – India. Reptiles – snakes.

Rikki-tikki-tavi adapt. & ill. by Jerry Pinkney. Morrow, 1997. ISBN 0-688-14321-0 Subj: Animals – mongooses. Character traits – bravery. Character traits – cleverness. Foreign lands – India. Reptiles – snakes.

The sing-song of old man kangaroo ill. by Michael C. Taylor. HarperCollins, 1986. ISBN 0-87226-073-9 Subj: Animals – kangaroos. Foreign lands – Australia.

Kirby, David K. *The bear who came to stay* (Woodman, Allen)

Cows are going to Paris by David Kirby & Allen Woodman; ill. by Chris L. Demarest. Boyds Mills, 1991. ISBN 0-878093-11-8 Subj: Animals – bulls, cows. Foreign lands – France. Trains.

Kirk, Barbara. *Grandpa, me and our house in the tree* ill. by author. Macmillan, 1978. ISBN 0-02-750750-5 Subj: Family life – grandfathers. Homes, houses. Trees.

Kirk, Daniel. *Bigger* ill. by author. Putnam, 1998. ISBN 0-399-23127-7 Subj: Behavior – growing up. Concepts – size. Self-concept.

Breakfast at the Liberty Diner ill. by author. Hyperion, 1997. ISBN 0-7868-2243-0 Subj: Handicaps – physical handicaps. Restaurants. Trains. U.S. history.

Bus stop, bus go ill. by author. Putnam, 2001. ISBN 0-399-23333-4 Subj: Animals – hamsters. Buses. Rhyming text.

Go! ill. by author. Hyperion, 2001. ISBN 0-7868-0305-3 Subj: Music. Songs. Transportation.

Hush, little alien ill. by author. Hyperion, 1999. ISBN 0-7868-2469-7 Subj: Aliens. Bedtime. Lullabies.

Jack and Jill ill. by author. Putnam, 2003. ISBN 0-399-23553-1 Subj: Behavior – wishing. Humorous stories. Nursery rhymes.

Lucky's twenty-four hour garage ill. by author. Hyperion, 1996. ISBN 0-7868-2168-X Subj: Automobiles. Careers – mechanics.

Moondogs ill. by author. Putnam, 1999. ISBN 0-399-23128-5 Subj: Animals – dogs. Moon. Rhyming text. Space & space ships.

The snow family ill. by author. Hyperion, 2000. ISBN 0-7868-2244-9 Subj: Family life – parents. Rhyming text. Snowmen.

Trash trucks! ill. by author. Putnam, 1997. ISBN 0-399-22927-2 Subj: Careers – sanitation workers. Rhyming text. Trucks.

Kirk, David. *Little bird, Biddle bird* ill. by author. Scholastic, 2001. ISBN 0-439-26092-2 Subj: Birds. Food. Rhyming text. Self-concept.

Little bunny, Biddle bunny ill. by author. Scholastic, 2002. ISBN 0-439-33819-0 Subj: Animals – rabbits. Rhyming text. Seasons.

Little Miss Spider ill. by author. Scholastic, 1999. ISBN 0-439-08389-3 Subj: Emotions – love. Family life – mothers. Rhyming text. Spiders.

Little Miss Spider at Sunny Patch School ill. by author. Scholastic, 2000. ISBN 0-439-08727-9 Subj: Insects. Rhyming text. School – first day. Spiders.

Little pig, Biddle pig ill. by author. Scholastic, 2001. ISBN 0-439-30575-6 Subj: Animals – pigs. Character traits – cleanliness. Rhyming text.

Miss Spider's ABC ill. by author. Scholastic, 1998. ISBN 0-590-28279-4 Subj: ABC books. Birthdays. Insects. Rhyming text. Spiders.

Miss Spider's new car ill. by author. Scholastic, 1997. ISBN 0-590-30713-4 Subj: Automobiles. Insects. Rhyming text. Spiders.

Miss Spider's tea party ill. by author. Scholastic, 1994. ISBN 0-590-47724-2 Subj: Emotions – fear. Parties. Rhyming text. Spiders.

Nova's ark ill. by author. Scholastic, 1999. ISBN 0-590-28208-5 Subj: Machines. Plants. Robots. School – field trips. Space & space ships.

Kirk, Heidi. *Carly* (Fuchshuber, Annegert)

Kirkpatrick, Rena K. *Leaves* ill. by Annabel Milne & Peter Stebbing. Raintree, 1991. Rev. ed. of: Look at leaves. ISBN 0-8172-2353-3 Subj: Plants. Science.

Look at flowers ill. by Annabel Milne & Peter Stebbing. Raintree, 1978. ISBN 0-8393-0061-1 Subj: Flowers. Science.

Magnets ill. by Ann Knight. Raintree, 1985. Rev. ed. of: Look at magnets. ISBN 0-8172-2354-1 Subj: Science.

Pond life ill. by Annabel Milne & Peter Stebbing. Raintree, 1985. Rev. ed. of: Look at pond life. ISBN 0-8172-2355-X Subj: Science.

Rainbow colors ill. by Anna Barnard. Raintree, 1978. Rev. ed. of: Look at rainbow colors. ISBN 0-8172-2356-8 Subj: Concepts – color. Science. Weather – rainbows.

Seeds and weeds ill. by Debbie King. Raintree, 1985. ISBN 0-8172-2357-6 Subj: Plants. Science.

Trees ill. by Jo Worth & Ann Knight. Raintree, 1985. Rev. ed. of: Look at trees. ISBN 0-8172-2359-2 Subj: Science. Trees.

Weather ill. by Janetta Lewin. Raintree, 1985. Rev. ed. of: Look at weather. ISBN 0-8172-2360-6 Subj: Science. Weather.

Kirn, Ann. *Beeswax catches a thief: from a Congo folktale* ill. by author. Norton, 1968. Subj: Animals. Ethnic groups in the U.S. – African Americans.

I spy ill. by author. Norton, 1965. Subj: Birds – owls. Crime.

The tale of a crocodile: from a Congo folktale ill. by author. Norton, 1968. Subj: Animals – rabbits. Fire. Folk & fairy tales. Foreign lands – Africa. Reptiles – alligators, crocodiles.

Kirschner, David. *Fievel's big showdown* (Herman, Gail)

Kirstein, Lincoln. *Puss in boots* (Perrault, Charles)

Kirtland, G. B. *see* Joslin, Sesyle

Kiser, Kevin. *The birthday thing* (Kiser, SuAnn)

Buzzy Widget ill. by John O'Brien. Cavendish, 1999. ISBN 0-7614-5057-2 Subj: Activities – making things. Behavior – needing someone. Emotions. Robots.

Sherman the sheep ill. by Rowan Barnes-Murphy. Macmillan, 1994. ISBN 0-02-750825-0 Subj: Animals – sheep.

Kiser, SuAnn. *The birthday thing* by SuAnn & Kevin Kiser; ill. by Yossi Abolafia. Greenwillow, 1989. ISBN 0-688-07773-0 Subj: Activities – making things. Birthdays. Family life.

The catspring somersault flying one-handed flip-flop ill. by Peter Catalanotto. Orchard, 1993. ISBN 0-531-08643-7 Subj: Behavior – running away. Family life. Farms. Sibling rivalry.

The hog call to end all! ill. by John Steven Gurney. Orchard, 1994. ISBN 0-531-08676-3 Subj: Animals – pigs. Country. Fairs, festivals. Farms.

Kishida, Eriko. *The hippo boat* ill. by Chiyoko Nakatani. Collins, 1967. Subj: Animals – hippopotamuses. Weather – floods. Weather – rain. Zoos.

The lion and the bird's nest ill. by Chiyoko Nakatani. Crowell, 1972. Subj: Animals – lions. Birds. Character traits – helpfulness. Friendship.

Kismaric, Carole. *A gift from Saint Nicholas* (Timmermans, Felix)

The rumor of Pavel and Paali: a Ukrainian folktale ill. by Charles Mikolaycak. HarperCollins, 1988. ISBN 0-06-023278-1 Subj: Behavior – greed. Character traits – meanness. Folk & fairy tales. Multiple births – twins.

Kitamura, Satoshi. *Captain Toby* ill. by author. Dutton, 1988. ISBN 0-525-44414-9 Subj: Animals – cats. Family life – grandparents. Sea & seashore. Weather – storms.

Comic adventures of Boots ill. by author. Farrar, 2002. ISBN 0-374-31455-1 Subj: Animals – cats.

From acorn to zoo and everything in between in alphabetical order ill. by author. Farrar, 1992. ISBN 0-374-32470-0 Subj: ABC books.

Lily takes a walk ill. by author. Dutton, 1987. ISBN 0-525-44333-9 Subj: Animals – dogs. Emotions – fear. Imagination.

Me and my cat? ill. by author. Farrar, 2000. ISBN 0-374-34906-1 Subj: Animals – cats. Magic. Witches.

Sheep in wolves' clothing ill. by author. Farrar, 1996. ISBN 0-374-36780-9 Subj: Animals – sheep. Animals – wolves. Behavior – trickery. Careers – detectives. Mystery stories.

What's inside? ill. by author. Farrar, 1985. ISBN 0-374-38306-5 Subj: ABC books.

When sheep cannot sleep ill. by author. Farrar, 1986. ISBN 0-374-38311-1 Subj: Animals – sheep. Bedtime. Counting, numbers.

Kitchen, Bert. *And so they build* ill. by author. Candlewick, 1993. ISBN 1-56402-217-X Subj: Animals. Homes, houses.

Animal alphabet ill. by author. Dial, 1984. ISBN 0-8037-0117-9 Subj: ABC books. Animals. Wordless.

Animal numbers ill. by author. Dial, 1987. ISBN 0-8037-0459-3 Subj: Animals. Counting, numbers.

Pig in a barrow ill. by author. Dial, 1991. ISBN 0-8037-0943-9 Subj: Animals. Rhyming text.

Somewhere today ill. by author. Candlewick, 1992. ISBN 1-56402-074-6 Subj: Activities. Animals.

Tenrec's twigs ill. by author. Putnam, 1989. ISBN 0-399-21720-7 Subj: Animals. Foreign lands – Africa. Jungle.

When hunger calls ill. by author. Candlewick, 1994. ISBN 1-56402-316-8 Subj: Animals. Food. Nature.

Kite, L. Patricia. *Dandelion adventures* ill. by Anca Hariton. Millbrook, 1998. ISBN 0-7613-0037-6 Subj: Plants. Seasons – spring. Seeds.

Down in the sea. The jellyfish ill. by author. A. Whitman, 1993. ISBN 0-8075-1712-7 Subj: Fish. Sea & seashore.

Down in the sea. The octopus ill. by author. A. Whitman, 1993. ISBN 0-8075-1715-1 Subj: Octopuses. Sea & seashore.

Kitt, Tamaram. *see* De Regniers, Beatrice Schenk

Klages, Simone. *Now, now Markus* (Auer, Martin)

Klein, Arthur Luce. *Puss in boots* (Perrault, Charles)

Klein, Leonore. *Henri's walk to Paris* ill. by Saul Bass. Addison-Wesley, 1962. Subj: Activities – walking. Foreign lands – France.

Just like you ill. by Audrey Walters. Harvey House, 1968. Subj: Ethnic groups in the U.S.

Old, older, oldest ill. by Leonard P. Kessler. Hastings House, 1983. ISBN 0-8038-5396-3 Subj: Old age.

Klein, Norma. *Girls can be anything* ill. by Roy Doty. Dutton, 1973. ISBN 0-525-30662-5 Subj: Careers.

Visiting Pamela ill. by Kay Chorao. Dial, 1979. ISBN 0-8037-9308-1 Subj: Behavior – sharing. Friendship.

Klein, Robin. *Thing* ill. by Alison Lester. Oxford Univ. Pr., 1983. ISBN 0-19-554330-0 Subj: Dinosaurs. Pets.

Klein, Suzanne. *An elephant in my bed* ill. by Sharleen Pederson. Follett, 1974. ISBN 0-695-40476-8 Subj: Animals – elephants. Furniture – beds.

Kleven, Elisa. *The dancing deer and the foolish hunter* ill. by author. Dutton, 2002. ISBN 0-525-46832-3 Subj: Activities – dancing. Animals – deer. Birds. Ecology. Forest, woods.

Ernst ill. by author. Tricycle, 2002. ISBN 1-58246-053-1 Subj: Birthdays. Reptiles – alligators, crocodiles.

The lion and the little red bird ill. by author. Dutton, 1992. ISBN 0-525-44898-5 Subj: Animals – lions. Birds. Careers – artists. Concepts – color.

A monster in the house ill. by author. Dutton, 1998. ISBN 0-525-45973-1 Subj: Babies. Family life – brothers. Monsters.

The paper princess ill. by author. Dutton, 1994. ISBN 0-525-45231-1 Subj: Activities – drawing. Activities – flying. Paper. Royalty – princesses.

The puddle pail ill. by author. Dutton, 1997. ISBN 0-525-45803-4 Subj: Behavior – collecting things. Family life – brothers. Reptiles – alligators, crocodiles.

Sun bread ill. by author. Dutton, 2001. ISBN 0-525-46674-6 Subj: Animals. Careers – bakers. Food. Rhyming text. Sun.

Kleven, Sandy. *The right touch: a read aloud story to help prevent child sexual abuse* ill. by Jody Bergsma. Illumination Arts, 1997. ISBN 0-935699-10-4 Subj: Child abuse. Family life.

Klimo, Kate. *Farm house* (Farm house)

Firehouse (Firehouse)

Gerald McBoing Boing (Seuss, Dr.)

Mother Goose house (Mother Goose)

Mouse house (Mouse house)

Sing a song of sixpence (Mother Goose)

Klimowicz, Barbara. *The strawberry thumb* ill. by Gloria Kamen. Abingdon, 1968. Subj: Problem solving. Puppets. Rhyming text. Thumb sucking.

Kline, Suzy. *Don't touch!* ill. by Dora Leder. A. Whitman, 1985. ISBN 0-8075-1707-0 Subj: Activities – playing. Behavior – misbehavior.

Ooops! ed. by Ann Fay; ill. by Dora Leder. A. Whitman, 1988. ISBN 0-8075-6122-3 Subj: Behavior – bad day. Behavior – carelessness.

Shhhh! ill. by Dora Leder. A. Whitman, 1984. ISBN 0-8075-7321-3 Subj: Noise, sounds.

Klingel, Cynthia Fitterer. *Crocodiles* by Cynthia Klingel & Robert B. Noyed; ill. with photos. Child's World, 2002. ISBN 1-56766-942-5 Subj: Reptiles – alligators, crocodiles.

Dancers by Cynthia Klingel & Robert B. Noyed; ill. with photos. Child's World, 2002. ISBN 1-56766-939-5 Subj: Activities – dancing. Careers – dancers.

Deserts by Cynthia Klingel & Robert B. Noyed; ill. with photos. Child's World, 2001. ISBN 1-56766-972-7 Subj: Animals. Desert. Nature. Science.

Farmers by Cynthia Klingel & Robert B. Noyed; ill. with photos. Child's World, 2002. ISBN 1-56766-940-9 Subj: Careers – farmers. Farms.

Firefighters by Cynthia Klingel & Robert B. Noyed; ill. with photos. Child's World, 2002. ISBN 1-56766-938-7 Subj: Careers – firefighters. Fire.

Forests by Cynthia Klingel & Robert B. Noyed; ill. with photos. Child's World, 2002. ISBN 1-56766-973-5 Subj: Animals. Forest, woods. Nature. Plants.

Grizzly bears by Cynthia Klingel & Robert B. Noyed; ill. with photos. Child's World, 2002. ISBN 1-56766-943-3 Subj: Animals – bears.

Halloween by Cynthia Klingel & Robert B. Noyed; ill. with photos. Child's World, 2002. ISBN 1-56766-955-7 Subj: Holidays – Halloween.

Manatees by Cynthia Klingel & Robert B. Noyed; ill. with photos. Child's World, 2002. ISBN 1-56766-944-1 Subj: Animals – manatees.

Oceans by Cynthia Klingel & Robert B. Noyed; ill. with photos. Child's World, 2002. ISBN 1-56766-974-3 Subj: Animals. Plants. Sea & seashore.

Paul Revere's ride by Cynthia Klingel & Robert B. Noyed; ill. with photos. Child's World, 2002. ISBN 1-56766-960-3 Subj: U.S. history. War.

Postal workers by Cynthia Klingel & Robert B. Noyed; ill. with photos. Child's World, 2002. ISBN 1-56766-941-7 Subj: Careers – postal workers. Letters, cards.

Rosa Parks by Cynthia Klingel & Robert B. Noyed; ill. with photos. Child's World, 2002. ISBN 1-56766-951-4 Subj: Ethnic groups in the U.S. – African Americans. Prejudice. U.S. history.

Soccer by Cynthia Klingel & Robert B. Noyed; ill. with photos. Child's World, 2001. ISBN 1-56766-805-4 Subj: Sports – soccer.

Thanksgiving by Cynthia Klingel & Robert B. Noyed; ill. with photos. Child's World, 2003. ISBN 1-56766-956-5 Subj: Holidays – Thanksgiving.

Timber wolves by Cynthia Klingel & Robert B. Noyed; ill. with photos. Child's World, 2002. ISBN 1-56766-945-X Subj: Animals – wolves.

Underground by Cynthia Klingel & Robert B. Noyed; ill. with photos. Child's World, 2002. ISBN 1-56766-975-1 Subj: Ecology.

Klinting, Lars. *Regal the golden eagle* trans. by Alan Bernstein; ill. by author. Farrar, 1988. ISBN 91-2958-774-3 Subj: Behavior – growing up. Birds – eagles. Emotions – fear.

Kliphuis, Christine. *Robbie and Ronnie* ill. by Charlotte Dematons. North-South, 2002. ISBN 0-7358-1627-1 Subj: Behavior – bullying. Concepts – size. Friendship. Sports – swimming.

Kliros, Thea. *The three bears [board book]* (The three bears)

The velveteen rabbit (Bianco, Margery Williams)

Klockner, Karen M. *The black sheep* (Heck, Elisabeth)

The Christmas train (Gantschev, Ivan)

Otto the bear (Gantschev, Ivan)

Klove, Lars. *I see a sign* photos by author. S&S, 1996. ISBN 0-689-80800-3 Subj: Communication. Concepts.

Klugmann, Judith. *The happy apple* (Bruna, Dick)

Klyce, Katherine P. *Kenya, jambo!* (McLean, Virginia O.)

Knab, Linda Z. *The day is waiting* (Freeman, Don)

Knaff, Jean Christian. *Manhattan* ill. by author. Knopf, 1989. ISBN 0-571-14653-8 Subj: Emotions – loneliness. Friendship. Imagination.

Knapp, Jennifer. *The go go dogs* ill. by author. Chronicle, 1998. ISBN 0-8118-2028-9 Subj: Activities – traveling. Animals – dogs.

Knapp, John, II. *A pillar of pepper and other Bible nursery rhymes* ill. by Dianne Turner Deckert. Cook, 1982. ISBN 0-89191-559-1 Subj: Nursery rhymes. Religion.

Kneen, Maggie. *The Christmas surprise* ill. by author. Chronicle, 2001. ISBN 0-8118-3210-4 Subj: Animals – pigs. Holidays – Christmas. Rhyming text. Weather – snow.

"Too many cooks . . ." and other proverbs ill. by author. Green Tiger Pr., 1992. ISBN 0-671-78120-0 Subj: Proverbs.

When you're not looking ill. by author. S&S, 1996. ISBN 0-689-80026-6 Subj: Counting, numbers. Puzzles.

Knight, Bertram T. *Working at a zoo* ill. with photos. Childrens Pr., 1998. ISBN 0-516-20751-2 Subj: Animals. Careers – zookeepers. Zoos.

Knight, David C. *Dinosaur days* ill. by Joel Schick. McGraw-Hill, 1977. ISBN 0-07035-102-3 Subj: Dinosaurs. Prehistory. Science.

Knight, Hilary. *Angels and berries and candy canes* ill. by author. HarperCollins, 1963. Subj: Angels. Holidays – Christmas. Santa Claus.

A firefly in a fir tree ill. by author. Tegen, 2004. ISBN 0-06-000992-6 Subj: Animals – mice. Holidays – Christmas. Music. Nature. Songs.

Hilary Knight's Cinderella ill. by author. Random House, 1978. ISBN 0-394-93759-7 Subj: Family life – stepfamilies. Folk & fairy tales. Royalty – princes. Sibling rivalry.

Hilary Knight's the owl and the pussy-cat ill. by author. Macmillan, 1983. Based on The owl and the pussy-cat by Edward Lear. ISBN 0-02-750900-1 Subj: Imagination. Magic. Poetry.

Sylvia the sloth ill. by author. HarperCollins, 1969. Subj: Animals – sloths. Concepts – up & down.

Where's Wallace? ill. by author. HarperCollins, 1964. ISBN 0-06-023171-8 Subj: Animals – monkeys. Behavior – running away. Zoos.

Knight, Joan. *Bon appetit, Bertie!* ill. by Penny Dann. DK, 1993. ISBN 1-56458-195-0 Subj: Behavior – misunderstanding. Family life. Food. Foreign lands – France. Hotels.

Opal in the closet ill. by Pau Estrada. S&S, 1992. ISBN 0-88708-174-6 Subj: Babies. Emotions. Family life – new sibling. Sibling rivalry.

Tickle-toe rhymes ill. by John Wallner. Watts, 1988. ISBN 0-531-08373-X Subj: Games. Nursery rhymes. Poetry.

Knight, Margy Burns. *Africa is not a country* by Margy Burns Knight & Mark Melnicove; ill. by Anne Sibley O'Brien. Millbrook, 2000. ISBN 0-7613-1266-8 Subj: Foreign lands – Africa.

Talking walls ill. by Anne Sibley O'Brien. Tilbury House, 1992. ISBN 0-88448-102-6 Subj: Foreign lands.

Welcoming babies ill. by Anne Sibley O'Brien. Tilbury House, 1994. ISBN 0-88448-123-9 Subj: Babies. Family life.

Knotts, Howard. *Great-grandfather, the baby and me* ill. by author. Atheneum, 1978. ISBN 0-689-30656-3 Subj: Family life – great-grandparents.

The lost Christmas ill. by author. Harcourt, 1978. ISBN 0-15-249361-1 Subj: Dreams. Holidays – Christmas. Illness.

The summer cat ill. by author. HarperCollins, 1981. ISBN 0-06-023179-3 Subj: Animals – cats. Seasons – summer.

The winter cat ill. by author. HarperCollins, 1972. ISBN 0-06-023167-X Subj: Animals – cats. Seasons – winter.

Knowles, Sheena. *Edward the emu* ill. by Rod Clement. HarperTrophy, 1998. ISBN 0-06-443499-0 Subj: Animals. Birds – emus. Character traits – individuality. Zoos.

Knowlton, Laurie Lazzaro. *God be in my heart* ill. by autnolr. Boyds Mills, 1999. ISBN 1-56397-646-3 Subj: Religion.

The Nativity: Mary remembers ill. by Kasi Kubiak. Boyds Mills, 1998. ISBN 1-56397-714-1 Subj: Babies. Holidays – Christmas. Religion – Nativity.

Why cowgirls are such sweet talkers ill. by James Rice. Pelican, 2000. ISBN 1-56554-698-9 Subj: Behavior. Cowboys, cowgirls.

Knox-Wagner, Elaine. *The best mom in the world* (Delton, Judy)

My grandpa retired today ill. by Charles Robinson. A. Whitman, 1982. ISBN 0-8075-5334-4 Subj: Emotions. Family life – grandfathers. Old age.

The oldest kid ill. by Gail Owens. A. Whitman, 1981. ISBN 0-8075-5986-5 Subj: Activities – picnicking. Sibling rivalry.

Knüppel, Helga. *The adventures of Christabel Crocodile* ill. by author. Interlink, 1991. ISBN 0-940793-74-1 Subj: Animals. Behavior – lost. Reptiles – alligators, crocodiles.

Christabel Crocodile's birthday egg ill. by author. Crocodile, 1992. ISBN 1-56656-113-2 Subj: Animals – rats. Behavior – lost. Birds – penguins. Birthdays. Eggs. Reptiles – alligators, crocodiles.

Knutson, Barbara. *How the guinea fowl got her spots: a Swahili tale of friendship* ill. by adapt. Carolrhoda, 1990. ISBN 0-87614-416-4 Subj: Animals. Birds – guinea fowl. Folk & fairy tales – pourquoi tales. Friendship.

Love and roast chicken ill. by author. Lerner, 2004. ISBN 1-57505-657-7 Subj: Animals – guinea pigs. Behavior – trickery. Folk & fairy tales. Foreign lands – South America. Indians of South America.

Why the crab has no head: an African tale ill. by author. Carolrhoda, 1987. ISBN 0-87614-322-2 Subj: Behavior – boasting. Crustaceans – crabs. Folk & fairy tales. Foreign lands – Africa. Foreign lands – Zaire.

Knutson, Kimberley. *Beach babble* ill. by author. Cavendish, 1998. ISBN 0-7614-5026-2 Subj: Noise, sounds. Sea & seashore – beaches.

Bed bouncers ill. by author. Macmillan, 1995. ISBN 0-02-750871-4 Subj: Bedtime. Furniture – beds. Rhyming text.

Jungle jamboree ill. by author. Cavendish, 1998. ISBN 0-7614-5032-7 Subj: Imagination. Music. Rhyming text. Weather – rain.

Muddigush ill. by author. Macmillan, 1992. ISBN 0-02-750843-9 Subj: Activities – playing. Rhyming text. Weather – rain.

Ska-tat! ill. by author. Macmillan, 1993. ISBN 0-02-750846-3 Subj: Noise, sounds. Seasons – fall. Senses – smell.

Kobayashi, Masako Matsuno. *see* Matsuno, Masako

Kobayashi, Robert. *Maria Mazaretti loves spaghetti* ill. by author. Knopf, 1991. ISBN 0-679-91659-8 Subj: Animals. Careers – butchers. Food. Magic.

Kobayashi, Yuji. *Miss Josephine's secret walk* ill. by author. Green Tiger Pr., 1991. ISBN 0-88138-096-2 Subj: Activities – playing. Animals.

Kobrin, Janet. *Coyote goes hunting for fire: a California Indian myth* (Bernstein, Margery)

Earth namer: a California Indian myth (Bernstein, Margery)

The first morning: an African myth (Bernstein, Margery)

How the sun made a promise and kept it: a Canadian Indian myth (Bernstein, Margery)

Koch, Dorothy Clarke. *Gone is my goose* ill. by Doris Lee. Holiday, 1956. Subj: Birds – geese.

I play at the beach ill. by Feodor Rojankovsky. Random House, 1955. Subj: Family life. Games. Sea & seashore – beaches.

When the cows got out ill. by Paul Lantz. Holiday, 1958. Subj: Animals – bulls, cows. Farms.

Koch, Michelle. *By the sea* ill. by author. Greenwillow, 1991. ISBN 0-688-09550-X Subj: Concepts – opposites. Language. Sea & seashore.

Hoot, howl, hiss ill. by author. Greenwillow, 1991. ISBN 0-688-09652-2 Subj: Animals. Nature. Noise, sounds.

Just one more ill. by author. Greenwillow, 1989. ISBN 0-688-08128-2 Subj: Counting, numbers. Language.

World water watch ill. by author. Greenwillow, 1993. ISBN 0-688-11465-2 Subj: Ecology. Water.

Kocí, Marta. *Blackie and Marie* trans. from German by Elizabeth D. Crawford; ill. by author. Morrow, 1981. ISBN 0-688-00236-6 Subj: Animals – dogs. Friendship.

Katie's kitten ill. by author. Alphabet Pr., 1982. ISBN 0-907234-21-6 Subj: Animals – cats. Behavior – lost.

Sarah's bear ill. by author. Picture Book Studio, 1987. ISBN 0-88708-038-3 Subj: Emotions – love. Toys – bears.

Koda-Callan, Elizabeth. *The squiggly Wigglys* ill. by author. Workman, 2003. ISBN 0-7611-2821-2 Subj: Family life. Food. Format, unusual – toy & movable books. Parties. Rhyming text.

Koehler, Phoebe. *The day we met you* ill. by author. Bradbury, 1990. ISBN 0-02-750901-X Subj: Adoption. Babies. Family life.

Making room ill. by author. Bradbury, 1993. ISBN 0-02-750875-7 Subj: Animals – cats. Animals – dogs. Babies. Behavior – sharing. Family life.

Koelling, Caryl. *Animal mix and match* ill. by Roger Beerworth. Delacorte, 1980. ISBN 0-440-00015-7 Subj: Animals. Format, unusual – board books.

Mad monsters mix and match ill. by Linda Griffith. Delacorte, 1980. ISBN 0-440-05141-X Subj: Format, unusual – board books. Monsters.

Silly stories mix and match ill. by Carroll Andrus. Delacorte, 1980. ISBN 0-440-07845-8 Subj: Format, unusual – board books. Humorous stories.

Koenig, Marion. *The little black hen* (Hille-Brandts, Lene)

Poor fish (Beisert, Heide Helene)

The tale of fancy Nancy: a Spanish folktale ill. by Klaus Ensikat. Merrimack, 1979. ISBN 0-7011-5100-5 Subj: Animals – cats. Animals – mice. Folk & fairy tales.

The wonderful world of night ill. by David Parry. Grosset, 1969. Subj: Animals – cats. Behavior – misbehavior. Night.

Koenner, Alfred. *Be quiet quiet beside the lake* trans. from German by Georgia Peet; ill. by Karl-Heinz Appelmann. Imported Pubs., 1981. ISBN 0-8285-1837-8 Subj: Format, unusual – board books. Noise, sounds.

High flies the ball by Alfred Koenner & Siegfried Linke; trans. from German by Georgia Peet; ill. by Siegfried Linke. Imported Pubs., 1983. ISBN 0-8285-2553-6 Subj: Format, unusual – board books. Poetry.

Koffler, Camilla. *see* Ylla

Kohlenberg, Sherry. *Sammy's mommy has cancer* ill. by Lauri Crow. G. Stevens, 1994. ISBN 0-8368-1071-6 Subj: Emotions – love. Family life – mothers. Illness – cancer.

Koide, Tan. *May we sleep here tonight?* ill. by Yasuko Koide. Atheneum, 1983. ISBN 0-689-50261-3 Subj: Animals. Bedtime.

Koike, Kay. *Left or right?* (Rehm, Karl)

Kojima, Naomi. *The flying grandmother* ill. by author. Crowell, 1981. ISBN 0-690-04143-8 Subj: Activities – flying. Behavior – wishing. Family life – grandmothers. Imagination.

Kolar, Bob. *Do you want to play?* ill. by author. Dutton, 1999. ISBN 0-525-45938-3 Subj: Friendship. Parks.

Racer dogs ill. by author. Dutton, 2003. ISBN 0-525-45939-1 Subj: Animals – dogs. Automobiles. Sports – racing.

Stomp, stomp! ill. by author. North-South, 1997. ISBN 1-55858-633-4 Subj: Animals. Dinosaurs. Family life – mothers. Rhyming text.

Koller, Jackie French. *Baby for sale* ill. by Janet Pedersen. Cavendish, 2002. ISBN 0-7614-5106-4 Subj: Babies. Family life – brothers & sisters. Sibling rivalry.

Bouncing on the bed ill. by Anna Gossnickle Hines. Orchard, 1999. ISBN 0-531-33138-5 Subj: Activities. Rhyming text.

Fish fry tonight ill. by Catharine O'Neill. Crown, 1992. ISBN 0-517-57815-8 Subj: Animals. Animals – mice. Food. Friendship. Rhyming text. Sports – fishing.

Mole and Shrew ill. by Stella Ormai. Atheneum, 1991. ISBN 0-689-31611-9 Subj: Animals – moles. Animals – shrews. Friendship. Homes, houses. Moving.

Mole and Shrew are two ill. by Anne Reas. Random House, 2000. ISBN 0-375-90690-8 Subj: Animals – moles. Animals – shrews. Friendship.

Mole and Shrew step out ill. by Stella Ormai. Atheneum, 1992. ISBN 0-689-31713-1 Subj: Animals. Animals – moles. Animals – shrews. Friendship. Parties.

Nickommoh! a Thanksgiving celebration ill. by Marcia Sewall. Atheneum, 1999. ISBN 0-689-81094-6 Subj: Holidays – Thanksgiving. Indians of North America – Narragansett. Seasons – fall.

No such thing ill. by Betsy Lewin. Boyds Mills, 1997. ISBN 1-56397-490-8 Subj: Bedtime. Emotions – fear. Family life – mothers. Monsters.

One monkey too many ill. by Lynn Munsinger. Harcourt, 1999. ISBN 0-15-200006-2 Subj: Animals – monkeys. Counting, numbers. Rhyming text.

Komaiko, Leah. *Annie Bananie* ill. by Laura Cornell. HarperCollins, 1987. ISBN 0-06-023261-7 Subj: Friendship. Moving. Rhyming text.

Aunt Elaine does the dance from Spain ill. by Petra Mathers. Doubleday, 1992. ISBN 0-385-30674-1 Subj: Activities – dancing. Careers – dancers. Rhyming text. Theater.

Broadway Banjo Bill ill. by Franz Spohn. Doubleday, 1993. ISBN 0-385-30524-9 Subj: Birthdays. Careers – musicians. Music. Musical instruments – banjos. Rhyming text.

Earl's too cool for me ill. by Laura Cornell. HarperCollins, 1988. ISBN 0-06-023282-X Subj: Behavior – misunderstanding. Friendship. Rhyming text.

Fritzi Fox flew in from Florida ill. by Thacher Hurd. HarperCollins, 1995. ISBN 0-060-21507-0 Subj: Animals – foxes. Magic. Rhyming text.

Great Aunt Ida and her Great Dane, Doc ill. by S. D. Schindler. Doubleday, 1994. ISBN 0-385-30682-2 Subj: Activities – walking. Animals – dogs. Family life – aunts, uncles. Rhyming text.

I like the music ill. by Barbara Westman. HarperCollins, 1987. ISBN 0-06-023272-2 Subj: Music. Rhyming text.

Just my dad and me ill. by Jeffrey Greene. HarperCollins, 1995. ISBN 0-06-024574-3 Subj: Family life – fathers. Fish. Rhyming text. Sea & seashore.

Lenora O'Grady ill. by Laura Cornell. HarperCollins, 1992. ISBN 0-06-021767-7 Subj: Homeless. Rhyming text.

A million moms and mine written & ill. by Leah Komaiko & kids. L. Claiborne, 1992. ISBN 0-9634893-0-5 Subj: Activities – working. Children as authors. Children as illustrators. Family life – mothers.

My perfect neighborhood ill. by Barbara Westman. HarperCollins, 1990. ISBN 0-06-023288-9 Subj: Communities, neighborhoods. Rhyming text.

On Sally Perry's farm ill. by Cat Bowman Smith. S&S, 1996. ISBN 0-689-80083-5 Subj: Activities – working. Farms. Gardens, gardening.

Shoeshine Shirley ill. by Franz Spohn. Doubleday, 1993. ISBN 0-385-30526-5 Subj: Clothing – shoes. Rhyming text.

Where can Daniel be? ill. by Denys Cazet. Orchard, 1994. ISBN 0-531-08700-X Subj: Babies. Behavior – lost. Behavior – worrying. Family life – brothers & sisters.

Komoda, Beverly. *Simon's soup* ill. by author. Parents' Magazine Pr., 1978. ISBN 0-8193-0951-6 Subj: Animals – cats. Animals – monkeys. Food.

The too hot day ill. by author. HarperCollins, 1991. ISBN 0-06-021612-3 Subj: Animals – rabbits. Family life. Seasons – summer.

The winter day ill. by author. HarperCollins, 1991. ISBN 0-06-023302-8 Subj: Animals – rabbits. Illness. Seasons – winter. Snowmen.

Komori, Atsushi. *Animal mothers* ill. by Masayuki Yabuuchi. Putnam, 1983. ISBN 0-399-20980-8 Subj: Animals. Science.

Konigsburg, E. L. (Elaine Lobl). *Amy Elizabeth explores Bloomingdale's* ill. by author. Atheneum, 1992. ISBN 0-689-31766-2 Subj: Activities. Cities, towns. Family life – grandmothers.

Samuel Todd's book of great colors ill. by author. Atheneum, 1990. ISBN 0-689-31593-7 Subj: Concepts – color.

Samuel Todd's book of great inventions ill. by author. Atheneum, 1991. ISBN 0-689-31680-1 Subj: Family life.

Kooharian, David. *Sammy's story* ill. by author. DK, 1997. ISBN 0-7894-2466-5 Subj: Death. Family life. Illness.

Koontz, Robin Michal. *Chicago and the cat* ill. by author. Cobblehill, 1993. ISBN 0-525-65097-0 Subj: Animals – cats. Animals – rabbits. Friendship.

Chicago and the cat, the camping trip ill. by author. Cobblehill, 1994. ISBN 0-525-65137-3 Subj: Animals – cats. Animals – rabbits. Camps, camping. Friendship.

Chicago and the cat, the family reunion ill. by author. Cobblehill, 1996. ISBN 0-525-65202-7 Subj: Animals – cats. Animals – rabbits. Family life. Friendship. Parties.

Dinosaur dream ill. by author. Putnam, 1988. ISBN 0-399-21669-3 Subj: Dinosaurs. Dreams. Prehistory. Wordless.

I see something you don't see ill. by author. Dutton, 1992. ISBN 0-525-65077-6 Subj: Riddles & jokes.

Pussycat ate the dumplings: cat rhymes from Mother Goose ill. by author. Dodd, 1987. ISBN 0-396-08899-6 Subj: Animals – cats. Nursery rhymes.

This old man: the counting song ill. by author. Putnam, 1988. ISBN 0-396-09120-2 Subj: Counting, numbers. Farms. Music. Songs.

Koopmans, Loek. *The woodcutter's mitten* ill. by author. Interlink, 1990. ISBN 0-940793-67-9 Subj: Animals. Clothing.

Kopczynski, Anna. *Jerry and Ami* ill. by author. Scribners, 1963. Subj: Animals – dogs. Friendship.

Kopelke, Lisa. *Excuse me!* ill. by author. S&S, 2003. ISBN 0-689-85111-1 Subj: Behavior. Etiquette. Frogs & toads.

Koplow, Lesley. *Tanya and the tobo man = Tanya y el hombre tobo* trans. into Spanish by Alexander Contos; ill. by Eric Velasquez. Magination Pr., 1991. ISBN 0-945354-34-7 Subj: Ethnic groups in the U.S. – African Americans. Foreign languages. Illness.

Kopper, Lisa. *Daisy is a mommy* ill. by author. Dutton, 1997. ISBN 0-525-45722-4 Subj: Animals – babies. Animals – dogs. Babies. Family life.

Daisy knows best ill. by author. Dutton, 1999. ISBN 0-525-45915-4 Subj: Activities – bathing. Animals – babies. Animals – dogs. Babies.

Daisy thinks she is a baby ill. by author. Knopf, 1994. ISBN 0-679-94723-X Subj: Animals – dogs. Babies.

An elephant came to swim (Lewin, Hugh)

Good dog, Daisy ill. by author. Dutton, 2001. ISBN 0-525-46661-4 Subj: Animals – babies. Animals – dogs. Babies.

I'm a baby, you're a baby ill. by author. Viking, 1995. ISBN 0-670-85813-7 Subj: Animals – babies. Babies. Language.

Ten little babies ill. by author. Dutton, 1990. ISBN 0-525-44643-5 Subj: Babies. Counting, numbers. Format, unusual – toy & movable books. Rhyming text.

Koralek, Jenny. *The boy and the cloth of dreams* ill. by James Mayhew. Candlewick, 1994. ISBN 1-56402-349-4 Subj: Dreams. Emotions – fear. Family life – grandmothers. Night. Quilts. Sleep.

Cat and Kit ill. by Patricia MacCarthy. Hyperion, 1994. ISBN 0-7868-2030-6 Subj: Animals – cats. Behavior – growing up. Cities, towns. Farms.

The cobweb curtain: a Christmas story ill. by Pauline Baynes. Holt, 1989. Based on a legend told by William Barclay. ISBN 0-8050-1051-3 Subj: Behavior – hiding. Holidays – Christmas. Spiders.

The friendly fox ill. by Beverley Gooding. Little, 1988. ISBN 0-316-50179-4 Subj: Animals. Animals – foxes. Farms. Friendship.

Hanukkah: the festival of lights ill. by Juan Wijngaard. Lothrop, 1990. ISBN 0-688-09329-9 Subj: Holidays – Hanukkah. Jewish culture. Religion.

Night ride to Nanna's ill. by Mandy Sutcliffe. Candlewick, 2000. ISBN 0-7636-1192-1 Subj: Activities – traveling. Automobiles. Family life – grandmothers.

Koren, Edward. *Behind the wheel* ill. by author. Holt, 1972. ISBN 0-03-080232-6 Subj: Transportation.

Very hairy Harry ill. by author. Cotler, 2003. ISBN 0-06-050908-2 Subj: Careers – barbers. Hair. Tall tales.

Korman, Susan. *Box turtle at Silver Pond Lane* ill. by Stephen Marchesi. Soundprints, 2000. ISBN 1-56899-860-0 Subj: Reptiles – turtles, tortoises.

Kornblatt, Marc. *Eli and the Dimplemeyers* ill. by Jack Ziegler. Macmillan, 1994. ISBN 0-02-750947-8 Subj: Family life. Imagination – imaginary friends.

Korth-Sander, Irmtraut. *Will you be my friend?* trans. from German by Rosemary Lanning; ill. by author. Holt, 1986. ISBN 0-8050-0039-9 Subj: Animals – pigs. Friendship.

Koscielniak, Bruce. *Bear and Bunny grow tomatoes* ill. by author. Knopf, 1993. ISBN 0-679-93687-4 Subj: Animals – bears. Animals – rabbits. Character traits – laziness. Gardens, gardening.

Euclid Bunny delivers the mail ill. by author. Knopf, 1991. ISBN 0-679-91069-7 Subj: Animals. Animals – rabbits. Behavior – carelessness. Careers – postal workers. Post office.

Geoffrey Groundhog predicts the weather ill. by author. Houghton Mifflin, 1995. ISBN 0-395-70933-4 Subj: Animals – groundhogs. Holidays – Groundhog Day. Seasons – spring. Weather.

Hector and Prudence ill. by author. Knopf, 1990. ISBN 0-394-94514-X Subj: Animals – pigs. Family life.

Hector and Prudence – all aboard! ill. by author. Knopf, 1990. ISBN 0-679-90486-7 Subj: Animals – pigs. Holidays – Christmas. Trains.

Koski, Mary. *Impatient Pamela asks, "Why are my feet so huge?"* ill. by Dan Brown. Trellis Pub., 1999. ISBN 0-966328-12-4 Subj: Anatomy – feet. Concepts – size. Self-concept.

Impatient Pamela calls 9-1-1 ill. by Dan Brown. Trellis Pub., 1998. ISBN 0-966328-19-1 Subj: Careers – emergency medical technicians. Character traits – patience. Telephone.

Impatient Pamela wants a bigger family ill. by Dan Brown. Trellis Pub., 2002. ISBN 1-930650-04-3 Subj: Adoption. Character traits – patience. Family life – only child. Self-concept.

Kosowsky, Cindy. *Wordless counting book* ill. by author. Greene Bark Press, 1992. ISBN 1-880851-00-8 Subj: Counting, numbers. Wordless.

Kottke, Jan. *From seed to pumpkin* ill. by author. Childrens Pr., 2000. ISBN 0-51623-309-2 Subj: Plants. Seeds.

Kotzwinkle, William. *The day the gang got rich* ill. by Joe Servello. Viking, 1970. ISBN 0-670-25943-8 Subj: Clubs, gangs. Friendship.

The nap master ill. by Joe Servello. Harcourt, 1979. ISBN 0-15-256704-6 Subj: Bedtime. Dreams. Sleep.

Up the alley with Jack and Joe ill. by Joe Servello. Macmillan, 1974. ISBN 0-02-750940-0 Subj: Friendship.

Walter, the farting dog by William Kotzwinkle & Glenn Murray; ill. by Audrey Colman. Frog, Ltd., 2001. ISBN 1-58394-053-7 Subj: Animals – dogs.

Walter, the farting dog: rough weather ahead by William Kotzwinkle & Glenn Murray; ill. by Audrey Colman. Dutton, 2005. ISBN 0-525-47218-5 Subj: Activities – flying. Animals – dogs. Insects – butterflies, caterpillars.

Walter, the farting dog: trouble at the yard sale by William Kotzwinkle & Glenn Murray; ill. by Audrey Colman. Dutton, 2004. ISBN 0-525-47217-7 Subj: Animals – dogs. Clowns, jesters. Crime. Garage sales, rummage sales. Toys – balloons.

Kouts, Anne. *Kenny's rat* ill. by Betty Fraser. Viking, 1970. ISBN 0-670-41263-5 Subj: Animals – rats. Pets.

Kovacs, Deborah. *Beaver gets lost* (Chottin, Ariane)

A home for Little Turtle (Chottin, Ariane)

Moonlight on the river ill. by William Shattuck. Viking, 1993. ISBN 0-670-84463-2 Subj: Boats, ships. Family life – brothers. Night. Rivers. Sports – fishing. Weather – storms.

Kovalski, Maryann. *Brenda and Edward* ill. by author. Kids Can, 1984. ISBN 0-919964-77-X Subj: Animals – dogs. Behavior – lost. Friendship.

Jingle bells ill. by adapt. Little, 1988. Originally published in 1859 as "Jingle bells or the one horse open sleigh, song and chorus," by J. Pierpont. ISBN 0-316-50258-8 Subj: Cities, towns. Holidays – Christmas. Music. Seasons – winter. Songs. Weather – snow.

Pizza for breakfast ill. by author. Kids Can, 1991. ISBN 0-688-10410-X Subj: Behavior – wishing. Food.

Queen Nadine ill. by author. Orca, 1998. ISBN 1-55143-093-2 Subj: Animals – bulls, cows. Farms.

Take me out to the ball game ill. by author. Fitzhenry & Whiteside, 2004. ISBN 1-55041-897-1 Subj: Family life – grandmothers. Music. Sports – baseball.

The wheels on the bus ill. by author. Little, 1987. ISBN 0-316-50256-1 Subj: Buses. Family life – grandmothers. Music. Musical instruments – guitars. Songs.

Kowall, Barbara. *Squaps the moonling* (Ziegler, Ursina)

Kozielski, Dolores. *On Halloween night* (Wolff, Ferida)

On Halloween night (Ziefert, Harriet)

Krahn, Fernando. *Amanda and the mysterious carpet* ill. by author. Clarion, 1985. ISBN 0-89919-258-0 Subj: Imagination. Magic. Wordless.

April fools ill. by author. Dutton, 1974. ISBN 0-525-25825-6 Subj: Holidays – April Fools' Day. Humorous stories. Wordless.

Arthur's adventure in the abandoned house ill. by author. Dutton, 1981. ISBN 0-525-25945-7 Subj: Mystery stories. Wordless.

The biggest Christmas tree on earth ill. by author. Little, 1978. ISBN 0-316-50309-6 Subj: Animals. Holidays – Christmas. Toys – balls. Trees. Wordless.

Catch that cat! ill. by author. Dutton, 1978. ISBN 0-525-27555-X Subj: Animals – cats. Wordless.

The creepy thing ill. by author. Houghton Mifflin, 1982. ISBN 0-89919-099-5 Subj: Imagination – imaginary friends. Wordless.

A funny friend from heaven ill. by author. Lippincott, 1977. ISBN 0-397-31760-3 Subj: Angels. Clowns, jesters. Wordless.

The great ape: being the true version of the famous saga of adventure and friendship newly discovered ill. by author. Viking, 1978. ISBN 0-670-34840-6 Subj: Animals – gorillas. Friendship. Islands. Wordless.

Here comes Alex Pumpernickel! ill. by author. Little, 1981. ISBN 0-316-50311-8 Subj: Behavior – bad day. Wordless.

How Santa Claus had a long and difficult journey delivering his presents ill. by author. Delacorte, 1970. Holidays – Christmas. Subj: Gifts. Santa Claus. Wordless.

Little love story ill. by author. Lippincott, 1976. ISBN 0-397-31700-X Subj: Holidays – Valentine's Day. Wordless.

Mr. Top ill. by author. Morrow, 1983. ISBN 0-688-02369-X Subj: Crime. Traffic, traffic signs.

The mystery of the giant footprints ill. by author. Dutton, 1977. ISBN 0-525-35595-2 Subj: Cumulative tales. Monsters. Mystery stories. Wordless.

Robot-bot-bot ill. by author. Dutton, 1979. ISBN 0-525-38545-2 Subj: Activities – playing. Activities – working. Robots. Wordless.

Sebastian and the mushroom ill. by author. Delacorte, 1976. ISBN 0-440-07695-1 Subj: Dreams. Wordless.

The secret in the dungeon ill. by author. Houghton Mifflin, 1983. ISBN 0-89919-148-7 Subj: Behavior – secrets. Dragons. Wordless.

Sleep tight, Alex Pumpernickel ill. by author. Little, 1982. ISBN 0-316-50312-6 Subj: Bedtime. Sleep. Wordless.

Who's seen the scissors? ill. by author. Dutton, 1975. ISBN 0-525-42710-4 Subj: Wordless.

Krajnc, Anton C. *For the sake of a cake* (Nobisso, Josephine)

Kramer, Anthony Penta. *Numbers on parade: 0 to 10* ill. by author. Lothrop, 1987. ISBN 0-688-05555-9 Subj: Animals. Counting, numbers.

Kramer, Sydelle. *Wagon train* ill. by Deborah Kogan Ray. Grosset, 1997. ISBN 0-448-41335-3 Subj: Family life. U.S. history – frontier & pioneer life.

Kramlich, Carolyn Walz. *Mary's treasure box* ill. by Walter Porter. Tommy Nelson, 1998. ISBN 0-8499-5834-2 Subj: Memories, memory. Religion – Nativity.

Kramsky, Jerry. *The cranky sun* ill. by Lorenzo Mattotti. Little, 1995. ISBN 0-316-50361-4 Subj: Bedtime. Clocks, watches. Sun.

Kranendonk, Anke. *Just a minute* ill. by Jung-Hee Spetter. Front St., 1998. ISBN 1-886910-29-4 Subj: Animals – pigs. Behavior – misbehavior. Family life – mothers.

Kranking, Kathy. *The ocean is . . .* photos by Norbert Wu. Holt, 2003. ISBN 0-8050-7097-4 Subj: Animals. Plants. Rhyming text. Sea & seashore.

Krasilovsky, Phyllis. *The cow who fell in the canal* ill. by Peter Spier. Doubleday, 1957. ISBN 0-385-07740-8 Subj: Animals – bulls, cows. Cumulative tales. Foreign lands – Holland.

The girl who was a cowboy ill. by Cyndy Szekeres. Doubleday, 1965. Subj: Clothing. Cowboys, cowgirls.

The man who cooked for himself ill. by Mamoru Funai. Parents' Magazine Pr., 1994. ISBN 0-8368-0984-X Subj: Activities – baking, cooking. Food.

The man who didn't wash his dishes ill. by Barbara Cooney. Doubleday, 1950. Subj: Character traits – cleanliness. Character traits – laziness.

The man who entered a contest ill. by Yuri Salzman. Doubleday, 1980. ISBN 0-385-13352-9 Subj: Activities – baking, cooking. Behavior – misbehavior.

The man who tried to save time ill. by Marcia Sewall. Doubleday, 1979. ISBN 0-385-12999-8 Subj: Character traits – laziness. Time.

The man who was too lazy to fix things ill. by John Emil Cymerman. Morrow, 1992. ISBN 0-688-10395-2 Subj: Character traits – laziness.

Scaredy cat ill. by Ninon. Macmillan, 1959. ISBN 0-02-750930-3 Subj: Animals – cats.

The shy little girl ill. by Trina Schart Hyman. Houghton Mifflin, 1970. Subj: Character traits – shyness. Friendship.

The very little boy ill. by Karen Gundersheimer. Scholastic, 1992. ISBN 0-590-44762-9 Subj: Activities. Babies. Behavior – growing up. Family life. Family life – new sibling.

The very little girl ill. by Karen Gundersheimer. Scholastic, 1992. ISBN 0-590-44761-0 Subj: Babies. Behavior – growing up. Family life – new sibling.

The very tall little girl ill. by Olivia Cole. Doubleday, 1969. Subj: Character traits – being different. Family life.

The woman who saved things ill. by John Emil Cymerman. Tambourine, 1993. ISBN 0-688-11163-7 Subj: Behavior – collecting things. Old age.

Kratka, Suzanne C. *Hi, new baby: a book to help your child learn about the new baby* (Andry, Andrew C.)

Kratky, Lada Josefa. *Out the door = Sal y entra: Out the door* (Matthias, Catherine)

Over and under = Arriba y abajo (Matthias, Catherine)

Too many balloons = Demasiados globos (Matthias, Catherine)

Kraus, Bruce. *The detective of London* (Kraus, Robert)

Kraus, Robert. *The adventures of Wise Old Owl* ill. by author. Troll, 1993. ISBN 0-8167-2943-3 Subj: Activities – writing. Animals. Birds – owls. Character traits – wisdom.

All my chickens ill. by author. Western, 1993. ISBN 0-307-30125-7 Subj: Animals – foxes. Birds – chickens.

Animal families ill. by José Aruego & Ariane Dewey. Windmill, 1980. ISBN 0-671-41532-8 Subj: Animals. Family life. Format, unusual – board books.

Another mouse to feed ill. by José Aruego & Ariane Dewey. S&S, 1989. ISBN 0-671-66522-7 Subj: Animals – mice. Family life.

Big brother ill. by author. Parents' Magazine Pr., 1973. ISBN 0-8193-0649-5 Subj: Animals – rabbits. Babies. Family life.

Big Squeak, Little Squeak ill. by Kevin O'Malley. Orchard, 1996. ISBN 0-531-08774-3 Subj: Animals – cats. Animals – mice. Character traits – cleverness. Food.

Boris bad enough ill. by José Aruego & Ariane Dewey. S&S, 1988. ISBN 0-671-66894-3 Subj: Animals – elephants. Behavior – misbehavior. Careers – doctors.

Buggy Bear cleans up ill. by author. Silver Pr., 1989. ISBN 0-671-68608-9 Subj: Animals. Animals – bears. Character traits – cleanliness. Emotions – love. School.

The Christmas cookie sprinkle snitcher ill. by author. Windmill, 1980. ISBN 0-671-41199-3 Subj: Character traits – meanness. Food. Holidays – Christmas. Rhyming text.

Come out and play, little mouse ill. by José Aruego & Ariane Dewey. Delmar, 1991. ISBN 0-8273-4504-6 Subj: Activities – playing. Animals – cats. Animals – mice. Behavior – trickery.

Daddy Long Ears ill. by author. Little Simon, 1990. ISBN 0-671-67415-3 Subj: Animals – rabbits. Family life – fathers. Holidays – Easter.

Dance, Spider, dance! ill. by author. Western, 1993. ISBN 0-307-65656-X Subj: Activities – dancing. Spiders.

The detective of London by Robert & Bruce Kraus; ill. by Robert Byrd. Windmill, 1978. ISBN 0-525-61568-7 Subj: Animals – dogs. Careers – detectives. Crime. Mystery stories.

Dr. Mouse, Bungle Jungle doctor ill. by author. Western, 1992. ISBN 0-307-69550-6 Subj: Animals – mice. Careers – doctors.

Ella the bad speller ill. by author. Silver Pr., 1989. ISBN 0-671-68606-2 Subj: Animals. Animals – elephants. Language. School.

The first robin ill. by author. Windmill, 1965. ISBN 0-671-44565-0 Subj: Birds – robins. Character traits – kindness. Illness. Seasons – spring.

Freddy, the fire engine ill. by author. Grosset, 1985. ISBN 0-448-10219-6 Subj: Fire. Format, unusual – board books. Trucks.

Good morning, Miss Gator ill. by author. Silver Pr., 1989. ISBN 0-671-68605-4 Subj: Animals. Careers – teachers. Reptiles – alligators, crocodiles. School.

Good night little one by Robert Kraus & N. M. Bodecker; ill. by N. M. Bodecker. Dutton, 1972. ISBN 0-525-61500-8 Subj: Bedtime. Counting, numbers. Night. Sleep.

Good night Richard Rabbit by Robert Kraus & N. M. Bodecker; ill. by N. M. Bodecker. Dutton, 1972. ISBN 0-525-61502-4 Subj: Animals – rabbits. Bedtime. Counting, numbers. Night. Sleep.

Here comes Tardy Toad ill. by author. Silver Pr., 1989. ISBN 0-671-68607-0 Subj: Animals. Behavior – promptness, tardiness. Frogs & toads. School.

Herman the helper ill. by José Aruego & Ariane Dewey. S&S, 1987. ISBN 0-671-66270-8 Subj: Character traits – helpfulness. Octopuses. Sea & seashore.

How Spider saved Easter ill. by author. Scholastic, 1988. ISBN 0-590-41092-X Subj: Animals. Holidays – Easter. Insects – flies. Insects – ladybugs. Spiders.

How Spider saved Halloween ill. by author. S&S, 1988. ISBN 0-671-66888-9 Subj: Holidays – Halloween. Insects. Spiders.

How Spider saved Turkey ill. by author. Windmill, 1991. ISBN 0-590-44411-5 Subj: Birds – turkeys. Friendship. Holidays – Thanksgiving. Spiders.

How Spider saved Valentine's Day ill. by author. Scholastic, 1986. ISBN 0-590-33743-2 Subj: Friendship. Holidays – Valentine's Day. Insects. Spiders.

I, Mouse ill. by author. Windmill, 1978. Subj: Animals – mice.

Jack O'Lantern's scary Halloween ill. by author. Western, 1993. ISBN 0-307-10016-2 Subj: Holidays – Halloween.

The king's trousers ill. by Fred Gwynne. Windmill, 1981. ISBN 0-671-42259-6 Subj: Behavior – trickery. Clothing – pants. Royalty – kings.

Klunky Monkey, new kid in class ill. by author. Silver Pr., 1990. ISBN 0-671-70853-8 Subj: Animals. Animals – monkeys. Food. School.

Ladybug, ladybug! ill. by author. Windmill, 1977. ISBN 0-525-62326-4 Subj: Behavior – misunderstanding. Friendship. Insects – ladybugs. Rhyming text.

Leo the late bloomer ill. by José Aruego. S&S, 1987. ISBN 0-671-96078-4 Subj: Animals – tigers. Behavior – growing up.

The little giant ill. by author. Windmill, 1977. ISBN 0-525-62322-1 Subj: Concepts – size. Giants.

Little Louie the baby bloomer ill. by José Aruego & Ariane Dewey. HarperCollins, 1998. ISBN 0-06-026294-X Subj: Animals – tigers. Family life – brothers.

The littlest rabbit ill. by author. HarperCollins, 1961. Subj: Animals – rabbits. Character traits – smallness.

Ludwig the dog who snored symphonies ill. by author. Windmill, 1981. ISBN 0-671-43411-X Subj: Animals – dogs. Music. Sleep – snoring.

Mert the blurt ill. by José Aruego & Ariane Dewey. S&S, 1989. ISBN 0-671-66537-5 Subj: Behavior – gossip. Frogs & toads.

Milton the early riser ill. by José Aruego & Ariane Dewey. S&S, 1987. ISBN 0-671-66272-4 Subj: Animals – pandas. Sleep.

Mort the sport ill. by John Himmelman. Orchard, 2000. ISBN 0-531-33247-0 Subj: Games. Musical instruments – violins. Sports – baseball.

Mouse in love ill. by José Aruego and Ariane Dewey. Orchard, 2000. ISBN 0-531-33297-7 Subj: Animals – mice. Communities, neighborhoods. Emotions – love. Rhyming text.

Mouse work ill. by author. Windmill, 1980. Subj: Animals – mice. Format, unusual – board books. Rhyming text.

Mummy knows best ill. by author. Warner, 1988. ISBN 1-55782-057-0 Subj: Ghosts. Mystery stories.

Musical Max ill. by José Aruego & Ariane Dewey. S&S, 1990. ISBN 0-671-68681-X Subj: Animals – hippopotamuses. Music. Musical instruments.

Noel the coward ill. by José Aruego & Ariane Dewey. S&S, 1988. ISBN 0-671-66845-5 Subj: Emotions – fear.

Owliver ill. by José Aruego & Ariane Dewey. Prentice-Hall, 1987, 1974. ISBN 0-13-647538-8 Subj: Birds – owls. Careers. Character traits – individuality.

The phantom of Creepy Hollow ill. by author. Warner, 1988. ISBN 1-5578-2060-0 Subj: Monsters.

Phil the ventriloquist ill. by author. Greenwillow, 1989. ISBN 0-688-07988-1 Subj: Animals – rabbits. Family life.

Rebecca Hatpin ill. by Robert Byrd. Dutton, 1974. ISBN 0-525-61520-2 Subj: Careers – nurses. Character traits – helpfulness. Character traits – selfishness. Family life – grandmothers.

Robert Kraus' a sunny day in Babytown ill. by author. Little Simon, 1987. ISBN 0-671-63300-7 Subj: Animals. Babies. Family life. Format, unusual – board books.

Robert Kraus' Babytown express ill. by author. Little Simon, 1987. ISBN 0-671-63301-5 Subj: Babies. Country. Format, unusual – board books.

Robert Kraus' meet the babies ill. by author. Little Simon, 1987. ISBN 0-671-63299-X Subj: Babies. Format, unusual – board books.

Robert Kraus' welcome to Babytown ill. by author. Little Simon, 1987. ISBN 0-671-63298-1 Subj: Babies. Format, unusual – board books.

Screamy Mimi ill. by Hilary Knight. S&S, 1987. ISBN 0-671-44471-9 Subj: Activities – singing. Noise, sounds.

See the Christmas lights ill. by Pam Kraus. Windmill, 1981. ISBN 0-671-44407-7 Subj: Format, unusual – toy & movable books. Holidays – Christmas. Poetry.

See the moon ill. by author. Windmill, 1980. ISBN 0-671-41206-X Subj: Format, unusual – toy & movable books. Moon. Night. Sleep.

Springfellow ill. by Sam Savitt. Dutton, 1978. ISBN 0-525-61577-6 Subj: Activities – playing. Animals – horses, ponies.

Springfellow's parade ill. by author. Windmill, 1982. ISBN 0-671-44564-2 Subj: Animals. Animals – horses, ponies. Parades. Seasons – spring.

Squirmy's big secret ill. by author. Silver Pr., 1990. ISBN 0-671-70851-1 Subj: Animals. Animals – worms. Names. School.

Strudwick, a sheep in wolf's clothing ill. by author. Viking, 1995. ISBN 0-670-85887-0 Subj: Animals – sheep. Animals – wolves. Behavior – trickery. Clothing. Disguises.

The three friends ill. by José Aruego & Ariane Dewey. Windmill, 1980. ISBN 0-671-96061-X Subj: Animals. Friendship.

Tony, the tow truck ill. by author. Grosset, 1985. ISBN 0-448-10220-X Subj: Format, unusual – board books. Friendship. Trucks.

The tree that stayed up until next Christmas ill. by Edna Eicke. Windmill, 1977. ISBN 0-525-61001-4 Subj: Holidays – Christmas. Toys. Trees.

The trouble with spider ill. by author. HarperCollins, 1962. Subj: Friendship. Insects – flies. Spiders.

Where are you going, little mouse? ill. by José Aruego & Ariane Dewey. Greenwillow, 1986. ISBN 0-688-04295-3 Subj: Animals – mice. Behavior – running away. Behavior – seeking better things.

Whose mouse are you? ill. by José Aruego. Aladdin, 1986. ISBN 0-02-751190-1 Subj: Animals – mice. Rhyming text.

Wise Old Owl's canoe trip adventure ill. by author. Troll, 1993. ISBN 0-8167-2947-6 Subj: Birds – owls. Canoes & canoeing. Character traits – wisdom. Reptiles – turtles, tortoises.

Wise Old Owl's Christmas adventure ill. by Robert & Pamela Kraus. Troll, 1994. ISBN 0-8167-2945-X Subj: Animals. Birds – owls. Character traits – wisdom. Holidays – Christmas.

Krause, Ute. *Nora and the great bear* ill. by author. Dial, 1989. ISBN 0-8037-0685-5 Subj: Animals – bears. Behavior – lost. Sports – hunting.

Pig surprise ill. by author. Dial, 1989. ISBN 0-8037-0714-2 Subj: Animals – pigs. Behavior – misbehavior. Behavior – misunderstanding. Pets.

Krauss, Ronnie. *Take a look, it's in a book* photos by Christopher Hornsby. Walker, 1997. ISBN 0-8027-8489-5 Subj: Television. Theater.

Krauss, Ruth. *The backward day* ill. by Marc Simont. HarperCollins, 1950. Subj: Family life.

Bears ill. by Phyllis Rowand. HarperCollins, 1948. Subj: Animals – bears. Poetry.

Big and little ill. by Mary Szilagyi. Scholastic, 1988. ISBN 0-590-41707-X Subj: Concepts – size. Emotions – love.

A bouquet of littles ill. by Jane Flora. HarperCollins, 1963. Subj: Concepts – size. Poetry.

The bundle book ill. by Helen Stone. HarperCollins, 1951. Subj: Emotions. Family life – mothers. Games.

The carrot seed ill. by Crockett Johnson. Scholastic, 1974, c1945. ISBN 0-06-023351-6 Subj: Character traits – optimism. Gardens, gardening. Plants. Self-concept.

Charlotte and the white horse ill. by Maurice Sendak. HarperCollins, 1955. ISBN 0-06-023361-3 Subj: Animals – horses, ponies.

Everything under a mushroom ill. by Margot Tomes. Four Winds, 1974. Subj: Imagination. Little people. Rhyming text.

Eyes, nose, fingers, toes ill. by Elizabeth Schneider. HarperCollins, 1964. Subj: Anatomy.

A good man and his good wife ill. by Marc Simont. Harper, 1962. Subj: Behavior – boredom. Friendship.

Goodnight, goodnight, sleepyhead ill. by Jane Dyer. HarperCollins, 2004. ISBN 0-06-028895-7 Subj: Bedtime. Rhyming text.

The growing story ill. by Helen Oxenbury. HarperCollins, 2000. ISBN 0-06-024717-7 Subj: Behavior – growing up.

The happy day ill. by Marc Simont. HarperCollins, 1949. ISBN 0-06-023396-6 Subj: Caldecott award honor books. Hibernation. Seasons – spring. Seasons – winter. Weather – snow.

The happy egg ill. by Crockett Johnson. HarperCollins, 2005. ISBN 0-06-076006-0 Subj: Birds. Eggs.

A hole is to dig: a first book of first definitions ill. by Maurice Sendak. HarperCollins, 1952. ISBN 0-06-023406-7 Subj: Activities – digging. Language.

I can fly ill. by Mary Blair. Golden Bks., 1999. ISBN 0-307-20320-4 Subj: Activities – flying. Activities – playing. Format, unusual – board books. Imagination. Rhyming text.

I write it ill. by Mary Chalmers. HarperCollins, 1970. Subj: Activities – writing.

I'll be you and you be me ill. by Maurice Sendak. HarperCollins, 1954. ISBN 0-06-023431-8 Subj: Friendship. Humorous stories.

Mama, I wish I was snow. Child, you'd be very cold ill. by Ellen Raskin. Atheneum, 1962. Subj: Behavior – wishing. Games.

A moon or a button ill. by Remy Charlip. HarperCollins, 1959. Subj: Imagination.

Open house for butterflies ill. by Maurice Sendak. HarperCollins, 1960. ISBN 0-06-023446-6 Subj: Imagination.

Somebody else's nut tree, and other tales from children ill. by Maurice Sendak. Linnet Books, 1990. ISBN 0-208-02264-3 Subj: Children as authors. Imagination.

This thumbprint ill. by author. HarperCollins, 1967. Subj: Humorous stories. Imagination.

A very special house ill. by Maurice Sendak. HarperCollins, 1953. ISBN 0-06-023456-3 Subj: Caldecott award honor books. Homes, houses. Imagination.

You're just what I need ill. by Julia Noonan. HarperCollins, 1998. ISBN 0-06-027515-4 Subj: Emotions. Family life – mothers. Games.

Krauze, Andrzej. *What's so special about today?* ill. by author. Lothrop, 1984. ISBN 0-688-02835-7 Subj: Animals. Birthdays. Character traits – questioning.

Krebs, Laurie. *The Beeman* ill. by Melissa Iwai. National Geographic, 2002. ISBN 0-7922-7224-2 Subj: Careers – beekeepers. Family life – grandfathers. Insects – bees. Rhyming text.

We all went on safari ill. by Julia Cairns. Barefoot, 2003. ISBN 1-84148-478-4 Subj: Counting, numbers. Foreign lands – Tanzania. Foreign languages.

Krementz, Jill. *Benjy goes to a restaurant* photos by author. Crown, 1986. ISBN 0-517-56166-2 Subj: Careers – waiters, waitresses. Family life. Format, unusual – board books. Restaurants.

Jack goes to the beach photos by author. Random House, 1986. ISBN 0-394-88001-3 Subj: Family life. Format, unusual – board books. Sand. Sea & seashore – beaches.

Jamie goes on an airplane photos by author. Random House, 1986. ISBN 0-394-88196-6 Subj: Activities – traveling. Airplanes, airports. Careers – airplane pilots. Format, unusual – board books.

Katharine goes to nursery school photos by author. Random House, 1986. ISBN 0-394-88195-8 Subj: Activities. Format, unusual – board books. School – first day. School – nursery.

Lily goes to the playground photos by author. Random House, 1986. ISBN 0-394-87999-6 Subj: Activities – playing. Family life. Format, unusual – board books.

Taryn goes to the dentist photos by author. Crown, 1986. ISBN 0-517-56168-9 Subj: Careers – dentists. Family life. Format, unusual – board books.

A very young actress photos by author. Knopf, 1991. ISBN 0-679-40637-9 Subj: Careers – actors. Theater.

A very young gardener photos by author. Dial, 1991. ISBN 0-8037-0875-0 Subj: Gardens, gardening.

A very young musician photos by author. S&S, 1991. ISBN 0-671-72687-0 Subj: Careers – musicians. Music. Musical instruments – trumpets.

A very young skier photos by author. Dial, 1990. ISBN 0-8037-0823-8 Subj: Seasons – winter. Sports – skiing.

A visit to Washington, D.C. photos by author. Scholastic, 1987. ISBN 0-500-40582-9 Subj: Activities – traveling. Cities, towns. Museums.

Krensky, Stephen. *Ben Franklin and his first kite* ill. by Bert Dodson. Aladdin, 2002. ISBN 0-689-84985-0 Subj: Careers – inventors. Careers – scientists. Kites.

The big time bears ill. by Maryann Cocca-Leffler. Little, 1989. ISBN 0-316-50375-4 Subj: Animals – bears. Time.

Children of the wind and water: five stories about Native American children ill. by James Watling. Scholastic, 1994. ISBN 0-590-46963-0 Subj: Behavior – growing up. Indians of North America.

Dinosaurs, beware! a safety guide (Brown, Marc Tolon)

Fraidy Cats ill. by Betsy Lewin. Scholastic, 1993. ISBN 0-590-46438-8 Subj: Animals – cats. Bedtime. Emotions – fear. Imagination. Night. Rhyming text.

A good knight's sleep ill. by Renée Williams-Andriani. Candlewick, 1996. ISBN 1-56402-769-4 Subj: Behavior – wishing. Knights.

How Santa got his job ill. by S. D. Schindler. S&S, 1998. ISBN 0-689-80697-3 Subj: Careers. Holidays – Christmas. Santa Claus.

How Santa lost his job ill. by S. D. Schindler. S&S, 2001. ISBN 0-689-83173-0 Subj: Careers. Holidays – Christmas. Mythical creatures – elves. Santa Claus.

The lion upstairs ill. by Leigh Grant. Atheneum, 1983. ISBN 0-689-30969-4 Subj: Imagination – imaginary friends.

The missing Mother Goose ill. by Chris L. Demarest. Doubleday, 1991. ISBN 0-385-26273-6 Subj: Nursery rhymes.

My first dictionary ill. by George Ulrich. Houghton Mifflin, 1980. ISBN 0-395-29210-7 Subj: Dictionaries.

My loose tooth ill. by Hideko Takahashi. Random House, 1998. ISBN 0-679-98847-5 Subj: Rhyming text. Teeth.

My teacher's secret life ill. by JoAnn Adinolfi. S&S, 1996. ISBN 0-689-80271-4 Subj: Careers – teachers. Communities, neighborhoods. School.

Perfect pigs: an introduction to manners (Brown, Marc Tolon)

The pizza book ill. by R. W. Alley. Scholastic, 1992. ISBN 0-590-44844-7 Subj: Activities – baking, cooking. Food.

Shooting for the moon ill. by Bernie Fuchs. Kroupa, 2001. ISBN 0-374-36843-0 Subj: Theater. U.S. history. Weapons.

We just moved! ill. by Larry DiFiori. Scholastic, 1998. ISBN 0-590-33127-2 Subj: Castles. Middle Ages. Moving.

What a mess! ill. by Joe Mathieu. Random House, 2001. ISBN 0-375-90220-1 Subj: Character traits – cleanliness.

The youngest fairy godmother ever ill. by Diana Cain Bluthenthal. S&S, 2000. ISBN 0-689-82011-9 Subj: Behavior – wishing. Fairies.

Kress, Camille. *Purim* ill. by author. UAHC Pr., 1998. ISBN 0-8074-0654-6 Subj: Format, unusual – board books. Holidays – Purim. Jewish culture. Religion.

Tot Shabbat ill. by author. UAHC Pr., 1996. ISBN 0-8074-0607-4 Subj: Format, unusual – board books. Holidays. Jewish culture.

Kreye, Walter. *The giant from the little island* ill. by Tomasz Bogacki. North-South, 1990. ISBN 1-55858-085-9 Subj: Activities – making things. Behavior – wishing. Friendship. Giants.

Kriegman, Mitchell. *The book of boo!* (Kennedy, Marge M.)

Krings, Antoon. *Oliver's bicycle* ill. by author. Walt Disney, 1992. ISBN 1-56282-161-X Subj: Animals – koalas. Sports – bicycling. Weather – rain.

Oliver's pool ill. by author. Walt Disney, 1992. ISBN 1-56282-161-X Subj: Animals – koalas. Sports – swimming.

Oliver's strawberry patch ill. by author. Walt Disney, 1992. ISBN 1-56282-163-6 Subj: Animals – koalas. Food. Gardens, gardening. Plants.

Krischanitz, Raoul. *Nobody likes me!* ill. by author; trans. by Rosemary Lanning. North-South, 1999. ISBN 0-7358-1055-9 Subj: Animals. Animals – dogs. Friendship.

Krisher, Trudy. *Kathy's hats: a story of hope* ill. by Nadine Bernard Westcott. A. Whitman, 1992. ISBN 0-8075-4116-8 Subj: Clothing – hats. Hair. Illness – cancer.

Krishnaswami, Uma. *Chachaji's cup* ill. by Soumya Sitaraman. Children's Book Pr., 2003. ISBN 0-89239-178-2 Subj: Ethnic groups in the U.S. – Indian Americans. Family life – aunts, uncles. Memories, memory.

Holi ill. with photos. Childrens Pr., 2003. ISBN 0-516-22863-3 Subj: Fairs, festivals. Religion.

Kroll, Steven. *Amanda and the giggling ghost* ill. by Dick Gackenbach. Holiday, 1980. ISBN 0-8234-0408-0 Subj: Behavior – stealing. Ghosts.

Annie's four grannies ill. by Eileen Christelow. Holiday, 1986. ISBN 0-8234-0605-9 Subj: Family life – grandmothers. Family life – stepfamilies. Rhyming text.

Are you pirates? ill. by Marylin Hafner. Pantheon, 1982. ISBN 0-394-93936-0 Subj: Imagination. Pirates.

The big bunny and the Easter eggs ill. by Janet Stevens. Holiday, 1982. ISBN 0-8234-0436-6 Subj: Animals – rabbits. Holidays – Easter. Illness.

The big bunny and the magic show ill. by Janet Stevens. Holiday, 1986. ISBN 0-8234-0589-3 Subj: Animals – rabbits. Holidays – Easter. Magic.

Big Jeremy ill. by Donald Carrick. Holiday, 1989. ISBN 0-8234-0759-4 Subj: Friendship. Giants.

Branigan's cat and the Halloween ghost ill. by Carolyn Ewing. Holiday, 1990. ISBN 0-8234-0822-1 Subj: Animals – cats. Ghosts. Holidays – Halloween.

By the dawn's early light: the story of the Star spangled banner ill. by Dan Andreasen. Scholastic, 1994. ISBN 0-590-45054-9 Subj: Music. Songs. U.S. history.

The candy witch ill. by Marylin Hafner. Holiday, 1979. ISBN 0-8234-0359-9 Subj: Behavior – unnoticed, unseen. Holidays – Halloween. Magic. Witches.

Doctor on an elephant ill. by Michael Chesworth. Holt, 1994. ISBN 0-8050-2876-5 Subj: Animals – elephants. Careers – doctors. Foreign lands – India. Weather – rain.

Don't get me in trouble ill. by Marvin Glass. Crown, 1987. ISBN 0-517-56724-5 Subj: Animals – dogs. Friendship.

Fat magic ill. by Tomie de Paola. Holiday, 1978. ISBN 0-823-40327-0 Subj: Magic. Royalty.

The goat parade ill. by Tim Kirk. Parents' Magazine Pr., 1983. ISBN 0-8193-1100-6 Subj: Animals – goats. Parades.

The hand-me-down doll ill. by Evaline Ness. Holiday, 1983. ISBN 0-8234-0495-1 Subj: Toys – dolls.

Happy Father's Day ill. by Marylin Hafner. Holiday, 1987. ISBN 0-5234-0671-7 Subj: Family life – fathers. Holidays – Father's Day.

Happy Mother's Day ill. by Marylin Hafner. Holiday, 1985. ISBN 0-8234-0504-4 Subj: Family life. Holidays – Mother's Day.

The Hokey-Pokey man ill. by Deborah Kogan Ray. Holiday, 1989. ISBN 0-8234-0728-4 Subj: Food.

Howard and Gracie's luncheonette ill. by Michael Sours. Holt, 1991. ISBN 0-8050-1305-9 Subj: Activities – working. Careers.

I love spring! ill. by Kathryn E. Shoemaker. Holiday, 1987. ISBN 0-8234-0634-2 Subj: Seasons – spring.

If I could be my grandmother ill. by Tasha Tudor. Pantheon, 1977. ISBN 0-394-93554-3 Subj: Family life – grandmothers.

It's April Fools' Day! ill. by Jeni Bassett. Holiday, 1990. ISBN 0-8234-0747-0 Subj: Animals – cats. Behavior – bullying. Holidays – April Fools' Day.

It's Groundhog Day! ill. by Jeni Bassett. Holiday, 1987. ISBN 0-8234-0643-1 Subj: Activities – picnicking. Animals. Holidays – Groundhog Day.

Lewis and Clark: explorers of the American West ill. by Richard Williams. Holiday, 1994. ISBN 0-8234-1034-X Subj: Careers – explorers. U.S. history.

Looking for Daniela ill. by Anita Lobel. Holiday, 1988. ISBN 0-8234-0695-4 Subj: Crime. Foreign lands – Italy. Problem solving.

Loose tooth ill. by Tricia Tusa. Holiday, 1984. ISBN 0-8234-0518-4 Subj: Fairies. Teeth.

The magic rocket ill. by Will Hillenbrand. Holiday, 1992. ISBN 0-8234-0916-3 Subj: Animals – dogs. Imagination. Space & space ships. Toys.

Mary McLean and the St. Patrick's Day parade ill. by Michael Dooling. Scholastic, 1991. ISBN 0-590-43701-1 Subj: Cities, towns. Ethnic groups in the U.S. – Irish Americans. Holidays – St. Patrick's Day. Parades.

Oh, Tucker! ill. by Scott Nash. Candlewick, 1998. ISBN 0-7636-0429-1 Subj: Animals – dogs. Character traits – clumsiness.

Oh, what a Thanksgiving! ill. by S. D. Schindler. Scholastic, 1988. ISBN 0-590-40613-2 Subj: Holidays – Thanksgiving. Imagination. U.S. history.

One tough turkey: a Thanksgiving story ill. by John Wallner. Holiday, 1982. ISBN 0-8234-0457-9 Subj: Birds – turkeys. Holidays – Thanksgiving. Pilgrims. Sports – hunting.

Otto ill. by Ned Delaney. Parents' Magazine Pr., 1983. ISBN 0-8193-1106-5 Subj: Behavior – misbehavior. Robots.

Patches: an art story ill. by Barry Gott. Winslow, 2001. ISBN 1-8908-1753-8 Subj: Activities – drawing. Animals – guinea pigs. Behavior – lost & found possessions. Children as authors. Children as illustrators.

Patches lost and found ill. by Barry Gott. Cavendish, 2005. ISBN 0-7614-5217-6 Subj: Activities – drawing. Animals – guinea pigs. Behavior – lost & found possessions. Pets. School.

The pigrates clean up ill. by Jeni Bassett. Holt, 1993. ISBN 0-8050-2368-2 Subj: Activities – bathing. Animals – pigs. Boats, ships. Character traits – cleanliness. Pirates. Rhyming text. Weddings.

Pigs in the house ill. by Tim Kirk. Parents' Magazine Pr., 1983. ISBN 0-8193-1111-1 Subj: Animals – pigs. Behavior – misbehavior. Homes, houses. Rhyming text.

Princess Abigail and the wonderful hat ill. by Patience Brewster. Holiday, 1991. ISBN 0-8234-0853-1 Subj: Clothing – hats. Folk & fairy tales. Royalty – princesses.

Queen of the May ill. by Patience Brewster. Holiday, 1993. ISBN 0-8234-1004-8 Subj: Animals. Character traits – kindness to animals. Fairs, festivals. Family life – stepfamilies. Folk & fairy tales.

Santa's crash-bang Christmas ill. by Tomie de Paola. Holiday, 1977. ISBN 0-8234-0302-5 Subj: Holidays – Christmas. Santa Claus.

The squirrels' Thanksgiving ill. by Jeni Bassett. Holiday, 1991. ISBN 0-8234-0823-X Subj: Animals – squirrels. Family life. Holidays – Thanksgiving. Sibling rivalry.

That makes me mad ill. by Christine Davenier. SeaStar, 2002. ISBN 1-58717-184-8 Subj: Behavior. Emotions – anger. Family life – mothers.

Toot! Toot! ill. by Anne F. Rockwell. Holiday, 1983. ISBN 0-8234-0471-4 Subj: Family life – grandparents. Imagination. Toys – trains. Trains.

The tyrannosaurus game ill. by Tomie de Paola. Holiday, 1976. ISBN 0-8234-0275-4 Subj: Cumulative tales. Dinosaurs. Games. Imagination.

Will you be my valentine? ill. by Lillian Hoban. Holiday, 1993. ISBN 0-8234-0925-2 Subj: Activities – making things. Behavior – indifference. Holidays – Valentine's Day. School.

Woof, woof! ill. by Nicole Rubel. Dial, 1983. ISBN 0-8037-9651-X Subj: Animals – dogs. Crime.

Kroll, Virginia L. *Africa brothers and sisters* ill. by Vanessa French. Four Winds, 1993. ISBN 0-02-751166-9 Subj: Ethnic groups in the U.S. – African Americans. Family life – fathers. Foreign lands – Africa.

Beginnings: how families come to be ill. by Stacey Schuett. A. Whitman, 1994. ISBN 0-8075-0602-8 Subj: Adoption. Family life.

Boy, you're amazing! ill. by Sachiko Yoshikawa. A. Whitman, 2004. ISBN 0-8075-0868-3 Subj: Activities. Rhyming text. Self-concept.

Butterfly boy ill. by Gerardo Suzán. Boyds Mills, 1997. ISBN 1-56397-371-5 Subj: Family life – grandfathers. Foreign lands – Mexico. Illness. Insects – butterflies, caterpillars.

Can you dance, Dalila? ill. by Nancy Carpenter. S&S, 1996. ISBN 0-689-80551-9 Subj: Activities – dancing. Ballet. Ethnic groups in the U.S. – African Americans.

A carp for Kimiko ill. by Katherine Roundtree. Charlesbridge, 1993. ISBN 0-8810-6413-0 Subj: Family life. Fish. Foreign lands – Japan. Gender roles. Holidays. Kites.

The Christmas cow ill. by author. Players Pr., 1996. ISBN 0-8873-4481-X Subj: Animals – bulls, cows. Holidays – Christmas. Religion – Nativity. Self-concept.

Faraway drums ill. by Floyd Cooper. Little, 1998. ISBN 0-316-50449-1 Subj: Cities, towns. Ethnic groups in the U.S. – African Americans. Family life – sisters. Foreign lands – Africa. Imagination.

Fireflies, peach pies, and lullabies ill. by Nancy Cote. S&S, 1995. ISBN 0-02-751001-8 Subj: Death. Family life. Illness – Alzheimer's. Memories, memory. Old age.

Girl, you're amazing! ill. by Mélisande Potter. A. Whitman, 2001. ISBN 0-8075-2930-3 Subj: Gender roles. Rhyming text.

Hands! ill. by Cathryn Falwell. Boyds Mills, 1997. ISBN 1-56397-051-1 Subj: Anatomy – hands.

Helen the fish ill. by Teri Weidner. A. Whitman, 1992. ISBN 0-8075-3194-4 Subj: Death. Family life – brothers. Fish. Pets.

Jaha and Jamil went down the hill: an African Mother Goose ill. by Katherine Roundtree. Charlesbridge, 1995. ISBN 0-88106-867-5 Subj: Foreign lands – Africa. Nursery rhymes.

Lunching and munching ill. by Jesse Sweetwater. S&S, 1999. ISBN 0-689-81564-6 Subj: Animals. Food. Rhyming text.

Masai and I ill. by Nancy Carpenter. Four Winds, 1992. ISBN 0-02-751165-0 Subj: Ethnic groups in the U.S. – African Americans. Family life. Foreign lands – Africa.

Motherlove ill. by Lucia Washburn. Dawn, 1998. ISBN 1-8832-2080-7 Subj: Animals – babies. Family life – mothers. Rhyming text.

My sister, then and now ill. by Mary Worcester. Carolrhoda, 1992. ISBN 0-8761-4718-X Subj: Family life – sisters. Illness.

Naomi knows it's springtime ill. by Jill Kastner. Caroline House, 1993. ISBN 1-56397-006-6 Subj: Handicaps – blindness. Seasons – spring.

New friends, true friends, stuck-like-glue friends ill. by Rose Rosely. Eerdmans, 1994. ISBN 0-8028-5085-5 Subj: Ethnic groups in the U.S. Friendship. Rhyming text.

Pink paper swans ill. by Nancy L. Clouse. Eerdmans, 1994. ISBN 0-8028-5081-2 Subj: Ethnic groups in the U.S. – Japanese Americans. Illness. Paper.

The seasons and someone ill. by Tatsuro Kiuchi. Harcourt, 1994. ISBN 0-15-271233-X Subj: Eskimos. Foreign lands – Arctic. Indians of North America. Names. Seasons.

She is born: a celebration of daughters ill. by John Rowe. Beyond Words, 1999. ISBN 1-8852-2394-3 Subj: Babies. Family life – daughters.

Sweet Magnolia ill. by Laura Jacques. Charlesbridge, 1995. ISBN 0-8810-6416-5 Subj: Animals. Birds. Character traits – kindness to animals. Ethnic groups in the U.S. – African Americans. Family life – grandmothers.

Wood-hoopoe Willie ill. by Katherine Roundtree. Charlesbridge, 1992. ISBN 0-88106-410-6 Subj: Birds – wood-hoopoes. Ethnic groups in the U.S. – African Americans. Family life. Holidays – Kwanzaa. Music. Musical instruments – drums.

Kroninger, Stephen. *If I crossed the road* ill. by author. Atheneum, 1997. ISBN 0-689-81190-X Subj: Imagination. Roads.

Kropf, Latifa Berry. *It's Hanukkah time!* photos by Tod Cohen. Kar-Ben Copies, 2004. ISBN 1-58013-120-4 Subj: Family life – grandparents. Holidays – Hanukkah. Jewish culture. Parties. Religion.

It's seder time! photos by Tod Cohen. Kar-Ben Copies, 2004. ISBN 1-58013-092-5 Subj: Holidays – Passover. Holidays – Seder. Jewish culture. Religion.

Krosoczka, Jarrett J. *Annie was warned* ill. by author. Knopf, 2003. ISBN 0-375-91567-2 Subj: Holidays – Halloween. Homes, houses.

Baghead ill. by author. Del Dragonfly, 2004. ISBN 0-375-91566-4 Subj: Hair. Humorous stories.

Bubble bath pirates ill. by author. Viking, 2003. ISBN 0-670-03599-8 Subj: Activities – bathing. Family life – mothers. Pirates.

Good night, Monkey Boy ill. by author. Knopf, 2001. ISBN 0-375-91121-9 Subj: Bedtime. Family life – mothers. Family life – sons.

Max for president ill. by author. Knopf, 2004. ISBN 0-375-92428-0 Subj: Friendship. School. Sportsmanship.

Krudop, Walter Lyon. *Blue claws* ill. by author. Atheneum, 1993. ISBN 0-689-31787-5 Subj: Crustaceans – crabs. Family life – grandfathers. Sports – fishing.

The man who caught fish ill. by author. Farrar, 2000. ISBN 0-374-34786-7 Subj: Behavior – greed. Folk & fairy tales. Foreign lands – Thailand. Royalty – kings. Sports – fishing.

Something is growing ill. by author. Atheneum, 1995. ISBN 0-689-31940-1 Subj: Behavior – unnoticed, unseen. Cities, towns. Gardens, gardening.

Krudwig, Vickie Leigh. *Cucumber soup* ill. by Craig McFarland Brown. Fulcrum Kids, 1998. ISBN 1-55591-380-6 Subj: Counting, numbers. Food. Insects.

Kruglik, Gerald. *Pish and Posh* (Bottner, Barbara)

Krulik, Nancy E. *Is it Hanukkah yet?* ill. by DyAnne DiSalvo-Ryan. Random House, 2003. ISBN 0-375-90286-4 Subj: Holidays – Hanukkah. Jewish culture. Religion.

Krull, Kathleen. *Autumn* (Allington, Richard L.)

The boy on Fairfield Street: how Ted Geisel grew up to become Dr. Seuss ill. by Steve Johnson & Lou Fancher; with decorative ill. by Dr. Seuss. Random House, 2004. ISBN 0-375-92298-9 Subj: Books, reading. Careers – authors. Careers – illustrators.

It's my earth too ill. by Melanie Hope Greenberg. Doubleday, 1992. ISBN 0-385-42088-9 Subj: Ecology. Nature.

M is for music ill. by Stacy Innerst. Harcourt, 2003. ISBN 0-15-201438-1 Subj: ABC books. Music.

Maria Molina and the Days of the Dead ill. by Enrique O. Sánchez. Macmillan, 1994. ISBN 0-02-750999-0 Subj: Family life. Foreign lands – Mexico. Holidays – Day of the Dead.

Measuring (Allington, Richard L.)

Reading (Allington, Richard L.)

Science (Allington, Richard L.)

Songs of praise ill. by Kathryn Hewitt. Harcourt, 1989. ISBN 0-15-277108-5 Subj: Music. Religion. Seasons. Songs.

Spring (Allington, Richard L.)

Summer (Allington, Richard L.)

Supermarket ill. by Melanie Hope Greenberg. Holiday, 2001. ISBN 0-8234-1546-5 Subj: Food. Stores.

Talking (Allington, Richard L.)

Thinking (Allington, Richard L.)

Time (Allington, Richard L.)

Winter (Allington, Richard L.)

Words (Allington, Richard L.)

Writing (Allington, Richard L.)

Krum, Charlotte. *The four riders* ill. by Katherine Evans. Follett, 1953. Subj: Animals – horses, ponies.

Krupinski, Loretta. *Best friends* ill. by author. Hyperion, 1998. ISBN 0-7868-0332-0 Subj: Friendship. Indians of North America – Nez Perce. Toys – dolls. U.S. history.

Celia's island journal (Thaxter, Celia)

Christmas in the city ill. by author. Hyperion, 2002. ISBN 0-7868-2652-5 Subj: Animals – mice. Cities, towns. Holidays – Christmas. Trees.

Into the woods: a woodland scrapbook ill. by author. HarperCollins, 1997. ISBN 0-06-026444-6 Subj: Activities – walking. Forest, woods. Nature. Science.

Lost in the fog (Bacheller, Irving)

A New England scrapbook: a journey through poetry, prose, and pictures ill. by author. HarperCollins, 1994. ISBN 0-06-022951-9 Subj: Poetry.

Krupp, E. C. (Edwin C.). *The comet and you* ill. by Robin Rector Krupp. Macmillan, 1985. ISBN 0-02-751250-9 Subj: Science.

The rainbow and you ill. by Robin Rector Krupp. HarperCollins, 2000. ISBN 0-688-15602-9 Subj: Weather – rainbows.

Krupp, Robin Rector. *Get set to wreck!* ill. by author. Macmillan, 1988. ISBN 0-02-751140-5 Subj: Activities – playing. Imagination. Language.

Let's go traveling in Mexico ill. by author. Morrow, 1996. ISBN 0-688-12368-6 Subj: Foreign lands – Mexico. Mythical creatures. Seasons.

Krüss, James. *Johnny Longnose* by James Krüss & Naomi Lewis; ill. by Stasys Eidrigevicius. North-South, 1990. ISBN 1-55858-023-9 Subj: Anatomy – noses. Poetry.

3 X 3: Three by three ill. by Eva Johanna Rubin; English text by Geoffrey Strachan. Macmillan, 1963. Subj: Animals. Counting, numbers. Poetry.

Krylov, Ivan Andreevich. *The cat and the cook and other fables of Krylov* (Heins, Ethel L.)

Kubler, Susanne. *The three friends* ill. by author. Macmillan, 1985. ISBN 0-02-751150-2 Subj: Animals. Friendship.

Kübler-Ross, Elisabeth. *Remember the secret* ill. by Heather Preston. Celestial Arts, 1982. Subj: Death. Memories, memory.

Kuchalla, Susan. *All about seeds* ill. by Jane McBee. Troll, 1982. Subj: Plants. Science. Seeds.

Baby animals ill. by Joel Snyder. Troll, 1982. Subj: Animals.

Bears ill. by Kathie Kelleher. Troll, 1982. Subj: Animals – bears.

Birds ill. by Gary Britt. Troll, 1982. Subj: Birds.

What is a reptile? ill. by Paul Harvey. Troll, 1982. Subj: Reptiles.

Kudler, David. *The Seven Gods of Luck* ill. by Linda Finch. Houghton Mifflin, 1997. ISBN 0-395-78830-7 Subj: Family life – brothers & sisters. Folk & fairy tales. Foreign lands – Japan. Holidays – New Year's. Poverty.

Kudrna, C. Imbior. *To bathe a boa* ill. by author. Carolrhoda, 1986. ISBN 0-87614-306-0 Subj: Activities – bathing. Behavior – hiding. Reptiles – snakes. Rhyming text.

Kuei, Ye Ping. *Monkey and the white bone demon* (Shi, Zhang Xiu)

Kuhn, Dwight. *Hungry little frog* photos by Dwight Kuhn; text by Ron Hirschi. Cobblehill, 1992. ISBN 0-525-65109-8 Subj: Animals. Counting, numbers. Frogs & toads.

Kühner, Peter. *The circus of mystery* (Fazzi, Maura)

Kuiper, Nannie. *Bailey the bear cub* ill. by Jeska Verstegen; trans. by J. Alison James. North-South, 2002. ISBN 0-7358-1625-5 Subj: Animals – babies. Animals – bears. Behavior – growing up. Family life – mothers.

Bravo, brave beavers ill. by Jeska Verstegen; trans. by J. Alison James. North-South, 2004. ISBN 0-7358-1916-5 Subj: Animals – beavers. Character traits – cooperation. Family life. Weather – storms.

Kuklin, Susan. *Dance* (Jones, Bill T.)

From head to toe: how a doll is made photos by author. Hyperion, 1994. ISBN 1-56282-667-0 Subj: Activities – making things. Toys – dolls.

Going to my ballet class photos by author. Bradbury, 1989. ISBN 0-02-751235-5 Subj: Activities – dancing. Ballet.

Going to my gymnastics class photos by author. Bradbury, 1991. ISBN 0-02-751236-3 Subj: Sports – gymnastics.

Going to my nursery school photos by author. Bradbury, 1990. ISBN 0-02-751237-1 Subj: School – nursery.

How my family lives in America photos by author. Bradbury, 1992. ISBN 0-02-751239-8 Subj: Ethnic groups in the U.S. Family life.

Lighting fires photos by author. Bradbury, 1993. ISBN 0-02-751238-X Subj: Careers – firefighters. Fire. Trucks.

Taking my dog to the vet photos by author. Bradbury, 1988. ISBN 0-02-751234-7 Subj: Animals. Careers – veterinarians. Pets.

Thinking big: the story of a young dwarf photos by author. Lothrop, 1986. ISBN 0-688-05827-2 Subj: Character traits – being different. Handicaps.

When I see my dentist photos by author. Bradbury, 1988. ISBN 0-02-751231-2 Subj: Careers – dentists. Health & fitness.

When I see my doctor photos by author. Bradbury, 1988. ISBN 0-02-751232-0 Subj: Careers – doctors.

Kulling, Monica. *Waiting for Amos* ill. by Vicky Lowe. Bradbury, 1993. ISBN 0-02-751245-2 Subj: Animals. Character traits – patience. Friendship. Frogs & toads. Reptiles – turtles, tortoises.

Kulman, Andrew. *Red light stop, green light go* ill. by author. S&S, 1993. ISBN 0-671-79493-0 Subj: Concepts. Traffic, traffic signs.

Kumin, Maxine W. *The beach before breakfast* ill. by Leonard Weisgard. Putnam, 1964. Subj: Sea & seashore – beaches.

Eggs of things ill. by Leonard W. Shortall. Putnam, 1963. Subj: Eggs. Frogs & toads. Humorous stories. Science.

Follow the fall ill. by Artur Marokvia. Putnam, 1961. Subj: Holidays. Imagination. Rhyming text. Seasons – fall.

Joey and the birthday present by Maxine W. Kumin & Anne Sexton; ill. by Evaline Ness. McGraw-Hill, 1971. Subj: Animals – mice. Birthdays.

Mittens in May ill. by Eliott Gilbert. Putnam, 1962. Subj: Birds. Character traits – kindness to animals. Clothing – gloves, mittens.

Sebastian and the dragon ill. by William D. Hayes. Putnam, 1960. Subj: Character traits – smallness. Dragons. Rhyming text.

Speedy digs downside up ill. by Ezra Jack Keats. Putnam, 1964. Subj: Activities – digging. Character traits – ambition. Humorous stories. Rhyming text.

What color is Caesar? ill. by Evaline Ness. McGraw-Hill, 1978. Subj: Animals – dogs. Concepts – color.

A winter friend ill. by Artur Marokvia. Putnam, 1961. Subj: Poetry. Seasons – winter.

Kunhardt, Dorothy. *Billy the barber* ill. by William Pène Du Bois. HarperCollins, 1961. Subj: Careers – barbers. Hair. Old age.

Kitty's new doll ill. by Lucinda McQueen. Golden Pr., 1984. Subj: Animals – cats. Toys – dolls.

Kunhardt, Edith. *Danny and the Easter egg* ill. by author. Greenwillow, 1989. ISBN 0-688-08036-7 Subj: Holidays – Easter. Reptiles – alligators, crocodiles.

Danny's birthday ill. by author. Greenwillow, 1986. ISBN 0-688-06177-X Subj: Birthdays. Parties. Reptiles – alligators, crocodiles.

Danny's Christmas star ill. by author. Greenwillow, 1989. ISBN 0-688-07906-7 Subj: Activities – making things. Holidays – Christmas. Reptiles – alligators, crocodiles.

Danny's mystery Valentine ill. by author. Greenwillow, 1987. ISBN 0-688-06854-5 Subj: Family life – grandmothers. Holidays – Valentine's Day. Reptiles – alligators, crocodiles.

I'm going to be a farmer photos by author. Scholastic, 1996. Originally published: I want to be a farmer. New York: Grosset & Dunlap, c1989. ISBN 0-590-25482-0 Subj: Careers – farmers. Farms.

I'm going to be a fire fighter photos by author. Scholastic, c1989, (1995 printing). Originally published: I want to be a fire fighter. New York: Grosset & Dunlap, 1989. ISBN 0-590-25483-9 Subj: Careers – firefighters.

I'm going to be a police officer photos by author. Scholastic, 1995. Originally published: I want to be a police officer. New York: Grosset & Dunlap, 1989. ISBN 0-590-25485-5 Subj: Careers – police officers.

I'm going to be a vet photos by author. Scholastic, 1996. ISBN 0-590-25484-7 Subj: Animals. Careers – veterinarians.

Pat the cat ill. by author. Golden Pr., 1984. Subj: Animals – cats. Format, unusual – toy & movable books. Pets.

Pat the puppy ill. by author. Western, 1993. ISBN 0-307-12004-X Subj: Animals – dogs. Family life – grandparents. Format, unusual – toy & movable books.

Red day, green day ill. by Marylin Hafner. Greenwillow, 1992. ISBN 0-688-09400-7 Subj: Concepts – color. School. Weather – rainbows.

Trick or treat, Danny! ill. by author. Greenwillow, 1988. ISBN 0-688-07311-5 Subj: Holidays – Halloween. Illness. Reptiles – alligators, crocodiles.

Where's Peter? ill. by author. Greenwillow, 1988. ISBN 0-688-07205-4 Subj: Babies. Family life. Games.

Which one would you choose? ill. by author. Greenwillow, 1989. ISBN 0-688-07908-3 Subj: Activities. Participation.

Which pig would you choose? ill. by author. Greenwillow, 1990. ISBN 0-688-08982-8 Subj: Activities. Farms. Participation.

Kunhardt, Katharine. *Let's count the puppies* photos by author. HarperCollins, 2004. ISBN 0-06-054337-X Subj: Animals – babies. Animals – dogs. Counting, numbers.

Kunkel, Jeff. *Noah, build your boat: Old Testament stories & pictures by kids* (Noah, build your boat)

Kunnas, Mauri. *The nighttime book* by Mauri Kunnas with Tarja Kunnas; trans. from Finnish by Tim Steffa; ill. by author. Crown, 1985. ISBN 0-517-55819-X Subj: Activities. Night.

One spooky night and other scary stories by Mauri Kunnas with Tarja Kunnas; trans. by Tim Steffa; ill. by author. Crown, 1986. ISBN 0-517-56253-7 Subj: Ghosts. Holidays – Halloween. Monsters.

Santa Claus and his elves by Mauri Kunnas; assisted by Tarja Kunnas; ill. by authors. Harmony, 1982. Translation of Joulupukki. Subj: Holidays – Christmas. Mythical creatures – elves. Santa Claus.

Twelve gifts for Santa Claus by Mauri & Tarja Kunnas; trans. by Tim Steffa; ill. by authors. Crown, 1988. ISBN 0-517-56631-1 Subj: Character traits – generosity. Gifts. Holidays – Christmas. Mythical creatures – elves. Santa Claus.

Kunnas, Tarja. *The nighttime book* (Kunnas, Mauri)

One spooky night and other scary stories (Kunnas, Mauri)

Santa Claus and his elves (Kunnas, Mauri)

Twelve gifts for Santa Claus (Kunnas, Mauri)

Kunstler, James Howard. *Annie Oakley* ill. by Fred Warter. Rabbit Ears, 1996. ISBN 0-689-80605-1 Subj: U.S. history – frontier & pioneer life.

Kupfer, Andrew. *Night city* (Wellington, Monica)

Kuratomi, Chizuko. *Mr. Bear and the robbers* ill. by Kozo Kakimoto. Dial, 1970. Subj: Animals – bears. Animals – rabbits.

Kurjian, Judi. *In my own backyard* ill. by David Wagner. Charlesbridge, 1993. ISBN 0-88106-443-2 Subj: Imagination.

Kurokawa, Mitsuhiro. *Dinosaur valley* ill. by author. Chronicle, 1992. ISBN 0-8118-0257-4 Subj: Dinosaurs. Format, unusual – toy & movable books. Prehistory.

Kurt, Kemal. *The five fingers and the moon* ill. by Aljoscha Blau; trans. by Anthea Bell. North-South, 1997. ISBN 1-55858-802-7 Subj: Magic. Moon. Mythical creatures.

Kurtz, Christopher. *Only a pigeon* (Kurtz, Jane)

Kurtz, Jane. *Faraway home* ill. by E.B. Lewis. Harcourt, 2000. ISBN 0-15-200036-4 Subj: Ethnic groups in the U.S. – African Americans. Family life – fathers. Foreign lands – Ethiopia. Memories, memory.

Fire on the mountain ill. by E. B. Lewis. S&S, 1994. ISBN 0-671-88268-6 Subj: Family life – brothers & sisters. Folk & fairy tales. Foreign lands – Ethiopia.

Miro in the kingdom of the sun ill. with woodcuts by David Frampton. Houghton Mifflin, 1996. ISBN 0-395-69181-8 Subj: Character traits – bravery. Folk & fairy tales. Indians of South America – Incas. Magic. Royalty.

Only a pigeon by Jane & Christopher Kurtz; ill. by E. B. Lewis. S&S, 1997. ISBN 0-689-80077-0 Subj: Birds – pigeons. Foreign lands – Ethiopia. Pets. Sports – racing.

Rain romp: stomping away a grouchy day ill. by Dyanna Wolcott. Greenwillow, 2002. ISBN 0-06-029806-5 Subj: Behavior. Family life – parents. Rhyming text. Weather – rain.

River friendly, river wild ill. by Neil Brennan. S&S, 2000. ISBN 0-689-82049-6 Subj: Family life. Rivers. U.S. history. Weather – floods.

Kushner, Donn. *Peter's pixie* ill. by Sylvie Daigneault. Tundra, 2003. ISBN 0-88776-603-X Subj: Family life – brothers. Family life – new sibling. Magic. Mythical creatures – pixies.

Kushner, Karen. *Because Nothing Looks Like God* (Kushner, Lawrence)

Kushner, Lawrence. *Because Nothing Looks Like God* by Lawrence Kushner & Karen Kushner; ill. by Dawn Majewski. Jewish Lights, 2000. ISBN 1-58023-092-X Subj: Religion.

Kushner, Tony. *Brundibar* ill. by Maurice Sendak. Hyperion, 2003. ISBN 0-7868-0904-3 Subj: Activities – singing. Behavior – bullying. Family life – brothers & sisters.

Kuskin, Karla. *ABCDEFGHIJKLMNOPQRSTUVWXYZ* ill. by author. HarperCollins, 1963. Subj: ABC books.

All sizes of noises ill. by author. HarperCollins, 1962. Subj: Concepts. Noise, sounds. Poetry.

The animals and the ark ill. by author. HarperCollins, 1958. Subj: Animals. Boats, ships. Poetry. Religion – Noah. Weather – floods. Weather – rain.

A boy had a mother who bought him a hat ill. by author. Houghton Mifflin, 1976. Subj: Cumulative tales. Rhyming text.

City dog ill. by author. Clarion, 1994. ISBN 0-395-66138-2 Subj: Animals – dogs. Country. Rhyming text. Sea & seashore.

City noise ill. by Renee Flower. HarperCollins, 1994. ISBN 0-06-021076-1 Subj: Cities, towns. Noise, sounds. Poetry.

The Dallas Titans get ready for bed ill. by Marc Simont. HarperCollins, 1986. ISBN 0-06-023563-2 Subj: Bedtime. Clothing. Sports – football.

A great miracle happened there: a Chanukah story Robert Andrew Parker ill. by Robert Andrew Parker. Willa Perlman Books, 1993. ISBN 0-06-023618-3 Subj: Family life. Holidays – Hanukkah. Jewish culture. Religion.

Herbert hated being small ill. by author. Houghton Mifflin, 1979. ISBN 0-395-26462-6 Subj: Character traits – smallness. Concepts – size. Rhyming text.

I am me ill. by Dyanna Wolcott. S&S, 2000. ISBN 0-689-81473-9 Subj: Character traits – individuality. Family life. Sea & seashore.

In the flaky frosty morning ill. by author. HarperCollins, 1969. Subj: Rhyming text. Seasons – winter. Snowmen. Weather – snow.

James and the rain ill. by author. HarperCollins, 1957. ISBN 0-671-88808-0 Subj: Animals. Rhyming text. Weather – rain.

Jerusalem, shining still ill. by David Frampton. HarperCollins, 1987. ISBN 0-06-023549-7 Subj: Cities, towns. Foreign lands – Israel. Religion.

Just like everyone else ill. by author. HarperCollins, 1959. ISBN 0-06-443032-4 Subj: Activities – flying.

Night again ill. by author. Little, 1981. ISBN 0-316-50721-0 Subj: Bedtime.

Patchwork island ill. by Petra Mathers. HarperCollins, 1994. ISBN 0-06-021284-5 Subj: Activities – sewing. Poetry. Quilts.

Paul ill. by Milton Avery. HarperCollins, 1994. ISBN 0-06-023573-X Subj: Family life – grandmothers. Imagination. Magic. Songs.

The Philharmonic gets dressed ill. by Marc Simont. HarperCollins, 1982. ISBN 0-06-023622-1 Subj: Clothing.

Roar and more ill. by author. HarperCollins, 1956. ISBN 0-06-023619-1 Subj: Animals. Noise, sounds. Participation. Rhyming text.

Sand and snow ill. by author. HarperCollins, 1965. Subj: Poetry. Sea & seashore. Seasons – summer. Seasons – winter.

The sky is always in the sky ill. by Isabelle Dervaux. Geringer, 1998. ISBN 0-06-027084-5 Subj: Poetry.

Soap soup and other verses ill. by author. HarperCollins, 1992. ISBN 0-06-023572-1 Subj: Poetry.

Something sleeping in the hall ill. by author. HarperCollins, 1985. ISBN 0-06-023634-5 Subj: Animals. Pets. Poetry.

A space story ill. by Marc Simont. HarperCollins, 1978. ISBN 0-06-023542-X Subj: Bedtime. Space & space ships. Stars.

Under my hood I have a hat ill. by Fumi Kosaka. Geringer, 2004. ISBN 0-06-057243-4 Subj: Clothing. Rhyming text. Seasons – winter.

The upstairs cat ill. by Howard Fine. Clarion, 1997. ISBN 0-395-70146-5 Subj: Animals – cats. Poetry.

Watson, the smartest dog in the U.S.A. ill. by author. HarperCollins, 1968. Subj: Animals – dogs. Books, reading.

What did you bring me? ill. by author. HarperCollins, 1973. ISBN 0-06-023653-1 Subj: Animals – mice. Behavior – greed. Self-concept. Witches.

Which horse is William? ill. by author. Greenwillow, 1992. ISBN 0-688-10638-2 Subj: Character traits – individuality. Imagination.

Kusugak, Michael. *A promise is a promise* (Munsch, Robert N.)

Kutner, Merrily. *Z is for zombie* ill. by John Manders. A. Whitman, 1999. ISBN 0-8075-9490-3 Subj: ABC books. Holidays – Halloween. Rhyming text.

Kvasnosky, Laura McGee. *One, two, three, play with me!* ill. by author. Dutton, 1994. ISBN 0-525-45234-6 Subj: Activities – playing. Counting, numbers. Format, unusual – board books. Poetry.

Pink, red, blue, what are you? ill. by author. Dutton, 1994. ISBN 0-525-45233-8 Subj: Animals. Concepts – color. Format, unusual – board books. Poetry.

What shall I dream? ill. by Judith Byron Schachner. Dutton, 1996. ISBN 0-525-45207-9 Subj: Dreams. Royalty – princes.

Zelda and Ivy ill. by author. Candlewick, 1998. ISBN 0-7636-0469-0 Subj: Animals – foxes. Family life – sisters.

Zelda and Ivy and the boy next door ill. by author. Candlewick, 1999. ISBN 0-7636-0672-3 Subj: Animals – foxes. Family life – sisters.

Zelda and Ivy one Christmas ill. by author. Candlewick, 2000. ISBN 0-7636-1000-3 Subj: Animals – foxes. Character traits – generosity. Family life – sisters. Holidays – Christmas. Old age.

Kwitz, Mary DeBall. *Little chick's breakfast* ill. by Bruce Degen. HarperCollins, 1983. ISBN 0-06-023675-2 Subj: Birds – chickens. Farms. Food.

Little chick's story ill. by Cyndy Szekeres. HarperCollins, 1978. ISBN 0-06-023666-3 Subj: Birds – chickens. Eggs.

Mouse at home ill. by author. HarperCollins, 1966. Subj: Animals – mice. Seasons.

Rabbits' search for a little house ill. by Lorinda Bryan Cauley. Crown, 1977. ISBN 0-517-52867-3 Subj: Animals – rabbits. Homes, houses.

When it rains ill. by author. Follett, 1974. ISBN 0-695-40411-3 Subj: Animals. Rhyming text. Weather – rain. Weather – rainbows.

Kwon, Holly H. *The moles and the mireuk: a Korean folktale* ill. by Woodleigh Hubbard. Houghton Mifflin, 1993. ISBN 0-395-64347-3 Subj: Animals – moles. Behavior – seeking better things. Folk & fairy tales. Foreign lands – Korea.

Kyle, Kathryn. *Honesty* ill. with photos. Child's World, 2003. ISBN 1-56766-089-4 Subj: Character traits – honesty.

Respect ill. with photos. Child's World, 2003. ISBN 1-56766-092-4 Subj: Behavior.

Kyte, Dennis. *Mattie and Cataragus* ill. by author. Doubleday, 1988. ISBN 0-385-24404-5 Subj: Animals – cats. Friendship.

L. M. C. *see* Child, Lydia Maria

Labatt, Mary. *A friend for Sam* ill. by Marisol Sarrazin. Kids Can, 2003. ISBN 1-55337-374-X Subj: Animals – dogs. Emotions – loneliness. Friendship.

Pizza for Sam ill. by Marisol Sarrazin. Kids Can, 2003. ISBN 1-55337-329-4 Subj: Animals – babies. Animals – dogs. Food.

Sam finds a monster ill. by Marisol Sarrazin. Kids Can, 2003. ISBN 1-55337-351-0 Subj: Animals – dogs. Monsters.

Sam gets lost ill. by Marisol Sarrazin. Kids Can, 2004. ISBN 1-55337-562-9 Subj: Animals – dogs. Behavior – lost.

Sam goes to school ill. by Marisol Sarrazin. Kids Can, 2004. ISBN 1-55337-564-5 Subj: Animals – dogs. School.

Sam's first Halloween ill. by Marisol Sarrazin. Kids Can, 2003. ISBN 1-55337-355-3 Subj: Animals – dogs. Holidays – Halloween.

Lacapa, Michael. *Antelope Woman: an Apache folktale* ill. by author. Northland, 1992. ISBN 0-87358-543-7 Subj: Animals – antelopes. Folk & fairy tales. Indians of North America – Apache. Sports – hunting.

Lach, William. *I imagine angels* (I imagine angels)

Lachner, Dorothea. *Andrew's angry words* ill. by The Tjong-Khing. North-South, 1995. ISBN 1-55858-436-6 Subj: Communication. Emotions – anger. Language.

Danny, the angry lion ill. by Gusti; trans. by J. Alison James. North-South, 2000. ISBN 0-7358-1387-6 Subj: Emotions – anger.

The gift from Saint Nicholas ill. by Maja Dusíková. North-South, 1995. ISBN 1-55858-457-9 Subj: Holidays – Christmas. Weather – snow.

Look out, Cinder! ill. by Eugen Sopko; trans. by Rosemary Lanning. North-South, 1996. ISBN 1-55858-521-4 Subj: Animals – cats. Emotions – loneliness. Friendship.

Meredith, the witch who wasn't ill. by Christa Unzner; trans. by J. Alison James. North-South, 1997. ISBN 1-55858-781-0 Subj: Character traits – individuality. Magic. Witches.

Meredith's mixed-up magic ill. by Christa Unzner; trans. by J. Alison James. North-South, 2000. ISBN 0-7358-1190-3 Subj: Magic. Witches.

Smoky's special Easter present ill. by Christa Unzner; trans. by Marianne Martens. North-South, 1996. ISBN 1-55858-574-5 Subj: Activities. Animals – rabbits. Holidays – Easter. Pets.

Lachtman, Ofelia Dumas. *Pepita takes time = Pepita, siempre tarde* ill. by Alex Pardo DeLange; Spanish trans. by Alejandra Balestra. Piñata, 2001. ISBN 1-55885-304-9 Subj: Behavior – promptness, tardiness. Ethnic groups in the U.S. – Hispanic Americans. Foreign languages.

Lackner, Michelle Myers. *Toil in the soil* ill. by Daniel Powers. Millbrook, 2001. ISBN 0-7613-1807-0 Subj: Animals – worms.

Lacoe, Addie. *Just not the same* ill. by Pau Estrada. Houghton Mifflin, 1992. ISBN 0-395-59347-6 Subj: Behavior – sharing. Birthdays. Multiple births – triplets. Sibling rivalry.

Lacome, Julie. *Funny business* ill. by author. Morrow, 1991. ISBN 0-688-10159-3 Subj: Animals – dogs. Circus. Clowns, jesters. Concepts – color. Concepts – shape. Format, unusual – toy & movable books.

Garden ill. by author. Candlewick, 1995. ISBN 1-56402-478-4 Subj: Animals. Format, unusual – toy & movable books. Gardens, gardening.

Hocus pocus ill. by author. Morrow, 1991. ISBN 0-688-10158-5 Subj: Animals – rabbits. Format, unusual – toy & movable books. Magic.

I'm a jolly farmer ill. by author. Candlewick, 1994. ISBN 1-56402-318-4 Subj: Activities – playing. Animals – dogs. Imagination. Rhyming text.

My first book of words ill. by author. 2nd ed. Candlewick, 1996. ISBN 1-56402-749-1 Subj: Language.

On the farm ill. by author. Candlewick, 1995. ISBN 1-56402-706-6 Subj: Farms.

Ruthie's big old coat ill. by author. Candlewick, 2000. ISBN 0-7636-0969-2 Subj: Activities – playing. Animals – rabbits. Clothing – coats.

Seashore ill. by author. Candlewick, 1995. ISBN 1-56402-479-2 Subj: Animals. Format, unusual – board books. Sea & seashore.

Walking through the jungle ill. by author. Candlewick, 1993. ISBN 1-56402-137-8 Subj: Animals. Jungle. Noise, sounds. Nursery rhymes.

Lacy, Donna. *The music box: the story of Cristofori* (Guy, Suzanne)

Laden, Nina. *Bad dog* ill. by author. Walker, 2000. ISBN 0-8027-8748-7 Subj: Animals – dogs. Behavior – misbehavior. Humorous stories.

Clowns on vacation ill. by author. Walker, 2002. ISBN 0-8027-8781-9 Subj: Activities – vacationing. Clowns, jesters. Rhyming text.

Peek-a-who? ill. by author. Chronicle, 2000. ISBN 0-8118-2602-3 Subj: Format, unusual – board books. Rhyming text.

Private I. Guana, the case of the missing chameleon ill. by author. Chronicle, 1995. ISBN 0-8118-0940-4 Subj: Humorous stories. Mystery stories. Reptiles – chameleons. Reptiles – iguanas. Reptiles – lizards.

Roberto, the insect architect ill. by author. Chronicle, 2000. ISBN 0-8118-2465-9 Subj: Careers – architects. Insects – termites.

When Pigasso met Mootisse ill. by author. Chronicle, 1998. ISBN 0-8118-1121-2 Subj: Animals – bulls, cows. Animals – pigs. Careers – artists.

Ladwig, Tim. *The Lord's prayer* (Bible New Testament)

Psalm twenty-three (Bible Old Testament Psalms)

Lady Eden's School. *Just how stories* ill. by Derek Steele. Merrimack, 1981. ISBN 0-224-01713-6 Subj: Animals. Children as authors.

Ladybug, ladybug, and other nursery rhymes ill. by Eloise Wilkin. Random House, 1979. ISBN 0-394-84282-0 Subj: Format, unusual. Nursery rhymes.

La Farge, Phyllis. *Joanna runs away* ill. by Trina Schart Hyman. Holt, 1973. ISBN 0-03-091306-3 Subj: Animals – horses, ponies. Behavior – running away.

La Farge, Sheila. *The boy who ate more than the giant and other Swedish folktales* (Löfgren, Ulf)

Peter's adventures in Blueberry Land (Beskow, Elsa Maartman)

La Fontaine, Jean de. *The fox and the stork* (McDermott, Gerald)

The hare and the tortoise ill. by Brian Wildsmith. Watts, 1963. Subj: Animals – rabbits. Folk & fairy tales. Reptiles – turtles, tortoises. Sports – racing.

The lion and the rat ill. by Brian Wildsmith. Oxford Univ. Pr., 1984 printing, c1963. ISBN 0-19-279607-0 Subj: Animals – lions. Animals – rats. Character traits – helpfulness. Folk & fairy tales.

The miller, the boy and the donkey adapt. & ill. by Brian Wildsmith. Watts, 1969. Based on a fable by La Fontaine. ISBN 0-19-279652-6 Subj: Animals – donkeys. Character traits – practicality. Folk & fairy tales. Humorous stories.

The north wind and the sun ill. by Brian Wildsmith. Watts, 1964. ISBN 0-19-272168-2 Subj: Folk & fairy tales. Sun. Weather – wind.

The turtle and the two ducks: animal fables (Plante, Patricia)

Lafontaine, Pascale Claude. *see* ClaudeLafontaine, Pascale

Lage, Ida De. *see* DeLage, Ida

Lager, Claude. *A tale of two rats* ill. by Nicole Rutten. Stewart, Tabori & Chang, 1991. ISBN 1-55670-228-0 Subj: Animals – rats. Careers – artists. Foreign lands – Italy. Friendship.

Lagercrantz, Rose. *Brave little Pete of Geranium Street* by Rose & Samuel Lagercrantz; trans. by Jack Prelutsky; ill. by Eva Eriksson. Greenwillow, 1986. ISBN 0-688-06181-8 Subj: Behavior – bullying. Character traits – bravery. Rhyming text.

Lagercrantz, Samuel. *Brave little Pete of Geranium Street* (Lagercrantz, Rose)

Lagerlöf, Selma. *The changeling* trans. from Swedish by Susanna Stevens; ill. by Jeanette Winter. Knopf, 1992. ISBN 0-679-91035-2 Subj: Babies. Emotions – love. Fairies. Format, unusual – toy & movable books. Mythical creatures – trolls.

The legend of the Christmas rose retold by Ellin Greene; ill. by Charles Mikolaycak. Holiday, 1990. ISBN 0-8234-8021-3 Subj: Flowers. Folk & fairy tales. Holidays – Christmas.

Laidlaw, Ken. *The amazing I spy ABC* ill. by author. Dial, 1996. ISBN 0-8037-1992-2 Subj: ABC books. Format, unusual – toy & movable books. Picture puzzles.

Laimgruber, Monika. *Susannah and the Sandman: a good-night story* ill. by author. North-South, 1996. ISBN 1-55858-602-4 Subj: Bedtime. Dreams. Mythical creatures – sandman. Sleep.

Laird, Donivee Martin. *The three little Hawaiian pigs and the magic shark* ill. by Carol Jossem. Bess Pr., 1981. ISBN 0-940350-01-7 Subj: Animals – pigs. Fish – sharks. Hawaii.

Laird, Elizabeth. *A book of promises* ill. by Michael Frith. DK, 2000. ISBN 0-7894-2547-5 Subj: Emotions – love. Family life.

The day Patch stood guard ill. by Colin Reeder. Morrow, 1991. ISBN 0-688-10240-9 Subj: Animals – dogs. Farms. Foreign lands – England. Tractors.

The day Sidney ran off ill. by Colin Reeder. Morrow, 1991. ISBN 0-688-10242-5 Subj: Animals – pigs. Farms. Foreign lands – England. Tractors.

The day the ducks went skating ill. by Colin Reeder. Morrow, 1991. ISBN 0-688-10247-6 Subj: Animals. Birds – ducks. Careers – farmers. Character traits – kindness to animals. Farms. Tractors.

The day Veronica was nosy ill. by Colin Reeder. Morrow, 1991. ISBN 0-688-10249-2 Subj: Animals. Careers – farmers. Farms. Insects – hornets. Tractors.

Lairla, Sergio. *Abel and the wolf* ill. by Alessandra Roberti; trans. by Marianne Martens. North-South, 2004. ISBN 0-7358-1903-3 Subj: Animals – wolves. Emotions. Forest, woods. Friendship.

Lake, Mary Dixon. *The royal drum: an Ashanti tale* ill. by Carol O'Malia. Mondo, 1996. ISBN 1-57255-125-9 Subj: Animals. Folk & fairy tales. Foreign lands – Ghana. Spiders.

Lakin, Pat (Patricia). *Aware and alert* ill. by Doug Cushman. Raintree, 1995. ISBN 0-8114-8261-8 Subj: Careers – police officers. Communities, neighborhoods. Crime. Safety.

Dad and me in the morning ill. by Robert Gantt Steele. A. Whitman, 1994. ISBN 0-8075-1419-5 Subj: Family life – fathers. Family life – sons. Handicaps – physical handicaps. Morning. Sea & seashore.

Don't forget ill. by Ted Rand. Tambourine, 1994. ISBN 0-688-12076-8 Subj: Behavior – secrets. Birthdays. Holocaust. Jewish culture.

Don't touch my room ill. by Patience Brewster. Little, 1985. ISBN 0-316-51230-3 Subj: Babies. Behavior – sharing. Emotions – fear. Family life – new sibling. Sibling rivalry.

Family: around the world ill. by author. Blackbirch, 1995. ISBN 1-56711-143-2 Subj: Family life. World.

A good sport ill. by Doug Cushman. Raintree, 1995. ISBN 0-8114-3870-8 Subj: Behavior. Sports – soccer.

Grandparents: around the world ill. by author. Blackbirch, 1999. ISBN 1-56711-146-7 Subj: Family life – grandparents. Old age. World.

Growing up: around the world ill. by author. Blackbirch, 1995. ISBN 1-56711-144-0 Subj: Behavior – growing up. Behavior – sharing. Family life.

Hurricane! ill. by Vanessa Lubach. Millbrook, 2000. ISBN 0-7613-1616-7 Subj: Family life – fathers. Weather – hurricanes.

Information, please ill. by Doug Cushman. Raintree, 1995. ISBN 0-8114-8260-X Subj: Careers – librarians. Communities, neighborhoods.

Jet black pickup truck ill. by Rosekrans Hoffman. Orchard, 1990. ISBN 0-531-08485-X Subj: Family life – grandmothers. Rhyming text. Trucks.

Just like me ill. by Patience Brewster. Little, 1989. ISBN 0-316-51233-8 Subj: Family life – brothers. School.

The mystery illness ill. by Doug Cushman. Raintree, 1995. ISBN 0-8114-3867-8 Subj: Careers – nurses. Illness. School.

Oh, brother! ill. by Patience Brewster. Little, 1987. ISBN 0-316-51231-1 Subj: Family life. Sibling rivalry. Trees.

The palace of stars ill. by Kimberly Bulcken Root. Tambourine, 1993. ISBN 0-688-11177-7 Subj: Family life – aunts, uncles. Friendship. Theater.

Play: around the world ill. by author. Blackbirch, 1995. ISBN 1-56711-141-6 Subj: Activities – playing.

Red letter day ill. by Doug Cushman. Raintree, 1995. ISBN 0-8114-8264-2 Subj: Careers – postal workers. Communities, neighborhoods. School.

Snow day! ill. by Scott Nash. Dial, 2002. ISBN 0-8037-2642-2 Subj: School. Weather – snow.

Subway sonata ill. by Heather Harms Maione. Millbrook, 2001. ISBN 0-7613-1464-4 Subj: Careers – artists. Cities, towns. Trains.

Trash and treasure ill. by Doug Cushman. Raintree, 1995. ISBN 0-8114-3865-1 Subj: Behavior – lost & found possessions. Careers – custodians, janitors. School.

Up a tree ill. by Doug Cushman. Raintree, 1995. ISBN 0-8114-3868-6 Subj: Careers – bus drivers. Pets. School.

Lakin, Patricia. *Clarence the copy cat* ill. by John Manders. Doubleday, 2002. ISBN 0-385-32747-1 Subj: Animals – cats. Animals – mice. Libraries.

Fat chance Thanksgiving. A. Whitman, 2001. ISBN 0-8075-2288-0 Subj: Books, reading. Communities, neighborhoods. Holidays – Thanksgiving. Homes, houses.

Lakota, Philomine. *Shota and the star quilt* (Bateson-Hill, Margaret)

Lalicki, Barbara. *If there were dreams to sell* ill. by Margot Tomes. 2nd ed. Four Winds, 1994. ISBN 0-02-751251-7 Subj: ABC books. Poetry.

Lalli, Judy. *Feelings alphabet: an album of emotions from A to Z* photos by Douglas L. Mason-Fry. Jalmar, 1984. ISBN 0-935266-15-1 Subj: ABC books. Emotions.

LaMarche, Jim. *The raft* ill. by author. HarperCollins, 2000. ISBN 0-688-13978-7 Subj: Animals. Boats, ships. Family life – grandmothers. Rivers.

The walloping window-blind (Carryl, Charles E. [Charles Edward])

La Mare, Walter De. *see* De La Mare, Walter (Walter John)

Lambert, Martha Lewis. *I won't get lost* ill. by Kate Duke. HarperCollins, 2003. ISBN 0-06-028961-9 Subj: Behavior – lost. Dragons. School.

Why do you love me? (Schlessinger, Laura)

Lambert, Paulette Livers. *Evening: an Appalachian lullaby* ill. by adapt. Roberts Rinehart, 1995. ISBN 1-57098-012-8 Subj: Lullabies. Music. Songs.

Lamborn, Florence. *Christmas in noisy village* (Lindgren, Astrid)

Laminack, Lester L. *Saturdays and teacakes* ill. by Chris Soentpiet. Peachtree, 2004. ISBN 1-56145-303-X Subj: Activities – baking, cooking. Character traits – helpfulness. Family life – grandmothers.

The sunsets of Miss Olivia Wiggins ill. by Constance R. Bergum. Peachtree, 1998. ISBN 1-56145-139-8 Subj: Family life – grandparents. Memories, memory. Old age.

Trevor's wiggly-wobbly tooth ill. by Kathi Garry McCord. Peachtree, 1998. ISBN 1-56145-175-4 Subj: Emotions – fear. Family life – grandmothers. School. Teeth.

Lamm, C. Drew. *Anniranni and Mollymishi, the wild-haired doll* ill. by Ruth Ohi. Firefly, 1990. ISBN 1-55037-105-3 Subj: Animals – dogs. Toys – dolls.

Gauchada ill. by Fabian Negrin. Knopf, 2001. ISBN 0-375-91267-3 Subj: Foreign lands – Argentina. Jewelry.

Pirates ill. by Stacey Schuett. Hyperion, 2001. ISBN 0-7868-0392-4 Subj: Books, reading. Emotions – fear. Family life – brothers & sisters. Pirates.

Screech Owl at Midnight Hollow ill. by Joel Snyder. Soundprints, 1996. ISBN 1-56899-265-3 Subj: Birds – owls. Family life. Nature.

Lamont, Priscilla. *Out to lunch* ill. by author. Kingfisher, 1995. ISBN 1-85697-564-9 Subj: Animals – dogs. Behavior – promptness, tardiness.

The troublesome pig (The old woman and her pig)

Lampert, Emily. *A little touch of monster* ill. by Victoria Chess. Atlantic Monthly, 1986. ISBN 0-87113-022-X Subj: Character traits – individuality. Family life.

Lamstein, Sarah Marwil. *Annie's Shabbat* ill. by Cecily Lang. A. Whitman, 1997. ISBN 0-8075-0376-2 Subj: Jewish culture. Religion.

I like your buttons! ill. by Nancy Cote. A. Whitman, 1999. ISBN 0-8075-3510-9 Subj: Character traits – kindness. School.

Landa, Norbert. *Cubs* by Norbert Landa, Ona Pans, Victoria Seix. Barron's, 2000. ISBN 0-7641-1480-8 Subj: Animals – babies.

How does it feel? ill. by Karin Littlewood. Thomasson-Grant, 1993. ISBN 1-56566-032-3 Subj: Imagination.

Kittens by Norbert Landa & Ona Pans. Barron's, 2000. ISBN 0-7641-1481-6 Subj: Animals – babies. Animals – cats.

Little Bear's Christmas ill. by Marlis Scharff-Kniemeyer; trans. by Anna Trenter. Little Tiger, 1999. ISBN 1-888444-60-6 Subj: Animals – bears. Holidays – Christmas. Santa Claus. Weather – snow.

Puppies by Norbert Landa, Ona Pans, Victoria Seix. Barron's, 2000. ISBN 0-7641-1482-4 Subj: Animals – babies. Animals – dogs.

Rabbit and chicken count eggs ill. by Hanne Türk. Tambourine, 1992. ISBN 0-688-09971-8 Subj: Animals – rabbits. Birds – chickens. Counting, numbers. Eggs. Format, unusual – board books. Friendship.

Rabbit and chicken find a box ill. by Hanne Türk. Morrow, 1992. ISBN 0-688-09968-8 Subj: Animals – rabbits. Birds – chickens. Character traits – helpfulness. Format, unusual – board books. Friendship.

Rabbit and chicken play hide and seek ill. by Hanne Türk. Morrow, 1992. ISBN 0-688-09970-X Subj: Activities – playing. Animals – rabbits. Birds – chickens. Friendship. Games.

Rabbit and chicken play with colors ill. by Hanne Türk. Tambourine, 1992. ISBN 0-688-09969-6 Subj: Animals – rabbits. Birds – chickens. Concepts – color. Eggs. Format, unusual – board books. Friendship. Holidays – Easter.

Landalf, Helen. *The secret night world of cats* ill. by author. Smith & Kraus, 1997. ISBN 1-57525-117-5 Subj: Animals – cats. Magic. Night.

Landau, Elaine. *Mardi Gras* ill. with photos. Enslow, 2002. ISBN 0-7660-1776-1 Subj: Fairs, festivals. Holidays. Mardi Gras.

St. Patrick's Day ill. with photos. Enslow, 2002. ISBN 0-7660-1777-X Subj: Holidays – St. Patrick's Day. Mythical creatures – leprechauns. Parades.

Valentine's Day ill. with photos. Enslow, 2002. ISBN 0-7660-1779-6 Subj: Holidays – Valentine's Day.

Landau, Terry. *Butterflies and rainbows* (Berger, Judith)

Landry, Leo. *Eat your peas, Ivy Louise!* ill. by author. Houghton, 2005. ISBN 0-618-44886-1 Subj: Circus. Food. Imagination.

The snow ghosts ill. by author. Houghton, 2003. ISBN 0-618-19655-2 Subj: Ghosts. Weather – snow.

Landshoff, Ursula. *Cats are good company* ill. by author. HarperCollins, 1983. ISBN 0-06-023677-9 Subj: Animals – cats. Pets. Science.

Landström, Lena. *Boo and Baa at sea* (Landström, Olof)

Boo and Baa get wet (Landström, Olof)

Boo and Baa in a party mood (Landström, Olof)

Boo and Baa in windy weather (Landström, Olof)

Boo and Baa on a cleaning spree (Landström, Olof)

The little hippos' adventure ill. by author; trans. by Joan Sandin. Farrar, 2002. ISBN 91-29-65500-5 Subj: Animals – hippopotamuses.

Will gets a haircut (Landström, Olof)

Will goes to the beach (Landström, Olof)

Will goes to the post office (Landström, Olof)

Will's new cap (Landström, Olof)

Landström, Olof. *Boo and Baa at sea* written & ill. by Olof & Lena Landström; trans. by Joan Sandin. R&S Books, 1997. ISBN 91-29-63921-2 Subj: Animals – sheep. Boats, ships. Humorous stories. Sea & seashore.

Boo and Baa get wet Olof & Lena Landström; ill. by authors; trans. by Joan Sandin. Farrar, 2000. ISBN 91-29-64752-5 Subj: Animals – sheep. Humorous stories. Weather – storms.

Boo and Baa in a party mood written & ill. by Olof & Lena Landström; trans. by Joan Sandin. Farrar, 1996. ISBN 91-29-63918-2 Subj: Activities – dancing. Animals – sheep. Birthdays. Humorous stories. Parties.

Boo and Baa in the woods Olof & Lena Landström; ill. by authors; trans. by Joan Sandin. Farrar, 2000. ISBN 91-29-64754-1 Subj: Activities – picnicking. Animals – sheep. Forest, woods. Humorous stories. Insects – ants.

Boo and Baa in windy weather written & ill. by Olof & Lena Landström; trans. by Joan Sandin. Farrar, 1996. ISBN 91-29-63920-4 Subj: Animals – sheep. Food. Humorous stories. Weather – snow. Weather – storms.

Boo and Baa on a cleaning spree written & ill. by Olof & Lena Landström; trans. by Joan Sandin. R&S Books, 1997. ISBN 91-29-63919-0 Subj: Animals – sheep. Character traits – cleanliness. Humorous stories.

Will gets a haircut written & ill. by Olof & Lena Landström; trans. by Elizabeth Dyssegaard. R&S Books, 1993. ISBN 91-29-62075-9 Subj: Hair.

Will goes to the beach written & ill. by Olof & Lena Landström. R&S Books, 1995. ISBN 91-29-65305-3 Subj: Sea & seashore – beaches.

Will goes to the post office written & ill. by Olof & Lena Landström; trans. by Elisabeth Dyssegaard. Farrar, 1994. ISBN 91-29-62950-0 Subj: Post office.

Will's new cap written & ill. by Olof & Lena Landström; trans. by Richard E. Fisher. Farrar, 1992. ISBN 91-29-62062-7 Subj: Clothing – hats.

Lane, Daniel. *The Animal Mall* (Edens, Cooper)

Lane, E. I. *Mother Goose's rhymes and melodies* (Mother Goose)

Lane, Judith. *Buster, where are you?* ill. by Nancy Lane. Benefactory, 1998. ISBN 1-58021-019-8 Subj: Animals – dogs. Behavior – lost.

Lane, Marcia. *Christoph wants a party* (Lobe, Mira)

Lane, Margaret. *The frog* ill. by Grahame Corbett. Dial, 1981. ISBN 0-8037-2711-9 Subj: Frogs & toads. Science.

The squirrel ill. by Kenneth Lilly. Dial, 1981. ISBN 0-8037-8230-6 Subj: Animals – squirrels. Science.

Lane, Megan Halsey. *Something to crow about* ill. by author. Dial, 1990. ISBN 0-8037-0698-7 Subj: Birds – chickens. Gender roles. Self-concept.

Lang, Andrew. *The flying ship* ill. by Dennis McDermott. Morrow, 1995. ISBN 0-688-11405-9 Subj: Activities – flying. Boats, ships. Folk & fairy tales. Foreign lands – Russia. Royalty – kings. Royalty – princesses.

Nursery rhyme book (Mother Goose)

Snow White and Rose Red (Grimm, Jacob)

Lang, Aubrey. *The adventures of Baby Bear* photos by Wayne Lynch. Fitzhenry & Whiteside, 2001. ISBN 1-55041-670-7 Subj: Animals – babies. Animals – bears.

Baby elephant photos by Wayne Lynch. Fitzhenry & Whiteside, 2002. ISBN 1-55041-715-0 Subj: Animals – babies. Animals – elephants.

Baby fox photos by Wayne Lynch. Fitzhenry & Whiteside, 2002. ISBN 1-55041-688-X Subj: Animals – babies. Animals – foxes.

Baby lion photos by Wayne Lynch. Fitzhenry & Whiteside, 2002. ISBN 1-55041-711-8 Subj: Animals – babies. Animals – lions.

Baby penguin photos by Wayne Lynch. Fitzhenry & Whiteside, 2001. ISBN 1-55041-675-8 Subj: Animals – babies. Birds – penguins.

Lang, Glenna. *Looking out for Sarah* ill. by author. Talewinds, 2001. ISBN 0-88106-647-8 Subj: Animals – dogs. Animals – service animals. Handicaps – blindness.

Langdo, Bryan. *The dog who loved the good life* ill. by author. Holt, 2001. ISBN 0-8050-6494-X Subj: Animals – dogs.

Lange, Willem. *John and Tom* ill. by Bert Dodson. Vermont Folklife Center, 2001. ISBN 0-916718-17-4 Subj: Accidents. Animals – horses, ponies. Careers – lumberjacks.

Langford, Sondra Gordon. *Mishka and Plishka* ill. by Debrah Santini. S&S, 1995. ISBN 0-689-80244-7 Subj: Careers – bakers. Foreign lands – Russia. Money.

Langham, Tony. *The amazing adventures of Teddy Tum Tum* (Breese, Gillian)

Langley, Jonathan. *Rumpelstiltskin* (Grimm, Jacob)

Shine (Langley, Karen)

The three billy goats Gruff (Asbjørnsen, P. C. [Peter Christen])

Langley, Karen. *Shine* by Karen & Jonathan Langley; ill. by Jonathan Langley. Cavendish, 2002. ISBN 0-7614-5127-7 Subj: Family life – fathers. Holidays – Christmas. School. Stars. Theater.

Langner, Nola. *By the light of the silvery moon* ill. by author. Lothrop, 1983. ISBN 0-688-01663-4 Subj: Behavior – running away. Imagination – imaginary friends. Royalty.

Freddy my grandfather ill. by author. Four Winds, 1979. ISBN 0-890-07577-2 Subj: Family life – grandfathers.

Langreuter, Jutta. *Little Bear and the big fight* by Jutta Langreuter & Vera Sobat; ill. by Vera Sobat. Millbrook, 1998. ISBN 0-7613-0403-7 Subj: Animals – bears. Behavior – misbehavior. Emotions – anger. Friendship. School.

Little Bear brushes his teeth by Jutta Langreuter & Vera Sobat; ill. by Vera Sobat. Millbrook, 1997. ISBN 0-7613-0190-9 Subj: Animals – bears. Family life. Hygiene.

Little Bear goes to kindergarten by Jutta Langreuter & Vera Sobat; ill. by Vera Sobat. Millbrook, 1997. ISBN 0-7613-0191-7 Subj: Animals – bears. Friendship. School – first day.

Little Bear won't go to bed ill. by Vera Sobat. Millbrook, 2000. ISBN 0-7613-1872-0 Subj: Animals – bears. Bedtime.

Langsen, Richard C. *When someone in the family drinks too much* ill. by Nicole Rubel. Dial, 1996. ISBN 0-8037-1687-7 Subj: Animals – bears. Family life. Illness – alcoholism.

Langstaff, John M. *Frog went a-courtin'* (A frog he would a-wooing go [folk-song])

Hot cross buns, and other old street cries (Hot cross buns, and other old street cries)

Oh, a-hunting we will go ill. by Nancy Winslow Parker. Atheneum, 1974. ISBN 0-689-50007-6 Subj: Folk & fairy tales. Music. Songs. Sports – hunting.

Ol' Dan Tucker ill. by Joe Krush. Harcourt, 1963. Subj: Folk & fairy tales. Music. Songs.

On Christmas day in the morning ill. by Antony Groves-Raines. Harcourt, 1959. Piano settings by Marshall Woodbridge. Subj: Folk & fairy tales. Holidays – Christmas. Music. Songs.

Over in the meadow ill. by Feodor Rojankovsky. Harcourt, 1957. Includes Over in the meadow (for voice and piano) by Marshall Woodbridge. ISBN 0-15-258854-X Subj: Animals. Counting, numbers. Folk & fairy tales. Songs.

Soldier, soldier, won't you marry me? ill. by Anita Lobel. Doubleday, 1972. Subj: Careers – military. Folk & fairy tales. Music. Songs.

The swapping boy ill. by Beth & Joe Krush. Harcourt, 1960. ISBN 0-15-283358-7 Subj: Activities – trading. Folk & fairy tales. Music. Songs.

The two magicians ill. by Fritz Eichenberg. Atheneum, 1973. Adapt. by John Langstaff from an ancient ballad. ISBN 0-689-30319-X Subj: Folk & fairy tales. Magic. Music. Songs. Witches.

What a morning! the Christmas story in Black spirituals (What a morning!)

Langstaff, Nancy. *A tiny baby for you* ill. by Suzanne Szasz. Harcourt, 1955. Subj: Babies.

Langston, Laura. *The fox's kettle* ill. by Victor Bosson. Orca, 1998. ISBN 1-55143-132-7 Subj: Animals – foxes. Folk & fairy tales. Foreign lands – Japan. Magic.

Langton, Jane. *The hedgehog boy: a Latvian folktale* ill. by Ilse Plume. HarperCollins, 1985. ISBN 0-06-023697-3 Subj: Character traits – honesty. Folk & fairy tales. Foreign lands – Latvia. Royalty. Weddings.

The queen's necklace: a Swedish folktale ill. by Ilse Plume. Hyperion, 1994. ISBN 0-7868-2007-1 Subj: Birds. Folk & fairy tales. Foreign lands – Sweden. Jewelry. Royalty.

Salt: from a Russian folktale (Afanas'ev, Aleksandr N.)

Lankford, Mary D. *Is it dark? Is it light?* ill. by Stacey Schuett. Knopf, 1991. ISBN 0-679-91579-6 Subj: Concepts – opposites. Moon.

Lanning, Rosemary. *Annie's dancing day* (Moers, Hermann)

The bear's Christmas (Moret, Brigitte Frey)

The blue monster (Ostheeren, Ingrid)

Camomile heads for home (Moers, Hermann)

Can we help you, Saint Nicholas? (Scheidl, Gerda Marie)

The Christmas visitor (Lussert, Anneliese)

The circus of mystery (Fazzi, Maura)

Coriander's Easter adventure (Ostheeren, Ingrid)

The emperor's new clothes (Andersen, H. C. [Hans Christian])

Happy birthday, Davy (Weninger, Brigitte)

Hare's Christmas gift (Schmid, Eleonore)

Hopper hunts for spring (Pfister, Marcus)

Hopper's treetop adventure (Pfister, Marcus)

I'm the real Santa Claus! (Ostheeren, Ingrid)

Jonathan Mouse (Ostheeren, Ingrid)

Jonathan Mouse and the baby bird (Ostheeren, Ingrid)

Jonathan Mouse and the magic box (Ostheeren, Ingrid)

Jonathan Mouse, detective (Ostheeren, Ingrid)

Laura (Schroeder, Binette)

Little Man's lucky day (Velthuijs, Max)

Little polar bear and the husky pup (De Beer, Hans)

Look out, Cinder! (Lachner, Dorothea)

Lullaby for a newborn king (Wilkon, Józef)

Merry Christmas, Davy! (Weninger, Brigitte)

Nobody likes me! (Krischanitz, Raoul)

Penguin Pete and Little Tim (Pfister, Marcus)

Pickle and Patch (Scheidl, Gerda Marie)

The seed (Pin, Isabel)

Snail started it! (Reider, Katja)

The special gifts (Grosz, Peter)

The squirrel and the moon (Schmid, Eleonore)

The star tree (Cölle, Gisela)

What's the matter, Davy? (Weninger, Brigitte)

When I grow up . . . (Horn, Peter)

Why are you fighting, Davy? (Weninger, Brigitte)

Will you be my friend? (Korth-Sander, Irmtraut)

Will you mind the baby, Davy? (Weninger, Brigitte)

Lansdown, Brenda. *Galumph* ill. by Ernest Crichlow. Houghton Mifflin, 1963. Subj: Animals – cats. Ethnic groups in the U.S. Ethnic groups in the U.S. – African Americans. Pets.

Lansky, Bruce. *Sweet dreams* ill. by Vicki Wehrman. Meadowbrook Press, 1996. ISBN 0-671-53479-3 Subj: Bedtime. Lullabies. Songs.

Lansky, Vicki. *It's not your fault, KoKo Bear: a read-together book for parents and young children during divorce* ill. by Jane Prince. Book Peddlers, 1998. ISBN 0-916-77346-9 Subj: Animals – bears. Divorce. Family life.

Lanteigne, Helen. *The seven chairs* ill. by Maryann Kovalski. Orchard, 1998. ISBN 0-531-30110-9 Subj: Activities – making things. Furniture – chairs.

Lanton, Sandy. *Daddy's chair* ill. by Shelly O. Haas. Kar-Ben Copies, 1991. ISBN 0-929371-51-8 Subj: Death. Emotions – grief. Family life – fathers. Furniture – chairs.

Lapp, Carolyn. *The dentists' tools* ill. by George Overlie. Lerner, 1961. Subj: Careers – dentists.

Lapp, Eleanor. *The blueberry bears* ill. by Margot Apple. A. Whitman, 1983. ISBN 0-8075-0796-2 Subj: Animals – bears. Food.

In the morning mist ill. by David Cunningham. A. Whitman, 1978. ISBN 0-8075-3634-2 Subj: Family life – grandfathers. Morning. Sports – fishing.

The mice came in early this year ill. by David Cunningham. A. Whitman, 1976. ISBN 0-8075-5111-2 Subj: Animals. Farms. Seasons – fall. Seasons – winter.

La Prise, Larry. *The hokey pokey* by Larry La Prise, Charles P. Macak, & Taftt Baker; ill. by Sheila Hamanaka. S&S, 1996. ISBN 0-689-80519-5 Subj: Activities – dancing. Music.

Lapsley, Susan. *I am adopted* ill. by Michael Charlton. Bradbury, 1974. ISBN 0-8788-8075-5 Subj: Adoption. Family life.

Larios, Julie Hofstrand. *On the stairs* ill. by Mary Hofstrand Cornish. Front St., 1999. ISBN 1-886910-34-0 Subj: Animals – mice. Counting, numbers. Rhyming text.

Laroche, Michel. *The snow rose* ill. by Sandra Laroche. Holiday, 1986. ISBN 0-8234-0594-X Subj: Character traits – cleverness. Folk & fairy tales. Royalty – princesses.

LaRochelle, David. *A Christmas guest* ill. by Martin Skoro. Carolrhoda, 1988. ISBN 0-87614-325-7 Subj: Character traits – kindness. Holidays – Christmas. Rhyming text.

The evening king ill. by Catherine Stock. Atheneum, 1993. ISBN 0-689-31640-2 Subj: Activities – playing. Imagination.

LaRose, Linda. *Jessica takes charge* ill. by Leanne Franson. Annick, 1999. ISBN 1-55037-563-6 Subj: Emotions – fear. Family life. Monsters. Night.

Larrick, Nancy. *Cats are cats* ill. by Ed Young. Putnam, 1988. ISBN 0-399-21517-4 Subj: Animals – cats. Poetry.

When the dark comes dancing: a bedtime poetry book ill. by John Wallner. Putnam, 1983. ISBN 0-399-20807-0 Subj: Bedtime. Night. Poetry.

Larry, Charles. *Peboan and Seegwun* ill. by author. Farrar, 1993. ISBN 0-374-35773-0 Subj: Folk & fairy tales. Indians of North America – Ojibwa. Seasons – spring. Seasons – winter.

Larsen, Hanne. *Don't forget Tom* ill. with photos. Crowell, 1978. ISBN 0-381-99554-2 Subj: Handicaps.

Larson, Bonnie. *When animals were people = Cuando los animales eran personas* ill. by Modesto Rivera Lemus. Clear Light, 2002. ISBN 1-57416-051-6 Subj: Animals. Folk & fairy tales – pourquoi tales. Foreign lands – Mexico. Foreign languages. Indians of North America – Huichol.

Larson, Kirby. *The magic kerchief* ill. by Rosanne Litzinger. Holiday, 2000. ISBN 0-8234-1473-6 Subj: Clothing. Folk & fairy tales. Magic.

Laschütza, Susanne. *Nat the bat* ill. by author. G. Stevens, 2003. ISBN 0-8368-3573-5 Subj: Animals – bats. Animals – dogs.

Lasell, Fen. *Fly away goose* ill. by author. Houghton Mifflin, 1965. Subj: Birds – geese. Eggs. Imagination.

Michael grows a wish ill. by author. Houghton Mifflin, 1974. ISBN 0-395-06880-0 Subj: Animals – horses, ponies. Behavior – wishing. Birthdays.

Laser, Michael. *The rain* ill. by Jeffrey Greene. S&S, 1997. ISBN 0-689-80506-3 Subj: Memories, memory. Weather – rain.

Lasher, Faith B. *Hubert Hippo's world* ill. by Leonard Lee Rue, III. Childrens Pr., 1971. ISBN 0-516-03489-8 Subj: Animals – hippopotamuses.

Lasker, David. *The boy who loved music* ill. by Joe Lasker. Viking, 1979. ISBN 0-670-18385-7 Subj: Careers – composers. Music. Royalty.

Lasker, Joe. *The do-something day* ill. by author. Viking, 1982. ISBN 0-670-27503-4 Subj: Behavior – running away.

He's my brother ill. by author. A. Whitman, 1974. ISBN 0-8075-3218-5 Subj: Character traits – loyalty. Family life. Handicaps.

Lentil soup ill. by author. A. Whitman, 1977. ISBN 0-8075-4438-8 Subj: Activities – baking, cooking. Counting, numbers. Days of the week, months of the year. Food.

Mothers can do anything ill. by author. A. Whitman, 1972. ISBN 0-8075-5287-9 Subj: Activities – working. Careers. Family life – mothers.

Nick joins in ill. by author. A. Whitman, 1980. ISBN 0-8075-5612-2 Subj: Handicaps – physical handicaps. School – first day.

Rabbit finds a way (Delton, Judy)

A tournament of knights ill. by author. Crowell, 1986. ISBN 0-690-04542-5 Subj: Behavior – fighting, arguing. Knights.

Laskin, Pamela L. *Wish upon a star: a story for children with a parent who is mentally ill* by Pamela L. Laskin & Addie Alexander Moskowitz; ill. by Margo Lemieux. Magination Pr., 1991. ISBN 0-945354-30-4 Subj: Emotions. Family life. Illness.

Laskowski, Janina Domanska. *see* Domanska, Janina

Laskowski, Jerzy. *Master of the royal cats* ill. by Janina Domanska. Seabury Pr., 1965. Subj: Animals – cats. Animals – dogs. Foreign lands – Africa. Foreign lands – Egypt. Royalty.

Lasky, Kathryn. *Agatha's alphabet, with her very own dictionary* (Floyd, Lucy)

A baby for Max photos by Christopher G. Knight. Scribners, 1984. ISBN 0-684-18064-2 Subj: Babies. Family life – new sibling. Sibling rivalry.

Baby love ill. by Jennifer Plecas. Candlewick, 2001. ISBN 1-56402-679-5 Subj: Babies.

The emperor's old clothes ill. by David Catrow. Harcourt, 1999. ISBN 0-15-200384-3 Subj: Careers – farmers. Clothing. Folk & fairy tales. Humorous stories. Royalty – emperors.

Fourth of July bear ill. by Helen Cogancherry. Morrow, 1991. ISBN 0-688-08288-2 Subj: Animals – bears. Friendship. Holidays – Fourth of July. Parades.

The Gates of the Wind ill. by Janet Stevens. Harcourt, 1995. ISBN 0-15-204264-4 Subj: Activities – traveling. Mountains. Weather – wind.

I have an aunt on Marlborough Street ill. by Susan Guevara. Macmillan, 1992. ISBN 0-02-751701-2 Subj: Cities, towns. Family life – aunts, uncles. Friendship.

I have four names for my grandfather ill. by Christopher G. Knight. Little, 1976. ISBN 0-316-51520-5 Subj: Emotions – love. Family life – grandfathers.

Lucille camps in ill. by Marylin Hafner. Knopf, 2003. ISBN 0-517-80042-X Subj: Animals – pigs. Camps, camping. Family life.

Lucille's snowsuit ill. by Marylin Hafner. Crown, 2000. ISBN 0-517-80038-1 Subj: Animals – pigs. Clothing. Family life – brothers & sisters. Weather – snow.

Lunch bunnies ill. by Marylin Hafner. Little, 1996. ISBN 0-316-51525-6 Subj: Animals – rabbits. Behavior – worrying. School – first day.

Marven of the Great North Woods ill. by Kevin Hawkes. Harcourt, 1997. ISBN 0-15-200104-2 Subj: Careers – accountants. Careers – lumberjacks. Forest, woods. Friendship. Illness.

Mommy's hands Kathryn Lasky & Jane Kamine; ill. by Darcia Labrosse. Hyperion, 2002. ISBN 0-7868-2225-2 Subj: Anatomy – hands. Family life – mothers. Seasons.

My island grandma ill. by Emily Arnold McCully. Warne, 1979. ISBN 0-7232-6159-8 Subj: Family life – grandmothers. Islands. Seasons – summer.

My island grandma ill. by Amy Schwartz. Morrow, 1993. ISBN 0-688-07948-2 Subj: Family life – grandmothers. Islands. Seasons – summer.

Pond year ill. by Mike Bostock. Candlewick, 1995. ISBN 1-56402-187-4 Subj: Activities – playing. Friendship. Lakes, ponds. Nature.

Science fair bunnies ill. by Marylin Hafner. Candlewick, 2000. ISBN 0-7636-0729-0 Subj: Animals – rabbits. Fairs, festivals. School. Science.

Sea swan ill. by Catherine Stock. Macmillan, 1988. ISBN 0-02-751700-4 Subj: Behavior – seeking better things. Old age. Sports – swimming.

Show and tell bunnies ill. by Marylin Hafner. Candlewick, 1998. ISBN 0-7636-0396-1 Subj: Animals – rabbits. School. Spiders.

The solo ill. by Bobette McCarthy. Macmillan, 1994. ISBN 0-02-751664-4 Subj: Activities – dancing. Character traits – confidence. Friendship. School.

Sophie and Rose ill. by Wendy Anderson Halperin. Candlewick, 1998. ISBN 0-7636-0459-3 Subj: Family life. Toys – dolls.

Starring Lucille ill. by Marylin Hafner. Crown, 2001. ISBN 0-517-80038-1 Subj: Activities – dancing. Animals – pigs. Ballet. Birthdays. Family life – brothers & sisters.

The tantrum ill. by Bobette McCarthy. Macmillan, 1993. ISBN 0-02-751661-X Subj: Emotions – anger. Family life.

Laslett, Stephanie. *The monster party: with six spooky holograms* ill. by Nigel McMullen. Dutton, 1996. ISBN 0-525-45691-0 Subj: Monsters. Parties. Witches.

Lass, Bonnie. *Who took the cookies from the cookie jar?* by Bonnie Lass & Philemon Sturges; ill. by Ashley Wolff. Little, 2000. ISBN 0-316-82016-4 Subj: Animals. Food. Insects – ants. Mystery stories. Rhyming text.

Lassen, Cary Pillo. *The big busy building* (Reasoner, Charles)

Lasson, Robert. *Orange Oliver: the kitten who wore glasses* ill. by Chuck Hayden. McKay, 1957. Subj: Animals – cats. Farms. Glasses. Senses – sight.

LaTeef, Nelda. *The hunter and the ebony tree* ill. by Nelda LaTeef. Moon Mt., 2002. ISBN 0-9677929-9-1 Subj: Folk & fairy tales. Foreign lands – Africa. Weddings.

Latham, Hugh. *Mother Goose in French: Poesies de la vraie Mere Oie* (Mother Goose)

Lathrop, Dorothy Pulis. *An angel in the woods* ill. by author. Macmillan, 1947. Subj: Angels. Holidays – Christmas.

Puppies for keeps ill. by author. Macmillan, 1943. Subj: Animals – dogs. Pets.

Who goes there? ill. by author. Macmillan, 1935. Subj: Activities – picnicking. Animals. Character traits – kindness to animals. Seasons – winter.

Latimer, Jim. *The fox under first base* ill. by Lisa McCue. Scribners, 1991. ISBN 0-684-19053-2 Subj: Animals – bears. Animals – foxes. Careers – detectives. Sports – baseball.

Going the moose way home ill. by Donald Carrick. Scribners, 1988. ISBN 0-684-18890-2 Subj: Animals – moose. Forest, woods. Friendship.

The Irish piper ill. by John O'Brien. Scribners, 1991. ISBN 0-684-19130-X Subj: Animals – rats. Behavior – trickery. Folk & fairy tales. Foreign lands – Germany. Poetry.

James Bear and the goose gathering ill. by Betsy Franco-Feeney. Scribners, 1994. ISBN 0-684-19526-7 Subj: Activities – singing. Animals. Animals – bears. Behavior – trickery. Birds – geese.

James Bear's pie ill. by Betsy Franco-Feeney. Scribners, 1992. ISBN 0-684-19226-8 Subj: Activities – baking, cooking. Animals – bears. Animals – skunks. Birds – crows.

Moose and friends ill. by C. S. Ewing. Scribners, 1993. ISBN 0-684-19335-3 Subj: Animals. Animals – moose.

Snail and Buffalo ill. by Tom Curry. Orchard, 1995. ISBN 0-531-08790-5 Subj: Animals – buffaloes. Animals – snails. Character traits – individuality.

When moose was young ill. by Donald Carrick. Scribners, 1990. ISBN 0-684-18932-1 Subj: Animals. Animals – moose.

Lattimore, Deborah Nourse. *Cinderhazel: the Cinderella of Halloween* ill. by author. Scholastic, 1997. ISBN 0-590-20232-4 Subj: Character traits – cleanliness. Royalty – princes. Witches.

The dragon's robe ill. by author. HarperCollins, 1990. ISBN 0-06-023723-6 Subj: Activities – weaving. Character traits – generosity. Character traits – selfishness. Dragons. Folk & fairy tales. Foreign lands – China.

Frida Maria: a story of the Old Southwest ill. by author. Browndeer, 1994. ISBN 0-15-276636-7 Subj: Family life. Gender roles.

I wonder what's under there? ill. by author; paper engineering by David A. Carter. Browndeer, 1998. ISBN 0-15-276652-9 Subj: Clothing. Format, unusual – toy & movable books.

The lady with the ship on her head ill. by author. Harcourt, 1990. ISBN 0-15-243525-5 Subj: Clothing – hats. Contests. Humorous stories.

The prince and the golden ax: a Minoan tale ill. by author. HarperCollins, 1988. ISBN 0-06-023716-3 Subj: Character traits – willfulness. Folk & fairy tales. Royalty – princes.

Punga the goddess of ugly ill. by author. Harcourt, 1993. ISBN 0-15-292862-6 Subj: Activities – dancing. Behavior – misbehavior. Family life – sisters. Folk & fairy tales. Foreign lands – New Zealand. Multiple births – twins.

The sailor who captured the sea: a story of the Book of Kells ill. by author. HarperCollins, 1991. ISBN 0-06-023711-2 Subj: Activities – writing. Books, reading. Character traits – persistence. Foreign lands – Ireland. Religion. Sailors.

Why there is no arguing in heaven: a Mayan myth ill. by author. Harper, 1989. ISBN 0-06-023718-X Subj: Creation. Folk & fairy tales. Indians of Central America – Maya.

Lattin, Anne. *Peter's policeman* ill. by Gertrude E. Espenscheid. Follett, 1958. Subj: Careers – police officers.

Lauber, Patricia. *Be a friend to trees* ill. by Holly Keller. HarperCollins, 1994. ISBN 0-06-021529-1 Subj: Ecology. Science. Trees.

Get ready for robots! ill. by True Kelley. HarperCollins, 1987. ISBN 0-690-04578-6 Subj: Robots.

How we learned the earth is round ill. by Megan Lloyd. Crowell, 1990. ISBN 0-690-04863-3 Subj: Earth. Science.

An octopus is amazing ill. by Holly Keller. Crowell, 1990. ISBN 0-690-04862-9 Subj: Octopuses.

Snakes are hunters ill. by Holly Keller. HarperCollins, 1988. ISBN 0-690-04630-8 Subj: Reptiles – snakes. Science.

What you never knew about tubs, toilets and showers ill. by John Manders. S&S, 2001. ISBN 0-689-82420-3 Subj: Activities – bathing. Character traits – cleanliness.

What's hatching out of that egg? ill. with photos. Crown, 1979. ISBN 0-517-53724-9 Subj: Eggs. Science.

Who eats what? ill. by Holly Keller. HarperCollins, 1995. ISBN 0-06-022982-9 Subj: Ecology. Food. Science.

You're aboard spaceship Earth ill. by Holly Keller. HarperCollins, 1996. ISBN 0-06-024408-9 Subj: Earth. Space & space ships.

Laurence, Margaret. *The Christmas birthday story* ill. by Helen Lucas. Knopf, 1980. ISBN 0-394-94361-9 Subj: Birthdays. Holidays – Christmas. Religion – Nativity.

Laurencin, Geneviève. *I wish I were* trans. from German by Andrea Mernan; ill. by Ulises Wensell. Putnam, 1987. ISBN 0-399-21416-X Subj: Animals. Behavior – bullying. Behavior – wishing.

Laurin, Anne. *Little things* ill. by Marcia Sewall. Atheneum, 1978. ISBN 0-689-30623-7 Subj: Activities – knitting. Character traits – patience. Humorous stories.

Perfect crane ill. by Charles Mikolaycak. HarperCollins, 1981. ISBN 0-06-023744-9 Subj: Birds – cranes. Foreign lands – Japan. Magic.

Lauture, Denizé. *Father and son* ill. by Jonathan Green. Philomel, 1992. ISBN 0-399-21867-X Subj: Ethnic groups in the U.S. – African Americans. Family life – fathers. Family life – sons. Poetry.

Running the road to ABC ill. by Reynold Ruffins. S&S, 1996. ISBN 0-689-80507-1 Subj: ABC books. Foreign lands – Haiti. School.

Laverde, Arlene. *Alaska's three pigs* ill. by Mindy Dwyer. Sasquatch, 2000. ISBN 1-57061-229-3 Subj: Alaska. Animals – pigs. Folk & fairy tales. Homes, houses.

Lavies, Bianca. *Lily pad pond* photos by author. Dutton, 1989. ISBN 0-525-44483-1 Subj: Animals. Nature. Trees.

Tree trunk traffic photos by author. Dutton, 1989. ISBN 0-525-44495-5 Subj: Animals. Insects. Nature. Trees.

Lavis, Steve. *Cock-a-doodle-doo: a farmyard counting book* ill. by author. Dutton, 1997. ISBN 0-525-67542-6 Subj: Animals. Counting, numbers. Noise, sounds.

Jump! ill. by author. Lodestar, 1998. ISBN 0-525-67578-7 Subj: Activities. Animals. Behavior – imitation. Birds.

On the farm ill. by author. Ragged Bears, 2001. ISBN 1-929927-23-1 Subj: Animals. Farms. Format, unusual – toy & movable books.

Lawlor, Laurie. *The biggest pest on Eighth Avenue* ill. by Cynthia Fisher. Holiday, 1997. ISBN 0-8234-1321-7 Subj: Family life – brothers & sisters. Theater.

Old Crump ill. by John Winch. Holiday, 2002. ISBN 0-8234-1608-9 Subj: Activities – traveling. Animals – oxen. Desert. Moving. U.S. history.

Second-grade dog ill. by Gioia Fiammenghi. A. Whitman, 1990. ISBN 0-8075-7280-2 Subj: Animals – dogs. Behavior – boredom. School.

Lawrence, James. *Binky Brothers and the fearless four* ill. by Leonard P. Kessler. HarperCollins, 1970. Subj: Careers – detectives. Multiple births – twins. Mystery stories.

Binky Brothers, detectives ill. by Leonard P. Kessler. Harper-Collins, 1968. ISBN 0-06-023759-7 Subj: Careers – detectives. Multiple births – twins. Mystery stories.

Lawrence, Jennifer B. *Sad doggy* ill. by Timothy Basil Ering. Piggy Toes, 2001. ISBN 1-58117-066-1 Subj: Animals – dogs. Emotions – sadness. Format, unusual – toy & movable books. Rhyming text.

Lawrence, John. *The giant of Grabbist* ill. by author. White, 1969. Subj: Foreign lands – England. Giants.

Pope Leo's elephant ill. by author. Collins-World, 1970, 1969. Subj: Animals – elephants. Cities, towns. Fire.

Rabbit and pork: rhyming talk ill. by author. Crowell, 1976. ISBN 0-690-00973-9 Subj: Animals – cats. Animals – pigs. Animals – rabbits. Rhyming text.

This little chick ill. by author. Candlewick, 2002. ISBN 0-7636-1716-4 Subj: Animals. Animals – babies. Birds – chickens. Noise, sounds. Rhyming text.

Lawrence, Mary. *What's that sound?* ill. by Lynn Adams. Kane Pr., 2002. ISBN 1-57565-118-1 Subj: Country. Family life. Noise, sounds.

Lawrence, Michael (Michael C.). *Baby loves* ill. by Adrian Reynolds. DK, 1999. ISBN 0-7894-3410-5 Subj: Babies. Emotions – love. Format, unusual – board books.

The caterpillar that roared ill. by Alison Bartlett. DK, 2000. ISBN 0-7894-5618-4 Subj: Animals. Behavior – imitation. Insects – butterflies, caterpillars. Self-concept.

Lawson, Annetta. *The lucky yak* ill. by Allen Say. Houghton Mifflin, 1980. ISBN 0-395-29523-8 Subj: Activities – babysitting. Animals – yaks. Birds – puffins.

Lawson, Barbara Spilman. *Jambo, watoto!* (Heatwole, Marsha)

Lawson, Carol. *Teddy bear, teddy bear* ill. by author. Dial, 1991. ISBN 0-8037-0970-6 Subj: Activities. Nursery rhymes. Toys – bears.

Lawson, Janet (Janet M.). *Audrey and Barbara* ill. by author. Atheneum, 2002. ISBN 0-689-83896-4 Subj: Animals – cats. Imagination.

Lawson, Julie. *Arizona Charlie and the Klondike Kid* ill. by Kasia Charko. Orca, 2003. ISBN 1-55143-250-1 Subj: Cowboys, cowgirls. Crime. Foreign lands – Canada. Theater.

Bear on the train ill. by Brian Dienes. Kids Can, 1999. ISBN 1-55074-560-3 Subj: Animals – bears. Hibernation. Trains.

The dragon's pearl ill. by Paul Morin. Clarion, 1993. ISBN 0-395-63623-X Subj: Dragons. Folk & fairy tales. Foreign lands – China.

Emma and the silk train ill. by Paul Mombourquette. Kids Can, 1998. ISBN 1-55074-388-0 Subj: Accidents. Trains. Transportation.

Midnight in the mountains ill. by Sheena Lott. Orca, 1999. ISBN 1-55143-113-0 Subj: Activities – vacationing. Family life. Mountains. Noise, sounds. Seasons – winter.

A morning to polish and keep ill. by Sheena Lott. Red Deer Pr., 1992. ISBN 0-613-23371-9 Subj: Animals – whales. Boats, ships. Family life – brothers. Sports – fishing.

Lawson, Robert. *They were strong and good* ill. by author. Viking, 1940. ISBN 0-670-69949-7 Subj: Caldecott award books. Family life. U.S. history – frontier & pioneer life.

Lawston, Lisa. *Can you hop?* ill. by Ed Vere. Orchard, 1999. ISBN 0-53130-131-1 Subj: Activities. Animals – rabbits. Friendship. Frogs & toads.

A pair of red sneakers ill. by B. B. Sams. Orchard, 1998. ISBN 0-531-33104-0 Subj: Clothing – shoes. Rhyming text.

Layne, Steven L. *My brother Dan's delicious* ill. by Chuck Galey. Pelican, 2003. ISBN 1-58980-071-0 Subj: Emotions – fear. Family life – brothers. Monsters.

Layton, Aviva. *The squeakers* ill. by Louise Scott. Mosaic Pr., 1982. Subj: Animals – mice. Family life. Theater.

Layton, Neal. *Hot, hot, hot* ill. by author. Candlewick, 2004. ISBN 0-7636-2148-X Subj: Animals. Behavior – resourcefulness. Seasons – summer.

Smile if you're human ill. by author. Dial, 1998. ISBN 0-8037-2381-4 Subj: Aliens. Animals. Animals – gorillas. Family life.

Lazard, Naomi. *What Amanda saw* ill. by Paul O. Zelinsky. Greenwillow, 1981. ISBN 0-688-84272-0 Subj: Activities – vacationing. Animals. Parties.

Lazy Jack. *Lazy Jack* ill. by Bert Dodson. Troll, 1979. ISBN 0-89375-123-5 Subj: Character traits – laziness. Cumulative tales. Folk & fairy tales.

Lazy Jack ill. by Tony Ross. Dial, 1986. ISBN 0-8037-0275-2 Subj: Character traits – laziness. Cumulative tales. Folk & fairy tales.

Lazy Jack ill. by Kurt Werth. Viking, 1970. ISBN 0-670-42146-4 Subj: Character traits – laziness. Cumulative tales. Folk & fairy tales.

Lazy Jack ill. by Barry Wilkinson. World, 1969. Story from Joseph Jacob's English fairy tales. Subj: Character traits – foolishness. Character traits – laziness. Folk & fairy tales.

Leach, Aroline Arnett Beecher. *The miracle of the mountain* (Kipling, Rudyard)

Leach, Michael. *Rabbits* ill. with photos. Global Lib. Mktg. Serv., 1984. ISBN 0-7136-2387-X Subj: Animals – rabbits. Nature. Science.

Leach, Norman. *My wicked stepmother* ill. by Jane Browne. Macmillan, 1993. ISBN 0-02-754700-0 Subj: Behavior – misbehavior. Family life – stepfamilies. Folk & fairy tales.

Leaf, Margaret. *Eyes of the dragon* ill. by Ed Young. Lothrop, 1987. ISBN 0-688-06156-7 Subj: Activities – painting. Careers – artists. Character traits – stubbornness. Dragons. Foreign lands – China.

Leaf, Munro. *Boo, who used to be scared of the dark* ill. by author. Random House, 1948. Subj: Bedtime. Emotions – fear. Night.

A flock of watchbirds ill. by author. Lippincott, 1946. Subj: Behavior – misbehavior. Etiquette.

Gordon, the goat ill. by author. Lippincott, 1944. Subj: Animals – goats.

Grammar can be fun ill. by author. Lippincott, 1934. Subj: Language.

Health can be fun ill. by author. Stokes, 1943. Subj: Health & fitness.

How to behave and why ill. by author. Lippincott, 1946. Subj: Etiquette.

Manners can be fun ill. by author. 3rd ed. Lippincott, 1985. ISBN 0-397-32118-X Subj: Etiquette.

Noodle ill. by author. Four Winds, 1965. Subj: Animals – dogs. Self-concept.

Robert Francis Weatherbee ill. by author. Lippincott, 1935. ISBN 0-208-02211-2 Subj: School.

Safety can be fun ill. by author. 3rd ed. Lippincott, 1961. ISBN 0-06-443111-8 Subj: Safety.

The story of Ferdinand the bull ill. by Robert Lawson. Viking, 1936. Subj: Animals – bulls, cows. Character traits – individuality. Foreign lands – Spain. Violence, nonviolence.

Wee Gillis ill. by Robert Lawson. Puffin, 1985, c1938. ISBN 0-14-050535-0 Subj: Caldecott award honor books. Foreign lands – Scotland.

Leaf by leaf sel. by Barbara Rogasky; photos by Marc Tauss. Scholastic, 2001. ISBN 0-590-25347-6 Subj: Poetry. Seasons – fall.

Leander, Ed. *Q is for crazy* ill. by Jözef Sumichrast. Dial-Delacorte, 1977. ISBN 0-8252-7512-1 Subj: ABC books.

Lear, Edward. *A was once an apple pie* ill. by Julie Lacome. Candlewick, 1992. ISBN 1-56402-000-2 Subj: ABC books. Poetry.

ABC ill. by author. McGraw-Hill, 1965. Subj: ABC books. Poetry.

A book of nonsense ill. by author. Metropolitan Museum of Art-Viking, 1980. ISBN 0-670-18011-4 Subj: Humorous stories. Poetry.

The dong with a luminous nose ill. by Edward Gorey. Adama, 1986. ISBN 0-915-36146-9 Subj: Humorous stories. Poetry.

An Edward Lear alphabet ill. by Carol Newsom. Lothrop, 1983. ISBN 0-688-00965-4 Subj: ABC books. Poetry.

An Edward Lear alphabet ill. by Vladimir Radunsky. HarperCollins, 1999. ISBN 0-06-028114-6 Subj: ABC books. Poetry.

Edward Lear's ABC: alphabet rhymes for children ill. by Carol Pike. Merrimack, 1986. ISBN 0-88162-219-2 Subj: ABC books. Poetry.

Edward Lear's nonsense book ill. by Tony Palazzo. Doubleday, 1956. Subj: Humorous stories. Music. Poetry.

Hilary Knight's the owl and the pussy-cat (Knight, Hilary)

The jumblies ill. by Emma Crosby. Merrimack, 1986. ISBN 0-88162-185-4 Subj: Poetry.

The jumblies ill. by Ted Rand. Putnam, 1989. ISBN 0-399-21632-4 Subj: Poetry.

A Learical lexicon comp. by Myra Cohn Livingston; ill. by Joseph Low. Atheneum, 1985. ISBN 0-689-50318-0 Subj: Humorous stories. Poetry.

Lear's nonsense verses ill. by Tomi Ungerer. Grosset, 1967. Subj: Humorous stories. Poetry.

Limericks ill. by Lois Ehlert. Collins-World, 1965. Subj: Poetry.

The new vestments ill. by DeLoss McGraw. S&S, 1995. ISBN 0-671-50089-9 Subj: Clothing. Food. Poetry.

Nonsense alphabet ill. by Richard Scarry. Doubleday, 1962. Subj: ABC books. Poetry.

The nutcrackers and the sugar-tongs ill. by Marcia Sewall. Little, 1978. ISBN 0-316-78181-9 Subj: Humorous stories. Poetry.

Of pelicans and pussycats ill. by Jill Newton. Dial, 1990. ISBN 0-8037-0728-2 Subj: Animals – cats. Birds – pelicans. Clothing – hats. Poetry.

The owl and the pussy cat ill. by Ian Beck. Atheneum, 1996. ISBN 0-689-81032-6 Subj: Animals – cats. Birds – owls. Poetry.

The owl and the pussycat ill. by Jan Brett. Putnam, 1991. ISBN 0-399-21925-0 Subj: Animals – cats. Birds – owls. Poetry.

The owl and the pussycat ill. by Lorinda Bryan Cauley. Putnam, 1986. ISBN 0-399-21254-X Subj: Animals – cats. Birds – owls. Poetry.

The owl and the pussy-cat ill. by Barbara Cooney. Little, 1969. First pub. in 1961. Subj: Animals – cats. Birds – owls. Poetry.

The owl and the pussycat ill. by Emma Crosby. Merrimack, 1986. ISBN 0-88162-183-8 Subj: Animals – cats. Birds – owls. Poetry.

The owl and the pussy-cat ill. by William Pène Du Bois. Doubleday, 1961. Subj: Animals – cats. Birds – owls. Poetry.

The owl and the pussy-cat ill. by Lori Farbanish. Putnam, 1988. ISBN 0-448-10229-3 Subj: Animals – cats. Birds – owls. Poetry.

The owl and the pussycat ill. by Gwen Fulton. Atheneum, 1977. ISBN 0-224-01400-5 Subj: Animals – cats. Birds – owls. Poetry.

The owl and the pussycat ill. by Paul Galdone. Houghton Mifflin, 1987. ISBN 0-89919-505-9 Subj: Animals – cats. Birds – owls. Poetry.

The owl and the pussy-cat ill. by Elaine Muis. Grosset, 1977. ISBN 0-448-13006-8 Subj: Animals – cats. Birds – owls. Poetry.

The owl and the pussycat ill. by Erica Rutherford. Tundra, 1986. ISBN 0-88776-181-X Subj: Animals – cats. Birds – owls. Poetry.

The owl and the pussycat ill. by Janet Stevens. Holiday, 1983. ISBN 0-8231-0474-9 Subj: Animals – cats. Birds – owls. Poetry.

The owl and the pussycat ill. by Louise Voce. Lothrop, 1991. ISBN 0-688-09537-2 Subj: Animals – cats. Birds – owls. Poetry.

The owl and the pussycat ill. by Colin West. Warne, 1988. ISBN 0-7232-3541-4 Subj: Animals – cats. Birds – owls. Poetry.

The owl and the pussy-cat: and other nonsense ill. by Owen Wood. Viking, 1979. ISBN 0-670-53314-9 Subj: Animals – cats. Birds – owls. Poetry.

The pelican chorus ill. by Harold Berson. Parents' Magazine Pr., 1967. Subj: Birds – pelicans. Humorous stories. Music. Poetry. Songs.

The pelican chorus and the quangle wangle's hat ill. by Kevin W. Maddison. Viking, 1981. ISBN 0-670-54613-5 Subj: Birds – pelicans. Humorous stories. Music. Poetry. Songs.

The pobble who has no toes ill. by Emma Crosby. Merrimack, 1986. ISBN 0-88162-184-6 Subj: Humorous stories. Poetry.

The pobble who has no toes ill. by Kevin W. Maddison. Viking, 1977. ISBN 0-904-06912-5 Subj: Humorous stories. Poetry.

The quangle wangle's hat ill. by Emma Crosby. Merrimack, 1986. ISBN 0-88162-182-X Subj: Clothing – hats. Humorous stories. Poetry.

The quangle wangle's hat ill. by Helen Oxenbury. Watts, 1969. ISBN 0-434-95596-5 Subj: Clothing – hats. Humorous stories. Poetry.

The quangle wangle's hat ill. by Janet Stevens. Harcourt, 1988. ISBN 0-15-264450-4 Subj: Clothing – hats. Humorous stories. Poetry.

Two laughable lyrics: The pobble who has no toes, [and] The quangle wangle's hat ill. by Paul Galdone. Putnam, 1966. Subj: Clothing – hats. Humorous stories. Poetry.

Whizz! ill. by Janina Domanska. Macmillan, 1973. Completed by Ogden Nash. Subj: Cumulative tales. Humorous stories. Poetry.

Lears, Laurie. *Becky the brave: a story about epilepsy* ill. by Gail Piazza. A. Whitman, 2002. ISBN 0-8075-0601-X Subj: Character traits – bravery. Family life – sisters. Illness – epilepsy. School.

Ben has something to say: a story about stuttering ill. by Karen Ritz. A. Whitman, 2000. ISBN 0-8075-0633-8 Subj: Animals – dogs. Emotions – fear. Handicaps – stuttering.

Ian's walk: a story about autism ill. by Karen Ritz. A. Whitman, 1998. ISBN 0-8075-3480-3 Subj: Behavior – lost. Family life – brothers & sisters. Handicaps – autism. Senses.

Waiting for Mr. Goose ill. by Karen Ritz. A. Whitman, 1999. ISBN 0-8075-8628-5 Subj: Birds – geese. Character traits – kindness to animals. Handicaps.

Leatham, E. Rutter (Mrs.). *A child's grace* (Burdekin, Harold)

Leavitt, Melvin. *Grena and the magic pomegranate* ill. by Beth Wright. Carolrhoda, 1994. ISBN 0-87614-760-0 Subj: Folk & fairy tales. Food.

Leavy, Una. *Good-bye, Papa* ill. by Jennifer Eachus. Orchard, 1996. ISBN 0-531-09545-2 Subj: Death. Emotions – grief. Family life – grandfathers.

Harry's stormy night ill. by Peter Utton. McElderry, 1995. ISBN 0-689-50625-2 Subj: Activities. Power failures. Rhyming text. Weather – storms.

Lebentritt, Julia. *The Kooken* by Julia Lebentritt & Richard Ploetz; ill. by Clément Oubrerie. Holt, 1992. ISBN 0-8050-1749-6 Subj: Animals – dogs. Family life – grandparents. Music. Musical instruments – cellos. Problem solving.

Leblanc, Anne. *Benjamin finds a friend* ill. by author. Sterling, 1999. ISBN 0-8069-1923-X Subj: Animals – bears. Friendship. Toys – bears.

Benjamin in the snow ill. by author. Sterling, 1999. ISBN 0-8069-1931-0 Subj: Animals – bears. Family life – fathers. Format, unusual – board books. Weather – snow.

Benjamin takes care of Mommy ill. by author. Sterling, 1999. ISBN 0-8069-1933-7 Subj: Animals – bears. Family life – mothers. Format, unusual – board books.

Benjamin's busy day ill. by author. Sterling, 1999. ISBN 0-8069-1935-3 Subj: Activities. Animals – bears. Format, unusual – board books.

Shopping with Benjamin ill. by author. Sterling, 1997. ISBN 0-8069-0395-3 Subj: Food. Format, unusual – board books. Shopping. Toys – bears.

LeBox, Annette. *Salmon Creek* ill. by Karen Reczuch. Douglas & McIntyre, 2002. ISBN 0-88899-458-3 Subj: Fish. Poetry.

Wild bog tea ill. by Harvey Chan. Douglas & McIntyre, 2001. ISBN 0-88899-406-0 Subj: Family life – grandfathers. Nature. Swamps.

Lebrun, Claude. *Little Brown Bear does not want to eat* ill. by Danièle Bour. Childrens Pr., 1995. ISBN 0-516-07823-2 Subj: Animals – bears. Behavior – growing up. Behavior – sharing. Food.

Little Brown Bear learns to share ill. by Danièle Bour. Childrens Pr., 1995. ISBN 0-516-07822-4 Subj: Activities – playing. Animals – bears. Behavior – growing up. Behavior – sharing.

Lecher, Doris. *Angelita's magic yarn* ill. by author. Farrar, 1992. ISBN 0-374-30332-0 Subj: Activities – knitting. Character traits – luck. Magic.

Lechner, Susan. *Followers of the north star: rhymes about African American heroes, heroines, and historical times* (Altman, Susan)

Lecourt, Nancy. *Abracadabra to zigzag* ill. by Barbara Lehman. Lothrop, 1991. ISBN 0-688-09481-3 Subj: ABC books.

Ledwon, Peter. *Midnight math twelve terrific math games* ill. by Marilyn Mets. Holiday, 2000. ISBN 0-8234-1530-9 Subj: Animals. Counting, numbers. Games.

Lee, Chinlun. *Good dog, Paw* ill. by author. Candlewick, 2004. ISBN 0-7636-2178-1 Subj: Animals. Animals – dogs. Careers – veterinarians. Emotions – love.

The very kind rich lady and her one hundred dogs ill. by author. Candlewick, 2001. ISBN 0-7636-1290-1 Subj: Animals – dogs. Pets.

Lee, Dennis. *Alligator pie* ill. by Frank Newfeld. Houghton Mifflin, 1975. ISBN 0-395-21596-X Subj: Nursery rhymes. Poetry.

Bubblegum delicious ill. by David McPhail. HarperCollins, 2001. ISBN 0-06-623709-2 Subj: Foreign lands – Canada. Poetry.

Lee, Hector Viveros. *I had a hippopotamus* ill. by author. Lee & Low, 1996. ISBN 1-880000-28-8 Subj: Animals – hippopotamuses. Food.

Lee, Ho Baek. *While we were out* ill. by author. Kane/Miller, 2002. ISBN 1-929132-44-1 Subj: Activities. Animals – rabbits. Pets.

Lee, Huy Voun. *1, 2, 3 go!* Holt, 2000. ISBN 0-8050-6205-X Subj: Counting, numbers. Foreign languages.

Lee, Jeanne M. *Ba-Nam* ill. by author. Holt, 1987. ISBN 0-8050-0169-7 Subj: Character traits – kindness. Foreign lands – Vietnam. Weather – storms.

I once was a monkey: stories Buddha told ill. by author. Farrar, 1999. ISBN 0-374-33548-6 Subj: Animals. Folk & fairy tales. Religion.

Legend of the Li River: an ancient Chinese tale ill. by author. Holt, 1983. ISBN 0-03-063523-3 Subj: Folk & fairy tales. Foreign lands – China. Rocks.

The legend of the milky way ill. by author. Holt, 1982. ISBN 0-03-060439-7 Subj: Folk & fairy tales. Foreign lands – China. Stars.

Silent lotus ill. by author. Farrar, 1991. ISBN 0-374-36911-9 Subj: Activities – dancing. Foreign lands – Cambodia. Handicaps – deafness. Handicaps – physical handicaps.

The song of Mu Lan ill. by author. Front St., 1995. ISBN 1-886910-00-6 Subj: Careers – military. Character traits – bravery. Folk & fairy tales. Foreign lands – China.

Toad is the uncle of heaven: a Vietnamese folk tale ill. by reteller. Holt, 1985. ISBN 0-03-004652-1 Subj: Animals. Folk & fairy tales. Frogs & toads. Royalty. Weather – rain.

Lee, Milly. *Earthquake* ill. by Yangsook Choi. Frances Foster, 2001. ISBN 0-374-39964-6 Subj: Earthquakes. Ethnic groups in the U.S. – Chinese Americans. U.S. history.

Nim and the war effort ill. by Yangsook Choi. Farrar, 1997. ISBN 0-374-22262-2 Subj: Ethnic groups in the U.S. – Chinese Americans. Family life. U.S. history. War.

Lee, Quinlan B. *Crazy Christmas chaos* ill. by Clive Scruton. HarperFestival, 2002. ISBN 0-694-01683-7 Subj: Holidays – Christmas. Santa Claus.

Lee, Sandra. *Giant pandas* ill. by author. Child's World, 1993. ISBN 1-56766-009-6 Subj: Animals – endangered animals. Animals – pandas.

Lee, Stan. *Stan Lee's superhero Christmas* ill. by Tim Jessell. Tegen, 2004. ISBN 0-06-056560-8 Subj: Holidays – Christmas. Santa Claus.

Lee, Tzexa Cherta. *Jouanah: a Hmong Cinderella* (Coburn, Jewell Reinhart)

Leech, Bryan Jeffery. *John Jeremy Colton* designed & ill. by Byron Glaser & Sandra Higashi. Hyperion, 1994. ISBN 1-56282-651-4 Subj: Character traits – being different. Fire. Rhyming text.

Leech, Jay. *Bright Fawn and me* by Jay Leech & Zane Spencer; ill. by Glo Coalson. Crowell, 1979. ISBN 0-690-03938-7 Subj: Fairs, festivals. Family life – sisters. Indians of North America – Cheyenne (Sioux). Sibling rivalry.

Leedahl, Shelley A. (Shelley Ann). *The bone talker* ill. by Bill Slavin. Red Deer Pr., 2000. ISBN 0-88995-214-0 Subj: Activities – sewing. Communities, neighborhoods. Family life – grandmothers. Memories, memory. Old age. Quilts.

Leedy, Loreen. *Blast off to Earth!* ill. by author. Holiday, 1992. ISBN 0-8234-0973-2 Subj: Activities – traveling. School. Space & space ships.

The bunny play ill. by author. Holiday, 1988. ISBN 0-8234-0679-2 Subj: Animals – rabbits. Theater.

A dragon Christmas: things to make and do ill. by author. Holiday, 1988. ISBN 0-8234-0716-0 Subj: Activities. Activities – making things. Dragons. Holidays – Christmas. Rhyming text.

The dragon Halloween party ill. by author. Holiday, 1986. ISBN 0-8234-0611-3 Subj: Dragons. Holidays – Halloween. Parties. Rhyming text.

The dragon Thanksgiving feast ill. by author. Holiday, 1990. ISBN 0-8234-0828-0 Subj: Dragons. Food. Holidays – Thanksgiving. Rhyming text.

The edible pyramid: good eating every day ill. by author. Holiday, 1994. ISBN 0-8234-1126-5 Subj: Food. Health & fitness.

Follow the money ill. by author. Holiday, 2002. ISBN 0-8234-1587-2 Subj: Money.

Fraction action ill. by author. Holiday, 1994. ISBN 0-8234-1109-5 Subj: Animals. Counting, numbers. School.

The Furry News ill. by author. Holiday, 1990. ISBN 0-8234-0793-4 Subj: Activities – writing. Animals. Careers – journalists. Communication. Communities, neighborhoods.

The great trash bash ill. by author. Holiday, 1991. ISBN 0-8234-0869-8 Subj: Animals. Ecology.

How humans make friends ill. by author. Holiday, 1996. ISBN 0-8234-1223-7 Subj: Friendship. Space & space ships.

Mapping Penny's world ill. by author. Holt, 2000. ISBN 0-8050-6178-9 Subj: Animals – dogs. Maps.

Messages in the mailbox ill. by author. Holiday, 1991. ISBN 0-8234-0889-2 Subj: Activities – writing. Letters, cards. School.

Mission – addition ill. by author. Holiday, 1997. ISBN 0-8234-1307-1 Subj: Animals. Counting, numbers. School.

The monster money book ill. by author. Holiday, 1992. ISBN 0-8234-0922-8 Subj: Clubs, gangs. Money. Monsters.

A number of dragons ill. by author. Holiday, 1985. ISBN 0-8234-0568-0 Subj: Counting, numbers. Dragons. Rhyming text.

Pingo the plaid panda ill. by author. Holiday, 1989. ISBN 0-8234-0727-6 Subj: Animals – pandas. Character traits – being different. Friendship.

Postcards from Pluto ill. by author. Holiday, 1993. ISBN 0-8234-1000-5 Subj: Astronomy. Space & space ships.

The potato party and other troll tales ill. by author. Holiday, 1989. ISBN 0-8234-0761-6 Subj: Mythical creatures – trolls.

The race ill. by author. Scott Foresman, 1993. ISBN 0-673-80337-6 Subj: Animals – rabbits. Animals – raccoons. Sports – racing.

There's a frog in my throat: 312 animal sayings from the horse's mouth by Loreen Leedy & Pat Street; ill. by Loreen Leedy. Winslow, 2001. ISBN 1-89081-724-4 Subj: Animals. Language.

Tracks in the sand ill. by author. Doubleday, 1993. ISBN 0-385-30658-X Subj: Eggs. Reptiles – turtles, tortoises. Sea & seashore.

2 x 2 = boo! a set of spooky multiplication stories ill. by author. Holiday, 1995. ISBN 0-8234-1190-7 Subj: Counting, numbers. Holidays – Halloween. Witches.

Who's who in my family? ill. by author. Holiday, 1995. ISBN 0-8234-1151-6 Subj: Animals. Family life.

Leemis, Ralph. *Mister Momboo's hat* ill. by Jeni Bassett. Dutton, 1991. ISBN 0-525-65045-8 Subj: Animals – hippopotamuses. Circular tales. Clothing – hats. Rhyming text. Weather – wind.

Smart dog ill. by Chris L. Demarest. Caroline House, 1993. ISBN 1-56397-109-7 Subj: Animals – dogs. Behavior – wishing. Imagination.

Leeson, Christine. *Molly and the storm* ill. by Gaby Hansen. Tiger Tales, 2003. ISBN 1-58925-027-3 Subj: Animals. Animals – mice. Friendship. Weather – storms.

Leeton, Will C. *The Tower of Babel* ill. by Jeffrey K. Lindberg. Dandelion, 1979. ISBN 0-89799-141-9 Subj: Language. Religion.

Le Gallienne, Eva. *The little mermaid* (Andersen, H. C. [Hans Christian])

The nightingale (Andersen, H. C. [Hans Christian])

The snow queen (Andersen, H. C. [Hans Christian])

Legg, Gerald. *From caterpillar to butterfly* ill. by Carolyn Scrace; created & designed by David Salariya. Watts, 1998. ISBN 0-531-14493-3 Subj: Insects – butterflies, caterpillars. Metamorphosis.

From egg to chicken ill. by Carolyn Scrace; created & designed by David Salariya. Watts, 1998. ISBN 0-531-14490-9 Subj: Birds – chickens. Eggs. Science.

From seed to sunflower ill. by Carolyn Scrace; created & designed by David Salariya. Watts, 1998. ISBN 0-531-14492-5 Subj: Flowers. Gardens, gardening. Science. Seeds.

From tadpole to frog ill. by Carolyn Scrace; created & designed by David Salariya. Watts, 1998. ISBN 0-531-15335-5 Subj: Frogs & toads.

Legge, David. *Bamboozled* ill. by author. Scholastic, 1994. ISBN 0-5904-7989-X Subj: Family life – grandfathers.

Le Guin, Ursula K. *Fish soup* ill. by Patrick Wynne. Atheneum, 1992. ISBN 0-689-31733-6 Subj: Family life. Gender roles. Imagination. Prejudice.

A ride on the red mare's back ill. by Julie Downing. Watts, 1992. ISBN 0-531-08591-0 Subj: Animals – horses, ponies. Character traits – bravery. Family life – brothers & sisters. Folk & fairy tales. Mythical creatures – trolls.

Solomon Leviathan's nine hundred and thirty-first trip around the world ill. by Alicia Austin. Putnam, 1988. ISBN 0-399-21491-7 Subj: Animals – giraffes. Animals – whales. Behavior – seeking better things. Reptiles – snakes.

Tom Mouse ill. by Julie Downing. DK, 1998. ISBN 0-7894-2554-8 Subj: Activities – traveling. Animals – mice. Friendship. Trains.

A visit from Dr. Katz ill. by Ann Barrow. Atheneum, 1988. ISBN 0-689-31332-2 Subj: Animals – cats. Illness.

Lehan, Daniel. *This is not a book about dodos* ill. by author. Dutton, 1992. ISBN 0-525-44878-0 Subj: Art. Birds – dodos. Careers – artists.

Lehman, Barbara. *The red book* ill. by author. Houghton, 2004. ISBN 0-618-42858-5 Subj: Books, reading. Caldecott award honor books. Friendship. Wordless.

Lehman-Wilzig, Tami. *Keeping the promise: a Torah's journey* ill. by Craig Orback. Kar-Ben Copies, 2004. ISBN 1-58013-117-4 Subj: Holocaust. Jewish culture. Religion.

Lehn, Barbara. *What is a scientist?* photos by Carol Krauss. Millbrook, 1998. ISBN 0-7613-1272-2 Subj: Careers – scientists. Science.

What is a teacher? photos by Carol Krauss. Millbrook, 2000. ISBN 0-7613-1713-9 Subj: Careers – teachers.

What is an athlete? photos by Carol Krauss. Millbrook, 2002. ISBN 0-7613-2258-2 Subj: Sports.

Leichman, Seymour. *Shaggy dogs and spotty dogs and shaggy and spotty dogs* ill. by author. Harcourt, 1973. ISBN 0-15-278020-3 Subj: Animals – dogs. Rhyming text.

The wicked wizard and the wicked witch ill. by author. Harcourt, 1972. ISBN 0-15-296455-X Subj: Magic. Rhyming text. Witches. Wizards.

Leigh, Oretta. *The merry-go-round* ill. by Kathryn E. Shoemaker. Holiday, 1985. ISBN 0-8234-0544-3 Subj: Animals. Merry-go-rounds. Rhyming text.

Leighton, Maxinne Rhea. *An Ellis Island Christmas* ill. by Dennis Nolan. Viking, 1992. ISBN 0-670-83182-4 Subj: Activities – traveling. Ethnic groups in the U.S. – Polish Americans. Holidays – Christmas. Moving.

Leiner, Katherine. *Both my parents work* photos by Steve Sax. Watts, 1986. ISBN 0-531-10101-0 Subj: Activities – working. Family life.

Halloween ill. with photos sel. by author. Atheneum, 1993. ISBN 0-689-31769-7 Subj: Clothing. Holidays – Halloween.

Mama does the mambo ill. by Edel Rodriguez. Hyperion, 2001. ISBN 0-7868-2533-2 Subj: Activities – dancing. Emotions – grief. Foreign lands – Cuba.

Leisk, David Johnson. *see* Johnson, Crockett

Leister, Mary. *The silent concert* ill. by Yoko Mitsuhashi. Bobbs-Merrill, 1970. Subj: Forest, woods. Noise, sounds.

Lemaître, Pascal. *Emily the giraffe* ill. by author. Hyperion, 1993. ISBN 1-56282-404-X Subj: Animals – giraffes. Character traits – bravery. Fire.

Zelda's secret ill. by author. BridgeWater, 1994. ISBN 0-8167-3309-0 Subj: Activities – dancing. Animals. Animals – elephants. Ballet. Behavior – secrets.

Leman, Jill. *Ten little pussy cats* ill. by Martin Leman. Trafalgar Square, 1996. ISBN 0-575-05979-6 Subj: Animals – cats. Counting, numbers.

Lember, Barbara Hirsch. *A book of fruit* ill. by author. Ticknor & Fields, 1994. ISBN 0-395-66989-8 Subj: Concepts. Food. Plants.

Lemberg, Stephen H. *Scaredy dog* ill. by Cat Bowman Smith. Knopf, 1994. ISBN 0-679-93175-9 Subj: Animals – dogs. Birds – swans. Emotions – fear. Seasons – summer.

Lemerise, Bruce. *Sheldon's lunch* ill. by author. Parents' Magazine Pr., 1980. ISBN 0-8193-1026-3 Subj: Activities – baking, cooking. Food. Reptiles – snakes.

Lemieux, Margo. *The fiddle ribbon* ill. by Francis Livingston. Silver Pr., 1996. ISBN 0-382-39096-2 Subj: Activities – dancing. Family life – grandparents. Farms. Music. Musical instruments – violins.

Lemieux, Michèle. *What's that noise?* ill. by author. Morrow, 1985. ISBN 0-688-04140-X Subj: Animals – bears. Noise, sounds.

Lemke, Horst. *Places and faces* ill. by author. Scroll Pr., 1971. Translation of Vielerlei aus Stadt und Land. ISBN 0-87592-041-1 Subj: Wordless.

L'Engle, Madeleine. *The other dog* ill. by Christine Davenier. SeaStar, 2001. ISBN 1-58717-041-8 Subj: Animals – dogs. Babies.

Lenski, Lois. *Animals for me* ill. by author. Walck, 1941. Subj: Animals.

At our house ill. by author. Walck, 1959. Music by Clyde Robert Bulla. Subj: Family life. Music. Songs.

Big little Davy ill. by author. Walck, 1956. Subj: Animals.

Cowboy Small ill. by author. Walck, 1960, c1949. ISBN 0-8098-1021-2 Subj: Cowboys, cowgirls.

Davy and his dog ill. by author. Walck, 1957. Subj: Animals – dogs. Music. Songs.

Davy goes places ill. by author. Walck, 1961. Subj: Activities – traveling. Music. Songs. Transportation.

Debbie and her dolls ill. by author. Walck, 1970. ISBN 0-8098-1159-6 Subj: Animals – dogs. Toys – dolls.

Debbie and her family ill. by author. Walck, 1969. ISBN 0-8098-1156-1 Subj: Family life.

Debbie and her grandma ill. by author. Walck, 1967. Subj: Family life – grandmothers. Music. Songs.

Debbie goes to nursery school ill. by author. Walck, 1970. ISBN 0-8098-1161-8 Subj: School – nursery.

A dog came to school ill. by author. Oxford Univ. Pr., 1955. Subj: Animals – dogs. Music. School. Songs.

The Easter Rabbit's parade ill. by author. Random House, 2004. ISBN 0-375-92748-4 Subj: Animals. Holidays – Easter. Parades.

I like winter ill. by author. Random House, 2000, c1950. ISBN 0-375-91068-9 Subj: Music. Poetry. Seasons – winter. Songs.

I went for a walk ill. by author. Walck, 1958. Subj: Activities – walking. Music. Songs.

Let's play house ill. by author. Walck, 1961, c1944. Subj: Activities – playing. Toys – dolls.

The life I live: collected poems ill. by author. Walck, 1966. Subj: Poetry. Songs.

The little airplane ill. by author. Random House, 2003, c1938. ISBN 0-375-91079-4 Subj: Airplanes, airports. Careers – airplane pilots.

The little auto ill. by author. Oxford Univ. Pr., 1934. ISBN 0-8098-1001-8 Subj: Automobiles.

The little family ill. by author. Random House, 2002, c1932. ISBN 0-375-91077-8 Subj: Family life.

The little farm ill. by author. Walck, 1959, c1942. ISBN 0-8098-1009-3 Subj: Farms.

The little fire engine ill. by author. Random House, 2000, c1946. ISBN 0-375-82263-1 Subj: Careers – firefighters.

The little sailboat ill. by author. Random House, 2003. ISBN 0-375-91078-6 Subj: Animals – dogs. Boats, ships. Sailors.

The little train ill. by author. Random House, 2002, c1940. ISBN 0-375-82264-X Subj: Careers – railroad engineers. Trains.

Lois Lenski's big book of Mr. Small ill. by author. Walck, 1979. ISBN 0-8098-6026-0 Subj: Careers. Transportation.

Mr. and Mrs. Noah ill. by author. Random House, 2002. ISBN 0-375-91076-X Subj: Animals. Boats, ships. Religion – Noah. Weather – floods. Weather – rain. Weather – rainbows.

Now it's fall ill. by author. Random House, 2000, c1948. ISBN 0-375-91069-7 Subj: Poetry. Seasons – fall.

On a summer day ill. by author. Oxford Univ. Pr., 1953. Subj: Poetry. Seasons – summer.

Papa Small ill. by author. Random House, 2004, c1951. ISBN 0-375-92749-2 Subj: Family life. Family life – fathers.

Policeman Small ill. by author. Random House, 2001, c1962. ISBN 0-375-91072-7 Subj: Careers – police officers. Cities, towns.

Sing a song of people ill. by Giles Laroche. Little, 1987. ISBN 0-316-52074-8 Subj: Cities, towns. Format, unusual. Rhyming text.

Spring is here ill. by author. Walck, 1960, c1945. Subj: Poetry. Seasons – spring.

A surprise for Davy ill. by author. Walck, 1959, c1947. Subj: Birthdays. Parties.

Susie Mariar ill. by author. Walck, 1968, c1967. First pub. in 1939. Subj: Cumulative tales. Folk & fairy tales. Poetry.

Lenssen, Ann. *A rainbow balloon* photos by author. Cobblehill, 1992. ISBN 0-525-65093-8 Subj: Activities – ballooning. Language.

Lent, Blair. *Bayberry Bluff* ill. by author. Houghton Mifflin, 1987. ISBN 0-395-35384-X Subj: Cities, towns. Islands.

John Tabor's ride ill. by author. Little, 1966. Subj: Animals – whales. Folk & fairy tales. Humorous stories. Tall tales.

Molasses flood ill. by author. Houghton Mifflin, 1992. ISBN 0-395-45314-3 Subj: Cities, towns. Food. U.S. history.

Pistachio ill. by author. Little, 1964. Subj: Animals – bulls, cows. Circus. Clowns, jesters.

Ruby and Fred ill. by author. Holt, 2000. ISBN 0-8050-6117-7 Subj: Animals – cats. Animals – dogs. Birds.

Leodhas, Sorche Nic. *see* Alger, Leclaire Gowans

Leonard, Alain. *Barnaby and the big gorilla* ill. by author. Morrow, 1992. ISBN 0-688-11292-7 Subj: Animals – rabbits. Character traits – bravery. Toys.

Leonard, Marcia. *Alphabet bandits: an ABC book* ill. by Maryann Cocca-Leffler. Troll, 1990. ISBN 0-8167-1718-4 Subj: ABC books. Animals – raccoons. Food.

Angry ill. by Wendy Watson. Fitzgerald, 1998. ISBN 1-887238-13-1 Subj: Emotions – anger. Family life.

Animal talk photos by Dorothy Handelman. HarperFestival, 2000. ISBN 0-694-01363-3 Subj: Animals. Noise, sounds.

Babies help out by Marcia Leonard, Dorothy Handelman; ed. by Suzanne Daghlian; photos by Dorothy Handelman. HarperCollins, 2001. ISBN 0-694-01369-2 Subj: Babies.

Bear's busy year: a book about seasons ill. by Bari Weissman. Troll, 1990. ISBN 0-8167-1720-6 Subj: Animals – bears. Seasons.

Best friends photos by Dorothy Handelman. Millbrook, 1999. ISBN 0-7613-2064-4 Subj: Character traits – individuality. Friendship. Rhyming text.

The best snowman ever ill. by Nancy Rainsford, Pistone. Troll, 1989. ISBN 0-8167-1488-6 Subj: Format, unusual – toy & movable books. Holidays – Christmas. Snowmen.

Big Ben photos by Dorothy Handelman. Millbrook, 1998. ISBN 0-7613-2013-X Subj: Careers – musicians. Rhyming text.

Birthday in a bathtub ill. by John Wallner. Silver Pr., 1989. ISBN 0-671-08588-0 Subj: Animals – pigs. Birthdays. Problem solving. Rhyming text.

Busy babies photos by Dorothy Handelman. HarperFestival, 2000. ISBN 0-694-01364-1 Subj: Activities. Babies.

Bye-bye, Baby-boo ill. by Dana Regan. C.R. Gibson, 1992. ISBN 0-8378-2521-1 Subj: Activities – traveling. Babies. Format, unusual – board books.

Counting kangaroos: a book about numbers ill. by Diane Palmisciano. Troll, 1990. ISBN 0-8167-1722-2 Subj: Animals – kangaroos. Counting, numbers.

Dan and Dan photos by Dorothy Handelman. Millbrook, 1998. ISBN 0-7613-2003-2 Subj: Family life – grandfathers. Rhyming text.

Dress-up photos by Dorothy Handelman. Millbrook, 1999. ISBN 0-7613-2053-9 Subj: Activities – playing. Imagination. Rhyming text.

The elves and the shoemaker (Grimm, Jacob)

Favorite colors by Marcia Leonard, Dorothy Handleman; ed. by Suzanne Daghlian; photos by Dorothy Handleman. HarperCollins, 2001. ISBN 0-694-01370-6 Subj: Concepts – color.

Food is fun! pictures by Dorothy Handelman. HarperFestival, 2000. ISBN 0-694-01366-8 Subj: Activities – baking, cooking. Food.

Get the ball, Slim photos by Dorothy Handelman. Millbrook, 1998. ISBN 0-7613-2000-8 Subj: Animals – dogs. Ethnic groups in the U.S. – African Americans. Family life – brothers & sisters. Multiple births – twins.

Getting dressed ill. by Deborah Michel. Bantam, 1988. ISBN 0-553-05467-8 Subj: Clothing. Family life.

Goldilocks and the three bears (The three bears)

Gregory and Mr. Grump ill. by Maxie Chambliss. Silver Pr., 1990. ISBN 0-671-70402-8 Subj: Gardens, gardening. Old age.

Hannah the hamster hunter ill. by Maxie Chambliss. Silver Pr., 1990. ISBN 0-671-70399-4 Subj: Animals – hamsters. School – first day.

Hop, skip, run photos by Dorothy Handelman. Millbrook, 1998. ISBN 0-7613-2015-6 Subj: Activities – playing. Rhyming text.

I like mess photos by Dorothy Handelman. Millbrook, 1998. ISBN 0-7613-2002-4 Subj: Character traits – orderliness. Family life – mothers. Rhyming text.

Jeffrey Lee, future fireman ill. by Ann Iosa. Silver Pr., 1990. ISBN 0-671-70403-6 Subj: Careers – firefighters.

King Lionheart's castle ill. by Alexandra Wallner. Silver Pr., 1992. ISBN 0-671-72974-8 Subj: Animals. Castles. Participation. Royalty – kings.

The kitten twins ill. by Maryann Cocca-Leffler. Troll, 1990. ISBN 0-8167-1724-9 Subj: Animals – cats. Concepts – opposites. Multiple births – twins.

Laura Jean the yard sale queen ill. by Ann Iosa. Silver Pr., 1990. ISBN 0-671-70401-X Subj: Animals – dogs.

Little owl leaves the nest ill. by Carol Newsom. Bantam, 1984. ISBN 0-533-15266-1 Subj: Birds – owls. Problem solving.

My camp-out photos by Dorothy Handelman. Millbrook, 1999. ISBN 0-7613-2052-0 Subj: Camps, camping. Ethnic groups in the U.S. – African Americans. Family life – mothers. Rhyming text.

My pal Al photos by Dorothy Handelman. Millbrook, 1998. ISBN 0-7613-2001-6 Subj: Ethnic groups in the U.S. – African Americans. Rhyming text. Toys.

Night-night, Baby-boo ill. by Dana Regan. C.R. Gibson, 1992. ISBN 0-8378-2522-9 Subj: Babies. Bedtime.

No new pants! photos by Dorothy Handelman. Millbrook, 1999. ISBN 0-7613-2063-6 Subj: Clothing. Family life – mothers. Rhyming text. Shopping.

Noisy neighbors ill. by Bari Weissman. Troll, 1990. ISBN 0-8167-1726-5 Subj: Animals. Noise, sounds.

The opposite of stop is go photos by Dorothy Handelman. HarperCollins, 2000. ISBN 0-694-01368-4 Subj: Concepts – opposites.

Paintbox penguins: a book about colors ill. by Diane Palmisciano. Troll, 1990. ISBN 0-8167-1716-8 Subj: Activities – painting. Birds – penguins. Concepts – color.

Peek-a-boo, baby! by Marcia Leonard, Dorothy Handelman; ed. by Mary-Alice Moore; photos by Dorothy Handelman. Harper-Collins, 2000. ISBN 0-694-01373-0 Subj: Babies. Games.

The pet vet photos by Dorothy Handelman. Millbrook, 1999. ISBN 0-7613-2050-4 Subj: Careers – veterinarians. Rhyming text.

Rainboots for breakfast ill. by John Himmelman. Silver Pr., 1989. ISBN 0-671-68587-2 Subj: Food. Frogs & toads.

Shopping for snowflakes ill. by John Himmelman. Silver Pr., 1989. ISBN 0-671-68590-2 Subj: Animals – rabbits. Shopping.

Spots photos by Dorothy Handelman. Millbrook, 1998. ISBN 0-7613-2016-4 Subj: Concepts. Multiple births – twins. Rhyming text.

Swimming in the sand ill. by John Wallner. Silver Pr., 1989. ISBN 0-671-68589-9 Subj: Animals – hippopotamuses. Sea & seashore.

The three little pigs (The three little pigs)

The tin can man photos by Dorothy Handelman. Millbrook, 1998. ISBN 0-7613-2012-1 Subj: Family life – daughters. Family life – fathers. Parades. Rhyming text.

Violet and the pirates ill. by John Wallner. Silver Pr., 1992. ISBN 0-671-72975-6 Subj: Activities – sewing. Animals – cats. Boats, ships. Pirates.

What's that, Baby-boo? ill. by Dana Regan. C.R. Gibson, 1992. ISBN 0-8378-2519-9 Subj: Animals. Babies. Format, unusual – board books.

Where's Baby-boo? ill. by Dana Regan. C.R. Gibson, 1992. ISBN 0-8378-2520-2 Subj: Babies. Format, unusual – board books. Games.

Léonard, Marie. *Tibili, the little boy who didn't want to go to school* ill. by Andrée Prigent. Kane/Miller, 2002. ISBN 1-929132-20-4 Subj: Animals. Books, reading. Foreign lands – Africa. School – first day.

Lepon, Shoshana. *Hillel builds a house* ill. by Marilynn G. Barr. Kar-Ben Copies, 1993. ISBN 0-92937-141-0 Subj: Holidays – Sukkot. Homes, houses. Jewish culture. Religion.

Lerman, Rory S. *Charlie's checklist* ill. by Alison Bartlett. Orchard, 1997. ISBN 0-531-30001-3 Subj: Animals – dogs. Cities, towns. Farms. Foreign lands – England.

Lerner, Carol. *Flowers of a woodland spring* ill. by author. Morrow, 1979. ISBN 0-688-32190-9 Subj: Flowers. Forest, woods. Seasons – spring.

Lerner, Harriet Goldhor. *Franny B. Kranny, there's a bird in your hair* Harriet Lerner & Susan Goldhor; ill. by Helen Oxenbury. HarperCollins, 2000. ISBN 0-06-024683-3 Subj: Birds. Family life. Hair.

What's so terrible about swallowing an apple seed? by Harriet Goldhor Lerner & Susan Henne Goldhor; ill. by Catharine O'Neill. HarperCollins, 1996. ISBN 0-06-024524-7 Subj: Behavior – worrying. Family life – sisters. Seeds. Sibling rivalry.

Lerner, Marguerite Rush. *Dear little mumps child* ill. by George Overlie. Lerner, 1959. ISBN 0-8225-0003-5 Subj: Illness – mumps. Rhyming text.

Doctors' tools ill. by George Overlie. Rev. 2nd ed. Lerner, 1960. Subj: Careers – doctors. Tools.

Lefty, the story of left-handedness ill. by Roy André. Lerner, 1960. Subj: Character traits – being different. Left-handedness.

Michael gets the measles ill. by George Overlie. Lerner, 1959. Subj: Illness.

Peter gets the chickenpox ill. by George Overlie. Lerner, 1959. ISBN 0-8225-0002-7 Subj: Illness.

Lerner, Sharon. *Big Bird's copycat day* featuring Jim Henson's Sesame Street Muppets; ill. by Jean-Pierre Jacquet. Random House, 1984. ISBN 0-394-86912-5 Subj: Puppets.

Follow the monsters! ill. by Tom Cooke. Random House, 1985. ISBN 0-394-97126-4 Subj: Monsters. Puppets. Rhyming text.

LeRoy, Gen. *Billy's shoes* ill. by J. Winslow Higginbottom. McGraw-Hill, 1981. ISBN 0-07-037201-2 Subj: Clothing – shoes. Sibling rivalry.

Lucky stiff! ill. by J. Winslow Higginbottom. McGraw-Hill, 1981. ISBN 0-07-037203-9 Subj: Humorous stories. Sibling rivalry.

LeSieg, Theo. *see* Seuss, Dr.

Lesikin, Joan. *Down the road* ill. by author. Prentice-Hall, 1978. ISBN 0-13-218909-7 Subj: Behavior – sharing. Reptiles – snakes. Reptiles – turtles, tortoises.

Leslie, Amanda. *Alfie and Betty Bug* ill. by author. Handprint, 2001. ISBN 1-929766-33-5 Subj: Animals. Animals – elephants. Format, unusual – toy & movable books. Insects.

Animal noises ill. by author. Candlewick, 1995. ISBN 1-56402-702-3 Subj: Animals. Noise, sounds.

Are chickens stripy? ill. by author. Handprint, 2000. ISBN 1-929766-09-2 Subj: Animals. Birds – chickens. Format, unusual – toy & movable books.

Do crocodiles moo? ill. by author. Handprint, 2000. ISBN 1-929766-08-4 Subj: Animals. Concepts – color. Format, unusual – toy & movable books. Noise, sounds.

Flappy, waggy, wiggly ill. by author. Dutton, 1999. ISBN 0-525-46182-5 Subj: Animals. Format, unusual – toy & movable books.

Hidden toys ill. by author. Dial, 1989. ISBN 0-8037-0568-9 Subj: Games. Toys.

Let's look inside the red car ill. by author. Candlewick, 1997. ISBN 0-7636-0089-X Subj: Automobiles. Format, unusual – toy & movable books.

Let's look inside the yellow truck ill. by author. Candlewick, 1997. ISBN 0-7636-0104-7 Subj: Format, unusual – toy & movable books. Trucks.

Play kitten play ill. by author. Candlewick, 1992. ISBN 1-56402-088-6 Subj: Animals. Animals – cats. Format, unusual – toy & movable books. Games.

Play puppy play ill. by author. Candlewick, 1992. ISBN 1-56402-087-8 Subj: Animals. Animals – dogs. Format, unusual – toy & movable books. Games.

Who's that scratching at my door? ill. by author. Handprint, 2001. ISBN 1-929766-19-X Subj: Activities – playing. Animals. Animals – dogs. Format, unusual – toy & movable books.

LeSourd, Nancy. *Christy, Christmastime at Cutter Gap* ill. by Bill Farnsworth. Zonderkidz, 2003. Based on the novel by Catherine Marshall. ISBN 0-310-70571-1 Subj: Holidays – Christmas. Religion. School.

Lessac, Frané. *Caribbean canvas* comp. & ill. by Frané Lessac. Wordsong, 1994, 1989. ISBN 1-56397-390-1 Subj: Art. Foreign lands – Caribbean Islands. Poetry.

My little island ill. by author. Lippincott, 1985. ISBN 0-397-32115-5 Subj: Foreign lands – Caribbean Islands. Islands.

Lesser, Carolyn. *The goodnight circle* ill. by Lorinda Bryan Cauley. Harcourt, 1984. ISBN 0-15-232158-6 Subj: Animals. Bedtime. Night.

Great crystal bear ill. by William Noonan. Harcourt, 1996. ISBN 0-15-200667-2 Subj: Animals – polar bears. Seasons.

What a wonderful day to be a cow ill. by Melissa Bay Mathis. Knopf, 1995. ISBN 0-679-92430-2 Subj: Animals. Days of the week, months of the year. Farms. Poetry. Seasons.

Lesser, Rika. *Hansel and Gretel* (Grimm, Jacob)

My sister Lotta and me (Dahlbäck-Lutteman, Helena)

Lester, Alison. *Alice and Aldo* ill. by author. Houghton Mifflin, 1997. ISBN 0-395-87092-5 Subj: ABC books. Activities – playing.

Celeste sails to Spain ill. by author. Houghton Mifflin, 1999. ISBN 0-395-97395-3 Subj: Activities. Character traits – individuality. Imagination.

Clive eats alligators ill. by author. Houghton Mifflin, 1986. ISBN 0-395-40775-3 Subj: Activities. Character traits – individuality.

Ernie dances to the didgeridoo ill. by author. Houghton Mifflin, 2001. ISBN 0-618-10442-9 Subj: Australian aborigines. Foreign lands – Australia. Letters, cards.

Imagine ill. by author. Houghton Mifflin, 1990. ISBN 0-395-53753-3 Subj: Animals.

Isabella's bed ill. by author. Houghton Mifflin, 1993. ISBN 0-395-65565-X Subj: Dreams. Family life – grandmothers. Imagination. Magic. Songs.

The journey home ill. by author. Houghton Mifflin, 1991. ISBN 0-395-53355-4 Subj: Activities – traveling. Family life – brothers & sisters.

Magic beach ill. by author. Little, 1992. ISBN 0-316-52177-9 Subj: Activities – vacationing. Family life. Imagination. Rhyming text. Sea & seashore – beaches.

My farm ill. by author. Houghton Mifflin, 1994. ISBN 0-395-68193-6 Subj: Family life. Farms. Foreign lands – Australia.

Rosie sips spiders ill. by author. Houghton Mifflin, 1989. ISBN 0-395-51526-2 Subj: Family life. Foreign lands – Australia.

Ruby ill. by author. Houghton Mifflin, 1988. ISBN 0-395-46477-3 Subj: Bedtime. Dreams.

Tessa snaps snakes ill. by author. Houghton Mifflin, 1991. ISBN 0-395-59505-3 Subj: Activities. Character traits – individuality.

When Frank was four ill. by author. Houghton Mifflin, 1996. ISBN 0-395-74275-7 Subj: Behavior – growing up. Counting, numbers.

Yikes! in seven wild adventures, who would you be? ill. by author. Houghton Mifflin, 1995. ISBN 0-395-71252-1 Subj: Activities. Rhyming text.

Lester, Helen. *Author: a true story* ill. by author. Houghton Mifflin, 1997. ISBN 0-395-82744-2 Subj: Careers – writers. Handicaps.

Help! I'm stuck! ill. by Paulette Bogan. Celebration Pr., 1996. ISBN 0-673-75716-1 Subj: Activities – storytelling. Family life – brothers & sisters. Pets.

Hooway for Wodney Wat ill. by Lynn Munsinger. Houghton Mifflin, 1999. ISBN 0-395-92392-1 Subj: Animals. Animals – rats. Behavior – bullying. Handicaps. School.

Hurty feelings ill. by Lynn Munsinger. Houghton, 2004. ISBN 0-618-41082-1 Subj: Animals – elephants. Animals – hippopotamuses. Behavior. Emotions. Sports – soccer.

It wasn't my fault ill. by Lynn Munsinger. Houghton Mifflin, 1985. ISBN 0-395-35629-6 Subj: Animals. Cumulative tales.

Lin's backpack ill. by Lynn Munsinger. Scott Foresman, 1993. ISBN 0-673-80339-2 Subj: Animals. Sports – hiking.

Listen, Buddy ill. by Lynn Munsinger. Houghton Mifflin, 1995. ISBN 0-395-72361-2 Subj: Animals – rabbits.

Me first ill. by Lynn Munsinger. Houghton Mifflin, 1992. ISBN 0-395-58706-9 Subj: Animals – pigs. Behavior. Character traits – selfishness. Witches.

Pookins gets her way ill. by Lynn Munsinger. Houghton Mifflin, 1987. ISBN 0-395-42636-7 Subj: Character traits – willfulness. Mythical creatures – gnomes.

A porcupine named Fluffy ill. by Lynn Munsinger. Houghton Mifflin, 1986. ISBN 0-395-36895-2 Subj: Animals – porcupines. Names.

Princess Penelope's parrot ill. by Lynn Munsinger. Houghton Mifflin, 1996. ISBN 0-395-78320-8 Subj: Birds – parakeets, parrots. Character traits – selfishness. Emotions – anger. Royalty – princes. Royalty – princesses.

The revenge of the magic chicken ill. by Lynn Munsinger. Houghton Mifflin, 1990. ISBN 0-395-50929-7 Subj: Birds – chickens. Magic.

Roy Foy's special name (Lester, Robin)

Score one for the sloths ill. by Lynn Munsinger. Houghton, 2001. ISBN 0-618-10857-2 Subj: Animals – pigs. Animals – sloths. Character traits – ambition. Character traits – laziness. School.

The shy people's picnic ill. by Nadine Bernard Westcott. Celebration Pr., 1996. ISBN 0-673-75739-0 Subj: Character traits – shyness.

Something might happen ill. by Lynn Munsinger. Houghton, 2003. ISBN 0-618-25406-4 Subj: Animals – lemurs. Behavior – worrying. Emotions – fear. Family life – aunts, uncles.

Tacky and the Emperor ill. by Lynn Munsinger. Houghton Mifflin, 2000. ISBN 0-395-98120-4 Subj: Birds – penguins. Clothing.

Tacky in trouble ill. by Lynn Munsinger. Houghton Mifflin, 1998. ISBN 0-395-86113-6 Subj: Animals – elephants. Behavior. Birds – penguins.

Tacky the penguin ill. by Lynn Munsinger. Houghton Mifflin, 1988. ISBN 0-395-45536-7 Subj: Animals – wolves. Birds – penguins. Character traits – individuality.

Tackylocks and the three bears ill. by Lynn Munsinger. Houghton, 2002. ISBN 0-618-22490-4 Subj: Birds – penguins. School. Theater.

Three cheers for Tacky ill. by Lynn Munsinger. Houghton Mifflin, 1994. ISBN 0-395-66841-7 Subj: Birds – penguins. Character traits – individuality. Cheerleading. Friendship. School.

The wizard, the fairy and the magic chicken ill. by Lynn Munsinger. Houghton Mifflin, 1983. ISBN 0-395-33885-9 Subj: Behavior – sharing. Birds – chickens. Fairies. Friendship. Wizards.

Wuzzy takes off (Lester, Robin)

Lester, Julius. *Ackamarackus: Julius Lester's sumptuously silly fantastically funny fables* ill. by Emilie Chollat. Scholastic, 2001. ISBN 0-590-48913-5 Subj: Animals. Folk & fairy tales.

Albidaro and the mischievous dream ill. by Jerry Pinkney. Fogelman, 2000. ISBN 0-8037-1987-6 Subj: Animals. Behavior. Dreams.

Black cowboy, wild horses ill. by Jerry Pinkney. Dial, 1998. ISBN 0-8037-1788-1 Subj: Animals – horses, ponies. Cowboys, cowgirls. Ethnic groups in the U.S. – African Americans.

John Henry ill. by Jerry Pinkney. Dial, 1994. ISBN 0-8037-1607-9 Subj: Caldecott award honor books. Character traits – perseverance. Character traits – pride. Ethnic groups in the U.S. – African Americans. Folk & fairy tales. Tall tales.

The knee-high man and other tales ill. by Ralph Pinto. Dial, 1972. ISBN 0-8037-4593-1 Subj: Ethnic groups in the U.S. – African Americans. Folk & fairy tales.

Sam and the tigers: a new telling of Little Black Sambo ill. by Jerry Pinkney. Dial, 1996. ISBN 0-8037-2029-7 Subj: Animals – tigers. Character traits – cleverness. Clothing. Family life. Foreign lands – India. Humorous stories.

Shining ill. by Terea Shaffer. Silver Whistle, 2000. ISBN 0-15-200773-3 Subj: Foreign lands – Africa. Handicaps.

What a truly cool world ill. by Joe Cepeda. Scholastic, 1999. ISBN 0-590-86468-8 Subj: Angels. Creation. Ethnic groups in the U.S. – African Americans. Religion.

Why heaven is far away ill. by Joe Cepeda. Scholastic, 2002. ISBN 0-439-17871-1 Subj: Angels. Ethnic groups in the U.S. – African Americans. Folk & fairy tales – pourquoi tales. Religion. Reptiles – snakes.

Lester, Mike. *A is for salad* ill. by author. Putnam, 2000. ISBN 0-399-23388-1 Subj: ABC books. School – first day.

Lester, Robin. *Roy Foy's special name* by Robin & Helen Lester; ill. by Diana Cain Bluthenthal. Candlewick, 1996. ISBN 1-56402-798-8 Subj: Names. School.

Wuzzy takes off by Robin & Helen Lester; ill. by Miko Imai. Candlewick, 1995. ISBN 1-56402-498-9 Subj: Moon. Toys – bears.

Lesynski, Loris. *Dirty dog boogie* ill. by author. Annick, 1999. ISBN 1-55037-573-3 Subj: Foreign lands. Humorous stories. Music. Poetry.

Night school ill. by author. Firefly, 2001. ISBN 1-55037-585-7 Subj: Bedtime. Monsters. Night. School.

Rocksy ill. by author. Annick, 2002. ISBN 1-55037-751-5 Subj: Behavior – wishing. Rhyming text. Rocks.

Let me call you sweetheart ill. by Amanda Haley. HarperFestival, 2002. ISBN 0-694-01556-3 Subj: Animals – dogs. Holidays – Valentine's Day. Pets. Songs.

Let there be light: poems and prayers for repairing the world comp. & ill. by Jane Breskin Zalben. Dutton, 2002. ISBN 0-525-46995-8 Subj: Poetry. Religion.

Le-Tan, Pierre. *The afternoon cat* ill. by author. Pantheon, 1977. ISBN 0-394-93095-9 Subj: Activities. Animals – cats.

Timothy's dream book ill. by author. Farrar, 1978. ISBN 0-374-37598-4 Subj: Careers. Imagination.

Visit to the North Pole ill. by author. Crown, 1983. ISBN 0-517-54893-3 Subj: Dreams. Imagination. Toys – bears.

Le Tord, Bijou. *A bird or two: a story about Henri Matisse* ill. by author. Eerdmans, 1999. ISBN 0-8028-5184-3 Subj: Art. Careers – artists. Concepts – color. Foreign lands – France.

A brown cow ill. by author. Little, 1989. ISBN 0-316-52166-3 Subj: Animals – bulls, cows.

The deep blue sea ill. by author. Orchard, 1990. ISBN 0-531-08453-1 Subj: Creation. Religion.

God's little seeds: a book of parables ill. by author. Eerdmans, 1998. ISBN 0-8028-5169-X Subj: Activities – storytelling. Religion. Seeds.

Good wood bear ill. by author. Bradbury, 1985. ISBN 0-02-756440-1 Subj: Animals – bears. Birds – geese. Homes, houses.

Joseph and Nellie ill. by author. Bradbury, 1986. ISBN 0-02-756450-9 Subj: Careers – fishermen. Sea & seashore.

My Grandma Leonie ill. by author. Bradbury, 1987. ISBN 0-02-756490-8 Subj: Death. Emotions – grief. Family life – grandmothers.

Noah's trees ill. by author. HarperCollins, 1999. ISBN 0-06-028527-3 Subj: Animals. Boats, ships. Religion – Noah. Trees. Weather – floods. Weather – rain.

Picking and weaving ill. by author. Four Winds, 1980. ISBN 0-590-07642-6 Subj: Activities – weaving. Plants.

Rabbit seeds ill. by author. Four Winds, 1984. ISBN 0-590-07797-X Subj: Animals – rabbits. Gardens, gardening.

The river and the rain: the Lord's prayer ill. by author. Doubleday, 1994. ISBN 0-385-32034-5 Subj: Ecology. Forest, woods. Religion.

Sing a new song: a book of Psalms ill. by author. Eerdmans, 1997. ISBN 0-8028-5139-8 Subj: Gardens, gardening. Religion. Seeds.

Let's count and count out comp. by Marion F. Grayson; ill. by Deborah Derr McClintock. Luce, 1975. ISBN 0-8833-1073-2 Subj: Counting, numbers. Games. Poetry.

Let's count the raindrops ill. by Fumi Kosaka. Viking, 2001. ISBN 0-670-89689-6 Subj: Poetry. Weather.

Let's talk about race ill. by Karen Barbour. HarperCollins, 2005. ISBN 0-06-028598-2 Subj: Ethnic groups in the U.S. Prejudice.

Leuck, Laura. *Goodnight, baby monster* ill. by Nigel McMullen. HarperCollins, 2002. ISBN 0-06-029152-4 Subj: Bedtime. Monsters. Rhyming text.

My baby brother has ten tiny toes ill. by Clara Vulliamy. A. Whitman, 1997. ISBN 0-8075-5310-7 Subj: Babies. Counting, numbers. Family life – brothers & sisters. Rhyming text.

My beastly brother ill. by Scott Nash. HarperCollins, 2003. ISBN 0-06-029548-1 Subj: Family life – brothers. Monsters. Rhyming text.

My monster mama loves me so ill. by Mark Buehner. Lothrop, 1999. ISBN 0-688-16867-1 Subj: Family life – mothers. Monsters. Rhyming text.

One witch ill. by S. D. Schindler. Walker, 2003. ISBN 0-8027-8860-2 Subj: Counting, numbers. Holidays – Halloween. Rhyming text. Witches.

Leupold, Nancy S. *Little ghost Godfry* (Sandberg, Inger)

Leutscher, Alfred. *Earth* ill. by John Butler. Dial, 1983. ISBN 0-8037-2109-9 Subj: Earth. Science.

Water ill. by Nick Hardcastle. Dial, 1983. ISBN 0-8037-9390-1 Subj: Ecology. Science. Water.

Levens, George. *Kippy the koala* ill. by Crosby Newell Bonsall. HarperCollins, 1960. Subj: Animals – koalas. Poetry. Seasons – spring.

Levenson, George. *Pumpkin circle: the story of a garden* photos by Shmuel Thaler. Tricycle, 1999. ISBN 1-58246-004-3 Subj: Gardens, gardening. Rhyming text.

Leventhal, Debra. *What is your language?* song by Debra Leventhal; ill. by Monica Wellington. Dutton, 1994. ISBN 0-525-45133-1 Subj: Activities – traveling. Foreign languages. Songs.

Leverich, Kathleen. *The hungry fox and the foxy duck* ill. by Paul Galdone. Parents' Magazine Pr., 1979. ISBN 0-8193-0988-5 Subj: Animals – foxes. Birds – ducks. Character traits – cleverness.

Levert, Mireille. *An island in the soup* ill. by author. Douglas & McIntyre, 2001. ISBN 0-88899-403-6 Subj: Food. Imagination.

Little Red Riding Hood (Grimm, Jacob)

Levete, Sarah. *Being jealous* ill. by Chrisopher O'Neill. Copper Beech, 1999. ISBN 0-7613-0911-X Subj: Emotions – envy, jealousy.

Looking after myself ill. by author. Copper Beech, 1998. ISBN 0-7613-0809-1 Subj: Emotions. Health & fitness. Safety.

Making friends ill. by author. Copper Beech, 1998. ISBN 0-7613-0808-3 Subj: Emotions – loneliness. Friendship.

Rain and shine (Kespert, Deborah)

When people die ill. by Chrisopher O'Neill. Copper Beech, 1998. ISBN 0-7613-0870-9 Subj: Death. Emotions – grief.

Levi, Dorothy Hoffman. *A very special sister* ill. by Ethel Gold. Gallaudet Univ. Pr., 1992. ISBN 0-930323-96-3 Subj: Babies. Family life – new sibling. Family life – sisters. Handicaps – deafness. Multiple births – twins. Sibling rivalry.

Levin, Isadora. *The scarlet flower* (Aksakov, Sergei)

Levin, Miriam Ramsfelder. *In the beginning* ill. by Katherine Janus Kahn. Kar-Ben Copies, 1996. ISBN 0-929371-94-1 Subj: Creation. Emotions – loneliness.

Levine, Abby. *Daddies give you horsey rides* ill. by John Bendall-Brunello. A. Whitman, 2004. ISBN 0-8075-1429-2 Subj: Activities. Family life – fathers. Rhyming text.

Gretchen Groundhog, it's your day! ill. by Nancy Cote. A. Whitman, 1998. ISBN 0-8075-3058-1 Subj: Animals – groundhogs. Holidays – Groundhog Day.

Ollie knows everything ill. by Lynn Munsinger. A. Whitman, 1994. ISBN 0-8075-6020-0 Subj: Activities – trading. Animals – rabbits. Behavior – lost. Sibling rivalry.

Sometimes I wish I were Mindy by Abby & Sarah Levine; ill. by Blanche Sims. A. Whitman, 1986. ISBN 0-8075-7542-9 Subj: Emotions – envy, jealousy.

This is the pumpkin ill. by Paige Billin-Frye. A. Whitman, 1997. ISBN 0-8075-7886-X Subj: Cumulative tales. Holidays – Halloween. Rhyming text.

This is the turkey ill. by Paige Billin-Frye. A. Whitman, 2000. ISBN 0-8075-7888-6 Subj: Family life. Holidays – Thanksgiving. Rhyming text.

Too much mush! ill. by Kathy Parkinson. A. Whitman, 1989. ISBN 0-8075-8025-2 Subj: Folk & fairy tales. Food. Magic. Poverty.

What did mommy do before you? ill. by DyAnne DiSalvo-Ryan. A. Whitman, 1988. ISBN 0-8075-8819-9 Subj: Babies. Behavior – growing up. Family life – mothers.

You push, I ride ill. by Margot Apple. A. Whitman, 1989. ISBN 0-8075-9444-X Subj: Animals – pigs. Family life. Rhyming text.

Levine, Arthur A. *All the lights in the night* ill. by James E. Ransome. Morrow, 1991. ISBN 0-688-10108-9 Subj: Family life – brothers. Foreign lands – Russia. Holidays – Hanukkah. Jewish culture. Religion.

The boardwalk princess ill. by Susan Guevara. Tambourine, 1993. ISBN 0-688-10307-3 Subj: Animals – mice. Family life – brothers & sisters. Folk & fairy tales. Witches.

Bono and Nonno ill. by Judy Lanfredi. Tambourine, 1995. ISBN 0-688-13234-0 Subj: Animals. Family life – grandfathers. Rhyming text.

The boy who drew cats ill. by Frédéric Clément. Dial, 1994. ISBN 0-8037-1173-5 Subj: Activities – drawing. Animals – cats. Careers – artists. Folk & fairy tales. Foreign lands – Japan. Religion.

On Cat Mountain (Richard, Françoise)

Pearl Moscowitz's last stand ill. by Robert Roth. Tambourine, 1993. ISBN 0-688-10754-0 Subj: Cities, towns. Trees.

Sheep dreams ill. by Judy Lanfredi. Dial, 1993. ISBN 0-8037-1195-6 Subj: Animals – sheep. Character traits – shyness. Theater.

Levine, Deb. *Parker picks* ill. by Pedro Martin. S&S, 2002. ISBN 0-689-83456-X Subj: Anatomy – noses. Behavior.

Levine, Ellen. *I hate English!* ill. by Steve Björkman. Scholastic, 1989. ISBN 0-590-42305-3 Subj: Ethnic groups in the U.S. – Chinese Americans. Language.

Levine, Evan. *Not the piano, Mrs. Medley!* ill. by S. D. Schindler. Watts, 1991. ISBN 0-531-08556-2 Subj: Animals – dogs. Family life – grandmothers. Music. Musical instruments – pianos. Sea & seashore.

Levine, Gail Carson. *Betsy who cried wolf* ill. by Scott Nash. HarperCollins, 2002. ISBN 0-06-028764-0 Subj: Animals – sheep. Animals – wolves. Careers – shepherds.

Levine, Joan. *A bedtime story* ill. by Gail Owens. Dutton, 1975. ISBN 0-525-26290-3 Subj: Bedtime.

Levine, Michelle. *Ambulances* ill. with photos. Lerner, 2004. ISBN 0-8225-0769-2 Subj: Careers – emergency medical technicians. Trucks.

Red foxes ill. with photos. Lerner, 2004. ISBN 0-8225-3774-5 Subj: Animals – foxes.

Levine, Rhoda. *Harrison loved his umbrella* ill. by Karla Kuskin. Atheneum, 1964. Subj: Character traits – being different. Character traits – individuality. Umbrellas.

Levine, Sarah. *Sometimes I wish I were Mindy* (Levine, Abby)

Levinson, Nancy Smiler. *Clara and the bookwagon* ill. by Carolyn Croll. HarperCollins, 1988. ISBN 0-06-023838-0 Subj: Books, reading. Libraries. U.S. history.

Death Valley ill. by Diane Dawson Hearn. Holiday, 2001. ISBN 0-8234-1566-X Subj: Desert. Ecology.

Levinson, Riki. *Country dawn to dusk* ill. by Kay Chorao. Dutton, 1992. ISBN 0-525-44957-4 Subj: Animals – dogs. Concepts – color. Country. Pets.

The emperor's new clothes (Andersen, H. C. [Hans Christian])

Grandpa's hotel ill. by David Soman. Orchard, 1995. ISBN 0-531-08775-1 Subj: Family life. Family life – grandparents. Hotels.

I go with my family to Grandma's ill. by Diane Goode. Dutton, 1990. ISBN 0-525-44261-8 Subj: Activities – photographing. Family life. Family life – grandmothers. Transportation.

Me baby! ill. by Marylin Hafner. Dutton, 1991. ISBN 0-525-44693-1 Subj: Babies. Behavior – unnoticed, unseen. Family life. Family life – new sibling. Sibling rivalry.

Our home is the sea ill. by Dennis Luzak. Dutton, 1988. ISBN 0-525-44406-8 Subj: Cities, towns. Family life. Foreign lands – China.

Soon, Annala ill. by Julie Downing. Orchard, 1993. ISBN 0-531-08644-5 Subj: Ethnic groups in the U.S. – Polish Americans. Immigrants. Jewish culture. Language.

Touch! Touch! ill. by True Kelley. Dutton, 1987. ISBN 0-525-44309-6 Subj: Behavior – misbehavior. Family life.

Watch the stars come out ill. by Diane Goode. Dutton, 1985. ISBN 0-525-44205-7 Subj: Family life. Family life – grandmothers. U.S. history.

Levitin, Sonia. *All the cats in the world* ill. by Charles Robinson. Harcourt, 1982. ISBN 0-15-202396-8 Subj: Animals – cats. Character traits – kindness to animals.

Boom town ill. by Cat Bowman Smith. Orchard, 1998. ISBN 0-531-33043-5 Subj: Careers – bakers. Careers – miners. Cities, towns. U.S. history – frontier & pioneer life.

The man who kept his heart in a bucket ill. by Jerry Pinkney. Dial, 1991. ISBN 0-8037-1030-5 Subj: Emotions – love.

Nine for California ill. by Cat Bowman Smith. Orchard, 1996. ISBN 0-531-08877-4 Subj: Activities – traveling. Family life. U.S. history – frontier & pioneer life.

Nobody stole the pie ill. by Fernando Krahn. Harcourt, 1980. ISBN 0-15-257469-7 Subj: Activities – baking, cooking. Crime. Food.

A piece of home ill. by Juan Wijngaard. Dial, 1996. ISBN 0-8037-1626-5 Subj: Behavior – worrying. Ethnic groups in the U.S. – Russian Americans. Family life – cousins.

A single speckled egg ill. by John M. Larrecq. Parnassus, 1976. ISBN 0-874-66075-0 Subj: Behavior – worrying. Eggs. Farms.

Taking charge ill. by Cat Bowman Smith. Orchard, 1999. ISBN 0-531-33149-0 Subj: Babies. U.S. history – frontier & pioneer life.

When Elephant goes to a party ill. by Jeff Seaver. Rising Moon, 2001. ISBN 0-87358-751-0 Subj: Animals – elephants. Etiquette. Humorous stories. Parties.

When Kangaroo goes to school ill. by Jeff Seaver. Rising Moon, 2001. ISBN 0-87358-791-X Subj: Animals – kangaroos. Etiquette. School – first day.

Who owns the moon? ill. by John M. Larrecq. Parnassus, 1973. ISBN 0-395-27656-X Subj: Behavior – fighting, arguing. Moon. Problem solving.

Levoy, Myron. *The Hanukkah of Great-Uncle Otto* ill. by Donna Ruff. Jewish Publication Society, 1984. ISBN 0-8276-0242-1 Subj: Family life – aunts, uncles. Holidays – Hanukkah. Jewish culture.

Levy, Elizabeth. *Cleo and the coyote* ill. by Diana Bryer. HarperCollins, 1996. ISBN 0-06-024272-8 Subj: Animals – coyotes. Animals – dogs. Desert. Friendship.

Nice little girls ill. by Mordicai Gerstein. Delacorte, 1974. ISBN 0-440-06193-8 Subj: School.

Levy, Janice. *Abuelito eats with his fingers* ill. by Layne Johnson. Eakin, 1998. ISBN 1-57168-177-9 Subj: Ethnic groups in the U.S. – Mexican Americans. Family life – grandfathers.

The man who lived in a hat ill. by Dave Brown. Hampton Roads, 2000. ISBN 1-57174-211-5 Subj: Behavior – greed. Clothing – hats. Humorous stories. Insects – ants. Magic.

Totally uncool ill. by Chris Monroe. Carolrhoda, 1999. ISBN 1-57505-306-3 Subj: Ethnic groups in the U.S. Family life – fathers. Friendship.

Levy, Miriam F. *Adam's world, San Francisco* (Fraser, Kathleen)

Levy, Sara G. *Mother Goose rhymes for Jewish children* ill. by Jessie B. Robinson. Bloch, 1945. ISBN 0-8197-0254-4 Subj: Jewish culture. Nursery rhymes.

Lewandowski, Frrich. *It's Christmas again* ill. by Kathryn H. Delisle. Ambassador, 2000. ISBN 1-929039-04-2 Subj: Animals. Holidays – Christmas. Religion – Nativity.

Lewin, Betsy. *Animal snackers* ill. by author. Dodd, 1980. ISBN 0-396-07782-X Subj: Animals. Food. Poetry.

Booby hatch ill. by author. Clarion, 1995. ISBN 0-395-68703-9 Subj: Birds – boobys. Islands. Nature.

Cat count ill. by author. Dodd, 1981. ISBN 0-396-07928-8 Subj: Animals – cats. Counting, numbers. Poetry.

Chubbo's pool ill. by author. Clarion, 1996. ISBN 0-395-72807-X Subj: Animals – elephants. Animals – hippopotamuses. Character traits – selfishness. Foreign lands – Botswana.

Groundhog day ill. by author. Scholastic, 2000. ISBN 0-439-10802-0 Subj: Animals – groundhogs. Holidays – Groundhog Day. Shadows.

Hip, hippo, hooray! ill. by author. Dodd, 1982. ISBN 0-396-08032-4 Subj: Animals – hippopotamuses. Counting, numbers. Illness. Weather.

What's the matter, Habibi? ill. by author. Clarion, 1997. ISBN 0-395-85816-X Subj: Animals – camels. Foreign lands – Egypt.

Wiley learns to spell ill. by author. Scholastic, 1998. ISBN 0-590-10835-2 Subj: Language. Monsters.

Lewin, Hugh. *An elephant came to swim* by Hugh Lewin & Lisa Kopper; ill. by authors. David & Charles, 1986. ISBN 0-241-11432-2 Subj: Animals – elephants. Foreign lands – Africa.

Jafta ill. by Lisa Kopper. Carolrhoda, 1983. ISBN 0-87614-207-2 Subj: Emotions. Family life. Foreign lands – Africa.

Jafta and the wedding ill. by Lisa Kopper. Carolrhoda, 1983. ISBN 0-87614-210-2 Subj: Family life. Foreign lands – Africa. Weddings.

Jafta – the homecoming ill. by Lisa Kopper. Knopf, 1994. ISBN 0-679-84722-7 Subj: Emotions. Family life – fathers. Foreign lands – South Africa.

Jafta – the journey ill. by Lisa Kopper. Carolrhoda, 1984. ISBN 0-87614-265-X Subj: Activities – traveling. Emotions. Foreign lands – Africa.

Jafta – the town ill. by Lisa Kopper. Carolrhoda, 1984. ISBN 0-87614-266-8 Subj: Cities, towns. Emotions. Foreign lands – Africa.

Jafta's father ill. by Lisa Kopper. Carolrhoda, 1983. ISBN 0-87614-209-9 Subj: Family life – fathers. Foreign lands – Africa.

Jafta's mother ill. by Lisa Kopper. Carolrhoda, 1983. ISBN 0-87614-208-0 Subj: Family life – mothers. Foreign lands – Africa.

Lewin, Ted. *Amazon boy* ill. by author. Macmillan, 1993. ISBN 0-02-757383-4 Subj: Birthdays. Boats, ships. Cities, towns. Ecology. Foreign lands – Brazil. Rivers.

Big Jimmy's Kum Kau Chinese take out ill. by author. HarperCollins, 2002. ISBN 0-688-16027-1 Subj: Activities – baking, cooking. Family life – fathers. Family life – sons. Restaurants. Stores.

Fair! ill. by author. Lothrop, 1997. ISBN 0-688-12851-3 Subj: Country. Fairs, festivals.

Market! ill. by author. Lothrop, 1996. ISBN 0-688-12162-4 Subj: Foreign lands. Stores.

Nilo and the tortoise ill. by author. Scholastic, 1999. ISBN 0-590-96004-0 Subj: Animals. Boats, ships. Careers – fishermen. Emotions – loneliness. Foreign lands – Galapagos Islands. Islands.

The storytellers ill. by author. Lothrop, 1998. ISBN 0-688-15179-5 Subj: Activities – storytelling. Foreign lands – Morocco.

When the rivers go home ill. by author. Macmillan, 1992. ISBN 0-02-757382-6 Subj: Animals. Ecology. Foreign lands – Brazil.

Lewis, Bobby. *Home before midnight: a traditional verse;* retold & ill. by Bobby Lewis. Lothrop, 1984. ISBN 0-688-00731-7 Subj: Animals – pigs. Cumulative tales.

Lewis, C. S. (Clive Staples). *Edmund and the White Witch* (Edmund and the White Witch)

Lucy steps through the wardrobe (Lucy steps through the wardrobe)

Lewis, Claudia Louise. *When I go to the moon* ill. by Leonard Weisgard. Macmillan, 1961. Subj: Earth. Moon.

Lewis, Eils Moorhouse. *The snug little house* ill. by Elise Primavera. Atheneum, 1981. ISBN 0-689-50177-3 Subj: Character traits – helpfulness. Homes, houses.

Lewis, J. Patrick. *Arithme-tickle* ill. by Frank Remkiewicz. Harcourt, 2002. ISBN 0-15-216418-9 Subj: Counting, numbers. Rhyming text. Riddles & jokes.

At the wish of the fish ill. by Katya Krenina. Atheneum, 1999. ISBN 0-689-81336-8 Subj: Behavior – wishing. Fish. Folk & fairy tales. Foreign lands – Russia.

The boat of many rooms ill. by Reg Cartwright. Atheneum, 1997. ISBN 0-689-80118-1 Subj: Animals. Boats, ships. Religion – Noah. Rhyming text. Weather – floods. Weather – rain.

The bookworm's feast ill. by John O'Brien. Dial, 1999. ISBN 0-8037-1693-1 Subj: Games. Humorous stories. Poetry.

The Christmas of the reddle moon ill. by Gary Kelley. Dial, 1994. ISBN 0-8037-1567-6 Subj: Behavior – lost. Foreign lands – England. Holidays – Christmas. Imagination. Magic. Santa Claus.

Doodle dandies: poems that take shape ill. by Lisa Desimini. Atheneum, 1998. ISBN 0-689-81075-X Subj: Poetry.

Earth and me, our family tree ill. by Christopher Canyon. Dawn, 2002. ISBN 1-58469-031-3 Subj: Animals. Earth. Nature. Rhyming text.

Earth and you, a closer view ill. by Christopher Canyon. Dawn, 2001. ISBN 1-58469-016-X Subj: Earth. Ecology. Geography. Nature. Rhyming text.

The Fat-Cats at sea ill. by Victoria Chess. Knopf, 1994. ISBN 0-679-82639-4 Subj: Animals – cats. Boats, ships. Poetry.

The frog princess ill. by Gennady Spirin. Dial, 1994. ISBN 0-8037-1624-9 Subj: Folk & fairy tales. Foreign lands – Russia. Frogs & toads. Magic. Royalty – princesses. Witches.

Good mousekeeping ill. by Lisa Desimini. Atheneum, 2001. Subj: Animals. Homes, houses. Poetry.

A hippopotamusn't ill. by Victoria Chess. Dial, 1990. ISBN 0-8037-0519-0 Subj: Animals. Poetry.

The house of Boo ill. by Katya Krénina. Atheneum, 1998. ISBN 0-689-80356-7 Subj: Ghosts. Holidays – Halloween. Rhyming text.

Isabella Abnormella and the very, very finicky Queen of Trouble ill. by Kyrsten Brooker. DK, 2000. ISBN 0-7894-2605-6 Subj: Furniture – beds. Rhyming text. Royalty – queens. Sleep.

July is a mad mosquito ill. by Melanie W. Hall. Atheneum, 1994. ISBN 0-689-31813-8 Subj: Days of the week, months of the year. Nature. Poetry. Seasons.

The la-di-da hare ill. by Diana Cain Bluthenthal. Atheneum, 1997. ISBN 0-689-31925-8 Subj: Activities – picnicking. Animals. Islands. Poetry.

The little buggers: insect and spider poems ill. by Victoria Chess. Dial, 1998. ISBN 0-8037-1770-9 Subj: Insects. Poetry. Spiders.

Long was the winter road they traveled: a tale of the nativity ill. by Drew Bairley. Dial, 1997. ISBN 0-8037-1815-2 Subj: Animals. Holidays – Christmas. Poetry. Religion – Nativity.

The moonbow of Mr. B. Bones ill. by Dirk Zimmer. Knopf, 1992. ISBN 0-394-95365-7 Subj: Careers – peddlers. Magic. Moon.

The night of the goat children ill. by Alexi Natchev. Dial, 1999. ISBN 0-8037-1871-3 Subj: Animals – goats. Crime. Disguises. Royalty – princesses.

Riddle-icious ill. by Debbie Tilley. Knopf, 1996. ISBN 0-679-94011-1 Subj: Poetry. Riddles & jokes.

Riddle-lightful: oodles of little riddle-poems ill. by Debbie Tilley. Knopf, 1998. ISBN 0-679-98760-6 Subj: Rhyming text. Riddles & jokes.

The tsar and the amazing cow ill. by Friso Henstra. Dial, 1988. ISBN 0-8037-0411-9 Subj: Behavior – greed. Folk & fairy tales. Old age.

Two-legged, four-legged, no-legged rhymes ill. by Pamela Paparone. Knopf, 1991. ISBN 0-679-90771-8 Subj: Animals. Poetry.

Lewis, Jacqueline Janette. *You are so wonderful* ill. by Jeremy Tugeau. Augsburg Fortress, 2003. ISBN 0-8066-4553-9 Subj: Creation. Religion. Rhyming text. Self-concept.

Lewis, Kevin. *Chugga-chugga choo-choo* ill. by Daniel Kirk. Hyperion, 1999. ISBN 0-7868-2379-8 Subj: Rhyming text. Toys – trains.

The lot at the end of my block ill. by Reg Cartwright. Hyperion, 2001. ISBN 0-7868-2512-X Subj: Buildings. Careers – construction workers. Cumulative tales. Rhyming text.

The runaway pumpkin ill. by S. D. Schindler. Orchard, 2003. ISBN 0-439-43974-4 Subj: Holidays – Halloween. Rhyming text.

Lewis, Kim. *Emma's lamb* ill. by author. Four Winds, 1991. ISBN 0-02-758821-1 Subj: Animals – sheep. Behavior – needing someone. Farms.

First snow ill. by author. Candlewick, 1993. ISBN 1-56402-194-7 Subj: Animals – dogs. Animals – sheep. Behavior – lost & found possessions. Farms. Toys – bears. Weather – snow.

Floss ill. by author. Candlewick, 1992. ISBN 1-56402-010-X Subj: Activities – playing. Activities – working. Animals – dogs.

Friends ill. by author. Candlewick, 1997. ISBN 0-7636-0346-5 Subj: Emotions – anger. Farms. Friendship.

Good night, Harry ill. by author. Candlewick, 2004. ISBN 0-7636-2206-0 Subj: Animals – elephants. Bedtime. Friendship. Sleep. Toys.

Here we go Harry ill. by author. Candlewick, 2005. ISBN 0-7636-2549-3 Subj: Activities – flying. Animals. Animals – elephants. Friendship. Toys.

Just like Floss ill. by author. Candlewick, 1998. ISBN 0-7636-0684-7 Subj: Animals – babies. Animals – dogs. Farms.

The last train ill. by author. Candlewick, 1994. ISBN 1-56402-343-5 Subj: Family life. Foreign lands – England. Imagination. Trains.

Little Baa ill. by author. Candlewick, 2001. ISBN 0-7636-1447-5 Subj: Animals – babies. Animals – sheep. Farms.

Little calf ill. by author. Candlewick, 2000. ISBN 0-7636-0899-8 Subj: Animals – babies. Animals – bulls, cows. Farms.

Little lamb ill. by author. Candlewick, 2000. ISBN 0-7636-0900-5 Subj: Animals – babies. Animals – sheep. Farms.

Little puppy ill. by author. Candlewick, 2000. ISBN 0-7636-0901-3 Subj: Animals – babies. Animals – dogs. Farms.

My friend Harry ill. by author. Candlewick, 1995. ISBN 1-56402-617-5 Subj: Animals – elephants. School. Toys.

One summer day ill. by author. Candlewick, 1996. ISBN 1-56402-883-6 Subj: Activities – walking. Country. Seasons – summer. Tractors.

The shepherd boy ill. by author. Four Winds, 1990. ISBN 0-02-758581-6 Subj: Animals – sheep. Careers – shepherds.

Lewis, Lucia Z. *see* Anderson, Lucia Z.

Lewis, Naomi. *The butterfly collector* ill. by Fulvio Testa. Prentice-Hall, 1979. ISBN 0-13-108852-1 Subj: Behavior – collecting things. Insects – butterflies, caterpillars. Rhyming text. Riddles & jokes.

The frog prince: or Iron Henry (Grimm, Jacob)

Hare and badger go to town ill. by Tony Ross. David & Charles, 1987. ISBN 0-905478-94-0 Subj: Animals. Ecology.

Johnny Longnose (Krüss, James)

Jorinda and Joringel (Grimm, Jacob)

Leaves ill. by Fulvio Testa. HarperCollins, 1983. ISBN 0-911-74501-7 Subj: Plants. Seasons. Trees.

The nightingale (Andersen, H. C. [Hans Christian])

Once upon a rainbow ill. by Gabriele Eichenauer. Jonathan Cape, 1981. ISBN 0-224-01842-6 Subj: Concepts – color. Rhyming text. Toys – bears.

Puffin ill. by Deborah King. Lothrop, 1984. ISBN 0-688-03783-6 Subj: Birds – puffins. Foreign lands – Scotland.

Puss in boots (Perrault, Charles)

The snow queen (Andersen, H. C. [Hans Christian])

The steadfast tin soldier (Andersen, H. C. [Hans Christian])

The stepsister ill. by Allison Reed. Dial, 1987. ISBN 0-8037-0430-5 Subj: Animals – cats. Family life – stepfamilies.

Swan ill. by Deborah King. Lothrop, 1986. ISBN 0-688-05535-4 Subj: Birds – swans. Nature. Science.

The tale of the vanishing rainbow (Rupprecht, Siegfried P.)

The wild swans (Andersen, H. C. [Hans Christian])

Lewis, Paeony. *I'll always love you* ill. by Penny Ives. Tiger Tales, 2002. ISBN 0-613-52270-2 Subj: Animals – bears. Behavior – worrying. Family life – mothers.

Lewis, Paul Owen. *Frog girl* ill. by author. G. Stevens, 1999. ISBN 0-8368-2228-5 Subj: Character traits – kindness to animals. Ecology. Folk & fairy tales. Frogs & toads. Indians of North America – Tlingit. Volcanoes.

Grasper ill. by author. Beyond Words, 1993. ISBN 0-941831-85-X Subj: Crustaceans – crabs. Self-concept.

Storm boy ill. by author. G. Stevens, 1999. ISBN 0-8368-2229-3 Subj: Animals – whales. Sea & seashore. Weather – storms.

Lewis, Richard. *In a spring garden* ill. by Ezra Jack Keats. Dial, 1965. A collection of haiku. ISBN 0-8037-4024-7 Subj: Poetry.

In the night, still dark ill. by Ed Young. Atheneum, 1988. ISBN 0-689-31310-1 Subj: Hawaii. Poetry.

Lewis, Rob. *Aunt Armadillo* ill. by author. Firefly, 1985. ISBN 0-920303-38-2 Subj: Animals – armadillos. Family life – aunts, uncles. Libraries.

Friends ill. by author. Holt, 2001. ISBN 0-8050-6691-8 Subj: Animals – rabbits. Communities, neighborhoods. Friendship.

Friska, the sheep that was too small ill. by author. Farrar, 1988. ISBN 0-374-32461-1 Subj: Animals – sheep. Animals – wolves. Character traits – bravery.

Hello, Mr. Scarecrow ill. by author. Farrar, 1987. ISBN 0-374-32947-8 Subj: Days of the week, months of the year. Scarecrows.

Lewis, Rose A. *I love you like crazy cakes* ill. by Jane Dyer. Little, 2002. ISBN 0-316-52576-6 Subj: Adoption. Babies. Family life. Foreign lands – China.

Lewis, Shari. *Baby Lamb Chop loves animals* ill. by Cathy Beylon. Random House, 1991. ISBN 0-679-81723-9 Subj: Animals. Format, unusual – board books. Puppets.

Baby Lamb Chop loves numbers ill. by Cathy Beylon. Random House, 1991. ISBN 0-679-81724-7 Subj: Counting, numbers. Format, unusual – board books. Puppets.

Baby Lamb Chop loves nursery school ill. by Cathy Beylon. Random House, 1991. ISBN 0-679-81725-5 Subj: Format, unusual – board books. Puppets. School – nursery.

Baby Lamb Chop loves the beach ill. by Cathy Beylon. Random House, 1991. ISBN 0-679-81726-3 Subj: Format, unusual – board books. Puppets. Sea & seashore – beaches.

Baby Lamb Chop loves words ill. by Cathy Beylon. Random House, 1991. ISBN 0-679-81722-0 Subj: Format, unusual – board books. Language. Puppets.

Lewis, Sharon. *Orca! The killer whale* ill. by Linda Roberts. HarperCollins, 1990. ISBN 0-694-00295-X Subj: Animals – whales.

Tiger! ill. by Linda Roberts. HarperCollins, 1990. ISBN 0-694-00296-8 Subj: Animals – tigers.

Lewis, Stephen (Stephen Paul). *Zoo city* ill. by author. Greenwillow, 1976. ISBN 0-688-86000-1 Subj: Animals. Cities, towns. Format, unusual. Imagination. Wordless. Zoos.

Lewis, Thomas P. *Call for Mr. Sniff* ill. by Beth Weiner Lipson. HarperCollins, 1981. ISBN 0-06-023815-1 Subj: Animals – dogs. Birthdays. Mystery stories.

Clipper ship ill. by Joan Sandin. HarperCollins, 1978. ISBN 0-06-023809-7 Subj: Activities – traveling. Boats, ships.

Hill of fire ill. by Joan Sandin. HarperCollins, 1971. ISBN 0-06-023803-8 Subj: Foreign lands – Mexico. Volcanoes.

Mr. Sniff and the motel mystery ill. by Beth Weiner Lipson. HarperCollins, 1984. ISBN 0-06-023825-9 Subj: Animals – dogs. Mystery stories.

Lewis, Wendy A. *In Abby's hands* ill. by Marilyn Mets & Peter Ledwon. Red Deer Pr., 2003. ISBN 0-88995-282-5 Subj: Animals – dogs. Character traits – confidence.

Lewis, Zoe. *Disney's Beauty and the beast teacup mix-up* ill. by Phil Wilson. Walt Disney, 1994. ISBN 0-7868-3013-1 Subj: Concepts.

Lewison, Wendy Cheyette. *Baby has a boo-boo* ill. by Bettina Paterson. Grosset, 1994. ISBN 0-448-40583-0 Subj: Babies. Format, unusual – board books. Illness.

Baby's first Mother Goose (Mother Goose)

"Buzz," said the bee ill. by Hans Wilhelm. Scholastic, 1992. ISBN 0-590-44185-X Subj: Animals. Cumulative tales. Noise, sounds. Rhyming text.

Bye-bye, baby ill. by True Kelley. Scholastic, 1992. ISBN 0-590-45172-3 Subj: Babies. Format, unusual – toy & movable books.

Don't wake the baby! ill. by Jerry Smath. Grosset, 1996. ISBN 0-448-41293-4 Subj: Babies. Rebuses.

Going to sleep on the farm ill. by Juan Wijngaard. Dial, 1992. ISBN 0-8037-1097-6 Subj: Animals. Bedtime. Cumulative tales. Farms. Rhyming text. Sleep.

Happy Thanksgiving! ill. by Mary Morgan. Grosset, 1993. ISBN 0-448-40552-0 Subj: Animals – mice. Format, unusual – board books. Rhyming text.

Hello, snow! ill. by Maryann Cocca-Leffler. Grosset, 1994. ISBN 0-448-40486-9 Subj: Rhyming text. Weather – snow.

I am a flower girl photos by Elizabeth Hathon. Grosset, 1999. ISBN 0-448-41956-4 Subj: Family life – aunts, uncles. Weddings.

I wear my tutu everywhere! ill. by Mary Morgan. Grosset, 1996. ISBN 0-448-40877-5 Subj: Activities – dancing. Ballet.

Mud ill. by Maryann Cocca-Leffler. Random House, 2001. ISBN 0-679-80251-7 Subj: Activities – playing. Rhyming text.

My baby brother ill. by Stephen Cartwright. Warner, 1990. ISBN 1-55782-102-X Subj: Family life – brothers & sisters. Format, unusual – toy & movable books.

My favorite doll ill. by Stephen Cartwright. Warner, 1990. ISBN 1-55782-116-X Subj: Bedtime. Format, unusual – toy & movable books. Toys – dolls.

My new puppy ill. by Stephen Cartwright. Warner, 1990. ISBN 1-55782-119-4 Subj: Animals – dogs. Format, unusual – toy & movable books.

Nighty-night ill. by Giulia Orecchia. Grosset, 1992. ISBN 0-448-40391-9 Subj: Format, unusual – board books. Moon. Night. Rhyming text.

Our new baby ill. by Nancy Sheehan. Grosset, 1996. ISBN 0-448-41147-4 Subj: Babies. Family life – brothers & sisters. Family life – new sibling.

The princess and the potty ill. by Rick Brown. S&S, 1994. ISBN 0-671-87284-2 Subj: Behavior – growing up. Royalty – princesses. Toilet training.

Princess Buttercup ill. by Jerry Smath. Grosset, 2001. ISBN 0-448-42473-8 Subj: Behavior – lost. Flowers. Royalty – princesses. Seasons – spring.

Raindrop, plop ill. by Pam Paparone. Viking, 2004. ISBN 0-670-03620-X Subj: Animals – dogs. Counting, numbers. Rhyming text. Weather – rain.

The rooster who lost his crow ill. by Thor Wickstrom. Dial, 1995. ISBN 0-8037-1546-3 Subj: Animals. Birds – chickens. Farms.

Say thank you, Theodore: a book about manners ill. by Juli Kangas. Platt, 1992. ISBN 0-448-40476-1 Subj: Animals – rabbits. Etiquette. Family life – brothers & sisters.

Shy Vi ill. by Stephen John Smith. S&S, 1993. ISBN 0-671-76968-5 Subj: Animals – mice. Character traits – individuality. Character traits – shyness. Theater.

So many boots ill. by Tony Griego. Scholastic, 2000. ISBN 0-439-09865-3 Subj: Clothing – boots. Insects. Rhyming text. Weather – rain.

Ten little ballerinas ill. by Joan Holub. Grosset, 1996. ISBN 0-448-41491-0 Subj: Activities – dancing. Ballet. Format, unusual – toy & movable books. Rhyming text.

A trip to the firehouse ill. by Elizabeth Hathon. Grosset, 1998. ISBN 0-448-41740-5 Subj: Careers – firefighters. Communities, neighborhoods.

Uh oh, baby ill. by True Kelley. Scholastic, 1992. ISBN 0-590-45171-5 Subj: Babies. Format, unusual – toy & movable books.

Where is Sammy's smile? ill. by Katy Bratun. Grosset, 1989. ISBN 0-448-40150-9 Subj: Animals – raccoons. Format, unusual.

Where's baby? ill. by True Kelley. Scholastic, 1992. ISBN 0-590-45170-7 Subj: Babies. Format, unusual – toy & movable books.

Where's my teddy? ill. by Stephen Cartwright. Warner, 1990. ISBN 1-55782-052-X Subj: Behavior – lost & found possessions. Format, unusual – toy & movable books. Toys – bears.

Lewiton, Mina. *see* Simon, Mina Lewiton

Lexau, Joan M. *Benjie* ill. by Don Bolognese. Dial, 1964. Subj: Character traits – shyness. Ethnic groups in the U.S. – African Americans. Family life. Family life – grandmothers. Problem solving.

Benjie on his own ill. by Don Bolognese. Dial, 1970. Subj: Cities, towns. Ethnic groups in the U.S. – African Americans. Family life – grandmothers. Illness. Problem solving.

Cathy is company ill. by Aliki. Dial, 1961. Subj: Etiquette. Friendship.

Come here, cat ill. by Steven Kellogg. HarperCollins, 1973. ISBN 0-06-024558-1 Subj: Animals – cats. Cities, towns.

Crocodile and hen ill. by Joan Sandin. HarperCollins, 1969. Adapt. of Why the crocodile does not eat the hen, from Notes on the folklore of the Fjort (French Congo), by R. E. Dennett. Subj: Birds – chickens. Cumulative tales. Folk & fairy tales. Foreign lands – Africa. Reptiles – alligators, crocodiles.

The dog food caper ill. by Marylin Hafner. Dial, 1985. ISBN 0-8037-0108-X Subj: Animals – dogs. Animals – mice. Mystery stories. Witches.

Every day a dragon ill. by Ben Shecter. HarperCollins, 1967. Subj: Family life. Family life – fathers. Games.

Finders keepers, losers weepers ill. by Tomie de Paola. Lippincott, 1967. Subj: Babies. Behavior – lost & found possessions. Behavior – lying. Family life.

Go away, dog ill. by Crosby Newell Bonsall. HarperCollins, 1963. ISBN 0-06-024556-5 Subj: Animals – dogs. Birthdays. Character traits – persistence.

Go away, dog ill. by Paul Meisel. HarperCollins, 1997. ISBN 0-06-027503-0 Subj: Animals – dogs. Birthdays. Character traits – persistence.

The homework caper ill. by Syd Hoff. HarperCollins, 1966. ISBN 0-06-023856-9 Subj: Sibling rivalry.

A house so big ill. by Syd Hoff. HarperCollins, 1968. Subj: Character traits – generosity. Emotions – love. Family life – mothers. Imagination.

I hate red rover ill. by Gail Owens. Dutton, 1979. ISBN 0-525-32527-1 Subj: Behavior – growing up. Games.

I should have stayed in bed ill. by Syd Hoff. HarperCollins, 1965. Subj: Behavior – bad day. Emotions – embarrassment. Ethnic groups in the U.S. – African Americans.

I'll tell on you ill. by Gail Owens. Dutton, 1981. ISBN 0-525-32542-5 Subj: Animals – dogs. Behavior – misbehavior. Sports – baseball.

It all began with a drip, drip, drip ill. by Joan Sandin. McCall, 1970. ISBN 0-8415-2019-4 Subj: Behavior – mistakes. Character traits – bravery. Folk & fairy tales. Foreign lands – India.

Me day ill. by Robert Weaver. Dial, 1971. Subj: Birthdays. Cities, towns. Divorce. Ethnic groups in the U.S. – African Americans. Family life. Family life – fathers.

Millicent's ghost ill. by Ben Shecter. Dial, 1962. Subj: Ghosts. Night.

More beautiful than flowers ill. by Don Bolognese. Lippincott, 1966. Subj: Poetry. Religion.

Olaf reads ill. by Harvey Weiss. Dial, 1961. ISBN 0-8037-6559-2 Subj: Books, reading.

The rooftop mystery ill. by Syd Hoff. HarperCollins, 1968. ISBN 0-06-023865-8 Subj: Ethnic groups in the U.S. – African Americans. Moving. Mystery stories. Toys – dolls.

Who took the farmer's hat? ill. by Fritz Siebel. HarperCollins, 1963. ISBN 0-06-024566-2 Subj: Clothing – hats. Farms. Weather – wind.

L'Hommedieu, Arthur John. *Working at a museum* ill. with photos. Childrens Pr., 1998. ISBN 0-516-20748-2 Subj: Careers – museum workers. Museums.

Lia, Simone. *Red's great chase* ill. by author. Dutton, 2000. ISBN 0-525-46213-9 Subj: Activities – playing. Monsters.

Liatsos, Sandra Olson. *Bicycle riding and other poems* ill. by Karen Dugan. Wordsong, 1997. ISBN 1-56397-235-2 Subj: Activities. Poetry. Sports.

Libby, Barbara. *I rode the red horse: Secretariat's Belmont race* ill. by author. Eclipse, 2003. ISBN 1-58150-096-3 Subj: Animals – horses, ponies. Sports – racing.

Libney, Varda. *What I like about Passover* ill. by author. Little Simon, 2002. ISBN 0-689-84491-3 Subj: Format, unusual – board books. Holidays – Passover. Jewish culture. Religion.

Lichtenheld, Tom. *Everything I know about monsters* ill. by autnor. S&S, 2002. ISBN 0-689-84381-X Subj: Monsters.

Everything I know about pirates ill. by author. S&S, 2000. ISBN 0-689-82625-7 Subj: Pirates.

Lichtveld, Noni. *I lost my arrow in a kankan tree* ill. by author. Lothrop, 1993. ISBN 0-688-12748-7 Subj: Activities – trading. Circular tales. Foreign lands – Suriname.

Liddell, Janice. *Imani and the Flying Africans* ill. by Linda Nickens. Africa World, 1994. ISBN 0-86543-365-8 Subj: Activities – flying. Activities – traveling. Ethnic groups in the U.S. – African Americans. Folk & fairy tales.

Lidz, Jane. *Zak, the one-of-a-kind dog* ill. by author. Abrams, 1997. ISBN 0-8109-3995-9 Subj: Animals – dogs. Character traits – individuality.

Lieberman, Deborah. *The Wooodles: stretching your imagination* (Fox, Perla)

Lieberman, Syd. *The wise shoemaker of Studena* ill. by Martin Lemelman. Jewish Publication Society, 1994. ISBN 0-8276-0509-9 Subj: Behavior – misbehavior. Careers – shoemakers. Character traits – appearance. Character traits – cleverness. Character traits – wisdom. Foreign lands – Hungary. Jewish culture.

Liebler, John. *Frog counts to ten* ill. by author. Millbrook, 1994. ISBN 1-56294-436-3 Subj: Counting, numbers. Frogs & toads. Sports – bicycling.

Liebman, Daniel. *I want to be a builder* ill. with photos. Firefly, 2003. ISBN 1-55297-758-7 Subj: Careers – construction workers.

I want to be a cowboy ill. with photos. Firefly, 1999. ISBN 1-55209-447-2 Subj: Careers. Cowboys, cowgirls.

I want to be a doctor ill. with photos. Firefly, 2000. ISBN 1-55209-463-4 Subj: Careers – doctors.

I want to be a firefighter ill. with photos. Firefly, 1999. ISBN 1-55209-448-0 Subj: Careers – firefighters. Communities, neighborhoods. Fire.

I want to be a librarian ill. with photos. Firefly, 2001. ISBN 1-55297-691-2 Subj: Careers – librarians.

I want to be a mechanic ill. with photos. Firefly, 2003. ISBN 1-55297-695-5 Subj: Careers – mechanics.

I want to be a musician ill. with photos. Firefly, 2003. ISBN 1-55297-760-9 Subj: Careers – musicians.

I want to be a nurse ill. with photos. Firefly, 2001. ISBN 1-55209-568-1 Subj: Careers – nurses.

I want to be a police officer ill. with photos. Firefly, 2000. ISBN 1-55209-467-7 Subj: Careers – police officers. Communities, neighborhoods.

I want to be a teacher ill. with photos. Firefly, 2001. ISBN 1-55209-572-X Subj: Careers – teachers.

I want to be a truck driver ill. with photos. Firefly, 2001. ISBN 1-55209-576-2 Subj: Careers – truck drivers.

I want to be a vet ill. with photos. Firefly, 2000. ISBN 1-55209-471-5 Subj: Careers – veterinarians.

I want to be a zookeeper ill. with photos. Firefly, 2003. ISBN 1-55297-699-8 Subj: Careers – zookeepers.

Liersch, Anne. *A house is not a home* ill. by Christa Unzner; trans. by J. Alison James. North-South, 1999. ISBN 0-7358-1157-1 Subj: Animals. Animals – badgers. Behavior – bullying. Friendship. Homes, houses.

Nell and Fluffy ill. by Christa Unzner; trans. by J. Alison James. North-South, 2001. ISBN 0-7358-1424-4 Subj: Animals – guinea pigs. Character traits – responsibility. Pets.

Lies, Brian. *Hamlet and the enormous Chinese dragon kite* ill. by author. Houghton Mifflin, 1994. ISBN 0-395-68391-2 Subj: Activities – flying. Animals – pigs. Animals – porcupines. Friendship. Kites.

Hamlet and the magnificent sandcastle ill. by author. Moon Mt., 2001. ISBN 0-9677929-2-4 Subj: Animals – pigs. Animals – porcupines. Sand.

The Lifesize animal counting book ill. with photos. DK, 1994. ISBN 1-56458-517-4 Subj: Animals. Counting, numbers.

Lifton, Betty Jean. *Goodnight orange monster* ill. by Cyndy Szekeres. Atheneum, 1972. Subj: Bedtime. Emotions – fear. Monsters. Night.

Joji and the Amanojaku ill. by Eiichi Mitsui. Norton, 1965. Subj: Birds. Foreign lands – Japan. Mythical creatures – goblins. Scarecrows.

Joji and the dragon ill. by Eiichi Mitsui. Morrow, 1989, c1957. Reprint. Originally published: New York: Morrow, 1957. ISBN 0-208-02245-7 Subj: Birds. Dragons. Foreign lands – Japan. Scarecrows.

Joji and the fog ill. by Eiichi Mitsui. Morrow, 1959. Subj: Birds. Scarecrows. Weather – fog.

The many lives of Chio and Goro ill. by Yasuo Segawa. Norton, 1968. Subj: Animals – foxes. Birds – chickens. Foreign lands – Japan.

The rice-cake rabbit ill. by Eiichi Mitsui. Norton, 1966. Subj: Animals – rabbits. Foreign lands – Japan. Moon.

The secret seller ill. by Etienne Delessert & Norma Holt. Norton, 1967. Subj: Behavior – secrets. Imagination.

Tell me a real adoption story ill. by Claire A. Nivola. Knopf, 1993. ISBN 0-679-90629-0 Subj: Activities – dancing. Insects. Parties. Rhyming text.

Light, Steve. *Puss in boots* (Perrault, Charles)

The shoemaker extraordinaire ill. by author. Abrams, 2003. ISBN 0-8109-4236-4 Subj: Careers – shoemakers. Clothing – shoes. Folk & fairy tales. Giants.

Lillegard, Dee. *The Big Bug Ball* ill. by Rex Barron. Putnam, 1999. ISBN 0-399-23121-8 Subj: Activities – dancing. Parties. Rhyming text.

The day the daisies danced ill. by Rex Barron. Putnam, 1996. ISBN 0-399-22661-3 Subj: Flowers. Rhyming text. Weddings.

The hee-haw river ill. by Allan Eitzen. Holt, 1995. ISBN 0-8050-2375-5 Subj: Animals. Noise, sounds. Rivers.

Hello school! ill. by Don Carter. Knopf, 2001. ISBN 0-375-91020-4 Subj: Poetry. School.

I can be a baker ill. with photos. Childrens Pr., 1986. ISBN 0-516-01892-2 Subj: Careers – bakers.

I can be a carpenter ill. with photos. Childrens Pr., 1986. ISBN 0-516-01884-1 Subj: Careers – carpenters.

I can be a welder by Dee Lillegard & Wayne Stoker. Childrens Pr., 1986. ISBN 0-516-01895-7 Subj: Careers – welders.

I can be an electrician ill. with photos. Childrens Pr., 1986. ISBN 0-516-01896-5 Subj: Careers – electricians.

My yellow ball ill. by Sarah Chamberlain. Dutton, 1993. ISBN 0-525-45078-5 Subj: Animals. Animals – dogs. Behavior – wishing. Toys – balls.

Sitting in my box ill. by Jon Agee. Dutton, 1989. ISBN 0-525-44528-5 Subj: Animals. Books, reading. Cumulative tales.

Tortoise brings the mail ill. by Jillian Lund. Dutton, 1997. ISBN 0-525-45156-0 Subj: Animals. Careers – postal workers. Letters, cards. Reptiles – turtles, tortoises.

Wake up house! rooms full of poems ill. by Don Carter. Knopf, 2000. ISBN 0-679-98351-1 Subj: Furniture. Homes, houses. Poetry.

The wild bunch ill. by Rex Barron. Putnam, 1997. ISBN 0-399-22826-8 Subj: Food. Poetry.

Lillie, Patricia. *Everything has a place* ill. by Nancy Tafuri. Greenwillow, 1993. ISBN 0-688-10083-X Subj: Character traits – orderliness.

Floppy teddy bear ill. by Karen Lee Baker. Greenwillow, 1995. ISBN 0-688-12570-0 Subj: Emotions – anger. Family life – sisters. Sibling rivalry. Toys – bears.

Jake and Rosie ill. by author. Greenwillow, 1989. ISBN 0-688-07625-4 Subj: Animals – cats. Ethnic groups in the U.S. – African Americans. Friendship.

One very, very quiet afternoon ill. by author. Greenwillow, 1986. ISBN 0-688-04323-2 Subj: ABC books. Behavior – misbehavior. Parties.

When the rooster crowed ill. by Nancy Winslow Parker. Greenwillow, 1991. ISBN 0-688-09379-5 Subj: Animals. Cumulative tales. Farms. Noise, sounds.

When this box is full ill. by Donald Crews. Greenwillow, 1993. ISBN 0-688-12017-2 Subj: Behavior – collecting things. Days of the week, months of the year.

Lilly, Kenneth. *Animal builders* ill. by author. Random House, 1984. ISBN 0-394-86373-9 Subj: Activities. Animals. Format, unusual – board books. Science.

Animal climbers ill. by author. Random House, 1984. ISBN 0-394-86374-7 Subj: Activities. Animals. Format, unusual – board books. Science.

Animal jumpers ill. by author. Random House, 1984. ISBN 0-394-86375-5 Subj: Activities. Animals. Format, unusual – board books. Science.

Animal runners ill. by author. Random House, 1984. ISBN 0-394-86376-3 Subj: Activities. Animals. Format, unusual – board books. Science.

Animal swimmers ill. by author. Random House, 1984. ISBN 0-394-86377-1 Subj: Activities. Animals. Format, unusual – board books. Science.

Animals at the zoo ill. by author. S&S, 1982. ISBN 0-671-45152-9 Subj: Animals. Format, unusual – board books. Zoos.

Animals in the country ill. by author. S&S, 1982. ISBN 0-671-45153-7 Subj: Animals. Format, unusual – board books. Wordless.

Animals in the jungle ill. by author. S&S, 1982. ISBN 0-671-45154-5 Subj: Animals. Format, unusual – board books. Jungle.

Animals of the ocean ill. by author. S&S, 1982. ISBN 0-671-45155-3 Subj: Animals – dolphins. Animals – polar bears. Animals – seals. Animals – whales. Birds – penguins. Format, unusual – board books. Sea & seashore.

Animals on the farm ill. by author. S&S, 1982. ISBN 0-671-45151-0 Subj: Animals. Farms. Format, unusual – board books.

Baby animals text by Kate Hayden; ill. by Kenneth Lilly. Candlewick, 1996. ISBN 0-7636-0067-9 Subj: Animals – babies.

Lilly, Melinda. *From slavery to freedom* ill. by Lori McElrath-Eslick. Rourke, 2003. ISBN 1-58952-363-6 Subj: Slavery. U.S. history.

Limb, Sue. *Come back, Grandma* ill. by Claudio Muñoz. Knopf, 1993. ISBN 0-679-84720-0 Subj: Death. Emotions – grief. Family life. Family life – grandmothers.

Lin, Grace. *Dim sum for everyone* ill. by author. Knopf, 2001. ISBN 0-375-91082-4 Subj: Activities – baking, cooking. Ethnic groups in the U.S. – Chinese Americans. Food. Restaurants.

Fortune cookie fortunes ill. by author. Knopf, 2004. ISBN 0-375-91521-4 Subj: Character traits – luck. Ethnic groups in the U.S. – Chinese Americans. Food.

Kite flying ill. by author. Knopf, 2002. ISBN 0-375-91520-6 Subj: Kites.

Okie-dokie, Artichokie ill. by author. Viking, 2003. ISBN 0-670-03623-4 Subj: Animals – giraffes. Animals – monkeys. Friendship. Holidays – Christmas. Homes, houses. Noise, sounds.

Olvina flies ill. by author. Holt, 2003. ISBN 0-8050-6711-6 Subj: Activities – traveling. Airplanes, airports. Animals – pigs. Birds – chickens. Emotions – fear.

The ugly vegetables ill. by author. Charlesbridge, 1999. ISBN 0-88106-336-3 Subj: Ethnic groups in the U.S. – Chinese Americans. Flowers. Food. Gardens, gardening.

Linch, Elizabeth Johanna. *Samson* ill. by author. HarperCollins, 1964. Subj: Animals – mice. Holidays – Christmas. Seasons – winter.

Linch, Tanya. *My duck* ill. by author. Scholastic, 2000. ISBN 0-439-20670-7 Subj: Activities – writing. Birds – ducks. Careers – teachers.

Lind, Mecka. *Cackle goes a-courting* ill. by Lars Rudebjer. Carolrhoda, 1992. ISBN 0-87614-715-5 Subj: Animals. Birds – chickens.

Lind, Michael. *Bluebonnet girl* ill. by Kate Kiesler. Holt, 2003. ISBN 0-8050-6573-3 Subj: Behavior – greed. Flowers. Folk & fairy tales. Indians of North America – Comanche. Weather – droughts.

Lindaman, Jane. *Read anything good lately?* (Allen, Susan)

Lindbergh, Anne. *Tidy lady* ill. by Susan Ramsay Hoguet. Harcourt, 1989. ISBN 0-15-287150-0 Subj: Character traits – cleanliness. Cumulative tales.

Lindbergh, Reeve. *The awful aardvarks go to school* ill. by Tracey Campbell Pearson. Viking, 1997. ISBN 0-670-85920-6 Subj: ABC books. Animals – aardvarks. Behavior – misbehavior. Rhyming text. School.

The awful aardvarks shop for school ill. by Tracey Campbell Pearson. Viking, 2000. ISBN 0-670-88763-3 Subj: Animals – aardvarks. Behavior – misbehavior. Rhyming text. Shopping.

Benjamin's barn ill. by Susan Jeffers. Dial, 1990. ISBN 0-8037-0614-6 Subj: Animals. Barns. Farms. Imagination. Rhyming text.

Bridget and the gray wolves ill. by Pija Lindenbaum; trans. by Kjersti Board. R&S Books, 2001. ISBN 91-29-65395-9 Subj: Animals – wolves. Behavior – lost. Emotions – fear.

The circle of days ill. by Cathie Felstead. Candlewick, 1998. ISBN 0-7636-0357-0 Subj: Creation. Religion.

The day the goose got loose ill. by Steven Kellogg. Dial, 1990. ISBN 0-8037-0409-7 Subj: Animals. Behavior – misbehavior. Birds – geese. Farms.

Grandfather's lovesong ill. by Rachel Isadora. Viking, 1993. ISBN 0-670-84842-5 Subj: Emotions – love. Family life – grandfathers. Poetry.

The hippie grandmother ill. by Aby Carter. Candlewick, 2002. ISBN 0-7636-0671-5 Subj: Family life – grandmothers. Rhyming text.

If I'd known then what I know now ill. by Bulcken Root Kimberly. Viking, 1994. ISBN 0-670-85351-8 Subj: Behavior – mistakes. Family life – fathers. Homes, houses. Rhyming text.

Johnny Appleseed ill. by Kathy Jakobsen. Little, 1990. ISBN 0-316-52618-5 Subj: Activities – traveling. Gardens, gardening. Rhyming text. Tall tales. Trees. U.S. history – frontier & pioneer life.

Midnight farm ill. by Susan Jeffers. Dial, 1987. ISBN 0-8037-0333-3 Subj: Animals. Counting, numbers. Farms. Night.

Nobody owns the sky: the story of "brave Bessie" Coleman ill. by Pamela Paparone. Candlewick, 1996. ISBN 1-56402-533-0 Subj: Activities – flying. Airplanes, airports. Ethnic groups in the U.S. – African Americans. Rhyming text.

North country spring ill. by Liz Sivertson. Houghton Mifflin, 1997. ISBN 0-395-82819-8 Subj: Animals. Nature. Rhyming text. Seasons – spring.

On morning wings ill. by Holly Meade. Candlewick, 2002. ISBN 0-7636-1106-9 Subj: Religion. Rhyming text.

Our nest ill. by Jill McElmurry. Candlewick, 2004. ISBN 0-7636-1286-3 Subj: Homes, houses. Rhyming text.

There's a cow in the road! ill. by Tracey Campbell Pearson. Dial, 1993. ISBN 0-8037-1336-3 Subj: Animals. Rhyming text.

A view from the air: Charles Lindbergh's earth and sky photos by Richard Brown. Viking, 1992. ISBN 0-670-84660-0 Subj: Careers – airplane pilots. Ecology. Nature. Rhyming text.

What is the sun? ill. by Stephen Lambert. Candlewick, 1994. ISBN 1-56402-146-7 Subj: Character traits – questioning. Moon. Sun. Weather – rain. Weather – wind.

Lindbloom, Steven. *Let's give kitty a bath!* ill. by True Kelley. Addison-Wesley, 1982. ISBN 0-201-10712-0 Subj: Activities – bathing. Animals – cats.

Linden, Ann Marie. *One smiling grandma* ill. by Lynne Russell. Dial, 1992. ISBN 0-8037-1132-8 Subj: Counting, numbers. Family life – grandmothers. Foreign lands – Caribbean Islands.

Linden, Madelaine Gill. *Under the blanket* ill. by author. Little, 1987. ISBN 0-316-52626-6 Subj: Rhyming text. Toys.

Lindenbaum, Pija. *Boodil, my dog* retold by Gabrielle Charbonnet; ill. by author. Holt, 1992. ISBN 0-8050-2444-1 Subj: Animals – dogs. Character traits – appearance.

Else-Marie and her seven little daddies ill. by author. Holt, 1991. ISBN 0-8050-1752-6 Subj: Behavior – worrying. Family life – fathers.

Linders, Clara. *The very best door of all* by Clara Linders & Marijke ten Cate; ill. by Marijke ten Cate. Front St., 2001. ISBN 1-886910-64-2 Subj: Animals – badgers. Animals – porcupines. Birthdays. Friendship. Gifts.

Lindgren, Astrid. *A calf for Christmas* trans. from Swedish by Barbara Lucas; ill. by Marit Tornqvist. Farrar, 1991. ISBN 91-29-59920-2 Subj: Animals – bulls, cows. Foreign lands – Sweden. Holidays – Christmas.

Christmas in noisy village by Astrid Lindgren & Ilon Wikland; trans. by Florence Lamborn; ill. by Ilon Wikland. Viking, 1964. ISBN 0-670-22106-6 Subj: Foreign lands – Sweden. Holidays – Christmas.

Christmas in the stable ill. by Harald Wiberg. Coward, 1962. ISBN 0-698-20677-0 Subj: Foreign lands – Sweden. Holidays – Christmas. Religion – Nativity.

Do you know Pippi Longstocking? ill. by Ingrid Nyman; trans. by Elisabeth Kallick Dyssegaard. R&S Books, 1999. ISBN 91-29-64661-8 Subj: Foreign lands – Sweden. Friendship. Humorous stories.

The dragon with red eyes ill. by Ilon Wikland; trans. by Patricia Crampton. Viking, 1987. ISBN 0-670-81620-5 Subj: Dragons. Farms.

The ghost of Skinny Jack ill. by Ilon Wikland. Viking, 1988. ISBN 0-670-81913-1 Subj: Emotions – fear. Family life – grandmothers. Folk & fairy tales. Ghosts.

I want a brother or sister trans. from Swedish by Barbara Lucas; ill. by Ilon Wikland. Farrar, 1988. ISBN 91-29-58778-6 Subj: Babies. Emotions – envy, jealousy. Family life – new sibling. Sibling rivalry.

I want to go to school, too trans. by Barbara Lucas; ill. by Ilon Wikland. Farrar, 1987. ISBN 91-29-58328-4 Subj: School. Sibling rivalry.

Lotta's Christmas surprise ill. by Ilon Wikland. Farrar, 1990. ISBN 91-29-59782-X Subj: Foreign lands – Sweden. Holidays – Christmas. Trees.

Most beloved sister ill. by Hans Arnold; trans. by Elisabeth Kallick Dyssegaard. Farrar, 2002. ISBN 91-29-65502-1 Subj: Family life – sisters. Friendship. Imagination. Multiple births – twins.

My nightingale is singing trans. by Patricia Crampton; ill. by Svend Otto S. Viking, 1986. ISBN 0-670-80997-7 Subj: Behavior – seeking better things. Emotions – sadness. Poverty.

Of course Polly can do almost everything ill. by Ilon Wikland. Follett, 1978. ISBN 0-695-40967-0 Subj: Character traits – optimism. Character traits – perseverance. Holidays – Christmas. Trees.

Pippi Longstocking in the park ill. by Ingrid Nyman. R&S Books, 2001. ISBN 91-29-65307-X Subj: Foreign lands – Sweden. Parks.

Pippi Longstocking's after-Christmas party ill. by Michael Chesworth. Viking, 1996. ISBN 0-679-86790-X Subj: Character traits – assertiveness. Foreign lands – Sweden. Holidays – Christmas. Parties.

The tomten ill. by Harald Wiberg. Coward, 1961. Adapt. from a poem by Victor Rydberg. ISBN 0-698-20147-7 Subj: Farms. Foreign lands – Sweden. Mythical creatures – trolls. Seasons – winter.

The tomten and the fox adapt. from a poem by Karl-Erik Forsslund; ill. by Harald Wiberg. Coward, 1965. ISBN 0-698-30371-7 Subj: Animals – foxes. Foreign lands – Sweden. Mythical creatures – trolls. Seasons – winter.

Lindgren, Barbro. *Andrei's search* ill. by Eva Eriksson; trans. by Elisabeth Kallick Dyssegaard. R&S Books, 2000. ISBN 91-29-64756-8 Subj: Behavior – needing someone. Foreign lands – Russia.

Benny and the binky ill. by Olof Landström; trans. by Elisabeth Kallick Dyssegaard. Farrar, 2002. ISBN 91-29-65497-1 Subj: Animals – pigs. Babies. Sibling rivalry.

Benny's had enough ill. by Olof Landström; trans. by Elisabeth Kallick Dyssegaard. R&S Books, 1999. ISBN 91-29-64563-8 Subj: Animals – pigs. Behavior – running away. Family life – mothers.

Rosa ill. by Eva Eriksson. Firefly, 1996. ISBN 1-55054-241-9 Subj: Activities – playing. Animals – dogs.

Rosa goes to daycare ill. by Eva Eriksson. Douglas & McIntyre, 2000. ISBN 0-88899-391-9 Subj: School – nursery.

Sam's ball ill. by Eva Eriksson. Morrow, 1983. ISBN 0-688-02359-2 Subj: Animals – cats. Toys – balls.

Sam's bath ill. by Eva Eriksson. Morrow, 1983. ISBN 0-688-02362-2 Subj: Activities – bathing. Animals – dogs.

Sam's car ill. by Eva Eriksson. Morrow, 1982. ISBN 0-688-01263-9 Subj: Behavior – sharing. Toys.

Sam's cookie ill. by Eva Eriksson. Morrow, 1982. ISBN 0-688-01267-1 Subj: Behavior – sharing. Pets.

Sam's lamp ill. by Eva Eriksson. Morrow, 1983. ISBN 0-688-02356-8 Subj: Safety.

Sam's potty ill. by Eva Eriksson. Morrow, 1986. ISBN 0-688-06603-8 Subj: Behavior – growing up. Toilet training.

Sam's teddy bear ill. by Eva Eriksson. Morrow, 1982. ISBN 0-688-01270-1 Subj: Toys – bears.

Sam's wagon ill. by Eva Eriksson. Morrow, 1986. ISBN 0-688-05803-5 Subj: Animals – dogs. Toys – wagons.

Shorty takes off trans. by Richard E. Fisher; ill. by Olof Landström. Farrar, 1990. ISBN 91-29-59770-6 Subj: Activities – flying. Character traits – smallness.

The wild baby adapt. from Swedish by Jack Prelutsky; ill. by Eva Eriksson. Greenwillow, 1981. ISBN 0-688-00601-9 Subj: Behavior – misbehavior. Family life – mothers. Rhyming text.

The wild baby gets a puppy ill. by Eva Eriksson; adapt. from the Swedish by Jack Prelutsky. Greenwillow, 1988. ISBN 0-688-06712-

3 Subj: Animals – dogs. Dreams. Family life – mothers. Night. Rhyming text.

The wild baby goes to sea adapt. from Swedish by Jack Prelutsky; ill. by Eva Eriksson. Greenwillow, 1983. ISBN 0-688-01931-7 Subj: Activities – playing. Family life – mothers. Imagination. Toys.

A worm's tale ill. by Cecilia Torudd. Farrar, 1988. ISBN 91-29-59068-X Subj: Animals – worms. Friendship.

Lindman, Maj. *Flicka, Ricka, Dicka and a little dog* ill. by author. A. Whitman, 1995. ISBN 0-8075-2486-7 Subj: Animals – dogs. Family life. Foreign lands – Sweden. Multiple births – triplets.

Flicka, Ricka, Dicka and the big red hen ill. by author. A. Whitman, 1995. ISBN 0-8075-2493-X Subj: Birds – chickens. Family life. Farms. Multiple births – triplets.

Flicka, Ricka, Dicka and the new dotted dress ill. by author. A. Whitman, 1994. ISBN 0-8075-2494-8 Subj: Character traits – helpfulness. Family life. Foreign lands – Sweden. Multiple births – triplets.

Flicka, Ricka, Dicka and the three kittens ill. by author. A. Whitman, 1994. ISBN 0-8075-2500-6 Subj: Animals – cats. Family life. Multiple births – triplets.

Flicka, Ricka, Dicka bake a cake ill. by author. A. Whitman, 1995. ISBN 0-8075-2480-8 Subj: Activities – baking, cooking. Birthdays. Family life. Foreign lands – Sweden. Multiple births – triplets.

Sailboat time ill. by author. A. Whitman, 1951. Subj: Boats, ships. Foreign lands – Sweden.

Snipp, Snapp, Snurr and the buttered bread ill. by author. A. Whitman, 1995. ISBN 0-8075-7504-6 Subj: Cumulative tales. Family life. Farms. Foreign lands – Sweden. Multiple births – triplets.

Snipp, Snapp, Snurr and the magic horse ill. by author. A. Whitman, 1935. Subj: Family life. Foreign lands – Sweden. Magic. Multiple births – triplets. Toys – rocking horses.

Snipp, Snapp, Snurr and the red shoes ill. by author. A. Whitman, 1994. ISBN 0-8075-7496-1 Subj: Activities – vacationing. Birthdays. Character traits – generosity. Character traits – helpfulness. Family life. Foreign lands – Lapland. Multiple births – triplets. Sports – skiing.

Snipp, Snapp, Snurr and the reindeer ill. by author. A. Whitman, 1995. ISBN 0-8075-7497-X Subj: Animals – deer. Family life. Foreign lands – Sweden. Multiple births – triplets.

Snipp, Snapp, Snurr and the seven dogs ill. by author. A. Whitman, 1959. Subj: Animals – dogs. Family life. Foreign lands – Sweden. Multiple births – triplets.

Snipp, Snapp, Snurr and the yellow sled ill. by author. A. Whitman, 1995. ISBN 0-8075-7499-6 Subj: Animals – dogs. Family life. Foreign lands – Sweden. Multiple births – triplets. Sports – ice skating.

Lindsay, Elizabeth. *A letter for Maria* ill. by Alex de Wolf. Watts, 1988. ISBN 0-531-08375-6 Subj: Activities – painting. Toys – bears.

Lindsay, Jeanne Warren. *Do I have a daddy?* ill. by Jami Moffett. Morning Glory Pr., 2000. ISBN 1-885356-62-5 Subj: Family life. Family life – fathers. Family life – mothers.

Lindsey, Treska. *When Batistine made bread* ill. by author. Macmillan, 1985. ISBN 0-02-759120-4 Subj: Activities – baking, cooking. Activities – working. Food.

Lines, Kathleen. *Dick Whittington* (Dick Whittington and his cat)

Lavender's blue (Mother Goose)

The old ballad of the babes in the woods (The babes in the woods)

Once in royal David's city: a picture book of the Nativity, retold from the Gospels ill. by Harold Jones. Watts, 1956. Subj: Holidays – Christmas. Religion.

Ling, Mary. *Butterfly* ill. by Kim Taylor. DK, 1992. ISBN 1-56458-112-8 Subj: Insects – butterflies, caterpillars.

Calf photos by Gordon Clayton. DK, 1993. ISBN 1-564582-05-1 Subj: Animals – bulls, cows. Farms.

Foal photos by Gordon Clayton. DK, 1992. ISBN 1-56458-113-6 Subj: Animals – horses, ponies. Farms.

Fox photos by Jane Burton. DK, 1992. ISBN 1-56458-114-4 Subj: Animals – foxes. Nature.

Pig photos by Bill Ling. DK, 1993. ISBN 1-56458-204-3 Subj: Animals – pigs. Farms.

Lingo, Susan L. *Do you see the star?* (Nappa, Mike)

Link, Martin A. *The goat in the rug* (Blood, Charles L.)

Linke, Siegfried. *High flies the ball* (Koenner, Alfred)

Linn, Margot. *A trip to the dentist* ill. by Catherine Siracusa. HarperCollins, 1988. ISBN 0-06-025834-9 Subj: Careers – dentists.

A trip to the doctor ill. by Catherine Siracusa. HarperCollins, 1988. ISBN 0-06-025843-8 Subj: Careers – doctors.

Linscott, Jody. *Once upon A to Z* ill. by Claudia Porges Holland. Doubleday, 1991. ISBN 0-385-41907-4 Subj: ABC books. Careers – musicians.

Linzer, Jeff. *The fire station book* (Bundt, Nancy)

Lionni, Leo. *Alexander and the wind-up mouse* ill. by author. Pantheon, 1969. ISBN 0-394-90914-3 Subj: Animals – mice. Caldecott award honor books. Emotions – envy, jealousy. Friendship. Toys.

The alphabet tree ill. by author. Knopf, 2004. ISBN 0-394-91016-8 Subj: ABC books. Activities – writing. Insects – butterflies, caterpillars.

The biggest house in the world ill. by author. Pantheon, 1968. ISBN 0-394-90944-5 Subj: Animals. Behavior – greed.

A busy year ill. by author. Knopf, 1992. ISBN 0-679-92464-7 Subj: Animals – mice. Nature. Seasons. Trees.

A color of his own ill. by author. Delmar, 1990. ISBN 0-8273-4114-8 Subj: Character traits – individuality. Concepts – color. Reptiles – lizards.

Colors to talk about ill. by author. Pantheon, 1985. ISBN 0-394-87003-4 Subj: Animals – mice. Concepts – color. Format, unusual – board books.

Cornelius ill. by author. Pantheon, 1983. ISBN 0-394-95419-X Subj: Character traits – being different. Reptiles – alligators, crocodiles.

An extraordinary egg ill. by author. Knopf, 1994. ISBN 0-679-95840-1 Subj: Eggs. Friendship. Frogs & toads. Reptiles – alligators, crocodiles.

Fish is fish ill. by author. Pantheon, 1970. ISBN 0-394-90440-0 Subj: Behavior – misunderstanding. Fish. Friendship. Frogs & toads.

Frederick ill. by author. Random House, 1973, c1967. ISBN 0-394-82614-0 Subj: Animals – mice. Caldecott award honor books. Music.

Frederick's fables ill. by author. Pantheon, 1985. ISBN 0-394-87710-1 Subj: Animals.

Geraldine, the music mouse ill. by author. Pantheon, 1979. ISBN 0-394-94238-8 Subj: Animals – mice. Music. Musical instruments – flutes.

The greentail mouse ill. by author. Pantheon, 1973. ISBN 0-394-92678-1 Subj: Animals – mice. Mardi Gras.

In the rabbitgarden ill. by author. Pantheon, 1975. ISBN 0-394-93089-4 Subj: Animals – foxes. Animals – mice. Reptiles – snakes.

Inch by inch ill. by author. Astor-Honor, 1960. ISBN 0-8392-3010-9 Subj: Birds. Caldecott award honor books. Concepts – measurement. Insects.

It's mine! a fable ill. by author. Knopf, 1986. ISBN 0-394-97000-X Subj: Behavior – fighting, arguing. Frogs & toads.

Let's make rabbits ill. by author. Knopf, 1992. Originally published: New York: Pantheon Books, c1982. ISBN 0-679-82640-8 Subj: Activities. Animals – rabbits. Art. Imagination.

Letters to talk about ill. by author. Pantheon, 1985. ISBN 0-394-87001-8 Subj: ABC books. Animals – mice. Format, unusual – board books.

Little blue and little yellow ill. by author. Mulberry, 1994. ISBN 0-688-13285-5 Subj: Concepts – color. Friendship.

Matthew's dream ill. by author. Knopf, 1991. ISBN 0-679-91075-1 Subj: Animals – mice. Careers – artists. Museums.

Mr. McMouse ill. by author. Knopf, 1992. ISBN 0-679-93890-7 Subj: Animals – mice. Friendship. Self-concept.

Mouse days ill. by author. Pantheon, 1981. ISBN 0-394-84548-X Subj: Animals – mice. Seasons.

Nicholas, where have you been? ill. by author. Knopf, 1987. ISBN 0-394-98370-X Subj: Animals – mice. Friendship.

Numbers to talk about ill. by author. Pantheon, 1985. ISBN 0-394-87002-6 Subj: Animals – mice. Counting, numbers. Format, unusual – board books.

On my beach there are many pebbles ill. by author. Astor-Honor, 1961. ISBN 0-8392-3024-9 Subj: Rocks. Sea & seashore – beaches.

Pezzettino ill. by author. Pantheon, 1975. ISBN 0-394-93156-4 Subj: Character traits – individuality. Concepts – shape. Self-concept.

Six crows ill. by author. Knopf, 1988. ISBN 0-394-99572-4 Subj: Birds – crows. Birds – owls. Farms.

Swimmy ill. by author. Random House, 1973, c1963. ISBN 0-394-82620-5 Subj: Caldecott award honor books. Fish. Sea & seashore.

Theodore and the talking mushroom ill. by author. Pantheon, 1971. ISBN 0-394-82312-5 Subj: Animals – mice. Character traits – optimism.

Tico and the golden wings ill. by author. Knopf, 1975, c1964. ISBN 0-394-83078-4 Subj: Birds. Character traits – generosity. Character traits – individuality. Character traits – questioning. Folk & fairy tales.

Tillie and the wall ill. by author. Knopf, 1989. ISBN 0-394-92155-0 Subj: Animals – mice. Behavior – seeking better things.

What? pictures to talk about ill. by author. Pantheon, 1983. ISBN 0-394-86031-4 Subj: Animals – mice. Format, unusual – board books. Senses – hearing. Senses – sight. Senses – smell. Senses – taste. Senses – touch. Wordless.

When? ill. by author. Pantheon, 1983. ISBN 0-394-86032-2 Subj: Animals – mice. Format, unusual – board books. Night. Seasons. Wordless.

Where? pictures to talk about ill. by author. Pantheon, 1983. ISBN 0-394-86033-0 Subj: Animals – mice. Format, unusual – board books. Humorous stories. Wordless.

Who? pictures to talk about ill. by author. Pantheon, 1983. ISBN 0-394-86030-6 Subj: Animals – mice. Format, unusual – board books. Wordless.

Words to talk about ill. by author. Pantheon, 1985. ISBN 0-394-87004-2 Subj: Animals – mice. Format, unusual – board books. Language.

Lions by Gallimard Jeunesse & Pierre de Hugo; ill. by Pierre de Hugo. Scholastic, 2000. ISBN 0-439-14825-1 Subj: Animals – lions. Format, unusual – toy & movable books.

Lipkind, William. *Billy the kid* by William Lipkind & Nicolas Mordvinoff; ill. by Nicolas Mordvinoff. Harcourt, 1964. Subj: Animals – goats.

The boy and the forest by William Lipkind & Nicolas Mordvinoff; ill. by Nicolas Mordvinoff. Harcourt, 1964. Subj: Animals. Character traits – kindness to animals. Forest, woods. Magic.

Chaga by William Lipkind & Nicolas Mordvinoff; ill. by Nicolas Mordvinoff. Harcourt, 1955. Subj: Animals – elephants. Concepts – size.

The Christmas bunny by William Lipkind & Nicolas Mordvinoff; ill. by Nicolas Mordvinoff. Harcourt, 1953. Subj: Animals – foxes. Animals – rabbits. Holidays – Christmas. Parties.

Circus ruckus by William Lipkind & Nicolas Mordvinoff; ill. by Nicolas Mordvinoff. Harcourt, 1954. Subj: Circus.

Even Steven by William Lipkind & Nicolas Mordvinoff; ill. by Nicolas Mordvinoff. Harcourt, 1952. Subj: Animals – dogs. Character traits – selfishness.

Finders keepers by William Lipkind & Nicolas Mordvinoff; ill. by Nicolas Mordvinoff. Harcourt, 1951. ISBN 0-15-227529-0 Subj: Animals – dogs. Caldecott award books. Character traits – selfishness.

Four-leaf clover by William Lipkind & Nicolas Mordvinoff; ill. by Nicolas Mordvinoff. Harcourt, 1959. Subj: Ethnic groups in the U.S. – African Americans.

The little tiny rooster by William Lipkind & Nicolas Mordvinoff; ill. by Nicolas Mordvinoff. Harcourt, 1960. ISBN 0-15-247578-8 Subj: Animals – foxes. Birds – chickens. Character traits – smallness. Self-concept.

The magic feather duster by William Lipkind & Nicolas Mordvinoff; ill. by Nicolas Mordvinoff. Harcourt, 1958. Subj: Character traits – kindness. Folk & fairy tales. Magic.

Nubber bear ill. by Roger Antoine Duvoisin. Harcourt, 1966. Subj: Animals – bears. Behavior – misbehavior.

Professor Bull's umbrella by William Lipkind & Georges Schreiber; ill. by Georges Schreiber. Viking, 1954. Subj: Umbrellas.

Russet and the two reds by William Lipkind & Nicolas Mordvinoff; ill. by Nicolas Mordvinoff. Harcourt, 1962. Subj: Animals – cats.

Sleepyhead by William Lipkind & Nicolas Mordvinoff; ill. by Nicolas Mordvinoff. Harcourt, 1957. Subj: Activities – playing. Games. Rhyming text.

The two reds by William Lipkind & Nicolas Mordvinoff; ill. by Nicolas Mordvinoff. Harcourt, 1950. Subj: Animals – cats. Caldecott award honor books. Friendship.

Lipniacka, Ewa. *To bed . . . or else!* ill. by Basia Bogdanowicz. Interlink, 1992. ISBN 0-940793-85-7 Subj: Bedtime. Friendship. Night. Sleepovers.

Lipp, Frederick. *The caged birds of Phnom Penh* ill. by Ronald Himler. Holiday, 2001. ISBN 0-8234-1534-1 Subj: Behavior – wishing. Birds. Foreign lands – Canada.

Lippert, Margaret H. *Head, body, legs* (Paye, Won-Ldy)

Mrs. Chicken and the hungry crocodile (Paye, Won-Ldy)

Lippman, Peter. *The Know-It-Alls go to sea* ill. by author. Doubleday, 1982. ISBN 0-385-17396-2 Subj: Behavior – misbehavior. Boats, ships.

The Know-It-Alls help out ill. by author. Doubleday, 1982. ISBN 0-385-17397-0 Subj: Behavior – misbehavior. Homes, houses.

The Know-It-Alls mind the store ill. by author. Doubleday, 1982. ISBN 0-385-17399-7 Subj: Behavior – misbehavior. Stores.

The Know-It-Alls take a winter vacation ill. by author. Doubleday, 1982. ISBN 0-385-17398-9 Subj: Activities – vacationing. Behavior – misbehavior.

New at the zoo ill. by author. HarperCollins, 1969. Subj: Animals. Bedtime. Zoos.

Peter Lippman's numbers ill. by author. Grosset, 1988. ISBN 0-448-19105-9 Subj: Counting, numbers. Format, unusual – toy & movable books.

Peter Lippman's opposites ill. by author. Grosset, 1988. ISBN 0-448-19106-7 Subj: Concepts – opposites. Format, unusual – toy & movable books.

Lippman, Sidney. *A you're adorable* words & music by Sidney Lippman, Buddy Kaye, & Fred Wise; ill. by Martha Alexander. Candlewick, 1994. ISBN 1-56402-237-4 Subj: ABC books. Babies. Ethnic groups in the U.S. Music. Songs.

Lipson, Beth Weiner. *Benjamin's perfect solution* ill. by author. Warner, 1979. ISBN 0-7232-6160-1 Subj: Animals – porcupines. Animals – possums. Behavior – mistakes. Self-concept.

Lipson, Michael. *How the wind plays* ill. by Daniel Kirk. Hyperion, 1994. ISBN 1-56282-326-4 Subj: Weather – wind.

Lish, Ted. *The three little puppies and the big bad flea* ill. by Charles Jordan. Munchweiler, 2001. ISBN 0-7940-0001-0 Subj: Animals – dogs. Family life – mothers. Homes, houses. Insects – fleas.

Lishak, Anthony. *Row your boat* ill. by Graham Percy. DK, 1999. ISBN 0-7894-3489-X Subj: Animals. Birthdays. Format, unusual – toy & movable books. Songs. Transportation.

Lisker, Sonia O. *Lost* ill. by author. Harcourt, 1975. ISBN 0-15-249363-8 Subj: Behavior – lost. Wordless. Zoos.

Two special cards by Sonia O. Lisker & Leigh Dean; ill. by Sonia O. Lisker. Harcourt, 1976. Subj: Divorce. Family life.

Lisowski, Gabriel. *How Tevye became a milkman* ill. by author. Holt, 1976. ISBN 0-03-016636-5 Subj: Foreign lands – Ukraine. Jewish culture.

Roncalli's magnificent circus ill. by author. Doubleday, 1980. ISBN 0-685-14856-9 Subj: Animals – bears. Behavior – running away. Circus.

Listen to the storyteller: *a trio of musical tales from around the world* ill. by Kristen Balouch. Viking, 1999. ISBN 0-670-88054-X Subj: Folk & fairy tales. Foreign lands. Music.

Lister, Clare. *My first Passover [board book]* ill. with photos. KD, 2002. ISBN 0-7894-8452-8 Subj: Format, unusual – board books. Holidays – Passover. Jewish culture. Religion.

Lister, Mary. *The Winter King and the Summer Queen* ill. by Diana Mayo. Barefoot, 2002. ISBN 1-84148-357-5 Subj: Behavior – sharing. Seasons. Seasons – summer. Seasons – winter.

Litchfield, Ada B. *A button in her ear* ill. by Eleanor Mill. A. Whitman, 1976. ISBN 0-8075-0987-6 Subj: Handicaps – deafness. Senses – hearing.

A cane in her hand ill. by Eleanor Mill. A. Whitman, 1977. ISBN 0-8075-1056-4 Subj: Handicaps – blindness. Senses – sight.

Litchfield, Jo. *The Usborne book of everyday words* designer & model-maker Jo Litchfield; ed. by Rebecca Treays, Kate Needham & Lisa Miles; photos Howard Allman. EDC, 1999. ISBN 1-58086-190-3 Subj: Games. Language.

Lithgow, John. *Carnival of the animals* ill. by Boris Kulikov. S&S, 2004. ISBN 0-689-86721-2 Subj: Animals. Imagination. Museums. Rhyming text. School – field trips.

I'm a manatee ill. by Ard Hoyt. S&S, 2003. ISBN 0-689-85427-7 Subj: Animals – manatees. Imagination. Rhyming text.

Marsupial Sue ill. by Jack E. Davis. S&S, 2001. ISBN 0-689-84394-1 Subj: Animals – kangaroos. Rhyming text. Self-concept. Songs.

Marsupial Sue presents "The Runaway Pancake" ill. by Jack E. Davis. S&S, 2005. ISBN 0-689-87847-8 Subj: Animals – kangaroos. Theater.

Micawber ill. by C. F. Payne. S&S, 2002. ISBN 0-689-83341-5 Subj: Animals – squirrels. Careers – artists. Museums. Rhyming text.

The remarkable Farkle McBride ill. by C. F. Payne. S&S, 2000. ISBN 0-689-83340-7 Subj: Careers – conductors (music). Careers – musicians. Format, unusual – toy & movable books. Musical instruments. Rhyming text.

Litowinsky, Olga. *Boats for bedtime* ill. by Melanie Hope Greenberg. Clarion, 1999. ISBN 0-395-89128-0 Subj: Bedtime. Boats, ships.

Little, Debbie. *The potluck adventures of Mrs. Marmalade* (Swendson, Patsy)

Little, Emily. *David and the giant* (Bible Old Testament David)

Little, Jean. *Bats about baseball* by Jean Little & Clair Mackay; ill. by Kim LaFave. Viking, 1995. ISBN 0-670-85270-8 Subj: Family life – grandmothers. Language. Sports – baseball.

Gruntle Piggle takes off ill. by Johnny Wales. Viking, 1996. ISBN 0-670-86340-8 Subj: Animals – pigs. Books, reading. Cities, towns. Family life – grandfathers. Farms.

Jess was the brave one ill. by Janet Wilson. Viking, 1992. ISBN 0-670-83495-5 Subj: Behavior – bullying. Character traits – bravery. Emotions – fear. Family life – sisters. Toys – bears.

Once upon a golden apple by Jean Little & Maggie De Vries; ill. by Phoebe Gilman. Viking, 1991. ISBN 0-670-82963-3 Subj: Activities – picnicking. Books, reading. Folk & fairy tales.

Pippin the Christmas pig ill. by H. Werner Zimmermann. Scholastic, 2004. ISBN 0-439-65062-3 Subj: Animals. Animals – pigs. Gifts. Holidays – Christmas.

Revenge of the small Small ill. by Janet Wilson. Viking, 1992. ISBN 0-670-84471-3 Subj: Concepts – size. Family life – brothers & sisters. Sibling rivalry.

Little, Lessie Jones. *Children of long ago* ill. by Jan Spivey Gilchrist. Putnam, 1988. ISBN 0-399-21473-9 Subj: Ethnic groups in the U.S. – African Americans. Poetry.

I can do it by myself by Lessie Jones Little & Eloise Greenfield; ill. by Carole M. Byard. Crowell, 1978. ISBN 0-690-03851-8 Subj: Birthdays. Character traits – bravery. Plants.

Little, Mary E. *ABC for the library* ill. by author. Atheneum, 1975. ISBN 0-689-30467-6 Subj: ABC books. Libraries.

Ricardo and the puppets ill. by author. Scribners, 1958. Subj: Animals – mice. Libraries. Puppets.

Little, Mimi Otey. *Blue moon soup spoon* ill. by author. Farrar, 1993. ISBN 0-374-30851-9 Subj: Moon. Rhyming text.

Daddy has a pair of striped shorts ill. by author. Farrar, 1990. ISBN 0-374-31675-9 Subj: Clothing. Family life – fathers.

Yoshiko and the foreigner ill. by author. Farrar, 1996. ISBN 0-374-32448-4 Subj: Careers – military. Ethnic groups in the U.S. – African Americans. Foreign lands – Japan. Weddings.

A little ABC book. S&S, 1980. ISBN 0-671-41342-2 Subj: ABC books. Format, unusual – board books.

Little Bear's Valentine ill. by Heather Green. HarperCollins, 2003. ISBN 0-06-052244-5 Subj: Animals. Animals – bears. Family life – mothers. Holidays – Valentine's Day.

The little book of cats ill. by Diane Goode. Dutton, 1993. ISBN 0-525-45160-9 Subj: Animals – cats. Nursery rhymes.

A little book of colors. S&S, 1982. ISBN 0-671-45570-2 Subj: Concepts – color. Format, unusual – board books.

The Little book of mice ill. by Diane Goode. Dutton, 1993. ISBN 0-525-45158-7 Subj: Animals – mice. Nursery rhymes.

A little book of numbers. S&S, 1980. ISBN 0-671-41346-5 Subj: Counting, numbers. Format, unusual – board books.

The Little book of pigs ill. by Diane Goode. Dutton, 1993. ISBN 0-525-45159-5 Subj: Animals – pigs. Nursery rhymes.

Little book of prayers ill. by Roma Bishop. Little, 1987. ISBN 0-316-09660-1 Subj: Religion.

Little old lady who swallowed a fly. *Fancy that!* retold & ill. by Jan Pieńkowski. Orchard, 1989. ISBN 1-8521-3345-7 Subj: Cumulative tales. Folk & fairy tales. Foreign lands – England. Format, unusual – toy & movable books. Insects – flies. Songs.

Golly Gump swallowed a fly retold by Joanna Cole; ill. by Bari Weisman. G. Stevens, 1992. ISBN 0-8368-0881-9 Subj: Cumulative tales. Folk & fairy tales. Insects – flies. Songs.

I know an old lady retold by Rose Bonne; ill. by Abner Graboff; music by Alan Mills. Rand McNally, 1961. Subj: Cumulative tales. Folk & fairy tales. Foreign lands – Canada. Insects – flies. Music. Songs.

I know an old lady retold & ill. by G. Brian Karas. Scholastic, 1994. ISBN 0-590-46575-9 Subj: Cumulative tales. Folk & fairy tales. Foreign lands – England. Insects – flies. Rhyming text. Songs. Witches.

I know an old lady adapt. by Amy Bauman & Margaret Snyder; ill. by Steve McInturff. Western, 1993. ISBN 0-307-74818-9 Subj: Cumulative tales. Folk & fairy tales. Foreign lands – England. Format, unusual – toy & movable books. Insects – flies. Songs.

I know an old lady retold & ill. by Albert Miller. Rand McNally, 1961. Subj: Cumulative tales. Folk & fairy tales. Insects – flies. Songs.

I know an old lady who swallowed a fly ill. by Stephen Gulbis. Scholastic, 2001. ISBN 0-439-24328-9 Subj: Cumulative tales. Folk & fairy tales. Foreign lands – England. Format, unusual – toy & movable books. Insects – flies. Songs.

I know an old lady who swallowed a fly retold & ill. by Glen Rounds. Holiday, 1990. ISBN 0-8234-0814-0 Subj: Cumulative tales. Folk & fairy tales. Foreign lands – England. Insects – flies. Songs.

I know an old lady who swallowed a fly retold by Rose Bonne; ill. by William Stobbs. Oxford Univ. Pr., 1987. ISBN 0-19-279837-5 Subj: Cumulative tales. Folk & fairy tales. Foreign lands – Canada. Insects – flies. Songs.

I know an old lady who swallowed a fly retold & ill. by Nadine Bernard Westcott. Little, 1980. ISBN 0-316-93128-4 Subj: Cumulative tales. Folk & fairy tales. Foreign lands – England. Insects – flies. Songs.

There was an old lady retold & ill. by Nick Bantock. Viking, 1990. ISBN 0-670-83194-8 Subj: Cumulative tales. Folk & fairy tales. Foreign lands – England. Format, unusual – toy & movable books. Insects – flies. Songs.

There was an old lady who swallowed a fly ill. by Pam Adams. Child's Play, 1990. ISBN 0-85953-021-3 Subj: Cumulative tales. Folk & fairy tales. Foreign lands – Canada. Format, unusual – toy & movable books. Insects – flies. Songs.

There was an old lady who swallowed a fly retold & ill. by Colin Hawkins. Putnam, 1987. ISBN 0-399-21484-4 Subj: Cumulative tales. Folk & fairy tales. Foreign lands – England. Format, unusual – toy & movable books. Insects – flies. Songs.

There was an old lady who swallowed a fly retold & ill. by Simms Taback. Viking, 1997. ISBN 0-670-86939-2 Subj: Caldecott award honor books. Cumulative tales. Folk & fairy tales. Format, unusual. Insects – flies. Rhyming text. Songs.

There was an old woman retold & ill. by Steven Kellogg. Four Winds, 1980, 1974. ISBN 0-590-07779-1 Subj: Cumulative tales. Folk & fairy tales. Insects – flies. Songs.

The little red hen. *The cock, the mouse and the little red hen* adapt. & ill. by Lorinda Bryan Cauley. Putnam, 1982. ISBN 0-399-20740-6 Subj: Activities – baking, cooking. Animals. Behavior – sharing. Birds – chickens. Character traits – laziness. Cumulative tales. Farms. Folk & fairy tales. Plants.

The cock, the mouse and the little red hen ill. by Graham Percy. Candlewick, 1992. ISBN 1-56402-008-8 Subj: Activities – baking, cooking. Animals. Behavior – sharing. Birds – chickens. Character traits – laziness. Cumulative tales. Farms. Folk & fairy tales. Plants.

The little red hen ill. by Byron Barton. HarperCollins, 1993. ISBN 0-06-021676-X Subj: Activities – baking, cooking. Animals. Behavior – sharing. Birds – chickens. Character traits – laziness. Cumulative tales. Farms. Folk & fairy tales. Plants.

The little red hen retold by Harriet Ziefert; ill. by Emily Bolam. Viking, 1995. ISBN 0-670-86050-6 Subj: Activities – baking, cooking. Animals. Behavior – sharing. Birds – chickens. Character traits – laziness. Cumulative tales. Farms. Folk & fairy tales. Plants.

The little red hen ill. by Janina Domanska. Macmillan, 1973. ISBN 0-02-732820-1 Subj: Activities – baking, cooking. Animals. Behavior – sharing. Birds – chickens. Character traits – laziness. Cumulative tales. Farms. Folk & fairy tales. Plants.

The little red hen ill. by Paul Galdone. Seabury Pr., 1973. ISBN 0-8164-3099-3 Subj: Activities – baking, cooking. Animals. Behavior – sharing. Birds – chickens. Character traits – laziness. Cumulative tales. Farms. Folk & fairy tales. Plants.

The little red hen by Patricia C. & Fredrick McKissack; ill. by Dennis Hockerman. Childrens Pr., 1985. ISBN 0-516-02363-2 Subj: Activities – baking, cooking. Animals. Behavior – sharing. Birds – chickens. Character traits – laziness. Cumulative tales. Farms. Folk & fairy tales. Plants.

Little red hen by Alan Garner; ill. by Norman Messenger. DK, 1997. ISBN 0-7894-1171-1 Subj: Activities – baking, cooking. Animals. Behavior – sharing. Birds – chickens. Character traits – laziness. Cumulative tales. Farms. Folk & fairy tales. Plants.

The little red hen retold by Jean Horton Berg; reading consultant: Morton Betel; ill. by Mel Pekarsky. Follett, 1963. Subj: Activities – baking, cooking. Animals. Behavior – sharing. Birds – chickens. Character traits – laziness. Cumulative tales. Farms. Folk & fairy tales. Plants.

The little red hen adapt. & ill. by William Stobbs. Oxford Univ. Pr., 1985. ISBN 0-19-279807-3 Subj: Activities – baking, cooking. Animals. Behavior – sharing. Birds – chickens. Character traits – laziness. Cumulative tales. Farms. Folk & fairy tales. Plants.

The little red hen retold by John Escott; ill. by Annie West. Gingham Dog, 2003. ISBN 1-57768-492-3 Subj: Activities – baking, cooking. Animals. Behavior – sharing. Birds – chickens. Character traits – laziness. Cumulative tales. Farms. Folk & fairy tales. Plants.

The little red hen retold & ill. by Margot Zemach. Farrar, 1983. ISBN 0-374-34621-6 Subj: Activities – baking, cooking. Animals. Behavior – sharing. Birds – chickens. Character traits – laziness. Cumulative tales. Farms. Folk & fairy tales. Plants.

The little red hen and the ear of wheat Retold by Mary Finch; ill. by Elisabeth Bell. Barefoot, 1999. ISBN 1-902283-47-3 Subj: Activities – baking, cooking. Animals – mice. Behavior – sharing. Birds – chickens. Character traits – laziness. Cumulative tales. Farms. Folk & fairy tales. Plants.

The Little Red Hen makes a pizza retold by Philemon Sturges; ill. by Amy Walrod. Dutton, 1999. ISBN 0-525-45953-7 Subj: Activities – baking, cooking. Animals. Behavior – sharing. Birds – chickens. Character traits – laziness. Cumulative tales. Farms. Folk & fairy tales. Plants.

Little Robin Redbreast: a Mother Goose rhyme ill. by Shari Halpern. North-South, 1994. ISBN 1-55858-248-7 Subj: Animals – cats. Birds – robins. Nursery rhymes.

Little Tom Tucker ill. by Paul Galdone. McGraw-Hill, 1970. This version was published by J. Kendrew, York, England, ca. 1820. Subj: Nursery rhymes.

Little Tuppen: an old tale ill. by Paul Galdone. Seabury Pr., 1967. ISBN 0-395-28804-5 Subj: Birds – chickens. Cumulative tales. Folk & fairy tales.

Littledale, Freya. *The farmer in the soup* ill. by Molly Delaney. Scholastic, 1987. ISBN 0-590-40194-7 Subj: Behavior – sharing. Farms. Folk & fairy tales.

The little mermaid (Andersen, H. C. [Hans Christian])

The magic plum tree ill. by Enrico Arno. Crown, 1981. ISBN 0-517-54166-1 Subj: Character traits – individuality. Plants. Royalty.

Peter and the north wind ill. by Troy Howell. Scholastic, 1988. ISBN 0-590-40756-2 Subj: Folk & fairy tales. Weather – wind.

The snow child ill. by Leon Steinmetz. Scholastic, 1978. Subj: Behavior – wishing. Old age. Seasons – winter.

Littlefield, William. *The whiskers of Ho Ho* ill. by Vladimir Bobri. Lothrop, 1958. Subj: Animals – rabbits. Birds – chickens. Folk & fairy tales. Foreign lands – China. Holidays – Easter.

Littlesugar, Amy. *Freedom school, yes!* ill. by Floyd Cooper. Philomel, 2001. ISBN 0-399-23006-8 Subj: Ethnic groups in the U.S. – African Americans. School.

Jonkonnu: a story from the sketchbook of Winslow Homer ill. by Ian Schoenherr. Philomel, 1997. ISBN 0-399-22831-4 Subj: Careers – artists. Ethnic groups in the U.S. – African Americans. Prejudice.

Josiah True and the art maker by Amy Littlesugar & Barbara Garrison; ill. by Barbara Garrison. S&S, 1995. ISBN 0-671-88354-2 Subj: Activities – drawing. Art. Careers – artists.

Lisette's angel ill. by Max Ginsburg. Dial, 2002. ISBN 0-8037-2435-7 Subj: Careers – military. Foreign lands – France. War.

Marie in fourth position: the story of Degas's "The little dancer" ill. by Ian Schoenherr. Philomel, 1996. ISBN 0-399-22794-6 Subj: Art. Ballet. Careers – artists. Careers – models.

Shake Rag: from the life of Elvis Presley ill. by Floyd Cooper. Philomel, 1998. ISBN 0-399-23005-X Subj: Careers – singers. Ethnic groups in the U.S. – African Americans. Music.

Tree of hope ill. by Floyd Cooper. Philomel, 1999. ISBN 0-399-23300-8 Subj: Careers – actors. Ethnic groups in the U.S. – African Americans. Poverty. Theater. U.S. history.

Littlewood, Valerie. *The season clock* ill. by author. Viking, 1987. ISBN 0-670-81433-4 Subj: Behavior – misbehavior. Character traits – bravery. Seasons. Time.

Litzinger, Rosanne. *The old woman and her pig* (The old woman and her pig)

Liu, Jae Soo. *Yellow umbrella* ill. by author. Kane/Miller, 2002. ISBN 1-929132-36-0 Subj: Concepts – color. Music. Umbrellas. Weather – rain. Wordless.

Lively, Penelope. *The cat, the crow, and the banyan tree* ill. by Terry Milne. Candlewick, 1994. ISBN 1-56402-325-7 Subj: Animals – cats. Birds – crows. Imagination.

Good night, sleep tight ill. by Adriano Gon. Candlewick, 1995. ISBN 1-56402-417-2 Subj: Bedtime. Night. Sleep. Toys.

One, two, three, jump! ill. by Jan Ormerod. McElderry, 1999. ISBN 0-689-82201-4 Subj: Character traits – helpfulness. Frogs & toads. Insects – dragonflies.

Livermore, Elaine. *Find the cat* ill. by author. Houghton Mifflin, 1973. ISBN 0-395-14756-5 Subj: Animals – cats. Games.

Follow the fox ill. by author. Houghton Mifflin, 1981. ISBN 0-395-31672-3 Subj: Animals – foxes. Behavior – lost. Behavior – needing someone.

Looking for Henry ill. by author. Houghton Mifflin, 1988. ISBN 0-395-44240-0 Subj: Animals – leopards. Behavior – hiding. Sports – hunting.

Lost and found ill. by author. Houghton Mifflin, 1975. ISBN 0-395-20279-5 Subj: Behavior – lost & found possessions. Games.

One to ten, count again ill. by author. Houghton Mifflin, 1973. ISBN 0-395-17514-3 Subj: Counting, numbers. Games.

Three little kittens lost their mittens ill. by author. Houghton Mifflin, 1979. ISBN 0-395-28379-5 Subj: Animals – cats. Behavior – lost & found possessions. Clothing – gloves, mittens. Games. Nursery rhymes.

Livingston, Carole. *"Why am I going to the hospital?"* (Ciliotta, Claire)

"Why was I adopted?" ill. by Arthur Robins; designed by Paul Walter. Lyle Stuart, 1978. ISBN 0-8184-0257-1 Subj: Adoption. Family life.

Livingston, Irene. *Finklehopper Frog* ill. by Brian Lies. Tricycle, 2003. ISBN 1-58246-075-2 Subj: Activities – running. Animals – rabbits. Character traits – individuality. Frogs & toads. Rhyming text.

Finklehopper Frog cheers ill. by Brian Lies. Tricycle, 2004. ISBN 1-58246-138-4 Subj: Activities – picnicking. Animals – rabbits. Friendship. Frogs & toads. Rhyming text.

Livingston, Myra Cohn. *Abraham Lincoln: a man for all the people* ill. by Samuel Byrd. Holiday, 1993. ISBN 0-8234-1049-8 Subj: Poetry. U.S. history.

B is for baby: an alphabet of verses photos by Steel Stillman. McElderry, 1996. ISBN 0-689-80950-6 Subj: ABC books. Babies. Poetry.

Birthday poems ill. by Margot Tomes. Holiday, 1989. ISBN 0-8234-0783-7 Subj: Birthdays. Poetry.

Cat poems ill. by Trina Schart Hyman. Holiday, 1987. ISBN 0-8234-0631-8 Subj: Animals – cats. Poetry.

Celebrations ill. by Leonard Everett Fisher. Holiday, 1985. ISBN 0-8234-0550-8 Subj: Holidays. Poetry.

Dog poems ill. by Leslie Holt Morrill. Holiday, 1990. ISBN 0-8234-0776-4 Subj: Animals – dogs. Poetry.

Festivals ill. by Leonard Everett Fisher. Holiday, 1996. ISBN 0-8234-1217-2 Subj: Fairs, festivals. Poetry.

Higgledy-Piggledy: verses and pictures by Myra Cohn Livingston & Peter Sis; ill. by Peter Sis. Macmillan, 1986. ISBN 0-689-50407-1 Subj: Behavior. Rhyming text.

If you ever meet a whale: poems (If you ever meet a whale)

Keep on singing: a ballad of Marian Anderson ill. by Samuel Byrd. Holiday, 1994. ISBN 0-8234-1098-6 Subj: Ethnic groups in the U.S. – African Americans. Poetry. U.S. history.

A Learical lexicon (Lear, Edward)

Poems for brothers, poems for sisters ill. by Jean Zallinger. Holiday, 1991. ISBN 0-8234-0861-2 Subj: Family life – brothers & sisters. Poetry.

Poems for fathers ill. by Robert Casilla. Holiday, 1989. ISBN 0-5234-0729-2 Subj: Family life – fathers. Holidays – Father's Day. Poetry.

Poems for mothers ill. by Deborah Kogan Ray. Holiday, 1988. ISBN 0-8234-0678-4 Subj: Family life – mothers. Holidays – Mother's Day. Poetry.

Valentine poems ill. by Patience Brewster. Holiday, 1987. ISBN 0-8234-0587-7 Subj: Animals. Holidays – Valentine's Day.

Livingstone, Star. *Harley* ill. by Molly Bang. SeaStar, 2001. ISBN 1-58717-049-3 Subj: Animals – llamas. Animals – sheep.

Livinson, Nancy Smiler. *North Pole, South Pole* ill. by Diane Dawson Hearn. Holiday, 2002. ISBN 0-8234-1737-9 Subj: Animals. Foreign lands – Antarctic. Foreign lands – Arctic. Weather.

Ljungkvist, Laura. *Snow White and the seven dwarfts* retold & ill. by Laura Ljungkvist. Abrams, 2003. ISBN 0-8109-4241-0 Subj: Dwarfs, midgets. Emotions – envy, jealousy. Folk & fairy tales. Magic. Witches.

Toni's topsy-turvy telephone day ill. by author. Abrams, 2001. ISBN 0-8109-4486-3 Subj: Food. Humorous stories. Parties.

Llewellyn, Claire. *The best book of bugs* ill. by Chris Forsey, Andrea Ricciardi di Gaudesi & David Wright. Kingfisher, 1998. ISBN 0-7534-5118-2 Subj: Insects. Science. Spiders.

The best book of sharks ill. by Ray Grinaway & Roger Stewart. Kingfisher, 1999. ISBN 0-7534-5173-5 Subj: Fish – sharks. Science. Sea & seashore.

Crocodile ill. by Simon Mendez. NorthWord, 2004. ISBN 1-55971-900-1 Subj: Animals – babies. Format, unusual. Reptiles – alligators, crocodiles.

Duck ill. by Simon Mendez. NorthWord, 2004. ISBN 1-55971-878-1 Subj: Animals – babies. Birds – ducks. Format, unusual.

Ladybug ill. by Simon Mendez. NorthWord, 2004. ISBN 1-55971-892-7 Subj: Format, unusual. Insects – ladybugs.

My first book of time ill. by Julie Carpenter; photos by Paul Bricknell. DK, 1992. ISBN 1-879431-78-5 Subj: Clocks, watches. Days of the week, months of the year. Format, unusual – toy & movable books. Seasons. Time.

Some bugs glow in the dark ill. by Myke Taylor, Rob Shone, & Jo Moore. Copper Beech, 1997. ISBN 0-7613-0562-9 Subj: Insects. Nature. Spiders.

Spiders have fangs ill. by Myke Taylor & Jo Moore. Copper Beech, 1997. ISBN 0-7613-0610-2 Subj: Spiders.

Tree ill. by Simon Mendez. NorthWord, 2004. ISBN 1-55971-879-X Subj: Food. Format, unusual. Trees.

Lloyd, David. *Air* ill. by Peter Visscher. Dial, 1982. ISBN 0-8037-0143-8 Subj: Science.

Cat and dog ill. by Clive Scruton. Lothrop, 1987. ISBN 0-688-07268-2 Subj: Animals – cats. Animals – dogs.

Duck ill. by Charlotte Voake. Lippincott, 1988. ISBN 0-397-32275-5 Subj: Animals. Birds – ducks. Family life – grandmothers.

Grandma and the pirate ill. by Gill Tomblin. Crown, 1986. ISBN 0-517-56023-2 Subj: Family life – grandmothers. Imagination. Pirates. Sand. Sea & seashore.

Hello, goodbye ill. by Louise Voce. Lothrop, 1988. ISBN 0-688-07699-8 Subj: Animals. Trees. Weather – rain.

Polly Molly Woof Woof ill. by Charlotte Hard. Candlewick, 2000. ISBN 0-7636-0755-X Subj: Animals – dogs. Emotions – happiness.

The ridiculous story of Gammer Gurton's needle ill. by Charlotte Voake. Potter/Crown, 1987. ISBN 0-517-56513-7 Subj: Behavior – lying. Folk & fairy tales. Humorous stories.

The stopwatch ill. by Penny Dale. Lippincott, 1986. ISBN 0-397-32193-7 Subj: Clocks, watches. Family life – grandmothers. Sibling rivalry.

Lloyd, Errol. *Nandy's bedtime* ill. by author. Merrimack, 1983. ISBN 0-370-30395-4 Subj: Bedtime. Night.

Nini at carnival ill. by author. Crowell, 1979. ISBN 0-690-03892-5 Subj: Character traits – helpfulness. Clothing.

Lloyd, Megan. *Chicken tricks* ill. by author. HarperCollins, 1983. ISBN 0-06-023985-9 Subj: Birds – chickens. Eggs. Humorous stories. Rhyming text.

Lobato, Arcadio. *The greatest treasure* ill. by author. Picture Book Studio, 1991. Originally published in Spanish. ISBN 0-88708-093-6 Subj: Animals – whales. Friendship. Royalty – queens. Sea & seashore. Witches.

Just one wish ill. by author. Picture Book Studio, 1989. ISBN 0-88708-134-7 Subj: Behavior – wishing. Magic.

Paper bird ill. by Emilio Urberuaga. Carolrhoda, 1994. ISBN 0-87614-817-8 Subj: Activities – flying. Art. Birds. Kites. Paper.

Lobb, Janice. *Color and noise! Let's play with toys!* ill. by Peter Utton & Ann Savage. Kingfisher, 2001. ISBN 0-7534-5362-2 Subj: Concepts – color. Noise, sounds. Science. Toys.

Counting sheep! How do we sleep? ill. by Peter Utton & Ann Savage. Kingfisher, 2001. ISBN 0-7534-5361-4 Subj: Science. Sleep.

Dig and sow! How do plants grow? ill. by Peter Utton & Ann Savage. Kingfisher, 2000. ISBN 0-7534-5245-6 Subj: Plants. Science.

Listen and see! What's on TV? ill. by Peter Utton & Ann Savage. Kingfisher, 2001. ISBN 0-7534-5336-3 Subj: Science. Television.

Splish! Splosh! Why do we wash? ill. by Peter Utton & Ann Savage. Kingfisher, 2000. ISBN 0-7534-5244-8 Subj: Activities – bathing. Character traits – cleanliness. Health & fitness. Riddles & jokes. Water.

Lobe, Mira. *Christoph wants a party* retold by Marcia Lane, ill. by Winfried Opgenoorth. Kane/Miller, 1995. ISBN 0-916291-59-6 Subj: Birthdays. Parties.

The snowman who went for a walk trans. from German by Peter Carter; ill. by Winfried Opgenoorth. Morrow, 1984. ISBN 0-688-03866-2 Subj: Activities – walking. Snowmen.

Valerie and the good-night swing trans. from German by Peter Carter; ill. by Winfried Opgenoorth. Oxford Univ. Pr., 1983. ISBN 0-19-279769-7 Subj: Bedtime. Rhyming text.

Lobel, Anita. *Alison's zinnia* ill. by author. Greenwillow, 1990. ISBN 0-688-08866-X Subj: ABC books. Flowers.

Away from home ill. by author. Greenwillow, 1994. ISBN 0-688-10355-3 Subj: ABC books. Activities – traveling.

A birthday for the princess ill. by author. HarperCollins, 1973. ISBN 0-06-023944-1 Subj: Behavior – needing someone. Birthdays. Royalty – princesses.

The dwarf giant ill. by author. Greenwillow, 1996. ISBN 0-688-14407-1 Subj: Dwarfs, midgets. Folk & fairy tales. Foreign lands – Japan. Giants.

King Rooster, Queen Hen ill. by author. Greenwillow, 1975. ISBN 0-688-84008-6 Subj: Animals. Birds – chickens. Foreign lands – Denmark.

One lighthouse, one moon ill. by author. Greenwillow, 2000. ISBN 0-688-15540-5 Subj: Animals – cats. Counting, numbers. Days of the week, months of the year. Lighthouses.

The pancake ill. by author. Greenwillow, 1978. ISBN 0-688-84125-2 Subj: Cumulative tales. Food.

Pierrot's ABC garden ill. by author. Western, 1993. ISBN 0-307-17551-0 Subj: ABC books. Clowns, jesters. Gardens, gardening.

Potatoes, potatoes ill. by author. Greenwillow, 1967. Subj: Violence, nonviolence.

The straw maid ill. by author. Greenwillow, 1983. ISBN 0-688-00330-3 Subj: Character traits – cleverness. Crime.

Sven's bridge ill. by author. Greenwillow, 1992. Newly illustrated. ISBN 0-688-11252-8 Subj: Bridges. Royalty.

The troll music ill. by author. HarperCollins, 1966. Subj: Magic. Music. Mythical creatures – trolls.

Lobel, Arnold. *Arnold Lobel book of Mother Goose* (Mother Goose)

Days with Frog and Toad ill. by author. HarperCollins, 1979. ISBN 0-06-023964-6 Subj: Friendship. Frogs & toads.

Fables ill. by author. HarperCollins, 1980. ISBN 0-06-023974-3 Subj: Animals. Caldecott award books.

Frog and Toad all year ill. by author. HarperCollins, 1976. ISBN 0-06-023951-4 Subj: Friendship. Frogs & toads. Seasons.

Frog and Toad are friends ill. by author. HarperCollins, 1970. ISBN 0-06-023958-1 Subj: Caldecott award honor books. Friendship. Frogs & toads.

The frog and toad pop-up book ill. by author. HarperCollins, 1986. ISBN 0-06-023986-7 Subj: Format, unusual – toy & movable books. Frogs & toads.

Frog and Toad together ill. by author. HarperCollins, 1971. ISBN 0-06-023959-X Subj: Friendship. Frogs & toads.

Giant John ill. by author. HarperCollins, 1964. ISBN 0-06-022946-2 Subj: Giants.

Grasshopper on the road ill. by author. HarperCollins, 1978. ISBN 0-06-023962-X Subj: Insects. Insects – grasshoppers.

The great blueness and other predicaments ill. by author. HarperCollins, 1968. ISBN 0-06-023938-7 Subj: Concepts – color. Wizards.

Gregory Griggs and other nursery rhyme people (Mother Goose)

A holiday for Mister Muster ill. by author. HarperCollins, 1963. ISBN 0-06-023956-5 Subj: Animals. Illness. Zoos.

How the rooster saved the day ill. by Anita Lobel. Greenwillow, 1977. ISBN 0-688-84063-9 Subj: Birds – chickens. Character traits – cleverness. Crime.

Lucille ill. by author. HarperCollins, 1964. ISBN 0-06-023966-2 Subj: Animals – horses, ponies. Humorous stories.

The man who took the indoors out ill. by author. HarperCollins, 1974. ISBN 0-06-023947-6 Subj: Behavior – running away.

Martha, the movie mouse ill. by author. HarperCollins, 1966. Subj: Animals – mice. Rhyming text. Theater.

Ming Lo moves the mountain ill. by author. Greenwillow, 1982. ISBN 0-688-00611-6 Subj: Foreign lands – China. Moving.

Mouse soup ill. by author. HarperCollins, 1977. ISBN 0-06-023968-9 Subj: Animals – mice. Animals – weasels. Character traits – cleverness.

Mouse tales ill. by author. HarperCollins, 1972. ISBN 0-06-023942-5 Subj: Animals – mice. Humorous stories. Tall tales.

On Market Street ill. by Anita Lobel. Greenwillow, 1981. ISBN 0-688-84309-3 Subj: ABC books. Caldecott award honor books. Rhyming text. Shopping. Stores.

On the day Peter Stuyvesant sailed into town ill. by author. HarperCollins, 1971. ISBN 0-06-023972-7 Subj: Problem solving. Rhyming text. U.S. history.

Owl at home ill. by author. HarperCollins, 1975. ISBN 0-06-023949-2 Subj: Birds – owls.

Prince Bertram the bad ill. by author. HarperCollins, 1963. ISBN 0-06-023976-X Subj: Behavior – misbehavior. Dragons. Royalty – princes. Witches.

The rose in my garden ill. by Anita Lobel. 1st Mulberry ed. Mulberry, 1993. ISBN 0-688-12265-5 Subj: Animals – cats. Animals – mice. Cumulative tales. Flowers. Gardens, gardening. Insects – bees. Rhyming text.

Small pig ill. by author. HarperCollins, 1969. ISBN 0-06-023932-8 Subj: Animals – pigs. Behavior – running away. Farms.

A treeful of pigs ill. by Anita Lobel. Greenwillow, 1979. ISBN 0-688-84177-5 Subj: Animals – pigs. Character traits – laziness. Farms. Humorous stories.

The turnaround wind ill. by author. HarperCollins, 1988. ISBN 0-06-023988-3 Subj: Weather – wind.

Uncle Elephant ill. by author. HarperCollins, 1981. ISBN 0-06-023980-8 Subj: Animals – elephants. Behavior – lost. Family life – aunts, uncles. Sea & seashore.

Whiskers and rhymes ill. by author. Greenwillow, 1985. ISBN 0-688-03836-0 Subj: Animals – cats. Poetry.

A zoo for Mister Muster ill. by author. HarperCollins, 1962. ISBN 0-06-023991-3 Subj: Animals. Zoos.

Lobel, Gillian. *Does anybody love me?* ill. by Rosalind Beardshaw. Good Bks., 2002. ISBN 1-56148-368-0 Subj: Behavior – running away. Family life – grandfathers. Family life – parents. Self-concept.

Locker, Thomas. *Anna and the bagpiper* ill. by author. Philomel, 1994. ISBN 0-399-22546-3 Subj: Music. Musical instruments – bagpipes. Senses – hearing.

Cloud dance ill. by author. Harcourt, 2000. ISBN 0-15-202231-7 Subj: Weather – clouds.

Family farm ill. by author. Dial, 1988. ISBN 0-8037-0490-9 Subj: Farms.

The land of gray wolf ill. by author. Dial, 1991. ISBN 0-8037-0937-4 Subj: Ecology. Indians of North America. Nature.

The man who paints nature photos by Tim Holmstrom. R.C. Owen, 1999. ISBN 1-57274-328-X Subj: Careers – artists. Careers – illustrators. Nature.

The mare on the hill ill. by author. Dial, 1985. ISBN 0-8037-0208-6 Subj: Animals – horses, ponies. Family life – grandfathers. Farms.

Miranda's smile ill. by author. Dial, 1994. ISBN 0-8037-1689-3 Subj: Careers – artists. Family life – daughters. Family life – fathers.

Mountain dance ill. by author. Harcourt, 2001. ISBN 0-15-202622-3 Subj: Mountains. Poetry.

Rip Van Winkle (Irving, Washington)

Sailing with the wind ill. by author. Dial, 1986. ISBN 0-8037-0312-0 Subj: Activities – traveling. Boats, ships. Sailors.

Sky tree ill. by Candice Christiansen. HarperCollins, 1995. ISBN 0-06-024884-X Subj: Science. Seasons. Trees.

Water dance ill. by author. Harcourt, 2002. ISBN 0-15-216396-4 Subj: Nature. Poetry. Water. Weather.

Where the river begins ill. by author. Dial, 1984. ISBN 0-8937-0090-3 Subj: Family life – grandfathers. Rivers.

The young artist ill. by author. Dial, 1989. ISBN 0-8037-0627-8 Subj: Careers – artists. Royalty.

Lockwood, Primrose. *Cat boy!* ill. by Clara Vulliamy. Houghton Mifflin, 1991. ISBN 0-395-55208-7 Subj: Animals – cats.

Cissy Lavender ill. by Emma Chichester Clark. Little, 1989. ISBN 0-316-14497-5 Subj: Activities – working. Activities – writing.

One winter's night ill. by Elaine Mills. Macmillan, 1991. ISBN 0-02-759235-9 Subj: Animals – dogs. Pets.

Lodge, Bernard. *Cloud Cuckoo Land (and other odd spots)* ill. by author. Houghton Mifflin, 1999. ISBN 0-395-96318-4 Subj: Activities – traveling. Humorous stories. Rhyming text.

Door to door ill. by Maureen Roffey. Lothrop, 1980. ISBN 0-688-41966-6 Subj: Foreign lands – England. Format, unusual.

How scary ill. by author. Houghton, 2001. ISBN 0-618-11547-1 Subj: Counting, numbers. Monsters.

Mouldylocks ill. by author. Houghton Mifflin, 1998. ISBN 0-395-90945-7 Subj: Birthdays. Magic. Parties. Witches.

Rhyming Nell ill. by Maureen Roffey. Lothrop, 1979. ISBN 0-688-51898-2 Subj: Format, unusual. Rhyming text. Witches.

Shoe Shoe Baby ill. by Katherine Lodge. Random House, 2000. ISBN 0-375-81084-6 Subj: Clothing – shoes.

Lodge, Jo. *Happy birthday, Moo Moo* ill. by autnor. Little, 2001. ISBN 0-316-66644-0 Subj: Animals. Birthdays. Format, unusual – toy & movable books. Parties.

Moo Moo goes to the city ill. by autnor. Little, 2002. ISBN 0-316-65582-1 Subj: Animals – bulls, cows. Cities, towns. Format, unusual – toy & movable books.

Loewen, Nancy. *Bicycle safety* ill. by Penny Dann. Child's World, 1997. ISBN 1-56766-260-9 Subj: Safety. Sports – bicycling.

Busy buzzers ill. by Brandon Reibeling. Picture Window, 2004. ISBN 1-4048-0143-X Subj: Insects – bees. Science.

Emergencies ill. by Penny Dann. Child's World, 1997. ISBN 1-56766-259-5 Subj: Accidents. Safety.

Hungry hoppers ill. by Brandon Reibeling. Picture Window, 2004. ISBN 1-4048-0146-4 Subj: Insects – grasshoppers.

Living lights ill. by Brandon Reibeling. Picture Window, 2004. ISBN 1-4048-0145-6 Subj: Insects – fireflies.

Night fliers ill. by Brandon Reibeling. Picture Window, 2004. ISBN 1-4048-0144-8 Subj: Insects – moths.

School safety ill. by Penny Dann. Child's World, 1997. ISBN 1-56766-255-2 Subj: Health & fitness. Safety. School.

Spotted beetles ill. by Melissa Voda. Picture Window, 2004. ISBN 1-4048-0142-1 Subj: Insects – ladybugs.

Tiny workers ill. by Brandon Reibeling. Picture Window, 2004. ISBN 1-4048-0141-3 Subj: Insects – ants.

Traffic safety ill. by Penny Dann. Child's World, 1997. ISBN 1-56766-254-4 Subj: Safety. Traffic, traffic signs.

Loewer, H. Peter. *The moonflower* by Peter & Jean Loewer; ill. by Jean Loewer. Peachtree, 1997. ISBN 1-56145-314-5 Subj: Animals. Flowers. Night.

Loewer, Jean. *The moonflower* (Loewer, H. Peter)

Lofa, Denize (pseud.). *see* Lauture, Denizé

Löfgren, Ulf. *Alvin the Knight* ill. by author. Carolrhoda, 1992. ISBN 0-8761-4698-1 Subj: Knights. Middle Ages. Museums.

Alvin the pirate ill. by author. Carolrhoda, 1990. ISBN 0-87614-402-4 Subj: Imagination. Pirates.

Alvin the zookeeper ill. by author. Carolrhoda, 1991. ISBN 0-87614-689-2 Subj: Animals. Careers – zookeepers. Zoos.

The boy who ate more than the giant and other Swedish folktales trans. from Swedish by Sheila La Farge; ill. by author. Collins-World, 1978. ISBN 0-529-05451-5 Subj: Folk & fairy tales. Giants. Humorous stories.

The color trumpet ill. by author. Addison-Wesley, 1973. English text by Alison Winn; adapt. by Ray Broekel. ISBN 0-340-17649-0 Subj: Concepts – color.

The flying orchestra ill. by author. Addison-Wesley, 1973. English text by Alison Winn; adapt. by Ray Broekel. ISBN 0-340-17650-4 Subj: Music. Musical instruments – orchestras.

One-two-three ill. by author. Addison-Wesley, 1973. English text by Alison Winn; adapt. by Ray Brockel. Subj: Animals. Counting, numbers. Participation.

The traffic stopper that became a grandmother visitor ill. by author. Addison-Wesley, 1973. English text by Alison Winn; adapt. by Ray Broekel. Subj: Animals – elephants. Automobiles. Machines.

The wonderful tree ill. by author. Delacorte, 1969. Subj: Imagination. Trees.

Logue, Christopher. *The magic circus* ill. by Wayne Anderson. Viking, 1979. ISBN 0-670-44809-5 Subj: Character traits – cleverness. Circus. Monsters.

Lohans, Alison. *Sundog rescue* ill. by Vladyana Krykorka. Annick, 1999. ISBN 1-55037-571-7 Subj: Animals – dogs. Family life – grandparents.

Waiting for the sun ill. by Marilyn Mets & Peter Ledwon. Red Deer Pr., 2002. ISBN 0-88995-240-X Subj: Babies. Birth. Family life – new sibling.

Lohf, Sabine. *Things I can make with buttons* ill. by author. Chronicle, 1990. ISBN 0-87701-687-9 Subj: Activities – making things.

Things I can make with cloth ill. by author. Chronicle, 1989. ISBN 0-87701-666-6 Subj: Activities – making things.

Things I can make with cork ill. by author. Chronicle, 1990. ISBN 0-87701-726-3 Subj: Activities – making things.

Things I can make with paper ill. by author. Chronicle, 1989. ISBN 0-87701-671-2 Subj: Activities – making things. Paper.

Loki. *Jake Greenthumb* ill. by Jason Gaillard. Mondo, 2002. ISBN 1-590-34186-4 Subj: Character traits – helpfulness. Gardens, gardening. Plants.

Lomas Garza, Carmen. *In my family* ill. by author. Children's Book Pr., 1996. ISBN 0-8923-9138-3 Subj: Ethnic groups in the U.S. – Hispanic Americans. Family life. Foreign languages.

LoMonaco, Palmyra. *Night letters* ill. by Normand Chartier. Dutton, 1995. ISBN 0-525-45387-3 Subj: Communication. Nature. Night.

London, Jonathan. *Ali, child of the desert* ill. by Ted Lewin. Lothrop, 1997. ISBN 0-688-12561-1 Subj: Behavior – lost. Desert. Foreign lands – Morocco. Shopping. Weather – sandstorms.

At the edge of the forest ill. by Barbara Frith. Candlewick, 1998. ISBN 0-7636-0014-8 Subj: Animals – coyotes. Animals – sheep. Family life – fathers. Family life – sons. Farms.

Baby whale's journey ill. by Jon Van Zyle. Chronicle, 1999. ISBN 0-8118-2496-9 Subj: Animals – babies. Animals – whales.

Candystore man ill. by Malcolm Brown. Lothrop, 1999. ISBN 0-688-13242-1 Subj: Food. Rhyming text. Stores.

Condor's egg ill. by James Chaffee. Chronicle, 1994. ISBN 0-8118-0260-4 Subj: Animals – endangered animals. Birds – condors. Eggs.

Count the ways, Little Brown Bear ill. by Margie Moore. Dutton, 2002. ISBN 0-525-46097-7 Subj: Animals – bears. Counting, numbers. Emotions – love. Family life – mothers.

Crunch munch ill. by Michael Rex. Silver Whistle, 2001. ISBN 0-15-202603-7 Subj: Animals. Food.

Dream weaver ill. by Rocco Baviera. Silver Whistle, 1997. ISBN 0-15200-944-2 Subj: Nature. Spiders.

The eyes of Gray Wolf ill. by Jon Van Zyle. Chronicle, 1993. ISBN 0-8118-0285-X Subj: Animals – wolves.

Fall rap ill. by author. Lothrop, 1995. ISBN 0-688-13995-5 Subj: Poetry. Seasons – fall.

Fire race: a Karuk coyote tale about how fire came to the people ill. by Sylvia Long. Chronicle, 1993. ISBN 0-8118-0241-8 Subj: Animals – coyotes. Fire. Folk & fairy tales. Indians of North America – Karok.

Fireflies, fireflies, light my way ill. by Linda Messier. Viking, 1996. ISBN 0-670-85442-5 Subj: Animals. Indians of North America. Lullabies. Night. Rhyming text.

Froggy eats out ill. by Frank Remkiewicz. Viking, 2001. ISBN 0-670-89686-1 Subj: Behavior – misbehavior. Family life – parents. Food. Frogs & toads. Restaurants.

Froggy gets dressed ill. by Frank Remkiewicz. Viking, 1992. ISBN 0-670-84249-4 Subj: Clothing. Frogs & toads. Hibernation. Seasons – winter. Weather – snow.

Froggy goes to bed ill. by Frank Remkiewicz. Viking, 2000. ISBN 0-670-88860-5 Subj: Bedtime. Frogs & toads.

Froggy goes to school ill. by Frank Remkiewicz. Viking, 1996. ISBN 0-670-86726-8 Subj: Clothing. Dreams. Frogs & toads. School – first day.

Froggy goes to the doctor ill. by Frank Remkiewicz. Viking, 2002. ISBN 0-670-03578-5 Subj: Careers – doctors. Frogs & toads. Humorous stories.

Froggy learns to swim ill. by Frank Remkiewicz. Viking, 1995. ISBN 0-670-85551-0 Subj: Emotions – fear. Frogs & toads. Sports – swimming.

Froggy plays in the band ill. by Frank Remkiewicz. Viking, 2002. ISBN 0-670-03532-7 Subj: Animals. Contests. Frogs & toads. Musical instruments – bands. Parades.

Froggy plays soccer ill. by Frank Remkiewicz. Viking, 1999. ISBN 0-670-88257-7 Subj: Animals. Frogs & toads. Sports – soccer.

Froggy's first Christmas ill. by Frank Remkiewicz. Viking, 2000. ISBN 0-670-89220-3 Subj: Animals. Frogs & toads. Holidays – Christmas.

Froggy's first kiss ill. by Frank Remkiewicz. Viking, 1998. ISBN 0-670-87064-1 Subj: Emotions – love. Frogs & toads. Holidays – Valentine's Day. School.

Froggy's Halloween ill. by Frank Remkiewicz. Viking, 1999. ISBN 0-670-88449-9 Subj: Clothing – costumes. Frogs & toads. Holidays – Halloween.

Gone again ptarmigan ill. by Jon Van Zyle. National Geographic, 2001. ISBN 0-7922-7561-6 Subj: Animals. Birds – ptarmigans. Ecology. Foreign lands – Arctic.

Gray fox ill. by Robert Sauber. Viking, 1993. ISBN 0-670-84490-X Subj: Animals – foxes. Death. Nature.

Hip cat ill. by Woodleigh Hubbard. Chronicle, 1993. ISBN 0-8118-0315-5 Subj: Activities – working. Animals – cats. Careers – musicians. Cities, towns.

Honey Paw and Lightfoot ill. by Jon Van Zyle. Chronicle, 1994. ISBN 0-8118-0533-6 Subj: Animals – bears. Nature.

Hurricane! ill. by Henri Sorensen. Lothrop, 1998. ISBN 0-688-12978-1 Subj: Family life. Foreign lands – Puerto Rico. Weather – hurricanes.

I see the moon and the moon sees me adapt. & expanded by Jonathan London; ill. by Peter Fiore. Viking, 1996. ISBN 0-670-85918-4 Subj: Nature. Nursery rhymes. Rhyming text.

Ice Bear and Little Fox ill. by Daniel San Souci. Dutton, 1998. ISBN 0-525-45907-3 Subj: Animals – foxes. Animals – polar bears. Foreign lands – Arctic. Indians of North America – Inuit.

If I had a horse ill. by Brooke Scudder. Chronicle, 1997. ISBN 0-8118-1112-3 Subj: Animals – horses, ponies. Imagination.

Into this night we are rising ill. by G. Brian Karas. Viking, 1993. ISBN 0-670-84905-7 Subj: Dreams. Folk & fairy tales. Jewish culture. Night. Religion.

Jackrabbit ill. by Deborah Kogan Ray. Crown, 1996. ISBN 0-517-59658-X Subj: Animals – rabbits. Character traits – kindness to animals.

A koala for Katie: an adoption story ill. by Cynthia Jabar. A. Whitman, 1993. ISBN 0-8075-4209-1 Subj: Adoption. Animals – koalas. Emotions – love. Family life. Zoos.

Let the lynx come in ill. by Patrick Benson. Candlewick, 1996. ISBN 1-56402-531-4 Subj: Animals – lynx. Imagination. Moon. Night. Northern lights. Sky.

Let's go, Froggy! ill. by Frank Remkiewicz. Viking, 1994. ISBN 0-670-85055-1 Subj: Activities – picnicking. Behavior – lost & found possessions. Frogs & toads. Sports – bicycling.

Like butter on pancakes ill. by G. Brian Karas. Viking, 1995. ISBN 0-670-85130-2 Subj: Farms. Sun.

The lion who had asthma ill. by Nadine Bernard Westcott. A. Whitman, 1992. ISBN 0-8075-4559-7 Subj: Illness – asthma. Imagination.

Liplap's wish ill. by Sylvia Long. Chronicle, 1994. ISBN 0-8118-0505-0 Subj: Animals – rabbits. Death. Emotions – grief. Family life – grandmothers. Stars.

Little Red Monkey ill. by Frank Remkiewicz. Dutton, 1997. ISBN 0-525-45642-2 Subj: Animals – monkeys. Circus. Jungle. Rhyming text.

Loon Lake ill. by Susan Ford. Chronicle, 2001. ISBN 0-8118-2003-3 Subj: Animals. Birds – loons. Canoes & canoeing. Family life – fathers. Family life – sons. Lakes, ponds.

Moshi moshi ill. by Yoshi Miyake. Millbrook, 1998. ISBN 0-76130-110-0 Subj: Activities – traveling. Family life – brothers. Foreign lands – Japan.

Mustang canyon ill. by Daniel San Souci. Dutton, 2000. ISBN 0-525-45596-5 Subj: Animals – horses, ponies. Canyons.

Old salt, young salt ill. by Todd L. W. Doney. Lothrop, 1997. ISBN 0-688-12976-5 Subj: Behavior – growing up. Boats, ships. Family life – fathers. Sports – fishing.

The owl who became the moon ill. by Ted Rand. Dutton, 1993. ISBN 0-525-45054-8 Subj: Animals. Birds – owls. Night. Trains.

Panther, shadow of the swamp ill. by Paul Morin. Candlewick, 2000. ISBN 1-56402-623-X Subj: Animals – cougars.

Park beat: rhyming through the seasons ill. by Woodleigh Hubbard. HarperCollins, 2000. ISBN 0-688-13995-7 Subj: Rhyming text. Seasons.

Phantom of the prairie: year of the black footed ferret ill. by Barbara Bash. Sierra Club, 1997. ISBN 0-8715-6387-8 Subj: Animals – ferrets. Nature.

Puddles ill. by G. Brian Karas. Viking, 1997. ISBN 0-670-87218-0 Subj: Activities – playing. Clothing – boots. Weather – rain.

Red wolf country ill. by Daniel San Souci. Dutton, 1996. ISBN 0-525-45191-9 Subj: Animals – wolves. Nature.

Shawn and Keeper and the birthday party ill. by Renée Williams-Andriani. Dutton, 1999. ISBN 0-525-46115-9 Subj: Animals – dogs. Birthdays. Food. Parties.

Shawn and Keeper: show-and-tell ill. by Renée Williams-Andriani. Dutton, 2000. ISBN 0-525-46114-0 Subj: Animals – dogs. Behavior – misbehavior. Friendship. School.

Snuggle wuggle ill. by Michael Rex. Silver Whistle, 2000. ISBN 0-15-202159-0 Subj: Animals – babies.

The sugaring-off party ill. by Gilles Pelletier. Dutton, 1995. ISBN 0-525-45187-0 Subj: Family life – grandmothers. Food. Foreign lands – Canada. Trees.

Sun dance, water dance ill. by Greg Couch. Dutton, 2001. ISBN 0-525-46682-7 Subj: Activities – playing. Poetry. Seasons – summer.

Tell me a story photos by Sherry Shahan. R.C. Owen, 1998. ISBN 1-57274-194-5 Subj: Careers – writers.

Thirteen moons on turtle's back (Bruchac, Joseph)

The village basket weaver ill. by George Crespo. Dutton, 1996. ISBN 0-525-45314-8 Subj: Activities – weaving. Family life – grandfathers. Foreign lands – Belize. Indians of Central America – Black Carib.

The waterfall ill. by Jill Kastner. Viking, 1999. ISBN 0-670-87617-8 Subj: Camps, camping. Family life. Sports – hiking. Sports – rock climbing.

What do you love? ill. by Karen Lee Schmidt. Harcourt, 2000. ISBN 0-15-201919-7 Subj: Animals – dogs. Emotions – love. Family life – mothers. Rhyming text.

What do you love? [board book] ill. by Karen Lee Schmidt. Harcourt, 2004. ISBN 0-15-205054-X Subj: Animals – dogs. Emotions – love. Family life – mothers. Format, unusual – board books. Rhyming text.

What Newt could do for Turtle ill. by Louise Voce. Candlewick, 1996. ISBN 1-56402-259-5 Subj: Friendship. Reptiles – lizards. Reptiles – turtles, tortoises. Seasons. Swamps.

What the animals were waiting for ill. by Paul Morin. Scholastic, 2002. ISBN 0-439-33630-9 Subj: Animals. Foreign lands – Africa. Weather – rain.

Where the big fish are ill. by Adam Gustavson. Candlewick, 2001. ISBN 0-7636-0922-6 Subj: Boats, ships. Character traits – perseverance. Fish. Sports – fishing.

White water ill. by Jill Kastner. Viking, 2001. ISBN 0-670-89286-6 Subj: Rivers. Sports.

Who bop ill. by Henry Cole. HarperCollins, 2000. ISBN 0-06-027918-4 Subj: Activities – dancing. Animals. Rhyming text.

Wiggle, waggle ill. by Michael Rex. Harcourt, 1999. ISBN 0-15-201940-5 Subj: Activities – walking. Animals. Noise, sounds.

London, Sara. *Firehorse Max* ill. by Ann Arnold. HarperCollins, 1997. ISBN 0-06-205094-X Subj: Animals – horses, ponies. Careers – peddlers. Music. Musical instruments – violins. Problem solving.

Long, Claudia. *Albert's story* ill. by Judy Glasser. Delacorte, 1978. ISBN 0-440-00080-7 Subj: Dragons. Imagination.

Long, Earlene. *Gone fishing* ill. by Richard Eric Brown. Houghton Mifflin, 1984. ISBN 0-395-35570-2 Subj: Concepts – size. Family life – fathers. Sports – fishing.

Johnny's egg photos by Neal Slavin & Charles Mikolaycak. Addison-Wesley, 1980. ISBN 0-201-04153-7 Subj: Activities – baking, cooking. Eggs.

Long, Jan Freeman. *The bee and the dream* ill. by Kaoru Ono. Dutton, 1996. ISBN 0-525-45287-7 Subj: Character traits – luck. Folk & fairy tales. Foreign lands – Japan. Insects – bees.

Long, Kathy. *Hallelujah the clown: a story of blessing and discovery* ill. by Joe Boddy. Augsburg Fortress, 1992. ISBN 0-8066-2560-0 Subj: Clowns, jesters. Religion.

Long, Melinda. *Hiccup snickup* ill. by Thor Wickstrom. S&S, 2001. ISBN 0-689-82245-6 Subj: Family life. Hiccups.

When Papa snores ill. by Holly Meade. S&S, 2000. ISBN 0-689-81943-9 Subj: Family life – grandparents. Sleep – snoring.

Long, Sylvia. *Deck the hall* ill. by author. Chronicle, 2000. ISBN 0-8118-2821-2 Subj: Animals – rabbits. Foreign lands – England. Holidays – Christmas. Music. Songs.

Long, Willabel L. *Mystery manor* (Mystery manor)

Longfellow, Henry Wadsworth. *The birds of Killingworth* (San Souci, Robert D.)

Hiawatha ill. by Susan Jeffers. Dial, 1983. ISBN 0-8037-0014-8 Subj: Indians of North America – Iroquois. Poetry.

Hiawatha's childhood ill. by Errol Le Cain. Farrar, 1984. ISBN 0-374-33065-4 Subj: Indians of North America – Iroquois. Poetry.

Paul Revere's ride ill. by Paul Galdone. Crowell, 1963. Subj: Poetry. U.S. history. War.

Paul Revere's ride ill. by Nancy Winslow Parker. Mulberry, 1993. ISBN 0-688-12387-2 Subj: Poetry. U.S. history. War.

Paul Revere's ride: the landlord's tale ill. by Charles Santore. HarperCollins, 2003. ISBN 0-688-16552-4 Subj: Poetry. U.S. history. War.

Longfellow, Layne. *Imaginary menagerie* ill. by Woodleigh Marx Hubbard. Chronicle, 1997. ISBN 0-8118-0797-5 Subj: Animals. Format, unusual – toy & movable books. Imagination. Rhyming text.

Loo, Sanne te. *Ping-Li's kite* ill. by author. Front St., 2002. ISBN 1-886910-75-8 Subj: Folk & fairy tales. Foreign lands – China.

Lööf, Jan. *Uncle Louie's fantastic sea voyage* ill. by author. Random House, 1978. ISBN 0-394-93860-7 Subj: Activities – traveling. Boats, ships. Family life – aunts, uncles. Zoos.

Look, Lenore. *Henry's first-moon birthday* ill. by Yumi Heo. Atheneum, 2001. ISBN 0-689-82294-4 Subj: Babies. Birthdays. Ethnic groups in the U.S. – Chinese Americans. Family life – brothers & sisters. Family life – grandmothers.

Love as strong as ginger ill. by Stephen T. Johnson. Atheneum, 1999. ISBN 0-689-81248-5 Subj: Activities – working. Ethnic groups in the U.S. – Chinese Americans. Family life – grandmothers.

Loomans, Diane. *The lovables in the kingdom of self-esteem* ill. by Kim Howard. Starseed Pr., 1991. ISBN 0-915811-25-1 Subj: Animals. Rhyming text. Self-concept.

Loomis, Christine. *Across America, I love you* ill. by Kate Kiesler. Hyperion, 2000. ISBN 0-7868-2314-3 Subj: Family life. Nature. U.S. history.

Astro Bunnies ill. by Ora Eitan. Putnam, 1998. ISBN 0-399-23175-7 Subj: Animals – rabbits. Rhyming text. Space & space ships.

At the laundromat ill. by Nancy Poydar. Scholastic, 1993. ISBN 0-590-72830-X Subj: Activities. Clothing. Communities, neighborhoods. Rhyming text.

At the library ill. by Nancy Poydar. Scholastic, 1993. ISBN 0-590-72829-6 Subj: Libraries. Rhyming text.

At the mall ill. by Nancy Poydar. Scholastic, 1994. ISBN 0-590-72832-6 Subj: Communities, neighborhoods. Shopping. Stores.

The cleanup surprise ill. by Julie Brillhart. Scholastic, 1993. ISBN 0-590-72774-5 Subj: Character traits – cleanliness. Ecology. Rhyming text. Robots. School.

Cowboy bunnies ill. by Ora Eitan. Putnam, 1997. ISBN 0-399-22625-7 Subj: Activities – playing. Animals – rabbits. Country. Cowboys, cowgirls. Rhyming text.

The Hippo Hop ill. by Nadine Bernard Westcott. Houghton Mifflin, 1995. ISBN 0-395-69702-6 Subj: Animals. Jungle. Parties. Rhyming text.

In the diner ill. by Nancy Poydar. Scholastic, 1994. ISBN 0-590-46716-6 Subj: Activities – baking, cooking. Careers – chefs, cooks. Careers – waiters, waitresses. Friendship. Restaurants.

My new baby-sitter photos by George Ancona. Morrow, 1991. ISBN 0-688-09626-3 Subj: Activities – babysitting.

One cow coughs: a counting book for the sick and miserable ill. by Pat Dypold. Ticknor & Fields, 1994. ISBN 0-395-67899-4 Subj: Animals. Counting, numbers. Illness. Rhyming text.

Rush hour ill. by Mari Takabayashi. Houghton Mifflin, 1996. ISBN 0-395-69129-X Subj: Activities – working. Cities, towns. Rhyming text. Transportation.

Scuba bunnies ill. by Ora Eitan. Putnam, 2004. ISBN 0-399-23465-9 Subj: Animals. Animals – rabbits. Rhyming text. Sea & seashore. Sports – skin diving.

We're going on a trip ill. by Maxie Chambliss. Morrow, 1994. ISBN 0-688-10173-9 Subj: Activities – traveling. Activities – vacationing. Airplanes, airports. Automobiles. Trains.

Loomis, Jennifer A. *A duck in a tree* photos by author. Stemmer House, 1996. ISBN 0-88045-136-X Subj: Birds – ducks. Nature.

Lopez, Loretta. *The birthday swap* ill. by author. Lee & Low, 1997. ISBN 1-880000-47-4 Subj: Birthdays. Ethnic groups in the U.S. – Mexican Americans. Family life. Parties.

Lopshire, Robert. *The biggest, smallest, fastest, tallest things you've ever heard of* ill. by author. Crowell, 1980. ISBN 0-690-04014-8 Subj: Concepts.

How to make snop snappers and other fine things ill. by author. Greenwillow, 1977. ISBN 0-688-84066-3 Subj: Activities – making things. Games.

I am better than you ill. by author. HarperCollins, 1968. ISBN 0-06-023997-2 Subj: Behavior – boasting. Reptiles – lizards.

I want to be somebody new! ill. by author. Random House, 1986. ISBN 0-394-97616-9 Subj: Behavior – seeking better things. Character traits – individuality. Rhyming text.

It's magic ill. by author. Macmillan, 1969. Subj: Magic.

New tricks I can do! ill. by author. Beginner Books, 1996. ISBN 0-679-97715-5 Subj: Activities – playing. Animals – dogs. Circus. Concepts – color. Concepts – shape. Rhyming text.

Put me in the zoo ill. by author. Random House, 1960. ISBN 0-394-90017-0 Subj: Animals – dogs. Circus. Concepts – color. Rhyming text.

Lorbiecki, Marybeth. *Louisa May and Mr. Thoreau's flute* (Dunlap, Julie)

Sister Anne's hands ill. by K. Wendy Popp. Dial, 1998. ISBN 0-8037-2039-4 Subj: Careers – teachers. Ethnic groups in the U.S. – African Americans. Prejudice. Rhyming text. School.

Lorca, Federico García. *see* García Lorca, Federico

Lord, Beman. *The days of the week* ill. by Walter Erhard. Walck, 1968. Subj: Days of the week, months of the year. Nursery rhymes. Poetry. Songs.

Lord, John Vernon. *Mr. Mead and his garden* ill. by author. Houghton Mifflin, 1975. ISBN 0-395-20278-7 Subj: Animals – snails. Gardens, gardening. Rhyming text.

Lord, Nancy. *see* Titus, Eve

Loredo, Elizabeth. *Boogie Bones* ill. by Kevin Hawkes. Putnam, 1997. ISBN 0-399-22763-6 Subj: Activities – dancing. Anatomy – skeletons. Contests.

Lorenz, Albert. *Jack and the beanstalk* (Jack and the beanstalk)

Lorenz, Konrad. *The goose family book* (Kalas, Sybille)

Lorenz, Lee. *Big Gus and Little Gus* ill. by author. Prentice-Hall, 1982. ISBN 0-03-077875-3 Subj: Character traits – laziness. Cumulative tales. Folk & fairy tales.

Dinah's egg ill. by author. S&S, 1990. ISBN 0-671-68685-2 Subj: Dinosaurs. Eggs.

The feathered ogre ill. by author. Prentice-Hall, 1983. ISBN 0-13-308296-2 Subj: Character traits – cleverness. Folk & fairy tales. Magic. Mythical creatures – ogres. Royalty.

Hugo and the spacedog ill. by author. Prentice-Hall, 1983. ISBN 0-13-444497-3 Subj: Animals. Animals – dogs. Farms. Space & space ships.

Pig and duck buy a truck ill. by author. Little Simon, 2000. ISBN 0-689-83780-1 Subj: Animals – pigs. Birds – ducks. Concepts – color. Rhyming text. Trucks.

Pinchpenny John ill. by author. Prentice-Hall, 1981. ISBN 0-13-676254-9 Subj: Behavior – greed. Folk & fairy tales.

Scornful Simkin ill. by author. Prentice-Hall, 1980. ISBN 0-13-796664-4 Subj: Folk & fairy tales.

A weekend in the city ill. by author. Pippin Pr., 1991. ISBN 0-945912-15-3 Subj: Animals. Cities, towns. Country.

A weekend in the country ill. by author. Prentice-Hall, 1984. ISBN 0-13-947961-9 Subj: Animals – pigs. Birds – ducks. Country.

Lorenzini, Carlo. *see* Collodi, Carlo

Loretan, Sylvia. *Bob the snowman* ill. by Jan Lenica. Viking, 1991. ISBN 0-670-83677-X Subj: Snowmen. Weather – snow.

Lorian, Nicole. *A birthday present for Mama* ill. by J. P. Miller. Random House, 1984. ISBN 0-394-96755-0 Subj: Animals. Animals – rabbits. Birthdays.

Lorimer, Janet. *The biggest bubble in the world* ill. by Diane Paterson. Watts, 1982. ISBN 0-531-04378-9 Subj: Behavior – misbehavior. Bubbles.

Lorimer, Lawrence T. *Noah's ark* (Martin, Charles E.)

Loriot. *Peter and the wolf* (Prokofiev, Sergei Sergeievitch)

Losi, Carol A. *The 512 ants on Sullivan Street* ill. by Jerry Zimmerman; math activities by Marilyn Burns. Scholastic, 1997. ISBN 0-590-30876-9 Subj: Activities – picnicking. Counting, numbers. Cumulative tales. Food. Insects – ants.

Losordo, Stephen. *Cow moo me* ill. by Jane Conteh-Morgan. HarperFestival, 1998. ISBN 0-694-01108-8 Subj: Animals. Format, unusual – board books. Noise, sounds. Rhyming text.

Lottridge, Celia Barker. *Berta, a remarkable dog* ill. by Elsa Myotte. Groundwood, 2002. ISBN 0-88899-461-3 Subj: Adoption. Animals. Animals – dogs. Behavior – needing someone. Farms.

The little rooster and the diamond button ill. by Joanne Fitzgerald. Douglas & McIntyre, 2001. ISBN 0-88899-443-5 Subj: Birds – chickens. Clothing. Folk & fairy tales. Foreign lands – Hungary. Royalty – sultans.

Music for the Tsar of the Sea ill. by Harvey Chan. Douglas & McIntyre, 1998. ISBN 0-88899-328-5 Subj: Folk & fairy tales. Foreign lands – Russia. Music. Musical instruments – gusli . Royalty – tsars. Sea & seashore.

Something might be hiding ill. by Jill Zwolak. Douglas & McIntyre, 1994. ISBN 0-88899-176-2 Subj: Emotions – fear. Family life. Monsters. Moving.

Lotz, Karen E. *Can't sit still* ill. by Colleen Browning. Dutton, 1993. ISBN 0-525-45066-1 Subj: Cities, towns. Ethnic groups in the U.S. – African Americans. Family life. Seasons. Weather.

Snowsong whistling ill. by Ehsa Kleven. Dutton, 1993. ISBN 0-525-45145-5 Subj: Noise, sounds. Rhyming text. Seasons – fall. Seasons – winter.

Louie, Ai-Ling. *Yeh Shen: a Cinderella story from China* ill. by Ed Young. Putnam, 1990. ISBN 0-399-20900-X Subj: Folk & fairy tales. Foreign lands – China.

Louie, Therese On. *Raymond's perfect present* ill. by Suling Wang. Lee & Low, 2002. ISBN 1-58430-055-8 Subj: Birds. Communities, neighborhoods. Ethnic groups in the U.S. – Chinese Americans. Flowers. Gifts. Illness.

Loupy, Christophe. *Don't worry, Wags* ill. by Eve Tharlet; trans. by J. Alison James. North-South, 2003. ISBN 0-7358-1850-9 Subj: Animals – dogs. Behavior – lost. Behavior – worrying. Stores.

Lourie, Helen. *see* Storr, Catherine (Cole)

Loux, Lynn C. *The day I could fly* ill. by Guy Porfirio. NorthWord, 2003. ISBN 1-55971-866-8 Subj: Activities – flying. Birds – crows. Imagination.

Love, Ann. *Farming* by Ann Love with Jane Drake; ill. by Pat Cupples. Kids Can, 1998. ISBN 1-55074-451-8 Subj: Careers – farmers. Farms. Machines.

Fishing by Ann Love with Jane Drake; ill. by Pat Cupples. Kids Can, 1999. ISBN 1-55074-457-7 Subj: Activities – working. Careers – fishermen. Fish. U.S. history.

Ice cream at the castle ill. by Toni Goffe. Child's Play, 1999. ISBN 0-8595-3677-7 Subj: Castles. Food. Money. Royalty – kings. Royalty – princes.

The prince who wrote a letter ill. by Toni Goffe. Child's Play, 1992. ISBN 0-85953-398-0 Subj: Behavior – gossip. Royalty – kings. Royalty – princesses.

Love, Pamela. *A loon alone* ill. by Shannon Sycks. Down East, 2002. ISBN 0-89272-517-0 Subj: Behavior – hiding. Birds – loons.

Love to mamá ed. by Pat Mora; ill. by Paula S. Barragán. Lee & Low, 2001. ISBN 1-58430-019-1 Subj: Family life – grandmothers. Family life – mothers. Foreign languages. Poetry.

Lovell, Patty. *Stand tall, Molly Lou Melon* ill. by David Catrow. Putnam, 2001. ISBN 0-399-23416-0 Subj: Behavior – bullying. Family life – grandmothers. Self-concept.

Loverseed, Amanda. *The thunder king: a Peruvian folk tale* ill. by author. Peter Bedrick, 1991. ISBN 0-87226-450-5 Subj: Folk & fairy tales. Foreign lands – Peru.

Tikkatoo's journey ill. by author. Peter Bedrick, 1990. ISBN 0-87226-420-3 Subj: Eskimos. Folk & fairy tales.

Low, Alice. *Aunt Lucy went to buy a hat* ill. by Laura Huliska-Beith. HarperCollins, 2004. ISBN 0-06-008972-5 Subj: Behavior – lost & found possessions. Clothing – hats. Humorous stories. Rhyming text.

The charge of the mouse brigade (Stone, Bernard)

David's windows ill. by Tomie de Paola. Putnam, 1974. ISBN 0-399-60883-4 Subj: Animals – horses, ponies. Cities, towns. Family life – grandmothers.

Taro and the bamboo shoot: a Japanese tale (Matsuno, Masako)

The witch who was afraid of witches ill. by Karen Gundersheimer. Pantheon, 1978. ISBN 0-394-93718-X Subj: Holidays – Halloween. Sibling rivalry. Witches.

Witch's holiday ill. by Tony Walton. Pantheon, 1971. ISBN 0-394-92165-8 Subj: Holidays – Halloween. Rhyming text. Witches.

Low, Joseph. *Adam's book of odd creatures* ill. by author. Atheneum, 1962. Subj: ABC books. Animals. Names. Poetry.

Benny rabbit and the owl ill. by author. Greenwillow, 1978. ISBN 0-688-84117-1 Subj: Birds – geese. Character traits – bravery. Emotions – fear. Farms.

Boo to a goose ill. by author. Atheneum, 1975. ISBN 0-689-50009-2 Subj: Birds – geese. Character traits – bravery. Emotions – fear. Farms.

The Christmas grump ill. by author. Atheneum, 1977. ISBN 0-689-50092-0 Subj: Animals – mice. Emotions – happiness. Emotions – sadness. Holidays – Christmas.

Don't drag your feet . . . ill. by author. Atheneum, 1983. ISBN 0-689-50271-0 Subj: Behavior. Dreams. Toys.

Five men under one umbrella ill. by author. Macmillan, 1975. ISBN 0-02-761460-3 Subj: Riddles & jokes.

A mad wet hen and other riddles ill. by author. Greenwillow, 1977. ISBN 0-688-84082-5 Subj: Riddles & jokes.

Mice twice ill. by author. Aladdin, 1986, c1980. ISBN 0-689-71060-7 Subj: Animals – mice. Caldecott award honor books.

My dog, your dog ill. by author. Macmillan, 1978. ISBN 0-02-761400-X Subj: Animals – dogs. Behavior.

What if . . . ? fourteen encounters — some frightful, some frivolous — that might happen to anyone ill. by author. Atheneum, 1976. ISBN 0-689-50064-5 Subj: Problem solving.

Low, Robert. *Peoples of the Arctic* ill. by author. Rosen, 1996. ISBN 0-8239-2294-4 Subj: Foreign lands – Arctic.

Peoples of the rain forest ill. by author. Rosen, 1996. ISBN 0-8239-2297-9 Subj: Foreign lands. Forest, woods.

Low, William. *Chinatown* ill. by author. Holt, 1997. ISBN 0-8050-4214-8 Subj: Communities, neighborhoods. Ethnic groups in the U.S. – Chinese Americans. Family life – grandmothers. Holidays – Chinese New Year.

Lowell, Susan. *The bootmaker and the elves* ill. by Tom Curry. Orchard, 1997. ISBN 0-531-33044-3 Subj: Careers – shoemakers. Character traits – helpfulness. Clothing – boots. Cowboys, cowgirls. Folk & fairy tales. Humorous stories. Mythical creatures – elves. U.S. history – frontier & pioneer life.

Cindy Ellen: a wild western Cinderella ill. by Jane Manning. HarperCollins, 2000. ISBN 0-06-027447-6 Subj: Fairies. Family life – stepfamilies. Folk & fairy tales. Sibling rivalry. U.S. history – frontier & pioneer life.

Dusty Locks and the three bears ill. by Randy Cecil. Holt, 2001. ISBN 0-8050-5862-1 Subj: Animals – bears. U.S. history – frontier & pioneer life.

Little Red Cowboy Hat ill. by Randy Cecil. Holt, 1997. ISBN 0-8050-3508-7 Subj: Animals – bulls, cows. Animals – wolves. Clothing – hats. Family life – grandmothers. Folk & fairy tales.

The three little javelinas ill. by Jim Harris. Northland, 1992. ISBN 0-87358-542-9 Subj: Animals – coyotes. Animals – pigs. Character traits – cleverness. Folk & fairy tales.

The tortoise and the jackrabbit ill. by Jim Harris. Northland, 1994. ISBN 0-87358-586-0 Subj: Animals. Animals – rabbits. Desert. Folk & fairy tales. Reptiles – turtles, tortoises. Sports – racing.

Lowery, Linda. *see* Keep, Linda Lowery

Lowitz, Anson. *The pilgrims' party* (Lowitz, Sadyebeth)

Lowitz, Sadyebeth. *The pilgrims' party* by Sadyebeth & Anson Lowitz; ill. by Anson Lowitz. Lerner, 1967, c1931. Subj: Holidays – Thanksgiving. Pilgrims. U.S. history.

Lowrey, Janette Sebring. *Six silver spoons* ill. by Robert M. Quackenbush. HarperCollins, 1971. Subj: Birthdays. U.S. history.

Lozoff, Bo. *The wonderful life of a fly who couldn't fly* ill. by Beth Stover. Hampton Roads, 2002. ISBN 1-57174-286-7 Subj: Insects – flies. Self-concept.

Lubach, Peter. *Harry and the singing fish* ill. by author. Walt Disney, 1992. ISBN 1-56282-159-8 Subj: Fish. Songs. Theater. Wordless.

Lubell, Cicil. *Rosalie, the bird market turtle* (Lubell, Winifred)

Lubell, Winifred. *Here comes daddy: a book for twos and threes* ill. by author. Addison-Wesley, 1944. Subj: Family life – fathers.

I wish I had another name (Williams, Jay)

Rosalie, the bird market turtle by Winifred & Cicil Lubell; ill. by Winifred Lubell. Rand McNally, 1962. Subj: Behavior – lost. Birds. Foreign lands – France. Reptiles – turtles, tortoises.

Lubin, Leonard B. *Christmas gift-bringers* ill. by author. Lothrop, 1989. ISBN 0-688-07020-5 Subj: Animals – mice. Gifts. Holidays – Christmas. Santa Claus.

Lucado, Max. *Alabaster's song: Christmas through the eyes of an angel* ill. by Michael Garland. Word Pub., 1996. ISBN 0-8499-1307-1 Subj: Activities – singing. Angels. Holidays – Christmas.

All you ever need ill. by Douglas Klauba. Crossway, 2000. ISBN 1-58134-134-2 Subj: Behavior. Character traits – generosity. Water.

Jacob's gift ill. by Robert Hunt. Tommy Nelson, 1998. ISBN 0-8499-5830-X Subj: Careers – carpenters. Religion – Nativity.

Small gifts in God's hands ill. by Cheri Bladholm. Tommy Nelson, 2000. ISBN 0-8499-5842-3 Subj: Fish. Food. Religion.

You are mine ill. by Sergio Martinez. Crossway, 2003. ISBN 1-58134-468-6 Subj: Self-concept.

Lucas, Barbara (Barbara M.). *A calf for Christmas* (Lindgren, Astrid)

Cats by Mother Goose (Mother Goose)

I want a brother or sister (Lindgren, Astrid)

I want to go to school, too (Lindgren, Astrid)

Sleeping over ill. by Stella Ormai. Macmillan, 1986. ISBN 0-02-761360-7 Subj: Animals – bears. Frogs & toads. Sleep. Sleepovers.

Snowed in ill. by Catherine Stock. Bradbury, 1993. ISBN 0-02-761465-4 Subj: Family life. Farms. School. Seasons – winter. Weather – snow.

Lucas, David. *Halibut Jackson* ill. by author. Knopf, 2004. ISBN 0-375-92690-9 Subj: Character traits – individuality. Character traits – shyness. Clothing.

Lucas, Victoria. *see* Plath, Sylvia

Lucht, Irmgard. *In this night* ill. by author; trans. by Frank Jacoby-Nelson; adapt. by Elizabeth Hollow. Hyperion, 1993. ISBN 1-56282-408-2 Subj: Night. Seasons – spring.

The red poppy ill. by author; trans. by Frank Jacoby-Nelson. Hyperion, 1995. ISBN 0-7868-2043-8 Subj: Flowers. Nature.

Luciani, Brigitte. *Those messy Hempels* ill. by Vannessa Hié; trans. by J. Alison James. North-South, 2004. ISBN 0-7358-1910-6 Subj: Behavior – lost & found possessions. Character traits – cleanliness. Food.

Lucy steps through the wardrobe adapt. from The chronicles by C. S. Lewis; ill. by Deborah Maze. HarperCollins, 1997. ISBN 0-06-027451-4 Subj: Imagination. Magic. Witches.

Ludwig, Warren. *Good morning, Granny Rose: an Arkansas folktale* ill. by reteller. Putnam, 1990. ISBN 0-399-21950-1 Subj: Animals – bears. Animals – dogs. Folk & fairy tales. Hibernation. Weather – snow.

Old Noah's elephants ill. by adapt. Putnam, 1991. ISBN 0-399-22256-1 Subj: Animals – elephants. Boats, ships. Folk & fairy tales. Religion – Noah. Weather – floods. Weather – rain. Weather – rainbows.

Ludy, Mark. *The farmer* ill. by author. Green Pastures, 1999. ISBN 0-9664276-0-2 Subj: Careers – farmers. Character traits – helpfulness. Character traits – patience. Character traits – perseverance. Farms.

Luenn, Nancy. *The dragon kite* ill. by Michael Hague. Harcourt, 1982. ISBN 0-15-224196-5 Subj: Folk & fairy tales. Foreign lands – Japan. Kites.

A gift for Abuelita ill. by Robert Chapman. Rising Moon, 1998. ISBN 0-8735-8688-3 Subj: Death. Ethnic groups in the U.S. – Mexican Americans. Family life – grandmothers. Foreign languages. Holidays – Day of the Dead.

Miser on the mountain: a Nisqually legend of Mount Rainier ill. by Pierr Morgan. Sasquatch, 1997. ISBN 1-57061-082-7 Subj: Behavior – greed. Folk & fairy tales. Indians of North America – Nisqually. Mountains.

Mother earth ill. by Neil Waldman. Atheneum, 1992. ISBN 0-689-31668-2 Subj: Earth. Ecology.

Nessa's fish ill. by Neil Waldman. Atheneum, 1990. ISBN 0-689-31477-9 Subj: Eskimos. Family life – grandmothers. Indians of North America. Sports – fishing.

Nessa's story ill. by Neil Waldman. Atheneum, 1994. ISBN 0-689-31782-4 Subj: Eskimos. Family life – grandmothers. Foreign lands – Arctic. Imagination.

Otter play ill. by Anna Vojtech. Atheneum, 1998. ISBN 0-689-81126-8 Subj: Activities – playing. Animals – otters.

Song for the ancient forest ill. by Jill Kastner. Atheneum, 1993. ISBN 0-689-31719-0 Subj: Behavior – trickery. Birds – ravens. Ecology. Forest, woods.

Squish! a wetland walk ill. by Ronald Himler. Atheneum, 1994. ISBN 0-689-31842-1 Subj: Activities – walking. Ecology. Nature.

Luján, Jorge. *Beyond my hand* ill. by Georgina Quintana. Groundwood, 2002. ISBN 0-88899-460-5 Subj: Poetry.

Lukasewich, Lori. *The night fire* ill. by autor. Stoddart, 2001. ISBN 0-7737-3296-9 Subj: Careers – firefighters. Rhyming text.

Lukesová, Milena. *Julian in the autumn woods* ill. by Jan Kudlácek. Holt, 1977. ISBN 0-03-021151-4 Subj: Forest, woods.

The little girl and the rain ill. by Jan Kudlácek. Holt, 1978. ISBN 0-03-021146-8 Subj: Emotions – loneliness. Weather – rain.

Lullaby and goodnight coll. & ill. by Ilse Plume. HarperCollins, 1994. ISBN 0-06-023502-0 Subj: Bedtime. Lullabies. Poetry. Songs.

Lullaby moons and a silver spoon ill. by Brooke Dyer. Little, 2003. ISBN 0-316-17474-2 Subj: Lullabies. Night. Poetry.

Lum, Kate. *Princesses are not quitters!* ill. by Sue Hellard. Bloomsbury, 2003. ISBN 1-58234-762-X Subj: Activities – working. Royalty – princesses.

What! cried Granny ill. by Adrian Johnson. Dial, 1999. ISBN 0-8037-2382-2 Subj: Activities – making things. Bedtime. Family life – grandmothers. Furniture – beds.

Lumley, Katheryn Wentzel. *I can be an animal doctor.* Childrens Pr., 1985. ISBN 0-516-01836-1 Subj: Careers – veterinarians.

Lumry, Amanda. *Safari in South Africa* by Amanda Lumry & Laura Hurwitz; ill. by Sarah McIntyre. Eaglemont, 2003. ISBN 0-9662257-8-3 Subj: Animals. Ecology. Foreign lands – Africa.

Lund, Deb. *Dinosailors* ill. by Howard Fine. Harcourt, 2003. ISBN 0-15-204609-7 Subj: Dinosaurs. Rhyming text. Sailors. Sports – sailing.

Tell me my story, Mama ill. by Hiroe Nakata. HarperCollins, 2004. ISBN 0-06-028877-9 Subj: Babies. Birth. Family life – parents.

Lund, Doris Herold. *The paint-box sea* ill. by Symeon Shimin. McGraw-Hill, 1971. ISBN 0-07-039098-3 Subj: Rhyming text. Sea & seashore. Seasons – summer.

You ought to see Herbert's house ill. by Steven Kellogg. McGraw-Hill, 1973. ISBN 0-531-02595-0 Subj: Behavior – boasting. Friendship.

Lund, Jillian. *Two cool coyotes* ill. by author. Dutton, 1999. ISBN 0-525-46151-5 Subj: Animals – coyotes. Emotions – loneliness. Friendship.

Lundell, Margo. *The furry bedtime book: Lovey Bear's story* ill. by David McPhail. Scholastic, 1996. ISBN 0-590-86371-1 Subj: Animals – bears. Bedtime. Format, unusual – toy & movable books. Rhyming text.

Teddy bear's birthday ill. by Dee deRosa. Platt, 1985. ISBN 0-448-40876-7 Subj: Birthdays. Format, unusual – board books. Toys – bears.

Lundgren, Mary Beth. *Seven scary monsters* ill. by Howard Fine. Clarion, 2003. ISBN 0-395-88913-8 Subj: Bedtime. Monsters. Rhyming text.

Lundy, Charlotte. *Thank you, Esther* ill. by Evelyn Diane Overcash. Bay Light, 2002. ISBN 0-9670280-4-3 Subj: Religion. School. Self-concept.

Thank you, Ruth and Naomi ill. by Miriam Sagasti. Bay Light, 2004. ISBN 0-9741817-0-6 Subj: Friendship. Religion.

Lunge-Larsen, Lise. *The legend of the lady slipper: an Ojibwe tale* retold by Lise Lunge-Larsen & Margi Preus; ill. by Andrea Arroyo. Houghton Mifflin, 1999. ISBN 0-395-90512-5 Subj: Character traits – bravery. Clothing – shoes. Flowers. Folk & fairy tales – pourquoi tales. Indians of North America – Ojibwa.

The race of the Birkebeiners ill. by Mary Azarian. Houghton, 2001. ISBN 0-618-10313-9 Subj: Folk & fairy tales. Foreign lands – Norway. Royalty – princes.

Lunn, Carolyn. *A buzz is part of a bee* ill. by Tom Dunnington. Childrens Pr., 1990. ISBN 0-516-02062-5 Subj: Rhyming text.

Lunn, Janet Louise Swoboda. *Amos's sweater* ill. by Kim LaFave. Firefly, 1991. ISBN 0-88899-074-X Subj: Animals – sheep. Clothing – sweaters.

Come to the fair ill. by Gilles Pelletier. Tundra, 1997. ISBN 0-88776-409-6 Subj: Careers – farmers. Country. Fairs, festivals.

Duck cakes for sale ill. by Kim LaFave. Firefly, 1991. ISBN 0-88899-094-4 Subj: Birds – ducks.

Lunsford, Annie. *What will I become?* ill. by Annie Lunsford; written by Dorothea DePrisco; designed by Treesha Runnells. Piggy Toes, 2002. ISBN 1-58117-160-9 Subj: Animals – babies. Format, unusual – toy & movable books.

Who lives here? ill. by Annie Lunsford; written by Dorothea DePrisco; designed by Treesha Runnells. Piggy Toes, 2002. ISBN 1-58117-159-5 Subj: Animals. Format, unusual – toy & movable books. Homes, houses.

Lupton, Hugh. *The gingerbread man* (The gingerbread boy)

Pirican Pic and Pirican Mor ill. by Yumi Heo. Barefoot, 2003. ISBN 1-84148-070-3 Subj: Cumulative tales. Folk & fairy tales. Foreign lands – Scotland.

Lurie, Morris. *The story of Imelda, who was small* ill. by Terry Denton. Houghton Mifflin, 1988, c1984. ISBN 0-395-48863-7 Subj: Character traits – smallness. Food.

Lussert, Anneliese. *The Christmas visitor* ill. by Loek Koopmans; trans. by Rosemary Lanning. North-South, 1995. ISBN 1-55858-450-1 Subj: Character traits – generosity. Holidays – Christmas. Religion – Nativity.

The farmer and the moon trans. by Anthea Bell; ill. by Józef Wilkon. Holt, 1987. ISBN 0-8050-0281-2 Subj: Behavior – greed. Magic. Moon.

Lustig, Esther. *Willy Whyner, cloud designer* (Lustig, Michael)

Lustig, Michael. *Willy Whyner, cloud designer* by Michael & Esther Lustig; ill. by Michael Lustig. Four Winds, 1994. ISBN 0-02-761365-8 Subj: Careers – inventors. Machines. Weather – clouds.

Luthardt, Kevin. *Hats* ill. by author. A. Whitman, 2004. ISBN 0-8075-3171-5 Subj: Clothing – hats. Friendship.

Mine ill. by author. Atheneum, 2001. ISBN 0-689-83237-0 Subj: Behavior – sharing. Family life – brothers. Toys.

Lüton, Mildred. *Little chicks' mothers and all the others* ill. by Mary Maki Rae. Viking, 1983. ISBN 0-670-43113-3 Subj: Animals. Farms. Poetry.

Luttrell, Ida. *Be nice to Marilyn* ill. by Lonni Sue Johnson. Atheneum, 1992. ISBN 0-689-31716-6 Subj: Family life – cousins. Farms.

Lonesome Lester ill. by Megan Lloyd. HarperCollins, 1984. ISBN 0-06-024030-X Subj: Animals – prairie dogs. Behavior – solitude. Emotions – loneliness.

Mattie and the chicken thief ill. by Thacher Hurd. Putnam, 1988. ISBN 0-396-09126-1 Subj: Animals. Behavior – misbehavior. Birds – chickens.

Mattie's little possum pet ill. by Betsy Lewin. Atheneum, 1993. ISBN 0-689-31786-7 Subj: Animals – cats. Animals – dogs. Animals – possums. Farms. Pets.

Milo's toothache ill. by Enzo Giannini. Dial, 1992. ISBN 0-8037-1035-6 Subj: Animals – pigs. Careers – dentists. Teeth.

Ottie Slockett ill. by Ute Krause. Dial, 1990. ISBN 0-8037-0711-8 Subj: Behavior. Friendship.

The star counters ill. by Korinna Pretro. Tambourine, 1994. ISBN 0-688-12150-0 Subj: Animals. Behavior – greed. Counting, numbers. Royalty – kings. Stars.

Three good blankets ill. by Michael McDermott. Atheneum, 1990. ISBN 0-689-31586-4 Subj: Animals. Behavior – sharing.

Lyfick, Warren. *Animal tales* ill. by Joe Kohl. Harvey House, 1980. ISBN 0-933258-01-1 Subj: Animals. Riddles & jokes.

The little book of fowl jokes ill. by Chris Cummings. Harvey House, 1980. ISBN 0-8178-5198-7 Subj: Birds. Riddles & jokes.

Lynch, Marietta. *Mommy and daddy are divorced* (Perry, Patricia)

Lynch, Tom. *Fables from Æsop* (Æsop)

Lynch, Wendy. *Bach* ill. with photos. Heinemann, 2000. ISBN 1-57572-214-3 Subj: Careers – composers. Foreign lands – Germany. Music.

Dr. Seuss ill. with photos. Heinemann, 2000. ISBN 1-57572-216-X Subj: Careers – authors. Careers – illustrators.

Janet and Allan Ahlberg ill. with photos. Heinemann, 2000. ISBN 1-57572-218-6 Subj: Careers – authors. Careers – illustrators.

Lyndon, Kerry Raines. *A birthday for Blue* ill. by Michael Hays. A. Whitman, 1989. ISBN 0-8075-0774-1 Subj: Activities – traveling. Birthdays. Family life. U.S. history – frontier & pioneer life.

Lyne, Alice. *A, my name is . . .* ill. by Lynne Cravath. Whispering Coyote, 1997. ISBN 1-879085-40-2 Subj: ABC books. Activities – jumping. Names. Rhyming text.

Lynn, Patricia. *see* Watts, Mabel (Pizzey)

Lynn, Sara. *Big animals* ill. by author. Aladdin, 1987. ISBN 0-689-71098-4 Subj: Animals. Format, unusual – board books.

Clothes ill. by author. Macmillan, 1986. ISBN 0-689-71095-X Subj: Clothing. Format, unusual – board books.

Colors ill. by author. Little, 1986. ISBN 0-316-54002-1 Subj: Clowns, jesters. Concepts – color.

Farm animals ill. by author. Aladdin, 1987. ISBN 0-689-71100-X Subj: Animals. Format, unusual – board books.

Food ill. by author. Candlewick, 1996. ISBN 1-56402-766-X Subj: Food. Format, unusual – board books.

Garden animals ill. by author. Aladdin, 1987. ISBN 0-689-71101-8 Subj: Animals. Format, unusual – board books. Gardens, gardening.

Home ill. by author. Macmillan, 1986. ISBN 0-689-71097-6 Subj: Format, unusual – board books. Homes, houses.

Jungle friends ill. by author. Candlewick, 1996. ISBN 0-7636-0042-3 Subj: Animals. Format, unusual – board books. Jungle.

1 2 3 ill. by author. Little, 1986. ISBN 0-316-54004-8 Subj: Animals. Counting, numbers.

Small animals ill. by author. Aladdin, 1987. ISBN 0-689-71099-2 Subj: Animals. Format, unusual – board books.

Toys ill. by author. Macmillan, 1986. ISBN 0-689-71096-8 Subj: Format, unusual – board books. Toys.

Wheels ill. by author. Candlewick, 1996. ISBN 1-56402-947-6 Subj: Format, unusual – board books. Wheels.

Lyon, David. *The biggest truck* ill. by author. Lothrop, 1988. ISBN 0-688-05514-1 Subj: Activities – working. Night. Trucks.

The brave little computer ill. by R. W. Alley. S&S, 1984. ISBN 0-671-52455-0 Subj: Computers. Problem solving.

The crumbly coast ill. by author. Doubleday, 1995. ISBN 0-385-32079-5 Subj: Animals – bears. Animals – minks. Food. Orphans.

The runaway duck ill. by author. Lothrop, 1985. ISBN 0-688-04002-0 Subj: Toys.

Lyon, George Ella. *A B Cedar: an alphabet of trees* designed & ill. by Tom Parker. Watts, 1989. ISBN 0-531-08395-0 Subj: ABC books. Trees.

Ada's pal ill. by Marguerite Casparian. Orchard, 1996. ISBN 0-531-08878-2 Subj: Animals – dogs. Death. Emotions – grief. Pets.

Basket ill. by Mary Szilagyi. Watts, 1990. ISBN 0-531-08486-8 Subj: Behavior – lost & found possessions. Family life – grandfathers.

Book ill. by Peter Catalanotto. DK, 1999. ISBN 0-7894-2560-2 Subj: Books, reading. Poetry.

Cecil's story ill. by Peter Catalanotto. Watts, 1991. ISBN 0-531-08512-0 Subj: Emotions – fear. Family life. Illness. U.S. history. War.

Come a tide ill. by Stephen Gammell. Watts, 1990. ISBN 0-531-08454-X Subj: Family life. Weather – floods.

Counting on the woods photos by Ann W. Olson. DK, 1998. ISBN 0-7894-2480-0 Subj: Counting, numbers. Forest, woods. Nature. Poetry.

A day at damp camp ill. by Peter Catalanotto. Orchard, 1996. ISBN 0-531-08854-5 Subj: Camps, camping. Friendship. Rhyming text.

Dreamplace ill. by Peter Catalanotto. Orchard, 1993. ISBN 0-531-08616-X Subj: Dreams. Indians of North America – Pueblo. Poetry.

Father Time and the day boxes ill. by Robert Andrew Parker. Bradbury, 1985. ISBN 0-02-761370-4 Subj: Time.

Five live bongos ill. by author. Scholastic, 1994. ISBN 0-590-44993-1 Subj: Family life. Music. Musical instruments – drums. Noise, sounds.

Mama is a miner ill. by Peter Catalanotto. Orchard, 1994. ISBN 0-531-08703-4 Subj: Activities – working. Careers – miners. Family life – mothers. Gender roles. Rhyming text.

Mother to tigers ill. by Peter Catalanotto. Atheneum, 2003. ISBN 0-689-84221-X Subj: Animals. Careers – zookeepers.

One lucky girl ill. by Irene Trivas. DK, 2000. ISBN 0-7894-2613-7 Subj: Family life. Homes, houses. Weather – tornadoes.

The outside inn ill. by Vera Rosenberry. Watts, 1991. ISBN 0-531-08536-8 Subj: Food. Nature. Rhyming text.

A regular rolling Noah ill. by Stephen Gammell. Bradbury, 1986. ISBN 0-02-761330-5 Subj: Activities – traveling. Animals. Trains.

A sign ill. by Chris K. Soentpiet. Orchard, 1998. ISBN 0-531-33073-7 Subj: Activities. Careers – writers. Memories, memory. Poetry.

Together ill. by Vera Rosenberry. Watts, 1989. ISBN 0-531-08431-0 Subj: Friendship. Poetry.

A traveling cat ill. by Paul Brett Johnson. Orchard, 1998. ISBN 0-531-33102-4 Subj: Activities – traveling. Animals – cats.

Who came down that road? ill. by Peter Catalanotto. Orchard, 1992. ISBN 0-531-08587-2 Subj: Imagination. Roads.

Lystad, Mary H. *That new boy* ill. by Emily Arnold McCully. Crown, 1973. ISBN 0-517-50259-3 Subj: Character traits – individuality. Friendship. Moving.

M. M. D. *see* Dodge, Mary Mapes

Maass, Robert. *Garbage* ill. by author. Holt, 2000. ISBN 0-8050-5951-2 Subj: Careers – sanitation workers. Ecology.

Garden ill. by author. Holt, 1998. ISBN 0-8050-5477-4 Subj: Gardens, gardening. Plants.

Tugboats ill. by author. Holt, 1997. ISBN 0-8050-3116-2 Subj: Boats, ships. Sailors. Transportation.

When autumn comes photos by author. Holt, 1990. ISBN 0-8050-1259-1 Subj: Seasons – fall.

When spring comes photos by author. Holt, 1994. ISBN 0-8050-2085-3 Subj: Seasons – spring.

When summer comes photos by author. Holt, 1993. ISBN 0-8050-2087-X Subj: Seasons – summer.

When winter comes photos by author. Holt, 1993. ISBN 0-8050-2086-1 Subj: Seasons – winter.

Mabey, Richard. *Oak and company* ill. by Clare Roberts. Greenwillow, 1983. ISBN 0-688-01993-5 Subj: Ecology. Science. Trees.

McAfee, Annalena. *Kirsty knows best* ill. by Anthony Browne. Knopf, 1987. ISBN 0-394-99478-7 Subj: Imagination. Rhyming text.

The visitors who came to stay ill. by Anthony Browne. Viking, 1985. ISBN 0-670-74714-9 Subj: Behavior – trickery. Family life – fathers. Sea & seashore.

Macak, Charles P. *The hokey pokey* (La Prise, Larry)

McAlinden, Paul. *Old MacDonald had a farm* (Old MacDonald had a farm)

McAllister, Angela. *The babies of Cockle Bay* by Angela McAllister & Susie Jenkin-Pearce; ill. by Susie Jenkin-Pearce. Barron's, 1994. ISBN 0-8120-6424-0 Subj: Activities – babysitting. Babies. Pirates.

The battle of Sir Cob and Sir Filbert ill. by author. Crown, 1992. ISBN 0-517-58730-0 Subj: Behavior – sharing. Emotions – envy, jealousy. Middle Ages. War.

The Christmas wish ill. by Susie Jenkin-Pearce. Viking, 1991. ISBN 0-670-84107-2 Subj: Behavior – wishing. Holidays – Christmas.

The clever cowboy ill. by Katherine Lodge. DK, 1998. ISBN 0-7894-3491-1 Subj: Cowboys, cowgirls. Family life – brothers & sisters. Tall tales.

The enchanted flute ill. by Margaret Chamberlain. Delacorte, 1991. ISBN 0-385-30327-0 Subj: Birthdays. Magic. Music. Musical instruments – flutes. Self-concept.

Harry's box ill. by Jenny Jones. Bloomsbury, 2003. ISBN 1-58234-772-7 Subj: Activities – playing. Animals – dogs. Imagination.

The ice palace ill. by Angela Barrett. Putnam, 1994. ISBN 0-399-22784-9 Subj: Concepts – cold & heat. Dreams. Family life – fathers. Illness.

Jessie's journey ill. by Anne Magill. Macmillan, 1992. ISBN 0-02-765366-8 Subj: Activities – traveling. Imagination. Trains. Transportation.

The little blue rabbit ill. by Jason Cockcroft. Bloomsbury, 2003. ISBN 1-58234-834-0 Subj: Animals – rabbits. Behavior – needing someone. Emotions. Toys.

Matepo ill. by Jill Newton. Dial, 1991. ISBN 0-8037-0838-6 Subj: Activities – trading. Animals. Animals – monkeys. Circular tales. Jungle.

Nesta, the little witch ill. by Susie Jenkin-Pearce. Viking, 1990. ISBN 0-670-83376-2 Subj: School. Witches.

Night-night, little one ill. by Maggie Kneen. Random House, 2003. ISBN 0-385-90861-X Subj: Animals – rabbits. Bedtime. Family life – mothers.

Sleepy Ella ill. by Susan Winter. Delacorte, 1994. ISBN 0-385-32050-7 Subj: Bedtime. Behavior – wishing. Imagination. Rhyming text.

Snail's birthday problem ill. by Susie Jenkin-Pearce. Viking, 1989. ISBN 0-670-82991-9 Subj: Animals – snails. Birthdays. Parties.

The snow angel ill. by Claire Fletcher. Lothrop, 1993. ISBN 0-688-04569-3 Subj: Angels. Family life – brothers & sisters. Weather – snow.

The whales' tale ill. by Michaela Bloomfield. Aurum, 1990. ISBN 1-85406-053-8 Subj: Animals – whales.

The wind garden ill. by Claire Fletcher. Lothrop, 1995. ISBN 0-688-13280-4 Subj: Family life – grandparents. Gardens, gardening. Weather – wind.

MacArthur-Onslow, Annette Rosemary. *Minnie* ill. by author. Rand McNally, 1971. ISBN 0-528-82278-0 Subj: Animals – cats.

Macaulay, David. *Angelo* ill. by author. Houghton, 2002. ISBN 0-618-16826-5 Subj: Birds – pigeons. Character traits – kindness to animals. Friendship.

Black and white ill. by author. Houghton Mifflin, 1990. ISBN 0-395-52151-3 Subj: Animals – bulls, cows. Caldecott award books. Family life. Trains.

Castle ill. by author. Houghton Mifflin, 1977. ISBN 0-395-25784-0 Subj: Caldecott award honor books.

Cathedral ill. by author. Houghton Mifflin, 1973. ISBN 0-395-17513-5 Subj: Caldecott award honor books.

Why the chicken crossed the road ill. by author. Houghton Mifflin, 1987. ISBN 0-395-44241-9 Subj: Cumulative tales. Humorous stories.

MacBean, Dilla Wittemore. *Picture book dictionary* ill. by Pauline B. Adams. Childrens Pr., 1962. Subj: Dictionaries.

MacBeth, George. *Jonah and the Lord* ill. by Margaret Gordon. Holt, 1970. ISBN 0-03-081612-2 Subj: Folk & fairy tales. Religion – Jonah.

Noah's journey ill. by Margaret Gordon. Viking, 1966. Subj: Boats, ships. Religion – Noah. Rhyming text. Weather – floods. Weather – rain. Weather – rainbows.

McBratney, Sam. *The caterpillow fight* ill. by Jill Barton. Candlewick, 1996. ISBN 1-56402-804-6 Subj: Bedtime. Behavior – misbehavior. Insects – butterflies, caterpillars. Rhyming text.

The dark at the top of the stairs ill. by Ivan Bates. Candlewick, 1996. ISBN 1-56402-640-X Subj: Animals – cats. Animals – mice. Bedtime. Character traits – curiosity. Emotions – fear.

Guess how much I love you ill. by Anita Jeram. Candlewick, 1995. ISBN 1-56402-473-3 Subj: Animals – rabbits. Bedtime. Emotions – love. Family life – fathers.

I'll always be your friend ill. by Kim Lewis. HarperCollins, 2001. ISBN 0-06-029485-X Subj: Animals – foxes. Emotions – anger. Family life – mothers.

I'm sorry by Sam McBratney & Jennifer Eachus; ed. by Robert Warren; ill. by Jennifer Eachus. HarperCollins, 2000. ISBN 0-06-028686-5 Subj: Behavior – fighting, arguing. Emotions – anger. Friendship. School.

In the light of the moon and other bedtime stories ill. by Kady MacDonald Denton. Kingfisher, 2001. ISBN 0-7534-5224-3 Subj: Bedtime.

Just one! ill. by Ivan Bates. Candlewick, 1997. ISBN 0-7636-0223-X Subj: Animals – squirrels. Character traits – generosity.

Just you and me ill. by Ivan Bates. Candlewick, 1998. ISBN 0-7636-0436-4 Subj: Animals. Birds – geese. Weather – storms.

Once there was a Hoodie ill. by Paul Hess. Putnam, 2001. ISBN 0-399-23581-7 Subj: Behavior – needing someone. Emotions – happiness. Mythical creatures.

McBrier, Page. *Beatrice's goat* ill. by Lori Lohstoeter. Atheneum, 2001. ISBN 0-689-82460-2 Subj: Animals – goats. Foreign lands – Uganda.

McCain, Becky R. (Becky Ray). *Grandmother's dreamcatcher* ill. by Stacey Schuett. A. Whitman, 1998. ISBN 0-8075-3031-X Subj: Activities – making things. Dreams. Family life – grandmothers. Indians of North America – Chippewa.

Nobody knew what to do: a story about bullying ill. by Todd Leonard. A. Whitman, 2001. ISBN 0-8075-5711-0 Subj: Behavior – bullying. School.

McCall, Francis X. *A huge hog is a big pig* by Francis McCall & Patricia Keeler; ill. with photos. Greenwillow, 2002. ISBN 0-06-029766-2 Subj: Animals. Games. Rhyming text.

Maccarone, Grace. *Baby visits grandma and grandpa* ill. by Carol Hudson. Scholastic, 1999. ISBN 0-590-43092-0 Subj: Babies. Family life – grandparents. Format, unusual – board books.

Baby's toys ill. by Carol Hudson. Scholastic, 1990. ISBN 0-590-43098-X Subj: Babies. Format, unusual – board books. Toys.

Cars! Cars! Cars! ill. by David A. Carter. Scholastic, 1995. ISBN 0-590-47572-X Subj: Automobiles. Rhyming text.

A child was born ill. by Sam Williams. Scholastic, 2000. ISBN 0-439-18296-4 Subj: Holidays – Christmas. Religion – Nativity. Rhyming text.

A child's good night prayer ill. by Sam Williams. Scholastic, 2001. ISBN 0-439-23505-7 Subj: Bedtime. Religion.

The class trip ill. by Besty Lewin. Scholastic, 1999. ISBN 0-439-06755-3 Subj: Animals. Behavior – lost. Rhyming text. School – field trips. Zoos.

The classroom pet ill. by Betsy Lewin. Scholastic, 1995. ISBN 0-590-26264-5 Subj: Crustaceans – crabs. Pets. Rhyming text. School.

Dinosaurs ill. by Richard Courtney. Scholastic, 2001. ISBN 0-439-20060-1 Subj: Dinosaurs. Prehistory.

I have a cold ill. by Betsy Lewin. Scholastic, 1998. ISBN 0-590-39638-2 Subj: Illness – cold (disease). Rhyming text.

I shop with my daddy ill. by Denise Brunkus. Scholastic, 1998. ISBN 0-590-50196-8 Subj: Family life. Rhyming text. Shopping.

Itchy, itchy chicken pox ill. by Betsy Lewin. Scholastic, 1992. ISBN 0-590-44948-6 Subj: Illness – chicken pox. Rhyming text.

The lunch box surprise ill. by Betsy Lewin. Scholastic, 1995. ISBN 0-590-26267-X Subj: Emotions. Food. School.

Martin and the tooth fairy (Chardiet, Bernice)

My tooth is about to fall out ill. by Betsy Lewin. Scholastic, 1995. ISBN 0-590-48376-5 Subj: Behavior – growing up. Teeth.

Oink! moo! how do you do? ill. by Hans Wilhelm. Scholastic, 1994. ISBN 0-590-48161-4 Subj: Animals. Careers – farmers. Farms. Noise, sounds. Rhyming text.

Pizza party ill. by Emily Arnold McCully. Cartwheel, 1994. ISBN 0-590-47563-0 Subj: Activities – baking, cooking. Food. Rhyming text.

Pumpkin faces ill. by author. Scholastic, 1997. ISBN 0-590-13454-X Subj: Animals. Concepts – opposites. Format, unusual – toy & movable books. Holidays – Halloween. Plants.

Sharing time troubles ill. by Betsy Lewin. Cartwheel, 1996. ISBN 0-590-73879-8 Subj: Behavior – sharing. Family life – brothers. Rhyming text. School.

McCarthy, Bobette. *Buffalo girls* ill. by author. Crown, 1987. ISBN 0-517-65568-4 Subj: Animals – buffaloes. Music. Songs.

Dreaming ill. by author. Candlewick, 1994. ISBN 1-56402-184-X Subj: Animals. Bedtime. Boats, ships. Dreams. Rhyming text. Sleep.

Happy hiding hippos ill. by author. Bradbury, 1994. ISBN 0-02-765446-X Subj: Animals – hippopotamuses. Behavior – hiding. Games.

See you later, alligator ill. by author. Macmillan, 1995. ISBN 0-02-765447-8 Subj: Moving. Reptiles – alligators, crocodiles. Rhyming text.

Ten little hippos ill. by author. Bradbury, 1992. ISBN 0-02-765445-1 Subj: Animals – hippopotamuses. Counting, numbers. Rhyming text.

McCarthy, Meghan. *The adventures of Patty and the big red bus* ill. by author. Knopf, 2005. ISBN 0-375-92939-8 Subj: Activities – traveling. Buses. Family life – sisters. Imagination. Moon. Mountains. Sea & seashore. Space & space ships.

George upside down ill. by author. Viking, 2003. ISBN 0-670-03608-0 Subj: Behavior. Character traits – individuality.

McCarthy, Michael. *The story of Daniel in the lions' den* ill. by Giuliano Ferri. Barefoot, 2005. ISBN 1-84148-209-9 Subj: Animals – lions. Religion – Daniel. Rhyming text.

The story of Noah and the ark ill. by Giuliano Ferri. Barefoot, 2001. ISBN 1-84148-361-3 Subj: Animals. Boats, ships. Religion – Noah. Rhyming text. Weather – floods. Weather – rain.

MacCarthy, Patricia. *Herds of words* ill. by author. Dial, 1991. ISBN 0-8037-0892-0 Subj: Language.

McCarthy, Ruth. *Katie and the smallest bear* ill. by Emilie Boon. Knopf, 1986. ISBN 0-394-97855-2 Subj: Activities – playing. Animals – bears. Zoos.

McCarty, Peter. *Baby steps* ill. by author. Holt, 2000. ISBN 0-8050-5953-9 Subj: Babies. Behavior – growing up.

Hondo and Fabian ill. by author. Holt, 2002. ISBN 0-8050-6352-8 Subj: Animals – cats. Animals – dogs. Caldecott award honor books. Sea & seashore.

Little bunny on the move ill. by author. Holt, 1999. ISBN 0-8050-4620-8 Subj: Activities – traveling. Animals. Animals – rabbits. Homes, houses.

McCaughrean, Geraldine. *Beauty and the beast* ill. by Gary Blythe. Carolrhoda, 2000. ISBN 1-57505-491-4 Subj: Emotions – love. Folk & fairy tales. Foreign lands – France. Royalty – princes.

The cherry tree (Ikeda, Daisaku)

Grandma Chickenlegs ill. by Moira Kemp. Carolrhoda, 2000. ISBN 1-57505-415-9 Subj: Family life – stepfamilies. Folk & fairy tales. Foreign lands – Russia. Magic. Witches.

How the reindeer got their antlers ill. by Heather Holland. Holiday, 2000. ISBN 0-8234-1562-7 Subj: Animals – reindeer. Character traits – individuality. Character traits – pride. Holidays – Christmas. Santa Claus. Self-concept.

My grandmother's clock ill. by Stephen Lambert. Clarion, 2002. ISBN 0-618-21695-2 Subj: Clocks, watches. Family life – grandmothers. Time.

One bright Penny. Viking, 2002. ISBN 0-670-03588-2 Subj: Behavior – trickery. Family life – fathers. Money.

The princess and the moon (Ikeda, Daisaku)

Saint George and the dragon ill. by Nicki Palin. Doubleday, 1989. ISBN 0-385-26529-8 Subj: Dragons. Folk & fairy tales.

The snow country prince (Ikeda, Daisaku)

The story of Noah and the ark ill. by Helen Ward. Ideals, 1989. ISBN 0-8249-8403-X Subj: Animals. Boats, ships. Religion – Noah. Weather – floods. Weather – rain. Weather – rainbows.

The story of the Nativity conceived & ill. by Ruth Wickings. Doubleday, 1998. ISBN 0-385-32631-9 Subj: Holidays – Christmas. Religion – Nativity.

Unicorns! Unicorns! ill. by Sophie Windham. Holiday, 1997. ISBN 0-8234-1319-5 Subj: Folk & fairy tales. Imagination. Mythical creatures – unicorns. Religion – Noah.

McCauley, Jane R. *Baby birds and how they grow* ill. with photos. National Geographic, 1983. ISBN 0-87044-492-1 Subj: Birds. Science.

The way animals sleep ill. with photos. National Geographic, 1983. ISBN 0-87044-494-8 Subj: Animals. Sleep.

Animals showing off (Chen, Tony)

McClenathan, Louise. *The Easter pig* ill. by Rosekrans Hoffman. Morrow, 1982. ISBN 0-688-01446-1 Subj: Animals – pigs. Character traits – generosity. Holidays – Easter.

My mother sends her wisdom ill. by Rosekrans Hoffman. Morrow, 1979. ISBN 0-688-32193-3 Subj: Behavior – greed. Character traits – cleverness. Character traits – wisdom.

McClintock, Barbara. *Animal fables from Æsop* (Æsop)

The battle of Luke and Longnose ill. by author. Houghton Mifflin, 1994. ISBN 0-395-65751-2 Subj: Animals – cats. Dreams. Magic. Theater. Toys.

Dahlia ill. by author. Farrar, 2002. ISBN 0-374-31678-3 Subj: Activities – playing. Family life – aunts, uncles. Toys – dolls.

The fantastic drawings of Danielle ill. by author. Houghton Mifflin, 1996. ISBN 0-395-73980-2 Subj: Activities – drawing. Activities – painting. Activities – photographing. Careers – artists. Imagination.

Molly and the magic wishbone ill. by author. Farrar, 2000. ISBN 0-374-34999-1 Subj: Behavior – wishing. Fairies. Family life – brothers & sisters.

McClintock, Marshall. *A fly went by* ill. by Fritz Siebel. Random House, 1958. ISBN 0-394-90003-0 Subj: Behavior – misunderstanding. Cumulative tales. Insects – flies.

Stop that ball ill. by Fritz Siebel. Random House, 1959. ISBN 0-394-90010-3 Subj: Toys – balls.

What have I got? ill. by Leonard P. Kessler. HarperCollins, 1961. ISBN 0-06-024141-1 Subj: Clothing. Imagination. Poetry.

McClintock, Mike. *see* McClintock, Marshall

McCloskey, Kevin. *Mrs. Fitz's flamingos* ill. by author. Lothrop, 1992. ISBN 0-688-10474-6 Subj: Birds – flamingos. Cities, towns. Emotions – love.

McCloskey, Robert. *Bert Dow, deep-water man: a tale of the sea in the classic tradition* ill. by author. Viking, 1963. Subj: Animals – whales. Boats, ships. Sea & seashore.

Blueberries for Sal ill. by author. Viking, 1948. ISBN 0-670-17591-9 Subj: Animals – bears. Behavior – lost. Caldecott award honor books. Family life. Food.

Lentil ill. by author. Viking, 1940. ISBN 0-670-42357-2 Subj: Music. Musical instruments – harmonicas. Noise, sounds. Problem solving.

Make way for ducklings ill. by author. Viking, 1941. ISBN 0-670-45149-5 Subj: Birds – ducks. Caldecott award books. Careers – police officers. Cities, towns.

One morning in Maine ill. by author. Viking, 1952. ISBN 0-670-52627-4 Subj: Caldecott award honor books. Family life. Sea & seashore. Teeth.

Time of wonder ill. by author. Viking, 1957. ISBN 0-670-71512-3 Subj: Caldecott award books. Islands. Sea & seashore. Seasons – summer. Weather.

McClung, Robert. *How animals hide* ill. with photos. National Geographic, 1973. ISBN 0-87044-144-2 Subj: Animals. Behavior – hiding. Science.

Sphinx: the story of a caterpillar ill. by Carol Lerner. Rev. ed. Morrow, 1981. ISBN 0-688-00465-2 Subj: Insects – butterflies, caterpillars. Metamorphosis. Science.

McClure, Gillian. *Fly home McDoo* ill. by author. Dutton, 1980. ISBN 0-233-97108-4 Subj: Behavior – running away. Birds – pigeons.

Prickly pig ill. by author. Elsevier-Dutton, 1980. ISBN 0-233-96780-X Subj: Animals – hedgehogs. Hibernation.

Selkie ill. by author. Farrar, 1999. ISBN 0-374-36709-4 Subj: Animals – seals. Character traits – kindness to animals. Folk & fairy tales. Islands. Mythical creatures – selkies. Sea & seashore.

Tom Finger ill. by author. Bloomsbury, 2002. ISBN 1-58234-782-4 Subj: Animals – cats. Gifts. Pets.

What's the time, Rory Wolf? ill. by author. Dutton, 1982. Subj: Animals – wolves. Emotions – loneliness. Friendship.

McConnachie, Brian. *Elmer and the chickens vs. the big league* ill. by Harvey Stevenson. Crown, 1992. ISBN 0-517-57617-1 Subj: Birds – chickens. Farms. Imagination. Sports – baseball.

Flying boy ill. by Jack Ziegler. Crown, 1988. ISBN 0-517-55980-3 Subj: Activities – flying. Character traits – helpfulness. Character traits – individuality.

Lily of the forest ill. by Jack Ziegler. Crown, 1987. ISBN 0-517-56595-1 Subj: Animals. Behavior – boredom. Behavior – running away. Family life. Forest, woods.

McCord, David. *Every time I climb a tree* ill. by Marc Simont. Little, 1967. ISBN 0-316-55514-2 Subj: Activities – playing. Poetry. Trees.

The star in the pail ill. by Marc Simont. Little, 1976. ISBN 0-316-55515-0 Subj: Poetry.

McCormack, John E. *Rabbit tales* ill. by Jenni Oliver. Dutton, 1980. ISBN 0-525-38005-1 Subj: Animals – rabbits. Character traits – cleverness. Character traits – individuality. Character traits – vanity. Friendship. Imagination.

Rabbit travels ill. by Lynne Cherry. Dutton, 1984. ISBN 0-525-44087-9 Subj: Activities – traveling. Animals – rabbits. Friendship.

McCormick, Wendy. *Daddy, will you miss me?* ill. by Jennifer Eachus. S&S, 1999. ISBN 0-689-81898-X Subj: Behavior – needing someone. Emotions – loneliness. Family life – fathers. Foreign lands – Africa.

The night you were born ill. by Sophy Williams. Peachtree, 2000. ISBN 1-56145-225-4 Subj: Babies. Family life – aunts, uncles. Family life – brothers & sisters. Family life – new sibling.

McCourt, Lisa. *Chicken soup for little souls: Della Splatnuk birthday girl* ill. by Pat Grant Porter. Health Communications, 1999. Based on the . . . best-selling series Chicken soup for the soul by Jack Canfield and Mark Victor Hansen. ISBN 1-55874-600-5 Subj: Birthdays. Friendship. Parties. Prejudice.

Chicken soup for little souls: The best night out with Dad story adapt. by Lisa McCourt; ill. by Bert Dodson. Health Communications, 1997. Based on the . . . best-selling series Chicken soup for the soul by Jack Canfield and Mark Victor Hansen. ISBN 1-55874-508-4 Subj: Character traits – generosity. Circus. Family life – fathers.

Chicken soup for little souls: The Goodness Gorillas story adapt. by Lisa McCourt; ill. by Pat Grant Porter. Health Communications, 1997. Based on the . . . best-selling series Chicken soup for the soul by Jack Canfield and Mark Victor Hansen. ISBN 1-55874-505-X Subj: Character traits – kindness. Clubs, gangs. School.

Chicken soup for little souls: The never-forgotten doll story adapt. by Lisa McCourt; ill. by Mary O'Keefe Young. Health Communications, 1997. Based on the . . . best-selling series Chicken soup for the soul by Jack Canfield and Mark Victor Hansen. ISBN 1-55874-507-6 Subj: Activities – babysitting. Behavior – lost & found possessions. Birthdays. Character traits – kindness. Gifts.

Chicken soup for little souls: The new kid and the cookie thief ill. by Mary O'Keefe Young. Health Communications, 1998. Inspired by . . . 'Chicken soup for the soul' by Jack Canfield and Mark Victor Hansen. ISBN 1-55874-588-2 Subj: Character traits – shyness. Friendship. School.

Good night, Princess Pruney Toes ill. by Cyd Moore. BridgeWater, 2001. ISBN 0-8167-5205-2 Subj: Bedtime. Family life – daughters. Family life – fathers. Imagination. Royalty – princesses.

I love you, Stinky Face ill. by Cyd Moore. Troll, 1997. ISBN 0-8167-4392-4 Subj: Bedtime. Emotions – love. Family life – mothers. Imagination.

I miss you, Stinky Face ill. by Cyd Moore. BridgeWater, 1999. ISBN 0-8167-5647-3 Subj: Activities – traveling. Family life – mothers. Transportation.

It's time for school, Stinky Face ill. by Cyd Moore. BridgeWater, 2000. ISBN 0-8167-6961-3 Subj: Family life – mothers. Imagination. School.

The long and short of it (Nathan, Cheryl)

The rainforest counts! ill. by Cheryl Nathan. Troll, 1997. ISBN 0-8167-4388-6 Subj: Animals. Counting, numbers. Forest, woods.

McCoy, Karen Kawamoto. *Bon Odori dancer* ill. by Carolina Yao. Polychrome Pub., 1998. ISBN 1-879965-16-X Subj: Activities – dancing. Ethnic groups in the U.S. – Japanese Americans.

McCrea, James. *The king's procession* by James & Ruth McCrea; ill. by authors. Atheneum, 1963. Subj: Animals – donkeys. Character traits – loyalty. Poverty. Royalty – kings.

The magic tree by James & Ruth McCrea; ill. by authors. Atheneum, 1965. Subj: Character traits – meanness. Emotions. Emotions – happiness. Royalty.

The story of Olaf by James & Ruth McCrea; ill. by authors. Atheneum, 1964. Subj: Dragons. Knights. Wizards.

McCrea, Lilian. *Mother hen* ill. by Edda Reinl. Picture Book Studio, 1987. ISBN 0-88708-037-5 Subj: Animals. Birds – chickens. Counting, numbers. Eggs. Farms.

McCrea, Ruth. *The king's procession* (McCrea, James)

The magic tree (McCrea, James)

The story of Olaf (McCrea, James)

McCready, Lady. *see* Tudor, Tasha

McCready, Tasha Tudor. *see* Tudor, Tasha

McCue, Lisa. *Corduroy's best Halloween ever!* ill. by Lisa McCue. Grosset, 2001. Based on the character by Don Freeman. ISBN 0-448-42499-1 Subj: Clothing – costumes. Holidays – Halloween. Toys – bears.

Corduroy's party ill. by Lisa McCue. Viking, 1985. ISBN 0-670-80520-3 Subj: Birthdays. Format, unusual – board books. Parties. Toys. Toys – bears. Wordless.

Corduroy's toys ill. by author. Viking, 1985. ISBN 0-670-80522-X Subj: Format, unusual – board books. Toys. Toys – bears. Wordless.

The little chick ill. by author. Random House, 1986. ISBN 0-394-88017-X Subj: Birds – chickens. Farms. Format, unusual – board books.

McCullough, Sharon Pierce. *Bunbun at bedtime* ill. by author. Barefoot, 2001. ISBN 1-84148-438-5 Subj: Animals – rabbits. Bedtime.

Bunbun, the middle one ill. by author. Barefoot, 2001. ISBN 1-84148-377-X Subj: Animals – rabbits. Family life – brothers & sisters.

McCully, Emily Arnold. *The ballot box battle* ill. by author. Knopf, 1996. ISBN 0-679-97938-7 Subj: Behavior – growing up. Character traits – persistence. U.S. history.

The Christmas gift ill. by author. HarperCollins, 1988. ISBN 0-06-024212-4 Subj: Animals – mice. Family life – grandfathers. Gifts. Holidays – Christmas. Toys. Wordless.

Crossing the new bridge ill. by author. Putnam, 1994. ISBN 0-399-22618-4 Subj: Bridges. Emotions – happiness.

The evil spell ill. by author. HarperCollins, 1992. ISBN 0-06-024154-3 Subj: Animals – bears. Emotions – fear. Theater.

First snow ill. by author. HarperCollins, 1985. ISBN 0-06-623853-6 Subj: Activities – playing. Animals – mice. Seasons – winter. Weather – snow. Wordless.

Four hungry kittens ill. by author. Dial, 2001. ISBN 0-8037-2505-1 Subj: Animals – cats. Wordless.

The grandma mix-up ill. by author. HarperCollins, 1988. ISBN 0-06-024202-7 Subj: Activities – babysitting. Family life – grandmothers.

Grandmas trick-or-treat ill. by author. HarperCollins, 2001. ISBN 0-06-028731-4 Subj: Behavior – bullying. Behavior – fighting, arguing. Family life – grandmothers. Holidays – Halloween.

Hurry! ill. by author. Harcourt, 2000. ISBN 0-15-201579-5 Subj: Animals – endangered animals. Behavior – hurrying.

Little Kit, or, The Industrious Flea Circus girl ill. by author. Dial, 1995. ISBN 0-8037-1674-5 Subj: Character traits – meanness. Circus. Insects – fleas. Orphans.

Mirette and Bellini cross Niagara Falls ill. by author. Putnam, 2000. ISBN 0-399-23348-2 Subj: Careers – aerialists. Ethnic groups in the U.S. – French Americans. Immigrants.

Mirette on the high wire ill. by author. Putnam, 1992. ISBN 0-399-22130-1 Subj: Caldecott award books. Emotions – fear. Foreign lands – France.

Monk camps out ill. by author. Scholastic, 2000. ISBN 0-439-09976-5 Subj: Animals – mice. Camps, camping. Family life.

Mouse practice ill. by author. Scholastic, 1999. ISBN 0-590-68220-2 Subj: Animals – mice. Character traits – persistence. Sports – baseball.

My real family ill. by author. Browndeer, 1994. ISBN 0-15-277698-2 Subj: Adoption. Animals – bears. Animals – sheep. Behavior – running away. Family life. Theater.

New baby ill. by author. HarperCollins, 1988. ISBN 0-06-024131-4 Subj: Animals – mice. Sibling rivalry. Wordless.

The orphan singer ill. by author. Scholastic, 2001. ISBN 0-439-19274-9 Subj: Activities – singing. Foreign lands – Italy. Music. Orphans.

An outlaw Thanksgiving ill. by author. Dial, 1998. ISBN 0-8037-2198-6 Subj: Crime. Holidays – Thanksgiving. Trains. U.S. history. Weather – snow.

Picnic ill. by author. HarperCollins, 1984. ISBN 0-06-024099-7 Subj: Activities – picnicking. Animals – mice. Behavior – lost. Wordless.

The pirate queen ill. by author. Putnam, 1995. ISBN 0-399-22657-5 Subj: Boats, ships. Foreign lands – Ireland. Pirates.

Popcorn at the palace ill. by author. Browndeer, 1997. ISBN 0-15-277699-0 Subj: Family life – fathers. Food. Foreign lands – England.

School ill. by author. HarperCollins, 1987. ISBN 0-06-024133-0 Subj: Animals – mice. School. Wordless.

Speak up, Blanche! ill. by author. HarperCollins, 1991. ISBN 0-06-024228-0 Subj: Animals – bears. Animals – sheep. Character traits – shyness. Theater.

Zaza's big break ill. by author. HarperCollins, 1989. ISBN 0-06-024224-8 Subj: Animals – bears. Careers – actors. Television. Theater.

McCunn, Ruthanne L. *Pie-Biter* ill. by You-Shah Tang. Design Ent., 1983. ISBN 0-932538-09-6 Subj: Activities – working. Behavior – seeking better things. Ethnic groups in the U.S. – Chinese Americans.

McCurdy, Michael. *An Algonquian year: the year according to the full moon* ill. by author. Houghton, 2000. ISBN 0-618-00705-9 Subj: Days of the week, months of the year. Food. Indians of North America – Algonquin.

The devils who learned to be good ill. by author. Little, 1987. ISBN 0-316-55527-4 Subj: Character traits – cleverness. Devil. Folk & fairy tales.

The old man and the fiddle ill. by author. Putnam, 1992. ISBN 0-399-21812-2 Subj: Music. Musical instruments – violins. Rhyming text.

The sailor's alphabet ill. by author. Houghton Mifflin, 1998. ISBN 0-395-84167-4 Subj: ABC books. Poetry. Sailors. Sea & seashore.

McCurry, Kristen. *Ocean babies* written & ed. by Kristen McCurry & Aimee Jackson; photos by Anup Shah. NorthWord, 2004. ISBN 1-55971-898-6 Subj: Animals. Animals – babies. Format, unusual – board books. Sea & seashore.

Safari babies written & ed. by Kristen McCurry & Aimee Jackson; photos by Anup Shah. NorthWord, 2004. ISBN 1-55971-899-4 Subj: Animals. Animals – babies. Format, unusual – board books. Science.

McCutcheon, John. *Happy adoption day!* lyrics by John McCutcheon; ill. by Julie Paschkis. Little, 1996. ISBN 0-316-55455-3 Subj: Adoption. Family life. Songs.

McCutcheon, Marc. *Grandfather's Christmas camp* ill. by Kate Kiesler. Clarion, 1995. ISBN 0-395-69626-7 Subj: Animals – dogs. Camps, camping. Family life – grandfathers. Holidays – Christmas. Weather – snow.

McDaniel, Becky Bring. *Katie did it* ill. by Lois Axeman. Childrens Pr., 1983. ISBN 0-516-02043-9 Subj: Sibling rivalry.

McDermott, Beverly Brodsky. *The crystal apple: a Russian tale* ill. by author. Viking, 1974. ISBN 0-670-25052-X Subj: Folk & fairy tales. Foreign lands – Russia. Imagination.

The dreamtime ill. by author. Blue Sky, 1995. ISBN 0-590-48518-0 Subj: Creation. Folk & fairy tales. Foreign lands – Australia.

The Golem: a Jewish legend ill. by author. Lippincott, 1976. ISBN 0-397-31674-7 Subj: Folk & fairy tales. Jewish culture.

Jonah: an Old Testament story ill. by author. Lippincott, 1977. ISBN 0-397-31711-6 Subj: Animals – whales. Religion – Jonah.

McDermott, Dennis. *The golden goose* (Grimm, Jacob)

McDermott, Gerald. *Anansi the spider: a tale from the Ashanti* ill. by author. Holt, 1972. ISBN 0-03080-236-9 Subj: Caldecott award honor books. Folk & fairy tales. Foreign lands – Africa. Moon. Spiders.

Arrow to the sun: a Pueblo Indian tale ill. by author. Viking, 1974. ISBN 0-670-13369-8 Subj: Caldecott award books. Folk & fairy tales. Indians of North America – Pueblo.

The Brambleberrys animal book of colors (Mayer, Marianna)

Coyote: a trickster tale from the American Southwest ill. by author. Harcourt, 1994. ISBN 0-15-220724-4 Subj: Activities – flying. Animals – coyotes. Birds – crows. Folk & fairy tales. Indians of North America – Southwest.

Daniel O'Rourke: an Irish tale ill. by author. Viking, 1986. ISBN 0-670-80924-1 Subj: Dreams. Folk & fairy tales. Foreign lands – Ireland. Mythical creatures – pooka spirit.

Daughter of earth: a Roman myth ill. by author. Delacorte, 1984. ISBN 0-385-29295-3 Subj: Folk & fairy tales. Seasons.

The fox and the stork retold from La Fontaine's fable & ill. by Gerald McDermott. Harcourt, 1999. ISBN 0-15-202343-7 Subj: Animals – foxes. Birds – storks. Folk & fairy tales.

Jabutí the tortoise ill. by author. Harcourt, 2001. ISBN 0-15-200496-3 Subj: Behavior – trickery. Folk & fairy tales – pourquoi tales. Foreign lands – South America. Reptiles – turtles, tortoises.

The light of the world: the story of the Nativity ill. by author. S&S, 1998. ISBN 0-689-80707-4 Subj: Holidays – Christmas. Religion – Nativity.

The magic tree: a tale from the Congo ill. by author. Holt, 1994. ISBN 0-8050-3080-8 Subj: Character traits – appearance. Magic. Multiple births – twins.

Musicians of the sun ill. by author. S&S, 1997. ISBN 0-689-80706-6 Subj: Folk & fairy tales. Foreign lands – Mexico. Indians of North America – Aztec. Music. Sun.

Papagayo, the mischief maker ill. by author. Windmill, 1980. ISBN 0-671-96084-9 Subj: Birds – parakeets, parrots. Moon.

Raven: a trickster tale from the Pacific Northwest ill. by author. Harcourt, 1993. ISBN 0-15-265661-8 Subj: Behavior – trickery. Birds – ravens. Caldecott award honor books. Folk & fairy tales. Indians of North America.

The stonecutter: a Japanese folk tale ill. by author. Viking, 1975. ISBN 0-670-67074-X Subj: Behavior – dissatisfaction. Folk & fairy tales. Foreign lands – Japan.

Tim O'Toole and the wee folk ill. by author. Viking, 1990. ISBN 0-670-80393-6 Subj: Behavior – trickery. Cities, towns. Folk & fairy tales. Magic.

The voyage of Osiris: a myth of ancient Egypt ill. by author. Windmill, 1977. ISBN 0-525-61567-9 Subj: Folk & fairy tales. Foreign lands – Egypt. Religion. Royalty.

Zomo the rabbit ill. by author. Harcourt, 1992. ISBN 0-15-299967-1 Subj: Animals – rabbits. Behavior – trickery. Foreign lands – Africa.

MacDonald, Alan. *Beware of the bears!* ill. by Gwyneth Williamson. Little Tiger, 1998. ISBN 1-888444-28-2 Subj: Animals – bears. Character traits – orderliness.

The not-so-wise man ill. by Andrew Rowland. Eerdmans, 1999. ISBN 0-8028-5196-7 Subj: Holidays – Christmas. Religion – Nativity. Royalty – kings.

MacDonald, Allan. *The pig in a wig* ill. by Paul Hess. Peachtree, 1999. ISBN 1-56145-197-5 Subj: Animals – pigs. Hair. Self-concept.

MacDonald, Amy. *Cousin Ruth's tooth* ill. by Marjorie Priceman. Houghton Mifflin, 1996. ISBN 0-395-71253-X Subj: Behavior – growing up. Behavior – lost & found possessions. Family life. Rhyming text. Teeth.

Let's do it ill. by Maureen Roffey. Candlewick, 1992. ISBN 1-56402-024-X Subj: Activities. Format, unusual – board books. Games.

Let's go ill. by Maureen Roffey. Candlewick, 1994. ISBN 1-56402-202-1 Subj: Activities – playing. Format, unusual – board books.

Let's make a noise ill. by Maureen Roffey. Candlewick, 1992. ISBN 1-56402-025-8 Subj: Format, unusual – board books. Noise, sounds.

Let's play ill. by Maureen Roffey. Candlewick, 1992. ISBN 1-56402-023-1 Subj: Activities – playing. Format, unusual – board books. Toys.

Let's pretend ill. by Maureen Roffey. Candlewick, 1994. ISBN 1-56402-201-3 Subj: Activities – playing. Format, unusual – board books. Imagination.

Let's try ill. by Maureen Roffey. Candlewick, 1992. ISBN 1-56402-022-3 Subj: Activities. Format, unusual – board books.

Little Beaver and the echo ill. by Sarah Fox-Davies. Putnam, 1990. ISBN 0-399-22203-0 Subj: Animals – beavers. Cumulative tales. Friendship. Noise, sounds.

Please, Malese! a trickster tale from Haiti ill. by Emily Lisker. DK, 2001. ISBN 0-7894-2647-1 Subj: Behavior – trickery. Folk & fairy tales. Foreign lands – Haiti.

Quentin Fenton Herter three ill. by Giselle Potter. Farrar, 2002. ISBN 0-374-36170-3 Subj: Behavior. Behavior – misbehavior. Humorous stories. Rhyming text. Shadows.

Rachel Fister's blister ill. by Marjorie Priceman. Houghton Mifflin, 1990. ISBN 0-395-52152-1 Subj: Illness. Rhyming text.

The spider who created the world ill. by G. Brian Karas. Orchard, 1996. ISBN 0-531-08855-3 Subj: Creation. Spiders.

Macdonald, Anne. *Wickiup walkingstick* ill. by Elaine Blier. Red Deer Pr., 1991. ISBN 0-88995-063-6 Subj: Behavior. Concepts – color. Ecology.

MacDonald, Elizabeth. *Dilly-Dally and the nine secrets* ill. by Ken Brown. Dutton, 1999. ISBN 0-525-46006-3 Subj: Animals – babies. Birds – ducks. Counting, numbers. Rivers.

John's picture ill. by David McTaggart. Viking, 1991. ISBN 0-670-83579-X Subj: Art.

Mike's kite ill. by Robert Kendall. Watts, 1990. ISBN 0-531-08476-0 Subj: Counting, numbers. Cumulative tales. Kites.

Miss Poppy and the honey cake ill. by Claire Smith. Dial, 1989. ISBN 0-8037-0578-6 Subj: Activities – baking, cooking. Animals – pigs. Rhyming text.

Mr. Badger's birthday pie ill. by Claire Smith. Dial, 1989. ISBN 0-8037-0579-4 Subj: Activities – baking, cooking. Animals – badgers. Birthdays.

Mr. MacGregor's breakfast egg ill. by Alex Ayliffe. Viking, 1990. ISBN 0-670-83256-1 Subj: Eggs. Food.

My aunt and the animals by Elizabeth MacDonald & Annie Owen; ill. by Annie Owen. Barron's, 1985. ISBN 0-8120-5641-8 Subj: Animals. Counting, numbers. Days of the week, months of the year. Family life – aunts, uncles.

The very windy day ill. by Lesley Summers. Tambourine, 1992. ISBN 0-688-11045-2 Subj: Circular tales. Weather – wind.

The wolf is coming! ill. by Ken Brown. Dutton, 1998. ISBN 0-525-45952-9 Subj: Animals. Animals – rabbits. Animals – wolves. Cumulative tales.

MacDonald, George. *The light princess* ill. by Maurice Sendak. Farrar, 1969. ISBN 0-374-34455-8 Subj: Folk & fairy tales.

The light princess adapt. by Robin McKinley; ill. by Katie Thamer Treherne. Harcourt, 1987. ISBN 0-15-245300-8 Subj: Concepts – weight. Folk & fairy tales. Royalty – princesses. Witches.

Little Daylight ill. by Dorothée Duntze. Holt, 1987. ISBN 0-8050-0493-9 Subj: Fairies. Folk & fairy tales. Magic. Royalty – princes. Royalty – princesses.

McDonald, Golden. *see* Brown, Margaret Wise

MacDonald, Greville. *see* MacDonald, George

McDonald, Jamie. *see* Heide, Florence Parry

MacDonald, Margaret Read. *Fat cat* ill. by Julie Paschkis. August House, 2001. ISBN 0-87483-616-6 Subj: Animals – cats. Animals – mice. Folk & fairy tales. Foreign lands – Denmark.

The girl who wore too much Thai text by Supaporn Vathanaprida; ill. by Yvonne LeBrun Davis. August House, 1998. ISBN 0-8748-3503-8 Subj: Character traits – vanity. Clothing. Folk & fairy tales. Foreign lands – Thailand.

Mabela the clever ill. by Tim Coffey. A. Whitman, 2001. ISBN 0-8075-4902-9 Subj: Animals – cats. Animals – mice. Folk & fairy tales. Foreign lands – Africa.

The old woman who lived in a vinegar bottle ill. by Nancy Dunaway Fowlkes. August House, 1995. ISBN 0-87483-415-5 Subj: Behavior – dissatisfaction. Folk & fairy tales. Foreign lands – England.

Pickin' peas ill. by Pat Cummings. HarperCollins, 1998. ISBN 0-06-027970-2 Subj: Animals – rabbits. Behavior – trickery. Ethnic groups in the U.S. – African Americans. Folk & fairy tales. Gardens, gardening.

Slop! a Welsh folktale ill. by Yvonne LeBrun Davis. Fulcrum Kids, 1997. ISBN 1-55591-352-0 Subj: Character traits – kindness. Fairies. Folk & fairy tales. Foreign lands – Wales.

Tuck-me-in tales ill. by Yvonne Davis. August House, 1996. ISBN 0-87483-461-9 Subj: Bedtime. Folk & fairy tales.

McDonald, Mary Ann. *Leopards* photos by author. Child's World, 1996. ISBN 1-56766-211-0 Subj: Animals – leopards.

Mosquitoes ill. with photos. Child's World, 2001. ISBN 1-56766-635-3 Subj: Insects – mosquitoes.

MacDonald, Maryann. *Ben at the beach* ill. by David McTaggart. Viking, 1991. ISBN 0-670-83920-5 Subj: Family life – brothers & sisters. Sand. Sea & seashore – beaches.

Hedgehog bakes a cake ill. by Lynn Munsinger. G. Stevens, 1996. ISBN 0-8368-1619-6 Subj: Activities – baking, cooking. Animals. Animals – hedgehogs. Food.

Little Hippo gets glasses ill. by Anna King. Dial, 1992. ISBN 0-8037-0964-1 Subj: Animals – hippopotamuses. Glasses. Senses – sight.

Little Hippo starts school ill. by Anna King. Dial, 1990. ISBN 0-8037-0720-7 Subj: Animals – hippopotamuses. School – first day.

The pink party ill. by Abby Carter. Hyperion, 1994. ISBN 1-56282-621-2 Subj: Concepts – color. Emotions – envy, jealousy. Friendship.

Rabbit's birthday kite ill. by Lynn Munsinger. Bantam, 1991. ISBN 0-553-05876-2 Subj: Animals – hedgehogs. Animals – rabbits. Birthdays. Kites.

Rosie and the poor rabbits ill. by Melissa Sweet. Atheneum, 1994. ISBN 0-689-31832-4 Subj: Animals – rabbits. Behavior – sharing. Character traits – generosity. Dreams.

Rosie runs away ill. by Melissa Sweet. Atheneum, 1990. ISBN 0-689-31625-9 Subj: Animals – rabbits. Behavior – running away. Family life.

Rosie's baby tooth ill. by Melissa Sweet. Atheneum, 1991. ISBN 0-689-31626-7 Subj: Animals – rabbits. Fairies. Teeth.

Sam's worries ill. by Judith Riches. Walt Disney, 1991. ISBN 1-56282-082-6 Subj: Behavior – worrying. Toys – bears.

McDonald, Megan. *Ant and Honey Bee* ill. by G. Brian Karas. Candlewick, 2001. ISBN 0-7636-1265-0 Subj: Clothing – costumes. Insects – ants. Insects – bees. Parties.

Bedbugs ill. by Paul Brett Johnson. Orchard, 1999. ISBN 0-531-33193-8 Subj: Activities – bathing. Bedtime. Emotions – fear. Family life – fathers. Imagination. Insects. Monsters. Rhyming text.

The bone keeper ill. by G. Brian Karas. DK, 1999. ISBN 0-7894-2559-9 Subj: Anatomy – skeletons. Animals – wolves. Desert. Magic. Mythical creatures.

The great pumpkin switch ill. by Ted Lewin. Watts, 1992. ISBN 0-531-08600-3 Subj: Family life – grandfathers. Mystery stories. Plants.

Insects are my life ill. by Paul Brett Johnson. Orchard, 1995. ISBN 0-531-08724-7 Subj: Behavior – collecting things. Family life. Insects. School.

Is this a house for Hermit Crab? ill. by S. D. Schindler. Watts, 1990. ISBN 0-531-08455-8 Subj: Crustaceans – crabs. Sea & seashore.

Lucky star ill. by Andrea Wallace. St. Martin's, 2000. ISBN 0-307-46329-X Subj: Books, reading. Friendship.

My house has stars ill. by Peter Catalanotto. Orchard, 1996. ISBN 0-531-08879-0 Subj: Foreign lands. Homes, houses. Night. Stars.

The night Iguana left home ill. by Ponder Goembel. DK, 1999. ISBN 0-7894-2581-5 Subj: Activities – traveling. Behavior – dissatisfaction. Friendship. Reptiles – iguanas.

Penguin and Little Blue ill. by Katherine Tillotson. Atheneum, 2003. ISBN 0-689-84415-8 Subj: Birds – penguins. Foreign lands – Antarctic. Theater.

The potato man ill. by Ted Lewin. Watts, 1991. ISBN 0-531-08514-7 Subj: Careers – peddlers. Family life – grandfathers.

Reptiles are my life ill. by Paul Brett Johnson. Orchard, 2001. ISBN 0-439-29306-5 Subj: Friendship. Insects. Reptiles. School.

Tundra mouse ill. by S. D. Schindler. Orchard, 1997. ISBN 0-531-33047-8 Subj: Activities – storytelling. Animals – mice. Eskimos. Indians of North America – Yupik.

Whoo-oo is it? ill. by S. D. Schindler. Watts, 1992. ISBN 0-531-08574-0 Subj: Birds – owls. Night. Noise, sounds.

MacDonald, Ross. *Achoo! Bang! Crash!* ill. by author. Roaring Brook, 2003. ISBN 0-7613-2900-5 Subj: ABC books. Language. Noise, sounds.

Another perfect day ill. by author. Roaring Brook, 2002. ISBN 0-7613-2659-6 Subj: Dreams.

MacDonald, Suse. *Alphabatics* ill. by author. Bradbury, 1986. ISBN 0-02-761520-0 Subj: ABC books. Caldecott award honor books.

Elephants on board ill. by author. Harcourt, 1999. ISBN 0-15-200951-5 Subj: Animals – elephants. Circus. Machines. Rhyming text. Transportation. Trucks.

Look whooo's counting ill. by author. Scholastic, 2000. ISBN 0-590-68320-9 Subj: Animals. Counting, numbers. Picture puzzles.

Nanta's lion ill. by author. Morrow, 1995. ISBN 0-688-13125-5 Subj: Animals. Animals – lions. Foreign lands – Africa. Format, unusual. Jungle. Sports – hunting.

Numblers by Suse MacDonald & Bill Oakes; ill. by authors. Dial, 1988. ISBN 0-8037-0548-4 Subj: Counting, numbers.

Once upon another by Suse MacDonald & Bill Oakes; ill. by authors. Dial, 1990. ISBN 0-8037-0787-8 Subj: Folk & fairy tales. Format, unusual.

Peck, slither and slide ill. by author. Harcourt, 1997. ISBN 0-15-200079-8 Subj: Animals. Behavior. Picture puzzles.

Sea shapes ill. by author. Harcourt, 1997. ISBN 0-15-201700-3 Subj: Animals. Concepts – shape. Sea & seashore.

Space spinners ill. by author. Dial, 1991. ISBN 0-8037-1009-7 Subj: Space & space ships. Spiders.

McDonnell, Flora. *Flora McDonnell's ABC* ill. by author. Candlewick, 1997. ISBN 0-7636-0118-7 Subj: ABC books.

Giddy-up! Let's ride! ill. by author. Candlewick, 2002. ISBN 0-7636-1778-4 Subj: Animals. Animals – horses, ponies.

I love animals ill. by author. Candlewick, 1994. ISBN 1-56402-387-7 Subj: Animals. Character traits – kindness to animals. Farms.

I love boats ill. by author. Candlewick, 1995. ISBN 1-56402-539-X Subj: Activities – bathing. Boats, ships. Toys.

Sparky ill. by author. Candlewick, 2004. ISBN 0-7636-2208-7 Subj: Animals – dogs. Pets.

Splash! ill. by author. Candlewick, 1999. ISBN 0-7636-0481-X Subj: Animals. Animals – elephants. Water.

McDonough, Yona Zeldis. *Eve and her sisters: women of the Old Testament* by Yona Zeldis McDonough & Malcah Zeldis; ill. by Malcah Zeldis. Greenwillow, 1994. ISBN 0-688-12513-1 Subj: Religion.

McElmurry, Jill. *Mad about plaid* ill. by author. Morrow, 2000. ISBN 0-688-16952-X Subj: Behavior – lost & found possessions. Clothing – handbags, purses. Concepts – patterns.

Mess pets. SeaStar, 2002. ISBN 1-58717-175-9 Subj: Character traits – cleanliness. Character traits – orderliness. Family life – sisters. Health & fitness. Multiple births – twins.

McElroy, Lisa Tucker. *Meet my grandmother. She's a children's book author* by Lisa Tucker McElroy & Abigail Jane Cobb; photos by Joel Benjamin. Millbrook, 2001. ISBN 0-7613-1972-7 Subj: Activities – writing. Careers – authors. Family life – grandmothers.

McFall, Gardner. *Jonathan's cloud* ill. by Steven Guarnaccia. HarperCollins, 1986. ISBN 0-06-024124-1 Subj: Weather – clouds.

Naming the animals ill. by Steven Guarnaccia. Viking, 1994. ISBN 0-670-84814-X Subj: Animals. Creation. Names.

MacFarland, Cynthia. *Cows in the parlor* photos by author. Atheneum, 1990. ISBN 0-689-31584-8 Subj: Animals – bulls, cows. Farms.

McFarland, John. *The exploding frog and other fables from Æsop* retold by John McFarland; ill. by James Marshall. Little, 1981. ISBN 0-316-55576-2 Subj: Folk & fairy tales.

McFarland, Lyn Rossiter. *The pirate's parrot* ill. by Jim McFarland. Tricycle, 2000. ISBN 1-58246-014-0 Subj: Behavior – fighting, arguing. Behavior – mistakes. Birds – parakeets, parrots. Pirates. Toys – bears.

Widget & the puppy ill. by Jim McFarland. Farrar, 2004. ISBN 0-374-38429-0 Subj: Animals – cats. Animals – dogs. Behavior – lost.

McFarlane, Sheryl. *Eagle dreams* ill. by Ron Lightburn. Philomel, 1994. ISBN 0-399-22695-8 Subj: Animals – endangered animals. Birds – eagles. Character traits – kindness to animals.

Going to the fair ill. by Sheena Lott. Orca, 1996. ISBN 1-55143-062-2 Subj: Fairs, festivals.

In the city ill. by Kim LaFave. Fitzhenry & Whiteside, 2004. ISBN 1-55041-812-2 Subj: Cities, towns. Format, unusual – board books. Noise, sounds.

On the farm ill. by Kim LaFave. Fitzhenry & Whiteside, 2004. ISBN 1-55041-814-9 Subj: Animals. Farms. Format, unusual – board books. Noise, sounds.

Waiting for the whales ill. by Ron Lightburn. Philomel, 1993. ISBN 0-399-22515-3 Subj: Animals – whales. Death. Family life – grandfathers.

McGaw, Wayne T. *T-boy of the bayou* ill. by George Crespo. Carolrhoda, 2002. ISBN 0-87614-648-5 Subj: Birds – herons. Careers – fishermen. Crustaceans – shrimp. Fish. Magic.

McGee, Barbara. *Counting sheep* ill. by author. Firefly, 1991. ISBN 1-55037-157-6 Subj: Animals – sheep. Counting, numbers.

McGee, Marni. *The colt and the king* ill. by John Winch. Holiday, 2002. ISBN 0-8234-1695-X Subj: Animals – donkeys. Holidays. Religion.

The noisy farm ill. by Leonie Shearing. Bloomsbury, 2004. ISBN 1-58234-879-0 Subj: Animals. Day. Farms. Noise, sounds.

The quiet farmer ill. by Lynne Dennis. Atheneum, 1991. ISBN 0-689-31678-X Subj: Animals. Farms. Noise, sounds.

Sleepy me ill. by Sam Williams. S&S, 2001. ISBN 0-689-82378-9 Subj: Bedtime. Family life – fathers. Rhyming text.

Wake up, me! ill. by Sam Williams. S&S, 2002. ISBN 0-689-83163-3 Subj: Behavior. Family life – parents. Morning. Rhyming text.

McGee, Shelagh. *I'm a little teapot* ill. by author. Doubleday, 1992. ISBN 0-385-30324-6 Subj: Games. Nursery rhymes. Songs.

McGeorge, Constance W. *Boomer goes to school* ill. by Mary Whyte. Chronicle, 1996. ISBN 0-8118-1117-4 Subj: Animals – dogs. Pets. School.

Boomer's big day ill. by Mary Whyte. Chronicle, 1994. ISBN 0-8118-0526-3 Subj: Animals – dogs. Moving. Pets.

Boomer's big surprise ill. by Mary Whyte. Chronicle, 1999. ISBN 0-8118-1977-9 Subj: Animals – babies. Animals – dogs. Emotions – envy, jealousy.

McGhee, Alison. *Countdown to kindergarten* ill. by Harry Bliss. Harcourt, 2002. ISBN 0-15-202516-2 Subj: Emotions – fear. School – first day.

In the hollow of your hand ill. by Michael Cummings. Houghton, 2000. ISBN 0-395-85755-4 Subj: Ethnic groups in the U.S. – African Americans. Lullabies. Slavery. Sleep.

McGill, Alice. *Molly Bannaky* ill. by Chris K. Soentpiet. Houghton Mifflin, 1999. ISBN 0-395-72287-X Subj: Books, reading. Ethnic groups in the U.S. – African Americans. Farms. Immigrants. Marriage, interracial. Slavery. U.S. history.

Sure as sunrise: stories of Bruh Rabbit & his walkin' talkin' friends ill. by Don Tate. Houghton, 2004. ISBN 0-618-21196-9 Subj: Animals. Ethnic groups in the U.S. – African Americans. Folk & fairy tales. Tall tales.

MacGill-Callahan, Sheila. *And still the turtle watched* ill. by Barry Moser. Dial, 1991. ISBN 0-8037-0932-3 Subj: Art. Family life – grandfathers. Folk & fairy tales. Indians of North America – Delaware. Progress. Reptiles – turtles, tortoises.

The children of Lir ill. by Gennady Spirin. Dial, 1993. ISBN 0-8037-1122-0 Subj: Birds – swans. Folk & fairy tales. Foreign lands – Ireland. Magic. Royalty – kings.

Finn MacCool and the talking fish ill. by John Thompson. Dial, 1998. ISBN 0-8037-1537-4 Subj: Fish. Folk & fairy tales. Foreign lands – Ireland.

The last snake in Ireland ill. by Will Hillenbrand. Holiday, 1999. ISBN 0-8234-1425-6 Subj: Folk & fairy tales. Foreign lands – Ireland. Monsters. Reptiles – snakes. Tall tales.

The seal prince ill. by Kris Waldherr. Dial, 1995. ISBN 0-8037-1487-4 Subj: Animals – seals. Folk & fairy tales. Foreign lands – Scotland. Mythical creatures – selkies.

To capture the wind ill. by Gregory Manchess. Dial, 1997. ISBN 0-8037-1542-0 Subj: Boats, ships. Folk & fairy tales. Foreign lands – Ireland. Inventions. Pirates.

When Solomon was king ill. by Stephen T. Johnson. Dial, 1995. ISBN 0-8037-1590-0 Subj: Animals. Folk & fairy tales. Jewish culture. Royalty – kings.

McGillicuddy, Mr. *see* Abisch, Roz

McGinley, Phyllis. *All around the town* ill. by Helen Stone. Lippincott, 1948. Subj: ABC books. Caldecott award honor books. Cities, towns. Rhyming text.

The horse who lived upstairs ill. by Helen Stone. Lippincott, 1944. Subj: Animals – horses, ponies. Behavior – dissatisfaction.

How Mrs. Santa Claus saved Christmas ill. by Kurt Werth. Lippincott, 1963. Subj: Holidays – Christmas. Rhyming text. Santa Claus.

Lucy McLockett ill. by Helen Stone. Lippincott, 1958. Subj: Behavior – lost & found possessions. Family life. Rhyming text. Teeth.

The most wonderful doll in the world ill. by Helen Stone. Lippincott, 1950. ISBN 0-590-43476-4 Subj: Caldecott award honor books. Toys – dolls.

Wonderful time ill. by John Alcorn. Lippincott, 1966. Subj: Clocks, watches. Rhyming text. Time.

McGinley-Nally, Sharon. *The friendly beasts* ill. by author. Greenwillow, 2000. ISBN 0-688-17422-1 Subj: Animals. Holidays – Christmas. Music. Religion – Nativity. Songs.

McGinnis, Lila Sprague. *If Daddy only knew me* ill. by Diane Paterson. A. Whitman, 1995. ISBN 0-8075-3537-0 Subj: Behavior – needing someone. Family life – fathers. Family life – sisters.

McGinty, Alice B. *Ten little lambs* ill. by Melissa Sweet. Dial, 2002. ISBN 0-8037-2596-5 Subj: Animals – sheep. Counting, numbers. Night. Rhyming text. Sleep.

McGough, Roger. *Counting by numbers* ill. by Marketa Prachaticka. Viking, 1990. ISBN 0-670-82671-5 Subj: Counting, numbers. Rhyming text.

Until I met Dudley: how everyday things really work ill. by Chris Riddell. Walker, 1997. ISBN 0-8027-8624-3 Subj: Animals – dogs. Homes, houses. Machines.

What on earth can it be? ill. by Lydia Monks. Little Simon, 2002. ISBN 0-689-85351-3 Subj: Humorous stories. Poetry. Rhyming text.

McGovern, Ann. *Black is beautiful* photos by Hope Wurmfeld. Four Winds, 1969. Subj: Ethnic groups in the U.S. – African Americans.

Eggs on your nose ill. by Maxie Chambliss. Macmillan, 1987. ISBN 0-02-765750-7 Subj: Eggs. Food. Rhyming text.

Feeling mad, feeling sad, feeling bad, feeling glad photos by Hope Wurmfeld. Walker, 1977. ISBN 0-8027-6295-6 Subj: Emotions. Poetry.

Mr. Skinner's skinny house ill. by Mort Gerberg. Four Winds, 1980. ISBN 0-590-07620-5 Subj: Character traits – being different. Emotions – loneliness. Homes, houses.

Nicholas Bentley Stoningpot III ill. by Tomie de Paola. Holiday, 1982. ISBN 0-8234-0443-9 Subj: Behavior – boredom. Boats, ships. Emotions – loneliness. Islands.

Too much noise ill. by Simms Taback. Houghton Mifflin, 1967. ISBN 0-590-02435-3 Subj: Humorous stories. Noise, sounds.

Zoo, where are you? ill. by Ezra Jack Keats. HarperCollins, 1965. Subj: Zoos.

McGowan, Alan. *Sailing ships* by Alan McGowan & Ron van der Meer; ill. by Borje Svensson. Viking, 1984. ISBN 0-670-61529-3 Subj: Boats, ships. Format, unusual – toy & movable books.

McGowen, Tom (Thomas). *The only glupmaker in the U.S. Navy* ill. by author. A. Whitman, 1966. Subj: Activities – working. Careers – military.

McGrath, Barbara Barbieri. *Kellogg's froot loops color fun book* ill. by Frank Mazzola, Jr. HarperFestival, 2001. ISBN 0-694-01577-6 Subj: Concepts – color. Food. Format, unusual – board books. Picture puzzles. Rhyming text.

Kellogg's froot loops counting fun book ill. by Rob Bolster & Frank Mazzola, Jr. HarperCollins, 2000. ISBN 0-694-01506-7 Subj: Counting, numbers. Food. Rhyming text.

McGraw, Sheila. *Pussycats everywhere* ill. by author. Firefly, 2000. ISBN 1-55209-346-8 Subj: Animals – cats. Behavior – lost. Humorous stories.

MacGregor, Ellen. *Mr. Pingle and Mr. Buttonhouse* ill. by Paul Galdone. McGraw-Hill, 1957. Subj: Friendship.

Theodor Turtle ill. by Paul Galdone. McGraw-Hill, 1955. Subj: Behavior – forgetfulness. Participation. Reptiles – turtles, tortoises.

MacGregor, Marilyn. *Baby takes a trip* ill. by author. Macmillan, 1985. ISBN 0-02-761940-0 Subj: Babies. Character traits – curiosity. Wordless.

Helen the hungry bear ill. by author. Four Winds, 1987. ISBN 0-02-761950-8 Subj: Activities – picnicking. Animals – bears. Family life. Food.

On top ill. by author. Morrow, 1988. ISBN 0-688-07491-X Subj: Animals – sheep. Character traits – individuality. Wordless.

McGrory, Anik. *Mouton's impossible dream* ill. by author. Harcourt, 2000. ISBN 0-15-202195-7 Subj: Activities – ballooning. Animals – sheep. Behavior – wishing. Birds. Royalty – queens.

McGuinness-Kelly, Tracy-Lee. *Bad Cat puts on his top hat* ill. by author. Little, 2005. ISBN 0-316-60547-6 Subj: Animals – cats. Behavior – trickery.

McGuire, Leslie. *Baby night owl* ill. by Mary Szilagyi. Random House, 1989. ISBN 0-394-99986-X Subj: Bedtime. Birds – owls.

Who will play with Little Dinosaur? ill. by Norman Gorbaty. Random House, 1989. ISBN 0-394-82129-7 Subj: Dinosaurs. Prehistory.

McGuire, Paula. *Me and Clara and Baldwin the pony* (Inkiow, Dimiter)

Me and Clara and Casimir the cat (Inkiow, Dimiter)

Me and Clara and Snuffy the dog (Inkiow, Dimiter)

Me and my sister Clara (Inkiow, Dimiter)

McGuire, Richard. *Night becomes day* ill. by author. Viking, 1994. ISBN 0-670-85547-2 Subj: Time.

The orange book ill. by author. Rizzoli, 1992. ISBN 0-8478-1465-3 Subj: Counting, numbers. Food.

What goes around comes around ill. by author. Viking, 1995. ISBN 0-670-86396-3 Subj: Behavior – misbehavior. Circular tales. Toys – dolls.

What's wrong with this book? ill. by author. Viking, 1997. ISBN 0-670-86852-3 Subj: Clowns, jesters. Format, unusual – toy & movable books. Picture puzzles. Rhyming text.

McGuire-Turcotte, Casey A. *How Honu the turtle got his shell* ill. by Dick Sakahara. Raintree, 1991. ISBN 0-8172-2783-0 Subj: Folk & fairy tales – pourquoi tales. Hawaii. Reptiles – turtles, tortoises.

McGuirk, Leslie. *Snail boy* ill. by author. Candlewick, 2003. ISBN 0-7636-1259-6 Subj: Animals – snails. Behavior – needing someone. Concepts – size.

Tucker flips! ill. by author. Dutton, 1999. ISBN 0-525-46259-7 Subj: Activities – playing. Animals – dogs. Weather – snow.

Tucker off his rocker ill. by author. Dutton, 2000. ISBN 0-525-46398-4 Subj: Activities. Animals – dogs.

Tucker over the top ill. by author. Dutton, 2000. ISBN 0-525-46465-4 Subj: Animals – dogs. Circus.

McGurn, Patty. *Me and Marie* ill. by author. Crown, 1989. ISBN 0-517-57218-4 Subj: Animals – cats. Pets.

Machado, Ana Maria. *Nina Bonita* ill. by Rosana Faria; trans. from Spanish by Elena Iribarren. Kane/Miller, 1996. ISBN 0-916291-63-4 Subj: Animals – rabbits. Character traits – being different. Foreign lands – Brazil.

McHale, Ethel Kharasch. *Son of thunder: an old Lapp tale* ill. by Ruth Lercher Bornstein. Childrens Pr., 1974. ISBN 0-516-08856-4 Subj: Folk & fairy tales. Foreign lands – Lapland.

McHargue, Georgess. *Private zoo* ill. by Michael Foreman. Viking, 1975. ISBN 0-670-57859-2 Subj: Imagination. Shadows.

McHenry, E. B. *Poodlena* ill. by author. Bloomsbury, 2004. ISBN 1-58234-824-3 Subj: Activities – playing. Animals – dogs. Character traits – cleanliness. Rhyming text.

Machetanz, Fred. *A puppy named Gia* (Machetanz, Sara)

Machetanz, Sara. *A puppy named Gia* by Sara & Fred Machetanz; ill. by Fred Machetanz. Scribners, 1957. Subj: Animals – dogs. Eskimos.

Machotka, Hana. *Breathtaking noses* photos by author. Morrow, 1992. ISBN 0-688-09527-5 Subj: Anatomy – noses. Animals. Games.

Outstanding outsides ill. by author. Morrow, 1993. ISBN 0-688-11753-8 Subj: Anatomy – skin. Animals.

Pasta factory ill. by author. Houghton Mifflin, 1992. ISBN 0-395-60197-5 Subj: Food. Machines.

Terrific tails ill. by author. Morrow, 1994. ISBN 0-688-04563-4 Subj: Anatomy – tails. Animals.

What do you do at a petting zoo? photos by author. Morrow, 1990. ISBN 0-688-08738-8 Subj: Animals. Zoos.

What neat feet! photos by author. Morrow, 1990. ISBN 0-688-09475-9 Subj: Anatomy – feet. Animals. Games.

McIntire, Alta. *Follett beginning to read picture dictionary* ill. by Janet La Salle. Follett, 1959. Subj: Dictionaries.

Mack, Gail. *Yesterday's snowman* ill. by Erik Blegvad. Pantheon, 1979. ISBN 0-394-93662-0 Subj: Family life. Snowmen.

Mack, Stanley (Stan). *Ten bears in my bed: a goodnight countdown* ill. by author. Pantheon, 1974. ISBN 0-394-92902-0 Subj: Animals – bears. Bedtime. Counting, numbers. Songs.

Mack, Todd. *Princess Penelope* ill. by Julia Gran. Scholastic, 2003. ISBN 0-439-22436-5 Subj: Family life – parents. Royalty – princesses.

Mackall, Dandi Daley. *Off to Bethlehem!* ill. by R. W. Alley. HarperCollins, 2002. ISBN 0-694-01505-9 Subj: Religion – Nativity. Rhyming text.

McKaughan, Larry. *Why are your fingers cold?* ill. by Joy Dunn Keenan. Herald Pr., 1992. ISBN 0-8361-3604-7 Subj: Character traits – questioning. Family life.

Mackay, Claire. *Bats about baseball* (Little, Jean)

McKay, George. *Marny's ride with the wind* (McKay, Louise)

McKay, Hilary. *Pirates ahoy!* ill. by Alex Ayliffe. McElderry, 2000. ISBN 0-689-83114-5 Subj: Activities – playing. Family life – cousins. Family life – grandmothers. Imagination.

Where's bear? ill. by Alex Ayliffe. McElderry, 1998. ISBN 0-689-82271-5 Subj: Character traits – cleanliness. Family life. Toys – bears.

MacKay, Jed. *The big secret* ill. by Heather Collins. Firefly, 1984. ISBN 0-920236-88-X Subj: Adoption. Family life. Parties.

McKay, Lawrence. *Caravan* ill. by Darryl Ligasan. Lee & Low, 1995. ISBN 1-880000-23-7 Subj: Activities – trading. Activities – traveling. Family life – fathers. Family life – sons. Foreign lands – Afghanistan.

Journey home ill. by Dom & Keunhee Lee. Lee & Low, 1998. ISBN 1-880000-65-2 Subj: Activities – traveling. Ethnic groups in the U.S. – Vietnamese Americans. Family life – mothers. Foreign lands – Vietnam. Orphans.

McKay, Louise. *Marny's ride with the wind* by Louise & George McKay; ill. by Margaret Smetana. New Harbinger, 1979. Subj: Friendship. Weather – wind.

McKay, Sindy. *About the rain forest* (Johanasen, Heather)

Jack and the beanstalk (Jack and the beanstalk)

McKean, Thomas. *Hooray for Grandma Jo!* ill. by Chris L. Demarest. Crown, 1994. ISBN 0-517-57843-3 Subj: Animals – lions. Behavior – lost & found possessions. Crime. Family life – grandmothers. Glasses. Zoos.

McKee, David. *The day the tide went out and out and out* ill. by author. Abelard-Schuman, 1975. Subj: Animals – camels. Desert. Sea & seashore.

Elmer ill. by author. Lothrop, 1989. ISBN 0-688-09172-5 Subj: Animals – elephants. Character traits – being different.

Elmer again ill. by author. Lothrop, 1991. ISBN 0-688-11597-7 Subj: Animals – elephants. Behavior – boredom.

Elmer and the kangaroo ill. by author. HarperCollins, 2000. ISBN 0-688-17951-7 Subj: Animals – elephants. Animals – kangaroos. Self-concept.

Elmer and the lost teddy ill. by author. Lothrop, 1999. ISBN 0-688-16912-0 Subj: Animals – elephants. Behavior – lost & found possessions. Toys – bears.

Elmer and the wind ill. by author. Lothrop, 1998. Subj: Activities – flying. Animals – elephants. Weather – wind.

Elmer and Wilbur ill. by author. Lothrop, 1996. ISBN 0-688-14934-0 Subj: Animals – elephants. Behavior – lost. Friendship.

Elmer in the snow ill. by author. Lothrop, 1995. ISBN 0-688-14596-5 Subj: Activities – playing. Animals – elephants. Friendship. Weather – snow.

Elmer takes off ill. by author. Lothrop, 1998. ISBN 0-688-15785-8 Subj: Activities – flying. Animals – elephants. Weather – wind.

Elmer's colors ill. by author. Lothrop, 1994. ISBN 0-688-13762-8 Subj: Animals – elephants. Concepts – color. Format, unusual – board books.

Elmer's day ill. by author. Lothrop, 1994. ISBN 0-688-13759-8 Subj: Animals – elephants. Format, unusual – board books.

Elmer's friends ill. by author. Lothrop, 1994. ISBN 0-688-13761-X Subj: Animals. Animals – elephants. Format, unusual – board books. Friendship.

Elmer's weather ill. by author. Lothrop, 1994. ISBN 0-688-13760-1 Subj: Animals – elephants. Format, unusual – board books. Weather.

The hill and the rock ill. by author. Ticknor & Fields, 1985. ISBN 0-89919-341-2 Subj: Behavior – seeking better things. Rocks.

I can too! an Elmer pop-up book ill. by author. Lothrop, 1997. ISBN 0-688-15547-2 Subj: Animals. Animals – elephants. Format, unusual – toy & movable books.

King Rollo and the birthday ill. by author. Little, 1979. Subj: Birthdays. Royalty – kings.

King Rollo and the bread ill. by author. Little, 1979. Subj: Food. Royalty – kings.

King Rollo and the new shoes ill. by author. Little, 1979. Subj: Clothing – shoes. Royalty – kings.

The man who was going to mind the house: a Norwegian folk-tale ill. by author. Abelard-Schuman, 1973. ISBN 0-200-71946-7 Subj: Folk & fairy tales.

The monster and the teddy bear ill. by author. Trafalgar Square, 1998. ISBN 0-86264-762-2 Subj: Behavior – wishing. Monsters. Toys – bears.

123456789 Benn ill. by author. McGraw-Hill, 1970. Subj: Crime. Mystery stories. Prisons.

Prince Peter and the teddy bear ill. by author. Farrar, 1997. ISBN 0-374-36123-1 Subj: Birthdays. Family life – fathers. Family life – mothers. Gifts. Royalty – princes. Toys – bears.

The sad story of Veronica who played the violin ill. by author. Kane/Miller, 1991. ISBN 0-916291-37-5 Subj: Animals. Careers – musicians. Music. Musical instruments – violins.

The school bus comes at eight o'clock ill. by author. Hyperion, 1994. ISBN 1-56282-663-8 Subj: Clocks, watches. Family life. Time.

Snow woman ill. by author. Lothrop, 1988. ISBN 0-688-07675-0 Subj: Family life. Snowmen.

Tusk tusk ill. by author. Kane/Miller, 1990, c1978. ISBN 0-916291-28-6 Subj: Animals – elephants. Behavior – fighting, arguing. War.

Two can toucan ill. by author. Abelard-Schuman, 1964. Subj: Birds – toucans. Names.

Two monsters ill. by author. Bradbury, 1986. ISBN 0-02-765760-4 Subj: Behavior – fighting, arguing. Monsters.

Zebra's hiccups ill. by author. S&S, 1993. ISBN 0-671-79440-X Subj: Animals. Animals – zebras. Hiccups.

McKee, Douglas. *Good night, Veronica* (Trez, Denise)

Maila and the flying carpet (Trez, Denise)

The royal hiccups (Trez, Denise)

MacKeen, Leslie Ann. *Who can fix it?* ill. by author. Landmark Editions, 1989. ISBN 0-933849-19-2 Subj: Animals. Automobiles. Children as authors. Children as illustrators.

McKeever, Katherine. *A family for Minerva* photos by author. Greey de Pencier Books, 1981. ISBN 0-910872-50-6 Subj: Birds – owls. Science.

McKelvey, David. *Bobby the mostly silky* ill. by author. Corona, 1984. ISBN 0-931722-28-4 Subj: Birds – chickens. Character traits – being different.

McKelvey, Douglas Kaine. *A child's Christmas at St. Nicholas Circle* ill. by Thomas Kinkade. Tommy Nelson, 1999. ISBN 0-8499-5883-0 Subj: Behavior – lost. Holidays – Christmas.

Locust pocus ill. by Richard Egielski. Philomel, 2001. ISBN 0-399-23452-7 Subj: Insects. Rhyming text.

Macken, JoAnn Early. *Cats on Judy* ill. by Judith DuFour Love. Whispering Coyote, 1997. ISBN 1-879085-73-9 Subj: Animals – cats. Emotions – love. Pets.

Goldfish ill. with photos. Weekly Reader, 2004. ISBN 0-8368-3797-5 Subj: Fish. Pets.

Guinea pigs ill. with photos. Weekly Reader, 2004. ISBN 0-8368-3798-3 Subj: Animals – guinea pigs. Pets.

Kittens ill. with photos. Weekly Reader, 2004. ISBN 0-8368-3799-1 Subj: Animals – babies. Animals – cats. Pets.

Parakeets ill. with photos. Weekly Reader, 2004. ISBN 0-8368-3800-9 Subj: Birds – parakeets, parrots. Pets.

Puppies ill. with photos. Weekly Reader, 2004. ISBN 0-8368-3801-7 Subj: Animals – babies. Animals – dogs. Pets.

Rabbits ill. with photos. Weekly Reader, 2004. ISBN 0-8368-3802-5 Subj: Animals – rabbits. Pets.

McKenna, Laura. *The giantess* (Hasler, Eveline)

The gift (Keselman, Gabriela)

Idora (Godard, Alex)

McKenna, Virginia. *Back to the blue* ill. by Ian Andrew. Millbrook, 1998. ISBN 0-7613-0409-6 Subj: Animals – dolphins. Character traits – freedom. Sea & seashore.

McKenzie, Ellen Kindt. *The perfectly orderly house* ill. by Megan Lloyd. Holt, 1994. ISBN 0-8050-1946-4 Subj: ABC books. Character traits – orderliness.

Mackie, Maron. *see* McNeely, Jeannette

McKié, Roy. *Noah's ark* ill. by author. Random House, 1984. ISBN 0-394-96584-1 Subj: Animals. Boats, ships. Religion – Noah. Weather – floods. Weather – rain. Weather – rainbows.

The riddle book ill. by author. Random House, 1978. ISBN 0-394-93732-5 Subj: Humorous stories. Riddles & jokes.

Snow by Roy McKié & P. D. Eastman; ill. by P. D. Eastman. Random House, 1962. ISBN 0-394-90027-8 Subj: Activities. Rhyming text. Weather – snow.

McKinley, Cindy. *One smile* ill. by Mary Gregg Byrne. Illumination, 2002. ISBN 0-935699-23-6 Subj: Character traits – kindness. Circular tales.

McKinley, Robin. *The light princess* (MacDonald, George)

My father is in the Navy ill. by Martine Gourbault. Greenwillow, 1992. ISBN 0-688-10640-4 Subj: Careers – military. Family life – fathers. Sailors.

Rowan ill. by Donna Ruff. Greenwillow, 1992. ISBN 0-688-10683-8 Subj: Animals – dogs. Pets.

McKinney, Barbara Shaw. *Pass the energy, please* ill. by Chad Wallace. Dawn, 1999. ISBN 1-58469-002-X Subj: Ecology. Food. Rhyming text.

MacKinnon, Debbie. *All about me* photos by Anthea Sieveking. Barron's, 1994. ISBN 0-8120-6348-1 Subj: Anatomy.

Baby's first year photos by Anthea Sieveking. Barron's, 1993. ISBN 0-8120-6334-1 Subj: Babies. Behavior – growing up.

Billy's boots photos by Anthea Sieveking. Dial, 1996. ISBN 0-8037-1905-1 Subj: Behavior – lost & found possessions. Clothing – boots. Format, unusual – toy & movable books.

Cathy's cake photos by Anthea Sieveking. Dial, 1996. ISBN 0-8037-1904-3 Subj: Behavior – lost & found possessions. Birthdays. Food. Format, unusual – toy & movable books. Parties.

Daniel's duck photos by Anthea Sieveking. Dial, 1997. ISBN 0-8037-2102-1 Subj: Activities – bathing. Birds – ducks. Format, unusual – toy & movable books. Toys.

Eye spy colors photos by Anthea Sieveking. Charlesbridge, 1998. ISBN 0-88106-334-7 Subj: Concepts – color. Format, unusual.

Eye spy shapes photos by Anthea Sieveking. Charlesbridge, 2000. ISBN 0-8810-6135-2 Subj: Concepts – shape. Format, unusual.

Find monkey! photos by Anthea Sieveking. Frances Lincoln, 1996. ISBN 0-7112-0923-5 Subj: Bedtime. Format, unusual – toy & movable books. Toys.

Find my boots! photos by Anthea Sieveking. Frances Lincoln, 1996. ISBN 0-7112-0922-7 Subj: Babies. Clothing. Format, unusual – toy & movable books.

Find my cake! photos by Anthea Sieveking. Frances Lincoln, 1996. ISBN 0-7112-0920-0 Subj: Birthdays. Food. Format, unusual – toy & movable books. Parties.

How many? photos by Anthea Sieveking. Dial, 1993. ISBN 0-8037-1253-7 Subj: Counting, numbers.

Ken's kitten photos by Anthea Sieveking. Dial, 1996. ISBN 0-8037-1903-5 Subj: Animals – cats. Behavior – lost & found possessions. Format, unusual – toy & movable books.

Let's play: I can do it! photos by Anthea Sieveking; paper engineered by Ania Mochlinska. Little, 1999. ISBN 0-316-64897-3 Subj: Activities – playing. Family life. Format, unusual – toy & movable books.

Meg's monkey photos by Anthea Sieveking. Dial, 1996. ISBN 0-8037-1907-8 Subj: Animals – monkeys. Behavior – lost & found possessions. Format, unusual – toy & movable books.

My day: I can do it! photos by Anthea Sieveking; paper engineered by Ania Mochlinska. Little, 1999. ISBN 0-316-64898-1 Subj: Activities. Format, unusual – toy & movable books.

My first ABC photos by Anthea Sieveking. Barron's, 1992. ISBN 0-8120-6331-7 Subj: ABC books. Ethnic groups in the U.S.

My kitty! photos by Anthea Sieveking. Frances Lincoln, 1996. ISBN 0-7112-0921-9 Subj: Animals – cats. Format, unusual – toy & movable books. Games.

Pippa's puppy photos by Anthea Sieveking. Dial, 1997. ISBN 0-8037-2104-8 Subj: Animals – dogs. Format, unusual – toy & movable books.

Sarah's shovel photos by Anthea Sieveking. Dial, 1997. ISBN 0-8037-2101-3 Subj: Format, unusual – toy & movable books. Sea & seashore. Toys.

The seasons: spring, summer, autumn, winter photos by Anthea Sieveking. Barron's, 1995. ISBN 0-8120-6422-4 Subj: Seasons.

Tom's train photos by Anthea Sieveking. Dial, 1997. ISBN 0-8037-2105-6 Subj: Family life – brothers. Format, unusual – toy & movable books. Multiple births – twins. Trains.

What am I? photos by Anthea Sieveking. Dial, 1996. ISBN 0-8037-1826-8 Subj: Activities – playing. Careers. Toys.

What noise? photos by Anthea Sieveking. Dial, 1994. ISBN 0-8037-1510-2 Subj: Noise, sounds.

What shape? photos by Anthea Sieveking. Dial, 1992. ISBN 0-8037-1244-8 Subj: Concepts – shape. Concepts – size.

What size? photos by Anthea Sieveking. Dial, 1995. ISBN 0-8037-1745-8 Subj: Concepts – size.

McKissack, Fredrick. *Big bug book of counting* (McKissack, Patricia C.)

Big bug book of opposites (McKissack, Patricia C.)

Big bug book of places to go (McKissack, Patricia C.)

Big bug book of the alphabet (McKissack, Patricia C.)

Booker T. Washington: leader and educator (McKissack, Patricia C.)

Cinderella (McKissack, Patricia C.)

Country mouse and city mouse (McKissack, Patricia C.)

King Midas and his gold (McKissack, Patricia C.)

The king's new clothes (McKissack, Patricia C.)

The little red hen (The little red hen)

Messy Bessey (McKissack, Patricia C.)

Messy Bessey = Ada, la desordenada (McKissack, Patricia C.)

Messy Bessey and the birthday overnight (McKissack, Patricia C.)

Messy Bessey's closet (McKissack, Patricia C.)

Messy Bessey's family reunion (McKissack, Patricia C.)

Messy Bessey's holidays (McKissack, Patricia C.)

My Bible ABC book (McKissack, Patricia C.)

Paul Robeson: a voice to remember (McKissack, Patricia C.)

Three billy goats Gruff (Asbjørnsen, P. C. [Peter Christen])

The ugly little duck (Andersen, H. C. [Hans Christian])

Who is coming? (McKissack, Patricia C.)

McKissack, Patricia C. *Big bug book of counting* by Patricia C. & Fredrick McKissack; ill. by Bartholomew. Milliken, 1987. ISBN 0-88335-762-3 Subj: Counting, numbers. Insects.

Big bug book of opposites by Patricia C. & Fredrick McKissack; ill. by Bartholomew. Milliken, 1987. ISBN 0-88335-763-1 Subj: Concepts – opposites. Insects.

Big bug book of places to go by Patricia C. & Fredrick McKissack; ill. by Bartholomew. Milliken, 1987. ISBN 0-88335-765-8 Subj: Activities – traveling. Insects.

Big bug book of the alphabet by Patricia C. & Fredrick McKissack; ill. by Bartholomew. Milliken, 1987. ISBN 0-88335-764-X Subj: ABC books. Insects.

Booker T. Washington: leader and educator by Patricia C. & Fredrick McKissack; photos by Michael Bryant. Enslow, 1992. ISBN 0-89490-314-4 Subj: Careers – clergy. Careers – teachers. Ethnic groups in the U.S. – African Americans. U.S. history.

Cinderella by Patricia C. & Fredrick McKissack; ill. by Tom Dunnington. Childrens Pr., 1985. ISBN 0-516-02361-6 Subj: Family life – stepfamilies. Folk & fairy tales. Royalty – princes. Sibling rivalry.

Country mouse and city mouse by Patricia C. & Fredrick McKissack; ill. by Anne Sikorski. Childrens Pr., 1985. ISBN 0-516-02362-4 Subj: Animals – mice. Cities, towns. Country.

Flossie and the fox ill. by Rachel Isadora. Dial, 1986. ISBN 0-8037-0251-5 Subj: Animals – foxes. Ethnic groups in the U.S. – African Americans.

Goin' someplace special ill. by Jerry Pinkney. Atheneum, 2001. ISBN 0-689-81885-8 Subj: Ethnic groups in the U.S. – African Americans. Prejudice. U.S. history.

The honest-to-goodness truth ill. by Giselle Potter. Atheneum, 2000. ISBN 0-689-82668-0 Subj: Behavior – lying. Character traits – honesty. Ethnic groups in the U.S. – African Americans.

King Midas and his gold by Patricia C. & Fredrick McKissack; ill. by Tom Dunnington. Childrens Pr., 1986. ISBN 0-516-03984-9 Subj: Behavior – greed. Behavior – wishing. Royalty – kings.

The king's new clothes by Patricia C. & Fredrick McKissack; ill. by Gwen Connelly. Childrens Pr., 1987. ISBN 0-516-02365-9 Subj: Character traits – pride. Character traits – vanity. Clothing. Humorous stories. Imagination. Royalty – kings.

The little red hen (The little red hen)

Ma Dear's aprons ill. by Floyd Cooper. Atheneum, 1997. ISBN 0-689-81051-2 Subj: Careers – housekeepers. Clothing – aprons. Ethnic groups in the U.S. – African Americans.

Messy Bessey by Patricia C. & Frederick McKissack; ill. by Dana Regan. Childrens Pr., 1999. ISBN 0-516-21650-3 Subj: Behavior – messy. Character traits – cleanliness. Character traits – orderliness. Ethnic groups in the U.S. – African Americans.

Messy Bessey = Ada, la desordenada by Patricia C. & Fredrick McKissack; ill. by Richard Hackney. Childrens Pr., 1988. ISBN 0-516-32083-1 Subj: Behavior – messy. Character traits – cleanliness. Ethnic groups in the U.S. – African Americans. Foreign languages.

Messy Bessey and the birthday overnight by Patricia C. & Fredrick McKissack; ill. by Dana Regan. Childrens Pr., 1998. ISBN 0-516-20828-4 Subj: Birthdays. Character traits – cleanliness. Character traits – helpfulness. Friendship. Rhyming text. Sleepovers.

Messy Bessey's closet by Patricia C. & Fredrick McKissack; ill. by Richard Hackney. Childrens Pr., 1989. ISBN 0-516-02091-9 Subj: Behavior – messy. Ethnic groups in the U.S. – African Americans. Rhyming text.

Messy Bessey's family reunion by Patricia & Fredrick McKissack; ill. by Dana Regan. Childrens Pr., 2000. ISBN 0-516-20830-6 Subj: Character traits – cleanliness. Ethnic groups in the U.S. – African Americans. Family life. Parks.

Messy Bessey's holidays by Patricia C. & Fredrick McKissack; ill. by Dana Regan. Childrens Pr., 1999. ISBN 0-516-20829-2 Subj: Activities – baking, cooking. Character traits – cleanliness. Ethnic

groups in the U.S. – African Americans. Holidays – Christmas. Holidays – Hanukkah. Holidays – Kwanzaa. Rhyming text.

A million fish . . . more or less ill. by Dena Schutzer. Knopf, 1992. ISBN 0-679-90692-4 Subj: Folk & fairy tales. Sports – fishing. Tall tales.

Mirandy and brother wind ill. by Jerry Pinkney. Knopf, 1988. ISBN 0-394-88765-4 Subj: Activities – dancing. Caldecott award honor books. Ethnic groups in the U.S. – African Americans. Folk & fairy tales.

My Bible ABC book by Patricia C. & Fredrick McKissack; ill. by Reed Merrill. Augsburg Fortress, 1987. ISBN 0-8066-2271-7 Subj: ABC books. Religion.

Nettie Jo's friends ill. by Scott Cook. Knopf, 1989. ISBN 0-394-99158-3 Subj: Clothing. Family life. Toys – dolls.

Paul Robeson: a voice to remember by Patricia C. & Fredrick McKissack; photos by Michael David Biegel. Enslow, 1992. ISBN 0-89490-310-1 Subj: Careers – actors. Careers – singers. Ethnic groups in the U.S. – African Americans. U.S. history.

Three billy goats Gruff (Asbjørnsen, P. C. [Peter Christen])

The ugly little duck (Andersen, H. C. [Hans Christian])

Who is coming? by Patricia C. & Fredrick McKissack; ill. by Clovis Martin. Childrens Pr., 1986. Prepared under the direction of Robert Hillerick. ISBN 0-516-02073-0 Subj: Animals – monkeys. Behavior – running away. Foreign lands – Africa. Safety.

Who is who? ill. by Elizabeth M. Allen. Childrens Pr., 1983. ISBN 0-516-02042-0 Subj: Multiple births – twins.

McKissack, Robert L. *Try your best* ill. by Joe Cepeda. Harcourt, 2004. ISBN 0-15-205089-2 Subj: Careers – teachers. School. Self-concept. Sports.

MacLachlan, Emily. *Bittle* (MacLachlan, Patricia)

Painting the wind (MacLachlan, Patricia)

MacLachlan, Patricia. *All the places to love* ill. by Mike Wimmer. HarperCollins, 1994. ISBN 0-06-021099-0 Subj: Babies. Birth. Country. Family life. Farms.

Bittle by Patricia MacLachlan & Emily MacLachlan; ill. by Dan Yaccarino. Cotler, 2004. ISBN 0-06-000962-4 Subj: Animals – cats. Animals – dogs. Babies. Pets.

Mama one, Mama two ill. by Ruth Lercher Bornstein. HarperCollins, 1982. ISBN 0-06-024082-2 Subj: Family life – mothers. Illness.

Moon, stars, frogs and friends ill. by Tomie de Paola. Pantheon, 1980. ISBN 0-394-94138-1 Subj: Friendship. Frogs & toads. Witches.

Painting the wind by Patricia MacLachlan & Emily MacLachlan; ill. by Katy Schneider. Cotler, 2003. ISBN 0-06-029799-9 Subj: Activities – painting. Careers – artists. Islands.

The sick day ill. by Jane Dyer. Random House, 2001. ISBN 0-385-90007-4 Subj: Family life – fathers. Illness.

Three names ill. by Alexander Pertzoff. HarperCollins, 1991. ISBN 0-06-024036-9 Subj: Animals – dogs. Family life – great-grandparents. Names. School.

What you know first ill. with engravings by Barry Moser. HarperCollins, 1995. ISBN 0-06-024414-3 Subj: Country. Emotions. Farms. Moving. U.S. history – frontier & pioneer life.

Who loves me? ill. by Amanda Shepherd. Cotler, 2005. ISBN 0-06-027977-X Subj: Animals – cats. Animals – dogs. Emotions – love. Family life.

McLaren, Chesley. *Zat cat* ill. by author. Scholastic, 2002. ISBN 0-439-27316-1 Subj: Animals – cats. Foreign lands – France. Rhyming text.

McLarey, Kristina Thermaenius. *When you take a pig to a party* Kristina Thermaenius McLarey & Myra McLarey; ill. by Marjory Wunsch. Orchard, 2000. ISBN 0-531-33257-8 Subj: Animals – pigs. Humorous stories. Parties.

McLarey, Majorie. *When you take a pig to a party* (McLarey, Kristina Thermaenius)

McLaughlin, Lissa. *Why won't winter go?* ill. by author. Lothrop, 1983. ISBN 0-688-02381-9 Subj: Behavior – boredom. Seasons – winter.

McLean, Dirk. *Play mas'! a carnival ABC* ill. by author. Tundra, 2000. ISBN 0-88776-486-X Subj: ABC books. Fairs, festivals. Foreign lands – Caribbean Islands. Foreign languages. Language.

McLean, Janet. *Dog tales* ill. by Andrew McLean. Ticknor & Fields, 1995. ISBN 0-395-72288-8 Subj: Animals – dogs. Rhyming text.

Josh ill. by Andrew McLean. Allen & Unwin, 1997. ISBN 1-86448-362-8 Subj: Animals – dogs. Day. Friendship. Pets.

MacLean, Kerry Lee. *Peaceful piggy meditation* ill. by author. A. Whitman, 2004. ISBN 0-8075-6380-3 Subj: Animals – pigs. Careers – artists. Careers – authors.

McLean, Virginia O. *Kenya, jambo!* by Virginia O. McLean & Katherine P. Klyce; ill. with photos & black-and-white drawings. Redbird Pr., 1989. Accompanying cassette by Regina and Evans Okuth. ISBN 0-9606046-4-2 Subj: Foreign lands – Kenya.

McLean-Carr, Carol. *Fairy dreams* ill. by author. Scholastic, 1999. ISBN 0-439-19257-9 Subj: Behavior – lost & found possessions. Fairies. Picture puzzles. Rhyming text.

McLeish, Kenneth. *Chicken Licken* (Chicken Little)

McLellan, Stephanie Simpson. *The chicken cat* ill. by Sean Cassidy. Fitzhenry & Whiteside, 2000. ISBN 1-55041-531-X Subj: Activities – flying. Animals – babies. Animals – cats. Birds – chickens. Ethnic groups in the U.S. – African Americans. Friendship.

McLenighan, Valjean. *I know you cheated* photos by Brent Jones. Raintree, 1977. ISBN 0-8172-0962-X Subj: Character traits – honesty. School.

One whole doughnut, one doughnut hole ill. by Steven Roger Cole. Childrens Pr., 1982. ISBN 0-516-02031-5 Subj: Books, reading.

Stop-go, fast-slow ill. by Margrit Fiddle. Childrens Pr., 1982. ISBN 0-516-03617-3 Subj: Concepts – opposites.

Three strikes and you're out ill. by Laurie Hamilton. Follett, 1980. ISBN 0-695-41462-3 Subj: Behavior – greed. Magic.

Turtle and rabbit ill. by Vernon McKissack. Follett, 1980. ISBN 0-695-41461-5 Subj: Animals – rabbits. Folk & fairy tales. Reptiles – turtles, tortoises. Sports – racing.

What you see is what you get ill. by Dev Appleyard. Four Winds, 1980. ISBN 0-695-41370-8 Subj: Character traits – pride. Clothing. Folk & fairy tales. Humorous stories. Imagination. Royalty.

You are what you are ill. by Jack Reilly. Follett, 1977. ISBN 0-695-40748-1 Subj: Folk & fairy tales. Frogs & toads. Royalty.

You can go jump ill. by Jared D. Lee. Follett, 1977. ISBN 0-695-40744-9 Subj: Emotions – envy, jealousy. Folk & fairy tales. Magic. Mythical creatures. Witches.

McLeod, Elaine. *Lessons from Mother Earth* ill. by Colleen Wood. Douglas & McIntyre, 2002. ISBN 0-88899-312-9 Subj: Family life – grandmothers. Gardens, gardening. Indians of North America. Nature.

MacLeod, Elizabeth. *I heard a little baa* ill. by Louise Phillips. Kids Can, 1998. ISBN 1-55074-496-8 Subj: Animals. Noise, sounds. Rhyming text. Toys – bears.

What did dinosaurs eat? ill. by Gordon Sauvé. Kids Can, 2001. ISBN 1-55337-460-6 Subj: Dinosaurs.

McLeod, Emilie Warren. *The bear's bicycle* ill. by David McPhail. Little, 1975. ISBN 0-316-56203-3 Subj: Safety. Sports – bicycling. Toys – bears.

One snail and me: a book of numbers and animals and a bathtub ill. by Walter Lorraine. Little, 1961. ISBN 0-316-56198-3 Subj: Activities – bathing. Animals. Counting, numbers. Imagination.

McLerran, Alice. *Dreamsong* ill. by Valery Vasiliev. Morrow, 1992. ISBN 0-688-10106-2 Subj: Dreams. Songs.

The ghost dance ill. by Paul Morin. Clarion, 1995. ISBN 0-395-63168-8 Subj: Activities – dancing. Indians of North America. Religion.

Hugs ill. by Mary Morgan. Scholastic, 1993. ISBN 0-590-44637-1 Subj: Emotions. Rhyming text.

I want to go home ill. by Jill Kastner. Morrow, 1992. ISBN 0-688-10145-3 Subj: Animals – cats. Moving.

Kisses ill. by Mary Morgan. Scholastic, 1993. ISBN 0-590-44711-4 Subj: Kissing. Rhyming text.

The mountain that loved a bird ill. by Eric Carle. Alphabet Pr., 1985. ISBN 0-88708-000-6 Subj: Behavior – needing someone. Birds. Character traits – loyalty. Emotions – sadness.

Roxaboxen ill. by Barbara Cooney. Lothrop, 1991. ISBN 0-688-07593-2 Subj: Activities – playing. Desert. Imagination.

The year of the ranch ill. by Kimberly Bulcken Root. Viking, 1996. ISBN 0-670-85131-0 Subj: Desert. Dreams. Family life. U.S. history – frontier & pioneer life.

McMahon, Patricia. *Listen for the bus: David's story* photos by John Godt. Boyds Mills, 1995. ISBN 1-56397-368-5 Subj: Buses. Handicaps – blindness. School – first day.

McMillan, Bruce. *The alphabet symphony: an ABC book* photos by author. Greenwillow, 1977. ISBN 0-688-84112-0 Subj: ABC books. Music. Musical instruments – orchestras.

Beach ball – left, right photos by author. Holiday, 1992. ISBN 0-8234-0946-5 Subj: Concepts – left & right. Toys – balls.

Becca backward, Becca forward photos by author. Lothrop, 1986. ISBN 0-688-06283-0 Subj: Concepts. Concepts – opposites.

Counting wildflowers ill. by author. Lothrop, 1986. ISBN 0-688-02860-8 Subj: Counting, numbers. Flowers. Science.

Days of the ducklings photos by author. Houghton, 2001. ISBN 0-618-04878-2 Subj: Birds – ducks. Ecology. Foreign lands – Iceland. Islands.

Dry or wet? photos by author. Lothrop, 1988. ISBN 0-688-07101-5 Subj: Concepts.

Eating fractions photos by author. Scholastic, 1991. ISBN 0-590-43770-4 Subj: Counting, numbers.

Fire engine shapes photos by author. Lothrop, 1988. ISBN 0-688-07843-5 Subj: Concepts – shape.

Ghost doll ill. by author. Houghton Mifflin, 1983. ISBN 0-395-33073-4 Subj: Ghosts. Toys – dolls.

Gletta the foal ill. by author. Cavendish, 1998. ISBN 0-7614-5039-4 Subj: Animals – horses, ponies. Foreign lands – Iceland. Noise, sounds.

Going on a whale watch ill. by author. Scholastic, 1992. ISBN 0-590-45768-3 Subj: Animals – whales. Boats, ships.

Grandfather's trolley photos by author. Candlewick, 1995. ISBN 1-56402-633-7 Subj: Cable cars, trolleys. Family life – grandfathers.

Growing colors photos by author. Lothrop, 1988. ISBN 0-688-07845-1 Subj: Concepts – color.

Here a chick, there a chick photos by author. Lothrop, 1983. ISBN 0-688-02001-1 Subj: Concepts – opposites.

Jelly beans for sale photos by author. Scholastic, 1996. ISBN 0-590-86584-6 Subj: Counting, numbers. Money.

Kitten can . . . photos by author. Lothrop, 1984. ISBN 0-688-02669-9 Subj: Animals – cats.

Mouse views: what the class pet saw ill. by author. Holiday, 1993. ISBN 0-8234-1008-0 Subj: Animals – mice. Picture puzzles. School.

Nights of the pufflings photos by author. Houghton Mifflin, 1995. ISBN 0-395-70810-9 Subj: Birds – puffins. Character traits – kindness to animals. Foreign lands – Iceland.

One sun: a book of terse verse photos by author. Holiday, 1990. ISBN 0-8234-0810-8 Subj: Language. Poetry. Sea & seashore.

One, two, one pair! photos by author. Scholastic, 1991. ISBN 0-590-43767-4 Subj: Concepts. Counting, numbers.

Play day: a book of terse verse photos by author. Holiday, 1991. ISBN 0-8234-0894-9 Subj: Activities – playing. Language. Poetry.

Puffins climb, penguins rhyme photos by author. Harcourt, 1995. ISBN 0-15-200362-2 Subj: Birds – penguins. Birds – puffins. Rhyming text.

Sense suspense: a guessing game for the five senses photos by author. Scholastic, 1994. ISBN 0-590-47904-0 Subj: Concepts. Foreign lands – Caribbean Islands. Senses.

Step by step photos by author. Lothrop, 1987. ISBN 0-688-07234-8 Subj: Activities. Babies.

Super, super, superwords photos by author. Lothrop, 1989. ISBN 0-688-08099-5 Subj: Language.

Time to . . . photos by author. Lothrop, 1989. ISBN 0-688-08856-2 Subj: Clocks, watches. Time.

McMullan, Jim. *No no Jo* (McMullan, Kate [Hall])

McMullan, Kate (Hall). *Baby Goose* ill. by Pascal Lemaître. Hyperion, 2002. ISBN 0-7868-2380-1 Subj: Nursery rhymes.

Batty riddles by Katy Hall & Lisa Eisenberg; ill. by Nicole Rubel. Dial, 1993. ISBN 0-8037-1218-9 Subj: Animals – bats. Riddles & jokes.

Bunny riddles by Katy Hall & Lisa Eisenberg; ill. by Nicole Rubel. Dial, 1997. ISBN 0-8037-1521-8 Subj: Animals – rabbits. Riddles & jokes.

Chickie riddles by Katy Hall & Lisa Eisenberg; ill. by Thor Wickstrom. Dial, 1997. ISBN 0-8037-1779-2 Subj: Birds – chickens. Riddles & jokes.

Creepy riddles by Katy Hall & Lisa Eisenberg; ill. by S. D. Schindler. Dial, 1998. ISBN 0-8037-1685-0 Subj: Ghosts. Monsters. Riddles & jokes. Witches.

Dinosaur riddles by Katy Hall & Lisa Eisenberg; ill. by Nicole Rubel. Dial, 2002. ISBN 0-8037-2239-7 Subj: Dinosaurs. Prehistory. Riddles & jokes.

Fishy riddles by Katy Hall & Lisa Eisenberg; ill. by Simms Taback. Puffin, 1993. ISBN 0-14-036546-X Subj: Fish. Riddles & jokes.

Good night, Stella ill. by Emma Chichester Clark. Candlewick, 1994. ISBN 1-56402-065-7 Subj: Bedtime. Emotions – fear. Imagination. Sleep.

Hearty har har: Valentine riddles you'll love by Katy Hall & Lisa Eisenberg; ill. by R. W. Alley. HarperFestival, 1997. ISBN 0-694-00691-2 Subj: Format, unusual – toy & movable books. Holidays – Valentine's Day. Riddles & jokes.

Hey, Pipsqueak! ill. by Jim McMullan. HarperCollins, 1995. ISBN 0-06-205101-6 Subj: Behavior – bullying. Mythical creatures – trolls. Parties.

I stink! by Kate and Jim McMullan; ill. by Jim McMullan. Colter, 2002. ISBN 0-06-029849-9 Subj: Careers – sanitation workers. Trucks.

If you were my bunny ill. by David McPhail. Scholastic, 1996. ISBN 0-590-52749-5 Subj: Animals – babies. Babies. Bedtime. Family life – mothers. Lullabies.

Kitty riddles by Katy Hall & Lisa Eisenberg; ill. by R. W. Alley. Dial, 2000. ISBN 0-8037-2121-8 Subj: Animals – cats. Riddles & jokes.

Mummy riddles by Katy Hall & Lisa Eisenberg; ill. by Nicole Rubel. Dial, 1997. ISBN 0-8037-1847-0 Subj: Foreign lands – Egypt. Riddles & jokes.

No no Jo by Kate & Jim McMullan; ill. by Jim McMullan. HarperCollins, 1997. ISBN 0-694-00904-0 Subj: Animals – cats. Character traits – helpfulness. Format, unusual – toy & movable books.

Noel the first ill. by Jim McMullan. HarperCollins, 1996. ISBN 0-06-205142-3 Subj: Activities – dancing. Ballet. Character traits – pride.

The noisy giant's tea party ill. by Jim McMullan. HarperCollins, 1992. ISBN 0-06-205018-4 Subj: Dreams. Imagination. Sleep.

Nutcracker Noel ill. by Jim McMullan. HarperCollins, 1993. ISBN 0-06-205040-0 Subj: Activities – dancing. Ballet. Careers – toy makers. Emotions – envy, jealousy.

Papa's song ill. by Jim McMullan. Farrar, 2000. ISBN 0-374-35732-3 Subj: Animals – bears. Babies. Family life – fathers. Sleep.

Puppy riddles by Katy Hall & Lisa Eisenberg; ill. by Thor Wickstrom. Dial, 1998. ISBN 0-8037-2129-3 Subj: Animals – dogs. Riddles & jokes.

Rock-a-baby band ill. by Janie Bynum. Little, 2003. ISBN 0-316-60858-0 Subj: Babies. Music. Musical instruments – bands. Rhyming text.

Sheepish riddles by Katy Hall & Lisa Eisenberg; ill. by R. W. Alley. Dial, 1996. ISBN 0-8037-1536-6 Subj: Animals – sheep. Riddles & jokes.

Skeletons! Skeletons! All about bones ill. by Paige Billin-Frye. Grosset, 1991. ISBN 0-448-40108-8 Subj: Anatomy – skeletons.

Snakey riddles by Katy Hall & Lisa Eisenberg; ill. by Simms Taback. Dial, 1990. ISBN 0-8037-0670-7 Subj: Reptiles – snakes. Riddles & jokes.

Spacey riddles by Katy Hall & Lisa Eisenberg; ill. by Simms Taback. Dial, 1992. ISBN 0-8037-0815-7 Subj: Riddles & jokes. Space & space ships.

Supercat ill. by Pascal Lemaître. Workman, 2002. ISBN 0-7611-2644-9 Subj: Animals. Animals – babies. Animals – cats. Format, unusual – board books.

Supercat to the rescue ill. by Pascal Lemaître. Workman, 2003. ISBN 0-7611-2734-8 Subj: Animals – cats. Animals – mice. Babies.

Trick or eeek! by Katy Hall & Lisa Eisenberg; ill. by R. W. Alley. HarperFestival, 1996. ISBN 0-694-00693-9 Subj: Format, unusual – toy & movable books. Holidays – Halloween. Riddles & jokes.

McMullen, Eunice. *Dragon for breakfast* by Eunice & Nigel McMullen; ill. by authors. Carolrhoda, 1990. ISBN 0-87614-650-7 Subj: Dragons. Royalty – kings.

McMullen, Nigel. *Dragon for breakfast* (McMullen, Eunice)

McNally, Darcie. *In a cabin in a wood* ill. by Robin Michal Koontz. Dutton, 1991. ISBN 0-525-65035-0 Subj: Animals. Character traits – kindness to animals. Music. Songs.

McNally, John. *Northern lights* ill. with photos. Washington Writers, 1977. Subj: Northern lights. Poetry.

McNaught, Harry. *Baby animals* ill. by author. Random House, 1976. ISBN 0-394-83241-8 Subj: Animals. Format, unusual – board books.

The truck book ill. by author. Random House, 1978. ISBN 0-394-93703-1 Subj: Transportation. Trucks.

Words to grow on ill. by author. Random House, 1984. ISBN 0-394-96103-X Subj: Language.

McNaughton, Colin. *At home* ill. by author. Putnam, 1982. ISBN 0-399-20878-X Subj: Concepts – opposites. Format, unusual – board books.

At playschool ill. by author. Putnam, 1982. ISBN 0-399-20875-5 Subj: Concepts – opposites. Format, unusual – board books. School – nursery.

At the park ill. by author. Putnam, 1982. ISBN 0-399-20879-8 Subj: Concepts – opposites. Format, unusual – board books. Parks.

At the party ill. by author. Putnam, 1982. ISBN 0-399-20877-1 Subj: Concepts – opposites. Format, unusual – board books. Parties.

At the stores ill. by author. Putnam, 1982. ISBN 0-399-20876-3 Subj: Concepts – opposites. Format, unusual – board books. Stores.

Autumn ill. by author. Dutton, 1983. ISBN 0-8037-0043-1 Subj: Activities. Format, unusual – board books. Seasons – fall.

Big bad pig (Ahlberg, Allan)

Boo! ill. by author. Harcourt, 1996. ISBN 0-15-200834-9 Subj: Animals – pigs. Disguises.

Captain Abdul's pirate school ill. by author. Candlewick, 1994. ISBN 1-56402-429-6 Subj: Behavior – misbehavior. Pirates. School.

Don't step on the crack! ill. by author. Dial, 2001. ISBN 0-8037-2611-2 Subj: Superstition.

Fee fi fo fum (Ahlberg, Allan)

Guess who's just moved in next door? ill. by author. Random House, 1991. ISBN 0-679-81802-2 Subj: Family life. Folk & fairy tales. Format, unusual. Moving.

Happy worm (Ahlberg, Allan)

Help! (Ahlberg, Allan)

Here come the aliens! ill. by author. Candlewick, 1995. ISBN 1-56402-642-6 Subj: Aliens. Space & space ships.

If dinosaurs were cats and dogs ill. by author. Four Winds, 1991. ISBN 0-02-765785-X Subj: Animals. Dinosaurs. Prehistory. Rhyming text.

Jolly Roger and the pirates of Captain Abdul ill. by author. Candlewick, 1995. ISBN 1-56402-512-8 Subj: Pirates.

Little boo! ill. by author. Harcourt, 2000. ISBN 0-15-202671-1 Subj: Animals – pigs.

Little goal! ill. by author. Harcourt, 2001. ISBN 0-15-202525-1 Subj: Animals – pigs.

Little oops! ill. by author. Harcourt, 2001. ISBN 0-15-202537-5 Subj: Animals – pigs.

Little suddenly! ill. by author. Harcourt, 2000. ISBN 0-15-202531-6 Subj: Animals – pigs.

Oomph! ill. by author. Harcourt, 2001. ISBN 0-15-216463-4 Subj: Animals – pigs. Animals – wolves. Emotions – love. Sea & seashore.

Oops! ill. by author. Harcourt, 1997. ISBN 0-15-201588-4 Subj: Animals – pigs. Animals – wolves. Character traits – cleverness.

Preston's goal! ill. by author. Harcourt, 1998. ISBN 0-15-201816-6 Subj: Animals – pigs. Animals – wolves. Character traits – clumsiness. Humorous stories. Sports – soccer.

The rat race: the amazing adventures of Anton B. Stanton ill. by author. Doubleday, 1978. ISBN 0-385-13620-X Subj: Animals – rats. Royalty. Sports – racing.

Shh! (Don't tell Mr. Wolf!) ill. by author. Harcourt, 1999. ISBN 0-15-202341-0 Subj: Animals – pigs. Animals – wolves. Behavior – hiding. Format, unusual – toy & movable books.

Spring ill. by author. Dial, 1984. ISBN 0-8037-0044-X Subj: Format, unusual – board books. Seasons – spring.

Suddenly! ill. by author. Harcourt, 1995. ISBN 0-15-200308-8 Subj: Animals – pigs. Animals – wolves. Humorous stories.

Summer ill. by author. Dial, 1984. ISBN 0-8037-0042-3 Subj: Format, unusual – board books. Seasons – summer.

Walk rabbit walk by Colin McNaughton & Elizabeth Attenborough; ill. by Colin McNaughton. Tambourine, 1992. ISBN 0-688-11375-3 Subj: Activities – walking. Animals – rabbits. Transportation.

Who's that banging on the ceiling? ill. by author. Candlewick, 1992. ISBN 1-56402-105-X Subj: Format, unusual – toy & movable books. Homes, houses. Imagination. Noise, sounds.

Winter ill. by author. Dutton, 1983. ISBN 0-8037-0040-7 Subj: Activities. Format, unusual – board books. Seasons – winter.

Yum! ill. by author. Harcourt, 1999. ISBN 0-15-202064-0 Subj: Animals – pigs. Animals – wolves. Careers.

McNaughton, Janet. *Brave Jack and the unicorn* ill. by Susan Tooke. Tundra, 2005. ISBN 0-88776-677-3 Subj: Character traits – kindness. Folk & fairy tales. Foreign lands – Canada. Magic. Mythical creatures – unicorns. Royalty – princesses.

McNeal, Laura. *The dog who lost his Bob* (McNeal, Tom)

McNeal, Tom. *The dog who lost his Bob* by Tom & Laura McNeal; ill. by John Sandford. A. Whitman, 1996. ISBN 0-8075-1662-7 Subj: Activities – bathing. Animals – dogs. Behavior – running away.

McNeely, Jeannette. *Where's Izzy?* ill. by Bill Morrison. Follett, 1972. ISBN 0-695-40318-4 Subj: Behavior – lost & found possessions. Pets. Reptiles – lizards.

McNeer, May Yonge. *Little Baptiste* ill. by Lynd Ward. Houghton Mifflin, 1954. Subj: Animals. Farms.

My friend Mac: the story of Little Baptiste and the moose ill. by Lynd Ward. Houghton Mifflin, 1960. ISBN 0-395-24371-8 Subj: Animals – moose. Emotions – loneliness.

McNeil, Florence. *Sail away* ill. by David McPhail. Orca, 2000. ISBN 1-55143-147-5 Subj: Boats, ships. Imagination. Pirates. Sports – sailing. Toys.

McNeill, Janet. *The giant's birthday* ill. by Walter Erhard. Walck, 1964. Subj: Birthdays. Giants.

McNulty, Faith. *The lady and the spider* ill. by Bob Marstall. HarperCollins, 1986. ISBN 0-06-024192-6 Subj: Character traits – kindness to animals. Spiders.

Mouse and Tim ill. by Marc Simont. HarperCollins, 1978. ISBN 0-06-024157-8 Subj: Animals – mice. Character traits – kindness to animals. Pets.

When a boy wakes up in the morning ill. by Leonard Weisgard. Knopf, 1962. Subj: Activities – playing. Morning. Noise, sounds.

Woodchuck ill. by Joan Sandin. HarperCollins, 1974. ISBN 0-06-024167-5 Subj: Animals – groundhogs. Science.

Maconie, Robin. *Alice and her fabulous teeth* ill. by Catherine Myler Fruisen. Cedco, 2000. ISBN 0-7683-2176-X Subj: Dreams. Fairies. Mythical creatures – elves. Rhyming text. Teeth.

McPartland, Suzy. *Good morning, sun* ill. by William Neeper. S&S, 1994. ISBN 0-689-71747-4 Subj: Format, unusual – toy & movable books. Morning. Rhyming text. Sun.

Sleepy-time moon ill. by William Neeper. S&S, 1994. ISBN 0-689-71748-2 Subj: Bedtime. Format, unusual – toy & movable books. Moon. Night. Rhyming text. Sleep.

Toy-shop surprise ill. by William Neeper. S&S, 1994. ISBN 0-689-71749-0 Subj: Format, unusual – toy & movable books. Rhyming text. Stores. Toys.

Zoom, car, zoom ill. by William Neeper. S&S, 1994. ISBN 0-689-71740-4 Subj: Automobiles. Country. Format, unusual – toy & movable books. Rhyming text.

McPhail, David M. *Adam's smile* ill. by author. Dutton, 1987. ISBN 0-525-44327-4 Subj: Dreams. Illness. Night.

Alligators are awful (and they have terrible manners, too) ill. by author. Doubleday, 1980. ISBN 0-385-13583-1 Subj: Humorous stories. Reptiles – alligators, crocodiles.

Andrew's bath ill. by author. Little, 1984. ISBN 0-316-56319-6 Subj: Activities – bathing. Animals. Behavior – misbehavior.

Animals A to Z ill. by author. Scholastic, 1988. ISBN 0-590-40715-5 Subj: ABC books. Animals.

Annie and Co. ill. by author. Holt, 1991. ISBN 0-8050-1686-4 Subj: Activities – working.

The bear's toothache ill. by author. Puffin, 1978, c1972. ISBN 0-14-050263-7 Subj: Animals – bears. Character traits – kindness to animals. Illness. Teeth.

Big brown bear ill. by author. Harcourt, 1999. ISBN 0-15-201999-5 Subj: Accidents. Activities – painting. Animals – bears. Concepts – color. Rhyming text.

Big Pig and Little Pig ill. by author. Harcourt, 2001. ISBN 0-15-216516-9 Subj: Animals – pigs. Friendship.

The blue door ill. by John O'Connor. Fitzhenry & Whiteside, 2001. ISBN 1-55041-647-2 Subj: Animals – foxes. Animals – rabbits. Behavior – lost. Cities, towns. Family life – aunts, uncles.

A bug, a bear, and a boy ill. by author. Scholastic, 1998. ISBN 0-590-14904-0 Subj: Activities. Animals – bears. Concepts – size. Friendship. Insects.

A bug, a bear, and a boy go to school ill. by author. Scholastic, 1999. ISBN 0-439-07783-4 Subj: Animals – bears. Insects. School.

Captain Toad and the motorbike ill. by author. Atheneum, 1978. ISBN 0-689-50118-8 Subj: Frogs & toads. Motorcycles.

The cereal box ill. by author. Little, 1974. ISBN 0-316-56313-7 Subj: Family life. Humorous stories. Imagination. Shopping.

The day the dog said, "Cock-a-doodle doo!" ill. by author. Scholastic, 1996. ISBN 0-590-73887-9 Subj: Animals. Noise, sounds. Weather – wind.

The day the sheep showed up ill. by author. Scholastic, 1998. ISBN 0-59084-910-7 Subj: Animals. Animals – sheep. Farms.

Drawing lessons from a bear ill. by author. Little, 2000. ISBN 0-316-56345-5 Subj: Activities – drawing. Animals – bears. Careers – artists.

The dream child ill. by author. Dutton, 1985. ISBN 0-525-44109-3 Subj: Bedtime. Dreams. Night. Sleep. Toys – bears.

Ed and me ill. by author. Harcourt, 1990. ISBN 0-15-224888-9 Subj: Country. Family life – fathers. Trucks.

Edward and the pirates ill. by author. Little, 1997. ISBN 0-316-56344-7 Subj: Books, reading. Imagination. Pirates.

Edward in the jungle ill. by author. Little, 2001. ISBN 0-316-56391-9 Subj: Animals. Imagination. Jungle.

Emma's pet ill. by author. Dutton, 1987. ISBN 0-525-44210-3 Subj: Activities – vacationing. Animals – bears. Behavior – needing someone. Family life. Pets.

Emma's vacation ill. by author. Dutton, 1987. ISBN 0-525-44315-0 Subj: Activities – vacationing. Animals – bears. Family life.

Farm boy's year ill. by author. Atheneum, 1992. ISBN 0-689-31679-8 Subj: Farms. U.S. history.

Farm morning ill. by author. Harcourt, 1985. ISBN 0-15-227299-2 Subj: Animals. Birds. Farms.

First flight ill. by author. Little, 1987. ISBN 0-316-56323-4 Subj: Activities – flying. Airplanes, airports. Toys – bears.

Fix-it ill. by author. Dutton, 1984. ISBN 0-525-44093-3 Subj: Books, reading. Television.

A girl, a goat, and a goose ill. by author. Scholastic, 2000. ISBN 0-439-09978-1 Subj: Activities. Animals – goats. Birds – geese. Friendship.

The Glerp ill. by author. Silver Pr., 1995. ISBN 0-382-24668-3 Subj: Animals. Monsters.

Goldilocks and the three bears (The three bears)

Great cat ill. by author. Dutton, 1982. ISBN 0-525-45102-1 Subj: Animals – cats. Behavior – needing someone. Islands.

The great race ill. by author. Scholastic, 1997. ISBN 0-590-84909-3 Subj: Animals. Sports – racing.

Henry Bear's Christmas ill. by author. Atheneum, 2001. ISBN 0-689-82198-0 Subj: Animals – bears. Animals – raccoons. Holidays – Christmas. Trees.

Henry Bear's park ill. by author; coloring by John O'Connor. Atheneum, 2001. ISBN 0-689-83967-7 Subj: Activities – ballooning. Animals – bears. Family life – fathers. Parks.

Jack and Rick ill. by author. Harcourt, 2002. ISBN 0-15-216552-5 Subj: Animals – bears. Animals – rabbits. Character traits – cooperation.

Little Red Riding Hood (Grimm, Jacob)

Lorenzo ill. by author. Doubleday, 1984. ISBN 0-385-15591-3 Subj: Activities – painting. Animals. Homes, houses.

Lost ill. by author. Little, 1990. ISBN 0-316-56329-3 Subj: Animals – bears. Behavior – lost.

The magical drawings of Moony B. Finch ill. by author. Doubleday, 1978. ISBN 0-385-12104-0 Subj: Art. Magic.

Mistletoe ill. by author. Dutton, 1978. ISBN 0-525-35040-3 Subj: Dreams. Holidays – Christmas. Imagination. Santa Claus. Toys.

Mole music ill. by author. Holt, 1999. ISBN 0-8050-2819-6 Subj: Animals – moles. Music. Musical instruments – violins.

Moony B. Finch, fastest draw in the West ill. by author. Artists & Writers Guild, 1994. ISBN 0-307-17554-5 Subj: Activities – drawing. Crime. Imagination. Magic. Trains.

The party ill. by author. Little, 1990. ISBN 0-316-56330-7 Subj: Animals. Family life – fathers. Parties. Toys.

Pig Pig and the magic photo album ill. by author. Dutton, 1986. ISBN 0-525-44238-3 Subj: Activities – photographing. Animals – pigs. Imagination.

Pig Pig gets a job ill. by author. Dutton, 1990. ISBN 0-525-44619-2 Subj: Activities – working. Animals – pigs. Careers.

Pig Pig goes to camp ill. by author. Dutton, 1983. ISBN 0-525-44064-X Subj: Animals – pigs. Camps, camping.

Pig Pig grows up ill. by author. Dutton, 1980. ISBN 0-525-37027-7 Subj: Animals – pigs. Behavior – growing up.

Pig Pig rides ill. by author. Dutton, 1982. ISBN 0-525-44024-0 Subj: Activities – playing. Animals – pigs. Imagination.

Pigs ahoy ill. by author. Dutton, 1995. ISBN 0-525-45334-2 Subj: Animals – pigs. Boats, ships. Rhyming text.

Pigs aplenty, pigs galore! ill. by author. Dutton, 1993. ISBN 0-525-45079-3 Subj: Animals – pigs. Food. Rhyming text.

The puddle ill. by author. Farrar, 1998. ISBN 0-374-36148-7 Subj: Animals. Toys. Weather – rain.

Santa's book of names ill. by author. Little, 1993. ISBN 0-316-56335-8 Subj: Books, reading. Character traits – helpfulness. Holidays – Christmas. Santa Claus.

Sisters ill. by author. Harcourt, 1984. ISBN 0-15-275319-2 Subj: Emotions – love. Sibling rivalry.

Snow lion ill. by author. Parents' Magazine Pr., 1983. ISBN 0-8193-1097-2 Subj: Weather – snow.

Something special ill. by author. Little, 1988. ISBN 0-316-56324-2 Subj: Activities – painting. Animals – raccoons.

Stanley: Henry Bear's friend ill. by author. Little, 1979. ISBN 0-316-56318-8 Subj: Animals – bears. Animals – raccoons. Behavior – running away. Crime.

The teddy bear ill. by author. Holt, 2002. ISBN 0-8050-6414-1 Subj: Behavior – lost & found possessions. Emotions – love. Homeless. Toys – bears.

Those can-do pigs ill. by author. Dutton, 1996. ISBN 0-525-45495-0 Subj: Activities. Animals – pigs. Rhyming text.

The three little pigs (The three little pigs)

Tinker and Tom and the Star Baby ill. by author. Little, 1998. ISBN 0-316-56349-8 Subj: Aliens. Animals – bears. Imagination. Space & space ships.

The train ill. by author. Little, 1977. ISBN 0-316-56316-1 Subj: Dreams. Imagination. Toys – trains. Trains.

Where can an elephant hide? ill. by author. Doubleday, 1979. ISBN 0-385-12941-6 Subj: Animals. Animals – elephants. Behavior – hiding.

A wolf story ill. by author. Scribners, 1981. ISBN 0-684-16713-1 Subj: Animals – wolves. Character traits – freedom. Character traits – kindness to animals.

McQuade, Jacqueline. *At preschool with Teddy Bear* ill. by author. Dial, 1999. ISBN 0-8037-2394-6 Subj: Family life – fathers. Format, unusual – board books. School – first day. School – nursery. Toys – bears.

At the petting zoo with Teddy Bear ill. by author. Dial, 1999. ISBN 0-8037-2395-4 Subj: Animals. Format, unusual – board books. Toys – bears. Zoos.

Big babies ill. by author. Sterling, 2000. ISBN 0-8069-7537-7 Subj: Animals. Animals – babies. Names.

Christmas with Teddy Bear ill. by author. Dial, 1996. ISBN 0-8037-2075-0 Subj: Holidays – Christmas. Toys – bears.

Farm babies ill. by author. Sterling, 2000. ISBN 0-8069-7539-3 Subj: Animals – babies. Farms.

Good times with Teddy Bear ill. by author. Dial, 1997. ISBN 0-8037-2076-9 Subj: Activities. Animals – cats. Family life. Toys – bears.

Small babies ill. by author. Sterling, 2000. ISBN 0-8069-7541-5 Subj: Animals. Animals – babies. Science.

Snow babies ill. by author. Sterling, 2000. ISBN 1-8560-2366-4 Subj: Animals. Animals – babies. Foreign lands – Antarctic. Foreign lands – Arctic. Weather – snow.

McQueen, John Troy. *A world full of monsters* ill. by Marc Brown. Crowell, 1986. ISBN 0-690-04546-8 Subj: Family life – grandmothers. Monsters. Night.

McQueen, Lucinda. *Tidy pig* by Lucinda McQueen & Jeremy Guitar; ill. by authors. Random House, 1989. ISBN 0-394-90573-3 Subj: Animals – pigs. Character traits – cleanliness.

Macsolis. *Dance moon = Baile de luna: Dance moon* ill. by author. Donars Spanish Books, 1991. ISBN 84-261-2583-2 Subj: Animals – cats. Foreign languages. Moon.

McToots, Rudi. *The kid's book of games for cars, trains and planes* ill. by author. Bantam, 1980. ISBN 0-553-01230-4 Subj: Activities – traveling. Games.

Madden, Don. *Lemonade serenade, or, the thing in the garden* ill. by author. A. Whitman, 1966. Subj: Noise, sounds.

The Wartville wizard ill. by author. Macmillan, 1986. ISBN 0-02-762100-6 Subj: Character traits – cleanliness. Wizards.

Maddern, Eric. *Curious clownfish* ill. by Adrienne Kennaway. Little, 1990. ISBN 0-316-48894-1 Subj: Fish. Sea & seashore.

The fire children: a West African creation tale ill. by Frané Lessac. Dial, 1993. ISBN 0-8037-1477-7 Subj: Creation. Folk & fairy tales. Foreign lands – Africa.

Madenski, Melissa. *Some of the pieces* ill. by Deborah Kogan Ray. Little, 1991. ISBN 0-316-54324-1 Subj: Death. Emotions – grief. Family life – fathers.

Madgwick, Wendy. *Animaze! a collection of amazing nature mazes* ill. by Lorna Hussey. Knopf, 1992. ISBN 0-679-92665-8 Subj: Animals. Mazes.

Up in the air ill. by author. Raintree, 1999. ISBN 0-8172-5325-4 Subj: Science.

Water play ill. by author. Raintree, 1999. ISBN 0-8172-5326-2 Subj: Science. Water.

Mado, Michio. *The animals* trans. by The Empress Michiko of Japan; ill. by Mitsumasa Anno. Macmillan, 1992. ISBN 0-689-50574-4 Subj: Animals. Poetry.

The magic pocket trans. by Empress Michiko of Japan; ill. by Mitsumasa Anno. McElderry, 1998. ISBN 0-689-82137-9 Subj: Foreign lands – Japan. Foreign languages. Poetry.

Madonna. *Yakov and the seven thieves* ill. by Gennady Spirin. Callaway, 2004. ISBN 0-670-05887-4 Subj: Careers – shoemakers. Crime. Illness. Religion.

Madrigal, Antonio Hernandez. *Erandi's braids* ill. by Tomie de Paola. Putnam, 1999. ISBN 0-399-23212-5 Subj: Birthdays. Family life – mothers. Foreign lands – Mexico. Hair.

Maestro, Betsy. *All aboard overnight* ill. by Giulio Maestro. Houghton Mifflin, 1992. ISBN 0-395-51120-8 Subj: Language. Trains.

Around the clock with Harriet: a book about telling time ill. by Giulio Maestro. Crown, 1984. ISBN 0-517-55118-7 Subj: Animals – elephants. Clocks, watches. Time.

Bats ill. by Giulio Maestro. Scholastic, 1994. ISBN 0-590-46150-8 Subj: Animals – bats.

Big city port by Betsy Maestro & Ellen Del Vecchio; ill. by Giulio Maestro. Four Winds, 1983. ISBN 0-590-07869-0 Subj: Boats, ships. Cities, towns.

Bike trip ill. by Giulio Maestro. HarperCollins, 1992. ISBN 0-06-022732-X Subj: Family life. Safety. Sports – bicycling.

Busy day: a book of action words by Betsy & Giulio Maestro; ill. by Giulio Maestro. Crown, 1978. ISBN 0-517-53288-3 Subj: Activities. Circus.

Camping out: a book of action words by Betsy & Giulio Maestro; ill. by authors. Crown, 1985. ISBN 0-517-55119-5 Subj: Camps, camping. Language.

Coming to America ill. by Susannah Ryan. Scholastic, 1996. ISBN 0-590-44151-5 Subj: Ethnic groups in the U.S.

Delivery van ill. by Giulio Maestro. Houghton Mifflin, 1990. ISBN 0-395-51119-4 Subj: Cities, towns. Country. Language.

Dollars and cents for Harriet ill. by Giulio Maestro. Crown, 1988. ISBN 0-517-56958-2 Subj: Counting, numbers. Money.

Fat polka-dot cat and other haiku ill. by Giulio Maestro. Dutton, 1976. ISBN 0-525-29625-5 Subj: Poetry.

Ferryboat by Betsy & Giulio Maestro; ill. by authors. Crowell, 1986. ISBN 0-690-04520-4 Subj: Activities – traveling. Boats, ships.

The guessing game ill. by Giulio Maestro. Grosset, 1983. ISBN 0-488-21701-5 Subj: Animals – pigs. Problem solving.

Harriet at home ill. by Giulio Maestro. Crown, 1984. ISBN 0-517-55417-8 Subj: Animals – elephants. Format, unusual – board books. Homes, houses.

Harriet at play ill. by Giulio Maestro. Crown, 1984. ISBN 0-517-55420-8 Subj: Activities – playing. Animals – elephants. Format, unusual – board books.

Harriet at school ill. by Giulio Maestro. Crown, 1984. ISBN 0-517-55419-4 Subj: Animals – elephants. Format, unusual – board books. School.

Harriet at work ill. by Giulio Maestro. Crown, 1984. ISBN 0-517-55418-6 Subj: Activities – working. Animals – elephants. Format, unusual – board books.

Harriet goes to the circus by Betsy & Giulio Maestro; ill. by Giulio Maestro. Crown, 1977. ISBN 0-517-52844-4 Subj: Animals – elephants. Circus. Counting, numbers.

Harriet reads signs and more signs ill. by Giulio Maestro. Crown, 1981. ISBN 0-517-54167-X Subj: Animals – elephants. Books, reading.

How do apples grow? ill. by Giulio Maestro. HarperCollins, 1992. ISBN 0-06-020056-1 Subj: Food. Science. Trees.

On the go: a book of adjectives by Betsy & Giulio Maestro; ill. by authors. Crown, 1979. ISBN 0-517-53596-3 Subj: Animals – elephants. Language.

On the town: a book of clothing words by Betsy & Giulio Maestro; ill. by authors. Crown, 1983. ISBN 0-517-54749-X Subj: Animals – elephants. Character traits – appearance. Clothing.

The pandas take a vacation ill. by Giulio Maestro. Western, 1986. ISBN 0-307-68258-7 Subj: Activities – vacationing. Animals – pandas.

The perfect picnic ill. by Giulio Maestro. Western, 1986. ISBN 0-307-10266-1 Subj: Activities – picnicking.

The story of the Statue of Liberty by Betsy & Giulio Maestro; ill. by Giulio Maestro. Lothrop, 1986. ISBN 0-688-05773-X Subj: Art. U.S. history.

Taxi ill. by Giulio Maestro. Clarion, 1989. ISBN 0-89919-528-8 Subj: Cities, towns. Language. Taxis.

Temperature and you ill. by Giulio Maestro. Dutton, 1990. ISBN 0-525-67271-0 Subj: Concepts. Weather.

Through the year with Harriet by Betsy & Giulio Maestro; ill. by authors. Crown, 1985. ISBN 0-517-55613-8 Subj: Animals – elephants. Days of the week, months of the year. Seasons. Weather.

Traffic: a book of opposites by Betsy & Giulio Maestro; ill. by authors. Crown, 1981. ISBN 0-517-54427-X Subj: Concepts – opposites. Traffic, traffic signs.

Where is my friend? ill. by Giulio Maestro. Crown, 1976. ISBN 0-517-55304-X Subj: Animals – elephants. Concepts.

Why do leaves change color? ill. by Loretta Krupinski. HarperCollins, 1994. ISBN 0-06-022874-1 Subj: Nature. Science. Seasons – fall. Trees.

Maestro, Giulio. *Busy day: a book of action words* (Maestro, Betsy)

Camping out: a book of action words (Maestro, Betsy)

Ferryboat (Maestro, Betsy)

Geese find the missing piece (Maestro, Marco)

Halloween howls: riddles that are a scream ill. by author. Dutton, 1983. ISBN 0-525-44059-3 Subj: Holidays – Halloween. Riddles & jokes.

Harriet goes to the circus (Maestro, Betsy)

Just enough Rosie ill. by author. Grosset, 1983. ISBN 0-448-21702-3 Subj: Animals – rhinoceros. Humorous stories.

Leopard is sick ill. by author. Greenwillow, 1978. ISBN 0-688-84162-7 Subj: Animals. Animals – leopards. Friendship. Illness.

On the go: a book of adjectives (Maestro, Betsy)

On the town: a book of clothing words (Maestro, Betsy)

One more and one less ill. by author. Crown, 1974. ISBN 0-517-51575-X Subj: Animals. Counting, numbers.

A raft of riddles ill. by author. Dutton, 1982. ISBN 0-525-44017-8 Subj: Humorous stories. Riddles & jokes.

The remarkable plant in apartment 4 ill. by author. Bradbury, 1973. Subj: Cities, towns. Humorous stories. Plants.

Riddle romp ill. by author. Houghton Mifflin, 1983. ISBN 0-89919-180-0 Subj: Riddles & jokes.

The story of the Statue of Liberty (Maestro, Betsy)

Through the year with Harriet (Maestro, Betsy)

The tortoise's tug of war ill. by author. Bradbury, 1971. ISBN 0-8788-8030-5 Subj: Animals – tapirs. Animals – whales. Folk & fairy tales. Foreign lands – South America. Games. Reptiles – turtles, tortoises.

Traffic: a book of opposites (Maestro, Betsy)

Maestro, Marco. *Geese find the missing piece* by Marco & Giulio Maestro; ill. by Giulio Maestro. HarperCollins, 1999. ISBN 0-06-026221-4 Subj: Animals. Rhyming text. Riddles & jokes. School.

What do you hear when cows sing? and other silly riddles ill. by Giulio Maestro. HarperCollins, 1996. ISBN 0-06-024949-8 Subj: Riddles & jokes.

Magdanz, James S. *Go home, river* ill. by Dianne Widom. Alaska Northwest Bks., 1996. ISBN 0-88240-476-8 Subj: Alaska. Eskimos. Family life. Rivers. U.S. history.

Magee, Doug. *All aboard ABC* by Doug Magee & Robert Newman; photos by authors. Dutton, 1990. ISBN 0-525-65036-9 Subj: ABC books. Trains.

Let's fly from A to Z by Doug Magee & Robert Newman; ill. by Robert Newman. Cobblehill, 1992. ISBN 0-525-65105-5 Subj: ABC books. Airplanes, airports. Language.

Trucks you can count on photos by author. Dodd, 1985. ISBN 0-396-08507-5 Subj: Counting, numbers. Trucks.

Maggi, María Elena. *The great canoe* ill. by Gloria Calderón. Douglas & McIntyre, 2001. ISBN 0-88899-444-3 Subj: Animals. Canoes & canoeing. Folk & fairy tales. Indians of South America – Karina. Weather – floods. Weather – rain.

Maggs, Catherine. *Goodbye Rune* (Kaldhol, Marit)

Magloff, Lisa. *Bear* ill. by author. DK, 2003. ISBN 0-7566-0194-0 Subj: Animals – babies. Animals – bears. Behavior – growing up.

Butterfly ill. with photos. DK, 2003. ISBN 0-7566-0193-2 Subj: Animals – babies. Behavior – growing up. Insects – butterflies, caterpillars.

Duckling ill. with photos. DK, 2003. ISBN 0-7894-9628-3 Subj: Animals – babies. Behavior – growing up. Birds – ducks.

Elephant ill. with photos. DK, 2005. ISBN 0-7566-1155-5 Subj: Animals – babies. Animals – elephants. Behavior – growing up.

Frog ill. with photos. DK, 2003. ISBN 0-7894-9629-1 Subj: Animals – babies. Behavior – growing up. Frogs & toads.

Kitten ill. with photos. DK, 2005. ISBN 0-7566-1156-3 Subj: Animals – babies. Animals – cats. Behavior – growing up.

Penguin ill. with photos. DK, 2004. ISBN 0-7566-0263-7 Subj: Animals – babies. Behavior – growing up. Birds – penguins.

Rabbit ill. with photos. DK, 2004. ISBN 0-7566-0262-9 Subj: Animals – babies. Animals – rabbits. Behavior – growing up.

Magnier, Thierry. *Isabelle and the angel* ill. by Georg Hallensleben. Chronicle, 2000. ISBN 0-8118-2526-4 Subj: Angels. Animals – pigs. Careers – artists. Museums.

Magnus, Erica. *Around me* ill. by author. Lothrop, 1992. ISBN 0-688-09753-7 Subj: Concepts. Format, unusual.

The boy and the devil ill. by author. Carolrhoda, 1986. ISBN 0-87614-305-2 Subj: Behavior – trickery. Devil. Folk & fairy tales. Foreign lands – Norway.

My secret place ill. by author. Lothrop, 1994. ISBN 0-688-11860-7 Subj: Imagination. Toys – bears.

Old Lars ill. by author. Carolrhoda, 1984. ISBN 0-87614-253-6 Subj: Folk & fairy tales. Foreign lands – Norway.

Magorian, Michelle. *Who's going to take care of me?* ill. by James Graham Hale. HarperCollins, 1990. ISBN 0-06-024106-3 Subj: Behavior – worrying. Family life – brothers & sisters. School.

Maguire, Arlene H. *Special people, special ways* ill. by Sheila Bailey. Portunus Pub., 1999. ISBN 1-886440-00-X Subj: Character traits – individuality. Handicaps. Rhyming text.

Maguire, Gregory. *Crabby Cratchitt* ill. by Andrew Glass. Clarion, 2000. ISBN 0-395-60485-0 Subj: Birds – chickens. Careers – farmers. Farms. Rhyming text.

Lucas Fishbone ill. by Frank Gargiulo. HarperCollins, 1990. ISBN 0-06-024090-3 Subj: Death. Emotions – grief. Family life – grandmothers. Gardens, gardening. Rhyming text.

Maguire, John. *People* ill. by Pauline Bewick. Collins, 2001. ISBN 1-903464-06-4 Subj: Character traits – individuality. Poetry.

Magyar, Sabina. *Mrs. Meyer, the bird* (Erlbruch, Wolf)

Mahiri, Jabari. *The day they stole the letter J* ill. by Dorothy Carter. Third World Pr., 1981. Subj: Behavior – misbehavior. Careers – barbers. Magic.

Mahler, Michael. *My everyday Spanish word book* (Kahn, Michèle)

Mählqvist, Stefan. *I'll take care of the crocodiles* ill. by Tord Nygren. Atheneum, 1979. ISBN 0-689-50124-2 Subj: Bedtime. Dreams.

Mahoney, Daniel J. *The perfect clubhouse* ill. by author. Clarion, 2004. ISBN 0-618-34672-4 Subj: Animals. Character traits – cooperation. Clubs, gangs. Friendship.

The Saturday escape ill. by author. Clarion, 2002. ISBN 0-618-13326-7 Subj: Activities – storytelling. Animals. Behavior. Books, reading. Character traits – responsibility. Libraries.

Mahony, Elizabeth Winthrop. *see* Winthrop, Elizabeth

Mahood, Kenneth. *The laughing dragon* ill. by author. Scribners, 1970. Subj: Dragons. Fire. Humorous stories. Royalty.

Why are there more questions than answers, Grandad? ill. by author. Bradbury, 1974. ISBN 0-87888-101-8 Subj: Character traits – questioning. Family life – grandfathers.

Mahurin, Tim. *Jeremy Kooloo* ill. by author. Dutton, 1995. ISBN 0-525-45203-6 Subj: ABC books. Animals – cats.

Mahy, Margaret. *Beaten by a balloon* ill. by Jonathan Allen. Viking, 1998. ISBN 0-670-87697-6 Subj: Behavior – bullying. Crime. Emotions – anger. Emotions – fear. Humorous stories.

Boom Baby boom, boom ill. by Patricia MacCarthy. Viking, 1997. ISBN 0-670-87314-4 Subj: Animals. Babies. Family life – mothers. Food. Noise, sounds.

The boy who was followed home ill. by Steven Kellogg. Watts, 1975. ISBN 0-531-02834-8 Subj: Animals – hippopotamuses. Humorous stories. Witches.

The boy with two shadows ill. by Jenny Williams. Lippincott, 1988, 1971. ISBN 0-397-32271-2 Subj: Behavior – misbehavior. Character traits – meanness. Shadows. Witches.

Bubble trouble and other poems and stories ill. by author Francisco Ordaz. McElderry, 1992. ISBN 0-689-50557-4 Subj: Foreign lands – New Zealand. Humorous stories. Poetry.

A busy day for a good grandmother ill. by Margaret Chamberlain. McElderry, 1993. ISBN 0-689-50595-7 Subj: Activities – traveling. Babies. Family life – grandmothers. Food. Transportation.

The Christmas tree tangle ill. by Anthony Kerins. McElderry, 1994. ISBN 0-689-50616-3 Subj: Animals. Animals – cats. Cumulative tales. Holidays – Christmas. Rhyming text. Trees.

Down the dragon's tongue ill. by Patricia MacCarthy. Orchard, 2000. ISBN 0-531-30272-5 Subj: Family life – fathers. Multiple births – twins. Parks.

The dragon of an ordinary family ill. by Helen Oxenbury. Watts, 1969. ISBN 0-434-95000-9 Subj: Dragons.

The great white man-eating shark ill. by Jonathan Allen. Dial, 1990. ISBN 0-8037-0749-5 Subj: Behavior – trickery. Fish – sharks.

The horrendous hullabaloo ill. by Patricia MacCarthy. Viking, 1992. ISBN 0-670-84547-7 Subj: Birds – parakeets, parrots. Family life – aunts, uncles. Pirates.

Jam: a true story ill. by Helen Craig. Atlantic Monthly, 1986. ISBN 0-87113-048-3 Subj: Family life. Food.

Keeping house ill. by Wendy Smith. Macmillan, 1991. ISBN 0-689-50515-9 Subj: Character traits – cleanliness.

A lion in the meadow ill. by Jenny Williams. Watts, 1969. ISBN 0-87951-446-9 Subj: Animals – lions. Dragons.

Making friends ill. by Wendy Smith. Macmillan, 1990. ISBN 0-689-50498-5 Subj: Animals – dogs. Friendship.

The man whose mother was a pirate ill. by Margaret Chamberlain. Viking, 1986. ISBN 0-670-81070-3 Subj: Behavior – seeking better things. Pirates. Sea & seashore.

Mrs. Discombobulous ill. by Jan Brychta. Watts, 1969. ISBN 0-460-05796-0 Subj: Behavior – nagging. Family life. Gypsies.

Pillycock's shop ill. by Carol Baker. Watts, 1969. ISBN 0-234-77473-8 Subj: Fairies. Values.

The pumpkin man and the crafty creeper ill. by Helen Craig. Lothrop, 1991. ISBN 0-688-10347-2 Subj: Gardens, gardening. Plants.

The queen's goat ill. by Emma Chichester Clark. Dial, 1991. ISBN 0-8037-0938-2 Subj: Animals – goats. Pets. Royalty – queens.

The rattlebang picnic ill. by Steven Kellogg. Dial, 1994. ISBN 0-8037-1319-3 Subj: Activities – picnicking. Automobiles. Family life.

Rooms for rent ill. by Jenny Williams. Watts, 1974. ISBN 0-531-02590-X Subj: Behavior – greed. Hotels.

Sailor Jack and the twenty orphans ill. by Robert Bartelt. Watts, 1970. ISBN 0-531-01863-6 Subj: Boats, ships. Careers – military. Orphans. Pirates. Sailors. Sea & seashore.

The seven Chinese brothers ill. by Jean & Mou-Sien Tseng. Scholastic, 1990. ISBN 0-590-42055-0 Subj: Character traits – cleverness. Family life. Folk & fairy tales. Foreign lands – China.

17 kings and 42 elephants ill. by Patricia MacCarthy. Dial, 1987. ISBN 0-8037-0458-5 Subj: Animals. Jungle. Rhyming text. Royalty – kings.

Simply delicious! ill. by Jonathan Allen. Orchard, 1999. ISBN 0-531-33181-4 Subj: Animals. Food. Jungle. Tongue twisters.

A summery Saturday morning ill. by Selina Young. Viking, 1998. ISBN 0-670-87943-6 Subj: Animals. Birds – geese. Humorous stories. Rhyming text. Sea & seashore. Seasons – summer.

The three-legged cat ill. by Jonathan Allen. Viking, 1993. ISBN 0-670-85015-2 Subj: Activities – traveling. Animals – cats. Humorous stories.

When the king rides by ill. by Betina Ogden. Mondo, 1995. ISBN 1-57255-003-1 Subj: Animals. Cumulative tales. Parades. Rhyming text. Royalty – kings.

Maier, Paul L. *The very first Christmas* ill. by Francisco Ordaz. Concordia, 1998. ISBN 0-570-05064-2 Subj: Format, unusual – board books. Holidays – Christmas. Religion – Nativity.

Mainwaring, Jane. *My feather* photos by Fiona Pragoff. Doubleday, 1990. ISBN 0-385-41197-9 Subj: Activities. Concepts – perspective. Science.

Maiorano, Robert. *Backstage* ill. by Rachel Isadora. Greenwillow, 1978. ISBN 0-688-84130-9 Subj: Theater.

Francisco ill. by Rachel Isadora. Macmillan, 1978. ISBN 0-02-762170-7 Subj: Foreign lands – South America. Poverty. Problem solving.

A little interlude ill. by Rachel Isadora. Coward, 1980. ISBN 0-698-20496-4 Subj: Activities – dancing. Ballet. Behavior – sharing. Music. Musical instruments – pianos.

Maisner, Heather. *Find Mouse in the house* ill. by Charlotte Hard. Candlewick, 1994. ISBN 1-56402-351-6 Subj: Animals – mice. Behavior – lost. Format, unusual – toy & movable books.

Find Mouse in the yard ill. by Charlotte Hard. Candlewick, 1994. ISBN 1-56402-350-8 Subj: Animals – mice. Format, unusual – toy & movable books. Games.

Planet monster ill. by Alan Rowe. Candlewick, 1996. ISBN 0-763-60057-1 Subj: Concepts – color. Concepts – shape. Counting, numbers. Space & space ships.

Save Brave Ted ill. by Charlotte Hard. Candlewick, 1996. ISBN 1-56402-878-X Subj: Monsters. Picture puzzles. Toys. Toys – bears.

Maitland, Antony. *Idle Jack* ill. by author. Farrar, 1979. ISBN 0-374-33628-8 Subj: Character traits – foolishness. Folk & fairy tales.

Maitland, Barbara. *The bear who didn't like honey* ill. by Odilon Moraes. Orchard, 1997. ISBN 0-531-09546-0 Subj: Animals – bears. Character traits – bravery. Emotions – fear. Night.

The bookstore burglar ill. by Nadine Bernard Westcott. Dutton, 2001. ISBN 0-525-46684-3 Subj: Animals – cats. Animals – mice. Books, reading. Crime. Stores.

The bookstore ghost ill. by Nadine Bernard Westcott. Dutton, 1998. ISBN 0-525-46049-7 Subj: Animals – cats. Animals – mice. Ghosts. Stores.

The bookstore valentine ill. by David LaRochelle. Dutton, 2002. ISBN 0-525-46913-3 Subj: Animals – cats. Books, reading. Ghosts. Holidays – Valentine's Day. Stores.

Moo in the morning ill. by Andrew Kulman. Farrar, 2000. ISBN 0-374-35038-8 Subj: Animals. Cities, towns. Farms. Noise, sounds.

My bear and me ill. by Lisa Flather. McElderry, 1999. ISBN 0-689-82085-2 Subj: Activities. Bedtime. Toys – bears.

Maizlish, Lisa. *The ring* photos by author. Greenwillow, 1996. ISBN 0-688-14217-6 Subj: Activities – flying. Cities, towns. Imagination. Wordless.

Majewski, Joe. *A friend for Oscar Mouse* ill. by Maria Majewska. Dial, 1988. ISBN 0-8037-0348-1 Subj: Animals – mice. Friendship.

Major, Beverly. *Playing sardines* ill. by Andrew Glass. Scholastic, 1988. ISBN 0-590-41153-5 Subj: Activities – playing. Behavior – hiding. Games. Twilight.

Major, Kevin. *Eh to zed?* ill. by Alan Daniel. Red Deer Pr., 2002. ISBN 0-88995-272-8 Subj: ABC books. Foreign lands – Canada.

Major League Baseball (Organization). *Baseball ABC* (Baseball ABC)

Baseball 1-2-3 (Baseball 1-2-3)

Mak, Kam. *My Chinatown* ill. by author. HarperCollins, 2002. ISBN 0-06-029191-5 Subj: Cities, towns. Ethnic groups in the U.S. – Chinese Americans. Immigrants. Poetry.

Makower, Sylvia. *Samson's breakfast* ill. by author. Watts, 1961. Subj: Animals – lions.

Malecki, Maryann. *Mom and dad and I are having a baby!* ill. by author. Pennypress, 1982. ISBN 0-937604-03-8 Subj: Babies. Family life – new sibling.

Maley, Anne. *Have you seen my mother?* ill. by Yutaka Sugita. Carolrhoda, 1969. ISBN 0-8761-4001-0 Subj: Circus. Family life – mothers. Toys – balls.

Malfatti, Patrizia. *Look inside an airplane* (Mantegazza, Giovanna)

Malkin, Michele. *Pinky's sweet tooth* ill. by author. Dutton, 2003. ISBN 0-525-47088-3 Subj: Activities – baking, cooking. Reptiles – alligators, crocodiles.

Malkovych, Ivan. *The cat and the rooster* ill. by Kost' Lavro; trans. by Motria Onyschuk. Knopf, 1995. ISBN 0-679-86964-6 Subj: Animals – cats. Animals – foxes. Birds – chickens. Folk & fairy tales. Foreign lands – Soviet Union. Foreign lands – Ukraine.

Mallat, Kathy. *Brave bear* ill. by author. Walker, 1999. ISBN 0-8027-8705-3 Subj: Animals – bears. Birds. Character traits – bravery. Emotions – fear.

Just ducky ill. by author. Walker, 2001. ISBN 0-8027-8824-6 Subj: Activities – playing. Birds – ducks. Friendship. Optical illusions.

Seven stars, more! ill. by author. Walker, 1998. ISBN 0-8027-8676-6 Subj: Animals – sheep. Bedtime. Counting, numbers. Sleep. Stars.

Trouble on the tracks ill. by author. Walker, 2001. ISBN 0-8027-8773-8 Subj: Activities – playing. Animals – cats. Toys – trains.

Mallett, Anne. *Here comes Tagalong* ill. by Steven Kellogg. Parents' Magazine Pr., 1971. ISBN 0-8193-0496-4 Subj: Family life. Friendship. Sibling rivalry.

Mallett, David. *Inch by inch: the garden song* ill. by Ora Eitan. HarperCollins, 1995. ISBN 0-06-024304-X Subj: Gardens, gardening. Music. Songs.

Mallory, Kenneth. *Families of the deep blue sea* ill. by Marshall H. Peck, III. Charlesbridge, 1995. ISBN 0-88106-887-X Subj: Animals. Fish. Sea & seashore.

Malloy, Judy. *Bad Thad* ill. by Martha G. Alexander. Dutton, 1980. ISBN 0-525-26148-6 Subj: Behavior – misbehavior. Family life. School.

Malone, Nola Langner. *A home* ill. by author. Bradbury, 1988. ISBN 0-02-751440-4 Subj: Friendship. Homes, houses. Moving.

Maloney, Peter (1955–). *Belly button boy* story & pictures by Peter Maloney & Felicia Zekauskas. Dial, 2000. ISBN 0-8037-2542-6 Subj: Anatomy – navels. Character traits – cleanliness. Rhyming text.

His mother's nose story & pictures by Peter Maloney & Felicia Zekauskas. Dial, 2001. ISBN 0-8037-2545-0 Subj: Anatomy. Character traits – individuality. Family life. Self-concept.

The magic hockey stick by Peter Maloney & Felicia Zekauskas; ill. by authors. Dial, 1999. ISBN 0-8037-2476-X Subj: Rhyming text. Sports – hockey.

Redbird at Rockefeller Center by Peter Maloney & Felicia Zekauskas; ill. by authors. Dial, 1997. ISBN 0-8037-2257-5 Subj: Birds – cardinals. Holidays – Christmas. Magic. Rhyming text. Santa Claus. Trees.

Malotki, Ekkehart. *The magic hummingbird* ill. by Michael Lomatuway'ma. Kiva, 1996. ISBN 1-885772-04-1 Subj: Folk & fairy tales. Indians of North America – Hopi. Weather – droughts.

Mamchur, Carolyn Marie. *The popcorn tree* ill. by Laurie McGaw. Stoddart, 1998. ISBN 0-7737-2896-1 Subj: Holidays – Christmas. Trees.

Mamin-Sibiryak, D. N. *Grey Neck* adapt. & trans. from Russian by Marguerita Rudolph; ill. by Leslie Shuman Kronz. Stemmer House, 1988. ISBN 0-88045-068-1 Subj: Birds – ducks. Character traits – kindness to animals. Folk & fairy tales. Seasons – winter.

Mammano, Julie. *Rhinos who play soccer* ill. by author. Chronicle, 2001. ISBN 0-8118-2779-8 Subj: Animals – rhinoceros. Sports – soccer.

Rhinos who skateboard ill. by author. Chronicle, 1999. ISBN 0-8118-2356-3 Subj: Animals – rhinoceros. Sports – skateboarding.

Rhinos who snowboard ill. by author. Chronicle, 1997. ISBN 0-8118-1715-6 Subj: Animals – rhinoceros. Sports – snowboarding.

Mandel, Peter. *Say hey: a song of Willie Mays* ill. by Don Tate. Hyperion, 2000. ISBN 0-7868-2417-4 Subj: Ethnic groups in the U.S. – African Americans. Rhyming text. Sports – baseball.

Mandry, Kathy. *The cat and the mouse and the mouse and the cat* ill. by Joe Toto. Pantheon, 1972. ISBN 0-394-92401-0 Subj: Animals – cats. Animals – mice. Friendship.

Manes, Esther. *The bananas move to the ceiling* by Esther & Stephen Manes; ill. by Barbara Samuels. Watts, 1983. ISBN 0-531-04517-X Subj: Family life. Humorous stories.

Manes, Stephen. *The bananas move to the ceiling* (Manes, Esther)

Mangan, Anne. *Browny, the smallest bear of all* ill. by Joanne Moss. Crocodile, 1998. ISBN 1-56656-266-X Subj: Animals – bears. Concepts – size. Self-concept.

The monkey who wanted the moon ill. by Catherine Walters. Crocodile, 2001. ISBN 1-56656-376-3 Subj: Animals – monkeys. Behavior – greed. Jungle. Moon.

Mangas, Brian. *A nice surprise for Father Rabbit* ill. by Sidney Levitt. S&S, 1989. ISBN 0-671-67194-4 Subj: Animals – rabbits. Emotions – love. Family life – fathers.

Mangin, Marie-France. *Suzette and Nicholas and the seasons clock* trans. from French by Joan Chevalier; ill. by Satomi Ichikawa. Putnam, 1982. ISBN 0-399-20832-1 Subj: Activities. Seasons.

Mangold, Paul. *Whose tracks are these?* (Gipson, Morrell)

Manheim, Ralph. *Dear Mili* (Grimm, Wilhelm)

The marvelous journey through the night (Heine, Helme)

Mollywoop (Heine, Helme)

The nutcracker (Hoffmann, E. T. A.)

Mann, Pamela. *The frog princess?* ill. by author. G. Stevens, 1995. ISBN 0-83681-352-9 Subj: Careers – librarians. Folk & fairy tales. Frogs & toads. Royalty – princes.

Mann, Peggy. *King Laurence, the alarm clock* ill. by Ray Cruz. Doubleday, 1976. ISBN 0-385-04972-2 Subj: Animals. Animals – lions. Illness. Morning.

Manna, Anthony L. *Mr. Semolina-Semolinus* retold by Anthony L. Manna & Christodoula Mitakidou; ill. by Giselle Potter. Atheneum, 1997. ISBN 0-689-81093-8 Subj: Emotions – love. Folk & fairy tales. Foreign lands – Greece. Magic. Royalty – princesses. Royalty – queens.

Manniche, Lise. *The prince who knew his fate: an ancient Egyptian tale* (The prince who knew his fate)

Manning, Jane K. *My first baby games* ill. by author. HarperFestival, 2001. ISBN 0-694-01435-4 Subj: Babies. Games.

Manning, Linda. *Animal hours* ill. by Vlasta van Kampen. Oxford Univ. Pr., 1991. ISBN 0-19-540771-7 Subj: Animals. Cumulative tales. Rhyming text. Time.

Dinosaur days ill. by Vlasta van Kampen. BridgeWater, 1994. ISBN 0-8167-3315-5 Subj: Behavior – misbehavior. Days of the week, months of the year. Dinosaurs. Prehistory.

Manning, Maurie J. *The aunts go marching* ill. by author. Boyds Mills, 2003. ISBN 1-59078-026-4 Subj: Counting, numbers. Cumulative tales. Family life – aunts, uncles. Rhyming text. Weather – rain.

Manning, Mick. *Honk! honk!* by Mick Manning & Brita Granström; ill. by authors. Kingfisher, 1997. ISBN 0-7534-5103-4 Subj: Birds – geese. Dreams. Migration.

My body, your body by Mick Manning & Brita Granström; ill. by authors. Watts, 1997. ISBN 0-531-14486-0 Subj: Anatomy. Animals. Character traits – individuality.

A ruined house ill. by author. Candlewick, 1994. ISBN 1-56402-453-9 Subj: Foreign lands – Scotland. Homes, houses. Nature.

Supermom ill. by Brita Granström. A. Whitman, 2001. ISBN 0-8075-7666-2 Subj: Animals. Family life – mothers.

What a Viking! ill. by Brita Granström. R&S Books, 2000. ISBN 91-29-64883-1 Subj: Foreign lands – Scandinavia. Sailors. Vikings.

Mannis, Celeste Davidson. *One leaf rides the wind* ill. by Susan Kathleen Hartung. Viking, 2002. ISBN 0-670-03525-4 Subj: Counting, numbers. Gardens, gardening. Nature. Poetry.

Mansell, Dom. *If dinosaurs came to town* ill. by author. Little, 1991. ISBN 0-316-54584-8 Subj: Dinosaurs. Imagination. Prehistory.

My old teddy ill. by author. Candlewick, 1992. ISBN 1-56402-035-5 Subj: Toys – bears.

Manson, Ainslie. *Ballerinas don't wear glasses* ill. by Dean Griffiths. Orca, 2000. ISBN 1-55143-176-9 Subj: Activities – dancing. Ballet. Family life – brothers & sisters. Self-concept.

Manson, Beverlie. *The fairies' alphabet book* ill. by author. Doubleday, 1982. ISBN 0-385-17544-2 Subj: ABC books. Fairies.

Manson, Christopher. *The crab prince* ill. by reteller. Holt, 1991. ISBN 0-8050-1215-X Subj: Crustaceans – crabs. Folk & fairy tales. Foreign lands – Italy. Royalty – princes. Witches.

A farmyard song ill. by author. North-South, 1992. ISBN 1-55858-170-7 Subj: Animals. Cumulative tales. Farms. Noise, sounds. Nursery rhymes. Songs.

A gift for the king ill. by author. Holt, 1989. ISBN 0-8050-0951-5 Subj: Folk & fairy tales. Foreign lands – Persia. Gifts. Royalty – kings.

Here begins the tale of the marvellous blue mouse ill. by author. Holt, 1992. ISBN 0-8050-1622-8 Subj: Animals – mice. Behavior – greed. Behavior – trickery. Foreign lands – France. Middle Ages. Problem solving. Royalty – emperors.

The tree in the wood: an old nursery song ill. by adapt. North-South, 1993. ISBN 1-55858-193-6 Subj: Cumulative tales. Folk & fairy tales. Songs. Trees.

Two travelers ill. by author. Holt, 1990. ISBN 0-8050-1214-1 Subj: Activities – traveling. Animals – elephants. Friendship.

Mantegazza, Giovanna. *The cat* ill. by Cristina Mesturini. Boyds Mills, 1992. ISBN 1-56397-032-5 Subj: Animals – cats. Format, unusual – board books.

The hippopotamus ill. by Cristina Mesturini. Boyds Mills, 1992. ISBN 1-56397-033-3 Subj: Animals – hippopotamuses. Foreign lands – Africa. Format, unusual – board books.

Look how a baby grows trans. from Italian by Alexandra E. Fischer; ill. by Anna Curti. Grosset, 1995. ISBN 0-448-40925-9 Subj: Babies. Birth. Format, unusual – board books. Format, unusual – toy & movable books.

Look inside a car trans. from Italian by Alexandra E. Fischer; ill. by Gianna Ronco. Grosset, 1996. ISBN 0-448-41315-9 Subj: Automobiles. Format, unusual – toy & movable books. Transportation.

Look inside a farm trans. from Italian by Alexandra E. Fischer; ill. by Cristina Mesturini. Grosset, 1994. ISBN 0-448-40958-5 Subj: Farms. Format, unusual – toy & movable books.

Look inside a rainforest trans. from Italian by Alexandra E. Fischer; ill. by Carlo A. Michelini. Grosset, 1993. ISBN 0-448-40489-3 Subj: Ecology. Forest, woods. Format, unusual – toy & movable books.

Look inside an airplane trans. from Italian by Patrizia Malfatti; ill. by Carlo A. Michelini. Grosset, 1994. ISBN 0-448-40543-1 Subj: Airplanes, airports. Transportation.

Mantinband, Gerda. *Blabbermouths* ill. by Paul Borovsky. Greenwillow, 1992. ISBN 0-688-10602-1 Subj: Behavior – gossip. Folk & fairy tales. Money.

Three clever mice ill. by Martine Gourbault. Greenwillow, 1993. ISBN 0-688-11370-2 Subj: Animals – mice. Character traits – cleverness.

Manuel, Lynn. *Camels always do* ill. by Kasia Charko. Orca, 2004. ISBN 1-55143-284-6 Subj: Animals – camels. Foreign lands – British Columbia.

Lucy Maud and the Cavendish cat ill. by Janet Wilson. Tundra, 1997. ISBN 0-88776-397-9 Subj: Animals – cats. Careers – authors.

The night the moon blew kisses ill. by Robin Spowart. Houghton Mifflin, 1996. ISBN 0-395-73979-9 Subj: Activities – walking. Family life – grandmothers. Moon. Seasons – winter. Weather – snow.

Manushkin, Fran. *Baby* ill. by Ronald Himler. HarperCollins, 1972. ISBN 0-06-024062-8 Subj: Babies. Family life.

Baby, come out! ill. by Ronald Himler. HarperCollins, 1972. Orig. entitled Baby. ISBN 0-06-024062-8 Subj: Babies. Birth.

Be brave, baby rabbit ill. by Diane de Groat. Crown, 1990. ISBN 0-517-57574-4 Subj: Animals – rabbits. Character traits – bravery. Family life – brothers & sisters. Holidays – Halloween.

The best toy of all ill. by Robin Ballard. Dutton, 1992. ISBN 0-525-44897-7 Subj: Activities – playing. Family life. Seasons. Toys.

Bubblebath! ill. by Ronald Himler. HarperCollins, 1974. ISBN 0-06-024059-8 Subj: Activities – bathing. Bubbles. Family life.

Hocus and Pocus at the circus ill. by Geoffrey Hayes. HarperCollins, 1983. ISBN 0-06-024092-X Subj: Character traits – meanness. Holidays – Halloween. Witches.

Hooray for Hanukkah! ill. by author. Random House, 2001. ISBN 0-375-91043-3 Subj: Holidays – Hanukkah. Jewish culture. Religion.

Latkes and applesauce ill. by Robin Spowart. Scholastic, 1990. ISBN 0-590-42261-8 Subj: Holidays – Hanukkah. Jewish culture. Religion.

Let's go riding in our strollers ill. by Benrei Huang. Hyperion, 1993. ISBN 1-56282-391-4 Subj: Cities, towns. Rhyming text.

Little rabbit's baby brother ill. by Diane de Groat. Crown, 1986. ISBN 0-517-56251-0 Subj: Animals – rabbits. Babies. Emotions – envy, jealousy. Family life – new sibling. Sibling rivalry.

The matzah that Papa brought home ill. by Ned Bittinger. Scholastic, 1995. ISBN 0-590-47146-5 Subj: Cumulative tales. Food. Holidays – Passover. Jewish culture. Religion.

Miriam's cup: a Passover story ill. by Bob Dacey. Scholastic, 1998. ISBN 0-590-67720-9 Subj: Holidays – Passover. Jewish culture. Religion.

Moon dragon ill. by Geoffrey Hayes. Macmillan, 1982. ISBN 0-02-762210-X Subj: Animals – mice. Dragons. Food. Moon.

My Christmas safari ill. by R. W. Alley. Dial, 1993. ISBN 0-8037-1295-2 Subj: Animals. Counting, numbers. Cumulative tales. Foreign lands – Africa. Holidays – Christmas. Music.

Peeping and sleeping ill. by Jennifer Plecas. Clarion, 1994. ISBN 0-395-64339-2 Subj: Family life – fathers. Frogs & toads. Night. Noise, sounds.

The perfect Christmas picture ill. by Karen Ann Weinhaus. HarperCollins, 1980. ISBN 0-06-024069-5 Subj: Activities – photographing. Family life. Holidays – Christmas.

Shirleybird ill. by Carl Stuart. HarperCollins, 1975. ISBN 0-06-024064-4 Subj: Character traits – individuality.

Starlight and candles: the joys of the Sabbath ill. by Jacqueline Chwast. S&S, 1995. ISBN 0-671-88333-X Subj: Family life. Jewish culture. Religion.

Swinging and swinging ill. by Thomas di Grazia. HarperCollins, 1976. ISBN 0-06-024067-9 Subj: Activities – playing. Activities – swinging. Weather – clouds.

Walt Disney's one hundred one dalmations ill. by Russell Hicks. Walt Disney, 1991. ISBN 1-56282-032-X Subj: Animals – dogs. Counting, numbers.

Many, Paul. *The great pancake escape* ill. by Scott Goto. Walker, 2002. ISBN 0-8027-8796-7 Subj: Activities – baking, cooking. Careers – magicians. Food. Magic. Rhyming text.

Manzano, Sonia. *No dogs allowed* ill. by Jon J. Muth. Atheneum, 2004. ISBN 0-689-83088-2 Subj: Activities – picnicking. Animals – dogs. Automobiles. Ethnic groups in the U.S. – Puerto Rican Americans. Family life.

Maple, Marilyn J. *On the wings of a butterfly: a story about life and death* ill. by Sandy Haight. Parenting Pr., 1992. ISBN 0-943990-69-6 Subj: Death. Emotions – grief. Illness – cancer. Insects – butterflies, caterpillars. Metamorphosis.

Mara, Wil. *Amelia Earhart* ill. with photos. Childrens Pr., 2002. ISBN 0-516-22522-7 Subj: Activities – flying. Careers – airplane pilots. U.S. history.

Jackie Robinson ill. with photos. Childrens Pr., 2002. ISBN 0-516-22520-0 Subj: Careers. Ethnic groups in the U.S. – African Americans. Sports – baseball.

Laura Ingalls Wilder ill. with photos. Childrens Pr., 2003. ISBN 0-516-22855-2 Subj: Careers – authors. U.S. history – frontier & pioneer life.

Marceau, Marcel. *The Marcel Marceau counting book* (Mendoza, George)

The story of Bip ill. by author. HarperCollins, 1976. ISBN 0-06-024053-9 Subj: Clowns, jesters. Imagination.

Marcellino, Fred. *I, crocodile* ill. by author. HarperCollins, 1999. ISBN 0-06-205199-7 Subj: Food. Foreign lands – Egypt. Foreign lands – France. Humorous stories. Reptiles – alligators, crocodiles. Royalty – emperors.

Marciano, John Bemelmans. *Delilah* ill. by author. Viking, 2002. ISBN 0-670-03523-8 Subj: Animals – babies. Animals – sheep. Careers – farmers. Character traits – individuality. Farms. Friendship.

Madeline says merci ill. by author. Viking, 2001. ISBN 0-670-03505-X Subj: Etiquette. Rhyming text.

Marcin, Marietta. *A zoo in her bed* ill. by Sofia. Coward, 1963. Subj: Bedtime. Rhyming text. Toys.

Marco, Chris. *Bee* (Hartley, Karen)

Cockroach (Hartley, Karen)

Hearing in living things (Hartley, Karen)

Ladybug (Hartley, Karen)

Seeing in living things (Hartley, Karen)

The sixth sense and other special senses (Hartley, Karen)

Smelling in living things (Hartley, Karen)

Snail (Hartley, Karen)

Tasting in living things (Hartley, Karen)

Touching in living things (Hartley, Karen)

Marcos, subcomandante. *The story of colors = La historia de los colores* ill. by Domitila Domínguez; trans. by Anne Bar Din. Cinco Puntos, 1999. ISBN 0-938317-45-8 Subj: Concepts – color. Folk & fairy tales – pourquoi tales. Foreign lands – Mexico. Foreign languages. Indians of Central America – Maya.

Marcus, Susan. *Casey visits the doctor* ill. by Deborah Drew-Brook. CBC Merchandising, 1982. ISBN 0-88794-101-X Subj: Careers – doctors. Health & fitness.

The missing button adventure ill. by Hajime Sawada. CBC Merchandising, 1981. ISBN 0-88794-102-8 Subj: Behavior – lost & found possessions. Character traits – helpfulness. Toys – bears.

Mare, Walter De La. see De La Mare, Walter (Walter John)

Margalit, Avishai. *The Hebrew alphabet book: Me-Alef+8:ad Tav* ill. by author. Funk & Wagnalls, 1968. Subj: ABC books. Jewish culture.

Margalith, Joan. *The babies are landing* ill. by Linda Bronson. Chronicle, 2000. ISBN 0-81182-674-0 Subj: Babies. Rhyming text.

Margolin, H. Ellen. *Goin' to Boston* ill. by Emily Bolam. Handprint, 2002. ISBN 1-929766-45-9 Subj: Activities – traveling. Cumulative tales. Music. Songs.

Margolis, Matthew. *Some swell pup: or Are you sure you want a dog?* (Sendak, Maurice)

Margolis, Richard J. *Big bear, spare that tree* ill. by Jack Kent. Greenwillow, 1980. ISBN 0-688-80248-6 Subj: Animals – bears. Birds – bluejays. Ecology. Trees.

Secrets of a small brother ill. by Donald Carrick. Macmillan, 1984. ISBN 0-02-762280-0 Subj: Poetry. Sibling rivalry.

Mari, Iela. *Eat and be eaten* ill. by author. Barron's, 1980. ISBN 0-8120-5396-6 Subj: Animals. Format, unusual. Sports – hunting. Wordless.

The magic balloon ill. by author. S. G. Phillips, 1970. Subj: Toys – balloons. Wordless.

Mariana. *Doki, the lonely papoose* ill. by author. Lothrop, 1955. Subj: Indians of North America.

The journey of Bangwell Putt ill. by author. Lothrop, 1965. Subj: Holidays – Christmas. Toys – dolls.

Marie, Geraldine. *The magic box* ill. by Michele Chessare. Elsevier-Nelson, 1981. ISBN 0-525-66721-0 Subj: Animals – dogs. Birthdays. Magic. Problem solving.

Maril, Lee. *Mr. Bunny paints the eggs* ill. by Irena Lorentowicz. Roy Pub., 1945. Subj: Animals – rabbits. Concepts – color. Holidays – Easter. Music. Songs.

Marino, Barbara Pavis. *Eric needs stitches* photos by Richard Rudinski. Addison-Wesley, 1979. ISBN 0-201-04401-3 Subj: Hospitals.

Marino, Dorothy. *Buzzy Bear and the rainbow* ill. by author. Watts, 1962. Subj: Animals – bears. Weather – rainbows.

Buzzy Bear goes camping ill. by author. Watts, 1964. Subj: Animals – bears. Camps, camping.

Buzzy Bear in the garden ill. by author. Watts, 1963, 1961. Subj: Animals – bears. Gardens, gardening.

Buzzy Bear's busy day ill. by author. Watts, 1965. Subj: Animals – bears.

Edward and the boxes ill. by author. Lippincott, 1957. Subj: Activities – playing. Sleep.

Good-bye thunderstorm ill. by author. Lippincott, 1958. Subj: Weather – lightning, thunder. Weather – rain. Weather – storms.

Mario, Heidi Stetson. *I'd rather have an iguana* ill. by author. Charlesbridge, 1999. ISBN 0-88106-357-6 Subj: Babies. Emotions – envy, jealousy. Family life – brothers & sisters. Family life – new sibling.

Marion, Jeff Daniel. *Hello, Crow* ill. by Leslie Bowman. Orchard, 1992. ISBN 0-531-08575-9 Subj: Birds – crows.

Mariotti, Mario. *Hand games* photos by author. Kane/Miller, 1992. ISBN 0-916291-43-X Subj: Sports – Olympics.

Hands off! photos by Roberto Marchiori. Kane/Miller, 1990. ISBN 0-916291-29-4 Subj: Imagination.

Hanimations photos by Roberto Marchiori. Kane/Miller, 1989. Original title: Rimani. ISBN 0-916291-22-7 Subj: Imagination.

Maris, Ron. *Are you there, bear?* ill. by author. Greenwillow, 1984. ISBN 0-688-03998-7 Subj: Behavior – lost. Toys. Toys – bears.

Bernard's boring day ill. by author. Delacorte, 1990. ISBN 0-385-29948-6 Subj: Animals. Behavior – boredom. Format, unusual – toy & movable books. Mythical creatures – gnomes. Sports – fishing.

Better move on, frog! ill. by author. Watts, 1982. ISBN 0-531-04575-7 Subj: Animals. Frogs & toads. Homes, houses. Nature.

Ducks quack ill. by author. Candlewick, 1992. ISBN 1-56402-080-0 Subj: Animals. Farms. Format, unusual – board books. Noise, sounds. Scarecrows.

Frogs jump ill. by author. Candlewick, 1992. ISBN 1-56402-081-9 Subj: Animals. Format, unusual – board books. Frogs & toads.

Hold tight, bear! ill. by author. Delacorte, 1989. ISBN 0-440-50152-0 Subj: Animals – bears. Animals – donkeys. Forest, woods. Problem solving. Toys – dolls. Wordless.

I wish I could fly ill. by author. Greenwillow, 1986. ISBN 0-688-06655-0 Subj: Animals. Behavior – wishing. Reptiles – turtles, tortoises.

In my garden ill. by author. Greenwillow, 1988. ISBN 0-688-07631-9 Subj: Activities – picnicking. Animals. Counting, numbers. Flowers. Gardens, gardening.

Is anyone home? ill. by author. Greenwillow, 1985. ISBN 0-688-05899-X Subj: Family life – grandparents. Farms. Format, unusual – toy & movable books.

My book ill. by author. Watts, 1983. ISBN 0-531-04610-9 Subj: Animals – cats. Bedtime.

Runaway rabbit ill. by author. Delacorte, 1989. ISBN 0-385-29764-5 Subj: Animals. Animals – rabbits. Behavior – running away.

Mark, Jan. *Fun with Mrs. Thumb* ill. by Nicola Bayley. Candlewick, 1993. ISBN 1-56402-247-1 Subj: Animals – cats. Rhyming text. Toys. Toys – dolls.

Fur ill. by Charlotte Voake. Walker, 1986. ISBN 0-7445-0478-3 Subj: Animals – cats. Birth. Pets.

The Midas touch ill. by Juan Wijngaard. Candlewick, 1999. ISBN 0-7636-0488-7 Subj: Behavior – greed. Behavior – wishing. Folk & fairy tales. Royalty – kings.

The tale of Tobias ill. by Rachel Merriman. Candlewick, 1996. ISBN 1-56402-692-2 Subj: Folk & fairy tales. Religion.

Markert, Jenny. *Giraffes* ill. with photos. Child's World, 2001. ISBN 1-56766-879-8 Subj: Animals – giraffes. Nature.

Markes, Julie. *Good thing you're not an octopus!* ill. by Maggie Smith. HarperCollins, 2001. ISBN 0-06-028466-8 Subj: Activities. Animals. Self-concept.

Sidewalk ABC ill. by Jennifer Markes. HarperFestival, 2001. ISBN 0-694-01455-9 Subj: ABC books. Format, unusual – board books.

Sidewalk 1 2 3 ill. by Jennifer Markes. HarperFestival, 2001. ISBN 0-694-01500-8 Subj: Counting, numbers. Format, unusual – board books.

Thanks for Thanksgiving ill. by Doris Barrette. HarperCollins, 2004. ISBN 0-06-051097-8 Subj: Holidays – Thanksgiving. Rhyming text.

Markle, Sandra. *Creepy, crawly baby bugs* ill. with photos. Walker, 1996. ISBN 0-8027-8444-5 Subj: Animals – babies. Insects. Science.

Outside and inside alligators ill. by author. Atheneum, 1998. ISBN 0-689-81457-7 Subj: Anatomy. Reptiles – alligators, crocodiles.

Outside and inside bats ill. by author. Atheneum, 1997. ISBN 0-689-81165-9 Subj: Anatomy. Animals – bats.

Outside and inside dinosaurs ill. by author. Atheneum, 2000. ISBN 0-689-82300-2 Subj: Anatomy. Dinosaurs. Fossils. Science.

Outside and inside you ill. by Susan Kuklin. Bradbury, 1991. ISBN 0-02-762311-4 Subj: Anatomy.

Markoe, Merrill. *The day my dogs became guys* ill. by Eric Brace. Viking, 1999. ISBN 0-670-85344-5 Subj: Animals – dogs. Astronomy. Behavior. Sun.

Marks, Alan. *Nowhere to be found* ill. by author. Picture Book Studio, 1988. ISBN 0-88708-062-6 Subj: Behavior – lost. Behavior – lost & found possessions. Language.

Marks, Burton. *Animals* ill. by Paul Harvey. Troll, 1991. ISBN 0-8167-2415-6 Subj: Animals.

Colors and numbers ill. by Paul Harvey. Troll, 1991. ISBN 0-8167-2411-3 Subj: Concepts – color. Counting, numbers.

Marks, J. *see* Highwater, Jamake

Marks, Marcia Bliss. *Swing me, swing tree* ill. by David Berger. Little, 1959. Subj: Activities – swinging. Poetry.

Marlowe, Pete. *One Arabian morning* ill. by Charles Bell. Annick, 2000. ISBN 1-55037-659-4 Subj: Foreign lands. Imagination. Royalty.

Marokvia, Merelle. *A French school for Paul* ill. by Artur Marokvia. Lippincott, 1963. Subj: Circus. Foreign lands – France. School.

Marol, Jean-Claude. *Vagabul and his shadow* ill. by author. Creative Ed., 1983. ISBN 0-87191-889-7 Subj: Shadows. Wordless.

Vagabul escapes ill. by author. Creative Ed., 1983. ISBN 0-87191-888-9 Subj: Behavior – running away. Wordless.

Vagabul goes skiing ill. by author. Creative Ed., 1983. ISBN 0-87191-886-2 Subj: Sports – skiing. Wordless.

Vagabul in the clouds ill. by author. Creative Ed., 1983. ISBN 0-87191-887-0 Subj: Weather – clouds. Wordless.

Marron, Carol A. *Gretchen's grandma* (Root, Phyllis)

No trouble for Grandpa ill. by Chaya M. Burstein. Raintree, 1983. ISBN 0-940742-27-6 Subj: Family life – grandfathers. Handicaps. Sibling rivalry.

Marsh, Gwen. *My everyday Spanish word book* (Kahn, Michèle)

Marsh, Jeri. *Hurrah for Alexander* ill. by Joan Hanson. Carolrhoda, 1977. ISBN 0-8761-4092-4 Subj: Character traits – persistence. Humorous stories.

Marsh, T. J. *Somewhere in the ocean* (Ward, Jennifer)

Way out in the desert by T. J. Marsh & Jennifer Ward; ill. by Kenneth J. Spengler. Rising Moon, 1998. ISBN 0-8735-8687-5 Subj: Animals. Animals – babies. Counting, numbers. Desert. Picture puzzles. Rhyming text.

Marshak, S. (Samuil). *The absentminded fellow* trans. from Russian by Richard Pevear; ill. by Marc Rosenthal. Farrar, 1999. ISBN 0-374-30013-5 Subj: Behavior – forgetfulness. Humorous stories. Memories, memory. Rhyming text.

Hail to mail trans. from Russian by Richard Pevear; ill. by Vladimir Radunsky. Holt, 1990. ISBN 0-8050-1132-3 Subj: Careers – postal workers. Poetry. Post office.

In the van trans. from Russian by Margaret Wettlin; ill. by V. Lebedev. Imported Pubs., 1983. ISBN 0-8285-2289-8 Subj: Animals – dogs. Moving. Poetry.

The merry starlings by Samuel Marshak with D. Harms; trans. from Russian by Dorian Rottenberg; ill. by Arieh Zeldich. HarperCollins, 1983. Subj: Birds. Nursery rhymes. Poetry.

The Month-Brothers: a Slavic tale trans. from Russian by Thomas P. Whitney; ill. by Diane Stanley. Morrow, 1983. ISBN 0-688-01510-7 Subj: Foreign lands – Czechoslovakia. Rhyming text. Seasons. Weather.

The pup grew up! trans. by Richard Pevear; ill. by Vladimir Radunsky. Holt, 1989. ISBN 0-8050-0952-3 Subj: Activities – traveling. Animals – dogs. Behavior – growing up. Behavior – lost & found possessions. Rhyming text. Trains.

The tale of a hero nobody knows trans. from Russian by Peter Tempest; ill. by Vassili Shulzhenko. Imported Pubs., 1983. ISBN 0-8285-2291-X Subj: Character traits – bravery. Foreign lands – Russia. Poetry.

Marshall, Catherine. *Christy, Christmastime at Cutter Gap* (LeSourd, Nancy)

Marshall, Douglas. *see* McClintock, Marshall

Marshall, Edward. *Four on the shore* ill. by James Marshall. Dial, 1985. ISBN 0-8037-0142-X Subj: Monsters. Sibling rivalry.

Fox all week ill. by James Marshall. Dial, 1984. ISBN 0-8037-0066-0 Subj: Animals. Animals – foxes. Friendship.

Fox and his friends ill. by James Marshall. Dial, 1982. ISBN 0-8037-2669-4 Subj: Animals – foxes. Behavior – misbehavior.

Fox at school ill. by James Marshall. Dial, 1983. ISBN 0-8037-2675-9 Subj: Animals – foxes. Humorous stories. School.

Fox in love ill. by James Marshall. Dial, 1982. ISBN 0-8037-2433-0 Subj: Animals – foxes. Emotions – love.

Fox on wheels ill. by James Marshall. Dial, 1983. ISBN 0-8037-0002-4 Subj: Animals – foxes. Behavior – misbehavior. Sports – racing.

Space case ill. by James Marshall. Dial, 1980. ISBN 0-8037-8007-9 Subj: Holidays – Halloween. Robots. Space & space ships.

Three by the sea ill. by James Marshall. Dial, 1981. ISBN 0-8037-8671-9 Subj: Activities – picnicking. Friendship.

Troll country ill. by James Marshall. Dial, 1980. ISBN 0-8037-6211-9 Subj: Forest, woods. Mythical creatures – trolls.

Marshall, Frances. *Princess Kalina and the hedgehog* (Flot, Jeannette B.)

Marshall, James. *The Cut-Ups* ill. by author. Viking, 1984. ISBN 0-670-25195-X Subj: Behavior – misbehavior. Humorous stories. Toys.

The Cut-Ups at Camp Custer ill. by author. Viking, 1989. ISBN 0-670-82051-2 Subj: Behavior – misbehavior. Camps, camping. Humorous stories.

The Cut-Ups carry on ill. by author. Viking, 1990. ISBN 0-670-81645-0 Subj: Activities – dancing. Contests. Humorous stories.

The Cut-Ups crack up ill. by author. Viking, 1992. ISBN 0-670-84486-1 Subj: Automobiles. Behavior – misbehavior. Humorous stories. School.

The Cut-Ups cut loose ill. by author. Viking, 1987. ISBN 0-670-80740-0 Subj: Behavior – misbehavior. Friendship. Humorous stories. School.

Eugene Ill. by author. Houghton, 2000. ISBN 0-618-07319-1 Subj: Animals. Careers – teachers. Format, unusual – board books. Reptiles – turtles, tortoises. School – first day.

Four little troubles ill. by author. Houghton Mifflin, 1975. ISBN 0-395-19880-1 Subj: Animals. Problem solving. Reptiles – turtles, tortoises.

Fox on the job ill. by author. Dial, 1988. ISBN 0-8037-0351-1 Subj: Activities – working. Animals – foxes. Behavior – misbehavior.

George and Martha ill. by author. Houghton Mifflin, 1972. ISBN 0-395-13732-2 Subj: Animals – hippopotamuses. Friendship.

George and Martha back in town ill. by author. Houghton Mifflin, 1984. ISBN 0-395-35386-6 Subj: Animals – hippopotamuses. Behavior – misbehavior. Friendship.

George and Martha encore ill. by author. Houghton Mifflin, 1973. ISBN 0-395-17512-7 Subj: Activities – dancing. Animals – hippopotamuses. Friendship.

George and Martha one fine day ill. by author. Houghton Mifflin, 1978. ISBN 0-395-27154-1 Subj: Animals – hippopotamuses. Friendship.

George and Martha rise and shine ill. by author. Houghton Mifflin, 1976. ISBN 0-395-24738-1 Subj: Animals – hippopotamuses. Friendship.

George and Martha 'round and 'round ill. by author. Houghton Mifflin, 1988. ISBN 0-395-46763-2 Subj: Activities – vacationing. Animals – hippopotamuses. Friendship. Imagination.

George and Martha, tons of fun ill. by author. Houghton Mifflin, 1980. ISBN 0-395-29524-6 Subj: Animals – hippopotamuses. Character traits – vanity.

Goldilocks and the three bears (The three bears)

The guest ill. by author. Houghton Mifflin, 1975. ISBN 0-395-20277-9 Subj: Animals – moose. Animals – snails. Friendship.

Hansel and Gretel ill. by reteller. Dial, 1990. ISBN 0-8037-0828-9 Subj: Behavior – lost. Folk & fairy tales. Forest, woods. Witches.

Hey, diddle, daddle ill. by author. Heath, 1989. ISBN 0-669-13293-4 Subj: Animals. Animals – horses, ponies. Format, unusual. Frogs & toads. Rhyming text. Sea & seashore.

Hey, diddle, diddle ill. by author. Farrar, 1994. ISBN 0-374-33061-1 Subj: Format, unusual – toy & movable books. Nursery rhymes.

James Marshall's Mother Goose (Mother Goose)

Merry Christmas, space case ill. by author. Dial, 1986. ISBN 0-8037-0216-7 Subj: Holidays – Christmas. Space & space ships.

Miss Dog's Christmas ill. by author. Houghton Mifflin, 1973. ISBN 0-395-18154-2 Subj: Animals – dogs. Food. Holidays – Christmas.

Miss Nelson is back (Allard, Harry)

Miss Nelson is missing! (Allard, Harry)

Pocketful of nonsense ill. by author. Artists & Writers Guild, 1993. ISBN 0-307-17552-9 Subj: Poetry.

Portly McSwine ill. by author. Houghton Mifflin, 1979. ISBN 0-395-28003-6 Subj: Animals – pigs. Behavior – worrying.

Rapscallion Jones ill. by author. Viking, 1983. ISBN 0-670-58965-9 Subj: Animals – foxes. Behavior – seeking better things.

Red Riding Hood ill. by adapt. Dial, 1987. ISBN 0-8037-0345-7 Subj: Animals – wolves. Behavior – talking to strangers. Folk & fairy tales.

Sing out, Irene ill. by author. Houghton, 2000. ISBN 0-618-07321-3 Subj: Animals. Format, unusual – board books. Humorous stories. Reptiles – turtles, tortoises. School – first day.

Snake, his story ill. by author. Houghton, 2000. ISBN 0-618-07320-5 Subj: Reptiles – snakes.

Speedboat ill. by author. Houghton Mifflin, 1976. ISBN 0-395-24384-X Subj: Animals – dogs. Boats, ships. Friendship.

The Stupids have a ball (Allard, Harry)

The Stupids take off (Allard, Harry)

Swine lake ill. by Maurice Sendak. HarperCollins, 1999. ISBN 0-06-205171-7 Subj: Activities – dancing. Animals – pigs. Animals – wolves. Ballet. Theater.

The three little pigs (The three little pigs)

Three up a tree ill. by author. Dutton, 1986. ISBN 0-8037-0329-5 Subj: Activities – playing. Imagination. Monsters. Trees.

What's the matter with Carruthers? ill. by author. Houghton Mifflin, 1972. ISBN 0-395-13895-7 Subj: Animals – bears. Bedtime. Character traits – helpfulness. Friendship. Hibernation.

Willis ill. by author. Houghton Mifflin, 1974. ISBN 0-395-19494-6 Subj: Animals. Friendship. Glasses.

Wings: a tale of two chickens ill. by author. Viking, 1986. ISBN 0-670-80961-6 Subj: Animals – foxes. Birds – chickens. Books, reading.

Yummers! ill. by author. Houghton Mifflin, 1973. ISBN 0-395-14757-3 Subj: Animals – pigs. Food. Illness.

Yummers too: the second course ill. by author. Houghton Mifflin, 1986. ISBN 0-395-38990-9 Subj: Animals – pigs. Behavior – greed. Food. Reptiles – turtles, tortoises.

Marshall, Janet Perry. *Baby sharks* (Gentle, Victor)

Banana moon ill. by author. Greenwillow, 1998. ISBN 0-688-15768-8 Subj: Food. Format, unusual – toy & movable books. Sea & seashore. Sports – sailing.

A honey of a day ill. by author. Greenwillow, 2000. ISBN 0-688-16917-1 Subj: Animals. Flowers. Weddings.

Killer sharks, killer people (Gentle, Victor)

My camera: at the zoo ill. by author. Little, 1989. ISBN 0-316-54687-9 Subj: Activities – photographing. Animals. Games. Zoos.

Ohmygosh, my pocket ill. by author. Boyds Mills, 1992. ISBN 1-56397-044-9 Subj: Clothing. Rhyming text. School.

Orcas, killer whales (Gentle, Victor)

Shark camouflage and armor (Gentle, Victor)

Very big sharks (Gentle, Victor)

The world's strangest shark (Gentle, Victor)

Marshall, Lyn. *Yoga for your children* ill. with photos. Schocken, 1979. ISBN 0-8052-0630-2 Subj: Health & fitness. Religion.

Marshall, Margaret. *Mike* ill. by Lorraine Spiro. Merrimack, 1983. ISBN 0-370-30934-0 Subj: Bedtime. Problem solving.

Marshall, Ray. *Pop-up numbers #1* by Ray Marshall & Korky Paul; ill. by authors. Dutton, 1984. ISBN 0-525-44088-7 Subj: Counting, numbers. Format, unusual – toy & movable books.

Pop-up numbers #2 by Ray Marshall & Korky Paul; ill. by authors. Dutton, 1984. ISBN 0-525-44089-5 Subj: Counting, numbers. Format, unusual – toy & movable books.

Pop-up numbers #3 by Ray Marshall & Korky Paul; ill. by authors. Dutton, 1984. ISBN 0-525-44090-9 Subj: Counting, numbers. Format, unusual – toy & movable books.

Pop-up numbers #4 by Ray Marshall & Korky Paul; ill. by authors. Dutton, 1984. ISBN 0-525-44091-7 Subj: Counting, numbers. Format, unusual – toy & movable books.

The train: watch it work by operating the moving diagrams! ill. by John Bradley. Viking, 1986. ISBN 0-670-81134-3 Subj: Format, unusual – toy & movable books. Trains.

Marston, Elsa. *Cynthia and the runaway gazebo* ill. by Friso henstra. Tambourine, 1992. ISBN 0-688-10283-2 Subj: Boats, ships. Pirates. Sea & seashore.

The fox maiden ill. by Tatsuro Kiuchi. S&S, 1996. ISBN 0-689-80107-6 Subj: Animals – foxes. Folk & fairy tales. Foreign lands – Japan. Magic.

A griffin in the garden ill. by Larry Daste. Tambourine, 1993. ISBN 0-688-10982-9 Subj: Gardens, gardening. Mythical creatures – griffins. Rocks.

Marston, Hope Irvin. *Big rigs* ill. with photos. Dodd, 1979. ISBN 0-396-07785-4 Subj: Transportation. Trucks.

Fire trucks ill. with photos. Dodd, 1984. ISBN 0-396-08451-6 Subj: Careers – firefighters. Trucks.

Martchenko, Michael. *Bird feeder banquet* ill. by author. Firefly, 1990. ISBN 1-55037-147-9 Subj: Birds. Character traits – assertiveness. Character traits – kindness to animals. Food. Seasons – winter.

Martel, Cruz. *Yagua days* ill. by Jerry Pinkney. Dial, 1976. ISBN 0-8037-9766-4 Subj: Family life. Foreign lands – Puerto Rico.

Martens, Marianne. *Abel and the wolf* (Lairla, Sergio)

Bernard Bear's amazing adventure (De Beer, Hans)

Evie to the rescue! (Moers, Hermann)

Just the way you are (Pfister, Marcus)

Katie and the big, brave bear (Moers, Hermann)

The little seahorse and the Christmas pearl (Damjan, Mischa)

Milo and the magical stones (Pfister, Marcus)

The ox and the Donkey (Spang, Günter)

Smoky's special Easter present (Lachner, Dorothea)

Timid Timmy (Dierssen, Andreas)

Martin, Ann M. *Fire truck to the rescue* ill. by Steven James Petruccio. Scholastic, 1994. ISBN 0-590-48854-6 Subj: Careers – firefighters. Trucks.

Leo the Magnificat ill. by Emily Arnold McCully. Scholastic, 1996. ISBN 0-590-48498-2 Subj: Animals – cats. Homeless. Religion.

Rachel Parker, kindergarten show-off ill. by Nancy Poydar. Holiday, 1992. ISBN 0-8234-0935-X Subj: Character traits – conceit. Emotions – envy, jealousy. Ethnic groups in the U.S. – African Americans. Friendship. School.

Martin, Antoinette Truglio. *Famous seaweed soup* ill. by Nadine Bernard Westcott. A. Whitman, 1993. ISBN 0-8075-2263-5 Subj: Character traits – laziness. Food. Sea & seashore.

Martin, Bernard H. *Brave little Indian* (Martin, Bill [William Ivan])

Chicken Chuck (Martin, Bill [William Ivan])

Smoky Poky (Martin, Bill [William Ivan])

Martin, Bill (William Ivan). *Adam, Adam, what do you see?* by Bill Martin, Jr. & Michael Sampson; ill. by Cathie Felstead. Tommy Nelson, 2000. ISBN 0-8499-7614-6 Subj: Religion. Rhyming text.

Barn dance! ill. by Ted Rand. Holt, 1986. ISBN 0-8050-0089-5 Subj: Activities – dancing. Barns. Country. Dreams. Night. Rhyming text. Scarecrows.

A beasty story by Bill Martin, Jr. & Steven Kellogg; ill. by Steven Kellogg. Harcourt, 1999. ISBN 0-15-201683-X Subj: Animals – mice. Forest, woods. Monsters.

A beautiful feast for a big king cat (Archambault, John)

Brave little Indian by Bill Martin, Jr. & Bernard H. Martin; ill. by Bernard H. Martin. Holt, 1967, c1951. Subj: Indians of North America. Participation.

Brown bear, brown bear, what do you see? ill. by Eric Carle. Holt, 1992. ISBN 0-8050-1744-5 Subj: Animals – bears. Concepts – color. Cumulative tales. Rhyming text.

Chicka chicka boom boom by Bill Martin, Jr. & John Archambault; ill. by Lois Ehlert. S&S, 1989. ISBN 0-617-67949-X Subj: ABC books. Rhyming text. Trees.

Chicka chicka boom boom [board book] by Bill Martin, Jr. & John Archambault; ill. by Lois Ehlert. S&S, 1993. ISBN 0-671-87893-X Subj: ABC books. Format, unusual – board books. Rhyming text. Trees.

Chicka chicka sticka sticka: an ABC sticker book by Bill Martin, Jr. & John Archambault; ill. by Lois Ehlert. Little Simon, 1995. ISBN 0-689-80096-7 Subj: ABC books. Format, unusual – toy & movable books. Rhyming text. Trees.

Chicken Chuck by Bill Martin, Jr. & Bernard H. Martin; ill. by Steven Salerno. Winslow, 2000. ISBN 1-8908-1731-7 Subj: Animals. Animals – horses, ponies. Birds – chickens. Character traits – individuality. Circus. Farms.

Fire! Fire! said Mrs. McGuire ill. by Richard Egielski. Harcourt, 1996. ISBN 0-15-227562-2 Subj: Birthdays. Careers – firefighters. Fire. Nursery rhymes.

The happy hippopotami ill. by Betsy Everitt. Harcourt, 1990, c1970. ISBN 0-15-233380-0 Subj: Animals – hippopotamuses. Rhyming text.

Here are my hands by Bill Martin, Jr. & John Archambault; ill. by Ted Rand. Holt, 1998. ISBN 0-8050-5911-3 Subj: Anatomy. Rhyming text.

I pledge allegiance commentary by Bill Martin Jr. & Michael Sampson; ill. by Chris Reschka. Candlewick, 2002. ISBN 0-7636-2527-2 Subj: Format, unusual – board books. U.S. history.

Knots on a counting rope by Bill Martin, Jr. & John Archambault; ill. by Ted Rand. Holt, 1987. ISBN 0-8050-0571-4 Subj: Character traits – bravery. Emotions – love. Family life – grandfathers. Handicaps – blindness. Indians of North America. Senses – sight.

Listen to the rain by Bill Martin, Jr. & John Archambault; ill. by James R. Endicott. Holt, 1988. ISBN 0-8050-0682-6 Subj: Rhyming text. Weather – rain.

Little granny quarterback Bill Martin, Jr. & Michael Sampson; ill. by Michael Chesworth. Boyds Mills, 2001. ISBN 1-56397-930-6 Subj: Dreams. Family life – grandmothers. Old age. Rhyming text. Sports – football.

The little squeegy bug by Bill Martin, Jr. & Michael Sampson; ill. by Pat Corrigan. Winslow, 2001. ISBN 1-8908-1790-2 Subj: Insects.

Maestro plays ill. by Vladimir Radunsky. Holt, 1994. ISBN 0-8050-1746-1 Subj: Careers – musicians. Rhyming text.

The magic pumpkin by Bill Martin, Jr. & John Archambault; ill. by Robert J. Lee. Holt, 1989. ISBN 0-8050-1134-X Subj: Holidays – Halloween. Magic. Rhyming text.

My days are made of butterflies adapt. by William Ivan Martin, Jr.; written by Sano M. Galea'i Fa'apouli; ill. by Vic Herman. Holt, 1970. ISBN 0-030-84599-8 Subj: Foreign lands – Mexico.

Old devil wind ill. by Barry Root. Harcourt, 1993. ISBN 0-15-257768-8 Subj: Cumulative tales. Ghosts. Holidays – Halloween. Weather – wind.

Polar bear, polar bear, what do you hear? ill. by Eric Carle. Holt, 1991. ISBN 0-8050-1759-3 Subj: Animals. Noise, sounds. Rhyming text. Zoos.

Rock it, sock it, number line by Bill Martin, Jr. & Michael Sampson; ill. by Heather Cahoon. Holt, 2001. ISBN 0-8050-6304-8 Subj: Counting, numbers. Food. Parties. Plants. Royalty.

Smoky Poky by Bill Martin, Jr. & Bernard H. Martin; ill. by Bernard H. Martin. Tell-Well Pr., 1947. Subj: Animals – elephants. Trains.

Sounds around the clock comp. by Bill Martin, Jr. in collaboration with Peggy Brogan; ill. by various authors & artists. Holt, 1972. ISBN 0-03-086194-2 Subj: Noise, sounds. Poetry.

Sounds I remember comp. by Bill Martin, Jr. in collaboration with Peggy Brogan; ill. by various artists. Holt, 1974. ISBN 0-03-089259-7 Subj: Counting, numbers. Memories, memory. Noise, sounds. Nursery rhymes.

Sounds of home comp. by Bill Martin, Jr. in collaboration with Peggy Brogan; ill. by various authors & artists. Holt, 1972. ISBN 0-03-083351-5 Subj: Noise, sounds. Poetry.

Sounds of laughter comp. by Bill Martin, Jr. in collaboration with Peggy Brogan; ill. by various artists. Holt, 1972. ISBN 0-03-086195-0 Subj: Folk & fairy tales. Humorous stories. Noise, sounds. Poetry.

Sounds of numbers comp. by Bill Martin, Jr. in collaboration with Peggy Brogan; ill. by various artists. Holt, 1972. ISBN 0-03-086193-4 Subj: Counting, numbers. Noise, sounds. Poetry.

Swish! by Bill Martin, Jr. & Michael Sampson; ill. by Michael Chesworth. Holt, 1997. ISBN 0-8050-4498-1 Subj: Sports – basketball.

Trick or treat? by Bill Martin, Jr. & Michael Sampson; ill. by Paul Meisel. S&S, 2002. ISBN 0-689-84968-0 Subj: Behavior – trickery. Food. Holidays – Halloween. Magic.

The turning of the year ill. by Greg Shed. Harcourt, 1998. ISBN 0-15-201085-8 Subj: Days of the week, months of the year. Rhyming text. Seasons.

Up and down on the merry-go-round by Bill Martin, Jr. & John Archambault; ill. by Ted Rand. Holt, 1988. ISBN 0-8050-0681-8 Subj: Merry-go-rounds.

White Dynamite and Curly Kidd by Bill Martin, Jr. & John Archambault; ill. by Ted Rand. Holt, 1986. ISBN 0-03-008399-0 Subj: Animals – bulls, cows. Family life. Sports.

The wizard ill. by Alex Schaefer. Harcourt, 1994. ISBN 0-15-298926-9 Subj: Magic. Rhyming text. Wizards.

Words by Bill Martin, Jr. & John Archambault; ill. by Lois Ehlert. Little Simon, 1993. ISBN 0-671-87174-9 Subj: Language.

Martin, C. L. G. *The blueberry train* ill. by Angela Trotta Thomas. Atheneum, 1995. ISBN 0-689-80304-4 Subj: Activities – traveling. Behavior – growing up. Family life. Trains. Transportation.

Down Dairy Farm Road ill. by Diane Dawson Hearn. Macmillan, 1994. ISBN 0-02-762450-1 Subj: Animals. Careers – veterinarians. Family life – grandfathers. Farms.

The dragon nanny ill. by Robert Rayevsky. Aladdin, 1991. ISBN 0-689-71451-3 Subj: Activities – babysitting. Dragons. Royalty – kings.

Three brave women ill. by Peter Elwell. Macmillan, 1991. ISBN 0-02-762445-5 Subj: Emotions – fear. Family life – grandmothers. Family life – mothers.

Martin, Charles E. *Dunkel takes a walk* ill. by author. Greenwillow, 1983. ISBN 0-688-01816-5 Subj: Animals – dogs. Character traits – cleverness.

For rent ill. by author. Greenwillow, 1986. ISBN 0-688-05717-9 Subj: Activities – painting. Islands. School. Seasons – summer.

Island rescue ill. by author. Greenwillow, 1985. ISBN 0-688-04258-9 Subj: Hospitals. Islands. Seasons – spring.

Island winter ill. by author. Greenwillow, 1984. ISBN 0-688-02592-7 Subj: Islands. Seasons – winter.

Noah's ark retold by Lawrence T. Lorimer; ill. by Charles E. Martin. Random House, 1978. ISBN 0-394-93861-5 Subj: Boats, ships. Religion – Noah. Weather – floods. Weather – rain. Weather – rainbows.

Sam saves the day ill. by author. Greenwillow, 1987. ISBN 0-688-06815-4 Subj: Activities – traveling. Activities – vacationing. Seasons – summer.

Martin, Claire. *Boots and the glass mountain* ill. by Gennady Spirin. Dial, 1992. ISBN 0-8037-1111-5 Subj: Folk & fairy tales. Foreign lands – Norway. Mythical creatures – trolls. Royalty – princesses.

The race of the golden apples ill. by Leo & Diane Dillon. Dial, 1991. ISBN 0-8037-0249-3 Subj: Animals – bears. Folk & fairy tales. Royalty – princesses.

Martin, David. *Five little piggies* ill. by Susan Meddaugh. Candlewick, 1998. ISBN 1-56402-918-2 Subj: Animals – pigs. Family life. Shopping.

Little Chicken Chicken ill. by Sue Heap. Candlewick, 1996. ISBN 1-56402-381-8 Subj: Birds – chickens. Imagination. Weather – lightning, thunder. Weather – storms.

Lizzie and her dolly ill. by Debi Gliori. Candlewick, 1993. ISBN 1-56402-060-6 Subj: Games. Rhyming text. Toys – dolls.

Lizzie and her friend ill. by Debi Gliori. Candlewick, 1993. ISBN 1-56402-061-4 Subj: Activities – playing. Friendship. Rhyming text. Water.

Lizzie and her kitty ill. by Debi Gliori. Candlewick, 1993. ISBN 1-56402-058-4 Subj: Animals – cats. Rhyming text.

Lizzie and her puppy ill. by Debi Gliori. Candlewick, 1993. ISBN 1-56402-059-2 Subj: Activities – playing. Animals – dogs. Rhyming text.

Monkey business ill. by Scott Nash. Candlewick, 2000. ISBN 0-7636-1178-6 Subj: Animals – monkeys. Birthdays. Family life – mothers.

Monkey trouble ill. by Scott Nash. Candlewick, 2000. ISBN 0-7636-1179-4 Subj: Animals – monkeys. Behavior – misbehavior.

Piggy and Dad ill. by Frank Remkiewicz. Candlewick, 2001. ISBN 0-7636-1326-6 Subj: Activities. Animals – pigs. Family life – fathers.

Piggy and Dad go fishing ill. by Frank Remkiewicz. Candlewick, 2005. ISBN 0-7636-2506-X Subj: Animals – pigs. Animals – worms. Family life – fathers. Fish. Sports – fishing.

We've all got bellybuttons ill. by Randy Cecil. Candlewick, 2005. ISBN 0-7636-1775-X Subj: Anatomy. Anatomy – navels. Animals. Rhyming text.

Martin, Diane. *Mister Mole* (Murschetz, Luis)

Martin, Francesca. *Clever Tortoise: a traditional African tale* ill. by author. Candlewick, 2000. ISBN 0-7636-0506-9 Subj: Animals. Folk & fairy tales. Foreign lands – Tanzania. Reptiles – turtles, tortoises.

The honey hunters ill. by reteller. Candlewick, 1992. ISBN 1-56402-086-X Subj: Animals. Behavior – fighting, arguing. Folk & fairy tales. Foreign lands – Africa.

Martin, Jacqueline Briggs. *Bizzy Bones and Moosemouse* ill. by Stella Ormai. Lothrop, 1986. ISBN 0-688-05746-2 Subj: Animals – mice. Behavior – lost. Friendship.

Bizzy Bones and the lost quilt ill. by Stella Ormai. Lothrop, 1988. ISBN 0-688-07408-1 Subj: Animals – mice. Behavior – lost & found possessions. Friendship. Quilts.

Bizzy Bones and Uncle Ezra ill. by Stella Ormai. Lothrop, 1984. ISBN 0-688-03782-8 Subj: Animals – mice. Emotions – fear. Family life – aunts, uncles.

Button, bucket, sky ill. by Vicki Jo Redenbaugh. Carolrhoda, 1998. ISBN 1-57505-244-X Subj: Gardens, gardening. Seeds. Trees.

The finest horse in town ill. by Susan Gaber. HarperCollins, 1992. ISBN 0-06-024152-7 Subj: Animals – horses, ponies. Family life – sisters. Memories, memory.

Good times on Grandfather Mountain ill. by Susan Gaber. Watts, 1992. ISBN 0-531-08577-5 Subj: Activities – making things. Character traits – optimism.

Grandmother Bryant's pocket ill. by Petra Mathers. Houghton Mifflin, 1996. ISBN 0-395-68984-8 Subj: Dreams. Emotions – fear. Emotions – grief. Family life – grandparents. Fire. Pets. Sleep.

The green truck garden giveaway: a neighborhood story and almanac ill. by Alec Gillman. S&S, 1997. ISBN 0-689-80498-9 Subj: Cities, towns. Communities, neighborhoods. Gardens, gardening.

On Sand Island ill. by David Johnson. Houghton, 2003. ISBN 0-618-23151-X Subj: Activities – trading. Boats, ships. Family life. Islands. Lakes, ponds.

Snowflake Bentley ill. by Mary Azarian. Houghton Mifflin, 1998. ISBN 0-395-86162-4 Subj: Caldecott award books. Careers – photographers. Careers – scientists. Nature. U.S. history. Weather – snow.

Washing the willow tree loon ill. by Nancy Carpenter. S&S, 1995. ISBN 0-02-762442-0 Subj: Birds – loons. Character traits – kindness to animals. Ecology.

The water gift and the pig of the pig ill. by Linda Wingerter. Houghton Mifflin, 2002. ISBN 0-618-07436-8 Subj: Animals – pigs. Family life – grandfathers. Orphans.

Martin, Jane Read. *Now everybody really hates me* by Jane Read Martin & Patricia Marx; ill. by Roz Chast. HarperCollins, 1993. ISBN 0-06-021294-2 Subj: Behavior – bad day. Character traits – selfishness. Sibling rivalry.

Now I will never leave the dinner table by Jane Read Martin & Patricia Marx; ill. by Roz Chast. HarperCollins, 1996. ISBN 0-06-024795-9 Subj: Behavior – bad day. Sibling rivalry.

Martin, Janet. *see* Allen, Robert

Martin, Jerome. *Carrot/parrot* ill. by author. S&S, 1991. ISBN 0-671-69555-X Subj: Format, unusual. Language. Rhyming text.

Mitten/kitten ill. by author. S&S, 1991. ISBN 0-671-69556-8 Subj: Format, unusual. Language. Rhyming text.

Martin, Judith. *The tree angel* by Judith Martin & Remy Charlip; ill. by Remy Charlip. Knopf, 1962. ISBN 0-440-40726-7 Subj: Angels. Holidays – Christmas. Theater.

Martin, Linda. *When dinosaurs go to school* ill. by author. Chronicle, 1999. ISBN 0-8118-2089-0 Subj: Dinosaurs. Prehistory. Rhyming text. School.

Martin, Mary Jane. *From Anne to Zach* ill. by Michael Grejniec. Boyds Mills, 1996. ISBN 1-56397-573-4 Subj: ABC books. Names. Rhyming text.

Martin, Nora. *The stone dancers* ill. by Jill Kastner. Atheneum, 1995. ISBN 0-689-80312-5 Subj: Activities – dancing. Character traits – kindness.

Martin, Patricia Miles. *see* Miles, Miska

Martin, Rafe. *The eagle's gift* ill. by Tatsuro Kiuchi. Putnam, 1997. ISBN 0-399-22923-X Subj: Alaska. Birds – eagles. Eskimos. Folk & fairy tales. Indians of North America – Inuit.

Foolish rabbit's big mistake ill. by Ed Young. Putnam, 1985. ISBN 0-399-21178-0 Subj: Animals – rabbits. Behavior – mistakes. Folk & fairy tales.

The hungry tigress: and other traditional Asian tales ill. by Richard Wehrman. Shambhala, 1984. ISBN 0-394-53698-3 Subj: Folk & fairy tales.

The language of birds ill. by Susan Gaber. Putnam, 2000. ISBN 0-399-22925-6 Subj: Character traits – kindness to animals. Folk & fairy tales. Foreign lands – Russia.

The monkey bridge ill. by Fahimeh Amiri. Knopf, 1997. ISBN 0-679-98106-3 Subj: Animals – monkeys. Character traits – bravery. Foreign lands – India. Royalty – kings.

The rough-face girl ill. by David Shannon. Putnam, 1992. ISBN 0-399-21859-9 Subj: Family life – sisters. Folk & fairy tales. Indians of North America – Algonquin.

The Shark God ill. by David Shannon. Levine, 2001. ISBN 0-590-39500-9 Subj: Character traits – kindness to animals. Fish – sharks. Folk & fairy tales. Hawaii. Royalty – kings.

The storytelling princess ill. by Kimberly Bulcken Root. Putnam, 2001. ISBN 0-399-22924-8 Subj: Activities – storytelling. Royalty – princes. Royalty – princesses.

The twelve months ill. by Vladyana Langer Krykorka. Stoddart, 2000. ISBN 0-7737-3249-7 Subj: Days of the week, months of the year. Folk & fairy tales. Foreign lands.

Will's mammoth ill. by Stephen Grammell. Putnam, 1989. ISBN 0-399-21627-8 Subj: Animals. Imagination.

Martin, Sarah Catherine. *The comic adventures of Old Mother Hubbard and her dog* ill. by Arnold Lobel. Bradbury, 1968. Subj: Animals – dogs. Nursery rhymes.

Old Mother Hubbard retold and ill. by Jane Cabrera. Holiday, 2001. Based on The comic adventures of Old Mother Hubbard and her dog, originally published in London, 1805, by John Harris. ISBN 0-8234-1659-3 Subj: Animals – dogs. Nursery rhymes.

Old Mother Hubbard adapt. by Colin & Jacqui Hawkins; ill. by Colin Hawkins. Putnam, 1985. ISBN 0-399-21162-4 Subj: Animals – dogs. Format, unusual – toy & movable books. Nursery rhymes.

Old Mother Hubbard and her dog ill. by Lisa Amoroso. Knopf, 1987. ISBN 0-394-98922-8 Subj: Animals – dogs. Nursery rhymes.

Old Mother Hubbard and her dog ill. by Paul Galdone. McGraw-Hill, 1960. Subj: Animals – dogs. Nursery rhymes.

Old Mother Hubbard and her dog ill. by Evaline Ness. Holt, 1972. ISBN 0-03-091360-8 Subj: Animals – dogs. Nursery rhymes.

Old Mother Hubbard and her wonderful dog ill. by James Marshall. Farrar, 1991. ISBN 0-374-35621-1 Subj: Animals – dogs. Nursery rhymes.

Martinez, Alba Nora. *Delicious hullabaloo = Pachanga deliciosa* (Mora, Pat)

Martinez, Ruth. *Mrs. McDockerty's knitting* ill. by Catherine O'Neill. Houghton Mifflin, 1990. ISBN 0-395-51591-2 Subj: Activities – knitting. Animals – cats. Animals – dogs. Animals – pigs. Cumulative tales. Problem solving.

Martin-James, Kathleen. *Soaring bald eagles* ill. with photos. Lerner, 2001. ISBN 0-8225-3636-6 Subj: Birds – eagles.

Martín Larrañaga, Ana. *The big wide-mouthed frog* ill. by author. Candlewick, 1999. ISBN 0-7636-0807-6 Subj: Frogs & toads. Self-concept.

Pepo and Lolo and the red apple ill. by author. Candlewick, 2004. ISBN 0-7636-2036-X Subj: Animals – pigs. Birds – chickens. Character traits – cooperation. Food.

Pepo and Lolo are friends ill. by author. Candlewick, 2004. ISBN 0-7636-1982-5 Subj: Animals – pigs. Birds – chickens. Friendship.

Woo! The not-so-scary Ghost ill. by author. Levine, 2000. ISBN 0-439-16958-5 Subj: Behavior – running away. Emotions – fear. Ghosts.

Marton, Jirina. *Flowers for mom* ill. by author. Firefly, 1991. ISBN 1-55037-155-X Subj: Behavior – bullying. Character traits – generosity. Flowers.

I'll do it myself ill. by author. Firefly, 1989. ISBN 1-55037-063-4 Subj: Dreams. Family life – mothers. Hair.

Midnight visit at Molly's house ill. by author. Firefly, 1988. ISBN 0-920303-99-4 Subj: Dreams. Moon. Night.

Marx, David F. *Canada* ill. with photos. Childrens Pr., 2000. ISBN 0-516-21550-7 Subj: Foreign lands – Canada.

Ramadan ill. with photos. Childrens Pr., 2002. ISBN 0-516-22269-4 Subj: Holidays – Ramadan. Religion.

Marx, Patricia (Patricia A.). *Meet my staff* ill. by Roz Chast. HarperCollins, 1998. ISBN 0-06-027485-9 Subj: Imagination – imaginary friends.

Now everybody really hates me (Martin, Jane Read)

Now I will never leave the dinner table (Martin, Jane Read)

Marzollo, Claudio. *Jed and the space bandits* (Marzollo, Jean)

Jed's junior space patrol (Marzollo, Jean)

Marzollo, Jean. *Amy goes fishing* ill. by Ann Schweninger. Dial, 1980. ISBN 0-8037-0109-8 Subj: Family life – fathers. Sports – fishing.

Baby's alphabet photos by Nancy Sheehan. Roaring Brook, 2002. ISBN 0-7613-2760-6 Subj: ABC books. Babies.

Baseball brothers by Jean, Dan, Dave Marzollo; ill. by True Kelley. Scholastic, 1999. ISBN 0-590-38398-1 Subj: Family life – brothers. Sports – baseball.

Christmas cats ill. by Hans Wilhelm. Scholastic, 1997. ISBN 0-590-37212-2 Subj: Animals – cats. Holidays – Christmas. Rhyming text.

Close your eyes ill. by Susan Jeffers. Dial, 1978. ISBN 0-8037-1610-9 Subj: Bedtime. Family life – fathers. Lullabies.

Daniel in the lion's den ill. by reteller. Little, 2003. ISBN 0-316-74132-9 Subj: Animals – lions. Religion – Daniel.

Do you know new? ill. by Mari Takabayashi. HarperCollins, 1997. ISBN 0-694-00870-2 Subj: Babies. Format, unusual – board books. Rhyming text.

Home sweet home ill. by Ashley Wolff. HarperCollins, 1997. ISBN 0-06-027353-4 Subj: Animals. Homes, houses. Nature. Rhyming text.

I love you: a rebus poem ill. by Suse MacDonald. Scholastic, 2000. ISBN 0-590-37656-X Subj: Concepts. Emotions – love. Poetry. Rebuses.

I see a star ill. by Suse MacDonald. Scholastic, 2002. ISBN 0-439-26616-5 Subj: Holidays – Christmas. Rebuses. Stars.

I spy a book of picture riddles (Wick, Walter)

I spy Christmas: a book of picture riddles (Wick, Walter)

I spy extreme challenger! a book of picture riddles (Wick, Walter)

I spy fantasy: a book of picture riddles (Wick, Walter)

I spy gold challenger! a book of picture riddles (Wick, Walter)

I spy little animals photos by Walter Wick. Scholastic, 1998. ISBN 0-590-11711-4 Subj: Animals. Format, unusual – board books. Picture puzzles. Rhyming text.

I spy little book photos by Walter Wick. Scholastic, 1997. ISBN 0-590-34129-4 Subj: Format, unusual – board books. Picture puzzles. Rhyming text.

I spy little bunnies photos by Walter Wick. Scholastic, 2001. ISBN 0-439-22158-7 Subj: Animals – rabbits. Picture puzzles. Rhyming text.

I spy little Christmas photos by Walter Wick. Scholastic, 1999. ISBN 0-439-08331-1 Subj: Holidays – Christmas. Picture puzzles. Rhyming text.

I spy little letters photos by Walter Wick. Scholastic, 2000. ISBN 0-439-11496-9 Subj: ABC books. Picture puzzles. Rhyming text.

I spy little numbers photos by Walter Wick. Scholastic, 1999. ISBN 0-590-68714-X Subj: Counting, numbers. Picture puzzles. Rhyming text.

I spy little wheels photos by Walter Wick. Scholastic, 1998. ISBN 0-590-04706-X Subj: Format, unusual – board books. Picture puzzles. Rhyming text. Toys.

I spy, mystery photos by Walter Wick. Scholastic, 1993. ISBN 0-590-46294-6 Subj: Picture puzzles. Rhyming text. Riddles & jokes.

I spy school days (Wick, Walter)

I spy spooky night: a book of picture riddles (Wick, Walter)

I spy super challenger! (Wick, Walter)

I spy treasure hunt (Wick, Walter)

I spy ultimate challenger! (Wick, Walter)

I spy, year-round challenger! photos by Walter Wick. Scholastic, 2001. ISBN 0-439-31634-0 Subj: Days of the week, months of the year. Picture puzzles. Rhyming text. Riddles & jokes.

I'm a caterpillar ill. by Judith Moffatt. Scholastic, 1997. ISBN 0-590-84779-1 Subj: Insects – butterflies, caterpillars. Metamorphosis. Science.

I'm a seed ill. by Judith Moffatt. Scholastic, 1996. ISBN 0-590-26586-5 Subj: Flowers. Plants. Seeds.

Jed and the space bandits by Jean & Claudio Marzollo; ill. by Peter Sis. Dial, 1987. ISBN 0-8037-0136-5 Subj: Crime. Pets. Robots. Space & space ships.

Jed's junior space patrol by Jean & Claudio Marzollo; ill. by David S. Rose. Dial, 1982. ISBN 0-8037-4288-6 Subj: Robots. Space & space ships. Toys – bears.

Mama, Mama ill. by Laura Regan. HarperFestival, 1999. ISBN 0-694-01245-9 Subj: Animals. Family life – mothers. Format, unusual – board books. Rhyming text.

Miriam and her brother Moses ill. by reteller. Little, 2003. ISBN 0-316-74131-0 Subj: Religion. Religion – Moses.

Once upon a springtime ill. by Jacqueline Rogers. Scholastic, 1997. ISBN 0-590-46017-X Subj: Animals – deer. Seasons.

Papa, papa ill. by Simone Kaplan. HarperFestival, 2000. ISBN 0-694-01246-7 Subj: Animals. Family life – fathers. Format, unusual – board books. Rhyming text.

Pretend you're a cat ill. by Jerry Pinkney. Dial, 1990. ISBN 0-8037-0774-6 Subj: Animals. Behavior – imitation. Imagination. Rhyming text.

The rebus treasury ill. by Carol D. Carson. Dial, 1986. ISBN 0-8037-0255-8 Subj: Nursery rhymes. Rebuses.

Shanna's ballerina show ill. by Shane W. Evans. Hyperion, 2002. ISBN 0-7868-0634-6 Subj: Activities – dancing. Ballet. Ethnic groups in the U.S. – African Americans. Games. Rhyming text.

Shanna's teacher show ill. by Shane W. Evans. Hyperion, 2002. ISBN 0-7868-0635-4 Subj: Careers – teachers. Rhyming text.

The silver bear ill. by Susan Meddaugh. Dial, 1987. ISBN 0-8037-0369-4 Subj: Imagination.

Snow angel ill. by Jacqueline Rogers. Scholastic, 1995. ISBN 0-590-48748-5 Subj: Angels. Behavior – lost. Weather – snow.

Sun song ill. by Laura Regan. HarperCollins, 1995. ISBN 0-06-020788-4 Subj: Animals. Plants. Rhyming text. Sun.

The teddy bear book ill. by Ann Schweninger. Dial, 1989. ISBN 0-8037-0632-4 Subj: Poetry. Toys – bears.

Ten cats have hats: a counting book ill. by David McPhail. Scholastic, 1994. ISBN 0-590-46968-1 Subj: Animals. Counting, numbers. Rhyming text.

Ten little eggs ill. by author. HarperFestival, 2004. ISBN 0-06-053052-9 Subj: Birds. Counting, numbers. Eggs. Format, unusual – toy & movable books. Rhyming text.

Thanksgiving cats ill. by Hans Wilhelm. Scholastic, 1999. ISBN 0-590-03714-5 Subj: Animals – cats. Holidays – Thanksgiving. Rhyming text.

The three little kittens (Mother Goose)

Uproar on Hollercat Hill ill. by Steven Kellogg. Dial, 1980. ISBN 0-8037-9028-7 Subj: Animals – cats. Behavior – misbehavior. Rhyming text.

Valentine cats ill. by Hans Wilhelm. Scholastic, 1996. ISBN 0-590-47596-7 Subj: Animals – cats. Holidays – Valentine's Day. Rhyming text.

Welcome to the Shanna show ill. by Shane Evans. Hyperion, 2001. ISBN 0-7868-2549-9 Subj: Rhyming text. Royalty – princesses.

What's the matter with Mother Goose? ill. by Irene Trivas. HarperCollins, 2000. ISBN 0-06-027277-5 Subj: Accidents. Animals. Rhyming text.

Maschler, Fay. *T. G. and Moonie go shopping* ill. by Sylvie Selig. Doubleday, 1978. ISBN 0-385-14148-3 Subj: Animals – cats. Birds – owls. Shopping. Stores.

T. G. and Moonie have a baby ill. by Sylvie Selig. Doubleday, 1979. ISBN 0-385-15333-3 Subj: Animals – cats. Birds – owls. Family life.

T. G. and Moonie move out of town ill. by Sylvia Selig. Doubleday, 1978. ISBN 0-395-14146-7 Subj: Animals – cats. Birds – owls. Moving.

Masini, Beatrice. *A brave little princess* ill. by Octavia Monaco; trans. by Diana Handley. Barefoot, 2000. ISBN 1-84148-267-6 Subj: Character traits – bravery. Concepts – patterns. Folk & fairy tales. Problem solving. Royalty – princesses. Royalty – queens.

Masks and puppets ill. by Louise Nevett. Watts, 1984. ISBN 0-531-04771-7 Subj: Activities. Masks. Puppets.

Mason, Adrienne. *Lu and Clancy sound off* ill. by Pat Cupples. Kids Can, 2002. ISBN 1-55337-058-9 Subj: Animals – dogs. Careers – detectives. Noise, sounds. Science.

Lu and Clancy's spy stuff ill. by Pat Cupples. Kids Can, 2000. ISBN 1-55074-693-6 Subj: Animals – dogs. Careers – detectives. Disguises.

Snakes ill. by Nancy Gray Ogle. Kids Can, 2005. ISBN 1-55337-627-7 Subj: Reptiles – snakes. Science.

Mason, Ann Maree. *The weird things in Nanna's house* ill. by Cathy Wilcox. Watts, 1992. ISBN 0-531-08570-8 Subj: Family life – grandmothers. Homes, houses.

Mason, Jane B. *The flying horse* ill. by Susan Swan. Grosset, 1999. ISBN 0-448-42051-1 Subj: Folk & fairy tales. Foreign lands – Greece. Monsters. Mythical creatures – Pegasus.

Hello, two-wheeler! ill. by David Monteith. Grosset, 1995. ISBN 0-448-40854-6 Subj: Behavior – growing up. Sports – bicycling.

River day ill. by Henri Sorensen. Macmillan, 1994. ISBN 0-02-762869-8 Subj: Birds – eagles. Canoes & canoeing. Family life – grandfathers.

The shadow stealer ill. by Aristides Ruiz. Scholastic, 1996. ISBN 0-590-50205-0 Subj: Mystery stories.

The wee puppy who wouldn't go to sleep ill. by Karen Lee Schmidt. Grosset, 1995. ISBN 0-448-40485-0 Subj: Animals – dogs. Bedtime.

Mason, Lura. *A book of boxes* ill. by author. S&S, 1989. ISBN 0-671-67801-9 Subj: Format, unusual – toy & movable books. Holidays.

Massey, Ed. *Milton* ill. by Kristy Chu. RDR/Wetlands, 1996. ISBN 1-57143-047-4 Subj: Art. Imagination.

Massey, Jeanne. *The littlest witch* ill. by Adrienne Adams. Knopf, 1959. Subj: Holidays – Halloween. Witches.

Massie, Diane Redfield. *The baby beebee bird* ill. by author. HarperCollins, 1963. Subj: Animals. Birds. Noise, sounds. Sleep.

Cockle stew and other rhymes ill. by author. Atheneum, 1967. Subj: Poetry.

Tiny pin ill. by author. HarperCollins, 1964. Subj: Animals – porcupines. Behavior – growing up. Poetry.

Walter was a frog ill. by author. S&S, 1970. ISBN 0-671-65158-7 Subj: Behavior – dissatisfaction. Frogs & toads.

Massie, Elizabeth. *Jambo, watoto!* (Heatwole, Marsha)

Masters, Anthony. *Ricky's rat gang* ill. by Chris Fisher. Kingfisher, 2004. ISBN 0-7534-5800-4 Subj: Animals – mice. Behavior – bullying. Stores.

Masurel, Claire. *A cat and a dog* ill. by Bob Kolar. North-South, 2001. ISBN 1-55858-950-3 Subj: Animals – cats. Animals – dogs. Behavior – fighting, arguing. Friendship.

Christmas is coming ill. by Marie H. Henry. Chronicle, 1998. ISBN 0-8118-2106-4 Subj: Behavior – sharing. Holidays – Christmas. Toys.

No, no, Titus! ill. by Shari Halpern. North-South, 1999. ISBN 1-55858-726-8 Subj: Animals – dogs. Behavior. Farms.

Ten dogs in the window ill. by Pamela Paparone. North-South, 1997. ISBN 1-55858-755-1 Subj: Animals – dogs. Counting, numbers. Pets. Rhyming text.

Too big! ill. by Hanako Wakiyama. Chronicle, 1999. ISBN 0-8118-2090-4 Subj: Concepts – size. Dinosaurs. Toys.

Two homes ill. by Kady MacDonald Denton. Candlewick, 2001. ISBN 0-7636-0511-5 Subj: Divorce. Emotions – love. Family life – parents. Homes, houses.

Mathers, Petra. *A cake for Herbie* ill. by author. Atheneum, 2000. ISBN 0-689-83017-3 Subj: Animals. Birds – ducks. Contests. Poetry.

Dodo gets married ill. by author. Atheneum, 2001. ISBN 0-689-83018-1 Subj: Birds – dodos. Weddings.

Herbie's secret Santa ill. by author. Atheneum, 2002. ISBN 0-689-83550-7 Subj: Birds. Careers – bakers. Character traits – honesty. Friendship. Holidays – Christmas.

Lottie's new beach towel ill. by author. Atheneum, 1998. ISBN 0-689-81606-5 Subj: Birds – chickens. Character traits – cleverness. Gifts. Sea & seashore – beaches.

Lottie's new friend ill. by author. Atheneum, 1999. ISBN 0-689-82014-3 Subj: Birds. Emotions – envy, jealousy. Friendship.

Maria Theresa ill. by author. HarperCollins, 1992. ISBN 0-06-443282-3 Subj: Birds – chickens. Cities, towns.

Sophie and Lou ill. by author. HarperCollins, 1991. ISBN 0-06-024072-5 Subj: Activities – dancing. Animals – mice. Character traits – shyness.

Theodor and Mr. Balbini ill. by author. HarperCollins, 1988. ISBN 0-06-024144-6 Subj: Animals – dogs. Pets.

Mathews, Judith. *An egg and seven socks* ill. by Marylin Hafner. HarperCollins, 1993. ISBN 0-06-020208-4 Subj: Clothing – socks. Dragons. Family life – sisters.

Nathaniel Willy, scared silly retold by Judith Mathews & Fay Robinson; ill. by Alexi Natchev. Bradbury, 1994. ISBN 0-02-765285-8 Subj: Animals. Bedtime. Emotions – fear. Family life – grandmothers. Folk & fairy tales. Rhyming text.

There's nothing to d-o-o-o! ill. by Kurt Cyrus. Harcourt, 1999. ISBN 0-15-201647-3 Subj: Animals – bulls, cows. Behavior – lost.

Tuti, Blue Horse, and the Nipnope Man ill. by Daniel Powers. A. Whitman, 1993. ISBN 0-8075-8130-5 Subj: Behavior – lost. Toys.

Mathews, Louise. *Bunches and bunches of bunnies* ill. by Jeni Bassett. Dodd, 1978. ISBN 0-396-07601-7 Subj: Animals – rabbits. Counting, numbers. Rhyming text.

Cluck one ill. by Jeni Bassett. Dodd, 1982. ISBN 0-396-08029-4 Subj: Animals – weasels. Birds – chickens. Counting, numbers. Eggs.

The great take-away ill. by Jeni Bassett. Dodd, 1980. ISBN 0-396-07846-X Subj: Animals – pigs. Character traits – laziness. Counting, numbers. Crime.

Mathias, Beverly. *Reader's Digest children's book of poetry* (Reader's Digest children's book of poetry)

Mathiesen, Egon. *Oswald, the monkey* adapt. from Danish by Nancy & Edward Maze; ill. by author. Astor-Honor, 1959. Subj: Animals – monkeys.

Mathis, Melissa Bay. *Animal house* ill. by author. S&S, 1999. ISBN 0-689-81594-8 Subj: Animals. Homes, houses. Rhyming text. Trees.

Matje, Martin. *Celeste: a day in the park* ill. by author. S&S, 1999. ISBN 0-689-82100-X Subj: Activities – picnicking. Birds – ducks. Parks. Toys – bears.

Matsui, Susan. *The bears' autumn* (Tejima, Keizaburo)

The sea and I (Nakawatari, Harutaka)

Matsuno, Masako. *A pair of red clogs* ill. by Kazue Mizumura. Philomel, 1981, c1960. ISBN 0-399-20796-1 Subj: Character traits – honesty. Clothing – shoes. Foreign lands – Japan.

Taro and the bamboo shoot: a Japanese tale ill. by Yasuo Segawa; adapt. from the Japanese by Alice Low. Pantheon, 1964. ISBN 0-394-91727-8 Subj: Folk & fairy tales. Foreign lands – Japan.

Taro and the Tofu ill. by Kazue Mizumura. Collins-World, 1962. Subj: Character traits – honesty. Foreign lands – Japan.

Matsutani, Miyoko. *The fisherman under the sea* English version by Alvin Tresselt; ill. by Chihiro Iwasaki. Parents' Magazine Pr., 1969. Translation of Urashima Tar+8.o. Subj: Careers – fishermen. Folk & fairy tales. Foreign lands – Japan. Reptiles – turtles, tortoises. Royalty. Sea & seashore.

How the withered trees blossomed ill. by Yasuo Segawa. Lippincott, 1969. Subj: Behavior – greed. Foreign lands – Japan. Foreign languages.

The witch's magic cloth English version by Alvin Tresselt; ill. by Yasuo Segawa. Parents' Magazine Pr., 1969. Subj: Character traits – bravery. Folk & fairy tales. Foreign lands – Japan. Witches.

Mattern, Joanne. *Safety at school* ill. by author. ABCO Pub., 1999. ISBN 1-57765-070-0 Subj: Safety. School.

Safety in public places ill. by author. ABCO Pub., 1999. ISBN 1-57765-074-3 Subj: Accidents. Safety.

Safety in the water ill. by author. ABCO Pub., 1999. ISBN 1-57765-072-7 Subj: Safety. Sports – swimming. Water.

Matthews, Caitlin. *The blessing seed: a creation myth for the new millennium* ill. by Alison Dexter. Barefoot, 1998. ISBN 1-901223-28-0 Subj: Creation. Religion.

Matthews, Wendy. *The gift of a traveler* ill. by Robert Van Nutt. BridgeWater, 1995. ISBN 0-8167-3656-1 Subj: Family life – great-grandparents. Foreign lands – Romania. Holidays – Christmas.

Matthias, Catherine. *I can be a computer operator* ill. with photos. Childrens Pr., 1985. ISBN 0-516-01838-8 Subj: Careers. Computers.

I love cats ill. by Tom Dunnington. Childrens Pr., 1983. ISBN 0-516-02041-2 Subj: Animals – cats.

Out the door ill. by Eileen Mueller Neill. Childrens Pr., 1982. ISBN 0-516-03560-6 Subj: Buses. School.

Out the door = Sal y entra: Out the door trans. Lada Josefa Kratky; ill. by Eileen Mueller Neill. Childrens Pr., 1989. ISBN 0-516-33560-X Subj: Concepts – in & out. Concepts – up & down. Foreign languages.

Over and under = Arriba y abajo trans. by Lada Josefa Kratky; ill. by Gene Sharp. Childrens Pr., 1989. ISBN 0-516-32048-3 Subj: Concepts. Foreign languages.

Over-under ill. by Gene Sharp. Childrens Pr., 1984. ISBN 0-516-02048-X Subj: Concepts – opposites.

Too many balloons ill. by Gene Sharp. Childrens Pr., 1982. ISBN 0-516-03633-5 Subj: Counting, numbers. Toys – balloons. Zoos.

Too many balloons = Demasiados globos trans. by Lada Josefa Kratky; ill. by Gene Sharp. Childrens Pr., 1989. ISBN 0-516-33633-9 Subj: Foreign languages. Toys – balloons.

Matthiesen, Thomas. *Things to see: a child's world of familiar objects* photos by author. Platt, 1968. ISBN 0-448-41051-6 Subj: Concepts. Senses – sight.

Mattingley, Christobel. *The angel with a mouth-organ* ill. by Astra Lacis. Holiday, 1984. ISBN 0-8234-0593-1 Subj: Death. Holidays – Christmas. War.

Matunis, Joe. *This home we have made* (Hammond, Anna)

Matura, Mustapha. *Moon jump* ill. by Jane Gifford. Knopf, 1988. ISBN 0-394-91976-9 Subj: Bedtime. Imagination. Moon.

Matus, Greta. *Where are you, Jason?* ill. by author. Lothrop, 1974. ISBN 0-688-51584-3 Subj: Behavior – hiding. Imagination. Night.

Matze, Claire Sidhom. *The stars in my Geddoh's sky* ill. by Bill Farnsworth. A. Whitman, 1999. ISBN 0-8075-5332-8 Subj: Family life – grandfathers. Foreign lands – Middle East. Stars.

Maugham, W. Somerset (William Somerset). *Princess September and the nightingale* ill. by Richard C. Jones. Oxford Univ. Pr., 1998. ISBN 0-19-512480-4 Subj: Birds – nightingales. Character traits – freedom. Folk & fairy tales. Foreign lands – Thailand. Royalty – princesses.

Mauner, Claudia. *Zoe Sophia's scrapbook* by Claudia Mauner & Elisa Smalley; ill. by Claudia Mauner. Chronicle, 2003. ISBN 0-8118-3606-1 Subj: Activities – traveling. Animals – dogs. Behavior – lost. Family life – aunts, uncles. Foreign lands – Italy.

Maupassant, Guy de. *When chickens grow teeth: a story from the French of Guy de Maupassant* (Halperin, Wendy Anderson)

Maurer, Tracy. *Growing flowers* ill. with photos. Rourke, 2001. ISBN 1-55916-251-1 Subj: Flowers. Gardens, gardening.

Maurer-Mathison, Diane V. *Make your own spectacular Valentines* photos by Michael Grand. Little, 1995. ISBN 0-316-45447-0 Subj: Activities – making things. Holidays – Valentine's Day.

Maury, Inez. *My mother the mail carrier = Mi mama la cartera* trans. by Norah E. Alemany; ill. by Tasha Tudor. Feminist Pr., 1976. ISBN 0-91267-023-1 Subj: Careers – postal workers. Foreign languages. Post office.

Mauver, Judy A. *Dusty wants to help* (Sandberg, Inger)

Mavor, Salley. *You and me: poems of friendship* (You and me)

Mawdsley, Ruth. *My first pop-up book of dinosaurs* (Bishop, Roma)

My first pop-up book of prehistoric animals (Bishop, Roma)

Maxfield, Christine. *Christmas in Water Village* ill. by Jean Colquhoun. Prima Design, 1989. ISBN 0-9621029-0-3 Subj: Holidays – Christmas. U.S. history.

Maxner, Joyce. *Lady Bugatti* ill. by Kevin Hawkes. Lothrop, 1991. ISBN 0-688-10341-3 Subj: Insects. Parties. Rhyming text.

Nicholas Cricket ill. by William Joyce. HarperCollins, 1989. ISBN 0-06-024222-1 Subj: Animals. Insects – crickets. Music. Musical instruments – bands. Rhyming text.

May, Charles Paul. *High-noon rocket* ill. by Brinton Turkle. Holiday, 1966. Subj: Activities – traveling. Science. Space & space ships. Time.

May, Daryl. *Rachael's splendifilous adventure* (Bansemer, Roger)

May, Julian. *Why people are different colors* ill. by Symeon Shimin. Holiday, 1971. ISBN 0-8234-0180-4 Subj: Ethnic groups in the U.S.

May, Kara. *Big brave brother Ben* ill. by Gus Clarke. Lothrop, 1992. ISBN 0-688-11235-8 Subj: Behavior – boasting. Character traits – bravery. Family life – brothers & sisters.

Creepy crawly caterpillar ill. by Emily Bolam. Doubleday, 1995. ISBN 0-385-32166-X Subj: Behavior – dissatisfaction. Insects – butterflies, caterpillars. Metamorphosis.

Joe Lion's big boots ill. by Jonathan Allen. Kingfisher, 2000. ISBN 0-7534-5318-5 Subj: Animals – lions. Clothing – boots. Concepts – size. Self-concept.

May, Kathy. *Molasses man* ill. by Felicia Marshall. Holiday, 2000. ISBN 0-8234-1438-8 Subj: Ethnic groups in the U.S. – African Americans. Family life. Family life – grandfathers.

May, Robert Lewis. *Rudolph the red-nosed reindeer* ill. by Diana Magnuson. Four Winds, 1980. ISBN 0-695-81471-0 Subj: Anatomy – noses. Animals – reindeer. Holidays – Christmas. Mythical creatures – elves. Santa Claus. Weather – fog.

Rudolph the red-nosed reindeer ill. by David Wenzel. Grosset, 2001. ISBN 0-448-42534-3 Subj: Anatomy – noses. Animals – reindeer. Holidays – Christmas. Mythical creatures – elves. Rhyming text. Santa Claus. Weather – fog.

Mayer, Gina. *This is my family* ill. by Mercer Mayer. Western, 1992. ISBN 0-307-00137-7 Subj: Family life.

Mayer, Marianna. *The adventures of Tom Thumb* (Tom Thumb)

Alley oop! ill. by Gerald McDermott. Holt, 1985. ISBN 0-03-070496-0 Subj: Animals – mice. Counting, numbers. Reptiles – alligators, crocodiles.

Baba Yaga and Vasilisa the Brave ill. by K. Y. Craft. Morrow, 1994. ISBN 0-688-08501-6 Subj: Folk & fairy tales. Foreign lands – Russia. Royalty. Toys – dolls. Witches.

Beauty and the beast ill. by Mercer Mayer. SeaStar, 2000. ISBN 1-58717-018-3 Subj: Animals. Character traits – appearance. Character traits – loyalty. Emotions – love. Folk & fairy tales. Magic.

The black horse ill. by Katie Thamer. Dial, 1984. ISBN 0-8037-0076-8 Subj: Animals – horses, ponies. Behavior – trickery. Folk & fairy tales. Magic. Royalty.

The Brambleberrys animal alphabet ill. by Gerald McDermott. Boyds Mills, 1991. ISBN 1-878093-78-9 Subj: ABC books. Animals.

The Brambleberrys animal book of big and small shapes ill. by Gerald McDermott. Boyds Mills, 1991. ISBN 1-878093-77-0 Subj: Animals. Concepts – shape. Concepts – size.

The Brambleberrys animal book of colors by Marianna Mayer & Gerald McDermott; ill. by Gerald McDermott. St. Martin's, 1991. ISBN 1-8780-9376-2 Subj: Animals. Animals – pandas. Concepts – color.

The Brambleberrys animal book of counting ill. by Gerald McDermott. Boyds Mills, 1991. ISBN 1-878093-75-4 Subj: Animals. Counting, numbers.

Iron John (Grimm, Jacob)

The little jewel box ill. by Margot Tomes. Dial, 1986. ISBN 0-8037-0149-7 Subj: Animals. Birds. Character traits – kindness. Character traits – luck. Folk & fairy tales. Magic.

Marcel the pastry chef ill. by Gerald McDermott. Bantam, 1991. ISBN 0-553-05192-X Subj: Activities – baking, cooking. Animals – hippopotamuses. Careers – bakers. Royalty – kings. Weddings.

Mine! (Mayer, Mercer)

My first book of nursery tales: five favorite bedtime tales ill. by William Joyce. Random House, 1983. ISBN 0-394-95396-7 Subj: Folk & fairy tales.

One frog too many (Mayer, Mercer)

Pegasus ill. by K. Y. Craft. Morrow, 1998. ISBN 0-688-13382-7 Subj: Folk & fairy tales. Foreign lands – Greece. Monsters. Mythical creatures – Pegasus.

Perseus ill. by Joel Spector. Fogelman, 2002. ISBN 0-8037-2619-8 Subj: Folk & fairy tales. Foreign lands – Greece. Religion.

The prince and the pauper adapt. by Marianna Mayer from the Mark Twain novel; ill. by Gary A. Lippincott. Dial, 1999. ISBN 0-8037-2099-8 Subj: Behavior – growing up. Behavior – misunderstanding. Character traits – individuality. Royalty – kings.

Rapunzel (Grimm, Jacob)

The spirit of the blue light ill. by Gerald McDermott. Macmillan, 1990. ISBN 0-02-765350-1 Subj: Behavior – wishing. Folk & fairy tales. Foreign lands – Germany. Magic. Royalty.

The twelve dancing princesses (Grimm, Jacob)

The twelve dancing princesses (Grimm, Jacob)

The ugly duckling (Andersen, H. C. [Hans Christian])

The unicorn alphabet ill. by Michael Hague. Dial, 1989. ISBN 0-8037-0373-2 Subj: ABC books. Mythical creatures – unicorns.

The unicorn and the lake ill. by Michael Hague. Dial, 1982. ISBN 0-8037-9338-3 Subj: Character traits – bravery. Mythical creatures – unicorns.

Mayer, Mercer. *Ah-choo* ill. by author. Dial, 1976. ISBN 0-8037-4895-7 Subj: Animals – elephants. Illness. Wordless.

Appelard and Liverwurst ill. by Steven Kellogg. Four Winds, 1978. ISBN 0-590-07506-3 Subj: Animals. Behavior – misbehavior. Farms.

Astronaut critter ill. by author. S&S, 1986. ISBN 0-671-61142-9 Subj: Format, unusual – board books. Space & space ships.

A boy, a dog, a frog and a friend ill. by author. Dial, 1971. ISBN 0-8037-0755-X Subj: Animals – dogs. Friendship. Frogs & toads. Sports – fishing. Wordless.

A boy, a dog and a frog ill. by author. Dial, 1967. ISBN 0-8037-0767-3 Subj: Animals – dogs. Friendship. Frogs & toads. Sports – fishing. Wordless.

Bubble bubble ill. by author. Four Winds, 1980, c1973. ISBN 0-590-07759-7 Subj: Bubbles. Imagination. Wordless.

Bun Bun's birthday ill. by author. Random House, 1996. ISBN 0-679-87368-6 Subj: Behavior – growing up. Behavior – misunderstanding. Birthdays.

Cowboy critter ill. by author. S&S, 1986. ISBN 0-671-61141-0 Subj: Cowboys, cowgirls. Format, unusual – board books.

Fireman critter ill. by author. S&S, 1986. ISBN 0-671-61143-7 Subj: Careers – firefighters. Format, unusual – board books.

Frog goes to dinner ill. by author. Dial, 1974. ISBN 0-8037-3381-X Subj: Food. Frogs & toads. Wordless.

Frog on his own ill. by author. Dial, 1973. ISBN 0-8037-2695-3 Subj: Frogs & toads. Wordless.

Frog, where are you? ill. by author. Dial, 1969. ISBN 0-8037-2732-1 Subj: Friendship. Frogs & toads. Wordless.

The great cat chase ill. by author. Four Winds, 1974. ISBN 0-590-07400-8 Subj: Animals – cats. Wordless.

Hiccup ill. by author. Dial, 1976. ISBN 0-8037-3592-8 Subj: Animals – hippopotamuses. Hiccups. Wordless.

How the trollusk got his hat ill. by author. Golden Pr., 1979. ISBN 0-307-13733-3 Subj: Character traits – appearance. Character traits – honesty.

I am a hunter ill. by author. Dial, 1969. Subj: Imagination.

Just big enough ill. by author. HarperFestival, 2004. ISBN 0-06-053964-X Subj: Behavior – bullying. Behavior – growing up. Concepts – size. Family life – grandfathers. Problem solving.

Just for you ill. by author. Golden Pr., 1975. ISBN 0-307-12542-4 Subj: Character traits – helpfulness. Emotions – love. Family life – mothers.

Just me and my dad ill. by author. Golden Pr., 1977. ISBN 0-307-61839-0 Subj: Camps, camping. Family life – fathers.

Little Monster at home ill. by author. Golden Pr., 1978. ISBN 0-307-61846-3 Subj: Homes, houses. Monsters.

Little Monster at school ill. by author. Golden Pr., 1978. ISBN 0-307-11845-2 Subj: Monsters. School.

Little Monster at work ill. by author. Golden Pr., 1978. ISBN 0-307-63736-0 Subj: Careers. Family life – grandfathers. Monsters.

Little Monster's alphabet book ill. by author. Golden Pr., 1978. ISBN 0-307-11847-9 Subj: ABC books. Monsters.

Little Monster's bedtime book ill. by author. Golden Pr., 1978. ISBN 0-307-61848-X Subj: Bedtime. Monsters. Poetry.

Little Monster's counting book ill. by author. Golden Pr., 1978. ISBN 0-307-61844-7 Subj: Counting, numbers. Monsters.

Little Monster's neighborhood ill. by author. Golden Pr., 1978. ISBN 0-307-61849-8 Subj: Cities, towns. Monsters.

Liverwurst is missing ill. by Steven Kellogg. Four Winds, 1981. ISBN 0-590-07793-7 Subj: Character traits – bravery. Circus. Crime.

Liza Lou and the Yeller Belly Swamp ill. by author. Parents' Magazine Pr., 1976. ISBN 0-81-930802-1 Subj: Character traits – bravery. Ethnic groups in the U.S. – African Americans. Monsters.

Mine! by Mercer & Marianna Mayer; ill. by Mercer Mayer. S&S, 1970. ISBN 0-671-65146-5 Subj: Concepts. Emotions.

Mrs. Beggs and the wizard ill. by author. Parents' Magazine Pr., 1973. ISBN 0-819-30693-2 Subj: Magic. Monsters. Wizards.

One frog too many by Mercer & Marianna Mayer; ill. by Mercer Mayer. Dial, 1975. ISBN 0-8037-4858-2 Subj: Emotions – envy, jealousy. Frogs & toads. Wordless.

Oops ill. by author. Dial, 1977. ISBN 0-8037-6567-3 Subj: Animals – hippopotamuses. Behavior – carelessness. Wordless.

The pied piper of Hamelin adapt. & ill. by Mercer Mayer. Macmillan, 1987. Adapt. of the poem The pied piper of Hamelin by Robert Browning. ISBN 0-02-765361-7 Subj: Animals – rats. Behavior – trickery. Folk & fairy tales. Foreign lands – Germany.

Policeman critter ill. by author. S&S, 1986. ISBN 0-671-61140-2 Subj: Careers – police officers. Format, unusual – board books.

The queen always wanted to dance ill. by author. S&S, 1971. ISBN 0-671-65143-9 Subj: Activities – dancing. Humorous stories. Music. Royalty – queens.

The rocking horse angel ill. by author. Cavendish, 2000. ISBN 0-7614-5072-6 Subj: Dreams. Family life. Illness. Toys – rocking horses. Weather – storms.

Shibumi and the kitemaker ill. by author. Cavendish, 1999. ISBN 0-7614-5054-8 Subj: Family life – fathers. Foreign lands – Japan. Kites. Royalty – emperors. Royalty – princesses.

The sleeping beauty (Grimm, Jacob)

A special trick ill. by author. Dial, 1976. ISBN 0-8037-8103-2 Subj: Magic.

Terrible troll ill. by author. Dial, 1968. ISBN 0-8037-8621-2 Subj: Imagination. Knights. Monsters. Mythical creatures. Mythical creatures – trolls.

There's a nightmare in my closet ill. by author. Dial, 1990. ISBN 0-8037-0843-2 Subj: Bedtime. Emotions – fear. Monsters.

There's an alligator under my bed ill. by author. Dial, 1987. ISBN 0-8037-0375-9 Subj: Bedtime. Emotions – fear. Reptiles – alligators, crocodiles.

There's something in my attic ill. by author. Dial, 1988. ISBN 0-8037-0415-1 Subj: Dreams. Emotions – fear. Night.

Two moral tales ill. by author. Four Winds, 1974. Bear's new clothes / Bird's new hat. ISBN 0-590-07366-4 Subj: Animals – bears. Birds. Clothing. Clothing – hats. Wordless.

What do you do with a kangaroo? ill. by author. Four Winds, 1973. ISBN 0-590-72851-2 Subj: Animals. Humorous stories. Problem solving.

Whinnie the lovesick dragon ill. by Diane Dawson Hearn. Macmillan, 1986. ISBN 0-02-765180-0 Subj: Behavior – needing someone. Dragons. Emotions – love. Magic. Middle Ages.

You're the scaredy cat ill. by author. Parents' Magazine Pr., 1974. ISBN 0-8193-0763-7 Subj: Camps, camping. Emotions – fear. Night.

Mayer, Pamela. *The scariest monster in the whole wide world* ill. by Lydia Monks. Putnam, 2001. ISBN 0-399-23459-4 Subj: Clothing – costumes. Family life – grandmothers. Holidays – Halloween. Monsters.

Mayers, Florence Cassen. *Egyptian art from the Brooklyn Museum: ABC* designed by Florence Cassen Mayers; ed. by Sheila Franklin. Abrams, 1988. ISBN 0-8109-1888-3 Subj: ABC books. Art. Foreign lands – Egypt. Museums.

The Museum of Fine Arts, Boston: ABC designed by Florence Cassen Mayers; ed. by Sheila Franklin. Abrams, 1986. ISBN 0-8109-1847-1 Subj: ABC books. Art. Museums.

The Museum of Modern Art, New York: ABC designed by Florence Cassen Mayers; ed. by Sheila Franklin. Abrams, 1986. ISBN 0-8109-1849-8 Subj: ABC books. Art. Museums.

The National Air and Space Museum: ABC designed by Florence Cassen Mayers; ed. by Sheila Franklin. Abrams, 1988. ISBN 0-8109-1859-5 Subj: ABC books. Museums. Space & space ships.

Mayers, Patrick. *Just one more block* ill. by Lucy Hawkinson. A. Whitman, 1970. ISBN 0-8075-4081-1 Subj: Activities – playing. Emotions. Sibling rivalry. Toys – blocks.

Mayhew, James. *Katie and the dinosaurs* ill. by author. Bantam, 1992. ISBN 0-553-08129-2 Subj: Dinosaurs. Museums. Prehistory.

Katie and the Mona Lisa ill. by author. Orchard, 1999. ISBN 0-531-30177-X Subj: Art. Careers – artists. Museums.

Katie and the sunflowers ill. by author. Orchard, 2001. ISBN 0-531-30325-X Subj: Art. Family life – grandmothers. Imagination. Museums.

Katie meets the Impressionists ill. by author. Orchard, 1999. ISBN 0-531-30151-6 Subj: Art. Careers – artists. Museums.

Miranda the explorer ill. by author. Orion Children's Books, 2002. ISBN 1-84255-000-4 Subj: Activities – ballooning. Activities – traveling. Careers – explorers. Imagination.

Mayle, Peter. *Divorce can happen to the nicest people* ill. by Arthur Robins. Macmillan, 1980. ISBN 0-02-582500-3 Subj: Divorce. Family life.

Why are we getting a divorce? ill. by Arthur Robins. Crown, 1988. ISBN 0-517-56527-7 Subj: Divorce. Family life.

Maynard, Bill. *Incredible Ned* ill. by Frank Remkiewicz. Putnam, 1997. ISBN 0-399-23023-8 Subj: Careers – artists. Rhyming text.

Quiet, Wyatt! ill. by Frank Remkiewicz. Putnam, 1999. ISBN 0-399-23217-6 Subj: Language. Noise, sounds. Rhyming text.

Santa's time off ill. by Tom Browning. Putnam, 1997. ISBN 0-399-23138-2 Subj: Activities – vacationing. Rhyming text. Santa Claus.

Maynard, Christopher. *The best book of dinosaurs* ill. by author. Kingfisher, 1998. ISBN 0-7534-5116-6 Subj: Dinosaurs.

Jobs people do ill. with photos. DK, 1997. ISBN 0-7894-1492-9 Subj: Careers.

Maynard, Joyce. *Camp-out* ill. by Steve Bethel. Harcourt, 1985. ISBN 0-15-214077-8 Subj: Camps, camping. Family life.

New house ill. by Steve Bethel. Harcourt, 1987. ISBN 0-15-257042-X Subj: Activities – working. Homes, houses. Trees.

Mayne, William. *Barnabas walks* ill. by Barbara Firth. Prentice-Hall, 1987. ISBN 0-13-057001-X Subj: Animals – guinea pigs. School.

The blue book of Hob stories ill. by Patrick Benson. Putnam, 1984. ISBN 0-399-20137-7 Subj: Character traits – helpfulness. Mythical creatures.

Come, come to my corner ill. by Kenneth Lilly. Prentice-Hall, 1987. ISBN 0-13-152497-6 Subj: Animals. Animals – rabbits.

The green book of Hob stories ill. by Patrick Benore. Putnam, 1984. ISBN 0-399-21039-3 Subj: Character traits – helpfulness. Fairies. Mythical creatures.

A house in town ill. by Sarah Fox-Davies. Prentice-Hall, 1988. ISBN 0-13-395880-9 Subj: Animals – foxes.

Lady Muck ill. by Jonathan Heale. Houghton Mifflin, 1997. ISBN 0-395-75281-7 Subj: Animals – pigs. Behavior – greed.

Mousewing ill. by Martin Baynton. Prentice-Hall, 1988. ISBN 0-13-604240-6 Subj: Animals – mice.

Pandora ill. by Dietlind Blech. Knopf, 1995. ISBN 0-679-94183-5 Subj: Animals – cats. Behavior – running away. Emotions – envy, jealousy.

The patchwork cat ill. by Nicola Bayley. Knopf, 1981. ISBN 0-394-95021-6 Subj: Animals – cats. Behavior – saving things. Emotions – love.

The red book of Hob stories ill. by Patrick Benson. Putnam, 1984. ISBN 0-399-21047-4 Subj: Character traits – helpfulness. Fairies. Mythical creatures.

Tibber ill. by Jonathan Heale. Prentice-Hall, 1987. ISBN 0-13-921214-0 Subj: Animals – cats. Farms.

The yellow book of Hob stories ill. by Patrick Benson. Putnam, 1984. ISBN 0-399-21050-4 Subj: Character traits – helpfulness. Fairies. Mythical creatures.

Mayo, Margaret. *Choo choo clickety-clack* ill. by Alex Ayliffe. Carolrhoda, 2005. ISBN 1-57505-819-7 Subj: Format, unusual – board books. Noise, sounds. Transportation.

Dig dig digging ill. by Alex Ayliffe. Holt, 2002. ISBN 0-8050-6840-6 Subj: Rhyming text. Tractors. Trucks.

Emergency! ill. by Alex Ayliffe. Carolrhoda, 2002. ISBN 0-8761-4922-0 Subj: Careers – emergency medical technicians. Careers – firefighters. Rhyming text. Safety. Trucks.

Wiggle waggle fun ill. by 24 illustrators. Knopf, 2002. ISBN 0-375-91529-X Subj: Poetry. Rhyming text. Songs.

Mayper, Monica. *After good-night* ill. by Peter Sis. HarperCollins, 1987. ISBN 0-06-024121-7 Subj: Bedtime. Dreams. Family life.

Come and see: a Christmas story ill. by Stacey Schuett. Harper-Collins, 1999. ISBN 0-06-023527-6 Subj: Holidays – Christmas. Religion – Nativity.

Oh snow ill. by June Otani. HarperCollins, 1991. ISBN 0-06-024204-3 Subj: Activities – playing. Rhyming text. Weather – snow.

Mayr, Diane. *Littlebat's Halloween story* ill. by Gideon Kendall. A. Whitman, 2001. ISBN 0-8075-7629-8 Subj: Activities – storytelling. Animals – bats. Holidays – Halloween. Libraries.

Out and about at the apple orchard ill. by Anne McMullem. Picture Window, 2003. ISBN 1-4048-0036-0 Subj: Farms. Food. School – field trips. Trees.

Maze, Edward. *Oswald, the monkey* (Mathiesen, Egon)

Maze, Nancy. *Oswald, the monkey* (Mathiesen, Egon)

Mazer, Anne. *The Fixits* ill. by Paul Meisel. Hyperion, 1998. ISBN 0-7868-2202-3 Subj: Behavior – misbehavior. Careers – handymen. Family life – brothers & sisters. Humorous stories.

The No-Nothings and their baby ill. by Ross Collins. Levine, 2000. ISBN 0-590-68051-X Subj: Babies. Family life. Humorous stories.

The salamander room ill. by Steve Johnson. Knopf, 1991. ISBN 0-394-92945-4 Subj: Ecology. Imagination. Pets. Reptiles – salamanders.

Watch me ill. by Stacey Schuett. Knopf, 1990. ISBN 0-394-92946-2 Subj: Activities. Family life.

The yellow button ill. by Judy Pedersen. Knopf, 1990. ISBN 0-394-92935-7 Subj: Concepts.

Mazzola, Frank. *Counting is for the birds* ill. by author. Charlesbridge, 1997. ISBN 0-88106-952-3 Subj: Birds. Counting, numbers. Rhyming text.

M'Bane, Phumla. *see* Phumla

McClintock, Barbara. *A little princess* (Burnett, Frances Hodgson)

McMullan, Kate (Hall). *Back-to-school belly busters* by Katy Hall & Lisa Eisenberg; ill. by Stephen Carpenter. HarperFestival, 2002. ISBN 0-694-01358-7 Subj: Format, unusual – toy & movable books. Humorous stories. Riddles & jokes. School.

Hanukkah ha-has by Katy Hall & Lisa Eisenberg; ill. by Stephen Carpenter. HarperFestival, 2001. ISBN 0-694-01361-7 Subj: Format, unusual – toy & movable books. Holidays – Hanukkah. Humorous stories. Riddles & jokes.

Ho ho ho, ha ha ha by Katy Hall & Lisa Eisenberg; ill. by Stephen Carpenter. HarperFestival, 2001. ISBN 0-694-01362-5 Subj: Format, unusual – toy & movable books. Holidays – Christmas. Riddles & jokes.

Ribbit riddles by Katy Hall & Lisa Eisenberg; ill. by Stephen Carpenter. Dial, 2001. ISBN 0-8037-2525-6 Subj: Frogs & toads. Riddles & jokes.

Mead, Alice. *Billy and Emma* ill. by Christy Hale. Farrar, 2000. ISBN 0-374-30705-9 Subj: Birds. Birds – macaws. Crime. Friendship. Zoos.

Mead, Katherine. *How spiders got eight legs* ill. by Carol O'Malia. Steck-Vaughn, 1998. ISBN 0-8172-7272-0 Subj: Anatomy – legs. Folk & fairy tales. Spiders.

Meade, Holly. *John Willy and Freddy McGee* ill. by author. Cavendish, 1998. ISBN 0-7614-5033-5 Subj: Animals – guinea pigs. Behavior – running away. Character traits – freedom.

A place to sleep ill. by author. Cavendish, 2001. ISBN 0-7614-5096-3 Subj: Animals. Bedtime. Rhyming text. Sleep.

The rabbit's bride (Grimm, Jacob)

Meddaugh, Susan. *Beast* ill. by author. Houghton Mifflin, 1981. ISBN 0-395-30349-4 Subj: Character traits – kindness. Monsters.

The best place ill. by author. Houghton Mifflin, 1999. ISBN 0-395-97994-3 Subj: Animals. Animals – wolves. Behavior – dissatisfaction. Homes, houses.

Cinderella's rat ill. by author. Houghton Mifflin, 1997. ISBN 0-395-86833-5 Subj: Animals – rats. Family life – brothers & sisters. Humorous stories. Magic.

Harry on the rocks ill. by author. Houghton, 2003. ISBN 0-618-27603-3 Subj: Boats, ships. Dragons. Eggs. Islands.

Hog-eye ill. by author. Houghton Mifflin, 1995. ISBN 0-395-74276-5 Subj: Activities – baking, cooking. Animals – pigs. Animals – wolves. Books, reading.

Martha and Skits ill. by author. Houghton Mifflin, 2000. ISBN 0-618-05776-5 Subj: Animals – dogs. Behavior – growing up.

Martha blah blah ill. by author. Houghton Mifflin, 1996. ISBN 0-395-79755-1 Subj: Animals – dogs. Food.

Martha calling ill. by author. Houghton Mifflin, 1994. ISBN 0-395-69825-1 Subj: Activities – vacationing. Animals – dogs.

Martha speaks ill. by author. Houghton Mifflin, 1992. ISBN 0-395-63313-3 Subj: Animals – dogs.

Martha walks the dog ill. by author. Houghton Mifflin, 1998. ISBN 0-395-90494-3 Subj: Animals – dogs. Behavior – bullying. Birds – parakeets, parrots.

Maude and Claude go abroad ill. by author. Houghton Mifflin, 1980. ISBN 0-395-29162-3 Subj: Activities – traveling. Animals – foxes. Boats, ships. Foreign lands – France.

Perfectly Martha ill. by author. Houghton, 2004. ISBN 0-618-37857-X Subj: Animals – dogs. Careers – detectives.

Too short Fred ill. by author. Houghton Mifflin, 1978. ISBN 0-395-27155-X Subj: Animals – cats. Character traits – smallness.

Tree of birds ill. by author. Houghton Mifflin, 1990. ISBN 0-395-53147-0 Subj: Birds. Character traits – kindness to animals.

The witches' supermarket ill. by author. Houghton Mifflin, 1991. ISBN 0-395-57034-4 Subj: Animals – dogs. Holidays – Halloween. Stores. Witches.

Medearis, Angela Shelf. *The adventures of Sugar and Junior* ill. by Nancy Poydar. Holiday, 1995. ISBN 0-8234-1182-6 Subj: Ethnic groups in the U.S. – African Americans. Ethnic groups in the U.S. – Hispanic Americans. Friendship.

Annie's gifts ill. by Anna Rich. Just Us Books, 1994. ISBN 0-940975-30-0 Subj: Ethnic groups in the U.S. – African Americans. Gifts. Self-concept.

Barry and Bennie ill. by Pat Cummings. Celebration Pr., 1996. ISBN 0-673-75753-6 Subj: Animals. Animals – bats. Animals – bears.

Best friends in the snow ill. by Ken Wilson-Max. Scholastic, 1999. ISBN 0-590-52284-1 Subj: Friendship. Rhyming text. Weather – snow.

Bye-bye, babies! ill. by Patrice Aggs. Candlewick, 1995. ISBN 1-56402-258-7 Subj: Babies. Format, unusual – board books. Rhyming text.

Daisy and the doll (Medearis, Michael)

Dancing with the Indians ill. by Samuel Byrd. Holiday, 1991. ISBN 0-8234-0893-0 Subj: Activities – dancing. Ethnic groups in the U.S. – African Americans. Indians of North America – Seminole. Rhyming text.

Eat, babies, eat! ill. by Patrice Aggs. Candlewick, 1995. ISBN 1-56402-257-9 Subj: Babies. Food. Format, unusual – board books.

The freedom riddle ill. by John Ward. Dutton, 1995. ISBN 0-525-67469-1 Subj: Ethnic groups in the U.S. – African Americans. Folk & fairy tales. Riddles & jokes. Slavery. U.S. history.

The friendship garden ill. by Marcy Dunn Ramsey. Celebration Pr., 1996. ISBN 0-673-75742-0 Subj: Gardens, gardening.

The ghost of Sifty-Sifty Sam ill. by Jacqueline Rogers. Scholastic, 1997. ISBN 0-590-48290-4 Subj: Careers – chefs, cooks. Ethnic groups in the U.S. – African Americans. Ghosts. Homes, houses. Rhyming text.

Here comes the snow ill. by Maxie Chambliss. Scholastic, 1996. ISBN 0-590-26266-1 Subj: Activities – playing. Rhyming text. Weather – snow.

Kyle's first Kwanzaa ill. by Gershom Griffith. Celebration Pr., 1996. ISBN 0-673-75745-5 Subj: Ethnic groups in the U.S. – African Americans. Holidays – Kwanzaa.

The 100th day of school ill. by Joan Holub. Scholastic, 1996. ISBN 0-590-25944-X Subj: Counting, numbers. Rhyming text. School.

Our people ill. by Michael Bryant. Atheneum, 1994. ISBN 0-689-31826-X Subj: Ethnic groups in the U.S. – African Americans. Family life – fathers.

Picking peas for a penny ill. by author. State House Press, 1990. ISBN 0-938349-54-6 Subj: Activities – working. Ethnic groups in the U.S. – African Americans. Farms. U.S. history.

Poppa's itchy Christmas ill. by John Ward. Holiday, 1998. ISBN 0-8234-1298-9 Subj: Clothing. Holidays – Christmas. Sports – ice skating.

Poppa's new pants ill. by John Ward. Holiday, 1995. ISBN 0-8234-1155-9 Subj: Behavior – mistakes. Clothing. Ethnic groups in the U.S. – African Americans.

Rum-a-tum-tum ill. by James Ransome. Holiday, 1997. ISBN 0-8234-1143-5 Subj: Communities, neighborhoods. Ethnic groups in the U.S. – African Americans. Noise, sounds. Rhyming text.

Seeds grow ill. by Jill Dubin. Scholastic, 1999. ISBN 0-590-37974-7 Subj: Flowers. Plants. Rhyming text. Seeds.

Seven spools of thread: a Kwanzaa story ill. by Daniel Minter. A. Whitman, 2000. ISBN 0-8075-7315-9 Subj: Activities – weaving. Folk & fairy tales. Foreign lands – Ghana. Holidays – Kwanzaa.

The singing man: adapted from a West African folktale ill. by Terea Shaffer. Holiday, 1994. ISBN 0-8234-1103-6 Subj: Folk & fairy tales. Foreign lands – Nigeria. Music.

Tailypo: a newfangled tall tale ill. by Sterling Brown. Holiday, 1996. ISBN 0-8234-1249-0 Subj: Ethnic groups in the U.S. – African Americans. Folk & fairy tales. Monsters.

Too much talk ill. by Stefano Vitale. Candlewick, 1995. ISBN 1-56402-323-0 Subj: Cumulative tales. Folk & fairy tales. Foreign lands – Ghana. Royalty – kings.

We eat dinner in the bathtub ill. by Jacqueline Rogers. Scholastic, 1996. ISBN 0-590-73886-0 Subj: Friendship. Homes, houses.

We play on a rainy day ill. by Sylvia Walker. Scholastic, 1995. ISBN 0-590-26265-3 Subj: Activities – playing. Rhyming text. Weather – rain.

The zebra-riding cowboy ill. by María Cristina Brusca. Holt, 1992. ISBN 0-8050-1712-7 Subj: Animals – horses, ponies. Cowboys, cowgirls. Ethnic groups in the U.S. Music. Songs. U.S. history – frontier & pioneer life.

Medearis, Michael. *Daisy and the doll* by Michael Medearis & Angela Shelf Medearis; ill. by Larry Johnson. Vermont Folklife Center, 2000. ISBN 0-916718-15-8 Subj: Ethnic groups in the U.S. – African Americans. Prejudice. School. Self-concept. Toys – dolls.

Medicine Crow, Joseph. *Brave Wolf and the Thunderbird* ill. by Linda R. Martin. National Museum of the American Indian, 1998. Developed under the auspices of the Smithsonian's National Museum of the American Indian. ISBN 0-7892-0160-7 Subj: Folk & fairy tales. Indians of North America – Crow. Monsters. Mythical creatures.

Medina, Nina. *Have you ever noticed that rabbits don't sing?* ill. by author. Harpswell Pr., 1989. ISBN 0-88448-061-5 Subj: Activities – dancing. Animals – rabbits. Poetry.

Medina, Tony. *Christmas makes me think* ill. by Chandra Cox. Lee & Low, 2001. ISBN 1-58430-024-8 Subj: Behavior – sharing. Ethnic groups in the U.S. – African Americans. Holidays – Christmas. Religion.

DeShawn days ill. by Gregory Christie. Lee & Low, 2001. ISBN 1-58430-022-1 Subj: Cities, towns. Ethnic groups in the U.S. – African Americans. Family life. Poetry.

Medoff, Francine. *The mouse in the matzah factory* ill. by Nicole in den Bosch. Kar-Ben Copies, 2003. ISBN 1-58013-048-8 Subj: Animals – mice. Food. Jewish culture.

Mee, Charles L. *Noah* ill. by Ken Munowitz. HarperCollins, 1978. ISBN 0-06-024184-5 Subj: Boats, ships. Religion – Noah. Weather – floods. Weather – rain. Weather – rainbows.

Meeker, Clare Hodgson. *A tale of two rice birds: a folktale from Thailand* ill. by Christine Lamb. Sasquatch, 1994. ISBN 1-57061-008-8 Subj: Birds. Death. Emotions – love. Royalty – princesses.

Who wakes rooster? ill. by Megan Halsey. S&S, 1996. ISBN 0-689-80541-1 Subj: Animals. Birds – chickens. Farms. Morning. Sun.

Meeks, Esther K. *The curious cow* ill. by Mel Pekarsky. Follett, 1960. Also published in German as "Die neugierige Kuh"; in French as "La vache curieuse"; and in Spanish as "La Vaca curiosa." Subj: Animals – bulls, cows. Character traits – curiosity.

Friendly farm animals. Follett, 1965. Subj: Animals. Farms.

The hill that grew ill. by Lazlo Roth. Follett, 1959. Subj: Activities – playing.

One is the engine ill. by Ernie King. Follett, 1956. Subj: Counting, numbers. Trains.

One is the engine: a counting book ill. by Joe Rogers. Follett, 1947, 1972. ISBN 0-695-40236-6 Subj: Counting, numbers. Trains.

Playland pony ill. by Mary Miller Salem. Follett, 1951. Subj: Animals – horses, ponies.

Something new at the zoo ill. by Hazel Hoecker. Follett, 1957. Subj: Animals. Zoos.

Meeuwissen, Tony. *Remarkable animals: 1,000 amazing amalgamations* ill. by author. Orchard, 1998. ISBN 0-531-30066-8 Subj: Animals. Format, unusual – toy & movable books. Humorous stories.

Meggendorfer, Lothar. *The genius of Lothar Meggendorfer* ill. by Jim Deesing. Random House, 1985. ISBN 0-394-54690-3 Subj: Format, unusual – toy & movable books. Rhyming text. Toys.

Meggs, Libby Phillips. *Go home! the true story of James the cat* ill. by author. A. Whitman, 2000. ISBN 0-8075-2975-3 Subj: Animals – cats. Behavior – needing someone. Homeless.

Meigs, Mildred Plew. *Moon song* ill. by Chris Conover. Morrow, 1990. ISBN 0-688-08707-8 Subj: Lullabies.

Meijer, Marie. *The bake-a-cake book* ill. by Charlotte Ramel. Chronicle, 1994. ISBN 0-8118-0693-6 Subj: Activities – baking, cooking. Food. Format, unusual.

Meisel, Paul. *Zara's hats* ill. by autor. Dutton, 2003. ISBN 0-525-45465-9 Subj: Behavior – resourcefulness. Clothing – hats. Family life – fathers.

Meister, Cari. *Busy, busy city street* ill. by Steven Guarnaccia. Viking, 2000. ISBN 0-670-88944-X Subj: Automobiles. Cities, towns. Noise, sounds. Rhyming text. Traffic, traffic signs. Trucks.

Skinny and fats, best friends ill. by Steve Björkman. Holiday, 2002. ISBN 0-8234-1692-5 Subj: Activities – baking, cooking. Animals – pigs. Animals – rabbits. Friendship.

Tiny goes to the library ill. by Rich Davis. Viking, 2000. ISBN 0-670-88556-8 Subj: Animals – dogs. Books, reading. Concepts – size. Libraries.

Tiny the snow dog ill. by Rich Davis. Viking, 2001. ISBN 0-670-89117-7 Subj: Animals – dogs. Weather – snow.

Tiny's bath ill. by Rich Davis. Viking, 1998. ISBN 0-670-87962-2 Subj: Activities – bathing. Animals – dogs. Concepts – size.

When Tiny was tiny ill. by Rich Davis. Viking, 1999. ISBN 0-670-88058-2 Subj: Animals – dogs. Behavior – growing up. Concepts – size.

Melcher, Mary. *Mommy, who does God love?* ill. by Mary Melcher. Little Simon, 1997. ISBN 0-689-81036-9 Subj: Format, unusual – toy & movable books. Religion.

Mellage, Nanette. *Coming home* ill. by Cornelius Van Wright & Ying-Hwa Hu. BridgeWater, 2001. ISBN 0-8167-7009-3 Subj: Careers. Ethnic groups in the U.S. – African Americans. Sports – baseball.

See me grow, head to toe ill. by Keaf Holliday. Golden Bks., 1996. ISBN 0-307-10036-7 Subj: Babies. Behavior – growing up. Ethnic groups in the U.S. – African Americans. Rhyming text.

Mellings, Joan. *It's fun to go to school* ill. by Sandra Laroche. Lippincott, 1986. ISBN 0-694-00125-2 Subj: Rhyming text. School.

Mellor, Corinne. *Bruce the balding moose* ill. by Jonathan Allen; paper engineering by Richard Ferguson. Dial, 1996. ISBN 0-8037-2064-5 Subj: Activities – dancing. Animals. Animals – moose. Format, unusual – toy & movable books. Friendship.

Clark the toothless shark ill. by Jonathan Allen. Western, 1994. ISBN 0-307-17606-1 Subj: Fish – sharks. Format, unusual – toy & movable books. Teeth.

Melmed, Laura Krauss. *Capital! Washington D.C. from A to Z* ill. by Frané Lessac. HarperCollins, 2003. ISBN 0-688-17562-7 Subj: ABC books. Cities, towns. Rhyming text.

The first song ever sung ill. by Ed Young. Lothrop, 1993. ISBN 0-688-08231-9 Subj: Bedtime. Foreign lands – Japan. Poetry. Songs.

Fright night flight ill. by Henry Cole. HarperCollins, 2002. ISBN 0-06-029702-6 Subj: Holidays – Halloween. Rhyming text. Witches.

A hug goes around ill. by Betsy Lewin. HarperCollins, 2002. ISBN 0-688-14681-3 Subj: Day. Emotions. Family life. Rhyming text.

I love you as much . . . ill. by Henri Sorensen. 1st Tupelo board books ed. Tupelo, 1998. ISBN 0-688-15978-8 Subj: Animals. Family life – mothers. Format, unusual – board books. Rhyming text.

Jumbo's lullaby ill. by Henri Sorensen. Lothrop, 1999. ISBN 0-688-16996-1 Subj: Animals – elephants. Bedtime. Dreams. Foreign lands – Africa. Lullabies. Rhyming text.

Little Oh ill. by Jim LaMarche. Lothrop, 1997. ISBN 0-688-14209-5 Subj: Behavior – lost. Family life. Paper.

The Marvelous Market on Mermaid ill. by Maryann Kovalski. Lothrop, 1995. ISBN 0-688-13054-2 Subj: Careers – storekeepers. Cumulative tales. Family life – grandmothers. Rhyming text. Stores.

Moishe's miracle ill. by David Slonim. HarperCollins, 2000. ISBN 0-688-14683-X Subj: Folk & fairy tales. Holidays – Hanukkah. Jewish culture. Magic.

1-2-3 Thanksgiving ill. by Robin Kramer. HarperCollins, 2000. ISBN 0-688-14555-8 Subj: Counting, numbers. Holidays – Thanksgiving. Poetry. U.S. history.

Prince Nautilus ill. by Henri Sorensen. Lothrop, 1994. ISBN 0-688-04567-7 Subj: Character traits – laziness. Folk & fairy tales.

The rainbabies ill. by Jim LaMarche. Lothrop, 1992. ISBN 0-688-10756-7 Subj: Babies. Folk & fairy tales.

This first Thanksgiving ill. by Mark Buehner. HarperCollins, 2001. ISBN 0-688-14555-8 Subj: Counting, numbers. Holidays – Thanksgiving. Poetry.

Melnicove, Mark. *Africa is not a country* (Knight, Margy Burns)

Meltzer, Lisa. *The three billy goats Gruff* (Asbjørnsen, P. C. [Peter Christen])

Melville, Herman. *Catskill eagle* ill. by Thomas Locker. Putnam, 1991. ISBN 0-399-21857-2 Subj: Birds – eagles.

Melville, Kristy. *Splash! a penguin counting book* (Chester, Jonathan)

Memling, Carl. *What's in the dark?* ill. by John E. Johnson. Parents' Magazine Pr., 1971. ISBN 0-8193-0445-X Subj: Monsters. Night.

Mendel, Lydia J. *All dressed up and nowhere to go* (Joseph, Daniel M.)

Mendell, Olga Karman. *This home we have made* (Hammond, Anna)

Mendelson, S. T. *Stupid Emilien* ill. by author. Stewart, Tabori & Chang, 1991. ISBN 1-55670-213-2 Subj: Animals – rabbits. Folk & fairy tales. Foreign lands – Russia.

Mendes, Valerie. *Look at me, Grandma!* ill. by Claire Fletcher. Scholastic, 2001. ISBN 0-439-29654-4 Subj: Babies. Dreams. Family life – aunts, uncles. Family life – brothers & sisters. Family life – grandmothers. Family life – new sibling.

Mendoza, George. *The alphabet boat: a seagoing alphabet book* ill. by author. American Heritage, 1972. ISBN 0-07-041425-4 Subj: ABC books. Boats, ships.

Alphabet sheep ill. by Kathleen Reidy. Grosset, 1982. ISBN 0-448-12220-0 Subj: ABC books. Animals – sheep. Behavior – lost.

The gillygoofang ill. by Mercer Mayer. Dial, 1982. ISBN 0-8037-2875-1 Subj: Fish.

Henri Mouse ill. by Joelle Boucher. Viking, 1985. ISBN 0-670-36689-7 Subj: Animals – mice. Art.

Henri Mouse, the juggler ill. by Joelle Boucher. Viking, 1986. ISBN 0-670-80945-4 Subj: Animals – mice. Foreign lands – France. Magic.

The hunter I might have been photos by De Wayne Dalrymple. Astor-Honor, 1968. ISBN 0-8392-3064-8 Subj: Death. Emotions – grief. Poetry. Sports – hunting.

The Marcel Marceau counting book photos by Milton H. Greene. Doubleday, 1971. Subj: Clowns, jesters.

Need a house? Call Ms. Mouse ill. by Doris Susan Smith. Grosset, 1981. ISBN 0-448-16575-9 Subj: Animals. Animals – mice. Homes, houses.

Norman Rockwell's Americana ABC ill. by Norman Rockwell. Abrams, 1975. ISBN 0-440-05944-5 Subj: ABC books.

The scribbler ill. by Robert M. Quackenbush. Holt, 1971. ISBN 0-03-086359-7 Subj: Birds – sandpipers. Poetry. Sea & seashore.

The Sesame Street book of opposites with Zero Mostel photos by Sheldon Secunda; book design by Nicole Sekora-Mendoza. Platt, 1974. ISBN 0-8228-7701-5 Subj: Concepts – opposites.

Silly sheep and other sheepish rhymes ill. by Kathleen Reidy. Grosset, 1982. ISBN 0-448-12219-7 Subj: Animals – sheep. Nursery rhymes.

Traffic jam ill. by David Stoltz. Stewart, Tabori & Chang, 1990. ISBN 1-55670-135-7 Subj: Animals. Automobiles. Rhyming text. Traffic, traffic signs.

Were you a wild duck, where would you go? ill. by Jane Osborn-Smith. Stewart, Tabori & Chang, 1990. ISBN 1-55670-136-5 Subj: Birds – ducks. Ecology. Rhyming text.

Mennen, Ingrid. *Somewhere in Africa* by Ingrid Mennen & Niki Daly; ill. by Nicolaas Maritz. Dutton, 1992. ISBN 0-525-44848-9 Subj: Cities, towns. Foreign lands – South Africa.

Menter, Ian. *The Albany Road mural* photos by Will Guy. David & Charles, 1984. ISBN 0-241-11032-7 Subj: Activities – painting. Art.

Carnival photos by Will Guy. David & Charles, 1983. ISBN 0-241-10833-0 Subj: Foreign lands – England. Holidays.

Merberg, Julie. *In the garden with Van Gogh* by Julie Merberg & Suzanne Bober. Chronicle, 2002. ISBN 0-8118-3415-8 Subj: Art. Careers – artists. Format, unusual – board books. Rhyming text.

A magical day with Matisse by Julie Merberg & Suzanne Bober. Chronicle, 2002. ISBN 0-8118-3414-X Subj: Art. Careers – artists. Format, unusual – board books. Rhyming text.

Mercer, Lynn. *Schubert's snowflakes* ill. by author. Sagebrush, 2001. ISBN 0-9535413-6-3 Subj: Animals – polar bears. Weather – snow.

Meredith, Carol. *Jamie Anderson wouldn't . . .* ill. by Lorrie Szekat. Annick, 1998. ISBN 1-55037-457-5 Subj: Emotions – fear. Family life – fathers. Illness. School – first day.

Meredith, Lucy. *The princess on the nut: or, the curious courtship of the son of the princess on the pea* (Nikly, Michelle)

Meredith, Susan. *Hamsters* ill. by Christyan Fox; photos by Tom Flach & Howard Allman. EDC, 1999. ISBN 1-580-86167-9 Subj: Animals – hamsters.

Meres, Jonathan. *The big bad rumor* ill. by Jacqueline East. Orchard, 2000. ISBN 0-531-30292-X Subj: Animals. Behavior – gossip. Birds. Communication.

Mernan, Andrea. *Ben finds a friend* (Chapouton, Anne-Marie)

I wish I were (Laurencin, Geneviève)

A kitten is born (Fischer-Nagel, Heiderose)

A puppy is born (Fischer-Nagel, Heiderose)

A walk in the rain (Scheffler, Ursel)

Meroux, Felix. *The prince of the rabbits* ill. by Cooper Edens. Green Tiger Pr., 1985. ISBN 0-88138-030-X Subj: Animals – rabbits. Behavior – boredom.

Merriam, Eve. *Bam, bam, bam* ill. by Dan Yaccarino. Holt, 1995. ISBN 0-8050-3527-3 Subj: Buildings. Cities, towns. Machines. Poetry.

The birthday cow ill. by Guy Michel. Knopf, 1978. ISBN 0-394-93808-9 Subj: Animals. Humorous stories. Poetry.

The birthday door ill. by Peter J. Thornton. Morrow, 1986. ISBN 0-688-06194-X Subj: Animals – cats. Birthdays. Homes, houses. Problem solving.

Blackberry ink ill. by Hans Wilhelm. Morrow, 1985. ISBN 0-688-04151-5 Subj: Poetry.

Boys and girls, girls and boys ill. by Harriet Sherman. Holt, 1972. ISBN 0-03-005716-7 Subj: Activities – playing. Ethnic groups in the U.S. Friendship.

Christmas (Bruna, Dick)

The Christmas box ill. by David Small. Morrow, 1985. ISBN 0-688-05256-8 Subj: Family life. Holidays – Christmas.

Epaminondas ill. by Trina Schart Hyman. Follett, 1968. Originally published in 1938 as "Epaminondas and his Aunty" by Sara Cone Bryant. Subj: Ethnic groups in the U.S. – African Americans. Family life – aunts, uncles. Folk & fairy tales. Humorous stories.

Fighting words ill. by David Small. Morrow, 1992. ISBN 0-688-09677-8 Subj: Behavior – fighting, arguing. Behavior – name calling. Cities, towns. Country.

Goodnight to Annie ill. by Carol Schwartz. Four Winds, 1992. ISBN 1-56282-206-3 Subj: ABC books. Animals. Bedtime. Lullabies. Sleep.

Goodnight to Annie ill. by John Wallner. Four Winds, 1980. ISBN 0-590-07485-7 Subj: ABC books. Bedtime.

Halloween ABC ill. by Lane Smith. Macmillan, 1987. ISBN 0-02-766870-3 Subj: ABC books. Holidays – Halloween. Poetry.

Higgle wiggle ill. by Hans Wilhelm. Morrow, 1994. ISBN 0-688-11949-2 Subj: Poetry.

The hole story designed & ill. by Ivan Chermayeff. S&S, 1995. ISBN 0-671-88353-4 Subj: Format, unusual – board books. Poetry.

Low song ill. by Pam Paparone. McElderry, 2001. ISBN 0-689-82820-9 Subj: Nature. Rhyming text.

Mommies at work ill. by Eugenie Fernandes. S&S, 1989. ISBN 0-671-64386-X Subj: Activities – working. Careers. Family life – mothers.

On my street ill. by Melanie Hope Greenberg. HarperCollins, 2000. ISBN 0-694-01258-0 Subj: Cities, towns. Communities, neighborhoods. Family life – mothers. Rhyming text.

A poem for a pickle: funnybone verses ill. by Sheila Hamanaka. Morrow, 1989. ISBN 0-688-08138-X Subj: Poetry.

Ten rosy roses ill. by Julia Gorton. HarperCollins, 1999. ISBN 0-06-027888-9 Subj: Counting, numbers. Flowers. Rhyming text.

Train leaves the station ill. by Dale Gottlieb. Holt, 1992. ISBN 0-8050-1934-0 Subj: Counting, numbers. Rhyming text. Time. Toys – trains.

12 ways to get to 11 ill. by Bernie Karlin. S&S, 1993. ISBN 0-671-75544-7 Subj: Counting, numbers.

What in the world? ill. by Barbara J. Phillips-Duke. HarperCollins, 1997. ISBN 0-694-01036-7 Subj: Animals. Format, unusual – toy & movable books. Rhyming text.

Where is everybody? ill. by Diane de Groat. S&S, 1989. ISBN 0-671-64964-7 Subj: ABC books. Animals.

Where's that cat? by Eve Merriam & Pam Pollack; ill. by Joanna Harrison. McElderry, 2000. ISBN 0-689-82904-3 Subj: Animals – cats. Parks. Rhyming text.

Merrick, Patrick. *Biting flies* ill. with photos. Child's World, 2001. ISBN 1-56766-631-0 Subj: Insects – flies.

Centipedes ill. with photos. Child's World, 2003. ISBN 1-56766-978-6 Subj: Crustaceans – centipedes, millipedes.

Cockroaches ill. with photos. Child's World, 2003. ISBN 1-56766-206-4 Subj: Insects – cockroaches.

Easter bunnies ill. by author. Child's World, 1999. ISBN 1-56766-639-6 Subj: Animals – rabbits. Eggs. Holidays – Easter.

Leeches ill. with photos. Child's World, 2001. ISBN 1-56766-633-7 Subj: Animals – leeches.

Merrill, Bob. *How much is that doggie in the window?* (Trapani, Iza)

Merrill, Jean. *Emily Emerson's moon* by Jean Merrill & Ronni Solbert; ill. by Ronni Solbert. Little, 1960. Subj: Family life. Moon.

The girl who loved caterpillars ill. by Floyd Cooper. Philomel, 1992. ISBN 0-399-21871-8 Subj: Foreign lands – Japan. Insects – butterflies, caterpillars. Nature. Science.

How many kids are hiding on my block? by Jean Merrill & Frances Gruse Scott; ill. by Frances Gruse Scott. A. Whitman, 1970. ISBN 0-807-53418-8 Subj: Counting, numbers. Ethnic groups in the U.S. Games.

Tell about the cowbarn, Daddy ill. by Lili Cassel-Wronker. Addison-Wesley, 1963. Subj: Animals – bulls, cows. Barns. Farms.

Merritt, Jane Hamilton. *see* HamiltonMerritt, Jane

Merski, P. K. *Roaring, boring, Alice* ill. by Mark Weber. Skeezel, 2004. ISBN 0-9747217-0-0 Subj: Animals – mice. Foreign lands – Arctic. Northern lights. Rhyming text.

Meryl, Debra. *Baby's peek-a-boo album* ill. by True Kelley. Putnam, 1989. ISBN 0-448-15375-0 Subj: Activities – playing. Format, unusual – toy & movable books. Games.

Meserve, Adria. *Smog, the city dog* ill. by author. Chronicle, 2002. ISBN 0-8118-3551-0 Subj: Animals – dogs. Behavior – sharing. Folk & fairy tales.

Meshover, Leonard. *The guinea pigs that went to school* by Leonard Meshover & Sally Feistel; photos by Eve Hoffmann. Follett, 1968. Subj: Animals – guinea pigs. School. Science.

The monkey that went to school by Leonard Meshover & Sally Feistel; photos by Eve Hoffmann. Follett, 1978. ISBN 0-695-40878-X Subj: Animals – monkeys. School. Science.

Messenger, Jannat. *Lullabies and baby songs* ill. by author. Dial, 1988. ISBN 0-8037-0491-7 Subj: Lullabies. Poetry.

Metaxas, Eric. *Bible ABC* ill. by Jim Harris. Tommy Nelson, 1998. ISBN 0-8499-1524-4 Subj: ABC books. Religion. Rhyming text.

The birthday ABC by Eric Metaxas & Tim Raglin; ill. by Tim Raglin. S&S, 1995. ISBN 0-671-88306-2 Subj: ABC books. Animals. Birthdays. Rhyming text.

The boy and the whale: a Christmas fairy tale ill. by Paul Lopez. Third Story Books, 1994. ISBN 1-884506-15-1 Subj: Animals – whales. Fairies. Folk & fairy tales. Holidays – Christmas. Lighthouses.

David and Goliath ill. by Douglas Fraser. Rabbit Ears, 1996. ISBN 0-88708-294-7 Subj: Foreign lands – Israel. Giants. Jewish culture. Religion. Royalty – kings.

The emperor's new clothes (Andersen, H. C. [Hans Christian])

The fool and the flying ship ill. by Henrik Drescher. Rabbit Ears, 1997. ISBN 0-689-81582-4 Subj: Activities – flying. Boats, ships. Character traits – cleverness. Folk & fairy tales. Foreign lands – Russia. Royalty – tsars.

The gardener's apprentice ill. by Rodica Prato. Creative Ed., 1997. ISBN 1-56846-154-2 Subj: Animals – horses, ponies. Folk & fairy tales. Foreign lands – Romania. Magic.

The monkey people ill. by Diana Bryan. Rabbit Ears, 1995. ISBN 0-689-80191-2 Subj: Animals – monkeys. Character traits – laziness. Folk & fairy tales. Foreign lands – Colombia. Indians of South America.

Pinocchio (Collodi, Carlo)

Princess Scargo and the birthday pumpkin ill. by Karen Barbour. Rabbit Ears, 1996. ISBN 0-689-80231-5 Subj: Fish. Indians of North America – Nobscusset. Royalty – princesses. Weather – droughts.

Puss in boots ill. by Pierre Le-Tan. Rabbit Ears, 1992. ISBN 0-88708-285-8 Subj: Animals – cats. Character traits – cleverness. Folk & fairy tales. Royalty – kings.

Squanto and the miracle of Thanksgiving ill. by Shannon Stirnweis. Nelson, 1999. ISBN 0-8499-5864-4 Subj: Holidays – Thanksgiving. Indians of North America – Wampanoag. Pilgrims. U.S. history.

Stormalong, the legendary sea captain ill. by Don Vanderbeek. Rabbit Ears, 1995. ISBN 0-689-80194-7 Subj: Boats, ships. Sailors. Sea & seashore. Tall tales.

Uncle Mugsy and the terrible twins of Christmas ill. by Tim Raglin. Madison Square Pr., 1995. ISBN 0-942604-53-9 Subj: Holidays – Christmas. Multiple births – twins. Rhyming text.

The white cat ill. by Barbara McClintock. S&S, 2000. ISBN 0-689-80140-8 Subj: Animals – cats. Folk & fairy tales. Royalty – princes.

Metcalf, Paula. *Norma No Friends* ill. by author. Barefoot, 1999. ISBN 1-902283-87-2 Subj: Character traits – shyness. Friendship.

Métral, Yvette. *The turtle* ill. by Charlotte Knox. Rourke, 1983. ISBN 0-86592-856-8 Subj: Reptiles – turtles, tortoises.

Metropolitan Museum of Art. *The Christmas story* (The Christmas story)

Metzger, Barbara. *Elizabeth Cady Stanton* (Schlank, Carol Hilgartner)

Meyer, Brigit. *Easter bunny saves the day* ill. by Anne Mussenbrock. Little Simon, 2004. ISBN 1-59384-037-3 Subj: Animals – rabbits. Eggs. Format, unusual – toy & movable books. Holidays – Easter.

Little Easter surprise ill. by Anne Mussenbrock. Parklane, 2004. ISBN 1-59384-038-1 Subj: Animals. Birds. Eggs. Format, unusual. Holidays.

Meyer, Dennis K. *Anything cuddly will do!* (Inkpen, Mick)

Pat the beastie: a pull-and-poke book (Drescher, Henrik)

Meyer, Eleanor Walsh. *The keeper of ugly sounds* ill. by Vlad Guzner. Winslow, 1998. ISBN 1-890817-02-3 Subj: Behavior. Noise, sounds.

Meyer, Elizabeth C. *The blue china pitcher* ill. by author. Abingdon, 1974. ISBN 0-687-03625-9 Subj: Holidays. Parties.

Meyer, June. *see* Jordan, June

Meyer, Linda D. *Safety zone* ill. by Marina Megale. Chas. Franklin Pr., 1984. ISBN 0-960-35168-X Subj: Behavior – talking to strangers. Safety.

Meyer, Louis A. *The clean air and peaceful contentment dirigible airline* ill. by author. Little, 1972. Subj: Ecology. Humorous stories. Noise, sounds.

Meyers, Susan. *Everywhere babies* ill. by Marla Frazee. Harcourt, 2004. ISBN 0-15-205315-8 Subj: Activities. Babies. Rhyming text.

The truth about gorillas ill. by John Hamberger. Dutton, 1980. ISBN 0-525-41564-5 Subj: Animals – gorillas. Science.

Mianowski, Marie. *Zee is not scared* (Gay, Michel)

Michael, Emory H. *Androcles and the lion* ill. by Mia Hatchem. Winston-Derek, 1988. ISBN 1-55523-132-2 Subj: Animals – lions. Character traits – helpfulness. Character traits – kindness to animals. Folk & fairy tales. Foreign lands – Italy. Religion.

Michaels, Ruth. *The family that grew* (Rondell, Florence)

Michaels, William. *Clare and her shadow* ill. by author. Linnet Books, 1991. ISBN 0-208-02301-1 Subj: Family life – grandfathers. Shadows.

Michel, Anna. *Little wild lion cub* ill. by Tony Chen. Pantheon, 1981. ISBN 0-394-84352-5 Subj: Animals – lions.

Michels, Tilde. *At the frog pond* trans. by Nina Ignatowicz; ill. by Reinhard Michl. Lippincott, 1989. ISBN 0-397-32315-8 Subj: Ecology. Frogs & toads. Science.

Rabbit spring ill. by Käthi Bhend. Harcourt, 1989. ISBN 0-15-200568-4 Subj: Animals – rabbits. Nature.

What a beautiful day! ill. by Thomas Müller. Carolrhoda, 1992. ISBN 0-87614-739-2 Subj: Nature. Seasons – summer.

Who's that knocking at my door? ill. by Reinhard Michl. Barron's, 1986. ISBN 0-8120-5732-5 Subj: Animals. Rhyming text. Seasons – winter. Sports – hunting.

Michels-Gualtieri, Akaela S. *I was born to be a sister* ill. by Marcy Dunn Ramsey. Platypus Media, 2001. ISBN 1-930775-03-2 Subj: Babies. Children as authors. Family life – brothers & sisters. Sibling rivalry.

Michelson, Richard. *Animals that ought to be: poems about imaginary pets* ill. by Leonard Baskin. S&S, 1996. ISBN 0-689-80635-3 Subj: Animals. Imagination. Poetry.

Did you say ghosts? ill. by Leonard Baskin. Macmillan, 1993. ISBN 0-02-766915-7 Subj: Bedtime. Emotions – fear. Ghosts. Monsters. Night. Rhyming text.

Ten times better ill. by author. Cavendish, 2001. ISBN 0-7614-5070-X Subj: Animals. Counting, numbers. Format, unusual – toy & movable books. Rhyming text.

Too young for Yiddish ill. by Neil Waldman. Talewinds, 2002. ISBN 0-88106-118-2 Subj: Family life – grandfathers. Jewish culture. Language.

Michl, Reinhard. *A day on the river* ill. by author. Barron's, 1986. ISBN 0-8120-5715-5 Subj: Rivers.

Micklethwait, Lucy. *Spot a cat* ill. by author. DK, 1995. ISBN 0-7894-0144-4 Subj: Animals – cats. Art. Behavior – hiding things.

Spot a dog ill. by author. DK, 1995. ISBN 0-789-40145-2 Subj: Animals – dogs. Art. Behavior – hiding things.

Micklos, John. *Daddy poems* ill. by Robert Casilla; forword by Jim Trelease. Boyds Mills, 2000. ISBN 1-56397-735-4 Subj: Family life – fathers. Poetry.

Mommy poems ill. by Lori McElrath-Eslick. Boyds Mills, 2001. ISBN 1-56397-849-0 Subj: Family life – mothers. Poetry.

Micucci, Charles. *A little night music* ill. by author. Morrow, 1989. ISBN 0-688-07901-6 Subj: Animals – cats. Music. Musical instruments – violins. Night.

Midge, Tiffany. *Buffalo* retold by Tiffany Midge; additional text & book design by Vic Warren; ill. by Diana Magnuson. Scholastic, 1995. ISBN 0-590-22489-1 Subj: Animals – buffaloes. Folk & fairy tales. Indians of North America.

Mike, Jan M. *The bird maiden* ill. by Dave Albers. Troll, 1996. ISBN 0-8167-4023-2 Subj: Folk & fairy tales. Foreign lands – Serbia. Magic. Royalty – princes. Royalty – princesses. Witches.

Clever Karlis ill. by Charles Reasoner. Troll, 1996. ISBN 0-8167-4024-0 Subj: Folk & fairy tales. Foreign lands – Latvia. Royalty – princesses.

Gift of the Nile: an Ancient Egyptian legend ill. by Charles Reasoner. Troll, 1993. ISBN 0-8167-2813-5 Subj: Folk & fairy tales. Foreign lands – Egypt. Royalty – pharaohs.

Juan Bobo and the horse of seven colors ill. by Charles Reasoner. Troll, 1995. ISBN 0-8167-3745-2 Subj: Behavior – wishing. Character traits – foolishness. Folk & fairy tales. Foreign lands – Puerto Rico. Royalty – princesses.

Opossum and the great firemaker ill. by Charles Reasoner. Troll, 1993. ISBN 0-8167-3055-5 Subj: Fire. Folk & fairy tales. Foreign lands – Mexico. Indians of North America – Cora.

Miklowitz, Gloria D. *Bearfoot boy* ill. by Jim Collins. Follett, 1964. Subj: Birthdays. Clothing.

Save that raccoon! ill. by St. Tamara. Harcourt, 1978. ISBN 0-15-270241-5 Subj: Animals – raccoons. Character traits – kindness to animals. Fire. Forest, woods.

The zoo that moved ill. by Don Madden. Follett, 1968. Subj: Animals. Zoos.

Miles, Betty. *Around and around . . . love* ill. with photos. Knopf, 1975. ISBN 0-394-93111-4 Subj: Emotions – love. Poetry.

Having a friend ill. by Erik Blegvad. Knopf, 1958. Subj: Friendship.

A house for everyone ill. by Jo Lowery. Knopf, 1958. Subj: Homes, houses.

The sky is falling (Chicken Little)

The three little pigs (The three little pigs)

Miles, Calvin. *Calvin's Christmas wish* ill. by Dolores Johnson. Viking, 1993. ISBN 0-670-84295-8 Subj: Ethnic groups in the U.S. – African Americans. Family life. Farms. Holidays – Christmas. Santa Claus.

Miles, Elizabeth J. *Ears* ill. with photos. Heinemann, 2003. ISBN 1-4034-0014-8 Subj: Anatomy – ears. Animals.

Mouths and teeth ill. with photos. Heinemann, 2003. ISBN 1-4034-0018-0 Subj: Anatomy – mouths. Animals. Teeth.

Noses ill. with photos. Heinemann, 2003. ISBN 1-4034-0019-9 Subj: Anatomy – noses. Animals.

Wings, fins, and flippers ill. with photos. Heinemann, 2003. ISBN 1-4034-0023-7 Subj: Anatomy – fins. Anatomy – wings. Animals.

Miles, Miska. *Apricot ABC* ill. by Peter Parnall. Little, 1969. Subj: ABC books. Rhyming text. Trees.

Chicken forgets ill. by Jim Arnosky. Little, 1976. ISBN 0-316-56972-0 Subj: Behavior – forgetfulness. Birds – chickens. Humorous stories.

The fox and the fire ill. by John Schoenherr. Little, 1966. Subj: Animals – foxes. Fire. Forest, woods.

Friend of Miguel ill. by Genia. Rand McNally, 1967. Subj: Animals – horses, ponies. Foreign lands – Mexico.

The horse and the bad morning (Clymer, Ted)

Jump frog jump ill. by Earl Thollander. Putnam, 1965. Subj: Fairs, festivals. Frogs & toads.

Mouse six and the happy birthday ill. by Leslie Holt Morrill. Dutton, 1978. ISBN 0-525-35230-9 Subj: Animals – mice. Birthdays. Family life – mothers.

No, no, Rosina ill. by Earl Thollander. Putnam, 1964. Subj: Boats, ships. Careers – fishermen. Character traits – smallness. Cities, towns. Sports – fishing.

Noisy gander ill. by Leslie Holt Morrill. Dutton, 1978. ISBN 0-525-36026-3 Subj: Animals. Birds – ducks. Farms. Noise, sounds.

The pointed brush . . . ill. by Roger Antoine Duvoisin. Lothrop, 1959. Subj: Activities – writing. Foreign lands – China.

Rabbit garden ill. by John Schoenherr. Little, 1967. Subj: Animals – rabbits. Ecology. Gardens, gardening.

The raccoon and Mrs. McGinnis ill. by Leonard Weisgard. Putnam, 1961. ISBN 0-399-60530-4 Subj: Animals – raccoons. Barns. Crime.

The rice bowl pet ill. by Ezra Jack Keats. Crowell, 1962. Subj: Pets.

Rolling the cheese ill. by Alton Raible. Atheneum, 1966. Subj: Cities, towns. Games.

Show and tell . . . ill. by Thomas Arthur Hamil. Putnam, 1962. Subj: Animals – dogs. School.

Small rabbit ill. by Jim Arnosky. Little, 1977. ISBN 0-316-56973-9 Subj: Animals – rabbits.

Somebody's dog ill. by John Schoenherr. Little, 1973. ISBN 0-316-56965-8 Subj: Animals – dogs. Pets.

Sylvester Jones and the voice in the forest ill. by Leonard Weisgard. Lothrop, 1958. Subj: Animals. Forest, woods.

This little pig ill. by Leslie Holt Morrill. Dutton, 1980. ISBN 0-525-41145-3 Subj: Animals – pigs. Behavior – lost. Behavior – running away. Farms.

Wharf rat ill. by John Schoenherr. Little, 1972. Subj: Animals – rats.

Miles, Sally. *Alfi and the dark* ill. by Errol Le Cain. Chronicle, 1988. ISBN 0-87701-527-9 Subj: Bedtime. Friendship. Night.

Milgram, Mary. *Brothers are all the same* ill. by Rosmarie Hausherr. Dutton, 1978. ISBN 0-525-27243-7 Subj: Adoption. Family life. Sibling rivalry.

Milgrim, David. *Cows can't fly* ill. by author. Viking, 1998. ISBN 0-670-87475-2 Subj: Animals – bulls, cows. Imagination. Rhyming text.

Dog brain ill. by author. Viking, 1996. ISBN 0-670-86935-X Subj: Animals – dogs. Behavior – misbehavior.

Here in space ill. by author. BridgeWater, 1997. ISBN 0-8167-4393-2 Subj: Earth. Rhyming text.

My friend Lucky ill. by author. Atheneum, 2002. ISBN 0-689-84253-8 Subj: Animals – dogs. Concepts – opposites. Language.

Why Benny barks ill. by author. Random House, 1994. ISBN 0-679-86157-2 Subj: Animals – dogs. Noise, sounds. Rhyming text.

Milgrom, Harry. *Egg-ventures: first science experiments* ill. by Giulio Maestro. Dutton, 1974. ISBN 0-525-29160-1 Subj: Eggs. Science.

Milhous, Katherine. *The egg tree* ill. by author. Aladdin, 1992, c1950. ISBN 0-689-71568-4 Subj: Caldecott award books. Eggs. Holidays – Easter.

The turnip by Katherine Milhouse & Alice Dalgliesh; ill. by Pierr Morgan. Putnam, 1990. From: Once on a time by Katherine Milhouse and Alice Dalgliesh (1938). ISBN 0-399-22229-4 Subj: Character traits – cooperation. Cumulative tales. Farms. Folk & fairy tales. Foreign lands – Russia. Plants. Problem solving.

Milich, Melissa. *Can't scare me!* ill. by Tyrone Geter. Doubleday, 1995. ISBN 0-385-31052-8 Subj: Emotions – fear. Ethnic groups in the U.S. – African Americans. Ghosts.

Miz Fannie Mae's fine new Easter hat ill. by Yong Chen. Little, 1997. ISBN 0-316-57159-8 Subj: Cities, towns. Clothing – hats. Ethnic groups in the U.S. – African Americans. Family life – fathers. Family life – mothers. Holidays – Easter.

Milich, Zoran. *The city ABC book* ill. by author. Kids Can, 2001. ISBN 1-55074-942-0 Subj: ABC books. Cities, towns.

City colors ill. by author. Kids Can, 2004. ISBN 1-55337-542-4 Subj: Cities, towns. Concepts – color.

City 1 2 3 ill. by author. Kids Can, 2005. ISBN 1-55337-540-8 Subj: Cities, towns. Counting, numbers.

City signs ill. by author. Kids Can, 2002. ISBN 1-55337-003-1 Subj: Cities, towns. Communication.

Milios, Rita. *Sneaky Pete* ill. by Clovis Martin. Childrens Pr., 1989. ISBN 0-516-02092-7 Subj: Behavior – hiding. Rhyming text.

Yo soy = I am ill. by Clovis Martin. Childrens Pr., 1990. ISBN 0-516-32081-5 Subj: Activities. Concepts – opposites. Foreign languages. Self-concept.

Milius, Winifred. *see* Lubell, Winifred

Mill, Garrett. *see* Miller, Margaret

Millais, Raoul. *Elijah and Pin-Pin* ill. by author. S&S, 1992. ISBN 0-671-75543-9 Subj: Animals – hedgehogs. Animals – moles. Friendship. Parties.

Millen, C. M. *Blue bowl down* ill. by Holly Meade. Candlewick, 2004. ISBN 0-7636-1817-9 Subj: Activities – baking, cooking. Food. Lullabies. Rhyming text.

The low-down laundry line blues ill. by Christine Davenier. Houghton Mifflin, 1999. ISBN 0-395-87497-1 Subj: Emotions. Family life – sisters. Sports.

Miller, Albert. *see* Mills, Alan

I know an old lady (Little old lady who swallowed a fly)

Miller, Alice P. *The little store on the corner* ill. by John Lawrence. Abelard-Schuman, 1961. Subj: Stores.

The mouse family's blueberry pie ill. by Carol Bloch. Elsevier-Nelson, 1981. ISBN 0-525-66745-8 Subj: Activities – baking, cooking. Animals – mice.

Miller, Cameron. *Woodlore* by Cameron Miller & Dominique Falla; ill. by authors. Ticknor & Fields, 1995. ISBN 0-395-72034-6 Subj: Activities – making things.

Miller, David. *Just like you and me* ill. by author. Dial, 1999. ISBN 0-8037-2586-8 Subj: Animals.

Miller, Debbie S. *Are trees alive?* ill. by Stacey Schuett. Walker, 2002. ISBN 0-8027-8801-7 Subj: Ecology. Forest, woods. Trees.

A caribou journey ill. by Jon Van Zyle. Little, 1994. ISBN 0-316-57380-9 Subj: Alaska. Animals – reindeer. Nature.

River of life ill. by Jon Van Zyle. Clarion, 2000. ISBN 0-395-96790-2 Subj: Alaska. Ecology. Rivers.

Woolly mammoth journey ill. by Jon Van Zyle. Little, 2001. ISBN 0-316-57212-8 Subj: Animals – woolly mammoths.

Miller, Edna. *Jumping bean* ill. by author. Prentice-Hall, 1980. ISBN 0-13-512384-4 Subj: Science.

Mousekin finds a friend ill. by author. Prentice-Hall, 1967. ISBN 0-13-604413-1 Subj: Animals – mice. Friendship.

Mousekin takes a trip ill. by author. Prentice-Hall, 1976. ISBN 0-13-604363-1 Subj: Activities – traveling. Animals – mice.

Mousekin's ABC ill. by author. Prentice-Hall, 1972. ISBN 0-136-04389-5 Subj: ABC books. Animals – mice. Forest, woods. Rhyming text.

Mousekin's Christmas eve ill. by author. Prentice-Hall, 1965. ISBN 0-13-604454-9 Subj: Animals – mice. Holidays – Christmas.

Mousekin's close call ill. by author. Prentice-Hall, 1978. ISBN 0-13-604207-4 Subj: Animals – mice. Forest, woods.

Mousekin's Easter basket ill. by author. Prentice-Hall, 1987. ISBN 0-13-604141-8 Subj: Animals – mice. Holidays – Easter. Seasons – spring.

Mousekin's fables ill. by author. Prentice-Hall, 1982. ISBN 0-13-604165-5 Subj: Animals – mice. Folk & fairy tales. Seasons.

Mousekin's family ill. by author. Prentice-Hall, 1969. ISBN 0-13-604462-X Subj: Animals – mice. Family life.

Mousekin's frosty friend ill. by author. S&S, 1990. ISBN 0-671-70445-1 Subj: Animals – mice. Character traits – kindness to animals. Food. Snowmen.

Mousekin's golden house ill. by author. Prentice-Hall, 1964. ISBN 0-13-604232-5 Subj: Animals – mice. Hibernation. Holidays – Halloween. Seasons – winter.

Mousekin's lost woodland ill. by author. S&S, 1992. ISBN 0-671-74938-2 Subj: Animals – mice. Ecology. Forest, woods.

Mousekin's mystery ill. by author. Prentice-Hall, 1983. ISBN 0-13-604330-5 Subj: Animals – mice. Mystery stories.

Mousekin's Thanksgiving ill. by author. Prentice-Hall, 1985. ISBN 0-13-604299-6 Subj: Animals. Animals – mice. Forest, woods. Holidays – Thanksgiving.

Patches finds a new home ill. by author. S&S, 1989. ISBN 0-671-66266-X Subj: Animals – cats. Nature.

Pebbles, a pack rat ill. by author. Prentice-Hall, 1976. ISBN 0-13-655399-0 Subj: Animals – pack rats. Scarecrows.

Scamper: a gray tree squirrel ill. by author. Pippin Pr., 1991. ISBN 0-915912-12-9 Subj: Animals – squirrels. Nature.

Miller, Edward. *The curse of Claudia* ill. by author. Crown, 1989. ISBN 0-517-57409-8 Subj: Character traits – cleanliness. Emotions – happiness. Monsters.

Frederick Ferdinand Fox ill. by author. Crown, 1987. ISBN 0-517-56356-8 Subj: Animals – foxes. War.

Miller, Elizabeth I. *Just like home = Como en mi tierra* ill. by Mira Reisberg; Spanish trans. by Teresa Mlawer. A. Whitman, 1999. ISBN 0-8075-4068-4 Subj: Ethnic groups in the U.S. – Hispanic Americans. Foreign languages. Homes, houses. Immigrants.

Miller, Heather. *Cowboy* ill. by author. Heinemann, 2003. ISBN 1-4034-0366-X Subj: Careers. Cowboys, cowgirls.

Librarian ill. with photos. Heinemann, 2003. ISBN 1-4034-0369-4 Subj: Careers – librarians. Libraries.

My chickens ill. by author. Childrens Pr., 2000. ISBN 0-516-23105-7 Subj: Birds – chickens. Farms.

My goats ill. by author. Childrens Pr., 2000. ISBN 0-516-23107-3 Subj: Animals – goats. Farms.

My horses ill. by author. Childrens Pr., 2000. ISBN 0-516-23108-1 Subj: Animals – horses, ponies. Farms.

My pigs ill. by author. Childrens Pr., 2000. ISBN 0-516-23109-X Subj: Animals – pigs. Farms.

Zookeeper ill. with photos. Heinemann, 2003. ISBN 1-4034-0373-2 Subj: Careers – zookeepers.

Miller, J. P. (John Parr). *Do you know colors?* by J. P. Miller & Katherine Howard; ill. by J. P. Miller. Random House, 1979. ISBN 0-394-93957-3 Subj: Concepts – color.

Farmer John's animals ill. by author. Random House, 1979. ISBN 0-394-84270-7 Subj: Animals. Farms.

Good night, Little Rabbit ill. by author. Random House, 1986. ISBN 0-394-87992-9 Subj: Animals – rabbits. Bedtime. Family life. Format, unusual – board books.

Learn about colors with Little Rabbit ill. by author. Random House, 1984. ISBN 0-394-86671-1 Subj: Concepts – color.

Learn to count with Little Rabbit ill. by author. Random House, 1984. ISBN 0-394-96149-8 Subj: Animals – rabbits. Counting, numbers.

Miller, J. Philip. *We all sing with the same voice* by Philip Miller & Sheppard M. Greene; ill. by Paul Meisel. HarperCollins, 2001. ISBN 0-06-027475-1 Subj: Ethnic groups in the U.S. Music. Rhyming text. Songs.

Miller, Jane. *Farm alphabet book* photos by author. Prentice-Hall, 1984. ISBN 0-13-304767-9 Subj: ABC books. Farms.

Farm counting book photos by author. Prentice-Hall, 1983. ISBN 0-13-304790-3 Subj: Counting, numbers. Farms.

Farm noises photos by author. S&S, 1989. ISBN 0-671-67450-1 Subj: Animals. Farms. Noise, sounds.

Seasons on the farm ill. by author. Prentice-Hall, 1986. ISBN 0-13-797275-X Subj: Animals. Farms. Seasons.

Miller, Judith Ransom. *Nabob and the geranium* ill. by Marilyn Neuhart. Golden Gate, 1967. Subj: Plants. Science.

Miller, Kathryn Ann. *Did my first mother love me? a story for an adopted child, with a special section for adoptive parents* ill. by Jami Moffett. Morning Glory Pr., 1994. ISBN 0-930934-85-7 Subj: Adoption. Emotions. Family life.

Miller, M. L. *Dizzy from fools* ill. by Eve Tharlet. Alphabet Pr., 1985. ISBN 0-88708-004-9 Subj: Character traits – questioning. Clowns, jesters. Royalty. Royalty – princesses.

The enormous snore ill. by Kevin Hawkes. Putnam, 1995. ISBN 0-399-22650-8 Subj: Behavior – lost. Character traits – helpfulness. Noise, sounds. Royalty – kings. Sleep – snoring.

Those Bottles! ill. by Barry Root. Putnam, 1994. ISBN 0-399-22607-9 Subj: Family life. Prejudice. Weather – floods.

Miller, Margaret. *At my house* ill. by author. Crowell, 1989. ISBN 0-694-00276-3 Subj: Babies. Family life. Format, unusual – board books.

At the shore photos by author. Little Simon, 1996. ISBN 0-689-80052-5 Subj: Format, unusual – board books. Sea & seashore.

Baby faces ill. by author. Little Simon, 1998. ISBN 0-689-81911-0 Subj: Anatomy – faces. Babies. Format, unusual – board books.

Big and little ill. by author. Greenwillow, 1998. ISBN 0-688-14749-6 Subj: Concepts – opposites. Concepts – size.

Can you guess? ill. by author. Greenwillow, 1993. ISBN 0-688-11181-5 Subj: Character traits – questioning.

Every day photos by author. HarperCollins, 1991. ISBN 0-694-00304-2 Subj: Activities. Format, unusual – board books. Language.

Family time photos by author. Little Simon, 1996. ISBN 0-689-80051-7 Subj: Family life. Format, unusual – board books.

Guess who? photos by author. Little Simon, 1996. ISBN 0-688-12784-3 Subj: Format, unusual – board books.

Happy days photos by author. Little Simon, 1996. ISBN 0-689-80050-9 Subj: Activities. Format, unusual – board books.

Here we go! ill. by author. Little Simon, 1998. ISBN 0-689-80041-X Subj: Format, unusual – board books. Sports.

I can help ill. by author. Little Simon, 1998. ISBN 0-689-80044-4 Subj: Family life. Format, unusual – board books.

I can make it! ill. by author. Little Simon, 1997. ISBN 0-689-80048-7 Subj: Activities – making things. Format, unusual – board books.

I love colors ill. by author. Little Simon, 1999. ISBN 0-689-82356-8 Subj: Animals. Babies. Concepts – color. Family life. Format, unusual – board books.

I'm grown up! ill. by author. Little Simon, 1998. ISBN 0-689-80043-6 Subj: Family life. Format, unusual – board books. Language.

In my room ill. by author. Crowell, 1989. ISBN 0-694-00271-2 Subj: Babies. Family life. Format, unusual – board books.

Let's play! ill. by author. Little Simon, 1997. ISBN 0-689-80047-9 Subj: Activities – playing. Format, unusual – board books.

Let's pretend! ill. by author. Little Simon, 1998. ISBN 0-689-80042-8 Subj: Format, unusual – board books. Imagination.

Me and my bear ill. by author. Little Simon, 1999. ISBN 0-689-82355-X Subj: Animals – babies. Animals – bears. Concepts – color. Format, unusual – board books.

My best friends photos by author. Little Simon, 1996. ISBN 0-689-80049-5 Subj: Format, unusual – board books. Pets.

My birthday photos by author. HarperCollins, 1991. ISBN 0-694-00302-6 Subj: Birthdays. Format, unusual – board books. Language. Parties.

My first words: me and my clothes ill. by author. Crowell, 1989. ISBN 0-694-00272-0 Subj: Babies. Clothing. Family life. Format, unusual – board books.

My five senses photos by author. S&S, 1994. ISBN 0-671-79168-0 Subj: Senses.

Now I'm big photos by author. Greenwillow, 1996. ISBN 0-688-14078-5 Subj: Babies. Concepts – size. School.

On my street photos by author. HarperCollins, 1991. ISBN 0-694-00303-4 Subj: Communities, neighborhoods. Format, unusual – board books. Language.

Playtime photos by author. HarperCollins, 1991. ISBN 0-694-00301-8 Subj: Activities – playing. Concepts – opposites. Format, unusual – board books. Language.

Time to eat ill. by author. Crowell, 1989. ISBN 0-87449-618-7 Subj: Babies. Family life. Food. Format, unusual – board books.

Water play ill. by author. Little Simon, 1997. ISBN 0-689-80046-0 Subj: Activities – playing. Format, unusual – board books. Sports. Water.

What's on my head? ill. by author. Little Simon, 1998. ISBN 0-689-81912-9 Subj: Anatomy – heads. Clothing – hats. Format, unusual – board books.

Wheels go 'round ill. by author. Little Simon, 1997. ISBN 0-689-80045-2 Subj: Format, unusual – board books. Wheels.

Where does it go? photos by author. Greenwillow, 1992. ISBN 0-688-10929-2 Subj: Character traits – orderliness. Clothing. Toys.

Where's Jenna? photos by author. S&S, 1994. ISBN 0-671-79167-2 Subj: Activities – bathing. Language.

Who uses this? photos by author. Greenwillow, 1990. ISBN 0-688-08279-3 Subj: Careers. Tools.

Whose hat? photos by author. Greenwillow, 1988. ISBN 0-688-06907-X Subj: Careers. Clothing – hats.

Whose shoe? photos by author. Greenwillow, 1991. ISBN 0-688-10009-0 Subj: Clothing – shoes. Games.

Miller, Michaela. *Guinea pigs* ill. with photos. Heinemann, 1998. ISBN 1-57572-575-4 Subj: Animals – guinea pigs. Pets.

Miller, Moira. *The moon dragon* ill. by Ian Deuchar. Dial, 1989. ISBN 0-8037-0566-2 Subj: Behavior – boasting. Folk & fairy tales. Foreign lands – China. Kites.

Oscar Mouse finds a home ill. by Maria Majewska. Dial, 1985. ISBN 0-8037-0229-9 Subj: Animals – mice. Behavior – seeking better things.

The proverbial mouse ill. by Ian Deuchar. Dial, 1987. ISBN 0-8037-0195-0 Subj: Animals – mice. Rhyming text. Toys.

The search for spring ill. by Ian Deuchar. Dial, 1988. ISBN 0-8037-0445-3 Subj: Seasons.

Miller, Robert H. (Robert Henry). *The story of Nat Love* by Robert Miller & Michael Bryant; ill. by Michael Bryant. Silver Pr., 1995. ISBN 0-382-24389-7 Subj: Cowboys, cowgirls. Slavery. U.S. history – frontier & pioneer life.

Miller, Ruth. *The bear on the bed* ill. by Bill Slavin. Kids Can, 2002. ISBN 1-55337-036-8 Subj: Animals – bears. Rhyming text.

I went to the bay ill. by Martine Gourbault. Kids Can, 1998. ISBN 1-55074-498-4 Subj: Animals. Boats, ships. Frogs & toads. Sea & seashore.

I went to the farm ill. by Per-Henrik Gurth. Kids Can, 2000. ISBN 1-55074-705-3 Subj: Activities – playing. Animals. Farms. Rhyming text.

Miller, Sara Swan. *Cat in the bag* ill. by Benton Mahan. Childrens Pr., 2001. ISBN 0-516-22014-4 Subj: Activities – traveling. Animals – cats.

Miller, Thomas Patton. *Can a coal scuttle fly?* by Tomas Patton Miller & Camay Calloway Murphy; ill. by Tomas Patton Miller. Maryland Historical Society, 1996. ISBN 0-938420-55-0 Subj: Art. Concepts – color. Ethnic groups in the U.S. – African Americans.

Miller, Virginia. *Be gentle!* ill. by author. Candlewick, 1997. ISBN 0-7636-0251-5 Subj: Animals – bears. Animals – cats. Pets.

Eat your dinner! ill. by author. Candlewick, 1992. ISBN 1-56402-121-1 Subj: Animals – bears. Food.

Go to bed! ill. by author. Candlewick, 1993. ISBN 1-56402-244-7 Subj: Animals – bears. Bedtime.

I love you just the way you are ill. by author. Candlewick, 1998. ISBN 0-7636-0664-2 Subj: Animals – bears. Behavior – bad day.

In a minute! ill. by author. Candlewick, 2000. ISBN 0-7636-1270-7 Subj: Activities – playing. Animals – bears.

On your potty! ill. by author. Greenwillow, 1991. ISBN 0-688-10618-8 Subj: Animals – bears. Behavior – growing up. Etiquette. Toilet training.

Ten red apples ill. by author. Candlewick, 2002. ISBN 0-7636-1901-9 Subj: Animals – bears. Animals – cats. Counting, numbers. Food.

Miller, Warren. *The goings on at Little Wishful* ill. by Edward Sorel. Little, 1959. Subj: Behavior – boasting. Emotions – envy, jealousy.

Pablo paints a picture ill. by Edward Sorel. Little, 1959. Subj: Activities – painting. Careers – artists.

Miller, William. *The bus ride* ill. by John Ward; intro. by Rosa Parks. Lee & Low, 1998. ISBN 1-880000-60-1 Subj: Ethnic groups in the U.S. – African Americans. Prejudice. U.S. history.

The conjure woman ill. by Terea D. Shaffer. Atheneum, 1996. ISBN 0-689-31962-2 Subj: Ethnic groups in the U.S. – African Americans. Illness. Magic.

Frederick Douglass: the last day of slavery ill. by Cedric Lucas. Lee & Low, 1995. ISBN 1-880000-17-2 Subj: Ethnic groups in the U.S. – African Americans. Slavery. U.S. history.

A house by the river ill. by Cornelius Van Wright & Ying-Hwa Hu. Lee & Low, 1997. ISBN 1-880000-48-2 Subj: Emotions – fear. Ethnic groups in the U.S. – African Americans. Family life – mothers. Homes, houses. Weather – storms.

Jenny and the peddler ill. by Rod Brown. Dial, 2000. ISBN 0-8037-2046-7 Subj: Careers – peddlers. Country. Ethnic groups in the U.S. – African Americans. Jewish culture.

The knee-high man ill. by Roberta Glidden. Gibbs Smith, 1996. ISBN 0-8790-5634-7 Subj: Character traits – foolishness. Ethnic groups in the U.S. – African Americans. Folk & fairy tales.

Night golf ill. by Cedric Lucas. Lee & Low, 1999. ISBN 1-880000-79-2 Subj: Ethnic groups in the U.S. – African Americans. Prejudice. Sports – golf.

The piano ill. by Susan Keeter. Lee & Low, 2000. ISBN 1-880000-98-9 Subj: Ethnic groups in the U.S. – African Americans. Music. Musical instruments – pianos. Old age.

Rent party jazz ill. by Charlotte Riley-Webb. Lee & Low, 2001. ISBN 1-58430-025-6 Subj: Ethnic groups in the U.S. – African Americans. Music. U.S. history.

Richard Wright and the library card ill. by Gregory Christie. Lee & Low, 1997. ISBN 1-880000-57-1 Subj: Books, reading. Ethnic groups in the U.S. – African Americans. Libraries.

Millhouse, Nicholas. *Blue-footed booby: bird of the Galápagos* ill. by Margret Bowman. Walker, 1986. ISBN 0-8027-6629-3 Subj: Animals. Birds. Islands. Science.

Milligan, Bryce. *Brigid's cloak* ill. by Helen Cann. Eerdmans, 2002. ISBN 0-8028-5224-6 Subj: Clothing – coats. Folk & fairy tales. Foreign lands – Ireland. Religion – Nativity.

The prince of Ireland and the three magic stallions ill. by Preston McDaniels. Holiday, 2003. ISBN 0-8234-1573-2 Subj: Emotions – envy, jealousy. Folk & fairy tales. Foreign lands – Ireland. Royalty – princes.

Millman, Isaac. *Moses goes to a concert* ill. by author. Farrar, 1998. ISBN 0-374-35067-1 Subj: Communication. Handicaps – deafness. Language. Music. Musical instruments – orchestras. School – field trips. Sign language.

Moses goes to school ill. by autor. Farrar, 2000. ISBN 0-374-35069-8 Subj: Handicaps – deafness. Language. School – first day. Senses – hearing.

Moses goes to the circus ill. by author. Frances Foster, 2003. ISBN 0-374-35064-7 Subj: Circus. Communication. Handicaps – deafness. Language.

Mills, Alan. *The hungry goat* ill. by Abner Graboff. Rand McNally, 1964. Subj: Animals – goats. Humorous stories. Music. Songs.

I know an old lady (Little old lady who swallowed a fly)

Mills, Claudia. *Gus and Grandpa and show-and-tell* ill. by Catherine Stock. Farrar, 2000. ISBN 0-374-32819-6 Subj: Family life – grandfathers. School.

Gus and Grandpa ride the train ill. by Catherine Stock. Farrar, 1998. ISBN 0-374-32826-9 Subj: Family life – grandfathers. Trains. Transportation.

One small lost sheep ill. by Walter Lyon Krudop. Farrar, 1997. ISBN 0-374-35649-1 Subj: Animals – sheep. Careers – shepherds. Religion – Nativity.

Phoebe's parade ill. by Carolyn Ewing. Macmillan, 1994. ISBN 0-02-767012-0 Subj: Family life – brothers & sisters. Parades. Sibling rivalry.

A visit to Amy-Claire ill. by Sheila Hamanaka. Macmillan, 1992. ISBN 0-02-766991-2 Subj: Emotions – envy, jealousy. Family life. Family life – sisters. Sibling rivalry.

Mills, Dorothy Jane. *see* Seymour, Dorothy Z.

Mills, Elaine. *Marinetta at the ballet* ill. by author. Andersen, 2001. ISBN 1-59019-439-X Subj: Ballet. Theater. Toys. Toys – dolls.

Mills, Joyce C. *Gentle Willow: a story for children about dying* ill. by Michael Chesworth. G. Stevens, 1994. ISBN 0-8368-1070-8 Subj: Animals – squirrels. Death. Trees.

Little Tree: a story for children with serious medical problems ill. by Michael Chesworth. Magination Pr., 1992. ISBN 0-945354-52-5 Subj: Illness. Self-concept. Trees.

Mills, Judith Christine. *The painted chest* ill. by author. Key Porter Kids, 2000. ISBN 1-55263-015-3 Subj: Activities – dancing. Activities – playing. Activities – working. Music.

The stonehook schooner ill. by author. Key Porter Books, 1995. ISBN 1-55013-653-4 Subj: Boats, ships. Lakes, ponds. Rocks. Sailors. U.S. history.

Mills, Lauren A. *The dog prince* ill. by Lauren Mills & Dennis Nolan. Little, 1996. ISBN 0-316-57417-1 Subj: Animals – dogs. Behavior. Magic. Monsters. Royalty – princes.

Fairy wings ill. by Lauren Mills & Dennis Nolan. Little, 1995. ISBN 0-316-57397-3 Subj: Activities – flying. Fairies. Folk & fairy tales. Mythical creatures – trolls. Royalty – princes.

Fin and the imp by Lauren Mills & Dennis Nolan; ill. by authors. Little, 2002. ISBN 0-316-57412-0 Subj: Character traits – being different. Fairies. Mythical creatures – imps. Royalty – queens.

The goblin baby ill. by author. Dial, 1999. ISBN 0-8037-2172-2 Subj: Babies. Emotions – envy, jealousy. Family life – brothers & sisters. Family life – new sibling. Imagination.

The rag coat ill. by author. Little, 1991. ISBN 0-316-57407-4 Subj: Behavior – sharing. Clothing. Friendship. Poverty.

Tatterhood and the hobgoblins ill. by reteller. Little, 1993. ISBN 0-316-57406-6 Subj: Character traits – individuality. Folk & fairy tales. Foreign lands – Norway. Mythical creatures – goblins. Royalty – princesses.

Mills, Patricia. *On an island in the bay* photos by author. North-South, 1994. ISBN 1-55858-334-3 Subj: Careers – fishermen. Islands. Sea & seashore.

Millward, David Wynn. *Jenny and Bob* ill. by Kady MacDonald Denton. Delacorte, 1991. ISBN 0-385-30431-5 Subj: Emotions. Family life.

Milne, A. A. (Alan Alexander). *Disney's Pooh's grand adventure: the search for Christopher Robin* (Henderson, Kathy)

Eeyore loses a tail ill. by Ernest H. Shepard. Dutton, 2001. ISBN 0-525-46703-3 Subj: Anatomy – tails. Toys. Toys – bears.

House at Pooh corner [a pop-up book] with ill. after the style of Ernest H. Shepard. Dutton, 1986. ISBN 0-525-44245-6 Subj: Format, unusual – toy & movable books. Homes, houses. Toys – bears.

The magic hill ill. by Isabel Bodor Brown. Dutton, 2000. Subj: Flowers. Folk & fairy tales. Royalty – princesses.

Pooh and some bees ill. by Robert Cremins. Dutton, 1987. ISBN 0-525-44339-8 Subj: Format, unusual – toy & movable books. Insects. Toys – bears.

Pooh goes visiting ill. by Robert Cremins. Dutton, 1987. ISBN 0-525-44337-1 Subj: Format, unusual – toy & movable books. Toys – bears.

Pooh's alphabet book ill. by E. H. Shepard. Dutton, 1976. ISBN 0-525-37370-5 Subj: ABC books. Toys – bears.

Pooh's counting book ill. by E. H. Shepard. Dutton, 1982. ISBN 0-525-44016-X Subj: Counting, numbers. Toys – bears.

Pooh's quiz book ill. by E. H. Shepard. Dutton, 1977. ISBN 0-525-37485-X Subj: Games. Toys – bears.

Prince Rabbit: and, The princess who could not laugh ill. by Mary Shepard. Dutton, 1966. Subj: Animals – rabbits. Folk & fairy tales. Royalty – princes.

Tigger comes to the forest and has breakfast ill. by Ernest H. Shepard. Dutton, 1999. ISBN 0-525-46822-6 Subj: Food. Forest, woods. Toys.

Tigger tales ill. by Ernest H. Shepard. Dutton, 2002. ISBN 0-525-46941-9 Subj: Toys. Toys – bears.

Winnie-the-Pooh: a pop-up book ill. by Chuck Murphy; engineering by Keith Moseley. Dutton, 1984. ISBN 0-525-44119-0 Subj: Character traits – bravery. Format, unusual – toy & movable books. Toys – bears.

Winnie-the-Pooh's ABC (Shepard, E. H. [Ernest Howard])

Winnie-the-Pooh's ABC (Winnie-the-Pooh's ABC)

Milord, Jerry. *Maggie and the goodbye gift* (Milord, Sue)

Milord, Sue. *Maggie and the goodbye gift* by Sue & Jerry Milord; ill. by authors. Lothrop, 1979. ISBN 0-688-51912-1 Subj: Family life. Gifts. Moving.

Milord, Susan. *The ghost on the hearth* ill. by Lydia Dabcovich. Vermont Folklife Center, 2003. ISBN 0-916718-18-2 Subj: Farms. Foreign lands – Canada. Ghosts.

Willa the wonderful ill. by author. Houghton, 2003. ISBN 0-618-27522-3 Subj: Animals – pigs. Fairies. Royalty – princesses. School.

Milstein, Linda Breiner. *Amanda's perfect hair* ill. by Susan Meddaugh. Tambourine, 1993. ISBN 0-688-11154-8 Subj: Behavior – dissatisfaction. Hair.

Coconut mon ill. by Cheryl Munro Taylor. Tambourine, 1995. ISBN 0-688-12862-9 Subj: Counting, numbers. Ethnic groups in the U.S. – African Americans. Foreign lands – Caribbean Islands.

Grandma's jewelry box ill. by Jean Hirashima. Random House, 1992. ISBN 0-679-81973-8 Subj: Family life – grandmothers. Format, unusual – toy & movable books.

Miami-Nanny stories ill. by Oki S. Han. Tambourine, 1994. ISBN 0-688-11152-1 Subj: Family life – grandmothers. Jewish culture.

Milton, John. *Comus* (Hodges, Margaret)

Milton, Joyce. *Big cats* ill. by Silvia Duran. Grosset, 1994. ISBN 0-448-40565-2 Subj: Animals – cheetahs. Animals – cougars. Animals – jaguars. Animals – leopards. Animals – lions. Animals – tigers.

Dinosaur days ill. by Richard Roe. Random House, 1985. ISBN 0-394-97023-3 Subj: Dinosaurs. Prehistory.

Milton, Nancy. *The giraffe that walked to Paris* ill. by Roger Roth. Crown, 1992. ISBN 0-517-58133-7 Subj: Activities – traveling. Animals – giraffes. Foreign lands – France. Royalty – kings.

Milway, Katie Smith. *Cappuccina goes to town* ill. by Eugenie Fernandes. Kids Can, 2002. ISBN 1-55074-807-6 Subj: Animals – bulls, cows. Cities, towns. Farms. Self-concept.

Min, Laura. *Mrs. Sato's hens* ill. by Benrei Huang. Scott Foresman, 1994. ISBN 0-673-36193-4 Subj: Birds – chickens. Counting, numbers. Days of the week, months of the year. Eggs. Ethnic groups in the U.S. – Asian Americans.

Min, Willemien. *Peter's patchwork dream* ill. by author. Barefoot, 1999. ISBN 1-902283-45-7 Subj: Friendship. Illness. Imagination. Quilts.

Minarik, Else Holmelund. *Am I beautiful?* ill. by Yossi Abolafia. Greenwillow, 1992. ISBN 0-688-09912-2 Subj: Animals. Animals – hippopotamuses. Family life – mothers. Self-concept.

Cat and dog ill. by Fritz Siebel. HarperCollins, 1960. ISBN 0-06-024221-3 Subj: Animals – cats. Animals – dogs.

Father Bear comes home ill. by Maurice Sendak. HarperCollins, 1959. ISBN 0-06-024231-0 Subj: Animals – bears. Family life – fathers.

Father's flying flapjacks ill. by David T. Wenzel. HarperFestival, 2002. ISBN 0-694-01687-X Subj: Animals – bears. Family life. Food. Format, unusual – board books.

It's spring! ill. by Margaret Bloy Graham. Greenwillow, 1989. ISBN 0-688-07620-3 Subj: Animals – cats. Seasons – spring.

A kiss for Little Bear ill. by Maurice Sendak. HarperCollins, 1959. ISBN 0-06-024299-X Subj: Animals – bears.

Little Bear ill. by Maurice Sendak. HarperCollins, 1957. ISBN 0-06-024241-8 Subj: Animals – bears. Birthdays.

Little Bear's friend ill. by Maurice Sendak. HarperCollins, 1960. ISBN 0-06-024256-6 Subj: Animals – bears. Friendship.

Little Bear's new friend ill. by Heather Green. HarperCollins, 2002. ISBN 0-06-623688-6 Subj: Animals – bears. Behavior – lost. Friendship.

Little Bear's visit ill. by Maurice Sendak. HarperCollins, 1961. ISBN 0-06-024266-3 Subj: Animals – bears. Caldecott award honor books. Family life – grandparents.

The little giant girl and the elf boys ill. by Garth Williams. HarperCollins, 1963. Subj: Giants. Mythical creatures – elves.

The little girl and the dragon ill. by Martine Gourbault. Greenwillow, 1991. ISBN 0-688-09914-9 Subj: Animals. Behavior – bullying. Character traits – stubbornness. Dragons.

No fighting, no biting! ill. by Maurice Sendak. HarperCollins, 1958. ISBN 0-06-024291-4 Subj: Behavior – fighting, arguing. Reptiles – alligators, crocodiles.

Percy and the five houses ill. by James Stevenson. Greenwillow, 1989. ISBN 0-688-08105-3 Subj: Animals – beavers. Homes, houses.

Minier, Nelson. *see* Baker, Laura Nelson

Minor, Wendell. *Pumpkin heads* ill. by author. Blue Sky, 2000. ISBN 0-590-52105-5 Subj: Holidays – Halloween.

Minsberg, David. *The book monster* ill. by Shelley Matheis. Littlebee Pr., 1982. ISBN 0-940674-00-9 Subj: Books, reading. Monsters.

Minshull, Evelyn White. *Eaglet's world* ill. by Andrea Gabriel. A. Whitman, 2002. ISBN 0-8075-8929-2 Subj: Activities – flying. Behavior – growing up. Birds – eagles.

Minters, Frances. *Cinder-Elly* ill. by G. Brian Karas. Viking, 1994. ISBN 0-670-84417-9 Subj: Folk & fairy tales. Rhyming text. Royalty – prince. Sibling rivalry.

Princess Fishtail ill. by G. Brian Karas. Viking, 2002. ISBN 0-670-03529-7 Subj: Humorous stories. Mythical creatures – mermaids, mermen. Mythical creatures – trolls. Rhyming text. Sports – surfing.

Sleepless Beauty ill. by G. Brian Karas. Viking, 1996. ISBN 0-670-87033-1 Subj: Folk & fairy tales. Rhyming text. Witches.

Too big, too small, just right ill. by Janie Bynum. Harcourt, 2001. ISBN 0-15-202157-4 Subj: Animals – rabbits. Concepts – opposites. Rhyming text.

Mintzberg, Yvette. *Sally, where are you?* ill. by author. David & Charles, 1988. ISBN 0-434-95158-7 Subj: Behavior – hiding. Family life.

Mintzer, Jo. *With my brother = Con mi hermano* (Roe, Eileen)

Miranda, Anne. *Alphabet fiesta* ill. by young children. Turtle, 2001. ISBN 1-890515-29-9 Subj: ABC books. Animals. Animals – zebras. Birthdays. Children as illustrators. Parties.

Baby talk ill. by Dorothy M. Stott. Dutton, 1987. ISBN 0-525-44319-3 Subj: Babies. Family life. Format, unusual – toy & movable books.

Baby walk ill. by Dorothy M. Stott. Dutton, 1988. ISBN 0-525-44421-1 Subj: Activities – playing. Babies. Format, unusual.

Baby-sit ill. by Dorothy M. Stott. Little, 1990. ISBN 0-316-57454-6 Subj: Activities – babysitting. Family life – mothers. Format, unusual – toy & movable books.

Beep! beep! ill. by David Murphy. Turtle Books, 1999. ISBN 1-890515-14-0 Subj: Automobiles. Imagination. Noise, sounds. Rhyming text. Trucks.

Counting ill. by Barbara Leonard Gibson. Time-Life, 1994. ISBN 0-7835-4502-9 Subj: Animals – bulls, cows. Birthdays. Counting, numbers. Rhyming text.

Does a mouse have a house? ill. by author. Bradbury, 1994. ISBN 0-02-767251-4 Subj: Animals. Homes, houses. Insects. Rhyming text.

The elephant at the Waldorf ill. by Don Vanderbeek. BridgeWater, 1995. ISBN 0-8167-3452-6 Subj: Animals – elephants. Circus. Rhyming text.

Monster math ill. by Polly Powell. Harcourt, 1999. ISBN 0-15-201835-2 Subj: Birthdays. Counting, numbers. Monsters. Parties. Rhyming text.

Night songs ill. by author. Bradbury, 1993. ISBN 0-02-767250-6 Subj: Lullabies. Night. Noise, sounds.

Pignic ill. by Rosekrans Hoffman. Boyds Mills, 1996. ISBN 1-56397-558-0 Subj: ABC books. Activities – picnicking. Animals – pigs.

To market, to market ill. by Janet Stevens. Harcourt, 1997. ISBN 0-15-200035-6 Subj: Animals. Animals – pigs. Nursery rhymes. Stores.

Vroom, chugga, vroom-vroom ill. by David Murphy. Turtle Books, 1998. ISBN 1-8905-1507-8 Subj: Automobiles. Counting, numbers. Sports – racing. Transportation.

Mirkovic, Irene. *The greedy shopkeeper* ill. by Harold Berson. Harcourt, 1980. Translated and adapt. from a Serbian folk tale. ISBN 0-15-232551-4 Subj: Behavior – trickery. Careers – judges. Folk & fairy tales.

Miryam. *The happy man and his dump truck* ill. by Tibor Gergely. Golden Bks., 1999. ISBN 0-307-10218-1 Subj: Animals. Emotions – happiness. Trucks.

Mitakidou, Christodoula. *Mr. Semolina-Semolinus* (Manna, Anthony L.)

Mitchard, Jacquelyn. *Baby bat's lullaby* ill. by Julia Noonan. HarperCollins, 2004. ISBN 0-06-050761-6 Subj: Animals – bats. Bedtime. Family life – mothers. Lullabies.

Mitchell, Adrian. *Nobody rides the unicorn* ill. by Stephen Lambert. Levine, 2000. ISBN 0-439-11204-4 Subj: Mythical creatures – unicorns. Royalty – kings.

Our mammoth ill. by Priscilla Lamont. Harcourt, 1987. ISBN 0-15-258838-8 Subj: Animals. Humorous stories.

Twice my size ill. by Daniel Pudles. Millbrook, 1999. ISBN 0-7613-1423-7 Subj: Animals. Birds. Concepts – size. Insects. Rhyming text.

Mitchell, Barbara. *Down Buttermilk Lane* ill. by John Sandford. Lothrop, 1993. ISBN 0-688-10115-1 Subj: Ethnic groups in the U.S. – Amish.

Red Bird ill. by Todd L. W. Doney. Lothrop, 1996. ISBN 0-688-10860-1 Subj: Fairs, festivals. Family life. Indians of North America – Nanticoke.

Waterman's child ill. by Daniel San Souci. Lothrop, 1997. ISBN 0-688-10862-8 Subj: Careers – fishermen. Family life. U.S. history.

Mitchell, Cynthia. *Halloweena Hecatee* ill. by Eileen Browne. Crowell, 1979. ISBN 0-690-03926-3 Subj: Activities – playing. Games. Poetry.

Here a little child I stand: poems of prayer and praise for children ill. by Satomi Ichikawa. Putnam, 1985. ISBN 0-399-21244-2 Subj: Foreign lands. Poetry. Religion.

Playtime ill. by Satomi Ichikawa. Collins-World, 1978. ISBN 0-434-94364-9 Subj: Activities – playing. Emotions. Poetry.

Under the cherry tree ill. by Satomi Ichikawa. Collins-World, 1979. ISBN 0-529-05544-9 Subj: Poetry.

Mitchell, Joyce Slayton. *My mommy makes money* ill. by True Kelley. Little, 1984. ISBN 0-316-57501-1 Subj: Activities – working. Careers. Family life – mothers.

Tractor-trailer trucker: a powerful truck book photos by Steven Borns. Tricycle, 2000. ISBN 1-58246-010-8 Subj: Careers – truck drivers. Trucks.

Mitchell, Lori. *Different just like me* ill. by author. Charlesbridge, 1999. ISBN 0-88106-975-2 Subj: Character traits – individuality. Family life – grandmothers.

Mitchell, Lucy Sprague. *The taxi that hurried* by Lucy Sprague Mitchell, Irma Simonton Black, & Jessie Stanton; ill. by Tibor Gergely. Western, 1992. ISBN 0-307-00144-X Subj: Taxis. Traffic, traffic signs.

Mitchell, Margaree King. *Granddaddy's gift* ill. by Larry Johnson. BridgeWater, 1996. ISBN 0-8167-4010-0 Subj: Character traits – bravery. Ethnic groups in the U.S. – African Americans. Family life – grandfathers. U.S. history.

Susie Mae ill. by Melodye Benson Rosales. Lothrop, 2000. ISBN 0-688-15222-8 Subj: Ethnic groups in the U.S. – African Americans. Prejudice. School.

Uncle Jed's barbershop ill. by James Ransome. S&S, 1993. ISBN 0-671-76969-3 Subj: Careers – barbers. Character traits – perseverance. Ethnic groups in the U.S. – African Americans. Family life – aunts, uncles.

Mitchell, Marianne. *Gullywasher gulch* ill. by Normand Chartier. Boyds Mills, 2002. ISBN 1-56397-123-2 Subj: Character traits – generosity. Weather – rain.

Joe Cinders ill. by Bryan Langdo. Holt, 2002. ISBN 0-8050-6529-6 Subj: Clothing – boots. Cowboys, cowgirls. Folk & fairy tales.

Mitchell, Rhonda. *The talking cloth* ill. by author. Orchard, 1997. ISBN 0-531-33004-4 Subj: Ethnic groups in the U.S. – African Americans. Family life – aunts, uncles. Foreign lands – Africa.

Mitchell, Robin. *Windy* by Robin Mitchell & Judith Steedman; photos by Mia Cunningham. Simply Read Bks., 2002. ISBN 0-9688768-2-X Subj: Kites. Weather – wind.

Mitgutsch, Ali. *From gold to money* ill. by author. Carolrhoda, 1985. ISBN 0-87614-230-7 Subj: Science.

From graphite to pencil ill. by author. Carolrhoda, 1985. ISBN 0-87614-231-5 Subj: Science.

From lemon to lemonade ill. by author. Carolrhoda, 1986. ISBN 0-87614-298-6 Subj: Food.

From rubber tree to tire ill. by author. Carolrhoda, 1986. ISBN 0-87614-297-8 Subj: Automobiles.

From sea to salt ill. by author. Carolrhoda, 1985. ISBN 0-87614-232-3 Subj: Science.

From swamp to coal ill. by author. Carolrhoda, 1985. ISBN 0-87614-233-1 Subj: Science.

From wood to paper ill. by author. Carolrhoda, 1986. ISBN 0-87614-296-X Subj: Paper.

Mitra, Annie. *Penguin moon* ill. by author. Holiday, 1989. ISBN 0-8234-0749-7 Subj: Behavior – wishing. Birds – penguins. Moon.

Tusk! Tusk! ill. by author. Holiday, 1990. ISBN 0-8234-0819-1 Subj: Animals – elephants. Careers – dentists. Teeth.

Mitter, Matt. *ABC: alphabet rhymes* ill. by Doug Cushman. G. Stevens, 2004. ISBN 0-8368-4095-X Subj: ABC books. Animals. Rhyming text.

Once upon a rhyme ill. by Susan Banta. G. Stevens, 2004. ISBN 0-8368-4096-8 Subj: Animals. Humorous stories. Rebuses. Rhyming text.

1, 2, 3, counting rhymes ill. by Doug Cushman. G. Stevens, 2004. ISBN 0-8368-4094-1 Subj: Animals. Counting, numbers. Farms. Rhyming text.

Mitton, Jacqueline. *Zoo in the sky: a book of animal constellations* ill. by Christina Balit; star maps by Wil Tirion. National Geographic, 1998. ISBN 0-7922-7069-X Subj: Stars.

Mitton, Tony. *Dinosaurumpus* ill. by Guy Parker-Rees. Orchard, 2003. ISBN 0-439-39514-3 Subj: Activities – dancing. Dinosaurs. Rhyming text.

Down by the cool of the pool ill. by Guy Parker-Rees. Orchard, 2002. ISBN 0-439-30915-8 Subj: Activities – dancing. Animals. Frogs & toads. Lakes, ponds. Rhyming text.

Flashing fire engines by Tony Mitton & Ant Parker; ill. by Ant Parker. Kingfisher, 1998. ISBN 0-7534-5104-2 Subj: Careers – firefighters. Noise, sounds. Rhyming text. Trucks.

Riddledy piggledy ill. by Paddy Mounter. Fickling, 2003. ISBN 0-385-75033-1 Subj: Nursery rhymes. Riddles & jokes.

Miyoshi, Sekiya. *Singing David* ill. by author. Watts, 1969. ISBN 0-531-01936-5 Subj: Religion.

Mizumura, Kazue. *If I built a village* ill. by author. Crowell, 1971. ISBN 0-690-42903-7 Subj: Character traits – kindness. Cities, towns. Ecology. Homes, houses.

If I were a cricket . . . ill. by author. Crowell, 1973. ISBN 0-690-00076-6 Subj: Animals. Emotions – love. Insects – crickets. Poetry.

If I were a mother ill. by author. Crowell, 1967. Subj: Family life – mothers.

Mlawer, Teresa. *Just like home = Como en mi tierra* (Miller, Elizabeth I.)

Moak, Allan. *A big city ABC* ill. by author. Tundra, 1984. ISBN 0-88776-161-5 Subj: ABC books. Cities, towns. Foreign lands – Canada.

Mobley, Jane. *The star husband* ill. by Anna Vojtech. Doubleday, 1979. ISBN 0-385-14283-8 Subj: Folk & fairy tales. Indians of North America – Great Plains. Stars.

Moché, Dinah L. *The astronauts* ill. with photos from NASA. Random House, 1979. ISBN 0-394-93901-8 Subj: Moon. Science. Space & space ships.

Mochizuki, Ken. *Baseball saved us* ill. by Dom Lee. Lee & Low, 1993. ISBN 1-880000-01-6 Subj: Ethnic groups in the U.S. – Japanese Americans. Sports – baseball. U.S. history. War.

Heroes ill. by Dom Lee. Lee & Low, 1995. ISBN 1-880000-16-4 Subj: Ethnic groups in the U.S. – Japanese Americans. U.S. history. War.

Mockford, Caroline. *Cleo and Caspar* ill. by Caroline Mockford; text by Stella Blackstone. Barefoot, 2001. ISBN 1-84148-440-7 Subj: Animals – cats. Animals – dogs. Friendship. Rhyming text.

Cleo in the snow ill. by Caroline Mockford; text by Stella Blackstone. Barefoot, 2002. ISBN 1-84148-951-4 Subj: Animals – cats. Animals – dogs. Friendship. Rhyming text. Weather – snow.

Cleo on the move ill. by Caroline Mockford; text by Stella Blackstone. Barefoot, 2002. ISBN 1-84148-898-4 Subj: Animals – cats. Animals – dogs. Friendship. Moving. Rhyming text.

Cleo the cat ill. by Caroline Mockford; text by Stella Blackstone. Barefoot, 2000. ISBN 1-84148-259-5 Subj: Animals – cats. Friendship. Rhyming text.

Cleo's alphabet book ill. by Caroline Mockford; text by Stella Blackstone. Barefoot, 2003. ISBN 1-84148-008-8 Subj: ABC books. Animals – cats. Rhyming text.

Cleo's counting book ill. by Caroline Mockford; text by Stella Blackstone. Barefoot, 2003. ISBN 1-84148-207-2 Subj: Animals – cats. Counting, numbers. Rhyming text.

Come here, Cleo ill. by Caroline Mockford; text by Stella Blackstone. Barefoot, 2001. ISBN 1-84148-329-X Subj: Animals – cats. Rhyming text.

What's this? ill. by author. Barefoot, 2000. ISBN 1-84148-018-5 Subj: Flowers. Gardens, gardening. Seeds.

Modarressi, Mitra. *The beastly visits* ill. by author. Orchard, 1996. ISBN 0-531-09530-4 Subj: Behavior – bullying. Character traits – being different. Friendship. Monsters.

The dream pillow ill. by author. Orchard, 1994. ISBN 0-531-08705-0 Subj: Birthdays. Character traits – conceit. Dreams. Friendship.

The parent thief ill. by author. Orchard, 1995. ISBN 0-531-08776-X Subj: Behavior – boredom. Behavior – running away. Boats, ships. Family life. Sea & seashore.

Yard sale ill. by author. DK, 2000. ISBN 0-7894-2651-X Subj: Communities, neighborhoods. Magic. Stores.

Modell, Frank. *Goodbye old year, hello new year* ill. by author. Greenwillow, 1984. ISBN 0-688-03939-1 Subj: Holidays – New Year's.

Ice cream soup ill. by author. Greenwillow, 1988. ISBN 0-688-07771-4 Subj: Birthdays. Parties.

Look out, it's April Fools' Day ill. by author. Greenwillow, 1985. ISBN 0-688-04017-9 Subj: Holidays – April Fools' Day. Riddles & jokes.

One zillion valentines ill. by author. Greenwillow, 1981. ISBN 0-688-00569-1 Subj: Character traits – practicality. Holidays – Valentine's Day.

Seen any cats? ill. by author. Greenwillow, 1979. ISBN 0-688-84229-1 Subj: Animals – cats. Circus.

Skeeter and the computer ill. by author. Greenwillow, 1988. ISBN 0-688-03706-2 Subj: Animals – dogs. Computers.

Tooley! Tooley! ill. by author. Greenwillow, 1979. ISBN 0-688-84092-2 Subj: Animals – dogs. Behavior – lost. Humorous stories.

Modesitt, Jeanne. *It's Hanukkah!* ill. by Robin Spowart. Holiday, 1999. ISBN 0-8234-1451-5 Subj: Animals – mice. Holidays – Hanukkah. Jewish culture. Religion.

Little Bunny's Easter surprise ill. by Robin Spowart. S&S, 1999. ISBN 0-689-82491-2 Subj: Animals – rabbits. Behavior – hiding things. Holidays – Easter.

Lunch with Milly ill. by Robin Spowart. BridgeWater, 1995. ISBN 0-8167-3388-0 Subj: Activities – working. Animals. Food. Sea & seashore.

Mama, if you had a wish ill. by Robin Spowart. Green Tiger Pr., 1993. ISBN 0-671-75437-8 Subj: Animals – rabbits. Behavior – wishing. Character traits – individuality. Family life – mothers.

The night call ill. by Robin Spowart. Viking, 1989. ISBN 0-670-82500-X Subj: Animals. Night. Stars. Toys.

Sometimes I feel like a mouse: a book about feelings ill. by Robin Spowart. Scholastic, 1992. ISBN 0-590-44835-8 Subj: Emotions. Imagination.

Songs of Chanukah ill. by Robin Spowart; music arranged by Uri Ophir. Little, 1992. ISBN 0-316-57739-1 Subj: Holidays – Hanukkah. Jewish culture. Music. Religion. Songs.

The story of Z ill. by Lonni Sue Johnson. Picture Book Studio, 1990. ISBN 0-88708-105-3 Subj: Emotions.

Vegetable soup ill. by Robin Spowart. Macmillan, 1991. ISBN 0-689-71523-4 Subj: Animals. Animals – rabbits. Communities, neighborhoods. Food.

Moe, J. E. *The man who kept house* (Asbjørnsen, P. C. [Peter Christen])

Moerbeek, Kees. *The diary of Hansel and Gretel* ill. by author. Little Simon, 2002. ISBN 0-689-84602-9 Subj: Behavior – lost. Folk & fairy tales. Forest, woods. Format, unusual – toy & movable books. Witches.

Moeri, Louise. *Star Mother's youngest child* ill. by Trina Schart Hyman. Houghton Mifflin, 1975. ISBN 0-395-21406-8 Subj: Folk & fairy tales. Holidays – Christmas.

The unicorn and the plow ill. by Diane Goode. Dutton, 1982. ISBN 0-525-45116-1 Subj: Character traits – luck. Farms. Mythical creatures – unicorns.

Moers, Hermann. *Annie's dancing day* ill. by Christa Unzner-Fischer; trans. by Rosemary Lanning. North-South, 1992. ISBN 1-55858-161-8 Subj: Activities – dancing. Ballet. Behavior – lost. Imagination.

Camomile heads for home trans. by Rosemary Lanning; ill. by Marcus Pfister. Holt, 1987. ISBN 0-8050-0280-4 Subj: Animals – bulls, cows. Behavior – growing up.

Evie to the rescue! ill. by Gusti; trans. by Marianne Martens. North-South, 1997. ISBN 1-55858-794-2 Subj: Animals – lions. Dreams. Foreign lands – Africa.

Hugo's baby brother ill. by Józef Wilkon. North-South, 1991. ISBN 1-55858-146-4 Subj: Animals – lions. Family life. Sibling rivalry.

Katie and the big, brave bear ill. by Józef Wilkon; trans. by Marianne Martens. North-South, 1995. ISBN 1-55858-398-X Subj: Animals – bears. Emotions – fear. Friendship. Imagination – imaginary friends.

Little Ben ill. by Jean-Pierre Corderoch; trans. by Rosemary Lanning. North-South, 1991. ISBN 1-55858-105-7 Subj: Behavior – growing up. Concepts – size.

Lullaby for a newborn king (Wilkon, Józef)

Rufus and Max ill. by Philippe Goossens; trans, by Kathryn Grell. North-South, 2003. ISBN 0-7358-1798-7 Subj: Activities – playing. Animals – dogs. Imagination.

Moffatt, Judith. *Christmas lights* ill. by author. Little Simon, 1999. ISBN 0-689-82269-3 Subj: Format, unusual. Holidays – Christmas.

Halloween frights ill. by author. Little Simon, 1999. ISBN 0-689-82270-7 Subj: Format, unusual. Holidays – Halloween.

The pumpkin man ill. by author. Scholastic, 1998. ISBN 0-590-63865-3 Subj: Holidays – Halloween. Rhyming text.

Snow shapes ill. by author. Scholastic, 2000. ISBN 0-439-09858-0 Subj: Activities – making things. Art. Paper. Seasons – winter.

Trick-or-treat faces: a glowing book you can read in the dark! ill. by author. Scholastic, 2000. ISBN 0-439-18299-9 Subj: Format, unusual. Holidays – Halloween. Monsters. Rhyming text.

Who stole the cookies? ill. by author. Grosset, 1996. ISBN 0-448-41127-X Subj: Animals. Behavior – stealing. Food. Rhyming text.

Moffett, Martha A. *A flower pot is not a hat* ill. by Susan Perl. Dutton, 1972. ISBN 0-525-29920-3 Subj: Activities – playing. Humorous stories.

Mogensen, Jan. *The forty-six little men* ill. by author. Greenwillow, 1991. ISBN 0-688-09284-5 Subj: Imagination. Little people. Wordless.

The Land of the Big ill. by author. Crocodile, 1992. ISBN 1-56656-111-6 Subj: Concepts – size. Family life – aunts, uncles. Insects.

Lost and found Teddy ill. by author. G. Stevens, 1990. ISBN 0-8368-0432-5 Subj: Behavior – lost. Toys – bears. Trains.

Teddy and the Chinese dragon ill. by author. G. Stevens, 1985. ISBN 1-55532-002-3 Subj: Dragons. Toys – bears.

Teddy in the undersea kingdom ill. by author. G. Stevens, 1985. ISBN 1-55532-000-7 Subj: Crustaceans – crabs. Sea & seashore. Toys – bears.

Teddy runs away ill. by author. G. Stevens, 1990. ISBN 0-8368-0371-X Subj: Behavior – running away. Toys. Toys – bears.

Teddy's birthday bugle ill. by author. G. Stevens, 1990. ISBN 0-8368-0372-8 Subj: Animals. Birthdays. Toys. Toys – bears.

Teddy's Christmas gift ill. by author. G. Stevens, 1985. ISBN 1-55532-004-X Subj: Character traits – kindness to animals. Gifts. Holidays – Christmas. Santa Claus. Toys – bears.

The tiger's breakfast ill. by author. Interlink, 1991. ISBN 0-940793-83-0 Subj: Animals – elephants. Animals – mice. Behavior – trickery. Character traits – cleverness.

When Teddy woke early ill. by author. G. Stevens, 1985. ISBN 1-55532-006-6 Subj: Behavior – lost. Toys – bears.

Mohr, Joseph. *Silent night* verses by Joseph Mohr; ill. by Susan Jeffers. Dutton, 1984. Orig. title: Stille Nacht, heilige Nacht. ISBN 0-525-44144-1 Subj: Holidays – Christmas. Songs.

Molarsky, Osmond. *A sky full of kites* ill. by Helen D. Hipshman. Tricycle, 1996. ISBN 1-883672-26-0 Subj: Activities – painting. Ethnic groups in the U.S. – Asian Americans. Kites.

Mole, John. *Copy cat* ill. by Bee Willey. Kingfisher, 1997. ISBN 0-7534-5008-9 Subj: Animals – cats. Behavior – imitation.

Molk, Laurel. *Good job, Oliver!* ill. by author. Crown, 1999. ISBN 0-517-70976-7 Subj: Animals – rabbits. Gardens, gardening.

Mollel, Tololwa M. (Tololwa Marti). *Ananse's feast: an Ashanti tale* ill. by Andrew Glass. Clarion, 1997. ISBN 0-395-67402-6 Subj: Behavior – trickery. Country. Folk & fairy tales. Foreign lands – Ghana. Reptiles – turtles, tortoises. Spiders.

Big boy ill. by E. B. Lewis. Clarion, 1995. ISBN 0-395-67403-4 Subj: Behavior – wishing. Folk & fairy tales. Foreign lands – Tanzania. Giants.

Dume's roar ill. by Kathy Blankley Roman. Stoddart, 1998. ISBN 0-7737-3003-6 Subj: Animals. Animals – lions. Folk & fairy tales. Foreign lands – Africa. Royalty – kings.

The flying tortoise: an Igbo tale ill. by Barbara Spurll. Oxford Univ. Pr., 1993. ISBN 0-395-68845-0 Subj: Behavior – greed. Behavior – trickery. Folk & fairy tales. Foreign lands – Nigeria. Reptiles – turtles, tortoises.

Kele's secret ill. by Catherine Stock. Dutton, 1997. ISBN 0-525-67500-0 Subj: Birds – chickens. Family life – grandparents. Foreign lands – Tanzania.

The king and the tortoise ill. by Kathy Blankley. Clarion, 1993. ISBN 0-395-64480-1 Subj: Animals. Folk & fairy tales. Foreign lands – Cameroon. Reptiles – turtles, tortoises. Royalty – kings.

Kitoto the mighty ill. by Kristi Frost. Stoddart, 1998. ISBN 0-7737-3019-2 Subj: Animals – mice. Folk & fairy tales. Foreign lands – Africa.

My rows and piles of coins ill. by E. B. Lewis. Clarion, 1999. ISBN 0-395-75186-1 Subj: Foreign lands – Tanzania. Money. Sports – bicycling.

Orphan boy ill. by Paul Morin. Clarion, 1991. ISBN 0-89919-985-2 Subj: Folk & fairy tales. Foreign lands – Kenya. Magic. Orphans.

The princess who lost her hair: an Akamba legend ill. by Charles Reasoner. Troll, 1993. ISBN 0-816-72815-1 Subj: Character traits – selfishness. Folk & fairy tales. Foreign lands – Africa. Hair. Royalty – princesses.

A promise to the sun ill. by Beatriz A. Vidal. Little, 1992. ISBN 0-316-57813-4 Subj: Animals – bats. Birds. Foreign lands – Kenya. Sun. Weather.

Rhinos for lunch and elephants for supper ill. by Barbara Spurll. Houghton Mifflin, 1992. ISBN 0-395-60734-5 Subj: Animals. Cumulative tales. Emotions – fear. Foreign lands – Kenya.

Shadow dance ill. by Donna Perrone. Clarion, 1998. ISBN 0-395-82909-7 Subj: Behavior – trickery. Folk & fairy tales. Foreign lands – Tanzania. Reptiles – alligators, crocodiles.

Song bird ill. by Rosanne Litzinger. Clarion, 1999. ISBN 0-395-82908-9 Subj: Birds. Folk & fairy tales. Foreign lands – Tanzania. Magic. Monsters.

Subira subira ill. by Linda Saport. Clarion, 2000. ISBN 0-395-91809-X Subj: Character traits – patience. Folk & fairy tales. Foreign lands – Tanzania.

To dinner, for dinner ill. by Synthia Saint James. Holiday, 2000. ISBN 0-8234-1527-9 Subj: Animals. Animals – leopards. Animals – rabbits. Foreign lands – Africa.

Molnar, Dorothy E. *Who will pick me up when I fall?* by Dorothy E. Molnar & Stephan H. Fenton; ill. by Irene Trivas. A. Whitman, 1991. ISBN 0-8075-9072-X Subj: Days of the week, months of the year. Family life.

Molnar, Joe. *Graciela: a Mexican-American child tells her story* photos by author. Watts, 1972. ISBN 0-531-02023-1 Subj: Ethnic groups in the U.S. – Mexican Americans.

Molnar-Fenton, Stephan. *An Mei's strange and wondrous journey* ill. by Vivienne Flesher. DK, 1998. ISBN 0-7894-2477-0 Subj: Adoption. Ethnic groups in the U.S. – Chinese Americans.

Moncure, Jane Belk. *Happy healthkins* ill. by Lois Axeman. Childrens Pr., 1982. ISBN 0-516-06314-6 Subj: Health & fitness. Rhyming text.

The healthkin food train ill. by Lois Axeman. Childrens Pr., 1982. ISBN 0-516-06311-1 Subj: Health & fitness. Rhyming text.

Healthkins exercise! ill. by Lois Axeman. Childrens Pr., 1982. ISBN 0-516-06312-X Subj: Health & fitness – exercise. Rhyming text.

Healthkins help ill. by Lois Axeman. Childrens Pr., 1982. ISBN 0-516-06313-8 Subj: Health & fitness. Rhyming text.

The look book ill. by Lois Axeman. Childrens Pr., 1982. ISBN 0-516-03251-8 Subj: Senses – sight.

Now I am five! ill. by Helen Endes. Childrens Pr., 1984. ISBN 0-516-01879-5 Subj: Activities. Behavior – growing up.

Now I am four! ill. by Kathryn Hutton. Childrens Pr., 1984. ISBN 0-516-01878-7 Subj: Activities. Behavior – growing up.

Now I am three! ill. by Linda Hohag. Childrens Pr., 1984. ISBN 0-516-01877-9 Subj: Activities. Behavior – growing up.

Riddle me a riddle ill. by Marc Belenchia. Childrens Pr., 1977. ISBN 0-913778-80-X Subj: Animals. Magic. Riddles & jokes.

Sounds all around ill. by Lois Axeman. Childrens Pr., 1982. ISBN 0-516-03252-6 Subj: Senses – hearing.

The talking tabby cat: a folk tale from France ill. by Helen Endres. Childrens Pr., 1980. ISBN 0-516-06483-5 Subj: Animals – cats. Folk & fairy tales.

A tasting party ill. by Viki Woodworth. Child's World, 1998. ISBN 1-56766-283-8 Subj: Food. Senses – taste.

The touch book ill. by Lois Axeman. Childrens Pr., 1982. ISBN 0-516-03254-2 Subj: Senses – touch.

What your nose knows! ill. by Lois Axeman. Childrens Pr., 1982. ISBN 0-516-03255-0 Subj: Anatomy – noses. Senses – smell.

Where? ill. by Lois Axeman. Childrens Pr., 1983. ISBN 0-516-06593-9 Subj: Character traits – curiosity. Character traits – questioning.

Word Bird's fall words ill. by Linda Hohag. Childrens Pr., 1985. ISBN 0-89565-308-7 Subj: Language. Seasons – fall.

Word Bird's spring words ill. by Vera Gohman. Childrens Pr., 1985. ISBN 0-89565-310-9 Subj: Language. Seasons – spring.

Word Bird's summer words ill. by Linda Hohag. Childrens Pr., 1985. ISBN 0-89565-311-7 Subj: Language. Seasons – summer.

Word Bird's winter words ill. by Vera Gohman. Childrens Pr., 1985. ISBN 0-89565-309-5 Subj: Language. Seasons – winter.

Monfried, Lucia. *Baby's world* ill. by Stephen Shott. Dutton, 1990. ISBN 0-525-44617-6 Subj: Babies. Format, unusual. Language.

The Daddies Boat ill. by Michele Chessare. Dutton, 1990. ISBN 0-525-44584-6 Subj: Activities – vacationing. Boats, ships. Family life – mothers. Islands.

Dishes all done ill. by Jon Agee. Dutton, 1989. ISBN 0-525-44433-5 Subj: Activities. Format, unusual – toy & movable books. Rhyming text.

Grizzly bear (Cherry, Lynne)

Orangutan (Cherry, Lynne)

Seal (Cherry, Lynne)

Snow leopard (Cherry, Lynne)

Monjo, F. N. *The drinking gourd: a story of the underground railroad* ill. by Fred Brenner. HarperCollins, 1993. ISBN 0-06-024330-9 Subj: Ethnic groups in the U.S. – African Americans. Slavery. U.S. history.

The one bad thing about father ill. by Rocco Negri. HarperCollins, 1970. ISBN 0-06-024334-1 Subj: Family life – fathers. U.S. history.

Poor Richard in France ill. by Brinton Turkle. Holt, 1973. ISBN 0-03-088597-3 Subj: U.S. history.

Rudi and the distelfink ill. by George Kraus. Windmill, 1972. ISBN 0-525-61002-2 Subj: Family life.

Monk, Isabell. *Blackberry stew* ill. by Janice Lee Porter. Carolrhoda, 2005. ISBN 1-57505-605-4 Subj: Death. Emotions – grief. Emotions – sadness. Family life – grandfathers. Memories, memory.

Family ill. by Janice Lee Porter. Carolrhoda, 2001. ISBN 1-57505-485-X Subj: Ethnic groups in the U.S. – African Americans. Family life. Food.

Hope ill. by Janice Lee Porter. Carolrhoda, 1999. ISBN 1-57505-230-X Subj: Ethnic groups in the U.S. – African Americans. Family life – aunts, uncles. Names.

Monks, Lydia. *Aaaarrgghh! spider!* ill. by author. Houghton, 2004. ISBN 0-618-43250-7 Subj: Pets. Spiders.

The cat barked? ill. by author. Dial, 1999. ISBN 0-8037-2338-5 Subj: Animals – cats. Animals – dogs. Rhyming text. Self-concept.

Monnier, Miriam. *Just right* ill. by author; trans. by J. Alison James. North-South, 2001. ISBN 0-7358-1522-4 Subj: Behavior – growing up. Family life – mothers. Self-concept.

Monsell, Helen Albee. *Paddy's Christmas* ill. by Kurt Wiese. Knopf, 1942. Subj: Animals – bears. Holidays – Christmas.

Monsell, Mary Elise. *Armadillo* ill. by Sylvie Wickstrom. Macmillan, 1991. ISBN 0-689-31676-3 Subj: Animals – armadillos. Friendship.

Crackle Creek ill. by Kathleen Garry McCord. Atheneum, 1990. ISBN 0-689-31564-3 Subj: Animals – mice. Careers – printers. Character traits – helpfulness. Paper.

Underwear! ill. by Lynn Munsinger. A. Whitman, 1988. ISBN 0-8075-8308-1 Subj: Animals. Clothing. Humorous stories.

Monson, A. M. *Wanted . . . best friend* ill. by Lynn Munsinger. Dial, 1997. ISBN 0-8037-1485-8 Subj: Animals – cats. Animals – mice. Friendship. Games.

Monster poems ed. by Daisy Wallace; ill. by Kay Chorao. Holiday, 1976. ISBN 0-8234-0268-1 Subj: Monsters. Poetry. Tongue twisters.

Monster soup and other spooky poems ill. by Jacqueline Rogers; comp. by Dilys Evans. Scholastic, 1992. ISBN 0-590-45208-8 Subj: Monsters. Poetry.

Montanari, Donata. *Children around the world* ill. by author. Kids Can, 2001. ISBN 1-55337-064-3 Subj: Etiquette. Foreign lands.

Montanari, Eva. *The crocodile's true colors* ill. by author. Watson-Guptill, 2002. ISBN 0-8230-2435-0 Subj: Animals. Concepts. Foreign lands – Africa. Reptiles – alligators, crocodiles. School.

Dino bikes ill. by author; trans. by J. Alison James. North-South, 2004. ISBN 0-7358-1918-1 Subj: Behavior – bullying. Dinosaurs. Sports – bicycling.

Tiff, Taff, and Lulu ill. by author. Houghton, 2004. ISBN 0-618-40238-1 Subj: Family life – sisters. Sibling rivalry.

Montenegro, Laura Nyman. *A bird about to sing* ill. by author. Houghton, 2003. ISBN 0-618-18865-7 Subj: Character traits – shyness. Poetry.

One stuck drawer ill. by author. Houghton Mifflin, 1991. ISBN 0-395-57319-X Subj: Furniture – dressers.

Sweet Tooth ill. by author. Houghton Mifflin, 1995. ISBN 0-395-68078-6 Subj: Animals – lions. Character traits – loyalty. Circus. Friendship.

Montgomerie, Norah. *This little pig went to market: play rhymes* ill. by Margery Gill. Watts, 1967. Subj: Games. Nursery rhymes. Participation.

Montgomery, Lee. *Ant* (Hawcock, David)

Bee (Hawcock, David)

Beetle (Hawcock, David)

Fly (Hawcock, David)

Spider (Hawcock, David)

Wasp (Hawcock, David)

Montgomery, Michael G. *'Night, America* ill. by author. Contemporary Books, 1989. ISBN 0-8092-4397-0 Subj: Bedtime. Night. Rhyming text.

Over the candlestick: classic nursery rhymes and the real stories behind them col. by Michael G. Montgomery & Wayne Montgomery; ill. by Michael G. Montgomery. Peachtree, 2002. ISBN 1-56145-259-9 Subj: Nursery rhymes.

Montgomery, Wayne. *Over the candlestick: classic nursery rhymes and the real stories behind them* (Montgomery, Michael G.)

Montresor, Beni. *A for angel: Beni Montresor's ABC picture-stories* ill. by author. Knopf, 1969. ISBN 0-394-90883-X Subj: ABC books.

Bedtime! ill. by author. HarperCollins, 1978. ISBN 0-06-024354-6 Subj: Bedtime. Dreams.

Hansel and Gretel ill. by author. Atheneum, 2001. ISBN 0-689-84144-2 Subj: Behavior – lost. Folk & fairy tales. Forest, woods. Witches.

The witches of Venice ill. by author. Doubleday, 1989. ISBN 0-385-26355-4 Subj: Dreams. Flowers. Royalty. Witches.

Moodie, Fiona. *Nabulela* ill. by reteller. Farrar, 1997. ISBN 0-374-35486-3 Subj: Emotions – envy, jealousy. Foreign lands – South Africa. Monsters.

Noko and the night monster ill. by author. Cavendish, 2001. ISBN 0-7614-5093-9 Subj: Animals – aardvarks. Animals – porcupines. Emotions – fear. Monsters. Night.

Moodie, Prudence. *Little Mop lost* (Kanome, Kayoko)

Moon, Carl. *One little Indian* (Moon, Grace Purdie)

Moon, Cliff. *Pigs on the farm* ill. by Anna Jupp. Watts, 1983. ISBN 0-531-04696-6 Subj: Animals – pigs. Farms.

Moon, Dolly M. *My very first book of cowboy songs: 21 favorite songs in easy piano arrangements* ill. by Frederic Remington. Dover, 1982. ISBN 0-486-24311-7 Subj: Cowboys, cowgirls. Folk & fairy tales. Songs.

Moon, Grace Purdie. *One little Indian* by Grace & Carl Moon; ill. by Carl Moon. A. Whitman, 1950. Subj: Birthdays. Indians of North America.

Moon, Nicola. *Alligator tails and crocodile cakes* ill. by Andy Ellis. Kingfisher, 1997. ISBN 0-7534-5080-1 Subj: Activities – baking, cooking. Character traits – cleanliness. Friendship. Games. Reptiles – alligators, crocodiles.

At the beginning of a pig ill. by Andy Ellis. Kingfisher, 1994. ISBN 1-85697-977-6 Subj: Anatomy. Animals. Format, unusual – toy & movable books.

Lucy's picture ill. by Alex Ayliffe. Dial, 1995. ISBN 0-8037-1833-0 Subj: Activities – making things. Art. Family life – grandfathers. Handicaps – blindness.

Something special ill. by Alex Ayliffe. Peachtree, 1997. ISBN 1-56145-137-1 Subj: Babies. Family life – brothers & sisters. School.

Tick-tock, drip-drop ill. by Eleanor Taylor. Bloomsbury, 2004. ISBN 1-58234-944-4 Subj: Animals – moles. Animals – rabbits. Bedtime. Noise, sounds. Sleep.

Moon, Pat. *This is the earth* ill. by Lisa Flather. Viking, 1994. ISBN 0-670-85488-3 Subj: Cumulative tales. Ecology. Poetry.

The moon's the north wind's cooky: night poems comp. & ill. by Susan Russo. Lothrop, 1979. ISBN 0-688-51879-6 Subj: Bedtime. Night. Poetry.

Moorat, Joseph. *Thirty old-time nursery songs* (Mother Goose)

Moore, Chevelle. *Getting dressed* (Moore, Dessie)

Good morning (Moore, Dessie)

Good night (Moore, Dessie)

Let's pretend (Moore, Dessie)

Moore, Christopher J. *Ishtar and Tammuz: a Babylonian myth of the seasons* ill. by Christina Balit. Kingfisher, 1996. ISBN 0-7534-5012-7 Subj: Mythical creatures. Seasons.

Moore, Clement Clarke. *The night before Christmas* ill. by Jan Brett. Putnam, 1998. ISBN 0-399-23190-0 Subj: Holidays – Christmas. Poetry. Santa Claus.

The night before Christmas ill. by Tomie de Paola. Holiday, 1980. ISBN 0-8234-0414-5 Subj: Holidays – Christmas. Poetry. Santa Claus.

The night before Christmas comp. by Cooper Edens & Harold Darling; ill. by various 19th- & 20th-century artists. A classic illustrated ed. Chronicle, 1998. ISBN 0-8118-1712-1 Subj: Holidays – Christmas. Poetry. Santa Claus.

The night before Christmas ill. by Mary Engelbreit. HarperCollins, 2002. ISBN 0-06-008161-9 Subj: Holidays – Christmas. Poetry. Santa Claus.

The night before Christmas ill. by Michael Foreman. Viking, 1988. ISBN 0-670-82388-0 Subj: Holidays – Christmas. Poetry. Santa Claus.

The night before Christmas ill. by Gyo Fujikawa. Grosset, 1961. ISBN 0-448-02935-9 Subj: Holidays – Christmas. Poetry. Santa Claus.

The night before Christmas ill. by Scott Gustafson. Knopf, 1985. ISBN 0-394-54809-4 Subj: Holidays – Christmas. Poetry. Santa Claus.

The night before Christmas ill. by Cheryl Harness. Random House, 1990. ISBN 0-394-92698-6 Subj: Holidays – Christmas. Poetry. Santa Claus.

The night before Christmas ill. by Raquel Jaramillo. Atheneum, 2001. ISBN 0-689-84053-5 Subj: Holidays – Christmas. Poetry. Santa Claus.

The night before Christmas ill. by Loretta Krupinski. Hyperion, 1998. ISBN 0-7868-2252-X Subj: Animals – mice. Holidays – Christmas. Poetry. Santa Claus.

The night before Christmas ill. by Anita Lobel. Knopf, 1984. ISBN 0-394-96863-8 Subj: Holidays – Christmas. Poetry. Santa Claus.

The night before Christmas ill. by James Marshall. Scholastic, 1989. ISBN 0-590-33805-6 Subj: Holidays – Christmas. Poetry. Santa Claus.

The night before Christmas ill. by Ted Rand. North-South, 1995. ISBN 1-55858-466-8 Subj: Holidays – Christmas. Poetry. Santa Claus.

The night before Christmas ill. by Jacqueline Rogers. Platt, 1987. ISBN 0-448-19097-4 Subj: Holidays – Christmas. Poetry. Santa Claus.

The night before Christmas ill. by Ruth Sanderson. Little, 1997. ISBN 0-316-57963-7 Subj: Holidays – Christmas. Poetry. Santa Claus.

The night before Christmas: a pop-up paper-engineering & ill. by Robert Sabuda. Little Simon, 2002. ISBN 0-689-83899-9 Subj: Format, unusual – toy & movable books. Holidays – Christmas. Poetry. Santa Claus.

The night before Christmas ill. by Robin Spowart. Dodd, 1986. ISBN 0-396-08798-1 Subj: Holidays – Christmas. Poetry. Santa Claus.

The night before Christmas ill. by Gustaf Tenggren. S&S, 1951. Subj: Holidays – Christmas. Poetry. Santa Claus.

The night before Christmas ill. by Tasha Tudor. Little, 1999. ISBN 0-316-85579-0 Subj: Holidays – Christmas. Poetry. Santa Claus.

The night before Christmas ill. by Wendy Watson. Houghton Mifflin, 1990. ISBN 0-395-53624-3 Subj: Holidays – Christmas. Poetry. Santa Claus.

The night before Christmas ill. by Bruce Whatley. HarperCollins, 1999. ISBN 0-06-026609-0 Subj: Holidays – Christmas. Poetry. Santa Claus.

The night before Christmas ill. by Jody Wheeler. Ideals, 1988. ISBN 0-8249-8279-7 Subj: Holidays – Christmas. Poetry. Santa Claus.

The night before Christmas in signed English ill. by Ralph R. Miller, Sr. Prepated under the supervision of the staff of the Pre-School Signed English Project by Barbara M. Kannapell. Gallaudet Univ. Pr., 1973. ISBN 0-913580-15-5 Subj: Handicaps – deafness. Holidays – Christmas. Poetry. Santa Claus. Sign language.

The teddy bears' night before Christmas photos by Monica Stevenson. Scholastic, 1999. ISBN 0-590-03243-7 Subj: Holidays – Christmas. Poetry. Santa Claus. Toys. Toys – bears.

'Twas the night before Christmas ill. by Matt Tavares. Candlewick, 2002. ISBN 0-7636-1585-4 Subj: Holidays – Christmas. Poetry. Santa Claus.

A visit from St. Nicholas: 'Twas the night before Christmas ill. by Paul Galdone. McGraw-Hill, 1968. Subj: Holidays – Christmas. Poetry. Santa Claus.

Moore, Dessie. *Getting dressed* by Dessie & Chevelle Moore; ill. by Chevelle Moore. HarperCollins, 1994. ISBN 0-694-00590-8 Subj: Clothing. Ethnic groups in the U.S. – African Americans. Format, unusual – board books.

Good morning by Dessie & Chevelle Moore; ill. by Chevelle Moore. HarperCollins, 1994. ISBN 0-694-00593-2 Subj: Ethnic groups in the U.S. – African Americans. Format, unusual – board books. Morning.

Good night by Dessie & Chevelle Moore; ill. by Chevelle Moore. HarperCollins, 1994. ISBN 0-694-00592-4 Subj: Ethnic groups in the U.S. – African Americans. Format, unusual – board books. Night.

Let's pretend by Dessie & Chevelle Moore; ill. by Chevelle Moore. HarperCollins, 1994. ISBN 0-694-00591-6 Subj: Ethnic groups in the U.S. – African Americans. Format, unusual – board books. Rhyming text.

Moore, Elaine. *Deep river* ill. by Henri Sorensen. S&S, 1994. ISBN 0-671-87278-8 Subj: Family life – grandfathers. Sports – fishing.

Good morning, city ill. by William Low. BridgeWater, 1995. ISBN 0-8167-3654-5 Subj: Careers. Cities, towns. Morning.

Grammy, do you love me? ill. by Kathy Wilburn. Longmeadow, 1994. ISBN 0-681-00442-8 Subj: Animals – rabbits. Emotions – love. Family life – grandmothers.

Grandma's garden ill. by Dan Andreasen. Lothrop, 1990. ISBN 0-688-08694-2 Subj: Family life – grandmothers. Gardens, gardening. Seasons – spring. Weather.

Grandma's house ill. by Elise Primavera. Lothrop, 1985. ISBN 0-688-04116-7 Subj: Animals. Country. Family life – grandmothers. Seasons – summer.

Grandma's promise ill. by Elise Primavera. Lothrop, 1988. ISBN 0-688-06741-7 Subj: Country. Family life – grandmothers. Seasons – winter.

Grandma's smile ill. by Dan Andreasen. Lothrop, 1995. ISBN 0-688-11076-2 Subj: Fairs, festivals. Family life – grandmothers. Seasons – fall.

Roly-poly puppies ill. by Jacqueline Rogers. Scholastic, 1996. ISBN 0-590-46665-8 Subj: Animals – dogs. Counting, numbers. Rhyming text.

Moore, Elizabeth. *Mimi and Jean-Paul's Cajun Mardi Gras* by Elizabeth Moore & Alice W. Couvillon; ill. by Marilyn Carter Rougelot. Pelican, 1996. ISBN 1-56554-069-7 Subj: Mardi Gras.

Moore, Eva. *Dick Whittington and his cat* (Dick Whittington and his cat)

Franklin and the baby ill. by Nelvana. Kids Can, 1999. Based on the characters created by Paulette Bourgeois & Brenda Clark. ISBN 1-55074-706-1 Subj: Animals. Animals – bears. Babies. Family life – new sibling. Reptiles – turtles, tortoises.

Moore, Inga. *Aktil's big swim* ill. by author. Oxford Univ. Pr., 1981. ISBN 0-19-554250-9 Subj: Animals – rats. Sports – swimming.

A big day for Little Jack ill. by author. Candlewick, 1994. ISBN 1-56402-418-0 Subj: Animals – rabbits. Character traits – shyness. Emotions – fear. Parties.

Fifty red night-caps ill. by Linda Moore. Chronicle, 1988. ISBN 0-87701-520-1 Subj: Animals – monkeys. Behavior – imitation. Behavior – stealing. Clothing – hats. Forest, woods.

Little dog lost ill. by author. Macmillan, 1991. ISBN 0-02-767648-X Subj: Animals – dogs. Behavior – running away. Country. Friendship. Moving.

Oh, little Jack ill. by author. Candlewick, 1992. ISBN 1-56402-028-2 Subj: Animals – rabbits. Character traits – smallness. Family life.

The reluctant dragon (Grahame, Kenneth)

Rose and the nightingale ill. by author. Knopf, 1990. ISBN 0-679-80197-9 Subj: Birds – nightingales. Character traits – kindness to animals.

Six dinner Sid ill. by author. S&S, 1991. ISBN 0-671-73199-8 Subj: Animals – cats. Pets.

The sorcerer's apprentice ill. by author. Macmillan, 1989. ISBN 0-02-767645-5 Subj: Folk & fairy tales. Magic.

The truffle hunter ill. by author. Kane/Miller, 1987. ISBN 0-916291-09-X Subj: Animals – pigs. Behavior – seeking better things. Country. Foreign lands – France.

The vegetable thieves ill. by author. Viking, 1984. ISBN 0-670-74380-1 Subj: Animals – mice. Gardens, gardening. Orphans.

Moore, John. *Granny Stickleback* by John Moore & Martin Wright; ill. by authors. Hamish Hamilton, 1982. ISBN 0-241-10635-4 Subj: Animals. Crime. Sports – racing.

Moore, Julia. *While you sleep* ill. by Lyn Gilbert. Dutton, 1996. ISBN 0-525-45462-4 Subj: Babies. Bedtime. Rhyming text. Sleep.

Moore, Karen Ann. *The baby king: fun fur to touch!* ill. by Bev Luedecke. Chariot Victor, 1999. ISBN 0-7814-3253-7 Subj: Animals. Format, unusual – toy & movable books. Holidays – Christmas. Religion – Nativity.

Moore, Lilian. *Adam Mouse's book of poems* ill. by Kathleen Garry-McCord. Atheneum, 1992. ISBN 0-689-31765-4 Subj: Animals – mice. Nature. Poetry.

Hooray for me! (Charlip, Remy)

I feel the same way ill. by Robert M. Quackenbush. Atheneum, 1967. Subj: Poetry.

I never did that before ill. by Lillian Hoban. Atheneum, 1995. ISBN 0-689-31889-8 Subj: Poetry.

I'm small and other verses ill. by Jill McElmurry. Candlewick, 2001. ISBN 0-7636-1169-7 Subj: Poetry.

Little Raccoon and no trouble at all ill. by Gioia Fiammenghi. McGraw-Hill, 1972. ISBN 0-07-042909-X Subj: Activities – babysitting. Animals – chipmunks. Animals – raccoons. Multiple births – twins.

Little Raccoon and the outside world ill. by Gioia Fiammenghi. McGraw-Hill, 1965. Subj: Animals – raccoons.

Little Raccoon and the thing in the pool ill. by Gioia Fiammenghi. McGraw-Hill, 1963. Subj: Animals – raccoons. Emotions – fear.

Mural on Second Avenue, and other city poems ill. by Roma Karas. Candlewick, 2004. ISBN 0-7636-1987-6 Subj: Cities, towns. Poetry.

Papa Albert ill. by Gioia Fiammenghi. Atheneum, 1964. Subj: Careers – taxi drivers. Family life. Foreign lands – France. Foreign languages. Taxis.

See my lovely poison ivy, and other verses about witches, ghosts and things ill. by Diane Dawson. Atheneum, 1975. ISBN 0-689-30468-4 Subj: Animals – cats. Monsters. Poetry. Witches.

The ugly duckling (Andersen, H. C. [Hans Christian])

While you were chasing a hat ill. by Rosanne Litzinger. HarperFestival, 2001. ISBN 0-694-01342-0 Subj: Clothing – hats. Family life – grandfathers. Weather – wind.

Moore, Liz. *Zizi and Tish* ill. by Liz Milkau. Orca, 2003. ISBN 1-55143-254-4 Subj: Emotions – envy, jealousy. Family life – sisters.

Moore, Maggie. *Jack and the beanstalk* (Jack and the beanstalk)

Little Red Riding Hood ill. by Paula Knight. Picture Window, 2003. ISBN 1-4048-0064-6 Subj: Animals – wolves. Behavior – talking to strangers. Family life – grandmothers. Folk & fairy tales. Foreign lands – Germany.

The three little pigs (The three little pigs)

Moore, Mary-Alice. *Peek-a-boo, baby!* (Leonard, Marcia)

Moore, Miriam. *Peter and Susie find a family* (Hess, Edith)

Moore, Sheila. *Samson Svenson's baby* ill. by Karen Ann Weinhaus. HarperCollins, 1983. ISBN 0-06-022613-7 Subj: Birds – ducks. Character traits – appearance. Character traits – kindness to animals.

Moorman, Margaret. *Light the lights!* ill. by author. Scholastic, 1994. ISBN 0-590-47003-5 Subj: Family life. Holidays – Christmas. Holidays – Hanukkah. Religion.

Mooser, Stephen. *The fat cat* by Stephen Mooser & Lin Oliver; ill. by Susan Day. Warner, 1988. ISBN 1-55782-022-8 Subj: Animals – cats.

Funnyman and the penny dodo ill. by Tomie de Paola. Watts, 1984. ISBN 0-531-04393-2 Subj: Crime. Humorous stories. Mystery stories.

Funnyman meets the monster from outer space ill. by Maxie Chambliss. Scholastic, 1987. ISBN 0-590-33959-1 Subj: Aliens. Monsters. Space & space ships.

Funnyman's first case ill. by Tomie de Paola. Watts, 1981. ISBN 0-531-04300-2 Subj: Careers – waiters, waitresses. Mystery stories. Riddles & jokes.

The ghost with the Halloween hiccups ill. by Tomie de Paola. Watts, 1977. ISBN 0-531-01316-2 Subj: Ghosts. Hiccups. Holidays – Halloween.

Mora, Emma. *Animals of the forest* trans. from Italian by Jean Grasso Fitzpatrick; ill. by Kennedy. Barron's, 1986. ISBN 0-8120-5722-8 Subj: Animals. Forest, woods.

Gideon, the little bear cub trans. from Italian by Jean Grasso Fitzpatrick; ill. by Kennedy. Barron's, 1986. ISBN 0-8120-5728-7 Subj: Forest, woods. Rhyming text. Seasons.

Mora, Jo (Joseph Jacinto). *Budgee Budgee Cottontail* ill. by author. D.R. Stoecklein, 1995. ISBN 0-922029-23-7 Subj: Animals – rabbits. Behavior – running away. Cowboys, cowgirls. Holidays – Christmas. Rhyming text.

Mora, Pat. *The bakery lady = La señora de la panadería* ill. by pablo Torrecilla; trans. by Gabriela Baez Vantura & Pat Mora. Piñata, 2001. ISBN 1-55885-343-X Subj: Activities – baking, cooking. Ethnic groups in the U.S. – Mexican Americans. Food. Foreign languages. Holidays.

A birthday basket for Tía ill. by Cecily Lang. Macmillan, 1992. ISBN 0-0-02-767400-2 Subj: Animals – cats. Birthdays. Ethnic groups in the U.S. – Mexican Americans. Family life – aunts, uncles. Gifts.

Confetti ill. by Enrique O. Sánchez. Lee & Low, 1996. ISBN 1-880000-25-3 Subj: Ethnic groups in the U.S. – Mexican Americans. Foreign languages. Poetry.

Delicious hullabaloo = Pachanga deliciosa ill. by Francisco X. Mora; Spanish trans. by Alba Nora Martinez & Pat Mora. Piñata, 1998. ISBN 1-55885-246-8 Subj: Animals. Desert. Foreign languages. Night. Parties. Poetry. Reptiles – lizards.

A library for Juana: the world of Sor Juana Inés ill. by Beatriz Vidal. Knopf, 2002. ISBN 0-375-80643-1 Subj: Books, reading. Careers – authors. Careers – nuns. Foreign lands – Mexico. Libraries.

Listen to the desert = Oye al desierto ill. by Francisco X. Mora. Clarion, 1994. ISBN 0-395-67292-9 Subj: Animals. Desert. Foreign languages. Noise, sounds. Poetry.

Love to mamá (Love to mamá)

The night the moon fell: a Maya myth retold ill. by Domi. Douglas & McIntyre, 2000. ISBN 0-88899-398-6 Subj: Folk & fairy tales. Foreign lands – Mexico. Indians of Central America – Maya. Moon.

One, two, three = Uno, dos, tres ill. by Barbara Lavallee. Clarion, 1996. ISBN 0-395-67294-5 Subj: Birthdays. Counting, numbers. Foreign languages. Rhyming text.

Pablo's tree ill. by Cecily Lang. Macmillan, 1994. ISBN 0-02-767401-0 Subj: Adoption. Birthdays. Ethnic groups in the U.S. – Mexican Americans. Family life – grandfathers.

The race of toad and deer ill. by Maya Itzna Brooks. Orchard, 1995. ISBN 0-531-08777-8 Subj: Animals. Behavior – trickery. Folk & fairy tales. Foreign lands – Guatemala. Foreign languages. Sports – racing.

The rainbow tulip ill. by Elizabeth Sayles. Viking, 1999. ISBN 0-670-87291-1 Subj: Character traits – being different. Ethnic groups in the U.S. – Mexican Americans. Holidays – May Day. Parades. School.

The desert is my mother = El desierto es mi madre ill. by Daniel Lechón. Piñata, 1994. ISBN 1-55885-121-6 Subj: Desert. Foreign languages. Poetry.

The gift of the poinsettia = El regalo de la flor de nochebuena by Pat Mora & Charles Ramírez Berg; ill. by Charles Ramírez Berg. Piñata, 1995. ISBN 1-55885-137-2 Subj: Foreign lands – Mexico. Foreign languages. Gifts. Holidays – Christmas.

This big sky ill. by Steve Jenkins. Scholastic, 1998. ISBN 0-590-37120-7 Subj: Animals. Desert. Poetry.

Tomás and the library lady ill. by Raúl Colón. Knopf, 1997. ISBN 0-679-90401-8 Subj: Books, reading. Careers – librarians. Careers – migrant workers. Ethnic groups in the U.S. – Mexican Americans. Libraries.

Moran, Alex. *Boots for Beth* ill. by Lisa Campbell Ernst. Harcourt, 2002. ISBN 0-15-216558-4 Subj: Animals. Animals – pigs. Clothing – boots.

Come here, tiger ill. by Lisa Campbell Ernst. Harcourt, 2001. ISBN 0-15-216218-6 Subj: Animals. Animals – cats. Pets.

Sam and Jack ill. by Tim Bowers. Harcourt, 2001. ISBN 0-15-216240-2 Subj: Animals – cats. Animals – mice. Friendship.

Moran, George. *Imagine me on a sit-ski!* ill. by Nadine Bernard Westcott. A. Whitman, 1995. ISBN 0-8075-3618-0 Subj: Handicaps – cerebral palsy. Handicaps – physical handicaps. Sports – skiing.

Morck, Irene. *Old bird* by Irene Morck & Muriel Wood; ill. by Muriel Wood. Fitzhenry & Whiteside, 2003. ISBN 1-55041-695-2 Subj: Activities – working. Animals – horses, ponies. Friendship.

Tyler's new boots ill. by Georgia Graham. Chronicle, 1998. ISBN 0-8118-2248-6 Subj: Animals – bulls, cows. Clothing – boots. Cowboys, cowgirls.

Mordvinoff, Nicolas. *Billy the kid* (Lipkind, William)

The boy and the forest (Lipkind, William)

Chaga (Lipkind, William)

The Christmas bunny (Lipkind, William)

Circus ruckus (Lipkind, William)

Coral Island ill. by author. Doubleday, 1957. Subj: Behavior – growing up. Foreign lands – South Sea Islands. Islands.

Even Steven (Lipkind, William)

Finders keepers (Lipkind, William)

Four-leaf clover (Lipkind, William)

The little tiny rooster (Lipkind, William)

The magic feather duster (Lipkind, William)

Russet and the two reds (Lipkind, William)

Sleepyhead (Lipkind, William)

The two reds (Lipkind, William)

More, Caroline. *see* Cone, Molly

Morehead, Debby. *A special place for Charlee: a child's companion through pet loss* ill. by Karen Cannon. Partners in Publishing, 1996. ISBN 0-9654049-0-0 Subj: Animals. Death. Emotions – grief. Pets.

Moreillon, Judi. *Sing down the rain* ill. by Michael Chiago. Kiva, 1997. ISBN 1-885772-07-6 Subj: Desert. Indians of North America – Pima. Plants. Rhyming text.

Morel, Eve. *Fairy tales* ill. by Gyo Fujikawa. Grosset, 1980. ISBN 0-448-13144-7 Subj: Folk & fairy tales.

Fairy tales and fables ill. by Gyo Fujikawa. Grosset, 1970. Subj: Folk & fairy tales.

Moremen, Grace E. *No, no, Natalie* photos by Geoffrey P. Fulton. Childrens Pr., 1973. ISBN 0-516-07624-8 Subj: Animals – rabbits. Behavior – misbehavior. School.

Moret, Brigitte Frey. *The bear's Christmas* ill. by Alexander Reichstein; trans. by Rosemary Lanning. North-South, 1998. ISBN 1-55858-972-4 Subj: Animals – bears. Hibernation. Holidays – Christmas. Religion – Nativity.

Moreton, Daniel. *La Cucaracha Martina: a Caribbean folktale* ill. by reteller. Turtle Books, 1997. ISBN 1-890515-03-5 Subj: Animals. Cities, towns. Folk & fairy tales. Foreign lands – Caribbean Islands. Foreign languages. Insects – cockroaches. Noise, sounds.

Morgan, Allen. *Matthew and the midnight ball game* ill. by Michael Martchenko. Stoddart, 1997. ISBN 0-7737-5853-4 Subj: Birds – turkeys. Careers – postal workers. Sports – baseball.

Matthew and the midnight firemen ill. by Michael Martchenko. Stoddart, 2000. ISBN 0-7737-6090-3 Subj: Careers – firefighters.

Matthew and the midnight flood ill. by Michael Martchenko. Stoddart, 1998. ISBN 0-7737-5941-7 Subj: Careers – plumbers. Weather – floods.

Matthew and the midnight hospital ill. by Michael Martchenko. Stoddart, 1999. ISBN 0-7737-6014-8 Subj: Health & fitness. Hospitals.

Matthew and the midnight money van ill. by Michael Martchenko. Firefly, 1987. ISBN 0-920303-75-7 Subj: Behavior – lost & found possessions. Holidays – Mother's Day.

Matthew and the midnight pilot ill. by Michael Martchenko. Stoddart, 1997. ISBN 0-7737-5852-6 Subj: Airplanes, airports. Careers – airplane pilots.

Matthew and the midnight pirates ill. by Michael Martchenko. Stoddart, 1998. ISBN 0-7737-5940-9 Subj: Pirates.

Matthew and the midnight tow truck ill. by Michael Martchenko. Annick, 1984. ISBN 0-920303-00-5 Subj: Trucks.

Matthew and the midnight turkeys ill. by Michael Martchenko. Annick, 1985. ISBN 0-920303-36-6 Subj: Birds – turkeys.

Matthew and the midnight wrestlers ill. by Michael Martchenko. Stoddart, 2000. ISBN 0-7737-6053-9 Subj: Sports – wrestling.

Molly and Mr. Maloney ill. by Maryann Kovalski. Kids Can, 1982. ISBN 0-919964-41-9 Subj: Animals – raccoons. Behavior – misbehavior. Pets.

Nicole's boat ill. by Jirina Marton. Firefly, 1986. ISBN 0-920303-60-9 Subj: Bedtime. Boats, ships. Dreams. Family life – fathers. Sea & seashore.

Sadie and the snowman ill. by Brenda Clark. Kids Can, 1985. ISBN 0-919964-86-9 Subj: Seasons – winter. Snowmen.

Morgan, Justina. *see* Freeman, Jean Todd

Morgan, Mary. *see* MorganVanroyen, Mary

My good night book ill. by author. Dutton, 2003. ISBN 0-525-46987-7 Subj: Bedtime. Format, unusual – toy & movable books. Night. Rhyming text.

Morgan, Michaela. *Brave, brave mouse* ill. by Michelle Cartlidge. A. Whitman, 2004. ISBN 0-8075-0869-1 Subj: Animals – mice. Character traits – bravery. Emotions – fear. Rhyming text.

Dinostory ill. by True Kelley. Dutton, 1991. ISBN 0-525-44726-1 Subj: Dinosaurs.

Edward gets a pet ill. by Sue Porter. Dutton, 1987. ISBN 0-525-44349-5 Subj: Animals. Imagination. Pets.

Helpful Betty solves a mystery ill. by Moira Kemp. Carolrhoda, 1994. ISBN 0-87614-832-1 Subj: Animals – hippopotamuses. Character traits – helpfulness. Jungle. Mystery stories.

Helpful Betty to the rescue ill. by Moira Kemp. Carolrhoda, 1994. ISBN 0-87614-831-3 Subj: Animals – hippopotamuses. Animals – monkeys. Behavior – misunderstanding. Character traits – foolishness. Character traits – helpfulness. Jungle.

Visitors for Edward ill. by Sue Porter. Dutton, 1988. ISBN 0-525-44354-1 Subj: Family life – grandparents. Imagination.

Morgan, Richard. *Zoo poo* ill. by author. Barron's, 2004. ISBN 0-613-81357-X Subj: Behavior – growing up. Toilet training. Zoos.

Morgan-Vanroyen, Mary. *Benjamin's bugs* ill. by author. Bradbury, 1994. ISBN 0-02-767450-9 Subj: Animals – porcupines. Insects.

Curious Rosie ill. by author. Hyperion, 2000. ISBN 0-7868-0477-7 Subj: Animals – mice. Character traits – curiosity.

Gentle Rosie ill. by author. Hyperion, 1999. ISBN 0-7868-0474-2 Subj: Animals – mice. Behavior.

Guess who I love? ill. by author. Grosset, 1992. ISBN 0-448-40313-7 Subj: Animals – mice. Emotions – love. Family life. Format, unusual – board books. Rhyming text.

Night ride ill. by author. Atheneum, 1997. ISBN 0-689-80545-4 Subj: Family life – grandfathers. Night. Seasons – spring. Sports – bicycling.

Patient Rosie ill. by author. Hyperion, 2000. ISBN 0-7868-0476-9 Subj: Animals – mice. Character traits – patience.

The Pudgy Merry Christmas book ill. by author. Grosset, 1989. ISBN 0-448-02262-1 Subj: Animals – mice. Format, unusual – board books. Holidays – Christmas.

Sleep tight, little mouse ill. by author. Knopf, 2003. ISBN 0-375-92308-X Subj: Animals – mice. Bedtime. Family life – mothers.

Wild Rosie ill. by author. Hyperion, 1999. ISBN 0-7868-0475-0 Subj: Activities – playing. Animals – mice. Behavior.

Morgenstern, Aliyah. *The wedding of Brown Bear and White Bear* (Beck, Martine)

Morgenstern, Christian. *Lullabies, lyrics and gallows songs* ill. by Lisbeth Zwerger; trans. by Anthea Bell. North-South, 1995. ISBN 1-55858-365-3 Subj: Lullabies. Poetry. Songs.

Morgenstern, Constance. *Good night, feet* ill. by Cat Bowman Smith. Holt, 1991. ISBN 0-8050-1453-5 Subj: Anatomy – feet. Bedtime. Rhyming text.

Morgenstern, Elizabeth. *The little gardeners* trans. from German by Elizabeth Morgenstern; retold by Louise F. Encking; ill. by Marigard Bantzer. A. Whitman, 1933. Subj: Foreign lands – Germany. Gardens, gardening.

Morice, Dave. *Dot town* ill. by author. Toothpaste Pr., 1982. ISBN 0-915124-38-6 Subj: Poetry.

The happy birthday handbook ill. by author. Coffee House, 1982. ISBN 0-915-12467-X Subj: Birthdays.

A visit from St. Alphabet ill. by author. Coffee House, 1980. ISBN 0-915-12447-5 Subj: ABC books. Poetry.

Morimoto, Isao. *The two bullies* (Morimoto, Junko)

Morimoto, Junko. *The inch boy* ill. by author. Viking, 1986. ISBN 0-670-80955-1 Subj: Family life. Folk & fairy tales. Little people.

Mouse's marriage ill. by author. Viking, 1986. ISBN 0-670-81071-1 Subj: Animals – mice. Folk & fairy tales.

My Hiroshima ill. by author. Viking, 1990. ISBN 0-670-83181-6 Subj: War.

The two bullies trans. from an original Japanese story by Isao Morimoto; ill. by Junko Morimoto. Crown, 1999. ISBN 0-517-80062-4 Subj: Behavior – bullying. Folk & fairy tales. Foreign lands – China. Foreign lands – Japan.

Morley, Carol. *Dots and spots* ill. by author. Willa Perlman Books, 1993. ISBN 0-06-021527-5 Subj: Witches.

Farmyard song ill. by author. S&S, 1995. ISBN 0-671-89551-6 Subj: Animals. Cumulative tales. Farms. Music. Noise, sounds. Nursery rhymes. Songs.

A spider and a pig ill. by author. Little, 1993. ISBN 0-316-58405-3 Subj: Animals – pigs. Behavior – lost. Folk & fairy tales. Islands. Spiders. Weather – storms.

Moroney, Lynn. *Baby Rattlesnake* (Ata, Te)

The boy who loved bears: adapt. from a traditional Pawnee tale ill. by Charles W. Chapman. Childrens Pr., 1994. ISBN 0-516-05142-3 Subj: Animals – bears. Folk & fairy tales. Indians of North America – Pawnee.

Elinda who danced in the sky: an Estonian folktale ill. by Veg Reisberg. Children's Book Pr., 1990. ISBN 0-89239-066-2 Subj: Folk & fairy tales. Foreign lands – Estonia. Sky.

Moontellers: myths of the moon from around the world ill. by Gred Shed. Northland, 1995. ISBN 0-87358-601-8 Subj: Folk & fairy tales. Moon.

Morozumi, Atsuko. *Helping daddy* ill. by author. Knopf, 2000. ISBN 0-375-80593-1 Subj: Family life. Format, unusual – board books.

In the park ill. by author. Knopf, 2000. ISBN 0-375-80591-5 Subj: Format, unusual – board books. Parks.

My friend gorilla ill. by author. Farrar, 1998. ISBN 0-374-35458-8 Subj: Animals – gorillas. Foreign lands – Africa. Friendship. Pets. Zoos.

One gorilla ill. by author. Farrar, 1990. ISBN 0-374-35644-0 Subj: Animals. Animals – gorillas. Counting, numbers.

Playing ill. by author. Knopf, 2000. ISBN 0-375-80592-3 Subj: Activities – playing. Format, unusual – board books.

Time for bed ill. by author. Knopf, 2000. ISBN 0-375-80594-X Subj: Bedtime. Format, unusual – board books.

Morpurgo, Michael. *Jo-Jo the melon donkey* ill. by Chris Molan. Prentice-Hall, 1988. ISBN 0-13-510009-7 Subj: Animals – donkeys. Foreign lands – Italy. Weather – floods.

The silver swan ill. by Christian Birmingham. Fogelman, 2000. ISBN 0-8037-2543-4 Subj: Birds – swans. Seasons – winter.

Wombat goes walkabout ill. by Christian Birmingham. Candlewick, 2000. ISBN 0-7636-1168-9 Subj: Animals. Animals – wombats. Behavior – lost. Foreign lands – Australia.

Morris, Ann. *The animal book* ill. by author. Silver Pr., 1996. ISBN 0-382-24702-7 Subj: Animals.

The baby book photos by Ken Heyman. Silver Pr., 1996. ISBN 0-382-24699-3 Subj: Babies. Family life.

Bread, bread, bread photos by Ken Heyman. Lothrop, 1989. ISBN 0-688-06335-7 Subj: Food.

The Cinderella rebus book ill. by Ljiljana Rylands. Orchard, 1989. ISBN 0-531-08361-6 Subj: Fairies. Folk & fairy tales. Foreign lands – France. Rebuses. Royalty – princes.

Cuddle up ill. by Maureen Roffey. HarperCollins, 1986. ISBN 0-694-00072-8 Subj: Bedtime. Family life – mothers. Night.

The daddy book photos by Ken Heyman. Silver Pr., 1996. ISBN 0-382-24696-9 Subj: Family life – fathers.

Eleanora Mousie catches a cold ill. by Ruth Young. Macmillan, 1987. ISBN 0-02-767500-9 Subj: Animals – mice. Illness.

Eleanora Mousie in the dark ill. by Ruth Young. Macmillan, 1987. ISBN 0-02-767530-0 Subj: Animals – mice. Monsters. Night.

Eleanora Mousie makes a mess ill. by Ruth Young. Macmillan, 1987. ISBN 0-02-767520-3 Subj: Animals – mice. Character traits – cleanliness.

Eleanora Mousie's gray day ill. by Ruth Young. Macmillan, 1987. ISBN 0-02-767510-6 Subj: Animals – mice. Behavior – bad day. Friendship.

Families ill. with photos. HarperCollins, 2000. ISBN 0-688-17199-0 Subj: Character traits – individuality. Family life.

The grandma book photos by Ken Heyman. Silver Pr., 1999. ISBN 0-382-39838-6 Subj: Family life – grandmothers.

Grandma Esther remembers photos & ill. by Peter Linenthal. Millbrook, 2002. ISBN 0-7613-2318-X Subj: Family life – grandmothers. Holocaust. Jewish culture. Memories, memory.

Grandma Francisca remembers photos & ill. by Peter Linenthal. Millbrook, 2002. ISBN 0-7613-2315-5 Subj: Ethnic groups in the U.S. – Hispanic Americans. Family life – grandmothers. Memories, memory.

Grandma Lai Goon remembers photos & ill. by Peter Linenthal. Millbrook, 2002. ISBN 0-7613-2314-7 Subj: Ethnic groups in the U.S. – Chinese Americans. Family life – grandmothers. Foreign lands – China. Memories, memory.

Grandma Lois remembers photos & ill. by Peter Linenthal. Millbrook, 2002. ISBN 0-7613-2316-3 Subj: Ethnic groups in the U.S. – African Americans. Family life – grandmothers. Memories, memory. Prejudice.

Grandma Maxine remembers photos & ill. by Peter Linenthal. Millbrook, 2002. ISBN 0-7613-2317-1 Subj: Family life – grandmothers. Indians of North America – Shoshone. Memories, memory.

The grandpa book photos by Ken Heyman. Silver Pr., 1999. ISBN 0-382-39841-6 Subj: Family life – grandfathers.

Hats, hats, hats photos by Ken Heyman. Lothrop, 1989. ISBN 0-688-06339-X Subj: Clothing – hats.

Hello Peter = Bonjour, Rémy ill. by Deborah Melmon. Celebration Pr., 1996. ISBN 0-673-75895-8 Subj: Animals – cats. Foreign lands – France. Foreign languages.

Houses and homes photos by Ken Heyman. Lothrop, 1992. ISBN 0-688-10169-0 Subj: Foreign lands. Homes, houses.

I am six photos by Nancy Sheehan. Silver Burdett, 1995. ISBN 0-382-24759-0 Subj: School.

Karate boy ill. by David Katzenstein. Dutton, 1996. ISBN 0-525-45337-7 Subj: Sports – karate.

Kiss time ill. by Maureen Roffey. HarperCollins, 1986. ISBN 0-694-00073-6 Subj: Bedtime. Night.

Light the candle! Bang the drum! ill. by Peter Linenthal. Dutton, 1997. ISBN 0-525-45639-2 Subj: Holidays.

Little ballerinas photos by Nancy Sheehan. Grosset, 1997. ISBN 0-448-41607-7 Subj: Activities – dancing. Ballet.

The Little Red Riding Hood rebus book ill. by Ljiljana Rylands. Orchard, 1987. ISBN 0-531-08330-6 Subj: Animals – wolves. Behavior – talking to strangers. Folk & fairy tales. Rebuses.

Little skaters photos by Nancy Sheehan. Grosset, 1997. ISBN 0-448-41734-0 Subj: Sports – ice skating.

Loving photos by Ken Heyman. Lothrop, 1990. ISBN 0-688-06341-1 Subj: Emotions – love. Family life. Foreign lands.

The mommy book photos by Ken Heyman. Silver Pr., 1996. ISBN 0-382-24693-4 Subj: Family life – mothers.

Night counting ill. by Maureen Roffey. HarperCollins, 1986. ISBN 0-694-00074-4 Subj: Bedtime. Counting, numbers. Night.

On the go photos by Ken Heyman. Lothrop, 1990. ISBN 0-688-06337-3 Subj: Foreign lands. Transportation.

Play photos by Ken Heyman. Lothrop, 1998. ISBN 0-688-14553-1 Subj: Activities – playing. Foreign lands. Imagination.

700 kids on Grandpa's farm photos by Ken Heyman. Dutton, 1994. ISBN 0-525-45162-5 Subj: Animals – goats. Family life – grandfathers. Farms.

Shoes, shoes, shoes ill. by author. Lothrop, 1995. ISBN 0-688-13667-2 Subj: Clothing – shoes. Rhyming text.

Sleepy, sleepy ill. by Maureen Roffey. HarperCollins, 1986. ISBN 0-694-00075-2 Subj: Bedtime. Night.

This little baby goes out (Breeze, Lynn)

This little baby's bedtime (Breeze, Lynn)

This little baby's morning (Breeze, Lynn)

Tools photos by Ken Heyman. Lothrop, 1992. ISBN 0-688-10171-2 Subj: Tools.

Weddings photos by Ken Heyman. Lothrop, 1995. ISBN 0-688-13273-1 Subj: Clothing. Weddings.

Work photos by Ken Heyman. Lothrop, 1998. ISBN 0-688-14867-0 Subj: Activities – working. Careers. Foreign lands.

Morris, Bob. *Crispin the Terrible* ill. by Dasha Ziborova. Callaway, 2000. ISBN 0-935112-44-8 Subj: Animals – cats. Imagination.

Morris, Christopher G. *The magic world of words: a very first dictionary* (Halsey, William D.)

Morris, Dewi. *Sandy's street* ill. by author. Little, 2001. ISBN 0-316-83609-5 Subj: Animals – cats. Format, unusual – toy & movable books. Roads.

Morris, Jill. *The boy who painted the sun* ill. by Geoff Hocking. Viking, 1984. ISBN 0-7226-6052-9 Subj: Activities – painting. Behavior – solitude. Cities, towns. Moving.

Monkey creates havoc in heaven (P'an, Ts'ai-ying)

Morris, Johnny. *Animal-go-round* ill. with photos. DK, 1993. ISBN 1-56458-329-5 Subj: Animals. Behavior – growing up. Format, unusual – toy & movable books.

Morris, Linda Lowe. *Morning milking* ill. by David DeRan. Picture Book Studio, 1991. ISBN 0-88708-173-8 Subj: Animals. Animals – bulls, cows. Farms.

Morris, Neil. *Find the canary* by Neil & Ting Morris; ill. by Anna Clarke. Little, 1983. ISBN 0-316-58375-8 Subj: Games.

Hide and seek by Neil & Ting; Morris ill. by Anna Clarke. Little, 1983. ISBN 0-316-58376-6 Subj: Games.

Search for Sam by Neil & Ting Morris; ill. by Anna Clarke. Little, 1983. ISBN 0-316-58377-4 Subj: Games.

Where's my hat? by Neil & Ting Morris; ill. by Anna Clarke. Little, 1983. ISBN 0-316-58378-2 Subj: Clothing – hats. Games.

Morris, Terry Nell. *Good night, dear monster!* ill. by author. Knopf, 1980. ISBN 0-394-94221-3 Subj: Bedtime. Imagination – imaginary friends. Monsters.

Lucky puppy! Lucky boy! ill. by author. Knopf, 1980. ISBN 0-394-84220-0 Subj: Animals – dogs. Behavior – needing someone.

Morris, Ting. *Find the canary* (Morris, Neil)

Hide and seek (Morris, Neil)

Search for Sam (Morris, Neil)

Where's my hat? (Morris, Neil)

Morris, Winifred. *The future of Yen-Tzu* ill. by Friso Henstra. Atheneum, 1992. ISBN 0-689-31501-5 Subj: Folk & fairy tales. Foreign lands – China. Royalty – emperors.

Just listen ill. by Patricia Cullen-Clark. Atheneum, 1990. ISBN 0-689-31588-0 Subj: Family life – grandmothers. Noise, sounds. Senses – hearing.

The magic leaf ill. by Ju-Hong Chen. Atheneum, 1987. ISBN 0-689-31358-6 Subj: Folk & fairy tales. Foreign lands – China.

What if the shark wears tennis shoes? ill. by Betsy Lewin. Atheneum, 1990. ISBN 0-689-31587-2 Subj: Bedtime. Emotions – fear. Imagination.

Morrison, Bill. *Louis James hates school* ill. by author. Houghton Mifflin, 1978. ISBN 0-395-27156-8 Subj: Careers. School.

Squeeze a sneeze ill. by author. Houghton Mifflin, 1977. ISBN 0-395-25151-6 Subj: Poetry.

Morrison, Gordon. *Bald eagle* ill. by author. Houghton Mifflin, 1998. ISBN 0-395-87328-2 Subj: Birds – eagles.

Morrison, Sean. *Is that a happy hippopotamus?* ill. by Aliki. Crowell, 1966. Subj: Animals. Humorous stories. Noise, sounds. Poetry.

Morrison, Taylor. *Cheetah* ill. by author. Holt, 1998. ISBN 0-8050-5121-X Subj: Animals – cheetahs. Foreign lands – Africa.

Morrison, Toni. *The book of mean people* ill. by Pascal Lemaître. Hyperion, 2002. ISBN 0-7868-2471-9 Subj: Behavior – bullying. Behavior – fighting, arguing. Character traits – meanness. Emotions – anger.

Morrissey, Dean. *The Christmas ship* ill. by author. HarperCollins, 2000. ISBN 0-06-028576-1 Subj: Boats, ships. Gifts. Holidays – Christmas. Magic. Santa Claus. Toys.

Morrow, Barbara. *Edward's portrait* ill. by author. Macmillan, 1991. ISBN 0-02-767591-2 Subj: Activities – photographing. Family life. U.S. history.

Help for Mr. Peale ill. by author. Macmillan, 1990. ISBN 0-02-767590-4 Subj: Moving. Museums.

Morrow, Elizabeth Cutter. *The painted pig* ill. by René d'Harnoncourt. Knopf, 1930. Subj: Foreign lands – Mexico.

Morrow, Suzanne Stark. *Inatuck's friend* ill. by Ellen Raskin. Little, 1968. Subj: Eskimos. Friendship.

Morrow, Tara Jaye. *Mommy loves her baby; Daddy loves his baby* ill. by Tiphanie Beeke. HarperCollins, 2003. ISBN 0-06-029078-1 Subj: Animals. Babies. Emotions – love. Family life – parents. Format, unusual. Rhyming text.

Morse, Samuel French. *All in a suitcase* ill. by Barbara Cooney. Little, 1966. Subj: ABC books. Animals.

Sea sums ill. by Fuku Akino. Little, 1970. Subj: Counting, numbers. Poetry. Sea & seashore. Weather – fog.

Morton, Christine. *Picnic farm* ill. by Sarah Barringer. Holiday, 1998. ISBN 0-8234-1332-2 Subj: Activities – picnicking. Animals. Farms.

Morton, Lone. *Hurry up, Molly = Apúrate, Molly* ill. by Gill Scriven; Spanish by Thessa Judkins. Barron's, 2000. ISBN 0-7641-5286-6 Subj: Bedtime. Family life – fathers. Foreign languages.

Hurry up, Molly = Dépêche-toi, Molly ill. by Gill Scriven; French by Christophe Dillinger. Barron's, 2000. ISBN 0-7641-5287-4 Subj: Bedtime. Family life – fathers. Foreign languages.

Mosel, Arlene. *The funny little woman* ill. by Blair Lent. Dutton, 1972. Based on The old woman and her dumpling by Lafcadio Hearn. ISBN 0-525-30265-4 Subj: Caldecott award books. Foreign lands – Japan. Monsters.

Tikki Tikki Tembo ill. by Blair Lent. Holt, 1968. ISBN 0-8050-0662-1 Subj: Folk & fairy tales. Foreign lands – China. Names.

Moseley, Keith. *Big creatures from the past* (Watson, Claire)

Dinosaurs: a lost world ill. by Robert Cremins. Putnam, 1984. ISBN 0-399-21063-6 Subj: Dinosaurs. Format, unusual – toy & movable books. Prehistory. Science.

Prehistoric mammals (Berger, Melvin)

Winnie-the-Pooh: a pop-up book (Milne, A. A. [Alan Alexander])

Moser, Barry. *Tucker Pfeffercorn: an old story retold* ill. by author. Little, 1994. ISBN 0-316-58542-4 Subj: Activities. Folk & fairy tales. Names.

Moser, Erwin. *The crow in the snow and other bedtime stories* trans. from German by Joel Agee; ill. by author. Adama, 1986. ISBN 0-915361-49-3 Subj: Animals. Imagination.

Wilma the elephant ill. by author. Adama, 1986. ISBN 0-915361-45-0 Subj: Animals – elephants. Behavior – lost. Behavior – needing someone.

Moser, Madeline. *Ever heard of an aardwolf?* ill. by Barry Moser. Harcourt, 1996. ISBN 0-15-200474-2 Subj: Animals. Character traits – being different.

Moses, Amy. *At the hospital* ill. by Penny Dann; photos by Phil Martin. Child's World, 1998. ISBN 1-56766-291-9 Subj: Hospitals.

At the zoo ill. by Penny Dann; photos by Phil Martin. Child's World, 1998. ISBN 1-56766-287-0 Subj: Animals. Zoos.

Moses, Will. *Silent night* ill. by author. Philomel, 1997. ISBN 0-399-23100-5 Subj: Babies. Family life. Holidays – Christmas. Songs.

Will Moses Mother Goose (Mother Goose)

Mosimann, Odie. *How the mouse was hit on the head by a stone and so discovered the world* (Delessert, Etienne)

Moskin, Marietta D. *Lysbet and the fire kittens* ill. by Margot Tomes. Coward, 1973. ISBN 0-698-30522-1 Subj: Animals – cats. Behavior – carelessness. Fire. U.S. history.

Moskof, Martin Stephen. *Still another alphabet book* (Chwast, Seymour)

Still another children's book (Chwast, Seymour)

Still another number book (Chwast, Seymour)

Moskowitz, Addie Alexander. *Wish upon a star: a story for children with a parent who is mentally ill* (Laskin, Pamela L.)

Mosley, Francis. *The dinosaur eggs* ill. by author. Barron's, 1988. ISBN 0-8120-5910-7 Subj: Dinosaurs. Family life. Prehistory.

Moss, Elaine. *From morn to midnight* (From morn to midnight)

Polar ill. by Jeannie Baker. Elsevier-Dutton, 1979. ISBN 0-233-96695-1 Subj: Activities – playing. Illness. Safety. Toys – bears.

Moss, Jeffrey. *The Sesame Street ABC storybook* featuring Jim Henson's Muppets; by Jeffrey Moss, Norman Stiles & Daniel Wilcox; ill. by Peter Cross & others. Random House, 1974. ISBN 0-394-92921-7 Subj: ABC books. Puppets.

The Sesame Street song book (Raposo, Joe)

The songs of Sesame Street in poems and pictures by Jeffrey Moss & others; ill. by Normand Chartier. Random House, 1983. ISBN 0-394-95245-6 Subj: Poetry. Puppets. Songs.

Moss, Jenny Jackson. *Cajun night after Christmas* by Jenny Jackson Moss & Amy Jackson Dixon; ill. by James Rice. Pelican, 2000. ISBN 1-56554-779-9 Subj: Ethnic groups in the U.S. Holidays – Christmas. Poetry. Reptiles – alligators, crocodiles. Santa Claus.

Moss, Lloyd. *Our marching band* ill. by Diana Cain Bluthenthal. Putnam, 2001. ISBN 0-399-23335-0 Subj: Music. Musical instruments – bands. Rhyming text.

Zin! zin! zin! A violin ill. by Marjorie Priceman. S&S, 1995. ISBN 0-671-88239-2 Subj: Caldecott award honor books. Counting, numbers. Music. Musical instruments – violins. Rhyming text.

Moss, Marissa. *After-school monster* ill. by author. Lothrop, 1991. ISBN 0-688-10117-8 Subj: Character traits – assertiveness. Character traits – bravery. Emotions – fear. Ethnic groups in the U.S. Monsters.

But not Kate ill. by author. Lothrop, 1992. ISBN 0-688-10601-3 Subj: Animals – mice. Character traits – individuality. Magic. School. Self-concept.

In America ill. by author. Dutton, 1994. ISBN 0-525-45152-8 Subj: Activities – traveling. Ethnic groups in the U.S. – Lithuanian Americans. Family life – aunts, uncles. Family life – grandfathers. Jewish culture.

Knick knack paddywack ill. by author. Houghton Mifflin, 1992. ISBN 0-395-54701-6 Subj: Activities – making things. Animals – dogs. Counting, numbers. Cumulative tales. Songs. Space & space ships.

Mel's diner ill. by author. BridgeWater, 1994. ISBN 0-8167-3460-7 Subj: Activities – baking, cooking. Careers – chefs, cooks. Careers – waiters, waitresses. Ethnic groups in the U.S. – African Americans. Family life. Restaurants.

Regina's big mistake ill. by author. Houghton Mifflin, 1990. ISBN 0-395-55330-X Subj: Activities – drawing. Art. Careers – artists. School. Self-concept.

True heart ill. by C. F. Payne. Silver Whistle, 1999. ISBN 0-15-201344-X Subj: Careers – engineers. Gender roles. Trains.

The ugly menorah ill. by author. Farrar, 1996. ISBN 0-374-38927-9 Subj: Family life – grandparents. Holidays – Hanukkah. Jewish culture. Religion.

Want to play? ill. by author. Houghton Mifflin, 1990. ISBN 0-395-52022-3 Subj: Activities – playing. Sibling rivalry. Toys.

Who was it? ill. by author. Houghton Mifflin, 1989. ISBN 0-395-49699-3 Subj: Behavior – misbehavior. Character traits – honesty. Family life – mothers.

Moss, Miriam. *Bad hare day* ill. by Lynne Chapman. Bloomsbury, 2003. ISBN 1-58234-785-9 Subj: Animals. Animals – rabbits. Behavior – misbehavior. Family life – aunts, uncles. Hair.

I'll be your friend, Smudge ill. by Lynne Chapman. Gullane, 2001. ISBN 1-86233-207-X Subj: Animals – mice. Birthdays. Friendship. Moving.

It's my turn, Smudge ill. by Lynne Chapman. Gullane, 2001. ISBN 1-86233-287-8 Subj: Animals – mice. Behavior – sharing.

A new house for Smudge ill. by Lynne Chapman. Gullane, 2001. ISBN 1-86233-202-9 Subj: Animals – mice. Homes, houses. Moving.

Smudge's grumpy day ill. by Lynne Chapman. Gullane, 2001. ISBN 1-86233-282-7 Subj: Behavior – bad day. Behavior – running away. Emotions – anger.

The snow bear ill. by Maggie Kneen. Dutton, 2000. ISBN 0-525-46658-4 Subj: Activities – playing. Animals – polar bears. Behavior – lost. Family life – mothers. Foreign lands – Arctic.

This is the tree ill. by Adrienne Kennaway. Kane/Miller, 2000. ISBN 0-916291-98-7 Subj: Animals. Ecology. Foreign lands – Africa. Trees.

Wibble wobble ill. by Joanna Mockler. Tiger Tales, 2001. ISBN 1-58925-013-3 Subj: Behavior – lost & found possessions. School. Teeth.

Moss, P. Buckley (Pat Buckley). *Reuben and the quilt* text by Merle Good; ill. by author. Good Bks., 1999. ISBN 1-56148-234-X Subj: Crime. Ethnic groups in the U.S. – Amish. Quilts.

Moss, Peggy. *Say something* ill. by Lea Lyon. Tilbury, 2004. ISBN 0-88448-261-8 Subj: Behavior – bullying.

Moss, Thylias. *I want to be* ill. by Jerry Pinkney. Dial, 1993. ISBN 0-8037-1287-1 Subj: Behavior – growing up. Ethnic groups in the U.S. – African Americans.

Most, Bernard. *ABC T-Rex* ill. by author. Harcourt, 2000. ISBN 0-15-202007-1 Subj: ABC books. Dinosaurs.

Boo! ill. by author. Prentice-Hall, 1980. ISBN 0-13-079780-4 Subj: Emotions – fear. Monsters.

Catbirds and dogfish ill. by author. Harcourt, 1995. ISBN 0-15-292844-8 Subj: Animals. Names.

Catch me if you can! ill. by author. Harcourt, 1999. ISBN 0-15-202001-2 Subj: Dinosaurs. Family life – grandfathers.

Cock-a-doodle-moo! ill. by author. Harcourt, 1996. ISBN 0-15-201252-4 Subj: Animals. Birds – chickens. Careers – farmers. Farms. Morning.

The cow that went oink ill. by author. Harcourt, 1990. ISBN 0-15-220195-5 Subj: Animals. Noise, sounds.

Dinosaur cousins? ill. by author. Harcourt, 1987. ISBN 0-15-223497-7 Subj: Animals. Dinosaurs. Prehistory.

A dinosaur named after me ill. by author. Harcourt, 1991. ISBN 0-15-223494-2 Subj: Dinosaurs. Names. Prehistory.

Dinosaur questions ill. by author. Harcourt, 1995. ISBN 0-15-292885-5 Subj: Dinosaurs. Prehistory.

Four and twenty dinosaurs ill. by author. HarperCollins, 1990. ISBN 0-06-024377-5 Subj: Dinosaurs. Nursery rhymes. Poetry. Prehistory.

Happy holidaysaurus! ill. by author. Harcourt, 1992. ISBN 0-15-233386-X Subj: Dinosaurs. Holidays.

Hippopotamus hunt ill. by author. Harcourt, 1994. ISBN 0-15-234520-5 Subj: Animals – hippopotamuses. Jungle. Language.

How big were the dinosaurs? ill. by author. Harcourt, 1994. ISBN 0-15-236800-0 Subj: Concepts – size. Dinosaurs. Prehistory.

If the dinosaurs came back ill. by author. Harcourt, 1995. ISBN 0-15-238020-5 Subj: Dinosaurs. Imagination. Prehistory.

The littlest dinosaurs ill. by author. Harcourt, 1989. ISBN 0-15-248125-7 Subj: Dinosaurs. Prehistory.

Moo-ha! ill. by author. Harcourt, 1997. ISBN 0-15-201248-6 Subj: Animals – bulls, cows. Format, unusual – board books.

My very own octopus ill. by author. Harcourt, 1980. ISBN 0-05-256641-4 Subj: Octopuses. Pets.

Oink-ha! ill. by author. Harcourt, 1997. ISBN 0-15-201249-4 Subj: Animals – pigs. Format, unusual – board books.

A pair of protoceratops ill. by author. Harcourt, 1998. ISBN 0-15-201443-8 Subj: Activities. Dinosaurs.

Peek-a-moo! ill. by author. Harcourt, 1998. ISBN 0-15-201251-6 Subj: Animals. Animals – bulls, cows. Format, unusual – toy & movable books. Games.

Pets in trumpets and other word-play riddles ill. by author. Harcourt, 1991. ISBN 0-15-261210-6 Subj: Language. Pets. Riddles & jokes.

Row, row, row your goat ill. by author. Harcourt, 1998. ISBN 0-15-201250-8 Subj: Animals. Boats, ships. Songs.

There's an ant in Anthony ill. by author. Morrow, 1980. ISBN 0-688-62226-3 Subj: Books, reading.

There's an ape behind the drape ill. by author. Morrow, 1981. ISBN 0-688-00381-8 Subj: Animals – gorillas. Games. Language.

A trio of triceratops ill. by author. Harcourt, 1998. ISBN 0-15-201448-9 Subj: Activities. Dinosaurs.

The very boastful kangaroo ill. by author. Harcourt, 1999. ISBN 0-15-202349-6 Subj: Activities – jumping. Animals – kangaroos. Contests.

Whatever happened to the dinosaurs? ill. by author. Harcourt, 1995. ISBN 0-15-200378-9 Subj: Dinosaurs. Prehistory.

Where to look for a dinosaur ill. by author. Harcourt, 1993. ISBN 0-15-295616-6 Subj: Dinosaurs. Prehistory. Science.

Zoodles ill. by author. Harcourt, 1992. ISBN 0-15-299969-8 Subj: Animals. Birds. Riddles & jokes.

Z-Z-Zoink! ill. by author. Harcourt, 1999. ISBN 0-15-292845-6 Subj: Animals – pigs. Birds – owls. Noise, sounds. Sleep.

Mostacchi, Massimo. *The beast and the boy* ill. by Monica Miceli; adapt. by Andrew Clements. North-South, 1995. ISBN 1-55858-444-7 Subj: Animals – lions. Behavior – running away. Prejudice.

A dog's best friend ill. by Monica Miceli; adapt. by Andrew Clements. North-South, 1995. ISBN 1-55858-498-6 Subj: Animals – dogs. Behavior – running away. Friendship.

Mostel, Zero. *The Sesame Street book of opposites with Zero Mostel* (Mendoza, George)

Mother Goose. *ABC rhymes* ill. by Lulu Delacre. S&S, 1984. ISBN 0-671-49685-9 Subj: ABC books. Format, unusual – board books. Nursery rhymes.

Animals from Mother Goose: a question book (Hopkins, Lee Bennett)

The annotated Mother Goose arranged & explained by William S. & Ceil Baring-Gould; chapter decorations by E. M. Simon; ill. by Walter Crane & others. Potter/Crown, 1962. Subj: Nursery rhymes.

Arnold Lobel book of Mother Goose ill. by Arnold Lobel. Knopf, 1997. ISBN 0-679-98736-3 Subj: Nursery rhymes. Poetry.

As I was going up and down ill. by Nicola Bayley. Lothrop, 1986. ISBN 0-02-708590-2 Subj: Nursery rhymes.

The authentic Mother Goose fairy tales and nursery rhymes (Barchilon, Jacques)

Baa baa black sheep (Trapani, Iza)

Baa baa, black sheep adapt. & ill. by Marilyn Janovitz. Hyperion, 1991. ISBN 1-56282-086-9 Subj: Animals – dogs. Animals – sheep. Nursery rhymes.

Baa, baa, black sheep ill. by Moira Kemp. Lodestar, 1994. ISBN 0-525-67443-8 Subj: Animals – sheep. Format, unusual – board books. Nursery rhymes.

Baa baa black sheep ill. by Sue Porter. Peter Bedrick, 1984. ISBN 0-911745-26-2 Subj: Format, unusual – board books. Nursery rhymes.

Baa baa black sheep ill. by Ferelith Eccles Williams. David & Charles, 1985. ISBN 0-437-86003-5 Subj: Format, unusual – board books. Nursery rhymes.

Baa baa black sheep [board book] (Trapani, Iza)

Baby's first Mother Goose ill. by Mary Morgan; comp. by Wendy Lewison. Western, 1993. ISBN 0-307-06143-4 Subj: Format, unusual – board books. Nursery rhymes.

The baby's lap book ill. by Kay Chorao. Dutton, 1990. ISBN 0-525-44604-4 Subj: Nursery rhymes.

Beatrix Potter's nursery rhyme book ill. by Beatrix Potter. Warne, 1984. ISBN 0-7232-3254-7 Subj: Nursery rhymes.

Blessed Mother Goose: favorite nursery rhymes for today's children ill. by Kaye Luke. House-Warven, 1951. Subj: Nursery rhymes.

Brian Wildsmith's Mother Goose ill. by Brian Wildsmith. Watts, 1964. Subj: Nursery rhymes.

Carolyn Wells' edition of Mother Goose ill. by Margeria Cooper & others. Doubleday, 1946. Subj: Nursery rhymes.

Cats by Mother Goose sel. by Barbara Lucas; ill. by Carol Newsom. Lothrop, 1986. ISBN 0-688-04635-5 Subj: Animals – cats. Nursery rhymes.

The Charles Addams Mother Goose ill. by Charles Addams. Harper, 1967. Subj: Nursery rhymes.

A child's book of old nursery rhymes ill. by Joan Walsh Anglund. Atheneum, 1973. ISBN 0-689-30413-7 Subj: Nursery rhymes.

The Chinese Mother Goose rhymes sel. & ed. by Robert Wyndham; ill. by Ed Young. Putnam, 1982. Orig. pub. by World, 1968. ISBN 0-399-20866-6 Subj: Nursery rhymes.

The city and country Mother Goose ill. by Hilda Hoffmann. American Heritage, 1969. ISBN 0-8281-5007-9 Subj: Nursery rhymes.

The comic adventures of Old Mother Hubbard and her dog (Martin, Sarah Catherine)

Frank Baber's Mother Goose sel. by Ruth Spriggs; ill. by Frank Baber. Crown, 1976. ISBN 0-517-52819-3 Subj: Nursery rhymes.

The gay Mother Goose ill. by Françoise Seignobosc. Scribners, 1938. Subj: Nursery rhymes.

The glorious Mother Goose sel. by Cooper Edens; ill. by the best artists from the past. Atheneum, 1988. ISBN 0-689-31434-5 Subj: Nursery rhymes.

The golden goose (The golden goose)

The golden goose book ill. by L. Leslie Brooke. Warne, 1977, 1905. ISBN 0-7232-1979-6 Subj: Birds – geese. Folk & fairy tales. Humorous stories. Royalty.

Grafa' Grig had a pig ill. by Wallace Tripp. Little, 1976. ISBN 0-316-85282-1 Subj: Nursery rhymes.

Gray goose and gander and other Mother Goose rhymes coll. & ill. by Anne F. Rockwell. Crowell, 1980. ISBN 0-690-04049-0 Subj: Nursery rhymes.

Gregory Griggs and other nursery rhyme people sel. & ill. by Arnold Lobel. Greenwillow, 1978. ISBN 0-688-84128-7 Subj: Nursery rhymes.

Here's a ball for baby: finger rhymes for young children (Williams, Jenny [Jennifer])

Hey, diddle, diddle (Marshall, James)

Hey, diddle, diddle compiled & ill. by Linda Bronson. Holt, 2003. ISBN 0-8050-6754-X Subj: Animals. Moon. Nursery rhymes.

Hey, diddle, diddle ill. by Heather Collins. Kids Can, 2003. ISBN 1-55337-078-3 Subj: Animals. Moon. Nursery rhymes.

Hey, diddle, diddle adapt. & ill. by Marilyn Janovitz. Walt Disney, 1992. ISBN 1-56282-169-5 Subj: Animals. Moon. Music. Nursery rhymes.

Hey, diddle, diddle ill. by Moira Kemp. Lodestar, 1994. ISBN 0-525-67445-4 Subj: Animals. Format, unusual – board books. Moon. Nursery rhymes.

Hey, diddle, diddle adapt. by Leonard P. Kessler; ill. by Marc Mongeau. Delmar, 1991. ISBN 0-8273-4503-8 Subj: Animals. Moon. Nursery rhymes.

Hey, diddle, diddle ill. by Nita Sowter. Peter Bedrick, 1984. ISBN 0-911745-27-0 Subj: Animals. Format, unusual – board books. Moon. Nursery rhymes.

Hey, diddle, diddle ill. by Eleanor Wasmuth. S&S, 1986. ISBN 0-671-61726-5 Subj: Animals. Format, unusual – board books. Moon. Nursery rhymes.

Hey, diddle, diddle, and Baby bunting ill. by Randolph Caldecott. Warne, 1882. Subj: Nursery rhymes.

Hey, diddle, diddle picture book ill. by Randolph Caldecott. Warne, 1883. Subj: Animals. Format, unusual – board books. Moon. Nursery rhymes.

Hickory, dickory, dock ill. by Heather Collins. Kids Can, 1997. ISBN 1-55074-408-9 Subj: Format, unusual – board books. Nursery rhymes.

Hickory dickory dock adapt. by Leonard P. Kessler; ill. by Doug Cushman. Garrard, 1980. ISBN 0-8116-7400-2 Subj: Animals – cats. Animals – mice. Clocks, watches.

Hickory, dickory, dock adapt. by Robin Muller; ill. by Suzanne Duranceau. Scholastic, 1994. ISBN 0-590-47278-X Subj: Animals. Clocks, watches. Parties. Rhyming text.

Hickory dickory dock adapt. & ill. by Marilyn Janovitz. Hyperion, 1991. ISBN 1-56282-084-2 Subj: Animals – cats. Animals – mice. Clocks, watches. Nursery rhymes.

Hickory, dickory, dock ill. by Moira Kemp. Lodestar, 1993. ISBN 0-525-67444-6 Subj: Animals – mice. Clocks, watches. Format, unusual – board books. Nursery rhymes.

Hickory dickory dock and other nursery rhymes ill. by Carol Jones. Houghton Mifflin, 1992. ISBN 0-395-60834-1 Subj: Format, unusual. Nursery rhymes.

Humpty Dumpty: five fingerwiggle nursery rhymes ill. by Colin & Jacqui Hawkins. Candlewick, 1992. ISBN 1-56402-015-0 Subj: Format, unusual – board books. Nursery rhymes.

Humpty Dumpty ill. by Moira Kemp; paper engineering by Steve Augarde; designed by Herman Lelie. Lodestar, 1996. ISBN 0-525-67540-X Subj: Eggs. Format, unusual – toy & movable books. Nursery rhymes.

Humpty Dumpty and other first rhymes ill. by Betty Ferrell Youngs. Bodley Head, 1980. ISBN 0-370-30025-4 Subj: Nursery rhymes.

Humpty Dumpty and other rhymes ed. by Iona Opie; ill. by Rosemary Wells. Candlewick, 1997. ISBN 0-7636-0353-8 Subj: Format, unusual – board books. Nursery rhymes.

Hurrah, we're outward bound! ill. by Peter Spier. Doubleday, 1968. ISBN 0-440-40715-X Subj: Nursery rhymes.

Hush-a-bye baby ill. by Nicola Bayley. Lothrop, 1986. ISBN 0-02-708610-0 Subj: Bedtime. Nursery rhymes.

Ian Penney's book of nursery rhymes ill. by Ian Penney. Abrams, 1994. ISBN 0-8109-3733-6 Subj: Nursery rhymes.

In a pumpkin shell ill. by Joan Walsh Anglund. Harcourt, 1960. ISBN 0-15-238269-0 Subj: ABC books. Nursery rhymes.

Jack and Jill: and other nursery rhymes (Cousins, Lucy)

Jack and Jill ill. by Heather Collins. Kids Can, 2003. ISBN 1-55337-075-9 Subj: Format, unusual – board books. Nursery rhymes.

Jack and Jill ill. by Eleanor Wasmuth. S&S, 1986. ISBN 0-671-61729-X Subj: Format, unusual – board books. Nursery rhymes.

Jack Kent's merry Mother Goose ill. by Jack Kent. Golden Pr., 1977. ISBN 0-307-65798-1 Subj: Nursery rhymes.

James Marshall's Mother Goose ill. by James Marshall. Farrar, 1979. ISBN 0-374-33653-9 Subj: Nursery rhymes.

Kate Greenaway's Mother Goose ill. by Kate Greenaway. Dial, 1988. ISBN 0-8037-0479-8 Subj: Format, unusual – board books. Nursery rhymes.

Kitten rhymes ill. by Lulu Delacre. S&S, 1984. ISBN 0-671-49687-5 Subj: Animals – cats. Format, unusual – board books. Nursery rhymes.

The Larousse book of nursery rhymes ed. by Robert Owen; ill. with photos. Larousse, 1984. Ill. are full color photos. of tile pictures, painted during the late 19th and early 20th cents., created by the Royal Doulton Co., designed by Margaret Thompson, William Rowe and John H. McLennan. ISBN 0-88332-371-0 Subj: Nursery rhymes.

Lavender's blue comp. by Kathleen Lines; ill. by Harold Jones. Oxford Univ. Pr., 1982. ISBN 0-19-279537-6 Subj: Nursery rhymes.

Little Boy Blue ill. by Nita Sowter. Peter Bedrick, 1984. ISBN 0-911745-28-9 Subj: Format, unusual – board books. Nursery rhymes.

Little Boy Blue and other rhymes ed. by Iona Opie; ill. by Rosemary Wells. Candlewick, 1997. ISBN 0-7636-0354-6 Subj: Format, unusual – board books. Nursery rhymes.

Little Miss Muffet: and other nursery rhymes (Cousins, Lucy)

Little Miss Muffet ill. by Heather Collins. Kids Can, 2003. ISBN 1-55337-076-7 Subj: Format, unusual – board books. Nursery rhymes.

Little Miss Muffet ill. by Mary Morgan. Publications International, 1998. ISBN 0-7853-2633-2 Subj: Format, unusual – toy & movable books. Nursery rhymes.

The little Mother Goose ill. by Jessie Willcox Smith. Dodd, 1918. Subj: Nursery rhymes.

Little Robin Redbreast: a Mother Goose rhyme (Little Robin Redbreast)

London Bridge is falling down ill. by Ed Emberley. Little, 1967. Subj: Folk & fairy tales. Foreign lands – England. Games. Nursery rhymes. Songs.

London Bridge is falling down ill. by Peter Spier. Doubleday, 1989, c1967. ISBN 0-385-08025-5 Subj: Folk & fairy tales. Foreign lands – England. Games. Nursery rhymes. Songs.

The Margaret Tarrant nursery rhyme book (Tarrant, Margaret)

Michael Foreman's Mother Goose ill. by Michael Foreman. Harcourt, 1991. ISBN 0-15-255820-9 Subj: Nursery rhymes.

Mother Goose sel. & ill. by Scott Cook. Knopf, 1994. ISBN 0-679-90949-4 Subj: Nursery rhymes.

Mother Goose comp. by William Rose Benét; ill. by Roger Antoine Duvoisin. Heritage Pr., 1943. Subj: Nursery rhymes.

Mother Goose sel. by Phyllis Maurine Fraser; ill. by Miss Elliott. S&S, 1942. Subj: Nursery rhymes.

Mother Goose ill. by C. B. Falls. Doubleday, 1924. Subj: Nursery rhymes.

Mother Goose ill. by Gyo Fujikawa. Grosset, 1967. ISBN 0-448-01810-1 Subj: Nursery rhymes.

Mother Goose: as told by Kellogg's singing lady ill. by Vernon Grant. Kellogg Co., 1933. Subj: Nursery rhymes.

Mother Goose: or, the old nursery rhymes sel. by Phyllis Maurine Fraser; ill. by Kate Greenaway. Routledge, 1881. Illustrated as originally engraved and printed by Edmund Evans. Subj: Nursery rhymes.

Mother Goose sel. & ill. by Michael Hague. Holt, 1984. ISBN 0-03-070723-4 Subj: Nursery rhymes.

Mother Goose ill. by Violet La Mont. S&S, 1957. Subj: Nursery rhymes.

Mother Goose: the old nursery rhymes ill. by Arthur Rackham. Century, 1913. Subj: Nursery rhymes.

Mother Goose arranged & ed. by Eulalie Osgood Grover; ill. by Frederick Richardson. The Volland ed. Volland, 1915. ISBN 0-517-43619-1 Subj: Nursery rhymes.

Mother Goose re-arranged & ed. by Eulalie Osgood Grover; ill. by Frederick Richardson. The classic Volland ed. Rand McNally, 1976. Reprint of the 1971 ed. published by Hubbard Press, Northbrook, Ill. ISBN 0-528-88559-6 Subj: Nursery rhymes.

Mother Goose ill. by Gustaf Tenggren. Little, 1940. Subj: Nursery rhymes.

Mother Goose ill. by Tasha Tudor. Walck, 1944. Subj: Caldecott award honor books. Nursery rhymes.

Mother Goose abroad: nursery rhymes (Tucker, Nicholas)

Mother Goose and nursery rhymes ill. by Philip Reed. Regnery/Gateway, 1979, c1963. ISBN 0-8952-6098-0 Subj: Caldecott award honor books. Nursery rhymes.

A Mother Goose book ill. by Joan Walsh Anglund. Harcourt, 1991. ISBN 0-15-200529-3 Subj: Nursery rhymes.

The Mother Goose book ill. by Alice & Martin Provensen. Random House, 1976. ISBN 0-394-92122-4 Subj: Nursery rhymes.

The Mother Goose book ill. by Sonia Roetter. Peter Pauper Pr., 1985, 1946. ISBN 0-8808-8759-1 Subj: Nursery rhymes.

Mother Goose house ill. by Zokeisha; ed. by Kate Klimo. S&S, 1983. ISBN 0-671-46127-3 Subj: Format, unusual – board books. Homes, houses. Nursery rhymes.

Mother Goose in French: Poesies de la vraie Mere Oie trans. by Hugh Latham; ill. by Barbara Cooney. Crowell, 1964. Subj: Foreign languages. Nursery rhymes.

Mother Goose in hieroglyphics ill. by George S. Appleton. Houghton Mifflin, 1962. Reproduction of the 1st ed. published in 1849. ISBN 0-486-20745-5 Subj: Games. Hieroglyphics. Nursery rhymes. Rebuses.

Mother Goose in prose (Baum, L. Frank [Lyman Frank])

Mother Goose in Spanish: Poesias de la Madre Oca trans. by Alastair Reid & Anthony Kerrigan; ill. by Barbara Cooney. Crowell, 1968. Subj: Foreign languages. Nursery rhymes.

Mother Goose melodies intro. & bib. note by E. F. Bleiler; ill. with engravings. Facsimile ed. of the Munroe and Francis c.1833 version. Dover, 1970. ISBN 0-486-22659-X Subj: Nursery rhymes.

Mother Goose nursery rhymes ill. by Arthur Rackham. Watts, 1969. Reprint of the 1913 ed. Subj: Nursery rhymes.

Mother Goose nursery rhymes ill. by Arthur Rackham. Viking, 1975. ISBN 0-670-49003-2 Subj: Nursery rhymes.

Mother Goose remembers ill. by Clare Beaton. Barefoot, 2000. ISBN 1-84148-073-8 Subj: Nursery rhymes.

Mother Goose rhymes ed. by Watty Piper; ill. by Eulalie M. Banks & Lois Lenski. Platt, 1947, 1956. Subj: Nursery rhymes.

The Mother Goose songbook ill. by Jacqueline Sinclair. David & Charles, 1985. ISBN 0-434-92841-0 Subj: Music. Nursery rhymes. Songs.

The Mother Goose treasury ill. by Raymond Briggs. Coward, 1966. ISBN 0-698-20094-2 Subj: Nursery rhymes.

Mother Goose's melodies: or, songs for the nursery ed. by William A. Wheeler. Houghton Mifflin, 189?. Subj: Nursery rhymes. Songs.

Mother Goose's melody: or, sonnets for the cradle. Facsimile of John Newbery's collection of Mother Goose rhymes, reproduced from the earliest known perfect copy of the 1794 printing. Frederic G. Melcher, 1945. Subj: Nursery rhymes.

Mother Goose's nursery rhymes ill. by Allen Atkinson. Knopf, 1984. ISBN 0-394-53699-1 Subj: Nursery rhymes.

Mother Goose's rhymes and melodies ill. by J. L. Webb; music & melodies by E. I. Lane. Cassell, 1888. Subj: Music. Nursery rhymes.

The movable Mother Goose (Sabuda, Robert James)

My first real Mother Goose [board book] ill. by Blanche Fisher Wright. Scholastic, 2000. ISBN 0-439-14671-2 Subj: Format, unusual – board books. Nursery rhymes.

Nursery rhyme book ed. by Andrew Lang; ill. by L. Leslie Brooke. Warne, 1897. Subj: Nursery rhymes.

Nursery rhymes sel. by Marie Gorsline; ill. by Douglas W. Gorsline. Random House, 1977. ISBN 0-394-83550-6 Subj: Nursery rhymes.

Nursery rhymes ill. by Eloise Wilkin. Random House, 1979. ISBN 0-394-94129-8 Subj: Nursery rhymes.

Nursery rhymes from Mother Goose in signed English Prepared under the supervision of the staff of the Pre-School Signed English Project: Barbara M. Kanapell & others. Gallaudet Univ. Pr., 1972. Subj: Handicaps – deafness. Nursery rhymes. Sign language.

Old Mother Hubbard and her dog (Martin, Sarah Catherine)

The old woman in a shoe ill. by Eleanor Wasmuth. S&S, 1986. ISBN 0-671-61728-1 Subj: Format, unusual – board books. Nursery rhymes.

One I love, two I love, and other loving Mother Goose rhymes ill. by Nonny Hogrogian. Dutton, 1972. ISBN 0-525-36420-X Subj: Nursery rhymes.

One misty moisty morning ill. by Mitchell Miller. Farrar, 1971. ISBN 0-374-35647-5 Subj: Nursery rhymes.

1, 2 buckle my shoe ill. by Sherry Neidigh. Publications International, 1997. ISBN 0-7853-2364-3 Subj: Counting, numbers. Format, unusual – toy & movable books. Nursery rhymes.

One, two, buckle my shoe (Williams, Jenny [Jennifer])

One, two, buckle my shoe [board book] ill. by Heather Collins. Kids Can, 1997. ISBN 1-55074-410-0 Subj: Nursery rhymes.

The only true Mother Goose melodies intro. by Edward Everett Hale. Lothrop, 1905. An exact and full-size reproduction of the original edition published and copyrighted in Boston in the year 1833 by Munroe and Francis. Subj: Nursery rhymes.

Over the candlestick: classic nursery rhymes and the real stories behind them (Montgomery, Michael G.)

Over the moon: a book of nursery rhymes ill. by Charlotte Voake. Crown, 1985. ISBN 0-517-55873-4 Subj: Nursery rhymes.

Pat-a-cake adapt. & ill. by Marilyn Janovitz. Walt Disney, 1992. ISBN 1-56282-171-7 Subj: Animals. Birthdays. Music. Nursery rhymes.

Pat-a-cake [board book] ill. by Heather Collins. Kids Can, 2003. ISBN 1-55337-077-5 Subj: Format, unusual – board books. Nursery rhymes.

Pat-a-cake, pat-a-cake ill. by Moira Kemp. Lodestar, 1992. ISBN 0-525-67393-8 Subj: Format, unusual – board books. Games. Nursery rhymes.

People from Mother Goose: a question book (Hopkins, Lee Bennett)

The piper's son ill. by Emily Newton Barto. Longman, 1942. Subj: Nursery rhymes.

A pocket full of posies ill. by Marguerite De Angeli. Doubleday, 1961. First pub. in 1954. Subj: Nursery rhymes.

A pocket full of posies (Gerrard, Roy)

Pussy cat, pussy cat ill. by Ferelith Eccles Williams. David & Charles, 1985. ISBN 0-437-86009-4 Subj: Format, unusual – board books. Nursery rhymes.

Pussycat ate the dumplings: cat rhymes from Mother Goose (Koontz, Robin Michal)

Pussycat, pussycat and other rhymes ed. by Iona Opie; ill. by Rosemary Wells. Candlewick, 1997. ISBN 0-7636-0355-4 Subj: Format, unusual – board books. Nursery rhymes.

The rainbow Mother Goose ed. with an intro. by May Lamberton Becker; ill. by Lili Cassel-Wronker. Collins-World, 1947. Subj: Nursery rhymes.

The real Mother Goose ill. by Blanche Fisher Wright. Rand McNally, 1916. Subj: Nursery rhymes.

The real Mother Goose [board book] ill. by Diane Muldrow. Scholastic, 1998. ISBN 0-590-00368-2 Subj: Format, unusual – board books. Nursery rhymes.

The real Mother Goose clock book ill. by Jane Chambless. Rand McNally, 1984. ISBN 0-528-82329-9 Subj: Clocks, watches. Nursery rhymes. Time.

Richard Scarry's best Mother Goose ever ill. by Richard Scarry. Golden Pr., 1970. ISBN 0-307-15578-1 Subj: Nursery rhymes.

Richard Scarry's favorite Mother Goose rhymes ill. by Richard Scarry. Golden Pr., 1964. Subj: Nursery rhymes.

Ride a cockhorse: animal rhymes for young children (Williams, Jenny [Jennifer])

Ride a cock-horse (Williams, Sarah)

Rimes de la Mere Oie: Mother Goose rhymes rendered into French by Ormonde De Kay, Jr.; ill. by Seymour Chwast, Milton Glaser, & Barry Zaid. Little, 1971. Subj: Foreign languages. Nursery rhymes.

Ring around a rosy: action rhymes for young children (Williams, Jenny [Jennifer])

Ring o' roses ill. by L. Leslie Brooke. Warne, 1923. ISBN 0-7232-1980-X Subj: Nursery rhymes.

Rock-a-bye baby [board book] ill. by Heather Collins. Kids Can, 2000. ISBN 1-55074-572-7 Subj: Format, unusual – board books. Nursery rhymes.

The Sesame Street players present Mother Goose: featuring Jim Henson's Sesame Street Muppets ill. by Michael J. Smollin. Random House, 1982. ISBN 0-394-95223-5 Subj: Nursery rhymes. Puppets.

Sing a song of Mother Goose ill. by Barbara Reid. North Winds, 1987. ISBN 0-590-71781-2 Subj: Nursery rhymes.

Sing a song of sixpence comp. & ill. by Randolph Caldecott. Barron's, 1988. Reprint of 1888 ed. ISBN 0-8120-5900-X Subj: Nursery rhymes.

Sing a song of sixpence ill. by Randolph Caldecott. New ed. Hart, 1977. Reprint of orig. Warne pub. between 1876 and 1886. ISBN 0-8055-0359-5 Subj: Nursery rhymes.

Sing a song of sixpence ill. by Margaret Chamberlain. Peter Bedrick, 1984. ISBN 0-911745-29-7 Subj: Format, unusual – board books. Nursery rhymes.

Sing a song of sixpence ill. by Leonard B. Lubin. Lothrop, 1987. ISBN 0-688-00545-4 Subj: Nursery rhymes. Royalty.

Sing a song of sixpence ed. by Kate Klimo; ill. by Ray Marshall & Korky Paul. S&S, 1983. ISBN 0-671-46237-7 Subj: Format, unusual – toy & movable books. Nursery rhymes.

Sing a song of sixpence ill. by Ferelith Eccles Williams. David & Charles, 1985. ISBN 0-437-86002-7 Subj: Format, unusual – board books. Nursery rhymes.

Sing hey, diddle, diddle: 66 nursery rhymes with their traditional tunes comp. by Beatrice Harrop; ill. by Frank Francis & Bernard Cheese. Sterling, 1983. ISBN 0-7136-2334-9 Subj: Music. Nursery rhymes.

Songs for Mother Goose ill. by Maginel Wright Enright Barney; set to music by Sidney Homer. Macmillan, 1920. Subj: Nursery rhymes.

The tall Mother Goose ill. by Feodor Rojankovsky. HarperCollins, 1942. Subj: Nursery rhymes.

Thirty old-time nursery songs ed. by Joseph Moorat; ill. by Paul Woodroffe. Norton, 1980. Orig. pub. in 1912. ISBN 0-500-01242-3 Subj: Music. Nursery rhymes. Songs.

This little pig: a Mother Goose favorite ill. by Leonard B. Lubin. Lothrop, 1985. ISBN 0-688-04089-6 Subj: Animals – pigs. Nursery rhymes.

This little pig ill. by Eleanor Wasmuth. S&S, 1986. ISBN 0-671-61727-3 Subj: Format, unusual – board books. Nursery rhymes.

This little pig went to market ill. by L. Leslie Brooke. Warne, 1922. Subj: Animals – pigs. Nursery rhymes.

This little pig went to market ill. by Denise Fleming. Random House, 1985. ISBN 0-394-87030-1 Subj: Format, unusual – toy & movable books. Nursery rhymes.

This little pig went to market ill. by Ferelith Eccles Williams. David & Charles, 1985. ISBN 0-437-86004-3 Subj: Format, unusual – board books. Games. Nursery rhymes.

This little piggy ill. by Moira Kemp. Lodestar, 1993. ISBN 0-525-67446-2 Subj: Animals – pigs. Format, unusual – board books. Nursery rhymes.

This little piggy [board book] ill. by Heather Collins. Kids Can, 1997. ISBN 1-55074-404-6 Subj: Format, unusual – board books. Nursery rhymes.

The three jovial huntsmen ill. by Susan Jeffers. Bradbury, 1973. ISBN 0-8788-8023-2 Subj: Caldecott award honor books. Nursery rhymes.

Three little kittens (Siomades, Lorianne)

The three little kittens ill. by Lorinda Bryan Cauley. Putnam, 1982. ISBN 0-399-20855-0 Subj: Animals – cats. Behavior – lost & found possessions. Clothing – gloves, mittens. Games. Nursery rhymes.

The three little kittens ill. by Paul Galdone. Clarion, 1986. ISBN 0-89919-426-5 Subj: Animals – cats. Behavior – lost & found possessions. Clothing – gloves, mittens. Nursery rhymes.

The three little kittens ill. by Dorothy Stott. Putnam, 1984. ISBN 0-448-10216-1 Subj: Animals – cats. Behavior – lost & found possessions. Clothing – gloves, mittens. Format, unusual – board books. Nursery rhymes.

The three little kittens adapt. by Jean Marzollo; ill. by Shelley Thornton. Scholastic, 1986. ISBN 0-590-33370-4 Subj: Animals – cats. Behavior – lost & found possessions. Clothing – gloves, mittens. Games. Nursery rhymes.

To market! To market! ill. by Emma Lillian Brock. Knopf, 1930. Subj: Nursery rhymes. Shopping.

To market! To market! ill. by Peter Spier. Doubleday, 1989, c1967. ISBN 0-385-05352-5 Subj: Nursery rhymes.

Tom, Tom the piper's son ill. by Paul Galdone. McGraw-Hill, 1964. Subj: Nursery rhymes.

Tomie de Paola's Mother Goose (De Paola, Tomie [Thomas Anthony])

Twenty nursery rhymes ill. by Philip Van Aver. Grabhorn-Hoyem, 1970. Subj: Nursery rhymes.

Vernon Grant's Mother Goose ill. by Vernon Grant. Abrams, 1998. ISBN 0-8109-4128-7 Subj: Nursery rhymes.

Wee Willie Winkie and other nursery rhymes (Cousins, Lucy)

Wee Willie Winkie and other rhymes ed. by Iona Opie; ill. by Rosemary Wells. Candlewick, 1997. ISBN 0-7636-0356-2 Subj: Format, unusual – board books. Nursery rhymes.

Wee willie winkie [board book] ill. by Heather Collins. Kids Can, 2000. ISBN 1-55074-568-9 Subj: Format, unusual – board books. Nursery rhymes.

Wendy Watson's Mother Goose ill. by Wendy Watson. Lothrop, 1989. ISBN 0-688-05708-X Subj: Nursery rhymes.

Will Moses Mother Goose ill. by Will Moses. Philomel, 2003. ISBN 0-399-23744-5 Subj: Nursery rhymes.

Willy Pogány's Mother Goose (1928) ill. by Willy Pogany. Nelson, 1928. Subj: Nursery rhymes.

Willy Pogány's Mother Goose (2000) ill. by Willy Pogány. Reproduction of the 1928 edition. SeaStar, 2000. ISBN 1-58717-026-4 Subj: Nursery rhymes.

Motomora, Mitchell. *Specs: the true story of baseball player George Toporcer* ill. by Nina Barbaresi. Raintree, 1990. ISBN 0-8172-3585-X Subj: Glasses. Sports – baseball.

Mott, Evelyn Clarke. *Balloon ride* ill. by author. Walker, 1991. ISBN 0-8027-8126-8 Subj: Activities – ballooning.

Cool cat ill. by author. Random House, 1996. ISBN 0-679-86956-5 Subj: Animals – cats. Format, unusual – board books. Rhyming text.

Dancing rainbows: a Pueblo boy's story photos by author. Cobblehill, 1996. ISBN 0-525-65216-7 Subj: Fairs, festivals. Family life – grandfathers. Food. Indians of North America – Twa.

Hot dog ill. by author. Random House, 1996. ISBN 0-679-86955-7 Subj: Animals – dogs. Format, unusual – board books. Pets. Rhyming text.

Steam train ride ill. by author. Walker, 1991. ISBN 0-8027-6996-9 Subj: Trains.

Motyka, Sally Mitchell. *An ordinary day* ill. by Donna Ayers. S&S, 1989. ISBN 0-671-67118-9 Subj: Activities. Family life.

Mould, Wendy. *Ants in my pants* ill. by author. Clarion, 2001. ISBN 0-618-09640-X Subj: Clothing. Humorous stories. Imagination.

Mouse house ed. by Kate Klimo; ill. by Zokeisha. S&S, 1983. ISBN 0-671-46129-X Subj: Animals – mice. Format, unusual – board books. Homes, houses.

The moving adventures of Old Dame Trot and her comical cat ill. by Paul Galdone. McGraw-Hill, 1973. ISBN 0-07-022692-X Subj: Animals – cats. Nursery rhymes.

Mower, Nancy. *I visit my Tūtū and Grandma* ill. by Patricia A. Wozniak. Press Pacifica, 1984. ISBN 0-916630-41-2 Subj: Family life – grandmothers. Hawaii.

Moxley, Sheila. *ABCD an alphabet book of cats and dogs* ill. by author. Little, 2001. ISBN 0-316-59240-4 Subj: ABC books. Animals – cats. Animals – dogs.

Moxley, Susan. *Abdul's treasure* ill. by author. David & Charles, 1988. ISBN 0-340-38918-4 Subj: Careers – fishermen. Folk & fairy tales. Royalty.

Moyer, Marshall M. *Rollo Bones, canine hypnotist* ill. by author. Tricycle, 1998. ISBN 1-883672-65-1 Subj: Animals – dogs. Behavior – running away.

Mozelle, Shirley. *The pig is in the pantry, the cat is on the shelf* ill. by Jennifer Plecas. Clarion, 2000. ISBN 0-395-78627-4 Subj: Animals. Behavior – misbehavior. Farms. Homes, houses. Pets.

Mozley, Charles. *The first book of tales of ancient Araby* (Arabian Nights)

Mudd-Ruth, Maria. *The beetle* ill. by Wendy Smith-Griswold. Stewart, Tabori & Chang, 1992. ISBN 1-55670-255-8 Subj: Format, unusual – toy & movable books. Insects – beetles.

The ultimate ocean book ill. by Virge Kask & Beverly E. Benner. Artists & Writers Guild, 1995. ISBN 0-307-17628-2 Subj: Animals. Fish. Format, unusual – toy & movable books. Sea & seashore.

Mude, O. *see* Gorey, Edward (St. John)

Mueller, Doris L. *Small One's adventure* ill. by Parker Fulton. All About Kids, 2003. ISBN 0-9710278-1-1 Subj: Animals – elephants. Behavior – growing up. Concepts – size. Self-concept.

Mueller, Evelyn. *I'm deaf and it's okay* (Aseltine, Lorraine)

Mueller, Virginia. *A Halloween mask for Monster* ill. by Lynn Munsinger. A. Whitman, 1986. ISBN 0-8075-3134-0 Subj: Holidays – Halloween. Masks. Monsters.

In the morning ill. by Diane Jaquith. Houghton Mifflin, 1991. ISBN 0-395-55018-1 Subj: Birds – chickens. Morning.

Monster and the baby ill. by Lynn Munsinger. A. Whitman, 1985. ISBN 0-8075-5253-4 Subj: Activities – babysitting. Babies. Monsters.

Monster can't sleep ill. by Lynn Munsinger. A. Whitman, 1986. ISBN 0-8075-5261-5 Subj: Bedtime. Monsters. Sleep.

Monster goes to school ill. by Lynn Munsinger. A. Whitman, 1991. ISBN 0-8075-5264-X Subj: Clocks, watches. Monsters. School. Time.

Monster's birthday hiccups ill. by Lynn Munsinger. A. Whitman, 1991. ISBN 0-8075-5267-4 Subj: Birthdays. Hiccups. Monsters. Parties.

A playhouse for Monster ill. by Lynn Munsinger. A. Whitman, 1985. ISBN 0-8075-6541-5 Subj: Activities – playing. Monsters.

Mühlberger, Richard. *The Christmas story* (The Christmas story)

Müller, Birte. *Finn cooks* ill. by author; trans. by J. Alison James. North-South, 2004. ISBN 0-7358-1936-X Subj: Activities – baking, cooking. Family life – mothers. Food. Health & fitness.

Muller, Gerda. *Around the oak* ill. by author. Dutton, 1994. ISBN 0-525-45239-7 Subj: Careers – park rangers. Forest, woods. Seasons. Trees.

Circle of seasons ill. by author. Dutton, 1995. ISBN 0-525-45394-6 Subj: Seasons.

The garden in the city ill. by author. Dutton, 1992. ISBN 0-525-44697-4 Subj: Cities, towns. Gardens, gardening.

Muller, Robin. *Badger's new house* ill. by author. Holt, 2002. ISBN 0-8050-6383-8 Subj: Animals – badgers. Animals – mice. Homes, houses.

Hickory, dickory, dock (Mother Goose)

Little Wonder ill. by author. North Winds, 1994. ISBN 0-590-24225-3 Subj: Animals – dogs.

The lucky old woman. Kids Can, 1987. ISBN 0-921103-07-7 Subj: Folk & fairy tales.

The magic paintbrush ill. by author. Viking, 1990. ISBN 0-670-83167-0 Subj: Activities – painting. Behavior – greed. Magic. Royalty – kings.

Mollie Whuppie and the giant ill. by reteller. Scholastic, 1993. ISBN 0-590-74036-9 Subj: Behavior – trickery. Folk & fairy tales. Foreign lands – England. Giants.

The sorcerer's apprentice ill. by author. Silver Burdett, 1986. ISBN 0-382-09382-8 Subj: Folk & fairy tales. Magic. Royalty.

Mullins, Edward S. *Animal limericks* ill. by author. Follett, 1966. Subj: Animals. Poetry.

Mullins, Patricia. *Dinosaur encore* ill. by author. HarperCollins, 1993. ISBN 0-06-021073-7 Subj: Dinosaurs. Format, unusual – toy & movable books. Prehistory.

One horse waiting for me ill. by author. S&S, 1998. ISBN 0-689-81381-3 Subj: Animals – horses, ponies. Counting, numbers.

The Sea-Breeze Hotel (Vaughan, Marcia Kapok)

V for vanishing: an alphabet of endangered animals ill. by author. HarperCollins, 1994. ISBN 0-06-023557-8 Subj: ABC books. Animals – endangered animals.

Munari, Bruno. *ABC* ill. by author. Collins-World, 1960. Subj: ABC books.

Animals for sale ill. by author. W. Collins, 1980, c1959. ISBN 0-529-05567-8 Subj: Animals.

The birthday present ill. by author. Collins, 1980, c1959. ISBN 0-529-05565-1 Subj: Birthdays. Games. Transportation.

Bruno Munari's zoo ill. by author. Collins-World, 1963. Subj: Animals. Birds. Zoos.

The circus in the mist ill. by author. Collins, 1968. Subj: Circus. Format, unusual. Weather – fog.

The elephant's wish ill. by author. Collins, 1959. First pub. in 1945. ISBN 0-529-05562-7 Subj: Animals. Behavior – wishing. Format, unusual – toy & movable books.

Jimmy has lost his cap ill. by author. Collins, 1980, c1959. ISBN 0-529-05563-5 Subj: Behavior – lost & found possessions. Format, unusual – toy & movable books.

Tic, Tac and Toc ill. by author. Collins-World, 1980, c1957. ISBN 0-529-05564-3 Subj: Birds. Format, unusual – toy & movable books.

Who's there? Open the door trans. by Maria Cimino; ill. by author. Collins-World, 1980, c1957. ISBN 0-529-05568-6 Subj: Animals. Format, unusual – toy & movable books.

Munro, Roxie. *Christmastime in New York City* ill. by author. Dodd, 1987. ISBN 0-396-08909-7 Subj: Cities, towns. Holidays – Christmas.

The inside-outside book of libraries ill. by author; text by Julie Cummins. Dutton, 1996. ISBN 0-525-45608-2 Subj: Libraries.

The inside-outside book of London ill. by author. Dutton, 1989. ISBN 0-525-44522-6 Subj: Cities, towns. Foreign lands – England.

The inside-outside book of New York City ill. by author. Dodd, 1985. ISBN 0-396-08513-X Subj: Cities, towns.

The inside-outside book of Paris ill. by author. Dutton, 1992. ISBN 0-525-44863-2 Subj: Cities, towns. Foreign lands – France.

The inside-outside book of Texas ill. by author. SeaStar, 2001. Subj: Activities – traveling. Cities, towns. Country. Cowboys, cowgirls. Museums. Texas. U.S. history.

The inside-outside book of Washington, D.C. ill. by author. Dutton, 1987. ISBN 0-525-44298-7 Subj: Activities – traveling. Cities, towns. Museums.

Mazescapes ill. by author. SeaStar, 2001. ISBN 1-58717-060-4 Subj: Activities – traveling. Cities, towns. Country. Games. Mazes. Picture puzzles.

Munsch, Robert N. *Aaron's hair* ill. by Alan & Lea Daniel. Scholastic, 2000. ISBN 0-439-19258-7 Subj: Behavior – running away. Emotions. Hair.

Alligator baby ill. by Michael Martchenko. Scholastic, 1997. ISBN 0-590-21101-3 Subj: Animals. Babies. Family life – brothers & sisters. Family life – new sibling. Zoos.

Andrew's loose tooth ill. by Michael Martchenko. Scholastic, 1998. ISBN 0-590-21102-1 Subj: Behavior – growing up. Fairies. Teeth.

Angela's airplane ill. by Michael Martchenko. Firefly, 1988. ISBN 1-55037-027-8 Subj: Activities – flying. Airplanes, airports. Behavior – misbehavior.

David's father ill. by Michael Martchenko. Firefly, 1983. ISBN 0-920236-62-6 Subj: Character traits – kindness. Giants.

The fire station ill. by Michael Martchenko. Firefly, 1991. ISBN 1-55037-170-3 Subj: Careers – firefighters.

From far away by Robert Munsch & Saoussan Askar; ill. by Michael Martchenko. Firefly, 1995. ISBN 1-55037-397-8 Subj: Foreign lands – Canada. Foreign lands – Lebanon. Moving. Names. School. War.

Get me another one! ill. by Shawn Steffler. Doubleday Canada, 1992. ISBN 0-385-25337-0 Subj: Family life – fathers. Foreign lands – Canada. Sports – fishing.

Get out of bed! ill. by Alan Daniel. Scholastic, 1998. ISBN 0-590-21103-X Subj: School. Sleep.

Good families don't ill. by Alan Daniel. Doubleday Canada, 1990. ISBN 0-385-25267-6 Subj: Anatomy. Behavior – misbehavior. Etiquette. Family life. Foreign lands – Canada.

I have to go! ill. by Michael Martchenko. Firefly, 1987. ISBN 0-920303-77-3 Subj: Behavior – growing up. Family life.

Jonathan cleaned up – then he heard a sound: or, blackberry subway jam ill. by Michael Martchenko. Firefly, 1981. ISBN 0-920236-22-7 Subj: Machines. Problem solving. Trains.

Love you forever ill. by Sheila McGraw. Firefly, 1994, 1986. ISBN 0-920668-36-4 Subj: Emotions – love. Family life – mothers. Foreign lands – Canada.

Makeup mess ill. by Michael Martchenko. Scholastic, 2001. ISBN 0-439-18771-0 Subj: Beauty shops. Character traits – appearance. Self-concept.

Millicent and the wind ill. by Suzanne Duranceau. Firefly, 1984. ISBN 0-920236-98-7 Subj: Behavior – needing someone. Behavior – wishing. Friendship. Weather – wind.

Mmm, cookies! ill. by Michael Martchenko. Scholastic, 2000. ISBN 0-590-89603-2 Subj: Behavior – trickery. Family life. Food. School.

Moira's birthday ill. by Michael Martchenko. Firefly, 1987. ISBN 0-920303-85-4 Subj: Behavior – misbehavior. Birthdays. Parties.

More pies ill. by Michael Martchenko. Cartwheel, 2002. ISBN 0-439-18773-7 Subj: Contests. Food.

Mortimer ill. by Michael Martchenko. Firefly, 1985. ISBN 0-920303-12-9 Subj: Bedtime. Noise, sounds. Songs.

Mud puddle ill. by author. Firefly, 1982. ISBN 0-920236-47-2 Subj: Activities – playing. Character traits – cleanliness. Foreign lands – Canada. Weather – rain.

Murmel, Murmel, Murmel ill. by Michael Martchenko. Firefly, 1982. ISBN 0-920236-33-2 Subj: Foreign lands – Canada. Friendship.

The paper bag princess ill. by Michael Martchenko. Firefly, 1980. ISBN 0-920236-82-0 Subj: Character traits – appearance. Dragons.

Pigs ill. by Michael Martchenko. Firefly, 1989. ISBN 1-550370-39-1 Subj: Animals – pigs.

A promise is a promise by Robert N. Munsch & Michael Kusugak; ill. by Vladyana Krykorka. Firefly, 1988. ISBN 1-55037-009-X Subj: Eskimos. Folk & fairy tales. Foreign lands – Canada. Sea & seashore.

Purple, green and yellow ill. by Hélène Desputeaux. Firefly, 1992. ISBN 1-55037-255-6 Subj: Concepts – color.

Ribbon rescue ill. by Eugenie Fernandes. Scholastic, 1999. ISBN 0-590-89012-3 Subj: Character traits – generosity. Clothing – dresses. Weddings.

Show-and-tell ill. by Michael Martchenko. Firefly, 1991. ISBN 1-55037-195-9 Subj: School.

Something good ill. by Michael Martchenko. Firefly, 1990. ISBN 1-55037-099-5 Subj: Family life – fathers. Shopping. Stores.

Stephanie's ponytail ill. by Michael Martchenko. Firefly, 1996. ISBN 1-55037-485-0 Subj: Behavior – imitation. Character traits – appearance. Cumulative tales. Hair. School.

Thomas' snowsuit ill. by Michael Martchenko. Firefly, 1985. ISBN 0-920303-32-3 Subj: Careers – teachers. Clothing. Foreign lands – Canada. School. Seasons – winter. Weather – snow.

Up, up, down! ill. by Michael Martchenko. Scholastic, 2001. ISBN 0-439-18770-2 Subj: Activities. Trees.

Wait and see ill. by Michael Martchenko. Firefly, 1993. ISBN 1-55037-335-8 Subj: Behavior – wishing. Birthdays. Foreign lands – Canada. Friendship.

We share everything! ill. by Michael Martchenko. Scholastic, 1999. ISBN 0-590-89600-8 Subj: Behavior – sharing. School.

Where is Gah-Ning? ill. by Hélène Desputeaux. Annick, 1994. ISBN 1-55037-982-8 Subj: Family life – fathers. Foreign lands – Canada. Shopping. Toys – balloons.

Zoom ill. by Michael Martchenko. Cartwheel, 2003. ISBN 0-439-18774-5 Subj: Concepts – speed. Handicaps – physical handicaps.

Munson, Derek. *Enemy pie* ill. by Tara Calahan King. Chronicle, 2000. ISBN 0-8118-2778-X Subj: Family life – fathers. Food. Friendship.

Munsterberg, Peggy. *Beastly banquet: tasty treats for animal appetites* ill. by Tracy Gallup. Dial, 1997. ISBN 0-8037-1482-3 Subj: Animals. Food. Poetry.

Muntean, Michaela. *Alligator's garden* ill. by Nicole Rubel. Dial, 1984. ISBN 0-8037-0025-3 Subj: Gardens, gardening. Reptiles – alligators, crocodiles.

Bicycle bear ill. by Doug Cushman. Parents' Magazine Pr., 1983. ISBN 0-8193-1103-0 Subj: Animals – bears. Rhyming text. Sports – bicycling.

Bicycle Bear rides again ill. by Doug Cushman. G. Stevens, 1995. ISBN 0-8368-0964-5 Subj: Animals – bears. Family life – aunts, uncles. Rhyming text. Sports – bicycling.

The house that bear built ill. by Nicole Rubel. Dial, 1984. ISBN 0-8037-0026-1 Subj: Animals – bears. Homes, houses.

Kermit and Robin's scary story ill. by Tom Leigh. Viking, 1995. ISBN 0-670-86106-5 Subj: Bedtime. Careers – writers. Family life – aunts, uncles. Frogs & toads. Puppets.

Mokey and the festival of the bells ill. by Michael Adams. Holt, 1985. ISBN 0-03-004553-3 Subj: Character traits – generosity. Puppets.

Muppet babies through the year ill. by Bruce McNally. Random House, 1984. ISBN 0-394-86544-8 Subj: Puppets. Seasons.

The very bumpy bus ride ill. by Bernard Wiseman. G. Stevens, 1993. ISBN 0-8368-0980-7 Subj: Buses. Fairs, festivals.

Munthe, Adam John. *I believe in unicorns* ill. by Elizabeth Falconer. Merrimack, 1980. ISBN 0-7011-2437-7 Subj: Emotions – loneliness. Mythical creatures – unicorns.

The Muppet Show book ill. by Tudor Banus. Abrams, 1978. ISBN 0-8109-1328-3 Subj: Puppets.

Murawski, Darlyne A. *Bug faces* ill. with photos. National Geographic, 2000. ISBN 0-7922-7557-8 Subj: Insects. Spiders.

Murdocca, Sal (Salvatore). *Baby wants the moon* ill. by author. Lothrop, 1994. ISBN 0-688-13665-6 Subj: Babies. Family life – brothers & sisters. Family life – new sibling.

Christmas bear ill. by author. S&S, 1987. ISBN 0-671-64565-X Subj: Animals – bears. Holidays – Christmas. Santa Claus.

Lucy takes a holiday ill. by author. Mondo, 1998. ISBN 1-57255-560-2 Subj: Activities – vacationing. Animals – dogs.

Tuttle's shell ill. by author. Mondo, 1999. ISBN 1-57255-643-9 Subj: Animals. Behavior – lost & found possessions. Reptiles – turtles, tortoises.

Murdock, Laurette. *Someone is talking about Hortense* ill. by James Marshall. Houghton, 1975. ISBN 0-618-07318-3 Subj: Animals. Behavior – secrets. Birthdays. Emotions. Parties.

Murkoff, Heidi Eisenberg. *What to expect at a play date* ill. by Laura Rader. HarperFestival, 2001. ISBN 0-694-01330-7 Subj: Activities – playing. Behavior. Friendship.

What to expect at preschool ill. by Laura Rader. HarperFestival, 2001. ISBN 0-694-01326-9 Subj: Activities. Friendship. School – nursery.

What to expect when the new baby comes home ill. by Laura Rader. HarperFestival, 2001. ISBN 0-694-01327-7 Subj: Babies. Family life – brothers & sisters. Family life – new sibling.

What to expect when you go to the dentist ill. by Laura Rader. HarperFestival, 2002. ISBN 0-694-01328-5 Subj: Careers – dentists. Health & fitness. Teeth.

What to expect when you go to the doctor ill. by Laura Rader. HarperFestival, 2000. ISBN 0-694-01324-2 Subj: Careers – doctors. Health & fitness.

Murphey, Sara. *The animal hat shop* reading consultant: Morton Botel; ill. by Mel Pekarsky. Follett, 1964. Subj: Animals – cats. Birds – chickens. Clothing – hats.

The roly poly cookie reading consultant: Morton Botel; ill. by Leonard W. Shortall. Follett, 1963. Subj: Cumulative tales. Food.

Murphy, Andy. *Out and about at the dairy farm* ill. by Anne McMullen. Picture Window, 2003. ISBN 1-4048-0038-7 Subj: Animals – bulls, cows. Farms. Machines. School – field trips.

Murphy, Camay Calloway. *Can a coal scuttle fly?* (Miller, Thomas Patton)

Murphy, Chuck. *Black cat, white cat: a pop up book of opposites* ill. by author. Little Simon, 1998. ISBN 0-689-81415-1 Subj: Animals – cats. Concepts – opposites. Format, unusual – toy & movable books.

Chuck Murphy's alphabet magic ill. by author. Little Simon, 1997. ISBN 0-689-81286-8 Subj: ABC books. Format, unusual – toy & movable books.

Colors ill. by author. Little Simon, 1997. ISBN 0-689-81497-6 Subj: Concepts – color. Format, unusual – board books.

Murphy, Elspeth Campbell. *Do you see me God? prayers for young children* ill. by Bill Duca. David C. Cook, 1989. ISBN 1-55513-457-2 Subj: Poetry. Religion.

Happy Easter, God ill. by Jim Lewis. Bethany Backyard, 2001. ISBN 0-7642-2386-0 Subj: Holidays – Easter. Poetry. Religion.

Murphy, Jill. *All for one* ill. by author. Candlewick, 1999. ISBN 0-7636-0785-1 Subj: Activities – playing. Friendship. Monsters.

All in one piece ill. by author. Putnam, 1987. ISBN 0-399-21433-X Subj: Animals – elephants. Behavior – misbehavior. Family life.

Five minutes' peace ill. by author. Putnam, 1986. ISBN 0-399-21354-6 Subj: Animals – elephants. Family life.

The last noo-noo ill. by author. Candlewick, 1995. ISBN 1-56402-581-0 Subj: Babies. Behavior – growing up. Family life. Monsters.

Peace at last ill. by author. Dial, 1980. ISBN 0-8037-6758-7 Subj: Animals – bears. Noise, sounds. Sleep.

A piece of cake ill. by author. Candlewick, 1997. ISBN 0-7636-0572-7 Subj: Animals – elephants. Food. Self-concept.

A quiet night in ill. by author. Candlewick, 1994. ISBN 1-56402-248-X Subj: Animals – elephants. Bedtime. Family life.

What next, baby bear! ill. by author. Dial, 1984. ISBN 0-8037-0027-X Subj: Animals – bears. Bedtime. Imagination. Night. Space & space ships.

Murphy, Jim. *Backyard bear* ill. by Jeffrey Greene. Scholastic, 1993. ISBN 0-590-44375-5 Subj: Animals – bears. Night.

The call of the wolves ill. by Mark Alan Weatherby. Scholastic, 1989. ISBN 0-590-41941-2 Subj: Animals – wolves.

Dinosaur for a day ill. by Mark Alan Weatherby. Scholastic, 1992. ISBN 0-590-42866-7 Subj: Dinosaurs. Prehistory.

Murphy, Kelly. *The boll weevil ball* ill. by author. Holt, 2002. ISBN 0-8050-6712-4 Subj: Activities – dancing. Concepts – size. Insects – beetles.

Murphy, Mary. *The Alphabet Keeper* ill. by author. Knopf, 2003. ISBN 0-375-92347-0 Subj: ABC books. Character traits – freedom.

Caterpillar's wish ill. by author. DK, 1999. ISBN 0-7894-2593-9 Subj: Behavior – wishing. Insects – butterflies, caterpillars. Metamorphosis.

Here comes spring, and summer and fall and winter ill. by author. DK, 1999. ISBN 0-7894-3484-9 Subj: Animals – dogs. Seasons.

How kind ill. by author. Candlewick, 2002. ISBN 0-7636-1732-6 Subj: Animals. Character traits – kindness. Circular tales. Farms.

I feel happy, and sad, and angry, and glad ill. by author. DK, 2000. ISBN 0-7894-2680-3 Subj: Animals – dogs. Emotions.

I like it when . . . ill. by author. Harcourt, 1997. ISBN 0-15-200039-9 Subj: Activities. Birds – penguins. Family life – parents.

I like it when . . . ill. by author. Harcourt, 1997. ISBN 0-15-205649-1 Subj: Activities. Birds – penguins. Family life – parents. Format, unusual – board books.

Koala and the flower ill. by author. Roaring Brook, 2002. ISBN 0-7613-2674-X Subj: Animals. Animals – koalas. Character traits – curiosity. Character traits – questioning. Flowers. Libraries.

My puffer train ill. by author. Houghton Mifflin, 1999. ISBN 0-395-97105-5 Subj: Animals. Birds – penguins. Noise, sounds. Rhyming text. Trains.

Please be quiet! ill. by author. Houghton Mifflin, 1999. ISBN 0-395-97113-6 Subj: Birds – penguins. Family life – mothers. Noise, sounds.

Some things change ill. by author. Houghton, 2001. ISBN 0-618-00334-7 Subj: Activities. Birds – penguins. Concepts – change. Toys – bears.

You smell and taste and feel and see and hear ill. by author. DK, 1997. ISBN 0-7894-2471-1 Subj: Animals – dogs. Senses.

Murphy, Pat. *Pigasus* ill. by Graham Percy. Dial, 1996. ISBN 0-8037-1588-9 Subj: Activities – flying. Animals – pigs. Behavior – stealing. Birds – blackbirds. Character traits – being different.

Murphy, Patricia J. *Canada Day* ill. with photos. Childrens Pr., 2002. ISBN 0-516-22662-2 Subj: Foreign lands – Canada. Holidays – Canada Day.

Murphy, Patti Beling. *Elinor and Violet* ill. by author. Little, 2003. ISBN 0-316-91034-1 Subj: Behavior – misbehavior. Birds – chickens. Family life – grandmothers. Friendship. Sea & seashore – beaches.

Murphy, Shirley Rousseau. *Tattie's river journey* ill. by Tomie de Paola. Dial, 1983. ISBN 0-8037-8770-7 Subj: Homes, houses. Rivers. Weather – rain.

Valentine for a dragon ill. by Kay Chorao. Atheneum, 1984. ISBN 0-689-31016-1 Subj: Dragons. Emotions – loneliness. Holidays – Valentine's Day. Monsters.

Wind child ill. by Leo & Diane Dillon. HarperCollins, 1999. ISBN 0-06-024904-8 Subj: Activities – weaving. Folk & fairy tales. Royalty – princes. Weather – wind.

Murphy, Stuart J. *Animals on board* ill. by R. W. Alley. HarperCollins, 1998. ISBN 0-06-027443-3 Subj: Animals. Counting, numbers. Merry-go-rounds. Rhyming text.

Beep beep, vroom vroom! ill. by Chris Demarest. HarperCollins, 2000. ISBN 0-06-028017-4 Subj: Automobiles. Counting, numbers.

The best bug parade ill. by Holly Keller. HarperCollins, 1996. ISBN 0-06-025872-1 Subj: Counting, numbers. Insects.

The best vacation ever ill. by Nadine Bernard Westcott. HarperCollins, 1997. ISBN 0-06-026767-4 Subj: Activities – vacationing. Family life. Problem solving. Rhyming text.

Betcha! ill. by S. D. Schindler. HarperCollins, 1997. ISBN 0-06-026769-0 Subj: Counting, numbers. Friendship.

Bigger, better, best ill. by Marsha Winborn. HarperCollins, 2002. ISBN 0-06-028919-8 Subj: Concepts – measurement. Concepts – size.

Bug dance ill. by Christopher Santoro. HarperCollins, 2002. ISBN 0-06-446252-8 Subj: Counting, numbers. Insects.

Captain Invincible and the space shapes ill. by Rémy Simard. HarperCollins, 2001. ISBN 0-06-028023-9 Subj: Concepts – shape. Counting, numbers.

Circus shapes ill. by Edward Miller. HarperCollins, 1998. ISBN 0-06-027437-9 Subj: Circus. Concepts – shape. Rhyming text.

Dave's down-to-earth rock shop ill. by Cat Bowman Smith. HarperCollins, 2000. ISBN 0-06-028019-0 Subj: Counting, numbers.

Dinosaur deals ill. by Kevin O'Malley. HarperCollins, 2001. ISBN 0-06-028927-9 Subj: Activities – trading. Counting, numbers. Dinosaurs.

Earth Day – hooray! ill. by Renée Andriani. HarperCollins, 2004. ISBN 0-06-000127-5 Subj: Counting, numbers. Ecology. Holidays.

Elevator magic ill. by G. Brian Karas. HarperCollins, 1997. ISBN 0-06-446709-0 Subj: Counting, numbers. Elevators, escalators. Rhyming text.

Every buddy counts ill. by Fiona Dunbar. HarperCollins, 1997. ISBN 0-06-026773-9 Subj: Counting, numbers. Rhyming text.

A fair bear share ill. by John Speirs. HarperCollins, 1998. ISBN 0-06-446714-7 Subj: Activities – baking, cooking. Animals – bears. Counting, numbers. Food.

Game time ill. by Cynthia Jabar. HarperCollins, 2000. ISBN 0-06-028025-5 Subj: Clocks, watches. Sports – soccer. Time.

Get up and go! ill. by Diane Greenseid. HarperCollins, 1996. ISBN 0-06-025882-9 Subj: Animals – dogs. Morning. Rhyming text. School. Time.

Give me half! ill. by G. Brian Karas. HarperCollins, 1996. ISBN 0-06-025874-8 Subj: Behavior – sharing. Counting, numbers. Friendship. Sibling rivalry.

The greatest gymnast of all ill. by Cynthia Jabar. HarperCollins, 1998. ISBN 0-06-027609-6 Subj: Concepts. Counting, numbers.

Henry the fourth ill. by Scott Nash. HarperCollins, 1999. ISBN 0-06-027611-8 Subj: Animals – dogs. Counting, numbers.

Just enough carrots ill. by Frank Remkiewicz. HarperCollins, 1997. ISBN 0-06-026779-8 Subj: Animals – rabbits. Counting, numbers. Food. Shopping. Stores.

Let's fly a kite ill. by Brian Floca. HarperCollins, 2000. ISBN 0-06-028035-2 Subj: Behavior – sharing. Concepts. Kites.

Missing mittens ill. by G. Brian Karas. HarperCollins, 2001. ISBN 0-06-028027-1 Subj: Concepts. Counting, numbers.

Monster musical chairs ill. by Scott Nash. HarperCollins, 2000. ISBN 0-06-028021-2 Subj: Counting, numbers. Games.

More or less ill. by David T. Wenzel. HarperCollins, 2005. ISBN 0-06-053165-7 Subj: Activities – picnicking. Counting, numbers. Games.

100 days of cool ill. by John Bendall-Brunello. HarperCollins, 2004. ISBN 0-06-000121-6 Subj: Counting, numbers. School.

A pair of socks ill. by Lois Ehlert. HarperCollins, 1996. ISBN 0-06-025880-2 Subj: Clothing – socks.

The penny pot ill. by Lynne Cravath. HarperCollins, 1998. ISBN 0-06-027607-X Subj: Counting, numbers. Fairs, festivals. Money. School.

Pepper's journal ill. by Marsha Winborn. HarperCollins, 2000. ISBN 0-06-027619-3 Subj: Animals – babies. Animals – cats. Calendars.

Probably pistachio ill. by Marsha Winborn. HarperCollins, 2001. ISBN 0-06-028029-8 Subj: Behavior – bad day. Concepts.

Rabbit's pajama party ill. by Frank Remkiewicz. HarperCollins, 1999. ISBN 0-06-027617-7 Subj: Animals – rabbits. Family life – mothers. Rhyming text. Sleepovers.

Ready, set, hop! ill. by John Buller. HarperCollins, 1996. ISBN 0-06-025878-0 Subj: Activities – jumping. Counting, numbers. Frogs & toads.

Seaweed soup ill. by Frank Remkiewicz. HarperCollins, 2001. ISBN 0-06-446736-8 Subj: Behavior – sharing. Counting, numbers. Food.

Sluggers' car wash ill. by Barney Saltzberg. HarperCollins, 2002. ISBN 0-06-028921-X Subj: Activities – working. Counting, numbers. Money.

The sundae scoop ill. by Cynthia Jabar. HarperCollins, 2003. ISBN 0-06-028924-4 Subj: Counting, numbers.

Too many kangaroo things to do! ill. by Kevin O'Malley. HarperCollins, 1996. ISBN 0-06-025884-5 Subj: Animals – kangaroos. Birthdays. Counting, numbers. Parties.

Treasure map ill. by Tricia Tusa. HarperCollins, 2004. ISBN 0-06-028036-0 Subj: Clubs, gangs. Maps. Problem solving.

Murray, Andrew. *Have you seen Chester?* ill. by Nicola Slater. HarperCollins, 2003. ISBN 0-06-057187-X Subj: Animals – cats. Animals – dogs. Behavior – fighting, arguing. Behavior – running away.

Murray, Glenn. *Walter, the farting dog* (Kotzwinkle, William)

Walter, the farting dog: rough weather ahead (Kotzwinkle, William)

Walter, the farting dog: trouble at the yard sale (Kotzwinkle, William)

Murray, Marjorie Dennis. *Little Wolf and the moon* ill. by Stacey Shuett. Cavendish, 2002. ISBN 0-7614-5100-5 Subj: Animals – babies. Animals – wolves. Moon.

The stars are waiting ill. by Jacqueline Rogers. Cavendish, 1998. ISBN 0-7614-5024-6 Subj: Animals. Bedtime. Night. Rhyming text.

Murray, Martine. *A moose called Mouse* ill. by author. Allen & Unwin, 2001. ISBN 1-86508-495-6 Subj: Animals – moose. Friendship. Games. Nature. Night.

Murray, Peter. *Beetles* ill. with photos. Child's World, 2003. ISBN 1-56766-976-X Subj: Insects – beetles.

Sea otters ill. with photos. Child's World, 2001. ISBN 1-56766-892-5 Subj: Animals – otters.

Murrow, Liza Ketchum. *Good-bye, Sammy* ill. by Gail Owens. Holiday, 1989. ISBN 0-8234-0726-8 Subj: Behavior – lost & found possessions. Toys.

Murschetz, Luis. *Mister Mole* trans. by Diane Martin; ill. by author. Prentice-Hall, 1976. Translation of Der Maulwurf Grabowski. ISBN 0-13-585976-X Subj: Animals – moles. Ecology. Progress.

Musgrave, Susan. *Dreams are more real than bathtubs* ill. by Marie-Louise Gay. Orca, 1998. ISBN 1-55143-107-6 Subj: Dreams. Emotions. School – first day.

Musgrove, Margaret. *Ashanti to Zulu* ill. by Leo & Diane Dillon. Dial, 1976. ISBN 0-8037-0358-9 Subj: ABC books. Caldecott award books. Foreign lands – Africa.

The spider weaver: a legend of kente cloth ill. by Julia Cairns. Blue Sky, 2001. ISBN 0-590-98787-9 Subj: Activities – weaving. Careers – weavers. Folk & fairy tales. Foreign lands – Ghana. Spiders.

Musicant, Elke. *The night vegetable eater* by Elke & Ted Musicant; ill. by Jeni Bassett. Dodd, 1981. ISBN 0-396-07923-7 Subj: Animals. Gardens, gardening. Mystery stories.

Musicant, Ted. *The night vegetable eater* (Musicant, Elke)

Mussenbrock, Anne. *Easter Bunny saves the day* ill. by author. Parklane, 2004. ISBN 1-59384-037-3 Subj: Animals – rabbits. Eggs. Format, unusual – toy & movable books. Friendship.

The little Easter surprise ill. by author. Parklane, 2004. ISBN 1-59384-038-1 Subj: Animals – rabbits. Birds – chickens. Eggs. Format, unusual – toy & movable books. Holidays – Easter.

Little Easter surprise (Meyer, Brigit)

Muth, Jon J. *Stone soup* ill. by reteller. Scholastic, 2003. ISBN 0-439-33909-X Subj: Careers – clergy. Character traits – cleverness. Folk & fairy tales. Food. Foreign lands – China.

The three questions ill. by author. Scholastic, 2002. ISBN 0-439-19996-4 Subj: Animals. Behavior.

Muzik, Katharine. *At home in the coral reef* ill. by Katherine Brown-Wing. Charlesbridge, 1992. ISBN 0-88106-487-4 Subj: Ecology. Fish. Sea & seashore.

Mwalimu. *Awful aardvark* by Mwalimu & Adrienne Kennaway; ill. by Adrienne Kennaway. Little, 1989. ISBN 0-316-59218-8 Subj: Animals – aardvarks. Animals – mongooses. Folk & fairy tales. Foreign lands – Africa. Night. Sleep.

Mwenye Hadithi. *Crafty chameleon* ill. by Adrienne Kennaway. Little, 1987. ISBN 0-316-33723-4 Subj: Animals. Behavior – bullying. Behavior – unnoticed, unseen.

Greedy zebra ill. by Adrienne Kennaway. Little, 1984. ISBN 0-316-33721-8 Subj: Animals – zebras. Behavior – greed. Clothing. Folk & fairy tales. Foreign lands – Africa.

Hot hippo ill. by Adrienne Kennaway. Little, 1986. ISBN 0-316-33722-6 Subj: Animals – hippopotamuses. Foreign lands – Africa. Rivers.

Lazy lion ill. by Adrienne Kennaway. Little, 1990. ISBN 0-316-33725-0 Subj: Animals. Animals – lions. Character traits – laziness.

Tricky tortoise ill. by Adrienne Kennaway. Little, 1988. ISBN 0-316-33724-2 Subj: Animals. Behavior – bullying. Jungle.

My body ill. by Sue Porter. HarperCollins, 1985. ISBN 0-911745-96-3 Subj: Anatomy. Format, unusual – board books. Wordless.

My busy day photos by Steve Gorton & Gary Ombler. DK, 2001. ISBN 0-7894-7407-7 Subj: Activities. Format, unusual.

My doctor's bag. DK, 2002. ISBN 0-7894-8520-6 Subj: Careers – doctors. Format, unusual.

My first book of baby animals ill. by Karen Lee Schmidt. Platt, 1986. ISBN 0-448-10826-7 Subj: Animals. Format, unusual – board books.

My first Christmas [board book] ill. with photos. DK, 1999. ISBN 0-7894-4735-5 Subj: Format, unusual – board books. Holidays – Christmas.

My first farm ill. with photos. DK, 2002. ISBN 0-7894-8524-9 Subj: Farms. Format, unusual – board books. Language.

My first nursery rhymes ill. by Bruce Whatley. HarperFestival, 1999. ISBN 0-694-01205-X Subj: Nursery rhymes.

My first Raggedy Ann, Raggedy Ann and Andy and the camel with the wrinkled knees adapt. from the story by Johnny Gruelle; ill. by Jan Palmer. S&S, 1998. ISBN 0-689-81120-9 Subj: Pirates. Toys. Toys – dolls.

My first Raggedy Ann, Raggedy Ann and Andy and the nice police officer adapt. from the story by Johnny Gruelle; ill. by Jan Palmer. S&S, 1999. ISBN 0-689-82174-3 Subj: Careers – magicians. Careers – police officers. Toys – dolls.

My first Raggedy Ann, Raggedy Ann's wishing pebble adapt. from the story by Johnny Gruelle; ill. by Jan Palmer. S&S, 1999. ISBN 0-689-82173-5 Subj: Behavior – stealing. Behavior – wishing. Toys – dolls.

My first songs ill. by Jane Manning. HarperFestival, 1998. ISBN 0-694-00983-0 Subj: Nursery rhymes. Songs.

My first word, touch and feel ill. with photos. DK, 2001. ISBN 0-7894-7931-1 Subj: Format, unusual – board books. Language.

My potty book for boys ill. with photos. DK, 2001. ISBN 0-7894-4889-0 Subj: Behavior – growing up. Toilet training.

My potty book for girls ill. with photos. DK, 2001. ISBN 0-7894-4845-9 Subj: Behavior – growing up. Toilet training.

Myers, Amy. *I know a monster* ill. by author. Addison-Wesley, 1979. ISBN 0-201-04990-2 Subj: Character traits – appearance. Games. Monsters.

Myers, Arthur. *Kids do amazing things* ill. by Anthony Rao. Random House, 1980. ISBN 0-394-94271-X Subj: Activities.

Myers, Bernice. *Charlie's birthday present* ill. by author. Scholastic, 1981. ISBN 0-590-31992-2 Subj: Birthdays. Trees.

The flying shoes ill. by author. Lothrop, 1992. ISBN 0-688-10696-X Subj: Activities – flying. Animals. Clothing – shoes. Magic. Royalty – queens.

The gold watch ill. by author. Lothrop, 1991. ISBN 0-688-09889-4 Subj: Careers. Clocks, watches. Family life – fathers.

Herman and the bears and the giants ill. by author. Scholastic, 1978. Subj: Animals – bears. Circus. Sports – bicycling.

It happens to everyone ill. by author. Lothrop, 1990. ISBN 0-688-09082-6 Subj: Behavior – hurrying. Careers – teachers.

The millionth egg ill. by author. Lothrop, 1991. ISBN 0-688-09886-X Subj: Birds – chickens. Eggs.

Sidney Rella and the glass sneaker ill. by author. Macmillan, 1985. ISBN 0-02-767790-7 Subj: Behavior – wishing. Fairies. Sports – football.

Myers, Christopher A. *Sparrows* ill. by author. Hyperion, 2001. ISBN 0-7868-2373-9 Subj: Birds. Birds – sparrows. Cities, towns. Ethnic groups in the U.S. – African Americans. Homeless.

Turnip soup by Christopher A. Myers & Lynne Born Myers; ill. by Katie Keller. Hyperion, 1994. ISBN 1-56282-446-5 Subj: Emotions – fear. Food. Reptiles – Komodo dragons. Reptiles – lizards.

Wings ill. by author. Scholastic, 2000. ISBN 0-590-03377-8 Subj: Activities – flying. Anatomy – wings. Character traits – being different.

Myers, Edward. *Forri the baker* ill. by Alexi Natchev. Dial, 1995. ISBN 0-8037-1397-5 Subj: Activities – baking, cooking. Careers – chefs, cooks. Character traits – cleverness. Food. War.

Myers, Lynne Born. *Turnip soup* (Myers, Christopher A.)

Myers, Tim (Tim Brian). *Basho and the fox* ill. by Oki S. Han. Cavendish, 2000. ISBN 0-7614-5068-8 Subj: Animals – foxes. Poetry.

Myers, Walter Dean. *The blues of Flats Brown* ill. by Nina Laden. Holiday, 2000. ISBN 0-8234-1480-9 Subj: Animals – dogs. Music. Musical instruments – guitars.

Brown angels ill. with photos. HarperCollins, 1993. ISBN 0-06-022918-7 Subj: Angels. Ethnic groups in the U.S. – African Americans. Poetry.

The dragon takes a wife ill. by Fiona French. Scholastic, 1995. ISBN 0-590-46693-3 Subj: Dragons. Fairies. Folk & fairy tales. Knights.

Glorious angels: a celebration of children ill. with photos. HarperCollins, 1995. ISBN 0-06-024823-8 Subj: Angels. Ethnic groups in the U.S. – African Americans. Poetry.

The golden serpent ill. by Alice & Martin Provensen. Viking, 1980. ISBN 0-670-34445-1 Subj: Folk & fairy tales. Foreign lands – India. Problem solving. Royalty.

Harlem: a poem ill. by Christopher Myers. Scholastic, 1997. ISBN 0-590-54340-7 Subj: Caldecott award honor books. Careers – authors. Careers – illustrators. Cities, towns. Ethnic groups in the U.S. – African Americans. Poetry.

How Mr. Monkey saw the whole world ill. by Synthia Saint James. Doubleday, 1996. ISBN 0-385-32057-4 Subj: Activities – flying. Animals – monkeys. Birds – buzzards. Emotions – fear. Food.

The story of the three kingdoms ill. by Ashley Bryan. HarperCollins, 1995. ISBN 0-06-024287-6 Subj: Animals. Nature.

Young Martin's promise ill. by Barbara Higgins Bond; Alex Haley, general editor. Raintree, 1993. ISBN 0-8114-7210-8 Subj: Ethnic groups in the U.S. – African Americans. U.S. history.

Myller, Lois. *No! No!* ill. by Cyndy Szekeres. S&S, 1971. ISBN 0-671-65186-2 Subj: Animals – hedgehogs. Behavior. Behavior – misbehavior. Etiquette. Family life. Safety.

Myller, Rolf. *How big is a foot?* ill. by author. Atheneum, 1962. ISBN 0-689-20298-9 Subj: Birthdays. Concepts – measurement. Humorous stories. Royalty – kings.

Rolling round ill. by author. Atheneum, 1963. Subj: Royalty. Wheels.

A very noisy day ill. by author. Atheneum, 1981. ISBN 0-689-30853-1 Subj: Animals – dogs. Crime. Noise, sounds.

Myra, Harold Lawrence. *Thanksgiving: what makes it special?* ill. by Jane Kurisu. Nelson, 2002. ISBN 1-4003-0006-1 Subj: Holidays – Thanksgiving. Religion.

Myrick, Jean Lockwood. *Ninety-nine pockets* ill. by Haris Petie. Lantern Pr., 1966. ISBN 0-8313-0079-5 Subj: Birthdays. Clothing – pockets. Problem solving.

Mystery manor Willabel L. Tong, designer; Phil Wilson, ill.; José R. Seminario, paper engineer. Piggy Toes, 2000. ISBN 1-58117-108-0 Subj: Animals – dogs. Format, unusual – toy & movable books. Ghosts. Monsters. Witches.

Nagda, Anne Whitehead. *A home for panda* ill. by Jim Effler. Soundprints, 2003. ISBN 1-59249-045-X Subj: Animals – pandas. Foreign lands – China. Homes, houses.

A tiger tale ill. by Paul Kratter. Soundprints, 2003. ISBN 1-59249-042-5 Subj: Animals – tigers. Foreign lands – Nepal.

World above the clouds ill. by Paul Kratter. Soundprints, 2000. ISBN 1-56899-878-3 Subj: Animals – leopards. Foreign lands – Himalayas. Mountains. Science.

Nagel, Andreas Fischer. *see* FischerNagel, Andreas

Nagel, Heiderose Fischer. *see* FischerNagel, Heiderose

Nahas, Sylvaine. *Nicolo's unicorn* ill. by Bimba Landmann. Watson-Guptill, 2001. ISBN 0-8230-5580-9 Subj: Dreams. Mythical creatures – unicorns.

Nail, James T. *Whose tracks are these? a clue book of familiar forest animals* ill. by Hyla Skudder. Roberts Rinehart, 1994. ISBN 1-879373-89-0 Subj: Animals. Forest, woods. Games.

Nakabayashi, Ei. *The rainy day puddle* ill. by author. Random House, 1989. ISBN 0-394-82095-9 Subj: Animals. Concepts – size. Weather – rain.

Nakagawa, Rieko. *Guri and Gura* by Rieko Nakagawa & Yuriko Yamawaki; ill. by Yuriko Yamawaki; trans. by Peter Howlett & Richard McNamara. Tuttle, 2002. ISBN 0-8048-3352-4 Subj: Activities – baking, cooking. Animals – mice. Behavior – sharing. Eggs. Food. Problem solving.

Guri and Gura's special gift by Rieko Nakagawa & Yuriko Yamawaki; ill. by Yuriko Yamawaki; trans. by Peter Howlett & Richard McNamara. Tuttle, 2002. ISBN 0-8048-3357-5 Subj: Activities – baking, cooking. Animals – mice. Behavior – sharing. Food.

Nakamura, Katherine Riley. *Song of night* ill. by Linnea Riley. Blue Sky, 2002. ISBN 0-439-26678-5 Subj: Animals. Animals – babies. Bedtime.

Nakano, Hirotaka. *Elephant blue* trans. by Fukuinkan Shoten; ill. by author. Bobbs-Merrill, 1970. Subj: Animals. Animals – elephants. Character traits – helpfulness.

Nakao, Naomi Löw. *The adventures of Chester the chest* (Ayal, Ora)

Ugbu (Ayal, Ora)

Nakatani, Chiyoko. *The day Chiro was lost* ill. by author. Collins-World, 1969. ISBN 0-370-01501-0 Subj: Animals – dogs. Behavior – lost.

Fumio and the dolphins ill. by author. Addison-Wesley, 1970. First published in Japan by Fukuinkan-Shoten, Tokyo, 1969. ISBN 0-370-01519-3 Subj: Animals – dolphins. Character traits – kindness to animals. Foreign lands – Japan. Sea & seashore.

My day on the farm ill. by author. Crowell, 1976. ISBN 0-690-01075-3 Subj: Farms.

The zoo in my garden ill. by author. Crowell, 1973. ISBN 0-690-95905-2 Subj: Animals.

Nakawatari, Harutaka. *The sea and I* trans. by Susan Matsui; ill. by author. Farrar, 1992. ISBN 0-374-36428-1 Subj: Boats, ships. Careers – fishermen. Sea & seashore.

Namioka, Lensey. *Hungriest boy in the world* ill. by Aki Sogabe. Holiday, 2001. ISBN 0-8234-1542-2 Subj: Food. Foreign lands – Japan. Monsters.

The laziest boy in the world ill. by YongSheng Xuan. Holiday, 1998. ISBN 0-8234-1330-6 Subj: Character traits – laziness. Family life. Foreign lands – China.

The loyal cat ill. by Aki Sogabe. Harcourt, 1995. ISBN 0-15-200092-5 Subj: Animals – cats. Character traits – bravery. Emotions – fear. Folk & fairy tales. Foreign lands – Japan. Magic. Poverty. Religion.

Namm, Diane. *Bunny's bedtime* ill. by Kathy Wilburn. Grolier, 1991. ISBN 0-7172-8247-3 Subj: Animals – rabbits. Bedtime. Rhyming text.

Favorite nursery rhymes comp. by Diane Namm; ill. by Delana Bettoli. Little, 1986. ISBN 0-671-60264-0 Subj: Nursery rhymes.

Little bear ill. by Lisa McCue. Childrens Pr., 1990. ISBN 0-516-05356-6 Subj: Animals – bears. Poetry.

Monsters! ill. by Maxie Chambliss. Childrens Pr., 1990. ISBN 0-516-05358-2 Subj: Counting, numbers. Monsters.

Nanao, Jun. *Contemplating your bellybutton* ill. by Tomako Hasegawa. Kane/Miller, 1995. ISBN 0-916291-60-X Subj: Anatomy – navels. Babies. Birth.

Nanji, Shenaaz. *An alien in my house* ill. by Chum McLeod. Second Story, 2003. ISBN 1-896764-77-0 Subj: Character traits – being different. Family life – grandfathers. Old age.

Treasure for lunch ill. by Yvonne Cathcart. Second Story, 2000. ISBN 1-896764-32-0 Subj: Behavior – sharing. Food.

Nanovic, Kathryn. *The ghosts' trip to Loch Ness* (Duquennoy, Jacques)

Napier, Matt. *Z is for zamboni* ill. by Melanie Rose. Sleeping Bear, 2002. ISBN 1-58536-065-1 Subj: ABC books. Sports – hockey.

Napoli, Donna Jo. *Albert* ill. by Jim LaMarche. Harcourt, 2001. ISBN 0-15-201572-8 Subj: Birds. Homes, houses.

Flamingo dream ill. by Cathie Felstead. Greenwillow, 2002. ISBN 0-688-17863-4 Subj: Death. Emotions. Emotions – grief. Family life – fathers. Illness – cancer.

Rocky, the cat who barks ill. by Tamara Petrosino. Dutton, 2002. ISBN 0-525-46544-8 Subj: Animals – cats. Animals – dogs. Friendship.

Napoli, Guillier. *Adventure at Mont-Saint-Michel* ill. by author. McGraw-Hill, 1966. Subj: Careers – fishermen. Character traits – curiosity. Foreign lands – France. Sea & seashore.

Nappa, Mike. *Do you see the star?* by Mike Nappa & Susan L. Lingo; ill. by Tony Griego. Group Pub., 1996. ISBN 1-55945-617-5 Subj: Format, unusual – toy & movable books. Religion – Nativity. Rhyming text. Stars.

Narahashi, Keiko. *I have a friend* ill. by author. McElderry, 1987. ISBN 0-689-50432-2 Subj: Shadows.

Is that Josie? ill. by author. McElderry, 1994. ISBN 0-689-50606-6 Subj: Activities – playing. Animals. Imagination.

Two girls can! ill. by author. McElderry, 2000. ISBN 0-689-82618-4 Subj: Friendship.

Narayan, Maya. *Leela and the watermelon* (Hirsh, Marilyn)

Nash, Ogden. *The adventures of Isabel* ill. by Walter Lorraine. Little, 1963. Subj: Animals – bears. Character traits – bravery. Emotions – fear. Giants. Poetry. Witches.

The adventures of Isabel ill. by James Marshall. Little, 1991. ISBN 0-316-59874-7 Subj: Animals – bears. Character traits – bravery. Emotions – fear. Giants. Poetry. Witches.

The animal garden ill. by Hilary Knight. Lippincott, 1965. Subj: Humorous stories. Plants. Poetry.

A boy is a boy ill. by Arthur Shilstone. Watts, 1960. Subj: Humorous stories. Poetry.

Custard the dragon ill. by Linell Nash. Little, 1961. ISBN 0-316-59841-0 Subj: Animals. Character traits – bravery. Dragons. Pirates. Poetry.

Custard the dragon and the wicked knight ill. by Lynn Munsinger. Little, 1996. ISBN 0-316-59882-8 Subj: Character traits – bravery. Dragons. Knights. Poetry.

Custard the dragon and the wicked knight ill. by Linell Nash. Little, 1959. Subj: Character traits – bravery. Dragons. Knights. Poetry.

Nash, Scott. *Tuff Fluff: the case of Duckie's missing brain* ill. by author. Candlewick, 2004. ISBN 0-7636-1882-9 Subj: Activities – storytelling. Careers – detectives. Mystery stories. Toys.

Nast, Elsa Ruth. *see* Watson, Jane Werner

Nathan, Cheryl. *Bugs and beasties ABC* ill. by author. Cool Kids, 1995. ISBN 1-56790-516-1 Subj: ABC books. Animals. Insects.

The long and short of it by Cheryl Nathan & Lisa McCourt; ill. by Cheryl Nathan. BridgeWater, 1998. ISBN 0-8167-4545-5 Subj: Animals. Concepts – size.

Nathan, Emma. *What do you call a group of turkeys?* ill. with photos. Blackbirch, 2000. ISBN 1-56711-357-5 Subj: Birds. Birds – turkeys. Language.

National Geographic Society (U.S.). *National Geographic our world: a child's first picture atlas* ill. with photos. National Geographic, 2000. ISBN 0-7922-7576-4 Subj: Geography. Maps.

Native Americans created by Gallimard Jeunesse, Ute Fuhr & Raoul Sautai; ill. by Ute Fuhr & Raoul Sautai. Scholastic, 1998. ISBN 0-590-38153-9 Subj: Indians of North America.

Nave, Yolanda. *Goosebumps and butterflies* ill. by author. Watts, 1990. ISBN 0-531-08504-X Subj: Emotions. Poetry.

Nayer, Judy. *Bath* ill. by author. McClanahan, 1996. ISBN 1-56293-912-2 Subj: Activities – bathing. Babies. Format, unusual – board books.

The eight nights of Hanukka ill. by Yuri Salzman. Troll, 1998. ISBN 0-8167-4550-1 Subj: Holidays – Hanukkah. Jewish culture. Religion.

Funny bunnies ill. by Steve Henry. McClanahan, 1994. ISBN 1-56293-436-8 Subj: Animals – rabbits. Counting, numbers. Format, unusual – toy & movable books.

Games ill. by author. McClanahan, 1996. ISBN 1-56293-911-4 Subj: Babies. Games.

The happy little engine ill. by Roz Schanzer. McClanahan, 1990. ISBN 1-878624-43-1 Subj: Activities – traveling. Automobiles. Family life.

Jungle life ill. by Grace Goldberg. McClanahan, 1992. ISBN 1-56293-221-7 Subj: Animals. Format, unusual – board books. Jungle.

Little bear's first Christmas ill. by author. McClanahan, 1994. ISBN 1-56293-498-8 Subj: Animals – bears. Holidays – Christmas.

Mice are nice ill. by Paul Harvey. McClanahan, 1994. ISBN 1-56293-434-1 Subj: Animals – mice. Format, unusual – toy & movable books. Language.

Night animals ill. by Grace Goldberg. McClanahan, 1992. ISBN 1-56293-223-3 Subj: Animals. Format, unusual – board books. Night.

Pig in a wig ill. by Paul Harvey. McClanahan, 1994. ISBN 1-56293-433-3 Subj: Animals – pigs. Format, unusual – toy & movable books. Language.

Reptiles ill. by Grace Goldberg. McElderry, 1992. ISBN 1-56293-220-9 Subj: Format, unusual – board books. Reptiles.

Rhymes ill. by author. McClanahan, 1996. ISBN 1-56293-910-6 Subj: Babies. Nursery rhymes.

Sea creatures ill. by Grace Goldberg. McElderry, 1992. ISBN 1-56293-222-5 Subj: Animals. Fish. Format, unusual – board books. Sea & seashore.

Toys ill. by author. McClanahan, 1996. ISBN 1-56293-913-0 Subj: Babies. Toys.

Tricky puppies ill. by Steve Henry. McElderry, 1994. ISBN 1-56293-435-X Subj: Animals – dogs. Counting, numbers. Format, unusual – toy & movable books.

Naylor, Phyllis Reynolds. *The baby, the bed, and the rose* ill. by Mary Szilagyi. Clarion, 1987. ISBN 0-899-19459-1 Subj: Babies. Emotions – love. Family life – brothers & sisters.

Ducks disappearing ill. by Tony Maddox. Atheneum, 1997. ISBN 0-689-31902-9 Subj: Behavior – lost. Birds – ducks. Counting, numbers. Hotels.

"I can't take you anywhere!" ill. by Jef Kaminsky. Atheneum, 1997. ISBN 0-689-31966-5 Subj: Character traits – clumsiness. Family life – aunts, uncles. Weddings.

Jennifer Jean, the Cross-Eyed Queen ill. by Karen Ritz. Carolrhoda, 1994. ISBN 0-8761-4791-0 Subj: Anatomy – eyes. Handicaps. School.

Keeping a Christmas secret ill. by Lena Shiffman. Macmillan, 1993. ISBN 0-689-71760-1 Subj: Behavior – secrets. Gifts. Holidays – Christmas.

King of the playground ill. by Nola Langner Malone. Atheneum, 1991. ISBN 0-689-31558-9 Subj: Activities – playing. Behavior – bullying. Friendship.

Old Sadie and the Christmas bear ill. by Patricia Montgomery Newton. Atheneum, 1984. ISBN 0-689-31052-8 Subj: Animals – bears. Holidays – Christmas.

The picnic ill. by Ana López Escrivá. Atheneum, 2002. ISBN 0-689-82561-7 Subj: Activities – picnicking. Animals. Sea & seashore. Toys – bears.

Please do feed the bears ill. by Ana López Escrivá. Atheneum, 2002. ISBN 0-689-82561-7 Subj: Activities – picnicking. Animals – bears. Sea & seashore – beaches. Toys – bears.

Sweet strawberries ill. by Rosalind Charney Kaye. Atheneum, 1999. ISBN 0-689-81338-4 Subj: Behavior. Food. Stores.

Neale, J. M. (John Mason). *Good King Wenceslas* ill. by Jamichael Henterly. Dutton, 1988. ISBN 0-525-44420-3 Subj: Folk & fairy tales. Holidays – Christmas. Music. Songs.

Neasi, Barbara J. *Just like me* ill. by Lois Axeman. Childrens Pr., 1984. ISBN 0-516-02047-1 Subj: Multiple births – twins.

Listen to me ill. by Gene Sharp. Childrens Pr., 1986. ISBN 0-516-02072-2 Subj: Family life – grandmothers.

Neidigh, Sherry. *Creatures at my feet* ill. by author; text by Charles E. Davis. Northland, 1993. ISBN 0-8735-8560-7 Subj: Anatomy – feet. Animals. Clothing – shoes. Poetry.

Neitzel, Shirley. *The bag I'm taking to Grandma's* ill. by Nancy Winslow Parker. Greenwillow, 1995. ISBN 0-688-12961-7 Subj: Activities – traveling. Cumulative tales. Rebuses. Rhyming text.

The dress I'll wear to the party ill. by Nancy Winslow Parker. Greenwillow, 1992. ISBN 0-688-09960-2 Subj: Clothing. Cumulative tales. Rebuses. Rhyming text.

From the land of the white birch ill. by Daniel Powers. River Road Pub., 1997. ISBN 0-938682-44-X Subj: Creation. Folk & fairy tales. Indians of North America – Ojibwa.

The house I'll build for the wrens ill. by Nancy Winslow Parker. Greenwillow, 1997. ISBN 0-688-14974-X Subj: Activities – making things. Birds. Cumulative tales. Homes, houses. Rebuses. Rhyming text. Tools.

I'm not feeling well today ill. by Nancy Winslow Parker. Greenwillow, 2001. ISBN 0-688-17381-0 Subj: Cumulative tales. Illness. Rebuses. Rhyming text. School.

I'm taking a trip on my train ill. by Nancy Winslow Parker. Greenwillow, 1999. ISBN 0-688-15834-X Subj: Activities – playing. Cumulative tales. Imagination. Rebuses. Rhyming text. Trains.

The jacket I wear in the snow ill. by Nancy Winslow Parker. Greenwillow, 1989. ISBN 0-688-08030-8 Subj: Clothing. Cumulative tales. Rhyming text.

We're making breakfast for mother ill. by Nancy Winslow Parker. Greenwillow, 1997. ISBN 0-688-14576-0 Subj: Family life – mothers. Food. Rebuses. Rhyming text.

Nelson, Brenda. *Mud for sale* ill. by Richard Eric Brown. Houghton Mifflin, 1984. ISBN 0-395-36175-3 Subj: Activities. Friendship.

Nelson, Esther L. *The funny songbook* ill. by Joyce Behr. Sterling, 1984. Subj: Music. Songs.

Holiday singing and dancing games photos by Shirley Zeiberg. Sterling, 1980. ISBN 0-8069-4630-X Subj: Activities – dancing. Games. Music. Songs.

The silly songbook ill. by Joyce Behr. Sterling, 1982. ISBN 0-8069-4651-2 Subj: Music. Songs.

Nelson, Kristin L. *Busy ants* ill. with photos. Lerner, 2004. ISBN 0-8225-3775-3 Subj: Insects – ants.

Clever raccoons ill. with photos. Lerner, 2001. ISBN 0-8225-3763-X Subj: Animals – raccoons.

Farm tractors ill. with photos. Lerner, 2003. ISBN 0-8225-0690-4 Subj: Farms. Tractors.

Monster trucks photos by David & Beverly Huntoon. Lerner, 2003. ISBN 0-8225-0691-2 Subj: Sports – racing. Trucks.

Nelson, Nan Ferring. *My day with Anka* ill. by Bill Farnsworth. Lothrop, 1996. ISBN 0-688-11059-2 Subj: Activities – babysitting. Activities – baking, cooking. Ethnic groups in the U.S. – Czechoslovakian Americans. Friendship.

Nelson, Robert Lyn. *Ocean friends* ill. by author. NorthWord, 2003. ISBN 1-55971-840-4 Subj: Animals. Animals – dolphins. Sea & seashore.

Nelson, Robin. *A cloudy day* ill. by author. Lerner, 2002. ISBN 0-8225-0172-4 Subj: Weather – clouds.

A day ill. by author. Lerner, 2002. ISBN 0-8225-0177-5 Subj: Day. Days of the week, months of the year.

Hearing ill. with photos. Lerner, 2002. ISBN 0-8225-1264-5 Subj: Anatomy – ears. Senses – hearing.

Months ill. with photos. Lerner, 2002. ISBN 0-8225-0179-1 Subj: Days of the week, months of the year.

Pet fish ill. with photos. Lerner, 2003. ISBN 0-8225-1267-X Subj: Fish. Pets.

Pet frog ill. with photos. Lerner, 2003. ISBN 0-8225-1271-8 Subj: Frogs & toads. Pets.

Pet guinea pig ill. with photos. Lerner, 2003. ISBN 0-8225-1268-8 Subj: Animals – guinea pigs. Pets.

Pet hamster ill. with photos. Lerner, 2003. ISBN 0-8225-1269-6 Subj: Animals – hamsters. Pets.

Pet hermit crab ill. with photos. Lerner, 2003. ISBN 0-8225-1270-X Subj: Crustaceans – crabs. Pets.

A rainy day ill. with photos. Lerner, 2002. ISBN 0-8225-0173-2 Subj: Weather – rain.

Seeing ill. with photos. Lerner, 2002. ISBN 0-8225-1262-9 Subj: Anatomy – eyes. Senses – sight.

Smelling ill. with photos. Lerner, 2002. ISBN 0-8225-1263-7 Subj: Anatomy – noses. Senses – smell.

A snowy day ill. with photos. Lerner, 2002. ISBN 0-8225-0175-9 Subj: Seasons – winter. Weather – snow.

A sunny day ill. with photos. Lerner, 2002. ISBN 0-8225-0176-7 Subj: Sun. Weather.

Tasting ill. with photos. Lerner, 2002. ISBN 0-8225-1265-3 Subj: Anatomy – tongues. Senses – taste.

Touching ill. with photos. Lerner, 2002. ISBN 0-8225-1266-1 Subj: Senses – touch.

A week ill. with photos. Lerner, 2002. ISBN 0-8225-0178-3 Subj: Days of the week, months of the year.

A windy day ill. with photos. Lerner, 2001. ISBN 0-8225-0174-0 Subj: Weather – wind.

Nelson, S. D. *Gift horse: a Lakota story* ill. by author. Abrams, 1999. ISBN 0-8109-4127-9 Subj: Animals – horses, ponies. Behavior – growing up. Indians of North America – Dakota (Sioux).

The Star People ill. by author. Abrams, 2003. ISBN 0-8109-4584-3 Subj: Family life – brothers & sisters. Family life – grandmothers. Fire. Indians of North America – Lakota (Sioux). Stars.

Nelson, Vaunda Micheaux. *Almost to freedom* ill. by Colin Bootman. Carolrhoda, 2003. ISBN 1-57505-342-X Subj: Character traits – freedom. Ethnic groups in the U.S. – African Americans. Slavery. Toys – dolls.

Always Gramma ill. by Kimanne Uhler. Putnam, 1988. ISBN 0-399-21542-5 Subj: Family life. Family life – grandmothers. Illness – Alzheimer's. Old age.

Nerlove, Miriam. *Christmas* ill. by author. A. Whitman, 1990. ISBN 0-8075-1148-X Subj: Holidays – Christmas. Rhyming text.

Easter ill. by author. A. Whitman, 1989. ISBN 0-8075-1871-9 Subj: Family life. Holidays – Easter. Religion. Rhyming text.

Flowers on the wall ill. by author. McElderry, 1996. ISBN 0-689-50614-7 Subj: Activities – painting. Foreign lands – Poland. Holocaust. Jewish culture. War.

Halloween ill. by author. A. Whitman, 1989. ISBN 0-8075-3131-6 Subj: Holidays – Halloween. Rhyming text.

Hanukkah ill. by author. A. Whitman, 1989. ISBN 0-8075-3143-X Subj: Holidays – Hanukkah. Jewish culture. Religion. Rhyming text.

I made a mistake ill. by author. Atheneum, 1985. ISBN 0-689-50327-X Subj: Animals. Rhyming text.

I meant to clean my room today ill. by author. Macmillan, 1988. ISBN 0-689-50438-1 Subj: Character traits – cleanliness. Imagination. Rhyming text.

If all the world were paper ill. by author. A. Whitman, 1990. ISBN 0-8075-3535-4 Subj: Activities – painting. Imagination. Rhyming text.

Just one tooth ill. by author. Macmillan, 1989. ISBN 0-689-50465-9 Subj: Rhyming text. Teeth.

Passover ill. by author. A. Whitman, 1989. ISBN 0-8075-6360-9 Subj: Jewish culture. Religion. Rhyming text.

Purim ill. by author. A. Whitman, 1992. ISBN 0-8075-6682-9 Subj: Holidays – Purim. Jewish culture. Religion.

Shabbat ill. by author. A. Whitman, 1998. ISBN 0-8075-7324-8 Subj: Jewish culture. Religion.

The Ten Commandments for Jewish children ill. by author. A. Whitman, 1999. ISBN 0-8075-7770-7 Subj: Jewish culture. Religion.

Thanksgiving ill. by author. A. Whitman, 1990. ISBN 0-8075-7818-5 Subj: Holidays – Thanksgiving. Rhyming text.

Valentine's Day ill. by author. A. Whitman, 1992. ISBN 0-8075-8454-1 Subj: Holidays – Valentine's Day. Rhyming text.

Nesbit, Edith. *Beauty and the beast* ill. by Julia Christie. Warne, 1988. ISBN 0-7232-3540-6 Subj: Character traits – appearance. Character traits – loyalty. Emotions – love. Folk & fairy tales. Magic.

Cockatoucan ill. by Elory Hughes. Dial, 1988. ISBN 0-8037-0474-7 Subj: Birds. Imagination.

The ice dragon ill. by Carole Gray. Dial, 1988. ISBN 0-8037-0475-5 Subj: World.

The last of the dragons ill. by Peter Firmin. McGraw-Hill, 1980. ISBN 0-07-046285-2 Subj: Character traits – kindness. Dragons. Folk & fairy tales. Royalty.

Melisande ill. by P. J. Lynch. Harcourt, 1989. ISBN 0-15-253164-5 Subj: Fairies. Folk & fairy tales. Hair. Magic. Royalty – princesses.

Ness, Evaline. *Do you have the time, Lydia?* ill. by author. Dutton, 1971. ISBN 0-525-28790-6 Subj: Birds – seagulls. Character traits – completing things. Problem solving. Time.

Exactly alike ill. by author. Scribners, 1964. Subj: Family life.

Fierce: the lion ill. by author. Holiday, 1980. ISBN 0-8234-0412-9 Subj: Animals – lions. Circus.

The girl and the goatherd: or, this and that and thus and so ill. by author. Dutton, 1970. ISBN 0-52530-657-9 Subj: Character traits – appearance. Folk & fairy tales.

Josefina February ill. by author. Scribners, 1963. Subj: Animals – donkeys. Birthdays. Character traits – generosity. Foreign lands – Caribbean Islands.

Pavo and the princess ill. by author. Scribners, 1964. Subj: Birds. Character traits – helpfulness. Emotions. Royalty – princesses.

Sam, Bangs, and moonshine ill. by author. Holt, 1966. ISBN 0-606-01326-1 Subj: Caldecott award books. Imagination. Sports – fishing.

Nestrick, Nova. *Pelle's new suit* (Beskow, Elsa Maartman)

Nethery, Mary. *Hannah and Jack* ill. by Mary Morgan. Atheneum, 1996. ISBN 0-689-80533-0 Subj: Activities – vacationing. Activities – working. Animals – cats. Family life – grandmothers.

Mary Veronica's egg ill. by Paul Yalowitz. Orchard, 1999. ISBN 0-531-33134-2 Subj: Birds – ducks. Eggs.

Orange cat goes to market ill. by author. Candlewick, 1997. ISBN 0-7636-0028-8 Subj: Animals – cats. Shopping.

Nettleton, Pamela Hill. *Abraham Lincoln* ill. by Becky Shipe. Picture Window, 2004. ISBN 1-4048-0185-5 Subj: U.S. history.

Benjamin Franklin ill. by Jeff Yesh. Picture Window, 2004. ISBN 1-4048-0186-3 Subj: Careers – inventors. Careers – printers. Careers – scientists. U.S. history.

George Washington ill. by Jeff Yesh. Picture Window, 2004. ISBN 1-4048-0184-7 Subj: Careers. Careers – farmers. Careers – military. U.S. history.

Martin Luther King, Jr. ill. by Garry Nichols. Picture Window, 2004. ISBN 1-4048-0188-X Subj: Careers – clergy. Ethnic groups in the U.S. – African Americans. Religion. U.S. history.

Pocahontas ill. by Jeff Yesh. Picture Window, 2004. ISBN 1-4048-0187-1 Subj: Indians of North America – Powhatan. U.S. history.

Sally Ride ill. by Becky Shipe. Picture Window, 2004. ISBN 1-4048-0189-8 Subj: Careers – astronauts. U.S. history.

Neugebauer, Charise. *The real winner* ill. by Barbara Nascimbeni. North-South, 2000. ISBN 0-7358-1253-5 Subj: Animals – hippopotamuses. Animals – raccoons. Contests.

Santa's gift ill. by Barbara Nascimbeni. North-South, 1999. ISBN 0-7358-1146-6 Subj: Animals. Gifts. Holidays – Christmas. Santa Claus.

Neugroschel, Joachim. *The boy and the tree* (Driz, Ovsei)

Neuhaus, David. *His finest hour* ill. by author. Viking, 1984. ISBN 0-670-37260-9 Subj: Friendship. Sports – racing.

Neumeier, Marty. *Action alphabet* by Marty Neumeier & Byron Glaser; ill. by authors. Greenwillow, 1985. ISBN 0-688-05704-7 Subj: ABC books. Activities.

Neumeyer, Peter F. *Mischa and his brothers* (Baumann, Hans)

Sleep well, little bear (Buchholz, Quint)

Neuschwander, Cindy. *Amanda Bean's amazing dream* ill. by Liza Woodruff; math activities by Marilyn Burns. Scholastic, 1998. ISBN 0-590-30012-1 Subj: Counting, numbers. Dreams. School.

Neville, Emily Cheney. *The bridge* ill. by Ronald Himler. HarperCollins, 1988. ISBN 0-06-024386-4 Subj: Bridges. Family life. Machines.

Neville, Mary. *The Christmas tree ride* ill. by Megan Lloyd. Holiday, 1992. ISBN 0-8234-0956-2 Subj: Family life. Friendship. Holidays – Christmas. Trees.

Newberry, Clare Turlay. *April's kittens* ill. by author. HarperCollins, 1940. ISBN 0-06-024401-1 Subj: Animals – cats. Caldecott award honor books. Pets.

Barkis ill. by author. HarperCollins, 1938. Subj: Animals – dogs. Caldecott award honor books. Pets.

Cousin Toby ill. by author. HarperCollins, 1939. Subj: Babies.

Herbert the lion ill. by author. HarperCollins, 1956. First pub. in 1931. Subj: Animals – lions. Pets.

The kittens' ABC verse & pictures by Clare Turlay Newberry. New and rev. ed.; completely redrawn. HarperCollins, 1965. Subj: ABC books. Animals – cats. Rhyming text.

Marshmallow ill. by author. HarperCollins, 1942. Subj: Animals – cats. Animals – rabbits. Caldecott award honor books. Friendship.

Pandora ill. by author. HarperCollins, 1944. Subj: Animals – cats.

Percy, Polly and Pete ill. by author. HarperCollins, 1952. Subj: Animals – cats. Behavior – growing up. Character traits – kindness to animals. Pets.

Smudge ill. by author. HarperCollins, 1948. Subj: Animals – cats.

T-Bone, the baby-sitter ill. by author. HarperCollins, 1950. Subj: Activities – babysitting. Animals – cats. Babies. Caldecott award honor books.

Widget ill. by author. HarperCollins, 1958. Subj: Animals – cats.

Newbolt, Henry John, Sir. *Rilloby-rill* ill. by Susanna Gretz. O'Hara, 1973. ISBN 0-8795-5707-9 Subj: Fairies. Insects – grasshoppers. Music. Songs.

Newcome, Zita. *Animal fun* ill. by author. Candlewick, 1999. ISBN 0-7636-0803-3 Subj: Behavior – imitation. Health & fitness – exercise. Rhyming text.

Pop-up toddlerobics ill. by author. Candlewick, 2002. ISBN 0-7636-1838-1 Subj: Activities – playing. Health & fitness. Rhyming text. Sports – gymnastics.

Rosie goes exploring ill. by author. Trafalgar Square, 1992. ISBN 1-85681-170-0 Subj: Animals. Imagination. Plants.

Rosie goes shopping ill. by author. Trafalgar Square, 1992. ISBN 1-85681-160-3 Subj: Family life – mothers. Foreign lands – England. Shopping.

Toddlerobics ill. by author. Candlewick, 1996. ISBN 1-56402-809-7 Subj: Activities – playing. Health & fitness – exercise. Rhyming text. Sports – gymnastics.

Newell, Crosby. *see* Bonsall, Crosby Newell

Newell, Peter. *The slant book* ill. by author. Tuttle, 1967. ISBN 0-8048-0532-6 Subj: Format, unusual – toy & movable books. Rhyming text.

Topsys and turvys ill. by author. Dover, 1965. Subj: Format, unusual. Humorous stories.

Newfield, Marcia. *Iggy* ill. by Jacqueline Chwast. Houghton Mifflin, 1972. ISBN 0-395-13898-1 Subj: Pets. Reptiles – iguanas.

Newland, Mary Reed. *Good King Wenceslas: a legend in music and pictures* ill. by author. Seabury Pr., 1980. ISBN 0-8164-0474-7 Subj: Holidays – Christmas. Music. Songs.

Newman, Jeff. *Reginald* ill. by author. Doubleday, 2003. ISBN 0-385-74634-2 Subj: Animals. Animals – bulls, cows. Jungle. Sports – swimming.

Newman, Lesléa. *Belinda's bouquet* ill. by Michael Willhoite. Alyson Wonderland, 1991. ISBN 1-55583-154-0 Subj: Character traits – individuality. Flowers. Health & fitness.

Cats, cats, cats ill. by Erika Oller. S&S, 2001. ISBN 0-689-83077-7 Subj: Animals – cats. Night. Rhyming text.

Dogs, dogs, dogs ill. by Erika Oller. S&S, 2002. ISBN 0-698-84492-1 Subj: Activities. Animals – dogs. Counting, numbers. Rhyming text.

A fire engine for Ruthie ill. by Cyd Moore. Clarion, 2004. ISBN 0-618-15989-4 Subj: Activities – playing. Toys. Trucks.

Heather has two mommies ill. by Diana Souza. Alyson Wonderland, 2000. ISBN 1-55583-570-8 Subj: Family life – daughters. Family life – mothers. Homosexuality.

Matzo ball moon ill. by Elaine Greenstein. Clarion, 1998. ISBN 0-395-71530-X Subj: Family life – grandmothers. Food. Holidays – Passover. Jewish culture. Religion.

Pigs, pigs, pigs ill. by Erika Oller. S&S, 2003. ISBN 0-689-84979-6 Subj: Animals – pigs. Careers – entertainers. Rhyming text.

Remember that ill. by Karen Ritz. Clarion, 1996. ISBN 0-395-66589-2 Subj: Family life – grandmothers. Memories, memory. Old age.

Runaway dreidel ill. by Kyrsten Brooker. Holt, 2002. ISBN 0-8050-6237-8 Subj: Games. Holidays – Hanukkah. Jewish culture. Rhyming text.

Saturday is Pattyday ill. by Annette Hegel. New Victoria, 1993. ISBN 0-934678-52-9 Subj: Divorce. Family life – mothers. Family life – sons. Homosexuality.

Too far away to touch ill. by Catherine Stock. Clarion, 1995. ISBN 0-395-68968-6 Subj: Death. Emotions – grief. Family life – aunts, uncles. Illness – AIDS. Stars.

Newman, Marjorie. *Mole and the baby bird* ill. by Patrick Benson. Bloomsbury, 2002. ISBN 1-58234-784-0 Subj: Animals – moles. Birds. Emotions – love.

Mole and the baby bird [board book] ill. by Patrick Benson. Bloomsbury, 2002. ISBN 1-58234-914-2 Subj: Animals – moles. Birds. Emotions – love. Format, unusual – board books.

Newman, Nanette. *There's a bear in the bath!* ill. by Michael Foreman. Harcourt, 1994. ISBN 0-15-285512-2 Subj: Animals – bears.

Newman, Robert. *All aboard ABC* (Magee, Doug)

Let's fly from A to Z (Magee, Doug)

Newman, Shirlee. *Tell me, grandma; tell me, grandpa* ill. by Joan E. Drescher. Houghton Mifflin, 1979. ISBN 0-395-27815-5 Subj: Family life – grandparents.

Newsham, Ian. *The monster hunt* (Newsham, Wendy)

Newsham, Wendy. *The monster hunt* by Wendy & Ian Newsham; ill. by authors. Hamish Hamilton, 1983. ISBN 0-241-10859-4 Subj: Monsters.

Newsome, Effie Lee. *Wonders: the best children's poems of Effie Lee Newsome* ill. by Lois Mailou Jones; comp. by Rudine Sims Bishop. Wordsong, 1999. ISBN 1-56397-788-5 Subj: Poetry.

Newsome, Jill. *Dream dancer* ill. by Claudio Muñoz. HarperCollins, 2002. ISBN 0-06-000932-2 Subj: Activities – dancing. Ballet. Family life – grandmothers. Illness. Toys – dolls.

Shadow ill. by Claudio Muñoz. DK, 1999. ISBN 0-7894-2631-5 Subj: Animals – rabbits. Friendship. Moving.

Newth, Philip. *Roly goes exploring: a book for blind and sighted children, in Braille and standard type, with pictures to feel as well as see.* Putnam, 1981. ISBN 0-399-20815-1 Subj: Concepts – shape. Format, unusual. Handicaps – blindness. Senses – sight.

Newton, James R. *A forest is reborn* ill. by Susan Bonners. Crowell, 1982. ISBN 0-690-04232-9 Subj: Fire. Forest, woods. Science.

Forest log ill. by Irene Brady. Crowell, 1980. ISBN 0-690-04008-3 Subj: Ecology. Forest, woods. Science. Trees.

Newton, Jill. *Cat-fish* ill. by author. Lothrop, 1992. ISBN 0-688-11424-5 Subj: Animals – cats. Behavior – dissatisfaction. Fish. Sea & seashore.

Don't sit there! ill. by author. Lothrop, 1994. ISBN 0-688-13309-6 Subj: Family life. Furniture – couches, sofas.

Polar bear scare ill. by author. Lothrop, 1992. ISBN 0-688-11233-1 Subj: Animals – polar bears. Animals – rabbits. Foreign lands – Arctic.

Newton, Laura P. *Me and my aunts* ill. by Robin Oz. A. Whitman, 1986. ISBN 0-8075-5029-9 Subj: Emotions – love. Family life – aunts, uncles.

William the vehicle king ill. by Jacqueline Rogers. Bradbury, 1987. ISBN 0-02-768230-7 Subj: Automobiles. Imagination. Toys. Trucks.

Newton, Pam. *see* Newton, Patricia Montgomery

Newton, Patricia Montgomery. *The five sparrows* ill. by author. Atheneum, 1982. ISBN 0-689-30936-8 Subj: Character traits – kindness. Folk & fairy tales. Foreign lands – Japan.

The frog who drank the waters of the world ill. by author. Atheneum, 1983. ISBN 0-689-30993-7 Subj: Animals. Birds – bluejays. Frogs & toads. Reptiles – snakes.

The stonecutter ill. by reteller. Putnam, 1990. ISBN 0-399-22187-5 Subj: Folk & fairy tales. Foreign lands – India.

Vacation surprise ill. by author. Atheneum, 1986. ISBN 0-689-31264-4 Subj: Activities – vacationing. Animals – pigs.

Newton-John, Olivia. *A pig tale* by Olivia Newton-John & Brian Seth Hurst; ill. by Sal Murdocca. S&S, 1993. ISBN 0-671-78778-0 Subj: Animals – pigs. Ecology. Family life – fathers. Rhyming text.

Neye, Emily. *Butterflies* ill. by Ron Broda. Grosset, 2000. ISBN 0-448-42280-8 Subj: Insects – butterflies, caterpillars.

Honeybees ill. by Tom Leonard. Golden Bks., 2002. ISBN 0-307-46217-X Subj: Insects – bees.

Nez, Redwing T. *Forbidden talent* ill. by Kathryn Wilder. Northland, 1995. ISBN 0-87358-605-0 Subj: Activities – painting. Art. Family life – grandfathers. Indians of North America – Navajo.

Nic Leodhas, Sorche. *see* Alger, Leclaire Gowans

Nichol, B. P. *On the merry-go-round* ill. by Simon Ng. Red Deer Pr., 1991. ISBN 0-88995-076-8 Subj: Bedtime. Night. Rhyming text.

Once, a lullaby ill. by Anita Lobel. Greenwillow, 1986. ISBN 0-688-04285-6 Subj: Animals. Bedtime. Lullabies. Music. Night. Sleep.

Nichol, Barbara. *Biscuits in the cupboard* ill. by Philippe Béha. Stoddard Kids, 1997. ISBN 0-7737-3025-7 Subj: Animals – dogs. Foreign lands – Canada. Poetry.

Trunks all aboard ill. by Sir William Cornelius Van Horne. Tundra, 2001. ISBN 0-8877-6536-X Subj: ABC books. Animals – elephants. Rhyming text.

Nicholls, Judith. *Billywise* ill. by Jason Cockcroft. Bloomsbury, 2002. ISBN 1-58234-778-6 Subj: Behavior – growing up. Birds – owls. Family life – mothers.

Someone I like: poems about people comp. by Judith Nicholls; ill. by Giovanni Manna. Barefoot, 2000. ISBN 1-84148-004-5 Subj: Emotions. Family life. Friendship. Poetry.

Nichols, Cathy. *Tuxedo Sam: a penguin of a different color* ill. by Haruo Takahashi. Random House, 1983. ISBN 0-394-86107-8 Subj: Birds – penguins. Cities, towns.

Nichols, Grace. *Asana and the animals: a book of pet poems* ill. by Sarah Adams. Candlewick, 1997. ISBN 0-7636-0145-4 Subj: Animals. Nursery rhymes. Poetry. Rhyming text.

No hickory no dickory no dock: Caribbean nursery rhymes (Agard, John)

Nichols, Paul. *Big Paul's school bus* ill. by William Marshall. Prentice-Hall, 1981. ISBN 0-13-076091-9 Subj: Buses. Careers. School.

Nicholson, Nicholas B. A. *Little girl in a red dress with cat and dog* ill. by Cynthia von Buhler. Viking, 1998. ISBN 0-670-87183-4 Subj: Animals. Art. Careers – artists. Family life. Farms. U.S. history.

Mona Lisa: the secret of the smile (Galli, Letizia)

Nicholson, William, Sir. *Clever Bill* ill. by author. Doubleday, 1961. Subj: Toys – soldiers.

Nickens, Bessie. *Walking the log* ill. by author. Rizzoli, 1994. ISBN 0-8478-1794-6 Subj: Careers – artists. Ethnic groups in the U.S. – African Americans. Poverty. U.S. history.

Nickl, Peter. *Ra ta ta tam: the strange story of a little engine* by Peter Nickl & Binette Schroeder; ill. by authors. Merrimack, 1984. ISBN 0-224-00974-5 Subj: Character traits – meanness. Format, unusual – board books. Trains.

Nickle, John. *The ant bully* ill. by author. Scholastic, 1999. ISBN 0-590-39591-2 Subj: Behavior – bullying. Concepts – size. Insects – ants.

TV Rex ill. by author. Scholastic, 2001. ISBN 0-439-12043-8 Subj: Emotions – grief. Family life – grandfathers. Imagination. Television.

Nicolai, Margaret. *Kitaq goes ice fishing* ill. by David Rubin. Alaska Northwest Bks., 1998. ISBN 0-88240-504-7 Subj: Alaska. Eskimos. Family life – grandfathers. Sports – fishing.

Nicolas. *see* Mordvinoff, Nicolas

Nicoll, Helen. *Meg and Mog* by Helen Nicoll & Jan Pieńkowski; ill. by Jan Pieńkowski. Atheneum, 1972. ISBN 0-434-95420-9 Subj: Animals – cats. Holidays – Halloween. Magic. Witches.

Meg at sea by Helen Nicoll & Jan Pieńkowski; ill. by Jan Pieńkowski. Harvey House, 1974. ISBN 0-8178-5281-6 Subj: Animals – cats. Birds – owls. Magic. Sea & seashore. Witches.

Meg on the moon by Helen Nicoll & Jan Pieńkowski; ill. by Jan Pieńkowski. Harvey House, 1974. ISBN 0-8178-5271-9 Subj: Animals – cats. Magic. Moon. Witches.

Meg's eggs by Helen Nicoll & Jan Pieńkowski; ill. by Jan Pieńkowski. Atheneum, 1972. ISBN 0-434-95421-7 Subj: Animals – cats. Birds – owls. Dinosaurs. Eggs. Magic. Witches.

Mog's box ill. by Jan Pieńkowski. David & Charles, 1987. ISBN 0-434-95658-9 Subj: Animals – cats. Magic. Witches.

Nidey, Kelli. *When autumn falls* ill. by Susan Swan. A. Whitman, 2004. ISBN 0-8075-0490-4 Subj: Poetry. Seasons – fall.

Nielsen, Laura F. *Jeremy's muffler* ill. by Christine M. Schneider. Bradbury, 1994. ISBN 0-02-768135-1 Subj: Clothing. Family life – aunts, uncles.

Night time written & ill. by the first grade students of Nancy Dutil at Richmond Elementary School, Richmond, Vermont. Willowisp Pr., 1995. Kids are authors award. ISBN 0-87406-800-2 Subj: Children as authors. Children as illustrators. Night.

Nightingale, Sandy. *Cat's knees and bee's whiskers* ill. by author. Harcourt, 1993. ISBN 0-15-215364-0 Subj: Animals – cats. Witches.

Cider apples ill. by author. Harcourt, 1996. ISBN 0-15-201244-3 Subj: Fairies. Family life – grandmothers. Magic. Trees.

A giraffe on the moon ill. by author. Harcourt, 1992. ISBN 0-15-230950-0 Subj: Dreams. Rhyming text.

I'm a little monster ill. by author. Harcourt, 1995. ISBN 0-15-200309-6 Subj: Birthdays. Imagination. Monsters.

Pink pigs aplenty ill. by author. Harcourt, 1992. ISBN 0-15-261882-1 Subj: Animals – pigs. Circus. Counting, numbers.

The witch's spell ill. by author. Andersen, 1998. ISBN 0-86264-739-8 Subj: Behavior – dissatisfaction. Magic. Seasons. Witches.

Nikly, Michelle. *The emperor's plum tree* trans. from French by Elizabeth Shub; ill. by author. Greenwillow, 1982. ISBN 0-688-01244-2 Subj: Friendship. Royalty – emperors. Trees.

The perfume of memory ill. by Jean Claverie. Levine, 1998. ISBN 0-439-08206-4 Subj: Behavior – forgetfulness. Senses – smell.

The princess on the nut: or, the curious courtship of the son of the princess on the pea trans. by Lucy Meredith; ill. by Jean Claverie. Faber, 1981. ISBN 0-571-11846-1 Subj: Folk & fairy tales. Royalty – princesses.

Nikola-Lisa, W. *America: my land, your land, our land* ill. by 14 outstanding American artists. Lee & Low, 1997. ISBN 1-880000-37-7 Subj: Ethnic groups in the U.S. Poetry. U.S. history.

Bein' with you this way ill. by Michael Bryant. Lee & Low, 1994. ISBN 1-880000-05-9 Subj: Activities – playing. Ethnic groups in the U.S. Ethnic groups in the U.S. – African Americans. Friendship. Poetry.

Can you top that? ill. by Hector Viveros Lee. Lee & Low, 2000. ISBN 1-880000-99-7 Subj: Activities – drawing. Animals. Counting, numbers.

The dancin' fox ill. by Marcia Sewall. Atheneum, 2000. ISBN 0-689-82621-4 Subj: Animals – foxes. Behavior – trickery. Birds – turkeys. Folk & fairy tales.

Hallelujah! a Christmas celebration ill. by Synthia Saint James. Atheneum, 1999. ISBN 0-689-81673-1 Subj: Ethnic groups in the U.S. – African Americans. Holidays – Christmas. Religion – Nativity.

Night is coming ill. by Jamichael Henterly. Dutton, 1991. ISBN 0-525-44687-7 Subj: Country. Family life – grandfathers. Night. Noise, sounds.

No babies asleep ill. by Peter Palagonia. Atheneum, 1994. ISBN 0-689-31841-3 Subj: Animals. Babies. Counting, numbers. Rhyming text.

One hole in the road ill. by Dan Yaccarino. Holt, 1996. ISBN 0-8050-4285-7 Subj: Counting, numbers. Machines. Roads.

One, two, three Thanksgiving! ill. by Robin Kramer. A. Whitman, 1991. ISBN 0-8075-6109-6 Subj: Counting, numbers. Family life. Holidays – Thanksgiving.

Shake dem Halloween bones ill. by Mike Reed. Houghton Mifflin, 1997. ISBN 0-395-73095-3 Subj: Holidays – Halloween. Parties. Rhyming text.

Storm ill. by Michael Hays. Atheneum, 1993. ISBN 0-689-31704-2 Subj: Country. Weather – lightning, thunder. Weather – storms.

Summer sun risin' ill. by Don Tate. Lee & Low, 2002. ISBN 1-58430-034-5 Subj: Ethnic groups in the U.S. – African Americans. Family life. Farms. Rhyming text.

Tangletalk ill. by Jessica Clerk. Dutton, 1997. ISBN 0-525-45399-7 Subj: Humorous stories. Rhyming text.

Till year's good end: a calendar of medieval labors ill. by Christopher Manson. Atheneum, 1997. ISBN 0-689-80020-7 Subj: Country. Days of the week, months of the year. Farms. Foreign lands – England.

To hear the angels sing ill. by Jill Weber. Holiday, 2002. ISBN 0-8234-1627-5 Subj: Holidays – Christmas. Religion – Nativity. Rhyming text.

Wheels go round ill. by Jane Conteh-Morgan. Doubleday, 1994. ISBN 0-385-32069-8 Subj: Animals – bulls, cows. Fairs, festivals. Rhyming text. Transportation. Wheels.

The year with Grandma Moses sel. writings & paintings by Grandma Moses. Holt, 2000. ISBN 0-8050-6243-2 Subj: Art. Careers – artists. Seasons.

Niland, Deborah. *ABC of monsters* ill. by author. McGraw-Hill, 1978. ISBN 0-07-046560-6 Subj: ABC books. Monsters.

Niland, Kilmeny. *A bellbird in a flame tree* ill. by author. Morrow, 1991. ISBN 0-688-10798-2 Subj: Foreign lands – Australia. Holidays – Christmas. Music. Songs.

Nilsén, Anna. *Drive your car* ill. by Tony Wells. Candlewick, 1996. ISBN 1-56402-921-2 Subj: Automobiles. Format, unusual.

Drive your tractor ill. by Tony Wells. Candlewick, 1996. ISBN 1-56402-920-4 Subj: Farms. Format, unusual. Tractors.

Let's all hang and dangle ill. by Anni Axworthy. Zero to Ten, 1998. ISBN 1-84089-002-9 Subj: Animals. Format, unusual.

Where are Percy's friends? ill. by Dom Mansell. Candlewick, 1996. ISBN 0-76360-017-2 Subj: Animals. Animals – dogs. Format, unusual – toy & movable books. Friendship.

Where is Percy's dinner? ill. by Dom Mansell. Candlewick, 1996. ISBN 0-76360-019-9 Subj: Animals. Animals – dogs. Food. Format, unusual – toy & movable books.

Nilsson, Ulf. *Little sister rabbit* ill. by Eva Eriksson. Little, 1985. ISBN 0-87113-009-2 Subj: Activities – babysitting. Animals – rabbits. Family life.

Nimmo, Jenny. *Esmeralda and the children next door* ill. by Paul Howard. Houghton, 2000. ISBN 0-618-02902-8 Subj: Circus. Concepts – size. Friendship. Illness.

Something wonderful ill. by Debbie Boon. Harcourt, 2001. ISBN 0-15-216486-3 Subj: Birds – chickens. Character traits – being different.

Nims, Bonnie Larkin. *Just beyond reach and other riddle poems* photos by George Ancona. Scholastic, 1992. ISBN 0-590-44077-2 Subj: Poetry. Riddles & jokes.

Where is the bear? ill. by John Wallner. A. Whitman, 1988. ISBN 0-8075-8933-0 Subj: Behavior – lost. Rhyming text. Toys – bears.

Where is the bear at school? ill. by Madelaine Gill. A. Whitman, 1989. ISBN 0-8075-8935-7 Subj: Games. Picture puzzles. Rhyming text. School. Toys – bears.

Where is the bear in the city? ill. by Madelaine Gill. A. Whitman, 1992. ISBN 0-8075-8937-3 Subj: Animals – bears. Behavior – hiding. Cities, towns. Rhyming text.

Niner, Holly L. *Mr. Worry* ill. by Greg Swearingen. A. Whitman, 2004. ISBN 0-8075-5182-1 Subj: Behavior. Illness – mental illness.

Nipp, Susan Hagen. *Wee Sing if you're happy and you know it* (Beall, Pamela Conon)

Nishikawa, Osamu. *Alexander and the blue ghost* ill. by author. Morrow, 1986. ISBN 0-688-06267-9 Subj: Character traits – bravery. Ghosts. Royalty.

Nishimura, Kae. *Dinah* ill. by author. Clarion, 2004. ISBN 0-618-33612-5 Subj: Animals – cats. Behavior – lost. Humorous stories. Self-concept.

Nister, Ernest. *Little tales from long ago: Cat's cradle, The tale of a dog, Three friends, Three little maids* ill. by author. Delacorte, 1979. ISBN 0-440-04968-6 Subj: Folk & fairy tales.

Nivola, Claire A. *Elisabeth* ill. by author. Farrar, 1997. ISBN 0-374-32085-3 Subj: Ethnic groups in the U.S. – German Americans. Family life. Immigrants. Jewish culture. Toys – dolls. War.

The forest ill. by author. Frances Foster, 2002. ISBN 0-374-32452-2 Subj: Animals – mice. Emotions – fear. Forest, woods.

Nixon, Joan Lowery. *Beats me, Claude* ill. by Tracey Campbell Pearson. Viking, 1986. ISBN 0-670-80781-8 Subj: Activities – baking, cooking. Humorous stories.

Bigfoot makes a movie ill. by Syd Hoff. Putnam, 1979. ISBN 0-399-20684-1 Subj: Behavior – misunderstanding. Folk & fairy tales. Monsters.

Fat chance, Claude ill. by Tracey Campbell Pearson. Viking, 1987. ISBN 0-670-81459-8 Subj: Careers – miners.

Gus and Gertie and the missing pearl ill. by Diane de Groat. SeaStar, 2000. ISBN 1-58717-022-1 Subj: Animals. Birds – penguins. Careers – detectives. Crime. Mystery stories.

If you say so, Claude ill. by Lorinda Bryan Cauley. Warne, 1980. ISBN 0-7232-6183-0 Subj: Activities – traveling. Behavior – seeking better things. U.S. history – frontier & pioneer life.

If you were a writer ill. by Bruce Degen. Four Winds, 1988. ISBN 0-02-768210-2 Subj: Activities – writing.

The Thanksgiving mystery ill. by Jim Cummins. A. Whitman, 1980. ISBN 0-8075-7820-7 Subj: Ghosts. Holidays – Thanksgiving. Mystery stories.

That's the spirit, Claude ill. by Tracey Campbell Pearson. Viking, 1992. ISBN 0-670-83434-3 Subj: Adoption. Holidays – Christmas. Humorous stories. Santa Claus. U.S. history – frontier & pioneer life.

The Valentine mystery ill. by Jim Cummins. A. Whitman, 1979. ISBN 0-8075-8450-9 Subj: Holidays – Valentine's Day. Mystery stories.

When I am eight ill. by Dick Gackenbach. Dial, 1994. ISBN 0-8037-1499-8 Subj: Birthdays. Family life – brothers. Imagination. Sibling rivalry.

Will you give me a dream? ill. by Bruce Degen. Four Winds, 1994. ISBN 0-02-768211-0 Subj: Bedtime. Dreams. Family life – mothers.

You bet your britches, Claude ill. by Tracey Campbell Pearson. Viking, 1989. ISBN 0-670-82310-4 Subj: Adoption. Family life. Humorous stories. U.S. history – frontier & pioneer life.

Njeng, Pierre Yves. *Vacation in the village: a story from West Africa* ill. by author. Boyds Mills, 1999. ISBN 1-56397-768-0 Subj: Activities – vacationing. Foreign lands – Cameroon. Friendship. Seasons – summer.

Noah, build your boat: *Old Testament stories & pictures by kids* ed. by Jeff Kunkel. Augsburg Fortress, 2002. ISBN 0-8066-4402-8 Subj: Children as authors. Children as illustrators. Religion.

Nobens, C. A. *Montgomery's time zone* ill. by author. Carolrhoda, 1990. ISBN 0-87614-398-2 Subj: Dreams. Time.

Nobisso, Josephine. *For the sake of a cake* by Josephine Nobisso & Anton C. Krajnc. Rizzoli, 1993. ISBN 0-8478-1685-0 Subj: Animals – koalas. Character traits – laziness. Reptiles – alligators, crocodiles. Rhyming text.

Grandma's scrapbook ill. by Maureen Hyde. Green Tiger Pr., 1991. ISBN 0-671-74976-5 Subj: Family life – grandmothers. Memories, memory.

Grandpa loved ill. by Maureen Hyde. 2nd ed. Gingerbread House, 2000. ISBN 0-940112-01-9 Subj: Death. Emotions – grief. Emotions – love. Family life – grandfathers.

Hot-cha-cha! ill. by Joan Holub. Winslow, 1998. ISBN 1-890817-00-7 Subj: Activities – playing. Rhyming text.

John Blair and the great Hinckley fire ill. by Ted Rose. Houghton, 2000. ISBN 0-618-01560-4 Subj: Character traits – bravery. Ethnic groups in the U.S. – African Americans. Fire. Trains.

The moon's lullaby ill. by Glo Coalson. Orchard, 2001. ISBN 0-531-33319-1 Subj: Activities. Bedtime. Night. Sleep.

Shh! the whale is smiling ill. by Maureen Hyde. Green Tiger Pr., 1992. ISBN 0-671-74908-0 Subj: Animals – whales. Bedtime. Night. Sea & seashore.

The weight of a Mass ill. by Katalin Szegedi. Gingerbread House, 2002. ISBN 0-940112-09-4 Subj: Religion. Royalty – kings. Royalty – queens. Weddings.

The yawn ill. by Glo Coalson. Orchard, 2001. ISBN 0-531-33319-1 Subj: Sleep.

Noble, June. *Two homes for Lynn* ill. by Yuri Salzman. Holt, 1979. ISBN 0-03-046186-3 Subj: Behavior – sharing. Divorce. Family life. Imagination – imaginary friends.

Noble, Kate. *The blue elephant* ill. by Rachel Bass. Silver Seahorse, 1994. ISBN 0-9631798-3-7 Subj: Animals – elephants. Zoos.

Bubble gum ill. by Rachel Bass. Silver Seahorse, 1995. ISBN 0-9631798-0-2 Subj: Animals. Animals – baboons. Foreign lands – Africa.

The dragon of Navy Pier ill. by Rachel Bass. Silver Seahorse, 1996. ISBN 0-9631798-5-3 Subj: Dragons. Merry-go-rounds.

Oh look, it's a nosserus ill. by Rachel Bass. Silver Seahorse, 1993. ISBN 0-96317-982-9 Subj: Animals. Animals – rhinoceros. Foreign lands – Africa.

Noble, Sheilagh. *More* ill. by author. Zero to Ten, 2000. ISBN 1-84089-127-0 Subj: Animals – dogs. Family life – mothers. Parks.

Noble, Trinka Hakes. *Apple tree Christmas* ill. by author. Dial, 1984. ISBN 0-8037-0103-9 Subj: Farms. Holidays – Christmas. Trees. Weather – storms.

The day Jimmy's boa ate the wash ill. by Steven Kellogg. Dial, 1980. ISBN 0-8037-1724-5 Subj: Activities. Humorous stories. Reptiles – snakes. School – field trips.

Hansy's mermaid ill. by author. Dial, 1983. ISBN 0-8037-3606-1 Subj: Character traits – kindness. Mythical creatures – mermaids, mermen.

Jimmy's boa and the big splash birthday bash ill. by Steven Kellogg. Dial, 1989. ISBN 0-8037-0540-9 Subj: Birthdays. Humorous stories. Pets. Reptiles – snakes.

Jimmy's boa bounces back ill. by Steven Kellogg. Dial, 1984. ISBN 0-8037-0049-0 Subj: Humorous stories. Reptiles – snakes.

The king's tea ill. by author. Dial, 1979. ISBN 0-8037-4520-3 Subj: Cumulative tales. Royalty – kings.

Meanwhile back at the ranch ill. by Tony Ross. Dial, 1987. ISBN 0-8037-0354-6 Subj: Behavior – boredom. Humorous stories.

Nobles, Kristen M. *Drive this book* ill. by author. Chronicle, 2001. ISBN 0-8118-2861-1 Subj: Automobiles. Format, unusual – toy & movable books. Noise, sounds. Transportation. Trucks.

Noda, Takayo. *Dear world* ill. by author. Dial, 2002. ISBN 0-8037-2644-9 Subj: Nature. Poetry.

Nodar, Carmen Santiago. *Abuelita's paradise* ill. by Diane Paterson. A. Whitman, 1992. ISBN 0-8075-0129-8 Subj: Death. Emotions – grief. Family life – grandmothers. Farms. Foreign lands – Puerto Rico.

Nodset, Joan L. *see* Lexau, Joan M.

Noguchi, Rick. *Flowers from Mariko* by Rick Noguchi & Deneen Jenks; ill. by Michelle Reiko Kumata. Lee & Low, 2001. ISBN 1-58430-032-9 Subj: Ethnic groups in the U.S. – Japanese Americans. Gardens, gardening. U.S. history.

Noguere, Suzanne. *Little raccoon* ill. by Tony Chen. Holt, 1981. ISBN 0-03-054826-8 Subj: Animals – raccoons.

Nolan, Dennis. *Androcles and the lion* (Æsop)

The castle builder ill. by author. Macmillan, 1987. ISBN 0-02-768240-4 Subj: Dragons. Imagination. Knights. Sand. Sea & seashore.

Dinosaur dream ill. by author. Aladdin, 1994. ISBN 0-689-71832-2 Subj: Dinosaurs. Dreams. Prehistory.

Fin and the imp (Mills, Lauren A.)

Shadow of the dinosaurs ill. by author. S&S, 2001. ISBN 0-689-82974-4 Subj: Animals – dogs. Dinosaurs. Magic.

Witch Bazooza ill. by author. Prentice-Hall, 1979. ISBN 0-13-961573-3 Subj: Holidays – Halloween. Homes, houses. Witches.

Wizard McBean and his flying machine ill. by author. Prentice-Hall, 1977. ISBN 0-139-61607-1 Subj: Airplanes, airports. Cumulative tales. Magic. Rhyming text. Wizards.

Nolan, Janet. *The St. Patrick's Day shillelagh* ill. by Ben F. Stahl. A. Whitman, 2002. ISBN 0-8075-7344-2 Subj: Activities – storytelling. Ethnic groups in the U.S. – Irish Americans. Foreign lands – Ireland. Holidays – St. Patrick's Day. Immigrants.

Nolan, Lucy A. *Jack Quack* ill. by Andréa Wesson. Cavendish, 2001. ISBN 0-7614-5091-2 Subj: Animals – babies. Birds – ducks. Self-concept.

The Lizard Man of Crabtree County ill. by Jill Kastner. Cavendish, 1999. ISBN 0-7614-5049-1 Subj: Communities, neighborhoods. Country. Humorous stories. Monsters.

Nolan, Madeena Spray. *My daddy don't go to work* ill. by Jim LaMarche. Carolrhoda, 1978. ISBN 0-8761-4093-2 Subj: Ethnic groups in the U.S. – African Americans. Family life. Family life – fathers. Poverty.

Nolen, Jerdine. *Big Jabe* ill. by Kadir Nelson. Lothrop, 2000. ISBN 0-688-13663-X Subj: Ethnic groups in the U.S. – African Americans. Slavery. Tall tales.

Harvey Potter's balloon farm ill. by Mark Buehner. Lothrop, 1994. ISBN 0-688-07888-5 Subj: Farms. Magic. Tall tales. Toys – balloons.

In my momma's kitchen ill. by Colin Bootman. Lothrop, 1999. ISBN 0-688-12761-4 Subj: Activities – baking, cooking. Family life. Homes, houses.

Plantzilla ill. by David Catrow. Harcourt, 2002. ISBN 0-15-202412-3 Subj: Careers – teachers. Humorous stories. Letters, cards. Plants.

Plantzilla goes to camp ill. by David Catrow. S&S, 2005. ISBN 0-689-86803-0 Subj: Behavior – bullying. Camps, camping. Humorous stories. Letters, cards. Plants.

Raising dragons ill. by Elise Primavera. Silver Whistle, 1998. ISBN 0-15-201288-5 Subj: Careers. Dragons. Eggs. Farms. Friendship.

Thunder Rose ill. by Kadir Nelson. Harcourt, 2003. ISBN 0-15-216472-3 Subj: Ethnic groups in the U.S. – African Americans. Tall tales. U.S. history – frontier & pioneer life.

Noll, Sally. *I have a loose tooth* ill. by author. Greenwillow, 1992. ISBN 0-688-11192-0 Subj: Behavior – growing up. Family life – grandmothers. Teeth.

Jiggle wiggle prance ill. by author. Greenwillow, 1987. ISBN 0-688-06761-1 Subj: Activities. Animals.

Lucky morning ill. by author. Greenwillow, 1994. ISBN 0-688-12475-5 Subj: Activities – vacationing. Animals. Family life – grandfathers. Sports – fishing.

Off and counting ill. by author. Greenwillow, 1984. ISBN 0-688-02796-2 Subj: Counting, numbers. Frogs & toads. Rhyming text. Toys.

Surprise! ill. by author. Greenwillow, 1997. ISBN 0-688-15171-X Subj: Animals – cats. Birthdays. Counting, numbers. Holidays.

That bothered Kate ill. by author. Greenwillow, 1991. ISBN 0-688-10096-1 Subj: Behavior – growing up. Behavior – imitation. Family life – sisters. Sibling rivalry.

Watch where you go ill. by author. Greenwillow, 1990. ISBN 0-688-08499-0 Subj: Animals – mice. Optical illusions.

Nomura, Noriko S. *I am Shinto* photos by author. Rosen, 1996. ISBN 0-8239-2380-0 Subj: Religion.

Nomura, Takaaki. *Grandpa's town* ill. by author; trans. by Amanda Mayer Stinchecum. Kane/Miller, 1991. ISBN 0-916291-57-X Subj: Activities – bathing. Emotions – loneliness. Family life – grandfathers. Foreign lands – Japan. Foreign languages. Friendship.

Nones, Eric Jon. *Angela's wings* ill. by author. Farrar, 1995. ISBN 0-374-30331-2 Subj: Activities – flying. Character traits – being different.

Caleb's friend ill. by author. Farrar, 1993. ISBN 0-374-31017-3 Subj: Friendship. Mythical creatures – mermaids, mermen.

Canary prince ill. by author. Farrar, 1991. ISBN 0-374-31029-7 Subj: Birds – canaries. Folk & fairy tales. Foreign lands – Italy. Magic. Royalty – princes. Royalty – princesses.

Wendell ill. by author. Farrar, 1989. ISBN 0-374-38266-2 Subj: Animals – cats. Behavior – misbehavior. Family life. Mythical creatures.

Noonan, Diana. *The crocodile* ill. with photos. Chelsea, 2003. ISBN 0-7910-6964-8 Subj: Animals – endangered animals. Reptiles – alligators, crocodiles.

Noonan, Julia. *Bath day* ill. by author. Scholastic, 2000. ISBN 0-439-11492-6 Subj: Activities – bathing. Animals – dogs. Rhyming text.

Breakfast time ill. by author. Scholastic, 2000. ISBN 0-439-11490-X Subj: Animals – dogs. Food. Rhyming text.

Hare and Rabbit, friends forever ill. by author. Scholastic, 2000. ISBN 0-439-08753-8 Subj: Animals – rabbits. Character traits – cleanliness. Circus. Friendship.

Mouse by mouse ill. by author. Dutton, 2003. ISBN 0-525-46864-1 Subj: Animals – mice. Counting, numbers. Format, unusual – toy & movable books. Rhyming text.

Norac, Carl. *Hello, sweetie pie* ill. by Claude K. Dubois. Random House, 2000. ISBN 0-385-32733-1 Subj: Animals – hamsters. Names. School.

I love to cuddle ill. by Claude K. Dubois. Doubleday, 1999. ISBN 0-385-32646-7 Subj: Animals – hamsters. Emotions – loneliness. Format, unusual – board books.

I love you so much ill. by Claude K. Dubois. Doubleday, 1997. ISBN 0-385-32512-6 Subj: Animals – hamsters. Emotions – love. Family life.

My daddy is a giant ill. by Ingrid Godon. Clarion, 2005. ISBN 0-618-44399-1 Subj: Concepts – size. Family life – fathers.

Norby, Lisa. *The Herself the elf storybook.* Scholastic, 1983. ISBN 0-590-32911-1 Subj: Magic. Mythical creatures – elves.

Nordlicht, Lillian. *I love to laugh* ill. by Allen Davis. Raintree, 1980. ISBN 0-8172-1364-3 Subj: Behavior – growing up. Character traits – being different.

Nordqvist, Sven. *Festus and Mercury go camping* ill. by author. Carolrhoda, 1993. ISBN 0-87614-802-X Subj: Animals – cats. Birds – chickens. Camps, camping. Humorous stories.

Festus and Mercury: ruckus in the garden ill. by author. Carolrhoda, 1991. ISBN 0-87614-678-7 Subj: Animals – cats. Gardens, gardening. Seasons – spring.

Festus and Mercury wishing to go fishing ill. by author. Carolrhoda, 1991. ISBN 0-87614-658-2 Subj: Animals – cats. Humorous stories. Old age. Sports – fishing.

The fox hunt ill. by author. Morrow, 1988. ISBN 0-688-06882-0 Subj: Animals – cats. Animals – foxes. Behavior – trickery. Careers – farmers.

Pancake pie ill. by author. Morrow, 1985. ISBN 0-688-04142-6 Subj: Animals – cats. Food.

Porker finds a chair ill. by author. Carolrhoda, 1989. ISBN 0-87614-367-2 Subj: Animals – bears. Behavior – misunderstanding. Furniture – chairs.

Porker's taxi ill. by author. Carolrhoda, 1992. ISBN 0-87614-744-9 Subj: Animals – bears. Taxis.

Willie in the big world: adventures with numbers ill. by author. Morrow, 1986. ISBN 0-688-06143-5 Subj: Activities – traveling. Counting, numbers.

Norling, Beth. *Sister night and sister day* ill. by author. Allen & Unwin, 2000. Retelling of the Grimm's fairy tale Mother Holle. ISBN 1-86448-863-8 Subj: Family life – sisters. Folk & fairy tales. Foreign lands – Germany. Multiple births – twins.

The stone baby ill. by author. Lothian, 2004. ISBN 0-7344-0353-4 Subj: Activities – traveling. Birds. Emotions. Toys – dolls.

Norman, Charles. *The hornbean tree and other poems* ill. by Ted Rand. Holt, 1988. ISBN 0-8050-0417-3 Subj: Animals. Birds. Nature. Poetry.

Norman, Howard A. *The owl-scatterer* ill. by Michael McCurdy. Atlantic Monthly, 1986. ISBN 0-87113-058-0 Subj: Behavior – disbelief. Birds – owls. Foreign lands – Canada.

Who-Paddled-Backward-With-Trout ill. by Ed Young. Little, 1987. ISBN 0-316-61182-4 Subj: Folk & fairy tales. Foreign lands – Canada. Indians of North America – Cree. Names.

Norman, Philip Ross. *The carrot war* ill. by author. Little, 1992. ISBN 0-316-61200-6 Subj: Animals – rabbits. Food. War.

Dancing dogs ill. by author. Little, 1995. ISBN 0-316-61208-1 Subj: Activities – dancing. Animals – cats. Animals – dogs.

A mammoth imagination ill. by author. Little, 1992. ISBN 0-316-61201-4 Subj: Animals. Imagination. Weather – snow.

Norris, Kathleen. *The holy twins: Benedict and Scholastica* ill. by Tomie De Paola. Putnam, 2001. ISBN 0-399-23424-1 Subj: Careers – clergy. Careers – nuns. Family life – brothers & sisters. Foreign lands – Italy. Multiple births – twins. Religion.

Norris, Leslie. *Albert and the angels* ill. by Mordicai Gerstein. Farrar, 2000. ISBN 0-374-30192-1 Subj: Angels. Animals – dogs. Behavior – lost & found possessions. Holidays – Christmas.

Norris, Lori P. (Peters). *D is for divorce* ill. by author. Health Communications, 1991. ISBN 1-55874-140-2 Subj: Divorce.

North, George Captain. *see* Stevenson, Robert Louis

Northam, Leland. *Hansel and Gretel* (Grimm, Jacob)

Sleeping Beauty (Grimm, Jacob)

The ugly duckling (Andersen, H. C. [Hans Christian])

Northey, Lawrence. *I'm a hop hop hoppity frog* ill. by Julie Northey. Stoddart, 2002. ISBN 0-7737-3335-3 Subj: Frogs & toads. Poetry. Rhyming text.

Northrup, Mili. *The watch cat* ill. by Adrina Zanazanian; designed by Kent Salisbury. Bobbs-Merrill, 1968. Subj: Animals – cats. Foreign lands – Thailand.

Northway, Jennifer. *Get lost, Laura!* ill. by author. Artists & Writers Guild, 1995. ISBN 0-307-17520-0 Subj: Activities – playing. Family life – cousins. Family life – sisters. Sibling rivalry.

Lucy's day trip ill. by author. André Deutsch, 1991. ISBN 0-233-98423-2 Subj: Family life – cousins. Foreign lands – England. Marriage, interracial.

Norton, Natalie. *A little old man* ill. by Will Huntington. Rand McNally, 1959. Subj: Emotions – loneliness.

Norwich, William D. *Molly and the magic dress* ill. by M. Scott Miller. Doubleday, 2002. ISBN 0-385-32745-5 Subj: Animals – cats. Clothing – dresses. Emotions – loneliness. Imagination. Magic.

Norworth, Jack. *Take me out to the ballgame* ill. by Alec Gillman. Four Winds, 1993. ISBN 0-02-735991-3 Subj: Songs. Sports – baseball.

Nourse, Alan Edward. *Lumps, bumps and rashes: a look at kids' diseases.* Watts, 1990. ISBN 0-531-10865-1 Subj: Illness.

Novak, Matt. *Claude and Sun* ill. by author. Bradbury, 1987. ISBN 0-02-768151-3 Subj: Friendship. Sun.

Elmer Blunt's open house ill. by author. Orchard, 1992. ISBN 0-531-08598-8 Subj: Behavior – carelessness. Homes, houses.

Gertie and Gumbo ill. by author. Orchard, 1995. ISBN 0-531-08778-6 Subj: Emotions – loneliness. Family life – fathers. Music. Reptiles – alligators, crocodiles. Sports – wrestling.

Jazzbo and Googy ill. by author. Hyperion, 2000. ISBN 0-7868-2340-2 Subj: Animals – bears. Animals – pigs. Friendship. Toys – bears.

Jazzbo goes to school ill. by author. Hyperion, 1999. ISBN 0-7868-2339-9 Subj: Animals – bears. School – first day.

The last Christmas present ill. by author. Orchard, 1993. ISBN 0-531-08645-3 Subj: Holidays – Christmas. Mythical creatures – elves. Santa Claus.

Little Wolf, Big Wolf ill. by author. HarperCollins, 2000. ISBN 0-06-027487-5 Subj: Animals – wolves. Character traits – being different. Friendship.

Mr. Floop's lunch ill. by author. Watts, 1990. ISBN 0-531-08426-4 Subj: Animals. Behavior – sharing. Character traits – kindness to animals.

Mouse TV ill. by author. Orchard, 1994. ISBN 0-531-08706-9 Subj: Animals – mice. Family life. Television.

No zombies allowed ill. by author. Atheneum, 2001. ISBN 0-689-84130-2 Subj: Holidays – Halloween. Parties. Witches.

The Pillow War ill. by author. Orchard, 1998. ISBN 0-531-33048-6 Subj: Animals – dogs. Behavior – fighting, arguing. Family life – brothers & sisters. Rhyming text. Sleep.

The Robobots ill. by author. DK, 1999. ISBN 0-7894-2566-1 Subj: Communities, neighborhoods. Robots.

Rolling ill. by author. Bradbury, 1986. ISBN 0-02-768150-5 Subj: Weather – lightning, thunder.

While the shepherd slept ill. by author. Watts, 1991. ISBN 0-531-08515-5 Subj: Animals – sheep. Sleep. Theater.

Noyed, Robert B. *Crocodiles* (Klingel, Cynthia Fitterer)

Deserts (Klingel, Cynthia Fitterer)

Farmers (Klingel, Cynthia Fitterer)

Firefighters (Klingel, Cynthia Fitterer)

Forests (Klingel, Cynthia Fitterer)

Grizzly bears (Klingel, Cynthia Fitterer)

Halloween (Klingel, Cynthia Fitterer)

Manatees (Klingel, Cynthia Fitterer)

Oceans (Klingel, Cynthia Fitterer)

Paul Revere's ride (Klingel, Cynthia Fitterer)

Postal workers (Klingel, Cynthia Fitterer)

Rosa Parks (Klingel, Cynthia Fitterer)

Soccer (Klingel, Cynthia Fitterer)

Thanksgiving (Klingel, Cynthia Fitterer)

Timber wolves (Klingel, Cynthia Fitterer)

Underground (Klingel, Cynthia Fitterer)

Noyes, Alfred. *The highwayman* ill. by Neil Waldman. Harcourt, 1990. ISBN 0-15-234340-7 Subj: Crime. Emotions – love. Poetry. Royalty – kings.

Noyes, Deborah. *It's Vladimir!* ill. by Christopher Mills. Cavendish, 2001. ISBN 0-7614-5071-8 Subj: Activities – flying. Behavior. Monsters – vampires.

Numeroff, Laura Joffe. *Amy for short* ill. by author. Macmillan, 1976. ISBN 0-02-768180-7 Subj: Character traits – appearance. Friendship.

The Chicken sisters ill. by Sharleen Collicott. Geringer, 1997. ISBN 0-06-026680-5 Subj: Animals. Birds – chickens. Family life – sisters. Farms.

Chimps don't wear glasses ill. by Joseph Mathieu. S&S, 1995. ISBN 0-671-87007-6 Subj: Activities. Animals. Imagination. Rhyming text.

Emily's bunch by Laura Joffe Numeroff & Alice Numeroff Richter; ill. by Laura Joffe Numeroff. Macmillan, 1978. ISBN 0-02-768430-X Subj: Holidays – Halloween.

The hope tree Laura Numeroff and Wendy S. Harpham; ill. by David McPhail. S&S, 1999. ISBN 0-689-84526-X Subj: Animals. Emotions. Family life – mothers. Illness – cancer.

If you give a moose a muffin ill. by Felicia Bond. HarperCollins, 1991. ISBN 0-06-024406-2 Subj: Animals – moose. Character traits – kindness to animals. Circular tales.

If you give a mouse a cookie ill. by Felicia Bond. HarperCollins, 1985. ISBN 0-06-024587-5 Subj: Animals – mice. Behavior – imitation. Character traits – kindness to animals. Circular tales.

If you give a pig a pancake ill. by Felicia Bond. Geringer, 1998. ISBN 0-06-026687-2 Subj: Animals – pigs. Character traits – kindness to animals. Circular tales.

If you take a mouse to school ill. by Felicia Bond. Geringer, 2002. ISBN 0-06-028329-7 Subj: Animals – mice. School.

If you take a mouse to the movies ill. by Felicia Bond. Geringer, 2000. ISBN 0-06-027868-4 Subj: Activities. Animals – mice. Holidays – Christmas.

Laura Numeroff's 10-step guide to living with your monster ill. by Nate Evans. Geringer, 2002. ISBN 0-06-623823-4 Subj: Humorous stories. Monsters. Pets.

Monster munchies ill. by Nate Evans. Random House, 1998. ISBN 0-679-99163-8 Subj: Counting, numbers. Monsters. Rhyming text.

Phoebe Dexter has Harriet Peterson's sniffles ill. by author. Greenwillow, 1977. ISBN 0-688-84091-4 Subj: Illness.

Sherman Crunchley Laura Numeroff & Nate Evans; ill. by Tim Bowers. Dutton, 2003. ISBN 0-525-47130-8 Subj: Animals – dogs. Careers – police officers. Character traits – individuality. Clothing – hats.

Sometimes I wonder if poodles like noodles ill. by Tim Bowers. S&S, 1999. ISBN 0-689-80563-2 Subj: Humorous stories. Poetry.

What daddies do best ill. by Lynn Munsinger. S&S, 2002. ISBN 0-689-82554-4 Subj: Animals – foxes. Buildings. Cities, towns. Family life – fathers. Gender roles.

What grandmas do best; What grandpas do best ill. by Lynn Munsinger. S&S, 2000. ISBN 0-689-80552-7 Subj: Animals. Family life – grandfathers. Family life – grandmothers. Format, unusual.

What mommies do best ill. by Lynn Munsinger. S&S, 1998. ISBN 0-689-80577-2 Subj: Activities – picnicking. Animals – mice. Gender roles.

Why a disguise? ill. by David McPhail. S&S, 1996. ISBN 0-671-87006-8 Subj: Character traits – appearance.

You can't put braces on spaces (Richter, Alice Numeroff)

Nunes, Susan Miho. *Coyote dreams* ill. by Ronald Himler. Aladdin, 1994. ISBN 0-689-71804-7 Subj: Animals – coyotes. Desert. Dreams. Imagination.

The last dragon ill. by Chris K. Soentpiet. Clarion, 1995. ISBN 0-395-67020-9 Subj: Dragons. Ethnic groups in the U.S. – Chinese Americans. Family life – aunts, uncles.

Tiddalick the frog ill. by Ju-Hong chen. Atheneum, 1989. ISBN 0-689-31502-3 Subj: Folk & fairy tales. Foreign lands – Australia. Frogs & toads.

Nursery rhymes ill. by Gertrude Elliott. S&S, 1948. Subj: Nursery rhymes.

Nussbaumer, Mares. *Away in a manger: a story of the Nativity* by Mares & Paul Nussbaumer; ill. by Paul Nussbaumer. Harcourt, 1965. Translation of Ihr Kinderlein kommet. ISBN 0-15-204735-2 Subj: Holidays – Christmas. Music. Religion – Nativity.

Nussbaumer, Paul. *Away in a manger: a story of the Nativity* (Nussbaumer, Mares)

Nye, Naomi Shihab. *Benito's dream bottle* ill. by Yu Cha Pak. S&S, 1995. ISBN 0-02-768467-9 Subj: Dreams. Family life – grandmothers. Poetry.

Come with me: poems for a journey ill. by Dan Yaccarino. Greenwillow, 2000. ISBN 0-688-15947-8 Subj: Activities – traveling. Poetry.

Lullaby raft ill. by Vivienne Flesher. S&S, 1997. ISBN 0-689-80521-7 Subj: Animals. Family life – mothers. Lullabies. Night.

Sitti's secrets ill. by Nancy Carpenter. Four Winds, 1994. ISBN 0-02-768460-1 Subj: Ethnic groups in the U.S. – Arab Americans. Family life – grandmothers. Foreign lands – Palestine. Foreign languages.

Nygaard, Elizabeth. *Snake alley band* ill. by Betsy Lewin. Doubleday, 1998. ISBN 0-385-32323-9 Subj: Animals. Music. Musical instruments – bands. Noise, sounds. Reptiles – snakes.

Nygren, Tord. *The red thread* ill. by author. Farrar, 1988. ISBN 91-29-59005-1 Subj: Imagination. Wordless.

O Christmas tree ill. by Michael Hague. Holt, 1991. ISBN 0-8050-1538-8 Subj: Holidays – Christmas. Songs. Trees.

Oakes, Bill. *Numblers* (MacDonald, Suse)

Once upon another (MacDonald, Suse)

Oakley, Graham. *The church cat abroad* ill. by author. Atheneum, 1973. ISBN 0-333-14825-8 Subj: Animals – cats. Animals – mice. Foreign lands – England.

The church mice adrift ill. by author. Atheneum, 1976. ISBN 0-689-30562-1 Subj: Animals – mice. Animals – rats. Rivers.

The church mice and the moon ill. by author. Atheneum, 1974. ISBN 0-689-30437-4 Subj: Animals – cats. Animals – mice. Foreign lands – England. Moon.

The church mice and the ring ill. by author. Atheneum, 1992. ISBN 0-689-31790-5 Subj: Animals – cats. Animals – dogs. Animals – mice. Friendship. Homes, houses.

The church mice at bay ill. by author. Atheneum, 1978. ISBN 0-333-23235-6 Subj: Animals – cats. Animals – mice. Foreign lands – England.

The church mice at Christmas ill. by author. Atheneum, 1980. ISBN 0-689-30797-7 Subj: Animals – mice. Holidays – Christmas.

The church mice in action ill. by author. Atheneum, 1983. ISBN 0-689-30949-X Subj: Animals – mice. Problem solving.

The church mice spread their wings ill. by author. Atheneum, 1975. ISBN 0-689-30496-X Subj: Animals – cats. Animals – mice. Foreign lands – England.

The church mouse ill. by author. Aladdin, 1987, c1972. ISBN 0-689-70475-5 Subj: Animals – cats. Animals – mice. Foreign lands – England.

The diary of a church mouse ill. by author. Atheneum, 1987. ISBN 0-689-31334-9 Subj: Activities – writing. Animals – cats. Animals – mice.

Graham Oakley's magical changes ill. by author. Atheneum, 1980. ISBN 0-689-30732-2 Subj: Format, unusual – toy & movable books. Imagination. Wordless.

Hetty and Harriet ill. by author. Atheneum, 1982. ISBN 0-689-30888-4 Subj: Behavior – running away. Birds – chickens.

Oana, Kay D. *Robbie and the raggedy scarecrow* ill. by Jackie Stephens. Oddo, 1978. ISBN 0-87783-154-8 Subj: Birds. Scarecrows. Trees.

Shasta and the shebang machine ill. by Jackie Stephens. Oddo, 1978. ISBN 0-87783-152-1 Subj: Animals – cats. Behavior – misbehavior.

Oates, Eddie Hershel. *Making music: 6 instruments you can create* ill. by Michael Koelsch. HarperCollins, 1995. ISBN 0-06-021479-1 Subj: Activities – making things. Music. Musical instruments. Noise, sounds.

Oates, Joyce Carol. *Come meet Muffin!* ill. by Mark Graham. Ecco, 1998. ISBN 0-88001-556-X Subj: Animals – cats. Animals – deer. Behavior – lost.

Oberman, Sheldon. *The always prayer shawl* ill. by Ted Lewin. Boyds Mills, 1994. ISBN 1-878093-22-3 Subj: Clothing. Family life – grandfathers. Immigrants. Jewish culture.

By the Hanukkah light ill. by Neil Waldman. Boyds Mills, 1997. ISBN 1-56397-658-7 Subj: Family life – grandfathers. Holidays – Hanukkah. Holocaust. War.

King Solomon, Sheba, and the hoopoe bird ill. by Neil Waldman. Boyds Mills, 2000. ISBN 1-56397-816-4 Subj: Character traits – responsibility. Jewish culture. Religion. Royalty – kings.

Sound of the shofar ill. by Neil Waldman. Boyds Mills, 1997. ISBN 1-56397-557-2 Subj: Jewish culture. Religion.

The white stone in the castle wall ill. by Les Tait. Tundra, 1995. ISBN 0-88776-333-2 Subj: Castles. Foreign lands – Canada.

The wisdom bird: a tale of Solomon and Sheba ill. by Neil Waldman. Boyds Mills, 2000. ISBN 1-56397-816-4 Subj: Birds. Character traits – wisdom. Folk & fairy tales. Foreign lands – Africa. Foreign lands – Israel. Royalty – kings. Royalty – queens.

Obligado, Lilian. *Faint frogs feeling feverish and other terrifically tantalizing tongue twisters* ill. by author. Viking, 1983. ISBN 0-670-30477-8 Subj: ABC books. Animals. Tongue twisters.

O'Book, Irene. *Maybe my baby* photos by Paula Hible. Harper-Collins, 1997. ISBN 0-694-00872-9 Subj: Babies. Careers. Rhyming text.

Oborne, Martine. *One beautiful baby* ill. by Ingrid Godon. Little, 2002. ISBN 0-316-06562-5 Subj: Babies.

O'Brien, Anne Sibley. *Come play with us* ill. by author. Holt, 1985. ISBN 0-03-005008-1 Subj: Activities. Format, unusual – board books. School – nursery.

I want that! ill. by author. Holt, 1985. ISBN 0-03-005012-X Subj: Behavior – sharing. Format, unusual – board books.

I'm not tired ill. by author. Holt, 1985. ISBN 0-03-005009-X Subj: Character traits – stubbornness. Format, unusual – board books.

Where's my truck? ill. by author. Holt, 1985. ISBN 0-03-005013-8 Subj: Behavior – lost & found possessions. Format, unusual – board books.

O'Brien, Claire. *Sam's sneaker search* ill. by Charles Fuge. S&S, 1997. ISBN 0-689-80169-6 Subj: Activities. Animals. Behavior – lost & found possessions.

O'Brien, John. *The farmer in the dell* (The farmer in the dell)

O'Brien, John (1953–). *Mother Hubbard's Christmas* ill. by author. Boyds Mills, 1996. ISBN 1-56397-139-9 Subj: Animals – dogs. Holidays – Christmas. Rhyming text.

Poof! ill. by author. Boyds Mills, 1999. ISBN 1-56397-815-6 Subj: Babies. Family life. Magic. Witches. Wizards.

Sam and Spot ill. by author. Cool Kids, 1995. ISBN 1-56790-500-5 Subj: Animals – dogs. Language.

O'Brien, Mary. *Counting sheep to sleep* ill. by Bobette McCarthy. Little, 1992. ISBN 0-316-62206-0 Subj: Animals – sheep. Bedtime. Counting, numbers. Farms. Sleep.

O'Brien, Patrick. *Gigantic! how big were the dinosaurs?* ill. by author. Holt, 1999. ISBN 0-8050-5738-2 Subj: Concepts – size. Dinosaurs.

Megatooth ill. by author. Holt, 2001. ISBN 0-8050-6214-9 Subj: Fish – sharks. Teeth.

Steam, smoke, and steel ill. by author. Charlesbridge, 2000. ISBN 0-88106-969-8 Subj: Careers – railroad engineers. Family life. Trains.

Obrist, Jürg. *Bear business* ill. by author. Atheneum, 1986. ISBN 0-689-31149-4 Subj: Animals – bears. Behavior – misbehavior. Multiple births – twins.

Fluffy: the story of a cat ill. by author. Atheneum, 1981. ISBN 0-689-30722-5 Subj: Animals – cats. Moving.

The miser who wanted the sun ill. by author. Atheneum, 1984. ISBN 0-689-50294-X Subj: Behavior – greed. Character traits – cleverness. Sun.

They do things right in Albern ill. by author. Atheneum, 1978. ISBN 0-689-30671-7 Subj: Animals – moles. Problem solving.

O'Callahan, Jay. *Herman and Marguerite* ill. by Laura O'Callahan. Peachtree, 1996. ISBN 1-56145-103-7 Subj: Animals – worms. Friendship. Insects – butterflies, caterpillars.

Orange cheeks ill. by Patricia Raine. Peachtree, 1993. ISBN 1-56145-073-1 Subj: Behavior. Family life – grandmothers.

Tulips ill. by Debrah Santini. Picture Book Studio, 1992. ISBN 0-88708-223-8 Subj: Behavior – trickery. Family life – grandmothers. Flowers. Foreign lands – France. Gardens, gardening.

Ochiltree, Dianne. *Pillow pup* ill. by Mireille d'Allancé. McElderry, 2002. ISBN 0-689-83408-X Subj: Activities – playing. Animals – dogs. Rhyming text.

O'Connor, Francine M. *The ABC's of Christmas* ill. by Bartholomew. Liguori Pub., 1994. ISBN 0-8924-3581-X Subj: Holidays – Christmas. Religion – Nativity. Rhyming text.

O'Connor, Jane. *Benny's big bubble* ill. by Tomie de Paola. Grosset, 1997. ISBN 0-448-41303-5 Subj: Bubbles. Rebuses.

Kate skates ill. by DyAnne DiSalvo-Ryan. Grosset, 1995. ISBN 0-448-40936-4 Subj: Behavior – sharing. Family life – sisters. Sports – ice skating.

Nina, Nina and the copycat ballerina ill. by DyAnne DiSalvo-Ryan. Grosset, 2000. ISBN 0-448-42152-6 Subj: Activities – dancing. Ballet. Behavior – imitation.

Nina, Nina ballerina ill. by DyAnne DiSalvo-Ryan. Grosset, 1993. ISBN 0-448-40512-1 Subj: Accidents. Activities – dancing. Ballet.

Nina, Nina, star ballerina ill. by DyAnne DiSalvo-Ryan. Grosset, 1997. ISBN 0-448-41611-5 Subj: Activities – dancing. Ballet. Character traits – honesty.

The perfect puppy for me ill. by Jessie Hartland. Viking, 2003. ISBN 0-670-03614-5 Subj: Animals – dogs. Pets.

Sir Small and the dragonfly ill. by John O'Brien. Random House, 2003. ISBN 0-394-99625-9 Subj: Concepts – size. Insects – ants. Insects – dragonflies. Knights.

Snail City ill. by Rick Brown. Grosset, 2001. ISBN 0-448-42471-1 Subj: Animals – snails. Character traits – being different. Cities, towns. Concepts – speed.

The teeny tiny woman ill. by R. W. Alley. Random House, 1986. ISBN 0-394-98320-3 Subj: Folk & fairy tales. Ghosts.

O'Connor, Teddy. *A new brain for Igor* ill. by Bill Basso. Random House, 2003. ISBN 0-375-90626-6 Subj: Anatomy – brain. Careers – scientists.

O'Cuilleanain, Eilis Dillon. *see* Dillon, Eilis

O'Donnell, Elizabeth Lee. *I can't get my turtle to move* ill. by Maxie Chambliss. Morrow, 1989. ISBN 0-688-07324-7 Subj: Counting, numbers. Pets. Reptiles – turtles, tortoises.

Maggie doesn't want to move ill. by Amy Schwartz. Four Winds, 1987. ISBN 0-02-768830-5 Subj: Behavior – dissatisfaction. Behavior – running away. Emotions. Family life. Moving.

Patrick's day ill. by Jacqueline Rogers. Morrow, 1994. ISBN 0-688-07854-0 Subj: Birthdays. Foreign lands – Ireland. Holidays – St. Patrick's Day. Parades. Self-concept.

Sing me a window ill. by Melissa Sweet. Morrow, 1993. ISBN 0-688-09501-1 Subj: Bedtime. Family life – fathers. Poetry. Toys – bears.

The twelve days of summer ill. by Karen Lee Schmidt. Morrow, 1991. ISBN 0-688-08203-3 Subj: Counting, numbers. Poetry. Sea & seashore. Seasons – summer.

Winter visitors ill. by Carol Schwartz. Morrow, 1997. ISBN 0-688-13064-X Subj: Animals. Counting, numbers. Rhyming text. Seasons – winter.

O'Donnell, Peter. *Carnegie's excuse* ill. by author. Scholastic, 1992. ISBN 0-590-46435-3 Subj: Animals. Animals – tigers. Behavior – promptness, tardiness. Parks – amusement. School.

Dizzy ill. by author. Scholastic, 1992. ISBN 0-590-45475-7 Subj: Airplanes, airports. Animals – elephants.

Moonlit journey ill. by author. Scholastic, 1991. ISBN 0-590-44655-X Subj: Animals. Emotions – fear. Forest, woods. Night. Toys – bears.

Oscar ill. by author. ABC, 1992. ISBN 1-8540-6135-6 Subj: Animals – elephants. Cities, towns. Jungle.

Pinkie goes south ill. by author. ABC, 1991. ISBN 1-8540-6120-8 Subj: Birds – penguins. Friendship.

Odoyevsky, Vladimir. *Old Father Frost* trans. from Russian by James Riordan; ill. by Vassili Shulzhenko. Imported Pubs., 1983. ISBN 0-8285-2216-2 Subj: Folk & fairy tales. Foreign lands – Russia. Seasons – winter.

Oechsli, Helen. *Fly away!* by Helen & Kelly Oechsli; ill. by Kelly Oechsli. Macmillan, 1992. ISBN 0-02-768520-9 Subj: Activities – traveling. Airplanes, airports. Family life – grandparents.

In my garden: a child's gardening book by Helen & Kelly Oechsli; ill. by Kelly Oechsli. Macmillan, 1985. ISBN 0-02-768510-1 Subj: Gardens, gardening.

Oechsli, Kelly. *Fly away!* (Oechsli, Helen)

In my garden: a child's gardening book (Oechsli, Helen)

Offen, Hilda. *As quiet as a mouse* ill. by author. Dutton, 1994. ISBN 0-525-45309-1 Subj: Animals. Noise, sounds. Rhyming text.

Elephant pie ill. by author. Dutton, 1993. ISBN 0-525-45123-4 Subj: Animals – elephants. Behavior – lost. Food. Reptiles – alligators, crocodiles.

A fox got my socks ill. by author. Dutton, 1993. ISBN 0-525-44991-4 Subj: Animals. Clothing. Rhyming text.

Good girl, Gracie Growler! ill. by author. G. Stevens, 1996. ISBN 0-8368-1624-2 Subj: Animals – tigers. Babies. Family life – brothers & sisters. Sibling rivalry.

Nice work, little wolf! ill. by author. Dutton, 1992. ISBN 0-525-44880-2 Subj: Animals – pigs. Animals – wolves.

The sheep made a leap ill. by author. Dutton, 1994. ISBN 0-525-45174-9 Subj: Activities – playing. Animals. Games. Rhyming text.

Ó Flatharta, Antoine. *Hurry and the monarch* ill. by Meilo So. Knopf, 2005. ISBN 0-375-93003-5 Subj: Friendship. Insects – butterflies, caterpillars. Migration. Reptiles – turtles, tortoises.

The prairie train ill. by Eric Rohmann. Crown, 1999. ISBN 0-613-86679-7 Subj: Immigrants. Trains. U.S. history – frontier & pioneer life.

Ogburn, Jacqueline K. *The jukebox man* ill. by James Ransome. Dial, 1998. ISBN 0-8037-1430-0 Subj: Family life – grandfathers. Music.

The magic nesting doll ill. by Laurel Long. Dial, 2000. ISBN 0-8037-2414-4 Subj: Family life – grandmothers. Folk & fairy tales. Magic. Royalty – tsars. Toys – dolls.

The Masked Maverick ill. by Nancy Carlson. Lothrop, 1994. ISBN 0-688-11050-9 Subj: Character traits – individuality. Sports – wrestling.

Noise lullaby ill. by John Sandford. Lothrop, 1994. ISBN 0-688-10453-3 Subj: Bedtime. Lullabies. Noise, sounds.

The reptile ball ill. by John O'Brien. Dial, 1997. ISBN 0-8037-1732-6 Subj: Frogs & toads. Parties. Poetry. Reptiles.

Scarlett Angelina Wolverton-Manning ill. by Brian Ajhar. Dial, 1994. ISBN 0-8037-1377-0 Subj: Crime. Mythical creatures – werewolves.

Ogle, Lucille. *A B See* by Lucille Ogle & Tina Thoburn; ill. by Ralph Stobart. McGraw-Hill, 1973. ISBN 0-07-047498-2 Subj: ABC books.

I hear by Lucille Ogle & Tina Thoburn; ill. by Eloise Wilkin. American Heritage, 1971. ISBN 0-07-047543-1 Subj: Noise, sounds. Participation. Senses – hearing.

I spy ill. by Joe Kaufman. American Heritage, 1970. ISBN 0-07-047549-0 Subj: Senses – sight. Wordless.

Oh, Jiwon. *Cat and mouse* ill. by author. HarperCollins, 2003. ISBN 0-06-052744-7 Subj: Animals – cats. Animals – mice. Friendship.

O'Hagan, Caroline. *It's easy to have a caterpillar visit you* ill. by Judith Allan. Lothrop, 1980. ISBN 0-688-51847-4 Subj: Insects – butterflies, caterpillars. Metamorphosis. Pets.

It's easy to have a snail visit you ill. by Judith Allan. Lothrop, 1980. ISBN 0-688-51848-2 Subj: Animals – snails. Pets.

It's easy to have a worm visit you ill. by Judith Allan. Lothrop, 1980. ISBN 0-688-51846-6 Subj: Animals – worms. Pets.

O'Hare, Colette. *What do you feed your donkey on? rhymes from a Belfast childhood* (What do you feed your donkey on?)

O'Hearn, Michael. *Hercules the harbor tug* ill. by Mela Lyman. Charlesbridge, 1994. ISBN 0-88106-890-X Subj: Boats, ships.

Ohi, Ruth. *Beneath the bridge* (Hutchins, H. J. [Hazel J.])

Pants off first ill. by author. Fitzhenry & Whiteside, 2001. ISBN 1-55041-667-7 Subj: Bedtime. Clothing. Family life – mothers. Format, unusual – board books. Pets.

O Huigin, Sean. *King of the birds* ill. by Tim Dixon. Firefly, 1991. ISBN 0-88753-168-7 Subj: Birds. Folk & fairy tales. Giants. Poetry.

Oishi, Makoto. *E. H. Grieg's Peer Gynt* (Grieg, E. H. [Edvard Hagerup])

The sorcerer's apprentice (Dukas, P. [Paul Abraham])

O'Keefe, Susan Heyboer. *Angel prayers* ill. by Sofia Suzán. Boyds Mills, 1999. ISBN 1-56397-683-8 Subj: Religion. Rhyming text.

Good night, God bless ill. by Hideko Takahashi. Holt, 1999. ISBN 0-8050-6008-1 Subj: Bedtime. Religion. Rhyming text.

Love me, love you ill. by Robin Spowart. Boyds Mills, 2001. ISBN 1-56397-837-7 Subj: Animals – rabbits. Emotions – love. Family life – mothers. Rhyming text.

One hungry monster ill. by Lynn Munsinger. Little, 1989. ISBN 0-316-63385-2 Subj: Counting, numbers. Food. Monsters. Poetry.

O'Kelley, Mattie Lou. *Circus!* ill. by author. Atlantic Monthly, 1986. ISBN 0-87113-094-7 Subj: Behavior – misbehavior. Circus. Family life. Farms.

Moving to town ill. by author. Little, 1991. ISBN 0-316-63805-6 Subj: Activities – traveling. Cities, towns. Moving.

Okimoto, Jean Davies. *Blumpoe the grumpoe meets Arnold the cat* ill. by Howie Schneider. Little, 1990. ISBN 0-316-62811-0 Subj: Animals – cats.

No dear, not here ill. by Celeste Henriquez. Sasquatch, 1995. ISBN 1-57061-019-3 Subj: Birds. Homes, houses.

A place for Grace ill. by Doug Keith. Sasquatch, 1993. ISBN 0-912365-73-0 Subj: Animals – dogs. Character traits – helpfulness. Handicaps – deafness.

The White Swan express by Jean Davies Okimoto & Elaine M. Aoki; ill. by Meilo So. Clarion, 2002. ISBN 0-618-16453-7 Subj: Adoption. Babies. Ethnic groups in the U.S. – Chinese Americans. Family life – parents. Foreign lands – China.

Okrend, Elise. *Blintzes for Blitzen* ill. by Alice L. Oglesby. MixedBlessings, 1996. ISBN 0-9651475-0-9 Subj: Animals – reindeer. Food. Holidays – Christmas. Holidays – Hanukkah.

Oksner, Robert M. *The incompetent wizard* ill. by Janet McCaffery. Morrow, 1965. Subj: Dragons. Magic. Wizards.

Olaleye, Isaac. *Bikes for rent!* ill. by Chris Demarest. Orchard, 2001. ISBN 0-531-33290-X Subj: Foreign lands – Nigeria. Sports – bicycling.

Bitter bananas ill. by Ed Young. Caroline House, 1994. ISBN 1-56397-039-2 Subj: Animals – baboons. Character traits – cleverness. Food. Foreign lands – Africa. Foreign lands – Nigeria. Problem solving.

The distant talking drum ill. by Frané Lessac. Wordsong, 1995. ISBN 1-56397-095-3 Subj: Foreign lands – Nigeria. Poetry.

In the Rainfield: who is the greatest? ill. by Ann Grifalconi. Blue Sky, 2000. ISBN 0-590-48363-3 Subj: Contests. Folk & fairy tales. Foreign lands – Nigeria. Nature. Weather – rain. Weather – wind.

Lake of the Big Snake ill. by Claudia Shepard. Boyds Mills, 1998. ISBN 1-56397-096-1 Subj: Foreign lands – Africa. Forest, woods. Reptiles – snakes.

Old, Wendie C. *Stacy had a little sister* ill. by Judith Friedman. A. Whitman, 1995. ISBN 0-8075-7598-4 Subj: Babies. Death. Emotions – grief. Family life – new sibling. Family life – sisters.

Old MacDonald had a farm. *E I E I O: the story of Old MacDonald, who had a farm* ill. by Gus Clarke. Lothrop, 1993. ISBN 0-688-12215-9 Subj: Animals. Careers – farmers. Cumulative tales. Farms. Music. Songs.

Old MacDonald retold & ill. by Rosemary Wells. Scholastic, 1998. ISBN 0-590-76985-5 Subj: Animals. Careers – farmers. Cumulative tales. Farms. Songs.

Old MacDonald had a farm ill. by Holly Berry. North-South, 1994. ISBN 1-55858-282-7 Subj: Animals. Careers – farmers. Cumulative tales. Farms. Music. Songs.

Old MacDonald had a farm ill. by Lorinda Bryan Cauley. Putnam, 1989. ISBN 0-399-21628-6 Subj: Animals. Careers – farmers. Cumulative tales. Farms. Music. Songs.

Old MacDonald had a farm ill. by Mel Crawford. Golden Pr., 1967. Subj: Animals. Careers – farmers. Cumulative tales. Farms. Music. Songs.

Old MacDonald had a farm ill. by Tracey English. Western, 1993. ISBN 0-307-17601-1 Subj: Animals. Careers – farmers. Cumulative tales. Farms. Music. Songs.

Old MacDonald had a farm ill. by David Frankland. Merrill, 1980. ISBN 0-675-01065-9 Subj: Animals. Careers – farmers. Cumulative tales. Farms. Music. Songs.

Old MacDonald had a farm ill. by Abner Graboff. Four Winds, 1970. Subj: Animals. Careers – farmers. Cumulative tales. Farms. Music. Songs.

Old MacDonald had a farm ill. by Nancy Hellen. Watts, 1990. ISBN 0-531-05872-7 Subj: Animals. Careers – farmers. Cumulative tales. Farms. Music. Songs.

Old MacDonald had a farm ill. by Carol Jones. Houghton Mifflin, 1989. ISBN 0-395-49212-2 Subj: Animals. Careers – farmers. Cumulative tales. Farms. Format, unusual. Music. Songs.

Old MacDonald had a farm ill. by Tracey Campbell Pearson. Dial, 1984. ISBN 0-8037-0070-9 Subj: Animals. Careers – farmers. Cumulative tales. Farms. Music. Songs.

Old MacDonald had a farm ill. by Robert M. Quackenbush. Lippincott, 1972. ISBN 0-397-31218-0 Subj: Animals. Careers – farmers. Cumulative tales. Farms. Music. Songs.

Old MacDonald had a farm ill. by Glen Rounds. Holiday, 1989. ISBN 0-8234-0739-X Subj: Animals. Careers – farmers. Cumulative tales. Farms. Music. Songs.

Old McDonald had a farm retold by Frances Cony; ill. by Iain Smyth. Orchard, 1999. ISBN 0-531-30129-X Subj: Animals. Careers – farmers. Cumulative tales. Farms. Format, unusual – toy & movable books. Songs.

Old MacDonald had a farm retold & ill. by Jessica Souhami; designed by Paul McAlinden. Orchard, 1996. ISBN 0-531-09493-6 Subj: Animals. Careers – farmers. Cumulative tales. Farms. Format, unusual – toy & movable books. Songs. Transportation.

Old MacDonald had a farm ill. by William Stobbs. Oxford Univ. Pr., 1986. ISBN 0-19-279817-0 Subj: Animals. Careers – farmers. Cumulative tales. Farms. Music. Songs.

Old MacDonald had a farm ill. by Prue Theobalds. Peter Bedrick, 1991. ISBN 0-87226-452-1 Subj: Animals. Careers – farmers. Cumulative tales. Farms. Music. Songs.

The old woman and her pig. *The old woman and her pig* ill. by Paul Galdone. McGraw-Hill, 1960. Subj: Cumulative tales. Folk & fairy tales.

The old woman and her pig adapt. by Eric A. Kimmel; ill. by Giyora Karmi. Holiday, 1992. ISBN 0-8234-0970-8 Subj: Cumulative tales. Folk & fairy tales.

The old woman and her pig retold & ill. by Rosanne Litzinger. Harcourt, 1993. ISBN 0-15-257802-1 Subj: Cumulative tales. Folk & fairy tales.

The troublesome pig retold & ill. by Priscilla Lamont. Crown, 1985. ISBN 0-517-55546-8 Subj: Cumulative tales. Folk & fairy tales.

Older, Effin. *My two grandmothers* ill. by Nancy Hayashi. Harcourt, 2000. ISBN 0-15-200785-7 Subj: Family life – grandmothers. Holidays – Christmas. Holidays – Hanukkah. Parties.

Older, Jules. *Telling time: how to tell time on digital and analog clocks* ill. by Megan Halsey. Charlesbridge, 2000. ISBN 0-88106-396-7 Subj: Clocks, watches. Time.

The old-fashioned children's storybook. Wanderer, 1980. ISBN 0-671-41540-9 Subj: Folk & fairy tales.

Oldfield, Pamela. *Melanie Brown climbs a tree* ill. by Carolyn Dinan. Faber, 1980. ISBN 0-571-11488-1 Subj: Behavior – misbehavior. Foreign lands – England.

Oldfield, Wendy. *My apple* (Davies, Kay)

My balloon (Davies, Kay)

My drum (Davies, Kay)

My mirror (Davies, Kay)

Olds, Elizabeth. *Feather mountain* ill. by author. Houghton Mifflin, 1951. Subj: Birds. Caldecott award honor books.

Little Una ill. by author. Scribners, 1963. Subj: Cities, towns.

Plop plop ploppie ill. by author. Scribners, 1962. Subj: Animals – sea lions. Clowns, jesters.

Olds, Helen Diehl. *Miss Hattie and the monkey* ill. by Dorothy Marino. Follett, 1958. Subj: Animals – monkeys. Careers – seamstresses.

Oleson, Claire. *For Pipita, an orange tree* ill. by Margot Tomes. Doubleday, 1967. Subj: Foreign lands – Spain. Plants.

Oleson, Jens. *Snail* photos by Bo Jarner. Silver Burdett, 1986. ISBN 0-382-09289-9 Subj: Animals – snails. Science.

Olfers, Sibylle Von. *When the root children wake up* (Wood, Audrey)

When the root children wake up (Fish, Helen Dean)

When the root children wake up (Fish, Helen Dean)

Oliver, Dexter. *I want to be . . .* by Dexter & Patricia Oliver; photos by Dexter Oliver. Third World Pr., 1974. ISBN 0-8837-8041-0 Subj: ABC books. Careers.

Oliver, Lin. *The fat cat* (Mooser, Stephen)

Oliver, Patricia. *I want to be . . .* (Oliver, Dexter)

Oliver, Stephen. *Clothes* photos by Steve Gorton. Random House, 1991. ISBN 0-679-81806-5 Subj: Clothing.

My first look at colors photos by author. McKay, 1990. ISBN 0-679-80535-4 Subj: Concepts – color.

My first look at numbers photos by author. McKay, 1990. ISBN 0-679-80533-8 Subj: Counting, numbers.

My first look at shapes photos by author. McKay, 1990. ISBN 0-679-80534-6 Subj: Concepts – shape.

My first look at sizes photos by author. McKay, 1990. ISBN 0-679-80532-X Subj: Concepts – size.

Nature photos by Steve Gorton. Random House, 1991. ISBN 0-679-81805-7 Subj: Nature.

Opposites photos by author. Random House, 1990. ISBN 0-679-80620-2 Subj: Concepts – opposites.

Seasons photos by author. Random House, 1990. ISBN 0-679-80621-0 Subj: Seasons.

Shopping photos by Steve Gorton. Random House, 1991. ISBN 0-679-81803-0 Subj: Shopping. Stores.

Things that go photos by Steve Gorton. Random House, 1991. ISBN 0-679-81804-9 Subj: Toys. Transportation.

Touch photos by author. Random House, 1990. ISBN 0-679-80623-7 Subj: Senses – touch.

Oliver, Sy. *The Sesame Street song book* (Raposo, Joe)

Oliviero, Jamie. *The day Sun was stolen* ill. by Sharon Hitchcock. Hyperion, 1995. ISBN 0-7868-2026-8 Subj: Animals – bears. Creation. Folk & fairy tales. Indians of North America – Haida.

The fish skin ill. by Brent Morriseau. Hyperion, 1993. ISBN 1-56282-402-3 Subj: Folk & fairy tales. Indians of North America – Cree. Sun. Weather – clouds. Weather – droughts. Weather – rain.

Som See and the magic elephant ill. by Jo'Anne Kelly. Hyperion, 1995. ISBN 0-7868-2020-9 Subj: Death. Emotions – grief. Family life – aunts, uncles. Foreign lands – Thailand.

Olivo, Richard. *Close, closer, closest* (Rotner, Shelley)

Oller, Erika. *The cabbage soup solution* ill. by author. Dutton, 2004. ISBN 0-525-47005-0 Subj: Animals – cats. Animals – rabbits. Farms. Food. Humorous stories.

Olney, Ross R. *Construction giants* ill. with photos. Atheneum, 1984. ISBN 0-689-31067-6 Subj: Machines.

Farm giants ill. with photos. Atheneum, 1982. ISBN 0-689-30937-6 Subj: Farms. Machines.

Olofsdotter, Marie. *Frej the fearless: the secret world of Frej* ill. by Marie Olofsdotter. Free Spirit, 1995. ISBN 0-915793-86-5 Subj: Activities – babysitting. Behavior – secrets. Imagination.

Sofia and the Heartmender ill. by author. Free Spirit, 1993. ISBN 0-915793-50-4 Subj: Emotions – fear. Monsters. Night. Shadows.

Olofsson, Helena. *The little jester* ill. by author; trans. by Kjersti Board. R&S Books, 2002. ISBN 91-29-65499-8 Subj: Books, reading. Careers – clergy. Clowns, jesters. Foreign lands – France. Middle Ages.

Olschewski, Alfred. *We fly* ill. by author. Little, 1967. Subj: Airplanes, airports.

The wheel rolls over ill. by author. Little, 1962. Subj: Transportation. Wheels.

Olsen, Alfa-Betty. *Gabby the shrew* by Alfa-Betty Olsen & Marshall Efron; ill. by Roz Chast. Random House, 1994. ISBN 0-679-94467-2 Subj: Animals – shrews. Behavior – dissatisfaction. Character traits – individuality. Noise, sounds.

Olsen, Ib Spang. *The boy in the moon* ill. by author. Parents' Magazine Pr., 1977. Tr. of Dregen i manen from the Danish by Virginia Allen Jensen. ISBN 0-8193-0734-3 Subj: Moon.

Cat alley trans. by Virginia Allen Jensen; ill. by author. Coward, 1971. Translation of Kattehuset. Subj: Behavior – lost. Cities, towns.

The grown-up trap ill. by author. Thomasson-Grant, 1992. ISBN 0-934738-96-3 Subj: Behavior – needing someone. Emotions – loneliness. Family life. Imagination. Rhyming text.

Olson, Arielle North. *Hurry home, Grandma!* ill. by Lydia Dabcovich. Dutton, 1984. ISBN 0-525-44113-1 Subj: Family life – grandmothers. Holidays – Christmas.

The lighthouse keeper's daughter ill. by Elaine Wentworth. Little, 1987. ISBN 0-316-65053-6 Subj: Character traits – bravery. Flowers. Islands. Lighthouses. Weather – storms.

Noah's cats and the devil's fire ill. by Barry Moser. Watts, 1992. ISBN 0-531-08584-8 Subj: Animals – cats. Animals – mice. Boats, ships. Devil. Folk & fairy tales. Foreign lands – Romania. Religion – Noah. Weather – floods. Weather – rain.

Olson, Helen Kronberg. *The strange thing that happened to Oliver Wendell Iscovitch* ill. by Betsy Lewin. Dodd, 1983. ISBN 0-396-08147-9 Subj: Behavior – misbehavior. Ghosts. Humorous stories.

Olson, Laura. *Clayton's path* (Bishop, Brett)

Olson, Mary. *An alligator ate my brother* ill. by Tammie Lyon. Boyds Mills, 2000. ISBN 1-56397-803-2 Subj: Family life – brothers. Reptiles – alligators, crocodiles.

Nice try, Tooth Fairy ill. by Katherine Tillotson. S&S, 2000. ISBN 0-689-82422-X Subj: Fairies. Letters, cards. Teeth.

Olujic, Grozdana. *Rose of Mother-of-Pearl* trans. from Serbo-Croatian by Grozdana Olujic & Jascha Kessler; ill. by Kathy Jacobi. Toothpaste Pr., 1983. ISBN 0-915124-90-4 Subj: Behavior – dissatisfaction. Sea & seashore.

Olyff, Clotilde. *1, 2, 3. One, two, three* ill. by author. Ticknor & Fields, 1994. ISBN 0-395-70736-6 Subj: Counting, numbers. Format, unusual – toy & movable books.

O'Malley, Kevin. *The box* ill. by author. Stewart, Tabori & Chang, 1993. ISBN 1-55670-275-2 Subj: Activities – playing. Imagination. Toys – bears. Wordless.

Bud ill. by author. Walker, 2000. ISBN 0-8027-8719-3 Subj: Animals – rhinoceros. Character traits – orderliness. Family life – grandfathers. Gardens, gardening.

Carl caught a flying fish ill. by author. S&S, 1996. ISBN 0-689-80098-3 Subj: Behavior – misbehavior. Fish. Rhyming text. School.

Humpty Dumpty egg-splodes ill. by author. Walker, 2001. ISBN 0-8027-8757-6 Subj: Character traits – meanness. Emotions – anger. Nursery rhymes.

Leo Cockroach . . . toy tester ill. by author. Walker, 1999. ISBN 0-8027-8690-1 Subj: Insects – cockroaches. Toys.

Little buggy ill. by author. Harcourt, 2002. ISBN 0-15-216339-5 Subj: Activities – flying. Family life – fathers. Insects – ladybugs.

Little Buggy runs away ill. by author. Harcourt, 2003. ISBN 0-15-216550-9 Subj: Behavior – fighting, arguing. Behavior – running away. Family life – fathers. Insects – ants. Insects – ladybugs.

Roller coaster ill. by author. Lothrop, 1995. ISBN 0-688-13972-8 Subj: Fairs, festivals.

Straight to the pole ill. by author. Walker, 2003. ISBN 0-8027-8868-8 Subj: Imagination. School. Weather – snow.

Velcome ill. by author. Walker, 1997. ISBN 0-8027-8629-4 Subj: Activities – storytelling. Holidays – Halloween. Monsters.

Who killed Cock Robin? ill. by Keevin O'Malley. Lothrop, 1993. ISBN 0-688-12431-3 Subj: Birds – owls. Birds – robins. Birds – wrens. Careers – detectives. Crime. Mystery stories. Picture puzzles. Rhyming text.

O'Mara, Carmel. *Good morning* ill. by author. Harcourt, 2000. ISBN 0-15-202135-3 Subj: Activities. Animals – bears. Family life – parents. Morning.

Good night ill. by author. Harcourt, 2000. ISBN 0-15-202136-1 Subj: Activities. Animals – bears. Family life – parents.

Rainy day ill. by author. Harcourt, 2001. ISBN 0-15-201934-0 Subj: Activities – playing. Animals – bears. Animals – rabbits. Format, unusual – board books. Friendship. Weather – rain.

Sunny day ill. by author. Harcourt, 2001. ISBN 0-15-202066-7 Subj: Activities – playing. Animals – bears. Animals – rabbits. Format, unusual – board books. Weather.

O'Mara-Horwitz, Carmel. *see* O'Mara, Carmel

On the little hearth trans. by Miriam Chaikin; ill. by Gabriel Lisowski; score by Mark Warshawski. Holt, 1978. ISBN 0-03-039931-9 Subj: Foreign languages. Jewish culture. Music. Songs.

Onassis, Jacqueline. *The firebird: and other Russian fairy tales* (The firebird)

Once I was . . . ill. by Woodleigh Marx Hubbard. Putnam, 1999. ISBN 0-399-23105-6 Subj: Behavior – growing up. Concepts. Rhyming text.

100 words about transportation ill. by Richard Eric Brown. Harcourt, 1987. ISBN 0-15-200551-X Subj: Language. Transportation.

100 words about working ill. by Richard Eric Brown. Harcourt, 1988. ISBN 0-15-200553-6 Subj: Activities – working. Careers. Language.

One rubber duckie: a Sesame Street counting book photos by John E. Barrett. Random House, 1982. ISBN 0-394-85309-1 Subj: Counting, numbers. Puppets.

One, two, buckle my shoe comp. & ill. by Rowan Barnes-Murphy. S&S, 1988. ISBN 0-671-63791-6 Subj: Counting, numbers. Nursery rhymes.

One, two, buckle my shoe ill. by Gail E. Haley. Doubleday, 1964. Subj: Counting, numbers. Nursery rhymes.

One, two, skip a few! ill. by Roberta Arenson. Barefoot, 1998. ISBN 1-901223-99-X Subj: Counting, numbers. Nursery rhymes. Rhyming text.

O'Neil, Amanda. *I wonder why spiders spin webs: and other questions about creepy crawlies* ill. by author. Kingfisher, 1995. ISBN 1-85697-643-2 Subj: Insects. Spiders.

O'Neill, Alexis. *Estela's swap* ill. by Enrique O. Sánchez. Lee & Low, 2002. ISBN 1-58430-044-2 Subj: Activities – trading. Ethnic groups in the U.S. – Mexican Americans. Family life – fathers. Money. Stores.

Loud Emily ill. by Nancy Carpenter. S&S, 1998. ISBN 0-689-81078-4 Subj: Animals – whales. Boats, ships. Noise, sounds. Sailors.

The Recess Queen ill. by Laura Huliska-Beith. Scholastic, 2002. ISBN 0-439-20637-5 Subj: Behavior – bullying. School.

O'Neill, Catharine. *Mrs. Dunphy's dog* ill. by author. Viking, 1987. ISBN 0-670-81135-1 Subj: Animals – dogs. Books, reading.

O'Neill, Mary. *Big red hen* ill. by Judy Piussi-Campbell. Doubleday, 1971. Subj: Birds – chickens. Eggs. Rhyming text.

O'Neill, Rachael. *Can't, don't, won't* (Davies, Gill)

The Christmas story (Butterfield, Moira)

Tiny's big wish (Davies, Gill)

Wilbur waited (Davies, Gill)

Onyefulu, Ifeoma. *Grandfather's work: a traditional healer in Nigeria* ill. with photos. Millbrook, 1998. ISBN 0-7613-0412-6 Subj: Family life – grandfathers. Foreign lands – Nigeria. Health & fitness.

Ogbo: sharing life in an African village ill. by author. Gulliver, 1996. ISBN 0-15-200498-X Subj: Foreign lands – Nigeria.

Saying goodbye ill. with photos. Millbrook, 2001. ISBN 0-7613-1965-4 Subj: Death. Emotions – grief. Foreign lands – Nigeria.

A triangle for Adaora ill. with photos. Dutton, 2000. ISBN 0-525-46382-8 Subj: Concepts – shape. Foreign lands – Africa.

Onyefulu, Obi. *Chinye* ill. by Evie Safarewicz. Viking, 1994. ISBN 0-670-85115-9 Subj: Folk & fairy tales. Foreign lands – Africa.

Onyschuk, Motria. *The cat and the rooster* (Malkovych, Ivan)

Ooka, D. T. *The monkey and the crab* (Horio, Seishi)

The old man who made the trees bloom (Shibano, Tamizo)

Wally the whale who loved balloons (Watanabe, Yuichi)

Ophir, Uri. *Songs of Chanukah* (Modesitt, Jeanne)

Opie, Iona Archibald. *Humpty Dumpty and other rhymes* (Mother Goose)

I saw Esau (I saw Esau)

Little Boy Blue and other rhymes (Mother Goose)

Pussycat, pussycat and other rhymes (Mother Goose)

Wee Willie Winkie and other rhymes (Mother Goose)

Opie, Peter. *I saw Esau* (I saw Esau)

Oppel, Kenneth. *Peg and the whale* ill. by Terry Widener. S&S, 2000. ISBN 0-689-82423-8 Subj: Animals – whales. Boats, ships. Sports – fishing. Tall tales.

Oppenheim, Joanne. *The Christmas witch* ill. by Annie Mitra. G. Stevens, 1997. ISBN 0-8368-1697-8 Subj: Folk & fairy tales. Holidays – Christmas. Religion – Nativity. Witches.

Could it be? ill. by S. D. Schindler. G. Stevens, 1998. ISBN 0-8368-1770-2 Subj: Animals – bears. Noise, sounds. Seasons – spring.

Do you like cats? ill. by Carol Newsom. G. Stevens, 1998. ISBN 0-8368-1757-5 Subj: Animals – cats. Rhyming text.

Donkey's tale ill. by Chris L. Demarest. Bantam, 1991. ISBN 0-553-07090-8 Subj: Animals – donkeys. Character traits – practicality. Folk & fairy tales. Humorous stories. Rhyming text.

The eency weency spider ill. by S. D. Schindler. Bantam, 1991. ISBN 0-553-07316-8 Subj: Games. Songs. Spiders.

Have you seen birds? ill. by Barbara Reid. Scholastic, 1986. ISBN 0-590-40585-3 Subj: Birds.

Have you seen bugs? ill. by Ron Broda. Scholastic, 1997. ISBN 0-590-05963-7 Subj: Insects. Rhyming text. Spiders.

Have you seen roads? ill. by Gerard Nook. Addison-Wesley, 1969. Subj: Poetry. Transportation.

Have you seen trees? ill. by Irwin Rosenhouse. Addison-Wesley, 1967. Subj: Poetry. Seasons. Trees.

Have you seen trees? ill. by Jean & Mou-Sien Tseng. Scholastic, 1995. ISBN 0-590-46691-7 Subj: Poetry. Seasons. Trees.

How do you make a bubble? (Hooks, William H.)

James will never die ill. by True Kelley. Dodd, 1982. ISBN 0-396-08067-7 Subj: Activities – playing.

Left and right ill. by Rosanne Litzinger. Harcourt, 1989. ISBN 0-15-200505-6 Subj: Careers – shoemakers. Concepts – left & right. Family life – brothers.

Mrs. Peloki's class play ill. by Joyce Audy dos Santos. Dodd, 1984. ISBN 0-396-08178-9 Subj: School. Theater.

Mrs. Peloki's snake ill. by Joyce Audy dos Santos. Dodd, 1980. ISBN 0-396-07810-9 Subj: Reptiles – snakes. School.

Mrs. Peloki's substitute ill. by Joyce Audy Zarins. Dodd, 1987. ISBN 0-396-08918-6 Subj: Behavior – trickery. School.

No way, Slippery Slick! a child's first book about drugs by Joanne Oppenheim, Barbara A. Brenner, & William H. Hooks; ill. by Joan Auclair. HarperCollins, 1991. ISBN 0-06-107437-3 Subj: Animals – cats. Illness – alcoholism. Illness – drug addiction.

"Not now!" said the cow ill. by Chris L. Demarest. Bantam, 1989. ISBN 0-553-34691-1 Subj: Animals. Birds – crows. Character traits – laziness. Cumulative tales. Farms.

On the other side of the river ill. by Aliki. Watts, 1972. Subj: Behavior – needing someone. Bridges. Careers.

One gift deserves another (Grimm, Jacob)

Read-a-rebus (Hooks, William H.)

Rooter remembers ill. by Lynn Munsinger. Viking, 1991. ISBN 0-670-82865-3 Subj: Family life. Memories, memory.

The story book prince ill. by Rosanne Litzinger. Harcourt, 1987. ISBN 0-15-200590-0 Subj: Bedtime. Rhyming text. Royalty – princes. Sleep.

"Uh-oh!" said the crow ill. by Chris L. Demarest. G. Stevens, 1997. ISBN 0-8368-1753-2 Subj: Animals. Barns. Emotions – fear. Noise, sounds.

You can't catch me! ill. by Andrew Shachat. Houghton Mifflin, 1986. ISBN 0-395-41452-0 Subj: Animals. Behavior – boasting. Cumulative tales. Insects – flies. Rhyming text.

Oppenheim, Shulamith Levey. *Ali and the magic stew* ill. by Winslow Pels. Boyds Mills, 2002. ISBN 1-56397-869-5 Subj: Careers – beggars. Family life – fathers. Foreign lands – Iran. Illness.

And the earth trembled: the creation of Adam and Eve ill. by Neil Waldman. Harcourt, 1996. ISBN 0-15-200025-9 Subj: Creation. Religion – Islam.

Fireflies for Nathan ill. by John Ward. Tambourine, 1994. ISBN 0-688-12148-9 Subj: Ethnic groups in the U.S. – African Americans. Family life – grandparents. Insects – fireflies.

The hundredth name ill. by Michael Hays. Boyds Mills, 1995. ISBN 1-56397-183-6 Subj: Animals – camels. Behavior – secrets. Foreign lands – Egypt. Names. Religion.

I love you, Bunny Rabbit ill. by Cyd Moore. Boyds Mills, 1995. ISBN 1-56397-322-7 Subj: Emotions – love. Toys.

Iblis ill. by Ed Young. Harcourt, 1994. ISBN 0-15-238016-7 Subj: Creation. Devil. Religion.

The lily cupboard ill. by Ronald Himler. HarperCollins, 1992. ISBN 0-06-024670-7 Subj: Behavior – hiding. Character traits – bravery. Emotions – fear. Foreign lands – Holland. Friendship. Holocaust. Jewish culture. War.

The sea king (Yolen, Jane)

Waiting for Noah ill. by Lillian Hoban. Harper, 1999. ISBN 0-06-024634-0 Subj: Babies. Birth. Birthdays. Family life – grandmothers.

What is the full moon full of? ill. by Cyd Moore. Boyds Mills, 1997. ISBN 1-56397-479-7 Subj: Animals. Bedtime. Moon. Night.

Yanni rubbish ill. by Doug Chayka. Boyds Mills, 1999. ISBN 1-56397-668-4 Subj: Animals – donkeys. Careers. Family life – fathers. Foreign lands – Greece.

Oram, Hiawyn. *Angry Arthur* ill. by Satoshi Kitamura. Farrar, 1997. ISBN 0-374-40386-4 Subj: Emotions – anger.

Baba Yaga and the wise doll ill. by Ruth Brown. Dutton, 1998. ISBN 0-525-45947-2 Subj: Behavior – trickery. Folk & fairy tales. Foreign lands – Russia. Toys – dolls. Witches.

Badger's bad mood ill. by Susan Varley. Levine, 1998. ISBN 0-590-18920-4 Subj: Animals. Animals – badgers. Animals – moles. Behavior – bad day. Friendship.

Badger's bring something party ill. by Susan Varley. Lothrop, 1995. ISBN 0-688-14082-3 Subj: Animals. Animals – badgers. Friendship. Parties.

A boy wants a dinosaur ill. by Satoshi Kitamura. Farrar, 1991. ISBN 0-374-30939-6 Subj: Dinosaurs. Dreams. Family life – grandfathers. Pets. Prehistory.

Gerda the goose ill. by David Melling. Barron's, 2000. ISBN 0-7641-1484-0 Subj: Birds – geese.

Going to Grandpa's ill. by Frédéric Joos. Dutton, 2001. ISBN 0-525-46701-7 Subj: Animals – bears. Family life – grandfathers. Trains.

In the attic ill. by Satoshi Kitamura. Holt, 1985. ISBN 0-03-002462-5 Subj: Activities – playing. Behavior – boredom. Imagination.

Jenna and the troublemaker ill. by Tony Ross. Holt, 1986. ISBN 0-8050-0025-9 Subj: Behavior – dissatisfaction. Mythical creatures.

Just Dog ill. by Lisa Flather. Chronicle, 1998. ISBN 0-8118-2247-8 Subj: Animals – cats. Animals – dogs. Self-concept.

Kiss it better ill. by Frédéric Joos. Dutton, 2000. ISBN 0-525-46386-0 Subj: Animals – bears. Behavior – bad day. Emotions – love. Kissing.

Mine! ill. by Mary Rees. Barron's, 1992. ISBN 0-8120-6303-1 Subj: Behavior – sharing. Friendship.

Mole's moon ill. by Susan Varley. Andersen, 1997. ISBN 0-8626-4694-4 Subj: Animals. Animals – moles. Moon.

Ned and the Joybaloo ill. by Satoshi Kitamura. David & Charles, 1989, c1983. ISBN 0-86264-048-2 Subj: Behavior – misbehavior. Character traits – individuality. Imagination – imaginary friends.

Princess Chamomile gets her way ill. by Susan Varley. Dutton, 1999. ISBN 0-525-46148-5 Subj: Animals – mice. Character traits – freedom. Crime. Royalty – princesses.

Reckless Ruby ill. by Tony Ross. Crown, 1992. ISBN 0-517-58744-0 Subj: Behavior – carelessness. Family life.

The second princess ill. by Tony Ross. Artists & Writers Guild, 1994. ISBN 0-307-17513-8 Subj: Family life – sisters. Royalty – princesses. Sibling rivalry.

Skittlewonder and the wizard ill. by Jenny Rodwell. Dial, 1980. ISBN 0-8037-7834-1 Subj: Folk & fairy tales. Games. Gypsies. Royalty. Witches. Wizards.

Where are you hiding, little lamb? ill. by Jonathan Langley. Barron's, 1999. ISBN 0-7641-5196-7 Subj: Animals – sheep. Behavior – hiding.

The wrong overcoat ill. by Mark Birchall. Carolrhoda, 2000. ISBN 1-57505-453-1 Subj: Animals – chimpanzees. Character traits – individuality. Clothing – coats. Self-concept.

Orbach, Ruth. *Apple pigs* ill. by author. Collins-World, 1977. ISBN 0-529-05332-2 Subj: Food. Rhyming text. Trees.

Please send a panda ill. by author. Collins-World, 1978. ISBN 0-00-183749-4 Subj: Behavior – wishing. Family life – grandmothers. Pets.

Ørdal, Stina Langlo. *Princess Aasta* ill. by author. Bloomsbury, 2002. ISBN 1-58234-783-2 Subj: Animals – bears. Animals – polar bears. Behavior – resourcefulness. Friendship. Royalty – kings. Royalty – princesses.

O'Reilly, Edward. *Brown pelican at the pond* ill. by Florence Strange. Manzanita, 1979. ISBN 0-931644-01-1 Subj: Birds – pelicans. Children as authors.

Orgel, Doris. *Button soup* ill. by Pau Estrada. G. Stevens, 1998. ISBN 0-8368-1761-3 Subj: Folk & fairy tales. Food. Foreign lands – France.

The flower of Sheba by Doris Orgel & Ellen Schecter; ill. by Laura Kelly. Bantam, 1994. ISBN 0-553-09041-0 Subj: Jewish culture. Religion. Royalty.

Godfather Cat and Mousie (Grimm, Jacob)

Little John by Theodor Storm; retold from the German by Doris Orgel; ill. by Anita Lobel. Farrar, 1972. ISBN 0-374-34620-8 Subj: Bedtime. Dreams.

Merry merry FIBruary ill. by Arnold Lobel. Parents' Magazine Pr., 1978. ISBN 0-8193-0901-X Subj: Poetry.

On the sand dune ill. by Leonard Weisgard. HarperCollins, 1968. Subj: Character traits – smallness. Sea & seashore.

The lion and the mouse and other Æsop fables (Æsop)

Two crows counting ill. by Judith Moffatt. Bantam, 1995. ISBN 0-553-37573-3 Subj: Birds – crows. Counting, numbers. Rhyming text.

Orgill, Roxane. *If I only had a horn* ill. by Leonard Jenkins. Houghton, 1997. ISBN 0-395-75919-6 Subj: Careers – musicians. Ethnic groups in the U.S. – African Americans. Musical instruments – bands. Musical instruments – trumpets. U.S. history.

Ormerod, Jan. *Ben goes swimming* ill. by author. HarperCollins, 1999. ISBN 0-688-17714-X Subj: Format, unusual – toy & movable books. Imagination. Sports – swimming.

Bend and stretch ill. by author. Lothrop, 1987. ISBN 0-688-07272-0 Subj: Babies. Family life – mothers. Sports.

Come back, kittens ill. by author. Lothrop, 1992. ISBN 0-688-09134-2 Subj: Animals – cats. Counting, numbers. Format, unusual.

Come back, puppies ill. by author. Lothrop, 1992. ISBN 0-688-09135-0 Subj: Animals – dogs. Counting, numbers. Format, unusual.

Dad's back ill. by author. Lothrop, 1985. ISBN 0-688-04126-4 Subj: Babies. Clothing. Family life – fathers.

Emily dances ill. by author. Tupelo, 1999. ISBN 0-688-17713-1 Subj: Activities – dancing. Format, unusual – toy & movable books.

If you're happy and you know it! by Jan Ormerod & Lindsey Gardiner; ill. by Lindsey Gardiner. Star Bright, 2003. ISBN 1-932065-07-5 Subj: Animals. Emotions – happiness. Rhyming text.

Joe can count ill. by author. Mulberry, 1993. ISBN 0-688-04588-X Subj: Animals. Counting, numbers.

Just like me ill. by author. Lothrop, 1986. ISBN 0-688-04211-2 Subj: Babies. Character traits – appearance.

Kitten day ill. by author. Lothrop, 1989. ISBN 0-688-08537-7 Subj: Animals – cats. Pets.

Making friends ill. by author. Lothrop, 1987. ISBN 0-688-07270-4 Subj: Babies. Family life – mothers. Toys – dolls.

Messy baby ill. by author. Lothrop, 1985. ISBN 0-688-04128-0 Subj: Babies. Family life – fathers. Toys.

Midnight pillow fight ill. by author. Candlewick, 1993. ISBN 1-56402-169-6 Subj: Activities – playing. Night.

Miss Mouse takes off ill. by author. HarperCollins, 2001. ISBN 0-688-17871-5 Subj: Activities – traveling. Airplanes, airports. Toys – dolls.

Miss Mouse's day ill. by author. HarperCollins, 2001. ISBN 0-688-16334-3 Subj: Activities – playing. Animals – mice. Toys.

Mom's home ill. by author. Lothrop, 1987. ISBN 0-688-07274-7 Subj: Babies. Family life – mothers.

Moonlight ill. by author. Lothrop, 1982. ISBN 0-688-00847-X Subj: Bedtime. Family life. Sleep. Wordless.

Ms. MacDonald has a class ill. by author. Clarion, 1996. ISBN 0-395-77611-2 Subj: Animals. Cumulative tales. Farms. Rhyming text. School. Songs. Theater.

101 things to do with a baby ill. by author. Turtleback, 1993. ISBN 0-606-06153-3 Subj: Babies. Behavior – sharing. Sibling rivalry.

Our Ollie ill. by author. Lothrop, 1986. ISBN 0-688-04208-2 Subj: Babies. Character traits – appearance.

Reading ill. by author. Lothrop, 1985. ISBN 0-688-04127-2 Subj: Books, reading. Family life – fathers.

Rock-a-baby ill. by author. Dutton, 1998. ISBN 0-525-45935-9 Subj: Babies. Format, unusual – toy & movable books. Rhyming text.

The saucepan game ill. by author. Lothrop, 1989. ISBN 0-688-08519-9 Subj: Activities – playing. Animals – cats. Babies. Imagination.

Silly goose ill. by author. Lothrop, 1986. ISBN 0-688-04209-0 Subj: Babies. Character traits – appearance.

Sleeping ill. by author. Lothrop, 1985. ISBN 0-688-04129-9 Subj: Babies. Family life – fathers. Sleep.

The story of Chicken Licken (Chicken Little)

Sunshine ill. by author. Lothrop, 1981. ISBN 0-688-00553-5 Subj: Morning. Sun. Wordless.

This little nose ill. by author. Lothrop, 1987. ISBN 0-688-07276-3 Subj: Anatomy – noses. Babies. Family life – mothers. Illness.

To baby with love ill. by author. Lothrop, 1994. ISBN 0-688-12559-X Subj: Games. Nursery rhymes.

When we went to the zoo ill. by author. Lothrop, 1991. ISBN 0-688-09879-7 Subj: Animals. Zoos.

Who's whose? ill. by author. Lothrop, 1998. ISBN 0-688-14679-1 Subj: Activities. Family life.

Young Joe ill. by author. Lothrop, 1986. ISBN 0-688-04210-4 Subj: Babies. Counting, numbers.

Ormondroyd, Edward. *Broderick* ill. by John M. Larrecq. Parnassus, 1969. ISBN 0-686-86580-4 Subj: Animals – mice. Books, reading. Sports – surfing.

Johnny Castleseed ill. by Diana Thewlis. Houghton Mifflin, 1985. ISBN 0-395-38355-2 Subj: Sand. Sea & seashore.

Theodore ill. by John M. Larrecq. Parnassus, 1966. ISBN 0-87466-028-9 Subj: Character traits – appearance. Character traits – kindness. Laundry. Toys – bears.

Theodore's rival ill. by John M. Larrecq. Parnassus, 1971. ISBN 0-8746-6001-7 Subj: Emotions – envy, jealousy. Sibling rivalry. Toys – bears.

Ormsby, Virginia H. *Twenty-one children plus ten* ill. by author. Lippincott, 1971. Subj: Ethnic groups in the U.S. – Mexican Americans. School.

Orstadius, Brita. *The dolphin journey* trans. from Swedish by Eric Bibb; ill. by Lennart Didoff. Farrar, 1989. ISBN 9-12-959138-4 Subj: Animals – dolphins. Character traits – kindness to animals. Foreign lands.

Ortiz, Simon. *The people shall continue* ill. by Sharol Graves. Children's Book Pr., 1988. ISBN 0-89239-041-7 Subj: Creation. Indians of North America. U.S. history.

Osborne, Mary Pope. *The brave little seamstress* ill. by Giselle Potter. Atheneum, 2002. ISBN 0-689-84486-7 Subj: Careers – tailors. Character traits – bravery. Folk & fairy tales. Giants. Royalty – kings. Royalty – queens.

Happy birthday, America ill. by Peter Catalanotto. Roaring Brook, 2003. ISBN 0-7613-2761-4 Subj: Family life. Holidays – Fourth of July.

Kate and the beanstalk ill. by Giselle Potter. Atheneum, 2000. ISBN 0-689-82550-1 Subj: Folk & fairy tales. Giants. Plants.

Molly and the prince ill. by Elizabeth Sayles. Knopf, 1994. ISBN 0-679-91941-4 Subj: Animals – dogs. Forest, woods. Mythical creatures. Royalty – princes.

Moonhorse ill. by David McPhail. Knopf, 1988. ISBN 0-394-98960-0 Subj: Activities – flying. Animals – horses, ponies. Behavior – wishing. Night. Sky.

Moonhorse ill. by S. M. Saelig. Knopf, 1991. ISBN 0-679-86709-0 Subj: Activities – flying. Animals – horses, ponies. Behavior – wishing. Night. Sky. Space & space ships.

New York's bravest ill. by Steve Johnson & Lou Fancher. Knopf, 2002. ISBN 0-375-92196-6 Subj: Careers – firefighters. Character traits – bravery. Cities, towns.

Osborne, Valerie. *One big yo to go* ill. by Jiri Tibor Novak. Oxford Univ. Pr., 1981. ISBN 0-19-554265-7 Subj: Rhyming text.

Osborne, Victor. *Rex, the most special car in the world* ill. by Scoular Anderson. Carolrhoda, 1989. ISBN 0-87614-357-5 Subj: Automobiles.

O'Shell, Marcia. *Alphabet Annie announces an all-American album* by Marcia O'Shell & Susan Purviance; ill. by Ruth Brunner-Strosser. Houghton Mifflin, 1988. ISBN 0-395-48070-1 Subj: ABC books. Cities, towns.

Osofsky, Audrey. *Dreamcatcher* ill. by Ed Young. Watts, 1992. ISBN 0-531-08588-0 Subj: Babies. Dreams. Family life. Folk & fairy tales. Indians of North America – Ojibwa.

My buddy ill. by Ted Rand. Holt, 1992. ISBN 0-8050-1747-X Subj: Animals – dogs. Camps, camping. Handicaps – physical handicaps. Illness – muscular dystrophy.

Ostheeren, Ingrid. *The blue monster* ill. by Christa Unzner; trans. by Rosemary Lanning. North-South, 1996. ISBN 1-55858-557-5 Subj: Animals – dogs. Birthdays. Family life. Pets.

Coriander's Easter adventure ill. by Jean-Pierre Corderoc'h; trans. by Rosemary Lanning. North-South, 1992. ISBN 1-55858-150-2 Subj: Animals – rabbits. Behavior – wishing. Holidays – Easter.

Fabian Youngpig sails the world ill. by Serena Romanelli; trans. by J. Alison James. North-South, 1992. ISBN 1-55858-145-6 Subj: Animals – pigs. Boats, ships. Sea & seashore.

I'm the real Santa Claus! ill. by Christa Unzner-Fischer; trans. by Rosemary Lanning. North-South, 1994. ISBN 1-55858-318-1 Subj: Behavior – imitation. Holidays – Christmas. Santa Claus.

Jonathan Mouse ill. by Agnès Mathieu; trans. by Rosemary Lanning. Holt, 1986. ISBN 0-03-005848-1 Subj: Animals – mice. Concepts – color. Magic.

Jonathan Mouse and the baby bird trans. from German by Rosemary Lanning; ill. by Agnès Mathieu. North-South, 1991. ISBN 1-55858-108-1 Subj: Animals – mice. Birds – sparrows. Farms.

Jonathan Mouse and the magic box trans. by Rosemary Lanning; ill. by Agnès Mathieu. North-South, 1990. ISBN 1-55858-087-5 Subj: Animals – mice. Magic.

Jonathan Mouse at the circus ill. by Agnès Mathieu. North-South, 1988. ISBN 3-85539-001-0 Subj: Animals – mice. Circus.

Jonathan Mouse, detective ill. by Agnès Mathieu; trans. by Rosemary Lanning. North-South, 1993. ISBN 1-55858-164-2 Subj: Animals. Animals – mice. Careers – detectives. Mystery stories.

Martin and the Pumpkin Ghost ill. by Christa Unzner-Fischer; trans. & adapt. by J. Alison James. North-South, 1994. ISBN 1-55858-268-1 Subj: Emotions – fear. Ghosts.

The new dog ill. by Christa Unzner-Fischer; trans. & adapt. by J. Alison James. North-South, 1993. ISBN 1-55858-219-3 Subj: Animals – dogs. Farms. Foreign lands – Switzerland. Pets.

Ostrovsky, Vivian. *Mumps!* ill. by Rose Ostrovsky. Holt, 1978. ISBN 0-03-042126-8 Subj: Illness – mumps.

Ostrow, Vivian. *My brother is from outer space: the book of proof* ill. by Eric Brace. A. Whitman, 1996. ISBN 0-8075-5325-5 Subj: Character traits – being different. Sibling rivalry. Space & space ships.

Otey, Mimi. *see* Little, Mimi Otey

Otfinoski, Steven. *The truth about three billy goats Gruff* (Asbjørnsen, P. C. [Peter Christen])

Otsuka, Yuzo. *Suho and the white horse: a legend of Mongolia* trans. by Ann Herring; ill. by Suekichi Akaba. Viking, 1981. ISBN 0-670-68149-0 Subj: Animals – horses, ponies. Emotions – love. Sports – racing.

Ott, John. *Peter Pumpkin* originated by Peter Coley; ill. by Ivan Chermayeff. Doubleday, 1963. Subj: Holidays – Halloween. Holidays – Thanksgiving. Seasons – fall.

Otten, Charlotte F. *January rides the wind: a book of months* ill. by Todd L. W. Doney. Lothrop, 1997. ISBN 0-688-12557-3 Subj: Days of the week, months of the year. Poetry.

Ottley, Matt. *What Faust saw* ill. by author. Dutton, 1996. ISBN 0-525-45650-3 Subj: Animals – dogs. Imagination. Night. Space & space ships.

Otto, Carolyn. *Dinosaur chase* ill. by Thacher Hurd. HarperCollins, 1991. ISBN 0-06-021614-X Subj: Bedtime. Dinosaurs. Poetry. Prehistory.

Ducks, ducks, ducks ill. by Molly Coxe. HarperCollins, 1991. ISBN 0-06-024639-1 Subj: Birds – ducks. Cities, towns. Poetry.

I can tell by touching ill. by Nadine Bernard Westcott. HarperCollins, 1994. ISBN 0-06-023325-7 Subj: Senses – touch.

Our puppies are growing ill. by Mary Morgan. HarperCollins, 1998. ISBN 0-06-027272-4 Subj: Animals – babies. Animals – dogs. Behavior – growing up.

Pioneer church ill. by Megan Lloyd. Holt, 1999. ISBN 0-8050-2554-5 Subj: Buildings. Religion. U.S. history.

That sky, that rain ill. by Megan Lloyd. HarperCollins, 1990. ISBN 0-690-04765-7 Subj: Family life – grandfathers. Farms. Sky. Weather – rain.

What color is camouflage? ill. by Megan Lloyd. HarperCollins, 1996. ISBN 0-06-027099-3 Subj: Animals. Character traits – appearance.

Otto, Margaret Glover. *The little brown horse* ill. by Barbara Cooney. Knopf, 1959. Subj: Animals – cats. Animals – horses, ponies. Birds – chickens.

Oughton, Jerrie. *How the stars fell into the sky* ill. by Lisa Desimini. Houghton Mifflin, 1992. ISBN 0-395-58798-0 Subj: Folk & fairy tales. Indians of North America – Navajo. Sky. Stars.

The magic weaver of rugs ill. by Lisa Desimini. Houghton Mifflin, 1994. ISBN 0-395-66140-4 Subj: Activities – weaving. Folk & fairy tales. Indians of North America – Navajo.

Our house ill. by Roser Capdevila. Firefly, 1985. ISBN 0-920303-10-2 Subj: Cities, towns. Format, unusual – board books. Homes, houses.

Ovenell-Carter, Julie. *Adam's daycare* ill. by Ruth Ohi. Firefly, 1997. ISBN 1-55037-445-1 Subj: Activities – babysitting. Family life.

Over in the grasslands ill. by Alison Bartlett. Little, 2000. ISBN 0-316-93910-2 Subj: Animals. Counting, numbers. Foreign lands – Africa.

Over in the meadow: an old nursery counting rhyme adapt. & ill. by Paul Galdone. Prentice-Hall, 1986. ISBN 0-13-646654-0 Subj: Animals. Counting, numbers. Nursery rhymes.

Over in the meadow ill. by Ezra Jack Keats. Four Winds, 1971. Subj: Animals. Counting, numbers. Folk & fairy tales. Rhyming text. Songs.

Overbeck, Cynthia. *Rusty the Irish setter* rev. English text by Cynthia Overbeck; original French text by Anne Marie Pajot; trans. by Dyan Hammarberg; photos by Antoinette Barrère; ill. by L'Enc Matte. Carolrhoda, 1977. Original ed. published under title: Jimmy, le grand chien. ISBN 0-8761-4080-0 Subj: Animals – dogs.

The winds that blow (Thompson, Brenda)

Overend, Jenni. *Welcome with love* ill. by Julie Vivas. Kane/Miller, 2000. ISBN 0-916291-96-0 Subj: Babies. Birth. Family life.

Owen, Ann (1953–). *Caring for your pet* ill. by Eric Thomas. Picture Window, 2004. ISBN 1-4048-0087-5 Subj: Careers – veterinarians. Pets.

Delivering your mail ill. by Eric Thomas. Picture Window, 2004. ISBN 1-4048-0091-3 Subj: Careers – postal workers. Letters, cards.

Keeping you healthy ill. by Eric Thomas. Picture Window, 2004. ISBN 1-4048-0085-9 Subj: Careers – doctors. Health & fitness.

Keeping you safe ill. by Eric Thomas. Picture Window, 2003. ISBN 1-4048-0089-1 Subj: Careers – police officers.

Protecting your home ill. by Eric Thomas. Picture Window, 2004. ISBN 1-4048-0088-3 Subj: Careers – firefighters. Fire.

Taking your places ill. by Eric Thomas. Picture Window, 2004. ISBN 1-4048-0090-5 Subj: Buses. Careers – bus drivers. Communities, neighborhoods.

Owen, Annie. *Bumper to bumper* ill. by author. Knopf, 1991. ISBN 0-679-91448-X Subj: Activities – traveling. Automobiles. Birthdays. Noise, sounds.

From snowflakes to sandcastles ill. by author. Millbrook, 1996. ISBN 1-56294-086-4 Subj: Counting, numbers. Days of the week, months of the year. Language. Puzzles.

Goodnight bear! ill. by author. Grisewood & Dempsey, 1994. ISBN 1-85697-945-8 Subj: Animals – bears. Bedtime. Format, unusual – board books. Night.

Hungry panda ill. by author. Grisewood & Dempsey, 1994. ISBN 1-85697-946-6 Subj: Animals – pandas. Food. Format, unusual – board books.

My aunt and the animals (MacDonald, Elizabeth)

Playtime duck ill. by author. Grisewood & Dempsey, 1994. ISBN 1-85697-947-4 Subj: Activities – playing. Birds – ducks. Format, unusual – board books.

Wake up Frog! ill. by author. Grisewood & Dempsey, 1994. ISBN 1-85697-948-2 Subj: Format, unusual – board books. Frogs & toads.

Owen, Robert. *The Larousse book of nursery rhymes* (Mother Goose)

Owen, Roy. *The ibis and the egret* ill. by Robert Sabuda. Philomel, 1993. ISBN 0-399-22504-8 Subj: Birds – herons. Birds – ibis. Seasons.

My night forest ill. by Amy Córdova. Four Winds, 1994. ISBN 0-02-769005-9 Subj: Animals. Bedtime. Forest, woods. Sleep.

Owens, Mary Beth. *A caribou alphabet* ill. by Mark McCollough. Farrar, 1990. ISBN 0-374-41043-7 Subj: ABC books. Animals – reindeer. Rhyming text.

Counting cranes ill. by author. Little, 1993. ISBN 0-316-67719-1 Subj: Birds – cranes. Counting, numbers.

Oxenbury, Helen. *All fall down* ill. by author. Macmillan, 1987. ISBN 0-02-769040-7 Subj: Activities – playing. Babies. Format, unusual – board books. Games.

Beach day ill. by author. Dial, 1982. ISBN 0-8037-0439-9 Subj: Family life. Format, unusual – board books. Sea & seashore – beaches. Wordless.

The birthday party ill. by author. Dial, 1983. ISBN 0-8037-0717-7 Subj: Birthdays.

The car trip ill. by author. Dial, 1983. ISBN 0-8037-0009-1 Subj: Automobiles. Behavior – bad day. Behavior – misbehavior.

The checkup ill. by author. Dial, 1983. ISBN 0-8037-0010-5 Subj: Careers – doctors. Health & fitness.

Clap hands ill. by author. Macmillan, 1987. ISBN 0-02-769030-X Subj: Activities – playing. Babies. Format, unusual – board books.

The dancing class ill. by author. Dial, 1983. ISBN 0-8037-1651-6 Subj: Activities – dancing. Ballet.

Dressing ill. by author. S&S, 1981. ISBN 0-671-42113-1 Subj: Clothing. Format, unusual – board books.

Eating out ill. by author. Dial, 1983. ISBN 0-8037-2203-6 Subj: Food.

Family ill. by author. S&S, 1981. ISBN 0-671-42110-7 Subj: Family life. Format, unusual – board books.

First day of school ill. by author. Dial, 1983. ISBN 0-8037-0012-1 Subj: Friendship. School – first day.

Friends ill. by author. S&S, 1981. ISBN 0-671-42111-5 Subj: Animals. Format, unusual – board books. Friendship.

Good night, good morning ill. by author. Dial, 1982. ISBN 0-8037-2980-4 Subj: Bedtime. Morning. Wordless.

Grandma and Grandpa ill. by author. Dial, 1984. ISBN 0-8037-0128-4 Subj: Activities – playing. Family life – grandparents.

Helen Oxenbury's ABC of things ill. by author. Watts, 1971. ISBN 0-434-95598-1 Subj: ABC books.

I can ill. by author. Random House, 1985. ISBN 0-394-87482-X Subj: Activities. Babies. Format, unusual – board books.

I hear ill. by author. Random House, 1985. ISBN 0-394-87481-1 Subj: Babies. Format, unusual – board books. Noise, sounds. Senses – hearing.

I see ill. by author. Random House, 1985. ISBN 0-394-87479-X Subj: Babies. Format, unusual – board books. Senses – sight.

I touch ill. by author. Random House, 1985. ISBN 0-394-87480-3 Subj: Babies. Format, unusual – board books. Senses – touch.

The important visitor ill. by author. Dial, 1984. ISBN 0-8037-0125-X Subj: Behavior – misbehavior.

It's my birthday ill. by author. Candlewick, 1994. ISBN 1-56402-412-1 Subj: Activities – baking, cooking. Animals. Birthdays. Cumulative tales. Food.

Monkey see, monkey do ill. by author. Dial, 1982. ISBN 0-8037-5436-1 Subj: Animals. Wordless. Zoos.

Mother's helper ill. by author. Dial, 1982. ISBN 0-8037-5425-6 Subj: Character traits – helpfulness. Family life – mothers. Wordless.

Numbers of things ill. by author. Watts, 1968. Subj: Counting, numbers.

Our dog ill. by author. Dial, 1984. ISBN 0-8037-0127-6 Subj: Activities – walking. Animals – dogs. Family life. Pets.

Pig tale ill. by author. Morrow, 1974. ISBN 0-688-30092-8 Subj: Animals – pigs. Rhyming text.

Pippo gets lost ill. by author. Macmillan, 1989. ISBN 0-689-71336-3 Subj: Animals. Behavior – lost & found possessions. Toys.

Playing ill. by author. Wanderer, 1981. ISBN 0-671-42109-3 Subj: Activities – playing. Babies. Format, unusual – board books. Toys.

The queen and Rosie Randall by Helen Oxenbury from an idea by Jill Butterfield-Campbell; ill. by author. Morrow, 1979. ISBN 0-688-32171-2 Subj: Foreign lands – England. Games. Parties. Royalty – queens.

Say goodnight ill. by author. Macmillan, 1987. ISBN 0-02-769010-5 Subj: Activities – playing. Babies. Format, unusual – board books. Sleep.

729 curious creatures ill. by author. HarperCollins, 1980. ISBN 0-06-024598-5 Subj: Animals. Format, unusual – board books. Imagination.

729 merry mix-ups ill. by author. HarperCollins, 1980. ISBN 0-06-024599-3 Subj: Animals. Format, unusual – board books. Imagination.

729 puzzle people ill. by author. HarperCollins, 1980. ISBN 0-06-024597-7 Subj: Format, unusual – board books. Imagination.

The shopping trip ill. by author. Dial, 1982. ISBN 0-8037-7939-9 Subj: Format, unusual – board books. Shopping. Wordless.

Tickle, tickle ill. by author. Macmillan, 1987. ISBN 0-02-769020-2 Subj: Activities – playing. Babies. Format, unusual – board books.

Tiny Tim: verses for children chosen by Jill Bennett; ill. by author. Delacorte, 1982. ISBN 0-440-08970-7 Subj: Humorous stories. Poetry.

Tom and Pippo and the dog ill. by author. Macmillan, 1989. ISBN 0-689-71338-X Subj: Activities – playing. Animals – dogs. Animals – monkeys. Friendship. Toys.

Tom and Pippo go shopping ill. by author. Macmillan, 1989. ISBN 0-689-71278-2 Subj: Animals – monkeys. Shopping. Toys.

Tom and Pippo in the garden ill. by author. Macmillan, 1989. ISBN 0-689-71275-8 Subj: Animals – monkeys. Gardens, gardening. Toys.

Tom and Pippo on the beach ill. by author. Candlewick, 1993. ISBN 1-56402-181-5 Subj: Animals – monkeys. Sea & seashore – beaches. Toys.

Tom and Pippo see the moon ill. by author. Macmillan, 1989. ISBN 0-689-71277-4 Subj: Animals – monkeys. Moon. Space & space ships. Toys.

Tom and Pippo's day ill. by author. Macmillan, 1989. ISBN 0-689-71276-6 Subj: Activities. Animals – monkeys. Toys.

Oxford Scientific Films. *Danger colors* ed. by Jennifer Coldrey & Karen Goldie-Morrison. Putnam, 1986. ISBN 0-399-21341-4 Subj: Behavior – hiding. Concepts – color.

Grey squirrel photos by George Bernard & John Paling. Putnam, 1982. ISBN 0-399-20906-9 Subj: Animals – squirrels. Science.

Hide and seek ed. by Jennifer Coldrey & Karen Goldie-Morrison. Putnam, 1986. ISBN 0-399-21342-2 Subj: Behavior – hiding. Concepts – color.

The spider's web photos by John Cooke. Putnam, 1978. ISBN 0-399-20621-4 Subj: Science. Spiders.

Oyibo, Papa. *Big brother, little sister* ill. by John Clementson. Barefoot, 2000. ISBN 1-84148-117-3 Subj: Animals – elephants. Animals – mice. Character traits – helpfulness. Friendship.

Pace, David. *Shouting Sharon* ill. by author. Western, 1995. ISBN 0-307-17518-9 Subj: Behavior. Counting, numbers. Cumulative tales. Poetry.

Pace, Elizabeth. *Chris gets ear tubes* ill. by Kathryn Hutton. Gallaudet Univ. Pr., 1987. ISBN 0-930323-36-X Subj: Handicaps – deafness. Hospitals. Illness. Senses – hearing.

Pacheco, Miguel Angel. *Kangaroo* (Sanchez, Jose Louis Garcia)

Pacilio, V. J. *Ling Cho and his three friends* ill. by Scott Cook. Farrar, 2000. ISBN 0-374-34545-7 Subj: Behavior – sharing. Foreign lands – China. Friendship. Rhyming text.

Pacini, Kathy. *In a meadow, two hares hide* (Bartoli, Jennifer)

Pack, Robert. *How to catch a crocodile* ill. by Nola Langner. Knopf, 1964. ISBN 0-394-91251-9 Subj: Character traits – laziness. Imagination. Poetry. Reptiles – alligators, crocodiles.

Then what did you do? ill. by Nola Langner. Macmillan, 1961. Subj: Animals. Cumulative tales. Humorous stories. Poetry.

Packard, Edward. *Big numbers: and pictures that show just how big they are!* ill. by Sal Murdocca. Millbrook, 2000. ISBN 0-7613-1570-5 Subj: Concepts – size. Counting, numbers.

Packard, Mary. *Bubble trouble* ill. by Elena Kuckarik. Scholastic, 1995. ISBN 0-590-48513-X Subj: Activities – playing. Bubbles. Rhyming text.

Don't make a sound ill. by Lane Yerkes. G. Stevens, 2004. ISBN 0-8368-4099-2 Subj: Animals – rabbits. Family life – brothers & sisters. Noise, sounds. Sleep.

The kite ill. by Benrei Huang. Childrens Pr., 1990. ISBN 0-516-05355-8 Subj: Kites. Rhyming text.

Same and different ill. by Susan Banta. G. Stevens, 2004. ISBN 0-8368-4097-6 Subj: Animals. Humorous stories. Language. Rhyming text.

We are monsters ill. by John Magine. Scholastic, 1996. ISBN 0-590-68995-9 Subj: Bedtime. Emotions – fear. Monsters. Rhyming text.

When I am big ill. by Laura Rader. Reader's Digest, 1999. ISBN 1-57584-294-7 Subj: Behavior – growing up. Behavior – imitation. Family life – brothers.

Where is Jake? ill. by Carolyn Ewing. Childrens Pr., 1990. ISBN 0-516-05361-2 Subj: Activities – playing. Games.

Packard, Steven. *see* Kelley, True

Pacovská, Kveta. *Flying* ill. by author. North-South, 1995. ISBN 1-55858-496-X Subj: Activities – flying. Animals.

One, five, many ill. by author. Houghton Mifflin, 1990. ISBN 0-395-54997-3 Subj: Counting, numbers. Format, unusual. Rhyming text.

Padt, Maartje. *Shanti* by Maartje Padt & Mylo Freeman; ill. by Mylo Freeman. DK, 1998. ISBN 0-7894-2520-3 Subj: Animals – zebras. Birth. Foreign lands – Africa. Format, unusual.

Paek, Min. *Aekyung's dream* ill. by author. Children's Book Pr., 1989. ISBN 0-89239-042-5 Subj: Character traits – being different. Ethnic groups in the U.S. Ethnic groups in the U.S. – Korean Americans. School.

Page, Eleanor. *see* Coerr, Eleanor

Page, P. K. (Patricia Kathleen). *The traveling musicians of Bremen* (Grimm, Jacob)

Page, Robin. *The alphabet sticker book* ill. by author. Houghton Mifflin, 1995. ISBN 0-395-71543-1 Subj: ABC books. Format, unusual.

Animals in flight (Jenkins, Steve)

Paige, Rob. *Some of my best friends are monsters* ill. by Paul Yalowitz. Bradbury, 1988. ISBN 0-02-769640-5 Subj: Monsters.

Paine, Penelope Colville. *My way Sally* (Bingham, Mindy)

Pajot, Anne Marie. *Rusty the Irish setter* (Overbeck, Cynthia)

Pak, Soyung. *Dear Juno* ill. by Susan Kathleen Hartung. Viking, 1999. ISBN 0-670-88252-6 Subj: Ethnic groups in the U.S. – Korean Americans. Family life – grandmothers. Foreign languages. Letters, cards.

A place to grow ill. by Marcelino Truong. Levine, 2002. ISBN 0-439-13015-8 Subj: Ethnic groups in the U.S. – Korean Americans. Family life – fathers. Gardens, gardening. Immigrants. Seeds.

Sumi's first day of school ever ill. by Joung Un Kim. Viking, 2003. ISBN 0-670-03522-X Subj: Ethnic groups in the U.S. – Korean Americans. School – first day.

Paker, Josephine. *I wonder why flutes have holes* ill. by author. Kingfisher, 1995. ISBN 1-85697-583-5 Subj: Music.

Palacios, Argentina. *A Christmas surprise for Chabelita* ill. by Lori Lohstoeter. BridgeWater, 1993. ISBN 0-8167-3131-4 Subj: Family life – grandparents. Family life – mothers. Foreign lands – Panama. School.

This can lick a lollipop = esto goza chupando un caramelo (Rothman, Joel)

Paladino, Catherine. *Our vanishing farm animals* ill. with photos. Little, 1992. ISBN 0-316-68891-6 Subj: Animals – endangered animals. Farms.

Palatini, Margie. *Bedhead* ill. by Jack E. Davis. S&S, 2000. ISBN 0-689-82397-5 Subj: Hair. School.

Ding dong ding dong ill. by Howard Fine. Hyperion, 1999. ISBN 0-7868-2367-4 Subj: Animals – gorillas. Careers – salesmen. Humorous stories.

Earthquack ill. by Barry Moser. S&S, 2002. ISBN 0-689-84280-5 Subj: Animals. Birds – ducks. Earthquakes. Humorous stories.

Goldie is mad ill. by author. Hyperion, 2001. ISBN 0-7868-2490-5 Subj: Babies. Emotions – anger. Family life – brothers & sisters. Sibling rivalry.

Good as Goldie ill. by author. Hyperion, 2000. ISBN 0-7868-2435-2 Subj: Behavior – dissatisfaction. Family life – brothers & sisters. Sibling rivalry.

Moo who? ill. by Keith Graves. Tegen, 2004. ISBN 0-06-000106-2 Subj: Animals. Animals – bulls, cows. Noise, sounds.

Moosetache ill. by Henry Cole. Hyperion, 1997. ISBN 0-7868-2246-5 Subj: Animals – moose. Hair.

The perfect pet ill. by Bruce Whatley. HarperCollins, 2003. ISBN 0-06-000109-7 Subj: Character traits – persistence. Insects. Pets.

Piggie pie ill. by Howard Fine. Clarion, 1995. ISBN 0-395-71691-8 Subj: Animals – pigs. Animals – wolves. Character traits – appearance. Holidays – Halloween. Witches.

Tub-boo-boo ill. by Glin Dibley. S&S, 2001. ISBN 0-689-82394-0 Subj: Activities – bathing. Family life. Family life – brothers.

The web files ill. by Richard Egielski. Hyperion, 2001. ISBN 0-7868-2366-6 Subj: Careers – detectives. Farms. Humorous stories. Nursery rhymes.

Zak's lunch ill. by Howard Fine. Clarion, 1998. ISBN 0-395-81674-2 Subj: Family life – mothers. Food. Imagination.

Zoom Broom ill. by Howard Fine. Hyperion, 1998. ISBN 0-7868-0322-3 Subj: Animals – foxes. Witches.

Palazzo, Tony (Anthony D.). *Animal babies* ill. by author. Doubleday, 1960. Subj: Animals.

Animals 'round the mulberry bush ill. by author. Doubleday, 1958. Subj: Animals. Nursery rhymes.

Noah's ark ill. by author. Doubleday, 1955. Subj: Boats, ships. Religion – Noah. Weather – floods. Weather – rain. Weather – rainbows.

Waldo the woodchuck ill. by author. Duell, 1964. Subj: Animals – groundhogs. Holidays – Groundhog Day. Picture puzzles.

Palazzo-Craig, Janet. *Ballet dancer* ill. by Barbara Todd. Troll, 1988. ISBN 0-8167-1434-7 Subj: Activities – dancing. Ballet.

Little Danny Dinosaur ill. by Paul Harvey. Troll, 1988. ISBN 0-8167-1229-8 Subj: Animals. Concepts – size. Dinosaurs. Prehistory.

Muffy and Fluffy: the kittens who didn't agree ill. by Susan Hall. Troll, 1988. ISBN 0-8167-1227-1 Subj: Animals – cats. Behavior – sharing.

Our friend the sun ill. by Susan Hall. Troll, 1982. ISBN 0-89375-650-4 Subj: Science. Sun.

Turtles ill. by Kathie Kelleher. Troll, 1982. ISBN 0-89375-664-4 Subj: Reptiles – turtles, tortoises. Science.

What makes the weather ill. by Paul Harvey. Troll, 1982. ISBN 0-89375-654-7 Subj: Weather.

What's under the ocean? ill. by Paul Harvey. Troll, 1982. ISBN 0-89375-652-0 Subj: Sea & seashore.

Palecek, Libuse. *Brave as a tiger* ill. by Josef Palecek; English adapt. by Andrew Clements. North-South, 1995. ISBN 1-55858-396-3 Subj: Animals – tigers. Character traits – bravery. Emotions – fear. Family life – mothers. Illness.

Palecek, Phyllis. *The ugly duckling* (Andersen, H. C. [Hans Christian])

Paley, Joan. *One more river* ill. by adapt. Little, 2002. ISBN 0-316-60702-9 Subj: Animals. Boats, ships. Counting, numbers. Religion – Noah. Songs. Weather – floods. Weather – rain. Weather – rainbows.

Pallandt, Nicholas van. *The butterfly night of Old Brown Bear* ill. by author. Farrar, 1992. ISBN 0-374-31009-2 Subj: Animals – bears. Dreams. Insects – butterflies, caterpillars.

Pallotta, Jerry. *The airplane alphabet book* by Jerry Pallotta & Fred Stillwell; ill. by Rob Bolster. Charlesbridge, 1997. ISBN 0-8810-6908-6 Subj: ABC books. Airplanes, airports.

The crayon counting book (Ryan, Pam Muñoz)

The dory story ill. by David Biedrzycki. Talewinds, 2000. ISBN 0-8810-6075-5 Subj: Activities – bathing. Animals. Boats, ships. Fish. Imagination. Nature. Sea & seashore.

Going lobstering ill. by Rob Bolster. Charlesbridge, 1990. ISBN 0-88106-475-0 Subj: Careers – fishermen. Sea & seashore.

The jet alphabet book ill. by Rob Bolster. Charlesbridge, 1999. ISBN 0-88106-916-7 Subj: ABC books. Airplanes, airports.

Shapes and patterns ill. by Rob Bolster. Scholastic, 2002. ISBN 0-439-35796-9 Subj: Concepts – patterns. Concepts – shape.

Twizzlers percentages book ill. by Rob Bolster. Scholastic, 2001. ISBN 0-439-25407-8 Subj: Aliens. Counting, numbers. Space & space ships.

Underwater counting ill. by David Biedrzycki. Charlesbridge, 2001. ISBN 0-88106-952-3 Subj: Animals. Counting, numbers. Sea & seashore.

The palm of my heart: *poetry by African American children* ed. by Davida Adedjouma; ill. by Gregory Christie. Lee & Low, 1996. ISBN 1-880000-41-5 Subj: Children as authors. Ethnic groups in the U.S. – African Americans. Poetry.

Palmer, Carole. *Why does it fly?* (Arvetis, Chris)

Why does it thunder and lightning? (Arvetis, Chris)

Why is it dark? (Arvetis, Chris)

Palmer, Mary Babcock. *No-sort-of-animal* ill. by Abner Graboff. Houghton Mifflin, 1964. Subj: Animals. Behavior – dissatisfaction. Self-concept.

Palmer, Todd Starr. *Rhino and Mouse* ill. by Judy Lanfredi. Dial, 1994. ISBN 0-8037-1323-1 Subj: Animals – mice. Animals – rhinoceros. Friendship.

Palmisciano, Diane. *Garden partners* ill. by author. Atheneum, 1989. ISBN 0-689-31415-9 Subj: Family life – grandmothers. Gardens, gardening.

P'an, Ts'ai-ying. *Monkey creates havoc in heaven* adapt. by Pan Cai Ying from the novel The pilgrimage to the West by Wu Cheng En; ill. by Xin Kuan Liang . . . et al.; trans. by Ye Pin Kuei & rev. by Jill Morris. Viking, 1989. ISBN 0-670-81805-4 Subj: Animals – monkeys. Folk & fairy tales. Foreign lands – China.

Pancheri, Jan. *The twelve poodle princess* ill. by author. Hutchinson, 1995. ISBN 0-09-176710-5 Subj: Activities – dancing. Animals – dogs. Folk & fairy tales. Royalty – princesses.

Pandell, Karen. *I love you sun, I love you moon* ill. by Tomie de Paola. Putnam, 1994. ISBN 0-399-22628-1 Subj: Ecology. Nature.

Pandya, Meenal. *Here comes Diwali* ill. by author; recipes by Laxmi Jain. MeeRa, 2000. ISBN 0-9635539-3-3 Subj: Holidays. Religion – Hinduism.

Panek, Dennis. *Ba ba sheep wouldn't go to sleep* ill. by author. Watts, 1988. ISBN 0-531-08376-4 Subj: School. Sleep.

Catastrophe Cat ill. by author. Bradbury, 1978. ISBN 0-8788-8130-1 Subj: Animals – cats. Behavior – carelessness.

Catastrophe Cat at the zoo ill. by author. Bradbury, 1979. ISBN 0-8788-8147-6 Subj: Animals – cats. Wordless. Zoos.

Detective Whoo ill. by author. Bradbury, 1981. ISBN 0-87888-183-2 Subj: Birds – owls. Careers – detectives. Circus. Mystery stories. Noise, sounds.

Matilda Hippo has a big mouth ill. by author. Bradbury, 1980. ISBN 0-8788-8161-1 Subj: Animals – hippopotamuses. Behavior.

Pans, Ona. *Cubs* (Landa, Norbert)

Kittens (Landa, Norbert)

Puppies (Landa, Norbert)

Paola, Tomie (Thomas Anthony) de. *see* De Paola, Tomie (Thomas Anthony)

Paolilli, Paul. *Silver seeds* by Paul Paolilli & Dan Brewer; ill. by Steve Johnson & Lou Fancher. Viking, 2001. ISBN 0-670-88941-5 Subj: Imagination. Nature. Poetry.

Papajani, Janet. *Museums* ill. with photos. Childrens Pr., 1983. ISBN 0-516-01682-2 Subj: Museums.

Paparone, Pamela. *Five little ducks* ill. by author. North-South, 1995. ISBN 1-55858-474-9 Subj: Birds – ducks. Counting, numbers. Nursery rhymes.

Papas, William. *Taresh the tea planter* ill. by author. Collins-World, 1968. ISBN 0-19-279643-7 Subj: Character traits – laziness. Foreign lands – India.

Pape, D. L. (Donna Lugg). *Doghouse for sale* ill. by Tom Eaton. Garrard, 1979. ISBN 0-8116-4415-4 Subj: Animals – dogs. Homes, houses.

Snoino mystery ill. by William Hutchinson. Garrard, 1980. ISBN 0-8116-6410-4 Subj: Mystery stories.

Where is my little Joey? ill. by Tom Eaton. Garrard, 1978. ISBN 0-8116-4411-1 Subj: Animals – kangaroos.

A paper of pins ill. by Margaret Gordon. Seabury Pr., 1975. ISBN 0-8164-3131-0 Subj: Folk & fairy tales. Money. Songs.

Paradis, Susan. *My Daddy* ill. by author. Front St., 1998. ISBN 1-886910-30-8 Subj: Activities. Family life – fathers.

My mommy ill. by author. Front St., 2002. ISBN 1-886910-73-1 Subj: Emotions – love. Family life – mothers.

Paraskevas, Betty. *Cecil Bunions and the midnight train* ill. by Michael Paraskevas. Harcourt, 1996. ISBN 0-15-292884-7 Subj: Dreams. Monsters. Night. Rhyming text. Trains.

The ferocious beast with the polka-dot hide ill. by Michael Paraskevas. Harcourt, 1996. ISBN 0-15-200838-1 Subj: Animals – pigs. Behavior – greed. Food. Friendship. Rhyming text.

Gracie Graves and the kids from room 402 ill. by Michael Paraskevas. Harcourt, 1995. ISBN 0-15-200321-5 Subj: Careers – teachers. Poetry. School.

Hoppy and Joe ill. by Michael Paraskevas. S&S, 1999. ISBN 0-689-82199-9 Subj: Animals – dogs. Birds – seagulls. Friendship. Sea & seashore – beaches. Seasons – summer.

Junior Kroll and Company ill. by Michael Paraskevas. Harcourt, 1994. ISBN 0-15-292855-3 Subj: Animals. Birds. Music. Musical instruments – saxophones. Poetry.

Maggie and the Ferocious Beast, the big carrot ill. by Michael Paraskevas. S&S, 2000. ISBN 0-689-82490-4 Subj: Activities – digging. Animals – mice. Animals – pigs. Animals – rabbits. Character traits – helpfulness. Gardens, gardening. Monsters.

Maggie and the Ferocious Beast, the big scare ill. by Michael Paraskevas. S&S, 1999. ISBN 0-689-82489-0 Subj: Animals – mice. Animals – pigs. Emotions – fear. Monsters.

Marvin, the tap-dancing horse ill. by Michael Paraskevas. S&S, 2001. ISBN 0-689-82153-0 Subj: Activities – dancing. Animals – horses, ponies. Fairs, festivals. Friendship. Theater.

Monster Beach ill. by Michael Paraskevas. Harcourt, 1995. ISBN 0-15-292882-0 Subj: Family life – grandfathers. Monsters. Sea & seashore – beaches.

Nibbles O'Hare ill. by Michael Paraskevas. S&S, 2001. ISBN 0-689-82865-9 Subj: Animals – rabbits. Holidays – Easter.

On the day the tall ships sailed ill. by Michael Paraskevas. S&S, 2000. ISBN 0-689-82864-0 Subj: Birds – eagles. Boats, ships. Holidays – Fourth of July. Music. U.S. history.

The tangerine bear ill. by Michael Paraskevas. HarperCollins, 1997. ISBN 0-06-205146-6 Subj: Behavior – needing someone. Character traits – appearance. Family life. Stores. Toys – bears.

A very Kroll Christmas ill. by Michael Paraskevas. Harcourt, 1994. ISBN 0-15-292883-9 Subj: Animals – dogs. Holidays – Christmas. Holidays – Thanksgiving. Poetry.

Paré, Roger. *Animal capers* by Roger Paré with Bertrand Gauthier; trans. by David Homel; ill. by Roger Paré. Firefly, 1992. ISBN 1-55037-243-2 Subj: Animals. Poetry.

Circus days by Roger Paré with Bertrand Gauthier; trans. by David Homel; ill. by Roger Paré. Firefly, 1988. ISBN 1-55037-021-9 Subj: Animals. Circus. Poetry.

A friend like you trans. by David Homel; ill. by author. Firefly, 1984. ISBN 0-920303-04-8 Subj: Animals – cats. Friendship.

Play time by Roger Paré with Bertrand Gauthier; trans. by David Homel; ill. by Roger Paré. Firefly, 1990. ISBN 1-55037-087-1 Subj: Animals. Poetry.

Summer days by Roger Paré with Bertrand Gauthier; trans. by David Homel; ill. by Roger Paré. Firefly, 1989. ISBN 1-55037-043-X Subj: Activities – playing. Animals. Poetry.

Parenteau, Shirley. *I'll bet you thought I was lost* ill. by Lorna Tomei. Lothrop, 1981. ISBN 0-688-00259-5 Subj: Behavior – lost.

Parillo, Tony. *Michelangelo's surprise* ill. by author. Farrar, 1998. ISBN 0-374-34961-4 Subj: Careers – artists. Foreign lands – Italy. Snowmen. Weather – snow.

Paris, Lena. *Mom is single* ill. by Mark Christianson. Childrens Pr., 1980. ISBN 0-516-01477-3 Subj: Divorce. Family life – fathers. Family life – mothers.

Parish, Herman. *Good driving, Amelia Bedelia* ill. by Lynn Sweat. Greenwillow, 1995. ISBN 0-688-13359-2 Subj: Automobiles.

Parish, Peggy. *Be ready at eight* ill. by Leonard P. Kessler. Macmillan, 1979. ISBN 0-02-769830-0 Subj: Behavior – forgetfulness. Birthdays.

The cats' burglar ill. by Lynn Sweat. Greenwillow, 1983. ISBN 0-688-01826-2 Subj: Animals – cats. Crime.

Dinosaur time ill. by Arnold Lobel. HarperCollins, 1974. ISBN 0-06-024654-5 Subj: Dinosaurs. Prehistory. Science.

Good hunting, Blue Sky ill. by James Watts. HarperCollins, 1988. ISBN 0-06-024662-6 Subj: Indians of North America. Sports – hunting.

Good hunting, Little Indian ill. by Leonard Weisgard. Addison-Wesley, 1962. Subj: Indians of North America.

Granny and the desperadoes ill. by Steven Kellogg. Macmillan, 1970. ISBN 0-689-80878-X Subj: Crime. Family life – grandmothers. Humorous stories.

Granny and the Indians ill. by Brinton Turkle. Macmillan, 1969. Subj: Family life – grandmothers. Humorous stories. Indians of North America.

Granny, the baby and the big gray thing ill. by Lynn Sweat. Macmillan, 1972. Subj: Animals – wolves. Babies. Family life – grandmothers. Humorous stories. Indians of North America.

I can – can you? ill. by Marylin Hafner. Greenwillow, 1984. Set of 4 books: levels 1-4. ISBN 0-688-03888-2 Subj: Activities. Behavior – growing up. Format, unusual – board books.

Jumper goes to school ill. by Cyndy Szekeres. S&S, 1969. ISBN 0-671-65076-9 Subj: Animals – chimpanzees. School.

Little Indian ill. by John E. Johnson. S&S, 1968. Subj: Indians of North America. Names.

Mind your manners ill. by Marylin Hafner. Greenwillow, 1978. ISBN 0-688-84157-0 Subj: Etiquette.

No more monsters for me! ill. by Marc Simont. HarperCollins, 1981. ISBN 0-06-024658-8 Subj: Monsters. Pets.

Ootah's lucky day ill. by Mamoru Funai. HarperCollins, 1970. Subj: Eskimos. Sports – hunting.

Scruffy ill. by Kelly Oechsli. HarperCollins, 1988. ISBN 0-06-024660-X Subj: Animals – cats. Birthdays. Pets.

Snapping turtle's all wrong day ill. by John E. Johnson. S&S, 1970. ISBN 0-671-65094-7 Subj: Birthdays. Indians of North America.

Too many rabbits ill. by Leonard P. Kessler. Macmillan, 1974. ISBN 0-02-769850-5 Subj: Animals – rabbits.

Zed and the monsters ill. by Paul Galdone. Doubleday, 1979. ISBN 0-385-12949-1 Subj: Character traits – cleverness. Monsters.

Park, Barbara. *Pssst! It's me . . . the Bogeyman* ill. by Stephen Kroninger. Atheneum, 1998. ISBN 0-689-81667-7 Subj: Emotions – fear. Monsters.

Park, Frances. *Good-bye, 382 Shin Dang Dong* ill. by Yangsook Choi. National Geographic, 2002. ISBN 0-7922-7985-9 Subj: Ethnic groups in the U.S. – Korean Americans. Foreign lands – Korea. Moving.

My freedom trip by Frances Park & Ginger Park; ill. by Debra Reid Jenkins. Boyds Mills, 1998. ISBN 1-56397-468-1 Subj: Character traits – freedom. Foreign lands – Korea (North). Immigrants.

The royal bee by Frances Park & Ginger Park; ill. by Christopher Zhong-Yuan Zhang. Boyds Mills, 2000. ISBN 1-56397-614-5 Subj: Contests. Foreign lands – Korea. Poverty. School.

Where on earth is my bagel? by Frances Park & Ginger Park; ill. by Grace Lin. Lee & Low, 2001. ISBN 1-58430-033-7 Subj: Activities – baking, cooking. Food. Foreign lands – Korea. Imagination.

Park, Ginger. *My freedom trip* (Park, Frances)

The royal bee (Park, Frances)

Where on earth is my bagel? (Park, Frances)

Park, Linda Sue. *The firekeeper's son* ill. by Julie Downing. Clarion, 2003. ISBN 0-618-13337-2 Subj: Character traits – responsibility. Family life – fathers. Foreign lands – Korea.

Park, Ruth. *When the wind changed* ill. by Deborah Niland. Coward, 1981. ISBN 0-698-20525-1 Subj: Character traits – appearance.

Park, W. B. *Bakery business* ill. by author. Little, 1983. ISBN 0-316-69078-3 Subj: Animals. Birthdays.

The costume party ill. by author. Little, 1983. ISBN 0-316-69077-5 Subj: Animals. Emotions – loneliness. Parties.

Parke, Margaret B. *Young reader's color-picture dictionary* ill. by Cynthia & Alvin Koehler. Grosset, 1958. Subj: Dictionaries.

Parker, Ant. *Desmond the dog* (Denchfield, Nick)

Desmond the dog, a wag-the-tail pop-up book (Denchfield, Nick)

Flashing fire engines (Mitton, Tony)

Parker, Dorothy D. *Liam's catch* ill. by Robert Andrew Parker. Viking, 1972. ISBN 0-670-42744-6 Subj: Careers – fishermen. Foreign lands – Ireland. Sports – fishing.

Parker, Ed. *Jack and the beanstalk* (Jack and the beanstalk)

Parker, Kristy. *My dad the magnificent* ill. by Lillian Hoban. Dutton, 1987. ISBN 0-525-44314-2 Subj: Behavior – boasting. Family life – fathers.

Parker, Marjorie. *Jasper's day* ill. by Janet Wilson. Kids Can, 2002. ISBN 1-55074-957-9 Subj: Animals – dogs. Death. Emotions – grief. Memories, memory.

Parker, Nancy Winslow. *Bugs* by Nancy Winslow Parker & Joan Richards Wright; ill. by Nancy Winslow Parker. Greenwillow, 1987. ISBN 0-688-06624-0 Subj: Insects. Science.

The Christmas camel ill. by author. Dodd, 1983. ISBN 0-396-08220-3 Subj: Animals – camels. Holidays – Christmas.

Cooper, the McNallys' big black dog ill. by author. Dodd, 1981. ISBN 0-396-07914-8 Subj: Animals – dogs. Behavior – misbehavior. Character traits – helpfulness.

The crocodile under Louis Finneberg's bed ill. by author. Dodd, 1978. ISBN 0-396-07542-8 Subj: Behavior – running away. Behavior – trickery. Furniture – beds. Reptiles – alligators, crocodiles.

Love from Aunt Betty ill. by author. Dodd, 1983. ISBN 0-396-08135-5 Subj: Activities – baking, cooking. Family life – aunts, uncles. Monsters.

Love from Uncle Clyde ill. by author. Dodd, 1977. ISBN 0-396-07426-X Subj: Animals – hippopotamuses. Birthdays. Family life – aunts, uncles.

Poofy loves company ill. by author. Dodd, 1980. ISBN 0-396-00783-8 Subj: Animals – dogs. Behavior – misbehavior.

Puddums, the Cathcarts' orange cat ill. by author. Atheneum, 1980. ISBN 0-689-50159-5 Subj: Animals – cats. Behavior.

Working frog ill. by author. Greenwillow, 1992. ISBN 0-688-09919-X Subj: Animals. Frogs & toads. Zoos.

Parker, Steve. *I wonder why tunnels are round* ill. by author. Kingfisher, 1995. ISBN 1-85697-641-6 Subj: Activities – making things. Buildings. Character traits – curiosity. Concepts – shape. Machines.

Parker, Victoria. *Bearum scarum* ill. by Emily Bolam. Viking, 2002. ISBN 0-670-03546-7 Subj: Animals. Animals – bears. Counting, numbers. Jungle. Rhyming text.

Parkin, Rex. *The red carpet* ill. by author. Macmillan, 1988, 1948. ISBN 0-02-770010-0 Subj: Hotels. Humorous stories.

Parkinson, Curtis. *Emily's eighteen aunts* ill. by Andrea Wayne von Königslöw. Stoddart, 2002. ISBN 0-7737-3336-1 Subj: Character traits – individuality. Family life – aunts, uncles. Humorous stories.

Parkinson, Kathy. *The enormous turnip* ill. by adapt. A. Whitman, 1985. ISBN 0-8075-2062-4 Subj: Behavior – sharing. Character traits – cooperation. Cumulative tales. Folk & fairy tales. Foreign lands – Russia. Plants. Problem solving.

The paper chain (Blake, Claire)

Parkison, Jami. *Amazing Mallika* ill. by Itoko Maeno. MarshMedia, 1996. ISBN 1-55942-087-1 Subj: Animals – tigers. Emotions – anger. Family life – mothers. Foreign lands – India.

Parks, Carmen. *Farmers market* ill. by Edward Martinez. Harcourt, 2002. ISBN 0-15-216680-7 Subj: Careers – farmers. Country. Family life – parents. Stores.

Parks, Van Dyke. *Jump! the adventures of Brer Rabbit* (Harris, Joel Chandler)

Jump again! more adventures of Brer Rabbit (Harris, Joel Chandler)

Parlato, Stephen. *The world that loved books* ill. by author. Simply Read Bks., 2003. ISBN 1-894965-04-3 Subj: Books, reading. Imagination.

Parnall, Peter. *Alfalfa Hill* ill. by author. Doubleday, 1975. ISBN 0-385-02448-7 Subj: Animals. Birds. Seasons – winter. Weather – snow.

The great fish ill. by author. Doubleday, 1973. ISBN 0-385-07863-3 Subj: Ecology. Fish. Folk & fairy tales. Indians of North America.

The rock ill. by author. Macmillan, 1991. ISBN 0-02-770181-6 Subj: Ecology. Forest, woods. Rocks.

Winter barn ill. by author. Macmillan, 1986. ISBN 0-02-770170-0 Subj: Animals. Barns. Seasons – winter.

Parr, Letitia. *A man and his hat* ill. by Paul Terrett; photos by Bob Peters. Putnam, 1991. ISBN 0-399-22255-3 Subj: Behavior – lost & found possessions. Clothing – hats. Rhyming text.

Parr, Todd. *The best friends book* ill. by autnor. Little, 2000. ISBN 0-316-69201-8 Subj: Friendship.

Big and little ill. by autnor. Little, 2001. ISBN 0-316-69291-3 Subj: Concepts – size. Format, unusual – board books. Language.

Black and white ill. by autnor. Little, 2001. ISBN 0-316-69225-5 Subj: Concepts – color. Format, unusual – board books. Language.

The daddy book ill. by autnor. Little, 2002. ISBN 0-316-60799-1 Subj: Family life – fathers.

Do's and don'ts ill. by author. Little, 1999. ISBN 0-316-69213-1 Subj: Behavior. Etiquette.

The feel good book ill. by autnor. Little, 2002. ISBN 0-316-07206-0 Subj: Emotions – happiness.

The feelings book ill. by autnor. Little, 2000. ISBN 0-316-69131-3 Subj: Emotions.

The mommy book ill. by autnor. Little, 2002. ISBN 0-316-60827-0 Subj: Family life – mothers.

The okay book ill. by author. Little, 1999. ISBN 0-316-69220-4 Subj: Character traits – individuality. Self-concept.

Things that make you feel good, things that make you feel bad ill. by author. Little, 1999. ISBN 0-316-69270-0 Subj: Emotions.

This is my hair ill. by author. Little, 1999. ISBN 0-316-69236-0 Subj: Hair.

Underwear do's and don'ts ill. by autnor. Little, 2000. ISBN 0-316-69151-8 Subj: Clothing. Humorous stories.

Parry, Marian. *King of the fish* ill. by author. Macmillan, 1977. ISBN 0-02-770200-6 Subj: Animals – rabbits. Character traits – cleverness. Fish. Folk & fairy tales. Foreign lands – Korea. Reptiles – turtles, tortoises.

Parsons, Alexandra. *Amazing birds* photos by Jerry Young. Knopf, 1990. ISBN 0-679-90223-6 Subj: Birds. Science.

Amazing mammals photos by Jerry Young. Knopf, 1990. ISBN 0-679-90224-4 Subj: Animals. Science.

Amazing snakes photos by Jerry Young. Knopf, 1990. ISBN 0-679-90225-2 Subj: Reptiles – snakes. Science.

Amazing spiders photos by Jerry Young. Knopf, 1990. ISBN 0-679-90226-0 Subj: Science. Spiders.

Parsons, Virginia. *Pinocchio and Gepetto* ill. by adapt. McGraw-Hill, 1979. ISBN 0-07-048531-3 Subj: Behavior – lying. Behavior – misbehavior. Character traits – loyalty. Folk & fairy tales. Puppets.

Pinocchio and the money tree ill. by adapt. McGraw-Hill, 1979. ISBN 0-07-048533-X Subj: Folk & fairy tales. Puppets.

Pinocchio goes on the stage ill. by adapt. McGraw-Hill, 1979. ISBN 0-07-048532-1 Subj: Folk & fairy tales. Puppets.

Pinocchio plays truant ill. by adapt. McGraw-Hill, 1979. ISBN 0-07-048530-5 Subj: Folk & fairy tales. Puppets.

Partch, Virgil Franklin. *The Christmas cookie sprinkle snitcher* ill. by author. Windmill, 1969. ISBN 0-67-166513-8 Subj: Crime. Holidays – Christmas. Rebuses. Rhyming text.

Partis, Joanne. *Stripe* ill. by author. Carolrhoda, 2000. ISBN 1-57505-450-7 Subj: Animals – babies. Animals – tigers. Behavior – misbehavior.

Stripe's naughty sister ill. by author. Carolrhoda, 2002. ISBN 0-87614-466-0 Subj: Animals – tigers. Family life – brothers & sisters.

Parton, Dolly. *Coat of many colors* ill. by Judith Sutton. Harper-Collins, 1994. ISBN 0-06-023413-X Subj: Clothing – coats. Family life – mothers. Poverty. Religion. Songs.

Partridge, Elizabeth. *Moon glowing* ill. by Joan Paley. Dutton, 2002. ISBN 0-525-46873-0 Subj: Animals. Hibernation. Rhyming text. Seasons – winter.

Oranges on Golden Mountain ill. by Aki Sogabe. Dutton, 2001. ISBN 0-525-46453-0 Subj: Ethnic groups in the U.S. – Chinese Americans. Family life – aunts, uncles. Foreign lands – China. Immigrants. Sports – fishing.

Pig's eggs ill. by Martha Weston. Golden Bks., 2000. ISBN 0-307-10232-7 Subj: Activities – painting. Animals – pigs. Birds – chickens. Eggs.

Partridge, Jenny. *Colonel Grunt* ill. by author. Holt, 1982. ISBN 0-03-061511-9 Subj: Animals.

Grandma Snuffles ill. by author. Holt, 1983. ISBN 0-03-062974-8 Subj: Animals. Clothing.

Hopfellow ill. by author. Holt, 1982. ISBN 0-03-061512-7 Subj: Animals. Boats, ships. Frogs & toads. Problem solving.

Mr. Squint ill. by author. Holt, 1982. ISBN 0-03-061509-7 Subj: Animals. Problem solving.

Peterkin Pollensnuff ill. by author. Holt, 1982. ISBN 0-03-061508-9 Subj: Animals. Character traits – helpfulness. Problem solving.

Parvathi, Thampi. *Moon-uncle, moon-uncle: rhymes from India* (Cassedy, Sylvia)

Paschkis, Julie. *Play all day* ill. by author. Little, 1998. ISBN 0-316-69043-0 Subj: Activities – playing. Rhyming text.

So happy/So sad ill. by author. Holt, 1995. ISBN 0-8050-3862-0 Subj: Animals. Emotions – happiness. Emotions – sadness. Format, unusual.

Pascoe, Gwen. *Deep in a rainforest* ill. by Veronica Jefferis. G. Stevens, 1999. ISBN 0-8368-2149-1 Subj: Concepts – color. Ecology. Forest, woods. Science.

Passen, Lisa. *Attack of the 50-foot teacher* ill. by author. Holt, 2000. ISBN 0-8050-6100-2 Subj: Aliens. Careers – teachers. Concepts – size. Holidays – Halloween. School.

Fat, fat Rose Marie ill. by author. Holt, 1991. ISBN 0-8050-1653-8 Subj: Behavior – bullying. Character traits – being different. Friendship.

Grammy and Sammy ill. by author. Holt, 1990. ISBN 0-8050-1415-2 Subj: Animals – cats. Family life – grandmothers.

The incredible shrinking teacher ill. by author. Holt, 2002. ISBN 0-8050-6452-4 Subj: Careers – teachers. Concepts – size. Humorous stories. Parties. School.

Patchett, Fiona. *Rabbits* ill. by Christyan Fox. Usborne, 1999. ISBN 1-58086-588-7 Subj: Animals – rabbits. Pets.

Patent, Dorothy Hinshaw. *Babies!* photos by author. Holiday, 1988. ISBN 0-8234-0685-7 Subj: Babies.

Bold and bright, black-and-white animals ill. by Kendahl Jan Jubb. Walker, 1998. ISBN 0-8027-8673-1 Subj: Animals. Concepts – color.

Fabulous fluttering tropical butterflies ill. by Kendahl Jan Jubb. Walker, 2003. ISBN 0-8027-8839-4 Subj: Insects – butterflies, caterpillars.

Maggie, a sheep dog photos by William Muñoz. Dodd, 1986. ISBN 0-396-08617-9 Subj: Animals – dogs. Animals – sheep.

Slinky, scaly, slithery snakes ill. by Kendahl Jan Jubb. Walker, 2000. ISBN 0-8027-8744-4 Subj: Reptiles – snakes.

Paterson, A. B. (Andrew Barton). *The man from Ironbark* ill. by Quentin Hole. Collins-World, 1975. ISBN 0-529-05262-8 Subj: Character traits – cleverness. Poetry.

Mulga Bill's bicycle ill. by Kilmeny & Deborah Niland. Parents' Magazine Pr., 1975. ISBN 0-8193-0778-5 Subj: Animals – horses, ponies. Foreign lands – Australia. Poetry. Sports – bicycling.

Waltzing Matilda ill. by Desmund Digby. Holt, 1970. ISBN 0-03-086749-5 Subj: Foreign lands – Australia. Songs.

Paterson, Bettina. *Bun and Mrs. Tubby* ill. by author. Watts, 1987. ISBN 0-531-08300-4 Subj: Activities – babysitting. Animals – elephants.

Bun's birthday ill. by author. Watts, 1988. ISBN 0-531-08336-5 Subj: Animals – elephants. Behavior – sharing. Birthdays. Parties.

In my house ill. by author. Holt, 1992. ISBN 0-8050-1882-4 Subj: Format, unusual – board books.

In my yard ill. by author. Holt, 1992. ISBN 0-8050-1881-6 Subj: Format, unusual – board books.

My clothes ill. by author. Holt, 1992. ISBN 0-8050-1884-0 Subj: Clothing. Format, unusual – board books.

My first wild animals ill. by author. HarperCollins, 1991. ISBN 0-690-04773-8 Subj: Animals.

My toys ill. by author. Holt, 1992. ISBN 0-8050-1883-2 Subj: Format, unusual – board books. Toys.

Paterson, Brian. *Zigby camps out* ill. by author. HarperCollins, 2002. ISBN 0-06-052921-0 Subj: Animals. Animals – meerkats. Animals – zebras. Birds – guinea fowl. Camps, camping. Jungle.

Zigby dives in ill. by author. HarperCollins, 2004. ISBN 0-06-053799-X Subj: Animals – zebras. Octopuses. Sports – fishing.

Zigby hunts for treasure ill. by author. HarperCollins, 2003. ISBN 0-06-052922-9 Subj: Animals – meerkats. Animals – zebras. Canoes & canoeing. Jungle. Maps.

Paterson, Diane. *The bathtub ocean* ill. by author. Dial, 1979. ISBN 0-8037-0462-3 Subj: Activities – bathing. Imagination.

Eat ill. by author. Dial, 1975. ISBN 0-8037-4831-0 Subj: Food. Humorous stories.

Hey, cowboy! ill. by author. Knopf, 1983. ISBN 0-394-95341-X Subj: Family life – grandfathers. Sibling rivalry.

If I were a toad ill. by author. Dial, 1977. ISBN 0-8037-4804-3 Subj: Animals. Behavior – wishing. Participation.

Smile for auntie ill. by author. Dial, 1976. ISBN 0-8037-8067-2 Subj: Family life – aunts, uncles. Humorous stories.

Soap and suds ill. by author. Knopf, 1984. ISBN 0-394-96131-5 Subj: Activities – working. Behavior – misbehavior.

Wretched Rachel ill. by author. Dial, 1978. ISBN 0-8037-9695-1 Subj: Behavior. Emotions – love. Family life.

Paterson, John (John Barstow). *Blueberries for the queen* by John & Katherine Paterson; ill. by Susan Jeffers. HarperCollins, 2004. ISBN 0-06-623943-5 Subj: Food. Royalty – queens. U.S. history. War.

Paterson, Katherine. *The angel and the donkey* ill. by Alexander Koshkin. Clarion, 1996. ISBN 0-395-68969-4 Subj: Angels. Religion – Moses. Royalty – kings.

Blueberries for the queen (Paterson, John [John Barstow])

Celia and the sweet, sweet water ill. by Vladimir Vagin. Clarion, 1998. ISBN 0-525-67481-0 Subj: Animals – dogs. Character traits – kindness. Family life – mothers. Friendship. Water.

The crane wife (Yagawa, Sumiko)

Marvin one too many ill. by Jane Clark Brown. HarperCollins, 2001. ISBN 0-06-028770-5 Subj: Books, reading. Family life – fathers. School.

The tale of the Mandarin ducks ill. by Leo & Diane Dillon. Dutton, 1990. ISBN 0-525-67283-4 Subj: Birds – ducks. Folk & fairy tales. Foreign lands – Japan.

The tongue-cut sparrow (Ishii, Momoko)

Patkau, Karen. *In the sea* ill. by author. Firefly, 1989. ISBN 1-55037-067-7 Subj: Sea & seashore.

Paton, Priscilla. *Howard and the sitter surprise* ill. by Paul Meisel. Houghton Mifflin, 1996. ISBN 0-395-71814-7 Subj: Activities – babysitting. Activities – storytelling. Animals – bears. Behavior – misbehavior.

Paton Walsh, Jill. *see* Walsh, Jill Paton

Patrick, Denise Lewis. *Look inside a house* (Gomboli, Mario)

Look inside a ship (Gomboli, Mario)

No diapers for baby! ill. by Sylvia Walker. Western, 1995. ISBN 0-307-12870-9 Subj: Behavior – growing up. Ethnic groups in the U.S. – African Americans. Format, unusual – board books. Toilet training.

Patrick, Jean L. S. *If I had a snowplow* ill. by karen Dugan. Boyds Mills, 2001. ISBN 1-56397-746-X Subj: Family life – mothers. Machines. Rhyming text. Trucks.

Patron, Susan. *Burgoo stew* ill. by Mike Shenon. Watts, 1991. ISBN 0-531-08516-3 Subj: Activities – baking, cooking. Character traits – cleverness. Folk & fairy tales. Food. Foreign lands – France.

Dark cloud strong breeze ill. by Peter Catalanotto. Orchard, 1994. ISBN 0-531-08665-8 Subj: Automobiles. Cumulative tales. Family life – fathers. Rhyming text. Weather – rain. Weather – wind.

Five bad boys, Billy Que, and the dustdobbin ill. by Mike Shenon. Orchard, 1992. ISBN 0-531-05989-8 Subj: Character traits – generosity. Concepts – size.

Patschke, Steve. *The spooky book* ill. by Matthew McElligott. Walker, 1999. ISBN 0-8027-8693-6 Subj: Books, reading. Emotions – fear. Homes, houses.

Patterson, Elizabeth Burman. *Whose eyes are these?* ill. by author. Tommy Nelson, 1997. ISBN 0-8499-1464-7 Subj: Anatomy – eyes. Animals. Games. Nature. Rhyming text. Science.

Patterson, Geoffrey. *Jonah and the whale* ill. by author. Lothrop, 1992. ISBN 0-688-11239-0 Subj: Animals – whales. Religion – Jonah.

The lion and the gypsy ill. by author. Doubleday, 1991. ISBN 0-385-41536-2 Subj: Animals. Gypsies. Music.

The naughty boy and the strawberry horse ill. by author. Hutchinson, 1997. ISBN 0-09-176547-1 Subj: Animals – horses, ponies. Behavior. Etiquette.

A pig's tale ill. by author. Dutton, 1983. ISBN 0-233-97477-6 Subj: Animals – pigs. Behavior – running away. Farms.

Patterson, José. *Mazal-Tov: a Jewish wedding* photos by Liba Taylor. David & Charles, 1988. ISBN 0-241-12269-4 Subj: Jewish culture. Weddings.

Patterson, Pat. *Hickory dickory duck: a book of very funny rhymes and picture puzzles* by Pat Patterson & Joe Weissmann. Greey de Pencier Books, 1982. ISBN 0-919872-72-7 Subj: Games. Nursery rhymes.

Pattison, Darcy. *The journey of Oliver K. Woodman* ill. by Joe Cepeda. Harcourt, 2003. ISBN 0-15-202329-1 Subj: Activities – traveling. Letters, cards. Toys – dolls.

The river dragon ill. by Jean & Mou-Sien Tseng. Lothrop, 1991. ISBN 0-688-10427-4 Subj: Dragons. Folk & fairy tales. Foreign lands – China.

Patton, Don. *Armadillos* ill. by author. Child's World, 1996. ISBN 1-56766-182-3 Subj: Animals – armadillos.

Pythons ill. with photos. Child's World, 1996. ISBN 1-56766-180-7 Subj: Reptiles – snakes.

Sea turtles ill. with photos. Child's World, 1996. ISBN 1-56766-188-2 Subj: Reptiles – turtles, tortoises.

Pattou, Edith. *Mrs. Spitzer's garden* ill. by Tricia Tusa. Harcourt, 2001. ISBN 0-15-201978-2 Subj: Careers – teachers. Gardens, gardening. School.

Patz, Nancy. *Gina Farina and the Prince of Mintz* ill. by author. Harcourt, 1986. ISBN 0-15-230815-6 Subj: Activities – traveling. Character traits – meanness. Character traits – persistence. Royalty – princes. Theater.

Moses supposes his toeses are roses and 7 other silly old rhymes ill. by author. Harcourt, 1983. ISBN 0-15-255690-7 Subj: Nursery rhymes. Poetry.

No thumpin' no bumpin' no rumpus tonight! ill. by author. Atheneum, 1990. ISBN 0-689-31510-4 Subj: Animals – elephants. Birthdays. Family life – mothers. Food. Imagination – imaginary friends.

Pumpernickel tickle and mean green cheese ill. by author. Watts, 1978. ISBN 0-531-02221-8 Subj: Animals – elephants. Behavior – forgetfulness. Humorous stories. Shopping. Tongue twisters.

Sarah Bear and Sweet Sidney ill. by author. Four Winds, 1989. ISBN 0-02-770270-7 Subj: Animals – bears. Hibernation. Poetry. Seasons – spring. Seasons – winter.

To Annabella Pelican from Thomas Hippopotamus ill. by author. Four Winds, 1991. ISBN 0-02-770280-4 Subj: Animals – hippopotamuses. Birds – pelicans. Friendship. Moving.

Paul, Ann Whitford. *Eight hands round* ill. by Jeanette Winter. HarperCollins, 1991. ISBN 0-06-024704-5 Subj: ABC books. Quilts.

Everything to spend the night . . . from A to Z ill. by Maggie Smith. DK, 1999. ISBN 0-7894-2511-4 Subj: ABC books. Bedtime. Family life – grandfathers. Rhyming text.

Hello toes! Hello feet! ill. by Nadine Bernard Westcott. DK, 1998. ISBN 0-7894-2481-9 Subj: Activities – playing. Anatomy – feet. Anatomy – toes. Animals – dogs. Clothing – shoes.

The seasons sewn ill. by Michael McCurdy. Browndeer, 1996. ISBN 0-15-276918-8 Subj: Activities – sewing. Quilts. Seasons. U.S. history – frontier & pioneer life.

Paul, Anthony. *The tiger who lost his stripes* ill. by Michael Foreman. Harcourt, 1982. ISBN 0-15-287681-2 Subj: Animals – tigers. Character traits – cleverness. Forest, woods.

Paul, Jan S. *Hortense* ill. by Madelaine Gill Linden. HarperCollins, 1984. ISBN 0-690-04371-6 Subj: Animals. Behavior – lost. Farms.

Paul, Korky. *Dragon poems* (Dragon poems)

Pop-up numbers #1 (Marshall, Ray)

Pop-up numbers #2 (Marshall, Ray)

Pop-up numbers #3 (Marshall, Ray)

Pop-up numbers #4 (Marshall, Ray)

Tiny (Rogers, Paul [Patrick])

Winnie flies again by Korky Paul & Valerie Thomas; ill. by Valerie Thomas. Kane/Miller, 2000. ISBN 0-916291-94-4 Subj: Glasses. Humorous stories. Witches.

Winnie in winter by Korky Paul & Valerie Thomas; ill. by Valerie Thomas. Oxford Univ. Pr., 1996. ISBN 0-19-279004-8 Subj: Animals. Nature. Seasons – winter. Witches.

Paul, Sherry. *2-B and the rock 'n roll band* ill. by Bob Miller. Childrens Pr., 1981. ISBN 0-516-02355-1 Subj: Character traits – helpfulness. Robots.

2-B and the space visitor ill. by Bob Miller. Childrens Pr., 1981. ISBN 0-516-02356-X Subj: Holidays – Halloween. Robots. Space & space ships.

Paulsen, Gary. *Canoe days* ill. by Ruth Wright Paulsen. Doubleday, 1999. ISBN 0-385-32524-X Subj: Birds. Canoes & canoeing. Fish. Insects. Seasons – summer.

Worksong ill. by Ruth Wright Paulsen. Harcourt, 1997. ISBN 0-15-200980-9 Subj: Activities – working. Careers. Rhyming text.

Pavey, Peter. *I'm Taggarty Toad* ill. by author. Bradbury, 1980. ISBN 0-87888-172-7 Subj: Behavior – boasting. Frogs & toads. Imagination.

One dragon's dream ill. by author. Bradbury, 1979. ISBN 0-87888-148-4 Subj: Counting, numbers. Dragons. Dreams. Rhyming text.

Pavlova, Anna. *I dreamed I was a ballerina* ill. with art by Edgar Degas. Atheneum, 2001. ISBN 0-689-84676-2 Subj: Activities – dancing. Ballet. Careers – dancers. Character traits – ambition. Foreign lands – Russia.

Paxton, Tom. *Androcles and the lion: and other Æsop fables* (Æsop)

Belling the cat and other Æsop fables ill. by Robert Rayevsky. Morrow, 1990. ISBN 0-688-08159-2 Subj: Animals. Folk & fairy tales.

Engelbert the elephant ill. by Steven Kellogg. Morrow, 1990. ISBN 0-688-08936-4 Subj: Activities – dancing. Animals – elephants. Etiquette. Parties. Royalty – queens.

Going to the zoo ill. by Karen Schmidt. Morrow, 1996. ISBN 0-688-13801-2 Subj: Animals. Music. Songs. Zoos.

Jennifer's rabbit ill. by Donna Ayers. Morrow, 1988. ISBN 0-688-07432-4 Subj: Behavior – running away. Dreams. Poetry.

The jungle baseball game ill. by Karen Schmidt. Morrow, 1999. ISBN 0-688-13980-9 Subj: Animals – hippopotamuses. Animals – monkeys. Sports – baseball.

The marvelous toy ill. by Elizabeth Sayles. Morrow, 1996. ISBN 0-688-13879-9 Subj: Family life – fathers. Rhyming text. Songs. Toys.

The story of Santa Claus ill. by Michael Dooling. Morrow, 1995. ISBN 0-688-11365-6 Subj: Folk & fairy tales. Holidays – Christmas. Santa Claus.

The story of the Tooth Fairy ill. by Robert Sauber. Morrow, 1996. ISBN 0-688-12988-9 Subj: Fairies. Folk & fairy tales. Friendship. Teeth.

Paye, Won-Ldy. *Head, body, legs* retold by Won-Ldy Paye & Margaret H. Lippert; ill. by Julie Paschkis. Holt, 2002. ISBN 0-8050-6570-9 Subj: Character traits – cooperation. Folk & fairy tales. Foreign lands – Liberia.

Mrs. Chicken and the hungry crocodile retold by Won-Ldy Paye & Margaret H. Lippert; ill. by Julie Paschkis. Holt, 2003. ISBN 0-8050-7047-8 Subj: Birds – chickens. Folk & fairy tales. Foreign lands – Liberia. Reptiles – alligators, crocodiles.

Payne, Emmy. *Katy no-pocket* ill. by Hans Augusto Rey. Houghton Mifflin, 1944. ISBN 0-395-52141-6 Subj: Animals – kangaroos. Clothing – aprons. Clothing – pockets. Problem solving.

Payne, Joan Balfour. *The stable that stayed* ill. by author. Ariel, 1952. Subj: Animals. Careers – artists. Country.

Payne, Sherry Neuwirth. *A contest* ill. by Jeff Kyle. Carolrhoda, 1982. ISBN 0-87614-176-9 Subj: Character traits – being different. Handicaps – cerebral palsy. School.

Paz, Elena. *Las Navidades: popular Christmas songs from Latin America* (Delacre, Lulu)

Paz, Octavio. *My life with the wave* (Cowan, Catherine)

Peaceable kingdom: the Shaker abecedarius ill. by Alice & Martin Provensen. Viking, 1978. ISBN 0-670-54500-7 Subj: ABC books. Animals. Poetry.

Peaceful moments in the wild: animals and their homes ill. with photos. Moonstone, 2001. ISBN 0-9707768-1-0 Subj: Animals. Homes, houses.

Peacock, Carol Antoinette. *Mommy far, Mommy near* ill. by Shawn Costello Brownell. A. Whitman, 2000. ISBN 0-8075-5234-8 Subj: Adoption. Emotions. Ethnic groups in the U.S. – Chinese Americans. Family life – mothers.

Pilgrim cat ill. by Doris Ettlinger. A. Whitman, 2004. ISBN 0-8075-6532-6 Subj: Animals – cats. Boats, ships. Pilgrims. U.S. history.

Pearce, Philippa. *Emily's own elephant* ill. by John Lawrence. Greenwillow, 1988. ISBN 0-688-07679-3 Subj: Animals – elephants. Family life. Pets.

Pearce, Q. L. *In the African grasslands* by Q. L. & W. J. Pearce; ill. by Delana Bettoli. Silver Pr., 1990. ISBN 0-671-68827-8 Subj: Animals. Foreign lands – Africa.

In the desert by Q. L. & W. J. Pearce; ill. by Delana Bettoli. Silver Pr., 1990. ISBN 0-671-68825-1 Subj: Animals. Desert.

Pearce, W. J. *In the African grasslands* (Pearce, Q. L.)

In the desert (Pearce, Q. L.)

Pearson, Debora. *Alphabeep* ill. by Edward Miller. Holiday, 2003. ISBN 0-8234-1722-0 Subj: ABC books. Automobiles. Traffic, traffic signs. Trucks.

Leo's tree ill. by Nora Hilb. Annick, 2004. ISBN 1-55037-844-9 Subj: Behavior – growing up. Poetry. Trees.

Pearson, Kit. *The singing basket* ill. by Ann Blades. Firefly, 1990. ISBN 0-88899-104-5 Subj: Behavior – lying. Folk & fairy tales. Foreign lands – Canada.

Pearson, Susan. *Baby and the bear* ill. by Nancy Carlson. Viking, 1987. ISBN 0-670-81299-4 Subj: Format, unusual – board books. Toys – bears.

The drowsy hours: poems for bedtime (The drowsy hours)

Everybody knows that! ill. by Diane Paterson. Dial, 1978. ISBN 0-8037-2418-7 Subj: Friendship. Gender roles. School.

Happy birthday, Grampie ill. by Ronald Himler. Dial, 1987. ISBN 0-8037-3457-3 Subj: Birthdays. Family life – grandfathers.

Jack and the beanstalk (Jack and the beanstalk)

Karin's Christmas walk ill. by Trinka Hakes Noble. Dial, 1980. ISBN 0-8037-4432-3 Subj: Family life – aunts, uncles. Holidays – Christmas.

Lenore's big break ill. by Nancy Carlson. Viking, 1992. ISBN 0-670-83474-2 Subj: Birds. Self-concept. Theater.

My favorite time of year ill. by John Wallner. HarperCollins, 1988. ISBN 0-06-024682-0 Subj: Seasons.

Saturday, I ran away ill. by Susan Jeschke. HarperCollins, 1981. ISBN 0-397-31958-4 Subj: Behavior – running away. Family life.

Silver morning ill. by David Christiana. Harcourt, 1998. ISBN 0-15-274786-9 Subj: Activities – walking. Family life – mothers. Weather – fog.

That's enough for one day! ill. by Kay Chorao. Dial, 1977. ISBN 0-8037-8567-4 Subj: Activities – playing. Books, reading.

Well, I never! ill. by James Warhola. S&S, 1990. ISBN 0-671-69199-6 Subj: Farms.

When baby went to bed ill. by Nancy Carlson. Viking, 1987. ISBN 0-670-81300-1 Subj: Babies. Bedtime. Counting, numbers. Format, unusual – board books.

Pearson, Tracey Campbell. *A apple pie* ill. by author. Dial, 1986. ISBN 0-8037-0252-3 Subj: ABC books. Format, unusual – toy & movable books. Nursery rhymes. Poetry.

Bob ill. by author. Farrar, 2002. ISBN 0-374-39957-3 Subj: Animals. Birds – chickens. Humorous stories. Noise, sounds.

Hector Protector [board book] ill. by author. Farrar, 2004. ISBN 0-374-30860-8 Subj: Format, unusual – board books. Nursery rhymes.

The howling dog ill. by author. Farrar, 1991. ISBN 0-374-33502-8 Subj: Animals – dogs. Behavior – misbehavior. Emotions – loneliness. Night. Noise, sounds.

The purple hat ill. by author. Farrar, 1997. ISBN 0-374-36153-3 Subj: Birds. Clothing – hats. Forest, woods.

Sing a song of sixpence ill. by author. Dial, 1985. ISBN 0-8037-0152-7 Subj: Behavior – misbehavior. Humorous stories. Nursery rhymes.

The storekeeper ill. by author. Dial, 1988. ISBN 0-8037-0371-6 Subj: Animals – cats. Careers – storekeepers. Stores.

Where does Joe go? ill. by author. Farrar, 1999. ISBN 0-374-38319-7 Subj: Restaurants. Rhyming text. Santa Claus. Seasons – winter.

The peasant's pea patch trans. by Guy Daniels; ill. by Robert M. Quackenbush. Delacorte, 1971. Subj: Birds – cranes. Folk & fairy tales. Foreign lands – Russia.

Peavy, Linda. *Allison's grandfather* ill. by Ronald Himler. Scribners, 1981. ISBN 0-684-17017-5 Subj: Death. Emotions – grief. Family life – grandfathers.

Peck, Jan. *The giant carrot* ill. by Barry Root. Dial, 1998. ISBN 0-8037-1824-1 Subj: Behavior – sharing. Folk & fairy tales. Food. Foreign lands – Russia.

Peck, Richard. *Monster night at Grandma's house* ill. by Don Freeman. Dial, 2003. ISBN 0-8037-2904-9 Subj: Bedtime. Emotions – fear. Family life – grandmothers. Monsters. Night.

Peck, Robert Newton. *Hamilton* ill. by Laura Lydecker. Little, 1976. ISBN 0-316-69653-6 Subj: Animals – pigs. Animals – wolves. Farms. Rhyming text.

Peddle, Daniel. *Snow day* ill. by author. Doubleday, 2000. ISBN 0-385-32693-9 Subj: Nature. Snowmen. Weather – snow. Wordless.

Pedersen, Janet. *Millie wants to play* ill. by author. Candlewick, 2004. ISBN 0-7636-1993-0 Subj: Animals – bulls, cows. Morning. Noise, sounds.

Pedersen, Judy. *Out in the country* ill. by author. Knopf, 1991. ISBN 0-679-90630-4 Subj: Country. Family life. Homes, houses. Moving.

The tiny patient ill. by author. Knopf, 1989. ISBN 0-394-90170-3 Subj: Birds. Character traits – kindness to animals. Illness.

When night time comes near ill. by author. Viking, 2000. ISBN 0-670-88259-3 Subj: Bedtime. Communities, neighborhoods. Night.

Pedersen, Marika. *Mommy works, Daddy works* by Marika Pedersen & Mikele Hall; ill. by Deirdre Betteridge. Annick, 2000. ISBN 1-55037-657-8 Subj: Activities – working. Family life – parents.

Peek, Merle. *The balancing act: a counting book* ill. by author. Clarion, 1987. ISBN 0-89919-458-3 Subj: Animals. Animals – elephants. Counting, numbers. Music. Rhyming text. Songs.

Mary wore her red dress and Henry wore his green sneakers ill. by adapt. Clarion, 1985. ISBN 0-89919-324-2 Subj: Animals. Animals – bears. Birthdays. Concepts – color. Songs.

Roll over! a counting song ill. by author. Houghton Mifflin, 1981. ISBN 0-395-29438-X Subj: Counting, numbers. Songs.

Peet, Bill (William Bartlett). *The ant and the elephant* ill. by author. Little, 1972. ISBN 0-395-13734-9 Subj: Animals. Animals – elephants. Character traits – helpfulness. Character traits – selfishness. Cumulative tales. Insects – ants.

Big bad Bruce ill. by author. Houghton Mifflin, 1977. ISBN 0-395-25150-8 Subj: Animals – bears. Behavior – bullying. Forest, woods. Humorous stories. Witches.

Bill Peet: an autobiography ill. by author. Houghton Mifflin, 1989. ISBN 0-395-50932-7 Subj: Caldecott award honor books.

Buford the little bighorn ill. by author. Houghton Mifflin, 1967. Subj: Animals – sheep. Character traits – individuality. Humorous stories. Sports – hunting. Sports – skiing.

The caboose who got loose ill. by author. Houghton Mifflin, 1971. ISBN 0-395-12578-2 Subj: Behavior – dissatisfaction. Ecology. Trains.

Chester the worldly pig ill. by author. Houghton Mifflin, 1965. Subj: Animals – pigs. Circus. Humorous stories. World.

Cock-a-doodle Dudley ill. by author. Houghton Mifflin, 1990. ISBN 0-395-55331-8 Subj: Animals. Birds – chickens. Farms. Sun.

Countdown to Christmas ill. by author. Houghton Mifflin, 1972. ISBN 0-8746-4199-3 Subj: Holidays – Christmas. Humorous stories. Magic. Progress. Santa Claus.

Cowardly Clyde ill. by author. Houghton Mifflin, 1979. ISBN 0-395-27802-3 Subj: Animals – horses, ponies. Character traits – bravery. Humorous stories. Knights.

Cyrus the unsinkable sea serpent ill. by author. Houghton Mifflin, 1975. ISBN 0-395-20272-8 Subj: Character traits – helpfulness. Monsters. Mythical creatures. Sea & seashore.

Eli ill. by author. Houghton Mifflin, 1978. ISBN 0-606-03378-5 Subj: Animals – lions. Birds – vultures. Friendship. Humorous stories.

Ella ill. by author. Houghton Mifflin, 1964. ISBN 0-395-17577-1 Subj: Animals – elephants. Behavior – lost. Character traits – conceit. Circus. Rhyming text.

Encore for Eleanor ill. by author. Houghton Mifflin, 1981. ISBN 0-395-29860-1 Subj: Animals – elephants. Art.

Farewell to Shady Glade ill. by author. Houghton Mifflin, 1966. ISBN 0-395-18975-6 Subj: Animals. Ecology. Progress.

Fly, Homer, fly ill. by author. Houghton Mifflin, 1969. Subj: Birds – pigeons. Cities, towns. Ecology.

The gnats of knotty pine ill. by author. Houghton Mifflin, 1975. ISBN 0-395-21405-X Subj: Animals. Ecology. Insects – gnats. Sports – hunting.

How Droofus the dragon lost his head ill. by author. Houghton Mifflin, 1971. ISBN 0-395-15085-X Subj: Dragons. Knights. Royalty – kings.

Hubert's hair-raising adventures ill. by author. Houghton Mifflin, 1959. Subj: Animals – lions. Careers – barbers. Humorous stories. Rhyming text.

Huge Harold ill. by author. Houghton Mifflin, 1961. ISBN 0-395-32923-X Subj: Animals – rabbits. Character traits – kindness to animals. Concepts – size. Humorous stories. Rhyming text.

Jennifer and Josephine ill. by author. Houghton Mifflin, 1967. ISBN 0-395-18225-5 Subj: Animals – cats. Automobiles. Humorous stories.

Jethro and Joel were a troll ill. by author. Houghton Mifflin, 1987. ISBN 0-395-43081-X Subj: Humorous stories. Magic. Mythical creatures – trolls.

Kermit the hermit ill. by author. Houghton Mifflin, 1965. ISBN 0-395-15084-1 Subj: Behavior – greed. Crustaceans – crabs. Humorous stories. Rhyming text. Sea & seashore.

The kweeks of Kookatumdee ill. by author. Houghton Mifflin, 1985. ISBN 0-395-37902-4 Subj: Activities – flying. Behavior – greed. Birds. Rhyming text.

The luckiest one of all ill. by author. Houghton Mifflin, 1982. ISBN 0-395-31863-7 Subj: Behavior – dissatisfaction. Emotions – envy, jealousy. Rhyming text.

Merle the high flying squirrel ill. by author. Houghton Mifflin, 1974. ISBN 0-395-18452-5 Subj: Activities – flying. Animals – squirrels. Humorous stories. Kites. Trees.

No such things ill. by author. Houghton Mifflin, 1983. ISBN 0-395-33888-3 Subj: Animals. Mythical creatures. Rhyming text.

Pamela Camel ill. by author. Houghton Mifflin, 1984. ISBN 0-395-35975-9 Subj: Animals – camels. Behavior – running away. Self-concept.

The pinkish, purplish, bluish egg ill. by author. Houghton Mifflin, 1963. ISBN 0-395-18472-X Subj: Birds. Birds – doves. Eggs. Mythical creatures. Rhyming text. Violence, nonviolence.

Randy's dandy lions ill. by author. Houghton Mifflin, 1964. ISBN 0-395-18507-6 Subj: Animals – lions. Circus. Humorous stories. Rhyming text.

Smokey ill. by author. Houghton Mifflin, 1962. ISBN 0-395-15992-X Subj: Old age. Rhyming text. Trains.

The spooky tail of Prewitt Peacock ill. by author. Houghton Mifflin, 1973. ISBN 0-395-15494-4 Subj: Birds – peacocks, peahens. Character traits – being different. Character traits – individuality.

The Whingdingdilly ill. by author. Houghton Mifflin, 1970. ISBN 0-395-24729-2 Subj: Animals – dogs. Behavior – dissatisfaction. Character traits – optimism. Witches.

The wump world ill. by author. Houghton Mifflin, 1970. ISBN 0-395-19841-0 Subj: Ecology. Progress. Space & space ships.

Zella, Zack, and Zodiac ill. by author. Houghton Mifflin, 1986. ISBN 0-395-40567-5 Subj: Animals – zebras. Behavior – needing someone. Birds – ostriches. Rhyming text.

Peet, Georgia. *Be quite quiet beside the lake* (Koenner, Alfred)

High flies the ball (Koenner, Alfred)

Pegram, Laura. *Daughter's Day blues* ill. by Cornelius Van Wright & Ying-Hwa Hu. Dial, 2000. ISBN 0-8037-1557-9 Subj: Ethnic groups in the U.S. – African Americans. Family life – brothers & sisters. Family life – grandmothers.

Peguero, Leone. *Lionel and Amelia* ill. by Adrian Peguero & Gerard Peguero. Mondo, 1996. ISBN 1-57255-197-6 Subj: Animals – mice. Character traits – orderliness. Friendship.

Pelham, David. *A is for animals* ill. by author. S&S, 1991. ISBN 0-671-72495-9 Subj: ABC books. Animals. Format, unusual – toy & movable books.

Crawlies creep ill. by author. Dutton, 1996. ISBN 0-525-45576-0 Subj: Animals. Format, unusual – toy & movable books.

Sam's pizza ill. by author. Dutton, 1996. ISBN 0-525-45594-9 Subj: Activities – baking, cooking. Family life – brothers & sisters. Food. Format, unusual – toy & movable books. Rhyming text. Sibling rivalry.

Sam's sandwich ill. by author. Dutton, 1991. ISBN 0-525-44751-2 Subj: Family life – brothers & sisters. Food. Format, unusual – toy & movable books. Rhyming text.

Worms wiggle ill. by Michael Foreman. S&S, 1989. ISBN 0-671-67218-5 Subj: Activities. Animals. Format, unusual – toy & movable books.

Pellant, Chris. *The best book of fossils, rocks, and minerals* ill. by author. Kingfisher, 2000. ISBN 0-7534-5274-X Subj: Fossils. Rocks.

Pellegrini, Nina. *Families are different* ill. by author. Holiday, 1991. ISBN 0-8234-0887-6 Subj: Adoption. Ethnic groups in the U.S. Ethnic groups in the U.S. – Korean Americans. Family life.

Pelletier, David. *The graphic alphabet* ill. by author. Orchard, 1996. ISBN 0-531-36001-6 Subj: ABC books. Caldecott award honor books. Concepts.

Pellowski, Anne. *The nine crying dolls: a story from Poland* ill. by Charles Mikolaycak. Philomel, 1980. ISBN 0-399-61162-2 Subj: Folk & fairy tales. Foreign lands – Poland. Toys – dolls.

Stairstep farm: Anna Rose's story ill. by Wendy Watson. Putnam, 1981. ISBN 0-399-20814-3 Subj: Behavior – growing up. Family life. Farms.

Pellowski, Michael. *Clara joins the circus* ill. by True Kelley. Parents' Magazine Pr., 1981. ISBN 0-8193-1058-1 Subj: Animals – bulls, cows. Circus. Clowns, jesters.

Pelton, Mindy L. *When Dad's at sea* ill. by Robert G. Steele. A. Whitman, 2004. ISBN 0-8075-6339-0 Subj: Behavior – needing someone. Boats, ships. Careers – airplane pilots. Careers – military. Family life – fathers.

Pender, Lydia. *Barnaby and the horses* ill. by Alie Evers. Oxford Univ. Pr., 1980. ISBN 0-19-554216-9 Subj: Animals – horses, ponies. Behavior – carelessness. Country.

Pendery, Rosemary. *A home for Hopper* ill. by Robert M. Quackenbush. Morrow, 1971. Subj: Frogs & toads.

Pendziwol, Jean. *No dragons for tea: fire safety for kids (and dragons)* ill. by Martine Gourbault. Kids Can, 1999. ISBN 1-55074-569-7 Subj: Dragons. Fire. Friendship. Rhyming text. Safety.

A treasure at sea for dragon and me ill. by Martine Gourbault. Kids Can, 2005. ISBN 1-55337-721-4 Subj: Dragons. Rhyming text. Safety. Sea & seashore – beaches. Sports.

Pène Du Bois, William. *see* Du Bois, William Pène

Penn, Ruth Bonn. *see* Clifford, Eth

Penner, Fred. *Proud* ill. by Vickey Bolling. Longstreet, 1997. ISBN 1-56352-441-4 Subj: Behavior – collecting things. Poetry.

Penner, Lucille Recht. *Dinosaur babies* ill. by Peter Barrett. Random House, 1991. ISBN 0-679-91207-X Subj: Dinosaurs. Prehistory. Science.

Lights out! ill. by Jerry Smath. Kane Pr., 2000. ISBN 1-575650-92-4 Subj: Bedtime. Counting, numbers.

Monster bugs ill. by Pamela Johnson. Random House, 1996. ISBN 0-679-96974-8 Subj: Insects. Science. Spiders.

Slowpoke ill. by Gioia . Kane Pr., 2001. ISBN 1-57565-108-4 Subj: ABC books. Concepts – speed.

Where's that bone? ill. by Lynn Adams. Kane Pr., 2000. ISBN 1-57565-097-5 Subj: Animals – cats. Animals – dogs. Behavior – hiding things. Maps.

Penney, Ian. *Ian Penney's ABC* ill. by author. Abrams, 1998. ISBN 0-8109-4350-6 Subj: ABC books. Foreign lands – England.

Ian Penney's book of fairy tales comp. & ill. by Ian Penney. Abrams, 1995. ISBN 0-8109-3740-9 Subj: Folk & fairy tales.

Ian Penney's book of nursery rhymes (Mother Goose)

Pennington, Daniel. *Itse selu: Cherokee harvest festival* ill. by Don Stewart. Charlesbridge, 1994. ISBN 0-88106-852-7 Subj: Holidays. Indians of North America – Cherokee.

Pennypacker, Sara. *Stuart's cape* ill. by Martin Matje. Orchard, 2002. ISBN 0-439-30180-7 Subj: Behavior – worrying. Imagination. Moving. School – first day.

Penrose, Gordon. *More science surprises from Dr. Zed* ill. with photos; ed. by Marilyn Baillie. S&S, 1992. ISBN 0-671-77810-2 Subj: Science.

Peppé, Rodney. *The alphabet book* ill. by author. Four Winds, 1968. Subj: ABC books.

Cat and mouse: a book of rhymes comp. & ill. by Rodney Peppé. Holt, 1973. ISBN 0-03-010321-5 Subj: Animals – cats. Animals – mice. Nursery rhymes. Poetry.

Circus numbers: a counting book ill. by author. Delacorte, 1969. ISBN 0-440-01288-0 Subj: Circus. Counting, numbers.

The color catalog ill. by author. Peter Bedrick, 1992. ISBN 0-87226-472-6 Subj: Animals – cats. Character traits – vanity. Concepts – color.

Hey, riddle, diddle ill. by author. Holt, 1971. ISBN 0-03-086233-7 Subj: Nursery rhymes. Riddles & jokes.

The kettleship pirates ill. by author. Lothrop, 1983. ISBN 0-688-02077-1 Subj: Animals – mice. Birthdays. Boats, ships. Imagination. Pirates.

Little circus ill. by author. Viking, 1984. ISBN 0-670-43134-6 Subj: Animals. Circus. Format, unusual – board books. Toys.

Little dolls ill. by author. Viking, 1984. ISBN 0-670-43182-6 Subj: Clothing. Format, unusual – board books. Toys.

Little games ill. by author. Viking, 1984. ISBN 0-670-43187-7 Subj: Format, unusual – board books. Games. Toys.

Little numbers ill. by author. Viking, 1984. ISBN 0-670-43248-2 Subj: Counting, numbers. Format, unusual – board books. Toys.

Little wheels ill. by author. Viking, 1984. ISBN 0-670-43417-5 Subj: Automobiles. Format, unusual – board books. Toys. Trucks.

The magic toy box ill. by author. Candlewick, 1996. ISBN 0-7636-0010-5 Subj: Magic. Toys.

The mice and the clockwork bus ill. by author. Lothrop, 1987. ISBN 0-688-06543-0 Subj: Animals – mice. Animals – rats. Buses.

The mice and the flying basket ill. by author. Lothrop, 1985. ISBN 0-688-04252-X Subj: Activities – ballooning. Animals – mice. Animals – rats. Behavior – greed.

The mice who lived in a shoe ill. by author. Lothrop, 1982. ISBN 0-688-00844-5 Subj: Animals – mice. Homes, houses.

Odd one out ill. by author. Viking, 1974. ISBN 0-670-52029-2 Subj: Concepts. Games.

Rodney Peppé's puzzle book ill. by author. Viking, 1977. ISBN 0-722-65274-7 Subj: Concepts. Games.

Thumbprint circus ill. by author. Delacorte, 1989. ISBN 0-440-50154-7 Subj: Circus.

Percy, Graham. *Elephants never forget* comp. & ill. by Graham Percy. Chronicle, 1992. ISBN 0-8118-0239-6 Subj: Animals – elephants. Nursery rhymes.

24 strange little animals in a haunted house ill. by author. Chronicle, 1996. ISBN 0-8118-1035-6 Subj: Animals. Character traits – individuality. Night.

Perdorno, Willie. *Visiting Langston* ill. by Bryan Collier. Holt, 2002. ISBN 0-8050-6744-2 Subj: Careers – poets. Ethnic groups in the U.S. – African Americans. Poetry.

Perera, Lydia. *Frisky* ill. by Oscar Liebman. Random House, 1966. Subj: Cities, towns. Merry-go-rounds.

Peretz, Isaac Loeb. *The magician* (Shulevitz, Uri)

Pérez, Amada Irma. *My very own room = Mi propio cuartito* ill. by Maya Christina Gonzalez. Children's Book Pr., 2000. Subj: Ethnic groups in the U.S. – Mexican Americans. Family life. Foreign languages. Homes, houses.

My diary from here to there = Mi diario de aquí hasta allá ill. by Maya Christina Gonzalez. Children's Book Pr., 2002. ISBN 0-89239-175-8 Subj: Ethnic groups in the U.S. – Mexican Americans. Family life. Foreign languages. Immigrants. Moving.

Perez, Carla. *Your turn, doctor* (Robison, Deborah)

Pérez, L. King. *First day in grapes* ill. by Robert Casilla. Lee & Low, 2002. ISBN 1-58430-045-0 Subj: Careers – migrant workers. Character traits – confidence. Ethnic groups in the U.S. – Mexican Americans. School – first day.

Pericoli, Matteo. *See the city* ill. by author. Knopf, 2004. ISBN 0-375-82469-3 Subj: Activities – drawing. Cities, towns. Format, unusual.

Periwinkle, Tribulation. *see* Alcott, Louisa May

Perkins, Al. *The digging-est dog* ill. by Eric Gurney. Random House, 1967. Subj: Activities – digging. Animals – dogs. Poetry.

Don and Donna go to bat ill. by Barney Tobey. Random House, 1968. Subj: Multiple births – twins. Sports – baseball.

The ear book ill. by William O'Brian. Random House, 1968. ISBN 0-394-91199-7 Subj: Anatomy – ears. Rhyming text. Senses – hearing.

Hand, hand, fingers, thumb ill. by Eric Gurney. Random House, 1969. ISBN 0-394-91076-1 Subj: Anatomy – hands. Rhyming text.

King Midas and the golden touch ill. by Harold Berson. Random House, 1970. Subj: Behavior – greed. Behavior – wishing. Royalty – kings.

The nose book ill. by Roy McKié. Random House, 1970. ISBN 0-394-80623-9 Subj: Anatomy – noses. Rhyming text. Senses – smell.

Tubby and the lantern ill. by Rowland B. Wilson. Random House, 1971. ISBN 0-394-92297-2 Subj: Animals – elephants. Birthdays. Foreign lands – China. Pirates.

Tubby and the Poo-Bah ill. by Rowland B. Wilson. Random House, 1972. ISBN 0-394-92469-X Subj: Animals – elephants. Boats, ships.

Perkins, Charles. *Swinging on a rainbow* ill. by Thomas Hamilton. Africa World, 1993. ISBN 0-86543-286-4 Subj: Ethnic groups in the U.S. – African Americans. Imagination. Rhyming text.

Perkins, Lynne Rae. *The broken cat* ill. by author. Greenwillow, 2002. ISBN 0-06-029264-4 Subj: Animals – cats. Careers – veterinarians. Family life. Illness. Memories, memory.

Clouds for dinner ill. by author. Greenwillow, 1997. ISBN 0-688-14904-9 Subj: Character traits – orderliness. Family life. Family life – aunts, uncles.

Home lovely ill. by author. Greenwillow, 1995. ISBN 0-688-13688-5 Subj: Family life. Gardens, gardening.

Perlman, Janet. *The Emperor Penguin's new clothes* ill. by author. Viking, 1995. ISBN 0-670-85864-1 Subj: Birds – penguins. Character traits – pride. Character traits – vanity. Clothing. Folk & fairy tales. Imagination. Royalty – emperors.

The penguin and the pea ill. by reteller. Kids Can, 2004. ISBN 1-55074-832-7 Subj: Birds – penguins. Folk & fairy tales. Royalty – princesses. Sleep.

Perrault, Charles. *Cinderella* adapt. by John Fowles; ill. by Sheilah Beckett. Little, 1974. Adapt. from Perrault's Cendrillon of 1697. ISBN 0-316-29101-3 Subj: Family life – stepfamilies. Folk & fairy tales. Royalty – princes. Sibling rivalry.

Cinderella: or, The little glass slipper ill. by Marcia Brown. Aladdin, 1988, c1954. ISBN 0-689-71261-8 Subj: Caldecott award books. Family life – stepfamilies. Folk & fairy tales. Royalty – princes. Sibling rivalry.

Cinderella ill. by Paul Galdone. McGraw-Hill, 1978. ISBN 0-07-022684-9 Subj: Family life – stepfamilies. Folk & fairy tales. Royalty – princes. Sibling rivalry.

Cinderella trans. & ill. by Diane Goode. Knopf, 1988. ISBN 0-394-99603-8 Subj: Animals – dogs. Fairies. Family life – stepfamilies. Folk & fairy tales. Royalty – princes. Sibling rivalry.

Cinderella retold by Amy Ehrlich; ill. by Susan Jeffers. Dial, 1985. ISBN 0-8037-0206-X Subj: Family life – stepfamilies. Folk & fairy tales. Royalty – princes. Sibling rivalry.

Cinderella ill. by Loek Koopmans; trans. by Anthea Bell. North-South, 1999. ISBN 0-7358-1052-4 Subj: Family life – stepfamilies. Folk & fairy tales. Royalty – princes. Sibling rivalry.

Cinderella: the story of Rossini's opera adapt. by Alan Blyth; ill. by Emanuele Luzzati. Watts, 1982. ISBN 0-531-04061-5 Subj: Family life – stepfamilies. Folk & fairy tales. Music. Royalty – princes. Sibling rivalry.

Cinderella retold by Barbara Karlin; ill. by James Marshall. Little, 1989. ISBN 0-316-54654-2 Subj: Family life – stepfamilies. Folk & fairy tales. Royalty – princes. Sibling rivalry.

Cinderella ill. by Phil Smith. Troll, 1979. ISBN 0-89375-120-0 Subj: Family life – stepfamilies. Folk & fairy tales. Royalty – princes. Sibling rivalry.

Cinderella, an Art Deco love story (Roberts, Lynn [Lynn M.])

Cinderella = Cenicienta adpt. by Francesc Boada; ill. by Monse Fransoy. Chronicle, 2001. In Spanish and English. ISBN 0-8118-3084-5 Subj: Family life – stepfamilies. Folk & fairy tales. Foreign lands – France. Foreign languages. Royalty – princes. Sibling rivalry.

Dick Bruna's Cinderella (Bruna, Dick)

Puss in boots a free trans. from the French; ill. by Marcia Brown. Scribners, 1952. Subj: Animals – cats. Caldecott award honor books. Character traits – cleverness. Folk & fairy tales. Royalty – kings.

Puss in boots adapt. & ill. by Lorinda Bryan Cauley. Harcourt, 1986. ISBN 0-15-264227-7 Subj: Animals – cats. Character traits – cleverness. Folk & fairy tales. Royalty – kings.

Puss in boots retold by Kurt Baumann; ill. by Jean Claverie. Faber, 1982. ISBN 0-571-12511-5 Subj: Animals – cats. Character traits – cleverness. Folk & fairy tales. Royalty – kings.

Puss in boots ill. by Andrea Da Rif. Farrar, 1990. ISBN 0-89375-130-8 Subj: Animals – cats. Character traits – cleverness. Folk & fairy tales. Royalty – kings.

Puss in boots ill. by Stasys Eidrigevicius; trans. by Naoma Lewis. North-South, 1994. ISBN 1-55858-120-0 Subj: Animals – cats. Character traits – cleverness. Folk & fairy tales. Royalty – kings.

Puss in boots adapt. & ill. by Hans Fischer. Harcourt, 1959. Subj: Animals – cats. Character traits – cleverness. Folk & fairy tales. Royalty – kings.

Puss in boots ill. by Paul Galdone. Seabury Pr., 1976. ISBN 0-8164-3159-0 Subj: Animals – cats. Character traits – cleverness. Folk & fairy tales. Royalty – kings.

Puss in boots retold & ill. by John S. Goodall. Macmillan, 1990. ISBN 0-689-50521-3 Subj: Animals – cats. Character traits – cleverness. Folk & fairy tales. Royalty – kings. Wordless.

Puss in boots retold & ill. by Gail E. Haley. Dutton, 1991. ISBN 0-525-44740-7 Subj: Animals – cats. Character traits – cleverness. Folk & fairy tales. Royalty – kings.

Puss in boots retold & ill. by Steve Light. Abrams, 2002. ISBN 0-8109-4368-9 Subj: Animals – cats. Character traits – cleverness. Clothing – boots. Folk & fairy tales. Royalty – kings.

Puss in boots retold by Kurt Baumann; trans. by Anthea Bell; ill. by Giuliano Lunelli. North-South, 1999. ISBN 0-7358-1159-8 Subj: Animals – cats. Character traits – cleverness. Folk & fairy tales. Royalty – kings.

Puss in boots ill. by Fred Marcellino; trans. by Malcolm Arthur. Farrar, 1990. ISBN 0-374-36160-6 Subj: Animals – cats. Caldecott award honor books. Character traits – cleverness. Folk & fairy tales. Royalty – kings.

Puss in boots ill. by Fred Marcellino; trans. by Malcolm Arthur. Farrar, 1998. ISBN 0-374-46034-5 Subj: Animals – cats. Character traits – cleverness. Folk & fairy tales. Royalty – kings.

Puss in boots adapt. by Arthur Luce Klein; ill. by Julia Noonan. Doubleday, 1970. Adapt. of Le Chat botté. Subj: Animals – cats. Character traits – cleverness. Folk & fairy tales. Foreign lands – France. Royalty – kings.

Puss in boots: the story of a sneaky cat adapt. & ill. by Tony Ross. Delacorte, 1981. ISBN 0-440-07157-7 Subj: Animals – cats. Character traits – cleverness. Folk & fairy tales. Royalty – kings.

Puss in boots ill. by William Stobbs. McGraw-Hill, 1975. A retelling of Maître Chat. ISBN 0-07-061581-0 Subj: Animals – cats. Character traits – cleverness. Folk & fairy tales. Royalty – kings.

Puss in boots trans. by Anthea Bell; ill. by Yan Thomas. Kingfisher, 1995. ISBN 1-85697-624-6 Subj: Animals – cats. Character traits – cleverness. Folk & fairy tales. Royalty – kings.

Puss in boots retold by Lincoln Kirstein; ill. by Alain Vaës. Little, 1992. ISBN 0-316-89506-7 Subj: Animals – cats. Character traits – cleverness. Folk & fairy tales. Royalty – kings.

Puss in boots ill. by Barry Wilkinson. Collins-World, 1969. Subj: Animals – cats. Character traits – cleverness. Clothing – boots. Folk & fairy tales. Royalty – kings.

The sleeping beauty trans. & ill. by David Walker. Crowell, 1977. ISBN 0-690-01279-9 Subj: Fairies. Folk & fairy tales. Royalty – princes. Royalty – princesses. Sleep. Witches.

Smoky Mountain Rose: an Appalachian Cinderella (Schroeder, Alan)

Tom Thumb: a tale (Tom Thumb)

Perrine, Mary. *Salt boy* ill. by Leonard Weisgard. Houghton Mifflin, 1968. ISBN 0-395-17450-3 Subj: Indians of North America – Navajo.

Perrow, Angeli. *Captain's castaway* ill. by Emily Harris. Down East, 1998. ISBN 0-8927-2419-6 Subj: Accidents. Animals – dogs. Friendship. Lighthouses. Sea & seashore.

Lighthouse dog to the rescue ill. by Emily Harris. Down East, 2000. ISBN 0-8927-2487-0 Subj: Animals – dogs. Lighthouses. Weather – storms.

Sirius, the dog star ill. by Emily Harris. Down East, 2002. ISBN 0-89272-545-1 Subj: Animals – dogs. Behavior – resourcefulness. Boats, ships.

Perry, Andrea. *Here's what you do when you can't find your shoe* ill. by Alan Snow. Atheneum, 2003. ISBN 0-689-83067-X Subj: Inventions. Poetry.

Perry, Michael. *Daniel's ride* ill. by Lee Ballard. Free Will, 2001. ISBN 0-9701771-9-4 Subj: Automobiles. Family life – brothers.

Perry, Patricia. *Mommy and daddy are divorced* by Patricia Perry & Marietta Lynch; ill. by authors. Dial, 1978. ISBN 0-8037-5771-9 Subj: Divorce.

Perry, Robert. *Down at the Seaweed Café* ill. by Greta Guzek. Raincoast, 2002. ISBN 1-55192-473-0 Subj: Restaurants. Rhyming text. Sea & seashore – beaches.

Perry, Sarah. *If . . .* ill. by author. J. P. Getty Museum, 1995. ISBN 0-89236-321-5 Subj: Imagination.

Pershall, Mary K. *Hello, Barney!* ill. by Mark Wilson. Viking, 1989. ISBN 0-670-82406-2 Subj: Birds – cockatoos. Foreign lands – Australia. Pets.

A pet for me sel. by Lee Bennett Hopkins; ill. by Jane Manning. HarperCollins, 2003. ISBN 0-06-029112-5 Subj: Animals. Pets. Poetry.

Petach, Heidi. *Goldilocks and the three hares* ill. by author. Putnam, 1995. ISBN 0-399-22828-4 Subj: Animals – rabbits. Folk & fairy tales.

Wee three pigs ill. by author. Grosset, 2002. ISBN 0-448-42528-9 Subj: Animals – pigs. Holidays – Christmas. Homes, houses.

Peter, Beate. *The adventures of Marco and Polo* (Wiesmüller, Dieter)

Peters, Andrew. *Salt is sweeter than gold* ill. by Zdena Kabátová-Táborská. Barefoot, 1994. ISBN 1-56957-933-4 Subj: Folk & fairy tales. Foreign lands – Czechoslovakia. Royalty – kings. Royalty – princesses.

Peters, Lisa Westberg. *Cold little duck, duck, duck* ill. by Sam Williams. Greenwillow, 2000. ISBN 0-688-16179-0 Subj: Birds – ducks. Imagination. Seasons – spring.

Good morning, river! ill. by Deborah Kogan Ray. Arcade, 1990. ISBN 1-55970-011-4 Subj: Old age. Rivers. Seasons.

The hayloft ill. by K. D. Plum. Dial, 1995. ISBN 0-8037-1491-2 Subj: Animals. Animals – cats. Farms. Seasons – summer.

Meg and dad discover treasure in the air ill. by Deborah Durland DeSaix. Holt, 1995. ISBN 0-8050-2418-2 Subj: Forest, woods. Nature. Rocks.

October smiled back ill. by Ed Young. Holt, 1996. ISBN 0-8050-1776-3 Subj: Days of the week, months of the year. Rhyming text.

Purple delicious blackberry jam ill. by Barbara McGregor. Arcade, 1992. ISBN 1-55970-167-6 Subj: Family life – grandmothers. Food.

The sun, the wind and the rain ill. by Ted Rand. Holt, 1988. ISBN 0-8050-0699-0 Subj: Nature. Science. Sea & seashore. Weather.

This way home ill. by Normand Chartier. Holt, 1994. ISBN 0-8050-1368-7 Subj: Activities – traveling. Birds. Nature.

Water's way ill. by Ted Rand. Arcade, 1991. ISBN 1-55970-062-9 Subj: Nature. Science. Water. Weather.

Peters, Sharon. *Animals at night* ill. by Paul Harvey. Troll, 1983. ISBN 0-89375-903-1 Subj: Animals. Night.

Fun at camp ill. by Irene Trivas. Troll, 1980. ISBN 0-89375-378-5 Subj: Camps, camping.

Happy birthday ill. by Paul Harvey. Troll, 1980. ISBN 0-89375-379-3 Subj: Birthdays.

Happy Jack ill. by Paul Harvey. Troll, 1980. ISBN 0-89375-380-7 Subj: Careers – waiters, waitresses.

Messy Mark ill. by Bill Morrison. Troll, 1980. ISBN 0-89375-381-5 Subj: Character traits – cleanliness.

Puppet show ill. by Alana Lee. Troll, 1980. ISBN 0-89375-385-8 Subj: Puppets.

Ready, get set, go! ill. by Irene Trivas. Troll, 1980. ISBN 0-89375-386-6 Subj: Animals – rabbits.

Stop that rabbit ill. by Don Silverstein. Troll, 1980. ISBN 0-89375-388-2 Subj: Animals – rabbits.

Trick or treat Halloween ill. by Susan Hall. Troll, 1980. ISBN 0-89375-392-0 Subj: Holidays – Halloween.

Peters, Stephanie True. *Raggedy Ann and Andy and the magic potion* adapt. by Stephanie True Peters from the stories by Johnny Gruelle; ill. by Reg Sandland. S&S, 2001. ISBN 0-689-83180-3 Subj: Fairies. Magic. Toys – dolls.

Petersen, David. *Dinosaur National Monument* ill. by author. Childrens Pr., 1995. ISBN 0-516-01074-3 Subj: Dinosaurs. Prehistory.

Petersen-Fleming, Judy. *Kitten training and critters, too!* by Judy Peterson-Fleming & Bill Fleming; photos by Darryl Bush. Tambourine, 1996. ISBN 0-688-13387-8 Subj: Animals – cats. Pets.

Puppy training and critters, too! by Judy Peterson-Fleming & Bill Fleming; photos by Darryl Bush. Tambourine, 1996. ISBN 0-688-13385-1 Subj: Animals – dogs. Pets.

Petersham, Maud. *An American ABC* by Maud & Miska Petersham; ill. by authors. Macmillan, 1941. Subj: ABC books. Caldecott award honor books. U.S. history.

The circus baby by Maud & Miska Petersham; ill. by authors. Aladdin, 1989, c1950. ISBN 0-689-71295-2 Subj: Animals – elephants. Circus. Clowns, jesters. Etiquette.

Off to bed: 7 stories for wide-awakes by Maud & Miska Petersham; ill. by authors. Macmillan, 1954. Subj: Bedtime.

The rooster crows by Maud & Miska Petersham; ill. by authors. Macmillan, 1945. ISBN 0-02-773100-6 Subj: Caldecott award books. Nursery rhymes.

Petersham, Miska. *An American ABC* (Petersham, Maud)

The circus baby (Petersham, Maud)

Off to bed: 7 stories for wide-awakes (Petersham, Maud)

The rooster crows (Petersham, Maud)

Peterson, Cris. *Amazing grazing* photos by Alvis Upitis. Boyds Mills, 2002. ISBN 1-56397-942-X Subj: Animals – bulls, cows. Careers – ranchers. Ecology.

Extra cheese, please! photos by Alvis Upitis. Boyds Mills, 1994. ISBN 1-56397-177-1 Subj: Animals – bulls, cows. Careers – farmers. Farms. Food.

Horsepower: the wonder of draft horses photos by Alvis Upitis. Boyds Mills, 1997. ISBN 1-56397-626-9 Subj: Activities – working. Animals – horses, ponies.

Peterson, Esther Allen. *Frederick's alligator* ill. by Susanna Natti. Crown, 1979. ISBN 0-517-53597-1 Subj: Animals. Behavior – boasting. Reptiles – alligators, crocodiles.

Penelope gets wheels ill. by Susanna Natti. Crown, 1982. ISBN 0-517-54467-9 Subj: Birthdays. Sports.

Peterson, Franklynn. *I can use tools* (Kesselman, Judi R.)

Peterson, Hans. *Erik and the Christmas horse* trans. from Swedish by Christine Hyatt; ill. by Ilon Wikland. Lothrop, 1970. Translation of Magnus, Lindberg och hästen Mari. Subj: Character traits – kindness. Foreign lands – Sweden. Holidays – Christmas.

Erik has a squirrel trans. from Swedish by Christine Hyatt; ill. by Ilon Wikland. Farrar, 1989. ISBN 9-12-959140-6 Subj: Animals – squirrels. Friendship.

Peterson, Jeanne Whitehouse. *Don't forget Winona* ill. by Kimberly Bulcken Root. Cotler, 2004. ISBN 0-06-027198-1 Subj: Family life. Family life – sisters. U.S. history. Weather – droughts.

My mama sings ill. by Sandra Speidel. HarperCollins, 1994. ISBN 0-06-023859-3 Subj: Activities – singing. Ethnic groups in the U.S. – African Americans. Family life – mothers. Music.

Sometimes I dream horses ill. by Eleanor Schick. HarperCollins, 1987. ISBN 0-06-024713-4 Subj: Animals – horses, ponies. Family life – grandmothers.

That is that ill. by Deborah Kogan Ray. HarperCollins, 1979. ISBN 0-06-024709-6 Subj: Divorce.

Peterson, Julienne. *Caterina, the clever farm girl* ill. by Enzo Giannini. Dial, 1996. ISBN 0-8037-1182-4 Subj: Character traits – cleverness. Folk & fairy tales. Foreign lands – Italy. Royalty – kings.

Peterson, Melissa. *Hanna's Christmas* ill. by Melissa Iwai. HarperFestival, 2001. ISBN 0-694-01371-4 Subj: Ethnic groups in the U.S. – Swedish Americans. Format, unusual – board books. Holidays – Christmas.

Peterson, Scott K. *What's your name? jokes about names* ill. by Joan Hanson. Lerner, 1987. ISBN 0-8225-0994-6 Subj: Names. Riddles & jokes.

Peterson, Stephanie True. *Where do the animals live?* ill. by author. Innovative KIDS, 2001. ISBN 1-58476-076-1 Subj: Animals. Format, unusual – toy & movable books. Homes, houses.

Peterson, Sue H. *Swim with me* ill. by Rama. Tricycle, 1998. ISBN 1-883672-94-5 Subj: Format, unusual. Poetry. Sports – swimming.

Petie, Haris. *Billions of bugs* ill. by author. Prentice-Hall, 1975. ISBN 0-13-076240-7 Subj: Counting, numbers. Insects. Rhyming text.

The seed the squirrel dropped ill. by author. Prentice-Hall, 1976. ISBN 0-13-799627-6 Subj: Activities – baking, cooking. Cumulative tales. Food. Plants. Rhyming text. Seeds. Trees.

Petrides, Heidrun. *Hans and Peter* ill. by author. Harcourt, 1962. Subj: Activities – working. Character traits – completing things.

Petrie, Catherine. *Hot Rod Harry* ill. by Paul Sharp. Childrens Pr., 1982. ISBN 0-516-03493-6 Subj: Automobiles.

Joshua James likes trucks ill. by Jerry Warshaw. Childrens Pr., 1982. ISBN 0-516-43525-6 Subj: Toys. Trucks.

Pets ill. with photos. Macmillan, 1991. ISBN 0-689-71404-1 Subj: Nature. Pets.

Pettigrew, Eileen. *Night-time* ill. by William Kimber. Firefly, 1992. ISBN 1-55037-235-1 Subj: Family life – fathers. Night.

Pettit, Henry. *The authentic Mother Goose fairy tales and nursery rhymes* (Barchilon, Jacques)

Petty, Dini. *The queen, the bear and the bumblebee* ill. by Rose Cowles. Beyond Words, 2000. ISBN 1-58270-036-2 Subj: Animals – bears. Behavior – wishing. Friendship. Insects – bees. Self-concept. Space & space ships.

Petty, Kate. *Being careful with strangers* ill. by Lisa Kopper. Watts, 1988. ISBN 0-531-17107-8 Subj: Behavior – talking to strangers. Safety.

Dinosaurs ill. by Alan Baker. Watts, 1984. ISBN 0-531-04811-X Subj: Dinosaurs. Prehistory.

Gerbils photos by George Thompson. Watts, 1989. ISBN 0-531-17158-2 Subj: Animals – gerbils. Pets.

Hamsters photos by George Thompson. Watts, 1989. ISBN 0-531-17159-0 Subj: Animals – hamsters. Pets.

On a plane ill. by Aline Riquier. Watts, 1984. ISBN 0-531-04716-4 Subj: Activities – traveling. Airplanes, airports. Foreign lands – England.

Rabbits photos by George Thompson. Watts, 1989. ISBN 0-531-17160-4 Subj: Animals – rabbits. Pets.

Petty, Roberta. *see* Petie, Haris

Pevear, Richard. *The absentminded fellow* (Marshak, S. [Samuil])

First, second (Kharms, Daniil)

Hail to mail (Marshak, S. [Samuil])

Mister Cat-and-a-Half ill. by Robert Rayevsky. Macmillan, 1986. ISBN 0-02-773910-4 Subj: Animals. Animals – cats. Animals – foxes. Folk & fairy tales.

Our king has horns! ill. by Robert Rayevsky. Macmillan, 1987. ISBN 0-02-773920-1 Subj: Behavior – secrets. Folk & fairy tales. Foreign lands – Russia. Royalty – kings.

The pup grew up! (Marshak, S. [Samuil])

Peyo. *The Smurfs and their woodland friends* ill. by author. Random House, 1983. ISBN 0-394-85370-9 Subj: Animals. Forest, woods. Insects.

What do smurfs do all day? ill. by author. Random House, 1983. ISBN 0-394-96078-5 Subj: Activities. Rhyming text.

Pfanner, Louise. *Louise builds a boat* ill. by author. Watts, 1990. ISBN 0-531-08488-4 Subj: Activities – making things. Boats, ships.

Louise builds a house ill. by author. Watts, 1989. ISBN 0-531-08396-9 Subj: Activities – making things. Homes, houses. Imagination.

Pfeffer, Wendy. *The big flood* ill. by Vanessa Lubach. Millbrook, 2001. ISBN 0-7613-1653-1 Subj: Farms. Rivers. U.S. history. Weather – floods.

Dolphin talk ill. by Helen K. Davie. HarperCollins, 2003. ISBN 0-06-028802-7 Subj: Animals – dolphins. Communication. Noise, sounds.

From tadpole to frog ill. by Holly Keller. HarperCollins, 1994. ISBN 0-06-023117-3 Subj: Frogs & toads. Nature. Science.

Mallard duck at Meadow View Pond ill. by Taylor Oughton. Soundprints, 2001. ISBN 1-56899-956-9 Subj: Animals – babies. Behavior – growing up. Birds – ducks. Family life. Lakes, ponds.

Marta's magnets ill. by Gail Piazza. Silver Pr., 1995. ISBN 0-382-24930-5 Subj: Behavior – collecting things. Friendship.

What's it like to be a fish? ill. by Holly Keller. HarperCollins, 1996. ISBN 0-06-024429-1 Subj: Fish. Pets.

Wiggling worms at work ill. by Steve Jenkins. HarperCollins, 2004. ISBN 0-06-028449-8 Subj: Animals – worms. Science.

Pfister, Marcus. *Chris and Croc* ill. by author. North-South, 1994. ISBN 1-55858-274-6 Subj: Activities – playing. Friendship. Toys.

The Christmas star ill. by author; trans. by J. Alison James. North-South, 1993. ISBN 1-55858-204-5 Subj: Holidays – Christmas. Religion – Nativity. Stars.

Dazzle the dinosaur ill. by author; trans. by J. Alison James. North-South, 1994. ISBN 1-55858-338-6 Subj: Dinosaurs. Prehistory.

Hang on, Hopper! ill. by Rosemary Lanning. North-South, 1995. ISBN 1-55858-404-8 Subj: Animals – rabbits. Safety. Sports – swimming.

The happy hedgehog ill. by author; trans. by J. Alison James. North-South, 2000. ISBN 0-7358-1165-2 Subj: Animals – hedgehogs. Family life – grandfathers.

Hopper ill. by author. North-South, 1991. ISBN 1-55858-106-5 Subj: Animals – rabbits. Seasons – spring. Seasons – winter.

Hopper hunts for spring ill. by author; trans. by Rosemary Lanning. North-South, 1992. ISBN 1-55858-139-1 Subj: Animals. Animals – rabbits. Frogs & toads. Seasons – spring.

Hopper's treetop adventure ill. by author; trans. by Rosemary Lanning. North-South, 1997. ISBN 1-55858-681-4 Subj: Animals – rabbits. Animals – squirrels. Nature. Trees.

How Leo learned to be king ill. by author; trans. by J. Alison James. North-South, 1998. ISBN 1-55858-914-7 Subj: Animals. Animals – lions. Behavior. Royalty – kings.

I see the moon: good-night poems and lullabies comp. & ill. by Marcus Pfister. North-South, 1991. ISBN 1-55858-119-7 Subj: Bedtime. Lullabies. Moon. Night. Poetry. Songs.

Just the way you are ill. by author; trans. by Marianne Martens. North-South, 2002. ISBN 0-7358-1615-8 Subj: Animals. Format, unusual – toy & movable books. Parties. Self-concept.

Make a wish, Honey Bear! ill. by author; trans. by Sibylle Kazeroid. North-South, 1999. ISBN 0-7358-1244-6 Subj: Animals – bears. Behavior – wishing. Birthdays.

Milo and the magical stones ill. by author; trans. by Marianne Martens. North-South, 1997. ISBN 1-55858-682-2 Subj: Animals – mice. Behavior. Format, unusual – toy & movable books. Magic.

Milo and the mysterious island ill. by author; trans. by Marianne Martens. North-South, 2000. ISBN 0-7358-1352-3 Subj: Animals – mice. Islands. Prejudice. Sea & seashore.

Penguin Pete and Little Tim ill. by author; trans. by Rosemary Lanning. North-South, 1994. ISBN 1-55858-302-5 Subj: Activities – walking. Birds – penguins. Family life – fathers. Weather – snow.

The rainbow fish ill. by author. North-South, 1992. ISBN 0-7358-1748-0 Subj: Behavior – sharing. Character traits – appearance. Emotions – loneliness. Fish.

Rainbow fish ABC ill. by author. North-South, 2002. ISBN 0-7358-1714-6 Subj: ABC books. Fish. Sea & seashore.

Rainbow fish and the big blue whale ill. by author; trans. by J. Alison James. North-South, 1998. ISBN 0-7358-1010-9 Subj: Animals – whales. Behavior – fighting, arguing. Fish.

Rainbow fish and the sea monsters' cave ill. by author; trans. by J. Alison James. North-South, 2001. ISBN 0-7358-1537-2 Subj: Caves. Fish. Monsters. Sea & seashore.

Rainbow fish board book and finger puppet ill. by author. North-South, 1999. ISBN 0-7358-1238-1 Subj: Fish. Format, unusual – board books. Puppets.

The rainbow fish floor puzzle book ill. by author. North-South, 2003. ISBN 0-7358-1837-1 Subj: Fish. Format, unusual – toy & movable books. Puzzles.

Rainbow fish mini-book ill. by author. North-South, 2000. ISBN 0-7358-1232-2 Subj: Fish. Format, unusual.

Rainbow fish to the rescue! ill. by author; trans. by J. Alison James. North-South, 1995. ISBN 1-55858-487-0 Subj: Character traits – appearance. Emotions – fear. Fish. Fish – sharks. Friendship.

The sleepy owl trans. from German by Jock J. Curle; ill. by author. Holt, 1986. ISBN 0-03-008023-1 Subj: Birds – owls. Friendship. Sleep.

Wake up, Santa Claus! ill. by author; trans. by J. Alison James. North-South, 1996. ISBN 1-55858-606-7 Subj: Behavior – hurrying. Dreams. Holidays – Christmas. Santa Claus.

Where is my friend? ill. by author. Holt, 1986. ISBN 0-03-008033-9 Subj: Animals – porcupines. Format, unusual – board books. Friendship.

Pfloog, Jan. *Kittens* ill. by author. Random House, 1977. ISBN 0-394-83590-5 Subj: Animals – cats. Format, unusual – board books.

Puppies ill. by author. Random House, 1979. ISBN 0-394-84132-8 Subj: Animals – dogs. Format, unusual – board books.

Phang, Ruth. *Patchwork tales* (Roth, Susan L.)

Phifer, Martha Nelson. *The colors of Christmas* ill. by Judy I. Roberts. Herald Pr., 1995. ISBN 0-8361-9029-7 Subj: Concepts – color. Holidays – Christmas. Religion – Nativity. Rhyming text.

Philip, Neil. *The fish is me* (The fish is me)

The golden bird (Grimm, Jacob)

Hot potato: mealtime rhymes (Hot potato)

I have a news: rhymes from the Caribbean (Jekyll, Walter)

Mary Middling and other silly folk (Fyleman, Rose)

Noah and the devil ill. by Isabelle Brent. Clarion, 2001. ISBN 0-618-11754-7 Subj: Boats, ships. Devil. Folk & fairy tales. Foreign lands – Romania. Religion – Noah.

The snow queen (Andersen, H. C. [Hans Christian])

Phillips, Betty Lou. *Emily goes wild* ill. by Sharon Watts. Gibbs Smith, 2003. ISBN 1-58685-268-X Subj: Animals – monkeys. Behavior – misbehavior. Pets. Zoos.

Phillips, Jack. *see* Sandburg, Carl (Charles August)

Phillips, Joan. *Lucky bear* ill. by J. P. Miller. Random House, 1986. ISBN 0-394-97987-7 Subj: Toys – bears.

My new boy ill. by Lynn Munsinger. Random House, 1986. ISBN 0-394-98277-0 Subj: Animals – dogs. Pets.

Peek-a-boo! I see you! ill. by Kathy Wilburn. Putnam, 1983. ISBN 0-488-03092-6 Subj: Animals – bears. Format, unusual – board books. Rhyming text.

Phillips, Louis. *The brothers Wrong and Wrong Again* ill. by J. Winslow Higginbottom. McGraw-Hill, 1979. ISBN 0-07-049805-9 Subj: Character traits – foolishness. Dragons. Middle Ages. War.

The upside down riddle book ill. by Beau Gardner. Lothrop, 1982. ISBN 0-688-00932-8 Subj: Humorous stories. Rhyming text. Riddles & jokes.

Phillips, Mildred. *And the cow said, "moo"!* ill. by Sonja Lamut. Greenwillow, 2000. ISBN 0-688-16803-5 Subj: Animals. Farms. Noise, sounds.

The sign in Mendel's window ill. by Margot Zemach. Macmillan, 1985. ISBN 0-02-774600-3 Subj: Folk & fairy tales. Jewish culture.

Phillips, Tamara. *Day care ABC* ill. by Dora Leder. A. Whitman, 1989. ISBN 0-8075-1483-7 Subj: ABC books. School – nursery.

Philothea. *see* Child, Lydia Maria

Philpot, Graham. *Amazing Anthony Ant* (Philpot, Lorna)

Fabulous fairy tale follies ill. by author. Random House, 1994. ISBN 0-679-85316-2 Subj: Careers – actors. Folk & fairy tales. Games. Theater.

Where is Little Harry? ill. by author. Candlewick, 2001. ISBN 0-7636-1439-4 Subj: Animals – pigs. Behavior – hiding. Format, unusual – toy & movable books. Games.

Philpot, Lorna. *Amazing Anthony Ant* by Lorna & Graham Philpot; ill. by authors. Orion Children's Books, 1993. ISBN 1-8588-1005-1 Subj: Counting, numbers. Format, unusual – toy & movable books. Insects – ants. Songs.

Phipps, Inga. *Animal homes* (Hewitt, Sally)

Phumla. *Nomi and the magic fish: a story from Africa* ill. by Carole M. Byard. Doubleday, 1973. Subj: Children as authors. Folk & fairy tales. Foreign lands – Africa. Magic.

Pia Toya: a Goshute Indian legend retold & ill. by the children & teachers of Ibapah Elementary school. Univ. of Utah Pr., 2000. ISBN 0-87480-661-5 Subj: Animals – coyotes. Birds – hawks. Children as authors. Children as illustrators. Creation. Folk & fairy tales. Indians of North America – Goshute. Indians of North America – Great Basin.

Piatti, Celestino. *Celestino Piatti's animal ABC* English text by Jon Reid; ill. by author. Atheneum, 1966. Subj: ABC books. Animals. Poetry.

The happy owls ill. by author. Atheneum, 1964. ISBN 0-689-20337-3 Subj: Birds – owls. Character traits – optimism. Emotions – happiness.

Pickering, Jimmy. *It's fall* ill. by author. Smallfellow, 2002. ISBN 1-931290-15-6 Subj: Animals – dogs. Poetry. Rhyming text. Seasons – fall.

It's winter ill. by author. Smallfellow, 2002. ISBN 1-931290-16-4 Subj: Animals – dogs. Poetry. Seasons – winter. Weather – snow.

Pickett, Carla. *Calvin Crocodile and the terrible noise* ill. by Carroll Dolezal. Steck-Vaughn, 1972. ISBN 0-8114-7736-3 Subj: Noise, sounds. Reptiles – alligators, crocodiles.

Pickthall, Marjorie L. C. (Marjorie Lowry Christie). *The worker in sandalwood: a Christmas eve miracle* ill. by Frances Tyrrell. Dutton, 1994. ISBN 0-525-45332-6 Subj: Careers – carpenters. Foreign lands – Canada. Holidays – Christmas.

Piehl, Janet. *Formula One race cars* ill. with photos. Lerner, 2004. ISBN 0-8225-0693-9 Subj: Automobiles. Sports – racing.

Pieńkowski, Jan. *Bel and Bub and the baby bird* ill. by author. DK, 2000. ISBN 0-7894-6526-4 Subj: Angels. Birds.

Bel and Bub and the bad snowball ill. by author. DK, 2000. Subj: Angels. Behavior – bullying. Emotions – anger.

Bel and Bub and the big brown box ill. by author. DK, 2000. Subj: Angels. Behavior – sharing.

Bel and Bub and the black hole ill. by author. DK, 2000. ISBN 0-7894-6528-0 Subj: Angels. Character traits – bravery. Dragons. Friendship. Stores.

Colors ill. by author. Harvey House, 1974. ISBN 0-8178-5232-8 Subj: Concepts – color.

Easter ill. by author. Knopf, 1989. ISBN 0-394-82455-5 Subj: Holidays – Easter. Religion.

Faces ill. by author. S&S, 1991. ISBN 0-671-72846-6 Subj: Anatomy – faces. Format, unusual – board books.

Fancy that! (Little old lady who swallowed a fly)

Farm ill. by author. David & Charles, 1985. ISBN 0-434-95651-1 Subj: Animals. Farms.

Food ill. by author. S&S, 1991. ISBN 0-671-72845-8 Subj: Food. Format, unusual – board books.

Good night, a pop-up lullaby ill. by author; paper engineering by Helen Balmer & Martin Taylor. Candlewick, 1999. ISBN 0-7636-0763-0 Subj: Format, unusual – toy & movable books. Lullabies.

Haunted house ill. by Jane Walmsley. Dutton, 2001, 1979. ISBN 0-525-46802-1 Subj: Format, unusual – toy & movable books. Ghosts. Homes, houses. Monsters.

Homes ill. by author. Messner, 1983. ISBN 0-671-46935-5 Subj: Animals. Homes, houses.

Meg and Mog (Nicoll, Helen)

Meg at sea (Nicoll, Helen)

Meg on the moon (Nicoll, Helen)

Meg's eggs (Nicoll, Helen)

Numbers ill. by author. Harvey House, 1975. ISBN 0-8178-5241-7 Subj: Counting, numbers.

Pizza! ill. by author; asst. ill., David Walser; paper eng. by Helen Balmer & Martin Taylor. Candlewick, 2001. ISBN 0-7636-1626-5 Subj: Animals. Food. Format, unusual – toy & movable books. Insects. Royalty – kings. Spiders.

Shapes ill. by author. Harvey House, 1975. ISBN 0-671-44455-7 Subj: Concepts – shape.

Sizes ill. by author. Messner, 1983. Orig. pub. by Harvey House, 1974. ISBN 0-671-46936-3 Subj: Concepts – size.

Time ill. by author. Messner, 1980. ISBN 0-671-46933-9 Subj: Clocks, watches. Time.

Weather ill. by author. Messner, 1983. ISBN 0-671-46934-7 Subj: Weather.

Zoo ill. by author. David & Charles, 1985. ISBN 0-434-95652-X Subj: Animals. Zoos.

Piepmeier, Charlotte. *Lucy's journey to the wild west* ill. by author. Azro, 2002. ISBN 1-929115-07-5 Subj: Activities – traveling. Animals – dogs. Geography. Maps. Moving. U.S. history.

Pierce, Jack. *The freight train book* photos by author. Carolrhoda, 1980. ISBN 0-87614-123-8 Subj: Trains.

Pierce, Roxanne Heide. *Oh, grow up! poems to help you survive parents, chores, school, and other afflictions* (Heide, Florence Parry)

Timothy Twinge (Heide, Florence Parry)

Pierpont, James. *Jingle bells* ill. by Michael Hague. Holt, 1990. ISBN 0-8050-1413-6 Subj: Holidays – Christmas. Music. Songs.

Piers, Helen. *Grasshopper and butterfly* ill. by Pauline Baynes. McGraw-Hill, 1975. Subj: Hibernation. Insects – butterflies, caterpillars. Insects – grasshoppers.

Is there room on the bus? ill. by Hannah Giffard. S&S, 1996. ISBN 0-689-80610-8 Subj: Activities – traveling. Animals. Buses. Counting, numbers. Cumulative tales.

The mouse book photos by author. Watts, 1968. Subj: Animals – mice.

Puppy's ABC photos by author. Oxford Univ. Pr., 1987. ISBN 0-19-520606-1 Subj: ABC books. Animals – dogs.

Who's in my bed? ill. by Dave Saunders. Cavendish, 1999. ISBN 0-7614-5046-7 Subj: Animals. Bedtime. Character traits – orderliness. Cumulative tales. Farms. Format, unusual – toy & movable books.

Pierson, Judith Patterson. *The always moon* ill. by Karen Stormer Brooks. First Story Pr., 1998. ISBN 1-890326-17-8 Subj: Bedtime. Dreams. Moon. Night.

Piggy and Bear in their underwear ill. by Dara Goldman. Innovative KIDS, 2002. ISBN 1-58476-101-6 Subj: Behavior – growing up. Clothing – underwear. Format, unusual – toy & movable books. Toilet training.

Pike, Carol. *The nutty queen* ill. by author. Trafalgar Square, 1990. ISBN 0-09-173795-8 Subj: Rhyming text. Royalty – queens. Toys – bears.

Pike, Debi. *Like me and you* (Raffi)

Pike, Norman. *The peach tree* ill. by Robin & Patricia DeWitt. Stemmer House, 1983. ISBN 0-88045-014-2 Subj: Gardens, gardening. Trees.

Pilegard, Virginia Walton. *The warlord's beads* ill. by Nicolas Debon. Pelican, 2001. ISBN 1-56554-863-9 Subj: Counting, numbers. Foreign lands – China.

The warlord's puzzle ill. by Nicolas Debon. Pelican, 2000. ISBN 1-56554-495-1 Subj: Concepts – shape. Folk & fairy tales. Foreign lands – China.

Pilkey, Dav. *Dragon's fat cat* ill. by author. Orchard, 1992. ISBN 0-531-08582-1 Subj: Animals – cats. Dragons.

Dragon's merry Christmas ill. by author. Orchard, 1991. ISBN 0-531-08557-0 Subj: Character traits – generosity. Dragons. Holidays – Christmas.

A friend for Dragon ill. by author. Orchard, 1991. ISBN 0-531-05934-0 Subj: Dragons. Emotions – loneliness. Friendship. Reptiles – snakes.

The Hallo-wiener ill. by author. Blue Sky, 1995. ISBN 0-590-41703-7 Subj: Animals – dogs. Family life. Holidays – Halloween.

The Moonglow Roll-O-Rama ill. by author. Orchard, 1995. ISBN 0-531-08726-3 Subj: Animals. Night. Rhyming text. Sports – roller skating.

The paperboy ill. by author. Orchard, 1996. ISBN 0-531-08856-1 Subj: Activities – working. Caldecott award honor books. Morning.

The Silly Gooses ill. by author. Blue Sky, 1997. ISBN 0-590-94733-8 Subj: Behavior. Birds – geese. Humorous stories. Weddings.

The Silly Gooses build a house ill. by author. Blue Sky, 1998. ISBN 0-590-94741-9 Subj: Activities – making things. Behavior – mistakes. Birds – geese. Homes, houses. Humorous stories.

'Twas the night before Thanksgiving ill. by author. Watts, 1990. ISBN 0-531-08505-8 Subj: Birds – turkeys. Holidays – Thanksgiving. Rhyming text.

When cats dream ill. by author. Watts, 1992. ISBN 0-531-08597-X Subj: Animals – cats. Art. Dreams.

Pillar, Marjorie. *Join the band!* photos by author. HarperCollins, 1992. ISBN 0-06-021829-0 Subj: Music. Musical instruments – bands. Musical instruments – flutes. School.

Pizza man photos by author. HarperCollins, 1990. ISBN 0-690-04836-X Subj: Careers – chefs, cooks. Food.

Pin, Isabel. *The seed* ill. by author; trans. by Rosemary Lanning. North-South, 2001. ISBN 0-7358-1408-2 Subj: Insects. Seeds. War.

Pincus, Harriet. *Minna and Pippin* ill. by author. Farrar, 1972. ISBN 0-374-34991-6 Subj: Toys – dolls.

Pinczes, Elinor J. *Arctic fives arrive* ill. by Holly Berry. Houghton Mifflin, 1996. ISBN 0-395-73577-7 Subj: Counting, numbers. Foreign lands – Arctic. Northern lights. Rhyming text. Sky.

Inchworm and a half ill. by Randall Enos. Houghton, 2001. ISBN 0-395-82849-X Subj: Animals – worms. Concepts – measurement. Counting, numbers. Food. Gardens, gardening. Rhyming text.

My full moon is square ill. by Randall Enos. Houghton, 2002. ISBN 0-618-15489-2 Subj: Books, reading. Frogs & toads. Insects – fireflies. Rhyming text.

A remainder of one ill. by Bonnie MacKain. Houghton Mifflin, 1995. ISBN 0-395-69455-8 Subj: Counting, numbers. Insects. Rhyming text.

Pingry, Patricia. *Joseph's story* ill. by George Hinke. CandyCane, 1998. ISBN 0-8249-4092-X Subj: Family life – fathers. Holidays – Christmas. Religion – Nativity.

Pinkney, Andrea Davis. *Alvin Ailey* ill. by J. Brian Pinkney. Hyperion, 1993. ISBN 1-56282-414-7 Subj: Activities – dancing. Careers – dancers. Ethnic groups in the U.S. – African Americans.

Bill Pickett, rodeo ridin' cowboy ill. by J. Brian Pinkney. Harcourt, 1996. ISBN 0-15-200100-X Subj: Cowboys, cowgirls. Ethnic groups in the U.S. – African Americans.

Dear Benjamin Banneker ill. by J. Brian Pinkney. Harcourt, 1994. ISBN 0-15-200417-3 Subj: Careers – astronomers. Ethnic groups in the U.S. – African Americans. Slavery. U.S. history.

Duke Ellington: the piano prince and his orchestra ill. by Brian Pinkney. Hyperion, 1998. ISBN 0-7868-2150-7 Subj: Caldecott award honor books. Careers – musicians. Ethnic groups in the U.S. – African Americans. Music. Musical instruments – pianos.

Mim's Christmas jam ill. by Brian Pinkney. Harcourt, 2001. ISBN 0-15-201918-9 Subj: Ethnic groups in the U.S. – African Americans. Family life. Food. Holidays – Christmas.

Pinkney, Gloria Jean. *Back home* ill. by Jerry Pinkney. Dial, 1992. ISBN 0-8037-1169-7 Subj: Ethnic groups in the U.S. – African Americans. Family life. Farms.

The Sunday outing ill. by Jerry Pinkney. Dial, 1994. ISBN 0-8037-1199-9 Subj: Activities – traveling. Ethnic groups in the U.S. – African Americans. Family life. Farms. Trains.

Pinkney, J. Brian. *The adventures of sparrowboy* ill. by author. S&S, 1997. ISBN 0-689-81071-7 Subj: Activities – flying. Behavior – bullying. Communities, neighborhoods. Ethnic groups in the U.S. – African Americans. Humorous stories.

Cosmo and the robot ill. by author. Greenwillow, 2000. ISBN 0-688-15941-9 Subj: Monsters. Planets. Robots. Space & space ships.

Jojo's flying side kick ill. by author. S&S, 1995. ISBN 0-671-88111-6 Subj: Character traits – perseverance. Family life. Sports – Tae Kwon Do.

Pinkney, Jerry. *Noah's ark* ill. by author. SeaStar, 2002. ISBN 1-587-17202-X Subj: Animals. Boats, ships. Caldecott award honor books. Religion – Noah. Weather – floods. Weather – rain. Weather – rainbows.

Rikki-tikki-tavi (Kipling, Rudyard)

The ugly duckling (Andersen, H. C. [Hans Christian])

Pinkney, Sandra L. *A rainbow all around me* photos by Myles C. Pinkney. Scholastic, 2002. ISBN 0-439-30928-X Subj: Anatomy – skin. Concepts – color. Ethnic groups in the U.S. Weather – rainbows.

Shades of black photos by Myles C. Pinkney. Scholastic, 2000. ISBN 0-439-14892-8 Subj: Ethnic groups in the U.S. – African Americans.

Pinkwater, Daniel Manus. *At the Hotel Larry* ill. by Jill Pinkwater. Cavendish, 1997. ISBN 0-7614-5005-X Subj: Animals – polar bears. Careers – lifeguards. Hotels. Humorous stories.

Aunt Lulu ill. by author. Macmillan, 1988. ISBN 0-02-774661-5 Subj: Animals – dogs. Careers – librarians. Family life – aunts, uncles.

Bad bears and a bunny ill. by Jill Pinkwater. Houghton, 2005. ISBN 0-618-33926-4 Subj: Animals – polar bears. Animals – rabbits. Behavior. Hotels. Humorous stories. Parties.

Bad bears in the big city ill. by Jill Pinkwater. Houghton, 2003. ISBN 0-618-25208-8 Subj: Animals – polar bears. Behavior – misbehavior. Cities, towns. Food. Humorous stories. Zoos.

The bear's picture ill. by author. Dutton, 1984. ISBN 0-525-44102-6 Subj: Animals – bears. Art. Careers – artists. Concepts – color.

The big orange splot ill. by author. Hastings House, 1977. ISBN 0-8038-0777-5 Subj: Activities – painting. Character traits – individuality. Concepts – color. Homes, houses.

Bongo Larry ill. by Jill Pinkwater. Cavendish, 1998. ISBN 0-7614-5020-3 Subj: Animals – bears. Animals – polar bears. Careers – musicians. Humorous stories. Musical instruments – drums.

Devil in the drain ill. by author. Dutton, 1984. ISBN 0-525-44092-5 Subj: Character traits – curiosity. Devil.

Doodle flute ill. by author. Macmillan, 1991. ISBN 0-02-774635-6 Subj: Behavior – sharing. Friendship. Music. Musical instruments – pianos.

The Frankenbagel monster ill. by author. Dutton, 1986. ISBN 0-525-44260-X Subj: Careers – bakers. Monsters.

Guys from space ill. by author. Macmillan, 1989. ISBN 0-02-774672-0 Subj: Aliens. Space & space ships.

I was a second grade werewolf ill. by author. Dutton, 1983. ISBN 0-525-44038-0 Subj: Imagination. Monsters.

Ice-cream Larry ill. by Jill Pinkwater. Cavendish, 1999. ISBN 0-7614-5043-2 Subj: Animals – polar bears. Behavior – misbehavior. Food. Humorous stories.

Irving and Muktuk ill. by Jill Pinkwater. Houghton, 2001. ISBN 0-618-09334-6 Subj: Animals – polar bears. Animals – rabbits. Behavior – misbehavior. Zoos.

The phantom of the lunch wagon ill. by author. Macmillan, 1992. ISBN 0-02-774641-0 Subj: Animals – cats. Food. Ghosts.

Pickle creature ill. by author. Four Winds, 1979. ISBN 0-590-07579-9 Subj: Imagination – imaginary friends.

The picture of Morty and Ray ill. by Jack E. Davis. HarperCollins, 2003. ISBN 0-06-623786-6 Subj: Activities – painting. Behavior – misbehavior. Humorous stories.

Rainy morning ill. by Jill Pinkwater. Atheneum, 1998. ISBN 0-689-81143-8 Subj: Animals. Character traits – kindness to animals. Circus. Food. Homes, houses. Weather – rain.

Roger's umbrella ill. by James Marshall. Dutton, 1982. ISBN 0-525-38555-X Subj: Animals – cats. Umbrellas.

Tooth-gnasher superflash ill. by author. Four Winds, 1981. ISBN 0-590-07624-8 Subj: Automobiles. Imagination.

Wallpaper from space ill. by author. Atheneum, 1996. ISBN 0-689-80764-3 Subj: Dreams. Space & space ships.

Wempires ill. by author. Macmillan, 1991. ISBN 0-02-774411-6 Subj: Family life. Imagination.

Wolf Christmas ill. by Jill Pinkwater. Cavendish, 1998. ISBN 0-7614-5030-0 Subj: Animals – wolves. Holidays – Christmas.

Young Larry ill. by Jill Pinkwater. Cavendish, 1997. ISBN 0-7614-5004-1 Subj: Animals – polar bears. Behavior – growing up. Careers – lifeguards. Family life – brothers. Family life – mothers. Foreign lands – Canada. Humorous stories.

Pio peep! sel. by Alma Flor Ada & F. Isabel Campoy; English adaptations by Alice Schertle; ill. by Viví Escrivá. HarperCollins, 2003. ISBN 0-688-16020-4 Subj: Foreign languages. Nursery rhymes.

Pipe, Jim. *What makes it swing?* ill. by author. Copper Beech, 2002. ISBN 0-7613-2822-X Subj: Concepts. Science.

Piper, Watty. *The little engine that could* ill. by George & Doris Hauman. Platt, 1990. Retold from The pony engine, by Mable C. Bragg. This version first pub. in 1955. 60th anniversary ed. ISBN 0-448-40041-3 Subj: Character traits – perseverance. Trains.

Mother Goose rhymes (Mother Goose)

Pirani, Felix. *Abigail at the beach* ill. by Christine Roche. Dial, 1989. ISBN 0-8037-0561-1 Subj: Activities – playing. Imagination. Sea & seashore – beaches.

Triplets ill. by Christine Roche. Viking, 1991. ISBN 0-670-83375-4 Subj: Multiple births – triplets.

Pirner, Connie White. *Even little kids get diabetes* ill. by Nadine Bernard Westcott. A. Whitman, 1991. ISBN 0-8075-2158-2 Subj: Hospitals. Illness – diabetes.

Pirotta, Saviour. *Little bird* ill. by Stephen Butler. Morrow, 1992. ISBN 0-688-11290-0 Subj: Activities. Activities – flying. Animals. Birds.

Pistoia, Sara. *Counting* ill. by author. Child's World, 2003. ISBN 1-56766-114-9 Subj: Counting, numbers.

Money ill. by author. Child's World, 2003. ISBN 1-56766-116-5 Subj: Counting, numbers. Money.

Pitcher, Caroline. *Animals* ill. by Louise Nevett. Watts, 1983. ISBN 0-531-04656-7 Subj: Activities. Animals. Wordless.

Are you spring? ill. by Cliff Wright. DK, 2000. ISBN 0-7894-5614-1 Subj: Animals. Animals – bears. Seasons – spring.

Cars and boats ill. by Louise Nevett. Watts, 1983. ISBN 0-531-04657-5 Subj: Activities. Automobiles. Boats, ships. Wordless.

Mariana and the merchild: a folk tale from Chile ill. by Jackie Morris. Eerdmans, 2000. ISBN 0-8028-5204-1 Subj: Folk & fairy tales. Foreign lands – Chile. Mythical creatures – mermaids, mermen.

Nico's octopus ill. by Nilesh Mistry. Crocodile, 2003. ISBN 1-56656-483-2 Subj: Death. Octopuses. Pets.

Run with the wind ill. by Jane Chapman. Little Tiger, 1998. ISBN 1-888444-29-0 Subj: Animals – horses, ponies. Behavior – growing up. Family life – mothers.

The snow whale ill. by Jackie Morris. Sierra Club, 1996. ISBN 0-87156-915-9 Subj: Animals – whales. Family life – brothers & sisters. Water. Weather – snow.

The time of the lion ill. by Jackie Morris. Beyond Words, 1998. ISBN 1-885223-83-8 Subj: Animals – lions. Family life – fathers. Foreign lands – Africa. Friendship.

Pitre, Felix. *Paco and the witch* ill. by Christy Hale. Lodestar, 1995. ISBN 0-525-67501-9 Subj: Folk & fairy tales. Foreign lands – Puerto Rico. Names. Witches.

Pittau, Francisco. *Voyage under the stars* (Gervais, Bernadette)

Pittaway, Margaret. *The rainforest children: a story set in tropical Australia* ill. by Heather Philpott. Oxford Univ. Pr., 1980. ISBN 0-19-554238-X Subj: Behavior – running away. Behavior – seeking better things. Foreign lands – Australia.

Pittman, Helena Clare. *The angel tree* ill. by Jo Ellen McAllister Stammen. Dial, 1998. ISBN 0-8037-1941-8 Subj: Angels. Communities, neighborhoods. Friendship. Holidays – Christmas. Trees.

A dinosaur for Gerald ill. by author. Carolrhoda, 1990. ISBN 0-87614-431-8 Subj: Birthdays. Dinosaurs. Pets. Prehistory.

The gift of the willows ill. by author. Carolrhoda, 1988. ISBN 0-87614-354-0 Subj: Folk & fairy tales. Foreign lands – Japan.

A grain of rice ill. by author. Hastings House, 1986. ISBN 0-8038-9289-6 Subj: Character traits – cleverness. Folk & fairy tales. Foreign lands – China. Royalty.

Miss Hindy's cats ill. by author. Carolrhoda, 1990. ISBN 0-87614-368-0 Subj: ABC books. Animals – cats.

Once when I was scared ill. by Ted Rand. Dutton, 1988. ISBN 0-525-44407-6 Subj: Animals. Emotions – fear. Imagination. Night.

The snowman's path ill. by Raúl Colón. Dial, 2000. ISBN 0-8037-2170-6 Subj: Friendship. Snowmen.

Still-life stew ill. by Victoria Raymond. Hyperion, 1998. ISBN 0-7868-2206-6 Subj: Activities – painting. Art. Food. Gardens, gardening.

Sunrise ill. by Michael Rex. Silver Whistle, 1998. ISBN 0-15-201684-8 Subj: Counting, numbers. Morning. Rhyming text.

Uncle Phil's diner ill. by author. Carolrhoda, 1998. ISBN 1-57505-083-8 Subj: Family life – fathers. Food. Restaurants. Seasons – winter.

Piumini, Roberto. *Doctor Me Di Cin* ill. by Piet Grobler. Front St., 2001. ISBN 1-886910-67-7 Subj: Careers – doctors. Foreign lands – China. Royalty – princes.

The saint and the circus trans. from Italian by Olivia Holmes; ill. by Barrett V. Root. Morrow, 1991. ISBN 0-688-10377-4 Subj: Circus.

Piven, Hanokh. *The perfect purple feather* English text by Rachel Back; silhouettes by Janet Stein; photos by Adi Gilad. Little, 2002. ISBN 0-316-76657-7 Subj: Animals. Feathers. Rhyming text.

Pizer, Abigail. *Charlie the puppy* ill. by author. Carolrhoda, 1989. ISBN 0-87614-363-X Subj: Animals – dogs. Farms. Seasons.

Harry's night out ill. by author. Dial, 1987. ISBN 0-8037-0055-5 Subj: Activities. Animals – cats. Night.

Hattie the goat ill. by author. Carolrhoda, 1989. ISBN 0-87614-364-8 Subj: Animals – goats. Farms. Seasons.

It's a perfect day ill. by author. Lippincott, 1990. ISBN 0-397-32420-0 Subj: Animals. Farms. Noise, sounds. Rebuses.

Loppylugs ill. by author. Viking, 1990. ISBN 0-670-83209-X Subj: Animals – rabbits. Behavior – running away.

Nosey Gilbert ill. by author. Dial, 1987. ISBN 0-8037-0081-4 Subj: Animals – cats. Animals – dogs. Birds – geese. Emotions – fear. Insects – bees.

Penelope pig ill. by author. Carolrhoda, 1989. ISBN 0-87614-366-4 Subj: Animals – pigs. Farms. Seasons.

Percy the duck ill. by author. Carolrhoda, 1989. ISBN 0-87614-365-6 Subj: Birds – ducks. Farms. Seasons.

Planes ill. with photos. DK, 1993. ISBN 1-56458-135-7 Subj: Airplanes, airports.

Plante, Patricia. *The turtle and the two ducks: animal fables* retold from La Fontaine by Patricia Plante & David Bergman; ill. by Anne F. Rockwell. HarperCollins, 1981. ISBN 0-690-04147-0 Subj: Animals. Folk & fairy tales.

Plath, Sylvia. *The bed book* ill. by Emily Arnold McCully. HarperCollins, 1976. ISBN 0-06-024747-9 Subj: Bedtime. Poetry. Sleep.

Please, Mr. Crocodile! comp. by Tessa Strickland; ill. by Rosslyn Moran. Barefoot, 1999. ISBN 1-902283-62-7 Subj: Animals. Poetry.

Ploetz, Richard. *The Kooken* (Lebentritt, Julia)

Plotkin, Mark J. *The shaman's apprentice* (Cherry, Lynne)

Plotz, Helen. *A week of lullabies* comp. & ed. by Helen Plotz; ill. by Marisabina Russo. Greenwillow, 1988. ISBN 0-688-06653-4 Subj: Bedtime. Days of the week, months of the year. Lullabies. Poetry.

Plourde, Lynn. *Pigs in the mud in the middle of the rud* ill. by John Schoenherr. Blue Sky, 1997. ISBN 0-590-56863-9 Subj: Animals – pigs. Character traits – stubbornness. Humorous stories. Poetry. Roads. Weather – rain.

School picture day ill. by Thor Wickstrom. Dutton, 2002. ISBN 0-525-46886-2 Subj: Activities – photographing. School.

Spring's sprung ill. by Greg Couch. S&S, 2002. ISBN 0-689-84229-5 Subj: Family life – sisters. Rhyming text. Seasons – spring. Sibling rivalry.

Wild child ill. by Greg Couch. S&S, 1999. ISBN 0-689-81552-2 Subj: Bedtime. Mythical creatures. Rhyming text. Seasons – fall.

Winter waits ill. by Greg Couch. S&S, 2001. ISBN 0-689-83268-0 Subj: Mythical creatures. Rhyming text. Seasons – winter. Time.

Pluckrose, Henry Arthur. *Ants* ill. by Tony Swift & David Cook. Watts, 1981. ISBN 0-531-03452-6 Subj: Insects – ants. Science.

Bears ill. by Richard Orr. Watts, 1979. ISBN 0-531-03403-8 Subj: Animals – bears. Animals – pandas. Animals – polar bears. Science.

Bees and wasps ill. by Tony Swift & Norman Weaver. Watts, 1981. ISBN 0-531-03453-4 Subj: Insects – bees. Insects – wasps. Science.

Beginnings and endings photos by Steve Shott. Childrens Pr., 1996. ISBN 0-516-08236-1 Subj: Concepts.

Big and little photos by Chris Fairclough. Watts, 1987. ISBN 0-531-10373-0 Subj: Concepts – size.

Butterflies and moths ill. by Norman Weaver & others. Watts, 1981. ISBN 0-531-03454-2 Subj: Insects – butterflies, caterpillars. Insects – moths. Science.

China ill. with photos. Watts, 1999. ISBN 0-531-14500-X Subj: Foreign lands – China.

Counting photos by Chris Fairclough. Watts, 1988. ISBN 0-531-10524-5 Subj: Counting, numbers.

Elephants ill. by Peter Barrett. Watts, 1979. ISBN 0-531-03404-6 Subj: Animals – elephants. Science.

Floating and sinking photos by Chris Fairclough. Watts, 1987. ISBN 0-531-10294-7 Subj: Science.

Fur and feathers ill. with photos. Watts, 1989. ISBN 0-531-10720-5 Subj: Anatomy. Animals.

Hearing photos by Chris Fairclough. G. Stevens, 1995. ISBN 0-8368-1287-5 Subj: Senses – hearing.

Horses ill. by Peter Barrett & Maurice Wilson. Watts, 1979. ISBN 0-531-03405-4 Subj: Animals – horses, ponies. Science.

Hot and cold photos by Chris Fairclough. Watts, 1987. ISBN 0-531-10295-5 Subj: Science.

Join it! ill. with photos. Watts, 1989. ISBN 0-531-10730-2 Subj: Activities. Language.

Lions and tigers ill. by Eric Tenny & Maurice Wilson. Archon Pr., 1979. ISBN 0-531-03410-0 Subj: Animals – lions. Animals – tigers.

Numbers photos by Chris Fairclough. Watts, 1988. ISBN 0-531-10453-2 Subj: Counting, numbers.

On the farm photos by Teri Gower. Watts, 1998. ISBN 0-531-14496-8 Subj: Farms. Machines.

On the move photos by Teri Gower. Watts, 1998. ISBN 0-531-14497-6 Subj: Machines. Transportation.

Paws and claws ill. with photos. Watts, 1989. ISBN 0-531-10721-3 Subj: Anatomy. Animals.

Reptiles ill. by Gary Hincks & others. Watts, 1981. ISBN 0-531-03455-0 Subj: Reptiles. Science.

Seeing photos by Chris Fairclough. G. Stevens, 1995. ISBN 0-8368-1288-3 Subj: Senses – sight.

Shape photos by Chris Fairclough. Watts, 1987. ISBN 0-531-10374-9 Subj: Concepts – shape.

Skin, shell and scale ill. with photos. Watts, 1989. ISBN 0-531-10722-7 Subj: Anatomy – skin. Animals.

Smelling photos by Chris Fairclough. G. Stevens, 1995. ISBN 0-8368-1289-1 Subj: Senses – smell.

Tasting photos by Chris Fairclough. G. Stevens, 1995. ISBN 0-8368-1290-5 Subj: Senses – taste.

Things we cut ill. by G. W. Hales. Watts, 1976. ISBN 0-531-01216-6 Subj: Tools.

Things we hear ill. by G. W. Hales. Watts, 1976. ISBN 0-531-00363-9 Subj: Senses – hearing.

Things we see ill. by G. W. Hales. Watts, 1976. ISBN 0-531-01217-4 Subj: Senses – sight.

Things we touch ill. by G. W. Hales. Watts, 1976. ISBN 0-531-00364-7 Subj: Senses – touch.

Time photos by Chris Fairclough. Watts, 1988. ISBN 0-531-10452-4 Subj: Time.

Touching photos by Chris Fairclough. G. Stevens, 1995. ISBN 0-8368-1291-3 Subj: Senses – touch.

Walls photos by Steve Shott. Childrens Pr., 1996. ISBN 0-516-08239-6 Subj: Buildings.

Weight photos by Chris Fairclough. Watts, 1988. ISBN 0-531-10525-3 Subj: Concepts – weight.

Whales ill. by Norman Weaver. Watts, 1979. ISBN 0-531-03406-2 Subj: Animals – whales. Science.

Plume, Alice. *Salt: from a Russian folktale* (Afanas'ev, Aleksandr N.)

Plume, Ilse. *The Bremen town musicians* (Grimm, Jacob)

Lullaby and goodnight (Lullaby and goodnight)

The shoemaker and the elves (Grimm, Jacob)

The story of Befana: an Italian Christmas tale ill. by adapt. Godine, 1981. ISBN 0-87923-420-2 Subj: Folk & fairy tales. Foreign lands – Italy. Holidays – Christmas.

Plummer, David. *Counting kittens* by David Plummer & John Archambault; ill. by Liisa Chauncy Guida. Silver Pr., 1997. ISBN 0-382-39649-9 Subj: Animals – babies. Animals – cats. Counting, numbers. Rhyming text.

Plunkett, Stephanie Haboush. *Kongi and Potgi: a Cinderella story from Korea* (Han, Oki S.)

Sir Whong and the golden pig (Han, Oki S.)

Po, Lee. *The hare and the tortoise and the tortoise and the hare = La liebre y la tortuga and La tortuga y la liebre* (Du Bois, William Pène)

Pochocki, Ethel. *Rosebud and red flannel* ill. by Mary Beth Owens. Down East, 1999. ISBN 0-8927-2474-9 Subj: Clothing. Emotions – love.

A pocketful of stars: poems about the night ill. by Emma Shaw-Smith. Barefoot, 2000. ISBN 1-902283-84-8 Subj: Night. Poetry.

Pocock, Rita. *Annabelle and the big slide* ill. by author. Harcourt, 1989. ISBN 0-15-200407-6 Subj: Activities – playing. Character traits – confidence.

Podendorf, Illa. *Color* ill. by Wayne Stuart. Childrens Pr., 1971. ISBN 0-516-01572-9 Subj: Concepts – color.

Shapes, sides, curves and corners ill. by Frank Rakoncay. Childrens Pr., 1970. ISBN 0-516-01555-9 Subj: Concepts – shape.

Space ill. with photos. Childrens Pr., 1982. ISBN 0-516-01650-4 Subj: Space & space ships.

Podwal, Mark H. *Golem: a giant made of mud* ill. by author. Greenwillow, 1995. ISBN 0-688-13811-X Subj: Folk & fairy tales. Giants. Jewish culture.

The menorah story ill. by author. Greenwillow, 1998. ISBN 0-688-15759-9 Subj: Holidays – Hanukkah. Jewish culture. Religion.

A sweet year ill. by author. Random House, 2003. ISBN 0-385-90869-5 Subj: Food. Holidays. Jewish culture. Religion.

Poems for the very young sel. by Michael Rosen; ill. by Bob Graham. Kingfisher, 2004. ISBN 0-7534-5816-0 Subj: Children as authors. Poetry.

Poems go clang! *a collection of noisy verse* ill. by Debi Gliori. Candlewick, 1997. ISBN 0-76360-148-9 Subj: Noise, sounds. Poetry.

Poffenberger, Nancy M. *September 11, 2001* ill. by students from Lotspeich School. Fun Pub., 2002. ISBN 0-938293-12-5 Subj: Cities, towns. Crime. U.S. history. War.

Pogány, Willy. *Willy Pogány's Mother Goose* (1928) (Mother Goose)

Willy Pogány's Mother Goose (2000) (Mother Goose)

Pogorelsky, Antony. *The black hen, or, The underground inhabitants* retold by Morse Hamilton; ill. by Tatyana Yuditskaya. Cobblehill, 1994. ISBN 0-525-65133-0 Subj: Behavior – dissatisfaction. Birds – chickens. Folk & fairy tales. Foreign lands – Russia.

The little black hen retold by Elizabeth James; ill. by Gennady Spirin. Simply Read Bks., 2003. ISBN 1-894965-03-5 Subj: Behavior – dissatisfaction. Birds – chickens. Folk & fairy tales. Foreign lands – Russia.

Pohrt, Tom. *Coyote goes walking* ill. by author. Farrar, 1995. ISBN 0-374-31628-7 Subj: Animals – coyotes. Creation. Folk & fairy tales. Indians of North America – Great Plains.

Having a wonderful time ill. by author. Farrar, 1999. ISBN 0-374-32898-6 Subj: Activities – vacationing. Animals – cats. Desert. Foreign lands – Africa.

Points, Larry. *Assateague: island of the wild ponies* (Jauck, Andrea)

Pokornik, Brigitte. *Circus* (Blume, Karin)

My new friends (Blume, Karin)

POLA. *see* Watson, Pauline

Polacco, Patricia. *Appelemando's dreams* ill. by author. Putnam, 1991. ISBN 0-399-21800-9 Subj: Dreams. Imagination.

Aunt Chip and the great Triple Creek dam affair ill. by author. Philomel, 1996. ISBN 0-399-22943-4 Subj: Books, reading. Libraries. Television.

Babushka's doll ill. by author. S&S, 1990. ISBN 0-671-68343-8 Subj: Toys – dolls.

Babushka's Mother Goose ill. by author. Philomel, 1995. ISBN 0-399-22747-4 Subj: Family life – grandmothers. Folk & fairy tales. Foreign lands – Russia. Nursery rhymes.

Betty Doll ill. by author. Philomel, 2001. ISBN 0-399-23638-4 Subj: Family life – mothers. Illness – cancer. Memories, memory. Toys – dolls.

The butterfly ill. by author. Philomel, 2000. ISBN 0-399-23170-6 Subj: Behavior – hiding. Behavior – secrets. Character traits – freedom. Foreign lands – France. Insects – butterflies, caterpillars. War.

Chicken Sunday ill. by author. Putnam, 1992. ISBN 0-399-22133-6 Subj: Eggs. Ethnic groups in the U.S. – African Americans. Family life – grandmothers. Friendship. Holidays – Easter. Religion.

I can hear the sun ill. by author. Philomel, 1996. ISBN 0-399-22520-X Subj: Birds – geese. Character traits – being different. Ethnic groups in the U.S. – African Americans. Homeless. Sun.

In Enzo's splendid gardens ill. by author. Philomel, 1997. ISBN 0-399-23107-2 Subj: Accidents. Cumulative tales. Food. Humorous stories. Insects – bees. Restaurants.

Just plain Fancy ill. by author. Bantam, 1990. ISBN 0-553-07062-2 Subj: Birds – peacocks, peahens. Eggs. Farms.

The keeping quilt ill. by author. S&S, 1998. ISBN 0-689-82090-9 Subj: Immigrants. Jewish culture. Quilts.

Luba and the wren ill. by author. Philomel, 1999. ISBN 0-399-23168-4 Subj: Behavior – wishing. Birds – wrens. Folk & fairy tales. Foreign lands – Soviet Union. Magic.

Meteor! ill. by author. Dodd, 1987. ISBN 0-396-08910-0 Subj: Country. Science.

Mr. Lincoln's way ill. by author. Philomel, 2001. ISBN 0-399-23754-2 Subj: Behavior – bullying. Birds. Careers – school principals. Prejudice. School.

Mrs. Katz and Tush ill. by author. Bantam, 1992. ISBN 0-553-08122-5 Subj: Animals – cats. Ethnic groups in the U.S. – African Americans. Friendship. Jewish culture. Pets.

Mrs. Mack ill. by author. Philomel, 1998. ISBN 0-399-23167-6 Subj: Animals – horses, ponies. Memories, memory. Seasons – summer.

My ol' man ill. by author. Philomel, 1995. ISBN 0-399-22822-5 Subj: Family life – fathers. Imagination. Magic. Rocks.

My rotten redheaded older brother ill. by author. S&S, 1994. ISBN 0-671-72751-6 Subj: Family life – brothers & sisters. Family life – grandparents. Sibling rivalry.

Oh, look! ill. by author. Philomel, 2004. ISBN 0-399-24223-6 Subj: Animals – goats. Fairs, festivals. Mythical creatures – trolls.

Picnic at Mudsock Meadow ill. by author. Putnam, 1992. ISBN 0-399-21811-4 Subj: Activities – picnicking. Holidays – Halloween.

Rechenka's eggs ill. by author. Putnam, 1988. ISBN 0-399-21501-8 Subj: Birds – geese. Eggs. Folk & fairy tales.

Some birthday! ill. by author. S&S, 1991. ISBN 0-671-72750-8 Subj: Birthdays. Family life – fathers. Monsters. Parties.

Thank you, Mr. Falker ill. by author. Philomel, 1998. ISBN 0-399-23166-8 Subj: Books, reading. Careers – teachers. Handicaps. School.

Thunder cake ill. by author. Putnam, 1990. ISBN 0-399-22231-6 Subj: Emotions – fear. Family life – grandmothers. Weather – lightning, thunder. Weather – storms.

Tikvah means hope ill. by author. Doubleday, 1994. ISBN 0-385-32059-0 Subj: Animals – cats. Fire. Holidays – Sukkot. Jewish culture.

The trees of the dancing goats ill. by author. S&S, 1996. ISBN 0-689-80862-3 Subj: Ethnic groups in the U.S. – Russian Americans. Family life – grandparents. Holidays – Christmas. Holidays – Hanukkah. Jewish culture.

Welcome Comfort ill. by author. Philomel, 1999. ISBN 0-399-23169-2 Subj: Holidays – Christmas. Orphans. Santa Claus. School.

Polette, Nancy. *The little old woman and the hungry cat* ill. by Frank Modell. Greenwillow, 1989. ISBN 0-688-08315-3 Subj: Animals – cats. Cumulative tales.

Polhamus, Jean Burt. *Dinosaur do's and don'ts* ill. by Steve O'Neill. Prentice-Hall, 1975. ISBN 0-13-214643-6 Subj: Dinosaurs. Etiquette. Prehistory.

Doctor Dinosaur ill. by Steve O'Neill. Prentice-Hall, 1981. ISBN 0-13-217083-3 Subj: Careers – veterinarians. Dinosaurs. Illness. Prehistory.

Policoff, Stephen Phillip. *Cesar's amazing journey* ill. by David Catrow. Viking, 1999. ISBN 0-670-88753-6 Subj: Frogs & toads. Spiders. Zoos.

Polisar, Barry Louis. *Don't do that! a child's guide to bad manners, ridiculous rules, and inadequate etiquette* ill. by David Clark. Rainbow Morning Music, 1994. ISBN 0-938663-20-8 Subj: Etiquette.

The haunted house party ill. by David Clark. Rainbow Morning Music, 1995. ISBN 0-938663-21-6 Subj: Ghosts. Holidays – Halloween. Homes, houses. Monsters. Parties. Rhyming text.

Insect soup ill. by David Clark. Rainbow Morning Music, 1999. ISBN 0-938663-22-4 Subj: Humorous stories. Insects. Poetry.

A little less noise ill. by David Clark. Rainbow Morning Music, 2001. ISBN 0-938663-23-2 Subj: Noise, sounds. Poetry.

The trouble with Ben ill. by David Clark. Rainbow Morning Music, 1992. ISBN 0-938663-13-5 Subj: Animals – bears. Character traits – being different. School. Self-concept.

Politi, Leo. *Emmet* ill. by author. Scribners, 1971. ISBN 0-684-12320-7 Subj: Animals – dogs. Crime.

Juanita ill. by author. Scribners, 1948. Subj: Caldecott award honor books. Ethnic groups in the U.S. – Mexican Americans.

Lito and the clown ill. by author. Scribners, 1964. Subj: Animals – cats. Clowns, jesters. Foreign lands – Mexico. Pets.

Little Leo ill. by author. Scribners, 1951. Subj: Clothing. Family life. Foreign lands – Italy.

Moy Moy ill. by author. Scribners, 1960. Subj: Ethnic groups in the U.S. – Chinese Americans. Holidays – Chinese New Year.

The nicest gift ill. by author. Scribners, 1973. ISBN 0-684-13383-0 Subj: Animals – dogs. Behavior – lost. Gifts. Holidays – Christmas.

Pedro, the angel of Olvera Street ill. by author. Scribners, 1946. Subj: Caldecott award honor books. Ethnic groups in the U.S. – Mexican Americans. Holidays – Christmas.

Rosa ill. by author. Scribners, 1963. Subj: Babies. Foreign lands – Mexico. Holidays – Christmas. Sibling rivalry. Toys – dolls.

Song of the swallows ill. by author. Scribners, 1949. ISBN 0-684-18831-7 Subj: Birds – swallows. Caldecott award books. Ethnic groups in the U.S. – Mexican Americans. Missions.

Polivy, Betsy Bober. *My bye-bye bottle book* (Gelbard, Jane)

My dressing book (Gelbard, Jane)

My eating book (Gelbard, Jane)

My sharing book (Gelbard, Jane)

Polizzotti, Mark. *Star of fear, star of hope* (Hoestlandt, Jo)

Pollack, Eileen. *Whisper whisper Jesse, whisper whisper Josh* ill. by Bruce Gilfoy. Advantage/Aurora, 1992. ISBN 0-9624828-4-6 Subj: Death. Emotions – grief. Family life – aunts, uncles. Illness – AIDS.

Pollack, Pamela. *Where's that cat?* (Merriam, Eve)

Pollard, Nik. *The river* ill. by author. Roaring Brook, 2003. ISBN 0-7613-2858-0 Subj: Rhyming text. Rivers.

The tide ill. by authnor. Roaring Brook, 2002. ISBN 0-7613-2467-4 Subj: Nature. Sea & seashore.

Pollock, Penny. *Emily's tiger* ill. by author. Paulist Pr., 1985. ISBN 0-8091-6554-6 Subj: Pets. Toys.

The turkey girl: a Zuni Cinderella story ill. by Ed Young. Little, 1996. ISBN 0-316-71314-7 Subj: Birds – turkeys. Character traits – loyalty. Folk & fairy tales. Indians of North America – Zuni.

Water is wet photos by Barbara Beirne. Putnam, 1985. ISBN 0-399-21180-2 Subj: Activities – playing. Water.

When the moon is full ill. by Mary Azarian. Little, 2001. ISBN 0-316-71317-1 Subj: Folk & fairy tales. Indians of North America. Moon. Poetry. Seasons.

Poltarnhess, Welleran. *An ABC of fashionable animals* (Edens, Cooper)

Polushkin, Maria. *see* Robbins, Maria Polushkin

Pomeranc, Marion Hess. *The American Wei* ill. by DyAnne DiSalvo-Ryan. A. Whitman, 1998. ISBN 0-8075-0312-6 Subj: Ethnic groups in the U.S. – Chinese Americans. Fairies. Immigrants.

The can-do Thanksgiving ill. by Nancy Cote. A. Whitman, 1998. ISBN 0-8075-1054-8 Subj: Food. Holidays – Thanksgiving. School.

Pomerantz, Charlotte. *All asleep* ill. by Nancy Tafuri. Greenwillow, 1984. ISBN 0-688-03762-3 Subj: Bedtime. Lullabies. Poetry.

The ballad of the long-tailed rat ill. by Marian Parry. Macmillan, 1975. ISBN 0-02-774890-1 Subj: Animals – cats. Animals – rats. Character traits – pride. Rhyming text.

The birthday letters ill. by JoAnn Adinolfi. Greenwillow, 2000. ISBN 0-688-16336-X Subj: Animals. Parties. Pets.

Buffy and Albert ill. by Yossi Abolafia. Greenwillow, 1982. ISBN 0-688-00921-2 Subj: Animals – cats. Family life – grandfathers. Old age.

The chalk doll ill. by Frané Lessac. HarperCollins, 1989. ISBN 0-397-32319-0 Subj: Family life – mothers. Toys – dolls.

Flap your wings and try ill. by Nancy Tafuri. Greenwillow, 1989. ISBN 0-688-08020-0 Subj: Activities – flying. Birds. Rhyming text.

The half-birthday party ill. by DyAnne DiSalvo-Ryan. Houghton Mifflin, 1984. ISBN 0-89919-273-4 Subj: Birthdays.

Here comes Henny ill. by Nancy Winslow Parker. Greenwillow, 1994. ISBN 0-688-12356-2 Subj: Birds – chickens. Rhyming text.

How many trucks can a tow truck tow? ill. by R. W. Alley. Random House, 1987. ISBN 0-394-88775-1 Subj: Rhyming text. Trucks.

If I had a Paka: poems of eleven languages ill. by Nancy Tafuri. Greenwillow, 1982. ISBN 0-688-00837-2 Subj: Foreign languages. Poetry.

Mangaboom ill. by Anita Lobel. Greenwillow, 1997. ISBN 0-688-12957-9 Subj: Giants. Trees.

The mango tooth ill. by Marylin Hafner. Greenwillow, 1977. ISBN 0-688-84070-1 Subj: Family life. Teeth.

The mousery ill. by Kurt Cyrus. Harcourt, 2000. ISBN 0-15-202304-6 Subj: Animals – mice. Character traits – generosity. Orphans. Rhyming text.

One duck, another duck ill. by José Aruego & Ariane Dewey. Greenwillow, 1984. ISBN 0-688-03745-3 Subj: Birds – ducks. Counting, numbers.

The outside dog ill. by Jennifer Plecas. HarperCollins, 1993. ISBN 0-06-024783-5 Subj: Animals – dogs. Family life – grandfathers. Foreign lands – Puerto Rico.

The piggy in the puddle ill. by James Marshall. Macmillan, 1974. ISBN 0-02-774900-2 Subj: Animals – pigs. Rhyming text. Tongue twisters.

Posy ill. by Catherine Stock. Greenwillow, 1983. ISBN 0-688-02299-5 Subj: Bedtime. Family life.

Serena Katz ill. by R. W. Alley. Macmillan, 1992. ISBN 0-02-774901-0 Subj: Activities. Friendship.

The tamarindo puppy and other poems ill. by Byron Barton. Greenwillow, 1980. ISBN 0-688-84251-8 Subj: Foreign languages. Poetry.

Timothy Tall Feather ill. by Catherine Stock. Greenwillow, 1986. ISBN 0-688-04247-3 Subj: Family life – grandfathers. Imagination. Indians of North America.

Where's the bear? ill. by Byron Barton. Greenwillow, 1984. ISBN 0-688-01753-3 Subj: Animals – bears.

Whiff, sniff, nibble and chew: The Gingerbread boy (The gingerbread boy)

You're not my best friend anymore ill. by David Soman. Dial, 1998. ISBN 0-8037-1560-9 Subj: Birthdays. Friendship. Gifts.

Pomeroy, Diana. *One potato* ill. by author. Harcourt, 1996. ISBN 0-15-200300-2 Subj: Counting, numbers. Food.

Wildflower ABC ill. by author. Harcourt, 1997. ISBN 0-15-201041-6 Subj: ABC books. Activities. Flowers.

Ponti, Claude. *Adele's album* ill. by author. Dutton, 1988. ISBN 0-525-44412-2 Subj: Imagination. Wordless.

Poole, Amy Lowry. *The ant and the grasshopper* (Æsop)

How the rooster got his crown ill. by author. Holiday, 1999. ISBN 0-8234-1389-6 Subj: Birds – chickens. Creation. Folk & fairy tales – pourquoi tales. Foreign lands – China.

Poole, Josephine. *Joan of Arc* ill. by Angela Barrett. Knopf, 1998. ISBN 0-679-99041-0 Subj: Foreign lands – France. Religion. War.

Poole, Valerie. *Obadiah Coffee and the music contest* ill. by author. HarperCollins, 1991. ISBN 0-06-021620-4 Subj: Animals. Animals – rabbits. Careers – musicians. Music. Musical instruments – bands.

Pope, Billy N. *Your world: let's visit the hospital* by Billy N. Pope & Ramona Ware Emmons. Taylor, 1971. ISBN 0-8783-3023-2 Subj: Hospitals.

Pope, Geraldine. *The empty creel* ill. by Dennis Cunningham. Godine, 1995. ISBN 1-56792-044-6 Subj: Family life – grandfathers. Sports – fishing.

Popov, Nikolai. *Why?* ill. by author. North-South, 1996. ISBN 1-55858-535-4 Subj: Animals – mice. Frogs & toads. War. Wordless.

Poppy Bear ill. by Catherine Deeter. Beyond Words, 2001. ISBN 1-58270-042-7 Subj: Animals – bears. Ecology. Gardens, gardening. Rhyming text. Seasons – spring.

Porazinska, Janina. *The enchanted book: a tale from Krakow* ill. by Jan Brett; trans. by Bozena Smith. Harcourt, 1987. ISBN 0-15-225950-3 Subj: Books, reading. Family life – sisters. Folk & fairy tales. Foreign lands – Poland.

The porcupine ill. by Patrick Oxenham. Rourke, 1983. ISBN 0-86592-852-5 Subj: Animals – porcupines.

Porte, Barbara Ann. *Chickens! Chickens!* ill. by Greg Henry. Orchard, 1995. ISBN 0-531-08727-1 Subj: Art. Birds – chickens. Careers – artists.

Harry in trouble ill. by Yossi Abolafia. Greenwillow, 1989. ISBN 0-688-07722-6 Subj: Careers – librarians. Character traits – helpfulness.

Harry's dog ill. by Yossi Abolafia. Greenwillow, 1983. ISBN 0-688-02556-0 Subj: Animals – dogs. Family life – fathers. Illness.

Harry's mom ill. by Yossi Abolafia. Greenwillow, 1985. ISBN 0-688-04818-8 Subj: Death. Emotions – grief. Family life. Family life – fathers. Family life – grandparents. Family life – mothers. School.

Harry's visit ill. by Yossi Abolafia. Greenwillow, 1983. ISBN 0-688-01208-6 Subj: Behavior – sharing. Sports – basketball.

Ma Jiang and the orange ants ill. by Annie Cannon. Orchard, 2000. ISBN 0-531-33241-1 Subj: Foreign lands – China. Insects – ants.

When Aunt Lucy rode a mule and other stories ill. by Maxie Chambliss. Orchard, 1994. ISBN 0-531-08666-6 Subj: Family life – aunts, uncles. Family life – sisters.

Porter, David Lord. *Mine!* ill. by author. Houghton Mifflin, 1981. ISBN 0-395-31607-3 Subj: Behavior – greed.

Porter, Sue. *Little Wolf and the giant* ill. by author. S&S, 1990. ISBN 0-671-70363-3 Subj: Animals – wolves. Forest, woods. Giants.

My little rabbit tale ill. by author. DK, 1994. ISBN 1-56458-339-2 Subj: Animals – rabbits.

One potato ill. by author. Bradbury, 1989. ISBN 0-02-774910-X Subj: Animals. Food.

Parsnip ill. by author. DK, 1997. ISBN 0-7894-2470-3 Subj: Animals – babies. Animals – sheep. Format, unusual – toy & movable books. Seasons – winter.

Parsnip and the pink blanket ill. by author. DK, 2000. ISBN 0-7894-5619-2 Subj: Animals – babies. Animals – horses, ponies. Animals – sheep. Behavior – lost & found possessions. Format, unusual – toy & movable books.

Parsnip and the runaway tractor ill. by author. DK, 1999. ISBN 0-7894-2494-0 Subj: Accidents. Animals – babies. Animals – sheep. Format, unusual – toy & movable books. Tractors.

Porter-Gaylord, Laurel. *I love my daddy because . . .* ill. by Ashley Wolff. Dutton, 1991. ISBN 0-525-44624-9 Subj: Animals. Emotions – love. Family life – fathers.

I love my mommy because . . . ill. by Ashley Wolff. Dutton, 1991. ISBN 0-525-44625-7 Subj: Animals. Emotions – love. Family life – mothers.

Portlock, Rob. *Someone's trying to cut off my head* ill. by author. InterVarsity, 1992. ISBN 0-8308-1902-9 Subj: Careers – barbers. Hair. Imagination.

Portnoy, Mindy Avra. *Ima on the Bima: my mommy is a Rabbi* ill. by Steffi Karen Rubin. Kar-Ben Copies, 1986. ISBN 0-930494-55-5 Subj: Careers. Family life – mothers. Jewish culture.

Matzah ball: a Passover story ill. by Katherine Janus Kahn. Kar-Ben Copies, 1994. ISBN 0-929-37168-2 Subj: Food. Holidays – Passover. Jewish culture. Sports – baseball.

Mommy never went to Hebrew school ill. by Shelly O. Haas. Kar-Ben Copies, 1989. ISBN 0-930494-96-2 Subj: Family life. Jewish culture.

Where do people go when they die? ill. by Shelly O. Haas. Kar-Ben Copies, 2004. ISBN 1-58013-081-X Subj: Death. Family life.

Porto, Tony. *Blue aliens* conceived & designed by 3CD (Tony Porto, Mitch Rice, Glenn Deutsch). Little, 2003. ISBN 0-316-61359-2 Subj: Aliens. Concepts – color. School.

Get red conceived & designed by 3CD (Tony Porto, Mitch Rice, Glenn Deutsch). Little, 2002. ISBN 0-316-60940-4 Subj: Aliens. Concepts – color. School.

Posada, Mia. *Dandelions, stars in the grass* ill. by author. Carolrhoda, 2000. ISBN 1-575-05383-7 Subj: Flowers. Plants. Science.

Ladybugs ill. by author. Carolrhoda, 2002. ISBN 0-87614-334-6 Subj: Insects – ladybugs. Rhyming text.

Robins ill. by author. Carolrhoda, 2004. ISBN 1-57505-615-1 Subj: Birds – robins. Rhyming text.

Posey, Lee. *Night rabbits* ill. by Michael G. Montgomery. Peachtree, 1999. ISBN 1-56145-164-9 Subj: Animals – rabbits. Family life – fathers. Homes, houses. Night. Seasons – summer.

Poskanzer, Susan Cornell. *Dairy farmer* ill. by George Ulrich. Troll, 1989. ISBN 0-8167-1426-6 Subj: Animals – bulls, cows. Careers – farmers. Farms.

Puppeteer ill. by Diane Paterson. Troll, 1989. ISBN 0-8167-1432-0 Subj: Careers – puppeteers. Family life – grandmothers. Puppets.

Riddles about Hannukah photos by Rob Gray. Silver Pr., 1990. ISBN 0-671-70553-9 Subj: Holidays – Hanukkah. Rhyming text. Riddles & jokes.

What's it like to be a chef? ill. by Karen E. Pellaton. Troll, 1990. ISBN 0-8167-1797-4 Subj: Careers – chefs, cooks.

Post, Howard. *The magic boots* (Emerson, Scott)

Postgate, Daniel. *The richest crocodile in the world* ill. by author. Collins, 2003. ISBN 0-00-710388-3 Subj: Friendship. Reptiles – alligators, crocodiles.

Postgate, Oliver. *Noggin and the whale* by Oliver Postgate & Peter Firmin; ill. by Peter Firmin. White, 1967. Subj: Animals – whales. Humorous stories. Royalty – kings.

Noggin the king by Oliver Postgate & Peter Firmin; ill. by Peter Firmin. White, 1965. Subj: Birds. Character traits – kindness. Humorous stories. Royalty – kings.

Posthuma, Sieb. *Benny* ill. by author. Kane/Miller, 2002. ISBN 1-929132-43-3 Subj: Animals – dogs. Family life – mothers. Illness – cold (disease). Senses – smell.

Postma, Lidia. *The stolen mirror* ill. by author. McGraw-Hill, 1976. Translation of De gestolen Spiegel. ISBN 0-07-050534-9 Subj: Imagination. Magic. Sibling rivalry.

Tom Thumb: a tale (Tom Thumb)

Poston, Elizabeth. *Baby's song book* ill. by William Stobbs. Crowell, 1971. Subj: Music. Songs.

Potok, Chaim. *The sky of now* ill. by Tony Auth. Knopf, 1995. ISBN 0-679-86021-5 Subj: Activities – flying. Emotions – fear. Family life – aunts, uncles.

Potter, Beatrix. *Appley Dapply's nursery rhymes* ill. by author. Warne, 1917. ISBN 0-7232-0613-9 Subj: Animals. Nursery rhymes.

Beatrix Potter's nursery rhyme book (Mother Goose)

Cecily Parsley's nursery rhymes ill. by author. Warne, 1922. ISBN 0-7232-0614-7 Subj: Animals. Nursery rhymes.

The complete adventures of Peter Rabbit ill. by author. Warne, 1982. ISBN 0-7232-6165-2 Subj: Animals – rabbits. Behavior – misbehavior.

Ginger and Pickles ill. by author. Warne, 1937. First pub. in 1909. Subj: Animals. Stores.

More tales from Beatrix Potter ill. by author. Warne, 1987. ISBN 0-7232-3366-7 Subj: Animals.

Peter Rabbit's ABC ill. by author. Warne, 1999, c1987. ISBN 0-7232-3423-X Subj: ABC books. Animals.

Peter Rabbit's one two three ill. by author. Warne, 1999, c1988. ISBN 0-7232-3424-8 Subj: Animals – rabbits. Counting, numbers.

The pie and the patty-pan ill. by author. Warne, 1933. First pub. in 1905. Subj: Animals – cats. Animals – dogs. Behavior – trickery.

Rolly-polly pudding ill. by author. Warne, 1936. First pub. in 1908. Subj: Animals – cats.

The sly old cat ill. by author. Warne, 1971. ISBN 0-7232-1420-4 Subj: Animals – cats. Animals – rats. Character traits – cleverness. Etiquette. Parties.

The story of fierce bad rabbit ill. by author. Warne, 1906. Subj: Animals – rabbits.

The story of Miss Moppet ill. by author. Warne, 1906. ISBN 0-7232-0612-0 Subj: Animals – cats. Behavior – trickery.

The tailor of Gloucester ill. by author. Warne, 1931. Subj: Animals – mice. Careers – tailors. Character traits – helpfulness.

The tale of Benjamin Bunny ill. by author. Warne, 1904. ISBN 0-7232-0595-7 Subj: Animals – rabbits. Behavior – misbehavior.

The tale of Jemima Puddle-Duck ill. by author. Warne, 1936. First pub. in 1910. Subj: Birds – ducks. Eggs.

The tale of Jemima Puddle-Duck and other farmyard tales: The tale of Mr. Jeremy Fisher; The tale of Mrs. Tiggy-Winkle; The tale of Pigling Bland ill. by author. Large format ed. Warne, 1987. ISBN 0-7232-3425-6 Subj: Animals. Birds.

The tale of Johnny Town-Mouse ill. by author. Warne, 1918. ISBN 0-7232-0604-X Subj: Animals – mice.

The tale of Little Pig Robinson ill. by author. Warne, 1930. Subj: Animals – pigs. Behavior – talking to strangers. Boats, ships. Shopping.

The tale of Mr. Jeremy Fisher ill. by author. Warne, 1934. ISBN 0-7232-6231-4 Subj: Frogs & toads. Sports – fishing.

The tale of Mr. Jeremy Fisher ill. by David Jorgensen. Picture Book Studio, 1989. ISBN 0-88708-094-4 Subj: Frogs & toads. Sports – fishing.

The tale of Mr. Tod ill. by author. Warne, 1939. First pub. in 1911. Subj: Animals – badgers. Animals – foxes. Animals – rabbits.

The tale of Mrs. Tittlemouse ill. by author. Warne, 1910. ISBN 0-7232-6235-7 Subj: Animals – mice. Character traits – cleanliness.

The tale of Mrs. Tiggy-Winkle ill. by author. Warne, 1905. Subj: Animals – hedgehogs. Clothing.

The tale of Mrs. Tittlemouse and other mouse stories: The tale of Johnny Town-Mouse; The tale of two bad mice; The tailor of Gloucester ill. by author. Large format ed. Warne, 1985. ISBN 0-7232-3324-1 Subj: Animals – mice.

The tale of Peter Rabbit ill. by Margot Apple. Troll, 1979. ISBN 0-89375-124-3 Subj: Animals – rabbits. Behavior – misbehavior.

The tale of Peter Rabbit ill. by author. Warne, 1902. ISBN 0-7232-0592-2 Subj: Animals – rabbits. Behavior – misbehavior. Farms.

The tale of Peter Rabbit and other stories ill. by Allen Atkinson. Knopf, 1982. ISBN 0-394-52845-X Subj: Animals.

The tale of Pigling Bland ill. by author. Warne, 1941, 1913. ISBN 0-7232-0606-6 Subj: Animals – pigs.

The tale of Squirrel Nutkin ill. by author. Warne, 1903. ISBN 0-7232-0593-0 Subj: Animals – squirrels. Birds – owls. Riddles & jokes. Seasons – fall.

The tale of the faithful dove ill. by Marie Angel. Warne, 1970. Subj: Birds – doves. Character traits – loyalty.

The tale of the Flopsy Bunnies ill. by author. Warne, 1909, 1937. ISBN 0-7232-0601-5 Subj: Animals – rabbits. Character traits – cleverness.

The tale of Timmy Tiptoes ill. by author. Warne, 1911, 1939. ISBN 0-7232-0603-1 Subj: Animals – squirrels.

The tale of Tom Kitten ill. by author. Warne, 1907. ISBN 0-7232-0599-X Subj: Animals – cats. Humorous stories.

The tale of Tuppeny ill. by Marie Angel. Warne, 1971. Subj: Animals – guinea pigs.

The tale of two bad mice ill. by author. Warne, 1904, 1934. Subj: Animals – mice. Behavior – misbehavior. Toys.

A treasury of Peter Rabbit and other stories ill. by author. Watts, 1978. Subj: Animals.

The two bad mice: pop-up book ill. by author. Warne, 1986. ISBN 0-7232-3360-8 Subj: Animals – mice. Behavior – misbehavior. Format, unusual – toy & movable books.

Where's Peter Rabbit? ill. by Colin Twinn. Warne, 1988. ISBN 0-7232-3519-8 Subj: Animals – rabbits. Behavior – misbehavior. Format, unusual.

Yours affectionately, Peter Rabbit: miniature letters ill. by author. Warne, 1984. ISBN 0-7232-3178-8 Subj: Animals. Communication.

Potter, Giselle. *The year I didn't go to school* ill. by author. Atheneum, 2002. ISBN 0-689-84730-0 Subj: Activities – traveling. Foreign lands – Italy. Puppets. Theater.

Potter, Stephen. *Squawky, the adventures of a clasperchoice* ill. by George Him. Lippincott, 1964. Subj: Birds – parakeets, parrots.

Potter, Tessa. *Digger, the story of a mole in the fall* ill. by Ken Lilly. Raintree, 1997. ISBN 0-8172-4623-1 Subj: Animals – moles. Seasons – fall. Weather – rain.

Potter, Tony. *See how it works: cars* ill. by Robin Lawrie. Aladdin, 1989. ISBN 0-689-71303-7 Subj: Automobiles. Format, unusual.

See how it works: earth movers ill. by Robin Lawrie. Aladdin, 1989. ISBN 0-689-71302-9 Subj: Format, unusual. Machines.

See how it works: planes ill. by Robin Lawrie. Aladdin, 1989. ISBN 0-689-71304-5 Subj: Airplanes, airports. Format, unusual.

See how it works: trucks ill. by Robin Lawrie. Aladdin, 1989. ISBN 0-689-71301-0 Subj: Format, unusual. Trucks.

Poulin, Stéphane. *Ah! belle cité = A beautiful city* ill. by author. Tundra, 1985. ISBN 0-88776-175-5 Subj: ABC books. Cities, towns. Foreign lands – Canada.

Benjamin and the pillow saga ill. by author. Firefly, 1989. ISBN 1-55037-069-3 Subj: Magic. Music.

Can you catch Josephine? ill. by author. Tundra, 1987. ISBN 0-88776-198-4 Subj: Animals – cats. Behavior – misbehavior. Foreign lands – Canada. School.

Have you seen Josephine? ill. by author. Tundra, 1986. ISBN 0-88776-180-1 Subj: Animals – cats. Behavior – running away. Foreign lands – Canada.

My mother's loves: stories and lies from my childhood ill. by author. Firefly, 1990. ISBN 1-55037-149-5 Subj: Behavior – growing up. Family life.

Travels for two ill. by author. Firefly, 1991. ISBN 1-55037-205-X Subj: Activities – traveling. Family life. Islands. Sea & seashore.

Pouyanne, Rési. *What I see hidden by the pond* ill. by Gerda Muller. Two Continents, 1977. Subj: Animals. Plants. Science.

Pouyanne, Thérèse. *The hippo* ill. by Caroline Binch. Rourke, 1983. ISBN 0-86592-855-X Subj: Animals – hippopotamuses.

Pow, Tom. *Tell me one thing, Dad* ill. by Ian Andrew. Candlewick, 2004. ISBN 0-7636-2474-8 Subj: Bedtime. Emotions – love. Family life – daughters. Family life – fathers. Games.

Who is the world for? ill. by Robert Ingpen. Candlewick, 2000. ISBN 0-7636-1280-4 Subj: Animals. Family life – parents. World.

Powell, Alma. *America's promise* ill. by Marsha Winborn. HarperCollins, 2003. ISBN 0-06-052173-2 Subj: Clubs, gangs. Communities, neighborhoods.

My little wagon [board book] ill. by Marsha Winborn. HarperFestival, 2003. ISBN 0-06-052193-7 Subj: Activities – playing. Animals – bears. Format, unusual – board books. Toys – wagons.

Powell, Consie. *Amazing apples* ill. by author. A. Whitman, 2003. ISBN 0-8075-0399-1 Subj: Careers – farmers. Food. Poetry. Trees.

A bold carnivore ill. by author. Roberts Rinehart, 1995. ISBN 1-57098-023-3 Subj: ABC books. Animals. Birds. Nature.

Old dog Cora and the Christmas tree ill. by author. A. Whitman, 1999. ISBN 0-8075-5968-7 Subj: Animals – dogs. Family life. Holidays – Christmas. Old age. Trees.

Powell, E. Sandy. *A chance to grow* ill. by Zulma Davila. Carolrhoda, 1992. ISBN 0-87614-741-4 Subj: Family life. Homeless. Poverty.

Powell, Jillian. *Eggs* ill. by author. Raintree, 1997. ISBN 0-8172-4759-9 Subj: Activities – baking, cooking. Eggs. Food.

Jumpers photos by author. Carolrhoda, 1992. ISBN 0-87614-702-3 Subj: Activities – jumping. Animals.

Powell, Polly. *Just dessert* ill. by author. Harcourt, 1996. ISBN 0-15-200383-5 Subj: Emotions – fear. Food. Imagination. Night.

Powell, Roxanne Dyer. *Cat, mouse and moon* ill. by Will Hillenbrand. Houghton Mifflin, 1994. ISBN 0-395-59348-4 Subj: Animals – cats. Animals – mice. Moon. Night.

Power, Barbara. *I wish Laura's mommy was my mommy* ill. by Marylin Hafner. Lippincott, 1979. ISBN 0-397-31838-3 Subj: Behavior – growing up. Behavior – wishing. Family life – mothers.

Powers, Daniel. *Jiro's pearl* ill. by author. Candlewick, 1997. ISBN 1-56402-631-0 Subj: Family life – grandmothers. Folk & fairy tales. Foreign lands – Japan. Illness.

Powers, Mary E. *Our teacher's in a wheelchair* photos by author. A. Whitman, 1986. ISBN 0-8075-6240-8 Subj: Careers – teachers. Handicaps. School.

Powzyk, Joyce Ann. *Tasmania: a wildlife journey* ill. by author. Lothrop, 1987. ISBN 0-688-06460-4 Subj: Animals. Foreign lands – Australia. Nature. Science.

Poydar, Nancy. *Busy Bea* ill. by author. McElderry, 1994. ISBN 0-689-50592-2 Subj: Behavior – lost & found possessions. Ethnic groups in the U.S. – African Americans. Family life – grandmothers. School.

Cool Ali ill. by author. McElderry, 1996. ISBN 0-689-80755-4 Subj: Activities – drawing. Cities, towns. Concepts – shape. Concepts – size. Seasons – summer.

First day, hooray! ill. by author. Holiday, 1999. ISBN 0-8234-1437-X Subj: Careers – bus drivers. Careers – school principals. Careers – teachers. School – first day.

Mailbox magic ill. by author. Holiday, 2000. ISBN 0-8234-1525-2 Subj: Character traits – patience. Letters, cards.

The perfectly horrible Halloween ill. by author. Holiday, 2001. ISBN 0-8234-1592-9 Subj: Clothing – Costumes. Holidays – Halloween. Problem solving. School.

Rhyme time Valentine ill. by author. Holiday, 2003. ISBN 0-8234-1684-4 Subj: Ethnic groups in the U.S. – African Americans. Holidays – Valentine's Day. Rhyming text. School. Weather – wind.

Snip, snip . . . snow! ill. by author. Holiday, 1997. ISBN 0-8234-1328-4 Subj: Activities – playing. Nature. School. Seasons – winter. Weather – snow.

Prager, Annabelle. *The baseball birthday party* ill. by Marilyn Mets. Random House, 1995. ISBN 0-679-94171-1 Subj: Behavior – mistakes. Ethnic groups in the U.S. Parties. Sports – baseball.

The spooky Halloween party ill. by Tomie de Paola. Pantheon, 1981. ISBN 0-394-94370-8 Subj: Holidays – Halloween. Parties.

The surprise party ill. by Tomie de Paola. Random House, 1988. ISBN 0-394-93235-8 Subj: Birthdays. Parties.

Prager, Ellen J. *Earthquakes* ill. by Susan Greenstein. National Geographic, 2002. ISBN 0-7922-8202-7 Subj: Earthquakes.

Pragoff, Fiona. *It's fun to be one* photos by author. Aladdin, 1994. ISBN 0-689-71813-6 Subj: Activities – playing. Babies.

It's great to be two photos by author. Aladdin, 1994. ISBN 0-689-71814-4 Subj: Activities – playing. Babies.

Let's find Teddy photos by author. Random House, 1992. ISBN 0-679-83501-6 Subj: Concepts. Games.

Odd one out ill. by author. Doubleday, 1989. ISBN 0-385-26410-0 Subj: Concepts. Format, unusual – board books. Games.

Opposites ill. by author. Doubleday, 1989. ISBN 0-385-26409-7 Subj: Concepts – opposites. Format, unusual – board books.

Shapes ill. by author. Doubleday, 1989. ISBN 0-385-26408-9 Subj: Concepts – shape. Concepts – size. Format, unusual – board books.

Prall, Jo. *My sister's special* ill. with photos. Childrens Pr., 1985. ISBN 0-516-03862-1 Subj: Family life – sisters. Handicaps.

Prater, John. *Along came Tom* ill. by author. Trafalgar Square, 1992. ISBN 0-370-31411-5 Subj: Family life.

The gift ill. by author. Viking, 1986. ISBN 0-670-80952-7 Subj: Behavior – wishing. Gifts. Wordless.

The greatest show on earth ill. by author. Candlewick, 1995. ISBN 1-56402-563-2 Subj: Circus. Clowns, jesters. Family life. Self-concept.

Hold tight! ill. by author. Barron's, 2003. ISBN 0-7641-2304-1 Subj: Animals – bears. Family life – grandfathers.

"No!" said Joe ill. by author. Candlewick, 1992. ISBN 1-56402-037-1 Subj: Behavior – misbehavior. Rhyming text. Shopping.

On Friday something funny happened ill. by author. Random House, 1988. ISBN 0-370-30449-7 Subj: Behavior – misbehavior. Days of the week, months of the year.

On top of the world ill. by author. Mondo, 1998. ISBN 1-57255-649-8 Subj: Animals. Night. Toys.

Once upon a picnic conceived & ill. by John Prater; text by Vivian French. Candlewick, 1996. ISBN 1-56402-810-0 Subj: Activities – picnicking. Imagination. Rhyming text.

Once upon a time conceived & ill. by John Prater; text by Vivian French. Candlewick, 1993. ISBN 1-56402-177-7 Subj: Imagination. Rhyming text.

The perfect day ill. by author. Dutton, 1987. ISBN 0-525-44282-0 Subj: Behavior – bad day. Sea & seashore.

You can't catch me! ill. by author. Salem House, 1986. ISBN 0-370-30594-9 Subj: Behavior – misbehavior. Behavior – running away.

Prather, Ray. *Double dog dare* ill. by author. Macmillan, 1975. ISBN 0-02-775040-X Subj: Animals – dogs. Humorous stories.

The ostrich girl ill. by author. Scribners, 1978. ISBN 0-684-15889-2 Subj: Folk & fairy tales. Foreign lands – Africa. Forest, woods. Reptiles – snakes. Witches.

Pratt, Kristin Joy. *A fly in the sky* ill. by author. Dawn, 1996. ISBN 1-883220-40-8 Subj: ABC books. Animals. Birds. Insects. Insects – flies.

A swim through the sea ill. by author. Dawn, 1994. ISBN 1-883220-03-3 Subj: ABC books. Crustaceans. Fish. Sea & seashore.

Pratt, Pierre. *Car* ill. by author. Candlewick, 2001. ISBN 0-7636-1390-8 Subj: Animals. Animals – elephants. Animals – mice. Automobiles. Birds.

Home ill. by author. Candlewick, 2001. ISBN 0-7636-1389-4 Subj: Animals – elephants. Animals – mice. Format, unusual – board books. Friendship. Homes, houses.

I see . . . my mom/I see . . . my dad ill. by author. Annick, 2001. ISBN 1-55037-624-1 Subj: Anatomy. Family life – parents. Format, unusual.

I see . . . my sister/I see . . . my cat ill. by author. Annick, 2001. ISBN 1-55037-625-X Subj: Anatomy. Animals – cats. Family life – parents. Format, unusual.

Park ill. by author. Candlewick, 2001. ISBN 0-7636-1391-6 Subj: Animals. Animals – elephants. Animals – mice. Format, unusual – board books. Parks.

Shopping ill. by author. Candlewick, 2001. ISBN 0-7636-1392-4 Subj: Activities – shopping. Animals – elephants. Animals – mice. Clothing – shoes. Format, unusual – board books.

Prebeg, Rick A. *Jungle Jack Hanna's safari adventure* (Hanna, Jack)

Precek, Katharine Wilson. *Penny in the road* ill. by Patricia Cullen-Clark. Macmillan, 1989. ISBN 0-02-774970-3 Subj: Behavior – lost & found possessions. U.S. history.

Preiss, Byron. *The first crazy word book: verbs* by Byron Preiss & Ralph Reese; ill. by Ralph Reese. Watts, 1982. ISBN 0-531-04439-4 Subj: Language.

Preller, James. *Cardinal and sunflower* ill. by Huy Voun Lee. HarperCollins, 1998. ISBN 0-06-026223-0 Subj: Birds – cardinals. Flowers. Nature.

Prelutsky, Jack. *Awful Ogre's awful day* ill. by Paul O. Zelinsky. Greenwillow, 2001. ISBN 0-688-07779-X Subj: Mythical creatures – ogres. Poetry.

The baby uggs are hatching ill. by James Stevenson. Greenwillow, 1982. ISBN 0-688-00923-9 Subj: Humorous stories. Imagination. Monsters. Poetry.

Beneath a blue umbrella ill. by Garth Williams. Greenwillow, 1990. ISBN 0-688-06429-9 Subj: Animals. Poetry.

Brave little Pete of Geranium Street (Lagercrantz, Rose)

Circus ill. by Arnold Lobel. Macmillan, 1974. ISBN 0-02-775060-4 Subj: Circus. Poetry.

For laughing out louder: more poems to tickle your funnybone (For laughing out louder)

The frogs wore red suspenders ill. by Petra Mathers. Greenwillow, 2002. ISBN 0-688-16720-9 Subj: Poetry.

Halloween countdown ill. by Dan Yaccarino. HarperFestival, 2002. ISBN 0-06-000512-2 Subj: Counting, numbers. Format, unusual – board books. Ghosts. Holidays – Halloween. Poetry.

Imagine that! poems of never-was (Imagine that! poems of never-was)

The mean old mean hyena ill. by Arnold Lobel. Greenwillow, 1978. ISBN 0-688-84163-5 Subj: Animals – hyenas. Character traits – meanness. Rhyming text.

Monday's troll ill. by Peter Sis. Greenwillow, 1996. ISBN 0-688-09644-1 Subj: Fairies. Mythical creatures – trolls. Poetry. Witches.

The pack rat's day and other poems ill. by Margaret Bloy Graham. Macmillan, 1974. ISBN 0-02-775050-7 Subj: Animals. Poetry.

The queen of Eene ill. by Victoria Chess. Greenwillow, 1978. ISBN 0-688-84144-9 Subj: Humorous stories. Poetry.

Rainy rainy Saturday ill. by Marylin Hafner. Greenwillow, 1980. ISBN 0-688-84252-6 Subj: Poetry. Weather – rain.

The Random House book of poetry for children ill. by Arnold Lobel. Random House, 1983. ISBN 0-394-95010-0 Subj: Humorous stories. Poetry.

Read-aloud rhymes for the very young ill. by Marc Brown. Knopf, 1986. ISBN 0-394-97218-X Subj: Poetry.

Ride a purple pelican ill. by Garth Williams. Greenwillow, 1986. ISBN 0-688-04031-4 Subj: Imagination. Poetry.

The snopp on the sidewalk and other poems ill. by Byron Barton. Greenwillow, 1977. ISBN 0-688-84084-1 Subj: Humorous stories. Imagination. Poetry.

The terrible tiger ill. by Arnold Lobel. Macmillan, 1970. ISBN 0-689-71300-2 Subj: Animals – tigers. Cumulative tales. Rhyming text.

Tyrannosaurus was a beast ill. by Arnold Lobel. Greenwillow, 1988. ISBN 0-688-06443-4 Subj: Dinosaurs. Poetry.

The wild baby (Lindgren, Barbro)

The wild baby gets a puppy (Lindgren, Barbro)

The wild baby goes to sea (Lindgren, Barbro)

Wild witches' ball ill. by Kelly Asbury. HarperFestival, 2004. ISBN 0-06-052972-5 Subj: Counting, numbers. Holidays – Halloween. Rhyming text. Witches.

Presencer, Alain. *Roaring lion tales* ill. by Ron Van der Meer. HarperCollins, 1984. ISBN 0-216-91606-2 Subj: Animals – lions. Folk & fairy tales. Format, unusual – toy & movable books.

Preston, Edna Mitchell. *Horrible Hepzibah* ill. by Ray Cruz. Viking, 1971. ISBN 0-670-37877-1 Subj: Behavior – misbehavior. Humorous stories.

Monkey in the jungle ill. by Clement Hurd. Viking, 1968. Subj: Animals – monkeys. Bedtime. Night. Sleep.

One dark night ill. by Kurt Werth. Viking, 1969. ISBN 0-670-52585-5 Subj: Cumulative tales. Holidays – Halloween.

Pop Corn and Ma Goodness ill. by Robert Andrew Parker. Viking, 1969. Subj: Caldecott award honor books. Humorous stories. Rhyming text. Songs. Weather – rain.

Squawk to the moon, little goose ill. by Barbara Cooney. Viking, 1974. ISBN 0-670-66609-2 Subj: Animals – foxes. Behavior – misbehavior. Birds – geese. Moon.

Preston, Tim. *Pumpkin moon* ill. by Simon Bartram. Dutton, 2001. ISBN 0-525-46713-0 Subj: Holidays – Halloween. Moon.

Preus, Margi. *The legend of the lady slipper: an Ojibwe tale* (Lunge-Larsen, Lise)

Preussler, Otfried. *The tale of the unicorn* trans. by Lenny Hort; ill. by Gennady Spirin. Dial, 1989. ISBN 0-8037-0583-2 Subj: Folk & fairy tales. Mythical creatures – unicorns.

Price, Christine. *One is God: two old counting songs* ill. by author. Warne, 1970. Subj: Counting, numbers. Religion. Songs.

Price, Dorothy E. *Speedy gets around* ill. by Betsy Warren. Steck-Vaughn, 1965. Subj: Animals – chipmunks. Camps, camping.

Price, Hope Lynne. *These hands* ill. by Bryan Collier. Hyperion, 1999. ISBN 0-7868-2320-8 Subj: Anatomy – hands. Ethnic groups in the U.S. – African Americans. Family life – mothers. Rhyming text.

Price, Kathy (Kathy Z.). *The Bourbon Street musicians* ill. by Andrew Glass. Clarion, 2002. ISBN 0-618-04076-5 Subj: Animals. Careers – musicians. Crime. Folk & fairy tales. Old age.

Price, Leontyne. *Aïda* ill. by Leo & Diane Dillon. Harcourt, 1990. Retells the story of Giuseppe Verdi's opera. ISBN 0-15-200405-X Subj: Emotions – love. Foreign lands – Egypt. Music. Royalty.

Price, Mathew. *Do you see what I see?* ill. by Sue Porter. HarperCollins, 1986. ISBN 0-694-00002-7 Subj: Animals. Behavior – lost & found possessions. Circus. Format, unusual.

Don't worry, Alfie ill. by Emma Chichester Clark. Orchard, 1999. ISBN 0-531-30127-3 Subj: Animals. Animals – bears. Family life – mothers.

Dumbo ill. by Atsuko Morozumi. Disney Pr., 2000. ISBN 0-7868-3274-6 Subj: Animals – elephants. Circus.

Have you seen my sister? ill. by Errol Le Cain. Harcourt, 1992. ISBN 0-15-200467-X Subj: Family life – sisters. Format, unusual. Friendship. Imagination. Toys.

Patch and the rabbits ill. by Emma Chichester Clark. Orchard, 2000. ISBN 0-531-30265-2 Subj: Animals – dogs. Animals – rabbits. Dreams. Format, unusual – toy & movable books.

Patch finds a friend ill. by Emma Chichester Clark. Orchard, 2000. ISBN 0-531-30264-4 Subj: Animals – cats. Animals – dogs. Friendship.

Peekaboo! ill. by Jean Claverie. Knopf, 1985. ISBN 0-394-87142-1 Subj: Family life. Format, unusual – toy & movable books.

Where's Alfie? ill. by Emma Chichester Clark. Orchard, 1999. ISBN 0-531-30126-5 Subj: Animals – bears. Behavior – hiding. Family life – mothers.

Price, Michelle. *Mean Melissa* ill. by author. Bradbury, 1977. ISBN 0-87888-126-3 Subj: Character traits – meanness. School.

Price, Roger. *The last little dragon* ill. by Mamoru Funai. HarperCollins, 1969. Subj: Behavior – dissatisfaction. Dragons.

Priceman, Marjorie. *Emeline at the circus* ill. by author. Knopf, 1999. ISBN 0-679-87685-5 Subj: Careers – teachers. Circus. School.

Friend or frog ill. by author. Houghton Mifflin, 1989. ISBN 0-395-44523-X Subj: Friendship. Frogs & toads.

Froggie went a courting (A frog he would a-wooing go [folksong])

How to make an apple pie and see the world ill. by author. Knopf, 1994. ISBN 0-679-93705-6 Subj: Activities – baking, cooking. Activities – traveling. Food.

It's me, Marva! ill. by author. Knopf, 2001. ISBN 0-679-98993-5 Subj: Careers – inventors. Concepts – color. Optical illusions.

My nine lives / by Clio ill. by author. Atheneum, 1998. ISBN 0-689-81135-7 Subj: Animals – cats. Memories, memory.

Princess Picky ill. by author. Roaring Brook, 2002. ISBN 0-7613-2418-6 Subj: Activities – flying. Character traits – stubbornness. Food. Royalty – princesses.

Price-Thomas, Brian. *The magic ark* ill. by author. Crown, 1987. ISBN 0-517-56705-9 Subj: Animals. Imagination.

Priddy, Roger. *Baby's book of nature* ill. by author. DK, 1995. ISBN 0-7894-0003-0 Subj: Concepts – color. Concepts – shape. Nature.

My big book of everything ill. by author. DK, 1996. ISBN 0-7894-0998-4 Subj: Dictionaries.

Priest, Robert H. *The old pirate of Central Park* ill. by author. Houghton Mifflin, 1999. ISBN 0-395-90505-2 Subj: Activities – playing. Boats, ships. Toys.

The pirate's eye ill. by author. Houghton, 2005. ISBN 0-618-43990-0 Subj: Activities – drawing. Anatomy – eyes. Behavior – lost & found possessions. Character traits – generosity. Pirates.

Priestley, Alice. *Someone is reading this book* ill. by author. Firefly, 1998. ISBN 1-55037-448-6 Subj: Activities – flying. Format, unusual – toy & movable books. Giants. Royalty – princes.

Prigger, Mary Skillings. *Aunt Minnie and the twister* ill. by Betsy Lewin. Clarion, 2002. ISBN 0-618-11136-0 Subj: Family life – aunts, uncles. Farms. Homes, houses. Weather – tornadoes.

Aunt Minnie McGranahan ill. by Betsy Lewin. Clarion, 1999. Subj: Character traits – orderliness. Family life – aunts, uncles. Family life – brothers & sisters. Orphans.

Primavera, Elise. *Auntie Claus* ill. by author. Harcourt, 1999. ISBN 0-15-201909-X Subj: Family life – aunts, uncles. Foreign lands – Arctic. Holidays – Christmas. Santa Claus.

Auntie Claus and the key to Christmas ill. by author. Harcourt, 2002. ISBN 0-15-202441-7 Subj: Family life – aunts, uncles. Foreign lands – Arctic. Holidays – Christmas. Santa Claus.

Basil and Maggie ill. by author. Lippincott, 1983. ISBN 0-397-32028-0 Subj: Animals – horses, ponies. Character traits – appearance.

Plantpet ill. by author. Putnam, 1994. ISBN 0-399-22627-3 Subj: Gardens, gardening. Pets. Plants.

Prince, Pamela. *The secret world of teddy bears* photos by Elaine Faris Keenan. Crown, 1983. ISBN 0-517-55022-9 Subj: Poetry. Toys – bears.

The prince who knew his fate: *an ancient Egyptian tale* trans. from hieroglyphs & ill. by Lise Manniche. Putnam, 1982. ISBN 0-399-20850-X Subj: Folk & fairy tales. Foreign lands – Egypt. Hieroglyphics. Magic. Royalty – princes.

Pringle, Laurence P. *Bear hug* ill. by Kate Salley Palmer. Boyds Mills, 2003. ISBN 1-56397-876-8 Subj: Animals – bears. Camps, camping. Family life – fathers.

Crows ill. by Bob Marstall. Boyds Mills, 2002. ISBN 1-56397-899-7 Subj: Birds – crows. Science.

Everybody has a bellybutton ill. by Clare Wood. Boyds Mills, 1997. ISBN 1-56397-009-0 Subj: Anatomy – navels. Birth. Family life.

Jesse builds a road ill. by Leslie Holt Morrill. Macmillan, 1989. ISBN 0-02-775311-5 Subj: Imagination. Machines. Roads.

Naming the cat ill. by Katherine Potter. Walker, 1997. ISBN 0-8027-8622-7 Subj: Animals – cats. Names. Pets.

Octopus hug ill. by Kate Salley Palmer. Boyds Mills, 1993. ISBN 1-56397-034-1 Subj: Activities – playing. Family life.

One room school ill. by Barbara Garrison. Boyds Mills, 1998. ISBN 1-56397-583-1 Subj: School. U.S. history. War.

Snakes ill. by Meryl Henderson. Boyds Mills, 2004. ISBN 1-59078-003-5 Subj: Reptiles – snakes. Science.

Prins, Johanna H. *The princess in the kitchen garden* (Heymans, Annemie)

Prins, Johanna W. *The princess in the kitchen garden* (Heymans, Annemie)

Proimos, James. *Joe's wish* ill. by author. Harcourt, 1998. ISBN 0-15-201831-X Subj: Behavior – wishing. Family life – grandfathers. Old age.

The loudness of Sam ill. by author. Harcourt, 1999. ISBN 0-15-202087-X Subj: Cities, towns. Emotions. Family life – aunts, uncles.

Prokofiev, Sergei Sergeievitch. *Peter and the wolf* adapt. by Selina Hastings; ill. by Reg Cartwright. Holt, 1987. ISBN 0-8050-0408-4 Subj: Animals – wolves. Character traits – cleverness. Folk & fairy tales. Foreign lands – Russia. Music. Musical instruments.

Peter and the wolf ill. by Warren Chappell; foreword by Serge Koussevitsky; calligraphy by Hollis Holland. Schocken, 1981, c1940. ISBN 0-8052-0684-1 Subj: Animals – wolves. Character traits – cleverness. Folk & fairy tales. Foreign lands – Russia. Music. Musical instruments.

Peter and the wolf ill. by Barbara Cooney. Viking, 1986. ISBN 0-670-80849-0 Subj: Animals – wolves. Character traits – clever-ness. Folk & fairy tales. Foreign lands – Russia. Format, unusual – toy & movable books. Music. Musical instruments.

Peter and the wolf adapt. by Gerlinde Wiencirz; ill. by Julia Gukova; trans. by Anthea Bell. North-South, 1999. ISBN 0-7358-1189-X Subj: Animals – wolves. Character traits – cleverness. Folk & fairy tales. Foreign lands – Russia. Music. Musical instruments.

Peter and the wolf ill. by Frans Haacken. Watts, 1961. Subj: Animals – wolves. Character traits – cleverness. Folk & fairy tales. Foreign lands – Russia. Music. Musical instruments.

Peter and the wolf ill. by Alan Howard. Transatlantic, 1954. Subj: Animals – wolves. Character traits – cleverness. Folk & fairy tales. Foreign lands – Russia. Music. Musical instruments.

Peter and the wolf trans. by Maria Carlson; ill. by Charles Mikolaycak. Viking, 1982. ISBN 0-670-54919-3 Subj: Animals – wolves. Character traits – cleverness. Folk & fairy tales. Foreign lands – Russia. Music. Musical instruments.

Peter and the wolf adapt. by Loriot; ill. by Jörg Müller. Knopf, 1986. Book-cassette included. ISBN 0-394-88417-5 Subj: Animals – wolves. Character traits – cleverness. Folk & fairy tales. Foreign lands – Russia. Music. Musical instruments.

Peter and the wolf trans. by Patricia Crampton; ill. by Josef Palecek. Picture Book Studio, 1987. ISBN 0-88708-049-9 Subj: Animals – wolves. Character traits – cleverness. Folk & fairy tales. Foreign lands – Russia. Music. Musical instruments.

Peter and the wolf retold by Ann Herring; ill. by Kozo Shimizu; photos by Yasugi Yajima. Gakken, 1971. Subj: Animals – wolves. Character traits – cleverness. Folk & fairy tales. Foreign lands – Russia. Music. Musical instruments.

Peter and the wolf retold & ill. by Vladimir Vagin. Scholastic, 2000. ISBN 0-590-38608-5 Subj: Animals – wolves. Character traits – cleverness. Folk & fairy tales. Foreign lands – Russia. Music. Musical instruments.

Peter and the wolf ill. by Erna Voigt. Godine, 1980. ISBN 0-87923-331-1 Subj: Animals – wolves. Character traits – cleverness. Folk & fairy tales. Foreign lands – Russia. Music. Musical instruments.

Propp, James. *Tuscanini* ill. by Ellen Weiss. Bradbury, 1992. ISBN 0-02-774911-8 Subj: Animals – elephants. Crime. Zoos.

Prose, Francine. *The angel's mistake* ill. by Mark Podwal. Greenwillow, 1997. ISBN 0-688-14906-5 Subj: Angels. Behavior – mistakes. Folk & fairy tales. Jewish culture.

The demons' mistake ill. by Mark Podwal. Greenwillow, 2000. ISBN 0-688-17566-X Subj: Folk & fairy tales. Jewish culture. Monsters.

Dybbuk ill. by Mark Podwal. Greenwillow, 1996. ISBN 0-688-14308-3 Subj: Angels. Folk & fairy tales. Jewish culture. Weddings.

You never know ill. by Mark Podwal. Greenwillow, 1998. ISBN 0-688-15807-2 Subj: Behavior – secrets. Careers – shoemakers. Folk & fairy tales. Jewish culture.

Provencher, Rose-Marie. *Mouse cleaning* ill. by Bernadette Pons. Holt, 2001. ISBN 0-8050-6240-8 Subj: Animals – mice. Behavior – messy. Character traits – cleanliness. Homes, houses.

Provensen, Alice. *A book of seasons* by Alice & Martin Provensen; ill. by authors. Random House, 1976. ISBN 0-394-83242-6 Subj: Seasons.

The glorious flight: across the channel with Louis Blériot by Alice & Martin Provensen; ill. by authors. Viking, 1983. ISBN 0-14-050729-9 Subj: Activities – flying. Airplanes, airports. Caldecott award books.

Karen's opposites by Alice & Martin Provensen; ill. by authors. Golden Pr., 1963. Subj: Concepts – opposites. Rhyming text.

My little hen by Alice & Martin Provensen; ill. by authors. Random House, 1973. ISBN 0-394-92684-6 Subj: Birds – chickens.

Our animal friends at Maple Hill Farm by Alice & Martin Provensen; ill. by authors. Random House, 1992, 1974. ISBN 0-394-92123-2 Subj: Animals. Farms.

An owl and three pussycats by Alice & Martin Provensen; ill. by authors. Browndeer, 1994. ISBN 0-15-200183-2 Subj: Family life. Farms. Pets.

Punch in New York ill. by author. Viking, 1991. ISBN 0-670-82790-8 Subj: Behavior – misbehavior. Cities, towns. Puppets.

Shaker Lane by Alice & Martin Provensen; ill. by authors. Viking, 1987. ISBN 0-670-81568-3 Subj: Cities, towns. Moving. Poverty.

Town and country by Alice & Martin Provensen; ill. by authors. Crown, 1984. ISBN 0-15-200182-4 Subj: Cities, towns. Country.

The year at Maple Hill Farm by Alice & Martin Provensen; ill. by authors. Atheneum, 1978. ISBN 0-689-20494-9 Subj: Animals. Days of the week, months of the year. Farms. Seasons.

Provensen, Martin. *A book of seasons* (Provensen, Alice)

The glorious flight: across the channel with Louis Blériot (Provensen, Alice)

Karen's opposites (Provensen, Alice)

My little hen (Provensen, Alice)

Our animal friends at Maple Hill Farm (Provensen, Alice)

An owl and three pussycats (Provensen, Alice)

Shaker Lane (Provensen, Alice)

Town and country (Provensen, Alice)

The year at Maple Hill Farm (Provensen, Alice)

Prøysen, Alf. *Christmas eve at Santa's* ill. by author. Farrar, 1992. ISBN 91-29-62066-X Subj: Careers – carpenters. Family life. Holidays – Christmas. Santa Claus.

Mrs. Pepperpot and the moose trans. from Swedish by Richard E. Fisher; ill. by Björn Berg. Farrar, 1991. ISBN 91-29-59924-5 Subj: Animals – moose. Character traits – smallness. Concepts – size.

Prunier, James. *Trains* (Trains)

Prusski, Jeffrey. *Bring back the deer* ill. by Neil Waldman. Harcourt, 1988. ISBN 0-15-200418-1 Subj: Animals – deer. Animals – wolves. Family life. Forest, woods. Indians of North America. Seasons – winter. Sports – hunting.

Pryor, Ainslie. *The baby blue cat and the dirty dog brothers* ill. by author. Viking, 1987. ISBN 0-670-81781-3 Subj: Activities – bathing. Animals – cats. Animals – dogs.

The baby blue cat and the smiley worm doll ill. by author. Viking, 1990. ISBN 0-670-83531-5 Subj: Animals – cats. Behavior – lost & found possessions. Toys – dolls.

The baby blue cat and the whole batch of cookies ill. by author. Viking, 1989. ISBN 0-670-81782-1 Subj: Behavior – lost & found possessions. Toys – dolls.

The baby blue cat who said no ill. by author. Viking, 1988. ISBN 0-670-81780-5 Subj: Animals – cats. Bedtime.

Pryor, Bonnie. *Amanda and April* ill. by Diane de Groat. Morrow, 1986. ISBN 0-688-05870-1 Subj: Animals – pigs. Family life – sisters. Parties. Sibling rivalry.

The beaver boys ill. by Karen Lee Baker. Morrow, 1991. ISBN 0-688-08703-5 Subj: Animals – beavers. Homes, houses. Moving.

The dream jar ill. by Mark Graham. Morrow, 1996. ISBN 0-688-13062-3 Subj: Activities – working. Cities, towns. Ethnic groups in the U.S. – Russian Americans. Family life. Immigrants.

Greenbrook farm ill. by Mark Graham. S&S, 1991. ISBN 0-671-69205-4 Subj: Animals. Babies. Farms.

The house on Maple Street ill. by Beth Peck. Morrow, 1987. ISBN 0-688-06381-0 Subj: U.S. history.

Lottie's dream ill. by Mark Graham. S&S, 1992. ISBN 0-671-74774-6 Subj: Farms. Sea & seashore. U.S. history – frontier & pioneer life.

Louie and Dan are friends ill. by Elizabeth J. Miles. Morrow, 1997. ISBN 0-688-08561-X Subj: Animals – mice. Family life – brothers. Friendship.

Merry Christmas, Amanda and April ill. by Diane de Groat. Morrow, 1990. ISBN 0-688-07545-2 Subj: Animals – pigs. Family life – sisters. Holidays – Christmas.

Mr. Munday and the rustlers ill. by Wallop Manyum. Prentice-Hall, 1988. ISBN 0-13-604737-8 Subj: Crime. Farms.

Mr. Munday and the space creatures ill. by Lee Lorenz. S&S, 1989. ISBN 0-671-67114-6 Subj: Aliens. Careers – postal workers. Space & space ships.

The porcupine mouse ill. by Maryjane Begin. Morrow, 1988. ISBN 0-688-07154-6 Subj: Animals – mice. Character traits – bravery. Emotions – fear. Sibling rivalry.

The pudgy book of babies ill. by Kathy Wilburn. Putnam, 1984. ISBN 0-448-10207-2 Subj: Babies. Format, unusual – board books.

The pudgy book of farm animals ill. by Julie Durrell. Putnam, 1984. ISBN 0-448-10211-0 Subj: Animals. Farms. Format, unusual – board books.

The pudgy book of here we go ill. by Beth Weiner Lipson. Putnam, 1984. ISBN 0-448-10208-0 Subj: Format, unusual – board books.

The pudgy book of make-believe ill. by Andrea Brooks. Putnam, 1984. ISBN 0-448-10209-9 Subj: Format, unusual – board books. Imagination.

The pudgy book of Mother Goose ill. by Richard Walz. Putnam, 1984. ISBN 0-448-10212-9 Subj: Format, unusual – board books. Nursery rhymes.

The pudgy book of toys ill. by Julie Durrell. Grosset, 1983. ISBN 0-448-10201-3 Subj: Format, unusual – board books. Toys.

The pudgy bunny book ill. by Ruth Sanderson. Putnam, 1984. ISBN 0-448-10210-2 Subj: Animals – rabbits. Format, unusual – board books.

The pudgy fingers counting book ill. by Doug Cushman. Grosset, 1983. ISBN 0-448-10202-1 Subj: Birthdays. Counting, numbers. Format, unusual – board books.

The pudgy pals ill. by Kathy Wilburn. Grosset, 1983. Subj: Format, unusual – board books.

The pudgy pat-a-cake book ill. by Terri Super. Grosset, 1983. ISBN 0-448-10204-8 Subj: Format, unusual – board books. Games.

The pudgy peek-a-boo book ill. by Amye Rosenberg. Grosset, 1983. ISBN 0-448-10205-6 Subj: Format, unusual – board books. Games.

The pudgy rock-a-bye book ill. by Kathy Wilburn. Grosset, 1983. ISBN 0-448-10206-4 Subj: Format, unusual – board books.

Pullman, Philip. *Puss in boots: the adventures of that most enterprising feline* ill. by Ian Beck. Knopf, 2000. ISBN 0-375-81354-3 Subj: Animals – cats. Character traits – cleverness. Folk & fairy tales. Foreign lands – France. Royalty – kings.

Pulsifer, Marjorie P. *Bikes* (Baugh, Dolores M.)

Let's go (Baugh, Dolores M.)

Let's see the animals (Baugh, Dolores M.)

Let's take a trip (Baugh, Dolores M.)

Slides (Baugh, Dolores M.)

Supermarket (Baugh, Dolores M.)

Swings (Baugh, Dolores M.)

Trucks and cars to ride (Baugh, Dolores M.)

Pulver, Robin. *Alicia's tutu* ill. by Mark Graham. Dial, 1997. ISBN 0-8037-1933-7 Subj: Activities – dancing. Ballet. Behavior – wishing. Family life. Family life – grandmothers. Furniture – beds.

Axle Annie ill. by Tedd Arnold. Dial, 1999. ISBN 0-8037-2096-3 Subj: Careers – bus drivers. School. Weather – snow.

Christmas for a kitten ill. by Layne Johnson. A. Whitman, 2003. ISBN 0-8075-1151-X Subj: Animals – cats. Holidays – Christmas. Santa Claus.

Homer and the house next door ill. by Annie Levin. Four Winds, 1994. ISBN 0-02-775457-X Subj: Animals – dogs. Moving.

Mrs. Toggle and the dinosaur ill. by R. W. Alley. Four Winds, 1991. ISBN 0-02-775452-9 Subj: Careers – teachers. Dinosaurs. Prehistory. School.

Mrs. Toggle's beautiful blue shoe ill. by R. W. Alley. Four Winds, 1991. ISBN 0-02-775456-1 Subj: Careers – teachers. Clothing – shoes. School.

Mrs. Toggle's zipper ill. by R. W. Alley. Four Winds, 1990. ISBN 0-02-775451-0 Subj: Careers – teachers. Clothing – coats. Humorous stories. School.

Nobody's mother is in second grade ill. by G. Brian Karas. Dial, 1992. ISBN 0-8037-1211-1 Subj: Family life – mothers. Plants. School.

Way to go, Alex! ill. by Elizabeth Wolf. A. Whitman, 1999. ISBN 0-8075-1583-3 Subj: Family life – brothers & sisters. Handicaps. Sports – Special Olympics.

Pumphrey, Jerome. *Creepy things are scaring me* ill. by Rosanne Litzinger. HarperCollins, 2003. ISBN 0-06-028963-5 Subj: Bedtime. Emotions – fear. Rhyming text.

Puner, Helen Walker. *Daddys, what they do all day* ill. by Roger Antoine Duvoisin. Lothrop, 1946. Subj: Activities – working. Careers. Family life – fathers. Rhyming text.

The sitter who didn't sit ill. by Roger Antoine Duvoisin. Lothrop, 1949. Subj: Activities – babysitting. Humorous stories. Rhyming text.

Puppies and kittens photos by Walter Chandoha. Platt, 1983. ISBN 0-448-40874-0 Subj: Animals – cats. Animals – dogs. Format, unusual – board books. Rhyming text.

Purcell, John Wallace. *African animals* ill. with photos. Rev. ed. Childrens Pr., 1982. ISBN 0-516-01665-2 Subj: Animals. Foreign lands – Africa.

Purdy, Carol. *Iva Dunnit and the big wind* ill. by Steven Kellogg. Dial, 1985. ISBN 0-8037-0184-5 Subj: Family life. Weather – wind.

Least of all ill. by Tim Arnold. Macmillan, 1987. ISBN 0-689-50404-7 Subj: Activities – working. Books, reading. Family life. Self-concept.

Mrs. Merriwether's musical cat ill. by Petra Mathers. Putnam, 1994. ISBN 0-399-22543-9 Subj: Animals – cats. Music. Musical instruments – pianos.

Puricelli, Luigi. *In my garden* (Cristini, Ermanno)

In the pond (Cristini, Ermanno)

In the woods (Cristini, Ermanno)

Purmell, Ann. *Apple cider making days* ill. by Joanne Friar. Millbrook, 2002. ISBN 0-7613-2364-3 Subj: Careers – farmers. Family life – grandfathers. Farms. Food.

Where wild babies sleep ill. by Lorianne Siomades. Boyds Mills, 2003. ISBN 1-59078-049-3 Subj: Animals – babies. Bedtime. Night. Sleep.

Pursell, Margaret Sanford. *Jessie the chicken* orig. trans. by Dyan Hammarberg; photos by Claudie Fayn-Rodriguez; ill. by L'Enc Matte. Carolrhoda, 1977. Based on Anne Marie Pajot's Picota la poule. ISBN 0-8761-4074-6 Subj: Birds – chickens. Eggs.

A look at birth ill. by Maria S. Forrai. Lerner, 1976. ISBN 0-8225-1307-2 Subj: Babies. Birth. Science.

A look at divorce ill. by Maria S. Forrai. Lerner, 1976. ISBN 0-8225-1301-3 Subj: Divorce. Emotions.

Polly the guinea pig orig. trans. by Dyan Hammarberg; photos by Antoinette Barrère; ill. by L'Enc Matte. Carolrhoda, 1977. Original ed. published under title: Amilcar le cochon d'Inde. ISBN 0-8761-4077-0 Subj: Animals – guinea pigs. Pets. Science.

Shelley the sea gull trans. by Dyan Hammarberg; photos by Jean Christian David, Guy Dhuit, & Claudie Fayn-Rodriguez. Carolrhoda, 1977. Original ed. published under title: Gwelan le goeland. ISBN 0-8761-4083-5 Subj: Birds – seagulls. Pets. Science.

Sprig the tree frog trans. by Dyan Hammarberg; ill. by Yves Vial. Carolrhoda, 1976. ISBN 0-8761-4064-9 Subj: Eggs. Frogs & toads. Science.

Purviance, Susan. *Alphabet Annie announces an all-American album* (O'Shell, Marcia)

Pushkin, Aleksandr Sergeevich. *The tale of Tsar Saltan* ill. by Gennady Spirin. Dial, 1996. ISBN 0-8037-2001-7 Subj: Emotions – envy, jealousy. Folk & fairy tales. Foreign lands – Russia. Royalty.

Puttock, Simon. *Big bad wolf is good* ill. by Lynne Chapman. Sterling, 2002. ISBN 0-8069-0027-X Subj: Animals. Animals – wolves. Behavior. Friendship.

A ladder to the stars ill. by Alison Jay. Holt, 2001. ISBN 0-8050-6783-3 Subj: Activities – dancing. Behavior – wishing. Old age. Stars.

Squeaky clean ill. by Mary McQuillan. Little, 2002. ISBN 0-316-78816-3 Subj: Activities – bathing. Animals – pigs. Hygiene.

A story for Hippo ill. by Alison Jay. Scholastic, 2001. ISBN 0-439-26219-4 Subj: Animals – hippopotamuses. Animals – monkeys. Death. Emotions – grief. Friendship.

Pyle, Howard. *The Swan Maiden* ill. by Robert Sauber. Holiday, 1994. ISBN 0-8234-1088-9 Subj: Behavior – stealing. Birds – swans. Folk & fairy tales. Royalty – princes. Trees.

Quackenbush, Robert M. *Batbaby* ill. by author. Random House, 1997. ISBN 0-679-98541-7 Subj: Animals – bats. Animals – squirrels. Bedtime. Weather – storms.

Batbaby finds a home ill. by author. Random House, 2001. ISBN 0-375-80430-7 Subj: Animals – bats. Homes, houses.

Chuck lends a paw ill. by author. Clarion, 1986. ISBN 0-89919-363-3 Subj: Animals – mice. Character traits – helpfulness.

City trucks ill. by author. A. Whitman, 1981. ISBN 0-8075-1163-3 Subj: Cities, towns. Trucks.

Clementine ill. by author. Lippincott, 1974. ISBN 0-397-31506-6 Subj: Folk & fairy tales. Music. Songs. U.S. history.

First grade jitters ill. by author. Lippincott, 1982. ISBN 0-397-31981-9 Subj: Animals – rabbits. School – first day.

Funny bunnies ill. by author. Houghton Mifflin, 1984. ISBN 0-8991-9267-X Subj: Animals – rabbits. Humorous stories.

Funny bunnies on the run ill. by author. Clarion, 1989. ISBN 0-89919-771-X Subj: Animals – rabbits. Family life. Parties. Power failures.

Henry babysits ill. by author. Parents' Magazine Pr., 1983. ISBN 0-8193-1107-3 Subj: Activities – babysitting. Birds – ducks.

Henry's world tour ill. by author. Doubleday, 1992. ISBN 0-385-42010-2 Subj: Activities – traveling. Birds – ducks. Family life. Foreign lands.

I don't want to go, I don't know how to act ill. by author. Lippincott, 1983. ISBN 0-397-32034-5 Subj: Animals – koalas. Behavior. Etiquette. Family life.

The man on the flying trapeze: the circus life of Emmett Kelly, Sr., told with pictures and song! ill. by author. Lippincott, 1975. ISBN 0-397-31643-7 Subj: Circus. Clowns, jesters. Music. Songs.

Mouse feathers ill. by author. Clarion, 1988. ISBN 0-89919-527-X Subj: Behavior – misbehavior. Family life.

No mouse for me ill. by author. Watts, 1981. ISBN 0-531-04303-7 Subj: Cumulative tales. Pets.

Pete Pack Rat ill. by author. Lothrop, 1976. ISBN 0-688-51763-3 Subj: Animals. Animals – pack rats. Cowboys, cowgirls. Humorous stories. U.S. history – frontier & pioneer life.

Pop! goes the weasel and Yankee Doodle: New York in 1776 and today ill. by author. HarperCollins, 1988, 1976. ISBN 0-397-32265-8 Subj: Music. Songs. U.S. history.

She'll be comin' 'round the mountain ill. by author. Lippincott, 1973. ISBN 0-397-31480-9 Subj: Folk & fairy tales. Music. Songs.

Sheriff Sally Gopher and the Thanksgiving caper ill. by author. Lothrop, 1982. ISBN 0-688-01293-0 Subj: Holidays – Thanksgiving.

Skip to my Lou ill. by author. Lippincott, 1975. ISBN 0-397-31613-5 Subj: Folk & fairy tales. Music. Songs.

There'll be a hot time in the old town tonight: the great Chicago fire of 1871 ill. by author. HarperCollins, 1988, 1974. ISBN 0-397-32267-4 Subj: Fire. Folk & fairy tales. Music. Songs. U.S. history.

Quattlebaum, Mary. *In the beginning* ill. by Bryn Barnard. Time-Life, 1995. ISBN 0-7835-4627-0 Subj: Creation. Religion.

The shine man ill. by Tim Ladwig. Eerdmans, 2001. ISBN 0-8028-5181-9 Subj: Careers – shoe shiners. Character traits – generosity. Holidays – Christmas. Poverty. U.S. history.

Underground train ill. by Cat Bowman Smith. Doubleday, 1997. ISBN 0-385-32204-6 Subj: Activities – traveling. Trains. Transportation.

Quattrocki, Carolyn. *The little drummer boy* ill. by Susan Spellman. Publications International, 1992. ISBN 1-56674-023-1 Subj: Gifts. Holidays – Christmas. Music. Musical instruments – drums. Religion – Nativity. Songs.

Quigley, Lillian Fox. *The blind men and the elephant* ill. by Janice Holland. Scribners, 1959. Subj: Animals – elephants. Folk & fairy tales. Foreign lands – India. Handicaps – blindness. Senses – sight.

Quindlen, Anna. *The tree that came to stay* ill. by Nancy Carpenter. Crown, 1992. ISBN 0-517-58146-9 Subj: Family life. Holidays – Christmas. Trees.

Quin-Harkin, Janet. *Benjamin's balloon* ill. by Robert Censoni. Parents' Magazine Pr., 1979. ISBN 0-8193-0977-X Subj: Activities – ballooning. Character traits – willfulness.

Helpful Hattie ill. by Susanna Natti. Harcourt, 1983. ISBN 0-15-233756-3 Subj: Birthdays. Hair. Parties. Teeth.

Peter Penny's dance ill. by Anita Lobel. Dial, 1976. ISBN 0-8037-7184-3 Subj: Activities – dancing. Weddings. World.

Quinlan, Patricia. *Anna's red sled* ill. by Lindsay Grater. Firefly, 1989. ISBN 1-55037-073-1 Subj: Family life – mothers. Seasons – winter. Toys.

Emma's sea journey ill. by Jirina Marton. Firefly, 1991. ISBN 1-55037-179-7 Subj: Activities – playing. Sea & seashore.

My dad takes care of me ill. by Vlasta van Kampen. Firefly, 1987. ISBN 0-920303-79-X Subj: Activities – working. Family life – fathers. Family life – mothers.

Quinn, Daniel P. *I am Buddhist* ill. with photos. PowerKids, 1996. ISBN 0-8239-2379-7 Subj: Ethnic groups in the U.S. – Chinese Americans. Religion – Buddhism.

Quinsey, Mary Beth. *Why does that man have such a big nose?* photos by Wilson Chan. Parenting Pr., 1986. ISBN 0-943990-25-4 Subj: Character traits – appearance. Character traits – being different.

Quintero-Spongberg, Emily. *Hannibal and the king* ill. by Tim Spongberg. Rainbow House, 1999. ISBN 1-893659-00-3 Subj: Animals – donkeys. Friendship. Religion.

R. F. *see* Fyleman, Rose

Ra, Carol F. *The sun is up* (Smith, William Jay)

Trot, trot to Boston: play rhymes for baby ill. by Catherine Stock. Lothrop, 1987. ISBN 0-688-06191-5 Subj: Games. Poetry.

Raatma, Lucia. *Abraham Lincoln* ill. with photos. Compass Pt., 2000. ISBN 0-7565-0012-5 Subj: U.S. history.

Veterinarians ill. with photos. Compass Pt., 2003. ISBN 0-7565-0304-3 Subj: Animals. Careers – veterinarians.

Rabe, Berniece. *The balancing girl* ill. by Lillian Hoban. Dutton, 1981. ISBN 0-525-26160-5 Subj: Handicaps. School.

The first Christmas candy cane ill. by Kathy Wilburn. Longmeadow, 1994. ISBN 0-681-00441-X Subj: Food. Holidays – Christmas. Religion – Nativity.

A smooth move ill. by Linda Shute. A. Whitman, 1987. ISBN 0-8075-7486-4 Subj: Activities – traveling. Moving.

Where's Chimpy? photos by Diane Schmidt. A. Whitman, 1988. ISBN 0-8075-8928-4 Subj: Behavior – lost & found possessions. Family life – fathers. Handicaps. Toys.

Rabinowitz, Sandy. *A colt named mischief* ill. by author. Doubleday, 1979. ISBN 0-385-14629-9 Subj: Animals – horses, ponies. Behavior – misbehavior.

What's happening to Daisy? ill. by author. HarperCollins, 1977. ISBN 0-06-024835-1 Subj: Animals – horses, ponies. Birth. Science.

Racioppo, Larry. *Halloween* photos by author. Scribners, 1980. ISBN 0-684-16708-5 Subj: Holidays – Halloween.

Raczek, Linda Theresa. *The night the grandfathers danced* ill. by Katalin Olah Ehling. Northland, 1995. ISBN 0-87358-610-7 Subj: Activities – dancing. Family life – grandfathers. Indians of North America – Ute.

Raczka, Bob. *Art is . . .* ill. with photos. Millbrook, 2003. ISBN 0-7613-2874-2 Subj: Art. Rhyming text.

No one saw: ordinary things through the eyes of an artist ill. with famous 20th century works of art. Millbrook, 2002. ISBN 0-7613-2370-8 Subj: Art. Careers – artists.

Radabaugh, Melinda Beth. *Getting a haircut* ill. with photos. Heinemann, 2003. ISBN 1-4034-0225-6 Subj: Careers – barbers. Hair.

Going to a restaurant ill. with photos. Heinemann, 2003. ISBN 1-4034-0226-4 Subj: Careers – chefs, cooks. Careers – waiters, waitresses. Food. Restaurants.

Going to school ill. with photos. Heinemann, 2003. ISBN 1-4034-0227-2 Subj: Careers – teachers. School – first day.

Going to the library ill. with photos. Heinemann, 2003. ISBN 1-4034-0230-2 Subj: Books, reading. Careers – librarians. Libraries.

Sleeping over ill. with photos. Heinemann, 2003. ISBN 1-4034-0231-0 Subj: Parties. Sleepovers.

Radcliffe, Theresa. *Bashi, elephant baby* ill. by John Butler. Viking, 1997. ISBN 0-670-87054-4 Subj: Animals – babies. Animals – elephants. Family life – mothers. Foreign lands – Africa.

Nanu, penguin chick ill. by John Butler. Viking, 2000. ISBN 0-670-88638-6 Subj: Birds – penguins. Foreign lands – Antarctic.

The snow leopard ill. by John Butler. Viking, 1994. ISBN 0-670-85052-7 Subj: Animals – leopards.

Rader, Laura. *Santa's new suit* Rader, Laura. HarperCollins, 2000. ISBN 0-06-028439-0 Subj: Clothing – suits. Holidays – Christmas. Humorous stories. Shopping.

Tea for me, tea for you Rader, Laura. HarperCollins, 2003. ISBN 0-06-008634-3 Subj: Animals – pigs. Counting, numbers. Food. Parties. Rhyming text.

Radford, Derek. *Building machines and what they do* ill. by author. Candlewick, 1992. ISBN 1-56402-006-1 Subj: Machines.

Cargo machines and what they do ill. by author. Candlewick, 1992. ISBN 1-56402-005-3 Subj: Machines.

Harry at the garage ill. by author. Candlewick, 1995. ISBN 1-56402-564-0 Subj: Animals – hippopotamuses. Automobiles. Careers – mechanics.

Harry builds a house ill. by author. Aladdin, 1990. ISBN 0-689-71439-4 Subj: Activities – making things. Homes, houses.

Radin, Ruth Yaffe. *High in the mountains* ill. by Ed Young. Macmillan, 1989. ISBN 0-02-775650-5 Subj: Family life – grandfathers. Nature.

A winter place ill. by Mattie Lou O'Kelley. Little, 1982. ISBN 0-316-73218-4 Subj: Seasons – winter. Sports – ice skating.

Radlauer, Ruth Shaw. *Breakfast by Molly* ill. by Emily Arnold McCully. Prentice-Hall, 1988. ISBN 0-671-66165-5 Subj: Birthdays. Family life – mothers. Food.

Molly ill. by Emily Arnold McCully. Prentice-Hall, 1987. ISBN 0-13-599762-3 Subj: Activities – picnicking. Activities – walking.

Molly at the library ill. by Emily Arnold McCully. Prentice-Hall, 1988. ISBN 0-671-66166-3 Subj: Books, reading. Family life – fathers. Libraries.

Molly goes hiking ill. by Emily Arnold McCully. Prentice-Hall, 1987. ISBN 0-13-599770-4 Subj: Activities – picnicking. Activities – walking.

Of course, you're a horse! ill. by Abner Graboff & Sheila Greenwald. Abelard-Schuman, 1959. Subj: Health & fitness. Imagination.

Radley, Gail. *The night Stella hid the stars* ill. by John Wallner. Crown, 1978. ISBN 0-517-53256-5 Subj: Imagination. Stars.

Rainy day rhymes ill. by Ellen Kandoian. Houghton Mifflin, 1992. ISBN 0-395-59967-9 Subj: Poetry. Weather – rain.

The spinner's gift ill. by Paige Miglio. North-South, 1994. ISBN 1-55858-326-2 Subj: Activities – weaving. Clothing. Ecology. Gifts. Quilts. Royalty.

Radunsky, Eugenia. *Square, triangle, round, skinny* ill. by Vladimir Radunsky. Holt, 1992. ISBN 0-8050-2205-8 Subj: Concepts – shape. Format, unusual.

Yucka Drucka Droni by Eugenia Radunsky & Vladimir Radunsky; ill. by Vladimir Radunsky. Scholastic, 1998. ISBN 0-590-09837-3 Subj: Family life – brothers & sisters. Tongue twisters.

Radunsky, Vladimir. *Manneken pis* ill. by author. Atheneum, 2002. ISBN 0-689-83193-5 Subj: Folk & fairy tales. Foreign lands – Belgium. War.

One: a nice story about an awful braggart ill. by autor. Viking, 2003. ISBN 0-670-03564-5 Subj: Animals – armadillos. Character traits – pride. Character traits – vanity.

Ten: a wonderful story ill. by author. Viking, 2002. ISBN 0-670-03563-7 Subj: Animals – armadillos. Babies. Birth.

Yucka Drucka Droni (Radunsky, Eugenia)

Rae, Jennifer. *Dog tales* ill. by Rose Cowles. Tricycle, 1998. ISBN 1-58246-011-6 Subj: Animals – cats. Animals – dogs. Folk & fairy tales.

Raebeck, Lois. *Who am I?* ill. by June Goldsborough. Follett, 1970. Subj: Activities – playing. Games. Songs.

Rael, Elsa Okon. *Rivka's first Thanksgiving* ill. by Maryann Kovalski. McElderry, 2001. ISBN 0-689-83901-4 Subj: Holidays – Thanksgiving. Immigrants. Jewish culture.

When Zaydeh danced on Eldridge Street ill. by Marjorie Priceman. S&S, 1997. ISBN 0-689-80451-2 Subj: Emotions – fear. Family life – grandfathers. Jewish culture. Religion.

Rael, Rick. *Baseball brothers* (Rubin, Jeff)

Raff, Courtney Granet. *Giant of the sea* ill. by Shawn Gould. Soundprints, 2002. ISBN 1-931465-71-1 Subj: Animals – whales. Family life – mothers. Sea & seashore.

Raffi. *Baby beluga* ill. by Ashley Wolff. Crown, 1990. ISBN 0-517-57840-9 Subj: Animals – endangered animals. Animals – whales. Foreign lands – Arctic. Music. Songs.

Down by the bay ill. by Nadine Bernard Westcott. Crown, 1987. ISBN 0-517-56644-3 Subj: Music. Songs.

Everything grows photos by Bruce McMillan. Crown, 1989. ISBN 0-517-57275-3 Subj: Music. Songs.

Like me and you words & music by Raffi & Debi Pike; ill. by Lillian Hoban. Crown, 1994. ISBN 0-517-59588-5 Subj: Foreign lands. Letters, cards. Music. Songs.

One light, one sun ill. by Eugenie Fernandes. Crown, 1988. ISBN 0-517-56785-7 Subj: Family life. Music. Songs.

Rise and shine words & music by Raffi, Bonnie Simpson, & Bert Simpson; ill. by Eugenie Fernandes. Crown, 1996. ISBN 0-517-70940-6 Subj: Morning. Music. Songs.

Shake my sillies out ill. by David Allender. Crown, 1987. ISBN 0-517-56646-X Subj: Music. Songs.

Wheels on the bus ill. by Sylvie Wickstrom. Crown, 1988. ISBN 0-517-56784-9 Subj: Foreign lands – France. Music. Songs.

Ragged Bear's book of nursery rhymes sel. & ill. by Diz Wallis. Ragged Bears, 2001. ISBN 1-929927-36-3 Subj: Nursery rhymes.

Raglin, Tim. *The birthday ABC* (Metaxas, Eric)

Raglus, Jeff. *Schnorky the wave puncher* ill. by author. Crown, 1996. ISBN 0-517-70924-4 Subj: Character traits – bravery. Islands. Sports – surfing. Weather – storms.

Ragz, M. M. *Lost little angel* ill. by Jane Manning. S&S, 1998. ISBN 0-689-81067-9 Subj: Angels. Behavior – lost. Humorous stories. Religion.

Rahaman, Vashanti. *O Christmas tree* ill. by Frané Lessac. Boyds Mills, 1996. ISBN 1-56397-237-9 Subj: Foreign lands – Caribbean Islands. Foreign lands – West Indies. Holidays – Christmas. Islands.

Read for me, Mama ill. by Lori McElrath-Eslick. Boyds Mills, 1997. ISBN 1-56397-313-8 Subj: Books, reading. Family life – mothers. Libraries.

Rahn, Joan Elma. *Holes* photos by author. Houghton Mifflin, 1984. ISBN 0-395-35389-0 Subj: Concepts.

Rambeck, Richard. *Kristi Yamaguchi* ill. with photos. Child's World, 1997. ISBN 1-56766-411-3 Subj: Sports – ice skating.

Ramirez, Melissa Bourbon. *The flight of the sunflower* ill. by Nadine Takvorian. All About Kids, 2002. ISBN 0-9700863-0-X Subj: Flowers. Seeds. Weather – wind.

Rand, Ann. *Little 1* by Ann & Paul Rand; ill. by Paul Rand. Abrams, 1991. ISBN 0-8109-3558-9 Subj: Counting, numbers.

Sparkle and spin: a book about words by Ann & Paul Rand; ill. by Paul Rand. Harcourt, 1957. ISBN 0-8109-3822-7 Subj: Language.

Rand, Gloria. *Aloha, Salty!* ill. by Ted Rand. Holt, 1996. ISBN 0-8050-3429-3 Subj: Animals – dogs. Boats, ships. Hawaii. Sea & seashore. Weather – storms.

Baby in a basket ill. by Ted Rand. Cobblehill, 1997. ISBN 0-525-65233-7 Subj: Accidents. Alaska. Babies. Family life. U.S. history.

The cabin key ill. by Ted Rand. Harcourt, 1994. ISBN 0-15-213884-6 Subj: Activities – vacationing. Family life. Nature.

Little Flower ill. by R. W. Alley. Holt, 2002. ISBN 0-8050-6480-X Subj: Accidents. Animals – pigs. Pets.

Prince William ill. by Ted Rand. Holt, 1992. ISBN 0-8050-1841-7 Subj: Alaska. Animals – mice. Ecology. Oil.

Sailing home ill. by Ted Rand. North-South, 2001. ISBN 0-7358-1540-2 Subj: Boats, ships. Family life. Sailors. Sea & seashore.

Salty dog ill. by Ted Rand. Holt, 1989. ISBN 0-8050-0837-3 Subj: Animals – dogs. Boats, ships. Careers – boat builders. Character traits – individuality.

Salty sails north ill. by Ted Rand. Holt, 1990. ISBN 0-8050-1160-9 Subj: Alaska. Animals – dogs. Boats, ships. Sea & seashore.

Salty takes off ill. by Ted Rand. Holt, 1991. ISBN 0-8050-1159-5 Subj: Airplanes, airports. Alaska. Animals – dogs.

Willie takes a hike ill. by Ted Rand. Harcourt, 1996. ISBN 0-15-200272-3 Subj: Animals – mice. Behavior – lost. Safety. Sports – hiking.

Rand, Paul. *Little 1* (Rand, Ann)

Sparkle and spin: a book about words (Rand, Ann)

Rand McNally picturebook dictionary: *a thousand words to see and say* comp. by Robert L. Hillerich & others; ill. by Dan Siculan. Rand McNally, 1971. Subj: Dictionaries.

Randall, Ronne. *The Hanukkah mice* ill. by Maggie Kneen. Chronicle, 2002. ISBN 0-8118-3623-1 Subj: Animals – mice. Holidays – Hanukkah. Jewish culture. Rhyming text.

Raney, Ken. *Stick horse* ill. by author. Green Tiger Pr., 1991. ISBN 0-9625261-4-2 Subj: Activities – playing. Activities – traveling. Toys. Wordless.

Rankin, Joan. *First day* ill. by author. McElderry, 2002. ISBN 0-689-84563-4 Subj: Animals. Animals – dogs. School – first day. School – nursery.

The little cat and the greedy old woman ill. by author. McElderry, 1995. ISBN 0-689-50611-2 Subj: Animals – cats. Behavior – sharing. Character traits – selfishness. Emotions – anger.

Wow! It's great being a duck ill. by author. McElderry, 1998. ISBN 0-689-81756-8 Subj: Animals – foxes. Birds – ducks.

You're somebody special, Walliwigs! ill. by author. McElderry, 1999. ISBN 0-689-82230-8 Subj: Animals. Birds. Birds – chickens. Birds – parakeets, parrots. Character traits – being different. Character traits – individuality. Emotions – love.

Rankin, Laura. *The handmade counting book* ill. by author. Dial, 1998. ISBN 0-8037-2311-3 Subj: Counting, numbers. Handicaps – deafness. Language.

Ransom, Candice F. *The Christmas dolls* ill. by Moira Fain. Walker, 1998. ISBN 0-8027-8661-8 Subj: Family life – mothers. Holidays – Christmas. Toys – dolls.

Mother Teresa ill. by Elaine Verstraete. Carolrhoda, 2001. ISBN 1-57505-441-8 Subj: Careers – nuns. Religion.

The promise quilt ill. by Ellen Beier. Walker, 1999. ISBN 0-8027-8695-2 Subj: Activities – making things. Activities – sewing. Quilts. U.S. history.

When the whippoorwill calls ill. by Kimberly Bulcken Root. Tambourine, 1995. ISBN 0-688-12730-4 Subj: Emotions. Family life. Moving.

Ransom, Jeanie Franz. *I don't want to talk about it* ill. by Kathryn Kunz Finney. Magination Pr., 2000. ISBN 1-55798-664-9 Subj: Divorce. Emotions – love. Family life – parents.

Ransome, Arthur. *The fool of the world and the flying ship* ill. by Uri Shulevitz. Farrar, 1968. ISBN 0-374-32442-5 Subj: Activities – flying. Boats, ships. Caldecott award books. Character traits – cleverness. Folk & fairy tales. Foreign lands – Ukraine. Royalty – tsars.

Ranville, Myralene. *Tex* ill. by author. Firefly, 1999. ISBN 1-55209-294-1 Subj: Animals – dogs. Behavior – needing someone.

Raphael, Elaine. *Donkey and Carlo* by Elaine Raphael & Don Bolognese; ill. by authors. HarperCollins, 1978. ISBN 0-06-020553-9 Subj: Animals – donkeys. Farms. Friendship.

Donkey, it's snowing by Elaine Raphael & Don Bolognese; ill. by authors. HarperCollins, 1981. ISBN 0-06-020555-5 Subj: Animals – donkeys. Farms. Weather – snow.

Turnabout by Elaine Raphael & Don Bolognese; ill. by authors. Viking, 1980. ISBN 0-670-73281-8 Subj: Animals – bears. Behavior – boasting. Family life. Folk & fairy tales. Rhyming text.

Raposo, Joe. *The Sesame Street song book* words & music by Joe Raposo & Jeffrey Moss; arrangements by Sy Oliver; ill. by Loretta Trezzo. S&S, 1971. Published in conjunction with Children's Television Workshop. Subj: Music. Songs.

Rappaport, Doreen. *Dirt on their skirts* by Doreen Rappaport & Lyndall Callan; ill. by E. B. Lewis. Dial, 2000. ISBN 0-8037-2042-4 Subj: Sports – baseball.

Journey of Meng ill. by Yang Ming-Yi. Dial, 1991. ISBN 0-8037-0896-3 Subj: Death. Folk & fairy tales. Foreign lands – China.

The long-haired girl ill. by Yang Ming-Yi. Dial, 1995. ISBN 0-8037-1412-2 Subj: Behavior – secrets. Character traits – bravery. Folk & fairy tales. Foreign lands – China. Weather – droughts.

Martin's big words ill. by Bryan Collier. Hyperion, 2001. ISBN 0-7868-2591-X Subj: Caldecott award honor books. Careers – clergy. Ethnic groups in the U.S. – African Americans. Language. U.S. history.

The new king ill. by E. B. Lewis. Dial, 1995. ISBN 0-8037-1461-0 Subj: Death. Emotions – grief. Family life – fathers. Folk & fairy tales. Foreign lands – Madagascar. Royalty.

We are the many ill. by Cornelius Van Wright & Ying-Hwa Hu. HarperCollins, 2002. ISBN 0-06-001139-4 Subj: Indians of North America. U.S. history.

Rappus, Gerhard. *When the sun was shining* ill. by author. Imported Pubs., 1986. ISBN 0-8285-2269-3 Subj: Activities – picnicking. Animals – goats. Behavior – misbehavior. Wordless.

Rascal. *Oregon's journey* ill. by Louis Joos. BridgeWater, 1993. ISBN 0-816-73305-8 Subj: Animals – bears. Character traits – freedom. Circus. Clowns, jesters. Dwarfs, midgets.

Orson ill. by Mario Ramos. Lothrop, 1995. ISBN 0-688-13799-7 Subj: Animals – bears. Friendship. Hibernation. Toys – bears.

Socrates ill. by Gert Bogaerts. Chronicle, 1992. ISBN 0-8118-0314-7 Subj: Animals – dogs. Glasses. Homeless.

Raschka, Christopher. *Arlene sardine* ill. by author. Orchard, 1998. ISBN 0-531-33111-3 Subj: Fish. Food. Self-concept.

The blushful hippopotamus ill. by author. Orchard, 1996. ISBN 0-531-08882-0 Subj: Animals – hippopotamuses. Emotions – embarrassment. Family life – brothers & sisters. Sibling rivalry.

Can't sleep ill. by author. Orchard, 1995. ISBN 0-531-08779-4 Subj: Animals – dogs. Bedtime. Emotions – fear. Moon. Night.

Charlie Parker played be bop ill. by author. Watts, 1992. ISBN 0-531-08599-6 Subj: Careers – musicians. Ethnic groups in the U.S. – African Americans. Music. Musical instruments – saxophones.

Elizabeth imagined an iceberg ill. by author. Orchard, 1994. ISBN 0-531-08667-4 Subj: Behavior – talking to strangers. Imagination.

John Coltrane's giant steps ill. by author. Atheneum, 2002. ISBN 0-689-84598-7 Subj: Animals – cats. Music. Musical instruments – bands. Weather – rain. Weather – snow.

Moosey Moose ill. by author. Hyperion, 2000. ISBN 0-7868-0581-1 Subj: Animals. Animals – moose. Clothing – pants.

Mysterious Thelonious ill. by author. Orchard, 1997. ISBN 0-531-33057-5 Subj: Careers – musicians. Concepts – color. Ethnic groups in the U.S. – African Americans.

Ring! Yo? ill. by author. DK, 2000. ISBN 0-7894-2614-5 Subj: Emotions. Friendship. Telephone.

Simple gifts: a Shaker hymn (Simple gifts)

Sluggy Slug ill. by author. Hyperion, 2000. ISBN 0-7868-0584-6 Subj: Animals – slugs.

Talk to me about the alphabet ill. by author. Holt, 2003. ISBN 0-8050-6782-5 Subj: ABC books. Noise, sounds.

Waffle ill. by author. Atheneum, 2001. ISBN 0-689-83838-7 Subj: Behavior – worrying. Character traits – bravery. Emotions – fear. Self-concept.

Whaley Whale ill. by author. Hyperion, 2000. ISBN 0-7868-0583-8 Subj: Animals – whales. Behavior – hiding.

Wormy Worm ill. by author. Hyperion, 2000. ISBN 0-7868-0582-X Subj: Animals – worms.

Yo! Yes? ill. by author. Orchard, 1993. ISBN 0-531-08619-4 Subj: Caldecott award honor books. Emotions. Ethnic groups in the U.S. – African Americans. Friendship.

Rash, Andy. *Agent A to Agent Z* ill. by author. Levine, 2004. ISBN 0-439-36882-0 Subj: ABC books. Careers – detectives. Rhyming text.

Raskin, Ellen. *A & The: or, William T. C. Baumgarten comes to town* ill. by author. Atheneum, 1970. Subj: Friendship. Names.

And it rained ill. by author. Atheneum, 1969. Subj: Animals. Weather – rain.

Franklin Stein ill. by author. Atheneum, 1972. Subj: Cities, towns. Friendship. Humorous stories. Imagination.

Ghost in a four-room apartment ill. by author. Atheneum, 1969. ISBN 0-689-20354-3 Subj: Cumulative tales. Family life. Ghosts. Rhyming text.

Nothing ever happens on my block ill. by author. Atheneum, 1966. ISBN 0-689-20588-0 Subj: Behavior – boredom. Cities, towns. Humorous stories.

Spectacles ill. by author. Atheneum, 1968. ISBN 0-689-20352-7 Subj: Glasses. Imagination. Senses – sight.

Who, said Sue, said whoo? ill. by author. Atheneum, 1973. Subj: Animals. Noise, sounds. Rhyming text.

Rasmussen, Knud. *Magic words: poems* (Field, Edward)

Rassmus, Jens. *Farmer Enno and his cow* ill. by author. Orchard, 1998. ISBN 0-531-30081-1 Subj: Boats, ships. Dreams. Farms.

Rathmann, Peggy. *Good night, Gorilla* ill. by author. Putnam, 1994. ISBN 0-399-22445-9 Subj: Animals. Careers – zookeepers. Night. Zoos.

Officer Buckle and Gloria ill. by author. Putnam, 1995. ISBN 0-399-22616-8 Subj: Animals – dogs. Behavior – sharing. Caldecott award books. Careers – police officers. School.

Ruby the copycat ill. by author. Scholastic, 1991. ISBN 0-590-43747-X Subj: Animals – cats. Behavior – imitation. School.

10 minutes till bedtime ill. by author. Putnam, 1998. ISBN 0-399-23103-X Subj: Animals – hamsters. Bedtime. Pets.

Ratnett, Michael. *Jenny's bear* ill. by June Goulding. Putnam, 1992. ISBN 0-399-22325-8 Subj: Animals – bears. Behavior – wishing. Imagination. Toys – bears.

Marmaduke and the scary story ill. by June Goulding. Trafalgar Square, 1992. ISBN 0-09-174084-3 Subj: Animals – rabbits. Emotions – fear.

Rattigan, Jama Kim. *The woman in the moon* ill. by Carla Golembe. Little, 1996. ISBN 0-316-73446-2 Subj: Folk & fairy tales. Foreign languages. Hawaii. Moon.

Ratz de Tagyos, Paul. *A coney tale* ill. by author. Houghton Mifflin, 1992. ISBN 0-395-58834-0 Subj: Animals – rabbits. Communities, neighborhoods.

Rau, Dana Meachen. *Chilly Charlie* ill. by Martin Lemelman. Childrens Pr., 2001. ISBN 0-516-22210-4 Subj: Concepts – cold & heat. Rhyming text.

Clown around ill. by Nate Evans. Compass Pt., 2001. ISBN 0-7565-0074-5 Subj: Circus. Clowns, jesters. Rhyming text.

Dr. Seuss ill. with photos. Childrens Pr., 2003. ISBN 0-516-22593-6 Subj: Careers – authors. Careers – illustrators.

Explore in a cave photos by Romie Flanagan. Rourke, 2000. ISBN 1-57103-318-1 Subj: Caves.

I'll make you a card ill. by Jan Bryan-Hunt. Compass Pt., 2002. ISBN 0-7565-0172-5 Subj: Days of the week, months of the year. Holidays. Letters, cards. Rhyming text.

In the yard ill. by Elizabeth Wolf. Compass Pt., 2001. ISBN 0-7565-0116-4 Subj: Character traits – helpfulness. Family life – parents. Seasons.

Lots of balloons ill. by Jayoung Cho. Compass Pt., 2001. ISBN 0-7565-0117-2 Subj: Concepts – color. Toys – balloons.

Mars photos by author. Compass Pt., 2002. ISBN 0-7565-0199-7 Subj: Planets. Science.

Neil Armstrong ill. with photos. Childrens Pr., 2003. ISBN 0-516-22592-8 Subj: Careers – astronauts. Space & space ships.

Rubber duck ill. by Patrick Girouard. Compass Pt., 2002. ISBN 0-7565-0121-0 Subj: Rhyming text. Toys.

The secret code ill. by Bari Weissman. Childrens Pr., 1998. ISBN 0-516-20700-8 Subj: Books, reading. Handicaps – blindness.

Shoo crow, shoo! ill. by Mary Rojas. Compass Pt., 2001. ISBN 0-7565-0072-9 Subj: Rhyming text. Scarecrows.

Stroll by the sea photos by author. Rourke, 2000. ISBN 1-57103-320-3 Subj: Nature. Sea & seashore – beaches.

Ways to go ill. by Jane Conteh-Morgan. Compass Pt., 2001. ISBN 0-7565-0071-0 Subj: Transportation.

Rauch, Hans-Georg. *The lines are coming: a book about drawing* ill. by author. Scribners, 1978. ISBN 0-684-15989-9 Subj: Art.

Rauch, Jennifer. *see* Davis, Jennifer

Rauzon, Mark J. *Eyes and ears* ill. by author. Lothrop, 1994. ISBN 0-688-10238-7 Subj: Anatomy – ears. Anatomy – eyes. Animals. Senses – hearing. Senses – sight.

Feet, flippers, hooves, and hands ill. by author. Lothrop, 1994. ISBN 0-688-10235-2 Subj: Anatomy. Anatomy – feet. Anatomy – hands. Animals.

Water, water everywhere by Mark J. Rauzon & Cynthia Overbeck Bix; ill. with photos. Sierra Club, 1994. ISBN 0-87156-598-6 Subj: Water.

Raven, Margot Theis. *Angels in the dust* ill. by Roger Essley. BridgeWater, 1997. ISBN 0-8167-3806-8 Subj: Family life. Farms. Friendship. Memories, memory. U.S. history.

Mercedes and the chocolate pilot ill. by Gijsbert van Frankenhuyzen. Sleeping Bear, 2002. ISBN 1-58536-069-4 Subj: Airplanes, airports. Careers – airplane pilots. Foreign lands – Germany. War.

Ravilious, Robin. *The runaway chick* ill. by author. Macmillan, 1987. ISBN 0-02-775640-8 Subj: Behavior – running away. Birds – chickens. Character traits – curiosity.

Two in a pocket ill. by author. Little, 1991. ISBN 0-316-73449-7 Subj: Animals – dormice. Birds – wrens. Friendship.

Rawlins, Donna. *Digging to China* ill. by author. Watts, 1989. ISBN 0-531-08414-0 Subj: Activities – digging. Old age.

Ray, Deborah Kogan. *The cloud* ill. by author. HarperCollins, 1984. ISBN 0-06-024847-5 Subj: Activities – walking. Weather – clouds.

Fog drift morning ill. by author. HarperCollins, 1983. ISBN 0-06-023198-X Subj: Morning. Sea & seashore.

Lily's garden ill. by author. Roaring Brook, 2002. ISBN 0-7613-2653-7 Subj: Food. Gardens, gardening. Letters, cards.

Stargazing sky ill. by author. Crown, 1991. ISBN 0-517-57838-7 Subj: Family life – mothers. Night. Stars.

Sunday morning we went to the zoo ill. by author. HarperCollins, 1981. ISBN 0-06-024842-4 Subj: Family life. Sibling rivalry. Zoos.

Ray, Jane. *Hansel and Gretel* (Grimm, Jacob)

The twelve dancing princesses (Grimm, Jacob)

Ray, Karen. *Sleep song* ill. by Rhonda Mitchell. Orchard, 1995. ISBN 0-531-08728-X Subj: Activities. Bedtime. Games. Rhyming text.

Ray, Mary Lyn. *All aboard* ill. by Amiko Hirao. Little, 2002. ISBN 0-316-73507-8 Subj: Animals – rabbits. Toys. Trains.

Basket moon ill. by Barbara Cooney. Little, 1999. ISBN 0-316-73521-3 Subj: Activities – making things. Careers. Family life – fathers. Mountains.

Mud ill. by Lauren Stringer. Harcourt, 1996. ISBN 0-15-256263-X Subj: Poetry. Seasons – spring.

Pianna ill. by Bobbie Henba. Harcourt, 1994. ISBN 0-15-261357-9 Subj: Careers – musicians. Music. Musical instruments – pianos. U.S. history.

Pumpkins ill. by Barry Root. Harcourt, 1992. ISBN 0-15-252252-2 Subj: Ecology. Gardens, gardening. Plants. Progress.

Red rubber boot day ill. by Lauren Stringer. Harcourt, 2000. ISBN 0-15-213756-4 Subj: Activities – playing. Clothing – boots. Weather – rain.

Shaker boy ill. by Jeanette Winter. Harcourt, 1994. ISBN 0-15-276921-8 Subj: Ethnic groups in the U.S. – Shakers. Music. Religion. Songs. U.S. history.

Rayevsky, Inna. *The talking tree* ill. by Robert Rayevsky. Putnam, 1990. ISBN 0-399-21631-6 Subj: Folk & fairy tales. Foreign lands – Italy. Trees.

Rayner, Mary. *Crocodarling* ill. by author. Bradbury, 1986. ISBN 0-02-775770-6 Subj: Behavior – bullying. Behavior – needing someone. School. Toys.

Garth Pig and the ice cream lady ill. by author. Atheneum, 1977. ISBN 0-33-322040-4 Subj: Animals – pigs. Animals – wolves.

Marathon and Steve ill. by author. Dutton, 1989. ISBN 0-525-44456-4 Subj: Animals – dogs. Pets. Sports.

Mr. and Mrs. Pig's evening out ill. by author. Atheneum, 1976. ISBN 0-689-30530-3 Subj: Activities – babysitting. Animals – pigs. Animals – wolves.

Mrs. Pig gets cross and other stories ill. by author. Dutton, 1987. ISBN 0-525-44280-4 Subj: Animals – pigs. Family life.

Mrs. Pig's bulk buy ill. by author. Atheneum, 1981. ISBN 0-689-30831-0 Subj: Animals – pigs. Food.

One by one: Garth Pig's rain song ill. by author. Dutton, 1994. ISBN 0-525-45240-0 Subj: Animals – pigs. Counting, numbers. Music. Songs. Weather – rain.

The rain cloud ill. by author. Atheneum, 1980. ISBN 0-689-30763-2 Subj: Character traits – helpfulness. Weather – clouds.

Ten pink piglets: Garth Pig's wall song ill. by author. Dutton, 1994. ISBN 0-525-45241-9 Subj: Animals – pigs. Counting, numbers. Music. Songs.

Rayner, Shoo. *My first picture joke book* ill. by author. Viking, 1990. ISBN 0-670-82450-X Subj: Animals. Humorous stories.

Raynor, Dorka. *Grandparents around the world* ed. by Caroline Rubin; photos by author. A. Whitman, 1977. ISBN 0-8075-3037-9 Subj: Family life – grandparents.

Rea, Jesus Guerrero. *Atariba and Niguayona: a story from the Taino people of Puerto Rico* (Rohmer, Harriet)

Reader, Dennis. *Butterfingers* ill. by author. Houghton Mifflin, 1991. ISBN 0-395-57581-8 Subj: Babies. Behavior – carelessness. Family life – brothers & sisters. Family life – new sibling.

I want one! ill. by author. Ideals, 1990. ISBN 0-8249-8442-0 Subj: Character traits – selfishness.

Reader's Digest children's book of poetry sel. by Beverly Mathias; ill. by Alan Snow. Reader's Digest, 1992. ISBN 0-895-77442-9 Subj: Poetry.

Reardon, Maureen. *Feelings between brothers and sisters* (Conta, Marcia Maher)

Feelings between friends (Conta, Marcia Maher)

Feelings between kids and grownups (Conta, Marcia Maher)

Feelings between kids and parents (Conta, Marcia Maher)

Reasoner, Charles. *Ants, ants, ants* ill. by author. Price Stern Sloan, 2001. ISBN 0-8431-7613-X Subj: Format, unusual – board books. Insects – ants. Rhyming text.

The big busy building by Chuck Reasoner & Cary Pillo Lassen; ill. by authors. Price Stern Sloan, 1994. ISBN 0-8431-3659-6 Subj: Buildings. Elevators, escalators. Format, unusual – board books. Format, unusual – toy & movable books. Wordless.

Sleepy time bunny (Cosgrove, Stephen [Edward])

Who drives this? ill. by author. Price Stern Sloan, 1996. ISBN 0-8431-3939-0 Subj: Animals. Automobiles. Careers. Format, unusual – toy & movable books. Transportation. Trucks.

Who pretends? ill. by author. Price Stern Sloan, 1996. ISBN 0-8431-3940-4 Subj: Activities. Foreign languages. Format, unusual – toy & movable books. Imagination.

Reavin, Sam. *Hurray for Captain Jane!* ill. by Emily Arnold McCully. Parents' Magazine Pr., 1971. ISBN 0-8193-0511-1 Subj: Activities – bathing. Boats, ships. Imagination.

Rebek, Kathleen. *The story of a round loaf* (Froment, Eugène)

Rechner, Amy. *Out and about at the aquarium* ill. by Becky Shipe. Picture Window, 2004. ISBN 1-4048-0298-3 Subj: Animals. Aquariums. Fish. School – field trips.

Recknagel, Friedrich. *Meg's wish* ill. by Ilse van Garderen; trans. by Sibylle Kazeroid. North-South, 1999. ISBN 0-7358-1117-2 Subj: Behavior – wishing. Dreams. Friendship.

Sarah's willow ill. by Maja Dusíková; trans. by Anthea Bell. North-South, 2002. ISBN 0-7358-1528-3 Subj: Emotions – grief. Hope. Trees.

Recorvits, Helen. *My name is Yoon* ill. by Gabi Swiatkowska. Frances Foster, 2003. ISBN 0-374-35114-7 Subj: Ethnic groups in the U.S. – Korean Americans. Immigrants. Names. School – first day.

Reddix, Valerie. *Dragon kite of the autumn moon* ill. by Jean & Mou-Sien Tseng. Lothrop, 1992. ISBN 0-688-11031-2 Subj: Dragons. Family life – grandfathers. Foreign lands – Taiwan. Kites.

Millie and the mudhole ill. by Thor Wickstrom. Lothrop, 1992. ISBN 0-688-10213-1 Subj: Animals. Animals – pigs. Farms. Noise, sounds. Rhyming text.

Redies, Rainer. *The cats' party* ill. by Gerta Melle. Barron's, 1986. ISBN 0-8120-5720-1 Subj: Animals – cats. Character traits – individuality. Family life. Parties.

Reece, Colleen L. *What?* ill. by Lois Axeman. Childrens Pr., 1983. ISBN 0-516-06591-2 Subj: Character traits – curiosity. Character traits – questioning.

Reed, Allison. *Genesis: the story of creation* ill. by author. Schocken, 1981. ISBN 0-8052-3778-X Subj: Creation. Religion.

Reed, Jonathan. *Do armadillos come in houses?* ill. by Carol Nicklaus. Atheneum, 1981. ISBN 0-689-30858-2 Subj: Emotions – fear.

Reed, Kit. *When we dream* ill. by Yutaka Sugita. Hawthorn, 1966. Subj: Behavior – wishing. Dreams.

Reed, Lillian Craig. *see* Reed, Kit

Reed, Lynn Rowe. *Pedro, his perro, and the alphabet sombrero* ill. by author. Hyperion, 1995. ISBN 0-7868-2058-6 Subj: ABC books. Animals – dogs. Birthdays. Clothing – hats. Foreign languages.

Reed, Mary M. *Biddy and the ducks* (Sondergaard, Arensa)

Reed-Jones, Carol. *The tree in the ancient forest* ill. by Christopher Canyon. Dawn, 1995. ISBN 1-883220-32-7 Subj: Ecology. Forest, woods. Trees.

Rees, Mary. *Ten in a bed* ill. by adapt. Little, 1988. ISBN 0-316-73708-9 Subj: Bedtime. Counting, numbers. Family life.

Reese, Ralph. *The first crazy word book: verbs* (Preiss, Byron)

Reesink, Marijke. *The golden treasure* ill. by Jaap Tol. Harcourt, 1968. Translation of Het vrouwtje van Stavoren. Subj: Boats, ships. Character traits – selfishness. Folk & fairy tales. Foreign lands – Holland.

The princess who always ran away ill. by Françoise Trésy. McGraw-Hill, 1981. ISBN 0-07-051714-2 Subj: Behavior – solitude. Character traits – being different. Folk & fairy tales. Royalty – princesses. Sibling rivalry.

Reeves, Howard W. *There was an old witch* ill. by David Catrow. Hyperion, 1998. ISBN 0-7868-2387-9 Subj: Holidays – Halloween. Rhyming text. Witches.

Reeves, James. *Ragged Robin: poems from A to Z* ill. by Emma Chichester Clark. Little, 1990. ISBN 0-316-73829-8 Subj: ABC books. Poetry.

Reeves, Mona Rabun. *I had a cat* ill. by Julie Downing. Bradbury, 1989. ISBN 0-02-775731-5 Subj: Animals. Rhyming text.

The spooky eerie night noise ill. by Paul Yalowitz. Bradbury, 1989. ISBN 0-02-775732-3 Subj: Animals – skunks. Emotions – fear. Night. Rhyming text.

Regan, Dana. *Monkey see, monkey do* ill. by author. Grosset, 2000. ISBN 0-448-42414-2 Subj: Animals – monkeys. Rhyming text.

Regan, Dian Curtis. *Daddies* ill. by Mary Morgan-Vanroyen. Scholastic, 1996. ISBN 0-590-47973-3 Subj: Activities. Family life – fathers. Rhyming text.

How do you know it's Halloween? ill. by Fumi Kosaka. Little Simon, 2002. ISBN 0-689-84570-7 Subj: Format, unusual – toy & movable books. Holidays – Halloween. Humorous stories. Riddles & jokes.

Regan, Lara Jo. *What is Mr. Winkle?* photos by author. Random House, 2001. ISBN 0-375-81554-6 Subj: Animals – dogs. Humorous stories.

Regan, Lara Jo (Michael P.). *A Winkle in time* by Mr. Winkle, as told to Michael Regan; photos by Michael Regan. Random House, 2003. ISBN 0-375-92487-6 Subj: Activities. Animals – dogs.

Regan, Michael. *A Winkle in time* (Regan, Lara Jo [Michael P.])

Regniers, Beatrice De. *see* De Regniers, Beatrice Schenk

Rehm, Karl. *Left or right?* by Karl Rehm & Kay Koike; photos by authors. Houghton Mifflin, 1991. ISBN 0-395-58080-3 Subj: Concepts – left & right.

Rehnman, Mats. *The clay flute* ill. by author. Farrar, 1989. ISBN 91-29-59184-8 Subj: Foreign lands. Magic. Music. Musical instruments – flutes. Witches.

Reich, Hanns. *Animal babies* (Zoll, Max Alfred)

Reichmeier, Betty. *Potty time!* ill. by author. Random House, 1988. ISBN 0-394-89403-0 Subj: Behavior – growing up. Toilet training.

Reid, Alastair. *A balloon for a blunderbuss* (Gill, Bob)

Mother Goose in Spanish: Poesias de la Madre Oca (Mother Goose)

Supposing ill. by Abe Birnbaum. Little, 1960. Subj: Humorous stories. Imagination.

Reid, Barbara. *The party* ill. by author. Scholastic, 1999. ISBN 0-590-97801-2 Subj: Family life. Parties. Rhyming text.

Reid, Jon. *Celestino Piatti's animal ABC* (Piatti, Celestino)

Reid, Rob. *Wave goodbye* ill. by Lorraine Williams. Lee & Low, 1996. ISBN 1-880000-30-X Subj: Activities – playing. Rhyming text.

Reidel, Marlene. *Jacob and the robbers* ill. by author. Atheneum, 1967. Subj: Crime. Night. Sleep.

Reider, Katja. *The big little sneeze* ill. by Wolfgang Slawski. North-South, 2002. ISBN 0-7358-1629-8 Subj: Animals. Animals – bears. Character traits – helpfulness. Illness.

Snail started it! by Katja Reider & Angela von Roehl; ill. by Angela von Roehl; trans. by Rosemary Lanning. North-South, 1999. ISBN 1-55858-707-1 Subj: Animals. Animals – snails. Behavior. Cumulative tales.

Reidy, Hannah. *All sorts of clothes* ill. by Emma Dodd. Picture Window, 2005. ISBN 1-4048-1063-3 Subj: Clothing.

Crazy creature contrasts ill. by Clare Mackie. Stewart, Tabori & Chang, 1996. ISBN 1-899883-44-4 Subj: Animals. Character traits – being different. Format, unusual – board books.

Reimold, Mary Gallagher. *My mom is a runner* photos by Sid Dorris. Abingdon, 1987. ISBN 0-687-27545-8 Subj: Family life – mothers. Sports – racing.

Reinen, Judy. *Bow wow* ill. with photos. Little, 2001. ISBN 0-316-83290-1 Subj: Activities. Animals – dogs.

Meow ill. with photos. Little, 2001. ISBN 0-316-83342-8 Subj: Activities. Animals – cats.

Reiner, Carl. *Tell me a scary story – but not too scary!* ill. by James Bennett. Little, 2003. ISBN 0-316-83329-0 Subj: Ghosts. Monsters.

Reinhart, Matthew. *Animal popposites* ill. by author. Little Simon, 2002. ISBN 0-689-84423-9 Subj: Animals. Concepts – opposites. Format, unusual – toy & movable books. Language.

Reinl, Edda. *The little snake* ill. by author. Alphabet Pr., 1982. ISBN 0-907234-15-1 Subj: Emotions – love. Reptiles – snakes.

Reiser, Bob. *David gets his drum* (Francis, Panama)

Reiser, Lynn. *Any kind of dog* ill. by author. Greenwillow, 1992. ISBN 0-688-10915-2 Subj: Animals – dogs. Family life – mothers. Imagination. Pets. Toys.

Bedtime cat ill. by author. Greenwillow, 1991. ISBN 0-688-10026-0 Subj: Animals – cats. Bedtime.

Best friends think alike ill. by author. Greenwillow, 1997. ISBN 0-688-15200-7 Subj: Activities – playing. Concepts – color. Friendship. Imagination.

Cherry pies and lullabies ill. by author. Greenwillow, 1998. ISBN 0-688-13392-4 Subj: Activities – baking, cooking. Family life – grandmothers. Family life – great-grandparents. Family life – mothers.

Christmas counting ill. by author. Greenwillow, 1992. ISBN 0-688-10677-3 Subj: Counting, numbers. Cumulative tales. Holidays – Christmas. Trees.

Dog and cat ill. by author. Greenwillow, 1991. ISBN 0-688-09893-2 Subj: Animals – cats. Animals – dogs.

Earthdance ill. by author. Greenwillow, 1999. ISBN 0-688-16327-0 Subj: Earth. Plants. School.

Little clam ill. by author. Greenwillow, 1998. ISBN 0-688-15909-5 Subj: Activities – storytelling. Animals. Bedtime. Sea & seashore.

My cat Tuna ill. by author. Greenwillow, 2001. ISBN 0-688-16874-4 Subj: Animals – cats. Format, unusual – toy & movable books. Senses.

My dog Truffle ill. by author. Greenwillow, 2001. ISBN 0-688-16875-2 Subj: Animals – dogs. Format, unusual – toy & movable books. Seasons – winter. Senses.

Night thunder and the Queen of the Wild Horses ill. by author. Greenwillow, 1995. ISBN 0-688-11792-9 Subj: Animals. Bedtime. Noise, sounds. Sleep. Weather – lightning, thunder.

The surprise family ill. by author. Greenwillow, 1994. ISBN 0-688-11672-8 Subj: Birds – chickens. Birds – ducks. Emotions – love.

Two mice in three fables ill. by author. Greenwillow, 1995. ISBN 0-688-13390-8 Subj: Animals – mice. Friendship.

Reiss, John J. *Colors* ill. by author. Aladdin, 1987, c1969. ISBN 0-689-71119-0 Subj: Concepts – color.

Numbers ill. by author. Aladdin, 1987, c1971. ISBN 0-689-71120-4 Subj: Counting, numbers.

Shapes ill. by author. Aladdin, 1974. ISBN 0-689-71121-2 Subj: Concepts – shape.

Reiss, Mike. *How Murray saved Christmas* ill. by David Catrow. Price Stern Sloan, 2000. ISBN 0-8431-7610-5 Subj: Holidays – Christmas. Rhyming text. Santa Claus.

Late for school ill. by Michael Austin. Peachtree, 2003. ISBN 1-56145-286-6 Subj: Behavior – promptness, tardiness. Cities, towns. Humorous stories. Rhyming text.

Santa claustrophobia ill. by David Catrow. Price Stern Sloan, 2002. ISBN 0-8431-7756-X Subj: Activities – vacationing. Holidays. Holidays – Christmas. Humorous stories. Rhyming text. Santa Claus.

Reit, Seymour. *The king who learned to smile* ill. by Gordon Laite. Golden Pr., 1960. Subj: Behavior – boredom. Royalty – kings.

Rebus bears ill. by Kenneth Smith. Bantam, 1989. ISBN 0-553-34689-X Subj: Animals – bears. Folk & fairy tales. Rebuses.

Round things everywhere photos by Carol Basen. McGraw-Hill, 1969. Subj: Concepts – shape. Ethnic groups in the U.S.

Reitman, Andrea. *Mouse in the house* ill. by Karen Bell; paper engineering by Renée Jablow. Piggy Toes, 2001. ISBN 1-58117-156-0 Subj: Animals – mice. Format, unusual – toy & movable books. Rhyming text.

Reitveld, Jane Klatt. *Monkey island* ill. by author. Viking, 1963. Subj: Animals – monkeys. Zoos.

Relf, Patricia. *The magic school bus plants seeds: a book about how living things grow* ill. by John Speirs. Scholastic, 1995. Based on The magic school bus series written by Joanna Cole and illustrated by Bruce Degen. TV tie-in book adaptation by Patricia Relf ; TV script written by Ronnie Krauss, Brian Meehl, and Joycelyn Stevenson. ISBN 0-590-22296-1 Subj: Plants. Science. Seeds.

Tonka big book of trucks ill. by Thomas LaPadula. Scholastic, 1996. ISBN 0-590-84572-1 Subj: Toys. Trucks.

Tonka trucks night and day ill. by Thomas LaPadula. Scholastic, 2000. ISBN 0-439-12196-5 Subj: Activities – working. Careers. Transportation. Trucks.

Remkiewicz, Frank. *Greedyanna* ill. by author. Lothrop, 1992. ISBN 0-688-10295-6 Subj: Behavior. Character traits – selfishness. Family life.

The last time I saw Harris ill. by author. Lothrop, 1991. ISBN 0-688-10292-1 Subj: Behavior – lost. Birds – parakeets, parrots. Pets.

Renberg, Dalia Hardof. *Hello, clouds!* ill. by Alona Frankel. HarperCollins, 1985. ISBN 0-06-024839-4 Subj: Imagination. Weather – clouds.

King Solomon and the bee ill. by Ruth Heller. HarperCollins, 1994. ISBN 0-06-022902-0 Subj: Folk & fairy tales. Insects – bees. Jewish culture. Religion.

Reneaux, J. J. *Why Alligator hates Dog* ill. by Donnie Lee Green. August House, 1995. ISBN 0-87483-412-0 Subj: Animals – dogs. Character traits – cleverness. Reptiles – alligators, crocodiles.

Repchuk, Caroline. *The forgotten garden* ill. by Ian Andrew. Millbrook, 1997. ISBN 0-7613-0141-0 Subj: Family life – fathers. Gardens, gardening. Memories, memory.

The race ill. by Alison Jay. Chronicle, 2002. ISBN 0-8118-3500-6 Subj: Animals – rabbits. Folk & fairy tales. Reptiles – turtles, tortoises. Rhyming text. Sports – racing.

Ressmeyer, Roger. *Astronaut to zodiac: a young stargazer's alphabet* photos by author. Crown, 1992. ISBN 0-517-58806-4 Subj: ABC books. Astronomy.

Ressner, Phil. *August explains* ill. by Crosby Newell Bonsall. HarperCollins, 1963. Subj: Animals – bears.

Dudley Pippin ill. by Arnold Lobel. HarperCollins, 1965. Subj: Cities, towns. Imagination.

Retan, Walter. *The snowplow that tried to go south* by Walter Retan [i.e. George Walters]; ill. by John Resko. Atheneum, 1950. Subj: Machines. Seasons – winter. Weather – snow.

The steam shovel that wouldn't eat dirt ill. by Roger Antoine Duvoisin. Atheneum, 1948. Subj: Food. Machines.

Rettich, Margret. *The voyage of the jolly boat* trans. from German by Joy Backhouse; ill. by author. Methuen, 1981. ISBN 0-416-30791-4 Subj: Boats, ships. Careers – fishermen. Weather – storms.

Reuter, Margaret. *My mother is blind* ill. by Philip Lanier. Childrens Pr., 1979. ISBN 0-516-02021-8 Subj: Family life – mothers. Handicaps – blindness. Senses – sight.

Rex, Michael. *Brooms are for flying* ill. by author. Holt, 2000. ISBN 0-8050-6410-9 Subj: Holidays – Halloween. Witches.

My fire engine ill. by author. Holt, 1999. ISBN 0-8050-5391-3 Subj: Careers – firefighters. Fire. Imagination. Safety. Trucks.

My freight train ill. by author. Holt, 2002. ISBN 0-8050-6682-9 Subj: Careers – railroad engineers. Trains.

My race car ill. by author. Holt, 2000. ISBN 0-8050-6101-0 Subj: Automobiles. Careers – race car drivers. Sports – racing.

The pie is cherry ill. by author. Holt, 2001. ISBN 0-8050-6717-5 Subj: Activities – baking, cooking. Food.

Who builds? ill. by author. HarperFestival, 1999. ISBN 0-694-01249-1 Subj: Buildings. Careers – construction workers. Format, unusual – toy & movable books.

Who digs? ill. by author. HarperFestival, 1999. ISBN 0-694-01254-8 Subj: Activities – digging. Animals. Careers – construction workers. Format, unusual – toy & movable books.

Rey, H. A. (Hans Augusto). *Curious George in the big city* (Curious George in the big city)

Curious George takes a train (Curious George takes a train)

Curious George visits a toy store (Curious George visits a toy store)

Anybody at home? ill. by author. Houghton Mifflin, 1942. Subj: Format, unusual. Homes, houses.

Billy's picture (Rey, Margret [Margret Elisabeth Waldstein])

Cecily G and the nine monkeys ill. by author. Houghton Mifflin, 1989, c1942. ISBN 0-395-18430-4 Subj: Animals – giraffes. Animals – monkeys. Humorous stories.

Curious George ill. by author. Houghton Mifflin, 1941. Subj: Animals – monkeys. Careers – firefighters. Character traits – curiosity. Humorous stories.

Curious George and the dump truck (Curious George and the dump truck)

Curious George and the hot air balloon (Curious George and the hot air balloon)

Curious George and the puppies (Curious George and the puppies)

Curious George gets a medal ill. by author. Houghton Mifflin, 1957. Subj: Animals – monkeys. Character traits – curiosity. Humorous stories. Space & space ships.

Curious George goes camping (Curious George goes camping)

Curious George goes to a chocolate factory: based on the original character by Margret and H. A. Rey (Curious George goes to a chocolate factory)

Curious George goes to a movie: based on the original character by Margret and H. A. Rey (Curious George goes to a movie)

Curious George goes to the hospital (Rey, Margret [Margret Elisabeth Waldstein])

Curious George in the snow: based on the original character by Margret and H. A. Rey (Curious George in the snow)

Curious George learns the alphabet ill. by author. Houghton Mifflin, 1963. ISBN 0-395-16031-6 Subj: ABC books. Animals – monkeys. Character traits – curiosity.

Curious George makes pancakes (Curious George makes pancakes)

Curious George rides a bike ill. by author. Houghton Mifflin, 1952. ISBN 0-395-16964-X Subj: Animals – monkeys. Character traits – curiosity. Circus. Humorous stories. Sports – bicycling.

Curious George takes a job ill. by author. Houghton Mifflin, 1947. Subj: Animals – monkeys. Careers – window cleaners. Character traits – curiosity. Humorous stories. Zoos.

Elizabite: adventures of a carnivorous plant ill. by author. Houghton Mifflin, 1999. ISBN 0-395-97702-9 Subj: Humorous stories. Plants. Rhyming text.

Elizabite, adventures of a carnivorous plant ill. by author. HarperCollins, 1942. Subj: Humorous stories. Plants. Rhyming text.

Feed the animals ill. by author. Houghton Mifflin, 1944. Subj: Rhyming text. Zoos.

How do you get there? ill. by author. Houghton Mifflin, 1941. Subj: Format, unusual. Transportation.

Humpty Dumpty and other Mother Goose songs ill. by author. HarperCollins, 1943. Subj: Music. Nursery rhymes. Songs.

Look for the letters ill. by author. HarperCollins, 1942. Subj: ABC books.

The original Curious George ill. by author. Houghton Mifflin, 1998. Printed from H.A. Rey's original watercolors. ISBN 0-395-92272-0 Subj: Animals – monkeys. Careers – firefighters. Character traits – curiosity. Humorous stories.

See the circus ill. by author. Houghton Mifflin, 1956. Subj: Circus. Format, unusual. Rhyming text.

Tit for tat ill. by author. HarperCollins, 1942. Subj: Animals. Humorous stories.

Where's my baby? ill. by author. Houghton Mifflin, 1943. Subj: Animals. Format, unusual. Rhyming text.

Rey, Margret (Margret Elisabeth Waldstein). *Billy's picture* by Margret & Hans Augusto Rey; ill. by Hans Augusto Rey. Harper-Collins, 1948. Subj: Activities – drawing. Animals. Art. Humorous stories.

Curious George and the dinosaur (Curious George and the dinosaur)

Curious George and the dump truck (Curious George and the dump truck)

Curious George and the hot air balloon (Curious George and the hot air balloon)

Curious George and the puppies (Curious George and the puppies)

Curious George flies a kite ill. by Hans Augusto Rey. Houghton Mifflin, 1958. Subj: Animals – monkeys. Character traits – curiosity. Humorous stories. Kites. Sports – fishing.

Curious George goes camping (Curious George goes camping)

Curious George goes to a chocolate factory: based on the original character by Margret and H. A. Rey (Curious George goes to a chocolate factory)

Curious George goes to a movie: based on the original character by Margret and H. A. Rey (Curious George goes to a movie)

Curious George goes to an ice cream shop (Curious George goes to an ice cream shop)

Curious George goes to school (Curious George goes to school)

Curious George goes to the dentist (Curious George goes to the dentist)

Curious George goes to the hospital by Margret & Hans Augusto Rey in collaboration with the Children's Hospital Medical Center, Boston; ill. by Hans Augusto Rey. Houghton Mifflin, 1966. Subj: Animals – monkeys. Behavior – lost. Character traits – curiosity. Hospitals. Humorous stories.

Curious George in the big city (Curious George in the big city)

Curious George in the snow: based on the original character by Margret and H. A. Rey (Curious George in the snow)

Curious George makes pancakes (Curious George makes pancakes)

Curious George takes a train (Curious George takes a train)

Curious George visits a toy store (Curious George visits a toy store)

Pretzel ill. by Hans Augusto Rey. HarperCollins, 1941. Subj: Animals – dogs.

Pretzel and the puppies ill. by Hans Augusto Rey. HarperCollins, 1946. Subj: Animals – dogs.

Spotty ill. by Hans Augusto Rey. Houghton Mifflin, 1997. ISBN 0-395-83736-7 Subj: Animals – rabbits. Character traits – being different.

Whiteblack the penguin sees the world ill. by Hans Augusto Rey. Houghton, 2000. ISBN 0-618-07389-2 Subj: Activities – traveling. Animals. Birds – penguins.

Reyher, Rebecca (Hourwich). *My mother is the most beautiful woman in the world* ill. by Ruth S. Gannett. Lothrop, 1945. Subj: Caldecott award honor books. Family life – mothers.

Reynolds, Adrian. *Pete and Polo's farmyard adventure* ill. by author. Orchard, 2002. ISBN 0-439-30913-1 Subj: Birds – ducks. Counting, numbers. Family life – grandfathers. Farms. Toys – bears.

Reynolds, Jan. *Amazon* photos by author. Harcourt, 1993. ISBN 0-15-202832-3 Subj: Foreign lands – South America. Indians of South America. Rivers.

Down under photos by author. Harcourt, 1992. ISBN 0-15-224182-5 Subj: Foreign lands – Australia.

Far north photos by author. Harcourt, 1992. ISBN 0-15-227178-3 Subj: Foreign lands – Arctic. Foreign lands – Lapland. Foreign lands – Norway.

Himalaya photos by author. Harcourt, 1991. ISBN 0-15-234465-9 Subj: Foreign lands – Nepal.

Sahara photos by author. Harcourt, 1991. ISBN 0-15-269959-7 Subj: Desert. Foreign lands – Sahara Desert.

Reynolds, Marilynn. *The magnificent piano recital* ill. by Laura Fernandez & Rick Jacobson. Orca, 2001. ISBN 1-55143-180-7 Subj: Careers – teachers. Family life – mothers. Musical instruments – pianos.

The name of the child ill. by Don Kilby. Orca, 2002. ISBN 1-55143-221-8 Subj: Babies. Character traits – bravery. Emotions – fear. Foreign lands – Canada. Illness – influenza. Names.

The new land: a first year on the prairie ill. by Stephen McCallum. Orca, 1997. ISBN 1-55143-069-X Subj: Family life. Farms. Immigrants. U.S. history – frontier & pioneer life.

The prairie fire ill. by Don Kilby. Orca, 1999. ISBN 1-55143-137-8 Subj: Farms. Fire. U.S. history – frontier & pioneer life.

A present for Mrs. Kazinski ill. by Lynn Smith-Ary. Orca, 2001. ISBN 1-55143-196-3 Subj: Animals – cats. Birthdays. Old age. Pets.

Reynolds, Peter H. *Sydney's star* ill. by author. S&S, 2001. ISBN 0-689-83184-6 Subj: Animals – mice. Boats, ships. Careers – inventors. Contests. Stars. Weather – storms.

Rheingrover, Jean Sasso. *Veronica's first year* ill. by Kay Life. A. Whitman, 1996. ISBN 0-8075-8474-6 Subj: Babies. Family life – new sibling. Family life – sisters. Handicaps – Down syndrome.

Rhodes, Timothy. *The hummingbird's gift* (Czernecki, Stefan)

Pancho's piñata (Czernecki, Stefan)

The singing snake (Czernecki, Stefan)

The sleeping bread (Czernecki, Stefan)

Rhyme time around the day col. by John Foster; ill. by Carol Thompon. Oxford Univ. Pr., 2000. ISBN 0-19-276227-3 Subj: Activities. Poetry.

Ribke, Simone T. *The shapes we eat* ill. with photos. Childrens Pr., 2004. ISBN 0-516-24431-0 Subj: Concepts – shape. Counting, numbers. Food.

Rice, Christopher. *My first body book* (Rice, Melanie)

Rice, David L. *Because Brian hugged his mother* ill. by K. Dyble Thompson. Dawn, 1999. ISBN 1-883220-90-4 Subj: Behavior. Character traits – kindness. Cities, towns. Family life. School.

Rice, Eve. *Aren't you coming too?* ill. by Nancy Winslow Parker. Greenwillow, 1988. ISBN 0-688-06447-7 Subj: Activities. Family life – grandfathers.

At Grammy's house ill. by Nancy Winslow Parker. Greenwillow, 1990. ISBN 0-688-08875-9 Subj: Family life – grandparents.

Benny bakes a cake ill. by author. Greenwillow, 1993. ISBN 0-688-11580-2 Subj: Activities – baking, cooking. Animals – dogs. Behavior – misbehavior. Birthdays.

City night ill. by Peter Sis. Greenwillow, 1987. ISBN 0-688-06857-X Subj: Cities, towns. Family life. Night. Poetry.

Ebbie ill. by author. Greenwillow, 1975. ISBN 0-688-84017-5 Subj: Family life. Names.

Goodnight, goodnight ill. by author. Greenwillow, 1980. ISBN 0-688-84254-2 Subj: Bedtime. Night.

New blue shoes ill. by author. Macmillan, 1975. ISBN 0-02-775960-1 Subj: Clothing – shoes. Family life – mothers. Shopping.

Once in a wood: ten tales from Æsop (Æsop)

Papa's lemonade and other stories ill. by author. Greenwillow, 1976. ISBN 0-688-84041-8 Subj: Animals – dogs. Family life.

Peter's pockets ill. by Nancy Winslow Parker. Greenwillow, 1989. ISBN 0-688-07242-9 Subj: Clothing – pants. Clothing – pockets. Problem solving.

Sam who never forgets ill. by author. Greenwillow, 1977. ISBN 0-688-84088-4 Subj: Animals. Food. Zoos.

Swim! ill. by Marisabina Russo. Greenwillow, 1996. ISBN 0-688-14275-3 Subj: Family life – fathers. Sports – swimming.

What Sadie sang ill. by author. Greenwillow, 1976. ISBN 0-688-84038-8 Subj: Babies. Emotions – happiness.

Rice, Inez. *A long long time* ill. by Robert M. Quackenbush. Lothrop, 1964. Subj: Character traits – optimism. Imagination.

The March wind ill. by Vladimir Bobri. Lothrop, 1957. Subj: Clothing. Imagination. Weather – wind.

Rice, James. *Cajun alphabet* ill. by author. Pelican, 1991. ISBN 0-88289-822-1 Subj: ABC books.

Gaston goes to Texas ill. by author. Pelican, 1978. ISBN 0-88289-204-5 Subj: Reptiles – alligators, crocodiles. Rhyming text. Texas.

Rice, Judith. *Those itsy-bitsy teeny-tiny not-so-nice head lice = Esos pequeñines, chiquitines, para nada simpáticos piojos* ill. by Julie Ann Stricklin; photos by Petronella J. Ytsma. Redleaf, 1998. ISBN 1-884834-54-X Subj: Foreign languages. Health & fitness. Insects – lice.

Those ooey gooey winky-blinky but – invisible pinkeye germs = Esos pringosos viscosos pestañeantes parpadeantes pero – invisibles gérmenes que causan conjuntivitis ill. by Julie Ann Stricklen; trans. by Eida de la Vega. Redleaf, 2000. ISBN 1-884834-89-2 Subj: Anatomy – eyes. Foreign languages. Health & fitness. Illness.

Rice, Melanie. *My first body book* by Melanie & Chris Rice; ill. with photos. DK, 1995. ISBN 1-56458-893-9 Subj: Anatomy. Format, unusual.

Rice, Mitch. *Blue aliens* (Porto, Tony)

Get red (Porto, Tony)

Rich, Scharlotte. *Who made the wild woods?* ill. by Anna Currey. WaterBrook, 1999. ISBN 1-57856-027-6 Subj: Animals. Creation. Forest, woods. Plants. Religion.

Rich, Susan. *Mrs. Meyer, the bird* (Erlbruch, Wolf)

Richard, Françoise. *On Cat Mountain* adapt. by Arthur A. Levine; ill. by Anne Buguet. Putnam, 1994. ISBN 0-399-22608-7 Subj: Animals – cats. Character traits – kindness. Folk & fairy tales. Foreign lands – Japan.

Richards, Jane. *A horse grows up* ill. by Bert Hardy. Walker, 1972. ISBN 0-8027-6104-6 Subj: Animals – horses, ponies. Science.

Richards, Jean. *The first Olympic games: a gruesome Greek myth with a happy ending* ill. by Kat Thacker. Millbrook, 2000. ISBN 0-7613-1311-7 Subj: Mythical creatures. Sports – Olympics.

How the elephant got his trunk a retelling of the Rudyard Kipling tale; ill. by Norman Gorbaty. Holt, 2003. ISBN 0-8050-6699-3 Subj: Anatomy – noses. Animals. Animals – elephants. Character traits – curiosity. Folk & fairy tales – pourquoi tales. Foreign lands – Africa. Reptiles – alligators, crocodiles.

Richards, Jon. *Jetliners* ill. by Simon Tegg & Mike Saunders. Copper Beech, 1998. ISBN 0-7613-0744-3 Subj: Airplanes, airports. Transportation.

Trains ill. with photos. Copper Beech, 1998. ISBN 0-7613-0824-5 Subj: Trains. Transportation.

Richards, Kitty. *It's about time, Max!* ill. by Gioia Fiammenghi. Kane/Miller, 2000. ISBN 1-57565-088-6 Subj: Clocks, watches. Time.

Merry Christmas, Rugrats! ill. by Barry Goldberg. Simon Spotlight, 1998. ISBN 0-689-82179-4 Subj: Babies. Format, unusual – toy & movable books. Holidays – Christmas.

Richards, Laura Elizabeth Howe. *Jiggle joggle jee* ill. by Sam Williams. Greenwillow, 2001. ISBN 0-688-17833-2 Subj: Babies. Poetry. Toys – trains.

Richardson, Bill. *But if they do* ill. by Marc Mongeau. Firefly, 2003. ISBN 1-55037-787-6 Subj: Bedtime. Humorous stories. Rhyming text.

Sally Dog Little ill. by Céline Malépart. Annick, 2003. ISBN 1-55037-759-0 Subj: Animals – dogs. Ghosts. Pirates.

Richardson, Jack E. *Six in a mix* by Jack E. Richardson, Jr., & others; ill. by Carlos Alfonso & others. Benziger, 1971. Subj: Language.

Richardson, Jean. *The bear who went to the ballet* ill. by Susan Winter. DK, 1995. ISBN 0-7894-0318-8 Subj: Activities – dancing. Ballet. Toys – bears.

Clara's dancing feet ill. by Joanna Carey. Putnam, 1987. ISBN 0-399-21388-0 Subj: Activities – dancing. Ballet. Character traits – shyness.

The nutcracker (Hoffmann, E. T. A.)

The sleeping beauty: the story of Tchaikovsky's ballet ill. by Francesca Crespi. Arcade, 1991. ISBN 1-55970-142-0 Subj: Activities – dancing. Ballet. Folk & fairy tales. Royalty – princes. Royalty – princesses. Sleep. Witches.

Stephen's feast ill. by Alice Englander. Little, 1991. ISBN 0-316-74435-2 Subj: Holidays – Christmas. Middle Ages. Music. Songs.

Tall inside ill. by Alice Englander. Putnam, 1988. ISBN 0-399-21486-0 Subj: Clowns, jesters. Self-concept.

Thomas's sitter ill. by Dawn Holmes. Four Winds, 1991. ISBN 0-02-776146-0 Subj: Activities – babysitting. Behavior – misbehavior. Gender roles.

Richardson, John. *Grunt* ill. by author. Clarion, 2001. ISBN 0-618-15974-6 Subj: Animals – pigs. Character traits – individuality. Family life. Self-concept. Sibling rivalry.

Ten bears in a bed ill. by author. Hyperion, 1992. ISBN 1-56282-157-1 Subj: Animals. Animals – bears. Bedtime. Counting, numbers. Format, unusual – toy & movable books.

Where's Jack? ill. by author; paper engineering by David Hawcock. Aladdin, 1993. ISBN 0-689-71713-X Subj: Format, unusual – toy & movable books. Holidays – Christmas. Toys.

Richardson, Judith Benét. *Old winter* ill. by R. W. Alley. Orchard, 1996. ISBN 0-531-08883-9 Subj: Seasons – spring. Seasons – winter. Sleep.

The way home ill. by Salley Mavor. Macmillan, 1991. ISBN 0-02-776145-2 Subj: Animals – elephants. Sea & seashore.

Riches, Judith. *Giraffes have more fun* ill. by author. Morrow, 1992. ISBN 0-688-11043-6 Subj: Animals – giraffes. Imagination.

Richmond Elementary School (Richmond, Vt.). *Night time* (Night time)

Richter, Alice Numeroff. *Emily's bunch* (Numeroff, Laura Joffe)

You can't put braces on spaces by Alice Numeroff Richter & Laura Joffe Numeroff; ill. by Laura Joffe Numeroff. Greenwillow, 1979. ISBN 0-688-84190-2 Subj: Careers – dentists. Teeth.

Richter, Mischa. *Eric and Matilda* ill. by author. HarperCollins, 1967. Subj: Birds – ducks. Parades.

Quack? ill. by author. Harper, 1978. ISBN 0-06-025020-8 Subj: Animals. Birds – ducks. Noise, sounds. Wordless.

To bed, to bed! ill. by author. Prentice-Hall, 1981. ISBN 0-03-922922-1 Subj: Bedtime. Royalty.

Rickard, Graham. *Let's look at tractors* ill. by Clifford Meadway. Watts, 1990. ISBN 0-531-18256-8 Subj: Tractors.

Rickert, Janet Elizabeth. *Russ and the almost perfect day* photos by Pete McGahan. Woodbine, 2000. ISBN 1-890627-18-6 Subj: Behavior – lost & found possessions. Handicaps – Down syndrome. Handicaps – mental handicaps. School.

Ricketts, Michael. *Rain* ill. by author. Wonder Books, 1971. Subj: Weather – rain.

Teeth ill. by author. Grosset, 1971. Subj: Teeth.

Ricklen, Neil. *My clothes = Mi ropa* ill. by author. Aladdin, 1994. ISBN 0-689-71773-3 Subj: Clothing. Foreign languages. Format, unusual – board books.

My colors = Mis colores ill. by author. Aladdin, 1994. ISBN 0-689-71772-5 Subj: Concepts – color. Foreign languages. Format, unusual – board books.

My family = Mi familia photos by author. Aladdin, 1994. ISBN 0-689-71771-7 Subj: Family life. Foreign languages. Format, unusual – board books.

My numbers = Mis números photos by author. Aladdin, 1994. ISBN 0-689-71770-9 Subj: Counting, numbers. Foreign languages. Format, unusual – board books.

Riddell, Chris. *The bear dance* ill. by author. S&S, 1990. ISBN 0-671-70974-7 Subj: Activities – dancing. Animals – bears.

Ben and the bear ill. by author. Lippincott, 1986. ISBN 0-397-32194-5 Subj: Animals – bears. Behavior – sharing.

Bird's new shoes ill. by author. Holt, 1987. ISBN 0-8050-0326-6 Subj: Animals. Behavior – imitation. Character traits – being different. Clothing – shoes. Cumulative tales.

Mr. Underbed ill. by author. Holt, 1986. ISBN 0-8050-0026-7 Subj: Bedtime. Humorous stories. Monsters. Night. Toys.

Platypus ill. by author. Harcourt, 2001. ISBN 0-15-216493-6 Subj: Animals – platypuses. Crustaceans – crabs. Sea & seashore.

Platypus and the lucky day ill. by author. Harcourt, 2002. ISBN 0-15-216723-4 Subj: Animals – platypuses. Behavior – bad day. Character traits – luck.

The trouble with elephants ill. by author. Lippincott, 1988. ISBN 0-397-32273-9 Subj: Animals – elephants.

The wish factory ill. by author. Ideals, 1990. ISBN 0-8249-8482-X Subj: Behavior – wishing. Dreams. Monsters. Sleep.

Riddell, Edwina. *My first day at preschool* ill. by author. Barron's, 1992. ISBN 0-8120-6261-2 Subj: School – first day. School – nursery.

One hundred first words ill. by author. Barron's, 1988. ISBN 0-8120-5786-4 Subj: Language.

Riddle, Tohby. *Careful with that ball, Eugene!* ill. by author. Watts, 1991. ISBN 0-531-08517-1 Subj: Imagination. Sports.

The great escape from City Zoo ill. by author. Farrar, 1999. ISBN 0-374-32776-9 Subj: Animals. Character traits – freedom. Disguises. Zoos.

The singing hat ill. by author. Farrar, 2001. ISBN 0-374-36934-8 Subj: Birds. Clothing – hats.

Rider, Alex. *A la ferme = At the farm: learn-a-language book in French and English* ill. by Paul Davis. Doubleday, 1962. Subj: Farms. Foreign lands – France. Foreign languages.

At our house = Chez nous: learn-a-language book in French and English ill. by Isadore Seltzer. Doubleday, 1962. Subj: Family life. Foreign lands – France. Foreign languages.

Rider, Joanne. *First grade valentines* ill. by Betsy Lewin. Troll, 1993. ISBN 0-8167-3004-0 Subj: Character traits – kindness. Holidays – Valentine's Day. School.

Ridlon, Marcia. *Kittens and more kittens* ill. by Elizabeth Dauber. Follett, 1967. Subj: Animals – cats. Pets.

Riecken, Nancy. *Today is the day* ill. by Catherine Stock. Houghton Mifflin, 1996. ISBN 0-395-73917-9 Subj: Careers – farmers. Family life – fathers. Farms. Foreign lands – Mexico.

Riehecky, Janet. *Apatosaurus* ill. by Lydia Halverson. Child's World, 1988. ISBN 0-89565-423-7 Subj: Dinosaurs.

Rigby, Rodney. *Hello, this is your penguin speaking* ill. by author. Walt Disney, 1992. ISBN 1-56282-232-2 Subj: Activities – flying. Birds – penguins. Character traits – persistence.

There's a building on Sixth Avenue ill. by author. Walt Disney, 1992. ISBN 1-56282-156-3 Subj: Poetry.

Rigby, Shirley Lincoln. *Smaller than most* ill. by Debby L. Carter. HarperCollins, 1985. ISBN 0-06-025028-3 Subj: Animals – pandas. Babies. Character traits – smallness. Family life. Family life – grandfathers.

Riggio, Anita. *Beware the Brindlebeast* ill. by author. Caroline House, 1994. ISBN 1-56397-133-X Subj: Folk & fairy tales. Foreign lands – England. Holidays – Halloween. Monsters.

A moon in my teacup ill. by author. Boyds Mills, 1996. ISBN 1-56397-008-2 Subj: Ethnic groups in the U.S. – Italian Americans. Family life – grandparents. Holidays – Christmas.

Secret signs: along the underground railroad ill. by author. Boyds Mills, 1997. ISBN 1-56397-555-6 Subj: Behavior – secrets. Ethnic groups in the U.S. – African Americans. Slavery. U.S. history.

Smack dab in the middle ill. by author. Putnam, 2002. ISBN 0-399-23700-3 Subj: Emotions – sadness. Family life.

Wake up, William! ill. by author. Atheneum, 1987. ISBN 0-689-31344-6 Subj: Family life. Sleep.

Rikys, Bodel. *Red bear* ill. by author. Dial, 1992. ISBN 0-8037-1048-8 Subj: Animals – bears. Concepts – color.

Riley, James Whitcomb. *Little Orphan Annie* ill. by Diane Stanley. Putnam, 1983. ISBN 0-399-20904-2 Subj: Poetry.

Riley, Joelle. *Quiet owls* ill. with photos. Lerner, 2004. ISBN 0-8225-3771-0 Subj: Birds – owls. Science.

Riley, Linda Capus. *Elephants swim* ill. by Steve Jenkins. Houghton Mifflin, 1995. ISBN 0-395-73654-4 Subj: Animals. Sports – swimming. Water.

Riley, Linnea Asplind. *Mouse mess* ill. by author. Blue Sky, 1997. ISBN 0-590-10048-3 Subj: Animals – mice. Behavior – messy. Food. Night.

Rinder, Lenore. *A big mistake* ill. by Susan Horn. G. Stevens, 1994. ISBN 0-8368-0674-3 Subj: Activities – painting. Behavior – mistakes. Imagination. Rhyming text.

Ring, Elizabeth. *Lucky mouse* ill. by Dwight Kuhn. Millbrook, 1995. ISBN 1-56294-344-8 Subj: Animals – mice. Nature.

Some stuff ill. by Anne Canevari Green. Millbrook, 1995. ISBN 1-56294-466-5 Subj: Activities – playing. Behavior – sharing. Emotions – loneliness. Rhyming text.

Tiger lilies and other beastly plants ill. by Barbara Bash. Walker, 1996. ISBN 0-8027-7454-7 Subj: Character traits – appearance. Plants.

Ring, Susan. *Polar babies* ill. by Lisa McCue. Random House, 2000. ISBN 0-679-99387-8 Subj: Animals – babies. Animals – polar bears. Family life – mothers. Foreign lands – Arctic.

Ringgold, Faith. *Bonjour, Lonnie* ill. by author. Hyperion, 1996. ISBN 0-7868-2062-4 Subj: Birds. Ethnic groups in the U.S. – African Americans. Family life. Foreign lands – France. Imagination.

Cassie's word quilt ill. by author. Knopf, 2002. ISBN 0-375-91200-2 Subj: Ethnic groups in the U.S. – African Americans. Language. Picture puzzles. Quilts.

Dinner at Aunt Connie's house ill. by author. Hyperion, 1993. ISBN 1-56282-426-0 Subj: Art. Ethnic groups in the U.S. – African Americans. Family life. Food. U.S. history.

If a bus could talk ill. by author. S&S, 1999. ISBN 0-689-81892-0 Subj: Ethnic groups in the U.S. – African Americans. Prejudice. Transportation. U.S. history.

The invisible princesses ill. by author. Crown, 1999. ISBN 0-517-80025-X Subj: Ethnic groups in the U.S. – African Americans. Family life. Folk & fairy tales. Royalty – princesses. Slavery.

My dream of Martin Luther King ill. by author. Crown, 1995. ISBN 0-517-59977-5 Subj: Dreams. Ethnic groups in the U.S. – African Americans. U.S. history.

Tar Beach ill. by author. Crown, 1991. ISBN 0-517-58031-4 Subj: Activities – flying. Caldecott award honor books. Cities, towns. Dreams. Ethnic groups in the U.S. – African Americans. Quilts.

Ringi, Kjell (Arne Sorensen). *My father and I* by Kjell Ringi & Adelaide Holl; ill. by Kjell Ringi. Watts, 1972. ISBN 0-531-02560-8 Subj: Character traits – ambition. Family life – fathers. Imagination.

The sun and the cloud ill. by author. HarperCollins, 1971. ISBN 0-06-025032-1 Subj: Plants. Sun. Weather – clouds.

The winner ill. by author. HarperCollins, 1969. Subj: Behavior. Wordless.

Rink, Cindy. *Where does the wind blow?* ill. by author. Dawn, 2002. ISBN 1-58469-041-0 Subj: Nature. Rhyming text. Weather – wind.

Riordan, James. *The coming of Night: a Yoruba tale from West Africa* ill. by Jenny Stow. Millbrook, 1999. ISBN 0-7613-1358-3 Subj: Creation. Folk & fairy tales. Foreign lands – Africa. Night.

Little Bunny Bobkin ill. by Tim Warnes. Little Tiger, 1999. ISBN 1-8884-4438-X Subj: Animals – foxes. Animals – rabbits. Counting, numbers.

Old Father Frost (Odoyevsky, Vladimir)

The Snowmaiden ill. by Stephen Lambert. Trafalgar Square, 1992. ISBN 0-09-173861-X Subj: Folk & fairy tales. Foreign lands – Russia.

The three magic gifts ill. by Errol le Cain. Oxford Univ. Pr., 1980. ISBN 0-19-520194-9 Subj: Character traits – perseverance. Folk & fairy tales. Gifts. Magic. Sibling rivalry.

Thumbelina (Andersen, H. C. [Hans Christian])

Ripley, Catherine. *Two dozen dinosaurs* ill. by Bo-Kim Louie. Firefly, 1992. ISBN 0-920775-55-1 Subj: Dinosaurs. Games. Prehistory.

Why do stars twinkle? and other nighttime questions ill. by Scot Ritchie. Firefly, 1996. ISBN 1-895688-42-6 Subj: Bedtime. Character traits – questioning. Night.

Why is soap so slippery? and other bathtime stories ill. by Scot Ritchie. Firefly, 1995. ISBN 1-895688-34-5 Subj: Activities – bathing. Character traits – questioning.

Rippon, Penelope. *My day* ill. by author. Viking, 1990. ISBN 0-670-83459-9 Subj: Babies. Family life.

Rister, Claude. *see* Marshall, James

Rives. *If I were a polar bear* ill. & paper-eng. by author. Piggy Toes, 2001. ISBN 1-58117-046-7 Subj: Animals – polar bears. Foreign lands – Arctic. Format, unusual – toy & movable books. Rhyming text.

Rix, Jamie. *The last chocolate cookie* ill. by Arthur Robins. Candlewick, 1998. ISBN 0-7636-0411-9 Subj: Aliens. Etiquette. Food. Humorous stories. Monsters.

Roach, Marilynne K. *Dune fox* ill. by author. Little, 1977. ISBN 0-316-74870-6 Subj: Animals – foxes. Ecology. Sand. Seasons.

Two Roman mice by Horace (Quintus Horatius Flaccus); ill. by reteller. Crowell, 1975. Based on a version of Æsop's fable about the country mouse and the city mouse as it appeared in Horace's Satirae II, 6. ISBN 0-690-00771-X Subj: Animals – mice. Cities, towns. Country.

Roache, Gordon. *A Halifax ABC* ill. by author. Tundra, 1987. ISBN 0-88776-183-6 Subj: ABC books. Cities, towns. Foreign lands – Canada.

Robart, Rose. *The cake that Mack ate* ill. by Maryann Kovalski. Little, 1987. ISBN 0-87113-121-8 Subj: Cumulative tales. Farms. Food.

Robb, Brian. *My grandmother's djinn* ill. by author. Parents' Magazine Pr., 1978. ISBN 0-8193-0918-4 Subj: Family life. Foreign lands. Mythical creatures. Problem solving.

Robb, Diane Burton. *The alphabet war* ill. by Gail Piazza. A. Whitman, 2004. ISBN 0-8075-0302-9 Subj: Books, reading. Handicaps – dyslexia. School.

Robb, Laura. *Snuffles and snouts* ill. by Steven Kellogg. Dial, 1995. ISBN 0-8037-1598-6 Subj: Animals – pigs. Poetry.

Robberecht, Thierry. *Stolen smile* ill. by Philippe Goossens. Random House, 2002. ISBN 0-385-90850-4 Subj: Behavior – bullying. Emotions.

Robbins, Beth. *Tom, Ally, and the baby-sitter* ill. by Jon Stuart. DK, 2001. ISBN 0-7894-7426-3 Subj: Activities – babysitting. Animals – cats. Animals – rabbits. Emotions – fear.

Tom, Ally, and the new baby ill. by Jon Stuart. DK, 2001. ISBN 0-7894-7431-X Subj: Animals – cats. Babies. Family life – brothers & sisters. Family life – new sibling.

Tom and Ally visit the doctor ill. by Jon Stuart. DK, 2001. ISBN 0-7894-7429-8 Subj: Animals – cats. Careers – doctors. Emotions – fear. Family life – brothers & sisters.

Tom's afraid of the dark ill. by Jon Stuart. DK, 2001. ISBN 0-7894-7421-2 Subj: Animals – cats. Bedtime. Emotions – fear. Imagination. Night.

Tom's first day at school ill. by Jon Stuart. DK, 2001. ISBN 0-7894-7423-9 Subj: Animals. Animals – cats. School – first day.

Tom's new haircut ill. by Jon Stuart. DK, 2001. ISBN 0-7894-7425-5 Subj: Animals. Animals – cats. Careers – barbers. Emotions – fear. Hair.

Robbins, Ken. *Apples* photos by author. Atheneum, 2002. ISBN 0-689-83024-6 Subj: Activities – baking, cooking. Farms. Food. Trees.

Autumn leaves ill. by author. Scholastic, 1998. ISBN 0-590-29879-8 Subj: Plants. Seasons – fall. Trees.

Beach days photos by author. Viking, 1987. ISBN 0-670-80138-0 Subj: Sand. Sea & seashore – beaches.

City/country photos by author. Viking, 1985. ISBN 0-670-80743-5 Subj: Activities – traveling. Automobiles.

Seeds ill. by author. Atheneum, 2005. ISBN 0-689-85041-7 Subj: Plants. Seeds.

Trucks, giants of the highway photos by author. Atheneum, 1999. ISBN 0-689-82664-8 Subj: Traffic, traffic signs. Transportation. Trucks.

Trucks of every sort photos by author. Crown, 1981. ISBN 0-517-54164-5 Subj: Trucks.

Robbins, Maria Polushkin. *Baby brother blues* ill. by Ellen Weiss. Bradbury, 1987. ISBN 0-02-774780-8 Subj: Babies. Family life – new sibling. Sibling rivalry.

Bubba and Babba ill. by Diane de Groat. Crown, 1976. ISBN 0-517-52435-X Subj: Animals – bears. Character traits – cleanliness. Folk & fairy tales.

Here's that kitten ill. by Betsy Lewin. Bradbury, 1990. ISBN 0-02-774741-7 Subj: Animals – cats.

Kitten in trouble ill. by Betsy Lewin. Bradbury, 1988. ISBN 0-02-774740-9 Subj: Animals – cats. Behavior – misbehavior.

The little hen and the giant ill. by Yuri Salzman. HarperCollins, 1977. Subj: Birds – chickens. Character traits – bravery. Folk & fairy tales. Foreign lands – Russia. Giants.

Morning ill. by Bill Morrison. Four Winds, 1983. ISBN 0-590-07871-2 Subj: Farms. Morning.

Mother, Mother, I want another ill. by Diane Dawson. Crown, 1978. ISBN 0-517-53401-0 Subj: Animals – mice. Bedtime. Behavior – misunderstanding. Family life – mothers. Sleep.

Mother, Mother I want another ill. by Jon Goodell. Knopf, 2005. ISBN 0-375-92588-0 Subj: Animals – mice. Bedtime. Behavior – misunderstanding. Family life – mothers. Sleep.

Who said meow? ill. by Giulio Maestro. Crown, 1975. ISBN 0-517-51846-5 Subj: Animals – cats. Animals – dogs. Noise, sounds.

Who said meow? ill. by Ellen Weiss. Bradbury, 1988. ISBN 0-02-774770-0 Subj: Animals – cats. Animals – dogs. Noise, sounds.

Robbins, Ruth. *Baboushka and the three kings* ill. by Nicolas Sidjakov; verse by Edith R. Thomas; music by Mary Clement Sanks. Parnassus, 1960. Adapt. from a Russian folk tale. ISBN 0-395-27672-1 Subj: Caldecott award books. Folk & fairy tales. Foreign lands – Russia. Holidays – Christmas. Music. Rhyming text. Songs.

The harlequin and Mother Goose: or, The magic stick ill. by Nicolas Sidjakov. Parnassus, 1965. Subj: Nursery rhymes.

How the first rainbow was made ill. by author. Houghton Mifflin, 1980. ISBN 0-395-29082-1 Subj: Folk & fairy tales – pourquoi tales. Indians of North America. Weather – rain. Weather – rainbows.

Robbins, Sandra. *The firefly star* ill. by Iku Oseki. See-More's Workshop, 1995. ISBN 1-882601-23-8 Subj: Animals – horses, ponies. Animals – mice. Foreign lands – Latin America. Holidays. Insects – fireflies. Insects – ladybugs. Stars.

Roberts, Bethany. *Birthday mice* ill. by Doug Cushman. Clarion, 2002. ISBN 0-618-07772-3 Subj: Animals. Animals – mice. Birthdays. Cowboys, cowgirls. Parties. Rhyming text.

Camel caravan by Bethany Roberts & Patricia Hubbell; ill. by Cheryl Munro Taylor. Tambourine, 1996. ISBN 0-688-13940-X Subj: Activities – traveling. Animals – camels. Behavior – dissatisfaction. Desert. Rhyming text.

Christmas mice ill. by Doug Cushman. Clarion, 2000. ISBN 0-395-91204-0 Subj: Animals – cats. Animals – mice. Holidays – Christmas. Rhyming text.

Easter mice ill. by Doug Cushman. Clarion, 2003. ISBN 0-618-31367-2 Subj: Animals – mice. Eggs. Holidays – Easter. Rhyming text.

Fourth of July mice ill. by Doug Cushman. Clarion, 2004. ISBN 0-618-31367-2 Subj: Activities. Animals – mice. Holidays – Fourth of July. Rhyming text.

Gramps and the fire dragon ill. by Melissa Iwai. Clarion, 1997. ISBN 0-395-69849-9 Subj: Activities – storytelling. Bedtime. Family life – grandfathers. Fire. Imagination.

Rosie to the rescue ill. by Kay Chorao. Holt, 2003. ISBN 0-8050-6486-9 Subj: Animals – squirrels. Family life – aunts, uncles. Family life – parents. Imagination.

Valentine mice! ill. by Doug Cushman. Clarion, 1997. ISBN 0-395-77518-3 Subj: Animals. Animals – mice. Holidays – Valentine's Day. Rhyming text.

Waiting-for-Christmas stories ill. by Sarah Stapler. Clarion, 1994. ISBN 0-395-67324-0 Subj: Animals – rabbits. Bedtime. Holidays – Christmas.

Waiting-for-Papa stories ill. by Sarah Stapler. HarperCollins, 1990. ISBN 0-06-025051-8 Subj: Animals – rabbits. Family life – fathers.

Waiting-for-spring stories ill. by William Joyce. HarperCollins, 1984. ISBN 0-06-025062-3 Subj: Animals – rabbits. Seasons – winter.

The wind's garden ill. by Melanie Hope Greenberg. Holt, 2001. ISBN 0-8050-6367-6 Subj: Gardens, gardening. Weather – wind.

Roberts, Cliff. *The dot* ill. by author. Watts, 1960. Subj: Concepts – shape.

Start with a dot ill. by author. Watts, 1968, c1960. Subj: Concepts – shape. Rhyming text.

Roberts, David (1970–). *Dirty Bertie* ill. by author. Abrams, 2003. ISBN 0-8109-4259-3 Subj: Behavior. Character traits – cleanliness.

Roberts, Lynn (Lynn M.). *Cinderella, an Art Deco love story* ill. by David Roberts. Abrams, 2001. ISBN 0-8109-4168-6 Subj: Family life – stepfamilies. Folk & fairy tales. Royalty – princes. Sibling rivalry.

Rapunzel, a groovy fairy tale ill. by David Roberts. Abrams, 2003. ISBN 0-8109-4242-9 Subj: Character traits – meanness. Family life – aunts, uncles. Folk & fairy tales. Hair.

Roberts, Sarah. *Bert and the missing mop mix-up* ill. by Joseph Mathieu. Random House, 1983. ISBN 0-394-95752-0 Subj: Behavior – misunderstanding. Puppets.

Ernie's big mess ill. by Joseph Mathieu. Random House, 1981. ISBN 0-394-94847-5 Subj: Behavior – carelessness. Puppets.

I want to go home! ill. by Joseph Mathieu. Random House, 1985. ISBN 0-394-97027-6 Subj: Behavior – needing someone. Family life – grandmothers. Puppets. Sea & seashore.

Roberts, Thom. *Pirates in the park* ill. by Harold Berson. Crown, 1973. ISBN 0-517-50257-7 Subj: Imagination. Parks. Pirates. Toys – rocking horses.

Roberts, Tom. *The three billy goats Gruff* (Asbjørnsen, P. C. [Peter Christen])

Robertson, Janet. *Oscar's spots* ill. by author. BridgeWater, 1993. ISBN 0-8167-3133-0 Subj: Animals – leopards. Magic. Self-concept.

Robertson, Joanne. *Sea witches* ill. by László Gál. Dial, 1991. ISBN 0-8037-1070-4 Subj: Family life – grandmothers. Folk & fairy tales. Foreign lands – Scotland. Poetry. Witches.

Robertson, Lilian. *Picnic woods* ill. by author. Harcourt, 1949. Subj: Activities – picnicking.

Runaway rocking horse ill. by author. Harcourt, 1948. Subj: Toys – rocking horses.

Robertson, M. P. *The egg* ill. by author. Fogelman, 2001. ISBN 0-8037-2546-9 Subj: Behavior – needing someone. Dragons. Eggs.

The sandcastle ill. by author. Rising Moon, 2001. ISBN 0-87358-782-0 Subj: Behavior – wishing. Sand. Sea & seashore – beaches.

Robertson, Patrisha Grainger. *Cirque du Soleil* photos by Al Seib. Abrams, 2003. ISBN 0-8109-4515-0 Subj: Circus. Concepts – color. Rhyming text.

Robertus, Polly M. *The dog who had kittens* ill. by Janet Stevens. Holiday, 1991. ISBN 0-8234-0860-4 Subj: Animals – cats. Animals – dogs.

Robins, Arthur. *The teeny tiny woman: a traditional tale* ill. by author. Candlewick, 1998. ISBN 0-7636-0444-5 Subj: Folk & fairy tales. Foreign lands – England. Ghosts.

Robins, Joan. *Addie meets Max* ill. by Sue Truesdell. HarperCollins, 1985. ISBN 0-06-025064-X Subj: Animals – dogs. Friendship.

Addie runs away ill. by Sue Truesdell. HarperCollins, 1989. ISBN 0-06-025081-X Subj: Behavior – running away. Camps, camping. Seasons – summer.

Addie's bad day ill. by Sue Truesdell. HarperCollins, 1993. ISBN 0-06-021298-5 Subj: Behavior – bad day. Birthdays. Friendship. Hair.

Max, the stubborn little wolf (Judes, Marie-Odile)

My brother, Will ill. by Marylin Hafner. Greenwillow, 1986. ISBN 0-688-05223-1 Subj: Babies. Family life – brothers. Family life – new sibling. Sibling rivalry.

Robinson, Adjai. *Femi and old grandaddie* ill. by Jerry Pinkney. Coward, 1972. ISBN 0-698-20189-2 Subj: Folk & fairy tales. Foreign lands – Africa.

Robinson, Aminah Brenda Lynn. *A street called home* ill. by author. Harcourt, 1997. ISBN 0-15-201465-9 Subj: Careers. Communities, neighborhoods. Ethnic groups in the U.S. – African Americans. Format, unusual – toy & movable books. U.S. history.

Robinson, Bruce. *The obvious elephant* ill. by Sophie Windham. Bloomsbury, 2002. ISBN 1-58234-769-7 Subj: Animals – elephants. Humorous stories.

Robinson, Claire. *Crocodiles* photos by author. Heinemann, 1997. ISBN 1-57572-133-3 Subj: Reptiles – alligators, crocodiles. Science.

Penguins photos by author. Heinemann, 1997. ISBN 1-57572-137-6 Subj: Birds – penguins. Science.

Robinson, Earl. *Black and white* (Arkin, David)

Robinson, Fay. *Fantastic frog* ill. by Jean Cassels. Scholastic, 1999. ISBN 0-590-52269-8 Subj: Frogs & toads. Science.

Nathaniel Willy, scared silly (Mathews, Judith)

Where did all the dragons go? ill. by Victor Lee. BridgeWater, 1996. ISBN 0-8167-3808-4 Subj: Dragons. Folk & fairy tales. Rhyming text.

Robinson, Irene Bowen. *Picture book of animal babies* by Irene & W. W. Robinson; ill. by Irene Bowen Robinson. Macmillan, 1947. Subj: Animals.

Robinson, Nancy K. *Firefighters!* ill. with photos. Scholastic, 1979. Subj: Careers – firefighters.

Robinson, Sue. *I want to play* ill. by Andy Beckett. Barron's, 2002. ISBN 0-7641-5486-9 Subj: Animals – babies. Animals – cats. Family life – mothers. Friendship.

Robinson, Thomas P. *Buttons* ill. by Peggy Bacon. Viking, 1938. Subj: Animals – cats.

Robinson, Tim. *Tobias, the quig, and the rumplenut tree* ill. by author. Winslow, 2000. ISBN 1-890817-20-1 Subj: Birds. Ecology. Rhyming text. Trees.

Robinson, W. W. (William Wilcox). *On the farm* ill. by Irene Bowen Robinson. Macmillan, 1939. Subj: Animals. Farms.

Picture book of animal babies (Robinson, Irene Bowen)

Robison, Deborah. *Bye-bye, old buddy* ill. by author. Houghton Mifflin, 1983. ISBN 0-89919-185-1 Subj: Problem solving.

No elephants allowed ill. by author. Houghton Mifflin, 1981. ISBN 0-395-30078-9 Subj: Bedtime. Emotions – fear. Problem solving.

Your turn, doctor by Deborah Robison & Carla Perez; ill. by Deborah Robison. Dial, 1982. ISBN 0-8037-9788-5 Subj: Behavior – misbehavior. Careers – doctors.

Robison, Nancy. *Ten tall soldiers* ill. by Hilary Knight. Holt, 1991. ISBN 0-8050-0768-7 Subj: Monsters. Royalty – kings. Shadows.

UFO kidnap ill. by Edward Frascino. Lothrop, 1978. ISBN 0-688-51853-2 Subj: Space & space ships.

Robledo, Honorio. *Nico visits the moon* ill. by author. Cinco Puntos, 2001. ISBN 0-938317-57-1 Subj: Animals – cats. Family life – parents. Moon. Toys – balloons.

Roche, A. K. *see* Abisch, Roz

Roche, A. K. *see* Kaplan, Boche

Roche, Denis (Denis M.). *The best class picture ever* ill. by author. Scholastic, 2003. ISBN 0-439-26983-0 Subj: Activities – photographing. Careers – teachers. School.

Little Pig is capable ill. by author. Houghton, 2002. ISBN 0-395-91368-3 Subj: Animals – pigs. Animals – wolves. Behavior – worrying. Safety.

Mim, gym, and June ill. by author. Houghton, 2003. ISBN 0-618-15254-7 Subj: Behavior – bullying. Friendship. School. Sports – gymnastics.

Roche, Hannah. *Corey's kite* ill. by Pierre Pratt. Stewart, Tabori & Chang, 1996. ISBN 1-899883-48-7 Subj: Kites. Weather – wind.

Sandra's sun hat ill. by Pierre Pratt. Stewart, Tabori & Chang, 1996. ISBN 1-899883-47-9 Subj: Clothing – hats. Sun. Weather.

Roche, Harriet. *Pete's puddles* ill. by Pierre Pratt. Stewart, Tabori & Chang, 1996. ISBN 1-899883-46-0 Subj: Activities – playing. Clothing – boots. Weather – rain.

Roche, P. K. (Patrick K.). *Good-bye, Arnold!* ill. by author. Dial, 1979. ISBN 0-8037-3032-2 Subj: Animals – mice. Family life. Sibling rivalry.

Jump all the morning: a child's day in verses ill. by author. Viking, 1984. ISBN 0-670-41057-8 Subj: Poetry.

Plaid bear and the rude rabbit gang ill. by author. Dial, 1982. ISBN 0-8037-6990-3 Subj: Behavior – bullying. Toys.

Webster and Arnold go camping ill. by author. Viking, 1989. ISBN 0-670-81993-X Subj: Animals – mice. Camps, camping. Family life – brothers.

Rochelle, Belinda. *Jewels* ill. by Cornelius Van Wright & Ying-Hwa Hu. Lodestar, 1998. ISBN 0-525-67502-7 Subj: Activities – storytelling. Ethnic groups in the U.S. – African Americans. Family life – great-grandparents. Memories, memory. Slavery. U.S. history.

Rock, Lois. *God bless me, God bless you* ill. by John Bendall-Brunello. Baker Bks., 2001. ISBN 0-8010-4488-X Subj: Bedtime. Religion. Rhyming text.

I wish tonight ill. by Anne Wilson. Good Bks., 2000. ISBN 1-56148-315-X Subj: Behavior – wishing. Dreams. Rhyming text.

I wonder why? ill. by Christopher Corr. Chronicle, 2001. ISBN 0-8118-3169-8 Subj: Religion. Rhyming text.

Learning about prayer ill. by Maureen Galvani. Little, 2003. ISBN 0-316-60557-3 Subj: Religion.

The Lord's prayer ill. by Debbie Lush. Paulist Pr., 1999. ISBN 0-8091-6679-8 Subj: Religion.

Now we have a baby ill. by Jane Massey. Good Bks., 2004. ISBN 1-56148-451-2 Subj: Babies. Emotions – love. Family life. Family life – new sibling. Format, unusual – board books.

Rockhill, Dennis. *Polar slumber = Sueño polar* ill. by author. Raven Tree, 2004. ISBN 0-9724973-1-5 Subj: Animals – polar bears. Dreams. Wordless.

Rocklin, Joanne. *This book is haunted* ill. by JoAnn Adinolfi. HarperCollins, 2001. ISBN 0-06-028457-9 Subj: Ghosts. Holidays – Halloween. Homes, houses.

Rockwell, Anne F. *The acorn tree and other folktales* ill. by author. Greenwillow, 1995. ISBN 0-688-13723-7 Subj: Folk & fairy tales.

Apples and pumpkins ill. by Lizzy Rockwell. Macmillan, 1989. ISBN 0-02-777270-5 Subj: Food. Holidays – Halloween.

At the beach ill. by Harlow Rockwell. Macmillan, 1987. ISBN 0-02-777940-8 Subj: Activities – playing. Sea & seashore – beaches.

At the firehouse ill. by author. HarperCollins, 2003. ISBN 0-06-029816-2 Subj: Careers – firefighters. Trucks.

Bafana: a Christmas story ill. by author. Atheneum, 1974. ISBN 0-689-30417-X Subj: Folk & fairy tales. Holidays – Christmas.

A bear, a bobcat and three ghosts ill. by author. Macmillan, 1977. ISBN 0-02-777460-0 Subj: Animals – bears. Animals – bobcats. Careers – peddlers. Ghosts. Holidays – Halloween.

Bear Child's book of hours ill. by author. Crowell, 1987. ISBN 0-690-04551-4 Subj: Animals – bears. Time.

Becoming butterflies ill. by Megan Halsey. Walker, 2002. ISBN 0-8027-8798-3 Subj: Insects – butterflies, caterpillars. Metamorphosis. School.

Big bad goat ill. by author. Dutton, 1982. ISBN 0-525-45100-5 Subj: Animals. Character traits – helpfulness. Insects – bees.

Big boss ill. by author. Macmillan, 1975. ISBN 0-02-777570-4 Subj: Animals – foxes. Animals – tigers. Character traits – cleverness. Frogs & toads.

Big wheels ill. by author. Dutton, 1986. ISBN 0-525-44226-X Subj: Machines.

Bikes ill. by author. Dutton, 1987. ISBN 0-525-44287-1 Subj: Sports – bicycling.

Blackout by Anne F. & Harlow Rockwell; ill. by authors. Macmillan, 1979. ISBN 0-02-777610-7 Subj: Family life. Power failures. Weather.

Boats ill. by author. Dutton, 1982. ISBN 0-525-44004-6 Subj: Animals – bears. Boats, ships.

The boy who wouldn't obey: a Mayan legend ill. by author. Greenwillow, 2000. ISBN 0-688-14881-6 Subj: Behavior – misbehavior. Folk & fairy tales. Indians of Central America – Maya.

Bugs are insects ill. by Steve Jenkins. HarperCollins, 2001. ISBN 0-06-028569-9 Subj: Insects.

Bumblebee, bumblebee, do you know me? a garden guessing game ill. by author. HarperCollins, 1999. ISBN 0-06-028212-6 Subj: Flowers. Insects. Insects – bees.

The bump in the night ill. by author. Greenwillow, 1979. ISBN 0-688-84180-5 Subj: Character traits – cleverness. Character traits – helpfulness.

Buster and the bogeyman ill. by author. Four Winds, 1978. ISBN 0-590-07531-4 Subj: Bedtime. Dreams. Mythical creatures.

Can I help? by Anne F. & Harlow Rockwell; ill. by authors. Macmillan, 1982. ISBN 0-02-777720-0 Subj: Character traits – helpfulness.

Career day ill. by Lizzy Rockwell. HarperCollins, 2000. ISBN 0-06-027566-9 Subj: Careers. School.

Cars ill. by author. Dutton, 1984. ISBN 0-525-44079-8 Subj: Automobiles.

Chip and the karate kick ill. by Paul Meisel. HarperCollins, 2004. ISBN 0-06-028446-3 Subj: Animals. Animals – rabbits. Character traits – patience. Sports – karate.

Come to town ill. by author. Crowell, 1987. ISBN 0-690-04646-4 Subj: Animals – bears. Cities, towns.

Ducklings and pollywogs ill. by Lizzy Rockwell. Macmillan, 1994. ISBN 0-02-777452-X Subj: Family life – fathers. Lakes, ponds. Seasons.

The emergency room by Anne F. & Harlow Rockwell; ill. by authors. Macmillan, 1985. ISBN 0-02-777300-0 Subj: Hospitals. Illness.

Father's Day ill. by Lizzy Rockwell. HarperCollins, 2005. ISBN 0-06-051378-0 Subj: Activities – writing. Books, reading. Family life – fathers. Holidays – Father's Day. School.

Ferryboat ride! ill. by Maggie Smith. Crown, 1999. ISBN 0-517-70959-7 Subj: Boats, ships. Islands. Sea & seashore. Transportation.

Fire engines ill. by author. Dutton, 1986. ISBN 0-525-44259-6 Subj: Animals – dogs. Careers – firefighters. Trucks.

First comes spring ill. by author. Crowell, 1985. ISBN 0-690-04455-0 Subj: Animals – bears. Seasons.

The first snowfall by Anne F. & Harlow Rockwell; ill. by authors. Macmillan, 1987. ISBN 0-02-777770-7 Subj: Seasons – winter. Weather – snow.

Gogo's pay day ill. by author. Doubleday, 1978. ISBN 0-385-13046-5 Subj: Character traits – generosity. Clowns, jesters. Money.

The gollywhopper egg ill. by author. Macmillan, 1974. ISBN 0-02-777470-8 Subj: Behavior – trickery. Eggs. Farms.

The good llama ill. by author. World, 1963. Subj: Animals. Animals – llamas. Foreign lands – South America.

Growing like me ill. by Holly Keller. Harcourt, 2001. ISBN 0-15-202202-3 Subj: Behavior – growing up.

Halloween Day ill. by Lizzy Rockwell. HarperCollins, 1997. ISBN 0-06-027568-5 Subj: Clothing – costumes. Holidays – Halloween. School.

Handy Hank will fix it ill. by author. Holt, 1988. ISBN 0-8050-0697-4 Subj: Careers – handymen. Character traits – helpfulness.

Happy birthday to me by Anne F. & Harlow Rockwell; ill. by authors. Macmillan, 1981. ISBN 0-02-777680-8 Subj: Birthdays.

Honey in a hive ill. by S. D. Schindler. HarperCollins, 2005. ISBN 0-06-028567-2 Subj: Food. Insects – bees.

Honk honk! ill. by author. Dutton, 1980. ISBN 0-525-32120-9 Subj: Animals. Behavior – misbehavior. Birds. Cumulative tales.

How my garden grew by Anne F. & Harlow Rockwell; ill. by authors. Macmillan, 1982. ISBN 0-02-777660-3 Subj: Gardens, gardening.

Hugo at the park ill. by author. Macmillan, 1990. ISBN 0-02-777301-9 Subj: Animals – dogs. Parks.

Hugo at the window ill. by author. Macmillan, 1988. ISBN 0-02-777330-2 Subj: Animals – dogs. Birthdays. Cities, towns.

I like the library ill. by author. Dutton, 1977. ISBN 0-525-32528-X Subj: Libraries.

I love my pets by Anne F. & Harlow Rockwell; ill. by authors. Macmillan, 1982. ISBN 0-02-777710-3 Subj: Pets.

I play in my room by Anne F. & Harlow Rockwell; ill. by authors. Macmillan, 1981. ISBN 0-02-777670-0 Subj: Activities – playing.

In our house ill. by author. Crowell, 1985. ISBN 0-690-04488-7 Subj: Activities. Animals – bears. Family life.

Katie Catz makes a splash ill. by Paul Meisel. HarperCollins, 2003. ISBN 0-06-028445-5 Subj: Animals. Animals – cats. Emotions – fear. Sports – swimming.

Long ago yesterday ill. by author. Greenwillow, 1999. ISBN 0-688-14411-X Subj: Babies. Family life.

Machines by Anne F. & Harlow Rockwell; ill. by Harlow Rockwell. Macmillan, 1972. ISBN 0-02-777520-8 Subj: Machines.

Morgan plays soccer ill. by Paul Meisel. HarperCollins, 2001. ISBN 0-06-028444-7 Subj: Animals. Animals – bears. Sports – soccer.

The Mother Goose cookie-candy book ill. by author. Random House, 1983. ISBN 0-394-95500-5 Subj: Activities – baking, cooking. Food.

Mother's Day ill. by Lizzy Rockwell. HarperCollins, 2004. ISBN 0-06-051375-6 Subj: Holidays – Mother's Day. School.

My back yard by Anne F. & Harlow Rockwell; ill. by authors. Macmillan, 1984. ISBN 0-02-777690-5 Subj: Activities – playing.

My barber by Anne F. & Harlow Rockwell; ill. by authors. Macmillan, 1981. ISBN 0-02-777630-1 Subj: Careers – barbers. Hair.

My pet hamster ill. by Bernice Lum. HarperCollins, 2002. ISBN 0-06-028565-6 Subj: Animals – hamsters. Pets.

My spring robin ill. by Harlow Rockwell & Lizzy Rockwell. Macmillan, 1989. ISBN 0-02-777611-5 Subj: Birds – robins. Flowers. Seasons – spring.

Nice and clean by Anne F. & Harlow Rockwell; ill. by authors. Macmillan, 1984. ISBN 0-02-777290-X Subj: Character traits – cleanliness. Homes, houses.

The night we slept outside by Anne F. & Harlow Rockwell; ill. by authors. Macmillan, 1983. ISBN 0-02-777450-3 Subj: Camps, camping. Night.

No! No! No! ill. by author. Macmillan, 1995. ISBN 0-02-777782-0 Subj: Behavior – bad day. Family life.

The old woman and her pig and 10 other stories ill. by adapt. Crowell, 1979. ISBN 0-390-03928-X Subj: Folk & fairy tales.

On our vacation ill. by author. Dutton, 1989. ISBN 0-525-44487-7 Subj: Activities – vacationing. Animals – bears. Camps, camping. Islands.

Once upon a time this morning ill. by Suçie Stevenson. Greenwillow, 1997. ISBN 0-688-14707-0 Subj: Babies. Family life.

One bean ill. by Megan Halsey. Walker, 1998. ISBN 0-8027-8649-9 Subj: Plants. Science. Seeds.

100 school days ill. by Lizzy Rockwell. HarperCollins, 2002. ISBN 0-06-029145-1 Subj: Counting, numbers. School.

The one-eyed giant and other monsters from the Greek Myths ill. by author. Greenwillow, 1996. ISBN 0-688-13810-1 Subj: Monsters. Mythical creatures.

Our garage sale ill. by Harlow Rockwell. Greenwillow, 1984. ISBN 0-688-84278-X Subj: Garage sales, rummage sales.

Our yard is full of birds ill. by Lizzy Rockwell. Macmillan, 1992. ISBN 0-02-777273-X Subj: Birds.

Planes by Anne F. & Harlow Rockwell; ill. by authors. Dutton, 1985. ISBN 0-525-44159-X Subj: Airplanes, airports. Transportation.

Poor Goose: a French folktale ill. by author. Crowell, 1976. ISBN 0-690-01014-1 Subj: Animals. Birds – geese. Cumulative tales. Folk & fairy tales. Foreign lands – France.

Pumpkin day, pumpkin night ill. by Megan Halsey. Walker, 1999. ISBN 0-8027-8697-9 Subj: Family life – mothers. Holidays – Halloween. Plants.

Pur stars ill. by author. Harcourt, 1999. ISBN 0-15-201868-9 Subj: Astronomy. Planets. Stars.

Romulus and Remus ill. by author. S&S, 1997. ISBN 0-689-81291-4 Subj: Animals – wolves. Folk & fairy tales. Foreign lands – Italy. Multiple births – twins.

Root-a-toot-toot ill. by author. Macmillan, 1991. ISBN 0-02-777272-1 Subj: Animals. Cumulative tales. Noise, sounds.

Show and tell day ill. by Lizzy Rockwell. HarperCollins, 1997. ISBN 0-06-027301-1 Subj: Character traits – individuality. School.

Sick in bed by Anne F. & Harlow Rockwell; ill. by authors. Macmillan, 1982. ISBN 0-02-777730-8 Subj: Illness.

Space vehicles by Anne F. Rockwell & David Brion; ill. by authors. Dutton, 1994. ISBN 0-525-45270-2 Subj: Animals – cats. Space & space ships.

The stolen necklace: a picture story from India ill. by author. Collins-World, 1968. Based on a tale from the Jataka. Subj: Animals – monkeys. Character traits – cleverness. Foreign lands – India.

The storm ill. by Robert Sauber. Hyperion, 1994. ISBN 0-7868-2013-6 Subj: Family life. Sea & seashore. Weather – storms.

The story snail ill. by author. Macmillan, 1974. ISBN 0-02-777560-7 Subj: Animals – snails. Magic.

The supermarket by Anne F. & Harlow Rockwell; ill. by authors. Macmillan, 1979. ISBN 0-02-777580-1 Subj: Shopping. Stores.

Thanksgiving Day ill. by Lizzy Rockwell. HarperCollins, 1999. ISBN 0-06-027795-5 Subj: Holidays – Thanksgiving. School. Theater.

Things that go ill. by author. Dutton, 1986. ISBN 0-525-44266-9 Subj: Transportation.

The three bears and 15 other stories ill. by author. Crown, 1975. ISBN 0-690-00598-9 Subj: Folk & fairy tales.

Thump thump thump! ill. by author. Dutton, 1981. ISBN 0-525-41300-6 Subj: Folk & fairy tales. Monsters.

Toad by Anne F. & Harlow Rockwell; ill. by authors. Doubleday, 1972. Subj: Frogs & toads.

The toolbox by Anne F. & Harlow Rockwell; ill. by Harlow Rockwell. Macmillan, 1971. ISBN 0-02-777540-2 Subj: Tools.

Trains ill. by author. Dutton, 1988. ISBN 0-525-44377-0 Subj: Trains. Transportation.

Trucks ill. by author. Dutton, 1984. ISBN 0-525-44147-6 Subj: Trucks.

Two blue jays ill. by Megan Halsey. Walker, 2003. ISBN 0-8027-8841-6 Subj: Birds – bluejays. Family life – parents.

Valentine's Day ill. by Lizzy Rockwell. HarperCollins, 2001. ISBN 0-06-028515-X Subj: Holidays – Valentine's Day. Letters, cards. School.

The way to Captain Yankee's ill. by author. Macmillan, 1994. ISBN 0-02-777271-3 Subj: Animals – cats. Maps.

Welcome to kindergarten ill. by author. Walker, 2001. ISBN 0-8027-8746-0 Subj: Emotions – fear. School – first day.

What we like ill. by author. Macmillan, 1992. ISBN 0-02-777274-8 Subj: Activities – making things. Concepts. Language.

When Hugo went to school ill. by author. Macmillan, 1991. ISBN 0-02-777305-1 Subj: Animals – dogs. School.

When I go visiting by Anne F. & Harlow Rockwell; ill. by authors. Macmillan, 1984. ISBN 0-02-777740-5 Subj: Family life – grandmothers. Family life – grandparents.

Willy can count ill. by author. Little, 1989. ISBN 1-55970-013-0 Subj: Activities – walking. Counting, numbers. Country. Family life – mothers.

Willy runs away ill. by author. Dutton, 1978. ISBN 0-525-42795-3 Subj: Animals – dogs. Behavior – running away.

The wolf who had a wonderful dream ill. by author. Crowell, 1973. ISBN 0-690-89724-3 Subj: Animals – wolves. Dreams. Folk & fairy tales. Food. Foreign lands – France.

The wonderful eggs of Furicchia: a picture story from Italy ill. by author. Collins-World, 1969. Subj: Birds – chickens. Eggs. Folk & fairy tales. Foreign lands – Italy. Magic.

Rockwell, Harlow. *Blackout* (Rockwell, Anne F.)

Can I help? (Rockwell, Anne F.)

The compost heap ill. by author. Doubleday, 1974. ISBN 0-385-08989-9 Subj: Gardens, gardening. Plants.

The emergency room (Rockwell, Anne F.)

The first snowfall (Rockwell, Anne F.)

Happy birthday to me (Rockwell, Anne F.)

How my garden grew (Rockwell, Anne F.)

I did it ill. by author. Macmillan, 1974. ISBN 0-02-777550-X Subj: Activities.

I love my pets (Rockwell, Anne F.)

I play in my room (Rockwell, Anne F.)

Look at this ill. by author. Macmillan, 1978. ISBN 0-02-777590-9 Subj: Activities.

Machines (Rockwell, Anne F.)

My back yard (Rockwell, Anne F.)

My barber (Rockwell, Anne F.)

My dentist ill. by author. Greenwillow, 1975. ISBN 0-688-84004-3 Subj: Careers – dentists. Teeth.

My doctor ill. by author. Macmillan, 1973. ISBN 0-02-777480-5 Subj: Careers – doctors. Health & fitness.

My kitchen ill. by author. Greenwillow, 1980. ISBN 0-688-84236-4 Subj: Food.

My nursery school ill. by author. Greenwillow, 1976. ISBN 0-688-84025-6 Subj: School – nursery.

Nice and clean (Rockwell, Anne F.)

The night we slept outside (Rockwell, Anne F.)

Planes (Rockwell, Anne F.)

Sick in bed (Rockwell, Anne F.)

The supermarket (Rockwell, Anne F.)

Toad (Rockwell, Anne F.)

The toolbox (Rockwell, Anne F.)

When I go visiting (Rockwell, Anne F.)

Rockwell, Lizzy. *The busy body book* ill. by author. Crown, 2004. ISBN 0-375-92203-2 Subj: Health & fitness – exercise.

Hello baby! ill. by author. Crown, 1999. ISBN 0-517-80012-8 Subj: Babies. Birth. Family life – brothers & sisters. Family life – new sibling.

Rockwell, Norman. *Norman Rockwell's counting book* sel. by Glorina Taborin; ill. by author. Harmony, 1977. ISBN 0-517-53205-0 Subj: Counting, numbers. Games. Holidays – April Fools' Day.

Rodanas, Kristina. *The dragonfly's tale* ill. by author. Houghton Mifflin, 1992. ISBN 0-395-57003-4 Subj: Folk & fairy tales. Indians of North America – Zuni. Insects – dragonflies.

Follow the stars ill. by reteller. Little, 1998. ISBN 0-7614-5029-7 Subj: Creation. Folk & fairy tales. Indians of North America – Ojibwa.

The little drummer boy ill. by author. Clarion, 2001. Words & music by Katherine Davis, Henry Onorati & Harry Simeonne. ISBN 0-395-97015-6 Subj: Gifts. Holidays – Christmas. Music. Musical instruments – drums. Religion – Nativity. Songs.

The story of Wali Dâd ill. by author. Lothrop, 1988. ISBN 0-688-07363-1 Subj: Character traits – generosity. Foreign lands – India.

Rodda, Emily. *Power and glory* ill. by Geoff Kelly. Greenwillow, 1996. ISBN 0-688-14215-X Subj: Birthdays. Games. Television.

Where do you hide two elephants? ill. by Andrew McLean. G. Stevens, 2001. ISBN 0-8368-2898-4 Subj: Animals – elephants. Behavior – hiding things. Rhyming text.

Yay! ill. by Craig Smith. Greenwillow, 1997. ISBN 0-688-15255-4 Subj: Activities – vacationing. Family life. Foreign lands – Australia. Parks – amusement.

Roddie, Shen. *Animal stew* ill. by Patrick J. Gallagher. Houghton Mifflin, 1992. ISBN 0-395-57582-6 Subj: Animals. Cumulative tales. Format, unusual. Giants.

Hatch, egg, hatch! ill. by Frances Cony. Little, 1991. ISBN 0-316-75345-9 Subj: Babies. Birds – chickens. Birth. Eggs. Format, unusual – toy & movable books.

Help, Mama, help! ill. by Frances Cony. Little, 1995. ISBN 0-316-75357-2 Subj: Birds – chickens. Emotions – fear. Family life – mothers. Format, unusual – toy & movable books.

Not now, Mrs. Wolf ill. by Selina Young. DK, 2000. ISBN 0-7894-5613-3 Subj: Animals – babies. Animals – wolves. Birds – ducks. Family life – mothers.

Sandbear ill. by Jenny Jones. Childrens Bk., 2002. ISBN 1-58234-758-1 Subj: Animals – bears. Animals – rabbits. Friendship. Sand.

Toes are to tickle ill. by Kady MacDonald Denton. Tricycle, 1997. ISBN 1-883672-49-X Subj: Activities – playing. Babies. Family life – brothers & sisters. Games.

Rodell, Susanna. *Dear Fred* ill. by Kim Gamble. Ticknor & Fields, 1995. ISBN 0-395-71544-X Subj: Animals – mice. Behavior – needing someone. Divorce. Family life – brothers & sisters. Letters, cards. Moving.

Rodgers, Frank. *Who's afraid of the ghost train?* ill. by author. Harcourt, 1989. ISBN 0-15-200642-7 Subj: Emotions – fear. Family life – grandfathers. Ghosts. Imagination. Trains.

Rodgers, Richard. *My favorite things* ill. by Renée Graef. HarperCollins, 2001. ISBN 0-06-029233-4 Subj: Songs.

A real nice clambake by Richard Rodgers & Oscar Hammerstein; ill. by Nadine Bernard Westcott. Little, 1992. ISBN 0-316-75422-6 Subj: Activities – picnicking. Music. Sea & seashore. Songs.

Rodriguez, Anita. *Jamal and the angel* ill. by author. Crown, 1992. ISBN 0-517-59115-4 Subj: Activities – working. Angels. Behavior – wishing. Ethnic groups in the U.S. – African Americans.

Rodriguez, Bobbie. *Sarah's sleepover* ill. by Mark Graham. Viking, 2000. ISBN 0-670-87750-6 Subj: Family life – cousins. Games. Handicaps – blindness. Night. Power failures. Sleepovers.

Roe, Eileen. *All I am* ill. by Helen Cogancherry. Bradbury, 1990. ISBN 0-02-777372-8 Subj: Self-concept.

Staying with Grandma ill. by Jacqueline Rogers. Bradbury, 1989. ISBN 0-02-777371-X Subj: Country. Family life – grandmothers.

With my brother = Con mi hermano trans. to Spanish by Jo Mintzer; ill. by Robert Casilla. Bradbury, 1991. ISBN 0-02-777373-6 Subj: Ethnic groups in the U.S. – Mexican Americans. Family life – brothers. Foreign languages.

Roe, Richard. *Animal ABC* ill. by author. Random House, 1984. ISBN 0-394-96864-6 Subj: ABC books. Animals.

Roehl, Angela von. *Snail started it!* (Reider, Katja)

Roehrdanz, Barbro Eriksson. *Hocus-pocus* (Eriksson, Eva)

Jealousy (Eriksson, Eva)

One short week (Eriksson, Eva)

The tooth trip (Eriksson, Eva)

Roennfeldt, Robert. *A day on the avenue* ill. by author. Viking, 1984. ISBN 0-670-25940-3 Subj: Roads. Wordless.

Roffey, Maureen. *Bathtime* ill. by author. Four Winds, 1989. ISBN 0-02-777161-X Subj: Activities – bathing. Family life.

Family scramble ill. by author. Dutton, 1987. ISBN 0-525-44290-1 Subj: Family life. Format, unusual.

Here, kitty kitty! ill. by author. Houghton Mifflin, 1991. ISBN 0-395-57584-2 Subj: Animals – cats. Family life. Format, unusual. Pets.

Home sweet home ill. by author. Coward, 1983. ISBN 0-698-20595-2 Subj: Format, unusual – toy & movable books. Homes, houses.

I spy at the zoo ill. by author. Four Winds, 1988. ISBN 0-02-777150-4 Subj: Animals. Zoos.

I spy on vacation ill. by author. Four Winds, 1988. ISBN 0-02-777160-1 Subj: Activities – vacationing. Sea & seashore.

I'm brave! (Erickson, Karen)

Look, there's my hat! ill. by author. Putnam, 1985. ISBN 0-399-21192-6 Subj: Behavior – greed. Format, unusual.

Mealtime ill. by author. Four Winds, 1989. ISBN 0-02-777151-2 Subj: Activities – picnicking. Birthdays. Family life. Food.

Quick, catch Dan! ill. by author. Houghton Mifflin, 1991. ISBN 0-395-57583-4 Subj: Animals – dogs. Family life. Format, unusual. Pets.

Rogasky, Barbara. *Leaf by leaf* (Leaf by leaf)

Rapunzel (Grimm, Jacob)

The water of life ill. by Trina Schart Hyman. Holiday, 1986. Adapt. of Das Wasser des Lebens by Jacob and Wilhelm Grimm. ISBN 0-8234-0552-4 Subj: Character traits – pride. Folk & fairy tales. Magic. Royalty. Sibling rivalry.

Rogers, Anne. *Cinderella* (Grimm, Jacob)

The musicians of Bremen (Grimm, Jacob)

The wolf and the seven little kids (Grimm, Jacob)

Rogers, Edmund. *Elephants* ill. with photos. Raintree, 1978. ISBN 0-8172-1076-8 Subj: Animals – elephants.

Rogers, Emma. *Quacky Duck* (Rogers, Paul [Patrick])

Ruby's dinnertime (Rogers, Paul [Patrick])

Ruby's potty (Rogers, Paul [Patrick])

Rogers, Fred. *Adoption* photos by Jim Judkis. Putnam, 1994. ISBN 0-399-22432-7 Subj: Adoption. Emotions. Family life.

Divorce photos by Jim Judkis. Putnam, 1998. ISBN 0-399-22449-1 Subj: Divorce. Family life.

Extraordinary friends photos by Jim Judkis. Putnam, 2000. ISBN 0-399-23146-3 Subj: Friendship. Handicaps.

Going on an airplane photos by Jim Judkis. Putnam, 1989. ISBN 0-399-21635-9 Subj: Activities – traveling. Airplanes, airports.

Going to day care photos by Jim Judkis. Putnam, 1985. ISBN 0-399-21235-3 Subj: School – nursery.

Going to the doctor photos by Jim Judkis. Putnam, 1986. ISBN 0-399-21298-1 Subj: Careers – doctors.

Going to the hospital photos by Jim Judkis. Putnam, 1988. ISBN 0-399-21503-4 Subj: Hospitals. Illness.

Going to the potty photos by Jim Judkis. Putnam, 1986. ISBN 0-399-21296-5 Subj: Behavior – growing up. Toilet training.

If we were all the same ill. by Pat Sustendal. Random House, 1988. ISBN 0-394-98778-0 Subj: Character traits – individuality.

Making friends photos by Jim Judkis. Putnam, 1987. ISBN 0-399-21382-1 Subj: Activities – playing. Emotions. Friendship.

Moving photos by Jim Judkis. Putnam, 1987. ISBN 0-399-21383-X Subj: Communities, neighborhoods. Emotions. Family life. Friendship. Moving.

The new baby photos by Jim Judkis. Putnam, 1985. ISBN 0-399-21236-1 Subj: Babies. Family life – new sibling. Sibling rivalry.

When a pet dies photos by Jim Judkis. Putnam, 1988. ISBN 0-399-21504-2 Subj: Death. Emotions – grief. Pets.

Rogers, Hal. *Airplanes* ill. with photos. Child's World, 2001. ISBN 1-56766-962-X Subj: Airplanes, airports. Transportation.

Buses ill. with photos. Child's World, 2001. ISBN 1-56766-963-8 Subj: Buses. Transportation.

Cars ill. with photos. Child's World, 2001. ISBN 1-56766-964-6 Subj: Automobiles. Transportation.

Combines ill. with photos. Child's World, 2001. ISBN 1-56766-754-6 Subj: Farms. Machines.

Milking machines ill. with photos. Child's World, 2001. ISBN 1-56766-753-8 Subj: Animals – bulls, cows. Farms. Machines.

Plows ill. with photos. Child's World, 2001. ISBN 1-56766-755-4 Subj: Farms. Machines.

Trains ill. with photos. Child's World, 2001. ISBN 1-56766-965-4 Subj: Trains. Transportation.

Rogers, Helen Spelman. *Morris and his brave lion* ill. by Glo Coalson. McGraw-Hill, 1975. ISBN 0-07-053502-7 Subj: Divorce.

Rogers, Jacqueline. *Kindergarten ABC* ill. by author. Scholastic, 2002. ISBN 0-439-36837-5 Subj: ABC books. Books, reading. School.

Tiptoe into kindergarten ill. by author. Scholastic, 1999. ISBN 0-590-46653-4 Subj: Family life – brothers & sisters. School.

Rogers, Jean. *Runaway mittens* ill. by Rie Munoz. Greenwillow, 1988. ISBN 0-688-07054-X Subj: Behavior – lost & found possessions. Clothing – gloves, mittens.

Rogers, Margaret. *Green is beautiful* by Margaret Rogers & Bernadette Watts; ill. by Bernadette Watts. State Mutual Books, 1982. ISBN 0-905478-17-7 Subj: Concepts – color. Folk & fairy tales.

Rogers, Paul (Patrick). *Don't blame me!* ill. by Robin Bell Corfield. Trafalgar Square, 1992. ISBN 0-370-31204-X Subj: Activities – painting. Circular tales. Foreign lands – England.

Forget-me-not ill. by Celia Berridge. Viking, 1984. ISBN 0-670-32365-9 Subj: Behavior – forgetfulness. Behavior – lost & found possessions.

From me to you ill. by Jane Johnson. Watts, 1988. ISBN 0-531-08332-2 Subj: Family life – grandmothers. Rhyming text.

Lily's picnic ill. by John Prater. Bodley Head, 1988. ISBN 0-370-31098-5 Subj: Activities – picnicking. Family life.

Quacky Duck by Paul & Emma Rogers; ill. by Barbara Mullarney. Little, 1995. ISBN 0-316-37647-7 Subj: Animals. Birds – ducks. Farms. Noise, sounds.

Ruby's dinnertime by Paul & Emma Rogers; ill. by by Emma Rogers. Dutton, 2002. ISBN 0-525-46847-1 Subj: Animals – mice. Behavior – growing up. Family life. Food. Rhyming text.

Ruby's potty by Paul & Emma Rogers; ill. by by Emma Rogers. Dutton, 2001. ISBN 0-525-46816-1 Subj: Animals – mice. Behavior – growing up. Rhyming text. Toilet training.

The shapes game ill. by Sian Tucker. Holt, 1990. ISBN 0-8050-1280-X Subj: Concepts – shape. Games.

Sheepchase ill. by Celia Berridge. Viking, 1986. ISBN 0-670-80599-8 Subj: Animals – sheep. Behavior – running away. Rhyming text.

Somebody's awake ill. by Robin Bell Corfield. Atheneum, 1988. ISBN 0-689-31490-6 Subj: Family life. Food. Morning.

Somebody's sleepy ill. by Robin Bell Corfield. Atheneum, 1988. ISBN 0-689-31491-4 Subj: Bedtime. Family life.

Tiny by Paul Rogers & Korky Paul; ill. by Korky Paul . Dutton, 2002. ISBN 1-929132-26-3 Subj: Insects – fleas.

Tumbledown ill. by Robin Bell Corfield. Atheneum, 1988. ISBN 0-689-31392-6 Subj: Cities, towns. Royalty – princes.

What can you see? ill. by Kazuko. Doubleday, 1998. ISBN 0-385-32603-3 Subj: Activities – ballooning. Animals – dogs. Picture puzzles.

What will the weather be like today? ill. by Kazuko. Greenwillow, 1990. ISBN 0-688-08951-8 Subj: Rhyming text. Weather.

Rogow, Zak. *Oranges* ill. by Mary Szilagyi. Watts, 1988. ISBN 0-531-08343-8 Subj: Food. Trees.

Rohmann, Eric. *The cinder-eyed cats* ill. by author. Crown, 1997. ISBN 0-517-70897-3 Subj: Animals – cats. Bedtime. Boats, ships. Dreams. Islands. Night.

My friend Rabbit ill. by author. Roaring Brook, 2002. ISBN 0-7613-2420-8 Subj: Animals – mice. Animals – rabbits. Caldecott award books. Friendship.

Pumpkinhead ill. by author. Knopf, 2003. ISBN 0-375-92416-7 Subj: Activities – traveling. Character traits – being different. Character traits – individuality.

Time flies ill. by author. Crown, 1994. ISBN 0-517-59599-0 Subj: Birds. Caldecott award honor books. Dinosaurs. Museums. Time. Wordless.

Rohmer, Harriet. *Atariba and Niguayona: a story from the Taino people of Puerto Rico* adapt. by Harriet Rohmer & Jesus Guerrero Rea; ill. by Consuelo Mendez. Children's Book Pr., 1988. ISBN 0-89239-026-3 Subj: Character traits – kindness. Foreign lands – Puerto Rico. Illness.

How we came to the fifth world: a creation story from Ancient Mexico adapt. by Harriet Rohmer & Mary Anchondo; ill. by Graciela Carrillo. Children's Book Pr., 1988. ISBN 0-89239-024-7 Subj: Creation. Folk & fairy tales. Foreign lands – Mexico.

The invisible hunters by Harriet Rohmer, Octavio Chow & Morris Vidaure; ill. by Joe Sam. Children's Book Pr., 1987. ISBN 0-89239-031-X Subj: Behavior – greed. Folk & fairy tales. Foreign lands – Nicaragua. Sports – hunting.

Mother scorpion country by Harriet Rohmer & Dorminster Wilson; ill. by Virginia Stearns. Children's Book Pr., 1987. ISBN 0-89239-032-8 Subj: Emotions – love. Folk & fairy tales. Foreign lands – Nicaragua.

Rojankovsky, Feodor. *ABC, an alphabet of many things* ill. by author. Golden Pr., 1970. Subj: ABC books.

Animals in the zoo ill. by author. Random House, 1973, c1962. ISBN 0-394-82622-1 Subj: ABC books. Animals. Zoos.

Animals on the farm ill. by author. Knopf, 1967. Subj: Animals. Farms. Wordless.

The great big animal book ill. by author. S&S, 1950. Subj: Animals. Farms.

The great big wild animal book ill. by author. S&S, 1951. Subj: Animals.

Rollings, Susan. *New shoes, red shoes* ill. by author. Orchard, 2000. ISBN 0-531-30268-7 Subj: Birthdays. Clothing – shoes. Parties. Rhyming text.

Romain, Trevor. *Jemma's journey* ill. by Pat Lopez. Boyds Mills, 2002. ISBN 1-56397-937-3 Subj: Ethnic groups in the U.S. – African Americans. Family life – grandmothers. Trees. U.S. history.

Romanek, Enid Warner. *Teddy* ill. by author. Scribners, 1978. ISBN 0-684-15811-6 Subj: Toys – bears.

Romanelli, Serena. *Little Bobo saves the day* ill. by Hans De Beer. North-South, 1997. ISBN 1-55858-787-X Subj: Activities – painting. Animals – orangutans. Illness. Kites.

Romanoli, Robert. *What's so funny?!!* ill. by Jerry Zimmerman. Grosset, 1978. ISBN 0-448-16400-0 Subj: Riddles & jokes.

Ronay, Jadja. *Ginger* ill. by Anthony Accardo. Magnolia, 1981. ISBN 0-943516-00-5 Subj: Folk & fairy tales. Magic.

Ronco, Gianna. *Look inside a car* (Mantegazza, Giovanna)

Rondell, Florence. *The family that grew* by Florence Rondell & Ruth Michaels. Crown, 1965. Subj: Adoption.

Rong, Yu. *A lovely day for Amelia Goose* ill. by author. Candlewick, 2004. ISBN 0-7636-2309-1 Subj: Birds – geese. Day. Frogs & toads.

Roop, Connie. *Backyard beasties* (Burns, Diane L.)

Going buggy! (Roop, Peter)

Let's celebrate! jokes about holidays (Roop, Peter)

Let's celebrate Earth Day by Connie & Peter Roop; ill. by Gwen Connelly. Millbrook, 2001. ISBN 0-7613-1812-7 Subj: Ecology. Holidays – Earth Day.

Stick out your tongue! (Roop, Peter)

Roop, Peter. *Backyard beasties* (Burns, Diane L.)

The buffalo jump ill. by Bill Farnsworth. Northland, 1996. ISBN 0-87358-616-6 Subj: Animals – buffaloes. Emotions – envy, jealousy. Indians of North America – Blackfoot. Sports – hunting.

Going buggy! by Peter & Connie Roop; ill. by Joan Hanson. Lerner, 1986. ISBN 0-8225-0988-1 Subj: Insects. Riddles & jokes.

Holiday howlers Peter & Connie Roop; ill. by Brian Gable. Carolrhoda, 2004. ISBN 1-57505-645-3 Subj: Holidays. Riddles & jokes.

Let's celebrate! jokes about holidays by Peter & Connie Roop; ill. by Joan Hanson. Lerner, 1986. ISBN 0-8225-0989-X Subj: Holidays. Riddles & jokes.

Let's celebrate Earth Day (Roop, Connie)

Stick out your tongue! by Peter & Connie Roop; ill. by Joan Hanson. Lerner, 1986. ISBN 0-8225-0990-3 Subj: Careers – doctors. Riddles & jokes.

Roosa, Karen. *Beach day* ill. by Maggie Smith. Clarion, 2001. ISBN 0-618-02923-0 Subj: Rhyming text. Sea & seashore – beaches.

Roosevelt, Michelle Chopin. *Zoo animals* ill. by author. Random House, 1983. ISBN 0-394-85285-0 Subj: Format, unusual – board books. Zoos.

Root, Barry. *Gumbrella* ill. by author. Putnam, 2002. ISBN 0-399-23347-4 Subj: Animals. Animals – elephants. Character traits – kindness to animals.

Root, Phyllis. *All for the newborn baby* ill. by Nicola Bayley. Candlewick, 2000. ISBN 0-7636-0093-8 Subj: Holidays – Christmas. Lullabies. Religion – Nativity.

Aunt Nancy and Cousin Lazybones ill. by David Parkins. Candlewick, 1998. ISBN 1-56402-425-3 Subj: Character traits – laziness. Family life – cousins.

Aunt Nancy and Old Man Trouble ill. by David Parkins. Candlewick, 1996. ISBN 1-56402-347-8 Subj: Behavior – trickery. Folk & fairy tales.

Big Momma makes the world ill. by Helen Oxenbury. Candlewick, 2002. ISBN 0-7636-1132-8 Subj: Creation.

Contrary bear ill. by Laura Cornell. HarperCollins, 1996. ISBN 0-06-025086-0 Subj: Behavior – mistakes. Family life – fathers. Toys – bears.

Grandmother Winter ill. by Beth Krommes. Houghton Mifflin, 1999. ISBN 0-395-88399-7 Subj: Birds – geese. Folk & fairy tales. Foreign lands – Germany. Seasons – winter. Weather – snow.

Gretchen's grandma by Phyllis Root & Carol A. Marron; ill. by Deborah Kogan Ray. Raintree, 1983. ISBN 0-940742-16-0 Subj: Birthdays. Family life – grandmothers. Language.

The hungry monster ill. by Sue Heap. Candlewick, 1997. ISBN 0-7636-0060-1 Subj: Food. Monsters. Space & space ships.

If you want to see a caribou ill. by Jim Meyer. Houghton, 2004. ISBN 0-618-39314-5 Subj: Animals – reindeer. Nature.

Kiss the cow ill. by Will Hillenbrand. Candlewick, 2000. ISBN 0-7636-0298-1 Subj: Animals – bulls, cows. Kissing. Tall tales.

Moon tiger ill. by Ed Young. Holt, 1985. ISBN 0-03-000042-4 Subj: Animals. Animals – tigers. Imagination. Sibling rivalry.

Mrs. Potter's pig ill. by Russell Ayto. Candlewick, 1996. ISBN 1-56402-924-7 Subj: Animals – pigs. Babies. Character traits – cleanliness. Character traits – orderliness.

The name quilt ill. by Margot Apple. Farrar, 2003. ISBN 0-374-35484-7 Subj: Family life – grandmothers. Names. Quilts.

The old red rocking chair ill. by John Sanford. Little, 1992. ISBN 1-55970-063-7 Subj: Circular tales. Furniture – chairs.

Oliver finds his way ill. by Christopher Denise. Candlewick, 2002. ISBN 0-7636-1383-5 Subj: Animals – babies. Animals – bears. Behavior – lost. Family life – parents.

One duck stuck ill. by Jane Chapman. Candlewick, 1998. ISBN 0-7636-1566-8 Subj: Animals. Birds – ducks. Counting, numbers. Rhyming text.

One duck stuck [board book] ill. by Jane Chapman. Candlewick, 1998. ISBN 0-7636-1104-2 Subj: Animals. Birds – ducks. Counting, numbers. Format, unusual – board books. Rhyming text.

One windy Wednesday ill. by Helen Craig. Candlewick, 1996. ISBN 0-7636-0054-7 Subj: Animals. Farms. Noise, sounds. Weather – wind.

Rattletrap car ill. by Jill Barton. Candlewick, 2001. ISBN 0-7636-0919-6 Subj: Automobiles. Family life. Humorous stories. Lakes, ponds. Problem solving. Rhyming text.

Rattletrap car [board book] ill. by Jill Barton. Candlewick, 2001. ISBN 0-7636-2007-6 Subj: Automobiles. Family life. Format, unusual – board books. Humorous stories. Lakes, ponds. Problem solving. Rhyming text.

Rosie's fiddle ill. by Kevin O'Malley. Lothrop, 1997. ISBN 0-688-12853-X Subj: Contests. Devil. Music. Musical instruments – violins. Tall tales.

Sam, who was swallowed by a shark ill. by Axel Scheffler. Candlewick, 1994. ISBN 1-56402-198-X Subj: Animals – rats. Boats, ships. Character traits – ambition. Sea & seashore.

Soup for supper ill. by Sue Truesdell. HarperCollins, 1986. ISBN 0-06-025071-2 Subj: Folk & fairy tales. Food. Friendship. Giants. Music. Songs.

Ten sleepy sheep ill. by Susan Gaber. Candlewick, 2004. ISBN 0-7636-1545-5 Subj: Animals – sheep. Bedtime. Rhyming text. Sleep.

Turnover Tuesday ill. by Helen Craig. Candlewick, 1998. ISBN 0-7636-0447-X Subj: Activities – baking, cooking. Food.

What Baby wants ill. by Jill Barton. Candlewick, 1998. ISBN 0-7636-0207-8 Subj: Babies. Family life. Farms. Lullabies.

What's that noise? (Edwards, Michelle)

Roper, Janice M. *Dancing on the moon* ill. by Lauren Grimm. SIDS Ed. Services, 2001. ISBN 0-9641218-6-7 Subj: Babies. Death. Dreams. Emotions – envy, jealousy. Emotions – grief. Family life – brothers & sisters. Moon.

Ros, Saphan. *The two brothers* (Ho, Minfong)

Rosa-Casanova, Sylvia. *Mama Provi and the pot of rice* ill. by Robert Roth. Atheneum, 1997. ISBN 0-689-31932-0 Subj: Character traits – helpfulness. Ethnic groups in the U.S. Food. Illness – chicken pox.

Rosado, Ana-Maria. *Las Navidades: popular Christmas songs from Latin America* (Delacre, Lulu)

Rosales, Melodye Benson. *Double Dutch and the voodoo shoes* ill. by author. Childrens Pr., 1992. ISBN 0-516-05133-4 Subj: Ethnic groups in the U.S. – African Americans. Games. Magic.

Leola and the honeybears ill. by author. Scholastic, 1999. An African-American retelling of Goldilocks and the Three Bears. ISBN 0-590-38358-2 Subj: Animals – bears. Ethnic groups in the U.S. – African Americans. Folk & fairy tales.

'Twas the night b'fore Christmas: an African-American version ill. by author. Scholastic, 1996. Based on the original poem, A visit from St. Nicholas, by Clement C. Moore. ISBN 0-590-73944-1 Subj: Ethnic groups in the U.S. – African Americans. Holidays – Christmas. Poetry. Santa Claus.

Rosa-Mendoza, Gladys. *What time is it? = Qué hora es?* ill. by Susan Chapman Calitri. Me & Mi, 2001. ISBN 0-9679748-9-5 Subj: Foreign languages. Format, unusual – board books. Time.

Rosario, Idalia. *Idalia's project ABC: an urban alphabet book in English and Spanish* ill. by author. Holt, 1981. ISBN 0-03-044141-2 Subj: ABC books. Cities, towns. Foreign languages.

Roscoe, William. *The butterfly's ball and the grasshopper's feast* ill. by Don Bolognese. McGraw-Hill, 1967. Subj: Animals. Insects – butterflies, caterpillars. Poetry.

Rose, Agatha. *Hide-and-seek in the yellow house* ill. by Kate Spohn. Viking, 1992. ISBN 0-670-84383-0 Subj: Animals – cats.

Rose, Anne K. *Akimba and the magic cow: a folktale from Africa* ill. by Hope Meryman. Four Winds, 1979. ISBN 0-590-07492-X Subj: Folk & fairy tales. Foreign lands – Africa. Magic.

As right as right can be ill. by Arnold Lobel. Dial, 1976. ISBN 0-8037-0296-5 Subj: Behavior – seeking better things. Money.

How does a czar eat potatoes? ill. by Janosch. Lothrop, 1973. ISBN 0-688-51531-2 Subj: Poverty. Rhyming text. Royalty – tsars.

Pot full of luck ill. by Margot Tomes. Lothrop, 1982. ISBN 0-688-00393-1 Subj: Folk & fairy tales. Foreign lands – Africa.

Spider in the sky ill. by Gail Owens. HarperCollins, 1978. Based on the story How the Sun came from American Indian mythology by Alice Marriott and Carol K. Rachlin. ISBN 0-06-025074-7 Subj: Animals. Creation. Folk & fairy tales. Indians of North America. Spiders.

The talking turnip ill. by Paul Galdone. Parents' Magazine Pr., 1979. ISBN 0-8193-1006-9 Subj: Cumulative tales. Folk & fairy tales. Plants. Problem solving.

The triumphs of Fuzzy Fogtop ill. by Tomie de Paola. Dial, 1979. ISBN 0-8037-8647-6 Subj: Folk & fairy tales.

Rose, David S. *It hardly seems like Halloween* ill. by author. Lothrop, 1983. ISBN 0-688-02093-3 Subj: Holidays – Halloween.

Rose, Deborah Lee. *Birthday zoo* ill. by Lynn Munsinger. A. Whitman, 2002. ISBN 0-8075-0776-8 Subj: Animals. Birthdays. Parties. Rhyming text. Toys. Zoos.

Into the A, B, sea ill. by Steve Jenkins. Scholastic, 2000. ISBN 0-439-09696-0 Subj: ABC books. Animals. Sea & seashore.

Meredith's mother takes the train ill. by Irene Trivas. A. Whitman, 1990. ISBN 0-8075-5061-2 Subj: Activities – working. Family life – mothers. Rhyming text.

The twelve days of kindergarten ill. by Carey Armstrong-Ellis. Abrams, 2003. ISBN 0-8109-4512-6 Subj: Counting, numbers. Cumulative tales. Poetry. School.

Rose, Emma. *Ballet magic* ill. by Jan Palmer. Scholastic, 1996. ISBN 0-590-26242-4 Subj: Activities – dancing. Ballet. Format, unusual – toy & movable books.

Rose, Gerald. *The bird garden* ill. by author. Salem House, 1987. ISBN 0-370-30690-2 Subj: Birds. Language. Royalty.

The hare and the tortoise (Æsop)

The lion and the mouse (Æsop)

PB takes a holiday ill. by author. Bodley Head, 1981. ISBN 0-370-30314-8 Subj: Activities – traveling. Animals – polar bears.

The raven and the fox (Æsop)

Scruff ill. by author. Salem House, 1985. ISBN 0-370-30619-8 Subj: Animals – dogs. Senses – smell.

The tiger-skin rug ill. by author. Prentice-Hall, 1979. ISBN 0-13-921585-9 Subj: Animals – tigers. Crime.

Trouble in the ark ill. by author. Morehouse, 1989. ISBN 0-8192-1511-2 Subj: Animals. Behavior – fighting, arguing. Boats, ships. Religion – Noah. Weather – floods. Weather – rain.

Wolf! Wolf! (Æsop)

Rose, Mitchell. *Norman* ill. by author. S&S, 1970. ISBN 0-671-65107-2 Subj: Animals – dogs. Theater.

Rose, Tatin. *Olie's bedtime walk* (Hertz, Grete Janus)

Rosen, Anne. *A family Passover* by Anne Rosen & others; photos by Laurence Salzmann. Jewish Publication Society, 1980. ISBN 0-8276-0169-7 Subj: Holidays – Passover. Jewish culture.

Rosen, Michael. *Poems for the very young* (Poems for the very young)

Rosen, Michael (1946–). *Crow and Hawk* ill. by John Clementson. Harcourt, 1995. ISBN 0-15-200257-X Subj: Behavior – running away. Birds – crows. Birds – hawks. Folk & fairy tales. Indians of North America – Pueblo.

How the animals got their colors ill. by John Clementson. Harcourt, 1992. ISBN 0-15-236783-7 Subj: Animals. Concepts – color. Folk & fairy tales – pourquoi tales. Poetry.

Howler ill. by Neal Layton. Bloomsbury, 2004. ISBN 1-58234-851-0 Subj: Animals – dogs. Babies. Emotions – envy, jealousy. Humorous stories.

Little rabbit Foo Foo ill. by Arthur Robins. S&S, 1990. ISBN 0-671-70968-2 Subj: Animals. Animals – rabbits.

Mission Ziffoid ill. by Arthur Robins. Candlewick, 1999. ISBN 0-7636-0805-X Subj: Aliens. Space & space ships.

Smelly jelly smelly fish ill. by Quentin Blake. Prentice-Hall, 1987. ISBN 0-13-814567-9 Subj: Humorous stories. Poetry.

A Thanksgiving wish ill. by John Thompson. Blue Sky, 1999. ISBN 0-590-25563-0 Subj: Communities, neighborhoods. Death. Family life – grandparents. Holidays – Thanksgiving.

This is our house ill. by Bob Graham. Candlewick, 1996. ISBN 1-56402-870-4 Subj: Behavior – sharing. Character traits – selfishness. Homes, houses. Prejudice.

Under the bed ill. by Quentin Blake. Prentice-Hall, 1986. ISBN 0-13-935412-3 Subj: Bedtime. Furniture – beds. Poetry.

We're going on a bear hunt ill. by Helen Oxenbury. Aladdin, 1992. ISBN 0-689-71653-2 Subj: Animals – bears. Games. Participation. Sports – hunting.

You can't catch me! ill. by Quentin Blake. Elsevier-Dutton, 1982. ISBN 0-233-97345-1 Subj: Humorous stories. Poetry.

Rosen, Michael J. (1954–). *All eyes on the pond* ill. by Tom Leonard. Hyperion, 1994. ISBN 1-56282-476-7 Subj: Animals. Lakes, ponds. Nature.

Avalanche ill. by David Butler. Candlewick, 1998. ISBN 0-7636-0589-1 Subj: ABC books. Animals – dogs. Rhyming text. Weather – snow.

Bonesy and Isabel ill. by James Ransome. Harcourt, 1995. ISBN 0-15-209813-5 Subj: Adoption. Animals – dogs. Death. Emotions – grief. Farms. Pets.

Chanukah lights everywhere ill. by Melissa Iwai. Harcourt, 2001. ISBN 0-15-202447-6 Subj: Counting, numbers. Holidays – Hanukkah. Jewish culture. Religion.

The dog who walked with God ill. by Stan Fellows. Candlewick, 1998. ISBN 0-7636-0470-4 Subj: Animals – dogs. Creation. Indians of North America – Kato. Weather – floods.

Elijah's angel ill. by Aminah Brenda Lynn Robinson. Harcourt, 1992. ISBN 0-15-225394-7 Subj: Careers – woodcarvers. Ethnic groups in the U.S. – African Americans. Friendship. Holidays – Christmas. Holidays – Hanukkah. Jewish culture.

Home. HarperCollins, 1992. A collaboration of thirty authors and illustrators to aid the homeless. ISBN 0-06-021789-8 Subj: Homeless.

Our eight nights of Hanukkah ill. by DyAnne DiSalvo-Ryan. Holiday, 2000. ISBN 0-8234-1476-0 Subj: Holidays – Hanukkah. Jewish culture.

With a dog like that, a kid like me . . . ill. by Ted Rand. Dial, 2000. ISBN 0-8037-2059-9 Subj: Animals. Animals – dogs. Imagination.

Rosen, Sidney. *How far is a star?* ill. by Dean Lindberg. Carolrhoda, 1992. ISBN 0-87614-684-1 Subj: Concepts – distance. Space & space ships. Stars.

Where does the moon go? ill. by Dean Lindberg. Carolrhoda, 1992. ISBN 0-87614-685-X Subj: Moon. Space & space ships.

Where's the big dipper? ill. by Dean Lindberg. Carolrhoda, 1995. ISBN 0-87614-883-6 Subj: Astronomy. Sky. Stars.

Rosen, Winifred. *Dragons hate to be discreet* ill. by Edward Koren. Knopf, 1978. ISBN 0-394-95377-2 Subj: Dragons. Imagination.

Henrietta and the day of the iguana ill. by Kay Chorao. Four Winds, 1978. ISBN 0-590-07471-7 Subj: Behavior – wishing. Pets. Reptiles – iguanas.

Henrietta and the gong from Hong Kong ill. by Kay Chorao. Four Winds, 1981. ISBN 0-590-07657-4 Subj: Family life – grandparents. Sibling rivalry.

Rosenberg, David. *see* Clifford, David

Rosenberg, Ethel. *see* Clifford, Eth

Rosenberg, Liz. *Adelaide and the night train* ill. by Lisa Desimini. HarperCollins, 1989. ISBN 0-06-025103-4 Subj: Bedtime. Night. Sleep. Trains.

A big and little alphabet ill. by Vera Rosenberry. Orchard, 1997. ISBN 0-531-33050-8 Subj: ABC books. Animals.

The carousel ill. by Jim LaMarche. Harcourt, 1995. ISBN 0-15-200853-5 Subj: Animals – horses, ponies. Death. Emotions – grief. Family life – mothers. Family life – sisters. Imagination. Merry-go-rounds.

Eli's night-light ill. by Joanna Yardley. Orchard, 2001. ISBN 0-531-33316-7 Subj: Bedtime. Light, lights. Night. Rhyming text.

Grandmother and the runaway shadow ill. by Beth Peck. Harcourt, 1996. ISBN 0-15-200948-5 Subj: Activities – traveling. Ethnic groups in the U.S. – Russian Americans. Family life – grandmothers. Jewish culture. Shadows.

Mama Goose: a new Mother Goose ill. by Janet Street. Philomel, 1994. ISBN 0-399-22348-7 Subj: Nursery rhymes.

On Christmas eve ill. by John Clapp. Roaring Brook, 2002. ISBN 0-7613-2707-X Subj: Family life. Holidays – Christmas. Santa Claus. Weather – snow. Weather – storms.

The scrap doll ill. by Robin Ballard. HarperCollins, 1991. ISBN 0-06-024865-3 Subj: Activities – making things. Toys – dolls.

The silence in the mountains ill. by Chris Soentpiet. Orchard, 1999. ISBN 0-531-33084-2 Subj: Family life – grandparents. Immigrants. Noise, sounds.

We wanted you ill. by Peter Catalanotto. Roaring Brook, 2002. ISBN 0-7613-2661-8 Subj: Adoption. Family life – parents.

Window, mirror, moon ill. by Ruth Richardson. HarperCollins, 1990. ISBN 0-06-025076-3 Subj: Babies. Circular tales. Moon. Night. Rhyming text.

Rosenberg, Maxine B. *Being adopted* photos by George Ancona. Lothrop, 1984. ISBN 0-688-02673-7 Subj: Adoption. Ethnic groups in the U.S. Family life.

Brothers and sisters photos by George Ancona. Houghton Mifflin, 1991. ISBN 0-395-51121-6 Subj: Family life – brothers & sisters.

Mommy's in the hospital having a baby photos by Robert Maass. Clarion, 1997. ISBN 0-395-71813-9 Subj: Babies. Birth. Family life – new sibling. Hospitals.

My friend Leslie: the story of a handicapped child photos by George Ancona. Lothrop, 1983. ISBN 0-688-01691-X Subj: Handicaps. School.

Rosenberg, Nancy Sherman. *see* Sherman, Nancy

Rosenberry, Vera. *Run, jump, whiz, splash* ill. by author. Holiday, 1999. ISBN 0-8234-1378-0 Subj: Activities. Seasons.

Vera goes to the dentist ill. by author. Holt, 2002. ISBN 0-8050-6668-3 Subj: Careers – dentists. Health & fitness. Teeth.

Vera runs away ill. by author. Holt, 2000. ISBN 0-8050-6267-X Subj: Behavior – running away. Family life.

Vera's first day of school ill. by author. Holt, 1999. ISBN 0-8050-5936-9 Subj: Character traits – shyness. Emotions – fear. School – first day.

When Vera was sick ill. by author. Holt, 1998. ISBN 0-8050-5405-7 Subj: Illness – chicken pox.

Who is in the garden? ill. by author. Holiday, 2001. ISBN 0-8234-1529-5 Subj: Animals. Gardens, gardening.

Rosenbloom, Joseph. *Deputy Dan and the bank robbers* ill. by Tim Raglin. Random House, 1985. ISBN 0-394-97045-4 Subj: Crime.

The funniest joke book ever! ill. by Hans Wilhelm. Sterling, 1986. ISBN 0-8069-4724-1 Subj: Riddles & jokes.

Rosenblum, Richard. *Journey to the golden land* ill. by author. Jewish Publication Society, 1992. ISBN 0-8276-0405-X Subj: Activities – traveling. Ethnic groups in the U.S. – Russian Americans. Family life. Foreign lands – Russia. Jewish culture.

The old synagogue ill. by author. Jewish Publication Society, 1989. ISBN 0-8276-0322-3 Subj: Cities, towns. Jewish culture. Religion.

Rosenfeld, Dina Herman. *Five alive: my Yom Tov five senses* ill. by Tova Leff. Hachai, 2003. ISBN 1-929628-09-9 Subj: Holidays. Jewish culture. Senses.

Get well soon ill. by Rina Lyampe. Hachai, 2001. ISBN 1-929628-05-6 Subj: Illness. Jewish culture.

How in the world does bread come from the earth? ill. by Rina Lyampe. Hachai, 2002. ISBN 1-929628-06-4 Subj: Food. Religion. Rhyming text.

Rosman, Steven M. *Deena the damselfly* ill. by Giyora Karmi. UAHC Pr., 1992. ISBN 0-8074-0477-2 Subj: Behavior – growing up. Insects – damselflies. Nature.

Rosner, Ruth. *Arabba gah zee, Marissa and Me!* ill. by author. A. Whitman, 1987. ISBN 0-8075-0442-4 Subj: Activities – playing. Friendship. Imagination.

Nattie witch ill. by author. HarperCollins, 1989. ISBN 0-06-025099-2 Subj: Witches.

Ross, Anna. *I did it!* ill. by Norman Gorbaty. Random House, 1990. ISBN 0-394-86019-5 Subj: Behavior – growing up. Character traits – pride. Puppets.

I have to go ill. by Norman Gorbaty. Random House, 1990. ISBN 0-394-86051-9 Subj: Behavior – growing up. Puppets.

Naptime ill. by Norman Gorbaty. Random House, 1990. ISBN 0-394-85828-X Subj: Puppets. Sleep.

Say the magic word, please ill. by Norman Gorbaty. Random House, 1990. ISBN 0-394-85857-3 Subj: Etiquette. Puppets.

Ross, Blanche. *A strange servant: a Russian folktale* (Galdone, Paul)

Ross, Christine. *Lily and the bears* ill. by author. Houghton Mifflin, 1991. ISBN 0-395-55332-6 Subj: Animals – bears. Behavior – imitation. Zoos.

Lily and the present ill. by author. Houghton Mifflin, 1992. ISBN 0-395-61127-X Subj: Babies. Character traits – generosity. Family life – new sibling. Shopping. Toys – balloons.

Ross, Dave (David). *A book of friends* ill. by Laura Rader. HarperCollins, 1999. ISBN 0-06-028170-7 Subj: Friendship.

A book of hugs ill. by Laura Rader. HarperCollins, 1999. ISBN 0-06-028147-2 Subj: Emotions.

A book of kisses ill. by Laura Rader. HarperCollins, 2000. ISBN 0-06-028453-6 Subj: Emotions.

Gorp and the space pirates ill. by author. Walker, 1983. ISBN 0-8037-6494-0 Subj: Monsters. Pirates. Space & space ships.

More hugs! ill. by author. Crowell, 1984. ISBN 0-694-00147-3 Subj: Emotions.

Space monster ill. by author. Walker, 1981. Subj: Monsters. Space & space ships.

Space Monster Gorp and the runaway computer ill. by author. Walker, 1984. Subj: Computers. Monsters. Space & space ships.

Ross, Diana. *The story of the little red engine* ill. by Leslie Wood. Transatlantic, 1947. Subj: Foreign lands – England. Trains.

Ross, Eileen. *The Halloween showdown* ill. by Lynn Rowe Reed. Holiday, 1999. ISBN 0-8234-1395-0 Subj: Animals. Animals – cats. Holidays – Halloween. Witches.

Ross, Gayle. *How Turtle's back was cracked* ill. by Murv Jacob. Dial, 1995. ISBN 0-8037-1729-6 Subj: Animals – wolves. Behavior – boasting. Folk & fairy tales. Indians of North America – Cherokee. Reptiles – turtles, tortoises.

The legend of the Windigo: a tale from native North America ill. by Murv Jacob. Dial, 1996. ISBN 0-8037-1898-5 Subj: Folk & fairy tales. Indians of North America – Algonquin. Indians of North America – Windigos. Insects – mosquitoes. Monsters.

Ross, George Maxim. *When Lucy went away* ill. by Ingrid Fetz. Dutton, 1976. Subj: Animals – cats. Pets.

Ross, H. L. *Not counting monsters* ill. by Doug Cushman. Platt, 1978. Subj: Activities. Counting, numbers. Monsters.

Ross, Jessica. *Ms. Klondike* ill. by author. Viking, 1977. Subj: Activities – working. Careers – taxi drivers. Taxis.

Ross, Joel. *Your first airplane trip* (Ross, Pat)

Ross, Katharine (1954–). *When you were a baby* photos by Phoebe Dunn. Random House, 1988. ISBN 0-394-89897-4 Subj: Babies. Behavior – growing up. Family life.

Ross, Lillian Hammer. *Buba Leah and her paper children* ill. by Mary Morgan. Jewish Publication Society, 1991. ISBN 0-8276-0375-4 Subj: Jewish culture. Letters, cards. Moving.

The little old man and his dreams ill. by Deborah Healy. HarperCollins, 1990. ISBN 0-06-025095-X Subj: Dreams. Jewish culture. Old age. Weddings.

Ross, Michael Elsohn. *Earth cycles* ill. by Gustav Moore. Millbrook, 2001. ISBN 0-7613-1815-1 Subj: Concepts. Day. Earth. Night. Seasons.

Mexican Christmas photos by Felix Rigau. Carolrhoda, 2002. ISBN 0-87614-601-9 Subj: Foreign lands – Mexico. Holidays – Christmas.

Ross, Pat. *Meet M and M* ill. by Marylin Hafner. Pantheon, 1980. Subj: Friendship.

Molly and the slow teeth ill. by Jerry Milord. Lothrop, 1980. Subj: School. Teeth.

Your first airplane trip by Pat & Joel Ross; ill. by Lynn Wheeling. Lothrop, 1981. Subj: Activities – flying. Airplanes, airports. Emotions – fear.

Ross, Stacey. *The magic dogs of the volcanoes* (Argueta, Manlio)

Ross, Tom. *Eggbert, the slightly cracked egg* ill. by Rex Barron. Putnam, 1994. ISBN 0-399-22416-5 Subj: Careers – artists. Character traits – individuality. Eggs.

Ross, Tony. *The boy who cried wolf* ill. by author. Dial, 1991. ISBN 0-8037-0193-4 Subj: Animals – wolves. Behavior – lying. Behavior – trickery. Folk & fairy tales.

Centipede's 100 shoes. Holt, 2003. ISBN 0-8050-7298-5 Subj: Clothing – shoes. Crustaceans – centipedes, millipedes.

The enchanted pig: an old Rumanian tale ill. by author. HarperCollins, 1983. ISBN 0-911745-00-9 Subj: Animals – pigs. Folk & fairy tales. Magic. Witches.

A fairy tale ill. by author. Little, 1992. ISBN 0-316-75750-0 Subj: Fairies. Friendship.

Goldilocks and the three bears (The three bears)

The greedy little cobbler ill. by author. Barron's, 1980. ISBN 0-8120-5389-3 Subj: Behavior – greed. Careers – shoemakers.

Hansel and Gretel ill. by author. Trafalgar Square, 1990. ISBN 0-86264-210-8 Subj: Behavior – lost. Folk & fairy tales. Forest, woods. Witches.

Happy blanket ill. by author. Farrar, 1990. ISBN 0-374-32843-9 Subj: Emotions – fear. Format, unusual.

Hugo and Oddsock ill. by author. Rourke, 1982. ISBN 0-8659-2123-7 Subj: Animals – mice. Imagination – imaginary friends.

Hugo and the bureau of holidays ill. by author. Follett, 1982. ISBN 0-86592-129-6 Subj: Animals – mice. Holidays.

Hugo and the man who stole colors ill. by author. Follett, 1982. ISBN 0-86592-121-0 Subj: Animals – mice. Behavior – stealing. Concepts – color.

I want a cat ill. by author. Farrar, 1989. ISBN 0-374-33621-0 Subj: Animals – cats. Character traits – persistence. Pets.

I want my potty ill. by author. Kane/Miller, 1986. ISBN 0-916291-08-1 Subj: Behavior – growing up. Toilet training.

I'm coming to get you! ill. by author. Dial, 1984. ISBN 0-8037-0119-5 Subj: Emotions – fear. Monsters. Space & space ships.

Jack and the beanstalk (Jack and the beanstalk)

Jack the giantkiller (Jack and the beanstalk)

Oscar got the blame ill. by author. Dial, 1988. ISBN 0-8037-0499-2 Subj: Behavior – misbehavior.

The pied piper of Hamelin retold & ill. by Tony Ross. Lothrop, 1978. ISBN 0-688-51824-9 Subj: Animals – rats. Folk & fairy tales. Foreign lands – Germany.

Puss in boots: the story of a sneaky cat (Perrault, Charles)

Stone soup ill. by author. Dial, 1987. ISBN 0-8037-0401-1 Subj: Animals – wolves. Birds – chickens. Character traits – cleverness. Folk & fairy tales.

This old man: a musical counting book ill. by author; paper engineering by Rodger

Smith. Collins, 1990. ISBN 0-00-184559-4 Subj: Animals – dogs. Counting, numbers. Format, unusual – toy & movable books. Music. Songs.

Towser and the terrible thing ill. by author. Pantheon, 1984. ISBN 0-394-96541-8 Subj: Animals – dogs. Monsters. Royalty.

Treasure of Cozy Cove ill. by author. Farrar, 1990. ISBN 0-374-37744-8 Subj: Activities. Animals – cats. Pirates.

Rosselson, Leon. *Where's my mom?* ill. by Priscilla Lamont. Candlewick, 1994. ISBN 1-56402-392-3 Subj: Family life – mothers. Rhyming text.

Rossetti, Christina Georgina. *Color* ill. by Mary Teichman. HarperCollins, 1992. ISBN 0-06-022650-1 Subj: Concepts – color. Poetry.

Fly away, fly away over the sea ill. by Bernadette Watts. North-South, 1991. ISBN 1-55858-101-4 Subj: Birds. Poetry.

What is pink? ill. by José Aruego. Macmillan, 1971. Subj: Birds – flamingos. Concepts – color. Poetry.

Rossiter, Nan Parson. *Sugar on snow* ill. by author. Dutton, 2002. ISBN 0-525-46910-9 Subj: Family life – brothers. Farms. Food.

The way home ill. by author. Dutton, 1999. ISBN 0-525-45767-4 Subj: Birds – geese. Character traits – kindness to animals. Farms. Illness.

Rossner, Judith. *What kind of feet does a bear have?* ill. by Irwin Rosenhouse. Bobbs-Merrill, 1963. Subj: Humorous stories.

Rotenberg, Lisa. *Rodeo pup* ill. by author. Firefly, 1998. ISBN 1-55209-245-3 Subj: Animals – dogs. Sports.

Roth, Carol. *Little Bunny's sleepless night* ill. by Valeri Gorbachev. North-South, 1999. ISBN 0-7358-1070-2 Subj: Animals – rabbits. Behavior – dissatisfaction. Friendship. Sleep.

The little school bus ill. by Pamela Paparone. North-South, 2002. ISBN 0-7358-1647-6 Subj: Animals. Buses. Rhyming text. School.

Ten dirty pigs / Ten clean pigs ill. by Pamela Paparone. North-South, 1999. ISBN 0-7358-1090-7 Subj: Animals – pigs. Bedtime. Counting, numbers. Format, unusual.

Roth, Harold. *Autumn days* photos by author. Grosset, 1986. ISBN 0-448-10680-9 Subj: Format, unusual – board books. Seasons – fall.

A checkup photos by author. Grosset, 1986. ISBN 0-448-10683-3 Subj: Format, unusual – board books. Health & fitness.

Let's look all around the farm photos by author. Putnam, 1988. ISBN 0-448-10687-6 Subj: Farms. Format, unusual – toy & movable books.

Let's look all around the house photos by author. Putnam, 1988. ISBN 0-448-10685-X Subj: Format, unusual – toy & movable books. Homes, houses.

Let's look all around the town photos by author. Putnam, 1988. ISBN 0-448-10684-1 Subj: Cities, towns. Format, unusual – toy & movable books.

Let's look for surprises all around photos by author. Putnam, 1988. ISBN 0-448-10686-8 Subj: Format, unusual – toy & movable books.

Nursery school photos by author. Grosset, 1986. ISBN 0-448-10682-5 Subj: Format, unusual – board books. School – nursery.

Winter days photos by author. Grosset, 1986. ISBN 0-448-10681-7 Subj: Format, unusual – board books. Seasons – winter.

Roth, Roger. *Fishing for Methuselah* ill. by author. HarperCollins, 1998. ISBN 0-06-027592-8 Subj: Friendship. Sports – fishing. Tall tales.

The sign painter's dream ill. by author. Crown, 1993. ISBN 0-517-58921-4 Subj: Activities – painting. Careers – sign painters. Character traits – generosity. Dreams.

Roth, Susan L. *Another Christmas* ill. by author. Morrow, 1992. ISBN 0-688-09943-2 Subj: Death. Emotions – grief. Family life. Family life – grandmothers. Foreign lands – Puerto Rico. Holidays – Christmas.

The biggest frog in Australia ill. by author. S&S, 1996. ISBN 0-689-80490-3 Subj: Foreign lands – Australia. Frogs & toads. Tall tales.

Brave Martha and the dragon ill. by author. Dial, 1996. ISBN 0-8037-1853-5 Subj: Character traits – bravery. Dragons. Folk & fairy tales.

Cinnamon's day out: a gerbil adventure ill. by author. Dial, 1998. ISBN 0-8037-2323-7 Subj: Animals – gerbils. Behavior – running away.

Fire came to the earth people: a Dahomean folktale ill. by adapt. St. Martin's, 1988. ISBN 0-312-01723-5 Subj: Fire. Folk & fairy tales. Foreign lands – Africa.

Happy birthday Mr. Kang ill. by author. National Geographic, 2001. ISBN 0-7922-7723-6 Subj: Behavior – wishing. Birds. Character traits – freedom. Cities, towns. Ethnic groups in the U.S. – Chinese Americans. Family life – grandfathers.

Kanahena: a Cherokee story ill. by adapt. St. Martin's, 1988. ISBN 0-312-01722-7 Subj: Animals – wolves. Folk & fairy tales. Indians of North America – Cherokee.

Night-time numbers: a scary counting book ill. by author. Barefoot, 1999. ISBN 1-84148-001-0 Subj: Bedtime. Counting, numbers. Night. Rhyming text.

Patchwork tales by Susan L. Roth & Ruth Phang; ill. by authors. Atheneum, 1984. ISBN 0-689-31053-6 Subj: Family life – grandmothers.

The story of light ill. by author. Morrow, 1990. ISBN 0-688-08677-2 Subj: Folk & fairy tales. Indians of North America – Cherokee. Sun.

We'll ride elephants through Brooklyn ill. by author. Farrar, 1990. ISBN 0-374-38258-1 Subj: Family life – grandfathers. Illness. Parades.

Rothenberg, Joan Keller. *Inside-out grandma* ill. by author. Hyperion, 1995. ISBN 0-7868-2092-6 Subj: Clothing. Family life – grandmothers. Folk & fairy tales. Holidays – Hanukkah. Jewish culture. Religion.

Matzah ball soup ill. by author. Hyperion, 1999. ISBN 0-7868-2170-1 Subj: Family life – sisters. Food. Holidays – Passover. Jewish culture.

Rothman, Joel. *This can lick a lollipop = esto goza chupando un caramelo* English by Joel Rothman, Spanish by Argentina Palacios; photos by Patricia Ruben. Doubleday, 1979. ISBN 0-385-13072-4 Subj: Anatomy. Foreign languages.

Rothstein, Gloria. *Sheep asleep* ill. by Lizzy Rockwell. HarperCollins, 2003. ISBN 0-06-029106-0 Subj: Animals – sheep. Bedtime. Counting, numbers. Rhyming text.

Rotner, Ken. *Everybody works* (Rotner, Shelley)

Rotner, Shelley. *The A.D.D. book for kids* by Shelley Rotner & Sheila Kelly; photos by Shelley Rotner. Millbrook, 2000. ISBN 0-7613-1722-8 Subj: Behavior. Handicaps – ADD.

Boats afloat photos by author. Orchard, 1998. ISBN 0-531-33112-1 Subj: Boats, ships. Transportation.

The body book by Shelley Rotner & Steve Calcagnino; photos by Shelley Rotner. Orchard, 2000. ISBN 0-531-33256-X Subj: Anatomy.

Changes (Allen, Marjorie N.)

Citybook photos by Ken Kreisler. Orchard, 1994. ISBN 0-531-06837-4 Subj: Cities, towns. Rhyming text.

Close, closer, closest by Shelley Rotner & Richard Olivo; photos by Shelley Rotner. Atheneum, 1997. ISBN 0-689-80762-7 Subj: Concepts – perspective. Concepts – size.

Everybody works by Shelley Rotner & Ken Kreisler; photos by Shelley Rotner. Millbrook, 2003. ISBN 0-7613-1751-1 Subj: Activities – working. Careers.

Faces photos by Ken Kreisler. Macmillan, 1994. ISBN 0-02-777887-8 Subj: Anatomy – faces. Character traits – individuality.

Feeling thankful by Shelley Rotner & Sheila Kelly; photos by Shelley Rotner. Millbrook, 2000. ISBN 0-7613-1918-2 Subj: Emotions.

Hold the anchovies! by Shelley Rotner & Julia Pemberton Hellums; photos by Shelley Rotner. Orchard, 1996. ISBN 0-531-08857-X Subj: Activities – baking, cooking. Food.

Lots of grandparents by Shelley Rotner & Sheila Kelly; photos by Shelley Rotner. Millbrook, 2001. ISBN 0-7613-2313-9 Subj: Emotions – love. Family life – grandparents.

Lots of moms by Shelley Rotner & Sheila M. Kelly; photos by Shelley Rotner. Dial, 1996. ISBN 0-8037-1892-6 Subj: Ethnic groups in the U.S. Family life – mothers.

Parts photos by author. Walker, 2001. ISBN 0-8027-8754-1 Subj: Concepts. Picture puzzles. Rhyming text.

Pick a pet by Shelley Rotner & Cheo García; photos by Shelley Rotner. Orchard, 1999. ISBN 0-531-33147-4 Subj: Animals. Pets.

What can you do? by Shelley Rotner & Sheila Kelly; photos by Shelley Rotner. Millbrook, 2001. ISBN 0-7613-2119-5 Subj: Activities. Character traits – individuality. Self-concept.

Wheels around photos by author. Houghton Mifflin, 1995. ISBN 0-395-71815-5 Subj: Wheels.

Rottenberg, Dorian. *The merry starlings* (Marshak, S. [Samuil])

Rotter, Charles. *Seals* ill. with photos. Child's World, 2001. ISBN 1-56766-891-7 Subj: Animals – seals. Science.

Walruses ill. with photos. Child's World, 2001. ISBN 1-56766-894-1 Subj: Animals – walruses. Science.

Roughsey, Dick. *The giant devil-dingo* ill. by author. Macmillan, 1975. ISBN 0-02-777840-1 Subj: Animals. Folk & fairy tales. Foreign lands – Australia.

Rouillard, Wendy. *Barnaby's bunny* ill. by author. Scholastic, 2003. ISBN 0-439-33307-5 Subj: Animals. Animals – bears. Eggs. Pets. School.

Round, Graham. *Hangdog* ill. by author. Dial, 1987. ISBN 0-8037-0448-8 Subj: Animals – dogs. Animals – tigers. Boats, ships. Friendship. Islands. Sea & seashore.

Rounds, Glen. *The boll weevil* Ill. by author. Golden Gate, 1967. Subj: Folk & fairy tales. Insects. Music. Songs.

Casey Jones: the story of a brave engineer ill. by author. Golden Gate, 1968. Subj: Folk & fairy tales. Music. Songs. Trains.

Cowboys ill. by author. Holiday, 1991. ISBN 0-8234-0867-1 Subj: Cowboys, cowgirls. U.S. history – frontier & pioneer life.

The day the circus came to Lone Tree ill. by author. Holiday, 1973. ISBN 0-8234-0232-0 Subj: Circus. Humorous stories.

I know an old lady who swallowed a fly (Little old lady who swallowed a fly)

Once we had a horse ill. by author. Holiday, 1996. ISBN 0-8234-1241-5 Subj: Animals – horses, ponies.

Sod houses on the Great Plains ill. by author. Holiday, 1995. ISBN 0-8234-1162-1 Subj: Family life. Homes, houses. U.S. history – frontier & pioneer life.

The strawberry roan comp. & ill. by Glen Rounds. Golden Gate, 1970. ISBN 0-8746-4160-8 Subj: Animals – horses, ponies. Music. Songs.

Sweet Betsy from Pike comp. & ill. by Glen Rounds. Childrens Pr., 1973. ISBN 0-516-08855-6 Subj: Folk & fairy tales. Music. Songs.

The three billy goats Gruff (Asbjørnsen, P. C. [Peter Christen])

The three little pigs and the big bad wolf (The three little pigs)

Washday on Noah's ark ill. by author. Holiday, 1985. ISBN 0-8234-0555-9 Subj: Animals. Boats, ships. Character traits – cleanliness. Religion – Noah. Tall tales. Weather – floods. Weather – rain.

Rouss, Sylvia A. *The littlest frog* ill. by Holly Hannon. Pitspopany, 2001. ISBN 1-930143-12-5 Subj: Foreign lands – Egypt. Frogs & toads. Jewish culture.

The littlest pair ill. by Holly Hannon. Pitspopany, 2001. ISBN 1-930143-17-6 Subj: Character traits – cooperation. Insects – termites. Religion – Noah.

Sammy Spider's first Passover ill. by Katherine Janus Kahn. Kar-Ben Copies, 1995. ISBN 0-929371-81-X Subj: Holidays – Passover. Jewish culture. Religion. Spiders.

Sammy Spider's first Shabbat ill. by Katherine Janus Kahn. Kar-Ben Copies, 1997. ISBN 1-58013-007-0 Subj: Jewish culture. Religion. Spiders.

Routh, Jonathan. *The Nuns go to Africa* ill. by author. Bobbs-Merrill, 1971. Subj: Careers – nuns. Foreign lands – Africa.

Rovetch, Lissa. *Cora and the elephants* ill. by Martha Weston & Lissa. Viking, 1995. ISBN 0-670-84335-0 Subj: Activities – traveling. Adoption. Animals – elephants. Cities, towns.

Crocs in shirts, hippos in skirts ill. by Rob Hefferan. Cronicle, 2004. ISBN 0-8118-3769-6 Subj: Animals. Clothing. Rhyming text. Zoos.

Ook the book ill. by Shannon McNeill. Chronicle, 2001. ISBN 0-8118-2660-0 Subj: Humorous stories. Language. Poetry. Tongue twisters.

Sweet dreams, little one ill. by Betina Ogden. Random House, 2001. ISBN 0-375-80624-5 Subj: Animals – babies. Dreams. Poetry.

TLC grow with me ill. by Chum McLeod. Kindermusik, 2005. ISBN 1-58987-114-6 Subj: Gifts. Plants. Rhyming text.

Trigwater did it ill. by author. Morrow, 1989. ISBN 0-688-08058-8 Subj: Behavior – misbehavior. Imagination – imaginary friends.

Rowan, James P. *I can be a zoo keeper.* Childrens Pr., 1985. ISBN 0-516-01889-2 Subj: Animals. Careers. Zoos.

Rowan, Paula S. *Rick and Rocky* ill. by Catherine Myler Fruisen. Cedco, 2000. ISBN 0-7683-2175-1 Subj: Activities – playing. Animals – cats. Friendship. Rhyming text.

Rowand, Phyllis. *Every day in the year* ill. by author. Little, 1959. Subj: Emotions – love. Holidays – Christmas.

George ill. by author. Little, 1956. Subj: Animals – dogs.

George goes to town ill. by author. Little, 1958. Subj: Animals – dogs.

It is night ill. by author. HarperCollins, 1953. Subj: Night. Sleep.

Rowe, Jeanne A. *City workers.* Watts, 1969. Subj: Careers. Cities, towns.

A trip through a school. Watts, 1969. Subj: School.

Rowe, Jeannette. *Whose ears?* ill. by author. Little, 1998. ISBN 0-316-75932-5 Subj: Anatomy – ears. Animals. Format, unusual – toy & movable books.

Whose feet? ill. by author. Little, 1998. ISBN 0-316-75934-1 Subj: Anatomy – feet. Animals. Format, unusual – toy & movable books.

Whose nose? ill. by author. Little, 1998. ISBN 0-316-75933-3 Subj: Anatomy – noses. Animals. Format, unusual – toy & movable books.

Rowe, John A. *Baby Crow* ill. by author. North-South, 1994. ISBN 1-55858-278-9 Subj: Birds – crows. Food.

Jasper the terror ill. by author. North-South, 2001. ISBN 0-7358-1477-5 Subj: Animals. Dragons.

Monkey trouble ill. by author. North-South, 1999. ISBN 0-7358-1034-6 Subj: Animals – monkeys. Behavior – mistakes.

Rabbit moon ill. by author. Picture Book Studio, 1992. ISBN 0-8870-8246-7 Subj: Animals – rabbits. Moon.

Smudge ill. by author. North-South, 1997. ISBN 1-55858-789-6 Subj: Animals. Animals – rats. Birds. Family life – mothers. Memories, memory.

Tommy DoLittle ill. by author. North-South, 2002. ISBN 0-7358-1719-7 Subj: Books, reading. Character traits – laziness. School.

Rowinski, Kate. *Cats in the dark* ill. by Bonnie Bishop. Down East, 1998. ISBN 0-8927-2427-7 Subj: Animals – cats. Lighthouses. Night. Noise, sounds. Rhyming text.

L. L. Bear's island adventure ill. by Dawn Peterson. Down East, 1992. ISBN 0-89272-320-3 Subj: Activities – picnicking. Animals. Animals – bears. Sea & seashore. Seasons – winter. Weather – storms.

Roy, Indrapramit. *The very hungry lion* (Wolf, Gita)

Roy, Ronald. *Breakfast with my father* ill. by Troy Howell. Houghton Mifflin, 1980. ISBN 0-395-29430-4 Subj: Divorce. Family life.

A thousand pails of water ill. by Vo-Dinh Mai. Knopf, 1978. ISBN 0-394-93752-X Subj: Animals – whales. Character traits – kindness to animals. Foreign lands – Japan.

Three ducks went wandering ill. by Paul Galdone. Seabury Pr., 1979. ISBN 0-8164-3231-7 Subj: Behavior – indifference. Birds – ducks. Humorous stories.

Whose hat is that? ill. by Rosmarie Hausherr. Clarion, 1987. ISBN 0-89919-446-X Subj: Clothing – hats.

Whose shoes are these? photos by Rosmarie Hausherr. Clarion, 1988. ISBN 0-89919-445-1 Subj: Clothing – shoes.

Royston, Angela. *Baby animals* photos by Steve Shott; additional photos by Jane Burton; ill. by Jane Cradock-Watson & Dave Hopkins. Aladdin, 1992. ISBN 0-689-71563-3 Subj: Animals.

Big machines ill. by Terry Pastor. Little, 1994. ISBN 0-316-76070-6 Subj: Machines. Trucks.

Cars ill. by Jane Cradock-Watson & Dave Hopkins; photos by Tim Ridley. Macmillan, 1991. ISBN 0-689-71517-X Subj: Automobiles. Format, unusual – board books.

Chick (Burton, Jane)

Cow ill. by Bob Bampton. Watts, 1990. ISBN 0-531-19077-3 Subj: Animals – bulls, cows. Farms.

Diggers and dump trucks ill. by Jane Cradock-Watson & Dave Hopkins; photos by Tim Ridley. Macmillan, 1991. ISBN 0-689-71516-1 Subj: Activities – digging. Machines. Trucks.

Dinosaurs ill. by Jane Cradock-Watson & Dave Hopkins; photos by Colin Keates. Macmillan, 1991. ISBN 0-689-71518-8 Subj: Dinosaurs. Prehistory.

Duck (Watts, Barrie)

Fire fighters ill. with photos. DK, 1998. ISBN 0-7894-2960-8 Subj: Careers – firefighters. Fire. Safety.

Frog (Taylor, Kim)

The goat ill. by Eric Robson. Watts, 1990. ISBN 0-531-19078-1 Subj: Animals – goats. Farms.

Heavy and light ill. with photos. Heinemann, 2003. ISBN 1-4034-0853-X Subj: Concepts. Concepts – weight. Science.

The hen ill. by Dave Cook. Watts, 1990. ISBN 0-531-19079-X Subj: Birds – chickens. Farms.

Jungle animals ill. by Martine Blaney & Dave Hopkins; photos by Philip Dowell. Macmillan, 1991. ISBN 0-689-71519-6 Subj: Animals. Jungle.

Kitten (Burton, Jane)

Lamb (Clayton, Gordon)

Levers ill. with photos. Heinemann, 2001. ISBN 1-57572-319-0 Subj: Concepts – leverage. Science.

Life cycle of a guinea pig ill. with photos. Heinemann, 1998. ISBN 1-57572-614-9 Subj: Animals – guinea pigs. Science.

Life cycle of a mushroom ill. with photos. Heinemann, 2000. ISBN 1-57572-210-0 Subj: Food. Fungi, molds. Science.

Life cycle of a salmon ill. with photos. Heinemann, 2000. ISBN 1-57572-212-7 Subj: Fish. Science.

Life cycle of an oak tree ill. with photos. Heinemann, 2000. ISBN 1-57572-211-9 Subj: Science. Trees.

Monster road builders ill. by Graham Thompson. Barron's, 1989. ISBN 0-8120-6126-8 Subj: Machines. Roads.

Mouse (Watts, Barrie)

My body ill. by Richard Manning. DK, 1991. ISBN 1-879431-22-X Subj: Anatomy.

Night-time animals photos by Dave King. Aladdin, 1992. ISBN 0-689-71646-X Subj: Animals. Night.

The pig ill. by Jim Channel. Watts, 1990. ISBN 0-531-19080-3 Subj: Animals – pigs. Farms.

Planes photos by Tim Ridley. Aladdin, 1992. ISBN 0-689-71564-1 Subj: Airplanes, airports.

The pony ill. by Bob Bampton. Watts, 1990. ISBN 0-531-19081-1 Subj: Animals – horses, ponies. Farms.

Puppy (Burton, Jane)

Rabbit (Watts, Barrie)

Sea animals photos by Steve Shott; ill. by Jane Cradock-Watson & Dave Hopkins. Aladdin, 1992. ISBN 0-689-71565-X Subj: Animals. Crustaceans. Fish. Sea & seashore.

The sheep ill. by Josephine Martin. Watts, 1990. ISBN 0-531-19082-X Subj: Animals – sheep. Farms.

Shells ill. by Richard Manning. DK, 1991. ISBN 1-879431-25-4 Subj: Format, unusual. Sea & seashore.

Ships and boats photos by Tim Ridley. Aladdin, 1992. ISBN 0-689-71566-8 Subj: Boats, ships.

Small animals ill. by Richard Manning. DK, 1991. ISBN 1-879431-24-6 Subj: Animals. Format, unusual. Nature.

Smooth and rough ill. with photos. Heinemann, 2003. ISBN 1-4034-0859-9 Subj: Concepts. Science.

Strange plants ill. with photos. Heinemann, 1999. ISBN 1-57572-829-X Subj: Plants. Science.

Toys ill. by Richard Manning. DK, 1991. ISBN 1-879431-23-8 Subj: Toys.

Truck trouble ill. with photos. DK, 1998. ISBN 0-7894-2958-6 Subj: Careers – truck drivers. Trucks.

Rubel, Nicole. *Bruno Brontosaurus* ill. by author. Camelot, 1983. ISBN 0-380-81562-1 Subj: Dinosaurs.

A cowboy named Ernestine ill. by author. Dial, 2001. ISBN 0-8037-2152-8 Subj: Cowboys, cowgirls. Tall tales.

The ghost family meets its match ill. by author. Dial, 1992. ISBN 0-8037-1094-1 Subj: Ghosts.

Goldie ill. by author. HarperCollins, 1989. ISBN 0-06-025097-6 Subj: Birds – chickens. Shopping. Stores.

Goldie's nap ill. by author. HarperCollins, 1991. ISBN 0-06-025107-7 Subj: Behavior – misbehavior. Birds – chickens. School – nursery. Sleep.

It came from the swamp ill. by author. Dial, 1988. ISBN 0-8037-0515-8 Subj: Behavior – lost. Humorous stories. Reptiles – alligators, crocodiles.

Me and my kitty ill. by author. Macmillan, 1983. ISBN 0-02-777880-0 Subj: Activities. Animals – cats.

No more vegetables! ill. by author. Farrar, 2002. ISBN 0-374-36362-5 Subj: Family life – mothers. Food. Gardens, gardening. Plants.

Sam and Violet are twins ill. by author. Camelot, 1981. ISBN 0-380-76919-0 Subj: Animals – cats. Character traits – individuality. Multiple births – twins.

Sam and Violet go camping ill. by author. Camelot, 1981. ISBN 0-380-76927-1 Subj: Animals – cats. Camps, camping. Character traits – individuality. Multiple births – twins.

Uncle Henry and Aunt Henrietta's honeymoon ill. by author. Dial, 1986. ISBN 0-8037-0247-7 Subj: Activities – babysitting. Boats, ships. Family life – aunts, uncles.

Ruben, Patricia. *Apples to zippers: an alphabet book* ill. by author. Doubleday, 1976. ISBN 0-385-11443-5 Subj: ABC books.

True or false? ill. by author. Lippincott, 1978. ISBN 0-397-31791-3 Subj: Concepts.

Rubin, C. M. *Eleanor, Ellatony, Ellencake, and me* ill. by Christopher Fowler. Gingham Dog, 2003. ISBN 1-57768-412-5 Subj: Family life. Names. Rhyming text. Self-concept.

Rubin, Caroline. *Grandma is somebody special* (Goldman, Susan)

Grandparents around the world (Raynor, Dorka)

Snow on bear's nose: a story of a Japanese moon bear cub (Bartoli, Jennifer)

Tell them my name is Amanda (Wold, Jo Anne)

Wild Bill Hiccup's riddle book (Bishop, Ann)

Rubin, Cynthia Elyce. *ABC Americana from the National Gallery of Art* photos by Carleton Palmer. Harcourt, 1989. ISBN 0-15-200660-5 Subj: ABC books. Art.

Rubin, Jeff. *Baseball brothers* by Jeff Rubin & Rick Rael; ill. by Sandy Kossin. Lothrop, 1976. ISBN 0-688-51744-7 Subj: Friendship. Sports – baseball.

Rubin, Mark. *The orchestra* ill. by Alan Daniel. Firefly, 1992. ISBN 0-920668-99-2 Subj: Music. Musical instruments – orchestras.

Rubin, Susan Goldman. *The yellow house: Vincent van Gogh and Paul Gauguin side by side* ill. by Jos. A. Smith. Abrams, 2001. ISBN 0-8109-4588-6 Subj: Art. Careers – artists. Foreign lands – France.

Rubinetti, Donald. *Cappy the lonely camel* ill. by Liisa Chauncy Guida. Silver Pr., 1996. ISBN 0-382-39151-9 Subj: Animals – camels. Character traits – being different. Prejudice.

Ruby-Spears Enterprises. *The puppy's new adventures: hide and seek* ill. by Ruby-Spears Enterprises. Antioch, 1983. ISBN 0-89954-228-X Subj: Animals – dogs. Crime. Format, unusual – toy & movable books.

Rucki, Ani. *When the Earth wakes* ill. by author. Scholastic, 1998. ISBN 0-590-05951-3 Subj: Animals – bears. Earth. Nature. Seasons.

Ruck-Pauquèt, Gina. *Little hedgehog* ill. by Marianne Richter. Hastings House, 1959. Subj: Animals – hedgehogs.

Mumble bear trans. by Anthea Bell; ill. by Erika Dietzsch-Capelle. Putnam, 1980. ISBN 0-399-20712-0 Subj: Animals – bears. Character traits – individuality.

Oh, that koala! ill. by Anna Mossakowska. McGraw-Hill, 1979. ISBN 0-07-054192-2 Subj: Animals – koalas. Behavior – misbehavior.

Rudin, Ellen. *The three billy goats Gruff* (Asbjørnsen, P. C. [Peter Christen])

Rudolph, Marguerita. *The good stepmother* (Zakhoder, Boris Vladimirovich)

Grey Neck (Mamin-Sibiryak, D. N.)

How a piglet crashed the Christmas party (Zakhoder, Boris Vladimirovich)

How a shirt grew in the field adapt. from the Russian of Konstantin Ushinsky; ill. by Erika Weihs. Clarion, 1992. ISBN 0-395-59761-7 Subj: Clothing – shirts. Foreign lands – Ukraine. Plants.

How a shirt grew in the field adapt. from the Russian of Konstantin Ushinsky; ill. by Yaroslava. McGraw-Hill, 1967. Subj: Clothing – shirts. Foreign lands – Ukraine. Plants.

Rosachok (Zakhoder, Boris Vladimirovich)

Rudomin, Esther. see Hautzig, Esther (Rudomin)

Ruelle, Karen Gray. *April fool* ill. by author. Holiday, 2002. ISBN 0-8234-1686-0 Subj: Animals – cats. Behavior – trickery. Family life – brothers & sisters. Holidays – April Fools' Day.

The crunchy, munchy Christmas tree ill. by author. Holiday, 2003. ISBN 0-8234-1787-5 Subj: Family life. Holidays – Christmas. Trees. Weather – snow.

Easter egg disaster ill. by author. Holiday, 2004. ISBN 0-8234-1806-5 Subj: Animals – cats. Eggs. Family life – brothers & sisters. Holidays – Easter.

Easy as apple pie ill. by author. Holiday, 2002. ISBN 0-8234-1759-X Subj: Animals – cats. Family life – grandparents. Food. Sleepovers.

Mother's Day mess ill. by author. Holiday, 2003. ISBN 0-8234-1773-5 Subj: Family life – brothers & sisters. Holidays – Mother's Day. Humorous stories.

Snow Valentines ill. by author. Holiday, 2000. ISBN 0-8234-1533-3 Subj: Animals – cats. Family life – brothers & sisters. Holidays – Valentine's Day. Weather – snow.

Spookier than a ghost ill. by author. Holiday, 2001. ISBN 0-8234-1667-4 Subj: Animals – cats. Clothing – costumes. Family life – brothers & sisters. Holidays – Halloween.

Ruffins, Reynold. *My brother never feeds the cat* ill. by author. Scribners, 1979. ISBN 0-684-16211-3 Subj: Family life.

Rühmann, Karl. *Filbert flies* ill. by Rolf Siegenthaler. North-South, 2003. ISBN 0-7358-1830-4 Subj: Activities – flying. Animals – seals. Birds – penguins. Birds – seagulls. Self-concept.

Rukeyser, Muriel. *More night* ill. by Symeon Shimin. HarperCollins, 1981. ISBN 0-06-025128-X Subj: Activities. Night.

Uncle Eddie's moustache (Brecht, Bertolt)

Rumford, James. *The cloudmakers* ill. by author. Houghton Mifflin, 1996. ISBN 0-395-76505-6 Subj: Activities – making things. Family life – grandfathers. Folk & fairy tales. Foreign lands – China. Paper.

Dog-of-the-Sea-Waves ill. by author. Houghton, 2004. ISBN 0-618-35611-8 Subj: Animals – seals. Character traits – kindness to animals. Family life – brothers. Foreign languages. Friendship. Hawaii.

The Island-below-the-star ill. by author. Houghton Mifflin, 1998. ISBN 0-395-85159-9 Subj: Activities – traveling. Boats, ships. Family life – brothers. Hawaii. Islands.

Nine animals and the well ill. by author. Houghton, 2003. ISBN 0-618-30915-2 Subj: Animals. Character traits – pride. Character traits – vanity. Counting, numbers. Folk & fairy tales. Foreign lands – India. Gifts. Parties. Royalty – rajahs.

Sequoyah ill. by author. Houghton, 2004. ISBN 0-618-36947-3 Subj: ABC books. Foreign languages. Indians of North America – Cherokee.

There's a monster in the alphabet ill. by author. Houghton, 2002. ISBN 0-618-22140-9 Subj: ABC books. Foreign lands – Greece. Foreign languages. Language.

Runcie, Jill. *Cock-a-doodle-doo* ill. by Lee Lorenz. S&S, 1991. ISBN 0-671-72602-1 Subj: Animals. Circular tales. Farms. Noise, sounds.

Runnells, Treesha. *What will I become?* (Lunsford, Annie)

Who lives here? (Lunsford, Annie)

Rupprecht, Siegfried P. *The tale of the vanishing rainbow* trans. by Naomi Lewis; ill. by Józef Wilkon. North-South, 1989. ISBN 1-55858-001-8 Subj: Animals. War. Weather – rainbows.

Rusackas, Francesca. *Daddy all day long* ill. by Priscilla Burris. HarperCollins, 2004. ISBN 0-06-050285-1 Subj: Animals – pigs. Bedtime. Counting, numbers. Emotions – love. Family life – fathers. Family life – sons.

I love you all day long ill. by Priscilla Burris. HarperCollins, 2003. ISBN 0-06-050277-0 Subj: Animals – pigs. Family life – mothers. School – first day.

Ruschak, Lynette. *The counting zoo* ill. by May Rousseau. Aladdin, 1992. ISBN 0-689-71619-2 Subj: Animals. Counting, numbers. Format, unusual – toy & movable books.

Rush, Ken. *Friday's journey* ill. by author. Orchard, 1994. ISBN 0-531-08671-2 Subj: Activities – traveling. Cities, towns. Divorce. Family life – fathers. Imagination. Trains.

Ruskin, John. *Dame Wiggins of Lee and her seven wonderful cats* (Dame Wiggins of Lee and her seven wonderful cats)

Rusling, Albert. *The mouse and Mrs. Proudfoot* ill. by author. Prentice-Hall, 1985. ISBN 0-13-604265-1 Subj: Animals. Homes, houses. Humorous stories.

Russ, Lavinia. *Alec's sand castle* ill. by James Stevenson. HarperCollins, 1972. ISBN 0-06-020150-9 Subj: Activities – playing. Imagination. Sea & seashore.

Russell, Betty. *Big store, funny door* ill. by Mary Gehr. A. Whitman, 1955. Subj: Character traits – luck. Shopping.

Run sheep run ill. by Mary Gehr. A. Whitman, 1952. Subj: Animals – sheep.

Russell, Janice. *Goldilocks* (The three bears)

Russell, Joan Plummer. *Aero and Officer Mike* photos by Kris Turner Sinnenberg. Boyds Mills, 2001. ISBN 1-56397-931-4 Subj: Animals – dogs. Animals – service animals. Careers – police officers.

Russell, Naomi. *The stream* ill. by author. Dutton, 1991. ISBN 0-525-44729-6 Subj: Nature. Rivers. Water.

The tree ill. by author. Dutton, 1989. ISBN 0-525-44468-8 Subj: Format, unusual. Nature. Trees.

Russell, P. Craig. *Fairy tales of Oscar Wilde: The selfish giant, and The star child* (Wilde, Oscar)

Russell, Pamela. *Do you have a secret? how to get help for scary secrets* by Pamela Russell & Beth Stone; ill. by Mary McKee. CompCare, 1986. ISBN 0-89638-098-X Subj: Behavior – secrets. Safety.

Russell, Sandra Joanne. *A farmer's dozen* ill. by author. HarperCollins, 1982. ISBN 0-06-025144-1 Subj: Farms. Rhyming text.

Russell, Solveig Paulson. *What good is a tail?* ill. by Ezra Jack Keats. Bobbs-Merrill, 1962. Subj: Animals. Science.

Russo, Marisabina. *The big brown box* ill. by author. Greenwillow, 2000. ISBN 0-688-17097-8 Subj: Activities – playing. Behavior – sharing. Family life – brothers. Games. Imagination. Sibling rivalry.

Come back, Hannah ill. by author. Greenwillow, 2001. ISBN 0-688-17384-5 Subj: Babies. Family life – mothers.

Grandpa Abe ill. by author. Greenwillow, 1996. ISBN 0-688-14098-X Subj: Death. Emotions – grief. Family life – grandfathers.

Hannah's baby sister ill. by author. Greenwillow, 1998. ISBN 0-688-15832-3 Subj: Babies. Family life – brothers & sisters. Family life – new sibling.

The line up book ill. by author. Greenwillow, 1986. ISBN 0-688-06205-9 Subj: Activities – playing. Family life. Games.

Mama talks too much ill. by author. Greenwillow, 1999. ISBN 0-688-16412-9 Subj: Cities, towns. Communities, neighborhoods. Family life – mothers. Shopping.

Only six more days ill. by author. Greenwillow, 1988. ISBN 0-688-07072-8 Subj: Birthdays. Sibling rivalry.

The trouble with baby ill. by author. Greenwillow, 2003. ISBN 0-06-008925-3 Subj: Emotions – envy, jealousy. Family life – brothers & sisters. Toys – dolls.

Under the table ill. by author. Greenwillow, 1997. ISBN 0-688-14603-1 Subj: Activities – drawing. Behavior – misbehavior. Family life.

A visit to Oma ill. by author. Greenwillow, 1991. ISBN 0-688-09624-7 Subj: Family life – great-grandparents.

Waiting for Hannah ill. by author. Greenwillow, 1989. ISBN 0-688-08016-2 Subj: Babies. Birth. Family life – mothers. Gardens, gardening.

When mama gets home ill. by author. Greenwillow, 1998. ISBN 0-688-14986-3 Subj: Family life. Family life – mothers.

Where is Ben? ill. by author. Greenwillow, 1990. ISBN 0-688-08013-8 Subj: Activities – playing. Games.

Why do grownups have all the fun? ill. by author. Greenwillow, 1987. ISBN 0-688-06626-7 Subj: Bedtime. Behavior – dissatisfaction. Family life. Imagination.

Russo, Susan. *The ice cream ocean and other delectable poems of the sea* ill. by author. Lothrop, 1984. ISBN 0-688-02123-9 Subj: Poetry. Sea & seashore.

The moon's the north wind's cooky: night poems (The moon's the north wind's cooky)

Rutherford, Erica. *An Island alphabet* ill. by author. Ragweed, 1994. ISBN 0-921556-44-6 Subj: ABC books. Foreign lands – Canada. Islands.

Rutherford, Meg. *Animal poems* ill. by Polly Richardson. Barron's, 1992. ISBN 0-8120-6283-3 Subj: Animals. Poetry.

Ruthstrom, Dorotha. *The big kite contest* ill. by Lillian Hoban. Pantheon, 1980. ISBN 0-394-94430-5 Subj: Kites. Sibling rivalry.

Ruurs, Margriet. *Animal alphabet* ill. by Jennifer Emery. Boyds Mills, 2005. ISBN 1-59078-200-3 Subj: ABC books. Animals. Poetry.

Emma and the coyote ill. by Barbara Spurll. Stoddart, 1999. ISBN 0-7737-3140-7 Subj: Animals – coyotes. Birds – chickens. Character traits – cleverness. Humorous stories.

Emma's cold day ill. by Barbara Spurll. Stoddart, 2001. ISBN 0-7737-3314-0 Subj: Animals. Behavior – imitation. Birds – chickens. Farms. Seasons – winter. Weather – cold.

Emma's eggs ill. by Barbara Spurll. Stoddart, 1996. ISBN 0-7737-2972-0 Subj: Birds – chickens. Eggs. Farms. Humorous stories.

A mountain alphabet Ill. by Andrew Kiss. Tundra, 1996. ISBN 0-88776-374-X Subj: ABC books. Animals. Mountains. Plants.

Ms. Bee's magical bookcase ill. by Andrew Gooderham. Chustnut, 2004. ISBN 1-894601-10-6 Subj: Activities – storytelling. Books, reading. Careers – librarians. School.

A Pacific alphabet ill. by Dianna Bonder. Whitecap, 2001. ISBN 1-55285-264-4 Subj: ABC books. Language. Rhyming text.

When we go camping ill. by Andrew Kiss. Tundra, 2001. ISBN 0-88776-476-2 Subj: Camps, camping. Family life. Nature.

Wild babies ill. by Andrew Kiss. Tundra, 2003. ISBN 0-88776-627-7 Subj: Animals – babies.

Ruzzier, Sergio. *The little giant* ill. by author. Geringer, 2004. ISBN 0-06-052952-0 Subj: Concepts – size. Dwarfs, midgets. Friendship. Giants.

Ryan, Cheli Durán. *Hildilid's night* ill. by Arnold Lobel. Macmillan, 1986, c1971. ISBN 0-02-777260-8 Subj: Caldecott award honor books. Night.

Ryan, Cheryl. *Red are the apples* (Harshman, Marc)

Ryan, Pam Muñoz. *Amelia and Eleanor go for a ride* ill. by Brian Selznick. Scholastic, 1999. ISBN 0-590-96075-X Subj: Activities – flying. Airplanes, airports. U.S. history.

Armadillos sleep in dugouts: and other places animals live ill. by Diane De Groat. Hyperion, 1997. ISBN 0-7868-2222-8 Subj: Animals. Homes, houses. Rhyming text.

The crayon counting book by Pam Muñoz Ryan & Jerry Pallotta; ill. by Frank Mazzola, Jr. Charlesbridge, 1996. ISBN 0-88106-955-8 Subj: Concepts – color. Counting, numbers. Rhyming text.

The flag we love ill. by Ralph Masiello. Charlesbridge, 1996. ISBN 0-88106-846-2 Subj: Poetry. U.S. history.

Hello, Ocean! ill. by Mark Astrella. Charlesbridge, 2001. ISBN 0-88106-987-6 Subj: Rhyming text. Sea & seashore – beaches. Senses.

Hello ocean = Hola mar ill. by Mark Astrella; trans. by Yanitzia Canetti. Charlesbridge, 2003. ISBN 1-57091-372-2 Subj: Foreign languages. Rhyming text. Sea & seashore – beaches. Senses.

How do you raise a raisin? ill. by Craig Brown. Charlesbridge, 2003. ISBN 0-613-82657-4 Subj: Food. Science.

Mud is cake ill. by David McPhail. Hyperion, 2002. ISBN 0-7868-0501-3 Subj: Activities – playing. Family life – brothers & sisters. Imagination. Rhyming text.

One hundred is a family ill. by Benrei Huang. Hyperion, 1994. ISBN 1-56282-673-5 Subj: Counting, numbers. Family life. Rhyming text.

A pinky is a baby mouse, and other baby animal names ill. by Diane DeGroat. Hyperion, 1997. ISBN 0-7868-2190-6 Subj: Animals – babies. Names. Rhyming text.

Rydell, Katy. *Wind says good night* ill. by David Jorgensen. Houghton Mifflin, 1994. ISBN 0-395-60474-5 Subj: Bedtime. Cumulative tales. Night.

Ryden, Hope. *The raggedy red squirrel* photos by author. Dutton, 1992. ISBN 0-525-67400-4 Subj: Animals – squirrels.

Wild animals of Africa ABC photos by author. Dutton, 1989. ISBN 0-525-67290-7 Subj: ABC books. Foreign lands – Africa.

Ryder, Eileen. *Winklet goes to school* ill. by Stephanie Lang. John Godon Burke, 1982. ISBN 0-222-00732-X Subj: School.

Winston's new cap ill. by Stephanie Lang. John Godon Burke, 1982. ISBN 0-222-00735-4 Subj: Behavior – lost & found possessions. Clothing – hats.

Ryder, Joanne. *Beach party* ill. by Diane Stanley. Warne, 1982. ISBN 0-7232-6198-9 Subj: Animals – sheep. Family life. Parties. Sea & seashore – beaches.

Bears out there ill. by Jo Ellen McAllister Stammen. Atheneum, 1995. ISBN 0-689-31780-8 Subj: Animals – bears. Imagination. Seasons – summer.

Big bear ball ill. by Steven Kellogg. HarperCollins, 2002. ISBN 0-06-027956-7 Subj: Activities – dancing. Animals. Animals – bears. Rhyming text.

Catching the wind ill. by Michael Rothman. Morrow, 1989. ISBN 0-688-07171-6 Subj: Birds – geese. Nature.

Chipmunk song ill. by Lynne Cherry. Dutton, 1987. ISBN 0-525-67191-9 Subj: Animals – chipmunks. Nature. Rhyming text.

Dancers in the garden ill. by Judith Lopez. Sierra Club, 1992. ISBN 0-87156-578-1 Subj: Birds – humming birds. Gardens, gardening. Nature.

Each living thing ill. by Ashley Wolff. Harcourt, 2000. ISBN 0-15-201898-0 Subj: Animals. Character traits – kindness to animals. Rhyming text.

A fawn in the grass ill. by Keiko Narahashi. Holt, 2001. ISBN 0-8050-6236-X Subj: Animals. Rhyming text.

Fireflies ill. by Don Bolognese. HarperCollins, 1977. ISBN 0-06-025154-9 Subj: Insects – fireflies. Science.

First grade ladybugs ill. by Betsy Lewin. Troll, 1993. ISBN 0-8167-3006-7 Subj: Gardens, gardening. Insects – ladybugs. School.

Fog in the meadow ill. by Gail Owens. HarperCollins, 1979. ISBN 0-06-025149-2 Subj: Animals. Weather – fog.

Hello, first grade ill. by Betsy Lewin. Troll, 1993. ISBN 0-8167-3008-3 Subj: Animals – rabbits. Puppets. School.

Hello, tree! ill. by Michael Hays. Dutton, 1991. ISBN 0-525-67310-5 Subj: Nature. Rhyming text. Trees.

A house by the sea ill. by Melissa Sweet. Morrow, 1994. ISBN 0-688-12676-6 Subj: Animals. Homes, houses. Rhyming text. Sea & seashore.

Jaguar in the rain forest ill. by Michael Rothman. Morrow, 1996. ISBN 0-688-12991-9 Subj: Animals – jaguars. Foreign lands – French Guiana. Forest, woods.

Little panda ill. with photos. Aladdin, 2001. ISBN 0-689-84310-0 Subj: Animals – babies. Animals – pandas. Zoos.

Lizard in the sun ill. by Michael Rothman. Morrow, 1990. ISBN 0-688-07173-2 Subj: Nature. Reptiles – lizards.

Mockingbird morning ill. by Dennis Nolan. Four Winds, 1989. ISBN 0-02-777961-0 Subj: Birds – mockingbirds. Nature. Poetry.

Mouse tail moon ill. by Maggie Kneen. Holt, 2002. ISBN 0-8050-6404-4 Subj: Animals – mice. Poetry.

My father's hands ill. by Mark Graham. Morrow, 1994. ISBN 0-688-09190-3 Subj: Anatomy – hands. Family life – fathers. Gardens, gardening. Insects.

The night flight ill. by Amy Schwartz. Four Winds, 1985. ISBN 0-02-778020-1 Subj: Animals. Cities, towns. Dreams. Night.

Rainbow wings ill. by Victor Lee. Morrow, 2000. ISBN 0-688-14129-3 Subj: Activities – flying. Science.

Snail in the woods by Joanne Ryder with the assistance of Harold S. Feinberg; ill. by Jo Polseno. HarperCollins, 1979. ISBN 0-06-025169-7 Subj: Animals – snails. Science.

The snail's spell ill. by Lynne Cherry. Warne, 1982. ISBN 0-7232-6197-0 Subj: Animals – snails. Night.

The spiders dance ill. by Robert J. Blake. HarperCollins, 1981. ISBN 0-06-025134-4 Subj: Science. Spiders.

Step into the night ill. by Dennis Nolan. Four Winds, 1988. ISBN 0-02-777951-3 Subj: Nature. Night. Poetry.

Tyrannosaurus time ill. by Michael Rothman. Morrow, 1999. ISBN 0-688-13683-4 Subj: Dinosaurs. Imagination.

Under your feet ill. by Dennis Nolan. Macmillan, 1990. ISBN 0-02-777955-6 Subj: Nature. Poetry. Seasons.

The waterfall's gift ill. by Richard Jesse Watson. Sierra Club, 2001. ISBN 0-87156-579-X Subj: Ecology. Forest, woods. Nature. Water.

A wet and sandy day ill. by Donald Carrick. HarperCollins, 1977. ISBN 0-06-025159-X Subj: Sea & seashore. Weather – rain.

Where butterflies grow ill. by Lynne Cherry. Dutton, 1989. ISBN 0-525-67284-2 Subj: Insects – butterflies, caterpillars. Metamorphosis. Nature. Science.

White bear, ice bear ill. by Michael Rothman. Morrow, 1989. ISBN 0-688-07175-9 Subj: Animals – polar bears. Foreign lands – Arctic. Nature.

Wild birds ill. by Susan Estelle Kwas. HarperCollins, 2003. ISBN 0-06-027739-4 Subj: Birds.

Winter whale ill. by Michael Rothman. Morrow, 1991. ISBN 0-688-07177-5 Subj: Animals – whales. Nature. Seasons – winter.

Rylant, Cynthia. *All I see* ill. by Peter Catalanotto. Watts, 1988. ISBN 0-531-08377-2 Subj: Activities – painting. Art. Friendship.

Appalachia: the voices of sleeping birds ill. by Barry Moser. Harcourt, 1991. ISBN 0-15-201605-8 Subj: Country.

Bear day ill. by Jennifer Selby. Harcourt, 1998. ISBN 0-15-201090-4 Subj: Animals – bears. Rhyming text.

Best wishes photos by Carlo Ontal. R.C. Owen, 1992. ISBN 1-878450-20-4 Subj: Activities – writing. Careers – writers. Family life.

The bird house ill. by Barry Moser. Blue Sky, 1998. ISBN 0-590-47345-X Subj: Birds. Homes, houses. Orphans.

Birthday presents ill. by Suçie Stevenson. Watts, 1987. ISBN 0-531-08305-5 Subj: Behavior – sharing. Birthdays. Family life. Gifts.

Bless us all: a child's yearbook of blessings ill. by author. S&S, 1998. ISBN 0-689-82370-3 Subj: Days of the week, months of the year. Religion. Rhyming text.

The bookshop dog ill. by author. Blue Sky, 1996. ISBN 0-590-54331-8 Subj: Animals – dogs. Character traits – kindness to animals. Friendship. Weddings.

Bunny bungalow ill. by author. Harcourt, 1999. ISBN 0-15-201092-0 Subj: Animals – rabbits. Family life. Homes, houses. Rhyming text.

Christmas in the country ill. by Diane Goode. Blue Sky, 2002. ISBN 0-439-07334-0 Subj: Country. Family life – grandparents. Holidays – Christmas.

The cookie-store cat ill. by author. Blue Sky, 1999. ISBN 0-590-54329-6 Subj: Activities – baking, cooking. Animals – cats. Careers – bakers.

Dog Heaven ill. by author. Blue Sky, 1995. ISBN 0-590-41701-0 Subj: Angels. Animals – dogs. Death.

Give me grace: a child's daybook of prayers ill. by author. S&S, 1999. ISBN 0-689-82293-6 Subj: Days of the week, months of the year. Religion. Rhyming text.

The great Gracie chase ill. by Mark Teague. Blue Sky, 2001. ISBN 0-590-10041-6 Subj: Animals – dogs. Cumulative tales.

In November ill. by Jill Kastner. Harcourt, 2000. ISBN 0-15-201076-9 Subj: Activities. Seasons – fall.

Little Whistle ill. by Tim Bowers. Harcourt, 2001. ISBN 0-15-201087-4 Subj: Animals – guinea pigs. Stores. Toys.

Little Whistle's Christmas ill. by Tim Bowers. Harcourt, 2003. ISBN 0-15-204590-2 Subj: Animals – guinea pigs. Holidays – Christmas. Letters, cards. Santa Claus. Stores. Toys.

Little Whistle's dinner party ill. by Tim Bowers. Harcourt, 2001. ISBN 0-15-201079-3 Subj: Animals – guinea pigs. Parties. Stores. Toys.

Little Whistle's medicine ill. by Tim Bowers. Harcourt, 2002. ISBN 0-15-201086-6 Subj: Animals – guinea pigs. Illness. Stores. Toys. Toys – soldiers.

Miss Maggie ill. by Thomas di Grazia. Dutton, 1983. ISBN 0-525-44048-8 Subj: Character traits – curiosity. Friendship.

Mr. Griggs' work ill. by Julie Downing. Watts, 1989. ISBN 0-531-08369-1 Subj: Activities – working. Careers – postal workers. Character traits – pride. Post office.

Mr. Putter and Tabby bake the cake ill. by Arthur Howard. Harcourt, 1994. ISBN 0-15-200205-7 Subj: Activities – baking, cooking. Animals – cats. Food. Holidays – Christmas. Old age.

Mr. Putter and Tabby paint the porch ill. by Arthur Howard. Harcourt, 2000. ISBN 0-15-201787-9 Subj: Activities – painting. Animals – cats. Animals – dogs.

Mr. Putter and Tabby pick the pears ill. by Arthur Howard. Harcourt, 1995. ISBN 0-15-200245-6 Subj: Animals – cats. Food. Friendship. Old age.

Mr. Putter and Tabby pour the tea ill. by Arthur Howard. Harcourt, 1994. ISBN 0-15-256255-9 Subj: Animals – cats. Emotions – loneliness. Old age.

Mr. Putter and Tabby walk the dog ill. by Arthur Howard. Harcourt, 1994. ISBN 0-15-256259-1 Subj: Animals – cats. Animals – dogs. Character traits – helpfulness. Old age.

Moonlight, the Halloween cat ill. by Melissa Sweet. HarperCollins, 2003. ISBN 0-06-029712-3 Subj: Animals – cats. Holidays – Halloween.

Night in the country ill. by Mary Szilagyi. Bradbury, 1986. ISBN 0-02-777210-1 Subj: Animals. Country. Night.

The relatives came ill. by Stephen Gammell. Bradbury, 1985. ISBN 0-02-777220-9 Subj: Activities – traveling. Caldecott award honor books. Family life.

Scarecrow ill. by Lauren Stringer. Harcourt, 1998. ISBN 0-15-201084-X Subj: Country. Farms. Scarecrows.

Silver packages: an Appalachian Christmas story ill. by Chris K. Soentpiet. Orchard, 1997. ISBN 0-531-33051-6 Subj: Accidents. Careers – doctors. Character traits – generosity. Holidays – Christmas. Illness. Trains. Transportation.

This year's garden ill. by Mary Szilagyi. Bradbury, 1984. ISBN 0-02-777970-X Subj: Gardens, gardening.

The ticky-tacky doll ill. by Harvey Stevenson. Harcourt, 2002. ISBN 0-15-201078-5 Subj: Family life – grandmothers. School.

Tulip sees America ill. by Lisa Desimini. Blue Sky, 1998. ISBN 0-590-84744-9 Subj: Activities – traveling. Animals – dogs. Automobiles.

The whales ill. by author. Blue Sky, 1996. ISBN 0-590-58285-2 Subj: Animals – whales. Sea & seashore.

When I was young in the mountains ill. by Diane Goode. Dutton, 1982. ISBN 0-525-42525-X Subj: Caldecott award honor books. Family life.

The wonderful happens ill. by Coco Dowley. S&S, 2000. ISBN 0-689-83177-3 Subj: Emotions – happiness.

S. J. H. *see* Hale, Sara Josepha Buel

Sabraw, John. *I wouldn't be scared* ill. by author. Watts, 1989. ISBN 0-531-08418-3 Subj: Emotions – fear. Imagination. Monsters.

Sabuda, Robert James. *ABC Disney* ill. by author. Disney Pr., 1998. ISBN 0-7868-3132-4 Subj: ABC books. Format, unusual – toy & movable books.

The Blizzard's robe ill. by author. Atheneum, 1999. ISBN 0-689-31988-6 Subj: Activities – sewing. Foreign lands – Arctic. Mythical creatures. Northern lights. Sky.

The Christmas alphabet ill. by author. Orchard, 1994. ISBN 0-531-06857-9 Subj: ABC books. Format, unusual – toy & movable books. Holidays – Christmas.

The movable Mother Goose ill. by author. Little Simon, 1999. ISBN 0-689-81192-6 Subj: Animals. Format, unusual – toy & movable books. Insects. Nursery rhymes.

The mummy's tomb ill. by author. Western, 1994. ISBN 0-307-17627-4 Subj: Animals – mice. Foreign lands – Egypt. Format, unusual – toy & movable books. Rhyming text.

St. Valentine ill. by author. Macmillan, 1993. ISBN 0-689-31762-X Subj: Holidays – Valentine's Day. Religion.

Tutankhamen's gift ill. by author. Atheneum, 1994. ISBN 0-689-31818-9 Subj: Foreign lands – Egypt. Gifts. Royalty – pharaohs.

Sachar, Louis. *Monkey soup* ill. by Cat Bowman Smith. Knopf, 1992. ISBN 0-679-90297-X Subj: Family life – fathers. Illness. Toys.

Sachs, Marilyn. *Fleet-footed Florence* ill. by Charles Robinson. Doubleday, 1981. ISBN 0-385-12746-4 Subj: Behavior – wishing. Magic. Sports – baseball.

Matt's mitt ill. by Hilary Knight. Doubleday, 1975. ISBN 0-385-00266-1 Subj: Sports – baseball.

Sackett, Elisabeth. *Danger on the African grassland* ill. by Martin Camm. Little, 1991. ISBN 0-316-76596-1 Subj: Animals – endangered animals. Animals – rhinoceros. Foreign lands – Africa.

Danger on the Arctic ice ill. by Martin Camm. Little, 1991. ISBN 0-316-76598-8 Subj: Animals – endangered animals. Animals – seals. Foreign lands – Arctic.

Saddler, Allen. *The Archery contest* ill. by Joe Wright. Oxford Univ. Pr., 1983. ISBN 0-19-279760-3 Subj: Humorous stories. Magic. Royalty. Sports.

The king gets fit ill. by Joe Wright. Oxford Univ. Pr., 1983. ISBN 0-19-279761-1 Subj: Humorous stories. Royalty – kings.

Sadie. *see* Williams, Sarah

Sadler, Catherine Edwards. *A duckling is born* (Isenbart, Hans-Heinrich)

A flamingo is born (Zoll, Max Alfred)

Sadler, Judy Ann. *Sandwiches for Duke* ill. by Lorna Bennett. Stoddart, 2001. ISBN 0-7737-3313-2 Subj: Animals – dogs. Clothing – hats. Farms. Pets. Weather – storms.

Sadler, Marilyn. *Alistair in outer space* ill. by Roger Bollen. Prentice-Hall, 1984. ISBN 0-13-022369-7 Subj: Libraries. Space & space ships.

Alistair's elephant ill. by Roger Bollen. Prentice-Hall, 1983. ISBN 0-13-022756-0 Subj: Animals – elephants. Behavior – misbehavior.

Alistair's time machine ill. by Roger Bollen. Prentice-Hall, 1986. ISBN 0-317-39621-8 Subj: Machines. School. Science. Space & space ships. Time.

Elizabeth, Larry, and Ed ill. by Roger Bollen. S&S, 1992. ISBN 0-671-75956-6 Subj: Animals. Ecology. Friendship. Reptiles – alligators, crocodiles.

It's not easy being a bunny ill. by Roger Bollen. Random House, 1983. ISBN 0-394-96102-1 Subj: Animals – rabbits. Behavior – dissatisfaction. Self-concept.

Sadu, Itah. *Christopher changes his name* ill. by Roy Candy. Firefly, 1998. ISBN 1-55209-216-X Subj: Ethnic groups in the U.S. – African Americans. Names.

Sáenz, Benjamin Alire. *A gift from papá Diego = Un regalo de papá Diego* ill. by Geronimo Garcia. Cinco Puntos, 1998. ISBN 0-938317-33-4 Subj: Birthdays. Ethnic groups in the U.S. – Mexican Americans. Family life – grandfathers. Foreign languages.

Grandma Fina and her wonderful umbrellas = La abuelita Fina y sus sombrillas maravillosas. Cinco Puntos, 1999. ISBN 0-938317-46-6 Subj: Birthdays. Ethnic groups in the U.S. – Mexican Americans. Family life – grandmothers. Foreign languages. Umbrellas.

Safran, Sheri. *The musical cherub* ill. by Pete Bowman; paper engineering by David Hawcock. Tango, 1995. ISBN 1-8570-7128-X Subj: Angels. Careers – shepherds. Format, unusual – toy & movable books. Music. Religion – Nativity.

The painted cherub ill. by Pete Bowman; paper engineering by David Hawcock. S&S, 1995. ISBN 0-689-80334-6 Subj: Angels. Format, unusual – toy & movable books.

Sage, Alison. *Rumpelstiltskin* (Grimm, Jacob)

Teddy bears at the seaside (Gretz, Susanna)

Teddy bears cure a cold (Gretz, Susanna)

Teddy bears stay indoors (Gretz, Susanna)

Teddy bears take the train (Gretz, Susanna)

Teddybears cookbook (Gretz, Susanna)

Sage, Angie. *Happy baby* (Sage, Chris)

Molly and the birthday party ill. by author. Peachtree, 2001. ISBN 1-56145-248-3 Subj: Birthdays. Format, unusual – toy & movable books. Gifts. Parties.

Monkeys in the jungle ill. by author. Dutton, 1989. ISBN 0-525-44466-1 Subj: Animals. Jungle. Rhyming text.

Sleepy baby (Sage, Chris)

Sage, Chris. *Happy baby* by Chris & Angie Sage; ill. by Angie Sage. Dial, 1990. ISBN 0-8037-0883-1 Subj: Babies. Format, unusual – board books.

Sleepy baby by Chris & Angie Sage; ill. by Angie Sage. Dial, 1990. ISBN 0-8037-0888-2 Subj: Babies. Format, unusual – board books. Sleep.

That's mine, that's yours ill. by Angie Sage. Viking, 1991. ISBN 0-670-83746-6 Subj: Activities. Behavior – sharing. Family life – sisters.

The trouble with babies ill. by Angie Sage. Viking, 1990. ISBN 0-670-82392-9 Subj: Babies. Sibling rivalry.

Sage, James. *The boy and the dove* photos by Robert Doisneau. Workman, 1978. ISBN 0-89480-030-2 Subj: Birds – doves. Theater.

Coyote makes man ill. by Britta Teckentrup. S&S, 1995. ISBN 0-689-80011-8 Subj: Animals – coyotes. Creation. Folk & fairy tales. Indians of North America – Crow.

Farmer Smart's fat cat ill. by Russell Ayto. Chronicle, 2002. ISBN 0-8118-3502-2 Subj: Animals – cats. Animals – mice. Contests. Farms. Plants.

The little band ill. by Keiko Narahashi. Macmillan, 1991. ISBN 0-689-50516-7 Subj: Ethnic groups in the U.S. Music. Musical instruments – bands.

To sleep ill. by Warwick Hutton. Macmillan, 1990. ISBN 0-689-50497-7 Subj: Bedtime. Dreams. Sleep.

Sage, Juniper. *see* Brown, Margaret Wise

Sage, Juniper. *see* Hurd, Edith Thacher

Sage, Michael. *Dippy dos and don'ts* by Michael Sage & Arnold Spilka; ill. by Arnold Spilka. Viking, 1967. Subj: Humorous stories. Rhyming text.

If you talked to a boar ill. by Arnold Spilka. Lippincott, 1960. Subj: Humorous stories. Language.

Sahagun, Bernardino de. *Spirit child: a story of the Nativity* trans. from Aztec by John Bierhorst; ill. by Barbara Cooney. Morrow, 1984. ISBN 0-688-02610-9 Subj: Folk & fairy tales. Foreign lands – Mexico. Holidays – Christmas. Religion – Nativity.

St. George, Judith. *The Halloween pumpkin smasher* ill. by Margot Tomes. Putnam, 1978. ISBN 0-399-20617-5 Subj: Animals – raccoons. Holidays – Halloween. Imagination – imaginary friends.

So you want to be president? ill. by David Small. Philomel, 2000. ISBN 0-399-23407-1 Subj: Caldecott award books. U.S. history.

St. Germain, Sharon. *The terrible fight* ill. by Deborah Zemke. Houghton Mifflin, 1990. ISBN 0-395-50069-9 Subj: Behavior – fighting, arguing. Friendship.

Saint James, Synthia. *The gifts of Kwanzaa* ill. by author. A. Whitman, 1994. ISBN 0-8075-2907-9 Subj: Ethnic groups in the U.S. – African Americans. Gifts. Holidays – Kwanzaa.

Sunday ill. by author. A. Whitman, 1996. ISBN 0-8075-7658-1 Subj: Ethnic groups in the U.S. – African Americans. Family life – grandparents. Multiple births – twins.

St. Pierre, Stephanie. *Cheetahs* ill. with photos. Heinemann, 2001. ISBN 1-58810-106-1 Subj: Animals – cheetahs. Science.

Jaguars ill. with photos. Heinemann, 2001. ISBN 1-58810-108-8 Subj: Animals – jaguars. Science.

Leopards ill. with photos. Heinemann, 2001. ISBN 1-58810-105-3 Subj: Animals – leopards. Science.

Lynx ill. with photos. Heinemann, 2001. ISBN 1-58810-109-6 Subj: Animals – lynx. Science.

Siberian tigers ill. with photos. Heinemann, 2001. ISBN 1-58810-110-X Subj: Animals – tigers. Science.

St. Pierre, Wendy. *Henry finds a home* ill. by Barbara Eidlitz. Firefly, 1981. ISBN 0-919984-05-3 Subj: Children as authors. Reptiles – turtles, tortoises.

Sakai, Kimiko. *Sachiko means happiness* ill. by Tomie Arai. Children's Book Pr., 1990. ISBN 0-89239-065-4 Subj: Ethnic groups in the U.S. – Japanese Americans. Family life – grandmothers. Illness – Alzheimer's. Old age.

Salariya, David. *From caterpillar to butterfly* (Legg, Gerald)

From egg to chicken (Legg, Gerald)

From seed to sunflower (Legg, Gerald)

From tadpole to frog (Legg, Gerald)

Salat, Cristina. *Peanut's emergency* ill. by Tammie Lyon. Whispering Coyote, 2002. ISBN 1-57091-440-0 Subj: Behavior – lost. Ethnic groups in the U.S. – African Americans. Problem solving. Safety.

Salazar, Violet. *Squares are not bad* ill. by Harlow Rockwell. Golden Pr., 1967. Subj: Concepts – shape.

Saleh, Harold J. *Even tiny ants must sleep* ill. by Jerry Pinkney. McGraw-Hill, 1967. Subj: Animals. Poetry. Sleep.

Salley, Coleen. *Epossumondas* ill. by Janet Stevens. Harcourt, 2002. ISBN 0-15-216748-X Subj: Animals. Animals – possums. Behavior – misunderstanding. Clowns, jesters. Family life. Folk & fairy tales. Humorous stories.

Who's that tripping over my bridge? ill. by Amy Jackson Dixon. Pelican, 2002. ISBN 1-56554-890-6 Subj: Animals – goats. Character traits – cleverness. Mythical creatures – trolls.

Salt, Jane. *See and say picture word book* ill. by Sarah Pooley. Random House, 1989. ISBN 0-679-90099-3 Subj: Language.

Salter, Heidi. *Taddy McFinley and the great grey grimly* ill. by author. Landmark Editions, 1989. ISBN 0-933849-21-4 Subj: Children as authors. Children as illustrators. Family life – grandfathers. Imagination. Monsters.

Salter, Mary Jo. *The moon comes home* ill. by Stacey Schuett. Knopf, 1989. ISBN 0-394-99983-5 Subj: Activities – traveling. Moon. Night.

Saltzberg, Barney. *Baby animal kisses* ill. by author. Harcourt, 2001. ISBN 0-15-202635-5 Subj: Animals – babies. Format, unusual – toy & movable books. Kissing.

Crazy hair day ill. by author. Candlewick, 2003. ISBN 0-7636-1954-X Subj: Animals – hamsters. Behavior – mistakes. Hair. School.

Cromwell ill. by author. Atheneum, 1986. ISBN 0-689-31282-2 Subj: Animals – dogs. Humorous stories.

The Flying Garbanzos ill. by author. Crown, 1998. ISBN 0-517-70979-1 Subj: Birthdays. Careers – acrobats. Food.

Hip, hip, hooray day! ill. by author. Harcourt, 2002. ISBN 0-15-202495-6 Subj: Animals – hippopotamuses. Animals – rabbits. Birthdays. Friendship. Sports – roller skating.

It must have been the wind ill. by author. HarperCollins, 1982. ISBN 0-06-025177-8 Subj: Bedtime. Noise, sounds. Weather – wind.

Phoebe and the spelling bee ill. by author. Hyperion, 1996. ISBN 0-7868-2114-0 Subj: Behavior – lying. Contests. Friendship. School.

The problem with pumpkins ill. by author. Harcourt, 2001. ISBN 0-15-202489-1 Subj: Animals – hippopotamuses. Animals – rabbits. Clothing – costumes. Friendship. Holidays – Halloween.

Soccer mom from outer space ill. by author. Crown, 2000. ISBN 0-517-80064-0 Subj: Clothing – costumes. Family life – mothers. Sports – soccer.

The yawn ill. by author. Atheneum, 1985. ISBN 0-689-31073-0 Subj: Behavior – imitation. Wordless.

Saltzman, David. *The jester has lost his jingle* ill. by David Saltzman; afterword by Maurice Sendak. Jester Co., 1995. ISBN 0-9644563-0-3 Subj: Character traits – optimism. Clowns, jesters. Middle Ages. Rhyming text.

Salus, Naomi Panush. *My daddy's mustache* ill. by Tomie de Paola. Doubleday, 1979. ISBN 0-385-13189-5 Subj: Character traits – appearance.

Sammy Spider's first Tu B'Shevat ill. by Katherine Janus Kahn. Kar-Ben Copies, 2000. ISBN 1-58013-065-8 Subj: Holidays – Tu B'Shevat. Jewish culture. Spiders. Trees.

Sampson, Michael R. *Adam, Adam, what do you see?* (Martin, Bill [William Ivan])

Caddie, the golf dog ill. by Floyd Cooper. Tommy Nelson, 1999. ISBN 0-8499-5823-7 Subj: Animals – dogs. Character traits – kindness to animals. Weather – storms.

I pledge allegiance (Martin, Bill [William Ivan])

Little granny quarterback (Martin, Bill [William Ivan])

The little squeegy bug (Martin, Bill [William Ivan])

Rock it, sock it, number line (Martin, Bill [William Ivan])

Swish! (Martin, Bill [William Ivan])

Trick or treat? (Martin, Bill [William Ivan])

Samson, Suzanne M. *Fairy dusters and blazing stars* ill. by Preston Neel. Roberts Rinehart, 1994. ISBN 1-879373-81-5 Subj: Flowers. Science.

Samton, Sheila White. *Amazing Aunt Agatha* ill. by Yvette Banek. Raintree, 1990. ISBN 0-8172-3575-2 Subj: ABC books. Ethnic groups in the U.S. – African Americans.

Beside the bay ill. by author. Putnam, 1987. ISBN 0-399-21420-8 Subj: Rhyming text. Sea & seashore.

Frogs in clogs ill. by author. Crown, 1995. ISBN 0-517-59875-2 Subj: Animals – pigs. Clothing. Frogs & toads. Insects. Rhyming text.

Jenny's journey ill. by author. Viking, 1991. ISBN 0-670-83490-4 Subj: Boats, ships. Friendship. Imagination.

Moon to sun ill. by author. Boyds Mills, 1991. ISBN 1-878093-13-4 Subj: Counting, numbers.

On the river ill. by author. Boyds Mills, 1991. ISBN 1-878093-14-2 Subj: Activities – picnicking. Counting, numbers.

Ten tiny monsters ill. by author. Crown, 1997. ISBN 0-517-70942-2 Subj: Animals. Counting, numbers. Monsters. Rhyming text.

The world from my window ill. by author. Crown, 1985. ISBN 0-517-55645-6 Subj: Counting, numbers. Rhyming text.

Samuels, Barbara. *Aloha, Dolores* ill. by author. DK, 2000. ISBN 0-7894-2508-4 Subj: Activities – vacationing. Animals – cats. Contests. Family life – sisters. Hawaii.

Duncan and Dolores ill. by author. Bradbury, 1986. ISBN 0-02-778210-7 Subj: Activities. Animals – cats. Family life – sisters. Humorous stories.

Faye and Dolores ill. by author. Bradbury, 1985. ISBN 0-02-778120-8 Subj: Emotions – love. Sibling rivalry.

Happy birthday, Dolores ill. by author. Watts, 1989. ISBN 0-531-08391-8 Subj: Birthdays. Parties.

What's so great about Cindy Snappleby? ill. by author. Watts, 1992. ISBN 0-531-08579-1 Subj: Family life – sisters. Frogs & toads. Sibling rivalry.

Samuels, Jenny. *A nose like a hose* ill. by author. Scholastic, 2003. ISBN 0-439-37303-4 Subj: Anatomy – noses. Animals – elephants.

Samuels, Vyanne. *Carry go bring come* ill. by Jennifer Northway. Macmillan, 1989. ISBN 0-02-778121-6 Subj: Ethnic groups in the U.S. – African Americans. Family life. Weddings.

San Diego Zoological Society. *Families* photos by Ron Garrison & F. D. Schmidt of the Zoological Society of San Diego; captions ed. by Georgeanne Irvine. Heian Intl., 1983. ISBN 0-89346-218-7 Subj: Animals. Zoos.

A visit to the zoo photos by Ron Garrison & F. D. Schmidt of the Zoological Society of San Diego; captions ed. by Georgeanne Irvine. Heian Intl., 1983. ISBN 0-89346-219-5 Subj: Animals. Zoos.

SanAngelo, Ryan. *Eddie spaghetti* ill. by Jackie Urbanovic. Boyds Mills, 2002. ISBN 1-56397-974-8 Subj: Communities, neighborhoods. Crime. Food. Imagination. Problem solving.

Sánchez, Enrique O. *Saturday market* (Grossman, Patricia)

Sanchez, Jose Louis Garcia. *Kangaroo* by Jose Louis Garcia Sanchez & Miguel Angel Pacheco; ill. by Nella Bosnia. H P Books, 1983. ISBN 0-89586-286-7 Subj: Animals – kangaroos.

Sandberg, Inger. *Come on out, Daddy!* by Inger & Lasse Sandberg; ill. by Lasse Sandberg. Delacorte, 1971. Translation of Pappa, kom ut. Subj: Activities – working. Careers. Family life – fathers.

Dusty wants to borrow everything ill. by Lasse Sandberg. Farrar, 1988. ISBN 91-29-58782-4 Subj: Character traits – curiosity. Family life – grandparents.

Dusty wants to help trans. from Swedish by Judy A. Mauver; ill. by Lasse Sandberg. Farrar, 1987. ISBN 91-29-58336-5 Subj: Behavior – misbehavior. Family life – grandfathers.

Little Anna saved by Inger & Lasse Sandberg; ill. by Lasse Sandberg. Lothrop, 1965. Subj: Games.

Little ghost Godfry by Inger & Lasse Sandberg; trans. by Nancy S. Leupold; ill. by Lasse Sandberg. Delacorte, 1968. Subj: Ghosts.

Nicholas' favorite pet by Inger & Lasse Sandberg; ill. by Lasse Sandberg. Delacorte, 1969. Translation of Niklas' önskedjur. Subj: Animals. Animals – dogs. Birthdays. Pets.

Nicholas' red day by Inger & Lasse Sandberg; ill. by authors. Delacorte, 1964. Subj: Behavior – misbehavior. Concepts – color. Illness.

Sandberg, Lasse. *Come on out, Daddy!* (Sandberg, Inger)

Little Anna saved (Sandberg, Inger)

Little ghost Godfry (Sandberg, Inger)

Nicholas' favorite pet (Sandberg, Inger)

Nicholas' red day (Sandberg, Inger)

Sandburg, Carl (Charles August). *From daybreak to good night* ill. by Lynn Smith-Ary. Annick, 2001. ISBN 1-55037-681-0 Subj: Farms. Poetry.

The Huckabuck family and how they raised popcorn in Nebraska and quit and came back ill. by David Small. Farrar, 1999. The text was originally published in 1923 by Harcourt, Brace & Company in the book Rootabaga stories by Carl Sandburg. ISBN 0-374-33511-7 Subj: Careers – farmers. Family life. Farms. Fire. Humorous stories.

Not everyday an aurora borealis for your birthday ill. by Anita Lobel. Knopf, 1998. ISBN 0-679-98170-5 Subj: Birthdays. Emotions – love. Northern lights. Poetry.

The wedding procession of the rag doll and the broom handle and who was in it ill. by Harriet Pincus. Harcourt, 1978, c1922. ISBN 0-15-294930-5 Subj: Toys. Toys – dolls. Weddings.

Sandburg, Helga. *Anna and the baby buzzard* ill. by Brinton Turkle. Dutton, 1970. ISBN 0-525-25769-1 Subj: Birds – buzzards. Character traits – kindness to animals.

Sandeman, Anna. *Skin, teeth, and hair* ill. by Ian Thompson. Copper Beech, 1996. ISBN 0-7613-0489-4 Subj: Anatomy – skin. Hair. Science. Teeth.

Sanders, Eve. *What's your name?* (Sanders, Marilyn)

Sanders, Marilyn. *What's your name?* photos by Marilyn Sanders; text by Eve Sanders. Holiday, 1995. ISBN 0-8234-1209-1 Subj: ABC books. Names.

Sanders, Scott R. (Scott Russell). *Crawdad Creek* ill. by Robert Hynes. National Geographic, 1999. ISBN 0-7922-7097-5 Subj: Ecology. Family life – brothers & sisters. Rivers.

A place called Freedom ill. by Thomas B. Allen. Atheneum, 1997. ISBN 0-689-80470-9 Subj: Character traits – freedom. Ethnic groups in the U.S. – African Americans. Slavery. U.S. history – frontier & pioneer life.

Warm as wool ill. by Helen Cogancherry. Bradbury, 1992. ISBN 0-02-778139-9 Subj: Animals – sheep. Clothing. U.S. history – frontier & pioneer life.

Sanderson, Ruth. *Cinderella* ill. by reteller. Little, 2002. ISBN 0-316-77965-2 Subj: Family life – stepfamilies. Folk & fairy tales. Royalty – princes. Sibling rivalry.

The enchanted wood ill. by author. Little, 1991. ISBN 0-316-77018-3 Subj: Folk & fairy tales. Royalty – princes.

The golden mare, the firebird, and the magic ring ill. by reteller. Little, 2001. ISBN 0-316-76906-1 Subj: Animals – horses, ponies. Folk & fairy tales. Foreign lands – Russia. Magic. Royalty – tsars.

Papa Gatto ill. by author. Little, 1995. ISBN 0-316-77073-6 Subj: Animals – cats. Behavior – greed. Folk & fairy tales. Foreign lands – Italy. Royalty – princes.

Sandin, Joan. *Boo and Baa at sea* (Landström, Olof)

Boo and Baa get wet (Landström, Olof)

Boo and Baa in a party mood (Landström, Olof)

Boo and Baa in windy weather (Landström, Olof)

Boo and Baa on a cleaning spree (Landström, Olof)

Boris's glasses (Cohen, Peter Zachary)

The little hippos' adventure (Landström, Lena)

Who's scaring Alfie Atkins? (Bergström, Gunilla)

Sandman, Rochel. *Perfect porridge* ill. by Chana Zakashansky-Zverev. Hachai, 2000. ISBN 0-922613-92-3 Subj: Character traits – generosity. Food. Foreign lands – Uzbekistan. Immigrants. War.

Sandved, Kjell Bloch. *The butterfly alphabet* ill. by author. Scholastic, 1996. ISBN 0-590-48003-0 Subj: ABC books. Insects – butterflies, caterpillars. Insects – moths.

Sanfield, Steve. *Bit by bit* ill. by Susan Gaber. Philomel, 1995. ISBN 0-399-22736-9 Subj: Careers – tailors. Clothing. Cumulative tales. Folk & fairy tales. Jewish culture.

The girl who wanted a song ill. by Stephen T. Johnson. Harcourt, 1996. ISBN 0-15-200969-8 Subj: Birds – geese. Emotions – loneliness. Orphans. Songs.

The great turtle drive ill. by Dirk Zimmer. Knopf, 1996. ISBN 0-679-95834-7 Subj: Cowboys, cowgirls. Reptiles – turtles, tortoises.

Just rewards, or, Who is that man in the moon and what's he doing up there anyway? ill. by Emily Lisker. Orchard, 1996. ISBN 0-531-08885-5 Subj: Behavior – greed. Character traits – selfishness. Folk & fairy tales. Foreign lands – China. Moon.

Snow ill. by Jeanette Winter. Philomel, 1995. ISBN 0-399-22751-2 Subj: Rhyming text. Weather – snow.

Sanford, Doris. *David has AIDS* ill. by Graci Evans. Multnomah, 1989. ISBN 0-88070-299-0 Subj: Death. Emotions – grief. Illness.

Sanger, Amy Wilson. *First book of sushi* ill. by author. Tricycle, 2001. ISBN 1-58246-050-7 Subj: Activities – baking, cooking. Ethnic groups in the U.S. – Japanese Americans. Food. Format, unusual – board books. Rhyming text.

San José, Christine. *Sleeping Beauty* ill. by Dominic Catalano. Boyds Mills, 1997. ISBN 1-56397-636-6 Subj: Animals – dormice. Folk & fairy tales.

Sanromán, Susana. *Señora Reganoña* ill. by author. Douglas & McIntyre, 1998. ISBN 0-88899-320-X Subj: Bedtime. Emotions – fear. Foreign lands – Mexico. Friendship. Night.

Sansevere, John R. *Ooey gooey* (Farber, Erica)

Sansone, Adele. *The little green goose* ill. by Alan Marks; trans. by J. Alison James. North-South, 1999. ISBN 0-7358-1072-9 Subj: Birds – geese. Character traits – being different. Dinosaurs. Family life.

San Souci, Daniel. *In the moonlight mist* ill. by Eujin Kim Neilan. Boyds Mills, 1999. ISBN 1-56397-754-0 Subj: Animals – deer. Family life. Folk & fairy tales. Foreign lands – Korea. Magic.

The rabbit and the dragon king ill. by Eujin Kim Neilan. Boyds Mills, 2002. ISBN 1-56397-880-6 Subj: Animals – rabbits. Dragons. Folk & fairy tales. Foreign lands – Korea. Reptiles – turtles, tortoises. Sea & seashore.

San Souci, Robert D. *The birds of Killingworth* ill. by Kimberly Root. Dial, 2002. Based on a poem by Henry Wadsworth Longfellow. ISBN 0-8037-2111-0 Subj: Birds. Ecology. Nature.

The boy and the ghost ill. by J. Brian Pinkney. S&S, 1989. ISBN 0-671-67176-6 Subj: Ethnic groups in the U.S. – African Americans. Ghosts. Homes, houses.

The brave little tailor (Grimm, Jacob)

Brave Margaret: an Irish adventure ill. by Sally Wern Comport. S&S, 1999. ISBN 0-689-81072-5 Subj: Boats, ships. Folk & fairy tales. Foreign lands – Ireland. Gender roles. Giants. Sea & seashore.

Callie Ann and Mistah Bear ill. by Don Daily. Dial, 1999. ISBN 0-8037-1768-7 Subj: Character traits – cleverness. Ethnic groups in the U.S. – African Americans. Folk & fairy tales.

Cendrillon: a Caribbean Cinderella ill. by Brian Pinkney. S&S, 1998. ISBN 0-689-80668-X Subj: Folk & fairy tales. Foreign lands – Caribbean Islands.

Cinderella Skeleton ill. by David Catrow. Harcourt, 2000. ISBN 0-15-202003-9 Subj: Anatomy – skeletons. Family life – stepfamilies. Folk & fairy tales. Holidays – Halloween. Rhyming text. Royalty – princes. Sibling rivalry.

The enchanted tapestry ill. by László Gál. Dial, 1987. ISBN 0-8037-0306-6 Subj: Activities – weaving. Behavior – greed. Character traits – bravery. Family life – brothers. Folk & fairy tales. Foreign lands – China.

The faithful friend ill. by J. Brian Pinkney. S&S, 1995. ISBN 0-02-786131-7 Subj: Caldecott award honor books. Folk & fairy tales. Foreign lands – Caribbean Islands. Foreign lands – Martinique.

Feathertop: based on the tale by Nathaniel Hawthorne; ill. by reteller. Doubleday, 1992. ISBN 0-385-42045-5 Subj: Behavior – trickery. Magic. Scarecrows. Witches.

The firebird (The firebird)

The hired hand: an African-American folktale ill. by Jerry Pinkney. Dial, 1997. ISBN 0-8037-1297-9 Subj: Activities – working. Character traits – laziness. Ethnic groups in the U.S. – African Americans. Folk & fairy tales. Magic.

The Hobyahs ill. by Alexi Natchev. Doubleday, 1994. ISBN 0-385-30934-1 Subj: Animals – dogs. Folk & fairy tales. Foreign lands – England. Monsters. Rhyming text.

The house in the sky ill. by Wil Clay. Dial, 1996. ISBN 0-8037-1285-5 Subj: Folk & fairy tales. Foreign lands – Caribbean Islands. Homes, houses.

The legend of Scarface ill. by Daniel San Souci. Doubleday, 1987. ISBN 0-385-15874-2 Subj: Folk & fairy tales. Indians of North America – Blackfoot. Indians of North America – Siksika.

The legend of Sleepy Hollow adapt. by Robert D. San Souci; ill. by Daniel San Souci. Doubleday, 1986. Based on the story by Washington Irving. ISBN 0-385-23397-3 Subj: Folk & fairy tales. Holidays – Halloween.

Little gold star ill. by Sergio Martinez. Morrow, 2000. ISBN 0-688-14781-X Subj: Ethnic groups in the U.S. – Hispanic Americans. Family life – stepfamilies. Folk & fairy tales. Foreign languages. Religion. Sibling rivalry.

Little Pierre ill. by David Catrow. Harcourt, 2003. ISBN 0-15-202482-4 Subj: Character traits – cleverness. Concepts – size. Family life – brothers. Folk & fairy tales. Little people. Mythical creatures – ogres. Swamps.

Nicholas Pipe ill. by David Shannon. Dial, 1997. ISBN 0-8037-1765-2 Subj: Careers – fishermen. Emotions – love. Folk & fairy tales. Mythical creatures – mermaids, mermen. Sea & seashore.

Pedro and the monkey ill. by Michael Hays. Morrow, 1996. ISBN 0-688-13743-1 Subj: Animals – monkeys. Folk & fairy tales. Foreign lands – Philippines. Monsters.

Peter and the blue witch baby ill. by Alexi Natchev. Doubleday, 2000. ISBN 0-385-32269-0 Subj: Emotions – envy, jealousy. Folk & fairy tales. Foreign lands – Russia. Giants. Royalty – tsars. Sun. Witches.

The red heels ill. by Gary Kelley. Dial, 1995. ISBN 0-8037-1134-4 Subj: Careers – shoemakers. Folk & fairy tales. Magic. Witches.

The samurai's daughter ill. by Stephen T. Johnson. Dial, 1992. ISBN 0-8037-1136-0 Subj: Character traits – bravery. Family life – fathers. Folk & fairy tales. Foreign lands – Japan.

The secret of the stones ill. by James Ransome. Fogelman, 2000. ISBN 0-8037-1640-0 Subj: Ethnic groups in the U.S. – African Americans. Folk & fairy tales. Foreign lands – Africa. Magic. Orphans.

The silver charm ill. by Yoriko Ito. Doubleday, 2002. ISBN 0-385-32159-7 Subj: Animals – dogs. Animals – foxes. Animals – mice. Folk & fairy tales. Foreign lands – Japan. Magic. Mythical creatures – ogres. Pets.

Six foolish fishermen ill. by Doug Kennedy. Hyperion, 2000. ISBN 0-7868-2335-6 Subj: Character traits – foolishness. Sports – fishing.

The six swans (Grimm, Jacob)

The snow wife ill. by Stephen T. Johnson. Dial, 1993. ISBN 0-8037-1410-6 Subj: Behavior – secrets. Folk & fairy tales. Foreign lands – Japan.

Song of Sedna ill. by Daniel San Souci. Doubleday, 1981. ISBN 0-385-15866-1 Subj: Eskimos. Folk & fairy tales.

Sootface: an Ojibwa Cinderella story ill. by author. Delacorte, 1994. ISBN 0-385-31202-4 Subj: Character traits – meanness. Family life – sisters. Folk & fairy tales. Indians of North America – Ojibwa.

Sukey and the mermaid ill. by J. Brian Pinkney. Four Winds, 1992. ISBN 0-02-778141-0 Subj: Ethnic groups in the U.S. – African Americans. Folk & fairy tales. Mythical creatures – mermaids, mermen.

The talking eggs ill. by Jerry Pinkney. Dial, 1989. ISBN 0-8037-0619-7 Subj: Caldecott award honor books. Character traits – kindness. Eggs. Folk & fairy tales. Magic.

Two bear cubs: a Miwok legend from California's Yosemite Valley ill. by Daniel San Souci. Yosemite Assoc., 1997. ISBN 0-939666-87-1 Subj: Animals. Animals – bears. Animals – worms. Folk & fairy tales. Indians of North America – Miwok.

A weave of words ill. by Raúl Colón. Orchard, 1997. ISBN 0-531-33053-2 Subj: Activities – weaving. Folk & fairy tales. Foreign lands – Armenia. Gender roles. Royalty – kings. Royalty – queens.

The white cat ill. by Gennady Spirin. Watts, 1990. ISBN 0-531-08409-4 Subj: Animals – cats. Folk & fairy tales. Magic. Royalty.

Sant, Laurent Sauveur. *Dinosaurs* ill. by author. Wonder Books, 1971. Subj: Dinosaurs. Prehistory.

Santa Claus is coming to town ill. by Laura Blanken Merer. HarperFestival, 2001. ISBN 0-694-01559-8 Subj: Format, unusual – toy & movable books. Holidays – Christmas. Music. Santa Claus. Songs.

Santacruz, Daniel. *In out, a Disney book of opposites = Dentro fuera, un libro Disney de opuestos* (Duerrstein, Richard)

One Mickey Mouse, a Disney book of numbers = Un Ratón Mickey, un libro Disney de números: a Disney book of numbers = Un Ratón Mickey: un libro Disney de números (Duerrstein, Richard)

Santangelo, Colony Elliott. *Brother Wolf of Gubbio* ill. by author. Handprint, 2000. ISBN 1-929766-07-6 Subj: Animals – wolves. Cities, towns. Religion.

Santa's little library of Christmas stories ill. by Vincent Douglas. McGraw-Hill, 2002. ISBN 1-58845-235-2 Subj: Format, unusual – board books. Holidays – Christmas. Santa Claus.

Santella, Andrew. *George Washington* ill. with photos. Compass Pt., 2000. ISBN 0-7565-0014-1 Subj: U.S. history. War.

Santore, Charles. *A stowaway on Noah's Ark* ill. by Charles Santore. Random House, 2000. ISBN 0-679-98820-3 Subj: Animals. Animals – mice. Behavior – hiding. Boats, ships. Religion – Noah.

William the Curious: Knight of the Water Lilies ill. by author. Random House, 1997. ISBN 0-679-98742-8 Subj: Ecology. Folk & fairy tales. Frogs & toads. Royalty – kings.

Santoro, Christopher. *Book of shapes* ill. by author. Dutton, 1979. ISBN 0-525-69406-4 Subj: Concepts – shape.

Santoro, Scott. *Isaac the Ice Cream Truck* ill. by author. Holt, 1999. ISBN 0-8050-5296-8 Subj: Careers – firefighters. Trucks.

Santos, Joyce Audy Dos. *see* Dos Santos, Joyce Audy

Santos, Rosa. *Play date* ill. by Gioir Fiammenghi. Kane Pr., 2001. ISBN 1-57565-105-X Subj: Days of the week, months of the year. Family life.

Santucci, Barbara. *Anna's corn* ill. by Lloyd Bloom. Eerdmans, 2002. ISBN 0-8028-5119-3 Subj: Death. Emotions – grief. Family life – grandfathers. Memories, memory. Plants. Seeds.

Loon summer ill. by Andrea Shine. Eerdmans, 2001. ISBN 0-8028-5182-7 Subj: Birds – loons. Divorce. Family life – daughters. Family life – fathers.

Sapphire, Paula. *The toddler's potty book* (Allison, Alida)

Sara. *Across town* ill. by author. Watts, 1991. ISBN 0-531-08532-5 Subj: Animals – cats. Cities, towns. Wordless.

The rabbit, the fox, and the wolf ill. by author. Watts, 1991. ISBN 0-531-08553-8 Subj: Animals – foxes. Animals – rabbits. Animals – wolves. Wordless.

Sardegna, Jill. *K is for kiss good night* ill. by Michael Hayes. Doubleday, 1994. ISBN 0-385-31044-7 Subj: ABC books. Bedtime.

The roly-poly spider ill. by Tedd Arnold. Scholastic, 1994. ISBN 0-590-47119-8 Subj: Insects. Rhyming text. Spiders.

Sargent, Susan. *My favorite place* by Susan Sargent & Donna Aaron Wirt; ill. by Allan Eitzen. Abingdon, 1983. ISBN 0-687-27538-5 Subj: Handicaps – blindness. Senses – sight.

Sarnoff, Jane. *That's not fair* ill. by Reynold Ruffins. Scribners, 1980. ISBN 0-684-16714-X Subj: Behavior – dissatisfaction. Family life. Sibling rivalry.

Sarrazin, Johan. *Tootle* ill. by Aislin. Tundra, 1984. ISBN 0-88776-168-2 Subj: Animals – dogs. Behavior – misbehavior.

Sarton, May. *Punch's secret* ill. by Howard Knotts. HarperCollins, 1974. ISBN 0-06-025192-1 Subj: Emotions – loneliness. Friendship.

A walk through the woods ill. by Kazue Mizumura. HarperCollins, 1976. ISBN 0-06-025190-5 Subj: Activities – walking. Nature. Poetry.

Sasaki, Isao. *Snow* ill. by author. Viking, 1982. ISBN 0-670-65364-0 Subj: Trains. Weather – snow. Wordless.

Sasso, Sandy Eisenberg. *Cain and Abel: finding the fruits of peace* ill. by Joani Keller Rothberg. Jewish Lights, 2001. ISBN 1-58023-123-3 Subj: Emotions – anger. Family life – brothers. Religion.

For heaven's sake ill. by Kathryn Kunz Finney. Jewish Lights, 1999. ISBN 1-58023-054-7 Subj: Family life – grandmothers. Friendship. Religion.

God said amen ill. by Avi Katz. Jewish Lights, 2000. ISBN 1-58023-080-6 Subj: Behavior – sharing. Character traits – pride. Character traits – vanity.

God's paintbrush ill. by Annette C. Compton. Jewish Lights, 1992. ISBN 1-879045-22-2 Subj: Religion.

In God's name ill. by Phoebe Stone. Jewish Lights, 1994. ISBN 1-879045-26-5 Subj: Names. Religion.

Naamah, Noah's wife ill. by Bethanne Andersen. Skylight Paths, 2002. ISBN 1-89336-156-X Subj: Family life. Format, unusual – board books. Plants. Religion – Noah. Seeds.

A prayer for the earth: the story of Naamah ill. by Bethanne Andersen. Jewish Lights, 1996. ISBN 1-879045-60-5 Subj: Animals. Boats, ships. Religion – Noah. Weather – floods. Weather – rain.

Sathre, Vivian. *Carnival time* ill. by Kazu. S&S, 1992. ISBN 0-671-76963-4 Subj: Fairs, festivals.

On Grandpa's farm ill. by Anne Hunter. Houghton Mifflin, 1997. ISBN 0-395-76506-4 Subj: Activities – working. Family life – grandfathers. Farms.

Sato, Satoru. *I wish I had a big, big tree* trans. from Japanese by Hitomi Jitodai & Carol Eisman; ill. by Tsutomu Murakami. Lothrop, 1989. ISBN 0-688-07304-2 Subj: Activities – playing. Imagination. Trees.

Satoshi, Kako. *Little Daruma and little Tengu* ill. by author; trans. by Peter Howlett & Richard McNamara. Tuttle, 2002. ISBN 0-8048-3347-8 Subj: Emotions – envy, jealousy. Foreign lands – Japan. Friendship.

Satterfield, Barbara. *The story dance* ill. by Fran Gregory. Fairview, 1997. ISBN 1-57749-022-3 Subj: Activities – dancing. Family life – grandmothers. Memories, memory.

Sattgast, L. J. *Look what God made* ill. by Janet McDonnell. Chariot Books, 1994. ISBN 0-7814-0184-4 Subj: Creation. Religion.

Sattler, Helen Roney. *No place for a goat* ill. by Bari Weissman. Elsevier-Nelson, 1981. ISBN 0-525-66723-7 Subj: Animals – goats. Homes, houses.

Train whistles ill. by Giulio Maestro. Rev. ed. Lothrop, 1985. ISBN 0-688-03980-4 Subj: Language. Trains. Whistles.

Sauer, Julia Lina. *Mike's house* ill. by Don Freeman. Viking, 1954. Subj: Behavior – lost. Cities, towns. Libraries. Weather – snow.

Saul, Carol P. *Barn cat* ill. by Mary Azarian. Little, 1998. ISBN 0-316-76113-3 Subj: Animals – cats. Counting, numbers. Rhyming text.

Peter's song ill. by Diane de Groat. S&S, 1992. ISBN 0-671-73812-7 Subj: Activities – singing. Animals – pigs. Friendship. Frogs & toads.

Saunders, Dave. *Snowtime* by Dave & Julie Saunders; ill. by Dave Saunders. Bradbury, 1991. ISBN 0-02-781075-5 Subj: Animals. Birds – ducks. Birds – geese. Weather – snow.

So slow! by Dave & Julie Saunders; ill. by Dave Saunders. Cavendish, 2001. ISBN 0-7614-5080-7 Subj: Animals. Animals – snails. Character traits – perseverance. Concepts – speed.

Saunders, Julie. *Snowtime* (Saunders, Dave)

So slow! (Saunders, Dave)

Saunders, Susan. *Charles Rat's picnic* ill. by Robert Byrd. Dutton, 1983. ISBN 0-525-44067-4 Subj: Activities – picnicking. Animals – armadillos. Animals – rats. Friendship.

Fish fry ill. by S. D. Schindler. Viking, 1982. ISBN 0-670-31664-4 Subj: Activities – picnicking.

The golden goose (Grimm, Jacob)

A sniff in time ill. by Michael Mariano. Macmillan, 1982. ISBN 0-689-30890-6 Subj: Magic. Senses – smell. Wizards.

Wales' tale ill. by Marilyn Hirsh. Viking, 1980. ISBN 0-670-74870-6 Subj: Animals – dogs.

Sautai, Raoul. *Bees* (Bees)

Native Americans (Native Americans)

Whales (Whales)

Sava, Donna Lynn. *Teddy bear dreams* ill. by Scott Sava. Ipicturebooks, 2002. ISBN 1-59019-128-5 Subj: Careers. Dreams. Imagination. Rhyming text. Toys – bears.

Savage, Kathleen. *Bear hunt* (Siewert, Margaret)

Savage, Stephen. *Making tracks* ill. by author. Dutton, 1992. ISBN 0-525-67353-9 Subj: Animals. Format, unusual – toy & movable books.

Savageau, Cheryl. *Muskrat will be swimming* ill. by Robert Hynes. Northland, 1996. ISBN 0-87358-604-2 Subj: Animals – muskrats. Family life – grandfathers. Folk & fairy tales. Indians of North America – Seneca. Self-concept.

Saville, Lynn. *Horses in the circus ring* ill. by author. Dutton, 1989. ISBN 0-525-44417-3 Subj: Animals – horses, ponies. Circus.

Sawicki, Norma Jean. *The little red house* ill. by Toni Goffe. Lothrop, 1989. ISBN 0-688-07892-3 Subj: Concepts – color. Toys.

Something for mom ill. by Martha Weston. Lothrop, 1987. ISBN 0-688-05590-7 Subj: Birthdays. Family life – mothers.

Sawyer, Jean. *Our village shop* ill. by Faith Jaques. Putnam, 1984. ISBN 0-399-21023-7 Subj: Stores.

Sawyer, Ruth. *The Christmas Anna angel* ill. by Kate Seredy. Viking, 1944. Subj: Angels. Caldecott award honor books. Holidays – Christmas.

Journey cake, ho! ill. by Robert McCloskey. Viking, 1953. ISBN 0-670-40943-X Subj: Caldecott award honor books. Cumulative tales. Folk & fairy tales. Poverty.

The remarkable Christmas of the cobbler's sons ill. by Barbara Cooney. Viking, 1994. ISBN 0-670-84922-7 Subj: Behavior – sharing. Folk & fairy tales. Foreign lands – Tyrol. Holidays – Christmas. Royalty – kings.

Saxe, John Godfrey. *The blind men and the elephant* ill. by Paul Galdone. McGraw-Hill, 1963. Subj: Animals – elephants. Handicaps – blindness. Senses – sight.

Elephant? (Balian, Lorna)

Saxon, Charles D. *Don't worry about Poopsie* ill. by author. Dodd, 1958. Subj: Animals – dogs. Behavior – lost.

Saxon, Gladys Relyea. *see* Seyton, Marion

Saxon, Victoria. *Disney's Pooh's grand adventure: the search for Christopher Robin* (Henderson, Kathy)

Say, Allen. *Allison* ill. by author. Houghton Mifflin, 1997. ISBN 0-395-85895-X Subj: Adoption. Animals – cats. Behavior – misbehavior. Emotions. Family life.

The bicycle man ill. by author. Houghton Mifflin, 1982. ISBN 0-395-32254-5 Subj: Foreign lands – Japan. Sports – bicycling.

Emma's rug ill. by author. Houghton, 1996. ISBN 0-395-74294-3 Subj: Activities – drawing. Ethnic groups in the U.S. – Japanese Americans. Imagination.

Grandfather's journey ill. by author. Houghton Mifflin, 1993. ISBN 0-395-57035-2 Subj: Activities – traveling. Caldecott award honor books. Ethnic groups in the U.S. – Japanese Americans. Family life. Family life – grandfathers. Foreign lands – Japan.

Once under the cherry blossom tree: an old Japanese tale ill. by author. HarperCollins, 1974. ISBN 0-06-025217-0 Subj: Folk & fairy tales. Foreign lands – Japan.

A river dream ill. by author. Houghton Mifflin, 1988. ISBN 0-395-48294-1 Subj: Dreams. Family life. Illness. Sports – fishing.

Tea with milk ill. by author. Houghton, 1999. ISBN 0-395-90495-1 Subj: Ethnic groups in the U.S. – Japanese Americans. Foreign lands – Japan.

Tree of cranes ill. by author. Houghton Mifflin, 1991. ISBN 0-395-52024-X Subj: Family life – mothers. Foreign lands – Japan. Holidays – Christmas.

Sayre, April Pulley. *Army ant parade* ill. by Rick Chrustowski. Holt, 2002. ISBN 0-8050-6353-6 Subj: Foreign lands – Panama. Forest, woods. Insects – ants. Science.

Dig, wait, listen ill. by Barbara Bash. Greenwillow, 2001. ISBN 0-688-16615-6 Subj: Animals. Desert. Frogs & toads. Science.

Home at last: a song of migration ill. by Alix Berenzy. Holt, 1998. ISBN 0-8050-5154-6 Subj: Animals. Migration.

The hungry hummingbird ill. by Gay W. Holland. Millbrook, 2001. ISBN 0-7613-1951-4 Subj: Birds – humming birds. Food. Science.

If you should hear a honey guide ill. by S. D. Schindler. Houghton Mifflin, 1995. ISBN 0-395-71545-8 Subj: Animals. Birds. Foreign lands – Africa. Insects – bees.

It's my city ill. by Denis Roche. Greenwillow, 2001. ISBN 0-688-16916-3 Subj: Birthdays. Cities, towns. Family life – brothers & sisters. Rhyming text.

Noodle Man ill. by Stephen Costanza. Orchard, 2002. ISBN 0-439-29307-3 Subj: Food. Humorous stories.

The shape of Betts Meadow ill. by Joanne Friar. Millbrook, 2002. ISBN 0-7613-2115-2 Subj: Ecology. Poetry.

Splish! splash! animal baths ill. by author. Millbrook, 2000. ISBN 0-7613-1821-6 Subj: Activities – bathing. Animals.

Trout, trout, trout ill. by Trip Park. NorthWord, 2004. ISBN 1-55971-889-7 Subj: Fish. Rhyming text.

Turtle, turtle, watch out! ill. by Lee Christiansen. Orchard, 2000. ISBN 0-531-33285-3 Subj: Character traits – kindness to animals. Migration. Reptiles – turtles, tortoises.

Sazer, Nina. *What do you think I saw? a nonsense number book* ill. by Lois Ehlert. Pantheon, 1976. ISBN 0-394-93182-3 Subj: Counting, numbers. Humorous stories. Rhyming text.

Scamell, Ragnhild. *Solo plus one* ill. by Elizabeth Martland. Little, 1992. ISBN 0-316-77242-9 Subj: Animals – cats. Birds – ducks. Eggs.

Who likes Wolfie? ill. by Tim Warnes. Little, 1995. ISBN 0-316-77243-7 Subj: Animals – wolves. Birds. Emotions – loneliness. Self-concept. Teeth.

The wish come true cat ill. by Gaby Hansen. Barron's, 2001. ISBN 0-7641-5392-7 Subj: Animals – cats. Behavior – wishing. Pets.

Scanlon, Elizabeth Garton. *A sock is a pocket for your toes* ill. by Robin Preiss-Glasser. HarperCollins, 2004. ISBN 0-06-029527-9 Subj: Clothing – pockets. Poetry. Rhyming text.

Scarry, Huck. *Huck Scarry's steam train journey* ill. by author. Collins-World, 1979. ISBN 0-529-05550-3 Subj: Trains.

Looking into the Middle Ages ill. by author. HarperCollins, 1985. ISBN 0-06-025224-3 Subj: Format, unusual – toy & movable books. Knights. Middle Ages.

On the road ill. by author. Putnam, 1981. ISBN 0-399-61183-5 Subj: Automobiles.

Scarry, Richard. *Egg in the hole* ill. by author. Golden Pr., 1967. ISBN 0-307-12030-9 Subj: Birds – chickens. Eggs. Format, unusual.

The great big car and truck book ill. by author. Golden Pr., 1976. ISBN 0-307-10473-7 Subj: Automobiles. Trucks.

Is this the house of Mistress Mouse? ill. by author. Golden Pr., 1964. ISBN 0-307-12029-5 Subj: Animals. Homes, houses.

Mr. Frumble's worst day ever! ill. by author. Random House, 1992. ISBN 0-679-81616-X Subj: Animals – pigs. Behavior – bad day.

My first word book ill. by author. Random House, 1986. ISBN 0-394-88016-1 Subj: Activities – picnicking. Format, unusual – board books.

Pie rats ahoy! ill. by author. Random House, 1994. ISBN 0-679-94760-4 Subj: Animals. Boats, ships. Food. Pirates.

Pig Will and Pig Won't: a book of manners ill. by author. Random House, 1984. ISBN 0-394-96585-X Subj: Animals – pigs. Behavior.

Pig Will and Pig Won't: 2-in-1 turn-around books ill. by author. Random House, 1990. ISBN 0-679-80067-0 Subj: Animals – pigs. Behavior. Format, unusual.

Richard Scarry's ABC word book ill. by author. Random House, 1971. ISBN 0-394-92339-1 Subj: ABC books.

Richard Scarry's all around Busytown ill. by author. Little Simon, 2001. Paper engineered by Renée Jablow and José Seminario. ISBN 0-689-82573-0 Subj: Animals. Careers – postal workers. Cities, towns. Format, unusual – toy & movable books.

Richard Scarry's animal nursery tales ill. by author. Golden Pr., 1975. ISBN 0-307-66810-X Subj: Animals. Folk & fairy tales. Nursery rhymes.

Richard Scarry's best Christmas book ever! ill. by author. Random House, 1981. ISBN 0-394-94936-6 Subj: Holidays – Christmas.

Richard Scarry's best counting book ever! ill. by author. Random House, 1975. ISBN 0-394-92924-1 Subj: Counting, numbers.

Richard Scarry's best first book ever! ill. by author. Random House, 1979. ISBN 0-394-94250-7 Subj: Concepts. Days of the week, months of the year.

Richard Scarry's best Mother Goose ever (Mother Goose)

Richard Scarry's biggest word book ever! ill. by author. Random House, 1985. ISBN 0-394-87374-2 Subj: Dictionaries. Format, unusual. Language.

Richard Scarry's busiest people ever ill. by author. Random House, 1976. ISBN 0-394-93293-5 Subj: Careers.

Richard Scarry's busy houses ill. by author. Random House, 1981. ISBN 0-394-84937-X Subj: Animals – worms. Format, unusual – board books. Homes, houses.

Richard Scarry's great big mystery book ill. by author. Random House, 1969. ISBN 0-394-92431-2 Subj: Animals. Crime. Stores.

Richard Scarry's hop aboard! Here we go! ill. by author. Golden Pr., 1972. Subj: Transportation.

Richard Scarry's Lowly Worm word book ill. by author. Random House, 1981. ISBN 0-394-84728-8 Subj: Format, unusual – board books.

Richard Scarry's Mr. Frumble's biggest hat flap book ever ill. by author. Little Simon, 2002. ISBN 0-689-84844-7 Subj: Animals. Animals – pigs. Clothing – hats. Format, unusual – toy & movable books. Humorous stories.

Richard Scarry's mix or match storybook ill. by author. Random House, 1979. ISBN 0-394-84150-6 Subj: Animals. Format, unusual – toy & movable books.

Richard Scarry's Peasant Pig and the terrible dragon ill. by author. Random House, 1980. Subj: Animals – pigs. Character traits – bravery. Dragons. Middle Ages.

Richard Scarry's please and thank you book ill. by author. Random House, 1973. ISBN 0-394-92681-1 Subj: Etiquette.

Richard Scarry's Postman Pig and his busy neighbors ill. by author. Random House, 1978. ISBN 0-394-93898-4 Subj: Animals. Careers. Careers – postal workers. Cities, towns. Post office.

Richard Scarry's storybook dictionary ill. by author. Golden Pr., 1966. ISBN 0-307-65548-2 Subj: Dictionaries.

Schaaf, Peter. *An apartment house close up* photos by author. Four Winds, 1980. ISBN 0-590-07670-1 Subj: Homes, houses.

The violin close up photos by author. Four Winds, 1980. ISBN 0-590-07655-8 Subj: Music. Musical instruments – violins.

Schaap, Martine. *Mop and the birthday picnic* by Martine Schaap & Alex de Wolf; ill. by Alex de Wolf. McGraw-Hill, 2000. ISBN 1-57768-882-1 Subj: Activities – picnicking. Animals – dogs. Birthdays. Multiple births – twins.

Mop's backyard concert by Martine Schaap & Alex de Wolf; ill. by Alex de Wolf. McGraw-Hill, 2001. ISBN 1-57768-892-9 Subj: Animals – dogs. Multiple births – twins. Musical instruments – bands.

Mop's mountain adventure by Martine Schaap & Alex de Wolf; ill. by Alex de Wolf. McGraw-Hill, 2000. ISBN 1-57768-881-3 Subj: Activities – playing. Animals – dogs. Imagination. Multiple births – twins.

Mop's treasure hunt by Martine Schaap & Alex de Wolf; ill. by Alex de Wolf. McGraw-Hill, 2001. ISBN 1-57768-891-0 Subj: Animals – dogs. Family life – grandfathers. Maps. Multiple births – twins.

Schachner, Judith Byron. *The Grannyman* ill. by author. Dutton, 1999. ISBN 0-525-46122-1 Subj: Animals – cats. Character traits – responsibility. Old age.

Yo, Vikings ill. by author. Dutton, 2002. ISBN 0-525-46889-7 Subj: Birthdays. Boats, ships. Careers – explorers. Character traits – persistence. Vikings.

Schackburg, Richard. *Yankee Doodle* ill. by Ed Emberley. Prentice-Hall, 1965. Subj: Music. Songs. U.S. history.

Schade, Susan. *Toad on the road* (Buller, Jon)

Schaefer, A. R. (Adam Richard). *Alexander Calder* ill. with photos. Heinemann, 2003. ISBN 1-4034-0287-6 Subj: Art. Careers – artists. Careers – sculptors.

Diego Rivera ill. with photos. Heinemann, 2003. ISBN 1-4034-0288-4 Subj: Art. Careers – artists. Foreign lands – Mexico.

Grandma Moses ill. with photos. Heinemann, 2003. ISBN 1-4034-0289-2 Subj: Art. Careers – artists.

Schaefer, Carole Lexa. *The copper tin cup* ill. by Stan Fellows. Candlewick, 1999. ISBN 0-7636-0471-2 Subj: Family life. Memories, memory.

Down in the woods at sleepytime ill. by Vanessa Cabban. Candlewick, 2000. ISBN 0-7636-0843-2 Subj: Activities – storytelling. Animals. Bedtime. Dreams. Family life – mothers. Forest, woods.

Down in the woods at sleepytime [board book] ill. by Vanessa Cabban. Candlewick, 2004. ISBN 0-7636-2566-3 Subj: Activities – storytelling. Animals. Bedtime. Dreams. Family life – mothers. Forest, woods. Format, unusual – board books.

The little French whistle ill. by Emilie Chollat. Knopf, 2002. ISBN 0-375-91022-0 Subj: Family life – cousins. Family life – grandfathers. Whistles.

Snow pumpkin ill. by Pierr Morgan. Crown, 2000. ISBN 0-517-80016-0 Subj: Activities – playing. Ethnic groups in the U.S. Snowmen. Weather – snow.

Someone says ill. by Pierr Morgan. Viking, 2003. ISBN 0-670-03664-1 Subj: Bedtime. Day. Imagination. School – nursery.

Sometimes moon ill. by Pierr Morgan. Crown, 1999. ISBN 0-517-70981-3 Subj: Moon.

Two scarlet songbirds ill. by Elizabeth Rosen. Knopf, 2001. ISBN 0-375-91022-0 Subj: Birds. Careers – composers. Music.

Under the midsummer sky ill. by Pat Geddes. Putnam, 1994. ISBN 03-99-21858-0 Subj: Character traits – kindness. Folk & fairy tales. Foreign lands – Sweden. Holidays. Scarecrows.

Schaefer, Charles E. *Cat's got your tongue?* ill. by Judith Friedman. G. Stevens, 1993. ISBN 0-8368-0930-0 Subj: Character traits – shyness. Emotions – fear. School – first day.

Schaefer, Jackie Jasina. *Miranda's day to dance* ill. by author. Four Winds, 1994. ISBN 0-02-781111-5 Subj: Activities – dancing. Animals. Counting, numbers. Food. Foreign lands – South America.

Schaefer, Lola M. *Airport* ill. with photos. Heinemann, 2000. ISBN 1-575-72515-0 Subj: Airplanes, airports. Careers.

Apartment ill. with photos. Heinemann, 2002. ISBN 1-4034-0258-2 Subj: Homes, houses.

Chinese New Year ill. with photos. Pebble, 2001. ISBN 0-7368-0660-1 Subj: Ethnic groups in the U.S. – Chinese Americans. Foreign lands – China. Holidays – Chinese New Year.

Cinco de Mayo ill. with photos. Pebble, 2001. ISBN 0-7368-0661-X Subj: Ethnic groups in the U.S. – Mexican Americans. Foreign lands – Mexico. Holidays – Cinco de Mayo.

Construction site ill. with photos. Heinemann, 2000. ISBN 1-575-72516-9 Subj: Careers – construction workers.

Dental office ill. with photos. Heinemann, 2000. ISBN 1-57572-517-7 Subj: Careers – dentists. Teeth.

Hanukkah ill. with photos. Pebble, 2001. ISBN 0-7368-0662-8 Subj: Holidays – Hanukkah. Jewish culture. Religion.

Homes ABC ill. with photos. Heinemann, 2003. ISBN 1-4034-0260-4 Subj: ABC books. Homes, houses.

Homes 123 ill. with photos. Heinemann, 2003. ISBN 1-4034-0259-0 Subj: Counting, numbers. Homes, houses.

Hospital ill. with photos. Heinemann, 2000. ISBN 1-57572-519-3 Subj: Careers – doctors. Careers – nurses. Hospitals.

House ill. with photos. Heinemann, 2003. ISBN 1-4034-0261-2 Subj: Homes, houses.

Kwanzaa ill. with photos. Pebble, 2001. ISBN 0-7368-0663-6 Subj: Ethnic groups in the U.S. – African Americans. Holidays – Kwanzaa.

Loose tooth ill. by Sylvie Wickstrom. HarperCollins, 2004. ISBN 0-06-052777-3 Subj: Family life. Rhyming text. Teeth.

Mobile home ill. with photos. Heinemann, 2003. ISBN 1-4034-0263-9 Subj: Homes, houses.

Police station ill. with photos. Heinemann, 2000. ISBN 1-57572-520-7 Subj: Careers – detectives. Careers – police officers.

Supermarket ill. with photos. Heinemann, 2000. ISBN 1-57572-518-5 Subj: Careers – storekeepers. Food. Stores.

This is the sunflower ill. by Donald Crews. Greenwillow, 2000. ISBN 0-688-16414-5 Subj: Cumulative tales. Flowers. Nature. Plants. Rhyming text. Seeds.

Tugboats ill. with photos. Heinemann, 2003. ISBN 1-4034-0262-0 Subj: Boats, ships. Homes, houses.

The Wright brothers ill. with photos. Pebble, 2000. ISBN 0-7368-0549-4 Subj: Airplanes, airports. Careers – inventors. U.S. history.

Schaeffer, Cornelia. *The Holy Night: the story of the first Christmas* (Jüchen, Aurel von)

Schafer, Kevin. *Penguins A B C* ill. with photos. NorthWord, 2002. ISBN 1-55971-831-5 Subj: ABC books. Birds – penguins.

Penguins 1 2 3 ill. with photos. NorthWord, 2002. ISBN 1-55971-830-7 Subj: Birds – penguins. Counting, numbers.

Schafer, Milton. *That crazy Barb'ra* ill. by G. Brian Karas. Dial, 2003. ISBN 0-8037-2584-1 Subj: Behavior – bullying. Rhyming text. School.

Schaffer, Libor. *Arthur sets sail* ill. by Agnès Mathieu. Holt, 1987. ISBN 0-8050-0489-0 Subj: Animals – aardvarks. Animals – pigs. Boats, ships. Character traits – appearance.

Schaffer, Marion. *I love my cat* ill. by Kathy Vanderlinden. Kids Can, 1981. ISBN 0-919964-26-5 Subj: Animals – cats. Foreign languages. Pets.

Schami, Rafik. *Albert and Lila* ill. by Els Cools & Oliver Streich; trans. by Anthea Bell. North-South, 1999. ISBN 0-7358-1183-0 Subj: Animals – foxes. Animals – pigs. Birds – chickens. Character traits – individuality. Prejudice.

The crow who stood on his beak ill. by Els Cools & Oliver Streich; trans. by Anthea Bell. North-South, 1996. ISBN 1-55858-528-1 Subj: Birds – crows. Birds – peacocks, peahens. Character traits – individuality.

Fatima and the dream thief ill. by Els Cools & Oliver Streich; trans. by Anthea Bell. North-South, 1996. ISBN 1-55858-654-7 Subj: Dreams. Folk & fairy tales. Giants.

Schanzer, Rosalyn. *How Ben Franklin stole the lightning* ill. by author. HarperCollins, 2003. ISBN 0-688-16994-5 Subj: Careers – inventors. Careers – scientists. Science. Tall tales. U.S. history.

In the synagogue ill. by author. Kar-Ben Copies, 1991. ISBN 0-929371-60-7 Subj: Format, unusual – board books. Jewish culture. Religion.

The Old Chisholm Trail ill. by author. National Geographic, 2001. ISBN 0-7922-7559-4 Subj: Cowboys, cowgirls. Music. Songs. U.S. history.

Schären, Beatrix. *Tillo* trans. by Gwen Marsh; ill. by author. Addison-Wesley, 1974. Subj: Birds – owls.

Scharer, Niko. *Emily's house* ill. by Joanne Fitzgerald. Firefly, 1991. ISBN 0-88899-111-8 Subj: Animals. Homes, houses. Noise, sounds. Rhyming text.

Schatell, Brian. *Farmer Goff and his turkey Sam* ill. by author. Lippincott, 1982. ISBN 0-397-31983-5 Subj: Behavior – misbehavior. Birds – turkeys. Fairs, festivals.

The McGoonys have a party ill. by author. Lippincott, 1985. ISBN 0-397-32134-4 Subj: Behavior – forgetfulness. Behavior – misunderstanding. Handicaps.

Midge and Fred ill. by author. Lippincott, 1983. ISBN 0-397-32047-7 Subj: Fish. Humorous stories.

Sam's no dummy, Farmer Goff ill. by author. Lippincott, 1984. ISBN 0-397-32062-0 Subj: Birds – turkeys. Character traits – cleverness.

Schatschneider, Lori Ann. *Song of Chirimia = La Musica de la Chirimia* (Volkmer, Jane Anne)

Schatz, Letta. *The extraordinary tug-of-war* ill. by John Burningham. Follett, 1968. Subj: Animals. Character traits – cleverness. Folk & fairy tales. Foreign lands – Africa.

Whiskers, my cat ill. by Paul Galdone. McGraw-Hill, 1967. Subj: Animals – cats.

Schecter, Ellen. *The flower of Sheba* (Orgel, Doris)

Scheer, Julian. *By the light of the captured moon* ill. by Ronald Himler. Holiday, 2001. ISBN 0-8234-1624-0 Subj: Friendship. Moon. Seasons – summer.

Rain makes applesauce by Julian Scheer & Marvin Bileck; ill. by Marvin Bileck. Holiday, 1964. ISBN 0-8234-0091-3 Subj: Caldecott award honor books. Humorous stories. Weather – rain.

Scheffler, Ursel. *Be brave, little lion!* trans. & ill. by Ruth Scholte van Mast. North-South, 2000. ISBN 0-7358-1265-9 Subj: Animals – lions. Character traits – bravery. Emotions – fear. Family life. Foreign lands – Africa.

Stop your crowing, Kasimir! ill. by Silke Brix-Henker. Carolrhoda, 1988. ISBN 0-87614-323-0 Subj: Birds – chickens. Communities, neighborhoods. Country. Noise, sounds.

Taking care of Sister Bear ill. by Ulises Wensell. Doubleday, 1999. ISBN 0-385-32660-2 Subj: Animals – bears. Babies. Behavior – lost. Family life – brothers & sisters.

A walk in the rain trans. by Andrea Mernan; ill. by Ulises Wensell. Putnam, 1986. ISBN 0-399-21267-1 Subj: Family life – grandmothers. Family life – grandparents. Weather – rain.

Who has time for Little Bear? ill. by Ulises Wensell. Doubleday, 1998. ISBN 0-385-32536-3 Subj: Animals – bears. Family life. Friendship.

Scheffrin-Falk, Gladys. *Another celebrated dancing bear* ill. by Barbara Garrison. Scribners, 1991. ISBN 0-684-19164-4 Subj: Activities – dancing. Animals – bears. Circus. Friendship.

Scheidl, Gerda Marie. *Can we help you, Saint Nicholas?* trans. by Rosemary Lanning; ill. by Jean-Pierre Corderoc'h. North-South, 1992. ISBN 1-55858-155-3 Subj: Animals. Forest, woods. Holidays – Christmas.

The moon man trans. & adapt. by J. Alison James; ill. by Józef Wilkon. North-South, 1994. ISBN 1-55858-272-X Subj: Art. Moon.

Pickle and Patch ill. by Jean-Pierre Corderoc'h; trans. by Rosemary Lanning. North-South, 1994. ISBN 1-55858-270-3 Subj: Animals – dogs. Animals – horses, ponies. Farms. Friendship.

Scheller, Melanie. *My grandfather's hat* ill. by Keiko Narahashi. Macmillan, 1992. ISBN 0-689-50540-X Subj: Clothing – hats. Death. Emotions – grief. Family life – grandfathers.

Schenk, Esther M. *Christmas time* ill. by Vera Stone Norman. Follett, 1931. Subj: Holidays – Christmas.

Schepp, Steven. *How babies are made* (Andry, Andrew C.)

Schermbrucker, Reviva. *Charlie's house* ill. by Niki Daly. Viking, 1991. ISBN 0-670-84024-6 Subj: Family life. Foreign lands – South Africa. Homes, houses. Poverty.

Schermer, Judith. *Mouse in house* ill. by author. Houghton Mifflin, 1979. ISBN 0-395-27801-5 Subj: Animals – mice. Family life. Problem solving.

Schertle, Alice. *Advice for a frog and other poems* ill. by Norman Green. Lothrop, 1995. ISBN 0-688-13487-4 Subj: Animals. Animals – endangered animals. Frogs & toads. Poetry.

Bill and the google-eyed goblins ill. by Patricia Coombs. Lothrop, 1987. ISBN 0-688-06702-6 Subj: Activities – dancing. Holidays – Halloween. Mythical creatures – goblins.

Down the road ill. by E. B. Lewis. Browndeer, 1995. ISBN 0-15-276622-7 Subj: Country. Eggs. Ethnic groups in the U.S. – African Americans. Family life.

Goodnight, Hattie, my dearie, my dove ill. by Linda Strauss Edwards. Lothrop, 1985. ISBN 0-688-03934-0 Subj: Bedtime. Counting, numbers. Toys.

Goodnight, Hattie, my dearie, my dove ill. by Ted Rand. HarperCollins, 2002. ISBN 0-688-16023-9 Subj: Bedtime. Counting, numbers. Toys.

The gorilla in the hall ill. by Paul Galdone. Lothrop, 1977. ISBN 0-688-51781-1 Subj: Animals – gorillas. Character traits – bravery. Emotions – fear.

Hob Goblin and the skeleton ill. by Katherine Coville. Lothrop, 1982. ISBN 0-688-00282-X Subj: Holidays – Halloween. Mythical creatures – trolls.

How now, brown cow? ill. by Amanda Schaffer. Browndeer, 1994. ISBN 0-15-276648-0 Subj: Animals – bulls, cows. Poetry.

I am the cat ill. by Mark Buehner. Lothrop, 1999. ISBN 0-688-13154-9 Subj: Animals – cats. Poetry.

In my treehouse ill. by Meredith Dunham. Lothrop, 1983. ISBN 0-688-01639-1 Subj: Behavior – solitude. Homes, houses. Trees.

Jeremy Bean's St. Patrick's Day ill. by Linda Shute. Lothrop, 1987. ISBN 0-688-04814-5 Subj: Behavior – hiding. Character traits – being different. Holidays – St. Patrick's Day. Parties. School.

Keepers ill. by Ted Rand. Lothrop, 1996. ISBN 0-688-11635-3 Subj: Poetry.

Little Frog's song ill. by Leonard Everett Fisher. HarperCollins, 1992. ISBN 0-06-020060-X Subj: Behavior – lost. Frogs & toads.

Maisie ill. by Lydia Dabcovich. Lothrop, 1995. ISBN 0-688-09311-6 Subj: Behavior – growing up. Family life – grandmothers. Farms.

My two feet ill. by Meredith Dunham. Lothrop, 1985. ISBN 0-688-02677-X Subj: Anatomy – feet.

The skeleton in the closet ill. by Curtis Jobling. HarperCollins, 2003. ISBN 0-688-17739-5 Subj: Anatomy – skeletons. Clothing. Rhyming text.

That Olive! ill. by Cindy Wheeler. Lothrop, 1986. ISBN 0-688-04091-8 Subj: Animals – cats. Behavior – hiding.

That's what I thought ill. by John Wallner. HarperCollins, 1990. ISBN 0-06-025205-7 Subj: Character traits – questioning. Family life.

Witch Hazel ill. by Margot Tomes. HarperCollins, 1991. ISBN 0-06-025141-7 Subj: Family life – brothers. Moon. Plants. Scarecrows.

Schick, Alice. *Just this once* by Alice & Joel Schick; ill. by Joel Schick. Lippincott, 1978. ISBN 0-397-31803-0 Subj: Animals – wolves. Pets.

Schick, Eleanor. *Art lessons* ill. by author. Greenwillow, 1987. ISBN 0-688-05121-9 Subj: Art.

City green ill. by author. Macmillan, 1974. ISBN 0-02-781170-0 Subj: Cities, towns. Poetry.

City in the winter ill. by author. Macmillan, 1970. Subj: Cities, towns. Family life – only child. Seasons – winter. Weather – snow. Weather – wind.

I have another language: the language is dance ill. by author. Macmillan, 1992. ISBN 0-02-781209-X Subj: Activities – dancing.

The little school at Cottonwood Corners ill. by author. HarperCollins, 1965. Subj: Caldecott award honor books. School. Wordless.

Making friends ill. by author. Macmillan, 1969. Subj: Friendship. Wordless.

Mama ill. by author. Cavendish, 2000. ISBN 0-7614-5060-2 Subj: Death. Emotions – grief. Family life – mothers. Illness. Memories, memory.

My Navajo sister ill. by author. S&S, 1996. ISBN 0-02-781155-7 Subj: Friendship. Indians of North America – Navajo.

Navajo ABC (Tapahonso, Luci)

One summer night ill. by author. Greenwillow, 1977. Subj: Cities, towns. Music. Seasons – summer.

Peggy's new brother ill. by author. Macmillan, 1970. Subj: Babies. Emotions – envy, jealousy. Family life – new sibling. Sibling rivalry.

Peter and Mr. Brandon ill. by Donald Carrick. Macmillan, 1973. Subj: Activities – babysitting. Cities, towns.

A piano for Julie ill. by author. Greenwillow, 1984. Subj: Family life. Music. Musical instruments – pianos.

A surprise in the forest ill. by author. HarperCollins, 1964. Subj: Animals. Eggs. Forest, woods.

Schick, Joel. *Just this once* (Schick, Alice)

Schiller, Barbara. *The white rat's tale* ill. by Adrienne Adams. Holt, 1967. Subj: Animals – rats. Folk & fairy tales. Foreign lands – France. Royalty.

Schilling, Betty. *Two kittens are born: from birth to two months* photos by author. Holt, 1980. Subj: Animals – cats. Birth. Science.

Schimmel, Schim. *The family of earth* ill. by author. NorthWord, 2001. ISBN 1-55971-790-4 Subj: Animals. Nature. World.

Schindel, John. *Busy penguins* by John Schindel & Jonathan Chester; ill. with photos. Tricycle, 2000. ISBN 1-58246-016-7 Subj: Activities. Birds – penguins. Format, unusual – board books. Rhyming text.

Dear Daddy ill. by Dorothy Donohue. A. Whitman, 1995. ISBN 0-8075-1531-0 Subj: Behavior – needing someone. Divorce. Family life – fathers. Letters, cards.

Frog face, my little sister and me photos by Janet Delaney. Holt, 1998. ISBN 0-8050-5546-0 Subj: Family life – new sibling. Family life – sisters.

What did they see? ill. by Doug Cushman. Holt, 2003. ISBN 0-8050-6167-3 Subj: Animals. Format, unusual – toy & movable books. Mirrors.

Who are you? ill. by James Watts. Macmillan, 1991. ISBN 0-689-50523-X Subj: Animals – bears. Bedtime. Parties.

Schindler, Regina. *The bear's cave* trans. from German by Christopher Franceschelli; ill. by Sita Jucker. Dutton, 1990. ISBN 0-525-44553-6 Subj: Animals. Behavior – boasting. Seasons – winter.

Schlank, Carol Hilgartner. *Elizabeth Cady Stanton* by Carol Hilgartner Schlank & Barbara Metzger; ill. by Janice Bond. Gryphon, 1991. ISBN 0-87659-152-7 Subj: Gender roles. U.S. history.

Schleh, Joy. *Jack and the beanstalk* (Jack and the beanstalk)

Schlein, Miriam. *The amazing Mr. Pelgrew* ill. by Harvey Weiss. Abelard-Schuman, 1957. Subj: Careers – police officers.

Big talk ill. by Joan Auclair. Rev. ed. Bradbury, 1990. ISBN 0-02-781231-6 Subj: Animals – kangaroos. Behavior – boasting.

Big talk ill. by Laura Lydecker. A. Whitman, 1988. ISBN 0-8075-0729-6 Subj: Animals – kangaroos. Behavior – boasting.

Billy, the littlest one ill. by Lucy Hawkinson. A. Whitman, 1966. Subj: Behavior – growing up. Character traits – smallness. Family life.

Deer in the snow ill. by Leonard P. Kessler. Abelard-Schuman, 1956. Subj: Animals – deer. Character traits – kindness to animals. Seasons – winter. Weather – snow.

Elephant herd ill. by Symeon Shimin. Addison-Wesley, 1954. Subj: Animals – elephants.

Fast is not a ladybug ill. by Leonard P. Kessler. Addison-Wesley, 1953. Subj: Concepts – speed. Insects – ladybugs.

The four little foxes ill. by Louis Quintanilla. Addison-Wesley, 1953. Subj: Animals – foxes.

Go with the sun ill. by Symeon Shimin. Addison-Wesley, 1952. Subj: Family life – grandfathers. Seasons – winter.

Heavy is a hippopotamus ill. by Leonard P. Kessler. Addison-Wesley, 1954. Subj: Concepts – weight.

Hello, hello! ill. by Daniel Kirk. S&S, 2002. ISBN 0-689-83435-7 Subj: Animals. Communication.

Here comes night ill. by Harvey Weiss. A. Whitman, 1957. Subj: Night.

Herman McGregor's world ill. by Harvey Weiss. A. Whitman, 1959. Subj: Behavior – growing up. World.

Home, the tale of a mouse ill. by E. Harper Johnson. Abelard-Schuman, 1958. Subj: Animals – mice.

It's about time ill. by Leonard P. Kessler. Addison-Wesley, 1955. Subj: Time.

Laurie's new brother ill. by Elizabeth Donald. Abelard-Schuman, 1961. Subj: Babies. Family life – new sibling. Sibling rivalry.

Little Rabbit, the high jumper ill. by Theresa Sherman. Addison-Wesley, 1957. Subj: Animals – rabbits.

Little Red Nose ill. by Roger Antoine Duvoisin. Abelard-Schuman, 1955. Subj: Seasons – spring.

Lucky porcupine! ill. by Martha Weston. Four Winds, 1980. Subj: Animals – porcupines. Science.

My family ill. by Harvey Weiss. Abelard-Schuman, 1960. Subj: Family life.

My house ill. by Joe Lasker. A. Whitman, 1971. Subj: Family life. Homes, houses. Moving.

The pile of junk ill. by Harvey Weiss. Abelard-Schuman, 1962. Subj: Character traits – practicality. Values.

Shapes ill. by Sam Berman. Addison-Wesley, 1952. Subj: Concepts – shape.

Sleep safe, little whale: a lullaby ill. by Peter Sis. Greenwillow, 1997. ISBN 0-688-14757-7 Subj: Animals. Animals – whales. Bedtime. Format, unusual – toy & movable books. Lullabies.

Something for now, something for later ill. by Leonard Weisgard. HarperCollins, 1956. Subj: Farms.

The story about me ill. by Kristina Stephenson. A. Whitman, 2004. ISBN 0-8075-7631-X Subj: Babies. Birth. Family life. Family life – grandmothers.

The sun looks down ill. by Abner Graboff. Abelard-Schuman, 1954. Subj: Sun.

The sun, the wind, the sea and the rain ill. by Joe Lasker. Abelard-Schuman, 1960. Subj: Sea & seashore. Sun. Weather. Weather – rain. Weather – wind.

That's not Goldie! ill. by Susan Gough Magurn. S&S, 1990. ISBN 0-671-70005-7 Subj: Fish. Pets.

What's wrong with being a skunk? ill. by Ray Cruz. Four Winds, 1974. Subj: Animals – skunks. Science.

When will the world be mine? the story of a snowshoe rabbit ill. by Jean Charlot. Addison-Wesley, 1953. Subj: Behavior – growing up. Caldecott award honor books.

Schlessinger, Laura. *But I waaannt it!* ill. by Daniel McFeeley. HarperCollins, 2000. ISBN 0-06-028775-6 Subj: Behavior – greed.

Dr. Laura Schlessinger's Growing up is hard ill. by Daniel McFeeley. HarperCollins, 2001. ISBN 0-06-029201-6 Subj: Behavior – growing up. Family life – fathers. Family life – sons.

Dr. Laura Schlessinger's Where's God? ill. by Daniel McFeeley. HarperCollins, 2003. ISBN 0-06-051909-6 Subj: Family life – grandfathers. Religion.

Why do you love me? by Dr. Laura Schlessinger & Martha Lambert; ill. by Daniel McFeeley. HarperCollins, 1999. ISBN 0-06-027866-8 Subj: Emotions – love. Family life – mothers. Family life – sons.

Schmeltz, Susan Alton. *Pets I wouldn't pick* ill. by Ellen Appleby. Parents' Magazine Pr., 1982. Subj: Pets. Rhyming text.

Schmid, Eleonore. *Farm animals* ill. by author. Holt, 1986. ISBN 0-03-008032-0 Subj: Animals. Farms. Format, unusual – board books.

Hare's Christmas gift ill. by author; trans. by Rosemary Lanning. North-South, 2000. ISBN 0-7358-1377-9 Subj: Animals – rabbits. Character traits – bravery. Religion – Nativity.

The living earth ill. by author. North-South, 1994. ISBN 1-55858-299-1 Subj: Earth. Ecology.

The squirrel and the moon trans. by Rosemary Lanning; ill. by author. North-South, 1996. ISBN 1-55858-531-1 Subj: Animals – squirrels. Moon. Trees.

The water's journey ill. by author. North-South, 1990. ISBN 1-55858-013-1 Subj: Rivers. Science. Water. Weather – snow.

Schmidt, Eric von. *The young man who wouldn't hoe corn* ill. by author. Houghton Mifflin, 1964. Subj: Character traits – laziness. Farms. Humorous stories.

Schmidt, Gary D. *The Great Stone Face* a tale by Nathaniel Hawthorne; retold by Gary Schmidt; ill. by Bill Farnsworth. Eerdmans, 2002. ISBN 0-8028-5194-0 Subj: Folk & fairy tales.

Schneider, Antonie. *The birthday bear* ill. by Uli Waas; trans. by J. Alison James. North-South, 1996. ISBN 1-55858-656-3 Subj: Animals – bears. Birthdays. Family life – grandparents.

Good-bye, Vivi! ill. by Maja Dusíková; trans. by J. Alison James. North-South, 1998. ISBN 1-55858-986-4 Subj: Birds – canaries. Death. Family life – grandmothers.

Luke the Lionhearted ill. by Cristina Kadmon; trans. by J. Alison James. North-South, 1998. ISBN 1-55858-977-5 Subj: Animals – lions. Behavior – lost. Behavior – running away. Zoos.

Schneider, Christine M. *Horace P. Tuttle, magician extraordinaire* ill. by author. Walker, 2001. ISBN 0-8027-8789-4 Subj: Behavior – needing someone. Careers – magicians. Humorous stories.

Picky Mrs. Pickle ill. by author. Walker, 1999. ISBN 0-8027-8703-7 Subj: Food. Rhyming text. Self-concept.

Saxophone Sam and his snazzy jazz band ill. by author. Walker, 2002. ISBN 0-8027-8809-2 Subj: Activities – dancing. Family life – brothers & sisters. Music. Radios. Rhyming text.

Schneider, Elisa. *The merry-go-round dog* ill. by author. Knopf, 1988. ISBN 0-394-99069-2 Subj: Animals – dogs. Merry-go-rounds.

Schneider, Herman. *Follow the sunset* by Herman & Nina Schneider; ill. by Lucille Corcos. Doubleday, 1952. Subj: Science. Sun. World.

Schneider, Howie. *The amazing Amos and the greatest couch on earth* (Seligson, Susan)

Amos ahoy: a couch adventure on land and sea (Seligson, Susan)

Amos camps out: a couch adventure in the woods (Seligson, Susan)

Amos: the story of an old dog and his couch (Seligson, Susan)

Chewy Louie ill. by author. Rising Moon, 2000. ISBN 0-87358-765-0 Subj: Animals – babies. Animals – dogs. Pets.

Fast 'n Snappy ill. by Jane Manning. Carolrhoda, 2004. ISBN 1-57505-539-2 Subj: Careers – postal workers. Crime. Frogs & toads. Humorous stories. Post office. Reptiles – alligators, crocodiles. U.S. history.

No dogs allowed ill. by author. Putnam, 1995. ISBN 0-399-22612-5 Subj: Activities – traveling. Activities – vacationing. Animals – dogs. Hotels.

Schneider, Nina. *Follow the sunset* (Schneider, Herman)

While Susie sleeps ill. by Dagmar Wilson. Addison-Wesley, 1948. Subj: Bedtime. Night. Sleep.

Schnitter, Jane. *William is my brother* ill. by Gerald Kruck. Perspectives Pr., 1991. ISBN 0-944934-03-X Subj: Adoption. Family life – brothers.

Schnitzlein, Danny. *The monster who ate my peas* ill. by Matt Faulkner. Peachtree, 2001. ISBN 1-56145-216-5 Subj: Food. Monsters. Rhyming text.

Schnitzler, Pattie L. *Widdermaker* ill. by Rick Sealock. Carolrhoda, 2002. ISBN 0-87614-647-7 Subj: Animals – bulls, cows. Animals – horses, ponies. Cowboys, cowgirls. Humorous stories. Tall tales. U.S. history – frontier & pioneer life.

Schnur, Steven. *Autumn* ill. by Leslie Evans. Clarion, 1997. ISBN 0-395-77043-2 Subj: ABC books. Poetry. Seasons – fall.

Night lights ill. by Stacey Schuett. Farrar, 2000. ISBN 0-374-35522-3 Subj: Counting, numbers. Light, lights. Night. Rhyming text.

Spring ill. by Leslie Evans. Clarion, 1999. ISBN 0-395-82269-6 Subj: ABC books. Poetry. Seasons – spring.

Spring thaw ill. by Stacey Schuett. Viking, 2000. ISBN 0-670-87961-4 Subj: Farms. Nature. Seasons – spring.

Summer ill. by Leslie Evans. Clarion, 2001. ISBN 0-618-02372-0 Subj: ABC books. Poetry. Seasons – summer.

The tie man's miracle ill. by Stephen T. Johnson. Morrow, 1995. ISBN 0-688-13463-7 Subj: Character traits – kindness. Clothing. Holidays – Hanukkah. Holocaust. Jewish culture.

Winter ill. by Leslie Evans. Clarion, 2002. ISBN 0-618-02374-7 Subj: ABC books. Poetry. Seasons – winter.

Schoberle, Ceile. *Beyond the Milky Way* ill. by author. Crown, 1986. ISBN 0-517-55716-9 Subj: Imagination. Science. Sky. Space & space ships.

Schoen, Mark. *Bellybuttons are navels* ill. by M. J. Quay. Focus International, 1990. ISBN 0-87975-585-7 Subj: Anatomy – navels.

Schoenherr, John. *The barn* ill. by author. Little, 1968. Subj: Animals – mice. Animals – skunks. Barns. Birds – owls. Farms.

Bear ill. by author. Putnam, 1991. ISBN 0-399-22177-8 Subj: Alaska. Animals – bears. Nature.

Rebel ill. by author. Putnam, 1995. ISBN 0-399-22727-X Subj: Birds – geese. Character traits – curiosity. Family life. Lakes, ponds.

Schofield, Jennifer. *Animal babies in grasslands* ill. with photos. Kingfisher, 2004. ISBN 0-7534-5789-X Subj: Animals. Animals – babies.

Animal babies in polar lands ill. with photos. Kingfisher, 2004. ISBN 0-7534-5755-5 Subj: Animals. Animals – babies. Foreign lands – Antarctic. Foreign lands – Arctic.

Animal babies in ponds and rivers ill. with photos. Kingfisher, 2004. ISBN 0-7534-5790-3 Subj: Animals. Animals – babies. Lakes, ponds. Rivers.

Animal babies in rain forests ill. with photos. Kingfisher, 2004. ISBN 0-7534-5788-1 Subj: Animals. Animals – babies. Forest, woods.

Scholey, Arthur. *Baboushka* ill. by Ray Burrows. Good News, 1983. ISBN 0-89107-281-0 Subj: Music. Religion. Royalty. Toys.

Scholte van Mast, Ruth. *Be brave, little lion!* (Scheffler, Ursel)

Schomp, Virginia. *If you were a . . . ballet dancer* ill. with photos. Benchmark, 1998. ISBN 0-7614-0616-6 Subj: Activities – dancing. Ballet. Careers – dancers.

If you were a . . . ballplayer ill. with photos. Benchmark, 1999. ISBN 0-7614-0916-5 Subj: Careers. Sports.

If you were a . . . construction worker ill. with photos. Benchmark, 1998. ISBN 0-7614-0617-4 Subj: Careers – construction workers.

If you were a . . . doctor ill. with photos. Benchmark, 2001. ISBN 0-7614-1000-7 Subj: Careers – doctors.

If you were a . . . farmer ill. with photos. Benchmark, 2001. ISBN 0-7614-1001-5 Subj: Careers – farmers. Farms.

If you were a . . . musician ill. with photos. Benchmark, 2001. ISBN 0-7614-1002-3 Subj: Careers – musicians. Music.

If you were a . . . pilot ill. with photos. Benchmark, 1999. ISBN 0-7614-0919-X Subj: Activities – flying. Careers – airplane pilots. Transportation.

If you were a . . . police officer ill. with photos. Benchmark, 1997. ISBN 0-7614-0614-X Subj: Careers – police officers.

If you were a . . . teacher ill. with photos. Benchmark, 1999. ISBN 0-7614-0916-5 Subj: Careers – teachers. School.

If you were a . . . truck driver ill. with photos. Benchmark, 2001. ISBN 0-7614-1003-1 Subj: Careers – truck drivers. Trucks.

If you were a . . . veterinarian ill. with photos. Benchmark, 1998. ISBN 0-7614-0613-1 Subj: Animals. Careers – veterinarians.

If you were a . . . zookeeper ill. with photos. Benchmark, 2000. ISBN 0-7614-0918-1 Subj: Animals. Careers – zookeepers.

If you were an . . . astronaut ill. with photos. Benchmark, 1998. ISBN 0-7614-0618-2 Subj: Careers – astronauts. Space & space ships.

Schongut, Emanuel. *Look kitten* ill. by author. S&S, 1983. Subj: Animals.

Schories, Pat. *Mouse around* ill. by author. Farrar, 1991. ISBN 0-374-35080-9 Subj: Activities – traveling. Animals – mice. Circular tales. Wordless.

Schotter, Richard. *There's a dragon about* by Richard & Roni Schotter; ill. by R. W. Alley. Orchard, 1994. ISBN 0-531-08708-5 Subj: Dragons. Rhyming text.

Schotter, Roni. *Bunny's night out* ill. by Margot Apple. Little, 1989. ISBN 0-316-77465-0 Subj: Animals – rabbits. Bedtime. Night.

Captain Bob sets sail ill. by Joe Cepeda. Atheneum, 2000. ISBN 0-689-82081-X Subj: Activities – bathing. Imagination. Pirates.

Captain Bob takes flight ill. by Joe Cepeda. Atheneum, 2003. ISBN 0-689-83388-1 Subj: Activities – flying. Character traits – orderliness. Imagination.

Captain Snap and the children of Vinegar Lane ill. by Marcia Sewall. Watts, 1989. ISBN 0-531-08397-7 Subj: Character traits – being different. Character traits – generosity. Character traits – kindness.

Dreamland ill. by Kevin Hawkes. Orchard, 1996. ISBN 0-531-08858-8 Subj: Careers – tailors. Character traits – individuality. Imagination.

Hanukkah! ill. by Marylin Hafner. Little, 1990. ISBN 0-316-77466-9 Subj: Holidays – Hanukkah. Jewish culture. Religion.

In the piney woods ill. by Kimberly Bulcken Root. Farrar, 2003. ISBN 0-374-33623-7 Subj: Death. Family life – grandfathers. Forest, woods. Trees.

Nothing ever happens on 90th Street ill. by Kyrsten Brooker. Orchard, 1997. ISBN 0-531-08886-3 Subj: Activities – writing. Careers – writers. Cities, towns.

Passover magic ill. by Marylin Hafner. Little, 1995. ISBN 0-316-77468-5 Subj: Holidays – Passover. Jewish culture. Religion.

Purim play ill. by Marylin Hafner. Little, 1998. ISBN 0-316-77518-5 Subj: Holidays – Purim. Jewish culture. Religion. Theater.

Room for Rabbit ill. by Cyd Moore. Clarion, 2003. ISBN 0-618-18183-0 Subj: Divorce. Family life – fathers. Family life – stepfamilies. Toys.

That extraordinary pig of Paris ill. by Dominic Catalano. Philomel, 1994. ISBN 0-399-22023-2 Subj: Animals – pigs. Food. Foreign lands – France. Foreign languages.

There's a dragon about (Schotter, Richard)

Schreck, Karen Halvorsen. *Lucy's family tree* ill. by Stephen Gassler III. Tilbury, 2001. ISBN 0-88448-225-1 Subj: Adoption. Ethnic groups in the U.S. – Mexican Americans. Family life. Genealogy. School. Self-concept.

Schrecker, Judie. *Santa's new reindeer* ill. by Daniel Rodriguez. E.M. Pr., 1996. ISBN 1-880664-18-6 Subj: Animals. Animals – reindeer. Holidays – Christmas. Santa Claus.

Schreiber, Georges. *Bambino goes home* ill. by author. Viking, 1959. Subj: Clowns, jesters. Friendship.

Bambino the clown ill. by author. Viking, 1947. Subj: Animals – sea lions. Caldecott award honor books. Clowns, jesters.

Professor Bull's umbrella (Lipkind, William)

Schreier, Alta. *Cuba* ill. with photos. Heinemann, 2001. ISBN 1-57572-380-8 Subj: Foreign lands – Cuba. Foreign languages.

Schreier, Joshua. *Luigi's all-night parking lot* ill. by author. Dutton, 1990. ISBN 0-525-44626-5 Subj: Bedtime. Imagination. Toys.

Schrier, Jeffrey. *On the wings of eagles: an Ethiopian boy's story* ill. by author. Millbrook, 1998. ISBN 0-7613-0004-X Subj: Ethnic groups in the U.S. – African Americans. Foreign lands – Africa. Foreign lands – Ethiopia. Imagination. Jewish culture. Religion.

Schroder, William. *Pea soup and serpents* ill. by author. Lothrop, 1977. ISBN 0-688-51785-4 Subj: Monsters. Mythical creatures. Weather – fog.

Schroeder, Alan. *Ragtime Tumpie* ill. by Bernie Fuchs. Little, 1989. ISBN 0-316-77497-9 Subj: Activities – dancing. Ethnic groups in the U.S. – African Americans.

Smoky Mountain Rose: an Appalachian Cinderella ill. by Brad Sneed. Dial, 1997. ISBN 0-8037-1734-2 Subj: Animals – pigs. Family life – stepfamilies. Folk & fairy tales.

The stone lion ill. by Todd L. W. Doney. Scribners, 1994. ISBN 0-684-19578-X Subj: Behavior – greed. Character traits – honesty. Character traits – kindness. Character traits – selfishness. Folk & fairy tales. Foreign lands – Tibet.

Schroeder, Binette. *Laura* ill. by author; trans. by Rosemary Lanning. North-South, 1999. ISBN 0-7358-1171-7 Subj: Rhyming text. Self-concept. Toys – bears.

Ra ta ta tam: the strange story of a little engine (Nickl, Peter)

Tuffa and her friends ill. by author. Dial, 1983. ISBN 0-8037-9894-6 Subj: Animals – dogs. Format, unusual – board books. Friendship.

Tuffa and the bone ill. by author. Dial, 1983. ISBN 0-8037-9893-8 Subj: Animals – dogs. Format, unusual – board books.

Tuffa and the ducks ill. by author. Dial, 1983. ISBN 0-8037-9892-X Subj: Animals – dogs. Birds – ducks. Format, unusual – board books.

Tuffa and the picnic ill. by author. Dial, 1983. ISBN 0-8037-9896-2 Subj: Activities – picnicking. Animals – dogs. Behavior – misbehavior. Format, unusual – board books.

Tuffa and the snow ill. by author. Dial, 1983. ISBN 0-8037-9895-4 Subj: Animals – dogs. Format, unusual – board books. Weather – snow.

Schroeder, Glen W. *At the zoo* (Colonius, Lillian)

Schubert, Dieter. *Bear's eggs* (Schubert, Ingrid)

Beaver's lodge (Schubert, Ingrid)

Little big feet (Schubert, Ingrid)

The magic bubble trip (Schubert, Ingrid)

There's a crocodile under my bed! (Schubert, Ingrid)

There's always room for one more (Schubert, Ingrid)

Where's my monkey? ill. by author. Dial, 1987. ISBN 0-8037-0069-5 Subj: Animals – monkeys. Behavior – lost & found possessions. Behavior – needing someone. Wordless.

Schubert, Ingrid. *Bear's eggs* written & ill. by Ingrid & Dieter Schubert. Front St., 1999. ISBN 1-886910-46-4 Subj: Animals – bears. Animals – hedgehogs. Birds – geese. Eggs.

Beaver's lodge by Ingrid and Dieter Schubert; ill. by authors. Front St., 2001. ISBN 1-886910-68-5 Subj: Animals – bears. Animals – beavers. Animals – hedgehogs. Friendship. Homes, houses.

Little big feet written & ill. by Ingrid & Dieter Schubert; trans. from Dutch by Amy Gelman. Carolrhoda, 1990. ISBN 0-87614-426-1 Subj: Anatomy – feet. Witches.

The magic bubble trip written & ill. by Ingrid & Dieter Schubert. Kane/Miller, 1985. ISBN 0-916291-02-2 Subj: Bubbles. Foreign lands – Holland. Frogs & toads.

There's a crocodile under my bed! written & ill. by Ingrid & Dieter Schubert. McGraw-Hill, 1981. ISBN 0-07-055614-8 Subj: Bedtime. Furniture – beds. Reptiles – alligators, crocodiles.

There's always room for one more by Ingrid and Dieter Schubert; ill. by authors. Front St., 2002. ISBN 1-886910-77-4 Subj: Animals. Animals – beavers. Friendship. Insects – butterflies, caterpillars. Sports – sailing.

Schubert, Leda. *Winnie all day long* ill. by William Benedict. Candlewick, 2000. ISBN 0-7636-1041-0 Subj: Animals – dogs. Sleep.

Winnie plays ball ill. by William Benedict. Candlewick, 2000. ISBN 0-7636-1040-2 Subj: Animals – dogs. Birthdays. Toys – balls.

Schuch, Steve. *A symphony of whales* ill. by Peter Sylvada. Harcourt, 1999. ISBN 0-15-201670-8 Subj: Animals – whales. Character traits – helpfulness. Dreams. Foreign lands – Russia. Music.

Schuchman, Joan. *Two places to sleep* ill. by Jim LaMarche. Carolrhoda, 1979. ISBN 0-87614-108-4 Subj: Divorce. Family life.

Schuett, Stacey. *Somewhere in the world right now* ill. by author. Knopf, 1995. ISBN 0-679-96537-8 Subj: Geography. Time. World.

Schuh, Mari C. *Chickens on the farm* ill. with photos. Pebble, 2002. ISBN 0-7368-0991-0 Subj: Birds – chickens. Farms.

Cows on the farm ill. with photos. Pebble, 2002. ISBN 0-7368-0992-9 Subj: Animals – bulls, cows. Farms.

Pigs on the farm ill. with photos. Pebble, 2002. ISBN 0-7368-0993-7 Subj: Animals – pigs. Farms.

Sheep on the farm ill. with photos. Pebble, 2002. ISBN 0-7368-0994-5 Subj: Animals – sheep. Farms.

Schulman, Janet. *The big hello* ill. by Lillian Hoban. Greenwillow, 1976. ISBN 0-688-84036-1 Subj: Friendship. Moving. Toys – dolls.

A bunny for all seasons ill. by Meilo So. Knopf, 2003. ISBN 0-375-92256-3 Subj: Animals – rabbits. Gardens, gardening. Seasons.

Camp Kee Wee's secret weapon ill. by Marylin Hafner. Greenwillow, 1979. ISBN 0-688-84185-6 Subj: Camps, camping. Sports – baseball.

Countdown to spring ill. by Meilo So. Knopf, 2002. ISBN 0-375-81364-0 Subj: Animals. Counting, numbers. Seasons – spring.

The great big dummy ill. by Lillian Hoban. Greenwillow, 1979. ISBN 0-688-84208-9 Subj: Animals – dogs. Friendship. Toys – dolls.

Jungles (Wood, John Norris)

Schulson, Rachel Ellenberg. *Guns . . . what you should know* ill. by Mary Jones. A. Whitman, 1997. ISBN 0-8075-3093-X Subj: Safety. Weapons.

Schultz, Sam. *Animal antics: the beast jokes ever* ill. by Brian Gable. Carolrhoda, 2004. ISBN 1-57505-640-2 Subj: Animals. Riddles & jokes.

Monster mayhem ill. by Brian Gable. Carolrhoda, 2004. ISBN 0-8225-1169-X Subj: Monsters. Riddles & jokes.

Schulz, Charles M. *Bon voyage, Charlie Brown (and don't come back!!)* ill. by author. Random House, 1980. ISBN 0-394-84415-7 Subj: Activities – traveling. Foreign lands.

The Charlie Brown dictionary based on the rainbow dictionary by Wendell W. Wright; asst. by Helene Laird; ill. by author. Random House, 1973. ISBN 0-394-93041-X Subj: Dictionaries.

Life is a circus, Charlie Brown ill. by author. Random House, 1981. ISBN 0-394-94826-2 Subj: Circus.

Snoopy's facts and fun book about boats ill. by author. Random House, 1979. ISBN 0-394-94171-3 Subj: Animals – dogs. Boats, ships.

Snoopy's facts and fun book about farms ill. by author. Random House, 1980. ISBN 0-394-94300-7 Subj: Animals – dogs. Farms.

Snoopy's facts and fun book about houses ill. by author. Random House, 1979. ISBN 0-394-94151-9 Subj: Animals – dogs. Homes, houses.

Snoopy's facts and fun book about nature ill. by author. Random House, 1979. ISBN 0-394-94299-X Subj: Animals – dogs. Nature. Science.

Snoopy's facts and fun book about planes ill. by author. Random House, 1979. ISBN 0-394-94172-1 Subj: Airplanes, airports. Animals – dogs.

Snoopy's facts and fun book about seashores ill. by author. Random House, 1979. ISBN 0-394-94298-1 Subj: Animals – dogs. Sea & seashore.

Snoopy's facts and fun book about seasons ill. by author. Random House, 1979. ISBN 0-394-94173-X Subj: Animals – dogs. Seasons.

Snoopy's facts and fun book about trucks ill. by author. Random House, 1979. ISBN 0-394-94273-6 Subj: Animals – dogs. Trucks.

You're the greatest, Charlie Brown ill. by author. Random House, 1979. ISBN 0-394-94260-4 Subj: Sports – Olympics.

Schulz, Walter A. *Will and Orv* ill. by Janet Schulz. Carolrhoda, 1991. ISBN 0-87614-669-8 Subj: Activities – flying. Airplanes, airports. U.S. history.

Schumacher, Claire. *Alto and Tango* ill. by author. Morrow, 1984. ISBN 0-688-02740-7 Subj: Birds. Fish. Friendship. Sea & seashore.

Brave Lily ill. by author. Morrow, 1985. ISBN 0-688-04963-X Subj: Character traits – bravery. Family life. Frogs & toads.

King of the zoo ill. by author. Morrow, 1985. ISBN 0-688-04132-9 Subj: Animals. Behavior – misbehavior. Friendship. Zoos.

Nutty's birthday ill. by author. Morrow, 1986. ISBN 0-688-06496-5 Subj: Activities – flying. Animals. Animals – squirrels. Birthdays.

Nutty's Christmas ill. by author. Morrow, 1984. ISBN 0-688-03852-2 Subj: Animals – squirrels. Holidays – Christmas.

Tim and Jim ill. by author. Dodd, 1987. ISBN 0-396-09040-0 Subj: Animals. Behavior – lost. Friendship.

Tommy the winner ill. by author. HarperCollins, 1991. ISBN 0-06-026905-7 Subj: Animals – mice. Letters, cards.

Schumaker, Ward. *Dance!* ill. by author. Harcourt, 1996. ISBN 0-15-200046-1 Subj: Activities – dancing. Animals. Rhyming text.

In my garden ill. by author. Chronicle, 2000. ISBN 0-8118-2689-9 Subj: Counting, numbers. Gardens, gardening.

Schur, Maxine Rose. *Day of delight* ill. by J. Brian Pinkney. Dial, 1994. ISBN 0-8037-1414-9 Subj: Foreign lands – Ethiopia. Jewish culture. Religion.

Schurr, Cathleen. *The long and the short of it* ill. by Dorothy Maas. Vanguard, 1950. Subj: Problem solving.

Schuurmans, Hilde. *Sydney won't swim* ill. by author. Whispering Coyote, 2001. ISBN 1-57091-476-1 Subj: Animals – badgers. Emotions – fear. Sports – swimming.

Schwab, Eva. *Robert and the Robot* ill. by author. Front St., 2001. ISBN 1-886910-59-6 Subj: Character traits – orderliness. Robots.

Schwalje, Marjory. *Mr. Angelo* ill. by Abner Graboff. Abelard-Schuman, 1960. Subj: Activities – baking, cooking. Food. Humorous stories.

Schwartz, Alvin. *All of our noses are here and other stories* ill. by Karen Ann Weinhaus. HarperCollins, 1985. ISBN 0-06-025288-X Subj: Folk & fairy tales. Humorous stories.

Schwartz, Amy. *Annabelle Swift, kindergartner* ill. by author. Orchard, 1988. ISBN 0-531-08337-3 Subj: Character traits – pride. School – first day. Sibling rivalry.

Bea and Mr. Jones ill. by author. Bradbury, 1982. ISBN 0-87888-202-2 Subj: Behavior – imitation. Family life – fathers.

Begin at the beginning ill. by author. HarperCollins, 1983. ISBN 0-06-025228-6 Subj: Behavior – growing up.

The boys teams ill. by author. Atheneum, 2001. ISBN 0-689-84138-8 Subj: Activities. School – nursery.

Camper of the week ill. by author. Watts, 1991. ISBN 0-531-08542-2 Subj: Behavior – misbehavior. Camps, camping. Friendship.

Her Majesty, Aunt Essie ill. by author. Bradbury, 1984. ISBN 0-02-781450-5 Subj: Behavior – boasting. Family life – aunts, uncles. Royalty.

How to catch an elephant ill. by author. DK, 1999. ISBN 0-7894-2579-3 Subj: Animals – elephants.

The lady who put salt in her coffee (Hale, Lucretia)

Mrs. Moskowitz and the Sabbath candlesticks ill. by author. Jewish Publication Society, 1983. ISBN 0-8276-0231-6 Subj: Jewish culture. Religion.

Oma and Bobo ill. by author. Bradbury, 1987. ISBN 0-02-781500-5 Subj: Animals – dogs. Family life – grandmothers.

Some babies ill. by author. Orchard, 2000. ISBN 0-531-33287-X Subj: Activities – storytelling. Bedtime. Family life.

A teeny, tiny baby ill. by author. Orchard, 1994. ISBN 0-531-08668-2 Subj: Babies. Cities, towns.

Things I learned in second grade ill. by author. Tegen, 2004. ISBN 0-06-050937-6 Subj: Behavior – growing up. School.

Yossel Zissel and the wisdom of Chelm ill. by author. Jewish Publication Society, 1988. ISBN 0-8276-0258-8 Subj: Character traits – foolishness. Folk & fairy tales. Jewish culture.

Schwartz, David M. *How much is a million?* ill. by Steven Kellogg. Lothrop, 1985. ISBN 0-688-04050-0 Subj: Concepts – size. Counting, numbers.

If you hopped like a frog ill. by James Warhola. Scholastic, 1999. ISBN 0-590-09857-8 Subj: Animals. Concepts. Counting, numbers. Picture puzzles. Science.

Ready! set! measure! ill. by Steven Kellogg. HarperCollins, 2002. ISBN 0-06-623784-X Subj: Concepts – measurement. Concepts – weight. Counting, numbers.

Sugargrandpa ill. by Bert Dodson. Lothrop, 1991. ISBN 0-688-09899-1 Subj: Family life – grandfathers. Foreign lands – Sweden. Old age. Sports – bicycling. Sports – racing.

Schwartz, Delmore. *"I am Cherry Alive," the little girl sang* ill. by Barbara Cooney. HarperCollins, 1979. ISBN 0-06-025244-8 Subj: Poetry.

Schwartz, Ellen. *Mr. Belinsky's bagels* ill. by Stefan Czernecki. Charlesbridge, 1998. ISBN 0-8810-6256-1 Subj: Careers – bakers. Food.

Schwartz, Henry. *Albert goes Hollywood* ill. by Amy Schwartz. Watts, 1992. ISBN 0-531-08580-5 Subj: Dinosaurs. Pets. Theater.

How I captured a dinosaur ill. by Amy Schwartz. Watts, 1989. ISBN 0-531-08370-5 Subj: Camps, camping. Dinosaurs. Pets. Prehistory.

Schwartz, Lynne Sharon. *The four questions* ill. by Ori Sherman. Dial, 1989. ISBN 0-8037-0601-4 Subj: Holidays – Passover. Jewish culture. Religion.

Schwartz, Mary. *Spiffen: a tale of a tidy pig* ill. by Lynn Munsinger. A. Whitman, 1988. ISBN 0-8075-7580-1 Subj: Animals – pigs. Character traits – cleanliness.

Schwartz, Roslyn. *The mole sisters and the cool breeze* ill. by author. Annick, 2002. ISBN 1-55037-771-X Subj: Animals. Animals – moles. Concepts – cold & heat. Family life – sisters.

The mole sisters and the fairy ring ill. by author. Annick, 2003. ISBN 1-55037-819-8 Subj: Activities – playing. Animals – moles. Family life – sisters.

The mole sisters and the piece of moss ill. by author. Annick, 1999. ISBN 1-55037-583-0 Subj: Animals – moles. Character traits – helpfulness. Character traits – optimism. Family life – sisters.

The mole sisters and the question ill. by author. Annick, 2002. ISBN 1-55037-769-8 Subj: Animals. Animals – moles. Family life – sisters.

The mole sisters and the rainy day ill. by author. Annick, 1999. ISBN 1-55037-611-X Subj: Animals – moles. Family life – sisters. Sports – swimming. Weather – rain.

Rose and Dorothy ill. by author. Watts, 1991. ISBN 0-531-08518-X Subj: Animals – elephants. Animals – mice. Friendship.

Schwarz, Viviane. *The adventures of a nose* ill. by Joel Stewart. Candlewick, 2002. ISBN 0-7636-1674-5 Subj: Anatomy – noses. Emotions – happiness. Self-concept.

Schweiger-Dmi'el, Itzhak. *Hanna's Sabbath dress* ill. by Ora Eitan. S&S, 1996. ISBN 0-689-80517-9 Subj: Character traits – helpfulness. Clothing – dresses. Folk & fairy tales. Jewish culture. Religion.

Schweitzer, Iris. *Hilda's restful chair* ill. by author. Atheneum, 1982. ISBN 0-689-50230-3 Subj: Animals. Friendship. Furniture – chairs.

Schweninger, Ann. *Autumn days* ill. by author. Viking, 1991. ISBN 0-670-82758-4 Subj: Animals – dogs. Seasons – fall.

Birthday wishes ill. by author. Viking, 1986. ISBN 0-670-80742-7 Subj: Animals – rabbits. Behavior – wishing. Birthdays. Parties.

Christmas secrets ill. by author. Viking, 1984. ISBN 0-670-22109-0 Subj: Animals – rabbits. Holidays – Christmas.

Halloween surprises ill. by author. Viking, 1984. ISBN 0-670-35935-1 Subj: Animals – rabbits. Holidays – Halloween.

The hunt for rabbit's galosh ill. by Kay Chorao. Doubleday, 1976. ISBN 0-385-00274-2 Subj: Animals – rabbits. Behavior – forgetfulness. Holidays – Valentine's Day.

The man in the moon as he sails the sky and other moon verse ill. by author. Dodd, 1979. ISBN 0-396-07741-2 Subj: Moon. Poetry.

Off to school! ill. by author. Viking, 1987. ISBN 0-670-81447-4 Subj: Animals – rabbits. School – first day.

Summertime ill. by author. Viking, 1992. ISBN 0-670-83610-9 Subj: Activities. Animals – dogs. Family life. Nature. Sea & seashore. Seasons – summer. Weather.

Valentine friends ill. by author. Viking, 1988. ISBN 0-670-81448-2 Subj: Animals – rabbits. Family life. Holidays – Valentine's Day.

Wintertime ill. by author. Viking, 1990. ISBN 0-670-83420-3 Subj: Animals – dogs. Seasons – winter.

Scieszka, Jon. *Baloney, Henry P.* ill. by Lane Smith. Viking, 2001. ISBN 0-670-89248-3 Subj: Aliens. School. Space & space ships.

The book that Jack wrote ill. by Daniel Adel. Viking, 1994. ISBN 0-670-84330-X Subj: Cumulative tales. Nursery rhymes.

The frog prince, continued ill. by Steve Johnson. Viking, 1991. ISBN 0-670-83421-1 Subj: Folk & fairy tales. Frogs & toads. Royalty – princes. Royalty – princesses. Witches.

The Stinky Cheese Man and other fairly stupid tales by Jon Scieszka & Lane Smith; ill. by Lane Smith. Viking, 1992. ISBN 0-670-84487-X Subj: Caldecott award honor books. Folk & fairy tales.

The true story of the three little pigs by A. Wolf, as told to Jon Scieszka ill. by Lane Smith. Viking, 1989. ISBN 0-670-82759-2 Subj: Animals – pigs. Animals – wolves. Folk & fairy tales.

Scoppettone, Sandra. *Bang, bang, you're dead* (Fitzhugh, Louise)

Scott, Ann Herbert. *Big Cowboy Western* ill. by Richard Lewis. Lothrop, 1965. Subj: Clothing. Cowboys, cowgirls. Ethnic groups in the U.S. – African Americans. Imagination. U.S. history – frontier & pioneer life.

Grandmother's chair ill. by Meg Kelleher Aubrey. Houghton Mifflin, 1990. ISBN 0-395-52001-0 Subj: Family life – grandmothers. Furniture – chairs.

Hi! ill. by Glo Coalson. Philomel, 1994. ISBN 0-399-21964-1 Subj: Behavior – unnoticed, unseen. Post office.

Let's catch a monster ill. by H. Tom Hall. Lothrop, 1967. Subj: Cities, towns. Ethnic groups in the U.S. – African Americans. Holidays – Halloween.

On mother's lap ill. by Glo Coalson. Rev. ed. Houghton Mifflin, 1992. ISBN 0-395-58920-7 Subj: Behavior – needing someone. Emotions – love. Eskimos. Family life. Family life – mothers. Sibling rivalry.

On mother's lap [board book] ill. by Glo Coalson. Clarion, 2000. ISBN 0-618-05159-7 Subj: Behavior – needing someone. Emotions – love. Eskimos. Family life. Family life – mothers. Format, unusual – board books. Sibling rivalry.

One good horse ill. by Lynn Sweat. Greenwillow, 1990. ISBN 0-688-09147-4 Subj: Counting, numbers. Cowboys, cowgirls.

Sam ill. by Symeon Shimin. McGraw-Hill, 1992, c1967. ISBN 0-399-22104-2 Subj: Behavior – needing someone. Ethnic groups in the U.S. – African Americans. Family life.

Someday rider ill. by Ronald Himler. Houghton Mifflin, 1989. ISBN 0-89919-792-2 Subj: Animals – horses, ponies. Behavior – growing up. Cowboys, cowgirls.

Scott, C. Anne (Cynthia Anne). *Old Jake's skirts* ill. by David Slonim. Northland, 1998. ISBN 0-8735-8615-8 Subj: Behavior – lost & found possessions. Careers – farmers. Clothing. Farms.

Scott, Cora Annett. *see* Annett, Cora

Scott, Elaine. *Friends!* photos by Margaret Miller. Atheneum, 2000. ISBN 0-689-82105-0 Subj: Friendship.

Scott, Frances Gruse. *How many kids are hiding on my block?* (Merrill, Jean)

Scott, Geoffrey. *Memorial Day* ill. by Peter E. Hanson. Carolrhoda, 1983. ISBN 0-87614-219-6 Subj: Holidays – Memorial Day. Memories, memory.

Scott, Janine. *Let's eat* ill. with photos. Compass Pt., 2003. ISBN 0-7565-0365-5 Subj: Food.

Let's get dressed ill. with photos. Compass Pt., 2003. ISBN 0-7565-0366-3 Subj: Clothing.

Time to tell ill. with photos. Compass Pt., 2003. ISBN 0-7565-0455-4 Subj: Time.

Scott, Lesbia. *I sing a song of the saints of God* ill. by Judith Gwyn Brown. Seabury Pr., 1981. An ill. version of Lesbia Scott's hymn, "I sing a song of the saints of God" written in 1929. ISBN 0-8164-2339-3 Subj: Music. Religion. Songs.

Scott, Natalie (Anderson). *Firebrand, push your hair out of your eyes* ill. by Sandra Smith. Carolrhoda, 1969. ISBN 0-8761-4005-3 Subj: Character traits – appearance. Hair.

Scott, Peter David. *Dinosaur* ill. by author; text by Nicholas Harris. Barron's, 2003. ISBN 0-7641-5584-9 Subj: Dinosaurs.

Scott, Rochelle. *Colors, colors all around* ill. by Leonard P. Kessler. Grosset, 1965. Subj: Concepts – color.

Scott, Sally. *Little Wiener* ill. by Beth Krush. Harcourt, 1951. Subj: Animals – dogs.

The magic horse ill. by adapt. Greenwillow, 1985. Retold and adapted from "The Ebony Horse," a story from The Arabian Nights tr. by Sir Richard Burton. ISBN 0-688-05898-1 Subj: Folk & fairy tales. Foreign lands. Magic. Royalty. Wizards.

There was Timmy! ill. by Beth Krush. Harcourt, 1957. Subj: Animals – dogs.

The three wonderful beggars ill. by author. Greenwillow, 1988. ISBN 0-688-06657-7 Subj: Careers – beggars. Folk & fairy tales.

Scott, William R. *This is the milk that Jack drank* adapt. from Mother Goose; ill. by Charles Green Shaw. Addison-Wesley, 1944. Subj: Cumulative tales.

Scotton, Rob. *Russell the sheep* ill. by author. HarperCollins, 2005. ISBN 0-06-059849-2 Subj: Animals – sheep. Bedtime. Counting, numbers. Sleep.

Scribner, Charles. *The devil's bridge: a legend* retold by Charles Scribner, Jr.; ill. by Evaline Ness. Scribners, 1978. ISBN 0-684-15034-4 Subj: Devil. Folk & fairy tales. Foreign lands – France.

Hansel and Gretel (Grimm, Jacob)

Scrimger, Richard. *Eugene's story* ill. by Gillian Johnson. Tundra, 2003. ISBN 0-88776-544-0 Subj: Activities – storytelling. Family life – brothers & sisters. Sibling rivalry.

Princess Bun Bun ill. by Johnson, Gillian. Tundra, 2002. ISBN 0-88776-543-2 Subj: Family life – aunts, uncles. Family life – brothers & sisters. Monsters. Royalty – princesses.

The scrubbly-bubbly car wash ill. by Cynthia Jabar. HarperCollins, 2003. ISBN 0-06-029486-8 Subj: Automobiles. Family life – fathers. Rhyming text.

Scruggs, Afi. *Jump rope magic* ill. by David Diaz. Blue Sky, 2000. ISBN 0-590-69327-1 Subj: Activities – jumping. Ethnic groups in the U.S. – African Americans. Games. Noise, sounds. Rhyming text.

Scruton, Clive. *Bubble and squeak* ill. by author. Random House, 1985. ISBN 0-394-87101-4 Subj: Animals – mice. Birds – ducks. Friendship.

Circus cow ill. by author. Random House, 1985. ISBN 0-394-87102-2 Subj: Animals – bulls, cows. Character traits – foolishness.

Mary's pets ill. by author. Lothrop, 1989. ISBN 0-688-08520-2 Subj: Animals. Format, unusual. Games. Pets. Rhyming text.

Pig in the air ill. by author. Random House, 1985. ISBN 0-394-87103-0 Subj: Activities – flying. Animals – pigs.

Scaredy cat ill. by author. Random House, 1985. ISBN 0-394-87014-X Subj: Animals – cats. Emotions – fear.

Scuderi, Lucia. *To fly* ill. by author. Kane/Miller, 1998. ISBN 0-916291-79-0 Subj: Activities – flying. Behavior – growing up. Birds. Family life. Format, unusual – toy & movable books.

Scullard, Sue. *Miss Fanshawe and the great dragon adventure* ill. by author. St. Martin's, 1987. ISBN 0-312-00510-5 Subj: Dragons. Format, unusual.

The Sea World alphabet book concept by Sally & Alan Sloan. Sea World Pr., 1979. ISBN 0-15-004037-7 Subj: ABC books. Sea & seashore.

Seabrook, Elizabeth. *Cabbages and kings* ill. by Jamie Wyeth. Viking, 1997. ISBN 0-670-87462-0 Subj: Friendship. Gardens, gardening. Plants.

Seabrooke, Brenda. *The best burglar alarm* ill. by Loretta Lustig. Morrow, 1978. ISBN 0-688-32165-8 Subj: Crime. Pets.

The swan's gift ill. by Wenhai Ma. Candlewick, 1995. ISBN 1-56402-360-5 Subj: Birds – swans. Family life. Farms. Folk & fairy tales. Food. Gifts. Poverty.

Sears, Martha. *Baby on the way* (Sears, William,)

Eat healthy, feel great (Sears, William,)

What baby needs (Sears, William,)

You can go to the potty (Sears, William,)

Sears, William, M.D. *Baby on the way* by William Sears, Martha Sears, & Christie Watts Kelly; ill. by Renée Andriani. Little, 2001. ISBN 0-316-78767-1 Subj: Babies. Birth.

Eat healthy, feel great by William Sears, Martha Sears, & Christie Watts Kelly; ill. by Renée Andriani. Little, 2002. ISBN 0-316-78708-6 Subj: Food. Health & fitness.

What baby needs by William Sears, Martha Sears, & Christie Watts Kelly; ill. by Renée Andriani. Little, 2001. ISBN 0-316-78828-7 Subj: Babies. Family life – new sibling.

You can go to the potty by William Sears, Martha Sears, & Christie Watts Kelly; ill. by Renée Andriani. Little, 2002. ISBN 0-316-78888-0 Subj: Behavior – growing up. Toilet training.

Seaside poems collected by Jill Bennett; ill. by Nick Sharratt. Oxford Univ. Pr., 1998. ISBN 0-19-276173-0 Subj: Poetry. Sea & seashore.

Seattle, Chief. *Brother eagle, sister sky* ill. by Susan Jeffers. Puffin, 2002. ISBN 0-14-230132-9 Subj: Ecology. Indians of North America – Suquamish.

Sebuda, Robert. *The night before Christmas: a pop-up* (Moore, Clement Clarke)

The secret princess handbook; or, How to be a little princess ill. by author. Little Simon, 2001. ISBN 0-689-84373-9 Subj: Format, unusual – toy & movable books. Royalty – princesses.

Sedges, John. *see* Buck, Pearl S. (Pearl Sydenstricker)

See the dinosaurs ill. by Roma Bishop. S&S, 1993. ISBN 0-671-88308-9 Subj: Dinosaurs. Format, unusual – toy & movable books. Prehistory.

Seeber, Dorothea P. *A pup just for me . . . A boy just for me* ill. by Ed Young. Philomel, 2000. ISBN 0-399-23403-9 Subj: Animals – dogs. Behavior – needing someone. Format, unusual – toy & movable books. Pets. Rhyming text.

Seed, Jenny. *Ntombi's song* ill. by Anno Berry. Beacon, 1989. ISBN 0-8070-8318-6 Subj: Character traits – confidence. Foreign lands – South Africa.

Seeger, Charles Louis. *The foolish frog* (Seeger, Pete)

Seeger, Pete. *Abiyoyo* ill. by Michael Hays. Macmillan, 1986. ISBN 0-02-781490-4 Subj: Folk & fairy tales. Magic. Monsters.

Abiyoyo returns by Pete Seeger & Paul DuBois Jacobs; ill. by Michael Hays. S&S, 2001. ISBN 0-689-83271-0 Subj: Careers – magicians. Folk & fairy tales. Foreign lands – South Africa. Giants. Magic.

The foolish frog by Pete Seeger & Charles Louis Seeger; ill. by Miloslav Jágr; adapt. & designed from Firebird Film by Gene Deitch. Macmillan, 1973. ISBN 0-02-781480-7 Subj: Cumulative tales. Folk & fairy tales. Frogs & toads. Music. Songs.

Segal, Lore Groszmann. *All the way home* ill. by James Marshall. Farrar, 1973. Subj: Cumulative tales.

The bear and the kingbird (Grimm, Jacob)

Morris the artist ill. by Boris Kulikov. Farrar, 2003. ISBN 0-374-35063-9 Subj: Activities – painting. Birthdays. Careers – artists. Gifts.

The story of old Mrs. Brubeck and how she looked for trouble and where she found him ill. by Marcia Sewall. Pantheon, 1981. ISBN 0-394-94039-3 Subj: Behavior – worrying. Problem solving.

Tell me a Mitzi ill. by Harriet Pincus. Farrar, 1970. ISBN 0-374-37392-2 Subj: Family life. Jewish culture.

Tell me a Trudy ill. by Rosemary Wells. Farrar, 1977. ISBN 0-3743-7395-7 Subj: Family life. Jewish culture.

Segal, Sheila. *Joshua's dream* ill. by Jana Paiss. UAHC Pr., 1985. ISBN 0-8074-0272-9 Subj: Foreign lands – Israel. Jewish culture.

Seguin-Fontes, Marthe. *The cat's surprise* adapt. by Sandra Beris; ill. by author. Larousse, 1983. ISBN 0-88332-322-2 Subj: Animals – cats.

A wedding book adapt. by Sandra Beris; ill. by author. Larousse, 1983. ISBN 0-88332-321-4 Subj: Activities – photographing. Weddings.

Seibert, Patricia. *Mush! across Alaska in the world's longest sled-dog race* ill. by Jan Davey Ellis. Millbrook, 1992. ISBN 1-56294-705-2 Subj: Alaska. Animals – dogs. Sports – racing. Sports – sledding.

Seibold, J. Otto. *Mr. Lunch borrows a canoe* by J. Otto Seibold & Vivian Walsh; ill. by J. Otto Seibold. Viking, 1994. ISBN 0-670-85661-4 Subj: Animals – dogs. Boats, ships. Foreign lands – Italy.

Mr. Lunch takes a plane ride by J. Otto Seibold & Vivian Walsh; ill. by J. Otto Seibold. Viking, 1993. ISBN 0-670-84775-5 Subj: Activities – flying. Airplanes, airports. Transportation.

Penguin dreams by J. Otto Seibold & Vivian Walsh; ill. by J. Otto Seibold. Chronicle, 1999. ISBN 0-8118-2558-2 Subj: Activities – flying. Birds – penguins. Dreams. Foreign lands – Antarctic. Rhyming text.

Seiden, Art. *Trucks* ill. by Art Seiden. Platt, 1983. ISBN 0-448-40873-2 Subj: Trucks.

Seidler, Rosalie. *Grumpus and the Venetian cat* ill. by author. Atheneum, 1964. Subj: Animals – cats. Animals – mice. Birds. Foreign lands – Italy.

Seidler, Tor. *The steadfast tin soldier* (Andersen, H. C. [Hans Christian])

Seignobosc, Françoise. *The big rain* ill. by author. Scribners, 1961. Subj: Animals. Farms. Foreign lands – France. Weather – rain.

Biquette, the white goat ill. by author. Scribners, 1953. Subj: Animals – goats. Foreign lands – France. Illness.

Chouchou ill. by author. Scribners, 1958. Subj: Animals – donkeys. Foreign lands – France.

Jeanne-Marie at the fair ill. by author. Scribners, 1959. Subj: Fairs, festivals. Foreign lands – France.

Jeanne-Marie counts her sheep ill. by author. Scribners, 1951. Subj: Behavior – wishing. Counting, numbers. Foreign lands – France.

Jeanne-Marie in gay Paris ill. by author. Scribners, 1956. Subj: Character traits. Foreign lands – France.

Minou ill. by author. Scribners, 1962. Subj: Animals – cats. Behavior – lost. Foreign lands – France.

Noël for Jeanne-Marie ill. by author. Scribners, 1953. Subj: Foreign lands – France. Holidays – Christmas.

Small-Trot ill. by author. Scribners, 1952. Subj: Animals – mice. Circus.

Springtime for Jeanne-Marie ill. by author. Scribners, 1955. Subj: Animals – goats. Behavior – lost. Birds – ducks. Foreign lands – France. Seasons – spring.

The story of Colette ill. by author. Hale, 1940. Subj: Animals. Emotions – loneliness. Pets.

The thank-you book ill. by author. Scribners, 1947. Subj: Etiquette. Religion.

The things I like ill. by author. Scribners, 1960. Subj: Participation.

What do you want to be? ill. by author. Scribners, 1957. Subj: Careers. Character traits – ambition.

What time is it, Jeanne-Marie? ill. by author. Scribners, 1963. Subj: Time.

Seinfeld, Jerry. *Halloween* ill. by James Bennett. Little, 2002. ISBN 0-316-13454-6 Subj: Holidays – Halloween. Memories, memory.

Seix, Victoria. *Cubs* (Landa, Norbert)

Puppies (Landa, Norbert)

Selberg, Ingrid. *Nature's hidden world* ill. by Andrew Miller. Putnam, 1984. ISBN 0-399-20973-5 Subj: Animals. Format, unusual – toy & movable books. Plants. Riddles & jokes. Science.

Selby, Jennifer. *Beach bunny* ill. by author. Harcourt, 1996. ISBN 0-15-200840-3 Subj: Animals – rabbits. Family life – mothers. Sea & seashore – beaches.

Selden, George. *The mice, the monks and the Christmas tree* ill. by Jan Balet. Macmillan, 1963. Subj: Animals – mice. Holidays – Christmas.

Sparrow socks ill. by Peter Lippman. HarperCollins, 1965. Subj: Birds – sparrows. Clothing – socks.

Selig, Sylvie. *Kangaroo* ill. by author. Merrimack, 1980. ISBN 0-224-01746-2 Subj: Animals – kangaroos. Wordless.

Ten what? a mystery counting book (Hoban, Russell)

Seligman, Dorothy Halle. *Run away home* ill. by Christine Hoffmann. Golden Gate, 1969. Subj: Behavior – running away. Family life.

Seligson, Susan. *The amazing Amos and the greatest couch on earth* by Susan Seligson & Howie Schneider; ill. by Howie Schneider. Little, 1989. ISBN 0-316-78033-2 Subj: Animals – dogs. Circus. Furniture – couches, sofas. Humorous stories. Imagination.

Amos ahoy: a couch adventure on land and sea by Susan Seligson & Howie Schneider; ill. by Howie Schneider. Little, 1990. ISBN 0-316-77403-0 Subj: Animals – dogs. Furniture – couches, sofas. Imagination.

Amos camps out: a couch adventure in the woods by Susan Seligson & Howie Schneider; ill. by Howie Schneider. Little, 1992. ISBN 0-316-77402-2 Subj: Animals – dogs. Camps, camping. Forest, woods. Furniture – couches, sofas.

Amos: the story of an old dog and his couch by Susan Seligson & Howie Schneider; ill. by Howie Schneider. Little, 1987. ISBN 0-316-77404-9 Subj: Animals – dogs. Furniture – couches, sofas. Humorous stories. Imagination. Old age.

Selkowe, Valrie M. *Happy birthday to me!* ill. by John Sandford. HarperCollins, 2001. ISBN 0-688-16680-6 Subj: Animals. Animals – rabbits. Birthdays. Gardens, gardening.

Spring green ill. by Jeni Bassett. Lothrop, 1985. ISBN 0-688-04056-X Subj: Animals. Concepts – color. Parties. Seasons – spring.

Sellers, Ronnie. *My first day at school* ill. by Patti Stren. Caedmon, 1985. ISBN 0-89845-373-9 Subj: Rhyming text. School – first day.

Selsam, Millicent E. *All kinds of babies* ill. by Symeon Shimin. Four Winds, 1967. Subj: Animals. Science.

Egg to chick ill. by Barbara Wolff. Rev. ed. HarperCollins, 1970. ISBN 0-06-025290-1 Subj: Birds – chickens. Birth. Eggs. Science.

A first look at bird nests by Millicent E. Selsam & Joyce Hunt; ill. by Harriett Springer. Walker, 1985. ISBN 0-8027-6565-3 Subj: Birds. Science.

A first look at caterpillars by Millicent E. Selsam & Joyce Hunt; ill. by Harriett Springer. Walker, 1987. ISBN 0-8027-6702-8 Subj: Insects – butterflies, caterpillars. Metamorphosis. Science.

A first look at cats by Millicent E. Selsam & Joyce Hunt; ill. by Harriett Springer. Walker, 1981. ISBN 0-8027-6399-5 Subj: Animals – cats. Science.

A first look at dinosaurs by Millicent E. Selsam & Joyce Hunt; ill. by Harriett Springer. Walker, 1982. ISBN 0-8027-6456-8 Subj: Dinosaurs. Prehistory.

A first look at dogs by Millicent E. Selsam & Joyce Hunt; ill. by Harriett Springer. Walker, 1981. ISBN 0-8027-6409-6 Subj: Animals – dogs. Animals – foxes. Animals – wolves.

A first look at flowers by Millicent E. Selsam & Joyce Hunt; ill. by Harriett Springer. Walker, 1977. ISBN 0-8027-6282-4 Subj: Flowers. Science.

A first look at kangaroos, koalas and other animals with pouches by Millicent E. Selsam & Joyce Hunt; ill. by Harriett Springer. Walker, 1985. ISBN 0-8027-6579-3 Subj: Animals. Science.

A first look at monkeys by Millicent E. Selsam & Joyce Hunt; ill. by Harriett Springer. Walker, 1979. ISBN 0-8027-6359-6 Subj: Animals – gorillas. Animals – monkeys. Science.

A first look at owls, eagles and other hunters of the sky by Millicent E. Selsam & Joyce Hunt; ill. by Harriett Springer. Walker, 1986. ISBN 0-8027-6642-0 Subj: Birds. Science.

A first look at rocks by Millicent E. Selsam & Joyce Hunt; ill. by Harriett Springer. Walker, 1984. ISBN 0-8027-6531-9 Subj: Rocks. Science.

A first look at seashells by Millicent E. Selsam & Joyce Hunt; ill. by Harriett Springer. Walker, 1983. ISBN 0-8027-6503-3 Subj: Animals. Science. Sea & seashore.

A first look at sharks by Millicent E. Selsam & Joyce Hunt; ill. by Harriett Springer. Walker, 1979. ISBN 0-8027-6373-1 Subj: Fish – sharks. Science.

A first look at spiders by Millicent E. Selsam & Joyce Hunt; ill. by Harriett Springer. Walker, 1983. ISBN 0-8027-6481-9 Subj: Science. Spiders.

A first look at the world of plants by Millicent E. Selsam & Joyce Hunt; ill. by Harriett Springer. Walker, 1978. ISBN 0-8027-6299-9 Subj: Plants. Science.

A first look at whales by Millicent E. Selsam & Joyce Hunt; ill. by Harriett Springer. Walker, 1980. ISBN 0-8027-6388-X Subj: Animals – whales. Science.

Hidden animals ill. by David Shapiro. HarperCollins, 1969. First pub. in 1947. ISBN 0-06-025282-0 Subj: Animals.

How kittens grow photos by Esther Bubley. Four Winds, 1975. ISBN 0-590-07409-1 Subj: Animals – cats. Science.

How puppies grow photos by Esther Bubley. Four Winds, 1971. Subj: Animals – dogs. Science.

How to be a nature detective ill. by Marlene Hill Donnelly. Harper-Collins, 1995. ISBN 0-06-023448-2 Subj: Animals. Nature.

Is this a baby dinosaur? and other science picture puzzles ill. with photos. HarperCollins, 1972. ISBN 0-06-025303-7 Subj: Games. Science.

Keep looking! by Millicent E. Selsam & Joyce Hunt; ill. by Normand Chartier. Macmillan, 1988. ISBN 0-02-781840-3 Subj: Animals. Farms. Seasons – winter.

More potatoes! ill. by Ben Shecter. HarperCollins, 1972. ISBN 0-06-025323-1 Subj: Farms. Plants. School. Science.

Night animals ill. with photos. Four Winds, 1980. ISBN 0-590-07755-4 Subj: Animals. Night.

Sea monsters of long ago ill. by John Hamberger. Four Winds, 1978. ISBN 0-590-07567-5 Subj: Monsters. Sea & seashore.

Seeds and more seeds ill. by Tomi Ungerer. HarperCollins, 1959. Subj: Plants. Science. Seeds.

Where do they go? Insects in winter ill. by Arabelle Wheatley. Scholastic, 1984. ISBN 0-02-778080-5 Subj: Insects. Science. Seasons – winter.

Selway, Martina. *Don't forget to write* ill. by author. Ideals, 1992. ISBN 0-8249-8543-5 Subj: Emotions. Family life – aunts, uncles. Family life – grandfathers. Farms. Letters, cards.

Greedyguts ill. by author. Hutchinson, 1990. ISBN 0-09-174151-3 Subj: Behavior – greed. Giants.

Selzer, Meyer. *Here comes the recycling truck!* photos by author. A. Whitman, 1992. ISBN 0-8075-3235-5 Subj: Ecology. Trucks.

Sendak, Maurice. *Alligators all around: an alphabet* ill. by author. HarperCollins, 1962. ISBN 0-06-025530-7 Subj: ABC books. Reptiles – alligators, crocodiles.

Chicken soup with rice ill. by author. HarperCollins, 1962. ISBN 0-06-025535-8 Subj: Days of the week, months of the year.

Hector Protector, and As I went over the water ill. by author. Harper-Collins, 1993. ISBN 0-06-028643-1 Subj: Nursery rhymes.

In the night kitchen ill. by author. HarperCollins, 1970. ISBN 0-06-026669-4 Subj: Caldecott award honor books. Dreams. Imagination.

The jester has lost his jingle (Saltzman, David)

Maurice Sendak's Really Rosie: starring the Nutshell Kids ill. by author; music by Carole King; design by Jane Byers Bierhorst. HarperCollins, 1976. ISBN 0-06-025537-4 Subj: Activities – playing. Music. Theater.

One was Johnny: a counting book ill. by author. HarperCollins, 1962. ISBN 0-06-025540-4 Subj: Counting, numbers.

Outside over there ill. by author. HarperCollins, 1981. ISBN 0-06-025524-2 Subj: Activities – babysitting. Babies. Caldecott award honor books. Mythical creatures – goblins.

Pierre: a cautionary tale in five chapters and a prologue ill. by author. HarperCollins, 1962. ISBN 0-06-118009-2 Subj: Behavior – indifference. Character traits – individuality. Humorous stories. Rhyming text.

Seven little monsters ill. by author. HarperCollins, 1977. ISBN 0-06-025478-5 Subj: Counting, numbers. Monsters. Rhyming text.

The sign on Rosie's door ill. by author. HarperCollins, 1960. ISBN 0-06-025506-4 Subj: Activities – playing. Imagination.

Some swell pup: or Are you sure you want a dog? by Maurice Sendak & Matthew Margolis; ill. by Maurice Sendak. Farrar, 1976. ISBN 0-374-46963-6 Subj: Animals – dogs. Pets.

Very far away ill. by author. HarperCollins, 1957. ISBN 0-06-025515-3 Subj: Animals. Behavior – needing someone. Behavior – running away.

Where the wild things are ill. by author. HarperCollins, 1963. ISBN 0-06-025521-8 Subj: Behavior – misbehavior. Caldecott award books. Imagination. Monsters.

Senisi, Ellen B. *All kinds of friends, even green* photos by author. Woodbine, 2002. ISBN 1-890627-35-6 Subj: Handicaps – physical handicaps. Reptiles – iguanas. School.

For my family, love, Allie photos by author. A. Whitman, 1998. ISBN 0-8075-2539-1 Subj: Family life. Food. Marriage, interracial.

Hurray for pre-K! photos by author. HarperCollins, 2000. ISBN 0-06-028897-3 Subj: Activities. Emotions. School – nursery.

Just kids: visiting a class for children with special needs ill. by author. Dutton, 1998. ISBN 0-525-45646-5 Subj: Handicaps. School.

Kindergarten kids ill. by author. Cartwheel, 1994. ISBN 0-590-47614-9 Subj: School.

Secrets ill. by author. Dutton, 1995. ISBN 0-525-45393-8 Subj: Behavior – secrets.

Sensel, Joni. *Bears barge in* ill. by Christopher L. Bivins. Dream Factory, 2000. ISBN 0-9701195-0-X Subj: Animals. Ecology. Rhyming text.

Senshu, Noriko. *Sonny's dream* ill. by author. Hampton Roads, 2000. ISBN 1-57174-215-8 Subj: Alaska. Animals – bears. Behavior – growing up. Dreams. Emotions – fear. Hibernation.

Serfozo, Mary. *Dirty Kurt* ill. by Nancy Poydar. Macmillan, 1992. ISBN 0-689-50537-X Subj: Behavior – carelessness. Character traits – cleanliness. Rhyming text.

A head is for hats ill. by Katy Bratun. Scholastic, 1999. ISBN 0-439-09909-9 Subj: Anatomy. Rhyming text. Self-concept.

Rain talk ill. by Keiko Narahashi. Macmillan, 1990. ISBN 0-689-50496-9 Subj: Noise, sounds. Weather – rain.

There's a square ill. by David A. Carter. Scholastic, 1996. ISBN 0-590-54426-8 Subj: Concepts – shape. Rhyming text.

Welcome Roberto! Bienvenido, Roberto! ill. by John Serfozo. Follett, 1969. ISBN 0-695-89225-8 Subj: Ethnic groups in the U.S. – Mexican Americans. Foreign languages.

What's what? a guessing game ill. by Keiko Narahashi. McElderry, 1996. ISBN 0-689-80653-1 Subj: Animals – dogs. Concepts – opposites. Ethnic groups in the U.S. – African Americans. Language.

Who said red? ill. by Keiko Narahashi. Macmillan, 1988. ISBN 0-689-50455-1 Subj: Concepts – color.

Who wants one? ill. by Keiko Narahashi. Macmillan, 1989. ISBN 0-689-50474-8 Subj: Counting, numbers. Rhyming text.

Serraillier, Anne. *Florina and the wild bird* (Chönz, Selina)

Serraillier, Ian. *Florina and the wild bird* (Chönz, Selina)

Suppose you met a witch ill. by Ed Emberley. Little, 1973. ISBN 0-316-78125-8 Subj: Rhyming text. Witches.

Service, Pamela F. *The wizard of wind and rock* ill. by Laura Marshall. Macmillan, 1990. ISBN 0-689-31600-3 Subj: Folk & fairy tales. Foreign lands – England. Wizards.

Sesame Street. *Ernie and Bert can . . . can you?* ill. by Michael J. Smollin. Random House, 1982. ISBN 0-394-85150-1 Subj: Format, unusual – board books. Puppets.

The Sesame Street book of letters created in cooperation with the Children's Television Workshop, producers of Sesame Street. Designed by Charles I. Miller & James J. Harvin. Preschool Pr., 1970. Subj: ABC books.

The Sesame Street book of numbers created in cooperation with the Children's Television Workshop, producers of Sesame Street. Designed by Charles I. Miller & James J. Harvin. Preschool Pr., 1970. Subj: Counting, numbers.

The Sesame Street book of people and things created in cooperation with the Children's Television Workshop, producers of Sesame Street. Designed by Charles I. Miller & James J. Harvin. Preschool Pr., 1970. Subj: Careers. Concepts. Emotions.

The Sesame Street book of shapes created in cooperation with the Children's Television Workshop, producers of Sesame Street. Designed by Charles I. Miller & James J. Harvin. Preschool Pr., 1970. Subj: Concepts – shape.

Sesame Street sign language fun ill. with photos. Random House, 1980. ISBN 0-394-94212-4 Subj: Puppets. Sign language.

Sesame Street word book ill. by Tom Leigh. Golden Pr., 1983. ISBN 0-307-65549-0 Subj: Language. Puppets.

Seskin, Steve. *Don't laugh at me* by Steve Seskin & Allen Shamblin; ill. by Glin Dibley. Tricycle, 2002. ISBN 1-58246-058-2 Subj: Character traits – individuality. Music. Songs.

Seuling, Barbara. *Drip! drop!* ill. by Nancy Tobin. Holiday, 2000. ISBN 0-8234-1459-0 Subj: Water.

Flick a switch ill. by Nancy Tobin. Holiday, 2003. ISBN 0-8234-1729-8 Subj: Science.

From head to toe ill. by Edward Miller. Holiday, 2002. ISBN 0-8234-1699-2 Subj: Anatomy. Science.

Spring song ill. by Greg Newbold. Harcourt, 2001. ISBN 0-15-202317-8 Subj: Animals. Rhyming text. Seasons – spring.

The teeny tiny woman: an old English ghost tale ill. by author. Viking, 1976. ISBN 0-670-69505-X Subj: Folk & fairy tales. Foreign lands – England. Ghosts.

The triplets ill. by author. Houghton Mifflin, 1980. ISBN 0-395-29107-0 Subj: Character traits – individuality. Multiple births – triplets.

What kind of family is this? a book about step families ill. by Ellen Dolce. Childrens Pr., 1985. ISBN 0-307-62482-X Subj: Family life. Family life – stepfamilies. Sibling rivalry.

Winter lullaby ill. by Greg Newbold. Browndeer, 1997. ISBN 0-15-201403-9 Subj: Animals. Seasons – winter.

Seuss, Dr. *And to think that I saw it on Mulberry Street* ill. by author. Random House, 1989, c1937. ISBN 0-394-94494-1 Subj: Humorous stories. Imagination. Rhyming text.

Bartholomew and the Oobleck ill. by author. Random House, 1949. ISBN 0-394-90075-8 Subj: Caldecott award honor books. Humorous stories. Royalty.

The butter battle book ill. by author. Random House, 1984. ISBN 0-394-96580-9 Subj: Rhyming text. War.

The cat in the hat ill. by author. Random House, 1957. ISBN 0-394-90001-4 Subj: Animals – cats. Humorous stories. Rhyming text.

The cat in the hat comes back! ill. by author. Random House, 1958. ISBN 0-394-90002-2 Subj: Animals – cats. Humorous stories. Rhyming text.

The cat in the hat dictionary by the Cat himself & P. D. Eastman; ill. by Dr. Seuss. Random House, 1964. ISBN 0-394-91009-5 Subj: Dictionaries. Humorous stories.

The cat's quizzer ill. by author. Random House, 1976. ISBN 0-394-93296-X Subj: Humorous stories. Rhyming text. Riddles & jokes.

Come over to my house by Theo LeSeig; ill. by Richard Erdoes. Random House, 1966. ISBN 0-394-90044-8 Subj: Homes, houses. Rhyming text.

Did I ever tell you how high you can count? (Hayward, Linda)

Did I ever tell you how lucky you are? ill. by Richard Erdoes. Random House, 1973. ISBN 0-394-92719-2 Subj: Character traits – luck. Humorous stories. Problem solving. Rhyming text.

Dr. Seuss's ABC ill. by author. Random House, 1963. ISBN 0-394-90030-8 Subj: ABC books. Humorous stories. Rhyming text.

Dr. Seuss's sleep book ill. by author. Random House, 1962. ISBN 0-394-90091-X Subj: Humorous stories. Rhyming text. Sleep.

The eye book ill. by Roy McKié. Random House, 1968. ISBN 0-394-91094-X Subj: Anatomy – eyes. Animals – rabbits. Rhyming text.

The foot book ill. by author. Random House, 1968. ISBN 0-394-90937-2 Subj: Anatomy – feet. Humorous stories. Rhyming text.

Fox in socks ill. by author. Random House, 1965. ISBN 0-394-90038-3 Subj: Humorous stories. Rhyming text.

Gerald McBoing Boing ill. by author; ed. by Kate Klimo. Random House, 2000. ISBN 0-679-99140-9 Subj: Communication. Concepts. Humorous stories. Noise, sounds. Rhyming text. Senses.

Gerald McBoing Boing sound book ill. by author. Random House, 2003. ISBN 0-375-82443-X Subj: Communication. Concepts. Format, unusual. Humorous stories. Noise, sounds. Participation. Rhyming text.

A great day for up ill. by Quentin Blake. Random House, 1974. ISBN 0-394-92913-6 Subj: Concepts – up & down. Humorous stories. Rhyming text.

Green eggs and ham ill. by author. Random House, 1960. ISBN 0-394-90016-2 Subj: Cumulative tales. Food. Humorous stories. Rhyming text.

Happy birthday to you! ill. by author. Random House, 1959. ISBN 0-394-90076-6 Subj: Birthdays. Humorous stories. Rhyming text.

Hooper Humperdink . . . ? Not him! ill. by Charles E. Martin. Random House, 1976. ISBN 0-394-93286-2 Subj: ABC books. Birthdays. Humorous stories. Rhyming text.

Hop on Pop ill. by author. Random House, 1963. ISBN 0-394-90029-4 Subj: Humorous stories. Rhyming text.

Horton hatches the egg ill. by author. Random House, 1940. ISBN 0-394-90077-4 Subj: Animals – elephants. Birds. Character traits – helpfulness. Eggs. Humorous stories. Rhyming text.

Horton hears a Who! ill. by author. Random House, 1954. ISBN 0-394-90078-2 Subj: Animals – elephants. Character traits – kindness. Humorous stories. Rhyming text.

How the Grinch stole Christmas ill. by author. Random House, 1957. ISBN 0-394-90079-0 Subj: Character traits – meanness. Holidays – Christmas. Humorous stories. Rhyming text.

Hunches in bunches ill. by author. Random House, 1982. ISBN 0-394-95502-1 Subj: Problem solving. Rhyming text.

I am not going to get up today! ill. by James Stevenson. Random House, 1987. ISBN 0-394-99217-2 Subj: Humorous stories. Rhyming text. Sleep.

I can add upside down! (Hayward, Linda)

I can draw it myself: by me, myself, with a little help from my friend Dr. Seuss ill. by author. Random House, 1987. ISBN 0-394-08009-7 Subj: Art. Character traits – individuality.

I can lick 30 tigers today and other stories ill. by author. Random House, 1969. ISBN 0-394-90094-X Subj: Animals – tigers. Humorous stories. Rhyming text.

I can read with my eyes shut ill. by author. Random House, 1978. ISBN 0-394-93912-3 Subj: Books, reading. Humorous stories. Rhyming text.

I can write! a book by me, myself, with a little help from Theo LeSeig and Roy McKié ill. by Roy McKié. Random House, 1971. ISBN 0-679-84700-6 Subj: Activities – writing. Humorous stories. Rhyming text.

I had trouble getting to Solla Sollew ill. by author. Random House, 1965. Subj: Activities – traveling. Humorous stories. Rhyming text.

I wish that I had duck feet ill. by Barney Tobey. Random House, 1965. ISBN 0-394-90040-5 Subj: Behavior – wishing. Rhyming text.

If I ran the circus ill. by author. Random House, 1956. ISBN 0-394-90080-4 Subj: Circus. Humorous stories. Rhyming text.

If I ran the zoo ill. by author. Random House, 1950. ISBN 0-394-90081-2 Subj: Caldecott award honor books. Humorous stories. Rhyming text. Zoos.

In a people house ill. by Roy McKié. Random House, 1972. ISBN 0-394-92395-2 Subj: Homes, houses. Humorous stories. Rhyming text.

The king's stilts ill. by author. Random House, 1939. ISBN 0-394-90082-0 Subj: Humorous stories. Rhyming text. Royalty – kings. Toys.

The Lorax ill. by author. Random House, 1971. ISBN 0-394-92337-5 Subj: Ecology. Humorous stories.

McElligot's pool ill. by author. Random House, 1947. ISBN 0-394-90083-9 Subj: Caldecott award honor books. Fish. Humorous stories. Imagination. Rhyming text.

Marvin K. Mooney, will you please go now! ill. by author. Random House, 1972. ISBN 0-394-92490-8 Subj: Humorous stories. Rhyming text.

Mr. Brown can moo! Can you? ill. by author. Random House, 1970. ISBN 0-394-80622-0 Subj: Animals. Humorous stories. Noise, sounds. Participation. Rhyming text.

Oh say can you say? ill. by author. Random House, 1979. ISBN 0-394-94255-8 Subj: Humorous stories. Imagination. Rhyming text.

Oh, the places you'll go! ill. by author. Random House, 1990. ISBN 0-679-90527-8 Subj: Self-concept.

Oh, the things you can count from 1-10 (Hayward, Linda)

Oh, the thinks you can think! ill. by author. Random House, 1975. ISBN 0-394-93129-7 Subj: Humorous stories. Imagination. Rhyming text.

On beyond zebra ill. by author. Random House, 1955. ISBN 0-394-90084-7 Subj: Humorous stories. Letters, cards. Rhyming text.

One fish, two fish, red fish, blue fish ill. by author. Random House, 1960. ISBN 0-606-04238-5 Subj: Fish. Humorous stories. Rhyming text.

Please try to remember the first of Octember! ill. by Art Cumings. Random House, 1977. ISBN 0-394-93563-2 Subj: Behavior – wishing. Humorous stories. Memories, memory. Rhyming text.

Scrambled eggs super! ill. by author. Random House, 1953. ISBN 0-394-90085-5 Subj: Food. Humorous stories. Rhyming text.

The shape of me and other stuff ill. by author. Random House, 1973. ISBN 0-394-92687-0 Subj: Concepts – shape. Humorous stories. Rhyming text.

The Sneetches, and other stories ill. by author. Random House, 1961. ISBN 0-394-90089-8 Subj: Emotions – fear. Humorous stories. Rhyming text.

Ten apples up on top by Theo LeSieg; ill. by Roy McKié. Random House, 1961. ISBN 0-394-90019-7 Subj: Counting, numbers.

There's a wocket in my pocket ill. by author. Random House, 1974. ISBN 0-394-92920-9 Subj: Humorous stories. Rhyming text.

Thidwick, the big-hearted moose ill. by author. Random House, 1948. ISBN 0-394-90086-3 Subj: Animals – moose. Birds. Humorous stories. Rhyming text.

The tooth book ill. by Roy McKié. Random House, 1981. ISBN 0-394-94825-4 Subj: Health & fitness. Rhyming text. Teeth.

Wacky Wednesday ill. by George Booth. Random House, 1974. ISBN 0-394-92912-8 Subj: Humorous stories. Participation. Rhyming text.

Wet foot, dry foot, low foot, high foot (Hayward, Linda)

Would you rather be a bullfrog? ill. by Roy McKié. Random House, 1975. ISBN 0-394-93128-9 Subj: Animals. Character traits – optimism. Frogs & toads.

Seven spunky monkeys ill. by Lynn Munsinger. Harcourt, 2005. ISBN 0-15-202519-7 Subj: Activities. Animals – monkeys. Counting, numbers. Day. Rhyming text.

Severn, Jeffrey. *George and his giant shadow* ill. by author. Chronicle, 1990. ISBN 0-87701-634-8 Subj: Animals. Shadows.

Severo, Emöke de Papp. *The good-hearted youngest brother: an Hungarian folktale* (The good-hearted youngest brother)

Sévigny, Éric. *Caillou, new shoes* (Johnson, Marion)

Sewall, Marcia. *Animal song* ill. by author. Little, 1988. ISBN 0-316-78191-6 Subj: Animals. Folk & fairy tales. Songs.

The cobbler's song ill. by author. Dutton, 1982. ISBN 0-525-44005-4 Subj: Behavior – worrying.

The Green Mist ill. by adapt. Houghton Mifflin, 1999. ISBN 0-395-90013-1 Subj: Folk & fairy tales. Foreign lands – England. Seasons – spring. Superstition.

The little wee tyke: an English folktale ill. by author. Atheneum, 1979. ISBN 0-689-30724-1 Subj: Animals – dogs. Folk & fairy tales. Foreign lands – England.

Ridin' that strawberry roan ill. by adapt. Viking, 1985. ISBN 0-670-80623-4 Subj: Animals – horses, ponies. Cowboys, cowgirls. Rhyming text. U.S. history – frontier & pioneer life.

The wee, wee mannie and the big, big coo: a Scottish folk tale ill. by author. Little, 1977. ISBN 0-316-78180-0 Subj: Animals – bulls, cows. Folk & fairy tales. Foreign lands – Scotland.

Sewell, Helen Moore. *Birthdays for Robin* ill. by author. Macmillan, 1943. Subj: Animals – dogs. Birthdays.

Blue barns ill. by author. Macmillan, 1933. Subj: Barns. Birds – ducks. Birds – geese. Farms.

Jimmy and Jemima ill. by author. Macmillan, 1940. Subj: Character traits – bravery. Sibling rivalry.

Ming and Mehitable ill. by author. Macmillan, 1936. Subj: Animals – dogs.

Peggy and the pony ill. by author. Oxford Univ. Pr., 1936. Subj: Animals – horses, ponies. Behavior – wishing.

Sexton, Anne. *Joey and the birthday present* (Kumin, Maxine W.)

Sexton, Colleen A. *Let's meet Martin Luther King, Jr.* ill. with photos. Chelsea, 2004. ISBN 0-7910-7322-X Subj: Careers – clergy. Ethnic groups in the U.S. – African Americans. U.S. history.

Sexton, Gwain. *There once was a king* ill. by author. Scribners, 1959. Subj: Rhyming text. Royalty – kings.

Seymour, Dorothy Z. *Ann likes red* ill. by Nancy Meyerhoff. Purple House, 2001. ISBN 1-930900-12-0 Subj: Clothing – dresses. Concepts – color.

The tent ill. by Nancé Holman. Grosset, 1965. Subj: Cumulative tales.

Seymour, Peter S. *Animals in disguise* ill. by Jean Cassels Helmer. Macmillan, 1985. ISBN 0-02-782160-9 Subj: Animals. Format, unusual – toy & movable books.

How the weather works ill. by Sally Springer. Macmillan, 1984. ISBN 0-02-782110-2 Subj: Format, unusual – toy & movable books. Science. Weather.

Insects: a close-up look ill. by Jean Cassels Helmer. Macmillan, 1985. ISBN 0-02-782120-X Subj: Format, unusual – toy & movable books. Insects.

Pilots ill. by Norm Ingersoll. Lodestar, 1992. ISBN 0-525-67372-5 Subj: Airplanes, airports. Careers – airplane pilots. Format, unusual – toy & movable books.

The pop-up book of big trucks ill. by Chuck Murphy. Little, 1989. ISBN 0-316-78197-5 Subj: Format, unusual – toy & movable books. Trucks.

What lives in the sea? ill. by Pamela Johnson. Macmillan, 1985. ISBN 0-02-782170-6 Subj: Format, unusual – toy & movable books. Sea & seashore.

What's at the beach? ill. by David A. Carter. Holt, 1985. ISBN 0-03-002557-5 Subj: Monsters. Nature. Sea & seashore – beaches.

What's in the deep blue sea? ill. by David A. Carter. Holt, 1990. ISBN 0-8050-1449-7 Subj: Format, unusual – toy & movable books. Science. Sea & seashore.

What's in the prehistoric forest? ill. by David A. Carter. Holt, 1990. ISBN 0-8050-1450-0 Subj: Forest, woods. Format, unusual – toy & movable books. Prehistory. Science.

Seymour, Tres. *The gulls of the Edmund Fitzgerald* ill. by author. Orchard, 1996. ISBN 0-531-08859-6 Subj: Birds. Boats, ships. Lakes, ponds.

I love my buzzard ill. by S. D. Schindler. Orchard, 1994. ISBN 0-531-08669-0 Subj: Animals. Family life – mothers. Pets. Rhyming text.

Too quiet for these old bones ill. by Paul Brett Johnson. Orchard, 1997. ISBN 0-531-33052-4 Subj: Behavior – boredom. Family life – grandmothers. Noise, sounds. Rhyming text.

We played marbles ill. by Dan Andreasen. Orchard, 1998. ISBN 0-531-33074-5 Subj: Games. U.S. history. War.

Seyton, Marion. *The hole in the hill* ill. by Leonard W. Shortall. Follett, 1960. Subj: Cavemen. Family life.

Shafer, Dana. *Mud Pie Annie: God's recipe for doing your best* (Buchanan, Sue)

Shah, Idries. *The boy without a name* ill. by Mona Caron. Hoopoe, 2000. ISBN 1-883536-20-0 Subj: Dreams. Folk & fairy tales. Foreign lands – Middle East. Magic. Names.

The clever boy and the terrible, dangerous animal ill. by Rose Mary Santiago. Hoopoe, 2000. ISBN 1-883536-18-9 Subj: Character traits – helpfulness. Emotions – fear. Folk & fairy tales. Foreign lands – Middle East.

The silly chicken ill. by Jeff Jackson. Hoopoe, 2000. ISBN 1-883536-19-7 Subj: Birds – chickens. Folk & fairy tales. Foreign lands – Middle East.

Shahan, Sherry. *The jazzy alphabet* ill. by Mary Thelen. Philomel, 2002. ISBN 0-399-23453-5 Subj: ABC books. Musical instruments. Rhyming text.

Shakespeare, William. *Hamlet for kids* (Burdett, Lois)

Macbeth for kids (Burdett, Lois)

A midsummer night's dream for kids (Burdett, Lois)

Romeo and Juliet for kids (Burdett, Lois)

The tempest for kids (Burdett, Lois)

To sleep, perchance to dream ill. by James Mayhew. Scholastic, 2001. ISBN 0-439-29655-2 Subj: Poetry.

Twelfth night (Burdett, Lois)

Shalev, Meir. *My father always embarrasses me* trans. by Dagmar Herrmann; ill. by Yossi Abolafia. Wellington, 1990. ISBN 0-922984-02-6 Subj: Emotions – embarrassment. Family life – fathers.

Shalleck, Alan J. *Curious George and the dinosaur* (Curious George and the dinosaur)

Curious George goes to an ice cream shop (Curious George goes to an ice cream shop)

Curious George goes to school (Curious George goes to school)

Curious George goes to the dentist (Curious George goes to the dentist)

Shamblin, Allen. *Don't laugh at me* (Seskin, Steve)

Shange, Ntozake. *Whitewash* ill. by Michael Sporn. Walker, 1997. ISBN 0-8027-8491-7 Subj: Ethnic groups in the U.S. – African Americans. Prejudice.

Shank, Ned. *The sanyasin's first day* ill. by Catherine Stock. Cavendish, 1998. ISBN 0-7614-5055-6 Subj: Careers. Foreign lands – India.

Shannon, David. *The amazing Christmas extravaganza* ill. by author. Blue Sky, 1995. ISBN 0-590-48090-1 Subj: Emotions – anger. Holidays – Christmas.

A bad case of stripes ill. by author. Blue Sky, 1998. ISBN 0-590-92997-6 Subj: Behavior. Character traits – individuality.

David gets in trouble ill. by author. Blue Sky, 2002. ISBN 0-439-05022-7 Subj: Bedtime. Behavior – misbehavior.

David goes to school ill. by author. Blue Sky, 1999. ISBN 0-590-48087-1 Subj: Behavior – misbehavior. School.

Duck on a bike ill. by author. Blue Sky, 2002. ISBN 0-439-05023-5 Subj: Animals. Birds – ducks. Sports – bicycling.

No, David! ill. by author. Blue Sky, 1998. ISBN 0-590-93002-8 Subj: Behavior – misbehavior. Caldecott award honor books.

The rain came down ill. by author. Blue Sky, 2000. ISBN 0-439-05021-9 Subj: Behavior. Behavior – misunderstanding. Weather – rain. Weather – rainbows.

Shannon, George. *April showers* ill. by José Aruego & Ariane Dewey. Greenwillow, 1995. ISBN 0-688-13122-0 Subj: Activities – dancing. Frogs & toads. Weather – rain.

Beanboy ill. by Peter Sís. Greenwillow, 1984. ISBN 0-688-03780-1 Subj: Cities, towns. Cumulative tales. Humorous stories.

Dancing the breeze ill. by Jacqueline Rogers. Macmillan, 1991. ISBN 0-02-782190-0 Subj: Activities – dancing. Family life – fathers. Flowers. Poetry.

Frog legs: a picture book of action verse ill. by Amit Trynan. Greenwillow, 2000. ISBN 0-688-17047-1 Subj: Frogs & toads. Poetry.

Heart to heart ill. by Steve Björkman. Houghton Mifflin, 1995. ISBN 0-395-72773-1 Subj: Animals – moles. Animals – squirrels. Friendship. Holidays – Valentine's Day.

Laughing all the way ill. by Meg McLean. Houghton Mifflin, 1992. ISBN 0-395-62473-8 Subj: Animals – bears. Behavior – bad day. Birds – ducks. Character traits – cleverness.

Lizard's home ill. by José Aruego & Ariane Dewey. Greenwillow, 1999. ISBN 0-688-16003-4 Subj: Character traits – cleverness. Homes, houses. Reptiles – lizards. Reptiles – snakes.

Lizard's song ill. by José Aruego & Ariane Dewey. Greenwillow, 1981. ISBN 0-688-84310-7 Subj: Animals – bears. Reptiles – lizards. Songs.

Oh, I love! ill. by Cheryl Harness. Bradbury, 1988. ISBN 0-02-782180-3 Subj: Cumulative tales. Folk & fairy tales. Poetry. Songs.

The Piney Woods peddler ill. by Nancy Tafuri. Greenwillow, 1982. ISBN 0-688-84304-2 Subj: Activities – trading. Folk & fairy tales.

Spring: a haiku story ill. by Malcah Zeldis. Greenwillow, 1996. ISBN 0-688-13889-6 Subj: Foreign lands – Japan. Poetry. Seasons – spring.

The surprise ill. by José Aruego & Ariane Dewey. Greenwillow, 1983. ISBN 0-688-02314-2 Subj: Animals – squirrels. Birthdays.

Tippy-toe chick, go ill. by Laura Dronzek. Greenwillow, 2003. ISBN 0-06-029824-3 Subj: Animals – dogs. Birds – chickens. Character traits – bravery.

Tomorrow's alphabet ill. by Donald Crews. Greenwillow, 1995. ISBN 0-688-13505-6 Subj: ABC books. Concepts.

Shannon, Margaret. *Gullible's troubles* ill. by author. Houghton Mifflin, 1998. ISBN 0-395-83933-5 Subj: Animals – guinea pigs. Behavior – trickery. Family life. Monsters.

The red wolf ill. by author. Houghton, 2002. ISBN 0-618-05544-4 Subj: Activities – knitting. Folk & fairy tales. Royalty – princesses.

Shannon, Mark. *The acrobat and the angel* ill. by David Shannon. Putnam, 1999. ISBN 0-399-22918-3 Subj: Angels. Folk & fairy tales. Foreign lands – France. Illness. Middle Ages.

Gawain and the Green Knight ill. by David Shannon. Putnam, 1994. ISBN 0-399-22446-7 Subj: Folk & fairy tales. Foreign lands – England. Knights. Middle Ages. Monsters.

Shannon, Terry Miller. *Tub toys* by Terry Miller Shannon & Timothy Warner; ill. by Lee Calderon. Tricycle, 2002. ISBN 1-58246-066-3 Subj: Activities – bathing. Rhyming text. Toys.

Shapes: with Dib, Dab, and Dob. DK, 1998. ISBN 0-7894-2913-6 Subj: Birds – ducks. Concepts – shape.

Shapiro, Arnold L. *Circle* ill. by Bari Weissman. Dial, 1992. ISBN 0-8037-1144-1 Subj: Concepts – shape. Format, unusual – toy & movable books.

Square ill. by Bari Weissman. Dial, 1992. ISBN 0-8037-1146-8 Subj: Activities – picnicking. Concepts – shape. Format, unusual – toy & movable books.

Triangles ill. by Bari Weissman. Dial, 1992. ISBN 0-8037-1147-6 Subj: Concepts – shape. Format, unusual – toy & movable books.

Who says that? ill. by Monica Wellington. Dutton, 1991. ISBN 0-525-44698-2 Subj: Animals. Noise, sounds. Rhyming text.

Shapiro, Jody Fickes. *Up, up, up! It's apple-picking time* ill. by Kitty Harvill. Holiday, 2003. ISBN 0-8234-1610-0 Subj: Family life – grandparents. Farms. Food. Seasons – fall.

Shapp, Charles. *Let's find out about babies* (Shapp, Martha)

Let's find out about houses (Shapp, Martha)

Let's find out what's big and what's small (Shapp, Martha)

Shapp, Martha. *Let's find out about babies* by Martha & Charles Shapp & Sylvia Shepard; ill. by Jenny Williams. Watts, 1975. ISBN 0-531-00087-7 Subj: Babies. Science.

Let's find out about houses by Martha & Charles Shapp; ill. by Tomie de Paola. Watts, 1975. ISBN 0-531-00026-5 Subj: Homes, houses.

Let's find out what's big and what's small by Martha & Charles Shapp; ill. by Carol Nicklaus. Watts, 1975. ISBN 0-531-00005-2 Subj: Concepts – size.

Sharkey, Niamh. *The gigantic turnip* (Tolstoy, Aleksey Nikolayevich)

Sharmat, Andrew. *Smedge* ill. by Chris L. Demarest. Macmillan, 1989. ISBN 0-02-782261-3 Subj: Animals – dogs.

Sharmat, Marjorie Weinman. *Attila the angry* ill. by Lillian Hoban. Holiday, 1985. ISBN 0-8234-0545-1 Subj: Animals – squirrels. Emotions – anger.

Bartholomew the bossy ill. by Normand Chartier. Macmillan, 1984. ISBN 0-02-782520-5 Subj: Animals. Behavior – growing up. Friendship.

The best Valentine in the world ill. by Lilian Obligado. Holiday, 1982. ISBN 0-8234-0440-4 Subj: Animals – foxes. Holidays – Valentine's Day.

A big fat enormous lie ill. by David McPhail. Dutton, 1978. ISBN 0-525-26510-4 Subj: Behavior – lying.

Burton and Dudley ill. by Barbara Cooney. Holiday, 1975. ISBN 0-8234-0260-6 Subj: Activities – walking. Character traits – laziness. Friendship.

Gila monsters meet you at the airport ill. by Byron Barton. Macmillan, 1980. ISBN 0-02-782450-0 Subj: Behavior – misunderstanding. Moving.

Gladys told me to meet her here ill. by Edward Frascino. HarperCollins, 1970. ISBN 0-06-025550-1 Subj: Friendship.

Go to sleep, Nicholas Joe ill. by John Himmelman. HarperCollins, 1988. ISBN 0-06-025504-8 Subj: Bedtime. Family life.

Goodnight, Andrew. Goodnight, Craig ill. by Mary Chalmers. HarperCollins, 1969. Subj: Bedtime. Family life.

Grumley the grouch ill. by Kay Chorao. Holiday, 1980. ISBN 0-8234-0410-2 Subj: Behavior – dissatisfaction.

Helga high-up ill. by David Neuhaus. Scholastic, 1988. ISBN 0-590-40692-2 Subj: Anatomy. Animals – giraffes. Character traits – being different.

Hooray for Father's Day! ill. by John Wallner. Holiday, 1987. ISBN 0-8234-0637-7 Subj: Animals – mules. Holidays – Father's Day.

Hooray for Mother's Day! ill. by John Wallner. Holiday, 1986. ISBN 0-8234-0588-5 Subj: Birds – chickens. Holidays – Mother's Day.

I don't care ill. by Lillian Hoban. Macmillan, 1977. ISBN 0-02-782290-7 Subj: Behavior – indifference. Emotions – sadness. Ethnic groups in the U.S. – African Americans. Toys – balloons.

I want mama ill. by Emily Arnold McCully. HarperCollins, 1974. ISBN 0-06-025554-4 Subj: Family life – only child. Illness.

I'm not Oscar's friend any more ill. by Tony DeLuna. Dutton, 1975. Subj: Behavior – fighting, arguing. Emotions – anger. Friendship.

I'm Santa Claus and I'm famous ill. by Marylin Hafner. Holiday, 1990. ISBN 0-8234-0826-4 Subj: Careers. Holidays – Christmas. Santa Claus.

I'm terrific ill. by Kay Chorao. Holiday, 1977. ISBN 0-8234-0282-7 Subj: Animals – bears. Character traits – conceit. Character traits – pride. Self-concept.

I'm the best ill. by Will Hillenbrand. Holiday, 1991. ISBN 0-8234-0859-0 Subj: Animals – dogs. Pets.

Lucretia the unbearable ill. by Janet Stevens. Holiday, 1981. ISBN 0-8234-0395-5 Subj: Animals – bears. Behavior – worrying. Health & fitness.

Mitchell is moving ill. by José Aruego & Ariane Dewey. Macmillan, 1978. ISBN 0-02-782410-1 Subj: Dinosaurs. Friendship. Moving.

Mooch the messy ill. by Ben Shecter. HarperCollins, 1976. ISBN 0-06-025532-3 Subj: Animals – rats. Character traits – cleanliness.

My mother never listens to me ed. by Kathleen Tucker; ill. by Lynn Munsinger. A. Whitman, 1984. ISBN 0-8075-5347-6 Subj: Books, reading. Family life – mothers. Imagination.

Nate the Great ill. by Marc Simont. Coward, 1972. ISBN 0-698-30444-6 Subj: Careers – detectives. Food. Mystery stories.

Nate the Great and the fishy prize ill. by Marc Simont. Coward, 1985. ISBN 0-698-30745-3 Subj: Animals – dogs. Mystery stories. Pets.

Nate the Great and the lost list ill. by Marc Simont. Coward, 1975. ISBN 0-698-30593-0 Subj: Careers – detectives. Food. Mystery stories.

Nate the Great and the monster mess ill. by Martha Weston in the style of Marc Simont. Delacorte, 1999. ISBN 0-385-32114-7 Subj: Activities – baking, cooking. Behavior – lost & found possessions. Careers – detectives. Food. Mystery stories.

Nate the Great and the phony clue ill. by Marc Simont. Coward, 1977. ISBN 0-698-30650-3 Subj: Careers – detectives. Food. Mystery stories.

Nate the Great goes undercover ill. by Marc Simont. Coward, 1974. ISBN 0-698-30547-7 Subj: Careers – detectives. Food. Mystery stories.

Nate the Great, San Francisco detective by Marjorie Weinman Sharmat & Mitchell Sharmat; ill. by Martha Weston in the style of Marc Simont. Delacorte, 2000. ISBN 0-385-32605-X Subj: Behavior – lost & found possessions. Careers – detectives. Mystery stories.

The pizza monster by Marjorie & Mitchell Sharmat; ill. by Denise Brunkus. Delacorte, 1989. ISBN 0-385-29722-X Subj: Friendship. Monsters. Problem solving.

Rex ill. by Emily Arnold McCully. HarperCollins, 1967. Subj: Behavior – running away.

Rollo and Juliet . . . forever! ill. by Marylin Hafner. Doubleday, 1981. ISBN 0-385-15785-1 Subj: Behavior – fighting, arguing. Emotions – anger. Friendship.

Sasha the silly ill. by Janet Stevens. Holiday, 1984. ISBN 0-8234-0503-6 Subj: Animals – dogs. Character traits – vanity.

Scarlet Monster lives here ill. by Dennis Kendrick. HarperCollins, 1979. ISBN 0-06-025527-7 Subj: Behavior. Friendship. Monsters. Moving.

Sometimes mama and papa fight ill. by Kay Chorao. HarperCollins, 1980. ISBN 0-06-025612-5 Subj: Behavior – fighting, arguing. Family life.

Sophie and Gussie ill. by Lillian Hoban. Macmillan, 1973. Subj: Animals – squirrels. Friendship.

Taking care of Melvin ill. by Victoria Chess. Holiday, 1980. ISBN 0-8234-0368-8 Subj: Animals. Friendship. Self-concept.

Thornton, the worrier ill. by Kay Chorao. Holiday, 1978. ISBN 0-8234-0328-9 Subj: Animals – rabbits. Behavior – worrying.

The 329th friend ill. by Cyndy Szekeres. Four Winds, 1992. ISBN 0-02-782259-1 Subj: Animals. Animals – raccoons. Counting, numbers. Friendship. Self-concept.

The trip: and other Sophie and Gussie stories ill. by Lillian Hoban. Macmillan, 1976. ISBN 0-02-782300-8 Subj: Animals – squirrels. Behavior – lost & found possessions. Behavior – sharing. Clothing. Friendship.

Two ghosts on a bench ill. by Nola Langner. HarperCollins, 1982. ISBN 0-06-025519-6 Subj: Ghosts.

Walter the wolf ill. by Kelly Oechsli. Holiday, 1975. ISBN 0-8234-0253-3 Subj: Animals. Animals – wolves. Violence, nonviolence.

What are we going to do about Andrew? ill. by Ray Cruz. Macmillan, 1980. ISBN 0-02-782440-3 Subj: Character traits – individuality. Family life.

Sharmat, Mitchell. *Gregory, the terrible eater* ill. by José Aruego & Ariane Dewey. Four Winds, 1980. ISBN 0-590-07586-1 Subj: Animals – goats. Food.

Nate the Great, San Francisco detective (Sharmat, Marjorie Weinman)

The pizza monster (Sharmat, Marjorie Weinman)

The seven sloppy days of Phineas Pig ill. by Sue Truesdell. Harcourt, 1983. ISBN 0-15-272936-4 Subj: Animals – pigs. Character traits – cleanliness.

Sherman is a slowpoke ill. by David Neuhaus. Scholastic, 1988. ISBN 0-590-40938-7 Subj: Animals – sloths. Character traits – individuality. School – first day.

Sharon, Mary Bruce. *Scenes from childhood* ill. by author. Dutton, 1978. ISBN 0-525-38820-6 Subj: Art. Careers – artists.

Sharp, N. L. *Today I'm going fishing with my dad* ill. by Chris L. Demarest. Boyds Mills, 1993. ISBN 1-56397-107-0 Subj: Family life – fathers. Sports – fishing.

Sharpe, Sara. *Gardener George goes to town* ill. by Susan Moxley. HarperCollins, 1982. ISBN 0-06-025620-6 Subj: Gardens, gardening.

Sharr, Christine. *Homes* ill. by author. Wonder Books, 1971. ISBN 0-448-06372-7 Subj: Family life. Homes, houses.

Sharratt, Nick. *Ahoy, Pirate Pete* ill. by author. Candlewick, 2004. ISBN 0-7636-2197-8 Subj: Format, unusual – toy & movable books. Imagination. Pirates.

The green queen ill. by author. Candlewick, 1992. ISBN 1-56402-093-2 Subj: Concepts – color. Royalty – queens.

I look like this ill. by author. Candlewick, 1992. ISBN 1-56402-016-9 Subj: Emotions. Format, unusual. Games.

Ketchup on your cornflakes? a wacky mix and match book ill. by author. Scholastic, 1997. ISBN 0-590-93106-7 Subj: Food. Format, unusual – toy & movable books.

Look what I found! ill. by author. Candlewick, 1992. ISBN 1-56402-017-7 Subj: Format, unusual. Sea & seashore.

Machine poems (Bennett, Jill)

Monday run-day ill. by author. Candlewick, 1992. ISBN 1-56402-092-4 Subj: Animals – dogs. Days of the week, months of the year. Rhyming text.

Mouse moves house ill. by author. Candlewick, 2000. ISBN 0-7636-0959-5 Subj: Animals – mice. Counting, numbers.

Mrs. Pirate ill. by author. Candlewick, 1994. ISBN 1-56402-249-8 Subj: Activities – traveling. Pirates. Rhyming text. Sea & seashore.

Once upon a time . . . ill. by author. Candlewick, 2002. ISBN 0-7636-1695-8 Subj: Format, unusual – toy & movable books. Imagination. Royalty – princesses.

Pants (Andreae, Giles)

Rocket countdown ill. by author. Candlewick, 1995. ISBN 1-56402-622-1 Subj: Counting, numbers. Format, unusual – toy & movable books. Space & space ships.

Shark in the park ill. by author. Candlewick, 2002. ISBN 0-385-75008-0 Subj: Animals. Birds. Fish – sharks. Format, unusual – toy & movable books. Parks. Rhyming text.

Snazzy aunties ill. by author. Candlewick, 1994. ISBN 1-56402-214-5 Subj: Family life – aunts, uncles. Rhyming text.

The time it took Tom by Nick Sharratt & Stephen Tucker; ill. by Nick Sharratt. Little Tiger, 2000. ISBN 1-888444-63-0 Subj: Activities – painting. Behavior – misbehavior. Time.

Shavick, Andrea. *You'll grow soon, Alex* ill. by Russell Ayto. Walker, 2000. ISBN 0-8027-8736-3 Subj: Behavior – growing up.

Shaw, Alison. *Until I saw the sea* sel. & ill. by Alison Shaw. Holt, 1995. ISBN 0-8050-2755-6 Subj: Poetry. Sea & seashore.

Shaw, Charles Green. *The blue guess book* ill. by author. Addison-Wesley, 1942. Subj: Games.

The guess book ill. by author. Addison-Wesley, 1941. Subj: Games.

It looked like spilt milk ill. by author. HarperCollins, 1947. ISBN 0-06-025565-X Subj: Concepts – shape. Games. Imagination. Participation. Sky. Weather – clouds.

Shaw, Evelyn S. *Alligator* ill. by Frances Zweifel. HarperCollins, 1972. ISBN 0-06-025557-9 Subj: Reptiles – alligators, crocodiles. Science.

Fish out of school ill. by Ralph Carpentier. HarperCollins, 1970. Subj: Fish. Science. Sea & seashore.

Nest of wood ducks ill. by Cherryl Pape. HarperCollins, 1976. ISBN 0-06-025592-7 Subj: Birds – ducks. Science.

Octopus ill. by Ralph Carpentier. HarperCollins, 1971. ISBN 0-06-025558-7 Subj: Octopuses. Science. Sea & seashore.

Sea otters ill. by Cherryl Pape. HarperCollins, 1980. ISBN 0-06-025614-1 Subj: Animals – otters. Science.

Shaw, Mary. *Brady Brady and the big mistake* ill. by Chuck Temple. Fitzhenry & Whiteside, 2002. ISBN 0-7737-6304-X Subj: Behavior – lost & found possessions. Behavior – misbehavior. Sports – hockey.

Brady Brady and the great rink ill. by Chuck Temple. Stoddart, 2002. ISBN 0-7737-6224-8 Subj: Activities – making things. Activities – working. Sports – hockey.

Brady Brady and the runaway goalie ill. by Chuck Temple. Stoddart, 2001. ISBN 0-7737-6225-6 Subj: Sports – hockey.

Brady Brady and the Twirlin' Torpedo goalie ill. by Chuck Temple. Stoddart, 2002. Subj: Friendship. Gender roles. Sports – hockey.

Shaw, Nancy (Nancy E.). *Raccoon tune* ill. by Howard Fine. Holt, 2003. ISBN 0-8050-6544-X Subj: Animals – raccoons. Noise, sounds. Rhyming text.

Sheep in a jeep ill. by Margot Apple. Houghton Mifflin, 1986. ISBN 0-395-41105-X Subj: Animals – sheep. Rhyming text.

Sheep in a shop ill. by Margot Apple. Houghton Mifflin, 1991. ISBN 0-395-53681-2 Subj: Animals – sheep. Rhyming text. Shopping.

Sheep on a ship ill. by Margot Apple. Houghton Mifflin, 1989. ISBN 0-395-48160-0 Subj: Animals – sheep. Boats, ships. Rhyming text.

Sheep out to eat ill. by Margot Apple. Houghton Mifflin, 1992. ISBN 0-395-61128-8 Subj: Animals – sheep. Food. Rhyming text.

Sheep take a hike ill. by Margot Apple. Houghton Mifflin, 1994. ISBN 0-395-68394-7 Subj: Animals – sheep. Rhyming text. Sports – hiking.

Sheep trick or treat ill. by Margot Apple. Houghton Mifflin, 1997. ISBN 0-395-84168-2 Subj: Animals – sheep. Holidays – Halloween. Rhyming text.

Shaw, Richard. *The kitten in the pumpkin patch* ill. by Jacqueline Kahane. Warne, 1973. ISBN 0-72-326099-0 Subj: Animals – cats. Holidays – Halloween. Witches.

Shay, Arthur. *What happens when you go to the hospital* ill. by author. Reilly & Lee, 1969. Subj: Hospitals. Illness.

Shea, Kitty. *Out and about at the newspaper* ill. by Zachary Trover. Picture Window, 2006. ISBN 1-4048-1149-4 Subj: Careers – journalists.

Out and about at the post office ill. by Becky Shipe. Picture Window, 2004. ISBN 1-4048-0294-0 Subj: Careers – postal workers. Post office. School – field trips.

Out and about at the public library ill. by Zachary Trover. Picture Window, 2005. ISBN 1-4048-1150-8 Subj: Careers – librarians. Libraries.

Out and about at the science center ill. by Becky Shipe. Picture Window, 2004. ISBN 1-4048-0297-5 Subj: Museums. School – field trips. Science.

Out and about at the supermarket ill. by Becky Shipe. Picture Window, 2004. ISBN 1-4048-0295-9 Subj: Careers – storekeepers. Food. School – field trips. Stores.

Out and about at the vet clinic ill. by Becky Shipe. Picture Window, 2004. ISBN 1-4048-0296-7 Subj: Animals. Careers – veterinarians. Pets. School – field trips.

Shea, Pegi Deitz. *Bungalow fungalow* ill. by Elizabeth Sayles. Houghton Mifflin, 1991. ISBN 0-395-55387-3 Subj: Activities – vacationing. Poetry. Sea & seashore.

I see me! ill. by Lucia Washburn. HarperFestival, 2000. ISBN 0-694-01278-5 Subj: Babies. Family life. Format, unusual – board books. Rhyming text.

New moon ill. by Cathryn Falwell. Boyds Mills, 1996. ISBN 1-56397-410-X Subj: Ethnic groups in the U.S. – Hispanic Americans. Family life – brothers & sisters. Moon.

The whispering cloth ill. by Anita Riggio; stitched by You Yang. Caroline House, 1995. ISBN 1-56397-134-8 Subj: Activities – sewing. Ethnic groups in the U.S. – Hmong Americans. Family life – grandmothers. Foreign lands – Thailand. War.

Shearer, Marilyn J. *The crown of fools: based on: The tortoise and the hare* ill. by author. Lauren Ashley & Joshua Storybooks, 1993. ISBN 1-879567-19-9 Subj: Character traits – perseverance. Folk & fairy tales. Reptiles – turtles, tortoises. Sports – racing.

I like to play ill. by Tom Roberts. Lauren Ashley & Joshua Storybooks, 1993. ISBN 0-685-30097-8 Subj: Activities – playing.

The Nubian princess ill. by Larry Walker. Lauren Ashley & Joshua Storybooks, 1993. ISBN 0-685-30091-9 Subj: Royalty – princesses.

The original three little pigs re-told (The three little pigs)

Sheather, Allan. *Neptune's nursery* (Toft, Kim Michelle)

One less fish (Toft, Kim Michelle)

Shecter, Ben. *The big stew* ill. by author. HarperCollins, 1991. ISBN 0-06-025610-9 Subj: Activities – baking, cooking. Food. Witches.

Conrad's castle ill. by author. HarperCollins, 1967. Subj: Imagination.

The discontented mother ill. by author. Harcourt, 1980. ISBN 0-15-223574-4 Subj: Behavior – wishing.

Emily, girl witch of New York ill. by author. Dial, 1963. Subj: Cities, towns. Homes, houses. Magic. Progress. Witches.

Grandma remembers ill. by author. HarperCollins, 1989. ISBN 0-06-025618-4 Subj: Family life – grandmothers. Memories, memory. Moving.

Hester the jester ill. by author. HarperCollins, 1977. ISBN 0-06-025600-1 Subj: Character traits – ambition. Clowns, jesters.

If I had a ship ill. by author. Doubleday, 1970. Subj: Boats, ships. Character traits – generosity. Emotions – love. Imagination.

Partouche plants a seed ill. by author. HarperCollins, 1966. Subj: Animals – pigs. Foreign lands – France. Gardens, gardening. Plants. Seeds.

The stocking child ill. by author. HarperCollins, 1976. ISBN 0-06-025594-3 Subj: Senses – sight. Toys – dolls.

Sheehan, Angela. *The beaver* ill. by Graham Allen. Watts, 1979. ISBN 0-531-09151-1 Subj: Animals – beavers. Science.

The duck ill. by Maurice Pledger & Bernard Robinson. Warwick Pr., 1979. ISBN 0-531-09074-4 Subj: Birds – ducks. Science.

The otter ill. by Bernard Robinson. Warwick Pr., 1979. ISBN 0-531-09109-0 Subj: Animals – otters. Science.

The penguin ill. by Trevor Boyer. Watts, 1979. ISBN 0-531-09153-8 Subj: Birds – penguins. Science.

Sheehan, Patty. *Shadow and the ready time* ill. by Itoko Maeno. Advocacy Pr., 1994. ISBN 0-911655-13-1 Subj: Animals – wolves. Behavior – growing up.

Shefelman, Janice Jordan. *A peddler's dream* ill. by Tom Shefelman. Houghton Mifflin, 1992. ISBN 0-395-60904-6 Subj: Careers – peddlers. Careers – storekeepers. Character traits – ambition. Ethnic groups in the U.S. – Lebanese Americans.

Victoria House ill. by Tom Shefelman. Harcourt, 1988. ISBN 0-15-200630-3 Subj: Homes, houses. Moving.

Sheffield, Margaret. *Before you were born* ill. by Sheila Bewley. Knopf, 1984. ISBN 0-394-53734-3 Subj: Babies. Birth. Science.

Where do babies come from? ill. by Sheila Bewley. Knopf, 1973. ISBN 0-394-48482-7 Subj: Babies. Birth. Science.

Shelby, Anne. *Homeplace* ill. by Wendy Anderson Halperin. Orchard, 1995. ISBN 0-531-08732-8 Subj: Family life. Family life – grandmothers.

Potluck ill. by Irene Trivas. Watts, 1991. ISBN 0-531-08519-8 Subj: ABC books. Ethnic groups in the U.S. Food.

The someday house ill. by Rosanne Litzinger. Orchard, 1996. ISBN 0-531-08860-X Subj: Homes, houses. Imagination.

We keep a store ill. by John Ward. Watts, 1990. ISBN 0-531-08456-6 Subj: Careers – storekeepers. Ethnic groups in the U.S. – African Americans. Family life. Stores.

Sheldon, Aure. *Of cobblers and kings* ill. by Don Leake. Parents' Magazine Pr., 1978. ISBN 0-8193-0832-3 Subj: Careers – shoemakers. Character traits – cleverness.

Sheldon, Dyan. *Love, your bear, Pete* ill. by Tania Hurt-Newton. Candlewick, 1994. ISBN 1-56402-332-X Subj: Activities – traveling. Family life – mothers. Foreign lands. Toys – bears.

Under the moon ill. by Gary Blythe. Dial, 1994. ISBN 0-8037-1670-2 Subj: Dreams. Indians of North America – Sioux.

Unicorn dreams ill. by Neil Reed. Dial, 1997. ISBN 0-8037-2284-2 Subj: Imagination. Mythical creatures – unicorns. School.

The whales' song ill. by Gary Blythe. Dial, 1991. ISBN 0-8037-0972-2 Subj: Animals – whales. Character traits – kindness to animals. Family life – grandmothers.

Shepard, Aaron. *The baker's dozen* ill. by Wendy Edelson. Atheneum, 1995. ISBN 0-689-80298-6 Subj: Careers – bakers. Character traits – generosity. Folk & fairy tales.

The crystal heart: a Vietnamese legend ill. by Joseph Daniel Fiedler. Atheneum, 1998. ISBN 0-689-81551-4 Subj: Folk & fairy tales. Foreign lands – Vietnam.

Forty fortunes: a tale of Iran ill. by Alisher Dianov. Clarion, 1999. ISBN 0-395-81133-3 Subj: Careers – fortune tellers. Folk & fairy tales. Foreign lands – Iran.

The gifts of Wali Dad ill. by Daniel San Souci. Atheneum, 1995. ISBN 0-684-19445-7 Subj: Behavior – wishing. Folk & fairy tales. Foreign lands – India. Foreign lands – Pakistan. Gifts.

Master man ill. by David Wisniewski. Lothrop, 2000. ISBN 0-688-13784-9 Subj: Folk & fairy tales – pourquoi tales. Foreign lands – Nigeria. Tall tales. Weather – lightning, thunder.

The princess mouse ill. by Leonid Gore. Atheneum, 2003. ISBN 0-689-82912-4 Subj: Animals – mice. Folk & fairy tales. Foreign lands – Finland. Royalty – princesses. Songs.

The sea king's daughter ill. by Gennady Spirin. Atheneum, 1997. ISBN 0-689-80759-7 Subj: Careers – musicians. Folk & fairy tales. Foreign lands – Russia. Mythical creatures. Sea & seashore.

Shepard, E. H. (Ernest Howard). *Winnie-the-Pooh's ABC* ill. by author; inspired by A. A. Milne. Dutton, 1995. ISBN 0-525-45365-2 Subj: ABC books. Toys.

Shepard, Steve. *Elvis Hornbill, international business bird* ill. by author. Holt, 1991. ISBN 0-8050-1617-1 Subj: Birds – hornbills. Careers. Family life – fathers. Foreign lands – Africa.

Shepard, Sylvia. *Let's find out about babies* (Shapp, Martha)

Sheppard, Jeff. *The right number of elephants* ill. by Felicia Bond. HarperCollins, 1990. ISBN 0-06-025616-8 Subj: Animals – elephants. Counting, numbers.

Splash, splash ill. by Dennis Panek. Macmillan, 1994. ISBN 0-02-782455-1 Subj: Animals. Noise, sounds. Rhyming text. Water.

Shepperson, Rob. *The sandman* ill. by author. Farrar, 1990. ISBN 0-374-36405-2 Subj: Bedtime. Dreams. Mythical creatures – sandman. Sleep.

Sherman, Eileen Bluestone. *The odd potato: a Chanukah story* ill. by Katherine Janus Kahn. Kar-Ben Copies, 1984. ISBN 0-930494-36-9 Subj: Family life. Holidays – Hanukkah. Jewish culture.

Sherman, Elizabeth. *see* Friskey, Margaret (Margaret Richards)

Sherman, Ivan. *I am a giant* ill. by author. Harcourt, 1975. ISBN 0-15-237983-5 Subj: Giants. Imagination.

I do not like it when my friend comes to visit ill. by author. Harcourt, 1973. ISBN 0-15-238000-0 Subj: Behavior – sharing. Etiquette. Friendship.

Walking talking words ill. by author. Harcourt, 1980. ISBN 0-05-294511-3 Subj: Language. Poetry.

Sherman, Joanne. *Because it's my body* ill. by John Steven Gurney. S.A.F.E. for Children, 2002. ISBN 0-9711735-0-8 Subj: Child abuse. Communication. Senses – touch.

Sherman, Josepha. *Vassilisa the wise: a tale of medieval Russia* ill. by Daniel San Souci. Harcourt, 1988. ISBN 0-15-293240-2 Subj: Character traits – wisdom. Folk & fairy tales. Foreign lands – Russia. Royalty – princes.

Sherman, Nancy. *Gwendolyn and the weathercock* ill. by Edward Sorel. Golden Pr., 1961. Subj: Birds – chickens. Farms. Rhyming text. Weather – rain.

Gwendolyn the miracle hen ill. by Edward Sorel. Western, 1961. Subj: Birds – chickens. Dragons. Rhyming text.

Sherman, Pat. *The sun's daughter* ill. by Gregory Christie. Clarion, 2005. ISBN 0-618-32430-5 Subj: Folk & fairy tales – pourquoi tales. Indians of North America – Iroquois. Sun.

Sherrow, Victoria. *There goes the ghost* ill. by Megan Lloyd. Harper-Collins, 1985. ISBN 0-06-025510-2 Subj: Behavior – misbehavior. Ghosts. Homes, houses. Moving.

Wilbur waits ill. by James Watts. HarperCollins, 1990. ISBN 0-06-025484-X Subj: Birthdays. Friendship. Toys. Weather.

Shi, Zhang Xiu. *Monkey and the white bone demon* trans. by Ye Ping Kuei; rev. by Jill Morris; ill. by Lin Zheng & others. Viking, 1984. Adapt. from the 16th century novel, The pilgrimage to the west, by Wu Cheng En. ISBN 0-670-48574-8 Subj: Animals – monkeys. Folk & fairy tales. Foreign lands – China.

Shibano, Tamizo. *The old man who made the trees bloom* by Hanasaka Jijii; retold by Tamizo Shibano; trans. by D. T. Ooka; ill. by Bunshu Iguchi. Heian Intl., 1985. ISBN 0-89346-247-0 Subj: Animals – dogs. Behavior – greed. Character traits – kindness. Character traits – meanness.

Shiefman, Vicky. *Sunday potatoes, Monday potatoes* ill. by Louise August. S&S, 1994. ISBN 0-671-86596-X Subj: Activities – baking, cooking. Days of the week, months of the year. Family life. Food. Poverty.

Shields, Carol Diggory. *The bugliest bug* ill. by Scott Nash. Candlewick, 2002. ISBN 0-7636-0784-3 Subj: Contests. Insects. Poetry. Spiders.

Colors ill. by Svjetlan Junakoviâc. Handprint, 2000. ISBN 1-929766-04-1 Subj: Animals. Concepts – color. Format, unusual – toy & movable books. Rhyming text. Riddles & jokes.

Day by day a week goes round ill. by True Kelley. Dutton, 1998. ISBN 0-525-45457-8 Subj: Activities. Days of the week, months of the year. Rhyming text.

Homes ill. by Svjetlan Junakoviâc. Handprint, 2001. ISBN 1-929766-27-0 Subj: Animals. Ecology. Format, unusual – toy & movable books. Homes, houses. Poetry. Riddles & jokes.

I am really a princess ill. by Paul Meisel. Dutton, 1993. ISBN 0-525-45138-2 Subj: Behavior – imitation. Character traits – vanity. Family life. Imagination. Royalty – princesses. Self-concept.

I wish my brother was a dog ill. by Paul Meisel. Dutton, 1997. ISBN 0-525-45464-0 Subj: Animals – dogs. Babies. Behavior – wishing. Emotions – anger. Family life – brothers. Family life – new sibling. Sibling rivalry.

Lucky pennies and hot chocolate ill. by Hiroe Nakata. Dutton, 2000. ISBN 0-525-46450-6 Subj: Family life – grandfathers.

Lunch money and other poems about school ill. by Paul Meisel. Dutton, 1995. ISBN 0-525-45345-8 Subj: Poetry. School.

Martian rock ill. by Scott Nash. Candlewick, 2000. ISBN 0-7636-0598-0 Subj: Aliens. Birds – penguins. Plants. Rhyming text. Space & space ships.

Month by month a year goes round ill. by True Kelley. Dutton, 1998. ISBN 0-525-45458-6 Subj: Days of the week, months of the year. Rhyming text. Seasons.

On the go ill. by Svjetlan Junakoviâc. Handprint, 2001. ISBN 1-929766-14-9 Subj: Animals. Format, unusual – toy & movable books. Poetry. Riddles & jokes.

Patterns ill. by Svjetlan Junakoviâc. Handprint, 2001. ISBN 1-929766-15-7 Subj: Animals. Format, unusual – toy & movable books. Poetry. Riddles & jokes.

Saturday night at the dinosaur stomp ill. by Scott Nash. Candlewick, 1997. ISBN 1-56402-693-0 Subj: Activities – dancing. Dinosaurs. Prehistory. Rhyming text.

Shimin, Symeon. *I wish there were two of me* ill. by author. Warne, 1976. ISBN 0-723-26128-8 Subj: Behavior – wishing. Dreams. Imagination.

A special birthday ill. by author. McGraw-Hill, 1976. ISBN 0-07-056902-9 Subj: Birthdays. Wordless.

Shine, Deborah. *The little engine that could pudgy word book* ill. by Christina Ong. Putnam, 1988. ISBN 0-448-19054-0 Subj: Character traits – perseverance. Format, unusual – board books. Trains.

Shipton, Jonathan. *Busy! Busy! Busy!* ill. by Michael Foreman. Delacorte, 1991. ISBN 0-385-30306-8 Subj: Activities – working. Emotions – love. Family life – mothers.

How to be a happy hippo ill. by Sally Percy. Little Tiger, 1999. ISBN 1-888444-61-4 Subj: Animals – hippopotamuses. Family life – fathers.

In the night ill. by Gill Scriven. Little, 1992. ISBN 0-316-78586-5 Subj: Bedtime. Night.

No biting, horrible crocodile! ill. by Claudio Muñoz. Western, 1995. ISBN 0-307-17521-9 Subj: Behavior – bullying. Reptiles – alligators, crocodiles. School.

What if? ill. by Barbara Nascimbeni. Dial, 1999. ISBN 0-8037-2390-3 Subj: Imagination. Self-concept.

Shire, Ellen. *The mystery at number seven, Rue Petite* ill. by author. Random House, 1978. ISBN 0-394-93664-7 Subj: Character traits – bravery. Crime. Mystery stories.

Shirotani, Hideo. *Let's eat = Vamos a comer* ill. by author. Little Simon, 1992. ISBN 0-671-76927-8 Subj: Food. Foreign languages. Format, unusual – board books.

Let's play ill. by author. Little & Woods, 1991. ISBN 1-5618-0044-9 Subj: Activities – playing. Format, unusual – board books.

Let's take a walk = Vamos a caminar ill. by author. Little Simon, 1992. ISBN 0-671-76929-4 Subj: Activities – walking. Foreign languages. Format, unusual – board books.

Opposites ill. by author. Little & Woods, 1991. ISBN 1-5618-0041-4 Subj: Concepts – opposites.

Sounds ill. by author. Little & Woods, 1991. ISBN 1-5618-0042-2 Subj: Noise, sounds. Senses – hearing.

What color? = Qué color? ill. by author. Little Simon, 1992. ISBN 0-671-76930-8 Subj: Concepts – color. Foreign languages. Format, unusual – board books.

Shles, Larry. *Moths and mothers, feathers and fathers: a story about a tiny owl named Squib* ill. by author. Houghton Mifflin, 1984. ISBN 0-395-36695-X Subj: Birds – owls. Character traits – being different.

Shohet, Marti. *Market days* concept & ill. by Marti Shohet; text by Madhur Jaffrey. BridgeWater, 1995. ISBN 0-8167-3504-2 Subj: Activities – baking, cooking. Foreign lands. Shopping.

Shollar, Leah. *A thread of kindness* ill. by Shoshana Mekibel. Hachai, 2000. ISBN 1-929628-01-3 Subj: Character traits – generosity. Jewish culture. Religion.

Shopping ill. by Roser Capdevila. Firefly, 1986. ISBN 0-920303-43-9 Subj: Format, unusual – toy & movable books. Shopping. Wordless.

Short, Mayo. *Andy and the wild ducks* ill. by Paul M. Souza. Melmont, 1959. Subj: Animals. Ecology. Farms.

Shortall, Leonard W. *Andy, the dog walker* ill. by author. Morrow, 1968. Subj: Animals – dogs. Behavior – lost.

One way: a trip with traffic signs ill. by author. Prentice-Hall, 1975. ISBN 0-13-636142-0 Subj: Holidays – Fourth of July. Rhyming text. Safety. Traffic, traffic signs.

Tod on the tugboat ill. by author. Morrow, 1971. Subj: Boats, ships.

Tony's first dive ill. by author. Morrow, 1972. Subj: Emotions – fear. Sports – swimming.

Shostak, Myra. *Rainbow candles: a Chanukah counting book* ill. by Katherine Janus Kahn. Kar-Ben Copies, 1986. ISBN 0-930494-59-8 Subj: Counting, numbers. Format, unusual – board books. Holidays – Hanukkah. Jewish culture.

Shoten, Fukuinkan. *Elephant blue* (Nakano, Hirotaka)

Shott, Steve (Stephen). *Bathtime* photos by author. Dutton, 1991. ISBN 0-525-44754-7 Subj: Activities – bathing. Format, unusual – board books.

Look at me photos by author. Dutton, 1991. ISBN 0-525-44755-5 Subj: Anatomy. Format, unusual – board books. Self-concept.

Mealtime photos by author. Dutton, 1991. ISBN 0-525-44756-3 Subj: Food. Format, unusual – board books.

Playtime photos by author. Dutton, 1991. ISBN 0-525-44757-1 Subj: Activities – playing. Format, unusual – board books.

Shotwell, Nathaniel. *see* Dodge, Mary Mapes

Showalter, Jean B. *The donkey ride* ill. by Tomi Ungerer. Doubleday, 1967. Subj: Animals – donkeys. Folk & fairy tales. Humorous stories.

Showers, Kay Sperry. *Before you were a baby* (Showers, Paul)

Showers, Paul. *Before you were a baby* by Paul Showers & Kay Sperry Showers; ill. by Ingrid Fetz. Crowell, 1968. ISBN 0-690-12882-7 Subj: Babies. Birth. Science.

Columbus Day ill. by Ed Emberley. Crowell, 1965. ISBN 0-690-19982-1 Subj: Holidays – Columbus Day. U.S. history.

A drop of blood ill. by Don Madden. Rev. ed. HarperCollins, 1989. ISBN 0-690-04717-7 Subj: Anatomy. Science.

Ears are for hearing ill. by Holly Keller. HarperCollins, 1990. ISBN 0-690-04720-7 Subj: Anatomy – ears. Science. Senses – hearing.

Hear your heart ill. by Holly Keller. HarperCollins, 2001. ISBN 0-06-025411-4 Subj: Anatomy. Noise, sounds. Science.

How you talk ill. by Megan Lloyd. Rev. ed. HarperCollins, 1992. ISBN 0-06-022768-0 Subj: Anatomy. Communication. Language.

The listening walk ill. by Aliki. Rev. ed. HarperCollins, 1991. ISBN 0-06-021638-7 Subj: Activities – walking. Noise, sounds. Senses – hearing.

Look at your eyes ill. by True Kelley. Rev. ed. HarperCollins, 1992. ISBN 0-06-020188-6 Subj: Anatomy – eyes. Ethnic groups in the U.S. – African Americans. Science. Senses – sight.

No measles, no mumps for me ill. by Harriett Barton. Crowell, 1980. ISBN 0-690-04018-0 Subj: Illness – mumps. Science.

Sleep is for everyone ill. by Wendy Watson. HarperCollins, 1997. ISBN 0-06-025393-2 Subj: Animals. Bedtime. Dreams. Health & fitness. Science. Sleep.

Where does the garbage go? ill. by Randy Chewning. Rev. ed. HarperCollins, 1994. ISBN 0-06-021057-5 Subj: Careers – sanitation workers. Ecology. Science.

You can't make a move without your muscles ill. by Harriett Barton. Crowell, 1982. ISBN 0-690-04185-3 Subj: Anatomy. Science.

Your skin and mine ill. by Kathleen Kuchera. Rev. ed. HarperCollins, 1991. ISBN 0-06-022523-8 Subj: Anatomy – skin. Ethnic groups in the U.S. – African Americans.

Shriver, Maria. *What's wrong with Timmy?* ill. by Sandra Speidel. Little, 2001. ISBN 0-316-23337-4 Subj: Friendship. Handicaps – mental handicaps.

Shub, Elizabeth. *The Bremen town musicians* (Grimm, Jacob)

Clever Kate (Grimm, Jacob)

Dear Sarah (Borchers, Elisabeth)

Dragon Franz text by Josef Guggenmos; adapt. by Elizabeth Shub; ill. by Ursula Konopka. Greenwillow, 1976. Orig. pub. in German under the title Franz, der Drache. ISBN 0-688-84077-9 Subj: Character traits – being different. Concepts – color. Dragons.

The emperor's plum tree (Nikly, Michelle)

The fisherman and his wife (Grimm, Jacob)

Jorinda and Joringel (Grimm, Jacob)

Seeing is believing ill. by Rachel Isadora. Greenwillow, 1979. ISBN 0-688-84211-9 Subj: Folk & fairy tales. Mythical creatures – leprechauns.

Sir Ribbeck of Ribbeck of Havelland (Fontane, Theodor)

The twelve dancing princesses (Grimm, Jacob)

Why Noah chose the dove (Singer, Isaac Bashevis)

Shulevitz, Uri. *Dawn* ill. by author. Farrar, 1974. ISBN 0-374-31707-0 Subj: Camps, camping. Family life – grandfathers. Morning. Sun.

The magician adapt. from the Yiddish of Isaac Loeb Peretz by Uri Shulevitz; ill. by adapt. Macmillan, 1985, c1973. ISBN 0-02-782770-4 Subj: Holidays – Passover. Jewish culture. Magic. Religion.

One Monday morning ill. by author. Aladdin, 1986, c1967. ISBN 0-684-13195-1 Subj: Cities, towns. Days of the week, months of the year. Imagination. Royalty.

Rain rain rivers ill. by author. Farrar, 1969. ISBN 0-374-36171-1 Subj: Rhyming text. Weather – rain.

Snow ill. by author. Farrar, 1998. ISBN 0-374-37092-3 Subj: Caldecott award honor books. Cities, towns. Nature. Weather – snow.

The treasure ill. by author. Farrar, 1978. ISBN 0-374-37740-5 Subj: Caldecott award honor books. Dreams. Folk & fairy tales.

What is a wise bird like you doing in a silly tale like this? ill. by author. Farrar, 2000. ISBN 0-3743-8300-6 Subj: Birds. Character traits – freedom. Royalty – emperors. Tall tales.

Shulman, Milton. *Prep, the little pigeon of Trafalgar Square* ill. by Dale Maxey. Random House, 1964. Subj: Birds – pigeons. Foreign lands – England.

Shute, Linda. *Clever Tom and the leprechaun* ill. by author. Lothrop, 1988. ISBN 0-688-07489-8 Subj: Folk & fairy tales. Mythical creatures – leprechauns.

Halloween party ill. by author. Lothrop, 1994. ISBN 0-688-11715-5 Subj: Holidays – Halloween. Parties. Rhyming text. Witches.

Momotaro, the peach boy ill. by author. Lothrop, 1986. ISBN 0-688-05864-7 Subj: Behavior – fighting, arguing. Character traits – bravery. Devil. Folk & fairy tales. Foreign lands – Japan.

Shuter, Jane. *Henry Ford* ill. with photos. Heinemann, 2001. ISBN 1-57572-229-1 Subj: Automobiles. Careers – engineers.

Shuttlesworth, Dorothy Edwards. *ABC of buses* ill. by Leonard W. Shortall. Doubleday, 1965. Subj: ABC books. Buses.

Shyer, Marlene Fanta. *Here I am, an only child* ill. by Donald Carrick. Scribners, 1985. ISBN 0-684-18296-3 Subj: Family life – only child.

Stepdog ill. by Judith Schermer. Scribners, 1983. ISBN 0-684-17998-9 Subj: Animals – dogs. Emotions – envy, jealousy. Family life.

Sibbick, John. *Creatures of long ago: dinosaurs* ill. by John Sibbick; written by Peggy D. Winston. National Geographic, 1988. ISBN 0-87044-723-8 Subj: Dinosaurs. Format, unusual – toy & movable books.

Siberell, Anne. *A journey to paradise* ill. by author. Holt, 1990. ISBN 0-8050-1212-5 Subj: Folk & fairy tales. Foreign lands – India.

Whale in the sky ill. by author. Dutton, 1982. ISBN 0-525-44021-6 Subj: Animals – whales. Folk & fairy tales. Indians of North America.

Sicotte, Virginia. *A riot of quiet* ill. by Edward Ardizzone. Holt, 1969. ISBN 0-03-061289-5 Subj: Imagination. Noise, sounds. Poetry.

Siddals, Mary McKenna. *I'll play with you* ill. by David Wisniewski. Clarion, 2000. ISBN 0-395-90373-4 Subj: Activities – playing. Nature.

Millions of snowflakes ill. by Elizabeth Sayles. Clarion, 1998. ISBN 0-395-71531-8 Subj: Rhyming text. Weather – snow.

Morning song ill. by Elizabeth Sayles. Holt, 2001. ISBN 0-8050-6369-2 Subj: Morning.

Tell me a season ill. by Petra Mathers. Clarion, 1997. ISBN 0-395-71021-9 Subj: Concepts – color. Rhyming text. Seasons.

Siddiqui, Ashraf. *Bhombal Dass, the uncle of lion: a tale from Pakistan* ill. by Thomas Arthur Hamil. Macmillan, 1959. Subj: Animals – goats. Animals – lions. Character traits – cleverness. Folk & fairy tales. Foreign lands – Pakistan.

Sidman, Joyce. *Just us two* ill. by Susan Swan. Millbrook, 2000. ISBN 0-7613-1563-2 Subj: Animals. Animals – babies. Family life – fathers.

Son of the water boatman ill. by Beckie Prange. Houghton, 2005. ISBN 0-618-13547-2 Subj: Animals. Insects. Lakes, ponds. Plants. Poetry.

Siebert, Diane. *Cave* ill. by Wayne McLoughlin. HarperCollins, 2000. ISBN 0-688-16448-X Subj: Caves. Rhyming text.

Heartland ill. by Wendell Minor. HarperCollins, 1989. ISBN 0-690-04732-0 Subj: Poetry. U.S. history.

Mojave ill. by Wendell Minor. HarperCollins, 1988. ISBN 0-690-04569-7 Subj: Desert. Poetry.

Plane song ill. by Vincent Nasta. HarperCollins, 1993. ISBN 0-06-021467-8 Subj: Airplanes, airports. Rhyming text.

Sierra ill. by Wendell Minor. HarperCollins, 1991. ISBN 0-06-021640-9 Subj: Nature. Poetry.

Train song ill. by Mike Wimmer. HarperCollins, 1990. ISBN 0-690-04728-2 Subj: Rhyming text. Trains.

Truck song ill. by Byron Barton. Crowell, 1984. ISBN 0-690-04411-9 Subj: Rhyming text. Trucks.

Siegelson, Kim L. *In the time of the drums* ill. by Brian Pinkney. Hyperion, 1999. ISBN 0-7868-2386-0 Subj: Character traits – freedom. Ethnic groups in the U.S. – African Americans. Slavery.

Siekkinen, Raija. *Mister King* trans. from Finnish by Tim Steffa; ill. by Hannu Taina. Carolrhoda, 1987. ISBN 0-87614-315-X Subj: Animals – cats. Emotions – loneliness. Royalty – kings.

Siepmann, Jane. *The lion on Scott Street* ill. by Clement Hurd. Walck, 1952. Subj: Animals – lions. Imagination.

Sierra, Judy. *The beautiful butterfly* ill. by Victoria Chess. Clarion, 2000. ISBN 0-395-90015-8 Subj: Animals – mice. Folk & fairy tales. Foreign lands – Spain. Insects – butterflies, caterpillars. Royalty – kings. Weddings.

Counting crocodiles ill. by Will Hillenbrand. Harcourt, 1997. ISBN 0-15-200192-1 Subj: Animals – monkeys. Counting, numbers. Foreign lands – Asia. Reptiles – alligators, crocodiles.

The gift of the crocodile: a Cinderella story ill. by Reynold Ruffins. S&S, 2000. ISBN 0-689-82188-3 Subj: Fairies. Family life – step-families. Folk & fairy tales. Foreign lands – Indonesia. Reptiles – alligators, crocodiles.

The house that Drac built ill. by Will Hillenbrand. Harcourt, 1995. ISBN 0-15-200015-1 Subj: Cumulative tales. Holidays – Halloween. Homes, houses. Monsters. Rhyming text.

Monster Goose ill. by Jack E. Davis. Harcourt, 2001. ISBN 0-15-202034-9 Subj: Monsters. Nursery rhymes.

Preschool to the rescue ill. by Will Hillenbrand. Harcourt, 2001. ISBN 0-15-202035-7 Subj: Animals. Character traits – helpfulness. School – nursery.

Tasty baby belly buttons ill. by Meilo So. Knopf, 1998. ISBN 0-679-99369-X Subj: Folk & fairy tales. Foreign lands – Japan. Gender roles. Mythical creatures – ogres.

There's a zoo in room 22 ill. by Barney Saltzberg. Harcourt, 2000. ISBN 0-15-202033-0 Subj: ABC books. Animals. Pets. Rhyming text. School.

'Twas the fright before Christmas ill. by Will Hillenbrand. Harcourt, 2002. ISBN 0-15-201805-0 Subj: Animals – mice. Cumulative tales. Dragons. Holidays – Christmas. Homes, houses. Monsters. Mythical creatures. Rhyming text. Santa Claus.

Wild about books ill. by Marc Tolon Brown. Knopf, 2004. ISBN 0-375-92538-4 Subj: Animals. Books, reading. Careers – librarians. Libraries. Rhyming text. Zoos.

Wiley and the Hairy Man ill. by J. Brian Pinkney. Lodestar, 1996. ISBN 0-525-67477-2 Subj: Character traits – cleverness. Ethnic groups in the U.S. – African Americans. Folk & fairy tales. Monsters.

Sieveking, Anthea. *Mary had a little lamb and other animal rhymes* photos by author. Barron's, 1991. ISBN 0-8120-6217-5 Subj: Format, unusual – board books. Nursery rhymes.

Polly put the kettle on and other play rhymes photos by author. Barron's, 1991. ISBN 0-8120-6218-3 Subj: Format, unusual – board books. Nursery rhymes.

Rub-a-dub-dub and other splashy rhymes photos by author. Barron's, 1991. ISBN 0-8120-6219-1 Subj: Format, unusual – board books. Nursery rhymes.

Twinkle, twinkle, little star and other bedtime rhymes photos by author. Barron's, 1991. ISBN 0-8120-6220-5 Subj: Format, unusual – board books. Nursery rhymes.

What color? photos by author. Dial, 1991. ISBN 0-8037-0909-9 Subj: Concepts – color.

Siewert, Margaret. *Bear hunt* by Margaret Siewert & Kathleen Savage; ill. by Leonard W. Shortall. Prentice-Hall, 1976. ISBN 0-13-072660-5 Subj: Animals – bears. Games. Participation. Toys – bears.

Sikundar, Sylvia. *Forest singer* ill. by Alison Astill. Barefoot, 1999. ISBN 1-902283-60-0 Subj: Activities – singing. Dwarfs, midgets. Foreign lands – Africa. Forest, woods.

Silbaugh, Elizabeth. *Raggedy Ann's birthday party book* ill. by Laura Francesca Filippucci. S&S, 2001. ISBN 0-689-82850-0 Subj: Activities. Birthdays. Parties. Toys – dolls.

Sill, Cathryn P. *About amphibians* ill. by John Sill. Peachtree, 2000. ISBN 1-56145-234-3 Subj: Frogs & toads. Reptiles.

About fish ill. by John Sill. Peachtree, 2002. ISBN 1-56145-256-4 Subj: Fish.

About insects ill. by John Sill. Peachtree, 2000. ISBN 1-56145-207-6 Subj: Insects.

About mammals ill. by John Sill. Peachtree, 1997. ISBN 1-56145-141-X Subj: Animals.

Silsbe, Brenda. *Just one more color* ill. by Shawn Steffler. Firefly, 1991. ISBN 1-55037-133-9 Subj: Activities – painting. Concepts – color. Homes, houses.

Silvano, Wendi. *Counting coconuts = Contando cocos* ill. by Marty Granius. Raven Tree, 2004. ISBN 0-9720192-6-X Subj: Animals – monkeys. Counting, numbers. Foreign languages.

Silvano, Wendi J. *Just one more* ill. by Ricardo Gamboa. All About Kids, 2002. ISBN 0-9700863-7-7 Subj: Activities – traveling. Buses. Foreign lands – South America. Mountains.

Silver, Jody. *Isadora* ill. by author. Doubleday, 1981. ISBN 0-385-17099-8 Subj: Animals – donkeys. Clothing.

Silverman, Erica. *Fixing the crack of dawn* ill. by Sandra Spiedel. BridgeWater, 1994. ISBN 0-8167-3458-5 Subj: Desert. Family life. Morning.

Follow the leader ill. by G. Brian Karas. Farrar, 2000. ISBN 0-374-32423-9 Subj: Activities – playing. Bedtime. Family life – brothers. Rhyming text.

Gittel's hands ill. by Deborah Nourse Lattimore. BridgeWater, 1996. ISBN 0-8167-3798-3 Subj: Character traits – kindness. Character traits – meanness. Holidays – Passover. Jewish culture. Religion.

The Halloween house ill. by Jon Agee. Farrar, 1997. ISBN 0-374-16768-0 Subj: Counting, numbers. Ghosts. Holidays – Halloween. Monsters. Rhyming text. Witches.

Mrs. Peachtree and the Eighth Avenue cat ill. by Ellen Beier. Macmillan, 1994. ISBN 0-02-782684-8 Subj: Animals – cats. Cities, towns.

On Grandma's roof ill. by Deborah Kogan Ray. Macmillan, 1990. ISBN 0-02-782681-3 Subj: Cities, towns. Family life – grandmothers. Homes, houses.

On the morn of Mayfest ill. by Marla Frazee. S&S, 1998. ISBN 0-689-80674-4 Subj: Cumulative tales. Holidays – May Day. Parades. Rhyming text. Seasons – spring.

Warm in winter ill. by Michael J. Deraney. Macmillan, 1989. ISBN 0-02-782661-9 Subj: Animals – badgers. Animals – rabbits. Friendship. Seasons. Seasons – winter.

Silverman, Maida. *Bunny's ABC* ill. by Ellen Blonder. Grosset, 1986. ISBN 0-448-01464-5 Subj: ABC books. Animals – rabbits. Format, unusual – board books.

Dinosaur babies ill. by Carol Inouye. S&S, 1988. ISBN 0-671-65897-2 Subj: Dinosaurs. Prehistory. Science.

Ladybug's color book ill. by Nancy Duell. Grosset, 1986. ISBN 0-448-01461-0 Subj: Concepts – color. Format, unusual – board books. Insects – ladybugs.

The magic well ill. by Manuel Boix. S&S, 1989. ISBN 0-617-67885-X Subj: Emotions – love. Fairies. Family life – mothers. Magic. Royalty – queens.

Mouse's shape book ill. by Frederic Marvin. Grosset, 1986. ISBN 0-448-01463-7 Subj: Animals – mice. Concepts – shape. Format, unusual – board books.

My first book of Jewish holidays ill. by Barbara Garrison. Dial, 1994. ISBN 0-0837-1428-9 Subj: Holidays. Jewish culture. Religion.

Silverman, Martin. *My tooth is loose* ill. by Amy Aitken. Viking, 1992. ISBN 0-670-83862-4 Subj: Teeth.

Silverstein, Shel. *A giraffe and a half* ill. by author. HarperCollins, 1964. ISBN 0-06-025656-7 Subj: Cumulative tales. Humorous stories. Rhyming text.

The giving tree ill. by author. HarperCollins, 2003. ISBN 0-06-025666-4 Subj: Character traits – generosity. Rhyming text. Trees.

The missing piece ill. by author. HarperCollins, 1976. ISBN 0-06-025672-9 Subj: Character traits – individuality. Concepts – shape.

Simmie, Lois. *Mister got to go* ill. by Cynthia Nugent. Red Deer Pr., 1995. ISBN 0-88995-127-6 Subj: Animals – cats. Hotels. Weather – rain. Weather – storms.

Mister got to go and Arnie ill. by Cynthia Nugent. Raincoast, 2001. ISBN 1-55192-494-3 Subj: Animals – cats. Animals – dogs. Foreign lands – Canada. Hotels.

Simmonds, Posy. *The chocolate wedding* ill. by author. Knopf, 1991. ISBN 0-679-91447-1 Subj: Behavior – boasting. Behavior – misbehavior. Dreams. Weddings.

Fred ill. by author. Knopf, 1988. ISBN 0-394-98627-X Subj: Animals – cats. Death. Emotions – grief.

Lulu and the flying babies ill. by author. Knopf, 1988. ISBN 0-394-99597-X Subj: Family life – fathers. Imagination. Museums. Weather – snow.

Simmons, Al. *Counting feathers* ill. by author. Longstreet, 1997. ISBN 1-56352-440-6 Subj: Birds. Counting, numbers.

Simmons, Jane. *Bouncy bouncy Daisy* ill. by author. Little, 2003. ISBN 0-316-79570-4 Subj: Birds – ducks. Format, unusual – toy & movable books.

Come along, Daisy! ill. by author. Little, 1998. ISBN 0-316-79790-1 Subj: Behavior – lost. Birds – ducks. Family life. Nature.

Daisy and the Beastie ill. by author. Little, 2000. ISBN 0-316-79785-5 Subj: Animals. Birds – ducks. Family life – brothers & sisters. Farms.

Daisy and the egg ill. by author. Little, 1998. ISBN 0-316-79747-2 Subj: Birds – ducks. Eggs. Family life – brothers & sisters. Family life – new sibling.

Daisy says Coo! ill. by author. Little, 2000. ISBN 0-316-79764-2 Subj: Animals. Birds – ducks. Format, unusual – board books. Noise, sounds.

Daisy says, "Here we go round the mulberry bush" ill. by author. Little, 2002. ISBN 0-316-79811-8 Subj: Activities. Birds – ducks. Format, unusual – board books. Participation. Songs.

Daisy says, "If you're happy and you know it" ill. by author. Little, 2002. ISBN 0-316-79940-8 Subj: Birds – ducks. Format, unusual – board books. Noise, sounds. Participation. Songs.

Daisy, the little duck with big feet ill. by author. Little, 2001. ISBN 0-316-79454-6 Subj: Birds – ducks. Format, unusual. Noise, sounds.

Daisy's day out ill. by author. Little, 2000. ISBN 0-316-79763-4 Subj: Birds – ducks. Format, unusual – board books. Noise, sounds.

Daisy's favorite things ill. by author. Little, 1999. ISBN 0-316-79762-6 Subj: Animals. Birds – ducks. Format, unusual – board books. Night. Rhyming text.

Daisy's hide-and-seek ill. by author. Little, 2001. ISBN 0-316-79616-6 Subj: Animals. Birds – ducks. Format, unusual – toy & movable books. Games. Noise, sounds.

The dreamtime fairies ill. by author. Little, 2002. ISBN 0-316-79523-2 Subj: Bedtime. Fairies. Sleep. Toys.

Ebb and Flo and the greedy gulls ill. by author. McElderry, 2000. ISBN 0-689-82484-X Subj: Animals – dogs. Behavior – misunderstanding. Birds – seagulls. Sea & seashore.

Ebb and Flo and the new friend ill. by author. Little, 1999. ISBN 0-689-82483-1 Subj: Animals – dogs. Behavior – sharing. Birds – geese.

Go to sleep, Daisy ill. by author. Little, 1999. ISBN 0-316-79761-8 Subj: Bedtime. Birds – ducks. Dreams. Noise, sounds. Sleep.

Little Fern's first winter ill. by author. Little, 2001. ISBN 0-316-79667-0 Subj: Activities – playing. Animals. Animals – rabbits. Family life – brothers & sisters. Games. Weather – snow.

Quack, Daisy, quack! ill. by author. Little, 2002. ISBN 0-316-79587-9 Subj: Behavior – lost. Birds – ducks. Noise, sounds.

Splish splash Daisy ill. by author. Little, 2003. ISBN 0-316-79560-7 Subj: Birds – ducks. Format, unusual – board books. Puzzles.

Simmons, Steven J. *Alice and Greta: a tale of two witches* ill. by Cyd Moore. Charlesbridge, 1997. ISBN 0-8810-6974-4 Subj: Character traits – kindness. Character traits – meanness. Magic. Witches.

Alice and Greta's color magic ill. by Cyd Moore. Knopf, 2001. ISBN 0-375-81245-8 Subj: Behavior – misbehavior. Concepts – color. Magic. Witches.

Greta's revenge ill. by Cyd Moore. Crown, 1999. ISBN 0-517-80051-9 Subj: Behavior – misbehavior. Magic. Witches.

Simmons-Lynch, Julie. *Tom* (Torres, Daniel)

Simms, Laura. *The bone man: a Native American Modoc tale* ill. by Michael McCurdy. Hyperion, 1997. ISBN 0-7868-2074-8 Subj: Creation. Folk & fairy tales. Indians of North America – Modoc. Monsters. Weather – rain.

Moon and Otter and Frog ill. by Clifford Brycelea. Hyperion, 1995. ISBN 0-7868-2022-5 Subj: Animals – otters. Folk & fairy tales. Frogs & toads. Indians of North America – Modoc. Moon.

Rotten teeth ill. by David Catrow. Houghton Mifflin, 1998. ISBN 0-395-82850-3 Subj: Activities – storytelling. School. Teeth.

The squeaky door ill. by Sylvie Wickstrom. Crown, 1991. ISBN 0-517-57584-1 Subj: Bedtime. Cumulative tales. Emotions – fear. Folk & fairy tales. Noise, sounds.

Simon, Carly. *Amy the dancing bear* ill. by Margot Datz. Doubleday, 1989. ISBN 0-385-26721-5 Subj: Activities – dancing. Animals – bears.

Midnight farm ill. by David Delamare. S&S, 1997. ISBN 0-689-81237-X Subj: Animals. Bedtime. Dreams. Farms. Islands. Multiple births – twins. Plants.

Simon, Charnan. *Click and the kids go sailing* ill. by Richard Kolding. McGraw-Hill, 2001. ISBN 1-57768-885-6 Subj: Activities – babysitting. Animals – mice. Family life – brothers & sisters. Sports – sailing.

The good bad day photos by Dorothy Handelman. Millbrook, 1998. ISBN 0-7613-2017-2 Subj: Behavior – bad day. Illness.

Mud! ill. by Dorothy Handelman. Millbrook, 1999. ISBN 0-7613-2051-2 Subj: Activities – playing. Rhyming text.

Show-and-tell Sam ill. by Gary Bialke. Childrens Pr., 1998. ISBN 0-516-20945-0 Subj: Animals – dogs. School.

Simon, Francesca. *But what does the hippopotamus say?* ill. by Helen Floate. Harcourt, 1994. ISBN 0-15-200029-1 Subj: Animals. Noise, sounds. Rhyming text.

Calling all toddlers ill. by Susan Winter. Orchard, 1999. ISBN 0-531-30120-6 Subj: Activities – playing. Rhyming text.

Camels don't ski ill. by Ailie Busby. Levinson Books, 1999. ISBN 1-899607-59-5 Subj: Animals – camels. Behavior – dissatisfaction. Seasons – winter. Sports – skiing.

Spider school ill. by Peta Coplans. Dial, 1996. ISBN 0-8037-1975-2 Subj: Behavior – bad day. Dreams. School. Spiders.

Toddler time ill. by Susan Winter. Orchard, 2000. ISBN 0-531-30251-2 Subj: Activities. Poetry.

The Topsy-Turvies ill. by Karen Ludlow. Dial, 1996. ISBN 0-8037-1969-8 Subj: Activities – babysitting. Character traits – being different. Family life.

Simon, Howard. *If you were an eel, how would you feel?* (Simon, Mina Lewiton)

Simon, Mina Lewiton. *If you were an eel, how would you feel?* by Mina & Howard Simon; ill. by Howard Simon. Follett, 1963. Subj: Animals.

Is anyone here? ill. by Howard Simon. Atheneum, 1967. Subj: Rhyming text. Sea & seashore.

Simon, Norma. *All families are special* ill. by Teresa Flavin. A. Whitman, 2003. ISBN 0-8075-2175-2 Subj: Family life. School.

All kinds of children ill. by Diane Paterson. A. Whitman, 1999. ISBN 0-8075-0281-2 Subj: Character traits – individuality. Self-concept.

All kinds of families ill. by Joe Lasker. A. Whitman, 1976. ISBN 0-8075-0282-0 Subj: Family life.

Cats do, dogs don't ill. by Dora Leder. A. Whitman, 1986. ISBN 0-8075-1102-1 Subj: Animals – cats. Animals – dogs. Pets.

The daddy days ill. by Abner Graboff. Abelard-Schuman, 1958. Subj: Divorce. Family life – fathers.

How do I feel? ill. by Joe Lasker. A. Whitman, 1970. ISBN 0-8075-3414-5 Subj: Emotions. Family life. Multiple births – twins.

I am not a crybaby! ill. by Helen Cogancherry. A. Whitman, 1988. ISBN 0-8075-3447-1 Subj: Emotions. Ethnic groups in the U.S.

I know what I like ill. by Dora Leder. A. Whitman, 1971. ISBN 0-8075-3507-9 Subj: Character traits – individuality.

I was so mad! ill. by Dora Leder. A. Whitman, 1974. ISBN 0-8075-3520-6 Subj: Emotions – anger.

I wish I had my father ill. by Arieh Zeldich. A. Whitman, 1983. ISBN 0-8075-3522-2 Subj: Behavior – wishing. Family life – fathers. Holidays – Father's Day.

I'm busy, too ill. by Dora Leder. A. Whitman, 1980. ISBN 0-8075-3464-1 Subj: Activities. Activities – working. School.

Mama cat's year ill. by Dora Leder. A. Whitman, 1991. ISBN 0-8075-4958-4 Subj: Animals – cats. Pets. Seasons.

Oh, that cat! ill. by Dora Leder. A. Whitman, 1986. ISBN 0-8075-5919-9 Subj: Animals – cats. Family life. Pets.

The saddest time ill. by Jacqueline Rogers. A. Whitman, 1986. ISBN 0-8075-7203-9 Subj: Death. Emotions – grief.

The story of Hanukkah ill. by Leonid Gore. HarperCollins, 1997. ISBN 0-06-027420-4 Subj: Holidays – Hanukkah. Jewish culture. Religion.

The story of Passover ill. by Erika Weihs. HarperCollins, 1997. ISBN 0-06-027063-2 Subj: Holidays – Passover. Jewish culture. Religion.

The wet world ill. by Jane Miller. Lippincott, 1954. Subj: Weather – rain.

The wet world ill. by Alexi Natchev. Candlewick, 1995. ISBN 1-56402-190-4 Subj: Weather – rain.

What do I do? ill. by Joe Lasker. A. Whitman, 1969. ISBN 0-8075-8822-9 Subj: Activities. Character traits – helpfulness. Cities, towns. Ethnic groups in the U.S. – Puerto Rican Americans. School.

What do I say? ill. by Joe Lasker. A. Whitman, 1967. ISBN 0-8075-8826-1 Subj: Ethnic groups in the U.S. Ethnic groups in the U.S. – Puerto Rican Americans. Family life. Foreign languages. Participation. School.

Where does my cat sleep? ill. by Dora Leder. A. Whitman, 1982. ISBN 0-8075-8926-8 Subj: Animals – cats. Sleep.

Why am I different? ill. by Dora Leder. A. Whitman, 1976. ISBN 0-8075-9075-6 Subj: Character traits – being different. Character traits – individuality. Self-concept.

Simon, Paul. *At the zoo* ill. by Valerie Michaut. Doubleday, 1991. ISBN 0-385-41906-6 Subj: Animals. Songs. Zoos.

Simon, Seymour. *Amazing aircraft* ill. with photos. SeaStar, 2002. ISBN 1-58717-179-1 Subj: Airplanes, airports.

Animal fact – animal fable ill. by Diane de Groat. Crown, 1979. ISBN 0-517-53474-6 Subj: Animals.

Beneath your feet ill. by Daniel Nevins. Walker, 1977. ISBN 0-8027-6293-X Subj: Earth. Science.

Cats ill. with photos. HarperCollins, 2004. ISBN 0-06-028941-4 Subj: Animals – cats. Pets.

Danger! earthquakes ill. with photos. SeaStar, 2002. ISBN 1-58717-139-2 Subj: Earthquakes.

Danger! volcanoes ill. with photos. SeaStar, 2002. ISBN 1-58717-181-3 Subj: Volcanoes.

Destination, Mars ill. with photos. Morrow, 2000. ISBN 0-688-15771-8 Subj: Planets.

Dogs ill. with photos. HarperCollins, 2004. ISBN 0-06-028943-0 Subj: Animals – dogs. Pets.

Giant machines ill. with photos. SeaStar, 2002. ISBN 1-58717-126-0 Subj: Concepts – size. Machines.

Icebergs and glaciers ill. with photos. Morrow, 1987. ISBN 0-688-06187-7 Subj: Nature. Science.

The largest dinosaurs ill. by Pamela Carroll. Macmillan, 1986. ISBN 0-02-782910-3 Subj: Dinosaurs. Prehistory.

Let's try it out in the air by Seymour Simon & Nicole Fauteux; ill. by Doug Cushman. S&S, 2001. ISBN 0-689-82918-3 Subj: Science.

Let's try it out in the water by Seymour Simon & Nicole Fauteux; ill. by Doug Cushman. S&S, 2001. ISBN 0-689-82919-1 Subj: Science. Water.

Seymour Simon's book of trains ill. with photos. HarperCollins, 2002. ISBN 0-06-028476-5 Subj: Trains. Transportation.

Seymour Simon's book of trucks ill. by author. HarperCollins, 2000. ISBN 0-06-028481-1 Subj: Transportation. Trucks.

Shadow magic ill. by Stella Ormai. Lothrop, 1985. ISBN 0-688-02682-6 Subj: Shadows.

The smallest dinosaurs ill. by Anthony Rao. Crown, 1982. ISBN 0-517-54425-3 Subj: Dinosaurs. Prehistory.

Wild bears ill. with photos. SeaStar, 2002. ISBN 1-58717-143-0 Subj: Animals – bears. Science.

Simon, Sidney B. *The armadillo who had no shell* ill. by Walter Lorraine. Norton, 1966. Subj: Animals – armadillos. Character traits – being different.

Henry, the uncatchable mouse ill. by Nola Langner. Norton, 1964. Subj: Animals – mice. Character traits – cleverness.

Simons, Traute. *Paulino* trans. by Ebbitt Cutler; ill. by Susi Bohdal. Tundra, 1978. ISBN 0-88776-110-0 Subj: Dreams. Toys.

Simont, Marc. *The goose that almost got cooked* ill. by author. Scholastic, 1997. ISBN 0-590-69075-2 Subj: Activities – flying. Birds – geese. Character traits – individuality. Farms.

How come elephants? ill. by author. HarperCollins, 1965. Subj: Animals – elephants. Character traits – questioning.

The Lieutenant Colonel and the gypsy (García Lorca, Federico)

Nate the Great, San Francisco detective (Sharmat, Marjorie Weinman)

The stray dog ill. by author. HarperCollins, 2001. ISBN 0-06-028934-1 Subj: Animals – dogs. Caldecott award honor books. Character traits – kindness to animals.

Simple gifts: a Shaker hymn ill. by Chris Raschka. Holt, 1998. ISBN 0-8050-5143-0 Subj: Animals. Birds. Forest, woods. Music. Songs.

Simple Simon. *The adventures of Simple Simon* ill. by Chris Conover. Farrar, 1987. ISBN 0-374-36921-6 Subj: Nursery rhymes.

The history of Simple Simon ill. by Paul Galdone. McGraw-Hill, 1966. The version used in this book was published in London in 1840 by A. Park. Subj: Nursery rhymes.

Simple Simon ill. by Rodney Peppé. Holt, 1973. ISBN 0-03-091462-0 Subj: Nursery rhymes.

Simpson, Bert. *Rise and shine* (Raffi)

Simpson, Bonnie. *Rise and shine* (Raffi)

Simpson, Gretchen Dow. *Gretchen's ABC* ill. by author. HarperCollins, 1991. ISBN 0-06-025646-X Subj: ABC books. Art.

Simpson, Lesley. *The Purim surprise* ill. by Peter Church. Kar-Ben Copies, 2003. ISBN 1-58013-090-9 Subj: Birthdays. Family life – daughters. Family life – mothers. Holidays – Purim. Jewish culture. Moving.

Sing, Rachel. *Chinese New Year's dragon* ill. by Shao Wei Liu. Modern Curriculum, 1992. ISBN 0-81362-238-7 Subj: Ethnic groups in the U.S. – Chinese Americans. Family life. Holidays – Chinese New Year.

Singer, Isaac Bashevis. *Why Noah chose the dove* trans. by Elizabeth Shub; ill. by Eric Carle. Farrar, 1974. ISBN 0-374-38420-7 Subj: Animals. Birds – doves. Boats, ships. Religion – Noah. Weather – floods. Weather – rain. Weather – rainbows.

Singer, Marilyn. *All we needed to say: poems about school from Tanya and Sophie* ill. by Lorna Clark. Atheneum, 1996. ISBN 0-689-80667-1 Subj: Friendship. Poetry. School.

Archer Armadillo's secret room ill. by Beth Weiner Lipson. Macmillan, 1985. ISBN 0-02-782700-3 Subj: Animals – armadillos. Behavior – running away. Moving.

Boo hoo boo-boo ill. by Elivia Savadier. HarperFestival, 2002. ISBN 0-694-01566-0 Subj: Accidents. Illness. Rhyming text.

Chester, the out-of-work dog ill. by Cat Bowman Smith. Holt, 1992. ISBN 0-8050-1828-X Subj: Activities – working. Animals – dogs. Behavior – lost.

The company of crows ill. by Linda Saport. Clarion, 2002. ISBN 0-618-08340-5 Subj: Birds – crows. Poetry.

Creature carnival ill. by Gris Grimly. Hyperion, 2004. ISBN 0-7868-1877-8 Subj: Animals. Humorous stories. Mythical creatures. Poetry.

Didi and Daddy on the Promenade ill. by Marie-Louise Gay. Clarion, 2001. ISBN 0-618-04640-2 Subj: Activities – walking. Family life – daughters. Family life – fathers. Parks.

The dog who insisted he wasn't ill. by Kelly Oechsli. Dutton, 1976. ISBN 0-525-28815-5 Subj: Animals – dogs. Character traits – individuality. Humorous stories.

Fred's bed ill. by JoAnn Adinolfi. HarperFestival, 2001. ISBN 0-694-01451-6 Subj: Animals. Furniture – beds. Rhyming text.

In the palace of the Ocean King ill. by Ted Rand. Atheneum, 1995. ISBN 0-689-31755-7 Subj: Emotions – sadness. Ethnic groups in the U.S. – African Americans. Family life – fathers.

The maiden on the moor ill. by Troy Howell. Morrow, 1995. ISBN 0-688-08675-6 Subj: Character traits – kindness. Folk & fairy tales. Middle Ages. Songs.

Minnie's Yom Kippur birthday ill. by Ruth Rosner. HarperCollins, 1989. ISBN 0-06-025847-0 Subj: Birthdays. Holidays – Yom Kippur. Jewish culture. Religion.

The Morgans' dream ill. by Gary Drake. Holt, 1995. ISBN 0-8050-3004-2 Subj: Dreams. Family life. Poetry.

Nine o'clock lullaby ill. by Frané Lessac. HarperCollins, 1991. ISBN 0-06-025648-6 Subj: Foreign lands. Time.

On the same day in March ill. by Frané Lessac. HarperCollins, 2000. ISBN 0-06-443528-8 Subj: Maps. Weather. World.

The one and only me ill. by Nicole Rubel. HarperFestival, 2000. ISBN 0-694-01279-3 Subj: Anatomy. Character traits – individuality. Family life.

Pickle plan ill. by Steven Kellogg. Dutton, 1978. ISBN 0-525-37021-8 Subj: Behavior – needing someone. Character traits – individuality.

Quiet night ill. by John Manders. Clarion, 2002. ISBN 0-618-12044-0 Subj: Animals. Camps, camping. Counting, numbers. Night. Noise, sounds.

Solomon sneezes ill. by Brian Floca. HarperCollins, 1999. ISBN 0-694-01748-5 Subj: Humorous stories. Rhyming text.

Tough beginnings ill. by Anna Vojtech. Holt, 2001. ISBN 0-8050-6164-9 Subj: Animals – babies. Poetry. Science.

Turtle in July ill. by Jerry Pinkney. Macmillan, 1989. ISBN 0-02-782881-6 Subj: Animals. Days of the week, months of the year. Nature. Poetry.

Will you take me to town on strawberry day? ill. by Trinka Hakes Noble. HarperCollins, 1981. ISBN 0-06-025738-5 Subj: Fairs, festivals. Music. Songs.

Singh, Jacquelin. *Fat Gopal* ill. by Demi. Harcourt, 1984. ISBN 0-05-227372-7 Subj: Character traits – cleverness. Foreign lands – India. Problem solving. Rhyming text.

Siomades, Lorianne. *Cuckoo can't find you* ill. by author. Boyds Mills, 2002. ISBN 1-56397-778-8 Subj: Animals. Behavior – lost & found possessions. Rhyming text.

The itsy bitsy spider ill. by author. Boyds Mills, 1999. ISBN 1-56397-727-3 Subj: Character traits – persistence. Nursery rhymes. Spiders.

Kangaroo and cricket ill. by author. Boyds Mills, 1999. ISBN 1-56397-780-X Subj: Activities. Animals. Rhyming text.

My box of color ill. by author. Boyds Mills, 1998. ISBN 1-56397-711-7 Subj: Animals. Concepts – color.

A place to bloom ill. by author. Boyds Mills, 1997. ISBN 1-56397-656-0 Subj: Behavior – sharing. Earth. Ecology. Rhyming text.

Three little kittens ill. by reteller. Boyds Mills, 2000. ISBN 1-56397-845-8 Subj: Animals – cats. Animals – mice. Behavior – lost & found possessions. Clothing – gloves, mittens. Nursery rhymes.

Sipiera, Paul P. *I can be a geologist* ill. with photos. Childrens Pr., 1986. ISBN 0-516-01897-3 Subj: Careers – geologists.

Siracusa, Catherine. *No mail for Mitchell* ill. by author. McKay, 1990. ISBN 0-679-90476-X Subj: Animals. Careers – postal workers. Illness. Letters, cards.

Sirois, Allen. *Dinosaur dress up* ill. by Janet Street. Morrow, 1992. ISBN 0-688-10460-6 Subj: Clothing. Dinosaurs. Prehistory.

Sis, Peter. *Ballerina* ill. by author. Greenwillow, 2001. ISBN 0-688-17944-4 Subj: Activities – dancing. Ballet. Careers – dancers. Imagination.

Beach ball ill. by author. Greenwillow, 1990. ISBN 0-688-09182-2 Subj: Concepts. Sea & seashore – beaches.

Dinosaur! ill. by author. Greenwillow, 2000. ISBN 0-688-17049-8 Subj: Dinosaurs. Imagination. Prehistory. Wordless.

Fire truck ill. by author. Greenwillow, 1998. ISBN 0-688-15878-1 Subj: Careers – firefighters. Counting, numbers. Format, unusual – toy & movable books. Trucks.

Follow the dream ill. by author. Knopf, 1991. ISBN 0-679-90628-2 Subj: Careers – explorers.

Going up! ill. by author. Greenwillow, 1989. ISBN 0-688-08125-8 Subj: Birthdays. Concepts – color. Counting, numbers. Elevators, escalators.

Higgledy-Piggledy: verses and pictures (Livingston, Myra Cohn)

Madlenka ill. by author. Farrar, 2000. ISBN 0-374-39969-7 Subj: Behavior – growing up. Foreign lands. Imagination. Teeth.

An ocean world ill. by author. Greenwillow, 1992. ISBN 0-688-09068-0 Subj: Animals – whales. Sea & seashore. Wordless.

Rainbow Rhino ill. by author. Knopf, 1987. ISBN 0-394-99009-9 Subj: Animals – rhinoceros. Birds. Friendship.

Ship ahoy! ill. by author. Greenwillow, 1999. ISBN 0-688-16644-X Subj: Boats, ships. Imagination. Monsters. Sea & seashore. Wordless.

A small tall tale from the far Far North ill. by author. Farrar, 2001. ISBN 0-374-37075-3 Subj: Eskimos. Foreign lands – Arctic. Indians of North America – Inuit. Tall tales.

Starry messenger ill. by author. Farrar, 1996. ISBN 0-374-37191-1 Subj: Astronomy. Caldecott award honor books. Space & space ships. Stars.

Tibet through the red box ill. by author. Farrar, 1998. ISBN 0-374-37552-6 Subj: Activities – traveling. Caldecott award honor books. Foreign lands – Tibet.

Trucks, trucks, trucks ill. by author. Greenwillow, 1999. ISBN 0-688-16276-2 Subj: Format, unusual – toy & movable books. Trucks.

Waving ill. by author. Greenwillow, 1988. ISBN 0-688-07160-0 Subj: Counting, numbers.

Sitomer, Harry. *How did numbers begin?* (Sitomer, Mindel)

Sitomer, Mindel. *How did numbers begin?* by Mindel & Harry Sitomer; ill. by Richard Cuffari. Crowell, 1976. ISBN 0-690-00794-9 Subj: Counting, numbers.

Sivulich, Sandra Stroner. *I'm going on a bear hunt* ill. by Glen Rounds. Dutton, 1973. ISBN 0-525-32535-2 Subj: Animals – bears. Games. Participation.

Sizes: with Dib, Dab, and Dob. DK, 1998. ISBN 0-7894-2915-2 Subj: Birds – ducks. Concepts – size.

Skaar, Grace Marion. *Nothing but (cats) and all about (dogs)* ill. by author. Addison-Wesley, 1947. Subj: Animals – cats. Animals – dogs.

The very little dog: and, The smart little kitty by Grace Marion Skaar & Louise Phinney Woodcock; ill. by Grace Marion Skaar & Lucienne Bloch. Addison-Wesley, 1967. Subj: Animals – cats. Animals – dogs.

What do the animals say? ill. by author. Addison-Wesley, 1968. 1950 ed. published under title: What do they say! Subj: Animals. Noise, sounds. Participation.

Skinner, Daphne. *Henry keeps score* ill. by Page Eastburn O'Rourke. Kane Pr., 2001. ISBN 1-57565-102-5 Subj: Counting, numbers. Family life – brothers & sisters. Sibling rivalry.

Tightwad Tod ill. by John Nez. Kane Pr., 2001. ISBN 1-57565-109-2 Subj: Counting, numbers. Money.

Skipper, Mervyn. *The fooling of King Alexander* ill. by Gaynor Chapman. Atheneum, 1967. Originally published in The white man's garden, by Mervyn Skipper. London, Mathews, 1931. Subj: Foreign lands – China. Royalty – kings.

Sklansky, Amy E. *Where do chicks come from?* ill. by Pam Paparone. HarperCollins, 2005. ISBN 0-06-028893-0 Subj: Birds – chickens. Eggs. Science.

Skofield, James. *All wet! All wet!* ill. by Diane Stanley. Harper-Collins, 1984. ISBN 0-06-025752-0 Subj: Weather – rain.

Crow moon, worm moon ill. by Joyce Powzyk. Four Winds, 1990. ISBN 0-02-782915-4 Subj: Animals. Moon. Nature. Poetry. Seasons – spring.

Snow country ill. by Laura Jean Allen. HarperCollins, 1983. ISBN 0-06-025787-3 Subj: Family life – grandparents. Farms. Weather – snow.

Skolsky, Mindy Warshaw. *Hannah and the whistling tea kettle* ill. by Diane Palmisciano. DK, 2000. ISBN 0-7894-2602-1 Subj: Crime. Family life – grandparents. Gifts. Noise, sounds. Stores.

Skorpen, Liesel Moak. *All the Lassies* ill. by Bruce Martin Scott. Dial, 1970. Subj: Animals. Animals – dogs. Character traits – perseverance. Cumulative tales. Family life – only child. Participation. Pets.

Charles ill. by Martha G. Alexander. HarperCollins, 1971. ISBN 0-06-025712-1 Subj: Behavior – needing someone. Toys – bears.

Elizabeth ill. by Martha G. Alexander. HarperCollins, 1970. Subj: Toys – dolls.

His mother's dog ill. by M. E. Mullin. HarperCollins, 1978. ISBN 0-06-025723-7 Subj: Animals – dogs. Emotions – envy, jealousy. Family life. Sibling rivalry.

If I had a lion ill. by Ursula Landshoff. HarperCollins, 1967. Subj: Animals – lions. Imagination.

Old Arthur ill. by Wallace Tripp. HarperCollins, 1972. ISBN 0-06-025715-6 Subj: Animals – dogs. Old age.

Outside my window ill. by Mercer Mayer. HarperCollins, 1968. Subj: Animals – bears. Bedtime.

We were tired of living in a house ill. by Joe Cepeda. Putnam, 1999. ISBN 0-399-23016-5 Subj: Activities – painting. Cumulative tales. Family life – brothers & sisters. Homes, houses.

Skrypuch, Marsha Forchuk. *Enough* ill. by Michael Martchenko. Fitzhenry & Whiteside, 2000. ISBN 1-55041-509-3 Subj: Careers – farmers. Folk & fairy tales. Foreign lands – Ukraine.

Skulavik, Mary Alys. *Bert* ill. by Zofia Kostyrko. Walker, 1990. ISBN 0-8027-6963-2 Subj: Computers. Family life. Self-concept.

Skurzynski, Gloria. *Here comes the mail* ill. by author. Bradbury, 1992. ISBN 0-02-782916-2 Subj: Careers – postal workers. Letters, cards. Post office.

Martin by himself ill. by Lynn Munsinger. Houghton Mifflin, 1979. ISBN 0-395-28271-3 Subj: Activities – working. Emotions – loneliness. Family life – mothers.

Skutina, Vladimir. *Nobody has time for me* trans. by Dagmar Herrmann; ill. by Marie-Jose Sacre. Wellington, 1991. ISBN 0-922984-07-7 Subj: Time.

Skwarek, Skip. *The horrors of Howling Hall* art by Compass Production Staff. Dial, 1992. ISBN 0-8037-1185-9 Subj: Format, unusual – toy & movable books. Ghosts. Rhyming text.

Mystery of Maggoty Mill art by Compass Production Staff. Dial, 1992. ISBN 0-8037-1186-7 Subj: Format, unusual – toy & movable books. Ghosts. Monsters.

Slangerup, Erik Jon. *Dirt Boy* ill. by John Manders. A. Whitman, 2000. ISBN 0-8075-4424-8 Subj: Activities – bathing. Behavior – running away. Family life – mothers. Health & fitness.

Slate, Joseph. *The great big wagon that rang* ill. by Craig Spearing. Cavendish, 2002. ISBN 0-7614-5108-0 Subj: Careers – farmers. Rhyming text. U.S. history.

Little Porcupine's Christmas ill. by Felicia Bond. Geringer, 2001. ISBN 0-06-029533-3 Subj: Animals. Animals – porcupines. Holidays – Christmas.

Lonely Lula cat ill. by Bruce Degen. HarperCollins, 1985. ISBN 0-06-025807-1 Subj: Animals – cats. Emotions – loneliness. Friendship.

The mean, clean, giant canoe machine ill. by Lynn Munsinger. Crowell, 1983. ISBN 0-690-04294-9 Subj: Activities – bathing. Animals – pigs. Witches.

Miss Bindergarten celebrates the 100th day of kindergarten ill. by Ashley Wolff. Dutton, 1998. ISBN 0-525-46000-4 Subj: Animals. Counting, numbers. Rhyming text. School.

Miss Bindergarten gets ready for kindergarten ill. by Ashley Wolff. Dutton, 1996. ISBN 0-525-45446-2 Subj: ABC books. Animals. School – first day.

Miss Bindergarten stays home from kindergarten ill. by Ashley Wolff. Dutton, 2000. ISBN 0-525-46396-8 Subj: ABC books. Animals. Illness – cold (disease). Rhyming text. School.

Miss Bindergarten takes a field trip with kindergarten ill. by Ashley Wolff. Dutton, 2001. ISBN 0-525-46710-6 Subj: ABC books. Animals. Rhyming text. School. School – field trips.

The secret stars ill. by Felipe Dávalos. Cavendish, 1998. ISBN 0-7614-5027-0 Subj: Ethnic groups in the U.S. – Hispanic Americans. Family life – grandmothers. Royalty – kings. Stars.

The star rocker ill. by Dirk Zimmer. HarperCollins, 1982. ISBN 0-06-025749-0 Subj: Bedtime. Lullabies. Stars.

Story time for Little Porcupine ill. by Jacqueline Rogers. Cavendish, 2001. ISBN 0-7614-5073-4 Subj: Activities – storytelling. Animals – porcupines. Creation. Family life – fathers. Folk & fairy tales. Sun.

Who is coming to our house? ill. by Ashley Wolff. Putnam, 1988. ISBN 0-399-21537-9 Subj: Animals. Animals – mice. Religion. Rhyming text.

Slater, Teddy. *The cow that could tap dance* ill. by Sandra Forrest. Silver Pr., 1991. ISBN 0-671-70408-7 Subj: Behavior – boasting. Character traits – questioning.

The emperor's nightingale (Andersen, H. C. [Hans Christian])

The fabulous fish from Lake Wiggawalla ill. by Laura Rankin. Silver Pr., 1991. ISBN 0-671-70409-5 Subj: Activities – traveling. Behavior – boasting.

Jan and Dan and the super dads ill. by Sandra Forrest. Silver Pr., 1991. ISBN 0-671-70410-9 Subj: Family life – fathers.

Slavin, Bill. *The cat came back* ill. by adapt. A. Whitman, 1992. ISBN 0-8075-1097-1 Subj: Activities – traveling. Animals – cats. Music. Songs.

Slawski, Wolfgang. *Captain Jonathan sails the sea* ill. by author; trans. by Rosemary Lanning. North-South, 1997. ISBN 1-55858-814-0 Subj: Boats, ships. Character traits – helpfulness. Sailors. Sea & seashore.

Slawson, Michele Benoit. *Signs for sale* ill. by Bagram Ibatoulline. Viking, 2002. ISBN 0-670-03568-8 Subj: Family life – daughters. Family life – fathers. Signs & signboards.

Sleator, William. *The angry moon* ill. by Blair Lent. Little, 1970. ISBN 0-316-78737-5 Subj: Caldecott award honor books. Folk & fairy tales. Indians of North America – Tlingit. Moon.

That's silly ill. by Lawrence DiFiori. Dutton, 1981. ISBN 0-525-40981-5 Subj: Imagination. Magic.

Sleep, baby, sleep: an old cradle song ill. by Trudi Oberhänsli. Atheneum, 1967. Includes melody with words. Subj: Lullabies.

Sleigh bells and snowflakes comp. & ill. by Linda Bronson. Holt, 2002. ISBN 0-8050-6755-8 Subj: Holidays – Christmas. Poetry.

Slepian, Jan. *Emily just in time* ill. by Glo Coalson. Philomel, 1998. ISBN 0-399-23043-2 Subj: Behavior – growing up. Emotions – fear. Family life – grandmothers.

The hungry thing returns ill. by Richard E. Martin. Scholastic, 1990. ISBN 0-590-42890-X Subj: Food. Rhyming text.

Lost moose ill. by Ted Lewin. Philomel, 1995. ISBN 0-399-22749-0 Subj: Animals – babies. Animals – moose. Babies. Behavior – lost.

Slingsby, Janet. *Hush-a-bye babies* ill. by Andy Beckett. Barron's, 2001. ISBN 0-7641-5410-9 Subj: Animals. Bedtime. Noise, sounds. Sleep.

Sloan, Alan. *The Sea World alphabet book* (The Sea World alphabet book)

Sloan, Carolyn. *Carter is a painter's cat* ill. by Fritz Wegner. S&S, 1971. ISBN 0-671-65172-2 Subj: Animals – cats. Careers – artists.

Sloan, Sally. *The Sea World alphabet book* (The Sea World alphabet book)

Sloat, Robert. *Rib-ticklers* (Sloat, Teri)

Sloat, Teri. *Farmer Brown goes round and round* ill. by Nadine Bernard Westcott. DK, 1999. ISBN 0-7894-2512-2 Subj: Animals. Farms. Noise, sounds. Rhyming text. Weather – tornadoes.

Farmer Brown shears his sheep: a yarn about wool ill. by Nadine Bernard Westcott. DK, 2000. ISBN 0-7894-2637-4 Subj: Animals – sheep. Farms. Rhyming text.

From letter to letter ill. by author. Dutton, 1989. ISBN 0-525-44518-8 Subj: ABC books.

Hark! The aardvark angels sing ill. by author. Putnam, 2001. ISBN 0-399-23371-7 Subj: Angels. Animals – aardvarks. Holidays – Christmas. Music. Songs.

Patty's pumpkin patch ill. by author. Putnam, 1999. ISBN 0-399-23010-6 Subj: ABC books. Rhyming text.

Pieces of Christmas ill. by author. Holt, 2002. ISBN 0-8050-6355-2 Subj: Animals. Holidays – Christmas. Letters, cards. Rhyming text. Santa Claus.

Rib-ticklers by Teri & Robert Sloat; ill. by authors. Lothrop, 1995. ISBN 0-688-12520-4 Subj: Animals. Riddles & jokes.

There was an old lady who swallowed a trout ill. by Reynold Ruffins. Holt, 1998. ISBN 0-8050-4294-6 Subj: Animals. Cumulative tales. Fish. Folk & fairy tales. Humorous stories. Rhyming text.

The thing that bothered Farmer Brown ill. by Nadine Bernard Westcott. Orchard, 1995. ISBN 0-531-08733-6 Subj: Animals. Careers – farmers. Insects – mosquitoes. Night. Noise, sounds. Rhyming text. Sleep.

Slobodkin, Louis. *Clear the track for Michael's magic train* ill. by author. Macmillan, 1945. Subj: Family life. Imagination. Rhyming text. Trains.

Colette and the princess ill. by author. Dutton, 1965. Subj: Animals – cats. Folk & fairy tales. Foreign lands – France. Noise, sounds. Royalty – princesses.

Dinny and Danny ill. by author. Macmillan, 1951. Subj: Cavemen. Character traits – helpfulness. Dinosaurs. Friendship.

Friendly animals ill. by author. Vanguard, 1944. Subj: Animals. Rhyming text.

Hustle and bustle ill. by author. Macmillan, 1962. Subj: Animals – hippopotamuses. Behavior – fighting, arguing.

The late cuckoo ill. by author. Vanguard, 1962. Subj: Clocks, watches. Time.

Magic Michael ill. by author. Macmillan, 1944. Subj: Family life. Imagination. Magic. Self-concept.

Melvin, the moose child ill. by author. Vanguard, 1967, c1957. Subj: Animals. Animals – moose. Forest, woods.

Millions and millions and millions ill. by author. Vanguard, 1955. Subj: Character traits – individuality. Rhyming text.

Moon Blossom and the golden penny ill. by author. Vanguard, 1963. ISBN 0-8149-0399-1 Subj: Foreign lands – China. Money.

One is good, but two are better ill. by author. Vanguard, 1956. Subj: Rhyming text.

Our friendly friends ill. by author. Vanguard, 1951. Subj: Animals.

The polka-dot goat ill. by author. Macmillan, 1964. Subj: Animals – goats. Foreign lands – India.

The seaweed hat ill. by author. Macmillan, 1947. Subj: Rhyming text. Sea & seashore.

Thank you – you're welcome ill. by author. Vanguard, 1957. Subj: Etiquette.

Trick or treat ill. by author. Macmillan, 1959. Subj: Holidays – Halloween.

Up high and down low ill. by author. Macmillan, 1960. Subj: Animals – goats. Animals – sheep. Concepts – up & down. Rhyming text.

Wide-awake owl ill. by author. Macmillan, 1958. Subj: Birds – owls. Music. Sleep. Songs.

Yasu and the strangers ill. by author. Macmillan, 1965. Subj: Behavior – lost. Foreign lands – Japan.

Slobodkina, Esphyr. *Billy, the condominium cat* ill. by author. Addison-Wesley, 1980. ISBN 0-201-09204-2 Subj: Animals – cats. Old age.

Boris and his balalaika ill. by Vladimir Bobri. Abelard-Schuman, 1964. Subj: Foreign lands – Russia.

Caps for sale ill. by author. Addison-Wesley, 1940. ISBN 0-06-025778-4 Subj: Animals – monkeys. Careers – peddlers. Clothing – hats. Humorous stories. Participation.

Circus caps for sale ill. by author. HarperCollins, 2002. ISBN 0-06-029656-9 Subj: Animals – elephants. Careers – peddlers. Circus. Clothing – hats. Crime. Humorous stories. Participation.

Pezzo the peddler and the circus elephant ill. by author. Abelard-Schuman, 1967. Subj: Animals – elephants. Careers – peddlers. Circus. Clothing. Humorous stories. Parades. Participation.

Pezzo the peddler and the thirteen silly thieves ill. by author. Abelard-Schuman, 1970. ISBN 0-200-71675-1 Subj: Careers – peddlers. Clothing. Crime. Humorous stories. Participation.

Pinky and the petunias ill. by author. Abelard-Schuman, 1959. Based on a story by Tamara Schildkraut. Subj: Animals – cats. Flowers.

The wonderful feast ill. by author. Greenwillow, 1993. ISBN 0-688-12349-X Subj: Animals. Animals – horses, ponies. Farms. Food.

Slocum, Rosalie. *Breakfast with the clowns* ill. by author. Viking, 1937. Subj: Circus. Clowns, jesters. Food.

Slonim, David. *Oh, Ducky* ill. by author. Chronicle, 2003. ISBN 0-8118-3562-6 Subj: Behavior – lost & found possessions. Food. Toys.

Slote, Elizabeth. *Nelly's garden* ill. by author. Morrow, 1991. ISBN 0-688-10014-7 Subj: Dragons. Flowers. Gardens, gardening.

Slovenz-Low, Madeline. *Lion dancer: Ernie Wan's Chinese new year* (Waters, Kate)

Slyder, Ingrid. *The Fabulous Flying Fandinis* ill. by author. Cobblehill, 1996. ISBN 0-525-65212-4 Subj: Character traits – being different. Circus. Family life.

Small, David. *Eulalie and the hopping head* ill. by author. Macmillan, 1982. ISBN 0-02-786010-8 Subj: Animals – foxes. Character traits – kindness. Frogs & toads.

George Washington's cows ill. by author. Farrar, 1994. ISBN 0-374-32535-9 Subj: Animals. Rhyming text. U.S. history.

Imogene's antlers ill. by author. Crown, 1985. ISBN 0-517-55564-6 Subj: Animals. Character traits – appearance.

Paper John ill. by author. Farrar, 1987. ISBN 0-374-35738-2 Subj: Behavior – misbehavior. Character traits – cleverness. Emotions – anger. Mythical creatures. Paper.

Ruby Mae has something to say ill. by author. Crown, 1992. ISBN 0-517-58249-X Subj: Handicaps. Language. Machines.

Small, Ernest. *see* Lent, Blair

Small, Terry. *The legend of William Tell* ill. by author. Bantam, 1991. ISBN 0-553-07031-2 Subj: Character traits – bravery. Folk & fairy tales. Poetry.

A small treasury of Christmas poems and prayers ill. by Susan Spellman. Boyds Mills, 1997. ISBN 1-56397-680-3 Subj: Holidays – Christmas. Poetry. Religion – Nativity.

A small treasury of Easter poems and prayers ill. by Susan Spellman. Boyds Mills, 1997. ISBN 1-56397-647-1 Subj: Holidays – Easter. Poetry. Religion.

Smalley, Elisa. *Zoe Sophia's scrapbook* (Mauner, Claudia)

Smalley, Gary. *Mooki's secret* (Gibson, Kari Smalley)

Smallman, Clare. *Outside in* ill. by Edwina Riddell. Barron's, 1986. ISBN 0-8120-5760-0 Subj: Anatomy. Format, unusual – toy & movable books.

Smalls, Irene. *Don't say ain't* ill. by Colin Bootman. Charlesbridge, 2003. ISBN 1-57091-381-1 Subj: Books, reading. Ethnic groups in the U.S. – African Americans. Family life. Prejudice. School.

Smalls-Hector, Irene. *Because you're lucky* ill. by Michael Hays. Little, 1997. ISBN 0-316-79867-3 Subj: Behavior – sharing. Emotions – envy, jealousy. Ethnic groups in the U.S. – African Americans. Family life – cousins. Friendship.

Beginning school ill. by Toni Goffe. Silver Pr., 1996. ISBN 0-382-39328-7 Subj: Ethnic groups in the U.S. – African Americans. School – first day.

Irene and the big, fine nickel ill. by Tyrone Geter. Little, 1991. ISBN 0-316-79871-1 Subj: Cities, towns. Communities, neighborhoods. Ethnic groups in the U.S. – African Americans. Family life. Money.

Irene Jennie and the Christmas masquerade ill. by Melodye Rosales. Little, 1996. ISBN 0-316-79878-9 Subj: Ethnic groups in the U.S. – African Americans. Holidays – Christmas. Slavery.

Jenny Reen and the Jack Muh Lantern ill. by Keinyo White. Atheneum, 1996. ISBN 0-689-31875-8 Subj: Ethnic groups in the U.S. – African Americans. Holidays – Halloween. Slavery. U.S. history.

Jonathan and his mommy ill. by Michael Hays. Little, 1992. ISBN 0-316-79870-3 Subj: Activities – walking. Cities, towns. Communities, neighborhoods. Ethnic groups in the U.S. – African Americans. Family life – mothers.

Kevin and his dad ill. by Michael Hays. Little, 1999. ISBN 0-316-79899-1 Subj: Ethnic groups in the U.S. – African Americans. Family life – fathers. Rhyming text.

Louise's gift: or What did she give me that for? ill. by Colin Bootman. Little, 1996. ISBN 0-316-79877-0 Subj: Ethnic groups in the U.S. – African Americans. Family life. Gifts. Self-concept.

Smaridge, Norah. *Peter's tent* ill. by Brinton Turkle. Viking, 1965. Subj: Friendship.

Watch out! ill. by Susan Perl. Abingdon, 1965. Subj: Safety.

You know better than that ill. by Susan Perl. Abingdon, 1973. ISBN 0-687-46744-6 Subj: Etiquette. Poetry.

Smart, Christopher. *For I will consider my cat Jeoffry* ill. by Emily Arnold McCully. Atheneum, 1984. ISBN 0-689-31026-9 Subj: Animals – cats. Poetry.

Smath, Jerry. *The animals' Christmas carol* ill. by author. BridgeWater, 2000. An adaption of Charles Dickens' A Christmas Carol. ISBN 0-8167-6940-0 Subj: Animals. Behavior – greed. Holidays – Christmas.

But no elephants ill. by author. Parents' Magazine Pr., 1979. ISBN 0-8193-1008-5 Subj: Animals – elephants. Pets.

Elephant goes to school ill. by author. Parents' Magazine Pr., 1984. ISBN 0-8193-1126-X Subj: Animals – elephants. School.

A hat so simple ill. by author. BridgeWater, 1993. ISBN 0-8167-3016-4 Subj: Clothing – hats. Reptiles – alligators, crocodiles. Rhyming text.

Mr. Digby's bad day by Jerry & Valerie Smath; ill. by authors. S&S, 1989. ISBN 0-671-67802-7 Subj: Behavior – bad day. Umbrellas. Weather – rain.

Smath, Valerie. *Mr. Digby's bad day* (Smath, Jerry)

Smee, Nicola. *Finish the story, dad* ill. by author. S&S, 1991. ISBN 0-671-74478-X Subj: Bedtime. Dreams. Family life – fathers.

The Tusk Fairy ill. by author. BridgeWater, 1994. ISBN 0-8167-3311-2 Subj: Activities – knitting. Fairies. Family life – grandmothers. Toys.

Smith, Barry. *A child's guide to bad behavior* ill. by author. Houghton Mifflin, 1991. ISBN 0-395-57435-8 Subj: Behavior – misbehavior. Etiquette. Family life.

Cumberland Road ill. by author. Houghton Mifflin, 1989. ISBN 0-395-51739-7 Subj: Behavior – lost & found possessions. Communities, neighborhoods.

The first voyage of Christopher Columbus ill. by author. Viking, 1992. ISBN 0-670-84051-3 Subj: Activities – traveling. Boats, ships. U.S. history.

Grandma Rabbitty's visit ill. by author. DK, 1999. ISBN 0-7894-4839-4 Subj: Animals – rabbits. Family life – grandmothers. Noise, sounds.

Minnie and Ginger ill. by author. Crown, 1991. ISBN 0-517-58253-8 Subj: Family life. Foreign lands – England. Old age. Weddings.

Tom and Annie go shopping ill. by author. Houghton Mifflin, 1989. ISBN 0-395-51738-9 Subj: Shopping.

Smith, Bozena. *The enchanted book: a tale from Krakow* (Porazinska, Janina)

Smith, Cara Lockhart. *Twenty-six rabbits run riot* ill. by author. Little, 1990. ISBN 0-316-80185-2 Subj: Animals – rabbits. Behavior – lost. Behavior – misbehavior.

Smith, Catriona Mary. *The long dive* (Smith, Raymond Kenneth)

The long slide (Smith, Raymond Kenneth)

Smith, Charles R. *I'll be there* photos by author. Hyperion, 2001. composed by Hal Davis, Berry Gordy, Jr., Bob West, & Willie

Hutchinson. ISBN 0-7868-0785-7 Subj: Babies. Format, unusual – board books. Music. Songs.

Loki and Alex photos by author. Dutton, 2001. ISBN 0-525-46700-9 Subj: Animals – dogs. Ethnic groups in the U.S. – African Americans.

My gal photos by author. Hyperion, 2001. ISBN 0-7868-0782-2 Subj: Babies. Format, unusual – board books. Music. Songs.

Smith, Cynthia Leitich. *Jingle dancer* ill. by Cornelius Van Wright & Ying-Hwa Hu. Morrow, 2000. ISBN 0-688-16242-8 Subj: Activities – dancing. Family life. Indians of North America.

Smith, Dian G. *Hanukkah lights* ill. by JoAnn Kitchel. Chronicle, 2001. ISBN 0-8118-3257-0 Subj: Holidays – Hanukkah. Jewish culture.

Smith, Donald. *Farm numbers: a counting book* ill. by author. Abelard-Schuman, 1970. ISBN 0-20-071635-2 Subj: Counting, numbers. Farms.

Who's wearing my baseball cap? ill. by author. Dial, 1987. ISBN 0-8037-0396-1 Subj: Animals. Clothing – hats. Format, unusual – board books. Problem solving.

Who's wearing my bow tie? ill. by author. Dial, 1987. ISBN 0-8037-0395-3 Subj: Animals. Clothing. Format, unusual – board books. Problem solving.

Who's wearing my sneakers? ill. by author. Dial, 1987. ISBN 0-8037-0398-8 Subj: Animals. Clothing – shoes. Format, unusual – board books. Problem solving.

Who's wearing my sunglasses? ill. by author. Dial, 1987. ISBN 0-8037-0399-6 Subj: Animals. Format, unusual – board books. Glasses. Problem solving.

Smith, Edward Biko. *A lullaby for Daddy* ill. by Susan Anderson. Africa World, 1994. ISBN 0-86543-403-4 Subj: Bedtime. Ethnic groups in the U.S. – African Americans. Family life. Lullabies. Music.

Smith, Elmer Boyd. *The story of Noah's ark* ill. by author. Houghton Mifflin, 1904. Subj: Boats, ships. Religion – Noah. Weather – floods. Weather – rain. Weather – rainbows.

Smith, Henry Lee. *Frog fun* (Stratemeyer, Clara Georgeanna)

Pepper (Stratemeyer, Clara Georgeanna)

Tuggy (Stratemeyer, Clara Georgeanna)

Smith, Janice Lee. *Jess and the stinky cowboys* ill. by Lisa Thiesing. Dial, 2004. ISBN 0-8037-2641-4 Subj: Activities – bathing. Animals – dogs. Careers – police officers. Character traits – cleanliness. Cowboys, cowgirls. Tall tales. U.S. history – frontier & pioneer life.

The monster in the third dresser drawer and other stories about Adam Joshua ill. by Dick Gackenbach. HarperCollins, 1981. ISBN 0-06-025739-3 Subj: Behavior – misbehavior. Emotions – fear. Monsters.

Wizard and Wart in trouble ill. by Paul Meisel. HarperCollins, 1998. ISBN 0-06-027762-9 Subj: Animals. Magic. Wizards.

Smith, Jean Shannon. *Scooter and the magic star* (Gardner, Mercedes)

Smith, Jim. *The frog band and Durrington Dormouse* ill. by author. Little, 1977. ISBN 0-316-80155-0 Subj: Animals – mice. Frogs & toads.

The frog band and the onion seller ill. by author. Little, 1976. ISBN 0-316-80006-6 Subj: Animals. Frogs & toads. Humorous stories. Problem solving.

The frog band and the ownapper ill. by author. Little, 1981. ISBN 0-316-80163-1 Subj: Animals. Birds – owls. Frogs & toads.

Nimbus the explorer ill. by author. Little, 1981. ISBN 0-316-80168-2 Subj: Animals. Dinosaurs. Imagination. Jungle.

Smith, Joseph A. (Joseph Anthony). *Circus train* ill. by author. Abrams, 2001. ISBN 0-8109-4148-1 Subj: Circus. Moving. Trains.

Smith, Kathryn. *Little Donkey's Christmas story* ill. by Amanda Wood. Candle Bks., 2002. ISBN 1-8598-5441-9 Subj: Animals – donkeys. Format, unusual – toy & movable books. Holidays – Christmas. Participation. Religion – Nativity.

Little Lamb's Christmas story ill. by Amanda Wood. Candle Bks., 2002. ISBN 1-8598-5442-7 Subj: Animals – sheep. Format, unusual – toy & movable books. Holidays – Christmas. Participation. Religion – Nativity.

Smith, Lane. *The big pets* ill. by author. Viking, 1991. ISBN 0-670-83378-9 Subj: Animals. Dreams. Pets.

Flying Jake ill. by author. Macmillan, 1988. ISBN 0-02-785830-8 Subj: Activities – flying. Birds. Wordless.

Glasses . . . who needs 'em? ill. by author. Viking, 1991. ISBN 0-670-84160-9 Subj: Glasses. Senses – sight.

Pinocchio, the boy ill. by author. Viking, 2002. ISBN 0-670-03585-8 Subj: Fairies. Folk & fairy tales. Humorous stories. Puppets. Self-concept.

The Stinky Cheese Man and other fairly stupid tales (Scieszka, Jon)

Smith, Linda. *Mrs. Biddlebox* ill. by Marla Frazee. HarperCollins, 2002. ISBN 0-06-028690-3 Subj: Activities – baking, cooking. Emotions. Food. Rhyming text.

Sir Cassie to the rescue ill. by Karen Patkau. Orca, 2003. ISBN 1-55143-243-9 Subj: Family life – brothers & sisters. Imagination. Knights.

When Moon fell down ill. by Kathryn Brown. HarperCollins, 2001. ISBN 0-06-029497-3 Subj: Animals – bulls, cows. Moon. Rhyming text.

Smith, Lucia B. *A special kind of sister* ill. by Chuck Hall. Holt, 1979. ISBN 0-03-047121-4 Subj: Family life. Handicaps. Sibling rivalry.

Smith, Maggie (Margaret C.). *Counting our way to Maine* ill. by author. Orchard, 1995. ISBN 0-531-08734-4 Subj: Activities – traveling. Counting, numbers.

Dear Daisy, get well soon ill. by author. Crown, 2000. ISBN 0-517-80073-X Subj: Counting, numbers. Days of the week, months of the year. Family life – mothers. Friendship. Illness – chicken pox. Toys.

Desser, the best ever cat ill. by author. Knopf, 2001. ISBN 0-375-91056-5 Subj: Animals – cats. Death. Emotions. Pets.

My grandma's chair ill. by author. Lothrop, 1992. ISBN 0-688-10664-1 Subj: Family life – grandmothers. Furniture – chairs. Imagination.

Noly Poly Rabbit Tail and me ill. by author. Lothrop, 1990. ISBN 0-688-09571-2 Subj: Friendship. Toys – dolls.

Paisley ill. by author. Knopf, 2004. ISBN 0-375-92164-8 Subj: Animals – elephants. Behavior – needing someone. Toys.

There's a witch under the stairs ill. by author. Lothrop, 1991. ISBN 0-688-09885-1 Subj: Emotions – fear. Imagination. Witches.

This is your garden ill. by author. Crown, 1998. ISBN 0-517-70993-7 Subj: Gardens, gardening.

Smith, Mary. *Long ago elf* by Mary & Robert Alan Smith; ill. by authors. Follett, 1968. Subj: Mythical creatures – elves. Mythical creatures – gnomes.

Smith, Mavis. *Circles* ill. by author. Little, 1991. ISBN 1-55782-366-9 Subj: Concepts – shape. Concepts – size.

Fred, is that you? ill. by author. Little, 1992. ISBN 0-316-80241-7 Subj: Animals. Birds – ducks. Format, unusual – toy & movable books. Rhyming text.

Good night, Jessie! (Ziefert, Harriet)

A snake mistake ill. by author. HarperCollins, 1991. ISBN 0-06-026909-X Subj: Behavior – trickery. Eggs. Farms. Reptiles – snakes.

'Twas the day after Thanksgiving ill. by author. Little Simon, 2002. ISBN 0-689-85234-7 Subj: Animals – mice. Format, unusual – toy & movable books. Holidays – Thanksgiving. Rhyming text.

Smith, Patty. *Faces* ill. by James Lee Croft. Running Pr., 2001. ISBN 0-7624-0933-9 Subj: Anatomy – faces.

Smith, Peter. *Jenny's baby brother* ill. by Bob Graham. Viking, 1984. ISBN 0-670-40636-8 Subj: Babies. Family life – new sibling. Sibling rivalry.

Smith, Raymond Kenneth. *The long dive* by Raymond Kenneth & Catriona Mary Smith; ill. by authors. Atheneum, 1978. ISBN 0-689-30672-5 Subj: Sea & seashore. Toys.

The long slide by Raymond Kenneth & Catriona Mary Smith; ill. by authors. Atheneum, 1977. ISBN 0-689-30576-1 Subj: Toys.

Smith, Robert Alan. *Long ago elf* (Smith, Mary)

Smith, Robert Paul. *Jack Mack* ill. by Erik Blegvad. Coward, 1960. Subj: Humorous stories. Tongue twisters.

Nothingatall, nothingatall, nothingatall ill. by Alan E. Cober. HarperCollins, 1965. Subj: Bedtime.

When I am big ill. by Lillian Hoban. HarperCollins, 1965. Subj: Behavior – growing up.

Smith, Rodger. *This old man: a musical counting book* (Ross, Tony)

The very good dinosaur (Inkpen, Mick)

Smith, Roger. *The empty island* ill. by author. Interlink, 1991. ISBN 0-940793-69-5 Subj: Islands.

How the animals saved the ark and put two and two together ill. by author. S&S, 1989. ISBN 0-671-66560-X Subj: Animals. Boats, ships. Religion – Noah. Weather – floods. Weather – rain.

Runners, sliders, bouncers, climbers (Bantock, Nick)

Smith, Rosie. *Captain Pajamas* (Whatley, Bruce)

Smith, Theresa Kalab. *The fog is secret* ill. by author. Prentice-Hall, 1966. Subj: Sea & seashore. Weather – fog.

Smith, Wendy. *The lonely, only mouse* ill. by author. Viking, 1986. ISBN 0-670-81251-X Subj: Animals – mice. Behavior – sharing. Emotions – loneliness. Family life – only child.

Say hello, Tilly ill. by author. Bantam, 1991. ISBN 0-553-07160-2 Subj: Animals – bears. Birthdays. Character traits – shyness.

Twice mice ill. by author. Carolrhoda, 1989. ISBN 0-87614-371-0 Subj: Animals – mice. Emotions. Family life. Sibling rivalry.

Smith, Will (1968–). *Just the two of us* ill. by Kadir Nelson. Scholastic, 2001. ISBN 0-439-08792-9 Subj: Family life – fathers. Family life – sons. Music. Songs.

Smith, William Jay. *Children of the forest* (Beskow, Elsa Maartman)

The telephone (Chukovskii, Kornei Ivanovich)

Up the hill and down (Up the hill and down)

Smith, William Jay (1918–). *Around my room* ill. by Erik Blegvad. Farrar, 2000. ISBN 0-374-30406-8 Subj: Poetry.

Birds and beasts ill. by Jacques Hnizdovsky. Godine, 1990. ISBN 0-87923-865-8 Subj: Animals. Birds. Poetry.

Puptents and pebbles: nonsense ABC ill. by Juliet Kepes. Little, 1959. Subj: ABC books. Humorous stories. Poetry.

The sun is up by William Jay Smith & Carol Ra; ill. by Jane Chambless Wright. Boyds Mills, 1996. ISBN 1-56397-029-5 Subj: Days of the week, months of the year. Poetry. Seasons.

Smith-Ayala, Emilie. *Marisol and the yellow messenger* ill. by Sami Suomalainen. Firefly, 1994. ISBN 1-55037-973-9 Subj: Death. Emotions – grief. Family life – fathers. Foreign lands – Canada. Foreign lands – South America.

Smith-Moore, J. J. *Sally Small* ill. by author. Price Stern Sloan, 1989. ISBN 0-8431-2360-5 Subj: Concepts – shape. Concepts – size. Dreams. Rhyming text.

Smothers, Ethel Footman. *Auntee Edna* ill. by Wil Clay. Eerdmans, 2001. ISBN 0-8028-5154-1 Subj: Activities – baking, cooking. Ethnic groups in the U.S. – African Americans. Food.

Smucker, Anna Egan. *No star nights* ill. by Steve Johnson. Knopf, 1989. ISBN 0-394-99925-8 Subj: Cities, towns. Machines.

Smucker, Barbara Claasen. *Selina and the bear paw quilt* ill. by Janet Wilson. Crown, 1996. ISBN 0-517-70904-X Subj: Ethnic groups in the U.S. – Amish. Family life – grandmothers. Foreign lands – Canada. Quilts. U.S. history. War.

Smyth, Gwenda. *A pet for Mrs. Arbuckle* ill. by Ann James. Crown, 1981. ISBN 0-517-55434-8 Subj: Activities – traveling. Animals – cats. Pets.

Snape, Charles. *Frog odyssey* (Snape, Juliet)

Snape, Juliet. *Frog odyssey* by Juliet & Charles Snape; ill. by authors. S&S, 1992. ISBN 0-671-74741-X Subj: Ecology. Frogs & toads. Moving.

Sneed, Brad. *Lucky Russell* ill. by author. Putnam, 1992. ISBN 0-399-22329-0 Subj: Animals. Animals – cats. Farms. Pets.

Picture a letter ill. by author. Fogelman, 2002. ISBN 0-8037-2613-9 Subj: ABC books. Wordless.

Snell, Gordon. *'Twas the day after Christmas* ill. by Sean DeLonas. HarperCollins, 2003. ISBN 0-06-028952-X Subj: Animals – mice. Holidays – Christmas. Humorous stories. Rhyming text.

Twelve days, a Christmas countdown ill. by Kevin O'Malley. HarperCollins, 2002. ISBN 0-06-028955-4 Subj: Cumulative tales. Holidays – Christmas. Music. Songs.

Snell, Nigel. *A bird in hand . . . a child's guide to sayings* ill. by author. David & Charles, 1987. ISBN 0-241-11815-8 Subj: Language.

Sneve, Virginia Driving Hawk. *The Cherokees* ill. by Ronald Himler. Holiday, 1996. ISBN 0-8234-1214-8 Subj: Creation. Folk & fairy tales. Indians of North America – Cherokee. U.S. history.

The Nez Perce ill. by Ronald Himler. Holiday, 1994. ISBN 0-8234-1090-0 Subj: Creation. Indians of North America – Nez Perce. U.S. history.

Sniff, Mr. *see* Abisch, Roz

Snihura, Ulana. *I miss Franklin P. Shuckles* ill. by Leanne Franson. Annick, 1998. ISBN 1-55037-517-2 Subj: Friendship.

Snoopy on wheels ill. by Charles M. Schulz. Random House, 1983. ISBN 0-394-85630-9 Subj: Animals – dogs. Birds. Toys. Wheels.

Snow, Alan. *Cluck!* ill. by author. Bantam, 1994. ISBN 0-553-09764-4 Subj: Birds – chickens. Farms. Format, unusual – board books. Noise, sounds.

The monster book of ABC sounds ill. by author. Dial, 1991. ISBN 0-8037-0935-8 Subj: ABC books. Animals – rats. Monsters. Noise, sounds. Rhyming text.

My first atlas ill. by author. Troll, 1992. ISBN 0-8167-2517-9 Subj: World.

My first dictionary ill. by author. Troll, 1992. ISBN 0-8167-2515-2 Subj: Language.

Oink! ill. by author. Bantam, 1994. ISBN 0-553-09765-2 Subj: Animals – pigs. Farms. Format, unusual – board books. Noise, sounds.

Quack! ill. by author. Bantam, 1994. ISBN 0-553-09762-8 Subj: Birds – ducks. Farms. Format, unusual – board books. Noise, sounds.

The truth about cats ill. by author. Little, 1996. ISBN 0-316-80282-4 Subj: Animals – cats. Space & space ships.

Woof! ill. by author. Bantam, 1994. ISBN 0-553-09763-6 Subj: Animals – dogs. Farms. Format, unusual – board books. Noise, sounds.

Snow, Pegeen. *Mrs. Periwinkle's groceries* ill. by Jerry Warshaw. Childrens Pr., 1981. ISBN 0-516-03558-4 Subj: Character traits – helpfulness. Cumulative tales. Old age.

A pet for Pat ill. by Tom Dunnington. Childrens Pr., 1984. ISBN 0-516-02049-8 Subj: Pets. Rhyming text.

Snyder, Anne. *The old man and the mule* ill. by Mila Lazarevich. Holt, 1978. ISBN 0-03-022571-X Subj: Animals – mules. Character traits – meanness.

Snyder, Carol. *We're painting* ill. by Lisa Jahn-Clough. HarperFestival, 2002. ISBN 0-694-01445-1 Subj: Activities – painting. Concepts – color. Concepts – shape.

Snyder, Dianne. *The boy of the three-year nap* ill. by Allen Say. Houghton Mifflin, 1988. ISBN 0-395-44090-4 Subj: Behavior – trickery. Caldecott award honor books. Character traits – laziness. Folk & fairy tales.

Snyder, Dick. *One day at the zoo* photos by author. Scribners, 1960. Subj: Animals. Animals – koalas. Zoos.

Talk to me tiger photos by author; foreword by George H. Pournelle. Golden Gate, 1965. Subj: Animals. Zoos.

Snyder, Inez. *Building tools* ill. with photos. Childrens Pr., 2002. ISBN 0-516-23976-7 Subj: Careers – carpenters. Furniture. Tools.

Gardening tools ill. with photos. Childrens Pr., 2002. ISBN 0-516-23978-3 Subj: Gardens, gardening. Tools.

Snyder, Margaret. *I know an old lady* (Little old lady who swallowed a fly)

Snyder, Zilpha Keatley. *The changing maze* ill. by Charles Mikolaycak. Macmillan, 1985. ISBN 0-02-785900-2 Subj: Animals – sheep. Folk & fairy tales. Magic. Wizards.

Come on, Patsy ill. by Margot Zemach. Atheneum, 1982. ISBN 0-689-30892-2 Subj: Activities – playing. Behavior – growing up. Friendship.

So, Meilo. *The emperor and the nightingale* (Andersen, H. C. [Hans Christian])

Gobble, gobble, slip, slop ill. by author. Knopf, 2004. ISBN 0-375-92504-X Subj: Animals – cats. Behavior – greed. Folk & fairy tales. Foreign lands – India.

Sobat, Vera. *Little Bear and the big fight* (Langreuter, Jutta)

Little Bear brushes his teeth (Langreuter, Jutta)

Little Bear goes to kindergarten (Langreuter, Jutta)

Sobol, Harriet Langsam. *A book of vegetables* photos by Patricia Agre. Dodd, 1984. ISBN 0-396-08450-8 Subj: Food. Gardens, gardening.

Clowns photos by Patricia Agre. Coward, 1982. ISBN 0-698-20558-8 Subj: Clowns, jesters.

Jeff's hospital book photos by Patricia Agre. Walck, 1975. ISBN 0-8098-1229-0 Subj: Hospitals.

We don't look like our mom and dad photos by Patricia Agre. Coward, 1984. ISBN 0-698-20608-8 Subj: Adoption. Ethnic groups in the U.S. Family life.

Sobol, Richard. *Adelina's whales* photos by author. Dutton, 2003. ISBN 0-525-47110-3 Subj: Animals – whales. Family life. Foreign lands – Mexico.

Sohi, Morteza E. *Look what I did with a leaf!* ill. by author. Walker, 1993. ISBN 0-8027-8216-7 Subj: Activities – making things. Nature.

Sokol, Edward. *Meet Stinky Magee* ill. by author. HarperCollins, 2000. ISBN 0-688-17416-7 Subj: Food. Magic. Toys – rocking horses.

Sokolinsky, Martin. *Threadbear* (Gallaz, Christophe)

Solbert, Ronni (Romaine G.). *Emily Emerson's moon* (Merrill, Jean)

Solheim, James. *Santa's secrets revealed* ill. by Barry Gott. Carolrhoda, 2004. ISBN 1-575-05600-3 Subj: Holidays – Christmas. Santa Claus.

Solomon, Chuck. *Moving up from kindergarten to first grade* photos by author. Crown, 1989. ISBN 0-517-57286-9 Subj: Behavior – growing up. School.

Solomon, Joan. *A present for Mum* photos by Joan & Ryan Solomon. Hamish Hamilton, 1982. ISBN 0-241-10553-6 Subj: Foreign lands – England. Shopping. Stores.

Solotareff, Grégoire. *Don't call me little bunny* ill. by author. Farrar, 1988. ISBN 0-374-35012-4 Subj: Animals – rabbits. Behavior – misbehavior. Crime. Prisons.

Never trust an ogre ill. by author. Greenwillow, 1988. ISBN 0-688-07741-2 Subj: Animals. Behavior – greed. Mythical creatures – ogres.

The ogre and the frog king ill. by author. Greenwillow, 1988. ISBN 0-688-07079-5 Subj: Frogs & toads. Monsters. Mythical creatures – ogres.

Somary, Wolfgang. *Night and the candlemaker* ill. by Simon Bartram. Barefoot, 2000. ISBN 1-84148-137-8 Subj: Night. Sleep.

Somers, Kevin. *Meaner than meanest* ill. by Diana Cain Bluthenthal. Hyperion, 2001. ISBN 0-7868-2498-0 Subj: Character traits – meanness. Magic. Witches.

Somme, Lauritz. *The penguin family book* by Lauritz Somme & Sybille Kalas; trans. by Patricia Crampton; ill. with photos. Picture Book Studio, 1988. ISBN 0-88708-057-X Subj: Birds – penguins.

Sommers, Tish. *Bert and the broken teapot* ill. by Diane Dawson Hearn. Childrens Pr., 1985. ISBN 0-307-62114-6 Subj: Behavior – carelessness. Friendship.

Sonberg, Lynn. *A horse named Paris* ill. by Ken Robbins. Bradbury, 1986. ISBN 0-02-786260-7 Subj: Animals – horses, ponies.

Sondergaard, Arensa. *Biddy and the ducks* by Arensa Sondergaard & Mary M. Reed; ill. by Doris Henderson & Marion Henderson. Heath, 1941. Subj: Birds – chickens. Birds – ducks.

Sondheimer, Ilse. *The boy who could make his mother stop yelling* ill. by Dee deRosa. Rainbow Pr., 1982. ISBN 0-943156-00-9 Subj: Behavior – bad day. Family life – mothers.

The magic of Pomme ill. by Dee deRosa. Rainbow Pr., 1990. ISBN 0-943156-02-5 Subj: Food. Magic. Problem solving.

The song of the Three Holy Children ill. by Pauline Baynes. Holt, 1986. The text of this edition is taken from The Book of Common Prayer, 1662. ISBN 0-8050-0134-4 Subj: Nature. Religion. Songs.

Sonneborn, Ruth A. *Friday night is papa night* ill. by Emily Arnold McCully. Viking, 1970. ISBN 0-670-32938-X Subj: Cities, towns. Ethnic groups in the U.S. – Puerto Rican Americans. Family life – fathers. Poverty.

I love Gram ill. by Leo Carty. Viking, 1971. ISBN 0-670-39064-X Subj: Cities, towns. Family life – grandmothers. Hospitals. Illness. Old age.

Lollipop's party ill. by Brinton Turkle. Viking, 1967. Subj: Cities, towns. Emotions – loneliness. Ethnic groups in the U.S. – Puerto Rican Americans.

Seven in a bed ill. by Don Freeman. Viking, 1968. Subj: Ethnic groups in the U.S. – Puerto Rican Americans. Family life. Poverty. Sleep.

Sonnenschein, Harriet. *Harold's hideaway thumb* ill. by Jürg Obrist. S&S, 1991. ISBN 0-671-73568-3 Subj: Animals – rabbits. Behavior – growing up. Thumb sucking.

Harold's runaway nose ill. by Jürg Obrist. S&S, 1989. ISBN 0-671-66912-5 Subj: Animals – rabbits. Behavior – lost & found possessions. Illness.

Sopko, Eugen. *Townsfolk and countryfolk* ill. by author. Faber, 1982. ISBN 0-051-12515-8 Subj: Cities, towns. Country. Foreign lands – Europe.

Sorel, Edward. *The Saturday kid* by Edward Sorel in collab. with Cheryl Carlesimo; ill. by Edward Sorel. McElderry, 1999. ISBN 0-689-82399-1 Subj: Behavior – bullying. Music. Musical instruments – violins.

Sorensen, Henri. *New Hope* ill. by author. Lothrop, 1995. ISBN 0-688-13926-4 Subj: Activities – traveling. Family life. U.S. history – frontier & pioneer life.

Sorine, Stephanie Riva. *Our ballet class* photos by Daniel S. Sorine. Knopf, 1981. ISBN 0-394-94821-1 Subj: Activities – dancing. Ballet.

Soros, Barbara. *Tenzin's deer* ill. by Danuta Maya. Barefoot, 2003. ISBN 1-84148-811-9 Subj: Animals – deer. Character traits – kindness to animals. Foreign lands – Tibet. Illness.

Sosa-Masso, Carmen. *No fair to tigers = No es justo para los tigres* (Hoffman, Eric)

Play Lady = La Señora Juguetona (Hoffman, Eric)

Soto, Gary. *Chato and the party animals* ill. by Susan Guevara. Putnam, 2000. ISBN 0-399-23159-5 Subj: Animals – cats. Birthdays. Parties.

Chato's kitchen ill. by Susan Guevara. Putnam, 1995. ISBN 0-399-22658-3 Subj: Animals – cats. Animals – dogs. Animals – mice. Cities, towns. Food. Foreign languages.

The old man and his door ill. by Joe Cepeda. Putnam, 1996. ISBN 0-399-22700-8 Subj: Character traits – helpfulness. Ethnic groups in the U.S. – Mexican Americans. Food. Foreign lands. Parties. Senses – hearing.

Snapshots from the wedding ill. by Stephanie Garcia. Putnam, 1997. ISBN 0-399-22808-X Subj: Ethnic groups in the U.S. – Mexican Americans. Family life. Weddings.

Too many tamales ill. by Ed Martinez. Putnam, 1993. ISBN 0-399-22146-8 Subj: Ethnic groups in the U.S. – Mexican Americans. Food. Foreign languages. Holidays – Christmas.

Sotzek, Hannelore. *A koala is not a bear!* by Hannelore Sotzek & Bobbie Kalman; ill. with photos & drawings. Crabtree, 1997. ISBN 0-8650-5739-7 Subj: Animals – koalas.

Souhami, Jessica. *The leopard's drum: an Asante tale from West Africa* ill. by author. Little, 1995. ISBN 0-316-80466-5 Subj: Animals – leopards. Folk & fairy tales. Foreign lands – Africa.

Mrs. McCool and the giant Cuhullin ill. by author. Holt, 2002. ISBN 0-8050-6852-X Subj: Behavior – fighting, arguing. Character traits – cleverness. Folk & fairy tales. Foreign lands – Ireland. Giants.

No dinner! the story of the old woman and the pumpkin ill. by author. Cavendish, 2000. ISBN 0-7614-5059-9 Subj: Animals. Animals – wolves. Behavior – trickery. Folk & fairy tales. Foreign lands – India.

Old MacDonald had a farm (Old MacDonald had a farm)

Rama and the demon king ill. by reteller. DK, 1997. ISBN 0-7894-2450-9 Subj: Animals – monkeys. Folk & fairy tales. Foreign lands – India. Royalty – kings. Royalty – princes.

Southey, Robert. *The cataract of Lodore* ill. by Mordicai Gerstein. Dial, 1991. ISBN 0-8037-1026-7 Subj: Foreign lands – England. Poetry. Water.

Southwell, Jandelyn. *The little country town* ill. by Kay Chorao. Holt, 2000. ISBN 0-8050-5711-0 Subj: Country. Night. Noise, sounds. Rhyming text. Senses – smell.

Sowden, Henry. *The grand old Duke of York* photos by author. Trafalgar Square, 1989. ISBN 0-575-04081-5 Subj: Poetry. Toys – soldiers.

Sowler, Sandie. *Amazing animal disguises* ill. by Ruth Lindsay & Jane Gedye, & with photos by Jerry Young. Knopf, 1992. ISBN 0-679-92768-9 Subj: Animals. Behavior – hiding.

Amazing armored animals photos by Jerry Young & Jane Burton. Knopf, 1992. ISBN 0-679-92767-0 Subj: Animals.

Soya, Kiyoshi. *A house of leaves* ill. by Akiko Hayashi. Putnam, 1987. ISBN 0-399-21422-4 Subj: Insects. Weather – rain.

Spafford, Suzy. *Witzy's colors* ill. by author. Lyrick, 2001. ISBN 1-58668-055-2 Subj: Animals. Concepts – color. Format, unusual – toy & movable books.

Spagnoli, Cathy. *Judge Rabbit and the tree spirit* (Wall, Lina Mao)

Nine-in-one Grr! Grr! (Xiong, Blia)

Spalding, Andrea. *It's raining, it's pouring* ill. by Leslie Elizabeth Watts. Orca, 2001. ISBN 1-55143-186-6 Subj: Giants. Illness. Imagination. Weather – rain.

Me and Mr. Mah ill. by author. Orca, 1999. ISBN 1-55143-168-8 Subj: Flowers. Friendship. Gardens, gardening. Memories, memory. Old age.

Sarah May and the new red dress ill. by Janet Wilson. Orca, 1998. ISBN 1-55143-117-3 Subj: Clothing – dresses. Family life – grandmothers. Memories, memory. Old age.

Solomon's tree ill. by Janet Wilson; mask & Tsimshian designs by Victor Reece. Orca, 2002. ISBN 1-55143-217-X Subj: Activities – storytelling. Indians of North America – Tsimshian. Masks. Trees.

Spang, Günter. *Clelia and the little mermaid* ill. by Pepperl Ott. Abelard-Schuman, 1967. Translation of Clelia und die kleine Wassernixe. Subj: Emotions – loneliness. Foreign lands – Germany. Friendship. Mythical creatures – mermaids, mermen.

The ox and the Donkey ill. by Loek Koopmans; trans. by Marianne Martens. North-South, 2001. ISBN 0-7358-1516-X Subj: Animals – donkeys. Animals – oxen. Holidays – Christmas. Religion – Nativity.

Spangenburg, Judith Dunn. *see* Dunn, Judy

Spanner, Helmut. *I am a little cat* trans. from German by Robert Kimber; ill. by author. Barron's, 1983. ISBN 0-8120-5513-6 Subj: Animals – cats. Format, unusual – board books.

Spanyol, Jessica. *Carlo likes counting* ill. by author. Candlewick, 2002. ISBN 0-7636-1774-1 Subj: Animals – giraffes. Counting, numbers.

Speare, Jean. *A candle for Christmas* ill. by Ann Blades. Macmillan, 1987. ISBN 0-689-50417-9 Subj: Family life. Foreign lands – Canada. Holidays – Christmas. Indians of North America.

Speed, Toby. *Brave potatoes* ill. by Barry Root. Putnam, 2000. ISBN 0-399-23158-7 Subj: Activities – baking, cooking. Fairs, festivals. Plants.

Hattie baked a wedding cake ill. by Cathi Hepworth. Putnam, 1994. ISBN 0-399-22342-8 Subj: Activities – baking, cooking. Food. Weddings.

Two cool cows ill. by Barry Root. Putnam, 1995. ISBN 0-399-22647-8 Subj: Animals – bulls, cows. Moon. Rhyming text.

Watervoices ill. by Julie Downing. Putnam, 1998. ISBN 0-399-22631-1 Subj: Humorous stories. Nature. Poetry. Riddles & jokes. Water.

Speirs, John. *The little boy's Christmas gift* ill. by author. Abrams, 2001. ISBN 0-8109-4399-9 Subj: Gifts. Holidays – Christmas. Religion – Nativity. Trees.

Spelman, Cornelia Maude. *Mama and Daddy Bear's divorce* ill. by Kathy Parkinson. A. Whitman, 1998. ISBN 0-8075-5221-6 Subj: Animals – bears. Divorce. Emotions. Emotions – love.

When I care about others ill. by Kathy Parkinson. A. Whitman, 2002. ISBN 0-8075-8889-X Subj: Animals – bears. Behavior – sharing. Character traits – kindness. Emotions.

When I feel angry ill. by Nancy Cote. A. Whitman, 2000. ISBN 0-8075-8888-1 Subj: Animals – rabbits. Behavior. Emotions – anger.

When I feel sad ill. by Kathy Parkinson. A. Whitman, 2002. ISBN 0-8075-8891-1 Subj: Animals – guinea pigs. Emotions – sadness.

When I feel scared ill. by Kathy Parkinson. A. Whitman, 2002. ISBN 0-8075-8890-3 Subj: Animals – bears. Emotions – fear.

When I miss you ill. by Kathy Parkinson. A. Whitman, 2004. ISBN 0-8075-8910-1 Subj: Animals – guinea pigs. Emotions – loneliness. Family life – parents.

Your body belongs to you ill. by Teri Weidner. A. Whitman, 1997. ISBN 0-8075-9474-1 Subj: Child abuse. Health & fitness. Safety.

Spence, Robert, III. *Clickety clack* ill. by Margaret Spengler. Viking, 1999. ISBN 0-670-87946-0 Subj: Animals. Noise, sounds. Rhyming text. Trains.

Spencer, Zane. *Bright Fawn and me* (Leech, Jay)

Sper, Emily. *Hanukkah: a counting book in English, Hebrew, & Yiddish* ill. by author. Scholastic, 2001. ISBN 0-439-28291-8 Subj: Counting, numbers. Foreign languages. Holidays – Hanukkah. Jewish culture. Religion.

The Passover seder ill. by author. Scholastic, 2003. ISBN 0-439-44312-1 Subj: Format, unusual – toy & movable books. Holidays – Passover. Jewish culture. Language. Religion.

Sperberg, Roger. *Real soon, raccoon* ill. by Jill Kimball. Watchung Plaza, 2000. E Book. ISBN 0-9678578-6-4 Subj: Family life. Games. Language.

The story of the sleeping beauty, whose name was Briar Rose by Roger Sperberg, C.M. Sperberg-McQueen; ill. by authors. S Press, 2000. ISBN 0-9678578-0-5 Subj: Fairies. Folk & fairy tales. Royalty – princes. Royalty – princesses. Sleep. Witches.

Spetter, Jung-Hee. *Lily and Trooper's fall* ill. by author. Front St., 1998. ISBN 1-886910-38-3 Subj: Activities – playing. Animals – dogs. Seasons – fall.

Lily and Trooper's spring ill. by author. Front St., 1998. ISBN 1-886910-36-7 Subj: Activities – picnicking. Activities – playing. Animals – dogs. Seasons – spring.

Lily and Trooper's summer ill. by author. Front St., 1998. ISBN 1-886910-37-5 Subj: Activities – playing. Animals – dogs. Seasons – summer.

Lily and Trooper's winter ill. by author. Front St., 1998. ISBN 1-886910-39-1 Subj: Activities. Animals – dogs. Seasons – winter. Weather – rain. Weather – snow.

Spiegel, Doris. *Danny and Company 92* ill. by author. Coward, 1945. Subj: Careers – firefighters. Fire.

Spiegelman, Art. *I'm a dog!* ill. by author. HarperCollins, 1997. ISBN 0-06-027320-8 Subj: Animals – dogs. Format, unusual – toy & movable books. Magic.

Spier, Peter. *Bill's service station* ill. by author. Doubleday, 1981. ISBN 0-385-15727-4 Subj: Automobiles. Format, unusual – board books.

The Book of Jonah (Bible Old Testament Jonah)

Bored – nothing to do! ill. by author. Doubleday, 1978. ISBN 0-385-13178-X Subj: Airplanes, airports. Behavior – boredom. Humorous stories.

Crash! bang! boom! ill. by author. Doubleday, 1972. ISBN 0-385-26569-7 Subj: Noise, sounds. Parades. Participation.

Dreams ill. by author. Doubleday, 1986. ISBN 0-385-19336-X Subj: Dreams. Sky. Weather – clouds. Wordless.

The Erie Canal ill. by author. Doubleday, 1970. ISBN 0-385-05452-1 Subj: Folk & fairy tales. Music. Songs. U.S. history.

Fast-slow, high-low: a book of opposites ill. by author. Doubleday, 1972. ISBN 0-385-06781-X Subj: Concepts – opposites. Concepts – speed.

Firehouse ill. by author. Doubleday, 1981. ISBN 0-385-15728-2 Subj: Careers – firefighters. Format, unusual – board books.

Food market ill. by author. Doubleday, 1981. ISBN 0-385-15731-2 Subj: Food. Format, unusual – board books. Shopping. Stores.

Gobble, growl, grunt ill. by author. Doubleday, 1971. ISBN 0-385-24094-5 Subj: Animals. Noise, sounds. Participation.

The legend of New Amsterdam ill. by author. Doubleday, 1979. ISBN 0-385-13180-1 Subj: Folk & fairy tales. U.S. history.

Little cats ill. by author. Doubleday, 1984. ISBN 0-385-18197-3 Subj: Animals – cats. Format, unusual – board books.

Little dogs ill. by author. Doubleday, 1984. ISBN 0-385-18196-5 Subj: Animals – dogs. Format, unusual – board books.

Little ducks ill. by author. Doubleday, 1984. ISBN 0-385-18199-X Subj: Birds – ducks. Format, unusual – board books.

Little rabbits ill. by author. Doubleday, 1984. ISBN 0-385-18198-1 Subj: Animals – rabbits. Format, unusual – board books.

My school ill. by author. Doubleday, 1981. ISBN 0-385-15732-0 Subj: Format, unusual – board books. School.

Noah's ark ill. by author. Doubleday, 1977. Includes P. Spier's translation of The flood, by Jacobus Revius. ISBN 0-385-12730-8 Subj: Animals. Boats, ships. Caldecott award books. Religion – Noah. Rhyming text. Weather – floods. Weather – rain. Wordless.

Oh, were they ever happy! ill. by author. Doubleday, 1978. ISBN 0-385-13176-3 Subj: Activities – painting. Concepts – color. Humorous stories.

People ill. by author. Doubleday, 1980. ISBN 0-385-13182-8 Subj: World.

The pet store ill. by author. Doubleday, 1981. ISBN 0-385-15730-4 Subj: Animals. Format, unusual – board books. Pets. Stores.

Peter Spier's Christmas! ill. by author. Doubleday, 1983. ISBN 0-385-13183-6 Subj: Holidays – Christmas.

Peter Spier's circus! ill. by author. Doubleday, 1992. ISBN 0-385-41970-8 Subj: Circus.

Peter Spier's rain ill. by author. Doubleday, 1982. ISBN 0-385-15485-2 Subj: Weather – rain. Wordless.

The toy shop ill. by author. Doubleday, 1981. ISBN 0-385-15729-0 Subj: Format, unusual – board books. Stores. Toys.

We the people: the Constitution of the United States of America ill. by author. Doubleday, 1987. ISBN 0-385-23789-8 Subj: U.S. history.

Spilka, Arnold. *Dippy dos and don'ts* (Sage, Michael)

A lion I can do without ill. by author. Walck, 1964. Subj: Humorous stories. Rhyming text.

Little birds don't cry ill. by author. Viking, 1965. Subj: Animals. Rhyming text.

A rumbudgin of nonsense ill. by author. Scribners, 1970. Subj: Humorous stories. Poetry.

Spilsbury, Louise. *Carrots* ill. with photos. Heinemann, 2002. ISBN 1-58810-616-0 Subj: Activities – baking, cooking. Food. Plants.

Oranges ill. with photos. Heinemann, 2002. ISBN 1-58810-618-7 Subj: Activities – baking, cooking. Food. Trees.

Peas ill. with photos. Heinemann, 2002. ISBN 1-58810-620-9 Subj: Activities – baking, cooking. Food. Plants.

Spinelli, Eileen. *The best time of day* ill. by Bryan Langdo. Harcourt, 2005. ISBN 0-15-205051-5 Subj: Country. Day. Family life. Farms. Rhyming text.

Coming through the blizzard ill. by Jenny Tylden-Wright. S&S, 1999. ISBN 0-689-81490-9 Subj: Holidays – Christmas. Weather – blizzards.

Here comes the year ill. by Narahashi. Holt, 2002. ISBN 0-8050-6685-3 Subj: Days of the week, months of the year. Rhyming text.

I know it's autumn ill. by Nancy Hayashi. HarperCollins, 2004. ISBN 0-06-029423-X Subj: Rhyming text. Seasons – fall.

In my new yellow shirt ill. by Hideko Takahashi. Holt, 2001. ISBN 0-8050-6242-4 Subj: Birthdays. Clothing – shirts. Concepts – color. Gifts. Imagination.

Night shift daddy ill. by Melissa Iwai. Hyperion, 2000. ISBN 0-7868-2424-7 Subj: Activities – working. Family life – fathers. Night.

Rise the moon ill. by Raúl Colón. Dial, 2003. ISBN 0-8037-2601-5 Subj: Moon. Night. Rhyming text.

A safe place called home ill. by Christy Hale. Cavendish, 2001. ISBN 0-7614-5085-8 Subj: Emotions – fear. Homes, houses. Rhyming text. Safety.

Six hogs on a scooter ill. by Scott Nash. Orchard, 2000. ISBN 0-531-33212-8 Subj: Animals – pigs. Family life. Humorous stories. Theater. Transportation.

Somebody loves you, Mr. Hatch ill. by Paul Yalowitz. Aladdin, 1994. ISBN 0-689-71872-1 Subj: Behavior – mistakes. Careers – postal workers. Communities, neighborhoods. Emotions – loneliness. Friendship. Holidays – Valentine's Day.

Sophie's masterpiece ill. by Jane Dyer. S&S, 1998. ISBN 0-689-80112-2 Subj: Art. Character traits – perseverance. Homes, houses. Spiders.

Summerbath, winterbath ill. by Elsa Warnick. Eerdmans, 2001. ISBN 0-8028-5179-7 Subj: Activities – bathing. Family life. Poetry. Seasons.

Thanksgiving at the Tappletons' ill. by Maryann Cocca-Leffler. Addison-Wesley, 1982. ISBN 0-201-15892-2 Subj: Animals – wolves. Behavior – sharing. Family life. Holidays – Thanksgiving. Humorous stories.

Wanda's monster ill. by Nancy Hayashi. A. Whitman, 2002. ISBN 0-8075-8656-0 Subj: Emotions – fear. Family life – grandmothers. Monsters. Problem solving.

What do angels wear? ill. by Emily Arnold McCully. HarperCollins, 2003. ISBN 0-06-028887-6 Subj: Activities. Angels. Rhyming text.

When Mama comes home tonight ill. by Jane Dyer. S&S, 1998. ISBN 0-689-81065-2 Subj: Bedtime. Family life – mothers. Rhyming text.

Where is the night train going? ill. by Cyd Moore. Boyds Mills, 1996. ISBN 1-56397-171-2 Subj: Bedtime. Dreams. Poetry. Sleep.

Spinelli, Jerry. *My daddy and me* ill. by Seymour Chwast. Knopf, 2003. ISBN 0-375-90606-1 Subj: Activities. Family life – fathers. Family life – sons.

Spinner, Stephanie. *The adventures of Pinocchio* (Collodi, Carlo)

It's a miracle ill. by Jill McElmurry. Atheneum, 2003. ISBN 0-689-84493-X Subj: Family life – grandmothers. Holidays – Hanukkah. Jewish culture.

The pirates of Tarnoonga (Weiss, Ellen)

Spires, Elizabeth. *The big meow* ill. by Cynthia Jabar. Candlewick, 2002. ISBN 0-7636-0679-0 Subj: Animals – cats. Animals – dogs. Noise, sounds.

Spirin, Gennady. *Philipok* ill. by author; retold by Ann Keay Beneduce. Philomel, 2000. ISBN 0-399-23482-9 Subj: Character traits – ambition. Foreign lands – Russia. School.

Spirn, Michele. *I am the turkey* ill. by Joy Allen. HarperCollins, 2004. ISBN 0-06-053231-9 Subj: Birds – turkeys. Holidays – Thanksgiving. School. Theater.

The Know-Nothing Halloween ill. by R. W. Alley. HarperCollins, 2000. ISBN 0-06-028186-3 Subj: Holidays – Halloween. Humorous stories.

The Know-Nothings talk turkey ill. by R. W. Alley. HarperCollins, 2000. ISBN 0-06-028184-7 Subj: Friendship. Holidays – Thanksgiving. Humorous stories.

Spohn, David. *Nate's treasure* ill. by author. Lothrop, 1991. ISBN 0-688-10091-0 Subj: Anatomy – skeletons. Animals. Death. Seasons.

Starry night ill. by author. Lothrop, 1992. ISBN 0-688-11171-8 Subj: Camps, camping. Family life – brothers. Family life – fathers. Night.

Winter wood ill. by author. Lothrop, 1991. ISBN 0-688-10094-5 Subj: Family life – fathers. Forest, woods. Seasons – winter.

Spohn, Kate. *By word of mouse* ill. by author. Bloomsbury, 2004. ISBN 1-58234-867-7 Subj: Animals – mice. Careers – artists. Family life – sisters.

Clementine's winter wardrobe ill. by author. Watts, 1989. ISBN 0-531-08441-8 Subj: Animals – cats. Clothing.

Introducing Fanny ill. by author. Watts, 1991. ISBN 0-531-08520-1 Subj: Food. Friendship.

Piglet's bath ill. by author. Random House, 1998. ISBN 0-679-88677-X Subj: Activities – bathing. Animals – pigs. Format, unusual – board books.

Ruth's bake shop ill. by author. Watts, 1990. ISBN 0-531-08489-2 Subj: Activities – baking, cooking. Octopuses.

Snow play ill. by author. Scholastic, 2001. ISBN 0-439-26713-7 Subj: Animals – bears. Family life – grandmothers. Format, unusual – board books. Rhyming text. Weather – snow.

Turtle and Snake and the Christmas tree ill. by author. Viking, 2000. ISBN 0-670-88867-2 Subj: Holidays – Christmas. Reptiles – snakes. Reptiles – turtles, tortoises. Trees.

Turtle and Snake go camping ill. by author. Viking, 2000. ISBN 0-670-88866-4 Subj: Camps, camping. Emotions – fear. Noise, sounds. Reptiles – snakes. Reptiles – turtles, tortoises.

Turtle and Snake's Valentine's Day ill. by author. Viking, 2003. ISBN 0-670-03613-7 Subj: Animals. Holidays – Valentine's Day. Reptiles – snakes. Reptiles – turtles, tortoises.

The wet dry book ill. by author. Random House, 2002. ISBN 0-375-82186-4 Subj: Concepts. Rhyming text.

Spooner, J. B. *The story of the little Black Dog* ill. by Terre Lamb Seeley. Arcade, 1994. ISBN 1-55970-239-7 Subj: Animals – dogs. Boats, ships. Pets. Sea & seashore.

Spooner, Michael. *Old Meshikee and the little crabs: an Ojibwe story* retold by Michael Spooner & Lolita Taylor; ill. by John Hart. Holt, 1996. ISBN 0-8050-3487-0 Subj: Crustaceans – crabs. Folk & fairy tales. Indians of North America – Ojibwa. Noise, sounds. Reptiles – turtles, tortoises.

Sports! sports! sports! poetry sel. by Lee Bennett Hopkins; ill. by Brian Floca. HarperCollins, 1999. ISBN 0-06-027801-3 Subj: Poetry. Sports.

Spriggs, Ruth. *The fables of Æsop* (Æsop)

Frank Baber's Mother Goose (Mother Goose)

Springer, Margaret. *A royal ball* ill. by Tom O'Sullivan. Boyds Mills, 1992. ISBN 1-878093-64-9 Subj: Folk & fairy tales. Parties. Pets. Royalty – princes. Royalty – princesses.

Springer, Nancy. *Music of their hooves* ill. by Sandy Rabinowitz. Boyds Mills, 1994. ISBN 1-56397-182-8 Subj: Animals – horses, ponies. Poetry.

Springer, Sally. *Let's make latkes* ill. by author. Kar-Ben Copies, 1991. ISBN 0-929371-58-5 Subj: Food. Format, unusual – board books. Jewish culture. Religion.

Springstubb, Tricia. *The magic guinea pig* ill. by Bari Weissman. Morrow, 1982. ISBN 0-688-01152-7 Subj: Behavior – mistakes. Witches.

Sproule, Gail. *Singing the dark* ill. by Sheena Lott. Fitzhenry & Whiteside, 2001. ISBN 1-55041-648-0 Subj: Activities – singing. Bedtime. Night.

Spurling, Margaret. *Bilby moon* ill. by Danny Snell. Kane/Miller, 2001. ISBN 1-929132-06-9 Subj: Animals. Animals – mice. Desert. Foreign lands – Australia. Moon.

Spurr, Elizabeth. *The biggest birthday cake in the world* ill. by Rosanne Litzinger. Harcourt, 1991. ISBN 0-15-207150-4 Subj: Behavior – sharing. Birthdays. Food. Parties.

The gumdrop tree ill. by Julia Gorton. Hyperion, 1994. ISBN 0-7868-2004-7 Subj: Gardens, gardening. Trees.

The long, long letter ill. by David Catrow. Hyperion, 1996. ISBN 0-7868-2100-0 Subj: Activities – writing. Emotions – loneliness. Family life – aunts, uncles. Family life – mothers. Letters, cards. Tall tales.

Mrs. Minetta's car pool ill. by Blanche Sims. Atheneum, 1985. ISBN 0-689-31103-6 Subj: Activities – flying. Automobiles. School.

A pig named Perrier ill. by Martin Matje. Hyperion, 2002. ISBN 0-7868-0302-9 Subj: Animals – pigs. Pets.

Two bears beneath the stairs ill. by Nadine Bernard Westcott. Little Simon, 2002. ISBN 0-689-84759-9 Subj: Animals. Counting, numbers. Format, unusual – toy & movable books. Rhyming text.

The squire's bride: *a Norwegian folk tale* orig. told by P. C. Asbjørnsen; ill. by Marcia Sewall. Atheneum, 1975. ISBN 0-689-30463-3 Subj: Folk & fairy tales. Foreign lands – Norway. Weddings.

S-Ringi, Kjell. *see* Ringi, Kjell (Arne Sorensen)

Staake, Bob. *My little ABC book* ill. by author. Little Simon, 1998. ISBN 0-689-81659-6 Subj: ABC books. Format, unusual – board books.

My little color book ill. by author. Little Simon, 2001. ISBN 0-689-83486-1 Subj: Concepts – color. Format, unusual – board books.

My little 1 2 3 book ill. by author. Little Simon, 1998. ISBN 0-689-81660-X Subj: Counting, numbers. Format, unusual – board books.

My little opposites book ill. by author. Little Simon, 2001. ISBN 0-689-83487-X Subj: Animals. Concepts – opposites. Format, unusual – board books.

Stacy, Joel. *see* Dodge, Mary Mapes

Stadler, Alexander. *Beverly Billingsly borrows a book* ill. by author. Harcourt, 2000. ISBN 0-15-202510-3 Subj: Behavior – worrying. Books, reading. Careers – librarians. Libraries. Nightmares.

Beverly Billingsly takes a bow ill. by author. Harcourt, 2003. ISBN 0-15-216816-8 Subj: Music. School. Theater.

Stadler, John. *Animal café* ill. by author. Bradbury, 1980. ISBN 0-87888-166-2 Subj: Animals. Behavior – greed. Food. Restaurants.

The ballad of Wilbur and the moose ill. by author. Warner, 1990. ISBN 1-55782-047-3 Subj: Animals – moose. Animals – pigs. Cowboys, cowgirls. U.S. history – frontier & pioneer life.

Cat is back at bat ill. by author. Dutton, 1991. ISBN 0-525-44762-8 Subj: Animals. Rhyming text.

Catilda ill. by author. Atheneum, 2003. ISBN 0-689-84728-9 Subj: Animals – cats. Behavior – lost & found possessions. Toys – bears.

The cats of Mrs. Calamari ill. by author. Orchard, 1997. ISBN 0-531-33020-6 Subj: Animals – cats. Animals – dogs. Cities, towns. Glasses. Weddings.

Gorman and the treasure chest ill. by author. Bradbury, 1984. ISBN 0-02-786650-5 Subj: Animals. Behavior – sharing.

Hector, the accordion-nosed dog ill. by author. Macmillan, 1987. ISBN 0-02-786680-7 Subj: Animals – dogs. Music. Musical instruments – accordions.

Hooray for snail! ill. by author. Crowell, 1984. ISBN 0-06-443075-8 Subj: Animals – snails. Sports – baseball.

One seal ill. by author. Orchard, 1999. ISBN 0-531-33195-4 Subj: Animals. Behavior – lost & found possessions. Kites. Sea & seashore.

Ready, set, go! ill. by author. HarperCollins, 1996. ISBN 0-06-024947-1 Subj: Animals – dogs. Self-concept. Sports – ice skating.

Snail saves the day ill. by author. Crowell, 1985. ISBN 0-690-04469-0 Subj: Animals – snails. Sports – football.

Three cheers for hippo! ill. by author. Crowell, 1987. ISBN 0-690-04670-7 Subj: Activities – flying. Animals – hippopotamuses.

What's so scary? ill. by author. Orchard, 2001. ISBN 0-531-33301-9 Subj: Animals. Books, reading. Careers – artists.

Stafford, Kay. *Ling Tang and the lucky cricket* ill. by Louise Zibold. McGraw-Hill, 1944. Subj: Character traits – luck. Foreign lands – China.

Stafford, Kim Robert. *We got here together* ill. by Debra Frasier. Harcourt, 1994. ISBN 0-15-294891-0 Subj: Family life – fathers. Nature. Sea & seashore. Water.

Stafford, Liliana. *Just dragon* ill. by Margaret Power. Cygnet Books, 2000. ISBN 1-876268-02-6 Subj: Boats, ships. Death. Emotions – grief. Family life – grandfathers. Kites.

The snow bear ill. by Lambert Davis. Scholastic, 2000. ISBN 0-439-26977-6 Subj: Animals – polar bears. Friendship. Indians of North America – Inuit. Weather – snow.

Stafford, William. *The animal that drank up sound* ill. by Debra Frasier. Harcourt, 1992. ISBN 0-15-203563-X Subj: Animals. Insects – crickets. Noise, sounds. Seasons – spring. Seasons – winter.

Stage, Mads. *The greedy blackbird* ill. by author. John Godon Burke, 1981. ISBN 0-222-00808-3 Subj: Behavior – greed. Behavior – sharing. Birds.

The lonely squirrel ill. by author. John Godon Burke, 1980. ISBN 0-222-00738-9 Subj: Animals – squirrels. Emotions – loneliness.

Staines, Bill. *All God's critters got a place in the choir* ill. by Margot Zemach. Dutton, 1989. ISBN 0-525-44469-6 Subj: Animals. Farms. Music. Songs.

Stainton, Sue. *The lighthouse cat* ill. by Anne Mortimer. Tegen, 2004. ISBN 0-06-009605-5 Subj: Animals – cats. Lighthouses. Weather – storms.

Santa's snow cat ill. by Anne Mortimer. HarperCollins, 2001. ISBN 0-06-623828-5 Subj: Animals – cats. Behavior – lost & found possessions. Cities, towns. Holidays – Christmas. Santa Claus.

Stalder, Valerie. *Even the devil is afraid of a shrew: a folktale of Lapland* adapt. by Ray Brocket; ill. by Richard Eric Brown. Addison-Wesley, 1972. ISBN 0-20-107188-6 Subj: Behavior – nagging. Devil. Folk & fairy tales. Foreign lands – Lapland.

Stamaty, Mark Alan. *Minnie Maloney and Macaroni* ill. by author. Dial, 1976. ISBN 0-8037-5589-9 Subj: Food. Humorous stories.

Standiford, Natalie. *Dollhouse mouse* ill. by Denise Fleming. Random House, 1989. ISBN 0-394-99935-5 Subj: Animals – mice. Sky.

The headless horseman retold by Natalie Standford; ill. by Donald Cook. Random House, 1992. Based on 'The legend of Sleepy Hollow' by Washington Irving. ISBN 0-679-91241-X Subj: Ghosts. Holidays – Halloween.

Standon, Anna. *Little duck lost* by Anna & Edward Cyril Standon; ill. by Edward Cyril Standon. Delacorte, 1965. Subj: Behavior – lost. Birds – ducks. Eggs. Family life – mothers.

The singing rhinoceros ill. by Edward Cyril Standon. Coward, 1963. Subj: Animals – rhinoceros.

Three little cats by Anna & Edward Cyril Standon; ill. by authors. Delacorte, 1964. ISBN 0-87459-000-3 Subj: Activities – playing. Animals – cats. Behavior – misbehavior. Foreign languages.

Standon, Edward Cyril. *Little duck lost* (Standon, Anna)

Three little cats (Standon, Anna)

Stanek, Muriel. *All alone after school* ill. by Ruth Rosner. A. Whitman, 1985. ISBN 0-8075-0278-2 Subj: Character traits – bravery. Emotions – loneliness. Family life – mothers.

Left, right, left, right! ill. by Lucy Hawkinson. A. Whitman, 1969. ISBN 0-8075-4421-3 Subj: Concepts – left & right. Emotions – embarrassment.

My little foster sister ill. by Judith Cheng. A. Whitman, 1981. ISBN 0-8075-5365-4 Subj: Adoption. Behavior – sharing. Sibling rivalry.

One, two, three for fun ill. by Seymour Fleishman. A. Whitman, 1967. Subj: Counting, numbers. Ethnic groups in the U.S.

Stang, Judit. *see* Varga, Judy

Stanhope, Lavinia. *see* Schlein, Miriam

Stanley, Diane. *Birdsong lullaby* ill. by author. Morrow, 1985. ISBN 0-688-05805-1 Subj: Birds. Imagination. Lullabies. Night. Sleep.

Captain Whiz-Bang ill. by author. Morrow, 1987. ISBN 0-688-06227-X Subj: Animals – cats. Behavior – growing up.

The conversation club ill. by author. Macmillan, 1983. ISBN 0-02-786740-4 Subj: Animals – mice. Clubs, gangs. Communication. Noise, sounds.

A country tale ill. by author. Four Winds, 1985. ISBN 0-02-786780-3 Subj: Animals – cats. Behavior – seeking better things. Cities, towns. Country. Friendship.

The Giant and the beanstalk ill. by author. HarperCollins, 2004. ISBN 0-06-000011-2 Subj: Folk & fairy tales. Giants. Humorous stories. Nursery rhymes.

Goldie and the three bears ill. by author. HarperCollins, 2003. ISBN 0-06-000009-0 Subj: Animals – bears. Friendship. Homes, houses. Humorous stories.

The good-luck pencil ill. by Bruce Degen. Macmillan, 1986. ISBN 0-02-786800-1 Subj: Character traits – luck. Magic. School.

Joining the Boston Tea Party ill. by Holly Berry. HarperCollins, 2001. ISBN 0-06-027068-3 Subj: Activities – traveling. Time. U.S. history.

Raising Sweetness ill. by G. Brian Karas. Putnam, 1999. ISBN 0-399-23225-7 Subj: Books, reading. Letters, cards. Orphans.

Rumpelstiltskin's daughter ill. by author. Morrow, 1997. ISBN 0-688-14328-8 Subj: Behavior – greed. Folk & fairy tales. Humorous stories.

Siegfried ill. by John Sandford. Bantam, 1991. ISBN 0-553-07022-3 Subj: Animals – cats. Clocks, watches. Emotions – envy, jealousy.

Thanksgiving on Plymouth Plantation ill. by Holly Berry. Cotler, 2004. ISBN 0-06-027076-4 Subj: Activities – traveling. Holidays – Thanksgiving. Multiple births – twins. U.S. history.

Stanley, Fay. *The last princess* ill. by Diane Stanley. HarperCollins, 2001. ISBN 0-06-029215-6 Subj: Hawaii. Royalty – princes. Royalty – princesses. U.S. history.

Stanley, John. *It's nice to be little* ill. by Jean Tamburine. Rand McNally, 1965. Subj: Character traits – smallness.

Stanley, Mandy. *At the pool* ill. by author. Kingfisher, 2004. ISBN 0-7534-5747-4 Subj: Format, unusual – board books. Language. Sports – swimming.

Bloomer, the dog you can play with ill. by author. Orchard, 2001. ISBN 0-531-30311-X Subj: Activities. Animals – dogs. Format, unusual – toy & movable books.

First word book ill. by author. Kingfisher, 2000. ISBN 0-7534-5272-3 Subj: Dictionaries. Language.

In the park ill. by author. Kingfisher, 2004. ISBN 0-7534-5750-4 Subj: Format, unusual – board books. Language. Pets.

Lettice, the dancing rabbit ill. by author. S&S, 2002. ISBN 0-689-84797-1 Subj: Activities – dancing. Animals – rabbits. Ballet.

On the move ill. by author. Kingfisher, 2004. ISBN 0-7534-5749-0 Subj: Automobiles. Format, unusual – board books. Transportation.

Perfect pets ill. by author. Kingfisher, 2004. ISBN 0-7534-5748-2 Subj: Format, unusual – board books. Pets.

Stanley, Sanna. *Monkey Sunday* ill. by author. Farrar, 1998. ISBN 0-374-35018-3 Subj: Animals. Animals – monkeys. Family life – fathers. Foreign lands – Africa. Holidays.

The rains are coming ill. by author. Greenwillow, 1993. ISBN 0-688-10949-7 Subj: Weather – rain.

Stanovich, Betty Jo. *Big boy, little boy* ill. by Virginia Wright-Frierson. Lothrop, 1984. ISBN 0-688-03808-5 Subj: Family life – grandmothers.

Hedgehog adventures ill. by Chris L. Demarest. Lothrop, 1983. ISBN 0-688-01669-3 Subj: Animals – groundhogs. Animals – hedgehogs. Character traits – loyalty.

Stan-Padilla, Viento. *Dream Feather* ill. by author. Atheneum, 1980. ISBN 0-89742-035-7 Subj: Folk & fairy tales. Indians of North America. Religion.

Stansfield, Ian. *The legend of the whale* ill. by author. Godine, 1986. ISBN 0-87923-628-0 Subj: Animals – whales. Folk & fairy tales.

Stanton, Elizabeth. *Sometimes I like to cry* by Elizabeth & Henry Stanton; ill. by Richard Leyden. A. Whitman, 1978. ISBN 0-8075-7537-2 Subj: Emotions.

The very messy room by Elizabeth & Henry Stanton; ill. by Richard Leyden. A. Whitman, 1978. ISBN 0-8075-5077-9 Subj: Character traits – cleanliness. Family life.

Stanton, Henry. *Sometimes I like to cry* (Stanton, Elizabeth)

The very messy room (Stanton, Elizabeth)

Stanton, Jessie. *The taxi that hurried* (Mitchell, Lucy Sprague)

Stanton, Karen. *Mr. K and Yudi* ill. by author. Golden Bks., 2001. ISBN 0-307-10210-6 Subj: Animals – dogs. Old age. Pets.

Stapler, Sarah. *Cordellia, dance!* ill. by author. Dial, 1990. ISBN 0-8037-0793-2 Subj: Activities – dancing. Character traits – being different. Reptiles – alligators, crocodiles.

Spruce the moose cuts loose ill. by author. Putnam, 1992. ISBN 0-399-21861-0 Subj: Animals – moose. Birthdays. Parties.

Trilby's trumpet ill. by author. HarperCollins, 1988. ISBN 0-06-025827-6 Subj: Animals – bears. Format, unusual – toy & movable books. Music. Musical instruments – trumpets. Noise, sounds. Sibling rivalry.

Starbird, Kaye. *The covered bridge house and other poems* ill. by Jim Arnosky. Four Winds, 1979. ISBN 0-590-07544-6 Subj: Poetry.

Starke, Katherine. *Dogs and puppies* ed. by Fiona Watt; ill. by Christyan Fox; photos by Jane Burton. Usborne, 1999. ISBN 1-58086-159-8 Subj: Animals – babies. Animals – dogs. Pets.

Starr, Meg. *Alicia's happy day* ill. by Ying Hwa-hu & Cornelius Van Wright. Star Bright, 2002. ISBN 1-887734-85-6 Subj: Birthdays. Emotions – happiness. Ethnic groups in the U.S. – Hispanic Americans. Parties.

Starret, William. *see* McClintock, Marshall

Staub, Leslie. *Bless this house* ill. by author. Harcourt, 2000. ISBN 0-15-201984-7 Subj: Animals. Bedtime. Earth. Ecology. Lullabies.

Staunton, Ted. *Taking care of Crumley* ill. by Tina Holdcroft. Kids Can, 1984. ISBN 0-919964-75-3 Subj: Behavior – bullying. School.

Steadman, Ralph. *The bridge* ill. by author. Collins, 1974, c1972. ISBN 0-0019-5068-1 Subj: Behavior – fighting, arguing. Bridges. Friendship.

The little red computer ill. by author. McGraw-Hill, 1969. Subj: Computers. Space & space ships.

Stecher, Miriam B. *Daddy and Ben together* photos by Alice Kandell. Lothrop, 1981. ISBN 0-688-00736-8 Subj: Family life – fathers.

Max, the music-maker by Miriam B. Stecher & Alice Kandell; photos by Alice Kandell. Lothrop, 1980. ISBN 0-688-50958-X Subj: Music. Musical instruments. Science.

Steel, Barry. *Greek cities* ill. by Bernard Long. Watts, 1990. ISBN 0-531-18326-2 Subj: Cities, towns. Foreign lands – Greece.

Steel, Danielle. *Freddie's first night away* ill. by Jacqueline Rogers. Dell, 1992. ISBN 0-440-40574-2 Subj: Friendship. Sleep. Sleepovers.

Freddie's trip ill. by Jacqueline Rogers. Dell, 1992. ISBN 0-440-40573-4 Subj: Activities – traveling. Activities – vacationing. Automobiles. Family life.

Martha's best friend ill. by Jacqueline Rogers. Delacorte, 1989. ISBN 0-385-29801-3 Subj: Friendship.

Martha's new daddy ill. by Jacqueline Rogers. Delacorte, 1989. ISBN 0-385-29799-8 Subj: Divorce. Family life. Family life – stepfamilies.

Martha's new school ill. by Jacqueline Rogers. Delacorte, 1989. ISBN 0-385-29800-5 Subj: Friendship. Moving. School – first day.

Max and the baby sitter ill. by Jacqueline Rogers. Delacorte, 1989. ISBN 0-385-29796-3 Subj: Activities – babysitting. Animals – cats. Emotions – fear. Family life. Problem solving.

Max's daddy goes to the hospital ill. by Jacqueline Rogers. Delacorte, 1989. ISBN 0-385-29797-1 Subj: Careers – firefighters. Family life – fathers. Hospitals. Illness.

Max's new baby ill. by Jacqueline Rogers. Delacorte, 1989. ISBN 0-385-29798-X Subj: Babies. Family life – new sibling. Multiple births – twins. Sibling rivalry.

Steele, Mary Quintard Govan. *see* Gage, Wilson

Steele, Philip. *The blue whale* ill. by Ian Jackson. Kingfisher, 1994. ISBN 1-85697-509-6 Subj: Animals – endangered animals. Animals – whales.

The giant panda ill. by John Butler. Kingfisher, 1994. ISBN 1-85697-511-8 Subj: Animals – endangered animals. Animals – pandas.

Steelsmith, Shari. *When you're mad and you know it* (Crary, Elizabeth)

Steen, Sandra. *Car wash* by Sandra Steen & Susan Steen; ill. by G. Brian Karas. Putnam, 2001. ISBN 0-399-23369-5 Subj: Automobiles. Family life – fathers.

Steen, Susan. *Car wash* (Steen, Sandra)

Steer, Dougald. *Just one more story* ill. by Elisabeth Moseng. Dutton, 1999. ISBN 0-525-46215-5 Subj: Animals – pigs. Bedtime. Books, reading. Folk & fairy tales. Format, unusual.

Steers, Billy. *Tractor Mac* ill. by author. Golden Bks., 1999. ISBN 0-307-10224-6 Subj: Animals – horses, ponies. Farms. Self-concept. Tractors.

Steffa, Tim. *Mister King* (Siekkinen, Raija)

The nighttime book (Kunnas, Mauri)

One spooky night and other scary stories (Kunnas, Mauri)

Twelve gifts for Santa Claus (Kunnas, Mauri)

Steger, Hans-Ulrich. *Traveling to Tripiti* trans. by Elizabeth D. Crawford; ill. by author. Harcourt, 1967. Subj: Activities – traveling. Cumulative tales. Toys. Toys – bears.

Stehr, Frédéric. *Quack-quack* ill. by author. Farrar, 1987. ISBN 0-374-36161-4 Subj: Animals. Behavior – needing someone. Birds – ducks. Family life – mothers.

Steig, Jeanne. *Consider the lemming* ill. by William Steig. Farrar, 1988. ISBN 0-374-31536-1 Subj: Animals – lemmings. Poetry.

Steig, William. *Abel's Island* ill. by author. Farrar, 1976. ISBN 0-374-30010-0 Subj: Animals – mice. Islands.

The amazing bone ill. by author. Farrar, 1976. ISBN 0-374-30248-0 Subj: Animals – pigs. Caldecott award honor books. Magic.

The bad speller ill. by author. Windmill, 1970. ISBN 0-671-66526-X Subj: Games. Language.

Brave Irene ill. by author. Farrar, 1986. ISBN 0-374-30947-7 Subj: Character traits – bravery. Character traits – perseverance. Seasons – winter. Weather – snow. Weather – storms.

Caleb and Kate ill. by author. Farrar, 1977. ISBN 0-374-31016-5 Subj: Animals – dogs. Magic. Witches.

Doctor De Soto ill. by author. Farrar, 1982. ISBN 0-374-31803-4 Subj: Animals – foxes. Animals – mice. Character traits – cleverness.

Doctor De Soto goes to Africa ill. by author. HarperCollins, 1992. ISBN 0-06-205003-6 Subj: Animals – elephants. Animals – mice. Careers – dentists. Foreign lands – Africa.

An eye for elephants ill. by author. Windmill, 1970. ISBN 0-8780-7002-8 Subj: Animals – elephants. Poetry.

Farmer Palmer's wagon ride ill. by author. Farrar, 1974. ISBN 0-374-32288-0 Subj: Animals – donkeys. Animals – pigs. Humorous stories.

Gorky rises ill. by author. Farrar, 1980. ISBN 0-374-31752-1 Subj: Frogs & toads. Magic.

Pete's a pizza ill. by author. HarperCollins, 1998. ISBN 0-06-205157-1 Subj: Activities – playing. Family life – fathers. Food. Games. Imagination.

Potch and Polly ill. by Jon Agee. Farrar, 2002. ISBN 0-374-36090-1 Subj: Emotions – love.

Roland, the minstrel pig ill. by author. S&S, 1988, c1968. ISBN 0-671-66841-2 Subj: Animals – foxes. Animals – pigs. Music. Musical instruments – lutes. Royalty.

Rotten island ill. by author. Rev. ed. of The bad island issued in 1969. Godine, 1984. ISBN 0-87923-526-8 Subj: Flowers. Islands. Monsters.

Solomon the rusty nail ill. by author. Farrar, 1985. ISBN 0-374-37131-8 Subj: Animals – cats. Animals – rabbits. Behavior – trickery. Magic.

Spinky sulks ill. by author. Farrar, 1988. ISBN 0-374-38321-9 Subj: Character traits – stubbornness. Emotions – happiness. Family life.

Sylvester and the magic pebble ill. by author. Little Simon, 1995, c1969. ISBN 0-689-80417-2 Subj: Animals. Animals – donkeys. Caldecott award books. Family life. Magic.

Tiffky Doofky ill. by author. Farrar, 1987. ISBN 0-374-37542-9 Subj: Animals – dogs. Careers – sanitation workers. Emotions – love. Magic.

Toby, what are you? ill. by Teryl Euvremer. HarperCollins, 2001. ISBN 0-06-205170-9 Subj: Activities – playing. Animals. Behavior – imitation. Family life. Games.

Toby, where are you? ill. by author. HarperCollins, 1997. ISBN 0-06-205082-6 Subj: Activities – playing. Animals. Behavior – hiding. Family life.

Toby, who are you? ill. by Teryl Euvremer. Cotler, 2004. ISBN 0-06-000706-0 Subj: Activities – picnicking. Animals. Family life – parents. Imagination.

The toy brother ill. by author. HarperCollins, 1996. ISBN 0-06-205079-6 Subj: Family life – brothers. Middle Ages. Science. Sibling rivalry.

When everybody wore a hat ill. by author. Cotler, 2003. ISBN 0-06-009701-9 Subj: Careers – authors. Careers – illustrators. Clothing – hats. Immigrants. Memories, memory.

Which would you rather be? ill. by Harry Bliss. Colter, 2002. ISBN 0-06-029654-2 Subj: Animals – rabbits. Clothing – hats.

Wizzil ill. by author. Farrar, 2000. ISBN 0-374-38466-5 Subj: Birds – parakeets, parrots. Careers – farmers. Character traits – kindness. Witches.

Yellow and pink ill. by author. Farrar, 1984. ISBN 0-374-38670-6 Subj: Toys – dolls.

The Zabajaba Jungle ill. by author. Farrar, 1987. ISBN 0-374-38790-7 Subj: Dreams. Jungle.

Zeke Pippin ill. by author. HarperCollins, 1994. ISBN 0-06-205076-1 Subj: Animals – pigs. Behavior – running away. Magic. Music. Musical instruments – harmonicas.

Stein, Sara Bonnett. *About dying: an open family book for parents and children together* by Sara Bonnett Stein, in cooperation with Gilbert W. Kliman . . . et al.; photos by Dick Frank; graphic design by Michael Goldberg. Walker, 1974. ISBN 0-8027-6170-0 Subj: Death. Emotions – grief.

About handicaps: an open family book for parents and children together by Sara Bonnett Stein, in cooperation with Gilbert W. Kliman . . . et al.; photos by Dick Frank; graphic design by Michael Goldberg. Walker, 1974. ISBN 0-8027-6174-7 Subj: Handicaps.

The adopted one: an open family book for parents and children together Thomas R. Holman, consultant; photos by Erika Stone. Walker, 1979. ISBN 0-8027-6347-2 Subj: Adoption. Family life.

Cat ill. by Manuel Garcia. Harcourt, 1985. ISBN 0-15-215150-8 Subj: Animals – cats. Science.

A child goes to school photos by Don Connors. Doubleday, 1978. ISBN 0-385-12953-X Subj: School – first day.

A hospital story: an open family book for parents and children together photos by Doris Pinney; graphic design by Michel Goldberg. Walker, 1974. ISBN 0-8027-6173-9 Subj: Careers – doctors. Careers – nurses. Hospitals. Illness.

Mouse ill. by Manuel Garcia. Harcourt, 1985. ISBN 0-15-256021-1 Subj: Animals – mice. Science.

Oh, baby! photos by Holly Anne Shelowitz. Walker, 1993. ISBN 0-8027-8262-0 Subj: Babies. Family life.

On divorce: an open family book for parents and children together Thomas R. Holman, consultant; photos by Erika Stone. Walker, 1979. ISBN 0-8027-6345-6 Subj: Divorce. Family life.

That new baby: an open family book for parents and children together by Sara Bonnett Stein, in cooperation with Gilbert W. Kliman . . . et al.; photos by Dick Frank; graphic design by Michael Goldberg. Walker, 1974. ISBN 0-8027-6175-5 Subj: Babies. Family life.

Stein, Stephanie. *Lucy's feet* ill. by Kathryn A. Imler. Perspectives Pr., 1992. ISBN 0-944934-05-6 Subj: Adoption. Emotions – anger. Sibling rivalry.

Steiner, Barbara (Annette). *But not Stanleigh* photos by George & Ruth Cloven. Childrens Pr., 1980. ISBN 0-516-03454-5 Subj: Animals – raccoons.

The whale brother ill. by Gretchen Will Mayo. Walker, 1988. ISBN 0-8027-6805-9 Subj: Animals – whales. Art. Eskimos. Sea & seashore.

Steiner, Charlotte. *ABC* ill. by author. Watts, 1946. Subj: ABC books.

Birthdays are for everyone ill. by author. Doubleday, 1964. Subj: Birthdays.

The climbing book by Charlotte Steiner & Mary Burlingham; ill. by Charlotte Steiner. Vanguard, 1943. Subj: Format, unusual. Holidays – Christmas.

Daddy comes home ill. by author. Doubleday, 1944. Subj: Family life. Family life – fathers.

Five little finger playmates ill. by author. Grosset, 1951. Subj: Counting, numbers. Games. Participation.

A friend is "Amie" ill. by author. Knopf, 1956. Subj: Foreign languages. Friendship.

Kiki and Muffy ill. by author. Doubleday, 1943. Subj: Animals – cats. Family life – grandmothers.

Kiki is an actress ill. by author. Doubleday, 1958. Subj: Theater.

Kiki's play house ill. by author. Doubleday, 1962. Subj: Activities – playing.

Listen to my seashell ill. by author. Knopf, 1959. Subj: Noise, sounds. Sea & seashore.

Look what Tracy found ill. by author. Knopf, 1972. ISBN 0-394-92305-7 Subj: Activities – playing. Imagination.

Lulu ill. by author. Doubleday, 1939. Subj: Animals – dogs. Imagination – imaginary friends.

My bunny feels soft ill. by author. Knopf, 1958. Subj: Animals – rabbits.

My slippers are red ill. by author. Knopf, 1958. Subj: Concepts – color.

Pete and Peter ill. by author. Doubleday, 1941. Subj: Animals – dogs. Sports – hunting.

Pete's puppets ill. by author. Doubleday, 1952. Subj: Puppets.

Polka Dot ill. by author. Doubleday, 1947. Subj: Pets.

Red Ridinghood's little lamb ill. by author. Knopf, 1964. Subj: Animals – sheep. Games. Mythical creatures.

The sleepy quilt ill. by author. Doubleday, 1947. Subj: Bedtime. Quilts.

What's the hurry, Harry? ill. by author. Lothrop, 1968. Subj: Behavior – hurrying. Character traits – patience.

Steiner, Joan (Joan Catherine). *Look-alikes* photos by Thomas Lindley. Little, 1998. ISBN 0-316-81255-2 Subj: Picture puzzles. Rhyming text.

Look-alikes, Jr. photos by Thomas Lindley. Little, 1999. ISBN 0-316-81307-9 Subj: Picture puzzles. Rhyming text.

Steiner, Jörg. *The bear who wanted to be a bear* from an idea by Frank Tashlin; ill. by Jörg Müller. Atheneum, 1977. ISBN 0-689-50079-3 Subj: Animals – bears. Progress. Stores.

Rabbit Island ill. by Jörg Müller. Harcourt, 1978. ISBN 0-15-265034-2 Subj: Animals – rabbits. Character traits – freedom.

Steinmetz, Leon. *Clocks in the woods* ill. by author. HarperCollins, 1979. ISBN 0-06-025650-8 Subj: Animals. Clocks, watches. Time.

Stem, J. David. *Kay Thompson's Eloise in Hollywood* text by David Stem & David Weiss; ill. by Hilary Knight. S&S, 2005. ISBN 0-689-84289-9 Subj: Activities – traveling. Behavior. Hotels.

Stemp, Robin. *Guy and the flowering plum tree* ill. by Carolyn Dinan. Atheneum, 1981. ISBN 0-689-50188-9 Subj: Imagination. Trees.

Stemple, Adam. *Jane Yolen's Old MacDonald songbook* (Yolen, Jane)

The lap-time song and play book (Yolen, Jane)

Stenmark, Victoria. *The singing chick* ill. by Randy Cecil. Holt, 1999. ISBN 0-8050-5255-0 Subj: Activities – singing. Animals. Birds – chickens.

Stephens, Helen. *Ahoyty-toyty* ill. by author. Fickling, 2004. ISBN 0-385-75040-4 Subj: Activities – vacationing. Boats, ships. Etiquette. Friendship.

I'm too busy ill. by author. DK, 1999. ISBN 0-7894-2606-4 Subj: Animals – cats. Format, unusual – board books.

Poochie-poo ill. by author. Fickling, 2003. ISBN 0-385-75018-8 Subj: Animals – dogs. Behavior – misbehavior.

Ruby and the muddy dog ill. by author. Kingfisher, 2000. ISBN 0-7534-5225-1 Subj: Animals – dogs. Character traits – cleanliness. Character traits – honesty. Character traits – responsibility.

Ruby and the noisy hippo ill. by author. Kingfisher, 2000. ISBN 0-7534-5226-X Subj: Animals – hippopotamuses. Monsters. Noise, sounds.

What about me? ill. by author. DK, 1999. ISBN 0-7894-4840-8 Subj: Animals – cats. Emotions – envy, jealousy. Ethnic groups in the U.S. – African Americans. Friendship.

Stephens, J. Moria. *Persephone, the ladybug* ill. by author. Little, 2001. ISBN 0-316-81544-6 Subj: Family life – daughters. Family life – mothers. Flowers. Insects – ladybugs.

Stephens, Karen. *Jumping* ill. by George Wiggins. Grosset, 1965. ISBN 0-448-04949-X Subj: Activities – jumping.

Stephenson, Dorothy. *How to scare a lion* ill. by John E. Johnson. Follett, 1965. Subj: Animals – lions. Illness.

The night it rained toys ill. by John E. Johnson. Follett, 1963. Subj: Holidays – Christmas. Poetry. Royalty. Toys.

Stepto, Michele. *Snuggle Piggy and the magic blanket* ill. by John Himmelman. Dutton, 1987. ISBN 0-525-44308-8 Subj: Animals – pigs. Family life. Night.

Steptoe, Javaka. *The Jones family express* ill. by author. Lee & Low, 2003. ISBN 1-58430-047-7 Subj: Activities – traveling. Ethnic groups in the U.S. – African Americans. Family life – aunts, uncles. Gifts. Letters, cards. Parties.

Steptoe, John. *Baby says* ill. by author. Lothrop, 1988. ISBN 0-688-07424-3 Subj: Activities – playing. Babies. Sibling rivalry.

Birthday ill. by author. Holt, 1972. ISBN 0-0309-1308-X Subj: Birthdays. Ethnic groups in the U.S. – African Americans.

Creativity ill. by Earl B. Lewis. Clarion, 1997. ISBN 0-395-68706-3 Subj: Ethnic groups in the U.S. – African Americans. Ethnic groups in the U.S. – Puerto Rican Americans. Friendship. School.

Daddy is a monster . . . sometimes ill. by author. Lippincott, 1980. ISBN 0-397-31893-6 Subj: Family life – fathers. Monsters.

Jeffrey Bear cleans up his act ill. by author. Lothrop, 1983. ISBN 0-688-01642-1 Subj: Animals – bears. School.

Mufaro's beautiful daughters: an African tale ill. by author. Lothrop, 1987. ISBN 0-688-04046-2 Subj: Caldecott award honor books. Character traits – kindness. Character traits – meanness. Folk & fairy tales. Foreign lands – Africa. Royalty – kings.

My special best words ill. by author. Viking, 1974. ISBN 0-670-50118-2 Subj: Ethnic groups in the U.S. – African Americans. Family life. Language.

Stevie ill. by author. HarperCollins, 1969. ISBN 0-06-025764-4 Subj: Ethnic groups in the U.S. – African Americans. Friendship.

The story of jumping mouse: a Native American legend ill. by author. Lothrop, 1984. ISBN 0-688-01903-X Subj: Animals – mice. Caldecott award honor books. Folk & fairy tales. Frogs & toads. Magic.

Uptown ill. by author. HarperCollins, 1970. Subj: Cities, towns. Ethnic groups in the U.S. – African Americans. Poverty.

Sterling, Helen. *see* Hoke, Helen L.

Stern, Ellen. *I saw a bullfrog* ill. by author. Random House, 2003. ISBN 0-375-92173-7 Subj: Animals. Character traits – appearance. Imagination. Rhyming text.

Stern, Elsie-Jean. *Wee Robin's Christmas song* ill. by Elsie McKean. Nelson, 1945. Subj: Birds – robins. Holidays – Christmas. Music. Songs.

Stern, Maggie. *Acorn magic* ill. by Donna Ruff. Greenwillow, 1998. ISBN 0-688-15699-1 Subj: Animals. Animals – moose. Camps, camping.

The missing sunflowers ill. by Donna Ruff. Greenwillow, 1997. ISBN 0-688-14873-5 Subj: Animals – squirrels. Flowers. Mystery stories. Plants.

Stern, Mark. *It's a dog's life* ill. by author. Atheneum, 1978. ISBN 0-689-30643-1 Subj: Animals – dogs. Character traits – freedom.

Stern, Peter. *Floyd, a cat's story* ill. by author. HarperCollins, 1982. ISBN 0-06-025779-2 Subj: Animals – cats.

Max the dragon ill. by author. Crown, 1990. ISBN 0-517-57588-4 Subj: Animals – mice. Dragons. Monsters.

Stern, Ronnie. *Pop's secret* (Townsend, Maryann)

Stern, Simon. *Mrs. Vinegar* ill. by author. Prentice-Hall, 1979. ISBN 0-13-604488-3 Subj: Homes, houses.

Vasily and the dragon: an epic Russian fairy tale ill. by author. Merrimack, 1983. ISBN 0-7207-1331-5 Subj: Dragons. Folk & fairy tales. Foreign lands – Russia.

Steven, Kenneth C. *The bearer of gifts* ill. by Lily Moon. Dial, 1998. ISBN 0-8037-2374-1 Subj: Careers – woodcarvers. Gifts. Holidays – Christmas. Santa Claus.

Stevens, Bryna. *Borrowed feathers and other fables* ill. by Freire Wright & Michael Foreman. Random House, 1978. ISBN 0-394-83622-7 Subj: Folk & fairy tales.

Handel and the famous sword swallower of Halle ill. by Ruth Tietjen Councell. Putnam, 1990. ISBN 0-399-21548-4 Subj: Family life – fathers. Music. Musical instruments.

Stevens, Carla. *Hooray for pig!* ill. by Rainey Bennett. Seabury Pr., 1974. ISBN 0-8164-3114-0 Subj: Animals. Animals – pigs. Sports – swimming.

Pig and the blue flag ill. by Rainey Bennett. Seabury Pr., 1977. ISBN 0-8164-3192-2 Subj: Animals. Animals – pigs. School. Sports – gymnastics.

Stories from a snowy meadow ill. by Eve Rice. Seabury Pr., 1976. ISBN 0-8164-3161-2 Subj: Animals. Character traits – kindness. Death. Friendship.

Stevens, Cat. *Teaser and the firecat* ill. by author. Four Winds, 1974. ISBN 0-590-07372-9 Subj: Animals – cats. Foreign languages. Imagination. Moon. Night.

Stevens, Harry. *Fat mouse* ill. by author. Viking, 1987. ISBN 0-670-80529-7 Subj: Animals. Animals – mice. Circular tales. Format, unusual – board books.

Parrot told snake ill. by author. Viking, 1987. ISBN 0-670-80530-0 Subj: Animals. Behavior – gossip. Format, unusual – board books.

Stevens, Jan Romero. *Carlos and the skunk = Carlos y el zorrillo* ill. by Jeanne Arnold. Rising Moon, 1997. ISBN 0-87358-591-7 Subj: Animals – skunks. Farms. Foreign languages.

Carlos digs to China = Carlos excava hasta la China ill. by Jeanne Arnold. Rising Moon, 2001. ISBN 0-8735-8764-2 Subj: Activities – baking, cooking. Activities – digging. Foreign lands – China. Foreign languages. Hotels.

Twelve lizards leaping: a new Twelve days of Christmas ill. by Christine Mau. Rising Moon, 1999. ISBN 0-8735-8744-8 Subj: Cumulative tales. Holidays – Christmas. Music. Religion. Songs.

Stevens, Janet. *And the dish ran away with the spoon* Janet Stevens & Susan Stevens Crummel; ill. by Janet Stevens. Harcourt, 2001. ISBN 0-15-202298-8 Subj: Animals. Behavior – running away. Humorous stories. Nursery rhymes.

Androcles and the lion (Æsop)

Animal fair adapt. & ill. by Janet Stevens. Holiday, 1981. ISBN 0-8234-0388-2 Subj: Animals. Dreams. Fairs, festivals. Poetry.

The Bremen town musicians (Grimm, Jacob)

Cook-a-doodle-doo! by Janet Stevens & Susan Stevens Crummel; ill. by Janet Stevens. Harcourt, 1999. ISBN 0-15-201924-3 Subj: Activities – baking, cooking. Animals. Birds – chickens. Food.

The emperor's new clothes (Andersen, H. C. [Hans Christian])

Goldilocks and the three bears (The three bears)

The tortoise and the hare: an Æsop fable (Æsop)

It's perfectly true! (Andersen, H. C. [Hans Christian])

My big dog by Janet Stevens & Susan Stevens Crummel; ill. by Janet Stevens. Golden Bks., 1999. ISBN 0-307-10220-3 Subj: Animals – cats. Animals – dogs. Behavior – running away. Friendship.

Old bag of bones ill. by author. Holiday, 1996. ISBN 0-8234-1215-6 Subj: Animals. Animals – coyotes. Folk & fairy tales. Indians of North America – Shoshone. Old age.

The princess and the pea (Andersen, H. C. [Hans Christian])

The three billy goats Gruff (Asbjørnsen, P. C. [Peter Christen])

Tops and bottoms ill. by author. Harcourt, 1995. ISBN 0-15-292851-0 Subj: Animals – bears. Animals – rabbits. Behavior – trickery. Caldecott award honor books. Character traits – cleverness. Folk & fairy tales. Gardens, gardening.

The town mouse and the country mouse (Æsop)

Stevens, Kathleen. *Aunt Skilly and the stranger* ill. by Robert Andrew Parker. Ticknor & Fields, 1994. ISBN 0-395-68712-8 Subj: Birds – geese. Country. Crime. Quilts.

The beast in the bathtub ill. by Ray Bowler. G. Stevens, 1985. ISBN 0-918831-15-6 Subj: Activities – bathing. Bedtime. Monsters.

Stevens, Margaret (Dean). *When grandpa died* ill. by Kenneth Ualand. Childrens Pr., 1979. ISBN 0-516-02025-0 Subj: Death. Emotions – grief. Family life – grandfathers.

Stevens, Susanna. *The changeling* (Lagerlöf, Selma)

Stevenson, Drew. *The ballad of Penelope Lou . . . and me* ill. by Marcia Sewall. Crossing Pr., 1978. ISBN 0-89594-004-3 Subj: Character traits – bravery. Emotions – fear. Rhyming text. Sailors.

Stevenson, Harvey. *Big scary wolf* ill. by author. Clarion, 1997. ISBN 0-395-74213-7 Subj: Animals – wolves. Bedtime. Emotions – fear. Noise, sounds.

Grandpa's house ill. by author. Hyperion, 1994. ISBN 1-56282-589-5 Subj: Activities – traveling. Family life – grandfathers. Seasons – summer.

Looking at liberty ill. by author. HarperCollins, 2003. ISBN 0-06-000101-1 Subj: Careers – sculptors. Foreign lands – France. Immigrants. U.S. history.

Stevenson, James. *All aboard!* ill. by author. Greenwillow, 1995. ISBN 0-688-12439-9 Subj: Activities – traveling. Animals – mice. Fairs, festivals. Trains.

Are we almost there? ill. by author. Greenwillow, 1985. ISBN 0-688-04239-2 Subj: Activities – traveling. Animals – dogs. Behavior – fighting, arguing.

Brr! ill. by author. Greenwillow, 1991. ISBN 0-688-09211-X Subj: Family life – grandfathers. Seasons – winter.

The castaway ill. by author. Greenwillow, 2002. ISBN 0-688-16966-X Subj: Activities – flying. Activities – vacationing. Animals – mice. Animals – porcupines. Islands.

Christmas at Mud Flat ill. by author. Greenwillow, 2000. ISBN 0-688-17301-2 Subj: Animals. Holidays – Christmas.

Clams can't sing ill. by author. Greenwillow, 1980. ISBN 0-688-84280-1 Subj: Animals. Music. Noise, sounds. Sea & seashore.

"Could be worse!" ill. by author. Greenwillow, 1977. ISBN 0-688-84075-2 Subj: Family life. Family life – grandfathers. Farms. Monsters.

Don't make me laugh ill. by author. Farrar, 1999. ISBN 0-374-31827-1 Subj: Animals. Behavior. Humorous stories.

Emma ill. by author. Greenwillow, 1985. ISBN 0-688-04021-7 Subj: Behavior – trickery. Witches.

Fried feathers for Thanksgiving ill. by author. Greenwillow, 1986. ISBN 0-688-06676-3 Subj: Behavior – trickery. Character traits – meanness. Witches.

Fun, no fun ill. by author. Greenwillow, 1994. ISBN 0-688-11674-4 Subj: Careers – artists. Careers – writers. Concepts – opposites. Emotions.

Grandpa's great city tour: an alphabet book ill. by author. Greenwillow, 1983. ISBN 0-688-02324-X Subj: ABC books. Activities – flying. Cities, towns. Family life – grandfathers. Wordless.

Grandpa's too-good garden ill. by author. Greenwillow, 1989. ISBN 0-688-08486-9 Subj: Family life – grandfathers. Gardens, gardening.

The great big especially beautiful Easter egg ill. by author. Greenwillow, 1983. ISBN 0-688-01791-6 Subj: Eggs. Family life – grandfathers.

Happy Valentine's Day, Emma! ill. by author. Greenwillow, 1987. ISBN 0-688-07358-1 Subj: Animals. Character traits – meanness. Holidays – Valentine's Day. Humorous stories. Witches.

Heat wave at Mud Flat ill. by author. Greenwillow, 1997. ISBN 0-688-14206-0 Subj: Animals. Weather. Weather – rain.

Higher on the door ill. by author. Greenwillow, 1987. ISBN 0-688-06637-2 Subj: Behavior – growing up. Family life – grandparents.

Howard ill. by author. Greenwillow, 1980. ISBN 0-688-84255-0 Subj: Behavior – lost. Birds – ducks. Friendship.

I meant to tell you ill. by author. Greenwillow, 1996. ISBN 0-688-14178-1 Subj: Behavior – growing up. Careers – artists. Careers – writers. Family life – daughters. Family life – fathers.

July ill. by author. Greenwillow, 1990. ISBN 0-688-08823-6 Subj: Family life – grandparents. Sea & seashore. Seasons – summer.

Mr. Hacker ill. by author. Greenwillow, 1990. ISBN 0-688-09217-9 Subj: Animals. Emotions – loneliness. Pets.

Monty ill. by author. Greenwillow, 1992. ISBN 0-688-11241-2 Subj: Animals – rabbits. Birds – ducks. Frogs & toads. Reptiles – alligators, crocodiles.

The most amazing dinosaur ill. by author. Greenwillow, 2000. ISBN 0-688-16433-1 Subj: Anatomy – skeletons. Animals. Animals – rats. Dinosaurs. Museums. Prehistory.

National worm day ill. by author. Greenwillow, 1990. ISBN 0-688-08772-8 Subj: Animals. Friendship.

No friends ill. by author. Greenwillow, 1986. ISBN 0-688-06507-4 Subj: Family life – grandfathers. Friendship. Moving.

No need for Monty ill. by author. Greenwillow, 1987. ISBN 0-688-07084-1 Subj: Animals. Reptiles – alligators, crocodiles. Transportation.

Quick! Turn the page! ill. by author. Greenwillow, 1990. ISBN 0-688-09309-4 Subj: Problem solving.

Rolling Rose ill. by author. Greenwillow, 1992. ISBN 0-688-10675-7 Subj: Activities. Activities – walking. Babies.

Sam the Zamboni man ill. by Harvey Stevenson. Greenwillow, 1998. ISBN 0-688-14485-3 Subj: Careers. Family life – fathers. Machines. Sports – hockey. Sports – ice skating.

The Sea View Hotel ill. by author. Greenwillow, 1978. ISBN 0-688-84168-6 Subj: Activities – vacationing. Animals – mice. Hotels.

The stowaway ill. by author. Greenwillow, 1990. ISBN 0-688-08620-9 Subj: Animals – mice. Boats, ships. Friendship.

That dreadful day ill. by author. Greenwillow, 1985. ISBN 0-688-04036-5 Subj: Family life – grandfathers. School – first day.

That terrible Halloween night ill. by author. Greenwillow, 1980. ISBN 0-688-94281-X Subj: Family life – grandfathers. Holidays – Halloween.

That's exactly the way it wasn't ill. by author. Greenwillow, 1991. ISBN 0-688-09869-X Subj: Family life – brothers. Family life – grandfathers. Sibling rivalry.

There's nothing to do! ill. by author. Greenwillow, 1986. ISBN 0-688-04699-1 Subj: Behavior – boredom. Family life – grandfathers.

A village full of valentines ill. by author. Greenwillow, 1995. ISBN 0-688-13603-6 Subj: Animals. Holidays – Valentine's Day.

We can't sleep ill. by author. Greenwillow, 1982. ISBN 0-688-01214-0 Subj: Animals. Bedtime. Family life – grandfathers. Sleep.

What's under my bed? ill. by author. Greenwillow, 1983. ISBN 0-688-02327-4 Subj: Bedtime. Emotions – fear. Family life – grandfathers. Furniture – beds.

When I was nine ill. by author. Greenwillow, 1986. ISBN 0-688-05943-0 Subj: Family life.

Which one is Whitney? ill. by author. Greenwillow, 1990. ISBN 0-688-09062-1 Subj: Animals. Fish. Sea & seashore.

Wilfred the rat ill. by author. Greenwillow, 1977. ISBN 0-688-84103-1 Subj: Animals – chipmunks. Animals – rats. Animals – squirrels. Friendship.

Will you please feed our cat? ill. by author. Greenwillow, 1987. ISBN 0-688-06848-0 Subj: Character traits – helpfulness. Family life – grandfathers. Pets.

Winston, Newton, Elton, and Ed ill. by author. Greenwillow, 1978. ISBN 0-688-84152-X Subj: Animals – walruses. Birds – penguins. Sibling rivalry.

The wish card ran out! ill. by author. Greenwillow, 1981. ISBN 0-688-84305-0 Subj: Behavior – wishing.

Worse than the worst ill. by author. Greenwillow, 1994. ISBN 0-688-12250-7 Subj: Animals – dogs. Behavior – misbehavior. Family life – aunts, uncles.

Worse than Willy! ill. by author. Greenwillow, 1984. ISBN 0-688-02597-8 Subj: Babies. Family life – grandfathers. Family life – new sibling. Imagination. Sibling rivalry.

The worst person in the world ill. by author. Greenwillow, 1978. ISBN 0-688-84127-9 Subj: Friendship.

The worst person in the world at Crab Beach ill. by author. Greenwillow, 1988. ISBN 0-688-07299-2 Subj: Friendship. Humorous stories. Sea & seashore – beaches.

The worst person's Christmas ill. by author. Greenwillow, 1991. ISBN 0-688-10211-5 Subj: Character traits – meanness. Holidays – Christmas.

Yard sale ill. by author. Greenwillow, 1996. ISBN 0-688-14127-7 Subj: Animals. Garage sales, rummage sales.

Yuck! ill. by author. Greenwillow, 1984. ISBN 0-688-03830-1 Subj: Magic. Witches.

Stevenson, Jocelyn. *Jim Henson's Muppets at sea* ill. by Graham Thompson. Random House, 1980. ISBN 0-394-84571-4 Subj: Boats, ships. Puppets. Sea & seashore.

Red and the pumpkins ill. by Kelly Oechsli. Holt, 1983. ISBN 0-03-068679-2 Subj: Food. Imagination. Puppets.

Stevenson, Robert Louis. *Block city* ill. by Ashley Wolff. Dutton, 1988. ISBN 0-525-44399-1 Subj: Imagination. Poetry. Sea & seashore. Toys.

A child's garden of verses ill. by Erik Blegvad. Random House, 1978. ISBN 0-394-93739-2 Subj: Poetry.

A child's garden of verses ill. by Pelagie Doane. Doubleday, 1942. Subj: Poetry.

A child's garden of verses ill., sel. & arranged by Cooper Edens. DK, 1997. ISBN 0-7894-2068-6 Subj: Poetry.

A child's garden of verses ill. by Toni Frissell. U.S. Camera, 1944. Subj: Poetry.

A child's garden of verses ill. by Diane Goode. Morrow, 1998. ISBN 0-688-14584-1 Subj: Poetry.

A child's garden of verses ill. by Joan Hassall. HarperCollins, 1986. ISBN 0-87226-051-8 Subj: Poetry.

A child's garden of verses ill. by Joanna Isles. Abrams, 1994. ISBN 0-8109-3196-6 Subj: Poetry.

A child's garden of verses ill. by Thomas Kinkade; comp. by June Ford. Tommy Nelson, 1999. ISBN 0-8499-5869-5 Subj: Poetry.

A child's garden of verses ill. by Thea Kliros. Dover, 1992. ISBN 0-486-27301-6 Subj: Poetry.

A child's garden of verses ill. by Charles Robinson. Mainstream: Waterstone's, 1990. Reproduced from the 1896 edition. ISBN 1-85158-391-2 Subj: Poetry.

A child's garden of verses ill. by Jessie Willcox Smith. Children's Classics, 1995. ISBN 0-517-12397-5 Subj: Poetry.

A child's garden of verses ill. by Tasha Tudor. S&S, 1999. ISBN 0-689-81882-3 Subj: Poetry.

The little land ill. by Kim Fernandes. Kids Can, 2002. ISBN 1-55337-385-5 Subj: Imagination. Poetry.

The moon ill. by Denise Saldutti. HarperCollins, 1984. ISBN 0-06-025789-X Subj: Family life. Moon. Night. Poetry. Sports – fishing.

Where go the boats? ill. by Max Grover. Browndeer, 1998. ISBN 0-15-201711-9 Subj: Activities – playing. Poetry.

Stevenson, Suçie. *Christmas eve* ill. by author. Putnam, 1988. ISBN 0-399-21667-7 Subj: Animals – rabbits. Family life – sisters. Holidays – Christmas. Sibling rivalry.

Do I have to take Violet? ill. by author. Dodd, 1987. ISBN 0-396-08921-6 Subj: Activities – playing. Animals – rabbits. Sibling rivalry.

I forgot ill. by author. Watts, 1988. ISBN 0-531-08344-6 Subj: Animals. Behavior – forgetfulness. Birthdays.

Jessica the blue streak ill. by author. Watts, 1989. ISBN 0-531-08398-5 Subj: Animals – dogs. Behavior – misbehavior. Family life – fathers. Pets.

The princess and the pea (Andersen, H. C. [Hans Christian])

The twelve dancing princesses (Grimm, Jacob)

Stewart, Anne. *The ugly duckling* (Andersen, H. C. [Hans Christian])

Stewart, Charles P. *Dinosaurs and other creatures of long ago* (Stewart, Frances Todd)

Stewart, Dana. *Friends from Galilee: a Bible-times visit with Micah and Hannah* ill. by Kathy A. Couri. Standard, 1994. ISBN 0-7847-0003-6 Subj: Family life. Foreign lands – Galilee. Foreign lands – Palestine.

Stewart, Elizabeth Laing. *The lion twins* photos by Marlin & Carol Morse Perkins. Atheneum, 1964. Subj: Animals – lions. Multiple births – twins.

Stewart, Frances Todd. *Dinosaurs and other creatures of long ago* by Frances Todd Stewart & Charles P. Stewart, ill. by Forest Rogers & Kathy Borland. HarperCollins, 1988. ISBN 0-694-00229-1 Subj: Dinosaurs. Prehistory.

Stewart, Paul. *The birthday presents* ill. by Chris Riddell. HarperCollins, 2000. ISBN 0-06-028279-7 Subj: Animals – hedgehogs. Animals – rabbits. Behavior – sharing. Birthdays. Gifts.

A little bit of winter ill. by Chris Riddell. HarperCollins, 1999. ISBN 0-06-028278-9 Subj: Animals – hedgehogs. Animals – rabbits. Friendship. Hibernation. Seasons – winter.

Rabbit's wish ill. by Chris Ridell. HarperCollins, 2001. ISBN 0-06-029518-X Subj: Animals – hedgehogs. Animals – rabbits. Friendship. Weather – floods.

Stewart, Robert S. *The daddy book* ill. by Don Madden. American Heritage, 1972. ISBN 0-07-061348-6 Subj: Careers. Family life – fathers.

Stewart, Sarah. *The gardener* ill. by David Small. Farrar, 1997. ISBN 0-374-32517-0 Subj: Caldecott award honor books. Careers – bakers. Family life – aunts, uncles. Gardens, gardening. Letters, cards. U.S. history.

The journey ill. by David Small. Farrar, 2001. ISBN 0-374-33905-8 Subj: Activities – writing. Birthdays. Cities, towns. Ethnic groups in the U.S. – Amish.

The library ill. by David Small. Farrar, 1995. ISBN 0-374-34388-8 Subj: Books, reading. Libraries. Rhyming text.

The money tree ill. by David Small. Farrar, 1991. ISBN 0-374-35014-0 Subj: Money. Seasons. Trees.

Stewart, Shannon. *Sea crow* ill. by Liz Milkau. Orca, 2004. ISBN 1-55143-288-9 Subj: Emotions – fear. Family life – brothers & sisters. Handicaps – physical handicaps. Moving.

Stewig, John Warren. *Clever Gretchen* ill. by Patricia Wittmann. Cavendish, 2000. ISBN 0-7614-5066-1 Subj: Character traits – cleverness. Devil. Folk & fairy tales. Magic.

The fisherman and his wife (Grimm, Jacob)

King Midas ill. by Omar Rayyan. Holiday, 1999. ISBN 0-8234-1423-X Subj: Behavior – greed. Folk & fairy tales. Foreign lands – Greece. Royalty – kings.

Making plum jam ill. by Kevin O'Malley. Hyperion, 2002. ISBN 0-7868-2402-6 Subj: Activities – baking, cooking. Family life – aunts, uncles. Farms. Food.

Mother Holly: a retelling from the Brothers Grimm ill. by Johanna Westerman. North-South, 2001. ISBN 1-55858-926-0 Subj: Family life – sisters. Family life – stepfamilies. Folk & fairy tales. Foreign lands – Germany.

Stone soup ill. by Margot Tomes. Holiday, 1991. ISBN 0-8234-0863-9 Subj: Character traits – cleverness. Folk & fairy tales. Food.

Stickland, Henrietta. *Dinosaur roar!* (Stickland, Paul)

Stickland, Paul. *All about diggers* ill. by author. G. Stevens, 1990. ISBN 0-8368-0422-8 Subj: Activities – digging. Machines.

Bears ill. by author. Ragged Bears, 2001. ISBN 1-929927-34-7 Subj: Animals – bears. Animals – sheep. Bedtime. Parties. Rhyming text. Toys.

A child's book of things ill. by author. Watts, 1990. ISBN 0-531-08506-6 Subj: Activities. Family life.

Dinosaur roar! by Paul & Henrietta Stickland; ill. by Paul Stickland. Dutton, 1994. ISBN 0-525-45276-1 Subj: Concepts – opposites. Dinosaurs. Prehistory. Rhyming text.

Dinosaur stomp! ill. by author. Dutton, 1996. ISBN 0-525-45591-4 Subj: Activities – dancing. Dinosaurs. Format, unusual – toy & movable books. Prehistory. Rhyming text.

Machines as big as monsters ill. by author. Random House, 1989. ISBN 0-394-93913-1 Subj: Concepts – size. Machines.

Ten terrible dinosaurs ill. by author. Dutton, 1997. ISBN 0-525-45905-7 Subj: Counting, numbers. Dinosaurs. Prehistory. Rhyming text.

Truck jam ill. by author. Ragged Bears, 2000. ISBN 1-929927-03-7 Subj: Format, unusual – toy & movable books. Transportation. Trucks.

Stier, Catherine. *If I were president* ill. by DyAnne DiSalvo-Ryan. A. Whitman, 1999. ISBN 0-8075-3541-9 Subj: U.S. history.

Stihler, Chérie B. *The giant cabbage turnip* ill. by Jeremiah Trammell. Sasquatch, 2003. ISBN 1-57061-357-5 Subj: Alaska. Animals. Animals – moose. Character traits – cooperation. Cumulative tales. Fairs, festivals. Friendship. Plants. Problem solving.

Stiles, Martha Bennett. *Island magic* ill. by Daniel San Souci. Atheneum, 1999. ISBN 0-689-80588-8 Subj: Family life – grandfathers. Islands. Nature.

Stiles, Norman. *I'll miss you, Mr. Hooper* ill. by Joseph Mathieu. Random House, 1984. ISBN 0-394-96600-7 Subj: Death. Emotions – grief. Puppets.

The Sesame Street ABC storybook (Moss, Jeffrey)

Still, James. *Jack and the wonder beans* ill. by Margot Tomes. Putnam, 1977. ISBN 0-399-20498-9 Subj: Folk & fairy tales. Giants.

Stille, Darlene R. *Police cars* ill. with photos. Compass Pt., 2003. ISBN 0-7565-0290-X Subj: Automobiles. Careers – police officers. Transportation. Trucks.

Tractors ill. with photos. Compass Pt., 2003. ISBN 0-7565-0287-X Subj: Tractors. Transportation.

Stillerman, Marci. *Nine spoons* ill. by Pesach Gerber. Hachai, 1998. ISBN 0-922613-84-2 Subj: Holidays – Hanukkah. Holocaust. Jewish culture. Religion. War.

Stillwell, Fred. *The airplane alphabet book* (Pallotta, Jerry)

Stilz, Carol Curtis. *Grandma Buffalo, May, and me* ill. by Constance R. Bergum. Sasquatch, 1995. ISBN 1-57061-015-0 Subj: Animals – buffaloes. Family life – grandmothers. U.S. history – frontier & pioneer life.

Kirsty's kite ill. by Gwen Harrison. Albatross, 1988. ISBN 0-86760-089-6 Subj: Death. Emotions – grief. Family life – grandfathers. Family life – mothers. Kites.

Stimson, Joan. *Big Panda, Little Panda* ill. by Meg Rutherford. Barron's, 1994. ISBN 0-8120-6404-6 Subj: Animals – pandas. Babies. Behavior – growing up. Family life – brothers & sisters. Family life – mothers. Family life – new sibling.

Stinchecum, Amanda Mayer. *All about scabs* (Yagya, Genichiro)

The gas we pass: the story of farts (Cho, Shinta)

Girl from the snow country (Hidaka, Masako)

Grandpa's town (Nomura, Takaaki)

Stine, Jovial Bob. *Pork and beans: play date* ill. by José Aruego & Ariane Dewey. Scholastic, 1989. ISBN 0-590-41579-4 Subj: Activities – playing. Animals – pigs. Games. Sibling rivalry.

Sting (Musician). *Rock steady* ill. by Hugh Whyte. HarperCollins, 2001. ISBN 0-06-029231-8 Subj: Animals. Boats, ships. Religion – Noah. Rhyming text. Weather – floods. Weather – rain. Weather – rainbows.

Stinson, Kathy. *The bare naked book* ill. by Heather Collins. Firefly, 1986. ISBN 0-920303-52-8 Subj: Anatomy.

The dressed up book ill. by Heather Collins. Firefly, 1990. ISBN 1-55037-104-5 Subj: Activities – playing. Clothing. Imagination.

Mom and dad don't live together any more ill. by Nancy Lou Reynolds. Firefly, 1984. ISBN 0-920236-92-8 Subj: Divorce.

Red is best ill. by Robin Baird Lewis. Firefly, 1982. ISBN 0-920236-24-3 Subj: Concepts – color.

Teddy Rabbit ill. by Stéphane Poulin. Firefly, 1988. ISBN 1-55037-017-0 Subj: Toys. Trains.

Those green things ill. by Mary McLoughlin. Firefly, 1985. ISBN 0-920303-40-4 Subj: Imagination.

Stites, Clara. *The ugly duckling* (Andersen, H. C. [Hans Christian])

Stobbs, Joanna. *One sun, two eyes, and a million stars* by Joanna & William Stobbs; ill. by authors. Merrimack, 1983. ISBN 0-19-279747-6 Subj: Counting, numbers.

Stobbs, William. *Animal pictures* ill. by author. Bodley Head, 1982. ISBN 0-370-30341-5 Subj: Animals. Wordless.

A car called beetle ill. by author. Merrimack, 1979. ISBN 0-370-11144-3 Subj: Automobiles.

The hare and the frogs (Æsop)

Jack and the beanstalk (Jack and the beanstalk)

The little red hen (The little red hen)

One sun, two eyes, and a million stars (Stobbs, Joanna)

There's a hole in my bucket ill. by author. Merrimack, 1983. ISBN 0-19-279755-7 Subj: Seasons – summer. Songs.

This little piggy ill. by author. Bodley Head, 1981. ISBN 0-370-30428-4 Subj: Animals – pigs. Counting, numbers. Nursery rhymes. Rhyming text.

Stock, Catherine. *Alexander's midnight snack: a little elephant's ABC* ill. by author. Clarion, 1988. ISBN 0-89919-512-1 Subj: ABC books. Animals – elephants. Bedtime. Food.

The birthday present ill. by author. Bradbury, 1991. ISBN 0-02-788401-5 Subj: Birthdays. Parties.

Christmas time ill. by author. Bradbury, 1990. ISBN 0-02-788403-1 Subj: Family life – fathers. Holidays – Christmas.

Easter surprise ill. by author. Bradbury, 1991. ISBN 0-02-788371-X Subj: Family life – mothers. Holidays – Easter.

Emma's dragon hunt ill. by author. Lothrop, 1984. ISBN 0-688-02698-2 Subj: Dragons. Family life – grandfathers.

Gugu's house ill. by author. Clarion, 2001. ISBN 0-618-00389-4 Subj: Careers – artists. Family life – grandmothers. Foreign lands – Zimbabwe. Weather – rain.

Halloween monster ill. by author. Bradbury, 1990. ISBN 0-02-788404-X Subj: Activities. Emotions – fear. Holidays – Halloween.

An island summer ill. by author. Lothrop, 1999. ISBN 0-688-12781-9 Subj: Islands. Seasons – summer.

Sampson the Christmas cat ill. by author. Putnam, 1984. ISBN 0-399-21002-4 Subj: Animals – cats. Holidays – Christmas.

Secret Valentine ill. by author. Bradbury, 1991. ISBN 0-02-788372-8 Subj: Character traits – kindness. Holidays – Valentine's Day.

Sophie's bucket ill. by author. Lothrop, 1985. ISBN 0-688-04225-2 Subj: Family life. Sea & seashore.

Sophie's knapsack ill. by author. Lothrop, 1988. ISBN 0-688-06458-2 Subj: Camps, camping. Family life.

Thanksgiving treat ill. by author. Bradbury, 1990. ISBN 0-02-788402-3 Subj: Family life – grandfathers. Holidays – Thanksgiving.

Stockdale, Susan. *Some sleep standing up* ill. by author. S&S, 1997. ISBN 0-689-80509-8 Subj: Animals. Cumulative tales. Sleep.

Stockton, Frank Richard. *The bee-man of Orn* ill. by Maurice Sendak. Harper, 1964. ISBN 0-06-025819-5 Subj: Folk & fairy tales. Insects – bees. Self-concept. Wizards.

Stoddard, Sandol. *Bedtime for bear* ill. by Lynn Munsinger. Houghton Mifflin, 1985. ISBN 0-395-38811-2 Subj: Animals – bears. Bedtime. Rhyming text.

Bedtime mouse ill. by Lynn Munsinger. Houghton Mifflin, 1981. ISBN 0-395-31609-X Subj: Animals. Animals – mice. Bedtime. Cumulative tales. Rhyming text.

Curl up small ill. by Trina Schart Hyman. Houghton Mifflin, 1964. Subj: Concepts – shape. Concepts – size. Family life. Imagination.

My very own special particular private and personal cat ill. by Remy Charlip. Houghton Mifflin, 1963. Subj: Animals – cats. Pets. Rhyming text.

The thinking book ill. by Ivan Chermayeff. Little, 1960. Subj: Family life. Imagination.

Turtle time ill. by Lynn Munsinger. Houghton Mifflin, 1995. ISBN 0-395-56754-8 Subj: Bedtime. Pets. Reptiles – turtles, tortoises. Rhyming text.

Stoeke, Janet Morgan. *A friend for Minerva Louise* ill. by author. Dutton, 1997. ISBN 0-525-45869-7 Subj: Babies. Behavior – mistakes. Birds – chickens.

A hat for Minerva Louise ill. by author. Dutton, 1994. ISBN 0-525-45328-8 Subj: Behavior – misunderstanding. Birds – chickens. Clothing.

Hide and seek ill. by author. Dutton, 1999. ISBN 0-525-46189-2 Subj: Animals. Behavior – hiding. Birds – chickens. Farms. Format, unusual – board books. Games.

Minerva Louise ill. by author. Dutton, 1988. ISBN 0-525-44374-6 Subj: Behavior – misunderstanding. Birds – chickens.

Minerva Louise and the red truck ill. by author. Dutton, 2002. ISBN 0-525-46909-5 Subj: Birds – chickens. Careers – construction workers. Trucks.

Minerva Louise at school ill. by author. Dutton, 1996. ISBN 0-525-45494-2 Subj: Behavior – misunderstanding. Birds – chickens. School.

Minerva Louise at the fair ill. by author. Dutton, 2000. ISBN 0-525-46439-5 Subj: Behavior – mistakes. Birds – chickens. Fairs, festivals.

Stohs, Anita. *An Easter alleluia* ill. by Joel Snyder. Concordia, 2003. ISBN 0-7586-0116-6 Subj: Holidays – Easter. Music. Religion. Rhyming text. Songs.

Stojic, Manya. *Rain* ill. by author. Crown, 2000. ISBN 0-517-80086-1 Subj: Animals. Cumulative tales. Foreign lands – Africa. Weather – rain.

Snow ill. by author. Knopf, 2002. ISBN 0-375-92348-9 Subj: Animals. Forest, woods. Seasons – winter. Weather – snow.

Wet pebbles under our feet ill. by author. Knopf, 2002. ISBN 0-375-91519-2 Subj: Family life – grandparents. Islands. Sea & seashore – beaches.

Stoker, Wayne. *I can be a welder* (Lillegard, Dee)

Stolz, Mary (Mary Slattery). *Emmett's pig* ill. by Garth Williams & Rosemary Wells. HarperCollins, 2003. Subj: Animals – pigs. Birthdays. Cities, towns.

Storm in the night ill. by Pat Cummings. HarperCollins, 1988. ISBN 0-06-025912-4 Subj: Ethnic groups in the U.S. – African Americans. Family life – grandfathers. Night. Weather – storms.

Zekmet, the stone carver ill. by Deborah Nourse Lattimore. Harcourt, 1988. ISBN 0-15-299961-2 Subj: Activities – working. Foreign lands – Egypt.

Stone, A. Harris. *The last free bird* ill. by Sheila Heins. Prentice-Hall, 1967. Subj: Birds. Ecology.

Stone, Bernard. *The charge of the mouse brigade* by Bernard Stone with Alice Low; ill. by Tony Ross. Pantheon, 1980. ISBN 0-394-84390-8 Subj: Animals – cats. Animals – mice. War.

Emergency mouse ill. by Ralph Steadman. Prentice-Hall, 1978. ISBN 0-13-274555-0 Subj: Animals – mice. Hospitals.

Stone, Beth. *Do you have a secret? how to get help for scary secrets* (Russell, Pamela)

Stone, Jon. *Big Bird in China* photos by Victor DiNapoli. Random House, 1983. ISBN 0-394-95645-1 Subj: Foreign lands – China. Puppets.

Stone, Kazuko G. *Goodnight Twinklegator* ill. by author. Scholastic, 1990. ISBN 0-590-43183-8 Subj: Bedtime. Imagination. Night. Reptiles – alligators, crocodiles. Sky. Stars.

Stone, Lynn M. *Chickens have chicks* ill. with photos. Compass Pt., 2000. ISBN 0-7565-0000-1 Subj: Animals – babies. Birds – chickens.

Farm buildings ill. with photos. Rourke, 2002. ISBN 1-58952-091-2 Subj: Buildings. Farms.

Farms old and new ill. with photos. Rourke, 2002. ISBN 1-58952-094-7 Subj: Family life. Farms.

Getting around ill. with photos. Rourke, 2002. ISBN 1-58952-110-2 Subj: Animals. Sea & seashore.

Life of the kelp forest ill. with photos. Rourke, 2002. ISBN 1-58952-112-9 Subj: Ecology. Sea & seashore.

Partners ill. with photos. Rourke, 2002. ISBN 1-58952-114-5 Subj: Animals. Behavior – sharing. Ecology. Symbiosis.

Pigs and piglets ill. with photos. Compass Pt., 2000. ISBN 0-7565-0003-6 Subj: Animals – babies. Animals – pigs.

Stone, Marti. *The singing fir tree* ill. by Barry Root. Putnam, 1992. ISBN 0-399-22207-3 Subj: Folk & fairy tales. Foreign lands – Switzerland. Trees.

Stone, Phoebe. *Go away, Shelley Boo!* ill. by author. Little, 1999. ISBN 0-316-81677-9 Subj: Friendship. Imagination.

What night do the angels wander? ill. by author. Little, 1998. ISBN 0-316-81439-3 Subj: Angels. Holidays – Christmas. Rhyming text.

When the Wind Bears go dancing ill. by author. Little, 1997. ISBN 0-316-81701-5 Subj: Nature. Weather – storms. Weather – wind.

Stone, Rosetta. *Because a little bug went ka-choo!* ill. by Michael K. Frith. Random House, 1975. ISBN 0-394-93130-0 Subj: Cumulative tales. Humorous stories. Insects. Rhyming text.

Stonehouse, Bernard. *Kangaroos* ill. with photos. Raintree, 1978. ISBN 0-8172-1079-2 Subj: Animals – kangaroos.

Stonem, Tanya Lee. *D is for dreidel* ill. by Dawn Apperley. Price Stern Sloan, 2002. ISBN 0-8431-4576-5 Subj: ABC books. Holidays – Hanukkah. Jewish culture. Rhyming text.

Storm, Theodor. *Little Hobbin* trans. from German by Anthea Bell; ill. by Lisbeth Zwerger. North-South, 1995. ISBN 1-55858-461-7 Subj: Activities – traveling. Bedtime. Dreams. Folk & fairy tales. Furniture – beds. Moon. Sun.

Little John (Orgel, Doris)

Storr, Catherine (Cole). *Clever Polly and the stupid wolf* ill. by Marjorie-Ann Watts. Faber, 1979. ISBN 0-571-18011-6 Subj: Animals – wolves. Character traits – cleverness.

Hugo and his grandma ill. by Nita Sowter. Merrimack, 1980. ISBN 0-85122-136-X Subj: Activities – knitting. Family life – grandmothers.

King Midas ill. by Mike Codd. Raintree, 1985. ISBN 0-8172-2112-3 Subj: Behavior – greed. Behavior – wishing. Royalty – kings.

Rip Van Winkle (Irving, Washington)

Robin Hood ill. by Chris Collingwood. Raintree, 1984. ISBN 0-8172-2109-3 Subj: Foreign lands – England. Forest, woods. Middle Ages.

Stortz, Diane M. *Barnaby Mouse, detective, and the mystery of the big book* ill. by Patrick Girouard. Standard, 1994. ISBN 0-7847-0004-4 Subj: Animals – mice. Books, reading. Careers – detectives. Mystery stories. Religion.

Stott, Dorothy. *Little Duck's bicycle ride* ill. by author. Dutton, 1991. ISBN 0-525-44728-8 Subj: Birds – ducks. Farms. Sports – bicycling.

Too much ill. by author. Dutton, 1990. ISBN 0-525-44569-2 Subj: Birds – ducks. Sports – swimming.

Stott, Rowena. *The hedgehog feast* ill. by Edith Holden. Dutton, 1978. ISBN 0-525-61580-2 Subj: Animals – hedgehogs. Hibernation. Parties.

Stover, Jo Ann. *If everybody did* ill. by author. McKay, 1960. ISBN 0-89084-487-9 Subj: Behavior. Etiquette. Rhyming text.

Why? Because ill. by author. McKay, 1961. Subj: Character traits – questioning.

Stower, Adam. *Two left feet* ill. by author. Bloomsbury, 2004. ISBN 1-58234-884-7 Subj: Activities – dancing. Character traits – clumsiness. Contests. Monsters.

Strachan, Geoffrey. *3 X 3: Three by three* (Krüss, James)

Strahl, Rudi. *Sandman in the lighthouse* trans. & adapt. by Anthea Bell; ill. by Eberhard Binder. Childrens Pr., 1967, 1969. Subj: Bedtime. Lighthouses. Mythical creatures – sandman. Sea & seashore.

Straight, Susan. *Bear E. Bear* ill. by Marisabina Russo. Hyperion, 1995. ISBN 1-56282-527-5 Subj: Ethnic groups in the U.S. – African Americans. Family life. Laundry. Toys – bears.

Straker, Joan Ann. *Animals that live in the sea* ill. with photos. National Geographic, 1979. ISBN 0-8704-4264-3 Subj: Sea & seashore.

Strand, Keith. *Grandfather's Christmas tree* ill. by Thomas Locker. Silver Whistle, 1999. ISBN 0-15-201821-2 Subj: Birds – geese. Character traits – kindness to animals. Holidays – Christmas. U.S. history – frontier & pioneer life.

Strand, Mark. *The night book* ill. by William Pène Du Bois. Crown, 1985. ISBN 0-517-55047-4 Subj: Emotions – fear. Night.

The planet of lost things ill. by William Pène du Bois. Crown, 1983. ISBN 0-517-54184-X Subj: Bedtime. Dreams. Noise, sounds.

Strange, Florence. *Rock-a-bye whale: a story of the birth of a humpback whale* ill. by author. Manzanita, 1977. ISBN 0-931644-08-3 Subj: Animals – whales. Science.

Stratemeyer, Clara Georgeanna. *Frog fun* by Clara G. Stratemeyer & Henry Lee Smith, Jr.; ill. by Lucy Hawkinson. HarperCollins, 1963. Subj: Frogs & toads.

Pepper by Clara G. Stratemeyer & Henry Lee Smith, Jr. Benziger, 1971. Subj: Animals. Animals – cats.

Tuggy by Clara Georgeanna Stratemeyer & Henry Lee Smith, Jr. HarperCollins, 1971. Subj: Animals – dogs. Frogs & toads.

Strathdee, Jean. *The house that grew* ill. by Jessica Wallace. Oxford Univ. Pr., 1980. ISBN 0-19-558041-9 Subj: Family life. Homes, houses. Moving.

Strauss, Anna. *Hush, Mama loves you* ill. by Alice Priestley. Walker, 2002. ISBN 0-8027-8806-8 Subj: Character traits – helpfulness. Emotions. Family life – mothers.

Strauss, Gwen. *The night shimmy* ill. by Anthony Browne. Knopf, 1992. ISBN 0-679-92384-5 Subj: Behavior – needing someone. Dreams. Friendship. Imagination – imaginary friends. Kites.

Trail of stones ill. by Anthony Browne. Knopf, 1990. ISBN 0-679-90582-0 Subj: Emotions. Folk & fairy tales. Poetry.

Strauss, Susan. *When woman became the sea: a Costa Rican creation myth* ill. by Cristina Acosta. Beyond Words, 1998. ISBN 1-885223-85-4 Subj: Creation. Folk & fairy tales. Foreign lands – Costa Rica. Sea & seashore.

Streatfield, Noel. *Sleepy Nicholas* (Brande, Marlie)

Street, Pat. *There's a frog in my throat: 312 animal sayings from the horse's mouth* (Leedy, Loreen)

Stren, Patti. *Hug me* ill. by author. HarperCollins, 1977. ISBN 0-06-026081-5 Subj: Animals – porcupines. Emotions – loneliness.

Mountain Rose ill. by author. Dutton, 1982. ISBN 0-525-35228-7 Subj: Character traits – appearance. Self-concept. Sports – wrestling.

Strete, Craig Kee. *Big thunder magic* ill. by Craig McFarland Brown. Greenwillow, 1990. ISBN 0-688-08854-6 Subj: Animals – sheep. Friendship. Indians of North America – Pueblo.

How the Indians bought the farm by Craig Kee Strete & Michelle Netten Chacon; ill. by Francisco X. Mora. Greenwillow, 1996. ISBN 0-688-14131-5 Subj: Animals. Behavior – trickery. Farms. Indians of North America.

The lost boy and the monster ill. by Steve Johnson & Lou Fancher. Putnam, 1999. ISBN 0-399-22922-1 Subj: Animals. Character traits – kindness to animals. Folk & fairy tales. Indians of North America – Southwest. Monsters. Reptiles – snakes.

They thought they saw him ill. by José Aruego & Ariane Dewey. Greenwillow, 1996. ISBN 0-688-14195-1 Subj: Concepts – color. Reptiles – lizards.

Strickland, Tessa. *Please, Mr. Crocodile!* (Please, Mr. Crocodile!)

Strom, Maria Diaz. *Rainbow Joe and me* ill. by author. Lee & Low, 1999. ISBN 1-880000-93-8 Subj: Concepts – color. Ethnic groups in the U.S. – African Americans. Friendship. Handicaps – blindness. Music. Musical instruments – saxophones.

Strong, Stacie. *Runners, sliders, bouncers, climbers* (Bantock, Nick)

Stroud, Bettye. *Dance y'all* ill. by Cornelius Van Wright & Ying-Hwa Hu. Cavendish, 2001. ISBN 0-7614-5065-3 Subj: Activities – dancing. Emotions – fear. Ethnic groups in the U.S. – African Americans. Farms. Reptiles – snakes.

Down home at Miss Dessa's ill. by Felicia Marshall. Lee & Low, 1996. ISBN 1-880000-39-3 Subj: Character traits – kindness. Ethnic groups in the U.S. – African Americans. Family life – sisters. Illness. Old age. Seasons – summer.

The leaving ill. by Cedric Lucas. Cavendish, 2001. ISBN 0-7614-5067-X Subj: Ethnic groups in the U.S. – African Americans. Slavery.

The patchwork path ill. by Erin Susanne Bennett. Candlewick, 2005. ISBN 0-7636-2423-3 Subj: Character traits – freedom. Ethnic groups in the U.S. – African Americans. Maps. Quilts. Slavery.

Stroud, Virginia A. *A walk to the Great Mystery* ill. by author. Dial, 1995. ISBN 0-8037-1637-0 Subj: Family life – grandmothers. Indians of North America – Cherokee. Nature.

Stroyer, Poul. *It's a deal* ill. by author. Astor-Honor, 1960. Subj: Activities – trading. Humorous stories.

Strub, Susanne. *Lulu goes swimming* ill. by author. Viking, 1990. ISBN 0-670-83460-2 Subj: Behavior – growing up. Dreams. Sports – swimming.

Lulu on her bike ill. by author. Viking, 1990. ISBN 0-670-83461-0 Subj: Behavior – growing up. Dreams. Sports – bicycling.

Struges, Philemon. *I love planes* ill. by Shari Halpern. HarperCollins, 2003. ISBN 0-06-028899-X Subj: Airplanes, airports.

I love school ill. by Shari Halpern. HarperCollins, 2004. ISBN 0-06-009285-8 Subj: Family life – brothers & sisters. Rhyming text. School – nursery.

I love trains ill. by Shari Halpern. HarperCollins, 2001. ISBN 0-06-028901-5 Subj: Rhyming text. Trains.

Struppi ill. by Ingrid Graichen. Imported Pubs., 1983. ISBN 0-8285-2583-8 Subj: Animals. Format, unusual – board books. Wordless.

Stuart, Chad. *The Ballymara flood* ill. by George Booth. Harcourt, 1996. ISBN 0-15-205698-X Subj: Activities – bathing. Foreign lands – Ireland. Rhyming text. Weather – floods.

Stuart, Mary. *see* Graham, Mary Stuart Campbell

Stuart-Clark, Christopher. *Bright star shining: poems for Christmas* (Bright star shining)

Stubbs, Joanna. *Happy Bear's day* ill. by author. Elsevier-Dutton, 1979. ISBN 0-233-96999-3 Subj: Animals – bears. Behavior – solitude.

With cat's eyes you'll never be scared of the dark ill. by author. Dutton, 1983. ISBN 0-233-97485-7 Subj: Emotions – fear. Magic. Night.

Stuchner, Joan Betty. *The Kugel Valley Klezmer Band* ill. by Richard Row. Crocodile, 2001. ISBN 1-56656-430-1 Subj: Foreign lands – Canada. Jewish culture. Musical instruments – bands.

Sturges, Philemon. *I love bugs* ill. by Shari Halpern. HarperCollins, 2005. ISBN 0-06-056169-6 Subj: Insects. Rhyming text.

I love trucks! ill. by Shari Halpern. HarperCollins, 1999. ISBN 0-06-027819-6 Subj: Careers – truck drivers. Rhyming text. Trucks.

The Little Red Hen makes a pizza (The little red hen)

Marushka and the Month Brothers: a folktale (Vojtech, Anna)

Ten flashing fireflies ill. by Anna Vojtech. North-South, 1995. ISBN 1-55858-421-8 Subj: Counting, numbers. Insects – fireflies. Night. Rhyming text.

What's that sound, Woolly Bear? ill. by Joan Paley. Little, 1996. ISBN 0-316-82021-0 Subj: Insects. Insects – butterflies, caterpillars. Insects – moths. Metamorphosis. Noise, sounds.

Who took the cookies from the cookie jar? (Lass, Bonnie)

Sturgis, Matthew. *Tosca's surprise* ill. by Anne Mortimer. Dial, 1991. ISBN 0-8037-0946-3 Subj: Animals – cats.

Sturtzel, Howard A. *see* Annixter, Paul

Sturtzel, Jane Levington. *see* Annixter, Jane

Stutson, Caroline. *By the light of the Halloween moon* ill. by Kevin Hawkes. Lothrop, 1993. ISBN 0-688-12046-6 Subj: Cumulative tales. Holidays – Halloween. Rhyming text.

Cowpokes ill. by Daniel San Souci. Lee & Shepard, 1999. ISBN 0-688-13974-4 Subj: Cowboys, cowgirls. Rhyming text.

Night train ill. by Katherine Tillotson. Roaring Brook, 2002. ISBN 0-7613-1598-5 Subj: Rhyming text. Trains.

Prairie primer A to Z ill. by Susan Condie Lamb. Dutton, 1996. ISBN 0-525-45163-3 Subj: ABC books. Family life. Farms. Rhyming text. U.S. history – frontier & pioneer life.

Stuve-Bodeen, Stephanie. *Elizabeti's school* ill. by Christy Hale. Lee & Low, 2002. ISBN 1-58430-043-4 Subj: Family life. Foreign lands – Tanzania. School – first day.

Elizabeti's doll ill. by Christy Hale. Lee & Low, 1998. ISBN 1-880000-70-9 Subj: Emotions – love. Foreign lands – Tanzania. Imagination. Rocks. Toys – dolls.

Mama Elizabeti ill. by Christy Hale. Lee & Low, 2000. ISBN 1-58430-002-7 Subj: Babies. Family life – brothers. Family life – new sibling. Foreign lands – Tanzania.

We'll paint the octopus red ill. by Pam DeVito. Woodbine House, 1998. ISBN 1-890627-06-2 Subj: Family life – brothers & sisters. Handicaps – Down syndrome.

Stynes, Barbara White. *Walking with mama* ill. by author. Dawn, 1997. ISBN 1-883220-56-4 Subj: Activities – walking. Family life – mothers.

Suba, Susanne. *The monkeys and the pedlar* ill. by author. Viking, 1970. ISBN 0-670-48655-8 Subj: Animals – monkeys. Careers – peddlers. Humorous stories.

Suben, Eric. *Pigeon takes a trip* ill. by Tiziana Zanetti; graphic design by Giorgio Vanetti. Golden Bks., 1984. ISBN 0-307-17103-5 Subj: Activities – traveling. Birds – pigeons. Format, unusual – board books.

Suen, Anastasia. *Air show* ill. by Cecco Mariniello. Holt, 2001. ISBN 0-8050-4952-5 Subj: Airplanes, airports.

Baby born ill. by Chih-wei Chang. Lee & Low, 1998. ISBN 1-88000-068-7 Subj: Babies. Behavior – growing up. Rhyming text.

Baby born [board book] ill. by Chih-wei Chang. Lee & Low, 1999. ISBN 1-880000-95-4 Subj: Babies. Behavior – growing up. Format, unusual – board books. Rhyming text.

The clubhouse ill. by Allan Eitzen; based on characters of Ezra Jack Keats. Viking, 2002. ISBN 0-670-03537-8 Subj: Character traits – cooperation. Clubs, gangs. Communities, neighborhoods. Ethnic groups in the U.S. – African Americans.

Delivery ill. by Wade Zahares. Viking, 1999. ISBN 0-670-88455-3 Subj: Rhyming text. Transportation.

Hamster chase ill. by Allan Eitzen; based on characters of Ezra Jack Keats. Viking, 2001. ISBN 0-670-88942-3 Subj: Animals – hamsters. Ethnic groups in the U.S. – African Americans. School.

Loose tooth ill. by Allan Eitzen; based on characters of Ezra Jack Keats. Viking, 2002. ISBN 0-670-03536-X Subj: Ethnic groups in the U.S. – African Americans. Sports – basketball. Teeth.

Man on the moon ill. by Benrei Huang. Viking, 1997. ISBN 0-670-87393-4 Subj: Moon. Space & space ships. U.S. history.

Raise the roof ill. by Elwood H. Smith. Viking, 2003. ISBN 0-670-89282-3 Subj: Buildings. Careers – construction workers. Family life. Homes, houses. Rhyming text.

Red light, green light ill. by Ken Wilson-Max. Harcourt, 2005. ISBN 0-15-202582-0 Subj: Automobiles. Rhyming text. Traffic, traffic signs. Transportation. Trucks.

Subway ill. by Karen Katz. Viking, 2004. ISBN 0-670-03622-6 Subj: Rhyming text. Trains. Transportation.

Willie's birthday ill. by Allan Eitzen; based on characters created by Ezra Jack Keats. Viking, 2001. Subj: Animals – dogs. Ethnic groups in the U.S. – African Americans. Parties. Pets.

Window music ill. by Wade Zahares. Viking, 1998. ISBN 0-670-87287-3 Subj: Activities – trading. Family life – mothers. Rhyming text. Trains.

Suetake, Kunihiro. *Red dragonfly on my shoulder* (Cassedy, Sylvia)

Sueyoshi, Akiko. *Ladybird on a bicycle* ill. by Viv Allbright. Faber, 1983. ISBN 0-571-11802-X Subj: Insects – ladybugs. Sports – bicycling.

Sugar snow adapt. from the Little house books by Laura Ingalls Wilder; ill. by Doris Ettlinger. HarperCollins, 1998. ISBN 0-06-025933-7 Subj: Careers – farmers. U.S. history – frontier & pioneer life.

Sugita, Yutaka. *The flower family* ill. by author. McGraw-Hill, 1975. ISBN 0-07-061769-4 Subj: Flowers. Plants. Science.

Good night 1, 2, 3 ill. by author. Scroll Pr., 1971. ISBN 0-87592-022-5 Subj: Bedtime. Counting, numbers. Sleep.

Helena the unhappy hippopotamus ill. by author. McGraw-Hill, 1972. ISBN 0-07-061763-5 Subj: Animals – hippopotamuses. Behavior – needing someone. Emotions – loneliness. Emotions – sadness. Friendship.

My friend Little John and me ill. by author. McGraw-Hill, 1972. ISBN 0-07-062458-5 Subj: Animals – dogs. Wordless.

Suhl, Yuri. *The Purim goat* ill. by Kaethe Zemach. Four Winds, 1980. ISBN 0-590-07658-2 Subj: Animals – goats. Character traits – helpfulness. Holidays – Purim.

Simon Boom gives a wedding ill. by Margot Zemach. Four Winds, 1972. Subj: Cumulative tales. Humorous stories. Jewish culture. Weddings.

Sullivan, Charles. *Numbers at play* ill. by author. Rizzoli, 1992. ISBN 0-8478-1501-3 Subj: Art. Counting, numbers. Rhyming text.

Sullivan, Paula. *Todd's box* ill. by Nadine Bernard Westcott. Harcourt, 2004. ISBN 0-15-205093-0 Subj: Activities – walking. Behavior – collecting things. Family life – mothers. Family life – sons.

Sullivan, Silky. *Grandpa was a cowboy* ill. by Bert Dodson. Orchard, 1996. ISBN 0-531-08861-8 Subj: Cowboys, cowgirls. Family life – aunts, uncles. Family life – grandfathers. Old age. Orphans.

Sumiko. *Kittymouse* ill. by author. Harcourt, 1979. ISBN 0-15-243028-8 Subj: Animals – cats. Animals – mice.

Summers, Kate. *Milly and Tilly: the story of a town mouse and a country mouse* ill. by Maggie Kneen. Dutton, 1997. ISBN 0-525-45801-8 Subj: Animals – mice. Cities, towns. Country. Folk & fairy tales.

Milly's wedding ill. by Maggie Kneen. Dutton, 1999. ISBN 0-525-46046-2 Subj: Animals – mice. Emotions – love. Weddings.

Summers, Susan. *The fourth wise man* based on the story by Henry Van Dyke; ill. by Jackie Morris. Dial, 1998. ISBN 0-8037-2312-1 Subj: Religion – Nativity.

The sun, the moon, and the stars col., written, & ill. by Nancy Elizabeth Wallace. Houghton, 2003. ISBN 0-618-26353-5 Subj: Moon. Poetry. Stars. Sun.

Sunami, Kitoba. *How the fisherman tricked the genie* ill. by Amiko Hirao. Atheneum, 2002. ISBN 0-689-83399-7 Subj: Behavior – trickery. Careers – fishermen. Emotions – anger. Folk & fairy tales. Mythical creatures – genies.

Sundgaard, Arnold. *The bear who loved Puccini* ill. by Dominic Catalano. Putnam, 1992. ISBN 0-399-22135-2 Subj: Activities – singing. Animals – bears.

Jethro's difficult dinosaur ill. by Stanley Mack. Pantheon, 1977. ISBN 0-394-93391-X Subj: Dinosaurs. Eggs. Humorous stories. Prehistory. Rhyming text.

The lamb and the butterfly ill. by Eric Carle. Watts, 1988. ISBN 0-531-08379-9 Subj: Animals – sheep. Character traits – freedom. Insects – butterflies, caterpillars.

Meet Jack Appleknocker ill. by Sheila White Samton. Putnam, 1988. ISBN 0-399-21472-0 Subj: Imagination.

Sundvall, Viveca. *Mimi and the biscuit factory* trans. from Swedish by Eris Bibb; ill. by Eva Eriksson. Farrar, 1989. ISBN 9-12-959142-2 Subj: Careers – bakers. Foreign lands – Sweden. School. Teeth.

Super, Gretchen. *Family traditions* ill. by Kees de Kiefte. Twenty-first Century, 1992. ISBN 0-8050-2218-X Subj: Etiquette. Family life.

Sisters and brothers ill. by Kees de Kiefte. Twenty-first Century, 1992. ISBN 0-8050-2219-8 Subj: Family life. Family life – brothers & sisters. Sibling rivalry.

The Superman mix or match storybook ill. by Ross Andru & Joe Orlando. Random House, 1979. ISBN 0-394-84211-1 Subj: Format, unusual – toy & movable books.

Supraner, Robyn. *Giggly-wiggly, snickety-snick* ill. by Stan Tusan. Parents' Magazine Pr., 1978. ISBN 0-8193-0855-2 Subj: Concepts.

Sam Sunday and the mystery at the Ocean Beach Hotel ill. by Will Hillenbrand. Viking, 1996. ISBN 0-670-84797-6 Subj: Animals. Birthdays. Careers – detectives. Friendship. Hotels. Mystery stories.

Would you rather be a tiger? ill. by Barbara Cooney. Houghton Mifflin, 1973. ISBN 0-395-15495-2 Subj: Behavior. Imagination. Rhyming text. Self-concept.

Supree, Burton. *Harlequin and the gift of many colors* (Charlip, Remy)

"Mother, mother I feel sick" (Charlip, Remy)

Surany, Anico. *Kati and Kormos* ill. by Leonard Everett Fisher. Holiday, 1966. Subj: Animals – dogs. Emotions – loneliness. Foreign lands – Hungary.

Ride the cold wind ill. by Leonard Everett Fisher. Putnam, 1964. Subj: Boats, ships. Foreign lands – South America. Sports – fishing.

Surat, Michele Maria. *Angel child, dragon child* ill. by Vo-Dinh Mai. Raintree, 1983. ISBN 0-940742-12-8 Subj: Ethnic groups in the U.S. – Vietnamese Americans. School.

Sussman, Susan. *Hippo thunder* ill. by John C. Wallner. A. Whitman, 1982. ISBN 0-8075-3307-6 Subj: Bedtime. Emotions. Weather – lightning, thunder.

Sutcliff, Rosemary. *The minstrel and the dragon pup* ill. by Emma Chichester Clark. Candlewick, 1993. ISBN 1-56402-098-3 Subj: Dragons. Eggs.

Suteev, V. (Vladimir). *The adventures of Snowwoman* (Arnold, Katya)

Meow! (Arnold, Katya)

Three kittens (Ginsburg, Mirra)

Sutherland, Colleen. *Jason goes to show-and-tell* ill. by Linda Weller. Boyds Mills, 1992. ISBN 1-878093-89-4 Subj: Behavior – forgetfulness. Character traits – orderliness. Clothing. Cumulative tales. School. Seasons – winter. Toys – bears.

Sutherland, Harry A. *Dad's car wash* ill. by Maxie Chambliss. Atheneum, 1988. ISBN 0-689-31335-7 Subj: Activities – bathing. Bedtime. Imagination.

Sutherland, Marc. *MacMurtrey's wall* ill. by author. Abrams, 2001. ISBN 0-8109-4494-4 Subj: Communities, neighborhoods. Sea & seashore. Weather – storms.

The waiting place ill. by author. Abrams, 1998. ISBN 0-8109-3994-0 Subj: Dreams. Imagination. Rhyming text.

Sutherland, Tui. *Meet Mo and Ella* ill. by Rose Mary Berlin. Grosset, 2001. ISBN 0-448-42456-8 Subj: Animals – elephants. Animals – mice. Concepts – size. Friendship.

Sutton, Elizabeth Henning. *A pony for keeps* ill. by Mary Brant Gamma. Thomasson-Grant, 1991. ISBN 0-934738-77-7 Subj: Animals – horses, ponies. Birthdays.

Sutton, Eve. *My cat likes to hide in boxes* ill. by Lynley Dodd. Parents' Magazine Pr., 1973. ISBN 0-8193-0753-X Subj: Animals – cats. Cumulative tales. Participation. Rhyming text.

Sutton, Jane. *What should a hippo wear?* ill. by Lynn Munsinger. Houghton Mifflin, 1979. ISBN 0-395-27800-7 Subj: Activities – dancing. Animals. Animals – hippopotamuses. Clothing.

Suzuki, David. *Salmon forest* by David Suzuki & Sarah Ellis; ill. by Sheena Lott. Greystone, 2003. ISBN 1-55054-937-5 Subj: Ecology. Fish. Nature.

Svend Otto S (Svend Otto Sorensen). *The giant fish and other stories* trans. from Danish by Joan Tate; ill. by author. Larousse, 1982. ISBN 0-88332-287-0 Subj: Behavior – growing up. Foreign lands.

Taxi dog ill. by author. Parents' Magazine Pr., 1978. ISBN 0-8193-0916-8 Subj: Animals – dogs. Behavior – running away. Careers – taxi drivers.

The three billy goats Gruff (Asbjørnsen, P. C. [Peter Christen])

Svendsen, Carol. *Hulda* ill. by Julius Svendsen. Houghton Mifflin, 1974. ISBN 0-395-19497-0 Subj: Behavior. Mythical creatures – trolls. Rhyming text.

Swados, Elizabeth. *Lullaby* ill. by Faith Hubley. HarperCollins, 1980. ISBN 0-06-026085-8 Subj: Bedtime. Lullabies.

Swain, Gwenyth. *I wonder as I wander* ill. by Ron Himler. Eerdmans, 2003. ISBN 0-8028-5214-9 Subj: Careers – clergy. Careers – composers. Religion. Songs. U.S. history.

Johnny Appleseed ill. by Janice Lee Porter. Carolrhoda, 2001. ISBN 1-57505-519-8 Subj: Activities – traveling. Gardens, gardening. Tall tales. Trees. U.S. history – frontier & pioneer life.

Smiling ill. with photos. Carolrhoda, 1999. ISBN 1-57505-256-3 Subj: Anatomy – faces. Emotions – happiness. Ethnic groups in the U.S.

Swain, Ruth Freeman. *Bedtime!* ill. by Cat Bowman Smith. Holiday, 1999. ISBN 0-8234-1444-2 Subj: Bedtime. Behavior. Furniture – beds. Sleep.

How sweet it is (and was) ill. by John O'Brien. Holiday, 2003. ISBN 0-8234-1712-3 Subj: Food.

Swamp, Jake. *Giving thanks* ill. by Erwin Printup, Jr. Lee & Low, 1995. ISBN 1-880000-15-6 Subj: Ecology. Indians of North America – Mohawk. Nature. Religion.

Swan, Donald. *The hippopotamus song: a muddy love story* (Flanders, Michael)

Swan flyway: the tundra swan ill. by Jo-Ellen Bosson. Soundprints, 1993. ISBN 0-92448-395-4 Subj: Birds – swans. Migration.

Swann, Brian. *A basket full of white eggs: riddle-poems* ill. by Ponder Goembel. Watts, 1988. ISBN 0-531-08334-9 Subj: Poetry. Proverbs. Riddles & jokes.

The house with no door: African riddle-poems ill. by Ashley Bryan. Harcourt, 1998. ISBN 0-15-200805-5 Subj: Folk & fairy tales. Foreign lands – Africa. Poetry. Riddles & jokes.

Swanson, Diane. *The dentist and you* ill. with photos. Firefly, 2002. ISBN 1-55037-729-9 Subj: Careers – dentists. Health & fitness. Teeth.

The doctor and you ill. with photos. Firefly, 2001. ISBN 1-55037-673-X Subj: Careers – doctors. Health & fitness.

Headgear that hides and plays ill. by Rose Cowles. Greystone, 2001. ISBN 1-55054-819-0 Subj: Anatomy – heads. Animals.

Noses that plow and poke ill. with photos. Greystone, 1999. ISBN 1-55054-715-1 Subj: Anatomy – noses. Animals.

Skin that slimes and scares ill. with photos. Greystone, 2001. ISBN 1-55054-817-4 Subj: Anatomy – skin. Animals.

Swanson, June. *Punny places: jokes to make you mappy* ill. by Brian Gable. Carolrhoda, 2004. ISBN 1-57505-647-X Subj: Riddles & jokes.

Summit up ill. by Susan Slattery Burke. Lerner, 1994. ISBN 0-8225-2342-6 Subj: Mountains. Riddles & jokes.

Swanson, Susan Marie. *The first thing my mama told me* ill. by Christine Davenier. Harcourt, 2002. ISBN 0-15-201075-0 Subj: Birthdays. Family life – mothers. Names. Self-concept.

Swanson-Natsues, Lyn. *Days of adventure* ill. by Joy Dunn Keenan. Mondo, 1996. ISBN 1-57255-160-7 Subj: Activities – playing. Ethnic groups in the U.S. – African Americans. Ethnic groups in the U.S. – Asian Americans. Imagination.

Swartz, Leslie. *A first Passover* ill. by Jacqueline Chwast. Modern Curriculum, 1992. ISBN 0-8136-2305-7 Subj: Holidays – Passover. Jewish culture.

Swartz, Nancy Sohn. *In our image: God's first creatures* ill. by Melanie Hall. Jewish Lights, 1998. ISBN 1-879045-99-0 Subj: Animals. Behavior – sharing. Creation. Religion.

Sweeney, Jacqueline. *Katie and the night noises* ill. by Arden Johnson. BridgeWater, 1993. ISBN 0-816-73014-8 Subj: Bedtime. Imagination. Noise, sounds. Rhyming text.

What about Bettie? photos by G. K. & Vikki Hart; photo ill. by Blind Mice Studio. Benchmark, 2001. ISBN 0-7614-1118-6 Subj: Animals. Birds – ducks. Character traits – being different. Family life – brothers & sisters.

Sweeney, Joan. *Me and my family tree* ill. by Annette Cable. Crown, 1999. ISBN 0-517-70966-X Subj: Family life. Genealogy.

Me and my senses ill. by Annette Cable. Crown, 2003. ISBN 0-375-91102-2 Subj: Senses.

Me and the measure of things ill. by Annette Cable. Crown, 2001. ISBN 0-375-91101-4 Subj: Concepts – measurement. Concepts – weight.

Me counting time ill. by Annette Cable. Crown, 2000. ISBN 0-517-80056-X Subj: Concepts – measurement. Time.

Suzette and the puppy ill. by Jennifer Heyd Wharton. Barron's, 2000. ISBN 0-7641-5294-7 Subj: Animals – dogs. Careers – artists. Foreign lands – France. Parks.

Sweet, Melissa. *Fiddle-i-fee* ill. by adapt. Little, 1992. ISBN 0-316-82516-6 Subj: Animals. Cumulative tales. Farms. Music. Songs.

Sweeten, Sami. *Wolf* ill. by author. A. Whitman, 1994. ISBN 0-8075-9160-2 Subj: Animals – wolves.

Sweetland, Nancy Rose. *God's quiet things* ill. by Rick Stevens. Eerdmans, 1994. ISBN 0-8028-5082-0 Subj: Behavior – solitude. Nature. Rhyming text.

If I could = Si yo pudiera ill. by Robert Sweetland. Raven Tree, 2002. ISBN 0-9701107-7-4 Subj: Foreign languages. Imagination.

Yelly Kelly ill. by Robert Sweetland. Raven Tree, 2003. ISBN 0-9720192-0-0 Subj: Behavior. Etiquette.

Swendson, Patsy. *The potluck adventures of Mrs. Marmalade* by Patsy Swendson & Debbie Little; ill. by authors. Eakin, 1989. ISBN 0-89015-718-9 Subj: Activities – baking, cooking. Animals. Animals – possums.

Swift, Hildegarde Hoyt. *The little red lighthouse and the great gray bridge* by Hildegarde H. Swift & Lynd Ward; ill. by Lynd Ward. Harcourt, 1942. Subj: Boats, ships. Bridges. Lighthouses.

Swinburne, Stephen R. *Go, go, go!* photos by author. Boyds Mills, 2002. ISBN 1-59078-022-1 Subj: Activities.

Guess whose shadow? ill. by author. Boyds Mills, 1999. ISBN 1-56397-724-9 Subj: Activities – photographing. Light, lights. Shadows.

Lots and lots of zebra stripes photos by author. Boyds Mills, 1998. ISBN 1-56397-707-9 Subj: Animals. Concepts – color. Concepts – patterns. Disguises. Nature.

Safe, warm, and snug ill. by José Aruego & Ariane Dewey. Harcourt, 1999. ISBN 0-15-201734-8 Subj: Animals. Animals – babies. Family life – parents.

Swallows in the birdhouse ill. by Robin Brickman. Millbrook, 1996. ISBN 1-56294-182-8 Subj: Activities – making things. Birds – swallows. Homes, houses.

Water for one, water for everyone ill. by Melinda Levine. Millbrook, 1998. ISBN 0-7613-0269-7 Subj: Animals. Counting, numbers. Foreign lands – Africa.

What color is nature? photos by author. Boyds Mills, 2002. ISBN 1-56397-967-5 Subj: Concepts – color. Nature.

What's a pair? What's a dozen? ill. by author. Boyds Mills, 2000. ISBN 1-56397-827-X Subj: Concepts. Counting, numbers.

What's opposite? ill. by author. Boyds Mills, 2000. ISBN 1-56397-881-4 Subj: Concepts – opposites.

Switzer, Robert E. *My friend the babysitter* (Watson, Jane Werner)

My friend the dentist (Watson, Jane Werner)

My friend the doctor (Watson, Jane Werner)

Sometimes a family has to move (Watson, Jane Werner)

Sometimes a family has to split up (Watson, Jane Werner)

Sometimes I get angry (Watson, Jane Werner)

Sometimes I'm afraid (Watson, Jane Werner)

Sometimes I'm jealous (Watson, Jane Werner)

Swope, Sam. *The Araboolies of Liberty Street* ill. by Barry Root. Crown, 1989. ISBN 0-517-57411-X Subj: Behavior. Communities, neighborhoods.

Gotta go! Gotta go! ill. by Sue Riddle. Farrar, 2000. ISBN 0-374-32757-2 Subj: Foreign lands – Mexico. Insects – butterflies, caterpillars. Migration.

Sykes, Julie. *Careful, Santa* ill. by Tim Warnes. Tiger Tales, 2002. ISBN 1-58925-023-0 Subj: Accidents. Animals. Holidays – Christmas. Santa Claus.

Dora's chicks ill. by Jane Chapman. Tiger Tales, 2002. ISBN 1-58925-015-X Subj: Animals. Behavior – lost. Birds – chickens. Counting, numbers.

Dora's eggs ill. by Jane Chapman. Little Tiger, 1997. ISBN 1-888444-09-6 Subj: Animals. Birds – chickens. Birth. Eggs. Farms.

Hurry, Santa! ill. by Tim Warnes. Little Tiger, 1998. ISBN 1-888444-37-1 Subj: Behavior – promptness, tardiness. Holidays – Christmas. Santa Claus.

I don't want to take a bath! ill. by Tim Warnes. Little Tiger, 1997. ISBN 1-888444-20-7 Subj: Activities – bathing. Animals. Animals – tigers. Behavior – running away. Family life – mothers.

Little Rocket's special star ill. by Jack Tickle. Dutton, 2000. ISBN 0-525-46494-8 Subj: Astronomy. Birthdays. Science. Stars.

Little Tiger's big surprise ill. by Tim Warnes. Little Tiger, 1999. ISBN 1-888444-52-5 Subj: Animals – tigers. Emotions – anger. Emotions – envy, jealousy. Family life – new sibling.

Robbie Rabbit and the little ones ill. by Catherine Walters. Little Tiger, 1996. ISBN 1-888444-01-0 Subj: Activities – babysitting. Animals – rabbits. Behavior – misbehavior. Games.

Smudge ill. by Jane Chapman. Little Tiger, 1998. ISBN 1-888444-44-4 Subj: Animals. Animals – dogs. Weather – rain.

This and that ill. by Tanya Linch. Farrar, 1996. ISBN 0-374-37492-9 Subj: Animals – cats. Birth. Farms.

Wait for me, Little Tiger ill. by Tim Warnes. Tiger Tales, 2001. ISBN 1-58925-009-5 Subj: Activities – playing. Animals – tigers. Family life – brothers & sisters. Jungle.

Syme, Daniel B. *I'm growing* (Bogot, Howard)

Szekeres, Cyndy. *Cyndy Szekeres' counting book, 1 to 10* ill. by author. Golden Pr., 1984. ISBN 0-307-12141-0 Subj: Animals – mice. Counting, numbers.

Cyndy Szekeres' learn to count, funny bunnies ill. by author. Scholastic, 2000. ISBN 0-439-14994-0 Subj: Animals – rabbits. Counting, numbers. Format, unusual – board books. Rhyming text.

Good night, Sammy ill. by author. Western, 1991. ISBN 0-307-12238-7 Subj: Animals – foxes. Format, unusual – board books. Sleep.

Hide-and-seek duck ill. by author. Western, 1991. ISBN 0-307-12235-2 Subj: Animals – rabbits. Behavior – hiding. Birds – ducks. Format, unusual – board books.

I can count 100 bunnies, and so can you! ill. by author. Scholastic, 1998. ISBN 0-590-38361-2 Subj: Animals – rabbits. Counting, numbers.

Ladybug, ladybug, where are you? ill. by author. Western, 1991. ISBN 0-307-62340-8 Subj: Activities – picnicking. Animals – mice. Insects – ladybugs.

Long ago ill. by author. McGraw-Hill, 1977. ISBN 0-07-062665-0 Subj: Animals. Pilgrims. U.S. history.

The mouse that Jack built ill. by author. Scholastic, 1997. ISBN 0-590-69197-X Subj: Animals – mice. Clothing. Cumulative tales. Seasons – winter.

Nothing-to-do puppy ill. by author. Western, 1991. ISBN 0-307-12237-9 Subj: Animals – dogs. Format, unusual – board books.

Suppertime for Frieda Fuzzypaws ill. by author. Western, 1991. ISBN 0-307-12234-4 Subj: Animals – cats. Behavior – trickery. Food. Format, unusual – board books.

Toby! ill. by author. Little Simon, 2000. ISBN 0-689-82645-1 Subj: Animals – mice. Behavior – boredom.

Toby's please and thank you ill. by author. Little Simon, 2001. ISBN 0-689-84275-9 Subj: Animals – mice. Etiquette. Format, unusual – board books. Rhyming text.

Szilagyi, Mary. *Thunderstorm* ill. by author. Bradbury, 1985. ISBN 0-02-788580-1 Subj: Emotions – fear. Pets. Weather – lightning, thunder. Weather – storms.

Taback, Simms. *Joseph had a little overcoat* ill. by author. Viking, 1999. ISBN 0-670-87855-3 Subj: Caldecott award books. Clothing – coats.

On our way to the barn (Ziefert, Harriet)

On our way to the forest (Ziefert, Harriet)

On our way to the water (Ziefert, Harriet)

On our way to the zoo (Ziefert, Harriet)

There was an old lady who swallowed a fly (Little old lady who swallowed a fly)

Tabberner, Jeffrey. *The endless party* (Delessert, Etienne)

Tabby, Abigail. *Baby face* ill. by Dan Yaccarino. HarperFestival, 2001. ISBN 0-694-01530-X Subj: Babies. Emotions. Format, unusual – toy & movable books.

Taber, Anthony. *Cats' eyes* ill. by author. Dutton, 1978. ISBN 0-525-07814-2 Subj: Animals – cats. Old age.

Taberski, Sharon. *Morning, noon, and night* ill. by Nancy Doniger. Mondo, 1996. ISBN 1-57255-128-3 Subj: Activities. Emotions. Poetry.

Tabler, Judith. *The new puppy* ill. by Pat Sustendal. Random House, 1986. ISBN 0-394-88038-2 Subj: Animals – dogs. Format, unusual – board books. Pets. Toys.

Tabor, Nancy (Maria Grande). *Bottles break* ill. by author. Charlesbridge, 1998. ISBN 0-8810-6317-7 Subj: Behavior. Careers – teachers. Family life – mothers. Illness – alcoholism.

Taborin, Glorina. *Norman Rockwell's counting book* (Rockwell, Norman)

Tada, Joni Eareckson. *Forever friends* by Joni Eareckson Tada & Melody Carlson; ill. by Melody Carlson. Crossway, 2000. ISBN 1-58134-216-0 Subj: Friendship. Toys. Toys – dolls.

The incredible discovery of Lindsey Renee ill. by Irena Roman. Crossway, 2001. ISBN 1-58134-195-4 Subj: Character traits – generosity. Money. Religion.

Tada, Satoshi. *Mr. Beetle* ill. by author; trans. by Cathy Hirano. Carolrhoda, 2001. ISBN 1-57505-561-9 Subj: Character traits – kindness to animals. Friendship. Insects – beetles.

Tafolla, Carmen. *Baby Coyote and the old woman = El coyotito y la viejita* ill. by Matt Novak. New ed. designed & ed. by Bryce Milligan. Wings, 2000. ISBN 0-930324-48-X Subj: Animals – babies. Animals – coyotes. Ecology. Foreign languages. Format, unusual – board books. Old age.

Tafuri, Nancy. *All year long* ill. by author. Greenwillow, 1983. ISBN 0-688-01416-X Subj: Days of the week, months of the year.

The ball bounced ill. by author. Greenwillow, 1989. ISBN 0-688-07871-0 Subj: Babies. Toys – balls.

The barn party ill. by author. Greenwillow, 1995. ISBN 0-688-04617-7 Subj: Animals. Barns. Birthdays. Parties.

The brass ring ill. by author. Greenwillow, 1996. ISBN 0-688-14169-2 Subj: Activities – vacationing. Concepts – shape. Concepts – size.

Counting to Christmas ill. by author. Scholastic, 1998. ISBN 0-590-27143-1 Subj: Activities – making things. Animals. Counting, numbers. Holidays – Christmas.

Do not disturb ill. by author. Greenwillow, 1987. ISBN 0-688-06542-2 Subj: Activities. Animals. Camps, camping. Family life. Night. Noise, sounds. Wordless.

The donkey's Christmas song ill. by author. Scholastic, 2002. ISBN 0-439-27313-7 Subj: Animals. Animals – donkeys. Holidays – Christmas. Noise, sounds. Religion – Nativity.

Early morning in the barn ill. by author. Greenwillow, 1983. ISBN 0-688-02329-0 Subj: Farms. Morning. Wordless.

Follow me! ill. by author. Greenwillow, 1990. ISBN 0-688-08774-4 Subj: Animals – sea lions. Crustaceans – crabs.

Have you seen my duckling? ill. by author. Greenwillow, 1984. ISBN 0-688-02798-9 Subj: Birds – ducks. Caldecott award honor books. Character traits – individuality.

I love you, little one ill. by author. Scholastic, 1997. ISBN 0-590-92159-2 Subj: Animals. Animals – babies. Emotions – love. Family life – mothers.

In a red house ill. by author. Greenwillow, 1987. ISBN 0-688-07185-6 Subj: Concepts – color. Format, unusual – board books. Toys.

Junglewalk ill. by author. Greenwillow, 1988. ISBN 0-688-07183-X Subj: Animals. Dreams. Imagination. Jungle. Wordless.

Mama's little bears ill. by author. Scholastic, 2002. ISBN 0-439-27311-0 Subj: Animals – bears. Family life – mothers.

My friends ill. by author. Greenwillow, 1987. ISBN 0-688-07187-2 Subj: Animals. Babies. Format, unusual – board books. Friendship.

One wet jacket ill. by author. Greenwillow, 1988. ISBN 0-688-07465-0 Subj: Clothing – coats. Format, unusual – board books.

Rabbit's morning ill. by author. Greenwillow, 1985. ISBN 0-688-04064-0 Subj: Animals. Animals – rabbits. Wordless.

Silly little goose! ill. by author. Scholastic, 2001. ISBN 0-439-06304-3 Subj: Animals. Birds – geese. Clothing – hats. Homes, houses.

Snowy flowy blowy ill. by author. Scholastic, 1999. ISBN 0-590-18973-5 Subj: Days of the week, months of the year. Rhyming text. Seasons.

This is the farmer ill. by author. Greenwillow, 1994. ISBN 0-688-09469-4 Subj: Animals. Careers – farmers. Cumulative tales. Farms.

Two new sneakers ill. by author. Greenwillow, 1988. ISBN 0-688-07462-6 Subj: Clothing – shoes. Format, unusual – board books.

What the sun sees / What the moon sees ill. by author. Greenwillow, 1997. ISBN 0-688-14493-4 Subj: Bedtime. Dreams. Format, unusual. Moon. Nature. Night. Sun.

Where did Bunny go? ill. by author. Scholastic, 2001. ISBN 0-439-16959-3 Subj: Animals – rabbits. Behavior – hiding. Birds. Friendship. Games.

Where we sleep ill. by author. Greenwillow, 1987. ISBN 0-688-07189-9 Subj: Animals. Format, unusual – board books. Sleep.

Who's counting? ill. by author. Greenwillow, 1986. ISBN 0-688-06131-1 Subj: Animals. Animals – dogs. Counting, numbers. Farms.

Will you be my friend? ill. by author. Scholastic, 2000. ISBN 0-590-63782-7 Subj: Animals – rabbits. Birds. Friendship. Weather – storms.

Tagg, Christine. *Cinderlily* (Ellwand, David)

Who will you meet on Scary Street? ill. by Charles Fuge; paper engineering by Richard Ferguson & Mat Johnstone. Little, 2001. ISBN 0-316-25606-4 Subj: Format, unusual – toy & movable books. Holidays – Halloween. Monsters. School. Witches.

Tagholm, Sally. *The frog* ill. by Bert Kitchen. Kingfisher, 2000. ISBN 0-7534-5215-4 Subj: Frogs & toads. Science.

Tagore, Rabindranath. *Paper boats* ill. by Grayce Bochak. Boyds Mills, 1992. ISBN 1-878093-12-6 Subj: Boats, ships. Paper. Poetry. Toys.

Taha, Karen T. *A gift for Tia Rose* ill. by Dee deRosa. Dillon, 1986. ISBN 0-87518-306-9 Subj: Death. Ethnic groups in the U.S. – Mexican Americans. Family life. Friendship. Gifts.

Tait, Nancy. *I'm deaf and it's okay* (Aseltine, Lorraine)

Takabayashi, Mari. *I live in Brooklyn* ill. by author. Houghton, 2004. ISBN 0-618-30899-7 Subj: Cities, towns. Family life. Seasons.

I live in Tokyo ill. by author. Houghton, 2001. ISBN 0-618-07702-2 Subj: Cities, towns. Family life. Foreign lands – Japan.

Takamado no Miya Hisako. *Katie and the dream-eater* by Her Imperial Highness Princess Takamado; ill. by Brian Wildsmith. Oxford Univ. Pr., 1996. ISBN 0-19-279005-6 Subj: Bedtime. Dreams. Mythical creatures. Night. Sleep.

Takao, Yuko. *A winter concert* ill. by author. Millbrook, 1997. ISBN 0-7613-0301-4 Subj: Animals. Animals – mice. Concepts – color. Music. Musical instruments – pianos. Seasons – winter.

Takeshita, Fumiko. *The park bench* trans. by Ruth A. Kanagy; ill. by Mamoru Suzuki. Kane/Miller, 1988. ISBN 0-916291-15-4 Subj: Activities. Foreign lands – Japan. Foreign languages. Parks.

Takihara, Koji. *Rolli* ill. by author. Picture Book Studio, 1988. ISBN 0-88708-058-8 Subj: Animals – moles. Seeds.

Talbot, John. *Pins and needles* ill. by author. Dial, 1992. ISBN 0-8037-0942-0 Subj: Animals – elephants. Animals – mice. Problem solving.

Talbott, Hudson. *Going Hollywood! A dinosaur's dream* ill. by author. Crown, 1989. ISBN 0-517-57309-1 Subj: Dinosaurs. Friendship. Prehistory. Self-concept.

Tallarico, Tony. *At home* ill. by author. Tuffy Books, 1984. ISBN 0-89828-055-9 Subj: Family life. Homes, houses.

Talley, Carol. *Clarissa* ill. by Itoko Maeno. MarshMedia, 1992. From a story by Penelope C. Paine. ISBN 1-55942-014-6 Subj: Animals – bulls, cows. Fairs, festivals. Farms. Self-concept.

Talley, Linda. *Jackson's plan* ill. by Andra Chase. MarshMedia, 1998. ISBN 1-55942-104-5 Subj: Activities – photographing. Animals. Frogs & toads. Swamps.

Tallon, Robert. *Latouse my moose* ill. by author. Knopf, 1983. ISBN 0-394-96017-3 Subj: Animals – dogs. Pets.

Talus, Taylor. *The adventures of the three colors* (Tison, Annette)

Animal hide-and-seek (Tison, Annette)

Inside and outside (Tison, Annette)

Tamar, Erika. *Donnatalee: a mermaid adventure* ill. by Barbara Lambase. Harcourt, 1998. ISBN 0-15-200386-X Subj: Imagination. Mythical creatures – mermaids, mermen. Sea & seashore. Seasons – summer.

The garden of happiness ill. by Barbara Lambase. Harcourt, 1996. ISBN 0-15-230582-3 Subj: Activities – painting. Cities, towns. Communities, neighborhoods. Flowers. Gardens, gardening.

Tamburine, Jean. *I think I will go to the hospital* ill. by author. Abingdon, 1965. Subj: Hospitals.

Tan, Amy. *The Chinese Siamese cat* ill. by Gretchen Schields. Macmillan, 1994. ISBN 0-02-788835-5 Subj: Animals – cats. Foreign lands – China.

The moon lady ill. by Gretchen Schields. Macmillan, 1992. ISBN 0-02-788830-4 Subj: Behavior – wishing. Family life – grandmothers. Folk & fairy tales. Foreign lands – China. Moon.

Tan, Pierre Le. *see* LeTan, Pierre

Tanaka, Beatrice. *The chase: a Kutenai Indian tale* ill. by Michel Gay. Crown, 1991. ISBN 0-517-58624-X Subj: Animals. Cumulative tales. Folk & fairy tales. Indians of North America – Kutenai.

Tanaka, Hideyuki. *The happy dog* ill. by author. Atheneum, 1983. ISBN 0-689-50259-1 Subj: Animals – dogs. Wordless.

Tang, Greg. *Math appeal* ill. by Harry Briggs. Scholastic, 2003. ISBN 0-439-21046-1 Subj: Counting, numbers. Rhyming text.

Tangvald, Christine Harder. *The best thing about Christmas* ill. by Judy Hand. Standard, 1990 (1998 printing). ISBN 0-7847-0850-9 Subj: Holidays – Christmas. Religion – Nativity.

The best thing about Easter ill. by C. A. Nobens. Standard, 2003. ISBN 0-7847-1285-9 Subj: Format, unusual – board books. Holidays – Easter. Religion.

Hey, Mr. Angel! ill. by Jeff Carnehl. Concordia, 1998. ISBN 0-570-05058-8 Subj: Angels. Holidays – Christmas. Religion – Nativity. Rhyming text. Theater.

Mom and dad don't live together anymore ill. by Benton Mahan. Cook, 1988. ISBN 1-55513-502-1 Subj: Divorce.

The Rinky Dinky Donkey ill. by Kathleen Estes. Standard, 1995. ISBN 0-7847-0168-7 Subj: Animals – donkeys. Concepts – size. Religion – Nativity.

Taniuchi, Kota. *Trolley* ill. by author. Watts, 1969. ISBN 0-531-01937-3 Subj: Cable cars, trolleys. Imagination.

Tanner, Suzy-Jane. *Tinyflock Nursery School* ill. by author. HarperFestival, 2004. ISBN 0-06-055723-0 Subj: Animals – babies. Animals – sheep. School – first day. School – nursery.

Tapahonso, Luci. *Navajo ABC* by Luci Tapahonso & Eleanor Schick; ill. by Eleanor Schick. Macmillan, 1995. ISBN 0-689-

80316-8 Subj: ABC books. Indians of North America – Navajo. Language.

Tapio, Pat Decker. *The lady who saw the good side of everything* ill. by Paul Galdone. Seabury Pr., 1975. ISBN 0-8164-3145-0 Subj: Activities – traveling. Animals – cats. Character traits – optimism. Emotions – happiness. Humorous stories. Weather – floods. Weather – rain.

Tarbescu, Edith. *Annushka's voyage* ill. by Lydia Dabcovich. Clarion, 1998. ISBN 0-395-64366-X Subj: Ethnic groups in the U.S. – Russian Americans. Family life – fathers. Family life – sisters. Immigrants. Jewish culture. Religion.

The boy who stuck out his tongue: a Yiddish folk tale ill. by Judith Christine Mills. Barefoot, 2000. ISBN 1-84148-067-3 Subj: Character traits – stubbornness. Folk & fairy tales. Jewish culture.

Tarpley, Natasha Anastasia. *Bippity Bop barbershop* ill. by E. B. Lewis. Little, 2002. ISBN 0-316-52284-8 Subj: Careers – barbers. Ethnic groups in the U.S. – African Americans. Family life – fathers. Family life – sons. Hair.

I love my hair! ill. by E. B. Lewis. Little, 1997. ISBN 0-316-52275-9 Subj: Ethnic groups in the U.S. – African Americans. Family life – mothers. Hair.

Joe-Joe's first flight ill. by E. B. Lewis. Knopf, 2003. ISBN 0-375-91053-0 Subj: Activities – flying. Careers – airplane pilots. Ethnic groups in the U.S. – African Americans. Imagination. Moon. Prejudice.

Tarrant, Graham. *Rabbits* ill. by Tonny King. Putnam, 1984. ISBN 0-399-21005-9 Subj: Animals – rabbits. Format, unusual.

Tarrant, Margaret. *Fairy tales* ill. with photos. Crowell, 1978. ISBN 0-690-03920-4 Subj: Folk & fairy tales.

The Margaret Tarrant nursery rhyme book ill. by author. Merrimack, 1986. ISBN 0-00-183732-X Subj: Nursery rhymes.

Tarsky, Sue. *The busy building book* ill. by Alex Ayliffe. Putnam, 1998. ISBN 0-399-23137-4 Subj: Buildings.

Tatcheva, Eva. *Witch Zelda's birthday cake* ill. by author; paper engineering by Richard Ferguson. Abrams, 2001. ISBN 0-8109-4567-3 Subj: Birthdays. Food. Format, unusual – toy & movable books. Holidays – Halloween. Witches.

Tate, Joan. *A Christmas book* (A Christmas book)

The giant fish and other stories (Svend Otto S [Svend Otto Sorensen])

Tate, Suzanne. *Crabby's water wish* ill. by James Melvin. Nags Head Art, 1991. ISBN 1-878405-04-7 Subj: Ecology. Sea & seashore.

Tatham, Betty. *Penguin chick* ill. by Helen Davie. HarperCollins, 2002. ISBN 0-06-028595-8 Subj: Animals – babies. Birds – penguins.

Tatham, Campbell. *see* Elting, Mary

Taublieb, Paul. *Giff the scaredy bear* (Gifford, Kathie Lee)

Giff's big game (Gifford, Kathie Lee)

Moochie's surprise (Gifford, Kathie Lee)

Taulbert, Clifton L. *Little Cliff and the cold place* ill. by E. B. Lewis. Dial, 2002. ISBN 0-8037-2558-2 Subj: Concepts – cold & heat. Foreign lands – Arctic.

Little Cliff and the porch people ill. by E. B. Lewis. Dial, 1999. ISBN 0-8037-2175-7 Subj: Communities, neighborhoods. Ethnic groups in the U.S. – African Americans. Family life. Food. Friendship. Magic.

Little Cliff's first day of school ill. by E. B. Lewis. Dial, 2001. ISBN 0-8037-2557-4 Subj: Emotions – fear. Ethnic groups in the U.S. –

African Americans. Family life – great-grandparents. School – first day.

Tavares, Matt. *Mudball* ill. by author. Candlewick, 2005. ISBN 0-7636-2387-3 Subj: Sports – baseball.

Oliver's game ill. by author. Candlewick, 2004. ISBN 0-7636-1852-7 Subj: Family life – grandfathers. Sports – baseball.

Zachary's ball ill. by author. Candlewick, 2000. ISBN 0-7636-0730-4 Subj: Sports – baseball.

Tax, Meredith. *Families* ill. by Marylin Hafner. Feminist Pr., 1996. ISBN 1-55861-157-6 Subj: Family life.

Taylor, Alastair. *Swollobog* ill. by author. Houghton, 2001. ISBN 0-618-04348-9 Subj: Animals – dogs. Humorous stories. Toys – balloons.

Taylor, Alice. *A child's treasury of Irish rhymes* ill. by Nicola Emoe. Barefoot, 1999. ISBN 1-902283-18-X Subj: Foreign lands – Ireland. Nursery rhymes.

Taylor, Anelise. *Lights on, lights off* ill. by author. Oxford Univ. Pr., 1988. ISBN 0-19-279843-X Subj: Emotions – fear. Night.

Taylor, Ann. *Baby dance* ill. by Marjorie van Heerden. HarperFestival, 1999. ISBN 0-694-01206-8 Subj: Activities – dancing. Activities – singing. Babies. Ethnic groups in the U.S. – African Americans. Family life – fathers. Format, unusual – board books.

Taylor, Barbara. *Going, going, gone* ill. with photos. Bedrick, 2001. ISBN 0-87226-658-3 Subj: Animals. Animals – endangered animals. Fossils. Museums. Plants.

I wonder why zippers have teeth and other questions about inventions. Kingfisher, 1995. ISBN 1-85697-670-X Subj: Careers – inventors. Character traits – questioning. Inventions.

Zooming and creeping ill. with photos. Bedrick, 2001. ISBN 0-87226-657-5 Subj: Activities. Animals.

Taylor, Edgar. *King Grisly-Beard* (Grimm, Jacob)

Taylor, Harriet Peck. *Coyote and the laughing butterflies* ill. by author. Macmillan, 1995. ISBN 0-02-788846-0 Subj: Animals – coyotes. Indians of North America. Insects – butterflies, caterpillars. Lakes, ponds.

Secrets of the stone ill. by author. Farrar, 2000. ISBN 0-374-36648-9 Subj: Animals. Art. Caves. Indians of North America – Southwest. Petroglyphs.

Two days in May ill. by Leyla Torres. Farrar, 1999. ISBN 0-374-37988-2 Subj: Animals. Animals – deer. Cities, towns. Seasons – spring.

Ulaq and the northern lights ill. by author. Farrar, 1998. ISBN 0-374-38063-5 Subj: Animals. Animals – foxes. Foreign lands – Arctic. Northern lights. Sky.

Taylor, Jane. *Twinkle, twinkle little star* ill. by Heather Collins. Kids Can, 2000. ISBN 1-55074-566-2 Subj: Fairies. Format, unusual – board books. Nursery rhymes. Sky. Songs. Stars.

Twinkle, twinkle, little star ill. by Michael Hague. Morrow, 1992. ISBN 0-688-11169-6 Subj: Fairies. Nursery rhymes. Sky. Songs. Stars.

Twinkle, twinkle little star ill. by Julia Noonan. Scholastic, 1992. ISBN 0-590-45566-4 Subj: Holidays – Christmas. Nursery rhymes. Santa Claus. Sky. Songs. Stars.

Taylor, Joanne. *Full moon rising* ill. by Susan Tooke. Tundra, 2002. ISBN 0-88776-548-3 Subj: Careers – farmers. Days of the week, months of the year. Moon.

Taylor, John Edward. *Petrosinella: a Neapolitan Rapunzel* (Basile, Giambattista)

Taylor, Judy. *Dudley and the monster* ill. by Peter Cross. Putnam, 1986. ISBN 0-399-21329-5 Subj: Animals – mice. Monsters. Seasons – spring.

Dudley and the strawberry shake ill. by Peter Cross. Putnam, 1987. ISBN 0-399-21330-9 Subj: Animals – mice. Food.

Dudley goes flying ill. by Peter Cross. Putnam, 1986. ISBN 0-399-21328-7 Subj: Activities – flying. Animals – mice.

Dudley in a jam ill. by Peter Cross. Putnam, 1987. ISBN 0-399-21331-7 Subj: Animals – mice. Food.

Sophie and Jack ill. by Susan Gantner. Putnam, 1983. ISBN 0-399-20947-6 Subj: Activities – picnicking. Animals – hippopotamuses. Family life.

Sophie and Jack help out ill. by Susan Gantner. Putnam, 1984. ISBN 0-399-21059-8 Subj: Animals – hippopotamuses. Gardens, gardening. Weather – storms.

Taylor, Kim. *Frog* [written & ed. by Angela Royston] photos by Kim Taylor & Jane Burton. Dutton, 1991. ISBN 0-525-67345-8 Subj: Birth. Format, unusual – board books. Frogs & toads.

Too fast to see photos by author. Delacorte, 1991. ISBN 0-385-30219-3 Subj: Nature.

Too small to see photos by author. Delacorte, 1991. ISBN 0-385-30221-5 Subj: Nature.

Taylor, Livingston. *Pajamas* by Livingston & Maggie Taylor; ill. by Tim Bowers. Harcourt, 1988. ISBN 0-15-200564-1 Subj: Bedtime. Lullabies.

Taylor, Lolita. *Old Meshikee and the little crabs: an Ojibwe story* (Spooner, Michael)

Taylor, Maggie. *Pajamas* (Taylor, Livingston)

Taylor, Mark. *The bold fisherman* ill. by Graham Booth. Golden Gate, 1967. Subj: Folk & fairy tales. Music. Sea & seashore. Songs. Sports – fishing.

The case of the missing kittens ill. by Graham Booth. Atheneum, 1978. ISBN 0-689-30627-X Subj: Animals – cats. Animals – dogs. Behavior – lost. Mystery stories.

Henry explores the jungle ill. by Graham Booth. Atheneum, 1968. Subj: Animals – tigers. Character traits – bravery. Circus. Seasons – summer.

Henry explores the mountains ill. by Graham Booth. Atheneum, 1975. ISBN 0-689-30461-7 Subj: Character traits – bravery. Fire. Helicopters. Seasons – fall.

Henry the castaway ill. by Graham Booth. Atheneum, 1972. ISBN 0-689-30070-0 Subj: Behavior – lost. Boats, ships. Seasons – spring. Weather – rain.

Henry the explorer ill. by Graham Booth. Atheneum, 1988, c1966. ISBN 0-316-83384-3 Subj: Animals – bears. Behavior – lost. Character traits – bravery. Seasons – winter.

"Lamb," said the lion, "I am here." ill. by Anne Siberell. Golden Gate, 1971. ISBN 0-8746-4182-9 Subj: Animals. Religion.

Old Blue, you good dog you ill. by Gene Holtan. Golden Gate, 1970. ISBN 0-8746-4142-X Subj: Animals – dogs. Animals – possums. Folk & fairy tales. Friendship. Games. Music. Old age. Songs.

Taylor, Scott. *Dinosaur James* ill. by author. Morrow, 1990. ISBN 0-688-08577-6 Subj: Behavior – bullying. Dinosaurs. Prehistory. Rhyming text.

Taylor, Sean. *Boing!* ill. by Bruce Ingman. Candlewick, 2004. ISBN 0-7636-2475-6 Subj: Health & fitness. Sports – gymnastics.

Taylor, Shirley. *The cross in the egg* ill. by Wendell E. Hall. August House, 1999. ISBN 0-8748-3549-6 Subj: Animals – rabbits. Eggs. Holidays – Easter. Religion.

Taylor, Sydney. *The dog who came to dinner* ill. by John E. Johnson. Follett, 1966. Subj: Animals – dogs. Ethnic groups in the U.S. – African Americans.

Mr. Barney's beard ill. by Charles Geer. Follett, 1961. Subj: Birds. Character traits – laziness.

Taylor, Theodore. *Hello, Arctic!* ill. by Margaret Chodos-Irvine. Harcourt, 2002. ISBN 0-15-201577-9 Subj: Animals. Foreign lands – Arctic. Seasons.

Tazewell, Charles. *The littlest angel* ill. by Deborah Lanino. Childrens Pr., 1998. ISBN 0-516-20433-5 Subj: Angels. Gifts. Holidays – Christmas. Religion – Nativity. Stars.

The littlest angel ill. by Paul Micich. Ideals, 1991. ISBN 0-8249-8516-8 Subj: Angels. Gifts. Holidays – Christmas. Religion – Nativity. Stars.

The littlest angel ill. by Rebecca Thornburgh. CandyCane, 2002. ISBN 0-8249-4224-8 Subj: Angels. Gifts. Holidays – Christmas. Religion – Nativity. Stars.

Tchana, Katrin. *Sense Pass King* ill. by Trina Schart Hyman. Holiday, 2002. ISBN 0-8234-1577-5 Subj: Character traits – cleverness. Folk & fairy tales. Foreign lands – Cameroon. Royalty – kings.

Te Loo, Sanne. *see* Loo, Sanne te

Teague, Mark. *Baby tamer* ill. by author. Scholastic, 1997. ISBN 0-590-67712-8 Subj: Activities – babysitting. Behavior. Circus. Ethnic groups in the U.S. – African Americans.

Dear Mrs. LaRue ill. by author. Scholastic, 2002. ISBN 0-439-20663-4 Subj: Activities – writing. Animals – dogs. Humorous stories. Letters, cards. Pets.

Detective LaRue ill. by author. Scholastic, 2004. ISBN 0-439-45868-4 Subj: Activities – writing. Animals – cats. Animals – dogs. Careers – detectives. Letters, cards.

The Lost and found ill. by author. Scholastic, 1998. ISBN 0-590-84619-1 Subj: Behavior – lost & found possessions. Imagination. School.

One Halloween night ill. by author. Scholastic, 1999. ISBN 0-590-63803-3 Subj: Holidays – Halloween. Magic.

Pigsty ill. by author. Scholastic, 1994. ISBN 0-590-45915-5 Subj: Animals – pigs. Character traits – cleanliness. Character traits – orderliness.

The secret shortcut ill. by author. Scholastic, 1996. ISBN 0-590-67714-4 Subj: Behavior – promptness, tardiness. School.

The trouble with the Johnsons ill. by author. Scholastic, 1989. ISBN 0-590-42394-0 Subj: Animals – cats. Dinosaurs. Moving.

Teasdale, Sara. *Christmas carol* ill. by Dale Gottlieb. Holt, 1993. ISBN 0-8050-2695-9 Subj: Holidays – Christmas. Poetry.

Teddyland photomagic by John Russell; photos by Howard Allman. Usborne, 1999. ISBN 1-58086-186-5 Subj: Picture puzzles. Toys – bears.

Tedesco, Donna. *Do you know how much I love you?* ill. by author. Bradbury, 1994. ISBN 0-02-789120-8 Subj: Emotions – love. Family life.

Tegen, Katherine Brown. *Dracula and Frankenstein are friends* ill. by Doug Cushman. HarperCollins, 2003. ISBN 0-06-000116-X Subj: Friendship. Holidays – Halloween. Monsters. Parties.

The story of the Easter Bunny ill. by Sally Anne Lambert. HarperCollins, 2005. ISBN 0-06-050712-8 Subj: Animals – rabbits. Holidays – Easter.

Tejima, Keizaburo. *The bears' autumn* trans. from Japanese by Susan Matsui; ill. by author. Green Tiger Pr., 1986. ISBN 0-88138-080-6 Subj: Animals – bears. Seasons – fall.

Fox's dream ill. by author. Philomel, 1987. ISBN 0-399-21455-0 Subj: Animals – foxes. Dreams. Forest, woods. Seasons – winter.

Ho-limlim ill. by author. Putnam, 1990. ISBN 0-399-22156-5 Subj: Animals – rabbits. Foreign lands – Japan. Old age.

Owl lake ill. by author. Philomel, 1987. ISBN 0-399-21426-7 Subj: Birds – owls. Family life. Nature. Night.

Swan sky ill. by author. Putnam, 1988. ISBN 0-399-21547-6 Subj: Birds – swans. Death.

Woodpecker forest ill. by author. Putnam, 1989. ISBN 0-399-21618-9 Subj: Birds – woodpeckers. Forest, woods. Nature.

Teleki, Geza. *Aerial apes: gibbons of Asia* by Geza Teleki & others; ill. with photos. Coward, 1979. ISBN 0-698-20477-8 Subj: Animals – monkeys.

Telephones ill. by Christine Sharr. Wonder Books, 1971. Subj: Communication. Telephone.

Tellenbach, Margrit Haubensak. *see* Haubensak-Tellenbach, Margrit

Tempest, Peter. *The tale of a hero nobody knows* (Marshak, S. [Samuil])

Temple, Bob. *Ellis Island* ill. with photos. Child's World, 2001. ISBN 1-56766-762-7 Subj: Immigrants. U.S. history.

Randy Moss ill. with photos. Child's World, 2001. ISBN 1-56766-968-9 Subj: Sports – football.

Temple, Charles A. *Train* ill. by Larry Johnson. Houghton Mifflin, 1996. ISBN 0-395-69826-X Subj: Ethnic groups in the U.S. – African Americans. Rhyming text. Trains. Transportation.

Temple, Frances. *Tiger soup* ill. by author. Orchard, 1994. ISBN 0-531-08709-3 Subj: Animals – monkeys. Animals – tigers. Behavior – trickery. Folk & fairy tales. Foreign lands – Jamaica. Spiders.

Tender moments in the wild ill. with photos. Moonstone, 2001. ISBN 0-9707768-0-2 Subj: Animals – babies. Family life – parents.

Tennyson, Alfred, Baron. *The brook* ill. by Charles Micucci. Orchard, 1994. ISBN 0-531-08704-2 Subj: Farms. Foreign lands – England. Poetry. Rivers.

Tennyson, Noel. *The lady's chair and the ottoman* ill. by author. Lothrop, 1987. ISBN 0-688-04098-5 Subj: Behavior – needing someone. Furniture – chairs.

Tensen, Ruth M. *Come to the zoo!* Reilly, 1948. Subj: Animals. Zoos.

Terasaki, Stanley Todd. *Ghosts for breakfast* ill. by Shelly Shinjo. Lee & Low, 2002. ISBN 1-58430-046-9 Subj: Ethnic groups in the U.S. – Japanese Americans. Farms. Ghosts. Humorous stories.

Terry, Michael. *Rhino's horns* ill. by author. Bloomsbury, 2001. ISBN 0-7475-5051-4 Subj: Animals. Animals – rhinoceros. Self-concept.

Tessler, Stephanie Gordon. *Francis, the earthquake dog* (Enderle, Judith (Ann) Ross)

The good-for-something dragon (Enderle, Judith (Ann) Ross)

Nell Nugget and the cow caper (Enderle, Judith (Ann) Ross)

A pile of pigs (Enderle, Judith (Ann) Ross)

Six creepy sheep (Enderle, Judith (Ann) Ross)

Six sandy sheep (Enderle, Judith (Ann) Ross)

Six snowy sheep (Enderle, Judith (Ann) Ross)

Upstairs (Enderle, Judith (Ann) Ross)

What would Mama do? (Enderle, Judith (Ann) Ross)

Where are you, little Zack? (Enderle, Judith (Ann) Ross)

Testa, Fulvio. *The endless journey* ill. by author. North-South, 2001. ISBN 0-7358-1504-6 Subj: Concepts – perspective. Imagination.

The ideal home ill. by author. HarperCollins, 1986. ISBN 0-87226-055-0 Subj: Homes, houses.

If you look around ill. by author. Dial, 1983. ISBN 0-8037-0003-2 Subj: Concepts – shape.

If you take a paintbrush: a book of colors ill. by author. Dial, 1983. ISBN 0-8037-3829-3 Subj: Concepts – color.

If you take a pencil ill. by author. Dial, 1982. ISBN 0-8037-4023-9 Subj: Counting, numbers.

The land where the ice cream grows story & ill. by Fulvio Testa; told by Anthony Burgess. Doubleday, 1979. ISBN 0-510-00045-2 Subj: Food. Imagination.

A long trip to Z ill. by author. Harcourt, 1997. ISBN 0-15-201610-4 Subj: ABC books.

Never satisfied ill. by author. North-South, 1988. ISBN 3-85539-009-6 Subj: Behavior – dissatisfaction.

The paper airplane ill. by author. Holt, 1988. ISBN 0-8050-0743-1 Subj: Activities – flying. Airplanes, airports. Paper.

Too much garbage ill. by author. North-South, 2001. ISBN 0-7358-1452-X Subj: Careers – sanitation workers. Cities, towns. Ecology.

Wolf's favor ill. by author. Dial, 1986. ISBN 0-8037-0244-2 Subj: Animals. Character traits – generosity.

Tester, Sylvia Root. *Chase!* ill. by author. Childrens Pr., 1980. ISBN 0-516-06439-8 Subj: Animals.

Never monkey with a monkey: a book of homographic homophones ill. by John Keely. Childrens Pr., 1977. ISBN 0-913778-90-7 Subj: Language.

Parade! ill. by author. Childrens Pr., 1980. ISBN 0-516-06441-X Subj: Circus.

A visit to the zoo photos by author. Childrens Pr., 1987. ISBN 0-516-01494-3 Subj: Animals. Zoos.

What did you say? a book of homophones ill. by John Keely. Childrens Pr., 1977. ISBN 0-913778-91-5 Subj: Language.

Tether, Graham. *The hair book* ill. by Roy McKie. Random House, 1979. ISBN 0-3948-3665-0 Subj: Hair. Rhyming text.

Skunk and possum ill. by Lucinda McQueen. Houghton Mifflin, 1979. ISBN 0-395-28270-5 Subj: Activities – picnicking. Animals – possums. Animals – skunks. Friendship.

Tettelbaum, Michael. *The cave of the lost Fraggle* ill. by Peter Elwell. Holt, 1985. ISBN 0-03-004554-1 Subj: Caves. Character traits – pride. Puppets.

Tews, Susan. *Lizard sees the world* ill. by George Crespo. Clarion, 1997. ISBN 0-395-72662-X Subj: Activities – traveling. Animals. Reptiles – lizards.

Teyssèdre, Fabienne. *Joseph wants to read* ill. by author. Dutton, 2001. ISBN 0-525-46692-4 Subj: ABC books. Animals. Animals – monkeys. Careers – teachers. Jungle. School.

Thacher, Edith. *see* Hurd, Edith Thacher

Thaler, Mike. *Hippo lemonade* ill. by Maxie Chambliss. HarperCollins, 1986. ISBN 0-06-026162-5 Subj: Animals. Animals – hippopotamuses. Behavior – wishing.

It's me, hippo! ill. by Maxie Chambliss. HarperCollins, 1983. ISBN 0-06-026154-4 Subj: Animals. Animals – hippopotamuses. Friendship.

Madge's magic show ill. by Carol Nicklaus. Watts, 1978. ISBN 0-531-01450-9 Subj: Magic.

Moonkey ill. by Giulio Maestro. HarperCollins, 1981. ISBN 0-06-026125-0 Subj: Animals – monkeys. Friendship. Moon.

My puppy ill. by Madeleine Fishman. HarperCollins, 1980. ISBN 0-06-026079-3 Subj: Animals – dogs. Imagination – imaginary friends. Pets.

Owley ill. by David Wiesner. HarperCollins, 1982. ISBN 0-06-026152-8 Subj: Birds – owls. Character traits – questioning. Family life – mothers.

Pack 109 ill. by Normand Chartier. Dutton, 1988. ISBN 0-525-44393-2 Subj: Animals. Clubs, gangs. Humorous stories.

There's a hippopotamus under my bed ill. by Ray Cruz. Watts, 1977. ISBN 0-531-01318-9 Subj: Animals – hippopotamuses. Furniture – beds.

What could a hippopotamus be? ill. by Robert Grossman. S&S, 1990. ISBN 0-671-70847-3 Subj: Animals – hippopotamuses. Careers.

The yellow brick toad: funny frog cartoons, riddles, and silly stories ill. by author. Doubleday, 1978. ISBN 0-385-14255-2 Subj: Humorous stories. Riddles & jokes.

Tharlet, Eve. *The emperor's new clothes* (Andersen, H. C. [Hans Christian])

Little pig, big trouble trans. by Andrew Clements; ill. by author. Picture Book Studio, 1989. Translation of: Henri, le petit cochon bleu. ISBN 0-88708-073-1 Subj: Animals – pigs. Behavior – misbehavior. Friendship.

Thaxter, Celia. *Celia's island journal* adapt. & ill. by Loretta Krupinski. Little, 1992. Adapt. of: Among the Isles of Shoals. ISBN 0-316-83921-3 Subj: Islands. Lighthouses. Sea & seashore.

Thayer, Ernest Lawrence. *Casey at the bat: a ballad of the Republic, sung in the year 1888* ill. by Christopher Bing. Handprint, 2000. ISBN 1-929766-00-9 Subj: Caldecott award honor books. Poetry. Sports – baseball.

Casey at the bat ill. by Gerald Fitzgerald. Atheneum, 1995. ISBN 0-689-31945-2 Subj: Poetry. Sports – baseball.

Casey at the bat: a ballad of the Republic, sung in the year 1888 ill. by Patricia Polacco. Putnam, 1988. ISBN 0-399-21585-9 Subj: Poetry. Sports – baseball.

Thayer, Jane. *Andy and his fine friends* ill. by Meg Wohlberg. Morrow, 1960. Subj: Animals. Imagination – imaginary friends.

Andy and the runaway horse ill. by Meg Wohlberg. Morrow, 1963. Subj: Animals – horses, ponies. Traffic, traffic signs.

Andy and the wild worm ill. by Beatrice Darwin. Morrow, 1973, 1954. ISBN 0-688-30061-8 Subj: Animals – worms. Imagination.

The cat that joined the club ill. by Seymour Fleishman. Morrow, 1967. Subj: Animals – cats.

The clever raccoon ill. by Holly Keller. Morrow, 1981. ISBN 0-688-00239-0 Subj: Animals – raccoons. Behavior – trickery.

Gus and the baby ghost ill. by Seymour Fleishman. Morrow, 1972. Subj: Babies. Ghosts. Museums.

Gus loved his happy home ill. by Seymour Fleishman. Shoe String Pr., 1989. ISBN 0-208-02249-X Subj: Ghosts. Kites.

Gus was a friendly ghost ill. by Seymour Fleishman. Morrow, 1962. Subj: Friendship. Ghosts.

Gus was a gorgeous ghost ill. by Seymour Fleishman. Morrow, 1978. ISBN 0-688-32133-X Subj: Clothing. Ghosts. Holidays – Halloween.

Gus was a real dumb ghost ill. by Joyce Audy dos Santos. Morrow, 1982. ISBN 0-688-01443-7 Subj: Ghosts. School.

The horse with the Easter bonnet ill. by Jay Hyde Barnum. Morrow, 1953. Subj: Animals – horses, ponies. Clothing – hats. Holidays – Easter.

I like trains ill. by George Fonseca. HarperCollins, 1965. Subj: Trains. Transportation.

Mr. Turtle's magic glasses ill. by Mamoru Funai. Morrow, 1971. Subj: Behavior – boredom. Glasses. Magic. Reptiles – turtles, tortoises. Senses – sight.

Part-time dog ill. by Lisa McCue. HarperCollins, 2004. ISBN 0-06-029692-5 Subj: Animals – dogs. Behavior – sharing. Character traits – kindness to animals. Communities, neighborhoods.

The popcorn dragon ill. by Jay Hyde Barnum. Morrow, 1953. Subj: Dragons. Food. Friendship.

The popcorn dragon ill. by Lisa McCue. Morrow, 1989. ISBN 0-688-08876-7 Subj: Dragons. Food. Friendship.

The puppy who wanted a boy ill. by Seymour Fleishman. Morrow, 1958. ISBN 0-688-31631-X Subj: Animals – dogs. Holidays – Christmas.

The puppy who wanted a boy ill. by Lisa McCue. Morrow, 1986. ISBN 0-688-05945-7 Subj: Animals – dogs. Holidays – Christmas.

Quiet on account of dinosaur ill. by Seymour Fleishman. Mulberry, 1988. ISBN 0-688-08292-0 Subj: Dinosaurs. Noise, sounds. Prehistory.

What's a ghost going to do? ill. by Seymour Fleishman. Morrow, 1966. Subj: Ghosts. Homes, houses. Problem solving.

Thayer, Mike. *In the middle of the puddle* ill. by Bruce Degen. HarperCollins, 1988. ISBN 0-06-026054-8 Subj: Frogs & toads. Reptiles – turtles, tortoises. Weather – rain.

Thayer, Tanya. *Counting money* ill. by author. Lerner, 2002. ISBN 0-8225-1258-0 Subj: Counting, numbers. Money.

Earning money ill. by author. Lerner, 2002. ISBN 0-8225-1259-9 Subj: Activities – working. Money.

Fall ill. by author. Lerner, 2002. ISBN 0-8225-1987-9 Subj: Seasons – fall.

Saving money ill. by author. Lerner, 2002. ISBN 0-8225-1260-2 Subj: Behavior – saving things. Money.

Spending money ill. by author. Lerner, 2002. ISBN 0-8225-1261-0 Subj: Money. Shopping.

Spring ill. by author. Lerner, 2002. ISBN 0-8225-1986-0 Subj: Seasons – spring.

Summer ill. by author. Lerner, 2002. ISBN 0-8225-1984-4 Subj: Seasons – summer.

Winter ill. by author. Lerner, 2002. ISBN 0-8225-1985-2 Subj: Seasons – winter.

Thelen, Gerda. *The toy maker: how a tree becomes a toy village* retold by Louise F. Encking; ill. by Fritz Kukenthal. A. Whitman, 1935. Subj: Activities – making things. Toys. Trees.

Theobalds, Prue. *The teddy bears' Christmas* (Kennedy, Jimmy)

Theodorou, Rod. *Across the solar system* ill. with photos. Heinemann, 2000. ISBN 1-57572-486-3 Subj: Planets. Space & space ships. Sun.

Bengal tiger ill. with photos. Heinemann, 2001. ISBN 1-57572-267-4 Subj: Animals – endangered animals. Animals – tigers.

Black rhino ill. with photos. Heinemann, 2001. ISBN 1-57572-262-3 Subj: Animals – endangered animals. Animals – rhinoceros.

Blue whale ill. with photos. Heinemann, 2001. ISBN 1-57572-263-1 Subj: Animals – endangered animals. Animals – whales.

Florida manatee ill. with photos. Heinemann, 2001. ISBN 1-57572-265-8 Subj: Animals – endangered animals. Animals – manatees.

Giant panda ill. with photos. Heinemann, 2001. ISBN 1-57572-264-X Subj: Animals – endangered animals. Animals – pandas.

Mountain gorilla ill. with photos. Heinemann, 2001. ISBN 1-57572-266-6 Subj: Animals – endangered animals. Animals – gorillas.

Thermes, Jennifer. *When I was built* ill. by author. Holt, 2001. ISBN 0-8050-6532-6 Subj: Family life. Homes, houses.

Theroux, Phyllis. *Serefina under the circumstances* ill. by Marjorie Priceman. Greenwillow, 1999. ISBN 0-688-15942-7 Subj: Behavior – secrets. Birthdays. Family life – grandmothers. Imagination.

They followed a bright star ill. by Ulises Wensell; based on a poem by Joan Alavedra. Putnam, 1994. ISBN 0-399-22706-7 Subj: Religion – Nativity. Stars.

Thiele, Bob. *What a wonderful world* (Weiss, George [George David])

Thiele, Colin. *Farmer Schulz's ducks* ill. by Mary Milton. HarperCollins, 1988. ISBN 0-06-026183-8 Subj: Birds – ducks. Farms. Foreign lands – Australia.

Thien, Madeleine. *The Chinese violin* ill. by Joe Chang. Whitecap, 2001. ISBN 1-55285-205-9 Subj: Foreign lands – Canada. Music. Musical instruments – violins.

Thiesing, Lisa. *Me and you: a mother-daughter album* ill. by author. Hyperion, 1998. ISBN 0-7868-2338-0 Subj: Family life – daughters. Family life – mothers.

The Viper ill. by author. Dutton, 2002. ISBN 0-525-46892-7 Subj: Animals – pigs. Careers – window cleaners. Emotions – fear. Humorous stories.

This place I know poems sel. by Georgia Heard; ill. by by eighteen renowned picture book artists. Candlewick, 2002. ISBN 0-7636-1924-8 Subj: Emotions – fear. Emotions – grief. Poetry. U.S. history.

Thoburn, Tina. *A B See* (Ogle, Lucille)

I hear (Ogle, Lucille)

Thomas, Abigail. *Pearl paints* ill. by Margaret Hewitt. Holt, 1994. ISBN 0-8050-2976-1 Subj: Activities – painting. Art. Careers – artists.

Thomas, Art. *Merry-go-rounds* ill. by George Overlie. Carolrhoda, 1981. ISBN 0-87614-168-8 Subj: Merry-go-rounds.

Thomas, Frances. *The Bear and Mr. Bear* ill. by Ruth Brown. Dutton, 1995. ISBN 0-525-45362-8 Subj: Animals – bears. Character traits – kindness to animals.

One day, Daddy ill. by Ross Collins. Hyperion, 2001. ISBN 0-7868-0732-6 Subj: Careers – explorers. Family life – parents. Monsters. Space & space ships.

What if? by Frances Thomas & Ross Collins; ill. by Ross Collins. Hyperion, 1998. ISBN 0-7868-0482-3 Subj: Family life – mothers. Imagination. Monsters.

Thomas, Ianthe. *Lordy, Aunt Hattie* ill. by Thomas di Grazia. HarperCollins, 1973. ISBN 0-06-026115-3 Subj: Ethnic groups in the U.S. – African Americans. Family life – aunts, uncles. Seasons – summer.

Walk home tired, Billy Jenkins ill. by Thomas di Grazia. HarperCollins, 1974. ISBN 0-06-026109-9 Subj: Activities – walking. Cities, towns. Ethnic groups in the U.S. – African Americans. Imagination.

Willie blows a mean horn ill. by Ann Toulmin-Rothe. HarperCollins, 1981. ISBN 0-06-026107-2 Subj: Family life – fathers. Music.

Thomas, Iolette. *Janine and the new baby* ill. by Jennifer Northway. Dutton, 1987. ISBN 0-233-97916-6 Subj: Babies. Family life – new sibling. Sibling rivalry.

Thomas, Jane Resh. *Celebration!* ill. by Raúl Colón. Hyperion, 1997. ISBN 0-7868-2160-4 Subj: Activities – picnicking. Ethnic groups in the U.S. – African Americans. Family life. Holidays – Fourth of July.

Lights on the river ill. by Michael Dooling. Hyperion, 1994. ISBN 0-7868-2003-9 Subj: Careers – migrant workers. Emotions. Ethnic groups in the U.S. – Mexican Americans. Family life. Farms. Poverty.

Saying good-bye to grandma ill. by Marcia Sewall. Clarion, 1988. ISBN 0-89919-645-4 Subj: Death. Emotions – grief. Family life – grandmothers.

Scaredy dog ill. by Marilyn Mets. Hyperion, 1996. ISBN 0-7868-0278-2 Subj: Animals – dogs. Character traits – kindness to animals. Character traits – perseverance. Family life – mothers. Pets.

Wheels ill. by Emily Arnold McCully. Ticknor & Fields, 1986. ISBN 0-89919-410-9 Subj: Sports – bicycling.

Thomas, Joyce Carol. *Brown honey in broomwheat tea* ill. by Floyd Cooper. HarperCollins, 1993. ISBN 0-06-021088-5 Subj: Ethnic groups in the U.S. – African Americans. Poetry.

Cherish me ill. by Nneka Bennett. HarperFestival, 1998. ISBN 0-694-01097-9 Subj: Character traits – individuality. Ethnic groups in the U.S. – African Americans. Poetry.

Crowning glory ill. by Brenda Joysmith. Cotler, 2002. ISBN 0-06-023474-1 Subj: Ethnic groups in the U.S. – African Americans. Family life. Hair. Poetry.

Gingerbread days ill. by Floyd Cooper. HarperCollins, 1995. ISBN 0-06-023472-5 Subj: Days of the week, months of the year. Ethnic groups in the U.S. – African Americans. Folk & fairy tales. Poetry.

The gospel Cinderella ill. by David Diaz. Amistad, 2004. ISBN 0-06-025388-6 Subj: Ethnic groups in the U.S. – African Americans. Family life – stepfamilies. Folk & fairy tales. Music. Swamps.

Hush songs: African American lullabies (Hush songs)

Joy ill. by Pamela Johnson. Hyperion, 2001. ISBN 0-7868-0750-4 Subj: Emotions – happiness. Ethnic groups in the U.S. – African Americans. Family life – mothers. Family life – sons. Format, unusual – board books.

You are my perfect baby ill. by Nneka Bennett. HarperCollins, 1999. ISBN 0-694-01096-0 Subj: Babies. Ethnic groups in the U.S. – African Americans. Family life – new sibling.

Thomas, Karen. *The good thing . . . the bad thing* ill. by Yaroslava. Prentice-Hall, 1979. ISBN 0-13-360354-7 Subj: Behavior.

Thomas, Kathy. *The angel's quest* ill. by Jacqueline Seitz. Living Flame Pr., 1983. ISBN 0-914544-99-3 Subj: Angels. Character traits – perseverance. Orphans. Religion.

Thomas, Mark. *Clothes in Colonial America* ill. with photos. Childrens Pr., 2002. ISBN 0-516-23932-5 Subj: Clothing. U.S. history.

Fun and games in Colonial America ill. with photos. Childrens Pr., 2002. ISBN 0-516-23935-X Subj: Games. U.S. history.

Work in Colonial America ill. with photos. Childrens Pr., 2002. ISBN 0-516-23934-1 Subj: Activities – working. U.S. history.

Thomas, Naturi. *Uh-oh! It's Mama's birthday!* ill. by Keinyo White. A. Whitman, 1997. ISBN 0-8075-8268-9 Subj: Birthdays. Ethnic groups in the U.S. – African Americans. Family life – mothers. Gifts.

Thomas, Pat (1959–). *My family's changing* ill. by Lesley Harker. Barron's, 1999. ISBN 0-7641-0995-2 Subj: Divorce. Family life.

Thomas, Patricia. *The one and only, super-duper, golly-whopper, jim-dandy, really-handy clock-tock-stopper* ill. by John O'Brien. Lothrop, 1990. ISBN 0-688-09341-8 Subj: Animals – porcupines. Animals – rabbits. Clocks, watches. Noise, sounds. Rhyming text.

"Stand back," said the elephant, "I'm going to sneeze!" ill. by Wallace Tripp. Lothrop, 1971. ISBN 0-688-09339-6 Subj: Animals. Humorous stories. Rhyming text.

"There are rocks in my socks!" said the ox to the fox ill. by Mordicai Gerstein. Lothrop, 1979. ISBN 0-688-51851-6 Subj: Animals – bulls, cows. Animals – foxes. Problem solving. Rhyming text.

Thomas, Shelley Moore. *A baby's coming to your house* photos by Eric Futran. A. Whitman, 2001. ISBN 0-8075-0502-1 Subj: Babies. Family life – new sibling.

Get well, good knight ill. by Jennifer Plecas. Dutton, 2002. ISBN 0-525-46914-1 Subj: Dragons. Family life – mothers. Friendship. Illness. Knights.

Good night, Good Knight ill. by Jennifer Plecas. Dutton, 2000. ISBN 0-525-46326-7 Subj: Bedtime. Dragons. Knights. Magic. Royalty.

Putting the world to sleep ill. by Bonnie Christensen. Houghton Mifflin, 1995. ISBN 0-395-71283-1 Subj: Bedtime. Cumulative tales. Night. Rhyming text.

Somewhere today: a book of peace photos by Eric Futran. A. Whitman, 1998. ISBN 0-8075-7546-1 Subj: Character traits – helpfulness.

Thomas, Valerie. *Winnie flies again* (Paul, Korky)

Winnie in winter (Paul, Korky)

Thomas's big railway pop-up book ill. by Owain Bell; paper engineering by David Hawcock. Random House, 1992. ISBN 0-679-83465-6 Subj: Format, unusual – toy & movable books. Trains.

Thomassie, Tynia. *Cajun through and through* ill. by Andrew Glass. Little, 2000. ISBN 0-316-84189-7 Subj: Family life – cousins.

Feliciana Feydra LeRoux: a Cajun tall tale ill. by Cat Bowman Smith. Little, 1995. ISBN 0-316-84125-0 Subj: Reptiles – alligators, crocodiles.

Thompson, Brenda. *Famous planes* by Brenda Thompson & Rosemary Giesen; ill. by Andrew Martin & Rosemary Giesen. Lerner, 1977. ISBN 0-8225-1354-4 Subj: Airplanes, airports.

Pirates by Brenda Thompson & Rosemary Giesen; ill. by Simon Stern & Rosemary Giesen. Lerner, 1977. ISBN 0-8225-1359-5 Subj: Pirates.

The winds that blow by Brenda Thompson & Cynthia Overbeck; ill. by Simon Stern & Rosemary Giesen. Lerner, 1977. ISBN 0-8225-1366-8 Subj: Concepts – measurement. Sea & seashore. Weather – wind.

Thompson, Carol. *Baby days* ill. by author. Macmillan, 1991. ISBN 0-02-789325-1 Subj: Activities. Babies. Rhyming text.

Piggy goes to bed ill. by author. Candlewick, 1998. ISBN 0-7636-0428-3 Subj: Animals – pigs. Furniture.

Time ill. by author. Delacorte, 1989. ISBN 0-385-29765-3 Subj: Animals – bears. Clocks, watches. Time.

Thompson, Colin (Colin Edward). *Falling angels* ill. by author. Hutchinson, 2001. ISBN 0-09-176817-9 Subj: Activities – flying. Family life. Family life – grandmothers. Imagination.

Unknown ill. by Anna Pignataro. Walker, 2000. ISBN 0-8027-8731-2 Subj: Animals – dogs. Behavior – needing someone. Fire.

Thompson, Elizabeth. *The true book of time* (Ziner, Feenie)

Thompson, George Selden. *see* Selden, George

Thompson, Harwood. *The witch's cat* ill. by Quentin Blake. Addison-Wesley, 1971. ISBN 0-20-107574-1 Subj: Animals – cats. Folk & fairy tales. Foreign lands – England. Witches.

Thompson, Kathleen. *Paul Revere* (Gleiter, Jan)

Sacagawea (Gleiter, Jan)

Thompson, Kay. *Here comes Eloise!* (Cheshire, Marc)

Kay Thompson's Eloise ill. by Hilary Knight. 50th anniversary ed. S&S, 2005. ISBN 0-689-82795-4 Subj: Behavior. Hotels.

Kay Thompson's Eloise at Christmastime ill. by Hilary Knight. S&S, 1999. ISBN 0-689-83039-4 Subj: Holidays – Christmas. Hotels.

Kay Thompson's Eloise in Hollywood (Stem, J. David)

Kay Thompson's Eloise in Moscow ill. by Hilary Knight. 40th anniversary ed. S&S, 2000. ISBN 0-689-83211-7 Subj: Activities – traveling. Foreign lands – Russia. Hotels.

Kay Thompson's Eloise takes a bawth [sic] ill. by Hilary Knight & Mart Crowley. S&S, 2002. ISBN 0-689-84288-0 Subj: Activities – bathing. Hotels. Parties.

Kay Thompson's Eloise's what I absolutely love love love ill. by Hilary Knight. S&S, 2005. ISBN 0-689-84965-6 Subj: Emotions – love. Hotels. Self-concept.

Love & kisses, Eloise (Cheshire, Marc)

Thompson, Lauren. *Little Quack* ill. by Derek Anderson. S&S, 2003. ISBN 0-689-84723-8 Subj: Animals – babies. Birds – ducks. Character traits – bravery. Counting, numbers.

Little Quack [board book] ill. by Derek Anderson. Little Simon, 2005. ISBN 0-689-87645-9 Subj: Animals – babies. Birds – ducks. Character traits – bravery. Counting, numbers. Format, unusual – board books.

Little Quack's bedtime ill. by Derek Anderson. S&S, 2005. ISBN 0-689-86894-4 Subj: Bedtime. Birds – ducks. Family life – mothers. Night.

Little Quack's hide and seek ill. by Derek Anderson. S&S, 2004. ISBN 0-689-85722-5 Subj: Birds – ducks. Counting, numbers. Family life – mothers. Games.

Little Quack's new friend ill. by Derek Anderson. S&S, 2006. ISBN 0-689-86893-6 Subj: Activities – playing. Birds – ducks. Friendship. Frogs & toads. Lakes, ponds.

Love one another ill. by Elizabeth Uyehara. Scholastic, 2000. ISBN 0-590-31830-6 Subj: Holidays – Easter. Religion.

Mouse's first Christmas ill. by Buket Erdogan. S&S, 1999. ISBN 0-689-82325-8 Subj: Animals – mice. Holidays – Christmas. Santa Claus.

Mouse's first Christmas [board book] ill. by Buket Erdogan. Little Simon, 2002. ISBN 0-689-85141-3 Subj: Animals – mice. Format, unusual – board books. Holidays – Christmas. Santa Claus.

Mouse's first Halloween ill. by author. S&S, 2000. ISBN 0-689-83176-5 Subj: Animals – mice. Holidays – Halloween.

One riddle, one answer ill. by Linda S. Wingerter. Scholastic, 2001. ISBN 0-590-31335-5 Subj: Counting, numbers. Riddles & jokes. Royalty – princesses.

Thompson, Mary. *Gran's bees* ill. by Donna Peterson. Millbrook, 1996. ISBN 1-56294-652-8 Subj: Family life – grandmothers. Farms. Insects – bees.

Thompson, Richard. *Effie's bath* ill. by Eugenie Fernandes. Firefly, 1989. ISBN 1-55037-055-3 Subj: Activities – bathing. Friendship. Imagination.

The follower ill. by Martin Springett. Fitzhenry & Whiteside, 2000. ISBN 1-55041-532-8 Subj: Cumulative tales. Days of the week, months of the year. Mystery stories. Rhyming text. Witches.

Foo ill. by Eugenie Fernandes. Firefly, 1988. ISBN 1-55037-005-7 Subj: Emotions – love. Family life.

Gurgle, bubble, splash ill. by Eugenie Fernandes. Firefly, 1989. ISBN 1-55037-029-4 Subj: Family life. Imagination. Sea & seashore.

I have to see this ill. by Eugenie Fernandes. Firefly, 1988. ISBN 1-55037-015-4 Subj: Activities – walking. Family life – fathers. Night.

Jenny's neighbours ill. by Kathryn E. Shoemaker. Firefly, 1987. ISBN 0-920303-73-0 Subj: Activities – playing. Friendship. Imagination.

Jesse on the night train ill. by Eugenie Fernandes. Firefly, 1990. ISBN 1-55037-093-6 Subj: Imagination. Night. Trains.

The night walker ill. by Martin Springett. Fitzhenry & Whiteside, 2003. ISBN 1-55041-672-3 Subj: Behavior – collecting things. Emotions – fear. Imagination. Night. Noise, sounds.

Sky full of babies ill. by Eugenie Fernandes. Firefly, 1987. ISBN 0-920303-93-5 Subj: Family life. Imagination. Space & space ships.

Thompson, Susan L. *Diary of a monarch butterfly* graphic design by Sas Colby; ill. by Judy LaMotte. Walker, 1976. ISBN 0-8027-6267-0 Subj: Insects – butterflies, caterpillars. Metamorphosis. Science.

One more thing, dad ill. by Dora Leder. A. Whitman, 1980. ISBN 0-8075-6095-2 Subj: Counting, numbers.

Thompson, Vivian Laubach. *Camp-in-the-yard* ill. by Brinton Turkle. Holiday, 1961. Subj: Camps, camping. Multiple births – twins. Problem solving.

The horse that liked sandwiches ill. by Aliki. Putnam, 1962. Subj: Animals – horses, ponies. Food.

Thomson, Pat. *Beware of the aunts!* ill. by Emma Chichester Clark. Macmillan, 1992. ISBN 0-689-50538-8 Subj: Character traits – individuality. Family life – aunts, uncles.

Rhymes around the day ill. by Jan Ormerod. Lothrop, 1983. ISBN 0-688-02074-7 Subj: Family life. Nursery rhymes.

The squeaky, creaky bed ill. by Niki Daly. Random House, 2003. ISBN 0-385-90856-3 Subj: Animals. Cumulative tales. Family life – grandparents. Furniture – beds. Noise, sounds.

Thomson, Peggy. *The brave little tailor* (Grimm, Jacob)

The king has horse's ears ill. by David Small. S&S, 1988. ISBN 0-671-64953-1 Subj: Behavior – secrets. Character traits – appearance. Royalty – kings.

Thomson, Ruth. *Drawing* ill. by author. Childrens Pr., 1994. ISBN 0-516-07989-1 Subj: Activities – drawing. Art.

Eyes ill. by Mike Galletly. Watts, 1988. ISBN 0-531-10549-0 Subj: Anatomy – eyes. Senses – sight.

My bear: I can . . . can you? ill. by Ian Beck. Dial, 1985. ISBN 0-8037-0110-1 Subj: Activities. Rhyming text. Toys – bears.

My bear: I like . . . do you? ill. by Ian Beck. Dial, 1985. ISBN 0-8037-0105-5 Subj: Rhyming text. Toys – bears.

Painting ill. by author. Childrens Pr., 1994. ISBN 0-516-07990-5 Subj: Activities – painting. Art.

Peabody all at sea ill. by Ken Kirkwood. Lothrop, 1978. ISBN 0-688-51862-1 Subj: Activities – vacationing. Animals – dogs. Boats, ships. Careers – detectives. Crime. Mystery stories.

Peabody's first case ill. by Ken Kirkwood. Lothrop, 1978. ISBN 0-688-51861-3 Subj: Animals – dogs. Careers – detectives. Crime. Mystery stories.

Printing ill. by author. Childrens Pr., 1994. ISBN 0-516-07992-1 Subj: Activities – making things. Art.

The Rainforest Indians ill. by author. Childrens Pr., 1996. ISBN 0-516-08074-1 Subj: Activities – making things. Foreign lands – South America. Forest, woods. Indians of South America – Yanomamo.

Thomson, Sarah L. *Amazing whales* ill. with photos. Harper-Collins, 2005. ISBN 0-06-054466-X Subj: Animals – whales.

The nutcracker (Hague, Michael)

Stars and stripes ill. by Bob Dacey & Debra Bandelin. Harper-Collins, 2003. ISBN 0-06-050417-X Subj: U.S. history.

Tigers ill. with photos. HarperCollins, 2004. ISBN 0-06-054451-1 Subj: Animals – endangered animals. Animals – tigers.

Thong, Roseanne. *Round is a mooncake* ill. by Grace Lin. Chronicle, 2000. ISBN 0-8118-2676-7 Subj: Concepts – shape. Ethnic groups in the U.S. – Chinese Americans.

Thoreau, Henry D. *What befell at Mrs. Brooks's* ill. by George Overlie. Lerner, 1974. ISBN 0-8225-0284-4 Subj: Behavior – hurrying.

Thorne, Ian. *see* May, Julian

Thorne, Jenny. *Adam and Eve* ill. by author. Aladdin, 1989. ISBN 0-689-71305-3 Subj: Religion.

Jonah and the whale ill. by author. Aladdin, 1989. ISBN 0-689-71307-X Subj: Animals – whales. Religion – Jonah.

My uncle ill. by author. Atheneum, 1982. ISBN 0-689-50233-8 Subj: Activities. Dreams. Family life – aunts, uncles. Sports – fishing.

Noah's ark ill. by author. Aladdin, 1989. ISBN 0-689-71306-1 Subj: Animals. Boats, ships. Religion – Noah. Weather – floods. Weather – rain. Weather – rainbows.

The walls of Jericho ill. by author. Aladdin, 1989. ISBN 0-689-71308-8 Subj: Religion.

Thornhill, Jan. *The rumor* ill. by reteller. Maple Tree, 2002. ISBN 1-894379-39-X Subj: Animals. Animals – rabbits. Behavior – misunderstanding. Cumulative tales. Emotions – fear. Folk & fairy tales. Foreign lands – India.

A tree in a forest ill. by author. S&S, 1992. ISBN 0-671-75901-9 Subj: Ecology. Foreign lands – Canada. Forest, woods. Trees.

Wild in the city ill. by author. Sierra Club, 1996. ISBN 0-87156-910-8 Subj: Animals. Animals – cats. Birds. Cities, towns. Ecology. Night.

Wildlife ABC ill. by author. S&S, 1990. ISBN 0-671-67925-2 Subj: ABC books. Animals. Nature.

The wildlife 1-2-3 ill. by author. S&S, 1989. ISBN 0-671-67926-0 Subj: Animals. Counting, numbers. Nature.

Thorpe, Kiki. *A comfy, cozy Thanksgiving* ill. by Tom Brannon. Simon Spotlight, 2002. Based on the TV series Bear in the Big Blue House. ISBN 0-6898-5012-3 Subj: Animals. Animals – bears. Character traits – helpfulness. Holidays – Thanksgiving.

Time to cha-cha-cha! ill. by Barry Goldberg. Simon Spotlight, 2000. ISBN 0-689-83431-4 Subj: Activities – dancing. Animals. Animals – bears. Musical instruments.

Threadgall, Colin. *Proud rooster and the fox* ill. by author. Morrow, 1992. ISBN 0-688-11124-6 Subj: Animals – foxes. Birds – chickens. Character traits – cleverness. Character traits – pride. Farms.

The three bears.

The three bears. *Goldilocks* adapt. & ill. by Janice Russell. Boyds Mills, 1997. ISBN 1-56397-430-4 Subj: Animals – bears. Folk & fairy tales.

Goldilocks retold by Dom DeLuise; ill. by Christopher Santoro. S&S, 1992. ISBN 0-671-74690-1 Subj: Animals – bears. Folk & fairy tales.

Goldilocks and the three bears retold & ill. by H. Amery. E D C, 1988. ISBN 0-88110-318-7 Subj: Animals – bears. Folk & fairy tales.

Goldilocks and the three bears retold by Marcia Leonard; ill. by Yvette Banek. Silver Pr., 1990. ISBN 0-671-69346-8 Subj: Animals – bears. Folk & fairy tales.

Goldilocks and the three bears retold & ill. by Jan Brett. Dodd, 1987. ISBN 0-396-08925-9 Subj: Animals – bears. Folk & fairy tales.

Goldilocks and the three bears adapt. & ill. by Lorinda Bryan Cauley. Putnam, 1981. ISBN 0-399-20794-5 Subj: Animals – bears. Folk & fairy tales.

Goldilocks and the three bears ill. by Jane Dyer. Grosset, 1984. ISBN 0-448-10213-7 Subj: Animals – bears. Folk & fairy tales. Format, unusual – board books.

Goldilocks and the three bears adapt. by Armand Eisen; ill. by Lynn Bywaters Ferris. Knopf, 1987. ISBN 0-394-55882-0 Subj: Animals – bears. Folk & fairy tales.

Goldilocks and the three bears retold & ill. by Valeri Gorbachev. North-South, 2001. ISBN 0-7358-1438-4 Subj: Animals – bears. Folk & fairy tales.

Goldilocks and the three bears retold & ill. by Steven Guarnaccia. Abrams, 2000. ISBN 0-8109-4139-2 Subj: Animals – bears. Folk & fairy tales.

Goldilocks and the three bears adapt. by Linda Hayward; ill. by Madelaine Gill Linden. Random House, 1988. ISBN 0-394-89637-8 (package) Subj: Animals – bears. Folk & fairy tales. Format, unusual. Rebuses.

Goldilocks and the three bears retold & ill. by David McPhail. Scholastic, 1995. ISBN 0-590-48117-7 Subj: Animals – bears. Folk & fairy tales.

Goldilocks and the three bears adapt. & ill. by James Marshall. Dial, 1988. ISBN 0-8037-0543-3 Subj: Animals – bears. Caldecott award honor books. Folk & fairy tales.

Goldilocks and the three bears retold by Harriet Ziefert; ill. by Laura Rader. Putnam, 1981. ISBN 0-688-13258-8 Subj: Animals – bears. Folk & fairy tales.

Goldilocks and the three bears retold & ill. by Tony Ross. Overlook Pr., 1992. ISBN 0-87951-453-1 Subj: Animals – bears. Folk & fairy tales.

Goldilocks and the three bears retold & ill. by Janet Stevens. Holiday, 1985. ISBN 0-8234-0608-3 Subj: Animals – bears. Folk & fairy tales.

Goldilocks and the three bears by Barrie Wade; ill. by Kristina Stephenson. Picture Window, 2003. ISBN 1-4048-0057-3 Subj: Animals – bears. Folk & fairy tales.

Goldilocks and the three bears adapt. & ill. by Bernadette Watts. Knopf, 1985. ISBN 0-03-005737-X Subj: Animals – bears. Folk & fairy tales.

Goldilocks and the three bears retold by Betty Miles; ill. by Bari Weissman. S&S, 1998. ISBN 0-689-81787-8 Subj: Animals – bears. Folk & fairy tales.

The story of the three bears ill. by L. Leslie Brooke. Warne, 1934. Subj: Animals – bears. Folk & fairy tales.

The story of the three bears ill. by William Stobbs. McGraw-Hill, 1965. Subj: Animals – bears. Folk & fairy tales.

The three bears (Hillert, Margaret)

The three bears adapt. & ill. by Byron Barton. HarperCollins, 1991. ISBN 0-06-020424-9 Subj: Animals – bears. Folk & fairy tales.

The three bears ill. by Paul Galdone. Seabury Pr., 1972. Subj: Animals – bears. Folk & fairy tales.

The three bears adapt. by Kathleen N. Daly; ill. by Feodor Rojankovsky. Golden Pr., 1967. Subj: Animals – bears. Folk & fairy tales.

The three bears ill. by Robin Spowart. Knopf, 1987. ISBN 0-394-98862-0 Subj: Animals – bears. Folk & fairy tales.

The three bears [board book] ill. by Thea Kliros. HarperFestival, 2003. ISBN 0-06-008238-0 Subj: Animals – bears. Folk & fairy tales. Format, unusual – board books.

The three little pigs. *The original three little pigs re-told* adapt. by Marilyn J. Shearer; ill. by Jonathan Smith. Lauren Ashley & Joshua Storybooks, 1990. ISBN 0-685-33065-6 Subj: Animals – pigs. Animals – wolves. Character traits – cleverness. Folk & fairy tales.

The story of the three little pigs ill. by L. Leslie Brooke. Warne, 1934. Subj: Animals – pigs. Animals – wolves. Character traits – cleverness. Folk & fairy tales.

The story of the three little pigs ill. by William Stobbs. McGraw-Hill, 1965. Subj: Animals – pigs. Animals – wolves. Character traits – cleverness. Folk & fairy tales.

Three little pigs. Facsimile ed. Bragdon, 1987. Reprint of 1924 ed. ISBN 0-916410-38-2 Subj: Animals – pigs. Animals – wolves. Character traits – cleverness. Folk & fairy tales.

The three little pigs retold & ill. by Val Biro. Oxford Univ. Pr., 1991. ISBN 0-19-279880-4 Subj: Animals – pigs. Animals – wolves. Character traits – cleverness. Folk & fairy tales. Format, unusual – board books.

The three little pigs retold & ill. by Gavin Bishop. Scholastic, 1990. ISBN 0-590-43358-X Subj: Animals – pigs. Animals – wolves. Character traits – cleverness. Folk & fairy tales.

The three little pigs ill. by Erik Blegvad. Atheneum, 1980. ISBN 0-689-50139-0 Subj: Animals – pigs. Animals – wolves. Character traits – cleverness. Rhyming text.

The three little pigs adapt. & ill. by Caroline Bucknall. Dial, 1987. ISBN 0-8037-0100-4 Subj: Animals – pigs. Animals – wolves. Character traits – cleverness. Folk & fairy tales. Rhyming text.

The three little pigs retold by H. Amery; ill. by Stephen Cartwright. E D C, 1987. ISBN 0-88110-293-8 Subj: Animals – pigs. Animals – wolves. Character traits – cleverness. Folk & fairy tales.

The three little pigs ill. by Lorinda Bryan Cauley. Putnam, 1980. ISBN 0-399-20733-3 Subj: Animals – pigs. Animals – wolves. Character traits – cleverness. Folk & fairy tales.

The three little pigs trans. & adapt. by Elizabeth D. Crawford; ill. by Jean Claverie. North-South, 1989. ISBN 1-55858-004-2 Subj: Animals – pigs. Animals – wolves. Character traits – cleverness. Folk & fairy tales.

The three little pigs retold by Marcia Leonard; ill. by Doug Cushman. Silver Pr., 1990. ISBN 0-671-69345-X Subj: Animals – pigs. Animals – wolves. Character traits – cleverness. Folk & fairy tales. Picture puzzles.

The three little pigs: in verse ill. by William Pène Du Bois. Viking, 1962. Subj: Animals – pigs. Animals – wolves. Character traits – cleverness. Folk & fairy tales. Rhyming text.

The three little pigs ill. by Paul Galdone. Seabury Pr., 1970. Subj: Animals – pigs. Animals – wolves. Character traits – cleverness. Folk & fairy tales.

The three little pigs adapt. by Linda Hayward; ill. by Madelaine Gill. Random House, 1988. ISBN 0-394-89637-8 (package) Subj: Animals – pigs. Animals – wolves. Character traits – cleverness. Folk & fairy tales. Rebuses.

The three little pigs by Maggie Moore; ill. by Rob Hefferan. Picture Window, 2003. ISBN 1-4048-0071-9 Subj: Animals – pigs. Animals – wolves. Character traits – cleverness. Folk & fairy tales.

The three little pigs retold & ill. by Steven Kellogg. Morrow, 1997. ISBN 0-688-08732-9 Subj: Animals – pigs. Animals – wolves. Character traits – cleverness. Family life – mothers. Folk & fairy tales.

The three little pigs retold & ill. by David McPhail. Scholastic, 1995. ISBN 0-590-48118-5 Subj: Animals – pigs. Animals – wolves. Character traits – cleverness. Folk & fairy tales.

The three little pigs retold & ill. by James Marshall. Dial, 1989. ISBN 0-8037-0594-8 Subj: Animals – pigs. Animals – wolves. Character traits – cleverness. Folk & fairy tales.

The three little pigs by Betty Miles; ill. by Paul Meisel. S&S, 1998. ISBN 0-689-81788-6 Subj: Animals – pigs. Animals – wolves. Character traits – cleverness. Folk & fairy tales.

The three little pigs ill. by Rodney Peppé. Lothrop, 1980. ISBN 0-688-51923-7 Subj: Animals – pigs. Animals – wolves. Character traits – cleverness. Folk & fairy tales.

The three little pigs ill. by Edda Reinl. Picture Book Studio, 1983. ISBN 0-907234-32-1 Subj: Animals – pigs. Animals – wolves. Character traits – cleverness. Folk & fairy tales.

The three little pigs ill. by John Wallner. Viking, 1987. ISBN 0-670-81707-4 Subj: Animals – pigs. Animals – wolves. Character traits – cleverness. Folk & fairy tales. Format, unusual – toy & movable books.

The three little pigs retold by Margaret Hillert; ill. by Irma Wilde. Follett, 1963. Subj: Animals – pigs. Animals – wolves. Character traits – cleverness. Folk & fairy tales.

The three little pigs ill. by Margot Zemach. Farrar, 1988. ISBN 0-374-37527-5 Subj: Animals – pigs. Animals – wolves. Character traits – cleverness. Folk & fairy tales.

The three little pigs and the big bad wolf retold & ill. by Glen Rounds. Holiday, 1992. ISBN 0-8234-0923-6 Subj: Animals – pigs. Animals – wolves. Character traits – cleverness. Folk & fairy tales. Rhyming text.

The three little pigs and the fox adapt. by William H. Hooks; ill. by S. D. Schindler. Macmillan, 1989. ISBN 0-02-744431-7 Subj: Animals – foxes. Animals – pigs. Birds – chickens. Character traits – cleverness. Folk & fairy tales.

The three little pigs [board book] ill. by Thea Kliros. HarperFestival, 2003. ISBN 0-06-008236-4 Subj: Animals – pigs. Animals – wolves. Character traits – cleverness. Folk & fairy tales. Format, unusual – board books.

The three pigs ill. by Tony Ross. Pantheon, 1983. ISBN 0-394-96143-9 Subj: Animals – pigs. Animals – wolves. Character traits – cleverness. Folk & fairy tales.

Who's at the door? adapt. & ill. by Jonathan Allen. Tambourine, 1993. ISBN 0-688-12257-4 Subj: Animals – pigs. Animals – wolves. Character traits – cleverness. Disguises. Folk & fairy tales. Format, unusual – toy & movable books.

Thurber, James. *The great Quillow* ill. by Steven Kellogg. Harcourt, 1994. ISBN 0-15-232544-1 Subj: Careers – toy makers. Character traits – being different. Character traits – cleverness. Giants. Toys.

Many moons ill. by Marc Simont. Harcourt, 1990. ISBN 0-15-251872-X Subj: Clowns, jesters. Illness. Moon. Royalty – princesses.

Many moons ill. by Louis Slobodkin. Harcourt, 1943. ISBN 0-15-251873-8 Subj: Caldecott award books. Clowns, jesters. Illness. Moon. Royalty – princesses.

Thury, Frederick. *The last straw* ill. by Vlasta Van Kampen. Charlesbridge, 1999. ISBN 0-88106-152-2 Subj: Animals – camels. Gifts. Holidays – Christmas. Religion – Nativity.

Thuswaldner, Werner. *Æsop's fables* (Æsop)

Thwaite, Ann. *The day with the Duke* ill. by George Him. World, 1969. Subj: Games.

Thwaites, Lyndsay. *Super Adam and Rosie Wonder* ill. by author. André Deutsch, 1983. ISBN 0-233-97532-2 Subj: Activities – playing. Family life.

Tibo, Gilles. *The cowboy kid* ill. by Tom Kapas. Tundra, 2000. ISBN 0-88776-473-8 Subj: Activities – flying. Animals – horses, ponies. Cowboys, cowgirls. Homeless. Imagination. Magic.

The grand journey of Mr. Man ill. by Luc Melanson. Dominique & Friends, 2001. ISBN 1-894363-78-7 Subj: Activities – traveling. Behavior – needing someone. Death. Emotions – grief. Toys – bears. War.

Simon and the snowflakes ill. by author. Tundra, 1988. ISBN 0-88776-218-2 Subj: Friendship. Stars. Weather – snow.

Simon's disguise ill. by author; trans. by Sheila Fischman. Tundra, 1999. ISBN 0-88776-472-X Subj: Activities – playing. Clothing – costumes. Disguises. Imagination.

Tidd, Louise Vitellaro. *The best pet yet* photos by Dorothy Handelman. Millbrook, 1998. ISBN 0-7613-2006-7 Subj: Animals. Animals – rabbits. Pets.

I'll do it later photos by Dorothy Handelman. Millbrook, 1999. ISBN 0-7613-2066-0 Subj: Behavior – promptness, tardiness. School.

Tierney, Hanne. *Where's your baby brother, Becky Bunting?* ill. by Paula Winter. Doubleday, 1979. ISBN 0-385-08654-7 Subj: Behavior – misbehavior. Family life. Sibling rivalry.

Tilden, Ruth. *Freddie works out* ill. by author. Hyperion, 1995. ISBN 0-7868-0108-5 Subj: Format, unusual – toy & movable books. Frogs & toads. Health & fitness.

Sophie's dance class ill. by author. Hyperion, 1996. ISBN 0-7868-0239-1 Subj: Activities – dancing. Ballet. Format, unusual – toy & movable books.

Tildes, Phyllis Limbacher. *Animals in camouflage* ill. by author. Charlesbridge, 2000. ISBN 0-88106-120-4 Subj: Animals. Disguises. Picture puzzles.

Baby animals black and white ill. by author. Charlesbridge, 1998. ISBN 0-88106-313-4 Subj: Animals – babies. Format, unusual – board books. Wordless.

Billy's big-boy bed ill. by author. Whispering Coyote, 2002. ISBN 1-57091-475-3 Subj: Behavior – growing up. Toys – bears.

The magic babushka ill. by author. Charlesbridge, 1998. ISBN 0-88106-840-3 Subj: Eggs. Folk & fairy tales. Holidays – Easter.

Tiller, Ruth. *Cats vanish slowly* ill. by Laura L. Seeley. Peachtree, 1995. ISBN 1-56145-106-1 Subj: Animals – cats. Farms. Poetry.

The Timbertoes 1 2 3 counting book by the editors of Highlights for Children; ill. by Judith A. Hunt. Boyds Mills, 1997. ISBN 1-56397-627-7 Subj: Counting, numbers. Puppets.

The Timbertoes ABC alphabet book by the editors of Highlights for Children; ill. by Judith A. Hunt. Boyds Mills, 1997. ISBN 1-56397-604-8 Subj: ABC books. Puppets.

Timlock, Jason. *Basil, the loneliest boy* ill. by Brett Colquhoun. Viking, 1990. ISBN 0-670-83125-5 Subj: Emotions – loneliness.

Timmermans, Felix. *A gift from Saint Nicholas* adapt. by Carole Kismaric; ill. by Charles Mikolaycak. Holiday, 1988. ISBN 0-8234-0674-1 Subj: Character traits – generosity. Gifts. Holidays – Christmas.

Tinkelman, Murray. *Cowgirl* ill. by author. Greenwillow, 1984. ISBN 0-688-02883-7 Subj: Animals – horses, ponies. Cowboys, cowgirls. Sports.

Tippett, James Sterling. *Counting the days* ill. by Elizabeth Tyler Wolcott. HarperCollins, 1940. Subj: Holidays – Christmas. Rhyming text.

Tirabosco, Tom. *At the same time* ill. by author. Kane/Miller, 2001. ISBN 1-929132-17-4 Subj: Activities. Books, reading.

Tison, Annette. *The adventures of the three colors* by Annette Tison & Talus Taylor. Collins-World, 1971. Subj: Concepts – color. Format, unusual.

Animal hide-and-seek by Annette Tison & Talus Taylor; ill. by authors. Collins-World, 1972. ISBN 0-529-04543-5 Subj: Activities – photographing. Animals. Format, unusual. Games. Insects.

Animals in color magic ill. by author. Merrill, 1980. ISBN 0-675-01046-2 Subj: Animals. Format, unusual.

Inside and outside by Annette Tison & Taylor Talus. Collins-World, 1972. ISBN 9-06-151014-7 Subj: Format, unusual. Homes, houses.

Titherington, Jeanne. *Baby's boat* ill. by author. Greenwillow, 1992. ISBN 0-688-08556-3 Subj: Babies. Bedtime. Boats, ships. Lullabies. Sea & seashore.

Baby's boat [board book] ill. by author. 1st Tupelo board book ed. Tupelo, 1998. ISBN 0-688-15979-6 Subj: Babies. Bedtime. Boats, ships. Format, unusual – board books. Lullabies. Sea & seashore.

Big world, small world ill. by author. Greenwillow, 1985. ISBN 0-688-04023-3 Subj: Concepts – perspective. Family life – mothers. Self-concept.

Bonkers Fellini ill. by author. Greenwillow, 2001. ISBN 0-688-15029-2 Subj: Friendship. Imagination – imaginary friends.

A child's prayer ill. by author. Greenwillow, 1989. ISBN 0-688-08318-8 Subj: Bedtime. Religion.

A place for Ben ill. by author. Greenwillow, 1987. ISBN 0-688-06494-9 Subj: Babies. Emotions – loneliness. Family life – brothers. Family life – new sibling.

Pumpkin pumpkin ill. by author. Greenwillow, 1985. ISBN 0-688-50696-1 Subj: Gardens, gardening. Holidays – Halloween.

Where are you going, Emma? ill. by author. Greenwillow, 1988. ISBN 0-688-07082-5 Subj: Behavior – lost. Family life – grandfathers.

Titus, Eve. *Anatole* ill. by Paul Galdone. McGraw-Hill, 1957. Subj: Animals – mice. Caldecott award honor books. Foreign lands – France.

Anatole and the cat ill. by Paul Galdone. McGraw-Hill, 1957. Subj: Animals – cats. Animals – mice. Caldecott award honor books. Character traits – bravery. Foreign lands – France. Problem solving.

Anatole and the piano ill. by Paul Galdone. McGraw-Hill, 1966. Subj: Animals – mice. Foreign lands – France. Music. Musical instruments – pianos.

Anatole and the pied piper ill. by Paul Galdone. McGraw-Hill, 1979. ISBN 0-07-064897-2 Subj: Animals – mice. Foreign lands – France. Music. Problem solving.

Anatole and the poodle ill. by Paul Galdone. McGraw-Hill, 1965. Subj: Animals – dogs. Animals – mice. Foreign lands – France. Problem solving.

Anatole and the robot ill. by Paul Galdone. McGraw-Hill, 1960. Subj: Animals – mice. Foreign lands – France. Problem solving. Robots.

Anatole and the thirty thieves ill. by Paul Galdone. McGraw-Hill, 1969. Subj: Animals – mice. Crime. Foreign lands – France. Problem solving.

Anatole and the toyshop ill. by Paul Galdone. McGraw-Hill, 1970. Subj: Animals – mice. Foreign lands – France. Problem solving. Toys.

Anatole in Italy ill. by Paul Galdone. McGraw-Hill, 1973. ISBN 0-07-064899-9 Subj: Animals – mice. Foreign lands – Italy. Problem solving.

Anatole over Paris ill. by Paul Galdone. McGraw-Hill, 1961. Subj: Activities – flying. Animals – mice. Foreign lands – France. Kites.

The kitten who couldn't purr ill. by Amrei Fechner. Morrow, 1991. ISBN 0-688-09364-7 Subj: Animals. Animals – cats. Noise, sounds.

Tobias, Tobi. *At the beach* ill. by Gloria Singer. McKay, 1978. ISBN 0-679-20447-4 Subj: Activities – vacationing. Family life. Sea & seashore – beaches.

Chasing the goblins away ill. by Victor G. Ambrus. Warne, 1977. ISBN 0-7232-6144-X Subj: Bedtime. Mythical creatures – goblins. Night. Sleep.

The dawdlewalk ill. by Jeanette Swofford. Carolrhoda, 1983. ISBN 0-87614-190-4 Subj: Activities – walking.

A day off ill. by Ray Cruz. Putnam, 1973. ISBN 0-399-60762-5 Subj: Family life. Illness.

Jane wishing ill. by Trina Schart Hyman. Viking, 1977. ISBN 0-670-40565-5 Subj: Behavior – wishing. Emotions – happiness. Family life. Humorous stories. Self-concept.

Moving day ill. by William Pène du Bois. Knopf, 1976. ISBN 0-394-93115-7 Subj: Emotions. Moving. Toys – bears.

The quitting deal ill. by Trina Schart Hyman. Viking, 1975. ISBN 0-670-58582-3 Subj: Family life – mothers. Thumb sucking.

Serendipity ill. by Peter H. Reynolds. S&S, 2000. ISBN 0-689-83373-3 Subj: Character traits – luck.

Tobias catches trout (Hertz, Ole)

Tobias goes ice fishing (Hertz, Ole)

Tobias goes seal hunting (Hertz, Ole)

Tobias has a birthday (Hertz, Ole)

Wishes for you ill. by Henri Sorensen. HarperCollins, 2003. ISBN 0-688-10839-3 Subj: Behavior – wishing. Family life – parents.

A world of words: an ABC of quotations ill. by Peter Malone. Lothrop, 1997. ISBN 0-688-12130-6 Subj: ABC books. Language. Poetry.

Tobola, Deborah. *The big buck adventure* (Gill, Shelley)

Todaro, John. *Phillip the flower-eating phoenix* by John Todaro & Barbara Ellen; ill. by John Todaro. Abelard-Schuman, 1961. Subj: Mythical creatures – phoenix.

Todd, Barbara. *The rainmaker* ill. by Rogé. Annick, 2003. ISBN 1-55037-775-2 Subj: Mythical creatures. Umbrellas. Weather – rain.

Todd, Kathleen. *Snow* ill. by author. Addison-Wesley, 1982. ISBN 0-201-16280-6 Subj: Activities – playing. Family life. Weather – snow.

Todd, Mark. *Monster trucks* ill. by author. Houghton, 2003. ISBN 0-618-18208-X Subj: Rhyming text. Trucks.

Start your engines ill. by author. Callaway, 2000. ISBN 0-935112-48-0 Subj: Animals. Automobiles. Counting, numbers. Sports – racing.

What will you be for Halloween? ill. by author. Houghton, 2001. ISBN 0-618-08803-2 Subj: Clothing – costumes. Holidays – Halloween. Monsters. Rhyming text.

Todd, Sarah Manning. *see* Freeman, Jean Todd

Toft, Kim Michelle. *Neptune's nursery* Kim Michelle Toft & Allan Sheather; ill. by Kim Michelle Toft. Charlesbridge, 2000. ISBN 1-57091-391-9 Subj: Animals. Picture puzzles. Rhyming text. Science. Sea & seashore.

One less fish Kim Michelle Toft & Allan Sheather; ill. by Kim Michelle Toft. Charlesbridge, 1998. ISBN 0-88106-322-3 Subj: Counting, numbers. Fish. Picture puzzles. Rhyming text.

Tokuda, Wendy. *Humphrey the lost whale* by Wendy Tokuda & Richard Hall; ill. by Hanako Wakiyama. Heian Intl., 1986. ISBN 0-89346-270-5 Subj: Animals – whales. Behavior – lost. Behavior – needing someone. Sea & seashore.

Samson the hot tub bear ill. by Lokken Millis. Roberts Rinehart, 1998. ISBN 1-57098-209-0 Subj: Animals – bears. Zoos.

Tolan, Stephanie S. *Bartholomew's blessing* ill. by Margie Moore. HarperCollins, 2004. ISBN 0-06-001198-X Subj: Angels. Animals – foxes. Animals – mice. Holidays – Christmas. Religion – Nativity.

Tolhurst, Marilyn. *Somebody and the three Blairs* ill. by Simone Abel. Watts, 1991. ISBN 0-531-08478-7 Subj: Animals – bears. Folk & fairy tales.

Tolkien, Baillie. *The Father Christmas letters* (Tolkien, J. R. R. [John Ronald Reuel])

Tolkien, J. R. R. (John Ronald Reuel). *The Father Christmas letters* ed. by Baillie Tolkien; ill. by author. Houghton Mifflin, 1977. ISBN 0-395-24981-3 Subj: Communication. Holidays – Christmas.

Tolstoy, Aleksey Nikolayevich. *The enormous turnip* ill. by Scott Goto. Harcourt, 2002. ISBN 0-15-204585-6 Subj: Animals. Character traits – cooperation. Cumulative tales. Farms. Folk & fairy tales. Foreign lands – Russia. Plants. Problem solving.

The gigantic turnip by Aleksei Tolstoy & Niamh Sharkey; ill. by Niamh Sharkey. Barefoot, 1999. ISBN 1-902283-12-0 Subj: Character traits – cooperation. Cumulative tales. Farms. Folk & fairy tales. Foreign lands – Russia. Plants. Problem solving.

The great big enormous turnip ill. by Helen Oxenbury. Watts, 1968. Subj: Animals. Character traits – cooperation. Cumulative tales. Farms. Folk & fairy tales. Foreign lands – Russia. Plants. Problem solving.

Shoemaker Martin trans. from Russian by Michael Hale; adapt. by Brigitte Hanhart; ill. by Bernadette Watts. Holt, 1986. ISBN 0-8050-0040-2 Subj: Character traits – generosity. Character traits – kindness. Religion.

Tolstoy, Leo. *How much land does a man need?* ill. by Elena Abesinova. Crocodile, 2001. ISBN 1-56656-407-7 Subj: Behavior – greed. Folk & fairy tales. Foreign lands – Russia.

Tom Thumb. *The adventures of Tom Thumb* adapt. by Marianna Mayer; ill. by Kinuko Y. Craft. SeaStar, 2001. ISBN 1-58717-065-5 Subj: Folk & fairy tales. Giants. Little people. Royalty – kings. Wizards.

Dick Bruna's Tom Thumb (Bruna, Dick)

Grimm Tom Thumb by Jacob & Wilhelm Grimm; trans. by Anthea Bell; ill. by Svend Otto S. Larousse, 1976. Translation of Tommeliden. ISBN 0-8833-2043-6 Subj: Folk & fairy tales. Little people.

Tom Thumb ill. by L. Leslie Brooke. Warne, 1904. Subj: Folk & fairy tales. Little people.

Tom Thumb adapt. by Margaret Hillert; ill. by Dennis Hockerman. Follett, 1982. ISBN 0-695-41542-5 Subj: Folk & fairy tales. Little people.

Tom Thumb by the Brothers Grimm; ill. by Felix Hoffmann. Atheneum, 1973. Translation of Der Daumling. ISBN 0-689-30318-1 Subj: Folk & fairy tales. Little people.

Tom Thumb: a tale adapt. & ill. by Lidia Postma. Schocken, 1983. Based on a tale by Charles Perrault. ISBN 0-8052-3855-7 Subj: Folk & fairy tales. Little people.

Tom Thumb adapt. & ill. by Richard Jesse Watson. Harcourt, 1989. ISBN 0-15-289280-X Subj: Folk & fairy tales. Little people.

Tom Thumb ill. by William Wiesner. Walck, 1974. ISBN 0-8098-1215-0 Subj: Folk & fairy tales. Little people.

Tom Tit Tot. *Tom Tit Tot: an English folk tale* ill. by Evaline Ness. Scribners, 1965. Subj: Caldecott award honor books. Folk & fairy tales. Magic. Names.

Tomchek, Ann Heinrichs. *I can be a chef.* Childrens Pr., 1985. ISBN 0-516-01886-8 Subj: Activities – baking, cooking. Careers – chefs, cooks.

Tomecek, Steve. *Dirt* ill. by Nancy Woodman. National Geographic, 2002. ISBN 0-7922-8204-3 Subj: Nature. Science.

Stars ill. by Sachiko Yoshikawa. National Geographic, 2003. ISBN 0-7922-6955-1 Subj: Astronomy. Stars.

Tomfool. *see* Farjeon, Eleanor

Tomkins, Jasper. *The catalog* ill. by author. Green Tiger Pr., 1981. ISBN 0-914676-54-7 Subj: Animals. Humorous stories.

Tomlinson, Jill. *The owl who was afraid of the dark* ill. by Paul Howard. Candlewick, 2000. ISBN 0-7636-1562-5 Subj: Animals. Birds – owls. Emotions – fear. Night.

Tomlinson, Theresa. *Little stowaway* ill. by Jane Browne. Julia MacRae Books, 1998. ISBN 1-85681-691-5 Subj: Activities – traveling. Careers – fishermen. Sea & seashore.

Tompert, Ann. *Badger on his own* ill. by Diane de Groat. Crown, 1978. ISBN 0-517-53226-3 Subj: Animals – badgers. Birds – owls.

A carol for Christmas ill. by Laura Kelly. Macmillan, 1994. ISBN 0-02-789402-9 Subj: Animals – mice. Foreign lands – Austria. Holidays – Christmas. Songs.

Charlotte and Charles ill. by John Wallner. Crown, 1979. ISBN 0-517-53660-9 Subj: Giants. Middle Ages.

Grandfather Tang's story ill. by Robert Andrew Parker. Crown, 1990. ISBN 0-517-57272-9 Subj: Animals – foxes. Family life – grandfathers. Foreign lands – China.

The hungry black bag ill. by Jacqueline Chwast. Houghton Mifflin, 1999. ISBN 0-395-89418-2 Subj: Animals. Animals – goats. Behavior – greed. Behavior – stealing. Crime. Farms.

The jade horse, the cricket, and the peach stone ill. by Winson Trang. Boyds Mills, 1996. ISBN 1-56397-239-5 Subj: Folk & fairy tales. Foreign lands – China. Royalty – emperors.

Just a little bit ill. by Lynn Munsinger. Houghton Mifflin, 1993. ISBN 0-395-51527-0 Subj: Activities – playing. Animals – elephants. Animals – mice. Concepts. Cumulative tales.

Little Fox goes to the end of the world ill. by John Wallner. Crown, 1976. ISBN 0-517-52600-X Subj: Animals – foxes. Imagination.

Little Otter remembers and other stories ill. by John Wallner. Crown, 1977. ISBN 0-517-52751-0 Subj: Animals – otters. Family life – mothers. Memories, memory.

Nothing sticks like a shadow ill. by Lynn Munsinger. Houghton Mifflin, 1984. ISBN 0-395-35391-2 Subj: Animals – groundhogs. Animals – rabbits. Holidays – Groundhog Day. Shadows.

The pied piper of Peru ill. by Kestutis Kasparavicius. Boyds Mills, 2002. ISBN 1-56397-949-7 Subj: Animals – mice. Character traits – kindness to animals. Foreign lands – Peru. Religion.

Saint Nicholas ill. by Michael Garland. Boyds Mills, 2000. ISBN 1-56397-844-X Subj: Folk & fairy tales. Religion. Santa Claus.

Saint Patrick ill. by Michael Garland. Boyds Mills, 1998. ISBN 1-56397-659-5 Subj: Foreign lands – Ireland. Religion.

Savina, the gypsy dancer ill. by Dennis Nolan. Macmillan, 1991. ISBN 0-02-789205-0 Subj: Activities – dancing. Gypsies.

The silver whistle ill. by Beth Peck. Macmillan, 1988. ISBN 0-02-789160-7 Subj: Foreign lands – Mexico. Holidays – Christmas. Whistles.

The Tzar's bird ill. by Robert Rayevsky. Macmillan, 1990. ISBN 0-02-789401-0 Subj: Emotions – fear. Foreign lands – Russia. Royalty.

Will you come back for me? ill. by Robin Kramer. A. Whitman, 1988. ISBN 0-8075-9112-2 Subj: Behavior – needing someone. Dreams. Emotions – fear. School – first day. School – nursery.

Tooinsky, Izzi. *The turkey prince* ill. by Edwina White. Viking, 2001. ISBN 0-670-88872-9 Subj: Folk & fairy tales. Illness – mental illness. Royalty – princes. Self-concept.

Topek, Susan Remick. *A costume for Noah* ill. by Sally Springer. Kar-Ben Copies, 1995. ISBN 0-929371-91-7 Subj: Clothing. Family life – brothers & sisters. Family life – new sibling. Holidays – Purim. Jewish culture. School.

Shalom, Shabbat: a book for havdalah ill. by Shelly S. Ephraim. Kar-Ben Copies, 1998. ISBN 1-58013-010-0 Subj: Format, unusual – board books. Jewish culture. Religion. Senses.

Ten good rules ill. by Rosalyn Schanzer. Kar-Ben Copies, 1991. ISBN 0-929371-30-5 Subj: Religion – Moses.

Tord, Bijou Le. *see* Le Tord, Bijou

Torgersen, Don Arthur. *The girl who tricked the troll* ill. by Tom Dunnington. Childrens Pr., 1978. ISBN 0-516-03465-0 Subj: Farms. Mythical creatures – trolls.

The troll who lived in the lake ill. by Tom Dunnington. Childrens Pr., 1978. ISBN 0-516-03631-9 Subj: Ecology. Mythical creatures – trolls.

Tornborg, Pat. *The Sesame Street cookbook* ill. by Robert Dennis. Platt, 1978. ISBN 0-448-13035-1 Subj: Activities – baking, cooking. Puppets.

Tornqvist, Rita. *The Christmas carp* trans. from Swedish by Greta Kilburn; ill. by Marit Tornqvist. Farrar, 1990. ISBN 91-29-59784-6 Subj: Behavior – wishing. Family life. Holidays – Christmas.

Torre, Betty L. *The luminous pearl* ill. by Carol Inouye. Watts, 1990. ISBN 0-531-08490-6 Subj: Character traits – honesty. Character traits – kindness. Dragons. Folk & fairy tales. Foreign lands – China. Royalty.

Torres, Daniel. *Tom* ill. by author; English adapt. by Julie Simmons-Lynch. Viking, 1996. ISBN 0-670-86665-2 Subj: Cities, towns. Dinosaurs. Friendship.

Torres, Leyla. *Liliana's grandmothers* ill. by author. Farrar, 1998. ISBN 0-374-35105-8 Subj: Family life – grandmothers. Foreign lands – Latin America. Quilts.

Saturday sancocho ill. by author. Farrar, 1995. ISBN 0-374-36418-4 Subj: Activities – baking, cooking. Activities – trading. Family life – grandmothers. Food. Foreign lands – Colombia.

Torres, Melissa A. *The great Christmas tree celebration* ill. by Barbara Lanza. Scholastic, 2001. ISBN 0-439-28200-4 Subj: Format, unusual – toy & movable books. Holidays – Christmas. Trees.

Tortillas and lullabies = Tortillas y cancioncitas ill. by "Corazones Valientes"; trans. by Rebecca Hart. Greenwillow, 1998. ISBN 0-688-14629-5 Subj: Family life. Foreign lands – Central America. Foreign languages.

Towle, Faith M. *The magic cooking pot: a folktale of India* ill. by author. Houghton Mifflin, 1975. ISBN 0-395-20273-6 Subj: Folk & fairy tales. Food. Foreign lands – India. Magic.

Townley, Roderick. *Paul and Sebastian* (Escudie, René)

Townsend, Anita. *The kangaroo* ill. by Michael Atkinson. Watts, 1979. ISBN 0-531-09152-X Subj: Animals – kangaroos. Science.

Townsend, Emily Rose. *Arctic foxes* ill. with photos. Capstone, 2004. ISBN 0-7368-2356-5 Subj: Animals – foxes. Foreign lands – Arctic.

Deer ill. with photos. Capstone, 2004. ISBN 0-7368-2067-1 Subj: Animals – deer.

Owls ill. with photos. Capstone, 2004. ISBN 0-7368-2068-X Subj: Birds – owls.

Penguins ill. with photos. Capstone, 2004. ISBN 0-7368-2357-3 Subj: Birds – penguins. Foreign lands – Antarctic.

Polar bears ill. with photos. Capstone, 2004. ISBN 0-7368-2358-1 Subj: Animals – polar bears. Foreign lands – Arctic.

Seals ill. with photos. Capstone, 2004. ISBN 0-7368-2359-X Subj: Animals – seals. Sea & seashore.

Squirrels ill. with photos. Capstone, 2004. ISBN 0-7368-2069-8 Subj: Animals – squirrels.

Woodpeckers ill. with photos. Capstone, 2004. ISBN 0-7368-2070-1 Subj: Birds – woodpeckers.

Townsend, Kenneth. *Felix, the bald-headed lion* ill. by author. Delacorte, 1967. Subj: Animals – lions. Clothing. Emotions – embarrassment. Hair.

Townsend, Maryann. *Pop's secret* by Maryann Townsend & Ronnie Stern; ill. with photos. Addison-Wesley, 1980. ISBN 0-201-07707-8 Subj: Death. Emotions – grief. Family life – grandfathers.

Townson, Hazel. *Terrible Tuesday* ill. by Tony Ross. Morrow, 1986. ISBN 0-688-06244-X Subj: Emotions – fear. Family life. Imagination.

What on earth . . . ? ill. by Mary Rees. Little, 1991. ISBN 0-316-85138-8 Subj: Activities – playing. Family life – fathers. Imagination.

Toye, William. *Fire stealer* photos by Elizabeth Cleaver. Oxford Univ. Pr., 1988. ISBN 0-19-540515-3 Subj: Folk & fairy tales. Indians of North America – Algonquin.

How summer came to Canada photos by Elizabeth Cleaver. Walck, 1969. ISBN 0-8098-1153-7 Subj: Folk & fairy tales. Foreign lands – Canada. Indians of North America – Micmac. Seasons – summer. Seasons – winter.

The loon's necklace photos by Elizabeth Cleaver. Oxford Univ. Pr., 1988. ISBN 0-19-540278-2 Subj: Folk & fairy tales. Foreign lands – Canada. Indians of North America.

The mountain goats of Temlaham photos by Elizabeth Cleaver. Walck, 1969. ISBN 0-8098-1154-5 Subj: Folk & fairy tales. Foreign lands – Canada. Indians of North America – Tsimshian.

Tracqui, Valérie. *The dog* photos by Marie-Luce Hubert & Jean-Louis Klein. Charlesbridge, 2002. ISBN 1-57091-452-4 Subj: Animals – dogs. Pets.

The horse photos by Gilles Delaborde. Charlesbridge, 2001. Subj: Animals – horses, ponies. U.S. history – frontier & pioneer life.

The ladybug photos by Patrick Lorne. Charlesbridge, 2002. ISBN 1-57091-453-2 Subj: Insects – ladybugs. Science.

Trains created by Gallimard Jeunesse & James Prunier; ill. by James Prunier; American text by Wendy Barish. Scholastic, 1998. ISBN 0-590-38156-3 Subj: Trains.

Trân-Khánh-Tuyê. *The little weaver of Thái-Yên Village* trans. from Vietnamese by Christopher N. H. Jenkins & author; ill. by Nancy Hom. Children's Book Pr., 1987. ISBN 0-89239-030-1 Subj: Activities – weaving. Foreign lands – Vietnam. Language.

Trapani, Iza. *Baa baa black sheep* ill. by author. Whispering Coyote, 2001. ISBN 1-58089-070-9 Subj: Animals. Animals – sheep. Friendship. Humorous stories. Nursery rhymes.

Baa baa black sheep [board book] ill. by author. Whispering Coyote, 2002. ISBN 1-58089-089-X Subj: Animals. Animals – sheep. Format, unusual – board books. Friendship. Humorous stories. Nursery rhymes.

How much is that doggie in the window? ill. by author; words & music by Bob Merrill. G. Stevens, 1999. ISBN 0-8368-2486-5; 1-58089-031-8 [board book] Subj: Animals – dogs. Family life. Format, unusual – board books. Pets. Songs.

I'm a little teapot ill. by author. Whispering Coyote, 1996. ISBN 1-87908-599-2 Subj: Foreign lands. Imagination. Music. Participation. Songs.

The itsy bitsy spider ill. by author. G. Stevens, 1996. ISBN 0-8368-1550-5 Subj: Character traits – persistence. Music. Nursery rhymes. Songs. Spiders.

Mary had a little lamb (Hale, Sarah Josepha Buell)

Mary had a little lamb [board book] (Hale, Sarah Josepha Buell)

Row, row, row your boat ill. by author. Whispering Coyote, 1999. ISBN 1-58089-022-9 Subj: Animals. Animals – bears. Boats, ships. Family life. Pets. Rhyming text. Weather – storms.

Shoo fly! ill. by author. Whispering Coyote, 2000. ISBN 1-58089-052-0 Subj: Animals – mice. Family life. Insects – flies. Music. Songs.

What am I? ill. by author. Whispering Coyote, 1992. ISBN 1-879085-76-3 Subj: Animals. Games. Rhyming text.

Tredez, Alain. *see* Trez, Alain

Tredez, Denise. *see* Trez, Denise

Tregebov, Rhea. *What-if Sara* ill. by Leanne Franson. Second Story, 1999. ISBN 1-896764-22-3 Subj: Character traits – helpfulness. Imagination. Immigrants.

Treherne, Katie Thamer. *The little mermaid* (Andersen, H. C. [Hans Christian])

Trelease, Jim. *Daddy poems* (Micklos, John)

Trent, Robbie. *The first Christmas* ill. by Marc Simont. HarperCollins, 1990, c1948. Subj: Holidays – Christmas. Religion – Nativity. Rhyming text.

Trenter, Anna. *Little Bear's Christmas* (Landa, Norbert)

Tresselt, Alvin R. *Autumn harvest* ill. by Roger Antoine Duvoisin. Lothrop, 1951. ISBN 0-688-51155-4 Subj: Holidays – Thanksgiving. Seasons – fall.

The beaver pond ill. by Roger Antoine Duvoisin. Lothrop, 1970. Subj: Animals – beavers. Ecology.

The dead tree ill. by Charles Robinson. Parents' Magazine Pr., 1972. ISBN 0-819-30564-2 Subj: Ecology. Trees.

The fisherman under the sea (Matsutani, Miyoko)

Follow the wind ill. by Roger Antoine Duvoisin. Lothrop, 1950. Subj: Rhyming text. Weather – wind.

Frog in the well ill. by Roger Antoine Duvoisin. Lothrop, 1958. Subj: Frogs & toads.

The gift of the tree ill. by Henri Sorensen. Lothrop, 1992. Original title: The dead tree. ISBN 0-688-10685-4 Subj: Ecology. Forest, woods. Trees.

Hi, Mister Robin ill. by Roger Antoine Duvoisin. Lothrop, 1950. ISBN 0-688-51168-6 Subj: Birds – robins. Family life. Seasons – spring.

Hide and seek fog ill. by Roger Antoine Duvoisin. Lothrop, 1965. ISBN 0-688-51169-4 Subj: Caldecott award honor books. Sea & seashore. Weather – fog.

How far is far? ill. by Ward Brackett. Parents' Magazine Pr., 1964. Subj: Concepts – distance. Science.

I saw the sea come in ill. by Roger Antoine Duvoisin. Lothrop, 1954. Subj: Behavior – solitude. Sea & seashore.

It's time now! ill. by Roger Antoine Duvoisin. Lothrop, 1969. Subj: Cities, towns. Seasons.

Johnny Maple-Leaf ill. by Roger Antoine Duvoisin. Lothrop, 1948. Subj: Seasons. Seasons – fall. Trees.

The mitten: an old Ukrainian folktale ill. by Yaroslava. Lothrop, 1989, c1964. Adapt. by Alvin Tresselt from the version by E. Rachev. ISBN 0-606-04277-6 Subj: Animals. Folk & fairy tales. Foreign lands – Ukraine.

The rabbit story ill. by Carolyn Ewing. Lothrop, 1989. ISBN 0-688-08651-9 Subj: Animals – rabbits.

Rabbit story ill. by Leonard Weisgard. Lothrop, 1957. Subj: Animals – rabbits.

Rain drop splash ill. by Leonard Weisgard. Lothrop, 1946. ISBN 0-688-51165-1 Subj: Caldecott award honor books. Cumulative tales. Science. Weather – rain.

Smallest elephant in the world ill. by Milton Glaser. Knopf, 1959. ISBN 0-394-90763-9 Subj: Animals – elephants. Character traits – smallness. Circus.

Sun up ill. by Roger Antoine Duvoisin. Lothrop, 1949. Subj: Farms. Sun. Weather.

Sun up ill. by Henri Sorensen. Lothrop, 1991. ISBN 0-688-08657-8 Subj: Farms. Sun. Weather.

Wake up, city! ill. by Carolyn Ewing. Lothrop, 1989. ISBN 0-688-08653-5 Subj: Cities, towns. Morning.

Wake up, farm! ill. by Roger Antoine Duvoisin. Lothrop, 1955. ISBN 0-688-51162-7 Subj: Animals. Farms. Morning. Noise, sounds.

Wake up, farm! ill. by Carolyn Ewing. Lothrop, 1991. ISBN 0-688-08655-1 Subj: Animals. Farms. Morning. Noise, sounds.

What did you leave behind? ill. by Roger Antoine Duvoisin. Lothrop, 1978. ISBN 0-688-51829-X Subj: Emotions.

White snow, bright snow ill. by Roger Antoine Duvoisin. Lothrop, 1988, c1947. ISBN 0-688-51161-9 Subj: Caldecott award books. Weather – snow.

The wind and Peter ill. by Garry McKenzie. Oxford Univ. Pr., 1948. Subj: Weather – wind.

The witch's magic cloth (Matsutani, Miyoko)

The world in the candy egg ill. by Roger Antoine Duvoisin. Lothrop, 1967. Subj: Eggs. Holidays – Easter. Magic.

Trevelyan, Kathy. *Don't be surprised!* ill. by Haydn Cornner. Dial, 1997. ISBN 0-8037-2282-6 Subj: Activities – traveling. Dragons. Format, unusual – toy & movable books. Magic.

Trez, Alain. *Good night, Veronica* (Trez, Denise)

The little knight's dragon (Trez, Denise)

Maila and the flying carpet (Trez, Denise)

Rabbit country (Trez, Denise)

The royal hiccups (Trez, Denise)

Trez, Denise. *Good night, Veronica* by Denise & Alain Trez; trans. by Douglas McKee; ill. by authors. Viking, 1968. Subj: Bedtime. Dreams. Sleep.

The little knight's dragon by Denise & Alain Trez; ill. by authors. Collins-World, 1963. Subj: Dragons. Knights.

Maila and the flying carpet by Denise & Alain Trez; trans. by Douglas McKee; ill. by authors. Viking, 1969. ISBN 0-670-45107-X Subj: Activities – flying. Foreign lands – India. Magic. Royalty.

Rabbit country by Denise & Alain Trez; ill. by authors. Viking, 1966. Subj: Animals – rabbits.

The royal hiccups by Denise & Alain Trez; trans. by Douglas McKee; ill. by authors. Viking, 1965. Subj: Emotions – fear. Hiccups. Royalty.

Trimble, Marcia. *Flower Green* ill. by Jill Dubin. Images Pr., 2002. ISBN 1-891577-67-0 Subj: Concepts – color. Flowers. Seasons.

Hello sun ill. by Susan Arciero. Images Pr., 2000. ISBN 1-891577-50-6 Subj: Activities – photographing. Activities – traveling. Animals – lions. Foreign lands – Africa.

Malinda Martha and her stepping stones ill. by Susi Grell. Images Pr., 1999. ISBN 1-891577-72-7 Subj: Activities – playing. Rocks. Sea & seashore.

Moonbeams for Santa ill. by Sid Bingham. Images Pr., 2001. ISBN 1-891577-89-1 Subj: Holidays – Christmas. Moon. Rhyming text. Santa Claus.

Peppy's shadow ill. by Will Pellegrini. Images Pr., 2003. ISBN 1-891577-70-0 Subj: Animals – dogs. Puppets. Theater.

Trimble, Patti. *Lost!* ill. by Daniel Moreton. Harcourt, 2000. ISBN 0-15-202667-3 Subj: Behavior – lost. Insects – ants.

What day is it? ill. by Daniel Moreton. Harcourt, 2000. ISBN 0-15-202500-6 Subj: Birthdays. Friendship. Insects – ants. Parties.

Trimby, Elisa. *Mr. Plum's paradise* ill. by author. Lothrop, 1977. ISBN 0-688-51797-8 Subj: Cities, towns. Gardens, gardening.

Trinca, Rod. *One woolly wombat* by Rod Trinca & Kerry Argent; ill. by Kerry Argent. Kane/Miller, 1985. ISBN 0-916291-00-6 Subj: Animals. Counting, numbers. Foreign lands – Australia.

Tripp, Paul. *The strawman who smiled by mistake* ill. by Wendy Watson. Doubleday, 1967. Subj: Emotions – happiness. Farms. Friendship. Scarecrows.

Tripp, Valerie. *Happy, happy Mother's Day* ill. by Sandra Kalthoff Martin. Childrens Pr., 1989. ISBN 0-516-01521-4 Subj: Animals. Holidays – Mother's Day. Rhyming text.

Sillyhen's big surprise ill. by Sandra Kalthoff Martin. Childrens Pr., 1989. ISBN 0-516-01522-2 Subj: Birds – chickens. Rhyming text.

Tripp, Wallace. *My Uncle Podger* ill. by author. Little, 1975. Based on a passage from Three men in a boat (to say nothing of the dog) by Jerome Klapka Jerome. ISBN 0-316-46180-6 Subj: Animals – rabbits. Family life – aunts, uncles. Humorous stories.

The tale of a pig: a caucasian folktale adapt. & ill. by Wallace Tripp. McGraw-Hill, 1968. Subj: Animals – pigs. Folk & fairy tales.

Trist, Glenda. *A child's book of prayers* ill. with photos. DK, 1999. ISBN 0-7894-3976-X Subj: Religion.

Trivas, Irene. *Annie . . . Anya: a month in Moscow* ill. by author. Watts, 1992. ISBN 0-531-08602-X Subj: Foreign lands – Russia. Friendship.

Emma's Christmas ill. by author. Watts, 1988. ISBN 0-531-08380-2 Subj: Holidays – Christmas. Songs. Weddings.

Trivizas, Eugenios. *The three little wolves and the big bad pig* ill. by Helen Oxenbury. McElderry, 1993. ISBN 0-689-50569-8 Subj: Animals – pigs. Animals – wolves. Behavior – misbehavior. Folk & fairy tales. Homes, houses.

Troll, Ray. *Sharkabet* ill. by author. WestWinds, 2002. ISBN 1-55868-518-9 Subj: ABC books. Fish – sharks.

Trosclair. *Cajun night before Christmas* ed. by Howard Jacobs; ill. by James Rice. Pelican, 1992. ISBN 0-88289-940-6 Subj: Cumulative tales. Ethnic groups in the U.S. – Cajuns. Holidays – Christmas. Poetry. Reptiles – alligators, crocodiles. Santa Claus.

Trottier, Maxine. *Dreamstones* ill. by Stella East. Stoddart, 1999. ISBN 0-7737-3191-1 Subj: Animals. Bedtime. Behavior – lost. Dreams. Foreign lands – Arctic. Indians of North America – Inuit.

Flags ill. by Paul Morin. Stoddart, 1999. ISBN 0-7737-3136-9 Subj: Ethnic groups in the U.S. – Japanese Americans. Gardens, gardening. Plants. U.S. history. War.

Little dog Moon ill. by Laura Fernandez & Rick Jacobson. Stoddart, 2000. ISBN 0-7737-3220-9 Subj: Activities – traveling. Animals – dogs. Character traits – freedom. Character traits – helpfulness. Foreign lands – Tibet. Religion.

Prairie willow ill. by Laura Fernandez & Rick Jacobson. Stoddart, 1998. ISBN 0-7737-3067-2 Subj: Careers – farmers. Death. Dreams. Emotions – grief. Family life. Foreign lands – Canada. Trees.

A safe place ill. by Judith Friedman. A. Whitman, 1997. ISBN 0-8075-7212-8 Subj: Child abuse. Family life – fathers. Family life – mothers. Safety.

Storm at Batoche ill. by John Mantha. Stoddart, 2000. ISBN 0-7737-3248-9 Subj: Behavior – lost. Foreign lands – Canada. Weather – blizzards.

The tiny kite of Eddie Wing ill. by Al Van Mil. Kane/Miller, 1996. ISBN 0-916291-66-9 Subj: Ethnic groups in the U.S. – Chinese Americans. Imagination. Kites.

The walking stick ill. by Annouchka G. Galouchko. Stoddart, 1999. ISBN 0-7737-3101-6 Subj: Ethnic groups in the U.S. – Vietnamese Americans. Immigrants. Religion.

Troughton, Joanna. *How rabbit stole the fire* ill. by adapt. HarperCollins, 1986. ISBN 0-87226-040-2 Subj: Animals – rabbits. Fire. Folk & fairy tales – pourquoi tales. Indians of North America.

How the birds changed their feathers: a South American Indian folk tale ill. by adapt. HarperCollins, 1986. ISBN 0-87226-080-1 Subj: Birds. Concepts – color. Folk & fairy tales – pourquoi tales. Foreign lands – South America.

Make-believe tales ill. by reteller. Peter Bedrick, 1991. ISBN 0-87226-451-3 Subj: Animals. Folk & fairy tales. Foreign lands – Burma.

Mouse-Deer's market ill. by adapt. HarperCollins, 1984. ISBN 0-911745-63-7 Subj: Animals. Animals – deer. Character traits – cleverness.

The quail's egg: a folk tale from Sri Lanka ill. by author. Peter Bedrick, 1988. ISBN 0-87226-185-9 Subj: Birds – quail. Cumulative tales. Eggs. Folk & fairy tales. Foreign lands – Sri Lanka.

Tortoise's dream: an African folk tale ill. by adapt. HarperCollins, 1986. ISBN 0-87226-039-9 Subj: Dreams. Folk & fairy tales. Foreign lands – Africa. Reptiles – turtles, tortoises.

What made Tiddalik laugh: an Australian Aborigine folk tale ill. by adapt. HarperCollins, 1986. ISBN 0-87226-081-X Subj: Folk & fairy tales. Foreign lands – Australia. Frogs & toads.

Who will be the sun? ill. by adapt. HarperCollins, 1986. ISBN 0-87226-038-0 Subj: Creation. Folk & fairy tales. Indians of North America – Kutenai. Sun.

Troupe, Quincy. *Little Stevie Wonder* ill. by Lisa Cohen. Houghton, 2005. ISBN 0-618-34060-2 Subj: Careers – musicians. Ethnic groups in the U.S. – African Americans. Handicaps – blindness. Poetry.

Trucks ill. with photos. Macmillan, 1991. ISBN 0-689-71405-X Subj: Transportation. Trucks.

Trumbull, Suzanne. *Upside-downers: more pictures to stretch the imagination* (Anno, Mitsumasa)

Tryon, Leslie. *Albert's alphabet* ill. by author. Atheneum, 1991. ISBN 0-689-31642-9 Subj: ABC books. Activities – making things. Birds – ducks. School.

Albert's birthday ill. by author. Atheneum, 1999. ISBN 0-689-82296-0 Subj: Animals. Birds – ducks. Birthdays. Parties.

Albert's Christmas ill. by author. Atheneum, 1997. ISBN 0-689-81034-2 Subj: Animals. Birds – ducks. Holidays – Christmas. Rhyming text. Santa Claus.

Albert's Halloween: the case of the stolen pumpkins ill. by author. Atheneum, 1998. ISBN 0-689-81136-5 Subj: Animals. Birds – ducks. Careers – detectives. Holidays – Halloween. Mystery stories.

Albert's play ill. by author. Atheneum, 1992. ISBN 0-689-31525-2 Subj: Animals. Rhyming text. Theater.

Patsy says ill. by author. Atheneum, 2001. ISBN 0-689-82297-9 Subj: Animals. Animals – pigs. Etiquette. School.

Tschiegg, Anne-Sophie. *Mommy time* (Brami, Elisbeth)

Tseng, Grace. *White tiger, blue serpent* ill. by Jean & Mou-Sien Tseng. Lothrop, 1999. ISBN 0-688-12516-6 Subj: Activities – weaving. Animals – tigers. Folk & fairy tales. Foreign lands – China. Magic. Reptiles – snakes.

Tsow, Ming. *A day with Ling* photos by Christopher Cormack. Hamish Hamilton, 1983. ISBN 0-241-10828-4 Subj: Family life.

Tsubakiyama, Margaret (Holloway). *Mei-Mei loves the morning* ill. by Cornelius Van Wright & Ying-Hwa Hu. A. Whitman, 1999. ISBN 0-8075-5039-6 Subj: Family life – grandparents. Foreign lands – China. Health & fitness – exercise.

Tsultim, Yeshe. *The mouse king: a story from Tibet* ill. by Kusho Ralla. Penguin, 1979. ISBN 0-14-030804-0 Subj: Animals – mice. Folk & fairy tales. Foreign lands – Tibet.

Tsutsui, Yoriko. *Anna in charge* ill. by Akiko Hayashi. Viking, 1989. ISBN 0-670-81672-8 Subj: Activities – babysitting. Behavior – lost. Emotions – fear. Family life.

Anna's secret friend ill. by Akiko Hayashi. Viking, 1987. ISBN 0-670-81670-1 Subj: Family life. Friendship. Moving.

Before the picnic ill. by Akiko Hayashi. Putnam, 1987. ISBN 0-399-21458-5 Subj: Activities – picnicking. Family life.

Tuber, Joel. *The steadfast tin soldier* (Andersen, H. C. [Hans Christian])

The ugly duckling (Andersen, H. C. [Hans Christian])

Tucker, Kathleen. *The little bear who forgot* (Chevalier, Christa)

My mother never listens to me (Sharmat, Marjorie Weinman)

Tucker, Kathy. *Do cowboys ride bikes?* ill. by Nadine Bernard Westcott. A. Whitman, 1997. ISBN 0-8075-1693-7 Subj: Character traits – questioning. Country. Cowboys, cowgirls. Rhyming text.

Do knights take naps? ill. by Nick Sharratt. A. Whitman, 2000. ISBN 0-8075-1695-3 Subj: Knights. Middle Ages. Rhyming text. Sleep.

Do pirates take baths? ill. by Nadine Bernard Westcott. A. Whitman, 1994. ISBN 0-8075-1696-1 Subj: Pirates. Rhyming text. Sea & seashore.

The leprechaun in the basement ill. by John Sandford. A. Whitman, 1999. ISBN 0-8075-4450-7 Subj: Clothing – shoes. Holidays – St. Patrick's Day. Mythical creatures – leprechauns.

The seven Chinese sisters ill. by Grace Lin. A. Whitman, 2003. ISBN 0-8075-7309-4 Subj: Dragons. Family life – sisters. Foreign lands – China.

Tucker, Kiyoko. *The boy and the bird* (Fujita, Tamao)

Tucker, Nicholas. *Mother Goose abroad: nursery rhymes* ill. by Trevor Stubley. Crowell, 1974. ISBN 0-2410-2464-1 Subj: Nursery rhymes.

Tucker, Sian. *A is for astronaut* ill. by author. Orchard, 1995. ISBN 1-852138-19-X Subj: ABC books. Format, unusual – toy & movable books.

At home ill. by author. S&S, 1991. ISBN 0-671-73399-0 Subj: Babies. Family life. Format, unusual – board books.

Going out ill. by author. S&S, 1991. ISBN 0-671-73397-4 Subj: Babies. Format, unusual – board books. Nature.

My clothes ill. by author. S&S, 1991. ISBN 0-671-73396-6 Subj: Babies. Clothing. Format, unusual – board books.

My toys ill. by author. S&S, 1991. ISBN 0-671-73398-2 Subj: Babies. Format, unusual – board books. Toys.

Tucker, Stephen. *The time it took Tom* (Sharratt, Nick)

Tudor, Bethany. *Samuel's tree house* ill. by author. Collins-World, 1979. ISBN 0-529-05522-8 Subj: Birds – ducks. Friendship. Homes, houses. Toys. Trees.

Skiddycock Pond ill. by author. Lippincott, 1965. Subj: Birds – ducks. Boats, ships.

Tudor, Tasha. *Around the year* ill. by author. Walck, 1957. Subj: Days of the week, months of the year. Poetry. Seasons.

Corgiville fair ill. by author. Crowell, 1971. ISBN 0-690-21791-9 Subj: Animals – goats. Fairs, festivals. Mythical creatures – trolls.

The doll's Christmas ill. by author. S&S, 1999. ISBN 0-689-82809-8 Subj: Holidays – Christmas. Parties. Toys – dolls.

Junior's tune ill. by author. Holiday, 1980. ISBN 0-8234-0411-0 Subj: Music. Musical instruments – trumpets. Sibling rivalry.

Mildred and the mummy ill. by author. Holiday, 1980. ISBN 0-8234-0372-6 Subj: Libraries.

Miss Kiss and the nasty beast ill. by author. Holiday, 1979. ISBN 0-8234-0355-6 Subj: Emotions – love.

More prayers ill. by author. McKay, 1967. ISBN 0-8098-1954-6 Subj: Religion.

1 is one ill. by author. Walck, 1956. ISBN 0-02-688535-2 Subj: Caldecott award honor books. Counting, numbers.

Pumpkin moonshine ill. by author. S&S, 2000. ISBN 0-689-82846-2 Subj: Farms. Food. Holidays – Halloween.

Snow before Christmas ill. by author. Oxford Univ. Pr., 1941. Subj: Holidays – Christmas. Seasons – winter. Weather – snow.

A tale for Easter ill. by author. S&S, 2001, c1941. ISBN 0-689-82844-6 Subj: Animals. Dreams. Eggs. Holidays – Easter.

Tufts, Mary L. *The wee kitten who sucked her thumb* ill. by Lucinda McQueen. Platt, 1986. ISBN 0-448-19076-1 Subj: Animals. Animals – cats. Thumb sucking.

Tullet, Hervé. *Night / day* ill. by author. Little, 1999. ISBN 0-316-84244-3 Subj: Concepts – opposites. Format, unusual – toy & movable books. Language.

Tulloch, Richard. *Danny in the toybox* ill. by Armin Greder. Scholastic, 1990. ISBN 0-8689-6610-X Subj: Behavior – hiding. Emotions – anger. Family life.

Stories from our house ill. by Julie Vivas. Cambridge Univ. Pr., 1987. ISBN 0-521-33485-3 Subj: Family life. Humorous stories.

Tulloch, Shirley. *Who made me?* ill. by Cathie Felstead. Augsburg Fortress, 2000. ISBN 0-8066-4045-6 Subj: Animals. Foreign lands – Africa. Religion.

Tune, Suelyn Ching. *How Maui slowed the sun* ill. by Robin Yoko Burningham. Univ. of Hawaii Pr., 1988. ISBN 0-8248-1083-X Subj: Folk & fairy tales. Hawaii. Magic.

Tunnell, Michael O. *Halloween pie* ill. by Kevin O'Malley. Lothrop, 1999. ISBN 0-688-16805-1 Subj: Food. Holidays. Magic. Monsters. Witches.

The joke's on George ill. by Kathy Osborn. Boyds Mills, 2001. ISBN 1-56397-970-5 Subj: Careers – artists. Friendship. Museums.

Mailing May ill. by Ted Rand. Greenwillow, 1997. ISBN 0-688-12879-3 Subj: Careers – postal workers. Family life – grandparents. Trains. Transportation. U.S. history.

Turbak, Gary. *Mountain animals in danger* ill. by Lawrence Ormsby. Northland, 1994. ISBN 0-87358-573-9 Subj: Animals – endangered animals.

Ocean animals in danger ill. by Lawrence Ormsby. Northland, 1994. ISBN 0-87358-574-7 Subj: Animals – endangered animals. Sea & seashore.

Türk, Hanne. *Goodnight Max* ill. by author. Firefly, 1983. ISBN 0-907234-39-9 Subj: Animals – mice. Bedtime. Wordless.

Happy birthday Max ill. by author. Alphabet Pr., 1984. ISBN 0-907234-42-2 Subj: Animals – mice. Birthdays. Wordless.

Max packs ill. by author. Alphabet Pr., 1984. ISBN 0-907234-40-2 Subj: Activities – traveling. Animals – mice. Wordless.

Max the artlover ill. by author. Alphabet Pr., 1983. ISBN 0-907234-25-9 Subj: Animals – mice. Art. Wordless.

Max versus the cube ill. by author. Alphabet Pr., 1982. Subj: Animals – mice. Problem solving. Riddles & jokes. Wordless.

Merry Christmas Max ill. by author. Firefly, 1983. ISBN 0-907234-37-2 Subj: Animals – mice. Holidays – Christmas. Wordless.

Rainy day Max ill. by author. Alphabet Pr., 1983. ISBN 0-907234-24-0 Subj: Activities – walking. Animals – mice. Weather – rain. Wordless.

Raking leaves with Max ill. by author. Firefly, 1983. ISBN 0-907234-38-0 Subj: Activities – working. Animals – mice. Wordless.

The rope skips Max ill. by author. Alphabet Pr., 1982. Subj: Activities. Animals – mice. Wordless.

Snapshot Max ill. by author. Alphabet Pr., 1984. ISBN 0-907234-41-2 Subj: Activities – photographing. Animals – mice. Wordless.

A surprise for Max ill. by author. Alphabet Pr., 1982. ISBN 0-907234-18-6 Subj: Animals – mice. Problem solving. Wordless.

Turkel, Pauline. *see* Kesselman, Judi R.

Turkle, Brinton. *The adventures of Obadiah* ill. by author. Viking, 1977. ISBN 0-670-10614-3 Subj: Behavior – lying. Character traits – honesty. Ethnic groups in the U.S. – Amish. U.S. history.

Deep in the forest ill. by author. Dutton, 1976. ISBN 0-525-28617-9 Subj: Animals – bears. Folk & fairy tales. Wordless.

Do not open ill. by author. Dutton, 1981. ISBN 0-525-28785-X Subj: Animals – cats. Behavior – trickery. Behavior – wishing. Monsters. Sea & seashore.

The magic of Millicent Musgrave ill. by author. Viking, 1967. Subj: Magic.

Obadiah the Bold ill. by author. Viking, 1965. ISBN 0-14-050233-5 Subj: Activities – playing. Behavior – growing up. Ethnic groups in the U.S. – Amish. Sea & seashore. U.S. history.

Rachel and Obadiah ill. by author. Dutton, 1978. ISBN 0-525-38020-5 Subj: Behavior – sharing. Ethnic groups in the U.S. – Amish. Money. Sibling rivalry.

The sky dog ill. by author. Viking, 1969. ISBN 0-670-65049-8 Subj: Animals – dogs. Imagination. Sea & seashore. Weather – clouds.

Thy friend, Obadiah ill. by author. Viking, 1969. ISBN 0-670-71229-9 Subj: Birds – seagulls. Caldecott award honor books. Character traits – kindness to animals. Ethnic groups in the U.S. – Amish. Seasons – winter. U.S. history.

Turnage, Sheila. *Trout the magnificent* ill. by Janet Stevens. Harcourt, 1984. ISBN 0-15-290962-1 Subj: Behavior – dissatisfaction. Fish. Self-concept.

Turnbull, Ann. *Rob goes a-hunting* ill. by Denise Teasdale. Watts, 1990. ISBN 0-531-08477-9 Subj: Animals – dogs. Behavior – lost. Sports – hunting.

The sand horse ill. by Michael Foreman. Atheneum, 1989. ISBN 0-689-31581-3 Subj: Careers – artists. Sand. Sea & seashore.

The tapestry cats ill. by Carol Morley. Little, 1992. ISBN 0-316-85626-6 Subj: Animals – cats. Behavior – wishing. Birthdays. Fairies. Royalty – princesses. Royalty – queens.

Too tired ill. by Emma Chichester Clark. Harcourt, 1994. ISBN 0-15-200549-8 Subj: Animals. Animals – sloths. Religion – Noah. Weather – floods. Weather – rain.

Turner, Ann Warren. *Abe Lincoln remembers* ill. by Wendell Minor. HarperCollins, 2001. ISBN 0-06-027578-2 Subj: Memories, memory. U.S. history.

Angel hide and seek ill. by Lois Ehlert. HarperCollins, 1998. ISBN 0-06-027086-1 Subj: Angels. Picture puzzles. Religion. Rhyming text.

The Christmas house ill. by Nancy Edwards Calder. HarperCollins, 1994. ISBN 0-06-023429-6 Subj: Family life. Holidays – Christmas. Homes, houses. Poetry.

Dakota dugout ill. by Ronald Himler. Macmillan, 1985. ISBN 0-02-789700-1 Subj: Farms. U.S. history – frontier & pioneer life.

Dust for dinner ill. by Robert Barrett. HarperCollins, 1995. ISBN 0-06-023377-X Subj: Farms. Moving. Poverty. U.S. history.

Hedgehog for breakfast ill. by Lisa McCue. Macmillan, 1989. ISBN 0-02-789241-7 Subj: Animals – foxes. Animals – hedgehogs. Behavior – misunderstanding.

In the heart ill. by Salley Mavor. HarperCollins, 2001. ISBN 0-06-023731-7 Subj: Day. Poetry.

Let's be animals ill. by Rick Brown. HarperFestival, 1998. ISBN 0-694-01154-1 Subj: Activities – playing. Animals. Imagination.

Nettie's trip south ill. by Ronald Himler. Macmillan, 1987. ISBN 0-02-789240-9 Subj: Activities – traveling. Behavior – disbelief. Ethnic groups in the U.S. – African Americans. Family life.

Red flower goes West ill. by Dennis Nolan. Hyperion, 1999. ISBN 0-7868-2253-8 Subj: Family life. Flowers. U.S. history – frontier & pioneer life.

Secrets from the dollhouse ill. by Raúl Colón. HarperCollins, 2000. ISBN 0-06-024567-0 Subj: Poetry. Toys – dolls.

Shaker hearts ill. by Wendell Minor. HarperCollins, 1997. ISBN 0-06-025370-3 Subj: Religion. Rhyming text. U.S. history.

Stars for Sarah ill. by Mary Teichman. HarperCollins, 1991. ISBN 0-06-026187-0 Subj: Family life – mothers. Moving.

Through moon and stars and night skies ill. by James Graham Hale. HarperCollins, 1990. ISBN 0-06-026190-0 Subj: Adoption.

Tickle a pickle ill. by Karen Ann Weinhaus. Macmillan, 1986. ISBN 0-02-789280-8 Subj: Poetry.

When Mr. Jefferson came to Philadelphia ill. by Mark Hess. HarperCollins, 2003. ISBN 0-06-027580-4 Subj: U.S. history. War.

Turner, Barbara J. *Out and about at the orchestra* ill. by Anne McMullen. Picture Window, 2003. ISBN 1-4048-0040-9 Subj: Careers – musicians. Music. Musical instruments – orchestras.

Turner, Charles. *The turtle and the moon* ill. by Melissa Bay Mathis. Dutton, 1991. ISBN 0-525-44659-1 Subj: Activities – playing. Moon. Reptiles – turtles, tortoises.

Turner, Ethel. *Walking to school* ill. by Peter Gouldthorpe. Watts, 1989. ISBN 0-531-08399-3 Subj: Activities – walking. Emotions. Foreign lands – Australia. Poetry. School – first day.

Turner, Gwenda. *Colors* ill. by author. Viking, 1990. ISBN 0-670-82552-2 Subj: Concepts – color.

Once upon a time ill. by author. Viking, 1990. ISBN 0-670-82551-4 Subj: Family life. Time.

Over on the farm ill. by author. Viking, 1994. ISBN 0-670-85437-9 Subj: Animals. Counting, numbers. Farms. Foreign lands – New Zealand. Rhyming text.

Playbook ill. by author. Viking, 1986. ISBN 0-670-80660-9 Subj: School.

Shapes ill. by author. Viking, 1991. ISBN 0-670-83744-X Subj: Concepts – shape.

Turner, Josie. *see* Crawford, Phyllis

Turner, Nancy Byrd. *When young Melissa sweeps* ill. by Debrah Santini. Peachtree, 1998. ISBN 1-56145-157-6 Subj: Activities – dancing. Activities – working. Poetry.

Turner, Pamela S. *Hachiko* ill. by Yan Nascimbene. Houghton, 2004. ISBN 0-618-14094-8 Subj: Animals – dogs. Death. Foreign lands – Japan. Pets.

Turner, Priscilla. *Among the odds and evens* ill. by Whitney Turner. Farrar, 1999. ISBN 0-374-30343-6 Subj: ABC books. Counting, numbers. Etiquette.

Turner, Sandy. *Grow up* ill. by author. Cotler, 2003. ISBN 0-06-000954-3 Subj: Behavior – growing up. Careers. Imagination.

Otto's trunk ill. by author. Cotler, 2003. ISBN 0-06-000957-8 Subj: Animals – elephants. Concepts – size. Self-concept.

Silent night ill. by author. Atheneum, 2001. ISBN 0-689-84156-6 Subj: Animals – dogs. Holidays – Christmas. Noise, sounds. Santa Claus.

Turska, Krystyna. *The magician of Cracow* ill. by author. Greenwillow, 1975. ISBN 0-688-84010-8 Subj: Character traits – ambition. Devil. Folk & fairy tales. Foreign lands – Poland. Magic. Moon.

The woodcutter's duck ill. by author. Macmillan, 1972. Subj: Birds – ducks. Character traits – kindness to animals. Folk & fairy tales. Foreign lands – Poland. Frogs & toads.

Tusa, Tricia. *Bunnies in my head* ill. by author & young patients at the M.D. Anderson Cancer Center in Houston, Texas. Univ. of Texas M. D. Anderson Cancer Center, 1998. ISBN 0-9664551-8-5 Subj: Art. Children as illustrators. Illness – cancer. Imagination.

Camilla's new hairdo ill. by author. Farrar, 1991. ISBN 0-374-31021-1 Subj: Character traits – individuality. Hair. Imagination. Problem solving.

Chicken ill. by author. Macmillan, 1986. ISBN 0-02-789320-0 Subj: Behavior – misunderstanding. Birds – chickens. Pets. Self-concept.

Libby's new glasses ill. by author. Holiday, 1984. ISBN 0-8234-0523-0 Subj: Glasses. Self-concept. Senses – sight.

Maebelle's suitcase ill. by author. Macmillan, 1987. ISBN 0-02-789250-6 Subj: Birds. Clothing. Old age.

Miranda ill. by author. Macmillan, 1985. ISBN 0-02-789520-3 Subj: Character traits – stubbornness. Music. Musical instruments – pianos.

Sherman and Pearl ill. by author. Macmillan, 1989. ISBN 0-02-789542-4 Subj: Progress. Roads.

Sisters ill. by author. Crown, 1995. ISBN 0-517-70033-6 Subj: Behavior – fighting, arguing. Food. Sibling rivalry.

Stay away from the junkyard! ill. by author. Macmillan, 1988. ISBN 0-02-789541-6 Subj: Art. Behavior – collecting things.

Tutt, Kay Cunningham. *And now we call him Santa Claus* ill. by author. Lothrop, 1963. Subj: Holidays – Christmas. Santa Claus.

Twain, Mark. *The prince and the pauper* (Mayer, Marianna)

The twelve days of Christmas. English folk song. *Brian Wildsmith's The twelve days of Christmas* ill. by Brian Wildsmith. Watts, 1972. ISBN 0-531-01555-6 Subj: Cumulative tales. Holidays – Christmas. Music. Songs.

Jack Kent's twelve days of Christmas ill. by Jack Kent. Parents' Magazine Pr., 1973. ISBN 0-819-30697-5 Subj: Cumulative tales. Holidays – Christmas. Humorous stories. Music. Songs.

The twelve days of Christmas ill. by Jan Brett. Dodd, 1986. ISBN 0-396-08821-X Subj: Cumulative tales. Holidays – Christmas. Music. Songs.

The twelve days of Christmas ill. by Ilonka Karasz. HarperCollins, 1949. Subj: Cumulative tales. Holidays – Christmas. Music. Songs.

The twelve days of Christmas ill. by Ilse Plume. HarperCollins, 1990. ISBN 0-06-024738-X Subj: Cumulative tales. Holidays – Christmas. Music. Songs.

The twelve days of Christmas ill. by Erika Schneider. Alphabet Pr., 1984. ISBN 0-907234-62-3 Subj: Cumulative tales. Format, unusual. Holidays – Christmas. Music. Songs.

The twelve days of Christmas ill. by Vladimir Vagin. HarperCollins, 1998. ISBN 0-06-028399-8 Subj: Cumulative tales. Holidays – Christmas. Music. Songs.

The twelve days of Christmas ill. by Sophie Windham. Putnam, 1986. ISBN 0-399-21327-9 Subj: Cumulative tales. Holidays – Christmas. Music. Songs.

The twelve days of Christmas [board book] ill. by Jan Brett. Putnam, 2004. ISBN 0-339-24329-1 Subj: Cumulative tales. Format, unusual – board books. Holidays – Christmas. Music. Songs.

The twelve days of Christmas ill. by Rachel Griffin. Barefoot, 2002. ISBN 1-84148-940-9 Subj: Cumulative tales. Holidays – Christmas. Music. Songs.

Twinem, Neecy. *Changing colors* ill. by author. Charlesbridge, 1996. ISBN 0-88106-941-8 Subj: Animals. Farms. Problem solving.

High in the trees ill. by author. Charlesbridge, 1996. ISBN 0-88106-940-X Subj: Animals. Problem solving.

In the air ill. by author. Charlesbridge, 1997. ISBN 0-88106-943-4 Subj: Animals. Birds. Format, unusual – board books. Picture puzzles.

Twining, Edith. *Sandman* ill. by author. Doubleday, 1991. ISBN 0-385-41259-2 Subj: Bedtime. Boats, ships. Dreams. Mythical creatures – sandman. Sleep.

Two little eyes and other action rhymes sel. by Grace Cook; ill. by Carol Thompson. Candlewick, 2000. ISBN 0-7636-0952-8 Subj: Counting, numbers. Participation. Rhyming text.

Tworkov, Jack. *The camel who took a walk* ill. by Roger Antoine Duvoisin. Aladdin, 1951. ISBN 0-525-27393-X Subj: Activities – walking. Animals. Animals – camels. Animals – tigers. Cumulative tales. Morning.

Tyers, Jenny. *When it is night and when it is day* ill. by author. Houghton Mifflin, 1996. ISBN 0-395-71546-6 Subj: Animals. Night. Noise, sounds.

Tyger, Rory. *Newton* ill. by author. Barron's, 2001. ISBN 0-7641-5390-0 Subj: Emotions – fear. Noise, sounds. Toys – bears.

Tyler, Jenny. *Big Pig on a dig* ill. by author. Usborne, 1999. ISBN 1-58086-182-2 Subj: Activities – digging. Animals – pigs. Maps.

Tyler, Linda Wagner. *After Christmas tree* ill. by Susan Davis. Viking, 1990. ISBN 0-670-83045-3 Subj: Character traits – kindness to animals. Holidays – Christmas.

The sick-in-bed birthday book ill. by Susan Davis. Viking, 1988. ISBN 0-670-81823-2 Subj: Animals – pigs. Birthdays. Illness.

Waiting for mom ill. by Susan Davis. Viking, 1987. ISBN 0-670-81408-3 Subj: Animals – hippopotamuses. Behavior – worrying. Family life – mothers. School.

When daddy comes home ill. by Susan Davis. Viking, 1986. ISBN 0-670-80301-4 Subj: Animals – hippopotamuses. Family life – fathers.

Tyrrell, Anne. *Elizabeth Jane gets dressed* ill. by Caroline Castle. Barron's, 1987. ISBN 0-8120-5775-9 Subj: Clothing. Days of the week, months of the year. Rhyming text. Toys.

Mary Ann always can ill. by Caroline Castle. Barron's, 1988. ISBN 0-8120-5939-5 Subj: Character traits – individuality. Rhyming text. Sibling rivalry.

Tzannes, Robin. *Sanji and the baker* ill. by Korky Paul. Oxford Univ. Pr., 1998. ISBN 0-19-279960-6 Subj: Activities – baking, cooking. Activities – traveling. Careers – bakers.

Uchida, Yoshiko. *The bracelet* ill. by Joanna Yardley. Philomel, 1993. ISBN 0-399-22503-X Subj: Ethnic groups in the U.S. – Japanese Americans. Friendship. Slavery. U.S. history.

The magic purse ill. by Keiko Narahashi. McElderry, 1993. ISBN 0-689-50559-0 Subj: Character traits – bravery. Clothing – handbags, purses. Folk & fairy tales. Foreign lands – Japan.

Sumi's prize ill. by Kazue Mizumura. Scribners, 1964. Subj: Character traits – ambition. Foreign lands – Japan. Kites.

Sumi's special happening ill. by Kazue Mizumura. Scribners, 1966. Subj: Birthdays. Foreign lands – Japan. Old age.

The two foolish cats ill. by Margot Zemach. Macmillan, 1987. ISBN 0-689-50397-0 Subj: Animals – cats. Folk & fairy tales. Food.

The wise old woman ill. by Martin Springett. McElderry, 1994. ISBN 0-689-50582-5 Subj: Character traits – wisdom. Folk & fairy tales. Foreign lands – Japan. Old age.

Udry, Janice May. *Alfred* ill. by Judith S. Roth. A. Whitman, 1960. Subj: Animals – dogs. Behavior – animals, dislike of. Emotions – fear.

Emily's autumn ill. by Erik Blegvad. A. Whitman, 1969. ISBN 0-8075-1998-7 Subj: Farms. Seasons – fall. Toys – dolls.

How I faded away ill. by Monica De Bruyn. A. Whitman, 1976. ISBN 0-8075-3416-1 Subj: Behavior – unnoticed, unseen. Emotions – embarrassment. Self-concept.

Is Susan here? ill. by Peter Edwards. Abelard-Schuman, 1962. Subj: Animals. Character traits – helpfulness. Family life – mothers. Imagination.

Is Susan here? ill. by Karen Gundersheimer. Newly ill. ed. HarperCollins, 1993. ISBN 0-06-026143-9 Subj: Animals. Character traits – helpfulness. Family life – mothers. Imagination.

Let's be enemies ill. by Maurice Sendak. HarperCollins, 1961. ISBN 0-06-026131-5 Subj: Behavior – fighting, arguing. Emotions – hate. Friendship.

Mary Ann's mud day ill. by Martha G. Alexander. HarperCollins, 1967. Subj: Activities – playing. Ethnic groups in the U.S. – African Americans.

Mary Jo's grandmother ill. by Eleanor Mill. A. Whitman, 1970. ISBN 0-8075-4984-3 Subj: Ethnic groups in the U.S. – African Americans. Family life – grandmothers. Illness. Seasons – winter. Weather – snow.

The mean mouse and other mean stories ill. by Ed Young. HarperCollins, 1962. Subj: Character traits – meanness.

The moon jumpers ill. by Maurice Sendak. HarperCollins, 1959. ISBN 0-06-026145-5 Subj: Caldecott award honor books. Moon. Twilight.

"Oh no, cat!" ill. by Mary Chalmers. Coward, 1976. ISBN 0-698-30620-1 Subj: Animals – cats. Pets.

Theodore's parents ill. by Adrienne Adams. Lothrop, 1958. Subj: Adoption. Family life.

Thump and Plunk ill. by Geoffrey Hayes. Newly ill. ed. HarperCollins, 2000. ISBN 0-06-028528-1 Subj: Behavior – fighting, arguing. Birds – ducks. Family life – mothers. Sibling rivalry. Toys – dolls.

Thump and Plunk ill. by Ann Schweninger. HarperCollins, 1981. ISBN 0-06-026150-1 Subj: Animals – mice. Behavior – fighting, arguing. Family life – mothers. Sibling rivalry. Toys – dolls.

A tree is nice ill. by Marc Simont. HarperCollins, 1956. ISBN 0-06-026156-0 Subj: Caldecott award books. Poetry. Seasons. Trees.

What Mary Jo shared ill. by Eleanor Mill. A. Whitman, 1966. ISBN 0-8075-8842-3 Subj: Character traits – shyness. Ethnic groups in the U.S. Ethnic groups in the U.S. – African Americans. Family life – fathers. School.

What Mary Jo wanted ill. by Eleanor Mill. A. Whitman, 1968. Subj: Animals – dogs. Ethnic groups in the U.S. – African Americans. Family life. Pets.

Uegaki, Chieri. *Suki's kimono* ill. by Stéphane Jorisch. Kids Can, 2003. ISBN 1-55337-084-8 Subj: Character traits – being different. Clothing – kimonos. Ethnic groups in the U.S. – Japanese Americans. Family life – grandmothers. School – first day.

Ueno, Noriko. *Elephant buttons* ill. by author. HarperCollins, 1973. ISBN 0-06-026161-7 Subj: Animals. Circular tales. Concepts – in & out. Concepts – size. Games. Humorous stories. Participation. Wordless.

Uff, Caroline. *Happy birthday, Lulu* ill. by author. Walker, 2000. ISBN 0-8027-8751-7 Subj: Birthdays. Gifts. Parties.

Hello, Lulu ill. by author. Walker, 1999. ISBN 0-8027-8712-6 Subj: Clothing – shoes. Family life. Friendship. Pets.

Lulu's busy day ill. by author. Walker, 2000. ISBN 0-8027-8716-9 Subj: Activities. Family life.

Uhlberg, Myron. *Flying over Brooklyn* ill. by Gerald Fitzgerald. Peachtree, 1999. ISBN 1-56145-194-0 Subj: Activities – flying. U.S. history. Weather – snow.

Lemuel, the fool ill. by Sonja Lamut. Peachtree, 2001. ISBN 1-56145-220-3 Subj: Activities – traveling. Character traits – foolishness. Cities, towns. Sports – sailing.

Mad Dog McGraw ill. by Lydia Monks. Putnam, 2000. ISBN 0-399-23308-3 Subj: Animals – dogs. Problem solving.

The printer ill. by Henri Sorensen. Peachtree, 2003. Subj: Family life – fathers. Fire. Handicaps – deafness. Sign language.

Uhlig, Elizabeth. *Dog and cat* (Alcantara, Ricardo)

Ulmer, Wendy K. *A campfire for cowboy Billy* ill. by Kenneth J. Spengler. Northland, 1997. ISBN 0-8735-8681-6 Subj: Cowboys, cowgirls. Emotions – grief. Family life – grandfathers. Imagination.

Ulrich, George. *The spook matinee: and other scary poems for kids* ill. by author. Delacorte, 1992. ISBN 0-385-30552-4 Subj: Humorous stories. Poetry.

Umansky, Kay. *You can swim, Jim* by Kaye Umansky & Margaret Chamberlain; ill. by Margaret Chamberlain. Bodley Head, 1997. ISBN 0-370-32452-8 Subj: Poetry. Sports – swimming.

Umezawa, Rui. *Aiko's flowers* ill. by Yuji Ando. Tundra, 1999. ISBN 0-8877-6465-7 Subj: Flowers.

Uncle Gus. *see* Rey, H. A. (Hans Augusto)

Underhill, Liz. *The lucky coin* ill. by Liz Underhill; text by Margaret Greaves. Stewart, Tabori & Chang, 1989. ISBN 1-55670-129-2 Subj: Animals. Character traits – luck. Format, unusual – toy & movable books. Money.

Ungar, Richard. *Rachel captures the moon* ill. by author. Tundra, 2001. Adapt. from a story by Samuel Tenenbaum. ISBN 0-88776-505-X Subj: Folk & fairy tales. Jewish culture. Moon.

Rachel's gift ill. by author. Tundra, 2003. ISBN 0-88776-616-1 Subj: Activities – baking, cooking. Character traits – kindness. Holidays – Passover. Jewish culture. Religion.

Rachel's library ill. by author. Tundra, 2004. ISBN 0-88776-678-1 Subj: Cities, towns. Foreign lands – Poland. Jewish culture. Libraries.

Ungerer, Jean Thomas. *see* Ungerer, Tomi

Ungerer, Tomi. *Adelaide* ill. by author. TomiCo, 1999. ISBN 1-57098-296-1 Subj: Activities – flying. Activities – traveling. Animals – kangaroos. Foreign lands – France.

The beast of Monsieur Racine ill. by author. Farrar, 1971. ISBN 0-374-30640-0 Subj: Behavior – trickery. Foreign lands – France. Humorous stories. Monsters.

Christmas eve at the Mellops ill. by author. HarperCollins, 1960. ISBN 1-57098-227-9 Subj: Animals – pigs. Holidays – Christmas.

Crictor ill. by author. HarperCollins, 1958. ISBN 0-06-026181-1 Subj: Humorous stories. Reptiles – snakes.

Emile ill. by author. HarperCollins, 1960. ISBN 0-440-40593-9 Subj: Humorous stories. Octopuses.

Flix ill. by author. Roberts Rinehart, 1998. ISBN 1-57098-161-2 Subj: Animals – cats. Animals – dogs. Prejudice.

The hat ill. by author. Parents' Magazine Pr., 1970. ISBN 0-8193-0378-X Subj: Clothing – hats. Foreign lands – Italy. Magic. Weather – wind.

The Mellops go diving for treasure ill. by author. HarperCollins, 1957. Subj: Animals – pigs. Sea & seashore. Sports – skin diving.

The Mellops go flying ill. by author. HarperCollins, 1957. Subj: Activities – flying. Airplanes, airports. Animals – pigs.

The Mellops go spelunking ill. by author. HarperCollins, 1963. Subj: Animals – pigs. Caves. Character traits – perseverance.

The Mellops strike oil ill. by author. HarperCollins, 1958. Subj: Animals – pigs. Fire. Oil.

Moon man ill. by author. HarperCollins, 1967. ISBN 0-06-026235-4 Subj: Moon. Space & space ships.

No kiss for mother ill. by author. HarperCollins, 1973. ISBN 0-06-026237-0 Subj: Animals – cats. Family life – mothers.

One, two, where's my shoe? ill. by author. HarperCollins, 1964. Subj: Games. Wordless.

Orlando, the brave vulture ill. by author. HarperCollins, 1966. Subj: Birds – vultures. Desert. Foreign lands – Mexico.

Rufus ill. by author. HarperCollins, 1961. Subj: Animals – bats.

Snail, where are you? ill. by author. HarperCollins, 1962. Subj: Animals – snails. Games. Wordless.

The three robbers ill. by author. Atheneum, 1962. Subj: Crime. Orphans.

Tortoni Tremelo the cursed musician ill. by author. Roberts Rinehart, 1998. ISBN 1-57098-226-0 Subj: Careers – musicians. Magic. Music.

Warwick's 3 bottles (Hodeir, André)

Zeralda's ogre ill. by author. HarperCollins, 1967. Subj: Activities – baking, cooking. Character traits – kindness. Giants. Monsters. Mythical creatures – ogres.

Unobagha, Uzoamaka Chinyelu. *Off to the sweet shores of Africa and other talking drum rhymes* ill. by Julia Cairns. Chronicle, 2000. ISBN 0-8118-2378-4 Subj: Foreign lands – Africa. Poetry.

Untermeyer, Louis. *The kitten who barked* ill. by Lilian Obligado. Golden Pr., 1962. Subj: Animals – cats. Animals – dogs.

Unwin, Pippa. *The great zoo hunt!* ill. by author. Doubleday, 1990. ISBN 0-385-41107-3 Subj: Animals. Behavior – hiding. Zoos.

Tomcat takes a walk ill. by author. Andersen, 1998. ISBN 0-86264-705-3 Subj: Animals – cats. Foreign lands – England.

Up the hill and down comp. by William Jay Smith; ill. by Allan Eitzen. Boyds Mills, 2003. ISBN 1-56397-028-7 Subj: Poetry.

Updike, David. *An autumn tale* ill. by Robert Andrew Parker. Pippin Pr., 1988. ISBN 0-945912-02-1 Subj: Imagination. Night. Seasons – fall.

A winter's journey ill. by Robert Andrew Parker. Prentice-Hall, 1985. ISBN 0-13-961566-0 Subj: Animals – dogs. Dreams. Family life. Weather – snow.

Updike, John. *A helpful alphabet of friendly objects* ill. by David Updike. Knopf, 1995. ISBN 0-679-94324-2 Subj: Poetry.

Upham, Elizabeth. *Little brown bear loses his clothes* ill. by Normand Chartier. Platt, 1978. ISBN 0-448-46523-X Subj: Animals – bears. Behavior – lost & found possessions.

Upper, Jonathan. *Spin's really wild Africa tour* ill. by Barbara Gibson. National Geographic, 1996. ISBN 0-7922-3501-0 Subj: Animals. Desert. Foreign lands – Africa. Jungle.

Upton, Pat. *Who does this job?* ill. by Matt Novak. Boyds Mills, 1991. ISBN 1-878093-20-7 Subj: Careers.

Who lives in the woods? ill. by Karen Lee Schmidt. Boyds Mills, 1991. ISBN 1-878093-19-3 Subj: Animals. Forest, woods.

U'Ren, Andrea. *Pugdog* ill. by author. Farrar, 2001. ISBN 0-374-36149-5 Subj: Animals – dogs. Gender roles.

Uribe, Verónica. *Buzz buzz buzz* ill. by Glolria Calderón. Douglas & McIntyre, 2001. ISBN 0-88899-430-3 Subj: Animals. Insects – mosquitoes. Sleep.

Usher, Margo Scegge. *see* McHargue, Georgess

Ushinskii, K. D. (Konstantin Dmitrievich). *How a shirt grew in the field* (Rudolph, Marguerita)

How a shirt grew in the field (Rudolph, Marguerita)

Uslander, Arlene. *That's what grandparents are for* ill. by Freddie Levin. Peel Productions, 2002. ISBN 0-939217-60-0 Subj: Family life – grandparents. Poetry.

Uttley, Alice Jane. *see* Uttley, Alison

Uttley, Alison. *The Christmas box* ill. by Graham Percy. Faber, 1989. ISBN 0-571-15264-7 Subj: Animals – pigs. Holidays – Christmas.

Sam Pig and the dragon ill. by Graham Percy. Faber, 1989. ISBN 0-571-15294-5 Subj: Animals – pigs. Dragons.

Sam Pig and the hurdy-gurdy man ill. by Graham Percy. Faber, 1989. ISBN 0-571-15076-4 Subj: Animals – pigs. Music. Musical instruments – hurdy-gurdies.

Sam Pig and the wind ill. by Graham Percy. Faber, 1989. ISBN 0-571-15295-3 Subj: Animals – pigs. Clothing – pants. Weather – wind.

Utton, Peter. *Jennifer's room* ill. by author. Orchard, 1995. ISBN 0-531-06842-0 Subj: Imagination.

The witch's hand ill. by author. Farrar, 1989. ISBN 0-374-38463-0 Subj: Family life. Witches.

Uysal, Ahmet E. *New patches for old: a Turkish folktale* (Walker, Barbara K. [Barbara Kerlin])

Va, Leong. *A letter to the king* trans. from Norwegian by James Anderson; ill. by author. HarperCollins, 1991. ISBN 0-06-020070-7 Subj: Character traits – bravery. Character traits – loyalty. Folk & fairy tales. Foreign lands – China. Foreign languages. Royalty – kings.

Vaës, Alain. *The porcelain pepper pot* ill. by author. Puffin, 1987, c1982. ISBN 0-14-050727-2 Subj: Activities – picnicking. Emotions – love. Farms.

The princess and the pea ill. by author. Little, 2001. ISBN 0-316-89633-0 Subj: Behavior – greed. Folk & fairy tales. Humorous stories. Jewelry. Royalty – princesses. Sleep.

The wild hamster ill. by author. Little, 1985. ISBN 0-316-89504-0 Subj: Animals – hamsters. Pets.

Vagin, Vladimir Vasilévich. *Dear brother* (Asch, Frank)

The enormous carrot ill. by reteller. Scholastic, 1998. ISBN 0-590-45491-9 Subj: Animals. Cumulative tales. Farms. Folk & fairy tales. Foreign lands – Russia. Plants. Problem solving.

The flower faerie (Asch, Frank)

Here comes the cat by Vladimir Vagin & Frank Asch; ill. by authors. Scholastic, 1989. ISBN 0-590-41859-9 Subj: Animals – cats. Animals – mice. Foreign languages.

Insects from outer space (Asch, Frank)

The nutcracker ballet (Hoffmann, E. T. A.)

Peter and the wolf (Prokofiev, Sergei Sergeievitch)

Vail, Rachel. *Over the moon* ill. by Scott Nash. Orchard, 1998. ISBN 0-531-33068-0 Subj: Animals. Moon. Nursery rhymes. Theater.

Sometimes I'm Bombaloo ill. by Yumi Heo. Scholastic, 2002. ISBN 0-439-08755-4 Subj: Emotions – anger. Family life – brothers & sisters.

Vainio, Pirkko. *The best of friends* ill. by author; trans. by J. Alison James. North-South, 2000. ISBN 0-73581-151-2 Subj: Animals – bears. Animals – rabbits. Friendship.

The Christmas angel ill. by author; trans. by Anthea Bell. North-South, 1995. ISBN 1-55858-500-1 Subj: Angels. Holidays – Christmas. Homeless. Music. Poverty.

The dream house ill. by author; trans. by J. Alison James. North-South, 1997. ISBN 1-55858-750-0 Subj: Activities – making things. Animals – cats. Homes, houses. Magic. Weather – storms.

Valderrama, Candido A. *Mister North Wind* (De Posadas Mane, Carmen)

Valens, Amy. *Jesse's day care* ill. by Richard Eric Brown. Houghton Mifflin, 1990. ISBN 0-395-53357-0 Subj: Activities – working. Family life – mothers. School – nursery.

Valens, Evans G. *Wingfin and Topple* ill. by Clement Hurd. Collins-World, 1962. Subj: Activities – flying. Fish.

Valentine, Johnny. *The duke who outlawed jelly beans and other stories* ill. by Lynette Schmidt. Alyson Wonderland, 1991. ISBN 1-55583-199-0 Subj: Folk & fairy tales.

One dad, two dads, brown dad, blue dads ill. by Melody Sarecky. Alyson Wonderland, 1994. ISBN 1-55583-253-9 Subj: Ethnic groups in the U.S. Family life – fathers. Prejudice.

Valeri, M. Eulalia. *Hansel and Gretel* (Grimm, Jacob)

Sleeping Beauty (Grimm, Jacob)

The ugly duckling (Andersen, H. C. [Hans Christian])

Valfre, Edward. *Backseat buckaroo* ill. by author. Thomasson-Grant, 1995. ISBN 1-56566-078-1 Subj: Activities – traveling. Imagination.

Vacationers from outer space ill. by author. Chronicle, 1997. ISBN 0-8118-1717-2 Subj: Activities – vacationing. Aliens. Imagination.

Valgardson, W. D. *Winter rescue* ill. by Ange Zhang. McElderry, 1995. ISBN 0-689-80094-0 Subj: Family life – grandfathers. Foreign lands – Canada. Holidays – Christmas. Lakes, ponds. Seasons – winter. Sports – fishing.

Valzania, Kim. *Tennessee* ill. with photos. Childrens Pr., 2003. ISBN 0-516-22699-1 Subj: U.S. history.

Van Leeuwenm, Jean. *"Wait for me!" said Maggie McGee* ill. by Jacqueline Rogers. Fogelman, 2001. ISBN 0-8037-2357-1 Subj: Behavior – growing up. Concepts – size. Family life – brothers & sisters.

Van Aarle, Thomas. *see* Aarle, Thomas Van

Van Allsburg, Chris. *Bad day at Riverbend* ill. by author. Houghton Mifflin, 1995. ISBN 0-395-67347-X Subj: Activities – drawing. Imagination.

The garden of Abdul Gasazi ill. by author. Houghton Mifflin, 1979. ISBN 0-395-27804-X Subj: Animals – dogs. Behavior – misbehavior. Caldecott award honor books. Imagination. Magic.

Jumanji ill. by author. Houghton Mifflin, 1981. ISBN 0-395-30448-2 Subj: Caldecott award books. Games. Imagination. Jungle.

The mysteries of Harris Burdick ill. by author. Houghton Mifflin, 1984. ISBN 0-395-35393-9 Subj: Imagination.

The polar express ill. by author. Houghton Mifflin, 1985. ISBN 0-395-38949-6 Subj: Caldecott award books. Holidays – Christmas. Imagination. Night. Santa Claus. Trains.

The stranger ill. by author. Houghton Mifflin, 1986. ISBN 0-395-42331-7 Subj: Behavior – forgetfulness. Country. Seasons – fall.

Two bad ants ill. by author. Houghton Mifflin, 1988. ISBN 0-395-48668-8 Subj: Homes, houses. Insects – ants.

The widow's broom ill. by author. Houghton Mifflin, 1992. ISBN 0-395-64051-2 Subj: Magic. Prejudice. Witches.

The wreck of the Zephyr ill. by author. Houghton Mifflin, 1983. ISBN 0-395-33075-0 Subj: Boats, ships. Sailors. Weather – storms.

The Z was zapped ill. by author. Houghton Mifflin, 1987. ISBN 0-395-44612-0 Subj: ABC books.

Zathura ill. by author. Houghton, 2002. ISBN 0-618-25396-3 Subj: Activities – playing. Family life – brothers. Games. Space & space ships.

Van Anrooy, Frans. *see* Anrooy, Frans van

Van Camp, Richard. *What's the most beautiful thing you know about horses?* ill. by George Littlechild. Children's Book Pr., 1998. ISBN 0-89239-154-5 Subj: Animals – horses, ponies. Foreign lands – Canada. Indians of North America.

Van Caster, Nancy. *An alligator lives in Benjamin's house* ill. by Dale Gottlieb. Putnam, 1990. ISBN 0-399-21489-5 Subj: Animals. Behavior – imitation. Family life. Imagination.

Vance, Eleanor Graham. *Jonathan* ill. by Albert John Pucci. Follett, 1966. Subj: Character traits – questioning. Poetry. Weather.

Vande Griek, Susan. *The art room* ill. by Pascal Milelli. Douglas & McIntyre, 2002. ISBN 0-88899-449-4 Subj: Art. Careers – artists.

Van den Berg, Marinus. *The three birds: a story for children about the loss of a loved one* ill. by Sandra Ireland. G. Stevens, 1994. ISBN 0-8368-1072-4 Subj: Birds. Death. Emotions – grief. Illness – cancer.

Van den Honert, Dorry. *Demi the baby sitter* ill. by Meg Wohlberg. Morrow, 1961. Subj: Activities – babysitting. Animals – dogs.

Van der Beek, Deborah. *Alice's blue cloth* ill. by author. Putnam, 1989. ISBN 0-399-21622-7 Subj: Birthdays. Family life.

Superbabe! ill. by author. Putnam, 1988. ISBN 0-399-21507-7 Subj: Babies. Family life. Parks. Rhyming text. Sibling rivalry.

VanderKlipp, Michael A. *Joy to the world! a Christmas counting book* ill. by Nancy Munger. Zondervan, 1998. ISBN 0-310-97660-X Subj: Counting, numbers. Format, unusual – board books. Religion – Nativity. Rhyming text.

Van der Meer, Atie. *Oh Lord!* (Van der Meer, Ron)

Pigs at home (Van der Meer, Ron)

Van der Meer, Mara. *Can we play?* ill. by author. Abrams, 2002. ISBN 0-8109-0379-2 Subj: Activities – playing. Days of the week, months of the year. Family life. Format, unusual – toy & movable books.

Van der Meer, Ron. *Babette Cole's beastly birthday book* (Cole, Babette)

Funny hats ill. by Atie van der Meer. Random House, 1992. ISBN 0-679-82850-8 Subj: Clothing – hats. Counting, numbers. Format, unusual – toy & movable books.

Oh Lord! by Ron & Atie van der Meer; ill. by authors. Crown, 1980. ISBN 0-517-54006-1 Subj: Humorous stories. Religion.

Pigs at home by Ron & Atie Van der Meer; ill. by authors. Atheneum, 1988. ISBN 0-689-71232-4 Subj: Animals – pigs. Format, unusual – toy & movable books.

Sailing ships (McGowan, Alan)

Vande Velde, Vivian. *Troll teacher* ill. by Mary Jane Auch. Holiday, 2000. ISBN 0-8234-1503-1 Subj: Careers – teachers. Mythical creatures – trolls. School.

Van Dusen, Chris. *Down to the sea with Mr. Magee* ill. by author. Chronicle, 2000. ISBN 0-8118-2499-3 Subj: Animals – dogs. Animals – whales. Boats, ships. Rhyming text. Sea & seashore. Sports – sailing.

Van Dyke, Henry. *The fourth wise man* (Summers, Susan)

Van Eerbeek. *The world of baby animals* ill. with photos. Sterling, 2000. ISBN 0-8069-8058-3 Subj: Animals – babies.

The world of farm animals ill. with photos. Sterling, 2001. ISBN 0-8069-8461-9 Subj: Animals. Farms.

The world of wild animals ill. with photos. Sterling, 2001. ISBN 0-8069-8452-X Subj: Animals.

Van Emst, Charlotte. *Little Rabbit's big day* ill. by author. Little, 1990. ISBN 0-316-89623-3 Subj: Animals – rabbits. Concepts – size.

Van Fleet, Matthew. *Fuzzy yellow ducklings* ill. by author. Dial, 1995. ISBN 0-8037-1759-8 Subj: Animals. Birds. Concepts – color. Concepts – shape. Format, unusual – toy & movable books.

One yellow lion ill. by author. Dial, 1992. ISBN 0-8037-1099-2 Subj: Animals. Concepts – color. Counting, numbers. Format, unusual – toy & movable books.

Spotted yellow frogs ill. by author. Dial, 1998. ISBN 0-8037-2350-4 Subj: Animals. Concepts – color. Concepts – shape. Format, unusual – toy & movable books.

Van Gelder, Richard George. *Animals in winter* (Bancroft, Henrietta)

Van Haeringen, Annemarie. *The cats' tale* ill. by author. Oxford Univ. Pr., 1989. ISBN 0-19-279819-7 Subj: Animals – cats. Family life – grandparents. Gardens, gardening. Giants.

Van Horn, Grace. *Little red rooster* ill. by Sheila Perry. Abelard-Schuman, 1961. Subj: Birds – chickens. Farms.

Van Horn, William. *Harry Hoyle's giant jumping bean* ill. by author. Atheneum, 1978. ISBN 0-689-30636-9 Subj: Animals – cats. Animals – pack rats. Behavior – collecting things.

Twitchtoe, the beastfinder ill. by author. Atheneum, 1978. ISBN 0-689-30670-9 Subj: Problem solving.

Van Kampen, Vlasta. *Bear tales* ill. by author. Annick, 2000. ISBN 1-55037-619-5 Subj: Animals – bears. Creation. Folk & fairy tales. Foreign lands – Czechoslovakia. Foreign lands – Russia.

It couldn't be worse ill. by author. Annick, 2003. ISBN 1-55037-783-3 Subj: Animals. Behavior – fighting, arguing. Family life. Folk & fairy tales. Humorous stories. Problem solving.

Van Laan, Nancy. *The big fat worm* ill. by Marisabina Russo. Knopf, 1987. ISBN 0-394-98763-2 Subj: Animals. Birds. Circular tales.

La boda: a Mexican wedding celebration ill. by Andrea Arroyo. Little, 1996. ISBN 0-316-89626-8 Subj: Foreign lands – Mexico. Foreign languages. Indians of North America – Zapotec. Weddings.

The legend of El Dorado story & ill. by Beatriz A. Vidal; adapt. by Nancy Van Laan. Knopf, 1991. ISBN 0-679-90136-1 Subj: Folk & fairy tales. Foreign lands – South America. Indians of South America. Royalty – kings.

Little baby Bobby ill. by Laura Cornell. Knopf, 1997. ISBN 0-679-94922-4 Subj: Behavior – running away. Humorous stories. Rhyming text. Toys – bears.

Little Fish lost ill. by Jane Conteh-Morgan. Atheneum, 1998. ISBN 0-689-81331-7 Subj: Animals. Family life – mothers. Fish. Foreign lands – Africa. Rhyming text.

The magic bean tree ill. by Beatriz A. Vidal. Houghton Mifflin, 1998. ISBN 0-395-82746-9 Subj: Folk & fairy tales. Foreign lands – Argentina. Indians of South America – Quechua.

Mama rocks, Papa sings ill. by Roberta Smith. Knopf, 1995. ISBN 0-679-94016-2 Subj: Activities – babysitting. Babies. Counting, numbers. Cumulative tales. Foreign lands – Haiti. Rhyming text.

Moose tales ill. by Amy Rusch. Houghton, 1999. ISBN 0-395-90863-9 Subj: Animals. Animals – beavers. Animals – moose. Friendship. Weather – snow.

A mouse in my house ill. by Marjorie Priceman. Knopf, 1990. ISBN 0-679-90043-8 Subj: Animals. Behavior. Rhyming text.

People, people, everywhere ill. by Nadine Bernard Westcott. Knopf, 1992. ISBN 0-679-91063-8 Subj: Activities. Cities, towns. Rhyming text.

Possum come a-knocking ill. by George Booth. Knopf, 1990. ISBN 0-394-92206-9 Subj: Animals – possums. Cumulative tales. Family life. Rhyming text.

Rainbow crow ill. by Beatriz A. Vidal. Knopf, 1989. ISBN 0-394-99577-5 Subj: Birds – crows. Concepts – color. Creation. Fire. Folk & fairy tales. Indians of North America – Lenape.

Round and round again ill. by Nadine Bernard Westcott. Hyperion, 1994. ISBN 0-7868-2005-5 Subj: Ecology. Rhyming text.

Shingebiss: an Ojibwe legend ill. by Betsy Bowen. Houghton Mifflin, 1997. ISBN 0-316-89627-6 Subj: Birds – ducks. Folk & fairy tales. Indians of North America – Ojibwa. Seasons – winter.

Sleep, sleep, sleep ill. by Holly Meade. Little, 1995. ISBN 0-316-89732-9 Subj: Animals. Foreign lands. Foreign languages. Lullabies. Sleep.

So say the little monkeys ill. by Yumi Heo. Atheneum, 1998. ISBN 0-689-81038-5 Subj: Animals – monkeys. Folk & fairy tales. Foreign lands – Brazil. Rhyming text.

This is the hat ill. by Holly Meade. Hyperion, 1995. ISBN 0-7868-1030-0 Subj: Animals. Circular tales. Clothing – hats. Rhyming text.

Tickle tum ill. by Bernadette Pons. Atheneum, 2001. ISBN 0-689-83143-9 Subj: Family life – mothers. Food. Games.

A tree for me ill. by Sheila White Samton. Knopf, 2000. ISBN 0-679-99384-3 Subj: Animals. Counting, numbers. Rhyming text. Trees.

When winter comes: a lullaby ill. by Susan Gaber. Atheneum, 2000. ISBN 0-689-81778-9 Subj: Animals. Lullabies. Seasons – winter.

Van Leeuwen, Jean. *Across the wide dark sea: the Mayflower journey* ill. by Thomas B. Allen. Dial, 1995. ISBN 0-8037-1167-0 Subj: Activities – traveling. Boats, ships. Pilgrims. Religion. U.S. history.

The emperor's new clothes (Andersen, H. C. [Hans Christian])

The emperor's new clothes (Andersen, H. C. [Hans Christian])

Going west ill. by Thomas B. Allen. Dial, 1992. ISBN 0-8037-1028-3 Subj: Family life. Moving. U.S. history – frontier & pioneer life.

More tales of Oliver Pig ill. by Arnold Lobel. Dial, 1981. ISBN 0-8037-8714-6 Subj: Animals – pigs. Family life.

Nothing here but trees ill. by Phil Boatwright. Dial, 1998. ISBN 0-8037-2180-3 Subj: Careers – farmers. Trees. U.S. history – frontier & pioneer life.

Sorry ill. by Brad Sneed. Fogelman, 2001. ISBN 0-8037-2261-3 Subj: Behavior – fighting, arguing. Careers – farmers. Character traits – persistence. Family life – brothers.

The strange adventures of Blue Dog ill. by Marco Ventura. Dial, 1999. ISBN 0-8037-1878-0 Subj: Animals – dogs. Farms. Toys.

The tickle stories ill. by Mary Whyte. Dial, 1998. ISBN 0-8037-2049-1 Subj: Activities – storytelling. Bedtime. Family life. Family life – grandfathers.

Too hot for ice cream ill. by Martha G. Alexander. Dial, 1974. ISBN 0-8037-6077-9 Subj: Behavior – bad day. Sports – swimming. Weather.

Touch the sky summer ill. by Dan Andreasen. Dial, 1997. ISBN 0-8037-1820-9 Subj: Activities – vacationing. Family life. Family life – grandparents. Lakes, ponds. Seasons – summer.

Van Liew Foster, Doris. *see* Foster, Doris Van Liew

Van Nutt, Julia. *The monster in the shadows* ill. by Robert Van Nutt. Doubleday, 2000. ISBN 0-385-32565-7 Subj: Crime. Monsters. Shadows.

The mystery of Mineral Gorge ill. by Robert Van Nutt. Doubleday, 1998. ISBN 0-385-32562-2 Subj: Animals – pigs. Mystery stories.

Pignapped! ill. by Robert Van Nutt. Doubleday, 2000. ISBN 0-385-32559-2 Subj: Animals – pigs. Character traits – foolishness. Museums.

Pumpkins from the sky? ill. by Robert Van Nutt. Doubleday, 1999. ISBN 0-385-32568-1 Subj: Animals – pigs. Fairs, festivals. Weather – storms.

Skyrockets and snickerdoodles ill. by Robert Van Nutt. Doubleday, 2001. ISBN 0-385-32553-3 Subj: Activities – writing. Cities, towns. Holidays – Fourth of July. Sports – baseball.

Van Rynbach, Iris. *Five little pumpkins* ill. by author. Boyds Mills, 1995. ISBN 1-56397-452-5 Subj: Holidays – Halloween. Plants. Rhyming text.

The soup stone adapt. & ill. by Iris Van Rynbach. Greenwillow, 1988. ISBN 0-688-07255-0 Subj: Careers – military. Character traits – cleverness. Folk & fairy tales. Food.

Van Stockum, Hilda. *A day on skates: the story of a Dutch picnic* ill. by author. Bethlehem Books, 1994, c1934. ISBN 1-883937-00-0 Subj: Activities – picnicking. Foreign lands – Holland. Sports – ice skating.

Van Vorst, M. L. *A Norse lullaby* ill. by Margot Tomes. Lothrop, 1988. ISBN 0-688-05813-2 Subj: Animals. Lullabies. Poetry. Seasons – winter. Sleep.

Van West, Patricia E. *The crab man* ill. by Cedric Lucas. Turtle Books, 1998. ISBN 1-890515-08-6 Subj: Character traits – kindness to animals. Crustaceans – crabs. Foreign lands – Jamaica.

Van Woerkom, Dorothy. *Abu Ali counts his donkeys* ill. by Harry Horse. Candlewick, 2000. ISBN 0-7636-0956-0 Subj: Animals – donkeys. Counting, numbers.

Alexandra the rock-eater: an old Rumanian tale retold ill. by Rosekrans Hoffman. Knopf, 1978. ISBN 0-394-93536-5 Subj: Dragons. Family life. Folk & fairy tales. Food. Foreign lands.

Becky and the bear ill. by Margot Tomes. Putnam, 1975. ISBN 0-399-60924-5 Subj: Animals – bears. Character traits – bravery. U.S. history – frontier & pioneer life.

Donkey Ysabel ill. by Normand Chartier. Macmillan, 1978. ISBN 0-02-791280-9 Subj: Animals – donkeys. Humorous stories.

Harry and Shelburt ill. by Erick Ingraham. Macmillan, 1977. ISBN 0-02-791290-6 Subj: Animals – rabbits. Friendship. Reptiles – turtles, tortoises. Sports – racing.

Hidden messages ill. by Lynne Cherry. Crown, 1980. ISBN 0-517-53520-3 Subj: Communication. Insects. Science.

The queen who couldn't bake gingerbread ill. by Paul Galdone. Knopf, 1975. ISBN 0-394-93033-9 Subj: Folk & fairy tales. Foreign lands – Germany. Humorous stories. Royalty – queens.

The rat, the ox and the zodiac: a Chinese legend ill. by Errol Le Cain. Crown, 1976. ISBN 0-517-51849-X Subj: Animals. Animals – rats. Character traits – cleverness. Folk & fairy tales. Foreign lands – China. Zodiac.

Sea frog, city frog ill. by José Aruego & Ariane Dewey. Macmillan, 1975. ISBN 0-02-791300-7 Subj: Folk & fairy tales. Foreign lands – Japan. Frogs & toads.

Something to crow about ill. by Paul Harvey. A. Whitman, 1982. ISBN 0-8075-7534-8 Subj: Birds – chickens. Family life – fathers.

Varekamp, Marjolein. *Little Sam takes a bath* ill. by author. Watts, 1991. ISBN 0-531-05944-8 Subj: Activities – bathing. Animals – pigs. Format, unusual – toy & movable books.

Varga, Judy. *Circus cannonball* ill. by author. Morrow, 1975. ISBN 0-688-32026-0 Subj: Circus.

Janko's wish ill. by author. Morrow, 1969. Subj: Behavior – wishing. Foreign lands – Hungary. Magic. Weddings.

The mare's egg ill. by author. Morrow, 1972. Subj: Animals – foxes. Behavior – trickery. Folk & fairy tales. Foreign lands – Russia.

Miss Lollipop's lion ill. by author. Morrow, 1963. Subj: Animals – lions. Circus. Pets.

The monster behind Black Rock ill. by author. Morrow, 1971. Subj: Animals. Behavior – gossip. Cumulative tales.

Varley, Dimitry. *The whirly bird* ill. by Feodor Rojankovsky. Knopf, 1961. Subj: Birds. Character traits – kindness to animals.

Varley, Susan. *Badger's parting gifts* ill. by author. Lothrop, 1984. ISBN 0-688-02703-2 Subj: Animals – badgers. Death. Friendship. Gifts.

Vasiliu, Mircea. *A day at the beach* ill. by author. Random House, 1978. ISBN 0-394-93475-X Subj: Activities – playing. Family life. Sand. Science. Sea & seashore – beaches.

Everything is somewhere ill. by author. John Day, 1970. Subj: Religion.

What's happening? ill. by author. John Day, 1970. Subj: Activities. Cities, towns.

Vathanaprida, Supaporn. *The girl who wore too much* (MacDonald, Margaret Read)

Vaughan, Marcia Kapok. *Abbie against the storm* ill. by Bill Farnsworth. Beyond Words, 1999. ISBN 1-58270-007-9 Subj: Lighthouses. Sea & seashore. U.S. history.

The dancing dragon ill. by Stanley Wong Hoo Foon. Mondo, 1996. ISBN 1-57255-134-8 Subj: Dragons. Ethnic groups in the U.S. – Chinese Americans. Format, unusual. Holidays – Chinese New Year. Rhyming text.

The lemonade stand ill. by Thomas Payne. Grosset, 1999. ISBN 0-448-41977-7 Subj: Animals. Humorous stories. Money.

Night dancer ill. by Lisa Desimini. Orchard, 2002. ISBN 0-439-35248-7 Subj: Activities – dancing. Desert. Indians of North America. Night.

The Sea-Breeze Hotel by Marcia Kapok Vaughn & Patricia Mullins; ill. by Patricia Mullins. HarperCollins, 1992. ISBN 0-06-020504-0 Subj: Hotels. Kites. Weather – wind.

Snap! ill. by Sascha Hutchinson. Scholastic, 1996. ISBN 0-590-60377-9 Subj: Animals. Animals – kangaroos. Reptiles – alligators, crocodiles.

We're going on a ghost hunt ill. by Ann Schweninger. Harcourt, 2001. ISBN 0-15-202353-4 Subj: Ghosts. Holidays – Halloween. Imagination. Rhyming text.

Whistling Dixie ill. by Barry Moser. HarperCollins, 1995. ISBN 0-06-021029-X Subj: Animals. Pets. Swamps.

Wombat stew ill. by Pamela Lofts. Silver Burdett, 1986. ISBN 0-382-09211-2 Subj: Animals. Foreign lands – Australia. Music. Songs.

Vaughan, Richard Lee. *Eagle boy* ill. by Lee Christiansen. Sasquatch, 2000. ISBN 1-570611-71-8 Subj: Birds – eagles. Folk & fairy tales. Indians of North America.

Vaughn, Jenny. *On the moon* ed. by Jenny Vaughn; Angela Grunsell, consultant; ill. by Tessa Barwick & Elsa Godfrey. Watts, 1983. ISBN 0-531-04631-1 Subj: Moon. Space & space ships. U.S. history.

Vega, Eida de la. *Oh, crumps! = Ay, caramba!* (Bock, Lee)

Those ooey gooey winky-blinky but – invisible pinkeye germs = Esos pringosos viscosos pestañeantes parpadeantes pero – invisibles gérmenes que causan conjuntivitis (Rice, Judith)

Velasquez, Eric. *Grandma's records* ill. by author. Walker, 2001. ISBN 0-8027-8760-6 Subj: Activities – storytelling. Ethnic groups in the U.S. – Puerto Rican Americans. Family life – grandmothers. Music.

Veldkamp, Tjibbe. *The school trip* ill. by Philip Hopman. Front St., 2001. ISBN 1-886910-70-7 Subj: School – first day.

22 orphans ill. by Philip Hopman. Kane/Miller, 1998. ISBN 0-916291-81-2 Subj: Activities – playing. Behavior – misbehavior.

Velthuijs, Max. *Crocodile's masterpiece* ill. by author. Farrar, 1992. ISBN 0-374-31658-9 Subj: Animals – elephants. Careers – artists. Imagination. Reptiles – alligators, crocodiles.

Frog and the birdsong ill. by author. Farrar, 1991. ISBN 0-374-32467-0 Subj: Animals. Death. Frogs & toads.

Frog in love trans. from Dutch by Anthea Bell; ill. by author. Farrar, 1989. ISBN 0-374-32465-4 Subj: Birds – ducks. Emotions – love. Frogs & toads.

Frog is a hero ill. by author. Andersen, 1995. ISBN 0-86264-601-4 Subj: Animals. Friendship. Frogs & toads. Weather – floods.

Frog is frightened ill. by author. Tambourine, 1995. ISBN 0-688-14203-6 Subj: Animals. Bedtime. Birds. Friendship. Frogs & toads. Noise, sounds.

Little Man finds a home ill. by author. Holt, 1985. ISBN 0-03-005734-5 Subj: Homes, houses. Weather – rain.

Little Man to the rescue ill. by author. Holt, 1986. ISBN 0-8050-0036-4 Subj: Animals – rabbits. Character traits – kindness to animals. Emotions – envy, jealousy. Frogs & toads.

Little Man's lucky day trans. from German by Rosemary Lanning; ill. by author. Holt, 1986. ISBN 0-03-005847-3 Subj: Character traits – luck.

The painter and the bird trans. by Ray Broekel; ill. by author. Addison-Wesley, 1975. Translation of Der Maler und der Vogel. ISBN 0-20-108082-6 Subj: Birds. Careers – artists. Imagination.

Venable, Alan. *The checker players* ill. by Byron Barton. Lippincott, 1973. ISBN 0-397-31479-5 Subj: Animals – bears. Behavior – fighting, arguing. Boats, ships. Friendship. Games. Reptiles – alligators, crocodiles.

Venino, Suzanne. *Animals helping people* ill. with photos. National Geographic, 1983. ISBN 0-87044-493-X Subj: Animals. Character traits – helpfulness.

Ventura, Gabriela Baeza. *The bakery lady = La señora de la panadería* (Mora, Pat)

Magda's piñata magic = Magda y la piñata mágica (Chavarría-Cháirez, Becky)

Ventura, Marisa. *The painter's trick* (Ventura, Piero)

Ventura, Piero. *The painter's trick* by Piero & Marisa Ventura; ill. by Marisa Ventura. Random House, 1977. ISBN 0-394-93320-6 Subj: Careers – artists.

Venturo, Betty Lou Baker. *see* Baker, Betty

Ver Beck, Frank. *The Little Black Sambo story book* (Bannerman, Helen)

Verboven, Agnes. *Ducks like to swim* ill. by Anne Westerduin. Orchard, 1997. ISBN 0-531-30054-4 Subj: Animals. Birds – ducks. Farms. Noise, sounds. Water. Weather – rain.

Verdet, Andre. *All about time* created by Gallimard Jeunesse & Andre Verdet; ill. by Celine Bour-Chollet, Daniel Moignot, & Donald Grant. Scholastic, 1995. ISBN 0-590-42795-4 Subj: Clocks, watches. Days of the week, months of the year. Format, unusual – toy & movable books. Seasons. Time.

Verdi, Giuseppe. *Aïda* (Price, Leontyne)

VerDorn, Bethea. *Day breaks* ill. by Thomas Graham. Arcade, 1992. ISBN 1-55970-187-0 Subj: Animals. Friendship. Morning.

Moon glows ill. by Thomas Graham. Arcade, 1990. ISBN 1-55970-073-4 Subj: Animals. Moon. Night. Rhyming text.

Vere, Ed. *Everyone's little* ill. by author. Orchard, 2001. ISBN 0-531-30336-5 Subj: Animals – elephants. Concepts – size. Format, unusual – toy & movable books.

Verma, Jatinder Nath. *The story of Divaali* ill. by Nilesh Mistry. Barefoot, 2002. ISBN 1-84148-936-0 Subj: Folk & fairy tales. Foreign lands – India. Holidays – Divali. Religion – Hinduism. Royalty – princes.

Vern, Alex. *Where do frogs come from?* ill. with photos. Harcourt, 2001. ISBN 0-15-216304-2 Subj: Frogs & toads. Science.

Vernon, Adele. *The riddle* ill. by Robert Rayevsky & Vladimir Radunsky. Dodd, 1987. ISBN 0-396-08920-8 Subj: Folk & fairy tales. Foreign lands – Spain. Royalty.

Vernon, Tannis. *Little Pig and the blue-green sea* ill. by author. Crown, 1986. ISBN 0-517-56118-2 Subj: Animals – pigs. Behavior – running away. Boats, ships. Sea & seashore.

Vesey, A. *Merry Christmas, Thomas!* ill. by author. Little, 1986. ISBN 0-87113-096-3 Subj: Animals – cats. Family life. Holidays – Christmas.

The princess and the frog ill. by author. Little, 1985. ISBN 0-87113-038-6 Subj: Character traits – willfulness. Folk & fairy tales. Frogs & toads. Royalty – princesses.

Vessel, Matthew F. *My goldfish* (Wong, Herbert H.)

My ladybug (Wong, Herbert H.)

My plant (Wong, Herbert H.)

Our caterpillars (Wong, Herbert H.)

Our earthworms (Wong, Herbert H.)

Our tree (Wong, Herbert H.)

Vevers, Gwynne. *Animal homes* ill. by Wendy Bramall. Merrimack, 1982. ISBN 0-370-30245-1 Subj: Animals. Homes, houses.

Animal parents ill. by Colin Threadgall. Merrimack, 1982. ISBN 0-370-30172-2 Subj: Animals. Family life.

Animals of the dark ill. by Wendy Bramall. Merrimack, 1982. ISBN 0-370-30331-8 Subj: Animals. Night.

Animals that store food ill. by Joyce Bee. Merrimack, 1982. ISBN 0-370-30330-X Subj: Animals. Food.

Animals that travel ill. by Matthew Hillier. Merrimack, 1982. ISBN 0-370-30399-7 Subj: Activities – traveling. Animals.

Vickers, Rebecca. *Florence Nightingale* ill. with photos. Heinemann, 2000. ISBN 1-57572-402-2 Subj: Careers – nurses. Foreign lands – England.

Vidal, Beatriz A. *Federico and the Magi's gift* ill. by author. Knopf, 2004. ISBN 0-375-92518-X Subj: Behavior – misbehavior. Foreign lands – Latin America. Foreign languages. Holidays – Christmas.

The legend of El Dorado (Van Laan, Nancy)

Vidaure, Morris. *The invisible hunters* (Rohmer, Harriet)

Vidrine, Beverly Barras. *Easter Day alphabet* ill. by Alison Davis Lyne. Pelican, 2003. ISBN 1-58980-076-1 Subj: ABC books. Holidays – Easter. Religion.

Vieira, Linda. *The ever-living tree* ill. by Christopher Canyon. Walker, 1994. ISBN 0-8027-8278-7 Subj: Trees. U.S. history.

Vigil-Piñón, Evangelina. *Muffler man = El hombre mofle* (Compos, Tito)

Marina's muumuu = el muumuu de Marina ill. by Pablo Torrecilla. Piñata, 2001. ISBN 1-55885-350-2 Subj: Clothing. Ethnic groups in the U.S. Family life – grandmothers. Foreign languages. Hawaii.

Vigna, Judith. *Anyhow, I'm glad I tried* ill. by author. A. Whitman, 1978. ISBN 0-8075-0378-9 Subj: Behavior – misbehavior. Character traits – kindness. School.

Boot weather ed. by Ann Fay; ill. by author. A. Whitman, 1988. ISBN 0-8075-0837-3 Subj: Activities – playing. Clothing – shoes. Imagination. Seasons – winter. Weather.

Couldn't we have a turtle instead? ill. by author. A. Whitman, 1975. ISBN 0-8075-1312-1 Subj: Animals. Babies. Emotions – envy, jealousy. Family life – mothers. Family life – new sibling.

Daddy's new baby ill. by author. A. Whitman, 1982. ISBN 0-8075-1435-7 Subj: Divorce. Family life – fathers. Sibling rivalry.

Everyone goes as a pumpkin ill. by author. A. Whitman, 1977. ISBN 0-8075-2186-8 Subj: Family life – grandmothers. Holidays – Halloween.

Grandma without me ill. by author. A. Whitman, 1984. ISBN 0-8075-3030-1 Subj: Divorce. Family life – grandmothers.

The hiding house ill. by author. A. Whitman, 1979. ISBN 0-8075-3275-4 Subj: Behavior – hiding. Behavior – sharing. Friendship.

I wish my daddy didn't drink so much ed. by Ann Fay; ill. by author. A. Whitman, 1988. ISBN 0-8075-3523-0 Subj: Behavior – wishing. Family life – fathers. Illness.

Mommy and me by ourselves again ill. by author. A. Whitman, 1987. ISBN 0-8075-5232-1 Subj: Behavior – needing someone. Birthdays. Family life – mothers.

My two uncles ill. by author. A. Whitman, 1995. ISBN 0-8075-5507-X Subj: Birthdays. Family life – aunts, uncles. Family life – grandfathers. Homosexuality.

Nobody wants a nuclear war ill. by author. A. Whitman, 1986. ISBN 0-8075-5739-0 Subj: Emotions – fear. Family life. War.

Saying goodbye to daddy ill. by author. A. Whitman, 1990. ISBN 0-8075-7253-5 Subj: Death. Emotions. Emotions – grief. Family life – fathers.

She's not my real mother ill. by author. A. Whitman, 1980. ISBN 0-8075-7340-X Subj: Behavior – misbehavior. Divorce. Family life.

Villarejo, Mary. *The art fair* ill. by author. Knopf, 1960. Subj: Art.

The tiger hunt ill. by author. Knopf, 1959. Subj: Activities – photographing. Animals. Animals – tigers. Foreign lands – India.

Villoldo, Alberto. *The first story ever told* (Jendresen, Erik)

Skeleton woman ill. by Yoshi. S&S, 1995. ISBN 0-689-80279-X Subj: Anatomy – skeletons. Eskimos. Folk & fairy tales. Indians of North America – Aleuts.

Vincent, Gabrielle. *Bravo, Ernest and Celestine!* ill. by author. Greenwillow, 1982. ISBN 0-688-00858-5 Subj: Animals – bears. Animals – mice. Behavior – sharing. Money. Music. Musical instruments – violins.

Breakfast time, Ernest and Celestine ill. by author. Greenwillow, 1985. ISBN 0-688-04555-3 Subj: Animals – bears. Animals – mice. Behavior – misbehavior. Friendship. Wordless.

A day, a dog ill. by author. Front St., 1999. ISBN 1-886910-51-0 Subj: Animals – dogs. Behavior – needing someone. Character traits – kindness to animals. Wordless.

Ernest and Celestine ill. by author. Greenwillow, 1982. ISBN 0-688-00856-9 Subj: Animals – bears. Animals – mice. Toys.

Ernest and Celestine at the circus ill. by author. Greenwillow, 1989. ISBN 0-688-08685-3 Subj: Animals – bears. Animals – mice. Circus.

Ernest and Celestine's patchwork quilt ill. by author. Greenwillow, 1985. ISBN 0-688-04577-X Subj: Animals – bears. Animals – mice. Behavior – sharing. Friendship. Quilts. Wordless.

Ernest and Celestine's picnic ill. by author. Morrow, 1988, 1982. ISBN 0-688-07809-5 Subj: Activities – picnicking. Animals – bears. Animals – mice. Weather – rain.

Merry Christmas, Ernest and Celestine ill. by author. Greenwillow, 1984. ISBN 0-688-02606-0 Subj: Animals – bears. Animals – mice. Friendship. Holidays – Christmas. Parties.

Smile, Ernest and Celestine ill. by author. Greenwillow, 1982. ISBN 0-688-01249-3 Subj: Activities – photographing. Animals – bears. Animals – mice.

Where are you, Ernest and Celestine? ill. by author. Greenwillow, 1986. ISBN 0-688-06235-0 Subj: Animals – bears. Animals – mice. Behavior – lost. Museums.

Vinson, Pauline. *Willie goes to the seashore* ill. by author. Macmillan, 1954. Subj: Animals – mice. Sea & seashore.

Viorst, Judith. *Alexander and the terrible, horrible, no good, very bad day* ill. by Ray Cruz. Aladdin, 1987, c1972. ISBN 0-689-71173-5 Subj: Behavior – bad day. Family life.

Alexander, who used to be rich last Sunday ill. by Ray Cruz. Atheneum, 1978. ISBN 0-689-30602-4 Subj: Money.

Alexander, who's not (Do you hear me? I mean it!) going to move ill. by Robin Preiss-Glasser. Atheneum, 1995. ISBN 0-689-31958-4 Subj: Character traits – stubbornness. Family life. Moving.

The Alphabet from Z to A: (with much confusion on the way) ill. by Richard Hull. Atheneum, 1994. ISBN 0-689-31768-9 Subj: ABC books. Games. Language. Poetry.

The good-bye book ill. by Kay Chorao. Atheneum, 1988. ISBN 0-689-31308-X Subj: Activities – babysitting. Books, reading. Imagination.

I'll fix Anthony ill. by Arnold Lobel. HarperCollins, 1988, c1969. ISBN 0-689-71202-2 Subj: Family life. Sibling rivalry.

My mama says there aren't any zombies, ghosts, vampires, creatures, demons, monsters, fiends, goblins, or things ill. by Kay Chorao. Atheneum, 1973. ISBN 0-689-30102-2 Subj: Bedtime. Emotions – fear. Family life – mothers. Imagination. Monsters.

Rosie and Michael ill. by Lorna Tomei. Atheneum, 1974. ISBN 0-689-30418-8 Subj: Friendship.

Sunday morning ill. by Hilary Knight. HarperCollins, 1986, c1968. ISBN 0-689-70447-X Subj: Activities – playing. Family life. Humorous stories.

Super-completely and totally the messiest ill. by Robin Preiss-Glasser. Atheneum, 2001. ISBN 0-689-82941-8 Subj: Character traits – cleanliness. Character traits – orderliness. Family life – sisters.

The tenth good thing about Barney ill. by Erik Blegvad. Atheneum, 1987, c1971. ISBN 0-689-71203-0 Subj: Animals – cats. Careers – doctors. Death. Emotions – grief. Pets.

Try it again, Sam: safety when you walk ill. by Paul Galdone. Lothrop, 1970. Subj: Activities – walking. Character traits – individuality. Safety.

Vipont, Charles. *see* Foulds, Elfrida Vipont

Vipont, Elfrida. *see* Foulds, Elfrida Vipont

A visit to a pond ill. with photos. Imported Pubs., 1983. ISBN 0-8285-2360-6 Subj: Animals. Format, unusual – board books. Wordless.

Vizurraga, Susan. *Miss Opal's auction* ill. by Mark Graham. Holt, 2000. ISBN 0-8050-5891-5 Subj: Ethnic groups in the U.S. – African Americans. Homes, houses. Memories, memory. Moving. Old age.

Our old house ill. by Leslie Baker. Holt, 1997. ISBN 0-8050-3911-2 Subj: Homes, houses. Memories, memory.

Voake, Charlotte. *First things first: a baby's companion* ill. by author. Little, 1988. ISBN 0-316-90510-0 Subj: Activities. Poetry.

Ginger ill. by author. Candlewick, 1997. ISBN 0-7636-0108-X Subj: Animals – cats. Behavior – running away. Emotions – envy, jealousy.

Here comes the train ill. by author. Candlewick, 1998. ISBN 0-7636-0438-0 Subj: Family life. Trains.

Mr. Davies and the baby ill. by author. Candlewick, 1996. ISBN 1-56402-390-7 Subj: Animals – dogs. Babies. Family life.

Mrs. Goose's baby ill. by author. Little, 1989. ISBN 0-316-90511-9 Subj: Adoption. Birds – chickens. Birds – geese. Character traits – being different.

Pizza kittens ill. by author. Candlewick, 2002. ISBN 0-7636-1622-2 Subj: Animals – cats Family life. Food.

Tom's cat ill. by author. Lippincott, 1986. ISBN 0-397-32195-3 Subj: Animals – cats. Noise, sounds.

Voce, Louise. *Over in the meadow* ill. by author. Candlewick, 1994. ISBN 1-56402-428-8 Subj: Animals. Counting, numbers. Nursery rhymes.

Vogel, Amos. *How little Lori visited Times Square* ill. by Maurice Sendak. Harper, 1963. ISBN 0-06-028462-5 Subj: Cities, towns. Humorous stories. Reptiles – turtles, tortoises. Transportation.

Vogel, Carole Garbuny. *The dangers of strangers* by Carole Garbuny Vogel & Kathryn Allen Goldner; ill. by Lynette Schmidt. Dillon, 1983. ISBN 0-87418-253-4 Subj: Behavior – talking to strangers. Safety.

Vogel, Ilse-Margret. *The don't be scared book: scares, remedies and pictures* ill. by author. Atheneum, 1964. Subj: Emotions – fear. Imagination. Rhyming text.

Voigt, Hannelore. *Not now, Sara!* ill. by Olivier Corthésy & Nicolas Fossati; trans. by J. Alison James. North-South, 1995. ISBN 1-55858-394-7 Subj: Activities – painting. Art. Family life.

Vojtech, Anna. *Marushka and the Month Brothers: a folktale* retold by Anna Vojtech & Philemon Sturges; ill. by Anna Vojtech. North-South, 1996. ISBN 1-55858-629-6 Subj: Days of the week, months of the year. Family life – stepfamilies. Folk & fairy tales. Foreign lands – Czechoslovakia. Mythical creatures.

Volkmann, Roy. *Curious kittens* ill. by author. Random House, 2001. ISBN 0-385-32778-1 Subj: Animals – babies. Animals – cats. Sports – swimming.

Volkmer, Jane Anne. *Song of Chirimia = La Musica de la Chirimia* trans. by Lori Ann Schatschneider; ill. by adapt. Carolrhoda, 1990. ISBN 0-87614-423-7 Subj: Folk & fairy tales. Foreign lands – Mexico. Foreign languages. Indians of Central America – Maya. Religion.

Von Hippel, Ursula. *The craziest Halloween* ill. by author. Coward, 1957. Subj: Holidays – Halloween.

Von Jüchen, Aurel. *see* Jüchen, Aurel von

Von Königslöw, Andrea Wayne. *Bing and Chutney* ill. by author. Annick, 1999. ISBN 1-55037-609-8 Subj: Activities – baking, cooking. Activities – dancing. Animals – elephants. Animals – pigs. Friendship.

Bing and Chutney off to Moosonee ill. by author. Annick, 2001. ISBN 1-55037-679-9 Subj: Activities – picnicking. Animals. Animals – elephants. Animals – pigs. Friendship. Transportation.

Bing finds Chutney ill. by author. Firefly, 2001. ISBN 1-55037-669-1 Subj: Animals. Animals – elephants. Animals – pigs. Friendship.

That's my baby? ill. by author. Firefly, 1986. ISBN 0-920303-56-0 Subj: Babies. Family life. Sibling rivalry. Toys.

Would you love me? ill. by author. Annick, 1997. ISBN 1-55037-430-3 Subj: Animals. Family life – parents. Rhyming text.

Vorst, Rochel Groner. *The sukkah that I built* ill. by Elizabeth Victor-Elsby. Hachai, 2002. ISBN 1-929628-07-2 Subj: Holidays – Sukkot. Jewish culture. Religion.

Votry, Kim. *Baby's first signs* (Waller, Curt)

More baby's first signs (Waller, Curt)

Vozar, David. *M. C. Turtle and the hip hop hare: a nursery rap* ill. by Betsy Lewin. Doubleday, 1995. ISBN 0-385-32157-0 Subj: Animals. Animals – rabbits. Reptiles – turtles, tortoises. Rhyming text. Sports – racing.

Yo, hungry wolf! a nursery rap ill. by Betsy Lewin. Doubleday, 1993. ISBN 0-385-30452-8 Subj: Animals – wolves. Folk & fairy tales. Rhyming text.

Vreeken, Elizabeth. *The boy who would not say his name* ill. by Leonard W. Shortall. Follett, 1959. Subj: Behavior – lost. Careers – police officers. Imagination. Names.

Henry ill. by Polly Jackson. Follett, 1961. Subj: Animals – mice. Pets.

One day everything went wrong ill. by Leonard W. Shortall. Follett, 1966. Subj: Behavior – bad day.

Vries, Anke de. *Grey mouse* ill. by Willemien Min. Front St., 2002. ISBN 1-886910-76-6 Subj: Animals – mice. Emotions – loneliness. Self-concept.

My elephant can do almost anything ill. by Ilja Walraven. Front St., 1996. ISBN 1-886910-06-5 Subj: Animals – elephants. Imagination – imaginary friends. Pets.

Vrombaut, An. *Clarabella's teeth* ill. by author. Clarion, 2003. ISBN 0-618-33379-7 Subj: Animals. Friendship. Reptiles – alligators, crocodiles. Teeth.

Vulliamy, Clara. *Bang and shout* ill. by author. Candlewick, 1994. ISBN 1-56402-409-1 Subj: Activities – playing. Babies. Format, unusual – board books. Games. Rhyming text.

Blue hat, red coat ill. by author. Candlewick, 1994. ISBN 1-56402-361-3 Subj: Babies. Clothing. Format, unusual – board books. Rhyming text.

Boo baby boo! ill. by author. Candlewick, 1994. ISBN 1-56402-388-5 Subj: Activities – playing. Babies. Format, unusual – board books. Games. Rhyming text.

Ellen and Penguin and the new baby ill. by author. Candlewick, 1996. ISBN 1-56402-697-3 Subj: Babies. Family life – brothers. Family life – mothers. Family life – new sibling. Toys.

Good night, baby ill. by author. Candlewick, 1996. ISBN 1-56402-817-8 Subj: Babies. Bedtime. Family life. Format, unusual – board books. Rhyming text. Sleep.

If I were bigger than anyone and other poems ill. by author. Candlewick, 2000. ISBN 0-7636-0950-1 Subj: Poetry.

Small ill. by author. Clarion, 2001. ISBN 0-618-19459-2 Subj: Animals – mice. Family life – grandmothers. Sleepovers. Toys.

Wide awake ill. by author. Candlewick, 1996. ISBN 1-56402-816-X Subj: Activities. Family life. Format, unusual – board books. Rhyming text.

Yum yum ill. by author. Candlewick, 1994. ISBN 1-56402-408-3 Subj: Animals. Babies. Food. Format, unusual – board books. Rhyming text.

Vullo, Vera. *About things you find at the beach* ill. by author. Benchmark, 1999. ISBN 0-7614-0851-7 Subj: Sea & seashore – beaches.

Vyner, Sue. *The stolen egg* ill. by Tim Vyner. Viking, 1992. ISBN 0-670-84460-8 Subj: Birds. Circular tales. Eggs. Reptiles. Science.

Vyner, Tim. *World team* ill. by author. Roaring Brook, 2002. ISBN 0-7613-2409-7 Subj: Geography. Sports – soccer. Time.

Wabbes, Marie. *Good night, Little Rabbit* ill. by author. Little, 1987. ISBN 0-871-13127-7 Subj: Animals – rabbits. Bedtime.

Happy birthday, Little Rabbit ill. by author. Little, 1987. ISBN 0-87113-129-3 Subj: Animals – rabbits. Birthdays.

It's snowing, Little Rabbit ill. by author. Little, 1987. ISBN 0-87113-128-5 Subj: Animals – rabbits. Seasons – winter. Weather – snow.

Little Rabbit's garden ill. by author. Little, 1987. ISBN 0-871-13126-9 Subj: Animals – rabbits. Gardens, gardening.

Rose is hungry ill. by author. Messner, 1988. Subj: Animals – pigs. Food.

Rose is muddy ill. by author. Messner, 1988. ISBN 0-671-66610-X Subj: Animals – pigs. Character traits – cleanliness.

Rose's bath ill. by author. Messner, 1988. ISBN 0-671-66612-6 Subj: Activities – bathing. Animals – pigs. Toys.

Rose's picture ill. by author. Messner, 1988. ISBN 0-671-66613-4 Subj: Activities – painting. Animals – pigs. Art.

Waber, Bernard. *An anteater named Arthur* ill. by author. Houghton Mifflin, 1967. ISBN 0-395-20336-8 Subj: ABC books. Animals – anteaters.

Bearsie Bear and the surprise sleepover party ill. by author. Houghton Mifflin, 1997. ISBN 0-395-86450-X Subj: Animals. Bedtime. Seasons – winter. Sleepovers.

Bernard ill. by author. Houghton Mifflin, 1982. ISBN 0-395-31865-3 Subj: Animals – dogs. Behavior – running away. Behavior – sharing.

But names will never hurt me ill. by author. Houghton Mifflin, 1976. ISBN 0-395-24383-1 Subj: Behavior – name calling. Names.

Courage ill. by author. Houghton, 2002. ISBN 0-618-23855-7 Subj: Character traits – bravery.

Do you see a mouse? ill. by author. Houghton Mifflin, 1995. ISBN 0-395-72292-6 Subj: Animals – mice. Behavior – disbelief. Hotels. Puzzles.

Evie & Margie ill. by author. Houghton, 2003. ISBN 0-618-34124-2 Subj: Animals – hippopotamuses. Careers – actors. Emotions – envy, jealousy. Friendship. School. Theater.

Fast food! gulp! gulp! ill. by author. Houghton, 2001. ISBN 0-618-14189-8 Subj: Animals. Food. Restaurants. Rhyming text.

Funny, funny Lyle ill. by author. Houghton Mifflin, 1987. ISBN 0-395-43619-2 Subj: Behavior – misunderstanding. Family life. Reptiles – alligators, crocodiles.

Gina ill. by author. Houghton Mifflin, 1995. ISBN 0-395-74279-X Subj: Emotions – loneliness. Friendship. Moving. Rhyming text. Sports – baseball.

How to go about laying an egg ill. by author. Houghton Mifflin, 1963. Subj: Birds – chickens. Eggs. Humorous stories.

I was all thumbs ill. by author. Houghton Mifflin, 1975. ISBN 0-395-21404-1 Subj: Octopuses. Sea & seashore.

Ira says goodbye ill. by author. Houghton Mifflin, 1988. ISBN 0-395-48315-8 Subj: Emotions. Friendship. Moving.

Ira sleeps over ill. by author. Houghton Mifflin, 1972. ISBN 0-395-13893-0 Subj: Activities – playing. Bedtime. Friendship. Sleep. Toys – bears.

A lion named Shirley Williamson ill. by author. Houghton Mifflin, 1996. ISBN 0-395-80979-7 Subj: Animals – lions. Behavior – running away. Flowers. Names. Zoos.

Lorenzo ill. by author. Houghton Mifflin, 1961. Subj: Character traits – curiosity. Fish.

Lovable Lyle ill. by author. Houghton Mifflin, 1969. ISBN 0-395-25378-0 Subj: Friendship. Reptiles – alligators, crocodiles.

Lyle and the birthday party ill. by author. Houghton Mifflin, 1966. ISBN 0-395-15080-9 Subj: Birthdays. Emotions – envy, jealousy. Reptiles – alligators, crocodiles.

Lyle at Christmas ill. by author. Houghton Mifflin, 1998. ISBN 0-395-91304-7 Subj: Animals – cats. Holidays – Christmas. Reptiles – alligators, crocodiles.

Lyle at the office ill. by author. Houghton Mifflin, 1994. ISBN 0-395-70563-0 Subj: Activities – working. Reptiles – alligators, crocodiles.

Lyle finds his mother ill. by author. Houghton Mifflin, 1974. ISBN 0-395-19489-X Subj: Family life – mothers. Reptiles – alligators, crocodiles.

Lyle, Lyle Crocodile ill. by author. Houghton Mifflin, 1965. ISBN 0-395-13720-9 Subj: Character traits – helpfulness. Reptiles – alligators, crocodiles.

Mice on my mind ill. by author. Houghton Mifflin, 1977. ISBN 0-395-25935-5 Subj: Animals – cats. Animals – mice.

The mouse that snored ill. by author. Houghton Mifflin, 2000. ISBN 0-395-97518-2 Subj: Animals – mice. Noise, sounds. Rhyming text. Sleep – snoring.

Nobody is perfick ill. by author. Houghton Mifflin, 1971. ISBN 0-395-12582-0 Subj: Behavior – mistakes. Friendship. Humorous stories.

Rich cat, poor cat ill. by author. Houghton Mifflin, 1963. ISBN 0-590-43091-2 Subj: Animals – cats.

The snake: a very long story ill. by author. Houghton Mifflin, 1978. ISBN 0-395-27157-6 Subj: Format, unusual. Reptiles – snakes.

"You look ridiculous," said the rhinoceros to the hippopotamus ill. by author. Houghton Mifflin, 1979. ISBN 0-395-07156-9 Subj: Animals. Animals – hippopotamuses. Character traits – individuality. Self-concept.

You're a little kid with a big heart ill. by author. Houghton Mifflin, 1980. ISBN 0-395-29163-1 Subj: Behavior – growing up. Behavior – wishing. Magic.

Waboose, Jan Bourdeau. *Firedancers* ill. by C. J. Taylor. Stoddart, 2000. ISBN 0-7737-3138-5 Subj: Activities – dancing. Family life – grandmothers. Indians of North America – Ojibwa. Night.

Morning on the lake ill. by Karen Reczuch. Kids Can, 1998. ISBN 1-55074-373-2 Subj: Family life – fathers. Indians of North America – Ojibwa. Nature.

SkySisters ill. by Brian Deines. Kids Can, 2000. ISBN 1-55074-697-9 Subj: Family life – sisters. Indians of North America – Ojibwa. Night. Northern lights. Sky.

Waddell, Martin. *Alice the artist* ill. by Jonathan Langley. Dutton, 1988. ISBN 0-525-44385-1 Subj: Art. Careers – artists.

Amy said ill. by Charlotte Voake. Little, 1990. ISBN 0-316-91636-6 Subj: Behavior – misbehavior. Family life – grandmothers.

The big big sea ill. by Jennifer Eachus. Candlewick, 1994. ISBN 1-56402-066-5 Subj: Family life – mothers. Night. Sea & seashore.

Can't you sleep, Little Bear? ill. by Barbara Firth. Candlewick, 1992. ISBN 1-56402-007-X Subj: Animals – bears. Bedtime. Emotions – fear. Family life – fathers. Night. Sleep.

Farmer Duck ill. by Helen Oxenbury. Candlewick, 1992. ISBN 1-56402-009-6 Subj: Animals. Birds – ducks. Careers – farmers. Character traits – helpfulness. Farms.

Good job, Little Bear! ill. by Barbara Firth. Candlewick, 1999. ISBN 0-7636-0736-3 Subj: Animals – bears. Character traits – confidence. Character traits – helpfulness.

Grandma's Bill ill. by Jane Johnson. Watts, 1991. ISBN 0-531-08523-6 Subj: Family life – grandparents.

The happy hedgehog band ill. by Jill Barton. Candlewick, 1992. ISBN 1-56402-011-8 Subj: Animals. Animals – hedgehogs. Music. Musical instruments – bands.

The hidden house ill. by Angela Barrett. Candlewick, 1997. ISBN 0-7636-0335-X Subj: Emotions – loneliness. Homes, houses. Toys – dolls.

It's quacking time ill. by Jill Barton. Candlewick, 2005. ISBN 0-7636-2738-0 Subj: Animals – babies. Birds – ducks. Eggs.

A kitten called Moonlight ill. by Christian Birmingham. Candlewick, 2001. ISBN 0-7636-1176-X Subj: Animals – cats. Behavior – lost. Family life – mothers.

Let's go home, Little Bear ill. by Barbara Firth. Candlewick, 1993. ISBN 1-56402-131-9 Subj: Animals – bears. Emotions – fear. Family life – fathers. Forest, woods. Noise, sounds.

Mimi and the dream house ill. by Leo Hartas. Candlewick, 1998. ISBN 0-7636-0587-5 Subj: Animals – mice. Dreams. Family life. Homes, houses.

Mimi and the picnic ill. by Leo Hartas. Candlewick, 1996. ISBN 0-7636-0588-3 Subj: Activities – picnicking. Animals – mice.

Mimi's Christmas ill. by Leo Hartas. Candlewick, 1997. ISBN 0-7636-0413-5 Subj: Animals – mice. Behavior – worrying. Family life. Holidays – Christmas.

My great grandpa ill. by Dom Mansell. Putnam, 1990. ISBN 0-399-22155-7 Subj: Family life – great-grandparents. Handicaps – physical handicaps. Rhyming text.

Night night Cuddly Bear ill. by Penny Dale. Candlewick, 2000. ISBN 0-7636-1195-6 Subj: Animals – bears. Bedtime. Family life. Toys – bears.

Once there were giants ill. by Penny Dale. Delacorte, 1989. ISBN 0-385-29806-4 Subj: Behavior – growing up. Family life.

Owl babies ill. by Patrick Benson. Candlewick, 1992. ISBN 1-56402-101-7 Subj: Birds – owls. Emotions – fear. Family life – mothers. Night.

Owl babies [board book] ill. by Patrick Benson. Candlewick, 1996. ISBN 1-56402-965-4 Subj: Emotions – fear. Family life – mothers. Format, unusual – board books. Night.

The park in the dark ill. by Barbara Firth. Lothrop, 1989. ISBN 0-688-08517-2 Subj: Emotions – fear. Night. Parks. Rhyming text. Toys.

The pig in the pond ill. by Jill Barton. Candlewick, 1992. ISBN 1-56402-050-9 Subj: Animals. Animals – pigs. Careers – farmers. Cumulative tales. Lakes, ponds. Sports – swimming.

Rosie's babies ill. by Penny Dale. Candlewick, 1999. ISBN 0-7636-0718-5 Subj: Family life – mothers. Family life – new sibling. Toys.

Sailor Bear ill. by Virginia Austin. Candlewick, 1992. ISBN 1-56402-040-1 Subj: Behavior – lost. Boats, ships. Sailors. Sea & seashore. Toys – bears.

Sam Vole and his brothers ill. by Barbara Firth. Candlewick, 1992. ISBN 1-56402-082-7 Subj: Animals – mice. Emotions – loneliness. Family life – brothers. Sibling rivalry.

Small Bear lost ill. by Virginia Austin. Candlewick, 1996. ISBN 1-56402-871-2 Subj: Activities – traveling. Behavior – lost. Toys – bears.

Snow bears ill. by Sarah Fox-Davies. Candlewick, 2002. ISBN 0-7636-1906-X Subj: Activities – playing. Animals – bears. Family life – mothers. Weather – snow.

Squeak-a-lot ill. by Virginia Miller. Greenwillow, 1991. ISBN 0-688-10245-X Subj: Activities – playing. Animals – mice. Noise, sounds.

Tom Rabbit ill. by Barbara Firth. Candlewick, 2001. ISBN 0-7636-1089-5 Subj: Activities – playing. Animals – rabbits. Bedtime. Emotions – fear. Farms. Toys.

The tough princess ill. by Patrick Benson. Putnam, 1987. ISBN 0-399-21380-5 Subj: Fairies. Folk & fairy tales. Royalty – princesses.

The toymaker ill. by Terry Milne. Candlewick, 1992. ISBN 1-56402-103-3 Subj: Careers – toy makers. Emotions – love. Family life – fathers. Illness. Toys – dolls.

We love them ill. by Barbara Firth. Lothrop, 1990. ISBN 0-688-09332-9 Subj: Animals – dogs. Animals – rabbits. Friendship.

Webster J. Duck ill. by David Parkins. Candlewick, 2001. ISBN 0-7636-1506-4 Subj: Animals. Behavior – lost. Birds – ducks. Family life – mothers.

When the teddy bears came ill. by Penny Dale. Candlewick, 1995. ISBN 1-56402-529-2 Subj: Babies. Family life – brothers & sisters. Family life – new sibling. Toys – bears.

Who do you love? ill. by Camilla Ashforth. Candlewick, 1999. ISBN 0-7636-0586-7 Subj: Animals – cats. Bedtime. Emotions – love.

Yum, yum, yummy ill. by John Bendall-Brunello. Candlewick, 1998. ISBN 0-7636-0477-1 Subj: Animals – bears. Behavior – bullying. Behavior – greed. Family life – mothers. Food.

Wade, Alan. *I'm flying!* ill. by Petra Mathers. Knopf, 1990. ISBN 0-394-94510-7 Subj: Activities – ballooning.

Wade, Anne. *A promise is for keeping* ill. by Jon Petersson. Childrens Pr., 1979. ISBN 0-516-02024-2 Subj: Friendship.

Wade, Barrie. *Cinderella* ill. by Julie Monks. Picture Window, 2003. ISBN 1-4048-0052-2 Subj: Family life – stepfamilies. Folk & fairy tales. Royalty – princes. Sibling rivalry.

Goldilocks and the three bears (The three bears)

Little monster ill. by Katinka Kew. Lothrop, 1990. ISBN 0-688-09597-6 Subj: Behavior – misbehavior. Emotions – love. Family life.

The three billy goats gruff ill. by Nicola Evans. Picture Window, 2003. ISBN 1-4048-0070-0 Subj: Animals – goats. Character traits – cleverness. Folk & fairy tales. Foreign lands – Norway. Mythical creatures – trolls.

Wade, Mary Dodson. *Cinco de Mayo* ill. with photos. Childrens Pr., 2003. ISBN 0-516-22664-9 Subj: Foreign lands – Mexico. Holidays – Cinco de Mayo. War.

Wadhams, Margaret. *Anna* ill. by Michael Charlton. Salem House, 1987. ISBN 0-370-30612-0 Subj: Character traits – being different. Illness.

Wadsworth, Ginger. *One tiger growls: a counting book of animal sounds* ill. by James M. Needham. Charlesbridge, 1999. ISBN 0-88106-273-1 Subj: Animals. Counting, numbers. Noise, sounds.

Tomorrow is Daddy's birthday ill. by Maxie Chambliss. Caroline House, 1994. ISBN 1-56397-042-2 Subj: Behavior – secrets. Birthdays. Family life – fathers.

Wadsworth, Olive A. *Over in the meadow: a counting-out rhyme* ill. by Mary Maki Rae. Viking, 1985. ISBN 0-670-53276-2 Subj: Counting, numbers. Nursery rhymes.

Waechter, Friedrich Karl. *Three is company* trans. by Harry Allard; ill. by author. Doubleday, 1980. ISBN 0-385-14633-7 Subj: Animals – pigs. Birds. Fish. Friendship.

Wagener, Gerda. *Leo the lion* trans. from German by Nina Ignatowicz; ill. by Reinhard Michl. HarperCollins, 1991. ISBN 0-06-021657-3 Subj: Animals – lions. Emotions – loneliness.

Waggoner, Karen. *Dad Gummit and Ma Foot* ill. by Anita Riggio. Watts, 1990. ISBN 0-531-08491-4 Subj: Behavior – fighting, arguing. Family life.

The lemonade babysitter ill. by Dorothy Donohue. Little, 1992. ISBN 0-316-91711-7 Subj: Activities – babysitting. Behavior. Old age.

Wagner, Elaine Knox. *see* KnoxWagner, Elaine

Wagner, Jenny. *Amy's monster* ill. by Terry Denton. Viking, 1991. ISBN 0-670-82748-7 Subj: Behavior – bullying. Family life – cousins. Monsters. Multiple births – twins. Seasons – summer.

Aranea: a story about a spider ill. by Ron Brooks. Bradbury, 1978. ISBN 0-87888-138-7 Subj: Spiders. Weather – rain.

The bunyip of Berkeley's Creek ill. by Ron Brooks. Bradbury, 1977. ISBN 0-87888-122-0 Subj: Foreign lands – Australia. Monsters. Mythical creatures.

John Brown, Rose and the midnight cat ill. by Ron Brooks. Bradbury, 1978. ISBN 0-8788-8120-4 Subj: Animals – cats. Animals – dogs.

Wagner, Karen. *Bravo, Mildred and Ed!* ill. by Janet Pedersen. Walker, 2000. ISBN 0-8027-8735-5 Subj: Animals – mice. Character traits – confidence. Friendship.

Chocolate chip cookies ill. by Leah Palmer Preiss. Holt, 1990. ISBN 0-8050-1268-0 Subj: Activities – baking, cooking. Family life. Multiple births – twins.

A friend like Ed ill. by Janet Pedersen. Walker, 1998. ISBN 0-8027-8663-4 Subj: Animals – mice. Concepts – opposites. Friendship.

Silly Fred ill. by Normand Chartier. Macmillan, 1989. ISBN 0-02-792280-4 Subj: Animals. Animals – pigs. Self-concept.

Wahl, Jan. *The adventures of Underwater Dog* ill. by Tim Bowers. Putnam, 1989. ISBN 0-448-09313-8 Subj: Animals – dogs. Crime. Sea & seashore.

Button eye's orange ill. by Wendy Watson. Warne, 1980. ISBN 0-7232-6188-1 Subj: Handicaps. Toys.

Cabbage moon ill. by Adrienne Adams. Holt, 1965. Subj: Humorous stories. Moon. Royalty.

Carrot nose ill. by James Marshall. Farrar, 1978. ISBN 0-374-31122-6 Subj: Animals – rabbits.

Doctor Rabbit's foundling ill. by Cyndy Szekeres. Pantheon, 1977. ISBN 0-394-93275-7 Subj: Animals – rabbits. Careers – doctors. Frogs & toads.

Dracula's cat ill. by Kay Chorao. Prentice-Hall, 1978. ISBN 0-13-218933-X Subj: Animals – cats. Monsters.

Dracula's cat and Frankenstein's dog ill. by Kay Chorao. S&S, 1990. ISBN 0-671-70820-1 Subj: Animals – cats. Animals – dogs. Format, unusual. Monsters. Pets.

Elf night ill. by Peter Weevers. Carolrhoda, 2002. ISBN 1-57505-512-0 Subj: Bedtime. Dreams. Mythical creatures – elves. Rhyming text.

The field mouse and the dinosaur named Sue ill. by Bob Doucet. Scholastic, 2000. ISBN 0-439-09984-6 Subj: Animals – mice. Dinosaurs. Museums. Prehistory.

The fishermen ill. by Emily Arnold McCully. Norton, 1969. Subj: Family life – grandfathers. Sports – fishing.

The five in the forest ill. by Erik Blegvad. Follett, 1974. ISBN 0-695-40446-6 Subj: Animals – rabbits. Eggs. Forest, woods. Holidays – Easter.

Follow me cried Bee ill. by John Wallner. Crown, 1976. ISBN 0-517-52353-1 Subj: Cumulative tales. Insects – bees. Rhyming text. Weather – rain.

Frankenstein's dog ill. by Kay Chorao. Prentice-Hall, 1977. ISBN 0-13-330522-8 Subj: Animals – dogs. Monsters.

Hello, elephant ill. by Edward Ardizzone. Holt, 1964. Subj: Animals – elephants.

Humphrey's bear ill. by William Joyce. Holt, 1987. ISBN 0-8050-0332-0 Subj: Bedtime. Dreams. Toys – bears.

I met a dinosaur ill. by Chris Sheban. Harcourt, 1997. ISBN 0-15-201644-9 Subj: Dinosaurs. Imagination. Museums. Prehistory. Rhyming text.

"I remember," cried Grandma Pinky ill. by Arden Johnson. Bridge-Water, 1994. ISBN 0-8167-3456-9 Subj: Animals – polar bears. Behavior – forgetfulness. Family life – grandmothers. Memories, memory. Old age.

Jamie's tiger ill. by Tomie de Paola. Harcourt, 1978. ISBN 0-15-239500-8 Subj: Handicaps – deafness. Illness. Senses – hearing. Toys.

Little Eight John ill. by Wil Clay. Dutton, 1992. ISBN 0-525-67367-9 Subj: Behavior – misbehavior. Folk & fairy tales.

Little Johnny Buttermilk ill. by Jennifer Mazzucco. August House, 1999. ISBN 0-87483-559-3 Subj: Behavior. Character traits – cleverness. Folk & fairy tales. Foreign lands – England. Witches.

Mabel ran away with the toys ill. by Liza Woodruff. Whispering Coyote, 2000. ISBN 1-58089-059-8 Subj: Babies. Behavior – running away. Emotions – envy, jealousy. Family life – new sibling. Sibling rivalry.

Mrs. Owl and Mr. Pig ill. by Eileen Christelow. Dutton, 1991. ISBN 0-525-67311-3 Subj: Animals – pigs. Behavior – sharing. Birds – owls. Character traits.

The Muffletumps ill. by Edward Ardizzone. Holt, 1966. Subj: Toys – dolls.

The Muffletumps' Christmas party ill. by Cyndy Szekeres. Follett, 1975. ISBN 0-695-40617-5 Subj: Holidays – Christmas. Toys – dolls.

The Muffletumps' Halloween scare ill. by Cyndy Szekeres. Follett, 1977. ISBN 0-695-40754-6 Subj: Toys – dolls.

My cat Ginger ill. by Naava. Tambourine, 1992. ISBN 0-688-10723-0 Subj: Animals – cats. Imagination. Nature. Night. Pets.

Old Hippo's Easter egg ill. by Lorinda Bryan Cauley. Harcourt, 1980. ISBN 0-15-257835-8 Subj: Animals – hippopotamuses. Animals – mice. Birds – ducks. Emotions – love. Family life.

Once when the world was green ill. by Fabricio Vandenbroeck. Tricycle, 1996. ISBN 1-883672-12-0 Subj: Ecology. Family life – fathers. Indians of Central America – Maya.

Peter and the troll baby ill. by Erik Blegvad. Golden Pr., 1984. ISBN 0-307-16525-6 Subj: Activities – babysitting. Mythical creatures – trolls. Sibling rivalry.

Pleasant Fieldmouse ill. by Maurice Sendak. HarperCollins, 1964. Subj: Animals. Animals – mice.

Pleasant Fieldmouse's Halloween party ill. by Wallace Tripp. Putnam, 1974. ISBN 0-399-60885-0 Subj: Animals. Animals – mice. Holidays – Halloween.

Push Kitty ill. by Garth Williams. HarperCollins, 1968. Subj: Activities – playing. Animals – cats.

Rabbits on roller skates! ill. by David Allender. Crown, 1986. ISBN 0-517-55935-8 Subj: Animals – rabbits. Rhyming text. Sports – roller skating.

The singing geese ill. by Sterling Brown. Lodestar, 1998. ISBN 0-525-67499-3 Subj: Activities – singing. Birds – geese. Ethnic groups in the U.S. – African Americans. Tall tales.

The sleepytime book ill. by Arden Johnson. Morrow, 1992. ISBN 0-688-10276-X Subj: Animals. Babies. Bedtime. Night. Rhyming text. Sleep.

Sylvester Bear overslept ill. by Lee Lorenz. Parents' Magazine Pr., 1979. ISBN 0-8193-1003-4 Subj: Animals – bears. Circus. Family life. Sleep.

Three pandas ill. by Naava. Boyds Mills, 2000. ISBN 1-56397-749-4 Subj: Activities – working. Animals – pandas. Cities, towns.

Tiger watch ill. by Charles Mikolaycak. Harcourt, 1982. ISBN 0-15-287674-X Subj: Animals – tigers. Death. Foreign lands – India. Sports – hunting.

The toy circus ill. by Tim Bowers. Harcourt, 1986. ISBN 0-15-200609-5 Subj: Circus. Dreams. Sleep. Toys.

The woman with the eggs (Andersen, H. C. [Hans Christian])

Wahl, Mats. *Grandfather's laika* ill. by Tord Nygren. Carolrhoda, 1990. ISBN 0-87614-434-2 Subj: Animals – dogs. Death. Emotions – grief. Family life – grandfathers. Pets.

Wahl, Robert. *Pyxx* ill. by author. Price Stern Sloan, 1989. ISBN 0-8431-2347-8 Subj: Behavior. Imagination.

Waite, Judy. *Laura's secret* (Baumgart, Klaus)

Mouse, look out! ill. by Norma Burgin. Dutton, 1998. ISBN 0-525-42031-2 Subj: Animals – cats. Animals – dogs. Animals – mice. Homes, houses. Rhyming text.

The stray kitten ill. by Gavin Rowe. Crocodile, 2000. ISBN 1-56656-356-9 Subj: Animals – cats. Behavior – growing up. Behavior – lost.

Waite, Michael P. *Jojofu* ill. by Yoriko Ito. Lothrop, 1996. ISBN 0-688-13661-3 Subj: Animals – dogs. Character traits – loyalty. Folk & fairy tales. Foreign lands – Japan.

Wakefield, Joyce. *Ask a silly question* ill. by Mike Venezia. Childrens Pr., 1979. ISBN 0-516-03408-1 Subj: Rhyming text. Riddles & jokes.

From where you are ill. by Tom Dunnington. Childrens Pr., 1978. ISBN 0-516-03460-X Subj: Concepts – perspective. Rhyming text.

Walbrecker, Dirk. *Benny's hat* ill. by Hans Poppel. Atomium, 1991. ISBN 1-56182-028-8 Subj: Clothing – hats.

Walburg, Lori. *The legend of the candy cane* ill. by James Bernardin. Zondervan, 2002. ISBN 0-310-70447-2 Subj: Folk & fairy tales. Food. Holidays – Christmas. Religion – Nativity.

Waldherr, Kris. *Harvest* ill. by author. Walker, 2001. ISBN 0-8027-8792-4 Subj: Gardens, gardening.

Waldman, Neil. *The starry night* ill. by author. Boyds Mills, 1999. ISBN 1-56397-736-2 Subj: Art. Careers – artists. Imagination.

The never-ending greenness ill. by author. Morrow, 1997. ISBN 0-688-14480-2 Subj: Foreign lands – Israel. Jewish culture. Trees.

They came from the Bronx ill. by author. Boyds Mills, 2001. ISBN 1-56397-891-1 Subj: Animals – buffaloes. Ecology. Family life – grandmothers. Indians of North America – Comanche. U.S. history. Zoos.

Waldman, Sarah. *Light: the first seven days* ill. by Neil Waldman. Harcourt, 1993. ISBN 0-15-220870-4 Subj: Children as authors. Creation. Religion.

Waldron, Jan L. *Angel Pig and the hidden Christmas* ill. by David M. McPhail. Dutton, 2000. ISBN 0-525-45744-5 Subj: Animals – pigs. Holidays – Christmas. Rhyming text.

John Pig's Halloween ill. by David M. McPhail. Dutton, 1998. ISBN 0-525-45941-3 Subj: Animals – pigs. Emotions – fear. Holidays – Halloween. Monsters. Parties. Rhyming text.

Waldron, Kathleen Cook. *Loon Lake fishing derby* ill. by Dean Griffiths. Orca, 1999. ISBN 1-55143-142-4 Subj: Animals – squirrels. Sports – fishing.

Rough day at Loon Lake ill. by Dean Griffiths. Orca, 2002. ISBN 1-55143-195-5 Subj: Animals. Sports – golf.

Walker, Alice. *Finding the green stone* ill. by Catherine Deeter. Harcourt, 1991. ISBN 0-15-227538-X Subj: Behavior. Character traits. Ethnic groups in the U.S. – African Americans. Rocks.

To hell with dying ill. by Catherine Deeter. Harcourt, 1987. ISBN 0-15-289075-0 Subj: Death. Ethnic groups in the U.S. – African Americans. Friendship.

Walker, Barbara K. (Barbara Kerlin). *New patches for old: a Turkish folktale* retold by Barbara K. Walker & Ahmet E. Uysal; ill. by Harold Berson. Parents' Magazine Pr., 1974. ISBN 0-8193-0714-9 Subj: Behavior – mistakes. Folk & fairy tales.

Pigs and pirates: a Greek tale ill. by Harold Berson. White, 1969. Subj: Animals – pigs. Foreign lands – Greece. Pirates.

Teeny-Tiny and the witch-woman ill. by Michael Foreman. Pantheon, 1975. ISBN 0-394-93088-6 Subj: Character traits – cleverness. Foreign lands – Turkey. Witches.

Walker, David. *The sleeping beauty* (Perrault, Charles)

Walker, Jane. *Ten little penguins* ill. by author. Bantam, 1995. ISBN 0-553-09768-7 Subj: Birds – penguins. Counting, numbers. Format, unusual – toy & movable books.

Walker, Joni. *Tell me the Christmas story* ill. by author. Concordia, 2003. ISBN 0-7586-0508-0 Subj: Format, unusual – board books. Holidays – Christmas. Religion – Nativity.

Walker, Richard. *Jack and the beanstalk* (Jack and the beanstalk)

Walker, Sally M. *Levers* by Sally M. Walker & Roseann Feldmann; photos by Andy King. Lerner, 2002. ISBN 0-8225-2218-7 Subj: Concepts – leverage. Machines. Science.

Seahorse reef ill. by Steven James Petruccio. Soundprints, 2000. ISBN 1-56899-869-4 Subj: Animals. Fish – seahorses. Foreign lands – Philippines. Sea & seashore.

Walker, Sarah. *Birds* (Gray, Samantha)

Wall, Lina Mao. *Judge Rabbit and the tree spirit* adapt. by Cathy Spagnoli; ill. by Nancy Hom. Children's Book Pr., 1991. ISBN 0-89239-071-9 Subj: Character traits – vanity. Folk & fairy tales. Foreign lands – Cambodia. Language.

Wallace, Barbara Brooks. *Argyle* ill. by John Sandford. Abingdon, 1987. ISBN 0-687-01724-6 Subj: Animals – sheep. Character traits – being different.

Wallace, Daisy. *Fairy poems* ill. by Trina Schart Hyman. Holiday, 1980. ISBN 0-8234-0371-8 Subj: Fairies. Poetry.

Ghost poems ill. by Tomie de Paola. Holiday, 1979. ISBN 0-8234-0344-0 Subj: Ghosts. Night. Poetry.

Giant poems ill. by Margot Tomes. Holiday, 1978. ISBN 0-8234-0326-2 Subj: Giants. Poetry.

Monster poems (Monster poems)

Witch poems (Witch poems)

Wallace, Ian. *Chin Chiang and the dragon's dance* ill. by author. Atheneum, 1984. ISBN 0-689-50299-0 Subj: Emotions – fear. Ethnic groups in the U.S. – Chinese Americans. Family life – grandfathers. Holidays – Chinese New Year.

Duncan's way ill. by author. DK, 2000. ISBN 0-7894-2539-4 Subj: Activities – baking, cooking. Family life. Family life – fathers. Foreign lands – Newfoundland.

Morgan the magnificent ill. by author. Macmillan, 1988. ISBN 0-689-50441-1 Subj: Angels. Behavior – misbehavior. Circus.

The naked lady ill. by author. Roaring Brook, 2002. ISBN 0-7613-2660-X Subj: Art. Careers – artists. Farms.

The sparrow's song ill. by author. Viking, 1987. ISBN 0-670-81453-9 Subj: Behavior – misbehavior. Birds – sparrows. Character traits – kindness to animals. Death.

The true story of Trapper Jack's left big toe ill. by author. Roaring Brook, 2002. ISBN 0-7613-2405-4 Subj: Anatomy – toes. Foreign lands – Canada. Foreign lands – Yukon Territory.

Wallace, Ivy. *Pookie* ill. by author. Collins, 2000. ISBN 0-00-198377-6 Subj: Activities – traveling. Animals. Animals – rabbits. Character traits – being different. Fairies.

Pookie believes in Santa Claus ill. by author. Collins, 2000. ISBN 0-00-198380-6 Subj: Animals. Animals – rabbits. Holidays – Christmas. Santa Claus.

Pookie puts the world right ill. by author. Collins, 2001. ISBN 0-00-664735-9 Subj: Animals. Animals – rabbits. Behavior – wishing. Seasons – winter.

Wallace, John. *Anything for you* ill. by Harry Horse. HarperCollins, 2004. ISBN 0-06-058129-8 Subj: Animals – bears. Bedtime. Family life – mothers.

Building a house with Mr. Bumble ill. by author. Candlewick, 1996. ISBN 0-7636-0074-1 Subj: Activities – making things. Animals. Homes, houses. Insects – bees. Tools.

Little Bean's friend ill. by author. HarperFestival, 1997. ISBN 0-694-00973-3 Subj: Activities – playing. Animals – dogs. Behavior – lost & found possessions. Family life.

Tiny Rabbit goes to a birthday party ill. by author. Holiday, 2000. ISBN 0-8234-1489-2 Subj: Animals – rabbits. Birthdays. Gifts. Parties.

The twins ill. by author. Golden Bks., 2001. ISBN 0-307-10211-4 Subj: Character traits – individuality. Family life – sisters. Multiple births – twins. Self-concept.

Wallace, Joseph E. *Big and noisy Simon* ill. by Kevin O'Malley. Hyperion, 2001. ISBN 0-7868-2450-6 Subj: Animals – elephants. Behavior. Foreign lands – Africa. Noise, sounds.

Wallace, Karen. *Bears in the forest* ill. by Barbara Firth. Candlewick, 1994. ISBN 1-56402-336-2 Subj: Animals – bears. Forest, woods. Nature.

A bed for winter ill. with photos. DK, 2000. ISBN 0-7894-5706-7 Subj: Animals. Animals – dormice. Hibernation. Seasons – winter.

Big machines ill. with photos. DK, 2000. ISBN 0-7894-5412-2 Subj: Careers – construction workers. Machines. Trucks.

Born to be a butterfly ill. with photos. DK, 2000. ISBN 0-7894-5704-0 Subj: Insects – butterflies, caterpillars.

City pig ill. by Lydia Monks. Orchard, 2000. ISBN 0-531-30252-0 Subj: Activities – vacationing. Animals – pigs. Cities, towns.

Diving dolphin ill. with photos. DK, 2001. ISBN 0-7894-7356-9 Subj: Animals – dolphins. Behavior – growing up.

Imagine you are a tiger ill. by Peter Melnyczuk. Holt, 1996. ISBN 0-8050-4636-4 Subj: Animals – tigers. Behavior – growing up. Imagination.

My hen is dancing ill. by Anita Jeram. Candlewick, 1994. ISBN 1-56402-303-6 Subj: Birds – chickens.

Red fox ill. by Peter Melnyczuk. Candlewick, 1994. ISBN 1-56402-422-9 Subj: Animals – foxes.

Rockets and spaceships ill. with photos. DK, 2001. ISBN 0-7894-7360-7 Subj: Space & space ships.

Scarlette Beane ill. by Jon Berkeley. Dial, 2000. ISBN 0-8037-2475-6 Subj: Food. Gardens, gardening. Magic. Nature. Plants.

Wallace, Levy Pittle. *see* Wallace, Pittle

Wallace, Nancy Elizabeth. *Apples, apples, apples* ill. by author. Winslow, 2000. ISBN 1-890817-19-8 Subj: Activities – baking, cooking. Animals – rabbits. Family life. Farms. Music. Songs.

Count down to clean up ill. by author. Houghton, 2001. ISBN 0-618-10130-6 Subj: Animals – rabbits. Character traits – cleanliness. Counting, numbers.

Paperwhite ill. by author. Houghton Mifflin, 2000. ISBN 0-618-04283-0 Subj: Animals – rabbits. Flowers. Friendship. Gardens, gardening. Plants. Seasons – spring.

Pumpkin day ill. by author. Cavendish, 2002. ISBN 0-7614-5128-5 Subj: Animals – rabbits. Farms. Food. Plants.

Rabbit's bedtime ill. by author. Houghton Mifflin, 1999. ISBN 0-395-98266-9 Subj: Animals – rabbits. Bedtime. Rhyming text.

Snow ill. by author. Western, 1995. ISBN 0-307-17562-6 Subj: Animals – rabbits. Family life – grandfathers. Weather – snow.

The sun, the moon, and the stars (The sun, the moon, and the stars)

Tell-a-bunny ill. by author. Winslow, 2000. ISBN 1-890817-29-5 Subj: Animals – rabbits. Birthdays. Parties.

Wallace, Pittle. *Winnie-the Pooh's A B C* (Winnie-the-Pooh's A B C)

Wallace-Brodeur, Ruth. *Goodbye, Mitch* ill. by Kathy Mitter. A. Whitman, 1995. ISBN 0-8075-2996-6 Subj: Animals – cats. Death. Emotions – grief. Pets.

Home by five ill. by Mark Graham. McElderry, 1992. ISBN 0-689-50509-4 Subj: Behavior – promptness, tardiness. Cities, towns. Family life. Sports – ice skating.

Wallas, Ada. *Clean Peter and the children of Grubbylea* (Adelborg, Ottilia)

Wallen, Ila. *The moon in my room* ill. by Robert Sauber. Bent Willow, 2002. ISBN 0-9710627-0-6 Subj: Activities – storytelling. Animals. Animals – bears. Bedtime. Emotions – fear. Forest, woods. Problem solving. Rhyming text.

Waller, Barrett. *New feet for old* ill. by Harvey Stevenson. Four Winds, 1992. ISBN 0-02-792371-1 Subj: Anatomy – feet. Behavior – dissatisfaction. Careers – peddlers.

Waller, Curt. *Baby's first signs* by Curt Waller & Kim Votry; ill. by Kim Votry. Gallaudet Univ. Pr., 2001. ISBN 1-56368-114-5 Subj: Books, reading. Format, unusual – board books. Handicaps – deafness. Sign language.

More baby's first signs by Curt Waller & Kim Votry; ill. by Kim Votry. Gallaudet Univ. Pr., 2001. ISBN 1-56368-115-3 Subj: Books, reading. Format, unusual – board books. Handicaps – deafness. Sign language.

Wallis, Diz. *Battle of the beasts: a tale of epic proportions from the brothers Grimm* retold & ill. by Diz Wallis. Ragged Bears, 2000. ISBN 1-929927-15-0 Subj: Animals. Behavior – fighting, arguing. Birds. Folk & fairy tales.

Pip's adventure ill. by author. Boyds Mills, 1991. ISBN 1-878093-43-6 Subj: Activities – baking, cooking. Animals – cats. Animals – mice.

Ragged Bear's book of nursery rhymes (Ragged Bear's book of nursery rhymes)

Wallis, Lisa. *Island child* ill. by Deborah Haeffele. Dutton, 1992. ISBN 0-525-67324-5 Subj: Family life. Islands.

Wallner, Alexandra. *An Alcott family Christmas* ill. by author. Holiday, 1996. ISBN 0-8234-1265-2 Subj: Behavior – sharing. Character traits – generosity. Family life. Holidays – Christmas.

Beatrix Potter ill. by author. Holiday, 1995. ISBN 0-8234-1181-8 Subj: Activities – drawing. Animals. Art. Careers – writers. Emotions – loneliness. Imagination.

Betsy Ross ill. by author. Holiday, 1994. ISBN 0-8234-1071-4 Subj: Activities – sewing. U.S. history.

The first air voyage in the United States: the story of Jean-Pierre Blanchard ill. by author. Holiday, 1996. ISBN 0-8234-1224-5 Subj: Activities – ballooning. Animals – dogs. U.S. history.

Munch ill. by author. Crown, 1976. ISBN 0-517-52459-7 Subj: Food. Poetry.

Sergio and the hurricane ill. by author. Holt, 2000. ISBN 0-8050-6203-3 Subj: Family life. Foreign lands – Puerto Rico. Islands. Weather – hurricanes.

Wallner, John C. *Look and find* ill. by author. Putnam, 1988. ISBN 0-448-19068-0 Subj: Concepts. Counting, numbers. Format, unusual – toy & movable books. Picture puzzles.

Old MacDonald had a farm: a musical pop-up book ill. by author. Dutton, 1986. ISBN 0-525-44279-0 Subj: Animals. Cumulative tales. Farms. Format, unusual – toy & movable books. Music. Songs.

Sleeping Beauty (Grimm, Jacob)

Wallwork, Amanda. *Find the fish that looks like this: a hide-and-seek animal book* ill. by author. Puffin, 1997. ISBN 0-14-055909-4 Subj: Animals. Concepts – color. Concepts – shape. Concepts – size. Picture puzzles.

Sleep songs ill. by author. Ragged Bears, 2001. ISBN 1-929927-39-8 Subj: Bedtime. Format, unusual – toy & movable books. Nursery rhymes. Sleep.

Walsh, Ellen Stoll. *Dot and Jabber and the great acorn mystery* ill. by author. Harcourt, 2001. ISBN 0-15-202602-9 Subj: Animals – mice. Animals – squirrels. Seeds. Trees.

Dot and Jabber and the mystery of the missing stream ill. by author. Harcourt, 2002. ISBN 0-15-216512-6 Subj: Animals – mice. Rivers.

For Pete's sake ill. by author. Harcourt, 1998. ISBN 0-15-200324-X Subj: Birds – flamingos. Character traits – being different. Character traits – individuality. Reptiles – alligators, crocodiles.

Hamsters to the rescue ill. by author. Harcourt, 2005. ISBN 0-15-205202-X Subj: Animals – hamsters. Behavior – lost & found possessions. Birds – seagulls. Crustaceans – crabs. Friendship. Sea & seashore – beaches.

Jack's tale ill. by author. Harcourt, 1997. ISBN 0-15-200323-1 Subj: Activities – storytelling. Careers – authors. Character traits – cleverness. Folk & fairy tales. Frogs & toads. Mythical creatures – trolls. Royalty – princesses.

Mouse count ill. by author. Harcourt, 1991. ISBN 0-15-256023-8 Subj: Animals – mice. Counting, numbers. Reptiles – snakes.

Mouse magic ill. by author. Harcourt, 2000. ISBN 0-15-200326-6 Subj: Animals – mice. Concepts – color. Magic. Wizards.

Mouse paint ill. by author. Harcourt, 1989. ISBN 0-15-256025-4 Subj: Activities – painting. Animals – mice. Behavior – hiding. Concepts – color.

Pip's magic ill. by author. Harcourt, 1994. ISBN 0-15-292850-2 Subj: Animals. Emotions – fear. Magic. Night. Reptiles – salamanders.

Two too much ill. by Pat Cummings. Bradbury, 1990. ISBN 0-02-792290-1 Subj: Emotions. Ethnic groups in the U.S. – African Americans. Family life – brothers & sisters.

You silly goose ill. by author. Harcourt, 1992. ISBN 0-15-299865-9 Subj: Animals – foxes. Animals – mice. Birds – geese.

Walsh, Grahame L. *Didane the koala* ill. by John Morrison. Univ. of Queensland Pr., 1986. ISBN 0-7022-1889-8 Subj: Animals – koalas. Folk & fairy tales. Foreign lands – Australia.

The goori goori bird ill. by John Morrison. Univ. of Queensland Pr., 1986. ISBN 0-7022-1777-8 Subj: Birds. Folk & fairy tales. Foreign lands – Australia.

Walsh, Jill Paton. *Connie came to play* ill. by Stephen Lambert. Viking, 1996. ISBN 0-670-86210-X Subj: Activities – playing. Behavior – sharing. Imagination.

Lost and found ill. by Mary Rayner. André Deutsch, 1985. ISBN 0-233-97672-8 Subj: Behavior – lost & found possessions. Character traits – luck. Family life – grandfathers.

Pepi and the secret names ill. by Fiona French. Lothrop, 1995. ISBN 0-688-13428-9 Subj: Activities – painting. Animals. Careers – artists. Folk & fairy tales. Foreign lands – Egypt. Hieroglyphics. Names.

When Grandma came ill. by Sophy Williams. Viking, 1992. ISBN 0-670-83581-1 Subj: Family life – grandmothers.

When I was little like you ill. by Stephen Lambert. Viking, 1997. ISBN 0-670-87608-9 Subj: Family life – grandmothers. Memories, memory.

Walsh, Joanna. *What if?* ill. by author. Jonathan Cape, 2000. ISBN 0-224-04752-3 Subj: Imagination.

Walsh, Melanie. *Do donkeys dance?* ill. by author. Houghton Mifflin, 2000. ISBN 0-618-00330-4 Subj: Activities. Animals. Nature.

Do monkeys tweet? ill. by author. Houghton Mifflin, 1997. ISBN 0-395-85081-9 Subj: Animals. Noise, sounds.

Hide and sleep ill. by author. DK, 1999. ISBN 0-7894-4820-3 Subj: Bedtime. Behavior – hiding. Games.

Monster, monster ill. by author. Candlewick, 2002. ISBN 0-7636-1669-9 Subj: Format, unusual – toy & movable books. Monsters.

Ned's rainbow ill. by author. DK, 2000. ISBN 0-7894-5623-0 Subj: Activities – painting. Weather – rainbows.

Walsh, Patricia. *Cars* ill. by David Westerfield. Heinemann, 2001. ISBN 1-57572-348-4 Subj: Activities – drawing. Automobiles.

Dinosaurs ill. by David Westerfield. Heinemann, 2001. ISBN 1-57572-349-2 Subj: Activities – drawing. Dinosaurs.

Walsh, Vivian. *Mr. Lunch borrows a canoe* (Seibold, J. Otto)

Mr. Lunch takes a plane ride (Seibold, J. Otto)

Penguin dreams (Seibold, J. Otto)

Walt Disney Productions. *In out, a Disney book of opposites = Dentro fuera, un libro Disney de opuestos* (Duerrstein, Richard)

Mickey is happy: a Disney book of feelings (Duerrstein, Richard)

One Mickey Mouse, a Disney book of numbers = Un Ratón Mickey, un libro Disney de números: a Disney book of numbers = Un Ratón Mickey: un libro Disney de números (Duerrstein, Richard)

Tod and Copper. Random House, 1981. ISBN 0-394-94819-X Subj: Animals – dogs. Animals – foxes.

Tod and Vixey. Random House, 1981. ISBN 0-394-94904-8 Subj: Animals – dogs. Animals – foxes.

Walt Disney's Snow White and the seven dwarfs. Viking, 1979. ISBN 0-670-65381-0 Subj: Dwarfs, midgets. Emotions – envy, jealousy. Folk & fairy tales. Magic. Witches.

Walt Disney's The adventures of Mr. Toad. Random House, 1981. ISBN 0-394-94818-1 Subj: Animals – moles. Animals – rats. Frogs & toads.

Walter, Mildred Pitts. *Brother to the wind* ill. by Leo & Diane Dillon. Lothrop, 1985. ISBN 0-688-03811-5 Subj: Activities – flying. Foreign lands – Africa.

Darkness ill. by Marcia Jameson. S&S, 1995. ISBN 0-689-80305-2 Subj: Night. Shadows.

My mama needs me ill. by Pat Cummings. Lothrop, 1983. ISBN 0-688-01671-5 Subj: Emotions – loneliness. Ethnic groups in the U.S. – African Americans. Family life.

Ty's one-man band ill. by Margot Tomes. Four Winds, 1980. ISBN 0-02-792300-2 Subj: Folk & fairy tales. Music. Musical instruments – bands.

Walter, Villiam Christian. *see* Andersen, H. C. (Hans Christian)

Walter, Virginia. *"Hi, pizza man!"* ill. by Ponder Goembel. Orchard, 1995. ISBN 0-531-08735-2 Subj: Animals. Noise, sounds.

Walters, Catherine. *Are you there, Baby Bear?* ill. by author. Dutton, 1999. ISBN 0-525-46161-2 Subj: Animals – babies. Animals – bears. Family life – new sibling. Multiple births – twins.

Play gently, Alfie Bear ill. by author. Dutton, 2002. ISBN 0-525-46885-4 Subj: Animals – bears. Family life – brothers & sisters. Family life – mothers.

When will it be spring? ill. by author. Dutton, 1998. ISBN 0-525-45881-6 Subj: Animals – bears. Character traits – patience. Family life – mothers. Hibernation. Nature. Seasons – spring. Seasons – winter.

Walters, Julie. *God is like . . .* ill. by Thea Kliros. WaterBrook, 2000. ISBN 1-57856-246-5 Subj: Religion.

Walters, Marguerite. *The city-country ABC: My alphabet walk in the country, and My alphabet ride in the city* ill. by Ib Spang Olsen. Doubleday, 1966. The two stories are bound dos-á-dos. Subj: ABC books. Cities, towns. Country. Format, unusual.

Walters, Virginia. *Are we there yet, Daddy?* ill. by S. D. Schindler. Viking, 1999. ISBN 0-670-87402-7 Subj: Activities – traveling. Automobiles. Family life – fathers. Maps. Rhyming text.

Walton, Ann. *Dumb clucks!* (Walton, Rick)

Something's fishy! (Walton, Rick)

Walton, Rick. *The bear came over to my house* ill. by James Warhola. Putnam, 2001. ISBN 0-399-23415-2 Subj: Animals – bears. Rhyming text.

Bertie was a watchdog ill. by Arthur Robins. Candlewick, 2002. ISBN 0-7636-1385-1 Subj: Animals – dogs. Concepts – size. Crime.

Dance, pioneer, dance! ill. by Brad Teare. Deseret Book, 1997. ISBN 1-57345-243-2 Subj: Activities – dancing. U.S. history – frontier & pioneer life.

Dumb clucks! by Rick & Ann Walton; ill. by Joan Hanson. Lerner, 1987. ISBN 0-8225-0991-1 Subj: Birds – chickens. Riddles & jokes.

How can you dance? ill. by Ana López-Escrivá. Putnam, 2001. ISBN 0-399-23229-X Subj: Activities – dancing. Rhyming text.

How many? ill. by Cynthia Jabar. Candlewick, 2000. ISBN 0-7636-0948-X Subj: Counting, numbers. Nursery rhymes. Riddles & jokes.

Little dogs say "Rough!" ill. by Henry Cole. Putnam, 2000. ISBN 0-399-23228-1 Subj: Animals. Noise, sounds. Rhyming text.

My two hands, my two feet ill. by Julia Gorton. Putnam, 2000. ISBN 0-399-23338-5 Subj: Anatomy – feet. Anatomy – hands. Communication.

Noah's square dance ill. by Thor Wickstrom. Lothrop, 1995. ISBN 0-688-11187-4 Subj: Activities – dancing. Animals. Boats, ships.

Religion – Noah. Rhyming text. Weather – floods. Weather – rain.

One more bunny ill. by Paige Miglio. Lothrop, 2000. ISBN 0-688-16848-5 Subj: Animals – rabbits. Counting, numbers.

Pig, Pigger, Piggest ill. by Jimmy Holder. Gibbs Smith, 1997. ISBN 0-8790-5806-4 Subj: Animals – pigs. Castles. Witches.

So many bunnies ill. by Paige Miglio. Lothrop, 1998. ISBN 0-688-13657-5 Subj: ABC books. Counting, numbers. Rhyming text. Sleep.

Something's fishy! by Rick & Ann Walton; ill. by Joan Hanson. Lerner, 1987. ISBN 0-8225-0993-8 Subj: Fish. Riddles & jokes.

Walty, Margaret. *Rock-a-bye baby: lullabies for bedtime* ill. by author. Barefoot, 1998. ISBN 1-902283-03-1 Subj: Bedtime. Lullabies. Music.

Wan, Manyee. *Lao Lao of Dragon Mountain* (Bateson-Hill, Margaret)

Wandelmaier, Roy. *Clouds* ill. by John Jones. Troll, 1985. ISBN 0-8167-0338-8 Subj: Weather – clouds. Weather – rain.

Stars ill. by Irene Trivas. Troll, 1985. ISBN 0-8167-0339-6 Subj: Science. Stars.

Wang, Mary Lewis. *The ant and the dove* (Æsop)

Wang, Rosalind C. *The fourth question* ill. by Ju-Hong Chen. Holiday, 1991. ISBN 0-8234-0855-8 Subj: Character traits – generosity. Folk & fairy tales. Foreign lands – China.

The treasure chest ill. by Will Hillenbrand. Holiday, 1995. ISBN 0-8234-1114-1 Subj: Character traits – generosity. Folk & fairy tales. Foreign lands – China. Magic.

Wang, Xing Chu. *China's bravest girl: the legend of Hua Mu Lan* (Chin, Charlie)

Wangerin, Walter. *Angels and all children* ill. by Tim Ladwig. Augsburg Fortress, 2002. ISBN 0-8066-3712-9 Subj: Holidays – Christmas. Music. Religion.

Probity Jones and the Fear Not Angel ill. by Tim Ladwig. Paraclete, 2005. ISBN 1-55725-457-5 Subj: Angels. Ethnic groups in the U.S. – African Americans. Holidays – Christmas. Religion – Nativity.

Water come down ill. by Gerardo Suzan. Augsburg Fortress, 1999. ISBN 0-80663-711-0 Subj: Babies. Family life. Religion.

Warbler, J. M. *see* Cocagnac, A. M. (Augustin Maurice)

Warburton, Nick. *Mr. Tite's belongings* ill. by Alex Ayliffe. Viking, 1992. ISBN 0-670-84155-2 Subj: Character traits – selfishness.

Ward, Andrew. *Baby bear and the long sleep* ill. by John Walsh. Little, 1980. ISBN 0-316-92197-1 Subj: Animals – bears. Hibernation. Seasons – winter.

Ward, Barbara Briggs. *The really really hairy flight of Snarly Sally* ill. by author. Landauer, 2001. ISBN 1-890621-23-4 Subj: Animals – dogs. Behavior – messy. Humorous stories.

Ward, Cindy. *Cookie's week* ill. by Tomie de Paola. Putnam, 1988. ISBN 0-399-21498-4 Subj: Animals – cats. Behavior – misbehavior. Days of the week, months of the year.

Ward, Heather Patricia. *I promise I'll find you* ill. by Sheila McGraw. Firefly, 1994. ISBN 1-895565-40-5 Subj: Behavior – lost. Emotions – love. Family life – mothers. Rhyming text.

Ward, Helen. *The dragon machine* ill. by Wayne Anderson. Dutton, 2003. ISBN 0-525-47114-6 Subj: Activities – flying. Dragons. Emotions – loneliness. Imagination.

The golden pear ill. by author. Ideals, 1991. ISBN 0-8249-8471-4 Subj: Folk & fairy tales. Friendship.

The hare and the tortoise (Æsop)

The king of the birds ill. by author. Millbrook, 1997. ISBN 0-7613-0288-3 Subj: Activities – flying. Birds. Character traits – cleverness. Royalty – kings.

The moonrat and the white turtle ill. by author. Ideals, 1990. ISBN 0-8249-8467-6 Subj: Character traits – selfishness. Moon. Pirates. Reptiles – turtles, tortoises.

Old shell, new shell ill. by author. Millbrook, 2002. ISBN 0-7613-2708-8 Subj: Animals. Crustaceans – crabs. Foreign lands – Australia. Sea & seashore.

The rooster and the fox ill. by author. Millbrook, 2003. ISBN 0-7613-2920-X Subj: Animals – foxes. Birds – chickens. Character traits – cleverness. Character traits – pride. Character traits – vanity. Farms.

The tin forest ill. by Wayne Anderson. Dutton, 2001. ISBN 0-525-46787-4 Subj: Animals. Dreams. Ecology. Forest, woods. Jungle. Trees.

Ward, Jennifer. *Over in the garden* ill. by Kenneth J. Spengler. Rising Moon, 2002. ISBN 0-87358-793-6 Subj: Counting, numbers. Gardens, gardening. Insects. Music. Rhyming text. Songs.

Somewhere in the ocean by Jennifer Ward & T. J. Marsh; ill. by Ken Spengler. Rising Moon, 2000. ISBN 0-87358-748-0 Subj: Animals – babies. Counting, numbers. Rhyming text. Sea & seashore.

Way out in the desert (Marsh, T. J.)

Ward, Kathy. *Dogs and puppies* (Starke, Katherine)

Ward, Leila. *I am eyes, ni macho* ill. by Nonny Hogrogian. Greenwillow, 1978. ISBN 0-688-84161-9 Subj: Foreign lands – Africa. Nature.

Ward, Lynd. *The biggest bear* ill. by author. Houghton Mifflin, 1952. Subj: Animals – bears. Caldecott award books. Character traits – kindness to animals. Foreign lands – Canada. Pets.

The little red lighthouse and the great gray bridge (Swift, Hildegarde Hoyt)

Nic of the woods ill. by author. Houghton Mifflin, 1965. Subj: Animals. Animals – dogs. Foreign lands – Canada. Forest, woods.

The silver pony ill. by author. Houghton Mifflin, 1973. ISBN 0-395-14753-0 Subj: Animals – horses, ponies. Dreams. Wordless.

Ward, May McNeer. *see* McNeer, May Yonge

Ward, Nanda Weedon. *The black sombrero* ill. by Lynd Ward. Ariel, 1952. Subj: Animals. Clothing – hats. Cowboys, cowgirls.

The elephant that ga-lumped by Nanda Weedon Ward & Robert Haynes; ill. by Robert Haynes. Ariel, 1959. Subj: Animals. Animals – elephants. Foreign lands – India.

Ward, Nick. *Come on Baby Duck* ill. by author. Good Bks., 2004. ISBN 1-56148-447-4 Subj: Birds – ducks. Emotions – fear. Sports – swimming.

Don't eat the teacher ill. by author. Scholastic, 2002. ISBN 0-439-37465-0 Subj: Fish – sharks. School – first day.

Farmer George and the fieldmice ill. by author. Pavilion, 1999. ISBN 1-86205-203-4 Subj: Animals. Animals – mice. Careers – farmers. Farms. Homes, houses. Machines.

Farmer George and the hungry guests ill. by author. Pavilion, 2000. ISBN 1-86205-436-3 Subj: Animals. Animals – foxes. Careers – farmers. Food. Mystery stories.

Farmer George and the lost chick ill. by author. Pavilion, 1999. ISBN 1-86205-412-6 Subj: Animals. Behavior – lost. Birds – chickens. Careers – farmers. Farms.

Giant. Oxford Univ. Pr., 1983. ISBN 0-19-278201-0 Subj: Behavior – misbehavior. Giants. Toys.

Ward, Sally G. *Charlie and Grandma* ill. by author. Scholastic, 1986. ISBN 0-590-33954-0 Subj: Behavior – misbehavior. Family life – grandmothers.

Molly and Grandpa ill. by author. Scholastic, 1986. ISBN 0-590-33955-9 Subj: Character traits – persistence. Family life – grandfathers. Food.

Punky goes fishing ill. by author. Dutton, 1991. ISBN 0-525-44681-8 Subj: Family life – grandfathers. Sports – fishing.

What goes around comes around ill. by author. Doubleday, 1991. ISBN 0-385-41223-1 Subj: Character traits – generosity. Communities, neighborhoods. Family life – grandmothers.

Wardlaw, Lee. *Bow-wow birthday* ill. by Arden Johnson-Petrov. Boyds Mills, 1998. ISBN 1-56397-489-4 Subj: Animals – dogs. Birthdays. Family life – grandfathers. Parties.

The chair where bear sits ill. by Russell Benfanti. Winslow, 2001. ISBN 1-890817-85-6 Subj: Accidents. Animals. Animals – bears. Babies. Character traits – clumsiness. Cumulative tales. Food. Rhyming text.

Saturday night jamboree ill. by Barry Root. Dial, 2000. ISBN 0-8037-2189-7 Subj: Activities – babysitting. Activities – dancing. Family life.

The tales of Grandpa Cat ill. by Ronald Searle. Dial, 1994. ISBN 0-8037-1512-9 Subj: Animals – cats. Family life – grandparents.

Warfel, Elizabeth Stuart. *The blue pearls* ill. by Véronique Giarrusso. Barefoot, 2001. ISBN 1-902283-78-3 Subj: Angels. Death. Emotions – grief.

Warhola, James. *Uncle Andy's* ill. by author. Putnam, 2003. ISBN 0-399-23869-7 Subj: Careers – artists. Family life. Family life – aunts, uncles.

Waring, Richard (Richard M. N.). *Alberto the dancing alligator* ill. by Holly Swain. Candlewick, 2002. ISBN 0-7636-1953-1 Subj: Behavior – lost. Pets. Reptiles – alligators, crocodiles.

Hungry hen ill. by Caroline Church. HarperCollins, 2001. ISBN 0-06-623880-3 Subj: Animals – foxes. Birds – chickens.

Warner, Sunny. *Madison finds a line* ill. by author. Houghton Mifflin, 1999. ISBN 0-395-88508-6 Subj: Activities – dancing. Animals – cats. Imagination. Insects. Music. Rhyming text.

The magic sewing machine ill. by author. Houghton Mifflin, 1997. ISBN 0-395-82747-7 Subj: Activities – sewing. Family life – brothers & sisters. Orphans.

The moon quilt ill. by author. Houghton, 2001. ISBN 0-618-05583-5 Subj: Animals – cats. Death. Family life. Memories, memory. Quilts.

Warner, Timothy. *Tub toys* (Shannon, Terry Miller)

Warnes, Tim. *Who's that?* (Gamble, Isobel)

Warnick, Elsa. *Bedtime* ill. by author. Browndeer, 1998. ISBN 0-15-201471-3 Subj: Activities. Bedtime.

Warren, Cathy. *Fred's first day* ill. by Pat Cummings. Lothrop, 1984. ISBN 0-688-03814-X Subj: Friendship. School – first day.

Saturday belongs to Sara ill. by DyAnne DiSalvo-Ryan. Bradbury, 1988. ISBN 0-02-792491-2 Subj: Character traits – kindness. Family life – mothers.

Springtime bears ill. by Pat Cummings. Lothrop, 1987. ISBN 0-688-05906-6 Subj: Animals – bears. Behavior – hiding. Seasons – spring.

The ten-alarm camp-out ill. by Steven Kellogg. Lothrop, 1983. ISBN 0-688-02128-X Subj: Camps, camping. Counting, numbers.

Warren, Elizabeth. *see* Supraner, Robyn

Warren, Robert. *I'm sorry* (McBratney, Sam)

Warren, Vic. *Buffalo* (Midge, Tiffany)

Warrick, Karen Clemens. *If I had a tail* ill. by Sherry Neidigh. Rising Moon, 2001. ISBN 0-8735-8781-2 Subj: Anatomy – tails. Animals. Riddles & jokes.

Who needs that nose? ill. by Sherry Neidigh. NorthWord, 2004. ISBN 1-55971-887-0 Subj: Anatomy – noses. Animals. Riddles & jokes.

Warshofsky, Isaac. *see* Singer, Isaac Bashevis

Washington, Donna L. *The big, spooky house* ill. by Jacqueline Rogers. Hyperion, 2000. ISBN 0-7868-0349-5 Subj: Animals – cats. Mythical creatures.

The story of Kwanzaa ill. by Stephen Taylor. HarperCollins, 1996. ISBN 0-06-024819-X Subj: Ethnic groups in the U.S. – African Americans. Holidays – Kwanzaa. U.S. history.

Wasmuth, Eleanor. *An alligator day* ill. by author. Grosset, 1983. ISBN 0-448-21703-1 Subj: Activities – playing. Reptiles – alligators, crocodiles.

The picnic basket ill. by author. Grosset, 1983. ISBN 0-448-21704-X Subj: Activities – picnicking. Food. Reptiles – alligators, crocodiles.

Wasserberg, Esther. *Grandmother dear* (Finfer, Celentha)

Wasson, Valentina Pavlovna. *The chosen baby* ill. by Glo Coalson. 3rd ed. HarperCollins, 1977. ISBN 0-397-31738-7 Subj: Adoption.

Watanabe, Shigeo. *Daddy, play with me!* ill. by Yasuo Ohtomo. Putnam, 1985. ISBN 0-399-21211-6 Subj: Activities – playing. Animals – bears. Family life – fathers.

How do I put it on? ill. by Yasuo Ohtomo. Putnam, 1979. ISBN 0-529-05557-0 Subj: Animals – bears. Clothing. Participation.

I can build a house! ill. by Yasuo Ohtomo. Philomel, 1983. ISBN 0-399-20950-6 Subj: Activities – playing. Animals – bears. Character traits – perseverance. Homes, houses.

I can ride it! ill. by Yasuo Ohtomo. Putnam, 1982. ISBN 0-399-61194-0 Subj: Activities – playing. Animals – bears. Character traits – perseverance.

I can take a bath! ill. by Yasuo Ohtomo. Putnam, 1987. ISBN 0-399-21362-7 Subj: Activities – bathing. Animals – bears. Family life – fathers.

I can take a walk! ill. by Yasuo Ohtomo. Putnam, 1984. ISBN 0-399-21044-X Subj: Activities – walking. Animals – bears.

Ice cream is falling! ill. by Yasuo Ohtomo. Putnam, 1989. ISBN 0-399-21550-6 Subj: Animals – bears. Seasons – winter. Weather – snow.

I'm the king of the castle! ill. by Yasuo Ohtomo. Putnam, 1982. ISBN 0-399-61195-9 Subj: Activities – playing. Animals – bears. Sand.

It's my birthday ill. by Yasuo Ohtomo. Putnam, 1988. ISBN 0-399-21492-5 Subj: Animals – bears. Birthdays. Family life – grandparents.

Let's go swimming ill. by Yasuo, Ohtomo. Putnam, 1990. ISBN 0-399-21896-3 Subj: Animals – bears. Family life – fathers. Sports – swimming.

What a good lunch! ill. by Yasuo Ohtomo. Collins-World, 1980. ISBN 0-529-05580-5 Subj: Animals – bears. Food. Humorous stories.

Where's my daddy? ill. by Yasuo Ohtomo. Philomel, 1982. ISBN 0-399-20899-2 Subj: Animals – bears. Behavior – lost. Character traits – perseverance. Family life – fathers.

Watanabe, Yuichi. *Wally the whale who loved balloons* trans. from Japanese by D. T. Ooka; ill. by author. Heian Intl., 1982. ISBN 0-89346-150-4 Subj: Animals – whales. Behavior – misbehavior. Toys – balloons.

Waterhouse, Stephen A. *Engines, engines* (Bruce, Lisa)

Get busy this Christmas ill. by author. Bloomsbury, 2002. ISBN 1-58234-802-2 Subj: Birds – penguins. Format, unusual – board books. Holidays – Christmas.

Waters, Fiona. *The selfish giant* (Wilde, Oscar)

Waters, Jennifer. *All kinds of people* ill. by author. Compass Pt., 2002. ISBN 0-7565-0377-9 Subj: Anatomy. Character traits – individuality.

Harvest time ill. with photos. Compass Pt., 2002. ISBN 0-7565-0239-X Subj: Careers – farmers. Farms.

Right at home ill. by author. Compass Pt., 2003. ISBN 0-7565-0380-9 Subj: Homes, houses.

Summer fun ill. by author. Compass Pt., 2002. ISBN 0-7565-0244-6 Subj: Activities – playing. Seasons – summer.

Waters, Kate. *Lion dancer: Ernie Wan's Chinese new year* by Kate Waters & Madeline Slovenz-Low; photos by Martha Cooper. Scholastic, 1990. ISBN 0-590-43046-7 Subj: Activities – dancing. Ethnic groups in the U.S. – Chinese Americans. Holidays – Chinese New Year.

Waters, Tony. *Sailor's bride* ill. by author. Doubleday, 1991. ISBN 0-385-41441-2 Subj: Animals – mice. Behavior – lost. Boats, ships. Sailors. Sea & seashore.

Waterton, Betty. *Orff, 27 dragons (and a snarkel)* ill. by Karen Kulyk. Firefly, 1984. ISBN 0-920303-02-1 Subj: Activities – flying. Character traits – perseverance. Dragons. Dreams.

Pettranella ill. by Ann Blades. Vanguard, 1981. ISBN 0-8149-0844-6 Subj: Family life – grandmothers. Foreign lands – Canada. Seasons – spring.

A salmon for Simon ill. by Ann Blades. Atheneum, 1980. ISBN 0-689-50169-2 Subj: Character traits – kindness to animals. Sports – fishing.

Watkins, Hope (Brister). *The cunning fox and other tales* ill. by Henry C. Pitz. Knopf, 1943. Subj: Animals. Folk & fairy tales.

Watkins, Sherrin. *White Bead Ceremony* ill. by Kim Doner. Council Oak Books, 1994. ISBN 0-933031-92-0 Subj: Family life – grandmothers. Indians of North America – Shawnee. Names.

Watson, Carol. *Æsop's fables* (Æsop)

Opposites ill. by David Higham. Usborne, 1983. ISBN 0-86020-758-7 Subj: Concepts – opposites.

Rabbit by Carol Watson & Jane Burton; ill. by Jane Burton. Rooster Books, 1994. ISBN 0-553-09547-1 Subj: Animals – rabbits. Format, unusual – board books.

Shapes ill. by David Higham. Usborne, 1983. ISBN 0-86020-759-5 Subj: Concepts – shape.

Sizes ill. by David Higham. Usborne, 1983. ISBN 0-86020-760-9 Subj: Concepts – size.

Watson, Claire. *Big creatures from the past* ill. by Robert Cremins; design & paper engineering by Keith Moseley. Putnam, 1990. ISBN 0-399-22159-X Subj: Dinosaurs. Format, unusual – toy & movable books.

Watson, Clyde. *Applebet: an ABC* ill. by Wendy Watson. Farrar, 1982. ISBN 0-374-30384-3 Subj: ABC books. Fairs, festivals. Rhyming text.

Catch me and kiss me and say it again ill. by Wendy Watson. Collins-World, 1978. ISBN 0-529-05438-8 Subj: Family life. Poetry.

Father Fox's feast of songs ill. by Wendy Watson. Putnam, 1983. ISBN 0-399-20928-X Subj: Animals – foxes. Music. Poetry.

Fisherman lullabies ed. & ill. by Wendy Watson; music by Clyde Watson. Collins-World, 1968. Subj: Bedtime. Lullabies. Music.

Hickory stick rag ill. by Wendy Watson. Crowell, 1976. ISBN 0-690-00960-7 Subj: Activities – picnicking. Humorous stories. Rhyming text. School.

How Brown Mouse kept Christmas ill. by Wendy Watson. Farrar, 1980. ISBN 0-374-33494-3 Subj: Animals – mice. Holidays – Christmas.

Love's a sweet ill. by Wendy Watson. Viking, 1998. ISBN 0-670-83453-X Subj: Emotions – love. Poetry.

Midnight moon ill. by Susanna Natti. Collins-World, 1979. ISBN 0-529-05527-9 Subj: Activities – flying. Bedtime. Imagination. Moon.

Tom Fox and the apple pie ill. by Wendy Watson. Crowell, 1972. ISBN 0-690-82784-9 Subj: Animals – foxes. Behavior – sharing. Fairs, festivals. Food.

Valentine foxes ill. by Wendy Watson. Watts, 1988. ISBN 0-531-08400-0 Subj: Animals – foxes. Family life. Food. Holidays – Valentine's Day.

Watson, Esther (Pearl). *The adventures of Jules and Gertie* ill. by author. Harcourt, 1999. ISBN 0-15-201975-8 Subj: Animals – horses, ponies. Cowboys, cowgirls. Humorous stories.

Trouble at Sugar Dip Well ill. by author. Houghton, 2002. ISBN 0-618-11863-2 Subj: Animals – horses, ponies. Behavior – greed. Cowboys, cowgirls. Crime.

Watson, Jane Werner. *The fuzzy duckling* ill. by Alice & Martin Provensen. Random House, 2003. ISBN 0-307-10325-0 Subj: Birds – ducks. Counting, numbers. Family life. Farms.

My friend the babysitter by Jane Werner Watson, Robert E. Switzer & J. Cotter Hirschberg; ill. by Hilde Hoffmann. Golden Pr., 1971. Subj: Activities – babysitting.

My friend the dentist by Jane Werner Watson, Robert E. Switzer & J. Cotter Hirschberg; ill. by Cat Bowman Smith. Crown, 1987. ISBN 0-517-56485-X Subj: Careers – dentists. Health & fitness.

My friend the doctor by Jane Werner Watson, Robert E. Switzer & J. Cotter Hirschberg; ill. by Cat Bowman Smith. Crown, 1987. ISBN 0-517-56485-8 Subj: Careers – doctors. Health & fitness.

Sometimes a family has to move by Jane Werner Watson, Robert E. Switzer & J. Cotter Hirschberg; ill. by Cat Bowman Smith. Crown, 1988. ISBN 0-517-56593-5 Subj: Family life. Moving.

Sometimes a family has to split up by Jane Werner Watson, Robert E. Switzer & J. Cotter Hirschberg; ill. by Cat Bowman Smith. Crown, 1988. ISBN 0-517-56811-X Subj: Divorce. Family life.

Sometimes I get angry by Jane Werner Watson, Robert E. Switzer & J. Cotter Hirschberg; ill. by Irene Trivas. Crown, 1986. ISBN 0-517-56088-7 Subj: Emotions – anger.

Sometimes I'm afraid by Jane Werner Watson, Robert E. Switzer & J. Cotter Hirschberg; ill. by Irene Trivas. Crown, 1986. ISBN 0-517-56087-9 Subj: Emotions – fear.

Sometimes I'm jealous by Jane Werner Watson, Robert E. Switzer & J. Cotter Hirschberg; ill. by Irene Trivas. Crown, 1986. ISBN 0-517-56062-3 Subj: Emotions – envy, jealousy.

Which is the witch? ill. by Victoria Chess. Pantheon, 1979. ISBN 0-394-93978-6 Subj: Holidays – Halloween. Witches.

Watson, John. *We're the noisy dinosaurs!* ill. by author. Candlewick, 1992. ISBN 1-56402-089-4 Subj: Dinosaurs. Noise, sounds. Prehistory.

Watson, Mary. *The butterfly seeds* ill. by author. Tambourine, 1995. ISBN 0-688-14133-1 Subj: Activities – traveling. Ethnic groups in the U.S. Family life – grandparents. Insects – butterflies, caterpillars. Memories, memory. Seeds.

Watson, Nancy Dingman. *The birthday goat* ill. by Wendy Watson. Crowell, 1974. ISBN 0-690-00146-0 Subj: Animals – goats. Birthdays. Crime. Fairs, festivals.

Sugar on snow ill. by Aldren Auld Watson. Viking, 1964. Subj: Food. Weather – snow.

Tommy's mommy's fish ill. by Aldren Auld Watson. Viking, 1971. ISBN 0-670-71926-9 Subj: Birthdays. Family life – mothers. Sports – fishing.

Tommy's mommy's fish ill. by Thomas Aldren Dingman Watson. Viking, 1996. ISBN 0-670-85681-9 Subj: Birthdays. Family life – mothers. Sports – fishing.

What does A begin with? ill. by Aldren Auld Watson. Knopf, 1956. Subj: ABC books. Farms.

What is one? ill. by Aldren Auld Watson. Knopf, 1954. Subj: Counting, numbers. Farms.

When is tomorrow? ill. by Aldren Auld Watson. Knopf, 1955. Subj: Sea & seashore. Time.

Watson, Pauline. *Curley Cat baby-sits* ill. by Lorinda Bryan Cauley. Harcourt, 1977. ISBN 0-15-221110-1 Subj: Activities – babysitting. Animals – cats.

Days with Daddy ill. by Joanne Scribner. Prentice-Hall, 1977. ISBN 0-13-196907-2 Subj: Family life. Family life – fathers.

The walking coat ill. by Tomie de Paola. Walker, 1980. ISBN 0-8027-6351-0 Subj: Clothing – coats.

Wriggles, the little wishing pig ill. by Paul Galdone. Seabury Pr., 1978. ISBN 0-8164-3216-3 Subj: Animals – pigs. Behavior – wishing. Monsters.

Watson, Richard Jesse. *Tom Thumb* (Tom Thumb)

Watson, Wendy. *Boo! It's Halloween* ill. by author. Clarion, 1992. ISBN 0-395-53628-6 Subj: Family life. Holidays – Halloween.

The bunnies' Christmas eve ill. by author. Putnam, 1983. ISBN 0-399-20968-9 Subj: Animals – rabbits. Format, unusual – toy & movable books. Holidays – Christmas.

Fisherman lullabies (Watson, Clyde)

Happy Easter day! ill. by author. Clarion, 1993. ISBN 0-395-53629-4 Subj: Animals – cats. Family life. Holidays – Easter.

Has winter come? ill. by author. Collins-World, 1978. ISBN 0-529-05441-8 Subj: Animals – groundhogs. Hibernation. Seasons – winter.

Holly's Christmas eve ill. by author. HarperCollins, 2002. ISBN 0-688-17653-4 Subj: Character traits – helpfulness. Friendship. Holidays – Christmas. Machines. Santa Claus.

Hurray for the Fourth of July ill. by author. Houghton Mifflin, 1992. ISBN 0-395-53627-8 Subj: Family life. Holidays – Fourth of July. Poetry.

Lollipop ill. by author. Crowell, 1976. ISBN 0-690-00768-X Subj: Animals – rabbits. Behavior – misbehavior.

Moving ill. by author. Crowell, 1978. ISBN 0-690-01327-2 Subj: Moving.

Tales for a winter's eve ill. by author. Farrar, 1988. ISBN 0-374-37373-6 Subj: Animals – foxes. Illness. Seasons – winter.

Thanksgiving at our house ill. by author. Houghton Mifflin, 1991. ISBN 0-395-53626-X Subj: Family life. Holidays – Thanksgiving. Nursery rhymes.

A Valentine for you ill. by author. Houghton Mifflin, 1991. ISBN 0-395-53625-1 Subj: Emotions – love. Holidays – Valentine's Day. Poetry.

Wendy Watson's Mother Goose (Mother Goose)

Watt, Fiona. *Kittens* ill. by Rachel Wells. EDC, 2002. ISBN 0-7945-0099-4 Subj: Animals – babies. Animals – cats. Format, unusual – toy & movable books.

Watt, Mélanie. *Leon the chameleon* ill. by author. Kids Can, 2001. ISBN 1-55074-867-X Subj: Character traits – being different. Concepts – color. Reptiles – chameleons.

Wattenberg, Jane. *Henny-Penny* (Chicken Little)

Mrs. Mustard's baby faces photos by author. Chronicle, 1989. ISBN 0-87701-659-3 Subj: Babies. Format, unusual.

Watts, Barrie. *Apple tree* photos by author. Silver Burdett, 1987. ISBN 0-382-09436-0 Subj: Nature. Science. Trees.

Bird's nest photos by author. Silver Burdett, 1987. ISBN 0-382-09439-5 Subj: Animals. Birds. Science.

Butterfly and caterpillar photos by author. Silver Burdett, 1986. ISBN 0-382-09282-1 Subj: Insects – butterflies, caterpillars. Metamorphosis. Science.

Dandelion photos by author. Silver Burdett, 1987. ISBN 0-382-09438-7 Subj: Plants. Science.

Duck [written & ed. by Angela Royston] photos by author. Dutton, 1991. ISBN 0-525-67346-6 Subj: Birds – ducks. Birth. Format, unusual – board books.

Hamster photos by author. Silver Burdett, 1986. ISBN 0-382-09281-3 Subj: Animals – hamsters. Science.

Ladybug photos by author. Silver Burdett, 1987. ISBN 0-382-09437-9 Subj: Insects – ladybugs. Science.

Mouse photos by Barrie Watts; written by Angela Royston & ill. by Rowan Clifford. Lodestar, 1992. ISBN 0-525-67357-1 Subj: Animals – mice. Behavior – growing up.

Mushrooms photos by author. Silver Burdett, 1986. ISBN 0-382-09287-2 Subj: Plants. Science.

Rabbit [written & ed. by Angela Royston] ill. by Rowan Clifford; photos by author. Dutton, 1992. ISBN 0-525-67356-3 Subj: Animals – rabbits. Birth. Format, unusual. Science.

Tomato photos & ill. by author. Silver Burdett, 1990. ISBN 0-382-24008-1 Subj: Gardens, gardening. Plants. Science.

Watts, Bernadette. *The Christmas bird* ill. by author. North-South, 1996. ISBN 1-55858-603-2 Subj: Activities – whistling. Birds. Holidays – Christmas. Religion – Nativity. Whistles.

David's waiting day ill. by author. Prentice-Hall, 1978. ISBN 0-13-197178-6 Subj: Babies. Family life – new sibling.

The elves and the shoemaker (Grimm, Jacob)

The fir tree (Andersen, H. C. [Hans Christian])

Goldilocks and the three bears (The three bears)

Green is beautiful (Rogers, Margaret)

Harvey Hare, postman extraordinaire ill. by author. North-South, 1997. ISBN 1-55858-688-1 Subj: Animals – rabbits. Careers – postal workers. Gifts.

Harvey Hare's Christmas ill. by author. North-South, 1999. ISBN 0-7358-1059-1 Subj: Animals. Animals – rabbits. Careers – postal workers. Holidays – Christmas.

The lion and the mouse (Æsop)

Rapunzel (Grimm, Jacob)

St. Francis and the proud crow ill. by author. Watts, 1988. ISBN 0-531-08358-6 Subj: Behavior – seeking better things. Folk & fairy tales.

Snow White and Rose Red (Grimm, Jacob)

Tattercoats ill. by author. North-South, 1989. ISBN 1-55858-002-6 Subj: Gardens, gardening. Scarecrows. Seasons. Weather.

The town mouse and the country mouse: an Æsop fable (Æsop)

The ugly duckling (Andersen, H. C. [Hans Christian])

Watts, Jeri Hanel. *Keepers* ill. by Felicia Marshall. Lee & Low, 1997. ISBN 1-880000-58-X Subj: Activities – storytelling. Birthdays. Ethnic groups in the U.S. – African Americans. Family life – grandmothers. Gifts. Old age.

Watts, Leslie Elizabeth. *You can't rush a cat* (Bradford, Karleen)

Watts, Mabel (Pizzey). *The day it rained watermelons* ill. by Lee Albertson. Lantern Pr., 1964. Subj: Behavior – indifference.

Something for you, something for me ill. by Abner Graboff. Abelard-Schuman, 1960. Subj: Activities – trading. Behavior – sharing.

Weeks and weeks ill. by Abner Graboff. Abelard-Schuman, 1962. Subj: Activities – photographing.

Watts, Marjorie-Ann. *Crocodile medicine* ill. by author. Warne, 1978. ISBN 0-7232-6154-7 Subj: Behavior – boredom. Hospitals. Illness. Reptiles – alligators, crocodiles.

Crocodile plaster ill. by author. Dutton, 1984. ISBN 0-233-96962-4 Subj: Hospitals. Illness. Reptiles – alligators, crocodiles.

Zebra goes to school ill. by author. Elsevier-Dutton, 1981. ISBN 0-233-97241-2 Subj: Imagination – imaginary friends. School – first day.

Waugh, Peter. *The great cannon beach mouse caper* ill. by Don Sunderland. Educare, 2002. ISBN 0-944638-38-4 Subj: Activities – traveling. Animals – mice. Birds – seagulls. Family life. Sea & seashore – beaches.

Wax, Wendy. *A very mice Christmas* photos by Jon Holderer. HarperFestival, 2003. ISBN 0-06-052321-2 Subj: Animals – mice. Format, unusual – board books. Holidays – Christmas. Rhyming text.

Waxman, Laura Hamilton. *Diving dolphins* ill. with photos. Lerner, 2003. ISBN 0-8225-0684-X Subj: Animals – dolphins. Science.

Waxman, Stephanie. *What is a girl? What is a boy?* photos by author. HarperCollins, 1989. ISBN 0-690-04711-8 Subj: Anatomy. Behavior – growing up. Character traits – individuality.

Wayland, April Halprin. *To Rabbittown* ill. by Robin Spowart. Scholastic, 1989. ISBN 0-590-40852-6 Subj: Animals – rabbits. Imagination. Pets.

Wayne-von-Königslöw, Andrea. *see* Von Königslöw, Andrea Wayne

Waysman, Dvora. *My Jewish days of the week* ill. by Melanie Schmidt. Hachai, 2000. ISBN 1-929628-03-X Subj: Days of the week, months of the year. Jewish culture. Rhyming text.

We wish you a merry Christmas: a traditional Christmas carol ill. by Tracey Campbell Pearson. Dial, 1983. ISBN 0-8037-9400-2 Subj: Behavior – misbehavior. Holidays – Christmas. Songs.

Weare, Tim. *Hide-and-seek with Leo* ill. by author. Scholastic, 2001. ISBN 0-439-29717-2 Subj: Behavior – hiding. Format, unusual – toy & movable books. Games. Monsters. Puppets.

I'm a little giraffe ill. by author. Scholastic, 2002. ISBN 0-439-40641-2 Subj: Animals – giraffes. Format, unusual – toy & movable books. Puppets.

I'm a little penguin ill. by author. Scholastic, 2002. ISBN 0-439-33868-9 Subj: Animals – babies. Birds – penguins. Format, unusual – toy & movable books. Puppets.

I'm a little puppy ill. by author. Scholastic, 2002. ISBN 0-439-40642-0 Subj: Animals – babies. Animals – dogs. Format, unusual – toy & movable books. Puppets.

Weary, Ogdred. *see* Gorey, Edward (St. John)

Weatherby, Meredith. *Upside-downers: more pictures to stretch the imagination* (Anno, Mitsumasa)

Weatherford, Carole Boston. *Jazz baby* ill. by Laura Freeman. Lee & Low, 2002. ISBN 1-58430-039-6 Subj: Activities – playing. Music. Rhyming text.

Juneteenth jamboree ill. by Yvonne Buchanan. Lee & Low, 1995. ISBN 1-880000-18-0 Subj: Ethnic groups in the U.S. – African Americans. Holidays – Juneteenth. Slavery. U.S. history.

Weatherill, Stephen. *The very first Lucy Goose book* ill. by author. Prentice-Hall, 1987. ISBN 0-13-941410-X Subj: Birds. Birds – geese. Humorous stories.

Weaver, Tess. *Opera cat* ill. by Andréa Wesson. Clarion, 2002. ISBN 0-618-09635-3 Subj: Activities – singing. Animals – cats. Careers – opera singers. Foreign lands – Italy.

Webb, Angela. *Talkabout air* photos by Chris Fairclough. Watts, 1987. ISBN 0-531-10369-2 Subj: Science.

Talkabout light photos by Chris Fairclough. Watts, 1988. ISBN 0-531-10455-9 Subj: Concepts. Science.

Talkabout reflections photos by Chris Fairclough. Watts, 1988. ISBN 0-531-10457-5 Subj: Concepts. Science.

Talkabout sand photos by Chris Fairclough. Watts, 1987. ISBN 0-531-10370-6 Subj: Sand. Science.

Talkabout soil photos by Chris Fairclough. Watts, 1987. ISBN 0-531-10371-4 Subj: Science.

Talkabout sound photos by Chris Fairclough. Watts, 1988. ISBN 0-531-10456-7 Subj: Concepts. Noise, sounds. Science.

Talkabout water photos by Chris Fairclough. Watts, 1987. ISBN 0-531-10372-2 Subj: Science.

Webb, Clifford. *The story of Noah* ill. by author. Warne, 1932. Subj: Animals. Boats, ships. Religion – Noah. Weather – floods. Weather – rain. Weather – rainbows.

Webb, Denise. *The same sun was in the sky* ill. by Walter Porter. Northland, 1994. ISBN 0-87358-602-6 Subj: Family life – grandfathers. Indians of North America – Hohokam. Petroglyphs.

Webber, Christopher. *Praise the Lord, my soul* ill. by Preston McDaniels. Morehouse, 2002. ISBN 0-8192-1889-8 Subj: Religion.

Weber, Alfons. *Elizabeth gets well* ill. by Jacqueline Blass. Crowell, 1970. Translation of Elisabeth wird gesund. ISBN 0-690-25839-9 Subj: Hospitals. Illness.

Weber, Linda Kay. *Louie Larkey and the bad dream patrol* ill. by Nora Hilb. Moon Mt., 2001. ISBN 0-9677929-3-2 Subj: Dreams. Toys. Toys – bears.

Webster, Belinda. *On the move* (Fecher, Sarah)

Wild animals (Fecher, Sarah)

Wedeven, Carol. *The Easter cave* ill. by Len Ebert. Concordia, 2001. ISBN 0-570-07135-6 Subj: Holidays – Easter. Religion.

Weedn, Flavia. *The elephant prince* by Flavia Weedn & Lisa Weedn Gilbert; ill. by Flavia Weedn. Hyperion, 1995. ISBN 0-7683-2052-6 Subj: Animals – elephants. Character traits – perseverance. Folk & fairy tales. Foreign lands – Scandinavia.

The enchanted tree by Flavia Weedn & Lisa Weedn Gilbert; ill. by Flavia Weedn. Hyperion, 1995. ISBN 0-7868-0120-4 Subj: Animals – giraffes. Character traits – being different. Folk & fairy tales. Self-concept. Trees.

The giant's garden by Flavia Weedn & Lisa Weedn Gilbert; ill. by Flavia Weedn. Hyperion, 1995. Based on: The selfish giant by Oscar Wilde. ISBN 0-7868-0121-2 Subj: Character traits – kindness. Character traits – selfishness. Folk & fairy tales. Gardens, gardening. Giants. Seasons – spring.

I feel happy by Flavia & Lisa Weedn; ill. by Flavia Weedn. Cedco, 1999. ISBN 0-7683-2065-8 Subj: Bedtime. Emotions – happiness. Family life – mothers. Format, unusual – board books.

The little snow bear by Flavia Weedn & Lisa Weedn Gilbert; ill. by Flavia Weedn. Hyperion, 1995. ISBN 0-7868-0044-5 Subj: Animals – bears. Friendship. Snowmen.

The magic cap by Flavia Weedn & Lisa Weedn Gilbert; ill. by Flavia Weedn. Hyperion, 1995. ISBN 0-7868-0119-0 Subj: Clothing – hats. Folk & fairy tales. Foreign lands – Sweden. Magic.

The moon maiden by Flavia Weedn & Lisa Weedn Gilbert; ill. by Flavia Weedn. Hyperion, 1995. ISBN 0-7868-0045-3 Subj: Folk & fairy tales. Foreign lands – Japan. Insects – fireflies. Moon.

The ragged peddler by Flavia Weedn & Lisa Weedn Gilbert; ill. by Flavia Weedn. Hyperion, 1995. ISBN 0-7868-0046-1 Subj: Behavior – dissatisfaction. Emotions – happiness. Folk & fairy tales. Foreign lands – Middle East. Jewish culture.

The star gift by Flavia Weedn & Lisa Weedn Gilbert; ill. by Flavia Weedn. Hyperion, 1995. ISBN 0-7868-0122-0 Subj: Family life. Folk & fairy tales. Gifts. Orphans. Stars.

Weedn, Lisa. *see* Gilbert, Lisa Weedn

The weekend ill. by Roser Capdevila. Firefly, 1986. ISBN 0-920303-44-7 Subj: Activities – picnicking. Country. Sea & seashore.

Weeks, Sarah. *Baa-choo!* ill. by Jane Manning. HarperCollins, 2004. ISBN 0-06-029237-7 Subj: Animals – babies. Animals – sheep. Illness – cold (disease). Rhyming text.

Bite me, I'm a shape ill. by Jef Kaminsky. Random House, 2002. ISBN 0-375-81262-8 Subj: Babies. Concepts – shape. Format, unusual – board books. Rhyming text.

Bite me, I'm a book ill. by Jef Kaminsky. Random House, 2002. ISBN 0-375-81261-X Subj: Babies. Books, reading. Format, unusual – board books. Humorous stories. Rhyming text.

Crocodile smile ill. by Lois Ehlert. HarperCollins, 1994. ISBN 0-06-022867-9 Subj: Animals. Animals – endangered animals. Music. Songs.

Drip, drop ill. by Jane Manning. HarperCollins, 2000. ISBN 0-06-028524-9 Subj: Animals – mice. Homes, houses. Rhyming text. Weather – rain.

Happy birthday, Frankie ill. by Warren Linn. Geringer, 1999. ISBN 0-06-028522-2 Subj: Birthdays. Humorous stories. Monsters.

Mrs. McNosh and the great big squash ill. by Nadine Bernard Westcott. Geringer, 2000. ISBN 0-694-01202-5 Subj: Gardens, gardening. Homes, houses. Plants. Rhyming text.

Mrs. McNosh hangs up her wash ill. by Nadine Bernard Westcott. Geringer, 1998. ISBN 0-694-01076-6 Subj: Humorous stories. Laundry.

My somebody special ill. by Ashley Wolff. Harcourt, 2002. ISBN 0-15-202561-8 Subj: Animals. Character traits – questioning. Emotions. Family life – parents. Rhyming text. School – nursery.

Noodles ill. by David A. Carter. HarperCollins, 1996. ISBN 0-694-00842-7 Subj: Food. Format, unusual – toy & movable books.

Oh my gosh, Mrs. McNosh! ill. by Nadine Bernard Westcott. Geringer, 2002. ISBN 0-06-008858-3 Subj: Animals – dogs. Behavior – running away. Humorous stories. Parks. Rhyming text.

Splish splash ill. by Ashley Wolff. HarperCollins, 1999. ISBN 0-06-027893-5 Subj: Activities – bathing. Animals. Fish. Rhyming text.

Who's under that hat? (Carter, David A.)

Without you ill. by Suzanne Duranceau. Geringer, 2003. ISBN 0-06-027816-1 Subj: Birds – penguins. Family life – parents.

Weelen, Guy. *The little red train* ill. by Mamoru Funai. Lothrop, 1966. Subj: Foreign lands – France. Trains.

Wegen, Ron. *The balloon trip* ill. by author. Houghton Mifflin, 1981. ISBN 0-395-30370-2 Subj: Activities – ballooning. Family life. Wordless.

Billy Gorilla ill. by author. Lothrop, 1983. ISBN 0-688-01986-2 Subj: Behavior – trickery. Holidays – April Fools' Day.

The Halloween costume party ill. by author. Houghton Mifflin, 1983. ISBN 0-89919-184-3 Subj: Holidays – Halloween. Parties.

Sand castle ill. by author. Greenwillow, 1977. ISBN 0-688-84033-7 Subj: Sea & seashore.

Sky dragon ill. by author. Greenwillow, 1982. ISBN 0-688-01146-2 Subj: Weather – clouds.

Where can the animals go? ill. by author. Greenwillow, 1978. ISBN 0-688-84137-6 Subj: Animals. Ecology.

Weidt, Maryann N. *Daddy played music for the cows* ill. by Henri Sorensen. Lothrop, 1995. ISBN 0-688-10058-9 Subj: Animals – bulls, cows. Farms. Music.

Weigel, Jeff. *Atomic Ace (he's just my dad)* ill. by author. A. Whitman, 2004. ISBN 0-8075-3216-9 Subj: Family life – fathers. Rhyming text.

Weigelt, Udo. *Bear's last journey* ill. by Sibylle Kazeroid. North-South, 2003. ISBN 0-7358-1800-2 Subj: Animals. Animals – bears. Death. Emotions – grief.

Ben and the Buccaneers ill. by Julia Gukova. North-South, 2001. ISBN 0-7358-1405-8 Subj: Animals – cats. Behavior – trickery. Birds – sparrows. Clubs, gangs.

The Easter Bunny's baby ill. by Rolf Siegenthaler. North-South, 2001. ISBN 0-7358-1442-2 Subj: Animals – rabbits. Behavior – mistakes. Birds – ostriches. Eggs. Family life – parents. Holidays – Easter.

It wasn't me ill. by Julia Gukova; trans. by J. Alison James. North-South, 2001. ISBN 0-7358-1524-0 Subj: Animals – ferrets. Animals – mice. Behavior – stealing. Birds – ravens. Crime.

Miranda's ghosts ill. by Christa Unzner. North-South, 2002. ISBN 0-7358-1705-7 Subj: Character traits – bravery. Ghosts. Holidays – Halloween.

Mole's journey ill. by Jakob Kirchmayr; trans. by Sibylle Kazeroid. North-South, 2004. ISBN 0-7358-1880-0 Subj: Activities – trading. Animals – moles. Dreams. Friendship. Illness.

Old Beaver ill. by Bernadette Watts. North-South, 2002. ISBN 0-7358-1565-8 Subj: Animals. Animals – beavers. Old age. Self-concept.

The Sandman ill. by Sibylle Heusser. North-South, 2003. ISBN 0-7358-1790-1 Subj: Behavior – needing someone. Emotions – loneliness. Friendship. Moon. Mythical creatures – sandman. Sleep.

There's room in the forest for everyone ill. by Gianluca Garofalo. North-South, 2003. ISBN 0-7358-1682-4 Subj: Animals – squirrels. Behavior – sharing. Forest, woods.

Who stole the gold? ill. by Julia Gukova; trans. by J. Alison James. North-South, 2000. ISBN 0-7358-1373-6 Subj: Animals. Animals – hamsters. Behavior – stealing. Friendship.

Weihs, Erika. *Count the cats* ill. by author. Doubleday, 1976. ISBN 0-385-11088-X Subj: Animals – cats. Counting, numbers.

Weil, Ann. *Animal families* ill. by Roger Vernam. Childrens Pr., 1956. Subj: Animals.

Weil, Lisl. *The candy egg bunny* ill. by author. Holiday, 1975. ISBN 0-823-40250-9 Subj: Animals – rabbits. Holidays – Easter. Witches.

Gertie and Gus ill. by author. Parents' Magazine Pr., 1977. ISBN 0-8193-0912-5 Subj: Careers – fishermen. Family life.

Gillie and the flattering fox ill. by author. Atheneum, 1978. ISBN 0-689-30637-7 Subj: Animals – foxes. Birds – chickens. Friendship.

Let's go to the circus ill. by author. Holiday, 1988. ISBN 0-8234-0693-8 Subj: Circus.

Let's go to the library ill. by author. Holiday, 1990. ISBN 0-8234-0529-9 Subj: Libraries.

Let's go to the museum ill. by author. Holiday, 1989. ISBN 0-8234-0784-5 Subj: Museums.

The magic of music ill. by author. Holiday, 1989. ISBN 0-8234-0735-7 Subj: Music.

Mother Goose picture riddles: a book of rebuses ill. by author. Holiday, 1981. ISBN 0-5234-0393-9 Subj: Nursery rhymes. Rebuses.

Owl and other scrambles ill. by author. Dutton, 1980. ISBN 0-525-36527-3 Subj: Games. Participation.

Pandora's box ill. by adapt. Atheneum, 1986. ISBN 0-689-31216-4 Subj: Character traits – curiosity. Folk & fairy tales.

Santa Claus around the world ill. by author. Holiday, 1987. ISBN 0-8234-0665-2 Subj: Holidays – Christmas. Santa Claus.

To sail a ship of treasures ill. by author. Atheneum, 1984. ISBN 0-689-31059-5 Subj: Behavior – collecting things.

Weilerstein, Sadie Rose. *The best of K'tonton* ill. by Marilyn Hirsh. Jewish Publication Society, 1980. ISBN 0-8276-0184-0 Subj: Jewish culture.

K'tonton's Yom Kippur kitten ill. by Joe Boddy. Jewish Publication Society, 1995. ISBN 0-8276-0541-2 Subj: Animals – cats. Behavior – misbehavior. Holidays – Yom Kippur. Jewish culture. Religion.

Weinberg, Florence. *Grandmother dear* (Finfer, Celentha)

Weinberg, Larry (Lawrence). *The Forgetful Bears* ill. by Paula Winter. Houghton Mifflin, 1982. ISBN 0-89919-068-5 Subj: Animals – bears. Behavior – forgetfulness.

The Forgetful Bears help Santa ill. by Jason Wolff. Random House, 2002. ISBN 0-375-92291-1 Subj: Animals – bears. Behavior – forgetfulness. Holidays – Christmas. Humorous stories. Santa Claus.

The Forgetful Bears meet Mr. Memory ill. by Bruce Degen. Scholastic, 1987. ISBN 0-590-40781-3 Subj: Animals – bears. Animals – elephants. Behavior – forgetfulness. Memories, memory.

Weir, Alison. *Peter, good night* ill. by Deborah Kogan Ray. Dutton, 1989. ISBN 0-525-44464-5 Subj: Bedtime. Night. Sleep.

Weir, Bob. *Panther dream* by Bob & Wendy Weir; ill. by Wendy Weir. Walt Disney, 1991. ISBN 1-56282-075-3 Subj: Food. Foreign lands – Africa. Forest, woods.

Weir, Wendy. *Panther dream* (Weir, Bob)

Weird pet poems comp. by Dilys Evans; ill. by Jacqueline Rogers. S&S, 1997. ISBN 0-689-80734-1 Subj: Animals. Pets. Poetry.

Weisgard, Leonard. *Mr. Peaceable paints* ill. by author. Scribners, 1956. Subj: Activities – painting. Careers – artists.

Silly Willy Nilly ill. by author. Scribners, 1953. Subj: Animals – elephants. Behavior – forgetfulness.

Who dreams of cheese? ill. by author. Scribners, 1950. Subj: Behavior – wishing. Dreams. Sleep.

Weiss, Bernard P. *I am Jewish* ill. with photos. PowerKids, 1996. ISBN 0-8239-2349-5 Subj: Jewish culture. Religion.

Weiss, David. *Kay Thompson's Eloise in Hollywood* (Stem, J. David)

Weiss, Ellen. *Clara the fortune-telling chicken* ill. by author. Dutton, 1978. ISBN 0-525-61576-8 Subj: Animals – sheep. Birds – chickens. Careers – fortune tellers. Seasons – winter.

For every child, a better world (Gikow, Louise)

Kitten castle (Friedman, Mel)

Millicent Maybe ill. by author. Watts, 1979. ISBN 0-531-02299-4 Subj: Reptiles – alligators, crocodiles.

Mokey's birthday present ill. by Elizabeth Miles. Holt, 1985. ISBN 0-03-004559-2 Subj: Birthdays. Friendship. Puppets.

Pigs in space ill. by Alastair Graham. Random House, 1983. ISBN 0-394-85730-5 Subj: Animals – pigs. Puppets. Space & space ships.

The pirates of Tarnoonga ed. by Stephanie Spinner; ill. by Bunny Carter. Random House, 1986. ISBN 0-394-87926-0 Subj: Pirates.

Telephone time: a first book of telephone do's and don'ts ill. by Hilary Knight. Random House, 1986. ISBN 0-394-98252-5 Subj: Etiquette. Telephone.

You are the star of a Muppet adventure ill. by Benjamin Alexander. Random House, 1983. ISBN 0-394-85623-6 Subj: Puppets.

Weiss, George (George David). *What a wonderful world* by George David Weiss & Bob Thiele; ill. by Ashley Bryan. Atheneum, 1995. ISBN 0-689-80087-8 Subj: Nature. Poetry. Puppets. Songs.

Weiss, Harvey. *My closet full of hats* ill. by author. Abelard-Schuman, 1962. Subj: Clothing – hats.

The sooner hound: a tale from American folklore ill. by author. Putnam, 1959. Subj: Animals – dogs. Careers – firefighters. Folk & fairy tales.

Weiss, Leatie. *Funny feet!* ill. by Ellen Weiss. Watts, 1978. ISBN 0-531-01348-0 Subj: Anatomy – feet. Birds – penguins. Clothing – shoes.

My teacher sleeps in school ill. by Ellen Weiss. Warne, 1984. ISBN 0-7232-6253-5 Subj: Animals – elephants. Careers – teachers. School.

Weiss, Miriam. *see* Schlein, Miriam

Weiss, Monica. *Mmmm . . . cookies!* ill. by Rose Mary Berlin. Troll, 1992. ISBN 0-8167-2486-6 Subj: Counting, numbers. Food. Frogs & toads.

Weiss, Nicki. *Barney is big* ill. by author. Greenwillow, 1988. ISBN 0-688-07587-8 Subj: Behavior – growing up. Family life. School – first day.

Battle day at Camp Delmont ill. by author. Greenwillow, 1985. ISBN 0-688-04307-0 Subj: Camps, camping. Friendship.

Dog boy cap skate ill. by author. Greenwillow, 1989. ISBN 0-688-08276-9 Subj: Animals. Sports – ice skating.

A family story ill. by author. Greenwillow, 1987. ISBN 0-688-06505-8 Subj: Family life – sisters. Friendship.

If you're happy and you know it ill. by author. Greenwillow, 1987. ISBN 0-688-06444-2 Subj: Folk & fairy tales. Music. Songs.

Maude and Sally ill. by author. Greenwillow, 1983. ISBN 0-688-01638-3 Subj: Friendship.

On a hot, hot day ill. by author. Putnam, 1992. ISBN 0-399-22119-0 Subj: Activities. Ethnic groups in the U.S. – Hispanic Americans. Family life – mothers. Seasons.

Princess Pearl ill. by author. Greenwillow, 1986. ISBN 0-688-05895-7 Subj: Family life – sisters. Sibling rivalry.

Sun sand sea sail ill. by author. Greenwillow, 1989. ISBN 0-688-08271-8 Subj: Family life. Rhyming text. Sea & seashore.

Waiting ill. by author. Greenwillow, 1981. ISBN 0-688-00603-5 Subj: Character traits – patience.

Weekend at Muskrat Lake ill. by author. Greenwillow, 1984. ISBN 0-688-03768-2 Subj: Activities – vacationing. Family life.

Where does the brown bear go? ill. by author. Greenwillow, 1989. ISBN 0-688-07863-X Subj: Animals. Bedtime. Night. Sleep. Toys.

Where does the brown bear go? [board book] ill. by author. Tupelo, 1998. ISBN 0-688-16388-2 Subj: Animals. Bedtime. Format, unusual – board books. Night. Sleep. Toys.

The world turns round and round ill. by author. Greenwillow, 2000. ISBN 0-688-17214-8 Subj: Clothing. Ethnic groups in the U.S. Rhyming text. World.

Weissmann, Joe. *Hickory dickory duck: a book of very funny rhymes and picture puzzles* (Patterson, Pat)

Weitzman, Elizabeth. *I am Jewish American* ill. with photos. PowerKids, 1997. ISBN 0-8239-5006-9 Subj: Ethnic groups in the U.S. – Jewish Americans. Jewish culture. Religion.

Let's talk about when a parent dies ill. by author. Rosen, 1996. ISBN 0-8239-2309-6 Subj: Death. Emotions – grief. Family life.

Let's talk about when someone you love has Alzheimer's disease ill. by author. Rosen, 1996. ISBN 0-8239-2306-1 Subj: Family life. Illness – Alzheimer's.

Weitzman, Jacqueline Preiss. *You can't take a balloon into the Metropolitan Museum* ill. by Robin Preiss-Glasser. Dial, 1998. ISBN 0-8037-2302-4 Subj: Art. Cities, towns. Family life – grandmothers. Museums. Toys – balloons. Wordless.

You can't take a balloon into the National Gallery ill. by Robin Preiss-Glasser. Dial, 2000. ISBN 0-8037-2303-2 Subj: Art. Cities, towns. Family life – grandmothers. Museums. Picture puzzles. Toys – balloons. Wordless.

Welber, Robert. *Goodbye, hello* ill. by Cyndy Szekeres. Pantheon, 1974. ISBN 0-394-92770-2 Subj: Animals. Behavior – growing up. Rhyming text.

Song of the seasons ill. by Deborah Kogan Ray. Pantheon, 1973. ISBN 0-394-92413-4 Subj: Seasons.

Welch, Martha McKeen. *Will that wake mother?* photos by author. Dodd, 1982. ISBN 0-396-08090-1 Subj: Animals – cats.

Welch, Willy. *Dancing with Daddy* ill. by Liza Woodruff. Whispering Coyote, 1999. ISBN 1-58089-020-2 Subj: Activities – dancing. Animals. Family life – fathers. Rhyming text. Trees.

Grumpy Bunnies ill. by Tammie Lyon. Charlesbridge, 2000. ISBN 1-58089-053-9 Subj: Animals – rabbits. Rhyming text. School.

Playing right field ill. by Marc Simont. Scholastic, 1995. ISBN 0-590-48298-X Subj: Songs. Sports – baseball.

Weller, Frances Ward. *The angel of Mill Street* ill. by Robert J. Blake. Philomel, 1998. ISBN 0-399-23133-1 Subj: Accidents. Angels. Animals – dogs. Careers – musicians. Ethnic groups in the U.S. – Irish Americans. Holidays – Christmas. Weather – snow.

The closet gorilla ill. by Cat Bowman Smith. Macmillan, 1991. ISBN 0-02-792531-5 Subj: Animals – gorillas. Family life – aunts, uncles. Holidays – Halloween.

Madaket Millie ill. by Marcia Sewall. Philomel, 1997. ISBN 0-399-22785-7 Subj: Character traits – helpfulness. Character traits – perseverance. Sea & seashore. U.S. history.

Matthew Wheelock's wall ill. by Ted Lewin. Macmillan, 1992. ISBN 0-02-792612-5 Subj: Activities – making things. Rocks.

Riptide ill. by Robert J. Blake. Putnam, 1990. ISBN 0-399-21675-8 Subj: Animals – dogs. Sea & seashore.

Welling, Peter J. *Andrew McGroundhog and his shady shadow* ill. by author. Pelican, 2001. ISBN 1-56554-711-X Subj: Animals – groundhogs. Hibernation. Holidays – Groundhog Day. Shadows.

Shawn O'Hisser, the last snake in Ireland ill. by author. Pelican, 2002. ISBN 1-58980-014-1 Subj: Animals. Foreign lands – Ireland. Humorous stories. Mythical creatures – leprechauns. Reptiles – snakes.

Wellington, Anne. *Apple pie* ill. by Nita Sowter. Prentice-Hall, 1978. ISBN 0-13-038745-2 Subj: Seasons.

Wellington, Monica. *All my little ducklings* ill. by author. Dutton, 1989. ISBN 0-525-44459-9 Subj: Activities. Birds – ducks.

Apple farmer Annie ill. by author. Dutton, 2001. ISBN 0-525-46727-0 Subj: Careers – farmers. Farms. Food. Stores.

Baby at home ill. by author. Dutton, 1997. ISBN 0-525-45640-6 Subj: Babies. Format, unusual – board books. Homes, houses.

Baby in a buggy ill. by author. Dutton, 1995. ISBN 0-525-45295-8 Subj: Babies. Format, unusual – board books.

Baby in a car ill. by author. Dutton, 1995. ISBN 0-525-45296-6 Subj: Babies. Format, unusual – board books.

Bunny's first snowflake ill. by author. Dutton, 2000. ISBN 0-525-46464-6 Subj: Animals. Animals – rabbits. Format, unusual – board books. Seasons – winter. Weather – snow.

Bunny's rainbow day ill. by author. Dutton, 1999. ISBN 0-525-46047-0 Subj: Animals. Animals – rabbits. Format, unusual – board books. Weather – rain. Weather – rainbows. Weather – storms.

Mr. Cookie Baker ill. by author. Dutton, 1992. ISBN 0-525-44965-5 Subj: Activities – baking, cooking. Careers – chefs, cooks. Food.

Night city by Monica Wellington, with Andrew Kupfer; ill. by Monica Wellington. Dutton, 1998. ISBN 0-525-45948-0 Subj: Activities. Animals – cats. Animals – mice. Cities, towns. Night.

Night rabbits ill. by author. Dutton, 1995. ISBN 0-525-45335-0 Subj: Animals – rabbits. Night. Weather – storms.

The sheep follow ill. by author. Dutton, 1992. ISBN 0-525-44837-3 Subj: Animals – dogs. Animals – sheep. Careers – shepherds. Farms.

Squeaking of art, the mice go to the museum ill. by author. Dutton, 2000. ISBN 0-525-46165-5 Subj: Animals – cats. Animals – mice. Art. Museums.

Wells, Carolyn. *Carolyn Wells' edition of Mother Goose* (Mother Goose)

Wells, H. G. (Herbert George). *The adventures of Tommy* ill. by author. Knopf, 1967. Subj: Animals – elephants. Character traits – bravery. Character traits – kindness.

Wells, Joel. *The manger mouse: what she saw and did and got on the very first Christmas* ill. by Annette Boarini Anderson. Thomas More, 1990. ISBN 0-8834-7255-4 Subj: Animals – mice. Holidays – Christmas. Religion – Nativity.

Wells, Philip. *Daddy Island* ill. by Niki Daly. Barefoot, 2001. ISBN 1-84148-319-2 Subj: Activities – playing. Family life – fathers. Imagination. Islands. Rhyming text.

Wells, Rosemary. *Abdul* ill. by author. Dial, 1986. ISBN 0-8037-4462-5 Subj: Animals – camels. Animals – horses, ponies. Character traits – being different.

The bear went over the mountain ill. by author. Scholastic, 1998. ISBN 0-590-02910-X Subj: Animals – bears. Mountains. Songs.

Bingo ill. by author. Scholastic, 1999. ISBN 0-590-02913-4 Subj: Animals – dogs. Format, unusual – board books. Music. Songs.

Bunny cakes ill. by author. Dial, 1997. ISBN 0-8037-2144-7 Subj: Activities – baking, cooking. Animals – rabbits. Family life – brothers & sisters. Family life – grandmothers.

Bunny money ill. by author. HarperCollins, 1997. ISBN 0-06-027258-9 Subj: Animals – rabbits. Family life – brothers & sisters. Family life – grandmothers. Money.

Bunny party Ill. by author. Viking, 2001. ISBN 0-670-03501-7 Subj: Animals – rabbits. Birthdays. Family life – brothers & sisters. Family life – grandmothers. Parties. Toys.

Don't spill it again, James ill. by author. Dial, 1990. ISBN 0-8037-2118-8 Subj: Animals – foxes. Rhyming text. Trains. Weather – rain.

Emily's first 100 days of school ill. by author. Hyperion, 2000. ISBN 0-7868-2443-3 Subj: Animals – rabbits. Counting, numbers. School – first day.

First tomato ill. by author. Dial, 1992. ISBN 0-8037-1175-1 Subj: Animals – rabbits. Gardens, gardening. Rhyming text. School.

The fisherman and his wife (Grimm, Jacob)

Forest of dreams by Rosemary Wells & Susan Jeffers; ill. by Susan Jeffers. Dial, 1988. ISBN 0-8037-0570-0 Subj: Nature. Seasons – spring. Seasons – winter.

Fritz and the mess fairy ill. by author. Dial, 1991. ISBN 0-8037-0983-8 Subj: Animals – skunks. Behavior – misbehavior. Character traits – cleanliness. Fairies.

The germ busters ill. by Jody Wheeler. Hyperion, 2002. ISBN 0-7868-0728-8 Subj: Animals. Character traits – cleanliness. Illness. School.

Good night, Fred ill. by author. Dial, 1981. ISBN 0-8037-2992-8 Subj: Behavior – misbehavior. Imagination. Sibling rivalry.

Goodnight Max ill. by author. Viking, 2000. ISBN 0-670-88707-2 Subj: Animals – rabbits. Bedtime. Family life – brothers & sisters. Format, unusual – toy & movable books.

The Halloween parade ill. by Jody Wheeler. Hyperion, 2001. ISBN 0-7868-0723-7 Subj: Contests. Holidays – Halloween. Parades. School.

Hazel's amazing mother ill. by author. Dial, 1985. ISBN 0-8037-0210-8 Subj: Animals. Animals – badgers. Behavior – misbehavior. Family life – mothers.

Hooray for Max ill. by author. Dial, 1986. ISBN 0-8037-0202-7 Subj: Animals – rabbits. Format, unusual – board books.

The house in the mail ill. by Dan Andreasen. Viking, 2002. ISBN 0-7894-2603-X Subj: Family life. Homes, houses. U.S. history.

How many? How much? ill. by Michael Koelsch. Viking, 2001. ISBN 0-670-89652-7 Subj: Concepts. Counting, numbers. School – first day.

The island light ill. by author. Dial, 1992. ISBN 0-8037-1178-6 Subj: Animals – rabbits. Family life – fathers. Illness. Lighthouses.

The itsy-bitsy spider ill. by author. Scholastic, 1998. ISBN 0-590-02911-8 Subj: Birds – ducks. Format, unusual – board books. Songs. Spiders.

The language of doves ill. by Greg Shed. Dial, 1996. ISBN 0-8037-1471-8 Subj: Birds – doves. Birds – pigeons. Death. Family life – grandfathers. War.

Letters and sounds ill. by Michael Koelsch. Viking, 2001. ISBN 0-670-89651-9 Subj: ABC books. Communication. Language. School.

A lion for Lewis ill. by author. Dial, 1982. ISBN 0-8037-4686-5 Subj: Activities – playing. Imagination.

The little lame prince ill. by author. Dial, 1990. ISBN 0-8037-0789-4 Subj: Animals – pigs. Behavior – greed. Folk & fairy tales. Handicaps – physical handicaps. Royalty – princes.

Lucy comes to stay ill. by Mark Graham. Dial, 1994. ISBN 0-8037-1214-6 Subj: Animals – dogs. Pets.

McDuff and the baby ill. by Susan Jeffers. Hyperion, 1997. ISBN 0-7868-2258-9 Subj: Animals – dogs. Babies. Family life.

McDuff comes home ill. by Susan Jeffers. Hyperion, 1997. ISBN 0-7868-2259-7 Subj: Animals – dogs. Behavior – lost.

McDuff goes to school ill. by Susan Jeffers. Hyperion, 2001. ISBN 0-7868-2432-8 Subj: Animals – dogs. Communities, neighborhoods. Foreign languages. School.

McDuff moves in ill. by Susan Jeffers. Hyperion, 1997. ISBN 0-7868-2257-0 Subj: Animals – dogs. Behavior – needing someone.

McDuff saves the day ill. by Susan Jeffers. Hyperion, 2002. ISBN 0-7868-2311-9 Subj: Activities – picnicking. Animals – dogs. Family life. Food. Holidays – Fourth of July. Insects – ants.

McDuffs hide-and-seek ill. by Susan Jeffers. Hyperion, 2004. ISBN 0-7868-1935-9 Subj: Animals – dogs. Animals – rabbits. Format, unusual – toy & movable books. Games.

McDuff's new friend ill. by Susan Jeffers. Hyperion, 1998. ISBN 0-7868-2337-2 Subj: Animals – dogs. Holidays – Christmas. Santa Claus.

Mama, don't go! ill. by Jody Wheeler. Hyperion, 2001. ISBN 0-7868-0720-2 Subj: Animals – cats. Emotions. School.

Max and Ruby's Midas ill. by author. Dial, 1995. ISBN 0-8037-1783-0 Subj: Animals – rabbits. Behavior – greed. Family life – brothers & sisters. Food.

Max cleans up ill. by author. Viking, 2000. ISBN 0-670-89218-1 Subj: Animals – rabbits. Babies. Character traits – cleanliness. Family life – brothers & sisters.

Max's bath ill. by author. Dial, 1985. ISBN 0-8037-0162-4 Subj: Activities – bathing. Animals – rabbits. Format, unusual – board books.

Max's bedtime ill. by author. Dial, 1985. ISBN 0-8037-0160-8 Subj: Animals – rabbits. Bedtime. Format, unusual – board books. Sibling rivalry. Toys.

Max's birthday ill. by author. Dial, 1985. ISBN 0-8037-0163-2 Subj: Animals – rabbits. Birthdays. Format, unusual – board books. Toys.

Max's breakfast ill. by author. Dial, 1998. ISBN 0-8037-2273-7 Subj: Animals – rabbits. Character traits – patience. Format, unusual – board books. Sibling rivalry.

Max's chocolate chicken ill. by author. Dial, 1999. ISBN 0-8037-2351-2 Subj: Animals – rabbits. Holidays – Easter. Seasons – spring. Sibling rivalry.

Max's Christmas ill. by author. Dial, 1986. ISBN 0-8037-0290-6 Subj: Animals – rabbits. Holidays – Christmas. Santa Claus.

Max's dragon shirt ill. by author. Dial, 1991. ISBN 0-8037-0945-5 Subj: Activities – babysitting. Animals – rabbits. Behavior – lost. Clothing. Family life – brothers & sisters. Stores.

Max's first word ill. by author. Dial, 1979. ISBN 0-8037-6066-3 Subj: Animals – rabbits. Format, unusual – board books. Language.

Max's new suit ill. by author. Dial, 1979. ISBN 0-8037-6065-5 Subj: Animals – rabbits. Clothing. Format, unusual – board books.

Max's ride ill. by author. Dial, 1979. ISBN 0-8037-6069-8 Subj: Animals – rabbits. Format, unusual – board books. Language.

Max's toys: a counting book ill. by author. Dial, 1979. ISBN 0-8037-6068-X Subj: Animals – rabbits. Counting, numbers. Format, unusual – board books. Toys.

Morris's disappearing bag ill. by author. Viking, 1999. ISBN 0-670-88721-8 Subj: Animals – rabbits. Gifts. Holidays – Christmas.

Moss pillows ill. by author. Dial, 1992. ISBN 0-8037-1177-8 Subj: Animals – rabbits. Family life. Forest, woods. Rhyming text.

My kindergarten ill. by author. Hyperion, 2004. ISBN 0-7868-0833-0 Subj: Animals. Animals – rabbits. Days of the week, months of the year. Rhyming text. School.

Night sounds, morning colors ill. by David McPhail. Dial, 1994. ISBN 0-8037-1302-9 Subj: Activities. Family life. Seasons. Senses.

Noisy Nora ill. by author. Dial, 1997. ISBN 0-8037-1835-7 Subj: Animals – mice. Behavior – needing someone. Rhyming text.

Old MacDonald (Old MacDonald had a farm)

Peabody ill. by author. Dial, 1983. ISBN 0-8037-0005-9 Subj: Sibling rivalry. Toys – dolls.

Read to your bunny ill. by author. Scholastic, 1998. ISBN 0-590-30284-1 Subj: Animals – rabbits. Books, reading. Rhyming text.

Ruby's beauty shop ill. by author. Viking, 2002. ISBN 0-670-03553-X Subj: Animals – rabbits. Beauty shops. Family life – brothers & sisters. Family life – grandmothers.

The school play ill. by Jody Wheeler. Hyperion, 2001. ISBN 0-7868-0721-0 Subj: Animals. Animals – cats. Hygiene. School. Teeth. Theater.

Shy Charles ill. by author. Dial, 1988. ISBN 0-8037-0564-6 Subj: Activities – babysitting. Animals – mice. Character traits – individuality. Family life. Rhyming text.

Small world of Binky Braverman ill. by Richard Egielski. Viking, 2003. ISBN 0-670-03636-6 Subj: Emotions – loneliness. Family life – aunts, uncles. Imagination.

Stanley and Rhoda ill. by author. Dial, 1978. ISBN 0-8037-8249-7 Subj: Activities – babysitting. Animals – mice. Sibling rivalry.

Timothy goes to school ill. by author. Viking, 2000. ISBN 0-670-89182-7 Subj: Animals – raccoons. Behavior – growing up. School – first day.

Unfortunately Harriet ill. by author. Dial, 1972. ISBN 0-8037-9169-0 Subj: Behavior – bad day.

Yoko ill. by author. Hyperion, 1998. ISBN 0-7868-2345-3 Subj: Animals – cats. Animals – raccoons. Food. Prejudice. School.

Yoko's paper cranes ill. by author. Hyperion, 2001. ISBN 0-7868-2602-9 Subj: Animals – cats. Birds – cranes. Birthdays. Ethnic groups in the U.S. – Japanese Americans. Family life – grandmothers. Foreign lands – Japan.

Wells, Ruth. *The farmer and the poor god* ill. by Yoshi. S&S, 1996. ISBN 0-689-80214-5 Subj: Character traits – laziness. Clothing – shoes. Folk & fairy tales. Foreign lands – Japan. Poverty.

Wells, Tony. *Allsorts* ill. by author. Macmillan, 1988. ISBN 0-689-71185-9 Subj: Concepts – color. Concepts – shape. Games.

Puzzle doubles ill. by author. Macmillan, 1988. ISBN 0-689-71186-7 Subj: Concepts – color. Concepts – size. Games.

Wen, George. *The little Christmas soldier* (Dedieu, Thierry)

Uglypuss (Gregoire, Caroline)

Wende, Philip. *Bird boy* ill. by author. Cowles, 1970. ISBN 0-40-214201-2 Subj: Activities – flying. Dreams.

Weninger, Brigitte. *Davy in the middle* ill. by Eve Tharlet. North-South, 2004. ISBN 0-7358-1934-3 Subj: Activities – babysitting. Animals – rabbits. Behavior – growing up. Character traits – helpfulness. Family life. Family life – brothers & sisters.

The elf's hat ill. by John A. Rowe; trans. by J. Alison James. North-South, 2000. ISBN 0-7358-1255-1 Subj: Animals. Clothing – hats. Cumulative tales. Fairies. Insects – fleas. Rhyming text.

Good-bye, daddy! ill. by Alan Marks. North-South, 1995. ISBN 1-55858-383-1 Subj: Divorce. Emotions. Family life – fathers. Toys – bears.

Happy birthday, Davy ill. by Eve Tharlet; trans. by Rosemary Lanning. North-South, 2000. ISBN 0-7358-1346-9 Subj: Animals – rabbits. Birthdays. Parties.

Happy Easter, Davy ill. by Eve Tharlet. North-South, 2001. ISBN 0-7358-1436-8 Subj: Animals – rabbits. Gifts. Holidays – Easter.

A letter to Santa Claus ill. by Anne Möller. North-South, 2000. ISBN 0-7358-1360-4 Subj: Holidays – Christmas. Letters, cards. Santa Claus.

Little apple ill. by Anne Möller. North-South, 2001. ISBN 0-7358-1426-0 Subj: Food. Trees.

Lumina: a story for the dark time of the year ill. by Julie Wintz-Litty; trans. by Anthea Bell. North-South, 1997. ISBN 1-55858-791-8 Subj: Holidays – Christmas. Homeless. Light, lights. Orphans.

Merry Christmas, Davy! ill. by Eve Tharlet; trans. by Rosemary Lanning. North-South, 1998. ISBN 1-55858-981-3 Subj: Animals. Animals – rabbits. Behavior – sharing. Holidays – Christmas.

Precious water ill. by Anne Möller. North-South, 2002. ISBN 0-7358-1514-3 Subj: Ecology. Nature. Water.

Special delivery ill. by Alexander Reichstein; trans. by J. Alison James. North-South, 2000. ISBN 0-7358-1318-3 Subj: Family life – mothers. Format, unusual – toy & movable books. Games.

What's the matter, Davy? trans. by Rosemary Lanning; ill. by Eve Tharlet. North-South, 1998. ISBN 1-55858-900-7 Subj: Animals – rabbits. Behavior – lost & found possessions. Toys.

Why are you fighting, Davy? ill. by Eve Tharlet; trans. by Rosemary Lanning. North-South, 1999. ISBN 0-7358-1074-5 Subj: Animals – rabbits. Behavior – fighting, arguing. Character traits – individuality. Friendship.

Will you mind the baby, Davy? ill. by Eve Tharlet; trans. by Rosemary Lanning. North-South, 1997. ISBN 1-55858-732-2 Subj: Activities – babysitting. Animals – rabbits. Babies. Family life – new sibling.

Wenning, Elisabeth. *The Christmas mouse* ill. by Barbara Remington. Holt, [1983] 1959. ISBN 0-03-015066-3 Subj: Animals – mice. Foreign lands – Austria. Holidays – Christmas. Music. Musical instruments – organs. Songs.

Werner, Jane. *see* Watson, Jane Werner

Wersba, Barbara. *Amanda dreaming* ill. by Mercer Mayer. Atheneum, 1973. ISBN 0-689-30073-5 Subj: Dreams. Sleep.

Do tigers ever bite kings? ill. by Mario Rivoli. Atheneum, 1966. Subj: Animals – tigers. Character traits – kindness to animals. Poetry. Royalty – kings.

West, Colin. *Go tell it to the toucan* ill. by author. Bantam, 1990. ISBN 0-553-05889-4 Subj: Animals. Birthdays. Cumulative tales. Parties.

Have you seen the crocodile? ill. by author. Lippincott, 1986. ISBN 0-397-32172-4 Subj: Birds. Cumulative tales. Reptiles – alligators, crocodiles.

I brought my love a tabby cat ill. by Caroline Anstey. Chronicle, 1988. ISBN 0-87701-518-X Subj: Animals. Careers – tailors. Clothing. Weddings.

The king of Kennelwick castle ill. by Anne Dalton. Lippincott, 1987. ISBN 0-397-32197-X Subj: Cumulative tales. Royalty – kings.

The king's toothache ill. by Anne Dalton. Lippincott, 1988. ISBN 0-397-32252-6 Subj: Cumulative tales. Illness. Rhyming text. Royalty – kings. Teeth.

A moment in rhyme ill. by Julie Banyard. Dial, 1987. ISBN 0-8037-0259-0 Subj: Poetry.

One day in the jungle ill. by author. Candlewick, 1995. ISBN 1-56402-646-9 Subj: Animals. Cumulative tales. Jungle. Noise, sounds.

"Only joking!" laughed the lobster ill. by author. Candlewick, 1995. ISBN 1-56402-647-7 Subj: Crustaceans – lobsters. Fish – sharks.

"Pardon?" said the giraffe ill. by author. Lippincott, 1986. ISBN 0-397-32173-2 Subj: Animals. Character traits – persistence. Frogs & toads.

West, Emily. *see* Payne, Emmy

West, Ian. *Silas, the first pig to fly* ill. by author. Grosset, 1977. ISBN 0-448-14288-0 Subj: Activities – flying. Animals – pigs.

West, James. *see* Withers, Carl

West, Judy. *Have you got my purr?* ill. by Tim Warnes. Dutton, 2000. ISBN 0-525-46390-9 Subj: Animals. Animals – cats. Behavior – lost & found possessions. Noise, sounds.

West, Keith. *Little Pig's special day* ill. by author. Putnam, 1991. ISBN 0-399-22209-X Subj: Animals – pigs. Babies. Family life – new sibling.

West, Kipling. *A rattle of bones: a Halloween book of collective nouns* ill. by author. Orchard, 1999. ISBN 0-531-33196-2 Subj: Holidays – Halloween. Language. Rhyming text.

Westcott, Nadine Bernard. *Getting up* ill. by author. Little, 1987. ISBN 0-316-93131-4 Subj: Family life. Morning.

The giant vegetable garden ill. by author. Little, 1981. ISBN 0-316-93129-2 Subj: Activities – picnicking. Gardens, gardening.

Going to bed ill. by author. Little, 1987. ISBN 0-316-93132-2 Subj: Bedtime. Family life. Night. Toys.

I know an old lady who swallowed a fly (Little old lady who swallowed a fly)

The lady with the alligator purse ill. by author. Little, 1988. ISBN 0-316-93135-7 Subj: Clothing – handbags, purses. Games. Humorous stories. Poetry.

Peanut butter and jelly: a play rhyme ill. by author. Dutton, 1987. ISBN 0-525-44317-7 Subj: Animals – elephants. Careers – bakers. Family life. Food. Rhyming text.

Skip to my Lou ill. by adapt. Little, 1989. ISBN 0-316-93137-3 Subj: Farms. Folk & fairy tales. Music. Songs.

There's a hole in the bucket ill. by adapt. HarperCollins, 1990. ISBN 0-06-026423-3 Subj: Animals. Farms. Music. Songs.

Westell, Kerry. *Amanda's book* ill. by Ruth Ohi. Firefly, 1991. ISBN 1-55037-185-1 Subj: Animals – cats. Behavior – collecting things. Imagination.

Westerberg, Christine. *The cap that mother made* ill. by adapt. Prentice-Hall, 1977. ISBN 0-13-113365-9 Subj: Clothing – hats. Folk & fairy tales. Foreign lands – Sweden.

Westman, Barbara. *Dancing dogs: Charlotte and Emilio at the circus* ill. by author. HarperCollins, 1991. ISBN 0-06-022460-6 Subj: Activities – dancing. Animals – dogs. Circus.

The day before Christmas: a story of Charlotte and Emilio ill. by author. HarperCollins, 1990. ISBN 0-06-026429-2 Subj: Animals – dogs. Holidays – Christmas.

Weston, Martha. *Bad baby brother* ill. by author. Clarion, 1997. ISBN 0-395-72103-2 Subj: Babies. Emotions. Family life – new sibling.

Bea's four bears ill. by author. Houghton Mifflin, 1992. ISBN 0-395-57791-8 Subj: Activities – picnicking. Behavior – sharing. Counting, numbers. Toys – bears.

The dinosaurs meet Dr. Clock ill. by author. Holiday, 2002. ISBN 0-8234-1661-5 Subj: Activities – traveling. Careers – scientists. Dinosaurs. Machines.

Jack and Jill and Big Dog Bill ill. by author. Random House, 2001. ISBN 0-375-91248-7 Subj: Animals – dogs. Rhyming text. Sports – sledding.

Peony's rainbow ill. by author. Lothrop, 1981. ISBN 0-688-00541-1 Subj: Animals – pigs. Weather – rainbows.

Space guys! ill. by author. Holiday, 2000. ISBN 0-8234-1487-6 Subj: Aliens. Night. Rhyming text. Space & space ships.

Tuck in the pool ill. by author. Clarion, 1995. ISBN 0-395-65479-3 Subj: Animals – pigs. Emotions – fear. Sports – swimming.

Tuck's haunted house ill. by author. Clarion, 2002. ISBN 0-618-15966-5 Subj: Animals – pigs. Family life – brothers & sisters. Holidays – Halloween. Homes, houses. Monsters.

Westwood, Jennifer. *Going to Squintum's: a foxy folktale* ill. by Fiona French. Dial, 1985. ISBN 0-8037-0015-6 Subj: Animals – foxes. Character traits – cleverness. Folk & fairy tales.

The star child (Wilde, Oscar)

Wethered, Peggy. *Touchdown Mars! an ABC adventure* by Peggy Wethered & Ken Edgett; ill. by Michael Chesworth. Putnam, 2000. ISBN 0-399-23214-1 Subj: ABC books. Animals – cats. Planets. Space & space ships.

Wetterer, Charles M. *The snow walker* (Wetterer, Margaret K.)

Wetterer, Margaret K. *Kate Shelley and the midnight express* ill. by Karen Ritz. Carolrhoda, 1990. ISBN 0-87614-425-3 Subj: Character traits – bravery. Trains. U.S. history.

Patrick and the fairy thief ill. by Enrico Arno. Atheneum, 1980. ISBN 0-689-50160-0 Subj: Character traits – cleverness. Fairies. Family life – mothers.

The snow walker by Margaret K. & Charles M. Wetterer; ill. by Mary O'Keefe Young. Carolrhoda, 1996. ISBN 0-87614-891-7 Subj: Character traits – bravery. Character traits – helpfulness. U.S. history. Weather – blizzards.

Wettlin, Margaret. *In the van* (Marshak, S. [Samuil])

Wexler, Jerome (LeRoy). *Find the hidden insect* (Cole, Joanna)

Flowers, fruits, seeds photos by author. Prentice-Hall, 1988. ISBN 0-13-322397-3 Subj: Plants. Science.

Wonderful pussy willows photos by author. Dutton, 1992. ISBN 0-525-44867-5 Subj: Plants. Science.

Wezel, Peter. *The good bird* ill. by author. HarperCollins, 1964. Subj: Behavior – sharing. Birds. Fish. Wordless.

The naughty bird ill. by author. Follett, 1967. Translation of Der freche Vogel Figaro. Subj: Animals – cats. Birds. Wordless.

Whales created by Gallimard Jeunesse, Ute Fuhr & Raoul Sautai; ill. by Ute Fuhr & Raoul Sautai. Scholastic, 1993. ISBN 0-590-47130-9 Subj: Animals – whales. Format, unusual – toy & movable books.

Wharton, Thomas. *Hildegard sings* ill. by author. Farrar, 1991. ISBN 0-374-33242-8 Subj: Animals – hippopotamuses. Emotions – fear. Theater.

What a morning! the Christmas story in Black spirituals sel. & ed. by John M. Langstaff; ill. by Ashley Bryan; musical arrangements by John Andrew Ross. McElderry, 1987. ISBN 0-689-50422-5 Subj: Holidays – Christmas. Music. Religion. Songs.

What do babies do? ill. with photos. Random House, 1985. ISBN 0-394-87279-7 Subj: Babies. Format, unusual – board books.

What do toddlers do? ill. with photos. Random House, 1985. ISBN 0-394-87280-0 Subj: Babies. Format, unusual – board books.

What do you feed your donkey on? rhymes from a Belfast childhood col. by Colette O'Hare; ill. by Jenny Rodwell. Collins-World, 1978. ISBN 0-00183-734-6 Subj: Foreign lands – Ireland. Nursery rhymes.

What we do ill. by Roser Capdevila. Firefly, 1986. ISBN 0-920303-46-3 Subj: Activities.

What will we do with the baby-o? rhymes & songs sel. by Theo Heras; ill. by Jennifer Herbert. Tundra, 2004. ISBN 0-88776-689-7 Subj: Rhyming text. Songs.

Whatley, Bruce. *Captain Pajamas* by Bruce Whatley & Rosie Smith; ill. by Bruce Whatley. HarperCollins, 1999. ISBN 0-06-026614-7 Subj: Aliens. Animals – dogs. Imagination. Night. Sleep.

That magnetic dog ill. by author. HarperCollins, 1999. ISBN 0-207-18420-8 Subj: Animals – dogs. Pets. Rhyming text.

Wait! No paint! ill. by author. HarperCollins, 2001. ISBN 0-06-028271-1 Subj: Animals – pigs. Animals – wolves. Behavior – carelessness. Careers – illustrators.

Wheatley, Nadia. *Luke's way of looking* ill. by Matt Ottley. Kane/Miller, 2001. ISBN 1-929132-18-2 Subj: Art. Careers – artists. Careers – teachers. Character traits – individuality. Imagination. Museums.

Wheeler, Cindy. *Marmalade's Christmas present* ill. by author. Knopf, 1984. ISBN 0-394-96794-1 Subj: Animals – cats. Holidays – Christmas.

Marmalade's nap ill. by author. Knopf, 1983. ISBN 0-394-95022-4 Subj: Animals – cats. Noise, sounds. Sleep.

Marmalade's picnic ill. by author. Knopf, 1983. ISBN 0-394-95023-2 Subj: Activities – picnicking. Animals – cats.

Marmalade's snowy day ill. by author. Knopf, 1982. ISBN 0-394-95025-9 Subj: Animals – cats. Weather – snow.

Marmalade's yellow leaf ill. by author. Knopf, 1982. ISBN 0-394-95024-0 Subj: Animals – cats. Seasons – fall.

More simple signs ill. by author. Viking, 1998. ISBN 0-670-87477-9 Subj: Communication. Handicaps – deafness. Sign language.

Rose ill. by author. Knopf, 1985. ISBN 0-394-96233-8 Subj: Animals – pigs. Farms.

Simple signs ill. by author. Viking, 1995. ISBN 0-670-86282-7 Subj: Communication. Handicaps – deafness. Sign language.

Wheeler, Lisa. *Jam & jelly by Holly & Nellie* ill. by Gijsbert van Frankenhuyzen. Sleeping Bear, 2002. ISBN 1-58536-109-7 Subj: Activities – working. Clothing – coats. Family life – mothers. Food. Plants.

Jazz baby ill. by R. Gregory Christie. Harcourt, 2004. ISBN 0-15-202522-7 Subj: Babies. Music. Rhyming text.

Old Cricket ill. by Ponder Goembel. Atheneum, 2003. ISBN 0-689-84510-3 Subj: Behavior. Birds – crows. Character traits – helpfulness. Insects – crickets.

Porcupining ill. by Janie Bynum. Little, 2002. ISBN 0-316-98912-6 Subj: Animals – hedgehogs. Animals – porcupines. Behavior – needing someone. Emotions – loneliness.

Sixteen cows ill. by Kurt Cyrus. Harcourt, 2002. ISBN 0-15-202676-2 Subj: Animals – bulls, cows. Cowboys, cowgirls. Rhyming text.

Turk and Runt ill. by Frank Ansley. Atheneum, 2002. ISBN 0-689-84761-0 Subj: Birds – turkeys. Character traits – cleverness. Concepts – size. Family life – brothers. Food. Holidays – Thanksgiving.

Wool gathering ill. by Frank Ansley. Atheneum, 2001. ISBN 0-689-84369-0 Subj: Animals – sheep. Family life. Poetry.

Wheeler, M. J. (Mary Jane). *First came the Indians* ill. by James Houston. Atheneum, 1983. ISBN 0-689-50258-3 Subj: Indians of North America.

Wheeler, Opal. *Sing in praise: a collection of the best loved hymns* ill. by Marjorie Torrey. Dutton, 1946. Subj: Caldecott award honor books. Music. Religion. Songs.

Sing Mother Goose ill. by Marjorie Torrey; music by Opal Wheeler. Dutton, 1945. Subj: Caldecott award honor books. Music. Nursery rhymes. Songs.

Wheeler, William A. (Adolphus). *Mother Goose's melodies: or, songs for the nursery* (Mother Goose)

Wheeling, Lynn. *When you fly* ill. by author. Little, 1967. Subj: Activities – flying. Airplanes, airports. Poetry.

Whelan, Gloria. *Bringing the farmhouse home* ill. by Jada Rowland. S&S, 1992. ISBN 0-671-74984-6 Subj: Death. Family life. Family life – grandmothers. Quilts.

A week of raccoons ill. by Lynn Munsinger. Knopf, 1988. ISBN 0-394-98396-3 Subj: Animals – raccoons.

Whippo, Walt. *Little white duck* lyrics by Walt Whippo; music by Bernard Zaritzky; ill. by Joan Paley. Little, 2000. ISBN 0-316-03227-1 Subj: Animals. Birds – ducks. Music. Songs. Theater.

Whishaw, Iona. *Henry and the cow problem* ill. by Chum McLeod. Firefly, 1992. ISBN 1-55037-375-7 Subj: Animals – bulls, cows. Bedtime. Emotions – fear.

Whitcher, Susan. *The key to the cupboard* ill. by Andrew Glass. Farrar, 1997. ISBN 0-374-34127-3 Subj: Imagination. Magic. Witches. Wizards.

Something for everyone ill. by Barbara Lehman. Farrar, 1995. ISBN 0-374-37138-5 Subj: Activities – traveling. Family life – aunts, uncles. Friendship. Moving.

Whitcomb, Mary E. *Odd Velvet* ill. by Tara Calahan King. Chronicle, 1998. ISBN 0-8118-2004-1 Subj: Character traits – being different. School.

White, Amanda. *Rip and Rap* ill. by Debbie Harter. Barefoot, 2002. ISBN 1-84148-944-1 Subj: Animals – dogs. Character traits – individuality. Format, unusual – board books. Multiple births – twins. Self-concept.

White, Carolyn. *The adventure of Louey and Frank* ill. by Laura Dronzek. Greenwillow, 2001. ISBN 0-688-16605-9 Subj: Animals – bears. Animals – rabbits. Boats, ships. Friendship.

Whuppity Stoorie ill. by S. D. Schindler. Putnam, 1997. ISBN 0-399-22903-5 Subj: Animals – pigs. Folk & fairy tales. Foreign lands – Scotland. Names. Witches.

White, Ellen Emerson. *Santa paws* ill. by Robert J. Blake. Scholastic, 2003. ISBN 0-439-32438-6 Subj: Animals – dogs. Character traits – helpfulness. Holidays – Christmas.

White, Florence Meiman. *How to lose your lunch money* ill. by Chris Jenkyns. Ritchie, 1970. Subj: Behavior – lost & found possessions. Behavior – misbehavior. School.

White, Kathryn (Kathryn Ivy). *Nutty nut chase* ill. by Vanessa Cabban. Good Bks., 2004. ISBN 1-56148-446-6 Subj: Animals. Behavior – fighting, arguing. Behavior – sharing. Food.

When they fight ill. by Cliff Wright. Winslow, 2000. ISBN 1-890817-46-5 Subj: Behavior – fighting, arguing. Family life.

White, Keinyo. *see* Lockard, Jon (Jon Onye)

White, Linda Arms. *Comes a wind* ill. by Tom Curry. DK, 2000. ISBN 0-7894-2601-3 Subj: Birthdays. Contests. Family life – brothers. Family life – mothers. Tall tales. Weather – wind.

Too many pumpkins ill. by Megan Lloyd. Holiday, 1996. ISBN 0-8234-1245-8 Subj: Behavior – dissatisfaction. Food. Friendship.

White, Mark. *The ant and the grasshopper* (Æsop)

The fox and the grapes (Æsop)

The goose that laid the golden egg (Æsop)

The tortoise and the hare (Æsop)

The lion and the mouse (Æsop)

The wolf in sheep's clothing (Æsop)

White, Marsha. *Hooper has lost his owner* ill. by author. Little, 2002. ISBN 0-316-06561-7 Subj: Animals – dogs. Behavior – lost & found possessions. Format, unusual – toy & movable books.

White, Paul. *Janet at school* photos by Jeremy Finlay. Crowell, 1978. ISBN 0-381-99557-7 Subj: Handicaps. School.

White Deer of Autumn. *The great change* ill. by Carol Grigg. Beyond Words, 1992. ISBN 0-941831-79-5 Subj: Death. Family life – grandfathers. Indians of North America.

White is for blueberry ill. by Laura Dronzek. Greenwillow, 2005. ISBN 0-06-029276-8 Subj: Concepts – color.

Whitehead, Jenny. *Lunch box mail and other poems* ill. by author. Holt, 2001. ISBN 0-8050-6259-9 Subj: Poetry. School.

Whitehouse, Patricia. *Alligator* ill. with photos. Heinemann, 2003. ISBN 1-58810-903-8 Subj: Reptiles – alligators, crocodiles. Zoos.

Barn owls ill. with photos. Heinemann, 2003. ISBN 1-58810-877-5 Subj: Birds – owls.

Bats ill. with photos. Heinemann, 2003. ISBN 1-58810-878-3 Subj: Animals – bats.

Coyotes ill. with photos. Heinemann, 2003. ISBN 1-58810-879-1 Subj: Animals – coyotes.

Elephants ill. with photos. Heinemann, 2003. ISBN 1-58810-897-X Subj: Animals – elephants. Zoos.

Fall ill. with photos. Heinemann, 2003. ISBN 1-58810-892-9 Subj: Seasons – fall.

Flamingo ill. with photos. Heinemann, 2003. ISBN 1-58810-901-1 Subj: Birds – flamingos. Zoos.

Hippopotamus ill. with photos. Heinemann, 2003. ISBN 1-58810-899-6 Subj: Animals – hippopotamuses. Zoos.

Opossums ill. with photos. Heinemann, 2003. ISBN 1-58810-880-5 Subj: Animals – possums.

Ostrich ill. with photos. Heinemann, 2003. ISBN 1-58810-887-2 Subj: Birds – ostriches. Zoos.

Raccoons ill. with photos. Heinemann, 2003. ISBN 1-58810-882-1 Subj: Animals – raccoons.

Rats ill. with photos. Heinemann, 2003. ISBN 1-58810-881-3 Subj: Animals – rats.

Sea lion ill. with photos. Heinemann, 2003. ISBN 1-58810-902-X Subj: Animals – sea lions. Zoos.

Seasons ABC ill. with photos. Heinemann, 2003. ISBN 1-58810-895-3 Subj: ABC books. Seasons.

Seasons 1 2 3 ill. with photos. Heinemann, 2003. ISBN 1-58810-896-1 Subj: Counting, numbers. Seasons.

Spring ill. with photos. Heinemann, 2003. ISBN 1-58810-894-5 Subj: Seasons – spring.

Summer ill. with photos. Heinemann, 2003. ISBN 1-58810-891-0 Subj: Seasons – summer.

Tiger ill. with photos. Heinemann, 2003. ISBN 1-58810-904-6 Subj: Animals – tigers. Zoos.

What's awake? A B C ill. with photos. Heinemann, 2003. ISBN 1-58810-884-8 Subj: ABC books. Animals. Night.

What's awake? 1 2 3 ill. with photos. Heinemann, 2003. ISBN 1-58810-885-6 Subj: Animals. Counting, numbers. Night.

Winter ill. with photos. Heinemann, 2003. ISBN 1-58810-893-7 Subj: Seasons – winter.

Whiteley, Opal Stanley. *Only Opal: the diary of a young girl* by Opal Whiteley; sel. & adapt. by Jane Boulton; ill. by Barbara Cooney. Philomel, 1994. An adapt. of: The story of Opal. ISBN 0-399-21990-0 Subj: Family life. Poetry. U.S. history – frontier & pioneer life.

Whiteside, Karen. *Lullaby of the wind* ill. by Kazue Mizumura. HarperCollins, 1984. ISBN 0-06-026412-8 Subj: Bedtime. Lullabies. Sleep. Weather – wind.

Whitethorne, Baje. *Sunpainters* ill. by author. Northland, 1994. ISBN 0-87358-587-9 Subj: Folk & fairy tales. Indians of North America – Navajo. Sun.

Whitfield, Susan. *The animals of the Chinese zodiac* ill. by Philippa-Alys Browne. Crocodile, 1998. ISBN 1-56656-236-8 Subj: Animals. Foreign lands – China.

Whitlock, Susan Love. *Donovan scares the monsters* ill. by Yossi Abolafia. Greenwillow, 1987. ISBN 0-688-06439-6 Subj: Family life – grandmothers. Monsters.

Whitman, Candace. *The night is like an animal* ill. by author. Farrar, 1995. ISBN 0-374-35521-5 Subj: Bedtime. Night. Rhyming text.

Now it is morning ill. by author. Farrar, 1999. ISBN 0-374-35527-4 Subj: Morning.

Whitmore, Adam. *Max in America* ill. by Janice Poltrick Donato. Silver Burdett, 1986. ISBN 0-382-09244-9 Subj: Animals – cats. Character traits – being different.

Max in Australia ill. by Janice Poltrick Donato. Silver Burdett, 1986. ISBN 0-382-09246-5 Subj: Animals – cats. Character traits – being different. Foreign lands – Australia.

Max in India ill. by Janice Poltrick Donato. Silver Burdett, 1986. ISBN 0-382-09245-7 Subj: Animals – cats. Character traits – being different. Foreign lands – India.

Max leaves home ill. by Janice Poltrick Donato. Silver Burdett, 1986. ISBN 0-382-09243-0 Subj: Animals – cats. Behavior – running away. Character traits – being different.

Whitney, Alex. *Once a bright red tiger* ill. by Charles Robinson. Walck, 1973. ISBN 0-8098-1212-6 Subj: Animals – tigers. Character traits – pride.

Whitney, Alma Marshak. *Just awful* ill. by Lillian Hoban. Addison-Wesley, 1971. ISBN 0-20-108625-5 Subj: Careers – nurses. Illness. School.

Leave Herbert alone ill. by David McPhail. Addison-Wesley, 1972. ISBN 0-201-08623-9 Subj: Animals – cats. Character traits – kindness to animals.

Whitney, Dorothy B. *Creatures of an exceptional kind* ill. by author. Humanics, 1989. ISBN 0-89334-127-4 Subj: Animals. Character traits – individuality. Handicaps.

Whitney, Thomas P. *The Month-Brothers: a Slavic tale* (Marshak, S. [Samuil])

Whittaker, Nicola. *Feet* ill. with photos. G. Stevens, 2002. ISBN 0-8368-3163-2 Subj: Anatomy – feet. Animals. Rhyming text.

Hair ill. with photos. G. Stevens, 2002. ISBN 0-8368-3164-0 Subj: Animals. Hair. Rhyming text.

Noses ill. with photos. G. Stevens, 2002. ISBN 0-8368-3165-9 Subj: Anatomy – noses. Animals.

Tails ill. with photos. G. Stevens, 2002. ISBN 0-8368-3166-7 Subj: Anatomy – tails. Animals.

Whittier, John Greenleaf. *Barbara Frietchie* ill. by Paul Galdone. Crowell, 1965. ISBN 0-690-11532-6 Subj: Character traits – loyalty. U.S. history. War.

Whittington, Mary K. *Carmina, come dance!* ill. by Michael McDermott. Macmillan, 1989. ISBN 0-689-31554-6 Subj: Activities – dancing. Family life – great-grandparents. Imagination. Music. Musical instruments – pianos.

The patchwork lady ill. by Jane Dyer. Harcourt, 1991. ISBN 0-15-259580-5 Subj: Birthdays. Quilts.

Winter's child ill. by Sue Ellen Brown. Atheneum, 1992. ISBN 0-689-31685-2 Subj: Seasons – spring. Seasons – winter.

Whittle, Emily. *Sailor cats* ill. by Jeri Burdick. Green Tiger Pr., 1993. ISBN 0-671-79933-9 Subj: Animals – cats. Sailors. Sea & seashore. Sports – sailing.

Who took the cookie? ill. by Tom Brannon. Random House, 2002. ISBN 0-375-81606-2 Subj: Food. Format, unusual – board books. Puppets.

Whybrow, Ian. *A baby for Grace* ill. by Christian Birmingham. Kingfisher, 1998. ISBN 0-7534-5142-5 Subj: Babies. Family life – new sibling. Family life – sisters.

Good night, monster ill. by Ken Wilson-Max. Knopf, 2001. ISBN 0-375-81579-1 Subj: Animals. Format, unusual – toy & movable books. Monsters.

Harry and the bucketful of dinosaurs ill. by Adrian Reynolds. Random House, 2003. "First published in the U.S by Orchard Bks under the title Sammy and the dinosaurs in 1999" ISBN 0-375-82541-X Subj: Activities – playing. Dinosaurs. Imagination. Names. Toys.

Harry and the dinosaurs say "Raahh" ill. by Adrian Reynolds. Random House, 2004. ISBN 0-375-82542-8 Subj: Careers – dentists. Dinosaurs. Emotions – fear. Toys.

Harry and the snow king ill. by Adrian Reynolds. Levinson Books, 1997. ISBN 1-899607-85-4 Subj: Family life. Seasons – winter. Snowmen. Weather – snow.

Parcel for Stanley ill. by Sally Hobson. Levinson Books, 1997. ISBN 1-899607-53-6 Subj: Animals. Animals – bulls, cows. Animals – cats. Animals – rabbits. Birds – ducks. Magic. Rhyming text.

Quacky quack-quack! ill. by Russell Ayto. Four Winds, 1991. ISBN 0-02-792741-5 Subj: Animals. Circular tales. Noise, sounds. Rhyming text.

Sammy and the robots ill. by Adrian Reynolds. Orchard, 2001. ISBN 0-531-30327-6 Subj: Family life – grandmothers. Format, unusual – toy & movable books. Hospitals. Illness. Robots. Toys.

Wish, change, friend ill. by Tiphanie Beeke. McElderry, 2002. ISBN 0-689-84930-3 Subj: Animals – pigs. Behavior – wishing. Birds – penguins. Books, reading. Snowmen.

Wick, Walter. *Can you see what I see? Cool collections* photos by Walter Wick by author. Scholastic, 2004. ISBN 0-439-61772-3 Subj: Animals. Dinosaurs. Games. Picture puzzles. Rhyming text. Seasons.

Can you see what I see? Dream machine photos by author. Scholastic, 2003. ISBN 0-439-39950-5 Subj: Bedtime. Dreams. Morning. Picture puzzles. Rhyming text.

Can you see what I see? picture puzzles to search and solve photos by author. Scholastic, 2002. ISBN 0-439-16391-9 Subj: Picture puzzles. Rhyming text.

Can you see what I see? Seymour and the juice box boat photos by author. Scholastic, 2004. ISBN 0-439-61778-2 Subj: Animals. Boats, ships. Picture puzzles. Rhyming text.

Can you see what I see? Seymour makes new friends photos by author. Scholastic, 2006. ISBN 0-439-61780-4 Subj: Friendship. Picture puzzles. Rhyming text.

Can you see what I see? The night before Christmas photos by author. Scholastic, 2005. ISBN 0-439-76927-2 Subj: Holidays – Christmas. Picture puzzles. Poetry. Santa Claus.

I spy a book of picture riddles by Walter Wick & Jean Marzollo; photos by Walter Wick. Scholastic, 1992. ISBN 0-590-45087-5 Subj: Picture puzzles. Rhyming text.

I spy Christmas: a book of picture riddles by Walter Wick & Jean Marzollo; photos by Walter Wick. Scholastic, 1992. ISBN 0-590-45846-9 Subj: Holidays – Christmas. Picture puzzles. Rhyming text. Riddles & jokes.

I spy extreme challenger! a book of picture riddles by Walter Wick & Jean Marzollo; photos by Walter Wick. Scholastic, 2000. ISBN 0-439-19900-X Subj: Picture puzzles. Rhyming text. Riddles & jokes.

I spy fantasy: a book of picture riddles by Walter Wick & Jean Marzollo; photos by Walter Wick. Scholastic, 1994. ISBN 0-590-46295-4 Subj: Imagination. Picture puzzles. Rhyming text. Riddles & jokes.

I spy gold challenger! a book of picture riddles by Walter Wick & Jean Marzollo; photos by Walter Wick. Scholastic, 1998. ISBN 0-590-04296-3 Subj: Picture puzzles. Rhyming text. Riddles & jokes.

I spy school days by Walter Wick & Jean Marzollo; photos by Walter Wick. Scholastic, 1995. ISBN 0-590-48135-5 Subj: Picture puzzles. Rhyming text. Riddles & jokes. School.

I spy spooky night: a book of picture riddles by Walter Wick & Jean Marzollo; photos by Walter Wick. Scholastic, 1996. ISBN 0-590-48137-1 Subj: Ghosts. Holidays – Halloween. Picture puzzles. Rhyming text. Riddles & jokes.

I spy super challenger! by Walter Wick & Jean Marzollo; photos by Walter Wick. Scholastic, 1997. ISBN 0-590-34128-6 Subj: Picture puzzles. Rhyming text. Riddles & jokes.

I spy treasure hunt by Walter Wick & Jean Marzollo; photos by Walter Wick. Scholastic, 1999. ISBN 0-439-04244-5 Subj: Mystery stories. Picture puzzles. Pirates. Rhyming text. Riddles & jokes.

I spy ultimate challenger! by Walter Wick & Jean Marzollo; photos by Walter Wick. Scholastic, 2003. ISBN 0-439-45401-8 Subj: Picture puzzles. Rhyming text. Riddles & jokes.

Wickings, Ruth. *The story of the Nativity* (McCaughrean, Geraldine)

Wickstrom, Sylvie (Sylvie Kantrovitz). *I love you, Mister Bear* ill. by autor. HarperCollins, 2003. ISBN 0-06-029332-2 Subj: Family life. Toys – bears.

Mothers can't get sick ill. by author. Crown, 1989. ISBN 0-517-57181-1 Subj: Birthdays. Family life. Family life – mothers. Illness.

Turkey on the loose! ill. by author. Dial, 1990. ISBN 0-8037-0820-3 Subj: Birds – turkeys.

Widdecombe Fair: an old English folk song ill. by Christine Price. Warne, 1968. Subj: Fairs, festivals. Folk & fairy tales. Foreign lands – England. Music. Songs.

Widerberg, Siv. *The boy and the dog* trans. from Swedish by Richard E. Fisher; ill. by Jens Ahlbom. Farrar, 1991. ISBN 91-29-59926-1 Subj: Animals – dogs. Emotions – fear.

Widman, Christine. *Housekeeper of the wind* ill. by Lisa Desimini. HarperCollins, 1990. ISBN 0-06-026468-3 Subj: Behavior – fighting, arguing. Careers – housekeepers. Emotions – anger. Weather – wind.

The star grazers ill. by Robin Spowart. HarperCollins, 1989. ISBN 0-06-026473-X Subj: Animals – sheep. Stars.

Wiebe, Rudy. *Hidden buffalo* ill. by Michael Lonechild. Red Deer Pr., 2003. ISBN 0-88995-285-X Subj: Animals – buffaloes. Dreams. Foreign lands – Canada. Indians of North America – Cree.

Wiencirz, Gerlinde. *Peter and the wolf* (Prokofiev, Sergei Sergeievitch)

Wiener, Lori. *Be a friend: children who live with HIV speak* art & writing comp. by Lori Weiner & others. A. Whitman, 1994. ISBN 0-8075-0590-0 Subj: Children as authors. Children as illustrators. Illness – AIDS.

Wiese, Kurt. *The cunning turtle* ill. by author. Viking, 1956. Subj: Reptiles – turtles, tortoises.

The dog, the fox and the fleas ill. by author. McKay, 1953. Subj: Animals – dogs. Animals – foxes. Insects – fleas.

Fish in the air ill. by author. Viking, 1948. Subj: Caldecott award honor books. Foreign lands – China. Humorous stories. Kites.

The five Chinese brothers (Bishop, Claire Huchet)

Happy Easter ill. by author. Viking, 1952. Subj: Animals – rabbits. Holidays – Easter.

The story about Ping (Flack, Marjorie)

You can write Chinese ill. by author. Viking, 1945. Subj: Caldecott award honor books. Foreign languages.

Wiesmüller, Dieter. *The adventures of Marco and Polo* ill. by author; trans. from German by Beate Peter. Walker, 2000. ISBN 0-8027-8729-0 Subj: Activities – traveling. Animals – monkeys. Birds – penguins.

In the blink of an eye ill. by author. Walker, 2002. ISBN 0-8027-8855-6 Subj: Anatomy – eyes. Animals. Picture puzzles.

Wiesner, David. *Free fall* ill. by author. Lothrop, 1988. ISBN 0-688-05584-2 Subj: Bedtime. Books, reading. Caldecott award honor books. Dragons. Dreams. Wordless.

Hurricane ill. by author. Houghton Mifflin, 1990. ISBN 0-395-54382-7 Subj: Family life – brothers & sisters. Imagination. Weather – storms.

The loathsome dragon by David Wiesner & Kim Kahng; ill. by David Wiesner. Clarion, 2005. ISBN 0-618-54359-7 Subj: Dragons. Folk & fairy tales. Magic. Royalty.

Sector 7 ill. by author. Clarion, 1999. ISBN 0-395-74656-6 Subj: Caldecott award honor books. School. Weather – clouds. Wordless.

Tuesday ill. by author. Houghton Mifflin, 1991. ISBN 0-395-55113-7 Subj: Activities – flying. Caldecott award books. Frogs & toads. Magic. Night.

Wiesner, William. *Happy-Go-Lucky: a Norwegian tale* ill. by author. Seabury Pr., 1970. Subj: Character traits – optimism. Cumulative tales. Farms. Foreign lands – Norway. Humorous stories.

Noah's ark ill. by author. Dutton, 1966. Subj: Animals. Boats, ships. Religion – Noah. Weather – floods. Weather – rain.

Tops ill. by author. Viking, 1969. ISBN 0-670-72089-5 Subj: Friendship. Giants. Violence, nonviolence.

The Tower of Babel ill. by author. Viking, 1968. Based on the book of Genesis and on commentaries . . . in the book Hebrew myths by Robert Graves and Raphael Patai. Subj: Language. Religion.

Turnabout: a Norwegian tale ill. by author. Seabury Pr., 1972. This text has been adapted from the version of Edouard Laboulaye. ISBN 0-8164-3083-7 Subj: Behavior – dissatisfaction. Foreign lands – Norway. Humorous stories.

Wight, Tamra. *The three grumpies* ill. by Ross Collins. Bloomsbury, 2003. ISBN 1-58234-840-5 Subj: Behavior – bad day. Emotions.

Wijngaard, Juan. *Bear* ill. by author. Crown, 1991. ISBN 0-517-58201-5 Subj: Animals – bears. Format, unusual – board books.

Cat ill. by author. Crown, 1991. ISBN 0-517-58202-3 Subj: Animals – cats. Format, unusual – board books.

Dog ill. by author. Crown, 1991. ISBN 0-517-58203-1 Subj: Animals – dogs. Format, unusual – board books.

Duck ill. by author. Crown, 1991. ISBN 0-517-58204-X Subj: Birds – ducks. Format, unusual – board books.

The Nativity ill. by author. Candlewick, 1996. ISBN 1-56402-981-6 Subj: Holidays – Christmas. Religion – Nativity.

Wikland, Ilon. *Christmas in noisy village* (Lindgren, Astrid)

Wikler, Linda. *see* Berkowitz, Linda

Wikler, Madeline. *All about Hanukkah* (Groner, Judyth Saypol)

All about Sukkot (Groner, Judyth Saypol)

Let's build a Sukkah by Madeline Wikler & Judyth Groner; ill. by Katherine Janus Kahn. Kar-Ben Copies, 1986. ISBN 0-930494-58-X Subj: Format, unusual – board books. Holidays. Jewish culture.

My first seder by Madeline Wikler & Judyth Groner; ill. by Katherine Janus Kahn. Kar-Ben Copies, 1986. ISBN 0-930494-61-X Subj: Food. Format, unusual – board books. Holidays – Passover. Jewish culture.

My very own Jewish community (Groner, Judyth Saypol)

The Purim parade by Madeline Wikler & Judyth Groner; ill. by Katherine Janus Kahn. Kar-Ben Copies, 1986. ISBN 0-930494-60-1 Subj: Format, unusual – board books. Holidays – Purim. Jewish culture.

Thank you, God! a Jewish child's book of prayers (Groner, Judyth Saypol)

Where is the Afikomen? (Groner, Judyth Saypol)

Wilbur, Richard. *The disappearing alphabet* ill. by David Diaz. Harcourt, 1998. ISBN 0-15-201470-5 Subj: ABC books. Poetry.

Runaway opposites ill. by Henrik Drescher. Harcourt, 1995. ISBN 0-15-258722-5 Subj: Concepts – opposites. Poetry.

Wilcox, Brad. *Hip, hip, hooray for Annie McRae!* ill. by Julie Olson. Gibbs Smith, 2001. ISBN 1-58685-058-X Subj: Emotions – happiness.

Wilcox, Brian. *Full moon* by Brian Wilcox & Lawrence David; ill. by Brian Wilcox. Random House, 2001. ISBN 0-385-32792-7 Subj: Birthdays. Cities, towns. Family life – grandmothers. Moon.

Wilcox, Cathy. *Enzo the Wonderfish* ill. by author. Ticknor & Fields, 1994. ISBN 0-395-68382-3 Subj: Fish. Pets.

Wilcox, Daniel. *The Sesame Street ABC storybook* (Moss, Jeffrey)

Wild, Jocelyn. *The bears' ABC book* (Wild, Robin)

The bears' counting book (Wild, Robin)

Florence and Eric take the cake ill. by author. Dial, 1987. ISBN 0-8037-0305-8 Subj: Animals – sheep. Behavior – misunderstanding. Family life.

Little Pig and the big bad wolf (Wild, Robin)

Spot's dogs and the alley cats (Wild, Robin)

Wild, Margaret. *Big cat dreaming* ill. by Anne Spudvilas. Annick, 1997. ISBN 1-55037-493-1 Subj: Animals – cats. Animals – dogs. Family life – grandmothers.

Fox by Margaret Wild & Ron Brooks; ill. by Ron Brooks. Kane/Miller, 2001. ISBN 1-929132-16-6 Subj: Animals – dogs. Animals – foxes. Birds – magpies. Emotions – envy, jealousy. Emotions – loneliness. Friendship.

Going home ill. by Wayne Harris. Scholastic, 1994. ISBN 0-590-47958-X Subj: Activities – traveling. Dreams. Hospitals.

Let the celebrations begin! ill. by Julie Vivas. Watts, 1991. ISBN 0-531-08537-6 Subj: Toys. War.

Midnight babies ill. by Ann James. Clarion, 1999. ISBN 0-618-10412-7 Subj: Activities – dancing. Babies. Night.

Mr. Nick's knitting ill. by Dee Huxley. Harcourt, 1989. ISBN 0-15-200518-8 Subj: Activities – knitting. Friendship. Hospitals. Illness.

My dearest dinosaur ill. by Donna Rawlins. Orchard, 1992. ISBN 0-531-08603-8 Subj: Dinosaurs. Family life. Prehistory.

Nighty night ill. by Kerry Argent. Peachtree, 2001. ISBN 1-56145-246-7 Subj: Animals. Bedtime.

Old Pig ill. by Ron Brooks. Dial, 1996. ISBN 0-8037-1917-5 Subj: Animals – pigs. Death. Family life – grandmothers. Old age.

Our granny ill. by Julie Vivas. Ticknor & Fields, 1994. ISBN 0-395-67023-3 Subj: Family life – grandmothers.

The pocket dogs ill. by Stephen Michael King. Scholastic, 2001. ISBN 0-439-23973-7 Subj: Accidents. Animals – dogs. Behavior – lost. Clothing.

The queen's holiday ill. by Sue O'Loughlin. Orchard, 1992. ISBN 0-531-08573-2 Subj: Royalty – queens. Sea & seashore.

Remember me ill. by Dee Huxley. A. Whitman, 1995. ISBN 0-8075-6934-8 Subj: Behavior – forgetfulness. Family life – grandmothers. Memories, memory. Old age.

Rosie and Tortoise ill. by Ron Brooks. DK, 1999. ISBN 0-7894-2630-7 Subj: Animals – rabbits. Family life – new sibling.

Thank you, Santa ill. by Kerry Argent. Scholastic, 1992. ISBN 0-590-45805-1 Subj: Animals – polar bears. Foreign lands – Arctic. Foreign lands – Australia. Holidays – Christmas. Letters, cards.

Toby ill. by Noela Young. Ticknor & Fields, 1994. ISBN 0-395-67024-1 Subj: Animals – dogs. Behavior – misbehavior. Death. Emotions. Family life – brothers & sisters.

Tom goes to kindergarten ill. by David Legge. A. Whitman, 2000. ISBN 0-8075-8012-0 Subj: Animals – pandas. Family life. School – first day.

The very best of friends ill. by Julie Vivas. Harcourt, 1990. ISBN 0-15-200625-7 Subj: Animals – cats. Death. Farms. Friendship.

Wild, Robin. *The bears' ABC book* by Robin & Jocelyn Wild; ill. by authors. Lippincott, 1978. ISBN 0-397-31767-0 Subj: ABC books. Animals – bears.

The bears' counting book by Robin & Jocelyn Wild; ill. by authors. Lippincott, 1978. ISBN 0-397-31808-1 Subj: Animals – bears. Counting, numbers.

Little Pig and the big bad wolf by Robin & Jocelyn Wild; ill. by authors. Coward, 1972. Subj: Animals – pigs. Animals – wolves. Character traits – cleverness. Rhyming text.

Spot's dogs and the alley cats by Robin & Jocelyn Wild; ill. by authors. Lippincott, 1979. ISBN 0-397-31841-3 Subj: Animals – cats. Animals – dogs. Behavior – trickery.

Wilde, Oscar. *Fairy tales of Oscar Wilde: The selfish giant, and The star child* adapt. & ill. by P. Craig Russell. NBM, 1992. Vol. 1. ISBN 1-56163-056-X Subj: Character traits – kindness. Character traits – selfishness. Folk & fairy tales. Gardens, gardening. Giants. Seasons – spring.

The giant's garden (Weedn, Flavia)

The happy prince ill. by Jane Ray. Dutton, 1995. ISBN 0-525-45367-9 Subj: Cities, towns. Folk & fairy tales. Poverty. Royalty – kings.

The selfish giant ill. by S. Saelig Gallagher. Putnam, 1995. ISBN 0-399-22448-3 Subj: Character traits – kindness. Character traits – selfishness. Folk & fairy tales. Gardens, gardening. Giants. Seasons – spring.

The selfish giant ill. by Dom Mansell. Prentice-Hall, 1986. ISBN 0-13-803586-5 Subj: Character traits – kindness. Character traits – selfishness. Folk & fairy tales. Gardens, gardening. Giants. Seasons – spring.

The selfish giant retold by Fiona Waters; ill. by Fabian Negrin. Knopf, 2000. ISBN 0-375-90319-4 Subj: Character traits – kindness. Character traits – selfishness. Folk & fairy tales. Gardens, gardening. Giants. Seasons – spring.

The selfish giant ill. by Lisbeth Zwerger. Alphabet Pr., 1984. ISBN 0-907234-30-5 Subj: Character traits – kindness. Character traits – selfishness. Folk & fairy tales. Gardens, gardening. Giants. Seasons – spring.

The star child abridged by Jennifer Westwood; ill. by Fiona French. Four Winds, 1979. An abridged version of one chapter from the author's A house of Pomegranates. ISBN 0-590-07641-8 Subj: Character traits – pride. Character traits – selfishness. Folk & fairy tales.

Wilder, Laura Ingalls. *A farmer boy birthday* (A farmer boy birthday)

Going to town ill. by Renée Graef. HarperCollins, 1994. ISBN 0-06-023013-4 Subj: Cities, towns. Family life – sisters. U.S. history – frontier & pioneer life.

Laura Ingalls Wilder's fairy poems intro. & comp. by Stephen W. Hines; ill. by Richard Hull. Doubleday, 1998. ISBN 0-385-32533-9 Subj: Fairies. Poetry.

My little house songbook ill. by Holly Jones. HarperCollins, 1995. ISBN 0-06-024295-7 Subj: Music. Songs. U.S. history – frontier & pioneer life.

Santa comes to little house ill. by Renée Graef. HarperCollins, 2001. ISBN 0-06-025939-6 Subj: Family life. Holidays – Christmas. Santa Claus. U.S. history – frontier & pioneer life.

Sugar snow (Sugar snow)

Wilds, Kazumi Inose. *Hajime in the North Woods* ill. by author. Little, 1994. ISBN 1-55970-240-0 Subj: Animals. Babies. Forest, woods.

Wildsmith, Brian. *Animal games* ill. by author. Oxford Univ. Pr., 1980. ISBN 0-19-279731-X Subj: Animals. Games.

Animal homes ill. by author. Oxford Univ. Pr., 1980. ISBN 0-19-279732-8 Subj: Animals. Homes, houses.

Animal shapes ill. by author. Oxford Univ. Pr., 1980. ISBN 0-19-279733-6 Subj: Animals. Concepts – shape.

Animal tricks ill. by author. Oxford Univ. Pr., 1980. ISBN 0-19-279743-3 Subj: Animals. Rhyming text.

Bear's adventure ill. by author. Pantheon, 1982. ISBN 0-394-95295-2 Subj: Activities – ballooning. Animals – bears.

The Bremen town band (Grimm, Jacob)

Brian Wildsmith 1 2 3 ill. by author. Millbrook, 1995. ISBN 1-56294-905-5 Subj: Concepts – shape. Counting, numbers.

Brian Wildsmith's birds ill. by author. Watts, 1967. Subj: Birds.

Brian Wildsmith's circus ill. by author. Watts, 1970. ISBN 0-531-01541-6 Subj: Circus.

Brian Wildsmith's Mother Goose (Mother Goose)

Brian Wildsmith's puzzles ill. by author. Millbrook, 1996. ISBN 0-761-30052-X Subj: Games.

Carousel ill. by author. Knopf, 1988. ISBN 0-394-91937-8 Subj: Dreams. Fairs, festivals. Illness. Merry-go-rounds.

A Christmas story ill. by author. Eerdmans, 1998. ISBN 0-8028-5173-8 Subj: Animals – donkeys. Holidays – Christmas. Religion – Nativity.

The Easter story ill. by author. Eerdmans, 2000, c1993. ISBN 0-8028-5189-4 Subj: Animals – donkeys. Holidays – Easter. Religion.

Fishes ill. by author. Watts, 1968. Subj: Fish.

Give a dog a bone ill. by author. Pantheon, 1985. ISBN 0-394-97709-2 Subj: Animals – dogs. Format, unusual.

Goat's trail ill. by author. Knopf, 1986. ISBN 0-394-98276-2 Subj: Animals. Animals – goats. Cumulative tales. Format, unusual. Noise, sounds.

Hunter and his dog ill. by author. Oxford Univ. Pr., 1979. ISBN 0-19-279725-5 Subj: Animals – dogs. Character traits – kindness to animals. Sports – hunting.

Joseph ill. by author. Eerdmans, 1997. ISBN 0-8028-5161-4 Subj: Religion.

The lazy bear ill. by author. Watts, 1974. ISBN 0-531-01559-9 Subj: Animals – bears. Character traits – laziness. Friendship.

The little wood duck ill. by author. Watts, 1972. ISBN 0-19-279686-0 Subj: Birds – ducks.

Mary ill. by author. Eerdmans, 2002. ISBN 0-8028-5231-9 Subj: Religion.

The miller, the boy and the donkey (La Fontaine, Jean de)

The owl and the woodpecker ill. by author. Watts, 1971. ISBN 0-19-279676-3 Subj: Birds – owls. Birds – woodpeckers. Character traits – compromising.

Pelican ill. by author. Pantheon, 1983. ISBN 0-394-95668-0 Subj: Birds – pelicans. Format, unusual. Sports – fishing.

Professor Noah's spaceship ill. by author. Oxford Univ. Pr., 1980. ISBN 0-19-279741-7 Subj: Animals. Ecology. Space & space ships.

Python's party ill. by author. Watts, 1975. ISBN 0-531-02808-9 Subj: Animals. Behavior – trickery. Reptiles – snakes.

Seasons ill. by author. Oxford Univ. Pr., 1980. ISBN 0-19-279730-1 Subj: Nature. Seasons.

The true cross ill. by author. Oxford Univ. Pr., 1985, 1977. ISBN 0-19-279718-2 Subj: Folk & fairy tales. Religion.

What the moon saw ill. by author. Oxford Univ. Pr., 1978. ISBN 0-19-279724-7 Subj: Animals. Concepts – opposites. Language. Moon. Sun.

Wild animals ill. by author. Watts, 1967. ISBN 0-19-272103-8 Subj: Animals.

Wiles, Debbie. *Freedom summer* ill. by Jerome Lagarrigue. Atheneum, 2001. ISBN 0-689-82380-0 Subj: Ethnic groups in the U.S. – African Americans. Friendship. Prejudice.

Wilhelm, Hans. *All for the best* ill. by author. Hampton Roads, 2003. ISBN 1-57174-344-8 Subj: Careers – weavers. Character traits – optimism. Folk & fairy tales.

Bunny trouble ill. by author. Scholastic, 1991. ISBN 0-590-63153-5 Subj: Animals – rabbits.

A cool kid – like me! ill. by author. Crown, 1990. ISBN 0-517-57822-0 Subj: Character traits – confidence. Family life – grandmothers. Toys – bears.

Don't cut my hair ill. by author. Scholastic, 1997. ISBN 0-590-30700-2 Subj: Animals – dogs. Hair.

I lost my tooth! ill. by author. Scholastic, 1999. ISBN 0-590-64230-8 Subj: Animals – dogs. Behavior – growing up. Problem solving. Teeth.

I'll always love you ill. by author. Crown, 1985. ISBN 0-517-55648-0 Subj: Animals – dogs. Death. Emotions – grief. Pets.

It's too windy! ill. by author. Scholastic, 2000. ISBN 0-439-10849-7 Subj: Animals – dogs. Babies. Family life. Weather – wind.

Let's be friends again! ill. by author. Crown, 1986. ISBN 0-517-56252-9 Subj: Emotions – anger. Family life – sisters. Friendship.

More bunny trouble ill. by author. Scholastic, 1989. ISBN 0-590-41589-1 Subj: Animals – foxes. Animals – rabbits. Eggs. Family life – brothers. Family life – sisters. Holidays – Easter.

A new home, a new friend ill. by author. Random House, 1985. ISBN 0-394-97226-0 Subj: Animals – dogs. Family life. Friendship. Moving.

Oh, what a mess ill. by author. Crown, 1988. ISBN 0-517-56909-4 Subj: Animals – pigs. Character traits – cleanliness.

Quacky Ducky's Easter egg ill. by author. HarperCollins, 2004. ISBN 0-06-053430-3 Subj: Birds – ducks. Eggs. Format, unusual – board books. Friendship. Holidays – Easter.

Quacky Ducky's Easter fun ill. by author. HarperCollins, 2004. ISBN 0-06-053431-1 Subj: Activities – painting. Birds – ducks. Format, unusual – board books. Holidays – Easter.

Schnitzel's first Christmas ill. by author. S&S, 1991. ISBN 0-671-74494-1 Subj: Animals – dogs. Behavior – needing someone. Holidays – Christmas. Santa Claus.

Tyrone the horrible ill. by author. Scholastic, 1988. ISBN 0-590-41471-2 Subj: Behavior – bullying. Dinosaurs.

Wilkes, Angela. *Animal nursery rhymes* (Animal nursery rhymes)

The best book of ballet ill. by author. Kingfisher, 2000. ISBN 0-7534-5275-8 Subj: Activities – dancing. Ballet.

The big book of dinosaurs ill. by author. DK, 1994. ISBN 1-56458-718-5 Subj: Dinosaurs. Prehistory.

Me and my body ill. by author. Two-Can, 2000. ISBN 1-58728-603-3 Subj: Anatomy. Science.

My first word book ill. by author. New ed. DK, 1999. ISBN 0-7894-3977-8 Subj: Dictionaries. Language.

Rain forest animals ill. by author. World Book, 1999. ISBN 0-7166-7703-2 Subj: Animals. Forest, woods.

See how I grow ill. with photos. DK, 1994. ISBN 1-56458-464-X Subj: Babies. Behavior – growing up.

Tough trucks ill. by author. World Book, 1999. ISBN 0-7166-7713-X Subj: Trucks.

Wilkes, Larry. *The king's egg dance* ill. by author. Carolrhoda, 1990. ISBN 0-87614-446-6 Subj: Activities – dancing. Eggs. Royalty – kings.

Wilkin, Refna. *Just one apple* (Janosch)

Wilkins, Mary Huiskamp Calhoun. *see* Calhoun, Mary

Wilkinson, Bruce. *The prayer of Jabez for young hearts* ill. by Sergio Martinez. Tommy Nelson, 2001. ISBN 0-8499-7932-3 Subj: Religion. Rhyming text.

Wilkinson, Sylvia. *Automobiles* ill. with photos. Childrens Pr., 1982. ISBN 0-516-01608-3 Subj: Automobiles.

I can be a race car driver ill. with photos. Childrens Pr., 1986. ISBN 0-516-01898-1 Subj: Automobiles. Careers – race car drivers. Sports – racing.

Wilkon, Józef. *Lullaby for a newborn king* by Józef Wilkon & Hermann Moers; trans. from German by Rosemary Lanning; ill. by Józef Wilkon. North-South, 1991. ISBN 1-55858-123-5 Subj: Holidays – Christmas. Lullabies. Religion.

Wilkon, Piotr. *The brave little kittens* trans. by Helen Graves; ill. by Józef Wilkon. North-South, 1991. ISBN 1-55858-103-0 Subj: Animals – cats. Character traits – bravery.

Rosie the cool cat ill. by Józef Wilkon. Viking, 1991. ISBN 0-670-83707-5 Subj: Animals – cats. Behavior – running away. Character traits – being different.

Wilkowski, Susan. *Baby's Bris* ill. by Judith Friedman. Kar-Ben Copies, 1999. ISBN 1-58013-052-6 Subj: Babies. Family life – brothers & sisters. Jewish culture. Names. Religion.

Will. *see* Lipkind, William

Willard, Barbara. *To London! To London!* ill. by Antony Maitland. Weybright & Talley, 1968. Subj: Foreign lands – England.

Willard, Nancy. *The high rise glorious skittle skat roarious sky pie angel food cake* ill. by Richard Jesse Watson. Harcourt, 1990. ISBN 0-15-234332-6 Subj: Activities – baking, cooking. Angels. Birthdays. Family life – mothers.

The marzipan moon ill. by Marcia Sewell. Harcourt, 1981. ISBN 0-15-252962-4 Subj: Behavior – wishing. Birthdays. Food. Magic.

The Moon & Riddles Diner and the Sunnyside Café ill. by Chris Butler. Harcourt, 2001. ISBN 0-15-201941-3 Subj: Food. Poetry. Restaurants.

The mountains of quilt ill. by Tomie de Paola. Harcourt, 1987. ISBN 0-15-256010-6 Subj: Dreams. Family life – grandmothers. Magic. Quilts.

The mouse, the cat and Grandmother's hat ill. by Jenny Mattheson. Little, 2003. ISBN 0-316-94006-2 Subj: Animals – cats. Animals – mice. Birthdays. Family life – grandmothers. Parties. Rhyming text.

Night story ill. by Ilse Plume. Harcourt, 1986. ISBN 0-15-257348-8 Subj: Dreams. Night. Rhyming text.

The nightgown of the sullen moon ill. by David McPhail. Harcourt, 1983. ISBN 0-15-257429-8 Subj: Moon. Night.

Pish posh, said Hieronymous Bosch ill. by Leo & Diane Dillon. Harcourt, 1991. ISBN 0-15-262210-1 Subj: Careers – artists. Poetry.

Shadow story ill. by David Diaz. Harcourt, 1999. ISBN 0-15-201638-4 Subj: Folk & fairy tales. Mythical creatures – ogres. Orphans. Shadows.

Simple pictures are best ill. by Tomie de Paola. Harcourt, 1978. ISBN 0-15-682625-9 Subj: Activities – photographing. Humorous stories.

The tale I told Sasha ill. by David Christiana. Little, 1999. ISBN 0-316-94115-8 Subj: Family life – mothers. Imagination.

A visit to William Blake's inn: poems for innocent and experienced travelers ill. by Alice & Martin Provensen. Harcourt, 1981. ISBN 0-15-293822-2 Subj: Caldecott award honor books. Imagination. Poetry.

The voyage of the Ludgate Hill: travels with Robert Louis Stevenson ill. by Alice & Martin Provensen. Harcourt, 1987. ISBN 0-15-294464-8 Subj: Activities – traveling. Animals. Boats, ships. Poetry. Sea & seashore. Weather – storms.

The well-mannered balloon ill. by Haig & Regina Shekerjian. Harcourt, 1991. ISBN 0-15-294986-0 Subj: Behavior – misbehavior. Night. Toys – balloons.

Willems, Mo. *Don't let the pigeon drive the bus* ill. by author. Hyperion, 2003. ISBN 0-7868-1988-X Subj: Birds – pigeons. Caldecott award honor books. Careers – bus drivers. Humorous stories.

Time to pee ill. by author. Hyperion, 2003. ISBN 0-7868-1868-9 Subj: Animals – mice. Toilet training.

Willey, Margaret. *Clever Beatrice, an Upper Peninsula conte* ill. by Heather M. Solomon. Atheneum, 2001. ISBN 0-689-83254-0 Subj: Character traits – cleverness. Folk & fairy tales. Giants. Tall tales.

Clever Beatrice and the best little pony ill. by Heather M. Solomon. Atheneum, 2004. ISBN 0-689-85339-4 Subj: Animals. Animals – horses, ponies. Careers – bakers. Character traits – cleverness. Folk & fairy tales. Mythical creatures – lutins.

Clever Beatrice Christmas ill. by Heather M. Solomon. Atheneum, 2006. ISBN 0-689-87017-5 Subj: Character traits – cleverness. Holidays – Christmas. Santa Claus.

Thanksgiving with me ill. by Lloyd Bloom. Geringer, 1998. ISBN 0-06-027114-0 Subj: Family life – aunts, uncles. Holidays – Thanksgiving. Rhyming text.

Willhoite, Michael. *Daddy's roommate* ill. by author. Alyson Wonderland, 1990. ISBN 1-55583-178-8 Subj: Divorce. Family life – fathers. Homosexuality.

Williams, Arlene. *Dragon soup* ill. by Sally J. Smith. H. J. Kramer, 1996. ISBN 0-915811-63-4 Subj: Behavior – fighting, arguing. Dragons. Folk & fairy tales. Food.

Williams, Barbara. *Albert's toothache* ill. by Kay Chorao. Dutton, 1974. ISBN 0-525-25368-8 Subj: Illness. Reptiles – turtles, tortoises. Teeth.

Chester Chipmunk's Thanksgiving ill. by Kay Chorao. Dutton, 1974. ISBN 0-525-27655-6 Subj: Animals – chipmunks. Holidays – Thanksgiving.

Donna Jean's disaster ill. by Margot Apple. A. Whitman, 1986. ISBN 0-8075-1682-1 Subj: Family life. Poetry. School. Self-concept. Sibling rivalry.

Hello, dandelions! photos by author. Holt, 1979. ISBN 0-03-048326-3 Subj: Flowers. Plants.

I know a salesperson ill. by Frank E. Aloise. Putnam, 1978. ISBN 0-399-61118-5 Subj: Careers. Stores.

If he's my brother ill. by Tomie de Paola. Harvey House, 1976. ISBN 0-8178-5422-3 Subj: Character traits – questioning. Family life.

Jeremy isn't hungry ill. by Martha G. Alexander. Dutton, 1978. ISBN 0-525-32760-6 Subj: Activities – babysitting. Babies. Humorous stories.

Kevin's grandma ill. by Kay Chorao. Dutton, 1975. ISBN 0-525-33115-8 Subj: Family life – grandmothers. Friendship.

So what if I'm a sore loser? ill. by Linda Strauss Edwards. Harcourt, 1981. ISBN 0-15-277260-X Subj: Character traits – conceit. Family life.

Someday, said Mitchell ill. by Kay Chorao. Dutton, 1976. ISBN 0-525-39580-6 Subj: Behavior – wishing. Character traits – helpfulness. Character traits – smallness. Emotions – happiness.

Whatever happened to Beverly Bigler's birthday? ill. by Emily Arnold McCully. Harcourt, 1979. ISBN 0-15-295286-1 Subj: Behavior – misbehavior. Birthdays. Weddings.

Williams, Charles. *see* Collier, James Lincoln

Williams, David. *Walking to the creek* ill. by Thomas B. Allen. Knopf, 1990. ISBN 0-394-90598-9 Subj: Activities – walking. Country. Nature.

Williams, Garth. *Benjamin's treasure* ill. by author & Rosemary Wells. HarperCollins, 2001. ISBN 0-06-028741-1 Subj: Animals – rabbits. Islands. Sea & seashore. Sports – fishing. Weather – storms.

The big golden animal ABC ill. by author. S&S, 1957. First published under the title: The golden animal A.B.C. Subj: ABC books. Animals.

The chicken book ill. by author. Delacorte, 1970. ISBN 0-385-30110-3 Subj: Birds – chickens. Counting, numbers. Nursery rhymes.

The rabbits' wedding ill. by author. HarperCollins, 1958. ISBN 0-06-026496-9 Subj: Animals – rabbits. Weddings.

Williams, Gweneira Maureen. *Timid Timothy, the kitten who learned to be brave* ill. by Leonard Weisgard. Addison-Wesley, 1944. Subj: Emotions – fear. Food. Science.

Williams, Jay. *The city witch and the country witch* ill. by Ed Renfro. Macmillan, 1979. ISBN 0-02-793050-5 Subj: Activities – vacationing. Cities, towns. Country. Witches.

Everyone knows what a dragon looks like ill. by Mercer Mayer. Four Winds, 1976. ISBN 0-590-07284-6 Subj: Dragons. Foreign lands – China.

I wish I had another name by Jay Williams & Winifred Lubell; ill. by authors. Atheneum, 1962. Subj: Names. Rhyming text.

The practical princess ill. by Friso Henstra. Parents' Magazine Pr., 1969. Subj: Folk & fairy tales. Royalty – princesses.

School for sillies ill. by Friso Henstra. Parents' Magazine Pr., 1969. Subj: Character traits – cleverness. Humorous stories. Royalty.

The surprising things Maui did ill. by Charles Mikolaycak. Four Winds, 1980. ISBN 0-590-07553-5 Subj: Folk & fairy tales. Hawaii.

Williams, Jenny (Jennifer). *Here's a ball for baby: finger rhymes for young children* ill. by author. Dial, 1987. ISBN 0-8037-0388-0 Subj: Nursery rhymes.

One, two, buckle my shoe ill. by Jenny Williams. Dial, 1987. ISBN 0-8037-0390-2 Subj: Counting, numbers. Nursery rhymes.

Playtime 1 2 3 ill. by author. Dial, 1992. ISBN 0-8037-1077-1 Subj: Activities. Counting, numbers. Rhyming text.

Ride a cockhorse: animal rhymes for young children ill. by author. Dial, 1987. ISBN 0-8037-0389-9 Subj: Animals. Nursery rhymes.

Ring around a rosy: action rhymes for young children ill. by author. Dial, 1987. ISBN 0-8037-0391-0 Subj: Games. Nursery rhymes.

A wet Monday (Edwards, Dorothy)

Williams, Julie Stewart. *And the birds appeared* ill. by Robin Yoko Burningham. Univ. of Hawaii Pr., 1988. ISBN 0-8248-1194-1 Subj: Birds. Folk & fairy tales. Hawaii.

Williams, Juliet. *Mouse house* ill. by Todd Sutherland; photos by Phi LeGris & Bob Klassy. Handprint, 2002. ISBN 1-929766-42-4 Subj: Animals – mice. Homes, houses. Humorous stories.

Mouse house [board book] ill. by Todd Sutherland; photos by Phi LeGris & Bob Klassy. Handprint, 2002. ISBN 1-59354-082-5 Subj: Animals – mice. Format, unusual – toy & movable books. Homes, houses. Humorous stories.

Williams, Karen Lynn. *Galimoto* ill. by Catherine Stock. Lothrop, 1990. ISBN 0-688-08790-6 Subj: Foreign lands – Africa. Toys.

Painted dreams ill. by Catherine Stock. Lothrop, 1998. ISBN 0-688-13902-7 Subj: Activities – painting. Foreign lands – Haiti. Problem solving.

Tap-tap ill. by Catherine Stock. Clarion, 1994. ISBN 0-395-65617-6 Subj: Clothing – hats. Family life – mothers. Foreign lands – Haiti. Stores. Trucks.

When Africa was home ill. by Floyd Cooper. Watts, 1991. ISBN 0-531-08525-2 Subj: Family life. Foreign lands – Africa. Friendship.

Williams, Laura E. *ABC kids* ill. by author. Philomel, 2000. ISBN 0-399-23370-9 Subj: ABC books.

The long silk strand ill. by Grayce Bochak. Boyds Mills, 1995. ISBN 1-56397-236-0 Subj: Death. Family life – grandmothers. Folk & fairy tales. Foreign lands – Japan.

Torch fishing with the sun ill. by Fabricio Vandenbroeck. Boyds Mills, 1999. ISBN 1-56397-685-4 Subj: Careers – fishermen. Family life – grandfathers. Folk & fairy tales. Hawaii. Night. Sun.

Williams, Leslie. *A bear in the air* ill. by Carme Solé Vendrell. Stemmer House, 1980. ISBN 0-916144-54-2 Subj: Animals – bears. Weather – clouds. Weather – rainbows.

Williams, Linda. *Horse in the pigpen* ill. by Megan Lloyd. HarperCollins, 2002. ISBN 0-06-028548-6 Subj: Animals. Family life – mothers. Farms. Rhyming text.

The little old lady who was not afraid of anything ill. by Megan Lloyd. Crowell, 1986. ISBN 0-690-04586-7 Subj: Cumulative tales. Emotions – fear. Scarecrows.

Williams, Marcia. *The first Christmas* ill. by author. Random House, 1988. ISBN 0-394-80434-1 Subj: Holidays – Christmas. Religion – Nativity.

Jonah and the whale ill. by author. Random House, 1989. ISBN 0-394-92345-6 Subj: Animals – whales. Religion – Jonah.

Joseph and his magnificent coat of many colors ill. by author. Candlewick, 1992. ISBN 1-56402-019-3 Subj: Clothing – coats. Religion.

Not a worry in the world ill. by author. Crown, 1991. ISBN 0-517-58156-6 Subj: Behavior – worrying. Family life.

Williams, Margery. *see* Bianco, Margery Williams

Williams, Maria. *How Raven stole the sun* ill. by Felix Vigil. Abbeville, 2001. ISBN 0-7892-0163-1 Subj: Alaska. Behavior – trickery. Birds – ravens. Folk & fairy tales. Indians of North America – Tlingit.

Williams, Rozanne Lanczak. *The coin counting book* ill. by author. Charlesbridge, 2001. ISBN 0-88106-325-8 Subj: Counting, numbers. Money. Rhyming text.

The purple snerd ill. by Mary GrandPré. Harcourt, 2000. ISBN 0-15-202654-1 Subj: Imagination – imaginary friends. Rhyming text.

Williams, Sam. *Angel's Christmas cookies* ill. by author. HarperFestival, 2002. ISBN 0-06-029651-8 Subj: Angels. Animals – bears. Food. Holidays – Christmas. Mythical creatures – elves. Trees.

The baby's word book ill. by author. Greenwillow, 1999, c1993. ISBN 0-688-16834-5 Subj: Activities. Babies. Dictionaries.

Snowy magic ill. by author. HarperFestival, 2002. ISBN 0-06-029652-6 Subj: Angels. Holidays – Christmas. Magic. Mythical creatures – elves. Weather – snow.

Spots and slots ill. by Manya Stojic. Scholastic, 2001. ISBN 0-439-24064-6 Subj: Concepts – color. Format, unusual – toy & movable books.

Williams, Sarah. *Ride a cock-horse* ill. by Ian Beck. Oxford Univ. Pr., 1987. ISBN 0-19-279831-6 Subj: Nursery rhymes.

Williams, Sherley Anne. *Girls together* ill. by Synthia Saint James. Harcourt, 1999. ISBN 0-15-230982-9 Subj: Activities – playing. Cities, towns. Ethnic groups in the U.S. – African Americans. Friendship.

Working cotton ill. by Carole M. Byard. Harcourt, 1992. ISBN 0-15-299624-9 Subj: Activities – working. Caldecott award honor books. Careers – migrant workers. Ethnic groups in the U.S. – African Americans. Family life.

Williams, Sheron. *And in the beginning . . .* ill. by Robert Roth. Atheneum, 1992. ISBN 0-689-31650-X Subj: Creation. Folk & fairy tales. Foreign lands – Africa.

Williams, Sophy. *Nana's garden* ill. by author. Viking, 1994. ISBN 0-670-85287-2 Subj: Activities – playing. Family life – grandmothers. Gardens, gardening. Ghosts.

Williams, Sue. *Dinnertime* ill. by Kerry Argent. Harcourt, 2001. ISBN 0-15-216471-5 Subj: Animals – foxes. Animals – rabbits. Counting, numbers. Rhyming text.

I went walking ill. by Julie Vivas. Harcourt, 1990. ISBN 0-15-200471-8 Subj: Activities – walking. Animals. Concepts – color. Rhyming text.

I went walking [board book] ill. by Julie Vivas. Harcourt, 1990. ISBN 0-15-205626-2 Subj: Activities – walking. Animals. Concepts – color. Format, unusual – board books. Rhyming text.

Let's go visiting ill. by Julie Vivas. Harcourt, 1998. ISBN 0-15-201823-9 Subj: Animals. Counting, numbers. Pets. Rhyming text.

Williams, Susan. *Poppy's first year* ill. by author. Macmillan, 1989. ISBN 0-02-793031-9 Subj: Babies. Family life – brothers & sisters.

Williams, Suzanne. *Library Lil* ill. by Steven Kellogg. Dial, 1997. ISBN 0-8037-1698-2 Subj: Books, reading. Careers – librarians. Tall tales.

Mommy doesn't know my name ill. by Andrew Shachat. Houghton Mifflin, 1990. ISBN 0-395-54228-6 Subj: Family life – mothers. Names.

My dog never says please ill. by Tedd Arnold. Dial, 1997. ISBN 0-8037-1681-8 Subj: Animals – dogs. Behavior – wishing. Family life.

Old MacDonald in the city ill. by Thor Wickstrom. Golden Bks., 2002. ISBN 0-307-10685-3 Subj: Animals. Cities, towns. Counting, numbers. Insects. Rhyming text.

The witch casts a spell ill. by Barbara Olsen. Dial, 2002. ISBN 0-8037-2646-5 Subj: Holidays – Halloween. Music. Mythical creatures. Songs. Witches.

Williams, Terry Tempest. *Between cattails* ill. by Peter Parnall. Scribners, 1985. ISBN 0-684-18309-9 Subj: Ecology. Rhyming text.

Williams, Vera B. *A chair for my mother* ill. by author. Greenwillow, 1982. ISBN 0-688-00915-8 Subj: Behavior – seeking better things. Caldecott award honor books. Family life. Furniture – chairs.

Cherries and cherry pits ill. by author. Greenwillow, 1986. ISBN 0-688-05146-4 Subj: Art. Ethnic groups in the U.S. – African Americans. Imagination.

"More more more," said the baby ill. by author. Greenwillow, 1991. ISBN 0-688-09174-1 Subj: Babies. Caldecott award honor books. Ethnic groups in the U.S. Family life.

Music, music for everyone ill. by author. Greenwillow, 1984. ISBN 0-688-20604-4 Subj: Family life. Family life – grandmothers. Illness. Music. Musical instruments – accordions.

Something special for me ill. by author. Greenwillow, 1983. ISBN 0-688-01807-6 Subj: Birthdays. Family life. Gifts.

Three days on a river in a red canoe ill. by author. Greenwillow, 1981. ISBN 0-688-84307-7 Subj: Boats, ships. Camps, camping.

Williams-Garcia, Rita. *Catching the wild waiyuuzee* ill. by Mike Reed. S&S, 2000. ISBN 0-689-82601-X Subj: Ethnic groups in the U.S. – African Americans. Hair. Imagination.

Williamson, Hamilton. *Little elephant* ill. by Berta & Elmer Hader. Doubleday, 1930. Subj: Animals – elephants.

Monkey tale ill. by Berta & Elmer Hader. Doubleday, 1929. Subj: Animals – monkeys.

Williamson, Mel. *Walk on!* by Mel Williamson & George Ford; ill. by authors. Third Pr. Review, 1972. ISBN 0-8938-8042-6 Subj: Cities, towns. Ethnic groups in the U.S. – African Americans.

Williamson, Stan. *The no-bark dog* ill. by Tom O'Sullivan. Follett, 1962. Subj: Animals – dogs. Ethnic groups in the U.S. – African Americans.

Willington, Monica. *Seasons of swans* ill. by author. Dutton, 1990. ISBN 0-525-44621-4 Subj: Birds – swans. Birth. Nature.

Willis, Jeanne. *Be gentle, Python!* ill. by Mark Birchall. Carolrhoda, 2001. ISBN 1-57505-508-2 Subj: Animals. Behavior – misbehavior. Reptiles – snakes. School – first day.

Be quiet, Parrot! ill. by Mark Birchall. Carolrhoda, 2000. ISBN 1-57505-492-2 Subj: Behavior – misbehavior. Birds – parakeets, parrots. School – first day.

The boy who lost his bellybutton ill. by Tony Ross. DK, 2000. ISBN 0-7894-6164-1 Subj: Anatomy – navels. Animals. Animals – dogs. Jungle. Reptiles – alligators, crocodiles.

Do little mermaids wet their beds ill. by Penelope Jossen. A. Whitman, 2001. ISBN 0-8075-1668-6 Subj: Behavior. Behavior – bedwetting. Mythical creatures – mermaids, mermen. Rhyming text.

Earth mobiles as explained by Professor Xargle ill. by Tony Ross. Dutton, 1992. ISBN 0-525-44892-6 Subj: Activities – traveling. Space & space ships. Transportation.

Earth tigerlets as explained by Professor Xargle ill. by Tony Ross. Dutton, 1991. ISBN 0-525-44732-6 Subj: Animals – cats. Space & space ships.

Earthlets as explained by Professor Xargle ill. by Tony Ross. Dutton, 1989. ISBN 0-525-44465-3 Subj: Babies. Space & space ships.

The long blue blazer ill. by Susan Varley. Dutton, 1988. ISBN 0-525-44381-9 Subj: Aliens. Character traits – being different. School. Space & space ships.

The monster bed ill. by Susan Varley. Lothrop, 1987. ISBN 0-688-06805-7 Subj: Bedtime. Emotions – fear. Furniture – beds. Monsters. Rhyming text.

The monster storm ill. by Susan Varley. Lothrop, 1995. ISBN 0-688-13785-7 Subj: Emotions – fear. Monsters. Rhyming text. Weather – storms.

No biting, Puma! ill. by Mark Birchall. Carolrhoda, 2001. ISBN 1-575-05509-0 Subj: Animals. Behavior – misbehavior. School – first day.

Sloth's shoes ill. by Tony Ross. Kane/Miller, 1998. ISBN 0-916291-78-2 Subj: Animals. Animals – sloths. Behavior – promptness, tardiness. Birthdays. Rhyming text.

Susan laughs ill. by Tony Ross. Holt, 2000. ISBN 0-8050-6501-6 Subj: Activities. Emotions. Handicaps – physical handicaps. Rhyming text.

Take turns, Penguin! ill. by Mark Birchall. Carolrhoda, 2000. ISBN 1-57505-493-0 Subj: Animals. Behavior – misbehavior. Behavior – sharing. Birds – penguins. School – first day.

The tale of Georgie Grub ill. by Margaret Chamberlain. Holt, 1982. ISBN 0-03-061222-5 Subj: Activities – bathing. Character traits – cleanliness.

What did I look like when I was a baby? ill. by Tony Ross. Putnam, 2000. ISBN 0-399-23595-7 Subj: Babies. Behavior – growing up. Character traits – appearance.

Willis, Val. *The mystery in the bottle* ill. by John Shelley. Farrar, 1991. ISBN 0-374-35194-5 Subj: Format, unusual – board books. Mythical creatures. School.

The secret in the matchbox ill. by John Shelley. Farrar, 1988. ISBN 0-374-36603-9 Subj: Behavior – secrets. Dragons. School.

Silly little chick ill. by Judy Brook. Dutton, 1989. ISBN 0-233-98307-4 Subj: Behavior – growing up. Birds – chickens. Farms.

Willoughby, Elaine Macmann. *Boris and the monsters* ill. by Lynn Munsinger. Houghton Mifflin, 1980. ISBN 0-395-29067-8 Subj: Animals – dogs. Monsters.

Wilner, Isabel. *The baby's game book* ill. by Sam Williams. Greenwillow, 2000. ISBN 0-688-15916-8 Subj: Babies. Family life. Games.

A garden alphabet ill. by Ashley Wolff. Dutton, 1991. ISBN 0-525-44731-8 Subj: ABC books. Animals. Gardens, gardening. Rhyming text.

Wilson, Anna. *Over in the grasslands* ill. by Alison Bartlett. Little, 2000. ISBN 0-316-93910-2 Subj: Animals. Counting, numbers. Foreign lands – Africa. Poetry.

Wilson, Anne. *Masha and the firebird* (Bateson-Hill, Margaret)

Noah's ark ill. by author. Chronicle, 2002. ISBN 0-8118-3563-4 Subj: Animals. Boats, ships. Caldecott award honor books. Religion – Noah. Weather – floods. Weather – rain. Weather – rainbows.

Wilson, April. *April Wilson's magpie magic* ill. by author. Dial, 1999. ISBN 0-8037-2354-7 Subj: Activities – drawing. Birds – magpies. Concepts – color. Concepts – shape. Concepts – size. Wordless.

Wilson, Barbara Ker. *ABC and 123* ill. by Gisèle Daigle. Fitzhenry & Whiteside, 1981. ISBN 0-88878-165-2 Subj: ABC books. Counting, numbers. Foreign languages.

The turtle and the island ill. by Frané Lessac. Lippincott, 1990. ISBN 0-397-32439-1 Subj: Folk & fairy tales. Foreign lands – New Guinea. Islands. Reptiles – turtles, tortoises.

Wilson, Beth P. *Jenny* ill. by Dolores Johnson. Macmillan, 1990. ISBN 0-02-793120-X Subj: Ethnic groups in the U.S. – African Americans. Family life – grandmothers.

Wilson, Bob. *Stanley Bagshaw and the twenty-two ton whale* ill. by author. David & Charles, 1984. ISBN 0-241-10812-8 Subj: Animals – whales. Sports – fishing.

Wilson, Budge. *The fear of Angelina Domino* ill. by Eugenie Fernandes. Stoddart, 2000. ISBN 0-7737-3217-9 Subj: Animals – cats. Emotions – fear. Pets.

A fiddle for Angus ill. by Susan Tooke. Tundra, 2001. ISBN 0-88776-500-9 Subj: Family life. Foreign lands – Canada. Music. Musical instruments – violins.

Wilson, Christopher Bernard. *Hobnob* ill. by William Wiesner. Viking, 1968. Subj: Behavior – sharing.

Wilson, Dorminster. *Mother scorpion country* (Rohmer, Harriet)

Wilson, Gina. *Ignis* ill. by P. J. Lynch. Candlewick, 2001. ISBN 0-7636-1623-0 Subj: Behavior – growing up. Dragons. Fire. Self-concept.

Wilson, Hazel Hutchins. *see* Hutchins, H. J. (Hazel J.)

Wilson, Jacqueline. *Mr. Cool* ill. by Stephen Lewis. Kingfisher, 2000. ISBN 0-7534-5822-5 Subj: Friendship. Musical instruments – bands.

Wilson, Joyce Lancaster. *Tobi* ill. by Anne Thiess. Funk & Wagnalls, 1968. Subj: Animals – cats.

Wilson, Julia. *Becky* ill. by John Wilson. Crowell, 1966. Subj: Character traits – honesty. Ethnic groups in the U.S. – African Americans. Toys – dolls.

Wilson, Karma. *Bear stays up for Christmas* ill. by Jane Chapman. McElderry, 2004. ISBN 0-689-85278-9 Subj: Animals. Animals – bears. Forest, woods. Hibernation. Holidays – Christmas. Rhyming text.

Wilson, Lynn. *Baby whale* ill. by author. Putnam, 1991. ISBN 0-448-40073-1 Subj: Animals – whales.

Wilson, Margaret. *The dog show* (Gray, Nigel)

Wilson, Robina Beckles. *Merry Christmas! children at Christmastime around the world* ill. by Satomi Ichikawa. Putnam, 1983. ISBN 0-399-20921-2 Subj: Holidays – Christmas.

Wilson, Ron. *Mice* ill. with photos. Global Lib. Mktg. Serv., 1984. ISBN 0-7136-2388-8 Subj: Animals – mice. Nature. Science.

Wilson, Sarah. *Beware the dragons!* ill. by author. HarperCollins, 1985. ISBN 0-06-026509-4 Subj: Dragons. Folk & fairy tales. Weather – storms.

Big day on the river ill. by Randy Cecil. Holt, 2003. ISBN 0-8050-6787-6 Subj: Family life. Rivers. Sports – sailing.

The day that Henry cleaned his room ill. by author. S&S, 1990. ISBN 0-671-69202-X Subj: Character traits – cleanliness.

Elmo says, achoo! ill. by Tom Brannon; featuring Jim Henson's Sesame Street Muppets. Random House, 2000. ISBN 0-375-90311-9 Subj: Illness – allergies. Puppets. Rhyming text.

Good zap, little grog ill. by Susan Meddaugh. Candlewick, 1995. ISBN 1-56402-286-2 Subj: Family life. Names. Rhyming text.

June is a tune that jumps on a stair ill. by author. S&S, 1992. ISBN 0-671-73919-0 Subj: Poetry.

Love and kisses ill. by Melissa Sweet. Candlewick, 1999. ISBN 1-56402-792-9 Subj: Animals. Emotions – love. Rhyming text.

Muskrat, muskrat, eat your peas! ill. by author. S&S, 1989. ISBN 0-671-67515-X Subj: Animals – muskrats. Family life. Food.

Uncle Albert's flying birthday ill. by author. S&S, 1991. ISBN 0-671-72793-1 Subj: Activities – bathing. Birthdays. Parties.

Wilson, Toña. *The cook and the king* (Brusca, María Cristina)

When jaguars ate the moon: and other stories about animals and plants of the Americas (Brusca, María Cristina)

Wilson, Troy. *Perfect man* ill. by Dean Griffiths. Orca, 2004. ISBN 1-55143-286-2 Subj: Careers – teachers. Careers – writers.

Wilson-Kelly, Becky. *Mother Grumpy's dog biscuits* ill. by author. Holt, 1990. ISBN 0-8050-1287-7 Subj: Activities – baking, cooking. Animals – dogs. Character traits. Food.

Wilson-Max, Ken. *Big blue engine* ill. by author. Scholastic, 1996. ISBN 0-590-89801-9 Subj: Format, unusual – toy & movable books. Trains.

Big red fire truck ill. by author. Scholastic, 1997. ISBN 0-590-10082-3 Subj: Careers – firefighters. Fire. Format, unusual – toy & movable books.

A book of letters ill. by Manya Stojic. Scholastic, 2002. ISBN 0-439-32455-6 Subj: ABC books. Format, unusual – toy & movable books.

Faraha means happy: a book of Swahili words ill. by author. Hyperion, 2000. ISBN 0-7868-2480-8 Subj: Foreign lands – Kenya. Foreign languages.

Halala means welcome: a book of Zulu words ill. by author. Hyperion, 1998. ISBN 0-7868-0914-9 Subj: Foreign lands – South Africa. Foreign languages.

Little red plane ill. by author. Scholastic, 1995. ISBN 0-590-43008-4 Subj: Airplanes, airports. Format, unusual – toy & movable books.

Max loves sunflowers ill. by author. Hyperion, 1998. ISBN 0-7868-0413-0 Subj: Flowers. Format, unusual – toy & movable books. Plants. Science.

Max's starry night ill. by author. Hyperion, 2001. ISBN 0-7868-0553-6 Subj: Animals – elephants. Emotions – fear. Ethnic groups in the U.S. – African Americans. Stars.

Wake up; Sleep tight ill. by author. Scholastic, 1998. ISBN 0-590-76779-8 Subj: Format, unusual. Time.

Winch, John. *Keeping up with Grandma* ill. by auithor. Holiday, 2000. ISBN 0-8234-1563-5 Subj: Activities. Family life – grandfathers. Family life – grandmothers.

Winch, Madeleine. *Come by chance* ill. by author. Crown, 1990. ISBN 0-517-57667-8 Subj: Animals. Homes, houses. Seasons – winter.

Windham, Sophie. *Down in the marvelous deep* ill. by author. Scholastic, 1994. ISBN 0-590-20898-5 Subj: Poetry. Sea & seashore.

Noah's ark ill. by author. Putnam, 1989. ISBN 0-399-21564-6 Subj: Animals. Boats, ships. Food. Format, unusual. Religion – Noah. Weather – floods. Weather – rain.

Winer, Yvonne. *Birds build nests* ill. by Tony Oliver. Charlesbridge, 2002. ISBN 1-57091-500-8 Subj: Birds. Homes, houses.

Butterflies fly Ill. by Karen Lloyd-Jones. Charlesbridge, 2001. ISBN 1-57091-446-X Subj: Activities – flying. Insects – butterflies, caterpillars.

Frogs sing songs ill. by Tony Oliver. Charlesbridge, 2003. ISBN 1-57091-548-2 Subj: Behavior. Ecology. Frogs & toads. Noise, sounds.

Wing, Natasha. *Jalapeño bagels* ill. by Robert Casilla. Atheneum, 1996. ISBN 0-02-793077-7 Subj: Ethnic groups in the U.S. Family life. Food. School.

The night before the night before Christmas ill. by Mike Lester. Grosset, 2002. ISBN 0-448-42872-5 Subj: Holidays – Christmas. Rhyming text.

Winkelman, Barbara Gaines. *Puffer's surprise* ill. by Steven James Petruccio. Soundprints, 2003. ISBN 1-59249-032-8 Subj: Fish. Foreign lands – Galapagos Islands. Sea & seashore.

Sockeye's journey home ill. by Joanie Popeo. Soundprints, 2000. ISBN 1-56899-829-5 Subj: Ecology. Fish. Migration.

Winkleman, Katherine K. *Firehouse* ill. by John S. Winkleman. Walker, 1994. ISBN 0-8027-8317-1 Subj: Careers – firefighters. Trucks.

Winn, Chris. *Archie's acrobats* ill. by author. Trafalgar Square, 1990. ISBN 0-575-04481-0 Subj: Activities. Circus.

Helping ill. by author. Holt, 1986. ISBN 0-8050-0064-X Subj: Activities. Format, unusual – board books.

Holiday ill. by author. Holt, 1986. ISBN 0-8050-0067-4 Subj: Format, unusual – board books. Holidays.

My day ill. by author. Holt, 1986. ISBN 0-8050-0066-6 Subj: Family life. Format, unusual – board books. Shopping.

Playing ill. by author. Holt, 1986. ISBN 0-8050-0065-8 Subj: Activities – playing. Format, unusual – board books.

Winne, Joanne. *Blue in my world* ill. with photos. Childrens Pr., 2000. ISBN 0-516-23123-5 Subj: Concepts – color.

Green in my world ill. with photos. Childrens Pr., 2000. ISBN 0-516-23124-3 Subj: Concepts – color.

Let's get ready for Kwanzaa ill. with photos. Childrens Pr., 2001. ISBN 0-516-23175-8 Subj: Ethnic groups in the U.S. – African Americans. Holidays – Kwanzaa.

Red in my world ill. with photos. Childrens Pr., 2001. ISBN 0-516-23126-X Subj: Concepts – color.

Winnick, Karen B. *Barn sneeze* ill. by author. Childrens Pr., 2000. ISBN 1-56397-948-9 Subj: Animals. Noise, sounds.

Sybil's night ride ill. by author. Boyds Mills, 2000. ISBN 1-56397-697-8 Subj: Animals – horses, ponies. Night. U.S. history. War.

A year goes round ill. by author. Boyds Mills, 2001. ISBN 1-56397-898-9 Subj: Days of the week, months of the year. Poetry.

Winnie-the Pooh's A B C inspired by A. A. Milne; created with Gallaudet University Pr.; ill. by Ernest H. Shepard; sign language ill. by Lois A. Lehman; sign language consultant Lvey Pittle Wallace. Dutton, 2001. ISBN 0-525-46714-9 Subj: ABC books. Handicaps – deafness. Language. Senses – hearing. Sign language.

Winston, Clara. *Thumbelina* (Andersen, H. C. [Hans Christian])

Winston, Peggy D. *Creatures of long ago: dinosaurs* (Sibbick, John)

Winston, Richard. *Thumbelina* (Andersen, H. C. [Hans Christian])

Winter, Jeanette. *The Christmas tree ship* ill. by author. Philomel, 1994. ISBN 0-399-22693-1 Subj: Boats, ships. Holidays – Christmas. Trees. U.S. history.

Cowboy Charlie ill. by author. Harcourt, 1995. ISBN 0-15-200857-8 Subj: Activities – playing. Art. Careers – artists. Cowboys, cowgirls. U.S. history – frontier & pioneer life.

Follow the drinking gourd ill. by author. Dragonfly Books, 1992. ISBN 0-679-81997-5 Subj: Ethnic groups in the U.S. – African Americans. Sailors. Slavery. Stars. U.S. history.

The girl and the moon man: a Siberian folktale ill. by author. Pantheon, 1984. ISBN 0-394-96326-1 Subj: Animals. Folk & fairy tales. Foreign lands – Russia. Moon. Music.

The house that Jack built (The house that Jack built)

My baby ill. by author. Frances Foster, 2001. ISBN 0-374-35103-1 Subj: Art. Babies. Behavior – growing up. Clothing. Foreign lands – Africa.

Niño's mask ill. by author. Dial, 2003. ISBN 0-8037-2807-7 Subj: Clothing – costumes. Fairs, festivals. Foreign lands – Mexico.

Once upon a time in Chicago ill. by author. Hyperion, 2000. ISBN 0-7868-2404-2 Subj: Careers – musicians. Music. Musical instruments – bands.

Winter, Jonah. *Diego* ill. by Jeanette Winter. Knopf, 1991. ISBN 0-679-91987-2 Subj: Art. Careers – artists. Foreign languages.

Winter, Paula. *The bear and the fly* ill. by author. Crown, 1976. ISBN 0-517-52605-0 Subj: Animals – bears. Insects – flies. Wordless.

Sir Andrew ill. by author. Crown, 1980. ISBN 0-517-53911-X Subj: Animals – donkeys. Character traits – vanity. Wordless.

Winter, Rick. *Dirty birdy feet* ill. by Mike Lester. Rising Moon, 2000. ISBN 0-8735-8768-5 Subj: Animals. Birds. Cumulative tales. Family life.

Winter, Susan. *A baby just like me* ill. by author. DK, 1994. ISBN 1-56458-668-5 Subj: Babies. Emotions – envy, jealousy. Family life – new sibling. Family life – sisters. Sibling rivalry.

My shadow ill. by author. Doubleday, 1994. ISBN 0-385-31066-8 Subj: Shadows.

Winteringham, Victoria. *Penguin day* ill. by author. HarperCollins, 1982. ISBN 0-06-026514-0 Subj: Activities. Birds – penguins.

Winters, Kay. *Abe Lincoln, the boy who loved books* ill. by Nancy Carpenter. S&S, 2003. ISBN 0-689-82554-4 Subj: Books, reading. U.S. history.

Did you see what I saw? ill. by Martha Weston. Viking, 1996. ISBN 0-670-87118-4 Subj: Poetry. School.

The teeny tiny ghost ill. by Lynn Munsinger. HarperCollins, 1997. ISBN 0-06-025684-2 Subj: Emotions – fear. Ghosts. Holidays – Halloween.

The teeny tiny ghost and the monster ill. by Lynn Munsinger. HarperCollins, 2004. ISBN 0-06-028885-X Subj: Contests. Ghosts. Monsters. School.

Tiger trail ill. by Laura Regan. S&S, 2000. ISBN 0-689-82323-1 Subj: Animals – tigers. Behavior – growing up. Nature.

Whooo's haunting the teeny tiny ghost? ill. by Lynn Munsinger. HarperCollins, 1999. ISBN 0-06-027359-3 Subj: Emotions – fear. Ghosts. Holidays – Halloween.

Wolf watch ill. by Laura Regan. S&S, 1997. ISBN 0-689-80218-8 Subj: Animals. Animals – wolves. Behavior – growing up. Nature. Rhyming text.

Winthrop, Elizabeth. *As the crow flies* ill. by Joan Sandin. Clarion, 1998. ISBN 0-395-77612-0 Subj: Divorce. Family life – fathers.

Bear and Mrs. Duck ill. by Patience Brewster. Holiday, 1988. ISBN 0-8234-0687-3 Subj: Activities – babysitting. Animals – bears. Birds – ducks.

Bear and Roly-Poly ill. by Patience Brewster. Holiday, 1996. ISBN 0-8234-1197-4 Subj: Activities – babysitting. Family life – brothers & sisters. Toys.

Bear's Christmas surprise ill. by Patience Brewster. Holiday, 1991. ISBN 0-8234-0888-4 Subj: Activities – babysitting. Animals – bears. Birds – ducks. Holidays – Christmas.

The Best Friends Club ill. by Martha Weston. Lothrop, 1989. ISBN 0-688-07583-5 Subj: Character traits – selfishness. Clubs, gangs. Friendship.

Bunk beds ill. by Ronald Himler. HarperCollins, 1972. ISBN 0-06-026532-9 Subj: Activities – playing. Bedtime. Family life. Furniture – beds. Imagination.

A child is born: the Christmas story adapt. from the New Testament; ill. by Charles Mikolaycak. Holiday, 1983. ISBN 0-8234-0472-2 Subj: Holidays – Christmas. Religion – Nativity.

Halloween hats ill. by Sue Truesdell. Holt, 2002. ISBN 0-8050-6386-2 Subj: Clothing – hats. Holidays – Halloween. Parades. Rhyming text.

He is risen: the Easter story ill. by Charles Mikolaycak. Holiday, 1985. ISBN 0-8234-0547-8 Subj: Holidays – Easter. Religion.

I think he likes me ill. by Denise Saldutti. HarperCollins, 1980. ISBN 0-06-026552-3 Subj: Family life. Sibling rivalry.

I'm the Boss! ill. by Mary Morgan. Holiday, 1994. ISBN 0-8234-1113-3 Subj: Animals – dogs. Character traits – assertiveness. Family life.

Katharine's doll ill. by Marylin Hafner. Dutton, 1983. ISBN 0-525-44061-5 Subj: Friendship. Toys – dolls.

The little humpbacked horse ill. by Alexander Koshkin. Clarion, 1997. ISBN 0-395-65361-4 Subj: Animals – horses, ponies. Character traits – cleverness. Folk & fairy tales. Foreign lands – Russia. Royalty – tsars.

Lizzie and Harold ill. by Martha Weston. Lothrop, 1986. ISBN 0-688-02712-1 Subj: Friendship.

Maggie and the monster ill. by Tomie de Paola. Holiday, 1987. ISBN 0-8234-0639-2 Subj: Bedtime. Monsters. Problem solving.

Potbellied possums ill. by Barbara McClintock. Holiday, 1977. ISBN 0-8234-0289-4 Subj: Animals – possums. Emotions – fear. Food. Night.

Promises ill. by Betsy Lewin. Clarion, 2000. ISBN 0-395-82272-6 Subj: Emotions. Family life – daughters. Family life – mothers. Illness – cancer.

Shoes ill. by William Joyce. HarperCollins, 1986. ISBN 0-06-026592-2 Subj: Clothing – shoes. Rhyming text.

Sledding ill. by Sarah Wilson. HarperCollins, 1989. ISBN 0-06-026566-3 Subj: Rhyming text. Sports – sledding.

Sloppy kisses ill. by Anne Burgess. Macmillan, 1980. ISBN 0-02-793210-9 Subj: Animals – pigs. Friendship.

That's mine ill. by Emily Arnold McCully. Holiday, 1977. ISBN 0-8234-0308-4 Subj: Activities – playing. Behavior – fighting, arguing. Behavior – greed. Behavior – sharing. Sibling rivalry. Toys – blocks.

Tough Eddie ill. by Lillian Hoban. Dutton, 1985. ISBN 0-525-44364-6 Subj: Character traits – pride. Gender roles. School.

Vasilissa the beautiful ill. by Alexander Koshkin. HarperCollins, 1991. ISBN 0-06-021663-8 Subj: Folk & fairy tales. Foreign lands – Russia. Royalty. Toys – dolls. Witches.

A very noisy girl ill. by Ellen Weiss. Holiday, 1991. ISBN 0-8234-0858-2 Subj: Family life – mothers. Imagination. Noise, sounds.

Winton, Tim. *The deep* ill. by Karen Louise. Tricycle, 2000. ISBN 1-58246-024-8 Subj: Animals – dolphins. Emotions – fear. Nature. Sea & seashore. Sports – swimming.

Wirt, Donna Aaron. *My favorite place* (Sargent, Susan)

Wirth, Beverly. *Margie and me* ill. by Karen Ann Weinhaus. Four Winds, 1983. ISBN 0-590-07870-4 Subj: Animals – dogs. Pets.

Wisbeski, Dorothy Gross. *Pícaro, a pet otter* ill. by Edna Miller. Hawthorn, 1971. Subj: Animals – otters. Pets.

Wisdom, Jude. *Whatever Wanda wanted* ill. by author. Fogelman, 2002. ISBN 0-8037-2693-7 Subj: Behavior. Character traits – selfishness. Islands. Kites.

Wise, Fred. *A you're adorable* (Lippman, Sidney)

Wise, William. *Dinosaurs forever* ill. by Lynn Munsinger. Dial, 2000. ISBN 0-8037-2114-5 Subj: Dinosaurs. Humorous stories. Poetry.

Wiseman, Bernard. *Christmas with Morris and Borris* ill. by author. Little, 1983. ISBN 0-316-94855-1 Subj: Animals – bears. Animals – moose. Holidays – Christmas.

Doctor Duck and Nurse Swan ill. by author. Dutton, 1984. ISBN 0-525-44095-X Subj: Animals. Problem solving.

Don't make fun! ill. by author. Houghton Mifflin, 1982. ISBN 0-395-32086-0 Subj: Animals – pigs. Behavior – misbehavior.

Little new kangaroo ill. by Robert Lopshire. Macmillan, 1973. ISBN 0-02-793220-6 Subj: Animals. Animals – kangaroos. Foreign lands – Russia. Rhyming text.

Morris and Boris at the circus ill. by author. HarperCollins, 1988. ISBN 0-06-026478-0 Subj: Animals – bears. Animals – moose. Circus.

Morris has a birthday party! ill. by author. Little, 1983. ISBN 0-316-94854-3 Subj: Animals – bears. Animals – moose. Behavior – misunderstanding. Parties.

Morris the moose ill. by author. Rev. ed. HarperCollins, 1989. ISBN 0-06-026476-4 Subj: Animals – bulls, cows. Animals – moose. Behavior – misunderstanding.

Oscar is a mama ill. by author. Garrard, 1980. ISBN 0-8116-6081-8 Subj: Animals – bulls, cows. Toys – dolls.

Tails are not for painting ill. by author. Garrard, 1980. ISBN 0-8116-6078-8 Subj: Animals. Behavior – mistakes. Humorous stories. School.

Wishinsky, Frieda. *Give Maggie a chance* ill. by Dean Griffiths. Fitzhenry & Whiteside, 2002. ISBN 1-55041-682-0 Subj: Animals – cats. Behavior – bullying. Books, reading. Character traits – bravery. Emotions – fear. School.

Jennifer Jones won't leave me alone ill. by Neal Layton. Carolrhoda, 2003. ISBN 0-87614-921-2 Subj: Friendship. Moving. Rhyming text. School.

Nothing scares us ill. by Neal Layton. Carolrhoda, 2000. ISBN 1-57505-490-6 Subj: Emotions – fear. Friendship. Monsters. Spiders.

Oonga boonga ill. by Suçie Stevenson. Little, 1990. ISBN 0-316-94872-1 Subj: Babies. Family life – brothers & sisters.

Oonga boonga ill. by Carol Thompson. New ed. Dutton, 1998. ISBN 0-525-46095-0 Subj: Babies. Family life – brothers & sisters.

What's the matter with Albert? the story of Albert Einstein ill. by Jacques Lamontagne. Firefly, 2002. ISBN 1-894379-31-4 Subj: Careers – journalists. Careers – scientists.

Wisniewski, David. *Elfwyn's saga* ill. by author. Lothrop, 1990. ISBN 0-688-09590-9 Subj: Folk & fairy tales. Foreign lands – Iceland. Handicaps – blindness. Magic.

Golem ill. by author. Clarion, 1996. ISBN 0-395-72618-2 Subj: Caldecott award honor books. Folk & fairy tales. Foreign lands – Czechoslovakia. Jewish culture. Mythical creatures.

Rain player ill. by author. Houghton Mifflin, 1991. ISBN 0-395-55112-9 Subj: Foreign lands – Central America. Foreign lands – Mexico. Games. Indians of Central America – Maya.

Sumo Mouse ill. by author. Chronicle, 2002. ISBN 0-8118-3492-1 Subj: Animals – mice. Careers – storekeepers. Crime. Foreign lands – Japan. Toys.

Sundiata: lion king of Mali ill. by author. Clarion, 1992. ISBN 0-395-61302-7 Subj: Folk & fairy tales. Foreign lands – Mali. Handicaps. Royalty – kings.

Tough cookie ill. by author. Lothrop, 1999. ISBN 0-688-15338-0 Subj: Food. Humorous stories.

The warrior and the wise man ill. by author. Lothrop, 1989. ISBN 0-688-07890-7 Subj: Character traits – wisdom. Folk & fairy tales. Foreign lands – Japan. Multiple births – twins. Royalty.

Witch poems ed. by Daisy Wallace; ill. by Trina Schart Hyman. Holiday, 1976. ISBN 0-8234-0281-9 Subj: Poetry. Witches.

Withers, Carl. *The tale of a black cat* ill. by Alan E. Cober. Holt, 1966. Subj: Animals – cats. Games.

The wild ducks and the goose ill. by Alan E. Cober. Holt, 1968. Subj: Birds – ducks. Games. Sports – hunting.

Witt, Alexa. *It's great to skate* ill. by Nate Evans. S&S, 2000. ISBN 0-689-83109-9 Subj: Sports – roller skating.

Wittbold, Maureen. *Mending Peter's heart* ill. by Larry Salk. Portunus Pub., 1995. ISBN 0-9641330-2-4 Subj: Animals – dogs. Death. Emotions – grief. Friendship. Pets.

Witte, Anna. *The parrot Tico Tango* ill. by author. Barefoot, 2004. ISBN 1-84148-243-9 Subj: Animals. Behavior – greed. Birds – parakeets, parrots. Cumulative tales. Forest, woods. Rhyming text.

Wittels, Harriet. *Things I hate!* by Harriet Wittels & Joan Greisman; ill. by Jerry McConnel. Behavioral, 1973. ISBN 0-8770-5096-1 Subj: Behavior. Emotions. Rhyming text.

Wittington, Mary K. *Troll games* ill. by Betsy Day. Macmillan, 1991. ISBN 0-689-31630-5 Subj: Games. Mythical creatures – trolls. Night.

Wittman, Sally. *The boy who hated Valentine's Day* ill. by Chaya M. Burstein. HarperCollins, 1987. ISBN 0-06-026594-9 Subj: Character traits – kindness. Friendship. Holidays – Valentine's Day. School.

Pelly and Peak ill. by author. HarperCollins, 1978. ISBN 0-06-026560-4 Subj: Birds – peacocks, peahens. Birds – pelicans. Friendship.

Plenty of Pelly and Peak ill. by author. HarperCollins, 1980. ISBN 0-06-026563-9 Subj: Birds – peacocks, peahens. Birds – pelicans. Friendship.

A special trade ill. by Karen Gundersheimer. HarperCollins, 1978. ISBN 0-06-026554-X Subj: Behavior – growing up. Friendship. Old age.

The wonderful Mrs. Trumbly ill. by Margot Apple. HarperCollins, 1982. ISBN 0-06-026512-4 Subj: Friendship. School. Weddings.

Wittmann, Patricia. *Buffalo Thunder* ill. by Bert Dodson. Cavendish, 1997. ISBN 0-7614-5001-7 Subj: Animals – buffaloes. Family life. U.S. history – frontier & pioneer life.

Go ask Giorgio! ill. by Will Hillenbrand. Macmillan, 1992. ISBN 0-02-793221-4 Subj: Activities – working. Careers. Character traits – helpfulness. Clothing – hats.

Wodge, Dreary. *see* Gorey, Edward (St. John)

Woelfle, Gretchen. *Katje the windmill cat* ill. by Nicola Bayley. Candlewick, 2001. ISBN 0-7636-1347-9 Subj: Animals – cats. Foreign lands – Holland. Weather – floods.

Wohl, Lauren L. *Matzoh mouse* ill. by Pamela Keavney. HarperCollins, 1991. ISBN 0-06-026581-7 Subj: Family life. Holidays – Passover. Jewish culture. Religion.

Wohlrabe, Sarah C. *Helping you heal, a book about nurses* ill. by Eric Thomas. Picture Window, 2004. ISBN 1-4048-0086-7 Subj: Careers – nurses.

Helping you learn, a book about teachers ill. by Eric Thomas. Picture Window, 2004. ISBN 1-4048-0084-0 Subj: Careers – teachers.

Wojciechowski, Susan. *The best Halloween of all* ill. by Susan Meddaugh. 2nd ed. Candlewick, 1998. ISBN 0-7636-0458-5 Subj: Clothing – costumes. Holidays – Halloween.

The Christmas miracle of Jonathan Toomey ill. by P. J. Lynch. Candlewick, 1995. ISBN 1-56402-320-6 Subj: Careers – woodcarvers. Friendship. Holidays – Christmas. Religion.

A fine St. Patrick's Day ill. by Tom Curry. Random House, 2004. ISBN 0-375-92386-1 Subj: Character traits – kindness. Contests. Holidays – St. Patrick's Day.

Wojtowycz, David. *Animal antics from 1 to 10* ill. by author. Holiday, 2000. ISBN 0-8234-1552-X Subj: Animals. Counting, numbers. Hotels.

A cuddle for Claude ill. by author. Dutton, 2001. ISBN 0-525-46691-6 Subj: Animals – polar bears. Behavior – running away. Family life – grandmothers.

David Wojtowycz presents Animal ABC ill. by author. David & Charles, 2000. ISBN 1-86233-107-3 Subj: ABC books. Animals.

Dudley helps out ill. by author. Little Tiger, 1999. ISBN 1-888444-71-1 Subj: Animals – pigs. Character traits – cleanliness. Character traits – helpfulness. Family life. Format, unusual – toy & movable books.

Dudley's birthday party ill. by author. Little Tiger, 1999. ISBN 1-888444-72-X Subj: Animals. Animals – pigs. Birthdays. Character traits – selfishness. Format, unusual – toy & movable books. Parties.

Wolcott, Patty. *Double-decker, double-decker, double-decker bus* ill. by Bob Barner. Addison-Wesley, 1980. ISBN 0-201-08735-9 Subj: Buses. Friendship.

Eeeeeek! ill. by Ned Delaney. Random House, 1991. ISBN 0-679-91929-5 Subj: Animals. Sleep. Sports – hunting.

Wold, Jo Anne. *Tell them my name is Amanda* ed. by Caroline Rubin; ill. by Dennis Hockerman. A. Whitman, 1977. ISBN 0-8075-7768-5 Subj: Character traits – shyness. Names. Problem solving. Self-concept.

Well! Why didn't you say so? ill. by Unada. A. Whitman, 1975. ISBN 0-8075-8724-9 Subj: Animals – dogs. Behavior – lost. Behavior – misunderstanding. Cities, towns.

Wolde, Gunilla. *Betsy and Peter are different* ill. by author. Random House, 1979. Translation of Annorlunda Emma och Per. ISBN 0-394-94210-8 Subj: Family life. Friendship.

Betsy and the chicken pox ill. by author. Random House, 1976. Translation of Emmas lillebror ar sjuk. ISBN 0-394-83328-7 Subj: Behavior – needing someone. Illness. Sibling rivalry.

Betsy and the doctor ill. by author. Random House, 1978. Translation of Emma hos doktorn. ISBN 0-394-95382-7 Subj: Careers – doctors. Hospitals. Illness.

Betsy and the vacuum cleaner ill. by author. Random House, 1979. ISBN 0-394-94209-4 Subj: Family life. Machines.

Betsy's first day at nursery school ill. by author. Random House, 1976. Translation of Emmas första dag på dagis. ISBN 0-394-95381-9 Subj: School – first day. School – nursery.

Betsy's fixing day ill. by author. Random House, 1978. ISBN 0-394-93781-3 Subj: Character traits – helpfulness. Family life.

This is Betsy ill. by author. Random House, 1975. Translation of Emma tvärtimot. ISBN 0-394-93161-0 Subj: Emotions. Family life.

Wolf, Alex de. *Mop and the birthday picnic* (Schaap, Martine)

Mop's backyard concert (Schaap, Martine)

Mop's mountain adventure (Schaap, Martine)

Mop's treasure hunt (Schaap, Martine)

Wolf, Ann. *The rabbit and the turtle* ill. by author. Wonder Books, 1965. Subj: Animals – rabbits. Folk & fairy tales. Reptiles – turtles, tortoises.

Wolf, Bernard. *Adam Smith goes to school* photos by author. Lippincott, 1978. ISBN 0-397-31764-6 Subj: School – first day.

Anna's silent world photos by author. Lippincott, 1977. ISBN 0-397-31739-5 Subj: Handicaps – deafness. Senses – hearing.

Don't feel sorry for Paul photos by author. Lippincott, 1974. ISBN 0-397-31588-0 Subj: Handicaps.

Michael and the dentist photos by author. Four Winds, 1980. ISBN 0-590-07637-X Subj: Careers – dentists. Emotions – fear. Teeth.

Wolf, Gita. *The very hungry lion* adapt. & ill. by Indrapramit Roy. Firefly, 1996. ISBN 1-55037-461-3 Subj: Animals – lions. Behavior – trickery. Character traits – laziness. Folk & fairy tales. Foreign lands – India.

Wolf, Jake. *Daddy, could I have an elephant?* ill. by Marylin Hafner. Greenwillow, 1996. ISBN 0-688-13295-2 Subj: Animals. Family life – fathers. Pets.

Wolf, Janet. *Adelaide to Zeke* ill. by author. HarperCollins, 1987. ISBN 0-06-026598-1 Subj: ABC books. Names.

The best present is me ill. by author. HarperCollins, 1984. ISBN 0-06-026584-1 Subj: Art. Family life – grandmothers.

The rosy fat magenta radish ill. by author. Little, 1990. ISBN 0-316-95045-9 Subj: Gardens, gardening.

Wolf, Sallie. *Peter's trucks* ill. by Cat Bowman Smith. A. Whitman, 1992. ISBN 0-8075-6519-9 Subj: Circular tales. Rhyming text. Trucks.

Wolf, Susan. *The adventures of Albert, the running bear* (Isenberg, Barbara)

Albert the running bear gets the jitters (Isenberg, Barbara)

Wolf, Winfried. *The Easter bunny* ill. by Agnès Mathieu. Dial, 1986. ISBN 0-8037-0239-6 Subj: Animals – rabbits. Holidays – Easter.

Wolfe, Art. *Northwest animal babies* by Art Wolfe & Andrea Helman; photos by Art Wolf. Sasquatch, 1998. ISBN 1-57061-144-0 Subj: Animals – babies.

1, 2, 3 moose photos by author; text by Andrea Helman. Sasquatch, 1996. ISBN 1-57061-078-9 Subj: Animals. Counting, numbers.

Wolfe, Frances. *It is the wind* ill. by James E. Ransome. HarperCollins, 2003. ISBN 0-06-028192-8 Subj: Animals. Bedtime. Ethnic groups in the U.S. – African Americans. Noise, sounds. Sleep.

One wish ill. by authnor. Tundra, 2004. ISBN 0-88776-662-5 Subj: Behavior – wishing. Homes, houses. Old age. Sea & seashore.

Where I live ill. by author. Tundra, 2001. ISBN 0-88776-529-7 Subj: Foreign lands – Canada. Poetry. Sea & seashore.

Wolfe, Robert L. *The truck book* photos by author. Carolrhoda, 1981. ISBN 0-87614-125-4 Subj: Trucks.

Wolff, Ashley. *The bells of London* ill. by author. Dodd, 1985. ISBN 0-396-08485-0 Subj: Birds – doves. Emotions – sadness. Foreign lands – England. Songs.

Only the cat saw ill. by author. Dodd, 1985. ISBN 0-396-08727-2 Subj: Animals – cats. Family life. Night.

Stella and Roy go camping ill. by author. Dutton, 1999. ISBN 0-525-45864-6 Subj: Camps, camping. Family life. Sibling rivalry.

A year of beasts ill. by author. Dutton, 1986. ISBN 0-525-44240-5 Subj: Animals. Days of the week, months of the year. Farms.

A year of birds ill. by author. Dodd, 1984. ISBN 0-396-08313-7 Subj: Birds. Days of the week, months of the year. Seasons.

Wolff, Ferida. *The emperor's garden* ill. by Kathy Osborn. Tambourine, 1994. ISBN 0-688-11652-3 Subj: Behavior – sharing. Folk & fairy tales. Foreign lands – China. Gardens, gardening. Royalty – emperors.

On Halloween night by Ferida Wolff & Dolores Kozielski; ill. by Dolores Avendaño. Tambourine, 1994. ISBN 0-688-12973-0 Subj: Counting, numbers. Holidays – Halloween. Rhyming text. Witches.

The woodcutter's coat ill. by Anne Wilsdorf. Little, 1992. ISBN 0-316-95048-3 Subj: Circular tales. Clothing – coats. Crime.

Wolff, Patricia Rae. *A new, improved Santa* ill. by Lynne Cravath. Orchard, 2002. ISBN 0-439-35249-5 Subj: Holidays – Christmas. Santa Claus. Self-concept.

The toll-bridge troll ill. by Kimberly Bulcken Root. Browndeer, 1998. ISBN 0-15-277665-6 Subj: Mythical creatures – trolls. Riddles & jokes. School.

Wolff, Robert Jay. *Feeling blue* ill. by author. Scribners, 1968. Subj: Concepts – color.

Hello, yellow! ill. by author. Scribners, 1968. Subj: Concepts – color.

Seeing red ill. by author. Scribners, 1968. Subj: Concepts – color.

Wolfson, Margaret. *Turtle songs* ill. by Karla Sachi. Beyond Words, 1999. ISBN 1-885223-95-1 Subj: Folk & fairy tales. Foreign lands – Fiji. Reptiles – turtles, tortoises. Royalty – princesses. Sea & seashore.

Wolkstein, Diane. *The banza: a Haitian story* ill. by Marc Brown. Dial, 1981. ISBN 0-8037-0429-1 Subj: Animals – goats. Animals – tigers. Character traits – bravery. Folk & fairy tales. Music. Musical instruments – banjos.

Bouki dances the Kokioko: a comical tale from Haiti ill. by Jesse Sweetwater. Harcourt, 1997. ISBN 0-15-200034-8 Subj: Activities – dancing. Behavior – trickery. Folk & fairy tales. Foreign lands – Haiti. Royalty – kings.

The cool ride in the sky ill. by Paul Galdone. Knopf, 1973. ISBN 0-394-92489-4 Subj: Activities – flying. Animals – monkeys. Birds – buzzards. Birds – vultures. Character traits – cleverness. Folk & fairy tales.

The day Ocean came to visit ill. by Steve Johnson & Lou Fancher. Harcourt, 2001. ISBN 0-15-201774-7 Subj: Folk & fairy tales – pourquoi tales. Foreign lands – Africa. Moon. Sea & seashore. Sun.

The glass mountain (Grimm, Jacob)

The legend of Sleepy Hollow ill. by R. W. Alley. Morrow, 1987. Based on the story by Washington Irving. ISBN 0-688-06533-3 Subj: Folk & fairy tales. Ghosts. Holidays – Halloween. Humorous stories.

Little Mouse's painting ill. by Maryjane Begin. Morrow, 1992. ISBN 0-688-07610-6 Subj: Animals. Animals – mice. Careers – artists. Friendship.

The magic wings: a tale from China ill. by Robert Andrew Parker. Dutton, 1983. ISBN 0-525-44062-3 Subj: Activities – flying. Behavior – wishing. Cumulative tales. Folk & fairy tales. Foreign lands – China. Seasons – spring.

Oom razoom; or, Go I know not where, Bring back I know not what ill. by Dennis McDermott. Morrow, 1991. ISBN 0-688-09417-1 Subj: Folk & fairy tales. Foreign lands – Russia. Magic.

Step by step ill. by Jos. A. Smith. Morrow, 1994. ISBN 0-688-10316-2 Subj: Friendship. Insects – ants. Insects – grasshoppers.

Sun Mother wakes the world ill. by Bronwyn Bancroft. HarperCollins, 2004. ISBN 0-688-13916-7 Subj: Australian aborigines. Creation. Folk & fairy tales. Foreign lands – Australia.

White wave: a Chinese tale ill. by Ed Young. Crowell, 1979. ISBN 0-690-03894-1 Subj: Folk & fairy tales. Foreign lands – China.

Wolman, Bernice. *Taking turns* ill. by Catherine Stock. Atheneum, 1992. ISBN 0-689-31677-1 Subj: Poetry.

Wolski, Slawomir. *Tiger cat* trans. by Elizabeth D. Crawford; ill. by Józef Wilkon. Holt, 1988. ISBN 0-8050-0741-5 Subj: Animals – tigers. Pets.

Wondriska, William. *Mr. Brown and Mr. Gray* ill. by author. Holt, 1968. Subj: Animals – pigs. Emotions – happiness. Money.

Puff ill. by author. Pantheon, 1960. Subj: Self-concept. Trains.

The stop ill. by author. Holt, 1972. ISBN 0-03-091982-7 Subj: Animals – horses, ponies. Character traits – kindness to animals. Desert. Emotions – fear. Indians of North America. Weather – storms.

The tomato patch ill. by author. Holt, 1964. Subj: Plants. Violence, nonviolence. Weapons.

Wong, Benedict Norbert. *Lo & behold* ill. by author. Taiji, 2003. ISBN 0-9728192-0-7 Subj: Dragons. Ethnic groups in the U.S. – Chinese Americans. Family life. Food. Self-concept.

Lo & behold, good enough to eat ill. by author. Taiji, 2003. ISBN 0-9728192-1-5 Subj: Dragons. Ethnic groups in the U.S. – Chinese Americans. Family life. Food. Self-concept.

Wong, Herbert H. *My goldfish* by Herbert H. Wong & Matthew F. Vessel; ill. by Arvis L. Stewart. Addison-Wesley, 1969. Subj: Fish. Pets. Science.

My ladybug by Herbert H. Wong & Matthew F. Vessel; ill. by Marie Nonast Bohlen. Addison-Wesley, 1969. Subj: Insects – ladybugs. Science.

My plant by Herbert H. Wong & Matthew F. Vessel; ill. by Richard Cuffari. Addison-Wesley, 1976. ISBN 0-201-08760-X Subj: Plants. Science.

Our caterpillars by Herbert H. Wong & Matthew F. Vessel; ill. by Arvis L. Stewart. Addison-Wesley, 1977. ISBN 0-201-08764-2 Subj: Insects – butterflies, caterpillars. Metamorphosis. Science.

Our earthworms by Herbert H. Wong & Matthew F. Vessel; ill. by Bill Davis. Addison-Wesley, 1977. ISBN 0-201-08766-9 Subj: Animals – worms. Science.

Our tree by Herbert H. Wong & Matthew F. Vessel; ill. by Kenneth Longtemps. Addison-Wesley, 1969. Subj: Science. Trees.

Wong, Janet S. *Buzz* ill. by Margaret Chodos-Irvine. Harcourt, 2000. ISBN 0-15-201923-5 Subj: Family life. Insects – bees. Noise, sounds.

Grump ill. by John Wallace. McElderry, 2001. ISBN 0-689-83485-3 Subj: Babies. Family life – mothers. Rhyming text. Sleep.

This next New Year ill. by Yangsook Choi. Farrar, 2000. ISBN 0-374-35503-7 Subj: Ethnic groups in the U.S. Family life. Holidays – Chinese New Year.

The trip back home ill. by Bo Jia. Harcourt, 2000. ISBN 0-15-200784-9 Subj: Activities – traveling. Ethnic groups in the U.S. – Korean Americans. Family life. Foreign lands – Korea.

Wood, A. J. *Amazing animals* ill. by Helen Ward. Boyds Mills, 1991. ISBN 1-878093-46-0 Subj: Animals.

Beautiful birds ill. by Helen Ward. Boyds Mills, 1991. ISBN 1-878093-47-9 Subj: Birds.

Look! The ultimate spot-the-difference book ill. by April Wilson. Dial, 1990. ISBN 0-8037-0925-0 Subj: Concepts. Games. Wordless.

Wood, Audrey. *Alphabet adventure* ill. by Bruce Wood. Blue Sky, 2001. ISBN 0-439-08069-X Subj: ABC books. Behavior – lost & found possessions.

Birdsong ill. by Robert Florczak. Harcourt, 1997. ISBN 0-15-200014-3 Subj: Birds. Flowers. Songs.

The Bunyans ill. by David Shannon. Blue Sky, 1996. ISBN 0-590-48089-8 Subj: Mythical creatures. Nature. Tall tales. U.S. history – frontier & pioneer life.

The Christmas adventure of Space Elf Sam ill. by Bruce Robert Wood. Blue Sky, 1998. ISBN 0-590-03143-0 Subj: Aliens. Holidays – Christmas. Santa Claus. Space & space ships.

A cowboy Christmas ill. by Robert Florczak. S&S, 2000. ISBN 0-689-82190-5 Subj: Accidents. Cowboys, cowgirls. Family life. Holidays – Christmas.

Elbert's bad word ill. by author. Harcourt, 1988. ISBN 0-15-225320-3 Subj: Behavior – misbehavior. Family life. Language.

The flying dragon room ill. by Mark Teague. Blue Sky, 1996. ISBN 0-590-48193-2 Subj: Activities – making things. Imagination. Magic.

Heckedy Peg ill. by Don Wood. Harcourt, 1987. ISBN 0-15-233678-8 Subj: Behavior – talking to strangers. Character traits – cleverness. Days of the week, months of the year. Folk & fairy tales. Food. Witches.

Jubal's wish ill. by Don Wood. Blue Sky, 2000. ISBN 0-439-16964-X Subj: Behavior – wishing. Friendship. Frogs & toads. Reptiles – lizards.

King Bidgood's in the bathtub ill. by Don Wood. Harcourt, 1985. ISBN 0-15-242730-9 Subj: Activities. Activities – bathing. Caldecott award honor books. Humorous stories. Royalty – kings.

Little Penguin's tale ill. by author. Harcourt, 1989. ISBN 0-15-246475-1 Subj: Activities – dancing. Animals. Animals – whales. Birds. Birds – penguins. Foreign lands – Antarctic.

Merry Christmas, big hungry bear (Wood, Don)

Moonflute ill. by Don Wood. Harcourt, 1986. ISBN 0-15-255337-1 Subj: Bedtime. Moon. Night. Sleep.

The napping house ill. by Don Wood. Harcourt, 1984. ISBN 0-15-256708-9 Subj: Animals. Cumulative tales. Family life – grandmothers. Rhyming text. Sleep.

The napping house wakes up ill. by Don Wood. Harcourt, 1994. ISBN 0-15-200890-X Subj: Animals. Family life – grandmothers. Format, unusual – toy & movable books. Insects – fleas. Rhyming text. Sleep.

Oh my baby bear! ill. by author. Harcourt, 1990. ISBN 0-15-257698-3 Subj: Animals – bears. Bedtime. Behavior – growing up.

Piggies (Wood, David)

Piggies [board book] (Wood, David)

The rainbow bridge ill. by Robert Florczak. Harcourt, 1995. ISBN 0-15-265475-5 Subj: Animals – dolphins. Creation. Folk & fairy tales. Indians of North America – Chumash.

Silly Sally ill. by author. Harcourt, 1992. ISBN 0-15-274428-2 Subj: Activities – traveling. Animals. Cumulative tales. Rhyming text.

Sweet dream pie ill. by Mark Teague. Blue Sky, 1998. ISBN 0-590-96204-3 Subj: Bedtime. Dreams.

Ten little fish ill. by Bruce Wood. Blue Sky, 2004. ISBN 0-439-63569-1 Subj: Counting, numbers. Fish. Foreign lands – South Sea Islands. Rhyming text.

The Tickleoctopus ill. by Don Wood. Harcourt, 1994. ISBN 0-15-287000-8 Subj: Activities – playing. Cavemen. Family life. Mythical creatures.

Weird parents ill. by author. Dial, 1990. ISBN 0-8037-0649-9 Subj: Character traits – being different. Emotions – embarrassment. Family life.

When the root children wake up ill. by Ned Bittinger. Scholastic, 2002. Retelling of: Etwas von den Wurzelkindern by Sibylle Olfers. ISBN 0-590-42517-X Subj: Flowers. Insects. Nature. Seasons – spring. Songs.

Wood, David. *Happy birthday, Mouse!* (Fowler, Richard)

Piggies by Don & Audrey Wood; ill. by Don Wood. Harcourt, 1991. ISBN 0-15-256341-5 Subj: Animals – pigs. Games.

Piggies [board book] by Don & Audrey Wood; ill. by Don Wood. Harcourt, 1991. ISBN 0-15-205632-7 Subj: Animals – pigs. Format, unusual – board books. Games.

Silly spider! ill. by Richard Fowler. Harcourt, 1998. ISBN 0-15-201842-5 Subj: Format, unusual – toy & movable books. Spiders.

Wood, Don. *Merry Christmas, big hungry bear* by Don Wood & Audrey Wood; ill. by Don Wood. Blue Sky, 2002. ISBN 0-439-32092-5 Subj: Animals – mice. Behavior – sharing. Gifts. Holidays – Christmas. Shopping.

Wood, Douglas. *Grandad's prayers of the earth* ill. by P. J. Lynch. Candlewick, 1999. ISBN 0-7636-0660-X Subj: Death. Emotions – grief. Family life – grandfathers. Nature.

Making the world ill. by Yoshi & Hibiki Miyazaki. S&S, 1998. ISBN 0-689-81358-9 Subj: Creation. Nature. World.

Northwoods cradle song ill. by Lisa Desimini. S&S, 1996. ISBN 0-689-80503-9 Subj: Ethnic groups in the U.S. – Amish. Family life – mothers. Forest, woods. Indians of North America. Lullabies. Night. Poetry.

Old Turtle ill. by Cheng-Khee Chee. Pfeifer-Hamilton, 1991. ISBN 0-938586-48-3 Subj: Animals. Ecology. Religion.

Rabbit and the moon ill. by Leslie Baker. Muppet Pr., 1986. ISBN 0-689-80769-4 Subj: Animals – rabbits. Folk & fairy tales. Indians of North America – Cree. Moon.

What dads can't do ill. by Doug Cushman. S&S, 2000. ISBN 0-689-82620-6 Subj: Family life – fathers.

What moms can't do ill. by Doug Cushman. S&S, 2000. ISBN 0-689-83358-X Subj: Family life – mothers.

What teachers can't do ill. by Doug Cushman. S&S, 2002. ISBN 0-689-84644-4 Subj: Careers – teachers. Dinosaurs. School.

Wood, Jacqueline. *Never say boo to a goose!* ill. by Clare Beaton. Barefoot, 2002. ISBN 1-84148-255-2 Subj: Animals. Animals – cats. Birds – geese. Farms.

Wood, Jakki. *Across the big blue sea* ill. by author. National Geographic, 1998. ISBN 0-7922-7308-7 Subj: Animals. Boats, ships. Nature. Sea & seashore.

Dads are such fun ill. by Rog Bonner. S&S, 1992. ISBN 0-671-75342-8 Subj: Activities – playing. Animals. Family life – fathers.

Fiddle-i-fee ill. by author. Bradbury, 1994. ISBN 0-02-793396-2 Subj: Animals. Cumulative tales. Music. Noise, sounds.

Moo moo, brown cow ill. by Rog Bonner. Harcourt, 1992. ISBN 0-15-200533-1 Subj: Animals. Animals – cats. Concepts – color. Counting, numbers. Farms.

One bear with bees in his hair ill. by author. Dutton, 1991. ISBN 0-525-44695-8 Subj: Animals – bears. Counting, numbers. Rhyming text.

Wood, Jenny. *The animal kingdom* ill. by Andrew Bale. Macmillan, 1992. ISBN 0-02-793395-4 Subj: Animals. Nature.

I wonder why kangaroos have pouches and other questions about baby animals ill. by author. Kingfisher, 2003. ISBN 0-7534-5661-3 Subj: Animals. Animals – babies. Family life – parents.

Wood, John Norris. *Jungles* ed. by Janet Schulman; ill. by Kevin Dean. Knopf, 1987. ISBN 0-394-87802-7 Subj: Animals. Behavior – hiding. Format, unusual. Jungle.

Oceans ill. by Mark Harrison. Knopf, 1985. ISBN 0-394-87583-4 Subj: Behavior – hiding. Fish. Format, unusual. Sea & seashore.

Wood, Joyce. *Grandmother Lucy goes on a picnic* ill. by Frank Francis. Collins-World, 1976. ISBN 0-529-05288-1 Subj: Activities – picnicking. Activities – walking. Family life – grandmothers.

Grandmother Lucy in her garden ill. by Frank Francis. Collins-World, 1975. ISBN 0-529-05239-3 Subj: Family life – grandmothers. Foreign lands – England. Seasons. Seasons – spring.

Wood, Leslie. *A dog called Mischief* ill. by author. Oxford Univ. Pr., 1997. ISBN 0-19-849014-3 Subj: Animals – dogs. Behavior – hiding things. Food.

Wood, Michele. *Going back home* ill. by author; trans. by Toyomi Igus. Children's Book Pr., 1996. ISBN 0-89239-137-5 Subj: Art. Careers – artists. Ethnic groups in the U.S. – African Americans.

Wood, Muriel. *Old bird* (Morck, Irene)

Wood, Nancy C. *Little wrangler* ill. by Myron Wood. Doubleday, 1966. Subj: Cowboys, cowgirls.

Wood, Tim. *Gymnastics* photos by Chris Fairclough. Watts, 1989. ISBN 0-531-10826-0 Subj: Sports – gymnastics.

Motor racing ill. by Chris Fairclough. Watts, 1989. ISBN 0-531-10828-7 Subj: Automobiles. Sports – racing.

Motorcycling ill. by Chris Fairclough. Watts, 1989. ISBN 0-531-10827-9 Subj: Sports – racing.

Woodcock, Louise Phinney. *The very little dog: and, The smart little kitty* (Skaar, Grace Marion)

Woodhouse, Jayne. *Pieter Bruegel* ill. with photos. Heinemann, 2001. ISBN 1-57572-344-1 Subj: Activities – painting. Art. Careers – artists. Foreign lands – Belgium.

Wooding, Sharon L. *Arthur's Christmas wish* ill. by author. Atheneum, 1986. ISBN 0-689-31211-3 Subj: Animals – mice. Behavior – wishing. Holidays – Christmas.

The painter's cat ill. by author. Putnam, 1994. ISBN 0-399-22414-9 Subj: Animals – cats. Art. Behavior – running away. Careers – artists.

Woodman, Allen. *The bear who came to stay* by Allen Woodman & David Kirby; ill. by Harvey Stevenson. Bradbury, 1994. ISBN 0-02-793397-0 Subj: Animals – bears. Family life. Forest, woods.

Cows are going to Paris (Kirby, David K.)

Woodruff, Elvira. *Can you guess where we're going?* ill. by Cynthia Fisher. Holiday, 1998. ISBN 0-8234-1387-X Subj: Family life – grandfathers. Libraries.

The memory coat ill. by Michael Dooling. Scholastic, 1999. ISBN 0-590-67717-9 Subj: Clothing – coats. Ethnic groups in the U.S. – Russian Americans. Immigrants. Jewish culture. Memories, memory.

Mrs. McCloskey's monkeys ill. by Jill Kastner. Scholastic, 1991. ISBN 0-590-41233-7 Subj: Animals – monkeys. Behavior – misbehavior. Family life – brothers. Zoos.

Show and tell ill. by Denise Brunkus. Holiday, 1991. ISBN 0-8234-0883-3 Subj: Bubbles. Magic. School.

Tubtime ill. by Suçie Stevenson. Holiday, 1990. ISBN 0-8234-0777-2 Subj: Activities – bathing. Bubbles. Family life – brothers & sisters. Imagination.

The wing shop ill. by Stephen Gammell. Holiday, 1991. ISBN 0-8234-0825-6 Subj: Activities – flying. Moving.

Woods, Noah. *Tom cat* ill. by author. Random House, 2004. ISBN 0-375-92497-3 Subj: Animals – cats. Character traits – individuality. Self-concept.

Woods, Theresa. *Jaguars* ill. with photos. Child's World, 2001. ISBN 1-56766-885-2 Subj: Animals – jaguars.

Woodson, Jacqueline. *Coming on home soon* ill. by E. B. Lewis. Putnam, 2004. ISBN 0-399-23748-8 Subj: Caldecott award honor books. Ethnic groups in the U.S. – African Americans. Family life – grandmothers. Family life – mothers. U.S. history. War.

The other side ill. by Earl B. Lewis. Putnam, 2001. ISBN 0-399-23116-1 Subj: Cities, towns. Prejudice. Seasons – summer.

Sweet, sweet memory ill. by Earl B. Lewis. Hyperion, 2000. ISBN 0-7868-2191-4 Subj: Death. Emotions – grief. Ethnic groups in the U.S. – African Americans. Family life – grandparents. Memories, memory.

We had a picnic this Sunday past ill. by Diane Greenseid. Hyperion, 1997. ISBN 0-7868-2192-2 Subj: Activities – picnicking. Ethnic groups in the U.S. – African Americans. Family life.

Woodtor, Dee. *Big meeting* ill. by Dolores Johnson. Atheneum, 1996. ISBN 0-689-31993-9 Subj: Activities – traveling. Ethnic groups in the U.S. – African Americans. Family life – aunts, uncles. Family life – grandparents. Religion. Seasons – summer.

Woodworth, Viki. *Daisy the dancing cow* ill. by author. Boyds Mills, 2003. ISBN 1-59078-059-0 Subj: Animals – bulls, cows. Careers – dancers.

Daisy the firecow ill. by author. Boyds Mills, 2001. ISBN 1-56397-934-9 Subj: Animals – bulls, cows. Careers – firefighters.

Fairy tale jokes ill. by author. Child's World, 1993. ISBN 0-89565-862-3 Subj: Folk & fairy tales. Riddles & jokes.

Woolaver, Lance. *Christmas with the rural mail* ill. by Maud Lewis. Nimbus Pub., 1981. ISBN 0-920852-04-1 Subj: Foreign lands – Canada. Holidays – Christmas. Poetry.

From Ben Loman to the sea ill. by Maud Lewis. Nimbus Pub., 1981. ISBN 0-920852-05-X Subj: Behavior – running away. Poetry. Sea & seashore. Seasons – spring.

Wooldridge, Connie Nordhielm. *The legend of Strap Buckner* ill. by Andrew Glass. Holiday, 2001. ISBN 0-8234-1536-8 Subj: Devil. Folk & fairy tales. Tall tales.

When Esther Morris headed west ill. by Jacqueline Rogers. Holiday, 2001. ISBN 0-8234-1597-X Subj: Gender roles. U.S. history.

Wicked Jack ill. by Will Hillenbrand. Holiday, 1995. ISBN 0-8234-1101-X Subj: Behavior – wishing. Character traits – meanness. Devil. Folk & fairy tales.

Woolf, Virginia. *Nurse Lugton's curtain* ill. by Julie Vivas. Harcourt, 1982. ISBN 0-15-200545-5 Subj: Activities – sewing. Animals. Careers – nurses. Imagination. Sleep.

Woolley, Catherine. *see* Thayer, Jane

Worley, Daryl. *Billy and the attic adventure* ill. by John Daab. Tyke Corp., 1989. ISBN 0-924067-00-4 Subj: Family life – fathers. Homes, houses.

Wormell, Christopher. *The big ugly monster and the little stone rabbit* ill. by author. Knopf, 2004. ISBN 0-375-92891-X Subj: Animals – rabbits. Emotions – loneliness. Friendship. Monsters.

Blue Rabbit and friends ill. by author. Fogelman, 2000. ISBN 0-8037-2499-3 Subj: Animals. Animals – rabbits. Friendship. Homes, houses.

Blue Rabbit and the runaway wheel ill. by author. Fogelman, 2001. ISBN 0-8037-2508-6 Subj: Animals. Animals – rabbits. Sports – bicycling.

The new alphabet of animals ill. by author. Running Pr., 2002. ISBN 0-7624-1347-6 Subj: ABC books. Animals.

Puff, puff, chugga-chugga ill. by author. McElderry, 2001. ISBN 0-689-83986-3 Subj: Animals. Trains.

Wormell, Mary. *Bernard the angry rooster* ill. by author. Farrar, 2001. ISBN 0-374-30670-2 Subj: Animals. Behavior – bad day. Birds – chickens. Emotions – anger.

Hilda Hen's happy birthday ill. by author. Harcourt, 1995. ISBN 0-15-200299-5 Subj: Animals. Birds – chickens. Birthdays. Farms.

Hilda Hen's search ill. by author. Harcourt, 1994. ISBN 0-15-200069-0 Subj: Birds – chickens. Eggs. Farms.

Why not? ill. by author. Farrar, 2000. ISBN 0-374-38422-3 Subj: Animals. Animals – babies. Animals – cats. Character traits – questioning. Farms.

Worth, Bonnie. *Jumbo: the most famous elephant in the world* ill. by Christopher Santoro. Random House, 2001. ISBN 0-375-91014-X Subj: Animals – elephants. Circus.

Peter Cottontail's surprise ill. by Greg Hildebrandt. Unicorn Publishing House, 1985. ISBN 0-88101-015-4 Subj: Animals – rabbits. Birthdays. Parties. Seasons – spring.

Worth, Valerie. *At Christmastime* ill. by Antonio Frasconi. HarperCollins, 1992. ISBN 0-06-205020-6 Subj: Holidays. Holidays – Christmas. Poetry.

Worthington, Joan. *Teddy bear farmer* (Worthington, Phoebe)

Worthington, Phoebe. *Teddy bear baker* by Phoebe & Selby Worthington; ill. by authors. Warne, 1980. ISBN 0-7232-2339-4 Subj: Careers – bakers. Foreign lands – England. Toys – bears.

Teddy bear coalman: a story for the very young by Phoebe & Selby Worthington; ill. by authors. Warne, 1980. ISBN 0-7232-2052-2 Subj: Foreign lands – England. Toys – bears.

Teddy bear farmer by Phoebe & Joan Worthington; ill. by authors. Viking, 1985. ISBN 0-670-80342-1 Subj: Animals. Farms. Toys – bears.

Worthington, Selby. *Teddy bear baker* (Worthington, Phoebe)

Teddy bear coalman: a story for the very young (Worthington, Phoebe)

Worthy, Judith. *Eyes* ill. by Beba Hall. Doubleday, 1989. ISBN 0-385-24966-7 Subj: Anatomy – eyes. Animals.

Wouters, Anne. *This book is for us* ill. by author. Dutton, 1992. ISBN 0-525-44882-9 Subj: Animals – moles. Animals – polar bears. Night. Wordless.

This book is too small ill. by author. Dutton, 1992. ISBN 0-525-44881-0 Subj: Animals – moles. Animals – polar bears. Wordless.

Woychuk, Denis. *The other side of the wall* ill. by Kim Howard. Lothrop, 1991. ISBN 0-688-09895-9 Subj: Animals – hippopotamuses. Animals – mice. Emotions – love. Middle Ages.

Pirates ill. by Kim Howard. Lothrop, 1992. ISBN 0-688-10337-5 Subj: Animals – hippopotamuses. Animals – mice. Pirates.

Wright, Betty Ren. *The blizzard* ill. by Ronald Himler. Holiday, 2003. ISBN 0-8234-1656-9 Subj: Birthdays. School. Weather – blizzards.

The cat next door ill. by Gail Owens. Holiday, 1991. ISBN 0-8234-0896-5 Subj: Animals – cats. Death. Emotions – grief. Family life – grandmothers.

Pet detectives! ill. by Kevin O'Malley. BridgeWater, 1999. ISBN 0-8167-4952-3 Subj: Animals – cats. Animals – dogs. Crime. Rhyming text.

Wright, Catherine (Catherine E.). *Steamboat Annie and the thousand-pound catfish* ill. by Howard Fine. Philomel, 2001. ISBN 0-399-23331-8 Subj: Activities – singing. Fish. Tall tales.

Wright, Christine. *Bedtime prayers* ill. by Roma Bishop. Baker Bks., 2002. ISBN 0-8010-1226-0 Subj: Bedtime. Religion.

Wright, Cliff. *Santa's ark* ill. by author. Millbrook, 1997. ISBN 0-7613-0314-6 Subj: Animals – babies. Animals – reindeer. Holidays – Christmas. Santa Claus.

Wright, Courtni Crump. *Journey to freedom* ill. by Gershom Griffith. Holiday, 1994. ISBN 0-8234-1096-X Subj: Character traits – freedom. Ethnic groups in the U.S. – African Americans. Slavery. U.S. history.

Jumping the broom ill. by Gershom Griffith. Holiday, 1994. ISBN 0-8234-1042-0 Subj: Ethnic groups in the U.S. – African Americans. Slavery. U.S. history. Weddings.

Wagon train: a family goes west in 1865 ill. by Gershom Griffith. Holiday, 1995. ISBN 0-8234-1152-4 Subj: Activities – traveling. Ethnic groups in the U.S. – African Americans. U.S. history – frontier & pioneer life.

Wright, Dare. *The doll and the kitten* photos by author. Doubleday, 1960. Subj: Animals – cats. Toys – bears. Toys – dolls.

Edith and Midnight photos by author. Doubleday, 1978. ISBN 0-385-14156-4 Subj: Toys – bears. Toys – dolls.

Edith and Mr. Bear photos by author. Random House, 1964. ISBN 0-618-00332-0 Subj: Behavior – lying. Behavior – running away. Toys – bears. Toys – dolls.

Edith and the duckling photos by author. Doubleday, 1981. ISBN 0-385-17101-3 Subj: Birds – ducks. Eggs. Toys – bears. Toys – dolls.

A gift from the lonely doll ill. by author. Houghton, 2001. ISBN 0-618-07181-4 Subj: Clothing – scarves. Emotions – loneliness. Gifts. Holidays – Christmas. Toys – bears. Toys – dolls.

The lonely doll photos by author. Houghton Mifflin, 1998. ISBN 0-395-90112-X Subj: Emotions – loneliness. Toys – bears. Toys – dolls.

The lonely doll learns a lesson photos by author. Random House, 1961. Subj: Animals – cats. Pets. Toys – bears. Toys – dolls.

Look at a calf photos by author. Random House, 1974. ISBN 0-394-92776-1 Subj: Animals – bulls, cows. Farms.

Look at a colt photos by author. Random House, 1969. Subj: Animals – horses, ponies. Farms.

Look at a kitten photos by author. Random House, 1975. ISBN 0-394-93123-8 Subj: Animals – cats.

Wright, Freire. *Beauty and the beast* ill. by adapt. David & Charles, 1985. ISBN 0-7182-6091-0 Subj: Character traits – appearance. Character traits – loyalty. Emotions – love. Folk & fairy tales. Magic.

Wright, Jill. *The old woman and the jar of ums* ill. by Glen Rounds. Putnam, 1990. ISBN 0-399-21736-3 Subj: Behavior – misbehavior. Magic.

The old woman and the Willy Nilly Man ill. by Glen Rounds. Putnam, 1987. ISBN 0-399-21355-4 Subj: Activities – dancing. Behavior – trickery. Clothing. Folk & fairy tales. Humorous stories.

Wright, Joan Richards. *Bugs* (Parker, Nancy Winslow)

Wright, Josephine Lord. *Cotton Cat and Martha Mouse* ill. by John E. Johnson. Dutton, 1966. Subj: Animals – cats. Animals – mice. Behavior – sharing. Poetry.

Wright, Lesley. *A child's book of values* ill. by author. DK, 2001. ISBN 0-7894-6518-3 Subj: Religion.

Wright, Lillian. *Hearing* ill. by author. Raintree, 1995. ISBN 0-8114-5516-5 Subj: Senses – hearing.

Seeing ill. by author. Raintree, 1995. ISBN 0-8114-5515-7 Subj: Senses – sight.

Smelling and tasting ill. by author. Raintree, 1995. ISBN 0-8114-5518-1 Subj: Senses – smell. Senses – taste.

Touching ill. by author. Raintree, 1995. ISBN 0-8114-5517-3 Subj: Senses – touch.

Wright, Martin. *Granny Stickleback* (Moore, John)

Wright, Rachel. *My amazing body* ill. with photos. Two-Can, 2001. ISBN 1-58728-212-7 Subj: Anatomy. Science.

Plundering pirates: a where's Waldo? fun fact book ill. by author. Candlewick, 2000. Based on the characters created by Martin Handford. ISBN 0-7636-1300-2 Subj: Picture puzzles. Pirates.

Wright, Sue (Sue M.). *The Christmas path: a legend of the luminarias* ill. by David Wenzel. Scholastic, 1998. ISBN 0-590-04709-4 Subj: Folk & fairy tales. Holidays – Christmas. Light, lights. Religion – Nativity.

Wright-Frierson, Virginia. *An island scrapbook* ill. by author. S&S, 1998. ISBN 0-689-81563-8 Subj: Animals. Ecology. Islands. Plants.

Wundrow, Deanna. *Jungle drum* cut-paper ill. by Susan Swan. Millbrook, 1999. ISBN 0-7613-1270-6 Subj: Animals. Jungle. Noise, sounds.

Wyart, Peter. *The shepherds' tale* (Dowley, Tim)

The wise men's tale (Dowley, Tim)

Wyeth, Sharon Dennis. *Always my dad* ill. by Raúl Colón. Knopf, 1995. ISBN 0-679-93447-2 Subj: Behavior – needing someone. Country. Ethnic groups in the U.S. – African Americans. Family life – fathers. Family life – grandparents.

Something beautiful ill. by Chris K. Soentpiet. Doubleday, 1998. ISBN 0-385-32239-9 Subj: Cities, towns. Communities, neighborhoods. Ethnic groups in the U.S. – African Americans.

Wyler, Rose. *Puddles and ponds* ill. by Steven James Petruccio. Messner, 1990. ISBN 0-671-66348-8 Subj: Animals. Nature. Science. Water.

Raindrops and rainbows ill. by Steven James Petruccio. Messner, 1989. ISBN 0-671-66346-1 Subj: Science. Weather – rain. Weather – rainbows.

The starry sky ill. by Steven James Petruccio. Messner, 1989. ISBN 0-671-66345-3 Subj: Earth. Science. Sky. Stars.

Wyllie, Stephen. *Dinner with fox* ill. by Korky Paul. Dial, 1990. ISBN 0-8037-0796-7 Subj: Animals – foxes. Animals – wolves. Food. Format, unusual – toy & movable books.

Ghost train ill. by Brian Lee. Dial, 1992. ISBN 0-8037-1163-8 Subj: Format, unusual. Ghosts. Trains.

The great race ill. by Anni Axworthy. HarperCollins, 1987. ISBN 0-694-00126-0 Subj: Animals. Format, unusual. Rebuses. Sports – racing.

Snappity snap ill. by Maureen Roffey. HarperCollins, 1989. ISBN 0-06-026630-9 Subj: Activities – photographing. Animals. Counting, numbers. Format, unusual – toy & movable books.

White Rabbit builds a dream house ill. by Anni Axworthy. Ideals, 1990. ISBN 0-8249-8363-7 Subj: Animals – rabbits. Format, unusual. Homes, houses.

Wyndham, Robert. *The Chinese Mother Goose rhymes* (Mother Goose)

Wynne-Jones, Tim. *Builder of the moon* ill. by Ian Wallace. Macmillan, 1989. ISBN 0-689-50472-1 Subj: Moon. Problem solving. Space & space ships. Toys – blocks.

The hour of the frog ill. by Catharine O'Neill. Little, 1990. ISBN 0-316-96309-7 Subj: Frogs & toads. Night. Noise, sounds.

On Tumbledown Hill ill. by Du?an Petricic. Red Deer Pr., 1998. ISBN 0-88995-186-1 Subj: Animals – rabbits. Careers – artists. Emotions – fear. Language. Monsters. Picture puzzles. Rhyming text.

Zoom upstream ill. by Eric Beddows. HarperCollins, 1994. ISBN 0-06-022978-0 Subj: Animals – cats. Foreign lands – Egypt.

Wynot, Jillian. *The Mother's Day sandwich* ill. by Maxie Chambliss. Watts, 1990. ISBN 0-531-08457-4 Subj: Family life – mothers. Food. Holidays – Mother's Day.

Wyse, Lois. *How to take your grandmother to the museum* by Lois Wyse & Molly Rose Goldman; ill. by Marie-Louise Gay. Workman, [pub. in association with the] American Museum of Natural History, 1998. ISBN 0-7611-0990-0 Subj: Family life – grandmothers. Museums.

Two guppies, a turtle and Aunt Edna ill. by Roger Coast. Collins-World, 1966. Subj: Family life – aunts, uncles. Fish. Problem solving. Reptiles – turtles, tortoises. Telephone.

Xiong, Blia. *Nine-in-one Grr! Grr!* adapt. by Cathy Spagnoli; ill. by Nancy Hom. Childrens Pr., 1989. ISBN 0-89239-048-4 Subj: Animals – tigers. Folk & fairy tales. Foreign lands – Laos.

Yabuki, Seiji. *I love the morning* ill. by author. Collins-World, 1969. Subj: Emotions – happiness. Morning.

Yabuuchi, Masayuki. *Animals sleeping* ill. by author. Putnam, 1983. ISBN 0-399-20983-2 Subj: Animals. Science. Sleep.

Whose baby? ill. by author. Putnam, 1985. ISBN 0-399-21210-8 Subj: Animals.

Whose footprints? ill. by author. Putnam, 1985. ISBN 0-399-21209-4 Subj: Animals.

Yaccarino, Dan. *Deep in the jungle* ill. by author. Atheneum, 2000. ISBN 0-689-82235-9 Subj: Animals. Animals – lions. Behavior – dissatisfaction. Circus.

First day on a strange new planet ill. by author. Hyperion, 2000. ISBN 0-7868-2499-9 Subj: Aliens. Planets. School. Space & space ships.

Five little ducks ill. by author. HarperFestival, 2005. ISBN 0-06-073465-5 Subj: Animals. Birds – ducks. Format, unusual – board books. Rhyming text. Songs.

Good night, Mr. Night ill. by author. Harcourt, 1997. ISBN 0-15-201319-9 Subj: Bedtime. Dreams. Night.

If I had a robot ill. by author. Viking, 1996. ISBN 0-670-86936-8 Subj: Behavior. Family life. Robots.

The lima bean monster ill. by Adam McCauley. Walker, 2001. ISBN 0-8027-8777-0 Subj: Food. Monsters.

New pet ill. by author. Hyperion, 2001. ISBN 0-7868-2500-6 Subj: Aliens. Pets. Planets. Space & space ships.

An octopus followed me home ill. by author. Viking, 1997. ISBN 0-670-87401-9 Subj: Animals. Octopuses. Pets.

Oswald ill. by author. Atheneum, 2001. ISBN 0-689-84252-X Subj: Animals – dogs. Moving. Octopuses. Pets.

So big ill. by author. HarperFestival, 2001. ISBN 0-694-01509-1 Subj: Animals. Concepts – size. Format, unusual – toy & movable books. Games.

Unlovable ill. by author. Holt, 2001. ISBN 0-8050-6321-8 Subj: Animals – dogs. Friendship. Self-concept.

Zoom! Zoom! Zoom! I'm off to the moon! ill. by author. Scholastic, 1997. ISBN 0-590-95610-8 Subj: Moon. Rhyming text. Space & space ships.

Yacowitz, Caryn. *The jade stone* ill. by Ju-Hong Chen. Holiday, 1992. ISBN 0-8234-0919-8 Subj: Careers – artists. Folk & fairy tales. Foreign lands – China. Royalty – emperors.

Pumpkin fiesta ill. by Joe Cepeda. HarperCollins, 1998. ISBN 0-06-027659-2 Subj: Fairs, festivals. Foreign lands – Mexico. Gardens, gardening. Plants.

Yaffe, Alan. *The magic meatballs* ill. by Karen Born Andersen. Dial, 1979. ISBN 0-8037-5140-0 Subj: Behavior – dissatisfaction. Family life. Magic.

Yagawa, Sumiko. *The crane wife* trans. from Japanese by Katherine Paterson; ill. by Suekichi Akaba. Morrow, 1982. ISBN 0-688-00496-2 Subj: Activities – weaving. Birds – cranes. Character traits – kindness to animals. Folk & fairy tales. Foreign lands – Japan.

Yagelski, Robert. *The day the lifting bridge stuck* ill. by Jennifer Beck Harris. Bradbury, 1992. ISBN 0-02-793595-7 Subj: Bridges. Machines. Problem solving. Traffic, traffic signs.

Yagya, Genichiro. *All about scabs* ill. by author; trans. by Amanda Mayer Stinchecum. Kane/Miller, 1998. ISBN 0-916291-82-0 Subj: Health & fitness. Hygiene.

Yamaguchi, Tohr. *Two crabs and the moonlight* ill. by Marianne Yamaguchi. Holt, 1965. Subj: Crustaceans – crabs. Moon.

Yamashita, Haruo. *Mice at the beach* ill. by Kazuo Iwamura. Morrow, 1987. ISBN 0-688-07064-7 Subj: Animals – mice. Family life. Safety. Sea & seashore – beaches.

Yamate, Sandra S. *Char siu bao boy* ill. by Carolina Yao. Polychrome Pub., 2000. ISBN 1-879965-19-4 Subj: Ethnic groups in the U.S. – Chinese Americans. Food.

Yamawaki, Yuriko. *Guri and Gura* (Nakagawa, Rieko)

Guri and Gura's special gift (Nakagawa, Rieko)

Yardley, Joanna. *The red ball* ill. by author. Harcourt, 1991. ISBN 0-15-200894-2 Subj: Family life. Imagination. Toys – balls.

Yardley, Thompson. *Buy now, pay later* ill. by author. Millbrook, 1992. ISBN 1-56294-149-6 Subj: Ecology. Money. Shopping.

Yardumian, Miryam. *see* Miryam

Yaroshevskaya, Kim. *Little Kim's doll* ill. by Luc Melanson. Douglas & McIntyre, 1999. ISBN 0-88899-353-6 Subj: Birthdays. Foreign lands – Russia. Gender roles. Toys – dolls.

Yashima, Mitsu. *Momo's kitten* ill. by Taro Yashima. Viking, 1961. Subj: Animals – cats. Ethnic groups in the U.S. – Japanese Americans.

Plenty to watch ill. by Taro Yashima. Viking, 1954. Subj: Foreign lands – Japan.

Yashima, Taro. *Crow boy* ill. by author. Viking, 1955. ISBN 0-670-24931-9 Subj: Caldecott award honor books. Character traits – shyness. Emotions – loneliness. Foreign lands – Japan. School.

Momo's kitten (Yashima, Mitsu)

Seashore story ill. by author. Viking, 1967. Subj: Caldecott award honor books. Folk & fairy tales. Reptiles – turtles, tortoises. Sea & seashore.

Umbrella ill. by author. Viking, 1958. ISBN 0-670-73858-1 Subj: Birthdays. Caldecott award honor books. Cities, towns. Ethnic groups in the U.S. – Japanese Americans. Umbrellas. Weather – rain.

The village tree ill. by author. Viking, 1972, c1953. ISBN 0-670-05072-5 Subj: Foreign lands – Japan. Seasons – summer. Trees.

The youngest one ill. by author. Viking, 1962. Subj: Character traits – shyness. Ethnic groups in the U.S. – Japanese Americans. Friendship.

Yates, Irene. *All about color* ill. by Jill Newton. Benchmark, 1998. ISBN 0-761-40514-3 Subj: Concepts – color.

All about pattern ill. by Jill Newton. Benchmark, 1998. ISBN 0-761-40517-8 Subj: Concepts – shape.

All about shape ill. by Jill Newton. Benchmark, 1998. ISBN 0-761-40515-1 Subj: Concepts – shape.

All about touch ill. by Jill Newton. Benchmark, 1998. ISBN 0-761-40516-X Subj: Senses – touch.

My ABC dictionary ill. by Chris Fisher. Barron's, 2001. ISBN 0-7641-5433-8 Subj: Dictionaries.

Yates, Philip. *Ten little mummies* ill. by G. Brian Karas. Viking, 2003. ISBN 0-670-03641-2 Subj: Counting, numbers. Foreign lands – Egypt. Mummies. Rhyming text.

Ybáñez, Terry. *Hairs = Pelitos* (Cisneros, Sandra)

Ye, Ting-xing. *Share the sky* ill. by Suzane Langlois. Annick, 1999. ISBN 1-55037-579-2 Subj: Ethnic groups in the U.S. – Chinese Americans. Family life – grandfathers. Foreign lands – China. Kites.

Three monks, no water ill. by Harvey Chan. Annick, 1997. ISBN 1-55037-443-5 Subj: Activities – working. Folk & fairy tales. Foreign lands – China.

Ye Pin Kwei. *Monkey creates havoc in heaven* (P'an, Ts'ai-ying)

Yee, Brenda Shannon. *Sand castle* ill. by Thea Kliros. Greenwillow, 1999. ISBN 0-688-16194-4 Subj: Castles. Cumulative tales. Sand. Sea & seashore.

Yee, Patrick. *Baby bear* ill. by author. Viking, 1993. ISBN 0-670-85288-0 Subj: Animals – bears. Format, unusual – board books.

Baby lion ill. by author. Viking, 1993. ISBN 0-670-85289-9 Subj: Animals – lions. Format, unusual – board books.

Baby monkey ill. by author. Viking, 1993. ISBN 0-670-85290-2 Subj: Animals – monkeys. Format, unusual – board books.

Baby penguin ill. by author. Viking, 1993. ISBN 0-670-85291-0 Subj: Birds – penguins. Foreign lands – Antarctic. Format, unusual – board books.

Bedtime for Rosie Rabbit ill. by Patrick Yee; text by Lucy Coats. S&S, 1996. ISBN 0-689-80716-3 Subj: Animals – rabbits. Bedtime. Format, unusual – toy & movable books.

Let's go ill. by author. Viking, 1995. ISBN 0-670-85937-0 Subj: Food. Format, unusual – board books.

Let's make friends ill. by author. Viking, 1995. ISBN 0-670-85940-0 Subj: Format, unusual – board books. Friendship.

Let's play ill. by author. Viking, 1995. ISBN 0-670-85939-7 Subj: Activities – playing. Format, unusual – board books.

Little Buddy meets Bobo ill. by author. Viking, 1993. ISBN 0-670-84803-4 Subj: Animals – elephants. Animals – rabbits. Format, unusual – toy & movable books.

Rosie Rabbit's colors ill. by author. Little Simon, 1998. ISBN 0-689-81842-4 Subj: Animals – rabbits. Concepts – color. Format, unusual – board books.

Rosie Rabbit's numbers ill. by author. Little Simon, 1998. ISBN 0-689-81843-2 Subj: Animals – rabbits. Counting, numbers. Format, unusual – board books.

Rosie Rabbit's opposites ill. by author. Little Simon, 1998. ISBN 0-689-81844-0 Subj: Animals – rabbits. Concepts – opposites. Format, unusual – board books.

Rosie Rabbit's shapes ill. by author. S&S, 1998. ISBN 0-689-81845-9 Subj: Animals – rabbits. Concepts – shape. Format, unusual – board books.

Winter rabbit ill. by author. Viking, 1994. ISBN 0-670-85353-6 Subj: Animals – rabbits. Snowmen.

Yee, Paul. *The boy in the attic* ill. by Gu Xiong. Douglas & McIntyre, 1998. ISBN 0-88899-330-7 Subj: Friendship. Ghosts. Insects – butterflies, caterpillars.

The jade necklace ill. by Grace Lin. Crocodile, 2001. ISBN 1-56656-455-7 Subj: Family life. Foreign lands – Canada. Immigrants. Sea & seashore.

Let's eat ill. by author. Viking, 1995. ISBN 0-670-85938-9 Subj: Activities – traveling. Format, unusual – board books. Transportation.

Roses sing on new snow ill. by Harvey Chan. Macmillan, 1992. ISBN 0-02-793622-8 Subj: Activities – baking, cooking. Ethnic groups in the U.S. – Chinese Americans.

Yee, Wong Herbert. *Big black bear* ill. by author. Houghton Mifflin, 1993. ISBN 0-395-66359-8 Subj: Animals – bears. Behavior – misbehavior. Etiquette. Rhyming text.

Did you see Chip? ill. by Laura Ovresat. Harcourt, 2003. ISBN 0-15-205095-7 Subj: Animals – dogs. Behavior – lost & found possessions. Cities, towns. Friendship. Moving.

A drop of rain ill. by author. Houghton Mifflin, 1995. ISBN 0-395-71549-0 Subj: Babies. Behavior – mistakes. Ethnic groups in the U.S. – Chinese Americans. Rhyming text. Weather – rain.

Eek! There's a mouse in the house ill. by author. Houghton Mifflin, 1992. ISBN 0-395-62303-0 Subj: Animals. Cumulative tales. Homes, houses. Rhyming text.

Fireman Small ill. by author. Houghton Mifflin, 1994. ISBN 0-395-68987-2 Subj: Animals. Animals – pigs. Careers – firefighters. Fire. Rhyming text.

Fireman Small, fire down below ill. by author. Houghton Mifflin, 2001. ISBN 0-618-00707-5 Subj: Animals. Animals – pigs. Careers – firefighters. Fire. Hotels. Rhyming text.

Fireman Small to the rescue ill. by author. Houghton Mifflin, 1998. ISBN 0-395-88122-6 Subj: Animals. Animals – pigs. Careers – farmers. Careers – firefighters. Fire. Rhyming text.

Hamburger Heaven ill. by author. Houghton Mifflin, 1999. ISBN 0-395-87548-X Subj: Activities – working. Animals. Animals – pigs. Food. Restaurants.

Mrs. Brown went to town ill. by author. Houghton Mifflin, 1996. ISBN 0-395-75282-5 Subj: Animals. Homes, houses. Rhyming text.

The Officers' Ball ill. by author. Houghton Mifflin, 1997. ISBN 0-395-81182-1 Subj: Activities – dancing. Animals. Animals – hippopotamuses. Careers – police officers. Crime. Rhyming text.

A small Christmas ill. by author. Houghton, 2004. ISBN 0-618-32612-X Subj: Animals. Careers – firefighters. Holidays – Christmas. Rhyming text. Santa Claus.

Yektai, Niki. *Bears at the beach* ill. by author. Millbrook, 1996. ISBN 0-7613-0022-8 Subj: Animals – bears. Counting, numbers. Sea & seashore – beaches.

Bears in pairs ill. by Diane de Groat. Bradbury, 1987. ISBN 0-02-793691-0 Subj: Animals – bears. Concepts. Rhyming text.

Hi bears, bye bears ill. by Diane de Groat. Watts, 1990. ISBN 0-531-08458-2 Subj: Rhyming text. Toys – bears.

What's missing? ill. by Susannah Ryan. Clarion, 1987. ISBN 0-89919-510-5 Subj: Games. Problem solving.

Yen, Clara. *Why rat comes first* ill. by Hideo C. Yoshida. Children's Book Pr., 1991. ISBN 0-89239-072-7 Subj: Animals. Foreign lands – China. Royalty. Zodiac.

Yenne, Bill. *Joshua and the battle of Jericho* ill. by reteller. Tommy Nelson, 1994. ISBN 0-7852-8331-5 Subj: Religion. War.

Yeoman, John. *The bear's water picnic* ill. by Quentin Blake. Atheneum, 1987, 1970. ISBN 0-689-31386-1 Subj: Activities – picnicking. Animals – bears. Animals – hedgehogs. Animals – pigs. Animals – squirrels. Frogs & toads.

Mouse trouble ill. by Quentin Blake. Collier, 1976, c1972. ISBN 0-02-045610-7 Subj: Animals – cats. Animals – mice. Friendship. Windmills.

Old Mother Hubbard's dog dresses up ill. by Quentin Blake. Houghton Mifflin, 1990. ISBN 0-394-53358-9 Subj: Animals – dogs. Clothing. Rhyming text.

Old Mother Hubbard's dog learns to play ill. by Quentin Blake. Houghton Mifflin, 1990. ISBN 0-395-53360-0 Subj: Animals – dogs. Music. Musical instruments. Rhyming text.

Old Mother Hubbard's dog needs a doctor ill. by Quentin Blake. Houghton Mifflin, 1990. ISBN 0-395-53359-7 Subj: Animals – dogs. Rhyming text.

Old Mother Hubbard's dog takes up sport ill. by Quentin Blake. Houghton Mifflin, 1990. ISBN 0-395-53361-9 Subj: Animals – dogs. Rhyming text. Sports.

Our village ill. by Quentin Blake. Atheneum, 1988. ISBN 0-689-31451-5 Subj: Communities, neighborhoods. Poetry.

The wild washerwomen: a new folk tale ill. by Quentin Blake. Crown, 1986, c1979. ISBN 0-517-56255-3 Subj: Activities – working. Behavior – misbehavior. Folk & fairy tales.

The young performing horse ill. by Quentin Blake. Parents' Magazine Pr., 1979. ISBN 0-8193-0971-0 Subj: Animals – horses, ponies. Multiple births – twins. Theater.

Yeomans, Thomas. *For every child a star: a Christmas story* ill. by Tomie de Paola. Holiday, 1986. ISBN 0-8234-0526-5 Subj: Holidays – Christmas. Night. Stars.

Yep, Laurence. *The city of dragons* ill. by Jean & Mou-Sien Tseng. Scholastic, 1995. ISBN 0-590-47865-6 Subj: Anatomy – faces. Behavior – running away. Character traits – appearance. Character traits – being different. Giants.

Dragon prince ill. by Kam Mak. HarperCollins, 1997. ISBN 0-06-024393-7 Subj: Dragons. Emotions – envy, jealousy. Family life – sisters. Folk & fairy tales. Foreign lands – China. Sibling rivalry.

The junior thunder lord ill. by Robert Van Nutt. BridgeWater, 1994. ISBN 0-8167-3454-2 Subj: Character traits – generosity. Character traits – kindness. Folk & fairy tales. Foreign lands – China. Weather – droughts. Weather – rain.

The Khan's daughter ill. by Jean & Mou-Sien Tseng. Scholastic, 1997. ISBN 0-590-48389-7 Subj: Folk & fairy tales. Foreign lands – Mongolia. Monsters. Royalty – khans. Weddings.

The man who tricked a ghost ill. by Isadore Seltzer. BridgeWater, 1993. ISBN 0-816-73030-X Subj: Behavior – trickery. Foreign lands – China. Ghosts. Middle Ages.

The shell woman and the king ill. by Yang Ming-Yi. Dial, 1993. ISBN 0-8037-1394-0 Subj: Folk & fairy tales. Foreign lands – China. Magic. Royalty – kings.

Tiger woman ill. by Robert Roth. BridgeWater, 1994. ISBN 0-8167-3464-X Subj: Animals. Behavior – greed. Character traits – selfishness. Folk & fairy tales. Foreign lands – China. Rhyming text.

Yerkes, Andy. *The book of Pooh: Biglet* (The book of Pooh: Biglet)

Yerxa, Leo. *A fish tale, or, The little one that got away* ill. by author. Douglas & McIntyre, 1995. ISBN 0-88899-247-5 Subj: Behavior – trickery. Fish. Sports – fishing.

Last leaf first snowflake to fall ill. by author. Orchard, 1994. ISBN 0-531-08674-7 Subj: Indians of North America – Nishnawbe. Nature. Poetry. Seasons – fall. Seasons – winter. Weather – snow.

Yezback, Steven A. *Pumpkinseeds* ill. by Mozelle Thompson. Bobbs-Merrill, 1969. Subj: Behavior – solitude. Cities, towns. Ethnic groups in the U.S. – African Americans.

Yezerski, Thomas F. *A full hand* ill. by author. Farrar, 2002. ISBN 0-374-42502-7 Subj: Animals – mules. Boats, ships. Family life – fathers. Family life – sons. Sailors. U.S. history.

Queen of the world ill. by author. Farrar, 2000. ISBN 0-374-36165-7 Subj: Birthdays. Family life – mothers. Family life – sisters. Sibling rivalry.

Together in Pinecone Patch ill. by author. Farrar, 1998. ISBN 0-374-37647-6 Subj: Emotions – love. Ethnic groups in the U.S. – Irish Americans. Ethnic groups in the U.S. – Polish Americans. Immigrants. Prejudice. Weddings.

Yim, Natasha. *Otto's rainy day* ill. by Pamela R. Levy. Talewinds, 2000. ISBN 1-57091-400-1 Subj: Activities – playing. Family life – mothers. Weather – rain.

Yin. *Coolies* ill. by Chris K. Soentpiet. Philomel, 2001. ISBN 0-399-23227-3 Subj: Ethnic groups in the U.S. – Chinese Americans. Family life – brothers. Immigrants. Prejudice. Trains. U.S. history.

Dear Santa, please come to the 19th floor ill. by Chris K. Soentpiet. Philomel, 2002. ISBN 0-399-23636-8 Subj: Behavior – worrying. Ethnic groups in the U.S. – Hispanic Americans. Handicaps – physical handicaps. Holidays – Christmas. Homes, houses. Santa Claus.

Ylla. *Animal babies* by Ylla & Arthur S. Gregor; ill. by Ylla. HarperCollins, 1959. Designed by Luc Bouchage. Subj: Animals.

I'll show you cats by Ylla & Crosby Newell Bonsall; ill. by Ylla. HarperCollins, 1964. Planned by Charles Rado; designed by Luc Bouchage. Subj: Animals – cats.

Listen, listen! (Bonsall, Crosby Newell)

The little elephant by Ylla & Arthur S. Gregor; ill. by Ylla. HarperCollins, 1956. Designed by Luc Bouchage. Subj: Animals – elephants.

Look who's talking by Ylla & Crosby Newell Bonsall; ill. by Ylla. HarperCollins, 1962. Planned by Charles Rado; designed by Luc Bouchage. Subj: Birds – ostriches. Zoos.

Polar bear brothers by Ylla & Crosby Newell Bonsall; ill. by Ylla. HarperCollins, 1960. Designed by Luc Bouchage. Subj: Animals – polar bears.

Two little bears ill. by author. HarperCollins, 1954. Subj: Animals – bears. Behavior – lost.

Yoaker, Harry. *The view* by Harry Yoaker & Simon Henwood; ill. by Simon Henwood. Dial, 1992. ISBN 0-8037-1105-0 Subj: Communities, neighborhoods. Homes, houses.

Yoder, Carolyn P. *Filipino Americans* ill. with photos. Heinemann, 2003. ISBN 1-4034-0164-0 Subj: Ethnic groups in the U.S. – Filipino Americans. Immigrants.

Yohannes, Gebregeorgis. *Silly Mammo = Kilu Mammo* ill. by Bogale Belachew. African Sun, 2002. ISBN 1-883701-04-X Subj: Character traits – cleverness. Folk & fairy tales. Foreign languages.

Yolen, Jane. *All in the woodland early: an ABC book* ill. by Jane Breskin Zalben; music & lyrics by author. Collins-World, 1980. ISBN 0-529-05509-0 Subj: ABC books. Forest, woods.

All those secrets of the world ill. by Leslie A. Baker. Little, 1991. ISBN 0-316-96891-9 Subj: Concepts – perspective. Family life – fathers. War.

Alphabestiary: animal poems from A to Z (Alphabestiary)

Animal train ill. by Doug Cushman. Little Simon, 2002. ISBN 0-689-84838-2 Subj: Animals. Format, unusual – toy & movable books. Trains.

Baby Bear's bedtime book ill. by Jane Dyer. Harcourt, 1990. ISBN 0-15-205120-1 Subj: Activities – babysitting. Animals – bears. Bedtime.

Before the storm ill. by Georgia Pugh. Boyds Mills, 1995. ISBN 1-56397-240-9 Subj: Activities – playing. Seasons – summer. Weather – storms.

Beneath the ghost moon ill. by Laurel Molk. Little, 1994. ISBN 0-316-96892-7 Subj: Animals – mice. Character traits – bravery. Holidays – Halloween. Rhyming text.

Bird watch: a book of poetry ill. by Ted Lewin. Philomel, 1990. ISBN 0-399-21612-X Subj: Birds. Poetry.

Child of faerie, child of earth ill. by Jane Dyer. Little, 1997. ISBN 0-316-96897-8 Subj: Fairies. Folk & fairy tales. Holidays – Halloween. Poetry.

Dragon night and other lullabies ill. by Demi. Methuen, 1980. ISBN 0-416-30711-6 Subj: Animals. Bedtime. Lullabies. Sleep.

Eeny, meeny, miney mole ill. by Kathryn Brown. Harcourt, 1992. ISBN 0-15-225350-5 Subj: Animals – moles. Character traits – curiosity.

Elfabet ill. by Lauren Mills. Little, 1989. ISBN 0-316-96900-1 Subj: ABC books. Activities. Mythical creatures – elves.

The emperor and the kite ill. by Ed Young. Philomel, 1988, c1967. ISBN 0-399-21499-2 Subj: Caldecott award honor books. Character traits – smallness. Family life – fathers. Foreign lands – China. Kites. Royalty – emperors.

The firebird ill. by Vladimir Vasilévich Vagin. HarperCollins, 2002. ISBN 0-06-028539-7 Subj: Ballet. Folk & fairy tales. Foreign lands – Russia. Magic. Mythical creatures. Royalty – princes. Wizards.

The flying witch ill. by Vladimir Vasilévich Vagin. HarperCollins, 2003. ISBN 0-06-028537-0 Subj: Careers – farmers. Character traits – cleverness. Folk & fairy tales. Foreign lands – Russia. Witches.

The giant's farm ill. by Tomie de Paola. Seabury Pr., 1977. ISBN 0-8164-3193-0 Subj: Farms. Giants.

The giants go camping ill. by Tomie de Paola. Seabury Pr., 1979. ISBN 0-8164-3223-6 Subj: Camps, camping. Giants.

The girl in the golden bower ill. by Jane Dyer. Little, 1994. ISBN 0-316-96894-3 Subj: Folk & fairy tales. Orphans. Witches.

The girl who loved the wind ill. by Ed Young. Crowell, 1972. ISBN 0-690-33100-2 Subj: Behavior – running away. Weather – wind.

Greyling ill. by David Ray. Putnam, 1991. ISBN 0-399-22262-6 Subj: Animals – seals. Careers – fishermen. Folk & fairy tales. Foreign lands – Scotland. Mythical creatures.

Harvest home ill. by Greg Shed. Harcourt, 2000. ISBN 0-15-201819-0 Subj: Careers – farmers. Farms. Rhyming text.

How beastly! ill. by James Marshall. Boyds Mills, 1994. ISBN 1-56397-086-4 Subj: Animals. Poetry.

How do dinosaurs clean their rooms? ill. by Mark Teague. Blue Sky, 2004. ISBN 0-439-64950-1 Subj: Character traits – orderliness. Dinosaurs. Format, unusual – board books. Rhyming text.

How do dinosaurs count to ten? ill. by Mark Teague. Blue Sky, 2004. ISBN 0-439-64949-8 Subj: Counting, numbers. Dinosaurs. Format, unusual – board books. Rhyming text.

How do dinosaurs get well soon? ill. by Mark Teague. Blue Sky, 2003. ISBN 0-439-24100-6 Subj: Dinosaurs. Illness. Rhyming text.

How do dinosaurs say good night? ill. by Mark Teague. Blue Sky, 2000. ISBN 0-590-31681-8 Subj: Bedtime. Behavior. Dinosaurs. Rhyming text.

An invitation to the butterfly ball: a counting rhyme ill. by Jane Breskin Zalben. Parents' Magazine Pr., 1976. ISBN 0-819-30800-5 Subj: Animals. Counting, numbers. Rhyming text.

Jane Yolen's Old MacDonald songbook musical arrangements by Adam Stemple; ill. by Rosekrans Hoffman. Boyds Mills, 1994. ISBN 1-56397-281-6 Subj: Animals. Cumulative tales. Farms. Music. Songs.

King Long Shanks ill. by Victoria Chess. Harcourt, 1998. ISBN 0-15-200013-5 Subj: Character traits – pride. Character traits – vanity. Clothing. Folk & fairy tales. Frogs & toads. Imagination. Royalty – kings.

The lap-time song and play book musical arrangements by Adam Stemple; ill. by Margot Tomes. Harcourt, 1989. ISBN 0-15-243588-3 Subj: Games. Music. Nursery rhymes. Songs.

Letting Swift River go ill. by Barbara Cooney. Little, 1992. ISBN 0-316-96899-4 Subj: Country. U.S. history. Water.

Little Mouse and Elephant ill. by John Segal. S&S, 1996. ISBN 0-689-80493-8 Subj: Animals – mice. Behavior – boasting. Folk & fairy tales. Foreign lands – Turkey. Self-concept.

The lullaby songbook ill. by Charles Mikolaycak; scores by Adam Stemple. Harcourt, 1986. ISBN 0-15-249903-2 Subj: Bedtime. Lullabies. Music.

Milkweed days photos by Gabriel Amadeus Cooney. Crowell, 1976. ISBN 0-690-01140-7 Subj: Seasons – summer.

Miz Berlin walks ill. by Floyd Cooper. Philomel, 1997. ISBN 0-399-22938-8 Subj: Activities – storytelling. Activities – walking. Ethnic groups in the U.S. – African Americans. Old age.

Moon ball ill. by Greg Couch. S&S, 1999. ISBN 0-689-81095-4 Subj: Bedtime. Dreams. Space & space ships. Sports – baseball.

The musicians of Bremen (Grimm, Jacob)

My brothers' flying machine ill. by Jim Burke. Little, 2003. ISBN 0-316-97159-6 Subj: Airplanes, airports. Careers – airplane pilots. Careers – inventors. Family life – brothers. U.S. history.

No bath tonight ill. by Nancy Winslow Parker. Crowell, 1978. ISBN 0-690-03882-8 Subj: Activities – bathing. Days of the week, months of the year. Family life – grandmothers.

Nocturne ill. by Anne Hunter. Harcourt, 1997. ISBN 0-15-201458-6 Subj: Animals. Animals – dogs. Family life – mothers. Night. Poetry.

Off we go! ill. by Laurel Molk. Little, 2000. ISBN 0-316-90228-4 Subj: Animals – babies. Family life – grandparents. Rhyming text.

Old Dame Counterpane ill. by Ruth Tietjen Councell. Philomel, 1994. ISBN 0-399-22686-9 Subj: Activities – sewing. Counting, numbers. Creation. Quilts. Rhyming text.

Owl moon ill. by John Schoenherr. Philomel, 1987. ISBN 0-399-21457-7 Subj: Birds – owls. Caldecott award books. Family life – fathers. Forest, woods. Night.

Pegasus, the flying horse ill. by Ming Li. Dutton, 1998. ISBN 0-525-65244-2 Subj: Character traits – vanity. Folk & fairy tales. Mythical creatures. Mythical creatures – Pegasus.

Picnic with Piggins ill. by Jane Dyer. Harcourt, 1988. ISBN 0-15-261534-2 Subj: Activities – picnicking. Animals. Animals – pigs. Birthdays.

Piggins ill. by Jane Dyer. Harcourt, 1987. ISBN 0-15-261685-3 Subj: Animals. Animals – pigs. Behavior – stealing. Parties. Problem solving.

Raising Yoder's barn ill. by Bernie Fuchs. Little, 1998. ISBN 0-316-96887-0 Subj: Barns. Communities, neighborhoods. Ethnic groups in the U.S. – Amish. Farms.

Ring of earth: a child's book of seasons ill. by John Wallner. Harcourt, 1986. ISBN 0-15-267140-4 Subj: Poetry. Seasons.

The sea king by Jane Yolen & Shulamith Oppenheim; ill. by Stefan Czernecki. Crocodile, 2003. ISBN 1-56656-459-X Subj: Folk & fairy tales. Foreign lands – Russia. Royalty – kings. Royalty – princes. Sea & seashore.

The seeing stick ill. by Remy Charlip & Demetra Maraslis. Crowell, 1977. ISBN 0-690-00596-2 Subj: Foreign lands – China. Handicaps – blindness. Royalty. Senses – sight.

Sky dogs ill. by Barry Moser. Harcourt, 1990. ISBN 0-15-275480-6 Subj: Animals – horses, ponies. Folk & fairy tales. Indians of North America – Blackfoot. Indians of North America – Siksika.

The sleeping beauty (Grimm, Jacob)

Snow, snow: winter poems for children ill. by Jason Stemple. Wordsong, 1998. ISBN 1-56397-721-4 Subj: Poetry. Seasons – winter. Weather – snow.

Spider Jane ill. by Stefen Bernath. Coward, 1978. ISBN 0-698-30696-1 Subj: Behavior – sharing. Birds. Insects – flies. Spiders.

Street rhymes around the world ill. by 17 international artists. Boyds Mills, 1992. ISBN 1-878093-53-3 Subj: Counting, numbers. Foreign lands. Foreign languages. Games. Nursery rhymes.

The three bears holiday rhyme book ill. by Jane Dyer. Harcourt, 1995. ISBN 0-15-200932-9 Subj: Animals – bears. Holidays. Poetry.

The three bears rhyme book ill. by Jane Dyer. Harcourt, 1987. ISBN 0-15-286386-9 Subj: Animals – bears. Folk & fairy tales. Poetry.

Time for naps ill. by Hiroe Nakata. Little Simon, 2002. ISBN 0-689-85057-3 Subj: Format, unusual – board books. Rhyming text. Sleep. Toys.

Welcome to the icehouse ill. by Laura Regan. Putnam, 1998. ISBN 0-399-23011-4 Subj: Animals. Foreign lands – Arctic. Nature. Science. Seasons.

Welcome to the river of grass ill. by Laura Regan. Putnam, 2001. ISBN 0-399-23221-4 Subj: Animals. Birds. Ecology. Swamps.

Welcome to the sea of sand ill. by Laura Regan. Putnam, 1996. ISBN 0-399-22765-2 Subj: Animals. Desert. Ecology. Plants. Poetry.

Where have the unicorns gone? ill. by Ruth Sanderson. S&S, 2000. ISBN 0-689-82465-3 Subj: Ecology. Mythical creatures – unicorns. Rhyming text.

Wings ill. by Dennis Nolan. Harcourt, 1992. ISBN 0-15-297850-X Subj: Activities – flying. Mythical creatures. Royalty – princes.

Yoon, Salina. *Wild animals* ill. by author. Piggy Toes, 2002. ISBN 1-58117-157-9 Subj: Animals. Format, unusual – toy & movable books. Games.

Yorinks, Arthur. *Bravo, Minski* ill. by Richard Egielski. Farrar, 1988. ISBN 0-374-30951-5 Subj: Behavior – seeking better things. Problem solving.

Christmas in July ill. by Richard Egielski. HarperCollins, 1991. ISBN 0-06-020257-2 Subj: Behavior – lost & found possessions. Clothing. Holidays – Christmas. Santa Claus.

Company's coming ill. by David Small. Crown, 1988. ISBN 0-517-56751-2 Subj: Behavior – misunderstanding. Humorous stories. Space & space ships.

Company's going ill. by David Small. Hyperion, 2001. ISBN 0-7868-0415-7 Subj: Activities – baking, cooking. Aliens. Humorous stories. Planets. Space & space ships. Weddings.

Harry and Lulu ill. by Martin Matje. Hyperion, 1999. ISBN 0-7868-2276-7 Subj: Animals – dogs. Emotions – anger. Emotions – love. Foreign lands – France. Imagination. Toys.

Hey, Al ill. by Richard Egielski. Farrar, 1986. ISBN 0-374-33060-3 Subj: Animals – dogs. Behavior – running away. Caldecott award books. Dreams. Imagination.

Louis the fish ill. by Richard Egielski. Farrar, 1980. ISBN 0-374-34658-5 Subj: Careers – butchers. Fish. Imagination.

The Miami giant ill. by Maurice Sendak. HarperCollins, 1995. ISBN 0-06-205069-9 Subj: Careers – explorers. Foreign lands – Italy. Giants. Jewish culture.

Oh, brother ill. by Richard Egielski. Farrar, 1989. ISBN 0-374-35599-1 Subj: Behavior – fighting, arguing. Careers – tailors. Family life – brothers. Multiple births – twins. Orphans.

Quack! ill. with quilts by Adrienne Yorinks. Abrams, 2003. ISBN 0-8109-3548-1 Subj: Animals. Birds – ducks. Quilts. Space & space ships.

Ugh ill. by Richard Egielski. Farrar, 1990. ISBN 0-374-38028-7 Subj: Family life – brothers. Sibling rivalry. Sports – bicycling.

Whitefish Will rides again ill. by Mort Drucker. HarperCollins, 1994. ISBN 0-06-205037-0 Subj: Careers – sheriffs. U.S. history – frontier & pioneer life.

York, Penelope. *Bugs* ill. with photos. DK, 2002. ISBN 0-7894-8552-4 Subj: Insects.

Yoshi. *One, two, three* ill. by author. Picture Book Studio, 1991. ISBN 0-88708-159-2 Subj: Counting, numbers.

Who's hiding here? ill. by author. Picture Book Studio, 1987. ISBN 0-88708-041-3 Subj: Animals. Format, unusual – toy & movable books. Rhyming text.

Yoshida, Toshi. *Elephant crossing* ill. by author. Putnam, 1989. ISBN 0-399-21745-2 Subj: Animals. Animals – elephants. Foreign lands – Africa.

Rhinoceros mother ill. by author. Putnam, 1991. Original title: Quarrel. ISBN 0-399-22270-7 Subj: Animals. Animals – rhinoceros. Birds. Foreign lands – Africa. Nature.

Young lions ill. by author. Putnam, 1989. ISBN 0-399-21546-8 Subj: Animals – lions. Behavior – growing up. Foreign lands – Africa.

You and me: poems of friendship sel. & ill. by Salley Mavor. Orchard, 1997. ISBN 0-531-33045-1 Subj: Friendship. Poetry.

You can name 100 trucks! ill. by Randy Chewning. Scholastic, 1994. ISBN 0-590-46302-0 Subj: Format, unusual – board books. Trucks.

Youldon, Gillian. *Colors* ill. by author. Watts, 1979. ISBN 0-531-00439-2 Subj: Concepts – color. Format, unusual – toy & movable books.

Counting ill. by James Hodgson. Watts, 1980. ISBN 0-531-02142-4 Subj: Counting, numbers. Format, unusual.

Numbers ill. by author. Watts, 1979. ISBN 0-531-00440-6 Subj: Counting, numbers. Format, unusual – toy & movable books.

Shapes ill. by author. Watts, 1979. ISBN 0-531-00441-4 Subj: Concepts – shape. Format, unusual.

Sizes ill. by author. Watts, 1979. ISBN 0-531-00442-2 Subj: Concepts – size. Format, unusual.

Young, Amy. *Belinda, the ballerina* ill. by author. Viking, 2002. ISBN 0-670-03549-1 Subj: Activities – dancing. Anatomy – feet. Ballet.

Young, Ed (Edward). *Cat and Rat* ill. by author. Holt, 1995. ISBN 0-8050-2977-X Subj: Animals – cats. Animals – rats. Folk & fairy tales. Foreign lands – China. Royalty – emperors. Zodiac.

Donkey trouble ill. by author. Atheneum, 1995. ISBN 0-689-31854-5 Subj: Animals – donkeys. Behavior – misunderstanding. Desert. Folk & fairy tales. Stores.

High on a hill: a book of Chinese riddles ill. by the selector. Collins-World, 1980. ISBN 0-529-05554-6 Subj: Folk & fairy tales. Foreign lands – China. Riddles & jokes.

Little Plum ill. by author. Philomel, 1994. ISBN 0-399-22683-4 Subj: Character traits – cleverness. Character traits – smallness. Folk & fairy tales. Foreign lands – China.

Lon Po Po: a Red Riding Hood story from China ill. by author. Putnam, 1989. ISBN 0-399-21619-7 Subj: Animals – wolves. Caldecott award books. Folk & fairy tales. Foreign lands – China.

The lost horse ill. by author. Silver Whistle, 1998. ISBN 0-15-201016-5 Subj: Animals – horses, ponies. Folk & fairy tales. Foreign lands – China. Weather – storms.

Monkey King ill. by author. HarperCollins, 2001. ISBN 0-06-027950-8 Subj: Animals – monkeys. Behavior – trickery. Foreign lands – China.

Mouse match ill. by author. Silver Whistle, 1997. ISBN 0-15-201453-5 Subj: Animals – mice. Family life – fathers. Foreign lands – China. Format, unusual. Weddings.

Night visitors ill. by author. Philomel, 1995. ISBN 0-399-22731-8 Subj: Dreams. Folk & fairy tales. Foreign lands – China. Insects – ants.

The rooster's horns: a Chinese puppet play to make and perform by Ed Young & Hilary Beckett; ill. by Ed Young. Collins-World, 1978. ISBN 0-529-05447-7 Subj: Folk & fairy tales. Foreign lands – China. Puppets.

Seven blind mice ill. by author. Putnam, 1992. ISBN 0-399-22261-8 Subj: Animals – elephants. Animals – mice. Caldecott award honor books. Days of the week, months of the year. Foreign lands – India. Handicaps – blindness. Senses – sight.

The terrible Nung Gwama: a Chinese folktale ill. by author. Collins-World, 1978. ISBN 0-529-05445-0 Subj: Character traits – cleverness. Folk & fairy tales. Foreign lands – China. Monsters.

Up a tree ill. by author. HarperCollins, 1983. ISBN 0-06-026814-X Subj: Animals – cats. Trees. Wordless.

What about me? ill. by author. Philomel, 2002. ISBN 0-399-23624-4 Subj: Cumulative tales. Folk & fairy tales. Foreign lands – Middle East. Religion.

Young, Evelyn. *The tale of Tai* ill. by author. Oxford Univ. Pr., 1940. Subj: Behavior – lost. Foreign lands – China. Holidays – Chinese New Year.

Wu and Lu and Li ill. by author. Walck, 1959, c1939. Subj: Family life. Foreign lands – China.

Young, Helen. *A throne for Sesame* ill. by Shirley Hughes. Elsevier-Dutton, 1979. ISBN 0-233-96871-7 Subj: Behavior – growing up.

Young, James. *Everyone loves the moon* ill. by author. Little, 1992. ISBN 0-316-97130-8 Subj: Animals – possums. Animals – raccoons. Moon. Rhyming text. Weddings.

A million chameleons ill. by author. Little, 1990. ISBN 0-316-97129-4 Subj: Concepts – color. Rhyming text.

Penelope and the pirates ill. by author. Arcade, 1990. ISBN 1-55970-074-2 Subj: Animals – cats. Boats, ships. Pirates.

Young, Jay. *Magic world of learning* (Butterfield, Moira)

Young, Miriam Burt. *If I drove a bus* ill. by Robert M. Quackenbush. Lothrop, 1973. Subj: Buses. Careers – bus drivers. Transportation.

If I drove a car ill. by Robert M. Quackenbush. Lothrop, 1971. Subj: Automobiles. Transportation.

If I drove a tractor ill. by Robert M. Quackenbush. Lothrop, 1973. ISBN 0-688-50041-2 Subj: Tractors.

If I drove a train ill. by Robert M. Quackenbush. Lothrop, 1972. Subj: Trains. Transportation.

If I drove a truck ill. by Robert M. Quackenbush. Lothrop, 1967. Subj: Careers – truck drivers. Transportation. Trucks.

If I flew a plane ill. by Robert M. Quackenbush. Lothrop, 1970. Subj: Activities – flying. Airplanes, airports. Careers – airplane pilots. Transportation.

If I rode a horse ill. by Robert M. Quackenbush. Lothrop, 1973. ISBN 0-6885-0042-0 Subj: Animals – horses, ponies.

If I rode an elephant ill. by Robert M. Quackenbush. Lothrop, 1974. ISBN 0-688-51589-4 Subj: Animals – elephants.

If I sailed a boat ill. by Robert M. Quackenbush. Lothrop, 1971. Subj: Boats, ships.

Jellybeans for breakfast ill. by Beverly Komoda. Parents' Magazine Pr., 1968. Subj: Activities – playing. Imagination.

Miss Suzy's Easter surprise ill. by Arnold Lobel. Parents' Magazine Pr., 1972. ISBN 0-819-30556-1 Subj: Animals – squirrels. Holidays – Easter.

Please don't feed Horace ill. by Abner Graboff. Dial, 1961. Subj: Animals – hippopotamuses. Zoos.

The sugar mouse cake ill. by Margaret Bloy Graham. Scribners, 1964. Subj: Activities – baking, cooking. Animals – mice. Careers – bakers. Food. Royalty.

Young, Russell. *Dragonsong* ill. by Civi Cheng. Shen's Bks., 2000. ISBN 1-885008-12-0 Subj: Dragons. Foreign lands – China. Gifts. Songs.

Young, Ruth. *Daisy's taxi* ill. by Marcia Sewall. Watts, 1991. ISBN 0-531-08521-X Subj: Boats, ships. Concepts – opposites. Sea & seashore.

Golden Bear ill. by Rachel Isadora. Viking, 1992. ISBN 0-670-82577-8 Subj: Ethnic groups in the U.S. – African Americans. Friendship. Imagination. Rhyming text. Toys – bears.

My baby-sitter ill. by author. Viking, 1987. ISBN 0-670-81305-2 Subj: Activities – babysitting.

My blanket ill. by author. Viking, 1987. ISBN 0-670-81306-0 Subj: Babies.

My potty chair ill. by author. Viking, 1987. ISBN 0-670-81307-9 Subj: Behavior – growing up. Toilet training.

The new baby ill. by author. Viking, 1987. ISBN 0-670-81304-4 Subj: Babies. Family life – new sibling. Sibling rivalry.

A trip to Mars ill. by Maryann Cocca-Leffler. Watts, 1990. ISBN 0-531-08492-2 Subj: Imagination. Space & space ships.

Who says moo? ill. by Lisa Campbell Ernst. Viking, 1994. ISBN 0-670-85162-0 Subj: Animals. Character traits – questioning. Noise, sounds. Riddles & jokes.

Young animals in the zoo ill. with photos. Imported Pubs., 1983. ISBN 0-8285-2211-1 Subj: Animals. Format, unusual – board books. Wordless.

Young domestic animals ill. with photos. Imported Pubs., 1983. ISBN 0-8285-2428-9 Subj: Animals. Format, unusual – board books. Wordless.

Youngquist, Cathrene Valente. *The three Billygoats Gruff and Mean Calypso Joe* ill. by Kristin Sorra. Atheneum, 2002. ISBN 0-689-82824-1 Subj: Animals – goats. Character traits – cleverness. Folk & fairy tales. Foreign lands – Caribbean Islands. Mythical creatures – trolls.

Youngs, Betty Ferrell. *One panda: an animal counting book* ill. by author. Merrimack, 1985. ISBN 0-370-30150-1 Subj: Animals. Counting, numbers.

Pink pigs in mud: a color book ill. by author. Merrimack, 1985. ISBN 0-370-30344-X Subj: Animals. Concepts – color.

Yudell, Lynn Deena. *Make a face* ill. by author. Little, 1970. Subj: Anatomy – faces. Emotions. Games. Participation.

Yulya. *Bears are sleeping* ill. by Nonny Hogrogian. Scribners, 1967. Subj: Animals – bears. Hibernation. Music. Sleep. Songs.

Yummy! eating through a day poems sel. by Lee Bennett Hopkins; ill. by Renée Flower. S&S, 2000. ISBN 0-689-81755-X Subj: Food. Poetry.

Zabar, Abbie. *Fifty-five friends* ill. by author. Hyperion, 1994. ISBN 0-7868-2017-9 Subj: Animals. Counting, numbers. Cumulative tales. Friendship.

Zacharias, Thomas. *But where is the green parrot?* by Thomas & Wanda Zacharias; ill. by Wanda Zacharias. Delacorte, 1968. Translation of Und wo ist der grüne Papagei? Subj: Birds – parakeets, parrots. Concepts – color. Games.

Zacharias, Wanda. *But where is the green parrot?* (Zacharias, Thomas)

Zadrzynska, Ewa. *The peaceable kingdom* ill. by Tomek Olbinski; painting from the Brooklyn Museum. M.M. Art Books, 1993. ISBN 0-9638904-0-9 Subj: Animals. Art. Museums.

Zaffo, George J. *Big book of real fire engines* text by Elizabeth Cameron; ill. by author. Grosset, 1964, c1950. Subj: Careers – firefighters.

The book of real airplanes ill. by author. Grosset, 1966. Subj: Airplanes, airports. Helicopters. Transportation.

The giant book of things in space ill. by author. Doubleday, 1969. Subj: Space & space ships.

The giant nursery book of things that go: fire engines, trains, boats, trucks, airplanes ill. by author. Doubleday, 1959. Subj: Airplanes, airports. Boats, ships. Transportation. Trucks.

The giant nursery book of things that work ill. by author. Doubleday, 1967. Subj: Machines. Tools. Transportation.

Zager, Karen. *Bubbles* ill. by author. Price Stern Sloan, 1988. ISBN 0-8431-1873-3 Subj: Bubbles. Format, unusual – toy & movable books. Wordless.

Zagone, Theresa. *No nap for me* ill. by Lillian Hoban. Dutton, 1978. ISBN 0-525-35982-6 Subj: Behavior – growing up. Sleep.

Zagwÿn, Deborah Turney. *Apple batter* ill. by author. Tricycle, 1999. ISBN 1-883672-92-9 Subj: Character traits – persistence. Family life. Food. Gardens, gardening. Sports – baseball. Trees.

Papa's latkes ill. by author. Holt, 1994. ISBN 0-8050-3099-9 Subj: Family life – fathers. Food. Holidays – Hanukkah. Jewish culture. Religion.

The pumpkin blanket ill. by author. Celestial Arts, 1990. ISBN 0-89087-637-1 Subj: Behavior – growing up. Foreign lands – Canada. Gardens, gardening. Quilts.

The sea house ill. by author. Tricycle, 2002. ISBN 1-58246-030-2 Subj: Boats, ships. Family life – aunts, uncles. Seasons – summer.

Turtle spring ill. by author. Tricycle, 1998. ISBN 1-883672-53-8 Subj: Family life – new sibling. Hibernation. Reptiles – turtles, tortoises. Seasons.

The winter gift ill. by author. Tricycle, 2000. ISBN 1-883672-93-7 Subj: Family life – grandmothers. Holidays – Christmas. Memories, memory. Moving.

Zakhoder, Boris Vladimirovich. *The good stepmother* adapt. by Marguerita Rudolph; ill. by Darcy May. S&S, 1992. ISBN 0-671-68270-9 Subj: Character traits – cleverness. Family life – stepfamilies. Foreign lands – Russia. Royalty – princesses.

How a piglet crashed the Christmas party trans. by Marguerita Rudolph; ill. by Kurt Werth. Lothrop, 1971. Subj: Animals – pigs. Holidays – Christmas.

Rosachok trans. by Marguerita Rudolph; ill. by Yaroslava. Lothrop, 1970. Translation of Rusachok. ISBN 0-688-51113-9 Subj: Animals – rabbits. Behavior – dissatisfaction. Character traits – optimism. Frogs & toads.

Zalben, Jane Breskin. *Baby Babka* ill. by Victoria Chess. Clarion, 2004. ISBN 0-618-23489-6 Subj: Babies. Family life. Family life – aunts, uncles. Family life – brothers & sisters.

Basil and Hillary ill. by author. Macmillan, 1975. ISBN 0-02-793720-8 Subj: Animals. Animals – pigs. Farms.

Beni's first Chanukah ill. by author. Holt, 1988. ISBN 0-8050-0479-3 Subj: Animals – bears. Family life. Friendship. Holidays – Hanukkah. Jewish culture.

Beni's first wedding ill. by author. Holt, 1998. ISBN 0-8050-4846-4 Subj: Animals – bears. Family life. Jewish culture. Weddings.

Buster gets braces ill. by author. Holt, 1992. ISBN 0-8050-1682-1 Subj: Careers – dentists. Dinosaurs. Family life – brothers & sisters. Sibling rivalry. Teeth.

Happy Passover, Rosie ill. by author. Holt, 1990. ISBN 0-8050-1221-4 Subj: Animals – bears. Family life. Holidays – Passover. Jewish culture. Religion.

Leo and Blossom's Sukkah ill. by author. Holt, 1990. ISBN 0-8050-1226-5 Subj: Animals – bears. Family life. Holidays – Sukkot. Jewish culture. Religion.

Miss Violet's shining day ill. by author. Boyds Mills, 1995. ISBN 1-56397-234-4 Subj: Animals – rabbits. Character traits – shyness. Music. Musical instruments – trombones.

Norton's nighttime ill. by author. Collins-World, 1979. ISBN 0-529-05431-0 Subj: Animals. Bedtime. Forest, woods. Night. Noise, sounds.

Oliver and Alison's week ill. by Emily Arnold McCully. Farrar, 1980. ISBN 0-374-35535-8 Subj: Activities. Friendship.

Pearl plants a tree ill. by author. S&S, 1995. ISBN 0-689-80034-7 Subj: Animals – sheep. Family life – grandfathers. Gardens, gardening. Trees.

Pearl's eight days of Chanukah ill. by author. S&S, 1998. ISBN 0-689-81488-7 Subj: Animals – sheep. Holidays – Hanukkah. Jewish culture. Religion.

Pearl's marigolds for grandpa ill. by author. S&S, 1997. ISBN 0-689-80448-2 Subj: Animals – sheep. Death. Emotions – grief. Family life – grandfathers. Memories, memory.

Pearl's Passover ill. by author. S&S, 2002. ISBN 0-689-81487-9 Subj: Family life. Holidays – Passover. Jewish culture.

A perfect nose for Ralph ill. by John Wallner. Putnam, 1980. ISBN 0-399-61154-1 Subj: Emotions – love. Toys – bears.

Saturday night at the Beastro by Jane Breskin Zalben & Steven Zalben; ill. by authors. HarperCollins, 2004. ISBN 0-06-029228-8 Subj: Food. Monsters. Parties. Rhyming text.

Zallinger, Peter. *Dinosaurs* ill. by author. Random House, 1977. ISBN 0-394-83485-2 Subj: Dinosaurs. Prehistory. Rhyming text.

Zamorano, Ana. *Let's eat!* ill. by Julie Vivas. Scholastic, 1997. ISBN 0-590-13444-2 Subj: Family life. Food. Foreign lands – Spain. Health & fitness.

Zander, Hans. *My blue chair* ill. by author. Firefly, 1985. ISBN 0-920303-16-1 Subj: Behavior – lost & found possessions. Furniture – chairs.

Zarin, Cynthia. *Rose and Sebastian* ill. by Sarah Durham. Houghton Mifflin, 1997. ISBN 0-395-75920-X Subj: Cities, towns. Communities, neighborhoods. Emotions – fear. Friendship. Noise, sounds.

What do you see when you shut your eyes? ill. by Sarah Durham. Houghton Mifflin, 1998. ISBN 0-395-76507-2 Subj: Ethnic groups in the U.S. Imagination. Rhyming text. Senses.

Zarins, Joyce Audy. *see* Dos Santos, Joyce Audy

Zaritzky, Bernard. *Little white duck* (Whippo, Walt)

Zaslavsky, Claudia. *Count on your fingers African style* ill. by Jerry Pinkney. Crowell, 1980. ISBN 0-690-03865-8 Subj: Counting, numbers. Foreign lands – Africa.

Zero! Is it something? Is it nothing? ill. by Jeni Bassett. Watts, 1989. ISBN 0-531-10693-4 Subj: Concepts. Counting, numbers.

Zehler, Antonia. *Two fine ladies have a tiff* ill. by author. Random House, 2001. ISBN 0-375-91104-9 Subj: Activities – playing. Behavior – fighting, arguing. Family life – sisters. Friendship. Multiple births – twins.

Two fine ladies: tea for three ill. by author. Random House, 2002. ISBN 0-613-84579-X Subj: Activities – playing. Animals – bears. Family life – sisters. Friendship. Multiple births – twins.

Zekauskas, Felicia. *Belly button boy* (Maloney, Peter [1955–])

His mother's nose (Maloney, Peter [1955–])

The magic hockey stick (Maloney, Peter [1955–])

Redbird at Rockefeller Center (Maloney, Peter [1955–])

Zeldis, Malcah. *Eve and her sisters: women of the Old Testament* (McDonough, Yona Zeldis)

Zelinsky, Paul O. *The lion and the stoat* ill. by author. Greenwillow, 1984. ISBN 0-688-02563-3 Subj: Animals – lions. Animals – weasels. Art. Friendship.

The maid and the mouse and the odd-shaped house ill. by author. Dodd, 1981. ISBN 0-396-07938-5 Subj: Animals – mice. Folk & fairy tales. Homes, houses.

Rapunzel (Grimm, Jacob)

Rumpelstiltskin (Grimm, Jacob)

The wheels on the bus ill. by adapt.; paper engineering by Roger Smith. Dutton, 2000; 1990. ISBN 0-525-46506-5 Subj: Buses. Family life – grandmothers. Format, unusual – toy & movable books. Music. Songs.

Zelver, Patricia. *The wonderful Towers of Watts* ill. by Frané Lessac. Tambourine, 1994. ISBN 0-688-12650-2 Subj: Art. Behavior – collecting things. Buildings.

Zemach, Harve. *Duffy and the devil: a Cornish tale* ill. by Margot Zemach. Farrar, 1973. ISBN 0-374-31887-5 Subj: Caldecott award books. Devil. Folk & fairy tales. Foreign lands – England.

The judge: an untrue tale ill. by Margot Zemach. Farrar, 1969. ISBN 0-374-33960-0 Subj: Caldecott award honor books. Careers – judges. Monsters. Rhyming text.

Mommy, buy me a China doll ill. by Margot Zemach. Follett, 1966. Adapt. from an Ozark children's song. ISBN 0-374-35005-1 Subj: Music. Songs. Toys – dolls.

Nail soup: a Swedish folk tale ill. by Margot Zemach. Follett, 1964. Subj: Character traits – cleverness. Folk & fairy tales. Foreign lands – Sweden.

The tricks of Master Dabble ill. by Margot Zemach. Holt, 1965. Subj: Behavior – trickery. Humorous stories. Royalty.

Zemach, Kaethe. *The beautiful rat* ill. by author. Four Winds, 1979. ISBN 0-590-07584-5 Subj: Animals – rats. Folk & fairy tales.

The character in the book ill. by author. HarperCollins, 1998. ISBN 0-06-205060-5 Subj: Books, reading.

The funny dream ill. by author. Greenwillow, 1988. ISBN 0-688-07501-0 Subj: Dreams. Family life.

Zemach, Margot. *It could always be worse: a Yiddish folk tale* ill. by author. Farrar, 1976. ISBN 0-374-33650-4 Subj: Caldecott award honor books. Folk & fairy tales. Humorous stories. Jewish culture. Problem solving.

Jake and Honeybunch go to heaven ill. by author. Farrar, 1982. ISBN 0-374-33652-0 Subj: Animals – mules. Behavior – misbehavior. Ethnic groups in the U.S. – African Americans. Folk & fairy tales.

The little red hen (The little red hen)

The little tiny woman ill. by author. Bobbs-Merrill, 1965. Subj: Folk & fairy tales. Ghosts.

Some from the moon, some from the sun ill. by author. Farrar, 2001. ISBN 0-374-39960-3 Subj: Nursery rhymes. Songs.

The three wishes: an old story adapt. & ill. by Margot Zemach. Farrar, 1986. ISBN 0-374-37529-1 Subj: Behavior – wishing. Character traits – foolishness. Folk & fairy tales.

To Hilda for helping ill. by author. Farrar, 1977. ISBN 0-374-37663-8 Subj: Character traits – helpfulness. Emotions – envy, jealousy. Family life.

Zemach-Barsin, Kaethe. *see* Zemach, Kaethe

Zeman, Ludmila. *The first red maple leaf* ill. by author. Tundra, 1997. ISBN 0-88776-372-3 Subj: Birds – geese. Creation. Foreign lands – Canada. Indians of North America. Mythical creatures. Seasons.

Sindbad: from the tales of the Thousand and one nights ill. by author. Tundra, 1999. ISBN 0-88776-460-6 Subj: Folk & fairy tales. Foreign lands – Arabia. Sailors. Sea & seashore.

Sindbad in the land of giants ill. by reteller. Tundra, 2001. ISBN 0-88776-461-4 Subj: Activities – storytelling. Folk & fairy tales. Foreign lands – Arabia. Giants. Tall tales.

Sindbad's secret ill. by author. Tundra, 2003. ISBN 0-88776-462-2 Subj: Activities – storytelling. Animals – elephants. Folk & fairy tales. Foreign lands.

Zemke, Deborah. *The shadow of Matilda Hunt* ill. by author. Houghton Mifflin, 1991. ISBN 0-395-55334-2 Subj: Behavior – misbehavior. Imagination – imaginary friends. Shadows.

The way it happened ill. by author. Houghton Mifflin, 1988. ISBN 0-395-47984-3 Subj: Behavior – misunderstanding. Behavior – secrets.

Zhang, Song Nan. *The ballad of Mulan* ill. by reteller. Pan Asian Publications, 1998. ISBN 1-57227-056-X Subj: Foreign lands – China. Gender roles. War.

The five heavenly emperors and other Chinese myths from the creation ill. by author. Tundra, 1994. ISBN 0-88776-338-3 Subj: Creation. Folk & fairy tales. Foreign lands – China.

Ziefert, Harriet. *All clean!* ill. by Henrik Drescher. HarperCollins, 1986. ISBN 0-694-00100-7 Subj: Animals.

All gone! ill. by Henrik Drescher. HarperCollins, 1986. ISBN 0-694-00098-1 Subj: Animals.

Animal music ill. by Donald Saaf. Houghton Mifflin, 1999. ISBN 0-395-95294-8 Subj: Animals. Music. Musical instruments – bands. Rhyming text.

Animals of the Bible ill. by Letizia Galli. Doubleday, 1995. ISBN 0-385-32084-1 Subj: Animals. Format, unusual – toy & movable books. Religion.

April Fool ill. by Chris Demarest. Viking, 2000. ISBN 0-670-88762-5 Subj: Animals – elephants. Holidays – April Fools' Day. Rhyming text. Sports – skateboarding.

Baby Ben's bow-wow book ill. by Norman Gorbaty. Random House, 1984. ISBN 0-394-86821-8 Subj: Animals. Babies. Format, unusual – board books.

Baby Ben's busy book ill. by Norman Gorbaty. Random House, 1984. ISBN 0-394-86819-6 Subj: Activities. Babies. Format, unusual – board books.

Baby Ben's go-go book ill. by Norman Gorbaty. Random House, 1984. ISBN 0-394-86820-X Subj: Activities – playing. Babies. Format, unusual – board books. Toys.

Baby Ben's noisy book ill. by Norman Gorbaty. Random House, 1984. ISBN 0-394-86822-6 Subj: Activities. Babies. Format, unusual – board books.

Bear all year ill. by Arnold Lobel. HarperCollins, 1986. ISBN 0-694-00087-6 Subj: Animals – bears. Format, unusual – toy & movable books. Games. Seasons.

Bear gets dressed ill. by Arnold Lobel. HarperCollins, 1986. ISBN 0-694-00086-8 Subj: Animals – bears. Clothing. Format, unusual – toy & movable books. Games.

Bear goes shopping ill. by Arnold Lobel. HarperCollins, 1986. ISBN 0-694-00085-X Subj: Animals – bears. Format, unusual – toy & movable books. Games. Shopping.

Bear's busy morning ill. by Arnold Lobel. HarperCollins, 1986. ISBN 0-694-00084-1 Subj: Activities. Animals – bears. Format, unusual – toy & movable books. Games.

Before I was born ill. by Rufus Coes. Knopf, 1989. ISBN 0-394-95128-X Subj: Activities – making things. Babies. Family life. Quilts.

Birdhouse for rent ill. by Donald Dreifuss. Houghton, 2001. ISBN 0-618-04881-2 Subj: Birds – chickadees. Family life. Homes, houses.

Breakfast time! by Harriet Ziefert & Lisa Campbell Ernst; ill. by Lisa Campbell Ernst. Viking, 1988. ISBN 0-670-81579-9 Subj: Animals – rabbits. Babies. Food.

Bye-bye, daddy! by Harriet Ziefert & Lisa Campbell Ernst; ill. by Lisa Campbell Ernst. Viking, 1988. ISBN 0-670-81581-0 Subj: Animals – rabbits. Babies.

A car trip for Mole and Mouse ill. by David Prebenna. Viking, 1991. ISBN 0-670-83858-6 Subj: Activities – traveling. Animals – mice. Animals – moles. Automobiles.

Chocolate mud cake ill. by Karen Gundersheimer. HarperCollins, 1988. ISBN 0-06-026892-1 Subj: Family life – grandparents.

Clara Ann Cookie ill. by Emily Bolam. Houghton Mifflin, 1999. ISBN 0-395-92324-7 Subj: Clothing. Family life – mothers. Rhyming text.

Clara Ann Cookie go to bed! ill. by Emily Bolam. Houghton Mifflin, 2000. ISBN 0-395-97381-3 Subj: Bedtime. Rhyming text. Toys – bears.

A clean house for Mole and Mouse ill. by David Prebenna. Viking, 1988. ISBN 0-670-82032-6 Subj: Animals – mice. Animals – moles. Character traits – cleanliness.

Cock-a-doodle-doo! ill. by Henrik Drescher. HarperCollins, 1986. ISBN 0-694-00099-X Subj: Animals.

Come out, Jessie! ill. by Mavis Smith. HarperCollins, 1991. ISBN 0-06-107414-4 Subj: Activities – playing. Toys.

Cow in the house ill. by Emily Bolam. Viking, 1997. ISBN 0-670-86779-9 Subj: Animals. Animals – bulls, cows. Folk & fairy tales. Homes, houses. Noise, sounds. Sleep.

Daddies are for catching fireflies ill. by Cynthia Jabar. Puffin, 1999. ISBN 0-14-056553-1 Subj: Family life. Format, unusual – toy & movable books.

Dancing ill. by Laura Rader. HarperCollins, 1991. ISBN 0-06-107422-5 Subj: Activities – dancing. Animals. Ballet. Format, unusual – toy & movable books.

A dozen dogs: a read-and-count story ill. by Carol Nicklaus. Random House, 1985. ISBN 0-394-96935-9 Subj: Animals – dogs. Counting, numbers. Sea & seashore.

A dozen ducklings lost and found ill. by Donald Dreifuss. Houghton, 2003. ISBN 0-618-14175-8 Subj: Animals – babies. Birds – ducks. Counting, numbers.

Egad, alligator! ill. by Todd McKie. Houghton, 2002. ISBN 0-618-14171-5 Subj: Animals. Emotions – fear. Reptiles – alligators, crocodiles.

Elemenopeo ill. by Donald Saaf. Houghton Mifflin, 1998. ISBN 0-395-90493-5 Subj: Activities – painting. Animals – cats.

First He made the sun ill. by Todd McKie. Putnam, 2000. ISBN 0-399-23199-4 Subj: Creation. Religion. Rhyming text.

First Night ill. by S. D. Schindler. Putnam, 1999. ISBN 0-399-23120-X Subj: Holidays – New Year's. Parades. Rhyming text.

Getting ready for new baby ill. by Laura Rader. HarperCollins, 1990. ISBN 0-06-026897-2 Subj: Babies. Emotions – envy, jealousy. Family life – new sibling. Science. Sibling rivalry.

The gingerbread boy (The gingerbread boy)

Goldilocks and the three bears (The three bears)

Good luck, bad luck ill. by Lillie James. Viking, 1991. ISBN 0-670-84275-3 Subj: Character traits – luck.

Good morning, sun! by Harriet Ziefert & Lisa Campbell Ernst; ill. by Lisa Campbell Ernst. Viking, 1988. ISBN 0-670-81578-0 Subj: Animals – rabbits. Babies. Morning.

Good night everyone! ill. by Andrea Baruffi. Little, 1988. ISBN 0-316-98756-5 Subj: Bedtime. Sleep. Toys.

Good night, Jessie! by Harriet Ziefert & Mavis Smith; ill. by Mavis Smith. Random House, 1987. ISBN 0-394-89193-7 Subj: Behavior – lost & found possessions. Family life. Sea & seashore.

Happy birthday, Grandpa! ill. by Sidney Levitt. HarperCollins, 1988. ISBN 0-694-00242-9 Subj: Animals. Animals – rabbits. Birthdays. Family life – grandfathers.

Happy Easter, Grandma! ill. by Sidney Levitt. HarperCollins, 1988. ISBN 0-694-00225-9 Subj: Animals – rabbits. Birds. Eggs. Holidays – Easter.

Harry takes a bath ill. by Mavis Smith. Viking, 1987. ISBN 0-670-81721-X Subj: Activities – bathing. Animals – hippopotamuses.

Hats off for the Fourth of July! ill. by Gustaf Miller. Viking, 2000. ISBN 0-670-89118-5 Subj: Clothing – hats. Holidays – Fourth of July. Rhyming text.

Henny Penny (Chicken Little)

Home for Navidad ill. by Santiago Cohen. Houghton, 2003. ISBN 0-618-34976-6 Subj: Family life – mothers. Foreign lands – Mexico. Foreign languages. Holidays – Christmas.

Hurry up, Jessie! ill. by Mavis Smith. Random House, 1987. ISBN 0-394-89194-5 Subj: Character traits – cleanliness. Night.

I swapped my dog ill. by Emily Bolam. Houghton Mifflin, 1998. ISBN 0-395-89159-0 Subj: Animals. Animals – dogs. Cumulative tales. Farms. Rhyming text.

I want to sleep in your bed! ill. by Mavis Smith. HarperCollins, 1990. ISBN 0-06-026895-6 Subj: Bedtime. Family life. Sleep.

I won't go to bed! ill. by Andrea Baruffi. Little, 1987. ISBN 0-316-98768-9 Subj: Bedtime.

Jason's bus ride ill. by Simms Taback. Viking, 1987. ISBN 0-670-81718-X Subj: Buses.

Keeping daddy awake on the way home from the beach ill. by Seymour Chwast. HarperCollins, 1986. ISBN 0-694-00080-9 Subj: Activities – traveling. Family life. Sea & seashore – beaches.

Let's get dressed! by Harriet Ziefert & Lisa Campbell Ernst; ill. by Lisa Campbell Ernst. Viking, 1988. ISBN 0-670-81580-2 Subj: Animals – rabbits. Babies. Clothing.

Let's go! Piggety Pig ill. by David Prebenna. Little, 1986. ISBN 0-316-98760-3 Subj: Animals – mice. Animals – pigs. Concepts – opposites.

Lewis the fire fighter ill. by Carol Nicklaus. Random House, 1986. ISBN 0-394-97618-5 Subj: Activities – playing. Fire. Imagination.

Listen! Piggety Pig ill. by David Prebenna. Little, 1986. ISBN 0-316-98761-1 Subj: Animals. Noise, sounds.

The little red hen (The little red hen)

Little Red Riding Hood ill. by Emily Bolam. Viking, 2000. ISBN 0-670-88389-1 Subj: Animals – wolves. Behavior – talking to strangers. Family life – grandmothers. Folk & fairy tales.

Lunchtime for a purple snake ill. by Todd McKie. Houghton, 2003. ISBN 0-618-31133-5 Subj: Activities – painting. Careers – artists. Concepts – color. Family life – grandfathers.

Math riddles ill. by Andrea Baruffi. Viking, 1997. Subj: Counting, numbers. Humorous stories. Riddles & jokes.

Me, too! Me, too! ill. by Karen Gundersheimer. HarperCollins, 1988. ISBN 0-06-026893-X Subj: Behavior – sharing.

Mike and Tony: best friends ill. by Catherine Siracusa. Viking, 1987. ISBN 0-670-81719-8 Subj: Friendship.

Mommies are for counting stars ill. by Cynthia Jabar. Penguin Putnam, 1999. ISBN 0-14-056552-3 Subj: Family life – mothers. Format, unusual – toy & movable books.

Moonride by Harriet Ziefert & Seymour Chwast; ill. by Seymour Chwast. Houghton Mifflin, 2000. ISBN 0-618-00229-4 Subj: Bedtime. Dreams. Moon. Night.

Mother Goose math ill. by Emily Bolam. Viking, 1997. ISBN 0-670-87569-4 Subj: Counting, numbers. Nursery rhymes.

Murphy meets the treadmill ill. by Emily Bolam. Houghton, 2001. ISBN 0-618-11357-6 Subj: Health & fitness – exercise. Pets.

My getting-ready-for-school book ill. by Mavis Smith. Random House, 1989. ISBN 0-394-82248-X Subj: Concepts. Format, unusual – board books.

My sister says nothing ever happens when we go sailing ill. by Seymour Chwast. HarperCollins, 1986. ISBN 0-694-00081-7 Subj: Boats, ships. Family life.

A new coat for Anna ill. by Anita Lobel. Knopf, 1988. ISBN 0-394-97426-3 Subj: Clothing – coats. Family life. War.

A new house for Mole and Mouse ill. by Mavis Smith. Viking, 1987. ISBN 0-670-81720-1 Subj: Animals – mice. Animals – moles. Homes, houses. Moving.

Nicky upstairs and down ill. by Richard Eric Brown. Viking, 1987. ISBN 0-670-81717-1 Subj: Animals – cats.

Nicky's Christmas surprise ill. by Richard Eric Brown. Penguin, 1985. ISBN 0-14-050555-5 Subj: Animals – cats. Farms. Holidays – Christmas.

Nicky's friends ill. by Richard Eric Brown. Viking, 1986. ISBN 0-670-81298-6 Subj: Animals – cats. Farms. Format, unusual – board books. Friendship.

Nicky's noisy night ill. by Richard Brown. Puffin, 1986. ISBN 0-929766-79-3 Subj: Animals – cats. Format, unusual – toy & movable books. Night. Noise, sounds.

No kiss for Grandpa! ill. by Emilie Boon. Orchard, 2001. ISBN 0-531-30328-4 Subj: Animals – cats. Family life – grandfathers.

No more! Piggety Pig ill. by David Prebenna. Little, 1986. ISBN 0-316-98763-8 Subj: Animals – mice. Animals – pigs. Concepts – color.

No, no, Nicky! ill. by Richard Eric Brown. Viking, 1986. ISBN 0-670-81297-8 Subj: Animals – cats. Format, unusual – board books. Safety.

Ode to Humpty Dumpty ill. by Seymour Chwast. Houghton, 2001. ISBN 0-618-05047-7 Subj: Character traits – helpfulness. Emotions – grief. Nursery rhymes.

Oh, what a noisy farm! ill. by Emily Bolam. Tambourine, 1995. ISBN 0-688-13261-8 Subj: Animals. Farms. Noise, sounds.

On Halloween night ill. by Ferida Wolff & Dolores Kozielski; ill. by Dolores Avendaño. Tambourine, 1994. ISBN 0-688-12973-0 Subj: Clothing – costumes. Cumulative tales. Holidays – Halloween. Rhyming text.

On our way to the barn by Harriet Ziefert & Simms Taback; ill. by Simms Taback. HarperCollins, 1985. ISBN 0-06-026877-8 Subj: Animals. Farms. Format, unusual – board books. Noise, sounds. Rhyming text.

On our way to the forest by Harriet Ziefert & Simms Taback; ill. by Simms Taback. HarperCollins, 1985. ISBN 0-06-026878-6 Subj: Forest, woods. Format, unusual – board books. Noise, sounds. Rhyming text.

On our way to the water by Harriet Ziefert & Simms Taback; ill. by Simms Taback. HarperCollins, 1985. ISBN 0-06-026879-4 Subj: Format, unusual – board books. Noise, sounds. Rhyming text.

On our way to the zoo by Harriet Ziefert & Simms Taback; ill. by Simms Taback. HarperCollins, 1985. ISBN 0-06-026880-8 Subj: Animals. Format, unusual – board books. Noise, sounds. Rhyming text. Zoos.

People of the Bible ill. by author. Doubleday, 1996. ISBN 0-553-09766-0 Subj: Format, unusual – toy & movable books. Religion.

Piggety Pig from morn 'til night ill. by David Prebenna. Little, 1986. ISBN 0-316-98764-6 Subj: Activities. Animals – pigs.

A polar bear can swim: what animals can and cannot do ill. by Emily Bolam. Viking, 1998. ISBN 0-670-88056-6 Subj: Activities. Animals. Circular tales.

Presents for Santa ill. by Laura Radar. Viking, 2000. ISBN 0-670-88390-5 Subj: Animals – mice. Gifts. Holidays – Christmas. Rhyming text. Santa Claus.

The princess and the pea (Andersen, H. C. [Hans Christian])

Pumpkin Pie ill. by Donald Dreifuss. Houghton Mifflin, 2000. ISBN 0-618-04883-9 Subj: Animals – goats. Fairs, festivals. Farms.

Pushkin meets the bundle ill. by Donald Saaf. Atheneum, 1998. ISBN 0-689-81413-5 Subj: Animals – dogs. Babies. Family life.

Pushkin minds the bundle ill. by Donald Saaf. Atheneum, 2000. ISBN 0-689-83216-8 Subj: Activities – vacationing. Animals – dogs. Babies. Family life.

Rabbit and Hare divide an apple ill. by Emily Bolam. Viking, 1998. ISBN 0-670-87790-5 Subj: Animals – rabbits. Behavior – sharing. Concepts. Counting, numbers. Food.

Rockheads ill. by Todd McKie. Houghton, 2004. ISBN 0-618-34574-4 Subj: Activities. Counting, numbers. Rhyming text.

Run! Run! ill. by Henrik Drescher. HarperCollins, 1986. ISBN 0-694-00097-3 Subj: Animals.

Sam and Lucy ill. by Claire Schumacher. HarperCollins, 1992. ISBN 0-06-026974-X Subj: Animals – dogs. Behavior – running away.

Sarah's questions ill. by Susan Bonners. Lothrop, 1986. ISBN 0-688-05615-6 Subj: Character traits – questioning. Family life – mothers. Nature.

Say good night! ill. by Catherine Siracusa. Viking, 1987. ISBN 0-670-81722-8 Subj: Bedtime. Morning. Night. Sleep.

Sleepy dog ill. by Norman Gorbaty. Random House, 1984. ISBN 0-394-96877-8 Subj: Animals – dogs. Sleep.

The snow child ill. by Julia Zanes. Viking, 2000. ISBN 0-670-88748-X Subj: Emotions – happiness. Folk & fairy tales. Foreign lands – Russia. Snowmen.

Someday we'll have very good manners ill. by Chris Demarest. Putnam, 2001. ISBN 0-399-23558-2 Subj: Etiquette.

Squarehead ill. by Todd McKie. Houghton, 2001. ISBN 0-618-08378-2 Subj: Concepts – shape. Dreams. Self-concept.

Strike four! ill. by Mavis Smith. Viking, 1988. ISBN 0-670-82033-4 Subj: Activities – playing. Behavior – misbehavior. Family life.

Surprise! ill. by Mary Morgan. Viking, 1988. ISBN 0-670-82036-9 Subj: Birthdays. Family life – mothers. Food.

Talk, baby! ill. by Emily Bolam. Holt, 1999. ISBN 0-8050-6144-4 Subj: Activities – talking. Babies. Family life – new sibling. Format, unusual – toy & movable books.

39 uses for a friend ill. by Rebecca Doughty. Putnam, 2001. ISBN 0-399-23616-3 Subj: Friendship.

The three billy goats Gruff (Asbjørnsen, P. C. [Peter Christen])

Toes have wiggles, kids have giggles ill. by . Putnam, 2002. ISBN 0-399-23617-1 Subj: Activities. Rhyming text.

Train song ill. by Donald Saaf. Orchard, 2000. ISBN 0-531-30204-0 Subj: Rhyming text. Trains.

The turnip ill. by Laura Rader. Viking, 1996. ISBN 0-670-86053-0 Subj: Animals. Character traits – cooperation. Cumulative tales. Farms. Folk & fairy tales. Foreign lands – Russia. Plants. Problem solving.

Two little witches ill. by Simms Taback. Candlewick, 1996. ISBN 1-56402-621-3 Subj: Counting, numbers. Holidays – Halloween. Witches.

Waiting for baby ill. by Emily Bolam. Holt, 1998. ISBN 0-8050-5929-6 Subj: Babies. Family life – new sibling.

Wee G. ill. by Donald Saaf. Atheneum, 1997. ISBN 0-689-81064-4 Subj: Animals – cats. Behavior – lost.

What do ducks dream? ill. by Donald Saaf. Putnam, 2001. ISBN 0-399-23358-X Subj: Animals. Bedtime. Dreams. Farms. Rhyming text. Sleep.

When daddy had the chicken pox ill. by Lionel Kalish. HarperCollins, 1991. ISBN 0-06-026907-3 Subj: Family life – fathers. Illness.

When I first came to this land ill. by Simms Taback. Putnam, 1998. ISBN 0-399-23044-0 Subj: Cumulative tales. Folk & fairy tales. Immigrants. Poverty. Songs.

Where's daddy's car? ill. by Andrea Baruffi. HarperCollins, 1992. ISBN 0-694-00378-6 Subj: Automobiles. Format, unusual – toy & movable books.

Where's mommy's truck? ill. by Andrea Baruffi. HarperCollins, 1992. ISBN 0-694-00377-8 Subj: Family life – mothers. Format, unusual – toy & movable books. Trucks.

Where's the cat? ill. by Arnold Lobel. HarperCollins, 1987. ISBN 0-694-00185-6 Subj: Animals – cats. Behavior – hiding. Format, unusual. Format, unusual – board books.

Where's the dog? ill. by Arnold Lobel. HarperCollins, 1987. ISBN 0-694-00184-8 Subj: Animals – dogs. Behavior – hiding. Format, unusual. Format, unusual – board books.

Where's the guinea pig? ill. by Arnold Lobel. HarperCollins, 1987. ISBN 0-694-00182-1 Subj: Animals – guinea pigs. Behavior – hiding. Format, unusual. Format, unusual – board books.

Where's the turtle? ill. by Arnold Lobel. HarperCollins, 1987. ISBN 0-694-00183-X Subj: Behavior – hiding. Format, unusual. Format, unusual – board books. Reptiles – turtles, tortoises.

Who can boo the loudest? ill. by Claire Schumacher. HarperCollins, 1990. ISBN 0-06-026899-9 Subj: Ghosts. Moon.

With love from Grandma ill. by Deborah Kogan Ray. Viking, 1989. ISBN 0-670-83004-6 Subj: Activities – knitting. Emotions – love. Family life – grandmothers.

You can't buy a dinosaur with a dime ill. by Amanda Haley. Blue Apple, 2003. ISBN 1-929766-81-5 Subj: Counting, numbers. Money. Problem solving.

You can't taste a pickle with your ear ill. by Amanda Haley. Blue Apple, 2002. ISBN 1-929766-68-8 Subj: Senses.

Ziegler, Sandra. *A visit to the bakery* photos by author. Childrens Pr., 1987. ISBN 0-516-01495-1 Subj: Careers – bakers.

Ziegler, Ursina. *Squaps the moonling* trans. by Barbara Kowall Gollob; ill. by Sita Jucker. Atheneum, 1969. Translation of Squaps, der Mondling. Subj: Aliens. Moon. Space & space ships.

Zijlstra, Tjerk. *Benny and his geese* ill. by Ivo de Weerd. McGraw-Hill, 1975. Translation of Bennie en zijn ganzen. ISBN 0-07-072825-9 Subj: Birds – geese. Folk & fairy tales. Wizards.

Zimelman, Nathan. *The great adventure of Wo Ti* ill. by Julie Downing. Macmillan, 1992. ISBN 0-02-793731-3 Subj: Animals – cats. Behavior – trickery. Fish. Foreign lands – China.

How the second grade got $8,205.50 to visit the Statue of Liberty ill. by Bill Slavin. A. Whitman, 1992. ISBN 0-8075-3431-5 Subj: Activities. Money. School.

If I were strong enough . . . ill. by Diane Paterson. Abingdon, 1982. ISBN 0-687-18670-6 Subj: Behavior – growing up. Family life.

Mean Murgatroyd and the ten cats ill. by Tony Auth. Dutton, 1984. ISBN 0-525-44116-6 Subj: Animals – cats. Animals – dogs. Character traits – meanness.

Once when I was five ill. by Carol Rogers. Steck-Vaughn, 1967. Subj: Birthdays. Imagination.

Positively no pets allowed ill. by Pamela Johnson. Dutton, 1980. ISBN 0-525-37560-0 Subj: Animals – gorillas. Pets.

The star of Melvin ill. by Olivier Dunrea. Macmillan, 1987. ISBN 0-02-793750-X Subj: Angels. Holidays – Christmas. Stars.

To sing a song as big as Ireland ill. by Joseph Low. Follett, 1967. Subj: Behavior – wishing. Foreign lands – Ireland. Holidays – St. Patrick's Day. Music. Mythical creatures.

Treed by a pride of irate lions ill. by Toni Goffe. Little, 1990. ISBN 0-316-98802-2 Subj: Animals – lions. Family life – fathers. Foreign lands – Africa.

Walls are to be walked ill. by Donald Carrick. Dutton, 1977. ISBN 0-525-42175-0 Subj: Activities – playing.

Zimmer, Dirk. *The trick-or-treat trap* ill. by author. HarperCollins, 1982. ISBN 0-06-026861-1 Subj: Holidays – Halloween. Parties. Witches.

Zimmerman, Andrea Griffing. *My dog Toby* by Andrea Zimmerman & David Clemesha; ill. by True Kelley. Harcourt, 2000. ISBN 0-15-202014-4 Subj: Animals – dogs. Pets.

Trashy town by Andrea Zimmerman & David Clemesha; ill. by Dan Yaccarino. HarperCollins, 1999. ISBN 0-06-027140-X Subj: Careers – sanitation workers. Cities, towns.

Yetta, the trickster ill. by Harold Berson. Seabury Pr., 1978. ISBN 0-8164-3218-X Subj: Foreign lands – Russia. Humorous stories.

Zimmerman, Baruch. *A Japanese fairy tale* (Iké, Jane Hori)

Zimmermann, H. Werner (Heinz Werner). *Alphonse knows . . . a circle is not a Valentine* ill. by author. Oxford Univ. Pr., 1991. ISBN 0-19-540744-X Subj: Concepts – shape. Holidays – Valentine's Day. Wizards.

Alphonse knows . . . the colour of spring ill. by author. Oxford Univ. Pr., 1991. ISBN 0-19-540743-1 Subj: Seasons – spring. Wizards.

Alphonse knows . . . twelve months make a year ill. by author. Oxford Univ. Pr., 1990. ISBN 0-19-540798-9 Subj: Animals – mice. Days of the week, months of the year. Seasons. Wizards.

Alphonse knows . . . zero is not enough ill. by author. Oxford Univ. Pr., 1990. ISBN 0-19-540797-0 Subj: Counting, numbers. Wizards.

Zimmett, Debbie. *Eddie enough* ill. by Charlotte Murray Fremaux. Woodbine, 2001. ISBN 1-890627-25-9 Subj: Behavior. Handicaps – ADD. School.

Zimnik, Reiner. *The bear on the motorcycle* trans. by Cornelia Schaeffer; ill. by author. Atheneum, 1963. Translation of Der bär auf dem motorrad. Subj: Animals – bears. Behavior – running away. Circus. Motorcycles.

The proud circus horse ill. by author. Pantheon, 1957. Subj: Animals – horses, ponies. Behavior – running away. Character traits – pride. Circus.

Zindel, Paul. *I love my mother* ill. by John Melo. HarperCollins, 1975. ISBN 0-06-026836-0 Subj: Emotions – loneliness. Emotions – love. Family life – mothers.

Ziner, Feenie. *Counting carnival* by Feenie Ziner & Paul Galdone; ill. by Paul Galdone. Coward, 1962. Subj: Activities – playing. Counting, numbers. Cumulative tales. Ethnic groups in the U.S. – African Americans. Parades. Poetry.

The true book of time by Feenie Ziner & Elizabeth Thompson; ill. by Katherine Evans. Childrens Pr., 1956. Subj: Time.

Zinnemann-Hope, Pam. *Find your coat, Ned* ill. by Kady MacDonald Denton. Macmillan, 1988. ISBN 0-689-50426-9 Subj: Behavior – lost & found possessions. Clothing – coats. Pets. Weather – rain.

Let's go shopping, Ned ill. by Kady MacDonald Denton. Macmillan, 1987. ISBN 0-689-50416-0 Subj: Shopping.

Let's play ball, Ned ill. by Kady MacDonald Denton. Macmillan, 1988. ISBN 0-689-50427-6 Subj: Activities – playing. Family life.

Time for bed, Ned ill. by Kady MacDonald Denton. Macmillan, 1987. ISBN 0-689-50415-2 Subj: Bedtime. Family life – mothers.

Zion, Gene. *All falling down* ill. by Margaret Bloy Graham. HarperCollins, 1951. Subj: Caldecott award honor books. Concepts – up & down.

Dear garbage man ill. by Margaret Bloy Graham. HarperCollins, 1957. Subj: Careers – sanitation workers. Cities, towns.

Harry, the dirty dog ill. by Margaret Bloy Graham. HarperCollins, 1956. Subj: Activities – bathing. Animals – dogs. Behavior – running away.

Hide and seek day ill. by Margaret Bloy Graham. HarperCollins, 1954. Subj: Behavior – hiding. Cities, towns. Games.

Jeffie's party ill. by Margaret Bloy Graham. HarperCollins, 1957. Subj: Games. Parties.

The meanest squirrel I ever met ill. by Margaret Bloy Graham. Scribners, 1962. Subj: Animals – squirrels. Character traits – meanness. Friendship. Holidays – Thanksgiving.

No roses for Harry ill. by Margaret Bloy Graham. HarperCollins, 1958. ISBN 0-06-026891-3 Subj: Animals – dogs. Clothing.

The plant sitter ill. by Margaret Bloy Graham. HarperCollins, 1959. ISBN 0-06-443012-X Subj: Plants.

Really spring ill. by Margaret Bloy Graham. HarperCollins, 1956. Subj: Seasons – spring.

The summer snowman ill. by Margaret Bloy Graham. HarperCollins, 1955. Subj: Holidays – Fourth of July. Seasons – summer. Snowmen. Weather – snow.

Zirbes, Laura. *How many bears?* ill. by E. Harper Johnson. Putnam, 1960. Subj: Animals – bears. Counting, numbers.

Zirkel, Lynn. *The shell dragon* ill. by Pete Bowman. Oxford Univ. Pr., 1989. ISBN 0-19-279838-3 Subj: Birds. Dragons.

Zisk, Mary. *The best single mom in the world* ill. by author. A. Whitman, 2001. ISBN 0-8075-0666-4 Subj: Adoption. Family life – mothers.

Zoehfeld, Kathleen Weidner. *Apples, apples* ill. by Christopher Santoro. HarperFestival, 2004. ISBN 0-06-053787-6 Subj: Animals – bears. Food. Format, unusual – board books. Seasons – fall. Trees.

Dinosaurs big and small ill. by Lucia Washburn. HarperCollins, 2002. ISBN 0-06-027936-2 Subj: Concepts – size. Dinosaurs.

Great white shark, ruler of the sea ill. by Steven James Petruccio. Soundprints, 1995. ISBN 1-56899-122-3 Subj: Fish – sharks. Sea & seashore.

How mountains are made ill. by James Graham Hale. HarperCollins, 1995. ISBN 0-06-024510-7 Subj: Earth. Mountains. Science.

What lives in a shell? ill. by Helen Davie. HarperCollins, 1994. ISBN 0-06-022999-3 Subj: Animals. Science. Sea & seashore.

What's alive? ill. by Nadine Bernard Westcott. HarperCollins, 1995. ISBN 0-06-023444-X Subj: Animals. Plants. Science.

Zola, Meguido. *The dream of promise: a folktale in Hebrew and English* ill. by Ruben Zellermayer. Kids Can, 1981. ISBN 0-919964-31-1 Subj: Folk & fairy tales. Foreign languages. Jewish culture. Self-concept.

Only the best ill. by Valerie Littlewood. Watts, 1982. ISBN 0-531-04066-6 Subj: Emotions – love. Family life – fathers.

Zolkower, Edie Stoltz. *Too many cooks* ill. by Shauna Mooney Kawasaki. Kar-Ben Copies, 2000. ISBN 1-58013-063-1 Subj: Activities – baking, cooking. Holidays – Passover. Jewish culture.

Zoll, Max Alfred. *Animal babies* trans. by Violetta Castillo; ed. by Hanns Reich; ill. by author. Hill & Wang, 1971. Translation of Tierkinder. ISBN 0-8090-2001-7 Subj: Animals.

A flamingo is born trans. by Catherine Edwards Sadler; photos by Winifried Noack. Putnam, 1978. ISBN 0-399-20632-9 Subj: Birds – flamingos. Science.

Zoller, Arthur David. *Fish colors* ill. by author. Charlesbridge, 2000. ISBN 0-88106-073-9 Subj: Concepts – color. Fish. Format, unusual – board books.

Fish counting ill. by author. Charlesbridge, 2000. ISBN 0-88106-074-7 Subj: Counting, numbers. Fish. Format, unusual – board books.

Zolotow, Charlotte (Shapiro). *The beautiful Christmas tree* ill. by Yan Nacimbene. Houghton Mifflin, 1999. ISBN 0-395-91365-9 Subj: Holidays – Christmas. Trees.

Big sister and little sister ill. by Martha G. Alexander. HarperCollins, 1966. ISBN 0-06-026926-X Subj: Behavior – running away. Family life.

The bunny who found Easter ill. by Helen Craig. Houghton Mifflin, 1998. ISBN 0-395-86265-5 Subj: Animals – rabbits. Emotions – loneliness. Holidays – Easter.

But not Billy ill. by Kay Chorao. HarperCollins, 1983. ISBN 0-06-026964-2 Subj: Babies. Behavior – growing up.

Do you know what I'll do? ill. by Javaka Steptoe. HarperCollins, 2000. ISBN 0-06-027880-3 Subj: Babies. Behavior – growing up. Emotions – love. Ethnic groups in the U.S. – African Americans. Family life.

Flocks of birds ill. by Ruth Lercher Bornstein. Crowell, 1981. ISBN 0-690-04113-6 Subj: Bedtime. Birds.

The hating book ill. by Ben Shecter. HarperCollins, 1969. ISBN 0-06-443197-5 Subj: Behavior – gossip. Emotions – hate. Friendship.

Hold my hand ill. by Thomas di Grazia. HarperCollins, 1972. ISBN 0-06-026952-9 Subj: Friendship. Weather – snow.

I have a horse of my own ill. by Yoko Mitsuhashi. Crowell, 1980. ISBN 0-690-04047-4 Subj: Animals – horses, ponies. Dreams. Night.

I know a lady ill. by James Stevenson. Greenwillow, 1984. ISBN 0-688-03837-9 Subj: Character traits – kindness. Old age.

I like to be little ill. by Erik Blegvad. HarperCollins, 1987. ISBN 0-690-04674-X Subj: Behavior – growing up. Family life – mothers.

If it weren't for you ill. by Ben Shecter. HarperCollins, 1966. ISBN 0-06-026943-X Subj: Family life. Sibling rivalry.

If you listen ill. by Stefano Vitale. Running Pr., 2002. ISBN 0-7624-1335-2 Subj: Emotions – love. Family life – fathers.

In my garden ill. by Roger Antoine Duvoisin. Lothrop, 1960. Subj: Plants. Seasons.

It's not fair ill. by William Pène Du Bois. HarperCollins, 1976. ISBN 0-06-026935-9 Subj: Behavior – dissatisfaction. Emotions – envy, jealousy. Family life.

Janey ill. by Ronald Himler. HarperCollins, 1973. ISBN 0-06-026928-6 Subj: Emotions – loneliness. Friendship. Moving.

May I visit? ill. by Erik Blegvad. HarperCollins, 1976. ISBN 0-06-026933-2 Subj: Behavior – growing up. Emotions – love. Family life.

Mr. Rabbit and the lovely present ill. by Maurice Sendak. HarperCollins, 1962. ISBN 0-06-026946-4 Subj: Animals – rabbits. Birthdays. Caldecott award honor books. Concepts – color. Family life – mothers. Holidays – Easter.

The moon was the best ill. by Tana Hoban. Greenwillow, 1993. ISBN 0-688-09941-6 Subj: Moon.

My friend John ill. by Ben Shecter. HarperCollins, 1968. ISBN 0-06-026948-0 Subj: Friendship.

My grandson Lew ill. by William Pène Du Bois. HarperCollins, 1974. ISBN 0-06-026961-8 Subj: Death. Emotions – grief. Family life. Family life – grandfathers.

The new friend ill. by Emily Arnold McCully. Crowell, 1981. ISBN 0-690-04087-3 Subj: Behavior – sharing. Friendship.

The old dog ill. by James Ransome. HarperCollins, 1995. ISBN 0-06-024412-7 Subj: Animals – dogs. Death. Emotions – grief. Ethnic groups in the U.S. – African Americans. Pets.

One step, two . . . ill. by Roger Antoine Duvoisin. Lothrop, 1955. Subj: Activities – walking. Cities, towns. Counting, numbers.

Over and over ill. by Garth Williams. HarperCollins, 1957. ISBN 0-06-026956-1 Subj: Holidays. Time.

The park book ill. by Hans Augusto Rey. HarperCollins, 1944. ISBN 0-06-026973-1 Subj: Activities – playing. Cities, towns. Parks.

The poodle who barked at the wind ill. by Roger Antoine Duvoisin. Lothrop, 1964. Subj: Animals – dogs. Noise, sounds. Pets.

The quarreling book ill. by Arnold Lobel. HarperCollins, 1963. ISBN 0-06-026976-6 Subj: Behavior – fighting, arguing. Cumulative tales. Emotions – anger. Weather – rain.

The quiet mother and the noisy little boy ill. by Marc Simont. HarperCollins, 1989. ISBN 0-06-026979-0 Subj: Family life. Noise, sounds.

River winding ill. by Kazue Mizumura. Crowell, 1978. ISBN 0-690-03867-4 Subj: Poetry.

A rose, a bridge, and a wild black horse ill. by Robin Spowart. HarperCollins, 1987. ISBN 0-06-026939-1 Subj: Emotions – love. Family life.

Say it! ill. by James Stevenson. Greenwillow, 1980. Subj: Activities – walking. Emotions – love. Family life – mothers. Nature. Seasons – fall.

The seashore book ill. by Wendell Minor. HarperCollins, 1992. ISBN 0-06-020214-9 Subj: Family life – mothers. Imagination. Sea & seashore.

The sky was blue ill. by Garth Williams. HarperCollins, 1963. ISBN 0-06-027001-2 Subj: Emotions – love. Family life.

The sleepy book ill. by Vladimir Bobri. Lothrop, 1958. Subj: Animals. Bedtime. Sleep.

The sleepy book ill. by Ilse Plume. Rev. ed. HarperCollins, 1988. ISBN 0-06-026968-5 Subj: Animals. Bedtime. Sleep.

Some things go together ill. by Ashley Wolff. Newly illustrated ed. HarperFestival, 1999. ISBN 0-694-01197-5 Subj: Emotions – love. Family life. Poetry.

Someday ill. by Arnold Lobel. HarperCollins, 1965. ISBN 0-06-027016-0 Subj: Behavior – wishing. Dreams.

Someone new ill. by Erik Blegvad. HarperCollins, 1978. ISBN 0-06-027018-7 Subj: Behavior – growing up. Family life.

Something is going to happen ill. by Catherine Stock. HarperCollins, 1988. ISBN 0-06-027029-2 Subj: Morning. Weather – snow.

The song ill. by Nancy Tafuri. Greenwillow, 1982. ISBN 0-688-00817-8 Subj: Nature. Seasons. Songs.

The storm book ill. by Margaret Bloy Graham. HarperCollins, 1952. ISBN 0-06-027026-8 Subj: Caldecott award honor books. Emotions – fear. Weather. Weather – rain. Weather – rainbows.

Summer is . . . ill. by Ruth Lercher Bornstein. Crowell, 1983. ISBN 0-690-04304-X Subj: Rhyming text. Seasons – summer.

The summer night ill. by Ben Shecter. HarperCollins, 1974. Published in 1958 under the title The night when mother was away. ISBN 0-06-026960-X Subj: Activities – walking. Bedtime. Family life. Family life – fathers.

This quiet lady ill. by Anita Lobel. Greenwillow, 1992. ISBN 0-688-09306-X Subj: Family life – mothers.

Three funny friends ill. by Mary Chalmers. HarperCollins, 1961. Subj: Emotions – loneliness. Friendship. Imagination – imaginary friends.

A tiger called Thomas ill. by Catherine Stock. Lothrop, 1988. ISBN 0-688-06697-6 Subj: Character traits – shyness. Emotions – loneliness. Holidays – Halloween.

A tiger called Thomas ill. by Kurt Werth. Lothrop, 1963. Subj: Character traits – shyness. Emotions – loneliness. Holidays – Halloween.

Timothy too! ill. by Ruth Robbins. Houghton Mifflin, 1986. ISBN 0-395-39378-7 Subj: Friendship. Sibling rivalry.

The unfriendly book ill. by William Pène Du Bois. HarperCollins, 1975. ISBN 0-06-026931-6 Subj: Behavior – fighting, arguing. Friendship.

Wake up and goodnight ill. by Pamela Paparone. HarperCollins, 1998. ISBN 0-694-01032-4 Subj: Activities. Animals. Bedtime. Circular tales. Dreams. Format, unusual. Morning. Night.

When I have a little girl; When I have a little boy ill. by Hilary Knight. Callaway, 2000. ISBN 0-935112-45-6 Subj: Behavior. Family life – parents. Format, unusual.

When I have a son ill. by Hilary Knight. HarperCollins, 1967. ISBN 0-06-027051-9 Subj: Behavior – growing up. Family life. Imagination.

When the wind stops ill. by Stefano Vitale. HarperCollins, 1995. ISBN 0-06-026972-3 Subj: Bedtime. Nature. Night. Weather – wind.

The white marble ill. by Lilian Obligado. Abelard-Schuman, 1963. Subj: Activities – playing. Friendship. Night.

Who is Ben? ill. by Kathryn Jacobi. HarperCollins, 1997. ISBN 0-06-027352-6 Subj: Bedtime. Dreams. Night.

William's doll ill. by William Pène Du Bois. HarperCollins, 1972. ISBN 0-06-027048-9 Subj: Family life. Family life – grandmothers. Toys – dolls.

Zonta, Pat. *Jessica's x-ray* ill. by Clive Dobson. Firefly, 2002. ISBN 1-55297-578-9 Subj: Hospitals. Illness.

Zoo animals ill. with photos. Imported Pubs., 1983. Subj: Animals. Format, unusual – board books. Wordless.

Zoo animals ill. with photos & drawings. Macmillan, 1991. ISBN 0-689-71406-8 Subj: Animals. Nature.

Zuchora-Walske, Christine. *Spiny sea stars* ill. with photos. Lerner, 2001. ISBN 0-8225-3765-6 Subj: Animals – starfish. Sea & seashore.

Zucker, Jonny. *Apples and honey* ill. by Jan Barger Cohen. Barron's, 2002. ISBN 0-7641-2265-7 Subj: Holidays – Rosh Hashanah. Jewish culture.

Four special questions ill. by Jan Barger Cohen. Barron's, 2003. ISBN 0-7641-2267-3 Subj: Holidays – Passover. Jewish culture.

It's party time ill. by Jan Barger Cohen. Barron's, 2003. ISBN 0-7641-2268-1 Subj: Holidays – Purim. Jewish culture.

Zullo, Germano. *Marta and the bicycle* ill. by Albertine. Kane/Miller, 2002. ISBN 1-929132-35-2 Subj: Animals – bulls, cows. Humorous stories. Sports – bicycling. Sports – racing.

Zusman, Evelyn. *The Passover parrot* ill. by Katherine Janus Kahn. Kar-Ben Copies, 1984. ISBN 0-930494-29-6 Subj: Birds – parakeets, parrots. Family life. Holidays – Passover. Jewish culture.

Zweifel, Frances W. *Animal baby-sitters* ill. by Irene Brady. Morrow, 1981. ISBN 0-688-00444-X Subj: Activities – babysitting. Animals. Nature.

Bony ill. by Whitney Darrow, Jr. HarperCollins, 1977. ISBN 0-06-027071-3 Subj: Animals – squirrels. Pets.

The Make-Something Club ill. by Ann Schweninger. Viking, 1994. ISBN 0-670-82361-9 Subj: Activities – baking, cooking. Activities – making things. Animals – raccoons. Animals – squirrels. Food.

Zwerger, Lisbeth. *Swan Lake* ill. by reteller. North-South, 2002. Based on Pyotr I. Tchaikovsky's original 1877 ballet. ISBN 0-7358-1703-0 Subj: Activities – dancing. Ballet. Birds – swans. Folk & fairy tales. Magic.

Zwetchkenbaum, G. *The Peanuts shape circus puzzle book* ill. by author. Scholastic, 1983. ISBN 0-590-32905-7 Subj: Concepts – shape. Riddles & jokes.

The Peanuts sleepy time puzzle book ill. by author. Scholastic, 1983. ISBN 0-590-32906-5 Subj: Riddles & jokes. Sleep.

The Snoopy farm puzzle book ill. by author. Scholastic, 1983. ISBN 0-590-32907-3 Subj: Farms. Riddles & jokes.

Snoopy safari puzzle book ill. by author. Scholastic, 1983. ISBN 0-590-32908-1 Subj: Riddles & jokes.

Title Index

Titles appear in alphabetical sequence with the author's name in parentheses, followed by the page number of the full listing in the Bibliographic Guide. For identical title listings, the illustrator's name is given to further identify the version. In the case of variant titles, both the original and differing titles are listed.

A

A & The (Raskin, Ellen), 1149

A apple pie (Greenaway, Kate), 870

A apple pie (Pearson, Tracey Campbell), 1124

A, B, C, D, tummy, toes, hands, knee (Hennessy, B. G. [Barbara G.]), 908

A B Cedar (Lyon, George Ella), 1028

A B See! (Hoban, Tana), 920

A B See (Ogle, Lucille), 1108

A for angel (Montresor, Beni), 1078

A for the ark (Duvoisin, Roger Antoine), 809

A is for – ? (Horenstein, Henry), 929

A is for Africa (Bond, Jean Carey), 695

A is for alphabet, 621

A is for always (Anglund, Joan Walsh), 643

A is for Amos (Chandra, Deborah), 746

A is for angry (Boynton, Sandra), 700

A is for animals (Pelham, David), 1126

A is for anything (Barry, Katharina), 667

A is for artist (J. Paul Getty Museum), 944

A is for Asia (Chin-Lee, Cynthia), 751

A is for astronaut (Tucker, Sian), 1249

A is for salad (Lester, Mike), 1005

A la ferme = At the farm (Rider, Alex), 1156

A. Lincoln and me (Borden, Louise), 697

A, my name is . . . (Lyne, Alice), 1028

A my name is Alice (Bayer, Jane), 672

The A to Z beastly jamboree (Bender, Robert), 677

A to Z, do you ever feel like me? (Hausman, Bonnie), 898

A to Z picture book (Fujikawa, Gyo) *Gyo Fujikawa's A to Z picture book*, 843

A was an angler (Domanska, Janina), 801

A was once an apple pie (Lear, Edward), 998

A you're adorable (Lippman, Sidney), 1016

Aaaarrgghh! spider! (Monks, Lydia), 1077

Aani and the tree huggers (Atkins, Jeannine), 653

Aardvarks, disembark! (Jonas, Ann), 957

Aardvark's picnic (Higham, Jon Atlas), 912

Aaron awoke (Burton, Marilee Robin), 727

Aaron's awful allergies (Harrison, Troon), 895

Aaron's hair (Munsch, Robert N.), 1091

Aaron's shirt (Gould, Deborah), 866

Abbie against the storm (Vaughan, Marcia Kapok), 1257

Abby (Caines, Jeannette), 730

ABC (Burningham, John) *John Burningham's ABC*, 725

ABC (Burton, Jane), 726

ABC (Calmenson, Stephanie), 731

ABC (Cleaver, Elizabeth), 755

ABC (Emberley, Ed [Edward Randolph]) *Ed Emberley's ABC*, 816

ABC (Kightley, Rosalinda), 971

ABC (Lear, Edward), 998

ABC (Munari, Bruno), 1091

ABC (Steiner, Charlotte), 1222

ABC: alphabet rhymes (Mitter, Matt), 1075

ABC Americana from the National Gallery of Art (Rubin, Cynthia Elyce), 1172

ABC, an alphabet of many things (Rojankovsky, Feodor), 1164

ABC and 123 (Wilson, Barbara Ker), 1287

ABC animal riddles (Joyce, Susan), 959

ABC book (Falls, C. B. [Charles Buckles]), 822

ABC bunny (Gág, Wanda), 844

ABC cat (Jewell, Nancy), 952

ABC cats (Darling, Kathy [Mary Kathleen]), 783

ABC Christmas (DeLage, Ida), 788

ABC Disney (Sabuda, Robert James), 1176

ABC dogs (Darling, Kathy [Mary Kathleen]), 783

ABC Easter bunny (DeLage, Ida), 788

The ABC exhibit (Fisher, Leonard Everett), 830

ABC fire dogs (DeLage, Ida), 788

ABC for the library (Little, Mary E.), 1016

ABC for you and me (Girnis, Margaret), 858

ABC Halloween witch (DeLage, Ida), 788

ABC, I like me! (Carlson, Nancy L.), 736

ABC kids (Williams, Laura E.), 1286

The ABC mystery (Cushman, Doug), 779

ABC nature riddles (Joyce, Susan), 959

ABC of African American poetry Ashley Bryan's *abc of African American poetry*, 653

ABC of buses (Shuttlesworth, Dorothy Edwards), 1203

ABC of cars and trucks (Alexander, Anne [Anna Barbara Cooke]), 630

The ABC of cars, trucks and machines (Holl, Adelaide), 925

An ABC of fashionable animals (Edens, Cooper), 811

ABC of monsters (Niland, Deborah), 1102

ABC pigs go to market (DeLage, Ida), 789

ABC pirate adventure (DeLage, Ida), 789

ABC pop! (Isadora, Rachel), 942

ABC rhymes (Mother Goose), 1086

ABC Santa Claus (DeLage, Ida), 789

A B C, say with me (Gundersheimer, Karen), 884

ABC school riddles, 621

ABC T-Rex (Most, Bernard), 1085

ABC triplets at the zoo (DeLage, Ida), 789

ABC word book (Scarry, Richard) *Richard Scarry's ABC word book*, 1182

ABCD an alphabet book of cats and dogs (Moxley, Sheila), 1090

ABCDEFGHIJKLMNOPQRSTUVWXYZ in English and Spanish, 622

ABCDEFGHIJKLMNOPQRSTUVWXYZ (Kuskin, Karla), 988

ABCDrive! (Howland, Naomi), 932

A-B-C-ing (Beller, Janet), 676

The ABC's of Christmas (O'Connor, Francine M.), 1108

Abdul (Wells, Rosemary), 1275

Abdul's treasure (Moxley, Susan), 1090

Abe Lincoln remembers (Turner, Ann Warren), 1250

Abe Lincoln, the boy who loved books (Winters, Kay), 1289

Abel and the wolf (Lairla, Sergio), 991

Abel's Island (Steig, William), 1221

Abel's moon (Hughes, Shirley), 933

Abigail at the beach (Pirani, Felix), 1134

Abiyoyo (Seeger, Pete), 1192

Abiyoyo returns (Seeger, Pete), 1192

About amphibians (Sill, Cathryn P.), 1204

About dying (Stein, Sara Bonnett), 1221

About fish (Sill, Cathryn P.), 1204

About handicaps (Stein, Sara Bonnett), 1221

About insects (Sill, Cathryn P.), 1204

About mammals (Sill, Cathryn P.), 1204

About Nono, the baby elephant (Hogan, Inez), 924

About the rain forest (Johanasen, Heather), 953

About things you find at the beach (Vullo, Vera), 1260

Abracadabra to zigzag (Lecourt, Nancy), 999

Abracatabby (Hiller, Catherine), 914

Abraham Lincoln (Aulaire, Ingri Mortenson d'), 654

Abraham Lincoln (Livingston, Myra Cohn), 1018

Abraham Lincoln (Nettleton, Pamela Hill), 1099

Abraham Lincoln (Raatma, Lucia), 1146

The absentminded fellow (Marshak, S. [Samuil]), 1052

Absolutely angels, 622

The absolutely awful alphabet (Gerstein, Mordicai), 853

F

G

Lupatelli's favorite nursery tales (Armitage, Marcia), 647

Lyle and the birthday party (Waber, Bernard), 1261

Lyle at Christmas (Waber, Bernard), 1261

Lyle at the office (Waber, Bernard), 1261

Lyle finds his mother (Waber, Bernard), 1261

Lyle, Lyle Crocodile (Waber, Bernard), 1261

Lynn Hollyn's Christmas toyland (Hollyn, Lynn), 926

Lynx (St. Pierre, Stephanie), 1177

Lysbet and the fire kittens (Moskin, Marietta D.), 1085

M

M. C. Turtle and the hip hop hare (Vozar, David), 1260

M is for Minnesota (Chial, Debra), 749

M is for moving (Ilsley, Velma), 939

M is for music (Krull, Kathleen), 986

Ma Dear's aprons (McKissack, Patricia C.), 1040

Ma Jiang and the orange ants (Porte, Barbara Ann), 1138

Ma nDa La (Adoff, Arnold), 625

Mabel dancing (Hest, Amy), 911

Mabel ran away with the toys (Wahl, Jan), 1263

Mabel the Tooth Fairy and how she got her job (Davis, Katie [Katie I.]), 785

Mabela the clever (MacDonald, Margaret Read), 1034

Mable the whale (King, Patricia), 973

Mac and Marie and the train toss surprise (Howard, Elizabeth Fitzgerald), 931

Mac side up (Elsdale, Bob), 816

Macbeth for kids (Burdett, Lois), 724

Maccabee jamboree (Holland, Cheri), 926

McDuff and the baby (Wells, Rosemary), 1276

McDuff comes home (Wells, Rosemary), 1276

McDuff goes to school (Wells, Rosemary), 1276

McDuff moves in (Wells, Rosemary), 1276

McDuff saves the day (Wells, Rosemary), 1276

McDuffs hide-and-seek (Wells, Rosemary), 1276

McDuff's new friend (Wells, Rosemary), 1276

McElligot's pool (Seuss, Dr.), 1196

McGillycuddy could (Edwards, Pamela Duncan), 812

The McGoonys have a party (Schatell, Brian), 1184

MacGooses's grocery (Asch, Frank), 652

McGraw's Emporium (Aylesworth, Jim), 656

Machine poems (Bennett, Jill), 677

Machines (Rockwell, Anne F.), 1161

Machines as big as monsters (Stickland, Paul), 1226

Machines at work (Barton, Byron), 668

Mack made movies (Brown, Don), 710

The Macmillan picture wordbook (Daly, Kathleen N.), 781

MacMurtrey's wall (Sutherland, Marc), 1231

MacPelican's American adventure (Anderson, Scoular), 642

Mad about plaid (McElmurry, Jill), 1035

Mad Dog McGraw (Uhlberg, Myron), 1253

Mad monsters mix and match (Koelling, Caryl), 978

Mad summer night's dream (Brown, Ruth), 715

A mad wet hen and other riddles (Low, Joseph), 1025

Madaket Millie (Weller, Frances Ward), 1275

Madame LaGrande and her so high, to the sky, uproarious pompadour (Fleming, Candace), 833

Madeline (Bemelmans, Ludwig), 676

Madeline [pop-up book] (Bemelmans, Ludwig), 676

Madeline and the bad hat (Bemelmans, Ludwig), 676

Madeline and the gypsies (Bemelmans, Ludwig), 676

Madeline in London (Bemelmans, Ludwig), 676

Madeline says merci (Marciano, John Bemelmans), 1051

Madeline's Christmas (Bemelmans, Ludwig), 676

Madeline's rescue (Bemelmans, Ludwig), 676

Madge's magic show (Thaler, Mike), 1238

Madison finds a line (Warner, Sunny), 1268

Madlenka (Sis, Peter), 1208

Madoulina (Bognomo, Joel Eboueme), 694

Maebelle's suitcase (Tusa, Tricia), 1251

Maestro plays (Martin, Bill [William Ivan]), 1055

Mag the magnificent (Gackenbach, Dick), 844

Magda's piñata magic = Magda y la piñata mágica (Chavarría-Cháirez, Becky), 748

Magda's tortillas = Las tortillas de Magada (Chavarría-Cháirez, Becky), 748

Maggie, a sheep dog (Patent, Dorothy Hinshaw), 1122

Maggie and Silky and Joe (Ehrlich, Amy), 814

Maggie and the emergency room (Davison, Martine), 785

Maggie and the Ferocious Beast, the big carrot (Paraskevas, Betty), 1119

Maggie and the Ferocious Beast, the big scare (Paraskevas, Betty), 1119

Maggie and the goodbye gift (Milord, Sue), 1073

Maggie and the monster (Winthrop, Elizabeth), 1290

Maggie and the pirate (Keats, Ezra Jack), 964

The Maggie B (Haas, Irene), 885

Maggie doesn't want to move (O'Donnell, Elizabeth Lee), 1108

Maggie Mab and the bogey beast (Carey, Valerie Scho), 734

Maggie Simpson's alphabet book (Groening, Maggie), 882

Maggie Simpson's book of animals (Groening, Maggie), 882

Maggie Simpson's book of colors and shapes (Groening, Maggie), 882

Maggie Simpson's counting book (Groening, Maggie), 882

Maggie's moon (Alexander, Martha G.), 631

Maggie's whopper (Alexander, Sally Hobart), 631

Magic and the night river (Bunting, Eve [Anne Evelyn]), 722

The magic apple (Bliss, Corinne Demas), 692

The magic ark (Price-Thomas, Brian), 1142

Magic art class (Black, Harley), 689

The magic auto (Janosch), 949

The magic babushka (Tildes, Phyllis Limbacher), 1243

The magic balloon (Mari, Iela), 1051

Magic beach (Lester, Alison), 1004

The magic bean tree (Van Laan, Nancy), 1256

The magic beans (Hillert, Margaret), 914

The magic bed (Burningham, John), 725

The magic bird (Bolliger, Max), 695

The magic boat (Demi), 792

The magic boots (Emerson, Scott), 817

The magic box (Alexander, Martha G.) 3 magic flip books, 631

The magic box (Marie, Geraldine), 1051

The magic bubble trip (Schubert, Ingrid), 1189

The magic cap (Weedn, Flavia), 1272

Magic carpet (Brisson, Pat), 708

The magic circus (Logue, Christopher), 1021

The magic cooking pot (Towle, Faith M.), 1246

The magic dogs of the volcanoes (Argueta, Manlio), 647

The magic dreidels (Kimmel, Eric A.), 972

The magic fan (Baker, Keith), 660

The magic feather duster (Lipkind, William), 1015

Magic fort (Havill, Juanita), 899

The magic gourd (Diakité, Baba Wagué), 797

The magic guinea pig (Springstubb, Tricia), 1218

The magic hat (Alexander, Martha G.) 3 magic flip books, 631

The magic hat (Fox, Mem), 837

The magic hill (Milne, A. A. [Alan Alexander]), 1072

The magic hockey stick (Maloney, Peter), 1049

The magic honey jar (Bohdal, Susi), 695

The magic horse (Scott, Sally), 1191

The magic house (Eversole, Robyn Harbert), 821

The magic hummingbird (Malotki, Ekkehart), 1049

Magic in the mist (Kimmel, Margaret Mary), 973

The magic kerchief (Larson, Kirby), 995

The magic leaf (Morris, Winifred), 1084

The magic meatballs (Yaffe, Alan), 1297

Magic Michael (Slobodkin, Louis), 1210

The magic moonberry jump ropes (Hru, Dakari), 932

The magic nesting doll (Ogburn, Jacqueline K.), 1108

The magic of Millicent Musgrave (Turkle, Brinton), 1250

The magic of music (Weil, Lisl), 1273

The magic of Pomme (Sondheimer, Ilse), 1215

The magic of Spider Woman (Duncan, Lois), 808

The magic paintbrush (Muller, Robin), 1091

The magic picture (Alexander, Martha G.) 3 magic flip books, 631

The magic plum tree (Littledale, Freya), 1018

The magic pocket (Mado, Michio), 1045

The magic porridge pot (Galdone, Paul), 845

N

O

Q

R

U

Illustrator Index

Illustrators appear alphabetically in bold-face followed by their titles. Names in parentheses are authors of the titles when different from the illustrator. Page numbers refer to the full listing in the Bibliographic Guide.

Cressy, Mike. *Bubble trouble* (Hulme, Joy N.), 934
Cretien, Paul D. *Sir Henry and the dragon,* 774
Crews, Donald. *Bicycle race,* 774
Blue sea (Kalan, Robert), 961
Carousel, 774
Cloudy day/sunny day, 774
Each orange had eight slices (Giganti, Paul), 856
Eclipse (Branley, Franklyn M. [Mansfield]), 703
Flying, 774
Freight train, 774
Harbor, 774
How many snails? (Giganti, Paul), 856
Inside freight train, 774
Light, 774
Night at the fair, 774
Parade, 774
Rain (Kalan, Robert), 961
Sail away, 774
School bus, 774
School bus [board book], 774
Shortcut, 774
Ten black dots, 775
This is the sunflower (Schaefer, Lola M.), 1184
Tomorrow's alphabet (Shannon, George), 1198
Truck, 775
We read, 775
When this box is full (Lillie, Patricia), 1012
Crews, Nina. *A ghost story,* 775
A high, low, near, far, loud, quiet story, 775
I'll catch the moon, 775
One hot summer day, 775
Snowball, 775
When will Sarah come? (Howard, Elizabeth Fitzgerald), 931
You are here, 775
Crichlow, Ernest. *Galumph* (Lansdown, Brenda), 994
Two is a team (Beim, Lorraine), 675
Crichton, Michael *see* Douglas, Michael
Cristini, Ermanno. *In my garden,* 775
In the pond, 775
In the woods, 775
Crockett-Blassingame, Linda. *In the park with dad* (Ackerman, Karen), 622
See the ocean (Condra, Estelle), 765
Croft, James Lee. *Faces* (Smith, Patty), 1213
Croft, Priscilla. *Dealing with jealousy,* 775
Croll, Carolyn. *The bear on the doorstep* (Flory, Jane), 834
The big balloon race (Coerr, Eleanor), 758
Clara and the bookwagon (Levinson, Nancy Smiler), 1006
The little snowgirl, 775
Paul Gallico's The small miracle (Barton, Bob), 668
Questions (Hopkins, Lee Bennett), 929
Switch on, switch off (Berger, Melvin), 681
The three brothers, 775
Too many babas, 775
The unexpected grandchildren (Flory, Jane), 834
We'll have a friend for lunch (Flory, Jane), 834
What will the weather be? (DeWitt, Lyndia), 797
Crosby, Emma. *The jumblies* (Lear, Edward), 998

The owl and the pussycat (Lear, Edward), 998
The pobble who has no toes (Lear, Edward), 998
The quangle wangle's hat (Lear, Edward), 998
Cross, Peter. *Dudley and the monster* (Taylor, Judy), 1236
Dudley and the strawberry shake (Taylor, Judy), 1236
Dudley goes flying (Taylor, Judy), 1236
Dudley in a jam (Taylor, Judy), 1236
The Sesame Street ABC storybook (Moss, Jeffrey), 1085
Trumpets in Grumpetland (Dallas-Smith, Peter), 781
Crossland, Caroline. *Ten tall oaktrees* (Edwards, Richard), 813
Croswell, Volney. *How to hide a hippopotamus,* 775
Crow, Lauri. *Sammy's mommy has cancer* (Kohlenberg, Sherry), 978
Crowley, Mart. *Kay Thompson's Eloise takes a bawth (sic)* (Thompson, Kay), 1240
Crowther, Kitty. *Jack and Jim,* 776
Crowther, Robert. *All the fun of the fair,* 776
Animal rap! 776
Animal snap! 776
Colors, 776
Dump trucks and diggers, 776
Hide and seek counting book, 776
The most amazing hide-and-seek alphabet book, 776
The most amazing hide-and-seek opposites book, 776
My pop-up surprise ABC, 776
My pop-up surprise 1 2 3, 776
Pop goes the weasel! 776
Shapes, 776
Who lives in the country? 776
Who lives in the garden? 776
Who lives on the farm? 776
Croxford, Vera. *All kinds of animals,* 776
Crozat, François. *The egg and I* (Chausse, Sylvie), 748
I am a little cat, 776
I am a little caterpillar, 776
I am a little dog, 776
Crum, Anna-Maria. *The adventure of Paz in the land of numbers* (Bowden, Miriam), 699
Cruz, Ray. *Alexander and the terrible, horrible, no good, very bad day* (Viorst, Judith), 1259
Alexander, who used to be rich last Sunday (Viorst, Judith), 1259
A day off (Tobias, Tobi), 1244
The gorilla did it! (Hazen, Barbara Shook), 902
Horrible Hepzibah (Preston, Edna Mitchell), 1142
I hate to go to bed (Barrett, Judi), 667
King Laurence, the alarm clock (Mann, Peggy), 1049
There's a hippopotamus under my bed (Thaler, Mike), 1238
What are we going to do about Andrew? (Sharmat, Marjorie Weinman), 1199
What's wrong with being a skunk? (Schlein, Miriam), 1186
The woman with the eggs (Andersen, H. C. [Hans Christian]), 641
Words (Allington, Richard L.), 636
You think it's fun to be a clown! (Adler, David A.), 624

Cuetara, Mittie. *Baby business,* 777
The crazy crawler crane and other very short truck stories, 777
Terrible Teresa and other very short stories, 777
Cuffari, Richard. *How did numbers begin?* (Sitomer, Mindel), 1208
Little Yellow Fur (Hays, Wilma Pitchford), 901
My plant (Wong, Herbert H.), 1293
The wonderful box (Ames, Mildred), 637
Cullen-Clark, Patricia. *Just listen* (Morris, Winifred), 1084
Penny in the road (Precek, Katharine Wilson), 1141
Cumings, Art. *The cat's pajamas* (Chittum, Ida), 751
Please try to remember the first of Octember! (Seuss, Dr.), 1196
Cummings, Chris. *The little book of fowl jokes* (Lyfick, Warren), 1027
Cummings, Michael. *In the hollow of your hand* (McGhee, Alison), 1036
Cummings, Pat. *Ananse and the lizard,* 777
Angel baby, 777
Barry and Bennie (Medearis, Angela Shelf), 1063
C is for city (Grimes, Nikki), 875
Carousel, 777
Chilly stomach (Caines, Jeannette), 730
Clean your room, Harvey Moon! 777
C.L.O.U.D.S., 777
Fred's first day (Warren, Cathy), 1268
I need a lunch box (Caines, Jeannette), 730
Jimmy Lee did it, 777
Just us women (Caines, Jeannette), 730
My aunt came back, 777
My mama needs me (Walter, Mildred Pitts), 1267
Petey Moroni's Camp Runamok diary, 777
Pickin' peas (MacDonald, Margaret Read), 1034
Springtime bears (Warren, Cathy), 1268
Storm in the night (Stolz, Mary [Mary Slattery]), 1227
Two too much (Walsh, Ellen Stoll), 1266
Willie's not the hugging kind (Barrett, Joyce Durham), 666
Cummings, W. T. (Walter Thies). *The kid,* 777
Miss Esta Maude's secret, 777
Wickford of Beacon Hill, 777
Cummings, William Lahey. *Picture book theater* (De Regniers, Beatrice Schenk), 796
Cummins, Jim. *Daniel in the lions' den* (Bible Old Testament Daniel), 685
Jesus our friend (Daly, Kathleen N.), 781
Jonah and the great fish (Bible Old Testament Jonah), 685
Joseph and his brothers (Bible Old Testament Joseph), 685
Noah and the ark (Bible Old Testament Noah), 685
The Thanksgiving mystery (Nixon, Joan Lowery), 1103
A tooth for the tooth fairy (Gunther, Louise), 884
The Valentine mystery (Nixon, Joan Lowery), 1103
Who took the top hat trick? (Bowden, Joan Chase), 699
Cundiff, Meg. *Song of the circus* (Duncan, Lois), 808

Burnt toast on Davenport Street, 813
Chestnut Cove, 813
Distant Feathers, 813
The experiments of Doctor Vermin, 813
Friday night at Hodges' café, 813
Metropolitan cow, 813
A mile from Ellington station, 813
Serious farm, 813
The trial of Cardigan Jones, 813
Egielski, Richard. *Bravo, Minski* (Yorinks, Arthur), 1301
Buz, 813
Call me Ahnighito (Conrad, Pam), 765
Christmas in July (Yorinks, Arthur), 1301
The fierce yellow pumpkin (Brown, Margaret Wise), 713
Fire! Fire! said Mrs. McGuire (Martin, Bill [William Ivan]), 1055
The gingerbread boy (The gingerbread boy), 857
Hey, Al (Yorinks, Arthur), 1301
Jazper, 813
The little father (Burgess, Gelett), 724
Locust pocus (McKelvey, Douglas Kaine), 1038
The lost sailor (Conrad, Pam), 765
Louis the fish (Yorinks, Arthur), 1301
Mary's mirror (Aylesworth, Jim), 656
Oh, brother (Yorinks, Arthur), 1301
One present from Flekman's (Arkin, Alan), 647
Slim and Jim, 813
Small world of Binky Braverman (Wells, Rosemary), 1276
Three magic balls, 813
The Tub grandfather (Conrad, Pam), 765
The Tub People (Conrad, Pam), 765
The Tub People's Christmas (Conrad, Pam), 765
Ugh (Yorinks, Arthur), 1301
The web files (Palatini, Margie), 1118
Ehlert, Lois. *Angel hide and seek* (Turner, Ann Warren), 1250
Chicka chicka boom boom (Martin, Bill [William Ivan]), 1054
Chicka chicka boom boom [board book] (Martin, Bill [William Ivan]), 1054
Chicka chicka sticka sticka (Martin, Bill [William Ivan]), 1054
Circus, 813
Color farm, 813
Color zoo, 813
Crocodile smile (Weeks, Sarah), 1272
Cuckoo, a Mexican folktale = Cucú: un cuento folklórico mexicano, 813
Eating the alphabet, 813
Feathers for lunch, 813
Fish eyes, 813
Growing vegetable soup, 813
Hands, 813
In my world, 813
Leaf man, 813
Limericks (Lear, Edward), 998
Market day, 813
Mole's hill, 814
Moon rope = Un lazo a la luna, 814
Nuts to you! 814
A pair of socks (Murphy, Stuart J.), 1094
Planting a rainbow, 814
Red leaf, yellow leaf, 814
Shapes (Allington, Richard L.), 635
Snowballs, 814
Thump thump rat-a-tat-tat (Baer, Gene), 658
Top cat, 814
Waiting for wings, 814

What do you think I saw? (Sazer, Nina), 1182
Words (Martin, Bill [William Ivan]), 1055
Ehling, Katalin Olah. *The night the grandfathers danced* (Raczek, Linda Theresa), 1147
Ehrlich, Bettina *see* Bettina (Bettina Ehrlich)
Eichenauer, Gabriele. *Once upon a rainbow* (Lewis, Naomi), 1008
Eichenbaum, Rose. *The number on my grandfather's arm* (Adler, David A.), 624
Eichenberg, Fritz. *Ape in cape*, 814
Dancing in the moon, 814
A peaceable kingdom, and other poems (Coatsworth, Elizabeth), 757
The two magicians (Langstaff, John M.), 993
Eicke, Edna. *The tree that stayed up until next Christmas* (Kraus, Robert), 983
Eidlitz, Barbara. *Henry finds a home* (St. Pierre, Wendy), 1177
Eidrigevicius, Stasys. *Johnny Longnose* (Krüss, James), 987
Puss in boots (Perrault, Charles), 1128
Eiffers, Joost. *Dr. Pompo's nose* (Freymann, Saxton), 841
One lonely seahorse (Freymann, Saxton), 841
Eisner, Viv. *Totally polar* (Crisp, Marty), 775
Eisner, Will. *The princess and the frog* (Grimm, Jacob), 879
Sundiata, 815
Eitan, Ora. *Astro Bunnies* (Loomis, Christine), 1023
A-tisket, a-tasket (Fitzgerald, Ella), 830
Cowboy bunnies (Loomis, Christine), 1023
Dance, sing, remember (Kimmelman, Leslie), 973
Hanna's Sabbath dress (Schweiger-Dmi'el, Itzhak), 1190
Inch by inch (Mallett, David), 1048
Little wild parrot (Johnston, Tony), 956
No milk! (Ericsson, Jennifer A.), 819
Scuba bunnies (Loomis, Christine), 1024
Up bear, down bear (Harris, Trudy), 894
Eitzen, Allan. *Alphabestiary* (Alphabestiary), 636
Castles and mirrors and cities of sand (Bason, Lillian), 669
Cherry tree (Bond, Ruskin), 696
The clubhouse (Suen, Anastasia), 1230
Corduroy writes a letter (Inches, Alison), 940
Corduroy's garden (Inches, Alison), 940
Corduroy's hike (Inches, Alison), 940
Hamster chase (Suen, Anastasia), 1230
The hee-haw river (Lillegard, Dee), 1011
Loose tooth (Suen, Anastasia), 1230
My favorite place (Sargent, Susan), 1181
Pick a raincoat, pick a whistle (Bason, Lillian), 669
Totem poles (Frantz, Jennifer), 838
Up the hill and down (Up the hill and down), 1254
What's that noise? (Kauffman, Lois), 963
Willie's birthday (Suen, Anastasia), 1230
Ekoomiak, Normee. *Arctic memories*, 815
Elgar, Rebecca. *Tiger and the new baby* (French, Vivian), 840
Tiger and the temper tantrum (French, Vivian), 840
Elgin, Jill. *Baby mouse goes shopping* (Chase, Catherine), 748

Baby mouse learns his ABC's (Chase, Catherine), 748
Elgin, Kathleen. *All ready for school* (Adelson, Leone), 624
All ready for summer (Adelson, Leone), 624
All ready for winter (Adelson, Leone), 624
Speckles goes to school (Berquist, Grace), 683
Ups and down (Berkley, Ethel S.), 682
Elks, Wendy. *Charles B. Wombat and the very strange thing*, 815
Ellentuck, Shan. *Did you see what I said?* 815
A sunflower as big as the sun, 815
Elliott, Gertrude. *Nursery rhymes* (Nursery rhymes), 1106
Elliott, Ingrid Glatz. *Hospital roadmap*, 815
Elliott, Mark. *The candle in the window* (Johnson, Grace), 954
Elliott, Miss. *Mother Goose* (Mother Goose), 1088
Ellis, Andy. *Alligator tails and crocodile cakes* (Moon, Nicola), 1078
At the beginning of a pig (Moon, Nicola), 1078
Can we play too, Piglittle? (Grindley, Sally), 882
Piggo and the nosebag (Ayres, Pam), 656
Piggo has a train ride (Ayres, Pam), 656
Ellis, Jan Davey. *The autumn equinox* (Jackson, Ellen B.), 945
The book of slime (Jackson, Ellen B.), 945
Mush! (Seibert, Patricia), 1192
The spring equinox (Jackson, Ellen B.), 945
The summer solstice (Jackson, Ellen B.), 945
The winter solstice (Jackson, Ellen B.), 945
Ellis, Tim. *Chicken socks and other contagious poems* (Bagert, Brod), 658
The gooch machine (Bagert, Brod), 658
Ellison, Chris. *King of the stable* (Carlson, Melody), 736
Ellwand, David. *Alfred's camera*, 815
Alfred's party, 815
Cinderlily, 815
Midas Mouse, 816
Ten in the bed, 816
Elsdale, Bob. *Mac side up*, 816
Elson, Susan. *Hello day* (Aldis, Dorothy [Keeley]), 630
Elwell, Peter. *The cave of the lost Fraggle* (Tettelbaum, Michael), 1237
The king of the pipers, 816
Margaret Ziegler is horse-crazy (Dragonwagon, Crescent), 804
Three brave women (Martin, C. L. G.), 1055
Ely, Paul. *Eerie feary feeling* (Hulme, Joy N.), 934
Elzbieta. *Brave Babette and sly Tom*, 816
Dikou and the baby star, 816
Dikou and the mysterious moon sheep, 816
Dikou and the Snivelly Snoak, 816
Dikou the little troon who walks at night, 816
Jon-Jon and Annette, 816
Emberley, Barbara. *Flash, crash, rumble, and roll* (Branley, Franklyn M. [Mansfield]), 703
The moon seems to change (Branley, Franklyn M. [Mansfield]), 703
Emberley, Ed (Edward Randolph). *Animals*, 816
Cars, boats, and planes, 816
Columbus Day (Showers, Paul), 1203

Estrada, Pau. *Button soup* (Orgel, Doris), 1113
Just not the same (Lacoe, Addie), 990
Opal in the closet (Knight, Joan), 977

Ets, Marie Hall. *Another day,* 820
Bad boy, good boy, 820
Beasts and nonsense, 820
The cow's party, 820
Elephant in a well, 820
Gilberto and the wind, 820
In the forest, 820
Just me, 820
Little old automobile, 820
Mister Penny, 820
Mister Penny's circus, 820
Mr. Penny's race horse, 820
Mr. T. W. Anthony Woo, 820
Nine days to Christmas, 820
Play with me, 820
Talking without words, 820

Ettlinger, Doris. *Pilgrim cat* (Peacock, Carol Antoinette), 1124
Sugar snow (Sugar snow), 1230

Eugenie *see* Fernandes, Eugenie

Euvremer, Teryl. *After dark,* 820
Sun's up, 820
The thieves of Peck's pocket, 821
Toby, what are you? (Steig, William), 1221
Toby, who are you? (Steig, William), 1221
Triple whammy, 821

Evans, Graci. *David has AIDS* (Sanford, Doris), 1179

Evans, Katherine. *The boy who cried wolf,* 821
A bundle of sticks, 821
Chicken Little, count-to-ten (Friskey, Margaret [Margaret Richards]), 841
The four riders (Krum, Charlotte), 986
Indian Two Feet and his horse (Friskey, Margaret [Margaret Richards]), 841
Lucky and the giant (Elkin, Benjamin), 815
Mable the whale (King, Patricia), 973
The maid and her pail of milk, 821
The man, the boy and the donkey, 821
Mystery of the gate sign (Friskey, Margaret [Margaret Richards]), 841
Six foolish fishermen (Elkin, Benjamin), 815
The true book of time (Ziner, Feenie), 1308

Evans, Leslie. *Autumn* (Schnur, Steven), 1187
Grandpa and me on Tu B'Shevat (Gold-Vukson, Marji E.), 863
Summer (Schnur, Steven), 1187
Winter (Schnur, Steven), 1187

Evans, Mark. *Rabbit,* 821

Evans, Nate. *Clown around* (Rau, Dana Meachen), 1149
It's great to skate (Witt, Alexa), 1291
Laura Numeroff's 10-step guide to living with your monster (Numeroff, Laura Joffe), 1106
The mixed-up zoo of professor Yahoo, 821
Monster munchies (Numeroff, Laura Joffe), 1106

Evans, Nicola. *The three billy goats gruff* (Wade, Barrie), 1262

Evans, Richard. *The swan children* (Day, David), 786

Evans, Shane W. *Bintou's braids* (Diouf, Sylviane A, [Sylviane Anna]), 799
Down the winding road (Johnson, Angela), 953
Shanna's ballerina show (Marzollo, Jean), 1058

Shanna's teacher show (Marzollo, Jean), 1058
Welcome to the Shanna show (Marzollo, Jean), 1058

Eve, Esmé. *Eggs* (Eggs), 813

Everitt, Betsy. *The happy hippopotami* (Martin, Bill [William Ivan]), 1055
Mean soup, 821

Evers, Alie. *Barnaby and the horses* (Pender, Lydia), 1126

Everton, Macduff. *Finding the magic circus = El circo magico modelo,* 821

Evrard, Gaëtan. *On the move* (Fecher, Sarah), 826

Ewald, Wendy. *The best part of me* (The best part of me), 684

Ewart, Claire. *The biggest horse I ever did see* (Couture, Susan Arkin), 771
The giant, 821
The legend of the persian carpet (De Paola, Tomie [Thomas Anthony]), 794
Sister Yessa's story (Greenfield, Karen R.), 872
Time train (Fleischman, Paul), 832

Ewers, Joe. *The biggest cookie in the world* (Hayward, Linda), 901
I am Kermit (Gikow, Louise), 856
Sunny day – rainy day (Hayden, Lea), 900
What's in Oscar's trashcan? (Findlay, Lisa), 828

Ewing, C. S. (Carolyn S.). *Branigan's cat and the Halloween ghost* (Kroll, Steven), 984
Moose and friends (Latimer, Jim), 996
The nutcracker ballet (Hoffmann, E. T. A.), 924
Phoebe's parade (Mills, Claudia), 1072
The rabbit story (Tresselt, Alvin R.), 1247
Wake up, city! (Tresselt, Alvin R.), 1247
Wake up, farm! (Tresselt, Alvin R.), 1247
Where is Jake? (Packard, Mary), 1117

F

Fabrès, Oscar. *Who blew that whistle?* (Adelson, Leone), 624

Facklam, Paul. *The big bug book* (Facklam, Margery), 821

Faglia, Matteo. *Happy birthday, I'm 2* (Faglia, Maeto), 822

Fain, Moira. *The Christmas dolls* (Ransom, Candice F.), 1148
Snow day, 822

Fair, Sylvia. *The bedspread,* 822

Fairclough, Chris. *Big and little* (Pluckrose, Henry Arthur), 1135
Centipedes and millipedes (Greenaway, Theresa), 870
Counting (Pluckrose, Henry Arthur), 1135
Floating and sinking (Pluckrose, Henry Arthur), 1135
Gymnastics (Wood, Tim), 1294
Hearing (Pluckrose, Henry Arthur), 1135
Hot and cold (Pluckrose, Henry Arthur), 1135
Motor racing (Wood, Tim), 1294
Motorcycling (Wood, Tim), 1294
Numbers (Pluckrose, Henry Arthur), 1135
Seeing (Pluckrose, Henry Arthur), 1135
Shape (Pluckrose, Henry Arthur), 1135

Smelling (Pluckrose, Henry Arthur), 1135
Take a trip to China, 822
Take a trip to England, 822
Take a trip to Holland, 822
Take a trip to Israel, 822
Take a trip to Italy, 822
Take a trip to West Germany, 822
Talkabout air (Webb, Angela), 1272
Talkabout light (Webb, Angela), 1272
Talkabout reflections (Webb, Angela), 1272
Talkabout sand (Webb, Angela), 1272
Talkabout soil (Webb, Angela), 1272
Talkabout sound (Webb, Angela), 1272
Talkabout water (Webb, Angela), 1272
Tasting (Pluckrose, Henry Arthur), 1135
Time (Pluckrose, Henry Arthur), 1135
Touching (Pluckrose, Henry Arthur), 1135
Weight (Pluckrose, Henry Arthur), 1135

Falconer, Elizabeth. *I believe in unicorns* (Munthe, Adam John), 1092

Falconer, Ian. *Olivia,* 822
Olivia – and the missing toy, 822
Olivia counts, 822
Olivia saves the circus, 822
Olivia's opposites, 822

Falk, Barbara Bustetter. *Animal lingo* (Conrad, Pam), 765
Grusha, 822

Falla, Dominique. *Woodlore* (Miller, Cameron), 1069

Falls, C. B. (Charles Buckles). *ABC book,* 822
Mother Goose (Mother Goose), 1088

Faltermayr, Christine. *Do you know the difference?* (Bischhoff-Miersch, Andrea), 688

Falwell, Cathryn. *Christmas for 10,* 822
Clowning around, 822
David's drawing, 822
Dragon tooth, 822
Feast for ten, 822
Hands! (Kroll, Virginia L.), 985
New moon (Shea, Pegi Deitz), 1200
Nicky and Alex, 822
Nicky and grandpa, 822
Nicky loves daddy, 822
Nicky, 1-2-3, 822
Nicky's walk, 822
P.J. & Puppy, 822
Shape space, 822
Turtle splash! 822
We have a baby, 822
Where's Nicky? 823
Word wizard, 823

Fancher, Lou. *The boy on Fairfield Street* (Krull, Kathleen), 986
Cat, you better come home (Keillor, Garrison), 965
Coppélia (Fonteyn, Margot, Dame), 834
The day Ocean came to visit (Wolkstein, Diane), 1292
The first night (Hennessy, B. G. [Barbara G.]), 908
I walk at night (Duncan, Lois), 808
The lost and found house (Cadnum, Michael), 729
The lost boy and the monster (Strete, Craig Kee), 1229
New York's bravest (Osborne, Mary Pope), 1114
Peach and Blue (Kilborne, Sarah S.), 971
The quest for the One Big Thing, 823
The range eternal (Erdrich, Louise), 819

Panda's puzzle, and his voyage of discovery, 835

The perfect present, 835

Peter's place (Grindley, Sally), 882

Private zoo (McHargue, Georgess), 1037

Rock-a-doodle-do! 835

The sand horse (Turnbull, Ann), 1250

Seal surfer, 835

The sleeping beauty and other favourite fairy tales (Carter, Angela), 740

Surprise! Surprise! 835

Teeny-Tiny and the witch-woman (Walker, Barbara K. [Barbara Kerlin]), 1264

There's a bear in the bath! (Newman, Nanette), 1100

The tiger who lost his stripes (Paul, Anthony), 1123

The two giants, 835

War and peas, 835

Worms wiggle (Pelham, David), 1126

Forman, Laura. *Marvelous mouse man* (Hoberman, Mary Ann), 921

Forrai, Maria S. *A look at birth* (Pursell, Margaret Sanford), 1145

A look at death (Anders, Rebecca), 638

A look at divorce (Pursell, Margaret Sanford), 1145

A look at prejudice and understanding (Anders, Rebecca), 638

Forrest, Don. *Creatures that look alike* (Harris, Susan), 894

Forrest, Sandra. *The cow that could tap dance* (Slater, Teddy), 1209

Jan and Dan and the super dads (Slater, Teddy), 1209

Forrester, Victoria. *The magnificent moo,* 835

Oddward, 835

The touch said hello, 835

Words to keep against the night, 835

Fort, Patrick. *Redbird,* 835

Fosberg, John. *Cookie shapes,* 835

Ice cream colors, 835

Fosey, Christopher. *The best book of bugs* (Llewellyn, Claire), 1019

Fossati, Nicolas. *Not now, Sara!* (Voigt, Hannelore), 1260

Foster, Karen Sharp. *Good night my little chicks = Buenas noches mis pollitos,* 836

Foster, Marian Curtis see Mariana

Foster, Sally. *A pup grows up,* 836

Founds, George. *Pandas* (Grosvenor, Donna), 883

Fowler, Christine. *Shota and the star quilt* (Bateson-Hill, Margaret), 670

Fowler, Christopher. *Eleanor, Ellatony, Ellencake, and me* (Rubin, C. M.), 1172

Fowler, Jim. *Beautiful* (Fowler, Susi Gregg), 836

Fog (Fowler, Susi Gregg), 836

I'll see you when the moon is full (Fowler, Susi Gregg), 836

When Joel comes home (Fowler, Susi Gregg), 836

Fowler, Richard. *Cat's cake,* 836

Cat's car, 836

Cat's story, 836

Happy birthday, Mouse! 836

Honeybee's busy day, 836

Inspector Smart gets the message! 836

Ladybug on the move, 836

Little Chick's big adventure, 836

Mr. Little's noisy car, 836

Mr. Little's noisy fire engine, 836

Mr. Little's noisy truck, 836

Pop-up trucks, 836

Silly spider! (Wood, David), 1294

Fowlkes, Nancy Dunaway. *The old woman who lived in a vinegar bottle* (MacDonald, Margaret Read), 1034

Fox, Charles Philip. *Come to the circus,* 836

A fox in the house, 836

Mr. Stripes the gopher, 836

Fox, Christyan. *Astronaut PiggyWiggy,* 837

Count to ten, PiggyWiggy! 837

Dogs and puppies (Starke, Katherine), 1220

Fire fighter PiggyWiggy, 837

Hamsters (Meredith, Susan), 1066

Rabbits (Patchett, Fiona), 1122

What color is that, PiggyWiggy? 837

What shape is that, PiggyWiggy? 837

Fox, Dorothea Warren. *Follow me the leader,* 837

Fox, Perla. *The Wooodles,* 837

Fox-Davies, Sarah. *Bat loves the night* (Davies, Nicola), 784

A house in town (Mayne, William), 1062

Little Beaver and the echo (MacDonald, Amy), 1033

Moon frog (Edwards, Richard), 813

Snow bears (Waddell, Martin), 1262

Fradon, Dana. *Sir Dana – a knight,* 837

Fraifield, Denise. *Baby high, baby low* (Blackstone, Stella), 689

Frame, Paul. *Anna's snow day* (Gunther, Louise), 884

Frampton, David. *Jerusalem, shining still* (Kuskin, Karla), 989

Miro in the kingdom of the sun (Kurtz, Jane), 988

My beastie book of ABC, 837

My son John (Aylesworth, Jim), 656

Riding the tiger (Bunting, Eve [Anne Evelyn]), 723

The whole night through, 837

Francia, Silvia. *Roberta's vacation,* 837

Francis, Anna B. *Pleasant dreams,* 838

Francis, Frank. *Grandmother Lucy goes on a picnic* (Wood, Joyce), 1294

Grandmother Lucy in her garden (Wood, Joyce), 1294

The magic wallpaper, 838

Natasha's new doll, 838

Sing hey, diddle, diddle (Mother Goose), 1089

Franco-Feeney, Betsy. *James Bear and the goose gathering* (Latimer, Jim), 996

James Bear's pie (Latimer, Jim), 996

Françoise see Seignobosc, Françoise

Frank, Dick. *About dying* (Stein, Sara Bonnett), 1221

About handicaps (Stein, Sara Bonnett), 1221

That new baby (Stein, Sara Bonnett), 1221

Frankel, Adrian. *Hoang breaks the lucky teapot* (Breckler, Rosemary K.), 704

Frankel, Alona. *Hello, clouds!* (Renberg, Dalia Hardof), 1153

Frankenhuyzen, Gijsbert van. *Jam & jelly by Holly & Nellie* (Wheeler, Lisa), 1278

Mercedes and the chocolate pilot (Raven, Margot Theis), 1150

Frankland, David. *Old MacDonald had a farm* (Old MacDonald had a farm), 1109

Franklin, Jonathan. *Don't wake the baby,* 838

Franson, Leanne. *I miss Franklin P. Shuckles* (Snihura, Ulana), 1213

Jessica takes charge (LaRose, Linda), 994

What-if Sara (Tregebov, Rhea), 1247

Fransoy, Monse. *Cinderella = Cenicienta* (Perrault, Charles), 1127

Frascino, Edward. *Gladys told me to meet her here* (Sharmat, Marjorie Weinman), 1198

It'll all come out in the wash (Gray, Nigel), 869

The little mermaid (Andersen, H. C. [Hans Christian]), 639

My cousin the king, 838

Nanny Noony and the dust queen, 838

Nanny Noony and the magic spell, 838

UFO kidnap (Robison, Nancy), 1159

Frasconi, Antonio. *At Christmastime* (Worth, Valerie), 1295

The house that Jack built = la maison que Jacques a batie (The house that Jack built), 930

How the left-behind beasts built Ararat (Farber, Norma), 823

See again, say again, 838

See and say, 838

The snow and the sun = la nieve y el sol, 838

Fraser, Betty. *A house is a house for me* (Hoberman, Mary Ann), 921

Kenny's rat (Kouts, Anne), 980

Songs from around a toadstool table (Bennett, Rowena), 678

Fraser, Douglas. *David and Goliath* (Metaxas, Eric), 1067

Fraser, Mary Ann. *Forest fire!* 838

How animal babies stay safe, 838

I.Q. goes to school, 838

I.Q. goes to the library, 838

Where are the night animals? 838

Frasier, Debra. *The animal that drank up sound* (Stafford, William), 1219

On the day you were born, 838

Out of the ocean, 838

We got here together (Stafford, Kim Robert), 1219

Frazee, Marla. *Everywhere babies* (Meyers, Susan), 1067

Harriet, you'll drive me wild (Fox, Mem), 837

Hush, little baby (Hush little baby), 937

Mrs. Biddlebox (Smith, Linda), 1212

On the morn of Mayfest (Silverman, Erica), 1205

Roller coaster, 838

Santa Claus, the world's number one toy expert, 838

The seven silly eaters (Hoberman, Mary Ann), 921

World famous Muriel and the magic mystery (Alexander, Sue), 632

Frederick, Larry. *Rain! Rain!* (Greene, Carol), 871

Freedman, Russell. *Farm babies,* 839

Hanging on, 839

Tooth and claw, 839

Freeman-Hines, Laura. *Babies* (Heiligman, Deborah), 904

Jazz baby (Weatherford, Carole Boston), 1272

Freeman, Don. *Add-a-line alphabet,* 839

Beady Bear, 839

Bearymore, 839

Best friends (Brown, Myra Berry), 715

The chalk box story, 839

Come again, pelican, 839

Corduroy, 839

G

My day, 861
My dog, 861
Odds and evens, 861
Seasons, 861
Sometimes I like to be alone, 861
When I grow up . . . , 861
While I am little, 861
Goetzl, Robert F. *Many nations* (Bruchac, Joseph), 717
Goffe, Toni. *Beginning school* (Smalls-Hector, Irene), 1211
Clap your hands (Hayes, Sarah), 901
Ice cream at the castle (Love, Ann), 1025
The knight who was afraid to fight (Hazen, Barbara Shook), 902
Little boy soup (Harrison, David Lee), 894
The little red house (Sawicki, Norma Jean), 1181
Miss Fannie's hat (Karon, Jan), 963
Mother Halverson's new cat (Aylesworth, Jim), 656
The prince who wrote a letter (Love, Ann), 1025
Rocks in my pocket (Harshman, Marc), 895
The story of creation, 861
Toby's animal rescue service, 861
Treed by a pride of irate lions (Zimelman, Nathan), 1308
Goffin, Josse. *The Christmas story,* 861
Oh! 861
Silent Christmas, 862
Who is the boss? 862
Yes, 862
Goffstein, M. B. (Marilyn Brooke). *Across the sea,* 862
An actor, 862
An artist, 862
Artists' helpers enjoy the evening, 862
Family scrapbook, 862
Fish for supper, 862
A house, a home, 862
Laughing latkes, 862
A little Schubert, 862
Me and my captain, 862
My Noah's ark, 862
Natural history, 862
Neighbors, 862
Our prairie home, 862
Our snowman, 862
School of names, 862
Sleepy people, 862
A writer, 862
Gohman, Vera. *Word Bird's spring words* (Moncure, Jane Belk), 1077
Word Bird's winter words (Moncure, Jane Belk), 1077
Gold, Caroline. *The crooked apple tree* (Houghton, Eric), 930
Gold, Ethel. *A very special sister* (Levi, Dorothy Hoffman), 1005
Goldberg, Barry. *Merry Christmas, Rugrats!* (Richards, Kitty), 1155
Time to cha-cha-cha! (Thorpe, Kiki), 1241
Goldberg, Grace. *Jungle life* (Nayer, Judy), 1097
Night animals (Nayer, Judy), 1097
Reptiles (Nayer, Judy), 1097
Sea creatures (Nayer, Judy), 1097
Goldfinger, Jennifer P. *A fish named Spot,* 862
Goldin, David. *Go-Go-Go!* 862
Lost cat (Hardy, Tad), 892
Golding, Kim. *Alphababies,* 862

Goldman, Dara. *Piggy and Bear in their underwear* (Piggy and Bear in their underwear), 1132
There's no such thing! 862
Goldman, Susan. *Cousins are special,* 862
Grandma is somebody special, 862
Goldsborough, June. *An alphabet book* (Chase, Catherine), 748
Dolphins and porpoises (Gordon, Sharon), 866
It happened on Thursday (Delton, Judy), 790
Who am I? (Raebeck, Lois), 1147
Gold-Vukson, Marji E. *The colors of my Jewish Year,* 863
Golembe, Carla. *Annabelle's big move,* 863
Honeybees (Heiligman, Deborah), 904
Why the sky is far away (Gerson, Mary-Joan), 853
The woman in the moon (Rattigan, Jama Kim), 1149
Goloshapov, Sergei. *The six servants* (Grimm, Jacob), 879
Gomboli, Mario. *Look inside a house,* 863
Look inside a ship, 863
Gomi, Taro. *The big book of boxes,* 863
Bus stop, 863
Coco can't wait! 863
The crocodile and the dentist, 863
Everyone poops, 863
First comes Harry, 863
Guess what? 863
Guess who? 863
Hi, butterfly! 863
I lost my dad, 863
My friends, 863
Santa through the window, 863
Seeing, saying, doing, playing, 863
Spring is here, 863
Toot! 863
Where's the fish? 863
Who ate it? 863
Who hid it? 863
Gon, Adriano. *Good night, sleep tight* (Lively, Penelope), 1018
Gonzales, Edward. *Farolitos for Abuelo* (Anaya, Rudolfo A.), 637
Gonzales, Tomás. *I can use tools* (Kesselman, Judi R.), 969
Gonzalez, Maya Christina. *From the bellybutton of the moon and other summer poems / poems = Del ombligo de la luna y otros poemas de verano / poemas* (Alarcón, Francisco X.), 629
Iguanas in the snow and other winter poems / poemas = Iguanas en la nieve y otros poemas de invierno / poemas (Alarcón, Francisco X.), 629
My diary from here to there = Mi diario de aquí hasta allá (Pérez, Amada Irma), 1127
My very own room = Mi propio cuartito (Pérez, Amada Irma), 1127
Prietita and the ghost woman = Prietita y la llorona (Anzaldúa, Gloria), 645
Goodall, John S. *The adventures of Paddy Pork,* 864
The ballooning adventures of Paddy Pork, 864
Creepy castle, 864
An Edwardian Christmas, 864
An Edwardian summer, 864
Great days of a country house, 864
Jacko, 864

Little Red Riding Hood (Grimm, Jacob), 878
The midnight adventures of Kelly, Dot and Esmeralda, 864
Naughty Nancy, 864
Naughty Nancy goes to school, 864
Paddy goes traveling, 864
Paddy Pork, 864
Paddy Pork's holiday, 864
Paddy to the rescue, 864
Paddy under water, 864
Paddy's evening out, 864
Paddy's new hat, 864
Puss in boots (Perrault, Charles), 1128
Shrewbettina's birthday, 864
The story of a castle, 864
The story of a farm, 864
The story of a main street, 864
The story of an English village, 864
The surprise picnic, 864
Goode, Diane. *The adventures of Pinocchio* (Collodi, Carlo), 764
A child's garden of verses (Stevenson, Robert Louis), 1225
Christmas carols (Christmas carols), 753
Christmas in the barn (Brown, Margaret Wise), 713
Christmas in the country (Rylant, Cynthia), 1175
Cinderella (Perrault, Charles), 1127
The Diane Goode book of American folk tales and songs (Durell, Ann), 809
Diane Goode's book of silly stories & songs, 864
The dinosaur's new clothes, 864
The dream eater (Garrison, Christian), 849
The fir tree (Andersen, H. C. [Hans Christian]), 638
The good-hearted youngest brother (The good-hearted youngest brother), 864
The house Gobbaleen (Alexander, Lloyd), 630
I go with my family to Grandma's (Levinson, Riki), 1006
I hear a noise, 864
The little book of cats (The little book of cats), 1017
The little book of farm friends, 864
The Little book of mice (The Little book of mice), 1017
The Little book of pigs (The Little book of pigs), 1017
Little pieces of the west wind (Garrison, Christian), 849
Mama's perfect present, 864
Peter Pan (Barrie, J. M. [James M.]), 667
Tiger trouble, 864
The unicorn and the plow (Moeri, Louise), 1076
Watch the stars come out (Levinson, Riki), 1006
When I was young in the mountains (Rylant, Cynthia), 1176
Where's our mama? 864
Goodell, Jon. *The Alley Cat's Meow* (Appelt, Kathi), 645
Andiamo, Weasel (Grant, Rose Marie), 869
Little Salt Lick and the Sun King (Armstrong, Jennifer), 648
Mice are nice (Ghigna, Charles), 854
Mother, Mother I want another (Robbins, Maria Polushkin), 1158
One winter night (Kimmel, Eric A.), 972
Zigazak! (Kimmel, Eric A.), 973
Goodenow, Earle. *The last camel,* 864

Laura Jean the yard sale queen (Leonard, Marcia), 1002

What was the wicked witch's real name? (Bernstein, Joanne E.), 682

Ipcar, Dahlov. *Animal hide and seek* (Ipcar, Dahlov [Zorach]), 941

The biggest fish in the sea (Ipcar, Dahlov [Zorach]), 941

Black and white (Ipcar, Dahlov [Zorach]), 941

Bright barnyard (Ipcar, Dahlov [Zorach]), 941

Brown cow farm (Ipcar, Dahlov [Zorach]), 941

Bug city (Ipcar, Dahlov [Zorach]), 941

The calico jungle (Ipcar, Dahlov [Zorach]), 941

The cat at night (Ipcar, Dahlov [Zorach]), 941

The cat came back (Ipcar, Dahlov [Zorach]), 941

A flood of creatures (Ipcar, Dahlov [Zorach]), 941

Hard scrabble harvest (Ipcar, Dahlov [Zorach]), 941

I like animals (Ipcar, Dahlov [Zorach]), 942

I love my anteater with an A (Ipcar, Dahlov [Zorach]), 942

The land of flowers (Ipcar, Dahlov [Zorach]), 942

The little fisherman (Brown, Margaret Wise), 714

Lost and found (Ipcar, Dahlov [Zorach]), 942

My wonderful Christmas tree (Ipcar, Dahlov [Zorach]), 942

One horse farm (Ipcar, Dahlov [Zorach]), 942

Sir Addlepate and the unicorn (Ipcar, Dahlov [Zorach]), 942

The song of the day birds and the night birds (Ipcar, Dahlov [Zorach]), 942

Stripes and spots (Ipcar, Dahlov [Zorach]), 942

Ten big farms (Ipcar, Dahlov [Zorach]), 942

Wild and tame animals (Ipcar, Dahlov [Zorach]), 942

World full of horses (Ipcar, Dahlov [Zorach]), 942

Ireland, Sandra. *The three birds* (Van den Berg, Marinus), 1255

Irvine, Rex J. *Clementine and the cage* (Heller, Wendy), 906

Irwin, Michael. *Bears in my bed*, 942

Isadora, Rachel. *ABC pop!* 942

At the crossroads, 942

Babies, 942

Backstage (Maiorano, Robert), 1048

Ben's trumpet, 942

Bring on that beat, 942

Caribbean dream, 942

City seen from A to Z, 942

The firebird (The firebird), 828

Flossie and the fox (McKissack, Patricia C.), 1040

Francisco (Maiorano, Robert), 1048

Friends, 942

Golden Bear (Young, Ruth), 1302

Grandfather's lovesong (Lindbergh, Reeve), 1012

I hear, 942

I see, 942

I touch, 942

Jesse and Abe, 942

Lili at ballet, 942

Lili on stage, 942

Listen to the city, 942

A little interlude (Maiorano, Robert), 1048

The little match girl (Andersen, H. C. [Hans Christian]), 638

The little mermaid (Andersen, H. C. [Hans Christian]), 639

Max, 942

My ballet class, 943

My ballet diary, 943

Nick plays baseball, 943

No, Agatha! 943

Not just tutus, 943

The nutcracker (Hoffmann, E. T. A.), 924

123 pop! 943

Opening night, 943

Over the green hills, 943

Peekaboo morning, 943

The pirates of Bedford Street, 943

The Potters' kitchen, 943

The princess and the frog (Grimm, Jacob), 879

Seeing is believing (Shub, Elizabeth), 1203

Sophie skates, 943

A South African night, 943

The steadfast tin soldier (Andersen, H. C. [Hans Christian]), 640

Willaby, 943

Isami, Ikuyo. *The fox's egg*, 943

Ishi, Jim. *Bear hugs* (Capucilli, Alyssa Satin), 733

Ishida, Takeo. *In a meadow, two hares hide* (Bartoli, Jennifer), 668

Snow on bear's nose (Bartoli, Jennifer), 668

Isles, Joanna. *A child's garden of verses* (Stevenson, Robert Louis), 1225

The nutcracker (Hoffmann, E. T. A.), 924

Isom, Joan Shaddox. *The first starry night*, 943

Ito, Yoriko. *Jojofu* (Waite, Michael P.), 1264

The silver charm (San Souci, Robert D.), 1180

Ivanov, Anatoly. *The demon who would not die* (Cohen, Barbara), 758

Even higher (Cohen, Barbara), 759

Ol' Jake's lucky day, 943

The pied piper of Hamelin (Browning, Robert), 716

Ivenbaum, Elliot. *Noah's ark* (Chase, Catherine), 748

Iverson, Diane. *Discover the seasons*, 943

Ives, Penny. *The golden angel*, 943

Mrs. Santa Claus, 943

On Christmas eve, 943

The snow angel, 943

Ives, Ruth. *The bear who was too big* (Cooper, Letice Ulpha), 767

Ivory, Lesley Anne. *The birthday cat*, 944

Cats in the sun, 944

Cats know best (Eisler, Colin), 815

A day in London, 944

A day in New York, 944

Meet my cats, 944

Iwai, Melissa. *The Beeman* (Krebs, Laurie), 983

Chanukah lights everywhere (Rosen, Michael J.), 1166

Gramps and the fire dragon (Roberts, Bethany), 1158

Hanna's Christmas (Peterson, Melissa), 1129

Night shift daddy (Spinelli, Eileen), 1217

Iwamatsu, Jun *see* Yashima, Taro

Iwamura, Kazuo. *The fourteen forest mice and the harvest moon watch*, 944

The fourteen forest mice and the spring meadow picnic, 944

The fourteen forest mice and the summer laundry day, 944

The fourteen forest mice and the winter sledding day, 944

Mice at the beach (Yamashita, Haruo), 1297

Tan Tan's hat, 944

Tan Tan's suspenders, 944

Ton and Pon: big and little, 944

Ton and Pon: two good friends, 944

Iwasaki, Chihiro. *The birthday wish*, 944

The fisherman under the sea (Matsutani, Miyoko), 1059

The little mermaid (Andersen, H. C. [Hans Christian]), 639

The red shoes (Andersen, H. C. [Hans Christian]), 639

Snow White and the seven dwarves (Grimm, Jacob), 880

Staying home alone on a rainy day, 944

Swan Lake (Bell, Anthea), 675

What's fun without a friend? 944

Will you be my friend? 944

The wise queen (Bell, Anthea), 676

Izawa, Tadasu. *The ugly duckling* (Andersen, H. C. [Hans Christian]), 640

Izawa, Yohji. *One Christmas* (Funakoshi, Canna), 843

One evening (Funakoshi, Canna), 843

One morning (Funakoshi, Canna), 843

J

Jabar, Cynthia. *The big meow* (Spires, Elizabeth), 1217

Bored blue? Think what you can do! 944

Daddies are for catching fireflies (Ziefert, Harriet), 1305

The frog who wanted to be a singer (Goss, Linda), 866

Game time (Murphy, Stuart J.), 1094

Good morning, pond (Capucilli, Alyssa Satin), 734

The greatest gymnast of all (Murphy, Stuart J.), 1094

How many? (Walton, Rick), 1267

A koala for Katie (London, Jonathan), 1022

Mommies are for counting stars (Ziefert, Harriet), 1306

No hickory no dickory no dock (Agard, John), 627

Party day! 944

Rain song (Evans, Lezlie), 821

The scrubbly-bubbly car wash (The scrubbly-bubbly car wash), 1191

Shimmy shake earthquake, 944

The sundae scoop (Murphy, Stuart J.), 1094

Won't you come and play with me? (Donovan, Mary Lee), 801

Jablow, Renée. *Fuzzy bear* (Bentley, Dawn), 678

Mum (Cole, Babette), 760

Richard Scarry's all around Busytown (Scarry, Richard), 1182

Mouse in the house (Reitman, Andrea), 1152

Jacana *see* Jacana, Viäl

Melle, Gerta. *The cats' party* (Redies, Rainer), 1151

Melling, David. *Countdown to bedtime* (Haines, Mike), 887
Gerda the goose (Oram, Hiawyn), 1113

Melmon, Deborah. *Hello Peter = Bonjour, Rémy* (Morris, Ann), 1083

Melnyczuk, Peter. *Imagine you are a tiger* (Wallace, Karen), 1265
Red fox (Wallace, Karen), 1265
Sleeping Nanna (Crossley-Holland, Kevin), 775
While shepherds watched (Fleetwood, Jenni), 832

Melo, John. *I love my mother* (Zindel, Paul), 1308

Meloni, Maria Teresa. *Rosie's ballet slippers* (Hampshire, Susan), 890

Melvin, James. *Crabby's water wish* (Tate, Suzanne), 1235

Menchin, Scott. *Plenty of pockets* (Braybrooks, Ann), 703
Wiggle (Cronin, Doreen), 775

Mendelson, S. T. *Stupid Emilien*, 1065

Mendez, Consuelo. *Atariba and Niguayona* (Rohmer, Harriet), 1164

Mendez, Simon. *Crocodile* (Llewellyn, Claire), 1019
Duck (Llewellyn, Claire), 1019
Ladybug (Llewellyn, Claire), 1019
Tree (Llewellyn, Claire), 1019

Mendoza, George. *The alphabet boat*, 1065

Mercer, Lynn. *Schubert's snowflakes*, 1066

Merer, Laura Blanken. *Santa Claus is coming to town* (Santa Claus is coming to town), 1180

Merrick, Patrick. *Easter bunnies*, 1067

Merrill, Reed. *My Bible ABC book* (McKissack, Patricia C.), 1040

Merriman, Rachel. *Funny Ruby* (Friend, Catherine), 841
The tale of Tobias (Mark, Jan), 1052

Merritt, Jane Hamilton *see* Hamilton-Merritt, Jane

Merryweather, Jack. *Cattle drive* (Chandler, Edna Walker), 746
Pony rider (Chandler, Edna Walker), 746
Secret tunnel (Chandler, Edna Walker), 746

Meryman, Hope. *Akimba and the magic cow* (Rose, Anne K.), 1166

Meserve, Adria. *Smog, the city dog*, 1067

Meshi, Ita. *A child's picture English-Hebrew dictionary* (A child's picture English-Hebrew dictionary), 750

Messenger, Jannat. *Lullabies and baby songs*, 1067

Messenger, Norman. *Little red hen* (The little red hen), 1017
Once upon a time, though it wasn't in your time, and it wasn't in my time, and it wasn't in anybody else's time . . . (Garner, Alan), 848

Messier, Linda. *Fireflies, fireflies, light my way* (London, Jonathan), 1022

Mesturini, Cristina. *The cat* (Mantegazza, Giovanna), 1050
The hippopotamus (Mantegazza, Giovanna), 1050
Look inside a farm (Mantegazza, Giovanna), 1050

Metcalf, Paula. *Norma No Friends*, 1067

Metcalfe, Penny. *Mr. Percy's magic greenhouse* (Kemp, Anthea), 967

Mets, Marilyn. *The baseball birthday party* (Prager, Annabelle), 1140
In Abby's hands (Lewis, Wendy A.), 1009
Midnight math twelve terrific math games (Ledwon, Peter), 999
Scaredy dog (Thomas, Jane Resh), 1239
Waiting for the sun (Lohans, Alison), 1021

Meyer, Dennis K. *Fuzzy bear* (Bentley, Dawn), 678
Fuzzy Bear's potty book (Bentley, Dawn), 678
Old Bear, a pop-up book (Hissey, Jane), 918

Meyer, Elizabeth C. *The blue china pitcher*, 1067

Meyer, Jim. *If you want to see a caribou* (Root, Phyllis), 1165

Meyer, Louis A. *The clean air and peaceful contentment dirigible airline*, 1067

Meyerhoff, Nancy. *Ann likes red* (Seymour, Dorothy Z.), 1196

Meyerowitz, Rick. *Joshua and Bigtooth* (Childress, Mark), 750
Paul Bunyan (Gleeson, Brian), 859

Miceli, Monica. *The beast and the boy* (Mostacchi, Massimo), 1086
A dog's best friend (Mostacchi, Massimo), 1086

Michaels, Steve. *Count your way through Canada* (Haskins, Jim [James]), 896

Michaels, William. *Clare and her shadow*, 1068

Michaut, Valérie. *At the zoo* (Simon, Paul), 1207
You are much too small (Boegehold, Betty), 694

Michel, Deborah. *Getting dressed* (Leonard, Marcia), 1002

Michel, Guy. *The birthday cow* (Merriam, Eve), 1066
The butterfly book of birds (Dalmais, Anne-Marie), 781

Michelini, Carlo Alberto. *Look inside a rainforest* (Mantegazza, Giovanna), 1050
Look inside an airplane (Mantegazza, Giovanna), 1050

Michelson, Richard. *Ten times better*, 1068

Michl, Reinhard. *At the frog pond* (Michels, Tilde), 1068
A day on the river, 1068
Leo the lion (Wagener, Gerda), 1263
Mischa and his brothers (Baumann, Hans), 671
Who's that knocking at my door? (Michels, Tilde), 1068

Micich, Paul. *The littlest angel* (Tazewell, Charles), 1236

Micklethwait, Lucy. *Spot a cat*, 1068
Spot a dog, 1068

Micucci, Charles. *The brook* (Tennyson, Alfred), 1237
A little night music, 1068

Midgett, Morgan. *Oh, crumps! = Ay, caramba!* (Bock, Lee), 693

Migdale, Lawrence. *Celebrating Chinese New Year* (Hoyt-Goldsmith, Diane), 932

Miglio, Paige. *One more bunny* (Walton, Rick), 1267
So many bunnies (Walton, Rick), 1267
The spinner's gift (Radley, Gail), 1147

Mikau, Elizabeth. *Going on a journey to the sea* (Barclay, Jane), 665

Mikolaycak, Charles. *Bearhead* (Kimmel, Eric A.), 972
The binding of Isaac (Cohen, Barbara), 758
The changing maze (Snyder, Zilpha Keatley), 1214
A child is born (Winthrop, Elizabeth), 1289
Exodus (Chaikin, Miriam), 745
A gift from Saint Nicholas (Timmermans, Felix), 1244
He is risen (Winthrop, Elizabeth), 1289
The hero of Bremen (Hodges, Margaret), 922
Johnny's egg (Long, Earlene), 1023
The legend of the Christmas rose (Lagerlöf, Selma), 991
The lullaby songbook (Yolen, Jane), 1300
The man who could call down owls (Bunting, Eve [Anne Evelyn]), 722
The nine crying dolls (Pellowski, Anne), 1126
Perfect crane (Laurin, Anne), 996
Peter and the wolf (Prokofiev, Sergei Sergeievitch), 1143
The rumor of Pavel and Paali (Kismaric, Carole), 975
The surprising things Maui did (Williams, Jay), 1285
Tiger watch (Wahl, Jan), 1264

Milelli, Pascal. *The art room* (Vande Griek, Susan), 1255

Miles, Elizabeth J. *Louie and Dan are friends* (Pryor, Bonnie), 1144
Mokey's birthday present (Weiss, Ellen), 1274
Molly Limbo (Hodges, Margaret), 922
The velveteen rabbit (Bianco, Margery Williams), 685

Milgrim, David. *Cows can't fly*, 1069
Dog brain, 1069
Here in space, 1069
My friend Lucky, 1069
Patrick's dinosaurs on the Internet (Carrick, Carol), 739
Why Benny barks, 1069

Milhous, Katherine. *The egg tree*, 1069

Milich, Zoran. *The city ABC book*, 1069
City colors, 1069
City 1 2 3, 1069
City signs, 1069

Milius, Winifred Lubell *see* Lubell, Winifred

Milkau, Liz. *Sea crow* (Stewart, Shannon), 1225
Zizi and Tish (Moore, Liz), 1080

Mill, Eleanor. *A button in her ear* (Litchfield, Ada B.), 1016
A cane in her hand (Litchfield, Ada B.), 1016
Mary Jo's grandmother (Udry, Janice May), 1252
What Mary Jo shared (Udry, Janice May), 1253
What Mary Jo wanted (Udry, Janice May), 1253

Millais, Raoul. *Elijah and Pin-Pin*, 1069

Miller, Albert. *I know an old lady* (Little old lady who swallowed a fly), 1017

Miller, Andrew. *Nature's hidden world* (Selberg, Ingrid), 1193

Miller, Bob. *2-B and the rock 'n roll band* (Paul, Sherry), 1123
2-B and the space visitor (Paul, Sherry), 1123

Montanari, Eva. *The crocodile's true colors,* 1078
Dino bikes, 1078
Tiff, Taff, and Lulu, 1078
Monteith, David. *Hello, two-wheeler!* (Mason, Jane B.), 1058
Montenegro, Laura Nyman. *A bird about to sing,* 1078
One stuck drawer, 1078
Sweet Tooth, 1078
Montezinos, Nina. *Look! Snow!* (Galbraith, Kathryn Osebold), 845
Montgomery, Lee. *Ant* (Hawcock, David), 899
Bee (Hawcock, David), 899
Beetle (Hawcock, David), 899
Fly (Hawcock, David), 899
Spider (Hawcock, David), 899
Wasp (Hawcock, David), 899
Montgomery, Michael G. *'Night, America,* 1078
Night rabbits (Posey, Lee), 1138
Over the candlestick, 1078
Montresor, Beni. *A for angel,* 1078
Bedtime! 1078
Hansel and Gretel, 1078
May I bring a friend? (De Regniers, Beatrice Schenk), 795
The nightingale (Andersen, H. C. [Hans Christian]), 639
On Christmas eve (Brown, Margaret Wise), 714
Sounds of a summer night (Garelick, May), 848
Willy O'Dwyer jumped in the fire (De Regniers, Beatrice Schenk), 796
The witches of Venice, 1078
Montserrat, Pep. *The gift* (Keselman, Gabriela), 969
Moodie, Fiona. *Nabulela,* 1078
Noko and the night monster, 1078
Moon, Carl. *One little Indian* (Moon, Grace Purdie), 1078
Moon, Lily. *The bearer of gifts* (Steven, Kenneth C.), 1223
Mooney, David. *Say it again* (Cassie, Brian), 742
Moore, Chevelle. *Getting dressed* (Moore, Dessie), 1079
Good morning (Moore, Dessie), 1079
Good night (Moore, Dessie), 1079
Let's pretend (Moore, Dessie), 1079
Moore, Cyd. *Alice and Greta* (Simmons, Steven J.), 1206
Alice and Greta's color magic (Simmons, Steven J.), 1206
A fire engine for Ruthie (Newman, Lesléa), 1100
Good night, Princess Pruney Toes (McCourt, Lisa), 1031
Greta's revenge (Simmons, Steven J.), 1206
I love you, Bunny Rabbit (Oppenheim, Shulamith Levey), 1112
I love you, Stinky Face (McCourt, Lisa), 1031
I miss you, Stinky Face (McCourt, Lisa), 1032
It's time for school, Stinky Face (McCourt, Lisa), 1032
Room for Rabbit (Schotter, Roni), 1188
What is the full moon full of? (Oppenheim, Shulamith Levey), 1113
Where is the night train going? (Spinelli, Eileen), 1217

Moore, Gustav. *Earth cycles* (Ross, Michael Elsohn), 1168
Moore, Inga. *Aktil's big swim,* 1080
Away in a manger (Hayes, Sarah), 901
A big day for Little Jack, 1080
Little dog lost, 1080
Oh, little Jack, 1080
The reluctant dragon (Grahame, Kenneth), 868
Rose and the nightingale, 1080
Six dinner Sid, 1080
The sorcerer's apprentice, 1080
The truffle hunter, 1080
The vegetable thieves, 1080
Moore, Jo. *Some bugs glow in the dark* (Llewellyn, Claire), 1019
Spiders have fangs (Llewellyn, Claire), 1019
Moore, John. *Granny Stickleback,* 1080
Moore, Linda. *Fifty red night-caps* (Moore, Inga), 1080
Moore, Margie. *Bartholomew's blessing* (Tolan, Stephanie S.), 1245
Count the ways, Little Brown Bear (London, Jonathan), 1021
Ruby bakes a cake (Hill, Susan), 914
Moore, Robert. *Little Black Sambo* (Bannerman, Helen), 663
Moore, Sparky. *Disney's Pooh's grand adventure: the search for Christopher Robin* (Henderson, Kathy), 907
Moore, Yvette. *A prairie alphabet* (Bannatyne-Cugnet, Jo), 663
Moorman, Margaret. *Light the lights!* 1080
Mora, Francisco X. *Delicious hullabaloo = Pachanga deliciosa* (Mora, Pat), 1081
How the Indians bought the farm (Strete, Craig Kee), 1228
Listen to the desert = Oye al desierto (Mora, Pat), 1081
The little red ant and the great big crumb (Climo, Shirley), 757
Pablo and Pimienta (Covault, Ruth M.), 771
Mora, Jo. *Budgee Budgee Cottontail* (Mora, Jo [Joseph Jacinto]), 1080
Moraes, Odilon. *The bear who didn't like honey* (Maitland, Barbara), 1048
Morales, Vincent. *Bisnipian blast-off* (Arnold, Tedd), 649
Moran, Rosslyn. *Please, Mr. Crocodile!* (Please, Mr. Crocodile!), 1134
Mordan, C. B. *Lost!* (Fleischman, Paul), 832
Silent movie (Avi), 655
Mordvinoff, Nicolas. *Billy the kid* (Lipkind, William), 1015
The boy and the forest (Lipkind, William), 1015
Chaga (Lipkind, William), 1015
The Christmas bunny (Lipkind, William), 1015
Circus ruckus (Lipkind, William), 1015
Coral Island, 1081
Even Steven (Lipkind, William), 1015
Finders keepers (Lipkind, William), 1015
Four-leaf clover (Lipkind, William), 1015
The little tiny rooster (Lipkind, William), 1015
The magic feather duster (Lipkind, William), 1015
Russet and the two reds (Lipkind, William), 1015
Sleepyhead (Lipkind, William), 1015
The two reds (Lipkind, William), 1015

Moreno, Rene King. *Fiesta* (Guy, Ginger Foglesong), 885
Under the lemon moon (Fine, Edith Hope), 828
Moreton, Daniel. *La Cucaracha Martina,* 1081
Lost! (Trimble, Patti), 1248
What day is it? (Trimble, Patti), 1248
Morey, Jean W. *Seven diving ducks* (Friskey, Margaret [Margaret Richards]), 842
Morgan, Judy. *Little Harry* (Bröger, Achim), 709
Morgan, Mary. *My good night book,* 1082
What the baby hears (Godwin, Laura), 861
Morgan, Pierr. *The bells of Santa Lucia* (Cazzola, Gus), 744
Miser on the mountain (Luenn, Nancy), 1026
Snow pumpkin (Schaefer, Carole Lexa), 1183
Someone says (Schaefer, Carole Lexa), 1183
Sometimes moon (Schaefer, Carole Lexa), 1183
The turnip (Milhous, Katherine), 1069
Morgan, Richard. *Zoo poo,* 1082
Morgan-Vanroyen, Mary. *Baby's first Mother Goose* (Mother Goose), 1086
Benjamin's bugs, 1082
Bloomers! (Blumberg, Rhoda), 693
Buba Leah and her paper children (Ross, Lillian Hammer), 1168
Curious Rosie, 1082
Daddies (Regan, Dian Curtis), 1151
Gentle Rosie, 1082
Guess who I love? 1082
The guppies of Hilly Dale House (Baird, Anne), 659
Hannah and Jack (Nethery, Mary), 1099
Happy Thanksgiving! (Lewison, Wendy Cheyette), 1009
Hugs (McLerran, Alice), 1041
I wear my tutu everywhere! (Lewison, Wendy Cheyette), 1009
I'm the Boss! (Winthrop, Elizabeth), 1290
Jake baked the cake (Hennessy, B. G. [Barbara G.]), 908
Kisses (McLerran, Alice), 1041
Little Miss Muffet (Mother Goose), 1087
Night ride, 1082
Our puppies are growing (Otto, Carolyn), 1115
Patient Rosie, 1082
The Pudgy Merry Christmas book, 1082
Sleep tight, little mouse, 1082
Surprise! (Ziefert, Harriet), 1307
The way to Wyatt's house (Carlstrom, Nancy White), 737
Where do bears sleep? (Hazen, Barbara Shook), 903
Wild Rosie, 1082
Moriarty, William J. *Jonathan goes to the doctor* (Baggette, Susan K.), 658
Jonathan goes to the grocery store (Baggette, Susan K.), 658
Jonathan goes to the library (Baggette, Susan K.), 658
Morice, Dave. *Dot town,* 1082
The happy birthday handbook, 1082
A visit from St. Alphabet, 1082
Morimoto, Junko. *The inch boy,* 1082
Mouse's marriage, 1082
My Hiroshima, 1082
The two bullies, 1082

Tibo, Gilles. *The beast* (Bartels, Alice L.), 667
Simon and the snowflakes, 1243
Simon's disguise, 1243

Tickle, Jack. *Little Rocket's special star* (Sykes, Julie), 1232
The very lazy ladybug (Finn, Isobel), 828

Tidholm, Anna-Clara. *The rabbit who longed for home* (Edvall, Lilian), 811

Tiegreen, Alan. *Pat-a-cake and other play rhymes* (Cole, Joanna), 762
Pin the tail on the donkey and other party games (Cole, Joanna), 762
Why did the chicken cross the road? (Cole, Joanna), 762

Tien. *The velveteen rabbit* (Bianco, Margery Williams), 685

Tilden, Ruth. *Freddie works out*, 1243
Sophie's dance class, 1243

Tildes, Phyllis Limbacher. *Animals in camouflage*, 1243
Baby animals black and white, 1243
Billy's big-boy bed, 1243
The magic babushka, 1243

Tilley, Debbie. *The difference between babies and cookies* (Hanson, Mary Elizabeth), 892
Fribbity ribbit (Johnson, Suzanne C.), 955
Hey little ant (Hoose, Philip M.), 928
Never let your cat make lunch for you (Harris, Lee), 894
No ordinary Olive (Baker, Roberta), 661
Riddle-icious (Lewis, J. Patrick), 1008
Riddle-lightful (Lewis, J. Patrick), 1008

Tillotson, Katherine. *Nice try, Tooth Fairy* (Olson, Mary), 1111
Night train (Stutson, Caroline), 1229
Penguin and Little Blue (McDonald, Megan), 1035

Timmers, Leo. *Monkey see, monkey do* (Holsonback, Anita), 926

Tinkelman, Murray. *Cowgirl*, 1244
Dinosaurs (Hopkins, Lee Bennett), 928

Tirabosco, Tom. *At the same time*, 1244

Tirion, Wil. *Zoo in the sky* (Mitton, Jacqueline), 1075

Tison, Annette. *Animal hide-and-seek*, 1244
Animals in color magic, 1244

Titherington, Jeanne. *Baby's boat*, 1244
Baby's boat [board book], 1244
Big world, small world, 1244
Bonkers Fellini, 1244
A child's prayer, 1244
A place for Ben, 1244
Pumpkin pumpkin, 1244
Where are you going, Emma? 1244

Tobey, Barney. *Don and Donna go to bat* (Perkins, Al), 1127
I wish that I had duck feet (Seuss, Dr.), 1196

Tobin, Nancy. *Drip! drop!* (Seuling, Barbara), 1195
Flick a switch (Seuling, Barbara), 1195
How tall, how short, how far away (Adler, David A.), 624

Todaro, John. *Phillip the flower-eating phoenix*, 1244

Todd, Barbara. *Ballet dancer* (Palazzo-Craig, Janet), 1118

Todd, Kathleen. *Snow*, 1245

Todd, Mark. *Monster trucks*, 1245
Start your engines, 1245
What will you be for Halloween? 1245

Toddy, Irving. *Cheyenne again* (Bunting, Eve [Anne Evelyn]), 722

Toft, Kim Michelle. *Neptune's nursery*, 1245
One less fish, 1245

Tokunbo, Dimitrea. *Has anybody lost a glove?* (Johnson, G. Francis), 954

Tol, Jaap. *The golden treasure* (Reesink, Marijke), 1151
The sea horse (Anrooy, Frans van), 645

Tolford, Joshua. *Jack and the three sillies* (Chase, Richard), 748

Tolkien, J. R. R. (John Ronald Reuel). *The Father Christmas letters*, 1245

Tomblin, Gill. *Grandma and the pirate* (Lloyd, David), 1019

Tomei, Lorna. *I'll bet you thought I was lost* (Parenteau, Shirley), 1119
Rosie and Michael (Viorst, Judith), 1259

Tomes, Margot. *Becky and the bear* (Van Woerkom, Dorothy), 1257
Birthday poems (Livingston, Myra Cohn), 1018
The earth gnome (Grimm, Jacob), 876
Everyone is good for something (De Regniers, Beatrice Schenk), 795
Everything under a mushroom (Krauss, Ruth), 983
The fisherman and his wife (Grimm, Jacob), 877
For Pipita, an orange tree (Oleson, Claire), 1110
Giant poems (Wallace, Daisy), 1264
The Halloween pumpkin smasher (St. George, Judith), 1177
If there were dreams to sell (Lalicki, Barbara), 991
Jack and the wonder beans (Still, James), 1226
Jorinda and Joringel (Grimm, Jacob), 878
The lap-time song and play book (Yolen, Jane), 1300
The little jewel box (Mayer, Marianna), 1061
Little Sister and the Month Brothers (De Regniers, Beatrice Schenk), 795
Lysbet and the fire kittens (Moskin, Marietta D.), 1085
A Norse lullaby (Van Vorst, M. L.), 1257
Pot full of luck (Rose, Anne K.), 1166
Prize performance (Fisher, Aileen Lucia), 830
The six swans (Grimm, Jacob), 879
The sorcerer's apprentice (Gág, Wanda), 844
Soup bone (Johnston, Tony), 956
Stone soup (Stewig, John Warren), 1226
Tattercoats (Jacobs, Joseph), 946
Those foolish Molboes! (Bason, Lillian), 669
Ty's one-man band (Walter, Mildred Pitts), 1267
Witch Hazel (Schertle, Alice), 1185
The witch's hat (Johnston, Tony), 957

Tomkins, Jasper. *The catalog*, 1245

Tomova, Veselina. *A dozen silk diapers* (Kajpust, Melissa), 961
Three teeny tiny tales (Helmer, Marilyn), 906

Tooke, Susan. *Brave Jack and the unicorn* (McNaughton, Janet), 1043
A fiddle for Angus (Wilson, Budge), 1287
Full moon rising (Taylor, Joanne), 1235
A seaside alphabet (Grassby, Donna), 869

Tord, Bijou Le *see* Le Tord, Bijou

Tornquist, Suzanne. *Play Lady = La Señora Juguetona* (Hoffman, Eric), 923

Tornqvist, Marit. *A calf for Christmas* (Lindgren, Astrid), 1013
The Christmas carp (Tornqvist, Rita), 1246

Torrecilla, Pablo. *The bakery lady = La señora de la panadería* (Mora, Pat), 1080
Marina's muumuu = el muumuu de Marina (Vigil-Piñón, Evangelina), 1258

Torres, Daniel. *Tom*, 1246

Torres, Leyla. *Liliana's grandmothers*, 1246
Saturday sancocho, 1246
Two days in May (Taylor, Harriet Peck), 1235

Torrey, Marjorie. *Sing in praise* (Wheeler, Opal), 1279
Sing Mother Goose (Wheeler, Opal), 1279

Torudd, Cecilia. *A worm's tale* (Lindgren, Barbro), 1014

Toto, Joe. *The cat and the mouse and the mouse and the cat* (Mandry, Kathy), 1049

Toulmin-Rothe, Ann. *Willie blows a mean horn* (Thomas, Ianthe), 1239

Towle, Faith M. *The magic cooking pot*, 1246

Townsend, Kenneth. *Felix, the bald-headed lion*, 1246

Tracy, Libba. *Building a bridge* (Begaye, Lisa Shook), 674
It rained on the desert today (Buchanan, Ken), 719
This house is made of mud (Buchanan, Ken), 719

Trammell, Jeremiah. *The giant cabbage turnip* (Stihler, Chérie B.), 1226

Trang, Winson. *The jade horse, the cricket, and the peach stone* (Tompert, Ann), 1245

Trapani, Iza. *Baa baa black sheep*, 1247
Baa baa black sheep [board book], 1247
How much is that doggie in the window? 1247
I'm a little teapot, 1247
The itsy bitsy spider, 1247
Mary had a little lamb (Hale, Sarah Josepha Buell), 887
Mary had a little lamb [board book] (Hale, Sarah Josepha Buell), 887
Row, row, row your boat, 1247
Shoo fly! 1247
What am I? 1247

Tredez, Alain *see* Trez, Alain

Tredez, Denise *see* Trez, Denise

Treherne, Katie Thamer. *The light princess* (MacDonald, George), 1034
The little mermaid (Andersen, H. C. [Hans Christian]), 639

Trésy, Françoise. *The princess who always ran away* (Reesink, Marijke), 1151

Trez, Alain. *Good night, Veronica* (Trez, Denise), 1248
The little knight's dragon (Trez, Denise), 1248
Maila and the flying carpet (Trez, Denise), 1248
Rabbit country (Trez, Denise), 1248
The royal hiccups (Trez, Denise), 1248

Trez, Denise. *Good night, Veronica*, 1248
The little knight's dragon, 1248
Maila and the flying carpet, 1248
Rabbit country, 1248
The royal hiccups, 1248

Trezzo, Loretta. *The Sesame Street song book* (Raposo, Joe), 1148

U

About the Authors

CAROLYN W. LIMA is former Children's Librarian, San Diego Public Library, Branch Libraries Division, San Diego, California.

JOHN A. LIMA is former Supervising Librarian, San Diego Public Library, Branch Libraries Division.